·ALABAMA·COLORADO·ARIZONA·MAINE·TEXAS·UTAH·ALASKA·
·IOWA·LOUISIANA·WISCONSIN·TENNESSEE·IDAHO·

1817 1998

The Official Catholic Directory

Anno Domini
1998

Published Annually by
P. J. Kenedy & Sons

GEORGIA·DELAWARE·ILLINOIS·KANSAS·NORTH CAROLINA·OREGON·NEBRASKA·KENTUCKY
NEW HAMPSHIRE·NEW JERSEY·NEW MEXICO·CONNECTICUT·FLORIDA·MASSACHUSETTS
·INDIANA·OKLAHOMA·RHODE ISLAND·MONTANA·
·HAWAII·WASHINGTON·VIRGINIA·VERMONT·WYOMING·OHIO·
CALIFORNIA·MICHIGAN·MINNESOTA·MISSISSIPPI·MISSOURI·WEST VIRGINIA·NEW YORK·NEVADA
NORTH DAKOTA·PENNSYLVANIA·SOUTH CAROLINA·SOUTH DAKOTA·MARYLAND·ARKANSAS

John R. Agel
Publisher

FOREWORD

We are pleased to present the ***1998 edition of the Official Catholic Directory*** *and again wish to thank all the ecclesiastical authorities and diocesan officials involved for their cooperation and participation. We consistently strive to maintain the integrity and credibility of information and offer it in an easy to understand format.*

Packaged again this year with the Official Catholic Directory, the ***Pilgrimage Destination Guide*** *is presented with the coming of the Millennium in mind. As acknowledged by the Bishops Subcommittee on the Millennium, this celebration offers the Church the opportunity to reflect on the meaning of Christianity locally, nationally and internationally. Millions are expected to journey to pilgrimage areas significant both in historical and traditional value to the Christian faith. This booklet has been developed to provide information relative to the pilgrimage and surrounding regions. Containing maps and contact information, we believe you will find this guide to be interesting and useful.*

Part II of the Official Catholic Directory, *published in early Fall is included with your subscription.* ***Part II*** *contains revisions and updates unavailable for the main volume; more expanded data for the Pilgrimage section, and a complete list of the dioceses and archdioceses of the world reprinted with permission from the Vatican.*

We are proud to have the honor of presenting the Directory to The Holy Father and to carry on the rich tradition of providing a detailed and thorough portrait of the Catholic Church. It is our hope to continue to develop this portrayal on a more universal level as we endeavor to improve the quantity and quality of information.

John R. Agel
Publisher

Published by P.J. Kenedy & Sons
121 Chanlon Road ✦ New Providence, NJ 07974 ✦ 908-665-6680

Photo of His Holiness The Pope courtesy of Arturo Mari, L'Osservatore Romano.

His Holiness the Pope John Paul II

P. Sullivan
4 - III - 91

The Seal of P.J. Kenedy & Sons
The Official Catholic Directory

SIGNIFICANCE:

The shield is the central part of a heraldic device, which is more commonly known as a coat of arms. If that shield is enclosed within a body of text, or other type of surrounding configuration, the device becomes know as a seal, yet it is the shield portion of the design that is the most important, and that which is described technically as the blazon. As the design is examined, it must be remembered that by heraldic tradition the design is described (blazoned) as if being done by the bearer with the shield being worn on the arm. Therefore, the terms dexter and sinister will be reversed as the design is viewed from the front.

The shield of the seal for The Official Catholic Directory has been designed to reflect the character and heritage of this publication of P.J. Kenedy & Sons.

The shield is in two major portions. The right half (sinister impalement) is composed of the blue field on which are seen a silver tree, two candles (in silver or white) in their candleholders (of gold or yellow) and an open book, edged in gold and with a red bookmark. These symbols have been used over the years as the sign of the P.J. Kenedy and Sons publishing organization. These are the traditional symbols of knowledge and learning, so appropriate to a publisher.

The other side of the shield (the dexter impalement) is composed of a silver (white) field on which is seen a red cross, throughout, and a gold eagle. These symbols, combined with the field of the sinister impalement, are represented in the color of the flag of the United States of America and the eagle, the symbol of the United States. The cross represents Christianity and all of this combines to signify that The Official Catholic Directory annually reports on the Catholic Church in the United States.

The shield is surrounded by a laurel wreath of excellence and is enclosed within the legend that states the name of the company, the name of the publication and date (1817) of its founding.

by: Paul J. Sullivan

THE I.T. VERDIN CO., CINCINNATI, OHIO

Adrian Hamers®

One Hundred Years Serving the Clergy
Frappez Toujours
1887

Church Interiors

For those hard to find items, contact Adrian Hamers, Inc.

Since 1887, the Hamers name has been synonymous with expert silversmithing throughout the world in the field of Liturgical Art. We are also experts in: Chruch Interiors from design to execution, Renovations, Altars, Sacred Vessels, Appraisals, Gold and Silver Plating & Repairing, Tabernacles, Marble, Statuary, Woodwork & Woodcarving, Stained Glass, Pews and Chairs, Gold Leafing, Wall Murals, Heraldic Design and Bishop Regalia.

2 MADISON AVENUE • LARCHMONT, N.Y. 10538 • FAX: 914-834-0712 • TEL: (914) 834-7780

St. Maria Goretti Church Madison, Wisconsin

St. Stanislaus Church Cleveland, Ohio

Photo: Don DuBroff

Since 1889, the Conrad Schmitt Studios has acquired a nationally recognized reputation for providing timeless interiors and fine works of art. From the rural church to the urban cathedral, the Studio has assisted churches of varying sizes and styles across the country. The Studio offers a variety of services and resources to assist your project from its initial phases to completion. Please call for more information.

"By a sample we may judge of the whole piece"
Miguel De Cervantes

SCULPTWAX®
CHURCH CANDLES
Classical symbolism and expressive liturgical design in the luxurious hand decorated artistry of SCULPTWAX®. . . created and mastercrafted here, in the United States, exclusively at Cathedral Candle Company.
Wedding Candle Ensemble
Holy Trinity™ Christ Candle
199
Christ Victorious™ Paschal Candle
Holy Trinity™ Paschal Candle
The Christian Rites™ RCIA Candle
Now, In Stock At Your Nearest Church Goods Dealer.
SCULPTWAX®
Only from . . .
SINCE 1897
Cathedral
CANDLE COMPANY

Terra Sancta Guild

serves the Christian people in three different ways:

- custom designs, made-to-order, in answer to individual needs
- limited editions to serve a special public
- substantial inventory of popular, off-the-shelf pieces, always ready for immediate shipment

858 Sussex Boulevard
P.O. Box 300
Broomall, PA 19008
1-800-523-5155

:RA SANCTA GUILD®
is committed to fine design and workmanship in ?hristian insignia, :cognition awards ıd gifts expressive religious thought -all graphic signs of faith.

I. A. Serot

I.A. Serot
President

Over 30 years ago, Terra Sancta Guild®

came onto the market with its own original copyrighted designs. Through our renowned Art Department, we dedicated ourselves to bring forth significant items designed for home, church, and school – pieces that would not add to the glut of kitsch. "What I like about Terra Sancta Guild," said a prominent clergyman in 1965, "is that I can hand these items down to my grandchildren." That comment encouraged us at the time, and now we see succeeding generations who still cherish our products. Today, for example, our responsive clients are requesting us to produce more Celtic designs .

Right: Adé Bethune, Terra Sancta Guild Art Director, is a renowned liturgical artist. Her fame as writer and illustrator, and her expertise in church architecture, are based on a profound grasp of Christian symbolism spoken in the Biblical tradition, in the multi-layered dimensions of Christian worship. Abigail McCarthy says that Adé has done "more than any other artist to rescue twentieth century religious art from the saccharine and the vapid." *The Living Church* writes that Adé should be declared "a national treasure."

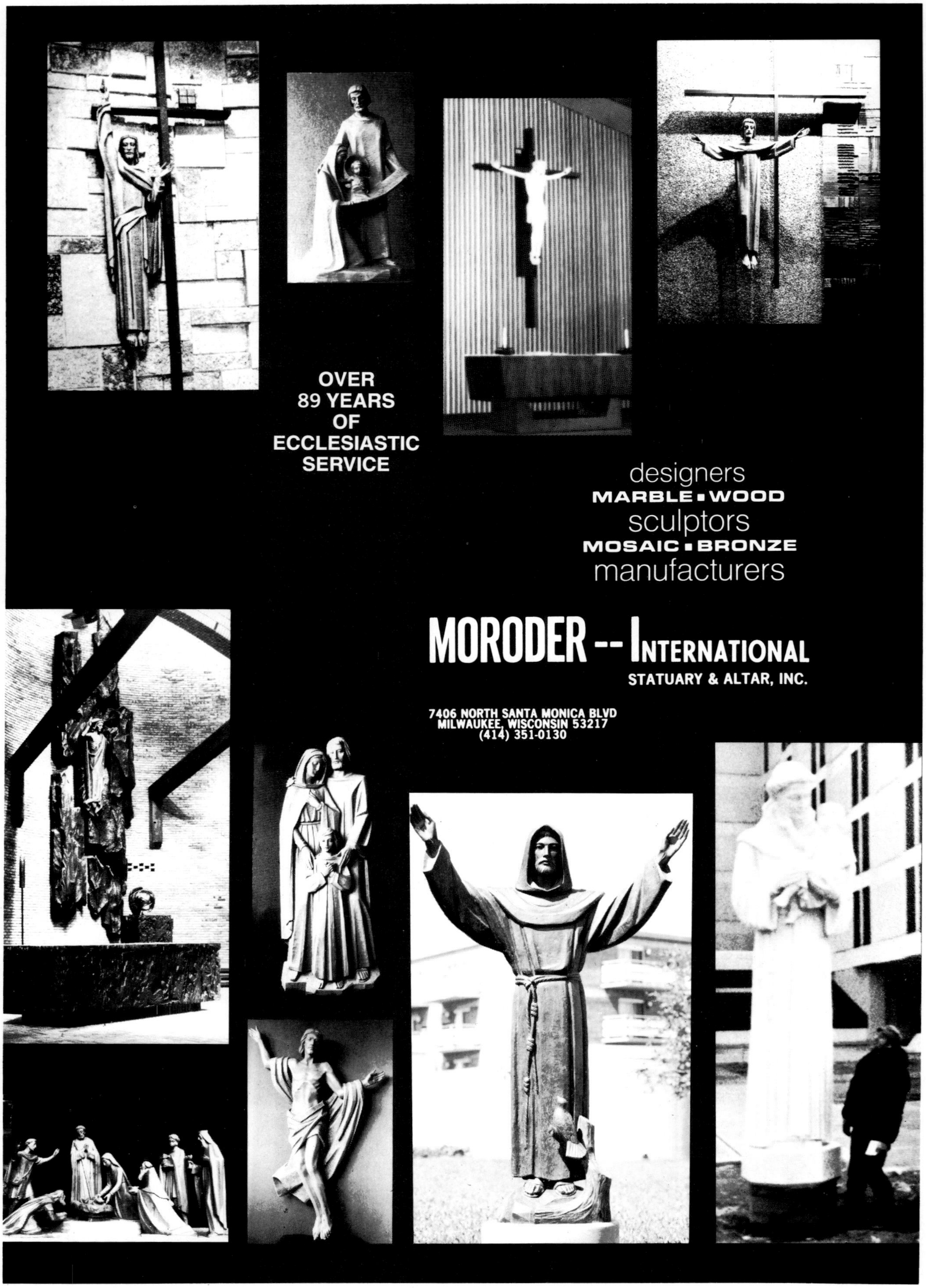
OVER
89 YEARS
OF
ECCLESIASTIC
SERVICE
designers
MARBLE ▪ WOOD
sculptors
MOSAIC ▪ BRONZE
manufacturers
MORODER -- INTERNATIONAL
STATUARY & ALTAR, INC.
7406 NORTH SANTA MONICA BLVD
MILWAUKEE, WISCONSIN 53217
(414) 351-0130

Baldwin C-470

Prestige G-505

Bevilacqua Pipe Organ

The Pontifical North American College

00120 Vatican City State
Europe
Rome Telephone: 011.39.6.684.931   Fax: 011.39.6.686.7561

Early in 1855, His Holiness Pope Pius IX advised the American hierarchy of his interest in seeing a national seminary established in Rome for the formation of candidates of the priesthood from the United States. On December 8, 1859, the feast of the Immaculate Conception of Mary, Pope Pius IX formally inaugurated the Pontifical North American College in a 16th century monastery building, which he had given to the bishops of America. Twelve young men were enrolled as the first class.

Today, nearly 200 seminarians and priests are studying in the Eternal City at the North American College, continuing the tradition of the initial twelve. And while the original 16th Century building is still in use, it is now the resident for our priests in graduate studies. Today's seminarians live, study, pray and are formed in a facility on the beautiful Janiculum Hill, overlooking St. Peter's Basilica. Allied with the North American in the intellectual and theological preparation of priests for the next millennium are a number of the finest theological universities, which are home of some of the world's foremost Catholic teachers and scholars.

The Institute for Continuing Theological Education

Twice a year, for three months in the Spring and Fall, the College offers a program of refreshment and renewal for those ordained a decade or more. Courses in theology, spirituality and pastoral care, among others, are offered along with sabbatical time for priests to share experiences and travel throughout Italy, other countries in Europe and the Holy Land. Applications are available for current and future sessions from the U.S.A. Development Office.

Administration

Rev. Msgr. Timothy M. Dolan, Ph.D., Rector; Rev. Msgr. Bernard E. Yarrish, S.T.L., Vice Rector for Administration; Rev. William Ogrodowski, Vice Rector for Student Life; Rev. Msgr. Charles W. Elmer, P.A., S.T.D., Director, Graduate Department; Rev. D. Terrence Morgan, S.T.L., Director, Institute for Continuing Theological Education.

Granda Liturgical Arts, Inc.

Quality Church Supplier from Europe, since 1891.

Manufacturers of:

- Chalices and ciboria.
- Tabernacles, monstrances.
- Candlesticks, lamps.
- Stations of the Cross, etc…

Statuary:

Wood carvings.

Vestments:

Chasubles, albs.

Interior design: Church decoration and renovation

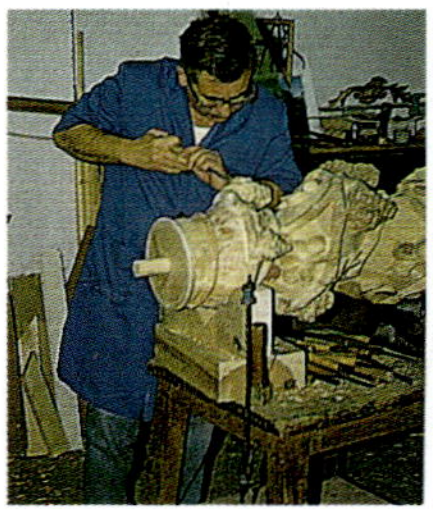

Wood carvings

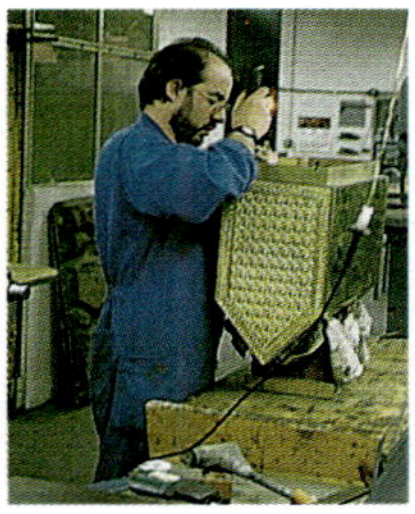

Silver work

Altars, church furniture, etc.

Vestments

Custom made orders: our specialty.

Some of our customers in USA:

- **Mother M. Angelica,** P.C.P.A., Abbess Our Lady of the Angels Monastery, Birmingham, Alabama.
- **St. Aloysius Church,** New Canaan, CT
- **St. John Fisher Seminary,** Stamford, CT
- **Christ the King Catholic Church,** Houston TX etc…

New Tabernacle for Holy Cross Cathedral Boston, MA.
Special design: gold plated finish, enamel decoration. The total height of the tabernacle is 42" and its square base measures 20" by 20". We also designed a matching sanctuary lamp.

GRANDA Liturgical Arts, Inc.
2525 Eastwood Avenue, Apt. 8-A
Evanston, Illinois 60201
Phone: 1-800-425.0828
Fax: (847) 492.1374
email: Ruf4granda@aol.com
http://www.hispacom.es/granda

FREE CATALOG (60 PAGES) OR CD-ROM AVAILABLE ON REQUEST

H3478

BC

BARTON~COTTON

DISTINCTIVE STATIONERY FOR THE RELIGIOUS AND CLERGY

FREE CATALOG NOW AVAILABLE!
FEATURING OVER 50 NEW PRODUCTS

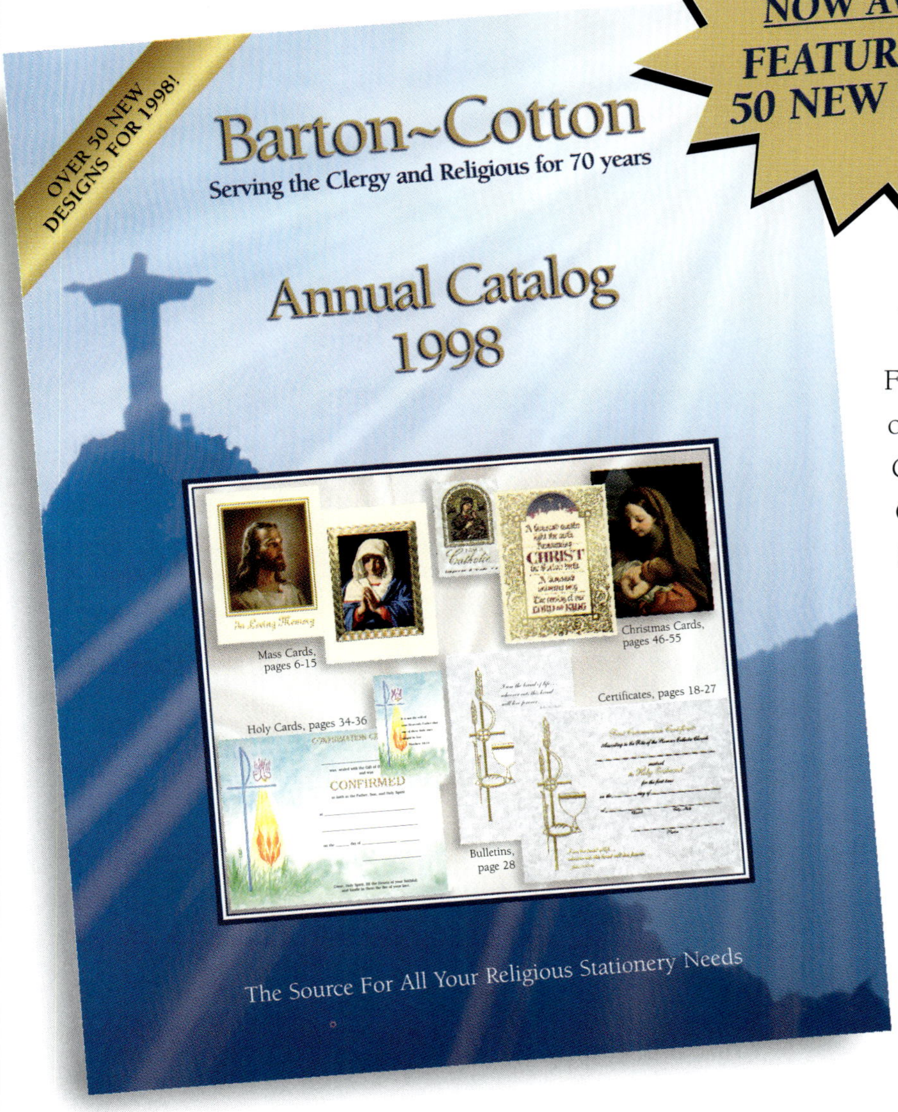

For 70 years, Barton~Cotton has offered quality Mass Cards, Certificates, Christmas Cards, Easter Cards, Mother's and Father's Day Sets, Devotional Booklets, Holy Cards, Letterhead, Bulletins, and Offering Envelopes!

- Time-saving imprinting options
- Friendly, professional customer service
- An **unconditional guarantee** for 100% satisfaction on over 300 products!

CALL TOLL-FREE **1-800-638-4652** TODAY
to request your FREE Catalog!

BARTON~COTTON • 1405 Parker Road • Baltimore, MD 21227 27F

Harvest Development, Inc.

We raise funds through Direct Solicitation and by Teaching the *Art of Solicitation* to our clients' Staff and Volunteers.

*And God will also supply you with all the seed you need and make it grow, to produce a rich **harvest** from your generosity.*

2 Corinthians 9:10

Harvest Development, Inc. is a national, full-service Catholic fundraising and professional consulting firm. We are *partners in development* and we are *fundraising educators.* Whatever your objective, **HDI** consultants cut to the heart of matters quickly and accurately with a keen eye for bottom line results.

Do you need a fresh independent perspective in your Fund Raising?...

- ❑ *Are you growing or declining rapidly?*
- ❑ *Looking to build your campaign on relationships rather than on slick sales presentations?*
- ❑ *Looking to properly match donors with your meaningful and worthwhile project?*
- ❑ *Failing to maintain donors or convert prospects?*
- ❑ *Opening new services to those you serve?*
- ❑ *Wanting to develop new ideas, strategies or plans?*
- ❑ *Experiencing a leadership change?*
- ❑ *In need of a Campaign Readiness Assessment?*

"

They assisted us with our 'Defining Moment Campaign' which raised $9.5-million in cash and pledges in one year. Their professionalism and willingness to roll up their sleeves and work side-by-side with us put both our staff and constituents at immediate ease.

Rev. Thomas A. Pesci, S.J., President
Rockhurst Jesuit High School

The highest standards of integrity, ethics, and honesty is what you will find when working with Harvest Development.

Mr. John E. Grimes, President/General Manager
Enterprise Rent-A-Car

Our Commitment

is to help our **non-profit, Catholic clients** to raise the funds that they need to fulfill their purpose and missions. It is our privilege to serve our clients who are seeking to raise **over $500,000.** Our clients success is HDI's success. When engaging HDI you're securing a development ally with positive beliefs, determination and high expectations. You're leveraging the talents, experience and resources of our firm for the highest return to your institution. You will receive:

- **Mutual Trust** and **Respect** given to you, your donors and your constituents;
- **Highest Quality Service** at the fairest investment;
- **Professionalism, Enthusiasm, Persistence** and a **Sense of Urgency**;
- **Action** – while maintaining a **Sensitivity** for all the people involved; realizing that personal relationships and common beliefs and values are at the heart of development work;
- **A belief** that people must be asked for support by the appropriate solicitor – be that a volunteer, board member President/Principal, development director, staff or HDI counsel.

Expect a trust-worthy, full-service partner when you contact us at

Harvest Development, Inc.
200 Executive Way
Ponte Vedra Beach, FL 32082 USA
or **888.828.9250** *or fax:* 904.285.1002
or e-mail: PaulDPVP@aol.com

Is your Parish ready for the coming millennium?

Our Parish Management Solutions Are!

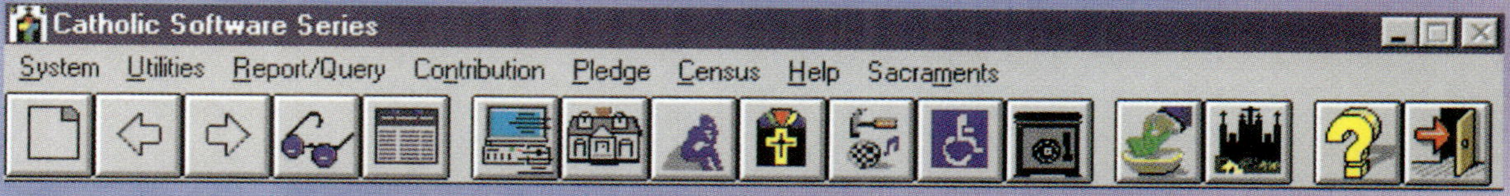

Intelligent, powerful, no training required, parish software

Very Simple

Conversions

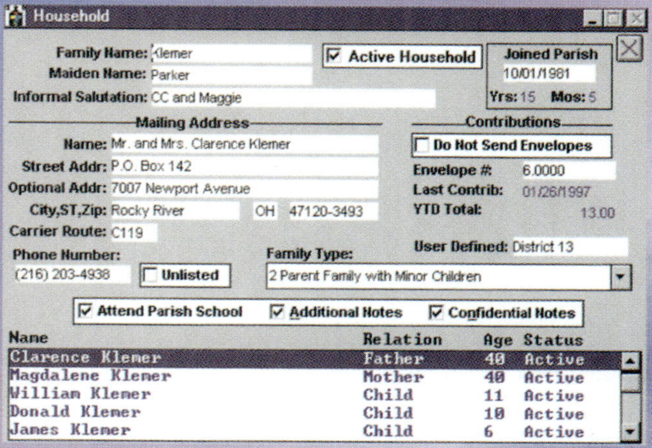

Affordable

Entry Wizard

Free Evaluation Software 1-800-428-3640

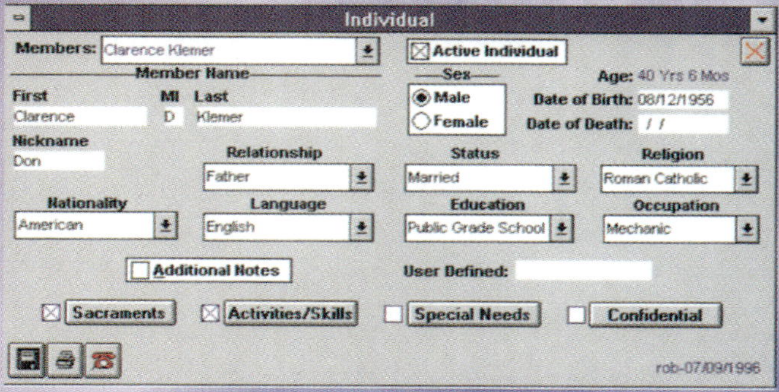

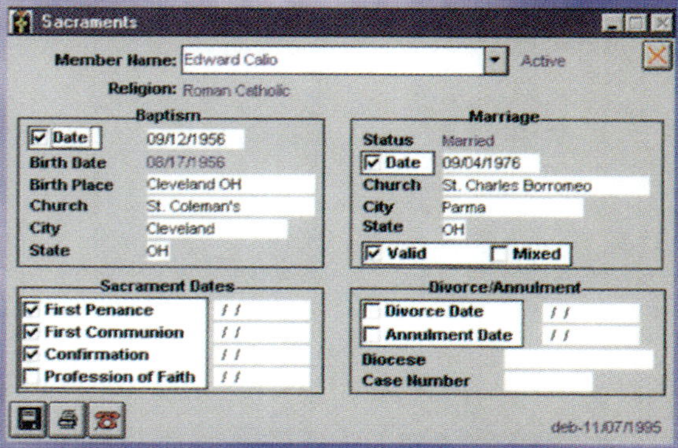

The Catholic
Software Co.

Suite 313, 3768 Rocky River Dr., Cleveland, OH 44111-4050 USA
800.428.3640 Fax: 216.671.1668 Web Site: www.catholicsoft.com

Next>>

See Alphabetical List of Priests section divider for more software information

CRUCIFIXION WINDOW - CIRCA 1908 44" X 156"
Attributed to D'Ascnzo Studio Philadelphia, PA
Outstanding example of superb workmanship in the Munich tradition.
Exquisitely hand painted and intricately multi-layered glass.

Catholic Travel Centre

'The Most Trusted Name in Religious Group Travel'

WHO IS CATHOLIC TRAVEL CENTRE?

Catholic Travel Centre has radically raised the definition of quality in religious group travel. We invite you to experience the quality and reliability that have christened us "the most trusted name in religious group travel!"

Our long list of repeat clientele includes prominent archdioceses, colleges, parishes and schools nationwide. Ask for our reference list!

HOW YOU CAN TRAVEL FOR FREE

As a group leader, with a minimum number of passengers, you travel FREE. And you'll 'sleep well' given our proven track record of high quality, legendary efficiency and excellent prices.

Call us to plan your trip to Rome, the Holy Land, Lourdes or any of the more than 20 countries we proudly serve for the Catholic community.

OBERAMMERGAU AND JUBILEE 2000

Call our Jubilee 2000 Specialty Department to begin planning your trip to:

- Oberammergau's Passion Play 2000
- Jubilee Pilgrimages to Rome
- Millennium Journeys to the Holy Land
- World Youth Day in Rome 2000
- Oberammergau & Rome Jubilee Combination

Catholic Travel Centre

Worldwide Tours and Pilgrimages

Los Angeles Headquarters

7100 Hayvenhurst Ave., Suite 107, Van Nuys, CA 91406

Tel: (818) 909-9910 Fax: (818) 909-0486

E-mail: CTCTWT@aol.com

800-553-5233

Ask for Scott, Inga or Yvonne.

Serenity®

Reverent

~

Enduring

~

Quality

Permanent Seating ♦ Flexible Design

Saint Clare's Church -- Santa Clara, California

Features

- ✓ Cushion-Loc Seating
  Replaceable Upholstery
- ✓ **Serenity**® Kneelers
  Hydraulically Silenced
- ✓ Open or Closed Back
- ✓ Pew Ends Available
- ✓ Bookracks
- ✓ Card & Pencil Inserts
- ✓ Prie Dieux - Frontals

WALTER JACOBI AND SONS, INC.

Phone: (800) 522 - 6241
Web Page: http://www.serenity-wjs.com

Belmont, CA 94002-0471

FAX (650) 592-2434
Email: sales@serenity-wjs.com

Church Chair Industries, Inc.

Cathedral Stacker

Free Chair Test Compare
(100+)

Plush, tall backs over 1/2" plywood.

Royal Stacker

Free Lumbar Back Support

Now Only
$24.25
100+

Now Only
$25.75
100+

Plush 4 & 5" deep foam seats over 1/2" plywood.

Design Stacker #1

Oak Pew Chair

*Call **1-800-331-5411***
For Free Catalog & Steel
Frame Sample Chair

GREAT PEW LIKE CHAIRS OAK OR STEEL FRAMES
LOCKS TOGETHER TO FORM A CONTINUOUS BENCH

DESIGN PATENT NO.
DES. 333,7333

OPTIONS
Arms
Kneelers
Book & Card Pockets

7007 New Calhoun Rd. • Rome, Georgia 30161 • 1-800-331-5411

JOIN A
GLOBAL MINISTRY
Air Force chaplains go where Air Force personnel are located around the world. Take the challenge of your ministry to a new level in the global military community. Your parish may be wherever our troops are called to serve — on the deserts of Iraq or the snow fields of Alaska. Now more than ever, we need qualified priests as a sign of the church for our military to provide sacramental and pastoral care to members and their families. Military in the next century will be shaped by unforeseen challenges and limitless opportunities. The Air Force is urgently looking for priests as chaplains. If you would be interested in the contemporary military opportunities in the Air Force and want to be part of creating a Global Ministry call 1-800-803-2452.
AIR FORCE
CHAPLAIN SERVICE

This complete catalog is available at your exclusive Stadelmaier dealer. Please see section devider, Catholic Church in U.S., for locations.

STADELMAIER
NIJMEGEN

Stadelmaier Nijmegen BV
Lagelandseweg 64, 6545 CG Nijmegen, Holland
tel. +31.24.3791170, fax +31.24.3791171
Email: stadelmaier@telebyte.nl

THE I.T. VERDIN CO., CINCINNATI, OHIO

TABLE OF CONTENTS

The Official Catholic Directory

for the Year of Our Lord

1998

GIVING STATUS OF THE CATHOLIC CHURCH AS OF JANUARY 1, 1998

Containing Ecclesiastical Statistics of

THE UNITED STATES, PUERTO RICO,
THE VIRGIN ISLANDS, AGANA, CAROLINE AND MARSHALL ISLANDS,
FOREIGN MISSIONARY ACTIVITIES, CANADA, AND MEXICO.

The information contained in this Directory is derived from reports submitted to the publishers by the ecclesiastical authorities of the countries concerned, and neither the publishers nor the ecclesiastical authorities assume responsibility for any errors or omissions.

THE OFFICIAL CATHOLIC DIRECTORY · P. J. KENEDY & SONS · 1817

P. J. KENEDY & SONS

Publishers to the Holy Apostolic See

For inquiries call: 908-665-3500
or write: 121 Chanlon Rd., New Providence, NJ 07974
To place an order call: 1-800-521-8110

The 1998 edition of *The Official Catholic Directory* was prepared by National Register Publishing's Database Publishing Group.

Publisher's Staff:
Publisher: John R. Agel
Managing Editor: Jeanne Hanline

Editorial Staff:
Senior Editorial Director: Thomas M. Bachmann
Managing Editor: Christina Fry Moxley
Senior Editor: Joseph C. Stewart
Associate Editor: Kathleen F. Jurcsek
Assistant Editor: Faith Shepherd
Editorial Assistants: Marlene Boyd, Stephanie Fragati, Michael Gianella, Linda Hummer, Melanie Koserowski, Elizabeth W. Marsh, Diane R. Moxley
Freelance Production Editor: Frank McDermott

Editorial Systems:
Vice-President, Information Technology: John Roney
Director, Biographical & Reference Systems: Carter McWilliams
Manager, Reference & Biographic Systems: Helene Davis

Photo of His Holiness The Pope courtesy of Arturo Mari, L'Osservatore Romano.

Published by P.J. Kenedy & Sons in association with National Register Publishing, a division of Reed Elsevier Inc.

Chief Operating Officer: Lou Andreozzi
Vice-President & Publisher: Randy H. Mysel
Vice-President, Database Production: Dean Hollister

Printed and bound in the United States of America
International Standard Book Number: 0-87217-963-X
International Standard Serial Number: 0078-3854
Library of Congress Catalog Card Number: 81-30961

CONTENTS

Part I

Part II
UNITED STATES

ARCHDIOCESES AND DIOCESES
(Archdioceses are in Boldface)

MISCELLANEOUS

EASTERN CHURCHES

TERRITORIAL SEES

Part III

CANADA AND MEXICO

Part IV

THE ARCHDIOCESES AND DIOCESES OF THE UNITED STATES—BY STATES

A—Indicates Archdiocese. The Archdiocese of Washington includes the District of Columbia and five Counties of Maryland. Dioceses traverse state lines in the following instances only: Cheyenne includes all of Yellowstone National Park;S Norwich includes Fisher's Island, NY; Wilmington includes the eastern shores of Maryland and Gallup includes parts of Arizona and New Mexico.

Religious Order Initials for Men

A.A.	Assumptionists	[0130]
B.C.S.	Brothers of Christian Service	[]
B.G.S.	Little Brothers of the Good Shepherd	[0580]
B.S.O.	Basilian Salvatorian Fathers	[0190]
C.F.A.	Alexian Brothers	[0120]
C.F.C.	Congregation of Christian Brothers	[0310]
C.F.M.M.	Brothers of Our Lady, Mother of Mercy	[0980]
C.F.P.	Brothers of the Poor of St. Francis	[0460]
C.F.R.	Franciscan Friars of the Renewal	[0535]
C.F.X.	Brothers of St. Francis Xavier	[1350]
C.I.C.M.	Missionhurst Congregation of the Immaculate Heart of Mary	[0860]
C.J.	Josephite Fathers	[0710]
C.J.M.	Congregation of Jesus and Mary	[0450]
C.M.	Congregation of the Mission	[1330]
C.M.C.	Congregation of Mother Coredemptrix	[]
C.M.F.	Claretian Missionaries	[0360]
C.M.I.	Carmelites of Mary Immaculate	[0275]
C.M.L.M.	The Congregation of Maronite Lebanese Missionaries	[0785]
C.M.M.	Congregation of Marianhill Missionaries, Marianhill Fathers & Brothers	[0750]
C.M.Vd.	Mekhitarist Fathers	[]
C.O.	Oratorians	[0950]
C.P.	Congregation of the Passion	[1000]
C.P.M.	Congregation of the Fathers of Mercy	[0820]
C.PP.S.	Society of the Precious Blood	[1060]
C.R.	Congregation of the Resurrection	[1080]
C.R.	Theatine Fathers	[1300]
C.R.I.C.	Canons Regular of the Immaculate Conception	[]
C.R.L.	Canons Regular of the Lateran	[0250]
C.R.M.	Adorno Fathers	[0100]
C.R.S.	Somascan Fathers	[1250]
C.R.S.P.	Clerics Regular of St. Paul	[0160]
C.S.	Missionaries of St. Charles-Scalabrinians	[1210]
C.S.B.	Basilian Fathers	[0170]
C.S.C.	Brothers of the Congregation of Holy Cross	[0600]
C.S.C.	Priests of the Congregation of Holy Cross	[0610]
C.S.J.	Congregation of St. Joseph	[1150]
C.S.J.B.	Congregation of St. John the Baptist	[]
C.S.P.	Paulist Fathers	[1030]
C.S.P.X.	Brothers of Saint Pius X	[1180]
C.S.S.	Stigmatine Fathers and Brothers	[1280]
C.S.Sp.	Holy Ghost Fathers	[0650]
C.SS.R.	Redemptorist Fathers	[1070]
C.S.V.	Clerics of St. Viator	[1320]
D.L.P.	Diocesan Labor Priests	[]
Er.Cam.	Camaldolese Hermits of the Congregation of Monte Corona	[0230]
F.C.	Brothers of Charity	[0290]
F.D.P.	Sons of Divine Providence	[0410]
F.F.I.	Franciscan Friars of the Immaculate	[0533]
F.F.S.C.	Franciscan Brothers of the Holy Cross	[0510]
F.I.C.	Brothers of Christian Instruction	[0320]
F.J.	Congregation of St. John	[]
F.M.M.	Brothers of Mercy	[0810]
F.M.M.	Missionary Fraternity of Mary	[]
F.M.S.	The Marist Brothers	[0770]
F.M.S.I.	Sons of Mary Missionary Society	[1270]
F.P.M.	Presentation Brothers	[]
F.S.C.	Brothers of the Christian Schools	[0330]
F.S.E.	Brothers of the Holy Eucharist	[0620]
F.S.P.	Brothers of St. Patrick	[1160]
F.S.R.	Brothers of the Congregation of Our Lady of the Holy Rosary	[0960]
F.S.S.P.	Priestly Fraternity of St. Peter	[1065]
Glmy.	The Glenmary Home Missioners	[0570]
H.J.D.	Los Hermanos de Juan Diego	[]
H.M.C.	Hermits of Mount Carmel	[]
I.C.	Institute of Charity	[0300]
I.C.	Incarnational Consecration	[]
I.H.M.	Brothers of the Immaculate Heart of Mary	[0680]
I.M.C.	Consolata Missionaries	[0390]
I.S.S.S.	Schoenstatt Institute of Secular Priests	[]
L.B.S.F.	Little Brothers of Saint Francis	[1144]
L.C.	Legionaries of Christ	[0730]
M.Afr.	Missionaries of Africa	[0850]
M.C.B.S.	Missionary Congregation of the Blessed Sacrament	[]
M.C.C.J.	Comboni Missionaries of the Heart of Jesus (Verona)	[0380]
M.Des.	Mercedarios Descalzos	[]
M.E.P.	Paris Foreign Mission Society	[0897]
M.G.	Guadalupe Missioners	[]
M.H.M.	Mill Hill Missionaries	[0830]
M.I.C.	Congregation of Marians of the Immaculate Conception	[0740]
M.J.	Missionaries of St. Joseph (Mexico)	[]
M.M.	Maryknoll	[0800]
M.S.	The Missionaries of Our Lady of La Salette	[0720]
M.S.C.	Missionaries of the Sacred Heart	[1110]
M.S.F.	Congregation of the Missionaries of the Holy Family	[0630]
M.S.P.	Missionaries of St. Paul	[]
M.Sp.S.	Missionaries of the Holy Spirit	[0660]
M.Ss.A.	Missionaries of the Holy Apostles	[0590]
M.SS.CC.	Missionaries of the Sacred Hearts of Jesus and Mary	[1120]
O.A.R.	Order of the Augustinian Recollects	[0150]
O.Carm.	Carmelite Fathers and Brothers	[0270]
O.Cart.	Order of Carthusians	[0280]
O.C.D.	Discalced Carmelite Fathers	[0260]
O.Cist.	Cistercian Fathers	[0340]
O.C.S.O.	The Cistercian Order of the Strict Observance (Trappists)	[0350]
O.de.M.	Order of Our Lady of Mercy	[0970]
O.F.M.	Franciscan Friars	[0520]
O.F.M.Cap.	The Capuchin Friars	[0470]
O.F.M.Conv.	Conventual Franciscans	[0480]
O.H.	Hospitaller Brothers of St. John of God	[0670]
O.I.C.	Order of the Imitation of Christ	[]
O.L.P.	Brothers of Our Lady of Providence	[]
O.M.	Minim Fathers	[0835]
O.Mar.	Congregation of Maronite Monks	[0790]
O.M.I.	Oblates of Mary Immaculate	[0910]
O.M.V.	Oblates of the Virgin Mary	[0940]
O.P.	Order of Preachers (Dominicans)	[0430]
O.Praem.	Canons Regular of Premontre	[0900]
O.R.C.	Operarios del Reina de Cristo	[]
O.S.A.	The Augustinians	[0140]
O.S.B.	Benedictine Monks	[0200]
O.S.B.Cam.	Camaldolese Hermits	[]
O.S.B.M.	Order of St. Basil the Great	[0180]
O.S.C.	Canons Regular of the Order of the Holy Cross	[0400]
O.S.Cam.	Camillian Fathers and Brothers	[0240]
O.S.F.	Congregation of the Religious Brothers of the Third Order Regular of St. Francis	[0490]
O.S.F.	Franciscan Brothers of Christ the King	[0500]
O.S.F.	Franciscan Brothers of the Third Order Regular	[0515]
O.S.F.	Franciscan Missionary Brothers of the Sacred Heart of Jesus	[0540]
O.S.F.S.	Oblates of St. Francis de Sales	[0920]
O.S.J.	Oblates of St. Joseph	[0930]
O.S.M.	Servites	[1240]
O.S.P.P.E.	Pauline Fathers	[1010]
O.Ss.S.	Brigittine Monks	[0895]
O.SS.T.	Order of the Holy Trinity	[1310]
P.I.M.E.	Pontifical Institute for Foreign Missions	[1050]
R.C.J.	Rogationist Fathers	[1090]
S.A.	Franciscan Friars of the Atonement	[0530]
S.A.C.	Society of the Catholic Apostolate	[0990]
S.C.	Brothers of the Sacred Heart	[1100]
S.C.	Servants of Charity	[1220]
S.Ch.	Society of Christ	[1260]
Sch.P.	Piarist Fathers	[1040]
S.C.J.	Congregation of the Priests of the Sacred Heart	[1130]
S.D.B.	Salesians of Don Bosco	[1190]
S.D.S.	Society of the Divine Savior	[1200]
S.D.V.	Vocationist Fathers	[1340]
S.F.	Sons of the Holy Family	[0640]
S.F.M.	Scarboro Foreign Missions	[]
S.J.	Jesuit Fathers and Brothers	[0690]
S.M.	Society of Mary (Marianists)	[0760]
S.M.	Marist Fathers	[0780]
S.M.A.	Society of African Missions	[0110]
S.M.M.	Montfort Missionaries	[0870]
S.M.P.	Society of Our Mother of Peace	[]
S.O.Cist.	Cistercian Monks of the Strict Observance	[]
S.O.L.T.	Society of Our Lady of the Most Holy Trinity	[0975]
s.P.	Servants of the Paraclete	[1230]
S.P.S.	St. Patrick Missionary Society	[1170]
S.S.	Society of the Priests of Saint Sulpice	[1290]
S.S.C.	Society of St. Columban	[0370]
SS.CC.	Congregation of the Sacred Hearts of Jesus and Mary	[1140]
S.S.E.	Society of Saint Edmund	[0440]
S.S.J.	St. Joseph's Society of the Sacred Heart	[0700]
S.S.P.	Pauline Fathers and Brothers	[1020]
S.S.S.	Congregation of the Blessed Sacrament	[0220]
S.S.T.	Missionary Society of St. Thomas the Apostle	[]
S.T.	Missionary Servants of the Most Holy Trinity	[0840]
S.X.	Xaverian Missionary Fathers	[1360]
S.V.D.	Society of the Divine Word	[0420]
T.O.R.	Third Order Regular of Saint Francis	[0560]
V.C.	Vincentian Congregation (India)	[]
V.D.C.	Verbum Dei Community	[]

Religious Order Initials for Women

A.B.S.	Auxiliaries of the Blessed Sacrament	[]
A.C.J.	Handmaids of the Sacred Heart of Jesus	[1870]
A.D.	Sisters of the Lamb of God	[2260]
A.I.M.	Association of Mary Immaculate	[]
A.N.G.	A New Genesis	[]
A.P.	Nuns of Perpetual Adoration of Blessed Sacrament	[3190]
A.P.B.	Adorers of the Precious Blood	[0110]
A.P.G.	Sisters of Perpetual Adoration	[3195]
A.R.	Handmaids of the Sacred Heart of Jesus for Reparation	[1880]
A.R.	Augustinian Recollects	[]
A.S.C.	Adorers of the Blood of Christ	[0100]
A.S.C.J.	Apostles of the Sacred Heart of Jesus	[0130]
B.C.	Notre Dame du Bon Conseil (Quebec)	[]
Bethl.	Bethlemita, Daughters of the Sacred Heart of Jesus	[0910]
B.V.M.	Sisters of Charity of Blessed Virgin Mary	[0430]
B.V.M.C.	Blessed Virgin Missionaries of Carmel	[]
C.ach.	Carmelite Sisters of Charity	[0340]
Carmel.D.C.J.	Carmelite Sisters of the Divine Heart of Jesus	[0360]
C.B.S.	Congregation of Bon Secours	[0270]
C.C.	Carmel Community	[0310]
C.C.V.I.	Sisters of Charity of Incarnate Word	[0460]
C.C.V.I.	Sisters of Charity of Incarnate Word, Houston, TX	[0470]
C.C.W.	Carmelite Community of the Word	[0315]
C.D.P.	Sisters of Divine Providence	[0990]
C.D.P.	Sisters of Divine Providence of Kentucky	[1000]
C.D.P.	Sisters of Divine Providence of San Antonio, TX	[1010]
C.D.P.	Capuchin Sisters (Spain)	[]
C.D.S.	Congregation of Divine Spirit	[1040]
C.F.M.M.	Minim Daughters of Mary Immaculate	[2675]
C.F.P.	Feminine Congregation of the Passion	[]
C.F.P.	Mexican Passionist Sisters	[]
C.G.S.	Contemplatives of Good Shepherd	[1830]
C.H.F.	Sisters of Holy Faith	[1940]
C.H.M.	Congregation of Humility of Mary	[2100]
C.H.S.	Community of the Holy Spirit	[2020]
C.I.C.	Sisters of Immaculate Conception	[2120]
C.I.J.	Congregation of Infant Jesus	[2230]
C.J.C.	Poor Sisters of Jesus Crucified and Sorrowful Mother	[3240]
C.K.	School Sisters of Christ the King	[]
C.L.H.C.	Congregation of Our Lady Help of the Clergy	[3090]
C.M.C.	Congregation of Mother of Carmel	[]
C.M.R.	Congregation of Mary Queen	[]
C.M.S.	Comboni Missionary Sisters	[0690]
C.M.S.	Cashel Mercy Sisters	[2515]
C.M.S.T.	Missionary Carmelites of St. Teresa	[0390]
C.N.D.	Congregation of Notre Dame	[2980]
C.O.C.	Companions of Christ	[]
C.P.	Religious of the Passion of Jesus Christ	[3170]
C.P.	Sisters of the Cross and Passion	[3180]
C.P.C.	Capuchin Poor Clares	[]
C.P.C.	St. Clare Capuchin Sisters	[]
C.PP.S.	Sisters of the Precious Blood (Dayton, Ohio)	[3260]
C.PP.S.	Sisters of the Most Precious Blood (O'Fallon, MO)	[3270]
C.P.S.	Missionary Sisters of the Precious Blood	[2850]
C.R.	Sisters of the Resurrection	[3480]
C.S.	Company of the Savior	[0710]
C.S.	The Christian Sisters (Pious Union)	[]
C.S.A.	Sisters of Charity of St. Augustine	[0580]
C.S.A.	Sisters of St. Agnes	[3710]
C.S.A.	Albertine Sisters (Krakow, Poland)	[]
C.S.A.C.	Sisters of the Catholic Apostolate (Pallottine)	[3140]
C.S.B.	Congregation of St. Brigid	[3735]
C.S.C.	Congregation of Sisters of Holy Cross	[1920]
C.S.C.	Sisters of Holy Cross	[1930]
C.S.C.	Sisters of Holy Cross and Seven Dolors	[]
C.S.E.	Carmelite Sisters of the Eucharist	[]
C.S.F.N.	Sisters of Holy Family of Nazareth	[1970]
C.S.J.	Sisters of St. Joseph (Boston, Brighton)	[3830-01]
C.S.J.	Sisters of St. Joseph (Chicago, Lagrange Park)	[3830-02]
C.S.J.	Sisters of St. Joseph (Orange)	[3830-03]
C.S.J.	Sisters of St. Joseph (Rockville Centre, Brentwood)	[3830-05]
C.S.J.	Sisters of St. Joseph (Cleveland)	[3830-08]
C.S.J.	Sisters of St. Joseph (Lafayette, IN)	[3830-10]
C.S.J.	Sisters of St. Joseph (Pittsburgh, Baden)	[3830-13]
C.S.J.	Sisters of St. Joseph (Salina, Concordia)	[3830-15]
C.S.J.	Sisters of St. Joseph (Wichita)	[3830-18]
C.S.J.	Sisters of St. Joseph of Carondelet	[3840]
C.S.J.	Sisters of St. Joseph of Chambery	[3850]
C.S.J.	Sisters of St. Joseph (Lyons, France)	[3870]
C.S.J.	Sisters of St. Joseph of Medaille	[3880]
C.S.J.B.	Sisters of St. John the Baptist	[3820]
C.S.J.P.	Sisters of St. Joseph of Peace	[3890]
C.S.M.	Sisters of St. Martha of Antigonish N.S.	[3937]
C.S.N.	Congregation of Sisters of Nazareth	[]
C.S.R.	Sisters of Holy Redeemer	[2000]
C.S.S.F.	Felician Sisters	[1170]
C.S.Sp.	Sisters of Holy Spirit	[2030]
C.S.S.T.	Carmelite Sisters of St. Teresa	[]
C.S.T.	Carmelite Sisters of St. Therese of Infant Jesus	[0380]
C.V.D.	Sisters of Bethany	[0250]
C.V.I.	Congregation of Incarnate Word and Blessed Sacrament	[2190]
C.V.I.	Religious of the Incarnate Word	[3449]
D.C.	Daughters of Charity of St. Vincent de Paul	[0760]
D.C.	Daughters of the Cross	[0770]
D.C.M.	Diocesan Carmelites of Maine	[]
D.C.P.B.	Daughters of Charity of Most Precious Blood	[0740]
D.H.M.	Daughters of Heart of Mary	[0810]
D.H.S.	Daughters of the Holy Spirit	[0820]
D.L.F.	Daughters of Our Lady of Fatima	[]
D.L.J.C.	Disciples of the Lord Jesus Christ	[0965]
D.M.	Daughters of Mary of the Immaculate Conception	[0860]
D.M.	Daughters of Our Lady of Mercy	[0890]
D.M.I.	Daughters of Mary Immaculate (Chaldean)	[]
D.M.J.	Daughters of Mary and Joseph	[0880]
D.O.M.	Daughters of Mercy (Croatian)	[]
D.S.F.	Daughters of St. Francis of Assisi	[0920]
D.S.M.P.	Daughters of St. Mary of Providence	[0940]
D.W.	Daughters of Wisdom	[0960]
E.F.M.S.	Eucharistic Franciscan Missionary Sisters	[1150]
E.M.S.	Eucharistic Missionary Society	[]
F.A.S.	Franciscan Apostolic Sisters	[]
F.C.	Daughters of the Cross of Liege	[0780]
F.C.J.	Society of Sisters Faithful Companions of Jesus	[4048]
F.C.S.C.J.	Daughters of Charity of the Sacred Heart of Jesus	[0750]
F.D.C.	Daughters of Divine Charity	[0790]
Fd.CC.	Canossian Daughters of Charity	[0730]
F.D.L.P.	Daughters of Providence	[]
F.D.N.S.C.	Daughters of Our Lady of the Sacred Heart	[0900]
F.D.P.	Daughters of Divine Providence	[0800]
F.D.Z.	Daughters of Divine Zeal	[0795]
F.H.I.C.	Franciscan Hospitaller Sisters of the Immaculate Conception	[1270]
F.H.M.	Franciscan Handmaids of the Most Pure Heart of Mary	[1260]
F.H.M.	Franciscan Sisters Daughters of Mercy	[1235]
F.I.	Daughters of Jesus	[0840]
F.J.	Congregation of the Daughters of Jesus	[0830]
F.L.G.	Franciscan Sisters of Our Lady of Grace	[]
F.M.A.	Daughters of Mary Help of Christians	[0850]
F.M.D.C.	Franciscan Missionaries of the Divine Child	[1340]
F.M.I.	Congregation of the Daughters of Mary Immaculate (Marianist Sisters)	[0870]
F.M.I.	Franciscan Sisters of Mary Immaculate of the Third Order of St. Francis of Assisi	[1500]
F.M.I.J.	Franciscan Missionaries of the Infant Jesus	[1365]
F.M.M.	The Franciscan Missionaries of Mary	[1370]
F.M.S.C.	Franciscan Missionary Sisters of the Sacred Heart	[1400]
F.M.S.J.	Mill Hill Sisters	[1410]
F.M.S.R.	Daughters of Our Lady of Holy Rosary	[]
F.N.S.S.C.	Franciscan Sisters of Our Lady of the Sacred Heart	[]
F.S.E.	The Institute of the Franciscan Sisters of the Eucharist	[1250]
F.S.J.	Religious Daughters of St. Joseph	[0930]
F.S.M.	Franciscan Sisters of Mary	[1415]
F.S.O.L.	Franciscan Sisters of Our Lady	[]
F.S.P.	Pious Society Daughters of St. Paul	[0950]
F.S.P.	Franciscan Sisters of Peace	[1425]
F.S.P.A.	Congregation of the Sisters of the Third Order of St. Francis of Perpetual Adoration	[1780]
F.S.R.	Franciscan Sisters of Ringwood	[1420]
F.S.S.C.	Franciscan Sisters of St. Clare (Pious Union)	[]
F.S.S.E.	Franciscan Sisters of St. Elizabeth	[1460]
F.S.S.J.	Franciscan Sisters of St. Joseph	[1470]
F.S.S.J.	Franciscan Sisters of St. Joseph	[1480]
F.S.S.M.	Franciscan Sisters of the Sorrowful Mother	[]
F.S.Sp.J.	Franciscan Sisters of the Spirit of Jesus	[]
G.H.M.S.	Home Mission Sisters of America (Glenmary)	[2080]
G.N.S.H.	Grey Nuns of the Sacred Heart	[1840]
H.B.S.	Hermanas Contemplativas del Buen Pastor	[]
H.C.G.	Hermanas Catequistas Guadalupanas	[1900]
H.F.deS.J.	Franciscan Sisters of St. Joseph (Mexico City)	[]
H.G.S.	Congregation de Hermanas Guadalupanas de la Salle	[]
H.H.S.	Society of Helpers	[1890]
H.J.	Hermanas Josefinas	[1910]
H.J.D.	Las Hermanas de Juan Diego	[]
H.M.	Sisters of the Humility of Mary	[2110]
H.M.C.	Hermits of Mount Carmel	[]
H.M.S.S.	Sisters of Mercy of the Blessed Sacrament	[2590]
H.M.S.S.	Religious Sisters of the Apostolate of the Blessed Sacrament	[3370]
H.O.Carm.	Hermits of Our Lady of Mt. Carmel	[]
H.P.B.	Congregation of the Handmaids of the Precious Blood	[1860]
H.R.F.	Sisters of the Holy Rosary of Fatima (Mexico)	[]
H.S.H.	Handmaids of the Sacred Heart of Pohang	[]
H.S.M.	Hermit Sisters of Mary	[]
H.Sp.S.	Daughters of the Holy Spirit Nazareth of the Good Shepherd	[]
H.S.S.	Hermanas del Servico Social	[]
H.S.S.R.	Hermit Sisters of Romuald	[]
H.T.	Handmaids of the Most Holy Trinity	[]
H.V.M.	Sisters, Home Visitors of Mary	[2090]
I.B.V.M.	Institute of the Blessed Virgin Mary (Loretto Sisters)	[2370]
I.B.V.M.	Institute of the Blessed Virgin Mary (Loretto Sisters)	[2380]
I.C.	Vietnamese Sisters Incarnational Consecration	[]
I.C.M.	Missionary Sisters of the Immaculate Heart of Mary	[2750]
I.H.M.	Sisters, Servants of the Immaculate Heart of Mary	[2150]
I.H.M.	Sisters, Servants of the Immaculate Heart of Mary	[2160]
I.H.M.	Sisters, Servants of the Immaculate Heart of Mary	[2170]
I.H.M.	Sisters, Servants of the Immaculate Heart of Mary	[2180]

I.H.M.	The California Institute of the Sisters of the Most Holy and Immaculate Heart of the Blessed Virgin Mary	[2930]
I.H.M.	Sisters of the Most Holy and Immaculate Heart of Blessed Virgin Mary (Wichita Foundation)	[]
I.J.	Sisters of the Infant Jesus	[2240]
I.M.	Sisters of Charity of the Infant Mary	[]
I.S.S.M.	Secular Institute of Schoenstatt Sisters of Mary	[]
I.W.B.S.	Congregation of the Incarnate Word and Blessed Sacrament	[2200]
I.W.B.S.	Congregation of the Incarnate Word and Blessed Sacrament	[2205]
J.S.O.P.	Dominican Oblates of Jesus (Spain)	[]
L.B.	Ladies of Bethany	[]
L.C.M.	Sisters of the Little Company of Mary	[2270]
L.H.C.	Lovers of the Holy Cross Sisters	[2390]
L.M.S.C.	Little Missionary Sisters of Charity	[2290]
L.S.	Lasallian Sisters (Vietnam)	[]
L.S.A.	Little Sisters of the Assumption	[2310]
L.S.G.	Little Sisters of the Gospel (France)	[]
L.S.I.C.	Little Servant Sisters of the Immaculate Conception	[2300]
L.S.J.	Little Sisters of Jesus	[2330]
L.S.J.M.	Little Sisters of Jesus and Mary	[2331]
L.S.P.	Little Sisters of the Poor	[2340]
M.C.	Consolata Missionary Sisters	[0720]
M.C.	Missionaries of Charity	[2710]
M.C.	Poor Clare Missionary Sisters	[2840]
M.C.D.P.	Missionary Catechists of Divine Providence, San Antonio, TX	[2690]
M.C.M.	Cordi Marian Sisters	[]
M.C.P.	Missioneras Catequestas de los Pobres	[]
M.C.S.	Missionary Sisters of the Sacred Side	[]
M.C.S.J.M.	Congregation of Missionary Catechists of the Sacred Heart of Jesus and Mary	[]
M.D.	Mothers of the Helpless	[]
M.D.P.V.M.	Missionary Daughters of the Most Pure Virgin Mary	[]
M.E.	Missionary Ecumenical (Rome)	[]
M.C.SS.CC.J.M.	Missionary Catechists of the Sacred Hearts of Jesus and Mary	[2700]
M.E.S.S.T.	Eucharistic Missionaries of the Most Holy Trinity	[]
M.E.S.T.	Eucharistic Missionaries of St. Theresa (Mexico)	[]
M.F.P.	Franciscan Missionaries Our Lady of Peace	[]
M.G.Sp.S.	Guadalupan Missionaries of the Holy Spirit	[1845]
M.H.S.	Sisters of the Most Holy Sacrament	[2940]
M.H.S.H.	Mission Helpers of the Sacred Heart	[2720]
M.I.C.	Missionary Sisters of the Immaculate Conception (Canada)	[]
M.J.	Missionary Sisters of Jesus	[]
M.J.M.J.	Missionaries of Jesus, Mary and Joseph	[2770]
M.M.	Maryknoll Sisters of St. Dominic	[2470]
M.M.D.	Servite Missionary Sisters of the Sorrowful Mother	[]
M.M.M.	Medical Missionaries of Mary	[2480]
M.M.S.	Medical Mission Sisters	[2490]
M.O.M.	Missionary Sisters of Our Lady of Mercy	[2830]
M.P.F.	Religious Teachers Filippini	[3430]
M.P.H.	Missionary Sisters of Our Lady of Perpetual Help	[]
M.P.S.	Misioneras del Perpetual Socorro	[]
M.P.S.	Missionary Sisters of Our Lady of Perpetual Help	[]
M.P.V.	Religious Venerini Sisters	[4180]
M.R.	Marianist Sisters	[]
M.S.	Marian Sisters of the Diocese of Lincoln	[2400]
M.S.B.T.	Missionary Servants of the Most Blessed Trinity	[2790]
M.S.C.	Congregation of the Marianites of the Holy Cross	[2410]
M.S.C.	Missionary Sisters of the Most Sacred Heart of Jesus of Hiltrup	[2800]
M.S.C.	Missionary Sisters of the Sacred Heart	[2860]
M.S.C.Gpe.	Missionaries of the Sacred Heart of Jesus and of Our Lady of Guadalupe	[2865]
M.S.C.K.	Missionary Sisters of Christ the King	[2715]
M.S.F.	Missionary Sisters of the Holy Family	[]
M.S.H.F.	Missionary Sisters of the Holy Family (Poland)	[]
M.S.H.R.	Missionary Sisters of the Holy Rosary	[2730]
M.S.J.	Medical Sisters of St. Joseph	[2500]
M.S.K.C.P.	Missionary Sisters of Christ the King of Polonia	[]
M.S.M.G.	Missionary Sisters of Mother of God	[2810]
M.S.O.L.A.	Missionary Sisters of Our Lady of Africa	[2820]
M.S.S.A.	Missionary Servants of St. Anthony	[2890]
M.S.S.C.B.	Missionary Sisters of St. Charles Borromeo	[2900]
M.S.S.J.	Missionary Servants of St. Joseph (Spain)	[]
M.S.Sp.	Mission Sisters of the Holy Spirit	[2740]
M.SS.S.	Missionary Sisters of the Most Blessed Sacrament	[2780]
M.X.Y.	The Yarumal Foreign Mission Institute (Colombia)	[]
N.A.U.-O.L.C.	North American Unions of Sisters of Our Lady of Charity	[3070]
N.D.	Notre Dame Sisters	[2960]
N.D.S.	Congregation of Notre Dame de Sion	[2950]
O.A.R.	Augustinian Recollect Sisters	[]
O.B.T.	Sisters Oblates to the Blessed Trinity	[3020]
O.C.A.	Carmelite Vietnamese of Our Lady of Mt. Carmel	[]
O.Carm.	Calced Carmelites	[0300]
O.Carm.	Carmelite Nuns of the Ancient Observance	[0320]
O.Carm.	Carmelite Sisters for Aged and Infirm	[0330]
O.Carm.	Carmelite Sisters (Corpus Christi)	[0350]
O.Carm.	Congregation of Our Lady of Mount Carmel	[0400]
O.Carm.	Institute of the Sisters of Our Lady of Mt. Carmel	[0410]
O.C.D.	Carmelite Sisters of the Most Sacred Heart of Los Angeles	[0370]
O.C.D.	Discalced Carmelite Nuns	[0420]
O.C.D.	Carmelitas del Sagrado Corazon	[]
O.Cist.	Cistercian Nuns	[0680]
O.C.S.O.	Cistercian Nuns of the Strict Observance	[0670]
O.D.N.	Company of Mary	[0700]
O.L.C.	Sisters of Our Lady of Charity	[3071]
O.L.C.	Sisters of Our Lady of Charity	[3073]
O.L.G.	Sisters of Our Lady of the Garden	[]
O.L.L.	Sisters of Our Lady of Lourdes	[]
O.L.M.	Sisters of Charity of Our Lady of Mercy	[0510]
O.L.S.	Sisters of Our Lady of Sorrows	[3120]
O.L.V.M.	Our Lady of Victory Missionary Sisters	[3130]
O.M.M.I.	Oblate Missionaries of Mary Immaculate	[]
O.M.O.	Oblates of the Mother of Orphans	[3035]
O.P.	Dominican Contemplative Nuns (Cloistered)	[1050]
O.P.	Dominican Contemplative Sisters (Cloistered)	[1060]
O.P.	Dominican Sisters (St. Catharine, KY)	[1070-01]
O.P.	Dominican Sisters (Columbus, OH)	[1070-02]
O.P.	Dominican Sisters (Sinsinawa, WI)	[1070-03]
O.P.	Dominican Sisters (San Rafael, CA)	[1070-04]
O.P.	Dominican Sisters (Amityville, NY)	[1070-05]
O.P.	Dominican Sisters (Newburgh, NY)	[1070-06]
O.P.	Dominican Sisters (Nashville, TN)	[1070-07]
O.P.	Dominican Sisters (New Orleans, LA)	[1070-08]
O.P.	Dominican Sisters (Racine, WI)	[1070-09]
O.P.	Dominican Sisters (Springfield, IL)	[1070-10]
O.P.	Dominican Sisters (Sparkill, NY)	[1070-11]
O.P.	Dominican Sisters (San Jose, CA)	[1070-12]
O.P.	Dominican Sisters (Adrian, MI)	[1070-13]
O.P.	Dominican Sisters (Grand Rapids, MI)	[1070-14]
O.P.	Dominican Sisters (Blauvelt, NY)	[1070-15]
O.P.	Dominican Sisters (Ossining, NY)	[1070-16]
O.P.	Dominican Sisters (Media, PA)	[1070-17]
O.P.	Dominican Sisters (Caldwell, PA)	[1070-18]
O.P.	Dominican Sisters (Houston, TX)	[1070-19]
O.P.	Dominican Sisters (Tacoma, WA)	[1070-20]
O.P.	Dominican Sisters (Edmonds, WA)	[1070-21]
O.P.	Dominican Sisters (Fall River, MA)	[1070-22]
O.P.	Dominican Sisters (Hawthorne, NY)	[1070-23]
O.P.	Dominican Sisters (Great Bend, KS)	[1070-24]
O.P.	Dominican Sisters (Kenosha, WI)	[1070-25]
O.P.	Dominican Sisters (Oxford, MI)	[1070-26]
O.P.	Dominican Sisters (Justice, IL)	[1070-27]
O.P.	Dominican Sisters (Akron, OH)	[1070-28]
O.P.	Dominican Sisters (Spokane, WA)	[1070-29]
O.P.	Dominican Sisters (Oxford, South Africa)	[1070-30]
O.P.	Marian Society of Dominican Catechists	[1090]
O.P.	Dominican Sisters of Charity of the Presentation of the Blessed Virgin	[1100]
O.P.	Dominican Sisters of Our Lady of the Rosary and of Saint Catherine of Siena, Cabra	[1110]
O.P.	Dominican Sisters of the Roman Congregation	[1120]
O.P.	Dominican Rural Missionaries	[1130]
O.P.	Eucharistic Missionaries of St. Dominic	[1140]
O.P.	Dominican Sisters of Carondelet	[]
O.P.	Religious Missionaries of St. Dominic (Spanish Prov.)	[]
O.P.	Dominican Sisters of Mt. Thabor	[]
O.P.	Dominican Sisters of Our Lady of the Most Holy Rosary	[]
O.P.	Dominican Sisters (Vietnam)	[]
O.P.	Dominican Contemplative Sisters	[]
O.P.	Dominican Sisters (Colombia)	[]
O.P.	Dominican Sisters (Ecuador)	[]
O.P.	Hermanas Dominicanas de la Doctrine Cristiana	[]
O.S.A.	Augustinian Nuns of Contemplative Life	[0160]
O.S.A.	Congregation of Augustinian Sisters Servants of Jesus and Mary	[2145]
O.S.A.	Sisters of St. Rita	[4010]
O.S.A.	Sisters of St. Augustine	[]
O.S.A.	Augustinian Sisters of Our Lady of Consolation	[]
O.S.B.	Benedictine Nuns of the Congregation of Solesmes	[0170]
O.S.B.	Benedictine Nuns of the Primitive Observance	[0180]
O.S.B.	Benedictine Sisters	[0190]
O.S.B.	Benedictine Sisters	[0200]
O.S.B.	Missionary Benedictine Sisters	[0210]
O.S.B.	Congregation of the Benedictine Sisters of Perpetual Adoration of Pontifical Jurisdiction	[0220]
O.S.B.	Benedictine Sisters of Pontifical Jurisdiction	[0230]
O.S.B.	Benedictine Nuns	[0233]
O.S.B.	Olivetan Benedictine Sisters	[0240]
O.S.B.	Congregation of Jesus Crucified	[2250]
O.S.B.	Benedictine Congregation of Our Lady of Monte	[]
O.S.B.	Benedictine Sisters of Sacred Heart	[]
O.S.B.	Contemplative Sisters of St. Benedict	[]
O.S.B.	Benedictine Sisters of Liberty	[]
O.S.B.	Congregation of the Benedictine Sisters of the Sacred Heart	[]
O.S.B.Cam.	Camaldolese Benedictine Sisters	[]
O.S.B.M.	Sisters of the Order of St. Basil the Great	[3730]
O.S.B.S.	Oblate Sisters of the Blessed Sacrament	[3010]
O.S.C.	Order of St. Clare	[3760]
O.S.C.	Sisters of St. Clare	[3770]
O.S.C.Cap.	Capuchin Poor Clares	[3765]
O.S.F.	Franciscan Sisters of Allegany, New York	[1180]
O.S.F.	The Franciscan Sisters of Baltimore	[1200]
O.S.F.	Franciscan Sisters of Chicago	[1210]
O.S.F.	Franciscan Sisters of Christian Charity	[1230]
O.S.F.	Franciscan Sister, Daughters of the Sacred Hearts of Jesus and Mary	[1240]
O.S.F.	Franciscan Sisters of the Immaculate Conception	[1280]
O.S.F.	Franciscan Sisters of the Immaculate Conception and St. Joseph for the Dying	[1300]
O.S.F.	Franciscan Sisters of Little Falls, Minnesota	[1310]
O.S.F.	Franciscan Missionary Sisters for Africa	[1320]
O.S.F.	Franciscan Missionary Sisters of the Immaculate Conception	[1350]
O.S.F.	Missionary Franciscan Sisters of the Immaculate Conception	[1360]
O.S.F.	Franciscan Missionaries of Our Lady	[1380]
O.S.F.	Franciscan Missionary Sisters of Our Lady of Sorrows	[1390]
O.S.F.	Franciscan Sisters of Our Lady of Perpetual Help	[1430]

O.S.F.	Franciscan Sisters of the Sacred Heart	[1450]
O.S.F.	Franciscan Sisters of St. Paul	[1485]
O.S.F.	Sisters of the Third Franciscan Order	[1490]
O.S.F.	St. Francis Mission Community	[1505]
O.S.F.	Sisters of St. Francis	[1510]
O.S.F.	Sisters of St. Francis of Christ the King	[1520]
O.S.F.	Sisters of St. Francis of the Congregation of Our Lady of Lourdes, Sylvania, Ohio	[1530]
O.S.F.	Sisters of Saint Francis, Clinton, Iowa	[1540]
O.S.F.	Sisters of St. Francis of the Holy Cross	[1550]
O.S.F.	Sisters of St. Francis of the Holy Eucharist	[1560]
O.S.F.	Sisters of St. Francis of the Holy Family	[1570]
O.S.F.	Sisters of St. Francis of the Immaculate Conception	[1580]
O.S.F.	Sisters of St. Francis of the Immaculate Heart of Mary (Hankinson, North Dakota)	[1590]
O.S.F.	Sisters of St. Francis of the Martyr St. George	[1600]
O.S.F.	Sisters of Saint Francis of Millvale, Pennsylvania	[1620]
O.S.F.	Sisters of St. Francis of Penance and Christian Charity	[1630]
O.S.F.	Sisters of St. Francis of Perpetual Adoration	[1640]
O.S.F.	The Sisters of St. Francis of Philadelphia	[1650]
O.S.F.	Sisters of Saint Francis of the Providence of God	[1660]
O.S.F.	Sisters of St. Francis of Savannah, MO	[1670]
O.S.F.	School Sisters of St. Francis	[1680]
O.S.F.	School Sisters of the Third Order of St. Francis (Pittsburgh, PA)	[1690]
O.S.F.	School Sisters of the Third Order of St. Francis (Panhandle, TX)	[1695]
O.S.F.	School Sisters of the Third Order of St. Francis (Bethlehem, PA)	[1700]
O.S.F.	The Sisters of St. Francis of Assisi	[1705]
O.S.F.	Congregation of the Third Order of St. Francis of Mary Immaculate, Joliet, IL	[1710]
O.S.F.	Sisters of the Third Order Regular of St. Francis of the Congregation of Our Lady of Lourdes	[1720]
O.S.F.	Congregation of the Sisters of the Third Order of St. Francis Oldenburg, IN	[1730]
O.S.F.	Sisters of the Third Order of St. Francis of Penance and Charity	[1760]
O.S.F.	Sisters of the Third Order of St. Francis (Peoria, IL)	[1770]
O.S.F.	Sisters of St. Francis of the Third Order Regular (Williamsville, New York)	[1800]
O.S.F.	Bernardine Sisters of the Third Order of St. Francis	[1810]
O.S.F.	Hospital Sisters of the Third Order of St. Francis	[1820]
O.S.F.	Servants of the Holy Infancy of Jesus	[1980]
O.S.F.	Consolation Sisters (Highland, CA)	[]
O.S.F.	Franciscan Sisters of Christ the Divine Teacher	[]
O.S.F.	St. Francis Mission Community	[]
O.S.F.S.	Oblate Sisters of St. Francis de Sales	[3060]
O.S.H.J.	Oblate Sisters of the Sacred Heart of Jesus	[3050]
O.S.M.	Mantellate Sisters, Servants of Mary of Blue Island	[3570]
O.S.M.	Servants of Mary	[3580]
O.S.M.	Servants of Mary (Servite Sisters)	[3590]
O.S.M.	Oblates of St. Martha	[]
O.S.P.	Oblate Sisters of Providence	[3040]
O.S.S.	Sacramentine Nuns	[3490]
O.SS.R.	Order of the Most Holy Redeemer	[2010]
O.SS.R.	Oblates of the Most Holy Redeemer	[3030]
O.SS.S.	The Brigittine Sisters	[0280]
O.SS.T.	Sisters of the Most Holy Trinity	[0260]
O.S.U.	Ursuline Nuns (Roman Union)	[4110]
O.S.U.	Ursuline Nuns of the Congregation of Paris (St. Martin, OH)	[4120]
O.S.U.	Ursuline Nuns of the Congregation of Paris (Cincinnati, OH)	[4120-01]
O.S.U.	Ursuline Nuns of the Congregation of Paris (Kansas City, KS)	[4120-02]
O.S.U.	Ursuline Nuns of the Congregation of Paris (Louisville, KY)	[4120-03]
O.S.U.	Ursuline Nuns of the Congregation of Paris (Cleveland, OH)	[4120-04]
O.S.U.	Ursuline Nuns of the Congregation of Paris (Owensboro, KY)	[4120-05]
O.S.U.	Ursuline Nuns of the Congregation of Paris (Toledo, OH)	[4120-06]
O.S.U.	Ursuline Nuns of the Congregation of Paris (Youngstown, OH)	[4120-07]
O.S.U.	Ursuline Sisters of the Congregation of Tildonk, Belgium	[4130]
O.S.U.	Ursuline Sisters of Belleville	[4140]
O.S.U.	Irish Ursuline Union	[4150]
P.B.V.M.	Presentation of the Blessed Virgin Mary Sisters	[3280]
P.B.V.M.	Sisters of the Presentation of the B.V.M.	[3320]
P.B.V.M.	Union of the Sisters of the Presentation of the Blessed Virgin Mary	[3330]
P.C.C.	Order of St. Clare	[3760]
P.C.I.	Pax Christi Institute	[]
P.C.J.	Sisters of the Poor Child Jesus	[3220]
P.C.P.A.	Poor Clares of Perpetual Adoration	[3210]
P.D.D.M.	Pious Disciples of the Divine Master	[0980]
P.F.M.	Little Franciscans of Mary	[2280]
P.H.J.C.	Poor Handmaids of Jesus Christ	[3230]
P.M.	Sisters of the Presentation of Mary	[3310]
P.O.S.C.	Little Workers of the Sacred Heart	[2345]
P.S.N.	Poor Sisters of Nazareth	[3242]
P.S.S.F.	The Little Sisters of the Holy Family	[2320]
P.S.S.J.	Poor Sisters of St. Joseph	[3250]
P.V.M.I.	The Parish Visitors of Mary Immaculate	[3160]
Q.M.H.C.	Quinhon Missionary Sisters of the Holy Cross	[]
R.A.	Religious of the Apostolate of the Sacred Heart	[3380]
R.A.	Religious of the Assumption	[3390]
R.A.	Antonine Sisters	[]
R.A.D.	Sisters of the Love of God	[]
R.C.	Congregation of Our Lady of Retreat in the Cenacle	[3110]
R.C.D.	Sisters of Our Lady of Christian Doctrine	[3080]
R.C.E.	Religious of Christian Education	[3410]
R.C.M.	Sisters of the Immaculate Conception	[2130]
R.C.S.C.J.	Sisters of the Cross of the Sacred Heart of Jesus (Mexico)	[]
R.D.C.	Sisters of the Divine Compassion	[0970]
R.E.	Religious of the Eucharist	[3420]
R.F.	Sisters of St. Philip Neri Missionary Teachers	[]
R.F.R.	Sisters of Our Lady of Refuge	[]
R.G.S.	The Sisters of the Good Shepherd	[1830]
R.H.S.J.	Religious Hospitallers of Saint Joseph	[3440]
R.J.M.	Religious of Jesus and Mary	[3450]
R.M.	Marianitas	[]
R.M.I.	Claretian Missionary Sisters	[0685]
R.M.I.	Religious of Mary Immaculate	[3460]
R.M.M.	Mercedarian Sisters	[]
R.O.D.A.	Sisters Oblates to Divine Love	[]
R.O.L.C.	Our Lady of Charity of Refuge	[3072]
R.S.C.	Religious Sisters of Charity	[3400]
R.S.C.J.	Society of the Sacred Heart	[4070]
R.S.H.M.	Religious of the Sacred Heart of Mary	[3465]
R.S.J.	Religious of St. Joseph of Australia	[]
R.S.M.	Religious Sisters of Mercy of Alma, Michigan	[2519]
R.S.M.	Sisters of Mercy	[2520]
R.S.M.	Sisters of Mercy of Ardagh & Clonmacnois	[2523]
R.S.M.	Sisters of Mercy (Galway)	[2535]
R.S.M.	Sisters of Mercy	[2540]
R.S.M.	Sisters of Mercy (Sligo)	[2549]
R.S.M.	Sisters of Mercy	[2550]
R.S.M.	Sisters of Mercy of the Americas	[2575]
R.S.M.	Sisters of Mercy (Ballyshannon, Ireland)	[]
R.S.M.	Sisters of Mercy (Mayo, Ireland)	[]
R.S.M.	Sisters of Mercy of Mississippi, Inc.	[]
R.S.M.	Sisters of Mercy of Portland	[2655]
R.S.M.	Diocesan Sisters of Mercy	[]
R.S.R.	Congregation of Our Lady of the Holy Rosary	[3100]
R.T.	Theatine Sisters of the Immaculate Conception	[]
R.V.M.	Religious of the Blessed Virgin Mary	[]
S.A.	Franciscan Sisters of the Atonement	[1190]
S.A.A.	Sisters Auxiliaries of the Apostolate.	[0140]
S.A.B.	Sisters of St. Anne Bangalone	[]
S.A.C.	Sisters of the Guardian Angel	[1850]
S.A.C.	Pallottine Missionary Sisters Queen of Apostles Prov.	[3150]
S.A.S.V.	Sisters of the Assumption	[0150]
S.B.S.	The Sisters of the Blessed Sacrament for Indians and Colored People	[0260]
S.C.	Sisters of Charity of Cincinnati, Ohio	[0440]
S.C.	Sisters of Charity of Seton Hill, Greensburg, PA.	[0570]
S.C.	Sisters of St. Elizabeth, Convent Station	[0590]
S.C.	Sisters of Charity of St. Vincent de Paul, Halifax	[0640]
S.C.	Sisters of Charity of St. Vincent de Paul, New York	[0650]
S.C.C.	Sisters of Christian Charity	[0660]
Sch.P.	Sisters of the Pious Schools	[3200]
S.C.I.C.	Sisters of Charity of the Immaculate Conception of Ivrea	[0450]
S.C.I.M.	Servants of the Immaculate Heart of Mary	[3550]
S.C.K.	Sisters of Christ the King	[]
S.C.L.	Sisters of Charity of Leavenworth, Kansas	[0480]
S.C.M.C.	Sisters of Charity of Our Lady, Mother of the Church	[0530]
S.C.M.M.	Sisters of Charity of Our Lady Mother of Mercy	[0520]
S.C.M.M.	Medical Mission Sisters	[2490]
S.C.N.	Sisters of Charity of Nazareth	[0500]
S.C.O.	Sisters of Charity of Ottawa (Grey Nuns of the Cross)	[0540]
S.C.O.	Sisters of Charity of Quebec (Grey Nuns)	[0560]
S.C.R.H.	Sisters of Charity of Rolling Meadows	[]
S.C.S.J.A.	Sisters of Charity of St. Joan Antida	[0600]
S.C.S.L.	Sisters of Charity of St. Louis	[0620]
S.C.S.H.	Sisters of Charity of St. Hyacinthe (Grey Nuns)	[0610]
S.deP.	Sister Servants of the Poor	[]
S.D.R.	Sisters of the Divine Redeemer	[1020]
S.D.S.	Sisters of the Divine Saviour	[1030]
S.D.S.H.	Sisters of the Society Devoted to the Sacred Heart	[4050]
S.D.V.	Vocationist Sisters	[4210]
S.E.	Sisters of Emanuel	[]
S.E.C.	Sisters of the Eucharistic Covenant	[]
S.F.C.C.	Sisters for Christian Community	[]
S.F.M.A.	Franciscan Missionary Sisters of Assisi	[1330]
S.F.P.	Franciscan Sisters of the Poor	[1440]
S.G.M.	Sisters of Charity of Montreal (Grey Nuns)	[0490]
S.G.S.	Hermanas del Buen Pastor	[]
S.H.C.J.	Society of the Holy Child Jesus	[4060]
S.H.F.	Sisters of the Holy Family	[1960]
S.H.J.M.	Sisters of the Sacred Hearts of Jesus and Mary	[3680]
S.H.S.	Sisters of the Holy Spirit	[2040]
S.H.Sp.	Sisters of the Holy Spirit and Mary Immaculate	[2050]
S.I.M.	Missionaries of the Kingship of Christ	[]
S.I.W.	Sisters of the Incarnate Word and the Blessed Sacrament	[2210]
S.J.	Servants of Jesus	[3560]
S.J.A.	Sisters of Ste. Jeanne D'Arc	[3815]
S.J.B.	Sisters of St. John Bosco (Taylor, TX)	[]
S.J.C.	Sisters of St. Joseph of Cluny	[3860]
S.J.S.	Servants of the Blessed Sacrament	[3499]
S.J.S.M.	Sisters of St. Joseph of St. Mark	[3910]
S.J.W.	Sisters of St. Joseph the Worker	[3920]
S.L.	Sisters of Loretto at the Foot of the Cross	[2360]
S.L.T.	Pious Society of Our Lady of the Most Holy Trinity	[]
S.L.W.	Sisters of the Living Word	[2350]
S.M.	Marist Sisters Congregation of Mary	[2430]
S.M.	Sisters of Mercy	[2516]
S.M.	Sisters of Mercy	[2518]
S.M.	Sisters of Mercy	[2570]
S.M.	Sisters of Mercy (Cork and Ross)	[2600]
S.M.	Misericordia Sisters	[2680]
S.M.	Sisters Servants of Mary	[3600]
S.M.	Sisters of Mercy (Loughrea, Ireland)	[]
S.M.	Sisters of Mercy of Tralee	[]
S.M.D.C.	Sisters of Mercy of Christian Charity of St. Vincent de Paul of Hungary	[2610]
S.M.G.	Poor Servants of the Mother of God	[3640]
S.M.I.	Sisters of Mary Immaculate	[2440]
S.M.I.C.	Missionary Sisters of the Immaculate Conception of the Mother of God	[2760]
S.M.M.G.	Sisters of Mary, Mother of God	[]
S.M.M.I.	Sisters Minor of the Mary Immaculate	[]
S.M.M.S.	Society of Mary Missionary Sisters	[]
S.M.P.	Sisters of Mary of the Presentation	[2450]
S.M.P.	Daughters of Our Mother of Peace	[]
S.M.P.	Society of Our Mother of Peace	[]

S.M.R.	Society of Mary Reparatrix	[2560]
S.M.S.H.	Sisters of Saint Marthe (of St. Hyacinthe)	[3940]
S.M.S.M.	Marist Missionary Sisters	[2420]
S.N.D.	Sisters of Notre Dame	[2990]
S.N.D.deN.	Sisters of Notre Dame de Namur	[3000]
S.N.J.M.	Sisters of the Holy Names of Jesus and Mary	[1990]
S.O.L.M.	Sisters of Our Lady of Mercy	[2670]
S.O.L.P.H.	Sisters of Our Lady of Perpetual Help	[]
S.O.L.T.	Our Lady of the Most Holy Trinity Convent	[3105]
S.P.	Sisters of Providence	[3340]
S.P.	Sisters of Providence	[3350]
S.P.	Sisters of Providence of Saint Mary-of-the-Woods, IN	[3360]
S.P.C.	Sisters of St. Paul of Chartres	[3980]
S.R.	Sisters of Reparation of the Sacred Wounds of Jesus	[]
S.R.C.	Servants of Our Lady, Queen of Clergy	[3650]
S.R.C.M.	Sisters of Reparation of the Congregation of Mary	[3470]
S.S.A.	Sisters of St. Ann	[3718]
S.S.A.	Sisters of St. Anne	[3720]
S.S.C.	Missionary Sisters of St. Columban	[2880]
S.S.C.	Sisters of St. Casimir	[3740]
S.S.C.	Society of the Sisters of the Church	[]
SS.CC.	Congregation of the Sacred Hearts and of Perpetual Adoration	[3690]
S.S.Ch.	Sisters of St. Chretienne	[3750]
S.S.C.J.	Servants of the Most Sacred Heart of Jesus	[3630]
S.S.C.J.	Sisters of the Sacred Heart of Jesus of Saint Jacut	[3670]
S.S.C.K.	Sisters Servants of Christ the King	[3510]
S.S.C.M.	Servants of the Holy Heart of Mary	[3520]
SS.C.M.	Sisters of Saints Cyril and Methodius	[3780]
S.S.D.	Institute of the Sisters of St. Dorothy	[3790]
S.S.E.	Sisters of St. Elizabeth	[3800]
S.S.F.	Congregation of the Sisters of the Holy Family	[1950]
S.S.H.	Sisters Servants of the Most Sacred Heart	[]
S.S.H.J.P.	Servants of the Sacred Heart of Jesus and of the Poor	[3660]
S.S.J.	Servants of St. Joseph	[3595]
S.S.J.	Sisters of St. Joseph (Buffalo)	[3830-06]
S.S.J.	Sisters of St. Joseph (Burlington)	[3830-07]
S.S.J.	Sisters of St. Joseph (Erie)	[3830-09]
S.S.J.	Sisters of St. Joseph (Kalamazoo, Nazareth)	[3830-11]
S.S.J.	Sisters of St. Joseph (Ogdensburg)	[3830-12]
S.S.J.	Sisters of St. Joseph (Rochester)	[3830-14]
S.S.J.	Sisters of St. Joseph (Springfield, MA)	[3830-16]
S.S.J.	Sisters of St. Joseph (Wheeling)	[3830-17]
S.S.J.	Sisters of Saint Joseph of Chestnut Hill, Philadelphia	[3893]
S.S.J.	Sisters of St. Joseph of St. Augustine, Florida	[3900]
S.S.J.C.	Sisters of St. Joseph Benedict Cottolengo	[]
S.S.J.-T.O.S.F.	Sisters of St. Joseph of the Third Order of St. Francis	[3930]
S.S.L.	Congregation of the Sisters of St. Louis, Juilly-Monaghan	[3935]
S.S.LOG.	Seton Sisters of Our Lady of Guadalupe, Tucson	[]
S.S.M.	Sisters of the Sorrowful Mother (Third Order of St. Francis)	[4100]
S.S.M.I.	Sisters Servants of Mary Immaculate	[3610]
S.S.M.I.	Sisters Servants of Mary Immaculate	[3620]
S.S.M.N.	Sisters of Saint Mary of Namur	[3950]
S.S.M.O.	Sisters of St. Mary of Oregon	[3960]
S.S.N.D.	School Sisters of Notre Dame	[2970]
S.S.P.C.	Missionary Sisters of St. Peter Claver	[3990]
S.Sp.S.	Missionary Sisters Servants of the Holy Spirit	[3530]
S.Sp.S.deA.P.	Sister Servants of the Holy Spirit of Perpetual Adoration	[3540]
S.S.S.	Servants of the Blessed Sacrament	[3500]
S.S.S.	Sisters of Social Service of Los Angeles, Inc.	[4080]
S.S.S.	Sisters of Social Service	[4090]
S.S.S.F.	School Sisters of St. Francis	[1680]
S.S.T.V.	Congregation of Sisters of St. Thomas of Villanova	[4030]
S.T.J.	Society of St. Teresa of Jesus	[4020]
S.U.	Society of St. Ursula	[4040]
S.U.S.C.	Sisters of the Holy Union	[2070]
S.V.M.	Sisters of the Visitation of the Congregation of the Immaculate Heart of Mary	[4200]
V.D.C.	Verbum Dei Community	[]
V.H.M.	Visitation Nuns	[4190]
V.S.	Vestiarski Sisters	[]
V.S.C.	Vincentian Sisters of Charity	[4160]
V.S.C.	Vincentian Sisters of Charity	[4170]
V.Z.	Sisters of Charity of St. Vincent de Paul	[0630]
X.M.M.	Xaverian Missionary Society of Mary, Inc.	[4230]
X.S.	Catholic Mission Sisters of St. Francis Xavier	[3810]

A USER'S GUIDE TO THE OFFICIAL CATHOLIC DIRECTORY

Each year the editors of *The Official Catholic Directory* seek added ways of serving their subscribers. Although the book may never answer every question, this is the conscientious goal; its format, arrangement and editorial features are directed toward the convenience and needs of the public. Comments and suggestions are welcome.

* * * *

GENERAL PLAN

For the benefit of the subscriber and a more efficient use of *The Official Catholic Directory* and its cross references, a summary of the contents and their meaning follows:

1. **Ecclesiastical forms of address** recognized in the United States.
   Formal forms of address for correspondence with the clergy in the United States.
2. ***The Official Catholic Directory* Glossary**
   A listing of some of the ecclesiastical terms and organizations found in the *Directory.*
3. **Religious Order Initials for Men** and **Religious Order Initials for Women**
   Indexes of abbreviations relevant to the religious institute name and the applicable identification number.
4. Part I: The Governing Bodies in Vatican City:
   A chronological table of the **Supreme Roman Pontiffs;** the **Pope,** and an alphabetical list of the **College of Cardinals;** the duties of each of the agencies of the **Roman Curia,** and other commissions and institutions associated with the Holy See, along with their officers; a list of the **Seminaries** and **National Colleges** in Rome; the **Apostolic Nunciature** and the **Permanent Observer Mission to the United Nations,** with their staff. As foreign organizations, these entities are not included in the USCC group tax exemption ruling ("Group Ruling").
5. **Part II: Alphabetical Place List**
   The cities, towns, and villages where there is a church with a resident priest, or a Catholic institution, or both, together with the abbreviations of the archdiocese or diocese to which it belongs. A key to the (arch)diocesan abbreviations precedes the *Religious Order Initials for Men* section and the *Alphabetical List of Diocesan and Religious Priests of the U.S.*
6. **The Catholic Church in the United States** (Provinces)
   The archdioceses and dioceses of the United States arranged under the provinces to which they belong, listed with their active archbishops and bishops.
7. **U.S. Cardinals, Archbishops, Bishops, Archabbots and Abbots**
   An alphabetical list of Cardinals, Archbishops, Bishops, Archabbots and Abbots, arranged within their specific title. Also listed is their address and status, followed by a hierarchical/chronological list by year.
8. **National Conference of Catholic Bishops [NCCB]**
   The national body of bishops, with headquarters in Washington, D.C. A listing of the NCCB offices and committees, with their officers.
9. **United States Catholic Conference [USCC]**
   The coordinating body of the American Catholic bishops, with their committees and officers. Also included are the **National Organizations** approved by the USCC and a brief description of their function, and the **National Association of State Catholic Conference Directors.**
10. **Dioceses and Archdioceses** in alphabetical sequence
    The most detailed information on the Catholic Church in the United States, including the Military Services, Eastern Churches, Personal Prelatures, and Apostolates to the Hungarians and Lithuani-

ans. Listings are in alphabetical order according to the name of the diocese/archdiocese and include the diocesan curia and administrative offices; a parish-by-parish listing of clergy, churches, missions, and parochial schools; information on institutions, and the religious institutes of men and women located in the diocese/archdiocese; and a statistical profile for each diocese/archdiocese.

11. **United States Territorial Sees**
This section contains information on U.S. territories similar to that found in the preceding section.

12. **Part III: The Catholic Church in Canada and Mexico**
A brief listing of the provinces, archdioceses, dioceses, and administrative organizations in Canada and Mexico. As foreign organizations, these entities are not included in the USCC Group Ruling.

13. **American Foreign Missions**
This section highlights the Religious working specifically in foreign countries. Each Province lists their U.S. members and the countries they serve in. For specific address requests, contact the mission office listed.

14. **Missionary Activities**
Organizations involved in missionary work in the U.S. and foreign countries.

15. **United States Conference of Secular Institutes**
An alphabetical list of secular organizations and their purposes.

16. **U.S. Catholic Mission Association**
An alphabetical list of countries served by the U.S. Catholic Mission Association, detailing the number and religious order or laity personnel working there.

17. **Mission Churches**
A list, by city, of mission churches in the U.S. and the parishes to which they are attached.

18. **Religious Institutes of Men and Women**
An alphabetical list of religious institutes of men and of women, using a P.J. Kenedy identification number. Each listing contains the general headquarters, provinces, provincialates, a summary of legal titles and holdings taken from the individual archdioceses and dioceses within the *Directory,* various forms of ministry and works, statistical data of personnel, and representation in the U.S. dioceses and archdioceses.

19. **Colleges and Universities**
An alphabetical list of colleges and universities by state and diocese, including detailed information on administrative officers, religious and lay faculty, and student body.

20. **Hospitals**
An alphabetical list of hospitals by state and diocese, including information on executive and administrative officers, religious and lay professional staff, bed capacity, and number of patients assisted annually.

21. **Special Care Facilities**
An alphabetical list of special care facilities by state and diocese, including administrators, type of care, religious and lay staff, beds, patients assisted annually, outpatients and residents.

22. **Diocesan and Religious Priests**
An alphabetical list of diocesan and religious priests denoting their year of ordination, the archdiocese or diocese they are assigned to or work in, and the church or institution with which they are affiliated.

23. **Necrology** of U.S. Cardinals, Archbishops, Bishops, Archabbots, Abbots, and Priests
An alphabetical list of the U.S. hierarchy and priests who have died since the last issue of the *Directory,* along with their date of death and last assignment.

24. **Alphabetical List of Institutions**
A list of institutions including the categorical letter indicating where an institution can be found in the *Dioceses and Archdioceses* section along with the diocese/archdiocese abbreviated code and the city and state of the institution.

25. **The General Summary**
A 40+ page general summary of statistics arranged alphabetically by state, listing the archdiocese first within each state, followed by the dioceses. This information, extracted from the Statistical Overview of each diocese/archdiocese, pertains to personnel, parishes, health and welfare, education, and specific sacramental figures, as well as Catholic and total population figures for each diocese/archdiocese. U.S. territories and Eastern Church statistics are also included.

26. **Map of Catholic Diocesan and Province Boundaries in the United States**
Map defining the diocesan, archdiocesan, provincial, and state boundaries.

27. **Products & Services Guide**
Includes a diverse array of products and services offered to the Catholic community.

The Official Catholic Directory Part II
Provides a comprehensive listing of archdioceses and dioceses of the world. Also contains mid-year updates to the U.S. (arch)dioceses. More information on *Official Catholic Directory Part II* can be obtained from the publisher.

* * * *

SPECIAL NOTATIONS USED IN THE DIRECTORY

An asterisk (*) denotes a tax-exempt organization that has its own IRS exemption status and is not covered by the USCC Group Ruling. The Group Ruling allows for the exemption from federal income tax of all Catholic institutions listed in *The Official Catholic Directory* for that year. The exemption was established in 1946 and has been extended every year since then.

[CEM] in a parish listing indicates that a cemetery is connected to the parish. [JC] indicates a joint cemetery, which is a cemetery being utilized by more than one parish. A number following [CEM] or [JC] indicates the number of cemeteries owned by the parish or joint cemeteries shared with other parishes.

A dagger (†) next to a name in the *Necrology* denotes a deceased priest. A Maltese cross (✠) denotes a deceased member of the hierarchy.

* * * *

THE GENERAL SUMMARY

Certain terms used in the General Summary may need additional explanation.

Extern Priests are priests who have not been incardinated into the diocese in which they are currently working and residing.

Health Care Centers include ancillary care systems, medical centers, sanitoriums, and hospices.

Specialized Homes refers to institutions which provide aid to abused children or adults, halfway homes, AIDS patients, ARC patients, ex-offenders, pregnant women, adjudicated delinquents, or runaway youths.

Special Centers for Social Services are institutions or services that provide assistance, such as hotline centers, food banks, homeless centers, legal aid services, or counseling services.

Residential Care of Children refers to orphanages, as opposed to day care centers.

Non-residential Schools for Handicapped are day schools which provide regular and religious education for physically and/or mentally handicapped students.

Received into Full Communion is used to describe people who have been baptized earlier in life and have now been received into full communion in the Catholic Church.

ECCLESIASTICAL FORMS OF ADDRESS RECOGNIZED IN THE UNITED STATES

(These are the formal forms of address used in correspondence.)

CARDINALS:

Address on envelope: His Eminence *(Christian name)* Cardinal *(Surname)*
Salutation: Your Eminence:
Concluding a letter: I have the honor to be, Your Eminence, *etc.*

ARCHBISHOPS:

Address on envelope: Most Reverend *N*_______ *N*_______
Salutation: Your Excellency:
Concluding a letter: I have the honor to be, Your Excellency, *etc.*

BISHOPS:

Address on envelope: Most Reverend *N*_______ *N*_______
Salutation: Your Excellency:
Concluding a letter: I have the honor to be, Your Excellency, *etc.*

ABBOTS:

Address on envelope: Right Reverend *N*_______ *N*_______ *(add religious order initials)*
Salutation: Right Reverend Abbot:
Concluding a letter: I have the honor to be, Right Reverend Abbot, *etc.*

PROTONOTARIES APOSTOLIC:

Address on envelope: Rev. Msgr. *N*_______ *N*_______
Salutation: Rev. Msgr.:
Concluding a letter: I am, Rev. Msgr., *etc.*

PRELATE OF HONOR OF HIS HOLINESS:

Address on envelope: Rev. Msgr. *N*_______ *N*_______
Salutation: Rev. Msgr.:
Concluding a letter: I am, Rev. Msgr., *etc.*

CHAPLAIN TO HIS HOLINESS:

Address on envelope: Rev. Msgr. *N*_______ *N*_______
Salutation: Rev. Msgr.:
Concluding a letter: I am, Rev. Msgr., *etc.*

SECULAR PRIESTS:

Address on envelope: Rev. *N*_______ *N*_______
Salutation: Dear Reverend Father:
Concluding a letter: I am, Reverend Father, *etc.*

RELIGIOUS ORDER PRIESTS:

Address on envelope: Rev. *N*_______ *N*_______ *(add religious order initials)*
Salutation: Dear Reverend Father:
Concluding a letter: I am, Reverend Father, *etc.*

BROTHERS:

Address on envelope: Brother *N*_______
Salutation: Dear Brother *N*_______
Concluding a letter: I am, Respectfully yours, *etc.*

SISTERS:

Address on envelope: Sister *N*_______
Salutation: Dear Sister *N*_______
Concluding a letter: I am, Respectfully yours, *etc.*

TRANSITIONAL DEACONS:

Address on envelope: Rev. Mr. *N*_______
Salutation: Dear Mr. *N*_______
Concluding a letter: I am, Respectfully yours, *etc.*

PERMANENT DEACONS:

Address on envelope: Mr. *N*_______
Salutation: Dear Mr. *N*_______
Concluding a letter: I am, Respectfully yours, *etc.*

THE OFFICIAL CATHOLIC DIRECTORY GLOSSARY

Abbot
The superior of an autonomous community of men religious. He has general and sacramental jurisdiction over his community. The head of a prominent monastery or a congregation consisting of several monasteries is an *archabbot.*

Advocate
An ecclesiastical advocate is someone approved by Church authority to safeguard the rights of a party in a canonical process by arguments regarding the law and the facts of the case. [Cf. c. 1481 and CLSA Comm., p. 967]

Apostolate
Apostolate is the mission of Christ and participation in it. Its object is to bring Christ to others, its goal is the greater glory of God, its scope is universal. The work is carried out by every human agency by which the life of grace may be given or increased in the soul. A mandate from the Church is essential to the Catholic apostolate.

Archbishop
A bishop of a main or metropolitan diocese in an ecclesiastical province. The term is equivalent to *metropolitan* in the Western Church. It may also be granted to other ordinaries and non-residential bishops, and to the ordinary of a diocese outside a province.

Auditor
An official of a diocesan court, who gathers evidence and testimony and draws up a record of an ecclesiastical case.

Bishop
A bishop, by divine institution, carries on the work of the apostles. By reason of episcopal consecration, he shares in the triple apostolic function of teacher of doctrine, priest of sacred worship, and minister of church government. Bishops are responsible for the pastoral care of their dioceses. In addition, bishops have a responsibility to act in council to guide the Church. The term *exarch* is used in Eastern-rite churches.

The bishop to whom a particular or local church is entrusted is called a *diocesan bishop* or a *residential bishop.* All other bishops receive *Titular Sees* over which they exercise no pastoral authority.

When the pastoral needs of a diocese or archdiocese warrant, an *auxiliary bishop* may be assigned to aid the residential bishop in governing his diocese. An auxiliary bishop is assigned when the residential bishop needs assistance in carrying out his duties because of ill health, advanced age, or amount of work. An auxiliary bishop does not have the right of succession within his diocese.

In special circumstances, such as the advanced age or ill health of a diocesan bishop, a *coadjutator bishop* may be appointed to assist the principal bishop of a diocese. Coadjutator bishops have the *right of succession* in the diocese of their appointment from the time the See becomes vacant upon the death or retirement of its bishop.

Brother
A man who is a member of a religious order, but is not ordained or studying for the priesthood.

Cana Conference
A Catholic family movement, originally designed to aid married couples and families in their spiritual and interpersonal relationships. The program is now divided into *Pre-Cana,* for couples engaged to be married, and *Cana Conferences,* programs for married people.

Censor Librorum
A theologian empowered by a bishop to judge a book's soundness in regard to Church teaching before publication.

Chancellor
The office of the chancellor (or the *chancery)* evolved from the practice in the early Church of appointing an official to sign and preserve the letters of the bishop. The first function of the chancellor in the present day is gathering, arranging, and safeguarding the acts of the diocesan curia. Dispensations and other official documents also originate from the chancery. In many dioceses, the chancellor continues to exercise ordinary jurisdiction as delegated by the diocesan bishop. He or she may be assisted by a separate official, the *vice-chancellor.*

Chapter
The *general chapter* of a religious order is an assembly of elected or appointed members and provincials. General chapters are convened for the election of officers, amendments to the constitution, and discussion and legislation of matters of concern to members and the order as a whole.

A *provincial chapter* conducts elections and handles legislation on a provincial level. The assembly is comprised of superiors and representatives of the religious.

A *chapter of canons* is a group of diocesan priests, appointed by the bishop of a diocese, with assigned authority or responsibilities.

College of Cardinals
The College of Cardinals is made up of the cardinals of the Church, who advise the Pope, assist in the central administration of the Church, head the various curial offices and congregations, administer the Holy See during a vacancy, and elect a new Pope. There are three ranks in the College of Cardinals, corresponding to the historical origins of cardinals in the Roman Catholic Church. All cardinals are bishops, but their rank within the College of Cardinals is characterized by one of the hierarchical ranks of bishop, priest, or deacon. Cardinals are given honorary title to churches in the city of Rome. [CF. c. 350; CLSA Comm., pp. 288-289]

1. Cardinal Bishops
There are two types of Cardinal Bishops: 1) those appointed by the Pope as titular bishops to one of the six suburban dioceses of Rome, and 2) Eastern-rite Patriarchs who are heads of Sees with apostolic origins that have been assigned to the College of Cardinals.

2. Cardinal Priests
Heads of Sees outside the city of Rome are assigned a "titular church," one of the churches in Rome. They have no pastoral authority over their titular church.

3. Cardinal Deacons
Cardinals of diaconal rank are bishops without Sees who head the various departments, offices, congregations, committees, and the Secretariat of State of the Roman Curia.

Confraternity of Christian Doctrine [CCD]
A lay organization established for religious education throughout a person's entire life. The term is currently used to describe Catholic parish-based religious education of children from kindergarten through high school. At the diocesan level, the offices are now more commonly known as offices of *religious education* or *Christian formation.* Nationally, the confraternity's religious education component has been taken over by the USCC's Department of Education. It still exists as a separate entity under the USCC Administrative Board, with responsibility for licensing religious and spiritual literature.

[Co]nsolidated School
[The t]erm, as used in the *Directory,* may refer to a [school th]at takes students from more than one par[ish, or a sc]hool that was formed by the consolida[tion of two or t]hree other schools. In both cases, it is a means of keeping a Catholic school in a given area open by taking students from the surrounding areas, regardless of parish boundaries.

Convent
In common usage, the term refers to a house of women religious. Originally, it referred to a building where members of religious institutes lived, and was not restricted to communities of women.

Cursillo
The *cursillo de cristianidad,* or "little course in Christianity," is a three-day program for achieving spiritual renewal or spiritual awakening. It seeks to convey a new sense of individual and organized apostolic action. The program, conducted by priests and laypeople, consists of a three-day weekend focused on prayer, study, and Christian action, and a follow-up program known as the *post-cursillo.*

Deacons
The diaconate is the first order or grade in ordained ministry. Its origins are in early apostolic times, when deacons preached and baptized under the direction of the presbyters or bishops. Any man who is to be ordained to the priesthood must first be ordained as a *transitional deacon.* Deacons serve in the ministry of liturgy, of the word, and of charity.

In 1967, Pope Paul VI reinstituted the *Permanent Diaconate* for men who do not plan to become ordained priests. Although men ordained as permanent deacons are sometimes referred to as "married deacons," the permanent diaconate is open to both married and unmarried men, with the understanding that after ordination, they may not marry even after the death of a spouse. Under the authority of the diocesan bishop, they perform the same functions as the transitional deacons while, at the same time, retaining their roles in society as family and business men.

Dean/Vicar Forane
The title of a priest appointed by the bishop to aid him in administering the parishes in a certain vicinity, called a "deanery," or "vicariates forane." The function of a dean, or vicar forane, involves promotion, coordination, and supervision of the common pastoral activity within the deanery or vicariate.

Defender of the Bond
A member of a diocesan tribunal, either a cleric or a lay person, holding a graduate degree in canon law, who is appointed by the diocesan bishop for cases concerning the nullity of sacred ordination or the nullity or dissolution of the marriage bond. The defender of the bond is responsible for a review of

the evidence, scrutiny of the briefs, examination of witnesses, and maintenance of proper procedures during the trial. The defender also deals with some situations concerning the content of the litigation rather than the legal procedures.

Diocesan Consultors
An advisory council of diocesan priests, as appointed by a diocesan bishop, that assists in the administrative affairs of the diocese.

Diocesan Curia
The personnel and offices assisting the diocesan bishop in directing the pastoral activity, administration, and the exercise of judicial power of his diocese. The curia includes among its officers laity and religious as well as clergy. Principal officers of a diocesan curia are the vicar general of the diocese, the chancellor, officials of the diocesan tribunal, examiners, consultors, auditors, the promoter of justice and the defender of the bond.

Diocese
The standard term for a territorial division of the Church, entrusted to a bishop who rules in his own name as local ordinary, and not as a delegate of another. The chief diocese of a province is an *archdiocese.* It is headed by an archbishop. A diocese is usually limited to a definite territory so that it comprises all the faithful who inhabit that territory. [Cf. cc. 369 and 372, #1] In Eastern-rite churches, the term eparchy is used.

Eastern-rite [Oriental] Church
The term used to describe the Catholic churches which developed in Eastern Europe, Asia, and Africa. The Eastern-rite churches have their own distinctive liturgical and organizational systems. Each is considered equal to the Latin rite within the Church.

Ecumenism/Ecumenical Movement
A movement for spiritual understanding and unity among Christians and their churches. The term is also extended to apply to efforts toward greater understanding and cooperation between Christians and members of other faiths.

Exarch/Exarchy
A church jurisdiction, similar to a diocese, established for Eastern-rite Catholics living outside their native land. The head of an exarchy, usually a bishop, is an *exarch.*

Hierarchy
In general, the term refers to the ordered body of clergy, divided into bishops, priests, and deacons. In Catholic practice, the term refers to the bishops of the world or of a particular region.

Holy Name Society
A lay organization which seeks to aid its members in living a genuinely Christian life. The society organizes retreats and other spiritual and devotional exercises.

Holy See
The term refers to the diocese of Rome. Used in reference to the governance of the Church, it refers to the Pontiff, the Roman Curia, and the Sacred College.

Knights of Columbus
A fraternal organization for Catholic men. Knights of Columbus engage in religious and charitable projects in the U.S., Canada, Puerto Rico, Mexico, and the Philippines.

Legion of Mary
A lay organization established to assist the clergy in the sanctification of its members' souls, and the spread of the Christian faith and spiritual service to others. Members participate in almost every form of social service and Catholic action, including evangelization. The organization was founded in 1921.

Metropolitan
The archbishop of an archdiocese in a province. He has limited supervisory powers and influence over the other dioceses and bishops in the province.

Military Ordinariate [Archdiocese for the Military Services, U.S.A.]
A nonterritorial diocese for American Catholics and their dependents who are in the military or affiliated with the armed forces. Personnel employed by or engaged in diplomatic missions for the U.S. government in countries where U.S. military forces are stationed also belong to the Military Ordinariate.

Mission
A mission, or *quasi-parish,* is a parish which has not been established because it lacks one or more of the following qualifications: a resident pastor; necessary financial resources; territorial boundaries; or a natural grouping by way of rite, nationality, or language. Missions are attached to some parishes under the care of their pastors.

Moderator of the Curia
A bishop or priest, appointed by the diocesan bishop, who is concerned primarily with administrative matters and with supervising those working in the curia.

Monastery
An autonomous community house of a religious order, which may or may not be a monastic order. The term is used more specifically to refer to a community house of men religious or women religious in which they lead a contemplative life separate from the world.

Monsignor
An honorary ecclesiastical title granted by the Pope to some diocesan priests. In the United States, the title is given to the vicar general of a diocese. In Europe, the title is also given to bishops.

National Conference of Catholic Bishops [NCCB]
The episcopal conference of U.S. bishops. The membership is comprised of diocesan bishops and their associate bishops. The conference decides matters of ecclesiastical law and issues policy statements on political and social issues.

Newman Apostolate
An apostolate to the Catholic college and university community, now commonly known as "campus ministry."

Notary
An elected or appointed ecclesiastical official who acts as a secretary in formal church proceedings. The notary records the minutes, testimony, etc., of the proceedings.

Opus Dei
A personal prelature dedicated to spreading through society an awareness of the call to Christian virtue, awareness, and witness in one's life and work. The organization was founded in 1928 and in 1950, it received Vatican approval as a secular institution. In 1982, it was designated a personal prelature, the *Prelature of the Holy Cross and Opus Dei*. Members are not members of a religious order, do not take vows, and do not live in community.

Ordinary
Diocesan bishops, religious superiors, and certain other diocesan authorities with jurisdiction over the clergy in a specific geographical area, or the members of a religious order.

Ordination/Ordain
The sacramental rite by which a "sacred order" is conferred (diaconate, priesthood, episcopacy).

Papal Audience
Request for attendance at papal audiences and similar functions may be addressed to: "Bishops' Office for United States Visitors to the Vatican." Postal address: Via dell 'Umilta 30, 00187 Rome, Italy. Tel.: 011-39-6-6678-9184; Fax: 011-39-6-679-1448. Rev. Msgr. Charles W. Elmer, Dir.

Papal Representatives
There are three types of representatives of the Roman Pontiff: 1) those who represent him to particular churches; 2) those who represent him to particular churches and civil government; 3) those who represent him in international organizations or at various conferences and meetings. [Cf. c. 363; CLSA Comm., p. 302]

1. Legate
An individual appointed by the Pope to be his personal representative to a nation, international conference, or local church. The legate may be chosen from the local clergy of a country.

2. Apostolic Pro-Nuncio
In the United States, the papal representative is sent by the Pope to both the local church and to the government. His title is Apostolic Pro-Nuncio. Although he holds the title of ambassador, in U.S. law he is not accorded the special privilege of being the dean of the diplomatic corps.

3. Permanent Observer to the United Nations
The Apostolic See maintains permanent legates below the ambassadorial level to several world organizations. Since the Papal Legate does not enjoy the right to vote within the organization, his title at the United Nations is that of *Observer*.

Parish
A specific community of the Christian faithful within a diocese, which has its own church building, under the authority of a *pastor* who is responsible for providing them with ministerial service. Most parishes are formed on a geographic basis, but they may be formed along national or ethnic lines.

Parish Coordinator
A deacon, religious, or lay person who is responsible for the pastoral care of parish. The parish coordinator is in charge of the day-to-day life of the parish in the areas of worship, education, pastoral service and administration.

Pastor
A priest in charge of a parish or congregation. He is responsible for administering the sacraments, instructing the congregation in the doctrine of the Church, and other services to the people of the parish.

Pastoral Associate
A member of the laity who is part of a parish ministry team.

Pastoral Council
A consultative body which the pastor or bishop consults concerning the pastoral activity within the diocese. Its members include laity, religious, and clergy. The pastoral council's purpose is to study practical situations, difficulties and problems, and make concrete recommendations and proposals to the diocesan bishop. The pastoral council is always subject to the final authority of the pastor or bishop.

Patriarch
The Pope is the traditional "Patriarch of the West." All other bishops in the Latin Rite, even those with the honorary title of "Patriarch," are subject to him. Similarly, patriarchs within nations have only an honorary title unless special provisions are made otherwise. Eastern-rite Patriarchs are subject to the Pope while serving as heads of the faithful belonging to their rites throughout the world.

Personal Prelature
In addition to the territorial arrangement of the Church into particular or local churches or dioceses, canon law also provides for non-territorial areas of religious jurisdiction, incorporating secular clergy and deacons. Membership is also open to lay persons. These *prelatures* are established to meet specific pastoral or missionary needs at the regional, national, or international level without infringing on the rights of the local bishops. A prelature is presided over by a *personal prelate,* who is an ordinary with the right to establish seminaries and ordain priests as members of the prelature.

Canon law also allows for laity to be associated in the works of prelatures without being withdrawn from the jurisdiction of their own diocesan bishop.

Presbyteral Council
Also known as the *priests' council,* the presbyteral council is the principal consultative body mandated by the Code of Canon Law to advise the diocesan bishop in matters of pastoral governance. It consists of bishops and priests serving the diocese.

Propagation of the Faith
An organization, headquartered in Rome, which distributes aid to Catholic missions and organizes the work of missionaries all over the world. The organization has responsibility for fostering missionary vocations, assigning missionaries to field work, defining ecclesiastical boundaries and assigning clergy to them, and encouraging training and installation of native-born clergy.

Promoter of Justice
A cleric or lay person, holding a graduate degree in canon law, who is appointed by the diocesan bishop to serve in the role of a "prosecuting attorney" in trials of crimes against church law and of other judicial litigations in the diocese. A promoter of justice may be appointed for a specific case by the bishop.

Province
A defined geographic area containing an archdiocese, or *Metropolitan See,* and at least one diocese, or *Suffragen See.* The archbishop of the archdiocese has no direct powers over the Suffragen Sees, but does have limited advisory and appellate authority and obligations. The term also refers to a territorial grouping of particular churches or communities, or a territory of a religious order.

Provincial
The superior of the communities of a religious order that constitute a province.

Provincial Council
An assembly of the bishops of an ecclesiastical province, called by the metropolitan archbishop. The term is also used in reference to the provincial superior of a province, along with his or her chief advisors.

Receptions into the Church
Can take two forms: baptism of those not previously validly baptized, or "reception into full communion" with the Church for those who have already been baptized, in which case a profession of faith affects the reception.

Religious Priest/Diocesan Priest
Religious, or regular, priests are those who are professed members of a religious order or institute. Religious clergy live according to the rule of their respective orders. In pastoral ministry, they are under the jurisdiction of their local bishop, as well as the superiors of their order. Diocesan, or secular, priests are under the direction of their local bishop. They commit to serving their congregations and other institutions.

Retreat
A period of time spent in meditation and religious exercise. Retreats may take various forms, from traditional closed forms, to open retreats, which do not disengage the participants from day-to-day life. Both clergy and lay people of all ages participate in retreats. Houses and centers providing facilities for retreats are *retreat houses.*

Rite of Christian Initiation of Adults [RCIA]
The liturgical book containing the norms and rituals of the Catholic Church for people who wish to join the Church. Part of the book is intended for baptized Christians who wish to become Catholics. The term is used in a general sense to refer to the process of entering the Catholic Church.

Roman Curia
The official collective name for the administrative agencies and courts, and their officials, who assist the Pope in governing the Church. Members are appointed and granted authority by the Pope.

St. Vincent DePaul Society
Originally known as the *Conference of Charity,* this is an organization of lay people who serve the poor through spiritual and material works of mercy. The society operates stores, rehabilitation workshops, food centers, shelters, criminal justice and other programs.

Scholastic
A member of a religious order who has completed his novitiate, but has not yet been ordained.

Scholastic Teaching
Usually refers to Scholastic Philosophy, which is the basis for much Catholic Theology. It comes from the canonical "schools" of the 12th-13th centuries, St. Thomas Aquinas, St. Bonaventure, St. Albert the Great, etc., who developed "scholasticism" based mainly on Aristotle. It is the semi-official philosophy of the Church.

Secular Institute
Canonically erected institute of consecrated life for single laity and clerics who strive for the perfection of charity and work for the sanctification of the world while remaining in a lifestyle within the world.

See
The word is taken from the Latin word "sedes" ("seat"), and is used to denote a diocese or ecclesiastical district. The term *Holy See* is reserved to the diocese of Rome whose bishop is the Pope.

Seminary
An educational institution for men preparing for *Holy Orders.* The term originates from the time of St. Augustine, when those preparing for the priesthood were educated in the "cathedral school." During the Middle Ages, the clergy were educated in a university setting where faculties of philosophy, theology, and canon law existed. Eventually individual dioceses or provinces came to establish their own schools for educating their clerical students. Traditional seminaries date from the Council of Trent in the 16th century.

A school for the spiritual, academic, and pastoral education and formation of priesthood candidates is known as a *major seminary* in which the focus is on philosophical and theological education. To prepare for entrance into a major seminary, a period of study is set aside for the required courses in the humanities and the sciences in institutions called *minor seminaries.*

Serra Club
Local units of *Serra International,* an organization which promotes vocations to the priesthood and religious life, and offers instruction to lay leaders.

Sister
The term, in the strictest sense, refers to women religious who belong to institutes which have professed simple vows. However, in everyday usage, the term is used for any woman religious.

Sodality
A group of laity established for the promotion of Christian life and worship, or some other religious purpose.

Special Centers for Social Services
This would seem to overlap with Specialized Homes. Some of the categorization is fairly arbitrary. Catholic Charities might have its own proper distinctions for government or private funding purposes.

Specialized Homes
Includes such institutions as homes for handicapped (e.g., Misericordia Homes), youth homes (e.g., Maryville, Mercy Boys and Girls, Homes), homes for battered women, drug rehab centers, homes for unwed mothers, etc.

Superior
The head of a religious order or congregation. He or she may be the head of a province, or an individual house.

Synod
A gathering of designated officials and representatives of a church, that has legislative and policy-making powers.

1. Synod of Bishops
The Synod of Bishops is a consultative body, unless explicitly stated otherwise by His Holiness, expressing the communion of the hierarchy. A synod of bishops meets in general assembly, either in "Ordinary" or "Extraordinary" session, when the matter for treatment concerns the whole Church

and in "Special Assembly" when the matter deals directly with a definite region or regions.

2. Synod of Oriental Churches
The synods of the Oriental Churches enjoy various prerogatives including the right to elect bishops, regulate discipline and exercise pastoral authority in their respective churches.

3. Diocesan Synod
A diocesan synod is an expression of the communion of the particular church. A diocesan synod enjoys the participation of priests, women and men religious and laypersons; the bishop is the sole legislator.

Theologate
An institution which provides the last four years of study for candidates for the priesthood.

Titular See
A former diocese which no longer physically or geographically exists. Titular Sees are given as an honorary title to any bishop not serving as a chief pastor of a diocese, i.e., auxiliary bishops, papal representatives, and bishops of the Roman Curia.

Tribunal
A tribunal (court) is the name given to the person or persons who exercise the Church's judicial powers. By its very nature, this procedure involves the determination of a legal controversy. A major concern of tribunals is conducting the process leading to the dissolution or annulment of marriages. In ecclesiastical matters, definite procedural norms for conducting a trial are found in the Code of Canon Law to settle disputes. There are various grades of tribunals, including diocesan tribunals, the first court of trial for most cases; regional and metropolitan tribunals, located in an archdiocese, the appellate court for all cases tried within the province; and the tribunals of the Holy See, which act as the Church's central appellate court, try cases reserved to the Holy See, deal with questions of procedure and jurisdiction of the other courts, and act as the Church's supreme court.

United States Catholic Conference [USCC]
The civil corporation and executive agency of the National Conference of Catholic Bishops. The USCC acts as the national public policy organization of the NCCB. Its purpose is to organize and promote Catholic activity in the U.S. and abroad, and to carry out the religious and social action of the Catholic Church in the U.S. The major departments are education, communication, and social development and world peace.

Vicar
The appointment of a priest or a bishop as an *episcopal vicar* is an option given to a diocesan bishop when he needs a deputy for governing a specific territory within the diocese, a group of persons or a specific rite, or a type of apostolic work within the diocese.

By Church law, the diocesan bishop is the judge of all cases in the diocesan tribunal of first trial. He must appoint a priest with ordinary power to judge cases not reserved to the bishop himself. This priest must have a graduate degree in canon law. He is called the *judicial vicar,* and is sometimes referred to as the chief judge or "officialis." He may be given another priest as an assistant with the title of *adjutant judicial vicar.*

A bishop or priest appointed to participate in the executive (administrative) governance of the diocese with executive jurisdiction as a deputy of the diocesan bishop is a *vicar general.* The appointment of a vicar general is mandatory for every diocese. This office is designed to facilitate and unify diocesan administration.

Vicar for Religious
A priest appointed by a bishop to act as his representative in dealing with the religious communities in his diocese.

Information for this glossary was taken from the *Catholic News Service's Stylebook on Religion,* the *Modern Catholic Dictionary,* published by Doubleday and Company, Inc., the *Concise Oxford Dictionary of the Christian Church,* published by Oxford University Press, and the *Encyclopedic Dictionary of Religion,* published by the Sisters of St. Joseph of Philadelphia. The publishers of the *Official Catholic Directory* also wish to thank the Vice Chancellors of the Archdiocese of Chicago for their work in the preparation of this glossary.

The Supreme Roman Pontiffs

St. Peter of Bethsaida in Galilee, Prince of the Apostles, who received from Jesus Christ the Supreme Pontifical Power to be transmitted to his Successors, resided first at Antioch, then at Rome for twenty-five years where he was martyred in the year 64, or 67 of the common reckoning.

END OF PONTIFICATE,	A.D.
St. Linus, M.	76
St. Anacletus or Cletus, M.	88
St. Clement, I, M.	97
St. Evaristus, M.	105
St. Alexander I, M.	115
St. Sixtus I, M.	125
St. Telesphorus, M.	136
St. Hyginus, M.	140
St. Pius I, M.	155
St. Anicetus, M.	166
St. Soterus, M.	175
St. Eleuterius, M.	189
St. Victor I, M.	199
St. Zephyrinus, M.	217
St. Callistus I, M.	222
St. Urban I, M.	230
St. Pontian, M.	235
St. Anterus, M.	236
St. Fabian, M.	250
St. Cornelius, M.	253
St. Lucius I, M.	254
St. Stephen I, M.	257
St. Sixtus II, M.	258
St. Dionysius	268
St. Felix I, M.	274
St. Eutychian, M.	283
St. Caius, M.	296
St. Marcellinus, M.	304
St. Marcellus I, M.	309
St. Eusebius, M.	309
St. Melchiades, M.	314
St. Sylvester I	335
St. Mark	336
St. Julius I	352
Liberius	366
St. Damasus I	384
St. Siricius	399
St. Anastasius I	401
St. Innocent I	417
St. Zozimus	418
St. Boniface I	422
St. Celestine I	432
St. Sixtus III	440
St. Leo I (the Great)	461
St. Hilary	468
St. Simplicius	483
St. Felix III or II	492
St. Gelasius I	496
Anastasius II	498
St. Symmacus	514
St. Hormisdas	523
St. John I	526
St. Felix IV or III	530
Boniface II	532
John II	535
St. Agapitus	536
St. Silverius, M.	537
Vigilius	555
Pelagius I	561
John III	574
Benedict I	579
Pelagius II	590
St. Gregory I (the Great)	604
Sabinianus	606
Boniface III	607
St. Boniface IV	615
St. Deusdeditus or Adeodatus I	618
Boniface V	625
Honorius I	638
Severinus	640
John IV	642
Theodore I	649
St. Martin I, M.	655
St. Eugene I	657
St. Vitalian	672
Adeodatus II	676
Donus I	678
St. Agathonus	681
St. Leo II	683
St. Benedict II	685
John V	686
Conon	687
St. Sergius I	701
John VI	705
John VII	707
Sisinnius	708
Constantine	715
St. Gregory II	731
St. Gregory III	741
St. Zachary	752
Stephen III	757
St. Paul I	767
Stephen IV	772
Adrian I	795
St. Leo III	816
Stephen V	817
St. Paschal I	824
Eugene II	827
Valentine	827
Gregory IV	844
Sergius II	847
St. Leo IV	855
Benedict III	858
St. Nicholas I (the Great)	867
Adrian II	872
John VIII	882
Marinus I	884
St. Adrian III	885
Stephen VI	891
Formosus	896
Boniface VI	896
Stephen VII	897
Romanus	897
Theodore II	897
John IX	900
Benedict IV	903
Leo V	903
Sergius III	911
Anastasius III	913
Landus	914
John X	928
Leo VI	928
Stephen VIII	931
John XI	935
Leo VII	939
Stephen IX	942
Marinus II	946
Agapitus II	955
John XII	964
Leo VIII	965
Benedict V	966
John XIII	972
Benedict VI	974
Benedict VII	983
John XIV	984
John XV	996
Gregory V	999
Sylvester II	1003
John XVII	1003
John XVIII	1009
Sergius IV	1012
Benedict VIII	1024
John XIX	1032
Benedict IX	1044
Benedict IX	1045
Sylvester III	1045
Gregory VI	1046
Clement II	1047
Benedict IX	1048
Damasus II	1048
St. Leo IX	1054
Victor II	1057
Stephen X	1058
Nicholas II	1061
Alexander II	1073
St. Gregory VII	1085
B. Victor III	1087
B. Urban II	1099
Paschal II	1118
Gelasius II	1119
Callistus II	1124
Honorius II	1130
Innocent II	1143
Celestine II	1144
Lucius II	1145
B. Eugene III	1153
Anastasius IV	1154
Adrian IV	1159
Alexander III	1181
Lucius III	1185
Urban III	1187
Gregory VIII	1187
Clement III	1191
Celestine III	1198
Innocent III	1216
Honorius III	1227
Gregory IX	1241
Celestine IV	1241
Innocent IV	1254
Alexander IV	1261
Urban IV	1264
Clement IV	1268
B. Gregory X	1276
B. Innocent V	1276
Adrian V	1276
John XXI	1277
Nicholas III	1280
Martin IV	1285
Honorius IV	1287
Nicholas IV	1292
St. Celestine V	1296
Boniface VIII	1303
B. Benedict XI	1304
Clement V	1314
John XXII	1334
Benedict XII	1342
Clement VI	1352
Innocent VI	1362
B. Urban V	1370
Gregory XI	1378
Urban VI	1389
Boniface IX	1404
Innocent VII	1406
Gregory XII	1415
Martin V	1431
Eugene IV	1447
Nicholas V	1455
Callistus III	1458
Pius II	1464
Paul II	1471
Sixtus IV	1484
Innocent VIII	1492
Alexander VI	1503
Pius III	1503
Julius II	1513
Leo X	1521
Adrian VI	1523
Clement VII	1534
Paul III	1549
Julius III	1555
Marcellus II	1555
Paul IV	1559
Pius IV	1565
St. Pius V	1572
Gregory XIII	1585
Sixtus V	1590
Urban VII	1590
Gregory XIV	1591
Innocent IX	1591
Clement VIII	1605
Leo XI	1605
Paul V	1621
Gregory XV	1623
Urban VIII	1644
Innocent X	1655
Alexander VII	1667
Clement IX	1669
Clement X	1676
B. Innocent XI	1689
Alexander VIII	1691
Innocent XII	1700
Clement XI	1721
Innocent XIII	1724
Benedict XIII	1730
Clement XII	1740
Benedict XIV	1758
Clement XIII	1769
Clement XIV	1774
Pius VI	1799
Pius VII	1823
Leo XII	1829
Pius VIII	1830
Gregory XVI	1846
Pius IX	1878
Leo XIII	1903
St. Pius X	1914
Benedict XV	1922
Pius XI	1939
Pius XII	1958
John XXIII	1963
Paul VI	1978
John Paul I	1978
John Paul II, now reigning.	

PART I
Hierarchy of the Catholic Church

The Hierarchy, as the supreme governing body of the Catholic Church, consists of the Roman Pontiff, the successor of Peter, and the Bishops joined together with him and never without him (canons 330,331,336) in one apostolic college to provide for the common good of the Church. The Roman Pontiff in the exercise of his office is assisted by the College of Cardinals, and further by the departments also called "dicasteries" of the Roman Curia. The bishops, of whom some bear the titles of Patriarch and Archbishop, are united with the Roman Pontiff in the governance of the whole Church; the bishops, when assigned to particular Sees, are individually responsible for the teaching, sanctification and governance of their particular Church. Apostolic Vicars and Prefects together with certain Abbots and other Prelates are also joined in this work.

HIS HOLINESS THE POPE

Bishop of Rome and Vicar of Jesus Christ, Successor of St. Peter, Prince of the Apostles, Supreme Pontiff of the Universal Church. Patriarch of the West Primate of Italy. Archbishop and Metropolitan of the Roman Province, Sovereign of Vatican City State.

JOHN PAUL II

KAROL WOJTYLA

The present successor of St. Peter was born in Wadowice, Diocese of Krakow, May 18, 1920; ordained Priest, November 1, 1946; appointed Titular Bishop of Ombi July 4, 1958; Promoted to Archbishop of Krakow, January 13, 1964; Proclaimed and created Cardinal June 26, 1967. Elected Pope, October 16, 1978; installed October 22, 1978.

VATICAN CITY

Vatican City is the smallest state in the world, occupying 108.7 acres, of which about one third is covered with buildings and is situated on the right side of the Tiber river. Vatican City has territory, population, and sovereignity. This territory, limited as it is, suffices to guarantee the spiritual and temporal independence needed for the exercise of the Holy See's spiritual mission. In 1870 the Kingdom of Italy seized all Vatican possessions which for several centuries had constituted the papal temporal domain. But even after 1870 the Holy See continued to regard itself as a separate entity in international law, and was recognized as such by numerous states with which it retained normal diplomatic relations. After long discussions the Holy See and the then Kingdom of Italy signed the Lateran Pacts on February 11, 1929, so that the complete and independent authority of the Vatican State was and is recognized by the Italian state.

The Sovereign of this small state is His Holiness, the Pope.

The government presently is administered by a Pontifical Commission of which His Eminence Jose Cardinal Castillo Lara is President.

THE COLLEGE OF CARDINALS

The Cardinals constitute a special college and they assist the Roman Pontiff collegially when they are called together to deal with questions of major importance; they do so individually when they assist the Pope especially in the daily care of the universal Church by means of the different offices which they perform (canons 349-350). The Cardinals who are under eighty years of age elect his successor.

The College of Cardinals is divided into three ranks: Cardinal-Bishops, Cardinal-Priests, and Cardinal-Deacons. The College of Cardinals, when complete formerly consisted of 70 members: 6 Cardinal Bishops, 50 Cardinal Priests and 14 Cardinal Deacons, but the late Pontiffs, Pope John XXIII and Pope Paul VI enlarged the College of Cardinals. At the moment the maximum number of Cardinal electors (those under 80 years of age) must not exceed 120.

The Cardinal Bishops (except the Patriarch-Cardinals of the Oriental Rites), have as Titular Sees the Suburban Sees of Rome, which are: *Porto Santa Rufina, Albano, Palestrina, Sabina, Frascati, Velletri, Segni.* The Cardinal Dean has united to his See the See of *Ostia.* The Cardinal Priests take their title from the "Titular Churches" to which they are appointed: the Cardinal Deacons are appointed to other Churches called "Deaconries." The first Cardinal Bishop is *Dean*; the first Cardinal Priest is *First Priest*; and the first Cardinal Deacon is *First Deacon* of the Sacred College. The Dean has the right of ordaining the new Pope if he is not already a bishop; the First Deacon the right of proclaiming him and investing him with the sacred Pallium. On the death of the Pontiff, the Cardinal *Camerlengo* has the Administration of the affairs of the Holy See.

Sometimes the Roman Pontiff promotes a person to the dignity of Cardinal but does not make public his name and keeps it "in pectore." Upon the publication of his name, this Cardinal enjoys his right of precedence from the day on which his name was reserved "in pectore" by the Pope (cfr. Can. 351 3).

The Cardinals of the Holy Roman Church

Listed in Alphabetical Order

Agustoni, Gilberto (Cardinal Deacon), Prefect of the Supreme Tribunal of the Apostolic Signatura; born in Schaffhausen, Switzerland, Diocese of Basel, July 26, 1922. Created and proclaimed November 26, 1994. Address: Via Tiberina, 191, 00188 Rome, Italy.

Ambrozie, Aloysius Matthew (Cardinal Priest), Archbishop of Toronto Canada; born in Gabrje Archdiocese of Ljubljana January 27, 1930. Created and proclaimed February 21, 1998. Address: Chancery Office 1155 Yonge St., Toronto, Ontario.

Angelini, Fiorenzo (Cardinal Deacon), Titular of S. Spirito in Sassia; Former President of the Pontifical Council for Pastoral Assistance to Health Care Workers; in Rome, Italy, August 1, 1916. Created and proclaimed June 28, 1991. Address: 00120 Vatican City State, Europe.

Antonetti, Lorenzo (Cardinal Priest), Titular of Roselle; Pro-President of the Administration ofthe Patrimony of the Apostolic See. Born in Romagnano Sesia, diocese of Novara July 31, 1922. Created and proclaimed February 21, 1998. Address: 00120 Vatican City State, Europe.

Aponte Martinez, Luis (Cardinal Priest), Titular of S. Maria Madre della Provvidenza a Monte Verde, Archbishop of San Juan; born in Lajas, diocese of Mayaguez, August 4, 1922. Created and proclaimed March 5, 1973. Address: Arzobispado, Apartado S-1967, Calle del Cristo 50, San Juan, PR 00902.

Aramburu, Juan Carlos (Cardinal Priest), Titular of San Giovanni Battista dei Fiorentini, Archbishop Emeritus of Buenos Aires; born in Reduccion, Diocese of Rio Cuarto, February 11, 1912. Created and proclaimed May 24, 1976. Address: La Pampa 4022, 1430 Buenos Aires, Argentina.

Arinze, Francis (Cardinal Priest), Titular of San Giovanni della Pigna; President of the Pontifical Council for Inter-Religious Dialogue; born in Eziowelle, Archdiocese of Onitsha, November 1, 1932. Created and proclaimed May 25, 1985. Address: Largo del Colonnato 3, 00193 Rome, Italy.

Arns, Paul Evaristo, *o.f.m.* (Cardinal Priest), Titular of S. Antonio da Padova in Via Tuscolana, Archbishop of Sao Paulo; born in Forquilhinha, Diocese of Tubarao, September 14, 1921. Created and proclaimed March 5, 1973. Address: Caixa Postal 916, Rua Alfredo Maia, 195, 01106 Sao Paulo, SP, Brazil.

Bafile, Corrado (Cardinal Priest), Titular of Santa Maria in Portico; born in L'Aquila, July 4, 1903. Created and proclaimed May 24, 1976. Address: Via P. Pancrazio Pfeiffer 10, 00193 Rome, Italy.

Balland, Jean (Cardinal Priest), Archbishop of Lyons, France; born in Bue Archdiocese of Bourges July 26, 1934. Created and proclaimed February 21, 1998. Address: 1 Place de Fourviere, 69321 Lyon Cedex 05, France.

Ballestrero, Anastasio Alberto, *o.c.d.* (Cardinal Priest), Titular of S. Maria Sopra Minerva, Archbishop Emeritus of Turin; born in Genoa, October 3, 1913. Created and proclaimed June 30, 1979. Address: Fortino Santa Maria, 19030 Bocca di Magra (La Spezia), Italy.

Baum, William Wakefield (Cardinal Priest), Titular of Santa Croce in Via Flaminia; "Penitenziere Maggiore" born in Dallas, Texas, November 21, 1926. Created and proclaimed, May 24, 1976. Address: Via Rusticucci 13, 00193 Rome, Italy.

Bertoli, Paolo (Cardinal Bishop), Titular Bishop of Frascati; born in Poggio Garfagnana, Diocese of Massa Carrara-Pontremoli, February 1, 1908. Created and proclaimed April 28, 1969. Address: Piazza della Citta Leonina 1, 00193 Rome, Italy.

Bevilacqua, Anthony J. (Cardinal Priest), Titular of Ss. Redentore e S. Alfonso in Via Merulana, Archbishop of Philadelphia; born in Brooklyn, New York, June 17, 1923. Created and proclaimed June 28, 1991. Address: 222 N. 17th St., Philadelphia, PA 19103-1299, U.S.A.

Biffi, Giacomo (Cardinal Priest), Titular of Ss. Giovanni Evangelista e Petronio, Archbishop of Bologna; born in Milan, June 13, 1928. Created and proclaimed May 25, 1985. Address: Arcivescovado, Via Altabella 6, 40126 Bologna, Italy.

Bovone, Alberto (Cardinal Priest), Titular of Caesarea in Numidia, Pro-Prefect of the Congregation for the Causes of Saints. Born in Frugarolo, Diocese of Alessandria June 11, 1922. Created and proclaimed February 21, 1998. Address: 00120 Vatican City State, Europe.

Canestri, Giovanni (Cardinal Priest), Titular of St. Andrea della Valle, Archbishop Emeritus of Genoa; born in Castelspina, Diocese of Alessandria, September 30, 1918. Created and proclaimed June 28, 1988. Address: Via Cernaia 9, 00185 Rome, Italy.

Caprio, Giuseppe (Cardinal Priest), Titular of S. Maria Ausiliatrice in Via Tuscolana; born in Lapio, Archdiocese of Benevento, November 15, 1914. Created and proclaimed June 30, 1979. Address: 00120 Vatican City State, Europe.

Carberry, John J. (Cardinal Priest), Titular of S. Giovanni Battista de Rossi a Via Latina, Archbishop Emeritus of St. Louis; born in Brooklyn, New York, July 31, 1904. Created and proclaimed April 28, 1969. Address: 4445 Lindell Blvd., St. Louis, MO 63108, U.S.A.

Carles Gordo, Ricardo Maria (Cardinal Priest), Archbishop of Barcelona, Spain; born in Valencia, September 24, 1926. Created and proclaimed November 26, 1994. Address: Arzobispado, Carrer del Bisbe 5, 08002 Barcelona, Spain.

Carter, Gerald Emmett (Cardinal Priest), Titular of S. Maria in Traspontina, Archbishop Emeritus of Toronto; born in Montreal, March 1, 1912. Created and proclaimed June 30, 1979. Address: 355 Church St., Toronto, Ont., M5B 1Z8, Canada.

Casaroli, Agostino (Cardinal Bishop), Titular Bishop of Porto-Santa Rufina and "in commendam" Titular of SS. XII Apostoli; born in Castel S. Giovanni, Diocese of Piacenza-Bobbio, November 24, 1914. Created and proclaimed June 30, 1979. Address: 00120 Vatican City State, Europe.

Casoria, Giuseppe (Cardinal Deacon),Deacon of S. Giuseppe in via Trionfale; born in Acerra, October 1, 1908. Created and proclaimed February 2, 1983. Address: Via P. Pancrazio Pfeiffer 10, 00193 Rome, Italy.

Cassidy, Edward I. (Cardinal Deacon), Deacon of S. Maria in Via Lata, President of the Pontifical Council for Promoting Christian Unity; born in Sydney, Australia, July 5, 1924. Created and proclaimed June 28, 1991. Address: 00120 Vatican City State, Europe.

Castillo Lara, Rosalio Jose, *s.d.b.* (Cardinal Priest), Titular of Nostra Signora di Coromoto in S. Giovanni di Dio, President of the Pontifical Commission for Vatican City; born in San Casimiro, Diocese of Maracay, September 4, 1922. Born in Medellin July 4, 1929. Created and proclaimed May 25, 1985. Address: 00120 Vatican City State, Europe.

Castrillon Hoyos, Dario (Cardinal Priest), Archbishop of Bucaramanga, Colombia; Pro-Prefect of the Congregation of Clergy. Created and proclaimed February 21, 1998. Address: 00120 Vatican City State, Europe.

Ce', Marco (Cardinal Priest), Titular of S. Marco, Patriarch of Venice; born in Izano, Diocese of Crema, July 8, 1925. Created and proclaimed June 30, 1979. Address: S. Marco 318, 30124 Venezia, Italy.

Cheli, Giovanni (Cardinal Priest), Titular Archbishop of Santa Giusta, President6 of the Pontifical Council for the Pastoral Care of Migrants and Itinerant People; born in Torino October 4, 1918. Created and proclaimed February 21, 1998. Address: 00120 Vatican City State, Europe.

Clancy, Edward Bede (Cardinal Priest), Titular of S. Maria in Vallicella, Archbishop of Sydney; born in Lithgow, Diocese of Bathurst, December 13, 1923. Created and proclaimed June 28, 1988. Address: St. Mary Cathedral, St. Mary and College Sts., Sydney, NSW 2000, Australia.

Colasuonno, Francesco (Cardinal Priest), Titular Archbishop of Truentum, Apostolic Nuncio in Italy; born in Grumo, Appula Archdiocese of Bari-Bitonte January 2, 1925. Created and proclaimed February 21, 1998.

Corripio Ahumada, Ernesto (Cardinal Priest), Titular dell'Immacolata al Tiburtino, Archbishop Emeritus of Mexico City; born in Tampico, June 29, 1919. Address: Apolinar Nieto, 40, Tetlameya, 04730 Mexico, D.F. Mexico.

Daly, Cahal Brendan (Cardinal Priest), Titular of S. Patrizio, Archbishop Emeritus of Armagh; born in Loughguile, Diocese of Down and Connor, October 1, 1917. Created and proclaimed June 28, 1991. Address: Archbishop's House, Ara Coeli, Armagh BT61 7QY, Ireland.

Danneels, Godfried (Cardinal Priest), Titular of S. Anastasia, Archbishop of Malines-Bruxelles; born in Kanegem, Diocese of Brugge, June 4, 1933. Created and proclaimed February 2, 1983. Address: Aartsbisdom, Wollemarkt 15, B-2800 Mechelen, Belgium.

Darmaatmadja, Julius Riyadi, *s.j.* (Cardinal Priest), Archbishop of Jakarta, Indonesia; born in Muntilan, Archdiocese of Semarang, December 20, 1934. Created and proclaimed November 26, 1994. Address: Keus Kupan Agung, Jl. Katedral 7, Jakarta 10710, Indonesia.

De Giorgi, Salvatore (Cardinal Priest), Archbishop of Palermo; born in Vernole Aarchdiocese of Lecce September 6, 1930. Created and proclaimed February 21, 1998. Address: Corso Cittorio Emanuele 461, 90134 Palermo, Italy.

Deskur, Andrzej Maria (Cardinal Deacon), Deacon of S. Cesareo in Palatio; born in Sancygniow, Diocese of Kielce, February 29, 1924. Created and proclaimed May 25, 1985. Address: 00120 Vatican City State, Europe.

Dezza, Paolo, *s.j.* (Cardinal Deacon), Deacon of S. Ignazio di Loyola a Campo Marzio, Rector emeritus of Gregorian University; born in Parma, December 13, 1901. Created and proclaimed June 28, 1991. Address: Borgo S. Spirito, 5, 00193 Rome, Italy.

do Nascimento, Alexandre (Cardinal Priest), Titular of S. Marco in Agro Laurentino, Archbishop of Luanda; born in Malanje, March 1, 1925. Created and proclaimed February 2, 1983. Address: Arcebispado, C.P. 87, 1230-C Luanda, Angola.

Echeverria Ruiz, Bernardino, *o.f.m.* (Cardinal Priest), Archbishop Emeritus of Guayaquil; born in Cotacachi, Diocese of Ibarra, November 12, 1912. Created and proclaimed November 26, 1994. Address: Garcia Moreno 548 y Bolivar, Casilla 10-01-04, Ibarra, Ecuador.

Etchegaray, Roger (Cardinal Priest), Titular of S. Leone I, President of Pontifical Council for Justice and Peace, also President of the Central Committee of the Holy Year 2,000; born in Espelette, Diocese of Bayonne, September 25, 1922. Created and proclaimed June 30, 1979. Address: Piazza San Calisto 16, 00153 Rome, Italy.

Etsou-Nzabi-Bamungwabi, Frederic, *C.I.C.M.* (Cardinal Priest), Titular of S. Lucia a Piazza d'Armi, Archbishop of Kinshasa; born in Mazalonga, Diocese of Lisala, December 3, 1930. Created and proclaimed June 28, 1991. Address: Archeveche, B.P. 8431, Kinshasa 1, Rep. du Zaire.

Eyt, Pierre (Cardinal Priest), Archbishop of Bordeaux, France; born in Laruns, Diocese of Bayonne, June 4, 1934. Created and proclaimed November 26, 1994. Address: Archeveche, B.P. 79, 183 cours de la Somme, 33034 Bordeaux Cedex, France.

Fagiolo, Vincenzo (Cardinal Deacon), President of the Disciplinary Commission of the Roman Curia; born in Segni, Italy, February 5, 1918. Created and proclaimed November 26, 1994. Address: Via Rusticucci 13, 00193 Rome, Italy.

Falcao, Jose Freire (Cardinal Priest), Titular of S. Luca a Via Prenestina, Archbishop of Brasilia; born in Erere, Diocese of Limoeira do Norte, October 23, 1925. Created and proclaimed June 28, 1988. Address: QL 12-Cj12, Lote 1, Lago Sul, 71600-325 Brasilia, D.F., Brazil.

Felici, Angelo (Cardinal Deacon), Deacon of Ss. Biagio e Carlo ai Catinari, President of the Pontifical Commission "Ecclesia Dei"; born in Segni, July 27, 1919. Created and proclaimed June 28, 1988. Address: Piazza della Citta Leonina 9, 00193 Rome, Italy.

Fernandes de Arujo, Serafim (Cardinal Priest), Archbishop of Belo Horizone, Brazil; born in Minas Novas Diocese of Aracuai August 13, 1924. Created and proclaimed February 21, 1998. Address: Metropolitan Curia Av. Brazil 2079, C.P. 494, 30140-002 Belo Horizone, MG, Brazil.

Fresno Larrain, Juan Francisco (Cardinal Priest), Titular of S. Maria Immacolata di Lourdes a Boccea, Archbishop Emeritus of Santiago, Chile; born in Santiago, Chile on July 26, 1914. Created and proclaimed May 25, 1985. Address: Laura Tromben 5675, Vitacura, Santiago, Chile.

Furno, Carlo (Cardinal Deacon), Grand Master of the Equestrian Order of the Holy Sepulchre of Jerusalem; born in Bairo Canavese, Diocese of Ivrea, December 2, 1921. Created and proclaimed November 26, 1994. Address: Piazza della Citta Leonina 1, 00193 Rome, Italy.

Gagnon, Edouard, *p.s.s.* (Cardinal Priest), Titular of S. Marcello; President of the Pontifical Committee for International Eucharistic Congresses; born in Port-Daniel, Diocese of Gaspe, January 15, 1918. Created and proclaimed May 25, 1985. Address: Via di Porta Angelica 31, 00193 Rome, Italy.

Gantin, Bernardin (Cardinal Bishop), Titular Bishop of Palestrina; Prefect Congregation for the Bishops and President of the Pontifical Commission for Latin America & Dean of the College of Cardinals; born in Toffo, Archdiocese of Cotonou, May 8, 1922. Created and proclaimed June 27, 1977. Address: 00120 Vatican City State, Europe.

George, Francis E., *o.m.i.*, (Cardinal Priest) Archbishop of Chicago; born in Chicago, Illinois USA January 16, 1937. Created and proclaimed February 21, 1998. Address: Post Office Box 1979, Chicago, Illinois 60690.

Giordano, Michele (Cardinal Priest), Titular of S. Gioacchino ai Prati di Castello, Archbishop of Naples; born in S. Arcangelo, Diocese of Tursi-Lagonegro, September 26, 1930. Created and proclaimed June 28, 1988. Address: Largo Donnaregina 23, 80138 Napoli, Italy.

Glemp, Jozef (Cardinal Priest), Titular of S. Maria in Trastevere, Archbishop of Warsaw; born in Inowroclaw, Archdiocese of Gniezno, December 18, 1929. Created and proclaimed February 2, 1983. Address: ul. Miodowa 17-19, 00-246 Warsaw, Poland.

Gong, Pin-mei Ignatius (Cardinal Priest), Titular of S. Sisto, Bishop of Shanghai and Apostolic Administrator of Soochow; born in P'ou-tong, Diocese of Shanghai, August 2, 1901. Created and reserved "in pectore" in the Consistory of June 30, 1979; proclaimed in the Consistory of June 28, 1991. Address: Our Lady Queen of the Clergy Home, 128 Strawberry Hill Ave., Stamford, CT 06904-1222, U.S.A.

Gonzalez Martin, Marcelo (Cardinal Priest), Titular of S. Agostino, Archbishop Emeritus of Toledo; born in Villanubla, Archdiocese of Valladolid, January 16, 1918. Created and proclaimed March 5, 1973. Address: Arco de Palacio 3, 45002 Toledo, Spain.

Gouyon, Paul (Cardinal Priest), Titular of Nativita di N.S.G.C. a via Gallia, Archbishop Emeritus of Rennes; born in Bordeaux, October 24, 1910. Created and proclaimed April 28, 1969. Address: 181, rue Judaique, 33081 Bordeaux Cedex, France.

Grillmeier, Alois, *s.j.* (Cardinal Deacon), Deacon of S. Nicola in Carcere, Germany. Created and proclaimed November 26, 1994. Address: Kaulbachstr. 31a, D-80538 Munchen, Germany.

Groer, Hans Herrmann, *o.s.b.* (Cardinal Priest), Titular of Ss. Gioacchino ed Anna al Tuscolano, Archbishop Emeritus of Vienna; born in Vienna, October 13, 1919. Created and proclaimed June 28, 1988. Address: Wollzeile 2, A-1010 Vienna, Austria.

Gulbinowicz, Henryk Roman (Cardinal Priest), Titular dell'Immacolata Concezione di Maria a Grottarossa, Archbishop of Wroclaw; born in Szukiszki, Archdiocese of Wilno, October 17, 1928. Created and proclaimed May 25, 1985. Address: ul. Katedralna 11, 50-328 Wroclaw, Poland.

Hickey, James Aloysius (Cardinal Priest), Titular Maria Madre del Redentore a Tor Bellamonica, Archbishop of Washington; born in Midland, Michigan, Diocese of Saginaw, October 11, 1920. Created and proclaimed June 28, 1988. Address: Archdiocesan Pastoral Center, 5001 Eastern Ave., P.O. Box 29260, Washington, DC 20017, U.S.A.

Hume, George Basil, *o.s.b.* (Cardinal Priest), Titular of San Silvestro in Capite, Archbishop of Westminster; born in Newcastle-on-Tyne, Diocese of Hexham and Newcastle March 2, 1923. Created and proclaimed May 24, 1976. Address: Archbishop's House, Ambrosden Ave., Westminster, London, SW1P-1QJ England, Great Britain.

Innocenti, Antonio (Cardinal Priest), Titular of S. Maria in Aquiro, born in Poppi, Diocese of Fiesole, August 23, 1915. Created and proclaimed May 25, 1985. Address: Piazza della Citta Leonina 9, 00193 Rome, Italy.

Javierre Ortas, Antonio Maria, *s.d.b.* (Cardinal Deacon), Deacon of S. Maria Liberatrice a Monte Testaccio, Former Prefect of Congregation for Divine Worship and the Discipline of the Sacraments; born at Sietamo, Diocese of Huesca, February 21, 1921. Created and proclaimed June 28, 1988. Address: Via Rusticucci 13, 00193 Rome, Italy.

Keeler, William Henry (Cardinal Priest), Archbishop of Baltimore; born in San Antonio, Texas, March 4, 1931. Created and proclaimed November 26, 1994. Address: 320 Cathedral Street, Baltimore, Maryland 21201. U.S.A.

Kim, Stephen Sou Hwan (Cardinal Priest), Titular of S. Felice da Cantalice a Centocelle, Archbishop of Seoul; born in Tae Gu, May 8, 1922. Created and proclaimed April 28, 1969. Address: Archbishop's House, 2Ka-1 Myong Dong, Jung Ku, Seoul 100-022, Korea.

Kitbunchu, Michael Michai (Cardinal Priest), Titular of S. Lorenzo in Panisperna, Archbishop of Bangkok; born in Samphan, Archdiocese of Bangkok, January 29, 1929. Created and proclaimed February 2, 1983. Address: Assumption Cathedral, 51 Oriental Ave., Bangkok 10500, Thailand.

Konig, Franz (Cardinal Priest), Titular of S. Eusebio, Archbishop Emeritus of Vienna; born in Rabenstein, Diocese of St. Poelten, August 3, 1905. Created and proclaimed December 15, 1958. Address: Wollzeile 2, A-1010 Wien, Austria.

Korec, Jan Chryzostom (Cardinal Priest), Titular of Ss. Fabiano e Venanzio a Villa Fiorelli, Bishop of Nitra, born in Bosany, Diocese of Nitra, January 22, 1924. Created and proclaimed June 28, 1991. Address: Biskupsky urad, post. schranka 46A, 950 50 Nitra-Hrad, Slovakia.

Kozlowiecki, Adam, *s.j.*, (Cardinal Priest), Titular Archbishop of Potenza Picena; born in Huta Komorowska Diocese of Sandomierz April 1, 1911. Created and proclaimed February 21, 1998. Address: P.O. Box 50003, 15101 Ridgeway, Zambia.

Kuharic, Franjo (Cardinal Priest), Titular S. Girolamo dei Croati, Archbishop of Zagreb; born in Pribic, Archdiocese of Zagreb April 15, 1919. Created and proclaimed February 2, 1983. Address: Kaptol 31, p.p. 553, 10000, Zagreb, Croatia.

Laghi, Pio (Cardinal Deacon), Deacon of S. Maria Ausiliatrice in Via Tuscolana, Prefect of the Congregation for Catholic Education; born in Castiglione, Diocese of Forli-Bertinoro, May 21, 1922. Created and proclaimed June 28, 1991. Address: 00120 Vatican City State, Europe.

Law, Bernard Francis (Cardinal Priest), Titular of S. Susanna, Archbishop of Boston; born in Torreon, November 4, 1931. Created and proclaimed May 25, 1985. Address: 2101 Commonwealth Ave., Brighton, MA 02135, U.S.A.

Lebrun Moratinos, Jose Ali (Cardinal Priest), Titular of S. Pancrazio, Archbishop Emeritus of Caracas; born in Puerto Cabello, Archdiocese of Valencia, March 19, 1919. Created and proclaimed February 2, 1983. Address: Palacio Arzobispal, Qta. Silvestre, Calle Otama, Valle Arriba, Caracas 1060, Venezuela.

Lopez Rodriguez, Nicolas de Jesus (Cardinal Priest), Titular of S. Pio X alla Balduina, Archbishop of Santo Domingo; born in Barranca, Diocese of La Vega, October 31, 1936. Created and proclaimed June 28, 1991. Address: Arzobispado, Apartado 186, Calle Isabel la Catolica 55, Santo Domingo, Dominican Republic.

Lopez Trujillo, Alfonso (Cardinal Priest), Titular of S. Prisca, President of the Pontifical Council for the Family; born in Villahermosa, Archdiocese of Ibague, November 8, 1935. Created and proclaimed February 2, 1983. Address: Piazza S. Calisto 16, 00153 Rome, Italy.

Lorscheider, Aloisio, *o.f.m.* (Cardinal Priest), Titular of San Pietro in Montorio, Archbishop of Aparecida; born in Picada Geraldo, Archdiocese of Porto Alegre, October 8, 1924. Created and proclaimed May 24, 1976. Address: Curia Metropolitana, C.P. 05, Torre da Basilica 48 andar, 12570-000 Aparecida, S.P., Brazil.

Lourdusamy, D. Simon (Cardinal Priest), Titular of S. Maria delle Grazie alle Fornaci fuori Porta Cavalleggeri; born in Kalleri, Archdioccese of Pondicherry and Cuddalore, February 5, 1924. Created and proclaimed May 25, 1985. Address: Via dei Corridori 64, 00193 Rome, Italy.

Lubachivsky, Myroslav Ivan (Cardinal Priest), Titular of S. Sofia a via Boccea, Major Archbishop of Lviv of the Ukrainians; born in Dolyna, Archdiocese of Lviv of the Ukrainians, June 24, 1914. Created and proclaimed May 25, 1985. Address: Sobor Sviatoho Jura, Ploshcha Sviatoho Jura 5, 290000 Lviv, Ukraina.

Lustiger, Jean-Marie (Cardinal Priest), Titular of S. Luigi dei Francesi, Archbishop of Paris; born in Paris, September 17, 1926. Created and proclaimed February 2, 1983. Address: 8 rue de la Ville l'Eveque, 75384, Paris, Cedex 08, France.

Macharski, Franciszek (Cardinal Priest), Titular of S. Giovanni a Porta Latina, Archbishop of Krakow; born in Krakow, May 20, 1927. Created and proclaimed June 30, 1979. Address: ul. Franciszkanska 3, 31-004 Krakow, Poland.

Mahony, Roger M. (Cardinal Priest), Titular of Ss. Quattro Coronati, Archbishop of Los Angeles; born in Hollywood, California, Archdiocese of Los Angeles, February 27, 1936. Created and proclaimed June 28, 1991. Address: 1531 W. 9th St., Los Angeles, CA 90015-1194, U.S.A.

Maida, Adam Joseph (Cardinal Priest), Archbishop of Detroit; born in East Vandergrift, Pennsylvania, Diocese of Greensburg, March 18, 1930. Created and proclaimed November 26, 1994. Address: 1234 Washington Blvd., Detroit, Michigan 48226, U.S.A.

Margeot, Jean (Cardinal Priest), Titular of S. Gabriele Arcangelo all Acqua Traversa, Bishop Emeritus of Port-Louis; born at Quatre-Bornes, Diocese of Port Louis, February 3, 1916. Created and proclaimed June 28, 1988. Address: Eveche, rue 13 Mgr Gonin, Port-Louis, Ile Maurice.

Martinez Somalo, Eduardo (Cardinal Deacon), Protodeacon of SS. Nome di Gesu', Prefect of the Congregation for Institutes of Consecrated Life and for Societies of Apostolic Life; born at Banos de Rio Tobia, Diocese of Calahorra and Calzada-Logrono, March 3, 1927. Created and proclaimed June 28, 1988. Address: 00120 Vatican City State, Europe.

Martini, Carlo Maria, *s.j.* (Cardinal Priest), Titular of S. Cecilia, Archbishop of Milan; born in Turin, February 15, 1927. Created and proclaimed February 2, 1983. Address: Palazzo Arcivescovile, Piazza Fontana 2, 20122 Milan, Italy.

Mayer, Paul Augustin, *o.s.b.* (Cardinal Priest), Titular of S. Anselmo all' Aventino; born in Altotting, Diocese of Passau, May 23, 1911. Created and proclaimed May 25, 1985. Address: Via Rusticucci 13, 00193 Rome, Italy.

Medina Estevez, Jorge Arturo (Cardinal Priest), Archbishop Emeritus of Valparaiso, Chile, Pro-Prefect of the Congregation for Divine Worship and the Discipline of the Sacraments; born in Santiago de Chile December 23, 1926. Created and proclaimed February 21, 1998. Address: 00120 Vatican City State, Europe.

Meisner, Joachim (Cardinal Priest), Titular of S. Pudenziana, Archbishop of Cologne; born in Breslau, December 25, 1933. Created and proclaimed February 2, 1983. Address: Kardinal-Frings-Strasse 10, D-50668 Koln 1, Bundesrepublik, Germany.

Monduzzi, Dino (Cardinal Priest), Titular Bishop of Capri, Prefect of the Papal Household; born in Brisighell Diocese of Faenza-Modigliana April 2, 1922. Created and proclaimed February 21, 1998. Address: 00120 Vatican City State, Europe.

Neves, Lucas Moreira, *o.p.* (Cardinal Priest), Titular of Ss. Bonifacio e Alessio, Archbishop of Sao Salvador da Bahia; born in Sao Joao Del Rei, September 16, 1925. Created and proclaimed June 28, 1988. Address: Av. 7 de Setembro 1682, Campo Grande, 40080-001 Salvador, B.A., Brazil.

Noe', Virgilio (Cardinal Deacon), Deacon of S. Giovanni Bosco, Vicar General of Vatican City State, Archpriest of St. Peter Basilica; born in Zelata di Bereguardo, Diocese of Pavia, March 30, 1922. Created and proclaimed June 28, 1991. Address: 00120 Vatican City State, Europe.

Obando Bravo, Miguel, *s.d.b.* (Cardinal Priest), Titular of S. Giovanni Evangelista a Spinaceto, Archbishop of Managua; born in La Libertad of the Prelature of Juigalpa, February 2, 1926. Created and proclaimed May 25, 1985. Address: Arzobispado, Apartado 3058, Managua, Nicaragua.

O'Connor, John Joseph (Cardinal Priest), Titular of Ss. Giovanni e Paolo, Archbishop of New York; born in Philadelphia, January 15, 1920. Created and proclaimed May 25, 1985. Address: 452 Madison Ave., New York, NY 10022, U.S.A.

Oddi, Silvio (Cardinal Priest), Titular of S. Agata de'Goti; born in Morfasso, Diocese of Piacenza-Bobbio, November 14, 1910. Created and proclaimed April 28, 1969. Address: Via delle Grazie 3, 00193 Rome, Italy.

Ortega y Alamino, Jaime Lucas (Cardinal Priest), Archbishop of San Cristobal de La Habana, Cuba; born in Jaguey Grande, Diocese of Matanzas, October 18, 1936. Created and proclaimed November 26, 1994. Address: Calle Habana 152, Apartado 594, La Habana, 10100 Cuba.

Otunga, Maurice Michael (Cardinal Priest), Titular of San Gregorio Barbarigo, Archbishop of Nairobi; born in Chebukwa, Diocese of Kakamega, January 1923. Created and proclaimed March 5, 1973. Address: Arcibishop's House, P.O. Box 14231, Nairobi, Kenya.

Oviedo Cavada, Carlos, *O.de.M.* (Cardinal Priest), Titular of S. Maria della Scala, Archbishop of Santiago de Chile, Chile; born in Santiago de Chile, January 19, 1927. Created and proclaimed November 26, 1994. Address: Simon Bolivar 2843, Santiago, Chile.

Padiyara, Anthony (Cardinal Priest), Titular of S. Maria "Regina Pacis" a Monte Verde, Major Archbishop of Ernakulam of the Syro-Malabar Rite; born at Manimala, Archdiocese of Changanacherry, February 11, 1921. Created and proclaimed June 28, 1988. Address: Cardinal's House, P.O. Box 2580, Ernakulam, Kochi-682031, Kerala, India.

Palazzini, Pietro (Cardinal Priest), Titular of S. Girolamo della Carita'; born in Piobbico, Diocese of Fano-Fossombrone-Cagli-Pergola, May 19, 1912. Created and proclaimed March 5, 1973. Address: Via Proba Petronia 83, 00136 Rome, Italy.

Pappalardo, Salvatore (Cardinal Priest), Titular of S. Maria Odigitria dei Siciliani, Archbishop Emeritus of Palermo; born in Villafranca Sicula, diocese of Agrigento, September 23, 1918. Created and proclaimed March 5, 1973. Address: Arcivescovado, Via Matteo Bonello 2, 90134 Palermo, Italy.

Pengo, Polycarp (Cardinal Priest), Archbishop of Dar-es-Salaam, Tanzania; born in Mwazye Diocese of Sumbawanga August 5, 1944. Created and proclaimed February 21, 1998. Address: Archbishops House, P.O. Box 167, Dar-es-Salaam, Tanzania.

Paskai, Laszlo, *o.f.m.* (Cardinal Priest), Titular of S. Teresa al Corso d'Italia, Archbishop of Esztergom-Budapest; born at Szeged, May 8, 1927. Created and proclaimed June 28, 1988. Address: Uri utca 62, H-1014 Budapest, Hungary.

Pham Dinh Tung, Paul Joseph (Cardinal Priest), Archbishop of Ha Noi, Viet Nam; born in Binh Hoa, Diocese of Phat Diem, June 15, 1919. Created and proclaimed November 26, 1994. Address: Toa Tong Giam Muc, 40 Pho Nha Chung, Ha Noi, Viet Nam.

Pimenta, Simon Ignatius (Cardinal Priest), Titular of S. Maria "Regina Mundi" a Torre Spaccata, Archbishop of Bombay; born in Marol, Archdiocese of Bombay, March 1, 1920. Created and proclaimed June 28, 1988. Address: Archbishop's House, 21 Nathalal Parekh Marg, Bombay-400001, India.

Piovanelli, Silvano (Cardinal Priest), Titular of S. Maria delle Grazie a Via Trionfale, Archbishop of Florence; born in Ronta di Mugello, Archdiocese of Florence, February 21, 1924. Created and proclaimed May 25, 1985. Address: Arcivescovado, Piazza S. Giovanni 3, 50129 Firenze, Italy.

Poggi, Luigi (Cardinal Deacon), Librarian and Archivist of the Holy Roman Church; born in Piacenza, Italy, November 25, 1917. Created and proclaimed November 26, 1994. Address: 00120 Vatican City State, Europe.

Poupard, Paul (Cardinal Priest), Titular of S. Prassede, President of the Pontifical Council of Culture; born in Bouzille, Diocese of Angers, August 30, 1930. Created and proclaimed May 25, 1985. Address: Piazza San Calisto 16, 00153 Rome, Italy.

Primatesta, Raul Francisco (Cardinal Priest), Titular of S. Maria Vergine Addolorata a Piazza Buenos Aires, Archbishop of Cordoba; born in Capilla del Senor, Diocese of Zarate-Campana, April 14, 1919. Created and proclaimed March 5, 1973. Address: Arzobispado, Avda H. Irigoyen 98, 5000 Cordoba, Argentina.

Puljic, Vinko (Cardinal Priest), Archbishop of Vrhbosna- Sarajevo, Bosnia-Hercegovina; born in Prijecani, Diocese of Banja Luke, September 8, 1945. Created and proclaimed November 26, 1994. Address: Nadbiskupski Ordinarijat, Kaptol 7, 71000 Sarajevo, Bosnia Hercegovina.

Quarracino, Antonio (Cardinal Priest), Titular of S. Maria della Salute a Primavalle, Archbishop of Buenos Aires; born in Pollica, Diocese of Vallo della Lucania, August 8, 1923. Created and proclaimed June 28, 1991. Address: Arzobispado, Rivadavia 415, 1002 Buenos Aires, Argentina.

Ratzinger, Joseph (Cardinal Bishop), Titular of Velletri-Segni, Prefect Congregation for the Doctrine of the Faith and President of the Pontifical Bible

Commission; born in Marktl am Inn, Diocese of Passau, April 16, 1927. Created and proclaimed June 27, 1977. Address: 00120 Vatican City State, Europe.

Razafindratandra, Armand Gaetan (Cardinal Priest), Archbishop of Antananarivo, Madagascar; born in Ambohimalaza, Archdiocese of Antananarivo, August 7, 1925. Created and proclaimed November 26, 1994. Address: Archeveche, Andohalo, Antanarivo 101, Madagascar.

Ribeiro, Antonio (Cardinal Priest), Titular of S. Antonio da Padova in Via Merulana, Patriarch of Lisbon; born in Gandarela de Basto, Archdiocese of Braga, May 21, 1928. Created and proclaimed March 5, 1973. Address: Campo dos Martires da Patria 45, 1150 Lisboa Codex, Portugal.

Righi-Lambertini, Egano (Cardinal Priest), Titular of S. Maria in Via; born in Casalecchio di Reno, Archdiocese of Bologna, February 22, 1906. Created and proclaimed June 30, 1979. Address: Piazza della Citta Leonina 9, 00193 Rome, Italy.

Rivera Carrera, Norberto (Cardinal Priest), Archbishop of Mexico City; born in Tepehuanes Archdiocese of Durango June 6, 1942. Created and proclaimed February 21, 1998. Address: Apartado Postal 24-433, Durango 90, Col. Roma, 06700 Mexico D.F. Mexico.

Rossi, Opilio (Cardinal Priest), Titular of S. Lorenzo in Lucina; born in New York, May 14, 1910. Created and proclaimed May 24, 1976. Address: Via della Scrofa, 70, 00186 Rome, Italy.

Rouco Varela, Antonio Maria (Cardinal Priest), Archbishop of Madrid Spain; born in Villalba Diocese of Mondonedo-Ferrol August 24, 1936. Created and proclaimed February 21, 1998. Address: Bailen 8, 28071, Madrid, Spain.

Ruini, Camillo (Cardinal Priest), Titular of S. Agnese, Vicar General of His Holiness of the Diocese of Rome; born in Sassuolo, Diocese of Reggio Emilia-Guastalla, February 19, 1931. Created and proclaimed June 28, 1991. Address: Piazza San Giovanni in Laterano 4, 00184 Rome, Italy.

Sabattani, Aurelio (Cardinal Deacon), Deacon of S. Apollinare alle Terme Neroniane-Allessandrine; born in Casal Fiumanese, Diocese of di Imola, October 18, 1912. Created and proclaimed February 2, 1983. Address: Palazzo del Tribunale, Piazza S. Marta, 00120 Vatican City State, Europe.

Saldarini, Giovanni (Cardinal Priest), Titular S. Cuore di Gesu' a Castro Pretorio, Archbishop of Torino; born in Cantu, Archdiocese of Milan, December 11, 1924. Created and proclaimed June 28, 1991. Address: via Arcivescovado 12, 10121 Torino, Italy.

Sales, Eugenio De Araujo (Cardinal Priest), Titular of S. Gregorio VII, Archbishop of Sao Sebastiao do Rio de Janeiro; born in Acari, Diocese of Caico, November 8, 1920. Created and proclaimed April 28, 1969. Address: Rua da Gloria, 446, C.P. 1362, 20001-970 Rio de Janeiro, R.J., Brazil.

Sanchez, Jose T. (Cardinal Deacon), Titular of St. Pio V, Former Prefect of the Congregation for the Clergy; born in Pandan, Diocese of Virac, March 17, 1920. Created and proclaimed June 28, 1991. Address: 00120 Vatican City State, Europe.

Sandoval Iniguez, Juan (Cardinal Priest), Archbishop of Guadalajara, Mexico; born in Yahualica, Diocese of San Juan de los Lagos, March 28, 1933. Created and proclaimed November 26, 1994. Address: Arzobispado, Apartado Postal 1-331, Liceo 17, 44100 Guadalajara, Jal., Mexico.

Santos, Alexandre Jose Maria dos, *o.f.m.* (Cardinal Priest), Titular of S. Frumenzio ai Prati Fiscali, Archbishop of Maputo; born in Zavala, Diocese of Inhambane, March 18, 1924. Created and proclaimed June 28, 1988. Address: Paco Arquiepiscopal, Avenida Eduardo Mondlane 1448, C.P. 258, Maputo, Mozambique.

Schonborn, Christoph, *o.p.*, (Cardinal Priest), Archbishop of Vienna, Austria; born in Skalsko, Diocese of Litomerice January 22, 1945. Created and proclaimed February 21, 1998. Address: Wolzeile 2, Vienna, Austria A-1010.

Schotte, Jan P., *c.i.c.m.* (Cardinal Deacon), General Secretary of the Synod of Bishops; born in Beveren-Leie, Diocese of Brugge, April 20, 1928. Created and proclaimed November 26, 1994. Address: Palazzo del Bramante, Via della Conciliazione, 34, 00193 Rome, Italy.

Schwery, Henri (Cardinal Priest), Titular of Ss. Protomartiri a Via Aurelia Antica, Bishop Emeritus of Sion; born in Saint Leonard, Diocese of Sion, June 14, 1932. Created and proclaimed June 28, 1991. Address: C.P. 2334, rue Mathieu-Schiner 5, CH-1950 Sion 2, Switzerland.

Sensi, Giuseppe Maria (Cardinal Priest), Titular of "Regina Apostolorum;" born in Cosenza, May 27, 1907. Created and proclaimed May 24, 1976. Address: Piazza S. Calisto, 16, 00153 Rome, Italy.

Sfeir, Nasrallah Pierre (Cardinal Bishop), Patriarch of Antioch of the Maronites, Lebanon; born in Reyfoun, Lebanon, Diocese of Sarba dei Maronitit, May 15, 1929. Created and proclaimed November 26, 1994. Address: Patriarcat Maronite, Bkerke, Lebanon.

Shan Kuo-hsi, Paul, *s.j.*, (Cardinal Priest), Bishop of Kaohsiung, Taiwan; born in Puyang Diocese of Taming December 3, 1923. Created and proclaimed February 21, 1998. Address: Bishop's House, 125 Szu-wei 3rd Rd., Kaohsiung 80203 Taiwan.

Shirayanagi, Peter Seiichi (Cardinal Priest), Archbishop of Tokyo, Japan; born in Hachioji, Archdiocese of Tokyo, June 17, 1928. Created and proclaimed November 26, 1994. Address: Archbishop's House, 16-15 Sekiguchi, 3-chome, Bunkyoku, Tokyo, 112 Japan.

Silva Henriquez, Raul, *s.d.b.* (Cardinal Priest), Titular of S. Bernardo alle Terme, Archbishop Emeritus of Santiago; born in Talca, September 27, 1907. Created and proclaimed March 19, 1962. Address: Calle Los Pescadores 2260, Santiago, Chile.

Silvestrini, Achille (Cardinal Deacon), Deacon of S. Benedetto fuori Porta S. Paolo, Prefect of the Congregation for Oriental Churches; born in Brisighella, Diocese of Faenza-Modigliana, October 25, 1923. Created and proclaimed June 28, 1988. Address: Palazzina della Zecca, 00120 Vatican City State, Europe.

Simonis, Adrianus Johannes (Cardinal Priest), Titular of S. Clemente, Archbishop of Utrecht; born in Lisse, Diocese of Rotterdam, November 26, 1931. Created and proclaimed May 25, 1985. Address: Aartsbisdom, P.B. 14019, 3508 SB Utrecht, Netherlands.

Sin, Jaime L. (Cardinal Priest), Titular of Santa Maria ai Monti, Archbishop of Manila; born in New Washington, Diocese of Kalibo, August 31, 1928. Created and proclaimed May 24, 1976. Address: P.O. Box 132, 1099 Manila, Philippines.

Sladkevicius, Vincentas (Cardinal Priest), Titular of Spirito Santo alla Ferratella, Archbishop Emeritus of Kaunas; born in Zasliai, Diocese of Kaisiadorys, August 20, 1920. Created and proclaimed June 28, 1988. Address: Valanciaus 6, 3000 Kaunas, Lithuania.

Sodano, Angelo, (Cardinal Bishop), Titular of S. Maria Nuova, Secretary of State; born in Isola d'Asti, Diocese of Asti, November 23, 1927. Created and proclaimed June 28, 1991. Address: 00120 Vatican City State, Europe.

Stafford, James Francis (Cardinal Priest), Archbishop Emeritus of Denver, USA; President of the Pontifical Council for the Laity. Born in Baltimore, Maryland, USA July 26, 1932. Created and proclaimed February 21, 1998. Address: 00120 Vatican City State, Europe.

Sterzinsky, Georg M. (Cardinal Priest), Titular of S. Giuseppe all' Aurelio, Archbishop of Berlin; born in Warlack, Diocese of Warmia, February 9, 1936. Created and proclaimed June 28, 1991. Address: Wundstrasse 48-50, 14057 Berlin, Germany.

Stickler, Alfons Maria, *s.d.b.* (Cardinal Priest), Titular of S. Giorgio in Velabro; born in Neunkirchen, Archdiocese of Vienna, August 23, 1910. Created and proclaimed May 25, 1985. Address: Piazza del S. Uffizio 11, 00193 Rome, Italy.

Suarez Rivera, Adolfo Antonio (Cardinal Priest), Archbishop of Monterrey in Mexico; born in San Cristobal de las Casas, January 9, 1927. Created and proclaimed November 26, 1994. Address: Apartado Postal 7, Loma Larga 2429 con Sierra Madre, 64000 Monterrey, N.L., Mexico.

Suquia Goicoechea, Angel (Cardinal Priest), Titular of Gran Madre di Dio, Archbishop Emeritus of Madrid; born in Zaldivia, Diocese of San Sebastian October 2, 1916. Created and proclaimed May 25, 1985. Address: Javier Barcaiztegui 7-3, 20010 San Sebastian, Spain.

Swiatek, Kazimierz (Cardinal Priest), Archbishop of Minsk-Mohilev, Apostolic Administrator of Pinsk, Belarus; born in Walga, Amm. Ap. of Estonia, October 21, 1914. Created and proclaimed November 26, 1994. Address: ul. Szewczenki 12/1, 225710 Pinsk, Belarus.

Szoka, Edmund Casimir (Cardinal Priest), Titular of Ss. Andrea e Gregorio al Monte Celio, President of the Prefecture of the Economic Affairs of the Holy See; born in Grand Rapids, Michigan, September 14, 1927. Created and proclaimed June 28, 1988. Address: 00120 Vatican City State, Europe.

Taofinu'u, Pio, *s.m.* (Cardinal Priest), Titular of S. Onofrio, Archbishop of Samoa-Apia; born in Falealupo, Archdiocese of Samoa-Apia, December 9 1923. Created and proclaimed March 5, 1973. Address: Archbishop's House, P.O. Box 532, Apia, Western Samoa, Oceania.

Tettamanzi, Dionigi (Cardinal Priest), Archbishop of Genoa, Italy; born in Renate Archdiocese of Milan March 14, 1934. Created and proclaimed February 21, 1998. Address: Piazza Matteotti 4, 16123 Genoa, Italy.

Thiandoum, Hyacinthe (Cardinal Priest), Titular of Santa Maria del Popolo, Archbishop of Dakar; born in Poponguine, Archdiocese of Dakar, February 2, 1921. Created and proclaimed May 24, 1976. Address: B.P. 1908, Villa Les Badamiers, Dakar-Fann, Senegal.

Todea, Alexandru (Cardinal Priest), Titular of S. Atanasio, Archbishop Emeritus of Fagaras and Alba Julia; born in 1913. Created and proclaimed June 28, 1991. Address: Str. P.P. Aron 2, RO-3175 Blaj, A.B., Romania.

Tomko, Jozef (Cardinal Priest), Titular of S. Sabina, Prefect of the Congregation for the Evangelization of People; born in Udavske, Diocese of Kosice, March 11, 1924. Created and proclaimed May 25, 1985. Address: Villa Betania, Via Urbano VIII 16, 00165 Rome, Italy.

Tonini, Ersilio (Cardinal Priest), Titular of Ss. Redentore a Val Melaina, Archbishop Emeritus of Ravenna-Cervia, Italy; born in Centovera di San Giorgio Piacentino, Diocese of Piacenza-Bobbio, July 20, 1914. Created and proclaimed November 26, 1994. Address: Via Santa Teresa 8, 48100 Ravenna, Italy.

Tumi, Christian Wiyghan (Cardinal Priest), Titular of Ss. Martiri dell' Uganda a Poggio Ameno, Archbishop of Douala; born in Kikaikelaki, Diocese of Kumbo, October 15, 1930. Created and proclaimed June 28, 1988. Address: Archeveche, B.P. 179, Douala, Cameroon.

Turcotte, Jean-Claude (Cardinal Priest), Archbishop of Montreal, Canada; born in Montreal, June 26, 1936. Created and proclaimed November 26, 1994. Address: 1071 rue de la Cathedrale, Montreal, P.Q., H2B 2V4 Canada.

Tzadua, Paulos (Cardinal Priests), Titular of Ss. Nome di Maria a Via Latina, Archbishop of Addis Abeba; born in Addifini, Eparchy of Asmara, August 25, 1921. Created and proclaimed May 25, 1985. Address: P.O. Box 21903, Addis Abeba, Ethiopia.

Ursi, Corrado (Cardinal Priest), Titular of S. Callisto, Archbishop Emeritus of Naples; born in Andria, July 26, 1908. Created and proclaimed June 26, 1967. Address: Via Capodimonte 13, 80136 Napoli, Italy.

Vachon, Louis-Albert (Cardinal Priest), Titular of S. Paolo della Croce a Corviale, Archbishop Emeritus of Quebec; born in Saint Frederic-de -Beauce, Archdiocese of Quebec, February 4, 1912. Created and proclaimed May 25, 1985. Address: 1 rue des Remparts, Quebec, Qué., G1R 5L7, Canada.

Vargas Alzamora, Augusto, *s.j.* (Cardinal Priest), Archbishop of Lima, Peru; born in Lima, November 9, 1922. Created and proclaimed November 26, 1994. Address: Calle Los Nogales 249, San Isidro, Lima, Peru.

Vidal, Ricardo J. (Cardinal Priest), Titular of Ss. Pietro e Paolo a Via Ostiense, Archbishop of Cebu; born in Mogpoc, Diocese of Boac, February 6, 1931. Created and proclaimed May 25, 1985. Address: D. Jakosalem Str., P.O. Box 52, 6000 Cebu City, Philippines.

Vlk, Miloslav (Cardinal Priest), Archbishop of Prague, Czech Republic; born in Lisnice-Sepekov, Diocese of Ceske Budejovice, May 17, 1932. Created and proclaimed November 26, 1994. Address: Arcibiskupska Kurie, Hradcanske nam. 16, 119 02, Praha 1, Czech Republic.

Wamala, Emmanuel (Cardinal Priest), Archbishop of Kampala, Uganda; born in Kamaggwa, Diocese of Masaka, December 15, 1926. Created and proclaimed November 26, 1994. Address: Archbishop's House, P.O. Box 14125, Mengo, Kampala, Uganda.

Wetter, Friedrich (Cardinal Priest), Titular of S. Stefano al Monte Celio, Archbishop of Munich & Freising; born in Landau, Diocese of Speyer, February 20, 1928. Created and proclaimed May 25, 1985. Address: Kardinal-Faulhaber Str., 7, D-8000 Munchen 2, Bundesrepublik, Germany.

Willebrands, Johannes (Cardinal Priest), Titular S. Sebastiano alle Catacombe; born in Bovenkarspel, Diocese of Haarlem, September 4, 1909. Created and proclaimed April 28, 1969. Address: Piazza della Citta Leonina 1, 00193 Rome, Italy.

Williams, Thomas Stafford (Cardinal Priest), Titular of Gesu' Divin Maestro alla Pineta Sacchetti, Archbishop of Wellington; born in Wellington, March 20, 1930. Created and proclaimed February 2, 1983. Address: Archbishop's House, P.O. Box 1937, Wellington 6015, New Zealand.

Winning, Thomas Joseph (Cardinal Priest), Archbishop of Glasgow, Scotland; born in Wishaw, Diocese of Motherwell, June 3, 1925. Created and proclaimed November 26, 1994. Address: 40 Newlands Road, Glasgow G43 2JD, Scotland, Great Britain.

Wu Cheng-Chung, John Baptist (Cardinal Priest), Titular of Beata Vergine Maria del Monte Carmelo a Mostacciano, Bishop of Hong Kong; born in Shui-Tsai, Diocese of Kaying, March 26, 1925. Created and proclaimed June 28, 1988. Address: Caritas House, 2 Caine Rd., Hong Kong.

Zoungrana, Paul, *m.afr.* (Cardinal Priest), Titular of S. Camillo, Archbishop Emeritus of Ougadougou; born in Ougadougou, September 3, 1917. Created and proclaimed February 22, 1965. Address: Archeveche, 01 B.P. 1472, Ouagadougou 01, Burkina-Faso.

Patriarchs

Alexandria (Egypt), *Coptic Rite*—His Beatitude Stephanos II Ghattas, born January 16, 1920 in Cheikh Zein-el-Dine; ordained March 25, 1944; elected to Luqsor of the Copts June 9, 1967; consecrated June 16, 1967; elected Patriarch June 9, 1986.

Antioch (Syria), *Syriac Rite*—His Beatitude Ignatius Anthony II Hayek, born in Halab, Archdiocese of Aleppo, September 14, 1910; elected Patriarch, March 10, 1968. Address: Rue Damas, Beyrouth, Lebanon. *Maronite Rite*—His Beatitude Nasrallah Peter Cardinal Sfeir; born in Reyfoun, May 15, 1920; elected Patriarch April 19, 1986.

Melkite Greek Catholic—His Beatitude Maximos V Hakim, born in Tantah, Egypt, May 18, 1908; elected Patriarch, November 22, 1967. Address: Bab Touma, Damascus, Syria.

Jerusalem (Israel)—His Beatitude Michael Sabbah, born in Nazareth, Israel, March 19, 1933; elected Patriarch of Jerusalem of the Latins December 11, 1987; consecrated January 6, 1988.

Babylon of the Chaldeans—His Beatitude Raphael I Bidawid; born in Mossul, April 17, 1922; elected Patriarch, May 21, 1989.

Cilicia of the Armenians—His Beatitude John Peter XVIII Kasparian, born in Cairo, January 20, 1927; elected Patriarch August 5, 1982.

East Indies—Most Rev. Raoul Nicholas Gonsalves; born in Bambolim, Archdiocese of Goa, June 15, 1927; promoted Patriarch January 30, 1978.

Lisbon (Portugal)—His Eminence Antonio Cardinal Ribeiro, born in Gandarela, Archdiocese of Braga, May 21, 1928; appointed Patriarch May 10, 1971. Created and proclaimed Cardinal in the Consistory of March 5, 1973.

Venice (Italy)—His Eminence Cardinal Marco Ce', born in Izano Diocese of Crema, July 8, 1925; ordained March 27, 1948; elected Titular Bishop of Vulturia April 22, 1970; Patriarch December 7, 1978. Created and proclaimed Cardinal in the Consistory of June 30, 1979.

Synod of Bishops

Synodus Episcoporum President: The Holy Father. *Secretary General:* His Eminence Jan Cardinal Schotte, C.I.C.M. *General Secretariat:* Palazzo del Bramante, Via della Conciliazione, 34 00193 Rome, Italy. Tel: 69.88.48.21 or 69.88.43.24. Fax: 69.88.33.92.

Office of Labor of the Apostolic See

Officium Laboris Apostolicae Sedia President: His Eminence Jan Cardinal Schotte, C.I.C.M. *Vice President:* Most Rev. Archbishop Giovanni De Andrea. *Assessor of the Presidency:* Prof. Matteo Dell'Olio. *Assessor of the Presidency:* Prof. Gian Carlo Perone. *Office:* Via dell Conciliazione, 1 00193 Rome, Italy. Tel: 69.88.44.49. Fax: 69.88.38.00.

The Roman Curia

The present norms regarding the Roman Curia were publicly announced June 28, 1988, in the "Pastor Bonus - Constitutio Apostolica de Romana Curia," and published in A.A.S. LXXX/1988, Commentarium Officiale; pp. 841-934. The Supreme Pontiff usually conducts business of the universal Church by means of the Roman Curia, which fulfills its duty in his name and by his authority for the good and the service of the Churches; it consists of the Secretariat of State or the Papal Secretariat, congregations, tribunals and other institutions, whose structure and competency are defined in special law (can. 360). The Roman curia is the complex of departments and institutes which assist the Roman Pontiff in the exercise of his supreme pastoral function for the good and service of the universal Church and of the particular churches, by which the unity of faith and communion of the people of God is strengthened and the mission is promoted which is proper to the Church in the world.

I. THE SECRETARIAT OF STATE TO HIS HOLINESS

The Secretariat of State

The Secretariat of State closely assists the Supreme Pontiff in the exercise of his supreme function. The cardinal secretary of state presides over it. It includes two sections, namely the section for general affairs under the immediate direction of the substitute, assisted by an assessor, and the section for relations with states under the direction of its own secretary, with the assistance of a subsecretary. Attached to this latter section is a body of cardinals and some bishops.

Secretary of State: His Eminence Angelo Cardinal Sodano.

Office: Apostolic Palace, 00120 Vatican City State, Europe. Tel: 69.88.34.38; Fax: 69.88.50.88.

First Section: for General Affairs

The first section handles anything entrusted to it by the Holy Father, as well as matters of daily business which do not fall within the competence of other dicasteries. It fosters relations with these departments, with the bishops, and with the diplomatic missions of the Holy See.

Substitute: Archbishop Giovanni Battista Re.

Assessor: Rev. Msgr. Pedro Lopez Quintana.

Second Section: for Relations with States

The second section of the Secretariat of State handles all matters pertaining to civil governments, fostering diplomatic relations with nations, and maintaining contact with all the diplomatic missions of the Holy See. It takes care also of what concerns the presence and activity of the Holy See in international institutes.

Secretary: Archbishop Jean-Louis Tauran.

Under-Secretary: Rev. Msgr. Celestino Migliore.

II. THE CONGREGATIONS

By the name of "department" (dicasteria) is understood: the congregations, tribunals, councils and offices, namely the Apostolic Camera, the Administration of the Patrimony of the Apostolic See, and the Prefecture of Economic Affairs of the Holy See. The departments are juridically equal among themselves. Attached to the institutes of the Roman Curia are the Prefecture of the Papal Household and the Office of Liturgical Celebrations of the Supreme Pontiff.

The Congregation for the Doctrine of the Faith

The proper function of the Congregation on the Doctrine of the Faith is to promote and safeguard the doctrine of faith and morals in the whole Catholic world; therefore, those things belong to it which touch this matter in any way. Fulfilling the function of promoting doctrine, it fosters studies in order that the understanding of the faith might grow and that a response can be prepared under the light of faith for new questions arising from developments in science and human culture. It is a help to bishops, whether individually or gathered in assemblies, in the exercise of the function by which they are constituted authentic teachers and doctors of the faith as well as the office by which they are held to safeguard and promote the integrity of that faith. This Sacred Congregation reproves doctrines opposed to the principles of the faith after the interested Bishops of a region have been heard. It studies the books referred to it and, if necessary, reproves them after the author has been heard and has had an opportunity to defend himself and after the Ordinary has been forewarned. It also examines whatever concerns ""the privilege of the faith" whether in law and in fact. It is competent to pass judgement on errors about the faith according to the norms of an ordinary process. It safeguards the dignity of the sacrament of Penance. The Congregation proceeds administratively or judicially according to the nature of the question to be treated.

Cardinal Prefect: His Eminence Joseph Cardinal Ratzinger.

Secretary: Most Rev. Archbishop Tarcisio Bertone, S.D.B.

Office: Piazza del S. Uffizio 11, 00193 Rome, Italy. Tel: 69.88.33.57; 69.88.34.13; Fax: 69.88.34.09.

The Congregation for the Causes of Saints

The Congregation for the Causes of Saints is competent in all matters which in any way pertain to the Beatification of Servants of God or to the Canonization of the Blessed or to the Preservation of Relics.

This Congregation is divided into three offices.

Prefect: His Eminence Alberto Cardinal Bovone.

Secretary: Most Rev. Archbishop Edward Nowak.

Office: Piazza Pio XII 10, 00193 Rome, Italy. Tel: 011 39 6 69.88.42.47. Fax: 011 39 6 6988 1935

The Congregation for the Oriental Churches

This Congregation considers those matters, whether regarding persons or things, which touch on the Eastern Catholic Churches. It treats all questions which pertain either to persons, or to discipline, or to the rites of the Oriental Churches, even if they are mixed in that by the nature of the thing or of persons they involve Latins. Territories in which a major part of the Christians belong to Oriental rites are subject only to this Congregation. Even in Latin territories it carefully supervises the faithful of Oriental rites and provides as much as possible for their spiritual needs even by the establishment of their own hierarchy if the number of faithful and circumstances require this.

Cardinal Prefect: His Eminence Achille Cardinal Silvestrini.

Secretary: Most Rev. Archbishop Miroslav Stefan Marusyn, Titular Archbishop of Cadi.

Office: Via della Conciliazione 34, 00193 Rome, Italy. Tel: 69.88.42.82; Fax: 69.88.43.00.

The Congregation for Bishops

This congregation examines what pertains to the constitution and provision of particular churches as well as the exercise of the episcopal function in the Latin Church, except for the competence of the Congregation for the Evangelization of Peoples. It belongs to the Congregation for Bishops to propose to the Roman Pontiff, for approval, the constitution of new dioceses, provinces and regions; to divide, unite and realign them after consulting the interested Episcopal Conferences; it deals also with the erection of the military ordinariates and, after consulting the Episcopal Conference, prelacies for special pastoral ministries for various regions or social groups. This Congregation provides also for the naming of bishops, apostolic administrators, coadjutors and auxiliaries of bishops, military and other vicars and prelates enjoying personal jurisdiction.

It is competent for all things that have to do with bishops and publishes norms which, through the Episcopal Conference, provide for the more urgent needs of the faithful.

Cardinal Prefect: His Eminence Bernardin Cardinal Gantin.

Secretary: Most Rev Archbishop Jorge Maria Mejia.

Office: Piazza Pio XII 10, 00193 Rome, Italy. Tel: 69.88.42.17; Fax: 69.88.53.03.

Pontifical Commission for Latin America

(Directly responsible to Congregation for Bishops).

President: His Eminence Bernardin Cardinal Gantin.

Vice President: Most Rev. Bishop Calderon Polo Cipriano.

The Congregation for Divine Worship and the Discipline of the Sacraments

This congregation does those things which pertain to the Apostolic See as to the moderation and promotion of the sacred liturgy, especially the sacraments, with due regard for the competence of the Congregation on Doctrine of the Faith. It fosters and safeguards the discipline of the sacraments, especially what pertains to their valid and licit celebration; moreover, it concedes favors and dispensations for matters which are not contained in the facilities of diocesan bishops in this line. It alone examines the non-consummation of a marriage and the presence of causes for the granting of a dispensation and everything connected with them. It has competence with regard to the obligations connected with major orders and it examines questions about the validity of sacred ordination.

Prefect: His Eminence Jorge Cardinal Arturo Medina Estevez.

Secretary: Most Rev. Archbishop Geraldo Majella Agnelo.

Office: 10 Piazza Pio XII 10, 00193 Rome, Italy. Tel: 69.88.43.16; Fax: 69.88.34.99.

The Congregation for the Evangelization of Peoples or for the Propagation of the Faith

It belongs to this congregation to direct and coordinate throughout the world the work of the evangelization of peoples itself and missionary cooperation, while respecting the competence of the Congregation for Eastern Churches. It is competent for those things which pertain to all the missions established for the spread of the Kingdom of Christ throughout the world and therefore for whatever is connected with the assignment and transferral of the necessary ministers, for describing ecclesiastical boundaries and proposing those who will govern them. It encourages also the development of an indigenous clergy. The congregation sponsors missionary initiatives and promotes missionary vocations and spirituality. In the territories subject to it, the Congregation has charge of all that pertains to the holding of synods and councils, to the establishing of episcopal conferences and to the review of their statutes and decrees. The Congregation has a Supreme Council for the direction of Pontifical Missionary Works, on which depend the general Councils of the Missionary Union of the Clergy, the Society for the Propagation of the Faith, the Society of St. Peter the Apostole, and the Society of the Holy Childhood.

Cardinal Prefect: His Eminence Jozef Cardinal Tomko.

Adjunct Secretary: Most Rev. Archbishop Charles A. Schleck, C.S.C.

Office: Palazzo di Propaganda Fide, Piazza di Spagna 48, 00187 Rome, Italy. Tel: 011 39 6 6988.01.01; Fax: 011 39 6 6988.01.18

The Congregation for Institutes of Consecrated Life and for Societies of Apostolic Life

The principal function of this congregation is to promote and supervise, in the whole Latin Church, the practices of the evangelical counsels as they are exercised in approved forms of consecrated life and at the same time the activities of societies of apostolic life. The Congregation takes care of Religious Institutes of Consecrated Life and Secular Institutes.

Religious Institutes: the Congregation is entrusted with the affairs of all religious institutes of the Latin Rite and their members. It is also competent in matters which pertain to societies of common life, whose members live like religious, or to Third Orders as such.

Secular Institutes: the Congregation is competent in the same way, all else being equal, for Apostolic Societies which, although not religious, make a true and complete profession of the evangelical counsels in the world.

Cardinal Prefect: His Eminence Eduardo Cardinal Martinez Somalo.

Secretary: Most Rev. Archbishop Piergiorgio Silvano Nesti, C.P.

Office: Piazza Pio XII 3, 00193 Rome, Italy. Tel: 69.88.41.28; Fax: 69.88.45.26.

The Congregation for the Clergy

With due regard for the rights of bishops and their conferences, this congregation examines those things which concern priests and deacons of the secular clergy with regard to their persons, pastoral ministry, matters which are in support of the exercise of these things, and in all this provides opportune assistance to the bishops. The Congregation has many functions: studies, proposes and urges the means and aids by which priests strive for sanctity. This office also has charge of everything which concerns the work and discipline of the diocesan clergy. Particularly it promotes the preaching of the Word of God and the works of the apostolate and organization of catechesis, evaluates and approves pastoral and catechetical directories, fosters national and international Catechetical Congresses and indicates the opportune norms for religious instruction of children, young people and adults. The Congregation looks also to the preservation and administration of the temporal goods of the Church without prejudice to the other Congregations which have temporal goods committed to their vigilance.

Prefect: His Eminence Dario Cardinal Castrillon Hoyos.

Secretary: Most Rev. Archbishop Csaba Ternyak.

Office: Piazza Pio XII 3, 00193 Rome, Italy. Tel: 69.88.41.51; Fax: 69.88.48.45.

The Congregation for Catholic Education

This Congregation expresses and exercises the Apostolic See's solicitude for the formation of those who are called to holy orders as well as for the promotion and organization of Catholic education. It is competent for all that pertains to the formation of clerics and the Catholic education both of clerics and of the laity.

The Congregation has many functions and is charged with the direction, discipline and temporal administration of seminaries and whatever touches the education of the diocesan clergy and the scientific formation of religious and secular institutes.

The Congregation oversees universities, faculties, athenaea and any institute of higher learning which has the name "Catholic" in so far as they depend on the authority of the Church, not excluding those directed by religious or the laity.

The Congregation cares for the establishment of parochial and diocesan schools; watches over all Catholic schools below the level of a university and faculty, as well as all institutes of instruction or education dependent on the authority of the Church.

Also within the Congregation is located the Pontifical Work for Vocations, which is charged with coordinating and promoting the work of fostering all ecclesiastical vocations.

Prefect: His Eminence Pio Cardinal Laghi.

Secretary: Most Rev. Archbishop Jose Saraiva Martins.

Office: Piazza Pio XII 3, 00193 Rome, Italy. Tel: 69.88.41.67; Fax: 69.88.41.72.

III. TRIBUNALS

Apostolic Penitentiary

The competence of this Tribunal is concerned with those matters which pertain to the internal forum, for both the sacramental and non-sacramental internal forum. It is competent in matters pertaining to the granting and use of indulgences.

Major Penitentiary: His Eminence William Cardinal Baum.

Regent: Most Rev. Bishop Luigi De Magistris.

Office: Piazza della Cancelleria 1, 00186 Rome, Italy. Tel: 69.88.75.26.

Supreme Tribunal of the Apostolic Signatura

This department, in addition to the function which it exercises as Supreme Tribunal, consults that justice may be correctly administered in the Church.

With the many functions, the Apostolic Signatura judges the matters assigned to it in the Code of Canon Law; it prorogues the competence of tribunals; it extends the forum for strangers in Rome to cases of matrimonial nullity in extraordinary circumstances and for grave reasons; it supervises the proper administration of justice; it provides for the establishment of regional and interregional tribunals; it enjoys the rights assigned to it in concordats between the Holy See and the various nations.

The Tribunal settles questions about the exercise of administrative ecclesiastical power which are referred to it. It also passes on conflicts of competence among the departments of the Holy See; it examines administrative matters referred to it by the Congregations of the Roman Curia as well as questions committed to it by the Holy Father.

Prefect: His Eminence Gilberto Cardinal Agustoni.

Secretary: Most Rev. Archbishop Zenon Grocholewski.

Office: Piazza della Cancelleria 1, 00186 Rome, Italy. Tel: 69.88.75.20; Fax: 69.88.75.53.

Tribunal of the Roman Rota

This tribunal acts as a higher instance at the Apostolic See, usually in the grade of appeal, for safeguarding rights in the Church; it fosters the unity of jurisprudence and, through its own sentences, is a help to lower tribunals. It is also a court of first instance for cases specified in the law and for others committed to the Rota by the Roman Pontiff. The greater part of its decisions concern the nullity of marriage. In such cases its competence includes marriages between two Catholics, between a Catholic and non-Catholic, and between two non-Catholic parties whether one or both of the baptized parties belongs to a Latin or Oriental Rite.

Dean: Rev. Msgr. Francesco Pompedda.

Office: Piazza della Cancelleria 1, 00186 Rome, Italy. Tel: 69.88.75.02; Fax: 69.88.75.54.

IV. PONTIFICAL COUNCILS

Pontifical Council for the Laity

This council is competent in those matters which pertain to the Apostolic See in promoting and coordinating the apostolate of the lay persons and, generally, in those things which look to the Christian life of lay persons as such. The norms were published in the apostolic letter, "Catholicam Christi Ecclesiam" of January 6, 1967 (A.A.S., LIX, pp. 25-28).

President: His Eminence J. Francis Cardinal Stafford.

Secretary: Most Rev. Bishop Stanislaus Rylko.

Office: Piazza S. Calisto 16, 00153 Rome, Italy. Tel: 69.88.73.22; Fax: 69.88.72.14.

Pontifical Council for Promoting Christian Unity

The function of this Council is to concentrate in an appropriate way on initiatives and ecumenical activities for the restoration of unity among Christians. It has charge of relations with those of other communities; considers the correct interpretation and observance of the principles of ecumenism; promotes Catholic groups and coordinates the efforts at unity, both on the national and international levels; institutes colloquies on ecumenical questions and activities with Churches and ecclesial communities separated from the Holy See; deputes Catholic observers for Christian congresses; invites to Catholic gatherings observers of the separated brethren; orders into practice conciliar decrees on ecumenical matters. Furthermore, it is competent for all questions concerning religious relations with Judaism.

President: His Eminence Edward Cardinal Cassidy.

Secretary: Most Rev. Bishop Pierre Duprey.

President-Emeritus: His Eminence Johannes Cardinal Willebrands.

Office: Via dell' Erba 1, 00193 Rome, Italy. Tel: 69.88.30.71; Fax: 69.88.53.65.

Pontifical Council for the Family

This Council promotes the pastoral care of families and fosters their rights and dignity in the Church and in civil society, in order that they might ever more suitably fulfill their own functions.

President: His Eminence Alfonso Cardinal Lopez Trujillo.

Secretary: Most Rev. Bishop Francisco Gil Hellin.

Office: Piazza S. Calisto 16, 00153 Rome, Italy. Tel: 69.88.72.43; Fax: 69.88.72.72.

Pontifical Council for Justice and Peace

This Council looks to those things which will promote justice and peace in the world according to the gospel and the social teaching of the Church.

President: His Eminence Roger Cardinal Etchegaray.

Secretary: Rev. Msgr. Diarmuid Martin.

Office: Piazza S. Calisto 16, 00153 Rome, Italy. Tel: 69.88.71.91; Fax: 69.88.72.05.

Pontifical Council "Cor Unum"

This Council shows the solicitude of the Catholic Church toward the needy, in order that human fraternity might be fostered and the charity of Christ be made manifest.

President: Most. Rev. Archbishop Paul Josef Cordes.

Office: Piazza S. Calisto 16, 00153 Rome, Italy. Tel: 69.88.73.31; Fax: 69.88.73.01.

Pastoral Council for the Pastoral Care of Migrants and Itinerant People

This Council directs the pastoral concern of the Church toward the special needs of those who are forced to leave their own native land or who perhaps lack one; it also sees that there is appropriate study of the questions which touch on this matter.

President: His Eminence Giovanni Cardinal Cheli.

Secretary: Most Rev. Archbishop Francesco Gioia

Office: Piazza S. Calisto 16, 00153 Rome, Italy. Tel: 69.88.71.93; Fax: 69.88.71.11.

Pontifical Council for the Pastoral Assistance to Health Care Workers

This Council shows the solicitude of the Church for the sick by aiding those who carry out a ministry toward the sick and suffering, in order that the apostolate of mercy, which they carry out, may ever more suitably respond to new needs.

President: Most Rev. Bishop Javier Lozano Barragan.

Secretary: Rev. Jose Luis Redrado Marchite, O.H.

Office: Via della Conciliazione, 00193 Rome, Italy. Tel: 69.88.31.38; Fax: 69.88.31.39.

Pontifical Council for the Intepretation of Legal Texts

The function of this Council consists especially in interpreting the Church's laws.

President: Most Rev. Archbishop Julian Herranz Casado.

Secretary: Most Rev. Bishop Bruno Bertagna.

Office: Palazzo delle Congregazioni Piazza Pio XII 10, 00193 Rome, Italy. Tel: 69.88.4008; Fax: 69.88.47.10.

Pontifical Council for Inter-Religious Dialogue

This Council fosters and moderates relations with members and bodies of religions which do not carry the name of Christian, as well as with those who in any way possess a religious spirit. It fosters studies and promotes relations with non-Christians to bring about an increase in mutual respect and seeks ways to establish a dialogue with them; it receives and carefully weighs the wishes of the Ordinaries; it provides for the formation of those who participate in dialogue.

President: His Eminence Francis Cardinal Arinze.

Secretary: Most Rev. Bishop Michael Louis Fitzgerald.

Office: Via dell' Erba 1, 00193 Rome, Italy. Tel: 69.88.43.21; Fax: 69.88.44.94.

Pontifical Council for Culture

The Council embodies the Church's pastoral concern over the relationship between faith and cultures. Its tasks include: studying unbelief and religious indifference, as present in different cultures; supporting the Church's inculturation of the Gospel; promotion initiatives of dialogue between faith and culture, as well as dialogue with those who do not believe in God. Its activities include seminars, intercultural exchanges, and coordinating the activities of Pontifical Academies and the Pontifical Commission for the Cultural Patrimony of the Church. An important hope of the Council is to show faith as the inspiration of science, literature and the arts.

President: His Eminence Paul Cardinal Poupard.

Secretary: Rev. Bernard Ardura, O.Praem

Office: Piazza S. Calisto 16, 00120 Vatican City State, Europe. Tel: 69.88.73.21; Fax: 69.88.73.68.

Pontifical Council for Social Communications

This Council is involved in questions touching on the instruments of social communication so that the proclamation of salvation and human progress might be promoted even through them in order to foster civil culture.

President: Most Rev. Archbishop John Foley.

Secretary: Most Rev. Bishop Pierfranco Pastore.

President-Emeritus: His Eminence Andrej Cardinal Deskur.

Office: Palazzo S. Carlo, 00120 Vatican City State, Europe. Tel: 69.88.31.97; Fax: 69.88.53.73.

V. OFFICES

Apostolic Camera

The Apostolic Camera is presided over by the cardinal chamberlain of the Holy Roman Church, assisted by the vice-chamberlain together with certain prelates chamberlain. It chiefly exercises the function which is given to it in the special law on the vacancy of the Apostolic See.

Camerlengo: His Eminence Eduardo Cardinal Martinez Somalo.

Prefecture of the Papal Household

The Prefecture looks after the internal order of the pontifical household and supervises everything which pertains to discipline and service either by clergy or laity who constitute the pontifical chapel and family. It is in charge of the Apostolic Palace and is at the service of the Holy Father, both there and wherever he goes. It arranges audiences with His Holiness and supervises papal ceremonies other than the strictly liturgical.

Prefect: Most Reverend Bishop James M. Harvey.

Administration of the Patrimony of the Apostolic See

This Office is competent to administer the goods proper to the Holy See, the income from which is destined to support the expenditures necessary for the functions of the Roman Curia.

Extraordinary Section: Handles the duties committed to it by the Sovereign Pontiff.

President: His Eminence Lorenzo Cardinal Antonetti

Secretary: Most Rev. Archbishop Claudio Maria Celli.

Central Office of Statistics of the Church

This Office gathers and organizes the data which seems necessary or useful for a better understanding of the state of the Church and for assistance to its Bishops.

Director: Rev. Msgr. Vittorio Fornenti

Prefecture of the Economic Affairs of the Holy See

The Prefecture has the function of supervising and governing the administration of goods which belong to the Holy See or which it is in charge of, no matter what kind of autonomy they may perhaps enjoy. This is directed by a Commission of three Cardinals and coordinates and watches over the administration of the possessions of the Holy See. It receives the reports on the receipts and disbursements of the Church's goods and the various budgets.

President: Most Rev. Archbishop Sergio Sebastiani

Secretary: Most Rev. Bishop Francesco Saverio Salerno

Office: Largo del Colonnato 3, 00193 Rome, Italy. Tel: 69.88.42.63; Fax: 69.88.50.11.

Office of the Liturgical Celebrations of the Supreme Pontiff

This Office prepares whatever is necessary for liturgical and other sacred celebrations which are carried out by the Supreme Pontiff or in his name and, in keeping with existing prescription of liturgical law, to supervise them.

Master of Ceremonies: Rev. Msgr. Piero Marini.

Archives of the Second Vatican Council

Director: Rev. Msgr. Vincenzo Carbone.

Archivist: Rev. Msgr. Nazzareno Cinti.

VI. COMMISSIONS AND COMMITTEES

Pontifical Commission for the Cultural Heritage of the Church

President: Most Rev. Archbishop Francesco Marchisano.

Secretary: Rev. Carlo Chenis, S.D.B.

Pontifical Commission for Sacred Archeology

President: Most Rev. Archbishop Francesco Marchisano.

Secretary: Prof. Fabrizio Bisconti.

Commission "Ecclesia Dei"

President: His Eminence Angelo Cardinal Felici.

Council of Cardinals for the Study of Organizational and Economic Problems of the Apostolic See

American Members: His Eminence John Cardinal O'Connor; His Eminence Roger M. Cardinal Mahony.

International Theological Commission

President: His Eminence Joseph Cardinal Ratzinger.

General Secretary: Rev. Georges Cottier, O.P.

Commission of Cardinals for the Pontifical Shrines of Pompei, Loreto, and Bari

President: His Eminence Virgilio Cardinal Noe.

Pontifical Biblical Commission

President: His Eminence Joseph Cardinal Ratzinger.

Secretary: Rev. P. Albert Vanhoye, S.J.

Pontifical Committee for the International Eucharistic Congresses

President: His Eminence Edouard Cardinal Gagnon.

Pontifical Commission for the Revision and Emendation of the Vulgate

Director: Rev. Jean Mallet, O.S.B.

Pontifical Commission for the Vatican City State

President: His Eminence Edmund Casimir Cardinal Szoka.

Pontifical Committee for Historical Sciences

President: Rev. Msgr. Victor Saxer.

Secretary: Rev. Vittorino Grossi, O.S.A.

Central Committee of the Holy Year 2000

President: His Eminence Cardinal Roger Etchegaray.

Secretary: Most Rev. Archbishop Crescenzio Sepe.

VII. INSTITUTIONS CONNECTED WITH THE HOLY SEE

Vatican Secret Archives

Archivist: His Eminence Luigi Cardinal Poggi.

Prefect: Rev. Sergio B. Pagaro.

Vatican Apostolic Library

Librarian: His Eminence Luigi Cardinal Poggi.

Prefect: Rev. Leonard Boyle, O.P.

Pontifical Academy of Sciences

President: Prof. Nicola Cabibbo.

Pontifical Academy of Social Sciences

President: Prof. Edmond Malinvaud.

Pontifical Academy for Life

President: Prof. Juan de Dios Vial Correa.

Vice President: Most Rev. Bishop Elio Sgreccia.

Vatican Radio

President of the Coordinating Committee: Rev. Roberto Tucci, S.J.

Director General: Rev. Pasquale Borgomeo, S.J.

Vatican Television Centre

President of the Administrative Council: Dr. Emilio Rossi.

Vice President: Dr. Sandro Baldoni.

Fabric of St. Peter's

President: His Eminence Virgilio Cardinal Noe.

Office of Papal Charities

Almoner: Most Rev. Archbishop Oscar Rizzato.

Vatican Polyglot Press

Director General: Rev. Elio Torrigiani, S.D.B.

Administrative Director: Mr. Giacomo Bonassoli, S.D.B.

Vatican Publishing House

President: Most Rev. Archbishop Giovanni De Andrea.

Director: Rev. Nicolo' Suffi, S.D.B.

Institute for Works of Religion

Director General: Dr. Lelio Scaletti.

Prelate: Vacant.

L'Osservatore Romano

Director: Prof. Mario Agnes.

Secretary: Dr. Carlo DeLucia.

English Language Weekly - Contact Person: Rev. Robert Dempsey.

Translations of English, French, Spanish, German, Portuguese, and Polish editions available.

Press Office of the Holy See

Director: Dr. Joaquin Navarro-Valls.

VIII. AMERICANS WORKING IN THE ROMAN CURIA

Secretariats of State. Section for General Affairs: Rev. Msgr. William Millea; Rev. Reginald Foster, O.C.D.; Rev. Steven Zak; Sr. M. Louise Marecka, C.S.S.F.; Sr. Yvonne Mary Loucks, R.S.M.; Sr. Ruth Aubrey, A.S.C.J. *II. Section for Relations with States:* Rev. Msgr. Timothy Broglio; Rev. Msgr. Joseph Marino.

Congregation for the Doctrine of the Faith: Rev. Msgr. Michael O. Jackels; Rev. Charles Brown.

Congregation for the Oriental Churches: Rev. Eric Powell.

Congregation for Divine Worship and the Discipline of the Sacraments: Rev. Thomas Fucinaro.

Congregation for Causes of Saints: Rev. Msgr. Robert Sarno.

Congregation for Bishops: Rev. Msgr. Daniel Thomas; Rev. James D. Conley.

Congregation for the Evangelization of Peoples: Most Rev. Archbishop Charles Schleck, C.S.C.; Rev. Joseph McCabe, M.M.

Congregation for the Clergy: Rev. David Ricken; Rev. Anthony McDaid.

Congregation for The Institutes of Consecrated Life and for Societies of Apostolic Life: Sr. Sharon Holland, I.H.M.; Sr. Dionette Werner, C.S.S.F.; Rev. John Ferrin, O.P.

Congregation for Catholic Education: Rev. Msgr. Walter J. Edyvean; Rev. Robert Zapfel.

Apostolic Penitentiary: William Cardinal Baum; Rev. Msgr. James Gillen.

Supreme Tribunal of the Apostolic Signatura: Rev. Msgr. Joseph Punderson; Rev. Salvatore Cordileone.

Tribunal of the Roman Rota: Rev. Msgr. Kenneth Boccafola; Rev. Msgr. Robert Sable.

Pontifical Council For the Laity: His Eminence J. Francis Cardinal Stafford.

Pontifical Council For Promoting Christian Unity: Rev. Msgr. John Radano.

Pontifical Council for the Family: Ms. Joan E. Collemacine-Parenti, Ph.D.; Rev. Frank A. Pavone.

Pontifical Council for Justice and Peace: Sr. Marjorie Keenan, R.S.C.M.

Pontifical Council for the Pastoral Care of Migrants and Itinerant People: Rev. Msgr. Joseph DeAndrea.

Pontifical Council - "Cor Unum": Rev. Msgr. Frank Dewane.

Pontifical Council for the Interpretation of Legislative Texts: Rev. Bernard Hebda.

Pontifical Council for Social Communications: Most Rev.Archbishop John Foley; Dr. Marjorie Weeke.

Administration for the Patrimony of the Apostolic See: Sr. Catherine Danovich, O.S.B.M.; Sr. Judith Zoebelein, F.S.E.

Prefecture of the Papal Household: Prefect:—Most Rev. Bishop James M. Harvey.

Pontifical Commission for Vatican City State: His Eminence Edmund Cardinal Szoka; Rev. Todd J. Lajiness.

L'Osservatore Romano: Rev. Msgr. Robert Dempsey, Editor. For subscription information for North America please contact: The Cathedral Foundation, Inc., 320 Cathedral St., Baltimore, MD 21201.

Synod of Bishops: Rev. Msgr. John Abruzzese.

Pontifical Commission"Ecclesia Dei": Rev. Msgr. Arthur Calkins.

Residence for American Diocesan Priests working in the Roman Curia: Villa Stritch, Via della Nocetta 63, 00164 Rome, Italy. Tel: (011.39.6) 66.16.26.62; 66.16.26.76; Fax: 66.16.27.00.

INSTITUTES OF GRADUATE STUDIES IN ROME

***Pontifical Gregorian University*, with which are associated the *Pontifical Biblical Institute* and the *Pontifical Oriental Institute*—**Constituted in 1552. Address: Piazza della Pilotta 4, 00187 Rome, Italy. Grand Chancellor: Pio Cardinal Laghi; Vice Chancellor: Rev. Peter-Hans Kolvenbach, S.J.; Rector: Rev. Giuseppe Pittau, S.J.; Rector of the Biblical Institute: Rev. Robert O'Toole, S.J.; Rector of the Oriental Institute: Rev. Gilles Pelland, S.J.

***Pontifical Lateran University*—**Founded in 1824. Address: Piazza S. Giovanni 4, 00184 Rome, Italy. Grand Chancellor: Camillo Cardinal Ruini; Rector: Most Rev. Bishop Angelo Scola.

***Augustinianum Instituto Patristico at the Pontifical Lateran University*—**Founded in 1969. Address: Via Paolo VI 25, 00193 Rome, Italy. Rev. Angelo D. Berardino, O.S.A., Pres.

***Pontifical Urban University*—**Founded in 1627. Address: Via Urbano VIII 16, 00165 Rome, Italy. Grand Chancellor: Jozef Cardinal Tomko; Rector: Rev. Msgr. Eric Schmid.

***Pontifical University of St. Thomas Aquinas*—**Founded in 1580. Address: Largo Angelicum 1, 00184 Rome, Italy. Grand Chancellor: Very Rev. Timothy Radcliffe, Master General of the Order of Preachers; Rector: Very Rev. Edward Kaczynski, O.P.

***Pontifical International Institute of St. Anselm*—**Founded in 1687. Address: Piazza Cavalieri di Malta 5, 00152 Rome, Italy. Tel: (06) 57.9.11. Grand Chancellor: Very Rev. Marcel Rooney, Pro-Abbot Primate; Rector: Rev. Pius Tragan, O.S.B.

***Pontifical Salesian University*—**Founded in 1940. Address: Piazza Ateneo Salesiano 1, 00139 Rome, Italy. Grand Chancellor: Vacant. Rector: Rev. Raffaele Farina.

***Pontifical Antonianum Atheneum*—**Founded in 1933. Address: Via Merulana 124, 00185 Rome, Italy. Grand Chancellor: Very Rev. Schaluck Hermann, O.F.M., Minister General of the Order of Friars Minor; Rector: Rev. Jose Antonio Merino.

***Pontifical Institute of Sacred Music*—**Founded in 1911. Address: Via di Torre Rossa 21, 00165, Rome, Italy. Grand Chancellor: Pio Cardinal Laghi; President: Rev. Msgr. Valentin Miserachs Grau.

***Pontifical Institute of Christian Archeology*—**Founded in 1925. Address: Via Napoleone III 1, 00185 Rome, Italy. Grand Chancellor: Pio Cardinal Laghi; Rector: Rev. Msgr. Patrick Saint-Roch.

***Pontifical Theological Faculty of St. Bonaventure, of the Friars Minor Conventual*—**Erected in 1935. Address: Via del Serafico 1, 00142 Rome, Italy. Grand Chancellor: Very Rev. Gianfranco Gardin; President: Rev. Giovanni Iammarrone, O.F.M.Conv.

***Pontifical Theological Faculty "Teresianum"*—**Founded in 1935. Address: Piazza S. Pancrazio 5-A, 00152 Rome, Italy. Grand Chancellor: Very Rev. Camilo Maccise, O.C.D., Prepositor General of the Discalced Carmelites; President: Rev. Jesus Castellano Cervera, O.C.D.

***Pontifical Theological Faculty "Marianum"*—**Founded in 1955. Address: Viale 30 Aprile 6, 00153 Rome, Italy. Grand Chancellor: Rev. Hubert Moons, Prior General of the Servites; President: Very Rev. Ignacio M. Calabuig Adan.

***Roman Atheneum of the Holy Cross*—**Erected on January 9, 1990. Address: Piazza S. Apollinare 49, 00186, Rome, Italy. Grand Chancellor: Rev. Msgr. Javier Echevarria Rodriguez; Rector: Rev. Lluis Clavell Ortiz-Repisco.

SEMINARIES AND NATIONAL COLLEGES IN ROME

***Pontifical Roman Major Seminary*—**Founded in 1565 by Pius IV. Address: Piazza S. Giovanni in Laterano 4, 00184 Rome, Italy. Rev. Msgr. Luigi Conti, Rector.

***Pontifical Roman Minor Seminary*—**Address: Viale Vaticano 42, 00165 Rome, Italy. Rev. Msgr. Paolo Selvadagi, Rector.

***French Seminary (Pontifical)*—**Founded on October 2, 1853. Address: Via di S. Chiara 42, 00186, Rome, Italy. Rev. Bernard Tenailleau, Rector.

***Lombard Seminary of SS. Ambrose and Charles (Pontifical)*—**Founded in 1863. Address: Piazza S. Maria Maggiore 5, 00185 Rome, Italy. Rev. Msgr. Diego Coletti, Rector.

***North American College (Pontifical)*—**Corporate Title: *The American College of the Roman Catholic Church of the United States.* A Maryland Corporation. Founded in 1859 by Pope Pius IX.

Postal Address: Via del Gianicolo 14, 00120 Vatican City State, Europe. Rev. Msgr. Timothy M. Dolan, Rector. (See AMERICAN COLLEGES ABROAD on the next page for further details.)

***Armenian College (Pontifical)*—**Founded on March 1, 1883. Address: Salita S. Nicola da Tolentino 17, 00187 Rome, Italy. Rev. Andon Saroyan, Rector.

***Beda College (Pontifical)*—**Founded in 1852; separated from the English College in 1917. Address: Viale San Paolo 18, 00146 Rome, Italy. Rev. Msgr. Brian Dazeley
, Rector.

***Belgian College (Pontifical)*—**Founded in 1844. Rev. Address: Via G.B. Pagano 35, 00167 Rome, Italy. Rev Msgr. Werner Quintens, Rector.

***Canadian College (Pontifical)*—**Founded in 1888. Address: Via Crescenzio 75, 00193 Rome, Italy. Rev. Martin Belanger, P.S.S., Rector.

***Capranica College (Almo)*—**Founded in 1457 by Cardinal Capranica. Address: Piazza Capranica 98, 00186 Rome, Italy. Rev. Msgr. Michele Pennisi, Rector.

***Ethiopian College (Pontifical)*—**Founded on October 1, 1919. Address: 00120 Citta del Vaticano, Europe. Rev. P. Teodoro Ghebretensae, Rector.

***German-Hungarian College (Pontifical)*—**Founded on October 28, 1552. Address: Via S. Nicolo da Tolentino 13, 00187 Rome, Italy. Very Rev. Johannes Gunter Gerhartz, S.J., Rector.

***Greek College (Pontifical)*—**Founded on January 13, 1577. Address: Via del Babuino 149, 00187 Rome, Italy. Very Rev. Ambrogio Dolfini, O.S.B., Rector.

***English College (Venerabile)*—**Founded on April 23, 1578. Address: Via Monserrato 45, 00186 Rome, Italy. Rev. Adrian Toffolo, Rector.

***Irish College (Pontifical)*—**Founded in 1628. Address: Via dei Ss. Quattro 1, 00184 Rome, Italy. Rev. Msgr. John Fleming, Rector.

***Lithuanian College (Pontifical)*—**Founded in 1946. Address: Via Casalmonferrato 20, 00182 Rome, Italy. Rev. Msgr. Antanas Algimantas Bartkus, Rector.

***Maronite College*—**Founded on June 17, 1584. Address: Via Porta Pinciana 14, 00187 Rome, Italy.

***Nepomucene College (Pontifical)*—**Address: Via Concordia 1, 00183 Rome, Italy. Rev. Msgr. Karel Janousek, Rector.

***Philippine College (Pontifical)*—**Founded on June 29, 1961. Address: Via Aurelia 490, 00165 Rome, Italy. Rev. Msgr. Jesse Mercado, Rector.

***Pius XI Dutch College (Pontifical)*—**Founded on October 26, 1930. Address: Via Ercole Rosa 1, 00153 Rome, Italy. Rev. Rudolphus Smit, Rector.

***Brazilian College (Pontifical)*—**Founded in 1934 by Pius XI. Address: Via Aurelia 527, 00165 Rome, Italy. Very Rev. Matias Martinho Lenz, S.J., Rector.

***Latin American College (Pio Latino Americano) (Pontifical)*—**Founded in 1858. Address: Via Aurelia Antica 408, 00165 Rome, Italy. Rev. Luis Palomera, S.J., Rector.

***Polish College (Pontifical)*—**Founded on March 9, 1866. Address: Piazza Remuria 2-A, 00153 Rome, Italy. Rev. Msgr. Marian Rola, Rector.

***Portuguese College (Pontifical)*—**Founded on October 28, 1900. Address: Via Nicolo V 3, 00165 Rome, Italy. Rev. Msgr. Jose Tomas Amandio, Rector.

***Russian College of S. Theresa of the Child Jesus (Pontifical)*—**Founded on August 15, 1929. Address: Via Carlo Cattaneo 2, 00185 Rome, Italy. Rev. Richard Cemus, S.J., Rector.

***Ukrainian College of Saint Josephat (Pontifical)*—**Founded in 1897. Address: Passeggiata del Gianicolo 7, 00165 Rome, Italy. Rev. Genesio Viomar, O.S.B.M., Rector.

***College of St. Jerome of the Croatians (Pontifical)*—**Founded on August 1, 1901. Address: Via Tomacelli 132, 00186 Rome, Italy. Rev. Msgr. Jure Bogdah.

***St. Thomas Aquinas*—**Founded in 1948. Address: Via Degli Ibernesi 20, 00184 Rome, Italy. Very Rev. Glenn Morris, O.P., Rector.

***Scots College (Pontifical)*—**Founded on December 5, 1600. Address: Via Cassia 481, 00189 Rome, Italy. Rev. Christopher Joseph McElroy, Rector.

***Spanish College (Pontifical)*—**Founded on April 1, 1892. Address: Via Di Torrerrossa 2, 00165 Rome, Italy. Rev. Lope Rubio Parrado, Rector.

Teutonic College (S. Maria dell'Anima)—Founded in 1859. Address: Via della Pace 20, 00186 Rome, Italy. Rev. Msgr. Johannes Nedbal, Rector.

Teutonic College (S. Maria in Camposanto), for the study of Sacred Archaeology and Ecclesiastical History—Founded on November 21, 1876. Address: Via della Sagrestia 17, 00120 Citta del Vaticano, Europe. Rev. Msgr. Erwin Gatz, Rector.

Polish Ecclesiastical Institute (Pontifical)—Founded in 1910. Address: Piazza B. Cairoli 117, 00186 Rome, Italy. Rev. Zbighiew Kiernikowski, S.J., Rector.

American Church. Santa Susanna—Address: Via Venti Settembre 14. Postal Address: Via Antonio Salandra 6, 00187 Rome, Italy. Tel: 488.2748; Fax: 474.0236. Rev. John J. Foley, C.S.P., Rector.

AMERICAN COLLEGES ABROAD

American College. Louvain, Belgium. Corporate title: *The American College of the Immaculate Conception, Catholic University of Louvain,*— a corporation of the District of Columbia. Founded in 1857. Postal Address: Naamsestraat 100, B-3000 Leuven, Belgium. Tel: 32.16.32.00.11; Fax: 32.16.32.00.12. Very Rev. David E. Windsor, C.M., Psy. D., Rector/Pres.; Rev. Francis Kayatta, S.T.B., J.C.L., Vice Rector;

Rev. Msgr. John Scanlan, S.T.B., M.Div., Vice Pres. - Development; Rev. Daniel Tormey, S.T.B., M.A., Dir. - Spiritual Formation;

Rev. Aurelius Boberek, O.S.B., S.T.B., M.A./Dir.- Liturgy and Homiletics;

Sr. Rina Cappellazzo, O.P., M.A., Ph.D., Dir. - Pastoral Formation; Rev. Jan Lambrecht, S.J., S.T.D., Theological Advisor; Rev. Stephen Banet, S.T.B., M.A., Pastor, Our Lady of Mercy Parish, Brussels; Prof. John A. Dick, S.T.D., Dir. - Academic Formation; Mr. Daniel J. Frett, S.T.L., Ph.L., Business Mgr. The American College is operated under the auspices of a special committee of the National Conference of Catholic Bishops. Most Rev. Frank Rodimer, Bishop of Paterson, Chairman.

The American College operates in four areas, all in the English language, in conjunction with the Institute of Philosophy, the Faculty of Theology and the Faculty of Canon Law of the Katholieke Universiteit te Leuven (K.U. Leuven) and of the Universite Catholique de Louvain (U.C.L.). *The Seminary Program of Priestly Formation*—both on the level of Philosophy, Pre-theology and Theology; graduate studies in Canon Law, Theology and Philosophy; monthly and semester sabbatical programs; and a summer session for ministerial renewal.

Office for Development and Recruitment for the American College of Louvain—Postal Address: The Americal College, USCC/NCCB 3211 Fourth St., N.E., Washington, DC 20017-1194. Tel: 202-541-3108; Fax: 202-541-3133.

The American College founded and remains associated with the English-speaking Parish of Our Lady of Mercy in the Brussels area. Parish Postal Address: 64 Avenue Reine Astrid 1410, Waterloo, Belgium. Tel: 32.2.354.5343; Fax: 32.2.351.2314.

North American College, Rome, Italy. (Pontifical)—Corporate Title: *The American College of the Roman Catholic Church of the United States.* A Maryland Corporation. Operates under the auspices of a special committee of the National Conference of Catholic Bishops. Chairman: His Eminence William Cardinal Keeler. Founded in 1859 by Pope Pius IX, the express purpose being to bring American seminarians and student priests into close association with the Holy See. Seminarians live and take their priestly formation at the College, while studying at the theological universities in Rome. Three major departments: Seminary, Graduate and Institute for Continuing Theological Education.

Postal Address: North American College, 00120 Vatican City State, Europe. Rev. Msgr. Timothy M. Dolan, Rector; Rev. Msgr. Bernard E. Yarrish, Vice Rector for Administration.

Seminary Department: Postal Address: North American College, 00120 Vatican City State, Europe. Tel: 011.39.6.684.931; Fax: 011.39.6.686.7561. Student Fax: 011.39.6.686.9665. Rev. Msgr. Timothy M. Dolan, Rector; Rev. William M. Ogrowdowski, Vice Rector for Community Life; Rev. Michael J. Curran, Dir.-Studies & Admissions; Rev. Jon J. O'Brien, S.J., Staff Psychiatrist; Rev. Thomas Raddloff, S.J., Spiritual Dir.; Rev. Cornelius McRae, Spiritual Dir.; Rev. Joseph Henchey, C.S.S., Spiritual Dir.; Rev. Miles D. Walsh, Dir.- Pastoral Formation; Dr. Edward Smith, Dir.- Worship; Rev. Ferrando Minoggio, Philosophy Tutor; Sr. Rebecca Abel, O.S.B., Librarian; Rev. Msgr. Daniel E. Thomas, in residence. Students 151, representing 80 Dioceses and Archdioceses.

Institute for Continuing Theological Education: Postal Address: North American College, 00120 Vatican City State, Europe. Tel: 011.39.6.687-1529; Fax: 011.39.6.686.7561. Rev. D. Terrence Morgan, Dir. Fall & Spring 12-week sabbatical sessions for priests. Participants 38.

Graduate Department: Casa Santa Maria, Postal Address: Via dell'Umilta 30, 00187 Rome, Italy. Tel: (011.39.6)69-00-11; Fax: (011.39.6)69-00-18-23. Residence hall of North American College for postgraduate priests from the United States. Rev. Msgr. Charles W. Elmer, Dir. Graduate priests 89, representing 50 Dioceses and Archdioceses.

Bishops' Office for United States Visitors to the Vatican: Postal Address: Via dell'Umilta 30, 00187 Rome, Italy. Tel: (011.39.6)69-00-11; Fax: (011.39.6)6900-1823 or 679-1448. Request for attendance at Papal audiences and similar functions may be addressed to this office. Rev. Msgr. Roger C. Roensch, Dir.

Office for Development of the North American College: Postal Address: 2500 Brunswick Pike, Lawrenceville, New Jersey 08648. Tel: 609-671-1400; Fax: 609-671-9200. Mr. Patrick Kennedy, Dir. - Development.

The Apostolic Nunciature

Established As Apostolic Delegation January 24, 1893; Nunciature January 10, 1984.
Address: 3339 Massachusetts Ave., N.W., Washington, DC 20008-3687. Tel: 202-333-7121. Fax: 202-337-4036.

APOSTOLIC PRO-NUNCIO TO THE UNITED STATES

His Excellency
The Most Reverend

AGOSTINO CACCIAVILLAN, J.C.D., J.Civ.D., S.Soc.Lic.
Titular Archbishop of Amiterno
Apostolic Pro-Nuncio

Born in the province of Vicenza, Italy, August 14, 1926; ordained a priest for the Diocese of Vicenza, June 26, 1949. Entered the diplomatic service of the Holy See in 1959; served at the Vatican Secretariat of State, the Philippines, Spain, and Portugal; from 1969 through 1976 he was head of the Documentation and Information Office of the Secretariat of State. On January 19, 1976, he was appointed Apostolic Pro-Nuncio to Kenya, and Apostolic Delegate to the Seychelles. Received episcopal ordination on February 28, 1976. He was named Apostolic Pro-Nuncio to India on May 9, 1981, and, in addition, first Apostolic Pro-Nuncio to the Kingdom of Nepal on April 30, 1985. On June 13, 1990, Pope John Paul II appointed him Apostolic Pro-Nuncio to the United States and Permanent Observer of the Holy See to the Organization of American States.

Rev. Msgr. Renato Volante, S.T.D., J.C.L. *Counsellor;* Rev. Msgr. Francis Cao Minh Dung, J.C.D., *Counsellor;* Rev. Msgr. Giorgio Lingua, J.C.D., *Secretary.*

Rev. Msgr. John H. Maksymowicz, S.T.L., *Secretary;* Rev. Joseph C. Mulqueen, J.C.L., *Secretary;* Rev. Matthew E. Rzeczkowski, O.P., S.T.L., *Archivist.*

Former Apostolic Delegates:	
His Eminence Francesco Cardinal Satolli,	1893-1896.
His Eminence Sebastiano Cardinal Martinelli,	1896-1902.
His Eminence Diomede Cardinal Falconio,	1902-1911.
His Eminence Giovanni Cardinal Bonzano,	1911-1922.
His Eminence Pietro Cardinal Fumasoni-Biondi,	1922-1933.
His Eminence Amleto G. Cardinal Cicognani,	1933-1958.
His Eminence Egidio Cardinal Vagnozzi,	1958-1967.
His Eminence Luigi Cardinal Raimondi,	1967-1973.
His Excellency Most Reverend Jean Jadot,	1973-1980.
His Eminence Pio Cardinal Laghi,	1980-1984.
Apostolic Pro-Nuncios:	
His Eminence Pio Cardinal Laghi,	1984-1990.
His Excellency Most Reverend Agostino Cacciavillan,	1990-

The Permanent Observer Mission of the Holy See to the United Nations

Established January 26, 1964
Address: 25 E. 39th St., New York, NY 10016-0903. 212-370-9614. Fax: 212-370-9622.

PERMANENT OBSERVER
OF THE HOLY SEE TO THE UNITED NATIONS

His Excellency
The Most Reverend

RENATO R. MARTINO, J.C.D., D.D.,
Titular Archbishop of Segerme;
Apostolic Nuncio

Born in Salerno, Italy on November 23, 1932; ordained for the Archdiocese of Salerno, June 20, 1957; Entered the diplomatic service of the Holy See July 1, 1962; Served in Nicaragua 1962-64-- Philippines 1964-66-- Lebanon 1966-70-- Canada 1975-78-- Brazil 1978-80; From 1970 to 1975, he was head of the Department for International Organizations in the Vatican Secretariat of State. Appointed Apostolic Pro-Nuncio to Thailand and named Titular Archbishop of Segerme September 14, 1980. Ordained a Bishop on December 14, 1980. Served as Apostolic Pro-Nuncio to Thailand from 1980-86 and also as Apostolic Delegate to Singapore, Malaysia, Laos and Brunei. Apostolic Pro-Nuncio to Singapore June 24, 1981. Appointed Permanent Observer of the Holy See to the United Nations December 3, 1986. Office Address: 25 East 39th St., New York, NY 10016-0903. Tel: 212-370-7885; Fax: 212-370-9622. Residential Address: 20 East 72nd St., New York, NY 10021-4196. Tel: 212-734-2900; Fax: 212-988-3633.

Rev. Msgr. George Panikulam, S.S.D., S.T.L., L.C.L., *Counsellor;* Rev. Msgr. David J. Malloy, S.T.D., 1st. *Secretary*; Rev. Msgr. Carl J. Marucci, M.A.,*Attache*; Rev. Msgr. James M. Reinert, Ph.D, *Attache*; Mr. Karol Krcmery, *Attache*; Ms. Olivetta Danese, *Attache*; Ms. Ana Lucia De Campos Charnaux Serta, *Attache*.

Former Permanent Observers:

Rev. Msgr. Alberto Giovannetti, J.C.D.	1964-1973
Most Rev. Giovanni Cheli, J.C.D., D.D.	1973-1986

Path to Peace Foundation, Inc.--25 East 39th St., New York, NY 10016-0903. 212-370-7885; Fax: 212-370-9622. Board of Directors: Archbishop Renato R. Martino, Pres.; Rev. Msgr. Robert L. Charlebois, Vice Pres.; Rev. Msgr. Eugene V. Clark, Treas.; Mr. John P. Reiner, Sec.

PART II
Alphabetical List of Places in the United States

This comprehensive list includes all cities and towns in the United States in which a Catholic Institution is located.

The abbreviations identify each city or town to the corresponding Diocese or Archdiocese.

Abbeville, LA	LAF
SC	CHR
Abbotsford, WI	LC
Abbott, TX	FWT
Abbottstown, PA	HBG
Aberdeen, ID	B
MD	BAL
MS	JKS
SD	SFS
WA	SEA
Abilene, KS	SAL
TX	SAN
Abingdon, IL	PEO
MD	BAL
VA	RIC
Abington, MA	BO
PA	PH
Abiquiu, NM	SFE
Abita Springs, LA	NO
Abrams, WI	GB
Absecon, NJ	CAM
Ackley, IA	DUB
Acme, MI	GAY
Acoma, NM	GLP
Acosta, PA	ALT
Acton, MA	BO
Acushnet, MA	FR
Ada, MI	GR
MN	CR
OH	COL
OK	OKL
Adair, IA	DM
Adams, MA	SPR
MN	WIN
NY	OG
WI	LC
Adamstown, MD	BAL
Addison, IL	JOL
NY	ROC
Adel, IA	DM
Adelanto, CA	SB
Adell, WI	MIL
Adelphi, MD	WDC
Adena, OH	STU
Adjuntas, PR	PCE
Adona, AR	LR
Adrian, MI	LAN
MN	WIN
Advance, MO	SPC
Affton, MO	STL
Afton, IA	DM
MI	GAY
Agana, GU	AGN
Agana Heights, GU	AGN
Agat, GU	AGN
Agawam, MA	SPR
Agua Dulce, TX	CC
Aguada, PR	MGZ
Aguadilla, PR	MGZ
Aguas Buenas, PR	CGS
Aguilar, CO	PBL
Aguirre, PR	PCE
Ahmeek, MI	MAR
Ahoskie, NC	R
Aibonito, PR	CGS
Aiea, HI	HON
Aiken, SC	CHR
Ainsworth, NE	GI
Aitkin, MN	DUL
Ajo, AZ	TUC
Akeley, MN	CR
Akron, CO	DEN
IA	SC
NY	BUF
OH	CLV
OH	NTN
OH	PRM
OH	SJP
Alakanuk, AK	FBK
Alameda, CA	OAK
NM	SFE
Alamo, TX	BWN
Alamogordo, NM	LSC
Alamosa, CO	PBL
Albany, GA	SAV
KY	L
LA	BR
MN	SCL
NY	ALB
OR	P
TX	FWT
Albee, MI	SAG
Albemarle, NC	CHL
Albers, IL	BEL
Albert Lea, MN	WIN
Alberta, AL	MOB
Albertville, MN	STP
Albia, IA	DAV
Albion, IN	FTW
MI	KAL
NE	OM
NY	BUF
PA	E
Albuquerque, NM	SFE
NM	VNN
Alburg, VT	BUR
Alcoa, TN	KNX
Alden, NY	BUF
Alden Station, PA	PHU
Aledo, IL	PEO
Aleppo, KS	WCH
Aleppo Township, PA	PIT
Alexander, IL	SFD
Alexander City, AL	BIR
Alexandria, IN	LFT
KY	COV
LA	ALX
MN	SCL
SD	SFS
VA	ARL
VA	NTN
Alexandria Bay, NY	OG
Alexis, IL	PEO
Alfred, ME	PRT
Algoma, WI	GB
Algona, IA	SC
Algonac, MI	DET
Algonquin, IL	RCK
Alhambra, CA	LA
Alhambra, Ponce, PR	PCE
Alice, ND	FAR
TX	CC
Aliquippa, PA	PBR
PA	PIT
PA	SJP
Allegan, MI	KAL
Allegany, NY	BUF
Allegany State Park, NY	BUF
Allen, TX	DAL
Allen Park, MI	DET
MI	PRM
Allendale, NJ	NEW
Allenspark, CO	DEN
Allenstown, NH	MAN
Allenton, MI	DET
WI	MIL
Allentown, NJ	TR
PA	ALN
PA	PHU
PA	PSC
Alliance, NE	GI
OH	Y
Allison, IA	DUB
Allison Park, PA	PIT
Alma, KS	KCK
MI	SAG
MN	CR
NE	LIN
WI	LC
Alma Center, WI	LC
Almena, WI	SUP
Almond, NY	BUF
WI	LC
Aloha, OR	P
Aloys, NE	OM
Alpena, MI	GAY
Alpha, MI	MAR
NJ	MET
Alpharetta, GA	ATL
Alpine, AZ	GLP
CA	SD
MI	GR
TX	ELP
Alsip, IL	CHI
Alta Loma, CA	SB
Alta Vista, IA	DUB
Altadena, CA	LA
Altamont, IL	SFD
NY	ALB
Altamonte Springs, FL	ORL
Altdorf, WI	LC
Alton, IA	SC
IL	SFD
NH	MAN
TX	BWN
Altona, NY	OG
Altoona, IA	DM
PA	ALT
PA	SJP
WI	LC
Altura, MN	WIN
Alturas, CA	SAC
Altus, AR	LR
OK	OKL
Alva, FL	VEN
OK	OKL
Alvada, OH	TOL
Alverno, MI	GAY
WI	GB
Alvin, TX	GAL
Alviso, CA	SJ
Ama, LA	NO
Amargosa Valley, NV	LAV
Amarillo, TX	AMA
Amberg, WI	GB
Ambler, PA	PH
Amboy, IL	RCK
Ambridge, PA	PBR
PA	PIT
PA	SJP
Amelia, LA	HT
OH	CIN
Amenia, NY	NY
American Canyon, CA	SR
American Falls, ID	B
American Fork, UT	SLC
Americus, GA	SAV
Amery, WI	SUP
Ames, IA	DUB
TX	BEA
Amesbury, MA	BO
Amherst, MA	SPR
NY	BUF
NY	PSC
OH	CLV
WI	LC
Amite, LA	BR
Amity, OR	P
Amityville, NY	BRK
NY	RVC
Ammannsville, TX	VIC
Amory, MS	JKS
Amsterdam, NY	ALB
NY	STF
OH	STU
Anaconda, MT	HEL
Anacortes, WA	SEA
Anacostia, Washington, DC	WDC
Anadarko, OK	OKL
Anaheim, CA	OLL
CA	ORG
CA	VNN
Anahuac, TX	BEA
Anamoose, ND	FAR
Anamosa, IA	DUB
Anasco, PR	MGZ
Anchorage, AK	ANC
AK	VNN
Anchorville, MI	DET
Andale, KS	WCH
Andalusia, AL	MOB
IL	PEO
Anderson, CA	SAC
IN	LFT
SC	CHR
TX	GAL
Andice, TX	AUS
Andover, MA	BO
NJ	PAT
NY	BUF
OH	Y
SD	SFS
Andrew, IA	DUB
Andrews, NC	CHL
TX	SAN
Aneta, ND	FAR
Angaur, FM	CI
Angelica, NY	BUF
Angels Camp, CA	STO
Angelus, KS	SAL
Angleton, TX	GAL
Angola, IN	FTW
NY	BUF
Aniak, AK	FBK
Anita, IA	DM
PA	E
Aniwa, WI	GB
Ankeny, IA	DM
Ann Arbor, MI	LAN
Anna, IL	BEL
Annandale, MN	STP
VA	ARL
VA	PSC
Annapolis, MD	BAL
Annawan, IL	PEO
Anniston, AL	BIR
Annville, PA	HBG
Anoka, MN	STP
Anselmo, NE	GI
Anson, TX	LUB
Ansonia, CT	HRT
CT	STF
Antelope, CA	SAC
Anthon, IA	SC
Anthony, KS	WCH
NM	LSC
Antigo, WI	GB
Antioch, CA	OAK
IL	CHI
TN	NSH
Antlers, OK	TLS
Anton Chico, NM	SFE
Antonino, KS	SAL
Antwerp, NY	OG
OH	TOL
Anza, CA	SB
Apache Junction, AZ	TUC
Apalachicola, FL	PT
Apalachin, NY	ROC
Apex, NC	R
Apollo, PA	GBG
Apopka, FL	ORL
FL	SJP
Apple Creek, MO	STL
Apple River, IL	RCK
Apple Valley, CA	SB
Applegate, CA	SAC
Appleton, MN	NU
WI	GB
Appomattox, VA	RIC
Aptos, CA	MRY
Arabi, LA	NO
Aragon, NM	GLP
Aransas Pass, TX	CC
Arbor Vitae, WI	SUP
Arcade, NY	BUF
Arcadia, CA	LA
FL	VEN
IA	SC
PA	PBR
WI	LC
Arcata, CA	SR

Archbald, PA	SCR
Archbold, OH	TOL
Arco, ID	B
Arcola, IL	SFD
IN	FTW
Arden, NC	CHL
Ardmore, OK	OKL
PA	PH
Ardoch, ND	FAR
Ardon, IA	DAV
Ardsley, NY	NY
PA	PH
Arecibo, PR	ARE
Arenzville, IL	SFD
Argo, IL	CHI
Argonne, WI	GB
Argusville, ND	FAR
Argyle, MI	SAG
MN	CR
MO	JC
WI	MAD
Arkadelphia, AR	LR
Arkansas City, KS	WCH
Arkansaw, WI	LC
Arlington, IL	PEO
MA	BO
MN	NU
OR	BAK
SD	SFS
TX	FWT
VA	ARL
VT	BUR
WA	SEA
Arlington Heights, IL	CHI
Arma, KS	WCH
Armada, MI	DET
Armonk, NY	NY
Armour, SD	SFS
Armstrong, IA	SC
WI	MIL
Armstrong Creek, WI	GB
Arnaudville, LA	LAF
Arnheim, OH	CIN
Arnold, MO	STL
PA	GBG
Arpin, WI	LC
Arrow Bear Lake, CA	SB
Arroyo, PR	PCE
Arroyo Grande, CA	MRY
Arroyo Seco, NM	SFE
Artesia, CA	LA
NM	LSC
Artesian, SD	SFS
Arvada, CO	DEN
Arvin, CA	FRS
Asan, GU	AGN
Asbury, NJ	MET
Asbury Park, NJ	TR
Ashburn, VA	ARL
Ashburnham, MA	WOR
Asheboro, NC	CHL
Asherton, TX	SAT
Asheville, NC	CHL
Ashford, CT	NOR
WI	MIL
Ashkum, IL	JOL
Ashland, AL	BIR
IL	SFD
KS	DOD
KY	LEX
MA	BO
ME	PRT
MT	GF
NE	LIN
NH	MAN
OH	CLV
OR	P
PA	ALN
VA	RIC
WI	SUP
Ashland City, TN	NSH
Ashley, ND	FAR
PA	SCR
Ashtabula, OH	PBR
OH	Y
Ashton, IA	SC
NE	GI
WI	MAD
Ashville, PA	ALT
Askeaton, WI	GB
Aspen, CO	DEN
Aspinwall, PA	PIT
Assinins, MI	MAR
Assonet, MA	FR
Assumption, IL	SFD
OH	TOL
Aston, PA	PH
Astoria, NY	BRK
NY	ROM
OR	P
Atascadero, CA	MRY

Atchison, KS	KCK
Atco, NJ	CAM
Athens, AL	BIR
GA	ATL
IL	SFD
NY	ALB
OH	STU
PA	SCR
TN	KNX
TX	TYL
WI	LC
WV	WH
Atherton, CA	SFR
Athol, MA	WOR
SD	SFS
Athol Springs, NY	BUF
Atkins, AR	LR
Atkinson, IL	PEO
NE	OM
Atlanta, GA	ATL
GA	NTN
GA	SAM
MI	GAY
TX	TYL
Atlantic, IA	DM
Atlantic Beach, FL	STA
Atlantic City, NJ	CAM
Atlantic Highlands, NJ	TR
Atmore, AL	MOB
Attica, IN	LFT
NY	BUF
OH	TOL
Attleboro, MA	FR
Attleboro Falls, MA	FR
Atwater, CA	FRS
Atwood, KS	SAL
Au Sable Forks, NY	OG
Auburn, AL	MOB
CA	SAC
IA	SC
IL	SFD
IN	FTW
MA	WOR
ME	PRT
MI	SAG
NE	LIN
NH	MAN
NY	ROC
NY	STF
NY	SY
WA	SEA
WI	MIL
Auburn Hills, MI	DET
Auburndale, WI	LC
Audubon, IA	DM
NJ	CAM
PA	PH
AuGres, MI	SAG
Augusta, GA	NTN
GA	SAV
IA	DAV
KS	WCH
KY	COV
ME	PRT
MO	STL
WI	LC
Ault, CO	DEN
Auriesville, NY	ALB
Aurora, CO	DEN
IL	JOL
IL	RCK
IL	ROM
IN	IND
KS	SAL
KY	OWN
MN	DUL
MO	SPC
NE	LIN
NY	ROC
OH	Y
SD	SFS
WI	GB
Austin, MN	WIN
TX	AUS
TX	OLL
Austintown, OH	SJP
Ava, IL	BEL
MO	SPC
Avalon, CA	LA
NJ	CAM
PA	PIT
Avella, PA	PBR
PA	PIT
Avenal, CA	FRS
Avenel, NJ	MET
Avenue, MD	WDC
Averill Park, NY	ALB
Avilla, IN	FTW
Aviston, IL	BEL
Avoca, IA	DM
PA	SCR

Avon, CT	HRT
MA	BO
MN	SCL
NJ	TR
NY	ROC
OH	CLV
Avon Lake, OH	CLV
Avon Park, FL	VEN
Avondale, AZ	PHX
CO	PBL
LA	NO
Avonmore, PA	GBG
Awak, FM	CI
Awak, Pohnpei, FM	CI
Axtel, KY	OWN
Axtell, KS	KCK
Ayer, MA	BO
Aztec, NM	GLP
Azusa, CA	LA
Babbitt, MN	DUL
Babcock, WI	LC
Babeldaob, FM	CI
Babylon, NY	RVC
Bad Axe, MI	SAG
Baden, MD	WDC
PA	PIT
Badger, MN	CR
Bagdad, AZ	PHX
Bagley, MN	CR
Bailey, CO	COS
Baileys Harbor, WI	GB
Baileyville, KS	KCK
Bainbridge, GA	SAV
NY	SY
Bainbridge Island, WA	SEA
Bairdford, PA	PIT
Baker, LA	BR
MT	GF
OR	BAK
Baker City, OR	BAK
Bakersfield, CA	FRS
Bakerton, PA	ALT
Bakerville, WI	LC
Bal Harbour, FL	MIA
Bala Cynwyd, PA	PH
Baldwin, KS	KCK
LA	LAF
MI	GR
NY	RVC
Baldwin Boro, PA	PIT
Baldwin Park, CA	LA
Baldwinsville, NY	SY
Baldwinville, MA	WOR
Balfour, ND	FAR
Ball Club, MN	DUL
Ballinger, TX	SAN
Ballouville, CT	NOR
Ballston Lake, NY	ALB
Ballston Spa, NY	ALB
Balltown, IA	DUB
Ballwin, MO	STL
Bally, PA	ALN
Balmorhea, TX	ELP
Balsam Lake, WI	SUP
Balta, ND	FAR
Baltic, CT	NOR
Baltimore, MD	BAL
MD	PHU
MD	PSC
MD	WDC
Bancroft, IA	SC
NE	OM
Bandera, TX	SAT
Bandon, OR	P
Bangall, NY	NY
Bangor, ME	PRT
MI	KAL
PA	ALN
WI	LC
Bankston, IA	DUB
Banning, CA	SB
Bannister, MI	SAG
Bantam, CT	HRT
Bapchule, AZ	PHX
Baptistown, NJ	MET
Bar Harbor, ME	PRT
Baraboo, WI	MAD
Baraga, MI	MAR
Barberton, OH	CLV
OH	PRM
Barbourville, KY	LEX
Barceloneta, PR	ARE
Barclay, IA	DUB
Bardonia, NY	NY
Bardstown, KY	L
Bardwell, KY	OWN
Barefoot Bay, FL	ORL
Baring, MO	JC
Bark River, MI	MAR
Barker, NY	BUF
Barling, AR	LR

Barnegat, NJ	TR
Barnesboro, PA	ALT
PA	PBR
PA	SJP
Barnesville, MD	WDC
MN	CR
OH	STU
PA	ALN
Barnum, IA	SC
Barranquitas, PR	CGS
Barre, MA	WOR
VT	BUR
Barrenspot, VI	STV
Barrett Station, TX	GAL
Barrigada, GU	AGN
Barrington, IL	CHI
NJ	CAM
RI	PRO
Barrio Rio Canas, PR	CGS
Barron, WI	SUP
Barrow, AK	FBK
Barry, IL	SFD
MN	NU
Barrytown, NY	NY
Barryville, NY	NY
Barstow, CA	SB
Bartelso, IL	BEL
Bartlesville, OK	TLS
Bartlett, IL	CHI
Barton, OH	STU
VT	BUR
Bartonville, IL	PEO
Bartow, FL	ORL
Basalt, CO	DEN
Bascom, OH	TOL
Basehor, KS	KCK
Basile, LA	LAF
Basking Ridge, NJ	MET
Bass Lake, CA	FRS
Bassfield, MS	BLX
Bastress, PA	SCR
Bastrop, LA	SHP
TX	AUS
Batavia, IL	RCK
NY	BUF
OH	CIN
Batchtown, IL	SFD
Batesburg, SC	CHR
Batesville, AR	LR
IN	IND
MS	JKS
Bath, ME	PRT
NY	ROC
NY	STF
PA	ALN
Bathgate, ND	FAR
Baton Rouge, LA	BR
LA	OLL
Battle Creek, MI	KAL
NE	OM
Battle Ground, WA	SEA
Battle Lake, MN	SCL
Battle Mountain, NV	RNO
Baudette, MN	CR
Bauer, IA	DAV
Baxter Springs, KS	WCH
Bay City, MI	PRM
MI	SAG
TX	VIC
Bay Head, NJ	TR
Bay Mills, MI	MAR
Bay Minette, AL	MOB
Bay St. Louis, MS	BLX
Bay Settlement, WI	GB
Bay Shore, MI	GAY
NY	RVC
Bay Village, OH	CLV
Bayamon, PR	SJN
Bayard, IA	DM
NM	LSC
Bayfield, WI	SUP
Bayonne, NJ	NEW
NJ	PHU
NJ	PSC
Bayou Black, LA	HT
Bayou George, FL	PT
Bayou LaBatre, AL	MOB
Bayou Pigeon, LA	BR
Bayou Vista, LA	LAF
Bayport, MN	STP
Bayside, NY	BRK
Baytown, TX	GAL
Bayville, NJ	TR
NY	RVC
Beach, ND	BIS
Beachwood, OH	CLV
Beacon, NY	NY
Beacon Falls, CT	HRT
Beal City, MI	SAG
Beans Cove, PA	ALT
Bear, DE	WIL

Bear Creek, WI	GB
Bear Creek Township, PA	SCR
Bear Valley, WI	LC
Beardsley, KS	SAL
MN	NU
Beardstown, IL	SFD
Beasley, TX	GAL
Beatrice, NE	LIN
Beattie, KS	KCK
Beattyville, KY	LEX
Beaufort, SC	CHR
Beaulieu, MN	CR
Beaumont, CA	SB
TX	BEA
Beaver, KS	DOD
MI	SAG
PA	PBR
PA	PIT
Beaver Crossing, NE	LIN
Beaver Dam, KY	OWN
WI	MIL
Beaver Falls, PA	PIT
Beaver Island, MI	GAY
Beaver Meadows, PA	ALN
PA	PSC
Beaver Prairie, IL	BEL
Beavercreek, OH	CIN
Beaverdale, PA	ALT
PA	PBR
Beaverton, OR	P
Beaverville, IL	JOL
Bechyn, MN	NU
Bechyne, ND	FAR
Beckemeyer, IL	BEL
Becker, MN	SCL
Beckley, WV	WH
Bedford, IA	DM
IN	IND
MA	BO
NH	MAN
NY	NY
OH	CLV
OH	PRM
PA	ALT
TX	FWT
VA	RIC
Bedford Heights, OH	CLV
Bedford Village, NY	NY
Beech Bottom, WV	WH
Beech Grove, IN	IND
Beemer, NE	OM
Beeville, TX	CC
Bejou, MN	CR
Bel Air, MD	BAL
Belchertown, MA	SPR
Belcourt, ND	FAR
Belding, MI	GR
Belen, NM	SFE
Belfast, ME	PRT
NY	BUF
Belfield, ND	BIS
ND	STN
Belgique, MO	STL
Belgium, WI	MIL
Belgrade, MN	NU
MN	SCL
Belington, WV	WH
Bell City, LA	LKC
Bell Gardens, CA	LA
Bella Vista, AR	LR
Bellaire, MI	GAY
OH	STU
Belle, MO	JC
WV	WH
Belle Chasse, LA	NO
Belle Creek, MN	STP
Belle Fontaine, AL	MOB
Belle Fourche, SD	RC
Belle Glade, FL	PMB
Belle Plaine, IA	DUB
MN	STP
Belle Prairie, MN	SCL
Belle River, MN	SCL
Belle Rose, LA	BR
Belle Valley, OH	STU
Belle Vernon, PA	GBG
Belleair Bluffs, FL	SP
Bellechester, MN	STP
Belledeau, LA	ALX
Bellefontaine, OH	CIN
Bellefontaine Neighbors, MO	STL
Bellefonte, DE	WIL
PA	ALT
Belleview, FL	ORL
IL	SFD
Belleville, IL	BEL
KS	SAL
MI	DET
NJ	NEW
WI	MAD
Bellevue, IA	DUB

KY	COV
MI	LAN
NE	OM
OH	TOL
PA	PIT
WA	SEA
Bellflower, CA	LA
Bellingham, MA	BO
WA	SEA
Bellmawr, NJ	CAM
Bellmore, NY	RVC
Bellows Falls, VT	BUR
Bellport, NY	RVC
Bellville, TX	GAL
Bellwood, IL	CHI
NE	LIN
PA	ALT
Belmar, NJ	TR
Belmond, IA	DUB
Belmont, CA	SFR
MA	BO
MI	GR
NC	CHL
NH	MAN
NY	BUF
WI	MAD
Beloit, KS	SAL
WI	MAD
WI	MIL
Belpre, KS	DOD
OH	STU
Bel-Ridge, MO	STL
Belt, MT	GF
Belton, MO	KC
TX	AUS
Beltrees, IL	SFD
Beltsville, MD	PSC
MD	WDC
Belvidere, IL	RCK
NJ	MET
Belzoni, MS	JKS
Bement, IL	PEO
Bemidji, MN	CR
Bemus Point, NY	BUF
Ben Avon, PA	PIT
Benavides, TX	CC
The Bend, OH	TOL
Bend, OR	BAK
Bendena, KS	KCK
Benedict, MD	WDC
Benedicta, ME	PRT
Benet Lake, WI	MIL
Benicia, CA	SAC
Benkelman, NE	LIN
Benld, IL	SFD
Bennington, NH	MAN
VT	BUR
Bennington Center, NY	BUF
Bensalem, PA	PH
Bensenville, IL	JOL
Benson, AZ	TUC
IL	PEO
MN	NU
VT	BUR
Bentley Creek, PA	SCR
Bentleyville, PA	PIT
Benton, AR	LR
IL	BEL
MO	SPC
WI	MAD
Benton City, WA	YAK
Benton Harbor, MI	KAL
Bentonville, AR	LR
Benwood, MN	CR
WV	WH
Berea, KY	LEX
OH	CLV
Beresford, SD	SFS
Bergen, NY	BUF
Bergenfield, NJ	NEW
Berger, MO	STL
Berkeley, CA	OAK
MO	STL
Berkeley Heights, NJ	NEW
Berkeley Springs, WV	WH
Berkley, MI	DET
Berlin, MA	WOR
NH	MAN
NJ	CAM
NY	ALB
WI	MAD
Berlinsville, PA	ALN
Bernalillo, NM	SFE
Bernardsville, NJ	MET
Beroun, MN	DUL
Berryville, AR	LR
VA	ARL
Bertha, MN	SCL
Berwick, LA	LAF
ME	PRT
PA	HBG

PA	PHU
Berwyn, IL	CHI
PA	PH
Besancon, IN	FTW
Bessemer, AL	BIR
MI	MAR
PA	PIT
Bethalto, IL	SFD
Bethany, IL	SFD
MO	KC
WV	WH
Bethany Beach, DE	WIL
Bethel, AK	FBK
CT	BGP
OH	CIN
VT	BUR
Bethel Park, PA	PIT
Bethesda, MD	WDC
Bethlehem, CT	HRT
OH	TOL
PA	ALN
PA	PHU
PA	PSC
SD	RC
SD	SAM
Bethpage, NY	RVC
Betram, TX	AUS
Bettendorf, IA	DAV
Beulah, ND	BIS
Bevent, WI	LC
Beverly, MA	BO
NJ	TR
OH	STU
Beverly Hills, CA	LA
FL	SP
MI	DET
Beverly Shores, IN	GRY
Bicknell, IN	EVN
Biddeford, ME	PRT
Biehle, MO	STL
Big Bear, CA	SB
Big Bear Lake, CA	SB
Big Bend, SD	SFS
WI	MIL
Big Clifty, KY	OWN
Big Elbow Lake, MN	CR
Big Lake, LA	LKC
MN	SCL
TX	SAN
Big Long Lake, IN	FTW
Big Pine Key, FL	MIA
Big Rapids, MI	GR
Big River, WI	LC
Big Sandy, MT	GF
Big Spring, TX	SAN
Big Stone City, SD	SFS
Big Stone Gap, VA	RIC
Big Sur, CA	MRY
Big Timber, MT	GF
Big Wells, TX	SAT
Bigelow, AR	LR
Bigfork, MN	DUL
MT	HEL
Billerica, MA	BO
Billings, MO	SPC
MT	GF
Biloxi, MS	BLX
Bingham, ME	PRT
Binghamton, NY	PSC
NY	SY
Birch Coolie, MN	NU
Birch Run, MI	SAG
Birchwood, WI	SUP
Bird City, KS	SAL
Bird Island, MN	NU
Birdsboro, PA	ALN
Birmingham, AL	BIR
AL	NTN
AL	OLL
MI	DET
Birnamwood, WI	GB
Bisbee, AZ	TUC
ND	FAR
Bishop, CA	FRS
TX	CC
Bishop Creek, IL	SFD
Bismarck, ND	BIS
Bismark, OH	TOL
Bison, OK	OKL
SD	RC
Bissell Hills, MO	STL
Biwabik, MN	DUL
Bixby, OK	TLS
Black Brook, NY	OG
Black Canyon City, AZ	PHX
Black Creek, WI	GB
Black Diamond, WA	SEA
Black Eagle, MT	GF
Black Jack, IL	SFD
Black River, MI	GAY
NY	OG

Black River Falls, WI	LC
Blackduck, MN	CR
Blackfoot, ID	B
Blacksburg, VA	RIC
Blackstone, IL	PEO
MA	WOR
VA	RIC
Blackwell, OK	OKL
Blackwood, NJ	CAM
Bladensburg, MD	WDC
Blaine, KS	KCK
MN	STP
OH	STU
Blair, NE	OM
WI	LC
Blairstown, IA	DUB
NJ	MET
Blairsville, GA	ATL
PA	GBG
Blakely, GA	SAV
Blakeslee, OH	TOL
PA	SCR
Blanchester, OH	CIN
Blanco, NM	GLP
TX	AUS
Blasdell, NY	BUF
Blauvelt, NY	NY
Blawnox, PA	PIT
Blenker, WI	LC
Blessing, IA	DUB
TX	VIC
Bliss, NY	BUF
Blissfield, MI	LAN
Bloomer, WI	LC
Bloomfield, CT	HRT
IA	DAV
IN	EVN
NE	OM
NJ	NEW
NM	GLP
PA	PIT
Bloomfield Hills, MI	DET
Blooming Prairie, MN	WIN
Bloomingdale, IL	JOL
NY	OG
OH	STU
Bloomington, CA	SB
IL	PEO
IN	IND
MN	STP
TX	VIC
WI	MAD
Bloomsburg, PA	HBG
Bloomsbury, NJ	MET
Bloomsdale, MO	STL
Bloomville, WI	SUP
Blossburg, PA	SCR
Blossom, NY	BUF
Blountstown, FL	PT
Blue Anchor, NJ	CAM
Blue Creek, OH	CIN
Blue Earth, MN	WIN
Blue Grass, IA	DAV
Blue Island, IL	CHI
Blue Point, NY	RVC
Blue Rapids, KS	KCK
Blue Ridge, GA	ATL
Blue Ridge Summit, PA	HBG
Blue Springs, MO	KC
Bluefield, WV	WH
BlueGrass, MN	SCL
Bluffs, IL	SFD
Bluffton, IA	DUB
IN	FTW
MN	SCL
OH	TOL
SC	CHR
Blunt, SD	SFS
Blythe, CA	SB
Blytheville, AR	LR
Boardman, OH	PBR
OH	Y
Bobtown, PA	PIT
Boca Grande, FL	VEN
Boca Raton, FL	PMB
Bodija, Ibadan, Oyo State, Nigeria	CHI
Boerne, TX	SAT
Bogalusa, LA	NO
Bogota, NJ	NEW
Bohemia, NY	RVC
Boise, ID	B
Bokeelia, FL	VEN
Bolingbrook, IL	JOL
Bolivar, MO	SPC
NY	BUF
OH	COL
TN	MEM
Bolton, CT	NOR
MA	WOR
Bolton Landing, NY	ALB
Bombay, NY	OG

Bondsville, MA	SPR
Bonesteel, SD	RC
Bonham, TX	DAL
Bonifay, FL	PT
Bonita, CA	SD
Bonita Springs, FL	VEN
Bonne Terre, MO	STL
Bonneauville, PA	HBG
Bonner, MT	HEL
Bonner Springs, KS	KCK
Bonners Ferry, ID	B
Bonnots Mill, MO	JC
Bono, OH	TOL
Boone, IA	SC
NC	CHL
Booneville, AR	LR
MS	JKS
Boonton, NJ	PAT
Boonville, IN	EVN
MO	JC
NY	SY
Boothbay Harbor, ME	PRT
Boothwyn, PA	PH
Bordelonville, LA	ALX
Bordentown, NJ	TR
Borger, TX	AMA
Boron, CA	FRS
Borrego Springs, CA	SD
Boscobel, WI	MAD
Bossier City, LA	SHP
Boston, MA	ARM
MA	BO
MA	NTN
MA	STF
NY	BUF
Boswell, PA	ALT
Bothell, WA	SEA
Botkins, OH	CIN
Bottineau, ND	FAR
Boulder, CO	DEN
MT	HEL
Boulder City, NV	LAV
Boulder Creek, CA	MRY
Boulder Junction, WI	SUP
Boulevard, CA	SD
Bound Brook, NJ	MET
Bountiful, UT	SLC
Bourbon, MO	JC
Bourbonnais, IL	JOL
Bourg, LA	HT
Bovard, PA	GBG
Bovina, TX	AMA
Bow Valley, NE	OM
Bowbells, ND	BIS
Bowdle, SD	SFS
Bowie, MD	WDC
TX	FWT
Bowling Green, KY	OWN
OH	TOL
Bowlus, MN	SCL
Bowman, ND	BIS
Bowmansville, NY	BUF
Boyce, LA	ALX
Boyceville, WI	LC
Boyd, WI	LC
Boyers, PA	PIT
Boyertown, PA	ALN
Boyes Hot Springs, CA	SR
Boylston, MA	WOR
Boyne City, MI	GAY
Boyne Falls, MI	GAY
Boynton Beach, FL	PMB
Boys Town, NE	OM
Bozeman, MT	HEL
Brackett, WI	LC
Brackettville, TX	SAT
Braddock, PA	PBR
PA	PIT
Braddock Hills, PA	PIT
Bradenton, FL	VEN
Bradenville, PA	PBR
Bradford, IL	PEO
IN	IND
MA	BO
NY	ROC
OH	CIN
PA	E
VT	BUR
Bradley, IL	JOL
ME	PRT
Bradley Beach, NJ	TR
Bradshaw, MD	BAL
Brady, TX	SAN
Brady's Bend, PA	GBG
Braham, MN	SCL
Braidwood, IL	JOL
Brainard, NE	LIN
Brainerd, MN	DUL
Braintree, MA	BO
Branchdale, PA	ALN
Branchville, NJ	PAT
Brandamore, PA	PH
Brandenburg, KY	L
Brandon, FL	SP
MN	SCL
MS	JKS
SD	SFS
VT	BUR
WI	MIL
Brandy Camp, PA	E
Brandywood, DE	WIL
Branford, CT	HRT
FL	STA
Branson, MO	SPC
Brant, NY	BUF
Brant Beach, NJ	TR
Brasher Falls, NY	OG
Brattleboro, VT	BUR
Brawley, CA	SD
Brazil, IN	IND
Brazoria, TX	GAL
Brea, CA	ORG
Breaux Bridge, LA	LAF
Breckenridge, CO	DEN
MN	SCL
TX	FWT
Brecksville, OH	CLV
OH	PRM
Breda, IA	SC
Breese, IL	BEL
Bremen, IN	FTW
ND	FAR
OH	COL
Bremerton, WA	SEA
Bremond, TX	AUS
Brenham, TX	AUS
Brennyville, MN	SCL
Brentwood, CA	OAK
MO	STL
NY	BRK
NY	RVC
PA	PIT
TN	NSH
Brevard, NC	CHL
Brewer, ME	PRT
MO	STL
Brewerton, NY	SY
Brewster, MA	FR
MN	WIN
NY	NY
OH	Y
WA	SPK
Brewton, AL	MOB
Briarcliff Manor, NY	NY
Briarwood, NY	BRK
Brick, NJ	TR
Brick Town, NJ	TR
Bridal Veil, OR	P
Bridge City, LA	NO
TX	BEA
Bridgehampton, NY	RVC
Bridgeport, CT	BGP
CT	PSC
CT	STF
IL	BEL
MI	SAG
NE	GI
NY	SY
OH	STU
PA	PH
PA	PHU
TX	FWT
WA	YAK
WV	WH
Bridger, MT	GF
Bridgeton, MO	STL
NJ	CAM
Bridgeview, IL	CHI
Bridgeville, PA	PIT
Bridgewater, MA	BO
NJ	MET
SD	SFS
Bridgman, MI	KAL
Bridgton, ME	PRT
Brigantine, NJ	CAM
Briggsville, WI	MAD
Brigham City, UT	SLC
Brighton, CO	DEN
IL	SFD
MA	BO
MI	LAN
WI	MIL
Brilliant, OH	STU
Brillion, WI	GB
Brimfield, IL	PEO
MA	SPR
Brimley, MI	MAR
Brinkley, AR	LR
Brinktown, MO	JC
Bristol, CT	HRT
IN	FTW
NH	MAN
PA	PH
PA	PHU
RI	PRO
SD	SFS
VA	RIC
VT	BUR
WI	MIL
WI	PRM
Bristow, VA	ARL
Britt, IA	DUB
Britton, SD	SFS
Broad Brook, CT	HRT
Broad Run, VA	ARL
Broadalbin, NY	ALB
Broadus, MT	GF
Broadview Heights, OH	CLV
Broadwater, NE	GI
Brocket, ND	FAR
Brockport, NY	ROC
Brockton, MA	BO
MA	LIT
MA	SAM
PA	ALN
PA	PSC
Brockway, PA	E
Brocton, IL	SFD
NY	BUF
Brodhead, WI	MAD
Brodheadsville, PA	SCR
Broken Arrow, OK	TLS
Broken Bow, NE	GI
Bronson, MI	KAL
Bronx, NY	NY
NY	STF
Bronxville, NY	NY
Brook Park, OH	CLV
Brookeville, MD	WDC
Brookfield, CT	BGP
IL	CHI
MA	WOR
MO	JC
WI	MIL
Brookhaven, MS	JKS
PA	PH
Brookings, OR	P
SD	SFS
Brooklandville, MD	BAL
Brooklawn, NJ	CAM
Brookline, MA	BO
PA	PH
Brooklyn, CT	NOR
IA	DAV
MI	LAN
NY	ARM
NY	BRK
NY	LIT
NY	NTN
NY	PSC
NY	SAM
NY	STF
OH	CLV
OH	NTN
Brooklyn Center, MN	STP
Brooklyn Park, MN	STP
Brookneal, VA	RIC
Brooks, MN	CR
WI	LC
Brooksville, FL	SP
KY	COV
MS	JKS
Brookville, IN	IND
KS	SAL
NY	RVC
PA	E
Broomall, PA	PH
Broomfield, CO	DEN
Brooten, MN	SCL
Brouillette, LA	ALX
Broussard, LA	LAF
Browerville, MN	SCL
Brown Deer, WI	MIL
Brown's Valley, KY	OWN
MN	SCL
Brownfield, TX	LUB
Browning, MT	HEL
Browns Mills, NJ	TR
Browns Valley, MN	SCL
Brownsburg, IN	IND
Brownsdale, MN	WIN
Brownstown, IN	IND
Brownsville, MN	WIN
PA	GBG
PA	PBR
TN	MEM
TX	BWN
Brownville, NY	OG
Brownville Junction, ME	PRT
Brownwood, TX	SAN
Bruce, MS	JKS
WI	SUP
Bruno, NE	LIN
Brunswick, GA	SAV
MD	BAL
ME	PRT
MI	GR
MO	JC
OH	CLV
OH	PRM
Brush, CO	DEN
Brushton, NY	OG
Brusly, LA	BR
Brussels, IL	SFD
WI	GB
Bryan, OH	TOL
TX	AUS
Bryant, IA	DAV
IN	LFT
SD	SFS
Bryantown, MD	WDC
Bryn Mawr, PA	PH
Bryson City, NC	CHL
Buchanan, MI	KAL
ND	FAR
NY	NY
Buchanan Valley, PA	HBG
Buchtel, OH	STU
Buckeye, AZ	PHX
Buckeye Lake, OH	COL
Buckeystown, MD	BAL
Buckhannon, WV	WH
Buckingham, VA	RIC
Buckley, WA	SEA
Bucklin, KS	DOD
Buckman, MN	SCL
Buckner, MO	KC
VA	RIC
Bucksport, ME	PRT
Bucyrus, OH	TOL
Buda, TX	AUS
Budd, IL	PEO
Budd Lake, NJ	PAT
Buena Park, CA	ORG
Buena Vista, CO	COS
WI	LC
Buffalo, IA	DAV
IL	SFD
MN	STP
MO	SPC
ND	FAR
NY	BUF
NY	STF
SD	RC
WY	CHY
Buffalo Center, IA	DUB
Buffalo Grove, IL	CHI
Buford, GA	ATL
Buhl, ID	B
Bulger, PA	PIT
Bullhead City, AZ	PHX
Buna, TX	BEA
Bunker Hill, IL	SFD
Bunkie, LA	ALX
Bunnell, FL	STA
Buras, LA	NO
Burbank, CA	LA
IL	CHI
Burdett, KS	DOD
Burgaw, NC	R
Burgettstown, PA	PIT
Burkburnett, TX	FWT
Burke, NY	OG
SD	RC
VA	ARL
Burkettsville, OH	CIN
Burkhart, OH	STU
Burleson, TX	FWT
Burley, ID	B
Burlingame, CA	SFR
Burlington, CO	COS
IA	DAV
KS	KCK
KY	COV
MA	BO
NC	R
ND	BIS
NJ	TR
VT	BUR
WA	SEA
WI	MIL
Burnet, TX	AUS
Burney, CA	SAC
Burnham, IL	CHI
Burns, KS	WCH
OR	BAK
Burnstad, ND	FAR
Burnsville, MN	STP
Burr Ridge, IL	JOL
Burriliville, RI	PRO
Burrilleville, RI	PRO
Burrillville, RI	PRO
Burt Lake, MI	GAY
Burton, MI	LAN

OH	PRM
Burtonsville, MD	WDC
Burwell, NE	GI
Bushnell, FL	ORL
IL	PEO
Bushton, KS	WCH
Bushwood, MD	WDC
Butler, AL	MOB
MN	SCL
MO	KC
NJ	PAT
PA	PBR
PA	PIT
TN	KNX
WI	MIL
Butte, MT	HEL
NE	OM
Butternut, WI	SUP
Buttonwillow, CA	FRS
Buttonwood, PA	SCR
Buxton, NC	R
Buzzards Bay, MA	FR
Byers, CO	DEN
Byesville, OH	STU
Byrn Mawr, PA	PH
Byron, CA	OAK
IL	RCK
MN	WIN
WI	MIL
Byron Center, MI	GR
MI	KAL
Cabery, IL	JOL
Cable, WI	SUP
Cabo Rojo, PR	MGZ
Cabot, PA	PIT
Cadet, MO	STL
Cadillac, MI	GAY
Cadiz, KY	OWN
OH	STU
Cadogan, PA	GBG
Cadott, WI	LC
Cadyville, NY	OG
Caguas, PR	CGS
Cahokia, IL	BEL
Cairo, IL	BEL
NY	ALB
Calais, ME	PRT
Caldwell, ID	B
KS	WCH
NJ	NEW
OH	STU
TX	AUS
Caledonia, MI	GR
MN	WIN
NY	ROC
WI	MIL
Calexico, CA	SD
Calhan, CO	COS
Calhoun, GA	ATL
KY	OWN
Caliente, NV	LAV
Califon, NJ	MET
California, KY	COV
MO	JC
PA	PIT
Calimesa, CA	SB
Calipatria, CA	SD
Calistoga, CA	SR
Callahan, FL	STA
Callaway, MN	CR
Callicoon, NY	NY
Calmar, IA	DUB
Calumet, MI	MAR
OK	OKL
PA	GBG
Calumet City, IL	CHI
Calumet Park, IL	CHI
Calvary, KY	L
Calvert, TX	AUS
Calvert City, KY	OWN
Camanche, IA	DAV
Camarillo, CA	LA
Camas, WA	SEA
Cambria, CA	MRY
Cambridge, MA	BO
MD	WIL
MN	SCL
NE	LIN
NY	ALB
OH	STU
VT	BUR
WI	MAD
Cambridge City, IN	IND
Cambridge Springs, PA	E
Camden, AL	MOB
AR	LR
ME	PRT
MS	JKS
NJ	CAM
NY	SY
OH	CIN
SC	CHR
TN	MEM
WV	WH
Camdenton, MO	JC
Cameron, LA	LKC
MO	KC
TX	AUS
WI	SUP
WV	WH
Camillus, NY	SY
Camp Douglas, WI	LC
Camp Grove, IL	PEO
Camp Hill, PA	HBG
Camp Point, IL	SFD
Camp Springs, KY	COV
MD	WDC
Camp Verde, AZ	PHX
Campbell, CA	SJ
NE	LIN
OH	PBR
OH	Y
Campbellsport, WI	MIL
Campbellsville, KY	L
Campti, LA	ALX
Campus, IL	PEO
Camuy, PR	ARE
Canaan, CT	HRT
VT	BUR
Canadensis, PA	SCR
Canadian, TX	AMA
Canajoharie, NY	ALB
Canal Fulton, OH	Y
Canandaigua, NY	ROC
Canaseraga, NY	BUF
Canastota, NY	SY
Canby, MN	NU
OR	P
Candia, NH	MAN
Cando, ND	FAR
Caney, KS	WCH
Canfield, OH	Y
Canisteo, NY	ROC
Cankton, LA	LAF
Cannelburg, IN	EVN
Cannelton, IN	IND
Cannon Falls, MN	STP
Canoga Park, CA	LA
Canon City, CO	PBL
Canonsburg, PA	PBR
PA	PIT
Canovanas, PR	SJN
Canterbury, CT	NOR
Canton, GA	ATL
IL	PEO
MA	BO
MI	DET
MN	WIN
MO	JC
MS	JKS
NY	OG
OH	ROM
OH	SJP
OH	Y
OK	OKL
PA	SCR
SD	SFS
TX	TYL
Cantonment, FL	PT
Canutillo, TX	ELP
Canyon, TX	AMA
Canyon Country, CA	LA
Canyon Lake, TX	SAT
Capac, MI	DET
Capaldo, KS	WCH
Cape Charles, VA	RIC
Cape Coral, FL	VEN
Cape Elizabeth, ME	PRT
Cape Girardeau, MO	SPC
Cape May, NJ	CAM
Cape May Court House, NJ	CAM
Cape May Point, NJ	CAM
Cape Vincent, NY	OG
Capistrano Beach, CA	ORG
Capital Plaza, MD	WDC
Capitola, CA	MRY
Capulin, CO	PBL
Carbondale, IL	BEL
PA	SCR
Cardale, PA	GBG
Cardington, OH	COL
Carefree, AZ	PHX
Carencro, LA	LAF
Carey, OH	TOL
Caribou, ME	PRT
Carle Place, NY	RVC
Carleton, MI	DET
Carlin, NV	RNO
Carlinville, IL	SFD
Carlisle, AR	LR
IA	DM
KY	LEX
MA	BO
OH	STU
PA	HBG
Carlsbad, CA	SD
NM	LSC
TX	SAN
Carlton, MN	DUL
Carlyle, IL	BEL
Carmel, CA	MRY
IN	LFT
NY	NY
Carmel Valley, CA	MRY
Carmi, IL	BEL
Carmichael, CA	SAC
Carmichaels, PA	PIT
Carnegie, PA	PIT
PA	SJP
Carneys Point, NJ	CAM
Caro, MI	SAG
Carol Stream, IL	JOL
Carolina, PR	SJN
Carolina Beach, NC	R
Caroline County, VA	RIC
Carpentersville, IL	RCK
Carpinteria, CA	LA
Carrington, ND	FAR
Carrizo Springs, TX	SAT
Carrizozo, NM	LSC
Carroll, IA	SC
Carrollton, GA	ATL
IL	SFD
KY	COV
MI	SAG
MO	KC
OH	STU
TX	FWT
Carrolltown, PA	ALT
Carson, CA	LA
ND	BIS
Carson City, MI	GR
NV	RNO
Carter Lake, IA	DM
Carteret, NJ	MET
NJ	PHU
NJ	PSC
Cartersville, GA	ATL
Carterville, IL	BEL
Carthage, IL	PEO
MO	SPC
MS	JKS
NY	OG
TX	TYL
Carthagena, OH	CIN
Caruthersville, MO	SPC
Carver, MA	BO
MN	STP
Carverton, PA	SCR
Cary, IL	RCK
NC	PSC
NC	R
Casa Grande, AZ	TUC
Cascade, CO	COS
IA	DUB
NH	MAN
WI	MIL
Casco, ME	PRT
WI	GB
Caseville, MI	SAG
Casey, IA	DM
IL	SFD
Caseyville, IL	BEL
Cashion, AZ	PHX
Cashmere, WA	YAK
Cashton, WI	LC
Casper, WY	CHY
Caspian, MI	MAR
Cass City, MI	SAG
Cass Lake, MN	DUL
Cassadaga, NY	BUF
Cassandra, PA	ALT
Cassel, WI	LC
Casselberry, FL	ORL
Cassella, OH	CIN
Casselton, ND	FAR
Cassopolis, MI	KAL
Cassville, WI	MAD
Castaner, PR	PCE
Castine, ME	PRT
Castle Grove, IA	DUB
Castle Hayne, NC	R
Castle Rock, CO	COS
WA	SEA
Castle Shannon, PA	PIT
Castleton, KS	WCH
NY	ALB
VT	BUR
Castleton-on-Hudson, NY	ALB
Castlewood, SD	SFS
Castro Valley, CA	OAK
Castroville, CA	MRY
TX	SAT
Catahoula, LA	LAF
Catano, PR	SJN
Catasauqua, PA	ALN
Catawba, WI	SUP
Catawissa, MO	STL
Catharine, KS	SAL
Cathedral City, CA	SB
Cato, NY	ROC
Catonsville, MD	BAL
Catskill, NY	ALB
Cattaraugus, NY	BUF
Cavalier, ND	FAR
Cavour, SD	SFS
Cawker City, KS	SAL
Cayey, PR	CGS
Cayucos, CA	MRY
Cayuga, ND	FAR
NY	ROC
Cazenovia, NY	SY
WI	LC
Cecil, OH	TOL
PA	PIT
WI	GB
Cecilia, KY	L
LA	LAF
Cedar, MI	GAY
MN	STP
Cedar City, UT	SLC
Cedar Creek, TX	AUS
Cedar Falls, IA	DUB
Cedar Grove, IN	IND
NJ	NEW
WI	MIL
Cedar Knolls, NJ	PAT
Cedar Lake, IN	GRY
MN	STP
Cedar Park, TX	AUS
Cedar Rapids, IA	DUB
NE	OM
Cedar Vale, KS	WCH
Cedarburg, WI	MIL
Cedarhurst, NY	RVC
Cedartown, GA	ATL
Cedarville, NJ	CAM
Ceiba, PR	CGS
Celestine, IN	EVN
Celina, OH	CIN
Center, CO	PBL
ND	BIS
TX	TYL
Center Harbor, NH	MAN
Center Moriches, NY	RVC
Center Ossipee, NH	MAN
Center Ridge, AR	LR
Center Square, PA	PH
Center Township, PA	PIT
Center Valley, PA	ALN
Centereach, NY	RVC
Centerline, MI	DET
Centerport, NY	BRK
NY	RVC
Centerville, IA	DAV
LA	LAF
MA	FR
MN	STP
MO	STL
MT	GF
NY	NY
OH	CIN
SD	SFS
TN	NSH
Central City, IA	DUB
KY	OWN
NE	OM
PA	ALT
Central Falls, RI	NTN
RI	PRO
Central Islip, NY	RVC
Central Point, OR	P
Central Square, NY	SY
Centralia, IL	BEL
MO	JC
PA	HBG
PA	PHU
WA	SEA
Centreville, IL	BEL
MD	WIL
Centuria, WI	SUP
Ceres, CA	STO
Cerrillos, NM	SFE
Cestohowa, TX	SAT
Chacahoula, LA	HT
Chackbay, LA	HT
Chadds Ford, PA	PH
Chadron, NE	GI
Chadwicks, NY	SY
Chaffee, MO	SPC
Chagrin Falls, OH	CLV
Chalan Kanoa Village, MP	CHK
Chalan Pago, GU	AGN
Chalfont, PA	PH

Chalmette, LA	NO
Chama, NM	SFE
Chamberino, NM	LSC
Chamberlain, SD	SFS
Chambers Island, WI	GB
Chambersburg, PA	HBG
Chamblee, GA	ATL
Chamois, MO	JC
Champaign, IL	PEO
Champion, MI	MAR
OH	Y
WI	GB
Champlain, NY	OG
Chancellorsville, VA	ARL
Chandler, AZ	PHX
OK	OKL
Chandlerville, IL	SFD
Chanhassen, MN	STP
Channahon, IL	JOL
Channelview, TX	GAL
Channing, MI	MAR
TX	AMA
Chantilly, VA	ARL
Chanute, KS	WCH
Chapel Hill, NC	R
Chapel Point, MD	WDC
Chapin, SC	CHR
Chapman, KS	SAL
Chappaqua, NY	NY
Chapparal, NM	LSC
Chappell, NE	GI
Chappell Hill, TX	AUS
Chaptico, MD	WDC
Chardon, OH	CLV
Charenton, LA	LAF
Chariton, IA	DM
Charleroi, PA	PBR
PA	PIT
Charles City, IA	DUB
Charles Town, WV	WH
Charlesburg, WI	GB
Charleston, AR	LR
IL	SFD
MO	SPC
MS	JKS
SC	CHR
WV	WH
Charlestown, IN	IND
MA	BO
NH	MAN
RI	PRO
WI	GB
Charlevoix, MI	GAY
Charlotte, IA	DAV
MI	LAN
NC	CHL
TX	SAT
VT	BUR
Charlottesville, VA	RIC
Charlton City, MA	WOR
Charter Oak, IA	SC
Chase, KS	WCH
WI	GB
Chaska, MN	STP
Chasm Falls, NY	OG
Chassell, MI	MAR
Chastang, AL	MOB
Chataignier, LA	LAF
Chatawa, MS	JKS
Chateaugay, NY	OG
Chatfield, MN	WIN
Chatham, IL	SFD
MA	FR
NJ	PAT
NY	ALB
Chatham Township, NJ	PAT
Chatom, AL	MOB
Chatsworth, CA	LA
IL	PEO
Chattahoochee, FL	PT
Chattanooga, TN	KNX
Chaumont, NY	OG
Chauncey, OH	STU
Chauvin, LA	HT
Chazy, NY	OG
Cheat Lake, WV	WH
Chebanse, IL	JOL
Cheboygan, MI	GAY
Cheek, TX	BEA
Cheektowaga, NY	BUF
Chefornak, AK	FBK
Chehalis, WA	SEA
Chelan, WA	YAK
Chelmsford, MA	BO
Chelsea, IA	DUB
MA	BO
MI	LAN
NY	NY
SD	SFS
WI	SUP
Cheltenham, PA	PH

Chenango Forks, NY	SY
Cheney, NE	LIN
WA	SPK
Cheneyville, LA	ALX
Chenoa, IL	PEO
Cheraw, SC	CHR
Cherokee, IA	SC
KS	WCH
NC	CHL
OK	OKL
Cherokee Village, AR	LR
Cherry, IL	PEO
Cherry Creek, NY	BUF
Cherry Hill, NJ	CAM
NJ	PHU
Cherry Mound, IA	DUB
Cherry Valley, CA	SB
NY	ALB
Cherryvale, KS	WCH
Chesaning, MI	SAG
Chesapeake, OH	STU
VA	RIC
Chesapeake City, MD	PHU
Cheshire, CT	HRT
MA	SPR
Chest Springs, PA	ALT
Chester, CT	NOR
IA	DUB
IL	BEL
MT	GF
NJ	PAT
NY	NY
PA	PH
PA	PHU
SC	CHR
VT	BUR
WV	WH
Chester Heights, PA	PH
Chester, Kent Island, MD	WIL
Chesterfield, MO	STL
Chesterland, OH	CLV
OH	ROM
Chesterton, IN	GRY
Chestertown, MD	WIL
NY	ALB
Chestnut Hill, MA	BO
Chetek, WI	SUP
Chetopa, KS	WCH
Chevak, AK	FBK
Cheverly, MD	WDC
Chevy Chase, MD	WDC
Chewelah, WA	SPK
Cheyenne, WY	CHY
Cheyenne Wells, CO	COS
Chicago, IL	CHI
IL	EST
IL	LIT
IL	PRM
IL	ROM
IL	STN
Chicago Heights, IL	CHI
Chicago Ridge, IL	CHI
Chichiltah, NM	GLP
Chickasaw, AL	MOB
OH	CIN
Chickasha, OK	OKL
Chico, CA	SAC
Chicopee, KS	WCH
MA	SPR
Chicora, PA	PIT
Chiefland, FL	STA
Childress, TX	AMA
Childs, MD	WIL
Chili, WI	LC
Chillicothe, IL	PEO
MO	KC
OH	COL
Chillum, MD	WDC
Chiloquin, OR	BAK
Chilton, WI	GB
Chimayo, NM	SFE
China, TX	BEA
China Spring, TX	AUS
Chincoteague, VA	RIC
Chinle, AZ	GLP
Chino, CA	SB
Chino Hills, CA	SB
Chinook, MT	GF
Chipley, FL	PT
Chippewa Falls, WI	LC
Chippewa Lake, OH	CLV
Chippewa Township, PA	PIT
Chisholm, MN	DUL
Chittenango, NY	SY
Chittenden, VT	BUR
Chokio, MN	SCL
Choteau, MT	HEL
Chowchilla, CA	FRS
Chrisney, IN	EVN
Christiansburg, VA	RIC
Christiansted, VI	STV

Christopher, IL	BEL
Christoval, TX	SAN
Chubbuck, ID	B
Chula Vista, CA	SD
Church Point, LA	LAF
Church Rock, NM	GLP
Churchill, PA	PIT
Churchill Borough, PA	PIT
Churchtown, OH	STU
Churchville, IA	DM
NY	ROC
Churdan, IA	SC
Churubusco, IN	FTW
NY	OG
Chuuk, FM	CI
Ciales, PR	ARE
Cibecue, AZ	GLP
Cicero, IL	CHI
IN	LFT
NY	SY
Cidra, PR	CGS
Cimarron, NM	SFE
Cincinnati, OH	CIN
OH	OLL
Cinnaminson, NJ	TR
Circle, MT	GF
Circleville, OH	COL
Cisco, TX	FWT
Cistern, TX	VIC
Citronelle, AL	MOB
Citrus Heights, CA	SAC
Citrus Springs, FL	SP
Claflin, KS	DOD
Clairfield, TN	KNX
Clairton, PA	PBR
PA	PIT
Clam Lake, WI	SUP
Clara City, MN	NU
Clare, IA	SC
MI	SAG
Claremont, CA	LA
MN	WIN
NH	MAN
Claremore, OK	TLS
Clarence, MO	JC
NY	BUF
PA	ALT
PA	PBR
Clarence Center, NY	BUF
Clarendon, TX	AMA
Clarendon Hills, IL	JOL
Clarinda, IA	DM
Clarion, IA	DUB
PA	E
Clarissa, MN	SCL
Clark, NJ	NEW
SD	SFS
Clark Mills, NY	SY
Clarkesville, GA	ATL
Clarkfield, MN	NU
Clarklake, MI	LAN
Clarks, NE	OM
Clarks Green, PA	SCR
Clarks Mills, WI	GB
Clarks Summit, PA	PSC
PA	SCR
Clarksburg, CA	SAC
WV	WH
Clarksdale, MS	JKS
Clarkson, KY	OWN
NE	OM
Clarkston, MI	DET
WA	B
WA	SPK
Clarksville, AR	LR
IN	IND
MD	BAL
PA	PIT
TN	NSH
TX	TYL
VA	RIC
Claudell, KS	SAL
Clawson, MI	DET
Claxton, GA	SAV
Clay Center, KS	SAL
Claymont, DE	WIL
Clayton, MO	STL
NJ	CAM
NM	SFE
NY	OG
WA	SPK
Clayville, NY	SY
Cle Elum, WA	YAK
Clear Creek, IA	DAV
Clear Lake, IA	DUB
IN	FTW
MN	SCL
SD	SFS
WI	SUP
Clearfield, PA	E
SD	RC

Clearlake, CA	SR
Clearwater, FL	SP
MN	STP
Cleburne, TX	FWT
Clements, MN	NU
Clementsville, KY	L
Clemmons, NC	CHL
Clemson, SC	CHR
Clermont, FL	ORL
IA	DUB
Clermont Harbor, MS	BLX
Cleveland, MN	STP
MS	JKS
NY	SY
OH	CLV
OH	OLL
OH	PRM
OH	ROM
OH	SJP
OK	TLS
TN	KNX
TX	BEA
WI	GB
Cleveland Heights, OH	CLV
Clewiston, FL	VEN
Cliffside Park, NJ	NEW
NJ	NTN
Clifton, AZ	TUC
IL	JOL
KS	SAL
NJ	PAT
TX	FWT
VA	ARL
Clifton Forge, VA	RIC
Clifton Heights, PA	PH
PA	PHU
Clifton Park, NY	ALB
Clifton Springs, NY	ROC
Clint, TX	ELP
Clinton, CT	NOR
IA	DAV
IL	PEO
IN	IND
KY	OWN
MA	WOR
MD	WDC
MI	LAN
MO	KC
MS	JKS
NC	R
NJ	MET
NY	SY
OH	CLV
OK	OKL
SC	CHR
TN	KNX
WI	MAD
Clinton Heights, NY	ALB
Clinton Township, MI	DET
Clinton Twp., MI	DET
Clintonville, WI	GB
Clintwood, VA	RIC
Clio, MI	LAN
Clonmel, KS	WCH
Clontarf, MN	NU
Cloquet, MN	DUL
Closter, NJ	NEW
Cloutierville, LA	ALX
Clover Bottom, MO	STL
Cloverdale, CA	SR
OH	TOL
Cloverport, KY	OWN
Clovis, CA	FRS
NM	SFE
Clute, TX	GAL
Clutier, IA	DUB
Clyde, KS	SAL
MO	KC
NY	ROC
OH	TOL
Clyman, WI	MIL
Clymer, PA	GBG
PA	PBR
Coachella, CA	SB
Coal City, IL	JOL
Coal Run, PA	PBR
Coal Township, PA	HBG
Coal Valley, IL	PEO
Coaldale, PA	ALN
PA	PSC
Coalgate, OK	TLS
Coalinga, CA	FRS
Coalport, PA	E
Coalton, WV	WH
Coamo, PR	PCE
Coates, MN	STP
Coatesville, PA	PH
PA	PSC
Cobden, IL	BEL
Cobleskill, NY	ALB
Cockeysville, MD	BAL

Cocoa, FL	ORL
Cocoa Beach, FL	ORL
Coconut Creek, FL	MIA
FL	PSC
Coconut Grove, FL	MIA
Cody, WY	CHY
Coeur D'Alene, ID	B
Coffeen, IL	SFD
Coffeyville, KS	WCH
Coffman, MO	STL
Coggon, IA	DUB
Cogswell, ND	FAR
Cohasset, MA	BO
Cohocton, NY	ROC
Cohoes, NY	ALB
NY	STF
Colbert, WA	SPK
Colby, KS	SAL
WI	LC
Colchester, CT	NOR
CT	STF
VT	BUR
Cold Spring, KY	COV
MN	SCL
Cold Spring-on-Hudson, NY	NY
Cold Springs, MN	SCL
Colden, NY	BUF
Coldwater, KS	DOD
MI	KAL
OH	CIN
Colebrook, NH	MAN
Coleman, MI	SAG
TX	SAN
WI	GB
Colerain, OH	STU
Coleraine, MN	DUL
Coleridge, NE	OM
Colesburg, IA	DUB
KY	L
Colesville, PA	ALN
Colfax, CA	SAC
IA	DAV
IL	PEO
LA	ALX
WA	SPK
College Park, MD	WDC
College Point, NY	BRK
College Station, TX	AUS
Collegeville, MN	SCL
PA	PH
Colleyville, TX	FWT
Collingdale, PA	PH
Collings Lakes, NJ	CAM
Collingswood, NJ	CAM
Collins Center, NY	BUF
Collinsville, CT	HRT
IL	SFD
OK	TLS
Collyer, KS	SAL
Colma, CA	SFR
Colman, SD	SFS
Colo, IA	DUB
Cologne, MN	STP
Colome, SD	RC
Colon, NE	LIN
Colona, IL	PEO
Colonia, NJ	MET
NJ	NEW
Colonia, Yap, FM	CI
Colonial Beach, VA	ARL
Colonial Heights, VA	RIC
Colonie, NY	ALB
The Colony, TX	FWT
Colorado City, TX	SAN
Colorado Springs, CO	COS
CO	VNN
Colstrip, MT	GF
Colton, CA	SB
NY	OG
WA	SPK
Colts Neck, NJ	TR
Columbia, CT	NOR
IL	BEL
KY	L
MD	BAL
MO	JC
MO	OLL
MS	BLX
PA	HBG
SC	CHR
TN	NSH
VA	RIC
Columbia City, IN	FTW
Columbia Falls, MT	HEL
Columbia Heights, MN	STP
Columbia Station, OH	CLV
Columbiana, OH	Y
Columbus, GA	SAV
IN	IND
KS	WCH
MI	DET
MS	JKS
MT	GF
NE	OM
OH	COL
OH	NTN
OH	OLL
OH	PRM
TX	VIC
WI	MAD
Columbus Grove, OH	TOL
Columbus Junction, IA	DAV
Colusa, CA	SAC
Colver, PA	ALT
Colville, WA	SPK
Colwich, KS	WCH
Comanche, TX	FWT
Combermere, Ontario	OG
Combined Locks, WI	GB
Comerio, PR	CGS
Comfort, TX	SAT
Comfrey, MN	NU
Commack, NY	RVC
Commerce, TX	DAL
Commerce City, CO	DEN
Compton, CA	LA
Conception, MO	KC
Conception Junction, MO	KC
Concho, AZ	GLP
Concord, CA	OAK
MA	BO
MI	LAN
NC	CHL
NH	MAN
Concord Hill, MO	STL
Concord Twp., OH	CLV
Concord Village, MO	STL
Concordia, KS	SAL
Conde, SD	SFS
Condon, OR	BAK
Conejos, CO	PBL
Conemaugh, PA	ALT
PA	PBR
Conewago Township, PA	HBG
Congers, NY	NY
Conifer, CO	DEN
Conklin, MI	GR
Conneaut, OH	Y
Conneaut Lake, PA	E
Conneautville, PA	E
Connell, WA	SPK
Connellsville, PA	GBG
Connersville, IN	IND
Conrad, MT	HEL
Conroe, TX	GAL
Conshohocken, PA	PH
Constable, NY	OG
Constableville, NY	OG
Constance, NE	OM
Continental, OH	TOL
Convent, LA	BR
Convent Station, NJ	PAT
Converse, TX	SAT
Conway, AR	LR
MI	GAY
MO	SPC
ND	FAR
PA	PIT
SC	CHR
Conway Springs, KS	WCH
Conyers, GA	ATL
Conyngham, PA	SCR
Cook, MN	DUL
Cookeville, TN	NSH
Cooks, MI	MAR
Cooks Valley, WI	LC
Coolidge, AZ	TUC
Coon Rapids, IA	SC
MN	STP
Coon Valley, WI	LC
Coopersburg, PA	ALN
Cooperstown, ND	FAR
NY	ALB
WI	GB
Coopersville, MI	GR
Cooperville, NY	OG
Coos Bay, OR	P
Copake Falls, NY	ALB
Copemish, MI	GAY
Copenhagen, NY	OG
Copiague, NY	RVC
Coplay, PA	ALN
Copley, OH	CLV
Coppell, TX	DAL
Copperas Cove, TX	AUS
Copperhill, TN	KNX
Copperopolis, CA	STO
Copperton, UT	SLC
Coquille, OR	P
Coral, PA	GBG
Coral Gables, FL	MIA
Coral Springs, FL	MIA
Coram, NY	RVC
Coraopolis, PA	PIT
Corbett, OR	P
Corbin, KY	LEX
Corcoran, CA	FRS
MN	STP
Cordele, GA	SAV
Cordova, AK	ANC
TN	MEM
Corfu, NY	BUF
Corinth, MS	JKS
NY	ALB
Cornelius, OR	P
Cornell, WI	LC
Corning, CA	SAC
IA	DM
KS	KCK
NY	ROC
OH	COL
Cornucopia, WI	SUP
Cornwall, NY	NY
PA	HBG
Cornwall Bridge, CT	HRT
Cornwall-on-Hudson, NY	NY
Corona, CA	SB
Coronado, CA	SD
Corozal, PR	ARE
Corozal-Padilla, PR	ARE
Corozal-Palmarito, PR	ARE
Corozal-Palos Blancos, PR	ARE
Corpus Christi, TX	CC
Corrales, NM	SFE
Corralitos, CA	MRY
Corrigan, TX	BEA
Corry, PA	E
Corsicana, TX	DAL
Cortaro, AZ	TUC
Cortez, CO	PBL
Cortland, NE	LIN
NY	SY
OH	Y
Cortlandt Manor, NY	NY
Corvallis, OR	P
Corwith, IA	DUB
Corydon, IA	DM
IN	IND
Cosgrove, IA	DAV
Coshocton, OH	COL
Costa Mesa, CA	ORG
Cotati, CA	SR
Coteau, LA	LAF
Coteau Holmes, LA	LAF
Coto Laurel, PR	PCE
Cottage Grove, MN	STP
OR	P
WI	MAD
Cottleville, MO	STL
Cottonport, LA	ALX
Cottonwood, AZ	PHX
ID	B
MN	NU
Cotulla, TX	SAT
Coudersport, PA	E
Coulee Dam, WA	SPK
Coulterville, IL	BEL
Council, ID	B
Council Bluffs, IA	DM
Council Grove, KS	WCH
Country Club Hills, IL	CHI
Countryside, IL	CHI
Coupon, PA	ALT
Courtenay, ND	FAR
Coventry, CT	NOR
RI	PRO
Covina, CA	LA
Covington, GA	ATL
IN	LFT
KY	COV
LA	NO
OH	CIN
TN	MEM
VA	RIC
Cow Island, LA	LAF
Coweta, OK	TLS
Cowiche, WA	YAK
Coxsackie, NY	ALB
Coylesville, PA	PIT
Cozad, NE	GI
Crabtree, PA	GBG
Crafton, PA	PIT
Craig, AK	JUN
CO	DEN
Cranberry Prairie, OH	CIN
Cranberry Township, PA	PIT
Cranberry Twp., PA	PIT
Cranbury, NJ	MET
Crandon, WI	GB
Crane, TX	SAN
Cranford, NJ	NEW
Cranston, RI	PRO
Crawford, NE	GI
Crawfordsville, IN	LFT
Creighton, NE	OM
PA	PIT
Creole, LA	LKC
Cresaptown, MD	BAL
Crescent, NY	ALB
OH	STU
Crescent City, CA	SR
FL	STA
Crescent Lake, WI	SUP
Crescent Springs, KY	COV
Cresco, IA	DUB
PA	SCR
Cresskill, NJ	NEW
Cresson, PA	ALT
Crested Butte, CO	PBL
Crestline, CA	SB
OH	TOL
Creston, IA	DM
Crestone, CO	PBL
Crestview, FL	PT
Crestwood, IL	CHI
KY	L
MO	STL
NY	NY
Crete, IL	JOL
NE	LIN
Creve Coeur, IL	PEO
MO	STL
Crewe, VA	RIC
Crivitz, WI	GB
Crocker, MO	JC
Crockett, CA	OAK
TX	TYL
Crofton, MD	BAL
NE	OM
Croghan, NY	OG
Cromwell, CT	NOR
Crookston, MN	CR
Crooksville, OH	COL
Crosby, MN	DUL
ND	BIS
TX	GAL
Cross Plains, WI	MAD
Cross Village, MI	GAY
Crossett, AR	LR
Crossingsville, PA	E
Crosslake, MN	DUL
Crossville, TN	KNX
Croswell, MI	SAG
Croton Falls, NY	NY
Croton-on-Hudson, NY	NY
Crow Agency, MT	GF
Crow Hill, ND	FAR
Crowell, TX	FWT
Crowley, LA	LAF
TX	FWT
Crown, PA	E
Crown Butte, ND	BIS
Crown Point, IN	GRY
LA	NO
NY	OG
Crownpoint, NM	GLP
Croydon, PA	PH
Crozet, VA	RIC
Cruz Bay, VI	STV
Crystal, MN	STP
ND	FAR
Crystal City, MO	STL
TX	SAT
Crystal Falls, MI	MAR
Crystal Lake, IL	RCK
Crystal River, FL	SP
Crystal Springs, MS	JKS
Cuba, KS	SAL
MO	JC
NM	GLP
NY	BUF
OH	TOL
Cuba City, WI	MAD
Cudahy, CA	LA
WI	MIL
Cuero, TX	VIC
Culbertson, MT	GF
Culebra, PR	CGS
Cullman, AL	BIR
Cullom, IL	PEO
Culpeper, VA	ARL
Culver, IN	FTW
Culver City, CA	LA
Culvertown, KY	L
Cumberland, IA	DM
KY	LEX
MD	BAL
RI	PRO
WI	SUP
Cumbola, PA	ALN
Cumming, GA	ATL
IA	DM
Cunningham, KS	WCH
Cupertino, CA	SJ

Curdsville, KY	OWN
Curlew, WA	SPK
Currie, MN	WIN
Curtis, NE	LIN
Curtis Bay, MD	PHU
Curwensville, PA	E
Cushing, OK	TLS
Cusick, WA	SPK
Custar, OH	TOL
Custer, MI	GR
SD	RC
WI	LC
Cut Bank, MT	HEL
Cutchogue, NY	RVC
Cutler, CA	FRS
Cut-Off, LA	HT
Cuyahoga Falls, OH	CLV
Cuyahoga Heights, OH	CLV
Cyclone, TX	AUS
Cygnet, OH	TOL
Cynthiana, KY	COV
Cypress, CA	ORG
Czestochowa, WI	LC
D'Hanis, TX	SAT
Dacada, WI	MIL
Dade City, FL	SP
Daggett, MI	MAR
Daguscahonda, PA	E
Dahlgren, IL	BEL
Dahlonega, GA	ATL
Daigle, ME	PRT
Daingerfield, TX	TYL
Dakota, MN	WIN
Dale, IN	EVN
Dale City, VA	ARL
Dalhart, TX	AMA
Dallas, OR	P
PA	SCR
TX	DAL
Dallastown, PA	HBG
The Dalles, OR	BAK
Dalton, GA	ATL
MA	SPR
PA	SCR
Dalton City, IL	SFD
Daly City, CA	SFR
Dalzell, IL	PEO
Damar, KS	SAL
Damascus, MD	WDC
Damiansville, IL	BEL
Damon, TX	GAL
Dana Point, CA	ORG
Danbury, CT	BGP
CT	NTN
CT	PSC
CT	SAM
IA	SC
TX	GAL
WI	SUP
Dane, WI	MAD
Dania, FL	MIA
Danielson, CT	NOR
Dannemora, NY	OG
Dansville, NY	ROC
Dante, SD	SFS
Danvers, MA	BO
MN	NU
Danville, CA	OAK
IL	PEO
IN	IND
KS	WCH
KY	LEX
OH	COL
PA	HBG
VA	RIC
Daphne, AL	MOB
Darboy, WI	GB
Darby, PA	PH
Dardanelle, AR	LR
Dardenne, MO	STL
Darien, CT	BGP
IL	JOL
Darien Center, NY	BUF
Darlington, NJ	NEW
PA	PIT
WI	MAD
Darnestown, MD	WDC
Darrow, LA	BR
Darwin, MN	NU
Dauby, WI	SUP
Dauphin, PA	HBG
Dauphin Island, AL	MOB
Davenport, CA	MRY
IA	DAV
WA	SPK
Davey, NE	LIN
David City, NE	LIN
Davidsonville, MD	BAL
Davidsville, PA	ALT
Davie, FL	MIA
Davis, CA	SAC
Davis Park, NY	RVC
Davison, MI	LAN
Dawson, MN	NU
NE	LIN
Dawson Springs, KY	OWN
Dayton, IA	SC
KY	COV
MN	STP
NV	RNO
NY	BUF
OH	CIN
OH	OLL
OH	PRM
TN	KNX
TX	BEA
WA	SPK
WY	CHY
Daytona Beach, FL	ORL
Dayville, CT	NOR
Dazey, ND	FAR
De Forest, WI	MAD
De Funiak Springs, FL	PT
De Graff, MN	NU
De Kalb Junction, NY	OG
De Land, FL	ORL
De Leon, TX	FWT
De Motte, IN	LFT
De Pere, WI	GB
De Queen, AR	LR
De Quincy, LA	LKC
De Ridder, LA	LKC
De Smet, SD	SFS
De Soto, MO	STL
WI	LC
De Witt, MI	LAN
Deadwood, SD	RC
Deal, NJ	TR
Dearborn, MI	DET
MI	ROM
MI	STN
Dearborn Heights, MI	DET
MI	STN
DeBary, FL	ORL
Decatur, AL	BIR
GA	ATL
IL	SFD
IN	FTW
MI	KAL
TX	FWT
Decherd, TN	NSH
Decorah, IA	DUB
Dededo, GU	AGN
Dedham, IA	SC
MA	BO
Deep River, CT	NOR
Deephaven, MN	STP
Deer Lodge, MT	HEL
Deer Park, NY	RVC
TX	GAL
WA	SPK
Deer River, MN	DUL
Deerbrook, WI	GB
Deerfield, IL	CHI
KS	DOD
MI	LAN
MN	WIN
Deerfield Beach, FL	MIA
Deferiet, NY	OG
Defiance, IA	DM
OH	TOL
DeKalb, IL	RCK
Del Mar, CA	SD
Del Norte, CO	PBL
Del Rey, CA	FRS
Del Rio, TX	SAT
Delafield, WI	MIL
Delair, NJ	CAM
Delancey, PA	E
Delano, CA	FRS
MN	STP
Delanson, NY	ALB
Delavan, IL	PEO
MN	WIN
WI	MIL
Delaware, OH	COL
Delaware City, DE	WIL
Delcambre, LA	LAF
Delevan, NY	BUF
Delhi, IA	DUB
NY	ALB
Delia, KS	KCK
DeLisle, MS	BLX
Dell Rapids, SD	SFS
Delmar, IA	DAV
NY	ALB
Delmont, PA	GBG
Delphi, IN	LFT
PA	PH
Delphos, KS	SAL
OH	TOL
Delran, NJ	TR
Delray Beach, FL	NTN
FL	PMB
Delta, CO	PBL
Delta Junction, AK	FBK
Delton, MI	KAL
Deltona, FL	ORL
Demarest, NJ	NEW
Deming, NM	LSC
Demopolis, AL	BIR
Denham Springs, LA	BR
Denison, IA	SC
TX	DAL
Denmark, WI	GB
Dennison, OH	COL
Densmore, KS	SAL
Dent, MN	SCL
Denton, NE	LIN
TX	FWT
Denver, CO	DEN
CO	OLL
CO	STN
CO	VNN
Denver City, TX	LUB
Denville, NJ	PAT
Depew, NY	BUF
Deposit, NY	SY
Deptford, NJ	CAM
Depue, IL	PEO
Derby, CT	HRT
KS	WCH
NY	BUF
Derby Line, VT	BUR
Derry, NH	MAN
PA	GBG
Derwood, MD	WDC
Des Allemands, LA	NO
Des Moines, IA	DM
WA	SEA
Des Peres, MO	STL
Des Plaines, IL	CHI
Descanso, CA	SD
Desert Hot Springs, CA	SB
Deshler, OH	TOL
DeSmet, ID	B
Desoto, TX	DAL
Destin, FL	PT
Destrehan, LA	NO
DeTour, MI	MAR
Detroit, MI	ARM
MI	DET
MI	EST
MI	OLL
MI	PRM
MI	ROM
MI	STN
Detroit Lakes, MN	CR
Deville, LA	ALX
Devils Lake, ND	FAR
Devine, TX	SAT
Devon, PA	PH
Dewey, OK	TLS
DeWitt, IA	DAV
Dewitt, NY	SY
Dexter, ME	PRT
MI	LAN
MO	SPC
NM	LSC
Diamond, LA	NO
Diamond Bar, CA	LA
Diboll, TX	TYL
Dickey, ND	FAR
Dickeyville, WI	MAD
Dickinson, ND	BIS
TX	GAL
Dickson, TN	NSH
Dickson City, PA	SCR
Dieterich, IL	SFD
Dighton, KS	DOD
MA	FR
Dike, IA	DUB
Dilley, TX	SAT
Dillingham, AK	ANC
Dillon, MT	HEL
SC	CHR
Dillonvale, OH	STU
Dilly, WI	LC
Dilworth, MN	CR
Dime Box, TX	AUS
Dimmitt, TX	AMA
Dimock, SD	SFS
Dimondale, MI	LAN
Dinuba, CA	FRS
Dinwiddie County, VA	RIC
Dittmer, MO	STL
Divernon, IL	SFD
Dix Hills, NY	RVC
Dixon, CA	SAC
IL	RCK
MO	JC
NM	SFE
Dobbs Ferry, NY	NY
Dobie, WI	SUP
Dodge, NE	OM
Dodge Center, MN	WIN
Dodge City, KS	DOD
Dodgeville, IA	DAV
WI	MAD
Dodson Prairie, TX	FWT
Doland, SD	SFS
Dolgeville, NY	ALB
Dolton, IL	CHI
Dominican Republic, VA	ARL
Dona Ana, NM	LSC
Donaldson, IN	FTW
Donaldsonville, LA	BR
Donegal, PA	GBG
Doniphan, KS	KCK
MO	SPC
NE	LIN
Donna, TX	BWN
Donnelly, MN	SCL
Donora, PA	PBR
PA	PIT
Dorado, PR	SJN
Doraville, GA	ATL
Dorchester, IA	DUB
MA	BO
WI	LC
Dorothy, MN	CR
Dorr, MI	KAL
Dorrance, KS	SAL
PA	SCR
Dos Palos, CA	FRS
Dothan, AL	MOB
Dotyville, WI	MIL
Dougherty, IA	DUB
Douglas, AZ	TUC
GA	SAV
MI	KAL
WY	CHY
Douglas Co., NE	OM
Douglaston, NY	BRK
Douglasville, GA	ATL
Dousman, WI	MIL
Dover, DE	WIL
IN	IND
MA	BO
NH	MAN
NH	SAM
NJ	PAT
OH	COL
TN	NSH
Dover Plains, NY	NY
Dover-Foxcroft, ME	PRT
Dow City, IA	SC
Dowagiac, MI	KAL
Downers Grove, IL	JOL
Downey, CA	LA
Downieville, CA	SAC
Downingtown, PA	PH
Downs, IL	PEO
KS	SAL
Doylesburg, PA	HBG
Doylestown, OH	CLV
PA	PH
PA	PSC
WI	MAD
Dracut, MA	BO
Drake, ND	FAR
Drayton, ND	FAR
Dresden, OH	COL
Drexel Hill, PA	PH
Dripping Springs, TX	AUS
Drummond, MT	HEL
Drums, PA	SCR
Dryden, MI	DET
NY	ROC
Drywood, WI	LC
Du Bois, PA	E
PA	PBR
Du Quoin, IL	BEL
Duarte, CA	LA
Dublin, CA	OAK
GA	SAV
OH	COL
TX	FWT
Dublon, FM	CI
Dubois, IL	BEL
IN	EVN
Dubuque, IA	DUB
KS	DOD
Dudley, MA	WOR
PA	ALT
Due West, SC	CHR
Duelm, MN	SCL
Dufur, OR	BAK
Duluth, GA	ATL
MN	DUL
Dumas, TX	AMA
Dumont, IA	DUB
MN	SCL
NJ	NEW

Dunbar, PA	GBG
WV	WH
Duncan, IA	DUB
NE	OM
OK	OKL
SD	SFS
Duncan Mills, CA	SR
Duncansville, PA	ALT
Duncanville, TX	DAL
Duncombe, IA	SC
Dundee, IL	RCK
MI	DET
MN	WIN
Dunedin, FL	SP
Dunellen, NJ	MET
NJ	PSC
Dungannon, OH	Y
Dunkirk, IN	LFT
MD	BAL
MD	WDC
NY	BUF
Dunlap, IA	DM
IL	PEO
TN	KNX
Dunlo, PA	ALT
PA	PBR
Dunmore, PA	PSC
PA	SCR
Dunn, NC	R
Dunnellon, FL	ORL
Dunnington, IN	LFT
Dunseith, ND	FAR
Dunsmuir, CA	SAC
Dunwoody, GA	ATL
Dupo, IL	BEL
Dupont, LA	ALX
PA	SCR
Duquesne, PA	PBR
PA	PIT
Duralde, LA	LAF
Durand, IL	RCK
MI	LAN
WI	LC
Durango, CO	PBL
Durant, OK	TLS
Durham, CT	NOR
NC	R
NH	MAN
Durhamville, NY	SY
Durward's Glen, WI	MAD
Duryea, PA	SCR
Dushore, PA	SCR
Duson, LA	LAF
Dutton, MT	HEL
Dutzow, MO	STL
Duxbury, MA	BO
Dwight, IL	PEO
NE	LIN
Dyckesville, WI	GB
Dyer, IN	GRY
Dyersburg, TN	MEM
Dyersville, IA	DUB
Dysart, IA	DUB
Eagan, MN	STP
Eagle, CO	DEN
ID	B
WI	MIL
Eagle Butte, SD	RC
Eagle Center, IA	DUB
Eagle Grove, IA	DUB
Eagle Lake, ME	PRT
TX	VIC
Eagle Pass, TX	SAT
Eagle River, AK	ANC
WI	SUP
Eagle Township, IL	PEO
Earl Park, IN	LFT
Earlimart, CA	FRS
Earling, IA	DM
Earlington, KY	OWN
Earlville, IA	DUB
IL	PEO
Early, IA	SC
Earth City, MO	STL
East Alton, IL	SFD
East Arcade, NY	BUF
East Aurora, NY	BUF
East Bay, NY	ROC
East Berlin, CT	HRT
East Bernard, TX	VIC
East Bethany, NY	BUF
East Bloomfield, NY	ROC
East Boston, MA	BO
East Brady, PA	E
East Bridgewater, MA	BO
East Bristol, WI	MAD
East Brookfield, MA	WOR
East Brunswick, NJ	MET
NJ	PSC
East Carbon, UT	SLC
East Chain, MN	WIN
East Chicago, IN	GRY
IN	PRM
IN	ROM
East Cleveland, OH	CLV
East Dorset, VT	BUR
East Douglas, MA	WOR
East Dubuque, IL	RCK
East Eden, NY	BUF
East Elmhurst, NY	BRK
East Falmouth, MA	FR
East Freetown, MA	FR
East Gary, IN	GRY
East Goshen, PA	PH
East Grand Forks, MN	CR
East Greenbush, NY	ALB
East Greenville, PA	PH
East Greenwich, RI	PRO
East Hampton, CT	NOR
NY	RVC
East Hanover, NJ	NEW
NJ	PAT
East Hartford, CT	HRT
East Haven, CT	HRT
East Helena, MT	HEL
East Islip, NY	RVC
East Jordan, MI	GAY
East Kingston, NY	NY
East Lansdowne, PA	PH
East Lansing, MI	LAN
East Liverpool, OH	Y
East Longmeadow, MA	SPR
East Lyme, CT	NOR
East McKeesport, PA	PIT
East Meadow, NY	RVC
East Millinocket, ME	PRT
East Millstone, NJ	MET
East Moline, IL	PEO
East Newark, NJ	NEW
East Northport, NY	RVC
East Orange, NJ	NEW
East Otto, NY	BUF
East Palestine, OH	Y
East Palo Alto, CA	SFR
East Patchogue, NY	RVC
East Pembroke, NY	BUF
East Peoria, IL	PEO
East Pittsburgh, PA	PBR
PA	PIT
East Pleasant Plain, IA	DAV
East Povidence, RI	PRO
East Providence, RI	PRO
East Rochester, NY	ROC
East Rockaway, NY	RVC
East Rutherford, NJ	NEW
East St. Louis, IL	BEL
East Stroudsburg, PA	SCR
East Syracuse, NY	SY
East Taunton, MA	FR
East Tawas, MI	GAY
East Templeton, MA	WOR
East Troy, WI	MIL
East Vandergrift, PA	GBG
East Walpole, MA	BO
East Wenatchee, WA	YAK
East Windsor, CT	HRT
Eastgate, TX	BEA
Easthampton, MA	SPR
Eastlake, OH	CLV
Eastland, TX	FWT
Eastman, WI	LC
Easton, CA	FRS
CT	BGP
KS	KCK
MD	WIL
MN	WIN
MO	KC
PA	ALN
PA	SAM
Eastpointe, MI	DET
Eastport, ME	PRT
NY	RVC
Eaton, OH	CIN
WI	GB
Eaton Rapids, MI	LAN
Eatonton, GA	ATL
Eatontown, NJ	TR
Eau Claire, WI	LC
Eau Galle, WI	LC
Ebensburg, PA	ALT
Ebeye, MH	MI
Echo, LA	ALX
Ecorse, MI	DET
Edcouch, TX	BWN
Eddystone, PA	PH
Eddyville, IA	DAV
KY	OWN
Eden, NC	CHL
NY	BUF
SD	SFS
TX	SAN
WI	MIL
Eden Prairie, MN	STP
Eden Valley, MN	NU
MN	SCL
Edenton, NC	R
Edgar, WI	LC
Edgard, LA	NO
Edgartown, MA	FR
Edgefield, SC	CHR
Edgeley, ND	FAR
Edgemont, SD	RC
Edgerton, KS	KCK
OH	TOL
WI	MAD
Edgewater, MD	BAL
NJ	NEW
Edgewood, IA	DUB
IL	SFD
KY	COV
MD	BAL
Edina, MN	STP
MO	JC
Edinboro, PA	E
Edinburg, TX	BWN
Edinburgh, IN	IND
Edison, NJ	MET
NJ	PSC
Edisto Beach, SC	CHR
Edmond, OK	OKL
Edmonds, WA	SEA
Edmonton, KY	L
Edmore, MI	GR
Edna, TX	VIC
Edson, WI	LC
Edwards, CO	DEN
NY	OG
Edwardsburg, MI	KAL
Edwardsville, IL	SFD
PA	PHU
PA	SCR
Effingham, IL	SFD
KS	KCK
Ege, IN	FTW
Egg Harbor, WI	GB
Egg Harbor City, NJ	CAM
Eggertsville, NY	BUF
Egypt, OH	CIN
Ehrenfeld, PA	ALT
El Cajon, CA	EST
CA	SD
El Campo, TX	VIC
El Centro, CA	SD
El Cerrito, CA	OAK
El Dorado, AR	LR
KS	WCH
El Dorado Hills, CA	SAC
El Dorado Springs, MO	SPC
El Mirage, AZ	PHX
El Monte, CA	LA
CA	OLL
El Paso, IL	PEO
TX	ELP
TX	OLL
El Reno, OK	OKL
El Rito, NM	SFE
El Segundo, CA	LA
CA	NTN
El Sobrante, CA	OAK
El Toro, CA	ORG
Eland, WI	GB
Elba, MN	WIN
NY	BUF
WI	MIL
Elberon, NJ	TR
Elberta, AL	MOB
Elbow Lake, MN	SCL
Elburn, IL	RCK
Elcho, WI	GB
Eldon, IA	DAV
MO	JC
Eldora, IA	DUB
Eldorado, IL	BEL
TX	SAN
WI	MIL
Eldred, PA	E
Eldridge, IA	DAV
Electra, TX	FWT
Elgin, IL	RCK
NE	OM
OK	OKL
OR	BAK
TX	AUS
Elizabeth, IL	RCK
MN	SCL
NJ	NEW
NJ	PHU
NJ	PSC
PA	PIT
Elizabeth City, NC	R
Elizabethton, TN	KNX
Elizabethtown, IL	BEL
KY	L
NY	OG
PA	HBG
Elk, TX	AUS
Elk City, OK	OKL
Elk Grove, CA	SAC
Elk Grove Village, IL	CHI
Elk Mound, WI	LC
Elk Point, SD	SFS
Elk Rapids, MI	GAY
Elk River, MN	SCL
Elkader, IA	DUB
Elkhart, IA	DM
IL	PEO
IN	FTW
KS	DOD
Elkhart Lake, WI	MIL
Elkhorn, NE	OM
WI	MIL
Elkins, WV	WH
Elkins Park, PA	PH
Elkland, PA	SCR
Elko, NV	RNO
Elkton, FL	STA
KY	OWN
MD	WIL
SD	SFS
VA	RIC
Elkview, WV	WH
Ellenburg, NY	OG
Ellenburg Center, NY	OG
Ellendale, MN	WIN
ND	FAR
Ellengowan, PA	ALN
Ellensburg, WA	YAK
Ellenville, NY	NY
Ellicott City, MD	BAL
Ellicottville, NY	BUF
Ellington, CT	NOR
MO	SPC
Ellinwood, KS	DOD
Ellis, KS	SAL
Ellis Grove, IL	BEL
Ellisville, MO	STL
Ellsworth, KS	SAL
ME	PRT
MN	WIN
PA	PIT
WI	LC
Ellwood City, PA	PIT
Elm Creek, NE	GI
Elm Grove, WI	MIL
Elma, IA	DUB
NY	BUF
WA	SEA
Elmdale, MN	SCL
Elmendorf, TX	SAT
Elmer, NJ	CAM
Elmhurst, IL	JOL
NY	BRK
PA	LIT
PA	SCR
Elmira, MI	GAY
NY	ROC
Elmira Heights, NY	ROC
NY	STF
Elmo, KS	SAL
Elmont, NY	RVC
Elmora, PA	ALT
Elmsford, NY	NY
Elmwood, IL	PEO
WI	LC
Elmwood Park, IL	CHI
NJ	NEW
Elon College, NC	R
Eloy, AZ	TUC
Elrama, PA	PIT
Elrosa, MN	SCL
Elroy, WI	LC
Elsa, TX	BWN
Elsberry, MO	STL
Elsmere, DE	WIL
Elton, LA	LKC
Eltopia, WA	SPK
Elverson, PA	PH
Elwood, IN	LFT
Ely, MN	DUL
NV	LAV
Elyria, NE	GI
OH	CLV
Elyria Township, OH	CLV
Elysburg, PA	HBG
Elysian, MN	STP
Emeigh, PA	ALT
Emerald, KS	KCK
Emerson, NE	OM
NJ	NEW
Emery, SD	SFS
Emeryville, CA	OAK
Emily, MN	DUL
Emlenton, PA	E
Emmaus, PA	ALN

Emmetsburg, IA	SC
Emmett, ID	B
KS	KCK
MI	DET
Emmitsburg, MD	BAL
Emmonak, AK	FBK
Empire, MI	GAY
Emporia, KS	KCK
VA	RIC
Emporium, PA	E
Emsworth, PA	PIT
Encinal, TX	CC
Encinitas, CA	SD
Encino, CA	LA
Enderlin, ND	FAR
Enders Island, CT	NOR
Endicott, NY	PSC
NY	SY
Endwell, NY	SY
Enfield, CT	HRT
IL	BEL
NH	MAN
Engadine, MI	MAR
Engelberg, AR	LR
Englewood, CO	DEN
FL	VEN
NJ	NEW
OH	CIN
Englewood Cliffs, NJ	NEW
Englishtown, NJ	TR
Enhaut, PA	HBG
Enid, OK	OKL
Ennis, TX	DAL
Enochsburg, IN	IND
Enola, PA	HBG
Enosburg Falls, VT	BUR
Ensenada, PR	PCE
Enterprise, AL	MOB
OR	BAK
Enumclaw, WA	SEA
Ephraim, UT	SLC
Ephrata, PA	HBG
WA	YAK
Epiphany, SD	SFS
Epping, NH	MAN
Epworth, IA	DUB
Equality, IL	BEL
Erath, LA	LAF
Erie, CO	DEN
KS	WCH
MI	DET
PA	E
PA	MIL
PA	PBR
Erin, WI	SUP
Erlanger, KY	COV
Ernest, PA	GBG
PA	PBR
Esbon, KS	SAL
Escalon, CA	STO
Escanaba, MI	MAR
Escobares, TX	BWN
Escondido, CA	SD
Eskridge, KS	KCK
Esmond, ND	FAR
Esopus, NY	NY
Espanola, NM	SFE
Essex, CT	NOR
MA	BO
NY	OG
Essex Center, VT	BUR
Essex Junction, VT	BUR
Essexville, MI	SAG
Essington, PA	PH
Estacada, OR	P
Estate Elizabeth, VI	STV
Estate Tutu, VI	STV
Estelline, SD	SFS
Estes Park, CO	DEN
Estherville, IA	SC
Ethan, SD	SFS
Etna, PA	PIT
Ettrick, WI	LC
Euclid, MN	CR
OH	CLV
OH	PRM
Eudora, KS	KCK
Eufaula, AL	MOB
Eugene, OR	P
Eunice, LA	LAF
Eureka, CA	SR
IL	PEO
KS	WCH
MO	STL
MT	HEL
NV	RNO
SD	SFS
UT	SLC
Eureka Springs, AR	LR
Eustis, FL	ORL
Eutaw, AL	BIR
Evangeline, LA	LAF
Evans City, PA	PIT
Evans Mills, NY	OG
Evansdale, IA	DUB
Evanston, IL	CHI
WY	CHY
Evansville, IL	BEL
IN	EVN
WI	MAD
Evart, MI	GR
Eveleth, MN	DUL
Everett, MA	BO
PA	ALT
WA	SEA
Evergreen, CO	DEN
LA	ALX
Evergreen Park, IL	CHI
Everson, PA	GBG
Evesham Township, NJ	TR
Ewa, HI	HON
Ewa Beach, HI	HON
Ewen, MI	MAR
Ewing, MO	JC
NE	OM
Excelsior, MN	STP
Excelsior Springs, MO	KC
Excelsior, Lake Minnetonka, MN	STP
Exeter, CA	FRS
NE	LIN
NH	MAN
PA	SCR
Exira, IA	DM
Export, PA	GBG
Exton, PA	PH
Eynon, PA	SCR
Eyota, MN	WIN
Fabens, TX	ELP
Fair Haven, NJ	TR
VT	BUR
Fair Lawn, NJ	NEW
Fair Oaks, CA	SAC
Fair Oaks Ranch, TX	SAT
Fairbank, IA	DUB
Fairbanks, AK	FBK
Fairbault, MN	STP
Fairborn, OH	CIN
Fairburn, GA	ATL
Fairbury, IL	PEO
NE	LIN
Fairchance, PA	GBG
Fairchild, WI	LC
Fairdale, KY	L
Fairfax, CA	SFR
DE	WIL
IA	DUB
MN	NU
OK	TLS
SD	RC
VA	ARL
VT	BUR
Fairfax Station, VA	ARL
Fairfield, AL	BIR
CA	SAC
CT	BGP
IA	DAV
IL	BEL
KY	L
ME	PRT
MT	HEL
ND	STN
NJ	NEW
OH	CIN
PA	HBG
TX	TYL
VT	BUR
Fairfield Bay, AR	LR
Fairfield Glade, TN	KNX
Fairhaven, MA	FR
Fairhope, AL	MOB
Fairlawn, OH	CLV
OH	OLL
Fairless Hills, PA	PH
Fairmont, MN	WIN
WV	WH
Fairmont City, IL	BEL
Fairmount, ND	FAR
NY	SY
Fairmount Springs, PA	SCR
Fairpoint, OH	STU
Fairport, NY	ROC
Fairport Harbor, OH	CLV
OH	PRM
Fairview, NJ	NEW
PA	E
TN	NSH
WI	LC
Fairview Heights, IL	BEL
Fairview Park, OH	CLV
OH	PRM
Faith, SD	RC
Fajardo, PR	CGS
Falconer, NY	BUF
Falfurrias, TX	CC
Fall Creek, WI	LC
Fall River, MA	FR
MA	SAM
MA	STF
Fallbrook, CA	SD
Fallentimber, PA	ALT
Fallon, NV	RNO
Falls, PA	SCR
Falls Church, VA	ARL
Falls City, NE	LIN
TX	SAT
Falls Creek, PA	E
Fallsington, PA	PH
Fallston, MD	BAL
Falmouth, KY	COV
MA	FR
ME	PRT
Falun, MN	CR
Fancher, WI	LC
Fancy Farm, KY	OWN
Fannett, TX	BEA
Far Hills, NJ	MET
Fargo, ND	FAR
Faribault, MN	STP
Farley, IA	DUB
Farmer, SD	SFS
Farmer City, IL	PEO
Farmersville, CA	FRS
IL	SFD
Farming, MN	SCL
Farmingdale, NJ	TR
NY	BRK
NY	RVC
Farmington, CT	HRT
IA	DAV
IL	PEO
ME	PRT
MI	DET
MN	STP
MO	STL
NH	MAN
NM	GLP
PA	GBG
WI	MIL
WI	SUP
WV	WH
Farmington Hills, MI	DET
MI	GAY
MI	OLD
Farmingville, NY	RVC
Farmville, NC	R
VA	RIC
Farnham, NY	BUF
Farrell, PA	E
Farwell, NE	GI
Fatima, OH	STU
Faulkner, MD	WDC
Faulkton, SD	SFS
Faxon Township, MN	NU
Fayette, AL	BIR
IA	DUB
MO	JC
MS	JKS
OH	TOL
Fayette City, PA	GBG
Fayetteville, AR	LR
GA	ATL
IL	BEL
NC	R
NC	SAM
NY	SY
OH	CIN
TN	NSH
TX	AUS
Feasterville, PA	PH
Federal Way, WA	SEA
Feeding Hills, MA	SPR
Fefan, FM	CI
Felicity, OH	CIN
Fellsmere, FL	PMB
Felton, CA	MRY
MN	CR
Fennimore, WI	MAD
Fenton, LA	LKC
MI	LAN
MO	STL
Ferdinand, ID	B
IN	EVN
Fergus Falls, MN	SCL
Ferguson, MO	STL
Fernandina Beach, FL	STA
Ferndale, CA	SR
MI	DET
WA	SEA
Fernley, NV	RNO
Ferriday, LA	ALX
Ferris, TX	DAL
Fertile, MN	CR
Fessenden, ND	FAR
Festina, IA	DUB
Festus, MO	STL
Fidelity, KS	KCK
Fieldon, IL	SFD
Fife Lake, MI	GAY
Fifield, WI	SUP
Fifth Ward, LA	ALX
Fillmore, CA	LA
IA	DUB
NY	BUF
Fincastle, VA	RIC
Findlay, OH	TOL
Fingal, ND	FAR
Finley, KY	L
ND	FAR
Finleyville, PA	PIT
Firebaugh, CA	FRS
Fish Creek, WI	GB
Fish Lake, IN	GRY
Fisher, MN	CR
Fishers, IN	LFT
Fishers Island, NY	NOR
Fisherville, MI	SAG
Fishkill, NY	NY
Fiskdale, MA	WOR
Fitchburg, MA	WOR
Flagler Beach, FL	STA
Flagstaff, AZ	PHX
Flaherty, KY	L
Flambeau, WI	SUP
Flanders, NJ	PAT
NJ	PSC
Flandreau, SD	SFS
Flasher, ND	BIS
Flat Rock, MI	DET
Flatonia, TX	VIC
Fleming, NY	ROC
Flemingsburg, KY	COV
Flemington, NJ	MET
Flensburg, MN	SCL
Flint, MI	LAN
MI	OLL
MI	STN
Flint Hill, MO	STL
Flintville, WI	GB
Floodwood, MN	DUL
Flora, IL	BEL
Flora Vista, NM	GLP
Floral Park, NY	RVC
Florence, AL	BIR
AZ	TUC
CO	PBL
KS	WCH
KY	COV
NJ	TR
NY	SY
OR	P
SC	CHR
SD	SFS
WI	GB
Floresville, TX	SAT
Florham Park, NJ	PAT
Florian, MN	CR
Florida, NY	NY
PR	ARE
Florissant, LA	NO
MO	STL
Flossmoor, IL	CHI
Flourtown, PA	PH
Floydada, TX	LUB
Flush, KS	KCK
Flushing, MI	LAN
MI	PRM
NY	BRK
OH	STU
Foley, AL	MOB
MN	SCL
Folk, MO	JC
Follansbee, WV	WH
Folsom, CA	SAC
LA	NO
PA	PH
Fond du Lac, WI	MIL
Fonda, IA	SC
NY	ALB
Fontana, CA	SB
CA	VNN
WI	MIL
Footedale, PA	GBG
Footville, WI	MAD
Forbes Road, PA	GBG
Force, PA	E
Ford, WA	SPK
Ford City, PA	GBG
PA	SJP
Fords, NJ	MET
Fordsville, KY	OWN
Fordyce, AR	LR
NE	OM
Forest, MS	JKS
Forest City, IA	DUB

MN	NU
NC	CHL
PA	PSC
PA	SCR
Forest Grove, OR	P
Forest Hill, LA	ALX
Forest Hills, NY	BRK
PA	PIT
Forest Lake, MN	STP
Forest Park, IL	CHI
Forestburgh, NY	NY
Foreston, MN	SCL
Forestport, NY	SY
Forestville, CT	HRT
MD	WDC
NY	BUF
Forked River, NJ	TR
Forks, WA	SEA
Forman, ND	FAR
Forney, TX	DAL
Forrest City, AR	LR
Forsyth, MO	SPC
MT	GF
Fort Ann, NY	ALB
Fort Ashby, WV	WH
Fort Atkinson, IA	DUB
WI	MAD
Fort Bend Co., TX	GAL
Fort Benton, MT	GF
Fort Berthold Reservation, ND	BIS
Fort Bragg, CA	SR
Fort Branch, IN	EVN
Fort Calhoun, NE	OM
Fort Collins, CO	DEN
Fort Covington, NY	OG
Fort Davis, TX	ELP
Fort Defiance, AZ	GLP
Fort Dodge, IA	SC
Fort Edward, NY	ALB
Fort Fairfield, ME	PRT
Fort Hancock, TX	ELP
Fort Jennings, OH	TOL
Fort Jones, CA	SAC
Fort Kent, ME	PRT
Fort Lauderdale, FL	MIA
Fort Leavenworth, KS	KCK
Fort Lee, NJ	NEW
Fort Loramie, OH	CIN
Fort Lupton, CO	DEN
Fort Madison, IA	DAV
Fort Mitchell, KY	COV
Fort Monroe, VA	RIC
Fort Morgan, CO	DEN
Fort Myers, FL	SP
FL	VEN
Fort Myers Beach, FL	VEN
Fort Oglethorpe, GA	ATL
Fort Pierce, FL	PMB
FL	PSC
Fort Pierre, SD	RC
Fort Plain, NY	ALB
Fort Recovery, OH	CIN
Fort Riley, KS	SAL
Fort Scott, KS	WCH
Fort Shaw, MT	GF
Fort Smith, AR	LR
Fort Stockton, TX	SAN
Fort Sumner, NM	SFE
Fort Thomas, KY	COV
Fort Thompson, SD	SFS
Fort Totten, ND	FAR
Fort Totten Reservation, ND	FAR
Fort Walton Beach, FL	PT
Fort Washington, MD	WDC
PA	PH
Fort Wayne, IN	FTW
Fort Wingate, NM	GLP
Fort Worth, TX	FWT
Fort Yates, ND	BIS
Fortuna, CA	SR
Fortville, IN	IND
Forty Fort, PA	SCR
Fosston, MN	CR
Foster, RI	PRO
Foster City, CA	SFR
Fostoria, OH	TOL
Fountain, CO	COS
FL	PT
MN	WIN
Fountain City, WI	LC
Fountain Hill, PA	ALN
Fountain Hills, AZ	PHX
Fountain Valley, CA	ORG
Four Corners, LA	LAF
Fowler, CA	FRS
IN	LFT
KS	DOD
MI	LAN
Fowlerville, MI	LAN
Fox Chase Manor, PA	PH
PA	PHU
Fox Lake, IL	CHI
WI	MIL
Fox Point, WI	MIL
Foxboro, MA	BO
Foxholm, ND	BIS
Foxhome, MN	SCL
Frackville, PA	ALN
PA	PHU
Framingham, MA	BO
Framingham Centre, MA	BO
Francesville, IN	LFT
Francis Creek, WI	GB
Frankenmuth, MI	SAG
Frankenstein, MO	JC
Frankfort, IL	JOL
IN	LFT
KS	KCK
KY	LEX
MI	GAY
NY	ALB
SD	SFS
Franklin, IL	SFD
IN	IND
KY	OWN
LA	LAF
MA	BO
MN	NU
NC	CHL
NH	MAN
NJ	PAT
OH	CIN
PA	E
TN	NSH
VA	RIC
WI	MIL
WV	WH
Franklin Lakes, NJ	NEW
Franklin Park, IL	CHI
Franklin Park Borough, PA	PIT
Franklin Square, NY	RVC
Franklinton, LA	NO
Franklinville, NJ	CAM
NY	BUF
Fraser, MI	DET
Frazee, MN	CR
Frazier Park, CA	FRS
Frederic, WI	SUP
Frederick, CO	DEN
MD	BAL
OK	OKL
Fredericksburg, TX	SAT
VA	ARL
Fredericktown, MO	SPC
PA	PIT
Frederiksted, VI	STV
Fredonia, KS	WCH
NY	BUF
WI	MIL
Free Soil, MI	GR
Freeburg, IL	BEL
MO	JC
Freedom, PA	PIT
WI	GB
Freehold, NJ	TR
Freeland, MI	SAG
PA	PSC
PA	SCR
Freeport, FL	PT
IL	RCK
MN	SCL
NY	RVC
OH	STU
PA	GBG
TX	GAL
Freer, TX	CC
Frelsburg, TX	VIC
Fremont, CA	NTN
CA	OAK
MI	GR
NE	OM
OH	TOL
Fremont Center, IL	CHI
French Creek, NY	BUF
French Lick, IN	IND
French Settlement, LA	BR
Frenchburg, KY	LEX
Frenchtown, IN	IND
MT	HEL
OH	CIN
OH	TOL
PA	E
Frenchville, ME	PRT
PA	E
Frenstat, TX	AUS
Fresh Meadows, NY	BRK
NY	STF
Fresno, CA	FRS
CA	VNN
Frewsburg, NY	BUF
Friday Harbor, WA	SEA
Fridley, MN	STP
Fried, ND	FAR
Friend, NE	LIN
Friendship, NY	BUF
Friendsville, PA	SCR
Friendswood, TX	GAL
Friona, TX	AMA
Frisco, TX	DAL
Front Royal, VA	ARL
VA	WDC
Frontenac, KS	WCH
MN	STP
MO	STL
Frostburg, MD	BAL
Fruita, CO	PBL
Fryburg, OH	CIN
PA	E
Frydek, TX	GAL
Fulda, IN	IND
MN	WIN
ND	FAR
OH	STU
Fullerton, CA	NTN
CA	ORG
ND	FAR
NE	OM
Fulton, IL	RCK
KS	WCH
KY	OWN
MD	BAL
MO	JC
NY	SY
Fuquay-Varina, NC	R
Gackle, ND	FAR
Gadsden, AL	BIR
Gaffney, SC	CHR
Gagetown, MI	SAG
Gagil, FM	CI
Gahanna, OH	COL
Gaines, MI	LAN
Gainesville, FL	STA
GA	ATL
TX	FWT
Gaithersburg, MD	WDC
Galena, AK	FBK
IL	RCK
KS	WCH
MD	WIL
Galena Park, TX	GAL
Gales Ferry, CT	NOR
Galesburg, IL	PEO
Galesville, WI	LC
Galeton, PA	E
Galion, OH	TOL
Gallatin, TN	NSH
Galliano, LA	HT
Gallipolis, OH	STU
Gallitzin, PA	ALT
Galloway, WI	LC
Gallup, NM	GLP
Galt, CA	SAC
Galva, IL	PEO
Galveston, TX	GAL
Ganado, AZ	GLP
TX	VIC
Garapan Village, District 11, MP	CHK
Garber, IA	DUB
Garberville, CA	SR
Garden, MI	MAR
Garden City, KS	DOD
MI	DET
NY	RVC
SC	CHR
Garden Grove, CA	ORG
Garden Plain, KS	WCH
Garden Valley, ID	B
Gardena, CA	LA
Gardendale, AL	BIR
Gardenville, MO	STL
Gardiner, ME	PRT
NY	NY
Gardner, CO	PBL
KS	KCK
MA	WOR
Gardnerville, NV	RNO
Garfield, NJ	NEW
NM	LSC
Garfield Heights, OH	CLV
Garfield Park, DE	WIL
Garland, TX	DAL
Garnavillo, IA	DUB
Garner, IA	DUB
NC	R
Garnerville, NY	NY
Garnett, KS	KCK
Garretson, SD	SFS
Garrett, IN	FTW
Garrett Park, MD	WDC
Garrettsville, OH	Y
Garrison, MN	DUL
ND	BIS
NY	NY
Garryowen, IA	DUB
SD	SFS
Garwin, IA	DUB
Garwood, NJ	NEW
Gary, IN	GRY
SD	SFS
WV	WH
Gary-New Duluth, MN	DUL
Garyville, LA	NO
Gas City, IN	LFT
Gasport, NY	BUF
Gassaway, WV	WH
Gastonia, NC	CHL
Gate City, VA	RIC
Gates Mills, OH	CLV
Gatesville, TX	AUS
Gatlinburg, TN	KNX
Gautier, MS	BLX
Gaylord, MI	GAY
MN	NU
Gays Mills, WI	LC
Geddes, SD	SFS
Genesee, ID	B
Genesee Depot, WI	MIL
Geneseo, IL	PEO
ND	FAR
NY	ROC
Geneva, IA	DUB
IL	RCK
IN	FTW
MN	WIN
NE	LIN
NY	ROC
OH	Y
Genoa, IL	RCK
NE	OM
OH	TOL
WI	LC
Gentilly, MN	CR
George West, TX	CC
Georgetown, CA	SAC
CT	BGP
DE	WIL
IA	DAV
IL	PEO
KY	LEX
MA	BO
MN	CR
OH	CIN
SC	CHR
TX	AUS
WI	SUP
Gering, NE	GI
Germantown, IL	BEL
MD	WDC
NY	ALB
OH	CIN
TN	MEM
WI	LC
WI	MIL
Gervais, OR	P
Gettysburg, PA	HBG
SD	SFS
Getzville, NY	BUF
Gheens, LA	HT
Ghent, MN	NU
WV	WH
Gibbon, MN	NU
Gibbsboro, NJ	CAM
Gibbstown, NJ	CAM
Gibraltar, MI	DET
Gibson, LA	HT
Gibson City, IL	JOL
Gibsonburg, OH	TOL
Gibsonia, PA	PIT
Giddings, TX	AUS
Gig Harbor, WA	SEA
Gila Bend, AZ	PHX
Gilbert, AZ	PHX
AZ	VNN
IA	DUB
MN	DUL
Gilbertville, IA	DUB
MA	WOR
Gildehaus, MO	STL
Gilford, NH	MAN
Gillespie, IL	SFD
Gillett, WI	GB
Gillette, WY	CHY
Gills Pier, MI	GAY
Gilman, IL	JOL
MN	SCL
VT	BUR
WI	SUP
Gilmanton Iron Works, NH	MAN
Gilmore City, IA	SC
Gilroy, CA	SJ
Girard, IL	SFD
KS	WCH
OH	Y
PA	E

PA	PBR
Girardville, PA	ALN
Glade Mills, PA	PIT
Gladstone, MI	MAR
MO	KC
NJ	PAT
Gladwin, MI	SAG
Gladwyne, PA	PH
Glandorf, OH	TOL
Glasco, KS	SAL
NY	NY
Glasgow, KY	L
MO	JC
MT	GF
Glasgow Village, MO	STL
Glassboro, NJ	CAM
Glassport, PA	PIT
Glastonbury, CT	HRT
CT	STF
Glen Allen, VA	RIC
Glen Burnie, MD	BAL
Glen Campbell, PA	GBG
Glen Carbon, IL	SFD
Glen Cove, NY	RVC
NY	STF
Glen Dale, WV	WH
Glen Ellyn, IL	JOL
Glen Falls, NY	ALB
Glen Head, NY	RVC
Glen Lyon, PA	PHU
PA	SCR
Glen Owen, MO	STL
Glen Rock, NJ	NEW
Glen Rose, TX	FWT
Glen Spey, NY	STF
Glen Ullin, ND	BIS
Glenbeulah, WI	MIL
Glenburn, ND	BIS
Glencoe, MN	NU
MO	STL
Glendale, AZ	PHX
CA	ARM
CA	LA
CO	DEN
NY	BRK
Glendale Heights, IL	JOL
Glendive, MT	GF
Glendora, CA	LA
Glenfield, NY	OG
Glenmoore, PA	PH
Glenmora, LA	ALX
Glenmore, WI	GB
Glennallen, AK	ANC
Glennie, MI	GAY
Glennonville, MO	SPC
Glenns Ferry, ID	B
Glenolden, PA	PH
Glenrock, WY	CHY
Glens Falls, NY	ALB
Glenshaw, PA	PIT
Glenside, PA	PH
Glenview, IL	CHI
Glenville, NY	ALB
WV	WH
Glenwood, IA	DM
IL	CHI
MN	SCL
Glenwood City, WI	SUP
Glenwood Springs, CO	DEN
Glidden, WI	SUP
Globe, AZ	TUC
Glocester, RI	PRO
Gloucester, MA	BO
NJ	CAM
VA	RIC
Glouster, OH	STU
Gloversville, NY	ALB
Gloverville, SC	CHR
Glyndon, MD	BAL
Glynwood, OH	CIN
GMF, GU	AGN
Gobles, MI	KAL
Godfrey, IL	SFD
Goetzville, MI	MAR
Goffstown, NH	MAN
Gold Hill, OR	P
Golden, CO	DEN
Golden Gate, FL	VEN
Golden Meadow, LA	HT
Golden Valley, MN	STP
Goldendale, WA	YAK
Goldenrod, FL	ORL
Goldsboro, NC	R
Goldthwaite, TX	AUS
Goleta, CA	LA
Goliad, TX	VIC
Gonic, NH	MAN
Gonzales, CA	MRY
LA	BR
TX	SAT
Good Hart, MI	GAY

Good Thunder, MN	WIN
Gooding, ID	B
Goodland, IN	LFT
KS	SAL
Goodman, WI	GB
Goodrich, IL	JOL
MI	LAN
Goodridge, MN	CR
Goodyear, AZ	PHX
Goose Creek, SC	CHR
Gordon, NE	GI
PA	ALN
WI	SUP
Gordonsville, VA	ARL
Gorham, KS	SAL
ME	PRT
NH	MAN
Goshen, CA	FRS
CT	HRT
IN	FTW
KY	L
MA	SPR
NY	NY
Gouldsboro, PA	SCR
Gouverneur, NY	OG
Gowanda, NY	BUF
Graceville, MN	NU
Graettinger, IA	SC
Graford, TX	FWT
Grafton, IL	SFD
MA	WOR
ND	FAR
NE	LIN
NY	ALB
OH	CLV
WI	MIL
WV	WH
Graham, TX	FWT
Grainfield, KS	SAL
Grambling, LA	SHP
Gramercy, LA	BR
Grampian, PA	E
Granada Hills, CA	LA
Granbury, TX	FWT
Granby, CT	HRT
MA	SPR
Grand Bay, AL	MOB
Grand Blanc, MI	LAN
Grand Caillou, LA	HT
Grand Canyon, AZ	PHX
Grand Chain, IL	BEL
Grand Chenier, LA	LKC
Grand Coteau, LA	LAF
Grand Coulee, WA	YAK
Grand Forks, ND	FAR
Grand Haven, MI	GR
Grand Island, NE	GI
NY	BUF
Grand Isle, LA	HT
ME	PRT
Grand Junction, CO	PBL
IA	SC
Grand Lake, CO	DEN
Grand Ledge, MI	LAN
Grand Marais, MI	MAR
MN	DUL
Grand Meadow, MN	WIN
Grand Mound, IA	DAV
Grand Prairie, LA	LAF
TX	DAL
Grand Rapids, MI	GR
MI	STN
MN	DUL
Grand River, IA	DM
Grand Rivers, KY	OWN
Grand Ronde, OR	P
Grand Terrace, CA	SB
Grandview, ID	B
MO	KC
WA	YAK
Grandville, MI	GR
Granger, IA	DM
IN	FTW
TX	AUS
WA	YAK
Grangeville, ID	B
Granite City, IL	SFD
Granite Falls, MN	NU
Graniteville, VT	BUR
Grant, NE	LIN
Grant Town, WV	WH
Grantfork, IL	SFD
Grants, NM	GLP
Grants Pass, OR	P
Grantsburg, WI	SUP
Grants-Milan, NM	GLP
Grantsville, MD	BAL
Grantwood, MO	STL
Granville, IA	SC
IL	PEO
ND	FAR

NY	ALB
NY	PSC
OH	COL
Grapevine, TX	FWT
Grass Lake, MI	LAN
Grass Valley, CA	SAC
Gratiot, WI	MAD
Gray, ME	PRT
Grayling, MI	GAY
Graymoor, NY	NY
Grayslake, IL	CHI
Grayson, KY	LEX
Grayson Springs, KY	OWN
Great Barrington, MA	SPR
Great Bend, KS	DOD
PA	SCR
Great Falls, MT	GF
VA	ARL
Great Meadows, NJ	MET
NJ	PHU
Great Mills, MD	WDC
Great Neck, NY	RVC
Greater Cincinnati, OH	CIN
Greeley, CO	DEN
IA	DUB
KS	KCK
NE	GI
Green, OH	CLV
Green Bay, WI	GB
Green Cove Springs, FL	STA
Green Creek, IL	SFD
Green Island, NY	ALB
Green Isle, MN	NU
Green Lake, WI	MAD
Green Pond, NJ	PAT
Green River, WY	CHY
Green Springs, OH	TOL
Green Tree, PA	PIT
Green Valley, AZ	TUC
MN	NU
Greenbelt, MD	WDC
Greenbrae, CA	SFR
Greenburgh, NY	NY
Greenbush, KS	WCH
MN	CR
Greencastle, IN	IND
PA	HBG
Greencreek, ID	B
Greendale, WI	MIL
Greene, IA	DUB
NY	SY
Greene County, VA	RIC
Greeneville, TN	KNX
Greenfield, CA	MRY
IA	DM
IL	SFD
IN	IND
MA	SPR
OH	CIN
WI	MIL
Greenfield Center, NY	ALB
Greenlawn, NY	RVC
Greenleaf, KS	SAL
MN	NU
WI	GB
Greenport, NY	RVC
Greensboro, GA	ATL
NC	CHL
Greensboro Bend, VT	BUR
Greensburg, IN	IND
KS	DOD
KY	L
PA	GBG
PA	PBR
Greenup, IL	SFD
Greenville, AL	MOB
DE	WIL
IL	SFD
ME	PRT
MI	GR
MS	JKS
NC	R
NY	ALB
OH	CIN
PA	E
SC	CHR
TX	DAL
WI	GB
Greenwald, MN	SCL
Greenwell Springs, LA	BR
Greenwich, CT	BGP
NY	ALB
Greenwood, IN	IND
MS	JKS
SC	CHR
WI	LC
Greenwood Lake, NY	NY
Greer, SC	CHR
Gregory, SD	RC
TX	CC
Grenada, MS	JKS

Grenora, ND	BIS
Grenville, SD	SFS
Gresham, OR	P
WI	GB
Gretna, LA	NO
NE	OM
Grey Eagle, MN	SCL
Greybull, WY	CHY
Gridley, CA	SAC
Griffin, GA	ATL
Griffith, IN	GRY
Griggsville, IL	SFD
Grindstone, PA	GBG
Grinnell, IA	DAV
KS	SAL
Griswold, IA	DM
Groom, TX	AMA
Grosse Ile, MI	DET
Grosse Pointe, MI	DET
Grosse Pointe Farms, MI	DET
Grosse Pointe Park, MI	DET
Grosse Tete, LA	BR
Groton, CT	NOR
MA	BO
NY	ROC
SD	SFS
Grove, OK	TLS
Grove City, FL	VEN
OH	COL
PA	E
Grove Hill, AL	MOB
Groveland, MA	BO
Groveport, OH	COL
Grover, SD	SFS
Groves, TX	BEA
Groveton, NH	MAN
Grulla, TX	BWN
Grundy Center, IA	DUB
Gruver, TX	AMA
Grygla, MN	CR
Guadalupe, AZ	PHX
CA	LA
Guanica, PR	PCE
Guasti, CA	SB
Guayama, PR	PCE
Guayanilla, PR	PCE
Guaynabo, PR	SJN
Guckeen, MN	WIN
Guerneville, CA	SR
Guernsey, WY	CHY
Gueydan, LA	LAF
Guilderland, NY	ALB
Guilford, CT	HRT
Gulf Breeze, FL	PT
Gulf Shores, AL	MOB
Gulfport, FL	SP
MS	BLX
Gull Lake, MI	KAL
Gun Barrel City, TX	TYL
Gunnison, CO	PBL
Guntersville, AL	BIR
Gurabo, PR	CGS
Gurnee, IL	CHI
Gustine, CA	FRS
Guthrie, KY	OWN
OK	OKL
Guthrie Center, IA	DM
Guttenberg, IA	DUB
NJ	NEW
Guymon, OK	OKL
Gwinn, MI	MAR
Gwinner, ND	FAR
Gwynedd Valley, PA	PH
Gypsum, KS	SAL
Hacienda Heights, CA	LA
Hackberry, LA	LKC
Hackensack, NJ	NEW
Hackettstown, NJ	MET
Haddon Heights, NJ	CAM
Haddon Township, NJ	CAM
Haddonfield, NJ	CAM
Hadley, MA	SPR
Hagaman, IL	SFD
NY	ALB
Hagerman, ID	B
Hagerstown, MD	BAL
Hague, ND	BIS
NY	ALB
Hahnville, LA	NO
Haiku, HI	HON
Hailey, ID	B
Haines, AK	JUN
Haines City, FL	ORL
Haines Falls, NY	ALB
Hainesport, NJ	TR
Hainesville, NJ	PAT
Halbur, IA	SC
Halder, WI	LC
Hale, MI	GAY
Hale Center, TX	LUB
Haledon, NJ	PAT

Hales Corners, WI	MIL
Half Moon Bay, CA	SFR
Halifax, MA	BO
Hallandale, FL	MIA
Hallettsville, TX	VIC
Halliday, ND	BIS
Hallock, MN	CR
Hallowell, ME	PRT
Halstad, MN	CR
Halstead, KS	WCH
Ham Lake, MN	STP
Hamburg, AR	LR
IA	DM
IN	IND
MI	LAN
NJ	PAT
NY	BUF
PA	ALN
Hamden, CT	HRT
Hamel, MN	STP
Hamilton, AL	BIR
GA	SAV
KS	WCH
MA	BO
MO	KC
MT	HEL
NY	SY
OH	CIN
TX	AUS
VA	ARL
Hamilton Square, NJ	TR
Hamler, OH	TOL
Hamlet, IN	GRY
NC	CHL
Hamlin, ME	PRT
NY	ROC
Hammond, IN	GRY
IN	NTN
LA	BR
MN	WIN
NY	OG
WI	SUP
Hammondsport, NY	ROC
Hammondsville, OH	STU
Hammonton, NJ	CAM
Hampden, MA	SPR
ME	PRT
Hampshire, IL	RCK
Hampstead, NC	R
NH	MAN
Hampton, CT	NOR
IA	DUB
MN	STP
NH	MAN
NJ	MET
VA	RIC
Hampton Bays, NY	RVC
Hampton Beach, NH	MAN
Hamptonburgh, NY	STF
Hamptonville, NC	CHL
Hamtramck, MI	DET
MI	STN
Hana, HI	HON
Hancock, MD	BAL
MI	MAR
NY	ALB
Hancock Township, MN	STP
Hanford, CA	FRS
Hankinson, ND	FAR
Hannah, MI	GAY
Hannastown, PA	PBR
Hannibal, MO	JC
NY	SY
Hanover, IA	DUB
IL	RCK
KS	SAL
MA	BO
NH	MAN
PA	HBG
Hanover Park, IL	CHI
Hansboro, ND	FAR
Hanson, MA	BO
Hanston, KS	DOD
Hapeville, GA	ATL
Happy, TX	AMA
Harahan, LA	NO
Harbor Beach, MI	SAG
Harbor Springs, MI	GAY
Harborcreek, PA	E
Hardin, IL	SFD
MT	GF
Harding, MN	SCL
PA	SCR
Hardinsburg, KY	OWN
Hardwick, VT	BUR
Harietta, MI	GAY
Harker Heights, TX	AUS
Harlan, IA	DM
KY	LEX
Harleigh, PA	SCR
Harlingen, TX	BWN
Harlowton, MT	HEL
Harmarville, PA	PIT
Harmon, IL	RCK
Harmony, MN	WIN
Harper, IA	DAV
KS	WCH
TX	SAT
Harper Woods, MI	DET
Harpers Ferry, IA	DUB
WV	WH
Harrah, OK	OKL
Harriettsville, OH	STU
Harriman, NY	NY
TN	KNX
Harrington, WA	SPK
Harrington Park, NJ	NEW
Harris Hill, NY	BUF
Harrisburg, IL	BEL
PA	HBG
PA	PSC
Harrison, AR	LR
MI	SAG
NJ	NEW
NY	NY
WI	SUP
Harrison City, PA	GBG
Harrison Twp., MI	DET
Harrisonburg, VA	RIC
Harrisonville, MO	KC
Harrisville, MI	GAY
NH	MAN
NY	OG
WV	WH
Harrodsburg, KY	LEX
Harrold, SD	SFS
Harsens Island, MI	DET
Hart, MI	GR
Hartford, AR	LR
CT	HRT
CT	STF
KS	KCK
KY	OWN
MI	KAL
SD	SFS
WI	MIL
Hartford City, IN	LFT
Hartington, NE	OM
Hartland, IL	RCK
MI	LAN
WI	MIL
Hartline, WA	YAK
Hartsdale, NY	NY
Hartshorne, OK	TLS
Hartsville, SC	CHR
Hartwell, GA	ATL
Harvard, IL	RCK
MA	WOR
NE	LIN
Harvey, IL	CHI
LA	NO
ND	FAR
Harvey Cedars, NJ	TR
Harveys Lake, PA	SCR
Harwichport, MA	FR
Harwick, PA	PIT
Harwinton, CT	HRT
Harwood Heights, IL	CHI
Hasbrouck Heights, NJ	NEW
Haskell, NJ	PAT
Hassan Township, MN	STP
Hastings, MI	KAL
MN	STP
NE	LIN
PA	ALT
Hastings-on-Hudson, NY	NY
Hatboro, PA	PH
Hatch, NM	LSC
Hatfield, MA	SPR
PA	PH
Hathaway Manor, MO	STL
Hatillo, PR	ARE
Hatley, WI	LC
Hato Rey, PR	SJN
Hattiesburg, MS	BLX
Haubstadt, IN	EVN
Haugen, WI	SUP
Hauppauge, NY	RVC
Havana, IL	PEO
Havelock, NC	R
Haverford, PA	PH
Haverhill, IA	DUB
MA	BO
Haverstraw, NY	NY
Havertown, PA	PH
Havre, MT	GF
Havre de Grace, MD	BAL
Hawaiian Gardens, CA	LA
Hawarden, IA	SC
Hawesville, KY	OWN
Hawi, HI	HON
Hawk Point, MO	STL
Hawk Run, PA	PBR
Hawkeye, IA	DUB
Hawkins, WI	SUP
Hawley, MN	CR
PA	SCR
Haworth, NJ	NEW
Hawthorne, CA	LA
NJ	PAT
NV	RNO
NY	NY
Hayden, AZ	TUC
Haydenville, MA	SPR
Hayesville, NC	CHL
Hayfield, MN	WIN
Hayneville, AL	MOB
Hays, KS	SAL
MT	GF
Haysville, KS	WCH
Hayward, CA	OAK
WI	SUP
Hazard, KY	LEX
Hazel Crest, IL	CHI
Hazel Green, WI	MAD
Hazel Park, MI	DET
Hazelton, ND	BIS
Hazelwood, MN	STP
MO	STL
Hazen, ND	BIS
Hazlehurst, GA	SAV
Hazlet, NJ	TR
Hazleton, IA	DUB
PA	PHU
PA	PSC
PA	SCR
Healdsburg, CA	SR
Healy, AK	FBK
Hearne, TX	AUS
Heart Butte, MT	HEL
Heath, OH	COL
Hebbronville, TX	CC
Hebron, CT	NOR
IN	GRY
ND	BIS
NE	LIN
Hecker, IL	BEL
Heckscherville, PA	ALN
Hecla, SD	SFS
Hector, MN	NU
Heffron, WI	LC
Hegbert, MN	NU
Heidelberg, MN	STP
Heilwood, PA	GBG
Helena, AR	LR
MI	SAG
MT	HEL
Helenwood, TN	KNX
Hellertown, PA	ALN
Helmetta, NJ	MET
Helmville, MT	HEL
Helotes, TX	SAT
Helper, UT	SLC
Hemet, CA	SB
Hemingford, NE	GI
Hemlock, MI	SAG
Hemphill, TX	TYL
Hempstead, NY	RVC
NY	STF
TX	GAL
Henderson, KY	OWN
LA	LAF
MN	NU
NC	R
NV	LAV
TX	TYL
Hendersonville, NC	CHL
TN	NSH
Hennepin, IL	PEO
Hennessey, OK	OKL
Henniker, NH	MAN
Henning, MN	SCL
Henrietta, NY	ROC
TX	FWT
Henry, IL	PEO
LA	LAF
SD	SFS
Henryetta, OK	TLS
Henryville, IN	IND
Henshaw, KY	OWN
Heppner, OR	BAK
Herculaneum, MO	STL
Hereford, AZ	TUC
TX	AMA
Herington, KS	SAL
Herkimer, NY	ALB
Herman, MN	SCL
PA	PIT
Hermann, MO	JC
Hermansville, MI	MAR
Herminie, PA	GBG
PA	PBR
Hermiston, OR	BAK
Hermitage, MO	JC
PA	E
PA	PBR
Hermosa, SD	RC
Hermosa Beach, CA	LA
Hernando, MS	JKS
Herndon, KS	SAL
VA	ARL
Heron Bay, AL	MOB
Heron Lake, MN	WIN
Herreid, SD	SFS
Herrin, IL	BEL
Herron, MI	GAY
Herscher, IL	JOL
Hershey, PA	HBG
Hesperia, CA	SB
Hessen Cassel, IN	FTW
Hessmer, LA	ALX
Hettinger, ND	BIS
Heun, NE	OM
Heuvelton, NY	OG
Hewitt, NJ	PAT
WI	LC
Hewlett, NY	RVC
Hialeah, FL	MIA
Hialeah Gardens, FL	MIA
Hiawatha, IA	DUB
KS	KCK
Hibbing, MN	DUL
Hickman, KY	OWN
Hickory, MD	BAL
NC	CHL
Hickory Hills, IL	CHI
Hicksville, NY	RVC
OH	TOL
Hidalgo, TX	BWN
Higganum, CT	NOR
Higgins Lake, MI	GAY
Higginsville, MO	KC
High Bridge, NJ	MET
High Hill, TX	VIC
High Point, NC	CHL
High Ridge, MO	STL
High Springs, FL	STA
Highbridge, WI	SUP
Highgate Center, VT	BUR
Highland, CA	SB
IL	SFD
IN	GRY
MI	DET
NY	NY
WI	MAD
Highland Beach, FL	PMB
Highland Falls, NY	NY
Highland Heights, KY	COV
OH	CLV
Highland Lakes, NJ	PAT
Highland Mills, NY	NY
Highland Park, IL	CHI
MI	DET
NJ	MET
PA	PH
Highland Springs, VA	RIC
Highlands, NJ	TR
TX	GAL
Highlands Ranch, CO	COS
Highmore, SD	SFS
Hightstown, NJ	TR
Highwood, IL	CHI
Hilbert, WI	GB
Hill City, KS	SAL
MN	DUL
SD	RC
Hillcrest Heights, MD	WDC
Hilliard, OH	COL
Hillje, TX	VIC
Hillman, MI	GAY
MN	DUL
MN	SCL
Hills, IA	DAV
Hillsboro, IL	SFD
MO	STL
ND	FAR
OH	CIN
OR	P
TX	FWT
WI	LC
Hillsborough, NC	R
NH	MAN
NJ	MET
Hillsborough Township, NJ	PSC
Hillsdale, MI	LAN
NJ	NEW
Hillside, IL	CHI
IL	OLL
NJ	NEW
NJ	PHU
Hillsville, PA	PIT
Hilltop, MD	WDC
Hilltown, PA	PH
Hilmar, CA	FRS

Hilo, HI	HON
Hilton, NY	ROC
Hilton Head Island, SC	CHR
Hinckley, MN	DUL
NY	SY
OH	CLV
Hinesburg, VT	BUR
Hinesville, GA	SAV
Hingham, MA	BO
Hinsdale, IL	JOL
MA	SPR
NH	MAN
NY	BUF
Hinton, WV	WH
Hirlingen, MO	KC
Hitchcock, OK	OKL
TX	GAL
Hixson, TN	KNX
Hoban Heights, PA	SCR
Hobart, IN	GRY
Hobbs, NM	LSC
Hobe Sound, FL	PMB
Hoboken, NJ	NEW
Hobson, TX	SAT
Hockessin, DE	WIL
Hodge, LA	SHP
Hodgenville, KY	L
Hofa Park, WI	GB
Hoffman Estates, IL	CHI
Hogansburg, NY	OG
Hohenwald, TN	NSH
Hohokus, NJ	NEW
Hoisington, KS	DOD
Hokah, MN	WIN
Holbrook, AZ	GLP
IA	DAV
MA	BO
NY	RVC
Holden, MO	KC
WV	WH
Holdenville, OK	TLS
Holdingford, MN	SCL
Holdrege, NE	LIN
Holgate, OH	TOL
Holiday, FL	SP
Holiday Park, PA	PIT
Holland, MI	GR
NY	BUF
PA	LIT
PA	PH
Holland Patent, NY	SY
Hollandale, WI	MAD
Hollandtown, WI	GB
Holley, NY	BUF
Hollidaysburg, PA	ALT
Hollister, CA	MRY
Holliston, MA	BO
Holloway, MN	NU
Holly, CO	PBL
MI	DET
Holly Springs, MS	JKS
Hollywood, FL	MIA
MD	WDC
Holmdel, NJ	TR
Holmen, WI	LC
Holmes Beach, FL	VEN
Holstein, IA	SC
Holton, KS	KCK
Holts Summit, MO	JC
Holtville, CA	SD
Holualoa, HI	HON
Holy Cross, AK	FBK
IA	DUB
KY	L
WI	MIL
Holy Hill, WI	MIL
Holy Trinity, AL	MOB
Holyoke, CO	DEN
MA	SPR
Holyrood, KS	SAL
Homedale, ID	B
Homer, AK	ANC
NY	SY
Homer City, PA	PBR
Homestead, FL	MIA
PA	PIT
Hometown, IL	CHI
Homewood, IL	CHI
Homosassa, FL	SP
Honaunau, HI	HON
Hondo, TX	SAT
Honeoye, NY	ROC
Honeoye Falls, NY	ROC
Honesdale, PA	SCR
Honey Brook, PA	PH
Honokaa, HI	HON
Honolulu, HI	HON
Hood River, OR	BAK
Hooksett, NH	MAN
Hoonah, AK	JUN
Hoopa, CA	SR

Hooper, NE	OM
Hooper Bay, AK	FBK
Hoopeston, IL	PEO
Hooppole, IL	PEO
Hoosick Falls, NY	ALB
Hooversville, PA	ALT
Hopatcong, NJ	PAT
Hope, AR	LR
KS	SAL
ND	FAR
Hope Mills, NC	R
Hopedale, MA	WOR
OH	STU
Hopewell, NJ	TR
VA	RIC
Hopewell Junction, NY	NY
Hopewell Township, PA	PIT
Hopkins, MN	STP
Hopkins Park, IL	JOL
Hopkinsville, KY	OWN
Hopkinton, IA	DUB
MA	BO
NY	OG
RI	PRO
Hoquiam, WA	SEA
Horicon, WI	MIL
Horizon City, TX	ELP
Hormigueros, PR	MGZ
Hornell, NY	ROC
Hornick, IA	SC
Horseheads, NY	ROC
Horseshoe Bay, TX	AUS
Horseshoe Bend, AR	LR
ID	B
Horsham, PA	PH
Horton, KS	KCK
Hortonville, WI	GB
Hoschton, GA	ATL
Hosmer, SD	SFS
Hospers, IA	SC
Hostyn, TX	VIC
Hostyn Hill, TX	AUS
Hot Springs, AR	LR
NC	CHL
SD	RC
VA	RIC
Hot Springs National Park, AR	LR
Hot Springs Village, AR	LR
Houck, AZ	GLP
Houghton, IA	DAV
MI	MAR
Houghton Lake, MI	GAY
Houlton, ME	PRT
Houma, LA	HT
Housatonic, MA	SPR
House Springs, MO	STL
Houseville, NY	OG
Houston, MN	WIN
MO	SPC
TX	GAL
TX	OLL
TX	PBR
TX	STN
Houtzdale, PA	E
Hoven, SD	SFS
Howard, SD	SFS
WI	GB
Howard City, MI	GR
Howardstown, KY	L
Howell, MI	LAN
Howell Township, NJ	TR
Howells, NE	OM
Howes, SD	RC
Howland, ME	PRT
Hoxie, KS	SAL
Hoyt Lakes, MN	DUL
Hubbard, OH	Y
Hubbardston, MI	GR
Hubbell, MI	MAR
Hubertus, WI	MIL
Hudson, FL	SP
MA	BO
MI	LAN
NH	MAN
NY	ALB
NY	STF
OH	CLV
PA	SCR
WI	SUP
Hudson Falls, NY	ALB
Huffman, TX	GAL
Hughestown, PA	SCR
Hughson, CA	STO
Hugo, MN	STP
OK	TLS
Hugoton, KS	DOD
Hull, MA	BO
Humacao, PR	CGS
Humacao Playa, PR	CGS
Humble, TX	GAL
Humboldt, IA	SC

KS	WCH
SD	SFS
TN	MEM
WI	GB
Hume, IL	SFD
Humphrey, NE	OM
NY	BUF
Hungerford, TX	VIC
Hunt Valley, MD	BAL
Hunter, ND	FAR
NY	STF
Huntersville, NC	CHL
Huntimer, SD	SFS
Huntingburg, IN	EVN
Huntingdon, PA	ALT
TN	MEM
Huntingdon Valley, PA	PH
Huntington, CT	BGP
IN	FTW
MA	SPR
NY	RVC
WV	WH
Huntington Beach, CA	ORG
Huntington Park, CA	LA
Huntington Station, NY	RVC
Huntingtown, MD	WDC
Huntley, IL	RCK
Huntsville, AL	BIR
AR	LR
OH	CIN
TX	GAL
UT	SLC
Hurdsfield, ND	FAR
Hurley, NM	LSC
NY	NY
WI	SUP
Huron, CA	FRS
OH	TOL
SD	SFS
Hurricane, WV	WH
Hurt, VA	RIC
Hurtsboro, AL	MOB
Hutchinson, KS	WCH
MN	NU
Huttonsville, WV	WH
Hyannis, MA	FR
Hyattsville, MD	WDC
Hyde Park, NY	NY
VT	BUR
Hydes, MD	BAL
Ida, MI	DET
Ida Grove, IA	SC
Idabel, OK	TLS
Idaho City, ID	B
Idaho Falls, ID	B
Idaho Springs, CO	DEN
Idalou, TX	LUB
Idyllwild, CA	SB
Idylwilde, SD	SFS
Ignacio, CO	PBL
Ilasco, MO	JC
Iliff, CO	DEN
Ilion, NY	ALB
Illiopolis, IL	SFD
Imlay City, MI	DET
Immaculata, PA	PH
Immokalee, FL	VEN
Imogene, IA	DM
Imperial, CA	SD
MO	STL
NE	LIN
PA	PIT
Inarajan, GU	AGN
Inchelium, WA	SPK
Incline Village, NV	RNO
Independence, IA	DUB
KS	WCH
KY	COV
LA	BR
MO	KC
OH	CLV
OR	P
WI	LC
Indialantic, FL	ORL
Indian Creek, MA	SPR
MO	JC
WI	LC
Indian Grove, MO	JC
Indian Head, MD	WDC
Indian Island, ME	PRT
Indian Lake, NY	OG
Indian Orchard, MA	SPR
Indian River, MI	GAY
Indian Rocks Beach, FL	SP
Indian Township, ME	PRT
Indiana, PA	GBG
Indiana Harbor Co., IN	PRM
Indianapolis, IN	IND
IN	PRM
Indianola, IA	DM
MS	JKS

NE	LIN
Indiantown, FL	PMB
Indio, CA	SB
Industry, PA	PIT
Inez, TX	VIC
Ingalls, KS	DOD
Ingleside, IL	CHI
TX	CC
Inglewood, CA	LA
Ingram, PA	PIT
Inkerman, PA	SCR
Inkster, MI	DET
Inlet, NY	OG
Ino, WI	SUP
Institute, WI	GB
Interlachen, FL	STA
Interlaken, NY	ROC
International Falls, MN	DUL
Inver Grove Heights, MN	STP
Inverness, FL	SP
IL	CHI
Inwood, NY	RVC
WV	WH
Iola, KS	WCH
Iona, MN	WIN
Ione, CA	SAC
OR	BAK
WA	SPK
Ionia, IA	DUB
MI	GR
Iota, LA	LAF
Iowa, LA	LKC
Iowa City, IA	DAV
Iowa Falls, IA	DUB
Iowa Park, TX	FWT
Ipswich, MA	BO
SD	SFS
Ipwutek, FM	CI
Ireland, IN	EVN
Irish Settlement, IA	DM
Iron Mountain, MI	MAR
Iron River, MI	MAR
WI	SUP
Irons, MI	GR
Ironton, MO	SPC
OH	STU
Ironwood, MI	MAR
Iroquois, SD	SFS
Irvine, CA	ORG
KY	LEX
Irving, TX	DAL
TX	PBR
Irvington, KY	OWN
NJ	NEW
Irvington-on-the-Hudson, NY	NY
Irwin, IL	JOL
PA	GBG
Irwindale, CA	LA
Isaar, WI	GB
Isabela, PR	ARE
Isanti, MN	SCL
Iselin, NJ	MET
PA	GBG
Ishpeming, MI	MAR
Island Falls, ME	PRT
Island Grove, IL	SFD
Island Park, NY	RVC
Island Pond, VT	BUR
Isle Brevelle, LA	ALX
Isle La Motte, VT	BUR
Isleta, NM	SFE
Isleton, CA	SAC
Islip, NY	RVC
Islip Terrace, NY	RVC
Issaquah, WA	SEA
Issue, MD	WDC
Itasca, IL	JOL
Ithaca, MI	SAG
NY	ROC
Ivanhoe, MN	NU
Ivesdale, IL	PEO
Jackman, ME	PRT
Jacksboro, TN	KNX
TX	FWT
Jackson, CA	SAC
GA	ATL
KY	LEX
MI	LAN
MN	WIN
MO	SPC
MS	JKS
NE	OM
NJ	TR
OH	COL
PA	SCR
TN	MEM
WY	CHY
Jacksonport, WI	GB
Jacksonville, AL	BIR
AR	LR
FL	OLD

FL	PSC
FL	SAM
FL	STA
IL	SFD
NC	R
TX	TYL
Jacksonville Beach, FL	STA
Jacob's Prairie, MN	SCL
Jacumba, CA	SD
Jaffrey, NH	MAN
Jal, NM	LSC
Jamaica, IA	DM
NY	BRK
Jamaica Estates, NY	BRK
NY	NY
Jamaica Plain, MA	BO
MA	SAM
Jamesburg, NJ	MET
Jamestown, KS	SAL
KY	L
ND	FAR
NY	BUF
OH	CIN
RI	PRO
Jamesville, NY	SY
Jamison, PA	PH
Jamul, CA	SD
Janesville, MN	WIN
WI	MAD
Jarrell, TX	AUS
Jasonville, IN	EVN
Jasper, AL	BIR
IN	EVN
MN	WIN
TX	BEA
Java Center, NY	BUF
Jay, ME	PRT
Jayuya, PR	PCE
Jeanerette, LA	LAF
Jeannette, PA	GBG
PA	SJP
Jeffers, MN	WIN
Jefferson, IA	SC
LA	NO
MA	WOR
NC	CHL
OH	Y
SD	SFS
TX	TYL
WI	MAD
Jefferson Boro, PA	PIT
Jefferson City, MO	JC
TN	KNX
Jeffersontown, KY	L
Jeffersonville, IN	IND
NY	NY
Jellico, KY	LEX
TN	KNX
Jemez Pueblo, NM	SFE
Jemez Springs, NM	SFE
Jena, LA	ALX
Jenison, MI	GR
Jenkins, KY	LEX
Jenkintown, PA	PH
PA	PHU
Jennings, LA	LKC
MO	STL
Jensen Beach, FL	PMB
Jericho, WI	GB
Jermyn, PA	SCR
Jerome, AZ	PHX
ID	B
PA	PBR
Jersey City, NJ	NEW
NJ	PHU
NJ	PSC
Jersey Shore, PA	SCR
Jerseyville, IL	SFD
Jessenland, MN	NU
Jessie, ND	FAR
Jessup, MD	BAL
PA	PSC
PA	SCR
Jesup, GA	SAV
IA	DUB
Jetmore, KS	DOD
Jewell, IA	DUB
Jewett, OH	STU
Jewett City, CT	NOR
Jim Falls, WI	LC
Jim Thorpe, PA	ALN
Joanna, SC	CHR
Joelton, TN	NSH
Johannesburg, MI	GAY
John Day, OR	BAK
Johns Island, SC	CHR
Johnsburg, IL	RCK
MN	WIN
WI	MIL
Johnson, KS	DOD
Johnson City, NY	STF
NY	SY
TN	KNX
Johnsonburg, PA	E
Johnsonville, NY	ALB
Johnston, IA	DM
RI	PRO
Johnston City, IL	BEL
Johnstown, CO	DEN
NY	ALB
OH	COL
PA	ALT
PA	PBR
PA	SJP
Joliet, IL	JOL
IL	PRM
Jolon, CA	MRY
Jones, OK	OKL
Jonesboro, AR	LR
GA	ATL
Jonesborough, TN	KNX
Jonesburg, MO	JC
Joplin, MO	SPC
Joppa, MD	BAL
Jordan, MN	STP
NY	SY
OR	P
Jordan Valley, OR	BAK
Josephville, MO	STL
Joshua Tree, CA	SB
Jourdanton, TX	SAT
Juana Diaz, PR	PCE
Judice, LA	LAF
Julesburg, CO	DEN
Julian, CA	SD
Jump River, WI	SUP
Juncos, PR	CGS
Junction, OH	TOL
TX	SAN
Junction City, KS	SAL
OH	COL
OR	P
WI	LC
Juneau, AK	JUN
WI	MIL
Juno Beach, FL	PMB
Jupiter, FL	PMB
Justice, IL	CHI
Kadoka, SD	RC
Kahoka, MO	JC
Kahuku, HI	HON
Kahului, HI	HON
Kailua, HI	HON
Kalaheo, HI	HON
Kalamazoo, MI	KAL
Kalaupapa, HI	HON
Kalaupapa, Molokai, HI	HON
Kalida, OH	TOL
Kalispell, MT	HEL
Kalkaska, MI	GAY
Kaltag, AK	FBK
Kamiah, ID	B
Kampsville, IL	SFD
Kamuela, HI	HON
Kanab, UT	SLC
Kandiyohi, MN	NU
Kane, PA	E
Kaneohe, HI	HON
Kankakee, IL	JOL
Kanopolis, KS	SAL
Kansas, OH	TOL
Kansas City, KS	KCK
MO	KC
Kansas City North, MO	KC
Kansasville, WI	MIL
Kapaa, HI	HON
Kaplan, LA	LAF
Karlsruhe, ND	FAR
Karlstad, MN	CR
Karnes City, TX	SAT
Kaskaskia, IL	BEL
Kasson, MN	WIN
Katonah, NY	NY
Katy, TX	GAL
Kaufman, TX	DAL
Kaukauna, WI	GB
Kaunakakai, HI	HON
Kawkawlin, MI	SAG
Kayenta, AZ	GLP
Keams Canyon, AZ	GLP
Keansburg, NJ	TR
Kearney, MO	KC
NE	GI
Kearneysville, WV	WH
Kearns, UT	SLC
Kearny, AZ	TUC
NJ	NEW
Keaukaha, Hilo, HI	HON
Keene, NH	MAN
NY	OG
Keeseville, NY	OG
Keewatin, MN	DUL
Keizer, OR	P
Kekaha, HI	HON
Kelayres, PA	ALN
Keller, TX	FWT
WA	SPK
Kelley's Island, OH	TOL
Kelliher, MN	CR
Kellnersville, WI	GB
Kellogg, ID	B
MN	WIN
Kelly, KS	KCK
Kelso, MO	SPC
WA	SEA
Kemmerer, WY	CHY
Kenai, AK	ANC
Kendall, NY	BUF
WI	LC
Kendall Park, NJ	MET
Kendallville, IN	FTW
Kenedy, TX	SAT
Kenel, SD	RC
Kenesaw, NE	LIN
Kenilworth, NJ	NEW
Kenmare, ND	BIS
Kenmore, NY	BUF
NY	STF
Kennasaw, GA	ATL
Kennebec, SD	RC
Kennebunk, ME	PRT
Kennebunkport, ME	PRT
Kennedy Township, PA	PIT
Kenner, LA	NO
Kennesaw, GA	ATL
Kennett, MO	SPC
Kennett Square, PA	PH
Kennewick, WA	YAK
Kenosha, WI	MIL
Kensal, ND	FAR
Kensington, CA	OAK
CT	HRT
MD	WDC
MN	SCL
Kent, CT	HRT
MN	SCL
OH	Y
PA	GBG
WA	SEA
Kentfield, CA	SFR
Kentland, IN	LFT
Kenton, KY	COV
OH	COL
Kenton Hills, KY	COV
Kenyon, MN	STP
Keokuk, IA	DAV
Keota, IA	DAV
Kerhonkson, NY	STF
Kerman, CA	FRS
Kermit, TX	ELP
Kernersville, NC	CHL
Kerrville, TX	SAT
Kersey, PA	E
Keshena, WI	GB
Keswick, IA	DAV
Ketchikan, AK	JUN
Kettle Falls, WA	SPK
Keuterville, ID	B
Kew Gardens, NY	BRK
Kewanee, IL	PEO
Kewanna, IN	LFT
Kewaskum, WI	MIL
Kewaunee, WI	GB
Key Biscayne, FL	MIA
Key Largo, FL	MIA
Key West, FL	MIA
IA	DUB
Keyesville, WI	LC
Keyport, NJ	TR
Keyser, WV	WH
Keystone Heights, FL	STA
Kickapoo, IL	PEO
Kiel, WI	GB
Kieler, WI	MAD
Kihei, HI	HON
Kilgore, TX	TYL
Kilkenny, MN	STP
Kill Devil Hills, NC	R
Killdeer, ND	BIS
Killeen, TX	AUS
Killingworth, CT	NOR
Kilmarnock, VA	ARL
Kiln, MS	BLX
Kimball, MN	SCL
NE	GI
SD	SFS
Kimberling City, MO	SPC
Kimberly, WI	GB
Kimberton, PA	PH
Kimeo, KS	SAL
Kimmswick, MO	STL
Kincaid, IL	SFD
Kinde, MI	SAG
Kinder, LA	LKC
Kindred, ND	FAR
King, WI	GB
King City, CA	MRY
King Ferry, NY	ROC
King of Prussia, PA	PH
Kingfisher, OK	OKL
Kingman, AZ	PHX
KS	WCH
Kings Park, NY	RVC
Kingsburg, CA	FRS
Kingsford, MI	MAR
Kingsford Heights, IN	GRY
Kingsland, TX	AUS
Kingsley, IA	SC
Kingsport, TN	KNX
Kingston, MA	BO
NY	NY
PA	PSC
PA	SCR
Kingstree, SC	CHR
Kingsville, OH	Y
TX	CC
Kingwood, TX	GAL
WV	WH
Kinloch, MO	STL
Kinmundy, IL	BEL
Kinnelon, NJ	PAT
Kinross, IA	DAV
Kinsley, KS	DOD
Kinsman, IL	JOL
OH	Y
Kinston, NC	R
Kintyre, ND	FAR
Kiowa, KS	DOD
Kirby, OH	TOL
TX	SAT
Kirbyville, TX	BEA
Kirkland, WA	SEA
Kirksville, MO	JC
Kirkwood, MO	STL
NY	SY
Kirtland, OH	CLV
Kissimmee, FL	ORL
Kittanning, PA	GBG
Kittery, ME	PRT
Kitty Hawk, NC	R
Klacking Creek, MI	GAY
Klamath Falls, OR	BAK
Kleinwood, LA	ALX
Klondike, WI	GB
Kloten, WI	GB
Knapp Creek, NY	BUF
Knights Landing, CA	SAC
Knightstown, IN	IND
Knottsville, KY	OWN
Knowlton, WI	LC
Knox, IN	GRY
ND	FAR
Knox City, TX	FWT
Knoxville, IA	DAV
TN	KNX
Kodiak, AK	ANC
Koerth, TX	VIC
Kohler, WI	MIL
Kokomo, IN	LFT
Koloa, HI	HON
Kolonia, FM	CI
Kolonia, Pohnpei, FM	CI
Konawa, OK	OKL
Koppel, PA	PIT
Korona, FL	STA
Koror, FM	CI
Koror, Palau, PW	CI
Kosciusko, MS	JKS
Kosciuszko, TX	SAT
Kossuth, WI	GB
Kotlik, AK	FBK
Kotzebue, AK	FBK
Kountze, TX	BEA
Kouts, IN	GRY
Kovar, TX	AUS
Koyukuk, AK	FBK
Kraemer, LA	HT
Krakow, MO	STL
NE	OM
WI	GB
Kranzburg, SD	SFS
Krebs, OK	TLS
Kremmling, CO	DEN
Krok, WI	GB
Krotz Springs, LA	LAF
Kula, HI	HON
Kulpmont, PA	HBG
Kutztown, PA	ALN
Kwajalein, MH	MI
Kyle, SD	RC
TX	AUS
L'Anse, MI	MAR
La Canada Flintridge, CA	LA
La Crescent, MN	WIN

La Crescenta, CA	ARM
CA	LA
La Crosse, WI	LC
La Feria, TX	BWN
La Grande, OR	BAK
La Grange, IL	CHI
TX	AUS
La Grange Park, IL	CHI
La Habra, CA	ORG
La Jolla, CA	SD
La Joya, NM	SFE
TX	BWN
La Junta, CO	PBL
La Marque, TX	GAL
La Mesa, CA	SD
NM	LSC
La Mirada, CA	LA
La Motte, IA	DUB
La Moure, ND	FAR
La Pine, OR	BAK
La Place, LA	NO
La Plata, MD	WDC
La Porte, IN	GRY
TX	GAL
La Porte City, IA	DUB
La Pryor, TX	SAT
La Puente, CA	LA
La Quinta, CA	SB
La Rue, OH	COL
La Salle, IL	PEO
La Verne, CA	LA
La Vernia, TX	SAT
Labadieville, LA	BR
LaBelle, FL	VEN
Lac du Flambeau, WI	SUP
LaCenter, KY	OWN
Lacey, WA	SEA
Lackawanna, NY	BUF
NY	STF
Lacombe, LA	NO
Lacon, IL	PEO
Lacona, IA	DM
NY	SY
Laconia, NH	MAN
LaConner, WA	SEA
LaCoste, TX	SAT
LaCrosse, KS	DOD
Lacrosse, WA	SPK
LaCygne, KS	KCK
Ladd, IL	PEO
Ladue, MO	STL
Lady Lake, FL	ORL
Ladysmith, WI	SUP
Lafargeville, NY	OG
Lafayette, CA	OAK
CO	DEN
IN	LFT
LA	LAF
LA	OLL
MN	NU
NJ	PAT
NY	SY
OR	P
TN	NSH
Lafayette Hill, PA	PH
Lafferty, OH	STU
Lafitte, LA	NO
Laflin, PA	SCR
LaFollette, TN	KNX
Lago Vista, TX	AUS
LaGrange, GA	ATL
IN	FTW
KY	L
TX	AUS
LaGrange Park, IL	CHI
Lagro, IN	FTW
Laguna, NM	GLP
Laguna Beach, CA	ORG
Laguna Hills, CA	ORG
Laguna Niguel, CA	ORG
Lagunitas, CA	SFR
Lahaina, HI	HON
Laingsburg, MI	LAN
Lajas, PR	MGZ
Lake Andes, SD	SFS
Lake Ariel, PA	SCR
Lake Arrowhead, CA	SB
Lake Arthur, LA	LKC
Lake Benton, MN	NU
Lake Charles, LA	LKC
LA	OLL
Lake City, FL	STA
IA	SC
MI	GAY
MN	WIN
SC	CHR
SD	SFS
TN	KNX
Lake Clear, NY	OG
Lake Crystal, MN	WIN
Lake Dallas, TX	FWT
Lake Easton, VA	RIC
Lake Elmo, MN	STP
Lake Elsinore, CA	SB
Lake Eunice Township, MN	CR
Lake Five, WI	MIL
Lake Forest, CA	ORG
IL	CHI
Lake Geneva, WI	MIL
Lake George, NY	ALB
Lake Harmony, PA	ALN
Lake Havasu City, AZ	PHX
Lake Henry, MN	SCL
Lake Hopatcong, NJ	PAT
Lake Itasca, MN	CR
Lake Jackson, TX	GAL
Lake Katrine, NY	NY
Lake Leelanau, MI	GAY
Lake Lillian, MN	NU
Lake Linden, MI	MAR
Lake Luzerne, NY	ALB
Lake Mills, IA	DUB
WI	MAD
Lake Milton, OH	Y
Lake Nebagamon, WI	SUP
Lake Odessa, MI	GR
Lake Orion, MI	DET
Lake Oswego, OR	P
Lake Ozark, MO	JC
Lake Park, MN	CR
Lake Placid, FL	VEN
NY	OG
Lake Pleasant, NY	OG
Lake Providence, LA	SHP
Lake Reno, MN	SCL
Lake Ridge, VA	ARL
Lake Ronkonkoma, NY	RVC
Lake St. Croix Beach, MN	STP
Lake St. Louis, MO	STL
Lake San Marcos, CA	SD
Lake Silkworth, PA	SCR
Lake Station, IN	GRY
Lake Tamarisk, CA	SB
Lake Tomahawk, WI	SUP
Lake View, NY	BUF
Lake Villa, IL	CHI
Lake Village, AR	LR
IN	LFT
Lake Wales, FL	ORL
Lake Williams, ND	FAR
Lake Wilson, MN	WIN
Lake Winola, PA	SCR
Lake Worth, FL	PMB
FL	PSC
Lake Zurich, IL	CHI
Lakefield, MN	WIN
Lakehurst, NJ	TR
Lakeland, FL	ORL
GA	SAV
LA	BR
NY	SY
Lakeport, CA	SR
MI	DET
NH	MAN
Lakeside, CA	SD
Lakeview, MI	GR
OR	BAK
Lakeville, CT	HRT
IN	FTW
MA	BO
MN	STP
Lakewood, CA	LA
CO	DEN
NJ	TR
NY	BUF
OH	CLV
OH	PRM
WA	SEA
WI	GB
Lakewood Club, MI	GR
Lakin, KS	DOD
Lakota, ND	FAR
Lamar, CO	PBL
MO	SPC
Lamberton, MN	NU
Lambertville, NJ	MET
Lame Deer, MT	GF
Lamesa, TX	LUB
Lamoille, MN	WIN
Lamont, CA	FRS
IA	DUB
Lampasas, TX	AUS
Lanai City, HI	HON
Lanark, WI	LC
Lanark Village, FL	PT
Lancaster, CA	LA
KY	LEX
MA	WOR
MN	CR
NH	MAN
NY	BUF
NY	STF
OH	COL
PA	HBG
SC	CHR
TX	DAL
WI	MAD
Lancing, TN	KNX
Land O'Lakes, FL	SP
Landeck, OH	TOL
Lander, WY	CHY
Landisville, NJ	CAM
Land-O'-Lakes, WI	SUP
Landover Hills, MD	WDC
Lanesboro, MA	SPR
MN	WIN
Lanesville, IN	IND
Lanett, AL	BIR
Langdon, ND	FAR
Langford, NY	BUF
Langhorne, PA	PH
PA	PHU
Langlade, WI	GB
Langley, OK	TLS
WA	SEA
Lanham, MD	WDC
Lanham-Seabrook, MD	WDC
Lankin, ND	FAR
Lansdale, PA	PH
PA	PHU
Lansdowne, MD	BAL
PA	PH
Lansford, PA	ALN
PA	PSC
Lansford-Summit Hill, PA	ALN
Lansing, IA	DUB
IL	CHI
KS	KCK
MI	LAN
MI	NTN
NY	ROC
Lantana, FL	PMB
Laona, WI	GB
Lapeer, KS	KCK
MI	DET
LaPointe, WI	SUP
Laporte, MN	CR
Lapwai, ID	B
Laramie, WY	CHY
Larchmont, NY	NY
Larchwood, IA	SC
Laredo, TX	CC
Lares, PR	ARE
Largo, FL	SP
MD	WDC
Larimore, ND	FAR
Larks Lake, MI	GAY
Larkspur, CA	SFR
Larksville, PA	SCR
Larned, KS	DOD
Larose, LA	HT
Las Animas, CO	PBL
Las Cruces, NM	LSC
NM	VNN
Las Marias, PR	MGZ
Las Piedras, PR	CGS
Las Vegas, NM	SFE
NV	LAV
NV	OLL
NV	VNN
Lastrup, MN	SCL
Latham, NY	ALB
Latium, TX	AUS
Laton, CA	FRS
Latrobe, PA	GBG
PA	SJP
Lattimer Mines, PA	SCR
Laughlin, NV	LAV
LaUnion, NM	LSC
Laurel, MD	BAL
MD	WDC
MS	BLX
MT	GF
NE	OM
Laurence Harbor, NJ	MET
Laurens, IA	SC
Laurie, MO	JC
Laurinburg, NC	R
Lavallette, NJ	TR
Laveen, AZ	PHX
Laverock, PA	PH
Lawler, IA	DUB
Lawrence, KS	KCK
MA	BO
MA	NTN
MA	SAM
NE	LIN
PA	PIT
Lawrenceburg, IN	IND
KY	LEX
TN	NSH
Lawrenceton, MO	STL
Lawrenceville, GA	ATL
IL	BEL
NJ	TR
Lawtell, LA	LAF
Lawton, OK	OKL
Layton, UT	SLC
Le Center, MN	STP
Le Claire-Princeton, IA	DAV
Le Mars, IA	SC
Le Roy, MN	WIN
NY	BUF
WI	MIL
Le Sueur, MN	STP
Lead, SD	RC
Leadore, ID	B
Leadville, CO	COS
League City, TX	GAL
Leander, TX	AUS
Leavenworth, KS	KCK
MN	NU
WA	YAK
Leawood, KS	KCK
Lebanon, CT	NOR
IL	BEL
IN	LFT
KY	L
MO	SPC
NH	MAN
OH	CIN
OR	P
PA	HBG
TN	NSH
VA	RIC
Lebanon Junction, KY	L
Lebanon Township, WI	GB
Lebeau, LA	LAF
Lecanto, FL	SP
Leckrone, PA	GBG
Lecompte, LA	ALX
Ledyard, IA	SC
Lee, IL	RCK
MA	SPR
Lee Center, NY	SY
Lee's Summit, MO	KC
Leechburg, PA	GBG
Leeds, AL	BIR
MA	SPR
ND	FAR
Leesburg, FL	ORL
VA	ARL
Leesville, LA	ALX
Leetonia, OH	Y
Lefor, ND	BIS
Leggett, CA	SR
Lehigh Acres, FL	VEN
Lehighton, PA	ALN
Leicester, MA	WOR
NY	ROC
Leigh, NE	OM
Leipsic, OH	TOL
Leisenring, PA	GBG
PA	PBR
Leisure City, FL	MIA
Leitchfield, KY	OWN
Leland, MS	JKS
Lemay, MO	STL
Lemhi, ID	B
Lemmon, SD	RC
Lemon Grove, CA	SD
Lemont, IL	CHI
IL	LIT
Lemoore, CA	FRS
Lena, IL	RCK
WI	GB
Lenexa, KS	KCK
Lenni, PA	PH
Lennox, SD	SFS
Lenoir, NC	CHL
Lenoir City, TN	KNX
Lenox, IA	DM
MA	SPR
Lenox Dale, MA	SPR
Leo, MN	CR
Leola, SD	SFS
Leominster, MA	WOR
Leon, IA	DM
Leon Springs, TX	SAT
Leonardtown, MD	WDC
Leone, AS	SPP
Leonia, NJ	NEW
Leonore, IL	PEO
Leonville, LA	LAF
Leopold, IN	IND
MO	SPC
Leopolis, WI	GB
Leoti, KS	DOD
Leoville, KS	SAL
Lepua, AS	SPP
Lepuapua, AS	SPP
Leroy, LA	LAF
ND	FAR
LeRoy, NY	BUF

Leslie, MI	LAN
Lester Prairie, MN	NU
Lesterville, SD	SFS
Letcher, SD	SFS
Levelland, TX	LUB
Levittown, NY	RVC
PA	PH
PA	PSC
Lewis Center, OH	COL
Lewis Run, PA	E
Lewisburg, PA	HBG
TN	NSH
Lewisport, KY	OWN
Lewiston, ID	B
ME	PRT
MI	GAY
MN	WIN
NY	BUF
Lewistown, IL	PEO
MT	GF
PA	HBG
Lewisville, TX	FWT
TX	OLL
Lexington, KY	LEX
MA	ARM
MA	BO
MI	SAG
MN	STP
MO	KC
MS	JKS
NC	CHL
NE	GI
OH	TOL
SC	CHR
TN	MEM
TX	AUS
VA	RIC
Lexington Park, MD	WDC
Libby, MT	HEL
Liberal, KS	DOD
Liberty, IL	SFD
IN	IND
KS	WCH
MO	KC
NY	NY
OH	TOL
TN	NSH
TX	BEA
Liberty Boro, PA	PIT
Libertytown, MD	BAL
Libertyville, IL	CHI
Library, PA	PIT
Lidderdale, IA	SC
Lidgerwood, ND	FAR
Liebenthal, KS	DOD
Liftwood, DE	WIL
Lighthouse Point, FL	MIA
Ligonier, IN	FTW
PA	GBG
Liguori, MO	STL
Lihue, HI	HON
Lilburn, GA	ATL
Lillian, AL	MOB
Lillis, KS	KCK
Lilly, PA	ALT
Lillyville, IL	SFD
Lily, SD	SFS
Lima, NY	ROC
OH	TOL
WI	LC
WI	MIL
Lime Ridge, WI	MAD
Limeport, PA	ALN
Limerick, ME	PRT
Limestone, ME	PRT
NY	BUF
Limon, CO	COS
Lincoln, CA	SAC
IL	PEO
KS	SAL
MA	BO
ME	PRT
NE	LIN
NE	STN
NH	MAN
RI	PRO
WI	GB
Lincoln City, OR	P
Lincoln Park, MI	DET
NJ	PAT
Lincolndale, NY	NY
Lincolnton, NC	CHL
Lincroft, NJ	TR
Lind, WA	SPK
Linden, CA	STO
NJ	NEW
NJ	PSC
Lindenhurst, NY	RVC
Lindenwold, NJ	CAM
Lindsay, CA	FRS
NE	OM

TX	FWT
Lindsborg, KS	WCH
Lindstrom, MN	STP
Linesville, PA	E
Lineville, AL	BIR
Linfield, PA	PH
Linn, MO	JC
Lino Lakes, MN	STP
Linthicum, MD	BAL
Linthicum Heights, MD	BAL
Linton, IN	EVN
ND	BIS
Linwood, MA	WOR
MI	SAG
NJ	CAM
PA	PH
Lisbon, ME	PRT
ND	FAR
NH	MAN
NY	OG
OH	Y
Lisbon Falls, ME	PRT
Lisle, IL	JOL
Lismore, MN	WIN
Litchfield, CT	HRT
IL	SFD
ME	PRT
MN	NU
OH	CLV
Litchfield Park, AZ	PHX
Lithia Springs, GA	ATL
Lithonia, GA	ATL
Lititz, PA	HBG
Litomysl, MN	WIN
Little Canada, MN	STP
Little Chute, WI	GB
Little Compton, RI	PRO
Little Falls, MN	SCL
NJ	PAT
NY	ALB
NY	STF
Little Ferry, NJ	NEW
Little Kohler, WI	MIL
Little Meadows, PA	SCR
Little River, KS	WCH
Little Rock, AR	LR
Little Suamico, WI	GB
Little Turkey, IA	DUB
Little Valley, NY	BUF
Little York, NJ	MET
Littlefield, TX	LUB
Littlefork, MN	DUL
Littlestown, PA	HBG
Littleton, CO	DEN
MA	BO
NH	MAN
Live Oak, FL	STA
Lively Grove, IL	BEL
Livermore, CA	OAK
IA	SC
KY	OWN
Liverpool, NY	SY
Livingston, AL	BIR
CA	FRS
IL	SFD
MT	GF
NJ	NEW
TX	BEA
Livingston Manor, NY	NY
Livonia, LA	BR
MI	DET
MI	PRM
NY	ROC
Livonia Center, NY	ROC
Llano, TX	AUS
Lock Haven, PA	ALT
Lockbourne, OH	COL
Lockeford, CA	STO
Lockhart, TX	AUS
Lockport, IL	JOL
LA	HT
NY	BUF
Lockport South, IL	JOL
Locust Gap, PA	HBG
Locustdale, PA	HBG
Lodge Grass, MT	GF
Lodi, CA	STO
NJ	NEW
OH	CLV
WI	MAD
Logan, IA	DM
KS	SAL
OH	COL
UT	SLC
WV	WH
Logansport, IN	LFT
Lohrville, IA	SC
Loiza, PR	SJN
Loma, NE	LIN
Loma Linda, CA	SB
Lombard, IL	JOL

Lometa, TX	AUS
Lomice, ND	FAR
Lomira, WI	MIL
Lomita, CA	LA
Lompoc, CA	LA
Lonaconing, MD	BAL
London, KY	LEX
OH	COL
Londonderry, NH	MAN
Lone Pine, CA	FRS
Lone Rock, WI	LC
Lone Tree, IA	DAV
Lonedell, MO	STL
Long Beach, CA	LA
MS	BLX
NY	RVC
Long Branch, NJ	TR
Long Grove, IA	DAV
Long Island City, NY	BRK
NY	NY
NY	STF
Long Lake, MN	STP
NY	OG
WI	GB
Long Prairie, MN	SCL
Long Valley, NJ	PAT
Longbeach, CA	LA
Longboat Key, FL	VEN
Longmeadow, MA	SPR
Longmont, CO	DEN
Longport, NJ	CAM
Longview, TX	TYL
WA	SEA
Longville, MN	DUL
Longwood, FL	ORL
Lonsdale, MN	STP
Loogootee, IN	EVN
Lookout Mountain, GA	ATL
Loomis, CA	SAC
Loose Creek, MO	JC
Lopez, PA	PSC
Lorain, OH	CLV
OH	PRM
OH	ROM
OH	SJP
Lords Valley, PA	SCR
Lordsburg, NM	LSC
Lore City, OH	STU
Loreauville, LA	LAF
Loretto, IL	PEO
KS	DOD
KY	L
MN	STP
PA	ALT
TN	NSH
Los Alamitos, CA	ORG
Los Alamos, NM	SFE
Los Altos, CA	SJ
Los Altos Hills, CA	SJ
Los Angeles, CA	ARM
CA	LA
CA	OLL
CA	SB
CA	SFR
CA	STN
Los Banos, CA	FRS
Los Fresnos, TX	BWN
Los Gatos, CA	MRY
CA	SJ
CA	VNN
Los Lunas, NM	SFE
Los Nietos, CA	LA
Los Ojos, NM	SFE
Los Osos, CA	MRY
Losoya, TX	SAT
Lost Creek, PA	ALN
Lost Lake, WI	MIL
Lost Nation, IA	DAV
Lostant, IL	PEO
Lott, TX	AUS
Loudonville, NY	ALB
OH	CLV
Louisa, KY	LEX
LA	LAF
Louisburg, KS	KCK
Louisiana, MO	JC
Louisville, CO	DEN
KY	L
KY	OLL
MS	JKS
NY	OG
OH	Y
Loup City, NE	GI
Lourdes, IA	DUB
Loveland, CO	DEN
OH	CIN
Lovell, WY	CHY
Lovelock, NV	RNO
Loves Park, IL	RCK
Lovilia, IA	DAV
Loving, NM	LSC

Lovington, IL	SFD
NM	LSC
Lowell, IN	GRY
MA	BO
MI	GR
OH	STU
Lowellville, OH	Y
Lower Brule, SD	RC
Lower Burrell, PA	GBG
Lower Makefield, PA	PH
Lowville, NY	OG
Loyal, OK	OKL
WI	LC
Lubbock, TX	LUB
Lubec, ME	PRT
Lubeck, WV	WH
Lublin, WI	SUP
Lucan, MN	NU
Lucerne, IN	LFT
Lucerne Valley, CA	SB
Lucernemines, PA	GBG
Lucinda, PA	E
Ludington, MI	GR
Ludlow, KY	COV
MA	SPR
MA	STF
VT	BUR
Luebbering, MO	STL
Lufkin, TX	TYL
Lukachukai, AZ	GLP
Lukunor, FM	CI
Luling, LA	NO
TX	AUS
Lumberton, MS	BLX
NC	R
NM	GLP
TX	BEA
Lunenburg, MA	WOR
Luquillo, PR	SJN
Luray, VA	ARL
Lusk, WY	CHY
Lutherville, MD	BAL
Luverne, MN	WIN
Luxemburg, IA	DUB
MN	SCL
WI	GB
Luzerne, PA	SCR
Lycurgus, IA	DUB
Lydia, LA	LAF
Lyford, TX	BWN
Lykens, PA	HBG
Lyle, MN	WIN
Lyman, ME	PRT
Lynbrook, NY	RVC
Lynch, KY	LEX
NE	OM
Lynchburg, VA	RIC
Lynden, WA	SEA
Lyndhurst, NJ	NEW
OH	CLV
Lyndon Station, WI	LC
Lyndonville, NY	BUF
VT	BUR
Lyndora, PA	PBR
PA	PIT
PA	SJP
Lynn, MA	BO
Lynnfield, MA	BO
Lynnwood, WA	SEA
Lynwood, CA	LA
Lyon Mountain, NY	OG
Lyons, IL	CHI
KS	WCH
NE	OM
NY	ROC
OH	TOL
WI	MIL
Lyons Point, LA	LAF
Lytle, TX	SAT
Mabel, MN	WIN
Mabton, WA	YAK
Macclenny, FL	STA
Macdona, TX	SAT
Macedon, NY	ROC
Macedonia, OH	CLV
Machias, ME	PRT
NY	BUF
Mackinac Island, MI	MAR
Mackinaw City, MI	GAY
Mackville, WI	GB
Macomb, IL	PEO
MI	DET
Macon, GA	SAV
IL	SFD
MO	JC
Madawaska, ME	PRT
Maddock, ND	FAR
Madelia, MN	WIN
Madera, CA	FRS
Madison, AL	BIR
CT	HRT

FL	PT
IL	SFD
IL	STN
IN	IND
KS	WCH
ME	PRT
MN	NU
MS	JKS
MT	HEL
NE	OM
NJ	PAT
OH	CLV
SD	SFS
TN	NSH
VA	ARL
WI	MAD
WV	WH
Madison Heights, MI	DET
Madison Lake, MN	WIN
Madisonville, KY	OWN
LA	NO
TN	KNX
TX	GAL
Madonnaville, IL	BEL
Madras, OR	BAK
Madrid, IA	SC
NY	OG
Magee, MS	JKS
Maggie Valley, NC	CHL
Magna, UT	SLC
Magnolia, NJ	CAM
TX	GAL
Magnolia Springs, AL	MOB
Mahanoy City, PA	ALN
PA	PHU
PA	PSC
Mahanoy Plane, PA	ALN
Mahnomen, MN	CR
Mahomet, IL	PEO
Mahopac, NY	NY
Mahtomedi, MN	STP
Mahwah, NJ	NEW
NJ	PSC
Maina, GU	AGN
Maine, MN	SCL
NY	SY
Maizeville, PA	ALN
PA	PHU
Majuro, MH	MI
Makakilo, HI	HON
Makawao, HI	HON
Malaeloa, AS	SPP
Malaga, NJ	CAM
Malden, MA	BO
MO	SPC
Malibu, CA	LA
Mallard, IA	SC
Mallet, LA	LAF
Malojlo, GU	AGN
Malone, NY	OG
Maloy, IA	DM
Malta, MT	GF
Malvern, AR	LR
OH	STU
PA	PH
Malverne, NY	RVC
Mamaroneck, NY	NY
Mammoth, AZ	TUC
Mammoth Lakes, CA	STO
Mamou, LA	LAF
Man, WV	WH
Manahawkin, NJ	TR
Manalapan, NJ	TR
Manannah, MN	NU
Manasquan, NJ	TR
Manassas, VA	ARL
VA	PHU
Manati, PR	ARE
Manawa, WI	GB
Mancelona, MI	GAY
Manchaug, MA	WOR
Manchester, CT	HRT
IA	DUB
KY	LEX
MD	BAL
MI	LAN
MI	LIT
MO	STL
NH	MAN
NH	NTN
NH	STF
OH	CIN
PA	PIT
WA	SEA
Manchester by the Sea, MA	BO
Manchester Center, VT	BUR
Mancos, CO	PBL
Mandan, ND	BIS
Mandaree, ND	BIS
Manderson, SD	RC
Mandeville, LA	NO
Mangilao, GU	AGN
Mangum, OK	OKL
Manhasset, NY	RVC
Manhattan, IL	JOL
KS	SAL
Manhattan Beach, CA	LA
Manheim, PA	HBG
Manilla, IA	SC
Manistee, MI	GAY
Manistique, MI	MAR
Manito Station, WA	SPK
Manitou Beach, MI	LAN
Manitowish Waters, WI	SUP
Manitowoc, WI	GB
WI	MIL
Mankato, KS	SAL
MN	WIN
Manley, NE	LIN
Manlius, NY	SY
Manly, IA	DUB
Manning, IA	SC
Mannington, WV	WH
Manoa, PA	PH
Manor, TX	AUS
Manorhaven, NY	RVC
Manorville, NY	RVC
Mansfield, LA	SHP
MA	FR
MO	SPC
OH	TOL
PA	SCR
TX	FWT
Manson, IA	SC
Mansura, LA	ALX
Mantador, ND	FAR
Manteca, CA	STO
Manteno, IL	JOL
Manton, MI	GAY
Mantua, NJ	CAM
OH	Y
Manvel, ND	FAR
TX	GAL
Manville, NJ	MET
NJ	PHU
RI	PRO
Many, LA	SHP
Maple City, MI	GAY
Maple Glen, PA	PH
Maple Grove, MI	SAG
MN	STP
WI	GB
Maple Heights, OH	CLV
Maple Hill, KS	KCK
Maple Lake, MN	STP
Maple Mount, KY	OWN
Maple Park, IL	RCK
Maple River, IA	SC
Maple Shade, NJ	CAM
NJ	TR
Mapleton, IA	SC
MI	GAY
MN	WIN
WI	MIL
Maplewood, MN	STP
MO	STL
NJ	NEW
WI	GB
Maquoketa, IA	DUB
Marak, TX	AUS
Marana, AZ	TUC
Marathon, FL	MIA
NY	SY
Marathon City, WI	LC
Marble, MN	DUL
Marble Falls, TX	AUS
Marblehead, MA	BO
OH	PRM
OH	TOL
Marbury, AL	MOB
Marceline, MO	JC
Marcellus, NY	SY
Marchand, WI	GB
Marco Island, FL	VEN
Marcus, IA	SC
Marcus Hook, PA	PH
Marengo, IA	DAV
IL	RCK
Marfa, TX	ELP
Margaretville, NY	ALB
Margate, FL	MIA
NJ	CAM
Marguerite, PA	GBG
Maria Stein, OH	CIN
Mariah Hill, IN	EVN
Marianna, FL	PT
Maricao, PR	MGZ
Marienthal, KS	DOD
Marietta, GA	ATL
OH	STU
PA	HBG
Marina, CA	MRY
Marina Del Rey, CA	LA
Marine, IL	SFD
Marine City, MI	DET
Marine on St. Croix, MN	STP
Marinette, WI	GB
Maringouin, LA	BR
Marion, AL	BIR
IA	DUB
IL	BEL
IN	LFT
KS	WCH
KY	OWN
MA	FR
MI	GR
ND	FAR
NY	ROC
OH	COL
SD	SFS
VA	RIC
WI	GB
Marion Heights, PA	HBG
PA	PHU
Marionville, MO	SPC
Mariposa, CA	FRS
Markesan, WI	MAD
Markham, IL	CHI
Marks, MS	JKS
Marksville, LA	ALX
Marlboro, MA	BO
NJ	PHU
NJ	TR
NY	NY
Marlborough, CT	HRT
NH	MAN
Marlette, MI	SAG
Marlin, TX	AUS
Marlinton, WV	WH
Marlton, NJ	TR
Marmora, NJ	CAM
Marne, MI	GR
Marquette, MI	MAR
Marrero, LA	NO
Marriottsville, MD	BAL
Mars, PA	PIT
Mars Hill, ME	PRT
NC	CHL
Marseilles, IL	PEO
Marshall, AK	FBK
IL	SFD
MI	KAL
MN	NU
MO	JC
TX	TYL
WI	MAD
Marshalltown, IA	DUB
Marshfield, MA	BO
MO	SPC
WI	LC
Martin, KY	LEX
SD	RC
TN	MEM
Martindale, TX	AUS
Martinez, CA	OAK
TX	SAT
Martins Creek, PA	ALN
Martins Ferry, OH	STU
Martinsburg, MO	JC
WV	WH
Martinsville, IN	IND
NJ	MET
VA	RIC
WI	MAD
Martinton, IL	JOL
Marty, SD	SFS
Marvin, SD	SFS
Mary Esther, FL	PT
Mary's Home, MO	JC
Marydale, IL	BEL
Marydel, MD	WIL
Marygrove, OH	TOL
Maryhill, IA	SC
Maryknoll, NY	NY
Maryland Heights, MO	STL
Marylhurst, OR	P
Marysburg, MN	STP
Marysdale, OH	TOL
Marystown, MN	STP
Marysville, CA	SAC
KS	KCK
MI	DET
OH	COL
PA	HBG
WA	SEA
Marytown, WI	MIL
Maryville, IL	SFD
MO	KC
Marywood, OH	TOL
Masaryktown, FL	SP
Mascoutah, IL	BEL
Mashpee, MA	FR
Mason, MI	LAN
OH	CIN
TX	AUS
Mason City, IA	DUB
Masontown, PA	GBG
WV	WH
Masonville, IA	DUB
Massapequa, NY	RVC
Massapequa Park, NY	RVC
Massena, IA	DM
NY	OG
Massillon, OH	Y
Mastic Beach, NY	RVC
Masury, OH	Y
Matamoras, PA	SCR
Matawan, NJ	PSC
NJ	TR
Matherville, IL	PEO
Mathews, VA	RIC
Mathis, TX	CC
Mattapoisett, MA	FR
Mattawa, WA	YAK
Mattawan, MI	KAL
Mattese, MO	STL
Matteson, IL	CHI
Mattoon, IL	SFD
WI	GB
Mattydale, NY	SY
Mauldin, SC	CHR
Maumee, OH	TOL
Maunabo, PR	CGS
Maurepas, LA	BR
Maurice, LA	LAF
Mauriceville, TX	BEA
Mauston, WI	LC
Maximo, OH	Y
Maxwell, CA	SAC
PA	GBG
May's Lick, KY	COV
Mayaguez, PR	MGZ
Maybee, MI	DET
Maybrook, NY	NY
Mayetta, KS	KCK
Mayfield, KY	OWN
PA	SCR
SD	SFS
Mayhew Lake, MN	SCL
Maynard, MA	BO
OH	STU
Mays Landing, NJ	CAM
Maysel, WV	WH
Maysville, KY	COV
Maytown, IL	RCK
Mayville, MI	SAG
ND	FAR
NY	BUF
WI	MIL
Maywood, CA	LA
IL	CHI
NJ	NEW
Mazeppa, MN	WIN
Mazomanie, WI	MAD
McAdoo, PA	ALN
PA	PHU
PA	PSC
McAfee, NJ	PAT
McAlester, OK	TLS
McAllen, TX	BWN
McBain, MI	GAY
McCall, ID	B
McCamey, TX	SAN
McCartyville, OH	CIN
McCloud, CA	SAC
McClusky, ND	FAR
McComb, MS	JKS
McConchie, MD	WDC
McConnellsburg, PA	ALT
McConnelsville, OH	STU
McCook, NE	LIN
TX	BWN
McCool Junction, NE	LIN
McCracken, KS	DOD
McDonald, OH	Y
PA	PIT
McDonough, GA	ATL
McDowell, KS	SAL
McEwen, TN	NSH
McFarland, CA	FRS
WI	MAD
McGehee, AR	LR
McGrath, AK	FBK
McGregor, IA	DUB
MN	DUL
MN	STP
TX	AUS
McHenry, IL	RCK
ND	FAR
McIntire, IA	DUB
McIntosh, SD	RC
McKean, PA	E
McKees Rocks, PA	PBR
PA	PIT

PA	SJP
McKeesport, PA	PBR
PA	PIT
PA	ROM
PA	SJP
McKenzie Bridge, OR	P
McKinleyville, CA	SR
McKinney, TX	DAL
McLaughlin, SD	RC
McLean, VA	ARL
VA	NTN
McLeansboro, IL	BEL
McLoud, OK	OKL
McMechen, WV	WH
McMinnville, OR	P
TN	NSH
McNair, TX	GAL
McNary, AZ	GLP
McPherson, KS	WCH
McQuady, KY	OWN
McRae, GA	SAV
McSherrystown, PA	HBG
Mead, NE	LIN
Meade, KS	DOD
Meadowbrook, PA	PH
Meadowlands, PA	PIT
Meadville, PA	E
Mecca, CA	SB
Mechanic Falls, ME	PRT
Mechanicsburg, OH	CIN
PA	HBG
Mechanicsville, IA	DAV
MD	WDC
VA	RIC
Mechanicville, NY	ALB
Medart, FL	PT
Medaryville, IN	LFT
Medfield, MA	BO
Medford, MA	BO
MN	WIN
NJ	TR
NY	RVC
OK	OKL
OR	P
WI	SUP
Media, PA	PH
Mediania Alta Ward, Loiza, PR	SJN
Medical Lake, WA	SPK
Medicine Lodge, KS	DOD
Medina, ND	FAR
NY	BUF
OH	CLV
Medley's Neck, MD	WDC
Medora, IL	SFD
Medway, MA	BO
Meeker, CO	DEN
Megargel, TX	FWT
Mehlville, MO	STL
Meire Grove, MN	SCL
Melbourne, FL	ORL
KY	COV
Melbourne Beach, FL	ORL
Melcher, IA	DAV
Mellen, WI	SUP
Mellette, SD	SFS
Melrose, IA	DAV
MA	BO
MN	SCL
WI	LC
Melrose Park, IL	CHI
Melville, LA	LAF
NY	RVC
Melvindale, MI	DET
Memphis, MI	DET
MO	JC
TN	MEM
TX	AMA
Mena, AR	LR
Menahga, MN	SCL
Menands, NY	ALB
Menard, TX	SAN
Menasha, WI	GB
Mendham, NJ	PAT
Mendocino, CA	SR
Mendon, IL	SFD
MA	WOR
MI	KAL
NY	ROC
Mendota, CA	FRS
IL	PEO
MN	STP
Mendota Heights, MN	STP
Menlo Park, CA	SFR
CA	SJ
Menoken, ND	BIS
Menominee, IL	RCK
MI	MAR
NE	OM
Menomonee Falls, WI	MIL
Menomonie, WI	LC
Mentor, MN	CR

OH	CLV
Mentor-on-the-Lake, OH	PRM
Mentz, TX	VIC
Meppen, IL	SFD
Mequon, WI	MIL
Meraux, LA	NO
Merced, CA	FRS
Mercedes, TX	BWN
Mercer, PA	E
WI	SUP
Mercer Island, WA	SEA
Merchantville, NJ	CAM
Meredith, KS	SAL
NH	MAN
Meriden, CT	HRT
CT	PSC
KS	KCK
Meridian, ID	B
MS	JKS
PA	PIT
Merion, PA	PH
Merion Station, PA	PH
Merizo, GU	AGN
Mermentau, LA	LAF
Merrick, NY	RVC
Merrill, IA	SC
MI	SAG
OR	BAK
WI	SUP
Merrillville, IN	GRY
IN	PRM
Merrimac, MA	BO
Merrimack, NH	MAN
Merriman, NE	GI
Merritt Island, FL	ORL
Mesa, AZ	PHX
ID	B
Mescalero, NM	LSC
Meshoppen, PA	SCR
Mesilla, NM	LSC
Mesilla Park, NM	LSC
Meta, MO	JC
Metairie, LA	NO
Metaline Falls, WA	SPK
Metamora, IL	PEO
Methuen, MA	BO
MA	NTN
Metropolis, IL	BEL
Metuchen, NJ	MET
Metz, MI	GAY
Mexia, TX	AUS
Mexico, ME	PRT
MO	JC
NY	SY
Mexico Beach, FL	PT
Meyer, IA	DUB
Meyersdale, PA	ALT
Meyersville, TX	VIC
Miami, AZ	TUC
FL	MIA
FL	NTN
FL	PSC
FL	SAM
FL	SJP
OK	TLS
Miami Beach, FL	MIA
Miami Lakes, FL	MIA
Miami Shores, FL	MIA
Miami Springs, FL	MIA
Miamisburg, OH	CIN
Michael, IL	SFD
Michigan, ND	FAR
Michigan Center, MI	LAN
Michigan City, IN	GRY
Middle Lake, MN	NU
Middle Ridge, WI	LC
Middle River, MN	CR
Middle Village, NY	BRK
NY	NY
Middleboro, MA	BO
Middlebranch, OH	Y
Middleburg, FL	STA
VA	ARL
Middleburg Heights, OH	CLV
Middleburgh, NY	ALB
Middlebury, CT	HRT
VT	BUR
Middlefield, CT	NOR
OH	CLV
Middleport, NY	BUF
PA	PHU
Middlesboro, KY	LEX
Middlesex, NJ	MET
Middlesex County, VA	RIC
Middleton, MA	BO
WI	MAD
Middletown, CA	SR
CT	NOR
DE	WIL
MD	BAL
NJ	TR

NY	NY
NY	STF
OH	CIN
PA	HBG
RI	PRO
Middletown Springs, VT	BUR
Midland, MD	BAL
MI	SAG
PA	PIT
SD	RC
TX	SAN
Midland Park, NJ	NEW
Midlothian, IL	CHI
Midvale, UT	SLC
Midway City, CA	ORG
Miesville, MN	STP
Mifflintown, PA	HBG
Mikado, MI	GAY
Milaca, MN	SCL
Milan, IL	PEO
IN	IND
MI	LAN
MO	JC
NM	GLP
OH	TOL
TN	MEM
WI	LC
Milbank, SD	SFS
Mildred, PA	SCR
Miles, TX	SAN
Miles City, MT	GF
Milford, CT	HRT
DE	WIL
IA	SC
IN	FTW
MA	WOR
MI	DET
NH	MAN
NJ	MET
OH	CIN
PA	SCR
UT	SLC
Mililani Town, HI	HON
Mill Creek, WI	LC
Mill Valley, CA	SFR
Milladore, WI	LC
Millbrae, CA	OLL
CA	SFR
Millbrook, AL	MOB
NY	NY
Millbury, MA	WOR
Milledgeville, GA	ATL
Millen, GA	SAV
Miller, SD	SFS
Miller City, OH	TOL
Miller Heights, PA	ALN
Millers Falls, MA	SPR
Millersburg, OH	COL
PA	HBG
Millersville, MD	BAL
OH	TOL
PA	HBG
Millerville, MN	SCL
Millhousen, IN	IND
Millinocket, ME	PRT
Millis, MA	BO
Millstadt, IL	BEL
Milltown, NJ	MET
Millvale, PA	PIT
Millville, MA	WOR
NJ	CAM
NJ	PHU
OH	CIN
Millwood, MO	STL
Milmont Park, PA	PH
Milnor, ND	FAR
Milpitas, CA	SJ
Milroy, MN	NU
Milton, FL	PT
LA	LAF
MA	BO
ND	FAR
NY	NY
PA	HBG
VT	BUR
WI	MAD
Milton Freewater, OR	BAK
Miltonsburg, OH	STU
Miltonvale, KS	SAL
Milwaukee, WI	MIL
WI	NTN
WI	STN
Milwaukie, OR	P
Mims, FL	ORL
Minatare, NE	GI
Minden, LA	SHP
NE	LIN
Mineola, NY	RVC
TX	TYL
Mineral, VA	RIC
Mineral City, OH	COL

Mineral Point, WI	MAD
Mineral Ridge, OH	Y
Mineral Wells, TX	FWT
Minersville, PA	ALN
PA	PHU
PA	PSC
Minerva, OH	STU
Minetto, NY	SY
Mineville, NY	OG
Mingo Junction, OH	PBR
OH	STU
Minneapolis, KS	SAL
MN	OLL
MN	PRM
MN	STN
MN	STP
Minneiska, MN	WIN
Minneota, MN	NU
Minnesota City, MN	WIN
Minnesota Lake, MN	WIN
Minnetonka, MN	STP
Minnewaukan, ND	FAR
Minoa, NY	SY
Minocqua, WI	SUP
Minong, WI	SUP
Minonk, IL	PEO
Minooka, IL	JOL
Minot, ND	BIS
Minotola, NJ	CAM
Minster, OH	CIN
Minto, ND	FAR
Minturn, CO	DEN
Mio, MI	GAY
Miramar, FL	MIA
Mire, LA	LAF
Miriam, MI	GR
Mishawaka, IN	FTW
IN	LFT
IN	STN
Mishicot, WI	GB
Mission, KS	KCK
SD	RC
TX	BWN
Mission Hills, CA	LA
CA	ROM
Mission San Jose, CA	OAK
Mission Viejo, CA	ORG
Missoula, MT	HEL
Missouri City, TX	GAL
Missouri Valley, IA	DM
Mitchell, IN	IND
NE	GI
SD	SFS
WI	MIL
Mitchellville, MD	WDC
Moab, UT	SLC
Moberly, MO	JC
Mobile, AL	MOB
Mobridge, SD	SFS
Moca, PR	MGZ
Mocanaqua, PA	SCR
Mocksville, NC	CHL
Modesto, CA	STO
Modoc, IL	BEL
Moen, FM	CI
Mohall, ND	BIS
Mohawk, NY	ALB
Mohnton, PA	ALN
Mojave, CA	FRS
Mokane, MO	JC
Mokena, IL	JOL
Molalla, OR	P
Moline, IL	PEO
KS	WCH
Momence, IL	JOL
Mon Luis Island, AL	MOB
Monaca, PA	PIT
Monahans, TX	ELP
Monarch, MT	GF
Monches, WI	MIL
Moncks Corner, SC	CHR
Mondamin, IA	DM
Mondovi, WI	LC
Monee, IL	JOL
Monessen, PA	GBG
PA	PBR
Moneta, VA	RIC
Monett, MO	SPC
Mongmong, GU	AGN
Monmouth, IL	PEO
Monmouth Beach, NJ	TR
Monmouth Junction, NJ	MET
Monona, IA	DUB
Monongah, WV	WH
Monongahela, PA	PBR
PA	PIT
Monroe, CT	BGP
GA	ATL
LA	SHP
MI	DET
NC	CHL

NY	NY
OH	CIN
OR	P
WA	SEA
WI	MAD
Monroe City, MO	JC
Monroe-Duvall, WA	SEA
Monroeville, AL	MOB
IN	FTW
OH	TOL
PA	PBR
PA	PIT
Monrovia, CA	LA
Monsey, NY	NY
Monson, MA	SPR
Mont Belvieu, TX	BEA
Mont Clare, PA	PSC
Montague, MI	GR
NJ	PAT
TX	FWT
Montauk, NY	RVC
Montclair, CA	SB
NJ	NEW
Montdale, PA	SCR
Monte Vista, CO	PBL
Montebello, CA	LA
Montecito, CA	LA
Montegut, LA	HT
Montello, WI	MAD
Monterey, CA	MRY
IN	LFT
NE	OM
Monterey Park, CA	LA
Montevallo, AL	BIR
Montevideo, MN	NU
Montezuma, IN	IND
NY	ROC
OH	CIN
Montfort, WI	MAD
Montgomery, AL	MOB
IN	EVN
MN	STP
NY	NY
WV	WH
Montgomery Center, VT	BUR
Montgomery City, MO	JC
Monti, IA	DUB
Monticello, AR	LR
FL	PT
IA	DUB
IL	PEO
IN	LFT
KY	LEX
MN	STP
NY	NY
UT	SLC
Montoursville, PA	SCR
Montpelier, IN	LFT
OH	TOL
VA	RIC
VT	BUR
WI	GB
Montreal, WI	SUP
Montrose, CA	ARM
CA	LA
CO	PBL
IA	DAV
IL	SFD
MI	LAN
MO	KC
NY	NY
PA	SCR
SD	SFS
Montvale, NJ	NEW
Montville, CT	NOR
NJ	PAT
Monument, CO	COS
Moodus, CT	NOR
Moody, TX	AUS
Mooers, NY	OG
Mooers Forks, NY	OG
Moon Township, PA	PIT
Moonachie, NJ	NEW
Mooney Creek, KS	KCK
Moore, OK	OKL
Moore Haven, FL	VEN
Moorefield, WV	WH
Moorestown, NJ	TR
Mooresville, IN	IND
NC	CHL
Mooreton, ND	FAR
Moorhead, MN	CR
Moorland, IA	SC
Moorpark, CA	LA
Moose Lake, MN	DUL
Moosup, CT	NOR
Moquah, WI	SUP
Mora, MN	SCL
NM	SFE
Moraga, CA	OAK
Moran, MI	MAR
MN	SCL
Moravia, NY	ROC
Moreauville, LA	ALX
Morehead, KY	LEX
Morehead City, NC	R
Morenci, AZ	TUC
Moreno Valley, CA	SB
Morgan, MN	NU
TX	FWT
Morgan City, LA	HT
Morgan Hill, CA	SJ
Morganfield, KY	OWN
Morganton, NC	CHL
Morgantown, KY	OWN
WV	PBR
WV	WH
Morganza, LA	BR
MD	WDC
Morges, OH	STU
Moriarty, NM	SFE
Morongo Valley, CA	SB
Morovis, PR	ARE
Morrice, MI	LAN
Morrill, MN	SCL
Morrilton, AR	LR
Morris, IL	JOL
IN	IND
MN	SCL
NY	ALB
Morris Plains, NJ	PAT
Morrisdale, PA	E
Morrison, IL	RCK
MO	JC
Morrison Bluff, AR	LR
Morrisonville, IL	SFD
NY	OG
Morristown, NJ	PAT
NY	OG
SD	RC
TN	KNX
Morrisville, NY	SY
PA	PH
VT	BUR
Morro Bay, CA	MRY
Morrow, LA	LAF
OH	CIN
Morrowville, KS	SAL
Morse, LA	LAF
Morse Bluff, NE	LIN
Morton, IL	PEO
MN	NU
PA	PH
TX	LUB
WA	SEA
Morton Grove, IL	CHI
Moscow, ID	B
PA	PHU
PA	SCR
TN	MEM
Moselle, MO	STL
Moses Lake, WA	YAK
Mosinee, WI	LC
Moss Beach, CA	SFR
Moss Bluff, LA	LKC
Moss Point, MS	BLX
Motley, MN	SCL
Mott, ND	BIS
Moulton, AL	BIR
TX	VIC
Moultrie, GA	SAV
Mound, MN	STP
Mound Bayou, MS	JKS
Mound City, IL	BEL
KS	KCK
Moundsville, WV	WH
Mt. Airy, NC	CHL
Mt. Angel, OR	P
Mount Arlington, NJ	PAT
Mt. Ayr, IA	DM
Mount Calvary, WI	MIL
Mount Carbon, PA	ALN
Mount Carmel, IA	SC
IL	BEL
ND	FAR
OH	CIN
PA	HBG
PA	PHU
Mount Carroll, IL	RCK
Mount Clemens, MI	DET
Mount Dora, FL	ORL
Mount Ephraim, NJ	CAM
Mount Holly, NJ	TR
Mount Hope, NJ	PAT
Mount Horeb, WI	MAD
Mount Jewett, PA	E
Mount Joy, PA	HBG
Mt. Kisco, NY	NY
Mount Laurel, NJ	TR
Mt. Lebanon, PA	PIT
Mount Morris, MI	LAN
NY	ROC
Mount Olive, IL	SFD
Mount Orab, OH	CIN
Mount Pleasant, IA	DAV
MI	SAG
PA	GBG
TX	TYL
Mt. Pleasant, VI	STV
Mount Pocono, PA	SCR
Mt. Prospect, IL	CHI
Mount Rainier, MD	WDC
Mount Repose, OH	CIN
Mount Saint Francis, IN	IND
Mount St. Macrina, PA	PBR
Mount Savage, MD	BAL
Mount Shasta, CA	SAC
Mount Sinai, NY	RVC
Mount Sterling, IL	SFD
Mt. Sterling, KY	LEX
Mount Union, PA	ALT
Mount Vernon, AL	MOB
IA	DUB
IL	BEL
IN	EVN
KS	WCH
Mt. Vernon, KY	LEX
Mount Vernon, MO	SPC
Mt. Vernon, NY	NY
OH	COL
Mount Vernon, SD	SFS
WA	SEA
Mount Washington, KY	L
Mt. Zion, IL	SFD
Mountain City, TN	KNX
Mountain Grove, MO	SPC
Mountain Home, AR	LR
ID	B
TX	SAT
Mountain Home Air Force Base, ID	B
Mountain Lakes, NJ	PAT
Mountain Top, PA	SCR
Mountain View, CA	SFR
CA	SJ
HI	HON
MO	SPC
Mountain Village, AK	FBK
Mountainair, NM	SFE
Mountainside, NJ	NEW
Mountaintop, PA	SCR
Mountlake Terrace, WA	SEA
Moville, IA	SC
Mowata, LA	LAF
Moweaqua, IL	SFD
Moxee City, WA	YAK
Muenster, TX	FWT
Mukwonago, WI	MIL
Mulberry, KS	WCH
Muleshoe, TX	LUB
Mullen, NE	GI
Mullens, WV	WH
Mullica Hill, NJ	CAM
Mulvane, KS	WCH
Muncie, IN	LFT
Muncy, PA	SCR
Mundelein, IL	CHI
Munden, KS	SAL
Mundys Corner, PA	ALT
Munger, MI	SAG
Munhall, PA	PBR
PA	PIT
Munich, ND	FAR
Munising, MI	MAR
Munjor, KS	SAL
Munnsville, NY	SY
Munster, IN	GRY
IN	PRM
IN	STN
Murdo, SD	RC
Murdock, FL	VEN
MN	NU
Murfreesboro, TN	NSH
Murphy, NC	CHL
Murphy Village, SC	CHR
Murphysboro, IL	BEL
Murray, KY	OWN
UT	OLL
UT	SLC
Murray City, OH	COL
Murrayville, IL	SFD
Murrietta, CA	SB
Murrysville, PA	GBG
Muscatine, IA	DAV
Muscoda, WI	MAD
Muse, PA	PIT
Muskegan, MI	GR
Muskego, WI	MIL
Muskegon, MI	GR
Muskegon Heights, MI	GR
Muskogee, OK	TLS
Mustang, OK	OKL
Myerstown, PA	HBG
Myrtle Beach, SC	CHR
Myrtle Creek, OR	P
Mystic, CT	NOR
IA	DAV
Naalehu, HI	HON
Nabob, WI	MIL
Naches, WA	YAK
Nacogdoches, TX	TYL
Nada, TX	VIC
Nadeau, MI	MAR
Naguabo, PR	CGS
Nahant, MA	BO
Nahma, MI	MAR
Nampa, ID	B
Namur, WI	GB
Nanakuli, HI	HON
Nanticoke, PA	PHU
PA	PSC
PA	SCR
Nantucket, MA	FR
Nanty-Glo, PA	ALT
PA	PBR
Nanuet, NY	NY
Napa, CA	SR
Napanee, IN	FTW
Naperville, IL	JOL
Naples, FL	VEN
NY	ROC
Napoleon, IN	IND
ND	FAR
OH	TOL
Napoleonville, LA	BR
Naranja, FL	MIA
Naranjito, PR	CGS
Narberth, PA	PH
Narragansett, RI	PRO
Narrowsburg, NY	NY
Nashua, IA	DUB
NH	MAN
Nashville, IL	BEL
IN	IND
TN	NSH
Nashwauk, MN	DUL
Nasonville, RI	PRO
Nassau, MN	NU
NY	ALB
Nassau Bay, TX	GAL
Natchez, MS	JKS
Natchitoches, LA	ALX
Natick, MA	BO
National City, CA	SD
National Park, NJ	CAM
Natrona, PA	PIT
Natrona Heights, PA	PIT
Naugatuck, CT	HRT
WV	WH
Nauvoo, IL	PEO
Navajo, NM	GLP
Navarino, WI	GB
Navarre, FL	PT
OH	Y
Navasota, TX	GAL
Navilleton, IN	IND
Naytahwaush, MN	CR
Nazareth, KY	L
MI	KAL
PA	ALN
TX	AMA
Nebish, MN	CR
Nebraska City, NE	LIN
Necedah, WI	LC
Neche, ND	FAR
Nederland, TX	BEA
Needham, MA	BO
Needles, CA	SB
Needville, TX	GAL
Neenah, WI	GB
Neenah/Menasha, WI	GB
Neepwukos, Chuuk, FM	CI
Neffs, OH	STU
Negaunee, MI	MAR
Neier, MO	STL
Neillsville, WI	LC
Nekoma, ND	FAR
Nekoosa, WI	LC
Neligh, NE	OM
Nelsonville, OH	STU
Nemacolin, PA	PIT
Nemar, FM	CI
Nenana, AK	FBK
Nenno, WI	MIL
Neodesha, KS	WCH
Neoga, IL	SFD
Neola, IA	DM
Neopit, WI	GB
Neosho, MO	SPC
WI	MIL
Neptune, IA	SC
NJ	TR
Nerinx, KY	L
Nesbit, MS	JKS
Nesconset, NY	RVC

Neshannock, PA	PIT
Neshkoro, WI	MAD
Nespelem, WA	SPK
Nesquehoning, PA	ALN
PA	PSC
Ness City, KS	DOD
Netcong, NJ	PAT
Neva, WI	GB
Nevada, IA	DUB
MO	KC
Nevada City, CA	SAC
Nevis, MN	CR
New Albany, IN	IND
MS	JKS
OH	COL
New Albin, IA	DUB
New Alexandria, PA	GBG
PA	SJP
New Almelo, KS	SAL
New Alsace, IN	IND
New Athens, IL	BEL
New Auburn, WI	LC
New Baden, IL	BEL
New Baltimore, MI	DET
PA	ALT
New Bavaria, OH	TOL
New Bedford, MA	FR
MA	SAM
PA	PIT
New Berlin, IL	SFD
NY	SY
WI	MIL
New Bern, NC	R
New Bethlehem, PA	E
New Bloomfield, PA	HBG
New Boston, IN	EVN
MI	DET
NH	MAN
OH	COL
TX	TYL
New Braunfels, TX	SAT
New Bremen, OH	CIN
New Brighton, MN	STP
PA	PIT
New Britain, CT	HRT
CT	PSC
CT	STF
New Brunswick, NJ	MET
NJ	PHU
NJ	PSC
New Buffalo, MI	KAL
New Canaan, CT	BGP
New Canen, TX	GAL
New Caney, TX	GAL
New Carlisle, IN	FTW
OH	CIN
New Castle, DE	WIL
IN	IND
PA	PIT
PA	SAM
New Chicago, IN	GRY
New City, NY	NY
New Cleveland, OH	TOL
New Cumberland, PA	HBG
WV	WH
New Cuyama, CA	LA
New Denmark, WI	GB
New Derry, PA	GBG
New Douglas, IL	SFD
New Effington, SD	SFS
New Egypt, NJ	TR
New England, ND	BIS
New Fairfield, CT	BGP
New Florence, PA	GBG
New Franken, WI	GB
New Freedom, PA	HBG
New Garden Township, PA	PH
New Hamburg, MO	SPC
New Hampton, IA	DUB
New Harmony, IN	EVN
New Hartford, CT	HRT
NY	SY
New Haven, CT	HRT
CT	STF
IA	DUB
IN	FTW
KY	L
MI	DET
MO	STL
New Holland, PA	HBG
New Holstein, WI	GB
New Hope, KY	L
MN	STP
PA	PH
New Hradec, ND	BIS
New Hyde Park, NY	RVC
New Iberia, LA	LAF
New Ipswich, NH	MAN
New Kensington, PA	GBG
PA	SJP
New Lebanon, NY	ALB
New Lenox, IL	JOL
New Lexington, OH	COL
New Lisbon, WI	LC
New London, CT	NOR
NH	MAN
NY	SY
OH	TOL
WI	GB
New Madrid, MO	SPC
New Marion, IN	IND
New Market, MN	STP
New Martinsville, WV	WH
New Melle, MO	STL
New Melleray, IA	DUB
New Miami, OH	CIN
New Middletown, IN	IND
OH	Y
New Milford, CT	HRT
NJ	NEW
New Monmouth, NJ	TR
New Munich, MN	SCL
New Munster, WI	MIL
New Orleans, LA	NO
LA	OLL
New Oxford, PA	HBG
New Paltz, NY	NY
New Paris, OH	CIN
New Philadelphia, OH	COL
PA	ALN
New Plymouth, ID	B
New Port Richey, FL	PSC
FL	SP
New Post, WI	SUP
New Prague, MN	STP
New Providence, NJ	NEW
New Richland, MN	WIN
New Richmond, OH	CIN
WI	SUP
New Riegel, OH	TOL
New Ringgold, PA	ALN
New Roads, LA	BR
New Rochelle, NY	NY
New Rockford, ND	FAR
New Salem, ND	BIS
PA	GBG
PA	PBR
New Shoreham, RI	PRO
New Smyrna Beach, FL	ORL
New Taiton, TX	VIC
New Town, ND	BIS
New Trier, MN	STP
New Ulm, MN	NU
New Underwood, SD	RC
New Vernon, NJ	PAT
New Vienna, IA	DUB
OH	CIN
New Village, NJ	MET
New Washington, OH	TOL
New Waverly, TX	GAL
New Windsor, NY	NY
New York, NY	ARM
NY	BUF
NY	NTN
NY	NY
NY	PSC
NY	STF
New York Mills, NY	SY
Newald, WI	GB
Newark, CA	OAK
DE	WIL
NJ	NEW
NJ	OLD
NJ	PHU
NJ	PSC
NY	ROC
OH	COL
Newark Valley, NY	ROC
Newaygo, MI	GR
Newberg, OR	P
Newberry, MI	MAR
SC	CHR
Newberry Springs, CA	VNN
Newburg, WI	MIL
Newburgh, IN	EVN
NY	NY
Newbury, OH	CLV
Newbury Park, CA	LA
Newburyport, MA	BO
Newcastle, ME	PRT
NE	OM
WY	CHY
Newcomb, NY	OG
TN	KNX
Newcomerstown, OH	COL
Newell, SD	RC
Newfane, NY	BUF
Newfield, NJ	CAM
Newhall, IA	DUB
Newington, CT	HRT
Newkirk, OK	OKL
Newman, CA	STO
Newmarket, NH	MAN
Newnan, GA	ATL
Newport, AR	LR
IA	DAV
KY	COV
MD	WDC
MI	DET
NH	MAN
NY	ALB
OH	CIN
OR	P
RI	PRO
TN	KNX
VT	BUR
WA	SPK
Newport Beach, CA	ORG
Newport News, VA	RIC
Newry, PA	ALT
Newtok, AK	FBK
Newton, IA	DAV
IL	SFD
KS	WCH
MA	BO
MA	NTN
NC	CHL
NH	MAN
NJ	PAT
Newton Falls, OH	PBR
OH	Y
Newton Grove, NC	R
Newtown, CT	BGP
PA	ALN
PA	PH
Newtown Square, PA	PH
PA	SAM
Newtowne, MD	WDC
Nezperce, ID	B
Niagara, WI	GB
Niagara Falls, NY	BUF
NY	STF
Niagara University, NY	BUF
Niantic, CT	NOR
IL	SFD
Niceville, FL	PT
Nicholasville, KY	LEX
Nichols, IA	DAV
Nicholson, PA	SCR
Nicktown, PA	ALT
Nicollet, MN	NU
Nicoma Park, OK	OKL
Nightmute, AK	FBK
Niles, IL	CHI
KS	SAL
MI	KAL
OH	Y
Nine Mile, MI	SAG
Nipomo, CA	MRY
Niskayuna, NY	ALB
Nitro, WV	WH
Nix Settlement, IN	FTW
Nixon, TX	SAT
Noble, LA	SHP
Noblesville, IN	LFT
Nocona, TX	FWT
Nogales, AZ	TUC
Nokomis, IL	SFD
Nolan Settlement, IA	DAV
Nome, AK	FBK
Norbeck, MD	WDC
Norco, CA	SB
LA	NO
Norcross, GA	ATL
Norfolk, CT	HRT
MA	BO
NE	OM
NY	OG
VA	RIC
Norge, VA	RIC
Normal, IL	PEO
Norman, OK	OKL
WI	GB
Normandy, MO	STL
Normandy Beach, NJ	TR
Norridge, IL	CHI
Norris, SD	RC
TN	KNX
Norristown, PA	PH
North Adams, MA	SPR
North Andover, MA	BO
North Arlington, NJ	NEW
North Arm, IL	SFD
North Attleboro, MA	FR
North Auburn, OH	TOL
North Augusta, SC	CHR
North Aurora, IL	RCK
North Baltimore, OH	TOL
North Bangor, NY	OG
North Bay, NY	SY
North Beach, MD	WDC
North Bend, NE	OM
OR	P
North Bennington, VT	BUR
North Bergen, NJ	NEW
North Bethesda, MD	WDC
North Branch, MI	DET
MN	STP
North Branford, CT	HRT
North Brookfield, MA	SAM
MA	WOR
North Brunswick, NJ	MET
North Buena Vista, IA	DUB
North Caldwell, NJ	NEW
North Canton, OH	Y
North Cape May, NJ	CAM
North Chicago, IL	CHI
North Chili, NY	ROC
North Collins, NY	BUF
North Conway, NH	MAN
North Creek, NY	ALB
OH	TOL
WI	LC
North Dartmouth, MA	FR
North Dighton, MA	FR
North East, PA	E
North Easton, MA	FR
North Ellinwood, KS	DOD
North English, IA	DAV
North Evans, NY	BUF
North Falmouth, MA	FR
North Fond du Lac, WI	MIL
North Fort Myers, FL	PSC
North Grafton, MA	WOR
North Greenbush, NY	ALB
North Grosvenordale, CT	NOR
North Guilford, CT	HRT
North Haledon, NJ	PAT
North Haven, CT	HRT
North Highlands, CA	SAC
North Hills, CA	LA
North Hills-Gibsonia, PA	PBR
North Hollywood, CA	EST
CA	LA
CA	NTN
CA	OLD
North Huntingdon, PA	GBG
PA	PBR
North Jackson, OH	OLL
OH	Y
North Java, NY	BUF
North Judson, IN	GRY
North Kingstown, RI	PRO
North Kinsley, KS	DOD
North Lake, WI	MIL
North Las Vegas, NV	LAV
North Lauderdale, FL	MIA
North Lawrence, NY	OG
North Lewisburg, OH	CIN
North Lima, OH	Y
North Manchester, IN	FTW
North Mankato, MN	NU
North Merrick, NY	RVC
North Miami, FL	MIA
North Miami Beach, FL	MIA
North Muskegon, MI	GR
North Myrtle Beach, SC	CHR
North Oakland, PA	PIT
North Olmsted, OH	CLV
North Oxford, MA	WOR
North Palm Beach, FL	PMB
North Plainfield, NJ	MET
North Plains, OR	P
North Platte, NE	GI
North Pole, AK	FBK
North Port, FL	SJP
FL	VEN
MI	GAY
North Prairie, MN	SCL
North Providence, RI	PRO
North Reading, MA	BO
North Ridgeville, OH	CLV
North Riverside, IL	CHI
North Rochester, PA	PIT
North Royalton, OH	CLV
OH	PRM
North St. Paul, MN	STP
North Smithfield, RI	PRO
North Stamford, CT	BGP
North Star, OH	CIN
North Stonington, CT	NOR
North Stratford, NH	MAN
North Syracuse, NY	SY
North Tarrytown, NY	NY
North Tonawanda, NY	BUF
North Topsail Beach, NC	R
North Troy, VT	BUR
North Vassalboro, ME	PRT
North Vernon, IN	IND
North Wales, PA	PH
North Walpole, NH	MAN
North Washington, IA	DUB
North Wilkesboro, NC	CHL
Northampton, MA	SPR

PA	ALN
PA	PHU
Northboro, MA	WOR
Northbridge, MA	WOR
Northbrook, IL	CHI
Northeast Harbor, ME	PRT
Northeim, WI	GB
Northfield, IL	CHI
MA	SPR
MN	STP
NJ	CAM
OH	CLV
VT	BUR
Northford, CT	HRT
Northglenn, CO	DEN
Northhampton, PA	ALN
Northlake, IL	CHI
IL	NTN
Northome, MN	DUL
Northport, NY	RVC
WA	SPK
Northridge, CA	LA
Northumberland, PA	HBG
Northvale, NJ	NEW
Northville, MI	DET
NY	ALB
Northwood, OH	PRM
Norton, KS	SAL
MA	FR
OH	CLV
VA	RIC
Nortonville, KS	KCK
ND	FAR
Norwalk, CA	LA
CT	BGP
OH	TOL
WI	LC
Norway, IA	DUB
ME	PRT
MI	MAR
Norwell, MA	BO
Norwich, CT	NOR
NY	SY
Norwood, MA	BO
MN	STP
NJ	NEW
NY	OG
PA	PH
Notre Dame, IN	FTW
Novato, CA	SFR
Novi, MI	DET
Nulato, AK	FBK
Nunda, NY	ROC
Nutley, NJ	NEW
Nyack, NY	NY
Nyssa, OR	BAK
O'Donnell, TX	LUB
O'Fallon, IL	BEL
MO	STL
O'Hara Township, PA	PIT
O'Neill, NE	OM
Oak Bluffs, MA	FR
Oak Brook, IL	JOL
Oak Creek, CO	DEN
WI	MIL
Oak Forest, IL	CHI
IN	IND
Oak Grove, KY	OWN
LA	SHP
Oak Harbor, OH	TOL
WA	SEA
Oak Hill, WV	WH
Oak Lawn, IL	CHI
Oak Park, CA	LA
IL	CHI
MI	DET
MI	EST
Oak Ridge, MN	WIN
NJ	PAT
TN	KNX
Oak Ridge-Milton, NJ	PAT
Oakbrook Terrace, IL	JOL
Oakdale, CA	STO
CT	NOR
LA	LKC
MN	STP
NY	RVC
PA	PIT
Oakes, ND	FAR
Oakesdale, WA	SPK
Oakfield, NY	BUF
WI	MIL
Oakland, CA	NTN
CA	OAK
MD	BAL
ME	PRT
NJ	NEW
Oakland City, IN	EVN
Oakley, CA	OAK
KS	SAL
MI	SAG

Oaklyn, NJ	CAM
Oakmont, PA	PIT
Oakridge, OR	P
Oakville, CA	SR
CT	HRT
MO	STL
Oakwood, ND	FAR
Oberlin, KS	SAL
LA	LKC
OH	CLV
Obernburg, NY	NY
Oblong, IL	SFD
Ocala, FL	ORL
Occidental, CA	SR
Occum, CT	NOR
Ocean Beach, NY	RVC
Ocean City, MD	WIL
NJ	CAM
Ocean Shores, WA	SEA
Ocean Springs, MS	BLX
Oceanside, CA	SD
NY	RVC
Oconee, IL	SFD
Oconomowoc, WI	MIL
Oconto, WI	GB
Oconto Falls, WI	GB
Odanah, WI	SUP
Odebolt, IA	SC
Odell, IL	PEO
Odem, TX	CC
Odenton, MD	BAL
Odessa, MO	KC
NY	ROC
TX	SAN
WA	SPK
Odin, KS	DOD
Oelwein, IA	DUB
Offerle, KS	DOD
Ogallala, NE	GI
Ogden, IA	SC
KS	SAL
UT	SLC
Ogdensburg, NJ	PAT
NY	OG
Ogema, MN	CR
Ogilvie, MN	SCL
Oglala, SD	RC
Oglesby, IL	PEO
Ogletown, DE	WIL
Ohio, IL	PEO
Oil City, PA	E
Oildale, CA	FRS
Ojai, CA	LA
Okanogan-Omak, WA	SPK
Okarche, OK	OKL
Okawville, IL	BEL
Okeechobee, FL	PMB
Okeene, OK	OKL
Okemos, MI	LAN
Oklahoma City, OK	OKL
Oklee, MN	CR
Okmulgee, OK	TLS
Olathe, KS	KCK
Olcott, NY	BUF
Old Bridge, NJ	MET
Old Fields, WV	WH
Old Forge, NY	OG
PA	PSC
PA	SCR
Old Hickory, TN	NSH
Old Lyme, CT	NOR
Old Mines, MO	STL
Old Monroe, MO	STL
Old Orchard Beach, ME	PRT
Old Saybrook, CT	NOR
Old Tappan, NJ	NEW
Old Town, ME	PRT
Old Washington-on-the Brazos, TX	AUS
Old Westbury, NY	RVC
Oldenburg, IN	IND
Oldham, SD	SFS
Olean, NE	OM
NY	BUF
NY	PSC
NY	SAM
Olema, CA	SFR
Olfen, TX	SAN
Olga, ND	FAR
Olive Branch, MS	JKS
Olive Hill, KY	LEX
Olivia, MN	NU
Olmitz, KS	DOD
Olmsted Falls, OH	CLV
Olmstedville, NY	OG
Olney, IL	BEL
MD	WDC
TX	FWT
Olpe, KS	KCK
Olympia, WA	SEA
WA	VNN

Olympia Fields, IL	CHI
Olyphant, PA	PHU
PA	SCR
Omaha, NE	MIL
NE	OM
NE	STN
Omak, WA	SPK
Omer, MI	PRM
Omro, WI	GB
Ona, WV	WH
Onaga, KS	KCK
Onaka, SD	SFS
Onalaska, WI	LC
Onamia, MN	SCL
Onawa, IA	SC
Onaway, MI	GAY
Oneida, NY	SY
WI	GB
Oneida Township, WI	GB
Onekama, MI	GAY
Oneonta, AL	BIR
NY	ALB
Onida, SD	SFS
Onley, VA	RIC
Onondaga Hill, NY	SY
Onset, MA	FR
Onsted, MI	DET
Ontario, CA	SB
NY	ROC
OR	BAK
Ontonagon, MI	MAR
Opa Locka, FL	MIA
Opelika, AL	MOB
Opelousas, LA	LAF
Opole, MN	SCL
Oquossoc, ME	PRT
Oradell, NJ	NEW
Oran, MO	SPC
Orange, CA	ORG
CT	HRT
MA	SPR
NJ	NEW
TX	BEA
VA	ARL
Orange Beach, AL	MOB
Orange Cove, CA	FRS
Orange Grove, TX	CC
Orange Park, FL	STA
Orange Village, OH	CLV
Orangeburg, NY	NY
SC	CHR
Orangefield, TX	BEA
Orangevale, CA	SAC
Orchard Lake, MI	DET
Orchard Park, NY	BUF
Ord, NE	GI
Ordot, GU	AGN
Oreana, ID	B
Orefield, PA	ALN
Oregon, IL	RCK
OH	TOL
WI	MAD
Oregon City, OR	P
Oreland, PA	PH
Orient, IA	DM
SD	SFS
Orinda, CA	OAK
Orion, IL	PEO
Orion Township, MI	DET
Oriska, ND	FAR
Oriskany, NY	SY
Oriskany Falls, NY	SY
Orland, CA	SAC
ME	PRT
Orland Hills, IL	CHI
Orland Park, IL	CHI
Orlando, FL	ORL
FL	PSC
FL	SAM
Orleans, MA	FR
NE	LIN
VT	BUR
Ormond Beach, FL	ORL
FL	PSC
Orocovis, PR	ARE
Orofino, ID	B
Orono, ME	PRT
Oroville, CA	SAC
WA	SPK
Orr, MN	DUL
Orrin, ND	FAR
Orrville, AL	MOB
OH	CLV
Ortonville, MI	DET
MN	NU
Orwell, OH	Y
VT	BUR
Orwigsburg, PA	ALN
Osage, IA	DUB
Osage Bend, MO	JC
Osage City, KS	KCK

Osakis, MN	SCL
Osawatomie, KS	KCK
Osborne, KS	SAL
Osceola, AR	LR
IA	DM
NE	LIN
WI	SUP
Oscoda, MI	GAY
Osgood, IN	IND
OH	CIN
Oshkosh, WI	GB
Oskaloosa, IA	DAV
Oslo, MN	CR
Osman, WI	GB
Osmond, NE	OM
Osnabrock, ND	FAR
Osseo, MN	STP
Ossian, IA	DUB
Ossineke, MI	GAY
Ossining, NY	NY
Ost, KS	WCH
Osterville, MA	FR
Oswego, IL	JOL
KS	WCH
NY	SY
Othello, WA	SPK
Otis, IN	GRY
Otis Orchards, WA	SPK
Otisville, MI	LAN
NY	NY
Otsego, MI	KAL
Ottawa, IL	PEO
KS	KCK
OH	TOL
Ottenheim, KY	LEX
Otter Creek, IA	DUB
Otter River, MA	WOR
Otterbein, IN	LFT
Ottoville, OH	TOL
Ottsville, PA	PH
Ottumwa, IA	DAV
Otway, OH	COL
Ouray, CO	PBL
Overbrook, PA	PH
PA	PIT
Overgaard, AZ	GLP
Overland, MO	STL
Overland Park, KS	KCK
Overton, NV	LAV
Ovid, MI	LAN
NY	ROC
Owasso, OK	TLS
Owatonna, MN	WIN
Owego, NY	ROC
Owen, WI	LC
Owensboro, KY	OWN
Owensville, MD	BAL
MO	JC
OH	CIN
Owingsville, KY	LEX
Owosso, MI	LAN
Oxford, CT	HRT
IA	DAV
IN	LFT
KS	WCH
MA	WOR
MI	DET
MS	JKS
NJ	MET
NY	SY
OH	CIN
PA	PH
Oxford Junction, IA	DUB
Oxnard, CA	LA
Oxon Hill, MD	WDC
Oyens, IA	SC
Oyster Bay, NY	RVC
Ozark, AL	MOB
AR	LR
MO	SPC
Ozona, TX	SAN
Ozone Park, (1954)	STF
NY	BRK
Ozora, MO	STL
Pacific, MO	STL
Pacific City, OR	P
Pacific Grove, CA	MRY
Pacific Palisades, CA	LA
Pacifica, CA	SFR
Pacoima, CA	LA
Paden City, WV	WH
Paderborn, IL	BEL
Padua, MN	SCL
Paducah, KY	OWN
Page, AZ	GLP
ND	FAR
Pagedale, MO	STL
Pago Pago, AS	SPP
Pagosa Springs, CO	PBL
Pahala, HI	HON
Pahoa, HI	HON

Pahokee, FL	PMB
Pahrump, NV	LAV
Paia, HI	HON
Paincourtville, LA	BR
Painesville, OH	CLV
Painted Post, NY	ROC
Paintsville, KY	LEX
Pala, CA	SD
Pala Indian Missions, CA	SD
Palacios, TX	VIC
Palatine, IL	CHI
IL	STN
Palatka, FL	STA
Palau, PW	CI
Palenville, NY	ALB
Palestine, TX	TYL
Palikir, FM	CI
Palisades Park, NJ	NEW
Palm Bay, FL	ORL
Palm Beach, FL	PMB
Palm Beach Gardens, FL	PMB
Palm City, FL	PMB
Palm Coast, FL	STA
Palm Desert, CA	SB
Palm Harbor, FL	SP
Palm Springs, CA	SB
CA	VNN
Palmdale, CA	LA
Palmer, AK	ANC
MA	SPR
PA	GBG
PR	SJN
Palmerton, PA	ALN
PA	PHU
PA	PSC
Palmerton-Slatington, PA	ALN
Palmetto, FL	VEN
Palms, MI	SAG
Palmyra, IL	SFD
MO	JC
NE	LIN
NY	ROC
PA	HBG
VA	RIC
WI	MAD
Palo Alto, CA	SJ
Palo Cedro, CA	SAC
Palos Heights, IL	CHI
Palos Hills, IL	CHI
Palos Park, IL	CHI
IL	STN
Pampa, TX	AMA
Pana, IL	SFD
Panama, IA	DM
IL	SFD
Panama City, FL	PT
Panama City Beach, FL	PT
Panhandle, TX	AMA
Panna Maria, TX	SAT
Panora, IA	DM
Panorama City, CA	LA
Paola, KS	KCK
Paoli, IN	IND
PA	PH
Paonia, CO	PBL
Papaaloa, HI	HON
Papaikou, HI	HON
Papillion, NE	OM
Paradis, LA	NO
Paradise, CA	SAC
Paradox, NY	ALB
Paragould, AR	LR
Paramount, CA	LA
Paramus, NJ	NEW
Parchment, MI	KAL
Pardeesville, PA	SCR
Pardeeville, WI	MAD
Paris, AR	LR
IL	SFD
KY	LEX
TN	MEM
TX	TYL
WI	MIL
Parish, NY	SY
Parisville, MI	SAG
Park, KS	SAL
Park City, UT	SLC
Park Falls, WI	SUP
Park Forest, IL	CHI
IL	JOL
Park Hills, MO	STL
Park Rapids, MN	CR
Park Ridge, IL	CHI
NJ	NEW
Park River, ND	FAR
Parker, AZ	TUC
CO	COS
PA	GBG
SD	SFS
Parkers Prairie, MN	SCL
Parkersburg, IA	DUB
WV	WH
Parkesburg, PA	PH
Parkland, FL	MIA
Parkman, OH	CLV
Parks, LA	LAF
Parkston, SD	SFS
Parkton, MD	BAL
Parkville, MO	KC
Parlier, CA	FRS
Parlin, NJ	MET
Parma, ID	B
OH	CLV
OH	PRM
OH	SJP
Parma Heights, OH	CLV
Parmelee, SD	RC
Parnell, IA	DAV
MI	GR
MO	KC
Parrish, FL	VEN
Parshall, ND	BIS
Parsippany, NJ	PAT
Parsons, KS	WCH
Pasadena, CA	LA
MD	BAL
TX	GAL
Pasadina, CA	LA
Pascagoula, MS	BLX
Pasco, WA	SPK
Paso Robles, CA	MRY
Pass Christian, MS	BLX
Passaic, NJ	PAT
NJ	PHU
NJ	PSC
Patagonia, AZ	TUC
Pataskala, OH	COL
Patchogue, NY	RVC
Paterson, NJ	ARM
NJ	PAT
Patillas, PR	PCE
Patterson, CA	STO
LA	LAF
NY	NY
Pattison/Brookshire, TX	GAL
Patton, PA	ALT
PA	PBR
Paul, NE	LIN
Paulding, MS	JKS
OH	TOL
Paulina, LA	BR
Pauls Valley, OK	OKL
Paulsboro, NJ	CAM
Pavilion, NY	BUF
Paw Paw, MI	KAL
Pawcatuck, CT	NOR
Pawhuska, OK	TLS
Pawleys Island, SC	CHR
Pawling, NY	NY
Pawnee, IL	SFD
OK	TLS
Pawtucket, RI	PRO
RI	SAM
Paxico, KS	KCK
Paxton, IL	JOL
MA	WOR
Payette, ID	B
Payne, OH	TOL
Paynesville, MN	SCL
Payneville, KY	L
Payson, AZ	TUC
UT	SLC
Pe Ell, WA	SEA
Peabody, MA	BO
Peachtree City, GA	ATL
Peaks Island, ME	PRT
Peapack, NJ	MET
Pearisburg, VA	RIC
Pearl, MI	KAL
MS	JKS
Pearl City, HI	HON
Pearl Lake, MN	SCL
Pearl River, LA	NO
NY	NY
Pearland, TX	GAL
Pearlington, MS	BLX
Pearsall, TX	SAT
Pecatonica, IL	RCK
Peckville, PA	SCR
Pecos, NM	SFE
TX	ELP
Peebles, OH	CIN
Peekskill, NY	NY
NY	PSC
Peetz, CO	DEN
Pekin, IL	PEO
Pelham, NH	MAN
NY	NY
Pelham Manor, NY	NY
Pelican Lake, WI	SUP
Pelican Rapids, MN	SCL
Pell City, AL	BIR
Pell Lake, WI	MIL
Pella, IA	DAV
Pellston, MI	GAY
Pembina, ND	FAR
Pembine, WI	GB
Pembroke, MA	BO
Pembroke Pines, FL	MIA
Pen Argyl, PA	ALN
Pena Blanca, NM	SFE
Penacook, NH	MAN
Penasco, NM	SFE
Pence, WI	SUP
Pender, NE	OM
Pendleton, NY	BUF
OR	BAK
Penelope, TX	FWT
Penfield, IL	PEO
NY	ROC
Peninsula, OH	CLV
Penn, ND	FAR
PA	GBG
Penn Hills, PA	PIT
Penn Valley, PA	PH
Penn Yan, NY	ROC
Penndel, PA	PH
Penngrove, CA	SR
Pennington, MN	CR
NJ	TR
Pennington Gap, VA	RIC
Penns Grove, NJ	CAM
Penns Valley, PA	ALT
Pennsauken, NJ	CAM
Pennsville, NJ	CAM
Pensacola, FL	PT
Pensacola Beach, FL	PT
Penuelas, PR	PCE
Peonia, KY	OWN
Peoria, AZ	PHX
IL	OLL
IL	PEO
Peosta, IA	DUB
Peotone, IL	JOL
Peplin, WI	LC
Pepper Pike, OH	CLV
Pepperell, MA	BO
Pequannock, NJ	PAT
Pequot Lakes, MN	DUL
Peralta, NM	SFE
Perezville-Tamuning, GU	AGN
Perham, MN	SCL
Perkins, MI	MAR
Perris, CA	SB
Perronville, MI	MAR
Perry, FL	PT
GA	SAV
IA	DM
KS	KCK
ME	PRT
MO	JC
NY	BUF
OH	CLV
OK	OKL
Perryopolis, PA	GBG
PA	PBR
Perrysburg, NY	BUF
OH	TOL
Perrysville, PA	PIT
Perryton, TX	AMA
Perryville, MD	WIL
MO	STL
Perth Amboy, NJ	MET
NJ	PHU
NJ	PSC
Peru, IL	PEO
IN	LFT
NY	OG
OH	TOL
Peshabestown, MI	GAY
Peshtigo, WI	GB
Pesotum, IL	PEO
Petal, MS	BLX
Petaluma, CA	SFR
CA	SR
Peterborough, NH	MAN
Peters Township, PA	PIT
Petersburg, AK	JUN
IA	DUB
IL	SFD
IN	EVN
NE	OM
TX	LUB
VA	RIC
WV	WH
Petersham, MA	SAM
MA	WOR
Peterstown, IL	PEO
Petersville, IA	DAV
Petoskey, MI	GAY
Pevely, MO	STL
Pewamo, MI	GR
Pewaukee, WI	MIL
Pewee Valley, KY	L
Pfeifer, KS	SAL
Pflugerville, TX	AUS
Pharr, TX	BWN
Phelan, CA	SB
Phelps, NY	ROC
WI	SUP
Phenix City, AL	MOB
Philadelphia, MS	JKS
PA	ARM
PA	HBG
PA	PH
PA	PHU
PA	PSC
PA	SAM
Philip, SD	RC
Philippi, WV	OLL
WV	WH
Philipsburg, MT	HEL
PA	ALT
Phillips, WI	SUP
Phillipsburg, KS	SAL
NJ	MET
NJ	PSC
Philmont, NY	ALB
Philo, CA	SR
IL	PEO
Philothea, OH	CIN
Philpot, KY	OWN
Phlox, WI	GB
Phoenicia, NY	NY
Phoenix, AZ	NTN
AZ	OLL
AZ	PHX
AZ	STN
AZ	VNN
NY	SY
Phoenixville, PA	PH
PA	PHU
Picayune, MS	BLX
Pickens, SC	CHR
Pickerington, OH	COL
Pico Rivera, CA	LA
Piedmont, CA	OAK
MO	SPC
OK	OKL
Piedmont-Black Hawk, SD	RC
Pierce, NE	OM
Pierce City, MO	SPC
Pierceton, IN	FTW
Piermont, NY	NY
Pierre, SD	SFS
Pierre Part, LA	BR
Pierron, IL	SFD
Pier-Willow, WI	SUP
Pierz, MN	SCL
Piffard, NY	ROC
Pigeon, MI	SAG
Pikesville, MD	BAL
Pikeville, KY	LEX
Pilot Grove, MO	JC
Pilot Knob, MO	SPC
Pilot Point, TX	FWT
Pilot Rock, OR	BAK
Pilot Station, AK	FBK
Pilsen, KS	WCH
Pin Oak, TX	AUS
Pinckney, MI	LAN
Pinckneyville, IL	BEL
Pinconning, MI	SAG
Pine Apple, AL	MOB
Pine Bluff, AR	LR
WI	MAD
Pine Bluffs, WY	CHY
Pine Bush, NY	NY
Pine City, MN	DUL
NY	ROC
Pine Creek, WI	LC
Pine Grove, OH	STU
PA	SCR
WI	GB
Pine Hill, NJ	CAM
Pine Island, MN	STP
NY	NY
Pine Lawn, MO	STL
Pine Plains, NY	NY
Pine Prairie, LA	LAF
Pine Ridge, SD	RC
Pine River, MN	DUL
Pinedale, WY	CHY
Pinehaven, NM	GLP
Pinehurst, NC	R
Pinellas Park, FL	SP
Pinetop, AZ	GLP
Pineville, LA	ALX
MS	BLX
WV	WH
Piney Fork, OH	STU
Pingree, ND	FAR
Pinnebog, MI	SAG
Pinole, CA	OAK

Pinon, AZ	GLP
Piopolis, IL	BEL
Piper City, IL	JOL
Pipestone, MN	WIN
Piqua, KS	WCH
OH	CIN
Pirtleville, AZ	TUC
Piscataway, MD	WDC
NJ	MET
Pisek, ND	FAR
Pismo Beach, CA	MRY
Pitcairn, PA	PIT
Piti, GU	AGN
Pitman, NJ	CAM
Pittsburg, CA	OAK
KS	WCH
TX	TYL
Pittsburgh, PA	PBR
PA	PIT
PA	SAM
PA	SJP
Pittsfield, IL	SFD
MA	SPR
MA	STF
ME	PRT
NH	MAN
Pittsford, NY	ROC
VT	BUR
Pittsgrove, NJ	CAM
Pittston, PA	PSC
PA	SCR
Pittstown, NJ	MET
NY	ALB
Pittsville, WI	LC
Placentia, CA	ORG
Placerville, CA	SAC
Placid, IA	DUB
Plain, WI	MAD
Plain City, OH	COL
Plainfield, CT	NOR
IL	JOL
IN	IND
NJ	NEW
WI	GB
Plains, KS	DOD
MT	HEL
PA	SCR
Plainsboro, NJ	MET
Plainview, MN	WIN
NE	OM
NY	RVC
TX	LUB
Plainville, CT	HRT
KS	SAL
MA	BO
Plaisance, LA	LAF
Plaistow, NH	MAN
Planada, CA	FRS
Plankinton, SD	SFS
Plano, IL	JOL
TX	DAL
Plant City, FL	SP
Plantation, FL	MIA
Plantersville, TX	GAL
Plantsville, CT	HRT
Plaquemine, LA	BR
Plateau, AL	MOB
Platte, SD	SFS
Platte Center, NE	OM
Plattekill, NY	NY
Plattenville, LA	BR
Platteville, CO	DEN
WI	MAD
Plattsburg, MO	KC
Plattsburgh, NY	OG
Plattsmouth, NE	LIN
Plaucheville, LA	ALX
Playa De Ponce, PR	PCE
Playa Del Rey, CA	LA
Playa Ponce, PR	PCE
Pleasant City, OH	PBR
Pleasant Hill, CA	OAK
Pleasant Hills, PA	PIT
Pleasant Mount, PA	SCR
Pleasant Point, ME	PRT
Pleasant Prairie, WI	MIL
Pleasant Valley, NY	NY
Pleasanton, CA	OAK
NE	GI
TX	SAT
Pleasantville, NJ	CAM
NY	NY
Pleasure Ridge Park, KY	L
Plentywood, MT	GF
Plover, WI	LC
Plum, TX	VIC
Plum City, WI	LC
Plummer, MN	CR
Plymouth, IA	DUB
IN	FTW
MA	BO
MI	DET
MI	NTN
MN	STP
NC	R
NH	MAN
OH	TOL
PA	PHU
PA	SCR
WI	MIL
Plymouth Rock, IA	DUB
Pocahontas, AR	LR
IA	SC
IL	SFD
VA	RIC
Pocantico Hills, NY	NY
Pocasset, MA	FR
Pocatello, ID	B
Pocomoke City, MD	WIL
Pocono Pines, PA	SCR
Pohnpei, FM	CI
Poinciana, FL	ORL
Point Arena, CA	SR
Point Lookout, NY	RVC
Point Marion, PA	GBG
Point Pleasant, NJ	TR
WV	WH
Point Pleasant Beach, NJ	TR
Point Richmond, CA	OAK
Pointe a la Hache, LA	NO
Pointe-Aux-Chenes, LA	HT
Pojoaque, NM	SFE
Poland, OH	Y
Pollock Pines, CA	SAC
Polo, IL	RCK
SD	SFS
Polonia, WI	LC
Polson, MT	HEL
Pomeroy, IA	SC
OH	STU
WA	SPK
Pomfret, CT	NOR
MD	WDC
Pomona, CA	LA
NJ	CAM
Pompano Beach, FL	MIA
Pompey, NY	SY
Pompton Lakes, NJ	PAT
Pompton Plains, NJ	PAT
Ponca, NE	OM
Ponca City, OK	OKL
Ponce, PR	PCE
Ponchatoula, LA	BR
LA	NO
Pond Settlement, IL	BEL
Poniatowski, WI	LC
Ponsford, MN	CR
Ponte Vedra Beach, FL	STA
Pontiac, IL	PEO
MI	DET
Poolesville, MD	WDC
Poplar, MT	GF
Poplar Bluff, MO	SPC
Poplar Springs, MD	BAL
Poquonock, CT	HRT
Porcupine, SD	RC
Porrassapw, FM	CI
Port Allegany, PA	E
Port Allen, LA	BR
Port Angeles, WA	SEA
Port Aransas, TX	CC
Port Arthur, TX	BEA
Port Austin, MI	SAG
Port Barre, LA	LAF
Port Bolivar, TX	GAL
Port Carbon, PA	ALN
Port Charlotte, FL	VEN
Port Chester, NY	NY
Port Clinton, OH	TOL
Port Edwards, WI	LC
Port Ewen, NY	NY
Port Gibson, MS	JKS
Port Henry, NY	OG
Port Hudson, MO	STL
Port Huron, MI	DET
Port Isabel, TX	BWN
Port Jefferson, NY	RVC
Port Jervis, NY	NY
Port Lavaca, TX	VIC
Port Leyden, NY	OG
Port Murray, NJ	MET
Port Neches, TX	BEA
Port Orange, FL	ORL
Port Orchard, WA	SEA
Port Reading, NJ	MET
Port Richey, FL	SP
Port St. Joe, FL	PT
Port St. Lucie, FL	PMB
Port Sanilac, MI	SAG
Port Sulphur, LA	NO
Port Tobacco, MD	WDC
Port Townsend, WA	SEA
Port Vue, PA	PIT
Port Washington, NY	RVC
WI	MIL
Port Wentworth, GA	SAV
Portage, IN	GRY
MI	KAL
PA	ALT
PA	PBR
WI	MAD
Portage Des Sioux, MO	STL
Portageville, MO	SPC
NY	BUF
Portales, NM	SFE
Porterville, CA	FRS
Portland, CT	NOR
IN	LFT
ME	PRT
MI	GR
OR	OLL
OR	P
OR	VNN
TX	CC
Portola, CA	SAC
Portola Valley, CA	SFR
Portsmouth, IA	DM
NH	MAN
OH	COL
RI	PRO
VA	RIC
Portville, NY	BUF
Posen, IL	BEL
IL	CHI
MI	GAY
Poseyville, IN	EVN
Post, TX	LUB
Post Falls, ID	B
Postville, IA	DUB
Poteau, OK	TLS
Poteet, TX	SAT
Poth, TX	SAT
Potlatch, ID	B
Potomac, MD	WDC
Potosi, MO	STL
Potsdam, NY	OG
Pottstown, PA	PH
PA	PHU
PA	PSC
Pottsville, PA	ALN
Poughkeepsie, NY	NY
Poulsbo, WA	SEA
Poultney, VT	BUR
Poway, CA	SD
Powell, OH	COL
WY	CHY
Powhatan, LA	ALX
VA	RIC
WV	WH
Powhatan Point, OH	STU
Poy Sippi, WI	GB
Poynette, WI	MAD
Praga, MI	GAY
Prague, NE	LIN
OK	OKL
Praha, TX	VIC
Prairie du Chien, WI	LC
Prairie du Rocher, IL	BEL
Prairie du Sac, WI	MAD
Prairie View, TX	GAL
Prairie Village, KS	KCK
Prairieburg, IA	DUB
Prairieville, LA	BR
Pratt, KS	DOD
Prattville, AL	MOB
Premont, TX	CC
Prentice, WI	SUP
Prescott, AZ	PHX
MI	GAY
WI	LC
Prescott Valley, AZ	PHX
Presho, SD	RC
Presidio, TX	ELP
Presque Isle, ME	PRT
WI	SUP
Preston, CT	NOR
IA	DUB
MN	WIN
Prestonsburg, KY	LEX
Price, UT	SLC
Prichard, AL	MOB
Priest River, ID	B
Primos, PA	PH
Prince Frederick, MD	WDC
Prince George County, VA	RIC
Princess Anne, MD	WIL
Princeton, IL	PEO
IN	EVN
KY	OWN
MA	WOR
MN	SCL
NJ	TR
OH	CIN
WI	MAD
WV	WH
Princeville, IL	PEO
Prineville, OR	BAK
Prior Lake, MN	STP
Proctor, MN	DUL
VT	BUR
Progreso, TX	BWN
Prophetstown, IL	RCK
Prospect, CT	HRT
PA	PIT
Prospect Heights, IL	CHI
Prospect Park, NJ	PAT
PA	PH
Prosser, WA	YAK
Protivin, IA	DUB
Protovin, IA	DUB
Providence, KY	OWN
OH	TOL
RI	PRO
Provincetown, MA	FR
Provo, UT	SLC
Prudenville, MI	GAY
Pryor, MT	GF
OK	TLS
Pueblo, CO	PBL
Puerta De Tierra, PR	SJN
Pukwana, SD	SFS
Pulaski, NY	SY
TN	NSH
WI	GB
Pulaskifield, MO	SPC
Pullman, WA	SPK
Puluwat, FM	CI
Punta Gorda, FL	VEN
Punxsutawney, PA	E
PA	PBR
Purcell, KS	KCK
OK	OKL
Purcellville, VA	ARL
Purchase, NY	NY
Put-In-Bay, OH	TOL
Putnam, CT	LIT
CT	NOR
IL	LIT
Putney, VT	BUR
Puyallup, WA	SEA
Pylesville, MD	BAL
Quaker Hill, CT	NOR
Quakertown, PA	PH
Quanah, TX	FWT
Quarryville, PA	HBG
Quebradillas, PR	ARE
Queens, NY	BRK
Queens Village, NY	BRK
Queensbury, NY	ALB
Quemado, NM	GLP
Questa, NM	SFE
Quincy, CA	SAC
FL	PT
IL	SFD
MA	BO
WA	YAK
Quinebaug, CT	NOR
Quinnesec, MI	MAR
Quinton, VA	RIC
Raceland, LA	HT
Racine, WI	MIL
Radcliff, KY	L
Raddle, IL	BEL
Radford, VA	RIC
Radisson, WI	SUP
Radnor, PA	ARM
PA	PH
Radom, IL	BEL
Raeford, NC	R
Raeville, NE	OM
Rahway, NJ	NEW
NJ	PSC
Rainelle, WV	WH
Rainier, OR	P
Raleigh, NC	R
ND	BIS
Ralls, TX	LUB
Ralston, NE	OM
Rambin, LA	SHP
Ramey, PA	E
PA	SJP
Ramona, CA	SD
SD	SFS
Ramsay, MI	MAR
Ramsey, IL	SFD
NJ	NEW
NJ	PHU
Ranchito, TX	BWN
Rancho Cordova, CA	SAC
Rancho Cucamonga, CA	SB
Rancho Dominguez, CA	LA
Rancho Palos Verdes, CA	LA
Rancho Santa Fe, CA	SD
Rancho Santa Margarita, CA	ORG

Ranchos De Taos, NM	SFE
Randall, MN	SCL
Randallstown, MD	BAL
Randolph, MA	BO
NE	OM
NJ	PAT
NY	BUF
VT	BUR
WI	MIL
Randolph Township, OH	Y
Random Lake, WI	MIL
Rangely, CO	DEN
Ranger, TX	FWT
Rankin, PA	PBR
PA	PIT
Ranshaw, PA	HBG
Ransom, IL	PEO
KS	DOD
Ransomville, NY	BUF
Rantoul, IL	PEO
Rapid City, SD	RC
Rapid River, MI	MAR
Rapids City, IL	PEO
Rapson, MI	SAG
Raquette Lake, NY	OG
Raritan, IL	PEO
NJ	MET
Ratcliff, AR	LR
Rathbun, IA	DAV
Rathdrum, ID	B
Raton, NM	SFE
Ravena, NY	ALB
Ravenna, KY	LEX
MI	GR
NE	GI
OH	Y
Ravenswood, WV	WH
Rawlins, WY	CHY
Raymond, IA	DUB
IL	SFD
LA	LKC
MN	NU
MS	JKS
WA	SEA
Raymondville, NY	OG
TX	BWN
Rayne, LA	LAF
Raynham, MA	FR
Raytown, MO	KC
Rayville, LA	SHP
Raywick, KY	L
Raywood, TX	BEA
Reading, KS	KCK
MA	BO
PA	ALN
PA	PHU
Readsboro, VT	BUR
Reardan, WA	SPK
Red Bank, NJ	TR
TN	KNX
Red Bluff, CA	SAC
Red Brush, IN	EVN
Red Bud, IL	BEL
Red Cliff, WI	SUP
Red Cloud, NE	LIN
Red Feathers Lakes, CO	DEN
Red Hook, NY	NY
Red Lake, MN	CR
Red Lake Falls, MN	CR
Red Lodge, MT	GF
Red Oak, IA	DM
Red Wing, MN	STP
Redding, CA	SAC
CT	BGP
Redfield, SD	SFS
Redford, MI	DET
NY	OG
Redford Township, MI	DET
Redgranite, WI	GB
Redland, OR	P
Redlands, CA	SB
CA	VNN
Redmond, OR	BAK
WA	SEA
Redondo Beach, CA	LA
Redwood, NY	OG
Redwood City, CA	SFR
Redwood Falls, MN	NU
Redwood Valley, CA	STN
Reed, KY	OWN
OH	TOL
Reed City, MI	GR
Reedley, CA	FRS
Reedsburg, WI	MAD
Reedsport, OR	P
Reedsville, WI	GB
Reedsville/Maple Grove, WI	GB
Reese, MI	SAG
Reeseville, WI	MIL
Refugio, TX	CC
Regal, MN	NU

Regent, ND	BIS
Rego Park, NY	BRK
Rehoboth, DE	WIL
Reidsville, NC	CHL
Reinbeck, IA	DUB
Reliance, SD	RC
Remington, IN	LFT
Remsen, IA	SC
Remus, MI	GR
Renault, IL	BEL
Reno, NV	RNO
Renovo, PA	ALT
Rensselaer, IN	LFT
NY	ALB
Renton, PA	PIT
WA	SEA
Renville, MN	NU
Republic, MI	MAR
MO	SPC
OH	TOL
PA	GBG
WA	SPK
Reseda, CA	LA
Reserve, LA	NO
WI	SUP
Reserve Township, PA	PIT
Reston, VA	ARL
Revere, MA	BO
Revillo, SD	SFS
Revloc, PA	ALT
PA	SJP
Rexville, NY	ROC
Reynolds, IN	LFT
ND	FAR
Reynoldsburg, OH	COL
Reynoldsville, PA	E
Rhine, OH	CIN
Rhinebeck, NY	NY
Rhineland, MO	JC
TX	FWT
Rhinelander, WI	SUP
Rhodelia, KY	L
Rhodell, WV	WH
Rialto, CA	SB
Rib Lake, WI	SUP
Ribera, NM	SFE
Rice, MN	SCL
Rice Lake, WI	SUP
Riceville, IA	DUB
Rich Fountain, MO	JC
Richard, LA	LAF
Richardson, TX	DAL
Richardton, ND	BIS
Richboro, PA	PH
Richeyville, PA	PIT
Richfield, MN	STP
OH	CLV
UT	SLC
WI	MIL
Richfield Center, OH	TOL
Richfield Springs, NY	ALB
Richford, VT	BUR
Richland, IA	DAV
MO	JC
NJ	CAM
WA	YAK
Richland Center, WI	LC
Richland Township, PA	PIT
Richlands, VA	RIC
Richmond, CA	OAK
IA	DAV
IL	RCK
IN	IND
KS	KCK
KY	LEX
ME	PRT
MI	DET
MN	SCL
MO	KC
OH	STU
TX	GAL
VA	PHU
VA	RIC
VA	SAM
VT	BUR
Richmond Heights, MO	STL
Richmond Hill, GA	SAV
Richwood, TX	GAL
WV	WH
Richwoods, MO	STL
Rickardsville, IA	DUB
Ridge, MD	WDC
Ridge Manor, FL	SP
Ridgecrest, CA	FRS
Ridgefield, CT	BGP
NJ	NEW
Ridgefield Park, NJ	NEW
Ridgeland, SC	CHR
Ridgeley, WV	WH
Ridgely, MD	WIL
Ridgeville, SC	CHR

Ridgeway, WI	MAD
Ridgewood, NJ	NEW
NY	BRK
Ridgway, IL	BEL
PA	E
Ridley Park, PA	PH
Riegelsville, PA	PH
Riegelwood, NC	R
Rifle, CO	DEN
Riggsville, MI	GAY
Rincon, PR	MGZ
Rindge, NH	MAN
Ringtown, PA	ALN
Ringwood, NJ	PAT
Rio Grande, NJ	CAM
OH	STU
PR	SJN
Rio Grande City, TX	BWN
Rio Hondo, TX	BWN
Rio Piedras, PR	SJN
Rio Rancho, NM	SFE
Rio Rico, AZ	TUC
Rio Vista, CA	SAC
Ripley, MS	JKS
OH	CIN
Ripon, WI	MIL
Rising Sun, WI	LC
Rittman, OH	CLV
Ritzville, WA	SPK
River Aux Vases, MO	STL
River Edge, NJ	NEW
River Falls, WI	SUP
River Forest, IL	CHI
River Grove, IL	CHI
River Ridge, LA	NO
River Rouge, MI	DET
River Vale, NJ	NEW
Riverbank, CA	STO
Riverdale, CA	FRS
GA	ATL
IL	CHI
MD	WDC
NY	NY
Riverhead, NY	RVC
NY	STF
Riverside, CA	SB
CT	BGP
IA	DAV
IL	CHI
NJ	TR
Riverton, IL	SFD
NJ	TR
WY	CHY
Riverview, FL	SP
MI	DET
Riverview Gardens, MO	STL
Riviera Beach, FL	PMB
Roanoke, IL	PEO
IN	FTW
VA	RIC
VA	SAM
Roanoke Rapids, NC	R
Roaring Creek, PA	HBG
Roaring Spring, PA	ALT
Robbinsdale, MN	STP
Robert's Cove, LA	LAF
Robertsdale, AL	MOB
Robesonia, PA	ALN
Robinson, IL	SFD
Robinson Township, PA	PIT
Robinsonville, WI	GB
Robstown, TX	CC
Rochdale, MA	WOR
Rochelle, IL	RCK
Rochelle Park, NJ	NEW
Rochester, IL	SFD
IN	LFT
MA	BO
MI	DET
MN	WIN
NH	MAN
NY	NTN
NY	ROC
NY	STF
PA	PIT
Rochester Hills, MI	DET
Rock Creek, OH	Y
Rock Falls, IL	RCK
WI	LC
Rock Hill, SC	CHR
Rock Island, IL	PEO
Rock Lake, ND	FAR
PA	SCR
Rock Rapids, IA	SC
Rock Springs, WY	CHY
Rock Valley, IA	SC
Rockaway, NJ	PAT
OR	P
Rockaway Park, NY	BRK
Rockaway Township, NJ	PAT
Rockdale, IL	JOL

TX	AUS
Rockford, IA	DUB
IL	RCK
MI	GR
OH	CIN
WA	SPK
Rockland, MA	BO
ME	PRT
MI	MAR
Rockledge, FL	ORL
Rocklin, CA	SAC
Rockne, TX	AUS
Rockport, IN	EVN
MA	BO
TX	CC
Rocksprings, TX	SAT
Rockville, CT	NOR
IN	IND
MD	WDC
MN	SCL
VA	RIC
Rockville Centre, NY	BRK
NY	RVC
Rockwall, TX	DAL
Rockwell, IA	DUB
Rockwell City, IA	SC
Rockwood, MI	DET
Rocky Ford, CO	PBL
Rocky Hill, CT	HRT
Rocky Mount, NC	R
VA	RIC
Rocky Point, NY	RVC
Rocky River, OH	CLV
Rodeo, CA	OAK
Roebling, NJ	PSC
NJ	ROM
NJ	TR
Roeland Park, KS	KCK
Rogers, AR	LR
CT	NOR
MN	STP
TX	AUS
Rogers City, MI	GAY
Rogersville, TN	KNX
Roggen, CO	DEN
Rohnert Park, CA	SR
Rohrerstown, PA	HBG
Rolesville, NC	R
Rolette, ND	FAR
Rolfe, IA	SC
Rolla, MO	JC
ND	FAR
Rolling Ground, WI	LC
Rolling Hills, CA	LA
Rolling Meadows, IL	CHI
Rolling Prairie, IN	GRY
Rollingstone, MN	WIN
Rollinsford, NH	MAN
Roma, TX	BWN
Rome, GA	ATL
KY	OWN
NY	STF
NY	SY
Rome City, IN	FTW
Romeo, MI	DET
Romeoville, IL	JOL
Romney, WV	WH
Romulus, MI	DET
Ronan, MT	HEL
Ronceverte, WV	WH
Ronkonkoma, NY	RVC
Roosevelt, NY	RVC
UT	SLC
Rootstown, OH	Y
Rosalia, WA	SPK
Rosario, PR	MGZ
Rosaryville, MD	WDC
Rosati, MO	JC
Roscoe, MN	SCL
PA	PIT
SD	SFS
Roscommon, MI	GAY
Rose Creek, MN	WIN
Roseau, MN	CR
Rosebud, SD	RC
TX	AUS
Roseburg, OR	P
Rosebush, MI	SAG
Rosedale, MS	JKS
Roseland, NE	LIN
NJ	NEW
Roselle, IA	SC
IL	JOL
NJ	NEW
Roselle Park, NJ	NEW
Rosemead, CA	LA
Rosemont, PA	PH
Rosemont-Des Plaines, IL	CHI
Rosemount, MN	STP
Rosen, MN	NU
Rosenberg, TX	GAL

Rosencrans, IL	CHI
Rosendale, NY	NY
Rosenhayn, NJ	CAM
Roseto, PA	ALN
Roseville, CA	SAC
IA	DUB
MI	DET
MN	STP
Rosholt, SD	SFS
WI	LC
Rosiere, NY	OG
WI	GB
Roslyn, NY	RVC
PA	PH
WA	YAK
Rosman, NC	CHL
Ross Township, PA	PIT
Rossford, OH	SJP
OH	TOL
Rossiter, PA	GBG
Rossville, KS	KCK
Rostraver, PA	GBG
Roswell, GA	ATL
GA	PSC
NM	LSC
OH	COL
Rotan, TX	LUB
Rothbury, MI	GR
Rothschild, WI	LC
Rotterdam, NY	ALB
Rotterdam Junction, NY	ALB
Round Lake, IL	CHI
Round Rock, TX	AUS
Roundup, MT	GF
Rouses Point, NY	OG
Rouseville, PA	E
Rowena, TX	SAN
Rowland Heights, CA	LA
Rowlett, TX	DAL
Rowley, IA	DUB
MA	BO
Roxboro, NC	R
Roxbury, MA	BO
WI	MAD
Roy, NM	SFE
OR	P
Royal, IA	SC
PA	SCR
Royal City, WA	YAK
Royal Oak, MI	DET
Royal Palm Beach, FL	PMB
Royalton, IL	BEL
MN	SCL
Royersford, PA	PH
Rozellville, WI	LC
Rubicon, WI	MIL
Ruby, AK	FBK
Rudolph, WI	LC
Rudyard, MI	MAR
Rugby, ND	FAR
Ruidoso, NM	LSC
Rulo, NE	LIN
Ruma, IL	BEL
Rumford, ME	PRT
Rumson, NJ	TR
Runge, TX	SAT
Runnemede, NJ	CAM
Running Springs, CA	SB
Rupert, ID	B
Rush, NY	ROC
Rush City, MN	STP
Rush Lake, MN	SCL
Rushford, MN	WIN
NY	BUF
Rushville, IL	PEO
IN	IND
Ruskin, FL	SP
Russell, KS	SAL
MA	SPR
Russells Point, OH	CIN
Russellton, PA	PIT
Russellville, AL	BIR
AR	LR
KY	OWN
MO	JC
Russia, OH	CIN
Ruston, LA	SHP
Ruth, MI	SAG
Rutherford, NJ	NEW
NJ	PHU
Ruthven, IA	SC
Rutland, IL	PEO
MA	SAM
MA	WOR
VT	BUR
Rutten, ND	FAR
Ryan, IA	DUB
MI	SAG
Rydal, PA	PH
Rye, CO	PBL
NY	NY
Rye Beach, NH	MAN
Rynella, LA	LAF
Sabana Grande, PR	MGZ
Sabattus, ME	PRT
Sabetha, KS	KCK
Sabin, MN	CR
Sabinal, TX	SAT
Sabine Pass, TX	BEA
Sabula, IA	DUB
Sac City, IA	SC
Sacaton, AZ	PHX
Sackets Harbor, NY	OG
Saco, ME	PRT
Sacramento, CA	NTN
CA	SAC
CA	STN
CA	VNN
Saddle Brook, NJ	NEW
Saddle River, NJ	NEW
Saddle River Borough, NJ	NEW
Safety Harbor, FL	SP
Safford, AZ	TUC
Sag Harbor, NY	RVC
Sagamore, PA	GBG
PA	PBR
Saginaw, MI	SAG
St. Agatha, ME	PRT
St. Albans, ME	PRT
VT	BUR
WV	WH
St. Albans Bay, VT	BUR
St. Amant, LA	BR
St. Ann, MO	STL
St. Anna, MN	SCL
WI	GB
St. Anne, IL	JOL
IN	IND
St. Ansgar, IA	DUB
St. Anthony, IA	DUB
ID	B
IN	EVN
MN	SCL
MO	JC
ND	BIS
OH	CIN
St. Augusta, MN	SCL
St. Augustine, FL	STA
IL	PEO
PA	ALT
St. Augustine Shores, FL	STA
St. Benedict, IA	SC
KS	KCK
LA	NO
MN	STP
OR	P
St. Bernard, IN	EVN
LA	NO
St. Bonaventure, NY	BUF
St. Boniface, PA	ALT
St. Bonifacius, MN	STP
St. Catharine, KY	L
St. Catherine, IA	DUB
St. Cecilia, IA	DUB
St. Charles, IL	RCK
MI	SAG
MN	WIN
MO	STL
NE	OM
St. Clair, MI	DET
MN	WIN
MO	STL
Saint Clair, PA	ALN
St. Clair, PA	PHU
PA	PSC
St. Clair Shores, MI	DET
St. Clairsville, OH	STU
St. Clement, MO	JC
St. Cloud, FL	ORL
MN	SCL
WI	MIL
St. Columbans, NE	OM
St. Croix, IN	IND
VI	STV
St. David, AZ	TUC
St. Denis, IN	IND
St. Donatus, IA	DUB
St. Edward, NE	OM
St. Elizabeth, MO	JC
St. Elmo, IL	SFD
St. Francis, KS	SAL
KY	L
ME	PRT
MN	SCL
SD	RC
WI	MIL
St. Francisville, IL	BEL
LA	BR
St. Gabriel, LA	BR
St. George, IL	JOL
UT	SLC
WI	MIL
St. Hedwig, TX	SAT
St. Helen, MI	GAY
Saint Helena, CA	SR
St. Helena, NE	OM
St. Helena Island, SC	CHR
St. Helens, OR	P
St. Henry, IN	EVN
MN	STP
OH	CIN
St. Ignace, MI	MAR
St. Ignatius, MT	HEL
St. Inigoes, MD	WDC
St. Jacob, IL	SFD
St. James, IN	EVN
LA	BR
MI	GAY
MN	WIN
MO	JC
NE	OM
NY	RVC
St. Joe, WI	MIL
Saint John, IN	GRY
St. John, KS	DOD
KY	L
ME	PRT
ND	FAR
NE	OM
TX	VIC
WA	SPK
WI	GB
St. Johns, AZ	GLP
MI	LAN
St. Johnsbury, VT	BUR
St. Johnsville, NY	ALB
St. Joseph, FL	SP
IA	SC
IN	EVN
IN	IND
KS	SAL
KY	L
KY	OWN
LA	ALX
MI	KAL
MN	SCL
MO	KC
MO	STN
OH	CIN
Saint Joseph, TN	NSH
St. Joseph Hill, IN	IND
Saint Joseph Ridge, WI	LC
St. Joseph Settlement, WV	WH
St. Kilian, MN	WIN
WI	MIL
St. Lawrence, PA	ALT
TX	SAN
WI	MIL
St. Leo, FL	SP
KS	WCH
MN	NU
St. Leon, IN	IND
St. Libory, IL	BEL
NE	GI
St. Louis, KS	KCK
MI	SAG
MO	JC
MO	OLL
MO	PRM
MO	STL
MO	STN
OR	P
St. Louis County, MO	STL
St. Louis Park, MN	STP
St. Lucas, IA	DUB
Saint Maries, ID	B
St. Mark, IN	IND
St. Mark's, KS	WCH
St. Martin, IN	EVN
MN	SCL
Saint Martin, OH	CIN
St. Martins, MO	JC
WI	MIL
St. Martinville, LA	LAF
St. Mary, KS	DOD
KY	L
St. Mary's, MO	STL
St. Mary's City, MD	WDC
Saint Mary's Ridge, WI	LC
St. Mary-of-the-Knobs, IN	IND
St. Mary-of-the-Rock, IN	IND
St. Mary-of-the-Woods, IN	IND
St. Marys, AK	FBK
GA	SAV
IA	DM
KS	KCK
OH	CIN
PA	E
WV	WH
St. Mathias, MN	DUL
St. Maurice, IN	IND
St. Meinrad, IN	IND
St. Michael, AK	FBK
MN	STP
ND	BIS
ND	FAR
PA	ALT
WI	MIL
St. Michael's Ridge, OH	TOL
St. Michaels, AZ	GLP
St. Nazianz, WI	GB
St. Nicholas, IN	IND
MN	SCL
St. Paris, OH	CIN
St. Patrick, KS	KCK
MO	JC
OH	CIN
St. Paul, IA	DAV
KS	WCH
KY	OWN
MN	OLL
MN	STN
MN	STP
MO	STL
NE	GI
OR	P
VA	RIC
St. Paul Park, MN	STP
St. Pete Beach, FL	SP
St. Peter, IN	IND
KS	SAL
MN	NU
WI	MIL
St. Peters, MO	STL
St. Petersburg, FL	MIA
FL	PSC
FL	SJP
FL	SP
St. Philip, IN	EVN
St. Pius, IN	IND
Saint Regis Falls, NY	OG
St. Rosa, MN	SCL
St. Rose, IL	BEL
LA	NO
OH	CIN
St. Sebastian, IL	BEL
OH	CIN
St. Simons Island, GA	SAV
St. Stephen, MN	SCL
OH	TOL
St. Stephens, WY	CHY
St. Theresa, IA	DUB
St. Thomas, KY	L
MN	STP
MO	JC
ND	FAR
VI	STV
St. Vincent, AR	LR
St. Vincent de Paul, IN	IND
St. Wendel, IN	EVN
MN	SCL
St. Wendelin, OH	CIN
St. Xavier, MT	GF
Saipan, MP	CHK
Salado, TX	AUS
Salamanca, NY	BUF
Salem, IL	BEL
IN	IND
MA	BO
MA	STF
MO	SPC
NH	MAN
NJ	CAM
NY	ALB
OH	Y
OR	P
SD	SFS
VA	RIC
WV	WH
Salem Twp., OH	TOL
Salida, CO	COS
Salina, KS	SAL
Salinas, CA	MRY
PR	PCE
Saline, MI	LAN
Salineville, OH	Y
Salisbury, MA	BO
MD	WIL
MO	JC
NC	CHL
Salix, IA	SC
Sallisaw, OK	TLS
Salmon, ID	B
Salt Lake City, UT	SLC
UT	VNN
Saltaire, NY	RVC
Saltsburg, PA	GBG
Sam Rayburn, TX	BEA
Samuels, KY	L
San Andreas, CA	STO
San Angelo, TX	SAN
San Anselmo, CA	SFR
San Antonio, FL	SP
TX	CLV

TX	OLL
TX	PBR
TX	SAT
San Antonio Village, MP	CHK
San Benito, TX	BWN
San Bernardino, CA	NTN
CA	SB
San Bruno, CA	SFR
San Carlos, AZ	TUC
CA	SFR
TX	BWN
San Clemente, CA	ORG
San Diego, CA	NTN
CA	OLD
CA	OLL
CA	SD
CA	STN
CA	VNN
TX	CC
San Dimas, CA	LA
San Elizario, TX	ELP
San Fernando, CA	LA
San Fidel, NM	GLP
San Francisco, CA	SFR
CA	STN
San Gabriel, CA	LA
San German, PR	MGZ
San Isidro, TX	BWN
San Jacinto, CA	SB
San Jose, CA	EST
CA	SJ
San Jose Village, MP	CHK
San Jose Village, MP	CHK
San Juan, PR	SJN
Puerto Rico	SJN
TX	BWN
San Juan Bautista, CA	MRY
San Juan Capistrano, CA	ORG
San Juan Pueblo, NM	SFE
San Leandro, CA	OAK
San Lorenzo, CA	OAK
PR	CGS
San Luis, CO	PBL
San Luis Obispo, CA	MRY
CA	VNN
San Luis Rey, CA	SD
San Manuel, AZ	TUC
San Marcos, CA	SD
TX	AUS
San Marino, CA	LA
San Mateo, CA	SFR
CA	VNN
NM	GLP
San Miguel, CA	MRY
NM	LSC
San Pablo, CA	OAK
San Pedro, CA	LA
San Pierre, IN	GRY
San Rafael, CA	SFR
NM	GLP
San Ramon, CA	OAK
San Roque Village, MP	CHK
San Saba, TX	AUS
San Sebastian, PR	MGZ
San Vicente Village, MP	CHK
San Ysidro, CA	SD
Sanborn, IA	SC
MN	NU
ND	FAR
WI	SUP
Sanbornville, NH	MAN
Sand Lake, MI	GR
Sand Springs, IA	DUB
OK	TLS
Sanderson, TX	SAN
Sandia, TX	CC
Sandoval, IL	BEL
Sandpoint, ID	B
Sandstone, MN	DUL
Sandusky, MI	SAG
OH	TOL
Sandwich, IL	RCK
MA	FR
Sandy, OR	P
UT	SLC
Sandy Hook, KY	LEX
Sanford, FL	ORL
ME	PRT
MI	SAG
NC	R
Sanger, CA	FRS
Sanibel, FL	VEN
Sanitaria Springs, NY	SY
Santa Ana, CA	ORG
Santa Barbara, CA	LA
Santa Clara, CA	SJ
CA	STN
NM	LSC
Santa Clarita, CA	LA
Santa Claus, IN	EVN
Santa Cruz, CA	MRY

NM	SFE
Santa Fe, NM	SFE
Santa Fe Springs, CA	LA
Santa Isabel, PR	PCE
Santa Margarita, CA	MRY
Santa Maria, CA	LA
Santa Monica, CA	LA
Santa Paula, CA	LA
Santa Rita, GU	AGN
Santa Rosa, CA	SR
NM	SFE
TX	BWN
Santa Rosa Beach, FL	PT
Santa Ynez, CA	LA
Santa Ysabel, CA	SD
Santa Ysabel Indian Missions, CA	SD
Santee, CA	SD
Santurce, PR	SJN
Sappington, MO	STL
Sapulpa, OK	TLS
Saranac, MI	GR
Saranac Lake, NY	OG
Sarasota, FL	VEN
Saratoga, CA	SJ
NY	ALB
WY	CHY
Saratoga Springs, NY	ALB
Sarcoxie, MO	SPC
Sardinia, NY	BUF
OH	CIN
Sardis, OH	STU
Sarita, TX	CC
Sarona, WI	SUP
Sarpy Co., NE	OM
Sartell, MN	SCL
Satanta, KS	DOD
Satin, TX	AUS
Saugerties, NY	NY
Saugus, MA	BO
Sauk Centre, MN	SCL
Sauk City, WI	MAD
Sauk Rapids, MN	SCL
Sauk Village, IL	CHI
Saukville, WI	MIL
Sault Sainte Marie, MI	MAR
Sausalito, CA	SFR
Savage, MN	STP
Savanna, IL	RCK
Savannah, GA	SAV
MO	KC
TN	MEM
Saxon, WI	SUP
Saxonville, MA	BO
Sayner, WI	SUP
Sayre, PA	PHU
PA	SCR
Sayreville, NJ	MET
Sayville, NY	RVC
Scales Mound, IL	RCK
Scammon, KS	WCH
Scammon Bay, AK	FBK
Scappoose, OR	P
Scarborough, ME	PRT
NY	NY
Scarsdale, NY	NY
Schaffer, MI	MAR
Schaghticoke, NY	ALB
Schaller, IA	SC
Schaumburg, IL	CHI
Scheller, IL	BEL
Schenectady, NY	ALB
Schererville, IN	GRY
Schertz, TX	SAT
Schiller Park, IL	CHI
Schley, IA	DUB
Schnellville, IN	EVN
Schoenchen, KS	SAL
Schoharie, NY	ALB
School Hill, WI	GB
Schooley's Mountain, NJ	PAT
Schriever, LA	HT
Schroon Lake, NY	OG
Schulenburg, TX	VIC
Schulte, KS	WCH
Schuyler, NE	OM
Schuylerville, NY	ALB
Schuylkill Haven, PA	ALN
Scio, OR	P
Sciota, NY	OG
Scipio, KS	KCK
Scipio Center, NY	ROC
Scituate, MA	BO
RI	PRO
Scobey, MT	GF
Scotch Plains, NJ	NEW
Scotia, CA	SR
NY	ALB
Scotland, SD	SFS
TX	FWT
Scott, LA	LAF
Scott City, KS	DOD

MO	SPC
Scott Township, PA	PIT
Scottdale, PA	GBG
PA	PBR
Scotts Valley, CA	MRY
Scottsbluff, NE	GI
Scottsboro, AL	BIR
Scottsburg, IN	IND
Scottsdale, AZ	EST
AZ	PHX
Scottsville, KY	OWN
NY	ROC
VA	RIC
Scottville, MI	GR
Scranton, AR	LR
IA	SC
KS	KCK
PA	NTN
PA	PHU
PA	PSC
PA	SAM
PA	SCR
Sea Cliff, NY	BRK
NY	RVC
Sea Girt, NJ	TR
Sea Isle City, NJ	CAM
Seabrook, NH	MAN
Seaford, DE	WIL
NY	RVC
Seaforth, MN	NU
Seahurst, WA	SEA
Seal Beach, CA	ORG
Sealy, TX	GAL
Searcy, AR	LR
Searles, MN	NU
Seaside, CA	MRY
OR	P
Seaside Heights, NJ	TR
Seaside Park, NJ	TR
Seat Pleasant, MD	WDC
Seattle, WA	SEA
WA	VNN
Seaview, WA	SEA
Sebastian, FL	PMB
Sebastopol, CA	SR
Sebewaing, MI	SAG
Seboyeta, NM	GLP
Sebree, KY	OWN
Sebring, FL	VEN
OH	Y
Secane, PA	PH
Secaucus, NJ	NEW
Secretary, MD	WIL
Security, CO	COS
Sedalia, CO	COS
MO	JC
Sedan, KS	WCH
MN	SCL
Sedona, AZ	PHX
Sedro Woolley, WA	SEA
Seekonk, MA	FR
Seelyville, IN	IND
Seffner, FL	SP
Seguin, KS	SAL
TX	SAT
Seinwar, FM	CI
Selah, WA	YAK
Selby, SD	SFS
Selden, KS	SAL
NY	RVC
Selfridge, ND	BIS
Seligman, AZ	PHX
Selinsgrove, PA	HBG
Sellersburg, IN	IND
Sellersvile, PA	PH
Sellersville, PA	PH
Selma, AL	MOB
CA	FRS
TX	SAT
Selmer, TN	MEM
Selz, ND	FAR
Seminole, FL	SP
OK	OKL
TX	LUB
Semmes, AL	MOB
Senatobia, MS	JKS
Seneca, IL	PEO
KS	KCK
MO	SPC
SD	SFS
WI	LC
Seneca Falls, NY	ROC
Sentinel Butte, ND	BIS
Sepulveda, CA	LA
Sequim, WA	SEA
Sereno, MO	STL
Sesser, IL	BEL
Setauket, NY	RVC
Severn, MD	BAL
Severna Park, MD	BAL
Seville-Creston, OH	CLV

Seward, AK	ANC
KS	DOD
NE	LIN
PA	GBG
Sewickley, PA	PIT
Seymour, CT	HRT
IL	PEO
IN	IND
TN	KNX
TX	FWT
WI	GB
WI	MAD
Shade Gap, PA	ALT
Shady Cove, OR	P
Shadyside, OH	STU
Shafter, CA	FRS
Shaker Heights, OH	CLV
Shakopee, MN	STP
Shallotte, NC	R
Shallowater, TX	LUB
Shamokin, PA	HBG
PA	PHU
Shandon, OH	CIN
Shannon, IL	RCK
Sharon, CT	HRT
KS	DOD
MA	BO
PA	E
PA	ROM
WI	MIL
Sharon Hill, PA	PH
Sharon Springs, KS	SAL
Sharpsburg, OH	CIN
PA	PIT
Sharpsville, PA	E
Shavertown, PA	SCR
Shaw, MS	JKS
OR	P
Shaw Island, WA	SEA
Shawano, WI	GB
Shawnee, KS	KCK
OH	COL
OK	OKL
Shawneetown, IL	BEL
Sheboygan, WI	MIL
Sheboygan Falls, WI	MIL
Sheffield, IL	PEO
MA	SPR
OH	CLV
PA	E
PA	PBR
Sheffield Lake, OH	CLV
Shelbina, MO	JC
Shelburne, VT	BUR
Shelburne Falls, MA	SPR
Shelby, IN	GRY
MI	GR
MS	JKS
MT	HEL
NC	CHL
NE	LIN
OH	TOL
Shelby Twp., MI	DET
Shelbyville, IL	SFD
IN	IND
KY	L
TN	NSH
Sheldon, IA	SC
ND	FAR
NY	BUF
WI	SUP
Sheldon Springs, VT	BUR
Shell Knob, MO	SPC
Shell Lake, WI	SUP
Shell Rock, IA	DUB
Shelter Island, NY	RVC
Shelter Island Heights, NY	RVC
Shelton, CT	BGP
WA	SEA
Shenandoah, IA	DM
PA	ALN
PA	PHU
Shepherd, MI	SAG
Shepherdstown, WV	WH
Shepherdsville, KY	L
Sheppton, PA	ALN
PA	PSC
Sherborn, MA	BO
Sherburn, MN	WIN
Sherburne, NY	SY
VT	BUR
Sheridan, AR	LR
NY	BUF
OR	P
WY	CHY
Sherman, CT	BGP
IL	SFD
NY	BUF
TX	DAL
Sherman Oaks, CA	LA
Sherrill, IA	DUB

NY	SY
Sherwood, OR	P
Sherwood Park, DE	WIL
Sherwood/St. John, WI	GB
Shevlin, MN	CR
Shields, MI	SAG
Shieldsville, MN	STP
Shillington, PA	ALN
Shiloh, IL	BEL
Shiner, TX	VIC
Shinglehouse, PA	E
Shinnston, WV	WH
Shiocton, WI	GB
Shipman, IL	SFD
Shippensburg, PA	HBG
Shiprock, NM	GLP
Shiremanstown, PA	HBG
Shirley, MA	BO
Shoal Creek, AR	LR
Shoals, IN	EVN
Shohola, PA	SCR
Shoreham, NY	RVC
Shoreview, MN	STP
Short Hills, NJ	NEW
Shortsville, NY	ROC
Shoshone, ID	B
Show Low, AZ	GLP
Shreveport, LA	SHP
Shrewsbury, MA	WOR
MO	STL
Shrub Oak, NY	NY
Shullsburg, WI	MAD
Shumway, IL	SFD
Siberia, IN	IND
Sibley, IA	SC
Sicklerville, NJ	CAM
Sidney, MT	GF
NE	GI
NY	ALB
OH	CIN
Sierra Blanca, TX	ELP
Sierra Madre, CA	LA
Sierra Vista, AZ	TUC
Sigel, IL	SFD
SD	SFS
WI	LC
Signal Mountain, TN	KNX
Sigourney, IA	DAV
Sikeston, MO	SPC
Siler City, NC	R
Siloam Springs, AR	LR
Silsbee, TX	BEA
Silver Bay, MN	DUL
Silver City, NM	LSC
Silver Creek, MI	KAL
NE	OM
NY	BUF
Silver Lake, MN	NU
MO	STL
Silver Spring, MD	BAL
MD	PHU
MD	WDC
Silver Springs, NY	BUF
Silver Springs Shores, FL	LA
FL	ORL
Silverado, CA	ORG
Silverton, CO	PBL
OR	P
Silvis, IL	PEO
imi, CA	LA
imi Valley, CA	LA
immesport, LA	ALX
impson, PA	PHU
PA	SCR
impsonville, SC	CHR
imsbury, CT	HRT
inajana, GU	AGN
inclair, ME	PRT
inclairville, NY	BUF
inking Spring, PA	ALN
insinawa, WI	MAD
inton, TX	CC
ioux City, IA	SC
ioux Falls, SD	SFS
ioux Rapids, IA	SC
isseton, SD	SFS
ster Bay, WI	GB
isters, OR	BAK
istersville, WV	WH
tka, AK	JUN
verado, CA	ORG
kagway, AK	JUN
kaneateles, NY	SY
kiatook, OK	TLS
kidmore, TX	CC
kidway Lake, MI	GAY
killman, NJ	MET
kokie, IL	CHI
kowhegan, ME	PRT
later, MO	JC
latington, PA	ALN
Slaton, TX	LUB
Slayton, MN	WIN
Sleepy Eye, MN	NU
Slickville, PA	GBG
Slidell, LA	NO
Slinger, WI	MIL
Slingerlands, NY	ALB
Slippery Rock, PA	PIT
Sloan, NY	BUF
Sloatsburg, NY	NY
NY	STF
Slovak, AR	LR
Slovan, WI	GB
Smethport, PA	E
Smiley, TX	SAT
Smith Center, KS	SAL
Smithfield, NC	R
OH	STU
RI	PRO
VA	RIC
Smithton, IL	BEL
PA	GBG
Smithtown, NY	PSC
NY	RVC
Smithville, MO	KC
TN	NSH
TX	AUS
Smock, PA	GBG
Smyrna, DE	WIL
GA	ATL
TN	NSH
Sneedville, TN	KNX
Snellville, GA	ATL
Snohomish, WA	SEA
Snoqualmie, WA	SEA
Snow Shoe, PA	ALT
Snowflake, AZ	GLP
Snowmass, CO	DEN
Snyder, NE	OM
NY	BUF
TX	LUB
Sobieski, MN	SCL
WI	GB
Soboba Indian Reservation, CA	SB
Socorro, NM	SFE
Soda Springs, ID	B
Sodus, NY	ROC
Sokehs, FM	CI
Solana Beach, CA	SD
Soldotna, AK	ANC
Soledad, CA	MRY
Solomon, AZ	TUC
KS	SAL
Solomons, MD	WDC
Solon, IA	DAV
OH	CLV
OH	PRM
OH	SJP
Solon Springs, WI	SUP
Solvang, CA	LA
Solvay, NY	SY
Somerdale, NJ	CAM
Somers, NY	NY
Somers Point, NJ	CAM
Somerset, KY	LEX
MA	FR
NJ	MET
NJ	PSC
NJ	SAM
OH	COL
PA	ALT
TX	SAT
WI	SUP
Somersville, CT	NOR
Somersworth, NH	MAN
Somerton, AZ	TUC
Somerville, MA	BO
NJ	MET
TN	MEM
TX	AUS
Somonauk, IL	RCK
Songsong Village, MP	CHK
Sonoita, AZ	TUC
Sonoma, CA	SR
Sonora, CA	STO
TX	SAN
Soquel, CA	MRY
Sorgho, KY	OWN
Sorrento, LA	BR
Sound Beach, NY	RVC
Sour Lake, TX	BEA
South Amboy, NJ	MET
South Amherst, OH	CLV
South Ashburnham, MA	WOR
South Barre, MA	WOR
South Beloit, IL	RCK
South Bend, IN	FTW
IN	NTN
South Berwick, ME	PRT
South Boston, VA	RIC
South Bound Brook, NJ	MET
South Branch, WI	GB
South Burlington, VT	BUR
South Charleston, OH	CIN
WV	WH
South Coventry, PA	PH
South Dartmouth, MA	FR
South Dayton, NY	BUF
South Deerfield, MA	SPR
MA	STF
South Easton, MA	FR
South El Monte, CA	LA
South Euclid, OH	CLV
South Fork, PA	ALT
PA	PBR
South Gate, CA	LA
South Glastonbury, CT	HRT
South Glens Falls, NY	ALB
South Grafton, MA	WOR
South Hadley, MA	PSC
MA	SPR
South Haven, MI	KAL
South Heart, ND	BIS
South Hero, VT	BUR
South Hill, VA	RIC
South Holland, IL	CHI
South Houston, TX	GAL
South Huntington, NY	RVC
South Kingston, RI	PRO
South Kingstown, RI	PRO
South Kortright, NY	ALB
South Lake Tahoe, CA	SAC
South Lyon, MI	DET
South Mantoloking, NJ	TR
South Meriden, CT	HRT
South Milwaukee, WI	MIL
South Mountain, PA	HBG
South Onondaga, NY	SY
South Orange, NJ	NEW
South Ozone Park, NY	BRK
South Park Township, PA	PIT
South Pasadena, CA	LA
South Pittsburg, TN	KNX
South Plainfield, NJ	MET
South Portland, ME	PRT
South Range, MI	MAR
South River, NJ	MET
South St. Paul, MN	STP
South San Francisco, CA	SFR
South Sioux City, NE	OM
South Union, KY	OWN
South Waverly, PA	SCR
South Williamsport, PA	SCR
South Wilmington, IL	JOL
South Windsor, CT	HRT
South Yarmouth, MA	FR
Southampton, NY	RVC
PA	PH
Southborough, MA	WOR
Southbridge, MA	WOR
Southbury, CT	HRT
Southeastern Portage County, WI	LC
Southern Pines, NC	R
Southfield, MI	DET
MI	EST
Southgate, KY	COV
MI	DET
Southhaven, MS	JKS
Southington, CT	HRT
Southold, NY	RVC
Southport, NC	R
Southwick, MA	SPR
Spalding, MI	MAR
NE	GI
Spangler, PA	ALT
Spanish Lake, MO	STL
Sparkill, NY	NY
Sparks, MD	BAL
NV	RNO
Sparta, IL	BEL
MI	GR
NJ	PAT
TN	NSH
WI	LC
Spartanburg, SC	CHR
Spaulding-City Point, WI	LC
Spearfish, SD	RC
Spearman, TX	AMA
Spearville, KS	DOD
Speigletown, NY	ALB
Spencer, IA	SC
IN	IND
MA	WOR
NE	OM
OH	CLV
SD	SFS
WI	LC
WV	WH
Spencerport, NY	ROC
Spencerville, OH	TOL
Spicer, MN	NU
Spillville, IA	DUB
Spirit Lake, IA	SC
Splendora, TX	GAL
Spokane, WA	SPK
WA	VNN
Spooner, WI	SUP
Spotswood, NJ	MET
Spotsylvania, VA	ARL
Sprague, WA	SPK
Spreckels, CA	MRY
Spring, TX	GAL
Spring Branch, TX	SAT
Spring City, PA	PH
Spring Green, WI	MAD
Spring Grove, IL	RCK
PA	HBG
Spring Hill, FL	SJP
FL	SP
MN	SCL
Spring House, PA	PH
Spring Lake, MI	GR
NJ	TR
Spring Valley, CA	SD
IL	PEO
MN	WIN
NY	NY
NY	STF
WI	LC
Springbrook, IA	DUB
NY	BUF
Springdale, AR	LR
PA	PIT
WA	SPK
Springer, NM	SFE
Springerville, AZ	GLP
Springfield, CO	PBL
IL	SFD
KY	L
MA	SAM
MA	SPR
MN	NU
MO	SPC
NE	OM
NJ	NEW
OH	CIN
OR	P
OR	STN
PA	PH
SD	SFS
TN	NSH
VA	ARL
VT	BUR
WI	LC
Springfield Gardens, NY	BRK
Springvale, ME	PRT
WI	MIL
Springville, IA	DUB
NY	BUF
Spruce, WI	GB
Spruce Pine, NC	CHL
Spur, TX	LUB
Stacyville, IA	DUB
Stafford, VA	ARL
Stafford Springs, CT	NOR
Stamford, CT	BGP
CT	STF
NY	ALB
TX	LUB
Stamps, AR	LR
Stanberry, MO	KC
Standing Rock, SD	RC
Standish, ME	PRT
MI	SAG
Stanford, CA	SJ
MT	GF
Stangelville, WI	GB
Stanley, KY	OWN
ND	BIS
NY	ROC
WI	LC
Stanton, CA	ORG
MI	GR
NE	OM
TX	SAN
WI	SUP
Stanwood, WA	SEA
Staples, MN	SCL
Stapleton, NE	GI
Star City, AR	LR
IN	LFT
WV	WH
Star Lake, NY	OG
Starford, PA	GBG
Stark, WI	GB
Starke, FL	STA
Starkville, MS	JKS
Starkweather, ND	FAR
Starlight, IN	IND
State Center, IA	DUB
State College, PA	ALT
Staten Island, NY	BRK
NY	NY

NY	SAM
NY	STF
Statesboro, GA	SAV
Statesville, NC	CHL
Staunton, IL	SFD
VA	RIC
Stayton, OR	P
Ste. Genevieve, MO	STL
Ste. Marie, IL	SFD
Stead, NV	RNO
Steamboat Springs, CO	DEN
Stebbins, AK	FBK
Steele, ND	FAR
Steelton, PA	HBG
Steelville, MO	JC
Steger, IL	CHI
IL	JOL
Steinauer, NE	LIN
Stella Niagara, NY	BUF
Stephan, SD	SFS
Stephen, MN	CR
Stephenson, MI	MAR
Stephensville, WI	GB
Stephenville, TX	FWT
Sterling, CO	DEN
IL	RCK
MA	WOR
VA	ARL
Sterling Heights, MI	DET
MI	PRM
Stetsonville, WI	SUP
Steubenville, OH	STU
Stevens Point, WI	LC
Stevenson, MD	BAL
Stevensville, MT	HEL
Stewart, MN	NU
Stewartville, MN	WIN
Stickney, IL	CHI
SD	SFS
Stiles, WI	GB
Still River, MA	WOR
Stillwater, MN	STP
NY	ALB
OK	TLS
Stirling, NJ	PAT
Stirum, ND	FAR
Stockbridge, MA	SPR
WI	GB
Stockdale, TX	SAT
Stockholm, ME	PRT
NJ	PAT
Stockton, CA	OLL
CA	STO
CA	VNN
IL	RCK
KS	SAL
Stone Bank, WI	MIL
Stone Harbor, NJ	CAM
Stone Lake, WI	SUP
Stone Mountain, GA	ATL
Stone Park, IL	CHI
Stoneboro, PA	E
Stonefort, IL	BEL
Stoneham, CO	DEN
MA	BO
Stonelick, OH	CIN
Stonewall, TX	SAT
Stonewood, WV	WH
Stonington, CT	NOR
IL	SFD
ME	PRT
Stony Point, NY	NY
TX	AUS
Storm Lake, IA	SC
Storrs, CT	NOR
Stottville, NY	ALB
Stoughton, MA	BO
WI	MAD
Stoutsville, MO	JC
Stow, MA	BO
OH	CLV
Stowe, PA	PH
VT	BUR
Strafford, PA	PH
Strasburg, ND	BIS
OH	COL
Stratford, CT	BGP
NJ	CAM
TX	AMA
WI	LC
Stratton, CO	COS
Strawberry Point, IA	DUB
Strawn, TX	FWT
Streamwood, IL	CHI
Streator, IL	PEO
Streetsboro, OH	Y
Strickland, WI	SUP
String Prairie, IA	DAV
TX	AUS
Stringtown, IL	BEL
Strong City, KS	WCH
Strongsville, OH	CLV
Stroudsburg, PA	SCR
Struble, IA	SC
Struthers, OH	Y
Stryker, OH	TOL
Strykersville, NY	BUF
Stuart, FL	PMB
IA	DM
NE	OM
Studio City, CA	LA
Sturgeon Bay, WI	GB
Sturgis, KY	OWN
MI	KAL
SD	RC
Sturtevant, WI	MIL
Stuttgart, AR	LR
Stuyvesant, NY	ALB
Stuyvesant Falls, NY	ALB
Suamico, WI	GB
Subiaco, AR	LR
Sublette, IL	RCK
Sublimity, OR	P
Succasunna, NJ	PAT
Sudbury, MA	BO
Suffern, NY	NY
Suffield, CT	HRT
Suffolk, VA	RIC
Sugar Camp, WI	SUP
Sugar Creek, IA	DAV
MO	KC
MO	PRM
Sugar Grove, OH	COL
Sugar Island, MI	MAR
Sugar Land, TX	GAL
Sugar Notch, PA	SCR
Sugarloaf, PA	PSC
Suitland, MD	WDC
Sulligent, AL	BIR
Sullivan, IL	SFD
IN	EVN
MO	STL
WI	MAD
Sulphur, LA	LKC
OK	OKL
Sulphur Springs, TX	TYL
Summerfield, KS	KCK
Summerhill, PA	ALT
Summersville, WV	WH
Summerton, SC	CHR
Summerville, SC	CHR
Summit, IL	CHI
NJ	NEW
NY	ALB
WI	LC
Summit Hill, PA	ALN
Summitville, OH	Y
Sumner, IA	DUB
WA	SEA
Sumter, SC	CHR
Sun City, AZ	PHX
CA	SB
Sun City Center, FL	SP
Sun City West, AZ	PHX
Sun Lakes, AZ	PHX
Sun Prairie, WI	MAD
Sun Valley, CA	LA
ID	B
NV	RNO
Sunbury, OH	COL
PA	HBG
Suncook, NH	MAN
Sunfish, KY	OWN
Sunland, CA	LA
Sunland Park, NM	LSC
Sunny Hills, FL	PT
Sunnyside, WA	YAK
Sunnyvale, CA	SJ
Sunrise, FL	MIA
Sunset Hills, MO	STL
Sunsites, AZ	TUC
Superior, AZ	TUC
NE	LIN
WI	SUP
Suring, WI	GB
Susanville, CA	SAC
Susquehanna, PA	SCR
Sussex, NJ	PAT
Sutersville, PA	GBG
Sutherland, IA	SC
NE	GI
Sutherlin, OR	P
Sutter Creek, CA	SAC
Sutton, MA	WOR
NE	LIN
Suttons Bay, MI	GAY
Swainsboro, GA	SAV
Swainton, NJ	CAM
NJ	TR
Swampscott, MA	BO
Swan Lake, MN	NU
MT	HEL
Swan Valley, MT	HEL
Swannanoa, NC	CHL
Swansboro, NC	R
Swansea, MA	FR
Swanton, OH	TOL
VT	BUR
Swanville, MN	SCL
Swarthmore, PA	PH
Swartswood, NJ	PAT
Swartz Creek, MI	LAN
Swedesboro, NJ	CAM
Swedesburg, PA	PH
Sweeny, TX	GAL
Sweet Home, OR	P
TX	VIC
Sweetwater, TX	SAN
Swissvale, PA	PIT
Switzerland, FL	STA
Swormville, NY	BUF
Swoyersville, PA	PSC
PA	SCR
Sybertsville, PA	PHU
PA	PSC
Sycamore, IL	RCK
OH	TOL
Sykeston, ND	FAR
Sykesville, MD	BAL
PA	E
PA	PBR
Sylacauga, AL	BIR
Sylmar, CA	LA
Sylva, NC	CHL
Sylvania, GA	SAV
OH	TOL
Sylvia, IA	DUB
Syosset, NY	RVC
Syracuse, IN	FTW
KS	DOD
NE	LIN
NY	STF
NY	SY
Tabb, VA	RIC
Taberg, NY	SY
Tabernacle, NJ	TR
Tabor, MN	CR
SD	SFS
Tacoma, WA	SEA
Taft, CA	FRS
TX	CC
Taftville, CT	NOR
Tahlequah, OK	TLS
Tahoe City, CA	SAC
Tai, GU	AGN
Takoma Park, MD	WDC
Talkeetna, AK	ANC
Talladega, AL	BIR
Tallahassee, FL	PT
Tallassee, AL	MOB
Tallmadge, OH	CLV
Tallulah, LA	ALX
Talofofo, GU	AGN
Tamaqua, PA	ALN
Tamarac, FL	MIA
Tamaroa, IL	BEL
Tama-Toledo, IA	DUB
Tamoroi, FM	CI
Tampa, FL	SP
KS	WCH
Tampico, IL	RCK
Tamuning, GU	AGN
Tanana, AK	FBK
Tanapag Village, MP	CHK
Taneytown, MD	BAL
Tangipahoa, LA	BR
Tannersville, PA	SCR
Taos, MO	JC
NM	SFE
Tappahannock, VA	RIC
Tappan, NY	NY
Tappan Lake, OH	STU
Tappen, ND	FAR
Tarboro, NC	R
Tarentum, PA	PBR
PA	PIT
Tariffville, CT	HRT
Tarkio, MO	KC
Tarnov, NE	OM
Tarpon Springs, FL	SP
Tarrytown, NY	NY
Taunton, MA	FR
MN	NU
Tavernier, FL	MIA
Tawas City, MI	GAY
Taycheedah, WI	MIL
Taylor, MI	DET
MI	PRM
PA	PSC
PA	SCR
TX	AUS
Taylor Mill, KY	COV
Taylors, SC	CHR
Taylors Falls, MN	STP
Taylorsville, UT	SLC
Taylorville, IL	SFD
Tazewell, TN	KNX
VA	RIC
Tea, SD	SFS
Teaneck, NJ	NEW
Techny, IL	CHI
Tecumseh, MI	LAN
NE	LIN
Tehachapi, CA	FRS
Tekamah, NE	OM
Tekoa, WA	SPK
Tell City, IN	IND
Teller, AK	FBK
Telluride, CO	PBL
Temecula, CA	NTN
CA	SB
Tempe, AZ	PHX
Temperance, MI	DET
Temperanceville, OH	STU
Temple, TX	AUS
Temple City, CA	LA
Temple Hill, IA	DUB
Temple Terrace, FL	SP
Templeton, IA	SC
Tenafly, NJ	NEW
Tennessee Ridge, TN	NSH
Tennyson-Potosi, WI	MAD
Tequesta, FL	PMB
Terre Haute, IN	IND
Terrebonne, MN	CR
Terrell, TX	DAL
Terrytown, LA	NO
Terryville, CT	HRT
CT	STF
Teutopolis, IL	SFD
Tewksbury, MA	BO
Texarkana, AR	LR
TX	TYL
Texas City, TX	GAL
Thatcher, AZ	TUC
Theilman, MN	WIN
Theresa, WI	MIL
Theriot, LA	HT
Thermal, CA	SB
Thermopolis, WY	CHY
Thibodaux, LA	HT
Thief River Falls, MN	CR
Thiensville, WI	MIL
Thiry Daems, WI	GB
Thomas, WV	WH
Thomasboro, IL	PEO
Thomaston, CT	HRT
Thomasville, GA	SAV
NC	CHL
Thompson, CT	LIT
CT	NOR
ND	FAR
OH	CLV
WI	MIL
Thompson Falls, MT	HEL
Thomson, GA	ATL
Thoreau, NM	GLP
Thorndike, MA	SPR
ME	PRT
Thornwood, NY	NY
Thorp, WI	LC
Thousand Oaks, CA	LA
Thousand Palms, CA	SB
Three Bridges, NJ	MET
Three Forks, MT	HEL
Three Lakes, WI	SUP
Three Oaks, MI	KAL
Three Rivers, CA	FRS
MA	SPR
MI	KAL
TX	CC
Throckmorton, TX	FWT
Throop, PA	SCR
Thunderbolt, GA	SAV
Thurmont, MD	BAL
Tiburon, CA	SFR
Tickfaw, LA	BR
Ticonderoga, NY	OG
Tidioute, PA	E
Tierra Amarilla, NM	SFE
Tiff, MO	STL
Tiffin, OH	TOL
Tifton, GA	SAV
Tigard, OR	P
Tiger Point, FL	PT
Tigerton, WI	GB
Tijeras, NM	SFE
Tilden, NE	OM
WI	LC
Tillamook, OR	P
Tillman's Corner, AL	MOB
Tilton, NH	MAN
Tiltonsville, OH	STU
Timber Lake, SD	RC

Timken, KS	DOD
Timonium, MD	BAL
Tinaja, NM	GLP
Tinley Park, IL	CHI
Tintah, MN	SCL
Tioga, LA	ALX
ND	BIS
Tipp City, OH	CIN
Tipton, CA	FRS
IA	DAV
IL	BEL
IN	LFT
KS	SAL
MO	JC
Tisch Mills, WI	GB
Tiskilwa, IL	PEO
Titusville, FL	ORL
PA	E
Tiverton, RI	PRO
Tivoli, NY	NY
TX	CC
Toa Alta, PR	SJN
Toa Baja, PR	SJN
Tobyhanna, PA	SCR
Toccoa, GA	ATL
Todd's Mill, IL	BEL
Tohatchi, NM	GLP
Tokio, ND	FAR
Toksook Bay, AK	FBK
Tol, FM	CI
Toledo, OH	TOL
WA	SEA
Tolland, CT	NOR
Tolleson, AZ	PHX
Tolna, ND	FAR
Tolono, IL	PEO
Toluca, IL	PEO
Tomah, WI	LC
Tomahawk, WI	SUP
Tomales, CA	SFR
Tomball, TX	GAL
Tombstone, AZ	TUC
Tome, NM	SFE
Tomil, FM	CI
Tompkinsville, KY	L
Toms River, NJ	PHU
NJ	PSC
NJ	TR
Tonasket, WA	SPK
Tonawanda, NY	BUF
Tonet, WI	GB
Tonganoxie, KS	KCK
Tonkawa, OK	OKL
Tonopah, NV	LAV
Tontitown, AR	LR
Tony, WI	SUP
Tooele, UT	SLC
Topawa, AZ	TUC
Topeka, KS	KCK
Toppenish, WA	YAK
Topsfield, MA	BO
Toronto, IA	DAV
OH	PBR
OH	STU
Torrance, CA	LA
Torrington, CT	HRT
CT	SAM
WY	CHY
Torun, WI	LC
Toto, GU	AGN
Totowa, NJ	PAT
Totowa Borough, NJ	PAT
Tours, TX	AUS
Towanda, PA	SCR
Tower, MN	DUL
Tower City, PA	ALN
Town and Country, MO	STL
Town of Gates, NY	SY
Towner, ND	FAR
Townsend, MA	BO
MT	HEL
TN	KNX
Towson, MD	BAL
Tracy, CA	STO
MN	NU
Traer, IA	DUB
Trafford, PA	GBG
Tranquillity, CA	FRS
Trappist, KY	L
Trauger, PA	GBG
PA	PBR
Traverse City, MI	GAY
Tremont, PA	ALN
Trempealeau, WI	LC
Trenary, MI	MAR
Trenton, IL	BEL
MI	DET
MO	KC
NE	LIN
NJ	PHU
NJ	PSC

NJ	ROM
NJ	TR
OH	CIN
Tres Pinos, CA	MRY
Tresckow, PA	ALN
Trevorton, PA	HBG
Triangle, VA	ARL
Tribes Hill, NY	ALB
Tribune, KS	DOD
Trimont, MN	WIN
Trinidad, CO	PBL
Trinity, TX	TYL
Tripp, SD	SFS
Trona, CA	SB
Trooper, PA	PH
Trout River, NY	OG
Troy, AL	MOB
IL	SFD
IN	IND
KS	KCK
MI	DET
MI	EST
MO	STL
NH	MAN
NY	ALB
NY	SAM
NY	STF
OH	CIN
VT	BUR
Truckee, CA	SAC
Trujillo Alto, PR	SJN
Truman, MN	WIN
Trumansburg, NY	ROC
Trumbull, CT	BGP
CT	PSC
Truro, MA	FR
Trussville, AL	BIR
Truth or Consequences, NM	LSC
Truxton, NY	SY
Tryon, NC	CHL
Tualatin, OR	P
Tuba City, AZ	GLP
Tubac, AZ	TUC
Tuckahoe, NY	NY
Tuckerton, NJ	TR
Tucson, AZ	STN
AZ	TUC
AZ	VNN
Tucumcari, NM	SFE
Tujunga, CA	LA
Tukwila, WA	SEA
Tulare, CA	FRS
Tularosa, NM	LSC
Tulelake, CA	SAC
Tulia, TX	AMA
Tullahoma, TN	NSH
Tully, NY	SY
Tulsa, OK	TLS
Tum Tum, WA	SPK
Tumon Bay, GU	AGN
Tumwater, WA	SEA
Tunkhannock, PA	SCR
Tunnuk, Chuuk, FM	CI
Tununak, AK	FBK
Tupelo, MS	JKS
Tupper Lake, NY	OG
Tupper Plains, OH	STU
Turlock, CA	EST
CA	STO
Turners Falls, MA	SPR
Turtle Creek, PA	PIT
Turtle Lake, WI	SUP
Turtle Mountain Reservation, ND	FAR
Turton, SD	SFS
Tuscaloosa, AL	BIR
Tuscarora, PA	ALN
Tuscola, IL	SFD
Tuscumbia, AL	BIR
Tuskegee Institute, AL	MOB
Tustin, CA	ORG
CA	SB
Tutwiler, MS	JKS
Tuxedo, NY	NY
Twain Harte, CA	STO
Twenty Mile Stand, OH	CIN
Twentynine Palms, CA	SB
Twin Falls, ID	B
Twin Lakes, MN	WIN
WI	MIL
Twin Rocks, PA	ALT
Twin Valley, MN	CR
Twinsburg, OH	CLV
Twisp, WA	SPK
Two Harbors, MN	DUL
Two Inlets, MN	CR
Two Rivers, WI	GB
Tybee Island, GA	SAV
Tyler, MN	NU
TX	TYL
Tyndall, SD	SFS
Tyngsboro, MA	BO

Tyringham, MA	SPR
Tyrone, PA	ALT
Ubly, MI	SAG
Udot, FM	CI
Uhland, TX	AUS
Ukiah, CA	SR
Ulithi and Neighboring Islands, FM	CI
Ullin, IL	BEL
Ulul, FM	CI
Ulysses, KS	DOD
NE	LIN
Umatac, GU	AGN
Umbarger, TX	AMA
Unadilla, NY	ALB
Unalakleet, AK	FBK
Uncasville, CT	NOR
Underhill Center, VT	BUR
Underwood, ND	BIS
Union, KY	COV
MO	STL
NJ	NEW
OR	BAK
SC	CHR
Union Beach, NJ	TR
Union Center, WI	LC
Union City, CA	OAK
CT	HRT
IN	LFT
NJ	NEW
OK	OKL
PA	E
TN	MEM
Union Grove, WI	MIL
Union Grove-Gladewater, TX	TYL
Union Hill, MN	STP
Union Springs, NY	ROC
Uniondale, NY	RVC
Uniontown, KY	OWN
OH	Y
PA	GBG
PA	PBR
PA	SAM
WA	SPK
Unionville, CT	HRT
United, PA	GBG
Unity, PA	PIT
Universal, IN	IND
University City, MO	STL
University Heights, OH	CLV
University Park, MD	WDC
PA	ALT
Upland, CA	SB
Upper Darby, PA	PH
Upper Frenchville, ME	PRT
Upper Gwynedd, PA	PH
Upper Marlboro, MD	BAL
MD	WDC
Upper Montclair, NJ	NEW
Upper Saddle River, NJ	NEW
Upper St. Clair, PA	PBR
PA	PIT
Upper Sandusky, OH	TOL
Upsala, MN	SCL
Upton, MA	WOR
Urbana, IA	DUB
IL	PEO
MD	BAL
OH	CIN
Urbandale, IA	DM
Urbank, MN	SCL
Ushers, NY	ALB
Usk, WA	SPK
Utica, IL	PEO
MI	DET
NY	NTN
NY	SAM
NY	STF
NY	SY
OH	COL
Utuado, PR	ARE
Uvalde, TX	SAT
Uxbridge, MA	WOR
Vacaville, CA	SAC
Vacherie, LA	BR
Vail, AZ	TUC
CO	DEN
IA	SC
Valatie, NY	ALB
Valdez, AK	ANC
Valdosta, GA	SAV
Vale, NC	CHL
OR	BAK
Valentine, NE	GI
Valeria, IA	DAV
Valhalla, NY	NY
Valier, MT	HEL
Valinda, CA	LA
Vallejo, CA	SAC
Valley, NE	OM
WA	SPK
Valley Center, CA	SD

Valley City, ND	FAR
OH	CLV
Valley Falls, KS	KCK
Valley Forge, PA	PH
Valley Lee, MD	WDC
Valley Park, MO	STL
Valley Station, KY	L
Valley Stream, NY	RVC
Valley View, TX	FWT
Valmeyer, IL	BEL
Valparaiso, IN	GRY
NE	LIN
Valrico, FL	SP
Valyermo, CA	LA
Van Buren, AR	LR
ME	PRT
Van Etten, NY	ROC
Van Horn, TX	ELP
Van Horne, IA	DUB
Van Nuys, CA	LA
CA	VNN
Van Wert, OH	TOL
Vanceburg, KY	COV
Vancleave, MS	BLX
Vancouver, WA	SEA
Vandalia, IL	SFD
MO	JC
NY	BUF
OH	CIN
Vanderbilt, MI	GAY
TX	VIC
Vandergrift, PA	GBG
Varina, IA	SC
Varysburg, NY	BUF
Vashon, WA	SEA
Vassar, MI	SAG
Vattman, TX	CC
Vaughn, NM	SFE
Veblen, SD	SFS
Vega, TX	AMA
Vega Alta, PR	ARE
Vega-Baja, PR	ARE
Velva, ND	FAR
Veneta, OR	P
Venice, CA	LA
FL	VEN
IL	SFD
Ventnor, NJ	CAM
PA	PH
Ventura, CA	LA
Vera Cruz, OH	CIN
Verboort, OR	P
Verdigre, NE	OM
Verga, NJ	CAM
Vergennes, VT	BUR
Vermilion, OH	TOL
Vermillion, MN	STP
SD	SFS
Vernal, UT	SLC
Verndale, MN	SCL
Vernon, CA	LA
CT	NOR
NY	SY
TX	FWT
Vernon Center, MN	WIN
Vernon Hills, IL	CHI
Vernonia, OR	P
Vero Beach, FL	PMB
Verona, MO	SPC
ND	FAR
NJ	NEW
NY	SY
PA	PIT
WI	MAD
Verplanck, NY	NY
Versailles, KY	LEX
OH	CIN
PA	PIT
Veseleyville, ND	FAR
Veseli, MN	STP
Vesper, WI	LC
Vesta, MN	NU
Vestal, NY	SY
Vevay, IN	IND
Vicksburg, MI	KAL
MS	JKS
Victor, IA	DAV
NY	ROC
Victoria, KS	SAL
MN	STP
TX	VIC
Victorville, CA	SB
Vidalia, GA	SAV
LA	ALX
Vidor, TX	BEA
Vienna, IL	BEL
MO	JC
OH	Y
VA	ARL
WV	WH
Vieques, PR	CGS

Villa Grove, IL	SFD
Villa Hills, KY	COV
Villa Maria, PA	PIT
Villa Nova, IA	DAV
Villa Park, IL	JOL
Villa Ridge, IL	BEL
Villalba, PR	PCE
Villanova, PA	PH
Villanueva, NM	SFE
Villard, MN	SCL
Villas, NJ	CAM
Ville Platte, LA	LAF
Villisca, IA	DM
Vina, CA	SAC
Vincennes, IN	EVN
Vincent, KS	SAL
OH	STU
Vine Grove, KY	L
Vineland, CO	PBL
MN	SCL
NJ	CAM
Vineyard Haven, MA	FR
Vining, IA	DUB
Vinita, OK	TLS
Vinita Park, MO	STL
Vinton, IA	DUB
LA	LKC
Violet, LA	NO
TX	CC
Virden, IL	SFD
Virgil, IL	RCK
Virginia, IL	SFD
MN	DUL
Virginia Beach, VA	RIC
Virginia City, NV	RNO
Virginia Dale, CO	DEN
Viroqua, WI	LC
Visalia, CA	FRS
Vista, CA	SD
Vivian, LA	SHP
Vodnany, SD	SFS
Volga, IA	DUB
Volo, IL	CHI
Voluntown, CT	NOR
Von Ormy, TX	SAT
Voorheesville, NY	ALB
Vredenburgh, AL	MOB
Vulcan, MI	MAR
Wabash, IN	FTW
Wabasha, MN	WIN
Wabasso, MN	NU
Wabeno, WI	GB
Waco, TX	AUS
Waconia, MN	STP
Waddington, NY	OG
Wadena, MN	SCL
Wading River, NY	RVC
Wadsworth, IL	CHI
OH	CLV
Waggaman, LA	NO
Wagner, SD	SFS
WI	GB
Wagon Mound, NM	SFE
Wagoner, OK	TLS
Wahiawa, HI	HON
Wahkon, MN	SCL
Wahoo, NE	LIN
Wahpeton, ND	FAR
Waialua, HI	HON
Waialua, Oahu, HI	HON
Waianae, HI	HON
Waihee, HI	HON
Waikane, HI	HON
Wailuku, HI	HON
Wailuku, Maui, HI	HON
Waimanalo, HI	HON
Wainwright, OH	COL
Waipahu, HI	HON
Waite Park, MN	SCL
Waitsburg, WA	SPK
Waitsfield, VT	BUR
Wake Forest, NC	R
WaKeeney, KS	SAL
Wakefield, MA	BO
MI	MAR
RI	PRO
Wakeman, OH	TOL
Wakonda, SD	SFS
Walbridge, OH	TOL
Walden, CO	DEN
NY	NY
Waldorf, MD	WDC
MN	WIN
Waldport, OR	P
Waldron, AR	LR
Wales, ND	FAR
Walford, IA	DUB
Walhain, WI	GB
Walhalla, ND	FAR
Walker, IA	DUB
KS	SAL
MN	DUL
Walkersville, MD	BAL
Walkerton, IN	FTW
Walkerville, MT	HEL
Wall, PA	PBR
SD	RC
TX	SAN
Wall Lake, IA	SC
Walla Walla, WA	SPK
WA	VNN
Wallace, ID	B
KS	SAL
NE	LIN
Wallagrass, ME	PRT
Walled Lake, MI	DET
Wallingford, CT	HRT
PA	PH
VT	BUR
Wallington, NJ	NEW
Wallis, TX	GAL
Walls, MS	JKS
Walnut, CA	LA
IA	DM
IL	PEO
KS	WCH
Walnut Creek, CA	OAK
Walnut Grove, CA	SAC
MN	NU
Walnut Ridge, AR	LR
Walpole, MA	BO
Walsenburg, CO	PBL
Walsh, IL	BEL
WI	GB
Walston, PA	E
Walterboro, SC	CHR
Walters, OK	OKL
Waltham, MA	BO
Walthill, NE	OM
Walton, IL	RCK
KY	COV
NY	ALB
Wamego, KS	KCK
Wampum, PA	PIT
Wanamie, PA	SCR
Wanatah, IN	GRY
Wanblee, SD	RC
Wanda, MN	NU
Wantagh, NY	RVC
Wapakoneta, OH	CIN
Wapato, WA	YAK
Wapella, IL	PEO
Wapello, IA	DAV
Wappingers Falls, NY	NY
War, WV	WH
Ward, SC	CHR
Ward Springs, MN	SCL
Warden, WA	YAK
Wardsville, MO	JC
Ware, MA	SPR
Wareham, MA	FR
Warminster, PA	PH
Warner, NH	MAN
Warner Robins, GA	SAV
Warners, NY	SY
Warren, IL	RCK
MA	WOR
MI	DET
MI	NTN
MI	STN
MN	CR
NJ	MET
OH	PBR
OH	Y
PA	E
RI	PRO
Warrens, WI	LC
Warrensburg, MO	KC
NY	ALB
Warrensville Heights, OH	CLV
Warrenton, MO	STL
VA	ARL
Warrenville, CT	NOR
IL	JOL
Warrington, PA	PH
PA	PHU
Warroad, MN	CR
Warsaw, IL	PEO
IN	FTW
KY	COV
MO	JC
ND	FAR
NY	BUF
Warson Woods, MO	STL
Warwick, NY	NY
RI	PRO
Wasco, CA	FRS
OR	BAK
Waseca, MN	WIN
Washburn, IL	PEO
WI	SUP
Washington, DC	PHU
DC	SAM
DC	WDC
GA	ATL
IA	DAV
IL	PEO
IN	EVN
KS	SAL
LA	LAF
MI	DET
MO	STL
NC	R
NJ	MET
PA	PIT
VT	BUR
Washington Court House, OH	COL
Washington Crossing, NJ	TR
Washington Depot, CT	HRT
Washington Park, IL	BEL
Washington Township, NJ	CAM
NJ	NEW
Washingtonville, NY	NY
Washtunca, WA	SPK
Wasilla, AK	ANC
Wassaic, NY	NY
Watauga, SD	RC
Watchung, NJ	MET
Water Mill, NY	RVC
Waterbury, CT	HRT
CT	SAM
VT	BUR
Waterflow, NM	GLP
Waterford, CT	NOR
CT	NTN
MI	DET
NJ	CAM
NY	ALB
PA	E
WI	MIL
Waterloo, IA	DUB
IL	BEL
IN	FTW
KS	WCH
NY	ROC
WI	MAD
Watersmeet, MI	MAR
Watertown, CT	HRT
MA	BO
MN	STP
NY	OG
SD	SFS
WI	MAD
Waterville, KS	KCK
ME	PRT
ME	SAM
MN	STP
NY	SY
WA	YAK
Watervliet, MI	KAL
NY	ALB
NY	STF
Watford City, ND	BIS
Wathena, KS	KCK
Watkins, IA	DUB
MN	NU
Watkins Glen, NY	ROC
Watonga, OK	OKL
Watseka, IL	JOL
Watsonville, CA	MRY
Wattenberg, CO	DEN
Waubay, SD	SFS
Waubun, MN	CR
Wauchula, FL	VEN
Waucoma, IA	DUB
Wauconda, IL	CHI
Waukee, IA	DM
Waukegan, IL	CHI
Waukesha, WI	MIL
Waukon, IA	DUB
Waumandee, WI	LC
Waunakee, WI	MAD
Waupaca, WI	GB
Waupun, WI	MIL
Wauregan, CT	NOR
Wausau, WI	LC
Wausaukee, WI	GB
Wauseon, OH	TOL
Wautoma, WI	GB
Wauwatosa, WI	MIL
Wauzeka, WI	LC
Waveland, MS	BLX
Waverly, IA	DUB
IL	SFD
KS	KCK
KY	OWN
MN	STP
NE	LIN
NY	ROC
OH	COL
SD	SFS
Wax, KY	OWN
Waxahachie, TX	DAL
Waycross, GA	SAV
Wayland, MA	BO
MI	KAL
NY	ROC
Waymart, PA	SCR
Wayne, IL	JOL
MI	DET
NE	OM
NJ	PAT
PA	PH
WI	MIL
WV	WH
Waynesboro, GA	SAV
MS	BLX
PA	HBG
TN	NSH
VA	RIC
Waynesburg, OH	Y
PA	PIT
Waynesville, MO	JC
NC	CHL
OH	CIN
Wayside, NJ	TR
Wayzata, MN	STP
Wea, KS	KCK
Weare Twp., MI	GR
Weatherford, OK	OKL
TX	FWT
Weatherly, PA	ALN
Weaverville, CA	SAC
Webb City, MO	SPC
Webster, MA	WOR
NY	ROC
SD	SFS
WI	SUP
Webster City, IA	DUB
Webster Groves, MO	STL
Webster Springs, WV	WH
Wedron, IL	PEO
Weed, CA	SAC
Weedsport, NY	ROC
Weehawken, NJ	NEW
Weeno, Chuuk, FM	CI
Weimar, TX	VIC
Weiner, AR	LR
Weingarten, MO	STL
Weir, KS	WCH
Weirton, WV	PBR
WV	WH
Weiser, ID	B
Welch, WV	WH
Weldona, CO	DEN
Weller, IA	DAV
Wellesley, MA	BO
Wellfleet, MA	FR
Wellington, FL	PMB
KS	WCH
OH	CLV
SD	SFS
TX	AMA
Wellman, IA	DAV
Wellpinit, WA	SPK
Wells, ME	PRT
MI	MAR
MN	WIN
NY	OG
Wellsboro, PA	SCR
Wellsburg, WV	WH
Wellston, MO	STL
OH	COL
Wellsville, MO	JC
NY	BUF
OH	Y
Welsh, LA	LKC
Welton, IA	DAV
Wenatchee, WA	YAK
Wendelin, IL	BEL
Wendell, ID	B
NC	R
Wendover, UT	SLC
Wenham, MA	BO
Wenona, IL	PEO
Wentzville, MO	STL
Wernersville, PA	ALN
Weslaco, TX	BWN
Wesley, IA	SC
Wesley Hills, NY	NY
Wessington, SD	SFS
Wessington Springs, SD	SFS
West, TX	AUS
West Albany, MN	WIN
West Aliquippa, PA	PIT
West Allis, WI	MIL
West Alton, MO	STL
West Babylon, NY	RVC
West Bangor, PA	ALN
West Barnstable, MA	FR
West Bend, IA	SC
WI	MIL
West Bethesda, MD	WDC
West Bloomfield, MI	DET

MI	EST
West Boylston, MA	WOR
West Branch, IA	DAV
MI	GAY
West Brattleboro, VT	BUR
VT	LIT
West Bridgewater, MA	BO
West Brookfield, MA	WOR
West Brooklyn, IL	RCK
West Burke, VT	STF
West Burlington, IA	DAV
West Chazy, NY	OG
West Chester, OH	CIN
PA	PH
West Chicago, IL	JOL
West Clarksville, NY	BUF
West Collingswood, NJ	CAM
West Concord, MN	WIN
West Conshohocken, PA	PH
West Covina, CA	LA
West Des Moines, IA	DM
West Duluth, MN	DUL
West Easton, PA	PHU
West Falls, NY	BUF
West Fargo, ND	FAR
West Frankfort, IL	BEL
West Franklin, NH	MAN
West Greenwich, RI	PRO
West Grove, PA	PH
West Hartford, CT	HRT
West Harwich, MA	FR
West Haven, CT	HRT
West Haverstraw, NY	NY
West Hazleton, PA	SCR
West Hempstead, NY	RVC
West Hollywood, CA	LA
FL	MIA
West Hurley-Woodstock, NY	NY
West Hyattsville, MD	WDC
West Islip, NY	RVC
NY	STF
West Jefferson, OH	COL
West Jordan, UT	SLC
West Kewaunee, WI	GB
West Lafayette, IN	LFT
West Lake Forest, IL	CHI
West Lawn, PA	ALN
West Lebanon, NH	MAN
West Leechburg, PA	SJP
West Leyden, NY	OG
West Liberty, IA	DAV
KY	LEX
WV	WH
West Long Branch, NJ	TR
West Memphis, AR	LR
West Middlesex, PA	E
West Mifflin, PA	PIT
West Milford Township, NJ	PAT
West Milton, OH	CIN
West Mineral, KS	WCH
West Monroe, LA	SHP
West New York, NJ	NEW
West Newbury, MA	BO
West Newton, PA	GBG
West Newton Township, MN	NU
West Nyack, NY	NY
West Orange, NJ	NEW
West Overland, MO	STL
West Palm Beach, FL	PMB
FL	SAM
West Park, NY	NY
West Paterson, NJ	NTN
NJ	PAT
West Peoria, IL	PEO
West Pittsburg, PA	PIT
West Pittston, PA	SCR
West Plains, MO	SPC
West Point, IA	DAV
MS	JKS
NE	OM
NY	NY
VA	RIC
West Portsmouth, OH	COL
West Reading, PA	ALN
West Redding, CT	BGP
West Rutland, VT	BUR
West Sacramento, CA	SAC
West St. Paul, MN	STP
West Salem, OH	CLV
WI	LC
West Salisbury, PA	ALT
West Seneca, NY	BUF
West Simsbury, CT	HRT
West Springfield, MA	SPR
West Stewartstown, NH	MAN
West Stockbridge, MA	SPR
West Sunbury, PA	PIT
West Swanzey, NH	MAN
West Taghkanic, NY	ALB
West Terre Haute, IN	IND
West Union, IA	DUB

MN	SCL
OH	CIN
WV	WH
West Valley, NY	BUF
West Valley City, UT	SLC
West View, PA	PIT
West Warren, MA	WOR
West Warwick, RI	PRO
West Willington, CT	NOR
West Windsor, NJ	TR
West Winfield, NY	ALB
West Wyoming, PA	SCR
West Yellowstone, MT	HEL
Westboro, WI	SUP
Westborough, MA	WOR
Westbrook, CT	NOR
ME	PRT
MN	WIN
Westbury, NY	PSC
NY	RVC
Westchester, IL	CHI
Westcliffe, CO	PBL
Westend, WA	SPK
Westerly, RI	PRO
Western Springs, IL	CHI
Westernport, MD	BAL
Westerville, OH	COL
Westfield, IN	LFT
MA	SPR
NJ	NEW
NY	BUF
VT	BUR
Westford, MA	BO
Westhampton Beach, NY	RVC
Westhope, ND	FAR
Westlake, CA	LA
LA	LKC
OH	CLV
Westlake Village, CA	LA
Westland, MI	DET
Westminster, CA	ORG
CO	DEN
MA	WOR
MD	BAL
Westmont, IL	JOL
NJ	CAM
Westmorland, CA	SD
Weston, CT	BGP
IA	DM
MA	BO
MO	KC
NE	LIN
PA	SCR
VT	BUR
WI	LC
WV	WH
Westover, WV	WH
Westphalia, IA	DM
KS	KCK
MI	LAN
MO	JC
TX	AUS
Westport, CT	BGP
MA	FR
NY	OG
SD	SFS
WI	MAD
Westtown, PA	PH
Westville, IL	PEO
NJ	CAM
Westville Grove, NJ	CAM
Westwego, LA	NO
Westwood, CA	SAC
MA	BO
NJ	NEW
Wethersfield, CT	HRT
Wetmore, KS	KCK
Wewahitchka, FL	PT
Wexford, IA	DUB
PA	PIT
Weyauwega, WI	GB
Weyerhaeuser, WI	SUP
Weymouth, MA	BO
Wharton, TX	VIC
What Cheer, IA	DAV
Wheat Ridge, CO	DEN
Wheatfield, IN	LFT
Wheatland, IA	DAV
WY	CHY
Wheaton, IL	JOL
KS	KCK
MD	WDC
MN	SCL
Wheelersburg, OH	COL
Wheeling, IL	CHI
WV	OLL
WV	SJP
WV	WH
Whippany, NJ	PAT
NJ	PHU
Whistler, AL	MOB

White, SD	SFS
White Bear Lake, MN	STP
White Castle, LA	BR
White Cloud, MI	GR
White Cypress, MS	BLX
White Deer, TX	AMA
White Earth, MN	CR
White Hall, IL	SFD
White Haven, PA	SCR
White Lake, MI	DET
SD	SFS
WI	GB
White Mills, KY	L
PA	SCR
White Oak Boro, PA	PIT
White Pigeon, MI	KAL
White Pine, MI	MAR
White Plains, NY	NY
NY	PSC
White River, SD	RC
White River Junction, VT	BUR
White Salmon, WA	YAK
White Sulphur Springs, MT	HEL
WV	WH
White Swan, WA	YAK
Whitefield, ME	PRT
NH	MAN
Whitefish, MT	HEL
Whitefish Bay, WI	MIL
Whitehall, MT	HEL
NY	ALB
PA	ALN
PA	PIT
WI	LC
Whitehouse, OH	TOL
TX	TYL
Whitehouse Station, NJ	MET
Whitelaw, WI	GB
Whiteriver, AZ	GLP
Whitesboro, NY	SY
Whitestone, NY	BRK
Whitesville, KY	OWN
NY	BUF
WV	WH
Whitethorn, CA	SR
Whiteville, NC	R
Whitewater, CO	PBL
WI	MIL
Whiting, IN	GRY
IN	PRM
NJ	TR
Whitinsville, MA	WOR
Whitley City, KY	LEX
Whitman, MA	BO
Whitney, PA	GBG
Whitney Point, NY	SY
Whittemore, IA	SC
MI	GAY
Whittier, CA	LA
Whittlesey, WI	SUP
Wichita, KS	WCH
Wichita Falls, TX	FWT
Wickatunk, NJ	TR
Wickenburg, AZ	PHX
Wickliffe, OH	CLV
Wien, MO	JC
Wiggins, CO	DEN
MS	BLX
Wilber, NE	LIN
Wilberforce, OH	CIN
Wilbraham, MA	SPR
Wilbur, WA	SPK
Wilcox, PA	E
Wild Rice, ND	FAR
Wilder, KY	COV
Wildwood, NJ	CAM
PA	PIT
Wildwood Crest, NJ	CAM
Wilkes-Barre, PA	PHU
PA	PSC
PA	SAM
PA	SCR
Wilkinsburg, PA	PIT
Willacoochee, GA	SAV
Willard, OH	TOL
WI	LC
Willcox, AZ	TUC
Willey, IA	SC
Williams, AZ	PHX
IA	DUB
MN	CR
Williamsburg, IA	DAV
KY	LEX
OH	CIN
PA	ALT
VA	PSC
VA	RIC
Williamson, WV	WH
Williamsport, MD	BAL
PA	SCR
Williamston, MI	LAN

NC	R
Williamstown, KY	COV
MA	SPR
NJ	CAM
NJ	PHU
PA	HBG
PA	PSC
Williamsville, NY	BUF
NY	SAM
Willimantic, CT	NOR
CT	STF
Willingboro, NJ	TR
Williston, FL	STA
ND	BIS
VT	BUR
VT	SAM
Williston Park, NY	RVC
Willisville, IL	BEL
Willits, CA	SR
Willmar, MN	NU
Willoughby, OH	CLV
Willoughby Hills, OH	CLV
Willow City, ND	FAR
Willow Grove, PA	PH
Willow Lake, SD	SFS
Willow River, MN	DUL
Willow Springs, IL	CHI
MO	SPC
Willowburn, PA	PH
Willowdale, KS	WCH
Willowick, OH	CLV
Willows, CA	SAC
Willsboro, NY	OG
Wilmerding, PA	PIT
PA	SJP
Wilmette, IL	CHI
Wilmington, CA	LA
DE	PHU
DE	WIL
IL	JOL
MA	BO
NC	R
OH	CIN
VT	BUR
Wilmington Manor, DE	WIL
Wilmont, MN	WIN
Wilmore, PA	ALT
Wilmot, MI	SAG
SD	SFS
WI	MIL
Wilno, MN	NU
Wilson, KS	SAL
MN	WIN
NC	R
NY	BUF
WI	LC
WI	SUP
Wilsonville, IL	SFD
OR	P
Wilton, CT	BGP
IA	DAV
ME	PRT
MN	CR
ND	BIS
ND	STN
NH	MAN
WI	LC
Wilton Center, IL	JOL
Wimberley, TX	AUS
Wimbledon, ND	FAR
Winamac, IN	LFT
Winburne, PA	E
Winchendon, MA	WOR
Winchester, IL	SFD
IN	LFT
KY	LEX
MA	BO
NH	MAN
VA	ARL
Winchester Center, CT	HRT
Wind Lake, WI	MIL
Windber, PA	ALT
PA	PBR
Windham, CT	NOR
ME	PRT
NH	MAN
NY	ALB
OH	Y
Windom, MN	WIN
Windsor, CA	SR
CO	DEN
CT	HRT
ND	FAR
NY	SY
VT	BUR
Windsor Locks, CT	HRT
Windthorst, KS	DOD
TX	FWT
Winfield, AL	BIR
IL	JOL
KS	WCH

Winlock, WA	SEA
Winnebago, MN	WIN
NE	OM
Winneconne, WI	GB
Winnemucca, NV	RNO
Winner, SD	RC
Winnetka, IL	CHI
Winnfield, LA	ALX
Winnie, TX	BEA
Winnsboro, LA	ALX
Winona, MN	WIN
Winooski, VT	BUR
Winslow, AR	LR
AZ	GLP
ME	PRT
Winsted, CT	HRT
MN	NU
Winston-Salem, NC	CHL
Winter, WI	SUP
Winter Garden, FL	ORL
Winter Haven, FL	ORL
Winter Park, CO	DEN
FL	ORL
Winter Springs, FL	ORL
Winterhaven, CA	SD
Winterport, ME	PRT
Winters, CA	SAC
TX	SAN
Winterset, IA	DM
Wintersville, OH	STU
Winthrop, IA	DUB
MA	BO
ME	PRT
MN	NU
Wireton, PA	PIT
Wisconsin Dells, WI	MAD
Wisconsin Rapids, WI	LC
Wishek, ND	FAR
Wisner, NE	OM
Withamsville, OH	CIN
Witherbee, NY	OG
Witt, IL	SFD
Wittenberg, WI	GB
Woburn, MA	BO
Woden, IA	DUB
Wofford Heights, CA	FRS
Wolcott, CT	HRT
NY	ROC
Woleai and Neighboring Islands, FM	CI
Wolf Point, MT	GF
Wolfeboro, NH	MAN
Wolfforth, TX	LUB
Wonder Lake, IL	RCK
Wonewoc, WI	LC
Wood Dale, IL	JOL
Wood River, IL	SFD
NE	GI
Woodbine, IA	DM
NJ	CAM
NJ	PHU
Woodbourne, NY	NY
Woodbridge, CT	HRT
NJ	MET
VA	ARL
Woodburn, OR	P
Woodbury, CT	HRT
NJ	CAM
NY	RVC
Woodbury Heights, NJ	CAM
Woodcliff Lake, NJ	NEW
Woodcrest, DE	WIL
Woodhaven, MI	DET
Woodhull, IL	PEO
WI	MIL
Woodlake, CA	FRS
Woodland, CA	SAC
ME	PRT
WA	SEA
WI	MIL
Woodland Hills, CA	LA
Woodland Park, CO	COS
The Woodlands, TX	GAL
Woodlawn, NY	BUF
VA	RIC
Woodlynne, NJ	CAM
Woodmont, CT	HRT
Woodridge, IL	JOL
Wood-Ridge, NJ	NEW
Woodrow, TX	LUB
Woodruff, WI	SUP
Woods Hole, MA	FR
Woodsboro, TX	CC
Woodsfield, OH	STU
Woodside, CA	SFR
Woodson Terrace, MO	STL
Woodstock, CT	NOR
GA	ATL
IL	RCK
MD	BAL
MN	WIN
VA	ARL
VT	BUR
Woodstown, NJ	CAM
Woodsville, NH	MAN
Woodville, FL	PT
MS	JKS
TX	BEA
Woodward, IA	DM
IA	SC
OK	OKL
Woonsocket, RI	NTN
RI	PRO
RI	STF
SD	SFS
Wooster, OH	CLV
Worcester, MA	NTN
MA	SAM
MA	WOR
NY	ALB
Worland, WY	CHY
Worth, IL	CHI
Worthing, SD	SFS
Worthington, IA	DUB
KS	KCK
MN	WIN
OH	STU
Wrangell, AK	JUN
Wray, CO	DEN
Wrentham, MA	BO
Wright, KS	DOD
Wright Township, MI	GR
Wrightstown, WI	GB
Wrightsville Beach, NC	R
Wrightwood, CA	SB
Wuerzburg, WI	LC
Wurtsboro, NY	NY
Wyalusing, PA	SCR
Wyandanch, NY	RVC
Wyandotte, MI	DET
Wyckoff, NJ	NEW
Wykoff, MN	WIN
Wylie, TX	DAL
Wymore, NE	LIN
Wynantskill, NY	ALB
Wyncote, PA	PH
Wyndmere, ND	FAR
Wyndmoor, PA	PH
Wynne, AR	LR
Wynnewood, PA	PH
Wynot, NE	OM
Wyoming, DE	WIL
IL	PEO
PA	SCR
Wytheville, VA	RIC
Xenia, OH	CIN
Yabucoa, PR	CGS
Yakima, WA	YAK
Yakutat, AK	JUN
Yale, MI	DET
Yalesville, CT	HRT
Yamhill, OR	P
Yankton, SD	SFS
Yardley, PA	PH
Yarmouth, ME	PRT
Yates Center, KS	WCH
Yatesboro, PA	GBG
Yauco, PR	PCE
Yazoo City, MS	JKS
Yeadon, PA	PH
Yellow Springs, OH	CIN
Yelm, WA	SEA
Yerington, NV	RNO
Yigo, GU	AGN
Yoakum, TX	VIC
Yoder, IN	FTW
Yona, GU	AGN
Yonges Island, SC	CHR
Yonkers, NY	NTN
NY	NY
NY	PSC
NY	STF
Yorba Linda, CA	ORG
York, NE	LIN
PA	HBG
SC	CHR
York Harbor, ME	PRT
York Haven, PA	HBG
Yorktown, TX	VIC
VA	RIC
Yorktown Heights, NY	NY
Yorkville, IN	IND
NY	SY
OH	STU
Yosemite National Park, CA	FRS
Youngstown, NY	BUF
OH	OLL
OH	PBR
OH	ROM
OH	SJP
OH	Y
PA	GBG
Youngsville, LA	LAF
NY	NY
PA	E
Youngwood, PA	GBG
Yountville, CA	SR
Ypsilanti, MI	LAN
Yreka, CA	SAC
Yuba, WI	LC
Yuba City, CA	SAC
Yucaipa, CA	SB
Yucca Valley, CA	SB
Yukon, OK	OKL
PA	GBG
Yulan, NY	NY
Yuma, AZ	TUC
CO	DEN
Zachary, LA	BR
Zaleski, OH	COL
Zanesville, OH	COL
OH	NTN
Zapata, TX	CC
Zearing, IA	DUB
Zeeland, ND	FAR
Zeigler, IL	BEL
Zelienople, PA	PIT
Zell, MO	STL
SD	SFS
Zenda, KS	WCH
Zephyr Cove, NV	RNO
Zephyrhills, FL	SP
Zillah, WA	YAK
Zilwaukee, MI	SAG
Zimmerman, MN	SCL
Zion-Beach Park, IL	CHI
Zionsville, IN	LFT
Zumbrota, MN	STP
Zuni, NM	GLP
Zurich, KS	SAL
Zwolle, LA	SHP

- *Barbiconi, Roma, Italy.*
  Tel: 06.679.49.85
- *Watra's, Chicago, IL.*
  Tel: 773.247.2425
- *Watra Florida Div., Tampa, FL.*
  Tel: 813.969.0435
- *Meyer-Vogelpohl, CIncinnati, OH.*
  Tel: 513.241.1535
- *St. Jude Shop, Havertown, PA.*
  Tel: 610.789.1300
- *Philip et Cie, Los Angeles, CA.*
  Tel: 310.659.0313
- *Baker and Sons, Southington, CT.*
  Tel: 860.628.5566
- *Kaufer's Religious Supplies,*
  San Francisco, CA. Tel: 415.333.4494
- *Kaufer Company, Seattle, WA.*
  Tel: 206.622.3100
- *F.C. Ziegler Co., Tulsa, OK.*
  Tel: 918.582.0494
- *The King's House, Scottsdale, AZ.*
  Tel: 602.947.9205
- *T. Mohrman, Grand Blanc, MI.*
  Tel: 810.695.5151
- *Moroneys' Rel. Art, Ft. Lauderdale, FL.*
  Tel: 954.463.6211
- *Abbott Church Goods, Cherry Hill, NJ.*
  Tel: 609.662.6959
- *Cath. Supply of St. Louis, Inc.,*
  St. Louis, MO Tel: 314.351.0277
- *Ramada Imports, Richmond Hill,*
  Ontario, Canada Tel: 905.883.4242
- *New Day Designs, Ltd.*
  Newmarket, Ontario, Canada
  Tel: 905.853.7433

OLIC CHURCH IN U.S.

Excellence in Vestments.

World's Foremost Vestment Studios known for "Quality in Liturgy". Since Anno Domini 1930 recognized and inspiring leader in this field. Devoted designers of contemporary, elegant and graceful vesture. Please make an appointment with one of our exclusive dealers. Or write for our new documentation to:

SN®

STADELMAIER
NIJMEGEN

STADELMAIER NIJMEGEN BV
P.O. Box 7063
6503 GN Nijmegen
Tel.: 31.24.379.1170
Fax: 31.24.379.1171
e-mail: stadelmaier@telebyte.nl

estments, Tapestries, Diocesan Sets, Religious Antiques. Directly from Holland-Europe.

The United States Embassy to the Holy See

Established United States Embassy to the Holy See January 10, 1984.

Address: Via Delle Terme Deciane, 26 00153 Rome, Italy. Tel: 011-39-6-4674-3425; Fax: 011-39-6-575-8346. APO Address: U.S. Embassy to the Holy See, PSC 59, Box 66, APO AE 09624.

UNITED STATES AMBASSADOR TO THE HOLY SEE

Your Excellency
The Honorable

CORINNE C. BOGGS

Mrs. Boggs is a graduate of Newcomb College of Tulane University (New Orleans), where she also holds an honorary degree. She holds honorary degrees from various colleges and universities in the United States as well. During her political career Mrs. Boggs became the first woman to serve in the U.S. House of Representatives from Louisiana. As a member of Congress, she served on the Appropriations Committee. Her three Subcommittee assignments, Energy and Water Development, VA/H.U.D. - Independent Agencies, and Legislative Brance, permitted her to take a special interest in scientific research and technology development and housing issues. She also served on the Select Committee on Child, Youth and Families where she chaired the Crisis Intervention Task Force. In 1976 as a Chairperson of the Democratic National Convention, she was the first woman to chair a major political convention. She has received numerous awards: 1985 Tulane University Distinguished and Outstanding Alumni Award; 1986 Congressional Award of the Veterans of Foreign Wars; AMVETS Auxiliary National Humanitarian Award; Eleanor Roosevelt Centennial Award; the National Housing Conference's Housing Person of the Year; Bess Wallace Truman Award; the National Science Foundation Distinguished Public Service Award; National Advertising Council's Distinguished Service Award; Former Members of Congress Distinguished Service Award; the Notre Dame University Laetare Medal; 1994 American Mother of the Year, and the Louisiana library Association's Literary Award for her book "Washington Through a Purple Veil".

Former Ambassadors to the Holy See:

The Honorable William A. Wilson	1984-1986.
The Honorable Frank Shakespeare	1986-1989.
The Honorable Thomas P. Melady	1989-1993.
The Honorable Raymond L. Flynn	1993-1997.

The Catholic Church in the United States

The organizational structure of the Catholic Church in the United States consists of 33 Provinces with as many Archdioceses (Metropolitan Sees); 148 Suffragan Sees (Dioceses); The Military Archdiocese; four Eastern-Rite jurisdictions immediately subject to the Holy See in Rome. The Eparchies of St. Maron (Maronites), Newton (Melkites), St. Thomas the Apostle of Detroit (Chaldeans) and St. George Martyr of Canton, Ohio (Romanians). Each of these jurisdictions is under the direction of an Archbishop and Bishop called an Ordinary, who has apostolic responsibility and authority for the pastoral service of the people in his care.

The structure includes the territorial episcopal conference known as the National Conference of Catholic Bishops. In and through this body, which is strictly ecclesiastical and has defined juridical authority, the Bishops exercise their collegiate pastorate over the Church in the entire country.

Related to the NCCB is the United States Catholic Conference, a civil corporation and operational secretariat through which the Bishops, in cooperation with other members of the Church, act on a wider-than-ecclesiastical scale for the good of the Church and society in the United States.

The following is a list of the thirteen regions in the United States and provinces within those regions.

Region I: Includes the states of Maine, Vermont, New Hampshire, Massachusetts, Rhode Island, and Connecticut. Provinces of Boston and Hartford; Eparchy of Stamford and Eparchy for Melkites.

Region II: Includes the state of New York. Province of New York and Eparchy of St. Maron.

Region III: Includes the states of New Jersey and Pennsylvania. Provinces of Newark and Philadelphia; Archeparchy of Philadelphia, Ukrainian Archeparchy of Pittsburgh, Byzantine Eparchy of Passaic, and Apostolic Exarchate for Armenians.

Region IV: Includes the states of Delaware, District of Columbia, Florida, Georgia, Maryland, North Carolina, South Carolina, Virgin Islands, Virginia and West Virginia. Provinces of Atlanta, Baltimore, Miami, Washington, and the Military Archdiocese.

Region V: Includes the states of Alabama, Kentucky, Louisiana, Mississippi and Tennessee. Provinces of Louisville, Mobile and New Orleans.

Region VI: Includes the states of Michigan and Ohio. Provinces of Cincinnati, Detroit; Eparchy of Parma, Apostolic Exarchate for Chaldeans, and Apostolic Exarchate for Romanians.

Region VII: Includes the states of Illinois, Indiana and Wisconsin. Provinces of Chicago, Indianapolis, Milwaukee; Eparchy of St. Nicholas in Chicago-Ukrainian.

Region VIII: Includes the states of Minnesota, North Dakota and South Dakota. Provinces of St. Paul and Minneapolis.

Region IX: Includes the states of Kansas, Missouri and Nebraska. Provinces of Dubuque, Kansas City in Kansas, Omaha and St. Louis.

Region X: Includes the states of Arkansas, Oklahoma and Texas (excluding El Paso). Provinces of Oklahoma City and San Antonio.

Region XI: Includes the states of California, Hawaii and Nevada. Provinces of Los Angeles and San Francisco (excluding Salt Lake City); Eparchy of Van Nuys.

Region XII: Includes the states of Alaska, Idaho, Montana, Oregon and Washington. Provinces of Anchorage, Portland and Seattle.

Region XIII: Includes the states of Utah, Arizona, New Mexico, Colorado and Wyoming. Provinces of Denver, Santa Fe, part of San Francisco, Salt Lake City, and El Paso.

Please refer to individual Diocesan and Archdiocesan listing for complete and detailed information. The following list does not include the retired Archbishops or retired Bishops.

PROVINCE OF ANCHORAGE

Includes the State of Alaska.

Archdiocese of Anchorage, AK.—Most Rev. Francis T. Hurley, Archbishop of Anchorage.

Diocese of Fairbanks, AK.—Most Rev. Michael Kaniecki, S.J., Bishop of Fairbanks.

Diocese of Juneau, AK.—Most Rev. Michael Warfel.

PROVINCE OF ATLANTA

Includes the States of Georgia, North Carolina and South Carolina.

Archdiocese of Atlanta, GA.—Most Rev. John F. Donoghue, Archbishop of Atlanta.

Diocese of Charleston, SC.—Most Rev. David B. Thompson, Bishop of Charleston.

Diocese of Charlotte, NC.—Most Rev. William G. Curlin, Bishop of Charlotte.

Diocese of Raleigh, NC.—Most Rev. F. Joseph Gossman, Bishop of Raleigh.

Diocese of Savannah, GA.—Most Rev. John K. Boland, Bishop of Savannah.

PROVINCE OF BALTIMORE

Includes the States of Maryland (except Montgomery, Prince Charles, St. Mary's, Calvert and Charles Counties), Delaware, Virginia and West Virginia.

Archdiocese of Baltimore, MD.—His Eminence William Cardinal Keeler, Archbishop of Baltimore. Most Rev. William Newmann, Auxiliary Bishop. Most Rev. P. Francis Murphy, Auxiliary Bishop. Most Rev. Gordon D. Bennett, S.J., Auxiliary Bishop.

Diocese of Arlington, VA.—Most Rev. John R. Keating, Bishop of Arlington.

Diocese of Richmond, VA.—Most Rev. Walter F. Sullivan, Bishop of Richmond.

Diocese of Wheeling-Charleston, WV.—Most Rev. Bernard W. Schmitt, Bishop of Wheeling-Charleston.

Diocese of Wilmington, DE.—Most Rev. Michael A. Saltarelli, Bishop of Wilmington.

PROVINCE OF BOSTON

Includes the States of Maine, New Hampshire, Vermont and Massachusetts.

Archdiocese of Boston, MA.—His Eminence Bernard Cardinal Law, Archbishop of Boston. Most Rev. John P. Boles, Auxiliary Bishop. Most Rev. John R. McNamara, Auxiliary Bishop. Most Rev. John B. McCormack, Auxiliary Bishop. Most Rev. William F. Murphy, Auxiliary Bishop. Most Rev. Francis X. Irwin, Auxiliary Bishop. Most Rev. Emilio Allue, S.D.B.

Diocese of Burlington, VT.—Kenneth A. Angell, Bishop of Burlington.

Diocese of Fall River, MA.—Most Rev. Sean P. O'Malley, O.F.M.Cap., Bishop of Fall River.

Diocese of Manchester, NH.—Vacant See. Most Rev. Francis J. Christian, Auxiliary Bishop.

Diocese of Portland, ME.—Most Rev. Joseph Gerry, O.S.B., Bishop of Portland. Most Rev. Michael R. Cote, Auxiliary Bishop.

Diocese of Springfield, MA.—Most Rev. Thomas L. Dupre, Bishop of Springfield.

Diocese of Worcester, MA.—Most Rev. Daniel P. Reilly, Bishop of Worcester. Most Rev. George Rueger, Auxiliary Bishop.

PROVINCE OF CHICAGO

Includes the State of Illinois.

Archdiocese of Chicago, IL.—His Eminence Francis Cardinal George, O.M.I., Archbishop of Chicago. Most Most Rev. Most Rev. John R. Gorman, Auxiliary Bishop. Most Rev. Thad J. Jakubowski, Auxiliary Bishop. Most Rev. Raymond E. Goedert, Auxiliary Bishop. Most Rev. Gerald F. Kicanas, Auxiliary Bishop. Most Rev. Edwin M. Conway, Auxiliary Bishop. Most Rev. George V. Murry, S.J., Auxiliary Bishop. Most Rev. John R. Manz, Auxiliary Bishop.

Diocese of Belleville, IL.—Most Rev. Wilton D. Gregory, Bishop of Belleville.

Diocese of Joliet, IL.—Most Rev. Joseph L. Imesch, Bishop of Joliet. Most Rev. Roger L. Kaffer, Auxiliary Bishop.

Diocese of Peoria, IL.—Most Rev. John J. Myers, Bishop of Peoria.

Diocese of Rockford, IL.—Most Rev. Thomas G. Doran, Bishop of Rockford.

Diocese of Springfield, IL.—Most Rev. Daniel L. Ryan, Bishop of Springfield.

PROVINCE OF CINCINNATI

Includes the State of Ohio.

Archdiocese of Cincinnati, OH.—Most Rev. Daniel E. Pilarczyk, Archbishop of Cincinnati. Most Rev. Carl K. Moeddel, Auxiliary Bishop.

Diocese of Cleveland, OH.—Most Rev. Anthony M. Pilla, Bishop of Cleveland. Most Rev. A. Edward Pevec, Auxiliary Bishop. Most Rev. Alexander James Quinn, Auxiliary Bishop.

Diocese of Columbus, OH.—Most Rev. James A. Griffin, Bishop of Columbus.

Diocese of Steubenville, OH.—Most Rev. Gilbert I. Sheldon, Bishop of Steubenville.

Diocese of Toledo, OH.—Most Rev. James R. Hoffman, Bishop of Toledo. Most Rev. Robert Donnelly, Auxiliary Bishop.

Diocese of Youngstown, OH.—Most Rev. Thomas J. Tobin, Bishop of Youngstown.

PROVINCE OF DENVER

Includes the States of Colorado and Wyoming.

Archdiocese of Denver, CO.—Most Rev. Charles J. Chaput, O.F.M.Cap., Archbishop of Denver.

Diocese of Cheyenne, WY.—Most Rev. Joseph Hart, Bishop of Cheyenne.

Diocese of Colorado Springs, CO.—Most Rev. Richard C. Hanifen, Bishop of Colorado Springs.

Diocese of Pueblo, CO.—Most Rev Arthur N. Tafoya, Bishop of Pueblo.

PROVINCE OF DETROIT

Includes the State of Michigan.

Archdiocese of Detroit, MI.—His Eminence Adam Cardinal Maida, Archbishop of Detroit. Most Rev. Thomas J. Gumbleton, Auxiliary Bishop. Most Rev. Moses B. Anderson, S.S.E., Auxiliary Bishop. Most Rev. Kevin M. Britt, Auxiliary Bishop. Most Rev. Bernard J. Harrington, Auxiliary Bishop. Most Rev. John C. Nienstedt, Auxiliary Bishop. Most Rev. Allen H. Vigneron, Auxiliary Bishop.

Diocese of Gaylord, MI.—Most Rev. Patrick R. Cooney, Bishop of Gaylord.

Diocese of Grand Rapids, MI.—Most Rev. Robert J. Rose, Bishop of Grand Rapids. Most Rev. Joseph C. McKinney, Auxiliary Bishop.

Diocese of Kalamazoo, MI.—Most Rev. James A. Murray, Bishop of Kalamazoo.

Diocese of Lansing, MI.—Most Rev. Carl F. Mengeling, Bishop of Lansing.

Diocese of Marquette, MI.—Most Rev. James H. Garland, Bishop of Marquette.

Diocese of Saginaw, MI.—Most Rev. Kenneth E. Untener, Bishop of Saginaw.

PROVINCE OF DUBUQUE

Includes the State of Iowa.

Archdiocese of Dubuque, IA.—Most Rev. Jerome G. Hanus, O.S.B., Archbishop of Dubuque.

Diocese of Davenport, IA.—Most Rev. William E. Franklin, Bishop of Davenport.

Diocese of Des Moines, IA.—Most Rev. Joseph L. Charron, C.P.P.S., Bishop of Des Moines.

Diocese of Sioux City, IA.—Most Rev. Lawrence Soens, Bishop of Sioux City.

PROVINCE OF HARTFORD

Includes the States of Connecticut and Rhode Island.

Archdiocese of Hartford, CT.—Most Rev. Daniel A. Cronin, Archbishop of Hartford. Most Rev. Peter A. Rosazza, Auxiliary Bishop. Most Rev. Christie A. Macaluso, Auxiliary Bishop.

Diocese of Bridgeport, CT.—Most Rev. Edward M. Egan, Bishop of Bridgeport.

Diocese of Norwich, CT.—Most Rev. Daniel A. Hart, Bishop of Norwich.

Diocese of Providence, RI.—Most Rev. Robert E. Mulvee, Bishop of Providence.

PROVINCE OF INDIANAPOLIS

Includes the State of Indiana.

Archdiocese of Indianapolis, IN.—Most Rev. Daniel M. Buechlein, O.S.B., Archbishop of Indianapolis.

Diocese of Evansville, IN.—Most Rev. Gerald A. Gettelfinger, Bishop of Evansville.

Diocese of Fort Wayne-South Bend, IN.—Most Rev. John D'Arcy, Bishop of Fort Wayne-South Bend. Most Rev. Daniel R. Jenky, C.S.C., Auxiliary Bishop.

Diocese of Gary, IN.—Most Rev. Dale J. Melczek, Bishop of Gary.

Diocese of Lafayette in Indiana, IN.—Most Rev. William Higi, Bishop of Lafayette in Indiana.

PROVINCE OF KANSAS CITY, KANSAS

Includes the State of Kansas.

Archdiocese of Kansas City, KS.—Most Rev. James P. Keleher, Archbishop of Kansas City.

Diocese of Dodge City, KS.—Most Rev. Stanley Schlarman, Bishop of Dodge City.

Diocese of Salina, KS.—Most Rev. George K. Fitzsimons, Bishop of Salina.

Diocese of Wichita, KS.—Most Rev. Eugene J. Gerber, Bishop of Wichita.

PROVINCE OF LOS ANGELES

Includes Southern California and Central California.

Archdiocese of Los Angeles, CA.—His Eminence Roger Cardinal Mahony, Archbishop of Los Angeles. Most Rev. Stephen E. Blaire, Auxiliary Bishop. Most Rev. Thomas J. Curry, Auxiliary Bishop. Most Rev. Joseph M. Sartoris, Auxiliary Bishop. Most Rev. Gabino Zavala, Auxiliary Bishop. Most Rev. Gerald E. Wilkerson, Auxiliary Bishop.

Diocese of Fresno, CA.—Most Rev. John T. Steinbock, Bishop of Fresno.

Diocese of Monterey, CA.—Most Rev. Sylvester D. Ryan, Bishop of Monterey.

Diocese of Orange, CA.—Most Rev. Norman F. McFarland, Bishop of Orange. Most Rev. Michael P. Driscoll, Auxiliary Bishop.

Diocese of San Bernardino, CA.—Most Rev. Gerald R. Barnes, Bishop of San Bernardino.

Diocese of San Diego, CA.—Most Rev. Robert Brom, Bishop of San Diego. Most Rev. Gilbert Chavez, Auxiliary Bishop.

PROVINCE OF LOUISVILLE

Includes the States of Kentucky and Tennessee.

Archdiocese of Louisville, KY.—Most Rev. Thomas C. Kelly, O.P., Archbishop of Louisville.

Diocese of Covington, KY.—Most Rev. Robert W. Muench, Bishop of Covington.

Diocese of Knoxville, TN.—Most Rev. Anthony J. O'Connell, Bishop of Knoxville.

Diocese of Lexington, KY.—Most Rev. J. Kendrick Williams, Bishop of Lexington.

Diocese of Memphis, TN.—Most Rev. J. Terry Steib, S.V.D., Bishop of Memphis.

Diocese of Nashville, TN.—Most Rev. Edward U. Kmiec, Bishop of Nashville.

Diocese of Owensboro, KY.—Most Rev. John J. McRaith, Bishop of Owensboro.

PROVINCE OF MIAMI

Includes the State of Florida.

Archdiocese of Miami, FL.—Most Rev. John C. Favalora, Archbishop of Miami. Most Rev. Agustin A. Roman, Auxiliary Bishop. Most Rev. Gilberto Fernandez, Auxiliary Bishop. Most Rev. Thomas Wenski, Auxiliary Bishop.

Diocese of Orlando, FL.—Most Rev. Norbert Dorsey, C.P., Bishop of Orlando.

Diocese of Palm Beach, FL.—Most Rev. J. Keith Symons, Bishop of Palm Beach.

Diocese of Pensacola-Tallahassee, FL.—Most Rev. John Ricard, S.S.J., Bishop of Pensacola-Tallahassee.

Diocese of St. Augustine, FL.—Most Rev. John J. Snyder, Bishop of St. Augustine.

Diocese of St. Petersburg, FL.—Most Rev. Robert N. Lynch, Bishop of St. Petersburg.

Diocese of Venice, FL.—Most Rev. John J. Nevins, Bishop of Venice.

PROVINCE OF MILWAUKEE

Includes the State of Wisconsin.

Archdiocese of Milwaukee, WI.—Most Rev. Rembert G. Weakland, O.S.B., Archbishop of Milwaukee. Most Rev. Richard J. Sklba, Auxiliary Bishop.

Diocese of Green Bay, WI.—Most Rev. Robert Banks, Bishop of Green Bay. Most Rev. Robert F. Morneau, Auxiliary Bishop.

Diocese of La Crosse, WI.—Most Rev. Raymond L. Burke, Bishop of La Crosse.

Diocese of Madison, WI.—Most Rev. William H. Bullock, Bishop of Madison. Most Rev. George O. Wirz, Auxiliary Bishop.

Diocese of Superior, WI.—Most Rev. Raphael M. Fliss, Bishop of Superior.

PROVINCE OF MOBILE

Includes the states of Alabama and Mississippi.

Archdiocese of Mobile, AL.—Most Rev. Oscar H. Lipscomb, Archbishop of Mobile.

Diocese of Birmingham, AL.—Most Rev. David E. Foley, Bishop of Birmingham.

Diocese of Biloxi, MS.—Most Rev. Joseph L. Howze, Bishop of Biloxi.

Diocese of Jackson MS.—Most Rev. William R. Houck, Bishop of Jackson.

PROVINCE OF NEWARK

Includes the State of New Jersey.

Archdiocese of Newark, NJ.—Most Rev. Theodore McCarrick, Archbishop of Newark. Most Rev. Dominic A. Marconi, Auxiliary Bishop. Most Rev. David Arias, O.A.R., Auxiliary Bishop. Most Rev. Charles J. McDonnell, Auxiliary Bishop. Most Rev. Nicholas A. DiMarzio, Auxiliary Bishop. Most Rev. Paul G. Bootkoski, Auxiliary Bishop.

Diocese of Camden, NJ.—Most Rev. James T. McHugh, Bishop of Camden.

Diocese of Metuchen, NJ.—Most Rev. Vincent DePaul Breen, Bishop of Metuchen.

Diocese of Paterson, NJ.—Most Rev. Frank J. Rodimer, Bishop of Paterson.

Diocese of Trenton, NJ.—Most Rev. John M. Smith, Bishop of Trenton.

PROVINCE OF NEW ORLEANS

Includes the State of Louisiana.

Archdiocese of New Orleans, LA.—Most Rev. Francis B. Schulte, Archbishop of New Orleans. Most Rev. Dominic Carmon, Auxiliary Bishop. Most Rev. Gregory M. Aymond, Auxiliary Bishop.

Diocese of Alexandria, LA.—Most Rev. Sam Jacobs, Bishop of Alexandria.

Diocese of Baton Rouge, LA.—Most Rev. Alfred C. Hughes, Bishop of Baton Rouge.

Diocese of Houma-Thibodaux, LA.—Most Rev. Michael C. Jarrell.

Diocese of Lafayette, LA.—Most Rev. Edward J. O'Donnell, Bishop of Lafayette.

Diocese of Lake Charles, LA.—Most Rev. Jude Speyrer, Bishop of Lake Charles.

Diocese of Shreveport, LA. (1986)—Most Rev. William Friend, Bishop of Shreveport.

PROVINCE OF NEW YORK

Includes the State of New York.

Archdiocese of New York, NY.—His Eminence John Cardinal O'Connor, Archbishop of New York. Most Rev. Anthony F. Mestice, Auxiliary Bishop. Most Rev. Francisco Garmendia, Auxiliary Bishop. Most Rev. Austin B. Vaughan, Auxiliary Bishop. Most Rev. William J. McCormack, Auxiliary Bishop. Most Rev. Patrick J. Sheridan, Auxiliary Bishop. Most Rev. Robert A. Brucato, Auxiliary Bishop.

Diocese of Albany, NY.—Most Rev. Howard J. Hubbard, Bishop of Albany.

Diocese of Brooklyn, NY.—Most Rev. Thomas Daily, Bishop of Brooklyn. Most Rev. Joseph M. Sullivan, Auxiliary Bishop. Most Rev. Rene A. Valero, Auxiliary Bishop. Most Rev. Ignatius Catanello, Auxiliary Bishop. Most Rev. Gerald M. Barbarito, Auxiliary Bishop.

Diocese of Buffalo, NY.—Most Rev. Henry J. Mansell, Bishop of Buffalo. Most Rev. Edward M. Grosz, Auxiliary Bishop.

Diocese of Ogdensburg, NY.—Most Rev. Paul S. Loverde, Bishop of Ogdensburg.

Diocese of Rochester, NY.—Most Rev. Matthew H. Clark, Bishop of Rochester.

Diocese of Rockville Centre, NY.—Most Rev. John R. McGann, Bishop of Rockville Centre. Most Rev. John C. Dunne, Auxiliary Bishop. Most Rev. Emil A. Wcela, Auxiliary Bishop.

Diocese of Syracuse, NY.—Most Rev. James M. Moynihan, Bishop of Syracuse. Most Rev. Thomas J. Costello, Auxiliary Bishop.

PROVINCE OF OKLAHOMA CITY

Includes States of Arkansas and Oklahoma.

Archdiocese of Oklahoma City, OK.—Most Rev. Eusebius J. Beltran, Archbishop of Oklahoma City.

Diocese of Little Rock, AR.—Most Rev. Andrew J. McDonald, Bishop of Little Rock.

Diocese of Tulsa, OK.—Most Rev. Edward J. Slattery, Bishop of Tulsa.

PROVINCE OF OMAHA

Includes the State of Nebraska.

Archdiocese of Omaha, NE.—Most Rev. Elden F. Curtiss, Archbishop of Omaha.

Diocese of Grand Island, NE.—Most Rev. Lawrence J. McNamara, Bishop of Grand Island.

Diocese of Lincoln, NE.—Most Rev. Fabian W. Bruskewitz, Bishop of Lincoln.

PROVINCE OF PHILADELPHIA

Includes the State of Pennsylvania.

Archdiocese of Philadelphia, PA.—His Eminence Anthony Cardinal Bevilacqua, Archbishop of Philadelphia. Most Rev. Robert P. Maginnis, Auxiliary Bishop. Most Rev. Joseph F. Martino, Auxiliary Bishop.

Diocese of Allentown, PA.—Most Rev. Edward P. Cullen Bishop of Allentown.

Diocese of Altoona-Johnstown, PA.—Most Rev. Joseph V. Adamec, Bishop of Altoona-Johnstown.

Diocese of Erie, PA.—Most Rev. Donald W. Trautman, Bishop of Erie.

Diocese of Greensburg, PA.—Most Rev. Anthony G. Bosco, Bishop of Greensburg.

Diocese of Harrisburg, PA.—Most Rev. Nicholas Dattilo, Bishop of Harrisburg.

Diocese of Pittsburgh, PA.—Most Rev. Donald W. Wuerl, Bishop of Pittsburgh. Most Rev. William J. Winter, Auxiliary Bishop. Most Rev. David A. Zubik, Auxiliary Bishop.

Diocese of Scranton, PA.—Most Rev. James C. Timlin, Bishop of Scranton. Most Rev. John M. Dougherty, Auxiliary Bishop.

PROVINCE OF PORTLAND IN OREGON

Includes the States of Oregon, Idaho and Montana.

Archdiocese of Portland, OR.—Most Rev. John G. Vlazny, Archbishop of Portland in Oregon.Most Rev. Kenneth D. Steiner, Auxiliary Bishop.

Diocese of Baker, OR.—Most Rev. Thomas J. Connolly, Bishop of Baker.

Diocese of Boise, ID.—Most Rev. Tod D. Brown, Bishop of Boise.

Diocese of Great Falls-Billings, MT.—Most Rev. Anthony M. Milone, Bishop of Great Falls-Billings.

Diocese of Helena, MT.—Vacant See.

PROVINCE OF ST. LOUIS

Includes the State of Missouri.

Archdiocese of St. Louis, MO.—Most Rev. Justin F. Regali, Archbishop of St. Louis. Most Rev. Edward K. Braxton, Auxiliary Bishop. Most Rev. Joseph F. Naumann, Auxiliary Bishop. Most Rev. Michael J. Sheridan, Auxiliary Bishop.

Diocese of Jefferson City, MO.—Most Rev. John R. Gaydos, Bishop of Jefferson City.

Diocese of Kansas City-St. Joseph, MO.—Most Rev. Raymond J. Boland, Bishop of Kansas City-St. Joseph.

Diocese of Springfield-Cape Girardeau, MO.—Most Rev. John J. Leibrecht, Bishop of Springfield-Cape Girardeau.

PROVINCE OF ST. PAUL AND MINNEAPOLIS

Includes the States of Minnesota, South Dakota and North Dakota.

Archdiocese of St. Paul and Minneapolis, MN.—Most Rev. Harry J. Flynn, Archbishop of St. Paul and Minneapolis. Most Rev. Lawrence H. Welsh, Auxiliary Bishop.

Diocese of Bismarck, ND.—Most Rev. Paul A. Zipfel, Bishop of Bismarck.

Diocese of Crookston, MN.—Most Rev. Victor H. Balke, Bishop of Crookston.

Diocese of Duluth, MN.—Most Rev. Roger L. Schwietz, O.M.I., Bishop of Duluth.
Diocese of Fargo, ND.—Most Rev. James Sullivan, Bishop of Fargo.
Diocese of New Ulm, MN.—Most Rev. Raymond A. Lucker, Bishop of New Ulm.
Diocese of Rapid City, SD.—Vacant See.
Diocese of St. Cloud, MN.—Most Rev. John F. Kinney, Bishop of St. Cloud.
Diocese of Sioux Falls, SD.—Most Rev. Robert J. Carlson, Bishop of Sioux Falls.
Diocese of Winona, MN.—Vacant See.

PROVINCE OF SAN ANTONIO

Includes the State of Texas.
Archdiocese of San Antonio, TX.—Most Rev. Patrick F. Flores, Archbishop of San Antonio. Most Rev. Thomas J. Flanagan, Auxiliary Bishop. Most Rev. Patrick J. Zurek, Auxiliary Bishop.
Diocese of Amarillo, TX.—Most Rev. John W. Yanta, Bishop of Amarillo.
Diocese of Austin, TX.—Most Rev. John E. McCarthy, Bishop of Austin.
Diocese of Beaumont, TX.—Most Rev. Joseph A. Galante, Bishop of Beaumont.
Diocese of Brownsville, TX.—Most Rev. Raymundo J. Pena, Bishop of Brownsville.
Diocese of Corpus Christi, TX.—Most Rev. Roberto O. Gonzalez, O.F.M., Bishop of Corpus Christi.
Diocese of Dallas, TX.—Most Rev. Charles V. Grahmann, Bishop of Dallas.
Diocese of El Paso, TX.—Most Rev. Amando Ochoa, Bishop of El Paso.
Diocese of Fort Worth, TX.—Most Rev. Joseph P. Delaney, Bishop of Fort Worth.
Diocese of Galveston-Houston, TX.—Most Rev. Joseph A. Fiorenza, Bishop of Galveston-Houston. Most Rev. Curtis Guillory, Auxiliary Bishop. Most Rev. James A. Tamayo, Auxiliary Bishop.
Diocese of Lubbock, TX.—Most Rev. Placido Rodriguez, C.M.F., Bishop of Lubbock.
Diocese of San Angelo, TX.—Most Rev. Michael Pfeifer, O.M.I., Bishop of San Angelo.
Diocese of Tyler, TX.—Most Rev. Edmond Carmody, Bishop of Tyler.
Diocese of Victoria, TX.—Most Rev. David E. Fellhauer, Bishop of Victoria.

PROVINCE OF SAN FRANCISCO

Includes Northern California and the States of Nevada, Utah and Hawaii.
Archdiocese of San Francisco, CA.—Most Rev. William J. Levada, Archbishop of San Francisco. Most Rev. Patrick J. McGrath, Auxiliary Bishop.
Diocese of Honolulu, HI.—Most Rev. Francis X. DiLorenzo, Bishop of Honolulu.
Diocese of Las Vegas, NV.—Most Rev. Daniel F. Walsh, Bishop of Las Vegas.
Diocese of Oakland, CA.—Most Rev. John S. Cummins, Bishop of Oakland.
Diocese of Reno, NV.—Most Rev. Phillip F. Straling, Bishop of Reno.
Diocese of Sacramento, CA.—Most Rev. William K. Weigand, Bishop of Sacramento. Most Rev. Richard J. Garcia, Auxiliary Bishop of Sacramento.
Diocese of Salt Lake City, UT.—Most Rev. George H. Niederauer, Bishop of Salt Lake City.
Diocese of San Jose, CA.—Most Rev. Pierre DuMaine, Bishop of San Jose.
Diocese of Santa Rosa, CA.—Most Rev. G. Patrick Zieman, Bishop of Santa Rosa.
Diocese of Stockton, CA.—Most Rev. Donald Montrose, Bishop of Stockton.

PROVINCE OF SANTA FE

Includes the States of New Mexico, and Arizona.
Archdiocese of Santa Fe, NM.—Most Rev. Michael Sheehan, Archbishop of Santa Fe.
Diocese of Gallup, NM.—Most Rev. Donald E. Pelotte, S.S.S., Bishop of Gallup.
Diocese of Las Cruces, NM.—Most Rev. Ricardo Ramirez, C.S.B., Bishop of Las Cruces.
Diocese of Phoenix, AZ.—Most Rev. Thomas J. O'Brien, Bishop of Phoenix.
Diocese of Tucson, AZ.—Most Rev. Manuel D. Moreno, Bishop of Tucson.

PROVINCE OF SEATTLE

Includes the State of Washington.
Archdiocese of Seattle, WA.—Most Rev. Alexander J. Brunett, Archbishop of Seattle.
Diocese of Spokane, WA.—Most Rev. William S. Skylstad, Bishop of Spokane.
Diocese of Yakima, WA.—Most Rev. Carlos Sevilla, S.J., Bishop of Yakima.

PROVINCE OF WASHINGTON

Includes the District of Columbia, and Montgomery, Prince Georges, Charles, Calvert and St. Mary's Counties in Maryland, also Virgin Islands.
Archdiocese of Washington, DC.—His Eminence James Cardinal Hickey, Archbishop of Washington. Most Rev. Alvaro Corrada, Auxiliary Bishop. Most Rev. Leonard Olivier, S.V.D., Auxiliary Bishop. Most Rev. William E. Lori, Auxiliary Bishop.
Diocese of St. Thomas, V.I.—Most Rev. Elliot G. Thomas, Bishop of St. Thomas, Virgin Islands.
Military Archdiocese—Most Rev. Edwin F. O'Brien, Archbishop for the Military Services. Most Rev. Francis X. Roque, Auxiliary Bishop. Most Rev. Joseph J. Madera, M.Sp.S., Auxiliary Bishop. Most Rev. John J. Glynn, Auxiliary Bishop.

EASTERN CATHOLIC JURISDICTIONS

ANTIOCHENE TRADITION

Maronite Rite—
Diocese of Saint Maron of Brooklyn—Most Rev. Hector Doueihi, Bishop St. Maron.
Diocese of Our Lady of Lebanon—Most Rev. John Chedid, Bishop of Our Lady of Lebanon.

ARMENIAN TRADITION

Armenian Catholic Exarchate of U.S.A. and Canada—Most Rev. Hovhannes Tertzakian, O.M.Ven., Apostolic Exarch for the Armenians.

CHALDEAN TRADITION

Eparchy of St. Thomas the Apostle—Most Rev. Ibrahim Ibrahim, Eparch of St. Thomas the Apostle.

CONSTANTINOPOLITAN TRADITION

Melkite - Greek Rite—
Diocese of Newton—Most Rev. John A. Elya, B.S., Bishop of Newton. Most Rev. Nicholas J. Samra, Auxiliary Bishop.
Romanian Rite—
Diocese of St. George's in Canton—Most Rev. John M. Botean, Eparch of St. George's in Canton.
Ruthenian Rite—
Metropolitan Archdiocese of Pittsburgh—Most Rev. Judson M. Procyk, Archbishop of Pittsburgh Byzantine Rite.
Diocese of Parma—Most Rev. Basil Schott,O.F.M., Bishop of Parma
Diocese of Passaic—Most Rev. Andrew Pataki, Bishop of Passaic.
Diocese of Van Nuys—Most Rev. George M. Kuzma, Bishop of Van Nuys.
Russian Rite—
Two parishes
Ukrainian Rite—
Metropolitan Archdiocese of Philadelphia—Most Rev. Stephan Sulyk, Archbishop of Philadelphia. Most Rev. Walter Paska, Auxiliary Bishop.
Diocese of St. Josaphat in Parma—Most Rev. Robert Moskal, Bishop of St. Josaphat in Parma.
Diocese of St. Nicholas—Most Rev. Michael Wiwchar, C.S.S.R., Bishop of St. Nicholas in Chicago.
Diocese of Stamford—Most Rev. Basil Losten, Bishop of Stamford.
Syrian Rite—
Diocese of Our Lady of Deliverance of Syriac—Most Rev. Joseph Younan, Bishop of Our Lady of Deliverance.

AN ALPHABETICAL LIST OF THE

Cardinals, Archbishops, Bishops, Archabbots & Abbots of the United States

CARDINALS

His Eminence Luis Cardinal Aponte Martinez, Archbishop of San Juan, P.O. Box S-1967, San Juan, PR 00903
His Eminence William Cardinal Baum, Prefect of Sacred Congregation for Catholic Education, Piazza Pio XII Vatican City State
His Eminence Anthony Cardinal Bevilacqua, Archbishop of Philadelphia, 222 N. 17th St., Philadelphia, PA 19103.
His Eminence John Cardinal Carberry, Retired Archbishop of Archdiocese of St. Louis, 4445 Lindell Blvd., St. Louis, MO 63108
His Eminence James Cardinal Hickey, Archbishop of Washington DC, P.O. Box 29260, Washington, DC 20017
His Eminence Francis Cardinal George, *o.m.i.*, Archbishop of Chicago, 155 E. Superior St., Chicago, IL 60611.
His Eminence William Cardinal Keeler, Archbishop of Baltimore, 320 Cathedral St., Baltimore, MD 21201
His Eminence Bernard Cardinal Law, Archbishop of Boston, 2101 Commonwealth Ave., Boston, MA 02135
His Eminence Adam Cardinal Maida, Archbishop of Detroit, 1234 Washington Blvd., Detroit, MI 48226
His Eminence Roger Cardinal Mahony, Archbishop of Los Angeles, 3424 Wilshire Blvd., Los Angeles, CA 90010-2241
His Eminence John Cardinal O'Connor, Archbishop of New York, 452 Madison Ave., New York, NY 10022
His Eminence Francis Cardinal Stafford, President - Pontifical Council for the Laity, Piazza San Calisto 16, Vatican City State, Europe 00120.
His Eminence Edmund Cardinal Szoka, Pres. Prefecture for Economic Affairs of the Holy See, Vatican City State

ARCHBISHOPS

His Excellency,
The Most Reverend

Apuron, Anthony Sablan, *o.f.m.cap.*, Archbishop of Agana, Cuesta San Ramon Agana, Guam 96910.
Beltran, Eusebius J., Archbishop of Oklahoma City, P.O. Box 32180, Oklahoma City, OK 73123.
Borders, William D., Retired Archbishop of Baltimore, 320 Cathedral St., Baltimore, MD 21201.
Brunett, Alexander J., Archbishop of Seattle, 910 Marion St., Seattle, WA 98104.
Buechlein, Daniel, *o.s.b.*, Archbishop of Indianapolis, 1400 N. Meridian St., P.O. Box 1410, Indianapolis, IN 46206.
Chaput, Charles J., *o.f.m.cap.*, Archbishop of Denver, 1300 Steele St., Denver, CO 80210.
Cronin, Daniel A., Archbishop of Hartford, 134 Farmington Ave., Hartford, CT 06105.
Curtiss, Elden F., Archbishop of Omaha, 100 N. 62nd St., Omaha, NE 68132-2795.
Dimino, Joseph T., Retired Archbishop of Military Services, P.O. Box 4469, Washington, DC 20017-04692.
Donoghue, John F., Archbishop of Atlanta, 680 W. Peachtree St., N.W., Atlanta, GA 30308.
Favalora, John C., Archbishop of Miami, 9401 Biscayne Blvd., Miami Shore, FL 33138.
Flores, Patrick F., Archbishop of San Antonio, 2600 W. Woodlawn Ave., San Antonio, TX 78228.
Flynn, Harry J., Archbishop of St. Paul and Minneapolis, 226 Summit Ave., St. Paul, MN 55102.
Foley, John P., Archbishop, President of the Pontifical Council for Social Communications, 00120 Vatican City State Europe.
Gerety, Peter Leo, Retired Archbishop of Newark, 31 Mulberry St., Newark, NJ 07102.
Hannan, Philip M., Retired Archbishop of New Orleans, 2929 S. Carrollton Ave., New Orleans, LA 70118-4301.
Hanus, Jerome, *o.s.b.*, Archbishop of Dubuque, 1229 Mt. Loretto Ave., P.O. Box 479, Dubuque, IA 52004-0479.
Hunthausen, Raymond G., Retired Archbishop of Seattle, 910 Marion St., Seattle, WA 98104.
Hurley, Francis T., Archbishop of Anchorage, P.O. Box 2239, Anchorage, AK 99510.
Keleher, James P., Archbishop of Kansas City, Kansas, 12615 Parallel Parkway, Kansas City, KS 66109.
Kelly, Thomas, *o.p.*, Archbishop of Louisville, 212 E. College St., Louisville, KY 40201.
Kucera, Daniel W., *o.s.b.*, Retired Archbishop of Dubuque, 13952 E. Marina Dr. -#612, Aurora, CO 80014.
Levada, William J., Archbishop of San Francisco, 445 Church St., San Francisco, CA 94114.
Lipscomb, Oscar H., Archbishop of Mobile, 400 Government St., Mobile, AL 36633.
Marcinkus, Paul C., Working Outside Chicago Archdiocese, Vatican City State, Europe.
Marino, Eugene A., *s.s.j.*, Former Archbishop of Atlanta, Salesian Province House, 148 Main St., New Rochelle, NY 10802.
McCarrick, Theodore E. Archbishop of Newark, 171 Clifton Ave., P.O. Box 9500, Newark, NJ 07104-9500.

His Excellency,
The Most Reverend

McCarthy, Edward A., Retired Archbishop of Miami, 2900 S.W. 87th Ave., Miami, FL 33138.
McDonough, Thomas J., Retired Archbishop of Louisville, St. Francis Country Home, 1412 Lansdowne Ave., Darby, PA 19023.
O'Brien, Edwin F., Archbishop of the Military Services USA, P.O. Box 4469, Washington, DC 20017.
Pilarczyk, Daniel E., Archbishop of Cincinnati, 100 E. 8th St., Cincinnati, OH 45202.
Procyk, Judson M., Archbishop of Pittsburgh Byzantine, 66 Riverview Ave., Pittsburgh, PA 15214.
Quinn, John R., Retired Archbishop of San Francisco, 322 Middlefield Rd., Menlo Park, CA 94025.
Rigali, Justin F., Archbishop of St. Louis, 4445 Lindell Blvd., St. Louis, MO 63108.
Roach, John R., Retired Archbishop of St. Paul-Minneapolis, 226 Summit Ave., St. Paul, MN 55102.
Ryan, Joseph T., Retired Archbishop of the Military Services, Our Lady of Hope Residence, 1 Jeannine Jugan Ln., Latham, NY 12110.
Salatka, Charles A., Retired Archbishop of Oklahoma City, Box 23205, Oklahoma City, OK 73123.
Sanchez, Robert F., Former Archbishop of Santa Fe, Catholic Center, St. Joseph's Pl., N.W., Albuquerque, NM 87120.
Schleck, Charles A., *c.s.c.*, Titular Archbishop of Africa, Congregation for Evangelization, Palazzo di Propaganda Fide, Piazza di Spagna 48, 00187 Rome, Italy.
Schulte, Francis B., Archbishop of New Orleans, 7887 Walmsley Ave., New Orleans, LA 70125-3496.
Sheehan, Daniel E., Retired Archbishop of Omaha, 10412 Pacific St., Omaha, NE 68114.
Sheehan, Michael J., Archbishop of Santa Fe, Catholic Center, 4000 Saint Joseph's Place, N.W., Albuquerque, NM 87120.
Strecker, Ignatius J., Retired Archbishop of Kansas City in Kansas, 3408 Minnesota Ave.,, Kansas City, KS 66102.
Sulyk, Stephen, Archbishop of Philadelphia Ukrainian, 827 N. Franklin St., Philadelphia, PA 19123.
Vlazny, John G., Archbishop of Portland Oregon, 2838 E.Burnside St., Portland, OR 97214-1895.
Weakland, Rembert G., *o.s.b.* Archbishop of Milwaukee, 3501 S. Lake Dr., St. Francis, WI 53235-3703.

BISHOPS

His Excellency,
The Most Reverend

Abramowicz, Alfred L., Retired Auxiliary Bishop of Chicago, 6101 S. 75th Ave., Summit-Argo, IL 60501.
Adamec, Joseph V., Bishop of Altoona-Johnstown, 126 Logan Blvd., Hollidaysburg, PA 16648.
Ahern, Patrick V., Retired Auxiliary Bishop of New York, St. Thomas More, 65 E. 89th St., New York, NY 10128.
Allue, Emilio, *s.d.b.*, Auxiliary Bishop of Boston, 558 South Ave., Weston, MA 02193-2699.
Anderson, Moses B., *s.s.e.*, Auxiliary Bishop of Detroit, 14155 Abingdon Rd., Detroit, MI 48227.

His Excellency,
The Most Reverend

Angell, Kenneth A., Bishop of Burlington, 351 North Ave.-P.O. Box 526, Burlington, VT 05402-0526.
Arias, David, *o.a.r.*, Auxiliary Bishop of Newark, St. Joseph of the Palisade Rectory, 6401 Palisade Ave., West New York, NJ 07093.
Arzube, Juan, Retired Auxiliary Bishop of Los Angeles, Sacred Heart Church, 2889 N. Lincoln Ave., Altadena, CA 91001.
Aymond, Gregory M., Auxiliary Bishop of New Orleans, 2901 S. Carrollton Ave., New Orleans, LA 70118.
Balke, Victor, Bishop of Crookston, 1200 Memorial Dr., Crookston, MN 56716.
Baltakis, Paul A., *o.f.m.*, Titular Bishop of Egara & Lithuanian Catholics, 361 Highland Blvd., Brooklyn, NY 11207.
Banks, Robert J., Bishop of Green Bay, 1910 S. Webster Ave.-P.O. Box 23825, Green Bay, WI 54305-3825.
Barbarito, Gerald, Auxiliary Bishop of Brooklyn, 1956 Batchelder St., Brooklyn, NY 11229.
Barnes, Gerald R., Bishop of San Bernardino, 1201 E. Highland Ave., San Bernardino, CA 92405.
Begley, Michael J., Retired Bishop of Charlotte, 1315 Greensboro Rd., High Point, NC 27260.
Bennett, Gordon D., *s.j.*, Auxiliary Bishop of Baltimore, Pres.-Loyola High School, 1901 Venice Blvd., Los Angeles, CA 90006.
Blaire, Stephen E., Auxiliary Bishop of Los Angeles, 2636 S. Mansfield Ave., Los Angeles, CA 90016-3512.
Boland, J. Kevin, Bishop of Savannah, 601 E. Liberty St., Savannah, GA 31401.
Boland, Raymond J., Bishop of Kansas City-St. Joseph, P.O. Box 419037, Kansas City, MO 64141-6037.
Boles, John P., Auxiliary Bishop of Boston, 307 Bowdoin St., Dorchester, MA 02122.
Bootkoski, Paul G., Auxiliary Bishop of Newark, Sacred Heart, 89 Ridge St., Newark, NJ 01704.
Bosco, Anthony G., Bishop of Greensburg, 723 E. Pittsburgh St., Greensburg, PA 15601.
Botean, John M., Bishop of Romanian-rite St. George's in Canton, 1121 44th St., N.E., Canton, OH 44714
Boudreaux, Warren L., Retired Bishop of Houma-Thibodaux, 233 Rienzi Dr., Thimodaux, LA 70301.
Braxton, Edward K., Auxiliary Bishop of St. Louis, 4445 Lindell Blvd., St. Louis, MO 63108-2497.
Breen, Vincent DePaul, Bishop of Metuchen, Ten Library Pl., Metuchen, NJ 08840.
Breitenbeck, Joseph M., Retired Bishop of Grand Rapids, 660 Burton St., S.E. Grand Rapids, MI 49507.
Britt, Kevin M., Auxiliary Bishop of Detroit, 1234 Washington Blvd., Detroit, MI 48226.
Broderick, Edwin B., Former Bishop of Albany, 900 Park Ave., New York, NY 10021.
Brom, Robert H., Bishop of San Diego, P.O. Box 85728, San Diego, CA 92186-5728.
Brown, Tod D., Bishop of Boise, 303 Federal Way, Boise, ID 83705-5925.
Brucato, Robert A., Auxiliary Bishop of New York, 201 Seminary Ave., Yonkers, NY 10704-1896.
Bruskewitz, Fabian W., Bishop of Lincoln, 5301 A Street, Lincoln, NE 68510.
Brzana, Stanislaus J., Retired Bishop of Ogdensburg, P.O. Box 369, Ogdensburg, NY 13669.

His Excellency,
The Most Reverend

Bullock, William H., Bishop of Madison, 15 E. Wilson St., Madison, WI 53701.
Burke, Raymond L., Bishop of La Crosse, 3710 East Avenue, S., Box 4004, La Crosse, WI 54602-4004.
Buswell, Charles A., Retired Bishop of Pueblo, 13 Tartan Ln., Pueblo, CO 81003.
Camacho, Tomas A., Bishop of Chalan Kanoa, Our Lady of Mt. Carmel, P.O. Box 745, Saipan, CM 96950.
Carlson, Robert J., Bishop of Sioux Falls, 3100 West 41 St., Sioux Falls, SD 57117.
Carmody, Edmond, Bishop of Tyler, 1015 East Southeast Loop 323, Tyler TX 75701-9663.
Carmon, Dominic, *s.v.d.*, Auxiliary Bishop of New Orleans, 4111 St. Blase Dr., Kenner, LA 70065-1656.
Casiano-Vargas, Ulises, Bishop of Mayaguez, P.O. Box 2272, Mayaguez, PR 00708.
Catanello, Ignatius, Auxiliary Bishop of Brooklyn, 75 Green Ave., Brooklyn, NY 11202.
Charron, Joseph J., *c.pp.s.*, Bishop of of Des Moines, P.O. Box 1816, 601 Grand Ave., Des Moines, IA 50306-5071.
Chavez, Gilbert E., Auxiliary Bishop of San Diego, 2020 Alaquinas Dr., San Ysidro, CA 92073.
Chedid, John, Bishop of Our Lady of Lebanon of Los Angeles, 333 S. San Vicente Blvd., Los Angeles, CA 90048.
Christian, Francis J., Auxiliary Bishop of Manchester, St. Joseph Cathedral, 145 Lowell St., Manchester, NH 03105.
Clark, Matthew H., Bishop of Rochester, 1150 Buffalo Rd., Rochester, NY 14624.
Clinch, Harry A., Retired Bishop of Monterey, 3400 Paul Sweet Rd., #C-119, Santa Cruz, CA 95065.
Connolly, Thomas J., Bishop of Baker, P.O. Box 5999, Bend, OR 97708.
Conway, Edwin M., Auxiliary Bishop of Chicago, 126 N. Des Plaines St., Chicago, IL 60661-2357.
Cooney, Patrick R., Bishop of Gaylord, 1665 M-32 West, Seton Building, Gaylord, MI 49735.
Corrada, Alvaro, *s.j.*, Auxiliary Bishop of Washington, 826 Wayne Ave., Silver Spring, MD 20910.
Costello, Thomas J., Auxiliary Bishop of Syracuse, P.O. Box 511, Syracuse, NY 13201.
Cote, Michael R., Auxiliary Bishop of Portland in Maine, 510 Ocean Ave., P.O. Box 11559, Portland, OR 04104-7559.
Crowley, Joseph R., Retired Auxiliary Bishop of Fort Wayne-South Bend, 1701 Miami St., South Bend, IN 46613.
Cullen, Edward P., Bishop of Allentown, 202 N. 17th St.- P.O. Box F, Allentwon, PA 18105.
Cummins, John S., Bishop of Oakland, 634 21st St., Oakland, CA 94612.
Curlin, William G., Bishop of Charlotte, P.O. Box 36776, Charlotte, NC 28236.
Curry, Thomas J., Auxiliary Bishop of Los Angeles, Santa Barbara Pastoral Region, 3240 Calle Pinon, Santa Barbara, CA 93105.
Curtis, Walter W., Retired Bishop of Bridgeport, 128 Strawberry Hill Ave., Stamford, CT 06904.
Daily, Thomas V., Bishop of Brooklyn, P.O. Box C, Brooklyn, NY 11202.
Daly, James J., Former Auxiliary Bishop of Rockville Centre, 25 Lanes End, Blue Point, NY 11715.
D'Antonio, Nicholas, *o.f.m.*, Retired Vicar for Latin American Apostolate, Archdiocese of New Orleans, 1221 Mandeville St., New Orleans, LA 70117-8498.
D'Arcy, John M., Bishop of Fort Wayne-South Bend, P.O. Box 390, Fort Wayne, IN 46801.
Dattilo, Nicholas, Bishop of Harrisburg, 4800 Union Deposit Rd., P.O. Box 2153, Harrisburg, PA 17105.
Delaney, Joseph P., Bishop of Fort Worth, 800 West Loop 820 South, Fort Worth, TX 76108.
DeSimone, Louis A., Former Auxiliary Bishop of Philadelphia, 2422 S. 17th St., Philadelphia, PA 19145.
DiMarzio, Nicholas A., Auxiliary Bishop of Newark, 1160 Raymond Blvd., Newark, NJ 07102-4105.
DiLorenzo, Francis X., Bishop of Honolulu, 1184 Bishop St., Honolulu, HI 96813.
Donnelly, Robert, Auxiliary Bishop of Toledo, 2544 Parkwood Ave., Toledo, OH 43610.
Donovan, Paul V., Retired Bishop of Kalamazoo, 238 Falkirk, Kalamazoo, MI 49006.
Doran, Thomas G., Bishop of Rockford, 1245 North Court St., Rockford, IL 61103.
Dorsey, Norbert L., *c.p.*, Bishop of Orlando, 421 E. Robinson, P.O. Box 1800, Orlando, FL 32802-1800.
Doueihi, Hector, Bishop of the Maronite Eparchy of St. Maron of Brooklyn, Our Lady of Lebanon Cathedral, 113 Remsen St., Brooklyn, NY 11201.
Dougherty, John M., Auxiliary Bishop of Scranton, 300 Wyoming Ave., Scranton, PA 18503.
Driscoll, Michael P., Auxiliary Bishop of Orange, 2811 E. Villa Real Dr., Orange, CA 92867.
Dudick, Michael J., Retired Bishop of Passaic, 32 Lakeview Trail, Sugarloaf, PA 18249-1043.

His Excellency,
The Most Reverend

Dudley, Paul V., Retired Bishop of Sioux Falls, Church of St. Dominic, 116 North Linden, Northfield, MN 55057-1435.
DuMaine, R. Pierre, Bishop of San Jose, 900 Lafayette St., Suite 301, Santa Clara, CA 95050-4966.
Dunne, John C., Auxiliary Bishop of Rockville Centre, P.O. Box 39, Farmingdale, NY 11735-0039.
Dupre, Thomas L., Bishop of Springfield, P.O. Box 1730, Springfield, MA 01105.
Egan, Edward M., Bishop of Bridgeport, Office, 238 Jewett Ave., Bridgeport, CT 06606-2892.
Elya, John A. *b.s.o.*, Eparch of Newton, 19 Dartmouth St., West Newton, MA 02165.
Federal, Joseph Lennox, Retired Bishop of Salt Lake City, 27 C St., Salt Lake City, UT 84111.
Fellhauer, David E., Bishop of Victoria, P.O. Box 4070, Victoria, TX 77903.
Fernandez, Gilberto, Auxiliary Bishop of Miami, St. John Vianney College Seminary, 2900 S.W. 87th St., Miami, FL 33165.
Ferrario, Joseph A., Retired Bishop of Honolulu, 45 N. Kalaheo Ave., Kailua, HI 96734.
Fiorenza, Joseph A., Bishop of Galveston-Houston, 1700 San Jacinto, Houston, TX 77002.
Fitzpatrick, John J., Retired Bishop of Brownsville, P.O. Box 2279, Brownsville, TX 78522-2279.
Fitzsimons, George K., Bishop of Salina, P.O. Box 980, Salina, KS 67402-0980.
Flanagan, Thomas J., Auxiliary Bishop of San Antonio, c/o St. Brigids Church, 6907 Kitchener Rd., San Antonio, TX 78240-2718.
Fliss, Raphael M., Bishop of Superior, Gitchinadji Dr., P.O. Box 969, Superior, WI 54880.
Foley, David E., Bishop of Birmingham, P.O. Box 12047, Birmingham, AL 35202-2047.
Forst, Marion F., Retired Bishop of Dodge City, St. Joseph Care Center, 759 Vermont Ave., Kansas City, KS 66101-3470.
Franklin, William E., Bishop of Davenport, 2761 Scott St., Davenport, IA 52803.
Franzetta, Benedict C., Retired Auxiliary Bishop of Youngstown, 144 W. Wood St., Youngstown, OH 44503.
Freking, Frederick W., Retired Bishop of La Crosse, 3524 East Ave., Apt. 7-B, La Crosse, WI 54601.
Frey, Gerard L., Retired Bishop of Lafayette, P.O. Drawer 3387, Lafayette, LA 70502.
Friend, William B., Bishop of Shreveport, 2104 Chase Crossing, Shreveport, LA 71118.
Galante, Joseph A., Bishop of Beaumont, 6550 Lexinton - Apt. 259, Beaumont, TX 77706.
Garcia, Richard J., Auxiliary Bishop of Sacramento, St. Leo the Great Church, 88 Race St., San Jose, CA 95126.
Garland, James H., Bishop of Marquette, 300 Rock St., P.O. Box 550, Marquette, MI 49855.
Garmendia, Francis, Auxiliary Bishop of New York, St. Thomas Aquinas, 1900 Crotona Parkway, Bronx, NY 10460.
Garner, Robert F., Retired Auxiliary Bishop of Newark, St. Josephs Home, 140 Sheperd Ln., Totowa, NJ 07512.
Gaughan, Norbert F., Retired Bishop of Gary, 180 West Joliet Rd., Valparaiso, IN 46383.
Gaydos, John R., Bishop of Jefferson City, Bishops House, P.O. Box 417, Jefferson City, MO 65102.
Gelineau, Louis E., Retired Bishop of Providence, One Cathedral Square, Providence, RI 02903.
Gendron, Odore J., Retired Bishop of Manchester, St. Joseph Cathedral Rectory, 145 Lowell St., Manchester, NH 03104-6135.
Gerber, Eugene J., Bishop of Wichita, 307 E. Central Ave., Wichita, KS 67202.
Gerry, Joseph J., *o.s.b.*, Bishop of Portland (in Maine), 510 Ocean Ave., Portland, ME 04101.
Gettelfinger, Gerald A., Bishop of Evansville, 3980 Woodcastle, Evansville, IN 47711.
Glynn, John J., Auxiliary Bishop of the Military Services, P.O. Box 4469, Washington, DC 20017-0469.
Goedert, Raymond E., Auxiliary Bishop of Chicago, 155 E. Superior St., Chicago, IL 60690.
González, Roberto O., *o.f.m.*, Bishop of Corpus Christi, 4109 Ocean Dr., Corpus Christi, TX 78411.
Gorman, John R., Auxiliary Bishop of Chicago, 2330 W. 118th St., Chicago, IL 60643.
Gossman, F. Joseph, Bishop of Raleigh, 715 Nazareth, Raleigh, NC 27606.
Gottwald, George J., Retired Auxiliary Bishop of St. Louis, c-o General Delivery, P.O. Box 220, Valles Mines, MO 63087.
Gracida, Rene H., Retired Bishop of Corpus Christi, 620 Lipan St., Corpus Christi, TX 78403-2620.
Grady, Thomas J., Retired Bishop of Orlando, P.O. Box 1800, Orlando, FL 32802-1800.
Graham, John J., Retired Auxiliary Bishop of Philadelphia, 9172 New Falls Rd., Fallsington, PA 19054-1899.

His Excellency,
The Most Reverend

Grahmann, Charles V., Bishop of Dallas, 3725 Blackburn, P.O. Box 190507, Dallas, TX 75219.
Gregory, Wilton D., Bishop of Belleville, 222 South Third St., Belleville, IL 62220.
Griffin, James A., Bishop of Columbus, 198 E. Broad St., Columbus, OH 43215.
Grosz, Edward M., Auxiliary Bishop of Buffalo, St. Stanislaus Kostka Parish, 2437 Niagara St., Niagara Falls, NY 14303-1925.
Guillory, Curtis J., Auxiliary Bishop of Galveston-Houston, 1700 San Jacinto St., Houston, TX 77001.
Gumbleton, Thomas J., Auxiliary Bishop of Detroit, 4860 15th St., Detroit, MI 48208.
Ham, J. Richard, *m.m.*, Retired Auxiliary Bishop of St. Paul-Minneapolis, St. Teresa's Residence, Maryknoll Headquarters, Ossining, NY 10545.
Hanifen, Richard C., Bishop of Colorado Springs, 29 West Kiowa St., Colorado Springs, CO 80903-1498.
Harrington, Bernard J., Auxiliary Bishop of Detroit, 1315 N. Woodward Ave., Bloomfield Hills, MI 48304.
Harrington, Timothy J., Retired Bishop of Worcester, 30 Julio Dr., #105, Shrewsbury, MA 01545.
Harrison, Frank J., Retired Bishop of Syracuse, 6655 Kirkville Rd., East Syracuse, NY 13057.
Hart, Daniel A., Bishop of Norwich, 201 Broadway, P.O. Box 587, Norwich, CT 06360.
Hart, Joseph H., Bishop of Cheyenne, Box 468, Cheyenne, WY 82001.
Head, Edward D., Retired Bishop of Buffalo, 77 Oakland Place, Buffalo, NY 14222.
Herrmann, Edward J., Retired Bishop of Columbus, St. Raphael Home, 1550 Roxbury Rd., Columbus, OH 43212.
Hickey, Dennis W., Retired Auxiliary Bishop of Rochester, 415 Ames St., Rochester, NY 14611.
Higi, William L., Bishop of Lafayette in Indiana, 610 Lingle Ave., Lafayette, IN 47902.
Hoffman, James R., Bishop of Toledo, 2544 Parkwood Ave., OH 43610.
Hogan, James J., Retired Bishop of Altoona-Johnstown, 126 Logan Blvd., Hollidaysburg, PA 16648.
Hogan, Joseph L., Retired Bishop of Rochester, 4199 East Avenue, Rochester, NY 14618.
Houck, William R., Bishop of Jackson, Mailing Address: P.O. Box 2248, Jackson, MS 39225.
Howze, Joseph L., Bishop of Biloxi, P.O. Box 1189, Biloxi, MS 39533.
Hubbard, Howard J., Bishop of Albany, 125 Eagle St., Albany, NY 12203.
Hughes, Alfred C., Bishop of Baton Rouge, 1800 South Acadian Thruway, P.O. Box 2028, Baton Rouge LA 70821-2028.
Hughes, Edward T., Retired Bishop of Metuchen, 10 Library Pl., Metuchen, NJ 08840.
Hughes, William A., Retired Bishop of Covington, Catheral Basilica of the Assumption, 1140 Madison Ave., Covington, KY 41011-3116.
Hurley, Mark J., Former Bishop of Santa Rosa, 273 Ulloa St., San Francisco, CA 94127.
Ibrahim, Ibrahim, Bishop-Eparch to St. Thomas the Apostle, 25585 Berg Rd., Southfield, MI 48034.
Imesch, Joseph L., Bishop of Joliet, 425 Summit St., Joliet, IL 60435.
Irwin, Francis X., Auxiliary Bishop of Boston, 2 Gardner St., Peabody, MA 01960-1896.
Jacobs, Sam, Bishop of Alexandria, P.O. Box 7417, Alexandria, LA 71306.
Jakubowski, Thad J., Auxiliary Bishop of Chicago, 6002 W. Berteau Ave., Chicago, IL 60634-7720.
Jarrell, Charles Michael, Bishop of Houma Thibodaux, 1801 Hwy. 311, Schriever, LA 70395.
Jenky, Daniel R., *c.s.c.*, Auxiliary Bishop of Fort Wayne-South Bend, University of Notre Dame, Fisher Graduate Residences, Notre Dame, IN 46556-5676.
Kaffer, Roger L., Auxiliary Bishop of Joliet, 425 Summit St., Joliet, IL 60435.
Kaniecki, Michael J., *s.j.*, Bishop of Fairbanks, 1316 Peger Rd., Fairbanks, AK 99709.
Keating, John R., Bishop of Arlington, 4600 N. Carlin Springs Rd., Arlington, VA 22203.
Kicanas, Gerald F., Auxiliary Bishop of Chicago, 200 N. Milwaukee, Suite 200, Libertyville, IL 60048-2250.
Kinney, John F., Bishop of St. Cloud, 214 Third Ave., South, Box 1248, St. Cloud, MN 56302-1248.
Kmiec, Edward U., Bishop of Nashville, 2400 Twenty-First Ave., South, Nashville, TN 37212.
Krawczak, Arthur H., Retired Auxiliary Bishop of Detroit, Marywood Nursing Center, 36975 Five Mile Rd., Livonia, MI 48154.
Kuzma, George M., Bishop of Van Nuys, Byzantine Catholic Eparchy of Van Nuys, 8131 North 16th St., Phoenix, AZ 85020.
Larkin, W. Thomas, Retired Bishop of St. Petersburg, P.O. Box 40200, St. Petersburg, FL 33743.

His Excellency,
The Most Reverend

Leibrecht, John J., Bishop of Springfield-Cape Girardeau, The Catholic Center, 601 S. Jefferson, Springfield, MO 65806-3143.

Lessard, Raymond W., Retired Bishop of Savannah, St. Vincent de Paul Seminary, 10701 S. Military Trail, Boynton Beach, FL 33436-4899.

Lohmuller, Martin N., Retired Auxiliary Bishop of Philadelphia, Villa Maria House of Studies, King Rd., Immaculate, PA 19345.

Lori, William E., Auxiliary Bishop of Washington, 5001 Eastern Ave., (P.O. Box 29260) Washington, DC 20017.

Losten, Basil, Bishop of Stamford, 14 Peveril Rd., Stamford, CT 06902-3019

Lotocky, Innocent, *o.s.b.m.*, Retired Bishop of St. Nicholas in Chicago, 2245 W. Rice St., Chicago, IL 60622.

Loverde, Paul S., Bishop of Ogdensburg, P.O. Box 369, 622 Washington St., Ogdensburg, NY 13669.

Lucker, Raymond A., Bishop of New Ulm, 1400 Sixth North St., New Ulm, MN 56073-2099.

Lynch, George E., Retired Auxiliary Bishop of Raleigh, P.O. Box 130, Bronx, NY 10470-0130.

Lynch, Robert N., Bishop of St. Petersburg, P.O. Box 40200, St. Petersburg, FL 33743.

Lyne, Timothy J., Retired Auxiliary Bishop of Chicago, 730 N. Wabash, Chicago, IL 60611.

Macaluso, Christie A., Auxiliary Bishop of Hartford, 134 Farmington Ave., Hartford, CT 06105-3784.

Madera, Joseph J., *m.sp.s.*, Auxiliary Bishop of Military Services, P.O. Box 4469, Washington, DC 20017-0469.

Maguire, Joseph F., Retired Bishop of Springfield, 68 Elliot St., Springfield, MA 01101.

Maginnis, Robert P., Auxiliary Bishop of Philadelphia, St. Colman Rectory, 11 Simpson Rd., Ardmore, PA 19003-2812.

Mahoney, James P., Retired Auxiliary Bishop of New York, Assumption Parish, 131 Union Ave., Peekskill, NY 10566.

Malone, James W., Retired Bishop of Youngstown, 144 W. Wood St., Youngstown, OH 44503.

Maloney, Charles G., Retired Auxiliary Bishop of Louisville, P.O. Box 1073, Louisville, KY 40201.

Mansell, Henry J., Bishop of Buffalo, 795 Main St., Buffalo, NY 14203.

Manz, John R., Auxiliary Bishop of Chicago, 1820 S. Leavitt St., Chicago, IL 60608.

Marconi, Dominic A., Auxiliary Bishop of Newark, P.O. Box 1246, Linden, NJ 07036.

Martino, Joseph F., Auxiliary Bishop of Phildelphia, St. Charles Borromeo Seminary, Overbrook, 100 E. Wynnewood Rd., Wynnewood, PA 19096.

Matthiesen, Leroy T., Retired Bishop of Amarillo, P.O. Box 5644, Amarillo, TX 79117.

McAuliffe, Michael F., Retired Bishop of Jefferson City, Bishop's House, P.O. Box 417, Jefferson City, MO 65102.

McCarthy, John E., Bishop of Austin, P.O. Box 13327, Austin, TX 78711.

McCormack, John B., Auxiliary Bishop of Boston, 236 Pleasant St., Weymouth, MA 02190.

McCormack, William J., Auxiliary Bishop of New York, 142 E. 29th St., New York, NY 10016.

McDonald, Andrew J., Bishop of Little Rock, P.O. Box 7239, Little Rock, AR 72217.

McDonnell, Charles J., Auxiliary Bishop of Newark, 34 Maple Ave., Hackensack, NJ 07601.

McDowell, John B., Former Auxiliary Bishop of Pittsburgh, 1817 Red Coach Rd., Allison Park, PA 15101.

McFarland, Norman F., Bishop of Orange, Marywood Center, 2811 E. Villa Real Dr., Orange, CA 92867.

McGann, John R., Bishop of Rockville Centre, 29 Quealy Place, Rockville Centre, NY 11570.

McGrath, Patrick J., Auxiliary Bishop of San Francisco, 445 Church St., San Francisco, CA 94114.

McHugh, James T., Bishop of Camden, Marywood, 1600 Peter Cheeseman Rd., P.O. Box 577, Blackwood, NJ 08012.

McKinney, Joseph C., Auxiliary Bishop of Grand Rapids, 654 Davis, N.W., Grand Rapids, MI 49504.

McLaughlin, Bernard J., Retired Auxiliary Bishop of Buffalo, 204 Knoche Rd., Tonawand, NY 14150.

McNamara, John R., Auxiliary Bishop of Boston, 70 Lawrence St., Lowell, MA 01852.

McNamara, Lawrence J., Bishop of Grand Island, P.O. Box 1531, Grand Island, NE 68802.

McRaith, John J., Bishop of Owensboro, 501 W. Fifth St., Owensboro, KY 42301.

Melczek, Dale J., Bishop of Gary, 9292 Broadway, Merrillville, IN 46410.

Mengeling, Carl F., Bishop of Lansing, 300 West Ottawa St., Lansing, MI 48933.

Mestice, Anthony F., Auxiliary Bishop of New York, Resurrection, 910 Post Rd., Rye, NY 10580.

His Excellency,
The Most Reverend

Michaels, James E., *s.s.c.*, Resigned Auxiliary Bishop of Wheeling-Charleston, P.O. Box 606, Berryville, VA 22611.

Mikloshazy, Attila, *s.j.*, Bishop to Hungarians, St. Augustine's Seminary, 2661 Kingston Rd., Scarborough, Ontario, Canada, M1M 1M3.

Milone, Anthony M., Bishop of Great Falls-Billings, 2825 4th Ave., N. Great Falls, MT 59401-2911.

Moeddel, Carl K., Auxiliary Bishop of Cincinnati, 100 East 8th St., Cincinnati, OH 45202.

Montrose, Donald, Bishop of Stockton, 1105 N. Lincoln St., Stockton, CA 95204-0237.

Moreno, Manuel D., Bishop of Tucson, 192 S. Stone Ave., Tucson, AZ 85702.

Morneau, Robert F., Auxiliary Bishop of Green Bay, 1910 S. Webster, P.O. Box 23825, Green Bay, WI 54305-3825.

Moskal, Robert M., Bishop of St. Josaphat in Parma, 5720 State Rd., Parma, OH 44134.

Moynihan, James M., Bishop of Syracuse, 240 East Onondaga St. -P.O. Box 511, Syracuse, NY 13201.

Muench, Robert W., Bishop of Covington, P.O. Box 18548, Erlanger, KY 41018.

Mulvee, Robert E., Bishop of Providence, One Cathedral Sq., Providence, RI 02903.

Murphy, Michael J., Retired Bishop of Erie, 130 E. Fourth St., Erie, PA 16507.

Murphy, P. Francis, Auxiliary Bishop of Baltimore, 320 Cathedral St., Baltimore, MD 21201.

Murphy, William F., Auxiliary Bishop of Boston, 2121 Commonwealth Ave., Brighton, MA 02135.

Murray, James A., Bishop of Kalamazoo, 215 N. Westnedge Ave., Kalamazoo, MI 49007-3760.

Murry, George V., *s.j.*, Auxiliary Bishop of Chicago, Box 733, South Holland, IL 60473-0733.

Myers, John Joseph, Bishop of Peoria, 607 N.E. Madison, Peoria, IL 61603.

Naumann, Joseph F., Auxliliary Bishop of St. Louis, 8900 Clayton Rd., Richmond Heights, MO 63117.

Nevins, John J., Bishop of Venice, P.O. Box 2006, Venice, FL 34284.

Newman, William C., Auxiliary Bishop of Baltimore, 5300 N. Charles St., Baltimore, MD 21210.

Neylon, Martin J., *s.j.*, Retired Bishop of The Caroline Islands, P.O. Box 250, Truk, Caroline Islands 96942.

Niederauer, George H., Bishop of Salt Lake City, 27 C St., Salt Lake City, UT 84103.

Niedergeses, James D., Retired Bishop of Nashville, 2400 Twenty-First Ave., South, Nashville, TN 37212.

Nienstedt, John C., Auxiliary Bishop of Detroit, 1234 WashingtonBlvd., Detroit, MI 48226.

Ochoa, Armando, Bishop of El Paso, 499 St. Matthews St., El Paso TX 79907.

O'Brien, Thomas J., Bishop of Phoenix, 48 E. Wagon Wheel Dr., Phoenix, AZ 85020.

O'Connell, Anthony J., Bishop of Knoxville, 805 Northshore Dr., Knoxville, TN 37919-7551.

O'Donnell, Edward J., Bishop of Lafayette, P.O. Box Drawer 3387, Lafayette, LA 70502.

O'Keefe, Gerald, Former Bishop of Davenport, 2706 N. Gaines St., Davenport, IA 52804-1998.

O'Leary, Edward C., Retired Bishop of Portland (in Maine), 510 Ocean Ave., Portland, ME 04102.

Olivier, Leonard J., *s.v.d.*, Auxiliary Bishop of Washington, 3340 St. Peter's Dr., Waldorf, MD 20601-2359.

O'Malley, Sean, *o.f.m.cap.*, Bishop of Fall River, Box 2577, Fall River, MA 02722.

O'Neill, Arthur J., Retired Bishop of Rockford, 1245 North Court St., Rockford, IL 61103.

O'Rourke, Edward W., Retired Bishop of Peoria, St. Augustine Manor, 1301 N.E. Glendale, Peoria, IL 61603.

Ottenweller, Albert H., Retired Bishop of Steubenville, 609 North Seventh St., Steubenville, OH 43952.

Paschang, John L., Retired Bishop of Grand Island, St. Joseph's Home, 320 E. Decatur St., West Point, NE 68788.

Paska, Walter, Auxiliary Bishop of Philadelphia Ukraine, 827 N. Franklin St., Philadelphia, PA 19123.

Pataki, Andrew, Bishop of Passaic of the Ruthenians, 445 Lackawanna Ave., West Paterson, NJ 07424.

Paul, John J., Retired Bishop of La Crosse, P.O. Box 69, La Crosse, WI 54601.

Pelotte, Donald, *s.s.s.*, Bishop of Gallup, 711 S. Puerco Drive, Gallup, NM 87301.

Pena, Raymundo J., Bishop of Brownsville, 1910 E. Elizabeth St., Brownsville, TX 78522-2279.

Pevec, A. Edward, Auxiliary Bishop of Cleveland, 28700 Euclid Ave., Wickliffe, OH 44092.

Pfeifer, Michael D., *o.m.i.*, Bishop of San Angelo, 116 S. Oakes, San Angelo, TX 75902.

Pilla, Anthony M., Bishop of Cleveland, 1027 Superior Ave., Cleveland, OH 44114.

His Excellency,
The Most Reverend

Popp, Bernard F., Retired Auxiliary Bishop of San Antonio, 4535 Lord Rd., San Antonio, TX 78220-3543.

Povish, Kenneth J., Retired Bishop of Lansing, 401-A East Madison St., DeWitt, MI 48820.

Pursley, Leo A., Retired Bishop of Fort Wayne-South Bend, 2 Northway Dr., Huntington, IN 46750.

Puscas, Vasile Louis, Former Apostolic Eparch of St. George Martyr in Canton for Romanian-Byzantine Catholics, 609 N. Lincoln Ave., Aurora, IL 60505-2112.

Quinn, A. James, Auxiliary Bishop of Cleveland, 2500 Elyria Ave., Lorain, OH 44055.

Quinn, Francis A., Retired Bishop of Sacramento, 8840 East 22nd St., Tucson, AZ 85710.

Ramirez, Ricardo, *c.s.b.*, Bishop of Las Cruces, 1280 Med Park Dr., Las Cruces, NM 88005.

Reilly, Daniel P., Bishop of Worcester, 49 Elm St., Worcester, MA 01609.

Reiss, John C., Retired Bishop of Trenton, 701 Lawrence Rd., Trenton, NJ 08648.

Ricard, John H., *s.s.j.*, Bishop of Pensacola-Tallahassee, 11 N. B St., Pensacola, FL 32501.

Riley, Lawrence J., Retired Auxiliary Bishop of Boston, 43 Maple St., Hyde

Park, Boston, MA 02136.

Rivera, Enrique Hernandez, Bishop of Caguas, P.O. Box 8698, Caguas, PR 00626.

Rivera, Hector M., Auxiliary Bishop of San Juan, P.O. Box S-1967, San Juan, PR 00603.

Rodimer, Frank J., Bishop of Paterson, 178 Derrom Ave., Paterson, NJ 07504.

Rodriguez, Miguel, *c.ss.r*, Retired Bishop of Arecibo, Calle Comercio 32, P.O. Box 238, Aguadilla, PR 00605-0238.

Rodriguez, Placido, *c.m.f.*, Bishop of Lubbock, P.O. Box 98700 - 4620 4th St., Lubbock, TX 79416.

Roque, Francis X., Auxiliary Bishop Military Services, P.O. Box 4469, Washington, DC 20017-0469.

Roman, Agustin A., Auxiliary Bishop of Miami, 9401 Biscayne Blvd., Miami Shores, FL 33138.

Rosazza, Peter A., Auxiliary Bishop of Hartford, 1450 Chapel St., New Haven, CT 06511.

Rose, Robert J., Bishop of Grand Rapids, 660 Burton St., S.E., Grand Rapids, MI 49507.

Rueger, George E., Auxiliary Bishop of Worcester, 2 High Ridge Rd., Worcester, MA 01602.

Ryan, Daniel L., Bishop of Springfield in Illinois, P.O. Box 1667, Springfield, IL 62705.

Ryan, Sylvester D., Bishop of Monterey, 580 Fremont St., P.O. Box 2048, Monterey, CA 93942-2048.

Saltarelli, Michael A., Bishop of Wilmington, 1925 Delaware Ave., Suite 1-A, Wilmington, DE 19806.

Samo, Amando, Auxiliary Bishop of The Caroline Islands. P.O. Box 250, Truk, Caroline Islands FSM 96942.

Samra, Nicholas J., Auxiliary Bishop of Newton, 8525 Cole St., Warren, MI 48093.

Santana, Hermin Negron, Auxiliary Bishop of San Juan, Calle 6, D-9 Urb. Royal Town, Bayamon, PR 00956.

Sartoris, Joseph M., Auxiliary Bishop of Los Angeles, San Pedro Pastoral Region, 3555 St. Pancratius Plc., Lakewood, CA 90712-1416.

Schad, James L., Retired Auxiliary Bishop of Camden, Neumann House - St. Mary's Home, Suite 102, 1730 Kresson Rd., Cherry Hill, NJ 08003.

Schlarman, Stanley G., Bishop of Dodge City, 910 Central Ave., P.O. Box 0137, Dodge City, KS 67801-0137.

Schmitt, Bernard W., Bishop of Wheeling-Charleston, 1300 Byron St., Box 230, Wheeling, WV 26003.

Schmitt, Mark F., Retired Bishop of Marquette, HC01 Box 159, Marquette, MI 49855.

Schoenherr, Walter J., Retired Auxiliary Bishop of Detroit, 14465 Levan Rd.- Apt. A, Livonia, MI 48154-5022.

Schuster, Eldon B., Retired Bishop of Great Falls, 1325 Smelter Ave., Black Eagle, Great Falls, MT 59414.

Schwietz, Roger L., *o.m.i.*, Bishop of Duluth, 2830 E. 4th St., Duluth, MN 55812.

Schott, Basil, *o.f.m.*, Bishop of Parma of the Ruthenians

Setian, Nerses M., Former Apostolate Exarch for the Armenian Catholics, c/o Our Lady Queen of Martyrs Church, 1327 Pleasant Ave., Los Angeles, CA 90033.

Sevilla, Carlos, *s.j.*, Bishop of Yakima.

Sheets, John R., *s.j.*, Retired Auxiliary Bishop of Ft. Wayne-South Bend, St. Matthew Cathedral, 1701 Miami St., South Bend, IN 46613.

Sheldon, Gilbert I., Bishop of Steubenville, P.O. Box 969, Steubenville, OH 43952.

Sheridan, Michael J., Auxiliary Bishop of St. Louis.

Sheridan, Patrick J., Auxiliary Bishop of New York, 452 Madison Ave., New York, NY 10022.

Sklba, Richard J., Auxiliary Bishop of Milwaukee, 2491 N. Murray Ave., Milwaukee, WI 53211.

His Excellency,
The Most Reverend

Skylstad, William S., Bishop of Spokane, W. 1023 Riverside Ave., Spokane, WA 99201.
Slattery, Edward J., Bishop of Tulsa, P.O. Box 2009, Tulsa, OK 74101.
Smith, John M., Bishop of Trenton, 701 Lawrenceville Rd., Trenton, NJ 08638.
Snyder, John J., Bishop of St. Augustine, 35 Treasury St., St. Augustine, FL 32084.
Soens, Lawrence D., Bishop of Sioux City, P.O. Box 3379, Sioux City, IA 51102-1437.
Speltz, George H., Retired Bishop of St. Cloud, Box 1248, St. Cloud, MN 56301.
Speyrer, Jude, Bishop of Lake Charles, P.O. Box 3223, Lake Charles, LA 70602.
Steib, James Terry, *s.v.d.*, Bishop of Memphis, The Catholic Center, P.O. Box 341669, Memphis, TN 38184-1669.
Steinbock, John T., Bishop of Fresno, 1550 N. Fresno St., Fresno, CA 93703-3788.
Steiner, Kenneth D., Auxiliary Bishop of Portland in Oregon, 501-N.W. 25th St., Corvalis, OR 97330.
Straling, Phillip F., Bishop of Reno, P.O. Box 1211, Reno, NV 89504-1211.
Sullivan, James S., Bishop of Fargo, Box 1750, Fargo, ND 58107.
Sullivan, John J., Retired Bishop of Kansas City-St. Joseph, 8745 James A. Reed Rd., Kansas City, MO 64138.
Sullivan, Joseph M., Auxiliary Bishop of Brooklyn, 256 Clinton Ave., Brooklyn, NY 11205.
Sullivan, Walter F., Bishop of Richmond, 800 Cathedral Place, Richmond, VA 23220.
Surinach-Carreras, Ricardo, Auxiliary Bishop of Ponce, P.O. Box 205, Ponce, PR 00731.
Symons, J. Keith, Bishop of Palm Beach, 9995 N. Military Trail (P.O. Box 109650), Palm Beach Gardens, FL 33410-9650.
Tafoya, Arthur N., Bishop of Pueblo, 1001 N. Grand Ave., Pueblo, CO 81003.
Tamayo, James A., Auxiliary Bishop of Galveston-Houston, 1700 San Jacinto, Houston, TX 77002-8291.
Tawil, Joseph, Retired Eparch of Newton, 19 Dartmouth St., West Newton, MA 02165.
Tertzakian, Hovhannes, *O.M.Ven.*, Apostolic Exarch for Armenian Catholics in the United States and Canada, 110 E 12th St., New York, NY 10003-5395.
Thomas, Elliot G., Bishop of St. Thomas, in the Virgin Islands, P.O. Box 1825, Charlotte Amalie, VI 00803.
Thompson, David B., Bishop of Charleston, 119 Broad St., Charleston, SC 29401.
Timlin, James C., Bishop of Scranton, 300 Wyoming Ave., Scranton, PA 18503.
Tobin, Thomas J., Bishop of Youngstown, 144 W. Wood St., Youngstown, OH 44503.
Torres, Juan Fremiot, Bishop of Ponce, P.O. Box 205, Ponce, PR 00732.
Trautman, Donald W., Bishop of Erie, 205 West 9th St., Erie, PA 16501.
Tschoepe, Thomas, Retired Bishop of Dallas, 3915 Lemmon Ave, Box 19507, Dallas, TX 75219.
Txertudi, Inaki Mallona, *c.p.*, 206 Dr. Salas St. - Box 616, Arecibo, PR 00613-0616.
Untener, Kenneth E., Bishop of Saginaw, 5800 Weiss St., Saginaw, MI 48603.
Valero, Rene, Auxiliary Bishop of Brooklyn, 34-43 93rd St., Jackson Heights, NY 11372.
Vaughan, Austin B., Auxiliary Bishop of New York, Our Lady of Consolation Res., 3103 Arlington Ave., Bronx, NY 10463-3305.
Vigneron, Allen H., Auxiliary Bishop of Detroit, Sacred Heart Major Seminary, 2701 Chicago Blvd., Detroit, MI 48206.
Walsh, Daniel F., Bishop of Las Vegas, P.O. Box 18316, Las Vegas, NV 89114.
Ward, John J., Former Auxiliary Bishop of Los Angeles, 3424 Wilshire Blvd., Los Angeles, CA 90010-2241
Warfel, Michael, Bishop of Juneau, 419 6th St., Suite 200, Juneau, AK 99801.
Watters, Loras J., Retired Bishop of Winona, 618 Forest, Apt. D., Pacific Grove, CA 93950.
Wcela, Emil A., Auxiliary Bishop of Rockville Centre, Eastern Vicariate, P.O. Box 780, Riverhead, NY 11901.
Weigand, William K., Bishop of Sacramento, Pastoral Center, 2110 Broadway, Sacramento CA 95818-2541.
Weitzel, John Quinn, *m.m.*, Bishop of Samoa-Pago Pago, Fatuoaiga P.O. Box 596, Pago Pago, American Samoa 967.
Welsh, Lawrence H., Auxiliary Bishop of St. Paul-Minneapolis, 226 Summit Ave., St. Paul, MN 55102.
Welsh, Thomas J., Retired Bishop of Allentown, 1325 Prospect AVe., Bethlehem, PA 18018.

His Excellency,
The Most Reverend

Wenski, Thomas G., Auxiliary Bishop of Miami, Cathlic Relief Services, 9401 Biscayne Blvd., Miami, FL 33138.
Whelan, Robert L., *s.j.*, Retired Bishop of Fairbanks, Regis Community, 1107 N. Astor, Spokane, WA 99202.
Wilkerson, Gerald E., Auxiliary Bishop of Los Angeles, P.O. Box 7608, Mission Hills, CA 91316.
Williams, James Kendrick, Bishop of Lexington, 1310 Leestown Rd., P.O. Box 12350, Lexington, KY 40582-2350.
Winter, William J., Auxiliary Bishop of Pittsburgh, Sacred Heart Church, 310 Shady Ave., Pittsburgh, PA 15206-4389.
Wirz, George O., Auxiliary Bishop of Madison, 3577 S. High Point Rd., Madison WI 53719-4999.
Wiwchar, Michael, *c.s.s.r.*, Bishop of St. Nicholas in Chicago for Ukrainians, 224 W. Rice St., Chicago, IL 60622.
Wuerl, Donald W., Bishop of Pittsburgh, 111 Blvd. of the Allies, Pittsburgh, PA 15222-1618.
Wycislo, Aloysius J., Retired Bishop of Green Bay, 1910 S. Webster, P.O. Box 23835, Green Bay, WI 54305-3825.
Yanta, John W., Bishop of Amarillo.
Younan, Joseph,, Bishop of Our Lady of Deliverance of Newark of the Syrians, P.O. Box 8366, Union City, NJ 07087-8262.
Zayek, Francis M., Former Eparch (Bishop) of St. Maron of Brooklyn, 294 Howard Ave., 4010 Galt Ocean Dr.-Apt. 1230, Fort Lauderdale, FL 33308.
Zavala, Gabino, Auxiliary Bishop of Los Angeles, San Gabriel Pastoral Region, 16009 East Cypress Ave., Irwindale, CA 91706-2122
Ziemann, G. Patrick, Bishop of Santa Rosa, 547 B St., P.O. Box 1297, Santa Rosa, CA 95402.
Zipfel, Paul A., Bishop of Bismarck.
Zubik, David A., Auxiliary Bishop of Pittsburgh, 111 Blvd. of Allies, Pittsburgh, PA 15222.
Zurek, Patrick J., Auxiliary Bishop of San Antonio, c/o St. John Newmann Church, 105 Reveille Rd., Austin, TX 78746.

U.S. HIERARCHY SERVING IN OTHER COUNTRIES

Adams, Edward J., Archbishop Apostolic Nuncio in Bangladesh, P.O. Box 6003, Dhaka, Bangladesh.
Boyle, Paul M., *c.p.*, Apostolic Vicar of Mandeville, Jamaica, West Indies.
Brown, Charles A.,*m.m.*, Auxiliary Bishop of Santa Cruz, Arzobispado, Casilla 25, Calle Ingavi 49, Santa Cruz, Bolivia.
De Paoli, Ambrose, Apostolic Nuncio to Japan: 9-2 Sanban-cho, Chiyodku, Tokio.
Dion, George E., *o.m.i.*, Retired Bishop of Jolo, Oblates of Notre Dame Motherhouse, Sinsuat Ave., 9600 Cotabato City, Philippines.
Harvey, James M., Bishop/Prefect of the Papal Household, Titular Episcopal of Memfi, 00120 Vatican City State.
Lambert, Francis Roland, *s.m.*, Bishop of Port-Vila, Eveche, B.P. 59, Port-Vila, Vanuatu.
McGarry, Urban E., *t.o.r.*, Bishop of Bhagalpur, Chancery Office: Nawab Colony, P.O. Box 61, Bhagalpur 812001, Bihar, India.
McNaughton, William J., *m.m.*, Bishop of Inchon, 3 Tap Tong, P.O. Box 19, Chung Ku, Inchon 400-600, Korea.
Smith, Philip Francis, *m.m.*, Archbishop of Cotabato, Residence, P.O. Box 186, Sinsuat Ave., Cotabato City 9600, Philippines.

OTHER HIERARCHY RESIDING IN THE UNITED STATES

Cotey, Arnold R., *s.d.s.*, Former Bishop of Nachingwea, 3140 Hwy K, Random Lake WI 53075.
DePalma, Joseph A., *s.c.j.* Former Bishop of De Aar, South Africa, Sacred Heart Residence, 6701 82nd Ave., N., Pinellas Park, FL 34665.
Durning, Dennis V., *c.s.sp.*, Bishop Emeritus of Arusha Tanzania, East Africa, Holy Ghost Provincialate, 6230 Brush Run Rd., Bethel Park, PA 15102.
Dempsey, Michael J., *o.p.*, 3005 W. 29th Ave., Denver, CO 80211.
Kung, Ignatius Cardinal, Our Lady Queen of the Clergy Home, 128 Strawberry Hill Ave., Stamford, CT 06904.
Kupfer, William F., *m.m.*, Former Bishop of Taichung, Taiwan, Annunciation Rectory, 410 Walnut St., Williamsport, PA 17701.
Meeking, Basil, Retired Bishop from New Zealand, 4635 S.W. 148th Ave., Beaverton, OR 97007.
Nolker, Bernard J., *c.ss.r.*, Retired Bishop of Paranagua Brazil, 600 S. Conkling St., Baltimore, MD 21224.
Pearce, George H., *s.m.*, Former Archbishop of Suva, 30 Fenner St., Providence, RI 02903.
Reilly, Thomas, *c.ss.r.*, Retired Bishop of San Juan de la Maguana, Dominican Republic, 1545 Tremont St., Roxbury, MA 02120.
Schlotterback, Edward J., *o.s.f.s.*, Retired Bishop of Keetmanschoop-Namibia, The Salesianum, 1801 N. Broom St., Wilmington, DE 19802.
Schmidt, Firmin, *o.f.m.cap.*, Former Bishop of Papua, New Guinea, c/o Diocese of Salina, 103 N. Ninth, Salina, KS 67402-0980.
Secondo, Louis J., *t.o.r.*, St. Anthony, 124 Maple Ave., Johnstown, PA 15901.
Veigle, Adriano J., *t.o.r.*, Retired Bishop of Borba, Brazil, Mount Assisi Monastery, Loretto, PA 15940.

ARCHABBOTS

The Right Reverend

Donovan, Egbert, *o.s.b.*, Retired. St. Vincent Archabbey, Latrobe, PA 15650.
Knaebel, Bonaventure, *o.s.b.*, Resigned. St. Meinrad Archabbey, St. Meinrad, IN 47577.
Maher, Paul R., *o.s.b.*, St. Vincent Archabbey, Latrobe, PA 15650.
Nowicki, Douglas R., *o.s.b.*, St. Vincent Archabbey, Latrobe, PA 15650.
Reilly, Lambert, *o.s.b.*, St. Meinrad Archabbey, St. Meinrad, IN 47577.

ABBOTS

Abdo, Michael, *o.c.s.o.*, St. Benedict Monastery, 1012 Monastery Rd., Snowmass, CO 81654.
Anderson, Hugh R., *o.s.b.*, St. Procopius Abbey, 5601 College Rd., Lisle, IL 60532.
Balsavich, Marion E., *o.s.b.*, Retired. St. Bede Abbey, Peru, IL 61354.
Bamberger, John E., *o.c.s.o.*, Abbey of Genesee, Piffard, NY 14533.
Bataille, Vincent, *o.s.b.*, Marmion Abbey, Butterfield Rd., Aurora, IL 60504.
Benedict, Francis, *o.s.b.*, St. Andrew's Abbey, 31001 N. Valyermo Rd., Valyermo, CA 93563.
Benkert, Gerald, *o.s.b.*, Resigned. Marmion Abbey, Butterfield Rd., Aurora, IL 60504.
Berndt, Alan, *o.s.b.*, Retired. Blue Cloud Abbey, P.O. Box 98, Marvin, SD 57252.
Berning, Philip, *o.s.b.*, Retired. St. Gregory Abbey, Shawnee, OK 74801.
Bock, David R., *o.c.s.o.*, Retired. New Melleray Abbey, 6500 Melleray Circle, Peosta, IA 52068.
Boultwood, Alban, *o.s.b.*, St. Anselm Abbey, 4501 S. Dakota Ave., N.E., Washington, DC 20017.
Bowman, Marion, *o.s.b.*, Retired. St. Leo Abbey, St. Leo, FL 33574.
Boyle, Joseph, *o.s.b.*, St. Benedict Monastery, 1012 Monastery Rd., Snowmass, CO 81654.
Buergler, Luke, *o.s.b.*, Corpus Christi Abbey, HCR #2, Box 6300, Sandia, TX 78383.
Burne, Martin J., *o.s.b.*, Retired. St. Mary Abbey, Delbarton, Mendham Rd., Morristown, NJ 07960.
Burnett, Oscar, *o.s.b.*, Belmont Abbey, 100 Belmont - Mount Holly Rd., Belmont, NC 28012-2795.
Burns, Flavian, *o.c.s.o.*, Abbey of Our Lady of the Holy Cross, Rt. 2, Box 3870, Berryville, VA 22611.
Campbell, Edward C., *o.s.b.*, Retired. Glastonbury Abbey, 16 Hull St., Hingham, MA 02043.
Carr, Christian Aidan, *o.c.s.o.*, Retired. Our Lady of Mepkin Abbey, HC 69, Box 800, Moncks Corner, SC 29461. Serving as chaplain in Africa.
Cassell, Leonard G., *o.s.b.*, Retired. St. Mary Abbey, Delbarton, Mendham Rd., Morristown, NJ 07960.
Chassagne, M. Anthony, *o.c.s.o.*, Retired. Abbey of Our Lady of Mepkin, HC 69, Box 800, Moncks Corner, SC 29461.
Clark, Victor J., *o.s.b.*, St. Bernard Abbey, 1600 St. Bernard Dr., Cullman, AL 35055.
Clarke, Brian H., *o.s.b.*, St. Mary Abbey, Delbarton, Mendham Rd., Morristown, NJ 07960.
Coggin, Walter A., *o.s.b.*, Retired. Belmont Abbey, 100 Belmont - Mount Holly Rd., Belmont, NC 28012-2795.
Cole, Edwin J., *o.s.b.*, St. Anselm Church, 530 S. Mason Rd., St. Louis, MO 63141.
Connor, James, *o.c.s.o.*, Assumption Abbey, Rte 5 - Box 1056, Ava, MO 65660.
Coppersmith, Anselm, *o.s.b.*, Retired. Conception Abbey, Conception, MO 64433.
Coriston, Charles V., *o.s.b.*, Resigned. St. Paul Abbey, Newton, NJ 07860.
Corpus, Roger, *o.s.b.*, St. Bede Abbey, Peru, IL 61354.

Cyr, David J., *o.s.b.*, Marmion Abbey, Butterfield Rd., Aurora, IL 60504.
Dagher, George, *b.s.o.*, American Headquarters, 30 East St., Methuen, MA 01844.
Davis, Thomas X., *o.c.s.o.*, Our Lady of New Clairvaux Abbey, P.O. Box 80, Vina, CA 96092.
De Wane, Thomas E., *o.praem.*, St. Norbert Abbey, 1016 N. Broadway, De Pere, WI 54115-2697.
Dimitrijevich, Nicholas, Our Lady of the Valley, P.O. Box 419, Gloverville, SC 29828.
Dreaper, Hilary, *o.s.b.*, St. Bernard Abbey, 1600 St. Bernard Dr., Cullman, AL 35055.
Dzikowicz, Justin E., *o.s.b.*, St. Paul Abbey, Newton, NJ 07860.
Eberle, Peter, *o.s.b.*, Mount Angel Abbey, St. Benedict, OR 97373.
Ehringer, Claude, *o.s.b.*, Prince of Peace Abbey, Oceanside, CA 92054.
Eidenschink, John, *o.s.b.*, Chaplain. Mother of Mercy Nursing Home & Retirement Center, Albany, MN 56307.
Farkasfalvy, Denis, *o.cist.*, Abbey of Our Lady of Dallas, 1 Cistercian Rd., Irving, TX 75039.
Flaherty, Malachy, *o.c.s.o.*, Abbey of Our Lady of the Holy Trinity, 1250 S. 9500 E., Huntsville, UT 84317.
Freeman, Brendan J., *o.c.s.o.*, Abbey of Our Lady of New Melleray, 6500 Melleray Circle, Peosta, IA 52068.
Fuez, Blaise J. *o.cist.*, Our Lady of Spring Bank Abbey, Rt. 3, Box 211, Sparta, WI 54656.
Galvin, Anselm, *o.s.b.*, Resigned, Mt. Angel Abbey, St. Benedict, OR 97373.
Garber, Andrew V., *o.s.b.*, Resigned. St. Benedict Abbey, Benet Lake, WI 53102.
Geraets, David, *o.s.b.*, Our Lady of Guadalupe Abbey, Pecos, NM 87552.
Gibbs, Gabriel, *o.s.b.*, St. Benedict Abbey, 252 Still River Rd., P.O. Box 67, Still River (Harvard), MA 01467.
Gries, Roger, *o.s.b.*, St. Andrew Abbey, 10510 Buckeye Rd., Cleveland, OH 44104.
Harrison, Cyprian, *o.c.s.o.*, Assumption Abbey, Rt. 5, Box 1056, Ava, MO 65608.
Hartman, Thomas F., *o.s.b.*, Retired. St. Benedict Abbey, Atchison, KS 66002.
Havlik, Thomas J., *o.s.b.*, St. Procopius Abbey, 5601 College Rd., Lisle, IL 60532.
Hayes, Eugene, *o.praem.*,St. Michael Abbey, 19292 El Toro Rd., Silverado, CA 92676-9710.
Heidgen, Warren J., *o.s.b.*, Retired. Holy Cross Abbey, P.O. Box 1510, Canon City, CO 81215-1510.
Hess, Gilbert, *o.s.b.*, Retired. Blue Cloud Abbey, P.O. Box 98, Marvin, SD 57251.
Hillenbrand, Thomas, *o.s.b.*, Blue Cloud Abbey, P.O. Box 98, Marvin, SD 57251.
Hinches, Augustine J., *o.s.b.*, Resigned. St. Paul Abbey, Newton, NJ 07860.
Hoenig, Alfred, *o.s.b.*, Retired. Corpus Christi Abbey, HCR No. 2, P.O. Box 6300, Sandia, TX 78383.
Johnson, Bernard, *o.c.s.o.*, Retired. Monastery of the Holy Spirit, 2625 Hwy 212 S.W., Conyers, GA 30208.
Jones, James, *o.s.b.*, Retired. St. Gabriel Archangel, 4737 N. Cleveland Ave., Kansas City, MO 64117.
Keating, Thomas, *o.c.s.o.*, Contemplative Outreach, Chrysalis House, 21 Ball Rd., Warwick, NY 10990.
Kelly, Timothy, *o.s.b.*, St. John's Abbey, Collegeville, MN 56321.
Kelly, Timothy, *o.c.s.o.*, Abbey of Gethsemani, Trappist, KY 40051.
Kerndt, James J., *o.c.s.o.*, Retired. New Melleray Abbey, 6500 Melleray Circle, Dubuque, IA 52068.
Killeen, Sylvester M., *o.praem.*, Retired. St. Norbert Abbey, 1016 N. Broadway, De Pere, WI 54115-2697.
Kline, Francis, *o.c.s.o.*, Our Lady of Mepkin Abbey, HC 69, Box 800, Moncks Corner, SC 29461.
Kodell, Jerome, *o.s.b.*, New Subiaco Abbey, Subiaco, AR 72865.
Koehler, Ralph, *o.s.b.*, Retired. St. Benedict Abbey, Atchison, KS 66002.
Lawrence, Philip, *o.s.b.*, Monastery of Christ in the Desert, Abiquiu, NM 87510.
Leavy, Matthew, *o.s.b.*, St. Anselm Abbey, Manchester, NH 03102.
Logan, John M., *o.praem.*, Daylesford Abbey, 220 S. Valley Rd., Paoli, PA 19301.
Luykx, Boniface, Holy Transfiguration Monastery, 17001 Tomki Rd., Redwood Valley, CA 95470.
Mackin, Benjamin T., *o.praem.*, Retired, St. Norbert Abbey, 1016 N. Broadway, De Pere, WI 54115-2697.
Massoth, Charles, *o.s.b.*, St. Gregory Abbey, Shawnee, OK 74801.
Matter, Robert, *o.c.s.o.*, Retired. Assumption Abbey, Rt. 5, Box 1056, Ava, MO 65608.
McCarthy, Gerald, *o.s.b.*, Resigned. St. Anselm Abbey, Manchester, NH 03102.
McCorkell, Edward, *o.c.s.o.*, Retired. Abbey of Our Lady of the Holy Cross, Rt. 2, Box 3870, Berryville, VA 22611.
Macrae, Maurus, *o.s.b.*, Westminster Abbey Mission, British Columbia, Canada V2V 4J2.
McDermott, Benedict, *o.s.b.*, Mary Mother of Church Abbey, 304 N. Sheppard St., Richmond, VA 23221.
McGonigle, Kevin, *o.s.b.*, Retired. Conception Abbey, Conception, MO 64433.
McVeigh, Bernard, *o.c.s.o.*, Our Lady of Guadalupe Abbey, Lafayette, OR 97127.
Moore, Augustine J., *o.c.s.o.*, Retired. Monastery of the Holy Spirit, 2625 Hwy. 213 S.W., Conyers, GA 30208.
Moore, Patrick, *o.s.b.*, Assumption Abbey, P.O. Box A, Richardton, ND 58652.
Morcone, Nicholas J., *o.s.b.*, Glastonbury Abbey, 16 Hull St., Hingham, MA 02043.
Neitzel, John E., *o.praem.*, Retired. Daylesford Abbey, 220 S. Valley Rd., Paoli, PA 19301.
O'Connor, Philip J., *o.c.s.o.*, Retired. New Melleray Abbey, 6500 Melleray Circle, Peosta, IA 52068.
Odenbrett, Stephen, *o.s.b.*, Our Lady of Guadalupe Abbey, Pecos, NM 87552.
Parcher, Adrian, *o.s.b.*, Retired. St. Martin's Abbey, 5300 Pacific Ave. S.E., Lacey, WA 98503.
Parker, Ladislaus K., *o.praem.*, Retired, St. Michael Abbey, 19292 E. Toro Rd., Silverado, CA 92676-9710
Purcell, Owen, *o.s.b.*, St. Benedict Abbey, Atchison, KS 66002.
Quinkert, Denis, *o.s.b.*, Blue Cloud Abbey, P.O. Box 98, Marvin, SD 57251.
Rausch, Conrad, *o.s.b.*, Retired. St. Martin's Abbey, 5300 Pacific Ave. S.E., Lacey, WA 98503.
Regan, Patrick, *o.s.b.*, St. Joseph Abbey, St. Benedict, LA 70457.
Rigby, Luke, *o.s.b.*, Abbey of St. Mary and St. Louis, 500 S. Mason Rd., St. Louis, MO 63141.
Roberts, Augustine, *o.c.s.o.*, St. Joseph Abbey, Spencer, MA 01562.
Rodriguez-Santiago, Jose M., *o.s.b.*, Abbey of San Antonio, Box 729, Humacao, PR 00661.
Roettger, Gregory J., *o.s.b.*, Retired. St. Bernard Abbey, 1600 St. Bernard Dr., Cullman, AL 35055.
Rooney, Marcel, *o.s.b.*, Conception Abbey, Conception, MO 64433.
Roth, Neal G., *o.s.b.*, St. Martin's Abbey, 5300 Pacific Ave. S.E., Lacey, WA 98503.
Ryska, Leo M., *o.s.b.*, St. Benedict's Abbey and Retreat Center, Benet Lake, WI 53102.
Schoofs, Robert, *o.s.b.*, St. Benedict Abbey, Benet Lake, WI 53102.
Serna, Dom Mark, *o.s.b.*, Abbey of St. Gregory, Cory's Ln., Portsmouth, RI 02871.
Shea, Aidan, *o.s.b.*, St. Anselm Abbey, 4501 S. Dakota, N.E., Washington, DC 20017.
Shelton, Patrick, *o.s.b.*, St. Leo Abbey, St. Leo, FL 33574.
Skluzacek, Valentine, *o.s.b.*, St. Procopius Abbey, 5601 College Rd., Lisle, IL 60532.
Skutecky, Paschal, *o.c.s.o.*, Retired. St. Joseph Abbey, Spencer, MA 01562.
Spillane, M. Emmanuel, *o.c.s.o.*, Retired. Abbey of Our Lady of the Trinity, 1250 S. 9500 E. Huntsville, UT 84317.
Stark, Matthew, *o.s.b.*, Abbey of St. Gregory the Great, Portsmouth, RI 02871.
Tremel, Jerome G., *o.praem.*,Admin.- Daylesford Abbey Norbertine Canonry, 220 S. Valley Rd., Paoli, PA 19301-1900.
Valvano, Melvin J., *o.s.b.*, Newark Abbey, 528 Dr. Martin Luther King Jr. Blvd., Newark, NJ 07102.
Veilleux, Armand J., *o.s.c.o.*, Monastery of the Holy Spirit, 2625 Hwy. 213 S.W., Conyers, GA 30208.
Vollmer, Edward J., *o.s.b.*, Retired. Holy Cross Abbey, P.O. Box 1510, Canon City, CO 81215-1510.
Vorderlandwehr, Adrian R., *o.s.b.*, Retired. St. Gregory Abbey, Shawnee, OK 74801.
Wagner, Lawrence, *o.s.b.*, Retired. Assumption Abbey, P.O. Box A, Richardton, ND 58652.
Walsh, Raphael, *o.s.b.*, Mt. Michael Abbey, Elkhorn, NE 68022.
Wechter, David L., *o.s.c.o.*, Retired. New Melleray Abbey, 6500 Melleray Circle, Peosta, IA 52068.
Wendt, Gregory F. Monastery of the Exaltation of the Most Holy Cross, 12425 Sunset Dr., Miami, FL 33183.
West, Robert, *o.s.b.*, Retired. Assumption Abbey, P.O. Box A, Richardton, ND 58652.
Wiseman, James, *o.s.b.*, Resigned. St. Anselm Abbey, 4501 S. Dakota Ave., N.E., Washington, DC 20017.
Wolff, Theodore, *o.s.b.* Mount Michael Abbey, Elkhorn, NE 68022.

A LIST OF CARDINALS IN THE UNITED STATES IN THE ORDER OF THEIR SENIORITY

CARDINALS

His Eminence John Cardinal Carberry, St. Louis
His Eminence Luis Cardinal Aponte Martinez, San Juan
His Eminence William Cardinal Baum, Vatican City State
His Eminence Bernard Cardinal Law, Boston
His Eminence John Cardinal O'Connor, New York
His Eminence James Cardinal Hickey, Washington
His Eminence Edmund Cardinal Szoka, Vatican City State
His Eminence Roger Cardinal Mahony, Los Angeles
His Eminence Anthony Cardinal Bevilacqua, Philadelphia
His Eminence William Cardinal Keeler, Baltimore
His Eminence Adam Cardinal Maida, Baltimore
His Eminence Francis Cardinal Stafford, Vatican City State
His Eminence Francis Cardinal George, O.M.I., Chicago

A CHRONOLOGICAL LIST OF CARDINAL, ARCHBISHOP & BISHOP ACTIVITY BY YEAR

1947

Bishops

McDonough, Thomas J., Appointed March 10, Ordained May 26, 1938. Auxiliary Bishop of St. Augustine.

1950

Bishops

Pursley, Leo A., Appointed July 22, Ordained June 11, 1927. Auxiliary Bishop of Fort Wayne-South Bend.

1951

Bishops

Federal, Joseph Lennox, Appointed Feb. 5, Ordained Dec. 8, 1934. Auxiliary Bishop of Salt Lake City.
Paschang, John L., Appointed July 28, Ordained June 12, 1921. Retired Bishop of Grand Island.

1954

Bishops

Maloney, Charles G., Appointed Dec. 30, Ordained Dec. 8, 1937. Retired Auxiliary Bishop of Louisville.

1956

Bishops

Carberry, John J., Appointed May 3, Ordained July 28, 1929. Coadjutor Lafayette in Indiana.
Clinch, Harry A., Appointed Dec. 5, Ordained June 6, 1936. Auxiliary Bishop of Monterey-Fresno.
Hannan, Philip M., Appointed June 16, Ordained Dec. 8, 1939. Auxiliary Bishop of Washington.
Helmsing, Charles H., Appointed Aug. 24, Ordained June 10, 1933. Bishop of Springfield-Cape Girardeau.

1957

Bishops

Carberry, John J., Succeeded to See Nov. 20. Bishop of Lafayette in Indiana.
Curtis, Walter W., Appointed June 27, Ordained Dec. 8, 1937. Auxiliary Bishop of Newark.
Freking, Frederick W., Appointed Oct. 10, Ordained July 31, 1938. Bishop of Salina.
McDonough, Thomas J., Appointed Jan. 2, Ordained May 26, 1938. Auxiliary Bishop of Savannah.
Pursley, Leo A., Appointed Feb. 26. Retired Bishop of Fort Wayne-South Bend.

1958

Bishops

Federal, Joseph L., Appointed May 8, Ordained Dec. 8, 1934. Coadjutor of Salt Lake City.

1959

Bishops

Buswell, Charles A., Appointed Aug. 8, Ordained July 9, 1939. Retired Bishop of Pueblo.
Hogan, James J., Appointed Nov. 27, Ordained Dec. 8, 1937. Auxiliary Bishop of Trenton.

1960

Bishops

Aponte Martinez, Luis, Appointed July 23, Ordained April 10, 1950. Auxiliary of Ponce.
Federal, Joseph L., Succeeded to See March 31. Retired Bishop of Salt Lake City.
Forst, Marion F., Appointed Jan. 2, Ordained June 10, 1934. Former Bishop of Dodge City.
Malone, James W., Appointed Jan. 2, Ordained May 26, 1945. Auxiliary Bishop of Youngstown.
McDonough, Thomas J., Appointed March 2, Ordained May 26, 1938. Bishop of Savannah.
Wycislo, Aloysius J., Appointed Oct. 17, Ordained April 7, 1934. Auxiliary Bishop of Chicago.

1961

Archbishops

Bishops

Curtis, Walter W., Appointed Sept. 23, Ordained Dec. 8, 1937. Retired Bishop of Bridgeport.
Gottwald, George J., Appointed June 20, Ordained June 9, 1940. Retired Auxiliary Bishop of St. Louis.
O'Keefe, Gerald, Appointed May 5, Ordained Jan. 29, 1944. Auxiliary Bishop of St. Paul.
Salatka, Charles A., Appointed Dec. 9, Ordained Feb. 24, 1945. Auxiliary Bishop of Grand Rapids.
Schuster, Eldon B., Appointed Oct. 30, Ordained May 27, 1937. Titular Bishop of Amblada.

1962

Archbishops

Bishops

Boudreaux, Warren L., Appointed May 19, Ordained May 30, 1942. Auxiliary Bishop of Lafayette.
Helmsing, Charles H. Appointed Jan. 27, Ordained June 10, 1933. Retired Bishop of Kansas City-St. Joseph.
Hunthausen, Raymond G., Appointed July 8, Ordained June 1, 1946. Bishop of Helena.
Reh, Francis F., Appointed June 4, Ordained Dec. 8, 1935. Bishop of Charleston.
Strecker, Ignatius J., Appointed April 7, Ordained Dec. 19, 1942. Bishop of Springfield-Cape Girardeau.
Zayek, Francis M., Appointed May 30, Ordained March 17, 1946. Titular Bishop of Callinicum.

1963

Bishops

Aponte Martinez, Luis, Appointed Nov. 18, Ordained April 10, 1950. Coadjutor Bishop of Ponce.
D'Antonio, Nicholas, Appointed Dec. 31, Ordained June 7, 1942. Bishop of Olancho, Honduras.
Graham, John J., Appointed Nov. 25, Ordained Feb. 26, 1938. Retired Auxiliary Bishop of Philadelphia.
Speltz, George H., Appointed Feb. 13, Ordained June 2, 1940. Auxiliary Bishop of Winona.
Ward, John J., Appointed Oct. 16, Ordained May 4, 1946. Auxiliary Bishop of Los Angeles.

1964

Archbishops

Aponte Martinez, Luis, Appointed Nov. 11, Ordained April 10, 1950. Archbishop of San Juan.

Bishops

Brzana, Stanislaus J., Appointed May 24, Ordained June 7, 1941. Auxiliary Bishop of Buffalo.
Freking, Frederick W., Appointed Dec. 30, Ordained July 31, 1938. Retired Bishop of La Crosse.
Reh, Francis F., Appointed Sept. 5, Ordained Dec. 8, 1935. Titular Bishop of Macinna & Rector of North American College Rome.
Sheehan, Daniel E., Appointed Jan. 4, Ordained May 23, 1942. Auxiliary Bishop of Omaha.
Torres, Juan Fremiot, Appointed Nov. 4, Ordained April 10, 1950. Bishop of Ponce.

1965

Archbishops

Hannan, Philip M., Appointed Sept. 29, Ordained Dec. 8, 1939. Retired Archbishop of New Orleans.

Bishops

Breitenbeck, Joseph M., Appointed Oct. 18, Ordained May 30, 1942. Auxiliary Bishop of Detroit.
Carberry, John J., Appointed Jan. 16, Ordained July 28, 1929. Bishop of Columbus.
McCarthy, Edward A., Appointed April 21, Ordained May 29, 1943. Auxiliary Bishop of Cincinnati.
Watters, Loras J., Appointed June 23, Ordained June 7, 1941. Auxiliary Bishop of Dubuque.

1966

Archbishops

Ryan, Joseph T., Appointed Feb. 7, Ordained June 3, 1939. Archbishop of Anchorage.

Bishops

Gerety, Peter L., Appointed March 4, Ordained June 29, 1939. Coadjutor Bishop of Portland (in Maine).
Herrmann, Edward J., Appointed March 4, Ordained June 12, 1947. Auxiliary Bishop of Washington.
Hogan, James J., Appointed May 23, Ordained Dec. 8, 1937. Retired Bishop of Altoona-Johnstown.

Malone, James W., Appointed Jan. 22, Ordained May 26, 1945. Apostolic Administrator of Youngstown.
Michaels, James, *s.s.c.*, Appointed Feb. 15, Ordained Dec. 21, 1951. Resigned Auxiliary Bishop of Wheeling-Charleston.
McDowell, John B., Appointed July 18, Ordained Nov. 4, 1945. Auxiliary Bishop of Pittsburgh.
O'Keefe, Gerald F., Appointed Oct. 20, Ordained Jan. 29, 1944. Bishop of Davenport.
Schad, James L., Appointed Oct. 18, Ordained April 10, 1943. Auxiliary Bishop of Camden.
Speltz, George H., Appointed April 4, Ordained June 2, 1940. Coadjutor Bishop of St. Cloud.
Tschoepe, Thomas, Appointed Jan. 12, Ordained May 30, 1943. Retired Bishop of Dallas.

1967

Archbishops

McDonough, Thomas J., Appointed March 1, Ordained May 26, 1938. Retired Archbishop of Louisville.

Bishops

Broderick, Edwin B., Appointed March 4, Ordained May 30, 1942. Auxiliary Bishop of New York.
Clinch, Harry A., Appointed Dec. 14, Ordained June 6, 1936. Retired Bishop of Monterey.
Frey, Gerard L., Appointed May 31, Ordained April 2, 1938. Bishop of Savannah.
Gerety, Peter L., Appointed Feb. 18, Ordained June 29, 1939. Apostolic Administrator of Portland (in Maine).
Grady, Thomas J., Appointed June 21, Ordained April 23, 1938. Auxiliary Bishop of Chicago.
Ham, J. Richard *m.m.*, Appointed Nov. 28, Ordained June 12, 1948. Auxiliary Bishop of Guatemala.
Hickey, James A., Appointed April 14, Ordained June 15, 1946. Auxiliary Bishop of Saginaw.
Hurley, Mark J., Appointed Oct. 12, Ordained Sept. 23, 1944. Auxiliary Bishop of San Francisco.
Quinn, John R., Appointed Oct. 21, Ordained July 19, 1953. Auxiliary Bishop of San Diego.
Reiss, John C., Appointed Oct. 21, Ordained May 31, 1947. Auxiliary Bishop of Trenton.
Scanlon, John J., Appointed Nov. 10, Ordained June 22, 1930. Apostolic Administrator of Honolulu.
Schuster, Eldon B., Appointed Dec. 2; Ordained May 27, 1937. Retired Bishop of Great Falls.
Whelan, Robert L., *s.j.*, Appointed Dec. 6, Ordained June 17, 1944. Coadjutor Bishop of Fairbanks.

1968

Archbishop

Carberry, John J., Appointed Feb. 17, Ordained July 28, 1929. Retired Archbishop of St. Louis.

Bishops

Abramowicz, Alfred L., Appointed May 8, Ordained May 1, 1943. Auxiliary Bishop of Chicago.
Borders, William D., Appointed May 8, Ordained May 18, 1940. Bishop of Arlington.
Brzana, Stanislaus J., Appointed Oct. 22, Ordained June 7, 1941. Bishop of Ogdensburg.
Cronin, Daniel A., Appointed June 10, Ordained Dec. 20, 1952. Auxiliary Bishop of Boston.
Dudick, Michael J., Appointed Aug. 21, Ordained Nov. 13, 1945. Bishop of Passaic.
Fitzpatrick, John J., Appointed June 24, Ordained Dec 13, 1942. Auxiliary Bishop of Miami.
Gossman, F. Joseph, Appointed July 15, Ordained Dec. 17, 1955. Auxiliary Bishop of Baltimore.
Gumbleton, Thomas J., Appointed March 8, Ordained June 2, 1956. Auxiliary Bishop of Detroit.
Harrington, Timothy J., Appointed April 2, Ordained Jan. 19, 1946. Auxiliary Bishop of Worcester.
Hickey, Dennis W., Appointed Jan. 10, Ordained June 7, 1941. Retired Auxiliary Bishop of Rochester.
Malone, James W., Succeeded to See May 2. Bishop of Youngstown.
McKinney, Joseph C., Appointed July 24, Ordained Dec. 20, 1953. Auxiliary Bishop of Grand Rapids.
McLaughlin, Bernard J., Appointed Dec. 28, Ordained Dec. 21, 1935. Retired Auxiliary Bishop of Buffalo.
O'Neill, Arthur J., Appointed Aug. 19, Ordained March 27, 1943. Bishop of Rockford.
Reh, Francis F., Appointed Dec. 18, Ordained Dec. 8, 1935. Retired Bishop of Saginaw.
Salatka, Charles A., Appointed Jan. 10, Ordained Feb. 24, 1945. Bishop of Marquette.
Scanlon, John J., Succeeded to See March 6; Retired Bishop of Honolulu.
Schoenherr, Walter J., Appointed March 8; Ordained Oct. 27, 1945. Auxiliary Bishop of Detroit.
Shea, Robert L., *s.j.*, Succeeded to See Nov. 30; Retired Bishop of Fairbanks.
Speltz, George H., Succeeded to See Jan. 31; Retired Bishop of St. Cloud.
Wycislo, Aloysius J., Appointed March 8; Ordained April 7, 1934. Retired Bishop of Green Bay.

1969

Cardinals

Carberry, John Cardinal, Created April 28; Retired Archbishop of St. Louis.

Archbishops

Sheehan, Daniel E., Appointed June 11, Ordained May 23, 1942. Archbishop of Omaha.
Strecker, Ignatius J., Appointed Sept. 10, Ordained Dec 19, 1942. Archbishop of Kansas City in Kansas.

Bishops

Breitenbeck, Joseph, Appointed Oct. 15, Ordained May 30, 1942. Retired Bishop of Grand Rapids.
Broderick, Edwin B., Appointed March 19, Ordained May 30, 1942. Former Bishop of Albany.
Gerety, Peter L., Succeeded to See Sept. 15. Bishop of Portland (in Maine).
Hogan, Joseph L., Appointed Oct. 15, Ordained June 6, 1942. Retired Bishop of Rochester.
Hurley, Mark J., Appointed Nov. 4, Ordained Sept. 23, 1944. Resigned Bishop of Santa Rosa.
Lynch, George E., Appointed Oct. 20, Ordained May 29, 1943. Retired Auxiliary Bishop of Raleigh.
McAuliffe, Michael F., Appointed July 2, Ordained May 31, 1945. Bishop of Jefferson City.
McCarthy, Edward A., Appointed Aug. 25, Ordained May 29, 1943. Bishop of Phoenix.
Neylon, Martin J., *s.j.*, Appointed Oct. 2, Ordained June 18, 1950. Titular Bishop of Libertina.
Tawil, Joseph E., Appointed Oct. 29, Ordained July 20, 1936. Apostolic Exarch of Newton.
Tshoepe, Thomas, Appointed Aug. 27, Ordained May 30, 1943. Retired Bishop of Dallas.
Watters, Loras J., Appointed Jan. 8, Ordained June 7, 1941. Retired Bishop of Winona.

1970

Bishops

Ahern, Patrick V., Appointed Feb. 3, Ordained Jan. 27, 1945. Auxiliary Bishop of New York.
Baum, William, Appointed Feb. 18, Ordained May 12, 1951. Bishop of Springfield-Cape Girardeau.
Bosco, Anthony G., Appointed May 14, Ordained June 7, 1952. Auxiliary Bishop of Pittsburgh.
Cronin, Daniel A., Appointed Oct. 30, Ordained Dec. 20, 1952. Bishop of Fall River.
Flores, Patrick F., Appointed March 18, Ordained May 26, 1956. Auxiliary Bishop of San Antonio.
Head, Edward D., Appointed Jan. 27, Ordained Jan. 27, 1945. Auxiliary Bishop of New York.
Hurley, Francis T., Appointed Feb. 4, Ordained June 16, 1951. Auxiliary Bishop of Juneau.
Lohmuller, Martin N., Appointed Feb. 11, Ordained June 3, 1944. Auxiliary Bishop of Philadelphia.
McFarland, Norman F., Appointed June 5, Ordained June 15, 1946. Auxiliary Bishop of San Francisco.
McGann, John R., Appointed Nov. 12, Ordained June 3, 1950. Auxiliary Bishop of Rockville Centre.
O'Leary, Edward C., Appointed Nov. 17, Ordained June 15, 1946. Auxiliary Bishop of Portland (in Maine).
Povish, Kenneth J., Appointed July 28, Ordained June 3, 1950. Bishop of Crookston.
Schmitt, Mark F., Appointed May 5, Ordained May 22, 1948. Auxiliary Bishop of Green Bay.
Sullivan, Walter F., Appointed Oct. 20, Ordained May 9, 1953. Auxiliary Bishop of Richmond.
Welsh, Thomas J. Appointed Feb. 18, Ordained May 30, 1946. Auxiliary Bishop of Philadelphia.

1971

Bishops

Arzube, Juan, Appointed Feb. 9, Ordained May 5, 1954. Auxiliary Bishop of Los Angeles.
Begley, Michael J., Appointed Nov. 30, Ordained May 26, 1934. Retired Bishop of Charlotte.
Boudreaux, Warren L., Appointed June 4, Ordained May 30, 1942. Bishop of Beaumont.
Connolly, Thomas J., Appointed May 4, Ordained April 8, 1947. Bishop of Baker.
Crowley, Joseph R., Appointed June 16, Ordained May 1, 1953. Retired Auxiliary Bishop of Fort Wayne-South Bend.
Donovan, Paul V., Appointed June 15, Ordained May 20, 1950. Bishop of Kalamazoo.
Fitzpatrick, John J., Appointed April 21, Ordained Dec. 13, 1942. Retired Bishop of Brownsville.
Gelineau, Louis E., Appointed Dec 6, Ordained June 5, 1954. Bishop of Providence.
Gracida, Rene H., Appointed Dec. 6, Ordained May 23, 1959. Auxiliary Bishop of Miami.
Harrison, Frank J., Appointed March 1, Ordained June 4, 1937. Auxiliary Bishop of Syracuse.
Hurley, Francis T., Appointed July 20, Ordained June 16, 1951. Bishop of Juneau.
Losten, Basil, Appointed March 15, Ordained June 10, 1957. Auxiliary Bishop of Philadelphia Ukrainian.
Lucker, Raymond A., Appointed July 12, Ordained June 7, 1952. Auxiliary Bishop of St. Paul-Minneapolis.
Maguire, Joseph F., Appointed Dec. 1, Ordained June 29, 1945. Auxiliary Bishop of Boston.
Neylon, Martin J., *s.j.*, Appointed Sept. 20, Ordained June 18, 1950. Vicar Apostolic of The Carolines-Marshalls.
O'Rourke, Edward W., Appointed May 24, Ordained May 28, 1944. Retired Bishop of Peoria.
Riley, Lawrence J., Appointed Dec. 7, Ordained Sept. 21, 1940. Retired Auxiliary Bishop of Boston.
Roach, John R., Appointed July 12, Ordained June 8, 1946. Auxiliary Bishop of St. Paul-Minneapolis.
Szoka, Edmund, Appointed June 15, Ordained June 5, 1954. Bishop of Gaylord.
Zayek, Francis M., Appointed Nov. 11, Ordained March 17, 1946. Eparch of St. Maron.

1972

Archbishops

Quinn, John R., Appointed Dec. 13; Ordained July 19, 1953. Archbishop of Oklahoma City.

Bishops

Frey, Gerard L., Appointed Nov. 7, Ordained April 2, 1938. Retired Bishop of Lafayette.
Howze, Joseph L., Appointed Nov. 8, Ordained May 7, 1959. Auxiliary Bishop of Jackson.
Mahoney, James P., Appointed July 25, Ordained May 19, 1951. Auxiliary Bishop of New York.
McDonald, Andrew J., Appointed July 4, Ordained May 8, 1948. Bishop of Little Rock.
Snyder, John J., Appointed Dec. 19, Ordained June 9, 1951. Auxiliary Bishop of Brooklyn.
Sullivan, James S., Appointed July 25, Ordained June 4, 1955. Auxiliary Bishop of Lansing.
Sullivan, John J., Appointed July 25, Ordained Sept. 23, 1944. Bishop of Grand Island.

1973

Cardinals

Aponte Martinez, Luis Cardinal, Created March 5. Archbishop of San Juan.

Archbishops

Baum, William, Appointed May 9, Ordained May 12, 1951. Archbishop of Washington.

Bishops

Head, Edward D., Appointed Jan. 17, Ordained Jan. 27, 1945. Bishop of Buffalo.
Herrmann, Edward J., Appointed June 26, Ordained June 12, 1947. Retired Bishop and Apostolic Administrator of Columbus.
Imesch, Joseph L., Appointed Feb. 8, Ordained Dec. 16, 1956. Auxiliary Bishop of Detroit.
Krawczak, Arthur H., Appointed Feb. 8, Ordained May 18, 1940. Retired Auxiliary Bishop of Detroit.
Law, Bernard, Appointed Oct. 22, Ordained May 21, 1961. Bishop of Springfield-Cape Girardeau.
Lessard, Raymond W., Appointed March 5, Ordained Dec. 16, 1956. Bishop of Savannah.
Mestice, Anthony F., Appointed March 5, Ordained June 4, 1949. Auxiliary Bishop of New York.
Sullivan, Walter F., Appointed April 30, Ordained May 9, 1953. Apostolic Administrator of Richmond.

1974

Archbishops

Borders, William D., Appointed March 25; Ordained May 18, 1940. Retired Archbishop of Baltimore.
Gerety, Peter Leo, Appointed April 2, Ordained June 29, 1939. Retired Archbishop of Newark.
Sanchez, Robert F., Appointed June 1; Ordained Dec. 20, 1959. Archbishop of Santa Fe.

Bishops

Angell, Kenneth A., Appointed Aug. 9, Ordained May 26, 1956. Auxiliary Bishop of Providence.
Chavez, Gilbert E., Appointed April 19, Ordained March 19, 1960. Auxiliary Bishop of San Diego.
Cummins, John S., Appointed Feb. 26, Ordained Jan. 24, 1953. Auxiliary Bishop of Sacramento.
Daily, Thomas V., Appointed Dec. 31, Ordained Jan. 10, 1952. Auxiliary Bishop of Boston.

D'Arcy, John M., Appointed Dec. 31, Ordained Feb. 2, 1957. Auxiliary Bishop of Boston.
Gendron, Odore J., Appointed Dec. 12, Ordained May 31, 1947. Retired Bishop of Manchester.
Grady, Thomas J., Appointed Nov. 9, Ordained April 23, 1938. Retired Bishop of Arlington.
Hanifen, Richard C., Appointed July 6, 1974. Ordained June 6, 1959. Auxiliary Bishop of Denver.
Hickey, James A., Appointed June 4, Ordained June 15, 1946. Bishop of Cleveland.
Hughes, William A., Appointed July 23, Ordained April 6, 1946. Auxiliary Bishop of Youngstown.
Marino, Eugene, *s.s.j.*, Appointed July 15, Ordained June 6, 1962. Auxiliary Bishop of Washington.
McFarland, Norman F., Appointed Dec. 6, Ordained June 15, 1946. Apostolic Administrator of Reno-Las Vegas.
O'Leary, Edward C., Appointed Dec. 4, Ordained June 15, 1946. Retired Bishop of Portland (in Maine).
Ottenweller, Albert H., Appointed April 17, Ordained June 19, 1943. Auxiliary Bishop of Toledo.
Pilarczyk, Daniel E., Appointed Nov. 12, Ordained Dec. 20, 1959. Auxiliary Bishop of Cincinnati.
Rodriguez, Miguel, *c.ss.r.*, Appointed Jan. 21, Ordained June 22, 1958. Retired Bishop of Arecibo.
Sullivan, Walter F., Succeeded to See June 6. Bishop of Richmond.
Walsh, Nicolas E., Appointed Sept. 5, Ordained June 6, 1942. Bishop of Yakima.
Welsh, Thomas J., Appointed June 4. Bishop of Arlington.

1975

Archbishops

Hunthausen, Raymond G., Appointed Feb. 25, Ordained June 1, 1946. Archbishop of Seattle.
Roach, John R., Appointed May 21, Ordained June 8, 1946. Archbishop of St. Paul-Minneapolis.
Ryan, Joseph T., Appointed Oct. 24, Ordained June 3, 1939. Coadjutor Archbishop to the Military Vicar.

Bishops

Fitzsimons, George K., Appointed May 27, Ordained March 18, 1961. Auxiliary Bishop of Kansas City-St. Joseph.
Gaughan, Norbert F., Appointed April 2, Ordained Nov. 4, 1945. Auxiliary Bishop of Greensburg.
Gracida, Rene H., Appointed Oct. 1, Ordained May 23, 1959. Bishop of Pensacola-Tallahassee.
Gossman, F. Joseph, Appointed April 8, Ordained Dec. 17, 1955. Bishop of Raleigh.
Lucker, Raymond A., Appointed Dec. 23, Ordained June 7, 1952. Bishop of New Ulm.
Mahony, Roger M., Appointed Jan. 7, Ordained May 1, 1962. Auxiliary Bishop of Fresno.
Niedergeses, James D., Appointed April 8, Ordained May 20, 1944. Bishop of Nashville.
Povish, Kenneth J., Appointed Oct. 21, Ordained June 3, 1950. Bishop of Lansing.
Reilly, Daniel P., Appointed June 17, Ordained May 30, 1953. Bishop of Norwich.
Surinach Carreras, Ricardo, Appointed May 26, Ordained April 13, 1957. Auxiliary Bishop of Ponce.

1976

Cardinals

Baum, William Cardinal, Created May 24. Prefect of Sacred Congregation for Catholic Education, Vatican.

Archbishops

Hurley, Francis T., Appointed May 4, Ordained June 16, 1951. Archbishop of Anchorage.
McCarthy, Edward A., Appointed Sept. 17, Ordained May 29, 1943. Coadjutor Archbishop of Miami.

Bishops

Balke, Victor, Appointed July 7, Ordained May 24, 1958. Bishop of Crookston.
Broderick, Edwin B., Appointed June 3. Exec. Dir. Catholic Relief Services.
Casiano-Vargas, Ulises, Appointed March 4, Ordained May 30, 1967. Bishop of Mayaguez.
Curtiss, Elden F., Appointed March 4, Ordained May 24, 1958. Bishop of Helena.
Dudley, Paul V., Appointed Nov. 16, Ordained June 2, 1951. Auxiliary Bishop of St. Paul-Minneapolis.
Forst, Marion F., Appointed Oct. 16, Ordained June 10, 1934. Retired Auxiliary Bishop of Kansas City in Kansas.
Garner, Robert F., Appointed May 3, Ordained June 15, 1946. Auxiliary Bishop of Newark.
Gerber, Eugene J., Appointed Oct. 16, Ordained May 19, 1959. Bishop of Dodge City.
Harrison, Frank J., Appointed Nov. 16, Ordained June 4, 1937. Retired Bishop of Syracuse.
Hart, Daniel A., Appointed Aug. 30, Ordained Feb. 2, 1953. Auxiliary Bishop of Boston.
Hart, Joseph H., Appointed July 1, Ordained May 1, 1956. Bishop of Cheyenne.
Hughes, Edward T., Appointed June 14, Ordained May 31, 1947. Auxiliary Bishop of Philadelphia.
Kinney, John F., Appointed Nov. 16, Ordained Feb. 2, 1963. Auxiliary Bishop of St. Paul-Minneapolis.
Losten, Basil H., Appointed June 8, Ordained June 10, 1957. Apostolic Administrator Philadelphia Ukrainian.
Maguire, Joseph F., Appointed April 3, Ordained June 29, 1945. Coadjutor Bishop of Springfield.
Marconi, Dominic A., Appointed May 3, Ordained May 30, 1953. Auxiliary Bishop of Newark.
McFarland, Norman F., Appointed Feb. 10, Ordained June 15, 1946. Bishop of Reno-Las Vegas.
McGann, John R., Appointed May 3, Ordained June 3, 1950. Bishop of Rockville Centre.
Moreno, Manuel D., Appointed Dec. 20, Ordained April 25, 1961. Auxiliary Bishop of Los Angeles.
Murphy, Michael J., Appointed April 20, Ordained Feb. 28, 1942. Auxiliary Bishop of Cleveland.
Murphy, P. Francis, Appointed Jan. 27, Ordained Dec. 20, 1958. Auxiliary Bishop of Baltimore.
Pena, Raymundo, Appointed Oct. 16, Ordained May 25, 1957. Auxiliary Bishop of San Antonio.
Sheldon, Gilbert I., Appointed April 20, Ordained Feb. 28, 1953. Auxiliary Bishop of Cleveland.
Stafford, J. Francis, Appointed Jan. 27, Ordained Dec. 15, 1957. Auxiliary Bishop of Baltimore.
Tawil, Joseph, Appointed July 15, Ordained July 20, 1936. Eparch Emeritus of Newton.
Timlin, James C., Appointed Aug. 3, Ordained July 16, 1951. Auxiliary Bishop of Scranton.
Walsh, Nicolas, Appointed Aug. 10, Ordained June 6, 1942. Retired Auxiliary Bishop of Seattle.

1977

Archbishops

McCarthy, Edward A., Succeeded to See July 26. Archbishop of Miami.
Quinn, John R., Appointed Feb. 22, Ordained July 19, 1953. Archbishop of San Francisco.
Salatka, Charles A., Appointed Sept. 27, Ordained Feb. 24, 1945. Archbishop of Oklahoma City.
Weakland, Rembert, *o.s.b.*, Appointed Sept. 20, Ordained June 24, 1951.
Archbishop of Milwaukee.

Bishops

Boudreaux, Warren L., Appointed June 5, Ordained May 30, 1942. Bishop of Houma-Thibodaux.
Cummins, John S., Appointed May 3, Ordained Jan. 24, 1953. Bishop of Oakland.
Daly, James J., Appointed Feb. 28; Ordained May 22, 1948. Auxiliary Bishop of Rockville Centre.
D'Antonio, Nicholas, *o.f.m.*, Appointed Aug. 22. Retired Vicar for Spanish-speaking, New Orleans.
Ferrario, Joseph A., Appointed Nov. 8, Ordained May 19, 1951. Auxiliary Bishop of Honolulu.
Garmendia, Francis, Appointed May 24, Ordained June 28, 1947. Auxiliary Bishop of New York.
Howze, Joseph L., Appointed March 1, Ordained May 7, 1959. Bishop of Biloxi.
Hubbard, Howard J., Appointed Feb. 1, Ordained Dec. 18, 1963. Bishop of Albany.
Kelly, Thomas C., *o.p.*, Appointed July 12, Ordained June 5, 1958. Auxiliary Bishop of Washington.
Kucera, Daniel W., *o.s.b.*, Appointed June 6, Ordained May 26, 1949. Auxiliary Bishop of Joliet.
Losten, Basil H., Appointed Sept. 20, Ordained June 10, 1957. Bishop of Stamford.
Maguire, Joseph F., Succeeded to See Nov. 4. Bishop of Springfield.
McCarrick, Theodore E., Appointed May 24, Ordained May 31, 1958. Auxiliary Bishop of New York.
Mulvee, Robert E., Appointed Feb. 15, Ordained June 30, 1957. Auxiliary Bishop of Manchester.
Ottenweller, Albert H., Appointed Oct. 11, Ordained June 19, 1943. Retired Bishop of Steubenville.
Paul, John J., Appointed May 17, Ordained Jan. 24, 1943. Titular Bishop of Lambese.
Rodimer, Frank J., Appointed Dec. 13, Ordained May 19, 1951. Bishop of Paterson.
Skylstad, William, Appointed Feb. 22, Ordained May 21, 1960. Bishop of Yakima.
Steiner, Kenneth, Appointed Dec. 6, Ordained May 19, 1962. Auxiliary Bishop of Portland in Oregon.
Sullivan, John J., Appointed June 27, Ordained Sept. 23, 1944. Bishop of Kansas City-St. Joseph.
Vaughan, Austin B., Appointed May 24, Ordained Dec. 8, 1956. Auxiliary Bishop of New York.
Wirz, George O., Appointed Dec. 20, Ordained May 31, 1952. Auxiliary Bishop of Madison.

1978

Bishops

Beltran, Eusebius J., Appointed Feb. 28, Ordained May 14, 1960. Bishop of Tulsa.
Costello, Thomas J., Appointed Jan. 10, Ordained June 5, 1954. Auxiliary Bishop of Syracuse.
Dudley, Paul V., Appointed Sept. 26, Ordained June 2, 1951. Bishop of Sioux Falls.
DuMaine, R. Pierre, Appointed April 28, Ordained June 5, 1957. Auxiliary Bishop of San Francisco.
Flores, Patrick F., Appointed April 4, Ordained May 26, 1956. Bishop of El Paso.
Hoffman, James R., Appointed April 18, Ordained July 28, 1957. Auxiliary Bishop of Toledo.
McNamara, Lawrence J., Appointed Jan. 10, Ordained May 30, 1953. Bishop of Grand Island.
Morneau, Robert F., Appointed Dec. 19, Ordained May 28, 1966. Auxiliary Bishop of Green Bay.
Murphy, Michael J., Appointed Nov. 28, Ordained Feb. 28, 1942. Coadjutor Bishop of Erie.
Quinn, Francis A., Appointed April 28, Ordained June 15, 1946. Auxiliary Bishop of San Francisco.
Rosazza, Peter A., Appointed Feb. 28, Ordained June 29, 1961. Auxiliary Bishop of Hartford.
Schmitt, Mark F., Appointed March 21, Ordained May 22, 1948. Bishop of Marquette.
Straling, Phillip F., Appointed July 18, Ordained March 19, 1959. Bishop of San Bernardino.
Welsh, Lawrence H., Appointed Nov. 7, Ordained May 26, 1962. Retired Bishop of Spokane.

1979

Archbishops

Flores, Patrick F., Appointed Aug. 28; Ordained May 26, 1956. Archbishop of San Antonio.

Bishops

Clark, Matthew H., Appointed May 2, Ordained Dec. 19, 1962. Bishop of Rochester.
Fiorenza, Joseph A., Appointed Sept. 4, Ordained May 29, 1954. Bishop of San Angelo.
Fliss, Raphael M., Appointed Nov. 6, Ordained May 26, 1956. Coadjutor Bishop of Superior.
Friend, William B., Appointed Aug. 31, Ordained May 7, 1959. Auxiliary Bishop of Alexandria-Shreveport.
Griffin, James A., Appointed June 30, Ordained May 28, 1960. Auxiliary Bishop of Cleveland.
Houck, William R., Appointed March 28, Ordained May 19, 1951. Auxiliary Bishop of Jackson.
Hughes, William A., Appointed April 13, Ordained April 6, 1946. Bishop of Covington.
Imesch, Joseph L., Appointed June 30, Ordained Dec. 16, 1956. Bishop of Joliet.
Keeler, William H., Appointed July 24, Ordained July 17, 1955. Auxiliary Bishop of Harrisburg.
Larkin, W. Thomas, Appointed April 24, Ordained May 15, 1947. Retired Bishop of St. Petersburg.
Madera, Joseph J., *m.sp.s.*, Appointed Dec. 18, Ordained June 15, 1957. Coadjutor Bishop of Fresno.
McCarthy, John E., Appointed Jan. 23, Ordained May 26, 1956. Auxiliary Bishop of Galveston-Houston.
Nevins, John J., Appointed Feb. 6, Ordained June 6, 1959. Auxiliary Bishop of Miami.
Neylon, Martin J., *s.j.*, Appointed May 3, Ordained June 18, 1950. Bishop of The Carolines-Marshalls.
O'Connor, John J., Appointed April 24, Ordained Dec. 15, 1945. Auxiliary Bishop of Military Vicariate.
Pilla, Anthony M., Appointed June 30, Ordained May 23, 1959. Auxiliary Bishop of Cleveland.
Quinn, Francis A., Appointed Dec. 18, Ordained June 15, 1946. Bishop of Sacramento.
Rivera, Enrique Hernandez, Appointed June 11, Ordained June 8, 1968. Auxiliary Bishop of San Juan.
Rivera, Hector M., Appointed June 11, Ordained June 12, 1966. Auxiliary Bishop of San Juan.
Roman, Agustin A., Appointed Feb. 6, Ordained July 5, 1959. Auxiliary Bishop of Miami.
Schlarman, Stanley G., Appointed March 13, Ordained July 13, 1958. Auxiliary Bishop of Belleville.
Sklba, Richard J., Appointed Nov. 6, Ordained Dec. 20, 1959. Auxiliary Bishop of Milwaukee.
Snyder, John J., Appointed Oct. 2, Ordained June 9, 1951. Bishop of St. Augustine.

1980

Archbishops

Hickey, James A., Appointed June 17; Ordained June 15, 1946. Archbishop of Washington.
Lipscomb, Oscar H., Appointed July 29; Ordained July 15, 1956. Archbishop of Mobile.
Sulyk, Stephen, Appointed Dec. 29; Archbishop of Philadelphia Ukrainian.

Bishops

Bevilacqua, Anthony, Appointed Oct. 7, Ordained June 11, 1949. Auxiliary Bishop of Brooklyn.
Bullock, William H., Appointed June 3, Ordained June 7, 1952. Auxiliary Bishop of St. Paul-Minneapolis.
Chedid, John, Appointed Oct. 28, Ordained Dec. 21, 1951. Auxiliary Bishop of St. Maron.
Franzetta, Benedict C., Appointed July 29, Ordained April 29, 1950. Auxiliary Bishop of Youngstown.
Ham, J. Richard, *m.m.*, Appointed Oct. 7, Ordained June 12, 1948. Retired Auxiliary Bishop of St. Paul-Minneapolis.
Hoffman, James R., Appointed Dec. 16, Ordained July 28, 1957. Bishop of Toledo.
Kucera, Daniel W., *o.s.b.*, Appointed March 11, Ordained May 26, 1949. Bishop of Salina.
Madera, Joseph J., *m.sp.s.*, Succeeded to See July 1. Bishop of Fresno.
Mahony, Roger M., Appointed Feb. 26, Ordained May 1, 1962. Bishop of Stockton.
Matthiesen, Leroy T., Appointed March 25, Ordained March 10, 1946. Bishop of Amarillo.
Pena, Raymundo J., Appointed April 29, Ordained May 25, 1957. Bishop of El Paso.
Pilla, Anthony M., Appointed Nov. 18, Ordained May 23, 1959. Bishop of Cleveland.
Reiss, John C., Appointed March 4, Ordained May 31, 1947. Bishop of Trenton.
Speyrer, Jude, Appointed Jan. 29, Ordained July 25, 1953. Bishop of Lake Charles.
Sullivan, Joseph M., Appointed Oct. 7, Ordained June 2, 1956. Auxiliary Bishop of Brooklyn.
Tafoya, Arthur N., Appointed July 1, Ordained May 12, 1962. Bishop of Pueblo.
Untener, Kenneth E., Appointed Oct. 4, Ordained June 1, 1963. Bishop of Saginaw.
Valero, Rene, Appointed Oct. 7, Ordained June 2, 1956. Auxiliary Bishop of Brooklyn.
Weigand, William K., Appointed Sept. 3, Ordained May 25, 1963. Bishop of Salt Lake City.

1981

Archbishops

Kelly, Thomas C., *o.p.*, Appointed Dec. 29, Ordained June 5, 1958. Archbishop of Louisville.
Marcinkus, Paul C., Appointed Sept. 26, Ordained May 3,1947. Titular Archbishop of Orta, Vatican City State.
Szoka, Edmund C., Appointed March 28, Ordained June 5, 1954. Emeritus Archbishop of Detroit.

Bishops

Delaney, Joseph P., Appointed July 10, Ordained Dec. 18, 1960. Bishop of Fort Worth.
DeSimone, Louis A., Appointed June 27, Ordained May 10, 1952. Auxiliary Bishop of Philadelphia.
Dumaine, Pierre, Appointed Jan. 27, Ordained June 5, 1957. Bishop of San Jose.
Grahmann, Charles V., Appointed June 30, Ordained March 17, 1956. Auxiliary Bishop of San Antonio.
Hughes, Alfred C., Appointed July 21, Ordained Dec. 15, 1957. Auxiliary Bishop of Boston.
Lotocky, Innocent, *o.s.b.m.*, Appointed Jan. 29, Ordained Nov. 24, 1940. Bishop of St. Nicholas Chicago.
McCarrick, Theodore E., Appointed Nov. 24. Bishop of Metuchen.
Milone, Anthony M., Appointed Nov. 10, Ordained Dec. 15, 1957. Auxiliary Bishop of Omaha.
Moskal, Robert M., Appointed Aug. 3, Ordained March 25, 1963. Auxiliary Bishop of Philadelphia Ukrainian.
O'Brien, Thomas J., Appointed Nov. 24. Ordained May 7, 1961. Bishop of Phoenix.
Ramirez, Ricardo, *c.s.b.*, Appointed Oct. 27, Ordained Dec. 10, 1966. Auxiliary Bishop of San Antonio.
Rivera, Enrique Hernandez, Appointed Feb. 13, Ordained June 8, 1968. Bishop of Caguas.
Rose, Robert J., Appointed Oct. 13, Ordained Dec. 21, 1955. Bishop of Gaylord.
Ryan, Daniel L., Appointed Aug. 14, Ordained May 3, 1956. Auxiliary Bishop of Joliet.
Santana, Hermin Negron, Appointed June 30, Ordained May 30, 1969. Auxiliary Bishop of San Juan.
Schulte, Francis B., Appointed June 27, Ordained May 10, 1952. Auxiliary Bishop of Philadelphia.
Setian, Nerses Mikael, Appointed July 3, Ordained April 13, 1941. Bishop of Armenian Catholic Exarchate of U.S.A. and Canada.
Symons, J. Keith, Appointed Jan. 16, Ordained May 18, 1958. Auxiliary Bishop of St. Petersburg.
Walsh, Daniel F., Appointed June 30, Ordained March 30, 1963. Auxiliary Bishop of San Francisco.

1982

Archbishops

Pilarczyk, Daniel E., Appointed Nov 2, Ordained Dec. 20, 1959. Archbishop of Cincinnati.
Zayek, Francis M., Appointed Dec. 22, Ordained March 17, 1946. Archbishop of St. Maron, Brooklyn.

Bishops

Anderson, Moses B., *s.s.e.*, Appointed Dec. 3, Ordained May 30, 1958. Auxiliary Bishop of Detroit.
Cooney, Patrick, R., Appointed Dec. 7, Ordained Dec. 20, 1959. Auxiliary Bishop of Detroit.
Ferrario, Joseph A., Appointed May 13, Ordained May 13, 1951. Bishop of Honolulu.
Friend, William B., Appointed Nov. 23. Bishop of Alexandria-Shreveport.
Gerber, Eugene J., Appointed Nov. 23, Ordained May 19, 1959. Bishop of Wichita.
Grahmann, Charles V., Appointed April 14, Ordained March 17, 1956. Bishop of Victoria.
Kinney, John F., Appointed June 28, Ordained Feb. 2, 1963. Bishop of Bismarck.
Kmiec, Edward V., Appointed Aug. 26, Ordained Dec. 20, 1961. Auxiliary Bishop of Trenton.
McRaith, John J., Appointed Oct. 23, Ordained Feb. 21, 1960. Bishop of Owensboro.
Melczek, Dale J., Appointed Dec. 3, Ordained June 6, 1964. Auxiliary Bishop of Detroit.
Moreno, Manuel D., Appointed Jan. 12, Ordained April 25, 1961. Bishop of Tucson.
Murphy, Michael J., Succeeded to See July 16. Bishop of Erie.
Pevec, Edward A., Appointed April 13, Ordained April 29, 1950. Auxiliary Bishop of Cleveland.
Puscas, Louis, Appointed Dec. 4, Ordained May 14, 1942. Eparch of Romanian Diocese of Canton.
Ramirez, Ricardo, *c.s.b.*, Appointed Aug. 31, Ordained Dec. 10, 1966. Bishop of Las Cruces.
Stafford, J. Francis, Appointed Nov. 16, Ordained Dec. 15, 1957. Bishop of Memphis.

1983

Archbishops

Kucera, Daniel, Appointed Dec. 20. Archbishop of Dubuque.

Bishops

Apuron, Anthony, *o.f.m.cap.*, Appointed Dec. 8. Auxiliary Bishop of Agana.
Arias, David, *o.a.r.*, Appointed Jan. 25. Auxiliary Bishop of Newark.
Bevilacqua, Anthony, Appointed Oct. 7. Bishop of Pittsburgh.
Brom, Robert, Appointed March 25. Bishop of Duluth.
Carlson, Robert, Appointed Nov. 22. Auxiliary Bishop of St. Paul-Minneapolis.
Dimino, Joseph, Appointed March 29. Auxiliary Bishop of Military Services.
Gracida, Rene, Appointed May 19. Bishop of Corpus Christi.
Gregory, Wilton, Appointed Oct. 31. Auxiliary Bishop of Chicago.
Griffin, James, Appointed Feb. 7. Bishop of Columbus.
Hanifen, Richard, Appointed Nov. 10. Bishop of Colorado Springs.
Harrington, Timothy, Appointed Sept. 6. Bishop of Worcester.
Keating, John R., Appointed June 7. Bishop of Arlington.
Keeler, William, Appointed Nov. 10. Bishop of Harrisburg.
Levada, William, Appointed March 29. Auxiliary Bishop of Los Angeles.
Lyne, Timothy, Appointed Oct. 31. Auxiliary Bishop of Chicago.
Maida, Adam, Appointed Nov. 8. Bishop of Green Bay.
Montrose, Donald, Appointed March 25. Auxiliary Bishop of Los Angeles.
Moskal, Robert, Appointed Dec. 5. Bishop of St. Josaphat in Parma.
O'Connor, John, Appointed May 10. Bishop of Scranton.
O'Donnell, Edward, Appointed Dec. 6. Auxiliary Bishop of St. Louis.
Pataki, Andrew, Appointed May 30. Auxiliary Bishop of Passaic.
Paul, John J., Appointed Oct. 18. Bishop of LaCrosse.
Popp, Bernard, Appointed June 7. Auxiliary Bishop of San Antonio.
Quinn, A. James, Appointed Oct. 14. Auxiliary Bishop of Cleveland.
Rodriguez, Placido, *c.m.f.*, Appointed Oct. 31. Auxiliary Bishop of Chicago.
Roque, Francis, Appointed March 29. Auxiliary Bishop of Military Services.
Ryan, Daniel, Appointed Nov. 22. Bishop of Springfield in Illinois.
Schlarmann, Stanley, Appointed March 1. Bishop of Dodge City.
Sheehan, Michael, Appointed March 29. Bishop of Lubbock.
Soens, Lawrence, Appointed June 15. Bishop of Sioux City.
Steib, J. Terry, *s.v.d.*, Appointed Dec. 6. Auxiliary Bishop of St. Louis.
Symons, J. Keith, Appointed Sept. 29. Bishop of Pensacola-Tallahassee.
Vlazny, John, Appointed Oct. 31. Auxiliary Bishop of Chicago.
Welsh, Thomas, Appointed Feb. 8. Bishop of Allentown.

1984

Archbishops

Foley, John, Appointed April 9; Archbishop to the Pontifical Commission for Social Communication.
Law, Bernard, Appointed Jan. 24; Archbishop of Boston.
O'Connor, John J., Appointed Jan. 31; Archbishop of New York.

Bishops

Baltakis, Paul, Appointed June 1. Bishop for the Lithuanian Apostolate.
Camacho, Tomas A., Appointed Nov. 8. Bishop of Chalan Kanoa.
Daily, Thomas, Appointed July 17. Bishop of Palm Beach.
Donnelly, Robert, Appointed March 20. Auxiliary Bishop of Toledo.
Donoghue, John, Appointed Nov. 6. Bishop of Charlotte.
Fiorenza, Joseph, Appointed Dec. 18. Bishop of Galveston-Houston.
Fitzsimons, George, Appointed March 22. Bishop of Salina.
Garland, James, Appointed June 25. Auxiliary Bishop of Cincinnati.
Gaughan, Norbert, Appointed July 9. Bishop of Gary.
Higi, William, Appointed April 7. Bishop of Lafayette in Indiana.
Houck, William, Appointed April 24. Bishop of Jackson.
Kaniecki, Michael, *s.j.*, Appointed March 8. Coadjutor Bishop of Fairbanks.
Keleher, James, Appointed Oct. 23. Bishop of Belleville.
Leibrecht, John, Appointed Oct. 23. Bishop of Springfield-Cape Girardeau.
Nevins, John, Appointed July 17. Bishop of Venice.
Newman, William, Appointed July 2. Auxiliary Bishop of Baltimore.
O'Malley, Sean, *o.f.m.cap.*, Appointed May 30. Coadjutor Bishop of St. Thomas Virgin Islands.
Pataki, Andrew, Appointed June 19. Bishop of Parma.
Ricard, John, *s.s.j.*, Appointed May 29. Auxiliary Bishop of Baltimore.
Steinbock, John, Appointed May 29. Auxiliary Bishop of Orange.
Timlin, James, Appointed April 24. Bishop of Scranton.
Williams, J. Kendrick, Appointed April 15. Auxiliary Bishop of Covington.

1985

Cardinals

Law, Bernard Cardinal, Created May 25; Archbishop of Boston.
O'Connor, John Cardinal, Created May 25; Archbishop of New York.
Mahony, Roger, Appointed July 16; Archbishop of Los Angeles.

Archbishops

Ryan, Joseph T., Succeeded to See March 16, Retired Archbishop to the Military Services.

Bishops

Apuron, Anthony S., *o.f.m.cap.*, Appointed Oct. 27. Apostolic Administrator of Agana.
Banks, Robert J., Appointed June 26. Auxiliary Bishop of Boston.
Corrada, Alvaro, *s.j.*, Appointed Aug. 4. Auxiliary Bishop of Washington.
D'Arcy, John M., Appointed Feb. 26.Bishop of Fort Wayne-South Bend.
Egan, Edward M., Appointed April 1. Auxiliary Bishop of New York.
Fliss, Raphael M., Succeeded to See June 27. Bishop of Superior.
Ibrahim, Ibrahim, Appointed Sept. 14. Eparch of St. Thomas the Apostle.

Kaffer, Roger L., Appointed April 25. Auxiliary Bishop of Joliet.
Kaniecki, Michael J., *s.j.*, Succeeded to See July 28. Bishop of Fairbanks.
McCarthy, John E., Appointed Dec. 24. Bishop of Austin.
Montrose, Donald, Appointed Dec. 19. Bishop of Stockton.
Mulvee, Robert E., Appointed Feb. 16. Bishop of Wilmington.
O'Malley, Sean, *o.f.m.cap.*, Succeeded to See Oct. 16. Bishop of St. Thomas in the Virgin Islands.
Pfeifer, Michael, *o.m.i.*, Appointed July 26. Bishop of San Angelo.
Schulte, Francis B., Appointed June 4. Bishop of Wheeling-Charleston.
Sullivan, James S., Appointed April 2. Bishop of Fargo.
Trautman, Donald W., Appointed Feb. 27. Auxiliary Bishop of Buffalo.
Wuerl, Donald, Appointed Dec. 3. Auxiliary Bishop of Seattle.

1986

Archbishops

Apuron, Anthony S., *o.f.m.cap.*, Succeeded to See May 11; Archbishop of Agana.
Levada, William J., Appointed July 1; Archbishop of Portland in Oregon.
McCarrick, Theodore, Appointed June 1; Archbishop of Newark.
Stafford, J. Francis, Appointed June 3; Archbishop of Denver.

Bishops

Dorsey, Norbert, *c.p.*, Appointed Jan. 10. Auxiliary Bishop of Miami.
Elya, John A., *b.s.o.*, Appointed April 2. Auxiliary Bishop of Newton.
Favalora, John C., Appointed June 16. Bishop of Alexandria.
Flynn, Harry, Appointed April 19. Coadjutor Bishop of Lafayette.
Foley, David, Appointed May 3. Auxiliary Bishop of Richmond.
Friend, William, Appointed June 1. Bishop of Shreveport.
Gerry, Joseph, *o.s.b.*, Appointed April 21. Auxiliary Bishop of Manchester.
Hughes, Edward, Appointed Dec. 11. Bishop of Metuchen.
Kuzma, George M., Appointed Nov. 11. Auxiliary Bishop of Passaic.
Markiewicz, Alfred, Appointed July 7. Auxiliary Bishop of Rockville Centre.
McCormack, William J., Appointed Dec. 23. Auxiliary Bishop of New York.
McFarland, Norman F., Appointed Dec. 29. Bishop of Orange.
Ochoa, Armando, Appointed Dec. 29. Auxiliary Bishop of Los Angeles.
Pelotte, Donald E., *s.s.s.*, Appointed Feb. 24. Coadjutor Bishop of Gallup.
Watters, Loras J., Appointed Oct. 14. Apostolic Administrator of Winona.
Weitzel, John Q., *m.m.*, Appointed Oct. 29. Bishop of Samoa-Pago Pago.
Ziemann, G. Patrick, Appointed Dec. 29. Auxiliary Bishop of Los Angeles.

1987

Archbishops

Bishops

Adamec, Joseph V., Appointed March 12. Bishop of Altoona-Johnstown.
Bosco, Anthony G., Appointed April 14. Bishop of Greensburg.
Buechlein, Daniel, *o.s.b.*, Appointed Jan. 20. Bishop of Memphis.
Bullock, William, Appointed Feb. 10. Bishop of Des Moines.
Franklin, William, Appointed Jan. 29. Auxiliary Bishop of Dubuque.
Guillory, Curtis, Appointed Dec. 29. Auxiliary Bishop of Galveston-Houston.
Hanus, Jerome, *o.s.b.*, Appointed July 6. Bishop of St. Cloud.
McHugh, James T., Appointed Nov. 20. Auxiliary Bishop of Newark.
Milone, Anthony G., Appointed Dec. 14. Bishop of Great Falls-Billings.
Myers, John J., Appointed July 14. Coadjutor Bishop of Peoria.
Rueger, George, Appointed Jan. 19. Auxiliary Bishop of Worcester.
Samo, Amando, Appointed May 10. Auxiliary Bishop of The Carolines-Marshalls.
Smith, John M., Appointed Dec. 1. Auxiliary Bishop of Newark.
Steinbock, John, Appointed March 31. Bishop of Santa Rosa.
Vlazny, John, Appointed May 19. Bishop of Winona.
Walsh, Daniel F., Appointed June 9. Bishop of Reno-Las Vegas.

1988

Cardinals

Hickey, James Cardinal, Created June 29; Archbishop of Washington.
Szoka, Edmund Cardinal, Created June 29; Pres. Prefecture for Economic Affairs of the Holy See, Vatican.

Archbishops

Bevilacqua, Anthony J., Appointed Feb. 11; Archbishop of Philadelphia.
Marino, Eugene A., Appointed March 14; Resigned Archbishop of Atlanta.
Schulte, Francis B., Appointed Dec. 13; Archbishop of New Orleans.

Bishops

Boland, Raymond J., Appointed Feb. 2. Bishop of Birmingham.
Brown, Tod D., Appointed Dec. 27. Bishop of Boise.
Carmody, Edmond, Appointed Nov. 8. Auxiliary Bishop of San Antonio.
Chaput, Charles, *o.f.m.cap.*, Appointed April 11. Bishop of Rapid City.
Curlin, William G., Appointed Dec. 20. Auxiliary Bishop of Washington.
DiLorenzo, Francis, Appointed Jan. 26. Auxiliary Bishop of Scranton.
Dunne, John C., Appointed Oct. 21. Auxiliary Bishop of Rockville Centre.
Egan, Edward, Appointed Nov. 8. Bishop of Bridgeport.
Gerry, Joseph, *o.s.b.*, Appointed Dec. 27. Bishop of Portland (in Maine).
Gonzalez, Roberto, *o.f.m.*, Appointed July 19. Auxiliary Bishop of Boston.
Gorman, John R., Appointed Feb. 16. Auxiliary Bishop of Chicago.
Jakubowski, Thaddeus J., Appointed Feb. 16. Auxiliary Bishop of Chicago.
Loverde, Paul S., Appointed Feb. 3. Auxiliary Bishop of Hartford.
McGrath, Patrick, Appointed Dec. 6. Auxiliary Bishop of San Francisco.
O'Connell, Anthony J., Appointed June 7. Bishop of Knoxville.
Olivier, Leonard J., *s.v.d.*, Appointed Dec. 20. Auxiliary Bishop of Washington.
Schmitt, Bernard W., Appointed May 31. Auxiliary Bishop of Wheeling-Charleston.
Sevilla, Carlos A., *s.j.*, Appointed Dec. 6. Auxiliary Bishop of San Francisco.
Wcela, Emil A., Appointed Oct. 21. Auxiliary Bishop of Rockville Centre.
Williams, J. Kendrick, Appointed March 2. Bishop of Lexington.
Winter, William J., Appointed Dec. 27. Auxiliary Bishop of Pittsburgh.
Wuerl, Donald, Appointed Feb. 11. Bishop of Pittsburgh.

1989

Archbishops

Keeler, William, Appointed April 6. Archbishop of Baltimore.

Bishops

Brom, Robert, Appointed April 22. Coadjutor Bishop of San Diego.
Charron, Joseph, *c.pp.s.*, Appointed Nov. 6. Auxiliary Bishop of St. Paul-Minneapolis.
Cooney, Patrick, Appointed Nov. 21. Bishop of Gaylord.
Datillo, Nicholas, Appointed Nov. 21. Bishop of Harrisburg.
Driscoll, Michael P., Appointed Dec. 19. Auxiliary Bishop of Orange.
Favalora, John, Appointed March 7. Bishop of St. Petersburg.
Flynn, Harry J., Succeeded to the See May 13. Bishop of Lafayette.
Gettelfinger, Gerald A., Appointed March 11. Bishop of Evansville.
Grahmann, Charles V., Appointed Dec. 18. Coadjutor Bishop of Dallas.
Grosz, Edward, Appointed Nov. 22. Auxiliary Bishop of Buffalo.
Jacobs, Sam, Appointed July 1. Bishop of Alexandria.
McHugh, James T., Appointed May 13. Bishop of Camden.
Mikloshazy, Attila, *s.j.*, Appointed Aug. 12. Bishop for the Apostolate to the Hungarians.
Rose, Robert J., Appointed July 11. Bishop of Grand Rapids.
Samra, Nicholas J., Appointed June 29. Auxiliary Bishop of Newton.
Schmitt, Bernard W., Appointed March 30. Bishop of Wheeling-Charleston.
Schwietz, Roger L., *o.m.i.*, Appointed Dec. 12. Bishop of Duluth.
Thompson, David B., Appointed May 9. Coadjutor Bishop of Charleston.
Zipfel, Paul A., Appointed May 16. Auxiliary Bishop of St. Louis.

1990

Archbishops

Maida, Adam J., Appointed June 11. Archbishop of Detroit.

Bishops

Banks, Robert J., Appointed Oct. 16. Bishop of Green Bay.
Blaire, Stephen E., Appointed Feb. 17. Auxiliary Bishop of Los Angeles.
Brom, Robert H., Succeeded to the See July 10. Bishop of San Diego.
Daily, Thomas V., Appointed Feb. 20. Bishop of Brooklyn.
Dorsey, Norbert M., *c.p.*, Appointed March 20. Bishop of Orlando.
Dupre, Thomas L., Appointed April 19. Auxiliary Bishop of Springfield in Massachusetts.
Fellhauer, David E., Appointed April 19. Bishop of Victoria.
George, Francis E., *o.m.i.*, Appointed July 10. Bishop of Yakima.
Grahmann, Charles V., Succeeded to See July 14. Bishop of Dallas.
Kuzma, George M., Appointed Oct. 23. Bishop of Van Nuys.
Muench, Robert W., Appointed May 8. Auxiliary Bishop of New Orleans.
Myers, John J., Succeeded to See Jan. 23. Bishop of Peoria.
Pelotte, Donald E., *s.s.s.*, Succeeded to See March 20. Bishop of Gallup.
Ryan, Sylvester D., Appointed Feb. 17. Auxiliary Bishop of Los Angeles.
Saltarelli, Michael A., Appointed June 12. Auxiliary Bishop of Newark.
Sheridan, Patrick J., Appointed Dec. 12. Auxiliary Bishop of New York.
Skylstad, William S., Appointed April 17. Bishop of Spokane.
Symons, J. Keith, Appointed June 2. Bishop of Palm Beach.
Thompson, David B., Succeeded to See Feb. 22. Bishop of Charleston.
Trautman, Donald W., Appointed July 16. Bishop of Erie.

1991

Cardinals

Bevilacqua, Anthony Cardinal, Created June 28; Archbishop of Philadelphia.
Mahony, Roger Cardinal, Created June 28; Archbishop of Los Angeles.

Archbishops

Cronin, Daniel A., Appointed Dec. 9; Archbishop of Hartford.
Dimino, Joseph T., Succeeded to the See June 21; Archbishop of the Military Services.

Bishops

Glynn, John J., Appointed Dec. 10. Auxiliary Bishop of the Military Services.
Goedert, Raymond E., Appointed July 8. Auxiliary Bishop of Chicago.
Madera, Joseph J., *m.sp.s.*, Appointed May 28. Auxiliary Bishop of the Military Services.
Sheets, John R., *s.j.*, Appointed May 14. Auxiliary Bishop of Fort Wayne-South Bend.
Smith, John M., Appointed June 24. Bishop of Pensacola-Tallahassee.
Steinbock, John T., Appointed October 15. Bishop of Santa Rosa.
Welsh, Lawrence H., Appointed November 8. Auxiliary Bishop of St. Paul-Minneapolis.

1992

Archbishops

Beltran, Eusebius J., Appointed November 24; Archbishop of Oklahoma City, from Bishop of Tulsa.
Buechlein, Daniel M., *o.s.b.*, Appointed July 14; Archbishop of Indianapolis, from Bishop of Memphis.

Bishops

Angell, Kenneth A., Appointed October 10, Bishop of Burlington, from Auxiliary Bishop of Providence.
Barnes, Gerald R., Appointed January 28, Auxiliary Bishop of San Bernardino.
Boles, John P., Appointed April 14 Auxiliary Bishop of Boston.
Bruskewitz, Fabian W., Appointed March 24, Bishop of Lincoln.
Carmody, Edmond, Appointed March 24, Bishop of Tyler, from Auxiliary Bishop of San Antonio.
Carmon, Dominic, *s.v.d.*, Appointed December 16, Auxiliary Bishop of New Orleans.
Galante, Joseph A., Appointed October 13, Auxiliary Bishop of San Antonio.
Garland, James H., Appointed October 10, Bishop of Marquette, from Auxiliary Bishop of Cincinnati.
Jarrell, Michael Charles, Appointed December 29, Bishop of Houma-Thibodaux.
Kmiec, Edward Urban, Appointed October 13, Bishop of Nashville, from Auxiliary Bishop of Trenton.
McNamara, John R., Appointed April 14, Auxiliary Bishop of Boston.
Mansell, Henry J., Appointed November 24, Auxiliary Bishop of New York.
O'Malley, Sean P., *o.f.m.cap.*, Appointed July 16, Bishop of Fall River, from Bishop of St. Thomas Virgin Islands.
Paska, Walter, Appointed January 26, Auxiliary Bishop of Philadelphia Ukrainian.
Ryan, Sylvester D., Appointed January 21, Bishop of Monterey, from Auxiliary Bishop of Los Angeles.
Sheldon, Gilbert I., Appointed January 28, Bishop of Steubenville, from Auxiliary Bishop of Cleveland.
Tobin, Thomas J., Appointed November 3, Auxiliary Bishop of Pittsburgh.
Ziemann, G. Patrick, Appointed July 14, Bishop of Santa Rosa, from Auxiliary Bishop of Los Angeles.

1993

Archbishops

Curtiss, Elden F., Appointed May 4, Archbishop of Omaha, from Bishop of Helena.
Donoghue, John F., Appointed June 22, Archbishop of Atlanta, Bishop of Charlotte.
Keleher, James P., transferred Sept. 8, Archbishop of Kansas City in Kansas, from Bishop of Belleville.
Sheehan, Michael J., Appointed April 6, Archbishop of Santa Fe.

Bishops

Boland, Raymond J., Appointed June 22, Bishop of Kansas City St. Joseph, from Bishop of Birmingham.
Britt, Kevin M., Appointed November 23, Auxiliary Bishop of Detroit.
Bullock, William H., Appointed April 13, Bishop of Madison, from Bishop of Des Moines.
Charron, Joseph J., *c.pp.s. Appointed November 12, Bishop of Des Moines, from Auxiliary Bishop of St. Paul and Minneapolis.*
Elya, John A., *b.s.o. Appointed December 7, Bishop of Newton from Auxiliary Bishop of Newton.*
Franklin, William E., Appointed November 12, Bishop of Davenport, from Auxiliary Bishop of Dubuque.
Gregory, Wilton, Appointed December 29, Bishop of Belleville from Auxiliary Bishop of Chicago.
Harrington, Bernard J., Appointed November 23, Auxiliary Bishop of Detroit.
Hughes, Alfred C., Appointed September 7, Bishop of Baton Rouge, from Auxiliary Bishop of Boston.
Loverde, Paul S., Appointed November 11, Bishop of Ogdensburg, from Auxiliary Bishop of Hartford.
Moeddel, Carl K., Appointed June 15, Auxiliary Bishop of Cincinnati.
Slattery, Edward J., Appointed November 11, Bishop of Tulsa.
Steib, James Terry, *s.v.d. Appointed March 23, Bishop of Memphis, from Auxiliary Bishop of St. Louis.*
Tamayo, James A., Appointed January 26, Auxiliary Bishop of Galveston-Houston.
Thomas, Elliot G., Appointed October 10, Bishop of St. Thomas, Virgin Islands.
Weigand, William K., Appointed November 3, Bishop of Sacramento from Bishop of Salt Lake City.
Wiwchar, Michael, *c.ss.r. Appointed July 15, Bishop of St. Nicholas in Chicago for Ukrainians.*

1994

Cardinals

Keeler, William Cardinal, Created November 26; Archbishop of Baltimore.
Maida, Adam Cardinal, Created November 26; Archbishop of Detroit.

Archbishops

Favalora, John C., Appointed November 3, Archbishop of Miami.
Flynn, Harry J., Appointed February 2, Coadjutor Archbishop of St. Paul-Minneapolis.
Hanus, Jerome, *o.s.b. Appointed August 23, Coadjutor Archbishop of Dubuque.*
Procyk, Judson M., Appointed November 15, Archbishop of Pittsburgh Byzantine.
Rigali, Justin F., Appointed January 25, Archbishop of St. Louis.

Bishops

Barbarito, Gerald, Appointed June 28, Auxiliary Bishop of Brooklyn.
Brunett, Alexander J., Appointed April 19, Bishop of Helena.
Burke, Raymond L., Appointed December 10, Bishop of La Crosse.
Carlson, Robert J., Appointed January 13, Bishop Coadjutor of Sioux Falls, from Auxiliary Bishop of St. Paul-Minneapolis.
Catanello, Ignatius, Appointed June 28, Auxiliary Bishop of Brooklyn.
Chedid, John G., Appointed March 1, First Bishop of Our Lady of Lebanon in Los Angeles, from Auxiliary Bishop of St. Maron of Brooklyn.
Cullen, Edward P., Appointed February 8, Auxiliary Bishop of Philadelphia.
Curlin, William G., Appointed February 22, Bishop of Charlotte, from Auxiliary Bishop of Washington.
Curry, Thomas J., Appointed February 8, Auxiliary Bishop of Los Angeles.
Doran, Thomas G., Appointed April 19, Bishop of Rockford.
DiLorenzo, Francis X., Appointed October 4, Bishop of Honolulu.
Foley, David E., Appointed March 22, Bishop of Birmingham, from Auxiliary Bishop of Richmond.
Galante, Joseph A., Appointed April 5, Bishop of Beaumont, from Auxiliary Bishop of San Antonio.
Markiewicz, Alfred J., Appointed November 22, Bishop of Kalamazoo.
McDonnell, Charles J., Appointed March 15, Auxiliary Bishop of Newark.
Niederauer, George H., Appointed November 3, Bishop of Salt Lake City.
O'Donnell, Edward J., Appointed November 8, Bishop of Lafayette (Louisiana).
Reilly, Daniel P., Appointed October 27, Bishop of Worcester.
Rodriguez, Placido, *c.m.f.*, Appointed April 5, Bishop of Lubbock, from Auxiliary Bishop of Chicago.
Sartoris, Joseph M., Appointed February 8, Auxiliary Bishop of Los Angeles.
Yanta, John W., Appointed October 27, Auxiliary of San Antonio.
Zavala, Gabino, Appointed February 8, Auxiliary Bishop of Los Angeles.

1995

Archbishops

Flynn, Harry J., Appointed September 8, from Coadjutor to Archbishop of St. Paul-Minneapolis.
Hanus, Jerome G., O.S.B., Succeeding as Archbishop of Dubuque from status of Coadjutor.
Levada, William J., Succeeding as Archbishop of San Francisco December 1995.
Schleck, Charles A., C.S.C., Appointed February 10, Titular Archbishop of Africa, Adjunct Secretary of the Congregation for the Evangelization of Peoples.

Bishops

Barnes, Gerald R., Appointed December 28, 1995, Bishop of San Bernardino, from Auxiliary of same Diocese.
Boland, J. Kevin, Appointed February 7, 1995, Bishop of Savannah.
Braxton, Edward K., Appointed March 28, Auxiliary Bishop of St. Louis.
Carlson, Robert J., Succeeding as Bishop of Sioux Falls in March, from status of Coadjutor.
Conway, Edwin M., Appointed January 24, Auxiliary Bishop of Chicago.
Cote, Michael R., Appointed May 9, Auxiliary Bishop of Portland in Maine.
Dougherty, John M., Appointed February 7, 1995, Auxiliary Bishop of Scranton.
Dupre, Thomas L., Appointed March 14, Bishop of Springfield, from Auxiliary Bishop of Springfield.
Gonzalez, Roberto O., O.F.M., Appointed May 16, Coadjutor Bishop of Corpus Chrisit, from Auxiliary Bishop of Boston.
Hart, Daniel A., Appointed September 12, Bishop of Norwich, from Auxiliary Bishop of Boston.
Kicanas, Gerald F., Appointed January 24, Auxiliary Bishop of Chicago.
Kinney, John F., Appointed May 8, Bishop of St. Cloud from Bishop of Bismarck.
Lori, William E., Appointed February 27, Auxiliary Bishop of Washington.
Lynch, Robert N., Appointed Bishop of St. Petersburg December 4, 1995.
McCormack, John B., Appointed November Auxiliary Bishop of Boston.
Mansell, Henry J., Appointed April 18, effective June 12, Bishop of Buffalo, from Auxiliary Bishop of New York.
Melczek, Dale J., named Coadjutor Bishop of Gary November 9.
Mengeling, Carl F., Appointed November Bishop of Lansing.
Moynihan, James M., Appointed April 29, effective May 29, Bishop of Syracuse.
Mulvee, Robert Edward, Appointed February 7, Coadjutor Bishop of Providence from Bishop of Wilmington.
Murphy, William F., Appointed November Auxiliary Bishop of Boston.
Murry, George V., *s.j.* Appointed January 24, Auxiliary Bishop of Chicago.
Pataki, Andrew, Appointed Bishop of Passaic November, from Bishop of Parma.
Pena, Raymundo J., Appointed May 23, Bishop of Brownsville, from Bishop of El Paso.
Saltarelli, Michael A., Apponted Bishop of Wilmington, from Auxiliary of Newark.
Smith, John M., named Coadjutor of Trenton from Bishop of Pensacola-Tallahassee.
Straling, Phillip F., Appointed March 21, Bishop of Reno, from former Bishop of San Bernadino.
Tertzakian, Hovhannes, *o.m.ven.*, Appointed January 6, effective April 29, Apostolic Exarch for Armenian Catholics in the United States and Canada.
Tobin, Thomas J., Appointed Bishop of Youngstown, from Auxiliary of Pittsburg.
Walsh, Daniel F., Appointed March 21, Bishop of Las Vegas, formerly Bishop of Reno-Las Vegas.

1996

Archbishops

George, Francis, *o.m.i.*, Appointed Archbishop of Portland in Oregon from Bishop of Yakima.

Bishops

Allue, Emilio, *s.d.b.*, Appointed Auxiliary Bishop of Boston July 24.
Aymond, Gregory M., Appointed Auxiliary Bishop of New Orleans November 19.
Botean, John Michael, Appointed Bishop of Romanian Catholic Diocese of St. George in Canton.
DiMarzio, Nicholas A., Appointed Auxiliary Bishop of Newark September.
Doueihi, Hector, Appointed Bishop of St. Maron of Brooklyn.
Irwin, Francis X., Appointed Auxiliary Bishop of Boston July 24.
O'Brien, Edwin F., Appointed Auxiliary Bishop of New York.
Manz, John R., Appointed Auxiliary Bishop of Chicago January 23.
Maginnis, Robert P., Appointed Auxiliary Bishop of Philadelphia January 23.
Martino, Joseph F., Appointed Auxiliary Bishop of Philadelphia, January 23.
Muench, Robert W., Bishop of Covington from Auxiliary Bishop of New Orleans.
Nienstedt, John C., Appointed Auxiliary Bishop of Detroit June 11.
Ochoa, Armando, Appointed Bishop of El Paso from Auxiliary Bishop of Los Angeles.
Sevilla, Carlos A., *s.j.* Appointed Bishop of Yakima from Auxiliary Bishop of San Francisco December 31.
Schott, Basil, *o.f.m.*, Bishop of Parma (Ruthenians).
Steiner, Kenneth, Appointed Auxiliary Bishop of Portland in Oregon.
Vigneron, Allen H., Appointed Auxiliary Bishop of Detroit June 11.
Warfel, Michael, Appointed Bishop of Juneau November 19.
Younan, Joseph, Appointed Bishop of Our Lady of Deliverance of Newark.
Zipfel, Paul A., Appointed Bishop of Bismarck from Auxiliary Bishop of Saint Louis December 31.

1997

Archbishops

Chaput, Charles J., *o.f.m.cap.*, appointed Archbishop of Denver February 18, 1997, from Bishop of Rapid City.

George, Francis, *o.m.i.*, appointed Archbishop of Chicago from Archbishop of Portland in Oregon from Bishop of Yakima.

O'Brien, Edwin F., appointed Archbishop for the Military Services from Auxiliary Bishop of New York.

Bishops

Bootkoski, Paul G., appointed Auxiliary Bishop for the Archdiocese of Newark, July.

Breen, Vincent DePaul, appointed Bishop of Metuchen, July 8.

Brucato, Robert A., appointed Auxiliary Bishop for the Archdiocese of New York, July.

Cullen, Edward P., appointed Bishop of Allentown from Auxiliary Bishop of Philadelphia, December.

Fernandez, Gilberto, appointed Auxiliary Bishop for the Archdiocese of Miami, June 23.

Garcia, Richard J., appointed Auxiliary Bishop of Sacramento, November.

Gaydos, John R., Bishop of Jefferson City, appointed June 24.

Gonzalez, Roberto, appointed Bishop of Corpus Christi March 31.

Jenky, Daniel R., *c.s.c.*, appointed Auxiliary Bishop of Fort Wayne-South Bend,

Macaluso, Christie A., appointed Auxiliary Bishop of Hartford March 18.

Mulvee, Robert E., succeeds as Bishop of Providence from Coadjutor Bishop of Providence, June.

Murray, James A., appointed Bishop of Kalamazoo November.

Naumann, Joseph F., appointed Bishop of St. Louis, July.

Ricard, John H., *s.s.j.*, appointed Bishop of Pensacola-Tallahassee January.

Sheridan, Michael J., appointed Auxiliary Bishop of St. Louis, July.

Smith, John M., succeeds as Bishop of Trenton from Coadjutor Bishop of Trenton, July.

Wenski, Thomas G., appointed Auxiliary Bishop for the Archdiocese of Miami, June 23.

Yanta, John W., appointed Bishop of Amarillo, from Auxiliary of San Antonio in January.

Zubik, David A., appointed Auxiliary Bishop of Pittsburgh February 18, 1997.

1998

Cardinals

George, Francis Cardinal, *o.m.i.*, Created February 21. Archbishop of Chicago

Stafford, Francis Cardinal, Created February 21. Pres.-Pontifical Council for the Laity, Vatican

Archbishops

Bishops

Harvey, James M., Bishop and Prefect of the Papal Household

National Conference of Catholic Bishops

Address—3211 Fourth St., Washington, DC 20017-1194. Tel: 202-541-3000.

The National Conference of Catholic Bishops (NCCB) is a canonical entity operating in accordance with the Conciliar Decree *Christus Dominus*. Its purpose is to foster the Church's mission by providing the Bishops of the United States of America with an opportunity to exchange views and insights of prudence and experience and to exercise in a joint manner their pastoral office. (cf. *Christus Dominus*, # 38). The NCCB is the successor to the Annual Meeting of the Bishops of the United States, approved in the brief "Communes" issued by Pope Benedict XV, April 10, 1919 and in a special letter of Pius XI issued on August 10, 1927. The present NCCB statutes with some slight amendment are those originally approved by the Sacred Consistorial Congregation in a decree issued on June 22, 1922.

The National Conference of Catholic Bishops is composed of every Bishop, residential or titular, who serves the Church in the United States, its territories or possessions. Each Bishop has an active and passive voice in the Conference. Under certain conditions, enunciated in conciliar legislation, the National Conference of Catholic Bishops can initiate actions that are juridically binding on all the bishops of the country.

The National Conference of Catholic Bishops is presided over by a president who is elected by the general membership. Other officers of the organization are a vice president, secretary, treasurer and general secretary. The National Conference of Catholic Bishops is a distinct entity from the United States Catholic Conference. Its relationship to the USCC is that of a sponsoring organization.

NCCB OFFICES AND COMMITTEES

I. Officers

President—Bishop Anthony M. Pilla
Vice President—Bishop Joseph A. Fiorenza
Treasurer—Bishop Robert J. Banks
Secretary—Archbishop Harry J. Flynn

II. NCCB General Secretariat

General Secretary—Rev. Msgr. Dennis M. Schnurr
Associate General Secretary—Sr. Sharon A. Euart, R.S.M.
Associate General Secretary—Rev. Msgr. William P. Fay
Assistant General Secretary—Mr. Bruce E. Egnew

III. Staff Offices

Finance—Mr. Kenneth Korotky, Dir.
Accounting—Ms. Jennifer McGowan
General Counsel—Mr. Mark E. Chopko
Associate General Counsel—Ms. Deirdre A. Halloran
General Services—Mr. Douglas Cissel, Dir.
Printing & Mailing Services—Mr. Mark J. Bowen, Dir.
Government Liaison—Mr. Frank J. Monahan, Dir.
Human Resources—Mr. Thomas J. Meehan, Dir.
Library Services—Mr. Guy Wilson,Dir.
Management Information Systems—Mr. William Kissane, Dir.
Office of Public and Promotion Services—Mr. Richard W. Daw, Dir.

NCCB COMMITTEES

I. Executive Level

Administrative Committee

Chairman—Bishop Anthony M. Pilla
Members— Anthony Cardinal Bevilacqua (Region III)
Bernard Cardinal Law
Archbishop Alexander J. Brunett (Region I)
Archbishop Daniel A. Cronin (Region I)
Archbishop John C. Favalora (Region IX)
Archbishop Harry J. Flynn
Archbishop Jerome G. Hanus, O.S.B.
Archbishop Theodore E. McCarrick
Archbishop Daniel E. Pilarczyk
Archbishop Justin F. Rigali (Region IX)
Archbishop Francis B. Schulte
Archbishop Michael J. Sheehan
Bishop Robert J. Banks
Bishop Gerald R. Barnes
Bishop Alexander J. Brunett
Bishop Matthew H. Clark (Region II)
Bishop John S. Cummins
Bishop Thomas G. Doran (Region VII)
Bishop John C. Dunne
Bishop Edward M. Egan
Bishop David E. Fellhauer
Bishop Joseph A. Fiorenza
Bishop Joseph J. Gerry,O.S.B.
Bishop Charles V. Grahmann (Region X)
Bishop Richard C. Hanifen
Bishop William R. Houck
Bishop Joseph L. Imesch
Bishop John R. Keating, (Region IV)
Bishop John F. Kinney
Bishop Edward U. Kmiec
Bishop Paul S. Loverde
Bishop Henry J. Mansell
Bishop George V. Murry,S.J.
Bishop Thomas J. O'Brien
Bishop Edward J. O'Donnell (Region V)
Bishop Sean P. O'Malley, O.F.M.Cap.
Bishop Armando X. Ochoa (Region XIII)
Bishop Andrew Pataki
Bishop A. Edward Pevec (Region VI)
Bishop Richardo Ramirez
Bishop John H. Ricard, S.S.J.
Bishop Frank J. Rodimer
Bishop Placido Rodriquez, C.M.F.
Bishop William S. Skylstad
Bishop Edward J. Slattery
Bishop James A. Tamayo
Bishop Daniel F. Walsh (Region XI)
Bishop Lawrence H. Welsh (Region VIII)
Bishop G. Patrick Ziemann
Bishop Paul A. Zipfel

Executive Committee

Chairman—Bishop Anthony M. Pilla
Vice President—Bishop Joseph A. Fiorenza
Treasurer—Bishop Robert J. Banks
Secretary—Archbishop Harry J. Flynn
Ex-Officio—His EminenceBernard Cardinal Law
Staff—Rev. Msgr. Dennis Schnurr

Committee on Budget and Finance

Chairman—Bishop Robert J. Banks
Members—Bishop David E. Fellhauer
Bishop John H. Ricard, S.S.J.
Bishop Daniel F. Walsh
Rev. Msgr. Dennis Schnurr
Staff—Mr. Kenneth Korotky

Committee on Personnel

Chairman—Bishop Joseph A. Fiorenza
Members—Bishop Joseph L. Imesch
Bishop Henry J. Mansell
Rev. Msgr. Dennis Schnurr
Staff—Mr. Bruce E. Egnew

Committee on Priorities and Plans

Chairman—Bishop Anthony M. Pilla
Vice-President—Bishop Joseph A. Fiorenza
Treasurer—Bishop Robert J. Banks
Past President—William Cardinal Keeler
Members—Archbishop Justin F. Rigali
Bishop Henry J. Mansell
Rev. Msgr. Dennis Schnurr
Staff—Sr. Sharon A. Euart, R.S.M.

SubCommittee on the Millennium

Chairman—Bishop Joseph A. Fiorenza
Members—Archbishop Oscar H. Lipscomb
Archbishop John G. Vlazny
Bishop Stephen E. Blaire
Bishop Tod D. Brown
Bishop Wilton D. Gregory
Bishop William C. Newman
Bishop Armando X. Ochoa
Consultants—Rev. John E. Hurley,C.S.P., Special Assisant
Staff—Mr. Paul Henderson,Exec. Dir.
Ms. Emily Davis,Project Assistant

II. General Membership Level

Standing Committees

African American Catholics

Chairman—Bishop George V. Murry, S.J.
Members—Archbishop Thomas C. Kelly, O.P.
Bishop Joseph A. Galante
Bishop Michael A. Saltarelli
Bishop J. Terry Steib, S.V.D.
Bishop David B. Thompson
Consultants—James Cardinal Hickey
William Cardinal Keeler
Bishop Curtis J. Guillory, S.V.D.
Staff—Ms. Beverly A. Carroll, Exec. Dir.
Mrs. Stephanie Greenhouse

American College Louvain

Chairman—Bishop Frank J. Rodimer
Members by Region—
Region I Bishop Francis J. Christian
Region II Bishop Matthew H. Clark
Region III Bishop Frank J. Rodimer
Region IV Bishop Joseph J. Madera, M.Sp.S.
Region V Bishop Gregory M. Aymond
Region VI Bishop Allen H. Vigneron
Region VII Bishop Gerald A. Gettelfinger
Region VIII Bishop James S. Sullivan
Region IX Bishop Edward K. Braxton
Region X Bishop John W. Yanta
Region XI Bishop Thomas J. Curry
Region XII Bishop William S. Skylstad
Region XIII Bishop Thomas J. O'Brien
Consultants—Bishop Benedict C. Franzetta
Staff—Mr. Daniel J. Frett
Rev. Msgr. John J. Scanlan
Very Rev. David E. Windsor
Rev. Francis P. Kayatta

Bishops' Welfare Emergency Relief

Chairman—Bishop Anthony M. Pilla
Members—Administrative Committee Members

Boundaries of Dioceses and Provinces

Chairman—Bishop Anthony M. Pilla
Members by Region—Region I Bishop Michael R. Cote
Region II Bishop Thomas V. Daily
Region III Bishop Dominic A. Marconi
Region IV Archbishop John F. Donoghue
Region V Archbishop Francis B. Schulte
Region VI Bishop Moses B. Anderson, S.S.E.
Region VII Bishop Raymond E. Goedert
Region VIII Bishop Victor Balke
Region IX Bishop Joseph L. Charron, C.P.P.S.
Region X Bishop James A. Tamayo
Region XI Bishop John T. Steinbock
Region XII Bishop Thomas J. Connolly
Region XIII Bishop Donald E. Pelotte, S.S.S.
Staff—Rev. Msgr. Dennis M. Schnurr

Canonical Affairs

Chairman—Bishop David E. Fellhauer
Members—Archbishop Thomas C. Kelly, O.P.
Bishop Raymond L. Burke
Bishop Michael R. Cote
Bishop Thomas G. Doran
Bishop Raymond E. Goedert
Bishop John J. Myers
Advisors —Adam Cardinal Maida
Bishop Joseph A. Galante
Staff—Sr. Sharon A. Euart, R.S.M.

Church in Latin America

Chairman—Bishop Roberto O. Gonzalez,O.F.M.
Members—Archbishop James P. Keleher
Bishop David Arias, O.A.R.
Bishop Alvaro Corrado del Rio, S.J.
Bishop William F. Murphy
Bishop Raymundo J. Pena
Bishop Michael Warfel
Staff—Rev. James J. Ronan, Exec. Dir.
Ms. Amy E. Fleming
Mrs. E. Carolina Salvador
Mrs. Marta Torres-Reilly

Consecrated Life

Chairman—Bishop Joseph J. Gerry,O.S.B.
Members—Archbishop Thomas C. Kelly,O.P.
Archbishop John G. Vlazny
Bishop Joseph L. Charron,C.P.P.S.
Bishop Basil Schott,O.F.M.
Staff—Rev. Msgr. Dennis M. Schnurr
Sr. Sharon A. Euart,R.S.M.

Diaconate
Chairman—Bishop Edward U. Kmiec
Members—Bishop Dominic Carmon, S.V.D.
Bishop Howard J. Hubbard
Bishop William E. Lori
Bishop Thomas J. O'Brien
Bishop Frank J. Rodimer
Bishop Rene A. Valero
Consultants—Rev. Msgr. William A. Varvaro Rev. Kevin W. Irwin
Staff—Deacon John Pistone, Exec. Dir.

Doctrine
Chairman—Archbishop Daniel E. Pilarczyk
Members—Francis Cardinal George, O.M.I.
Archbishop William J. Levada
Bishop Francis X. DiLorenzo
Bishop Norbert M. Dorsey,C.P.
Bishop Wilton D. Gregory
Bishop Richard J. Sklba
Consultants—Rev. Avery Dulles, S.J.
Robin Darling Young, Ph.D.
Rev. Rick A. Marzheuser
Staff—Rev. J. Augustine DiNoia, O.P., Exec. Dir.
Ms. Siobhan M. Verbeek, Assoc. Dir.

Ecumenical and Interreligious Affairs
Chairman—Archbishop Alexander J. Brunett
Members—William Cardinal Keeler
Archbishop Rembert G. Weakland, O.S.B.
Bishop Joseph J. Gerry, O.S.B.
Bishop Donald E. Pelotte, S.S.S.
Bishop Placido Rodriguez, C.M.F.
Bishop Nicholas J. Samra
Bishop William S. Skylstad
Bishop John J. Snyder
Bishop J. Kendrick Williams
Consultants—John Cardinal O'Connor
Archbishop Oscar H. Lipscomb
Bishop John S. Cummins
Bishop Howard J. Hubbard
Bishop George V. Murry, S.J.
Bishop Richard J. Sklba
Bishop James C. Timlin
Staff—Rev. John F. Hotchkin, Exec. Dir.
John Borelli, Ph.D., Assoc. Dir.
Eugene Fisher, Ph.D., Assoc. Dir.
Bro. Jeffrey Gros, F.S.C., Assoc. Dir.
Rev. Ronald G. Roberson, C.S.P., Assoc. Dir.

Evangelization
Chairman—Archbishop Michael J. Sheehan
Members—Anthony Cardinal Bevilacqua
Bishop Stephen E. Blaire
Bishop Sam G. Jacobs
Bishop Raymond A. Lucker
Bishop Joseph F. Martino
Bishop Daniel F. Walsh
Staff—Dr. David M. Byers, Exec. Dir.
Rev. John E. Hurley, C.S.P., Assoc. Dir.

Hispanic Affairs
Chairman—Bishop Gerald R. Barnes
Members—Bishop Emilio Allue, S.D.B.
Bishop Curtis J. Guillory S.V.D.
Bishop James R. Hoffman
Bishop Ricardo Ramirez, C.S.B.
Bishop Placido Rodriguez, C.M.F.
Bishop Agustin A. Roman
Bishop Carlos A. Sevilla, S.J.
Bishop Gabino Zavala
Consultants—Rev. Msgr. Lorenzo Albacete
Sr. Maria Elena Gonzalez, R.S.M.
Mr. Gonzalo Saldana
Staff—Mr. Ronaldo M. Cruz, Exec. Dir.
Mr. Alejandro Aguilera-Titus, Assoc. Dir.

Home Missions
Chairman—Bishop Edward J. Slattery
Members—BishopSam G. Jacobs
Bishop Basil H. Losten
Bishop Anthony J. O'Connell
Bishop John H. Ricard, S.S.J.
Bishop Peter A. Rosazza
Consultants—BishopVictor Balke
Staff—Dr. David M. Byers, Ph.D., Exec. Dir.
Mrs. Patricia D. Boman, Special Asst.
Ms. Mary M. Campbell, Exec. Asst.

Laity
Chairman—Bishop G. Patrick Ziemann
Members—Archbishop Harry J. Flynn
Bishop Joseph P. Delaney
Bishop Gerald F. Kicanas
Bishop Manuel D. Moreno
Bishop Roger L. Schwietz, O.M.I.
Bishop Phillip F. Straling
Staff—Mr. H. Richard McCord, Exec. Dir.
Ms. Sheila Garcia, Asst. Dir.
Ms. Ana Villamil, Asst. Dir.
Sr. Amy Hoey, R.S.M., Project Coord.

Lay Ministry SubCommittee
Chairman—Bishop Phillip F. Straling
Members—Bishop Tod D. Brown
Bishop John C. Dunne
Bishop Bernard J. Harrington
Bishop James R. Hoffman
Bishop Gerald F. Kicanas
Bishop Edward U. Kmiec
Bishop Armando X. Ochoa
Bishop Emil A. Wcela
Advisors—
Zoila Diaz, D.Min.
Dr. Zeni Fox
Rev. Msgr. Phil Murnion
Staff—Mr. H. Richard McCord, Exec. Dir.
Ms. Ana Villamil, Asst. Dir.
Sr. Amy Hoey, R.S.M., Project Coord.

SubCommittee on Youth
Chairman—Bishop Roger L. Schwietz,O.M.I.
Members—Bishop Emilio Allue, S.D.B.
Bishop Kevin M. Britt
Bishop Patrick J. McGrath
Bishop John M. Smith
Advisors—Mr. Robert McCarty
Ms. Maritza Gamboa
Mr. Mitchel J. Zimmerman
Staff—Ms. Ana Villamil, Asst. Dir.

Liturgy
Chairman—Archbishop Jerome Hanus, O.S.B.
Members—Archbishop Justin F. Rigali
Archbishop Rembert G. Weakland, O.S.B.
Bishop Gerald F. Kicanas
Bishop Leonard J. Olivier, S.V.D.
Bishop Sylvester D. Ryan
Consultants—Roger Cardinal Mahony
Francis Cardinal George, O.M.I.
Bishop Roberto Gonzalez, O.F.M.
Bishop Frank J. Rodimer
Staff—Rev. James P. Moroney, Exec. Dir.
Mr. Dennis D. McManus, Assoc. Dir.
Sr. Ann F. Rehrauer, Assoc. Dir.
Ms. Annette Williams

Marriage and Family Life
Chairman—Bishop Thomas J. O'Brien
Members—Archbishop Elden F. Curtiss
Bishop John F. Kinney
Bishop Carl K. Moeddel
Bishop Richard J. Sklba
Bishop John M. Smith
Bishop John W. Yanta
Staff—Mr. H. Richard McCord, Exec. Dir.

Migration
Chairman—Bishop John S. Cummins
Members—Adam Cardinal Maida
Archbishop John C. Favalora
Bishop George V. Murry, S.J.
Bishop Peter A. Rosazza
Bishop John W. Yanta
Bishop Gabino Zavata
Consultants—Archbishop Theodore E. McCarrick
Archbishop Francis B. Schulte
Bishop R. Pierre DuMaine
Bishop John A. Elya, B.S.O.
Bishop Joseph L. Howze
Bishop James C. Timlin
Staff—Mr. Mark Franken, Interim Exec. Dir.
Rev. Msgr. William P. Fay

North American College Rome
Chairman—William Cardinal Keeler
Members—Region I Bishop Edward M. Egan
Region II Bishop Paul S. Loverde
Region III Bishop Donald W. Wuerl
Region IV William Cardinal Keeler
Region V Archbishop Oscar H. Lipscomb
Region VI Bishop John C. Nienstedt
Region VII Bishop Gerald F. Kicanas
Region VIII Bishop Robert J. Carlson
Region IX Bishop Fabian W. Bruskewitz
Region X Bishop Joseph A. Galante
Region XI Bishop Robert M. Brom
Region XII Bishop Tod D. Brown
Region XIII Bishop Richard C. Hanifen
Staff—Rev. Msgr. William P. Fay

Pastoral Practices
Chairman—Bishop Joseph L. Imesch
Members—Bishop Gerald R. Barnes
Bishop Stephen E. Blaire
Bishop J. Kevin Boland
Bishop Robert W. Donnelly
Bishop Stanley G. Schlarman
Bishop Emil A. Wcela
Staff—Rev. J. Augustine DiNoia, O.P., Exec. Dir.
Ms. Siobhan M. Verbee, Assoc. Dir.

Priestly Formation
Chairman—Archbishop John C. Favalora
Members—Archbishop Edwin F. O'Brien
Archbishop John G. Vlazny
Bishop Curtis J. Guillory, S.V.D.
Bishop Gerald F. Kicanas
Bishop Robert W. Muench
Bishop Gabino Zavala
Advisor—Bishop Norbert M. Dorsey, C.P.
Bishop Donald W. Wuerl
Staff—Rev. Timothy Reker, Exec.Dir.

Priestly Life and Ministry
Chairman—Bishop Richard C. Hanifen
Members—Bishop Francis J. Christian
Bishop John R. Gaydos
Bishop George H. Niederauer
Bishop William S. Skylstad
Bishop Arthur N. Tafoya
Bishop Paul A. Zipfel
Consultants—Rev. Donal Wolf
Rev. —Kevin Spiess
Rev. —Francis Tebbe, O.F.M.
Staff—Rev. Cletus Kiley, Exec. Dir.

Pro-Life Activities
Chairman—Bernard Cardinal Law
Members—William Cardinal Keeler
Adam Cardinal Maida
Archbishop Daniel Buechlein, O.S.B.
Bishop Roberto O. Gonzalez, O.F.M.
Bishop James T. McHugh
Bishop Andrew Pataki
Bishop John H. Ricard, S.S.J.
Bishop William K. Weigand
Consultants—Anthony Cardinal Bevilacqua
James Cardinal Hickey
Roger Cardinal Mahony
John Cardinal O'Connor
Archbishop John C. Favalora
Archbishop Charles J. Chaput, O.F.M.Cap.
Mr. Virgil Dechant
Ms. Frances X. Hogan, Esq.
Staff—Ms. Gail P. Quinn, Exec. Dir.
Ms. Helen Alvare, Dir. Information & Planning
Mr. Richard Doerflinger, Assoc. Dir. Policy Devel.
Mrs. Susan Wills, Asst. Dir. Programming
Ms. Theresa Notare, Spec. Asst. Natural Family Planning

Relationship Between Eastern and Latin Catholic Churches
Chairman—Bishop Andrew Pataki
Members—Bishop Gerald Barbarito
Bishop Kevin M. Britt
Bishop Ibrahim N. Ibrahim
Bishop Basil H. Losten
Bishop James M. Moynihan
Bishop Nicholas J. Samra
Bishop Joseph Younan
Staff—Rev. Msgr. William P. Fay

Religious Life and Ministry
Chairman—Bishop Joseph A. Galante
Members—Archbishop Francis George, O.M.I.
Bishop John C. Dunne
Bishop Carlos A. Sevilla, S.J.
Bishop John G. Vlazny
Staff—Rev. Msgr. Dennis M. Schnurr
Sr. Sharon A. Euart, R.S.M.

Science and Human Values
Chairman—Bishop Edward M. Egan
Members—Archbishop Daniel A. Cronin
Bishop Edward K. Braxton
Bishop John S. Cummins
Bishop Francis X. DiLorenzo
Bishop R. Pierre DuMaine
Bishop William E. Lori
Consultants—Dr. John Burris
Dr. Eric Fisher
Dr. John Haught
Rev. Ernan McMullin
Rev. James Salmon, S.J.
Dr. Robert White
Staff—Dr. David M. Byers, Ph.D., Exec. Dir.

Selection of Bishops
Chairman—Bishop Anthony M. Pilla
Members—Region I Bishop Michael R. Cote
Region II Bishop Thomas V. Daily
Region III Bishop Dominic A. Marconi

Region IV Archbishop John F. Donoghue
Region V Archbishop Francis B. Schulte
Region VI Bishop Moses B. Anderson, S.S.E.
Region VII Bishop Raymond E. Goedert
Region VIII Bishop Victor Balke
Region IX Bishop Joseph L. Charron, C.P.P.S.
Region X Bishop James A. Tamayo
Region XI Bishop John T. Steinbock
Region XII Bishop Thomas J. Connolly
Region XIII Bishop Donald E. Pelotte, S.S.S.
Staff—Rev. Msgr. Dennis M. Schnurr

Vocations

Chairman—Bishop Paul S. Loverde
Members—Bishop Kevin M. Britt
Bishop John J. McRaith
Bishop John J. Myers
Bishop Roger L. Schwietz, O.M.I.
Bishop Daniel F. Walsh
Bishop Gabino Zavala
Consultants—Bishop Robert J. Carlson
Bishop John J. Glynn
Bishop Donald E. Pelotte, S.S.S.
Bishop J. Terry Steib, S.V.D.
Sr. Catherine Bertrand, S.S.N.D.
Mrs. Dorothy Foss
Staff—Rev. Timothy Reker, Exec. Dir.

Women in Society and in the Church

Chairman—Bishop John C. Dunne
Members—Bishop F. Joseph Gossman
Bishop Richard C. Hanifen
Bishop Howard J. Hubbard
Bishop George V. Murry, S.J.
Bishop William C. Newman
Bishop Gabino Zavala
Advisors—Ms. Mary Ann Dantuono
Ms. Joan M. Finucci
Ms. Kathleen Henricks
Sr. Lynn Jarrell, O.S.U.
Ms. Joan F. Neal
Staff—Mr. H. Richard McCord, Exec. Dir.
Sr. Amy Hoey, R.S.M., Project Coord.
Ms. Sheila Garcia, Asst. Dir.

World Missions

Chairman—Bishop Sean P. O'Malley, O.F.M.Cap.
Members—Francis Cardinal George, O.M.I.
Archbishop William J. Levada
Bishop William E. Lori
Bishop Robert E. Mulvee
Bishop Edward J. Slattery
Bishop Elliott G. Thomas
Consultant—Bishop William J. McCormack
Sr. Mary Waskowiak, R.S.M.
Rev. John Converset
Mr. James Lindsay
Mr. Donald Mueller
Sr. Carole Marie Troskowski
Rev. Francis Wright
Staff—Dr. David M. Byers, Ph.D., Exec. Dir.
Mrs. Patricia D. Bowman, Special Asst.
Ms. Mary M. Campbell, Exec. Asst.

AD HOC COMMITTEES

1999 Special Assembly

Chairman—Bishop Robert N. Lynch
Members—Francis Cardinal George, O.M.I.
Bishop Gerald R. Barnes
Bishop Joseph P. Delaney
Bishop Howard J. Hubbard
Bishop Robert E. Mulvee
Bishop George V. Murry, S.J.
Bishop John M. Smith
Staff—Sr. Sharon Euart, R.S.M.

Aid to the Church in Central and Eastern Europe

Chairman—Adam Cardinal Maida
Members—Archbishop Theodore E. McCarrick
Archbishop Francis B. Schulte
Archbishop Judson M. Procyk
Archbishop Justin F. Rigali
Bishop John J. Myers
Bishop Michael Wiwchar, C.Ss.R.
Staff—Rev. Msgr. R. George Sarauskas, Exec. Dir.
Mr. James H. O'Beirne, Deputy Dir.
Ms. Margit Serenyi, Assoc. Dir.

Bishops' Life and Ministry

Chairman—Bishop William Skylstad
Members—Archbishop William S. Skylstad
Archbishop Edward A. McCarthy
Bishop John Michael Botean
Bishop Francis X. DiLorenzo
Bishop Joseph F. Maguire
Bishop Robert E. Mulvee
Bishop Leonard J. Olivier, S.V.D.
Bishop Ricardo Ramirez, C.S.B.
Bishop Thomas J. Tobin
Bishop Lawrence H. Welsh
Staff—Rev. Msgr. Dennis M. Schnurr

Catholic Charismatic Renewal

Chairman—Bishop Sam G. Jacobs
Members—Archbishop Harry J. Flynn
Archbishop George H. Pearce, S.M.
Bishop Francisco Garmendia
Bishop Raymond A. Lucker
Bishop Joseph C. McKinney
Bishop Donald W. Montrose
Bishop Kenneth J. Povish
Bishop Patrick G. Ziemann
Staff—Sr. Sharon A. Euart, R.S.M.

Economic Concerns of the Holy See

Chairman—Archbishop James P. Keleher
Members—James Cardinal Hickey
Bernard Cardinal Law
Archbishop Daniel A. Cronin
Archbishop Theodore E. McCarrick
Archbishop Justin F. Rigali
Archbishop Francis B. Schulte
Bishop Robert J. Banks
Bishop Edward M. Egan
Bishop Joseph A. Fiorenza
Bishop Henry J. Mansell
Bishop Thomas J. O'Brien
Bishop Edward J. Slattery
Staff—Mr. Bruce E. Egnew

Forum on the Principles of Translation

Chairman—Archbishop Jerome G. Hanus, O.S.B.
Members—Archbishop Alexander J. Brunett
Archbishop Justin F. Rigali
Bishop Victor Balke
Bishop Joseph J. Gerry, O.S.B.
Staff—Sr. Ann Rehrauer, O.S.F.
Mr. Dennis McManus

Health Care Issues and the Church

Chairman—Bishop Donald W. Wuerl
Members—Archbishop Justin F. Rigali
Bishop Henry J. Mansell
Bishop William F. Murphy
Bishop Joseph M. Sullivan
Consultants—Bishop James W. Malone
Staff—Rev. J. Augustine DiNoia, O.P. , Exec. Dir.

Implementation of Ex Corde Ecclesiae

Chairman—BishopJohn J. Leibrecht
Members—James Cardinal HickeyJ
Adam Cardinal Maida
Archbishop Oscar H. Lipscomb
Archbishop Francis B. Schulte
Bishop James A. Griffin
Consultants—Bishop James W. Malone
Staff—Rev. Msgr. Thomas J. McDade
Sr. Sharon Euart, R.S.M.

Interdicasterial Instruction

Chairman—BishopStephen E. Blaire
Members—BishopThomas G. Doran
Bishop John C. Dunne
Bishop Richard C. Hanifen
Bishop Gerald F. Kicanas
Bishop Richard J. Sklba
Bishop Emil A. Wcela
Staff—Rev. J. Cletus Kiley
Mrs. Siobhan M. Verbeek

Native American Catholics

Chairman—Bishop Donald E. Pelotte, S.S.S.
Members—Archbishop Charles J. Chaput, O.F.M.Cap.
Archbishop Alexander J. Brunett
Bishop Michael J. Kaniecki, S.J.
Bishop Anthony M. Milone
Consultants—Rev. Raymond Bucko, S.J.
Rev. John Hatcher
Rev. Msgr. Paul Lenz
Staff—Rev. Msgr. William P. Fay

Nomination of Conference Offices

Chairman—Bishop Dale J. Melczek
Members—Region I Bishop Michael R. Cote
Region II Bishop Thomas J. Costello
Region III Bishop Nicholas C. Dattilo
Region IV Bishop Robert N. Lynch
Region V Bishop William R. Houck
Region VI Bishop Kevin M. Britt
Region VII Bishop Dale J. Melczek
Region VIII Bishop Paul A. Zipfel
Region IX Bishop John J. Leibrecht
Region X Bishop Raymundo J. Pena
Region XI Bishop Michael P. Driscoll
Region XII Bishop Anthony M. Milone
Region XIII Bishop George H. Niederauer
Staff—Sr. Sharon A. Euart, R.S.M.

Oversee the Use of the Catechism

Chairman—Archbishop Daniel M. Buechlein, O.S.B.
Members—Bernard Cardinal Law
Francis Cardinal George, O.M.I.
Archbishop William Levada
Bishop Robert J. Banks
Bishop Alfred C. Hughes
Bishop Donald W. Wuerl
Staff—Rev. John E. Pollard, Exec. Dir.
Rev. Thomas D. DeVries, Coord.-Assessment & Research

Review of Scripture Translations

Chairman—Bishop Richard J. Sklba
Members—Archbishop John R. Quinn
Bishop Edward K. Braxton
Bishop Michael J. Murphy
Bishop Donald W. Trautman
Bishop Emil A. Wcela
Staff—Rev. J. Augustine DiNoia, O.P.
Ms. Siobhan M. Verbeek

Revision of Statues and Bylaws

Chairman—Archbishop Daniel E. Pilarczyk
Members—William Cardinal Keeler
Archbishop Thomas C. Kelly, O.P.
Archbishop John R. Roach
Bishop Michael R. Cote
Bishop Robert N. Lynch
Staff—Sr. Sharon A. Euart, R.S.M.

Sexual Abuse

Chairman—Bishop John F. Kinney
Members—Archbishop John C. Favalora
Archbishop Harry J. Flynn
Bishop Wilton D. Gregory
Bishop John B. McCormack
Bishop Robert F. Morneau
Consultants—Rev. Steven Henrich, O.S.C.
Dr. Frederick Berlin
Dr. James Gill, S.J.
Rev. Tomas Marin
Rev. Kevin McDonough
Mrs. Mary Margaret O'Neil
Dr. Elizabeth C. Piasecki
Advisor—Roger Cardinal Mahony
Staff—Rev. J. Cletus Kiley
Mr. Mark Chopko
Rev. Msgr. Francis Maniscalco

Shrines

Chairman—Archbishop James P. Keleher
Members—Archbishop Charles J. Chaput, O.F.M.Cap.
Francis Cardinal George, O.M.I.
Archbishop Charles J. Chaput, O.F.M.Cap.
Archbishop John G. Vlazny
Bishop John J. Myers
Bishop Sean O'Malley, O.F.M.Cap.
Consultant—Rev. Msgr. Anthony Czarnecki

Stewardship

Chairman—Bishop Sylvester D. Ryan
Members—Archbishop James P. Keleher
Bishop Eugene J. Gerber
Bishop James R. Hoffman
Bishop Joseph L. Imesch
Bishop John J. McRaith
Bishop Sylvester Ryan
Staff—Mr. Bruce E. Egnew

Subcommittee for Implementation of Ex Corde Ecclesiae

Chairman—Anthony Cardinal Bevilacqua
Members—Adam Cardinal Maida
Bishop Raymond L. Burke
Bishop Thomas G. Doran
Rev. Msgr. John Alesandro
Staff—Sr. Sharon A. Euart, R.S.M.

United States Catholic Conference

Address—*3211 Fourth St., N.E., Washington, DC 20017-1194. Tel: 202-541-3000.*

The United States Catholic Conference (USCC) is a civil entity of the American Catholic Bishops assisting them in their service to the Church in the United States of America by uniting the People of God where voluntary, collective action on a broad diocesan level is needed. The USCC provides an organizational structure and the resources needed to insure coordination, cooperation, and assistance in the public, educational, and social concerns of the Church at the national, regional, state, interdiocesan and, as appropriate, diocesan levels.

I. Officers

President—Bishop Anthony M. Pilla
Vice President—Bishop Joseph A. Fiorenza
Treasurer—Bishop Robert J. Banks
Secretary—Archbishop Harry J. Flynn

II. NCCB General Secretariat

General Secretary—Rev. Msgr. Dennis M. Schnurr
Associate General Secretary—Sr. Sharon A. Euart, R.S.M.
Associate General Secretary—Rev. Msgr. William P. Fay
Associate General Secretary—Rev. Msgr. Paul D. Theroux
Assistant General Secretary—Mr. Bruce E. Egnew

III. Staff Offices

Finance—Mr. Kenneth Korotky, Dir.
Accounting—Ms. Jennifer McGowan, Dir.
General Counsel—Mr. Mark E. Chopko
Associate General Counsel—Ms. Deirdre A. Halloran
Associate General Counsel—Mr. John A. Liekweg
General Services—Mr. Douglas Cissel, Dir.
Printing & Mailing Services—Mr. Mark J. Bowen, Dir.
Government Liaison—Mr. Frank J. Monahan, Dir.
Human Resources—Mr. Thomas J. Meehan, Dir.
Library Services—Mr. Guy Wilson, Dir.
Management Information Systems—Mr. William Kissane, Dir.
Office of Public & Promotional Services—Mr. Richard W. Daw, Dir.

USCC COMMITTEES

EXECUTIVE LEVEL

Administrative Board

Chairman—Bishop Anthony M. Pilla
Members—
Anthony Cardinal Bevilacqua (Region III); James Cardinal Hickey; Bernard Cardinal Law; Archbishop Daniel A. Cronin (Region I); Archbishop John C. Favalora; Archbishop Harry J. Flynn; Archbishop Jerome G. Hanus, O.S.B.; Archbishop Thomas C. Kelly, O.P.; Archbishop Theodore E. McCarrick; Archbishop Daniel E. Pilarczyk; Archbishop Justin F. Rigali, (Region IX); Archbishop Francis B. Schulte; Archbishop Michael J. Sheehan; Bishop Victor H. Balke; Bishop Robert J. Banks; Bishop Gerald R. Barnes; Bishop Alexander J. Brunett; Bishop Matthew H. Clark (Region II); Bishop Thomas J. Costello; Bishop John S. Cummins; Bishop John C. Dunne; Bishop Edward M. Egan; Bishop David E. Fellhauer; Bishop Joseph A. Fiorenza; Bishop Joseph A. Galante; Bishop William R. Houck; Bishop Joseph L. Imesch; Bishop John R. Keating (Region IV); Bishop John F. Kinney; Bishop Edward U. Kmiec; Bishop Paul S. Loverde; Bishop Henry J. Mansell; Bishop Anthony M. Milone (Region XII); Bishop Robert F. Morneau; Bishop George V. Murry, S.J.; Bishop John J. Myers (Region XII); Bishop Thomas J. O'Brien; Bishop Sean P. O'Malley, O.F.M.Cap.; Bishop Armando X. Ochoa (Region XIII); Bishop Andrew Pataki; Bishop Raymundo J. Pena; Bishop A. Edward Pevec (Region VI); Bishop Ricardo Ramirez, C.S.B.; Bishop John H. Ricard, S.S.J.; Bishop Frank J. Rodimer; Bishop Placido Rodriquez, C.M.F.; Bishop Roger L. Schwietz (Region VIII); Bishop William S. Skylstad; Bishop Edward J. Slattery (Region X); Bishop James A. Tamayo; Bishop Daniel F. Walsh (Region XI); Bishop G. Patrick Ziemann; Bishop Paul A. Zipfel
Regional Alternates—
Bishop John R. McNamara (Region I); Bishop James M. Moynihan (Region II); Bishop Charles J. Mc Donnell (Region III); Bishop William E. Lori (Region IV); Bishop Jude Speyrer (Region V); Bishop Bernard J. Harrington (Region VI); Vacant - (Region VII); Bishop John F. Kinney (Region VIII); Bishop Edward K. Braxton (Region IX); Bishop Charles V. Grahmann (Region X); Bishop Williwm K. Weigand (Region XI); Archbishop Francis George, O.M.I. (Region XII); Bishop George H. Niederauer (Region XIII)

Executive Committee

Chairman—Bishop Anthony M. Pilla
Members—Bishop Joseph A. Fiorenza, Vice Pres.; Bishop Robert J. Banks, Treas.; Archbishop Harry J. Flynn, Sec.
Members—Bernard Cardinal Law
Staff—Rev. Msgr. Dennis M. Schnurr

Committee on Budget and Finance

Chairman—Bishop Robert J. Banks
Members—Bishop David E. Fellhauer; Bishop John H. Ricard, S.S.J.; Bishop Daniel F. Walsh; Rev. Msgr. Dennis M. Schnurr
Staff—Mr. Kenneth Korotky

Committee on Personnel

Chairman—Bishop Joseph A. Fiorenza
Members—Bishop Joseph L. Imesch; Bishop Henry J. Mansell; Rev. Msgr. Dennis M. Schnurr
Staff—Mr. Bruce E. Egnew

Committee on Priorities and Plans

Chairman—Bishop Anthony A. Pilla.
Vice President—Bishop Joseph A. Fiorenza
Treasurer—Bishop Robert J. Bank
Past President—William Cardinal Keeler
Members—Bishop Henry J. Mansell; Rev. Msgr. Dennis M. Schnurr
Staff—Sr. Sharon A. Euart, R.S.M.

DEPARTMENTAL LEVEL

Campaign for Human Development

Chairman—Bishop Ricardo Ramirez, C.S.B.
Members—Bishop Stephen E. Blaire; Bishop Howard J. Hubbard; Bishop George V. Murry, S.J.; Bishop Placido Rodriguez, C.M.F.; Bishop Bernard W. Schmitt; Bishop John J. Snyder; Bishop Paul A. Zipfel; Mr. John A. Carlisi; Ms. Maureen Geddes; Mr. J. Gibbs MacVeigh; Sr. Peg Maloney, R.S.M.; Dr. William A. Mason; Ms. Kerry A. Robinson; Sr. Consuelo Tovar, D.C.
Staff—Rev. Robert J. Vitillo, Exec. Dir.; Mr. Timothy Collins, Deputy Exec. Dir.; Mr. Douglas M. Lawson, Assoc. Dir.- Field Operations; Ms. Barbara Stephenson, Assoc. Dir.- Communications

COMMUNICATIONS

Chairman—Bishop Thomas J. Costello
Members—Sr. Carol Hoverman, O.S.F.; Mr. Frank Morock; Bishop Michael R. Cote; Bishop William E. Franklin; Bishop Joseph A. Galante; Bishop Roberto O. Gonzalez, O.F.M.; Bishop Robert N. Lynch; Bishop Lawrence J. McNamara; Bishop Carl K. Moeddel; Bishop Edwin F. O'Brien; Bishop Paul A. Zipfel; Sr. Maria de la C. Aymes, S.H.; Mr. Gerald D'Avolio; Mr. Christopher Gunty; Mr. Greg Erlandson; Mr. William G. Halpin; Dr. Marti Tomas Izral; Rev. Paul A. Soukup, S.J.; Mrs. Marilyn Vydra; Mr. Joseph Zwilling
Consultant—William Cardinal Keeler
Staff—Rev. Msgr. Francis J. Maniscalco, Dir. for Communications; Mr. Ramon E. Rodriguez, Dir. Catholic Communication Campaign; Mr. Henry Herx, Dir. Film and Broadcasting; Mr. Thomas N. Lorsung, Dir. & Editor-in-Chief Catholic News Service.

DOMESTIC POLICY

Chairman—Bishop William S. Skylstad
Members—Archbishop John F. Donoghue; Bishop James W. Malone; Bishop John J. McRaith; Bishop Edward O'Donnell; Bishop John Ricard, S.S.J.; Bishop Carlos A. Sevilla, S.J.; Bishop Joseph M. Sullivan; Mr. W. Shepherdson Abell; Rev. Dennis J. Dease; Mr. Roger Lyons; Sr. Mary Roch Rocklage, R.S.M.; Ms. Mildred Shanley; Mr. John Sweeney
Observers—Bro. David Andrews, C.S.C.; Mr. J. Mark Brinkmoeller; Ms. Beverly Carroll; Mr. Tim Collins; Mr. John E. Curley, Jr.; Mr. Ronaldo Cruz; Rev. John Huebscher; Mr. John Huebscher; Rev. Fred Kammer, S.J.; Ms. Annette Kane

Department of Social Development and World Peace

Sec.-Social Development & World Peace—Mr. John Carr
Outreach Coord.—Mr. Richard Fowler

Office of Domestic Social Development

Director—Ms. Nancy Wisdo
Advisor-Health & Welfare Issues—Ms. Patricia King
Advisor-Food, Agriculture & Rural Devel.—Mr.DanielMisleh
Advisor-Urban & Economic Issues—Mr. Thomas Shellabuger

EDUCATION

Chairman—Archbishop Francis B. Schulte
Members—Bishop Edward K. Braxton; Bishop Edward M. Egan; Bishop Bernard J. Harrington; Bishop William E. Lori; Bishop Henry J. Mansell; Bishop G. Patrick Zieman; Sr. Joan Curtin, C.N.D.; Rev. Richard M. Jacobs, O.S.A., Ph.D.; Sr. Domenica Rocchio, S.C.; Dr. Elaine Schuster
Staff—Rev. Msgr. Thomas J. McDade

Advisory Committee on Public Policy and Catholic Schools

Chairman—Archbishop Francis B. Schulte
Members—BishopHenry J. Mannsell; Sr. Monica Kostielney; Dr. Michael McCarron; Sr. Dale McDonald; Dr. Jerome Porath; Dr. Elaine Schuster; Mr.George Solana; Dr. Leonard DeFiore (NCEA)
At Large—Rev. Philip Cribben; Sr. Dominica Rocchio, S.C.
Staff—Rev. Msgr. Thomas J. McDade; Rev. William Davis, O.S.F.S.

Committee of Bishops and Catholic College and Univeristy Presidents

Chairman—Archbishop Francis B. Schulte
Members—Bishop John P. Boles; Bishop Ignatius A. Catanello; Bishop John M. D'Arcy; Bishop Robert N. Lynch; Bishop George H. Niederauer.
Presidents—Sr. Barbara Doherty, S.P., (St. Mary's of the Woods, IN); Sr. Brigid Driscoll, R.S.H.M., (Marymount College, Tarrytown, NY); Bro. Patrick Ellis, F.S.C., (The Catholic University of America, Washington, DC); Sr. Maureen Fay, O.P., (Detroit-Mercy University, Detroit, MI); Rev. Paul L. Locatelli, S.J., (Santa Clara University, Santa Clara, CA); Rev. Joseph O'Hare, (Fordham University, New York, NY); Bro. Dietrich Reinhart, O.S.B., (St. John's University, New York, NY)
Representatives—Rev. Charles H. Hagan, Higher Education and Campus Ministry; Dr. Monika Hellwig, Exec. Dir., Association of Catholic Colleges and Universities
Staff—Rev. Msgr. Thomas J. McDade, Sec. for Education

SAPIENTIA CHRISTIANA

Chairman—Bishop John P. Boles
Members—Bishop Donald W. Trautman; Bishop Donald W. Wuerl
Staff—Rev. Charles H. Hagan, Rep.-Higher Education & Campus Ministry; Rev. Msgr. Thomas J. McDade, Sec. for Education

USCC Department of Education

Secretary for Education—Rev. Msgr. Thomas J. McDade

Representative for Catholic Schools and Federal Assistance—Rev. William Davis, O.S.F.S.

Representative for Higher Education and Campus Ministry—Rev. Charles H. Hagan

Representative for Catechesis and Multicultural Concerns—Sr. Elaine McCarron, S.C.N.

Representative for Catechesis and Leadership Development—Sr. Maureen Shaughnessy

Representative for Catholic School Parent Associations—Mr. Raymond J. Burnell

COMMITTEE ON INTERNATIONAL POLICY

Chairman—Archbishop Theodore E. McCarrick; *Members*—Adam Cardinal Maida; Bishop John S. Cummins; Bishop John J. Glynn; Bishop Wilton D. Gregory; Bishop James A. Griffin; Bishop William F. Murphy; Bishop Donald W. Wuerl; Bishop Ricardo Ramirez, C.S.B.; Bishop James A. Tamayo; Mr. James Bishop; Mr. Eugene Theroux, Esq.

Observers—Mr. J. Mark Brinkmoeller; Mr. Ken Hackett; Rev. Ted Keating, S.M.; Rev. Msgr. Robert L. Stern; Mr. John Swenson

Department of Social Development and World Peace

Secretary for Social Development and World Peace—Mr. John L. Carr

Outreach Coordinator—Mr. Richard Fowler

Office of International Justice and Peace

Director for International Justice and Peace—Rev. Drew Christiansen, S.J.

Policy Advisor, International Economic Affairs—Ms. Barbara Kohnen

Policy Advisor, Latin American, Caribbean, and Asian Affairs—Mr. Thomas Quigley

Policy Advisor, African Affairs—Mr. Kevin James Lee

Policy Advisor, Europe and Security Policies—Mr. Gerard F. Powers

Manager, Environmental Justice Project—Mr. Walter Grazer

SUBCOMMITTEE ON CATECHESIS

Chairman—Bishop G. Patrick Ziemann

Members—Bishop Edward K. Braxton; Dr. Maria de los Angeles Garcia; Dr. Mary Anne Boyarski; Sr. Joan Curtin, C.N.D.; Sr. Catherine Dooley, O.P.; Rev. Alfred McBride

Staff—Rev. Msgr. Thomas J. McDade, Sec. for Education; Sr. Elaine McCarron, S.C.N., Rep.- Catechesis and Multicultural Concerns; Sr. Maureen Shaughnessy, S.C., Rep.-Catechesis and Leadership Development

NATIONAL ADVISORY COUNCIL

Officers—Ms. Kathleen Dyer, Chm. (Fulton, NY); Mrs. Helen Boettcher, Chm.-Elect (Evansville, IN); Ms. Rita Wray, Sec. (Brandon, MS)

Members—Bishop Matthew H. Clark; Bishop George V. Murry, S.J.; Bishop G. Patrick Ziemamm; Bishop James A. Tamayo; Rev. John E. MacInnis; Rev. Richard G. Mohr; Rev. Martin M. Muller; Rev. Joseph Naumann; Rev. Lawrence J. O'Keefe; Rev. Msgr. Edward R. Sacks; Rev. Msgr. Donald Webber; Rev. Bernard Smith; Bro. Kevin Smith, O.F.S.; Sr. Theresa Kelly, F.M.A.; Sr. Mary Mollison, C.S.A.; Sr. Sean Peters, C.S.J.

Regional Representatives—

Region I: Mr. Matthew T. Boyle; Mrs. Lois E. McKinney

Region II: Mr. Joseph P. Schramm; Ms. Dolores B. Grierny

Region III: Mr. J. Brian Benestad; Mrs. Rita Martin

Region IV: Rev. Mr. Curtiss P. Todd; Ms. Mary M. Jeffcoat

Region V: Dr. Peter Pavlov, D.D.S.; Mrs. Rita Wray

Region VI: Mr. Kenneth Shepard; Mrs. Adele G. Salerno

Region VII: Mr. Joseph A. Russo; Mrs. Helen Boettcher

Region VIII: Mr. Justin W. Gullekson; Mrs. Elizabeth Mohr

Region IX: Mr. William B. Guyol; Mrs. Rhonda M. Lohkamp

Region X: Mr. Philip Verhalen; Mrs. Anne C. Dierks

Region XI: Mr. Justin K. Kwak; Mrs. Sharon Seitz

Region XII: Mr. Mario M. Villanueva; Mrs. Katherine Bishop

Region XIII: Mr. Antonio Gonzalez, Ph.D.; Mrs. Rachel Pineda

Members—Bishop Patrick R. Cooney; Bishop Joseph F. Martino; Deacon Ronald R. Ealey; Mrs. Graciela Contreras; Mrs. D. Phyllis DeCory; Ms. Kathleen Dyer; Sr. Teresa Gomez, H.M.S.S.; Ms. Carolyn C. Jenkins; Mr. Andrew Lyke, Jr.; Mr. Timothy D. McCauley; Bro. Donald Mouton, F.S.C.; Mrs. Nedra R. Robinson; Mrs. Olga Seim; Mr. Kenneth Wang; Rev. Msgr.Donald F. Zimmerman

Staff—Rev. Msgr. Paul D. Theroux

RELATED ORGANIZATIONS

*** Catholic Legal Immigration Network, Inc. (CLINIC)—**

Theological College, National Office, 401 Michigan Ave. N.E., First Flr., Washington, DC 20017. Tel: 202-635-2556; Fax: 202-635-2649.

Staff—Mr. John Swenson, Pres. & C.E.O.; Mr. Donald Kerwin, Vice Pres. & C.E.O.; Mr. Donald Kerwin, Vice Pres. & C.O.O.; Rev. Msgr. Dennis M. Schnurr, Sec.; Most Rev. George V. Murry, S.J., Treas.

Catholic Legal Immigration Network, Inc. (CLINIC) Board of Directors—

Chairman—Bishop John S. Cummins

Members—Anthony Cardinal Bevilacqua; Most Revs. Stephen E. Blaire; Nicolas A. DiMarzio; William F. Murphy; Armando X. Ochoa; Rev. Msgr. William P. Fay; Hon. Judge James Belson; Ms. Jane Golden Belford, Esq.; Mr. Edward L. Quinn

CLINIC was incorporated in 1988 as a non-profit tax-exempt subsidiary of the National Conference of Catholic Bishops. It is a unique legal services corporation charged with the mandate to serve as a national support and resource center and to assist diocesan programs in the provision of immigration services to their indigent and low-income clients, regardless of race, nationality, ethnicity, political or religious beliefs.

Catholic Relief Services—

CRS World Headquarters: 209 W. Fayette St., Baltimore, MD 21201. Tel: 410-625-2220; Fax: 410-685-1635. Each diocese has a local CRS representative, listed in this book. Mr. Kenneth F. Hackett, Exec. Dir.

Catholic Relief Services Board of Directors—

Chairman—Bishop John H. Ricard, S.S.J.

Members—Most Revs. Joseph L. Imesch; John F. Kinney; Dale J. Melczek; Donald E. Pelotte; William C. Newman; Anthony J. O'Connell; Sean P. O'Malley, O.F.M.Cap.; Michael A. Saltarelli; Roger L. Schwietz; John M. Smith; Rev. Msgr. Dennis M. Schnurr.

Catholic Relief Services-USCC The official overseas relief and development agency of U.S. Catholics; it is a separately incorporated organization of the U.S. Catholic Conference.

CRS was founded in 1943 by the bishops of the United States to assist the poor and disadvantaged outside this country.

CRS maintains programs and projects in 80 countries around the world. Help is given to all those in need regardless of race, creed or political affiliation.

In addition to its highly acclaimed disaster relief work, CRS carries on development and nutrition programs throughout the developing world. These include health projects, school feeding programs, agricultural development, water resource management, income-generating projects, and community promotion and are designed to help people help themselves and to raise the standard of living not only of the individual but of families and entire communities.

CRS operations are funded, in part, from the proceeds of an annual collection - American Bishops Overseas Appeal (also known as the Bishop's Welfare Emergency Fund) - held during the Lenten season in more than 18,000 Catholic churches in the U.S. - Support is also received from Operation Rice Bowl, a Lenten program of prayer, fasting, and almsgiving, and from individuals, church and school groups, foundations and corporations. Assistance from the federal government takes several forms: food available under Title II of Public Law 480; defrayment of ocean freight costs on U.S. government-donated foods and relief supplies generated by CRS itself; grants for some emergency operations.

Educational programs for parishes and dioceses, brochures, newsletters, and information on planned giving programs, including wills/bequests, and annuities, are available upon request.

In the year ending Dec. 31, 1996, the CRS global program in 80 countries had a total value of 213 million dollars.

CTNA Telecommunications, Inc.—

3211 Fourth St. N.E., Washington, DC 20017-1194. Tel: 202-541-3200. Rev. Msgr. Francis J. Maniscalco, President; Rev. Msgr. William P. Fay, Chairman, Board of Directors.

National Religious Retirement Office—

3211 Fourth St., N.E., Washington, DC 20017-1194. Tel: 202-541-3215. Sr. Mary A. Leahy, S.P., Dir.

NATIONAL ORGANIZATIONS

Listing in this category is not related to classification under Canon Law as a public juridic person.

American Catholic Correctional Chaplains Association—

13934 Lemoli Ave., Hawthorne, CA 90250. Tel: 310-676-2038. Most Rev. J. Kendrick Williams, D.D., Episcopal Advisor; Rev. Mark Santo, Pres.; Rev. John Wilkinson, O.M.I., Vice Pres. & Treas.; Edward Bryon, Sec.

The Board of Directors include the Episcopal Advisor, Elected Officers, Regional Vice Presidents, and Past Presidents. Address all Communications to the President or Secretary.

A non-profit organization for the purposes of unifying and implementing the Church's corrective and rehabilative efforts for the spiritual welfare of persons committed to the Catholic Chaplains' care, and to foster a Catholic approach to the problems and study of the correctional field in accord with the principles of Sacred Scriptures, Catholic philosophy and theology. Affiliated with the Social Development and World Peace Department, U.S. Catholic Conference, Inc., American Correctional Association, American Correctional Chaplains Association, National Council on Crime and Delinquency and Catholic University of America, it was established with approval of the American Bishops. Grants USCC recognized certification to qualified members.

Publications: *The Chap-lett.*

American Catholic Historical Association (1919)—

The Catholic University of America, Washington, DC 20064. Uta-Renate Blumenthal, Pres.; Rev. Msgr. Robert Trisco, Sec. & Treas.

A membership organization, founded to promote the study of church history understood in the broad sense and to assist American Catholics and other members in all fields of history.

The American College of the Roman Catholic Church of the United States—North American College (1859)—

Mailing Address, P.O. Box 29260, Washington, DC 20017-0260. His Eminence James Cardinal Hickey, Chm.; Very Rev. Timothy M. Dolan, Rector, 00120, Vatican City, Europe. Mr. Patrick W. Kennedy, Dir. Office for Devel. & Public Rels., 2500 Brunswick Pike, Lawrenceville, NJ 08648. Tel: 609-671-1400; Fax: 609-671-9200.

The College is owned and operated by the Bishops of the United States and is incorporated under the laws of the State of Maryland.

Association of Catholic Diocesan Archivists—

711 W. Monroe St., Chicago, IL 60661. Tel: 312-831-0711; Fax: 312-831-0610. Rev. Msgr. Francis J. Weber, Pres.; Mr. Charles Nolan, Vice Pres.; Sr. Catherine Louise LaCoste, C.S.J., Sec.

The Association of Catholic Diocesan Archivists was established in 1979 and is committed to the active promotion of professionalism in the management of diocesan archives in the United States.

Catholic Association of Teachers of Homiletics (CATH)—

Weston School of Theology, 3 Phillips Pl., Cambridge, MA 02138. Tel: 617-492-1960; Fax: 617-492-5833.

Officers: Rev. Thomas A. Kane, C.S.P., Pres.; Rev. Daniel E. Harris, C.M., Sec. & Treas.

Catholic Campus Ministry Association.

Executive Office, 300 College Park Ave., Dayton, OH 45469-2515. Tel: 937-229-4648; Fax: 937-229-4024. Donald R. McCrabb, Exec. Dir.

Founded in 1969 by campus ministers, the association promotes the mission of the Church in higher education and implements the 1985 Pastoral Letter on Campus Ministry through educational programs and services, leadership, the development of cooperative relationships with other organizations and development activities. Membership is open to individuals interested in campus ministry.

Publications: *Crossroads, the Association Newsletter; The Catholic Campus, Ministry Directory; The Journal of The Catholic Campus Ministry Association.*

Catholic Charities USA—

1731 King St., Ste. 200, Alexandria, VA 22314. Tel: 703-549-1390; Fax: 703-549-1656. Most Rev. Joseph M. Sullivan, Episcopal Liaison; Rev. Timothy Hogan, Chm.; Rev. Fred Kammer, S.J., Pres.

Catholic Charities USA is a national network of more than 1,200 agencies and institutions as well as thousands of concerned individuals who are dedicated to serving the most vulnerable members of American society. The nation's largest network of private, independent social service organizations aims to support families, strengthen communities, and reduce poverty.

Diocesan Catholic Charities agencies provide shelter, food, counseling and a host of other services to children, teen parents, adults, and the elderly. The services are offered to people of all religious, national, racial, social, and economic backgrounds. Each year, millions of people turn to Catholic Charities for everything from a hot meal at a soup kitchen to a new family through adoption.

The organization was founded in 1910 as the National Conference of Catholic Charities by the Most Rev. Thomas J. Shahan and Rt. Rev. Msgr. William J. Kerby in cooperation with lay leaders of the Society of St. Vincent de Paul. Today the network has several hundred thousand volunteers and staff members who provide services to people in need, advocate for justice in social structures, and call the entire Church and other people of good will to do the same.

Catholic Charities USA serves members through national and regional meetings and networking, training, literature, and social policy advocacy on the national level. It is commissioned by the U.S. Catholic Conference to represent the Catholic community when disasters strike in the United States. Catholic Charities USA's president represents North America before Caritas Internationalis, the international conference of Catholic Charities, and thus maintains contact with the Catholic Charities Movement throughout the world.

Publications: quarterly membership magazine, *Charities U.S.A.*, biannual, *Directory of Catholic Charities, Agencies and Organizations; Annual, Survey* of Catholic Charities services nationwide; annual report; and various books, pamphlets and studies.

The Catholic Communications Foundation (CCF)—

P.O. Box 374, Pawling, NY 12564. Tel: 203-746-6685. The Catholic Communications Foundation was established and is supported by Catholic Fraternal Benefit Societies. Its mission is to assist the communications apostolates of the Catholic Church in the United States, with particular emphasis at the diocesan level. The Foundation awards religious communications training scholarships; Most Rev. Anthony G. Bosco, Chm.; Most Rev. Daniel A. Cronin, Pres.; Bernard J. Lengerman, Exec. Vice Pres.; James R. Bastis, Sec.

The Catholic Health Association of the United States (1915)—

Headquarters, 4455 Woodson Rd., St. Louis, MO 63134. Tel: 314-427-2500; Fax: 314-427-0029. Rev. Michael Place, Pres. & CEO; William J. Cox, Exec. Vice Pres.; Timothy J. Eckels, Sr. Vice Pres. Planning & Policy Devel.; Sr. Jean deBlois, C.S.J., Vice. Pres., Mission, Ethics & Pastoral Svcs.; David J. Sauer, Vice Pres. Admin. Svcs.; Brian F. Camey, Chief Financial Officer; J. Fred Caesar, Dir. Media Svcs.; Jack Bresch, Congressional & Exec. Liaison; Joanne Elden Beale, Co.-Dir. Sponsor Svcs.; Peter M. Leibold, Gen. Counsel; Susan Hume, Communications Services.

The Catholic Health Association of the United States is the national leadership organization of more than 1,200 Catholic healthcare sponsors, systems, facilities, and related organizations and services. Founded in 1915, CHA enables its members to accomplish collectively what they could not achieve individually. The association participates in the life of the Church by advancing the healthcare ministry and by asserting leadership within the Church and the rest of society through programs of advocacy, facilitation, and education. Presents Achievement Citation Award. Sponsors continuing education for healthcare personnel. Conducts surveys; compiles statistics. Divisions: Government Services; Administrative Services; IDN Services; Ministry Services; and Information Services.

Publications: 6 times-year, *Health Progress,* bimonthly, *Catholic Health World,* annual, *Guidebook of Catholic Health Care Facilities,* booklets, books & audio-visual on healthcare, Church-related subjects, CHA's Web Site, *CHA Online,* can be found at http:\\www.chausa.org.

Catholic Kolping Society of America (1849)—

9 East 8th St., Clifton, NJ 07011-1101. (Please direct all correspondence to the National Secretary.) Patricia Farkas, Natl. Sec.

The Society was founded by Rev. Adolph Kolping in Cologne, Germany, and established in the United States in 1856. The Catholic Kolping Society of America is a part of the world-wide Kolping movement and belongs to the International Kolping Society. There are 13 branches in principal cities of the United States with a combined membership of approximately 2,500. The membership is open to men and women of all ages. The Society's mission statement reads: We, the members of the Catholic Kolping Society of America, extend the vision of our founder, Blessed Adolph Kolping, by promoting the development of the individual and family; we foster a sense of belonging and friendship through our program of spiritual, educational, charitable and social activities.

Catholic Network Of Volunteer Service—

4121 Harewood Rd., N.E., Washington, DC 20017. Tel: 202-529-1100; 800-543-5046; Fax: 202-526-1094. Most Rev. John J. Snyder, Episcopal Advisor; James G. Lindsay, Exec. Dir.

National Office Team: Margaret Weeks; Mary Ellen Moore; Jean Newell; Linda Iekel; Jennifer L. Schumacher; Theresa Deere.

The Catholic Network of Volunteer Service promotes, recruits and refers volunteers to missions in the United States and overseas. We represent over 180 faith-based volunteer programs worldwide and work with the U.S. dioceses, religious communities and the private sector to determine their needs for help. The Catholic Network of Volunteer Service (CNVS) is committed to the goal that every Catholic man and woman be invited to consider a period of service in the missions, as a vital and important manifestation of the baptismal call of all Catholic people to missionary life. Currently, 5,500 men and women are serving in CNVS member mission programs offering their gifts and abilities in full-time service to people in need and living their Catholic faith more fully than many had imagined possible. These volunteers are serving domestically for a summer, six months, a year or more, and they are serving internationally for two or more years at a time. They are single and married, recent college graduates and early retirees, doctors and teachers, parish ministers and social workers, community organizers, computer operators, legal aides and more Gatherings: Annual Conference; Formation Workshops, Training Seminars.

Publications: annual, cir. 70,000, *The Response,* bi-weekly, *How Can I Help?,* quarterly, *Mission Handbook, Awards: The Father George Mader Award, given annually to honor organizations and individuals who promote the value of lay mission service.*

The Catholic Theological Society of America—

Ursuline College, 2550 Lander Rd., Pepper Pike, OH 44124. Tel: 440-646-8194; Fax: 216-752-5841. Mary Ann Donovan, Pres., Berkeley, CA; Robert Schreiter, Pres.-Elect, Chicago, IL; Margaret A. Farley, Vice Pres., New Haven, CT; Mary Ann Hinsdale, Sec., Worcester, MA; Roger McGrath, Treas., Baltimore, MD; William Thompson, Past Pres., Pittsburgh, PA; Board Members: Jeffrey Gros, Washington, DC; Diana L. Hayes, Washington, DC; James Pambrun, Ottawa, Ontario; Susan Secker, Seattle, WA; Dolores Christie, Exec. Sec., Pepper Pike, OH; Judith Dwyer, Editor of Proceedings, Staten Island, NY.

An association of professional theologians. Its purpose is to promote studies and research in theology within the Roman Catholic tradition, to relate theological science to current problems, and to foster a more effective theological education by providing a forum for an exchange of views among theologians and with scholars in other disciplines.

The Center For Human Development (1972)—

National Office: St. Joseph Abbey, Spencer, MA 01562. Tel: 508-885-8720.

The Center for Human Development is established to provide service and support to the people of God. To achieve this end, the Center designs and administers programs to foster the holistic spiritual growth and development of clergy, religious and laity.

Conference of Diocesan Coordinators of Health Affairs.

417 N. Main St., Davenport, IA 52801. Tel: 319-322-3303. Rev. James Conroy, Chm.

Membership in this Conference is by direct appointment and authority from the Ordinary of the appointee and gives members an opportunity of maintaining mutually helpful relationships with the Catholic Health Association, with one another, and with all religious, professional and governmental organizations in the health and hospital field.

The Conference of Major Religious Superiors of Men's Institutes of the United States, Inc.—

8808 Cameron St., Silver Spring, MD 20910. Tel: 301-588-4030; Fax: 301-587-4575. Rev. Steven Henrich, O.S.C., Exec. Dir.; Bro. John Klein, F.M.S., Pres.; Bro. Stephen Glodek, S.M., Vice Pres.; Rev. Dennis D. Thiessen, S.D.S., Sec. & Treas.

An association of the major superiors of religious communities and institutes of men for the purpose of promoting the spiritual and apostolic welfare of priests and brothers.

The Confraternity of Christian Doctrine, Inc.—

3211 Fourth St. N.E., Washington, DC 20017. Tel: 202-541-3098. Mary Sperry, Permissions Mgr.

The Confraternity is a distinct entity, separately incorporated and directed by a Board of Trustees from the United States Catholic Conference of Bishops. The purpose of the Corporation is to foster and promote the teachings of Christ as understood and handed down by the Roman Catholic Church. To this end it licenses religious and spiritual literature especially the Lectionary for Mass and the New American Bible, a translation made from the original languages in accordance with the papal encyclical "Divino Afflante Spiritu" of Pope Pius XII and a revision of the New Testament and the Revised Psalms of the New American Bible.

Council of Major Superiors of Women Religious in the United States of America—

4200 Harewood Rd. N.E., P.O. Box 4467, Washington, DC 20017-0467. Tel: 202-832-2575; Fax: 202-832-6325. Mother Mary Bernard Nettle, L.S.P., Chm. A canonically erected conference of Major Superiors of women's religious communities established in 1992 to promote mutual support among them and to foster coordination and cooperation with the Bishops' conference and individual Bishops, under the governance of the Holy See.

Federation of Diocesan Liturgical Commissions—

National Office, 401 Michigan Ave. N.E., P.O. Box 29039, Washington, DC 20017. Tel: 202-635-6990. Rev. Michael Spillane, Exec. Dir.; Rev. Edward J. Hislop, Chm.; Ms. Anne Grycz, Vice Chm.; Mr. David Reilly, Treas.; Rev. James Field, Delegate-at-Large; Ms. Carolyn Lassek, Delegate-at-Large.

The FDLC is a voluntary association of all diocesan liturgical commissions/offices from the United States. Two members of each diocesan liturgical commission/office serve as diocesan representatives to the FDLC. From this membership are elected 24 representatives (two from each of the 12 episcopal regions) to serve as the National Board of Directors. The day-to-day activities of the FDLC are directed by the Executive Director. The FDLC relates closely to the Bishops because its membership consists of their appointees. The Federation serves the Bishops and local commissions in matters of ongoing liturgical renewal. It also serves through education and other coordinated services requested by individual commissions or through consultation and voting at national meetings. The FDLC is organized and operated exclusively for religious and educational purposes.

Diocesan Fiscal Management Conference—

National Office, 1910 Indian Wood Cir., Ste. 111, Maumee, OH 43537-4029. Tel: 800-505-3362. Tel: 419-897-7916; Fax: 419-897-0888. Most Rev. Donald W. Trautman, S.T.D., S.S.L., Episcopal Moderator; Rev. Robert J. Yeager, Ed.D., Exec. Dir.; David Malanowski, Pres.; David Castilleja, Vice Pres.; John Wettach, Sec. & Treas.

Mindful of their special ministry in the Roman Catholic Church as the extension of the Diocesan Bishop in fiscal matters, the members of the

DFMC unite to be of service to the Church in the ministry of fiscal management. In particular, this organization promotes the spiritual growth of its members; promotes financial and administrative knowledge and expertise in service to the local and national Church; facilitates the free exchange of ideas and information, and serves as a liaison among the fiscal managers of the Dioceses and Archdioceses of the Church.

Instituto de Liturgia Hispana—

P.O. Box 29387, Washington, DC 20017-0387. Tel: 202-319-6450; Fax: 202-319-6449. Rev. Heliodoro Lucatero, Pres.; Ms. Sylvia Sanchez, Vice Pres.; Mrs. Maria Perez Rudisill, Sec.; Rev. Agustin Escalante, Treas.; Sr. Doris Mary Turek, S.S.N.D., Exec. Dir.

The Instituto is a national organization committed to meeting the liturgical needs of Hispanic Catholic communities. Its aim is to study, reflect and celebrate more authentically our Catholic faith from the perspective of our religious traditions and in the light of the teachings of the Church. Its members cooperate and assist in national, regional, diocesan, and parish groups with regard to Hispanic liturgical needs and concerns. They give lectures, publish in Spanish and in bilingual editions, and translate liturgical materials. Membership is open to all persons and institutions interested in liturgy. Committees: Art and Environment, Music, Popular Religiosity, Sacraments and Sacramentals, and Texts. The Instituto sponsors a national conference every two years on liturgical topics. The members meet annually.

International Catholic Migration Commission (ICMC) & ICMC, Inc.—

ICMC, Inc. Headquarters, 1319 F St. N.W., Washington, DC 20004. Michael Whiteley, Pres.; William A. Canny, Sec. Gen.

Provides technical assistance and coordination in area of service to migrants and refugees. Nonprofit New York Corporation.

Jesuit Conference, Inc.—

1616 P St., N.W., Washington, DC 20036-1405. Tel: 202-462-0400; Fax: 202-328-9212. Rev. Daniel C. McDonald, S.J., Exec. Sec. & Treas.

Ladies of Charity of the United States of America (LCUSA)—

910 Carnoustie Dr., Kansas City, MS 64145-1250. Mrs. John E. Hoag, Pres.; Most Rev. Paul Zipfel, Episcopal Chm. Spiritual Advisors: Revs. Fred Kammer, S.J.; Richard Gielow.

LCUSA Service Center, Ladies of Charity in the United States of America, whose 17,500 members give personal service to the needy, sick (especially the poor sick), underprivileged, handicapped and elderly, and also assist the clergy in pastoral care. They also strive for social justice. LCUSA encourages activities of the current Associations and promotes the organization of new Associations. The Board of Directors is the governing body of LCUSA. Organizational information is provided to members and Bishops through its official publication "Servicette," published four times annually and through contact with the President. National Biennial Meetings are held in even-numbered years and Regional Meetings are held in alternate years. They also affiliate with the Association of International Charities of St. Vincent de Paul (AIC). Ladies of Charity was founded in 1617 by St. Vincent de Paul and has continued in existence longer than any other church-oriented volunteer group of lay persons. They work closely with the Daughters of Charity.

Leadership Conference of Women Religious in the United States of America—

Office, 8808 Cameron St., Silver Spring, MD 20910. Tel: 301-588-4955; Fax: 301-587-4575. Sr. Mary Christine Fellerhoff, C.S.A., Exec. Dir.; Sr. Anne Munley, I.H.M., Past Pres.; Sr. Mary Waskowiak, R.S.M., Pres.; Sr. Camille D'Arienzo, R.S.M., Vice Pres.; Sr. Anne Finnerty, S.H.Sp., Sec.; Sr. Frances Mlocek, I.H.M., Treas.

An association of the major superiors of Religious Communities of Women for the purpose of promoting the spiritual and apostolic welfare of the Sisterhoods of the United States.

Lithuanian Roman Catholic Federation of America—

4545 W. 63rd St., Chicago, IL 60629. Tel: 312-585-9500. Most Rev. Paulius Baltakis, O.F.M., Episcopal Advisor; Rev. Msgr. Joseph Prunskis, Spiritual Advisor; Saulius V. Kuprys, Pres., 150 S. Wacker Dr., Ste. 1050, Chicago, IL 60606. Tel: 312-346-5275; 708-243-0416; Fax: 312-346-5640; 708-243-0418.

A not-for-profit corporation founded in 1906 in Wilkes-Barre, PA, to promote and coordinate religious, educational and charitable activities among Lithuanian American Catholics, their organizations, institutions, religious communities, and parishes (for detailed information regarding religious institutions please refer to the Apostolate for Lithuanians).

Mariological Society of America (1949)—

Secretariat: Marian Library, University of Dayton, Dayton, OH 45469-1390. Tel: 937-229-4294; Fax: 937-229-4258. Rev. Thomas A. Thompson, S.M., Exec. Sec.; Most Rev. Austin B. Vaughan, Episcopal Chm.

The objects and purposes of this organization are to promote interest and research in the theology of the Virgin Mary. Professional and associate membership. Proceedings of annual meeting published in Marian Studies. Annual convention in late May or early June.

The Mexican American Cultural Center (1972)—

3019 West French Pl., San Antonio, TX 78228. Tel: 210-732-2156. Most Rev. Patrick F. Flores, Chm.; Sr. Maria Elena Gonzalez, R.S.M., Pres.

The Mexican American Cultural Center (MACC) is a National Catholic Institute for Pastoral Leadership and Language Studies for Hispanic ministry. MACC researches and responds to the religious and social needs of the Hispanic community in light of the Gospel and the social teachings of the Roman Catholic Church in light of the Gospel. MACC programs include: *Hispanic Pastoral Ministry:* A program that offers a creative response to the need for preparation for U.S. Hispanic ministry. Dates: January-April and September-December. *Mini-Pastoral:* An intense three-week preparation to meet the challenges of U.S. Hispanic ministry. Dates: January (in English), June (in English), July (in Spanish), and August (in English). Intensive Pastoral Spanish: A language program that concentrates on the needs of persons engaged in Hispanic ministry. *Intensive Pastoral English* for those whose first language is other than English; Cooperative Seminary Program, Masters degree in cooperation with Universities throughout the United States; Workshops and Weeks of Study. By Request, MACC faculty members serve dioceses, parishes and other groups by offering courses and workshops throughout the United States.

National Apostolate with People with Mental Retardation (1968)—

Mailing Address, 4516 30th Street, N.W., Washington, DC 20008. Tel: 800-736-1280; Fax: 202-686-6716. Dr. Michela M. Perrone, Exec. Dir.

Established in 1968 to promote the full participation and inclusion of Catholics with mental retardation in the life of their church community.

Publications: quarterly journal; newsletter; pamphlets; training materials.

The National Association of Religious Brothers—

National Office, 1337 W. Ohio St., Chicago, IL 60622-6490. Tel: 312-829-8525; Fax: 312-829-8915. Bros. Gerald Meegan, S.D.B., Pres.; Thomas J. Sullivan, F.S.C., Past Pres.; Dennis Wermert, S.C., Vice Pres.; Aquin Gauthier, S.C., Treas.; John Louis Collignon, S.C., Sec.; Sr. Emily Wollschlager, S.S.N.D., Exec. Sec.

The National Association of Religious Brothers is a membership organization of brothers from all religious orders in the U.S., Canada and around the world.

Publications: bi-monthly, *Brothers' Voice.*

National Assembly of Religious Women (NARW)—

National Office, 529 S. Wabash, Rm. 404, Chicago, IL 60605. Tel: 312-663-1980; Fax: 312-663-9161. Sr. Judith Vaughan, C.S.J., Natl. Coord.

A grassroots organization of Catholic women with a commitment to work inclusively for systemic change. NARW members commit themselves to a Ministry of Justice by the continuous use of their organized power for the liberation of all peoples from oppression; to work actively to promote respect for and dignity of all, and to ensure effective participation of people in decisions which affect their own lives. Their challenging and supportive action is based on Gospel values. NARW publishes books, periodicals, and other educational materials; sponsors training conferences and workshops; and collaborates with groups addressing similar issues, particularly but not exclusively, those of justice for women in society, the Church and the world.

National Association of African American Catholic Deacons, Inc.—

4323 Chaplin St. N.E., Washington, DC 20019. Tel: 202-575-1296; Fax: 202-678-3325. Deacon John P. Stewart, Pres.

National Association of Catholic Chaplains—

National Office, 3501 South Lake Dr., Milwaukee, WI 53207. Tel: 414-483-4898; Fax: 414-483-6712. Most Rev. Thomas Kelly, O.P., Episcopal Advisor; Sr. Monica Lucas, S.C., Pres.; Rev. Stephen R. Ryan, O.S.M., Pres.-Elect; Rev. Joseph J. Driscoll, Exec. Dir.

The purpose of this organization is to assist priests, religious, and lay institutional and parish professionals to attain the realization of progressively higher ideals and professional competency for ministry in specialized works and settings. Membership includes those who minister to the sick and dying, the mentally retarded, the aged, the incarcerated and confined; the families of the above and all who are a part of the faith and/or service communities in which the members serve in both public and private institutions. Certification as Chaplain and Supervisor is granted. Continuing education programs are presented on a national and a regional basis. The regions are coterminus with the Bishops' regions. Local associations are also encouraged.

Publications: 10 times-year, journal-newsletter, *Vision.*

The National Association of Catholic Family Life Ministers—

Univ. of Dayton, 300 College Park, Dayton, OH 45469-2512. Kay Ryan, C.S.J., Pres.; Pat McCarthy, Sec.

The National Association of Church Personnel Administrators (NACPA)—

Headquarters, 100 E. Eighth St., Cincinnati, OH 45202. Tel: 513-421-3134; Fax: 513-421-3085. Ms. Linda Bearie, Pres.; Sr. Ann White, S.L., Exec. Dir.

The National Association of Church Personnel Administrators (NACPA) is a membership association of lay, religious and clergy Personnel Directors, Assistant Directors, and Personnel Board Members serving dioceses, religious congregations and other church-related institutions. The purpose of the Association is to identify skills and competencies for human resource managers, develop personnel systems which integrate management and pastoral values, and advocate standards of just treatment for Church Personnel.

National Association of Deacon Organizations—

4410 89th St., Kenosha, WI 53142. Tel: 414-694-9143. Deacon Ron Lesjak, Pres.

National Association of Diocesan Directors of Campus Ministry—

6 Madbury Rd.-P.O. Box 620, Durham, NH 03824-0620. Tel: 603-862-1310. Rev. Frederick J. Pennett, Jr., Pres.

National Association of Diocesan Ecumenical Officers (NADEO)—

462 N. Taylor, St. Louis, MO 63108. Tel: 314-531-9700; Fax: 314-531-2269. Rev. Vincent A. Heier, Pres.; Mrs. Garland Pohl, Vice Pres.; Rev. Lawrence J. McNeil, Treas.; Deacon Thomas McGowan, Sec.

The purposes of NADEO are to stimulate an exchange of ideas, experiences and evaluations among the ecumenical officers of the (Arch)Dioceses in union with Rome; to promote programs which further the work of Christian unity and of interreligious cooperation; and to cooperate with the Bishops' Committee for Ecumenical and Interreligious Affairs of the National Conference of Catholic Bishops, and with other ecumenical and interreligious agencies.

Publications: quarterly Newsletter; annual booklets on various ecumenical topics, *Handbook for Catholic Ecumenical Officers.*

National Association of the Holy Name Society (1970)—

Office of Communications, P.O. Box 1292, Baltimore, MD 21281-2012. Most Rev. Michael A. Saltarelli, Episcopal Moderator, Newark, NJ; Rev. Thomas Dzurenda, National Spiritual Dir., Metuchen, NJ, Aaron X. Gilyard, Pres., New Orleans, LA, Felix Ad Sablad, Newsletter Editor, San Francisco, CA; Deacon Stephen Andrussian, Supply Officer, Minersville, PA.

Association of parochial and diocesan Holy Name units of the International Society, established to promote reverence for the Divine Name of Jesus and for the sanctification of its members through spiritual and social action programs.

National Association of Pastoral Musicians—
National Office, 225 Sheridan St. N.W., Washington, DC 20011. Tel: 202-723-5800; Fax: 202-723-2262. Rev. Virgil C. Funk, Exec. Dir.

A national membership organization for the improvement of music within the parish, with special emphasis on liturgical music. Membership includes parish musicians and parish clergy simultaneously, with a unique interest in the practical issues facing the practicing musician and parish clergy.

Publications: six times a year with membership, *Pastoral Music,* bi-monthly with membership, *Pastoral Music Notebook.*

Services: NPM Conventions—national and regional gatherings for clergy and musicians. Director of Music Ministries Division (DMMD)—division for members who are full-time, salaried music staff in a parish or diocese and have responsibility for managing the overall liturgical music program. NPM-ME—division for music educators working in Catholic schools. NPM Hotline assists musicians seeking positions, and parishes looking for musicians. Resources for Association members are issued under the name, NPM Publications. NPM Board and NPM Council: Dr. J. Michael McMahon, Chm. The Association has Sections for Clergy, Choir Directors, Organists, Cantors, Seminary Music Educators, Military Musicians, Campus Ministers, Young Musicians, Hispanic Musicians and Musicians serving African-American parishes. The NPM Council provides committee leadership in each of these areas. National Training programs: annually, for Choir Directors, Organists, Guitarists and Cantors with emphasis on developing musical skills, leadership abilities and ministerial skills.

National Association of Diaconate Directors (1977)—
National Office, 1204 N. Church St., Rockford, IL 61103. Tel: 815-965-5837. Deacon Thomas C. Welch, Exec. Dir.; Deacon Maury Reed, Pres.; Deacon Peter D'Heilly, Pres. Elect.

Directors, vicars of deacons, and others responsible for the formation of candidates and the ongoing growth and development of deacons in the U.S. Promotes communication and facilitates the exchange of information and resources among members. Seeks to develop professional expertise among members through research, dialogue, formation and self-evaluation procedures. Proposes ways and means for effective implementation of solutions to national and regional issues relating to the diaconate. Maintains library on related issues.

National Black Catholic Clergy Caucus—
Office, 343 N. Walnut St., P.O. Box 1088, Opelousas, LA 70571-1088. Tel: 318-942-2481; Fax: 318-942-9201. Rev. Albert J. McKnight, C.S.Sp., Exec. Dir.

National Catholic Cemetery Conference—
National Office, 710 North River Rd., Des Plaines, IL 60016. Tel: 708-824-8131. Mrs. Irene K. Pesce, Exec. Dir.; Most Rev. G. Patrick Ziemann, D.D., Episcopal Moderator.

The Conference is an organization of Diocesan Directors of Cemeteries and parish cemetery administrators from throughout the United States and Canada. Guided by the principle: "That burial of the dead is one of the Corporal Works of Mercy," the Conference promotes high standards of Catholic cemetery management, development, operation and maintenance consistent with Christian service to the Catholic community; and fosters and promotes the religious, charitable and educational interests of Catholic cemeteries and the people they serve.

Publications: monthly magazine, *Catholic Cemetery,* various booklets on cemetery management & evaluation service; funeral liturgy at the cemetery. Annual Convention.

National Catholic Conference of Airport Chaplains (NCCAC)—
Mailing Address, P.O. Box 2220, Newark, NJ 07114. Tel: 973-961-0260; Fax: 973-961-0260. Rev. David J. Baratelli, Pres., (Newark International Airport); Rev. James T. Devine, Vice Pres., (Kennedy International Airport); Deacon James A. O'Malley, Treas., (Chicago O'Hare International Airport); Deacon Donald A. Kelsey, Sec., (Atlanta Hartsfield International Airport); Most Rev. James C. Timlin, Bishop of Scranton, Episcopal Liaison.

This Conference provides support and communication for all Catholics performing pastoral ministry to airport & airline workers, and travelers; in affiliation with the Bishop's Committee on Migration of the National Conference of Catholic Bishops.

National Catholic Conference for Seafarers—
221 20th St., Galveston, TX 79550. Tel: 409-762-0026; Fax: 409-763-8112. Mrs. Karen Lai, Pres.; Mrs. Alice Charlotte Smith, Vice Pres.; Bro. Hugh Maguire, Sec.; Rev. James P. Keating, Treas.

An association of Chaplains, Seafarers and laity serving in the pastoral care of seafarers in the ports of the U.S. in affiliation with the Apostleship of the Sea in the United States.

National Catholic Committee on Scouting Executive Committee (1934)—
1325 W. Walnut Hill Lane, P.O. Box 152079, Irving, TX 75015-2079; Fax: 972-580-2502. Most Rev. Gerald A. Gettelfinger, Bishop of Evansville, IN, Episcopal Advisor; Robert Oldowski, Chm., (Bloomington, MN), Thomas T. Nishikubo, Vice Chm., (Gardena, CA), Joseph DeStefano, Vice Chm., (Providence, RI), John Ribar, Vice Chm., (Louisville, KY), Al Feliksa, Vice Chm., (St. Ignace, MI), Jack Deckenbach, Vice Chm., (Minneapolis, MN), Eleanore P. Starr, Admin. Sec., (Irving, TX); Revs. Dennis O'Rourke, Natl. Chap., (Scottsdale, AZ), Donald Hummerl, Assoc. Chap., (Westfield, NJ), Randy Cuevas, Past Natl. Chap., (Donaldson, IN).

A voluntary organization of clergy and laymen, members include a chaplain and lay chairman from all of the dioceses in the United States Conferences. It serves as an advisory committee to the Boy Scouts of America. It has the responsibility of promoting and guiding cooperative contracts between the proper authorities of the Catholic Church in the United States and the Boy Scouts of America.

National Catholic Conference for Total Stewardship, Inc. (NCCTS)—
Mailing Address, 1633 N. Cleveland Ave., Chicago, IL 60614. Tel: 773-363-8046; 800-572-CCLO (2250); Fax: 773-363-2123. Rev. Francis A. Novak, C.SS.R., Pres.; Margaret Ann Filipovich, Admin. Asst.

The goal of this organization is to provide parishes and dioceses with a Total Stewardship Process called THE CHRISTIAN CELEBRATION OF LIFE (CCL), an integrated, comprehensive, systematically carried out formation of laity and clergy in Evangelization, Discipleship and Stewardship. The NCCTS achieves its goal by conducting Schools of Evangelization in dioceses and parishes and on the Internet for clergy, religious and laity and by working with them to implement the CCL in the local church. Implementation takes place on three levels: 1) Information on the CCL for in-place *Leadership,* clergy and laity; 2)Formation in the CCL for both parish leadership and newly recruited lay leaders called the *Matrix and Associate Matrices* (Small Faith Communities); 3) Transformation of church-going people into responsible Stewards of their Gifts, who reach out to non-church-going people by Home Visitation and Evangelization to build up the faith community. Transformation climaxes with *Stewardship of Eucharist* in order to deepen belief in and love of the Holy Eucharist, the fountain and summit of holiness. Under the title *Giving in Thanksgiving,* tithing is introduced as an "act of worship" within the liturgy. The CCL is also a perfect instrument for implementing the Holy Father's universal plan of preparation of the Church for the Great Jubilee Year 2000.

National Catholic Council on Alcoholism and Related Drug Problems, Inc.—
Headquarters, 1550 Hendrickson St., Brooklyn, NY 11234-3514. Tel: 718-951-7177; Fax: 718-951-7233. Mr. Richard K. Frisch, Exec. Dir.; Rev. Msgr. Kieran Martin, Sec. & Treas.; His Eminence Anthony Cardinal Bevilacqua, Episcopal Moderator.

N.C.C.A. is an agency of the Church which is dedicated to the promotion of adequate treatment for all clergy, men and women religious, and laity who are suffering from alcoholism and other drug dependencies. N.C.C.A. also provides educational programs, especially through and an annual symposium and publication of the Blue Book, to reach all those engaged in pastoral ministry and (or) education concerning the problems associated with the use, misuse and abuse of alcohol and other drugs in our society.

National Catholic Development Conference (1968)—
86 Front St., Hempstead, NY 11550. Tel: 516-481-6000. Rev. Charles F. Shelby, C.M., Chm.; Mr. William J. Nixon, Vice Chm.; Ms. Carmelita Linden, Sec.; Sr. Ladonna Kassmeyer, F.S.P.A., Treas.; Mr. George T. Holloway, Pres.

Members, of one of the nation's largest association of religious fund raising organizations, include religious orders, colleges, high schools, hospitals, Catholic social service organizations and other institutions engaged in raising funds to support their activities. The function of the NCDC is to assist its members in developing effective, professional, ethical methods of raising funds. Members of the NCDC have subscribed to a code of ethics called Precepts of Stewardship. The national office serves as a center of information, issues special interest bulletins, conducts an annual conference and numerous seminars, workshops and regional meetings, maintains a library, follows and reports on legislative matters, conducts a special public information program, Giving is an Act of Faith, and maintains relations with a number of associations and organizations in related fields.

Publications: *Dimensions, Fund Raising Forum, Member Exchange,* frequently issued, *Monitor* on postal, regulatory and tax issues, A Guide for Preparing a Statement of Accountability.

National Catholic Educational Association (1904)—
National Headquarters, 1077-30th St. N.W., Ste. 100, Washington, DC 20007. Tel: 202-337-6232; Fax: 202-333-6706. Most Rev. John J. Leibrecht, D.D., Chm.; Dr. Leonard DeFiore, Pres.

The National Catholic Educational Association (NCEA) has been providing leadership and service to American Catholic educators since 1904. NCEA's institutional and individual memberships represent Catholic education at all levels and in a variety of settings: preschools, elementary and secondary schools, parish catechetical/religious education programs, diocesan offices, colleges, universities and seminaries. The Association advances the educational and catechetical mission of the Church; provides leadership and service to its members; articulates the contribution of Catholic education to the Church and society; proclaims the uniqueness of Catholic schools; advocates recognition of and support for Catholic education in parish, school, college and university communities; enhances and supports leadership among the members; and fosters local, national and international collaboration

National Catholic Office for the Deaf (1971)—
NCOD Office, 7202 Buchanan St., Landover Hills, MD 20784-2236. Tel: 301-577-1684 (Voice); 301-577-4184 (TTY only); Fax: 301-577-1690. Nora Letourneau, Exec. Dir.

The NCOD, established by the Catholic pastoral workers of the deaf in 1971 at Trinity College, Washington, DC is devoted to coordinating the Church's pastoral ministry to deaf and hard-of-hearing persons at the national level; developing special liturgies, catechetical texts and materials; organizing workshops, leadership programs, cursillos and marriage encounters, and national and regional pastoral workers meetings; coordinating a training program for ministers with the deaf; and serving as an information and referral center for all those involved in this special ministry as well as members of the deaf community and their families. Policy is established by a board of directors elected by the members.

Publications: pastoral journal, *Vision,* newsletter for members, *RADAR.*

National Catholic Office for Persons with Disabilities (NCPD) (1982)—
P.O. Box 29113, Washington, DC 20017. Tel: 202-529-2933 (TT-voice); Fax: 202-529-4678. Mary Jane Owen, Exec. Dir.; Sr. Bernadette Downes, C.I.J., Chm.

Established to implement the Bishops' Statement on ministry with persons with disabilites. Prime concern is the establishment of Diocesan offices, support and education of newly appointed personnel, collaborating with other national Catholic organizations relative to the need for inclusion of disability perspectives in their programs, and advocacy in religious and secular concerns. Provides training, national conferences, resources, in cooperation with other national organizations concerned with ministry in the area of disabilities.

National Catholic Rural Life Conference—
National Headquarters, 4625 Beaver Ave., Des Moines, IA 50310-2199. Tel: 515-270-2634; Fax: 515-270-9447. Bro. David G. Andrews, Esq., C.S.C., Exec. Dir.; Most Rev. Raymond Burke, Bishop of La-Crosse, Pres. of the Bd. of Directors of the National Catholic Rural Life Conference.

The National Catholic Rural Life Conference is a membership organization grounded in a spiritual tradition which brings together the Church, care for creation and care for community. The NCRLC fosters programs of direct service and systemic change. As an educator in the faith, the NCRLC seeks to relate religion to the rural world; develops support services for rural pastoral ministers; serves as a prophetic voice and as a catalyst and convener for social justice.

National Catholic Stewardship Council, Inc.
National Office, 1275 K St. N.W., Ste. 980, Washington, DC 20005. Tel: 202-289-1093; Fax: 202-682-9018. Most Rev. James P. Keleher, S.T.D.,

Archbishop of Kansas City, KS, Episcopal Moderator; Mr. Matthew R. Paratore, Natl. Dir.

The Stewardship Council promotes the concept of holistic Christian stewardship. It serves dioceses, parishes, professional firms, religious congregations, Catholic colleges/universities and Catholic associations from the U.S., Canada and the Caribbean through its seminars, summer institute, publications and annual international conference. It encourages the growing professionalism of diocesan development procedures and programs directed toward improving the long-term growth of diocesan funds. It also fosters the development of parish-centered stewardship programs aimed at increasing monies and personal service on the basis of the principles of stewardship as outlined in the 1992 NCCB Pastoral Letter: *Stewardship: A Disciple's Response.*

Publications: newsletter, *Commitment,* journal, *Resource,* guide for pastoral leaders, *Stewardship: Disciples Respond,* publications available for parish and diocesan use through, Liturgical Press; *Stewardship Kit, For a complete list of services and publications contact the National Office. Membership information available on request.*

National Catholic Student Coalition (1988)—
6801 N. Yates Rd.-Box 90A, Milwaukee, WI 53217. Tel: 414-410-4251; Fax: 414-410-4252. Ms. Sarah LaPlante, Exec. Dir.

The National Catholic Student Coalition (NCSC) is a national coalition of Catholic student communities in institutes of higher education. The coalition provides a platform for Catholic students to reflect, speak, and act on issues within the university, the Church and society. The NCSC promotes the development of campus ministry and Catholic lay and religious leaders for the Church and society. The NCSC is a member of the International Movement of Catholic Students. Membership is open to groups or individuals associated with Catholic student groups in higher education. The NCSC holds an annual leadership conference.

Publications: *The Catholic Collegian.*

The National Center for Urban Ethnic Affairs (1971)—
National Office, P.O. Box 20, Cardinal Station, Washington, DC 20064. Tel: 202-232-3600; 635-5128. Dr. John A. Kromkowski, Pres.; Rev. George F. McLean, Sec.; Rev. Msgr. Salvatore Polizzi, Chm.; Ruth Dee, Treas.

"The great task incumbent on all men of good will is to restore the relations of the human family in truth, in justice, in love, and in freedom." (Pope John XXIII, *Peace on Earth.*) The independent program of this non-profit organization has evolved from the efforts initiated by the former Task Force on Urban Problems of the United States Catholic Conference. Its aims and purposes are to continue the expression of the Catholic Church's concern for the problems facing our urban society. NCUEA promotes the celebration of cultural pluralism in America and bridges the gaps between groups of various ethnic and cultural traditions. The Center disseminates information, conducts research, develops and supports programs concerned with ethnic Americans and urban society. The Center in association with various community and church groups develops workshops, conferences and programs related to the quality of human life, national priorities and the development of an urban mission strategy. The Center is also associated with public and private agencies in developing urban economic, social, and intercultural programs, etc.

The National Conference of Catechetical Leadership (NCCL)—
3021 Fourth St. N.E., Washington, DC 20017-1102. Tel: 202-636-3826; Fax: 202-832-2712. Most Rev. Sylvester Ryan, Episcopal Moderator; Mr. Dan Kurre, Pres.; Mr. Neil Parent, Exec. Dir.

A voluntary organization composed of diocesan catechetical personnel, including vicars and secretaries of education, catechetical office directors and staff; academics specializing in religious education; representatives of diocesan parish DRE organizations and various associate and affiliated members, including publishers of catechetical texts. The Conference operates on three levels: national, regional and provincial. The purpose of the Conference is to assist its members in their roles as leaders in the Church's catechetical ministry through networking, resource development, research, training, consultation and advocacy. The Conference is also committed to collaboration with other national groups concerned with catechesis/religious education.

National Council for Catholic Evangelization (1983)—
905 E. 166th St., P.O. Box 1260, South Holland, 60473-2420 22111. Tel: 1-800-786-NCCE. Ms. Gloria Clark, Pres., Lafayette, LA; Sr. Priscilla Lemire, R.J.M., Vice Pres., San Diego, CA; Sr. Louise Alff, F.M.D.C., Sec., Buffalo, NY; Bro. Douglas Zlatis, C.F.C., Treas., Lisle, IL; Mr. John Simon, Exec. Dir., South Holland, IL; Most Rev. Michael J. Sheehan, Episcopal Liaison, Albuquerque, NM.

Established at the request of the Bishops' Committee on Evangelization, NCCE is an independent membership association which brings together (Arch)Dioceses, organizations, religious congregations, parishes and individuals to promote evangelization as the primary and essential mission of the Church. NCCE sponsors an Annual Conference and Evangelization Training Workshops and Seminars.

Publications: ten issues a year, *Newsletter; Resource Review, Resources: printed materials, audio and video tapes. Memberships are available to (Arch)Dioceses, religious congregations, organizations, parishes and individuals.*

National Council of the Catholic Men—
5664 Midforest Ln., Cincinnati, OH 45233. Mr. Fred Niehaus, Pres.

The NCCM, a federation of Catholic organizations of men, has pioneered in promoting parish councils and diocesan renewal.

National Council of Catholic Women—
1275 K St. N.W., Ste. 975, Washington, DC 20005. Tel: 202-682-0334; Fax: 202-682-0338. Joann Hillebrand, Pres.; Annette Kane, Exec. Dir.

The NCCW is a federation of Catholic women's organizations in the United States, numbering 7,000 local, diocesan and national organizations. It programs through its six commissions, Church, Family Concerns, Community Concerns, International Concerns, Legislation and Organization. The program of the Council is furthered through leadership training institutes and national conventions.

Publications: bimonthly, *Catholic Woman.*

National Federation of Catholic Physicians' Guilds (1932)—
850 Elm Grove Rd., Elm Grove, WI 53122. Tel: 414-784-3435; Fax: 414-782-8788.

Officers 1996-1997: Michael V. Rock, M.D., Pres., Paradise Valley, AZ, Paul A. Byrne, M.D., Pres.-Elect, Toledo, OH, Richard A. Watson, M.D., Vice Pres., Mountainside, NJ, Michael R. Aiello, M.D., Sec., Rochester, NY, Charles P. Prezzia M.D., Treas., Holland, OH; Most. Rev. Edwin O'Brien, S.T.D. D.D., Episcopal Advisor, Yonkers, NY, Robert H. Herzog, Exec. Dir.; Michael J. Herzog, Asst. Dir.

Directors:

Region I: John A. Roque, M.D., 1997, Saunderstown, RI, E. Joanne Angelo, M.D., 1998, Cambridge, MA.

Region II: Michael R. Aiello, M.D., 1997, Rochester, NY, Alfred W. Murphy, M.D., 1998, White Plains, NY.

Region III: Larry Lyons, M.D., 1997, N. Huntington, PA, John D. Lane, M.D., 1998, Philadelphia, PA.

Region IV: Dennis M. Doody, M.D., 1997, Columbus, OH, Felino Barnes, M.D., 1998, Zanesville, OH.

Region V: Robert J. Saxer, M.D., 1997, Ft. Walton Beach, FL, Patrick Mongan, M.D., 1998, Augusta, GA.

Region VI: Albert E. Gunn, M.D., 1997, Houston, TX.

Region VII: Donald J. Mehan, M.D., 1997, St. Louis, MO, Patrick D. Guinan, M.D., 1998, Chicago, IL.

Region VIII: John I. Lane, M.D., 1998, Great Falls, MT.

Region IX: Robert Hurt, M.D., 1997, Phoenix, AZ, William A. Brophy, M.D., 1998, Phoenix, AZ.

Region X: Thomas M. Goodwin, M.D., 1997, Monrovia, CA, Stephen G. Watson, M.D., 1998, Van Nuys, CA.

Military Guild: Richard A. Watson, M.D., 1998, Mountainside, NJ.

Upholding the principles of the Catholic faith and morality as related to the science and practice of medicine.

National Federation for Catholic Youth Ministry, Inc. (NFCYM) (1981)—
3700-A Oakview Terr. N.E., Washington, DC 20017-2591. Tel: 202-636-3825. Mr. Robert J. McCarty, Exec. Dir.; Ms. Nancy Werner, Chm.; Ms. Kathleen Carver, Assoc. Dir.; Ms. Therese Brown, Assoc. Dir.; Ruby Mikell, Admin. Asst.; Jane Parvis, Sec.

A membership association of diocesan youth offices, founded after a reorganization of the USCC Department of Education and the National CYO Federation (now defunct). The stated purpose is "In light of the Gospel message, the Federation will foster the development of youth ministry in the United States to, with, by, and for youth." Members of the Federation work through diocesan, regional and national structures to provide national leadership, support and direction for adults and youth in youth ministry. The biennial National Conference on Catholic Youth Ministry (a conference for adults working with youth); the biennial National Catholic Youth Conference (for teenagers and their adult chaperones); the writing and distributing of resource booklets for parish workers; religious recognitions for Catholic Girl Scouts/Camp Fire; position papers on current topics and issues in youth ministry; and regional and diocesan consultations.

National Foundation for Catholic Youth—
3700-A Oakview Terr., Washington, DC 20017. Tel: 202-636-3825. Mr. Robert J. McCarty, Exec. Dir.; Mrs. Irene Friend, Pres. of Board; His Eminence John Cardinal O'Connor, Honorary Pres.

National Office for Black Catholics (1972)—
The Paulist Center, 3025 Fourth St. N.E., Washington, DC 20017. Tel: 202-635-1778. Walter T. Hubbard, Exec. Dir.

The National Office for Black Catholics, organized in 1970, is a central agency with the general purpose of promoting active and full participation by Black Catholics in the Church and of making more effective the presence and ministry of the Church in the Black community. Its operations support the aspirations of Black Catholics for objectives that include: representation and voice among Bishops and other leaders of the Church; promotion of vocations to the priesthood and religious life; sponsorship of programs of evangelization, pastoral ministry, education and liturgy on national and regional levels; recognition of Black heritage in liturgy, community life, theology and education; and establishment of an Institute for Leadership Training Formation and Development.

National Organization for Continuing Education of Roman Catholic Clergy, Inc—
1337 W. Ohio St., Chicago, IL 60622-6490. Tel: 312-226-1890; Fax: 312-829-8915. Rev. Francis S. Tebbe, O.F.M., Pres.; Bro. Paul J. Murray, C.F.X., Exec. Dir.

A professional organization of those involved in the continuing education/formation of priests in the Catholic Church. Dioceses and religious communities in the U.S. are full members. Institutions and organizations that are concerned with continuing education/formation of priests are associate members. Dioceses and provinces outside the U.S. may be associate members. NOCERCC was founded in 1973 through the efforts of the National Federation of Priests Councils. It is governed by a Board of Directors that involves a president elected by the membership, elected members from the 13 NCCB Regions and two elected religious members. Its services include an Annual Convention, training for new and experienced directors, regional meetings, consultations and service to regional and interdiocesan programs.

Publications: *NewsNotes, Sabbatical Programs,* Handbook for Continuing Formation of Priests, other print and video resources.

National Pastoral Center for the Chinese Apostolate, Inc.—
234 Fairview Ave., Paramus, NJ 07652. Tel: 201-634-0709; Fax: 201-634-0801. Rev. Joseph Chiang, Dir.

National Pastoral Life Center—
Headquarters, 18 Bleecker St., New York, NY 10012-2404. Tel: 212-431-7825; Fax: 212-274-9786. Rev. Philip J. Murnion, Dir.; Ms. Karen Sue Smith, Editorial Dir.; Donna Ciangio, O.P., Project Dir.

The Center is an information, training, and consulting resource for diocesan and parish leaders. The Center works with bishops and diocesan directors as consultants for diocesan evaluation and reorganization and conducts and staffs educational and training programs for pastors and others in ministry. It also sponsors pastoral ministry conventions, conducts pastoral research, and serves as a resource and referral center for church ministers.

Publications: magazine and, *Church,* Center Papers and other publications.

North American Pastoral Center for Czech Catholics—
c/o St. Norbert Catholic Church, 300 E. Taft Ave., Orange, CA 92865-4388. Tel: 714-998-0251; Fax: 714-637-0201. Rev. Msgr. Peter Esterka, Pres.

The Papal Foundation—
Office, 222 North 17th St., Philadelphia, PA 19103. Tel: 215-587-2491. Rev. Msgr. Thomas J. Benestad, Exec. Dir. Board of Trustees; John Cardinal O'Connor, Chm.; Anthony Cardinal Bevilacqua, Vice Chm.; John Cardinal Carberry; Bernard Cardinal Law; James Cardinal Hickey; Roger Cardinal Mahony; William Cardinal Keeler; Adam Cardinal Maida. Trustees: Most Rev. Theodore E. McCarrick, Pres.; Mr. Arthur Birtcher; Mr. Geoffrey T. Boisi; Mr. John Brennan; Mr. William F. Connell; Most Rev. Thomas V. Daily; Mr. Thomas J. Flatley; Most Rev. Harry J. Flynn; His Eminence Francis

Cardinal George, O.M.I.; Most Rev. Charles V. Grahmann; Mr. E. F. Hansen; Most Rev. William J. Levada; Mr. Frank J. Lynch; Mr. William A. McIntosh; Mr. Thomas S. Monaghan; Mr. Robert J. Morrissey; Mr. Frank Pasquerilla; Mr. Gerald A. Rauenhorst; Most Rev. Justin Regali; Mr. John Saeman; Most Rev. Francis B. Schulte; Mr. Francis J. Sehn; Mr. Daniel J. Donohue, Trustee Emeritus.

The Parish Evaluation Project—
O'Hare Lake Office Plaza, 2200 E. Devon, Ste. 283, Des Plaines, IL 60018. Tel: 847-297-2080; Fax: 847-297-2107. Rev. Thomas P. Sweetser, S.J., Dir.; Ms. Mary Beth Vogel, Assoc. Dir.

The Parish Evaluation Project is a non-profit organization under the laws of Illinois, whose purpose is to provide religious and educational services to Catholic parishes in the United States in the areas of surveying, needs assessment, leadership skills, goal setting, evaluation techniques, staff development, pastoral council formation and other resources helpful in parish planning and renewal.

Pax Christi U.S.A., National Catholic Peace Movement—
532 W. 8th St., Erie, PA 16502-1343. Tel: 814-453-4955; Fax: 814-452-4784. Mr. Etienne de'Jonghe, Intl. Sec.; Most Rev. Walter F. Sullivan, Pres.; Colleen McHenry-Connell, Chm.; Ligory Fernandes, Treas.; Most Rev. Thomas J. Gumbleton.

Pax Christi has as its primary objective to work with all people for peace for all humankind, always witnessing to the peace of Christ. The Movement springs from a gospel vision of peace. It asks its members to ground their peacemaking in prayer, study and action on the message of Jesus. Pax Christi keeps as its priorities the Christian vision of spirituality, nonviolence and peacemaking, disarmament, demilitarization, reconciliation with justice, human rights and global restoration, and economic and interracial justice in the United States.

Publications: quarterly newspaper and peace education materials.

Religious Formation Conference—
National Office, 8820 Cameron St., Silver Spring, MD 20910-4152. Tel: 301-588-4938; Fax: 301-585-7649. Sr. Janet Mock, C.S.J., Exec. Dir.; Sr. Clare D'Auria, O.S.F., Assoc. Dir. Board Co-Chm.: Sr. Dorothy Batto, C.C.V.I.; Sr. Lyn Symkiewicz, C.S.J.

An association of women and men Religious engaged in Initial and On- going Formation ministry in their Communities. The Conference, through its National Office and Regional Conferences, seeks to be a forum for exchange and a center for communication and the sharing of resources.

Retreats International, Inc.—
National Office, Box 1067, Notre Dame, IN 46556. Tel: 219-631-5320; Fax: 219-631-6968. Rev. Thomas W. Gedeon, S.J., Dir.; Most Rev. Robert Morneau, Bishop Advisor; Sr. Mary Elizabeth Imler, O.S.F., Pres.; Ms. Geri Eitter, Vice Pres.; Mr. Tom Grant, Sec. & Treas. Trustees: Sr. Catherine Cahill, O.S.F.; Ms. Mary Ann Lewis; Sr. Marion Renkens, C.S.J.; Mr. Richard Wray; Rev. Ted Haag, O.F.M.

Created in 1928 under the guidance of the Archbishops and Bishops of the United States. The national headquarters for information and all phases of the retreat movement in the United States.

The Slovak Catholic Federation (1911)—
915 Cornell St., Youngstown, OH 44502. Tel: 330-788-5082; Fax: 330-788-2383. Rev. Msgr. Peter M. Polando, Pres.; Most Rev. Joseph V. Adamec, Episcopal Advisor; Rev. Andrew S. Hvozdovic, Spiritual Dir.; Mrs. Bernadette J. Demechko, Sec. & Treas.

Founded by Father Joseph Murgas at Wilkes-Barre, Pennsylvania as a non-profit corporation to promote and coordinate religious activities among Slovak Catholic fraternal societies, religious communities, and Slovak ethnic parishes in their effort to address themselves to the pastoral needs of Slovak Catholics in the United States and Canada.

UNDA-USA National Catholic Association for Communicators—
National Office, 901 Irving Ave., Dayton, OH 45409-2316. Tel: 937-229-2303; Fax: 937-229-2300. Mr. Frank Morock, Pres.; Mr. David Maloney, 1st Vice Pres.; Sr. Rose Pacatte, 2nd Vice Pres.; Marilyn Vydra, Treas.; Rev. James Gardiner, S.A., Sec.

UNDA-USA, the national Catholic association of communicators, includes more than 400 individual and organizational members: diocesan directors of communications, professional broadcasters, editors of regional and national publications, educators, religious community communications personnel, directors of closed-circuit educational television (ITFS) systems and staffs, and syndicators of national Catholic radio and television programs. UNDA-USA has on its Board of Directors representatives of local, regional and national Catholic communications agencies, including the Catholic Television Network (dioceses having ITFS systems), the Association of Catholic Television and Radio Syndicators and the U.S. Catholic Conference Department of Communications. UNDA-USA, organized in 1972 as successor to the Catholic Broadcasters Association (CBA), is a member of the international Catholic association for radio and television known as UNDA International (the Latin word for "Wave," symbolic of air waves of communication). UNDA-USA is dependent on annual individual and organizational membership fees for its operating expenses. Principal activities of UNDA-USA: annual General Assembly for all members, consisting of professional communication sessions; previews and ministry-related activities; annual Gabriel Awards for excellence in broadcasting on local and national levels.

Publications: quarterly newsletter, *White papers.*

The USCC Commission on Certification and Accreditation—
3501 S. Lake Dr., P.O. Box 07058, Milwaukee, WI 53207-0058. Tel: 414-486-0139; Fax: 414-489-0006. Stephanie Y. Mitchem, Board Chm.; Sr. Kay L. Sheskaitis, I.H.M., Exec. Dir.

Accredits post-secondary programs that offer pastoral formation or education for persons preparing for ministry. These programs may be offered or sponsored by colleges, dioceses, health institutions, retreat centers, universities, or other institutions that are authorized to conduct post- secondary programs and whose programs are in compliance with the USCC/CCA standards, accreditation policies, and procedures established by the Commission. The Commission also approves certification standards for national organizations of specialized ministers and certification procedures of dioceses utilizing the Commission-certification standards of national organizations and procedures established by the Commission.

United States Catholic Mission Association—
3029 Fourth St. N.E., Washington, DC 20017. Tel: 202-832-3112; Fax: 202-832-3688. Mr. William Morton, Pres.; Sr. Rosanne Rustemeyer, S.S.N.D., Exec. Dir.

The USCMA was juridically established September 1, 1981. Its members include U.S. missioners, mission organizations, diocesan mission offices, and others concerned about the mission of the Church and global solidarity. The Association seeks to help missioners to stay up-to-date on mission and world trends, to promote greater global awareness, sensibility, and solidarity in the U.S., and periodically to be a voice for U.S. missioners speaking out in defense of the poor and oppressed throughout the world. USCMA activities include a national conference and regional seminars that highlight specific mission themes and issues, liaison and cooperation with missionary bodies of other Christian churches. The USCMA is responsible for gathering statistical data on the U.S. missionary personnel, which is published bi-annually.

Publications: quarterly newsletter, *Mission Update,* reports, *U.S. Catholic Missionary Statistics, and education programs on mission and global awareness.*

NATIONAL ORGANIZATIONS WITH INDIVIDUAL I.R.S. RULINGS

Apostleship of the Sea in the United States—
3211 Fourth Street, N.W., Washington, DC 20017. Tel: 202-541-3226; Fax: 202-541-3351. Most Rev. Joseph L. Howze, D.D., Bishop Promoter; Deacon Robert Mario Balderas, National Dir.

Official Catholic agency for the religious, educational and charitable welfare of seafarers.

Publications: monthly, *The Catholic Maritime News.*

The Beginning Experience—
International Ministry Center, 1209 Washington Blvd., Detroit, MI 48226. Tel: 313-965-5110; Fax: 313-965-5557. Most Rev. A. Edward Pevec, Episcopal Moderator; Kathleen Murphy, Pres.; Dorothy Van Poppel-Ray, Vice Pres.; Rev. Robert Botthof, O.P., Sec. & Treas.

The Beginning Experience is a copyrighted weekend program to help divorced, separated and widowed persons, as well as their families, work through the trauma of the loss of their spouse and make a new beginning in life. The program was designed by and for Catholics and has its roots in sound Catholic tradition and the sacramental life of the Church. True to the ecumenical spirit in the Church since Vatican II, it has been open to persons of all faiths from the beginning. The BE Weekend was originated in 1974 by Sr. Josephine Stewart of Fort Worth, TX. It has spread throughout the United States as well as other countries. Trained teams make the Beginning Experience Weekend available on a regular basis. It also serves as an informational and materials resource for the establishment of support groups to minister to the needs of the divorced, separated and widowed and their families at various points in their growth process.

Canon Law Society of America—
Catholic University, Washington, DC 20064. Tel: 202-269-3491; Fax: 202-319-5719. Rev. Patrick J. Cogan, S.A., Exec. Coord.; Most Rev. Lawrence Di-Nardo, Pres., Pittsburgh, PA; Rev. Msgr. Frederick Easton, Vice Pres., Indianapolis, IN; Rev. Kevin McKenna, Treas., Rochester, NY; Rev. Paul Counce, Sec., Baton Rouge, LA.

A membership association of Bishops, Clergy, Religious and Laity for the purpose of promoting research and professional collaboration in the area of Ecclesiastical Law.

Catholic Coalition on Preaching, Inc.—
Madonna University, 36600 Schoolcraft Rd., Livonia, MI 48150-1173. Tel: 313-432-5538. Rev. Francis S. Tebbe, Pres.

Catholic Engaged Encounter, Inc.—
8699 Pinyon St., Buena Park, CA 90620. Tel: 714-821-8680. Mr. Michael Chavez; Mrs. Kathy Chavez.

Catholic Library Association—
461 W. Lancaster Ave., Haverford, PA 19041. Tel: 215-649-5250. Bro. Paul J. Osterdorf, Pres. Tel: 507-457-6935.

The Catholic Mutual Relief Society of America—
4223 Center St., Omaha, NE 68105. Tel: 402-551-8765. Mr. Donald E. Ruth, Pres. & CEO; Mr. Joseph T. Beveridge, Exec. Vice Pres. & Chief Oper. Officer.

The Catholic Relief Insurance Company of America—
4223 Center St., Omaha, NE 68105. Tel: 402-551-8765. Mr. Donald E. Ruth, Pres. & CEO; Mr. Joseph T. Beveridge, Exec. Vice Pres. & Chief Oper. Officer.

Conference for Pastoral Planning and Council Development—
320 E. Ripa Ave., St. Louis, MO 63125. Tel: 314-631-6797; Fax: 314-544-6754. Rev. Eugene Costa, Chm.; M. Frances Schumer, Exec Dir.

National Association for Lay Ministry (NALM)—
National Office, 5420 S. Cornell Ave., Ste. 103, Chicago, IL 60615-5604. Tel: 773-241-6050; Fax: 773-241-6061. Sr. Louise Bond, S.N.J.M., Exec. Dir. Executive Board; Barbara L. Castellano, Chair; Tom Germanson, Sec. & Treas.; Dennis Beeman; David Suley; Kathleen Heffern; Marti Jewell; Graziano Marcheschi; John Reid.

NALM is a professional organization that supports, educates and advocates for lay ministers and promotes the development of lay ministry in the Catholic Church. In accomplishing its mission, NALM is committed to: 1) the Gospel; 2) working for justice; 3) upholding the dignity of each person; 4) ongoing conversion of persons and structures; 5) collaboration in ministry and participative Church leadership; 6) on-going dialogue and consultation with national groups.

Publications: bimonthly, *Lay Ministry; National Competency-Based Standards for Pastoral, Ministers, Pastoral Associates, Parish Life Coordinators; No Turning Back: A Lay Perspective on Ministry in the Catholic Church of the United States; Focus Group Study of Career/Volunteer Lay Ministers; Formation of Laity for Ecclesial Ministry; The Gospel Call to Collaborative Ministry; Ministry Formation Self-Assessment Instrument; NALM Chapter Manual; Pastoral Annual Conference—1998 "Ministering in the Spirit: From Communion to Mission. Research, Chapters, Affiliations, Networking.*

National Catholic Conference for Interracial Justice NCCIJ (1959)—
Office, 1200 Varnum St., N.E., Washington, DC 20017-1102. Tel: 202-529-6480; Fax: 202-526-1262. Co-Chm.: Most Rev. Charles J. Chaput, O.F.M.; Hon. Lindy Boggs; Deacon Joseph M. Conrad, Jr., Exec. Dir.

Established to implement the teaching of the Catholic Church on cultural and racial justice and to promote the church's vision of multicultural, multiracial understanding, mutual respect and collaboration.

National Catholic Risk Retention Group, Inc.—
National Office, 36800 N. Woodward Ave., Ste. 209, P.O. Box 864, Bloomfield Hills, MI 48303-0864. Tel: 248-642-6676; Fax: 248-642-6412. Most Rev. Raymond J. Boland, Episcopal Moderator; Mr. Henry P. Devlin, Mng. Dir.; Rev. Kevin C. McCoy,

Chmn. Bd.; Mr. William H. Hinkes, Pres.; Mr. Joseph Frank, Vice. Pres.; Rev. Jay C. Haskin, Sec.; Mrs. Maryellen Connor, Treas.

The Company is wholly owned by 45 Catholic Dioceses and The Christian Brothers Risk Pooling Trust. It underwrites excess liability insurance for Diocese and other Church organizations listed in the Kenedy Directory. Coverage is always subject to a minimum self-insured retention or underlying coverage of $250,000. Maximum limits of coverage available are $5 million. The company has the capability to underwrite insurance in all states, Territories and Possessions of the U.S.

National Catholic Young Adult Ministry Association, Inc.—

Membership Office, 7541 W. Broadway Ave., Forest Lake, MN 55025. Tel: 888-629-2621; Fax: 402-554-8493. Lori Spanbauer, Pres.; Gary Ashby, Vice Pres.; Rev. Charles Pfeffer, Treas.; Christine Zieker, Sec.

Founded in 1982, NCYAMA is an organization for young adults (single or married, late teens, twenties or thirties) and those who are ministering to and with young adults in an intentional way. es of outreach to young adults and interpreting to Church constituencies the contemporary needs, concerns hopes and insights of young adults.

Publications: quarterly, *The Cutting Edge.*

National Conference of Diocesan Vocation Directors (1962)—

National Office, P.O. Box 1570, Little River, SC 29566. Tel: 803-280-7191. Revs. Robert Flagg, Pres.; William Kubacki, Vice Pres.; Sr. Judith Anne Haase, O.P., Sec.-Treas. Members at Large: Revs. Michael Kuse; Richard Martini; Carlos Velazquez; Mrs. Dorothy Foss, Exec. Dir.

This Conference serves as a resource-service to the personnel of vocation offices in dioceses associated with the USCC-NCCB. Besides direct service to its membership, this Conference also represents them to various related organizations and offers personal and ministerial support to the staffs of these diocesan vocation office members. The Conference is a member organization of the National Coalition for Church Vocations and represents members to the NCCB Committee on Vocations.

Publications: five times a year, *Newsletter,* documents of interest, Meetings annually for Regional Conferences and a National Convention.

The National Federation of Priests' Councils (1968)—

National Office, 1337 W. Ohio, Chicago, IL 60622. Tel: 312-226-3334; Fax: 312-829-8915. Rev. Donald Wolf, Pres.; Bro. Bernard F. Stratman, S.M., Exec. Dir.

The NFPC was organized to promote priestly fraternity by facilitating communication among priests' councils, to provide a forum for priests to discuss pastoral matters, to enable priests' councils to speak with a common voice, to promote and collaborate on programs of pastoral research, to further the spiritual renewal of priestly life, to collaborate with national lay and religious groups in ways that promote renewal in the Church, to collaborate with the NCCB in addressing the needs of the Church in the U.S.A., to encourage priests' councils to promote justice in light of the social teachings of the Church, and to participate in developing a national and universal perspective of church and ministry.

The NFPC represents 113 priests' councils, priests' associations and religious communities. Elected delegates of member councils meet annually to set policy, and a national executive board meets regularly to carry out the work of the NFPC, assisted by standing committees. Member councils represent approximately 26,000 priests.

Publications: quarterly newsletter, *Touchstone,* bimonthly, *NFPC Update,* books; occasional papers and studies concerned with various aspects, of ministry, the ministerial priesthood and the spiritual renewal of priests.

National Institute for the Word of God—

Headquarters, 487 Michigan Ave. N.E., Washington, DC 20017. Tel: 202-529-0001. Episcopal Advisory Board: Most Rev. John R. Quinn; Most Rev. David E. Foley; Most Rev. Juan A. Arzube; Most Rev. Patrick R. Cooney; Most Rev. William G. Curlin; Most Rev. Rene H. Gracida; Most Rev. James W. Malone. Staff: Rev. John Burke, O.P., Exec. Dir.; Mr. William H. Graham, Assoc. Dir.; Mary C. Graham, Sec.; Very Rev. Joseph P. Allen, O.P., Treas. Councilors; James R. Dimond, Jr.; Michael A. Graham; Francis Litz; Joseph A. Taney; Carol McCarty; Kay McDonald.

The Institute is an unaffiliated nonprofit organization incorporated under the laws of the District of Columbia, whose purpose is to promote, support, conduct and assist in any way whatsoever educational, liturgical, and remedial programs and activities, public and private, through the use of any and all media, to further effective communication of the revealed word of God, as the primary pastoral work of the Church. Ongoing efforts include the dissemination of scriptural, theological and pastoral aids such as books, films and tape albums, and the conducting of parish missions, conferences and retreats for clergy and laity.

National Service Committee of the Catholic Charismatic Renewal of the United States Inc.

P.O. Box 628, Locust Grove, VA 22508-0628. Rev. Patsy Iaquinta, Chm.; Mr. Walter Matthews, Dir.

Our focus is to foster baptism in the Holy Spirit in the life of the Church in the United States and throughout the world, to broaden and deepen the understanding that baptism in the Holy Spirit is the Christian inheritance of all, and to strengthen the Catholic Charismatic Renewal. The National Service Committee has established and supported numerous programs to help further our mission. Some of the activities and programs include the establishment of Chariscenter USA, which serves as the national headquarters for our committee and a national office for the Catholic Charismatic Renewal. The NSC offers a national newsletter, a Catholic Charismatic Renewal Directory and leadership training materials as well as an annual national conference, outreach to youth, and evangelization training. The NSC has supported the International Catholic Charismatic Renewal Office in Rome.

The North American Forum on the Catechumenate—

3033 Fourth St., N.E., Washington, DC 20017-1102. Tel: 202-529-9493; Fax: 202-529-9497. Thomas H. Morris, Exec. Dir.; Sr. Sheila O'Dea, R.S.M., Assoc. Dir.

The North American Forum on the Catechumenate is an international network committed to the implementation of the Order of Christian Initiation of Adults. The work of FORUM is overseen by a Board of Directors of 5 elected representatives. A variety of institutes are offered in co-sponsorship with a hosting diocese to serve the local Church. FORUM networks with other national groups, promotes research into issues raised by Christian Initiation (including outreach to the inactive through a process of Re-Membering Church), and provides a quarterly newsletter which focuses on the impact of Christian Initiation on the Church as well as key issues related to its implementation.

Worldwide Marriage Encounter (1969)—

National Office, 2210 E. Highland Ave., Ste. 106, San Bernardino, CA 92404. Tel: 909-863-9963; Fax: 909-863-9986. Most Rev. G. Patrick Ziemann, D.D., Episcopal Moderator. Secretariat Team: Rev. Richard O'Brien, C.M.; Dennis Battaglia; Alynn Battaglia.

Organized to foster a program of Christian information to instruct married couples in the means to find God's plan and matrimony in their lives, for their own spiritual development and the betterment of all humankind; and to develop, foster and disseminate an adult catechesis supporting, furthering and building upon such instruction. Worldwide Marriage Encounter offers the marriage encounter weekend experience in 150 dioceses in the United States as well as in 88 foreign countries. In the United States over 1,500,000 couples and over 5,000 priests and bishops have experienced the Worldwide weekend.

Publications: quarterly, *Matrimony - A Sign of Our Church.*

Catholic Committee for Refugees & Children—

3211 Fourth St. N.E., Washington, DC 20017-1194; Fax: 202-541-3399. Mr. John Swenson, Pres.

In operation since January 4, 1937, and incorporated since 1954, the Catholic Committee for Refugees and Children was founded to counsel and cooperate with European refugees during and after World War II. Since that time its mission has been expanded to include service to refugees worldwide. It has a special mandate from the bishops concerning its work with children through international child welfare, child care or placement, international adoption, and the coordination of services to refugee minors.

National Association of State Catholic Conference Directors

An Association of the Directors of the State Catholic Conference, organized in 1968 to facilitate and encourage the exchange of information among its members pertaining to the activities, programs and organization of the Conferences. A State Catholic Conference is a Church agency composed of the dioceses within a state to provide for the coordination of the public policy concerns of the Church. Thus a Conference of the Church communicates with state government, other Church Agencies, non-Catholic churches and secular agencies. Bishops, priests, religious and lay persons are involved in the work of the State Conferences. *National Association:* NCCB-USCC, 3211 4th St., N.E., Washington, DC 20017-1194.

ARIZONA

Arizona Catholic Conference.
400 E. Monroe St., Phoenix, AZ 85004-2376. Tel: 602-257-0030; Fax: 602-258-3425.
Chairman: Bishop Thomas J. O'Brien.
Executive Director: Rev. Msgr. Edward J. Ryle, M.A., M.S.W.

CALIFORNIA

California Catholic Conference.
Cathedral Square, 1010 11th St., Suite 200, Sacramento, CA 95814. Tel: 916-443-4851; Fax: 916-443-5629; Email: cacathcon@aol.com.
President: Bishop Sylvester D. Ryan.
Vice President: Bishop William K. Weigand.
Secretary-Treasurer: Bishop Michael P. Driscoll.
Executive Director: Mr. Edward E. Dolejsi.
Director of Catholic Charities of California, Inc.: Mr. Richard Mockler.
Associate Director for Public Policy: Mr. David A. Pollard.
Associate Director for Hispanic Affairs: Rev. Alejandro Castillo, S.V.D.
Associate Director for Communications: Mrs. Carol Hogan.
Associate Director for Education: Mr. Robert Teegarden.
Associate Director for Finances: Mr. Richard Strawn.
General Counsel: Mr. Raymond Leonardini, Esq.

COLORADO

Colorado Catholic Conference.
Catholic Pastoral Center, 1300 S. Steele St., Denver, CO 80210-2599. Tel: 303-715-3206; Fax: 303-715-2042.
Executive Director: Mr. James P. Tatten.

CONNECTICUT

Connecticut Catholic Conference.
134 Farmington Avenue, Hartford, CT 06105. Tel: 203-524-7882; Fax: 203-525-0750.
President and Chairman of the Board: Archbishop Daniel A. Cronin.
Secretary: Bishop Daniel A. Hart.
Executive Director: Dr. Marie T. Hilliard, J.C.L.

FLORIDA

Florida Catholic Conference.
P.O. Box 1638, Tallahassee, FL 32302. Tel: 850-222-3803; Fax: 850-681-9548.
President: Archbishop John Clement Favalora.
Executive Director: D. Michael McCarron, Ph.D.

GEORGIA

Georgia Catholic Conference.
Office Building, 3200 Deans Bridge Rd., Augusta, GA 30906. Tel: 404-798-1719; Fax: 706-798-6037.
Executive Director: Mr. Cheatham E. Hodges, Jr.

HAWAII

Hawaii Catholic Conference.
St. Stephen Diocesan Center, 6301 Pali Hwy., Kaneohe, HI 96744-5298. Tel: 808-263-8844, ext. 548; Fax: 808-261-7022; Email: malexander@compuserve.com.
Executive Director: Rev. Marc R. Alexander, S.T.D.

ILLINOIS

Catholic Conference of Illinois.
500 North Clark St., Chicago, IL 60610. Tel: 312-467-4375. and 200 Broadway, Springfield, IL 62701. Tel: 217-528-9200.
Chairman: Joseph Cardinal Bernardin.
Executive Director: Mr. Doug Delaney.
Associate Directors: Jura S. Scharf; Joan L. McKinney.

INDIANA

Indiana Catholic Conference.
1400 N. Meridian St., P.O. Box 1410, Indianapolis, IN 46206. Tel: 317-236-1455; Fax: 317-236-1456.
General Chairman: Archbishop Daniel M. Buechlein, O.S.B., D.D.
Executive Chairman: Bishop William L. Higi, D.D.
Executive Director: Dr. M. Desmond Ryan, Ph.D.

IOWA

Iowa Catholic Conference.
505 5th Ave., Ste. 818, Des Moines, IA 50309-2393. Tel: 515-243-6256; Fax: 515-243-6257.
President: Archbishop Jerome Hanus, O.S.B.
Vice President: Bishop Lawrence D. Soens.
Secretary-Treasurer: Bishop Joseph Charron, C.PP.S.
Executive Director: Timothy McCarthy.

KANSAS

Kansas Catholic Conference.
6301 Antioch, Merriam, KS 66202. Tel: 913-722-6633.
Chairman: Archbishop James P. Keleher.
Executive Director: Mr. Robert Runnels, Jr.
Program Director: Mrs. Beatrice Swoopes.

KENTUCKY

Catholic Conference of Kentucky.
1042 Burlington Ln., Frankfort, KY 40601. Tel: 502-875-4345; Fax: 502-875-2841.
Chairman: Archbishop Thomas C. Kelly, O.P.
Executive Director: Mrs. Jane J. Chiles.

LOUISIANA

Louisiana Catholic Conference.
3423 Hundred Oaks Ave., Baton Rouge, LA 70808. Tel: 504-344-7120; Fax: 504-383-9591.
Chairman: Archbishop Francis B. Schulte.
Executive Director: Mr. Kirby J. Ducote.
Assistant Director for Administrative Services: Mrs. Barbara Bovard.

MARYLAND

Maryland Catholic Conference.
188 Duke of Gloucester St., Annapolis, MD 21401-2515. Tel: 410-269-1155.
Chairman: William Cardinal Keeler.
Executive Director: Richard J. Dowling, Esq.

MASSACHUSETTS

Massachusetts Catholic Conference.
49 Franklin St., Boston, MA 02110. Tel: 617-574-0771.
Executive Director: Mr. Gerald D. D'Avolio, Esq.

MICHIGAN

Michigan Catholic Conference.
505 N. Capitol Ave., Lansing, MI 48933. Tel: 517-372-9310; Fax: 517-372-3940.
Chairman: His Eminence Adam Cardinal Maida.
President & CEO: Sr. Monica Kostielney, R.S.M.
Secretary-Treasurer: Most Rev. Patrick R. Cooney.

MINNESOTA

Minnesota Catholic Conference.
475 University Ave., W., Suite B, St. Paul, MN 55103-1996. Tel: 612-227-8777; Fax: 612-227-2675.
President: Archbishop Harry J. Flynn.
Vice President: Bishop Raymond A. Lucker.
Secretary/Treasurer: Bishop Roger L. Schwietz, O.M.I.
Executive Director: Rev. David F. McCauley.
Education Department Director: Mr. Thomas J. Pearson.

MISSOURI

Missouri Catholic Conference.
600 Clark Ave., P.O. Box 1022, Jefferson City, MO 65102. Tel: 573-635-7239; Fax: 573-635-7431.
General Chairman: Archbishop Justin Rigali.
Executive Chairman: Bishop John R. Gaydos.
General Counsel Executive Director: Louis C. DeFeo, Jr.
Assistant Director: Mike Hoey.
Administrative Assistant: Josetta M. Forck.

MONTANA

Montana Catholic Conference.
P.O. Box 1708, Helena, MT 59624. Tel: 406-442-5761; Fax: 406-442-9047.
President: Julie French.
Vice President: Myles Grotbo.
Treasurer: Linda McCauley.
Executive Director: Sharon Hoff.

NEBRASKA

Nebraska Catholic Conference.
215 Centennial Mall South, Ste. 410, Lincoln, NE 68508-1890. Tel: 402-477-7517.
President: Archbishop Eldin Francis Curtiss.
Director: Bishop Fabian W. Bruskewitz.
Director: Bishop Lawrence J. McNamara.
Executive Director: James R. Cunningham.

NEW JERSEY

New Jersey Catholic Conference.
211 N. Warren St., Trenton, NJ 08618. Tel: 609-599-2110.
President: Archbishop Theodore E. McCarrick.
Executive Director: William F. Bolan, Jr. J.D.

NEW YORK

New York State Catholic Conference.
465 State St., Albany, NY 12203. Tel: 518-434-6195.
President: John Cardinal O'Connor.
Vice President: Bishop John R. McGann.
Treasurer: Bishop Thomas V. Daily.
Chairman—Public Policy Committee: Bishop Howard J. Hubbard.
Executive Director: John M. Kerry.

NORTH DAKOTA

North Dakota Catholic Conference.
227 W. Broadway, Suite 2, Bismarck, ND 58501. Tel: 701-223-2519; Fax: 701-223-6075.
President: Bishop Paul A. Zipfel.
Secretary-Treasurer: Bro. Basil Atwell, O.S.B.
Executive Director: Christopher T. Dodson.

OHIO

Catholic Conference of Ohio.
9 East Long St. - Suite 201, Columbus, OH 43215. Tel: 614-224-7147.
President: Archbishop Daniel E. Pilarczyk.
Vice President: Bishop Anthony M. Pilla.
Secretary-Treasurer: Bishop James A. Griffin.
Executive Director: Timothy V. Luckhaupt.

OREGON

Oregon Catholic Conference.
2838 E. Burnside St., Portland, OR 97214. Tel: 503-233-8387; Fax: 503-235-2630.
President: Archbishop John G. Vlazny, O.M.I.
Vice President: Bishop Thomas J. Connolly.
Secretary-Treasurer: Very Rev. Gregory Moys.
General Counsel & Executive Director: Mr. Robert J. Castagna.

PENNSYLVANIA

Pennsylvania Catholic Conference.
223 North St., P.O. Box 2835, Harrisburg, PA 17105. Tel: 717-238-9613; Fax: 717-238-1473.
Chairman: Anthony Cardinal Bevilacqua.
President: Bishop Nicholas C. Dattilo.
Vice President: Rev. Msgr. George B. Flinn.
Secretary: Rev. Msgr. Joseph E. Kurtz.
Executive Director: Dr. Robert J. O'Hara, Jr.
Treasurer: Rev. Msgr. Michael E. Servinsky.

TEXAS

Texas Catholic Conference.
1625 Rutherford Ln., Bldg. D, Austin, TX 78754-5105. Tel: 512-339-9882.
Chairman: Archbishop Patrick F. Flores.
Executive Director: Brother Richard Daly, C.S.C.
Associate Director: Rev. Msgr. William L. Broussard.
Associate Director for Education: Mr. George Solana.
Director, Volunteers for Education and Social Services: Mr. Michael Guerra.
Director of Evangelization: Rev. John Duffy, C.S.P.
Director, Catholic Archives of Texas: Mrs. Kinga Perzynska.

WASHINGTON

Washington State Catholic Conference.
508 2nd Avenue West, Seattle, WA 98119. Tel: 206-301-0556; Fax: 206-301-0558.
President: Bishop William S. Skylstad.
Executive Director: Sister Sharon Park, O.P.
Administrative Assistant: Ms. Evelyn Tangalin.
Legislative Coordinator: Mr. Eric Paige.

WEST VIRGINIA

West Virginia State Catholic Conference.
1300 Byron St., P.O. Box 230, Wheeling, WV 26003. Tel: 304-233-0880 ext. 242; Fax: 304-233-0890.
Director: Rev. John R. Gallagher, V.G.

WISCONSIN

Wisconsin Catholic Conference.
30 W. Mifflin St., Room 302, Madison, WI 53703-2579. Tel: 608-257-0004; Fax: 608-257-0376.
Chairman: Archbishop Rembert G. Weakland, O.S.B.
Vice Chairman: Bishop William H. Bullock.
Executive Director: John A. Huebscher.
Associate Director: Sharon L. Schmeling.

Diocesan Abbreviations

ARCHDIOCESES AND DIOCESES

(ALB) .... Albany (New York)
(ALN) .... Allentown (Pennsylvania)
(ALT) .... Altoona-Johnstown (Pennsylvania)
(ALX) .... Alexandria (Louisiana)
(AGN) .... Agana (Guam)
(AMA) .... Amarillo (Texas)
(ANC) .... Anchorage (Alaska)
(ARE) .... Arecibo (Puerto Rico)
(ARL) .... Arlington (Virginia)
(ARM) .... Armenian Catholic Exarchate (Pennsylvania)
(ATH) .... Apostolate To Hungarians (Washington, DC)
(ATL) .... Atlanta (Georgia)
(AUS) .... Austin (Texas)
(B) .... Boise (Idaho)
(BAK) .... Baker (Oregon)
(BAL) .... Baltimore (Maryland)
(BEA) .... Beaumont (Texas)
(BEL) .... Belleville (Illinois)
(BGP) .... Bridgeport (Connecticut)
(BIR) .... Birmingham (Alabama)
(BIS) .... Bismarck (North Dakota)
(BLX) .... Biloxi (Mississippi)
(BO) .... Boston (Massachusetts)
(BR) .... Baton Rouge (Louisiana)
(BRK) .... Brooklyn (New York)
(BUF) .... Buffalo (New York)
(BUR) .... Burlington (Vermont)
(BWN) .... Brownsville (Texas)
(CAM) .... Camden (New Jersey)
(CC) .... Corpus Christi (Texas)
(CGS) .... Caguas (Puerto Rico)
(CHI) .... Chicago (Illinois)
(CHK) .... Chalan Kanoa
(CHL) .... Charlotte (North Carolina)
(CHR) .... Charleston (South Carolina)
(CHY) .... Cheyenne (Wyoming)
(CI) .... Caroline Islands
(CIN) .... Cincinnati (Ohio)
(CLV) .... Cleveland (Ohio)
(COL) .... Columbus (Ohio)
(COS) .... Colorado Springs (Colorado)
(COV) .... Covington (Kentucky)
(CR) .... Crookston (Minnesota)
(DAL) .... Dallas (Texas)
(DAV) .... Davenport (Iowa)
(DEN) .... Denver (Colorado)
(DET) .... Detroit (Michigan)
(DM) .... Des Moines (Iowa)
(DOD) .... Dodge City (Kansas)
(DUB) .... Dubuque (Iowa)
(DUL) .... Duluth (Minnesota)
(E) .... Erie (Pennsylvania)
(ELP) .... El Paso (Texas)
(EST) .... Eparchy of Saint Thomas the Apostle
(EVN) .... Evansville (Indiana)
(FAR) .... Fargo (North Dakota)
(FBK) .... Fairbanks (Alaska)
(FgM) .... Foreign Mission Section
(FR) .... Fall River (Massachusetts)
(FRS) .... Fresno (California)
(FTW) .... Fort Wayne-South Bend (Indiana)
(FWT) .... Fort Worth (Texas)
(GAL) .... Galveston-Houston (Texas)
(GAY) .... Gaylord (Michigan)
(GB) .... Green Bay (Wisconsin)
(GBG) .... Greensburg (Pennsylvania)
(GF) .... Great Falls-Billings (Montana)
(GI) .... Grand Island (Nebraska)
(GLP) .... Gallup (New Mexico)
(GR) .... Grand Rapids (Michigan)
(GRY) .... Gary (Indiana)
(HBG) .... Harrisburg (Pennsylvania)
(HEL) .... Helena (Montana)
(HON) .... Honolulu (Hawaii)
(HRT) .... Hartford (Connecticut)
(HT) .... Houma-Thibodaux (Louisiana)
(IND) .... Indianapolis (Indiana)
(JC) .... Jefferson City (Missouri)
(JKS) .... Jackson (Mississippi)
(JOL) .... Joliet in Illinois
(JUN) .... Juneau (Alaska)
(KAL) .... Kalamazoo (Michigan)
(KC) .... Kansas City-St. Joseph (Missouri)
(KCK) .... Kansas City in Kansas
(KNX) .... Knoxville (Tennessee)
(L) .... Louisville (Kentucky)
(LA) .... Los Angeles (California)
(LAF) .... Lafayette (Louisiana)
(LAN) .... Lansing (Michigan)
(LC) .... La Crosse (Wisconsin)
(LEX) .... Lexington (Kentucky)
(LFT) .... Lafayette in Indiana
(LIN) .... Lincoln (Nebraska)
(LIT) .... Lithuanian Apostolate for Lithuanian Catholics
(LKC) .... Lake Charles (Louisiana)
(LR) .... Little Rock (Arkansas)
(LSC) .... Las Cruces (New Mexico)
(LUB) .... Lubbock (Texas)
(LAV) .... Las Vegas (Nevada)
(MAD) .... Madison (Wisconsin)
(MAN) .... Manchester (New Hampshire)
(MAR) .... Marquette (Michigan)
(MEM) .... Memphis (Tennessee)
(MET) .... Metuchen (New Jersey)
(MGZ) .... Mayaguez (Puerto Rico)
(MI) .... Marshall Islands
(MIA) .... Miami (Florida)
(MIL) .... Milwaukee (Wisconsin)
(MO) .... Military Services (Maryland)
(MOB) .... Mobile (Alabama)
(MRY) .... Monterey in California
(NEW) .... Newark (New Jersey)
(NO) .... New Orleans (Louisiana)
(NOR) .... Norwich (Connecticut)
(NSH) .... Nashville (Tennessee)
(NTN) .... Newton (Melkite, United States)
(NU) .... New Ulm (Minnesota)
(NY) .... New York (New York)
(OAK) .... Oakland (California)
(OG) .... Ogdensburg (New York)
(OKL) .... Oklahoma City (Oklahoma)
(OLD) .... Our Lady of Deliverance *Syriac* (Union City, New Jersey)
(OLL) .... Our Lady of Lebanon of Los Angeles (California)
(OM) .... Omaha (Nebraska)
(ORG) .... Orange in California
(ORL) .... Orlando (Florida)
(OWN) .... Owensboro (Kentucky)
(P) .... Portland in Oregon
(PAT) .... Paterson (New Jersey)
(PBL) .... Pueblo (Colorado)
(PBR) .... Pittsburgh *Byzantine* (Pennsylvania)
(PCE) .... Ponce (Puerto Rico)
(PEO) .... Peoria (Illinois)
(PH) .... Philadelphia (Pennsylvania)
(PHU) .... Philadelphia *Ukrainian* (Pennsylvania)
(PHX) .... Phoenix (Arizona)
(PIT) .... Pittsburgh (Pennsylvania)
(PMB) .... Palm Beach (Florida)
(PP) .... Personal Prelatures
(PRM) .... Parma *Byzantine* (Ohio)
(PRO) .... Providence (Rhode Island)
(PRT) .... Portland (Maine)
(PSC) .... Passaic *Byzantine* (New Jersey)
(PT) .... Pensacola-Tallahassee (Florida)
(R) .... Raleigh (North Carolina)
(RC) .... Rapid City (South Dakota)
(RCK) .... Rockford (Illinois)
(RIC) .... Richmond (Virginia)
(RNO) .... Reno (Nevada)
(ROC) .... Rochester (New York)
(ROM) .... Romanian (Byzantine) (Ohio)
(RVC) .... Rockville Centre (New York)
(SAC) .... Sacramento (California)
(SAG) .... Saginaw (Michigan)
(SAL) .... Salina (Kansas)
(SAM) .... St. Maron of Brooklyn (U.S.A.), Eparchy of
(SAN) .... San Angelo (Texas)
(SAT) .... San Antonio (Texas)
(SAV) .... Savannah (Georgia)
(SB) .... San Bernadino (California)
(SC) .... Sioux City (Iowa)
(SCL) .... St. Cloud (Minnesota)
(SCR) .... Scranton (Pennsylvania)
(SD) .... San Diego (California)
(SEA) .... Seattle (Washington)
(SFD) .... Springfield in Illinois
(SFE) .... Santa Fe (New Mexico)
(SFR) .... San Francisco (California)
(SFS) .... Sioux Falls (South Dakota)
(SHP) .... Shreveport (Louisiana)
(SJ) .... San Jose in California
(SJN) .... San Juan (Puerto Rico)
(SJP) .... St. Josaphat in Parma (Ohio)
(SLC) .... Salt Lake City (Utah)
(SP) .... St. Petersburg (Florida)
(SPC) .... Sprgfld-Cape Girardeau (Missouri)
(SPK) .... Spokane (Washington)
(SPP) .... Samoa-Pago Pago
(SPR) .... Springfield in Massachusetts
(SR) .... Santa Rosa in California
(STA) .... St. Augustine (Florida)
(STF) .... Stamford *Ukrainian* (Connecticut)
(STL) .... St. Louis (Missouri)
(STN) .... St. Nicholas in Chicago *Ukrainian*
(STO) .... Stockton (California)
(STP) .... St. Paul and Minneapolis (Minnesota)
(STU) .... Steubenville (Ohio)
(STV) .... St. Thomas, Virgin Islands
(SUP) .... Superior (Wisconsin)
(SY) .... Syracuse (New York)
(TLS) .... Tulsa (Oklahoma)
(TOL) .... Toledo (Ohio)
(TR) .... Trenton (New Jersey)
(TUC) .... Tucson (Arizona)
(TYL) .... Tyler (Texas)
(VEN) .... Venice (Florida)
(VIC) .... Victoria in Texas
(VNN) .... Van Nuys *Byzantine* (California)
(WCH) .... Wichita (Kansas)
(WDC) .... Washington (District of Columbia)
(WH) .... Wheeling-Charleston (West Virginia)
(WIL) .... Wilmington (Delaware)
(WIN) .... Winona (Minnesota)
(WOR) .... Worcester (Massachusetts)
(Y) .... Youngstown (Ohio)
(YAK) .... Yakima (Washington)

Diocese of Albany

(Dioecesis Albanensis)

Most Reverend

HOWARD J. HUBBARD, D.D.

Bishop of Albany; ordained December 18, 1963; appointed February 1, 1977; ordained and installed March 27, 1977. *Res., 125 Eagle St., Albany, NY, 12202.* Tel.: 518-462-3804.

Chancery Office: Pastoral Center, 40 N. Main Ave., Albany, NY, 12203. Tel.: 518-453-6600; Fax: 518-453-6793.

ESTABLISHED APRIL 23, 1847.

Square Miles 10,419.

(Incorporated by a special act of the Legislature of the State of New York, April 12, 1941, with the title "The Roman Catholic Diocese of Albany, New York.")

Comprises the entire Counties of Albany, Columbia, Delaware, Fulton, Greene, Montgomery, Otsego, Rensselaer, Saratoga, Schenectady, Schoharie, Warren and Washington and that part of Herkimer and Hamilton Counties, south of the northern line of the townships of Ohio and Russia, as existing in 1872 in the State of New York.

For legal titles of parishes and diocesan institutions, consult the Chancery Office.

STATISTICAL OVERVIEW

Personnel	
Retired Archbishops	1
Bishop	1
Priests: Diocesan Active in Diocese	235
Priests: Active Outside Diocese	12
Priests: Diocesan in Foreign Missions	72
Number of Diocesan Priests	319
Religious Priests in Diocese	120
Extern Priests in Diocese	1
Ordinations:	
Diocesan Priests	2
Religious Priests	1
Transitional Deacons	2
Permanent Deacons	3
Permanent Deacons in Diocese	95
Total Brothers	90
Total Sisters	957
Parishes	
Parishes	187
With Resident Pastor:	
Resident Diocesan Priests	153
Resident Religious Priests	15
Without Resident Pastor:	
Administered by Priests	15
Administered by Women Religious	4
Missions	34
Pastoral Centers	43
Professional Ministry Personnel:	
Lay Ministers	1,202
Welfare	
Catholic Hospitals	4
Total Assisted	600,000
Health Care Centers	15
Total Assisted	35,000
Homes for the Aged	10
Total Assisted	1,600
Day Care and Extended Day Care Centers	7
Total Assisted	89
Specialized Homes	17
Total Assisted	1,500
Special Centers for Social Services	22
Total Assisted	179,500
Residential Care of Disabled	8
Total Assisted	200
Other Institutions	9
Total Assisted	530
Educational	
Diocesan Students in Other Seminaries	11
Total Seminarians	11
Colleges and Universities	4
Total Students	4,650
High Schools, Diocesan and Parish	4
Total Students	1,823
High Schools, Private	3
Total Students	1,192
Elementary Schools, Diocesan and Parish	38
Total Students	8,939
Elementary Schools, Private	2
Total Students	424
Catechesis/Religious Education:	
High School Students	10,194
Elementary Students	33,052
Total Students Under Catholic Instruction	60,285
Teachers in the Diocese:	
Priests	8
Brothers	19
Sisters	98
Lay Teachers	861
Vital Statistics	
Receptions into the Church:	
Infant Baptism Totals	5,859
Adult Baptism Totals	384
First Communions	5,774
Confirmations	4,059
Marriages:	
Catholic	1,995
Interfaith	188
Total Marriages	2,183
Deaths	5,204
Total Catholic Population	403,403
Total Population	1,340,388

Former Bishops—His Eminence JOHN CARDINAL MCCLOSKEY, D.D., appt. Bishop of Axiere and Coadjutor to the Bishop of New York, Nov. 21, 1843; cons. March 10, 1844; transferred to Albany, May 21, 1847; promoted to New York, May 6, 1864; created Cardinal Priest of the Holy Roman Church, March 15, 1875, under the title Sanctae Mariae supra Minervam; died Oct. 10, 1885.—Rt. Rev. JOHN J. CONROY, appt. Bishop July 7, 1865; cons. Oct. 15, 1865; resigned Oct. 16, 1877; transferred to the See of Curium, March 22, 1878; died Nov. 20, 1895.—Rt. Rev. Msgr. FRANCIS MCNEIRNY, D.D., appt. Bishop of Rhesina and Coadjutor to the Bishop of Albany, Dec. 22, 1871; cons. April 21, 1872; appt. Administrator of the Diocese of Albany, Jan. 18, 1874: Bishop of Albany, by right of succession, Oct. 16, 1877; died Jan. 2, 1894.—Rt. Rev. Msgr. THOMAS M. A. BURKE, D.D., preconized May 18, 1894; cons. July 1, 1894; died Jan 20, 1915.—Rt. Rev. Msgr. THOMAS F. CUSACK, D.D., cons. Titular Bishop of Themiscyra and Auxiliary to the Archbishop of New York, April 25, 1904; transferred to Albany, July 5, 1915; died July 12, 1918.—Most Rev. EDMUND F. GIBBONS, D.D., appt. Bishop, Feb. 1, 1919; cons. March 25, 1919; resigned Nov. 10, 1954; transferred to See of Verbe; died June 19, 1964.—Most Rev. WILLIAM A. SCULLY, D.D., appt. Coadjutor Bishop "cum jure successionis," Aug. 21, 1945; cons. Oct. 24, 1945; succeeded to See, Nov. 10, 1954; died Jan. 5, 1969.—Most Rev. EDWIN B. BRODERICK, D.D., appt. Titular Bishop of Tizica and Auxiliary of New York, March 8, 1967; cons. April 21, 1967; transferred Albany, March 19, 1969; resigned June 2, 1976; appt. Exec. Dir. Catholic Relief Services, June 3, 1976; retired September, 1985.

Chancery Office—Pastoral Center, 40 N. Main Ave., Albany, 12203. Tel: 518-453-6600; Fax: 518-453-6793. Office Hours: Mon.-Fri. 8:30-4:30.

Vicars General—Rev. LEO P. O'BRIEN, *900 Madison Ave., Albany, 12208.* Tel: 518-489-5408. Rev. MICHAEL A. FARANO, *23 Crumite Rd., Loudonville, 12211.* Rev. Msgr. JAMES G. HART, Vicar General Emeritus, *391 Delaware Ave., Albany, 12209.*

Chancellors—Pastoral Center, 40 N. Main Ave., Albany, 12203. Rev. GEOFFREY BURKE, Chancellor, Personnel & Public Information. Tel: 518-453-6612. Mr. JOHN FEENEY, Chancellor, Finance & Admin. Tel: 518-453-6612. Sr. KATHLEEN TURLEY, R.S.M., Chancellor, Planning & Pastoral Svcs. Tel: 518-453-6661.

Comptroller—RICHARD FARRELL, *40 N. Main Ave., Albany, 12203.* Tel: 518-453-6640.

Insurance Office—RONALD WATERS, Dir., *40 N. Main Ave., Albany, 12203.* Tel: 518-453-6790.

Office of Human Resources—JOHN COSGROVE, Dir., *40 N. Main Ave., Albany, 12203.* Tel: 518-453-6635. FRANK DUCHARME, Human Resource Assoc. Tel: 518-453-4461. MARY JO HELNARSKI, Personnel Asst. Tel: 518-453-6635. Sr. NOLA BRUNNER, Spec. Projects. Tel: 518-453-6662.

Pastoral Planning—Sr. KATHLEEN TURLEY, R.S.M., Dir., *40 N. Main Ave., Albany, 12203.* Tel: 518-453-6661.

Archivist—Sr. MARY BERCHMANS MAHONEY, R.S.M., *40 N. Main Ave., Albany, 12203.* Tel: 518-453-6633.

Office of Canonical Services—40 N. Main Ave., Albany, 12203. Tel: 518-453-6620; Fax: 518-453-6778. Office Hours: 8:30-4:30 (By appointment only).

Vicar Judicial—Rev. JAMES I. DONLON, J.C.D.

Adjutant Vicar Judicial—Rev. PETER J. SULLIVAN, III, J.C.L.

Judges—Revs. DAVID BERBERIAN; JAMES I. DONLON; PETER J. SULLIVAN, III; Sr. MARY ANN HAYES.

Defender of the Marriage Bond in First Instance—Vacant.

Promoter of Justice—Sr. MARY ANN HAYES, C.S.J.

Advocates—Revs. THOMAS KRUPA; THOMAS BERARDI; JAMES LEFEBVRE; JOSEPH O'BRIEN; JOHN MOYNA; ARTHUR BECKER; FRANK GILCHRIST.

Bishop's Delegate for Marriage Dispensations—Revs. JAMES I. DONLON, J.C.D.; PETER J. SULLIVAN, III, J.C.L.

Notaries—JOANNNE MONAHAN; MARTHA MCEWAN.

Inter Diocesan Tribunal for the Province of NY—(Second Instance Appeal Court), Rev. Msgr WALTER F. KENNY, Vicar Judicial; Sr. AILEEN KELLY, Admin. and Chief Exec. Sec., *201 Seminary Ave., Yonkers, 10704-1852.* Tel: 914-968-4301; 800-293-6598; Fax: 914-968-4466.

Presbyteral Council—Most Rev. HOWARD J. HUBBARD, Pres.; Revs. KENNETH J. DOYLE, Chm. MARTIN FISHER, Vice Chm. PETER RUSSO; BRIAN RAICHE;

PETER N. PAGONES; CHRISTOPHER J. DRENNAN, O.S.A.; JOSEPH O'BRIEN; LOUIS DEIMEKE; ANTHONY LIGATO; DONALD CZELUSNIAK; JAMES D. DALEY. Bishop's Staff (Non-Voting): Rev. Msgr. JAMES G. HART; Revs. LEO P. O'BRIEN; MICHAEL A. FARANO; GEOFFREY D. BURKE; JAMES I. DONLON; Mr. RICHARD N. FARRELL.

Diocesan Board of Consultors—Revs. MARTIN FISHER; LOUIS DEIMEKE; CHRISTOPHER J. DRENNAN, O.S.A.; ANTHONY LIGATO; DONALD CZELUSNIAK; KENNETH J. DOYLE; BRIAN RAICHE; JOSEPH O'BRIEN; PETER RUSSO; PETER N. PAGONES; JAMES D. DALEY; MICHAEL A. FARANO, Sec. JAMES I. DONLON, Canonical Consultant to the Board.

Deans—Albany Co.-City: Rev. ROBERT J. HOHENSTEIN, V.F.; *Northern:* Rev. LAWRENCE MCTAVEY, V.F.; *Suburban:* Rev. JOHN WALDRON; *Colombia:* Rev. THOMAS M. POWERS, V.F.; *Delaware:* Rev. ROBERT PURCELL, V.F.; *Fulton:* Rev. JOSEPH BARKER, V.F.; *Greene: Rev.* JEREMIAH NUNAN, V.F.; *Herkimer:* Rev. JOSEPH BENINTENDE; *Montgomery:* Rev. JAMES GULLEY; *Otsego:* Rev. PAUL ROMAN; *Rensselaer Co.-Northern:* Rev. DONALD OPHALS; *Southern:* Rev. GEORGE G. ST. JOHN; *Saratoga:* Rev. EDWARD PRATT; *Schenectady Co.:* Rev. JOHN PROVOST; *Schoharie:* Rev. THOMAS BERARDI; *Warren:* Rev. JOSEPH ANSELMENT; *Washington:* Rev. BARRY LONERGAN.

Diocesan Offices and Directors

All Diocesan Offices and Directors are located at *The Pastoral Center, 40 N. Main Ave., Albany, 12203.* Tel: 518-453-6600; Fax: 518-453-6793 unless otherwise indicated.

Office of Real Property—NOEL A. OLSEN, Dir. Tel: 518-453-6623.

Receptionist—Ms. SUZANNE SECOR; Ms. ZOE BOPP; Ms. PEG GILBRIDE.

Administrative Review Board (Due Process)—Rev. DAVID BERBERIAN, J.C.L., Chm. Tel: 518-453-6620.

Apostleship of Prayer—Rev. JOHN J. PARET, S.J., *Auriesville, 12016.* Tel: 518-853-3153.

Korean Catholic Apostolate—Rev. PIUS BIO JUNG, *10 Lodge St., Albany, 12207.*

Bishop's Appeal—JOHN MANNING, Dir. Tel: 518-453-6680.

Black Apostolate—Rev. KOFI NTSIFUL-AMISSAH, Admin., *St. George's Church, 50 Thornton St., Albany, 12206.* Tel: 518-462-9604.

Campus Ministry—Sr. MAUREEN O'LEARY, F.S.P., Diocesan Dir., *SUNY at Albany, P.O. Box 22225, Albany, 12222.* Tel: 518-489-8573.

Catholic Communication of Albany—ROBERT J. MURPHY, Dir., Media Office, *40 N. Main Ave., Albany, 12203.* Tel: 518-453-6690; Fax: 518-453-6793.

Catholic Deaf Ministry—Rev. JAMES E. CLARK, Chap., *24 Wells Ave., P.O. Box 311, Middleburgh, 12122-0311.* Tel: 518-827-5132; Fax: 518-827-7873.

Cemeteries—Rev. ROBERT BUCKLEY, Diocesan Dir., *St. Agnes Cemetery, 48 Cemetery Ave., Menands, Albany, 12204.* Tel: 518-432-4953., *Res., 18 Pearl St., Schuylerville, 12871.* RICHARD TOUCHETTE, Exec. Dir.

Censores Librorum—Rev. JOHN R. ROOS, J.C.D.

Catholic Office for Motion Pictures—Rev. ANTHONY D. GULLEY, Diocesan Dir., *Res., 607 Central Ave., Albany, 12205.* Tel: 518-482-3375.

Architecture and Building Commission—Rev. THOMAS PHELAN, Chm. CAROL FITZGERALD, Coord. Tel: 518-453-6622.

Communications Commission—Rev. GEOFFREY BURKE, Public Information Officer. Tel: 518-453-6612. ROBERT J. MURPHY, Dir. Media Operations & Devel. Tel: 518-453-6690.

Cursillos in Christianity Diocese of Albany—Rev. CHRISTOPHER J. DRENNEN, O.S.A., *Assumption/St. Paul, 52 William St., P.O. Box 308, Mechanicville, 12118.* Tel: 518-664-6196.

Diocesan Service Committee for Charismatic Renewal—Rev. MARTIN FISHER, Liaison, *62 Warren St., Glen Falls, 12801.* Tel: 518-792-0989. JAMES B. RYAN, Communications, *707 Pleasantview Ave., Scotia, 12302.*

Diocesan Stewardship Office—JOHN MANNING. Tel: 518-453-6680.

Department of Information Resources—MICHAEL R. SCHWAB, Dir. Tel: 518-453-6685; Fax: 518-453-6779.

Catholic Charities of Diocese of Albany, Inc.; St. Vincent's Child Care Society, Inc.—Sr. MAUREEN JOYCE, R.S.M., Exec. Dir. & Sec. to the Bishop for Health and Social Svcs. Tel: 518-453-6650; Fax: 518-453-6792. Sr. MAUREEN JOYCE, R.S.M., Sec., St. Vincent's Child Care Society, Inc. RICHARD MARINI, Chief Financial Officer; Sr. PEG SULLIVAN, R.S.M., Assoc. Exec. Dir. WILLIAM J. PRZYLUCKI, Assoc. Exec. Dir. KAREN DEHAIS, Assoc. Exec. Dir. ALBERT TURO, Assoc. Exec. Dir. Catholic Relief Svcs., Disaster Relief Svcs. & Staff.

Catholic Family Service Agencies—100 Slingerland St., Albany, 12202. Tel: 518-426-3511. DIGNA BETANCOURT-SWINGLE, Dir., Catholic Charities of Montgomery County, *1 Kimball St., Amsterdam, 12010.* Tel: 518-842-4202. AGNES DONLON, Dir., Catholic Charities of Colombia & Greene Counties, *431 E. Allen St., Hudson, 12534.* Tel: 518-828-8660. JOHN NASSO, Dir., Catholic Charities of Fulton County, *208 W. State St., Johnstown, 12095.* Tel: 518-762-8313. DAVID BRUCE, Dir., Catholic Charities of Herkimer County, *61 West St., Ilion, 13357.* Tel: 315-894-9917. JOSEPH WALKER, Dir., Catholic Charities, Delaware & Otsego Counties, *9-11 S. Main St., Oneonta, 13820.* Tel: 607-432-0061. Sr. CHARLA COMMINS, Dir., Catholic Charities of Saratoga, Warren & Washington Counties, *142 Regent St., Saratoga, 12866.* Tel: 518-587-5000. JOHN D. STEELE, Dir., Catholic Charities of Schenectady County, *818 Union St., Schenectady, 12308.* Tel: 518-372-5667. THOMAS MAYER, Dir., Family and Community Svcs., Schoharie Co., *41 W. Main St., Cobleskill, 12043.* Tel: 518-234-3541. LINDA BONESTEEL, Dir., Catholic Charities, Northern Albany & Rensselaer Cos., *1400 Eighth Ave., Watervliet, 12189.* Tel: 518-272-4964.

Other Agencies and Commissions—Sr. SERENA BRANSON, D.C., Staff, Commission on Aging, *40 N. Main Ave., Albany, 12203.* Tel: 518-453-6650. BARBARA DITOMMASO, Dir., Commission on Peace & Justice, *40 N. Main Ave., Albany, 12203.* Tel: 518-453-6650. Vacant; Staff, Task Force on Chemical Dependency, *40 N. Main Ave., Albany, 12203.* Tel: 518-453-6650. MARTHA HAASE, Dir., Caregivers Program, *100 Slingerland St., Albany, 12202.* Tel: 518-449-2001. Sr. MARY ANN LOGIUDICE, R.S.M., Dir., Community Maternity Svcs., *27 N. Main Ave., Albany, 12203.* Tel: 518-482-8836. GARY SIEGEL, Dir., Catholic Charities Disabilities Svcs., *15 Avis Dr., Latham, 12210.* Tel: 518-482-8904. Vacant; Catholic Charities Housing, *40 N. Main Ave., Albany, 12203.* Tel: 518-453-6650. Vacant; Supvr., Masterson Child Devel. Center, *50 Philip St., Albany, 12207.* Tel: 518-434-8585. DENISE KIRKLEY-CAIN, Dir., Neighborhood Community Centre, *340 1st St., Albany, 12206.* Tel: 518-465-5408. Sr. CLAUDETTE HARRIS, C.S.J., Dir., Sunnyside Center, *P.O. Box 1410, Troy, 12181.* Tel: 518-274-5986. PETER NAPOLITANO, Dir., St. Charles Lwanga Center, *115 Grand St., Albany, 12202.* Tel: 518-465-4973. Sr. ANNE TRANELLI, C.S.J., Dir., Hispanic Outreach Svcs., *40 N. Main Ave., Albany, 12203.* Tel: 518-453-6655. KAREN LAQUIDARA-DICKINSON, Dir., HIV/AIDS Svcs., *40 N. Main Ave., Albany, 12203.* Tel: 518-453-6650. JAMES J. MCCORMACK, Ph.D., Health Care Coord., *Diocesan Community Health Alliance, 40 N. Main Ave., Albany, 12203.* Tel: 518-453-6650. Bro. LARRY BACKUS, C.S.C., Dir., Diocesan Jail Ministry, *St. Joseph's Center, Valatie, 12184.* Tel: 518-784-9481.

Campaign for Human Development—ALBERT TURO. Tel: 518-453-6650.

Catholic Relief Services—See Catholic Charities of the Diocese of Albany.

Disaster Relief Services—See Catholic Charities of the Diocese of Albany.

Health and Hospitals Office—Sr. MAUREEN JOYCE, Bishop's Rep. Tel: 518-453-6650.

Catholic Women's Service League—ROSE E. CIANI, Pres., *c/o LaSalle, 391 Western Ave., Albany, 12203.* Tel: 518-426-8202.

Ladies of Charity—BETTY ELLIOTT, *107 Van Wies Point, Glenmont, 12077.* Tel: 518-449-8060.

Society of St. Vincent de Paul—EDWARD NARE, Diocesan Central Council Pres., *202 S. Ballston Ave., Scotia, 12302.* Tel: 518-374-2548. EMMET J. LYNCH, Pres. Emeritus; Rev. RICHARD DOWNS, Spiritual Dir., *12 Rosemont St., Albany, 12203.* Tel: 518-489-8197.

Consultation Center of the Diocese of Albany—A non-profit Mental Health Center, which provides quality professional psychological counseling services and educational programs in the area of mental health, to individuals and groups.

Office—Rev. ANTHONY J. CHIARAMONTE, Ph.D., Dir.; Sr. MARY FRANCES BECK, S.N.J.M., Admin. Dir.; Rev. JOHN J. MALECKI, Ph.D., Psychologist; KATHLEEN STIFFEN, Sec., *790 Lancaster St., Albany, 12203.* Tel: 518-489-4431.

Psychological Counseling—Provides individual therapy, psychological testing, and consultative services to individuals and groups in matters calling for psychological expertise.

Group Therapy—Provides a variety of different kinds of therapy groups.

Educational Programs—Offers lectures and workshops in the area of mental health and personal growth. The Center also offers specialized workshops and training programs to meet the needs of various groups.

Counseling for Laity—Sr. ANNE BRYAN SMOLLIN, C.S.J., Ph.D., Exec. Dir. ETTA JONES, Admin. Asst., *40 N. Main Ave., Albany, 12203.* Tel: 518-453-6625. Provides individual and group psychological counseling-therapy by certified trained therapists. The staff provides services for the Young Married program and assessments for second marriages. Consultation and training programs are offered upon request.

Diocesan Pastoral Council—PATRICIA MOUSAW, Staff; PAT BARR, Chm. JOANNE SCHEIBLY, Vice Chm. Tel: 518-453-6661.

Drug Education Ministry—JEANNE COTE, Prog. Dir., *40 N. Main Ave., Albany, 12203.* Tel: 518-453-6771; Fax: 518-453-6793.

Ecumenical and Interreligious Affairs of the Roman Catholic Diocese of Albany, Commission for—Sr. MAUREEN O'LEARY F.S.P.; AUDREY HUGHES; Deacons WILLIAM GAFFNEY; EARLE FLATT; Sr. JOAN NOLAN, O.P.; JOAN HOLMAN; JOAN LIPSCOMB; Rev. THOMAS PHELAN; Ms. PATRICIA CREWELL; Ms. MARGE MILANESE; Sr. MARY GEN SMYTHE, R.C.S.J.; JOAN DUNHAM; Sr. ELIZABETH HOYE, R.S.C.J.; FRANK M. PELL; Revs. MAURICE DROWN; JAMES KANE, Dir.; Mrs. ELLEN SERVISS, Sec. Tel: 518-453-6660.

"The Evangelist"—Diocesan Newspaper *Albany Catholic Press Assoc., Inc.,* JAMES P. BREIG, Editor. Tel: 518-453-6688.

Family Life Office—Sr. KAY RYAN, C.S.J., Dir. Assoc. Dirs.: MARY MORIARTY; LAURA WEBER; KAREN FONTANELLI, Admin. Asst. Tel: 518-453-6677. Bereavement Ministry; Catholic Singles; Family Perspective; Marriage & Remarriage Preparation; Marriage & Family Enrichment; Natural Family Planning; Parenting; Respect Life; Separated, Divorced & Widowed; Young Adult Ministry.

Natural Family Planning—MARGARET FURLONG MALLOY, Coord. Tel: 518-453-6610.

Education Sites—HELENE WALLINGFORD, *St. Peter's Hospital, 315 S. Manning Blvd., Albany, 12208.* Tel: 518-525-1388. LOIS HAGGERTY, *St. Mary's Hospital, 380 Guy Park Ave., Amsterdam, 12010.* Tel: 518-842-1900, Ext. 463.

Chancery Office—40 N. Main Ave., Albany, 12203. Tel: 518-453-6612.

Holy Name Societies—Rev. WILLIAM W. CRANDALL, Dir., *St. Joseph Rectory, 181 Main St., Worcester, 12197.* Tel: 607-397-9373.

Initial & Ongoing Formation—Rev. THOMAS POWERS, Dir., Continuing Education of Clergy and Ministry to Priests Program. Tel: 518-453-6670. ELIZABETH ROWE, Formation for Ministry Program. Tel: 518-453-6678. Rev. JOHN MOLYN, Dir., Vocations & Diaconate Formation Program. Tel: 518-453-6678.

Legion of Mary—Deacon WILLIAM J. BRETT, *197 Woods Edge Ct., Voorheesville, 12186.*

Office of Religious Education—JEANNE SCHREMPF, Diocesan Dir. CHRISTOPHER WEBER, Assoc. Dir., Catechist Formation; DAVID G. AMICO, Assoc. Dir., Persons with Developmental Disabilities; Sr. ANNA TANTSITS, I.H.M., Assoc. Dir., Adult Faith Formation; MARY HARRISON, Assoc. Dir., Youth Ministry; JOYCE SOLIMINI, Assoc. Dir., Children and Adolescents.

Permanent Diaconate Office—Co-Directors: Deacons FRANK LUKOVITS; TIMOTHY MCAULIFFE. Tel: 518-453-6670.

Catholic Foundation—Most Rev. HOWARD J. HUBBARD, Pres. JOHN MANNING, Exec. Dir. Tel: 518-453-6680.

Office of Prayer & Worship—CATHY ANN LAVENDER, Dir., *40 N. Main Ave., Albany, 12203.* Tel: 518-453-6645; Fax: 518-453-6793.

Priests Personnel Board—Revs. GEOFFREY BURKE, Chm. KENNETH DOYLE; JOHN BRADLEY; WILLIAM JILLISKY; JAMES WALSH.

Priests Retirement Board—Revs. GEOFFREY D. BURKE, Chm. MARTIN FISHER; JOSEPH E. ANSELMENT; JOHN T. PROVOST; MORRIS R. DWYER; MICHAEL A. FARANO; JOHN F. CONNOLLY; Rev. Msgr. HOWARD F. MANNY; Rev. Msgr. JAMES G. HART; Mr. RICHARD FARRELL. Tel: 518-453-6612.

Priests' Retirement Plan—Rev. GEOFFREY BURKE, Chancellor.

Propagation of the Faith-Pontifical Society—Revs. MICHAEL A. FARANO, Dir. Tel: 518-453-6675.

Schools: Diocesan School Board—ALBERT J. BROWN, JR. Tel: 518-453-6666.

Diocesan School Office—Sr. MARY JANE HERB, I.H.M., Supt. of Schools. Tel: 518-453-6666. THOMAS FITZGERALD, Asst. Supt., Admin. Svcs. NANCY MACHOLD, Dir. Devel. JEANNE COTE, Drug & Alcohol Education Prog. CURTIS A. MCEWAN, Business Mgr. SAL CARBONE, Coord., Special Projects - Asbestos; STEPHEN PARTISANO, Coord., Special Projects-Mandated Svcs. THOMAS BUCCINO, Technology Consultant.

Scouting—Rev. JOSEPH SCHUCK, Diocesan Chap., *c/o Gilead House of Prayer, 1101 State Hwy. 7, Unadilla, 13849-9771.* Tel: 607-369-2317.

St. Bernards Institute/Albany—Sr. MARGERY HALPIN, R.S.M., Dir., *40 N. Main Ave., Albany, 12203.* Tel: 518-453-6760; Fax: 518-453-6793.

Vicar for Religious—Sr. NOLA BRUNNER, C.S.J. Tel: 518-453-6662. Rev. JOHN ROOS, Asst. Vicar, *Res., St. Mary Rectory, 31 Elm St., Cooperstown, 13326.* Tel: 607-547-2213.

Vocations and Vocation Awareness Program—Rev. JOHN MOLYN, Diocesan Dir. Tel: 518-453-6678.

CLERGY, PARISHES, MISSIONS AND PAROCHIAL SCHOOLS

CITY OF ALBANY
(Albany County)

1—CATHEDRAL OF THE IMMACULATE CONCEPTION, Rev. William H. Pape, Rector; Deacon Arthur H. Egan. In res., Most Rev. Howard J. Hubbard Tel: 518-462-3804; Revs. Peter J. Sullivan, III Tel: 518-465-7244; Dennis P. Murphy.
Rectory Office: 125 Eagle St., 12202. Tel: 518-463-4447; Fax: 518-436-5177.
Religious Education Office—Tel: 518-436-7918.
Cathedral Social Services—Tel: 518-463-2279.
Convent—93 Park Ave., 12202. Tel: 518-436-7697. Sisters 13.

2—ST. JOHN-ST. ANN, Rev. John Kirwin.
Office: 157 Franklin St., 12202. Tel: 518-472-9091; Fax: 518-427-5983.

3—BLESSED SACRAMENT, Revs. John J. Bradley; Anthony Ligato; Sr. Ann Rose, C.S.J., Pastoral Assoc.; Deacon William Fitzgerald. In res., Rev. Anthony D. Gulley.
Res., 607 Central Ave., 12206. Tel: 518-482-3375.
School—605 Central Ave., 12206. Tel: 518-438-5854; Fax: 518-438-1532. Sr. Jane Somerville, Prin. Sisters of Mercy 1; Lay Teachers 18; Students 248.

4—ST. CASIMIR (Polish). Attended by Our Lady of Angels. Rev. Joseph Angelini, O.F.M.Conv., Admin. In res., Revs. Francis A. O'Connor; Frank Gilchrist.
Res., 324 Sheridan Ave., 12206. Tel: 518-463-7147.
School—Tel: 518-434-4264. Arthur Farrington, Prin. Sisters of the Resurrection 3; Lay Teachers 14; Students 290.
Convent—315 Sheridan Ave., 12206. Tel: 518-463-5440.

5—ST. CATHERINE OF SIENA, Rev. Kennth Doyle; Deacon Gerald Ladouceur. In res., Revs. John A. Keefe; Joseph Romano; Robert Donnelly; John Tallman.
Res., 40 Collins Pl., 12208. Tel: 518-489-3204; Fax: 518-482-3721.
School—35 Hurst Ave., 12208. Tel: 518-439-3111. Theresa L. Ewell, Prin.
Lay Teachers 17; Students 245.

6—ST. GEORGE (Lithuanian), Rev. Kofi Amissah, Admin. & Dir. Black Apostolate.
Res., 50 Thornton St., 12206. Tel: 518-463-3585.

7—CHURCH OF THE HOLY CROSS, Revs. Daniel J. Maher; Peter Sullivan; Sr. Helen Charles, Spiritual Growth Coord.
Res., 12 Rosemont St., 12203. Tel: 518-489-8197.
School—Rosement St., 12203. Tel: 518-438-0066. Sr. Mary Ellen Owens, Prin.
Sisters 1; Lay Teachers 16; Students 291.

8—ST. JAMES, Rev. Dominic Ingemie; Sr. Geraldine Kennah, C.S.J., Assoc. Pastoral Care; Deacon Bill Gorman. In res., Rev. Msgr. James Hart; Rev. Anthony Sidoti, Pastor Emeritus.
Res., 391 Delaware Ave., 12209. Tel: 518-434-4028.
School—50 Summit Ave., 12209. Tel: 518-465-1973. Mrs. Elizabeth Rubinstein, Prin.
Sisters 5; Lay Teachers 12; Students 208.
Convent—58 Summit Ave., 12209. Tel: 518-449-7993.
Mission—Albany, Albany Co., Child's Hospital & Eden Park Nursing Home.

9—ST. JOSEPH, Rev. Thomas Hayes, Admin.
Parish Office: 31 Walter St., 12204. Tel: 518-463-3286.

10—ST. MARGARET MARY, Rev. Thomas H. Chevalier; Deacons Richard D. Cioppa; J. Neil Hook. In res., Revs. Raymond Dlugos, O.S.A.; John Fitzpatrick; James Fitzmaurice, O.F.M.
Parish Office: 1168 Western Ave., 12203. Tel: 518-482-4497.

11—ST. MARY, Rev. James Lefebvre; Deacon George Witko. In res., Revs. Lloyd Rebeyro; Pius-Bio Jung.
Res., 10 Lodge St., 12207. Tel: 518-462-4254; Fax: 518-462-4255.
Chapel—111 Washington Ave., 12203.

12—OUR LADY OF ANGELS, Revs. Joseph Angelini, O.F.M.Conv., Guardian; Germain Williams, O.F.M.Conv. In res., Revs. Rufino Maloney, O.F.M.Conv., Guardian; Salvatore Pantano, O.F.M.Conv.; Evan Roche, O.F.M.; Nicholas Weiss, O.F.M.Conv.; Thomas Crimmins, O.F.M.Conv.; Bro. Leo Merriman, O.F.M.Conv.
Res., 183 Central Ave., 12206. Tel: 518-463-3262; Fax: 518-463-3264. [CEM]

13—OUR LADY HELP OF CHRISTIANS (German), Very Rev. Robert J. Hohenstein, V.F.
Res., 74 Second Ave., 12202. Tel: 518-463-7338; 434-4868. [CEM]

14—ST. PATRICK, Rev. Francis A. O'Connor.
Office: 283 Central Ave., 12206. Tel: 518-465-3685.

15—SACRED HEART OF JESUS, Revs. Thomas J. Hayes, Admin.; John Diem Dihn Tran, C.M.C.
Res., 31 Walter St., 12204. Tel: 518-463-3286.

16—ST. TERESA OF AVILA, Rev. William D. Turnbull; Deacon Raymond Sullivan. In res., Revs. John L. Close; John L. Jones, (Retired).
Res., 435 New Scotland Ave., 12208. Tel: 518-438-7851.
Schools—(Grades PreK-5) 433 New Scotland Ave., 12208. Tel: 518-438-5268.; (Grades 6-8) 8 Hollywood Ave., 12208. Tel: 518-482-3736; Fax: 518-482-3745. Sr. Patricia Houlihan, R.S.M., Prin.
Sisters of Mercy 4; Lay Teachers 10; Students 218.
Convent—401 New Scotland Ave., 12208. Tel: 518-482-8901.
Mission—Albany, Albany Co., Albany Medical Center.

17—ST. VINCENT DE PAUL, Rev. Leo P. O'Brien; Deacon William Gaffney.
Parish Office: 900 Madison Ave., 12208. Tel: 518-489-5408; Fax: 518-489-5474.
Res., 599 Hudson Ave., 12203. Tel: 518-489-0563.

OUTSIDE THE CITY OF ALBANY

Altamont, Albany Co., St. Lucy, Rev. Paul Smith; Sr. Mary Lou Liptak, R.S.M., Parish Life Dir.
Parish House: 109 Grand St., 12009. Tel: 518-861-8770.
Mission—Berne, Albany Co., St. Bernadette, 1763 Helderberg Trail, Berne, 12023. Tel: 518-872-1131.

Amsterdam, Montgomery Co.,

1—ST. CASIMIR, (Lithuanian), Rev. Joseph J. Grabys.
Res., 260 E. Main St., 12010. Tel: 518-842-5481. [CEM]

2—ST. JOHN THE BAPTIST, (Polish), Rev. Stanislaus J. Swierzowski.
Res., 40 Van Derveer St., 12010. Tel: 518-842-6851. [CEM]

3—ST. JOSEPH-ST. MICHAEL-OUR LADY OF MOUNT CARMEL. Canonically merged parishes in 1980. Rev. Lawrence J. Decker.
Mailing Address: P.O. Box 699, 12010.
Office: 39 St. John St. & 58 Grove St., 12010. Tel: 518-843-3250; Fax: 518-453-4070.
Res., 35 St. John St., 12010.

4—ST. JOSEPH. Canonically merged in 1980 into St. Joseph-St. Michael-Our Lady of Mount Carmel. All inquiries should be directed to the listed address, 39 St. John St. & 58 Grove St., Amsterdam, NY 12010.

5—ST. MICHAEL THE ARCHANGEL. Canonically merged in 1980 into St. Joseph-St. Michael-Our Lady of Mount Carmel. All inquiries should be directed to the listed address, 39 St. John St. & 58 Grove St., Amsterdam, NY 12010.

6—OUR LADY OF MT. CARMEL, (Italian). Canonically merged in 1980 into St. Joseph-St. Michael-Our Lady of Mount Carmel. All inquiries should be directed to the listed address, 39 St. John St. & 58 Grove St., Amsterdam, NY 12010.

7—ST. MARY, Rev. James Gulley.
Res., 156 E. Main St., 12010. Tel: 518-842-4500. [CEM]
School—St. Mary Institute, Upper Church St., 12010. Tel: 518-842-5452.
Sisters 2; Lay Teachers 28; Students 515.

8—ST. STANISLAUS, (Polish), Revs. Walter Czechowicz; Edward Sipperly.
Res., 73 Reid St., 12010. Tel: 518-842-2771. [CEM]
School—42-44 Cornell St., 12010. Tel: 518-842-6710. Sr. M. Bernice, C.S.S.F., Prin.
Felician Sisters 3; Lay Teachers 7; Students 212.
Convent—46 Cornell St., 12010. Tel: 518-842-2621.

Athens, Greene Co., St. Patrick, Rev. Richard J. Doyle.
Res., 19 N. Franklin St., 12015. Tel: 518-945-1656.

Averill Park, Rensselaer Co., St. Henry, Rev. Peter N. Pagones; Deacons Frank Lukovits; John W. Novak; Robert Pasquarelli.
Res., Crystal Lake Rd., P.O. Box 550, 12018. Tel: 518-674-3818. [CEM 2]

Ballston Lake, Saratoga Co., Our Lady of Grace, Rev. Anthony C. Diacetis.
Res., 73 Midline Rd., 12019. Tel: 518-399-5713; Fax: 518-399-5713.

Ballston Spa, Saratoga Co., St. Mary, Rev. John F. French.
Res., 167 Milton Ave., 12020. Tel: 518-885-7411; Fax: 518-885-6863. [CEM]
School—40 Thompson St., 12020. Tel: 518-885-7300; Fax: 518-855-7378. Sr. Annette M. Allard, C.S.J., Prin.
Sisters 2; Lay Teachers 8; Students 144.

Berlin, Rensselaer Co., Sacred Heart, Rev. Kenneth Gregory; Sr. Kenan McGowan, R.S.M., Parish Life Dir.
Res., P.O. Box 243, Main St., 12022. Tel: 518-658-2780.
Mission—Stephentown, St. Joseph. [CEM]

Bolton Landing, Warren Co., Blessed Sacrament, Rev. Peter G. Young.
Res., Goodman Ave., P.O. Box 266, 12814. Tel: 518-644-3861. [CEM]

Broadalbin, Fulton Co., St. Joseph, Rev. Timothy Mangan, S.S.S.
Res., 7 North St., 12025. Tel: 518-883-3774; Fax: 518-883-3774.
Mission—Galway, St. Mary. [CEM]

Cairo, Greene Co., Sacred Heart, Revs. Jeremiah Nunan; Sean McMahon. In res., Rev. John F. Mallon.
Res., Mountain Ave., 12413. Tel: 518-622-3319; Fax: 518-622-0131.
Missions—East Durham, Greene Co., Our Lady of Knock Shrine; East Durham, St. Mary.

Cambridge, Washington Co., St. Patrick, Revs. Thomas Konopka; Liam Condon; Sr. Anne Sheridan, C.S.J., Parish Life Dir.
Res., 17 S. Park St., 12816-1248. Tel: 518-677-2757. [CEM]

Canajoharie, Montgomery Co., St. Peter's and Paul's, Rev. William J. Gaffigan.
Res., 100 Cliff St., 13317-1199. Tel: 518-673-3333. [CEM]

Castleton-on-Hudson, Rensselaer Co., Sacred Heart, Rev. Thomas J. Krupa.
Res., 3 Catholic Way, 12033-1526. Tel: 518-732-2155; Fax: 518-732-4906. [CEM 2]
Missions—Schodack Landing, Assumption of B.V.M. [CEM]
Schodack Landing, Shrine of St. Jude. [CEM]

Catskill, Greene Co., St. Patrick, Revs. John J. Murphy; John Medwid, Assoc.
Res., 157 Bridge St., 12414. Tel: 518-943-3150.
School—80 Woodland Ave., 12414. Tel: 518-943-2952.
Franciscan Sisters of Allegany 1; Lay Teachers 10; Students 188.
Convent—82 Woodland Ave., 12414. Tel: 518-943-5341.
Missions—Leeds, St. Bridget; Smith's Landing, St. Mary's, 6104 Rte. 9W, Smith's Landing, 12415.

Chatham, Columbia Co., St. James, Rev. Gary Paul Gelfenbien; Deacon Peter Trawinski.
Res., 129 Hudson Ave., 12037. Tel: 518-392-4991.

Cherry Valley, Otsego Co., St. Thomas the Apostle, Rev. Santino Titta.
Res., 24 Maple Ave., 13320. Tel: 607-264-3779.
Mission—Springfield Center, Blessed Sacrament.

Chestertown, Warren Co., St. John the Baptist, Rev. Joseph O'Brien, Admin.
Res., Riverside Dr., P.O. Box 471, 12817. Tel: 518-494-2617.

Clifton Park, Saratoga Co., St. Edward the Confessor, Revs. John L. Cairns; John R. Lanese; Deacons Jerry Grigaitis; Walter MacKinnon.
Office: Tel: 518-371-7372; Fax: 518-371-1206.
Res., 21 Hemlock Dr., 12065-4845. Tel: 518-371-9595.

Clinton Heights, Rensselaer Co., St. Mary, Revs. Jerome R. Gingras; J. Joseph Delaney, Pastor Emeritus.
Res., 163 Columbia Tpke., East Greenbush, 12144. Tel: 518-449-2232; Fax: 518-449-2234.
School—Tel: 518-449-2498. Sr. Patricia Lynch, R.S.M., Supr.
Lay Teachers 16; Students 249.

Cobleskill, Schoharie Co., St. Vincent de Paul, Rev. Thomas F. Berardi; Deacon Gary Surman.
Res., One Washington Heights, 12043. Tel: 518-234-2892. [CEM]
Mission—Sharon Springs, St. Mary.

Cohoes, Albany Co.,

1—ST. AGNES-ST. PATRICK, Rev. Arthur J. Becker; Deacons Owen South; Albert Schrempf.
Office: 49 Johnston Ave., 12047. Tel: 518-237-6091.
Res., 122 Vliet Blvd., 12047-1842. Tel: 518-237-2373; Fax: 518-238-9427.
School—Cohoes Consolidated Catholic Schools. See separate listing.

2—ST. BERNARD, Revs. Lawrence G. McTavey; Marc L. Touchette; Deacon Walter MacKinnon; Sr. Margaret Totten, C.S.J., Pastoral Assoc. In res., Rev. John Phillips.
Res., P.O. Box 137, 107 Canvass St., 12047. Tel: 518-237-2721; Fax: 518-237-7980.

3—ST. JOSEPH, (French), Rev. Joseph S. Robitaille.

Res., 65 Congress St., 12047. Tel: 518-237-4241. [CEM]
School—Cohoes Consolidated Catholic Schools. See separate listing.

4—ST. MARIE, Rev. Arthur J. Becker; Deacons Owen South; Albert Schrempf.
Res., 122 Vliet Blvd., 12047. Tel: 518-237-2373; Fax: 518-238-9427.
School—Cohoes Consolidated Catholic Schools. See separate listing.

5—ST. MICHAEL, (Polish), Rev. Richard W. Dybas.
Res., 36 Page Ave., 12047. Tel: 518-237-5151. [CEM]

6—ST. RITA-SACRED HEART, Rev. John Facci, S.A.C.
Res., 50 St. Rita Ln., 12047. Tel: 518-237-4444.
Mission—Cohoes, Sacred Heart of Jesus.

Colonie, Albany Co., Our Lady of Mercy, Rev. John F. Waldron.
Res., 424 Shaker Run, 12205. Tel: 518-456-8269.
Parish Center: 26 Wilson Ave., 12205. Tel: 518-459-1272.

St. Clare, Rev. Michael T. Schmitt; Deacon George Nahm. In res., Rev. Michael Miller.
Res., 1947 Central Ave., 12205-4299. Tel: 518-456-3112; Fax: 518-456-1072.

Cooperstown, Otsego Co., St. Mary, Rev. John R. Roos.
Res., 31 Elm St., 13326. Tel: 607-547-2213. [CEM 2]

Copake Falls, Columbia Co., St. Bridget, Rev. Peter Russo; Deacon Martin Stosiek.
Res., 8074 State Rte. 22, 12517. Tel: 518-329-4711; Fax: 518-329-4240. [CEM]

Corinth, Saratoga Co., Immaculate Conception, Rev. Owen F. Shanley.
Res., 409 Palmer Ave., 12822. Tel: 518-654-2113. [CEM]

Coxsackie, Greene Co., St. Mary, Rev. John L. Moyna.
Res., 80 Mansion St., 12051. Tel: 518-731-8800; Fax: 518-731-8505. [CEM]

Crescent, Saratoga Co., St. Mary, Rev. Richard Broderick; Deacon Walter Srode.
Parish Center: 86 Church Hill Rd., Waterford, 12188. Tel: 518-371-9632; Fax: 518-371-7235.

Delanson, Schenectady Co., Our Lady of Fatima, Rev. John Connolly.
Res., 1735 Alexander Rd., P.O. Box 219, 12053. Tel: 518-895-2788.

Delhi, Delaware Co., St. Peter, Rev. Joseph Manerowski.
Res., 8 Franklin St., P.O. Box 71, 13753. Tel: 607-746-2503.

Delmar, Albany Co., St. Thomas the Apostle, Revs. James D. Daley; James J. Walsh; Deacon Alfred Manzella.
Res., 35 Adams Pl., 12054. Tel: 518-439-4951; Fax: 518-439-0108.
School—42 Adams Pl., 12054. Tel: 518-439-5573; Fax: 518-439-0108. Sr. Mary Frederick Coyne, S.N.J.M., Prin.
Lay Teachers 18; Students 271.

Dolgeville, Herkimer Co., St. Joseph, Rev. Leo F. Potvin; Deacon Peter Manno.
Res., 31 N. Helmer Ave., 13329. Tel: 315-429-8338. [CEM 2]

East Greenbush, Rensselaer Co., Holy Spirit, Rev. George G. St. John; Deacons William Dringus; Cyril Lavin. In res., Rev. Joseph M. Siniskey.
Res., 667 Columbia Tpke., 12061. Tel: 518-477-7925.
School—Highland Dr., 12061. Tel: 518-477-5739; Fax: 518-477-5743. Sr. Maureen Moffitt, C.S.J., Prin.
Sisters 1; Lay Teachers 17; Students 246.

Fonda, Montgomery Co., St. Cecilia, Rev. Kevin Kenny, O.F.M.Conv. In res., Rev. Andre Lambert, O.F.M.Conv.; Bro. Kenneth Lucas, O.F.M.Conv.
Res., 26 Broadway, P.O. Box 837, 12068. Tel: 518-853-4195. [CEM]

Fort Ann, Washington Co., St. Ann, Rev. William A. Gorman.
Res., 10 George St., P.O. Box 226, 12827. Tel: 518-639-5218.
Mission—South Hartford, St. Philip.

Fort Edward, Washington Co., St. Joseph, Rev. James Rosoh; Deacon Donald Webster. In res., Rev. Edward N. Leroux.
Res., 164 Broadway, 12828. Tel: 518-747-5117; Fax: 518-747-3444. [CEM]

Fort Plain, Montgomery Co., St. James, Rev. Kenneth J. Swain.
Parish Office: Tel: 518-993-3822.
Res., 119 Reid St., P.O. Box 287, 13339-0287. Tel: 518-993-5523.

Frankfort, Herkimer Co., Our Lady Queen of Apostles (1995), Rev. John Yanas.
Res., 414 Frankfort St., 13340. Tel: 315-894-2025; 894-2360; Fax: 315-894-2025. [CEM]

St. Mary. Merged with SS. Peter & Paul, Frankfort, to form Our Lady Queen of Apostles, Frankfort, Jan. 8, 1995.

SS. Peter & Paul. Merged with St. Mary, Frankfort, to form Our Lady Queen of Apostles, Frankfort, Jan. 8, 1995.

Germantown, Columbia Co., Resurrection, Rev. Theodore Gerken.
Res., 9 Church Ave., P.O. Box 96, 12526. Tel: 518-537-6136. [CEM]
Mission—Linlithgo, Nativity of Our Lord.

Glens Falls, Warren Co., St. Alphonsus, Rev. Robert W. Powhida; Deacon William F. Bazinet.
Res., 35 Broad St., P.O. Box 2088, 12801. Tel: 518-792-1574; Fax: 518-792-6056. [CEM]
School—Merged with St. Mary's Academy to form St Mary's/St. Alphonsus Regional School. Tel: 518-792-1574; Fax: 518-792-6056.

St. Mary, Revs. Martin Fisher; Thomas Holmes; Deacon F. David Powers. In res., Rev. O. Robert DeMartinis.
Res., 62 Warren St., 12801. Tel: 518-792-0989; Fax: 518-792-0251.
School—St. Mary's/St. Alphonsus Regional School, Tel: 518-792-3178; Fax: 518-792-6056.

Glenville, Schenectady Co., Immaculate Conception, Revs. J. Thomas Connery; R. Mansfield Starks, Pastor Emeritus; Michael Flannery; Deacons August Van Patten; Michael Melanson.
Res., 400 Saratoga Rd., 12302. Tel: 518-399-9168; Fax: 518-384-3278.

Gloversville, Fulton Co., St. Mary. Canonically merged with Our Lady of Mount Carmel in 1990. See St. Mary of Mount Carmel.

St. Mary of Mt. Carmel. Consolidated from Our Lady of Mount Carmel and St. Mary in 1990. Rev. Donald Czelusniak.
Res., 149 S. Main St., 12078. Tel: 518-725-3143; Fax: 518-725-7245. [CEM]
Mission—Caroga Lake, St. Barbara.

Sacred Heart, Rev. Thomas Boyle, Admin.
Res., 189 Kingsboro Ave., 12078. Tel: 518-725-9375.

Grafton, Rensselaer Co., St. John Francis Regis, Sr. Mary Kenan McGowan, R.S.M., Parish Life Dir.; Rev. Kenneth Gregory, Sacramental Min.
Mailing Address: P.O. Box 234, 12082. Tel: 518-279-4943.

Granville, Washington Co., Roman Catholic Community of Granville. Consolidated St. Mary's, All Saints, and Our Lady of Mount Carmel. Rev. Thomas Zelker.
Res., 23 Bulkley Ave., 12832. Tel: 518-642-1262.
Parish Center: All Saints House, Morrison Ave., 12832.

St. Mary. Closed. For inquiries for parish records contact the Chancery.

Greenfield Center, Saratoga Co., St. Joseph, Rev. John Weyand; Deacon Arthur Turcott.
Res., 3159 Rte. 9N, P.O. Box 168, 12833. Tel: 518-893-7680.
Mission—Rock City Falls, St. Paul, Tel: 518-885-4877.

Green Island, Albany Co., St. Joseph, Rev. Donald Kelly.
Res., 131 George St., 12183. Tel: 518-273-3552; Fax: 518-273-3978.

Greenville, Greene Co., St. John the Baptist, Rev. William M. Bauer; Deacon Peter Sedlmeir.
Mailing Address: P.O. Box 340, 12083.
Office: R.D. No. 2, Box 2, 12083. Tel: 518-966-8317; Fax: 518-966-4652.
Mission—Crystal Lake.

Greenwich, Washington Co., St. Joseph, Rev. Thomas Konopka; Deacons Herbert Howley; William Gaul.
Res., 36 Bleecker St., 12834. Tel: 518-692-2159; Fax: 518-692-8706.

Guilderland, Albany Co., Christ the King, Revs. Patrick J. Butler; Mark Allman; Deacons Timothy McAuliffe; Joseph Markham.
Res., 20 Sumpter Ave., Albany, 12203. Tel: 518-456-1644; Fax: 518-456-4696.
School—Tel: 518-456-5400. Mr. Thomas F. Gould, Prin.
Lay Teachers 14; Students 190.

St. Madeleine Sophie, Revs. James Belogi; Desmond Rossi; Sr. Frances Mesley, R.S.M., Pastoral Assoc.; Deacons Earle Flatt; Gary Beck.
Res., 3500 Carman Rd., Schenectady, 12303. Tel: 518-355-0421.
School—3510 Carman Rd., Schenectady, 12303. Tel: 518-355-3080. Miss Teresa Kovarovic, Prin.
Lay Teachers 13; Students 186.
Convent—3514 Carman Rd., Schenectady, 12303. Tel: 518-355-8052.

Hagaman, Montgomery Co., St. Stephen, Rev. Ronald Matulewicz.
Res., 51 Pawling, 12086. Tel: 518-843-2951. [CEM]

Hague, Warren Co., Blessed Sacrament, Rev. Joseph O'Brien, Admin.
Res., Hague Rd., P.O. Box 529, 12836. Tel: 518-543-8828.
Mission—Brant Lake, Warren Co., St. Teresa of Avila.

Haines Falls, Greene Co., Immaculate Conception, Rev. Anthony Motta.
Res., Mountain House Rd., 12436. Tel: 518-589-5577. [CEM]
Missions—Elka Park, Greene Co., St. Francis de Sales; Lexington, St. Francis de Sales; Hunter, Greene Co., St. Mary of the Mountains; Haines Falls, Greene Co., Wayside Shrine.

Hancock, Delaware Co., St. Paul the Apostle, Rev. James Cribbs.
Res., 60 W. Main St., 13783. Tel: 607-637-2571. [CEM 2]

Herkimer, Herkimer Co., St. Anthony-St. Joseph, Rev. Robert Shinos; Sr. Patricia Woolheater, C.S.J., Pastoral Assoc.
Res., 228 S. Main St., 13350. Tel: 315-866-2892; 866-6373 (Parish Office).

St. Francis de Sales, Rev. Peter J. Nabozny.
Parish Center: 219 N. Bellinger St., 13350. Tel: 315-866-4282.
Res., 25 Park Pl. S., 13350. Tel: 315-866-7301. [CEM]
School—220 Henry St., 13350. Tel: 315-866-4831. Sr. Rosalie Kelly, C.S.J., Prin.
Sisters of St. Joseph of Carondolet 4; Lay Teachers 8; Students 190.
Convent—One Park Pl., 13350. Tel: 315-866-4492.

Hoosick Falls, Rensselaer Co., Immaculate Conception, Rev. Philip M. Cioppa.
Res., Box 269, 67 Main St., 12090. Tel: 518-686-5064; Fax: 518-686-1625. [CEM]
School—St. Mary Academy, 4 Parsons Ave., 12090. Tel: 518-686-4314; Fax: 518-686-5957. Mrs. Anne Marie Donovan, Prin.
Lay Teachers 13; Students 179.

Hudson, Columbia Co., Church of St. Mary. Canonically merged with Our Lady of Mount Carmel and Our Lady of Perpetual Help-Sacred Heart in 1991. Rev. Winston L. Bath. In res., Rev. Edward F. Cantwell.
Mailing Address: P.O. Box 323, 12534.
Res., 429 E. Allen St., 12534. Tel: 518-828-1334; Fax: 518-828-2783.

Our Lady of Mt. Carmel. Canonically merged with Church of St. Mary in 1991. All inquiries should be directed to P.O. Box 323, Hudson, NY 12534. Tel: 518-828-1334.

Our Lady of Perpetual Help-Sacred Heart (Polish). Canonically merged with Church of St. Mary in 1991. All inquiries should be directed to P.O. Box 323, Hudson, NY 12534. Tel: 518-828-1334.

Hudson Falls, Washington Co., Church of St. Mary's/St. Paul's (Sandy Hill). The Roman Catholic Community of Hudson Falls/Kingsbury. Revs. James B. Lonergan, V.F.; Leo L. Marcil, (Retired); Deacon Frank Herlihy.
Res., 11 Wall St., 12839. Tel: 518-747-4823; Fax: 518-747-2265. [CEM 2]

Immaculate Heart of Mary (Sandy Hill) (French). Canonically merged with St. Paul, Hudson Falls. Now called Church of St. Mary's/St. Paul's, Roman Catholic Community of Hudson Falls/Kingsbury.

St. Paul (Sandy Hill) (French). Canonically merged with Immaculate Heart of Mary parish, Hudson Falls. Now called Church of St. Mary's/St. Paul's, Roman Catholic Community of Hudson Falls/Kingsbury.

Ilion, Herkimer Co., Annunciation, Rev. Joseph Benintende.
Res., 109 West St., 13357. Tel: 315-894-3766; Fax: 315-894-1550. [CEM]

Johnsonville, Rensselaer Co., St. Monica's Church, Rev. Bernard R. Turner.
Res., St. Monica's Rectory, 16 St. Monica Ln., 12094. Tel: 518-753-4003; Fax: 518-753-4003.

Johnstown, Fulton Co., St. Anthony (Slovak), Rev. Francis Dunbar.
Res., 4 Nicholas St., 12095. Tel: 518-762-8176. [CEM]

Immaculate Conception (Italian), Rev. Joseph F. DiMaggio.
Res., One Warren St., 12095. Tel: 518-762-3272. [CEM]

St. Patrick, Rev. Joseph F. Barker.
Res., 205 Glebe St., 12095. Tel: 518-762-8775. [CEM]

Lake George, Warren Co., Sacred Heart, Revs. Paul Cox; James I. Donlon.
Res., 50 Mohican St., 12845. Tel: 518-668-2046; Fax: 518-668-4377.
Mission—Queensbury, Warren Co., Our Lady of the Assumption, Tel: 518-668-2046.

Lake Luzerne, Warren Co., Holy Infancy, Rev. Charles A. Gaffigan.

Res., 323 Lake Ave., 12846. Tel: 518-696-2625. [JC]

Latham, Albany Co., Our Lady of the Assumption, Revs. John J. Hardiman; David L. Tressic; Deacon Robert Rucinski.
Res., 498 Watervliet-Shaker Rd., 12110. Tel: 518-785-0234.

St. Ambrose, Revs. Francis J. DuBois; John Bertolucci. In res., Rev. George Phillips.
Res., 347 Old Loudon Rd., 12110. Tel: 518-785-1351; Fax: 518-785-8370.
School—Tel: 518-785-6453. Sr. Mary Catherine, P.B.V.M., Prin.
Sisters 11; Lay Teachers 9; Students 293.

Little Falls, Herkimer Co.,

1—ST. JOSEPH. Consolidated with St. Mary and Sacred Heart to form Holy Family Parish, Little Falls.

2—ST. MARY. Consolidated with St. Joseph and Sacred Heart to form Holy Family Parish, Little Falls.

3—SACRED HEART, (Polish). Consolidated with St. Joseph and St. Mary to form Holy Family Parish, Little Falls.

4—HOLY FAMILY, Rev. Charles R. Celeste; Sr. Marilyn Hayes, C.S.J., Pastoral Assoc.
Office: 763 E. Main St., 13365. Tel: 315-823-3410; 823-2110; Fax: 315-823-2701. [CEM]

Loudonville, Albany Co., St. Pius X, Revs. Michael A. Farano, V.G.; James McDevitt.
Res., 2 Fairview Rd., 12211. Tel: 518-462-1336; Fax: 518-462-1338.
School—Upper Loudon Rd., 12211. Tel: 518-465-4539. Nicholas Audi, Prin.
Sisters 3; Lay Teachers 19; Students 316.
Convent—Upper Loudon Rd., 12211. Tel: 518-449-1658.

St. Francis de Sales (1972), Revs. David E. Noone; Christopher Welch.
Church & Offices: One Maria Dr., 12211. Tel: 518-489-8386; Fax: 518-489-6910.
Res., 15 Exchange St., Albany, 12205. Tel: 518-489-8386.
Old Church—15 Exchange St., Albany, 12205.

Margaretville, Delaware Co., Sacred Heart, Rev. Robert H. Purcell, V.F.
Res., Academy St., 12455. Tel: 914-586-2665.
Missions—Andes, St. Ann; Roxbury, Our Lady of Good Counsel.

Mechanicville, Saratoga Co., Assumption-St. Paul, Revs. Christopher J. Drennen, O.S.A.; David Kelly, O.S.A. In res., Rev. Joseph Getz, O.S.A.; Deacon Arthur Canary.
Res., 52 William St., P.O. Box 308, 12118. Tel: 518-664-6196; Fax: 518-664-6782.
Convent—77 Viall Ave., 12118. Tel: 518-664-4053. Sisters of St. Joseph

Menands, Albany Co., St. Joan of Arc, Rev. William F. Jillisky; Deacon Andy Cohen.
Parish Office & Res.: 76 Menand Rd., 12204. Tel: 518-463-0378; 462-2496.

Middleburgh, Schoharie Co., St. Catherine, Rev. James E. Clark, Admin.
Res., 24 Wells Ave., 12122. Tel: 518-827-5132; Fax: 518-827-7873.

Mohawk, Herkimer Co., Blessed Sacrament, Rev. James Steuer.
Res., 54 E. Main St., 13407. Tel: 315-866-1752.

Morris, Otsego Co., Holy Cross, Rev. Morris R. Dwyer.
Res., 43 W. Main St., P.O. Box 118, 13808. Tel: 607-263-5143.
Mission—Edmeston, Nativity of B.V.M.

Nassau, Rensselaer Co., St. Mary, Rev. Antone Kandrac, O.F.M.Conv.; Deacon John Skelly.
Res., 26 Church St., P.O. Box 435, 12123. Tel: 518-766-2701. [CEM]

New Lebanon, Columbia Co., Immaculate Conception, Rev. Joseph Halloran.
Church—Church and Shrine of Our Lady of Lourdes, U.S. Rte. 20, 12125. Tel: 518-794-7651; 766-5651. [CEM]
Mission—Stephentown, St. Joseph's.

Newport, Herkimer Co., St. John the Baptist, Rev. Leo F. Potvin.
Res., Main St., Box 475, 13416. Tel: 315-845-8017.
Mission—Middleville, St. Mary of the Assumption. [CEM]

North Creek, Warren Co., St. James, Rev. Joseph O'Brien.
Res., Main St., 12853. Tel: 518-251-2518. [CEM]
Mission—Pottersville, St. Pius X.

Northville, Fulton Co., St. Francis of Assisi, Rev. Augustine Kapinus, O.F.M.Conv.
Mailing Address: P.O. Box 126, 12134.
Res., 501 Bridge St., 12134. Tel: 518-863-4736.

Oneonta, Otsego Co., St. Mary, Revs. Paul A. Roman; Brian Raiche; Mrs. Barbara Dugan Lilly, Pastoral Ministry; Susan Nesbitt, Campus Ministry.
Res., 39 Walnut St., 13820. Tel: 607-432-3920; Fax: 607-432-0772. [CEM]
School—38 Walnut St., 13820. Tel: 607-432-1450; Fax: 607-432-4826. Sr. Mary Christopher Comproski, C.R., Prin.
Religious 2; Lay Teachers 13; Students 215.
Convent—10 Irving Pl., 13820. Tel: 607-433-2220.

Palenville, Greene Co., Sacred Heart, Rev. Paul R. Guido, O.F.M.
Mailing Address: Box 40, Rte. 32 A, 12463. Tel: 518-678-9937.

Philmont, Columbia Co., Sacred Heart, Rev. Raymond Ethier.
Res., 141 Main St., 12565. Tel: 518-672-4655. [CEM]
Mission—Philmont, Pine Haven Home.

Pittstown, Rensselaer Co., St. George, Revs. John F. Riley; Daniel J. Menihane, O.S.A.
Res., Immaculate Conception Friary, Box 343, Main St., Hoosick Falls, 12090.
Mission—Grafton, Rensselaer Co., St. John Francis Regis.

Queensbury, Warren Co., Our Lady of the Annunciation, Rev. Joseph Anselment.
Res., 448 Aviation Rd., 12804. Tel: 518-793-9677; Fax: 518-793-9678.

Ravena, Albany Co., St. Patrick, Rev. Vincent J. Ciotoli.
Res., 21 Main St., 12143. Tel: 518-756-3145. [CEM]

Rensselaer, Rensselaer Co., St. John, Rev. Joseph Cotugno, Admin. In res., Rev. Thomas J. Hiney. Pastoral Assocs.: Sr. M. Anastasia, R.S.M.; Sr. M. Andre, R.S.M.
Res., 50 Herrick St., 12144. Tel: 518-465-2209. [CEM]
Parish Office: P.O. Box 256, 12144. Tel: 518-465-0482.
Convent—20 Lawrence St., 12144. Tel: 518-465-1514. Sr. M. Kathleen Turley, R.S.M., Coord. Sisters 20.

St. Joseph (1915), Rev. R. Adam Forno, Admin.
Office: 1620 Third St., 12144. Tel: 518-463-4401; Fax: 518-463-3194.
School—St. Joseph-St. John, 1641 Third St., 12144. Tel: 518-465-1151. Sr. Kathleen Pritty R.S.M., Prin.
Lay Teachers 16; Students 155.
Catechesis/Religious Programs—Students 165.

Richfield Springs, Otsego Co., St. Joseph, Rev. Francis E. Husselbeck.
Res., 35 Canadarago St., 13439-0791. Tel: 315-858-1682. [CEM]

Rotterdam, Schenectady Co., St. Gabriel the Archangel, Rev. Leo F. Markert; Deacon Kenneth Baechel.
Res., 3040 Hamburg St., Schenectady, 12303. Tel: 518-355-6600; Fax: 518-355-6600.

Rotterdam Junction, Schenectady Co., St. Margaret of Cortona, Revs. Denis J. Brennan; Brian Gronin, Temporary Admin.
Res., 2 Putnam St., 12150. Tel: 518-887-5288.

St. Johnsville, Montgomery Co., St. Patrick, Rev. Pascal A. Iannotti.
Res., 30 Center St., 13452. Tel: 518-568-7418.

Salem, Washington Co., Holy Cross, Rev. Liam Condon.
Res., 26 N. Main St., 12865. Tel: 518-854-7626. [CEM]
Mission—Cossayuna Lake.

Saratoga Springs, Saratoga Co., St. Clement, Revs. James O'Blaney, C.SS.R.; James Cannon, C.SS.R.; Pierce Kenny, C.SS.R.; Arthur Tuttle, C.SS.R. Pastoral Assocs.: Sr. Carolyn Krebs, O.P.; Deacons Larry Willette; Arthur Turcotte.
Res., 231 Lake Ave., 12866. Tel: 518-584-6122; Fax: 518-584-2644.
School—Lake Ave., 12866. Tel: 518-584-7350; Fax: 518-587-2623. Michael Dillon, Prin.
Lay Teachers 22; Students 393.
Chapel—Gansevoort, St. Therese, Tel: 518-587-3180. Deacon Danny Boyd.

St. Peter, Rev. Robert J. LeFevre Tel: 518-584-6113. In res., Rev. Anthony J. Maione.
Res., 241 S. Broadway, 12866. Tel: 518-584-2375; Fax: 518-584-5471. [CEM]

Schaghticoke, Rensselaer Co., St. John the Baptist, Rev. Bernard Turner; Deacon Walter Rehder.
Mailing Address: P.O. Box 300, 12154.
Res., St. Monica Ln., Johnsonville, 12094. Tel: 518-753-4003. [CEM]
Mission—Valley Falls, Our Lady of Good Counsel.

Schenectady, Schenectady Co.,

1—CHURCH OF ST. ADALBERT, (Polish), Rev. Carl A. Urban; Sr. Bernadette Filter, C.R., Pastoral Assoc. for Elderly.
Res., 550 Lansing St., 12303-1195. Tel: 518-346-4204; Fax: 518-346-0348. [CEM]

2—ST. ANTHONY, (Italian), Revs. John M. Medwid; Anthony DeFranco, Pastor Emeritus; Sr. Maria Rose Querini, M.P.V., Pastoral Assoc.; Deacon August DiDonna.
Parish Office: 331 Seward Pl., 12305. Tel: 518-374-4591; Fax: 518-377-5245.
School—1840 Van Vranken Ave., 12305. Tel: 518-372-5961; Fax: 518-372-7337. Sr. Elisa Brasili, M.P.V., Prin.
Venerini Sisters 3; Lay Teachers 8; Students 149.
Convent—1834 Van Vranken Ave., 12305. Tel: 518-346-2060.

3—SACRED HEART-ST. COLUMBA, Rev. Michael Hogan; Mr. George Vielkind, Admin. Pastoral Assocs.: Sr. Rosemary Endres, C.S.J.; Sr. Joseph Andrew Dunham, C.S.J., Coord. of Food Pantry; Sr. Norina Mastro, M.P.V.; Sr. M. Therese Van de Mosselaer, I.C.M., Parish Visitor; Judy Fitzner-Atchinson, Artist-in-Residence.
Res., 801 Stanley St., 12307. Tel: 518-377-8559; 346-0261; Fax: 518-393-9265.

4—SS. CYRIL AND METHODIUS. Closed. For inquiries for parish records contact Our Lady of Mount Carmel, Schenectady.

5—ST. HELEN, Rev. James J. Kane.
Res., 1803 Union St., 12309. Tel: 518-346-6137; Fax: 518-346-5390.
School—1801 Union St., 12309. Tel: 518-382-8225; Fax: 518-382-2226. Sr. Anne Marie, P.B.V.M., Prin.
Sisters of Presentation 4; Lay Teachers 15; Students 248.
Convent—40 Ray St., 12309. Tel: 518-374-7055.

6—HOLY CROSS, Rev. John T. Provost.
Res., 19 N. College St., 12305. Tel: 518-374-1551.

7—IMMACULATE CONCEPTION, Rev. L. Edward Deimeke.
Res., 523 Thompson St., 12306. Tel: 518-382-0451; Fax: 518-370-1089.
School—520 Bradt St., 12306. Tel: 518-377-7470; Fax: 518-370-1089. Marjorie Edgar, Prin.
Lay Teachers 11; Students 185.

8—ST. JOHN THE BAPTIST, Rev. John Peter Rosson.
Res., 427 Franklin St., 12305. Tel: 518-374-9148; Fax: 518-374-9149. [CEM]

9—ST. JOHN THE EVANGELIST, Revs. John T. Provost; George Fleming; Anthony Curran. In res., Rev. Anthony DeFranco.
Res., 802 Union St., 12308. Tel: 518-377-9607; Fax: 518-374-4663.
Office: 816 Union St., 12308. Tel: 518-372-3381; Fax: 518-372-0992.
School—806 Union St., 12308. Tel: 518-393-5331. Marie Keenan, Prin.
Lay Teachers 15; Students 280.

10—ST. JOSEPH, (German), Rev. Bernard J. Gustas. In res., Rev. Joseph P. Biondino.
Res., 225 Lafayette St., 12305. Tel: 518-374-4466; Fax: 518-374-4466. [CEM 2]

11—ST. LUKE, Rev. Msgr. Howard F. Manny, Pastor Emeritus; Rev. Dominic Isopo.
Res., 1241 State St., 12304. Tel: 518-346-3405; Fax: 518-346-3406.
School—1252 Albany St., 12304. Tel: 518-377-7330; Fax: 518-377-7330. Sr. Ann Christi Brink, C.S.J., Prin.
Sisters of St. Joseph of Carondelet 5; Lay Teachers 10; Students 185.
Convent—1252 Albany St., 12304. Tel: 518-372-2182.
Mission—Schenectady, Schenectady Co., St. Teresa Carmelite Monastery, 428 Duane Ave., 12304.

12—ST. MARY, (Polish), Rev. John T. Provost. In res., Rev. Michael Zakens.
Res., 828 Eastern Ave., 12308. Tel: 518-374-2423;. [CEM]

13—OUR LADY OF THE ASSUMPTION, Revs. Richard A. Carlino; John Kostek.
Res., 3034 Ford Ave., 12306. Tel: 518-346-4926.

14—OUR LADY OF FATIMA, Rev. Alan D. Jupin.
Res., 2216 Rosa Rd., 12309. Tel: 518-370-3136.

15—OUR LADY OF MT. CARMEL, (Italian), Rev. Joseph A. Mancuso.
Res., 1255 Pleasant St., 12303. Tel: 518-393-4109; Fax: 518-393-4100.
School—1274 Pleasant St., 12303. Tel: 518-372-0336. Sr. Elizabeth Calello, M.P.F., Prin.
Religious Teachers Filippini 2; Lay Teachers 15; Students 197.
Convent—1383 Pleasant St., 12303. Tel: 518-393-6702.

16—ST. PAUL THE APOSTLE, Revs. George W. Brucker; Joseph A. McKay; Deacon Robert H. Stanton. In res., Rev. Kenneth J. Tunny.
Res., 2777 Albany St., 12304. Tel: 518-377-8886; Fax: 518-377-8887.
School—16 Van Zandt St., 12304. Tel: 518-377-0506. Mr. Claude Palczak, Prin.
Lay Teachers 8; Students 136.

17—ST. THOMAS THE APOSTLE, Rev. William J. Kelleher.
Res., 1228 Sixth Ave., 12303. Tel: 518-370-2066.

Schoharie, Schoharie Co., St. Joseph, Revs. Kenneth J. Tunny, Sacramental Min.; James Clark; Sr. Joan Curley, C.S.J., Parish Life Dir.
Res., P.O. Box 514, 12157. Tel: 518-295-8923.

Schuylerville, Saratoga Co., Notre Dame-Visitation, Rev. Robert L. Buckley.
Res., 18 Pearl St., 12871. Tel: 518-695-3391; Fax: 518-695-4651. [CEM 2]
Convent—127 Pearl St., 12871. Tel: 518-695-3318.
Visitation of the Blessed Virgin Mary. Closed. For inquiries for parish records contact Notre Dame de Lourdes Parish, Schuylerville.

Scotia, Schenectady Co., St. Joseph, Rev. Ronald A. Menty; Deacons Robert R. Brady; John P. Crane.
Res., 231 Second St., 12302. Tel: 518-346-4960.
Parish Center: 45 MacArthur Dr., 12302. Tel: 518-346-2316; Fax: 518-374-3383.

Sidney, Delaware Co., Sacred Heart, Revs. Gordon Polenz; Joseph J. Schuck; Deacons Thomas E. Luby; Michael R. Donnell.
Res., 15 Liberty St., 13838. Tel: 607-563-1591.
Convent—24 1/2 Grand St., 13838. Tel: 607-563-3301.
Missions—Unadilla, Otsego Co., St. Ambrose; Franklin, Delaware Co., St. Paul.

South Glens Falls, Saratoga Co., St. Michael the Archangel, Revs. Robert Nugent; M. Curtis Hughes, Pastor Emeritus.
Res., 80 Saratoga Ave., 12803. Tel: 518-792-5859.

South Kortright, Delaware Co., Church of the Most Precious Blood of Jesus, Rev. John R. Burns; Deacon George D. Sheehan.
Res., Main St., P.O. Box 186, 13842-0186. Tel: 607-538-9309. [JC]
Mission—Davenport Center, Delaware Co., Chapel of St. Theresa the Little Flower.

Speigletown, Rensselaer Co., St. Bonaventure, Rev. Salvatore A. Rodino.
Res., Hillview Dr., Troy, 12182. Tel: 518-235-0337.

Stamford, Delaware Co., Sacred Heart, Rev. Joseph S. Cebula.
Res., 27 Harper St., P.O. Box 38, 12167. Tel: 607-652-7170. [CEM]
Mission—Grand Gorge, Delaware Co., St. Philip Neri.

Stillwater, Saratoga Co., St. Peter the Apostle, Rev. James O'Neill.
Res., 271 N. Hudson Ave., 12170. Tel: 518-664-3354. [CEM]
Mission—Saratoga Lake, Saratoga Co., St. Isaac Jogues. (Summer).

Stottville, Columbia Co., Holy Family, Rev. William H. Kennedy.
Res., 2824 Atlantic Ave., 12172. Tel: 518-828-1889; Fax: 518-822-9238.

Stuyvesant, Columbia Co., Nativity of the Blessed Virgin Mary. Unassigned.
1820 Rte. 9, 12173.

Stuyvesant Falls, Columbia Co., St. Mary, Rev. Joseph Faletta.
Church—1820 Rte. 9, Stuyvesant, 12173. Tel: 518-799-5411; Fax: 518-799-3144. [CEM]

Summit, Schoharie Co., St. Anna, Rev. Edward Golding, Admin.
Res., Main St., P.O. Box 124, 12175. Tel: 518-287-1553.
Missions—Camp Summit, N.Y.S. Correctional Facility; Camp Summit, S.U.N.Y. Cobleskill College.

Tribes Hill, Montgomery Co., Sacred Heart, Rev. Conrad Somerville, O.F.M.Conv.
Res., Box 264 Third Ave., 12177. Tel: 518-829-7301.

Troy, Rensselaer Co.,

1—St. Anthony of Padua, (Italian), Revs. Isaac J. Calicchio, O.F.M.; Louis M. Pintye, O.F.M.; Bro. James Welch, III; Deacon Gerald Christiano.
Res., Friary, 28 State St., 12180. Tel: 518-273-8622; Fax: 518-273-2731.
Center—107 Fourth St., Tel: 518-273-8351; Fax: 518-273-6220.

2—St. Augustine, Revs. Thomas J. Meehan, O.S.A.; Joseph D. Keffer, O.S.A.; Bro. Joseph T. Spindler, O.S.A., Pastoral Assoc.
Res., 25 115th St., 12182. Tel: 518-235-3861; Fax: 518-233-0284.
School—525 Fourth Ave., 12182. Tel: 518-235-7287. Ms. Elizabeth Allard, Prin.
Sisters of St. Joseph 1; Lay Teachers 14; Students 182.
Convent—523 Fourth Ave., 12182. Tel: 518-235-5959.

3—St. Francis de Sales, Rev. Donald J. Ophals. In res., Rev. John Lysogorski.
Res., 316 Congress St., 12180. Tel: 518-274-4232.

4—Holy Trinity, (Polish), Rev. Romaeus Cooney, O.Carm., Admin.
Mailing Address: St. Joseph's Priory, 416 Third St., 12180. Tel: 518-274-6720.

5—St. Joseph, Revs. Albert Pavlik, O.Carm.; Romaeus Cooney, O.Carm.; Vincent McDonald, O.Carm.
Res., 416 Third St., 12180. Tel: 518-274-6720; Fax: 518-272-6503. [CEM]

6—St. Lawrence. Closed. For inquiries for parish records contact St. Joseph Parish, Troy.

7—St. Mary, Rev. Harry Donaghy.
Res., 331 Fourth St., 12180. Tel: 518-272-5820.

8—St. Michael the Archangel, Rev. James M. Mackey; Deacons Frank Yankowski; John Skelly.
Res., 26 Bridle Pl., East Greenbush, 12061. Tel: 518-477-5656.
Church—175 Williams Rd., 12180. Tel: 518-283-6110; Fax: 518-283-3938.
Missions—North Greenbush, Rensselaer Co., Van Rensselaer Manor, County Welfare Home; Troy, Rensselaer Co., Hallmark Nursing Home.

9—Our Lady of Victory, Rev. Randall P. Patterson. In res., Revs. David Berberian; Gregory Weider.
Res., 55 N. Lake Ave., 12180. Tel: 518-273-7609; 273-7602 (Office); Fax: 518-273-0310.
School—451 Marshland Ct., 12180. Tel: 518-274-6202.
Lay Teachers 15; Students 155.

10—St. Patrick, Revs. Thomas J. Kelly; Cyril F. Pereira.
Res., 3027 Sixth Ave., 12180. Tel: 518-272-4666.
School—762 River St., 12180. Tel: 518-274-6502.
Sisters 2; Lay Teachers 5; Students 160.
Convent—139 Fifth Ave., 12180. Tel: 518-274-6768.

11—St. Paul the Apostle, Rev. James McNerney.
Res., 138 Twelfth St., 12180. Tel: 518-274-4083.

12—St. Peter, Rev. Thomas K. Flanigan.
Res., 2310 Fifth Ave., 12180. Tel: 518-272-2750. [CEM]

13—Sacred Heart, Revs. James Vaughan; Gary Mercure.
Res., 310 Spring Ave., 12180. Tel: 518-274-1363; Fax: 518-274-8720.
School—308 Spring Ave., 12180. Tel: 518-274-3655; Fax: 518-274-8270. Susan Holland, Prin.
Sisters 3; Lay Teachers 20; Students 312.

14—St. Williams, Rev. Joseph E. Keyrouze.
Res., 1010 Madison Ave., 12180. Tel: 518-273-1680.

Ushers, Saratoga Co., Corpus Christi, Rev. Edward C. Pratt; Deacons Michael Sheppeck; John Tierney.
Mailing Address: P.O. Box 628, 12151-0628.
Res., 10 Southwood Dr., Ballston Lake, 12019-1302. Tel: 518-877-8506 (Office); Fax: 518-877-5620 (Office).

Valatie, Columbia Co., St. John the Baptist, Rev. Thomas M. Powers.
Res., 1025 Kinderhook St., 12184. Tel: 518-758-9401; Fax: 518-758-9409. [CEM]

Voorheesville, Albany Co., St. Matthew, Rev. Arthur A. Toole.
Res., 31 Mountain View St., 12186. Tel: 518-765-2805; Fax: 518-765-3701.

Walton, Delaware Co., St. John the Baptist, Rev. Eugene F. Willis.
Mailing Address: P.O. Box 315, 13856-0315.
Res., 15 Benton Ave., 13856-0315. Tel: 607-865-4720; Fax: 607-865-7394.
Mission—Downsville, Delaware Co., Holy Family.

Warrensburg, Warren Co., St. Cecilia, Rev. Nellis J. Tremblay.
Res., 3802 Main St., 12885-1629. Tel: 518-623-3021; Fax: 518-623-3021. [CEM]

Waterford, Saratoga Co., St. Anne, Rev. John Steven Kostek.
Res., 75 Grace St., 12188. Tel: 518-237-5211; Fax: 518-233-8292.
St. Mary of the Assumption, Revs. Marshall J. Halphen, O.S.A.; Daniel J. Menihane, O.S.A.; J. Riley Havener, O.S.A. In res., Rev. W. Howard McGraw, O.S.A.
Res., 119 Broad St., 12188-2397. Tel: 518-237-3131; Fax: 518-237-9625. [CEM]
School—Waterford Central Catholic School, 12 Sixth St., 12188. Tel: 518-237-0652. Sr. Geraldine Corkrey, C.S.J., Prin.
Lay Teachers 19; Students 283.

Watervliet, Albany Co.,

1—St. Brigid, Rev. Joseph Busch. In res., Rev. Timothy Harrison.
Res., 695 Fifth Ave., 12189. Tel: 518-273-2913.
School—(Regional) 700 Fifth Ave., 12189. Tel: 518-273-3321; Fax: 518-273-9355. Patricia Eldridge, Prin.
Sisters 4; Lay Teachers 20; Students 304.

2—Immaculate Conception, (Polish), Rev. Paul J. Antos. In res., Rev. Boleslaus M. Watroba, Pastor Emeritus.
Res., 2420 Seventh Ave., 12189. Tel: 518-273-3173. [CEM]
Convent—2425 Seventh Ave., 12189. Tel: 518-273-4423.

3—Our Lady of Mt. Carmel, (Italian), Revs. Emery Parillo, O.F.M.; Bonaventure Bionda, O.F.M.
Res., 410 23rd St., 12189. Tel: 518-273-2932.

4—St. Patrick, Rev. Erwin H. Schweigardt. In res., Rev. James I. Donlon.
Res., 515 19th St., Box 388, 12189. Tel: 518-273-2971; Fax: 518-273-2972.

5—Sacred Heart of Mary, Rev. John J. Rooney.
Res., 1511 Sixth Ave., 12189. Tel: 518-273-6252.

West Taghkanic, Columbia Co., Holy Cross, Rev. Peter V. Kranch.
Res., 880 Rte. 82, Elizaville, 12523. Tel: 518-851-7577.

West Winfield, Herkimer Co., St. Joseph, Rev. Terence P. Healy; Deacon Richard Brown.
Res., 305 W. Main St., P.O. Box 360, 13491-0360. Tel: 315-822-3191. [CEM]

Whitehall, Washington Co., Notre Dame des Victoires, Rev. George C. Gagnon.
Res., 9 Wheeler Ave., 12887. Tel: 518-499-1656.
Our Lady of Angels, Rev. William Esmond.
Res., 2 Boardman St., 12887. Tel: 518-499-1597. [CEM]

Windham, Greene Co., St. Theresa of Child Jesus, Revs. Donald E. Doyle; John G. O'Grady.
Res., Main St., 12496. Tel: 518-734-3352.
Mission—Ashland, St. Joseph's Chapel.

Worcester, Otsego Co., St. Joseph, Rev. William W. Crandall.
Res., 181 Main St., 12197. Tel: 607-397-9373.
Mission—Schenevus, Otsego Co., St. Mary. [CEM]

Wynantskill, Rensselaer Co., St. Jude the Apostle, Rev. John J. Varno.
Res., 6 Schuyler Ct., P.O. Box 347, 12198. Tel: 518-283-1162.
School—Brookside Ave., 12198. Tel: 518-283-0333. Mrs. Marcia Rosenfield, Admin.
Sisters 2; Lay Teachers 12; Students 190.

Chaplains of Public Institutions

Albany. *Albany County Jail*. Rev. Richard Shaw, Rensselaer, Schenectady.
Albany County Nursing Home. Ms. Sigh Buchanan, Chap.
Albany Medical Center Hospital. Revs. David Mickiewicz; Kenneth Gregory; John Lysogorski; Sr. Lucille Theroux, Chap.
Capital District Psychiatric Center. Rev. James R. Joslin.
Memorial Hospital. Rev. John T. Kelly; Sr. Frances Markham, R.G.S., Chap.; Deacon Cyril Lavin, Chap.
St. Peter's Hospital. Chaplains: Revs. John Tallman; Michael Miller.
University Heights Nursing Home. Sr. Jane Carr, R.S.M., Chap.
Veterans' Administration Hospital. Rev. John Minkler.

Comstock. *Great Meadows Correctional Institution*. Rev. James Hayes.

Coxsackie. *Greene County Correctional Institution*. Rev. Joseph Romano.
Regional Medical Unit. Rev. John L. Moyna.

Glens Falls. *Glens Falls Hospital*. Chaplains: Rev. O. Robert DeMartinis; Sr. Helen LeClerc, C.S.J.
Hudson Correctional Facility. Rev. Edward Cantwell, Chap.

Schenectady. *Ellis Hospital*. Sr. June Baker, O.P., Chap.; Sr. Elizabeth Hunter, R.S.C.J.; Deacons George Nahm, Chap.; August Van Patten, Chap.
Schenectady County Nursing Home. Sr. Clare Pelkey, C.S.J., Chap.
Silver Haven Nursing Home. Deacon Earle Flatt, Chap.

Troy. *Leonard Hospital*. Deacon Gerald Christiano, Chap.
Samaritan Hospital. Rev. Gregory Weider; Deacon Frank Lukovits.
Van Rensselaer Manor. Deacon John Skelly, Chap.

West Coxsackie. *Coxsackie Correctional Facility*. Revs. William H. Kennedy; Joseph Romano.

Wilton. *Mount McGregor Correctional Facility*. Rev. Richard Severson.
Wilton Developmental Center. Tel: 518-584-3110. Rev. Gerald D. Kampfer.

Special Assignment:
Reverend Fathers—
Bentley, David, 40 N. Main Ave., Albany, NY 12203
Berbian, David, Tribunal, 40 N. Main Ave., Albany, NY 12203
Burke, Geoffrey D., Chancellor Personnel & Public Information, 40 N. Main Ave., Albany, NY 12203
Chiaramonte, Anthony, Consultation Center, 790 Lancaster St., Albany, NY 12203
Close, John L., Computer Services, Pastoral Center, St. Teresa, Albany
DeGiovine, Christopher, College of St. Rose, 432 Western Ave., Albany, NY 12203
Donlon, James I., Judicial Vicar, Tribunal, Pastoral Center
Donnolly, Robert, St. Catherine of Siena, 40 Collins Pl., Albany, NY 12208

Dworak, Joseph J., Chap., St. Mary's Hospital, 427 Guy Park Ave., Amsterdam, NY 12010
Farano, Michael A., Vicar Gen. & Dir. Society of the Propagation of Faith, 2 Fairview Rd., Loudonville, NY 12211
Gregory, Kenneth, Chap., Albany Medical Center, Albany, NY 12208
Gulley, Anthony D., 607 Central Ave., Albany, NY 12206
Hayes, James, 23 Buckley Ave., Granville, NY 12832
Hiney, Thomas J., 50 Herrick St., Rensselaer, NY 12144
Joslin, James R., 1086 Regent St., Schenectady, NY 12308
Kacerguis, Edward, 2008 19th St., Troy, NY 12181
Kampher, Gerald D., Sonoma Pt., Loon Lake, Chestertown, NY 12817
Kane, James J., Dir., Pastoral Center, Ecumenical & Interreligious Affairs
Kelly, John T., 600 N. Blvd., Albany, NY 12010
Leskovar, Richard J., 600 McClellan St., Schenectady, NY 12304
Lysogorski, John, AIDS Ministries/Albany Med., 39 Grandview Dr., Latham, NY 12110
Maione, Anthony, Saratoga Catholic Central High, 247 S. Broadway, Saratoga Springs, NY 12866
Malecki, John, Consultation Ctr., 790 Lancaster St., Albany, NY 12203
Marbury, Cabell, 99 Slingerland St., Albany, NY 12202
McCloskey, Francis, Copake Falls, NY 12517
Mickiewicz, David, Chaplain, Albany Medical Hospital, New Scotland Ave., Albany, NY 12208
Molyn, John A., Dir., Vocations, Pastoral Center
Ntsiful-Amissah, Kofi, Black Apostolate, 50 Thornton St., Albany, NY 12206
O'Brien, Leo P., Vicar Gen., 900 Madison Ave., Albany, NY 12208
Pereira, Cyril F., 3027 Sixth Ave., Troy, NY 12180
Pius, Jung Bio, Korean Apostolate, 10 Lodge St., Albany, NY 12207-2196
Powers, Thomas, Continuing Education for Clergy, Pastoral Center
Romano, Joseph, 40 Collins Pl., Albany, NY 12208
Severson, Richard, P.O. Box 2264, Wilton, NY 12866
Shaw, Richard, St. Helen's Rectory, 1803 Union St., Schenectady, NY 12309
Smith, Paul, 37 Parkwood St. E., Albany, NY 12203
Sullivan, Peter J., III, Adjutant Vicar Judicial Tribunal, Pastoral Center
Testa, Richard, 512 Third Ave., Troy, NY 12182
Tunny, Kenneth J., St. Paul's Rectory, 277 Albany St., Schenectady, NY 12304
Vosko, Richard, 4611 Foxwood Dr., P.O. Box 2217, Clifton Park, NY 12605
Weider, Gregory, Chaplain Samaritan Hospital, Troy, NY 12180

On Duty Outside the Diocese:
Reverend Fathers—
Allie, Stanley J., Sacred Heart Church, 1201 Bogard Rd., Wasilla, AK 99654-6523
Casey, Liam C., St. Francis Hospital, 114 Woodland St., Hartford, CT 06105
Fragomeni, Richard, 5401 S. Cornell Ave., Chicago, IL 60615-5698
Nusbaum, Daniel C., Mt. St. Mary College, Emmitsburg, MD 21727
O'Grady, John F., Barry University, 11300 N.E. Second Ave., Miami, FL 33161
Polewczak, Michael J., Holy Trinity Parish, 2161 Griffith Dr., Orangeburg, SC 29118
Redmond, Paul, Mt. St. Mary College, Emmitsburg, MD 21727
Testa, David, Holy Spirit Monastery, Franciscan University, Steubenville, OH 43952-6701

Military Chaplains:
Reverend Fathers—
Estabrook, Joseph, Fleet Chap. (NOIC), Commander-in-Chief, Capt., CHC, USN, Pacific Fleet, Pearl Harbor, HI 96860-7000
Minkler, John, Chaplain's Office, V.A. Hospital, Holland Ave., Albany, NY 12208
O'Keeffe, L. Joseph, 2121 Columbia Pike, Apt. #167, Arlington, VA 22204
Rutherford, Donald L., 826 Kiln Ln., Hinesville, GA 31313

Unassigned:
Reverend Fathers—
Murphy, Dennis P., Cathedral Rectory, 125 Eagle St., Albany, NY 12205

Retired:
Most Rev.—
Ryan, Joseph T., D.D., Our Lady of Hope Residence, One Jeanne Jugan Ln., Latham, NY 12110
Reverend Monsignors—
Hart, James, 391 Delaware Ave., Albany, NY 12209
Jones, John L., St. Teresa's Rectory, 435 New Scotland Ave., Albany, NY 12208-2397
Manny, Howard F., St. Luke's Rectory, 1241 State St., Schenectady, NY 12304
Reverend Fathers—
Ahern, Bernard, 4418 Poppy Tree Ln., Jacksonville, FL 32223
Amato, Joseph, St. Martha's Church, 200 Orange Ave., P.O. Box 1706, Sarasota, FL 34230-1706
Baniak, Walter, 540 Second St., Troy, NY 12180
Batkiewicz, Joseph J., Teresian House, 200 Washington Ave. Ext., Albany, NY 12203-5894
Bondi, Paul, 167 Milton Ave., Ballston Spa, NY 12020
Caldara, John N., 3025 Myrtle Ave., Schenectady, NY 12306
Campagnone, Nicholas, Wesley Health Care Center, 131 Lawrence St., Hathorn Residence, Room 117, Saratoga Springs, NY 12866
Ciani, Francis P., 49 Warwick Rd., Elmont, NY 11003
Ciulek, Joseph, One Gorski St., Amsterdam, NY 12010
Clemente, Michael, 11570 - 64th Ter. N., Seminola, FL 34642
Clune, Gerald F., 9466 Navajo Tr., Morongo Valley, CA 92256
Collins, William, Villa Mary Immaculate, 301 Hackett Blvd., Albany, NY 12208
Cyvas, Matthew, 555 68th Ave., St. Petersburg Beach, FL 33706
D'Agostino, Joseph, 6 Bircher Ave., Poughkeepsie, NY 12601
De Caprio, John, 105 Florida Ave., Amsterdam, NY 12010
De Pasquale, Daniel, CDR, 2750 Blarrita Ct., Ponte Vedra Beach, FL 32802
DeFranco, Anthony, 802 Union St., Schenectady, NY 12308
Delos, Bernard M., 4044 N.W. 19th St., G 109, Lauderhill, FL 33313
Di Cerbo, Almerico F., McAuley Residence, 308 S. Manning Blvd., Albany, NY 12208
Donnelly, Elmer, Teresian House, 200 Washington Ave. Ext., Albany, NY 12203-5894
Douglas, Louis, 1880 Superfine Ln., #8, Wilmington, DE 19802
Downs, Richard J., 77 Crescent Dr., Albany, NY 12208
Engel, Paul, P.O. Box 506, Schoharie, NY 12157
Fitzpatrick, Edward, 32 Joseph St., Saratoga Springs, NY 12866
Girzone, Joseph, 8 Leesome Ln., Altamont, NY 12209
Guillaume, Lionel A., 11216B Pendleton Ave., Englewood, FL 34224
Halpin, Raymond J., 12 Van Buren Ave., East Greenbush, NY 12061
Hughes, M. Curtis, 80 Saratoga Ave., South Glens Falls, NY 12801
Jonaitis, Peter, 217 N. Kingsboro Ave., Gloversville, NY 12078
Keefe, John A., 40 Collins Pl., Albany, NY 12208
Keefe, John W., Our Lady of Hope, 1 Jeanne Jugan Ln., Latham, NY 12110
Kelly, Donald, St. Mary's Rectory, 156 E. Main St., Amsterdam, NY 12010
Kelly, James, P.O. Box 977, McGill, NV 89318
Kelly, Joseph Anthony, Our Lady of Hope Residence, 1 Jeanne Jugan Ln., Latham, NY 12110
Klementowicz, Chester, 30 William St., Amsterdam, NY 12010
Konisky, Edward, 64 Parkwin Dr., Delmar, NY 12054
Lamanna, Alfred, The Prospect Inn, 20 N. Prospect St., Apt. J, Herkimer, NY 13350
Lemoyne, William, 29 Burgoyne St., Schuylerville, NY 12871
Lerox, Edward, 8 Clark St., South Glens Falls, NY 12803
Lynch, Patrick J., P.O. Box 68, Lans Sta., Troy, NY 12182
Malin, Peter, 8104 San Bernardine Dr., Port Richey, FL 34688
Mallon, John F., St. Mary's Rectory, P.O. Box 351, East Durham, NY 12423-0223
Marcil, Leo L., 11 Wall St., Hudson Falls, NY 12839
McNamara, John, Our Lady of Hope Residence, 1 Jeanne Jugan Ln., Latham, NY 12110
Morrill, Giles, P.O. Box 6566, Delray Beach, FL 33482-6566
Mulcahy, Howard J., McAuley Residence, 308 S. Manning Blvd., Albany, NY 12208
Mulhall, J. Gregory, Our Lady of Hope, 1 Jeanne Jugan Ln., Lathan, NY 12110
Mullen, Francis, 103 Madison St., Troy, NY 12180
Nowak, Vincent A., King Park Apt., 125 Bldg. B., 4025 N. Federal Hwy., Ft. Lauderdale, FL 33308
Nowakowski, Francis M., c/o Stanley Zima, 17 Sixth St., Yorkville, NY 13495
O'Connor, Stephen, 26 Irving St., Albany, NY 12202
O'Grady, John G., Box 123, Windham, NY 12496
Petit, Roland, 1850 St. Joseph Blvd., E. #1, Montreal, Quebec H2H 1C7 Canada
Phillips, George, 347 Old Loudon Rd., Latham, NY 12110
Powers, John J., 1471 Greenwood Ave., Palo Alto, CA 94301
Roos, Robert E., 720 New Scotland Ave., Albany, NY 12208
Ryan, Edward, P.O. Box 277, Stamford, NY 12094
Sidoti, Anthony, 496 Delaware Ave., Albany, NY 12209
Sinisky, Joseph, 667 Columbia Tpke., East Greenbush, NY 12061
Sise, John, 64 Pioneer St., Apt. C., Box 293, Cooperstown, NY 13346
Starks, R. Mansfield, 400 Saratoga Rd., Scotia, NY 12302
Stone, Carl, P.O. Box Owlshead, Owlshead, NY 12969
Szarek, Joseph, St. Mary's Woodland Village, Upper Tibbits Ave., Troy, NY 12180
Tartaglia, Paul, (June-Nov.), 465 State St., Albany, NY 12203
Vail, Thomas, 76 Moreland St., Little Falls, NY 13365
Watroba, Boleslaus M., 2420 Seventh Ave., Watervliet, NY 12189
Whalen, John P., 1614 Pacham Rd., Silver Spring, MD 20903
Whalen, William F., Beverwyck Apartments, 40 Autumn Dr., Apt. 147, Slingerlands, NY 12159
Zakens, Michael W., St. Mary's Church, 828 Eastern Ave., Schenectady, NY 12308

Permanent Deacons:
Baechel, Kenneth, St. Gabriel, Rotterdam & Office of Prayer and Worship
Bazinet, William, St. Alphonsus, Glens Falls
Beck, Gary, Dioc. AIDS Task Force, St. Madeleine Sophie, Guilderland
Beckman, Martin L., Outside Diocese
Beuerman, David, St. Mary's, Cooperstown
Bickmore, Henry, Sacred Heart and Chancery, Albany
Boyd, Danny S., St. Therese Mission, Gansevoort
Brady, Robert, Glendale Nursing Home & St. Joseph, Scotia
Brett, William, Chap., Our Lady of Mercy Center, Guilderland; Legion of Mary
Brown, Richard, St. Joseph, West Winfield
Canary, Arthur, Assumption-St. Paul, Mechanicville
Chambers, Frank, Annunciation, Ilion
Christiano, Gerald, St. Anthony & Seton Health Care System, Troy
Cioppa, Richard, St. Margaret Mary, Albany
Cohen, Andrew, Office of Prayer & Worship & St. Joan of Arc, Menands
Crane, John, ARC Homes & St. Joseph, Scotia
Culkin, John J., Sr., Our Lady of Victory, Troy
DeLorenzo, Joseph, Holy Family, Little Falls
Desormeaux, David, Leave of Absence
Devine, Patrick, Holy Cross, Albany
Didonna, August, Dioc. Formation Team, St. Anthony, Schenectady
Dillon, Joseph, St. Mary's, Troy
Donnell, Michael, Sacred Heart, Sidney
Dringus, William, Holy Spirit Church, East Greenbush
Eagan, Arthur, Cathedral & Cathedral Social Services, Albany
Fitzgerald, William, Blessed Sacrament, Albany
Flatt, Earle, St. Madeleine Sophie & Hallmark Nursing Home, Rotterdam
Gaffney, William, St. Vincent de Paul, Albany
Gallipeo, Paul, St. Mary, Glens Falls
Gaul, William H., Jr., St. Joseph's Church, Greenwich; Diocesan Office of Scouting
Gil, Joseph, St. Vincent de Paul, Albany and Hispanic Outreach Services
Glennon, Dr. John E., Health Care Advocate for HIV/AIDS, Great Meadow Correctional Facility; St. Mary's, Granville
Gorman, William A., St. Helen's, Schenectady
Grigaitis, Jerry, St. Edward the Confessor, Clifton Park
Hall, Charles R., St. John the Baptist, Greenville
Herlihy, Frank, St. Mary, Glens Falls; St. Mary's/St. Paul's, Hudson Falls
Hewitt, William, St. Peter's, Saratoga
Hook, J. Neil, St. Margaret Mary, Albany
Howley, Herbert J., St. Joseph's, Greenwich
Hyland, Arnold K., Leave of Absence
Jones, Dennis, Annunciation, Ilion
Kratz, Russell J., Educational/Sacramental Preparation, St. John's/St. Ann's, Albany
Ladouceur, Gerald, St. Catherine of Siena, Albany

Lavin, Cyril, Holy Spirit, East Greenbush & Memorial Hospital
Luby, Thomas T., Rural Ministry, Sacred Heart, Sidney
Lukovits, Frank, St. Henry, Averill Park & Dir. Deacon Personnel
MacKinnon, Walter, St. Edward, Clifton Park; St. Bernard's, Cohoes
Manno, Peter, St. Joseph's, Dolgeville
Manzella, Alfred R., St. Thomas, Delmar
Markham, Joseph, Christ the King, Albany
McAuliffe, Timothy, Christ the King, Westmere & Permanent Diaconate Office
McGarry, Frank, Leave of Absence
McNamara, Eugene, Outside Diocese
Melanson, Michael, Immaculate Conception, Glenville
Monscko, Walter G., St. John the Baptist, Chestertown
Nahm, George H., St. Clare's, Colonie
Neurohr, Helmut N., St. Ambrose, Latham
Novak, John W., St. Henry, Averill Park
O'Connell, Thomas, Outside Diocese
O'Neill, Charles, St. Mary's, Hudson
Pasquarelli, Robert, St. Henry's, Averill Park
Powers, David F., St. Mary's, Glen Falls
Pudney, E. Jack, Leave of Absence
Raup, Konrad, St. Patrick's, Ravena
Rehder, Walter, St. John the Baptist, Schaghticoke
Robert, Joseph, Outside Diocese
Roemer, Paul W., St. Patrick's, Catskill
Rucinski, Robert, Our Lady of the Assumption, Latham; Family Life Office
Salamone, Samuel, Our Lady Queen of Apostles, Frankfort
Schickel, Frank, Outside Diocese
Schrempf, Albert G., St. Marie & St. Patrick's, Cohoes; St. Thomas, Delmar
Sedelmeir, Peter, St. John the Baptist, Greenville
Sheehan, George D., Rural Preaching, Delaware County
Sheppeck, Michael, Corpus Christi, Ushers
Skelly, John, St. Mary, Nassau & Van Rensselaer Manor Nursing Home
Solar, Richard, St. Anthony, Johnstown
South, Owen D., St. Agnes/St. Patrick/St. Marie, Cohoes
Sroda, Walter A., 375 Farm-to-Market Rd., Clifton Park, NY 12065
Stalter, William, Outside Diocese
Stanton, Robert, St. Paul the Apostle, Schenectady & Family Life Commission
Stosiek, Martin, St. Bridget, Copake Falls; Rural Affairs Coord., Diocese of Albany
Sullivan, Raymond, St. Teresa of Avila, Albany
Surman, Dr. Gary, St. Vincent, Cobleskill
Szarejko, Walter, St John the Baptist, Newport
Tapia, Raymon, Immaculate Conception, Glenville
Tierney, John, Corpus Christi, Ushers; County and State Prison
Trawinski, Peter, St. James, Chatham
Turcotte, Arthur W., St. Paul's, Rock City Falls
Vaillancourt, Leonard, St. Peter Hospital, Albany; St. Joseph, Rensselaer
VanPatten, August, Immaculate Conception, Glenville
Webster, Donald, St. Joseph, Fort Edward
Whalen, Charles, Outside Diocese
Willette, Lawrence, St. Clement, Saratoga Springs
Witko, George, St. Mary, Albany
Yankowski, Frank, Eden Park Nursing Home & St. Michael, Troy

INSTITUTIONS LOCATED IN THE DIOCESE

[A] SEMINARIES, RELIGIOUS OR SCHOLASTICATES

ALTAMONT. *La Salette Shrine and Seminary*, Leesome Ln., P.O. Box 680, 12009-0680. Tel: 518-861-8159. Rev. Jeffrey L'Arche, M.S., Dir.; Bro. Anthony Casso, M.S., Asst. Dir.
Corporate Titles: Missionaries of Our Lady of LaSalette, Inc., Altamont, NY; LaSalette Seminary, Altamont, NY.

CATSKILL. *St. Anthony Friary*, P.O. Box 487, Harrison St., 12414. Tel: 518-943-3451. Order of Friars Minor. Revs. Owen Angeloni, O.F.M., Guardian; Francis Solanus DeLorenzo, O.F.M., Vicar; Frederick Fusco, O.F.M.; Gregory Palma, O.F.M.; Bros. John Golisano, O.F.M.; Lawrence Stumpo, O.F.M.

RENSSELAER. *Conventual Franciscan Friars*. Immaculate Conception Province, Provincialate, Office of the Treasurer, P.O. Box 629, 12144. Tel: 518-472-1016; Fax: 518-472-1013. (Corporate Name: Order Minor Conventuals). 517 Washington Ave., 12144. Friars Minor Conventual. Mr. Peter Sheehan, Dir. Finance & Devel., Tel: 518-472-1000; Fax: 518-472-1013. In res. Revs. Canice Connors, O.F.M.Conv., Minister Prov.; Justin Biase, O.F.M.Conv., Vicar Prov.; Paul Lininger, O.F.M.Conv., Treas.; Bros. Andre Picotte, O.F.M.Conv., Dir. of Cemeteries; John Joseph Dolan, O.F.M.Conv., Guardian; Stephen Merrigan, O.F.M.Conv., Archivist. Priests 3; Brothers 3.

[B] COLLEGES AND UNIVERSITIES

ALBANY. *The College of Saint Rose*, 432 Western Ave., 12203. Tel: 518-454-5111; 800-657-8556; Fax: 518-458-5447
For a complete listing, refer to the Colleges and Universities section.
Maria College, 700 New Scotland Ave., 12208
For a complete listing, refer to the Colleges and Universities section.
St. Bernard's Institute at Albany, 40 N. Main Ave., 12203. Tel: 518-453-6760
For a complete listing, refer to the Colleges and Universities section.

LOUDONVILLE. *Siena College*, 12211. Tel: 518-783-2300
For a complete listing, refer to the Colleges and Universities section.

[C] HIGH SCHOOLS, DIOCESAN

ALBANY. *Bishop Maginn High School*, 99 Slingerland St., 12202. Mr. Joseph Grasso, Prin.; Rev. Cabell B. Marbury, Vice Prin. Priests 1; Sisters 7; Lay Teachers 28; Students 450.

AMSTERDAM. *Bishop Scully High School*, Upper Church St., 12010. Tel: 518-842-4100.

GLENS FALLS. *St. Mary-St. Alphonsus Regional Catholic School*, 10-12 Church St., 12801. Tel: 518-792-3178. Pastors: Revs. Martin Fisher; Robert W. Powhida. Lay Teachers 21; Students 254.

SARATOGA SPRINGS. *Saratoga Central Catholic High School*. (Grades 7-12), 247 South Broadway, 12866. Tel: 518-587-7070; Fax: 518-587-0678. Mr. Edwin Hammond, Jr., Prin. Lay Teachers 23; Students 232.

SCHENECTADY. *Notre Dame-Bishop Gibbons School*. (Coed Grades 6-12), 2600 Albany St., 12304. Tel: 518-393-3131. Bro. H. Mark Staniecki, C.F.C., Prin. Conducted by the Congregation of Christian Brothers. Brothers 5; Sisters 2; Lay Teachers 32; Students 470.

TROY. *Catholic Central High School*. (Grades 7-12), 625 Seventh Ave., 12182. Tel: 518-235-7100; Fax: 518-237-1796. Sr. Carolyn Schanz, C.S.J., Pres.; Sr. Katherine Arsenau, C.S.J., Prin. Sisters 8; Lay Teachers 43; Students 683.

[D] HIGH SCHOOLS, PRIVATE

ALBANY. *Academy of the Holy Names Upper, Middle and Lower Schools*, 1073 New Scotland Rd., 12208. Tel: 518-438-7895. Sr. Constance Casey, S.N.J.M., Pres. (PreK-12); Ms. Mary Anne Vigliante, Prin. (Grades 9-12); Sr. Virginia Dunn, S.N.J.M., Prin. (Grades PreK-8); Rev. Paul Smith. Sisters 8; Lay Teachers 47; Students 467.
Christian Brothers' Academy, De La Salle Rd., 12208. Tel: 518-462-5447. Brothers of the Christian Schools. Bro. Matthew Michelini, F.S.C., Prin. JROTC College Prep. Program. Brothers 8; Lay Teachers 31; Students 400.
The Doane Stuart School. (Grades PreK-12). Ecumenical Day School. Coed., 12202. Religious of the Sacred Heart and the Episcopal Diocese of Albany. Faculty 26; Students 224.
Mercy High, Private School for Girls, c/o 40 N. Main Ave., 12203.

TROY. *LaSalle Institute*, 174 Williams Rd., 12180. Tel: 518-283-2500; Fax: 518-283-6265. Brothers of the Christian Schools. Bro. James Romond, F.S.C., Prin. Brothers 10; Lay Teachers 47; Students 575.

[E] ELEMENTARY SCHOOLS, PRIVATE

LOUDONVILLE. *Saint Gregory's School*, 121 Old Niskayuna Rd., 12211-1399. Tel: 518-785-6621. Michael O'Donoghue, Headmaster. An independent Catholic day school for boys staffed by laity (Nursery-8). Girls admitted in Nursery and Kindergarten classes. Lay Teachers 24; Students 196.

[F] CONSOLIDATED ELEMENTARY SCHOOLS

ALBANY. *Cathedral Academy*, 75 Park Ave., 12202. Tel: 518-449-5232.

COHOES. *Cohoes Catholic School*, One St. Marie's Ln., 12047. Tel: 518-235-5202. Sr. Sandra Tripp, C.S.J., Prin. Convent, 5 Wilson Way, 12047. Tel: 518-237-1457.

WATERFORD. *Waterford Central Catholic School*. (Grades K-8), 12 Sixth St., 12188. Tel: 518-237-0652. Sr. Geraldine Corkrey, C.S.J., Prin. Lay Teachers 18; Students 283.

[G] RESIDENTIAL INSTITUTIONS FOR CHILDREN & ADOLESCENTS

ALBANY. *LaSalle School, Inc.*, 391 Western Ave., 12203. Tel: 518-242-4731; Fax: 518-242-4747
For a complete listing, refer to the Special Care Facilities section.
Saint Anne Institute, 160 N. Main Ave., 12206. Tel: 518-437-6500
For a complete listing, refer to the Special Care Facilities section.
Saint Catherine's Center for Children, 40 N. Main Ave., 12203. Tel: 518-453-6700; Fax: 518-453-6712
For a complete listing, refer to the Special Care Facilities section.

WATERVLIET. *St. Colman's Home*, 12189. Tel: 518-273-4911; Fax: 518-273-3312
For a complete listing, refer to the Special Care Facilities section.

[H] GENERAL HOSPITALS

ALBANY. *Mercycare Corporation*, 315 S. Manning Blvd., 12208. Tel: 518-454-1084; Fax: 518-454-1520
For a complete listing, refer to the Hospitals section.
Mercycare Corporation, St. Peter's Hospital, 315 S. Manning Blvd., 12208. Tel: 518-454-1540
For a complete listing, refer to the Hospitals section.

AMSTERDAM. *St. Mary's Hospital*, 427 Guy Park Ave., 12010. Tel: 518-842-1900
For a complete listing, refer to the Hospitals section.

SCHENECTADY. *St. Clare's Holding Company, Inc.*, 600 McClellan St., 12304
For a complete listing, refer to the Hospitals section.
St. Clare's Hospital, 600 McClellan St., 12304. Tel: 518-382-2000
For a complete listing, refer to the Hospitals section.

TROY. *Seton Health System, Inc.*, 1300 Massachusetts Ave., 12180. Tel: 518-272-5000
For a complete listing, refer to the Hospitals section.

[I] SERVICES FOR ELDERLY

ALBANY. *SMILE, Independent Living Services, Inc. at Catholic Charities*, 100 Slingerland St., 12202. Tel: 518-432-0089. James McCaffrey, Dir.

[J] NURSING AND AGED HOMES

ALBANY. *Teresian House*, (1974) 200 Washington Ave. Ext., 12203. Tel: 518-456-2000
For a complete listing, refer to the Special Care Facilities section.
Villa Mary Immaculate, 301 Hackett Blvd., 12208. Tel: 518-482-3363
For a complete listing, refer to the Special Care Facilities section.

AMSTERDAM. *Mt. Loretto Nursing Home*, 302 Swart Hill Rd., 12010. Tel: 518-842-6790; Fax: 518-843-5993
For a complete listing, refer to the Special Care Facilities section.

CASTLETON. *Resurrection Nursing Home*, 12033. Tel: 518-732-7617; Fax: 518-732-4211
For a complete listing, refer to the Special Care Facilities section.

CATSKILL. *St. Joseph's Villa*, 38 Prospect Ave., 12414. Tel: 518-943-5701
For a complete listing, refer to the Special Care Facilities section.

LATHAM. *Our Lady of Hope Residence* Little Sisters of the Poor, Jeanne Jugan Ln., 12110. Tel: 518-785-4551.
For a complete listing, refer to the Special Care Facilities section.

TROY. *St. Mary's Woodland Village, Inc.*, Upper Tibbits Ave., 12180. Tel: 518-273-2040
For a complete listing, refer to the Special Care Facilities section.

[K] APARTMENTS FOR ELDERLY

ALBANY. *Bishop Broderick Apartments Housing Development Fund Co., Inc.*, 50 Prescott St., 12205. Tel: 518-869-7441; Fax: 518-869-0443
For a complete listing, refer to the Special Care Facilities section.
C.S.C. Housing Development Fund Co., Inc., dba Sanderson Court Senior Apts. 6 Carondelet Dr. Watervliet, 12189. Tel: 518-436-0156; 782-1123; Fax: 518-782-1125.
For a complete listing, refer to the Special Care Facilities section.
DePaul Management Corp., 41 N. Main Ave., 12203. Tel: 518-459-0183; Fax: 518-459-0202
For a complete listing, refer to the Special Care Facilities section.
St. Vincent Apartments Housing Development Fund Co., Inc., 475 Yates St., 12208. Tel: 518-482-8915; Fax: 518-489-1220
For a complete listing, refer to the Special Care Facilities section.

CLIFTON PARK. *Halfmoon Housing Development Fund Co., Inc. dba Bishop Hubbard Senior Apartments / De Paul Management Corp.*, 54 Katherine Dr., 12065.

Tel: 518-383-2705
For a complete listing, refer to the Special Care Facilities section.

NORTH GREENBUSH. *S.J. Housing Development Fund Company, Inc. dba St. Jude's Apartments* 50 Dana Ave. Wynantskill, 12198. Tel: 518-283-5690; Fax: 518-283-5893.
For a complete listing, refer to the Special Care Facilities section.

RENSSELAER. *East Greenbush Housing Development Fund Co., Inc. dba Branson Manor Senior Apartment*, 3 Grandview Dr., 12144. Tel: 518-283-8280; Fax: 518-283-8292
For a complete listing, refer to the Special Care Facilities section.

SLINGERLANDS. *Marie-Rose Manor HDFCI*, 100 Marquis Dr., 12159 Fax: 518-459-0204
For a complete listing, refer to the Special Care Facilities section.

WATERVLIET. *Carondelet Commons Senior Apartments*, 2 Carondelet Dr., 12189. Tel: 518-783-0444; Fax: 518-783-0456
For a complete listing, refer to the Special Care Facilities section.

Italian-American Housing Development Fund Co., Inc. dba Cabrini Acers Senior Apts., 4 Carondelet Dr., 12189. Tel: 518-785-0050; Fax: 518-785-0110
For a complete listing, refer to the Special Care Facilities section.

[L] MONASTERIES AND RESIDENCES OF PRIESTS AND BROTHERS

ALBANY. *Vincentian Fathers Residence*, 110 Menands Rd., 12204-1499. Tel: 518-433-1003. Revs. Stephen J. India, C.M., Supr.; John A. Doyle, C.M.; James E. Smith, C.M., Dir. of Daughters of Charity. Priests 3.

LAKE GEORGE. *St. Mary of the Lake*, P.O. Box 31, 12845. Tel: 518-668-5594. Rev. Robert T. Scott, Dir. Summer retreat of the Paulist Fathers.

RENSSELAER. *Franciscan Mission House*, Washington Ave., 12144. Tel: 518-465-0062. Promotion Center for Order's Missions. Bro. James Amrhein, O.F.M.Conv., Dir. & Guardian; Revs. Antone Kandrac, O.F.M.Conv.; Simon Mohr, O.F.M.Conv.; Angelus Netzer, O.F.M.Conv.

Provincialate, Immaculate Conception Friary - Order of Friars Minor Conventual (1872). (Immaculate Conception Province), P.O. Box 629, 12144. Tel: 518-472-1000. Revs. Canice Connors, O.F.M.Conv., Min. Prov. & Pres.; Justin Biase, O.F.M.Conv., Vicar Prov. & Vice Pres.; Bros. Stephen Merrigan, O.F.M.Conv., Archivist; John Joseph Dolan, O.F.M.Conv., Guardian; Andre Picotte, O.F.M.Conv., Dir. Cemeteries; Paul Lininger, O.F.M.Conv., Treas.; Rev. Jude DeAngelo, O.F.M.Conv., Definitor.
(Corporate Name: Order Minor Conventuals, Inc.).

SARATOGA SPRINGS. *St. John Neumann Residence*, 233 Lake Ave., 12866. Tel: 518-584-7500. Redemptorist Priests and Brothers of the Baltimore Province. Revs. John O'Connor, C.SS.R.; George Bridge, C.SS.R.; Julian Nichols Helldorfen, C.SS.R.; Edward Rosa, C.SS.R.; Joseph Oberle, C.S.S.R.; Joseph Rowan, C.SS.R.; Alfred C. Rush, C.SS.R.; Thomas F. O'Toole, C.SS.R.; Arthur Finn, C.SS.R.; Owen Rice; Gerard Smith, C.SS.R.; Richard Knappik, C.SS.R.; John McGuire, C.SS.R.; John Guiniven, C.SS.R.; Carl J. Langhirt, C.SS.R.; Joseph Oberle, C.SS.R.; James Lacey; Joseph Noll, C.SS.R.; Charles Fehrenbach; James Ferris, C.SS.R.; Edward Tardiff, C.SS.R.; Adam Otterbein, C.SS.R.; Bro. Richard Driscoll, C.SS.R.

VALATIE. *St. Joseph*. Residence for retired Holy Cross Brothers and Priests. 495 Maple Ln., 12184. Tel: 518-784-9481; Fax: 518-784-9494. Bros. Richard Kiniry, Supr. & Dir.; John Thornton, C.S.C., Admin.; Rev. Gregory Roy, S.J., Chap.

[M] CONVENTS AND RESIDENCES FOR SISTERS

ALBANY. *Convent of Mercy*, 310 S. Manning Blvd., 12208. Tel: 518-437-3000; Fax: 518-437-3030. Motherhouse of Sisters of Mercy. Sr. Rosemary Sgroi, R.S.M., Pres.; Sr. Arlene Boyd, R.S.M., V.P. Internal Affairs; Sr. Marilyn Murray, V.P. Corporate Affairs. Sisters 178.

Convent of the Sacred Heart, Kenwood, 799 S. Pearl St., 12202. Tel: 518-465-3341. Convent and Retirement Center for Religious of the Sacred Heart. Sr. Elizabeth Shearman, R.S.C.J., Area Dir.; Sr. Joan Inglis, R.S.C.J., Admin. of Kenwood Campus & Coord. of the Pax Christi Community; Rev. Christopher DeGiovine, Chap.
(Corporate Name: Female Academy of the Sacred Heart of Albany). Sisters 75.

Franciscan House, Mill Hill Sisters. Regional House, 1006 Madison Ave., 12208-2600. Tel: 518-482-1991. Sr. Judith Dever, F.M.S.J. Sisters 5.

Franciscan Sisters of Mary, 4 Katherine St., 12801-3839. Tel: 518-761-0976.

Sisters of the Holy Names of Jesus and Mary, Province Center, 1061 New Scotland Ave., 12208-1198. Tel: 518-489-5469; Fax: 518-489-5804.
(Corporate Name: Sisters of the Holy Names of Jesus and Mary of the New York Province, Inc.).

Academy of the Holy Names of New York, 1075 New Scotland Ave., 12208. Tel: 518-489-2559.

CASTLETON-ON-HUDSON. *Provincial House, Juniorate and Novitiate of the Sisters of Resurrection*, Mount St. Joseph, 35 Boltwood Ave., 12033-1011. Tel: 518-732-2226; Fax: 518-732-2898. Sr. Jeanne Marie Harla, Prov. Sup.; Sr. M. Krystyna, C.R., Local Supr.; Sr. Dolores Palermo, C.R., Dir. Novices. Sisters 22. 34 Boltwood Ave. Tel: 518-732-7831.

CLIFTON PARK. *Sisters of Charity of St. Louis Convent*, 6 Secada Dr., 12065-5005. Tel: 518-371-0247; Fax: 518-371-1206. Sr. Louise Marceau, S.C.S.L., Vocation & Formation Dir.

GERMANTOWN. *St. Teresa's Motherhouse*, Avila on the Hudson, 600 Woods Rd., 12526-5617. Tel: 518-537-5000. Motherhouse and Novitiate. Carmelite Sisters for the Aged and Infirm. Mother M. Suzanne Sapa, O.Carm., Supr. Gen.; Rev. Joseph E. Finch, Chap. Sisters 29.

Postulation Office. Mother M. Angeline Teresa, O.Carm., Servant of God; Rev. Mario Esposito, O.Carm.; Sr. M. Gabriel, O.Carm., Coord. of the Cause.

GLEN FALLS. *Franciscan Sisters of Mary*, 4 Katherine St., 12801-5102. Tel: 518-761-0976.

LATHAM. *Provincial House of the Sisters of St. Joseph of Carondelet (Albany Province)*, 12110. Tel: 518-783-3500. Sr. Sean C. Peters, C.S.J., Prov. Dir.; Rev. Geoffrey D. Burke, Chap. Sisters 602.

MENANDS. *De Paul Provincial House*. (Corporate Name: Daughters of Charity of St. Vincent de Paul, N.E. Prov.), 96 Menands Rd., 12204. Tel: 518-462-5593. Sr. Louise Gallahue, D.C., Prov. Sup.; Rev. James E. Smith, Prov. Dir.

SCHENECTADY. *Monastery of St. Teresa of Jesus of Discalced Carmelites*, 428 Duane Ave., 12304. Mother Mary St. John of the Cross, O.C.D., Prioress. Professed Sisters 12; Postulants 1.

WATERVLIET. *St. Colman's Convent*, 12189. Tel: 518-273-4911; Fax: 518-273-3312. Motherhouse and Novitiate of Sisters of the Presentation of the B.V.M. Mother M. Carmel, P.B.V.M., Mother Gen.; Rev. John A. Molyn, Chap.

[N] TEEN CENTERS

GUILDERLAND. *Innovative Teen Services, Inc.*, 2333A Western Ave., 12084.

[O] HOUSES OF PRAYER AND RETREAT HOUSES

ALBANY. *Abba House of Prayer*. A nonprofit corporation. 647 Western Ave., 12203. Tel: 518-438-8320.

AURIESVILLE. *Jesuit Retreat House for Priests, Religious and Lay People*, 12016. Tel: 518-853-4496; Fax: 518-853-3051. Revs. John G. Marzolf, S.J., Supr. & Dir.; William B. Cogan, S.J.; Thomas E. Brady, S.J.; Vincent M. McNally, S.J.; Louis A. Mounteer, S.J.; William P. Poorten, S.J.; Bros. Theodore C. Bender, S.J.; Paul C. Acer, S.J.; John T. Gibbons, S.J.; Edward G. Lawniczak, S.J. Priests 6; Brothers 4.

Shrine of Our Lady of Martyrs, 12016. Tel: 518-853-3033.
E-mail: jesuit@klink.net
Web site: www.klink.net/~jesuit
National Shrine of the Jesuit Martyrs of North America. Revs. John G. Marzolf, S.J.; John J. Paret, S.J., Asst. Dir. & Vice-Postulator Cause of Kateri Tekakwitha; John M. Doolan, S.J.

CHESTERTOWN. *The Priory*, 12817. Tel: 518-494-3733. Sr. Constance M. Messitt, C.S.J., Dir.; Sr. Francis Anne Gilchrist, C.S.J., Co-Dir.

FONDA. *Blessed Kateri Retreat House*, Rte. 5, P.O. Box 627, 12068. Tel: 518-853-3646; Fax: 518-853-3371. Rev. Kevin Kenny, O.F.M.Conv., Dir.; Bro. Kenneth H. Lucas, O.F.M.Conv., Assoc. Shrine Dir.

GLENS FALLS. *Wellsprings*. A Program for Christian Ministers. 93 Maple St., 12801. Tel: 518-792-3183; Fax: 518-792-3184. A four-month holistic enrichment sabbatical program for men and women serving in the church. Sr. Margaret Picha, S.S.N.D., Dir.; Michael Laratonda, F.M.S., Assoc. Dir.

PARADOX. *Pyramid Life Center*. Corporation name: Albany Catholic Youth Association, Inc., 12858. Tel: 518-585-7545. Summer, fall and winter retreat house, located at Pyramid Lake.

SCHENECTADY. *Dominican Spiritual Life Center*. Corporation Name: Dominican Congregation of St. Catherine De Ricci. 1945 Union St., 12309. Tel: 518-393-4169. Jeanne Qualters, Admin. Residence Facilities for 45; Non-resident Facilities for 90 to 100.

STILLWATER. *Still Point House of Prayer*, Rte. 423, Box 53, 12170. Tel: 518-587-4967. House of Prayer operated by The Community of Still Point, Inc. Yearround hermitages, retreats, sabbaticals, holistic and interfaith programs. Sr. Lillian Needham, S.S.J., Dir.; Sr. Mary Ellen Curtin, C.S.J., Assoc. Dir.

UNADILLA. *Gilead, Inc.*, 1011 State Hwy. 7, 13849. Eucharistic Community.

VALATIE. *St. Joseph Spiritual Life Center*, 495 Maple Ln., 12184. Tel: 518-784-9481.

[P] SHELTERS FOR WOMEN

ALBANY. *Arbor House*, 302 Western Ave., 12203. Tel: 518-489-6030
For a complete listing, refer to the Special Care Facilities section.

[Q] YOUTH TREATMENT FACILITIES

ALBANY. *Hospitality House Therapeutic Community Inc.*, 271 Central Ave., 12206. Tel: 518-434-6468. A private, not-for-profit, residential treatment program for young people, 16 to 30 years old, with a history of drug and/or substance abuse.

ALTAMONT. *Bernard and Caroline Cobb Memorial School*. Day Care Center with day program for both preschool and school age children with special needs. Sisters of the Presentation Day Care Center, 100-300 Mt. Presentation Way., 12009. Tel: 518-861-6446.

[R] SHRINES

FONDA. *The National Shrine of Blessed Kateri Tekakwitha and Friary*, P.O. Box 627, 12068. Tel: 518-853-3646; Fax: 518-853-3371. Rev. Kevin Kenny, O.F.M.Conv., Shrine Dir. & Guardian; Bro. Kenneth Lucas, O.F.M.Conv., Assoc. Dir.

[S] CAMPUS MINISTRY

ALBANY. *New York State University at Albany*. (Albany Collegiate Interfaith Center, Inc.) with offices at SUNYA. Box 22225, 12222. Tel: 518-489-8573; Fax: 518-489-8573. Sr. Maureen O'Leary, F.S.P., Chap.

COBLESKILL. *State University of New York College of Agricultural & Technology at Cobleskill*, Main St., P.O. Box 124, 12175. Rev. Edward Golding.

DELHI. *State University of New York College of Agricultural & Technology at Delhi*, St. Peter Rectory, 8 Franklin St., 13753. Tel: 607-746-2503. Rev. Joseph Manerowski.

GLENS FALLS. *Adirondack Community College*, Annunciation, 12804. Tel: 518-793-9677. Rev. Gary Mercure.

HUDSON. *Columbia-Greene Community College*, P.O. Box 1000, 12534. Tel: 518-828-4181.

LOUDONVILLE. *Siena College*, 12211. Tel: 518-783-2332. Rev. Francis X. Gunn, O.F.M., Dir. Campus Ministry. Assoc. Campus Ministers: Revs. Kevin Daly, O.F.M.; Michael J. Harlan, O.F.M., Assoc. Campus Min.; Charlotte Tabor, Protestant Min.; Ms. Claire Morgan, Vol. Coord.; Ms. Judy Dougherty, Sec.

ONEONTA. *New York State University at Oneonta and Hartwick College*. Corporate Title: Oneonta Newman Foundation. Newman House, 77 Spruce St., 13820. Tel: 607-432-4400. Susan Resbitt, Campus Min. Tel: 607-432-4400; Vincent Fox, Pres. of Foundation, Bd. of Dir.; Rev. Brian Raiche, Sacramental Min.; Tracie Jones, Sec.

SARATOGA. *Skidmore College*, Broadway, 12866. Tel: 584-5000, Ext. 2175. Rev. Ronald J. Boccieri, M.M.

SCHENECTADY. *Union College, Catholic Campus Ministry*, 12308. Tel: 518-388-6087. Mr. Thomas J. Frieberg, Chap. Religious Programs Office of Union College, the College Center.

TROY. *Hudson Valley Community College*, 80 Vandenburgh Ave., 12180. Tel: 518-270-7168. Sr. Rosemary Ann Cuneo, C.R., Campus Min.

Rensselaer Polytechnic Institute. Office of the Resident Catholic Chaplain, 217 Rensselaer Union, 12180. Tel: 518-276-6518. Rev. Edward Kacerguis, Chap.; Catherine A. Waibel, Chap.

The Rensselaer Newman Foundation, 217 Rensselaer Union, 12180. Michael Duffy, Pres.

University Parish of Christ Sun of Justice. Rev. Thomas Phelan, Chapel & Cultural Center, 2008 19th St., 12180. Tel: 518-274-7793. William McQuiston, Dir.

Russell Sage College, Campus Ministry Office, Rm. #304 Student Center, 12180. Tel: 518-271-4507. Sr. Rosemary Cuneo, C.R.

[T] MISCELLANEOUS LISTINGS

ALBANY. *Birthright of Albany*, 586 Central Ave., 12206. Tel: 518-438-2978. Diane Koster, Dir.

Burke Community Service Corp., Inc., 40 N. Main Ave., 12203. Tel: 518-453-6600.

Diocesan HIV/AIDS Ministries, 40 N. Main Ave., 12203. Tel: 518-453-6650, Ext. 485; Fax: 518-453-6792. Rev. Bernard R. Turner, Dir.

Emmaus House. Albany Catholic Worker Community, 35 N. Main Ave., 12203.

The Family Rosary Worldwide Office. Sponsored by Congregation of Holy Cross (Eastern Prov.). (Corporate Name: The Family Rosary, Inc.), 4 Pine West

Plaza, 12205-5520. Tel: 518-452-3082; Fax: 518-452-3956. Revs. Hugh W. Cleary, C.S.C., Prov.; John P. Phalen, C.S.C., Pres.; Mr. Robert R. Klein, Vice Pres., Finance & Admin.

Crusade for Family Prayer, Inc. Sponsored by Congregation of Holy Cross (Eastern Prov.). Revs. Hugh W. Cleary, C.S.C., Prov.; John P. Phalen, C.S.C., Pres.; Mr. Robert P. Klein, Vice Pres., Finance & Admin.

The Foundation of the Roman Catholic Diocese of Albany, New York, Inc., 40 N. Main Ave., 12203. Tel: 518-453-6680; Fax: 518-453-6793. Mr. Jack Manning, Dir.

LaSalle Albany, Inc., De La Salle Rd., 12208. Bros. Michael Corry, F.S.C., Chm.; Stephen McCabe, F.S.C., Vice Chm.; E. James Stolz, F.S.C., Sec.

McCloskey Community Service Corporation, 40 N. Main Ave., 12203. Tel: 518-453-6683; Fax: 518-453-6792. Phyllis Hathaway, Exec. Dir.

New York State Catholic Conference, 465 State St., 12203. Tel: 518-434-6195; Fax: 518-434-9796. John M. Kerry, Exec. Dir.

New York State Catholic Healthcare Council, 465 State St., 12203. Tel: 518-434-8293. Richard N. McDevitt, Exec. Sec.

New York State Council of Catholic Charities Directors, 465 State St., 12203. Tel: 518-434-3482. Joseph Buttigieg, Exec. Sec.

New York State Council of Catholic School Superintendents. New York State Council of Diocesan Directors of Religious Education. 465 State St., 12203. Tel: 518-434-6195. James D. Cultrara, Exec. Sec.

St. Francis Chapel, 1440 Central Ave., Northway Mall, 12205. Tel: 518-459-2854. Order of Friars Minor Province of the Most Holy Name of Jesus.

Sisters of the Holy Names of Jesus & Mary of the New York Province, Inc. Continuing Support Charitable Trust to provide for the needs of the Tutwiler Clinic, Tutwiler, Mississippi. 1061 New Scotland Ave., 12208-1198. Tel: 601-345-8334.

Sisters of the Holy Names of Jesus and Mary. Community Support Charitable Trust. 1061 New Scotland Ave., 12208-1198; Fax: 518-489-5804.

Support Fund Trust of the Province of St. Thomas of Villanova, c/o 40 N. Main Ave., 12203.

CASTLETON-ON-HUDSON. *C.C.M. of Schodack, Inc.*, 92 S. Main St., 12033.

COHOES. *Apostolate for the Suffering*, c/o St. Rita Rectory, 50 St. Rita Pl., 12047. Tel: 518-237-4444. Rev. Mario Pacini, S.A.C.

GERMANTOWN. *Oneness in Peace Center, Inc.*, 49 Main St., 12526. Tel: 518-537-5678. Co-Directors: Sr. Vergilia Jim, O.S.F.; Claire Langie.

LATHAM. *The Sister M. Athanasia Gurry Trust Fund of the Sisters of St. Joseph*, 385 Watervliet-Shaker Rd., 12110-4799. Tel: 518-783-3538.

NISKAYUNA. *Villa Fusco Child Day Care Center*, 955 Balltown Rd., 12309. Tel: 518-377-1613. Sr. Josephine Alderuccio, D.C.P.B., Supr. Daughters of Charity of the Most Precious Blood. Capacity 14.

RENSSELAER. *Order of Friars Minor Conventual Immaculate Conception Province Charitable Trust.* (Established 1990), P.O. Box 629, 12144. Tel: 518-432-6623. Rev. Anthony Kall, O.F.M.Conv., Trustee.

SCHENECTADY. *St. Luke's Guild*, c/o St. Clare Hospital, 600 McClellan St., 12304. Tel: 518-347-5760. Paul Brisson, M.D., Pres.

Secular Order of Discalced Carmelites, 428 Duane Ave., 12304-2691. Ms. Mary Therese Thouin, Pres.

TROY. *Catholic School Administrators' Association of New York State*, 406 Fulton St., Ste. 512, 12180. Tel: 518-273-1205; Fax: 518-273-1206. Sr. Carol Cimino, S.S.J., Exec. Dir.; Sr. Jennifer Votraw, S.S.J., Dir.

[U] SUMMER CAMPS

ALBANY. *Camp Scully*, 100 Slingerland St., 12202. Tel: 518-426-3511; 283-1617 (Snyders Lake). Summer Address, 24 Camp Scully Way, Wynantskill, 12198. A program of Albany Catholic Family and Community Services. Summer Residential Camp for children 7-14. Under direction of Catholic Charities of the Diocese of Albany. Financed by local Youth Bureaus, the Albany Catholic Diocese, USDA Summer Program and by contributions. Capacity 110 per week for 7 weeks.

TROY. *Troy CYO Day Camp*, Box 867, 237 Fourth St., 12180. Tel: 518-274-2630. Sponsored by Troy Youth Organization, Inc. for Boys and Girls, ages 5-12 yrs. Raymond R. Piscitelli, Exec. Dir.; Mara A. Wager, Prog. Dir.; Jeanne Mailloux, Exec. Sec.

RELIGIOUS INSTITUTES OF MEN REPRESENTED IN THE DIOCESE

For further details refer to the corresponding bracketed number in the Religious Institutes of Men or Women section.

[0140]—*The Augustinians.*—O.S.A.
[0330]—*Brothers of the Christian Schools.* (New York Prov.).—F.S.C.
[0600]—*Brothers of the Congregation of Holy Cross.* (Eastern Prov.).—C.S.C.
[0270]—*Carmelite Fathers & Brothers.*—O.Carm.
[0310]—*Congregation of Christian Brothers.* (Eastern US).—C.F.C.
[0220]—*Congregation of the Blessed Sacrament.*—S.S.S.
[1330]—*Congregation of the Mission.* (Eastern Prov.).—C.M.
[0480]—*Conventual Franciscans.* (Prov. of Immaculate Conception).—O.F.M.Conv.
[0520]—*Franciscan Friars.* (Most Holy Name Prov.).—O.F.M.
[0690]—*Jesuit Fathers and Brothers.* (New York Prov.).—S.J.
[0720]—*The Missionaries of Our Lady of La Salette.* (Prov. of Our Lady of Seven Dolors).—M.S.
[1030]—*Paulist Fathers.* (New York).—C.S.P.
[0610]—*Priests of the Congregation of Holy Cross.* (Eastern Prov.).—C.S.C.
[1070]—*Redemptorist Fathers.* (Baltimore Prov.).—C.SS.R.
[0990]—*Society of the Catholic Apostolate.*—S.A.C.

RELIGIOUS INSTITUTES OF WOMEN REPRESENTED IN THE DIOCESE

[0330]—*Carmelite Sisters for the Aged and Infirm.*—O.Carm.
[2980]—*Congregation of Notre Dame.*—C.N.D.
[0760]—*Daughters of Charity of St. Vincent de Paul.*—D.C.
[0740]—*Daughters of Charity of the Most Precious Blood.*—D.C.P.B.
[0420]—*Discalced Carmelite Nuns.*—O.C.D.
[1070-17]—*Dominican Sisters - Congregation of St. Catherine de Ricci.*—O.P.
[]—*Dominican Sisters of Hope.*—O.P.
[1170]—*Felician Sisters.*—C.S.S.F.
[]—*Franciscan Missionaries of Jesus Crucified.*—F.M.J.C.
[1180]—*Franciscan Sisters of Allegany, New York.*—O.S.F.
[1415]—*Franciscan Sisters of Mary.*—F.S.M.
[1425]—*Franciscan Sisters of Peace.*—F.S.P.
[1190]—*Franciscan Sisters of the Atonement.*—S.A.
[2340]—*Little Sisters of the Poor.*—L.S.P.
[1410]—*Mill Hill Sisters (Franciscan Missionaries of St. Joseph).*—F.M.S.J.
[2070]—*Religious of the Holy Union of the Sacred Hearts.*—S.U.S.C.
[3430]—*Religious Teachers Filippini.*—M.P.F.
[4180]—*Religious Venerini Sisters.*—M.P.V.
[0620]—*Sisters of Charity of St. Louis.*—S.C.S.L.
[2560]—*Sisters of Mary Reparatrix.*—S.M.R.
[2575]—*Sisters of Mercy of the Americas.* (Albany).—R.S.M.
[1660]—*Sisters of St. Francis of the Providence of God.*—O.S.F.
[3840]—*Sisters of St. Joseph of Carondelet.*—C.S.J.
[0150]—*Sisters of the Assumption.*—S.A.S.V.
[2980]—*Sisters of the Congregation de Notre Dame.*—C.N.D.
[1990]—*Sisters of the Holy Names of Jesus and Mary.*—S.N.J.M.
[3320]—*Sisters of the Presentation of the B.V.M..*—P.B.V.M.
[3480]—*Sisters of the Resurrection.*—C.R.
[1490]—*Sisters of the Third Franciscan Order.*—O.S.F.
[4070]—*Society of the Sacred Heart.*—R.S.C.J.

DIOCESAN CEMETERIES

COHOES. *St. Agnes Cemetery*, St. Agnes Hwy., 12047. Tel: 518-463-0134.

GLENVILLE. *St. Anthony Cemetery*, Glenridge Rd., 12325. Tel: 518-374-5319.

MENANDS. *St. Agnes Cemetery*, 48 Cemetery Ave. Tel: 518-463-0134.

ROTTERDAM. *Holy Cross Cemetery.* Tel: 518-374-5319.

SCHENECTADY. *Most Holy Redeemer Cemetery*, 2501 Troy Rd.

St. Cyril & St. Methodius Cemetery. Tel: 518-374-5319.

TROY. *St. Jean Baptiste Cemetery*, 968 Spring Ave., 12180. Tel: 518-272-0931.

St. John Cemetery. Tel: 518-272-0931.

St. Mary's Cemetery of Troy, Inc., Brunswick Rd., 12180. Tel: 518-272-0931.

WATERVLIET. *St. Patrick Cemetery*, Troy Rd., 12189. Tel: 518-463-0134.

NECROLOGY

† Ashline, Alfred, (Retired). —Died March 30, 1997.
† Cekovsky, Andrew, (Retired). —Died May 24, 1997.
† Colburn, Harold, (Retired). —Died Nov. 13, 1996.
† Glavin, Rev. Msgr. Edward R., Amsterdam, NY, St. Mary. —Died June 21, 1997.
† Keeshan, Paul J., (Retired). —Died May 31, 1997.
† Lockwood, Charles, Altamont, NY, St. Lucy. —Died March 18, 1997.
† McManus, Edward A., (Retired). —Died March 7, 1997.
† Mealey, John H., Albany, NY, St. Teresa of Avila. —Died Aug. 25, 1997.
† Pritchard, James F., (Retired). —Died June 10, 1997.

Diocese of Alexandria

(Dioecesis Alexandrina in Louisiana)

Most Reverend

SAM G. JACOBS, D.D.

Bishop of Alexandria; ordained June 6, 1964; appointed Bishop of Alexandria July 1, 1989; ordained and installed August 24, 1989. *Mailing Address: P.O. Box 7417, Alexandria, LA, 71306.*

Chancery Office: 4400 Coliseum Blvd., P.O. Box 7417, Alexandria, LA, 71306. Tel.: 318-445-2401; Fax: 318-448-6121.

Web site address: www.diocesealex.org

E-mail address: info@diocesealex.org

ERECTED AS DIOCESE OF NATCHITOCHES JULY 29, 1853.

Square Miles 22,212.

TRANSFERRED TO ALEXANDRIA AUGUST 6, 1910 AND BECAME DIOCESE OF ALEXANDRIA.

REDESIGNATED DIOCESE OF ALEXANDRIA-SHREVEPORT ON JANUARY 12, 1977; SPLIT, FORMING TWO DIOCESES, THE DIOCESE OF ALEXANDRIA AND THE DIOCESE OF SHREVEPORT AS OF JUNE 16, 1986.

Square Miles 11,116.

Comprises the counties (parishes) of Rapides, Avoyelles, Concordia, Catahoula, LaSalle, Grant, Natchitoches, Vernon, Tensas, Caldwell, Winn, Franklin and Madison.

For legal titles of parishes and diocesan institutions, consult the Chancery Office.

STATISTICAL OVERVIEW

Personnel	
Bishop	1
Priests: Diocesan Active in Diocese	38
Priests: Active Outside Diocese	5
Priests: Retired, Sick or Absent	23
Number of Diocesan Priests	66
Religious Priests in Diocese	16
Extern Priests in Diocese	8
Ordinations:	
Diocesan Priests	3
Transitional Deacons	2
Permanent Deacons in Diocese	7
Total Brothers	3
Total Sisters	62
Parishes	
Parishes	48
With Resident Pastor:	
Resident Diocesan Priests	32
Resident Religious Priests	10
Without Resident Pastor:	
Administered by Priests	5
Administered by Women Religious	1
Missions	23
Pastoral Centers	1
Professional Ministry Personnel:	
Brothers	1
Sisters	10
Lay Ministers	11
Welfare	
Catholic Hospitals	1
Total Assisted	131,845
Health Care Centers	1
Total Assisted	312
Homes for the Aged	2
Total Assisted	164
Special Centers for Social Services	16
Total Assisted	125,650
Residential Care of Disabled	1
Total Assisted	152
Educational	
Diocesan Students in Other Seminaries	12
Total Seminarians	12
High Schools, Diocesan and Parish	3
Total Students	570
Elementary Schools, Diocesan and Parish	9
Total Students	2,546
Catechesis/Religious Education:	
High School Students	1,746
Elementary Students	3,116
Total Students Under Catholic Instruction	7,990
Teachers in the Diocese:	
Brothers	2
Sisters	20
Lay Teachers	182
Vital Statistics	
Receptions into the Church:	
Infant Baptism Totals	788
Adult Baptism Totals	84
Received into Full Communion	133
First Communions	760
Confirmations	568
Marriages:	
Catholic	156
Interfaith	116
Total Marriages	272
Deaths	674
Total Catholic Population	48,050
Total Population	393,880

Former Bishops—Rt. Rev. AUGUSTUS M. MARTIN, cons. Nov. 30, 1853; died Sept. 29, 1875.—Rt. Rev. FRANCIS XAVIER LERAY, cons. Bishop of Natchitoches, April 22, 1877; named Bishop of Janopolis, Coadjutor of New Orleans, and Administrator of Natchitoches, Oct. 23, 1879; promoted to the See of New Orleans, Dec., 1883; died Sept. 23, 1887.—Rt. Rev. ANTHONY DURIER, D.D., cons. March 19, 1885; died Feb. 28, 1904.—Most Rev. CORNELIUS VAN DE VEN, cons. Nov. 30, 1904; made assistant at the Pontifical Throne, Nov. 12, 1929; died May 8, 1932.—Most Rev. DANIEL FRANCIS DESMOND, D.D., cons. Bishop of Alexandria Jan. 5, 1933; died Sept. 11, 1945.—Most Rev. CHARLES P. GRECO, D.D., cons. Feb. 25, 1946; retired May 22, 1973; died Jan. 20, 1987.—Most Rev. LAWRENCE P. GRAVES, D.D., J.C.L., cons. April 25, 1969; retired July 20, 1982; died Jan. 15, 1994.—Most Rev. WILLIAM B. FRIEND, D.D., ord. Aug. 31, 1979; installed Bishop of Alexandria-Shreveport Jan. 11, 1983 then after Diocese of Alexandria-Shreveport was split into two dioceses June 16, 1986; installed Bishop of Shreveport July 30, 1986.—Most Rev. JOHN C. FAVALORA, D.D., ord. December 20, 1961; appt. Bishop of Alexandria June 16, 1986; ord. and installed July 29, 1986; installed Bishop of St. Petersburg May 16, 1989; installed Archbishop of Miami Dec. 20, 1994.

Vicar General—Rev. Msgr. RONALD C. HOPPE, *P.O. Box 7417, Alexandria, 71306.* Tel: 318-445-2401.

Chancery Office—*4400 Coliseum Blvd., P.O. Box 7417, Alexandria, 71306.* Tel: 318-445-2401; Fax: 318-448-6121. Office Hours: Mon.-Fri. 8-12 & 1-4:30.

Moderator of the Curia—Rev. Msgr. RONALD C. HOPPE, V.G.

Chancellor—Rev. Msgr. JOSEPH M. SUSI.

Ecclesiastical Notaries—Rev. Msgr. JOSEPH M. SUSI; Ms. ADDIE BUTLER; Ms. DEBORAH DEOROSAN; Mrs. PATRICIA LACAZE; Mrs. ETTA OHRT; Mrs. PATRICIA THOMAS.

Diocesan Tribunal—*P.O. Box 7417, Alexandria, 71306.* Tel: 318-445-2401.

Judicial Vicar—Rev. BRUCE MILLER, J.C.L.

Judges—Most Rev. SAM G. JACOBS; Rev. BRUCE MILLER, J.C.L.

Defenders of the Bond and Promoters of Justice—Rev. JAMES A. FERGUSON, J.C.L.

Chief Auditors—Ms. ADDIE BUTLER; Mrs. PATRICIA THOMAS.

College of Consultors—Rev. Msgr. RONALD C. HOPPE, V.G.; Rev. Msgr. JOSEPH M. SUSI; Rev. Msgr. STEVE J. TESTA, V.F.; Revs. GERARD M. FOLEY, V.F.; KENNETH J. ROY, V.F.; BERNARD L. ZAGST, V.F.

Finance Council—Mr. ROBERT CHAPPUIS; Mr. SHERMAN COOK; Mr. WILLIAM HAMLIN; Mr. TODD MARYE; Mrs. DOROTHY PUGH; Mr. GUS VOLTZ, JR.; Rev. Msgr. HENRY F. BECKERS; Rev. Msgr. RONALD C. HOPPE, V.G.; Rev. Msgr. JOSEPH M. SUSI.

Building Review Committee—Mr. GEORGE C. ADAMS; Mr. DONALD A. MANSOUR; Mr. LYNN MCCAIN; Mr. FINLEY L. PONTHIE; Mr. REX L. PONTHIE; Mr. WILLIE PUGH, JR.; Mr. WILLIAM O. ROLLINS; Mr. JOSEPH T. SIMMS, JR.; Mr. WILLIAM J. THEVENOTE.

Priests Council—Revs. JAMES A. FERGUSON, J.C.L., Chm.; KENNETH J. MICHIELS, Vice Chm.; SCOTT CHEMINO, Sec.-Treas.; Rev. Msgr. RONALD C. HOPPE, V.G.; Rev. Msgr. JOSEPH M. SUSI; Rev. Msgr. STEVE J. TESTA, V.F.; Rev. Msgr. FREDERICK J. LYONS; Revs. GERARD FOLEY, V.F.; BERNARD L. ZAGST, V.F.; AUGUST THOMPSON; ANGELO MESSINA; JAMES A. FOSTER; JACOB THOMAS; DAVID J. BRAQUET; VINCENT MANUEL.

Retirement Board—Rev. Msgr. FREDERICK J. LYONS; Rev. Msgr. JOHN M. TIMMERMANS; Rev. GERARD FOLEY, V.F.; Dr. VINCENT VINCENT; Mr. ROBERT LAWRENCE.

Rural Deans—Rev. Msgr. STEVE J. TESTA, V.F.; Revs. KENNETH J. ROY, V.F.; GERARD M. FOLEY, V.F.; BERNARD L. ZAGST, V.F.

The Catholic Foundation of North-Central Louisiana, Inc.—*P.O. Box 8021, Alexandria, 71306.* Tel: 318-487-9222. JOSEPH L. HEBERT, Pres.-Treas.; Mrs. BETTY CHOP, Corp. Sec. *Board of Directors:* Mr. GRAHAM KRAMER, Chm.; Rev. Msgr. FREDERICK J. LYONS, Vice Chm.; Rev. Msgr. HENRY F. BECKERS; Mr. SCOTT O. BRAME; Mrs. SUSAN CHADWICK; Mr. MARION J. CHANEY; Mr. ROBERT E. CHAPPUIS; Mrs. MARY CONVERSE; Mr. JAMES CURLEY; Mr. LEO P. DOBARD, JR.; Most Rev. SAM G. JACOBS; Rev. Msgr. J. CARSON LACAZE; Mrs. JO ANN NOEL; Rev. Msgr.

STEVE J. TESTA; Mrs. KAREN WILLIAMS.

Diocesan Offices and Directors

Archivist—Rev. Msgr. JOSEPH M. SUSI, *4400 Coliseum Blvd., P.O. Box 7417, Alexandria, 71306-0417.* Tel: 318-445-2401.

Black Affairs—Vacant.

Business Affairs—Mr. DAVID BROOK, Dir., *4400 Coliseum Blvd., P.O. Box 7417, Alexandria, 71306-0417.* Tel: 318-445-2401.

Campaign for Human Development—Sr. JOHN MARTIN EBROM, C.D.P., Dir., *4400 Coliseum Blvd., P.O. Box 7417, Alexandria, 71306-0417.* Tel: 318-445-2401.

Campus Ministry—Rev. EDWIN RODRIGUEZ-HERNANDEZ, Dir., *LSU-A, 8700 Hwy. 71-S, Alexandria, 71302-9633.* Tel: 318-473-6494.

Catholic Community Services—Sr. JOHN MARTIN EBROM, C.D.P., Dir., *4400 Coliseum Blvd., P.O. Box 7417, Alexandria, 71306-0417.* Tel: 318-445-2401.

Catholic Relief Services—Sr. JOHN MARTIN EBROM, C.D.P., Dir., *4400 Coliseum Blvd., P.O. Box 7417, Alexandria, 71306-0417.* Tel: 318-445-2401.

Cemeteries—Rev. Msgr. JOHN M. TIMMERMANS, Coord., *238 Mon Borde St., Moreauville, 71355.* Tel: 318-985-1774.

Charismatic Movement—Rev. H. GERALD BORDELON, Diocesan Liaison, *401 21st St., Alexandria, 71301.* Tel: 318-445-3693.

Church Financial Development—Mrs. ANN MASDEN, Dir., *4400 Coliseum Blvd., P.O. Box 7417, Alexandria, 71301.* Tel: 318-445-2401.

Church Vocations Board—Most Rev. SAM G. JACOBS; Revs. EDWIN RODRIGUEZ-HERNANDEZ; SHELDON L. ROY; KENNETH J. MICHIELS; GEORGE KROSFIELD; Mr. TOMMY RIGMAIDEN; Ms. GAIL BRODNAX; Sr. OLIVE BORDELON, C.C.V.I.

Clergy and Religious—Rev. SAMUEL J. POLIZZI, Vicar, *P.O. Box 7417, Alexandria, 71306-0417.* Tel: 318-445-2401.

Communications—Mr. AL NASSIF, Print Media; Mrs. ANN MASDEN, Electronic Media, *4400 Coliseum Blvd., P.O. Box 7417, Alexandria, 71306-0417.* Tel: 318-445-2401.

Continuing Formation of the Clergy—Rev. H. GERALD BORDELON, Dir., *401 21st St., Alexandria, 71301.* Tel: 318-445-3693.

Ecumenical—Rev. S. SCOTT CHEMINO, Liaison, *P.O. Box 8, Plaucheville, 71362.* Tel: 318-922-3131.

Eucharistic League, Priests—Rev. Msgr. JOSEPH M. SUSI, Dir., *4400 Coliseum Blvd., P.O. Drawer 7417, Alexandria, 71306-0417.* Tel: 318-445-2401.

Evangelization—Rev. JOSE A. ROBLES-SANCHEZ, Dir., *P.O. Box 31, Bordelonville, 71320-0031.* Tel: 318-997-2151.

Family Life Ministry—Sr. JOHN MARTIN EBROM, C.D.P., Dir., *4400 Coliseum Blvd., P.O. Box 7417, Alexandria, 71306-0417.* Tel: 318-445-2401.

Fiscal Management—Mr. DAVID BROOK, Dir. Business Affairs, *4400 Coliseum Blvd., P.O. Box 7417, Alexandria, 71306-0417.* Tel: 318-445-2401.

Hispanic Apostolate—Rev. PEDRO J. SIERRA-POSADA, *4400 Coliseum Blvd., P.O. Box 7417, Alexandria, 71306-0417.* Tel: 318-445-2401.

Holy Childhood Association—Rev. Msgr. STEVE J. TESTA, V.F., Dir., *4400 Coliseum Blvd., P.O. Box 7417, Alexandria, 71306-0417.* Tel: 318-445-2401.

Liturgy Committee—Rev. KENNETH MATHEWS, *626 Fourth St., Alexandria, 71301.* Tel: 318-445-1451.

Maryhill Renewal Center—Sr. RUTHANN WILLIAMS, O.P., Dir., *600 Maryhill Rd., Pineville, 71360.* Tel: 318-640-1378.

Newspaper "The Church Today"—Mr. AL NASSIF, Editor, *4400 Coliseum Blvd., P.O. Box 7417, Alexandria, 71306-0417.* Tel: 318-445-2401.

Permanent Deacons—Rev. D. MATHEW WOOLLETT, *P.O. Box 1123, Cottonport, 71327-1123.* Tel: 318-876-3681.

Personnel / Property Management—Mr. LONNIE DUFOUR, Dir., *P.O. Box 7417, Alexandria, 71306-0417.* Tel: 318-445-2401.

Print Media—(The Church Today and Digest of the News)—Mr. AL NASSIF, Dir. and Editor, *4400 Coliseum Blvd., P.O. Box 7417, Alexandria, 71306-0417.* Tel: 318-445-2401.

Propagation of the Faith and Foreign Mission Education—Rev. Msgr. STEVE J. TESTA, Dir., *4400 Coliseum Blvd., P.O. Box 7417, Alexandria, 71306-0417.* Tel: 318-445-2401.

Public Affairs—Mrs. ANN MASDEN, Dir., *4400 Coliseum Blvd., P.O. Box 7417, Alexandria, 71306-0417.* Tel: 318-445-0417.

Religious, Coordinator for—Bro. ANDRE M. LUCIA, F.S.E., *P.O. Box 25, Plaucheville, 71362.* Tel: 318-922-3630.

Religious Education—Sr. MARY ELLEN THERIOT, S.S.N.D., Dir., *4400 Coliseum Blvd., P.O. Box 7417, Alexandria, 71306-0417.* Tel: 318-445-2401.

Renew—Mr. TOM WEBB, Dir., *4400 Coliseum Blvd., P.O. Box 7417, Alexandria, 71306-0417.* Tel: 318-445-2401.

Rural Life Ministry—Rev. JAMES ROY, Coord., *P.O. Box 66, Hessmer, Alexandria, 71341.* Tel: 318-563-4550.

Schools—Sr. MARICE ELVEKROG, S.S.N.D., Supt., *4400 Coliseum Blvd., P.O. Box 7417, Alexandria, 71306-0417.* Tel: 318-445-2401.

Scouting—Rev. CHARLES MORGAN, Area 5 Chap., *1712 West St., Winnsboro, 71295.* Tel: 318-435-5658. Rev. DANIEL P. O'CONNOR, Diocesan and Attakapas Council Chap., *1315 Eggbend Rd., Marksville, 71351-4223.* Tel: 318-253-9936.

Seminarians—Rev. EDWIN RODRIGUEZ-HERNANDEZ, Dir., *P.O. Box 7417, Alexandria, 71306-0417.* Tel: 318-445-7120.

Social Ministry—Sr. JOHN MARTIN EBROM, C.D.P., Admin., *4400 Coliseum Blvd., P.O. Box 7417, Alexandria, 71306-0417.* Tel: 318-445-2401.

School Food Service—Mrs. DEBORAH M. PAYNE, C.N.P., Supvr., *4400 Coliseum Blvd., P.O. Box 7417, Alexandria, 71306-0417.* Tel: 318-445-2485.

The Beginning Experience—Rev. BRUCE MILLER, J.C.L., *4400 Coliseum Blvd., P.O. Box 7417, Alexandria, 71306-0417.* Tel: 318-445-2401.

Vocations Recruitment—Rev. EDWIN RODRIGUEZ-HERNANDEZ, Dir., *P.O. Box 7417, Alexandria, 71306-0417.* Tel: 318-445-7120.

Youth Ministry—Mr. WARREN DUNGEN, Dir., *4400 Coliseum Blvd., P.O. Box 7417, Alexandria, 71306-0417.* Tel: 318-445-2401.

CLERGY, PARISHES, MISSIONS AND PAROCHIAL SCHOOLS

CITY OF ALEXANDRIA (Rapides Parish)

1—ST. FRANCIS XAVIER CATHEDRAL (1834), Rev. Kenneth M. Mathews, Rector. In res., Rev. Pedro J. Sierra-Posada (Colombia).
Res., 626 Fourth St., 71301-8424. Tel: 318-445-1451; Fax: 318-445-1433.

2—OUR LADY OF PROMPT SUCCOR (1947), Revs. H. Gerald Bordelon; Michael Craig Scott. In res., Revs. Edwin Rodriguez-Hernandez; Thomas M. Jezak.
Res., 401 21st St., 71301-7022. Tel: 318-445-3693; Fax: 318-445-8471.
School—Tel: 318-487-1862; Fax: 318-473-9321.
Sisters of Divine Providence 3; Lay Teachers 26; Students 512.

3—ST. FRANCES XAVIER CABRINI (1947), Rev. Msgr. Ronald C. Hoppe, V.G.; Rev. Rusty P. Rabalais.
Office: 2211 E. Texas Ave., P.O. Box 5004, 71307-5004. Tel: 318-445-4588; Fax: 318-443-7156.
Res., 2012 Wedgewood Ave., 71301. Tel: 318-487-4413; Fax: 318-443-7156.
School—Tel: 318-448-3333; Fax: 318-448-3343.
Sisters of Charity of the Incarnate Word 2; Lay Teachers 21; Students 283.

4—ST. JAMES MEMORIAL (1911), Rev. Vincent Manuel, S.A.C. (India).
Mailing Address: 900 Daspit St., 71302-5343. Tel: 318-445-6700; Fax: 318-445-9826.
Church—714 Winn St., 71301. Tel: 318-487-9512.
Convent—Tel: 318-473-8601.
Handmaids of the Holy Child Jesus 2.

5—ST. JULIANA (1959), Rev. Vincent Manuel, S.A.C. (India).
Res., 900 Daspit St., 71302-5343. Tel: 318-445-6700; Fax: 318-445-9826.

6—ST. RITA (1940), Rev. Bruce Miller, J.C.L.
Res., 214 N. 17th St., P.O. Box 7056, 71306-0056. Tel: 318-445-7120; Fax: 318-448-0704.
School—Tel: 318-473-0538.
Sisters 4; Lay Teachers 15; Students 203.

OUTSIDE THE CITY OF ALEXANDRIA

Belledeau, Avoyelles Parish, St. Martin of Tours (1950), Rev. Timothy R. Marceau, O.S.B.
Res., 1981 Hwy. 114, Hessmer, 71341-4234. Tel: 318-563-4533; Fax: 318-563-4385. [CEM]

Bordelonville, Avoyelles Parish, St. Peter (1903), Rev. Jose' A. Robles-Sanchez (Puerto Rico).
Res., P.O. Box 31, 71320-0031. Tel: 318-997-2151. [CEM]

Boyce, Rapides Parish, St. Margaret (1936), Rev. Bernard L. Zagst, V.F.
Res., P.O. Box 367, 71409-0367. Tel: 318-793-8811; Fax: 318-793-8815.
Missions—Flatwoods, St. Cyril; Gorum, St. Margaret Mary.

Brouillette, Avoyelles Parish, St. Genevieve (1953), Rev. Morson Ravi Livingston, S.A.C. (India).
Res., 4052 Hwy. 452, Marksville, 71351-3530. Tel: 318-253-9237. [CEM]

Bunkie, Avoyelles Parish, St. Anthony of Padua (1904), Rev. Msgr. Steve J. Testa, V.F.
Res., 409 St. John St., P.O. Box 719, 71322-0719. Tel: 318-346-7274; Fax: 318-346-7275. [CEM]
School—Tel: 318-346-2739; Fax: 318-346-9191.
Daughters of Divine Providence 1; Lay Teachers 12; Students 246.

Campti, Natchitoches Parish, Nativity of The Blessed Virgin Mary (1831), Rev. Jacob Thomas (India); Deacons John Foster; Robert Daspit.
Res., 119 Tally St., P.O. Box 439, 71411-0439. Tel: 318-476-2116. [CEM 3]
Missions—Trichel, St. Joseph; Black Lake, Our Lady of the Holy Rosary.

Cheneyville, Rapides Parish, St. Joseph (1966), Rev. Msgr. Julius G. Walle.
Res., P.O. Box 446, 71325-0446. Tel: 318-279-2394; Fax: 318-279-2394. [CEM]

Cloutierville, Natchitoches Parish, St. John the Baptist (1816), Rev. Daniel Corkery (Ireland).
Res., P.O. Box 40, 71416-0040. Tel: 318-379-2231. [CEM]
Missions—Emmanuel, Holy Rosary; Monet Ferry, Holy Family.

Colfax, Grant Parish, St. Joseph (1897), Rev. James A. Foster.
Res., 801 Third St., P.O. Box 243, 71417-0243. Tel: 318-627-5442.
Mission—Montgomery, St. Patrick, P.O. Box 243, 71417.

Cottonport, Avoyelles Parish, St. Mary Assumption (1889), Rev. D. Mathew Woollett.
Res., P.O. Box 1123, 71327-1123. Tel: 318-876-3681. [CEM 3]
School—Tel: 318-876-3651.
Sisters 1; Lay Teachers 9; Students 212.

Deville, Rapides Parish, St. John the Baptist (1942), Rev. Joseph F. Pellettieri, C.SS.R.
Res., P.O. Box 7, 71328-0007. Tel: 318-466-5587; Fax: 318-466-5265. [CEM 2]
Missions—Kolin, Sts. Francis and Anne; Effie, St. Winifred.

Dupont, Avoyelles Parish, Immaculate Conception (1945), Rev. Abraham Kallarackal, C.M.I. (India); Deacon Norman Gremillion.
Res., P.O. Box 385, 71329-0385. Tel: 318-922-3243. [CEM]

Echo, Rapides Parish, St. Francis de Sales (1894), Rev. Raphael Karekatt, M.S.F.S. (India).
Res., P.O. Box 37, 71330-0037. Tel: 318-563-4530. [CEM]

Evergreen, Avoyelles Parish, Little Flower (1928), Rev. Harvey J. Fortier.
Res., P.O. Box 20, 71333-0020. Tel: 318-346-2840. [CEM 2]
Mission—Goudeau, St. Charles.

Ferriday, Concordia Parish, St. Patrick (1952), Revs. Paul Kunnumpuram, M.S.F.S. (India); Anthony Dharmaraj, M.S.F.S. (India).
Res., P.O. Box 369, 71334. Tel: 318-757-3834. [JC]
Mission—Jonesville, St. Gerard, P.O. Box 863, Jonesville, 71343. Tel: 318-339-6143.

Fifth Ward, Avoyelles Parish, Our Lady of Lourdes (1948), Rev. Daniel P. O'Connor.
Res., 1315 Eggbend Rd., 71351-4223. Tel: 318-253-9936. [CEM 4]
Mission—Moncla, St. John the Baptist.

Glenmora, Rapides Parish, St. Louis (1941), Rev. Msgr. Ronald C. Hoppe, V.G.; Revs. Thomas M. Jezak; Pedro J. Sierra-Posada (Colombia). In res., Sr. Marie T. Brogan, S.S.N.D., Parish Life Coord.
Res., 826 8th St., P.O. Box 636, 71433-0636. Tel: 318-748-8324; Fax: 318-748-8324. [CEM]
Missions—Elmer, St. Peter; Sieper, St. Jude.

Hessmer, Avoyelles Parish, St. Alphonsus (1898), Rev. James Roy.
Res., P.O. Box 66, 71341-0066. Tel: 318-563-4550. [CEM]

Isle Brevelle, Natchitoches Parish, St. Augustine's (1856), Rev. Victor P. Vead.
Res., 2262 Hwy. 484, Natchez, 71456-3622. Tel: 318-379-2521. [CEM]
Convent—Tel: 318-379-2325.
Sisters of Divine Providence 2.
Missions—Bermuda, St. Charles; Old River, St. Anne.

Jena, LaSalle Parish, St. Mary (1949), Rev. John H. Cunningham.
Mailing Address: Second St., P.O. Box 669, Pollock, 71467-0669. Tel: 318-765-3798.
Mission—Fishville, St. Edward, 71467.

Kleinwood, Avoyelles Parish, St. Michael (1964), Rev. Jose' A. Robles-Sanchez (Puerto Rico).

Res., P.O. Box 31, Bordelonville, 71320. Tel: 318-997-2151. [CEM]

Lecompte, Rapides Parish, St. Martin (1860), Rev. David J. Braquet.
Res., P.O. Box 459, 71346-0459. Tel: 318-776-9480; Fax: 318-776-9485. [CEM]
Mission—Woodworth, Mary, Mother of Jesus.

Leesville, Vernon Parish, St. Michael (1946), Rev. Angelo Messina.
Res., 604 S. Fifth St., P.O. Box 240, 71496-0240. Tel: 318-239-2656.

Mansura, Avoyelles Parish, Our Lady of Prompt Succor (1937), Rev. James Moran, C.O.
Res., Escude St., P.O. Box 67, 71350-0067. Tel: 318-964-2654.
St. Paul the Apostle (1796), Rev. Russell J. Lemoine.
Res., P.O. Box 130, 71350-0130. Tel: 318-964-2921. [CEM]

Marksville, Avoyelles Parish, Holy Ghost (1919), Rev. Kenneth J. Michiels.
Res., 121 S. Preston St., 71351-3034. Tel: 318-253-7131. [CEM 2]
Mission—Hickory Hill, St. Richard.
St. Joseph's (1869), Revs. James A. Ferguson, J.C.L.; Paul M. LaPalme.
Res., 141 S. Washington, 71351-3025. Tel: 318-253-5610; 253-7561 (Office); Fax: 318-253-8871. [CEM 2]

Moreauville, Avoyelles Parish, Our Lady of Sorrows (1944), Revs. Joseph E. Montalbano; Albert Nambiaparambil (India).
Res., P.O. Box 247, 71355-0247. Tel: 318-985-2968. [CEM]
Sacred Heart (1860), Rev. Joseph E. Montalbano.
Res., 9986 Bayou Des Glaise St., 71355-9702. Tel: 318-985-2774. [CEM]
School—Tel: 318-985-2772; Fax: 318-985-2164.
Sisters of Our Lady of Sorrows 3; Lay Teachers 14; Students 270.

Natchitoches, Natchitoches Parish, Holy Cross (1968), Rev. Sheldon L. Roy.
Res., 129 Second St., P.O. Box 211, Nachitoches, 71458-0211. Tel: 318-352-2615; Fax: 318-352-8989.
Mission—Spanish Lake, St. Anne. [CEM]
Immaculate Conception (1728), Revs. Kenneth J. Roy, V.F.; Patrick X. Braquet.
Res., 145 Church St., P.O. Box 13, Nachitoches, 71458-0013. Tel: 318-352-3422. [CEM]
School—St. Mary, (Grades PreK-8) 1101 E. Fifth St., P.O. Box 2070, 71458-0013. Tel: 318-352-8394; Fax: 318-352-5798.
Lay Teachers 13; Students 256.
High School—Lay Teachers 18; Students 200.
St. Anthony (1935), Rev. Norbert Rosso, C.S.Sp.
Res., 911 Fifth St., P.O. Box 432, Nachitoches, 71458-0432. Tel: 318-352-2559. [JC]

Pineville, Rapides Parish, Sacred Heart (1933), Rev. Terry E. Allen.
Res., 600 Lakeview, P.O. Drawer 3009, 71361-3009. Tel: 318-445-2496; Fax: 318-443-0808.

Plaucheville, Avoyelles Parish, Mater Dolorosa (1879), Revs. Stephen Scott Chemino; John W. Andries.
Res., P.O. Box 9, 71362-0009. Tel: 318-922-3131. [CEM]
School—Tel: 318-922-3401.
Brothers of the Holy Eucharist 2; Marianites of the Holy Cross 2; Lay Teachers 11; Students 365.
High School—Sisters 1; Brothers 1; Lay Teachers 6; Students 103.

Powhatan, Natchitoches Parish, St. Francis (1952), Revs. Kenneth J. Roy, V.F.; Patrick X. Braquet.
Mailing Address: P.O. Box 13, Natchitoches, 71458-0013. Tel: 318-352-3422. [JC]

St. Joseph, Tensas Parish, St. Joseph (1940), Rev. Antony Aelavanthara (India).
Res., P.O. Box 198, 71366-0198. Tel: 318-766-3565. [CEM]
Mission—Waterproof, St. Francis of Assisi, P.O. Box 198, 71366.

Simmesport, Avoyelles Parish, Christ the King (1935), Rev. George Krosfield (India).
Res., P.O. Box 186, 71369-0186. Tel: 318-941-2381. [CEM]

Tallulah, Madison Parish, St. Edward (1936), Rev. Msgr. Patrick J. Murphy (Ireland).
Res., Hwy. 80 E., P.O. Box 1308, 71282-1308. Tel: 318-574-1677.

Tioga, Rapides Parish, Immaculate Heart of Mary (1971), Rev. Gerard M. Foley, V.F.
Res., P.O. Box 687, 71477-0687. Tel: 318-640-5314; 640-9446 (Office).

Vidalia, Concordia Parish, Our Lady of Lourdes (1887), Revs. Paul Kunnumpuram, M.S.F.S. (India); Anthony Dharmaraj, M.S.F.S. (India).
Res., 503 Texas St., P.O. Box 460, 71373. Tel: 318-336-5450. [JC]

Winnfield, Winn Parish, Our Lady of Lourdes (1988), Rev. Peter J. Grant (South Africa).
Res., 772 Country Club Rd., 71483. Tel: 318-628-2561.
Mission—Olla, St. William.

Winnsboro, Franklin Parish, St. Mary (1945), Rev. Charles J. Morgan.
Res., 1712 West St., 71295-3240. Tel: 318-435-5658.
Mission—Columbia, St. John, 1712 West St., 71295.

Chaplains of Public Institutions

PINEVILLE. *Central Louisiana State Hospital*, W. Shamrock Ave., P.O. Box 5031, 71361. Tel: 318-484-6357; 484-6352. Revs. Stephen J. Brandow; Timothy Marceaux, O.S.B.

Special Assignment:
Reverend Monsignors—
Susi, Joseph M., Chancellor

On Duty Outside the Diocese:
Reverend Monsignors—
Bordelon, Roland, USCC Relief Services, New York, NY
Reverend Fathers—
Hasieber, Joseph S., Sacred Heart, Lancaster, PA
Matthews, Ron, Christ the King Church, Bossier City, LA
Viviano, Nino, St. Michael Church, Clearwater, FL

Military Chaplains:
Reverend Fathers—
Fey, Thomas J., U.S.A.F.

Absent on Leave:
Reverend Fathers—
Deevy, Edward

Retired:
Reverend Monsignors—
Anderson, Marcel
Beckers, Henry F.
Early, Thomas C.
Lyons, Frederick J.
Susi, Joseph M.
Timmermans, John
Wakeman, John J.
Walle, Julius G.
Reverend Fathers—
Cloutier, Wilbur G.
Cumella, Anthony N.
Deasy, Edward
Engelen, R. J.
Gagnard, Louis
Glasnovic, Serafin
Horacek, Mark
Polizzi, Samuel J.
Robitaille, Yves
Ryan, John
Thompson, August L.
Van-Hoorn, Leo
Villaverde, Antonio E.
Voorhies, Louis

Permanent Deacons:
Daigrepont, William, Avoyelles Prison Ministry
Daspit, Robert A., Jr., St. Joseph, Trichel
Foster, John, Our Lady of the Rosary, Black Lake
Giaco, Vincent, Chap., Rapides Regional Medical Center
Gremillion, Norman, Immaculate Conception, Dupont
Jones, Charles A., (Retired)
Peltier, Joseph, (Retired)

INSTITUTIONS LOCATED IN THE DIOCESE

[A] HIGH SCHOOLS, DIOCESAN

ALEXANDRIA. *Holy Savior Menard Central*, 4603 Coliseum Blvd., 71303. Tel: 318-445-8233; Fax: 318-448-8170. Junior & High School. Mr. Ronald Lemoine, Prin. Sisters 1; Lay Teachers 27; Students 388.

[B] ELEMENTARY SCHOOLS, INTERPAROCHIAL

MARKSVILLE. *Marksville Catholic School*, 320 E. Mark St., 71351. Tel: 318-253-6932; 253-7440; Fax: 318-253-7132.
Brig. Gen. Sheridan G. Cadoria, Prin. Sisters of the Holy Family 2; Lay Teachers 11; Students 146.

[C] GENERAL HOSPITALS

ALEXANDRIA. *St. Frances Cabrini Hospital*, 3330 Masonic Dr., 71301. Tel: 318-487-1122
For a complete listing, refer to the Hospitals section.

[D] PROTECTIVE INSTITUTIONS

ALEXANDRIA. *St. Mary's Residential Training School, Inc.*, P.O. Box Drawer 7768, 71306. Tel: 318-445-6443; Fax: 318-449-8520
For a complete listing, refer to the Special Care Facilities section.

FOREST HILL. *Our Lady of Guadalupe Mission*, 10 Butter Cemetery Rd., 71430
For a complete listing, refer to the Special Care Facilities section.

[E] HOMES FOR AGED

ALEXANDRIA. *Our Lady's Manor, Inc.*, 402 Monroe St., 71301. Tel: 318-473-2560
For a complete listing, refer to the Special Care Facilities section.

MOREAUVILLE. *St. John's Village*, 116 Beridon St., 71355-3004. Tel: 318-985-2948
For a complete listing, refer to the Special Care Facilities section.

[F] RESIDENCES OF PRIESTS AND BROTHERS

NATCHITOCHES. *Holy Ghost Fathers Home, Maison Brothier*, 911 Second St., 71457. Tel: 318-357-7940. Revs. John A. Burns, C.S.Sp.; Anthony F. Frommholz, C.S.Sp.; Henry J. Planinsek, C.S.Sp.

PLAUCHEVILLE. *Brothers of the Holy Eucharist*, P.O. Box 25, 71362. Tel: 318-922-3630. Bro. Andre M. Lucia, F.S.E., Supr. Brothers 3.

[G] CONVENTS AND RESIDENCES FOR SISTERS

ALEXANDRIA. *Congregation of the Marianites of Holy Cross*, St. Rita Convent, 1717 Ashley St., 71301. Tel: 318-448-8001. Sisters 4.
Congregation of the Sisters of Charity of the Incarnate Word, St. Francis Cabrini Hospital Convent, 3330 Masonic Dr., 71301. Tel: 318-443-5520; 487-1122. Sisters 11.
Disciples of the Lord Jesus Christ, 4609 Coliseum Blvd., 71303. Sisters 3.
Sisters of Divine Providence of San Antonio, Texas, Our Lady of Prompt Succor Convent, 580 Chester St., 71301-6516. Tel: 318-442-3315. Sisters 8.
Sisters of Our Lady of Sorrows, St. Mary's Convent, P.O. Box 7768, 71306. Tel: 318-445-6461. Sisters 8.
The Sisters of the Handmaids of the Holy Child Jesus (of Nigeria, Africa), 332 Avoyelles Drive, 71302. Tel: 318-473-8601.
E-mail: sisters7@juno.com
Sisters 2.

BUNKIE. *Daughters of Divine Providence*, St. Anthony Convent, 114 Knoll St., 71322. Tel: 318-346-4481. Sisters 2.

COTTONPORT. *Congregation of the Marianites of Holy Cross*, Holy Cross Convent, P.O. Box 1062, 71327-1062. Tel: 318-876-3794. Sisters 3.

GLENMORA. *School Sisters of Notre Dame*, Miryam House, P.O. Box 636, 71433. Tel: 318-748-8324. Sisters 2.

MARKSVILLE. *Congregation of the Sisters of the Holy Family*, Holy Ghost Convent, 304 E. Mark St., 71351. Tel: 318-253-7440. Sisters 3.

MOREAUVILLE. *Sisters of Our Lady of Sorrows*, Sacred Heart Convent, P.O. Box 179, 71355. Tel: 318-985-2772. Sisters 5.

[H] RETREAT HOUSES

PINEVILLE. *Maryhill Renewal Center*, 600 Maryhill Rd., 71360. Tel: 318-640-1378; Fax: 318-640-8604.
E-mail: info@diocesealex.org
Web site: diocesealex.org
Sr. Ruthann Williams, O.P., Exec. Dir.; Sr. Linda Anne Ranard, A.S.C., Asst. Dir.

[I] CATHOLIC COMMUNITY SERVICES

ALEXANDRIA. *Catholic Community Services*, 4400 Coliseum Blvd., P.O. Box 7417, 71306. Tel: 318-445-2401. Sr. John Martin Ebrom, C.D.P., Dir.

[J] NEWMAN CENTERS

ALEXANDRIA. *Louisiana State University at Alexandria*, Catholic Student Center, 8100 Hwy. 71-S, 71302-9633. Tel: 318-473-6494. Rev. Edwin Rodriguez-Hernandez, Dir.

NATCHITOCHES. *Northwestern State University*, Catholic Student Center, 129 Second St., P.O. Box 211, 71458. Tel: 318-352-2615. Rev. Sheldon L. Roy, Chap.

RELIGIOUS INSTITUTES OF MEN REPRESENTED IN THE DIOCESE

For further details refer to the corresponding bracketed number in the Religious Institutes of Men or Women section.

[0200]—*Benedictine Monks.* (Lisle, IL).—O.S.B.
[0620]—*Brothers of the Holy Eucharist.*—F.S.E.
[0275]—*Carmelites of Mary Immaculate.*—C.M.I.
[0650]—*Holy Ghost Fathers.* (Western Prov.).—C.S.Sp.
[]—*Missionaries of St. Francis de Sales (of India).*—M.S.F.S.
[0860]—*Missionhurst Congregation of the Immaculate Heart of Mary.*—C.I.C.M.
[0950]—*Oratorians.*—C.O.
[1070]—*Redemptorist Fathers.*—C.Ss.R.
[0990]—*Society of the Catholic Apostolate.*—S.A.C.

RELIGIOUS INSTITUTES OF WOMEN REPRESENTED IN THE DIOCESE

[0100]—*Adorers of the Blood of Christ.*—A.S.C.
[]—*Congregation of the Franciscan Religious of Our Lady of Refuge.* (Guadalajara, Mexico).—R.F.R.
[2410]—*Congregation of the Marianites of Holy Cross.* (Louisiana Prov.).—M.S.C.
[0470]—*Congregation of the Sisters of Charity of the Incarnate Word.*—C.C.V.I.
[1950]—*Congregation of the Sisters of the Holy Family.*—S.S.F.
[0800]—*Daughters of Divine Providence.*—F.D.P.
[0965]—*Disciples of the Lord Jesus Christ.*—D.L.J.C.
[1070-05]—*Dominican Sisters.*—O.P.
[]—*Handmaids of the Holy Child Jesus (of Nigeria, Africa).*—H.H.C.J.
[2970]—*School Sisters of Notre Dame.*—S.S.N.D.
[1010]—*Sisters of Divine Providence of San Antonio, Texas.*—C.D.P.
[3120]—*Sisters of Our Lady of Sorrows.*—O.L.S.
[4070]—*Society of the Sacred Heart.*—R.S.C.J.

DIOCESAN CEMETERIES

PINEVILLE. *Maryhill Cemetery for Clergy.*

NECROLOGY

† Provosty, William B., Cottonport, LA, St. Mary's Assumption. —Died April 3, 1997.
† Smith, Paul B., Chicago, IL, Holy Angels. —Died Nov. 23, 1996.

Diocese of Allentown

(Dioecesis Alanopolitana)

Most Reverend

EDWARD P. CULLEN, D.D., V.G.

Bishop of Allentown; ordained May 19, 1962; appointed Auxiliary Bishop of Philadelphia and Titular Bishop of Paria in Preconsilare February 8, 1994; consecrated April 14, 1994; appointed Bishop of Allentown December 16, 1997; installed Third Bishop of Allentown February 9, 1998. *Mailing Address: Chancery Office, 202 N. 17th St., P.O. Box F, Allentown, PA, 18105.*

Most Reverend

THOMAS J. WELSH, D.D., J.C.D.

Retired Bishop of Allentown; ordained May 30, 1946; appointed Titular Bishop of Scattery Island and Auxiliary Bishop of Philadelphia on February 18, 1970; consecrated April 2, 1970; appointed as First Bishop of Arlington on June 4, 1974; installed on August 13, 1974; appointed Bishop of Allentown February 8, 1983; installed Second Bishop of Allentown on March 21, 1983; resigned December 16, 1997. *Mailing Address: 1325 Prospect Ave., Bethlehem, PA, 18018.*

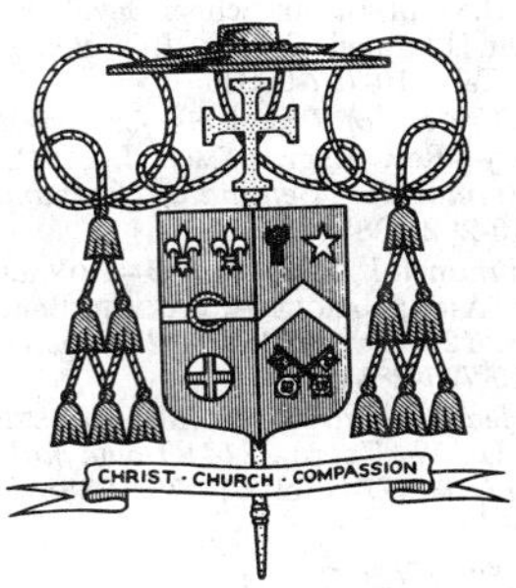

Chancery Office: 202 N. 17th St., P.O. Box F, Allentown, PA, 18105. Tel.: 610-437-0755; Fax: 610-433-7822.

ESTABLISHED JANUARY 28, 1961.

Square Miles 2,773.

Comprises the Counties of Berks, Carbon, Lehigh, Northampton and Schuylkill in the State of Pennsylvania.

STATISTICAL OVERVIEW

Personnel	
Bishop	1
Priests: Diocesan Active in Diocese	207
Priests: Active Outside Diocese	9
Priests: Diocesan in Foreign Missions	1
Priests: Retired, Sick or Absent	30
Number of Diocesan Priests	247
Religious Priests in Diocese	75
Extern Priests in Diocese	3
Ordinations:	
Diocesan Priests	3
Transitional Deacons	3
Permanent Deacons in Diocese	84
Total Brothers	11
Total Sisters	690
Parishes	
Parishes	153
With Resident Pastor:	
Resident Diocesan Priests	127
Resident Religious Priests	5
Without Resident Pastor:	
Administered by Priests	21
Missions	12
Welfare	
Catholic Hospitals	3
Total Assisted	672,650
Health Care Centers	1
Total Assisted	1,641
Homes for the Aged	11
Total Assisted	677
Day Care and Extended Day Care Centers	50
Total Assisted	1,988
Specialized Homes	3
Total Assisted	844
Special Centers for Social Services	14
Total Assisted	71,535
Residential Care of Disabled	2
Total Assisted	38
Educational	
Diocesan Students in Other Seminaries	28
Total Seminarians	28
Colleges and Universities	2
Total Students	3,508
High Schools, Diocesan and Parish	9
Total Students	4,140
Elementary Schools, Diocesan and Parish	55
Total Students	14,410
Non-residential Schools for the Disabled	3
Total Students	126
Catechesis/Religious Education:	
High School Students	1,732
Elementary Students	16,546
Total Students Under Catholic Instruction	40,490
Teachers in the Diocese:	
Priests	23
Sisters	98
Lay Teachers	905
Vital Statistics	
Receptions into the Church:	
Infant Baptism Totals	3,980
Adult Baptism Totals	181
Received into Full Communion	415
Confirmations	3,445
Marriages:	
Catholic	920
Interfaith	609
Total Marriages	1,529
Deaths	3,195
Total Catholic Population	259,729
Total Population	1,084,189

Former Bishops—Most Rev. JOSEPH MCSHEA, appt. Titular Bishop of Mina and Auxiliary Bishop of Philadelphia Feb. 9, 1952; cons. March 19, 1952; appt. Bishop of Allentown Feb. 15, 1961; installed April 11, 1961; retired Feb. 8, 1983; died Nov. 28, 1991.—Most Rev. THOMAS J. WELSH, D.D., J.C.D., appt. Titular Bishop of Scattery Island and Auxiliary Bishop of Philadelphia, Feb. 18, 1970; cons. April 2, 1970; appt. First Bishop of Arlington, June 4, 1974; installed Aug. 13, 1974; appt. Bishop of Allentown, Feb. 8, 1983; installed Second Bishop of Allentown, March 21, 1983; resigned Dec. 16, 1997.

Moderator of the Curia—Rev. Msgr. ANTHONY D. MUNTONE, P.A., V.G., S.T.L.

Vicar General—Rev. Msgr. ANTHONY D. MUNTONE, P.A., V.G., S.T.L.

Chancellor—Rev. Msgr. JOSEPH M. WHALEN, S.T.L.

Vice Chancellor—Rev. ALFRED A. SCHLERT, J.C.L.

Office of Vicar General and Chancery Office—202 N. 17th St., P.O. Box F, Allentown, 18105. Tel: 610-437-0755; Fax: 610-433-7822.

Canonical Consultant—Rev. Msgr. DAVID J. MORRISON, J.C.D., M.A., Diocesan Tribunal, *219 N. 18th St., Allentown, 18104.* Tel: 610-434-3200.

Secretary to the Bishop—Rev. ALFRED A. SCHLERT, J.C.L., *Bishop's Office, 202 N. 17th St., P.O. Box F, Allentown, 18105.* Tel: 610-437-0755.

Director of Information—Deacon JOHN W. MURPHY, JR., *Office of Information, 2141 Downyflake Ln., Allentown, 18103-4724.* Tel: 610-797-3845; Fax: 610-797-3941.

Assistant to the Diocesan Director for Radio and Television—BRIAN MULVIHILL, *"The A.D. Times", 2141 Downyflake Ln., Allentown, 18103-4724.* Tel: 610-797-3330.

Diocesan Financial Secretary—Rev. Msgr. JOHN J. MARTIN; RONALD J. JACOBS, M.B.A., Admin. Asst.; Rev. Msgr. WILLIAM F. BAVER, Th.M., Admin. Asst., *Diocesan Office, 1729 Turner St., P.O. Box F, Allentown, 18105.* Tel: 610-435-9527.

Vicar for Religious—Rev. Msgr. THOMAS E. HOBAN, *415 S. Sixth St., Emmaus, 18094.*

Diocesan Tribunal—219 N. 18th St., Allentown, 18104. Tel: 610-434-3200.

Judicial Vicar—Rev. Msgr. RONALD W. GAINER, M.Div., J.C.L.

Judges—Rev. Msgr. DAVID J. MORRISON, J.C.D.; Revs. JAMES J. WARD, M.Div.; JOHN PAUL, M.S.C., S.T.L., J.C.D.

Promoter of Justice—Rev. DAVID J. KOZAK, J.C.L.

Defenders of the Bond—Revs. DAVID J. KOZAK, J.C.L.; MICHAEL S. LAWRENCE, M.Div.; ALFRED A. SCHLERT, J.C.L.

Secretary—Deacon EUGENE J. WYRWA.

Advocates—Revs. JAMES J. BURDESS; EDWARD R. DOMIN, M.A.; VICTOR F. FINELLI, Th.M.; DAVID C. LIEBNER, M.Div.; FRANCIS P. STRAKA; ROBERT G. COFENAS, Ed.D.; DAVID J. LOEPER, M.A.; EDWARD J. O'CONNOR, M.Th., M.S.W.; EDWARD S. ZEMANIK, M.Div., B.A.; Rev. Msgr. STANLEY T. SOSNOWSKI, M.Div.; Deacon JOHN D. CUMMINGS.

Notaries—JUDY CHUSS; PATRICIA ECHTERNACH; DIANE SELDOMRIDGE; COLETTE SNYDER.

Diocesan Offices and Directors

Allentown Catholic Communications, Inc.—Most Rev. THOMAS J. WELSH, D.D., J.C.D., Pres.; Rev. Msgr.

JOHN J. MARTIN, Treas., *202 N. 17th St., P.O. Box F, Allentown, 18105.* Tel: 610-437-0755.

Apostolate for the Spanish Speaking—Rev. Msgr. ROBERT J. BISZEK, Diocesan Dir., *Holy Infancy Rectory, 312 E. Fourth St., Bethlehem, 18015.* Tel: 610-866-1121. Regional Directors: Berks Co.: Rev. CHARLES A. MARCIANO; Deacons LEOPOLDO ALVARADO; JESUS CENTENO; FRANCISCO COLON; JULIO COLON; FERNANDO TORRES; MARIANO TORRES, Lehigh Co.: Rev. Msgr. JOSEPH R. SOBIESIAK; Deacons JAIME DEJESUS; ROBERTO DEJESUS; JOSE GONZALEZ; VICTOR QUILES; ALFONSO D. SOLIS, Northampton Co.: Rev. Msgr. ROBERT J. BISZEK; Deacons RAFAEL CUEVAS; EDISON MORALES; NICASIO RODRIGUEZ; RODOBERTO MATOS.

Bishop's Annual Appeal—Rev. Msgr. EDWARD R. SACKS, M.Ed., Vicar Devel., *P.O. Box F, Allentown, 18105.* Tel: 610-797-6657.

Books, Censor of—Rev. Msgr. JAMES J. MULLIGAN, S.T.L., *300 Cherryville Rd., Northampton, 18067.* Tel: 610-262-1885.

Building Committee—Rev. Msgr. RICHARD J. LOEPER, M.A., Chm., *417 Carlton Ave., Bethlehem, 18015.* Tel: 610-867-9382.

Campus Ministry—Rev. LARRY J. HESS, M.A., Dir., *Newman Association for Kutztown University, 15207 Kutztown Rd., Kutztown, 19530.* Tel: 610-683-8380.

Catechumenate Office—CAROLE CHUK, Dir., *P.O. Box 20607, 2145 Madison Ave., Lehigh Valley, 18002-0607.* Tel: 610-866-4919.

Catholic Charities—Rev. Msgr. JOSEPH E. KURTZ, Dir., *2141 Downyflake Ln., Allentown, 18103-4774.* Tel: 610-791-3888.

Catholic Charities, Appeal Office—Rev. Msgr. EDWARD R. SACKS, M.Ed., Diocesan Dir., *P.O. Box F, Allentown, 18105.* Tel: 610-797-6657.

Catholic Housing Corporations—Rev. Msgr. DENNIS A. RIGNEY, Pres. & Chief Exec.; RONALD G. DELORENZO, Dir. of Housing, *1200 Spring St., Bethlehem, 18018.* Tel: 610-865-5595; Fax: 610-865-5866.

Catholic Social Agency-Family Life Bureau—Rev. Msgr. JOHN B. MCCANN, S.T.L., Dir.; Deacon BERNARD M. WISSER, *2141 Downyflake Ln., Allentown, 18103-4774.* Tel: 610-791-3888.

Catholic Youth Organization—(See Youth Ministry).

Cemeteries Office—Rev. Msgr. WILLIAM F. BAVER, Dir., *1729 Turner St., P.O. Box F, Allentown, 18105.* Tel: 610-435-9527.

Christian Doctrine, Confraternity of—BARBARA A. PENGITORE, Dir.; RITANNE PURSEL, Asst. Dir., *Dewberry & Madison Aves., P.O. Box 20607, Lehigh Valley, 18002-0607.* Regional Directors: Lehigh Co.: Rev. JAMES J. BURDESS; Carbon Co.: Rev. STEPHEN J. HALABURA; Northampton Co.: Rev. STEPHEN J. RADOCHA; North Schuylkill Co.: Rev. ROBERT J. KUZMANN.

Council of Priests/Diocesan Consultors—202 N. 17th St., P.O. Box F, Allentown, 18105. Tel: 610-437-0755.

Consultors—Rev. Msgr. ANTHONY D. MUNTONE, P.A., V.G., S.T.L.; Rev. Msgr. JOSEPH M. WHALEN; Rev. Msgr. RICHARD J. LOEPER, M.A.; Rev. Msgr. FRANCIS X. BARRETT; Rev. Msgr. WILLIAM E. HANDGES; Rev. Msgr. JOHN P. MURPHY; Rev. Msgr. JOHN J. MARTIN; Rev. Msgr. ALFRED R. OTT; Rev. Msgr. FRANCIS J. ZAVODNY; Rev. Msgr. GERALD E. GOBITAS; Rev. LADISLAUS J. DUDEK.

Ex Officio Members—Rev. Msgr. EDWARD R. SACKS, V.F.; Rev. Msgr. JAMES A. TRESTON, V.F.; Rev. Msgr. ALFRED R. OTT, V.F.; Rev. Msgr. WILLIAM E. JONES, V.F.; Rev. Msgr. JOHN G. CHIZMAR, V.F.; Rev. Msgr. DENNIS A. RIGNEY; Rev. Msgr. THOMAS E. HOBAN; Rev. Msgr. JOSEPH E. KURTZ; Rev. Msgr. WALTER T. SCHEAFFER; Rev. Msgr. JOHN B. MCCANN; Rev. Msgr. ROBERT J. BISZEK; Rev. LARRY J. HESS.

Elected Members—Rev. Msgr. ROBERT M. FORST; Rev. Msgr. JOHN A. AUCHTER; Revs. RICHARD H. CLEMENT; JOHN M. GIBBONS; ROBERT J. KUZMANN; RONALD C. BOCIAN; FRANCIS J. FOX; ALEXANDER T. POCETTO, O.S.F.S.; JAMES G. PRIOR, C.M.

Appointed Members—Rev. Msgr. JOSEPH P.T. SMITH; Rev. Msgr. WILLIAM E. HANDGES; Rev. Msgr. JOHN P. MURPHY.

Committee on Ecumenism—Rev. ROBERT C. QUINN, Chm., *St. Columbkill, 200 Indian Spring Rd., Boyertown, 19512-2008.* Tel: 610-367-2371. Revs. BERNARD O'CONNOR, O.S.F.S., Ph.D.; EDWIN J. SANDERS, S.J.

Department of Education—Rev. Msgr. WALTER T. SCHEAFFER, M.Ed., Vicar for Education; Dr. JAMES J. CUSIMANO, Esq., Supt.; Rev. JOHN S. MRAZ, M.A., Asst. Supt. Education; BARBARA A. PENGITORE, Dir. Religious Education; Asst. Dir. Religious Education; RITANNE PURSEL. Asst. Supts. Elementary Education: MARIANNE C. WHELAN; Sr. EILEEN DOROTHY MAGUIRE, I.H.M.; JOHN CLARK, Asst. Secondary Education; SUZANNE M. MELLO, Media Librarian; SUSAN DELAZARO, Marketing & Public Rels., *Dewberry & Madison Aves., P.O. Box 20607, Lehigh Valley, 18002-0607.* Tel: 610-866-0581.

Deposit and Loan Fund-Diocesan Review Board—Rev. Msgr. JOHN J. MARTIN, Chm.; Rev. Msgr. JOSEPH P. DOOLEY; Rev. Msgr. FELIX A. LOSITO; Rev. Msgr. FRANCIS J. ZAVODNY; Rev. MICHAEL J. STONE; BERNARDINE STANZ, *1729 Turner St., P.O. Box F, Allentown, 18105.* Tel: 610-435-9527.

Diocesan Board of Education—Voting Members: Mr. MICHAEL DEPAUL, Pres.; Mrs. ROSE YAVULLA, Vice Pres. PATRICIA AGGER; Dr. DWIGHT R. DAVIS; JOSEPH DOUGHERTY; KEVIN KANE; Rev. ROBERT J. MCCONAGHY, M.Th.; JOHN MORGANELLI, Esq.; Rev. BERNARD O'CONNOR, O.S.F.S.; Rev. Msgr. JOSEPH R. SOBIESIAK, Th.M.; Rev. MICHAEL J. STONE; Mrs. MARGARET M. SURDOVAL; Rev. VINCENT P. YORK. Non-voting Member: JAMES J. CUSIMANO, Esq. Non-voting Consultants: Sr. PATRICIA CULLEN, S.S.J.; Rev. Msgr. JOHN J. MARTIN, M.Div.; FRANCIS MCGOULDRICK; Rev. Msgr. ANTHONY D. MUNTONE, P.A., V.G., S.T.L.; RITA PURSEL; Rev. WILLIAM N. SEIFERT, M.Div.; Mrs. CAROL SONON. Executive Secretary: JAMES J. CUSIMANO, ESQ.

Diocesan Development Office—Rev. Msgr. EDWARD R. SACKS, M.Ed., Vicar Devel.; PAUL W. ZAMBO, Dir.; FRANK C. GODINO, Dir. School Devel.; ROBERT DESILVER, Dir. Planned Giving, *P.O. Box F, Allentown, 18105.* Tel: 610-797-9691.

Diocesan Director of Programs for Priestly Life and Ministry—Rev. Msgr. JAMES J. MULLIGAN, S.T.L., *Mary Immaculate Seminary, Northampton, 18067.* Tel: 610-262-1885.

Diocesan Financial Office Annex—RONALD J. JACOBS, Admin. Asst.; CAROLE A. SARMIR, Benefits Admin., *2222 S. 12th St., Suite D, Allentown, 18103-5648.* Tel: 610-797-2811.

Diocesan Health Affairs—Rev. Msgr. JOSEPH E. KURTZ, M.Div L.S.W., Coord., *2141 Downyflake Ln., Allentown, 18103-4774.* Tel: 610-791-3888; Fax: 610-791-1878.

Diocesan Newspaper—

"The A.D. Times"—The Allentown Diocese in the Year of Our Lord, Deacon JOHN W. MURPHY, JR., Editor; JILL M. CARAVAN, Mng. Editor; PAULINE PARKFINNEGAN, Production & Design Editor, *2141 Downyflake Ln., Allentown, 18103-4724.* Tel: 610-797-3330.

Diocesan Pastoral Planning Committee—Rev. Msgr. EDWARD R. SACKS, M.Ed., Chm., *3219 Santee Rd., Bethlehem, 18017.* Tel: 610-867-8409.

Diocesan Textbook Review Committee—Rev. JOHN S. MRAZ, Dept. Educ., *P.O. Box 20607, Lehigh Valley, 18002-0607.* Tel: 610-866-0581.

Directory—Deacon JOHN W. MURPHY, JR., Editor, *"The A.D. Times," 2141 Downyflake Ln., Allentown, 18103-4724.* Tel: 610-797-3845.

Family Life Bureau—(See Catholic Social Agency).

Finance Committee—Rev. Msgr. ANTHONY D. MUNTONE, P.A., V.G., S.T.L., Bishop's Delegate, *202 N. 17th St., P.O. Box F, Allentown, 18105.* Tel: 610-437-0755. Very Rev. DANIEL G. GAMBET, O.S.F.S.; CARL FEICHTEL; JOHN HORRIGAN, JR.; MARIANNE S. LAVELLE, Esq.; CARL S. FRENSKY; BERNARD F. MULLIGAN; Rev. Msgr. ALFRED R. OTT; THOMAS F. TRAUD, ESQ.; ALBERT BOVA.

Forward with Christ Allocation Committee—Rev. Msgr. WILLIAM E. HANDGES, Chm., *900 Washington St., Easton, 18042.* Tel: 610-253-7188. Rev. Msgr. RICHARD J. LOEPER, M.A.; Sr. FRANCIS BISLAND, C.P.S.; PAUL DOMALAKES, Esq.; FRANCIS HARTNETT; FRANK C. GODINO, M.P.A.

High School Budget Boards—Allentown Central Catholic High School: Rev. Msgr. JOSEPH R. SOBIESIAK; Rev. Msgr. JOHN P. MURPHY; Rev. Msgr. THOMAS E. HOBAN; Rev. Msgr. FRANCIS J. ZAVODNY. Bethlehem Catholic High School: Rev. Msgr. RICHARD J. LOEPER; Rev. Msgr. JOSEPH E. KURTZ; Rev. Msgr. RAYMOND F. MERMAN. Cardinal Brennan High School: Rev. ROBERT J. POTTS; Rev. Msgr. JAMES C. BECHTEL; EDWARD J. O'CONNOR; Rev. ANTHONY P. MONGIELLO. Holy Name High School: Rev. Msgr. JAMES A. TRESTON; Rev. DAVID C. GILLIS; Rev. Msgr. JAMES J. REICHERT, M.Div.; Rev. FRANCIS P. SCHOENAUER. Marian Catholic High School: Rev. JOSEPH L. GREMBOCKI; Rev. Msgr. JOHN G. CHIZMAR; Revs. THOMAS A. DERZACK; WILLIAM T. CAMPION. Nativity B.V.M. High School: Rev. Msgr. JOHN S. CAMPBELL; Rev. Msgr. WILLIAM E. JONES; Rev. MICHAEL J. STONE. Notre Dame High School: Rev. Msgr. WILLIAM E. HANDGES; Rev. THOMAS J. KING; Rev. Msgr. EDWARD R. SACKS, M.Ed.; Rev. Msgr. GERALD E. GOBITAS. Pius X High School: Rev. Msgr. JOSEPH P. DOOLEY; Rev. Msgr. CHARLES T. MOSS; Revs. JAMES G. PRIOR, C.M.; RICHARD A. SCHWARE, M.Div. Reading Central Catholic High School: Rev. Msgr. JOSEPH P.T. SMITH; Rev. Msgr. FRANCIS X. BARRETT; Rev. MICHAEL J. BRIGGMAN; Rev. Msgr. FELIX A. LOSITO.

Liturgical Commission—Rev. Msgr. EDWARD J. COYLE, Th.M., Chm., *Bishop's Office, 202 N. 17th St., P.O. Box F, Allentown, 18105.* Tel: 610-437-0755. Revs. FRANCIS J. BARANSKY, M.Div.; EDMUND J. BRENNAN, M.Div.; CAROLE C. CHUK; Rev. THOMAS A. DERZACK, M.Div.; ALETHA FASSI; RITA FERRONE; Rev. ERIC J. GRUBER, M.Div.; Sr. JANICE MARIE JOHNSON, R.S.M.; Revs. MARTIN F. KERN, M.Div.; EDWARD J. O'CONNOR; TERESA RODGERS; Deacon BERNARD J. SALABSKY; Rev. WILLIAM N. SEIFERT; Sr. REGINA STUPAK, I.H.M.

Millennium Preparation Committee—Rev. Msgr. ALFRED R. OTT, Chm., *1825 Turner St., Allentown, 18104.* Tel: 610-433-6461.

National Shrine of the Immaculate Conception—Rev. Msgr. JOHN G. CHIZMAR, Chm. Diocesan Pilgrimage Committee, *180 W. Broadway, Jim Thorpe, 18229.* Tel: 717-325-2791.

Nurses, Council of Catholic—Rev. Msgr. DENNIS A. RIGNEY, M.Div., A.C.S.W., N.H.A., Dir., *1200 Spring St., Bethlehem, 18018.* Tel: 610-865-5595. Regional Directors: Revs. JOSEPH A. ROCK, Lehigh Co. & Northampton Co.; WALTER J. HALL, South Schuylkill Co.; VINCENT I. CRONIN, Carbon Co.

Permanent Diaconate, Office of the—Rev. Msgr. JAMES J. MULLIGAN, S.T.L., Dir.; Deacon FRANCIS J. COSGROVE, Assoc. Dir., *P.O. Box 20607, Dewberry & Madison Aves., Lehigh Valley, 18002-0607.* Tel: 610-866-0581.

Project H.E.A.D.—Diocesan Golden Age Clubs, Rev. Msgr. DENNIS A. RIGNEY, M.Div., L.S.W., A.C.S.W., N.H.A., Dir., *1200 Spring St., Bethlehem, 18018.* Tel: 610-865-5595. Regional Directors: Rev. ROBERT J. REED, Lehigh Co.; Rev. FRANCIS P. SCHOENAUER, Berks Co.; Rev. Msgr. WILLIAM E. HANDGES, Northampton Co.; Rev. STEPHEN J. HALABURA, Carbon Co.; Rev. Msgr. ANTHONY F. WASSEL, Schuylkill Co.

Pro-Life Office—Rev. Msgr. STEPHEN T. FORISH, M.Div., Diocesan Dir.; Revs. GREGORY J. TAUBER, Asst. Dir.; RONALD P. BOWMAN, Asst. Dir.; JOHN J. GRABISH, Spanish Apostolate, *1135 Stefko Blvd., Bethlehem, 18017.* Tel: 610-691-0380; Fax: 610-691-0403.

Recruitment Committee for Encouraging Vocations to the Priesthood and Religious Life—Rev. WILLIAM F. GLOSSER, Chm., *900 W. Market St., Orwigsburg, 17961.* Tel: 717-366-1405.

Saint Francis Center—Deacon ALEX L. MAGGITTI, Dir., *900 W. Market St., Orwigsburg, 17961.* Tel: 717-366-1016.

Dept. of Youth Ministry and Youth and Adult Retreats—Tel: 717-366-1405.

Catholic Social Agency—Tel: 717-366-1403; 1404.

Holy Family Health Care—Tel: 717-366-0990.

Holy Family Residence—Tel: 717-366-2912.

St. Francis Adult Day Care Center—Tel: 717-366-2924.

Scouting—(See Youth Ministry).

Social Action Bureau—MARY ANN HAMMER, Exec. Dir., *2141 Downyflake Ln., Allentown, 18104-4774.* Tel: 610-791-3888. Advisory Board: JOHN B. SYLVESTER, Chm.; JAMES A. RITTER, Vice-Chm.; BARBARA PENGITORE, Sec.; ELBA APONTE; ROSE MARIE ARMON; DAVID BOWEN; ROBERT BROWN; LYDIA DASILVA; Sr. MIRIAM DENIS, S.S.J.; MARY BETH DOUGHERTY; Rev. ANTHONY M. DROUNCHECK; JANE GALLO; JOSEPHINE GARCIA; BRENNA GILBERT; JOSEPHINE HOZZA; DENNIS KEAN, M.D.; Rev. Msgr. FELIX A. LOSITO; TERRY QUAIN; Deacon DANIEL METZKER; Mrs. DANIEL METZKER; DONNA STESLOW MURACH, Esq.; Sr. ST. GREGORY, S.S.J.; Deacon LUIS R. VISOT, M.D.; Rev. GEORGE R. WINNE. Staff: MARY ANN HAMMER, Exec. Dir.; ROBIN DURSO, Sec./Bookkeeper; Rev. JOHN M. GIBBONS, M.Div.; MARYANN HARTZELL.

Social Services, Council of—Rev. Msgr. JOSEPH E. KURTZ, M.Div., A.C.S.W., Exec. Sec. & Moderator, *2141 Downyflake Ln., Allentown, 18104-4774.* Tel: 610-791-3888. Member Agencies: Catholic Social Agency; Department for the Aged; Diocesan Liaison for Ministry to the Elderly; Family Life Bureau; Holy Family Home Health Care; Holy Family Manor, Inc.; Pro-Life Office; Social Action Bureau; Spanish Apostolate.

Family Life Review Committee—Rev. JOHN S. MRAZ, Chm., *P.O. Box 20607, Lehigh Valley, 18002-0607.* Tel: 610-866-0581.

Vicars Forane—Rev. Msgr. JOHN G. CHIZMAR, V.F., Carbon Co.; Rev. Msgr. ALFRED R. OTT, V.F., Lehigh Co.; Rev. Msgr. JAMES A. TRESTON, V.F., Berks Co.; Rev. Msgr. EDWARD R. SACKS, V.F., Northampton Co.; Rev. Msgr. WILLIAM E. JONES, V.F., South Schuylkill Co.; Very Rev. WILLIAM CAMPION, V.F., North Schuylkill Co.

Vocations and Priestly Formation Committee—Rev. RONALD V. JANKAITIS, Chm., *St. Casimir Rectory, 441 S. Nichols St., St. Clair, 17970.* Tel: 717-429-2400. Revs. ERIC R. ARNOUT; ANDREW R. BAKER; Rev. Msgr. ROBERT J. BISZEK; Revs. DONALD W. CIENIEWICZ, M.Div.; Rev. Msgr. EDWARD J. COYLE; Rev. Msgr. JOHN P. MURPHY; Rev. ALFRED A. SCHLERT; Rev. Msgr. ROBERT J. WARGO.

Vocations Apostolate—Rev. Msgr. ROBERT J. WARGO, Dir.; Rev. ALFRED A. SCHLERT, Asst. Dir., *202 N. 17th St., P.O. Box F, Allentown, 18105.* Tel: 610-437-0755. Regional Directors: Lehigh Co.: Rev. ERIC A.

ARNOUT; Berks Co.: Rev. Msgr. EDWARD J. COYLE; Carbon Co.: Rev. THOMAS A. DERZACK; Northampton Co.: Rev. FRANCIS A. NAVE; North Schuylkill Co.: Rev. EDWARD J. ESSIG; South Schuylkill Co.: BERNARD A. FLANAGAN; For Hispanics: Rev. GEORGE R. WINNE.

Women Religious, Commission for—Sr. ANN MARIE COLL, O.S.F., Pres., *Sacred Heart Convent, 460 St. Bernadine St., Reading, 19607.* Tel: 610-777-6111.

Youth Ministry, Department of—Rev. WILLIAM F. GLOSSER, M.A., Dir.; LYNN PAPA, Retreat Coord.; MARY ELLEN JOHNS, Retreats & Young Adult Ministry; Rev. JOSEPH L. GREMBOCKI, Scouting Coord.; EDWARD TRAY, C.Y.O. Coord.; DENISE RYAN, Sec., *St. Francis Center, 900 W. Market St., Orwigsburg, 17961.* Tel: 717-366-1405. Regional Directors: Lehigh Co.: Rev. MARTIN F. KERN; Berks Co.: Rev. CHRISTOPHER L. WAKEFIELD; Carbon Co.: Rev. JAMES M. TORPEY; North Schuylkill Co.: Rev. DAVID J. KOZAK. High School Directors: Revs. GEORGE R. WINNE, Allentown Central Catholic; STEPHEN L. MACO, Bethlehem Catholic; ANTHONY P. MONGIELLO, Cardinal Brennan; THOMAS J. ORSULAK, Holy Name; WILLIAM N. SEIFERT, Marian Catholic; BERNARD A. FLANAGAN, Nativity; THOMAS J. KESSLER, Notre Dame; PATRICK H. LAMB, Reading Central Catholic; WAYNE E. KILLIAN, Saint Pius X. C.Y.O. Regional Directors: Carbon Co. and East Schuylkill Co.: Rev. JOHN G. HILFERTY; Berks Co.: Rev. RICHARD C. BRENSINGER; Lehigh Co.: Rev. ROBERT J. GEORGE; Mid-Schuylkill Co.: Rev. ANTHONY P. MONGIELLO; Northampton Co.: Rev. EDWARD R. DOMIN; West Schuylkill Co.: Rev. ERIC J. GRUBER. Catholic Scouting Area Chaplains: Minsi Trails Council: Carbon Co.: Rev. ROBERT J. MCCONAGHY; Lehigh Co.: Rev. VICTOR F. FINELLI; Northampton Co.: Rev. FRANCIS A. NAVE. Hawk Mountain Council Co-Chairpersons: ELIZABETH PAOLINI; ANNE MARIE HALCOVAGE. North Schuylkill Co. Area: Rev. VICTOR J. ANSELMI. Scouting (Girls): CAROLE YEAGER. Camp-Fire Inc.: ELIZABETH PAOLINI.

Affiliated Organizations

Apostleship of Prayer—Very Rev. EUGENE W. JUNG, M.S.C., Dir., *55 Rothermel St., Reading, 19605.* Tel: 610-929-2025.

American Catholic Overseas Aid Fund—Rev. RICHARD J. FORD, Diocesan Dir., *3121 Kutztown Rd., Reading, 19605.* Tel: 610-921-2729. Regional Directors: Lehigh Co.: Rev. Msgr. WILLIAM F. BAVER, Th.M.; Northampton Co.: Rev. DAVID J. LOEPER, M.A.; North Schuylkill Co.: Rev. FRANCIS M. GRUNDOWSKI; South Schuylkill Co.: Rev. JAMES R. BRADY.

Beginning Experience—Rev. Msgr. RONALD W. GAINER, Diocesan Spiritual Dir., *4102 S. Church St., Whitehall, 18052.* Tel: 610-262-9315.

Catholic Daughters of the Americas—Mrs. JOYCE TORPEY, Diocese Committee Chm., *501 Greenwood Ave., Pottsville, 17901.* Tel: 717-622-9967.

Charismatic Renewal—Rev. LARRY J. HESS, Bishop's Liaison, *Newman Association, 15207 Kutztown Rd., Kutztown, 19530.* Tel: 610-683-8380.

Courage—Rev. BERNARD J. EZAKI, Dir., *1861 Catasauqua Rd., Bethlehem, 18018.* Tel: 610-866-8938.

Cursillo Movement—Rev. ROBERT J. REED, Dir., *SS. Simon & Jude Rectory, 730 W. Broad St., Bethlehem, 18018.* Tel: 610-866-5582.

Dayspring Homes, Inc.—Sr. FRANCIS BISLAND, C.P.S., Dir. A program providing residential settings for adult persons with mental retardation. *Corporate Address: P.O. Box 172, Shillington, 19607.* Tel: 610-777-1624.

The Father Walter Ciszek Prayer League, Inc.—The official organization for the promotion of the cause of the Rev. Walter J. Ciszek, S.J. Co-Postulators: Rev. Msgr. ANTHONY D. MUNTONE; Rev. THOMAS SABLE, S.J., *The Ciszek Center, 231 N. Jardin St., Shenandoah, 17976.* Tel: 717-462-2270; Fax: 717-462-2274.

Holy Childhood Association—Rev. Msgr. JOHN P. MURPHY, Dir., *1040 Flexer Ave., Allentown, 18103.* Tel: 610-433-7413.

Holy Name Societies—Deacon STEPHAN ANDRUSISIAN, Dir., *516 N. Front St., Minersville, 17954.* Tel: 717-544-5339. Regional Directors: North Schuylkill Co.: Deacon JOHN A. SETLOCK; Northampton Co.: Rev. THOMAS J. KING; South Schuylkill Co.: Deacon STEPHEN ANDRUSISIAN; Carbon Co.: Rev. BRUNO M. TUCCI; Berks Co.: Rev. KEVIN P. GALLAGHER.

Legion of Mary—ELIZABETH PAOLINI, *414 Douglass St., Reading, 19601.*

Magnificat House—4530 Vera Cruz Rd., Center Valley, 18034. Tel: 610-797-1950.

Marriage Encounter—Rev. ROBERT A. DRESSLER, *33 Fourth St., P.O. Box G, Kelayres, 18231-0070.* Tel: 717-929-3670.

National Society for Shut-Ins—Rev. Msgr. FELIX A. LOSITO, Natl. Dir., *237 Franklin St., Reading, 19602.* Tel: 610-374-2930. MICHAEL SHEIDY, Pres.

Operation Rice Bowl—Rev. Msgr. JOHN P. MURPHY, Dir., *1040 Flexer Ave., Allentown, 18103.* Tel: 610-433-7413.

Priests' Eucharistic League—Rev. Msgr. THOMAS E. HOBAN, Dir., *415 S. Sixth St., Emmaus, 18049.* Tel: 610-965-2426.

Propagation of the Faith—Rev. Msgr. JOHN P. MURPHY, Dir., *1040 Flexer Ave., Allentown, 18103.* Tel: 610-433-7413.

Saint Vincent de Paul—Rev. Msgr. JOHN B. MCCANN, S.T.L., L.S.W., Spiritual Advisor; EDWARD BUTLER, Diocesan Council Pres., *2141 Downyflake Ln., Allentown, 18103-4774.* Tel: 610-791-3888.

Serra Clubs—Forks of the Delaware Serra, Rev. JOSEPH A. SHEEHAN; JOHN DALY, Pres., *723 Reeder St., Easton, 18042.* Serra Club of Allentown, Rev. Msgr. ALFRED R. OTT, Chap.; ELLWYN D. SPIKER, Pres., *1306 Russet Rd., Allentown, 18104.* Reading Serra, Rev. Msgr. JAMES J. REICHERT, Chap.; LEO W. MIKUS, Pres., *125 Gibralter Rd., Reading, 19606-3321.* Serra Club of Bethlehem, Rev. Msgr. ROBERT F. KOZEL, Chap.; ANTHONY F. ORTWEIN, Pres., *755 Johnston Dr., Bethlehem, 18017.*

CLERGY, PARISHES, MISSIONS AND PAROCHIAL SCHOOLS

CITY OF ALLENTOWN
(Lehigh County)

1—CATHEDRAL OF ST. CATHARINE OF SIENA (1919), Rev. Msgr. Alfred R. Ott, V.F.; Revs. Robert J. George; David L. James; Deacon Ralph Jaccodine.
Res., 1825 Turner St., 18104. Tel: 610-433-6461; Fax: 610-433-5452.
School—(Grades K-8) 210 N. 18th St., 18104. Tel: 610-434-8981; Fax: 610-437-4951. Mrs. H. Jacqueline Greco, Prin.
Lay Teachers 27; Students 500.
Catechesis/Religious Programs—Tel: 610-432-7655. Sr. Elizabeth Agnes, S.S.J., D.R.E.
Students 131.
Convent—215 N. 18th St., 18104. Tel: 610-434-9824.

2—ST. FRANCIS OF ASSISI (1928), Rev. Msgr. Dennis A. Rigney; Rev. Joseph McGarr; Deacons Alexander L. Maggitti, Sr.; Arthur L. Chin-Fatt.
Res., 801 N. 11th St., 18102. Tel: 610-434-8770; Fax: 610-434-6972.
School—(Grades PreK-8) 1035 Washington St., 18102. Tel: 610-435-0364.
Sisters of St. Francis of Philadelphia 2; Lay Teachers 11; Students 324.
Parish Center—1028 W. Cedar St., 18102. Tel: 610-433-6102.
Catechesis/Religious Programs—Tel: 610-434-8299.
Students 231.

3—IMMACULATE CONCEPTION (1857). (Declared National Shrine of Our Lady of Guadalupe, Mother of the Americas 1974). Rev. Harold F. Dagle; Deacon Brian J. Monahan. In res., Rev. Msgr. John B. McCann.
Res., 501 Ridge Ave., 18102. Tel: 610-433-4404; Fax: 610-433-8401. [CEM]
School—Holy Spirit Regional Catholic Elementary School, Allentown. See separate listing.
Catechesis/Religious Programs—Located at Holy Spirit Elementary School, Allentown.
Convent—508 Ridge Ave., 18102. Tel: 610-432-0838.

4—ST. JOHN THE BAPTIST (Slovak), Rev. Msgr. Francis J. Zavodny; Rev. Andrew Sroba.
Res., 924 N. Front St., 18102. Tel: 610-432-0034. [CEM]
School—Holy Spirit Regional Catholic Elementary School, Allentown. See separate listing.
Convent—920 N. Front St., 18102. Tel: 610-434-1471.

5—OUR LADY HELP OF CHRISTIANS (1927), Revs. Daniel J. Yenushosky; John M. Gibbons; Deacon Charles Coyle.
Res., 444 N. Jasper St., 18103. Tel: 610-432-9384; Fax: 610-782-9297.
School—934 Hanover Ave., 18103. Tel: 610-433-1592.
Sisters of Christian Charity 2; Lay Teachers 8; Students 193.
Catechesis/Religious Programs—Students 46.
Convent—922 Hanover Ave., 18103. Tel: 610-433-4915.

6—OUR LADY OF MT. CARMEL (1911) (Italian), Rev. Msgr. Joseph R. Sobiesiak; Deacon Dominick F. Amedeo.
Res., 177 Chew St., 18102. Tel: 610-434-5171; Fax: 610-434-2441. [CEM]
School—Sacred Heart Regional Catholic Elementary School, Allentown. See separate listing. Tel: 610-437-3031.
Catechesis/Religious Programs—Located at Sacred Heart, Allentown.

7—ST. PAUL (1928), Rev. Msgr. Robert M. Forst; Revs. Francis J. Fromholzer; Luigi Palmieri; Deacon Daniel A. Thomson. In res., Rev. Michael S. Lawrence.
Res., 920 S. Second St., 18103. Tel: 610-797-9733.
Church—Second St. & Susquehanna St., 18103.
School—(Grades K-8) Third St. & Susquehanna St., 18103. Tel: 610-797-5321. Rita Curran, Prin.
Lay Teachers 12; Students 285.
Catechesis/Religious Programs—Students 150.

8—SS. PETER AND PAUL (Polish), Rev. Ladislaus J. Dudek.
Res., 1065 Fullerton Ave., 18102. Tel: 610-432-2252.
School—Holy Spirit Regional Catholic Elementary School, Allentown. See separate listing.

9—SACRED HEART OF JESUS (1869) (German-Spanish), Rev. Msgr. Joseph R. Sobiesiak; Rev. Martin F. Kern; Deacons Jaime de Jesus; Victor M. Quiles; Alfonso Solis; Dominic Amadeo. In res., Rev. George R. Winne.
Res., 336 N. Fourth St., 18102. Tel: 610-434-5171; Fax: 610-434-2441. [CEM]
School—(Grades PreK-8) 321 N. Fourth St., 18102. Tel: 610-437-3031; Fax: 610-434-2441. James Krupka, Prin.
Lay Teachers 10; Students 216.
High School—Tel: 610-437-4601. James Hodrick, Prin.
Catechesis/Religious Programs—Parish Center, 417 Pine St., 18102. Tel: 610-434-5171; Fax: 610-434-2441. Sr. Regina Rosaii, D.R.E.
Students 363.

10—ST. STEPHEN OF HUNGARY (1915) (Hungarian), Rev. Msgr. William F. Baver, Th.M.
Res., 510 Union St., 18101-2307. Tel: 610-439-0111; Fax: 610-439-6048.
School—Sacred Heart Regional Catholic Elementary School, Allentown. See separate listing.

11—ST. THOMAS MORE (1966), Rev. Msgr. John P. Murphy; Rev. Eric R. Arnout, Jr.; Deacons James R. Duncan; Robert J. Tyson. In res., Rev. John S. Mraz.
Res., 1040 Flexer Ave., 18103. Tel: 610-433-7413; Fax: 610-433-2308.
School—Tel: 610-432-0396; Fax: 610-432-1395.
Bernardine Sisters 4; Lay Teachers 28; Students 610.
Catechesis/Religious Programs—Tel: 610-437-3491.
Students 573.
Convent—992 Flexer Ave., 18103. Tel: 610-437-9520.

OUTSIDE CITY OF ALLENTOWN

Ashland, Schuylkill Co., St. Joseph (1856), Rev. Floyd Caesar; Deacon Robert McManus. In res., Rev. Frans J. Berkhout.
Res., 1100 Walnut St., 17921. Tel: 717-875-1521; Fax: 717-875-2635. [CEM]
School—Immaculate Heart Regional Catholic Elementary School, Girardville. See separate listing. Tel: 717-276-6568.
Catechesis/Religious Programs—Students 100.
Convent—1123 Walnut St., 17921. Tel: 717-875-3553.

St. Mauritius (1856) (German), Rev. Floyd Caesar; Deacon Robert McManus. In res., Rev. Frans J. Berkhout.
Res., 802 Pine St., 17921. Tel: 717-875-2990; Fax: 717-875-2635. [CEM]
School—Immaculate Heart Regional Catholic Elementary School, Girardville. See separate listing. Tel: 717-276-6568.
Mission—Lavelle, Schuylkill Co., St. Elizabeth, Lavelle, 17943.

Bally, Berks Co., Most Blessed Sacrament (1741), Rev. Msgr. Edward J. Coyle; Rev. Michael J. Briggman, Pastor Emeritus; Deacon Thomas J. Murphy.
Res., 610 Pine St., Box C, 19503. Tel: 610-845-2460; Fax: 610-845-2660. [CEM]
School—St. Francis Academy, Bally. See separate listing. Tel: 610-845-7364; Fax: 610-845-2794.
Catechesis/Religious Programs—Barbara A. Seaman, D.R.E.
Students 196.

Bangor, Northampton Co., Our Lady of Good Counsel (1915), Revs. John B. Fitzgerald, C.M.; Emerick J. Hydo, C.M.
Res., 436 S. Second St., 18013. Tel: 610-588-5445; Fax: 610-588-5445. [CEM]
School—Our Lady of Mt. Carmel Regional Catholic Elementary School, Roseto. See separate listing.
Catechesis/Religious Programs—Elizabeth Thompson, D.R.E.
Students 120.

Mission—Portland, Northampton Co., St. Vincent de Paul, Church St., Portland, 18351.

Barnesville, Schuylkill Co., St. Richard (1950), Rev. Paul G. Puza.
Res., Park Crest, R.R. 2, Box 221, 18214-9747. Tel: 717-467-2315; Fax: 717-467-3803.
Catechesis/Religious Programs—Tel: 717-773-3687; Fax: 717-467-3803. Marcella Gill, D.R.E.
Students 50.

Bath, Northampton Co., Sacred Heart (1920), Rev. Francis A. Nave, Admin.
Res., 210 E. Northampton St., 18014. Tel: 610-837-7874; Fax: 610-837-4570. [CEM]
School—(Grades PreK-8) 115 Washington St., 18014. Tel: 610-837-6391. Patricia A. Wertman, Prin.
Lay Teachers 9; Students 177.
Catechesis/Religious Programs—Mrs. Helen Browne, D.R.E.
Students 275.

Beaver Meadows, Carbon Co., St. Mary (1841), Rev. John J. Duminiak.
Res., 121 Berwick St., P.O. Box 235, 18216. Tel: 717-455-2613; Fax: 717-455-3125. [CEM]
Catechesis/Religious Programs—Students 44.

Berlinsville, Northampton Co., St. Nicholas, Rev. Edward W. McElduff.
Res., 1152 Oak Rd., Walnutport, 18088. Tel: 610-767-3148.
School—St. John Neumann Regional Catholic Elementary School, Palmerton-Slatington. See separate listing.

Bethlehem, Northampton Co.,

1—St. Anne, (1929), Rev. Msgr. Robert F. Kozel; Revs. Richard H. Clement; William R. Dermott; Deacons Francis Cosgrove; Richard G. Scrak; Sr. Kathleen Mackerer, S.S.J., Pastoral Assoc. In res., Rev. Stephen L. Maco.
Res., 450 Washington Ave., 18017. Tel: 610-867-5039; Fax: 610-882-4094.
School—(Grades PreK-8) Easton Ave. & Hickory St., 18017. Tel: 610-868-4182. Mrs. Norma Romberger, Prin.
Lay Teachers 20; Students 451.
Catechesis/Religious Programs—Tel: 610-868-7514.
Students 186.

2—SS. Cyril and Methodius, (1891) (Slovak), Rev. Msgr. Michael J. Chaback, S.T.D.; Deacon Frank J. Danyi, Jr.
Res., 617 Pierce St., 18015. Tel: 610-866-3391; Fax: 610-866-6490. [CEM]
School—(Grades PreK-8) 551 Thomas St. & Pierce St., 18015. Tel: 610-866-0422. Mrs. Joan M. West, Prin.
Lay Teachers 11; Students 135.
Catechesis/Religious Programs—Students 33.
Convent—520 Buchanan St., 18015. Tel: 610-866-0275.

3—Holy Ghost, (1871) (German), Rev. Msgr. Richard J. Loeper; Deacon Franklin J. Chiles. In res., Rev. Ai Ba Do (Vietnam).
Res., 417 Carlton Ave., 18015. Tel: 610-867-9382; Fax: 610-867-6839. [CEM]
School—Holy Child Regional Catholic Elementary School, Bethlehem. See separate listing. Tel: 610-865-0861.
Convent—427 Carlton Ave., 18015. Tel: 610-867-3364.

4—Holy Infancy, Rev. Msgr. James M. Butler; Deacons Edison Morales; Alfonso D. Solis; Nicasio Rodriguez; Rafael Cuevas. In res., Rev. Msgr. Robert J. Biszek; Rev. Jose Dos Santos (Portugal).
Res., 312 E. Fourth St., 18015. Tel: 610-866-1121. [CEM]
School—(Grades PreK-8) 202 E. Fourth St., 18015. Tel: 610-868-2621. Sr. Joyce Valese, Prin.
Sisters of St. Joseph 4; Lay Teachers 8; Students 285.
Catechesis/Religious Programs—Stephanie Rivera, D.R.E.
Students 132.
Convents—202 E. Fourth St., 18015. Tel: 610-867-7384. Poor Sisters of St. Joseph; Casa Belen, 305 E. Fourth St., 18015. Tel: 610-867-4030.

5—St. John Capistrano, (1903) (Hungarian), Rev. Edward C. Bolez.
Res., 910 E. Fourth St., 18015. Tel: 610-866-2714; Fax: 610-317-8026.
School—SS. Cyril and Methodius Regional Catholic Elementary School, Bethlehem. See separate listing. Tel: 610-866-0042; Fax: 610-866-6490.

6—St. Joseph, (Slovenian), Rev. Joseph N. Galic, O.F.M.
Res., 416 E. Fifth St., 18015. Tel: 610-866-4102.
School—SS. Cyril and Methodius Regional Catholic Elementary School, Bethlehem. See separate listing.

7—Notre Dame of Bethlehem, Lehigh Co., (1954), Rev. Msgr. Joseph E. Kurtz, M.Div., L.S.W.; Revs. Paul L. Rothermel; Gregory Karpyn; Deacons Lemuel Von Leer; Richard Sewald. In res., Rev. Bernard J. Ezaki.
Res., 1861 Catasauqua Rd., 18018-1298. Tel: 610-866-4371; Fax: 610-866-9065.
School—(Grades K-8) 1835 Catasauqua Rd., 18018. Tel: 610-866-2231. Sr. Patricia A. Cullen, S.S.J., Prin.
Sisters of St. Joseph 1; Lay Teachers 23; Students 475.
Catechesis/Religious Programs—Tel: 610-866-1418. Mrs. Dawn Mayton, D.R.E.
Students 330.
Convent—1823 Catasauqua Rd., 18018. Tel: 610-866-4310.

8—Our Lady of Perpetual Help, (1963), Rev. Msgr. Edward R. Sacks; Rev. Fred F. Sattler; Deacon Bernard J. Salabsky, Jr. In res., Rev. Msgr. David J. Morrison.
Res., 3219 Santee Rd., 18020. Tel: 610-867-8409; Fax: 610-867-4870.
School—3221 Santee Rd., 18020. Tel: 610-868-6570; Fax: 610-868-7941.
Lay Teachers 12; Students 302.
Catechesis/Religious Programs—Students 310.

9—Our Lady of Pompeii, (1902) (Italian), Rev. Msgr. Paul B. della Picca.
Res., 826 E. Fourth St., 18015. Tel: 610-691-0719; Fax: 610-691-0719.
School—SS. Cyril and Methodius Regional Catholic Elementary School, Bethlehem. See separate listing. Tel: 610-866-0042; Fax: 610-866-6490.

10—SS. Simon and Jude, Lehigh Co., (1917), Revs. Robert J. Reed; David J. Loeper.
Res., 730 W. Broad St., 18018. Tel: 610-866-5582; Fax: 610-866-2992.
School—(Grades K-8) 6th & North St., 18018. Tel: 610-867-9530. Sr. Lisa Ann Golden, I.H.M., Prin.
Sisters of the Immaculate Heart of Mary 5; Lay Teachers 7; Students 215.
Catechesis/Religious Programs—Tel: 610-861-7507. Sr. Dolores Gordon, S.N.De.N., D.R.E.
Students 245.
Convent—714 W. Broad St., 18018. Tel: 610-867-9546.

11—St. Stanislaus, (1906) (Polish), Rev. Frederick Przydzial.
Res., 429 Hayes St., 18015. Tel: 610-867-9323.
School—SS. Cyril and Methodius Regional Catholic Elementary School, Bethlehem. See separate listing.

Birdsboro, Berks Co., Immaculate Conception, Rev. Msgr. Nevin J. Klinger, J.C.L., M.A.
Res., 640 Main St., 19508. Tel: 610-582-2411; Fax: 610-582-3866. [CEM]
School—St. Catharine of Siena Regional Catholic Elementary School, Birdsboro. See separate listing.

Boyertown, Berks Co., St. Columbkill (1921), Revs. Robert C. Quinn; Philip F. Rodgers.
Res., 200 Indian Spring Rd., 19512. Tel: 610-367-2371; Fax: 610-369-0242.
School—St. Francis Academy, Bally. See separate listing. Tel: 610-845-7364.
Catechesis/Religious Programs—Tel: 610-367-2371; Fax: 610-369-0242. D.R.E.: Sr. Nancy Kramer, S.S.J.; Constance Boyer.
Students 669.

Branchdale, Schuylkill Co., St. Mary Star of the Sea (1886), Rev. Edmund J. Brennan.
Res., State Rd., 17923. Tel: 717-544-2592. [CEM]
School—Good Shepherd Regional Catholic Elementary School, Minersville. See separate listing. Tel: 717-544-3766.

Brockton, Schuylkill Co., St. Bartholomew (1846), Rev. Francis M. Grundowski.
Res., 214 Green St., Box 292, 17925. Tel: 717-668-1500. [CEM]
School—St. Jerome Regional Catholic Elementary, Tamaqua. See separate listing.

Catasauqua, Northampton Co., St. Andrew (1902) (Slovac), Rev. Stephen J. Radocha.
Mailing Address: 2174 Lincoln Ave., Northampton, 18067. Tel: 610-262-2559; Fax: 610-262-1613. [CEM]
Church—Third St. & Cypress St., North Catasauqua, 18032. Tel: 610-264-0612.
School—Our Lady of Hungary Regional Catholic Elementary School, Northampton. See separate listing. Tel: 610-262-9171.
Catechesis/Religious Programs—Located at Assumption B.V.M., Northhampton.

Annunciation B.V.M. - St. Mary's, Lehigh Co., (1857) (German), Rev. Francis T. Gillespie.
Res., 122 Union St., 18032. Tel: 610-264-0332; Fax: 610-266-7133. [CEM]
Catechesis/Religious Programs—Tel: 610-264-9383.
Students 258.

St. Lawrence (Lehigh Co.) (1858), Rev. Joseph J. Campion. In res., Rev. Msgr. Francis C. Revak.
Res., 1001 Second St., 18032. Tel: 610-264-1972; Fax: 610-264-2105. [CEM]

Coaldale, Schuylkill Co., SS. Cyril and Methodius (1920) (Slovak), Rev. Francis J. Baransky.
Res., 41 E. Ruddle St., 18218. Tel: 717-645-4647. [CEM]
School—St. Michael Regional Catholic Elementary School, Lansford. See separate listing.

St. John the Baptist (1914) (Lithuanian), Rev. Francis J. Baransky.
Res., 41 E. Ruddle St., 18218. Tel: 717-645-4647. [JC]
School—St. Michael Regional Catholic Elementary School, Lansford. See separate listing.

St. Mary of the Assumption (1892), Rev. Francis J. Baransky.
Res., 41 E. Ruddle St., 18218. Tel: 717-645-4647. [JC]
School—St. Michael Regional Catholic Elementary School, Lansford. See separate listing.
Convent—231 Second St., 18218. Tel: 717-645-2310.

Colesville, Lehigh Co., Assumption B.V.M. (1927), Rev. Msgr. John J. Martin; Rev. James P. Finnegan, O.S.F.S.; Patricia Herbst, Pastoral Min.; Deacon Bernard M. Wisser.
Res., 4101 Old Bethlehem Pike, Bethlehem, 18015. Tel: 610-867-7424; Fax: 610-865-3021.
School—St. Michael the Archangel Regional Catholic Elementary School, Colesville-Limeport. See separate listing.
Catechesis/Religious Programs—Tel: 610-867-7424. Christina M. Bigatel, D.R.E.
Students 225.

Coplay, Lehigh Co., St. Peter (1927) (Austrian-Hungarian), Revs. Paul L. Bader; Michael E. Ahrensfield; Deacon Michael J. Laroche.
Res., 4 S. Fifth St., 18037. Tel: 610-262-2417; Fax: 610-262-0211. [CEM]
School—Christ the King Regional Catholic Elementary School, Coplay, Whitehall. See separate listing. Tel: 610-262-5822.
Catechesis/Religious Programs—Tel: 610-262-2417. Deacon Michale J. Laroche, D.R.E.
Students 75.

Cumbola, Schuylkill Co., St. Anthony of Padua (1907) (Polish), Rev. Msgr. Ronald C. Bocian.
Res., Market St., 17930. Tel: 717-277-0064. [CEM]
School—Holy Cross Regional Catholic Elementary School, New Philadelphia. See separate listing.

Easton, Northampton Co.,

1—St. Anthony of Padua, (1909) (Italian), Rev. Msgr. William E. Handges; Revs. David W. Karns; Joseph D. Hulko; Deacon Charles A. DeBellis; Fred A. Williams, Business Admin.
Res., 900 Washington St., 18042. Tel: 610-253-7188; Fax: 610-253-6184. [CEM]
Nursery School—138 E. Nesquehoning St., 18042. Tel: 610-242-4033.
School—Easton Catholic School, Easton. See separate listing. Tel: 610-252-1393; Fax: 610-253-6184.
Catechesis/Religious Programs—Tel: 610-253-7188; Fax: 610-253-6184. Mrs. Karen Donato, D.R.E.
Students 220.
Convent—770 Washington St., 18042. Tel: 610-258-7792.
Chapel—South Easton, St. Mary's.

2—St. Bernard, (1829), Revs. John J. Grabish; William J. Nahn; Deacons Henry Fleck, Jr.; Thomas C. Reichard.
Parish Center—123 S. Sixth St., 18042.
Res., 132 S. Fifth St., 18042. Tel: 610-252-7381; Fax: 610-252-6757. [CEM][JC]
School—Easton Catholic School, Easton. See separate listing. Tel: 610-252-1393; Fax: 610-253-6184.
Catechesis/Religious Programs—Tel: 610-258-4548. Patricia Pierson, D.R.E.
Students 180.

3—St. Jane Frances de Chantal, (1925), Rev. Msgr. Gerald Gobitas; Revs. Richard W. Campo; Edward Domin; Deacon Robert W. Rodgers.
Res., 1918 Washington Blvd., 18042. Tel: 610-253-3553; Fax: 610-253-5711. [JC]
Church—19th St. & Washington Blvd., 18042.
School—(Grades PreK-8) 1946 Washington Blvd., 18042. Tel: 610-253-8442.
Sisters of the Immaculate Heart of Mary 7; Lay Teachers 17; Students 514.
Catechesis/Religious Programs—Tel: 610-253-7794.
Students 480.
Convent—Tel: 610-253-4912.

4—St. Joseph, (1852) (German), Rev. Joseph A. Sheehan.
Res., 129 Davis St., 18042-6295. Tel: 610-252-0242; Fax: 610-253-7558. [CEM 2]
School—Easton Catholic School, Easton. See separate listing.
Catechesis/Religious Programs—Students 93.

5—St. Michael, (1915) (Lithuanian), Rev. John J. Grabish; Deacons Thomas C. Reichard; Henry Fleck, Jr.
Res., 132 S. Fifth, 18042. Tel: 610-252-7381; Fax: 610-252-6757. [CEM]
School—Easton Catholic School, Easton. See separate listing. Tel: 610-252-1393; Fax: 610-253-6184.
Catechesis/Religious Programs—Students 3.

Ellengowan, Schuylkill Co., St. Aidan. Closed. Parish from November 1919 to July 9, 1948. Records at the Annunciation B.V.M. Church, Shenandoah.

Emmaus, Lehigh Co., St. Ann (1931), Rev. Msgr. Thomas E. Hoban; Revs. John A. Frink; Thomas P. Koons; Deacon Richard B. Close.
Res., 415 S. Sixth St., 18049. Tel: 610-965-2426; Fax: 610-967-1099. [CEM]
School—(Grades PreK-8) 570 Wood St., 18049. Tel: 610-965-9220. Loretta Chapin, Prin.
Sisters 2; Lay Teachers 10; Students 325.
Catechesis/Religious Programs—Tel: 610-965-6888. Angela Faidley, D.R.E.
Students 540.
Convent—526 Fairview St., 18049. Tel: 610-965-6818.

Fountain Hill, Lehigh Co., St. Ursula (Bethlehem P.O.) (1919), Revs. Vincent P. York; Peter Jurcik.
Res., 1300 Broadway, 18015. Tel: 610-867-5122; Fax: 610-867-6569.
School—Holy Child Regional Catholic Elementary School, Bethlehem. See separate listing. Tel: 610-865-0861.

Frackville, Schuylkill Co., St. Ann (1924) (Polish), Rev. Dominik P. Kalata, M.Ed.; Deacon John A. Setlock.
Res., 7 S. Broad Mountain Ave., 17931. Tel: 717-874-0842; Fax: 717-874-2265.
School—Holy Family Regional Catholic Elementary School, Frackville. See separate listing. Tel: 717-874-0285.
Catechesis/Religious Programs—Located at St. Joseph, Frackville.

Annunciation B.V.M. (1917) (Lithuanian), Rev. Dominik P. Kalata, M.Ed.; Deacon John A. Setlock. In res., Rev. David J. Kozak, J.C.L.
Res., 7 S. Broad Mountain Ave., 17931. Tel: 717-874-0842; Fax: 717-874-2265. [CEM]
School—Holy Family Regional Catholic Elementary School, Frackville. See separate listing. Tel: 717-874-0285.
Catechesis/Religious Programs—Located at St. Joseph, Frackville.
Convent—25 S. Broad Mountain Ave., 17931. Tel: 717-874-0351.

St. Joseph (1909). St. Joseph's, Frackville administers over Our Lady of Siluva Parish, Maizeville. Rev. Albert J. Byrne; Deacon Joseph Burda.
Res., 14 N. Nice St., 17931. Tel: 717-874-0610; Fax: 717-874-0969. [CEM]
School—Holy Family Regional Catholic Elementary School, Frackville. See separate listing. Tel: 717-874-1921.
Catechesis/Religious Programs—Tel: 714-874-0610.
Students 81.

Girardville, Schuylkill Co., St. Joseph (1870), Rev. Anthony P. Mongiello.
Res., 211 W. Main St., 17935. Tel: 717-276-6239; Fax: 717-276-1444. [CEM]
School—Immaculate Heart Regional Catholic Elementary School, Girardville. See separate listing.
Catechesis/Religious Programs—Students 285.

St. Vincent de Paul (1907) (Lithuanian), Rev. David M. Liebner.
Res., 260 N. Second St., 17935. Tel: 717-276-6033. [CEM]
School—Immaculate Heart Regional Catholic Elementary School, Girardville. See separate listing.

Gordon, Schuylkill Co., Our Lady of Good Counsel (1922), Rev. James C. Bechtel.
Res., 220 W. Biddle St., 17936. Tel: 717-875-0774; Fax: 717-875-2443.
School—Immaculate Heart Regional Catholic Elementary School, Girardville. See separate listing. Tel: 717-276-6568.

Hamburg, Berks Co., St. Mary (1854), Rev. Joseph M. Braudis; Deacon Henry G. Gordon.
Res., 766 State St., 19526. Tel: 610-562-7657; Fax: 610-562-0379. [CEM]
Catechesis/Religious Programs—Parish Hall, 501 State St., 19526. Tel: 610-562-8110. Sr. Michele Fisher, C.S.F.N., D.R.E.
Students 246.
Station—Hamburg State School and Hospital, Tel: 610-562-6063.

Heckscherville, Schuylkill Co., St. Kieran (1857), Rev. Walter J. Hall.
Res., R.D. No. 2, Box 2401, Pottsville, 17901. Tel: 717-544-4857; Fax: 717-544-4854. [CEM]
School—St. Elizabeth Ann Seton Regional Catholic Elementary School, Minersville. See separate listing. Tel: 717-544-4360.

Hellertown, Northampton Co., St. Theresa of the Child Jesus, Rev. Msgr. Raymond F. Merman; Rev. Francis P. Straka.
Res., 1408 Easton Rd., 18055. Tel: 610-838-7045.
School—(Grades PreK-8) 300 Leonard St., 18055. Tel: 610-838-8161. Sr. Roseann Velas, O.S.F., Prin. Sisters of the Third Order of St. Francis 5; Lay Teachers 13; Students 244.
Catechesis/Religious Programs—Sr. S. M. Electa Barlok, O.S.F., D.R.E.
Students 141.
Convent—255 Wilson Ave., 18055. Tel: 610-838-7645.

Jim Thorpe, Carbon Co., Immaculate Conception, Rev. Msgr. John G. Chizmar, V.F.
Res., 180 W. Broadway, 18229. Tel: 717-325-2791. [CEM]
School—St. Joseph Regional Academy, Jim Thorpe. See separate listing.

St. Joseph (1871), Rev. John G. Hilferty.
Res., 526 North St., 18229. Tel: 717-325-3731; Fax: 717-325-2523. [CEM]
School—St. Joseph Regional Academy, Jim Thorpe. See separate listing. Tel: 717-325-3186.
Catechesis/Religious Programs—Tel: 717-722-0259; Fax: 717-325-2523.
Students 130.
Convent—27 W. Sixth St., 18229. Tel: 717-325-2212.

Kelayres, Schuylkill Co., Immaculate Conception (1899) (Italian), Rev. Robert A. Dressler.
Res., 33 Fourth St., P.O. Box G, 18231-0070. Tel: 717-929-3670; Fax: 717-929-2176. [CEM]
School—McAdoo Regional Catholic Elementary School, McAdoo. See separate listing.
Catechesis/Religious Programs—Students 42.

Kutztown, Berks Co., St. Mary (1919), Rev. Msgr. Walter T. Scheaffer.
Res., R.R. #4, Box 128D, 19530. Tel: 610-683-7443; 683-0740 (Church); Fax: 610-683-7625.
Catechesis/Religious Programs—44 Rose Alley, 19530. Tel: 610-683-3797.
Students 365.

Lake Harmony, Carbon Co., St. Peter the Fisherman (1989), Rev. Msgr. John A. Auchter.
Res., Lake Dr., P.O. Box 237, 18624. Tel: 717-722-2034; Fax: 717-722-1348.
Catechesis/Religious Programs—Students 155.

Lansford, Carbon Co., St. Ann, Rev. Stephen J. Halabura.
Res., 8 E. Bertsch St., 18232. Tel: 717-645-2575.
School—Our Lady of the Valley Regional Catholic Elementary School, Lansford-Summit Hill. See separate listing.
Convent—30 E. Bertsch St., 18232. Tel: 717-645-2750.

St. Michael (Slovak), Rev. Thomas A. Derzack.
Res., 124 E. Abbott St., 18232. Tel: 717-645-2282. [CEM]
School—St. Michael Regional Catholic Elementary School, Lansford. See separate listing.
Convent—124 E. Water St., 18232. Tel: 717-645-2484.

SS. Peter and Paul (Polish). Attended by St. Ann's Church. Rev. Stephen J. Halabura.
Mailing Address: 8 E. Bertsch St., 18232.
Church—225 W. Phillip St., Coaldale, 18218. Tel: 717-645-7605. [CEM]
School—St. Michael Regional Catholic Elementary School, Lansford. See separate listing.

Lehighton, Carbon Co., SS. Peter and Paul (1885), Rev. Robert J. McConaghy; Deacon William J. Wagner.
Res., 260 N. Third St., 18235-1595. Tel: 610-377-3690; Fax: 610-377-8881. [CEM]
School—307 Coal St., 18235. Tel: 610-377-4466. Mrs. Antoinette Collier, M.A., Prin.
Lay Teachers 6; Students 123.
Catechesis/Religious Programs—Students 105.

Limeport, Lehigh Co., St. Joseph (1926), Rev. Thomas R. Buckley.
Res., 5050 St. Joseph's Rd., 18060. Tel: 610-965-2877; Fax: 610-965-8317. [CEM]
School—St. Michael the Archangel Regional Catholic Elementary School, Colesville-Limeport. See separate listing. Tel: 610-965-4441; Fax: 610-965-1030.
Catechesis/Religious Programs—Students 221.

Lost Creek, Schuylkill Co., St. Mary Magdalen (1879), Rev. Edward J. O'Connor. In res., Rev. Charles J. Dene.
Res., P.O. Box 73, 17946. Tel: 717-462-1916. [JC]
School—Father Walter J. Ciszek Elementary School, Shenandoah. See separate listing. Tel: 717-462-9666.

Mahanoy City, Schuylkill Co.,

1—Assumption B.V.M., (1892) (Slovak), Rev. William J. Maslar.
Res., 728 W. Centre St., 17948. Tel: 717-773-1990. [CEM]
School—Mahanoy City Regional Catholic Elementary School, Mahanoy City. See separate listing.

2—St. Canicus, (1862), Very Rev. William T. Campion; Deacon Ted Koval. In res., Rev. Robert J. Kuzmann.
Res., 22 S. Catawissa St., 17948. Tel: 717-773-0550; Fax: 717-775-0668. [CEM]
School—Mahanoy City Regional Catholic Elementary School, Mahanoy City. See separate listing.

3—St. Casimir, (1893) (Polish), Rev. Lawrence J. Bukaty.
Res., 113 S. Catawissa St., 17948. Tel: 717-773-2461; Fax: 717-773-0610. [CEM]
School—Mahanoy City Regional Catholic Elementary School, Mahanoy City. See separate listing. Tel: 717-773-2668.

4—St. Fidelis, (1863) (German), Very Rev. William T. Campion; Deacon Ted Koval. In res., Rev. Robert J. Kuzmann.
Res., 22 S. Catawissa St., 17948. Tel: 717-773-2850; Fax: 717-773-0668. [CEM]
School—Mahanoy City Regional Catholic Elementary School, Mahanoy City. See separate listing.

5—St. Joseph, (Lithuanian), Rev. Msgr. Anthony F. Wassel.
Res., 614 W. Mahanoy Ave., 17948. Tel: 717-773-2771. [CEM]
School—Mahanoy City Regional Catholic Elementary School, Mahanoy City. See separate listing.

6—Sacred Heart, (Italian), Rev. William J. Maslar.
Res., 728 W. Centre St., 17948. Tel: 717-773-1990. [CEM]
School—Mahanoy City Regional Catholic Elementary School, Mahanoy City. See separate listing.

Mahanoy Plane, Schuylkill Co., Holy Rosary. Closed. 1988. Parish records at St. Joseph's Church, Girardville.

Maizeville, Schuylkill Co., Our Lady of Siluva (Gilberton P.O.) (1907) (Lithuanian). (Formerly St. Louis). Rev. Albert J. Byrne.
Res., c/o 14 N. Nice St., Frackville, 17931. Tel: 717-874-0610; Fax: 717-874-0969. [CEM]

Martins Creek, Northampton Co., St. Rocco (1937), Rev. Msgr. Joseph P. Dooley.
Res., Box 421, 18063-0010. Tel: 610-258-9059; Fax: 610-258-4780.
School—Immaculate Conception Regional Catholic Elementary School, Pen-Argyl. See separate listing. Tel: 610-863-4816.
Catechesis/Religious Programs—Tel: 610-258-9059.
Students 72.

McAdoo, Schuylkill Co.,

1—St. Kunegunda, (Polish), Rev. Joseph L. Grembocki.
Res., 36 E. Washington St., 18237. Tel: 717-929-2341; Fax: 717-929-2158. [CEM]
School—McAdoo Regional Catholic Elementary School, McAdoo. See separate listing. Tel: 717-929-1442.

2—St. Mary, (1893) (Slovak), Rev. Joseph Martinkovic (Slovakia).
Res., 101 E. Grant St., 18237. Tel: 717-929-1061. [CEM]
School—McAdoo Regional Catholic Elementary School, McAdoo. See separate listing.

3—St. Patrick, (1869) (Irish), Rev. Edward S. Zemanik.
Res., 17 N. Cleveland St., 18237. Tel: 717-929-1073; Fax: 717-929-3016. [CEM]
School—McAdoo Regional Catholic Elementary School, McAdoo. See separate listing. Tel: 717-929-1442.

4—St. Stephen of Hungary, (Hungarian). Attended by St. Kunegunda, McAdoo, 36 E. Washington St., 18237.

Miller Heights, Northampton Co., Sacred Heart of Jesus (1936), Rev. Thomas J. King; Deacon Hugh E. McShane. In res., Rev. Thomas J. Kessler.
Res., 1817 First St., Bethlehem, 18017. Tel: 610-865-5042; Fax: 610-865-1912.
School—(Grades K-8). Tel: 610-867-0221; Fax: 610-867-8351. Dr. Robert LaFrankie, Prin.
Lay Teachers 11; Students 253.
Catechesis/Religious Programs—Students 156.

Minersville, Schuylkill Co.,

1—St. Barbara, (1913) (Italian), Rev. David C. Liebner; Deacon Cyril Roth.
Res., 320 Spruce St., 17954. Tel: 717-544-2234; Fax: 717-544-5043. [CEM]
School—Holy Redeemer Regional Catholic Elementary School, Minersville. See separate listing under Regional Catholic Elemetary Schools, Diocesan. Tel: 717-544-4360 (Grades PreK-3) & 544-3766 (Grades 4-8); Fax: 717-544-4870 (Grades PreK-8).

2—St. Francis of Assisi, (1895) (Lithuanian), Rev. David C. Liebner; Deacon Cyril Roth.
Res., 320 Spruce St., 17954. Tel: 717-544-2234; Fax: 717-544-5043. [CEM]

School—Good Shepherd Regional School, (Grades PreK-3). No longer Holy Redeemer Regional Catholic Elementary School. Merged to form Good Shepherd Regional School, Minersville. 538 Sunbury St., 17954. Tel: 717-544-4360; Fax: 717-544-4870.
(Grades 4-8) 301 St. Francis St., 17954. Tel: 717-544-3766. Ms. Rosalie Novack, Prin.
Catechesis/Religious Programs—Tel: 717-544-2016. Sr. Catherine Therese, S.S.J., D.R.E. Students 78.
Convent—300 Oak St., 17954. Tel: 717-544-4534. Sisters of St. Casimir

3—OUR LADY OF MOUNT CARMEL, (1855) (German), Rev. John W. Bambrick.
Res., 519 School St., 17954. Tel: 717-544-2031; Fax: 717-544-4978. [CEM]
School—Good Shepherd Regional School, (Grades PreK-3) 538 Sunbury St., 17954. Tel: 717-544-4560. (Grades 4-8) 301 St. Francis St., 17954. Tel: 717-544-3766. Ms. Rosalie Novack, Prin.
Catechesis/Religious Programs—Students 350.

4—ST. STANISLAUS KOSTKA, (1905) (Polish), Rev. Leo J. Maletz.
Res., 139 Spruce St., 17954. Tel: 717-544-2211; Fax: 717-544-2317. [CEM 2]
School—Good Shepherd Regional School, (Grades PreK-3) 538 Sunbury St., 17954. Tel: 717-544-4360. (Grades 4-8) 301 St. Francis St., 17954. Tel: 717-544-3766; Fax: 717-544-4870. Ms. Rosalie Novack, Prin.
Catechesis/Religious Programs—Tel: 717-544-4360; 544-2016.
Students 53.

5—ST. VINCENT DE PAUL, (1842), Rev. Msgr. John S. Campbell.
Res., 541 Sunbury St., 17954. Tel: 717-544-4741; Fax: 717-544-4742. [CEM 2]
School—Good Shepherd Regional Catholic School, Minersville. See separate listing under Regional Catholic Elementary Schools, Diocesan.
Catechesis/Religious Programs—Students 295.
Convent—534 Sunbury St., 17954. Tel: 717-544-2016. Sisters of St. Joseph

Mohnton, Berks Co., St. Benedict's (1955), Rev. Dennis T. Hartgen.
Res., R.D. 1, Box 1346, 19540. Tel: 610-856-1006; Fax: 610-856-1035.
School—LaSalle Academy, Shillington. See separate listing.
Catechesis/Religious Programs—Tel: 610-370-0199; 856-5146; Fax: 610-856-1035. Ms. Valerie Christo, D.R.E.
Students 175.

Mount Carbon, Schuylkill Co., St. Francis de Sales (Pottsville P.O.), Rev. Edward B. Connolly.
Res., 49 Main St., Pottsville, 17901. Tel: 717-622-8270.
School—All Saints Regional Catholic Elementary School, Pottsville. See separate listing.

Nazareth, Northampton Co., Holy Family (1908), Revs. Norbert Weber, M.S.C.; John Schweikert, M.S.C.; Deacon Michael P. McGouldrick.
Res., 23 Forest Dr., 18064. Tel: 610-759-0870; Fax: 610-756-2026. [CEM 2]
School—(Grades PreK-8) 17 Convent Ave., 18064. Tel: 610-759-5642. Ms. Barbara Amabile, Prin.
Lay Teachers 21; Students 390.
Catechesis/Religious Programs—Tel: 610-759-7467. D.R.E.: Jeanine Breault; Eileen Boligitz.
Students 615.

Nesquehoning, Carbon Co., Immaculate Conception of B.V.M. (1914) (Slovak), Rev. Bruno M. Tucci.
Res., 15 E. Garibaldi Ave., 18240. Tel: 717-669-6321; Fax: 717-669-9440.
School—Our Lady of the Valley Regional Catholic Elementary School, Lansford-Summit Hill. See separate listing.

Our Lady of Mount Carmel (1913) (Italian), Rev. Bruno M. Tucci.
Res., 15 E. Garibaldi Ave., 18240. Tel: 717-669-6321; Fax: 717-669-9440. [CEM]
School—Our Lady of the Valley Regional Catholic Elementary School, Lansford-Summit Hill. See separate listing.

Sacred Heart (1887), Revs. Paul P. Welkie, Pastor Emeritus; Edward W. Coleman.
Res., 81 W. High St., 18240. Tel: 717-669-9008; Fax: 717-669-5091. [CEM]
School—Our Lady of the Valley Regional Catholic Elementary School, Lansford-Summit Hill. See separate listing. Tel: 717-645-4700.

New Philadelphia, Schuylkill Co., Holy Family (1866), Rev. William J. O'Donnell.
Res., 99 Valley St., 17959. Tel: 717-277-6800. [CEM]
School—Holy Cross Regional Catholic Elementary School, New Philadelphia. See separate listing. Tel: 717-277-0197.

Sacred Heart (Lithuanian), Rev. James J. Lofton.
Res., 41 Clay St., 17959. Tel: 717-277-6815. [CEM]
School—Holy Cross Regional Catholic Elementary School, New Philadelphia. See separate listing.
Convent—47 Wiggan St., 17959. Tel: 717-277-6820.
Mission—Middleport, Immaculate Heart of Mary Chapel.

Newtown, Schuylkill Co., Sacred Heart (1896) (German), Rev. Edmund J. Brennan.
Res., State Rd., Branchdale, 17923. Tel: 717-544-2592. [CEM]
School—Good Shepherd Regional School, (Grades PreK-3) 538 Sunbury St., Minersville, 17954. Tel: 717-544-4560.
(Grades 4-8) 301 St. Francis St., Minersville, 17954. Tel: 717-544-3766. Ms. Rosalie Novack, Prin.

Northampton, Northampton Co., Assumption of the Blessed Virgin Mary (1922) (Slovak), Rev. Stephen J. Radocha.
Res., 2174 Lincoln Ave., 18067. Tel: 610-262-2559; Fax: 610-262-1613. [CEM]
School—Our Lady of Hungary Regional Catholic Elementary School, Northampton. See separate listing. Tel: 610-262-9171.
Catechesis/Religious Programs—22nd & Washington Ave., 18067. Tel: 610-262-7343. Sr. Lorraine Molchanow, M.S.C., D.R.E.
Students 139.

St. Michael (1914) (Polish), Rev. John J. Pavlosky.
Res., 829 Main St., 18067. Tel: 610-262-2472; Fax: 610-262-2472. [JC]
School—Our Lady of Hungary Regional Catholic Elementary School, Northampton. See separate listing.

Our Lady of Hungary (German-Magyar), Revs. Edwin V. Schwartz; John J. L. Little. In res., Rev. Msgr. James J. Mulligan.
Res., 1324 Newport Ave., 18067. Tel: 610-262-2227. [CEM]
School—Our Lady of Hungary Regional Catholic Elementary School, Northampton. See separate listing.
Convent—1314 Newport Ave., 18067. Tel: 610-262-2427.

Orefield, Lehigh Co., St. Joseph The Worker (1948), Rev. Msgr. Robert J. Wargo; Rev. James J. Burdess; Sr. Mary Kathryn Quinn, S.S.J., Pastoral Assoc.; Deacon Daniel F. Metzker. In res., Rev. Donald Schaible.
Res., 1879 Applewood Dr., 18069-9507. Tel: 610-395-2876; Fax: 610-395-2616.
Preschool—Program for 3 & 4-year old children. Tel: 610-395-4010. Mrs. Stacy Gowell, Dir.
Students 95.
School—(Grades (K-8)) 1858 Applewood Dr., 18069. Tel: 610-395-7221; Fax: 610-395-7904. Mrs. Patricia L. Johnson, Prin.
Students 315.
Catechesis/Religious Programs—Tel: 610-395-4920; Fax: 610-395-7904.
Students 925.

Palmerton, Carbon Co., Sacred Heart (1908), Rev. Vincent I. Cronin; Deacons William P. Pitts; Andrew J. Mihalik.
Res., 243 Lafayette Ave., 18071-1597. Tel: 610-826-2335; Fax: 610-826-5360. [CEM]
School—St. John Neumann Regional Catholic Elementary School, Palmerton-Slatington. See separate listing.
Annex—252 Lafayette Ave., 18071. Tel: 610-826-2849.

Pen Argyl, Northampton Co., St. Elizabeth of Hungary (1929), Rev. Richard A. Schware. In res., Rev. Wayne E. Killian, M.A.
Res., 300 W. Babbitt Ave., P.O. Box 126, 18072-0126. Tel: 610-863-4777; Fax: 610-863-7449. [CEM]
School—Immaculate Conception Regional Catholic Elementary School, Pen Argyl. See separate listing.
Catechesis/Religious Programs—Students 179.
Convent—111-115 Lobb Ave., 18072. Tel: 610-863-9214.
Mission—Wind Gap, Northampton Co., St. Joseph, Lehigh Ave. & Genoga Ave., 18072.

Port Carbon, Schuylkill Co., St. Stephen, Rev. John J. McNamara.
Res., 218 Valley St., 17965. Tel: 717-622-6600. [CEM]
School—214 Valley St., 17965.
Sisters of the Immaculate Heart of Mary 3; Lay Teachers 7; Students 183.
Convent—Tel: 717-622-1461.

Pottsville, Schuylkill Co.,

1—ST. JOHN THE BAPTIST, (1841) (German), Rev. Gregory J. Tauber; Sr. Barbara J. Wojnicki, C.S.N.F., Pastoral Assoc.; Deacon Luis R. Visot.
Res., 913 Mahantongo St., 17901. Tel: 717-622-5470; Fax: 717-622-4589. [CEM 3]
School—All Saints Regional Catholic Elementary School, Pottsville. See separate listing. Tel: 717-622-0106.
Catechesis/Religious Programs—Lucilla Kochol, D.R.E.
Students 100.

2—ST. JOSEPH, (Italian), Rev. Edward B. Connolly.
Res., 321 W. Howard Ave., 17901. Tel: 717-622-3081. [CEM]
School—All Saints Regional Catholic Elementary School, Pottsville. See separate listing.

3—MARY QUEEN OF PEACE, (1920), Rev. Bernard F. Flanagan; Deacon Stephen Andrusisian.
Res., 728 N. Centre St., 17901. Tel: 717-622-7004; Fax: 717-622-4287.
School—All Saints Regional Catholic Elementary School, Pottsville. See separate listing. Tel: 717-622-0106.
Catechesis/Religious Programs—Peterine Wojcik, D.R.E.
Students 135.

4—ST. PATRICK, (1827), Rev. Msgr. William E. Jones, V.F.; Revs. Edward J. Essig, M.Div.; Frederick F. Sattler, M.Div. In res., Rev. Ronald P. Bowman.
Res., 319 Mahantongo St., 17901. Tel: 717-622-1802; Fax: 717-622-2593. [CEM]
Catechesis/Religious Programs—Students 244.
Convent—825 Mahantongo St., 17901. Tel: 717-622-0203.
Chapel—St. John Neumann, 2051 W. Norwegian St., 17901.

Reading, Berks Co.,

1—ST. ANTHONY, (Lithuanian). Attended by St. Peter, 322 S. Fifth St., 16902. Tel.: 610-372-9652.

2—ST. ANTHONY OF PADUA, (1914) (Polish), Rev. Richard E. Nachajski; Sr. Mary Joy Wasnesky, O.S.F., Pastoral Assoc.
Res., 501 Summit Ave., 19611. Tel: 610-374-1539; Fax: 610-374-0263.
School—LaSalle Academy & Early Childhood Center, Shillington. See separate listing. Tel: 610-777-7392; Fax: 610-777-1280.
Catechesis/Religious Programs—Students 54.
Convent—234 Grace St., 19611. Tel: 610-372-8578.

3—ST. CATHARINE OF SIENA, (1925), Rev. Msgr. Joseph P.T. Smith; Revs. Anthony M. Drouncheck; Robert G. Cofenas; Deacons George J. Faller; Richard A. Horst.
Res., 2427 Perkiomen Ave., 19606. Tel: 610-779-4005; Fax: 610-779-0859.
Church—4975 Boyertown Pike, 19606. Tel: 610-779-4090.
School—St. Catharine of Siena Regional Catholic Elementary School, Reading. See separate listing. Tel: 610-779-5810.
Catechesis/Religious Programs—Tel: 610-779-5810.
Students 458.
Convent—2328 Perkiomen Ave., 19606. Tel: 610-779-5583.

4—SS. CYRIL AND METHODIUS, (1895) (Slovak), Rev. Charles S. Sperlak; Deacon John J. Allison.
Res., 449 S. Sixth St., 19602. Tel: 610-373-0627.
Convent—502 S. Sixth St., 19602. Tel: 610-375-8001.

5—HOLY GUARDIAN ANGELS, (1929), Rev. Msgr. Francis X. Barrett; Revs. Richard J. Ford; Kevin P. Gallagher.
Res., 3121 Kutztown Rd., 19605. Tel: 610-921-2729; Fax: 610-921-8886.
School—(Grades PreK-8) 3125 Kutztown Rd., 19605. Tel: 610-929-4124. Mr. Philip Fromuth, Prin.
Lay Teachers 10; Students 304.
Catechesis/Religious Programs—Sr. Kathleen White, M.S.C., D.R.E.
Students 376.
Mission—Temple, Berks Co., St. Anthony, 8th & Columbia, Temple, 19560.

6—HOLY ROSARY, (1904) (Italian), Rev. Msgr. Felix A. Losito; Deacon Lawrence A. Dudeck.
Res., 237 Franklin St., 19602. Tel: 610-373-5579; Fax: 610-372-0130.
School—Cabrini Academy, (Grades PreK-8) 240 Franklin St., 19602. Tel: 610-374-8483.
Sisters 4; Lay Teachers 9; Students 300.
Catechesis/Religious Programs—Tel: 610-374-8483.
Students 102.
Convent—234 Franklin St., 19602. Tel: 610-375-9072.
Mission—Reading, Berks Co., Holy Rosary Chapel, Schuylkill Ave., 19601. Tel: 610-376-4383.

7—ST. JOSEPH, (1891), Revs. Thomas D. Baddick; Thomas G. Shanfelt; Deacon Peter LaFata.
Res., 1018 N. Eighth St., 19604. Tel: 610-376-2976; Fax: 610-376-2825.
School—(Grades K-8) 1040 N. Eighth St., 19604. Tel: 610-374-2951. Sr. Eileen Therese Gillespie, Prin.
Sisters of the Immaculate Heart of Mary 3; Lay

Teachers 7; Students 181.
Catechesis/Religious Programs—Students 68.
Convent—Tel: 610-372-1302.

8—ST. MARGARET, (1920), Revs. Francis P. Schoenauer; Ronald J. Yarrosh; John S. Pendzick; Deacon John P. Konopelski.
Res., 925 Centre Ave., 19601. Tel: 610-376-2919; Fax: 610-376-2462.
School—(Grades K-8) 233 Spring St., 19601. Tel: 610-375-1882. Sr. Diane Licordare, Prin.
Servants of Immaculate Heart of Mary 2; Lay Teachers 9; Students 250.
Catechesis/Religious Programs—Tel: 610-376-4584. William Davis, D.R.E.
Students 224.
Convent—233 Spring St., 19601. Tel: 610-372-1302.

9—ST. MARY, (1888) (Polish), Rev. Leo S. Stajkowski. In res., Rev. Donald W. Cieniewicz.
Res., 250 S. 12th St., 19602. Tel: 610-376-6321; Fax: 610-376-1378. [CEM]
School—1200 Spruce St., 19602. Tel: 610-375-9311; Fax: 610-375-1298.
Lay Teachers 12; Students 154.

10—ST. PAUL, (1860), Revs. Andrew A. Ulincy; Theodore S. Macunas; Aram Berard, S.J.
Res., 151 N. 9th St., 19601. Tel: 610-372-1531; Fax: 610-372-7478. [CEM]

11—ST. PETER, (1752) (Spanish American), Revs. Charles A. Marciano; Christopher L. Wakefield; Deacons Jesus Centeno; Mariano Torres; Julio Colon; Fernando L. Torres; Leopoldo Alvarado. In res., Rev. Thomas J. Orsulak.
Res., 322 S. Fifth St., 19602. Tel: 610-372-9652; Fax: 610-374-3351. [CEM]
School—218 S. Fifth St., 19602. Tel: 610-374-2447.
Sisters of the Immaculate Heart of Mary 5; Lay Teachers 7; Students 200.
Catechesis/Religious Programs—Tel: 610-378-1947.
Students 450.
Convent—Tel: 610-373-6185.

Ringtown, Schuylkill Co., St. Mary (1923), Rev. Victor J. Anselmi.
Mailing Address: 18 E. Oak St., Shenandoah, 17976.
Res., 86 N. Center St., 17967. Tel: 717-889-3850; Fax: 717-462-1747. [CEM]
School—Father Walter J. Ciszek Elementary School, Shenandoah. See separate listing. Tel: 717-462-3927; Fax: 717-462-4603.
Catechesis/Religious Programs—Students 45.

Robesonia, Berks Co., St. Francis de Sales (1982), Rev. James P. Byrne, O.S.F.S.; Sr. Mary Heffron, I.H.M., Pastoral Assoc.
Res., 321 N. Church St., 19551. Tel: 610-693-5851; Fax: 610-693-5852.
Catechesis/Religious Programs—Students 195.

Roseto, Northampton Co., Our Lady of Mt. Carmel (1897) (Italian), Revs. Daniel E. Donovan, C.M.; James G. Prior, C.M.
Res., P.O. Box 422, 18013. Tel: 610-588-2183; Fax: 610-588-2629. [CEM 2]
School—Our Lady of Mt. Carmel Regional Catholic Elementary School, Roseto. See separate listing. Tel: 610-588-2629.
Catechesis/Religious Programs—Students 344.
Convent—80 Ridge St., 18013. Tel: 610-588-2906.

Saint Clair, Schuylkill Co.,

1—ST. BONIFACE, (1854) (German), Rev. James J. Ward.
Parish Office: Tel: 717-429-0370.
Res., 250 E. Hancock St., 17970. Tel: 717-429-0701; Fax: 717-429-0630. [CEM]
School—St. Stephen Regional Catholic School, Port Carbon. See separate listing. Tel: 717-622-3063; Fax: 717-622-3689.

2—ST. CASIMIR, (Lithuanian), Rev. Ronald V. Jankaitis.
Res., 441 S. Nichols St., 17970. Tel: 717-429-2400. [CEM]
School—Saint Clair Regional Catholic Elementary School, Saint Clair. See separate listing.

3—IMMACULATE CONCEPTION, (1905) (Slovak), Rev. Paul E. Masiar.
Res., Caroline Ave., Diener's Hill, 17970-1361. Tel: 717-429-1315; Fax: 717-429-0369. [CEM]
Catechesis/Religious Programs—Located at St. Mary's Hall, St. Clair.

4—ST. MARY, (1864), Rev. James J. Ward; Deacon John F. Pogash. In res., Rev. Ronald C. Bowman.
Parish Office: Tel: 717-429-0370.
Res., 250 E. Hancock St., 17970. Tel: 717-429-0701; Fax: 717-424-0630. [CEM 2]
School—St. Stephen Regional Catholic School, Port Carbon. See separate listing. Tel: 717-622-3063; Fax: 717-622-3689.
Catechesis/Religious Programs—Tel: 717-429-1621.
Students 150.

5—SS. PETER AND PAUL, (1918) (Polish), Rev. James J. Ward.
Parish Office: Tel: 717-429-0370.
Res., 216 N. Mill St., 17970. Tel: 717-429-0701; Fax: 717-429-0630. [CEM]
School—St. Stephen Regional Catholic School, Port Carbon. See separate listing. Tel: 717-622-3063; Fax: 717-622-3689.

Schuylkill Haven, Schuylkill Co., St. Ambrose (1851), Revs. Michael J. Stone; Eric J. Gruber. In res., Rev. William F. Glosser.
Res., 201 Randel St., 17972. Tel: 717-385-1031; Fax: 717-385-1035. [CEM]
School—(Grades PreK-8) 302 Randel St., 17972. Tel: 717-385-2377; Fax: 717-385-2387. Mary Lou Michaels, Prin.
Lay Teachers 10; Students 210.
Catechesis/Religious Programs—Sr. Dolorita C.S.F.N., D.R.E.
Students 460.
Station—Schuylkill County Hospital and Home for Aged.

Shenandoah, Schuylkill Co.,

1—ANNUNCIATION, (1870), Revs. Edward J. O'Connor; James F. Gaffney.
Res., 218 W. Cherry St., 17976. Tel: 717-462-1916. [CEM]
School—Father Walter J. Ciszek Elementary School, Shenandoah. See separate listing. Tel: 717-462-9666.
Convent—229 W. Cherry St., 17976. Tel: 717-462-1024.

2—ST. CASIMIR, (Polish), Rev. Msgr. Edward W. Sarzynski.
Res., 108 W. Cherry St., 17976. Tel: 717-462-1968. [CEM]
School—St. Casimir-St. Stanislaus Regional Catholic Elementary School, Shenandoah. See separate listing.
Convent—233 N. Jardin St., 17976. Tel: 717-462-0877.

3—ST. GEORGE, (1891) (Lithuanian), Revs. Robert J. Potts; Peter A. Mushi, A.J.
Res., 129 S. Jardin St., 17976. Tel: 717-462-1989; Fax: 717-462-1980. [CEM 5]
School—Father Walter J. Ciszek Elementary School, Shenandoah. See separate listing.

4—HOLY FAMILY, (1870-1934). Closed. Records kept at Annunciation Church, Shenandoah.

5—OUR LADY OF MT. CARMEL, (1914) (Italian), Revs. Robert J. Potts; Peter A. Mushi, A.J.
Res., 129 S. Jardin St., 17976. Tel: 717-462-1989; Fax: 717-462-1980. [CEM]
School—Father Walter J. Ciszek Elementary School, Shenandoah. See separate listing.

6—ST. STANISLAUS, (Polish), Rev. Msgr. Edward W. Sarzynski.
Res., 108 W. Cherry St., 17976. Tel: 717-462-1968. [CEM]
School—Father Walter J. Ciszek Elementary School, Shenandoah. See separate listing.

7—ST. STEPHEN, (1899) (Slovak), Rev. Victor J. Anselmi.
Res., 18 E. Oak St., 17976. Tel: 717-462-0331; Fax: 717-462-1747. [CEM]
School—Father Walter J. Ciszek Elementary School, Shenandoah. See separate listing. Tel: 717-462-3927; Fax: 717-462-4603.
Catechesis/Religious Programs—Located at Fr. Ciszek School, Shenandoah.

Sheppton, Schuylkill Co., St. Joseph (1894), Rev. Raymond P. Slezak.
Res., E. Oak St., 18248. Tel: 717-384-4102; Fax: 717-384-4757. [CEM]
Mission—Oneida, Schuykill Co., St. John the Baptist, P.O. Box 118, 18248.

Shillington, Berks Co., St. John Baptist de la Salle (1948), Rev. Msgr. Thomas J. Birch, Pastor Emeritus; Revs. David C. Gillis; Kenneth A. Medve; John S. Pendzick; Deacon Sylvester F. Simchick. In res., Rev. Robert T. Finlan, Jr.
Res., 420 Holland St., 19607. Tel: 610-777-1697; Fax: 610-777-4468.
School—LaSalle Academy, Shillington. See separate listing.
Catechesis/Religious Programs—Bernadette H. Yohn, D.R.E.
Students 313.

Sinking Spring, Berks Co., St. Ignatius Loyola (1965), Rev. Msgr. James A. Treston, V.F.; Revs. Richard C. Brensinger; Francis J. McNelis; Deacons John A. Coffin; John W. Murphy, Jr.
Res., 2810 St. Alban's Dr., 19608-1028. Tel: 610-678-3767; Fax: 610-678-4483.
School—(Grades PreK-8). Tel: 610-678-0111; Fax: 610-670-5795. Mrs. Janice Bayerle, Prin.
Sisters of the Third Order of St. Francis 2; Lay Teachers 28; Students 609.
Catechesis/Religious Programs—2710 St. Alban's Dr., Reading, 19609. Tel: 610-678-0676.
Students 651.
Convent—2601 St. Alban's Dr., West Lawn, 19609. Tel: 610-678-2769.

Slatington, Lehigh Co., Assumption B.V.M. (1883). Unassigned.
Res., 633 W. Washington St., 18080. Tel: 610-767-2214; Fax: 610-767-2702. [CEM]
School—St. John Neumann Regional Catholic Elementary School, Palmerton-Slatington. See separate listing. Tel: 610-767-2935.
Catechesis/Religious Programs—Students 92.

Summit Hill, Carbon Co., St. Joseph (1850), Rev. James M. Torpey; Sr. Mary Florence, R.S.M., Pastoral Assoc.
Res., 118 N. Market St., 18250. Tel: 717-645-2664; Fax: 717-645-5655. [CEM]
School—Our Lady of the Valley Regional Catholic Elementary School, Lansford-Summit Hill. See separate listing.
Catechesis/Religious Programs—Students 68.

St. Stanislaus (1924) (Polish), Rev. James M. Torpey; Sr. Mary Florence, R.S.M., Pastoral Assoc.
Res., 118 N. Market St., 18250. Tel: 717-645-3037; Fax: 717-645-5655.
School—Our Lady of the Valley Regional Catholic Elementary School, Lansford-Summit Hill. See separate listing.

Tamaqua, Schuylkill Co., St. Jerome (1833), Revs. Robert R. Fagan; Henry E. Strassner. In res., Rev. William N. Seifert.
Res., 266 W. Broad St., 18252. Tel: 717-668-2301; Fax: 717-668-4406.
School—250 W. Broad St., 18252. Tel: 717-668-2757.
Sisters of the Immaculate Heart of Mary 2; Lay Teachers 8; Students 219.
Catechesis/Religious Programs—Tel: 717-668-4416.
Students 208.
Convent—Tel: 717-668-2730.
Mission—Coaldale, Schuylkill Co., St. Patrick (Seek), Miner St., Coaldale, 18218. [CEM][JC 2]

SS. Peter and Paul (1911) (Lithuanian), Rev. William J. Linkchorst.
Res., 307 Pine St., 18252. Tel: 717-668-1150; Fax: 717-668-1150. [CEM]
Catechesis/Religious Programs—Students 154.

Tower City, Schuylkill Co., SS. Peter and Paul (1896), Rev. Francis J. Opps.
Res., 825 E. Grand Ave., 17980. Tel: 717-647-9472.
School—St. Elizabeth Ann Seton Regional Catholic Elementary School, Minersville. See separate listing.
Catechesis/Religious Programs—Students 97.

Tremont, Schuylkill Co., Immaculate Conception (1853), Rev. James R. Brady; Deacon William Ahrensfield.
Res., 113 Clay St., P.O. Box 35, 17981. Tel: 717-695-3648. [CEM]
School—Good Shepherd Regional School, (Grades PreK-3) 538 Sunbury St., Minersville, 17954. Tel: 717-544-4560.
(Grades 4-8) 301 St. Francis St., Minersville, 17954. Tel: 717-544-3766. Ms. Rosalie Novack, Prin.
Catechesis/Religious Programs—Ann Starr, D.R.E.
Students 113.

Tresckow, Carbon Co., St. Bartholomew (1917) (Italian), Rev. John L. Ondic.
Res., 49 E. Maple St., P.O. Box 238, 18254-0238. Tel: 717-455-0922.
School—McAdoo Regional Catholic Elementary School, McAdoo. See separate listing. 717-929-1442. Tel: 717-929-3016.

St. Michael (1908), Rev. John L. Ondic.
Res., 18 S. Chestnut St., 18254. Tel: 717-454-2802; Fax: 717-454-1765. [CEM]
School—McAdoo Regional Catholic Elementary School, McAdoo. See separate listing. Tel: 717-929-1442; Fax: 717-929-3016.

Tuscarora, Schuylkill Co., St. Bertha (1922), Rev. Francis M. Grundowski; Deacon Leo F. Keenan.
Res., 214 Green St., Brockton, 17925. Tel: 717-668-1500. [CEM]
Church—710 Broad St., P.O. Box 245, 17982. Tel: 717-668-4465.
School—St. Jerome Regional Catholic Elementary School, Tamaqua. See separate listing.

Weatherly, Carbon Co., St. Nicholas (1874), Rev. William J. Onushco; Deacon Raymond W. Wilkinson.
Res., 318 Plane St., 18255. Tel: 717-427-4123; Fax: 717-427-4615. [CEM 2][JC]
School—McAdoo Regional Catholic Elementary School, McAdoo. See separate listing. Tel: 717-929-1442.
Catechesis/Religious Programs—Students 76.
Station—Weatherwood, Carbon County District Home, Tel: 717-427-8683.

West Bangor, Northampton Co., St. Roch (1937), Rev. Msgr. Charles T. Moss. In res., Rev. Joseph A. DeSantis.
Res., 1141 Verona Dr., Pen Argyl, 18072. Tel: 610-863-9055; Fax: 610-863-5971. [CEM]

School—Immaculate Conception Regional Catholic Elementary School, Pen Argyl. See separate listing. Tel: 610-863-4876.

West Reading, Berks Co., Sacred Heart (1917) (German), Rev. Msgr. James J. Reichert; Revs. Joseph J. Whalen; David J. Fick; E. Jerry Yoder, Business Admin.; Deacon William R. Kase.
Res., Lakeview Dr. and Cherry St., P.O. Box 6217, Reading, 19610. Tel: 610-372-4010; Fax: 610-372-4926.
School—701 Franklin St., 19611. Tel: 610-373-3316. Dr. Richard Flannery, Prin.
Lay Teachers 11; Students 208.
Catechesis/Religious Programs—Tel: 610-374-5430. Valerie Christo, D.R.E.
Students 235.

Whitehall, Lehigh Co., Holy Trinity (1928), Rev. Msgr. Ronald W. Gainer; Rev. Msgr. Stanley T. Sosnowski; Deacon Eugene J. Wyrwa.
Res., 4102 S. Church St., 18052. Tel: 610-262-9315.
School—Christ the King Regional Catholic Elementary School, Coplay, Whitehall. See separate listing.
Catechesis/Religious Programs—Mrs. Carole C. Chuk, D.R.E.
Students 262.

St. Elizabeth (1941), Rev. Msgr. Anthony D. Muntone, V.G.; Revs. Victor F. Finelli; Joseph J. Kweder; Deacon Alexander L. Maggitti, Sr.
Res., 618 Fullerton Ave., 18052. Tel: 610-266-0695; Fax: 610-266-1548.
School—(Grades PreK-8) 431 Pershing Blvd., 18052. Tel: 610-264-0143. Sr. Helen Ann Sharkey, R.S.M., Prin.
Sisters of Mercy 1; Lay Teachers 11; Students 269.
Catechesis/Religious Programs—Mrs. Carol O'Connor, D.R.E.
Students 181.

St. John the Baptist (1927), Rev. Francis J. Schuster, K.H.S.
Res., 3024 S. Ruch St., 18052. Tel: 610-262-2260; Fax: 610-262-1935. [CEM]
School—Christ the King Regional Catholic Elementary School, Coplay, Whitehall. See separate listing.
Catechesis/Religious Programs—Tel: 610-262-4177. Sr. Mary Dolora, D.R.E.
Students 69.

Chaplains of Public Institutions

ALLENTOWN. *Good Shepherd Home*. (St. Paul).
Lehigh County Prison. (Sacred Heart).
Lehigh Valley Hospital at 17th St. (St. Catharine of Siena).
Lehigh Valley Hospital at Cedar Crest. (St. Thomas More). Rev. Joseph P. Becker, O.S.F.S.; Deacon Richard B. Close.
Liberty Nursing Center. (St. Catharine of Siena).
Luthercrest. (St. Joseph, Orefield).
Osteopathic Hospital. (St. Catharine of Siena).
Phoebe Devitt Home. (St. Catharine of Siena).
State Hospital. (Our Lady Help of Christians).
Westminster Village. (Our Lady Help of Christians).

ASHLAND. *Ashland State Hospital*. Administered by St. Mauritius, Ashland; St. Joseph, Ashland; St. Joseph, Girardville; St. Vincent de Paul, Girardville.

BETHLEHEM. *Leader Nursing & Rehab Centers*. (Notre Dame of Bethlehem).
Lutheran Manor. (Notre Dame of Bethlehem).
Muhlenberg Medical Center. (Notre Dame of Bethlehem).
Muhlenberg Rehab Center. (Notre Dame of Bethlehem).

COALDALE. *Coaldale State Hospital*. Administered by SS. Cyril & Methodius, Coaldale; St. Michael, Lansford; St. Stanislaus, Summit Hill; SS. Peter and Paul, Lansford. Rev. Paul E. Masiar.

EASTON. *Easton Hospital*. (Priests of Easton Area).
Northampton County Prison. (St. Bernard). Deacon Robert W. Rodgers.

FOUNTAIN HILL. *Cedarbrook*. (Lehigh County Home) St. Ursula.

FRACKVILLE. *State Prison*. Rev. Ronald P. Bowman.

HAMBURG. *Hamburg State School and Hospital*. (St. Mary).

LEHIGHTON. *Gnaden Huetten Memorial Hospital*. (SS. Peter and Paul).
Gnaden Huetten Nursing Home. (SS. Peter & Paul).
Mahoning Valley Nursing Home. (SS. Peter & Paul).

MINERSVILLE. *FCI-Schuylkill, Federal Correctional Institute*. Rev. Charles J. Dene.

NAZARETH. *Gracedale*. (Northampton County Home) Holy Family. Deacon Michael P. McGouldrick.

NEW TRIPOLI. *Zimmerman Country Homestead*. (St. Joseph, Orefield).

ORWIGSBURG. *Orwigsburg Manor*. (St. Ambrose, Schuylkill Haven).

PALMERTON. *Palmerton Hospital*. (Sacred Heart).

PINEBROOK. *Personal Care Center*. (St. Ambrose, Schuylkill Haven).

POTTSVILLE. *Leader Nursing Home*. (Mary, Queen of Peace).
Pottsville Hospital and Warne Clinic. Sr. Marjorie S.S.J., Chap.
Schuylkill County Prison. (Mary, Queen of Peace).

READING. *Community Hospital*. (St. Peter).
Reading Hospital. (Sacred Heart). Deacon John P. Konopelski.

SCHUYLKILL HAVEN. *Rest Haven County Home*. (St. Ambrose).

TREXLERTOWN. *Mosser Nursing Home*. (St. Joseph, Orefield).

WEATHERWOOD. *Carbon County District Home*. (St. Nicholas, Weatherly).

WERNERSVILLE. *Berks County Prison*. (St. Ignatius Loyola, Reading; St. Joseph, Reading; St. Peter, Reading).
Berksheim. (Berks County Home; St. Ignatius Loyola, Reading).
State Hospital. Deacons Richard A. Horst; John J. Allison.

WESCOSVILLE. *Lehigh County Home*. (Cedarbrook) St. Catharine of Siena, Allentown.

Special Assignment:
Reverend Fathers—
Schlert, Alfred A., Bishop's Residence, 2920 Chew St., Allentown, PA 18104

On Duty Outside the Diocese:
Reverend Monsignors—
Bartkus, Algimantas A., Pontificio Collegio Lituano, Via Casal Monferrato, Rome, 00182 Italy
Benestad, Thomas J., The Papal Foundation, 222 N. 17th St., Philadelphia, PA 19103
Callaghan, Aloysius R., Moderator of the Curia & Chancellor, Archdiocese for the Military Services, P.O. Box 4469, Washington, DC 20017-0469
Reverend Fathers—
Baker, William T., Casilla 919, Santa Cruz, Bolivia
Beers, John Michael, S.S.L., Ph.D., Mt. St. Mary's Seminary, Emmitsburg, MD 21727-7797
Donahue, Edward J., Bishop Moore High School, 3901 Edgewater Dr., Orlando, FL 32804
Fanti, Joseph J.
Henry, Donald H., St. John the Evangelist, 10631 Regent Circle, Naples, FL 33942

Military Chaplains:
Reverend Fathers—
Connolly, James M., Chaplain's Office, Code 004, 4755 Pasture Rd., Fallon, NV 89496
Czartorynski, David F., 2730 Eagle Dr., Tyndall AFB, FL 32403
Thomas, James J., Chap. Lt. Col., PSC, Box 3226, Altus AFB, OK 73523

Unassigned:
Reverend Fathers—
Bender, Thomas J.
Conte, John P.
Czaus, Joseph C.
Galko, Joseph
Kean, Joseph H.
Kerestus, Thomas J.
Soderlund, David

Retired:
Reverend Monsignors—
Birch, Thomas J., 1315 Penn Forest Streams, Jim Thorpe, PA, 18229
Coll, Robert J., P.O. Box 1363, Marco, FL 34145
Messaros, Michael F., Fairways at Brookside, 2866 Whitemarsh Pl., Macungie, PA 18062
Seitzinger, John P., 122 W. 17th St., Ocean City, NJ 08226
Reverend Fathers—
Barnes, Joseph A., Holy Family Villa, 1325 Prospect Ave., Bethlehem, PA 18018
Briggman, Michael J., Holy Family Villa, 1325 Prospect Ave., Bethlehem, PA 18018
Carr, James M., Holy Family Villa, 1325 Prospect Ave., Bethlehem, PA 18018
Carroll, Joseph D., Holy Family Villa, 1325 Prospect Ave., Bethlehem, PA 18018
Edwards, Thomas L., Holy Family Villa, 1325 Prospect Ave., Bethlehem, PA 18018
Flynn, Stephen F.X., Holy Family Manor, 1200 Spring St., Bethlehem, PA 18018
Fox, Francis J., 331 Florida Ave., Whitehall, PA 18052
Graff, Edward R., P.O. Box 47, Silverton, TX 79257
Horan, Thomas A., 125 E. Main St., Girardville, PA 17935
Jones, William P., Holy Family Villa, 1325 Prospect Ave., Bethlehem, PA 18018
McKenna, F. Charles, Holy Family Villa, 1325 Prospect Ave., Bethlehem, PA 18018
McNulty, Charles L., Holy Family Villa, 1325 Prospect Ave., Bethlehem, PA 18018
Nave, Francis R., Holy Family Villa, 1325 Prospect Ave., Bethlehem, PA 18018
Paskowicz, Marian, 611 Caroline Dr., Norristown, PA 19401
Rapczynski, Joseph B., Holy Family Villa, 1325 Prospect Ave., Bethlehem, PA 18018
Sheridan, John F., Precious Blood Convent, P.O. Box 97, Reading, PA 19607
Sverchek, Michael P., 70 W. Juniper St., Box 301, Hazleton, PA 18201
Sweeney, James E., 1817 First St., Miller Heights, PA 18017
Vandergeest, Peter J., 1008 Hemlock Pl., Huntington Valley, PA 19006
Welkie, Paul P., Lake Hauto, R.R.1 Lake Dr., P.O. Box 34, Nesquehoning, PA 18240-0034

Permanent Deacons:
Ahrensfield, William L., Immaculate Conception, Tremont
Allison, John J., Wernersville State Hospital & SS. Cyril and Methodius, Reading
Alvarado, Leopoldo, Spanish Apostolate, Berks County & St. Peter, Reading
Amedeo, Dominick F., Sacred Heart & Our Lady of Mt. Carmel, Allentown
Andrusisian, Stephen, Mary, Queen of Peace, Pottsville
Bankos, Gregory J., Assumption B.V.M., Northampton, St. Andrew, Catasauqua, & Pro-Life Office, Bethlehem
Bogusky, Joseph H., Annunciation B.V.M., Catasauqua
Buragino, Joseph G., St. Ursula, Bethlehem
Burda, Joseph R., St. Joseph, Frackville
Cain, Leonard, St. Francis de Sales, Robesonia
Centeno, Jesus, Spanish Apostolate, Berks Co. & St. Peter, Reading
Chiles, Franklin J., Holy Ghost, Bethlehem
Chin-Fatt, Arthur L., St. Francis of Assisi, Allentown
Close, Richard B., Lehigh Valley Hospital Center, Allentown & St. Ann, Emmaus
Coffin, John A., St. Ignatius Loyola, Sinking Spring
Colon, Francisco, Hispanic Apostolate, Berks Co. & St. Peter, Reading
Colon, Julio, Hispanic Apostolate, Berks Co. & St. Peter, Reading
Cosgrove, Francis J., Office of the Permanent Diaconate & St. Anne, Bethlehem
Costa, Joseph J., Our Lady of Siluva, Gilberton
Coyle, Charles A., Our Lady Help of Christians, Allentown
Cuevas, Rafael, Spanish Apostolate, Northampton Co. & Holy Infancy, Bethlehem
Cummings, John D., Tribunal, Allentown
Danyi, Frank J., SS. Cyril and Methodius, Bethlehem
de Bellis, Charles A., St. Anthony of Padua, Easton
de Jesus, Jaime, Hispanic Apostolate, Lehigh Co. & Sacred Heart of Jesus, Allentown
de Jesus, Roberto, Spanish Apostolate, Northampton County & Holy Infancy, Bethlehem
Dudeck, Larry, Holy Rosary, Reading
Duncan, James R., Diocesan Tribunal & St. Thomas More, Allentown
Faller, George J., St. Catharine of Siena, Mt. Penn
Fessler, Lawrence J., Immaculate Conception, Birdsboro
Fleck, Henry, Jr., St. Bernard, Easton
Giltrap, James F., St. Joseph, Limeport
Godiska, Joseph F., Our Lady of Hungary, Northampton
Gonzalez, Jose, Spanish Apostolate, Lehigh Co. & Sacred Heart, Allentown
Gordon, Henry G., St. Mary, Hamburg
Gousie, Joseph N., Sr., St. Joseph, Reading
Horst, Richard A., St. Catharine of Siena, Reading & Wernersville State Hospital, Wernersville
Hunkele, Thomas H., Precious Blood Convent, Shillington
Jaccodine, Ralph J., St. Catharine of Siena, Allentown
Kase, William R., Holy Name High School, Reading & Sacred Heart, West Reading
Keenan, Leo F., Jr., St. Bertha, Tuscarora & St. Bartholomew, Brockton
Konopelski, John P., Reading Hospital & St. Margaret, Reading
Koval, Edward P., State Correctional Facility, Frackville & St. Canicus and St. Fidelis, Mahanoy City
Lafata, Peter M., St. Joseph, Reading
Laroche, Michael J., St. Peter, Coplay
Maggitti, Alexander L., Sr., St. Elizabeth, Whitehall & St. Francis Center, Orwigsburg
Matos, Rodoberto, Spanish Apostolate, Northampton Co. & Holy Infancy, Bethlehem; St. Bernard, Easton
McGouldirck, Michael P., Gracedale County Home

& Holy Family, Nazareth
McManus, Robert J., St. Mauritius & St. Joseph, Ashland
McShane, Hugh E., Sacred Heart, Miller Heights
Metzker, Daniel F., Cathedral, Allentown; St. Joseph the Worker, Orefield
Mihalik, Andrew J., Jr., Sacred Heart, Palmerton
Monahan, Brian, Immaculate Conception, Allentown
Morales, Edison, Hispanic Apostolate, Northampton Co. & Holy Infancy, Bethlehem
Murphy, John W., Jr., St. Ignatius Loyola, Sinking Spring; "The A.D. Times," Allentown
Murphy, Thomas J., Most Blessed Sacrament & St. Francis Academy, Bally
Pitts, William P., Sacred Heart, Palmerton
Pogash, John F., SS. Peter and Paul & St. Mary, St. Clair
Quiles, Victor M., Hispanic Apostolate, Lehigh Co. & Sacred Heart of Jesus, Allentown
Reichard, Thomas C., St. Bernard & St. Michael, Easton
Rodgers, Robert W., St. Jane Frances de Chantal, Wilson Borough
Rodriguez, Nicasio, Spanish Apostolate, Northampton Co. & Holy Infancy, Bethlehem
Roos, Carl J.
Roth, Cyril A., St. Barbara & St. Francis of Assisi, Minersville
Salabsky, Bernard J., Jr., Our Lady of Perpetual Help, Bethlehem
Scrak, Richard G., Catholic Social Agency, Ecumenical Soup Kitchen, Allentown & St. Anne, Bethlehem
Setlock, John A., Annunciation & St. Ann, Frackville
Sewald, Richard T., Notre Dame of Bethlehem, Bethlehem
Simchick, Sylvester, St. John Baptist de la Salle, Shillington
Solis, Alfonso D., Hispanic Apostolate, Lehigh Co. & Sacred Heart, Allentown
Thomson, Daniel, Good Shepherd Home and Rehabilitation Hospital & St. Paul, Allentown
Torres, Fernando L., Hispanic Apostolate, Berks Co. & St. Peter, Reading
Torres, Mariano, Spanish Apostolate, Berks Co. & St. Peter, Reading
Tyson, Robert J., St. Thomas More, Allentown
Visot, Luis R., St. John the Baptist, Pottsville
VonLeer, Lemuel, Catholic Social Agency, Allentown & Notre Dame, Bethlehem
Wagner, William J., S.S. Peter and Paul, Lehighton
Wilkinson, Raymond, St. Nicholas, Weatherly
Wisser, Bernard M., Family Life Bureau & Assumption B.V.M., Colesville
Wyrwa, Eugene, Holy Trinity, Whitehall; Diocesan Tribunal, Allentown

INSTITUTIONS LOCATED IN THE DIOCESE

[A] SEMINARIES, RELIGIOUS OR SCHOLASTICATES

CENTER VALLEY. *Missionaries of the Sacred Heart*, 3300 Station Ave., P.O. Box 9, 18034-0009. Tel: 610-282-1415; Fax: 610-282-0610. Revs. Anthony Ripp, M.S.C., Supr.; Raymond Costello, M.S.C.; Jacob Welle, M.S.C.; E. Michael Camilli, M.S.C.; Michael Vasti, M.S.C.; Stephen Geusic, M.S.C.; Henry Einhaus, M.S.C.; Bros. Lawrence Viele, M.S.C.; Richard Kuhl, M.S.C.

NORTHAMPTON. *Mary Immaculate Seminary*, 300 Cherryville Rd., Box 27, 18067-0027. Tel: 610-262-7866; Fax: 610-262-6766. Conducted by the Archdiocese of Philadelphia as a seminary for the Spirituality Year Program for the seminarians and for the ongoing formation of priests, and as a house of prayer and retreat for priests, religious, and laity. Rev. Thomas M. Mullin, M.Div., M.A., S.S.L., Dir. for Continuing Formation of Diocesan Priests, Spirituality Year Program. Tel: 610-262-9674. Revs. John M. Savinski, M.Div., M.A., Dir.; Edward L. Warnken, M.Div., M.A.; Peter J. Welsh, M.Div., Ph.D., Assoc., Vincentian Community in Residence. Tel: 610-262-7530; 262-7589; Fax: 610-262-7490. Bro. John P. McErlean, F.S.C., Retreat Admin.

WERNERSVILLE. *Novitiate of St. Isaac Jogues*, 19565. Tel: 610-678-8085; Fax: 610-678-8747. Very Rev. William F. Gavin, S.J., Rector; Rev. John T. McCaslin, S.J., Admin.; Mr. Joseph Rodolff, Treas. In res. Revs. George A. Aschenbrenner, S.J.; John P. Barron, S.J.; James A. Borbely, S.J.; Frederick A. Brew, S.J.; Ralph C. Campbell, S.J.; Gerald J. Fitzpatrick, S.J.; William F. Graham, S.J.; Joseph B. Hanzely, S.J.; Harold J. Hocking, S.J.; John J. Keenan, S.J.; Thomas J. Kuller, S.J.; Thomas J. Linsky, S.J.; Clarence A. Martin, S.J.; Robert J. McAllister, S.J.; Richard W. Norman, S.J.; Frank Mc G.A. Nugent, S.J.; Eugene J. Power, S.J.; Burton Proctor, S.J.; Edwin J. Sanders, S.J.; William E. Schaffner; D. Gilbert Sweeney, S.J.; Edward J. Tinney, S.J.; Francis A. Wallner, S.J.; Robert J. Whalen, S.J.; George S. Williams, S.J. Brothers 2.

[B] COLLEGES AND UNIVERSITIES

CENTER VALLEY. *Allentown College of St. Francis de Sales*, 2755 Station Ave., 18034-9568. Tel: 610-282-1100
For a complete listing, refer to the Colleges and Universities section.

READING. *Alvernia College*, 19607. Tel: 610-796-8200; Fax: 610-777-6632
For a complete listing, refer to the Colleges and Universities section.

[C] HIGH SCHOOLS, DIOCESAN

ALLENTOWN. *Allentown Central Catholic High School*, 301 N. Fourth St., 18102-3098. Tel: 610-437-4601. Rev. Msgr. Joseph R. Sobiesiak, Dir.; Mr. James M. Hodrick, M.Ed., Prin.; Mr. William F. Tielman, Vice Prin.; Rev. Msgr. Francis C. Revak; Revs. Peter J. Hosak, (Byzantine); Donald J. Schaible; John A. Krivak; George R. Winne. Priests 5; Sisters 3; Lay Teachers 46; Students 880.

ASHLAND. *Cardinal Brennan Jr./Sr. High School*, 130 Academy Ln., 17921. Tel: 717-874-3921. Rev. Frans Berkhout, Prin.; Mr. Daniel T. Demczko, Vice Prin.; Revs. David J. Kozak; Anthony P. Mongiello, Dir. of Spiritual Activities; James Betchel; Lawrence J. Bukaty. Lay Teachers 25; Students 258.

BANGOR. *Pius X High School*, 580 Third Ave., 18013-1399. Tel: 610-588-3291. Mr. Leonard D. Litzi, Jr., Prin.; Revs. Joseph A. DeSantis, Asst. Prin.; Wayne E. Killian, Dir. Spiritual Activities. Priests 2; Lay Teachers 18; Students 284.

BETHLEHEM. *Bethlehem Catholic High School*, 2133 Madison Ave., 18017-4699. Tel: 610-866-0791. Founded as two-year commercial high school, 1897. Founded as four-year comprehensive high school, 1925. Mr. Richard B. Culver, M.Ed., Prin.; Sr. Marjorie Keenan, S.S.J., Vice Prin.; Mr. Richard F. Mazza, Dir. Studies; Revs. Andrew R. Baker; Stephen L. Maco, Dir. Spiritual Activities; Bernard J. Ezaki. Sisters of St. Joseph 5; Lay Teachers 41; Students 845.

EASTON. *Notre Dame High School*, 3417 Church Rd., 18042. Tel: 610-868-1431. Mr. Joseph R. Kramer, Prin.; Rev. Thomas J. Kessler. Priests 1; Sisters 7; Lay Teachers 28; Students 501.

POTTSVILLE. *Nativity B.V.M. High School*, One Lawtons Hill, 17901. Tel: 717-622-8110. Rev. Msgr. Ronald C. Bocian; Revs. Bernard A. Flanagan; Ronald V. Jankaitis. Sisters 4; Lay Teachers 19; Students 293.

READING. *Holy Name High School*, 955 E. Wyomissing Blvd., 19611. Tel: 610-374-8361. Sr. Joseph Eleanor Murphy, I.H.M., Prin.; Deacon William R. Kase, Vice Prin.; Revs. Thomas J. Orsulak, Dir. of Spiritual Activities; Robert T. Finlan. Priests 2; Brothers 1; Sisters 3; Lay Teachers 26; Students 400.

Reading Central Catholic High School (Monsignor Bornemann Memorial), 1400 Hill Rd., 19602-1499. Tel: 610-373-4178. Mr. Vincent T. Shemanski, Prin.; Revs. Donald W. Cieniewicz, Vice Prin.; Patrick H. Lamb, O.F.M., Dir. Spiritual Activities. Priests 2; Sisters 11; Lay Teachers 17; Administrators 2; Students 452.

TAMAQUA. *Marian Catholic High School*, R.D. 4, Box 446, 18252. Tel: 717-467-3335; Fax: 717-467-0186. Mr. John P. Malarkey, Prin.; Revs. Robert J. Kuzmann, Vice Prin.; William Seifert; Paul G. Puza. Priests 2; Servants of the Immaculate Heart of Mary 2; Lay Teachers 27; Students 407.

[D] REGIONAL CATHOLIC ELEMENTARY SCHOOLS, DIOCESAN

ALLENTOWN. *Holy Spirit School*. Serving St. John the Baptist, Immaculate Conception, SS. Peter and Paul, Allentown. Enrollment 210 (Grades PreK-8).
Primary School. (Grades PreK-3), Front St. & Bridge St., 18102. Tel: 610-820-0220.
Middle School. (Grades 4-8), 508 Ridge Ave., 18102. Tel: 610-434-4044. Sr. Catherine Ortwein, S.S.J., Prin. Tel: 610-434-4044.
Sacred Heart School, 325 N. Fourth St., 18102. Tel: 610-437-3031. Mr. James Krupka, Prin. Lay Teachers 10; Students 210.
Serving Sacred Heart, Our Lady of Mt. Carmel, St. Stephen, Allentown.

BALLY. *St. Francis Academy*, 668 Pine St., 19503. Tel: 610-845-7364. Deacon Thomas J. Murphy, Prin. Lay Teachers 10; Students 250.
Serving Most Blessed Sacrament, Bally, and St. Columbkill, Boyertown.

BETHLEHEM. *Holy Child School*. (Grades K-8), 1301 Sioux St., 18015. Tel: 610-865-0861. Sr. Marie John Holland, O.S.F., Prin. Sisters 2; Lay Teachers 9; Students 240.
Serving Holy Ghost, St. Ursula, Bethlehem.
St. Michael the Archangel School. Primary Bldg. & Main Office. (Grades K-4), St. Joseph's Rd., Limeport, 18060. Tel: 610-965-4441. Middle School. (Grades PreK & 5-8), 4121 Old Bethlehem Pike, 18015. Tel: 610-867-8422. Carol Sonon, Prin. Priests 2; Lay Teachers 14; Students 328.
Serving Assumption B.V.M., Colesville; St. Joseph, Limeport.
SS. Cyril and Methodius Regional Catholic Elementary School. (Grades PreK-8), 551 Thomas St., 18015. Tel: 610-866-0042. Mrs. Joan M. West, Prin. Lay Teachers 10; Students 145.
Serving SS. Cyril and Methodius, St. Joseph, St. John Capistrano, Our Lady of Pompeii, St. Stanislaus.

EASTON. *Easton Catholic Elementary School*. (Grades K-3), Primary Bldg., 283 W. St. Joseph St., 18042. Tel: 610-253-0651. Middle Bldg. (Grades 4-8), 841 Washington St., 18042. Tel: 610-252-1393. Mary Frances Haluska, Prin. Lay Teachers 12; Students 204.
Serving St. Anthony, St. Joseph, St. Michael, St. Bernard.

FRACKVILLE. *Holy Family School*. (Grades PreK-6), 29 S. Broad Mountain Ave., 17931. Tel: 717-874-0285. Mr. Paul T. Coombe, Prin. Sisters 3; Lay Teachers 6; Students 167.
Serving Annunciation, B.V.M., St. Joseph, St. Ann.

GIRARDVILLE. *Immaculate Heart Elementary School*. (Grades PreK-8), Main St. & Richard St., 17935. Tel: 717-276-6568. Sr. Helene Joseph Kollar, I.H.M., Prin. Religious 2; Lay Teachers 8; Students 230.
Serving St. Joseph, St. Mauritius, Ashland; St. Joseph, St. Vincent, Girardville; Our Lady of Good Counsel, Gordon.

JIM THORPE. *St. Joseph Regional Academy*. (Grades K-8), Sixth St. & School St., 18229. Tel: 717-325-3186. Sr. Maria Electa Schulz, S.C.C., Prin. Sisters 2; Lay Teachers 9; Students 213.
Serving St. Joseph, Immaculate Conception and St. Peter the Fisherman.

LANSFORD. *St. Michael School*. (Grades PreK-8), 123 E. Water St., 18232. Tel: 717-645-7170. Miss Susan M. Klinger, Prin. Students 225.
Serving St. Michael, SS. Peter and Paul, Lansford; SS. Cyril and Methodius, St. John the Baptist, St. Mary of the Assumption, Coaldale.

LANSFORD-SUMMIT HILL. *Our Lady of the Valley School*. (Grades K-4), 118 W. Ludlow St., 18250. Tel: 717-645-4700. (Grades 5-8), 30 E. Bertsch St., 18232. Tel: 717-645-7101. Sr. Susan Joseph, I.H.M., Prin. Sisters 1; Lay Teachers 9; Students 172.
Serving St. Joseph, St. Stanislaus, Summit Hill; St. Ann, Lansford; Immaculate Conception, Our Lady of Mt. Carmel, Sacred Heart, Nesquehoning.

MAHANOY CITY. *Mahanoy City Catholic Elementary School*. (Grades K-8), S. Catawissa St. & Pine St., 17948. Tel: 717-773-2668. Sr. Anna Mae, O.S.F., Prin. Religious 1; Lay Teachers 7; Students 95.
Serving Assumption B.V.M., Sacred Heart, St. Canicus, St. Casimir, St. Fidelis, St. Joseph, Our Lady of Silva, St. Richard, and St. Mary Byzantine.

MCADOO. *McAdoo Catholic Elementary School*. (Grades K-8), 35 N. Cleveland St., 18237. Tel: 717-929-1442. Sr. Anne Francine Windle, I.H.M., Prin. Sisters 3; Lay Teachers 9; Students 199.
Serving St. Patrick, St. Kunegunda, St. Mary, McAdoo; St. Bartholomew, St. Michael, Tresckow; Immaculate Conception, Kelayres; St. Nicholas, Weatherly; St. Mary, Beaver Meadows.

MINERSVILLE. *Good Shepherd Regional School*. (Grades PreK-3). No longer Holy Redeemer Regional Catholic Elementary School. Merged to form Good Shepherd Regional School, Minersville. 538 Sunbury St., 17954. Tel: 717-544-4360. (Grades 4-8), 301 Heffner St., 17954. Tel: 717-544-3766. Ms. Rosalie Novack, Prin. Sisters 1; Lay Teachers 10; Students 196.
Serving St. Kieran, Heckscherville; St. Mary, Star of the Sea, Branchdale; Sacred Heart, Newtown; Immaculate Conception, Tremont; SS. Peter and Paul, Tower City; St. Barbara, St. Francis of Assisi, St. Stanislaus Kostka, St. Vincent de Paul, Our Lady of Mt. Carmel, Minersville.

NEW PHILADELPHIA. *Holy Cross Elementary School*. (Grades K-8), 37 Clay St., 17959. Tel: 717-277-0197. Mrs. Dolores Bartashus, Prin. Lay Teachers 6; Students 84.
Serving Holy Family, Sacred Heart, New Philadelphia; St. Anthony, Cumbola.

NORTHAMPTON. *Our Lady of Hungary Regional School*, 1300 Newport Ave., 18067. Tel: 610-262-9171. Mrs. Barbara J. Sullivan, M.Ed., Prin. Sisters 3; Lay Teachers 16; Students 375.
Serving Our Lady of Hungary, Assumption B.V.M., St. Michael, Northampton; St. Lawrence and St.

Andrew, Catasauqua.

PALMERTON-SLATINGTON. *St. John Neumann Regional School.* (Grades K-3), 641-645 W. Washington St., Slatington, 18080. Tel: 610-767-2935. (Grades 4-8), 259 Lafayette Ave., Palmerton, 18071. Tel: 610-826-2354. Mrs. Mary Ellen Chuss-Mirro, M.Ed., Prin. Lay Teachers 9; Students 168.
Serving St. Nicholas, Berlinsville; Sacred Heart, Palmerton; Assumption B.V.M., Slatington.

PEN ARGYL. *Immaculate Conception School.* (Grades K-6), Babbitt Ave. & Heller Ave., 18072. Tel: 610-863-4816. Sr. Maria Evelyn, O.P., Prin. Sisters 6; Lay Teachers 2; Students 152.
Serving St. Elizabeth, Pen Argyl; St. Rocco, Martins Creek; St. Roch, West Bangor.

PORT CARBON. *St. Stephen Regional School.* (Grades PreK-8), 214 Valley St., 17965. Tel: 717-622-3063. Sr. Mary Anne Hoesle, I.H.M., Prin. Sisters 5; Lay Teachers 10; Students 204.
Serving the following parishes: St. Stephen, St. Mary, Immaculate Conception & St. Casimir, Port Carbon; Ss. Peter & Paul & St. Boniface, St. Clair.

POTTSVILLE. *All Saints Elementary School.* (Grades K-8), 112 S. Seventh St., 17901. Tel: 717-622-0106; 622-1765. Sr. Mary Jane Hahner, C.S.F.N., Prin.
Serving St. Patrick, St. John the Baptist, Mary, Queen of Peace, St. Joseph and St. Francis. Sisters 1; Lay Teachers 17; Students 279.

Little Saints Preschool, 2051 W. Norwegian St., 17901. Tel: 717-622-1073. Sr. M. Leonore, S.S.J., Dir. Sisters 1; Lay Teachers 1; Students 50.
Serving the Pottsville area.

READING. *St. Catharine of Siena School*, 2330 Perkiomen Ave., 19606. Tel: 610-779-5810. Sr. Mary Ellen Tennity, I.H.M., Prin. Sisters 4; Lay Teachers 20; Students 537.
Serving St. Catharine of Siena, Reading, and Immaculate Conception, Birdsboro.

ROSETO. *Our Lady of Mt. Carmel School*, 80 Ridge St., 18013. Tel: 610-588-2629. Sr. Maria Pilar, O.P., Prin.; Dorothy Ruggiero, Asst. Prin. Lay Teachers 10; Students 232.
Serving Our Lady of Mt. Carmel, Roseto, and Our Lady of Good Counsel, Bangor.

SHENANDOAH. *Father Walter J. Ciszek Elementary School.* (Grades PreK-6), 233 W. Cherry St., 17976. Tel: 717-462-3927. Sr. Barbara Ann Browne, I.H.M., Prin. Sisters 1; Lay Teachers 9; Students 260.
Serving Annunciation, St. Casimir, St. George, Our Lady of Mt. Carmel, St. Stanislaus, St. Stephen, Shenandoah; St. Mary Magdalen, Lost Creek; St. Mary, Ringtown.

SHILLINGTON. *La Salle Academy and Early Childhood Center.* (Grades PreK-8), 440 Holland St., 19607. Tel: 610-777-7392. Miss Geraldine M. Williams, M.Ed., Prin. Lay Teachers 25; Students 402.
Serving St. John Baptist de La Salle, Shillington; St. Benedict, Plowville; St. Anthony, Millmont.

SINKING SPRING. *St. Ignatius Loyola School.* (Grades PreK-8), 2700 St. Alban's Dr., 19609. Tel: 610-678-0111. Mrs. Janice E. Bayerle, Prin. Sisters 2; Lay Teachers 27; Students 609.
Serving St. Ignatius Loyola, Sinking Spring; St. Francis de Sales, Robesonia.

TAMAQUA. *St. Jerome Regional School*, 250 W. Broad St., 18252. Tel: 717-668-2757. Sr. Honora Marie Johnston, I.H.M., Prin. Sisters 3; Lay Teachers 8; Students 221.
Serving St. Jerome, SS. Peter and Paul, Tamaqua; St. Bartholomew, Brockton; St. Bertha, Tuscarora.

WHITEHALL. *Christ the King School*, Primary Bldg., 3008 Ruch St., 18052. Tel: 610-262-4177. Middle Bldg., 22 S. Fifth St., Coplay, 18037. Tel: 610-262-5822. Dr. Mary C. Grosse, Prin. Lay Teachers 13; Students 340.

Preschool, 40 S. Fifth St., Coplay, 18037. Tel: 610-262-4064.
Serving St. Peter, Coplay; St. John the Baptist, Whitehall; Holy Trinity, Egypt.

St. Elizabeth School, 433 Pershing Blvd., 18052. Tel: 610-264-0143. Sr. Helen Ann Sharkey, R.S.M., Prin. Lay Teachers 10; Students 268.
Serving St. Elizabeth, Whitehall; Annunciation, Catasauqua.

[E] SPECIAL SCHOOLS

ALLENTOWN. *Mercy Special Learning Center*, 830 S. Woodward St., 18103. Tel: 610-797-8242. Mrs. Heidi Fritts, Prin. Ages: Newborn to 21. Lay Teachers 8; Students 80.

BETHLEHEM. *St. Francis Academy Kindergarten*, Monocacy Manor, 395 Bridle Path Rd., 18017. Tel: 610-866-5030. Sr. Carol Ann Papp, O.S.F., Prin. Sisters 2; Students 16.

St. Francis Day Care, Monocacy Manner, 395 Bridle Path Rd., 18017. Tel: 610-866-5030. Sr. Carol Ann Papp, O.S.F., Dir. Sisters 4; Lay Staff 9; Students 75.

POTTSVILLE. *St. Joseph Center*, 2075 W. Norwegian St., 17901. Tel: 717-622-4638. Sr. Grace Christi, S.S.J., Prin. Lay Teachers 4; Students 32.

READING. *Alvernia Montessori School.* (Grades PreK-K), Mt. Alvernia, 19607. Tel: 610-775-0250; Fax: 610-777-6029. Sr. Ann Marie Coll, Dir. Sisters 4; Students 65.

WEST READING. *John Paul II Center for Special Learning*, 200 Reading Ave., 19611. Tel: 610-373-5687. Lawrence P. O'Donnell, Prin. Lay Teachers 3; Students 16.

WHITEHALL. *National LEARNING CLUB Ministry*, Two Maryland Cir.-120, 18052. Tel: 610-437-4463; Fax: 610-437-8843. Outside-of-school education ministry for "at-risk" youth. Sisters 2; Lay Teachers 15; Students 550.

[F] CATHOLIC CHARITIES AND SOCIAL AGENCIES

ALLENTOWN. *Catholic Social Agency-Catholic Charities Administrative Office*, 2141 Downyflake Ln., 18103-4774. Tel: 610-791-3888. Rev. Msgr. Joseph E. Kurtz, L.S.W., M.S.W., Diocesan Dir. of Catholic Charities; Rev. Msgr. John B. McCann, L.S.W., S.T.L., Exec. Dir. of Catholic Social Agency.
Branch Offices:
Branch Office, 928 Union Blvd., 18103. Tel: 610-435-1541. (For Lehigh and Northampton Cos.).
Adult Outreach Center, 310 E. Mahanoy Ave., Mahanoy City, 17948. Tel: 717-773-2010.
St. Francis Center, 900 W. Market St., Orwigsburg, 17961. Tel: 717-366-1403. (For Schuylkill and Carbon Cos.).
Operation Plus, 913 Howard Ave., Pottsville, 17901. Tel: 717-622-6010. Day Treatment Center and Partial Hospitalization for Adolescents.
Berks County Branch Office, 2147 Perkiomen Ave., Reading, 19606. Tel: 610-370-3378.
Pastoral Visitor, 218 W. Cherry St., Shenandoah, 17976. Tel: 717-462-1154.
Pregnancy Crisis Center. (24-Hour Hotline). Bangor. Tel: 717-897-6060. Easton. Tel: 610-253-3373. Pen Argyl. Tel: 610-588-8400. Parish-Based Counseling Centers: Our Lady of Mt. Carmel, Bangor; Sacred Heart, Palmerton; St. Fidelis, Mahanoy City; St. Joseph, Summit Hill; St. Columbkill, Boyertown.

[G] GENERAL HOSPITALS

ALLENTOWN. *Sacred Heart Hospital*, 421 Chew St., 18102-3490. Tel: 610-776-4500
For a complete listing, refer to the Hospitals section.

POTTSVILLE. *Good Samaritan Regional Medical Center*, 700 E. Norwegian St., 17901. Tel: 717-621-4000; Fax: 717-622-7950
For a complete listing, refer to the Hospitals section.

READING. *Bornemann Health Corporation*, c/o Saint Joseph Hospital, 12th St. & Walnut St., P.O. Box 316, 19603. Tel: 610-378-2300
For a complete listing, refer to the Hospitals section.

CHI Community General Hospital, 215 N. 12th St., Box 316, 19603. Tel: 610-358-4215
For a complete listing, refer to the Hospitals section.

Saint Joseph Medical Center, 215 N. 12th St., P.O. Box 316, 19603. Tel: 610-378-2000
For a complete listing, refer to the Hospitals section.

[H] SKILLED NURSING FACILITIES

BETHLEHEM. *Holy Family Manor*, 1200 Spring St., 18018. Tel: 610-865-5595; Fax: 610-865-5866
For a complete listing, refer to the Special Care Facilities section.

ORWIGSBURG. *Holy Family Home Health and Hospice Care*, Schuylkill County and Admin. Office, 900 W. Market St., 17961. Tel: 717-366-0990; 800-726-8761
For a complete listing, refer to the Special Care Facilities section.

[I] HOMES AND SERVICES FOR THE ELDERLY AND CONVALESCENT

BETHLEHEM. *Grace Mansion Personal Care Residence of Holy Manor*, 1200 Spring St., 18018. Tel: 610-865-6748
For a complete listing, refer to the Special Care Facilities section.

Holy Family Adult Day Care, 1200 Spring St., 18018. Tel: 610-865-5595
For a complete listing, refer to the Special Care Facilities section.

Holy Family Apartments, 330-338 13th Ave., 18018. Tel: 610-866-4603
For a complete listing, refer to the Special Care Facilities section.

Trexler Pavilion, Personal Care Residence of Holy Family Manor, 1220 Prospect Ave., 18018. Tel: 610-868-7776
For a complete listing, refer to the Special Care Facilities section.

EASTON. *Antonian Towers*, 2405 Hillside Ave., 18042. Tel: 610-258-2033
For a complete listing, refer to the Special Care Facilities section.

NEW PHILADELPHIA. *Holy Family Apartments*, Valley St. & Clay St., 17959. Tel: 717-429-0699; Fax: 717-429-2368
For a complete listing, refer to the Special Care Facilities section.

ORWIGSBURG. *Holy Family Adult Day Care at St. Francis Center*, 900 W. Market St., 17961. Tel: 717-366-2924
For a complete listing, refer to the Special Care Facilities section.

Holy Family Residence, 900 W. Market St., 17961. Tel: 717-366-2912
For a complete listing, refer to the Special Care Facilities section.

POTTSVILLE. *Queen of Peace Apartments*, 777 Water St., 17901. Tel: 717-628-4504
For a complete listing, refer to the Special Care Facilities section.

READING. *Queen of Angels Apartment*, 22 Rothermel St., Hyde Park, 19605. Tel: 610-921-3115
For a complete listing, refer to the Special Care Facilities section.

SAINT CLAIR. *Neumann Apartments*, 25 N. Nichols St., 17970. Tel: 717-429-0699
For a complete listing, refer to the Special Care Facilities section.

[J] HOMES FOR PRIESTS

BETHLEHEM. *Holy Family Villa*, 1325 Prospect Ave., 18018. Tel: 610-694-0395. Rev. Msgr. Dennis A. Rigney, M.Div., L.S.W., A.C.S.W., Diocesan Dir. In res. Rev. Msgr. Stephen T. Forish; Revs. Joseph A. Barnes; Michael J. Briggman, S.T.B.; Joseph D. Carroll; Albert T. Cervella; Thomas L. Edwards; William P. Jones; Joseph H. Kean; Thomas J. Kerestus; F. Charles McKenna; Charles L. McNulty; Francis R. Nave; Joseph B. Rapczynski; Joseph A. Rock, Chap.; William J. Shields; James E. Sweeney; Rev. Msgr. Joseph M. Whalen, Chancellor.

[K] MONASTERIES AND RESIDENCES OF PRIESTS AND BROTHERS

BETHLEHEM. *The Barnabite Fathers Barnabite Spiritual Center*, R.D. 1, 4301 Hecktown Rd., 18017. Tel: 610-691-8648; Fax: 610-691-8649. Revs. Anthony M. Bianco, C.R.S.P., M.A., Local Supr., Moderator of Spiritual Center & House Sec.; Gabriel M. Patil, C.R.S.P., M.A., S.T.L., S.S.L., Theology College Professor & House Treasurer; Peter M. Calabrese, C.R.S.P., Seminarian, (Rome, Italy); Dick M. Delzingaro, C.R.S.P., M.A., Local Vicar, Prefect of Sacristy, Provincial Counselor & NACC Chap.

CENTER VALLEY. *Oblates of St. Francis de Sales*, Wills Hall, 2755 Station Ave., 18034-9568. Tel: 610-282-3300. In res. Very Rev. Bernard F. O'Connor, O.S.F.S., Ph.D., Supr.; Revs. Joseph P. Becker, O.S.F.S., M.A.; Thomas F. Dailey, O.S.F.S., S.T.D.; Bernard F. Donahue, O.S.F.S., Ph.D.; James P. Finnegan, O.S.F.S., S.T.D.; Daniel G. Gambet, O.S.F.S., Ph.D.; John A. Hanley, O.S.F.S., M.R.E.; John F. Harvey, O.S.F.S., S.T.D.; Peter J. Leonard, O.S.F.S., Ph.D.; A. Robert McGilvray, O.S.F.S., Ph.D.; John F. McGinley, O.S.F.S., M.Ed.; Alexander T. Pocetto, O.S.F.S., Ph.D.; Gerard H. Schubert, O.S.F.S., Ph.D.; Robert M. Rutledge, O.S.F.S. Total in Residence 14.

EASTON. *St. Francis Friary*, 3908 Chipman Rd., 18045. Tel: 610-258-3053; Fax: 610-258-2412. Franciscan Vice Province of the Holy Savior. Revs. William Reisteter, O.F.M., Dir. of Retreat Development; Michael Lenz, O.F.M., Guardian; Roland Maruscak, O.F.M.; Francis S. Duchala, O.F.M.; Bros. Michael Dubec, O.F.M.; Edward Skutka, O.F.M. Total in Residence 6. Brothers 2.

NEW RINGGOLD. *Cistercian Conventual Priory, St. Mary's Priory*, R.D. 1, Box 206, 17960. Tel: 717-943-2645. Very Rev. Luke Anderson, S.O.Cist., Th.M., Ph.D., Prior; Revs. Hugh Montague, S.O.Cist., M.A., Th.M.; Alphonsus Lachapelle, S.O.Cist., M.A., Th.M. Fathers 3.

READING. *Missionaries of the Sacred Heart*, 55 Rothermel St., 19605-2680. Tel: 610-929-2025; Fax: 610-929-4397. Very Rev. John J. Paul, M.S.C., Supr.; Revs. Philip DeRea, M.S.C.; Joseph W. Gaspar, M.S.C.; William Gies, M.S.C.; Eugene Jung, M.S.C.; Robert Tobolski, M.S.C.; Lawrence H. Wildonger, M.S.C.; Philip Yandrisevits, M.S.C.; Bros. Edward Baker, M.S.C.; George Farkas, M.S.C.; Warren Perrotto, M.S.C.

[L] CONVENTS AND RESIDENCES OF SISTERS

ALLENTOWN. *Missionary Sisters of the Most Sacred Heart of Jesus*, 425 Pine St., 18102. Tel: 610-776-4855. Staff Sacred Heart Hospital. Sr. M. Adella Lukac, M.S.C., Supr. Sisters 3.

Villa Maria Convent, 303 N. Sixth St., 18102. Tel: 610-433-3567. Faculty house of Sisters, Servants of the Immaculate Heart of Mary, who teach at Allentown Central Catholic High School and staff Centro Parroquial Sacred Heart Parish. Sr. Helene Thomas, I.H.M., Supr. Clergy of Sacred Heart Parish,

Chap., Tel: 610-434-5171 (Rectory at Sacred Heart). Sisters 4.

BETHLEHEM. *Casa Belen*, 305 E. Fourth St., 18015. Tel: 610-867-4030. Sr. Marta Munoz, P.S.S.J., Supr. Residence of the Poor Sisters of St. Joseph who minister to the Spanish speaking people of the area. Sisters 3.

Monocacy Manor, 395 Bridle Path Rd., 18017. Tel: 610-866-2597. Provincialate and Novitiate of the School Sisters of the Third Order Regular of St. Francis (Bethlehem Prov.). Sr. Mary Xavier Bomberger, O.S.F., Prov. Supr. Professed Sisters 28; Retreat Center Total Staff 7.

St. Joseph Convent, 2133 Madison Ave., 18017-4699. Tel: 610-865-4691. Sisters of St. Joseph. Sisters 15.

Ss. Cyril & Methodius Convent, 255 Buchanan St., 18015. Sisters 7.

COOPERSBURG. *Carmelite Monastery*. St. Therese of the Child Jesus and St. Mary Magdalen de Pazzi, St. Therese's Valley. 3551 Lanark Rd., 18036. Tel: 610-797-3721. Carmelite Nuns of the Ancient Observance. Mother Joseph Marie, O.Carm., Prioress; Rev. Michael S. Lawrence, Chap. Professed Nuns 12.

MAHANOY CITY. *St. Joseph Convent*, 536 W. South St., 17948. Tel: 717-773-1420. Missionaries of Charity. Sisters 4.

NESQUEHONING. *Our Lady of Perpetual Help House of Prayer*, 140 W. Mill St., 18240. Tel: 717-669-9858. Sister Servants of the Immaculate Heart of Mary. Sr. Katharine McCormack, I.H.M., Supr. Sisters 4.

PEN ARGYL. *Dominican Daughters of the Immaculate Mother*, 115 Lobb Ave., 18072. Sr. Marie, O.P., Supr. Sisters 7.

POTTSVILLE. *Sisters House*, 700 E. Norwegian St., 17901. Tel: 717-621-4000; 621-4651. Res. of the Daughters of Charity of St. Vincent de Paul, Northeast Province, who staff Good Samaritan Regional Medical Center and Nativity High School. Sr. Andrea Miller, D.C., Supr. Priests 1; Sisters 14.

READING. *Alvernia College Convent*, 19607. Tel: 610-796-8331. Residence for Bernardine Sisters on college faculty. Sr. M. Pacelli, Local Min. Tel: 610-796-8329.

Daughters of Divine Zeal, Inc., 1526 Hill Rd., 19602. Tel: 610-375-1738; 375-9072; Fax: 610-375-2188. Sr. Gesulmina Micali, F.D.Z., Supr. Sisters 6.

House of Nazareth (Casa Nazaret), 532 Spruce St., 19602. Tel: 610-378-1947. Sr. Maria Gonzalez, Supr. Residence of the Poor Sisters of St. Joseph who work in Spanish Apostolate of Berks County. Sisters 3.

MSC Province Center, 2811 Moyers Ln., 19605. Tel: 610-929-5944. Sr. Marie Clark, M.S.C., Prov. Sisters 3.

Neumann Convent Sisters of St. Francis of Philadelphia (Glen Riddle). Mailing Address: 1235 Elm St., 19603. Tel: 610-374-4974. Sisters 9.

Our Lady of the Assumption Convent, 1500 Eckert Ave., 19602. Tel: 610-373-8203. Faculty House of Sisters of Christian Charity, teaching in Central Catholic High School. Sr. Mary Joseph Schultz, S.C.C., Supr. Sisters 8.

Precious Blood Convent, 1094 Welsh Rd.P.O. Box 97, 19607. Tel: 610-777-1624; Fax: 610-777-3359.
E-mail: cpspa@aol.com
Web site: http://members.aol.com/cpspa/index.html
Residence for Missionary Sisters of the Precious Blood and Noviate. Sr. M. Francis Bisland, C.P.S., Supr. Sisters 24.

Sacred Heart Convent, Mt. Alvernia, 460 St. Bernardine St., 19607-1737. Tel: 610-777-6111; Fax: 610-777-6029. Residence for Bernardine Sisters of Third Order of St. Francis. Sr. Mary Maxine, O.S.F., Admin. Tel: 610-777-7221; Sr. Rosemary McGowan, O.S.F., Contact Person; Rev. Patrick H. Lamb, O.F.M., Chap.
U.S. Province Offices. Total Staff 10. Professed Sisters 34.

St. Clare Convent, 465 St. Bernardine St., 19607. Tel: 610-777-4590. Bernardine Franciscan Sisters. Sr. Claude Marie Jablonski, O.S.F., Local Min. Novices 2.

St. Joseph Villa, 464 Bernardine St., 19607. Tel: 610-777-5556. Home of the Retired Bernardine Sisters of the Third Order of St. Francis. Sr. M. Lorentia Kocon, O.S.F., Admin.; Sr. Myra Dziedzic, O.S.F.; Rev. Robert Reece, O.S.F.S., Chap. Sisters 110.

St. Michael Convent, 19605. Tel: 610-929-5751. Missionary Sisters of the Sacred Heart of Jesus. Sr. Theresa Lepera, M.S.C., Coord., Motherhouse Community; Sr. Joanne Leblanc, M.S.C., Coord., Motherhouse Community; Sr. Bernette Ball, M.S.C., Coord., Retirement Center Community.
Attended by M.S.C. Fathers from Sacred Heart Monastery, Hyde Park. Professed Sisters 80.

Sisters of St. Francis Residence, 502 S. Sixth St., 19602. Tel: 610-375-8001. Convent of the Sisters of St. Francis of Philadelphia who are on the staffs at Central Catholic High School, SS. Cyril and Methodius Parish, and St. Joseph Hospital. Sisters 4.

WEST LAWN. *Saint Ignatius Convent*, 2601 St. Alban Dr., 18015. Sisters 2.

WHITEHALL. *Sisters for Christian Community / Poor Servants*, Two Maryland Cir.-120, 18052. Sisters 2.

[M] RETREAT HOUSES

BETHLEHEM. *St. Francis Center for Renewal (Monocacy Manor)*, 395 Bridle Path Rd., 18017. Tel: 610-867-8890.
E-mail: peace@enter.net
Web site: www.catholic-church.org/st
School Sisters of St. Francis. Sr. M. Anita Kuchera, O.S.F., Dir. Weekend retreats (68) and days of recollection (150); retreats for men and women, marriage encounter; engaged encounters; parish retreats; workshops; youth groups; weekends; privately directed retreats; private retreats. Total Staff 5.

EASTON. *St. Francis Retreat House*, 3918 Chipman Rd., 18045. Tel: 610-258-3053. Rev. William Reisteter, O.F.M., Dir. of Retreat Development. Houses of Religious Men: Total in Residence 6; Total Staff 8; Retreat Centers: Total in Residence 6; Total Staff 10. Retreatants 80.

NORTHHAMPTON. *Mary Immaculate Seminary*, 300 Cherryville Rd., 18067-0027. Tel: 610-262-7866; Fax: 610-262-6766. Bro. John P. McErlean, F.S.C., Admin.

ORWIGSBURG. *St. Francis Center*, 900 W. Market St., 17961. Tel: 717-366-1016. Deacon Alex L. Maggitti, Dir.
Adult & Youth Retreats. Tel: 717-366-1405. Retreat Centers Total Staff 6. Overnight retreats, day retreats, weekend retreats and workshops.
Other Diocesan Agencies with Facilities in the St. Francis Center:
Catholic Social Agency. (Branch Office). Tel: 717-366-1403. Sr. Miriam Denis, S.S.J., M.B.A.
Department of Youth Ministry. Tel: 717-366-1405. Rev. William F. Glosser, M.A.
Holy Family Adult Day Care. Tel: 717-366-2924. Mrs. Linda Herb, Dir. Total Assisted Average 25/Day; Total Staff 5.
Holy Family Home Health Care. Tel: 717-366-0990. Mrs. Arlene Mongrain, R.N., B.S., Exec. Dir.
Holy Family Residence. Tel: 717-366-2912. Mr. James Polaski, Admin.

SHILLINGTON. *Mariawald Renewal Center-Precious Blood Convent*. 1094 Welsh Rd., P.O. Box 97, Reading, 19607. Tel: 610-777-0135; Fax: 610-777-3359. For women, men and mixed groups. Sr. M. Francis Bisland, C.P.S., Supr.; Sr. Theresa Bringazi, C.P.S., Dir. Total Staff 6; Total in Residence 2.

[N] CENTERS FOR SPIRITUAL GROWTH

WERNERSVILLE. *Jesuit Center for Spiritual Growth*, 19565. Tel: 610-678-8085; Fax: 610-678-8747. Revs. George A. Aschenbrenner, S.J., Dir.; John P. Barron, S.J.; George S. Williams, S.J.; James A. Borbely, S.J.; Gerald J. Fitzpatrick, S.J.; Sr. Susan Bowers, I.H.M.; Sr. Bernadette Duross, R.S.M.; Sr. Maria McCoy, S.S.J.; Sr. Barbara Weigand, I.H.M.; Bro. Renatus Foldenauer, C.S.C. Directed retreats, programs in prayer, discernment, psychology and spirituality.

[O] NEWMAN CENTERS

KUTZTOWN. *Christopher House*, 15207 Kutztown Rd., 19530. Tel: 610-683-8380; Fax: 610-683-8457.
E-mail: ljh99@kutztown.edu
Rev. Larry J. Hess, Diocesan Dir., Campus Ministry.
Albright College (Reading), St. Margaret Rectory, 925 Centre St., Reading, 19601. Tel: 610-376-2919. Rev. Ronald J. Yarrosh, M.S.
Allentown College of St. Francis de Sales (Center Valley), 2755 Station Ave., Center Valley, 18034-9568. Rev. John Hanley, O.S.F.S. Tel: 610-282-1100 Ext. 1389.
Alvernia College, Dept. of Campus Ministry, Mt. Alvernia, Reading, 19607. Tel: 610-796-8300; Fax: 610-796-8378. Mr. Bob Shearn.
Cedar Crest College (Allentown), Catholic Chaplaincy Center, 2400 Chew St., Allentown, 18104-5586. Tel: 610-821-3122; Fax: 610-821-3123. Rev. John A. Krivak, Ed.D.
Kutztown University (Kutztown), Christopher House, 15207 Kutztown Rd., 19530. Tel: 610-683-8380; Fax: 610-683-8457. Rev. Larry J. Hess, M.A.
Lafayette College (Easton), 119 McCartney St., Easton, 18042-7647. Tel: 610-253-5044; Fax: 610-253-1391. Rev. Charles Norman, O.S.F.S.
Lehigh University (Bethlehem), Newman Center at Lehigh University #41, 661 Taylor St., Bethlehem, 18015-3107. Tel: 610-758-4148; 866-0581; Fax: 610-758-6392. Rev. Andrew R. Baker, S.T.D.
Moravian College (Bethlehem), Koinonia House, 1130 Monocacy St., Bethlehem, 18018-6650. Tel: 610-861-3936; Fax: 610-253-1391. Rev. Charles Norman, O.S.F.S.
Muhlenberg College (Allentown), Catholic Chaplaincy Center, 2400 Chew St., Allentown, 18104-5586. Tel: 610-821-3122; Fax: 610-821-3123. Rev. John A. Krivak, Ed.D.
Penn State University (Sinking Spring), St. Ignatius Loyola, 2810 St. Alban Dr., Sinking Spring, 19608. Tel: 610-678-3767.
Penn State University (Schuylkill Haven Center, Schuylkill Haven), St. Ambrose Rectory, 201 Randel St., Schuylkill Haven, 17972. Tel: 717-385-1031. Rev. Eric J. Gruber.

[P] MISCELLANEOUS

READING, PA. *Mary's Shelter*, 325 S. 12th St., 19602. Tel: 610-376-1973; Fax: 610-376-1973. Sr. M. Joanna Monticello, M.S.C., Admin. A residence for homeless unwed pregnant women.

SHENANDOAH, PA. *Apostles of Jesus*, P.O. Box 215, 17976-0215. Tel: 717-462-2104. Rev. Paul O. Gaggawala, A.P., Coord.

RELIGIOUS INSTITUTES OF MEN REPRESENTED IN THE DIOCESE

For further details refer to the corresponding bracketed number in the Religious Institutes of Men or Women section.

[]—*Apostles of Jesus*.—A.J.
[]—*Cistercian Monks of the Strict Observance*.—S.O.Cist.
[0160]—*Clerics Regular of St. Paul*. (Bernabite Fathers).—C.R.S.P.
[1330]—*Congregation of the Mission*. (Eastern Prov.).—C.M.
[0520]—*Franciscan Friars*. (Custody of the Most Holy Savior; Croatian Custody of the Holy Family).—O.F.M.
[0690]—*Jesuit Fathers and Brothers*. (Maryland Prov.).—S.J.
[1110]—*Missionaries of the Sacred Heart*. (U.S. Prov.).—M.S.C.
[0860]—*Missionhurst Congregation of the Immaculate Heart of Mary*.—C.I.C.M.
[0920]—*Oblates of St. Francis De Sales*.—O.S.F.S.

RELIGIOUS INSTITUTES OF WOMEN REPRESENTED IN THE DIOCESE

[0120]—*Angelic Sisters of St. Paul*.—A.S.S.P.
[1810]—*Bernardine Sisters of the Third Order of St. Francis*.—O.S.F.
[0320]—*Carmelite Nuns of the Ancient Observance*.—O.Carm.
[]—*Congregation of Sisters of Holy Family Nazareth*.—C.S.F.N.
[]—*Congregation of St. Agnes*.—C.S.A.
[0760]—*Daughters of Charity of St. Vincent de Paul*.—D.C.
[0795]—*Daughters of Divine Zeal*.—F.D.Z.
[1065]—*Dominican Daughters of the Immaculate Mother*.—O.P.
[2575]—*Institute of the Sisters of Mercy of the Americas*. (Merion, PA).—R.S.M.
[2710]—*Missionaries of Charity*.—M.C.
[2800]—*Missionary Sisters of the Most Sacred Heart of Jesus of Hiltrup*.—M.S.C.
[2850]—*Missionary Sisters of the Precious Blood*.—C.P.S.
[3240]—*Poor Sisters of Jesus Crucified and the Sorrowful Mother*.—C.J.C.
[3250]—*Poor Sisters of St. Joseph*.—P.S.S.J.
[1700]—*School Sisters of the Third Order of St. Francis*. (Bethlehem, PA).—O.S.F.
[0660]—*Sisters of Christian Charity*.—S.C.C.
[3780]—*Sisters of Saints Cyril and Methodius*.—SS.C.M.
[3700]—*Sisters of St. Benedict*.—O.S.B.
[3740]—*Sisters of St. Casimir*.—S.S.C.
[1650]—*Sisters of St. Francis of Philadelphia*.—O.S.F.
[3830]—*Sisters of St. Joseph*.—S.S.J.
[2170]—*Sisters, Servants of the Immaculate Heart of Mary*.—I.H.M.

DIOCESAN CEMETERIES

ALLENTOWN. *Resurrection*, 547 N. Krocks Rd., 18106. Tel: 610-395-3819.

BETHLEHEM. *Holy Saviour*, 857 E. Langhorne Ave., 18017. Tel: 610-866-2372.

NECROLOGY

† Carr, James M., (Retired). —Died May 15, 1997.

† Carter, William H., Shenandoah, PA, Annunciation/ St. Mary Magdalen. —Died May 22, 1997.
† Luszczak, Francis J., (Retired). —Died Nov. 24, 1996.
† McHale, Rev. Msgr. James J., Bath, PA, Sacred Heart. —Died Oct. 25, 1997.
† Morrell, Joseph J., Allentown, PA, St. Francis of Assisi. —Died Dec. 11, 1996.
† Pasura, John G., (Retired). —Died Sept. 23, 1996.
† Romagno, Michael, (Retired). —Died Feb. 10, 1997.

Diocese of Altoona-Johnstown

(Dioecesis Altunensis-Johnstoniensis)

Most Reverend

JOSEPH V. ADAMEC, D.D., S.T.L.

Bishop of Altoona-Johnstown; ordained July 3, 1960; appointed Bishop of Altoona-Johnstown March 17, 1987; ordained and installed May 20, 1987. *Mailing Address: Chancery Office, 126 Logan Blvd., Hollidaysburg, PA, 16648.*

Most Reverend

JAMES J. HOGAN, D.D.

Retired Bishop of Altoona-Johnstown; ordained December 8, 1937; appointed Titular Bishop of Philomelium and Auxiliary of Trenton November 27, 1959; consecrated February 25, 1960; appointed to the See of Altoona-Johnstown May 23, 1966; installed July 6, 1966; retired October 17, 1986. *Office: 126 Logan Blvd., Hollidaysburg, PA, 16648.*

ESTABLISHED DIOCESE OF ALTOONA, MAY 27, 1901.

REDESIGNATED DIOCESE OF ALTOONA-JOHNSTOWN, OCTOBER 9, 1957.

Square Miles 6,674.

Comprises the Counties of Bedford, Blair, Cambria, Centre, Clinton, Fulton, Huntingdon and Somerset in the State of Pennsylvania.

For legal titles of parishes and diocesan institutions, consult the Chancery Office.

The Chancery: 126 Logan Blvd., Hollidaysburg, PA, 16648. Tel.: 814-695-5579; Fax: 814-695-8894.

STATISTICAL OVERVIEW

Personnel	
Bishop	1
Retired Bishops	1
Priests: Diocesan Active in Diocese	115
Priests: Active Outside Diocese	5
Priests: Retired, Sick or Absent	34
Number of Diocesan Priests	154
Religious Priests in Diocese	61
Ordinations:	
Diocesan Priests	1
Transitional Deacons	3
Permanent Deacons	2
Permanent Deacons in Diocese	18
Total Brothers	8
Total Sisters	155
Parishes	
Parishes	112
With Resident Pastor:	
Resident Diocesan Priests	86
Resident Religious Priests	14
Without Resident Pastor:	
Administered by Priests	12
Missions	5
Welfare	
Catholic Hospitals	2
Total Assisted	219,121
Homes for the Aged	3
Total Assisted	241
Special Centers for Social Services	2
Total Assisted	57,904
Educational	
Diocesan Students in Other Seminaries	9
Total Seminarians	9
Colleges and Universities	2
Total Students	3,953
High Schools, Diocesan and Parish	3
Total Students	1,194
Elementary Schools, Diocesan and Parish	31
Total Students	5,537
Catechesis/Religious Education:	
High School Students	4,794
Elementary Students	9,283
Total Students Under Catholic Instruction	24,770
Teachers in the Diocese:	
Priests	5
Brothers	2
Sisters	19
Lay Teachers	495
Vital Statistics	
Receptions into the Church:	
Infant Baptism Totals	1,613
Adult Baptism Totals	139
Received into Full Communion	173
First Communions	1,885
Confirmations	2,443
Marriages:	
Catholic	483
Interfaith	362
Total Marriages	845
Deaths	1,665
Total Catholic Population	117,493
Total Population	645,521

Former Bishops—Rt. Rev. EUGENE A. GARVEY, D.D., ord. Sept. 22, 1869; cons. Sept. 8, 1901; died Oct. 22, 1920.—Most Rev. JOHN JOSEPH MCCORT, D.D., ord. Oct. 14, 1883; cons. Titular Bishop of Azotus and Auxiliary to the Archbishop of Philadelphia, Sept. 17, 1912; appt. Coadjutor cum jure successionis to the Bishop of Altoona, Jan. 27, 1920; appt. Bishop of Altoona, Oct. 22, 1920; appt. Assistant at the Pontifical Throne, Oct. 5, 1933; died April 21, 1936.—Most Rev. RICHARD T. GUILFOYLE, D.D., ord. June 2, 1917; appt. Aug. 8, 1936; cons. Nov. 30, 1936; died June 10, 1957.—Most Rev. HOWARD J. CARROLL, D.D., ord. April 2, 1927; appt. Dec. 5, 1957; cons. Jan. 2, 1958; died March 21, 1960.—Most Rev. J. CARROLL MCCORMICK, D.D., ord. July 10, 1932; cons. April 20, 1947; appt. June 25, 1960; transferred to See of Scranton March 4, 1966; retired Feb. 15, 1983; died Nov. 2, 1996.—Most Rev. JAMES J. HOGAN, D.D., ord. Dec. 8, 1937; appt. Titular Bishop of Philomelium and Auxiliary of Trenton, Nov. 27, 1959; cons. Feb. 25, 1960; appt. to the See of Altoona-Johnstown May 23, 1966; retired Oct. 17, 1986.

Diocesan Officials

Bishop—Most Rev. JOSEPH V. ADAMEC, D.D., S.T.L., *126 Logan Blvd., Hollidaysburg, 16648.* Tel: 814-695-5579.

Secretary to the Bishop—126 Logan Blvd., Hollidaysburg, 16648. Tel: 814-695-5579.

Retired Bishop—Most Rev. JAMES J. HOGAN, D.D., J.C.D., *126 Logan Blvd., Hollidaysburg, 16648.* Tel: 814-696-0278.

Vicars General—Rev. Msgr. STANLEY B. CARSON, V.G., Admin. (Secretariats), *126 Logan Blvd., Hollidaysburg, 16648.* Tel: 814-695-5579; 943-8553 (Res.).; Rev. Msgr. GEORGE B. FLINN, V.G., S.T.L., Pastoral Life and Ministry, *126 Logan Blvd., Hollidaysburg, 16648.* Tel: 814-695-5579; 536-0117 (Res.).

Judicial Vicar—Rev. Msgr. MICHAEL E. SERVINSKY, S.T.L., J.C.L., *126 Logan Blvd., Hollidaysburg, 16648.* Tel: 814-695-5579; 943-8464 (Res.).

Bishop's Vicar for Religious—Very Rev. GILES SCHINELLI, T.O.R., *Our Lady of Mt. Carmel Rectory, 806 11th Ave., Altoona, 16602.* Tel: 814-942-8501.

Vicars Forane

Allegheny—Rev. Msgr. JOHN R. SASWAY, V.F.
Altoona—Very Rev. PAUL E. TURNBULL, V.F.
Barnesboro—Very Rev. CHARLES F. BODZIAK, V.F.
Cambria—Very Rev. CHARLES M. AMERSHEK, V.F.
Clinton-Centre—Very Rev. D. TIMOTHY GRIMME, V.F.
Ebensburg—Rev. Msgr. JOHN J. LITTLE, V.F.
Huntingdon-Blair—Rev. Msgr. DAVID A. LOCKARD, V.F.
Johnstown—Rev. Msgr. JOSEPH R. KINIRY, P.A., V.F.
Prince Gallitzin—Rev. Msgr. THOMAS J. MAHER, V.F.
Southern—Rev. Msgr. SAMUEL J. TOMASELLI, V.F.
Windber—Rev. Msgr. IGNATIUS C. WADAS, V.F.

Secretariats

CHANCERY—Rev. Msgr. DENNIS R. BOGGS, Sec., *126 Logan Blvd., Hollidaysburg, 16648.* Tel: 814-695-5579; Fax: 814-695-8894. Office Hours: Mon.-Fri. 9-4:30. Closed Holy Days.

Catholic Register—Rev. TIMOTHY P. STEIN, Editor. Tel: 814-695-7563; Fax: 814-695-7517.

Ecumenical Minister—Rev. HAROLD N. BILLER. Tel: 814-539-2186.

Information Officers—Rev. Msgr. DENNIS R. BOGGS; Rev. TIMOTHY P. STEIN. Tel: 814-695-5579.

Interfaith Minister—Rev. Msgr. ROY F. KLINE. Tel: 814-695-2337.

EVANGELIZATION—Sr. CHARMAINE GRILLIOT, C.PP.S., M.A., Sec., *126A Logan Blvd., Hollidaysburg, 16648.* Tel: 814-695-5579.

Education—Sr. CHARMAINE GRILLIOT, C.PP.S., M.A., Dir. Tel: 814-695-5579.

Youth / Campus Ministry—ROBERT SHERWIN. Tel: 814-695-5579.

Catholic Scouting—Rev. JOSEPH ORR. Tel: 717-485-3723.

MINISTERIAL & LEADERSHIP—Rev. ROBERT C. MAZUR, Sec., *124 Logan Blvd., Hollidaysburg, 16648.* Tel: 814-695-5579.

Christian Initiation—Mrs. JEANNE THOMPSON. Tel:

814-695-5579.
Diaconal Formation—Deacon JOHN J. CONCANNON. Tel: 814-695-5579.
Lay Ministries—Tel: 814-695-5579.
Liturgy & Worship—Rev. ROBERT C. MAZUR, Dir. Tel: 814-695-5579.
Ongoing Formation of the Clergy—Rev. ALAN THOMAS. Tel: 814-472-5441.
Pastoral Centers—Sr. MARJORIE MCGUIRE, C.C.W. Tel: 814-247-9954.
Propagation of the Faith—Rev. ROBERT J. KELLY. Tel: 814-695-5579.
Vocation—Rev. MICHAEL A. BECKER. Tel: 814-472-5441.

PASTORAL SERVICES—Rev. Msgr. ROBERT J. SALY, Sec., *1300 12th Ave., P.O. Box 1349, Altoona, 16603.* Tel: 814-944-9388.
Catholic Social Services—Rev. Msgr. ROBERT J. SALY. Tel: 814-944-9388.
Family Life Ministries—Sr. MARILYN WELCH, C.C.W. Tel: 814-886-5551.
Peace & Justice Commission—Mr. CHARLES LEIDEN. Tel: 814-946-9291.
Priests' Residence - Dmitri Manor—Rev. Msgr. ROBERT J. SALY. Tel: 814-944-9388.

TEMPORALITIES—LARRY R. SUTTON, Sec., *126 Logan Blvd., Hollidaysburg, 16648.* Tel: 814-695-5579.
Building Commission—Mr. JERRY KINIRY. Tel: 814-288-2663.
Building & Grounds—ERNEST ENEDY. Tel: 814-695-5579.
Comptroller—HERMAN NAGLE. Tel: 814-695-5579.
Computer Systems—RONALD MULDOON. Tel: 814-695-5579.
Cemetery Commission—Rev. RICHARD D. CLARK. Tel: 814-536-4622.
Development Office—JAMES EDWARDS. Tel: 814-695-5579.
Diocesan Shrines—Rev. MICHAEL BECKER. Tel: 814-472-5441.
Financial & Legal—LARRY R. SUTTON, Dir. Tel: 814-695-5579.

Diocesan Offices

Building Commission—Mr. JERRY KINIRY. Tel: 814-288-2663.
Campus Ministry—(For further details regarding Campus Ministries please refer to Institutions Located in the Diocese.).
Catholic Social Service—Rev. Msgr. ROBERT J. SALY, Dir. JOHN R. PRICHARD, M.S.W., A.C.S.W., Asst. Dir.; Sr. CAROL JEAN CZYRNIK, Intake Worker, *1300 12th Ave., P.O. Box 1349, Altoona, 16603.* Tel: 814-944-9388.
Johnstown Offices—232 Walnut St., 2nd Floor, Johnstown, 15901. Tel: 814-535-6538.
State College Offices—276 W. Hamilton Ave., P.O. Box 680, State College, 16801. Tel: 814-238-4937.
"The Catholic Register"—Rev. TIMOTHY P. STEIN, Editor, *P.O. Box 413, Hollidaysburg, 16648.* Tel: 814-695-7563.
Cemetery Commission—Rev. RICHARD D. CLARK, *Sacred Heart Rectory, 219 Oak St., Conemaugh, 15909.* Tel: 814-536-4622.
Chancery—Rev. Msgr. DENNIS R. BOGGS, Chancellor, *126 Logan Blvd., Hollidaysburg, 16648.* Tel: 814-695-5579; Fax: 814-695-8894.
Christian Initiation—Mrs. JEANNE THOMPSON, *126A Logan Blvd., Hollidaysburg, 16648.* Tel: 814-695-5579; Fax: 814-695-8894.
Computer Systems—RONALD MULDOON, *126 Logan Blvd., Hollidaysburg, 16648.* Tel: 814-695-5579; Fax: 814-695-8894.
Comptroller—HERMAN NAGLE, *126 Logan Blvd., Hollidaysburg, 16648.* Tel: 814-695-5579; Fax: 814-695-8894.
Development Office—JAMES EDWARDS, *P.O. Box 409, Hollidaysburg, 16648.* Tel: 814-696-4389; Fax: 814-695-8894.
Diaconal Formation—Deacon JOHN J. CONCANNON, *124 Logan Blvd., Hollidaysburg, 16648.* Tel: 814-695-5579; Fax: 814-695-8894.
Diocesan Shrines—Rev. MICHAEL BECKER, *Prince Gallitzin Chapel House, P.O. Box 99, Loretto, 15940.* Tel: 814-472-5441; Fax: 814-472-5446.
Education—Sr. CHARMAINE GRILLIOT, C.PP.S., M.A., Dir., *126A Logan Blvd., Hollidaysburg, 16648.* Tel: 814-695-5579; Fax: 814-695-8894. Asst. Directors: CHARLEEN BLUM, Religious Ed.; Sr. MARK PLESCHER, C.S.A., Elementary; ROBERT SHERWIN, Campus/Youth Ministry.
Ecumenical Minister—Rev. HAROLD N. BILLER, *609 Park Ave., Johnstown, 15902.* Tel: 814-539-2186.
Family Life Office—Sr. MARILYN WELCH, C.C.W., Dir., *5379 Portage St., Lilly, 15938.* Tel: 814-886-5551; Fax: 814-886-7697. SUSAN STITH, Prog. Coord. *Divorced/Separated & Bereaved Ministries; Parent & Marriage Preparation Ministries.* Programs: *Persons with Disabilities Ministry; Natural Family Planning; Respect Life.*
Finance Council—FRANK PASQUERILLA.
Finance Office—LARRY R. SUTTON, Dir., *126 Logan Blvd., Hollidaysburg, 16648.* Tel: 814-695-5579; Fax: 814-695-8894.
Holy Childhood Association—Rev. ROBERT J. KELLY, Dir., *124 Logan Blvd., Hollidaysburg, 16648.* Tel: 814-695-5579; Fax: 814-695-8894.
Information Office—Rev. Msgr. DENNIS R. BOGGS; Rev. TIMOTHY P. STEIN, *126 Logan Blvd., Hollidaysburg, 16648.* Tel: 814-695-5579; Fax: 814-695-8894.
Interfaith Minister—Rev. Msgr. ROY KLINE, *P.O. Box 88, Duncansville, 16635.* Tel: 814-695-2337.
Lay Ministries—124 Logan Blvd., Hollidaysburg, 16648. Tel: 814-695-5579; Fax: 814-695-8894.
Liturgical Commission—Mrs. DEBORAH HETRICK, *534 Pine St., Hollidaysburg, 16648.* Tel: 814-695-6181.
Liturgy & Worship—Rev. ROBERT C. MAZUR, *124 Logan Blvd., Hollidaysburg, 16648.* Tel: 814-695-5579; Fax: 814-695-8894.
Mission - Carmelite Community of the Word—110 S. Third St., McConnellsburg, 17233. Tel: 717-485-5917.
Ongoing Formation Clergy—Rev. ALAN THOMAS, Dir., *P.O. Box 99, Loretto, 15940.* Tel: 814-472-5441; Fax: 814-472-5446.
Pastoral Centers—
Altoona—Sr. JEANNE MARIE KLISIEWICZ, Dir., *1304 13th Ave., Altoona, 16601.* Tel: 814-942-7661.
Johnstown—Sr. MARTHA BURBULLA, Dir., *741 Railroad St., Johnstown, 15901.* Tel: 814-535-7005.
Permanent Deacons—Deacon JOHN J. CONCANNON, *124 Logan Blvd., Hollidasyburg, 16648.* Tel: 814-695-5579; Fax: 814-695-8894.
Peace & Justice Commission—Mr. CHARLES LEIDEN, *306 Coleridge Ave., Altoona, 16602.* Tel: 814-946-9291.
Presbyteral Council—Rev. GEORGE D. KOHARCHIK, Chm., *509 Caldwell Ave., Portage, 15946.* Tel: 814-736-4279.
Priests' Personnel Board—Rev. Msgr. GEORGE B. FLINN, V.G., S.T.L., *126 Logan Blvd., Hollidaysburg, 16648.* Tel: 814-695-5579; Fax: 814-695-8894.
Priests' Residence - Dmitri Manor—Rev. Msgr. ROBERT J. SALY, Dir., *St. Mary's Lane, Hollidaysburg, 16648.* Tel: 814-944-9338.
Retreat & Conference Center—St. John the Baptist Retreat Center, P.O. Box 10, New Baltimore, 15553. Tel: 814-733-2210.
Scouting—Rev. JOSEPH ORR, *303 Lincoln Way E., McConnellsburg, 17233.* Tel: 717-485-3723.
Self Insurance Program—JOSEPH WATT, *Gallagher Bassett Insurance - Berkshire Center, Ste. 302, Greensburg, 15601.* Tel: 800-831-3247; Fax: 412-836-8684.
Society for the Propagation of the Faith—Rev. ROBERT J. KELLY, Dir., *124 Logan Blvd., Hollidaysburg, 16648.* Tel: 814-695-5579; Fax: 814-695-8894.
St. Vincent de Paul Society—PAUL MCCONNELL, Pres.; Deacon JOHN E. SROKA, Exec. Dir., *566 Vine St., Johnstown, 15901.* Tel: 814-535-4357.
Tribunal Office—Rev. Msgr. MICHAEL E. SERVINSKY, S.T.L., J.C.L., *126 Logan Blvd., Hollidaysburg, 16648.* Tel: 814-695-5579; Fax: 814-695-8894.
Vocation Office—Rev. MICHAEL A. BECKER, *Prince Gallitzin Chapel House, P.O. Box 99, Loretto, 15940.* Tel: 814-472-5441; Fax: 814-472-5446.

CLERGY, PARISHES, MISSIONS AND PAROCHIAL SCHOOLS

CITY OF ALTOONA
(Blair County)

1—CATHEDRAL OF THE BLESSED SACRAMENT (1851), Revs. Robert C. Mazur; George M. Gulash; John J. Slovikovski; Rev. Msgr. Thomas E. Madden, P.A., (Retired); Deacon James F. Leap.
Res., 1331 13th Ave., P.O. Box 33, 16603. Tel: 814-944-4603.
School—Altoona Central Catholic School Cathedral Site. See Elementary Diocesan Schools under Institutions Located in the Diocese. Tel: 814-943-7423; Fax: 814-949-4794. Mr. Anthony Consiglio, Prin.
Catechesis/Religious Programs—Tel: 814-943-7423; Fax: 814-949-4794. Mrs. Jeanne Thompson, D.R.E.
Students 123.

2—IMMACULATE CONCEPTION (1860). (St. Mary's). Revs. Robert G. Neugebauer; Robert P. Reese. In res., Rev. Albert Anselmi.
Res., 1405 Fifth Ave., 16602. Tel: 814-942-2416. [CEM]
School—Altoona Central Catholic School Immaculate Conception Site. See Elementary Diocesan Schools under Institutions Located in the Diocese. 1400 Fourth Ave., 16602.
Lay Teachers 7; Students 157.
Catechesis/Religious Programs—Tel: 814-944-1250. Sr. Julia Zilka, V.S.C., D.R.E.
Students 173.

3—ST. MARK'S (1889), Rev. Msgr. Robert J. Saly; Rev. Henry Stange. In res., Rev. John Neugebaur.
Res., 416 Sixth Ave., 16602. Tel: 814-942-0364.
Catechesis/Religious Programs—Students 98.
Chapel—Valley View Home for the Aged, Tel: 814-944-0845.

4—SACRED HEART (1890), Rev. Msgr. Stanley B. Carson, V.G. In res., Rev. Leo A. Lynch.
Res., 511 20th St., 16602. Tel: 814-943-8553; Fax: 814-943-1556.
Formation Center—2009 Sixth Ave., 16602. Tel: 814-944-3922.
Catechesis/Religious Programs—Students 119.

5—HOLY ROSARY (1901), Revs. Carl A. Spishak; Edward J. Dabcosky.
Res., 900 Fourth St.-Juniata, 16601. Tel: 814-944-6676.
Catechesis/Religious Programs—Tel: 814-944-4611. Mrs. Margaret M. McCulloch, D.R.E.
Students 133.

6—OUR LADY OF FATIMA (1995) (Irish-Polish), Rev. Anthony J. Pollack.
Res., 2010 12th Ave., 16601. Tel: 814-942-0371. [CEM]
School—Altoona Central Catholic School Our Lady of Fatima Site. See Elementary Diocesan Schools under Institutions Located in the Diocese. Tel: 814-943-7423.
Catechesis/Religious Programs—1304 13th Ave., 16603. Tel: 814-943-7423.
Students 28.

7—OUR LADY OF MT. CARMEL (1905) (Italian), Revs. Giles A. Schinelli, T.O.R.; Terrence T. Smith, T.O.R.; Louis J. Secondo, T.O.R. In res., Rev. Alan Polimine, T.O.R., (Retired).
Res., 806 11th St., 16602. Tel: 814-942-8501; Fax: 814-944-2208.
School—Altoona Central Catholic School Our Lady of Mt. Carmel Site, 1012 Eighth Ave., 16602. Tel: 814-943-5931; Fax: 814-942-5787. Sr. Elizabeth Ann, O.S.F., Prin.
Franciscan Sisters of the Immaculate Conception 1; Lay Teachers 10; Students 180.
Catechesis/Religious Programs—Mr. Ronald Petak, D.R.E.
Students 140.
Convent—Tel: 814-942-8964.
Mission—Pleasant Valley, Blair Co., Our Lady of the Assumption, (1925) 15 1/2 Pierce St., Pleasant Valley, 16602.

8—ST. LEO THE GREAT (1911). Merged with SS. Peter & Paul to form Our Lady of Fatima, Altoona.

9—SS. PETER AND PAUL (1911) (Polish). Merged with St. Leo the Great to form Our Lady of Fatima, Altoona.

10—ST. JOHN THE EVANGELIST (1921), Very Rev. Paul E. Turnbull, V.F.; Deacon Gene Neral.
Res., 309 Lotz Ave., Lakemont, Altoona, 16602. Tel: 814-942-5503; Fax: 814-942-4514.
School—Tel: 814-943-4966; Fax: 814-943-8832. Gary Evangelisto, Prin.
Lay Teachers 9; Students 100.
Catechesis/Religious Programs—Ms. Joan Price, D.R.E.
Students 222.

11—OUR LADY OF LOURDES (1923), Revs. Robert C. Hall; Edward L. Eckenrod.
Res., 2716 Broad Ave., 16601. Tel: 814-943-6185; Fax: 814-943-1968.
School—2713 W. Chestnut Ave., 16601. Tel: 814-942-3421. Mrs. Catherine M. DiSabato, Prin.
Lay Teachers 9; Students 152.
Catechesis/Religious Programs—Tel: 814-943-1685.
Students 68.

12—ST. ROSE OF LIMA (1924), Revs. James F. Crookston; Peter Jacek Kuligowski. In res., Rev. Robert J. Kelly; Deacon Lubomir J. Strecok.
Res., 5514 Roselawn Ave., 16602. Tel: 814-944-8509.
School—5519 Sixth Ave., 16602. Tel: 814-942-7835; Fax: 814-942-1095. Joseph Maschue, Prin.
Lay Teachers 10; Students 236.
Catechesis/Religious Programs—Students 185.

13—ST. THERESE OF THE CHILD JESUS (1927), Rev. Msgr. Anthony B. Little; Rev. Allen P. Zeth.
Res., 2329 4th St., 16601. Tel: 814-943-4844; Fax: 814-942-1873.
School—Altoona Central Catholic Middle School, 424 Wopsononock Ave., 16601. Tel: 814-944-3751; Fax: 814-944-8283. Sr. Mary Kevin Breen, O.S.F., Prin.
Religious 1; Lay Teachers 8; Students 142.

Catechesis/Religious Programs—Andrew Callaghan, D.R.E.
Students 142.

CITY OF JOHNSTOWN
(Cambria County)

1—St. John Gualbert Cathedral (1835), Rev. Msgr. George B. Flinn, V.G., Rector; Revs. John F. Brezovec; Alan E. Thomas; Clarence S. Bridges; Deacon John J. Concannon.
Res., P.O. Box 807, 117 Clinton St., 15907. Tel: 814-536-0117; Fax: 814-535-6771. [CEM 2]
School—Central Catholic Elementary. See Elementary Diocesan Schools under Institutions Located in the Diocese. Tel: 814-536-1532.
Catechesis/Religious Programs—St. Anthony School, 124 Maple Ave., 15901. Tel: 814-535-4228.
Students 61.

2—St. Joseph's (1852) (German). Merged with Our Lady of Mercy to form St. John Gualbert Cathedral, Johnstown.
School—Central Catholic Elementary. See Elementary Diocesan Schools under Institutions Located in the Diocese. Tel: 814-536-1532.

3—Immaculate Conception (1859) (German), Rev. Andrew C. Stanko.
Res., 308 Broad St., 15906. Tel: 814-535-4407. [CEM]
School—West End Catholic. See Elementary Diocesan Schools under Institutions Located in the Diocese. Tel: 814-536-4722.

4—SS. Casimir & Emerich (Polish-Hungarian), Rev. John J. Marshall. Tel: 814-536-8534.
Res., 501 Power St., 15906. Tel: 814-535-2139. [CEM][JC]
School—West End Catholic. See Elementary Diocesan Schools under Institutions Located in the Diocese. Tel: 814-536-4722.
Catechesis/Religious Programs—Students 81.

5—St. Columba's (1888), Rev. Benjamin Dykas.
Res., 916 Broad St., 15906. Tel: 814-535-1627. [CEM]
School—West End Catholic. See Elementary Diocesan Schools under Institutions Located in the Diocese. Tel: 814-536-4722.

6—St. Stephen, First King of Hungary (1891) (Slovak), Rev. Lawrence L. Lacovic.
Res., 414 Fourth Ave., 15906. Tel: 814-539-6334. [CEM]
School—West End Catholic. See Elementary Diocesan Schools under Institutions Located in the Diocese. Tel: 814-536-4722.
Catechesis/Religious Programs—Students 68.

7—St. Rochus (1900) (Croatian), Rev. Charles M. Amershek, Jr., V.F.; Sr. Patricia Milko, C.D.P., Pastoral Min.
Res., 314 Eighth Ave., 15906. Tel: 814-539-1520; Fax: 814-539-8845. [CEM]
School—West End Catholic. See Elementary Diocesan Schools under Institutions Located in the Diocese. Tel: 814-536-4722.
Catechesis/Religious Programs—Tel: 814-535-5409. Theresa Marcus, D.R.E.
Students 190.

8—St. Patrick's (1904), Rev. Harold N. Biller; Deacon Leo A. Kist, P.D.
Res., 609 Park Ave., 15902. Tel: 814-539-2186; Fax: 814-539-2410.
School—617 Park Ave., 15902. Tel: 814-535-2926. Dr. Kevin J. Moran, Prin.
Sisters of St. Joseph 1; Lay Teachers 7; Students 174.
Catechesis/Religious Programs—Students 43.

9—St. Emerich's (1905) (Hungarian). Merged with St. Casimir's, Johnstown, to form Saints Casimir & Emerich's, Johnstown.

10—St. Anthony's (1905) (Italian), Revs. Patrick Seelman, T.O.R.; Leonard Blostic, T.O.R.; Bro. Stephen Baker, T.O.R.
Res., 124 Maple Ave., 15901. Tel: 814-535-4228. [CEM]
School—Central Catholic Elementary. See Elementary Diocesan Schools under Institutions Located in the Diocese. Tel: 814-536-1532.
Catechesis/Religious Programs—Tel: 814-535-2360.
Students 100.

11—St. Michael's (1910) (German), Rev. Andrew C. Stanko.
Res., 180 Gilbert St., 15906. Tel: 814-535-4407.

12—SS. Peter and Paul's (1918) (Slovak), Rev. Christopher Panagoplos, T.O.R.
Res., 218 Maple Ave., 15901. Tel: 814-535-1133. [CEM]
School—Central Catholic Elementary. See Elementary Diocesan Schools under Institutions Located in the Diocese. Tel: 814-536-1532.

13—Our Mother of Sorrows (1920), Rev. Msgr. Thomas K. Mabon; Revs. Donald W. Dusza; Leo F. Arnone.
Res., 415 Tioga St., 15905. Tel: 814-535-7646; Fax: 814-536-7850.
School—430 Tioga St., 15905. Tel: 814-539-5315. Mr. John Skubak, Prin.
Lay Teachers 20; Students 384.
Catechesis/Religious Programs—Tel: 814-255-1264. Mrs. Karen Fink, D.R.E.
Students 459.

14—Our Lady of Mercy (1921). Merged with St. Joseph to form St. John Gualbert Cathedral, Johnstown.

15—St. Francis of Assisi (1922) (Slovak), Rev. Francis P. Balestino.
Res., 120 Barron Ave., 15906. Tel: 814-539-1632. [CEM]
School—West End Catholic. See Elementary Diocesan Schools under Institutions Located in the Diocese.
Catechesis/Religious Programs—Students 91.

16—Visitation of the B.V.M. (1927), Rev. Martin A. Cingle; Deacon John E. Sroka.
Res., 1428 Coventry Ct., 15905.
Catechesis/Religious Programs—Tel: 814-536-6110.
Students 41.

17—St. Therese of the Child Jesus (1929) (Slovenian), Revs. Bernard Karmanocky, O.F.M.; Raphael Stragisher, O.F.M., (Retired).
Res., 536 Decker Ave., 15906. Tel: 814-539-7633. [CEM]
School—West End Catholic. See Elementary Diocesan Schools under Institutions Located in the Diocese. Tel: 814-536-4472.
Mission—Moxham, Cambria Co., St. Anne's, (1935) 533 Woodland Ave., Moxham, 15902. Tel: 814-539-7633.
Catechesis/Religious Programs—Tel: 814-536-2287.
Students 60.

18—St. Clement's (1956), Rev. William E. Rosenbaum; Very Rev. Robert Radasky.
Res., 114 Lindberg Ave., 15905. Tel: 814-255-4422.
School—110 Lindberg Ave., 15905. Tel: 814-255-1964. A. Ernest Papinchak, Prin.
Lay Teachers 10; Students 161.
Catechesis/Religious Programs—Ms. Mary Drager, D.R.E.
Students 191.

19—St. Andrew's (1956), Rev. Barry J. Baroni; Deacon Herman J. Lux. In res., Rev. John Byrnes.
Res., 1621 Ferndale Ave., 15905. Tel: 814-288-4324; Fax: 814-288-6750.
School—(Grades Nursery-8) 1629 Ferndale Ave., 15905. Tel: 814-288-1854.
Lay Teachers 10; Students 188.
Catechesis/Religious Programs—Students 115.

20—St. Gregory's (1919), Rev. Msgr. Daniel J. O'Neill.
Res., 120 Boltz St., 15902. Tel: 814-536-6818.
Catechesis/Religious Programs—Students 84.

21—St. Barnabas (1954) (Slovenian), Rev. Daniel J. O'Neill.
Res., 120 Boltz St., 15902. Tel: 814-536-6818. [CEM]

22—St. Benedict's (1930), Rev. Msgr. Joseph R. Kiniry, P.A., V.F.; Revs. James M. Dugan; David S. Peles.
Res., 2310 Bedford St., 15904. Tel: 814-266-9718.
School—2306 Bedford St., 15904. Tel: 814-266-3837; Fax: 814-266-7718. Gerald Brown, Prin.
Lay Teachers 28; Students 520.
Catechesis/Religious Programs—Tel: 814-266-2105. Dianne Brandle, D.R.E.
Students 705.

OUTSIDE THE CITIES OF ALTOONA AND JOHNSTOWN

Acosta, Somerset Co., St. John the Baptist's (1912). Merged with St. Joseph, Boswell, and St. Stanislaus, Boswell, to form All Saints Church, Boswell.

Ashville, Cambria Co., St. Thomas Aquinas (1889), Rev. James F. Bunn.
Res., 16613. Tel: 814-944-5615; 674-5416. [CEM]
Catechesis/Religious Programs—Mrs. Ann Bilko, D.R.E.
Students 104.

Bakerton, Cambria Co., Sacred Heart (1904). Merged with St. Patrick, Spangler, to form St. Jude, Elmora.

Barnesboro, Cambria Co.,

1—St. John the Baptist, (1896) (Slovak), Rev. Gerard M. Connolly, T.O.R.
Res., 811 Chestnut Ave., 15714. Tel: 814-948-6842. [CEM]
School—Northern Cambria Catholic, Nicktown. See Elementary Diocesan Schools under Institutions Located in the Diocese. Tel: 814-948-8900.
Catechesis/Religious Programs—Tel: 814-948-8391. Rita Switzler, D.R.E.
Students 75.

2—St. Stanislaus Kostka, (1906) (Polish), Very Rev. Charles F. Bodziak, V.F.
Res., 3805 Bigler Ave., 15714. Tel: 814-948-8582. [CEM]
School—Northern Cambria Catholic, Nicktown. See Elementary Diocesan Schools under Institutions Located in the Diocese. Tel: 814-948-8900.
Catechesis/Religious Programs—Tel: 814-948-9226. Valerie Hood, D.R.E.
Students 65.

3—Our Lady of Mt. Carmel, (1908) (Italian), Rev. Gerard M. Connolly, T.O.R.
Res., 606 Philadelphia Ave., 15714. Tel: 814-948-8391. [CEM]
Catechesis/Religious Programs—Rita Switzler, D.R.E.
Students 144.

4—Christ the King, (1993), Very Rev. Charles F. Bodziak, V.F.
Res., 1104 Maple Ave., 15714. Tel: 814-948-8582.
Catechesis/Religious Programs—Tel: 814-948-6622.
Students 93.

Beans Cove, Bedford Co., Seven Dolors B.V.M. (1878), Rev. Msgr. Charles D. Rager.
Mailing Address: R.D. 3, Box 158-B, Clearville, 15535. Tel: 814-696-7480.
Res., 4 St. Mary's Lane, Hollidaysburg, 16648. Tel: 814-696-7480. [CEM]

Beaverdale, Cambria Co., St. Joseph's (1904) (Slovak). Merged with St. Agnes, Beaverdale, and Corpus Christi, Dunlo, to form Holy Spirit Church, Beaverdale.
St. Agnes (1909). Merged with St. Joseph, Beaverdale, and Corpus Christi, Dunlo, to form Holy Spirit Church, Beaverdale.
Holy Spirit (1995), Rev. Nicholas J. Mancini.
Mailing Address: 727 Cameron Ave., P.O. Box 616, 15921. Tel: 814-487-5633. [CEM 2]
Catechesis/Religious Programs—Students 103.

Bedford, Bedford Co., St. Thomas (1816), Rev. John C. Vago.
Res., 215 E. Penn St., 15522. Tel: 814-623-5526. [CEM 2]
School—129 W. Penn St., 15522. Tel: 814-623-8873. Joyce Wityk, Prin.
Lay Teachers 8; Students 72.
Catechesis/Religious Programs—Tel: 814-652-5028. Mrs. Jane Cunard, D.R.E.
Students 154.

Bellefonte, Centre Co., St. John the Evangelist's (1828), Very Rev. D. Timothy Grimme; Rev. James M. Foster.
Res., 134 E. Bishop St., 16823. Tel: 814-355-3134; Fax: 814-355-4820. [CEM 2]
School—(Grades PreK-8) 116 E. Bishop St., 16823. Tel: 814-355-7859; Fax: 814-355-2939. Mrs. Carol Gouty, Prin.
Lay Teachers 15; Students 215.
Catechesis/Religious Programs—Students 228.

Bellwood, Blair Co., St. Joseph's (1890), Rev. David H. Roesch.
Res., 623 E. Third St., 16617. Tel: 814-742-7075.
Catechesis/Religious Programs—Tel: 814-742-7894.
Students 122.

Boswell, All Saints (1995), Rev. Blase Wegierski, O.F.M.Conv.
Res., 325 Quemahoning St., 15531. Tel: 814-629-5551. [CEM 3]
Catechesis/Religious Programs—Students 163.
St. Stanislaus, Somerset Co., (1901) (Polish). Merged with St. John the Baptist, Acosta, to form All Saints Church, Boswell.

Carrolltown, Cambria Co., St. Benedict's (1840), Revs. Kieran Rodgers, O.S.B.; Vincent E. Zidek, O.S.B.
Res., 15722. Tel: 814-344-6548; Fax: 814-344-8656. [CEM]
School—119 S. Benedict St., 15722. Tel: 814-344-6512.
Religious 1; Lay Teachers 7; Students 101.
Catechesis/Religious Programs—Tel: 814-674-5786. Bonnie Westrick, D.R.E.
Students 270.

Cassandra, Cambria Co., St. Agnes (1909), Rev. Robert L. Ruston.
Res., P.O. Box 56, 15925. Tel: 814-736-8314.

Central City, Somerset Co., Sacred Heart (1914) (Polish), Rev. Msgr. Ignatius C. Wadas, V.F.
Res., 738 Sunshine Ave., 15926. Tel: 814-754-5224. [CEM]
Catechesis/Religious Programs—Students 53.
St. John the Baptist (1917) (Slovak), Rev. Msgr. Ignatius C. Wadas, V.F.
Res., 164 Wheeler St., 15926. Tel: 814-754-5224. [CEM]
Catechesis/Religious Programs—Students 50.

Chest Springs, Cambria Co., St. Monica's (1859), Rev. Timothy P. Stein.
Res., 3037 Colonel Drake Hwy., 16624. Tel: 814-674-3712. [CEM]
Catechesis/Religious Programs—Tel: 814-674-5064.
Students 62.

Clarence, Centre Co., St. Michael's (1859) (Slovak), Rev. Sylvester J. Bendzella.
Res., 102 Church St., 16829. Tel: 814-387-6762. [CEM]
Catechesis/Religious Programs—Students 79.

Colver, Cambria Co., Holy Family (1912) (Polish), Rev. James B. Coveney.
Res., 562 Fifth St., 15927. Tel: 814-748-7054. [CEM]
Catechesis/Religious Programs—Sr. Anna Marie, S.A., D.R.E.
Students 87.

Conemaugh, Cambria Co., Sacred Heart (1902), Rev. Richard D. Clark.
Res., 219 Oak St., 15909. Tel: 814-536-4622. [CEM]
Catechesis/Religious Programs—Tel: 814-535-4450.
Students 103.

Assumption of B.V.M. (1910) (Polish), Rev. Bernard F. Grega.
Res., 340 Second St., 15909. Tel: 814-535-2250. [CEM]
Catechesis/Religious Programs—335 Second St., 15909. Tel: 814-539-5203.
Students 62.

Coupon, Cambria Co., St. Joseph's (1855), Rev. Msgr. Michael E. Servinsky.
Res., 16629. Tel: 814-943-8464. [CEM 2]
Catechesis/Religious Programs—Students 47.

Cresson, Cambria Co., St. Aloysius (1838), Rev. William E. Mullen.
Res., 7911 Admiral Peary Hwy., 16630. Tel: 814-886-2235. [CEM]
School—All Saints Catholic. See Elementary Diocesan Schools under Institutions Located in the Diocese. Tel: 814-886-7942.
Catechesis/Religious Programs—Tel: 814-886-2669. Margaret H. Eberhart, D.R.E.
Students 200.

St. Francis Xavier (1908), Rev. David W. Cronauer.
Res., 211 Powell Ave., 16630. Tel: 814-886-2374. [CEM]
School—All Saints Catholic. See Elementary Diocesan Schools under Institutions Located in the Diocese. Tel: 814-886-7942; Fax: 814-886-7942.
Catechesis/Religious Programs—Tel: 814-886-2374. Mrs. Janet Rickens, D.R.E.
Students 127.

Davidsville, Somerset Co., St. Anne (1911), Rev. Michael Lewandowski, O.F.M.Conv.
Mailing Address: P.O. Box 500, Woodstown Rd., 15928. Tel: 814-479-2664; Fax: 814-479-7702. [CEM]
Catechesis/Religious Programs—Students 81.

Dudley, Huntingdon Co., Immaculate Conception (1856), Rev. Patrick R. Leahey.
Res., P.O. Box 188, 16634. Tel: 814-635-2919. [CEM]
Catechesis/Religious Programs—Students 55.

Duncansville, Blair Co., St. Catherine of Siena (1963), Rev. Msgr. Roy F. Kline.
Res., 49 Woodland Terr., 16635. Tel: 814-695-2337.
Catechesis/Religious Programs—P.O. Box 88, 16635. Tel: 814-696-0616. Debra Terchanik, D.R.E.
Students 146.

Dunlo, Cambria Co., Corpus Christi (1903). Merged with St. Agnes, Beaverdale, and St. Joseph, Beaverdale, to form Holy Spirit Church, Beaverdale. Rev. Nicholas J. Mancini.

Ebensburg, Cambria Co., Holy Name (1816), Rev. Msgr. Arnold L. Gaus; Rev. Walter J. Moll. In res., Rev. Msgr. Faber J. Malloy.
Res., 500 N. Julian St., 15931. Tel: 814-472-7244; Fax: 814-472-7249. [CEM]
School—Tel: 814-472-8817. Sr. Jean Uzupis, Prin.
Sisters 2; Lay Teachers 20; Students 396.
Catechesis/Religious Programs—Sr. Nancy Spence, C.C.W., D.R.E.
Students 561.

Ehrenfeld, Cambria Co., Our Lady of Mt. Carmel (1892). Merged with St. James, South Fork, and St. Anthony's, South Fork, to form Most Holy Trinity, South Fork.

Elmora, St. Jude (1995), Rev. David J. Arseneault.
Res., 1274 Deveaux St., P.O. Box 10, 15737. Tel: 814-948-9241. [CEM]
Catechesis/Religious Programs—Tel: 814-948-6622.
Students 50.
Mission—Spangler, St. Jude Chapel, 15775.

Emeigh, Cambria Co., Most Precious Blood. See Christ the King, Barnesboro.

Everett, Bedford Co., St. John the Evangelist (1971), Rev. Angelo J. Patti.
Res., 161 E. First Ave., 15537. Tel: 814-652-5854.
Church—163 E. First Ave., 15537.
Catechesis/Religious Programs—Students 57.

Fallentimber, Cambria Co., St. Mary Magdalen's (Frugality) (1889). Merged with St. Richard's Mission, Blandburg, to form St. Joan of Arc Church, Fallentimber. Rev. James F. Bunn.
Res., 692 Glendale Valley Blvd., 16639. Tel: 814-943-5437.
Catechesis/Religious Programs—Students 57.

St. Joan of Arc (1995), Rev. James F. Bunn.
Res., 692 Glendale Valley Blvd., 16639. Tel: 814-943-5437.
Catechesis/Religious Programs—Tel: 814-941-3440. Mrs. Mary Lou Coloussy, D.R.E.
Students 56.

Gallitzin, Cambria Co., St. Patrick's (1850), Rev. Msgr. Bernard A. Przybocki.
Res., 811 Church St., 16641. Tel: 814-886-7941. [CEM]
School—825 Church St., 11641. Tel: 814-886-8772. Mrs. Helen Saylor, Prin.
Lay Teachers 8; Students 101.
Catechesis/Religious Programs—Students 135.

Our Lady of Czestochowa (1903) (Polish), Rev. Msgr. Bernard A. Przybocki.
Res., 811 Church St., 16641. Tel: 814-886-4203. [CEM]
Catechesis/Religious Programs—Tel: 814-886-8772.
Students 59.

Hastings, Cambria Co., St. Bernard (1890), Rev. Joachim R. Fatora, O.S.B. In res., Rev. Germain L. Lieb, O.S.B.
Res., Beaver St., P.O. Box 497, 16646. Tel: 814-247-6558. [CEM 2]
School—Tel: 814-247-6322. Jeffrey M. Rabish, Prin.
Lay Teachers 8; Students 87.
Catechesis/Religious Programs—Tel: 814-674-5841. Mrs. Aileen Ropp, D.R.E.
Students 190.
Mission—St. Boniface, Cambria Co., St. Boniface Chapel, 16675.

Hollidaysburg, Blair Co., St. Mary's (1841), Revs. John J. Palko; John A. Tiernan.
Res., 312 Clark St., P.O. Box 317, 16648. Tel: 814-695-0622; Fax: 814-696-9609. [CEM 2]
School—Hollidaysburg Consolidated Catholic Elementary. See Elementary Diocesan Schools under Institutions Located in the Diocese.
Catechesis/Religious Programs—Tel: 814-695-5678. Mrs. Connie Curfman, D.R.E.
Students 300.

St. Michael's (1862), Revs. Clement Gardner; George Valko.
Res., 301 Spruce St., 16648. Tel: 814-695-0912. [CEM]
School—Hollidaysburg Consolidated Catholic Elementary. See Elementary Diocesan Schools under Institutions Located in the Diocese. Tel: 814-695-6112; Fax: 814-695-1215.
Catechesis/Religious Programs—Tel: 814-695-6972. James G. Burke, D.R.E.
Students 238.

Hooversville, Somerset Co., Holy Family (1911), Rev. Romulus Roslowski, O.F.M. Conv.
Res., 15936. Tel: 814-798-2933; Fax: 814-798-8601. [CEM]
Catechesis/Religious Programs—Students 61.

Huntingdon, Huntingdon Co., Most Holy Trinity (1826), Rev. Msgr. David A. Lockard, V.F.
Res., 524 Mifflin St., 16652. Tel: 814-643-0160; Fax: 814-643-0160. [CEM]
Catechesis/Religious Programs—Students 197.

Lilly, Cambria Co., St. Brigid's (1883). Merged with Our Lady of Mount Carmel, Lilly, to form Our Lady of the Alleghenies, Lilly. Rev. Msgr. John R. Sasway.
Res., 608 Main St., 15938. Tel: 814-866-2504. [CEM]
Catechesis/Religious Programs—Tel: 814-886-2161. Barbara Pysher, D.R.E.
Students 172.

Our Lady of Mt. Carmel (1910) (Polish). Merged with St. Brigid, Lilly, to form Our Lady of the Alleghenies, Lilly.

Our Lady of the Alleghenies (1995), Rev. Msgr. John R. Sasway.
Res., 608 Main St., 15938. Tel: 814-886-2504. [CEM]
Catechesis/Religious Programs—Tel: 814-886-2161.
Students 212.

Lock Haven, Clinton Co., Immaculate Conception (1852), Rev. Msgr. Dennis R. Boggs.
Res., 310 W. Water St., 17745. Tel: 717-748-4535; Fax: 717-748-1674. [CEM]
School—Lock Haven Catholic School, Tel: 717-748-7252. Sr. Mary Joan Gibson, O.P., Prin.
Sisters of Sinsinawa Dominicans 3; Lay Teachers 18; Students 200.
Catechesis/Religious Programs—Tel: 717-748-4828.
Students 117.

St. Agnes (1873), Rev. Neil R. Dadey.
Res., 3 E. Walnut St., 17745. Tel: 717-748-4594. [CEM]
School—Lock Haven Catholic School. See Immaculate Conception for details. Tel: 717-742-7252.
Catechesis/Religious Programs—Tel: 717-748-4282.
Students 89.

Loretto, Cambria Co., Basilica of St. Michael the Archangel (1799), Very Rev. Msgr. Thomas J. Maher, V.F. In res., Rev. Michael Becker.
Res., 15940. Tel: 814-472-8551. [CEM]
School—Tel: 814-472-9117. Sr. Elizabeth Ann Brody, R.S.M., Prin.
Lay Teachers 6; Students 71.
Catechesis/Religious Programs—Tel: 814-472-2332. D.R.E.: Sr. Miriam Rita, R.S.M., (Elementary); Betty Seymour, (High School & Conf.), Tel: 717-472-6279.
Students 239.

McConnellsburg, Fulton Co., St. Stephen's (1962), Rev. Joseph T. Orr.
Res., 303 Lincoln Way E., 17233. Tel: 717-485-3723.

Meyersdale, Somerset Co., SS. Philip and James (1850), Rev. Msgr. Timothy J. Swope, Admin.
Res., 247 High St., 15552. Tel: 814-634-8150. [CEM 2]
Catechesis/Religious Programs—Students 129.
Mission—MacDonaldton, Somerset Co., St. Gregory, (1907) 247 High St., 15552. Tel: 814-634-8150.

Mount Union, Huntingdon Co., St. Catherine's (1912), Rev. Elwood F. Figurelle.
Res., 205 W. Market St., 17066. Tel: 814-542-4582. [CEM]
Catechesis/Religious Programs—Students 47.

Mundys Corner, Cambria Co., St. John Vianney's (1950), Rev. Paul M. Robine.
Res., 3513 William Penn Ave., Johnstown, 15909. Tel: 814-322-4789.
Catechesis/Religious Programs—Tel: 814-322-1109. Ms. Mary Ellen Broad, D.R.E.
Students 166.

Nanty-Glo, Cambria Co., St. Mary's (1902), Rev. Msgr. John J. Little, V.F.; Deacon Thomas M. Buige.
Res., 1020 Caroline St., 15943. Tel: 814-749-9103. [CEM]
School—1005 Caroline St., 15943. Tel: 814-749-9031. Mrs. Rosemary Conzo, Prin.
Sisters of St. Agnes 2; Lay Teachers 9; Students 119.
Catechesis/Religious Programs—Mrs. Patricia LaMantia, D.R.E.
Students 129.

New Baltimore, Somerset Co., St. John the Baptist (1829), Rev. Mark S. Begly.
Res., 15553. Tel: 814-733-2210; Fax: 814-733-2966. [CEM]
Catechesis/Religious Programs—Students 125.

Newry, Blair Co., St. Patrick's (1816), Rev. William A. Rosensteel; Rev. Msgr. Harold J. Burkardt.
Res., P.O. Box 398, 16665. Tel: 814-695-3413. [CEM 2]
School—Tel: 814-695-3819. Sr. Pauline Kastoski, C.C.W., Prin.
Sisters 2; Lay Teachers 8; Students 116.
Catechesis/Religious Programs—Tel: 814-695-3819. Mrs. Linda Guiffre, D.R.E.
Students 106.

Nicktown, Cambria Co., St. Nicholas (1861), Rev. Claude W. Pollak, O.S.B.
Res., 15762. Tel: 814-948-9614. [CEM]
School—Northern Cambria Catholic. See Elementary Diocesan Schools under Institutions Located in the Diocese. Tel: 814-948-8900; Fax: 814-948-8720.
Catechesis/Religious Programs—Tel: 814-948-8900. Nancy McKee, D.R.E.
Students 143.

Patton, Cambria Co., Our Lady of Perpetual Help (1892). Merged with St. George, Patton, and St. Lawrence to form Queen of Peace, Patton. Revs. Joseph Gerg, O.S.B.; Robert Roche, O.S.B.
Res., 907 Sixth Ave., 16668. Tel: 814-674-8983. [CEM]
Catechesis/Religious Programs—Tel: 814-674-8938. D.R.E.: Michelle Kirk; Rita Horne.
Students 239.

Queen of Peace (1995), Revs. Joseph Gerg, O.S.B.; Robert Roche, O.S.B.
Res., 907 Sixth Ave., 16668. Tel: 814-674-8983; Fax: 814-674-8805. [CEM]
Catechesis/Religious Programs—Tel: 814-674-5591. Joanne VanOrmer, D.R.E.

Students 220.
St. George (1907) (Slovak). Merged with Our Lady of Perpetual Help, Patton, and St. Lawrence to form Queen of Peace, Patton.

Penns Valley, Centre Co., Blessed Kateri Tekakwitha (1986), Rev. William S. Crouse.
Res., R.D. No. 1, Box 245A, Spring Mills, 16875. Tel: 814-422-8983.
Catechesis/Religious Programs—Students 97.

Philipsburg, Centre Co., SS. Peter and Paul (1868), Rev. Msgr. Philip P. Saylor.
Res., 400 S. Fourth St., 16866. Tel: 814-342-1700; Fax: 814-342-5480. [CEM]
Catechesis/Religious Programs—William J. Slother, Jr., D.R.E.
Students 210.

Portage, Cambria Co.,

1—St. Joseph's, (1898), Rev. George D. Koharchik.
Res., 509 Caldwell Ave., 15946. Tel: 814-736-4279; Fax: 814-736-4764.
School—Tel: 814-736-4033.
Lay Teachers 6; Students 57. Principals: Mrs. Teresa Koenigberg; Mrs. Deborah Boyko.
Catechesis/Religious Programs—Mary E. Heinrich, D.R.E.
Students 210.

2—Sacred Heart, (1909) (Polish), Rev. Ronald V. Osinski.
Res., 601 Mountain Ave., 15946. Tel: 814-736-4239. [CEM]
School—812 Orchard St., 15946. Tel: 814-736-3588. Sr. Miriam Joseph, S.S.C.J., Prin.
Pre-School & Kindergarten Students 17.
Convent—803 Orchard St., 15946. Tel: 814-736-3875.
Catechesis/Religious Programs—Students 228.

3—Assumption B.V.M., (1907) (Slovak), Rev. Ronald V. Osinski.
Res., 806 Hammers St., 15946. Tel: 814-736-9770. [CEM]
Catechesis/Religious Programs—Tel: 814-736-3588.
Students 228.

4—St. John the Baptist, (1923) (Hungarian), Rev. Ronald B. Yogus.
Res., 900 Johnson Ave., 15946. Tel: 814-736-9747. [CEM]

Renovo, Clinton Co., St. Joseph's (1869), Rev. Donald E. Boslett.
Res., 925 Huron Ave., 17764. Tel: 717-923-0172. [CEM 2]
Catechesis/Religious Programs—Judy M. Kurutz, D.R.E.
Students 171.

Revloc, Cambria Co., Most Holy Redeemer (1920), Rev. William J. Kovach.
Res., 553 Cambria Ave., 15948. Tel: 814-472-7928.

Roaring Spring, Blair Co., St. Thomas More (1969), Rev. Msgr. William E. Schultz.
Res., 825 Williams St., 16673. Tel: 814-224-4522.
Catechesis/Religious Programs—Students 74.

St. Augustine, Cambria Co., St. Augustine (1847), Rev. Joseph W. Fleming.
Res., 803 St. Augustine Rd., Dysart, 16636. Tel: 814-674-8550. [CEM]
Catechesis/Religious Programs—Students 170.

St. Boniface, Cambria Co., St. Boniface Chapel (1859). Merged to form St. Bernard, Hastings.

St. Lawrence, Cambria Co., St. Lawrence's (1853). Merged with Our Lady of Perpetual Help, Patton, and St. George, Patton, to form Queen of Peace, Patton.

St. Michael, Cambria Co., St. Michael's (1913), Rev. John P. Ellias.
Res., Box 103, 15951. Tel: 814-495-9640. [CEM]
Catechesis/Religious Programs—Students 192.

Shade Gap, Huntingdon Co., St. Mary's (1840), Rev. David R. Becker.
Res., Shade Gap, H.C. 62, Box 696, 17255. Tel: 814-447-3172. [CEM 2]

Snow Shoe, Centre Co., St. Mary's (1865) (Irish), Rev. Sylvester J. Bendzella.
Res., 522 Fourth St., 16874. Tel: 814-387-6793. [CEM]

Somerset, Somerset Co., St. Peter's (1920), Rev. Msgr. Samuel J. Tomaselli; Rev. Sean A. Code; Deacon Frederick F. Weaver. In res., Rev. Joseph Mazurkiewicz.
Res., 433 W. Church St., 15501. Tel: 814-443-6574; Fax: 814-445-7766. [CEM]
School—Tel: 814-445-6662. Mrs. Susan Dudley, Prin.
Lay Teachers 6; Students 110.
Catechesis/Religious Programs—Tel: 814-443-6574.
Students 364.
St. Peter in Chains (1995),
Mailing Address: S.C.I.-Somerset, 1590 Walters Mill Rd., 15501-0001. Tel: 814-443-8100.

South Fork, Cambria Co., Most Holy Trinity (1995), Rev. Louis J. Mulvehill.
Res., 550 Main St., 15956. Tel: 814-495-4419; Fax: 814-495-4419. [CEM 2]
Catechesis/Religious Programs—Tel: 814-495-4028. Mrs. Betty Rosmus, D.R.E.
Students 82.
St. Anthony's (1905) (Polish). Merged with St. James, South Fork, and Our Lady of Mt. Carmel, Ehrenfeld, to form Most Holy Trinity, South Fork.
St. James (1906). Merged with St. Anthony, South Fork, and Our Lady of Mt. Carmel, Ehrenfeld, to form Most Holy Trinity, South Fork.

Spangler, Cambria Co., Holy Cross (1893), Rev. David J. Arseneault.
Res., 2410 Campbell Ave., P.O. Box 507, 15775-0507. Tel: 814-948-8043; Fax: 814-948-7533. [CEM]
Catechesis/Religious Programs—Tel: 814-948-6622.
Students 118.
St. Patrick's (1902). Merged with Sacred Heart, Bakerton, to form St. Jude, Elmora.

State College, Centre Co., Good Shepherd (1989), Rev. Philip M. Bender.
Res., 867 Gray's Woods Blvd., P.O. Box 8186, 16803. Tel: 814-238-7463.
Church—Tel: 814-238-2110.
Catechesis/Religious Programs—Tel: 814-238-2110. Dorothy Kardohely, D.R.E.
Students 354.
Our Lady of Victory (1908), Revs. Martin Dugan McCamley; Anthony Petracca; James D. Zatalava.
Res., 820 Westerly Pkwy., 16801. Tel: 814-237-7832; Fax: 814-237-6709.
School—Tel: 814-238-1592; Fax: 814-238-4553. Kathleen Hershbine, Prin.
Lay Teachers 16; Students 347.
Pre School—Tel: 814-238-6616.
Lay Teachers 4; Students 60.
Catechesis/Religious Programs—Tel: 814-234-3315. Steve Kretschmer, D.R.E.
Students 575.

Summerhill, Cambria Co., St. John (1903), Rev. Daniel C. Wolfel, O.S.B.
Res., 538 Main St., P.O. Box 248, 15958. Tel: 814-495-5241. [CEM]
Mission—New Germany, Cambria Co., Immaculate Conception, (1855) 1640 New Germany Rd., P.O. Box 248, 15958.
Catechesis/Religious Programs—Students 248.

Twin Rocks, Cambria Co., St. Charles (1917). Merged with Immaculate Conception Mission, Vintondale, to form SS. Timothy & Mark Church, Twin Rocks & SS. Timothy & Mark Chapel, Vintondale.
SS. Timothy & Mark (1995),
Mailing Address: P.O. Box 275, 15960. Tel: 814-749-9331.
Catechesis/Religious Programs—Students 82.
Mission—Vintondale, SS. Timothy & Mark Chapel.

Tyrone, Blair Co., St. Matthew's (1853), Rev. Norman P. Imgrund.
Res., 406 W. 11th St., 16686. Tel: 814-684-1480. [CEM]
School—1107 Cameron Ave., 16686. Tel: 814-684-3510. Mrs. Kathleen Bechdel, Prin.
Lay Teachers 5; Students 76.
Catechesis/Religious Programs—Tel: 814-684-4808. Teresa Jeffries, D.R.E.
Students 162.

West Salisbury, Somerset Co., St. Michael's (1887), Rev. Bernard L. White.
Res., 15565. Tel: 814-662-2958. [CEM 2]
Mission—Pocahontas, Somerset Co., St. Mary's, (1906) P.O. Box 31, 15565. Tel: 814-662-2958.
Catechesis/Religious Programs—Students 63.

Williamsburg, Blair Co., St. Joseph (1861), Rev. Dennis M. Kurdziel.
Res., 628 W. First St., 16693. Tel: 814-832-2137. [CEM 2]
Catechesis/Religious Programs—Students 62.

Wilmore, Cambria Co., St. Bartholomew's (1840), Rev. Robert L. Ruston.
Res., P.O. Box 96, 15962. Tel: 814-495-5360; 736-8314. [CEM]
Catechesis/Religious Programs—Tel: 814-495-5360.
Students 107.

Windber, Somerset Co.,

1—St. John Cantius, (1898) (Polish), Rev. Leonard E. Voytek.
Res., 605 Graham Ave., 15963-1398. Tel: 814-467-7191. [CEM]
Catechesis/Religious Programs—D.R.E.: Paul Banjak, (High School), Tel: 814-467-8443; Sr. Evangelista Stronmier, (Elementary), Tel: 814-467-9670.
Students 168.

2—SS. Cyril and Methodius, (1906) (Slovak), Rev. James H. Conrad, S.T.L.
Res., 604 Graham Ave., 15963. Tel: 814-467-7042. [CEM 2]
Catechesis/Religious Programs—600 Graham Ave., 15963. Tel: 814-467-9670.
Students 67.

3—St. Anthony of Padua, (1908) (Italian), Very Rev. William Santre, T.O.R.; Revs. Adrian Tirpak, T.O.R.; Mark Reifel, T.O.R.; Deacon Joseph R. Dalla Valle.
Res., 2201 Graham Ave., 15963. Tel: 814-467-7292. [CEM]
Schools—St. Benedict School, Tel: 814-266-3837. Students 12; St. Andrew School.
Students 2.
Catechesis/Religious Programs—Tel: 814-467-9670;467-8443. D.R.E.: Sr. Evangelista R.S.M.; Roxann Newcomer.
Students 176.

4—St. Mary's, (1914) (Hungarian), Rev. Leonard E. Voytek.
Res., 605 Graham Ave., 15963-1398. Tel: 814-467-7191. [CEM]
Catechesis/Religious Programs—D.R.E.: Sr. Evangelista Stronmier, (Elementary), Tel: 814-467-9670; Paul Banjak, (High School), Tel: 814-467-8443.
Students 55.

5—Holy Child Jesus, (1921) (Irish), Rev. Charles F. Leonardis.
Res., 913 Graham Ave., 15963. Tel: 814-467-7097. [JC]
Catechesis/Religious Programs—Tel: 814-467-9670.
Students 31.

Chaplains of Public Institutions

Altoona. *Altoona Hospital.* Howard Ave. & Seventh St., 16601. Tel: 814-946-2011; 942-2416 (Res.). Chaplains: Revs. Edward L. Eckenrod; Albert Anselmi.
Veterans Medical Center. 2907 Pleasant Valley Blvd., 16602. Tel: 814-943-8164. Rev. Edward J. Dabcosky, Chap.

Johnstown. *Lee Hospital.* 320 Main St., 15901. Tel: 814-533-0123; 536-0117 (Res.). Chaplains: Revs. Andrew Stanko; Christopher Panagoplos, T.O.R.; Bernard V. Grattan.
Memorial Hospital. Franklin St., 15905. Tel: 814-533-9000; 536-0117 (Res.). Chaplains: Revs. Andrew C. Stanko; Christopher Panagoplos, T.O.R.; Bernard V. Grattan.

Bellefonte. *State Correctional Institution.* Our Lady of the Mount, Box A, 16823. Tel: 814-355-4874; 422-8983 (Res.). Rev. William S. Crouse.

Cresson. *State Correctional Institution.* Drawer A, 16630. Tel: 814-886-8181; 736-9497 (Res.). Rev. Ronald B. Yogus, Chap.

Ebensburg. *Laurel Crest Manor.* Vacant. P.O. Box 360, 15931. Tel: 814-472-8100.

Huntingdon. *State Correctional Institution.* St. Dismas, Drawer R, 16652. Tel: 814-643-2400; 447-3172 (Res.). Rev. David R. Becker.

Laural Highlands. *State Correctional Institution.* 5706 Glades Pike Rd., Tel: 814-445-6501. Deacon Frederick Weaver, Chap.

Loretto. *Federal Correctional Institution.* P.O. Box 1000, 15940. Tel: 814-472-4140; 472-9363 (Res.). Sr. Mary Ann Palko, C.C.W., Chap.

Smithfield. *State Correctional Institution.* 1120 Pike St., Huntingdon, 16652. Tel: 814-643-6520; 643-0160 (Res.). Rev. Dennis M. Kurdziel, Chap.

Somerset. *State Correctional Institution.* St. Peter in Chains, 1590 Walters Mill Rd., 15510. Tel: 814-443-8100; 443-6574 (Res.). Rev. Joseph Mazurkiewicz.

On Duty Outside the Diocese:
Reverend Monsignors—
Lenz, Paul A., Black and Indian Mission Office, 2021 H St., N.W., Washington, DC 20006. Tel: 202-331-8542
Reverend Fathers—
Ledoux, Albert H., 11007 Montgomery Rd., Beltsville, MD 20705. Tel: 301-937-7183

Military Chaplains:
Reverend Fathers—
Gergel, Stephen J., U.S. Navy
Gomulka, Eugene T., U.S. Navy
Legarski, Anthony J., U.S. Navy

Absent on Leave:
Reverend Fathers—
Christiana, Nicholas M.
Karr, Raymond E.
Mascherino, Alphonse
Norcavage, Albert R.

Retired:
Reverend Monsignors—
Ackerson, Francis A.

Beiter, Lambert M., 224 Main St., Conemaugh, PA
Burkardt, Harold J., 5509 5th Ave., Altoona, PA 16602
Fleming, Joseph H., 14408 Gallagher Rd., Delray Beach, FL 33484. Tel: 407-498-7646
Fleming, Patrick V., FL 33484. Tel: 407-498-7646
Lafferty, John J., Dmitri Manor, 3 St. Mary's Ln., Hollidaysburg, PA 16648
Madden, Thomas E., P.O. Box 33, Altoona, PA 16603
Malloy, Faber J., Bishop's Liaison, 500 N. Julian St., Ebensburg, PA 15931
McCaa, Francis B., 311 Lincoln Dr., Martinsburg, WV 25401
O'Toole, Anthony J., Dmitri Manor, 6 St. Mary's Ln., Hollidaysburg, PA 16648
O'Toole, Joseph M., Dmitri Manor, 7 St. Mary's Ln., Hollidaysburg, PA 16648
Panza, Paul D., P.A., Dmitri Manor, 1 St. Mary's Ln., Hollidaysburg, PA 16648
Pier, Joseph, 1776 Clapboard Run Rd., Johnstown, PA 15904
Rager, Charles D., Dmitri Manor, 4 St. Mary's Ln., Hollidaysburg, PA 16648
Walsh, Richard J., 1254 Lincoln Ave., P.O. Box 197, Tyrone, PA 16686. Tel: 814-684-2505

Reverend Fathers—
Bender, Joseph J., 72 Clover Dr., Hollidaysburg, PA 16648
Boyle, John J., P.O. Box 159, Mill Hall, PA 17751
Crosser, Raymond G., 100 Beckman Dr., 6F, Altoona, PA 16602
George, J. Clark, Dmitri Manor, 2 St. Mary's Ln., Hollidaysburg, PA 16648
Greiner, Kenneth A., REAR 319 Cherry Ave., Altoona, PA 16601
Inman, Leonard T., Garvey Manor, 128 Logan Blvd., Hollidaysburg, PA 16648
Joly, Henry L., P.O. Box 705, Hollidaysburg, PA 16648
Knapik, Andrew G., P.O. Box 111, Bellefonte, PA 16823
Mattiello, Lucian C., 121 E. 25th Ave., Altoona, PA 16601
Michaels, Emmett T., Box 94, Accomac, VA 23301
Myers, Regis F., Dmitri Manor, 10 St. Mary's Ln., Hollidaysburg, PA 16648
Orlando, John V., Garvey Manor Nursing Home, 128 Logan Blvd., Hollidaysburg, PA 16648
Ream, Gerard J., 351 Habicht St., Johnstown, PA 15906
Strittmatter, J. Joseph, Dmitri Manor, 8 St. Mary's Ln., Hollidaysburg, PA 16648
Thomas, Paul, Garvey Manor Nursing Home, 128 Logan Blvd., Hollidaysburg, PA 16648

Permanent Deacons:
Buige, Thomas M., St. Mary, Nanty Glo
Cammarata, Samuel M., Holy Spirit, Beaverdale
Cassidy, Joseph A., (Retired)
Concannon, John, St. John Gualbert, Johnstown
Condor, Michael, Jr., St. Francis Xavier, Cresson
Dalla Valle, Joseph R., St. Anthony, Windber
Ivantis, Laszlo P., Penn State Catholic Community
Janisko, Thaddeus J., St. John Cantius/St. Mary, Windber
Kist, Leo A., St. Patrick, Johnstown
Lapinski, David C., Our Lady of Victory, State College
Leap, James F., Blessed Sacrament Cathedral, Altoona
Lux, Herman J., St. Andrew, Johnstown
Mazurkiewicz, Joseph F., Sr., St. John Evangelist, Bellefonte
Neral, Gene, St. John the Evangelist, Lakemont
Rzewnicki, Philipe, St. Rose of Lima, Altoona
Sroka, John, Visitation, Johnstown
Tiernan, John A., St. Mary, Hollidaysburg
Weaver, Frederick F., St. Peter, Somerset

INSTITUTIONS LOCATED IN THE DIOCESE

[A] COLLEGES AND UNIVERSITIES
(NON-DIOCESAN)

CRESSON. *Mount Aloysius College*, 7373 Admiral Peary Hwy., 16630. Tel: 814-886-4131.
E-mail: cindymi@mtaloy.edu
Web site: www.mtaloy.edu
For a complete listing, refer to the Colleges and Universities section.

LORETTO. *St. Francis College*, P.O. Box 600, 15940-0600. Tel: 814-472-3000
For a complete listing, refer to the Colleges and Universities section.

[B] HIGH SCHOOLS, DIOCESAN

ALTOONA. *Bishop Guilfoyle High School*, 2400 Pleasant Valley Blvd., 16602. Tel: 814-944-4014; Fax: 814-944-8695.
E-mail: bghsl@penn.com
Web site: http://users.penn.com/~bghsl/index.htm
Sr. Beverly Hmel, I.H.M., Asst. Prin.; Rev. Leo Lynch, Chap. Sisters 3; Brothers 1; Lay Teachers 25; Students 372.

JOHNSTOWN. *Bishop McCort High School*, 25 Osborne St., 15905. Tel: 814-536-8991; Fax: 814-535-4118.
E-mail: mccort@third-wave.com
Sr. Donna Marie Leiden, S.C., Prin.; Revs. John D. Byrnes; Matthew E. Misurda; Bro. Steve Baker, T.O.R. Sisters 3; Lay Teachers 31; Students 478.

EBENSBURG. *Bishop Carroll High School*, 15931. Tel: 814-472-7500; Fax: 814-472-8020. Mr. Charles J. Koren, Prin.; Rev. Alan E. Thomas, Chap. Priests 1; Sisters 1; Lay Teachers 22; Students 344.

[C] ELEMENTARY DIOCESAN SCHOOLS

ALTOONA. *Altoona Central Catholic School.* (Grades K-5). Located at the Cathedral of the Blessed Sacrament. 1304 13th Ave., 16601. Tel: 814-943-7423. Mr. Anthony Consiglio, Prin.
Consolidation of the following parishes: Cathedral of the Blessed Sacrament; Our Lady of Fatima. Sisters 1; Lay Teachers 7; Students 157.

JOHNSTOWN. *Central Catholic Elementary School.* (Grades K-8), 751 Railroad St., 15901. Tel: 814-536-1532. Mrs. Lois Ryan, Prin.
Consolidation of the following parishes: St. Anthony; St. John Gualbert; Ss. Peter & Paul. Lay Teachers 9; Students 140.

West End Catholic School. (Grades K-8), 317 Power St., 15906. Tel: 814-536-4722. Mr. Louis Bennese, Prin.
Consolidation of the following parishes: St. Casimir; St. Columba; St. Emerich; St. Francis of Assisi; Immaculate Conception; St. Rochus; St. Stephen; St. Therese. Sisters 1; Lay Teachers 10; Students 177.

CRESSON. *All Saints Catholic School.* (Grades K-8), 220 Powell Ave., 16630. Tel: 814-886-7942. Mrs. Susan Glass, Prin.
Merger of the following parishes: St. Francis Xavier; St. Aloysius; St. Agnes; Our Lady of the Alleghenies. Sisters 1; Lay Teachers 8; Students 148.

HOLLIDAYSBURG. *Hollidaysburg Consolidated Catholic Elementary School.* (Grades PreK-8), Spruce & Wayne Sts., P.O. Box 599, 16648. Tel: 814-695-6112.
E-mail: hcs@soundcity.net
Mr. Edward DiSabato, Prin.
Consolidation of the following parishes: St. Michael's; St. Mary's. Lay Teachers 10; Students 165.

NICKTOWN. *Northern Cambria Catholic School*, P.O. Box 249, Rte. 271S, 15762. Tel: 814-948-8900. Sr. Jane Mary Prostko, C.S.S.F., Prin.
Consolidation of the following parishes: Holy Cross; Our Lady of Mount Carmel; St. John the Baptist; St. Nicholas; Christ the King; St. Stanislaus Kostka. Sisters 2; Lay Teachers 8; Students 132.

[D] GENERAL HOSPITALS
(NON-DIOCESAN)

ALTOONA. *Bon Secours Holy Family Regional Health System*, 2500 Seventh Ave., 16602.
Web site: www.mercynet.org
For a complete listing, refer to the Hospitals section.

JOHNSTOWN. *Good Samaritan Medical Center*, 1020 Franklin St., 15905. Tel: 814-533-1000; 533-1410; Fax: 814-533-1819.
E-mail: stucker@conemaugh.org
For a complete listing, refer to the Hospitals section.

[E] HOMES FOR AGED
(NON-DIOCESAN)

HOLLIDAYSBURG. *Garvey Manor*, Logan Blvd., 16648. Tel: 814-695-5571
For a complete listing, refer to the Special Care Facilities section.

St. Leonard's Home, Inc., 601 N. Montgomery St., 16648. Tel: 814-695-9581; Fax: 814-695-2606
For a complete listing, refer to the Special Care Facilities section.

(DIOCESAN)

HOLLIDAYSBURG. *Dmitri Manor Priests' Residence*, St. Mary's Ln., 16648
For a complete listing, refer to the Special Care Facilities section.

[F] MONASTERIES AND RESIDENCES OF PRIESTS AND BROTHERS
(NON-DIOCESAN)

HOLLIDAYSBURG. *St. Joseph Friary*, 501-503 Walnut St., 16648. Tel: 814-695-5802. Bros. Bernard Dougherty, T.O.R., Supr.; Alexis Nagle, T.O.R.; Very Rev. Canon Aloysius Hankinson, T.O.R.; Rev. Domenic R. Aversa, T.O.R.; Very Rev. Adalbert Wolski, T.O.R.

LORETTO. *Mount Assisi Friary*, P.O. Box 40, 15940. Tel: 814-472-5324. Revs. Marianus D. Lieb, T.O.R.; Damian L. Noel, T.O.R.; Bro. Mark McBride, T.O.R., Prov. Econome & Vicar Min.; Revs. Ronald Bodenschatz, T.O.R.; Thomas Edwards, T.O.R., Local Min. Tel: 814-472-5324 Ext. 302; John J. Wilger, T.O.R.; Vincent R. Negherbon; Daniel Mulkern, T.O.R.; Simon Engler, T.O.R.; Kenneth Flaherty, T.O.R.; Terence Henry, T.O.R.; Bros. Callistus Gerardi, T.O.R.; Bernard J. Nicolosi, T.O.R.; Damien W. Koehler, T.O.R. Priests 10; Brothers in Solemn Vows 4.

St. Bonaventure Friary, P.O. Box 155, 15940. Tel: 814-472-9422.
E-mail: mhiggins@csrlink.net
Rev. Michael J. Higgins, T.O.R., Dir. Novices. Priests 1; Novices 3.

St. Francis Friary, Third Order Regular of St. Francis of Penance. Province of the Most Sacred Heart of Jesus., 15940. Tel: 814-472-3362. Revs. Christian R. Oravec, T.O.R., Pres., St. Francis College; Joseph A. Chancler, T.O.R.; Bede F. Hines, T.O.R.; Emil C. Resconich, T.O.R.; Jude Ventiquattro, T.O.R.; Oliver Herbert, T.O.R.; Carl A. Szura, T.O.R.; Thomas Carapella, T.O.R.; Fabian McNichol, T.O.R.; Andre Strittmatter, T.O.R.; Patrick Donahoe, T.O.R.

NEWRY. *St. Bernardine Monastery*, P.O. Box 208, 16665. Tel: 814-695-3992; 695-8991. Revs. Frank Scornaienchi, T.O.R., Vicar & Dir. Devel. & Mass Assoc.; Martin D. Brady, T.O.R.; Eugene Kubina, T.O.R., Local Min. & Provincial Treas.; Camillus Angle, T.O.R.; Kenneth La Pan, T.O.R.; Bro. Christian Neetz, T.O.R. Priests 5; Brothers 1.

Novitiate of the Immaculate Conception Province of the T.O.R. of St. Francis. Franciscan Development Office, P.O. Box 139, Hollidaysburg, 16648. Tel: 814-695-3802; Fax: 814-695-1611. Province Treasurer's Office, P.O. Box 117, Hollidaysburg, 16648. Tel: 814-696-3321; Fax: 814-695-1611.

[G] CONVENTS AND RESIDENCES FOR SISTERS
(NON-DIOCESAN)

ALTOONA. *Carmelite Community of the Word*, Ss. Peter & Paul Convent, 1906 19th St., 16601. Tel: 814-942-5747. Total in Residence 4.

Carmelite Community of the Word Motherhouse and Diocesan Pastoral Center, 1304 13th Ave., 16601. Tel: 814-943-0088; 944-9070. Sr. Marilyn Welch, C.C.W., General Admin. Total in Residence 3.

Our Lady of Perpetual Help Convent, 601 Sixth Ave. Juniata, 16601. Tel: 814-942-3819. Sisters, Servants of the Immaculate Heart of Mary. Total in Residence 2; Total Staff 2.

Sisters of Charity, 2011 Second Ave., 16602. Tel: 814-942-8601. Total in Residence 3.

JOHNSTOWN. *Carmelite Community of the Word*, St. Joseph's Convent, 741 Railroad St., 15901. Tel: 814-535-7118. Total in Residence 5.

Sisters of Mercy, Mercy Convent, 972 Fritz St., 15905. Tel: 814-536-2610. Sr. Vincent de Paul Gibbon, R.S.M., Coord. Sisters 5.

CRESSON. *McAuley Hall*, 4 College Dr., 16630-1900. Tel: 814-886-4159. Institute of the Sisters of Mercy of the Americas (Silver Spring, MD). Sr. Ruth Hollen, R.S.M., Coord. Total in Residence 21; Total Staff 9.

Sisters Servants of the Sacred Heart, Provincial House, 866 Cambria St., 16630-1713. Tel: 814-886-4223. Sr. Theresa Marie, S.S.C.J., Provincial Sup.

Personal Care Home. Total in Residence 18; Total Staff 7.

EBENSBURG. *Carmelite Community of the Word*, St. Therese Convent, 218 W. Lloyd St., 15931. Tel: 814-472-9457. Total in Residence 3.

Family Life Office. 5379 Portage St., Lilly, 15938. Tel: 814-886-5551; Fax: 814-886-7697.

Mount St. Ann Retreat House and Novitiate, P.O. Box 328, 15931. Tel: 814-472-9354. Sisters of St. Ann. Sr. Melany Pereira, S.S.A., Supr. Total In Residence 5.

GALLITZIN. *Little Sisters of Jesus*, 347 Tunnel Hill St., 16641. Tel: 814-886-4679. Total in Residence 3.

HASTINGS. *Carmelite Community of the Word.* (Novitiate), Our Lady of Grace Convent, 197 Harvey St., P.O. Box 669, 16646. Tel: 814-247-9954; 247-9956. Total in Residence 4.

LILLY, 5379 Portage St., 15938. Tel: 814-886-5551; Fax: 814-886-7697.

LORETTO. *Carmel of St. Therese of Lisieux Monastery*, P.O. Box 57, 15940. Tel: 814-472-8620. Mother John of the Cross, O.C.D., Prioress. Discalced Carmelite Nuns. Nuns with Solemn Vows 8; Extern Professed 1; Novices 2; Postulants 1.

Our Lady of Loretto, Box 36, 15940. Tel: 814-886-5798. Sisters of Mercy. Total in Residence 5.

MCCONNELLSBURG. *Carmelite Community of the Word*, Fulton County Mission, 110 S. Third St., 17223. Tel: 717-485-5917; 485-5863. Total in Residence 2. Total in Residence 2.

PORTAGE. *Sisters Servants of the Sacred Heart Novitiate,* Sacred Heart Novitiate, 1872 Munster Rd., 15946. Tel: 814-886-7785. Sr. Jacinta Miryam, S.S.C.J., Novice Mistress.

[H] CAMPUS MINISTRY

HOLLIDAYSBURG. *Campus Ministry,* Altoona-Johnstown Diocese, 126A Logan Blvd., 16648.

Juniata College, 17th & Moore St., Huntington, 16648. Tel: 814-641-3361 (Office). Rev. Allen P. Zeth, Chap.; Cheryl Carson, Campus Min.

Lock Haven University (Lock Haven), Newman Center, 445 W. Main St., Lock Haven, 17745. Tel: 717-748-8592. Chaplains: Rev. Neil Dadey; Ms. Theresa Miller.

Mt. Aloysius Jr. College (Cresson), Wm. Penn Hwy., Cresson, 16630. Tel: 814-886-4131. Sr. Benedict Joseph Watters, R.S.M., M.S., Dir.; Rev. George J. Valko, M.A., M.Div., Chap.

Penn State University - Altoona Campus, 3000 Ivyside Park, Altoona, 16601. Tel: 814-949-5000; 949-5835 (Office). Rev. Allen P. Zeth, Chap.

St. Francis College (Loretto), Loretto, 15940. Tel: 814-472-7000. Campus Ministers: Revs. Carl A. Szura, T.O.R. Tel: 814-472-3390 (Office); Jude Ventiquattro, T.O.R. Tel: 814-472-3391 (Office); Thomas Carapella, T.O.R.

University of Pittsburgh at Johnstown, 450 Schoolhouse Rd., Johnstown, 15904. Tel: 814-266-9662, Ext. 336. Rev. Daniel J. O'Neill; Miss Theresa Miller.

[I] NEWMAN CENTERS
(NON-DIOCESAN)

UNIVERSITY PARK. *Penn State Catholic Community,* 207A Helen Eakin Eisenhower Chapel, 16802. Tel: 814-865-4281.
E-mail: mdm121@psu.edu
Web site: http://www.psu.edu/catholic
Campus Ministers: Revs. Conan E. Feigh, O.S.B.; Frederick Byrne, O.S.B.; Joseph Hlubik. Total in Residence 3; Total Staff 6. Catholic Students attending Penn State University 10,000.

[J] MISCELLANEOUS LISTINGS
(NON-DIOCESAN)

BEDFORD. *St. Mary's House of Greater Solitude,* Passionist Community, R.D. 1, Box 276, 15522. Tel: 814-623-1796; Fax: 814-623-2457. Revs. Silvan Rouse, C.P., Supr.; Malachy McGill, C.P.; Howard Chirdon, C.P.

LORETTO. *Prince Gallitzin Chapel House (Diocesan).*
E-mail: mbecker253@aol.com
Mailing Address: P.O. Box 99, 15940. Tel: 814-472-5441.
Office of Vocations.
Office of Ongoing Formation of Clergy.

NEW BALTIMORE. *St. John The Baptist Retreat Center,* P.O. Box 10, 15553. Total in Residence 1; Total Staff 7.

RELIGIOUS INSTITUTES OF MEN REPRESENTED IN THE DIOCESE

For further details refer to the corresponding bracketed number in the Religious Institutes of Men or Women section.

[0200]—*Benedictine Monks.*—O.S.B.
[0470]—*The Capuchin Friars.*—O.F.M.Cap.
[1000]—*Congregation of the Passion.*—C.P.
[0480]—*Conventual Franciscans.* (St. Anthony of Padua Prov.).—O.F.M.Conv.
[0520]—*Franciscan Friars.*—O.F.M.
[0560]—*Third Order Regular of Saint Francis.* (Provs. of Sacred Heart, Immaculate Conception).—T.O.R.

RELIGIOUS INSTITUTES OF WOMEN REPRESENTED IN THE DIOCESE

[0100]—*Adorers of the Blood of Christ.*—A.S.C.
[0315]—*Carmelite Community of the Word.*—C.C.W.
[0330]—*Carmelite Sisters for the Aged and Infirm.*—O.Carm.
[3710]—*Congregation of the Sisters of Saint Agnes.*—C.S.A.
[0420]—*Discalced Carmelite Nuns.*—O.C.D.
[1070-03]—*Dominican Sisters.*—O.P.
[1170]—*Felician Sisters.*—C.S.S.F.
[2330]—*Little Sisters of Jesus.*—L.S.J.
[3630]—*Servants of the Most Sacred Heart of Jesus.*—S.S.C.J.
[0570]—*Sisters of Charity of Seton Hill, Greensburg, Pennsylvania.*—S.C.
[2575]—*Sisters of Mercy of the Americas.*—R.S.M. (Dallas Regional Community).
[1620]—*Sisters of Saint Francis of Millvale, Pennsylvania.*—O.S.F.
[3780]—*Sisters of Ss. Cyril and Methodius.*—SS.C.M.
[3718]—*Sisters of St. Ann.* (Italy).—S.S.A.
[3830]—*Sisters of St. Joseph.*—C.S.J.
[1970]—*Sisters of the Holy Family of Nazareth.*—C.S.F.N.
[3260]—*Sisters of the Precious Blood. (Ohio).*—C.PP.S.
[2160]—*Sisters, Servants of the Immaculate Heart of Mary.* (Scranton, PA).—I.H.M.
[4160]—*Vincentian Sisters of Charity.*—V.S.C.

NECROLOGY

† Gorney, Rev. Msgr. Francis L., (Retired). —Died Feb. 19, 1997.
† Greinader, Rev. Msgr. Linford F., (Retired). —Died July 29, 1997.
† Ossowski, Rev. Msgr. Casimir B., Johnstown, PA, St. Casimir. —Died Jan. 28, 1997.
† Wolf, Benedict L., (Retired). —Died April 20, 1997.
† Zywicki, Francis S., (Retired). —Died Sept. 15, 1997.

Diocese of Amarillo

(Dioecesis Amarillensis)

Most Reverend

JOHN W. YANTA, D.D.

Bishop of Amarillo; ordained March 17, 1956; appointed Titular Bishop of Naratcata and Auxiliary Bishop of San Antonio October 27, 1994; consecrated December 30, 1994; appointed Bishop of Amarillo January 21, 1997.

Most Reverend

LEROY T. MATTHIESEN, D.D., M.A., LITT.D.

Retired Bishop of Amarillo; ordained March 10, 1946; appointed March 25, 1980; ordained May 30, 1980; retired January 21, 1997. *Mailing Address: P.O. Box 5644, Amarillo, TX, 79117-5664.*

ERECTED A DIOCESE BY POPE PIUS XI, AUGUST 25, 1926.

Square Miles Approximately 25,800.

Comprises that part of the State of Texas known as the Panhandle, and extending thence southward; bounded on the east by Oklahoma, and by the eastern county line of Childress and by the southern lines Childress, Hall, Briscoe, Swisher, Castro and Parmer Counties; the western boundary is the New Mexico state line from the southern line of Parmer County, Texas, northward to the northwestern corner of the Panhandle of Texas. There are 26 counties.

For legal titles of parishes and diocesan institutions, consult the Chancery Office.

Diocesan Pastoral Center: 1800 N. Spring St., P.O. Box 5644, Amarillo, TX, 79117-5644. Tel.: 806-383-2243; Fax: 806-383-8452.

STATISTICAL OVERVIEW

Personnel	
Bishop	1
Retired Bishops	1
Priests: Diocesan Active in Diocese	46
Priests: Active Outside Diocese	5
Priests: Retired, Sick or Absent	14
Number of Diocesan Priests	65
Religious Priests in Diocese	6
Extern Priests in Diocese	1
Ordinations:	
Diocesan Priests	1
Permanent Deacons in Diocese	45
Total Brothers	1
Total Sisters	148
Parishes	
Parishes	35
With Resident Pastor:	
Resident Diocesan Priests	29
Resident Religious Priests	3
Without Resident Pastor:	
Administered by Priests	3
Missions	13
Professional Ministry Personnel:	
Sisters	5
Lay Ministers	13
Welfare	
Catholic Hospitals	1
Total Assisted	22,300
Health Care Centers	1
Total Assisted	730
Homes for the Aged	1
Total Assisted	56
Day Care and Extended Day Care Centers	6
Total Assisted	493
Specialized Homes	2
Total Assisted	550
Special Centers for Social Services	4
Total Assisted	35,000
Other Institutions	1
Total Assisted	4
Educational	
Diocesan Students in Other Seminaries	16
Total Seminarians	16
High Schools, Diocesan and Parish	1
Total Students	134
Elementary Schools, Diocesan and Parish	8
Total Students	1,097
Catechesis/Religious Education:	
High School Students	1,792
Elementary Students	3,708
Total Students Under Catholic Instruction	6,747
Teachers in the Diocese:	
Sisters	15
Lay Teachers	104
Vital Statistics	
Receptions into the Church:	
Infant Baptism Totals	1,122
Adult Baptism Totals	114
Received into Full Communion	147
First Communions	1,047
Confirmations	1,066
Marriages:	
Catholic	154
Interfaith	63
Total Marriages	217
Deaths	305
Total Catholic Population	47,387
Total Population	396,914

Former Bishops—Most Rev. RUDOLPH ALOYSIUS GERKEN, D.D., ord. June 10, 1917; cons. April 26, 1927; installed Bishop of Amarillo, April 28, 1927; elevated to the Metropolitan See of Santa Fe, NM, June 2, 1933; died March 2, 1943.—Most Rev. ROBERT E. LUCEY, ord. May 14, 1916; cons. May 1, 1934; installed May 16, 1934; elevated to the Metropolitan See of San Antonio, Jan. 22, 1941.—Most Rev. LAURENCE J. FITZSIMON, D.D., ord. May 17, 1921; cons. Oct. 22, 1941; installed Nov. 5, 1941; died July 2, 1958.—Most Rev. JOHN L. MORKOVSKY, appt. Auxiliary of Amarillo, Dec. 22, 1955; named Bishop of Amarillo, Aug. 18, 1958; transferred as Coadjutor Bishop of Galveston-Houston *"cum jure successionis"*, April 16, 1963.—Most Rev. LAWRENCE M. DEFALCO, D.D., ord. June 11, 1942; appt. April 16, 1963; cons. May 30, 1963; installed June 13, 1963; retired Aug. 28, 1979; died Sept. 22, 1979.—Most Rev. LEROY T. MATTHIESEN, D.D., M.A., LITT.D, ord. March 10, 1946; appt. March 25, 1980; ord. Bishop, May 30, 1980; retired Jan. 21, 1997.

Diocesan Officials

Diocesan Pastoral Center—1800 N. Spring St., Amarillo, 79107. Tel: 806-383-2243; Fax: 806-383-8452., *P.O. Box 5644, Amarillo, 79117-5644.*

Vicar General—Rev. JOSEPH E. BIXENMAN.

Diocesan Tribunal—

Judicial Vicar—Rev. Msgr. JAMES C. GURZYNSKI, J.C.L.

Defender of the Bond—Rev. Msgr. HAROLD WALDOW.

Advocates—Rev. Msgr. JOSEPH TASH; Rev. Msgr. HAROLD WALDOW; Revs. MICHAEL COLWELL; PHU PHAN, J.C.L.

Notaries—Mrs. MADOLYN GUTIERREZ; Ms. SUSAN GARNER.

Chancellor—Rev. MICHAEL COLWELL, J.C.L.

Diocesan Advisory Councils

Presbyteral Council—Revs. RAYMOND CROSIER; JOSE E. GOMEZ; Rev. Msgr. ORVILLE R. BLUM; Rev. Msgr. HAROLD WALDOW; Revs. JOHN VALDEZ; NEAL DEE; JOHN SALAZAR; GREG MAYERS, C.S.S.R.; JOSEPH E. BIXENMAN.

College of Consultors—Revs. JOSEPH BIXENMAN; NEAL DEE; JOHN SALAZAR; Rev. Msgr. JAMES C. GURZYNSKI; Rev. Msgr. KEVIN HAND; Rev. Msgr. FRANCIS A. SMYER; Rev. Msgr. JOSEPH TASH.

Diocesan Pastoral Council—LEO LENERS; LAURENCE WALKER; PAULA BREEDING; THERESA LOPEZ; BRENDA SAUCEDO; MARGIE LONG; MARIA NEAL; ELODIA BRAVO; VENTURA RAMOS; AMPARO BECERRA; GEORGIA SCIACA; ANITA SUMNER; GLORIA MARTIN; MATILDA BACA; BETTY KOELZER; DOROTHY SCHERLEN; Deacon JOE SCHWERTNER.

Vocation Team—

Track I—Rev. Msgr. ORVILLE BLUM, *St. Anthony's Church, 115 N. 25 Mile Rd., Hereford, 79045.* Rev. KENNETH KELLER, *St. Mary's Church, 1200 S. Washington, Amarillo, 79102.* Rev. Msgr. NORBERT C. KUEHLER, *St. John's Church, 201 St. John's Rd., Borger, 79007.* Rev. GUILLERMO MORALES, *Immaculate Conception Church, Dimmitt, 79027.* Rev. MICHAEL COLWELL, Pastoral Center.

Track II—Revs. MICHAEL COLWELL, Coord.; PHU PHAN; JOHN VALDEZ; SCOTT RAEF; ROBERT BUSCH; JUAN CARLOS BARRAGAN.

Deacon Advisory Council—Deacon BLAINE WESTLAKE, Coord.; Revs. JOHN DALTON; PATRICK HOFFMAN; Deacons TIMOTHY REID; BILL DORSEY; Mrs. FRANCES DORSEY; MADOLYN GUTIERREZ.

Diocesan Departments

Youth and Young Adult Ministry—Deacon JESSIE GUERRERO, Dir.

Office for the Catholic Schools—Sr. CORNELIA MARIE KNEZEK, S.S.C.J., Supt.

Christian Formation Commission—CHARLOTTE PAETZOLD, Coord., *St. Anthony's Church, 115 N. 25 Mile Rd., Hereford, 79045.* Tel: 806-364-0969.
Department of Communications—CHRIS ALBRACHT, Dir. Information & Editor "The West Texas Catholic".
Department of Finances and Ecclesiastical Properties—Fiscal Manager—BEN R. SMART.
Director of Administrative Services—PATSY GRAHAM.
Office of Development and Stewardship—NANCY KOONS, Dir., *P.O. Box 1011, Canyon, 79015.* Tel: 806-655-2556.
United Catholic Appeal—NANCY KOONS.

General Auxiliary Pastoral Services

Diocesan Attorney—FREDERICK J. GRIFFIN, *504 S. Polk, Amarillo, 79101.*
Vicar for Canonical Affairs—(see Tribunal).
Coalition for Catholic Social Services - CCSS—Rev. KEN KELLER, Chm.
Catholic Historical Society—EDITH DANILE, Pres.
Diocesan Liturgical Commission—Rev. PHILIP LINDLEY, Chm.
Rural Life Director—Vacant.
Holy Childhood Association—Rev. Msgr. RICHARD F. VAUGHAN.
Propagation of the Faith—Rev. Msgr. RICHARD F. VAUGHAN.
Office of Worship—Rev. PATRICK CARATHERS, Dir.
Rite of Christian Initiation of Adults—Vacant.

Auxiliary Pastoral Services for the Laity

Institute for Pastoral Ministry—Rev. ROBERT BUSCH, Dir., *2610 4th Ave., Canyon, 79015.* Tel: 806-655-4345. THERESA UNRUH, Asst. to Dir.
Diocesan Council of Catholic Women—Rev. Msgr. FRANCIS A. SMYER, Moderator, *1200 S. Washington, Amarillo, 79102.*
Engaged Encounter—Directors:: BLAIN WESTLAKE; LOUISE WESTLAKE. Contact Couple:: JENNY BALLARD; AGNES BALLARD. Tel: 806-353-0907.
Beginning Experience—BECKY SONDERSON. Tel: 806-364-5813.
Catholic Student Center at West Texas A & M University—Rev. ROBERT BUSCH, Dir.-Chap., *2614 Fourth Ave., Canyon, 79015.* Tel: 806-655-4345.
Scouting—Deacon JESSIE GUERRERO, *1200 S. Washington, Amarillo, 79102.*
Serra Club—DAVID DZIK, Pres.
Natural Family Planning—Certified Teaching Couples: GERALD MARNELL; DENISE MARNELL, *Rte. 5, Box 117-A, Hereford, 79045.* JOHN BRADICICH; CALEY BRADICICH.

Auxiliary Pastoral Services for Clergy and Religious

Vicar for Priests—Rev. Msgr. RICHARD F. VAUGHAN.
Vicar for Religious—Sr. HELEN ANN COLLIER, C.C.V.I., *St. Anthony's Hospital, 200 N.W. Seventh St., Amarillo, 79176-0001.* Tel:
Office for the Permanent Diaconate—Deacon BLAINE WESTLAKE, Coord.
Continuing Education of Clergy—Rev. ROBERT BUSCH.
Priests' Retirement—PATSY GRAHAM.

CLERGY, PARISHES, MISSIONS AND PAROCHIAL SCHOOLS

CITY OF AMARILLO
(Potter County)

1—SACRED HEART CATHEDRAL. Closed. This parish ceased to exist 1/19/75. For inquiries contact the Diocese of Amarillo: P.O. Box 5644, Amarillo, TX 79117-5644. Tel: 806-383-2243.

2—ST. LAURENCE CATHEDRAL, Revs. Patrick Hoffman; Arnulfo Gradillas, C.S.Sp.; Deacon Leo Ramos.
Res., 2300 N. Spring St., 79107. Tel: 806-383-2261.
Kindergarten & Child Development Center—. Sisters 3; Lay Teachers 17; Students 110.
Catechesis/Religious Programs—Students 397.

3—BLESSED SACRAMENT, Rev. Phillip Lindley; Deacon Mark Seidlitz.
Res., 4112 S.E. 25th St., 79103. Tel: 806-374-1132.
Catechesis/Religious Programs—Carolina Searcy, D.R.E.
Students 75.

4—OUR LADY OF GUADALUPE, Rev. Hector Madrigal; Deacon Hector Gallegos.
Res., 1210 E. 11th Ave., 79102. Tel: 806-372-1128.
School—See Elementary Schools, City-Wide under Institutions Located in the Diocese.
Catechesis/Religious Programs—Martha Loza, D.R.E.
Students 485.

5—OUR LADY OF VIETNAM, Revs. Polycarp Ducthuan, C.M.C.; Joseph Le Van Canh; John Baptist Phan Van Chac.
Res., 1800 N. Spring Rd., 79107. Tel: 806-383-0467.

6—ST. FRANCIS, Rev. Theodore E. Podson, Sch.P.
Res., 5005 Klinke Rd., 79107-9628. Tel: 806-335-1872.
Catechesis/Religious Programs—Evelyn Detten, D.R.E.
Students 43.

7—ST. HYACINTH'S, Revs. Patrick Carathers; Bert Horvath; Sr. Hilary Decker, O.S.B., Pastoral Assoc. & D.R.E.
Res., 4500 W. Hills Tr., 79106. Tel: 806-358-1351; Fax: 806-467-1708.
Catechesis/Religious Programs—Students 77.

8—ST. JOSEPH'S, Rev. Neal Dee; Deacons James R. Ambs; Richard Riley; Bill Jordon; Robert Smith.
Res., 4122 Bonham St., 79110. Tel: 806-355-5621; Fax: 806-355-5622.
School—See Elementary Schools, City-Wide under Institutions Located in the Diocese.
St. Joseph Day Care Center—4108 Bonham, 79110. Tel: 806-353-7043.
Students 86.
Catechesis/Religious Programs—Mrs. Rosie Sisneros, D.R.E.
Students 219.

9—ST. MARTIN DE PORRES MISSION, Rev. Francis R. Crowe, O.P.
Res., 1501 N. Adams, P.O. Box 1951, 79105. Tel: 806-376-8871.

10—ST. MARY'S, Rev. Msgr. Francis A. Smyer; Rev. Ken Keller.
Res., 1200 Washington St., 79102. Tel: 806-376-7204; Fax: 806-376-4314.
School—See Elementary Schools, City-Wide under Institutions Located in the Diocese.
Catechesis/Religious Programs—Cindy Luginbill, D.R.E.
Students 493.

11—ST. THOMAS THE APOSTLE, Rev. Msgr. Joseph T. Tash; Deacons Terry Pevehouse; Timothy Reid; Blain Westlake. In res., Rev. Robert Busch.
Res., 4100 Coulter Dr., 79109. Tel: 806-358-2461; Fax: 806-358-2529.
Catechesis/Religious Programs—D.R.E.: Bernice Noggler, (Grades PreK-5); Amy Reid, (Grades 6-12).
Students 632.
Mission—Amarillo, Potter Co., Laotian Catholic Community. Rev. Phu T. Phan, J.C.L.

OUTSIDE THE CITY OF AMARILLO

Borger, Hutchinson Co., St. John the Evangelist, Rev. Msgr. Norbert Kuehler; Rev. Juan Carlos Barragan; Deacon Zeferino Jimenez.
Res., 201 St. John's Rd., 79007. Tel: 806-274-7064.
School—Linda Wright, Dir. Sisters 3; Lay Teachers 3; Students 65.
Catechesis/Religious Programs—Cathy Gregory, D.R.E.
Students 245.
Convent—Tel: 806-274-6504.
Mission—Stinnett, St. Ann's.

Bovina, Parmer Co., St. Ann's, Rev. Ed Kieran; Deacon Zeferino Villarreal.
Res., Box 657, 79009. Tel: 806-238-1511.
Catechesis/Religious Programs—Nancy Schwertner, D.R.E.
Students 200.

Canadian, Hemphill Co., Sacred Heart, Revs. James McGhee; John Valdez, Parochial Admin.; Deacon Jose Jesus Gutierrez.
Res., 721 Main, P.O. Box 786, 79014. Tel: 806-323-9705.

Canyon, Randall Co., St. Ann's, Rev. Phu T. Phan; Deacons Jerry Grossman; August Hesse, III; Mauro Hernandes; Gabriel Rivas.
Mailing Address: P.O. Box 59, 79015.
Res., 38th St. at Conner Dr., 79015. Tel: 806-655-3302; Fax: 806-655-3384.
Catechesis/Religious Programs—Carol Sanford, D.R.E.
Students 270.

Childress, Childress Co., Holy Angels, Rev. Dennis Boylan.
Res., 308 Ave. B, S.W., P.O. Box 608, 79201. Tel: 940-937-3946; Fax: 940-937-3946.
Catechesis/Religious Programs—Students 40.

Clarendon, Donley Co., St. Mary's, Rev. Jose Gomez; Deacon Bill Dorsey.
Res., 815 McClelland St., P.O. Drawer C, 79226. Tel: 806-874-3910.

Dalhart, Dallam Co., St. Anthony's, Revs. Dale Guidry; Rosendo Herrera; Deacon Ronald Hein.
Res., 411 Texas Blvd., Box 1029, 79022. Tel: 806-249-4811; Fax: 806-249-4811.
School—1302 Oak St., 79022. Tel: 806-249-2390. Mrs. Sandra Kelso, Prin.
School Sisters of the Third Order of St. Francis 2; Lay Teachers 3; Students 69.
Mission—Texline, Dallum Co., St. Mary's.

Dimmitt, Castro Co., Immaculate Conception, Rev. Guillermo Morales; Deacons Joseph Ortega; John Nino; Jose Luis Velo.
Res., 710 W. Halsell St., 79027. Tel: 806-647-4219 (Church); 647-0105 (Office).
Catechesis/Religious Programs—Mary Helen Flores, D.R.E.
Students 400.

Dumas, Moore Co., SS. Peter and Paul, Rev. Richard D. Scully; Deacons Joseph Schwertner; Jessie Ruiz; Vacilio Anaya.
Res., Box 503, 79029. Tel: 806-935-5002.
Catechesis/Religious Programs—D.R.E.: Rhonda Ollinger; Ann Easterling.
Students 300.
Missions—Sunray, Moore Co., Christ the King, Box 503, Dumas, 79029. Tel: 806-396-5687. Deacon Wayne Norrell.; Cactus, Our Lady of Guadalupe, Box 28, Stratford, 79084. Tel: 806-396-5687.

Friona, Parmer Co., St. Teresa of Jesus, Rev. Edward Sweeney; Deacons Zeferino Villarreal; Raymond Solano.
Res., HCR 2, Box 1A, P.O. Box 381, 79035-0381. Tel: 806-247-2871; Fax: 806-247-2871.
Catechesis/Religious Programs—D.R.E.: Diana Santella; Lisa Alaniz.
Students 142.

Groom, Carson Co., Immaculate Heart of Mary, Rev. Raymond Crosier.
Res., 411 Ware Ave., P.O. Box 130, 79039. Tel: 806-248-7584. [CEM]
Catechesis/Religious Programs—Students 67.

Gruver, Cristo Redentor, Rev. Scott Raef; Deacon Jesus Favela.
Res., 603 Main St., P.O. Box 238, 79040. Tel: 806-733-5236.
Catechesis/Religious Programs—Elena Salazar, D.R.E.
Students 51.

Happy, Swisher Co., Holy Name of Jesus, Revs. Jerry Stein; John Hickey; Deacon Amadeo Perez.
Res., 317 W. Main, P.O. Box 128, 79042. Tel: 806-558-2871. [CEM]
Catechesis/Religious Programs—Students 35.

Hereford, Deaf Smith Co., St. Anthony's, Rev. Msgr. Orville Blum; Deacon Jonay Cloud; Charlotte Paetzold, Pastoral Assoc.
Res., 115 N. 25 Mile Ave., 79045. Tel: 806-364-6150; 364-6152; Fax: 806-364-0969.
School—120 W. Park Ave., 79045. Tel: 806-364-1952. Ann Lueb, Prin.
Franciscan Sisters of Mary Immaculate 2; Lay Teachers 11; Students 139.
Catechesis/Religious Programs—Students 211.
Convent—114 Sunset, 79045. Tel: 806-364-3344.

San Jose, Rev. Domingo Castillo; Deacons Esteban Castillo; Emilio Fuentes; Vicente Garcia; Jessie Guerrero, Pastoral Assoc.
Res., 735 Brevard, 79045. Tel: 806-364-5053; Fax: 806-364-2880.
Preschool—.
Catechesis/Religious Programs—Tel: 806-364-4365.
Students 360.

Memphis, Hall Co., Sacred Heart, Rev. Jose Gomez.
Mailing Address: 213 N. Third St., P.O. Box 239, 79245. Tel: 806-259-2178.
Catechesis/Religious Programs—Mrs. Juanita Garza, D.R.E.
Students 24.

Nazareth, Castro Co., Holy Family, Revs. Jerry Stein; John Hickey; Deacons Jerome Brockman; Alfonse Mauer.
Res., 210 St. Joseph, P.O. Box 100, 79063. Tel: 806-945-2616.
Catechesis/Religious Programs—Gladys Fortenberry, D.R.E.
Students 192.
Mission—Hart, St. John's.

Pampa, Gray Co., St. Vincent de Paul, Rev. John Valdez; Sr. Nancy Dragotta, S.C.S.J.A., Pastoral Assoc.; Deacons Tony Campos; Daniel Rose.
Res., 810 W. 23rd St., 79065. Tel: 806-665-2840.
School—2300 N. Hobart, 79065.
Lay Teachers 10; Students 112.
Catechesis/Religious Programs—Students 204.

Panhandle, Carson Co., St. Theresa, Rev. Gary Sides.
Res., P.O. Box 366, 79068. Tel: 806-537-3677.
Catechesis/Religious Programs—Mother M. Valentina, D.R.E.
Students 140.

Perryton, Ochiltree Co., Immaculate Conception, Rev. Rex F. Nicholl.
Res., 1000 S.W. Fifth Ave., 79070. Tel: 806-435-3802.
Catechesis/Religious Programs—Daryla Allred, D.R.E.
Students 225.
Mission—Booker, St. Peter.

Spearman, Hansford Co., Sacred Heart, Rev. Scott Raef.
Res., 1109 Townsend, P.O. Box 127, 79081. Tel: 806-659-2166; Fax: 806-659-1042.
Catechesis/Religious Programs—David & Lisa Link, D.R.E.
Students 130.
Mission—Gruver, Iglesia Castro Redentor, P.O. Box 238, Gruver, 79040.

Stratford, Sherman Co., St. Joseph's, Rev. David Contreras; Deacon Willie Artho.
Mailing Address: Box 28, 79084. Tel: 806-396-5687.
Catechesis/Religious Programs—Johnny Garza, D.R.E.
Students 70.

Tulia, Swisher Co., Church of the Holy Spirit, Rev. John Salazar-Jimenez. Pastoral Assocs.: Mary Lou Moreno; Ventura Ramos.
Res., 513 S. Austin, P.O. Box 25, 79088. Tel: 806-995-3191; Fax: 806-995-3286.
Catechesis/Religious Programs—Martha Rocha, D.R.E.
Students 225.
Missions—Silverton, Briscoe Co., Our Lady of Loreto, P.O. Box 47, Silverton, 79257. Rev. Ed Graff, Parochial Admin.; Kress, Swisher Co., St. Paul's, P.O. Box 231, Kress, 79052. Ampara Becerra, Pastoral Assoc.
Station—Quitaque.

Umbarger, Randall Co., St. Mary's, Rev. James Hutzler.
Res., P.O. Box 105, 79091. Tel: 806-499-3531. [CEM]
Catechesis/Religious Programs—Karen Frimel, D.R.E.
Students 100.

Vega, Oldham Co., Immaculate Conception, Revs. Patrick Carathers; Bert Horvath.
Res., P.O. Box 250, 79092. Tel: 806-267-2343.
Catechesis/Religious Programs—Patty Frerich, D.R.E.
Students 88.

Wellington, Collingsworth Co., Our Mother of Mercy, Rev. Cal Stalter.
Church—1108 Floydada, P.O. Box 686, 79095.
Mission—Shamrock, St. Patrick. Rev. Cal Stalter, Admin.

White Deer, Carson Co., Sacred Heart, Rev. Msgr. Kevin Hand.
Res., Box 427, 79097. Tel: 806-883-4781.
Catechesis/Religious Programs—Ben Rapstine, D.R.E.
Students 67.

Absent on Leave:
Reverend Fathers—
Alvarez, Xavier
Madrigal, Hector
Rosolen, Emil
Sherry, Brendan

On Duty Outside the Diocese:
Reverend Fathers—
Afunugo, Emmanuel
Birkenfeld, Darryl
Greka, David
Malnar, Matthew
Meza, Arturo
Wood, Michael Bruce

On Special or Other Diocesan Assignment:
Reverend Monsignors—
Vaughan, Richard F., Vicar for Priests, Pastoral Services for Clergy and Religious

---

Military Chaplains:
Reverend Fathers—
Otto, Peter B., U.S. Air Force

Retired:
Reverend Monsignors—
Corcoran, Clifton J., P.O. Box 1179, Panhandle, TX 79068
Erpen, B. A., 318 S.E. Fifth, Tulia, TX 79088
Morsch, Peter, 1410 Peoria Dr., Slaton, TX 79364
Sonderman, James W., P.O. Box 1179, Panhandle, TX 79068
Reverend Fathers—
Brashears, Bill, 1505 Rusk, Amarillo, TX 79102
Carlson, J. Arnold, P.O. Box 1179, Panhandle, TX 79068
Chen, Raphael, 9170 Graham, Cypress, CA 90630
Choong, Norbert, 6303 Butte Ave., New Port Richey, FL 34653
Pawlak, Ed, 5431 Denise Ave., Orlando, FL 32810-3609
Stortz, Mario, Rte. 1, Box 174, Tulia, TX 79088

Permanent Deacons:
Ambs, James R., St. Joseph's Church, Amarillo
Anaya, Vacilio, Sts. Peter and Paul Church, Dumas
Artho, Kenneth, Inactive
Artho, Willie F., St. Joseph's Church, Stratford
Blunt, Orvel Ray, On Leave
Brockman, Jerome, Holy Family Church, Nazareth
Campos, Tony, St. Vincente de Paul Church, Pampa
Castillo, Esteban, On Leave
Cloud, Jonny E., St. Anthony Church, Hereford
Dollins, Belvin G., St. Hyacinth's
Dorsey, Bill, St. Mary's Church, Clarendon
Frausto, Joseph, Inactive
Fromm, Jeffery, St. Cloud Diocese
Fuentes, Emilio, Sr., San Jose Church, Hereford
Gallegos, Hector, Our Lady of Guadalupe Church, Amarillo
Garcia, Vicente H., San Jose Church, Hereford
Gonzales, Roberto, St. John Nepomucene Church, Hart
Grossman, Jerry, St. Ann's Church, Canyon
Guerrero, Jesse, San Jose Church, Hereford
Gutierrez, Jose Jesus, Sacred Heart Church, Canadian
Gutierrez, Robert, On Leave
Hein, Ronald, St. Anthony's Church, Dalhart
Hernandez, Mauro, St. Ann's Church, Canyon
Hesse, August, III, St. Ann's Church, Canyon
Jimenez, Zeferino, St. John's Church, Borger
Jordan, Bill, St. Joseph's Church, Amarillo
Keller, Robert C., Diocese of Galveston-Houston
Maurer, Alfons A., Diocese of Tyler
Nino, John, Immaculate Conception Church, Dimmitt
Norrell, Wayne, Christ the King Church, Sunray
Ortega, Joseph, (Retired)
Perez, Amadeo, Holy Name Church, Happy
Pevehouse, Terry, St. Thomas the Apostle Church, Amarillo
Ramos, Leo, St. Laurence Cathedral, Amarillo
Reid, Timothy, St. Thomas Church, Amarillo
Riley, Richard D., St. Joseph's Church, Amarillo
Rivas, Gabriel, St. Ann's Church, Canyon
Rose, Daniel, St. Vincente de Paul Church, Pampa
Ruiz, Jesse P., Diocese of Fort Worth
Schwertner, Joseph A., SS. Peter & Paul Church, Dumas
Seidlitz, Mark, Blessed Sacrament Church, Amarillo
Smith, Robert, St. Joseph's Church, Amarillo
Solano, Raymond, St. Theresa's Church, Friona
Stewart, Arthur Gerald, (Retired)
Thiele, William E., Sick Leave
Valdez, Pete, On Leave
Velo, Joe, Immaculate Conception Church, Dimmitt
Villarreal, Zeferino, St. Ann's Church, Bovina
Westlake, Blain, St. Thomas Church, Amarillo

INSTITUTIONS LOCATED IN THE DIOCESE

[A] HIGH SCHOOLS, CITY-WIDE

AMARILLO. *Alamo Catholic High School and Amarillo Catholic Middle School.* (Coed), 4114 S. Bonham, 79110-1113. Tel: 806-355-9637; 356-0550. Darla Mueller, Prin., 4110 S. Bonham, 79110-1113. High School. Priests 2; Lay Teachers 14; Students 61. *Middle School.* Sisters 2; Lay Teachers 14; Students 73.

[B] ELEMENTARY SCHOOLS, CITY-WIDE

AMARILLO. *Our Lady of Guadalupe School*, 1103 S. Houston, 79102. Tel: 806-372-2629. Lea Reynolds, Prin. Lay Teachers 4; Students 51. 1108 S. Houston, 79102.
St. Joseph's School, 4118 Bonham St., 79110. Tel: 806-359-1604. Mrs. Betty Keller, Prin. Priests 1; Lay Teachers 13; Students 80.
St. Laurence Cathedral School, 2300-B N. Spring St., 79107. Tel: 806-383-2261. Sr. Pauline Broman, O.S.F., Prin. Sisters 2; Lay Teachers 3; Students 35.
St. Mary School, 1200 S. Washington, 79102. Davlyn Duesterhaus, Prin. Sisters 2; Lay Teachers 21; Students 292.

[C] CATHOLIC CHILDREN'S DEVELOPMENT CENTERS

AMARILLO. *Amarillo Catholic Children's Development Centers.*
St. Joseph Campus, 4108 Bonham St., P.O. Box 19726, 79114. Tel: 806-383-4411. Theresa Pigott, Dir. Sisters 1; Teachers 2; Caregivers 11; Students 95.
St. Laurence Campus, 2300-B N. Spring St., 79107. Tel: 806-383-4411. Theresa Pigott, Dir. Sisters 1; Lay Teachers 2; Caregivers 13; Students 100.
Our Lady of Guadalupe Campus, 1108 S. Houston, 79102. Tel: 806-372-2629. Katrina Adams, Dir. Teachers 2; Caregivers 2; Students 30.
St. John Campus, 201 St. John's Rd., Borger, 79007. Tel: 806-273-3941.
San Jose Preschool, 725 Brevard, Hereford, 79045. Tel: 806-364-5053; Fax: 806-364-2880. Tomas Salazar, Dir. & Teacher.
St. Mary's Montessori School, 1200 S. Washington, 79102. Tel: 806-376-9155. Roe Fitzsimmons, Dir.

[D] HOMES FOR THE AGED

PANHANDLE. *St. Ann's Nursing Home*, P.O. Box 1179, 79068. Tel: 806-537-3194
For a complete listing, refer to the Special Care Facilities section.
St. Joseph's Home for Retired Priests, P.O. Box 1179, 79068
For a complete listing, refer to the Special Care Facilities section.

[E] COALITION OF CATHOLIC SOCIAL SERVICES

AMARILLO.
**Catholic Family Service, Inc.*, 200 S. Tyler, 79102. Tel: 806-376-4571; Fax: 806-345-7911. Mailing Address: Box 15127, 79105-5127. Al Bednorz, Dir.
Morning Star Hostel and Mark Schupp Center, 2501 W. Sixth, 79102. Tel: 806-371-0373. Rev. Terence Burke, Dir.
**Downtown Women's Center and Abba House, Inc.*, P.O. Box 1985, 79105. Tel: 806-372-3625. Sr. Mary Virginia Clarke, D.C., Dir.
**Another Chance Houses, Inc.*, 209 S. Jackson, 79101. Tel: 806-372-3344. Dale Botts, Dir.

[F] GENERAL HOSPITALS

*AMARILLO. *Baptist St. Anthony Health System*, 1600 Wallace Blvd., 79106. Tel: 806-358-3151
For a complete listing, refer to the Hospitals section.

[G] SPECIAL HOSPITALS

AMARILLO. *St. Anthony's Hospice and Life Enrichment Center*, 600 N. Tyler, P.O. Box 950, 79176. Tel: 806-378-6777; Fax: 806-378-5031
For a complete listing, refer to the Hospitals section.

[H] RETREAT HOUSE

AMARILLO. *Bishop DeFalco Retreat Center*, 2100 N. Spring St., 79107. Tel: 806-383-1811; Fax: 806-383-6919. The Redemptorist Fathers. Rev. Gregory Mayers, C.SS.R., Dir. Retreat Staff: Rev. Pat Hawk, C.SS.R.; Bro. Michael Rhodes, C.SS.R.
Bishop DeFalco Retreat Center Foundation.

[I] MONASTERIES AND RESIDENCES OF PRIESTS AND BROTHERS

AMARILLO. *Redemptorists Fathers*, 2100 N. Spring St., 79107. Tel: 806-383-1811. Priests 2; Brothers 1.

[J] CONVENTS AND RESIDENCES FOR SISTERS

AMARILLO. *Daughters of Charity of St. Vincent de Paul*, 1104 S. Washington, 79102. Tel: 806-734-7812. Sisters 4.
Madres Clarisas Capuchinas, Capuchin Nuns of St. Clare, 4201 N.E. 18th Ave., 79107.
Convent of the Blessed Sacrament and Our Lady of Guadalupe. Mother Rocio Hernandez, O.S.C., Abbess. Professed Nuns 12; Apostulants 3; Novices 1.
St. Francis Convent, Novitiate and U.S. Provincial House, 4301 N.E. 18th, 79107. Tel: 806-383-5769. Franciscan Sisters of Mary Immaculate of the Third Order of St. Francis. Sr. Geraldine Duran, F.M.I., Prov. Supr.; Rev. Bert Horvath, Chap. Sisters 47.
St. Francis Mission Community, O.S.F., LaVerna Convent, 203 S. Avondale, 79106. Tel: 806-352-2981. Sr. Celine Thames, O.S.F., Mission Community Coord. Sisters 5.
St. Martin's Convent, 1507 N. Adams St., P.O. Box 5398, 79117. Tel: 806-373-6024. Sisters of Charity of St. Jeanne Antide.

BORGER. *St. John's Convent*, 201 St. John's Rd., 79007. Tel: 806-274-6504. Franciscan Sisters of Mary Immaculate. Sisters 4.

CANYON. *St. Benedict's Monastery*, 2100 Fifth Ave., 79015. Tel: 806-655-9317. Sr. Mary Hawkins, O.S.B., Supr. Sisters 5.

CHANNING. *Disciples of the Lord Jesus Christ.* Mailing Address: Emmanuel Prayer Town, Motherhouse and Retreat Center, P.O. Box 17, 79018-0017. Tel: 806-534-2312. House of Prayer (Mission House), 4609 Coliseum Blvd., Alexandria, LA, 71303. Sr.

Bernadette Beamsley, Supr. Gen.; Rev. John Dalton, Chap. Members 42.

DALHART. *St. Anthony's Convent,* 1301 Oak Ave., 79022. Tel: 806-249-2390. School Sisters of St. Francis. Sisters 5.

HEREFORD. *St. Anthony's Convent,* 114 Sunset Dr., 79045. Tel: 806-364-3344. Franciscan Sisters of Mary Immaculate. Sisters 3.

PANHANDLE. *Sancta Maria Convent (North American Region and Novitiate),* P.O. Box 906, 79068-0906. Tel: 806-537-3182. School Sisters of the Third Order of St. Francis. Mother Bernadette Black, Regl. Supr. Sisters 26.

[K] CAMPUS MINISTRY

CANYON. *Catholic Student Center at West Texas A & M University,* 2610 Fourth Ave., 79015. Tel: 806-655-4345.
E-mail: frrabcsc@qrn.net
Web site: www.wtcsc.org
Rev. Robert Busch, Chap. & Dir.

[L] MISCELLANEOUS LISTINGS

AMARILLO. *Amarillo Catholic Education Foundation,* 1800 N. Spring St., 79107. Tel: 806-383-2243; Fax: 806-383-8452.

Amarillo Catholic School System, 1800 N. Spring St., 79109. Tel: 806-383-2243; Fax: 806-383-8452.
E-mail: amacathschof@connectInc.com

Amarillo Scholarship Endowment and Assistance Fund, 1800 N. Spring St., 79107. Tel: 806-383-2243; Fax: 806-383-8452.

Engaged Encounter, 3600 Torre, 79109. Tel: 806-352-2607. Directors: Blain Westlake; Louise Westlake. Contact Couple: Jenny Ballard. Tel: 806-353-0907; Agnes Ballard.

Marriage Encounter, 1800 N. Spring, 79107. Rev. Arnulfo Gradillas, C.S.Sp., Dir.

RELIGIOUS INSTITUTES OF MEN REPRESENTED IN THE DIOCESE

For further details refer to the corresponding bracketed number in the Religious Institutes of Men or Women section.

[]—*Congregation of Mother Coredemptrix.*—C.M.C.

[0430]—*Order of Preachers-Dominicans.*—O.P.

[1070]—*Redemptorist Fathers.* (New Orleans Vice Prov.).—C.SS.R.

RELIGIOUS INSTITUTES OF WOMEN REPRESENTED IN THE DIOCESE

[0230]—*Benedictine Sisters of Pontifical Jurisdiction.* (Little Rock, AR).—O.S.B.

[0460]—*Congregation of the Sisters of Charity of the Incarnate Word.*—C.C.V.I.

[0760]—*Daughters of Charity of St. Vincent De Paul.*—D.C.

[0965]—*Disciples of the Lord Jesus Christ.*—D.L.J.C.

[1500]—*Franciscan Sisters of Mary Immaculate of the Third Order of St. Francis of Assisi.*—F.M.I.

[]—*Franciscan Sisters of Perpetual Adoration.*—F.F.P.A.

[]—*St. Clare Capuchin Sisters.*—C.P.C.

[1695]—*School Sisters of the Third Order of St. Francis, (Panhandle, Texas).*—O.S.F.

[0600]—*Sisters of St. Jeanne Antide.*—S.C.S.J.A.

[3670]—*Sisters of the Sacred Heart of Jesus of St. Jacut.*—S.S.C.J.

[1705]—*Sisters of the Third Order of St. Francis of Assisi.*—O.S.F.

NECROLOGY

(No Deaths)

Archdiocese of Anchorage

(Archidioecesis Ancoragiensis)

Most Reverend

FRANCIS T. HURLEY, D.D.

Archbishop of Anchorage; ordained June 16, 1951; appointed Titular Bishop of Daimlaig and Auxiliary of Juneau February 4, 1970; consecrated March 19, 1970; appointed Bishop of Juneau July 20, 1971; installed September 8, 1971; appointed Archbishop of Anchorage May 4, 1976; installed July 8, 1976.

ESTABLISHED FEBRUARY 9, 1966.

Comprises the Third Judicial Division of Alaska.

Square Miles 138,985.

For legal titles of parishes and archdiocesan institutions, consult the Chancery Office.

Chancery Office: 225 Cordova St., Anchorage, AK, 99501. Tel.: 907-258-7898; Fax: 907-279-3885.

Web site address: http://www.cathanchornews.org

E-mail address: 71162.711@compuserve.com

STATISTICAL OVERVIEW

Personnel	
Archbishop	1
Retired Abbots	1
Priests: Diocesan Active in Diocese	12
Priests: Active Outside Diocese	1
Priests: Diocesan in Foreign Missions	1
Priests: Retired, Sick or Absent	6
Number of Diocesan Priests	20
Religious Priests in Diocese	10
Extern Priests in Diocese	8
Permanent Deacons in Diocese	12
Total Brothers	1
Total Sisters	44
Parishes	
Parishes	20
With Resident Pastor:	
Resident Diocesan Priests	11
Resident Religious Priests	3
Without Resident Pastor:	
Administered by Women Religious	3
Administered by Lay People	2
Administered by Pastoral Teams, etc.	1
Missions	8
Professional Ministry Personnel:	
Sisters	9
Lay Ministers	17
Welfare	
Catholic Hospitals	1
Total Assisted	287,000
Health Care Centers	1
Total Assisted	380
Homes for the Aged	2
Total Assisted	189
Specialized Homes	2
Total Assisted	4,172
Special Centers for Social Services	5
Total Assisted	13,600
Educational	
Diocesan Students in Other Seminaries	3
Total Seminarians	3
High Schools, Private	1
Total Students	60
Elementary Schools, Diocesan and Parish	2
Total Students	347
Elementary Schools, Private	1
Total Students	140
Catechesis/Religious Education:	
High School Students	899
Elementary Students	2,630
Total Students Under Catholic Instruction	4,079
Teachers in the Diocese:	
Sisters	6
Lay Teachers	43
Vital Statistics	
Receptions into the Church:	
Infant Baptism Totals	562
Adult Baptism Totals	67
Received into Full Communion	69
First Communions	610
Confirmations	326
Marriages:	
Catholic	82
Interfaith	77
Total Marriages	159
Deaths	121
Total Catholic Population	28,723
Total Population	384,209

Former Bishop—Most Rev. JOSEPH T. RYAN, D.D., Archbishop of Anchorage; ord. June 3, 1939; cons. March 25, 1966; installed April 14, 1966; transferred as Coadjutor Military Vicar of U.S. Armed Forces, Dec. 13, 1975; appt. First Archbishop of the Archdiocese for the Military Services, U.S.A., March 16, 1985.

Vicar General—Rev. STEVEN C. MOORE.

Chancery Office—225 Cordova St., Anchorage, 99501. Tel: 907-258-7898; Fax: 907-279-3885.

Chancellor—Vacant.

Assistant to Archbishop—Rev. TIMOTHY M. CROWLEY.

Secretary to Archbishop—JOANN WHITE.

Office of Stewardship/Development—Mr. JAMES CALDAROLA.

Tribunal—225 Cordova St., Box 102239, Anchorage, 99510-2239. Tel: 907-258-7898. Mr. GREG O'KEEFE, Treasurer.

Judicial Vicar—Rev. J. MICHAEL HORNICK, S.T.B., J.C.L.

Defenders of the Bond—Deacon WILLIAM FINNEGAN, J.C.L.; MIRIAM DONOHUE.

Advocate for Respondents—Sr. MAUREEN MCPARTLAND, O.P.

Notaries—MIRIAM DONOHUE; EILEEN T. KRAMER.

Diocesan Consultors—Rev. Msgr. FRANCIS A. COWGILL; Revs. STEVEN C. MOORE, Ex Officio; ALFRED W. GIEBEL; LEO DESSO; LASALLE HALLISSEY, O.P.; RICHARD D. TERO; FRED BUGARIN; DANIEL J. HEBERT.

Representatives for Pastoral Adminstrators—Sr. MARIE ANN BRENT, S.H.F.; Sr. JOYCE ROSS, R.S.M.

Archdiocesan Offices and Directors

Apostleship of the Sea—Port Chaplains: Anchorage: SALLY BOSTWICK; Cordova: Sr. PEGGY GLYNN, O.P.; Kodiak: Rev. FRED BUGARIN; Seward: Rev. RICHARD STRASS, C.SS.R.

A.R.E.A./RENEW Coordinator—KATHY BISHOP, *c/o Chancery Office.*

Campaign for Human Development—Rev. ERNEST H. MUELLERLEILE, Dir., *8147 Medellin Cir., Anchorage, 99507.* Tel: 907-349-3910.

Catholic Social Services—SUZANNE GOODRICH, Exec. Dir., *225 Cordova St., Anchorage, 99501.* Tel: 907-277-2554; Fax: 907-279-3885.

Board Members—DAVID GOTTSTEIN; JAMES PALMER; Mr. CHRIS SWALLING; Mr. DONALD STONEBURNER; Mr. JOE MORAN; FRAN MARGARGER; SUSAN ELLIOTT; BEN BARRERA; REGINA DEFRANCISCO; LISA MURKOWSKI.

Communications—Bro. CHARLES MCBRIDE, C.S.C., *c/o Chancery Office.*

Hispanic Ministry—Sr. VERONICA RIVAS, M.C.D.P., *c/o Our Lady of Guadalupe Parish, 3900 Wisconsin St., Anchorage, 99517.*

Korean Ministry—Rev. YOUCHUL PHILIP KIM; Sr. KOUNG JA MARIA BEDA KIM, S.P.C.; Sr. MYEONG SEON CLAIRA SEONG, S.P.C.; Sr. SOON HEE ROMANANA LEE, S.P.C., *St. Anthony's Parish, 825 S. Klevin St., Anchorage, 99508.* Tel: 907-337-5307.

Lay Leadership Program—Mrs. JOYCE D. SCHUTT, *c/o Chancery Office.*

Native Ministry—Sr. M. VICTOR NEGRETE, S.H.F., *c/o Chancery Office.*

Office of Finance—c/o Chancery Office.

Pastoral Administrator Mentor—Rev. LEROY CLEMENTICH, C.S.C., *c/o Chancery Office.*

Pastoral Leadership Formation Program—Deacon DAVID E. SCHUTT.

Permanent Diaconate—Rev. TIMOTHY M. CROWLEY, *c/o Chancery Office.*

Propagation of the Faith—JAMES CALDAROLA, *c/o Chancery Office.*

Retreats—Rev. VINCENT BEUZER, S.J., Dir., *Holy Spirit Retreat House, 10980 Hillside Dr., Anchorage, 99516.* Tel: 907-346-2343.

Superintendent of Schools—Sr. DIANE BARDOL, G.N.S.H., *St. Mary's School, 2932 Mill Bay Rd., Kodiak, 99615.* Tel: 907-486-3513.

Vocations—Rev. STEVEN MOORE, *c/o Chancery Office.*

Youth—Vacant, *c/o Chancery Office.*

CLERGY, PARISHES, MISSIONS AND PAROCHIAL SCHOOLS

CITY OF ANCHORAGE

1—HOLY FAMILY CATHEDRAL, Revs. LaSalle Hallissey, O.P.; John Adams, O.P. Pastoral Assocs.: Sr. Victor Negrete, S.H.F.; Deacon Felix Maguire. In res., Rev. Urban M. Bates, O.P.
Mailing Address: 811 W. 6th Ave., 99501-2093. Tel: 907-276-3455; Fax: 907-258-9785. [JC]
Catechesis/Religious Programs—Mrs. Jo Brosamer, D.R.E.
Students 242.

2—ST. ANTHONY, Rev. Msgr. Francis A. Cowgill; Revs. Leo A. Walsh, Jr.; Youchul Philip Kim; Deacon Theodore W. Greene, Pastoral Assoc.
Res., 825 S. Klevin St., 99508-2698. Tel: 907-333-5544; Fax: 907-338-3864.
Catechesis/Religious Programs—Students 256.

3—ST. BENEDICT, Rev. Alfred W. Giebel; Deacon Ray W. Allor.
Res., 8110 Jewel Lake Rd., 99502. Tel: 907-243-2195; Fax: 907-243-0088.
Catechesis/Religious Programs—Students 409.

4—ST. ELIZABETH ANN SETON, Revs. Justin Dzikowicz, O.S.B.; Scott Medlock; Sr. Loretta Luecke, C.PP.S., Pastoral Assoc.; Deacon Kenneth Donohue.
Res., 2901 E. Huffman Rd., 99516. Tel: 907-345-4466; Fax: 907-345-6361.
Catechesis/Religious Programs—Connie Ripley, D.R.E.
Students 728.

5—HOLY CROSS, Rev. Ernest H. Muellerleile; Sr. Joan Oberle, C.PP.S., Pastoral Assoc.; Deacon William Finnegan.
Res., 8147 Medellin Cir., 99507. Tel: 907-349-3910; Fax: 907-349-3910.
Catechesis/Religious Programs—Mrs. Janine Redding, D.R.E.
Students 250.

6—OUR LADY OF GUADALUPE, Rev. Daniel Hebert; Rev. Msgr. John A. Lunney, Pastor Emeritus; Rev. Art Lopilato, S.J. In res., Rev. Timothy Crowley (LAN).
Res., 3900 Wisconsin St., 99517. Tel: 907-248-2000; Fax: 907-245-1600.
Guadalupe Centre—Tel: 907-243-2657.
Catechesis/Religious Programs—Sr. M. Veronica Rivas, M.C.D.P., D.R.E.
Students 254.

7—ST. PAUL MIKI. Closed. For inquiries for parish records contact St. Elizabeth Ann Seton Parish, Anchorage.

8—ST. PATRICK, Very Rev. Steven C. Moore, V.G.
Res., 2111 Muldoon Rd., 99504-3699. Tel: 907-337-1538; Fax: 907-337-5460.
Catechesis/Religious Programs—Martha Rogers, D.R.E.
Students 281.

OUTSIDE THE CITY OF ANCHORAGE

Cordova, St. Joseph, Sr. Peggy Glynn, O.P., Pastoral Admin.
Res., 220 Adams Ave., P.O. Box 79, 99574. Tel: 907-424-3637; Fax: 907-424-3637.

Dillingham, Holy Rosary, Rev. James F. Kelley.
Res., P.O. Box 810, 99576. Tel: 907-842-5581; Fax: 907-842-5581.
Missions—Naknek, St. Theresa, P.O.Box 73, Naknek, 99633. Tel: 907-246-6652; Unalaska, St. Christopher, P.O. Box 405, Unalaska, 99685. Tel: 907-581-4022; Fax: 907-581-4022. Ms. Annemiek Brunklaus, Pastoral Admin.
Stations—Chignik Lagoon.; Chignik Lake.; Clarks Point.; Cold Bay.; Ekwok.; Igiugig.; Iliamna.; King Salmon.; Levelock.; Manokotak.; Naknek.; New Stuyohok.; Sand Point.; South Naknek.; Togiak.; Alexander.; Ekuk.; Port Moller.; New Koliganek.; Ivanof Bay.

Eagle River, St. Andrew, Rev. Leo C. Desso; Sr. Camilla Menting, S.S.S.F., Pastoral Assoc. & D.R.E.; Deacon James Hostman.
Res., 16601 Artillery Rd., 99577. Tel: 907-694-2170; Fax: 907-694-1385.
Catechesis/Religious Programs—Students 536.

Glennallen, Holy Family, Mrs. Tami Jindra, Pastoral Admin.
Res., P.O. Box 126, 99588. Tel: 907-822-3442; Fax: 907-822-3442.
Station—Kenny Lake.

Homer, St. John the Baptist, Mrs. Henri Leger, Pastoral Admin.
Res., 238 Jenny Way, 99603. Tel: 907-235-8436; Fax: 907-235-8436.
Missions—Seldovia, St. James the Apostle, Tel: 907-234-7478; Ninilchik, St. Peter, Box 290, Ninilchik, 99639. Tel: 907-567-3490.
Catechesis/Religious Programs—Ms. Maria Walli, D.R.E.
Students 110.

Kenai, Our Lady of the Angels, Sr. Joyce Ross, R.S.M., Admin.; Sr. Joan Barina, M.M.S., Pastoral Assoc.
Res., 225 S. Spruce Rd., 99611. Tel: 907-283-4555; Fax: 907-283-4555.
Catechesis/Religious Programs—Ms. Valarie Kwietniak, D.R.E.
Students 90.

Kodiak, St. Mary's of Kodiak and the Islands, Rev. Fred Bugarin; Mrs. Delores Ossowski, Pastoral Assoc.
Res., 2934 Mill Bay Rd., 99615. Tel: 907-486-5411.
School—Tel: 907-486-3513. Sr. Diane Bardol, G.N.S.H., Prin. & D.R.E.
Sisters 3; Lay Teachers 13; Students 181.
Catechesis/Religious Programs—Students 90.

Palmer, St. Michael, Rev. David Cowden.
Res., 432 E. Fireweed Ave., 99645. Tel: 907-745-3229; Fax: 907-746-7040.
Catechesis/Religious Programs—Mrs. Joanne Rousculp, D.R.E.
Students 230.

Seward, Sacred Heart, Rev. Richard Strass, C.Ss.R.
Res., 409 Fifth Ave., P.O. Box 207, 99664. Tel: 907-224-5414; Fax: 907-224-5093.
Catechesis/Religious Programs—Mrs. Diane Elhard, D.R.E.
Students 80.
Mission—Cooper Landing, St. John Neumann Church, P.O. Box 737, Cooper Landing, 99572. Tel: 907-595-1300.

Soldotna, Our Lady of Perpetual Help, Rev. Richard D. Tero.
Res., 222 Redoubt Ave., 99669. Tel: 907-262-4749; Fax: 907-262-4749.
Catechesis/Religious Programs—Marlys Verba, D.R.E.
Students 270.

Talkeetna, St. Bernard. Unassigned.
Res., P.O. Box 510, 99676. Tel: 907-733-2442.
Missions—Trapper Creek, St. Philip Benizi, Trapper Creek, 99683.; Willow, St. Christopher, Willow, 99688.

Valdez, St. Francis Xavier, Sr. Marie Ann Brent, S.H.F., Pastoral Admin.
Res., 341 Pioneer Dr., P.O. Box 908, 99686. Tel: 907-835-4556; Fax: 907-835-4556.
Catechesis/Religious Programs—Mrs. Linda Maguire, D.R.E.
Students 74.

Wasilla, Sacred Heart, Rev. Stanley J. Allie (ALB); Kathleen Agoff, Pastoral Assoc. & D.R.E.
Res., 1201 Bogard Rd., 99654-6523. Tel: 907-376-5087; Fax: 907-373-1156.
Catechesis/Religious Programs—Students 80.
Mission—Big Lake, Our Lady of the Lake, P.O. Box 520769, Big Lake, 99652-0769. Tel: 907-892-6492; Fax: 907-892-6497. Deacon Louis Hoffman, Admin.

On Duty Outside Archdiocese:
Reverend Fathers—
Abele, Alan Carl
Means, David (STL), Magadan, Russia
Shields, Michael, Magadan, Russia

Retired:
Reverend Monsignors—
Lunney, John A., 3900 Wisconsin St., Anchorage, AK 99517
Murphy, Francis A., P.O. Box 1625, Cuba, NM 87013
Reverend Fathers—
Daley, Neil, 100 4th Ave., Shalimar, FL 32579
Houck, Peter, 4611 Kupreanof St., Anchorage, AK 99507
Marx, John, 2200 First Ave. N., Apt. 208, Seattle, WA 98109
Power, Thomas E., 415 Maplewood Cir., Greer, SC 29651

Permanent Deacons:
Albert, Merle, Milan, NH
Allor, Raymond W., Anchorage
Donohue, Kenneth, St. Elizabeth Ann Seton, Anchorage
Finnegan, William, Anchorage
Foreman, Dennis, Anchorage
Gnerich, Otto, Anchorage
Greene, Theodore, St. Anthony Church, Anchorage
Hoffman, Louis, Our Lady of the Lake, Big Lake
Hostman, James, St. Andrew, Eagle River
Larroque, Robert, Port Angeles, WA
Maguire, Felix M., Cathedral, Anchorage
Schutt, David E., Wasilla

INSTITUTIONS LOCATED IN THE ARCHDIOCESE

[A] GRADE SCHOOLS, PAROCHIAL

ANCHORAGE. *St. Elizabeth Ann Seton School*, 2901 E. Huffman Rd., 99516. Tel: 907-345-3712; Fax: 907-345-2910.
E-mail: seas@alaska.net
Web site: www.alaska.net/~seas
Mr. John Fleming, Prin. Lay Teachers 10; Students 169.

KODIAK. *St. Mary's*, 2932 Mill Bay Rd., 99615. Tel: 907-486-3513.
E-mail: dbardol@kodiak.alaska.edu
Sr. Diane Bardol, G.N.S.H., Prin. Sisters 3; Lay Teachers 15; Students 181.

[B] PRIVATE SCHOOLS

ANCHORAGE. *Holy Rosary Academy*, 1010 W. Fireweed Ln., 99503. Tel: 907-276-5822; Fax: 907-258-1055. Mr. Jim Hickel, Headmaster.

Lumen Christi Jr./Sr. High School, 750 E. Fireweed Ln., 99503. Tel: 907-272-7692; Fax: 907-272-7641. Sr. M. Marie Parrino, R.S.M., Prin.

[C] GENERAL HOSPITALS

ANCHORAGE. *Providence Alaska Foundation*, 3200 Providence Dr., P.O. Box 196604, 99519. Tel: 907-261-3600; Fax: 907-261-3048
For a complete listing, refer to the Hospitals section.

Providence Alaska Medical Center, 3200 Providence Dr., P.O. Box 196604, 99519. Tel: 907-562-2211; Fax: 907-261-3041
For a complete listing, refer to the Hospitals section.

[D] NURSING HOME

ANCHORAGE. *Providence Extended Care Center*, 4900 Eagle St., 99503. Tel: 907-562-2281
For a complete listing, refer to the Special Care Facilities section.

[E] HOMES FOR AGED

*ANCHORAGE. *Mary Conrad Center*, 9100 Centennial Dr., 99504. Tel: 907-333-8100; Fax: 907-338-6789
For a complete listing, refer to the Special Care Facilities section.

[F] CATHOLIC SOCIAL SERVICES

ANCHORAGE. *Brother Francis Shelter*, 1021 E. Third Ave., 99501. Tel: 907-277-1731. Mrs. Cheryl Sheldon, Dir. Overnight shelter for homeless men and women.

Brother Francis Shelter, 411 Cedar St., P.O. Box 3421, Kodiak, 99615. Tel: 907-486-5610. Monte Hawver, Dir.

Catholic Social Services Center, Administrative Office, 225 Cordova St., Bldg. B, 99501. Tel: 907-277-2554. Ms. Suzanne Goodrich, Exec. Dir., Catholic Social Services Center, 3710 E. 20th Ave., 99508. Tel: 907-258-2673. Ms. Robin Bronen, Dir., Immigration & Refugee Svcs.; Ms. Karen Yesh, Pregnancy Support & Adoption Dir.; Karleen Jackson, Dir., Beyond Shelter Prog., St. Francis House; Lynn Caswell, Dir., Special Needs Respite Prog.

Clare House, 420 W. 54th Ave., 99518. Tel: 907-563-4545. Cheryl Sheldon, Dir. Temporary shelter for homeless women and women with children.

McAuley Manor, 3015 Yale Dr., 99508. Ms. Cheryl Sheldon, Dir. Residence for homeless teenage girls.

[G] MONASTERIES AND RESIDENCES OF PRIESTS AND BROTHERS

ANCHORAGE. *Holy Spirit Retreat House*, 10980 Hillside Dr., 99516. Tel: 907-346-2343; Fax: 907-346-2140. Revs. Vincent J. Beuzer, S.J.; J. Michael Hornick; William T. Burke, S.J.

Jesuit House, 1500 Birchwood, 99508. Tel: 907-279-4389. Revs. Art Lopilato, S.J.; Paul B. Macke, S.J. Alaska Region of OR Prov.

Jesuit Residence, 237 E. 3rd Ave. #1, 99501. Tel: 907-277-5933. Rev. Thomas Gallagher, S.J.

[H] CONVENTS AND RESIDENCES FOR SISTERS

ANCHORAGE. *Convent of Mercy*, 2627 Redwood St., 99508. Tel: 907-258-7802. Sisters 2.

Marian House Apartments, 3005 W. 34th Ave., 99517. Priests 1; Sisters 2.

Mary's House, 3424 E. 15th Ave., 99508. Tel: 907-276-4921. Sisters 3.

Providence Alaska Medical Center, 3200 Providence Dr., P.O. Box 196604, 99519. Tel: 907-562-2211. Sisters of Providence in Washington 2.

Sisters of Perpetual Adoration, 2645 E. 72nd Ave., 99507. Tel: 907-344-3330. Mother Maria de las Victorias Amezcua, A.P., Supr. Sisters 6.

Sisters of St. Joseph of Peace, 1441 E. 17th Ave., #16, 99501. 355 Donna Dr. #19, 99504.
Sisters of St. Paul de Chartres, 825 S. Klevin St., 99508. Tel: 907-258-3273. Sisters 3.

EAGLE RIVER. *School Sisters of St. Francis*, 16601 Artillery Rd., 99577. Tel: 907-694-8087.

KENAI. *Kenai Convent*, 1122 Walnut St., 99611. Tel: 907-283-6466. Sisters 2.

KODIAK. *St. Mary's Convent*, 2932 Mill Bay Rd., 99615. Tel: 907-486-5214. Sisters 4.

[I] RETREAT HOUSES

ANCHORAGE. *Holy Spirit Retreat House*, 10980 Hillside Dr., 99516. Tel: 907-346-2343; Fax: 907-346-2140. Rev. Vincent J. Beuzer, S.J., Dir.

[J] CAMPS

ANCHORAGE. *St. Theresa's Camp, Inc.* Sept-May: 225 Cordova St., 99501. Tel: 907-258-7898. June-Sept: Box 3144, Soldotna, 99669. Tel: 907-262-4215. Archdiocesan summer camp for boys and girls.

[K] MISCELLANEOUS

ANCHORAGE. *Catholic Foundation of Alaska*, 225 Cordova St., 99501.
Catholic Retreat House Ministries, Inc., 225 Cordova St., 99501.
Covenant House Alaska, 609 F St., 99501. Tel: 907-272-1255. Ms. Deirdre Phayer, Exec. Dir. Crisis center for homeless and runaway youth.
Providence Horizon House, 4140 Folker Ave., 99508.
St. Vincent de Paul Society, Holy Family Cathedral, 811 W. 6th Ave., 99501. Tel: 907-276-3455.

RELIGIOUS INSTITUTES OF MEN REPRESENTED IN THE ARCHDIOCESE

For further details refer to the corresponding bracketed number in the Religious Institutes of Men or Women section.

[0200]—*Benedictian Fathers.* (Newton, NJ).—O.S.B.
[0600]—*Brothers of the Congregation of Holy Cross.*—C.S.C.
[0690]—*Jesuit Fathers and Brothers.* (Oregon Prov.).—S.J.
[0780]—*Marist Fathers.* (Boston Prov.).—S.M.
[0430]—*Order of Preachers-Dominicans.* (Oakland Prov.).—O.P.
[1070]—*Redemptorist Fathers.* (Oakland Prov.).—C.Ss.R.

RELIGIOUS INSTITUTES OF WOMEN REPRESENTED IN THE ARCHDIOCESE

[1070-03]—*Dominican Sisters.*—O.P.
[1840]—*Grey Nuns of the Sacred Heart.*—G.N.S.H.
[2575]—*Institute of the Sisters of Mercy of the Americas.* (Albany, NY; Merion, PA; Providence, RI).—R.S.M.
[2330]—*Little Sisters of Jesus.*—L.S.J.
[2490]—*Medical Mission Sisters.*—M.M.S.
[2690]—*Missionary Catechists of Divine Providence.*—M.C.D.P.
[3190]—*Nuns of Perpetual Adoration of the Blessed Sacrament.* (Mexico).—A.P.
[1680]—*School Sisters of St. Francis.*—O.S.F.
[3350]—*Sisters of Providence.*—S.P.
[1570]—*Sisters of St. Francis of the Holy Family, Dubuque, IA.*—O.S.F.
[3890]—*Sisters of St. Joseph of Peace.* (Bellevue).—C.S.J.P.
[3980]—*Sisters of St. Paul de Chartres, South Korea.*—S.P.C.
[1960]—*Sisters of the Holy Family.*—S.H.F.
[1990]—*Sisters of the Holy Names of Jesus and Mary.*—S.N.J.M.
[3270]—*Sisters of the Most Precious Blood.* (O'Fallon, MO).—C.PP.S.
[4110]—*Ursuline Nuns.*—O.S.U.

NECROLOGY

(No Deaths)

Diocese of Arlington

(Dioecesis Arlingtonensis)

Most Reverend

JOHN R. KEATING

Bishop of Arlington; ordained December 20, 1958; appointed Bishop of Arlington June 7, 1983; consecrated and installed as Second Bishop of Arlington August 4, 1983. *Res., 4600 N. Carlin Springs Rd., Arlington, VA, 22203.*

ESTABLISHED AUGUST 13, 1974.

Square Miles 6,541.

Comprises the following 21 Counties in Northern Virginia: Arlington, Clarke, Culpeper, Fairfax, Fauquier, Frederick, King George, Lancaster, Loudoun, Madison, Northumberland, Orange, Page, Prince William, Rappahannock, Richmond, Shenandoah, Spotsylvania, Stafford, Warren and Westmoreland and the 7 independent cities of Alexandria, Fairfax City, Falls Church, Fredericksburg, Manassas, Manassas Park and Winchester.

For legal titles of parishes and diocesan institutions, consult the Chancery Office.

The Chancery: Ste. 704, 200 N. Glebe Rd., Arlington, VA, 22203. Tel.: 703-841-2500; Fax: 703-524-5028.

Web site address: www.rc.net/arlington

STATISTICAL OVERVIEW

Personnel	
Bishop	1
Priests: Diocesan Active in Diocese	120
Priests: Active Outside Diocese	8
Priests: Diocesan in Foreign Missions	2
Priests: Retired, Sick or Absent	12
Number of Diocesan Priests	142
Religious Priests in Diocese	76
Extern Priests in Diocese	16
Ordinations:	
Diocesan Priests	3
Transitional Deacons	3
Permanent Deacons in Diocese	50
Total Brothers	16
Total Sisters	215
Parishes	
Parishes	62
With Resident Pastor:	
Resident Diocesan Priests	52
Resident Religious Priests	10
Without Resident Pastor:	
Missions	6
New Parishes Created	1
Welfare	
Special Centers for Social Services	7
Total Assisted	30,991
Educational	
Diocesan Students in Other Seminaries	32
Total Seminarians	32
Colleges and Universities	2
Total Students	3,065
High Schools, Diocesan and Parish	3
Total Students	3,393
High Schools, Private	1
Total Students	150
Elementary Schools, Diocesan and Parish	32
Total Students	12,740
Elementary Schools, Private	2
Total Students	535
Non-residential Schools for the Disabled	1
Total Students	56
Catechesis/Religious Education:	
High School Students	9,235
Elementary Students	16,910
Total Students Under Catholic Instruction	46,116
Teachers in the Diocese:	
Priests	7
Scholastics	1
Brothers	1
Sisters	69
Lay Teachers	840
Vital Statistics	
Receptions into the Church:	
Infant Baptism Totals	5,250
Adult Baptism Totals	1,953
First Communions	7,702
Confirmations	4,997
Marriages:	
Catholic	1,058
Interfaith	753
Total Marriages	1,811
Deaths	1,382
Total Catholic Population	326,398
Total Population	2,115,700

Former Bishop—Most Rev. THOMAS J. WELSH, D.D., J.C.D., appt. Titular Bishop of Scattery Island and Auxiliary Bishop of Philadelphia on Feb. 18, 1970; cons. April 2, 1970; appt. as 1st Bishop of Arlington on June 4, 1974; installed on Aug. 13, 1974; transferred to the See of Allentown, Feb. 8, 1983.

The Chancery

The Chancery—200 N. Glebe Rd., Ste. 704, Arlington, 22203. Tel: 703-841-2500; Fax: 703-524-5028. Office Hours: Mon.-Fri. 8:30-4:30. Address all official business to this office.

Vicar General—Rev. Msgr. R. ROY COSBY, V.G., *905 Park Ave., Falls Church, 22046.* Tel: 703-532-8815.

Chancellor and Moderator of the Curia—Rev. ROBERT J. RIPPY, J.C.L., *The Chancery, 200 N. Glebe Rd., Ste. 704, Arlington, 22203.* Tel: 703-841-2508.

Diocesan Fiscal Manager—SUSAN D. HANDLON, Fiscal Mgr., *200 N. Glebe Rd., Ste. 704, Arlington, 22203.* Tel: 703-841-2577.

Director of Diocesan Charities—Rev. JOHN T. O'HARA, M.S.W., *Ste. 704.* Tel: 703-841-2500.

Deans—Rev. Msgr. JAMES W. MCMURTRIE, V.F.; Rev. Msgr. R. ROY COSBY, V.F.; Rev. Msgr. JOHN T. CILINSKI, V.F.; Revs. WILLIAM F. RUEHL, V.F.; FRANK J. READY, V.F.

Vicar for The Permanent Diaconate—Rev. ROBERT J. RIPPY, J.C.L., The Chancery. Tel: 703-841-2508; 684-9261 (Res.).

Vicar for Women Religious—Rev. GERVASE CAIN, T.O.R., *St. Joseph Parish, 750 Peachtree St., Herndon, 20170-3798.* Tel: 703-437-3737.

The Tribunal

The Tribunal—200 N. Glebe Rd., Ste. 620, Arlington, 22203. Tel: 703-841-2555.

Judicial Vicar—Rev. MARK S. MEALEY, O.S.F.S., J.C.D., Ph.D.

Diocesan Judges—Revs. ROBERT C. BROOKS; J. STEWART CULKIN, M.A.; JOHN C. CREGAN; HORACE H. GRINNELL; HILARY HAYDEN, O.S.B., S.T.L.; PATRICK HOLROYD; EUGENIO J. HOYOS, C.S.V.; MARK S. MEALY, O.S.F.S., J.C.D., Ph.D.; STEPHEN A. ROSZEL, J.C.L.; WILLIAM B. SCHARDT, J.C.L.; JAMES A. VERRECCHIA; LEO J. ZONNEVELD, C.I.C.M., Ph.D., V.F.

Defenders of the Bond—Revs. ROBERT E. AVELLA, M.A.; ROBERT C. CILINSKI; Rev. Msgr. R. ROY COSBY, M.A., V.G.; Rev. PAUL F. DELADURANTAYE, S.T.L.; Sr. PATRICK MARIE DOHERTY, I.H.M.; Revs. DANIEL E. HAMILTON; THOMAS J. LEHNING, S.T.L., Ph.D.; DANIEL L. MODE; LEE R. ROOS; DAVID H. WHITESTONE, J.C.L.; PETER W. NASSETTA; Deacon CHARLES A. COUTU.

Advocates—Revs. ALEXANDER R. DRUMMOND; JOHN H. MELMER; JOHN D. KELLY; STEPHEN F. LEVA; CHARLES W. MERKLE; JAMES R. GOULD.

Notaries—Revs. PAUL A. BERGHOUT; VINCENT P. BORK; CHRISTIAN T. CONNELLY; JOHN C. DE CELLES; ROBERT J. DEMARTINO; FRANCIS M. DE ROSA; RONALD S. ESCALANTE; WILHELM J. ETTNER; PAUL M. EVERSOLE; DANIEL N. GEE; RONALD J. GRIPSHOVER, JR.; RICHARD M. GUEST; MICHAEL C. KELLY; DENNIS J. KLEINMANN; KEVIN J. LARSEN; JOHN P. MOSIMANN; RICHARD A. MULLINS; CHRISTOPHER S. MURPHY; J. KEVIN O'KEEFE; MARCUS A. POLLARD; DAVID C. RAHN; SEAN K. ROUSSEAU; PAUL D. SCALIA; TERRY W. SPECHT; TERRENCE R. STAPLES; MICHAEL G. TAYLOR; EDWIN T. TEWES; THOMAS C. VANDER WOUDE; LAWRENCE M. VIOLETTE; JERRY A. WOOTEN; JOHN ZIEGLER; MATTHEW H. ZUBERBUELER.

Diocesan Offices

Diocesan Offices—Unless otherwise noted, all offices are located at, 200 N. Glebe Rd., Arlington, 22203.

Accounting Office—CLARE FARISS, Mgr., *Ste. 602.* Tel: 703-841-2582.

Archives—MAGGIE O'CONNOR, *80 N. Glebe Rd.* Tel: 703-524-2122.

Arlington Catholic Herald, Inc.—MICHAEL F. FLACH, Editor & Gen. Mgr., *Ste. 607, Arlington.* Tel: 703-841-2590.

Audio-Visual—MAGGIE O'CONNOR, Coord., *Ste. 608.* Tel: 703-841-2530.

Campaign for Human Development—Rev. JOHN T. O'HARA, M.S.W., Diocesan Dir., *3838 Cathedral Ln., Arlington, 22203.* Tel: 703-841-2531.

Campus Ministry—Rev. JAMES R. GOULD, Bishop's Liaison, *Ste. 619.* Tel: 703-841-2514.

Catholic Charities of the Diocese of Arlington—Rev. JOHN T. O'HARA, M.S.W., Exec. Dir.; MICHAEL J. O'ROURKE, Assoc. Dir. Admin.; ELIANA V. TURINA, Asst. to the Exec. Dir., *3838 N. Cathedral Ln., Arlington, 22203.* Tel: 703-841-2544.

Catholic Charities Fredericksburg Office—612 Lafayette Blvd., Ste. 50, Fredericksburg, 22401.

Catholic Charities Winchester Office—1011 Berryville Ave., Ste. 1, Winchester, 22601.

Children's Services—PATRICIA MUDD, Prog. Dir., *5294 Lyngate Ct., Burke, 22015.* Tel: 703-425-0100.

Christ House—ROSE MARIE LAROCCA, Prog. Dir., *131 S. West St., Alexandria, 22314.* Tel: 703-549-8644.

Development—TANIA HINDERT, Prog. Dir., *3838 Cathedral Ln., Arlington, 22203.* Tel: 703-841-2531.

Elderly Services—CAROL AUGUSTINE, Prog. Dir., *St. Martin de Porres Senior Center, 4650 Taney Ave., Alexandria, 22304.* Tel: 703-751-2766.

Emergency Assistance—ROSE MARIE LA ROCCA, Prog. Dir., *131 S. West St., Alexandria, 22314.* Tel: 703-548-4227.

Family Services—DAVID CAVANAUGH, M.S.W., Prog. Dir., *3838 N. Cathedral Ln., Arlington, 22203.* Tel: 703-841-2531.

Fredericksburg Office—DIANN KELLISON, M.S.W., Prog. Dir., *612 Lafayette Blvd., Ste. 50, Fredericksburg, 22401.* Tel: 540-371-1124.

Hogar Hispano-Assistance to Immigrants—CLAIRE CHERKARSKY-HACKETT, Esq., Prog. Dir., *2300 S. 9th St., Ste. 305, Arlington, 22204.* Tel: 703-979-1705.

Parish Outreach—BERNADETTE TRAVERS, *3838 N. Cathedral Ln., Arlington, 22203.* Tel: 703-841-2531.

Prison Ministry—Vacant, *3838 N. Cathedral Ln., Arlington, 22203.* Tel: 703-841-2531.

Services with Disabled Persons—HARRY BURKE, Prog. Dir., *3838 N. Cathedral Ln., Arlington, 22203.* Tel: 703-841-2531.

Winchester Office—LORETTA DUNN, Prog. Dir., *1011 Berryville Ave., Ste. 1, Winchester, 22601.* Tel: 540-667-7940.

Catholic Education, Office of Catechetics—Rev. PAUL F. DELADURANTAYE, Sec. for Religious Education, *Ste. 703.* Tel: 703-841-2554. MAGGIE O'CONNOR, Coord., Audio-Visual Materials. Tel: 703-841-2530. Mrs. M. PROVIE RYDSTROM, Coord.-Pastoral Ministry for the Hearing Impaired. Tel: 703-978-7997 (V-TTD). NADINE HALLUMS, Dir., Special Religious Education (SPRED). Tel: 703-569-2428.

Office of Catholic Schools—Dr. TIMOTHY J. MCNIFF, Supt. of Schools. Tel: 703-841-2519. Sr. PATRICIA HELENE EARL, I.H.M., Asst. Supt. for Secondary Education & Professional Educational Personnel. Tel: 703-841-2519. Sr. KARL ANN HOMBERG, S.S.J., Asst. Supt. for Elementary Education. Tel: 703-841-2519.

Catholic Mutual Relief Society of America—Vacant. Tel: 703-525-1460.

Catholic Relief Services—Rev. JOHN T. O'HARA, M.S.W., Dir., *3838 N. Cathedral Ln., Arlington, 22203.* Tel: 703-841-2531.

Central Purchasing—JOAN CANAN, Purchasing Agent, *Ste. 618.* Tel: 703-841-2571.

Communications Office—CONCHITA VALLECILLO, Coord., *Ste. 617.* Tel: 703-841-2517.

Management Information Systems—WILFREDO MALDONADO, Coord., *Ste. 606.* Tel: 703-841-2585.

Construction Management, Office of—*Ste. 625.* Tel: 703-841-2572. PETER B. FISHER, Supvr. Construction; PAUL E. MAY, Supvr. Construction.

Development Office—KATHLEEN WOZNIAK, Mgr., *Ste. 617.* Tel: 703-841-2570.

Ecumenical Affairs—Rev. Msgr. R. ROY COSBY, Coord., *St. James, Falls Church.* Tel: 703-532-8815; 8816.

Employee Benefits—LINDA HENNESSEY, Mgr., *Ste. 611.* Tel: 703-841-2588.

Family Life Office—Deacon ROGER T. OSTROM, Dir., *Ste. 700.* Tel: 703-841-2550.

Liturgy, Office of Sacred—Rev. PAUL F. DELADURANTAYE, Sec. for the Liturgy. Tel: 703-841-2587. RICHARD GIBALA, Chm., Diocesan Music Committee. Tel: 703-476-1697.

Permanent Diaconate—Rev. ROBERT J. RIPPY, J.C.L., *Ste. 704.* Tel: 703-841-2508.

Propagation of the Faith—Rev. DONALD C. GREENHALGH, Dir., *St. Mary of Sorrows, 5222 Sideburn Rd., Fairfax, 22032.* Tel: 703-978-4141.

Spanish Apostolate—Rev. OVIDIO PECHARROMAN, Dir., *80 N. Glebe Rd., Arlington, 22203.* Tel: 703-524-2122.

Office of Resettlement—DAVID HERRMANN, Refugee Program Coord., *80 N. Glebe Rd., Arlington, 22203.* Tel: 703-524-2130.

Vocations, Office of—Revs. JAMES R. GOULD, Dir. OVIDIO PECHARROMAN, Coord. Spanish Speaking Vocations, *Ste. 619.* Tel: 703-841-2514.

Youth Activities, Office of—Rev. CHARLES C. MCCOART, Dir., *Ste. 623.* Tel: 703-841-2559.

Scouting & Camp Fire, Diocesan Committee on—GENE WICHMANN, Chm., *7313 Mizzen Pl., Burke, 22015.* Tel: 703-455-3539.

Consultative Bodies

Clergy Personnel Board—Rev. ROBERT E. AVELLA, Chm., *St. Leo, Fairfax.* Tel: 703-273-7277.

Diaconal Council—Deacon WILLIAM J. DONOVAN, Chm. Tel: 703-276-8344.

Diocesan Consultors—Rev. Msgr. JOHN P. HANNAN; Rev. Msgr. JAMES W. MCMURTRIE; Rev. Msgr. JOHN T. CILINSKI; Rev. Msgr. R. ROY COSBY; Revs. FRANKLYN M. MCAFEE; STEWART CULKIN; STANLEY KREMPA; RICHARD J. LEY; FRANK J. READY; ROBERT J. RIPPY; LEO J. ZONNEVELD, C.I.C.M.

Diocesan Finance Committee—Most Rev. JOHN R. KEATING, Chm.; Rev. LEO J. ZONNEVELD, C.I.C.M., Vice Chm. Tel: 540-825-8945. Rev. DANIEL J. MAHER, Sec. Tel: 202-526-8300.

Diocesan School Board—MOLLIE ROY, Chm. Tel: 703-250-9121.

Priests' Council—Most Rev. JOHN R. KEATING, Pres. Tel: 703-841-2500. Rev. ROBERT E. AVELLA, Vice Pres. Tel: 703-273-5369.

Religious Education Committee—ROSE WAKEHAM, *St. Luke, McLean.* Tel: 703-356-8419.

Sisters' Council—Sr. DOROTHY MENNIS, R.C., Pres., *The Cenacle House, Great Falls.* Tel: 703-759-6901. Sr. CARLA PRZYBILLA, O.S.F., Vice Pres., *New Life Center, Middleburg.* Tel: 540-687-3809; 800-982-6216.

CLERGY, PARISHES, MISSIONS AND PAROCHIAL SCHOOLS

COUNTY OF ARLINGTON

1—CATHEDRAL OF ST. THOMAS MORE (1938), Revs. Dominic P. Irace, Rector; Christian T. Connelly; Deacons Samuel M. Taub, Jr.; Claudio F. Benedi. In res., Rev. Paul F. deLadurantaye.
Res., 3901 Cathedral Ln., 22203. Tel: 703-525-1300; 525-0450; Fax: 703-528-5760.
School—105 N. Thomas St., 22203. Tel: 703-528-6781; Fax: 703-528-5040. Sr. Carmel Regina Shields, I.H.M., Prin.
Sisters, Servants of the Immaculate Heart of Mary 1; Lay Teachers 21; Students 424.
Catechesis/Religious Programs—Tel: 703-528-7104. Sr. Maria Angelica I.H.M., D.R.E.
Students 487.

2—ST. AGNES (1936), Revs. James R. Gould; Wilhelm J. Ettner. In res., Rev. Msgr. Thomas P. Scannell; Rev. Paul Gaggawala, A.J.
Res., 1914 N. Randolph St., 22207. Tel: 703-525-1166; Fax: 703-243-2840.
School—2024 N. Randolph St., 22207. Tel: 703-527-5423; Fax: 703-527-6325. Ms. Sheila Tomlinson, Prin.
Sisters 2; Lay Teachers 21; Students 337.
Catechesis/Religious Programs—Tel: 703-522-7045. Sr. Mary Margaret Ann Schlather, S.N.D., D.R.E.
Students 340.

3—ST. ANN (1947), Revs. William B. Schardt; Stephen F. Leva; Deacons Eduardo Ramirez; William J. Donovan.
Res., 5312 10th St., N., 22205. Tel: 703-528-6276; Fax: 703-522-4758.
School—980 N. Frederick St., 22205. Tel: 703-525-7599; Fax: 703-525-2687. Mrs. Marlene Tennier, Prin.
Sisters of Notre Dame of Cleveland, Ohio 3; Lay Teachers 18; Students 235.
Catechesis/Religious Programs—Tel: 703-524-8377. Sr. Theresa Sullivan, S.N.D., D.R.E.
Students 244.
Convent—5307 N. Fairfax Dr., 22205. Tel: 703-525-8395.

4—ST. CHARLES BORROMEO (1909), Revs. Gerard Creedon; Francisco Mendez de Dios; Deacon John B. Mallon.
Res., 3304 N. Washington Blvd., 22201. Tel: 703-527-5500; Fax: 703-527-5505.
School—Tel: 703-527-0608; Fax: 703-526-0262. Sr. Benedict Kesock, O.S.B., Prin.
Sisters of St. Benedict 1; Lay Teachers 14; Students 240.
Catechesis/Religious Programs—Mrs. Marilyn Krause, M.R.E., D.R.E.
Students 216.

5—HOLY MARTYRS OF VIETNAM (1979) (Vietnamese), Rev. John T.B. Trong; Deacon Pham Minh Kien, D.R.E. In res., Rev. Anthony Hoang Minh Thu.
Res., 915 S. Wakefield St., 22204. Tel: 703-553-0370; Fax: 703-553-4326.
Catechesis/Religious Programs—Tel: 703-553-4326.
Students 459.

6—OUR LADY OF LOURDES (1946), Revs. Robert J. Rippy; David C. Rahn; Deacon James F. Ambury, Pastoral Assoc.
Res., 830 S. 23rd St., 22202. Tel: 703-684-9261; 684-9211; Fax: 703-684-6342.

7—OUR LADY, QUEEN OF PEACE (1945), Revs. Jeffrey T. Duaime, C.S.Sp.; Edward J. Kelly, C.S.Sp.; Deacon Eugene D. Betit. In res., Rev. Thomas P. Tunney.
Res., 2700 S. 19th St., 22204. Tel: 703-979-5580; Fax: 703-979-5590.
Catechesis/Religious Programs—Students 92.

OUTSIDE THE COUNTY OF ARLINGTON

Alexandria

1—BLESSED SACRAMENT (1946), Revs. John C. Cregan; John C. De Celles; Tarsicio Buitrago (Columbia); Charles W. Merkle, III.
Church—1427 W. Braddock Rd., 22302. Tel: 703-998-6100; Fax: 703-671-3219.
Res., 1407 W. Braddock Rd., 22302. Tel: 703-578-4707.
School—Tel: 703-998-4170. Maureen Dowling, Prin.
Lay Teachers 17; Students 360.
Catechesis/Religious Programs—Tel: 703-998-6100; Fax: 703-671-3219. Patrica Wheatley, D.R.E.
Students 485.

2—GOOD SHEPHERD (1965), Revs. George J. Griffin; Charles C. McCoart, Jr.; Deacons Lawrence B. Henry, Jr.; Thomas G. White. In res., Rev. Francisco Cristancho (Colombia) (Istima-Tado).
Church & Mailing Address—8710 Mount Vernon Hwy., 22309. Tel: 703-780-4055; Fax: 703-360-5385.
Res., 3321 Wessynton Way, 22309.
Catechesis/Religious Programs—Judi Ryerse, D.R.E.
Students 520.

3—QUEEN OF APOSTLES (1963), Revs. William P. Saunders; Tran Dinh Nhi; Franz Howscher, C.I.C.M.
Res., 4329 Sano St., 22312. Tel: 703-354-8711; Fax: 703-354-0766.
School—4409 Sano St., 22312. Tel: 703-354-0714; Fax: 703-354-1820. Mary West, Prin.
Lay Teachers 16; Students 279.
Catechesis/Religious Programs—Tel: 703-354-4360. D.R.E.: Philip Girardi; Sally Girardi.
Students 240.

4—ST. JOSEPH'S (1915), Rev. John J. McBrearty, S.S.J.
Res., 711 N. Columbus St., 22314. Tel: 703-836-3725.
Catechesis/Religious Programs—Mrs. Wilma Anderson, D.R.E.
Students 75.

5—ST. LAWRENCE (Franconia) (1967), Revs. William J. Erbacher; John Ziegler; Ronald Escalante; Deacons Joseph L. Bosch; Walter E. Classen; Joseph Benin.
Res., 6222 Franconia Rd., 22310. Tel: 703-971-4378; Fax: 703-313-0971.
Catechesis/Religious Programs—Tel: 703-971-8541. Deacon Anthony Barrasso, D.R.E.
Students 432.

6—ST. LOUIS (1949), Revs. Richard J. Ley; Marcus A. Pollard; Matthew Paul Richardson; Deacon Paul J. Plaisance.
Res., 2907 Popkins Ln., 22306. Tel: 703-765-4421; Fax: 703-765-4571.
School—2901 Popkins Ln., 22306. Tel: 703-768-7732; Fax: 703-768-3836. Mrs. Noreen M. Gilmour, Prin.
Lay Teachers 22; Students 450.
Catechesis/Religious Programs—Tel: 703-765-6600. Deacon Paul J. Plaisance, M.R.E., D.R.E.
Students 433.

7—ST. MARY'S (1795), Revs. Stanley J. Krempa; Christopher Murphy; Carroll L. Oubre; Dr. Betty McLaughlin, Pastoral Assoc.
Res., 310 Duke St., 22314. Tel: 703-549-3603; 836-4100; Fax: 703-549-3605. [CEM]
School—400 Green St., 22314. Tel: 703-549-1646; Fax: 703-519-0840. Mrs. Mary F. Davis, Prin.
Sisters 2; Lay Teachers 29; Students 650.
Catechesis/Religious Programs—Tel: 703-548-6833. Sr. Bernadette Snearinger, C.S.C., D.R.E.
Students 192.
Convent—309 S. Royal St., 22314. Tel: 703-548-3545. Sisters of the Holy Cross

8—ST. RITA'S (1914), Revs. Clarence N. Watkins; Kevin Walsh.
Res., 3815 Russell Rd., 22305. Tel: 703-836-1640.
School—3801 Russell Rd., 22305. Tel: 703-548-1888. Sr. Catherine Michael Fee, S.S.J., Prin.
Sisters of St. Joseph 3; Lay Teachers 12; Students 210.
Catechesis/Religious Programs—Tel: 703-836-1940.
Students 121.

Annandale, Fairfax Co., Holy Spirit (1964), Revs. Frank J. Ready; Jerry Pokorsky; Joseph J. Clark. In res., Rev. Msgr. Francis L. Bradican, V.F., (Retired).
Res., 5121 Woodland Way, 22003. Tel: 703-978-8074; Fax: 703-978-9671.
School—8800 Braddock Rd., 22003. Tel: 703-978-7117; Fax: 703-978-7438. Mrs. Deborah Mohney, Prin.
Lay Teachers 27; Students 492.
Catechesis/Religious Programs—Tel: 703-978-8925; Fax: 703-978-7438. Mrs. Margaret Whitehead, D.R.E.
Students 786.

St. Ambrose (1966), Revs. Mark A. Pilon; Lawrence Violette; Deacon Roger T. Ostrom.
Res., 3901 Woodburn Rd., 22003. Tel: 703-280-4400.

School—St. Ambrose.
Lay Teachers 14; Students 240.
Catechesis/Religious Programs—Tel: 703-280-1122. Mr. John Mallory, D.R.E.
Students 178.

St. Michael's (1953), Rev. Msgr. Edward P. Browne; Revs. Richard A. Mullins; Stefan P. Starzynski; Deacons Joseph W. Stasiak; Robert E. deLaduran-taye. In res., Rev. J. Eugene Poirier, S.J.
Res., 7401 St. Michael's Ln., 22003. Tel: 703-256-7822; Fax: 703-256-0446.
School—7421 St. Michael's Ln., 22003. Tel: 703-256-1222. Sr. Dorothy Mayer, I.H.M., Prin.
Servants of the Immaculate Heart of Mary 7; Lay Teachers 24; Students 490.
Catechesis/Religious Programs—Tel: 703-941-9403. Mrs. Ann Buckreis, D.R.E.
Students 415.

Ashburn, St. Theresa (1991), Rev. Msgr. James W. McMurtrie, V.F.; Rev. David P. Meng.
Mailing Address: P.O. Box 526, 20146-0526. Tel: 703-729-2287.
Rectory—43313 Dovetail Pl., 20147. Tel: 703-729-9036.
Church—21370 St. Theresa Ln., 20147. Tel: 703-729-2287.
School—Tel: 703-729-3577. Mrs. Jacqueline MacKenzie, Prin.
Lay Teachers 12; Students 220.
Catechesis/Religious Programs—Tel: 703-729-3714. Mrs. Denise Pope, D.R.E.
Students 714.

Burke, Fairfax Co., Church of the Nativity (W. Springfield) (1973), Revs. Richard B. Martin; Kevin J. Larsen; Sr. Vicky Bartkowski, Pastoral Min.
Mailing Address: 6400 Nativity Ln., 22015. Tel: 703-455-2400; Fax: 703-455-6832.
Res., 9523 Lyra Ct., 22015. Tel: 703-913-2306.
School—Tel: 703-455-2300. Sr. Lisa Marie DiSabatino, C.S.S.F., Prin.
Lay Teachers 16; Students 237.
Catechesis/Religious Programs—Tel: 703-455-0372. D.R.E.: Deacon Wilson I. Korpi; Sr. Donatella Merulla, M.R.E.; Sr. Mary Attilia Todaro, M.R.E.
Students 1,319.

Chancellorsville, Spotsylvania Co., St. Patrick's (1983), Revs. Philip S. Majka; William Aitcheson (RNO); John P. Peterson; Deacons David Conroy; David J. Geary; Edward Whelan.
Res., 8200 Robert E. Lee Dr., Spotsylvania, 22553. Tel: 540-582-5252; Fax: 540-582-8639.
Church—9151 Ely's Ford Rd., Fredericksburg, 22407.
School—9151 Ely's Ford Rd., Fredericksburg, 22407. Tel: 540-786-2277; Fax: 540-785-2213. Mrs. Patricia Marcus, Prin.
Lay Teachers 9; Students 160.
Catechesis/Religious Programs—Mrs. Corita O'Brien, D.R.E.
Students 500.
Convent—8208 Robert E. Lee Dr., Spotsylvania, 22553. Tel: 540-582-2653. Daughters of Charity of St. Vincent de Paul (Emmitsburg, MD) Sr. Carol Supr.; Sr. Rosalie Brocato, D.C.
Sisters 3.
Mission—Spotsylvania, Spotsylvania Co., St. Matthew, 8200 Robert E. Lee Dr., 22553. Tel: 540-582-5575.

Chantilly, Fairfax Co., St. Timothy (1969), Revs. Cornelius O'Brien; Matthew H. Zuberbueler; Alexander Drummond; James Mercer; Deacons David E. Conroy; William J. Pyrek.
Res., 13807 Poplar Tree Rd., 20151. Tel: 703-378-7461; 378-7646; Fax: 703-378-7552.
School—13809 Poplar Tree Rd., 20151. Tel: 703-378-6932; Fax: 703-378-1273. Mrs. Marilyn Valatka, Prin.
Lay Teachers 28; Students 629.
Catechesis/Religious Programs—Tel: 703-378-9143. Maria Garvey, D.R.E.
Students 1,273.

Clifton, Fairfax Co., St. Andrew the Apostle (1989), Revs. Jerome W. Fasano; Edward C. Hathaway; Robert J DeMartino. In res., Rev. Julius J. Cilinski, (Retired).
Res., 6720 Union Mill Rd., 20124. Tel: 703-817-1770.
School—Tel: 703-817-1774. Mrs. Cherie Geide, Prin.
Lay Teachers 15; Students 253.
Catechesis/Religious Programs—Tel: 703-817-1773. Mrs. Maura Rush, D.R.E.
Students 1,400.

St. Claire of Assisi, Rev. Msgr. Frank E. Mahler.
Res., 6720 Union Mill Rd., 20124-1115.
Church—12049 Henderson Rd., 20124. Tel: 703-266-1310.

Colonial Beach, Westmoreland Co., St. Elizabeth (1906), Revs. William J. Schopps; John H. Melmer; Deacons Robert Baker; Edward Cleary.
Res., 11 Irving Ave. S., P.O. Box 275, 22443. Tel: 804-224-7221; Fax: 804-224-7221. [JC]
Catechesis/Religious Programs—Rev. William J. Schopps, D.R.E.
Students 185.
Mission—King George, King George Co., St. Anthony's, P.O. Box 275, 22443. [CEM]
Chaplaincy—Naval Surface Weapons Center, Dahlgren, Tel: 540-653-8297; Fax: 540-653-7278.

Culpeper, Culpeper Co., Precious Blood (1880), Rev. Leo J. Zonneveld, C.I.C.M.
Res., 114 E. Edmondson St., 22701. Tel: 540-825-8945; Fax: 540-825-8987.
Catechesis/Religious Programs—Tel: 540-825-1339. Mrs. Kathleen Holter, D.R.E.
Students 256.
Mission—Washington, Rappahannock Co., St. Peter, P.O. Box 27, Washington, 22747. Tel: 540-675-3432. Rev. Robert A. Lange.

Dale City, Prince William Co., Holy Family (1970), Revs. Joseph P. Biniek; James S. Barkett; J. Armando Avellaneda, P., M.Ss.A. (Columbia); Andrew W.P. Krafcik, (Retired); Deacons Charles A. Coutu; Gerald J. Moore; Richard L. Demers; Vincent Einsmann. In res., Rev. John T. O'Hara.
Res., 14160 Ferndale Rd., 22193. Tel: 703-670-8161; Fax: 703-670-8323.
School—Bibiana Quiamba, Dir. Lay Teachers 4; Students 90.
Catechesis/Religious Programs—Jan Clark, D.R.E..
Students 877.

Fairfax, Fairfax Co., St. Leo's (1957), Revs. Robert E. Avella; Sean K. Rousseau; John P. Mosimann.
Res., 3700 Old Lee Hwy., 22030. Tel: 703-273-5369; Fax: 703-273-2371.
School—3704 Old Lee Hwy., 22030. Tel: 703-273-1211; Fax: 703-273-6913. Mrs. Diane Drews, Prin.
Lay Teachers 25; Students 566.
Catechesis/Religious Programs—Tel: 703-273-4868.
Students 444.
Station—Fairfax Nursing Home, Tel: 703-273-7705.

St. Mary of Sorrows (1858), Revs. Donald C. Greenhalgh; Terry W. Specht; Terrence R. Staples; Deacons John M. Ligon; Nicholas LaDuca.
Mailing Address & Parish Center—5222 Sideburn Rd., 22032-2640. Tel: 703-978-4141; Fax: 703-978-2568.
Historic Church—5612 Ox Rd., Fairfax Station, 22039.
Res., 11112 Fairfax Station Rd., Fairfax Station, 22039. [CEM]
Preschool—Tel: 703-978-9656. Elena Quartuccio, Dir.
Catechesis/Religious Programs—Tel: 703-978-4283. Maureen Kelly, D.R.E.
Students 1,293.

St. Paul Chung (1996), Revs. Simon Hyun-Man Shin (Wonju); Emmanuel Shin Chun, P.Y.O (Wonju); Deacon Paul Lee.
Res., 4708 Rippling Pond Dr., 22033. Tel: 703-968-3010; Fax: 703-968-3013.
Church—4712 Rippling Pond Dr., 22033.

Fairfax Station, St. Raymond of Penafort, Rev. Salvator L. Ciullo.
Res., 8900 Triple Ridge Ct., 22039. Tel: 703-690-6650; Fax: 703-690-7399.

Falls Church, Fairfax Co., St. Anthony's (1952), Revs. Horace H. Grinnell; Jose E. Hoyos; Dennis M. Donahue; Ben M. Opara (Nigeria); Deacons Robert Curtin; Mario Mendoza.
Res., 3305 Glen Carlyn Rd., 22041. Tel: 703-820-7111; Fax: 703-379-9195.
Catechesis/Religious Programs—Tel: 703-820-2158. Mary Lou Miller, D.R.E.
Students 697.

St. James (1892), Revs. R. Roy Cosby; Paul L. Dudzinski; Michael D. Kelly; J. Kevin O'Keefe; Deacons James A. Fishenden; Thomas M. Bello. In res., Rev. Peter W. Nassetta.
Res., 905 Park Ave., 22046. Tel: 703-532-8815; Fax: 703-532-8816. [CEM]
School—Tel: 703-533-1182; Fax: 703-532-8316. Sr. Janet Regina, I.H.M., Prin. & Supr.
Servants of the Immaculate Heart of Mary 8; Lay Teachers 25; Students 630.
Catechesis/Religious Programs—Tel: 703-532-4344. Sr. Michele I.H.M., D.R.E.
Students 350.
Convent—101 N. Spring St., 22046. Tel: 703-532-2388.

St. Philip (1963), Rev. David A. Whitestone. In res., Rev. Ovidio Pecharroman.
Res., 7500 St. Philip's Ct., 22042. Tel: 703-573-3808; Fax: 703-560-2832.
Catechesis/Religious Programs—Tel: 703-573-1899; Fax: 703-573-6832. Rev. Joseph J. Loftus, D.R.E.
Students 172.

Fredericksburg, St. Mary (1858), Revs. Christopher M. Buckner; Christopher J. Mould; John Edwin Thayer Tewes.
Res., 1009 Stafford Ave., 22401-5418. Tel: 540-373-6491; 373-6663; Fax: 540-371-0251.
Catechesis/Religious Programs—Tel: 540-373-7770.
Students 892.

Front Royal, Warren Co., St. John the Baptist (1884), Rev. William F. Ruehl; Deacon Paul J. Rees, (Retired).
Res., 123 W. Main St., 22630. Tel: 540-635-3780; Fax: 540-635-2683.
Catechesis/Religious Programs—Tel: 540-635-9493. Dr. Eleanor Kelly, D.R.E.
Students 242.

Gordonsville, Orange Co., St. Mark's (1972), Rev. David L. Martin, Admin.
Res., 317 Main St., P.O. Box 124, 22942. Tel: 540-832-3062.

Great Falls, Fairfax Co., St. Catherine of Siena (1979), Revs. Franklyn M. McAfee; Thomas Vander Woude.
Mailing Address: 1020 Springvale Rd., 22066. Tel: 703-759-4350; Fax: 703-759-3753.
Catechesis/Religious Programs—Tel: 703-759-3530. Mrs. Evanne Hoyt, D.R.E.
Students 731.

Herndon, Fairfax Co., St. Joseph (1950), Revs. David Bonarrigo, T.O.R.; Gervase Cain, T.O.R.; Christopher Dobson, T.O.R.; David Morrier T.O.R.; James Angert, T.O.R.; Deacon James A. Sheehan.
Res., 750 Peachtree St., 20170. Tel: 703-437-3737; Fax: 703-437-8745.
School—Tel: 703-437-3014; Fax: 703-437-0765. Mrs. Joan Cargill, Prin.
Lay Teachers 23; Students 547.
Catechesis/Religious Programs—Joan Harrington, D.R.E.
Students 1,048.

Kilmarnock, Lancaster Co., St. Francis de Sales (1966), Rev. James C. Bruse; Sr. Elizabeth Mary Allard, M.S.B.T., Pastoral Assoc.
Res., 151 E. Church St., P.O. Box 759, 22482-0759. Tel: 804-435-1511; Fax: 804-435-2362. [CEM 2]
Catechesis/Religious Programs—Tel: 804-435-1110.
Students 72.
Mission—Hague, Westmoreland Co., St. Paul.

Lake Ridge, Prince William Co., St. Elizabeth Seton (1976), Revs. Daniel E. Hamilton; Ronald J. Gripshover, Jr.; Deacon Emil P. Myskowski.
Mailing Address: 12805 Valleywood Dr., 22192. Tel: 703-690-1493; Fax: 703-494-1995.
Res., 12805A Valleywood Dr., 22192. Tel: 703-690-1493; Fax: 703-494-1995.
Catechesis/Religious Programs—Tel: 703-494-3966. Jackie Ezersky, D.R.E.
Students 1,011.

Leesburg, Loudoun Co., St. John the Apostle (1926), Revs. Robert C. Brooks; Jerry A. Wooton.
Mailing Address: 101 Oakcrest Manor Dr., N.E., 20176-2221. Tel: 703-777-1317; Fax: 703-771-9016. [CEM]
Res., 302 N. King St., 22075.
Catechesis/Religious Programs—Mrs. Kathleen A. Fridley, D.R.E.
Students 410.

Luray, Page Co., Our Lady of the Valley (1954), Rev. Andrew Draper, T.O.R.
Mailing Address: 200 Collins Ave., P.O. Box 462, 22835. Tel: 703-743-4919.
Catechesis/Religious Programs—Students 42.

McLean, Fairfax Co., St. John's (1913), Revs. Jerome R. Daly; Vincent P. Bork. In res., Rev. Daniel L. Mode.
Res., 6420 Linway Ter., 22101. Tel: 703-356-7916; Fax: 703-356-4517.
School—6422 Linway Ter., 22101. Tel: 703-356-7554; Fax: 703-448-3811. Mrs. Christine Wells, Prin.
Lay Teachers 16; Students 297.
Catechesis/Religious Programs—Tel: 703-356-5275. Ms. Laura Pennefather, D.R.E.
Students 292.

St. Luke's (1961), Revs. Martin McGuill; John D. Kelly. In res., Rev. Lee R. Roos.
Res., 7001 Georgetown Pike, 22101. Tel: 703-356-7481; 356-1255; Fax: 703-442-0848.
School—7005 Georgetown Pike, 22101. Tel: 703-356-1508; Fax: 703-356-1141. Margaret Cahill, Prin.
Lay Teachers 22; Students 250.
Catechesis/Religious Programs—Tel: 703-356-8419; Fax: 703-356-3543. Rose Wakeham, D.R.E.
Students 543.

Madison, Madison Co., Our Lady of the Blue Ridge (1974), Rev. John F. Morel, C.I.C.M.
Res., H.C.R. 4, Box 28, 22727. Tel: 540-948-4144.
Catechesis/Religious Programs—Tel: 540-547-3850. Mr. Bill Daley, D.R.E.
Students 60.

Manassas, Prince William Co., All Saints (1929), Revs.

James A. Verrecchia; James R. Haley; Paul A. Berghout; Daniel N. Gee; Deacons John W. Eberlein; Richard O'Connell.
Res., 9300 Stonewall Rd., 20110. Tel: 703-368-4500; Fax: 703-257-9299.
School—9294 Stonewall Rd., 20110. Tel: 703-368-4400; Fax: 703-361-8573. Mr. David E. Conroy, Jr., Prin.
Lay Teachers 26; Students 475.
Catechesis/Religious Programs—Tel: 703-361-7850. D.R.E.: Mrs. Maryann Riley, (Elementary); Carol A. Patterson, (Junior-Senior Education).
Students 1,288.

Sacred Heart (1984), Revs. Thomas J. Lehning; Michael T. Orlowsky; Deacon Thomas W. Wolter.
Church & Offices—12975 Purcell Rd., 20112-3217. Tel: 703-590-0030; Fax: 703-590-0141.
Res., 6258 Terrapin Dr., 20112. Tel: 703-791-5131. [CEM]
Catechesis/Religious Programs—Tel: 703-590-0030.
Students 496.

Middleburg, Loudoun Co., St. Stephen the Martyr (1975), Rev. James D. Muldowney.
Res., Route 748, P.O. Box 474, 22117. Tel: 540-687-6433. [JC]
Catechesis/Religious Programs—Tel: 703-754-8567. Julia Neely, D.R.E.
Students 112.

Orange, Orange Co., St. John's (1946), Rev. David L. Martin (ARL).
Res., 108 W. Nelson St., P.O. Box 350, 22960. Tel: 703-672-4933; Fax: 703-672-7416.
Catechesis/Religious Programs—Nancy Schleser, D.R.E.
Students 70.

Purcellville, Loudoun Co., St. Francis de Sales (1967), Rev. Msgr. Thomas J. Cassidy; Rev. Stephen A. Roszel.
Res., 37730 St. Francis Ct., 20132. Tel: 540-338-6381; Fax: 540-338-6431.
Catechesis/Religious Programs—Students 485.

Reston, Fairfax Co., St. John Neumann (1979), Revs. Robert A. Brown, O.S.F.S.; John T. Gavin, O.S.F.S.; William N. Dougherty, O.S.F.S. In res., Rev. Michael C. Connolly, O.S.F.S.
Res., 11900 Lawyers Rd., 22091. Tel: 703-860-8510; Fax: 703-860-2136.
Catechesis/Religious Programs—Tel: 703-860-2815. D.R.E.: Susan Merkel Hayden, M.R.E.; Corinne Butera.
Students 1,428.

St. Thomas a Becket (1970), Rev. Patrick Holroyd.
Res., 1421 Wiehle Ave., 20190. Tel: 703-437-7113; Fax: 703-689-3814.
Catechesis/Religious Programs—Tel: 703-689-3816. Maureen Riddel, D.R.E.
Students 420.

Springfield, Fairfax Co., St. Bernadette's (1959), Revs. John J. Hughes; Michael Taylor; Paul D. Scalia.
Res., 7600 Old Keene Mill Rd., 22152-2022. Tel: 703-451-8576; Fax: 703-451-6893.
School—7602 Old Keene Mill Rd., 22152-2099. Tel: 703-451-8696. Mrs. Catherine M. Gilbride, Prin.
Priests 2; Lay Teachers 22; Students 512.
Catechesis/Religious Programs—Tel: 703-569-0512.
Students 870.

Stafford, Fairfax Co., St. William of York (1971), Revs. Gerald Weymes; Richard Guest; Deacons Richard P. Smith; Donald K. McKaskill. In res., Rev. Anthony J. Pinizotto, O.S.F.S.
Mailing Address: P.O. Box 116, 22555. Tel: 540-659-1102; Fax: 540-659-5637.
Res., 3130 Jefferson Davis Hwy., 22554. Tel: 540-659-9190.
Catechesis/Religious Programs—Tel: 540-659-5705. Mrs. Martha Sallette, D.R.E.
Students 679.

Sterling, Loudoun Co., Christ the Redeemer (1972), Revs. C. Donald Howard, S.A.; Robert E. Langone, S.A.; Deacon Joseph Singer.
Res., 512 N. York Rd., 20164. Tel: 703-430-1686.
Church—46833 Harry Byrd Hwy., 20164. Tel: 703-430-0811; Fax: 703-430-1590.
Catechesis/Religious Programs—Tel: 703-430-0813. Mrs. Marie Kordes, D.R.E.
Students 1,016.

Triangle, Prince William Co., St. Francis of Assisi (1957), Revs. John F. O'Connor, O.F.M.; Robert Menard, O.F.M.; Joseph V. Kiernan, O.F.M.; Gene B. Pistacchio, O.F.M.
Res., 18825 Fuller Heights Rd., 22172. Tel: 703-221-4575.
Church—Tel: 703-221-4044; Fax: 703-221-3246.
School—Tel: 703-221-3868. Dr. Tricia Barber, Prin.
Lay Teachers 16; Students 347.
Catechesis/Religious Programs—Tel: 703-221-4978. Mrs. Margaret Bruni, D.R.E.
Students 800.

Vienna, Fairfax Co., Our Lady of Good Counsel (1956), Revs. John M. O'Neill, O.S.F.S.; Raymond G. Collins, O.S.F.S.; John J. Dolan, O.S.F.S.; Eugene J. McBride, O.S.F.S.; Deacon Leonard P. Malinowski. In res., Revs. Mark Mealey, O.S.F.S.; Edward Corcoran, O.S.F.S., (Retired).
Office: P.O. Box 97, 22183. Tel: 703-938-2828.
Res., 8601 Wolftrap Rd., 22182.
School—Tel: 703-938-3600; Fax: 703-255-1543. Sr. Ann McGreevy, O.S.B., Prin.
Benedictine Sisters of Virginia 2; Lay Teachers 23; Students 535.
Catechesis/Religious Programs—Tel: 703-938-2553; Fax: 703-938-2416. Ms. Patricia Jones, D.R.E.
Students 308.

St. Mark's (1965), Revs. J. Stewart Culkin; Mark E. Moretti; Francis DeRosa; Deacon Lawrence L. Ziemianski.
Res., 9970 Vale Rd., 22181. Tel: 703-281-9100; Fax: 703-281-0675. [CEM]
Catechesis/Religious Programs—Tel: 703-938-1948. D.R.E.: Sue Long; Alan Talley.
Students 1,388.

Warrenton, Fauquier Co., St. John the Evangelist (1874), Revs. Michael J. Bazan; John J. Riley; Deacons W. Bernard Ragan, Jr.; Richard A. Cronican.
Res., 271 Winchester St., 22186. Tel: 540-347-2922; Fax: 540-347-1274.
School—111 King St., 22186. Tel: 540-347-2458; Fax: 540-349-8007. Elizabeth Roach, Prin.
Lay Teachers 13; Students 315.
Catechesis/Religious Programs—Virginia Hilleary, D.R.E.
Students 462.

Winchester, Frederick Co., Sacred Heart of Jesus (1870), Revs. Daniel S. Spychala; Dennis W. Kleinmann; John W. Rea, (Retired); Deacon Edward L. Christianson.
Res., 1717 Amherst St., 22601-2806. Tel: 540-662-5858; Fax: 540-667-6156. [CEM]
School—1713 Amherst St., 22601-2800. Tel: 703-662-7177. Ms. Mariette L. Zucchi, Prin.
School Sisters of Notre Dame 3; Lay Teachers 12; Students 97.
Catechesis/Religious Programs—Tel: 703-665-1975. Mr. Thomas L. McFadden, D.R.E.
Students 400.
Mission—Berryville, Clark Co.

Woodbridge, Prince William Co., Our Lady of Angels (1959), Rev. Msgr. John T. Cilinski; Revs. Francis J. Peffley; Paul M. Eversole; Deacons Danny E. Johnson; Jose I. Pardo; Andrew Fisher.
Res., 13752 Mary's Way, 22191. Tel: 703-494-2444; 494-5015; Fax: 703-494-0005.
Catechesis/Religious Programs—Tel: 703-494-3696; Fax: 703-494-3605. Patricia Charron, D.R.E.
Students 637.

Woodstock, Shenandoah Co., St. John Bosco (1888), Rev. Robert L. Ruskamp.
Res., 315 N. Main St., 22664. Tel: 540-459-4448.
Catechesis/Religious Programs—Students 130.
Mission—Basye, Shenandoah Co., Our Lady of the Shenandoah, Basye, 22810. Tel: 703-459-4448.

DIOCESAN MISSION PARISH

Dominican Republic, San Francisco de Asis, Banica, Rev. Donald J. Rooney.
Mailing Address: c/o Lynx Air, P.O. Box 407052, Fort Lauderdale, FL 33340. Fax: 809-527-5665.

San Jose, Pedro Santana, Rev. Patrick L. Posey.
Mailing Address: c/o Lynx Air, P.O. Box 407052, Fort Lauderdale, FL 33340. Fax: 809-527-5665.

Special Assignment:
Reverend Fathers—
Cilinski, Robert C., George Mason University, Fairfax

On Duty Outside the Diocese:
Reverend Fathers—
Clark, Curtis L., Jr., St. Charles Borromeo Seminary, Overbrook, PA
Ferguson, Thomas P., Ottawa, Canada
Gross, Lee W., Mount St. Mary's Seminary, Emmitsburg, MD
Maher, Daniel J., Basilica of the National Shrine of the Immaculate Conception, Washington, DC
Planty, Donald J., Rome, Italy
Posey, Patrick L., St. Francis of Assisi Parish, Banica, Dominican Republic
Rooney, Donald J., Dominican Republic
Trinkle, Clarence M., Romney, WV

Military Chaplains:
Reverend Fathers—
Albertson, Eric, Capt., APO, AE
Duesterhaus, Michael R., Lt. MR, FPO, AP

Retired:
Reverend Monsignors—
Bradican, Francis L., Holy Spirit, Annandale
Hannan, John P., Gainsville
Hendrick, Frank J., Pinehurst, NC
Scannell, Thomas P., St. Agnes, Arlington
Reverend Fathers—
Cilinski, Julius J., St. Andrew the Apostle
Dair, Richard J., Fairfax
Gerloff, Charles W., Virginia Beach
Kollar, Edmund, Lecanto, FL
Krafcik, Andrew W.P., Holy Family, Dale City
Rea, John W., Sacred Heart of Jesus, Winchester
Slivonik, Stanley, Lovettsville
Snella, Adolph A., Little Sisters of the Poor, Richmond

Permanent Deacons:
Ambury, James F., Our Lady of Lourdes, Arlington
Arquette, Lester K., Leave of Absence
Bayne, James L., Leave of Absence
Bello, Thomas M., St. James, Falls Church
Benedi, Claudio F., Cathedral of St. Thomas More, Arlington
Benin, Joseph G., St. Catherine, Great Falls
Betit, Eugene D., Our Lady Queen of Peace, Arlington
Bidon, Patrick J., St. Paul, Colorado Springs, CO
Bosch, Joseph L., St. Lawrence, Alexandria
Braun, Richard L., Leave of Absence
Brodeur, Harold H., St. John, Atlantic Beach, FL
Burrell, Richard L., Leave of Absence
Canonica, Donald A., St. Mary, Opelika, AL
Christianson, Edward L., Sacred Heart, Winchester
Classen, Walter E., St. Lawrence, Alexandria
Conroy, David E., St. Timothy, Chantilly; St. Patrick, Chancellors
Coutu, Charles A., Holy Family, Dale City; St. Peter Mission, Washington
Curtin, Robert J., (Retired)
De Ladurantaye, Robert E., St. Michael, Annandale
Demers, Richard L., Holy Family, Dale City
Donovan, William J., St. Ann, Arlington
Dunn, Darryl A., St. Mark, Westminster, CO
Eberlein, John W., All Saints, Manassas
Einsmann, W. Vincent, Holy Family, Dale City
Fishenden, James A., St. James, Falls Church
Frank, John L., Leave of Absence
Galvez, Rene A., Leave of Absence
George, Paul J., Leave of Absence
Harding, Stanley L., (Retired)
Henry, Lawrence B., Good Shepherd, Alexandria
Johnson, Danny E., Our Lady of Angels, Woodbridge
Kenski, Frank G., Our Lady of Good Counsel, Marysville & St. Bernadette, Duncannon, PA
Korpi, Wilson I., Nativity, Burke
La Duca, Nicholas J., St. Mary of Sorrows, Fairfax
Lee, Jea Duck, Leave of Absence
Lee, Paul, St. Paul Chung, Fairfax
Ligon, Jack M., St. Mary of Sorrows, Fairfax
Malinowski, Leonard P., Our Lady of Good Counsel, Vienna
Mallon, John B., St. Charles Borromeo, Arlington
Melvin, Gerald A., Leave of Absence
Mendoza, Mario L., St. Anthony, Falls Church
Moore, Gerald J., Holy Family, Dale City
Myskowski, Emil P., St. Elizabeth Ann Seton, Lake Ridge
Nickle, Dennis E., Leave of Absence
O'Connell, Richard T., All Saints, Manassas
Ostrom, Roger T., St. Ambrose, Annandale
Pardo, Jose I., Our Lady of Angels, Woodbridge
Pham, Kien Minh, Holy Martyrs of Vietnam, Arlington
Pivarnik, William D., Immaculate Conception, Hendersonville, NC
Prien, Richard K., St. Francis of Xavier, Carbondale, IL
Pyrek, William J., St. Timothy, Chantilly
Ragan, W. Bernard, St. John the Evangelist, Warrenton
Ramirez, Eduardo A., St. Ann, Arlington
Rees, Paul J., Leave of Absence
Resendes, Daniel F., (Retired)
Sheehan, James A., St. Joseph, Herndon
Singer, Joseph R., Christ the Redeemer, Sterling
Smith, Richard P., St. William of York, Stafford
Soutuyo, Francisco R., Leave of Absence
Stasiak, Joseph W., St. Michael, Annandale
Taub, Samuel M., Cathedral of St. Thomas More, Arlington
Vivaldi, Noel, St. Philip, Falls Church
Ward, Albert P., (Retired)
Webb, Paul J., (Retired)
White, Thomas G., Good Shepherd, Alexandria
Wilbur, Carl A., Catholic Chapel, National Institute of Health
Wolter, Thomas W., Sacred Heart, Manassas

INSTITUTIONS LOCATED IN THE DIOCESE

[A] COLLEGES AND UNIVERSITIES

ARLINGTON. *Marymount University*, 2807 N. Glebe Rd., 22207. Tel: 703-522-5600.
E-mail: admissions@marymount.edu
Web site: www.marymount.edu
For a complete listing, refer to the Colleges and Universities section.

FRONT ROYAL. *Christendom College*. Tel: 540-636-2900
For a complete listing, refer to the Colleges and Universities section.

[B] CATECHETICAL INSTITUTE

ARLINGTON. *Notre Dame Graduate School of Christendom College*, 4407 Sano St., 22312. Tel: 703-658-4304. Rev. William P. Saunders, Ph.D., Dean; Sr. M. Timothy Prokes, F.S.E., Ph.D., Dean of Students; Sr. Mary St. Mark, I.H.M., Dean Summer School; Luther P. Niehoff, Admin. Dir.

[C] CORRESPONDENCE SCHOOL

HAMILTON. *The Catholic Distance University fka The Catholic Home Study Institute*, 120 E. Colonial Hwy., 20158-9012. Tel: 504-338-2700; Fax: 504-338-4788.
E-mail: cdu@cdu.edu
Web site: http://www.cdu.edu
Accredited Catechetical Institute for Adults; Catechetical Diploma; Continuing Education; and Optional College credit, Masters in Religious Studies. All programs through distance learning. Most Rev. Thomas J. Welsh, D.D., Bd. Chm., Pres. & Chancellor; Marianne Evans Mount, Exec.Vice Pres.

[D] HIGH SCHOOLS, DIOCESAN

ARLINGTON. *Bishop Denis J. O'Connell High School*, 6600 Little Falls Rd., 22213. Tel: 703-237-1400. Mr. Alward V. Burch, Prin. Assistant Principals: Sr. Marie laReine, I.H.M.; Mr. John J. Gutter; Mr. Richard J. Martin; Rev. Daniel L. Mode, Spiritual Dir.; Mr. Thomas McNichol, Guidance Dir. Sisters Servants of the Immaculate Heart of Mary 11; Lay Teachers 87; Students 1,440.

ALEXANDRIA. *Bishop Ireton High School*, 201 Cambridge Rd., 22314. Tel: 703-751-7606. (See separate listing for Oblates of St. Francis de Sales Residence). Rev. William J. Metzger, O.S.F.S., M.A., Prin.; Very Rev. Michael J. McCue, O.S.F.S., M.A., Supr.; Revs. Thomas J. Erbrick, O.S.F.S., B.A.; Edward J. Roszko, O.S.F.S., B.A.; John J. Muzdakis, O.S.F.S., B.S.; Manning C. Moore, O.S.F.S., M.A.; Mr. Michael Robinson. Oblates of St. Francis de Sales 6; Brothers 1; Sisters 2; Lay Teachers 63; Students 770.

FAIRFAX. *Paul VI High School*, 10675 Lee Hwy., 22030. Tel: 703-352-0925.
E-mail: paulVI@erols.com
Rev. John W. Lyle, O.S.F.S., Prin. Asst. Principals: Mr. David DiPippa; Mrs. Joan Grossel; Mrs. Marie Powell; Revs. Matthew J. Hillyard, O.S.F.S.; Michael Cavanaugh, O.S.F.S.; Mr. Derek Donnelly. Oblates of St. Francis de Sales 4; Lay Teachers 85; Students 1,190.

[E] HIGH SCHOOLS, PRIVATE

MIDDLEBURG. *Notre Dame Academy, Middleburg, VA*, 35321 Notre Dame Ln., 20117. Tel: 540-687-5581; Fax: 540-687-3103.
E-mail: nda@mnsinc.com
Web site: http://www.rc.net/arlington/nda
Sr. Cecilia Liberatore, S.N.D., Head of School. Sisters of Notre Dame 7; Lay Teachers 22; Students 166.

[F] ELEMENTARY SCHOOLS, PRIVATE

BRISTOW. *Linton Hall*, 9535 Linton Hall Rd., 22013. Tel: 703-368-3157.
E-mail: lintonhall@aol.com
Sr. Glenna Smith, O.S.B., Prin. Benedictine Sisters of Virginia 9; Lay Teachers 15; Students 180.

FREDERICKSBURG. *Montfort Academy, Inc.* (Grades K-8), 700 Sunken Rd., 22401. Tel: 703-373-9478.
E-mail: montfort@pipeline.com
Sr. Joan Rohan, D.W., Prin. Daughters of Wisdom 2; Lay Teachers 22; Students 350.

[G] INTERPAROCHIAL SCHOOLS

FALLS CHURCH. *Corpus Christi School*. (Grades 1-8), 3301 Glen Carlyn Rd., 22041. Tel: 703-820-7450.
E-mail: corpuse@mnsine.com
Sponsoring parishes: St. Anthony and St. Philip. Mr. George Chiplock, Prin. Lay Teachers 23; Students 465.

WOODBRIDGE. *Aquinas School*. (Grades K-8), 13750 Mary's Way, 22191. Tel: 703-491-4447.
E-mail: aquinas@erols.com
Sponsoring parishes: Our Lady of Angels, Woodbridge; Holy Family, Dale City; St. Elizabeth Ann Seton, Lake Ridge; and Sacred Heart, Manassas. Sr. Mary Anne, O.P., Prin.. Dominican Sisters, Congregation of St. Cecilia 2; Lay Teachers 19; Students 546.

[H] DAY CARE AND CHILD LEARNING CENTERS

ARLINGTON. *Holy Martyrs of Vietnam Church Child Enrichment Day Care Center*. (Children 2-5 years), 915 S. Wakefield St., 22204. Tel: 703-920-1049. Mrs. T. Mai Nguyen. Lay Teachers 5; Students 40.

ALEXANDRIA. *Blessed Sacrament Grade School and Early Childhood Center*. (Grades PreK-8), 1417 W. Braddock Rd., 22302. Tel: 703-998-4170. Ms. Maureen Dowling, Prin. Lay Teachers 44; Students 360.

St. Gabriel's, 4319 Sano St., 22312. Tel: 703-354-0395. Poor Sisters of St. Joseph (Buenos Aires). Sr. Margarita Quintero, P.S.S.J., Supr. Sisters 8; Students 90. Sisters 8; Students 90.

FALLS CHURCH. *Corpus Christi Early Childhood Center*. (Children 3-5 years), 7506 St. Philip's Ct., 22042. Tel: 703-573-4570. Mr. George Chiplock, Prin.; Mrs. Monique T. Myers, Dir.; Mrs. Mary Stevens, Daycare Dir. Sponsoring Parishes: St. Anthony and St. Philip. Lay Teachers 8; Students 184.

St. Joseph's Day Nursery & Kindergarten, 203 N. Spring St., 22046. Tel: 703-533-8441. Servants of St. Joseph (Salamanca, Spain). Sr. Jacinta Salazar, S.S.J., Dir. Sisters 3; Lay Teachers 7; Students 80.

[I] SCHOOLS FOR EXCEPTIONAL CHILDREN

ALEXANDRIA. *St. Coletta School*, 207 S. Peyton St., 22314. Tel: 703-683-3686; Fax: 703-683-9888. Ms. Sharon Raimo, Prin. Private, Non-residential School providing education and vocational training for students and young adults with mental retardation, autism and secondary disabilities ages 4 through 22. Medicaid waivered day program for adults, age 22 and up. Religious 1; Teachers 9; Teacher Aides 30; Speech Pathologists 3; Physical Therapists 2; Occupational Therapists 3; Music Teachers 1; Adaptive Physical Education Instructors 1; Psychologists 2; Adult Program Instructors 1; Students 80.

FALLS CHURCH. *Seton Centers, Inc.*, 115 Hillwood Ave., 22046. Tel: 703-533-7670. Elementary & High School Programs. School for children with learning disabilities. Mary K. Doherty, Exec. Dir. Teachers 6; Students 76.

[J] MONASTERIES AND RESIDENCES OF PRIESTS AND BROTHERS

ARLINGTON. *Missionary Servants of the Most Holy Trinity, S.T.*, 1215 N. Scott St., 22209-3097. Tel: 703-276-8646; Fax: 703-522-2656. Generalate of the Missionary Servants of the Most Holy Trinity. Revs. Domingo Rodriguez, S.T., Gen. Custodian; Jesus Rivera, S.T., Gen. Councilor & Vicar for Spanish-speaking Personnel & Apostolates; John McSpiritt, S.T., Gen. Councilor & Vicar for Personnel; Bro. Hilary Mettes, S.T., Sec. Gen. Legal Titles: *Missionary Servants Charitable Trust.*; *Father Judge Charitable Trust.*

Missionhurst, C.I.C.M.-Central House and Provincialate, 4651 N. 25th St., 22207. Tel: 703-528-3800; Fax: 703-528-5355.
E-mail: provcicm@aol.com
Congregation of the Immaculate Heart of Mary foreign and home missions. Legal Titles: *American I.H.M. Province, Inc.*; *Immaculate Heart Missions, Inc.*; *Missionhurst, Inc.* Revs. Joseph Lapauw, C.I.C.M., Prov. Supr.; Paul DeWolf, C.I.C.M., Rector; Leo J. Zonneveld, C.I.C.M., Prov. Treas.; Louis Tysmans, C.I.C.M., Dir. Prog. Svcs.; Bill Wyndaele, C.I.C.M., Editor of Missionhurst Magazine & Dir. Mission Ctr.; His Eminence Jan Cardinal Schotte, C.I.C.M.; Revs. Howard Picard, C.I.C.M.; Albert VanNuffelen, C.I.C.M.; Francis Loos, C.I.C.M.; Roger Van Cauwenburgh, C.I.C.M.; Joseph Dewaele, C.I.C.M.; John Van de Paer, C.I.C.M.; Frank Holscher, C.I.C.M.; Jerome Meersman, C.I.C.M.; Charles Denys, C.I.C.M.; Marcel Van Thillo, C.I.C.M.; Joseph Smits, C.I.C.M.

ALEXANDRIA. *Oblates of St. Francis de Sales Residence*, 101 Cambridge Rd., 22314. Tel: 703-751-7606. (See separate listing for Bishop Ireton High School regarding staff.). Revs. Michael J. McCue, O.S.F.S., Supr.; John W. Crossin, O.S.F.S.; William J. Metzger, O.S.F.S.; Manning C. Moore, O.S.F.S.; John J. Muzdakis, O.S.F.S.; Thomas J. Erbrick, O.S.F.S.; Edward J. Roszko, O.S.F.S.; Bro. Edward Ogden, O.S.F.S.

BERRYVILLE. *Cistercian Abbey of Our Lady of the Holy Cross*, Rte. 2, Box 3870, 22611-9526. Tel: 540-955-1425.
E-mail: HolyCross@shentel.net
Web site: http://www.MonasteryFruitcake.org
Order of Cistercians of the Strict Observance (Trappist). Rt. Revs. Flavian Burns, O.C.S.O., Chap., Our Lady of the Angels, Crozet; Edward McCorkell, O.C.S.O., Retired Abbot; Revs. Edmund Flynn, O.C.S.O., Treas.; Paschal Balkan, O.C.S.O.; Andrew Gries, O.C.S.O.; Rt. Rev. Mark Delery, O.C.S.O., Retreat House Counsellor and Retired Abbot; Revs. Maurice Flood, O.C.S.O.; Robert Barnes, O.C.S.O.; Joseph Wittstock, O.C.S.O., Prior; James Orthmann, O.C.S.O., Novice Master & Vocation Dir.; Malachy Marrion, O.C.S.O.; Bros. Benedict Simmonds, O.C.S.O., Supr.; Stephen Maguire, O.C.S.O., Guest Master. Community 25; Leave of Absence 1; Residents 24; Priests 12; Solemnly Professed Non-priest Monks 9; Novices 1; Temporarily Professed 2.

FAIRFAX. *Oblates of St. Francis de Sales Residence*. (See separate listing for Paul VI High School.), 10600 Cedar Ave., 22030. Tel: 703-273-8067. Very Rev. Michael Cavanaugh, O.S.F.S., Supr.; Revs. John W. Lyle, O.S.F.S.; Matthew J. Hillard, O.S.F.S.; Mr. Joseph Cullinan, Scholastic.

FALLS CHURCH. *Missionhurst-C.I.C.M.*, 3425 Annandale Rd., 22042. Tel: 703-560-0766. Rev. Louis Tysmans, C.I.C.M.

WINCHESTER. *Sacred Heart Friary*, Box 825, 22604. Tel: 540-869-1599. Third Order Regular of St. Francis. Revs. Patrick Boland, T.O.R.; Martin Brohead, T.O.R.; Marion Deck, T.O.R.; Bonaventure Kiley, T.O.R.; Francis McKinney, T.O.R.; Samuel Tiesi, T.O.R.; Christopher Petrosky, T.O.R.; James Cleary, T.O.R.; Bros. Richard Gates, T.O.R., Local Min.; Stephen Liebal, T.O.R.; Stan Prenatt, T.O.R.; Dominic Barkovich, T.O.R.; John Paul McMahon, T.O.R.; Finbar Gallagher, T.O.R.; Norman McNelis, T.O.R. Professed Brothers 5.

[K] CONVENTS AND RESIDENCES FOR SISTERS

ARLINGTON. *Religious of the Sacred Heart of Mary*, 2807 N. Glebe Rd., 22207-4299. Tel: 703-284-1495.
E-mail: sister.murphy@marymount.edu
Sr. Michelle Murphy, R.S.H.M., Coord. Sisters 12.

Sisters Servants of the Immaculate Heart of Mary, 6600 Little Falls Rd., 22213. Tel: 703-237-1410. Teachers at Bishop O'Connell High School. Sr. Mary Theresa McBride; Sr. Mary Lynn; Sr. St. Kathleen Blaston; Sr. Charles B. Harvey; Sr. Mary Raphael Hafner; Sr. Marie la Reine Spain; Sr. Joanna McKelvey; Sr. Maureen Chistopher Dusterhoff; Sr. Rose Harlan; Sr. Janice Urbanec; Sr. Ingrid Schwerkart; Sr. Susan Cronin; Sr. Dolores Quigley; Sr. Patricia Mary Hale; Sr. Marie DeLourdes Mates; Sr. Arleen McCann. Sisters 12.

ALEXANDRIA. *Poor Clare Monastery of Mary, Mother of the Church*, 2505 Stonehedge Dr., 22306. Tel: 703-768-4918. Observing the Primitive Rule of St. Clare. Solemnly Professed 11; Junior Professed 2; Novices 1; Postulants 4.

St. Gabriel's Convent, 4319 Sano St., 22312. Tel: 703-354-0395. Sr. Margarita Quintero, P.S.S.J., Supr. Poor Sisters of St. Joseph's Buenos Aires Regional House and Novitiate 8.

Sisters of the Holy Cross, 5582 First Statesman Ln., 22312. Tel: 703-658-9519. Legal Title: *Sisters of the Holy Cross, Inc.* Sisters 2.

BRISTOW. *St. Benedict Monastery*, 9535 Linton Hall Rd., 20136-1217. Tel: 703-361-0106. Sr. Cecilia Dwyer, O.S.B., Prioress. Tel: 703-368-4848; Rev. Mark Broski, O.S.B., Chap. Tel: 703-335-2195. Professed Sisters 43; Sisters in Temporary Commitment 1; Sisters Resident at Motherhouse 40.

FALLS CHURCH. *Holy Family House Convent, S.S.J.*, 3438 Charles St., 22041. Tel: 703-820-9785. Sisters 4.

Servants of St. Joseph Convent, 203 N. Spring St., 22046. Tel: 703-533-8441. Sr. Carmen Guerrero, S.S.J., Supr. Tel: 703-534-9549; Sr. Prudencia Gonzalo, S.S.J.; Sr. Josefina Laguno, S.S.J.; Sr. Jacinta Salazar, S.S.J.; Sr. Agustina Temprano, S.S.J. Sisters 5.

GREAT FALLS. *Sisters of the Cenacle*, 1033 Riva Ridge Dr., 22066. Tel: 703-759-6901. Religious of the Cenacle 2.

SPOTSYLVANIA. *Daughters of Charity of St. Vincent de Paul*, St. Matthew's House, 8208 Robert E. Lee Dr., 22553-3504. Tel: 540-582-2653. Sisters 3.

WOODBRIDGE. *Dominican Sisters Convent*. (Congregation of St. Cecilia), 2655 Falmouth Ct., 22192. Tel: 703-494-4488. Dominican Sisters. Sr. Mary Anne, O.P., Prin., Supr. Sisters 5.

[L] RETREAT HOUSES

BERRYVILLE. *Retreat House, Holy Cross Abbey*, Rte. 2, Box 3870, 22611. Tel: 540-955-3124. Retreat Masters: Rt. Rev. Mark Delery, O.C.S.O., Retreat Dir.; Rev. Maurice Flood, O.C.S.O.; Bro. Stephen Maguire, O.C.S.O., Guest Master.

MCLEAN. *Dominican Retreat*. Accommodations for 41 persons. 7103 Old Dominion Dr., 22101. Tel: 703-356-4243. Dominican Sisters of St. Catherine De

Ricci. Sr. Bartholomew VanDusky, O.P., Coord. Sisters 5.

[M] CAMPUS MINISTRY

FAIRFAX. *George Mason University, Catholic Campus Ministry House*, 4521 Roberts Rd., 22032. Tel: 703-425-0022.
E-mail: rcilinsk@gmu.edu
Rev. Robert C. Cilinski, Chap. & Dir. Campus Ministry.

St. Robert Bellarmine Chapel. Catholic Campus Ministry. George Mason University, 4515 Roberts Rd., 22032. Tel: 703-425-0022. Rev. Robert Cilinski; Ms. Michelle Miller, Assoc. Campus Min.; Dr. Elaine Rendler, Dir. Liturgical Music.

[N] MISCELLANEOUS

ARLINGTON. *Youth Apostles Institute, An Association of Christian Faithful*. 1600 Carlin Ln., McLean, 22101-4100. Tel: 703-556-0914.

ALEXANDRIA. *St. Paul Book & Media Center (Daughters of St. Paul)*, 1025 King St., 22314. Tel: 703-549-3806; 683-1741 (Convent).
E-mail: FSPDC@juno.com
Sr. Susan James Heady, F.S.P. Missionary Sisters of the Communications Media.

BROAD RUN. *National Association of Catholic Home Educators (NACHE)*, 6102 Saints Hill Ln., 20137. Tel: 703-349-4314. Mr. Bill Bales, Pres.

FRONT ROYAL. *Seton Home Study School*, 1350 Progress Dr., 22630. Tel: 540-636-9990. Dr. Mary K. Clark, Dir.

SPOTSYLVANIA. *St. Francis Catholic Worker West*, 9631 Peppertree Rd., 22553. Tel: 540-972-3218. Mr. John Mahoney. Total in Residence 2.

STAFFORD. *American Life League, Inc.*, P.O. Box 1350, 22555. Tel: 540-659-4171.
E-mail: jbrown@all.org
Web site: www.all.org
Mrs. Judie Brown, Pres.

VIENNA. *Mount Tabor Society, Inc.*, 2363 Hunter Mill Rd., 22181. Tel: 703-938-2564. A House of Prayer and Christian Community. Rev. Paul G. Wynants, C.I.C.M., Dir.

WOODBRIDGE. *Apostolate for Family Consecration*, St. Damien Center, 1410 Harrison St., 22191-2215. Tel: 703-491-6544. Jerome F. Coniker, Exec. Dir.

RELIGIOUS INSTITUTES OF MEN REPRESENTED IN THE DIOCESE

For further details refer to the corresponding bracketed number in the Religious Institutes of Men or Women section.

[0470]—*The Capuchin Friars.* (New Jersey Prov. of the Stigmata).—O.F.M.Cap.
[0350]—*Cistercians Order of the Strict Observance.* (Trappists).—O.C.S.O.
[0520]—*Franciscan Friars.* (Holy Name Prov.).—O.F.M.
[0650]—*Holy Ghost Fathers.*—C.S.Sp.
[0690]—*Jesuit Fathers and Brothers.*—S.J.
[0840]—*Missionary Servants of the Most Holy Trinity.*—S.T.
[0860]—*Missionhurst Congregation of the Immaculate Heart of Mary.*—C.I.C.M.
[0920]—*Oblates of St. Francis de Sales.* (Wilmington-Philadelphia Prov.).—O.S.F.S.
[0700]—*St. Joseph's Society of the Sacred Heart.* (Baltimore, MD).—S.S.J.
[0560]—*Third Order Regular of Saint Francis.* (Sacred Heart Prov.).—T.O.R.

RELIGIOUS INSTITUTES OF WOMEN REPRESENTED IN THE DIOCESE

[0230]—*Benedictine Sisters.* (Erie, PA).—O.S.B.
[0230]—*Benedictine Sisters.* (South Dakota).—O.S.B.
[0230]—*Benedictine Sisters.* (Virginia).—O.S.B.
[3110]—*Congregation of Our Lady of the Retreat in the Cenacle.*—R.C.
[1920]—*Congregation of the Sisters of the Holy Cross.*—C.S.C.
[0760]—*Daughters of Charity of St. Vincent de Paul.* (Emmitsburg Province).—D.C.
[0960]—*Daughters of Wisdom.*—D.W.
[1070-17]—*Dominican Sisters Congregation of St. Catherine deRicci.*—O.P.
[1070-07]—*Dominican Sisters Congregation of St. Cecilia.*—O.P.
[1070-21]—*Dominican Sisters of the Congregation of the Most Holy Trinity.*—O.P.
[1880]—*Handmaidens of Reparation of the Sacred Heart of Jesus.*—A.R.
[2790]—*Missionary Servants of the Most Blessed Trinity.*—M.S.B.T.
[3760]—*Order of St. Clare (Cloistered).*—P.C.C.
[0950]—*Pious Society of Daughters of St. Paul.*—F.S.P.
[3250]—*Poor Sisters of St. Joseph.*—P.S.S.J.
[3465]—*Religious of the Sacred Heart of Mary.* (Eastern North Amer. Prov.).—R.S.H.M.
[2970]—*School Sisters of Notre Dame.*—S.S.N.D.
[3595]—*Servants of St. Joseph.*—S.S.J.
[3830]—*Sisters of St. Joseph.* (Philadelphia).—S.S.J.
[2990]—*Sisters of Notre Dame.*—S.N.D.
[1650]—*Sisters of St. Francis of Philadelphia.*—O.S.F.
[8983]—*Sisters of St. Joseph.* (Chestnut Hill, PA).—S.S.J.
[2170]—*Sisters, Servants of the Immaculate Heart of Mary.*—I.H.M.

NECROLOGY

† Burke, Rev. Msgr. Richard J., Arlington, VA, Cathedral of St. Thomas More. —Died Nov. 30, 1996.
† Hammond, Henry E., Alexandria, VA, St. Lawrence. —Died Nov. 9, 1996.
† McLean, Edward J., Arlington, VA, St. Charles Borromeo. —Died Oct. 14, 1997.

Archdiocese of Atlanta

(Archidioecesis Atlantensis)

Most Reverend

JOHN FRANCIS DONOGHUE, D.D.

Archbishop of Atlanta; ordained June 4, 1955; appointed Bishop of Charlotte November 6, 1984; appointed Archbishop of Atlanta June 22, 1993; installed August 18, 1993.

Catholic Center Archdiocese of Atlanta: 680 W. Peachtree St., N.W., Atlanta, GA, 30308.

Web site address: http://www.archatl.com/

ESTABLISHED JULY 2, 1956.

CANONICALLY ERECTED NOVEMBER 8, 1956.

Created an Archdiocese February 21, 1962.

Square Miles 21,445.

Comprises the 69 Counties in the northern part of the State of Georgia, north of and including the following counties: Lincoln, McDuffie, Warren, Hancock, Baldwin, Putnam, Jasper, Monroe, Upson, Meriwether and Troup.

PATRONS OF THE ARCHDIOCESE: I. Our Blessed Lady under the title of the Immaculate Heart of Mary; II. Saint Pius X.

For legal titles of parishes and archdiocesan institutions, consult the Archbishop's Office.

STATISTICAL OVERVIEW

Personnel	
Archbishop	1
Retired Archbishops	1
Abbots	1
Retired Abbots	1
Priests: Diocesan Active in Diocese	99
Priests: Active Outside Diocese	4
Priests: Retired, Sick or Absent	8
Number of Diocesan Priests	111
Religious Priests in Diocese	99
Extern Priests in Diocese	8
Ordinations:	
Diocesan Priests	5
Transitional Deacons	6
Permanent Deacons in Diocese	136
Total Brothers	1
Total Sisters	123
Parishes	
Parishes	69
With Resident Pastor:	
Resident Diocesan Priests	54
Resident Religious Priests	15
Without Resident Pastor:	
Missions	22
Pastoral Centers	3
Professional Ministry Personnel:	
Sisters	15
Lay Ministers	147
Welfare	
Catholic Hospitals	2
Total Assisted	132,736
Health Care Centers	2
Total Assisted	20,202
Homes for the Aged	5
Total Assisted	150
Day Care and Extended Day Care Centers	2
Total Assisted	77
Specialized Homes	1
Total Assisted	70
Special Centers for Social Services	12
Total Assisted	46,500
Educational	
Diocesan Students in Other Seminaries	70
Total Seminarians	70
High Schools, Diocesan and Parish	1
Total Students	1,023
High Schools, Private	1
Total Students	1,025
Elementary Schools, Diocesan and Parish	12
Total Students	4,497
Elementary Schools, Private	2
Total Students	1,361
Catechesis/Religious Education:	
High School Students	4,731
Elementary Students	27,342
Total Students Under Catholic Instruction	40,049
Teachers in the Diocese:	
Priests	2
Sisters	8
Lay Teachers	364
Vital Statistics	
Receptions into the Church:	
Infant Baptism Totals	6,069
Adult Baptism Totals	469
Received into Full Communion	980
First Communions	4,111
Confirmations	3,086
Marriages:	
Catholic	799
Interfaith	834
Total Marriages	1,633
Deaths	789
Total Catholic Population	292,300
Total Population	4,896,392

Former Bishops—Most Rev. FRANCIS E. HYLAND, D.D., J.C.D., appt. Titular Bishop of Gomphi and Auxiliary Bishop of Savannah-Atlanta, Oct. 15, 1949; cons. Dec. 21, 1949; First Bishop of Atlanta, July 17, 1956; installed on Nov. 8, 1956; resigned and appointed Titular Bishop of Bisica, Oct. 11, 1961; died Jan. 31, 1968.—Most Rev. PAUL J. HALLINAN, D.D., appt. Bishop of Charleston, Sept. 9, 1958; cons. Oct. 28, 1958; elevated to the Archiepiscopal dignity, Feb. 21, 1962; installed First Archbishop of Atlanta, March 29, 1962; died March 27, 1968.—Most Rev. JOSEPH L. BERNARDIN, D.D., appt. Auxiliary of Atlanta, March 9, 1966; cons. April 26, 1966; appt. Gen. Sec. U.S.C.C., April 5, 1968.—Most Rev. THOMAS A. DONNELLAN, appt. Bishop of Ogdensburg, March 4, 1964; cons. April 9, 1964; appt. to Atlanta, May 29, 1968; installed July 16, 1968; died Oct. 15, 1987.—Most Rev. EUGENE A. MARINO, S.S.J., D.D., appt. Auxiliary of Washington, July 15, 1974; appt. Archbishop of Atlanta, March 14, 1988; installed May 5, 1988; resigned July 10, 1990.—Most Rev. JAMES P. LYKE, O.F.M., Ph.D., appt. Auxiliary Bishop of Cleveland and Titular Bishop of Fornos Maggiore, June 30, 1979; cons. Aug. 1, 1979; appt. Apostolic Administrator Archdiocese of Atlanta, July 10, 1990; appt. Archbishop of Archdiocese of Atlanta, April 30, 1991; installed June 24, 1991 Pallium conferred June 29, 1991; died Dec. 27, 1992.

Moderator of Religious—Sr. MARY PRINISKI, O.P., *235 E. Ponce de Leon Ave., Ste. 226, Decatur, 30030.*

Vicar for Clergy—Rev. Msgr. HENRY C. GRACZ.

Associate Vicar for Clergy—Rev. RICHARD MORROW.

Archdiocesan Offices and Directors

Catholic Center Archdiocese of Atlanta—680 W. Peachtree St., N.W., Atlanta, 30308.

Catholic Information—Tel: 404-888-7801.

Archbishop's Office—Tel: 404-888-7804; Fax: 404-885-7494.

Vicar General—Rev. Msgr. PETER A. DORA.

Chancellor—Rev. MARK W. LACEY. Tel: 404-888-7804. ANNO HARDAGE. Tel: 404-888-7804.

Secretariat for Finance & Administration—Tel: 404-888-7808. MICHAEL J. MCNAMARA, Sec. & Chief Financial Officer.

Secretariat for Education—Tel: 404-888-7833. BERTHA MARTIN, Sec. Education.

Continuing Education in Ministry—Rev. MARK W. LACEY. Tel: 404-888-7804.

Secretariat for Catholic Charities—Mr. CARROLL STERNE, Dir. Tel: 404-881-6571. See separate listing for detailed information.

Office for Black Catholic Ministry—Tel: 404-888-7843. HOWARD BROWN, Dept. Head (Secretariat Supvr. & Chancellor).

Office Of Communications—Tel: 404-888-7832; Fax: 404-888-7849. KATHI STEARNS.

"The Georgia Bulletin"—KATHI STEARNS, Exec. Editor; GRETCHEN KEISER, Editor.

Media Relations—Rev. Msgr. PETER A. DORA. Tel: 404-888-7804; Fax: 404-885-7494.

Metropolitan Tribunal—

Judicial Vicar—Rev. Msgr. LOUIS NAUGHTON, J.C.L., S.T.B., M.A.

Court Administrator—Deacon WHITNEY F. ROBICHAUX, B.S., M.A., M.P.S.

Auditor—Sr. FRANCES WHITMAN, G.N.S.H., M.A.

Archdiocesan Judges—Rev. STEPHEN T. CHURCHWELL, J.C.D., M.Div.; Rev. Msgr. EDWARD J. DILLON, J.C.D.; Revs. DAVID P. TALLEY, J.C.D., M.Div., B.A., M.S.W.; TIMOTHY A. GADZIALA, M.Th., M.Div.; MARK W. LACEY, S.T.B., B.B.A.

Defender of the Bond—Rt. Rev. DOM BERNARD M. JOHNSON, O.C.S.O., J.C.L.; Mr. ROBERT J. KAMPINE, J.C.L., S.T.B., B.A.; Mr. ROBERT G. WESSELMANN, J.C.L., S.T.L.

Notaries—Mrs. MARIANNE GEYER; Mrs. KIM M. DANIEL; Ms. ROBERTA I. SIEGWALD; Ms. JEAN M. SMITH.

Court of Appeals-Province of Atlanta—Tel: 404-888-7813; Fax: 404-885-7494.

Judicial Vicar—Very Rev. PAUL J. HACHEY, S.M., J.C.D.

Administrator—Sr. MARIE BREITENBECK, O.P., J.C.D.

Defenders of the Bond—Rev. Msgr. PETER A. DORA, M.Div.; Revs. JOHN R. HENLEY, M.Div.; DANIEL J. MCCORMICK, B.A.; LUIS ZARAMA, J.C.L.

Judges—Sr. MARIE BREITENBECK, O.P. J.C.D.; Revs. GREGORY D. GOOLSBY, M.Div.; ALBERT J. JOWDY, M.Div.; Rev. Msgr. R. DONALD KIERNAN, P.A., D.P.A.; Revs. JAMES A. MICELI, M.Div.; RICHARD B. MORROW, B.A.; Rev. Msgr. MICHAEL J. REGAN, J.C.D.; Revs. PAUL H. REYNOLDS; JAMES A. SCHILLINGER, S.T.L.

Notary—DOROTHY WESSELMANN, M.S.Ed.
Promoter of Justice—Rev. DANIEL J. MCCORMICK, B.A.
Office of Vocations—Rev. Msgr. DONALD A. KENNY, Dir. Tel: 770-422-5633. Rev. DAVID P. TALLEY. Tel: 770-888-7802.
Office for Permanent Diaconate—Deacons ALFRED MITCHELL, Dir. (Secretariat Supvr./Chancellor); LORIS SINANIAN, Dir. of Formation.
Office for Pro-Life—PEGGY SINANIAN, Dir. (Secretariat Supvr. & Chancellor).
Office of Family Concerns—Tel: 404-888-7819. MARY ELLEN HUGHES, Dir. (Secretariat Supvr./Catholic Charities).
Office of Hispanic Apostolate—Tel: 404-888-7839. Mr. GONZALO SALDANA, Dir. (Secretariat Supvr. & Chancellor).
Development Office—
Director—SUSAN KELLY. Tel: 404-888-7804.
Director of the Archdiocesan Annual Appeal and Archdiocesan Stewardship—SUSAN KELLY.
Archives—ANTHONY R. DEES. Tel: 404-888-7802.

Other Archdiocesan Offices

AACCW—DIEDRA HOLLER, *680 W. Peachtree St., N.W., Atlanta, 30308-1984.* Tel: 770-469-4123. Rev. PAUL W. BERNY, Spiritual Moderator. Tel: 404-885-7200.
Apostleship of Prayer—Rev. VINCENT R. MALATESTA, S.J., *Ignatius House, 6700 Riverside Dr., N.W., Atlanta, 30328.* Tel: 404-255-0503.
Girl and Boy Scouts—Deacon BRUCE C. PUBLICOVER, *P.O. Box 78, Woodstock, 30188.* Tel: 770-591-9200.
Cana Conferences—MARY ELLEN HUGHES, *680 W. Peachtree St., N.W., Atlanta, 30308.* Tel: 404-888-7819.
Consultors—Rev. Msgr. PETER A. DORA,Very Rev. Deans and Vicar for Clergy, Presbyteral Council Pres. & Chancellor.
Cursillo—Sr. MARGARET MCANOY, I.H.M., Dir., *680 W. Peachtree St., N.W., Atlanta, 30308.* Tel: 404-885-7413.
Deans—Northeast Metro: Very Rev. JAMES J. FENNESSY, V.F.; Northwest Metro: Very Rev. PAUL H. REYNOLDS, V.F.; South Metro: Very Rev. FRANK J. GIUSTA, V.F.; Northeast Rural: Very Rev. WALTER J. FOLEY, V.F.; Northwest Rural: Very Rev. JAMES A. MICELI, V.F.; South Rural: Very Rev. LEO P. HERBERT, V.F.
Georgia Catholic Conference—CHEATHAM E. HODGES, JR., Exec. Sec., *Office Bldg., 3200 Deans Bridge Rd., Augusta, 30906.* Tel: 706-798-1719.
Campus Ministry—Rev. MARK W. LACEY, *680 W. Peachtree St., N.W., Atlanta, 30308.* Tel: 404-888-7804.
Council of Priests—Rev. Msgr. HENRY C. GRACZ, *P.O. Box 32, McDonough, 30253.*
Atlanta Conference of Sisters—Sr. MARY PRINISKI, O.P., *235 E. Ponce de Leon Ave., Ste. 226, Decatur, 30030.* Tel: 404-377-7010.

Archdiocesan Councils, Boards, Commissions, and Committees

Boards—
Education—BERTHA MARTIN, Chm. & Sec. Education, *680 W. Peachtree St., N.W., Atlanta, 30308.* Tel: 404-888-7833.
Social Services—CARROLL P. STERNE, Sec. Catholic Charities, *680 W. Peachtree St., N.W., Atlanta, 30308.* Tel: 404-881-6571.
Clergy Retirement—Rev. Msgr. R. DONALD KIERNAN, P.A., *2443 Mt. Vernon Rd., Dunwoody, 30338.* Tel: 404-393-3255.
Commissions—
Liturgical—Rev. Msgr. LOUIS NAUGHTON, Sec., *680 W. Peachtree St., N.W., Atlanta, 30308.* Tel: 404-888-7815.

CLERGY, PARISHES, MISSIONS AND PAROCHIAL SCHOOLS

CITY OF ATLANTA
(Fulton County)

1—CATHEDRAL OF CHRIST THE KING (1936), Rev. Msgr. Thomas Kenny, Rector; Revs. Martin Ralph Kalu; Richard B. Morrow, (Retired); Hernan Quevedo-Rodriguez; Deacons Richard Narey; Whitney Robichaux. In res., Rev. Msgr. Louis Naughton.
Res., 2699 Peachtree Rd., N.E., 30305. Tel: 404-233-2145; Fax: 404-233-9711.
School—46 Peachtree Way, 30305. Tel: 404-233-0383; Fax: 404-266-0704. Mrs. Peggy Warner, Prin.
Lay Teachers 30; Students 505.
Catechesis/Religious Programs—Tel: 404-237-0564; Fax: 404-233-4984.
Students 500.

2—HOLY CROSS (1964), Revs. Paul Fogarty; Larry P. Niese; Alvaro D. Avendano; Peter Duc Vu; Deacons Lou Hettel; Bill Jindrich; Sam Mure; Cece Reimer; Dick Suever; Tom Silvestri.
Res., 3175 Hathaway Ct., 30341. Tel: 770-939-3501; Fax: 770-723-7013.
Catechesis/Religious Programs—Tel: 770-934-5757.
Students 650.

3—HOLY SPIRIT (1964), Rev. Msgr. Edward J. Dillon; Rev. Darragh W. Griffith; Deacon Thomas Shuler.
Church & Res.: 4465 Northside Dr., N.W., 30327. Tel: 404-252-4513; Fax: 404-252-1162.
Catechesis/Religious Programs—Tel: 404-252-2764.
Students 426.

4—IMMACULATE HEART OF MARY (1958), Revs. Alfred W. Wendel; James H. Sexstone; Carlos Carreras, S.J.; Jose D. Gonzalez-Florez; Deacons James Stewart; Thomas McGrane.
Res., 2855 Briarcliff Rd., N.E., 30329. Tel: 404-636-1418; Fax: 404-636-4394.
School—Tel: 404-636-4488; Fax: 404-636-1853. Mrs. Margo A. Wolke, Prin.
Lay Teachers 28; Students 480.
Catechesis/Religious Programs—Tel: 404-321-3175. Sr. Marietta Jansen, A.C.J., D.R.E.
Students 285.
Mission—Doraville, Dekalb Co., Our Lady of the Americas, 5918 New Peachtree Rd., Doraville, 30340. Tel: 770-454-8437; Fax: 770-454-4885.

5—MOST BLESSED SACRAMENT (1960), Rev. Bruce W. Wilkinson. In res., Rev. Raymond F. Horan.
Res., 1926 Austin Rd., S.W., 30331-4805. Tel: 404-349-0176; Fax: 404-349-0178.
Church—2971 Butner Rd. S.W., 30331.

6—OUR LADY OF THE ASSUMPTION (1951), Revs. James F. McGoldrick, S.M.; Eugene Hughes, S.M., Pastoral Assoc.; Deacons Douglas Anderson; Bill Bevacqua; Robert Gresher; Michael O'Brien; William Pond; John Shell.
Office: 1350 Hearst Dr., N.E., 30319. Tel: 404-261-7181; Fax: 404-364-1913.
Res., 1406 Hearst Dr., N.E., 30319. Tel: 404-364-1909.
School—1320 Hearst Dr., N.E., 30319. Tel: 404-364-1902; Fax: 404-364-1914. Mrs. Joan Tiernan, Prin.
Lay Teachers 28; Students 500.
Catechesis/Religious Programs—Tel: 404-364-1905; Fax: 404-364-1913.
Students 158.
Chapels—Marist School, Tel: 404-457-7201; Fax: 404-457-8402; St. Joseph's Hospital, Tel: 404-851-7001; Fax: 404-851-5901; Sisters of Mercy Convent at St. Joseph's Hospital, Tel: 404-255-6427.

7—OUR LADY OF LOURDES (1911), Rev. Frank Giusta. Pastoral Assocs.: Deacons Homer Woods; Thomas Zaworski.
Res., 25 Boulevard, N.E., 30312. Tel: 404-522-6776; Fax: 404-222-0202.
School—29 Boulevard, N.E., 30312. Tel: 404-581-0643.
Lay Teachers 15; Students 131.
Catechesis/Religious Programs—Students 116.

8—SACRED HEART OF JESUS (1880), Revs. Stephen T. Churchwell; Carlos Rocha-Sosa; Deacons Wayne D. Smith; Loris Sinanian. In res., Rev. Msgr. Walter J. Donovan, (Retired).
Res., 353 Peachtree St., N.E., 30308. Tel: 404-522-6800; Fax: 404-524-5440.
Catechesis/Religious Programs—Students 182.

9—ST. ANTHONY OF PADUA (1903) (African American), Rev. Hugh Marren; Deacon Joseph Barker. In res., Rev. John C.K. Fallon.
Res., 928 Ralph David Abernathy Blvd., S.W., 30310. Tel: 404-758-8861.
School—953 Ralph David Abernathy Blvd., S.W., 30310.
Sisters of St. Joseph of Carondelet 2; Lay Teachers 13; Students 130.
Child Care Center—.
Lay Teachers 10; Students 62.
Catechesis/Religious Programs—Fax: 404-755-6755.
Students 130.

10—ST. JUDE (1960), Rev. Msgr. Daniel J. O'Connor; Revs. Victor J. Reyes; William Williams.
Res., 7171 Glenridge Dr. N.E., 30328. Tel: 770-394-3896; Fax: 770-399-7866.
School—Tel: 770-394-2880; Fax: 770-804-9248.
Lay Teachers 40; Students 500.
Catechesis/Religious Programs—Tel: 770-394-4588.
Students 418.

11—ST. PAUL OF THE CROSS (1954) (African American), Revs. Melvin Shorter, C.P.; Michael Greene, C.P.; Deacons Joseph P. Goolsby; Hilliard M. Lee, Jr.; Leon Allain; Benjamin Petty, (Retired). In res., Rev. Joseph A. Fahy, C.P.
Res., 551 Harwell Rd. N.W., 30318. Tel: 404-696-6704; Fax: 404-696-4735.
Catechesis/Religious Programs—Tel: 404-696-6709.
Students 110.

12—SHRINE OF THE IMMACULATE CONCEPTION (1848), Revs. John S. Adamski; Alan M. Dillmann; Norberto Mateus (Columbia); T.J. Meehan; Deacon William Payne.
Res., 48 Martin Luther King, Jr. Dr., S.W., 30303-3599. Tel: 404-521-1866.
Mission—Atlanta, Fulton Co., San Felipe de Jesus Catholic Mission, 402 McDonough Blvd., S.E., Atlanta, 30315. Tel: 404-627-0821.

OUTSIDE CITY OF ATLANTA

Alpharetta, Fulton Co., St. Thomas Aquinas (1972), Revs. Albert W. Jowdy; John R. Anderson; Ricardo Espinosa, M.G. (Mexico); Deacons William W. Keeling; Edmund LaHouse; Donald N. Nadeau; John Strachan.
Res., 535 Rucker Rd., 30201. Tel: 770-475-4501; Fax: 770-772-0355.
Catechesis/Religious Programs—Tel: 770-475-4508.
Students 2051.

Athens, Clarke Co., St. Joseph's (1873), Revs. Joseph Chaloux; Joy Nellissery; Deacons Don Marchildon; Bill Lakin; Jim Gaudin.
Res., 134 Prince Ave., 30610. Tel: 706-548-6332; Fax: 706-354-1783.
School—Tel: 706-543-1621; Fax: 706-543-0149. Sr. Teresa Ballisty, I.H.M., Prin.
Servants of the Immaculate Heart of Mary 3; Missionary Sisters of the Sacred Heart 7; Lay Teachers 21; Students 370.
Catechesis/Religious Programs—Tel: 706-548-5487; Fax: 706-548-5487.
Students 435.
Chapels—St. Mary's Hospital, Tel: 706-548-7581; Fax: 706-355-7274; Catholic Student Center, Tel: 706-543-2293; Fax: 706-543-2541; University of Georgia.

Blairsville, Union Co., St. Francis of Assisi (1966), Rev. Timothy A. Gadziala,.; Sr. Rosemary Wickham, O.S.F., Pastoral Assoc.; Deacons Robert O'Neill; Lawrence Casey.
Res., 2839 Young Harris Hwy., 30512. Tel: 706-745-6400; Fax: 706-745-1468.
Catechesis/Religious Programs—Students 58.
Mission—Cleveland, White Co., St. Paul the Apostle, 1397 Helen Hwy., Cleveland, 30528. Tel: 706-865-4474; Fax: 706-219-3009. Deacon Daniel Bradach.

Blue Ridge, Fannin Co., St. Anthony's (1976), Rev. Christopher Williamson; Deacon John Stanley.
Res., P.O. Box 1448, 30513. Tel: 706-632-5970; Fax: 706-632-2120.
Mission—Ellijay, Gilmer Co., Good Samaritan Mission, (1982) 25 Church St., Ellijay, 30540. Tel: 706-636-2772.

Buford, Gwinnett Co., Prince of Peace (1975), Rev. James P. Adams; Deacon Michael R. Jones.
Mailing Address: P.O. Box 591, 30515-0591. Tel: 770-945-2244 (Office); 945-0200 (Rectory); Fax: 770-945-4599.
Res., 4300 S. Lee St., 30518-0591. Tel: 770-945-0200.
Catechesis/Religious Programs—Tel: 770-945-2244.
Students 600.

Calhoun, Gordon Co., St. Clements (1958), Rev. Leo B. Cummings, M.S.
Mailing Address: P.O. Box 1301, 30703-1301.
Res., 102 Greenbriar Cir., 30703. Tel: 706-625-0375; Fax: 706-625-5219.

Canton, Cherokee Co., Our Lady of LaSalette (1984), Revs. Neil G. Jones, M.S.; Denis Kolumber, M.S.
Res., 2942 Sam Nelson Rd., P.O. Box 1146, 30114. Tel: 770-479-8923; Fax: 770-479-8923.
Catechesis/Religious Programs—Students 184.
Mission—Jasper, Pickens Co., Our Lady of the Mountains, P.O. Box 248, Jasper, 30143. Tel: 706-692-3078.

Carrollton, Carroll Co., Church of Our Lady of Perpetual Help (1962), Rev. Msgr. Michael J. Regan, (Retired); Rev. John P. Farrelly; Deacon David Higgins.
Res., 210 Old Center Point Rd., 30117. Tel: 770-832-8977; Fax: 770-832-1666. [CEM]
Newman Center West Georgia College—Rev. Msgr. Michael J. Regan, J.C.D., Catholic Campus Min.
Catechesis/Religious Programs—Students 210.

Cartersville, Bartow Co., St. Francis of Assisi (1969), Rev. Peter McKeown, M.S.; Bro. Robert Russell, M.S.
850 Douthit Ferry Rd., P.O. Box 2048, 30120. Tel:

770-382-4549; Fax: 770-382-4506.
Res., 57 Pine Grove Rd., 30120. Tel: 770-386-7811.
Catechesis/Religious Programs—Students 189.

Cedartown, Polk Co., St. Bernadette's (1941), Rev. Richard K. Young.
Res., 101 S. College St., 30125. Tel: 770-748-1517; Fax: 770-748-1568.
Catechesis/Religious Programs—Students 90.

Clarkesville, Habersham Co., St. Mark's (1964), Rev. Luis Zarama; Deacon John F. Thompson.
Mailing Address: 5410 Hwy. 197 S., 30523. Tel: 706-754-4518.
Res., 151 Salome Dr., 30523. Tel: 706-754-6504; Fax: 706-754-9751.
Church—Rte. 5, Box 5058, 30523-9542.
Mission—Clayton, Rabun Co., St. Helena's, Box 534, Clayton, 30525. Tel: 706-782-5152. Deacon M. Robert Mulligan.
Station—Lee Arrendale Correctional Institute, Alto, Tel: 706-776-4700.

Conyers, Rockdale Co., St. Pius X Catholic (1974), Revs. John C. Kieran; Charles J. Kerscher, (Retired); Gordon L. Sidler.
Res., 2621 Hwy. 20, S.E., 30208. Tel: 770-483-3660; Fax: 770-483-7006.
Catechesis/Religious Programs—Tel: 770-929-1017.
Students 758.

Covington, Newton Co., St. Augustine Church (1959), Rev. Michael J. Redden; Deacon Herbert C. Berding.
Res., 11524 Hwy. 278 E., 30014. Tel: 770-787-0685; Fax: 770-787-0871.
Catechesis/Religious Programs—Students 107.
Mission—Madison, Morgan Co., St. James, 562 Vine St., Madison, 30650. Tel: 706-342-9661.

Cumming, Forsyth Co., Good Shepherd (1975), Rev. Peter J. Rau.
Church—3740 Holtzclaw Rd., 30041. Tel: 770-887-9861; Fax: 770-887-2241.
Catechesis/Religious Programs—Tel: 770-781-5378.
Students 500.

Dahlonega, Lumpkin Co., St. Luke Catholic (1960), Rev. Edward A. Danneker.
Catholic Center—75 Park St. N., 30533. Tel: 706-864-4779; Fax: 706-864-2568.
Res., 75 Park St. N., 30533.
Catechesis/Religious Programs—Students 66.
Mission—Dawsonville, Dawson Co., Christ Redeemer, P.O. Box 506, Dawsonville, 30534. Tel: 706-265-1361.
Station—Dahlonega, North Georgia College (Newman Club).

Dalton, Whitfield Co., St. Joseph's (1941), Revs. Daniel Stack; Samuel E. Porras-Gomez.
Res., 623 S. Thornton Ave., 30720. Tel: 706-278-3107; Fax: 706-278-6902. [JC]
Catechesis/Religious Programs—Students 311.

Decatur, DeKalb Co., Sts. Peter and Paul (1959) (African American), Rev. Richard P. Wise; Deacons Jerry Lett; Alfred Mitchell; J. Eugene Whitmeyer.
Res., 2372 Collier Dr., 30032. Tel: 404-241-5862; Fax: 404-241-5839.
School—2560 Tilson Rd., 30032. Tel: 404-241-3063; Fax: 404-241-4382. Sr. Mary Jane McDonnell, I.H.M., Prin.
Sister Servants of the Immaculate Heart of Mary 3; Lay Teachers 13; Students 138.
Catechesis/Religious Programs—Tel: 404-244-0598. Sr. Carol Tenerovich, C.D.P., D.R.E.
Students 179.

St. Thomas More (1949), Revs. Patrick F. Mulhern; Balappa Selvaraj; Ms. Ann Dugan, Pastoral Assoc.
Res., 624 W. Ponce de Leon Ave., 30030. Tel: 404-378-4588; Fax: 404-378-0506.
School—Tel: 404-373-8456; Fax: 404-377-8554. Dr. Thomas Collins, Prin.
Sisters Notre Dame de Namur 2; Lay Teachers 24; Students 475.
Catechesis/Religious Programs—Students 216.
Convent—636 W. Ponce de Leon Ave., 30030. Tel: 404-378-6119.

Douglasville, Douglas Co., St. Theresa (1985), Rev. Stewart A. Wilber.
Res., 3194 S. Elizabeth Dr., 30135.
Church—4401 Prestley Mill Rd., 30135. Tel: 770-489-7115; Fax: 770-489-4873.
Catechesis/Religious Programs—Tel: 770-942-9765.
Students 330.

Duluth, Fulton, St. Benedict (1987), Rev. Msgr. Terry W. Young; Rev. Daniel J. Fleming; Deacons John Stroop; William Monahan; Walker P. King; William Lange.
Res., 11085 Parsons Rd., 30097. Tel: 770-664-5099.
Office: 11045 Parsons Rd., 30097. Tel: 770-442-5903; Fax: 770-442-0744.
Catechesis/Religious Programs—Students 2,366.
Mission—Duluth, Gwinnett Co., St. Monica, 1925 Peach Bluff Dr., 30097. Tel: 770-495-9201; Fax: 770-495-9216. In res., Rev. Gregory D. Goolsby.

Dunwoody, DeKalb Co., All Saints Catholic (1977), Rev. Msgr. R. Donald Kiernan, P.A.; Revs. Daniel J. McCormick; David M. Dye; W. Joseph Corbett; Deacon Raymond F. Egan.
Res., 2443 Mount Vernon Rd., 30338-3099. Tel: 770-393-3255; Fax: 770-913-0140.
Catechesis/Religious Programs—Students 822.
Mission—Norcross, Gwinnett Co., Mary, Our Queen, 5875 Peachtree Industrial Blvd., Ste. 260, Norcross, 30092. Tel: 770-416-0002; Fax: 770-416-1846.

Eatonton, Putnam Co., Christ Our Savior Mission (1993). Merged with Christ Our King, Greensboro to form Christ Our King and Saviour, Greensboro.

Fairburn, Fulton Co., St. Matthew's (1979), Rev. Leo C. Holleran, M.S.
Res., 104 W. Campbellton St., P.O. Box 158, 30213. Tel: 770-964-5804; Fax: 770-964-1228.
Catechesis/Religious Programs—Students 130.

Fayetteville, Fayette Co., St. Gabriel (1993), Rev. Paul W. Berny; Deacons Al C. McHugh; I. Carl McBride; T.C. Meuninck.
Office: 135 Antioch Rd., 30215-5702. Tel: 770-461-0492; Fax: 770-461-0374.
Catechesis/Religious Programs—Tel: 770-461-0493.
Students 304.

Fort Oglethorpe, Catoosa Co., St. Gerard's (1947), Rev. Timothy M. Hepburn.
Res., 415 LaFayette Rd., P.O. Box 2217, 30742. Tel: 706-861-9410; Fax: 706-866-0574.
Catechesis/Religious Programs—Students 45.

Gainesville, Hall Co., St. Michael's (1945), Revs. William G. Hoffman; Jorge Christancho; Deacons Felix Cosme; Michael Kennedy.
Office: 1440 Pearce Cir., 30501. Tel: 770-534-3338; 536-1603 (Rectory); Fax: 770-535-2440.
Catechesis/Religious Programs—Students 522.

Greensboro, Greene Co., Christ Our King and Savior. Consolidation of Christ Our Savior, Eatonton, and Christ Our King, Greensboro. Rev. Serge E. Ward.
Office & Church—6341 Lake Oconee Pkwy., 30642. Tel: 706-453-1584 (Rectory).
Res., 307 S. Walnut St., 30642. Tel: 706-453-7292; 485-0102; Fax: 706-453-7095.

Griffin, Spalding Co., Sacred Heart (1941), Revs. John L. Smyth, C.SS.R.; James E. McGonagle, C.SS.R.; Thomas Burke, C.SS.R.; Deacons James Hedderman, (Retired); Felix Marrero. In res., Rev. Jerome Chavarriq, C.SS.R.
Res., 1323 MacArthur Dr., 30223. Tel: 770-227-2378; Fax: 770-227-6440.
Catechesis/Religious Programs—Tel: 770-227-2898.
Students 101.
Missions—Thomaston, Upson Co., St. John the Baptist, P.O. Box 897, Thomaston, 30286. Tel: 706-647-9993; Barnesville, Lamar Co., St. Ann, Hwy. 341, Barnesville, 30204. Tel: 706-358-0635.
Chapel—Redemptorist Fathers Residence, Tel: 404-227-0541.
Station—Forsyth.

Hapeville, Fulton Co., St. John the Evangelist (1950), Revs. Vincent J. Douglass, C.Ss.R.; Michael Dillon, C.Ss.R.; Joseph Gribbon, C.Ss.R.; Deacons Richard Beckman; Henry Akers; Michael K. Mobley.
Mailing Address: 230 Arnold St., 30354-1530. Tel: 404-768-5647 (Church); Fax: 404-767-6416.
School—Tel: 404-767-4312; Fax: 404-767-0359.
Lay Teachers 18; Students 165.
Catechesis/Religious Programs—Tel: 404-767-5877. Mrs. Barbara Nichols, D.R.E.
Students 256.

Hartwell, Hart Co., Sacred Heart of Jesus (1977), Rev. Walter W. Foley.
Res., 1009 Benson St., 30643. Tel: 404-376-4112; Fax: 404-376-1695.
Catechesis/Religious Programs—Students 88.

Jonesboro, Clayton Co., St. Philip Benizi (1965), Revs. Gregory J. Hartmayer, O.F.M.Conv.; John P. Krzyzanski, O.F.M.Conv.; John A. Koziol, O.F.M.Conv.; Deacons Joseph C. Anzalone; William F. McCarthy.
Res., 591 Flint River Rd., 30238-3452. Tel: 770-478-0178; Fax: 770-471-2079.
Catechesis/Religious Programs—Tel: 770-471-2881. Mary M. Mauldin, D.R.E.
Students 764.

Kennesaw, Cobb Co., St. Catherine of Siena (1981), Revs. James Harrison; Frank McNamee; Benneth Osigwe; Deacons Pat O'Connor; David Rauth; Martin Lampe.
Res., 1620 Overlook Ct., 30144. Tel: 770-419-9112.
Church—1618 Ben King Rd., N.W., 30144. Tel: 770-428-7139; Fax: 770-428-0131.
Catechesis/Religious Programs—Tel: 770-428-7440. D.R.E.: Rita Bek; Catherine Hackney; Lisa Fiamingo; Maureen Ingalls; Rose Robbins.
Students 1,200.

LaGrange, Troup Co., St. Peter's (1963), Rev. John M. Murphy; Deacon Jim Stagg, Pastoral Assoc.
Res., 200 LaFayette Pkwy., 30241. Tel: 706-884-0445 (Rectory); 884-4224 (Church); Fax: 706-884-1624.
Catechesis/Religious Programs—Students 230.
Mission—Warm Springs, Meriwether Co., St. Elizabeth Seton, P.O. Box 638, Warm Springs, 31830. Tel: 706-846-5223. Sr. Gloria Carpinello, F.F.M., Pastoral Assoc.

Lawrenceville, Gwinnett Co., St. Lawrence (1971), Revs. Anthony T. Curran; Christopher Williamson; Deacons Richard Johnson; Walter T. Bedard, Sr.
Res., 319 Grayson Hwy., 30045. Tel: 770-963-8992; Fax: 770-963-1710.
Catechesis/Religious Programs—Tel: 770-962-2765. Diane Mcguire, D.R.E.
Students 1,003.

St. Marguerite D'Youville (1995), Rev. Brendan Doyle.
Res., Hwy. 29 at Huff Rd., P.O. Box 464335, 30246. Tel: 770-513-4109; Fax: 770-513-1731.
Catechesis/Religious Programs—Students 340.

Lilburn, Gwinnett Co., St. John Neumann (1977), Revs. James J. Fennessy; Michael J. Campbell; Patrick H. Donaghey; Craig David; Deacons Rafael Cintron; Evelio Garcia; Jim O'Brien; Gary Womack; Larry French.
Res., 801 Tom Smith Rd., 30247. Tel: 770-923-6633; 923-6909; Fax: 770-381-7856.
School—(Grades K-8). (Regional). Tel: 404-381-0557; Fax: 404-381-0276. Mary Ann Radnovich, Prin.
Lay Teachers 35; Students 571.
Catechesis/Religious Programs—Students 1,237.
Mission—Lilburn, Gwinnet Co., St. Stephen the Martyr, 382 Rockbridge Rd., 30247. Tel: 770-925-2736.

Lithia Springs, Douglas Co., St. John Vianney (1958), Revs. Daniel Fink, O.F.M.Conv.; Carl Zdancewicz, O.F.M.Conv.; Deacon William Lyday. In res., Rev. Linus DeSantis, O.F.M.Conv.
Mailing Address: 1920 Skyview Dr., 30122. Tel: 770-941-2807; Fax: 770-941-5821.
Catechesis/Religious Programs—Students 400.
Mission—Dallas, Paulding Co., St. Vincent de Paul, 680 W. Memorial Dr., Dallas, 30132. Tel: 770-443-1533.

Lithonia, DeKalb Co., Christ Our Hope (1984), Rev. Paul A. Flood.
Res., 1786 Wellborn Rd., 30058. Tel: 770-482-5017; Fax: 770-482-9476.
Catechesis/Religious Programs—Tel: 770-482-5894.
Students 133.

Lookout Mountain, Walker Co., Our Lady of the Mount (1947), Rev. Francis X. Richardson.
Res., 1227 Scenic Hwy., P.O. Box 214, 30750. Tel: 706-820-0680; Fax: 706-820-2797. [JC]
Catechesis/Religious Programs—Students 125.

McDonough, Henry Co., St. James The Apostle (1979), Rev. Msgr. Henry C. Gracz; Rev. John T. Howren; Deacons Robert Rich; Robert Readdy. In res., Rev. Austin Fogarty.
Res., Georgia Hwy. 155, P.O. Box 32, 30253. Tel: 770-957-5441; Fax: 770-957-0383.
Catechesis/Religious Programs—Tel: 770-957-2990.
Students 470.
Mission—Jackson, Butts Co., St. Mary's, P.O. Box 901, Jackson, 30233. Tel: 770-775-4162; Fax: 770-775-4162.

Marietta, Cobb Co.,

1—HOLY FAMILY, (1973), Revs. Edward Thein; Paul D. Williams, Jr.; Juan de la Cruz; Deacons Paul Dietz; Al Gallagher.
Res., 3401 Lower Roswell Rd., 30068. Tel: 770-973-0038; Fax: 770-578-0475.
Catechesis/Religious Programs—Tel: 770-973-7400. Theresa Johnson, D.R.E.
Students 710.

2—CHURCH OF ST. ANN, (1978), Revs. Robert Susann, M.S.; Joseph Nolan, M.S.; James P. Hurley, M.S.; Deacons Edmund Grabowy; J. Nicholas Morning.
Res., 4905 Roswell Rd., N.E., 30062. Tel: 770-998-1373; Fax: 770-993-3022.
Catechesis/Religious Programs—Tel: 770-998-0444.
Students 2,300.

3—ST. JOSEPH, (1952), Rev. Msgr. Donald A. Kenny; Revs. Paul A. Burke; Thomas J. Hennessy; Tuan Quoc Tran; Deacons Thomas Shaver; Michael Esper.
Res., 87 Lacy St., N.W., 30060. Tel: 770-422-5633; Fax: 770-422-1148.
School—Tel: 770-428-3328; Fax: 770-424-2960. Sr. Patricia Baber, R.S.M., Prin.
Lay Teachers 26; Students 484.
Catechesis/Religious Programs—Tel: 770-428-1833. Linda Hughey, D.R.E.

Students 900.

4—CHURCH OF THE TRANSFIGURATION, (1977), Revs. Patrick A. Bishop; Joseph E. Morris; Sr. Barbara Baker, M.H.S.H., Pastoral Assoc.; Deacon Bruce Publicover.
Res., 1815 Blackwell Rd., N.E., 30066-2911. Tel: 770-977-1442; Fax: 770-578-1415.
Catechesis/Religious Programs—Rick Fehrenbach, D.R.E.
Students 1,660.

Milledgeville, Baldwin Co., Sacred Heart of Jesus (1874), Rev. Michael L. McWhorter.
Res., 110 N. Jefferson St., P.O. Box 754, 31061. Tel: 912-452-2421; Fax: 912-454-1110.
Chapel—Milledgeville, Central State Hospital.

Monroe, Walton Co., St. Anna's (1951), Rev. Richard A. Kieran; Deacon Jerry F. Connell.
Res., 836 E. Spring St., 30655. Tel: 770-267-7637; Fax: 770-267-0465.
Catechesis/Religious Programs—Tel: 770-267-0420.
Students 57.

Newnan, Coweta Co., St. George's (1952), Rev. Leo P. Herbert, V.F.; Deacons Ben Gross; John Myers.
Res., 771 Roscoe Rd., 30263. Tel: 770-253-0512; Fax: 770-251-2053. [JC]
Catechesis/Religious Programs—Tel: 770-251-5353.
Students 455.

Norcross, Gwinnett Co., Saint Patrick's (1968), Revs. Martin J. Kopchik, M.S.F.S.; Hrudaya Raj Patchala, M.S.F.S.; Joseph Mullakkara, M.S.F.S.; Deacons Jose Narvaez; Bob Tipton; Edwin Martinez; Tom Labat.
Res., 2140 Beaver Ruin Rd., 30071. Tel: 770-446-2041.
Church—Beaver Ruin Rd., 30071. Tel: 770-448-2028; Fax: 770-448-7046.
Catechesis/Religious Programs—Tel: 770-448-6386.
Students 482.

Peachtree City, Fayette Co., Holy Trinity Catholic (1972), Revs. Guyma Noel; John P. Walsh; Deacons Don Kelsey; Anthony F. Cuomo.
Res., 101 Walt Banks Rd., P.O. Box 2121, 30269. Tel: 770-487-7672; Fax: 770-486-9152.
Catechesis/Religious Programs—Tel: 770-487-0175. Mary Ann Cox, D.R.E.
Students 1,185.

Rome, Floyd Co., St. Mary's (1930), Very Rev. James A. Miceli, V.F.; Deacons Ronald A. Comeau; James Hopkins.
Res., 911 N. Broad St., 30161. Tel: 706-295-7014; Fax: 706-295-1717.
School—401 E. 7th St., 30161. Tel: 404-234-4953. Ms. Susan Odle, Prin.
Lay Teachers 15; Students 178.
Catechesis/Religious Programs—Students 228.

Roswell, Fulton Co., St. Andrew (1981), Revs. Paul H. Reynolds; William Keen; Robert Smith; John C. Druding.
Res., 115 River Lake Ct., 30075. Tel: 770-552-0485; Fax: 770-641-8584 (Office).
Catechesis/Religious Programs—Tel: 404-641-0261.
Students 1,050.

Smyrna, Cobb Co., St. Thomas the Apostle (1966), Revs. James Caffery, M.S.; Eugene Barrette, M.S.; John A. Welch, M.S.
Res., 4300 King Springs Rd., 30082. Tel: 770-432-8579; Fax: 770-432-8570.
Catechesis/Religious Programs—Tel: 770-432-5296.
Students 394.

Snellville, Gwinnett Co., St. Oliver Plunkett (1978), Revs. Thomas J. Carroll, M.S.; Michael J. Flanagan, M.S.; Clifford Hasler, M.S.; Deacon Michael Cappoza.
Res., 1318 Summit Chase Dr., 30078. Tel: 770-979-3827; Fax: 770-985-6590.
Church—3200 Brooks Dr., 30078. Tel: 770-979-2500; Fax: 770-985-6590.
Catechesis/Religious Programs—Tel: 770-978-6751.
Students 857.
Mission—Winder, Barrow Co., St. Matthew, c/o St. Oliver Plunkett, 30278.

Stone Mountain, DeKalb Co., Corpus Christi (1971), Revs. Gregory D. Kenny, C.M.F.; Ronald Stua, C.M.F.; Severino Lopez, C.M.F.; Raymond O'Connor, C.M.F.; Deacon Will MacDonald.
Res., 600 Mountain View Dr., 30083. Tel: 770-469-0395; Fax: 770-469-6822. [JC]
Catechesis/Religious Programs—Tel: 770-469-0597.
Students 408.

Thomson, McDuffie Co., Queen of Angels (1955), Rev. Edward O'Connor.
Res., 1326 Washington Rd., 30824. Tel: 706-595-2913; Fax: 706-595-2913.
Catechesis/Religious Programs—Students 78.

Toccoa, Stephens Co., St. Mary's (1956), Rev. Daniel R. Toof.
Res., 6388 Rothell Rd. Ext., 30577. Tel: 706-886-2819; Fax: 706-886-8770. [JC]
Catechesis/Religious Programs—Students 71.
Mission—Commerce, Jackson Co., St. Catherine Laboure, 708 State St., Commerce, 30529. Tel: 706-335-2622.

Washington, Wilkes Co., St. Joseph's (1840), Rev. G. Philip Ryan.
Res., P.O. Box 632, U.S. Hwy. 78, 30673. Tel: 706-678-2110; Fax: 706-678-3353. [CEM]
Missions—Elberton, Elbert Co., St. Mary's, Forest Ave., Elberton, 30635.; Sharon, Talifero Co., Purification, Hwy. 47, Sharon, 30631.

Woodstock, Cherokee Co., St. Michael the Archangel (1995), Rev. Patrick J. Kingery; Deacon Jim Eastwood.
Res., 490 Arnold Mill Rd., 30188. Tel: 770-516-0009; Fax: 770-516-4664.
Catechesis/Religious Programs—Students 705.

Chaplains of Public Institutions

ATLANTA. *Atlanta Veterans Administration Hospital*. Rev. Thad B. Rudd, Chap.
Dobbins Air Force Base. Vacant. 94 AW/HC, 1311 Patrol Rd., Dobbins Air Force Base, 30069-5003. Tel: 404-919-4955; 4956.
Fort McPherson. Office of the Garrison Chaplain, Vacant. Bldg. 51, Fort McPherson, 30330-5000. Tel: 404-752-2616. Office of the FORSCOM Chap., 6 W. Staff Row, 30310. Tel: 404-755-1487. Rev. Msgr. Kenneth A. Seifried.
U.S. Penitentiary 601 McDonough Blvd., S.E., 30315. Rev. John C.K. Fallon.

Special or Other Archdiocesan Assignment:
Reverend Monsignors—
Kenny, Donald A., Vocations Dir.

Released from Archdiocesan Assignment:
Reverend Fathers—
Fitzgerald, Cornelius J.
Zivic, Richard

On Duty Outside the Archdiocese:
Reverend Fathers—
Atkins, James P., Monastery of Our Savior, 711 North St., Steubenville, OH 43952
Kinast, Robert L., P.O. Box 86035, Maderia Beach, FL 33738-6035
McBrearity, Gerald D., Society of St. Sulpice, 5408 Roland Ave., Baltimore, MD 21210
Patterson, David L., Diocese of Savannah, GA
Sanches, Joseph A., Diocese of Nashville, TN
Scherer, James F., Diocese of Charlotte, NC
Talley, David P., Pontifical, North American College, Rome, Italy
Woods, Michael A., Diocese of Knoxville, TN

Military Chaplains:
Reverend Fathers—
McCormick, Patrick J., PSC 816, FPO AE 09612

Retired:
Reverend Monsignors—
Regan, Michael J., Pastor Emeritus
Reverend Fathers—
Donovan, Walter J., Sacred Heart Church, 353 Peachtree St., Atlanta, GA 30308
Drohan, Joseph W.
Henley, John R.
Kerscher, Charles J.
Morrow, Richard B.
O'Shea, John J., The Fountainview Center for Alzheimer's Disease, 2611 N. Druid Hills Rd., Atlanta, GA 30329
Ware, Joseph F., St. Francis Cabrini, 11500 Middleground Rd., Savannah, GA 31419

Permanent Deacons:
Akers, Henry, St. John the Evangelist, Hapeville
Allain, Leon G., St. Paul of the Cross, Atlanta
Anderson, Douglas J., Our Lady of the Assumption, Atlanta
Angelich, George D., Our Lady of Perpetual Help, Carrollton
Anzalone, Joseph C., St. Philip Benizi, Jonesboro
Anzalone, Joseph S., St. Peter the Apostle, Birmingham, AL
Appel, Charles M., Epiphany Byzantine, Roswell
Barker, Joseph J., St. Anthony's, Atlanta
Bathea, Val, All Saints, Dallas, TX
Beckman, Richard F., St. John the Evangelist, Hapeville
Bedard, Walter T., St. Lawrence, Lawrenceville
Berding, Herbert C., St. James Mission, Madison
Bevacqua, Bill J., Our Lady of the Assumption, Atlanta
Bidelman, William E., Jr., Unassigned
Borsavage, Charles T., St. Patrick's, Norcross
Bradach, Daniel D., St. Paul's Mission, Cleveland
Briesch, Forrest R., St. Raphael's, Glendale, AZ
Capozza, Michael A., St. Oliver Plunkett, Snellville
Casal, Matias A., St. Philip Benizi, Jonesboro
Casey, Lawrence B., St. Francis of Assisi, Blairsville
Cintron, Rafael, St. John Neumann, Lilburn
Comeau, Ronald A., St. Mary's, Rome
Connell, Jerry F., St. Anna's, Monroe
Cosme, Felix, St. Michael's, Gainesville
Coughlin, Frank F., St. Marguerite D'Youville, Lawrenceville
Cuomo, Anthony F., Holy Trinity, Peachtree City
DeSandre, Bart R., St. Marguerite D'Youville, Lawrenceville
Diehl, William P., St. Francis of Assisi, Blairsville
Dietz, Paul E., Holy Family, Marietta
Easterwood, James M., St. Michael the Archangel, Canton
Egan, Raymond F., All Saints, Dunwoody
Esper, Michael L., St. Joseph's, Marietta
French, Lawrence E., St. John Neumann, Lilburn
Gallagher, Alexander S., Holy Family, Marietta
Galvis, Enrique L., U.S. Penitentiary, Atlanta
Garcia-Carreras, Evelio, St. John Neumann, Lilburn
Gaudin, James M., Jr., St. Joseph's, Athens
Goolsby, Joseph B., St. Paul of the Cross, Atlanta
Gourgues, Harold W., Jr., Good Shepherd, Cumming
Grabowy, Edmund M., St. Ann's, Marietta
Gresher, Robert C., Our Lady of the Assumption, Atlanta
Gross, Benedict, St. George, Newnan
Hedderman, James J., Sr., (Retired)
Henrich, Robert A., Unassigned
Hettel, Louis A., Holy Cross, Atlanta
Higgins, David J., Our Lady of Perpetual Hope, Carrollton
Hopkins, James A., St. Mary's, Rome
Hughes, Thomas E., Catholic Center at Emory University, Atlanta
Jansen, John C., St. Pius X, Conyers
Jimenez, Arturo P., Immaculate Heart of Mary, Atlanta
Jindrich, William L., Holy Cross, Atlanta
Johnson, Richard M., St. Lawrence, Lawrenceville
Jones, Fredenuet, Holy Family, Marietta
Jones, Michael R., Prince of Peace, Buford
Keeling, William W., St. Thomas Aquinas, Alpharetta
Keen, William, St. Andrew's, Roswell
Kelsey, Donald A., Holy Trinity, Peachtree City
Kennedy, Michael L., St. Michael's, Gainesville
King, Walker P., St. Benedict, Duluth
Kirksey, Timothy K., Unassigned
Korte, Jerry R., Sacred Heart of Jesus, Hartwell
La House, Edmund J., St. Thomas Aquinas, Alpharetta
Labat, Thomas E., St. Patrick's, Norcross
Lakin, William P., St. Joseph's, Athens
Lampe, Martin J., St. Catherine of Siena, Kennesaw
Lange, William G., St. Benedict's, Duluth
Lee, Hilliard M., Jr., St. Paul of the Cross, Atlanta
Lett, Jerry M., Sts. Peter & Paul, Decatur
Leverett, Winston A., (Retired)
Lyday, William E., St. Vincent De Paul Mission, Dallas
Mac Donald, Will, Corpus Christi, Stone Mountain
Mackin, Thomas F., Christ Our King and Savior, Greensboro
Marchildon, Donald W., St. Joseph's, Athens
Marrero, Felix, Sacred Heart, Griffin
Martorell, Gerardo G., Unassigned
Mattox, William F., Jr., St. Marguerite D'Youville, Lawrenceville
Mc Bride, I. Carl, St. Gabriel's, Fayetteville
Mc Carthy, Kevin J., St. Joseph Mission, Madison, MS
Mc Carthy, William F., St. Philip Benizi, Jonesboro
Mc Grane, Thomas J., Immaculate Heart of Mary, Atlanta
Mc Hugh, Al C., St. Gabriel's, Fayetteville
Meuninck, Tilton C., St. Gabriel's, Fayetteville
Miller, Paul M., (Retired)
Mitchell, Alfred, Sts. Peter & Paul, Decatur
Mobley, Michael K., St. John the Evangelist, Hapeville
Moenk, Jean R., Deacon Emeritus, St. Matthew, Fairburn
Monahan, William J., St. Benedict's, Duluth
Morning, J. Nicholas, St. Ann, Marietta
Mulligan, M. Robert, St. Helena's Mission, Clayton
Mure, Samuel M., Holy Cross, Atlanta
Myers, John W., St. George's, Newnan

Nadeau, Donald N., St. Thomas Aquinas, Alpharetta
Narey, Richard D., Cathedral of Christ the King, Atlanta
Narvaez, Jose A., St. Patrick's, Norcross
O'Brien, James M., St. John Neumann, Lilburn
O'Brien, Michael J., Our Lady of Assumption, Atlanta
O'Connor, D. Patrick, St. Catherine of Siena, Kennesaw
O'Neill, Robert A., St. Francis of Assisi, Blairsville
Payne, William E., Jr., Shrine of the Immaculate Conception, Atlanta
Petty, Benjamin R., (Retired)
Pond, Billy, Our Lady of Assumption, Atlanta
Prawdzik, Stanley T., Unassigned
Publicover, Bruce C., Archdiocesan Scout Chap., Transfiguration, Marietta
Rauth, David W., St. Catherine of Siena, Kennesaw
Readdy, Robert G., St. James the Apostle, McDonough
Reimer, Cecil R., Holy Cross, Atlanta
Rich, Robert M., St. James the Apostle, McDonough
Robichaux, Whitney F., Jr., Cathedral of Christ the King, Atlanta
Rusmisel, William O., St. Bernadette, Cedartown
Sambrone, Fred J., Jr., Atlanta Catholic University Center
Santiago, Rigoberto A., St. Patrick's, Norcross
Shaver, Thomas R., St. Joseph's, Marietta
Shell, John B., Our Lady of the Assumption, Atlanta
Shoemaker, John W., Sacred Heart, Milledgeville
Shuler, Thomas B., Holy Spirit, Atlanta
Silvestri, Thomas D., Holy Cross, Atlanta; Chap., Georgia Diagnostic and Correctional Center, Jackson
Sinanian, Loris R., Asst. Vicar, Sacred Heart, Atlanta
Smith, Robert B., St. Andrew's, Roswell
Smith, Wayne D., Sacred Heart, Atlanta
Stagg, James A., Unassigned
Stanley, John C., St. Anthony's, Blue Ridge
Stewart, James M., Immaculate Heart of Mary, Atlanta
Stives, Edward C., Unassigned
Stone, James E., Mary Our Queen, Norcross
Strachan, John S., St. Thomas Aquinas, Alpharetta
Stroop, John, St. Benedict's, Duluth
Suever, Richard M., Holy Cross, Atlanta
Thompson, John F., St. Mark's, Clarkesville
Timme, William G., (Retired)
Tipton, Robert F., St. Patrick's, Norcross
Tolcher, Richard P., Chap., Federal Prison, Atlanta; St. Philip Benizi, Jonesboro
Weeks, Jim G., St. Matthew's, Fairburn
Whitmeyer, J. Eugene, Sts. Peter & Paul, Decatur
Womack, Gary D., St. John Neumann, Lilburn
Woods, Homer, Sr., Our Lady of Lourdes, Atlanta
Zaworski, Thomas E., Our Lady of Lourdes, Atlanta

INSTITUTIONS LOCATED IN THE ARCHDIOCESE

[A] SEMINARIES, RELIGIOUS OR SCHOLASTICATES

ATLANTA. *Aquinas Center of Theology at Emory University*, 1703 Clifton Rd., F-5, 30329. Tel: 404-727-8860; Fax: 404-727-8862. Dr. P. Lyndon Reynolds, Dir.

[B] HIGH SCHOOLS, ARCHDIOCESAN

ATLANTA. *St. Pius X Catholic High School.* (Coed), 2674 Johnson Rd., N.E., 30345. Tel: 404-636-3023.
E-mail: lion@atl.mindspring.com
Web site: http://www.atl.mindspring.com/~lion
Mr. Donald T. Sasso. Priests 2; Lay Teachers 76; Students 1,023.

[C] HIGH SCHOOLS, PRIVATE

ATLANTA. *Marist School.* (Grades 7-12), 3790 Ashford-Dunwoody, N.E., 30319-1899. Tel: 770-457-7201; 451-1316 (Res.); Fax: 770-457-8402.
E-mail: marist@marist.com
Web site: www.marist.com
A Private Catholic School. College Preparatory Day School conducted by The Marists. Corporate Title: Marist School, Inc. Mr. Michael F. Maher, Headmaster; Revs. Francis J. Kissel, S.M., Dir. Admissions; Ralph F. Olek, S.M., Supr.; James L. Hartnett, S.M., Pres.; Ronald J. Nikodem, S.M., Campus Pastor; Bro. Timothy McCoy, S.M.; Mr. Shaun Scully, S.M., Scholastic. In res. Revs. Thomas Gilroy, S.M., (Retired); James M. Cummings, S.M., (Retired); Paul J. Hachey, S.M., Metropolitan Tribunal; Thomas D. O'Donnell, S.M., (Retired); Charles Pfab, S.M., (Retired); Lawrence R. Schmuhl, S.M., (Retired). Priests 10; Lay Faculty 98; Students 1,025.

[D] ELEMENTARY SCHOOLS, PRIVATE

ATLANTA. *Archbishop Thomas A. Donnellan School*, 4820 Long Island Dr., 30342-2570. Tel: 404-255-0900; Fax: 404-255-0914.
E-mail: srdawn@donnellan.org
Sr. Dawn Gear, G.N.S.H., Prin. Lay Teachers 19; Students 186.

CUMMING. *Pinecrest Academy*, 955 Peachtree Pkwy., 30041. Tel: 770-888-4477; Fax: 770-888-0404. Priests 1; Brothers 1; Lay Teachers 5.

[E] RESIDENTIAL TREATMENT CENTER AND DAY SCHOOL

ATLANTA. *Village of St. Joseph.* (Children & Adolescents, Ages 11-16), 2969 Butner Rd., S.W., 30331. Tel: 404-349-2400. Charles L. Bright, M.A.Ed. Lay Teachers 5; Students 31.

[F] CATHOLIC SOCIAL SERVICES

Departmental Agencies

ATLANTA. *Catholic Social Services, Inc.*, 680 W. Peachtree St., N.W., 30308-1984. Tel: 404-881-6571. Pam Buckmaster, Exec. Dir.; Charles Prejean, CSS Chm. Bd.
Counseling Services, Crisis Pregnancy & Adoption, Immigration Services, Multicultural Services & Parish Social Ministry. Branch Offices outside the city of Atlanta. Dr. Jim Kantner, Program Dir.
Parish Social Ministry/Community Connections. Tel: 404-881-6571. Myles McCabe, Prog. Dir.
Pregnancy, Parenting & Adoption Services. Tel: 404-881-6571. Noreen Horrigan, Prog. Dir.
Immigration Services. Tel: 404-885-7454. Sue Colussy, Esq., Prog. Dir.
Multicultural Services. Tel: 404-885-7465. Bui Van Tam, Esq., Prog. Dir.
Community Centers:
Tri-Cities, 532 Cleveland Ave., 30315. Tel: 404-766-5553.
Grant Park, 570D Burroughs St., 30315. Tel: 404-624-9329.
Cobb Multicultural Center, 4300 Kingspring Rd., Smyrna, 30082. Tel: 770-432-6068.
CSS at Doraville, 5918 New Peachtree Rd., Doraville, 30082. Tel: 770-432-6880.
CSS/Athens, 160 Winston Dr., Ste. 1, Athens, 30607. Tel: 706-548-9421. Margaret Portillo Bell, Prog. Dir.
The Place, 1480 Bettis Tribble Gap Rd., P.O. Box 507, Cumming, 30130. Tel: 404-887-1098. Dolores Mitchell, Prog. Dir., Village of St. Joseph, Inc., 3409 Washington Rd., S.W., 30331. Tel: 404-349-2400. Charles I. Bright, M.A.Ed., Dir. Residential Child Care for Emotionally Disturbed Children, Catholic Personal Care Homes, Inc., 3409 Washington Rd., S.W., East Point, 30344. Tel: 404-669-0143. Sr. Helen Mick, Dir.
Marian Manor, 2801 Briarcliff Rd. N.E., 30329. Tel: 404-982-0606.
St. Thomas Manor, 3409 Washington Rd. S.W., East Point, 30344. Tel: 404-669-0143.
St. Teresa Manor, 227 Medical Way, Riverdale, 30274. Tel: 707-996-8707. Catholic Housing Initiatives, Inc., 680 W. Peachtree St. N.W., 30308-1984. Tel: 404-881-6571. Mary Lou Scruggs, Asst. Dir., Catholic Retirement Facilities, Inc. Carroll Sterne, Pres. Total Assisted 40,210; Total Staff 221.

[G] GENERAL HOSPITALS

ATLANTA. *Saint Joseph's Hospital of Atlanta, Inc.*, 5665 Peachtree Dunwoody Rd., N.E., 30342. Tel: 404-851-7001
For a complete listing, refer to the Hospitals section.

ATHENS. *St. Mary's Hospital*, 1230 Baxter St., 30606-3791. Tel: 706-354-3033; Fax: 706-354-3197
For a complete listing, refer to the Hospitals section.

[H] SPECIAL HOSPITALS

ATLANTA. *Our Lady of Perpetual Help Home*, 760 Washington St. S.W., 30315. Tel: 404-688-9515
For a complete listing, refer to the Special Care Facilities section.
Saint Joseph's Mercy Care Services, 60 Eleventh St., 30309-3970. Tel: 404-249-8600
For a complete listing, refer to the Special Care Facilities section.

ROME. *Mercy Senior Care, Inc.*, 212 W. Third St., 30165
For a complete listing, refer to the Special Care Facilities section.

[I] MONASTERIES AND RESIDENCES OF PRIESTS

CONYERS. *The Monastery of the Holy Spirit*, 2625 Hwy. 212 S.W., 30208. Tel: 770-483-8705; Fax: 770-760-0989.
E-mail: abbeystore@ga.monks.org
Web site: www.ga.monks.org
Rt. Revs. Dom Bernard Johnson, O.C.S.O.; Augustine J. Moore, O.C.S.O., Retired Abbot; Bro. Mark Dohle, O.C.S.O., Prior; Revs. Methodius Telnack, O.C.S.O., Procurator; James Stephen Behrens, O.C.S.O.; Clarence J. Biggers, O.C.S.O.; Edmund H. Brand, O.C.S.O.; Malachy Corley, O.C.S.O.; Philip R. Dehner, O.C.S.O.; Anthony Delisi, O.C.S.O., Prior; Richard Donarski, O.C.S.O.; Corentine J. Finnegan, O.C.S.O.; Jerome J. Hickey, O.C.S.O.; Francis X. Kavanagh, O.C.S.O.; Luke C. Kot, O.C.S.O.; John M. O'Brien, O.C.S.O.; Robert L. Pearson, O.C.S.O.; Eduardo Rodriguez, O.C.S.O.; Thomas F. Skonny, O.C.S.O.; Thomas F. Smith, O.C.S.O.; Lawrence Swartz, O.C.S.O.; Joachim Tierney, O.C.S.O.; Matt G. Torpey, O.C.S.O.; Damian C. Turk, O.C.S.O.; Joseph F. Tynan, O.C.S.O.; Charles Felix Zell, O.C.S.O.; Gerard Gross, C.SS.R.; Deacon Alberic Farbolin, Novice Master.
Located Elsewhere: Revs. Dom Armand Veilleux, O.C.S.O Italy, Generalate; Patrick Duffy, O.C.S.O.; George J. Evans, O.C.S.O., V.A. Hospital, San Antonio, TX; Edward T. Morley, O.C.S.O.; Manuel Rodriguez, Cistercian Monastery in Merida, Venezuela. Priests 33; Professed Brothers 16; Novices 5.

DUNWOODY. *Legionaries of Christ*, 225 Lack Land Ct., 30350-5076. Tel: 770-394-2158; Fax: 770-393-3688. Revs. John Hopkins, L.C., Supr.; Dean Stasell, L.C., Promotion, Retreats; Scott Rielly, L.C. Total In Residence 5.

[J] CONVENTS AND RESIDENCES OF SISTERS

ATLANTA. *Missionaries of Charity*, 995 St. Charles Ave., N.E., 30306-4211. Tel: 404-892-5111. Sr. M. Graynel, M.C., Supr.; Sr. Treslin, M.C.; Sr. Amabella, M.C.; Sr. M. Salvina, M.C. Sisters 4; Total Assisted 60.

CHAMBLEE. *Missionary Sisters of the Sacred Heart "Ad Gentes"*, 3152 Terramar Dr., 30341. Tel: 770-934-8939. To serve the Hispanic community. Sr. Beatriz Taneco, M.A.G., Supr., Atlanta Community. Sisters 5.

GAINESVILLE. *Adrian Dominican Sisters, Mid-Atlantic Mission Chapter*, 5735 Dawsonville Hwy., 30506-3889. Tel: 770-844-1370; Fax: 770-844-1371.
E-mail: midatla@aol.com
Web site: http://www.op.org/adrian/
Sr. Mary Kathryn Cliatt, O.P., Chapter Prioress.

SNELLVILLE. *Monastery of the Visitation* (Maryfield), 2055 Ridgedale Dr., 30278. Tel: 770-972-1060. Strictly cloistered contemplative Office of First Federation. Private retreats for women, no more than 3 at a time. Mother Mary Jozefa Kowalewski, V.H.M., Supr. Maryfield; Rev. Joseph Mendes, M.S.F.S., Chap. U.S. Professed Sisters 14; Novices 1; Postulants 1.

[K] RETREAT HOUSES

ATLANTA. *Ignatius House*, 6700 Riverside Dr., N.W., 30328-2710. Tel: 404-255-0503.
E-mail: rethouse@aol.com
Revs. James C. Babb, S.J., Assoc. Dir.; Vincent R. Malatesta, S.J., Assoc. Dir.; John L. Vessels, S.J., Dir. Total In Residence 3; Total Staff 8.
Maisha House of Prayer, Inc., 392 Glen Iris Dr., N.E., 30308. Tel: 404-688-8040.
E-mail: maishahouse@mindspring.com
Total in Residence 2; Total Staff 2.

GAINESVILLE. *Cedar Hill Enrichment Center, Inc.*, 5735 Dawsonville Hwy., 30506. Tel: 770-887-0051. Sr. June Racicot, O.P., Dir. Total In Residence 2.

HOSCHTON. *Sisters of the Cenacle*, 5913 Jackson Trail Rd., 30548. Tel: 706-654-3460. Congregation of Our Lady of the Retreat in the Cenacle.
Retreat Ministry, Spiritual Development Programs, Spiritual Direction, and Other Forms of Spiritual Ministry. Sisters 2.

[L] CAMPUS MINISTRY CENTERS

ATLANTA. *Campus Ministry*, 680 W. Peachtree St., N.W., 30308. Tel: 404-888-7804. Rev. Mark W. Lacey.
The Catholic Center at Atlanta University Center, 165 James P. Brawley Dr., S.W., 30314-3518. Tel: 404-524-0511. Rev. Edward Branch.
Berry College. 3457 Frey Lake Rd., Kennesaw, 30144. Tel: 770-423-9909; Fax: 770-423-9605. Rev. Linus De Santis, O.F.M.Conv.
Emory University, Agnes Scott College, 1753 N. Decatur Rd., N.E., 30307. Tel: 404-636-7237. Rev. James Schillinger.
Georgia Institute of Technology, 172 4th St., N.W., 30313. Tel: 404-892-6759. Rev. Mario Di Lella, O.F.M.
Oglethorpe University, 4484 Peachtree Rd., N.E., 30319. Tel: 404-261-1441. Our Lady of the Assumption Catholic Church, 1350 Hearst Dr., N.E., 30319. Tel: 404-261-7181. Rev. James F. McGoldrick, S.M.
Catholic Student Center - University of Georgia.

(Athens), 1344 S. Lumpkin St., Athens, 30605. Tel: 706-543-2293. Rev. Steven J. Pavignano, O.F.M., Dir.

West Georgia College. (Carrollton), Church of Our Lady of Perpetual Help, Center Point Rd., Rte. 5, Box 100, Carrollton, 30117. Tel: 706-832-8977. Rev. John Farrelly.

North Georgia College. (Dahlonega). St. Luke the Evangelist Church, 301 Hawkins St., Dahlonega, 30533. Tel: 706-864-2568. Rev. Edward A. Danneker.

Dalton Junior College. (Dalton). Church of St. Joseph, 623 S. Thornton Ave., Dalton, 30720. Tel: 706-278-3107. Rev. Daniel Stack.

Brenau College. (Gainesville), 440 Pearce Cir., N.E., Gainesville, 30501-2457. Tel: 706-534-3338. Rev. William G. Hoffman.

Kennesaw State University. (Kennesaw), 3487 Frey Lake Rd., Kennesaw, 30144. Tel: 770-423-9909; Fax: 770-423-9605. Rev. Linus DeSantis, O.F.M.Conv.

LaGrange Jr. College. (LaGrange), 200 LaFayette Pkwy., LaGrange, 30240. Tel: 706-884-4224. Rev. John M. Murphy.

Georgia College. (Milledgeville), 345 Glenhaven Dr., Milledgeville, 31061. Tel: 706-452-8628. Rev. Michael L. McWhorter.

Shorter College. (Rome). St. Mary's Church, 911 N. Broad St., Rome, 30161. Tel: 706-295-7014. Rev. James A. Miceli.

Dekalb Community College. (Stone Mountain). Corpus Christi Church, 600 Mountain View Dr., Stone Mountain, 30083. Tel: 770-469-0395. Rev. Gregory D. Kenny, C.M.F.

[M] MISCELLANEOUS LISTINGS

ATLANTA. *Atlanta Particular Council, St. Vincent de Paul Society, Inc.*, 26 Third St., N.W., 30308. Tel: 404-874-7014; 874-7140; 874-6990.
E-mail: sudp@mindspring.com
Web site: www.mindspring.com/~sudp
Ms. Sheila Bissonnette, Exec. Dir. Total Assisted 12,000; Total Staff 17.

Carlow College Bicentennial Fund, Inc., 680 W. Peachtree St., N.W., 30308. Tel: 708-888-7804. Rev. Msgr. Edward J. Dillon, Contact Person.

The Catholic Charismatic Renewal in Atlanta. St. Gerard's Catholic Church, P.O. Box 2217, Fort Oglethorpe, 30742. Tel: 706-861-9410. Rev. Timothy M. Hepburn; Paul Grutsch, Coord. Tel: 770-294-7596.

Catholic Construction Services, Inc., 680 W. Peachtree St, N.W., 30308. Tel: 404-888-7838; Fax: 404-885-7299. George Barrie, Pres. & CEO; Donna L. Worley, Office Mgr.; Glenn O. Anderson, Devel. Mgr. Preconstruction Svcs.; Deacon Bill Lyday. Project Managers: Allen Kronenberger; Carl Trevathan.

Catholic Foundation of North Georgia, Inc., 680 W. Peachtree St., N.W., 30308-1984. Tel: 404-888-7837.

Catholic Schools Properties, Inc., 680 W. Peachtree St., N.W., 30308. Tel: 404-888-7835; Fax: 404-885-7494. Bertha Martin, Pres.

Good Shepherd Services of Atlanta, Inc. (Incorporated as Good Shepherd Corporation). Main Office, 2430 Shallowford Terr., Chamblee, 30341. Tel: 770-445-1230; Fax: 770-455-6310. Phillip Bonner, Exec. Dir. Tel: 770-455-8420.

Good Shepherd Counseling Center, 2855 Briarcliff Rd., N.E., 30329. Tel: 404-636-0712; Fax: 770-908-8777.

Good Shepherd Outreach Center, 2426 Shallowford Ter., Chamblee, 30341. Tel: 770-455-9379; Fax: 770-908-8777. Sr. Mary Brigid Lawlor, Pres. Sisters 4.

National Catholic Association of Diocesan Directors for Hispanic Ministry, Inc., 680 W. Peachtree St., N.W., 30308. Total Staff 11; Total Assisted 6,500.

Renovacion Carismatica Catolica Hispana De Atlanta, 334-7 Henderson Mill Rd., 30341. Ms. Anais Arias.

Saint Joseph's Health System, Inc., 5671 Peachtree Dunwoody Rd., Ste. 700, 30342. Tel: 404-851-5700. Ronald P. Hogan, Pres. & CEO; Sr. Jane Gerety, R.S.M., Senior Vice Pres. for Sponsorship. Sponsorship. Holding Company Sponsored by Sisters of Mercy of Americas, Baltimore Regional Community, which operates: Saint Joseph's Hospital of Atlanta, Inc.; Saint Joseph's Mercy Foundation, Inc.; Saint Joseph's Mercy Care Services, Inc.; Saint Joseph's Care Management Corporation and Saint Joseph's Service Corporation.

Saint Joseph's Mercy Foundation, 5671 Peachtree Dunwoody Rd., Ste. 700, 30342. Tel: 404-851-5710. Ted D. Bayley, Pres.

Serra Club #120, Dis. 18. Metro Atlanta, 680 W. Peachtree St., N.W., 30308. Edward J. de St. Aubin, Pres.

Serra Club #684, Dis. 18. North Metro Atlanta, 680 W. Peachtree St., N.W., 30308. Mary D. Elkins, Pres.

ALPHARETTA. *St. Francis de Sales Latin Mass Community - Pastoral Center*, 3400 Old Alabama Rd., 30202-5525. Tel: 770-442-2511. Rev. Mark F. Fischer, F.S.S.P. Total in Residence 2.

DORAVILLE. *Korean Martyrs Pastoral Center*, 6003 Buford Hwy., N.E., 30340. Tel: 770-455-1380. Rev. Msgr. Donald Kiernan.

DUNWOODY. *Home and Family, Inc.*, 225 Lack Land Ct., 30350. Rev. John Hopkins, L.C.

Legion of Christ, Inc., 225 Lack Land Ct., 30350. Rev. John Hopkins, L.C.

GAINESVILLE. *Southern Dominican Ministries, Inc.*, 5735 Dawsonville Hwy., 30506. Southern Dominican Ministries is an organization designed to give technical assistance to grassroots groups wishing to incorporate to do ministry which addresses poverty and/or justice issues. All work is done by the volunteer board and volunteers from our congregations.

JACKSON. *Magnificat - Joyful Visitation Chapter, Inc.*, 198 Harris Rd., 30233. Tel: 770-775-3783; 504-8703. Olga Myers, Coord.

RIVERDALE. *Our Lady of Vietnam Catholic Church - Pastoral Center*, 91 Valley Hill Rd., 30274. Tel: 770-473-8453; Fax: 770-473-5211. Rev. Msgr. Francis Pham Van Phuong, Admin.

RELIGIOUS INSTITUTES OF MEN REPRESENTED IN THE ARCHDIOCESE

For further details refer to the corresponding bracketed number in the Religious Institutes of Men or Women section.

[0350]—*Cistercians Order of the Strict Observance-Trappists.*—O.C.S.O.
[0360]—*Claretian Missionaries.* (Eastern Province).—C.M.F.
[1000]—*Congregation of the Passion.* (Prov. of St. Paul of the Cross).—C.P.
[0480]—*Conventual Franciscans.* (Prov. of St. Anthony of Padua, Baltimore).—O.F.M.Conv.
[0520]—*Franciscan Friars.* (Prov. of the Most Holy Name of Jesus).—O.F.M.
[0570]—*Glenmary Home Missioners.*
[0690]—*Jesuit Fathers and Brothers.* (New Orleans Prov.).—S.J.
[0730]—*Legionaries of Christ.*—L.C.
[0780]—*Marist Fathers.* (Washington Prov.).—S.M.
[0720]—*The Missionaries of Our Lady of La Salette.*—M.S.
[]—*Missionaries of St. Francis de Sales.* (Annecy, France).—M.S.F.S.
[1065]—*The Priestly Fraternity of St. Peter.*—F.S.S.P.
[1070]—*Redemptorist Fathers.* (Baltimore Prov.).—C.SS.R.

RELIGIOUS INSTITUTES OF WOMEN REPRESENTED IN THE ARCHDIOCESE

[3110]—*Congregation of Our Lady of the Retreat in the Cenacle.*—R.C.
[]—*Daughters, Mary of the Mother Mary.*—D.M.M.M.
[1070-13]—*Dominican Sisters (Adrian, MI).*—O.P.
[1070-03]—*Dominican Sisters (Sinsinawa, WI).*—O.P.
[1070-23]—*Dominican Sisters of St. Rose of Lima (Hawthorne, NY).*—O.P.
[1370]—*The Franciscan Missionaries of Mary.*—F.M.M.
[1840]—*Grey Nuns of the Sacred Heart.*—G.N.S.H.
[1870]—*Handmaids of the Sacred Heart of Jesus.*—A.C.J.
[2575]—*Institute of the Sisters of Mercy of the Americas.* (Merion, PA; Rochester, NY; Baltimore, MD).—R.S.M.
[2720]—*Mission Helpers of the Sacred Heart.*—M.H.S.H.
[2710]—*Missionaries of Charity.*—M.C.
[2800]—*Missionary Sisters of the Most Sacred Heart of Jesus of Hiltrup.*—M.S.C.
[]—*Missionary Sisters of the Sacred Heart.* (Mexico).—M.A.G.
[]—*Religious Franciscan Sisters of Our Lady of Refuge.*—R.F.R.
[2970]—*School Sisters of Notre Dame.*—S.S.N.D.
[]—*Sisters for Christian Community.*—S.F.C.C.
[0650]—*Sisters of Charity of St. Vincent de Paul.* (New York).—S.C.
[0430]—*Sisters of Charity of the Blessed Virgin Mary.*—B.V.M.
[0990]—*Sisters of Divine Providence.*—C.D.P.
[2360]—*Sisters of Loretto.*—S.L.
[3000]—*Sisters of Notre Dame de Namur.*—S.N.D.deN.
[1580]—*Sisters of St. Francis (Sylvania, OH).*—O.S.F.
[1570]—*Sisters of St. Francis of the Holy Family.*—O.S.F.
[3830-01]—*Sisters of St. Joseph.*—C.S.J.
[3840]—*Sisters of St. Joseph of Carondelet.*—C.S.J.
[3830-15]—*Sisters of St. Joseph of Concordia.*—C.S.J.
[0260]—*Sisters of the Blessed Sacrament for Indians and Colored People.*—S.B.S.
[1830]—*The Sisters of the Good Shepherd.*—R.G.S.
[1990]—*Sisters of the Holy Names of Jesus and Mary.*—S.N.J.M.
[4190]—*Sisters of the Visitation.*—V.H.M.
[2170]—*Sisters, Servants of the Immaculate Heart of Mary.*—I.H.M.
[2150]—*Sisters, Servants of the Immaculate Heart of Mary.*—I.H.M.

ARCHDIOCESAN CEMETERIES

ATLANTA. *Washington.*

NECROLOGY

† Benassu, Gregory R., Kennasaw, GA, St. Catherine of Siena. —Died March 30, 1997.
† Calhoun, William E., (Retired). —Died Jan. 4, 1997.
† Peacock, Joseph L., Decatur, GA, St. Thomas More. —Died Sept. 31, 1997.

Diocese of Austin

(Dioecesis Austiniensis)

Most Reverend

JOHN E. McCARTHY, D.D.

Bishop of Austin; ordained May 26, 1956; appointed Titular Bishop of Padena and Auxiliary Bishop of Galveston-Houston January 23, 1979; consecrated March 14, 1979; appointed Bishop of Austin December 24, 1985; installed February 25, 1986. *Office: P.O. Box 13327, Austin, TX, 78711.*

ERECTED 1948.

Square Miles 19,511.

Comprises the Counties of Mills, Hamilton, San Saba, Lampasas, Coryell, McLennan, Limestone, Bell, Falls, Robertson, Mason, Llano, Burnet, Williamson, Milam, Brazos, Blanco, Travis, Bastrop, Lee, Burleson, Washington, Hays, Caldwell and the part of Fayette County north of the Colorado River in the State of Texas.

For legal titles of parishes and diocesan institutions, consult the Chancery Office.

Chancery Office: 1600 N. Congress Ave., P.O. Box 13327, Austin, TX, 78711. Tel.: 512-476-4888; Fax: 512-469-9537.

STATISTICAL OVERVIEW

Personnel	
Bishop	1
Priests: Diocesan Active in Diocese	103
Priests: Active Outside Diocese	9
Priests: Diocesan in Foreign Missions	1
Priests: Retired, Sick or Absent	12
Number of Diocesan Priests	125
Religious Priests in Diocese	57
Ordinations:	
Diocesan Priests	2
Permanent Deacons in Diocese	101
Total Brothers	40
Total Sisters	115
Parishes	
Parishes	105
With Resident Pastor:	
Resident Diocesan Priests	72
Resident Religious Priests	23
Without Resident Pastor:	
Administered by Permanent Deacons	9
Administered by Lay People	1
Missions	30
Pastoral Centers	1
New Parishes Created	2
Professional Ministry Personnel:	
Brothers	2
Sisters	24
Lay Ministers	78
Welfare	
Catholic Hospitals	4
Total Assisted	341,863
Health Care Centers	3
Total Assisted	64,000
Homes for the Aged	1
Total Assisted	242
Day Care and Extended Day Care Centers	4
Total Assisted	187
Specialized Homes	1
Total Assisted	250
Special Centers for Social Services	1
Total Assisted	210
Residential Care of Disabled	1
Total Assisted	1,900
Educational	
Diocesan Students in Other Seminaries	11
Total Seminarians	11
Colleges and Universities	1
Total Students	3,101
High Schools, Diocesan and Parish	1
Total Students	206
High Schools, Private	3
Total Students	403
Elementary Schools, Diocesan and Parish	16
Total Students	3,507
Elementary Schools, Private	1
Total Students	39
Catechesis/Religious Education:	
High School Students	5,559
Elementary Students	22,635
Total Students Under Catholic Instruction	35,461
Teachers in the Diocese:	
Priests	5
Sisters	13
Lay Teachers	302
Vital Statistics	
Receptions into the Church:	
Infant Baptism Totals	6,710
Adult Baptism Totals	560
Received into Full Communion	931
First Communions	5,594
Confirmations	3,368
Marriages:	
Catholic	979
Interfaith	497
Total Marriages	1,476
Deaths	1,514
Total Catholic Population	234,487
Total Population	1,915,392

Former Bishops—Most Rev. LOUIS J. REICHER, D.D., ord. Dec. 6, 1918; appt. first Bishop of Austin Nov. 29, 1947; cons. April 14, 1948; died Feb. 23, 1984.—Most Rev. VINCENT M. HARRIS, D.D., ord. March 19, 1938; appt. Bishop of Beaumont July 4, 1966; cons. Sept. 28, 1966; transferred to Austin April 21, 1971; succeeded to the See Nov. 16, 1971; retired Feb. 25, 1986; died March 31, 1988.

Vicar-General—Rev. Msgr. EDWARD C. MATOCHA, P.A.

Moderator of the Curia—Rev. Msgr. DONALD J. FRUGE, J.C.D.

Chancery Office—1600 N. Congress Ave., P.O. Box 13327, Austin, 78711. Tel: 512-476-4888; Fax: 512-469-9537. Office Hours: Mon.-Fri. 8:30-5.

Deans—Vacant, Austin; Rev. Msgr. LONNIE REYES, Central Austin; Rev. ELMER HOLTMAN, North Austin; Rev. JOHN KORCSMAR, C.S.C., South Austin; Rev. JOHN McCAFFREY, Brazos Valley; Rev. EDWARD DOKUPIL, Southern; Rev. WILLIAM DONAHUE, C.S.C., Temple; Rev. ANGELO BERTINI, Northern; Rev. Msgr. RALPH BRENNAN, Eastern; Rev. LONNIE URBAN, Central; Rev. EDWIN KADZIELAWSKI, C.S.C., Western.

Presbyteral Council—Rev. Msgr. EDWARD MATOCHA; Rev. Msgr. FRED BOMAR; Rev. Msgr. EDWARD JORDAN; Rev. Msgr. BEN MAZURKIEWICZ; Rev. Msgr. LOUIS WOZNIAK; Revs. DANIEL GARCIA; WILLIAM DONAHUE, C.S.C.; KIRBY GARNER; VICTOR GOERTZ; OLIVER JOHNSON; JOHN KORCSMAR, C.S.C.; JOSEPH MARTORELL, T.O.R.; JAMES McCABE, C.S.P.; LONNIE URBAN; DEAN WILHELM; PATRICK ZUREK.

Consultors—Rev. Msgr. FRED BOMAR; Rev. Msgr. LONNIE REYES; Rev. Msgr. MARK DEERING; Rev. Msgr. HARRY MAZURKIEWICS; Revs. KIRBY GARNER; ALBERT RUIZ.

Diocesan Tribunal—1625 Rutherford Ln., Austin, 78754. Tel: 512-832-0313; Fax: 512-832-0316; 832-0016. Direct all inquiries concerning marriage nullity, dispensation and permissions to this address.

Judicial Vicar—Rev. DAVID-MARIA A. JAEGER, O.F.M. J.C.D.

Adjutant Judicial Vicars—Revs. JOZEF MUSIOL, S.D.S. J.C.D.; RONNIE JENKINS, J.C.L.

Diocesan Judges—Rev. Msgr. DONALD J. FRUGE, J.C.D.; Revs. VICTOR GOERTZ, J.C.D.; GILES AMARASEKERA; ROBERT KINEL, J.C.L.

Defenders of the Bond—Rev. Msgr. EDWARD C. MATOCHA; Rev. KIRBY GARNER; TAMMY EDGERLY, J.C.L.

Administrator—Ms. GEORGIA LOVETT.

Notaries—Ms. GEORGIA LOVETT; Ms. PEGGY LEAZER; Mr. CHARLES COLLINS; Deacon PETER SCHWAB; Mr. FRANK MONROE, J.D.

Advocates—Priests or deacons exercising their ministry in the diocese.

Finance Office—Rev. Msgr. DONALD J. FRUGE, J.C.D., Finance Officer; PATRICIA RUSSELL, Business Mgr., *P.O. Box 13327, Austin, 78711.* Tel: 512-476-4888; Fax: 512-469-9537.

Finance Council—Rev. Msgr. DONALD J. FRUGE, J.C.D.; DON E. COX; SWITZER DEASON; CAMPBELL McGINNIS; PATRICIA RUSSELL; PHILIP JOSEPH; ROBERT GREENWOOD; JIM SMOLIK; CATHERINE GHIGLIERI.

Archives—KINGA PERZYNSKA, Archivist, *P.O. Box 13124, Austin, 78711-3124.* Tel: 512-476-6296; Fax: 512-476-3715.

Black Ministry—Mr. JOHNNY DORSEY, Dir., *P.O. Box 13327, Austin, 78711.* Tel: 512-388-1320; 472-3741.

Building Commission—Rev. Msgr. EDWARD C. MATOCHA, *P.O. Box 13327, Austin, 78711.* Tel: 512-476-4888; Fax: 512-469-9537.

Campaign for Human Development—Rev. JOHN KORCSMAR, C.S.C., *1111 Montopolis Dr., Austin, 78741.* Tel: 512-385-4333.

Campus Ministry—Rev. ALBERT PALERMO, Dir., *St. Albert the Great, 12041 Bittern Hollow, Austin, 78758.* Tel: 512-837-7825.

Catholic Charities—Rev. JIM EVANS, Dir., *P.O. Box 13327, Austin, 78711-3327.* Tel: 512-476-4888; Fax: 512-469-9537.

Catholic Schools Office—Sr. THECLA CAIN, O.S.F., Supt., *1625 Rutherford Ln., Austin, 78754.* Tel: 512-873-7771; Fax: 512-873-8338.

Catholic Services Appeal—LEANN POWERS, Dir., *P.O. Box 13327, Austin, 78711.* Tel: 512-476-4888; Fax: 512-469-9537.

"Catholic Spirit"—HELEN OSMAN, Editor, *P.O. Box 13327, Austin, 78711.* Tel: 512-476-4888; Fax: 512-469-9537.

Catholic Youth Ministry Office—LAURIE KISH, Dir., *1625 Rutherford Ln., Austin, 78754.* Tel: 512-873-7771; Fax: 512-873-8338.

Cemeteries—Rev. Msgr. JOHN MALINOWSKI, *2541 E. By-Pass, College Station, 77845.* Tel: 409-693-6994.

Charismatic Renewal—JESSE MARTINEZ, Dir., *1104 Turtle Creek, Austin, 78745.* Tel: 512-447-8977.

Communications—HELEN OSMAN, Dir., *P.O. Box 13327, Austin, 78711.* Tel: 512-476-4888.

Continuing Education Priests—Rev. ELMER HOLTMAN, *10205 R.R. 620 N., Austin, 78726.* Tel: 512-258-1161.

Council of Catholic Women—MARY ANN TILL, Pres.

Cursillo—Our Lady of Guadalupe Cursillo Center, Jarrell. Tel: 512-746-2041. Spanish: LOUIS RUIZ, Pres., *3201 Shady Hill, Temple, 76502.* Tel: 254-773-5905. English: MARGARET CAMACHO, *1505 Haskell, Austin, 78702.* Tel: 512-478-1719. Young Adults: Deacon WILLIE CORTEZ, *1816 E. Sixth St., Austin, 78762.* Tel: 512-322-0632.

Deaf Ministry—Sr. DENISE MARIE HACKETT, C.S.C., Dir., *St. Ignatius Church, 2309 Euclid St., Austin, 78704.* Tel: 512-444-5330.

Diaconate—Deacon JEROME KLEMENT, Dir., *St. Luke's, 2807 Oakdale, Temple, 76502.* Tel: 254-773-1561.

Diocesan Pastoral Center—Sr. MARY LOU BARBA, M.C.D.P., Dir., *1625 Rutherford Ln., Austin, 78754.* Tel: 512-873-7771; Fax: 512-873-8338.

Diocesan Social Concerns—Rev. JAMES L. EVANS, Dir., *P.O. Box 13327, Austin, 78711.* Tel: 512-476-4888; Fax: 512-469-9537.

Ecumenism—Rev. CHARLES L. COVINGTON, Dir., *St. Louis Church, 7601 Burnet Rd., Austin, 78757.* Tel: 512-454-0384.

Evangelization—Sr. MARY LOU BARBA, M.C.D.P., *1625 Rutherford Ln., Austin, 78754.* Tel: 512-873-7771; Fax: 512-873-8338.

Family Life Office—JANIS HRNCIR, Dir., *Diocesan Pastoral Center, 1625 Rutherford Ln., Austin, 78754.* Tel: 512-873-7771; Fax: 512-873-8338.

Health Care—Rev. Msgr. WILLIAM BROUSSARD, Dir., *1625 Rutherford Ln., Austin, 78754.* Tel: 512-339-1157.

Historical Commission—CHARLES HRNCIR, Dir., *7007 Bent Oak Cir., Austin, 78749.* Tel: 512-892-3704.

Holy Childhood—Bro. THEO FLYNN, C.S.C., *3001 S. Congress Ave., Austin, 78704.* Tel: 512-442-4534.

Criminal Justice Ministry—Deacon E. GENERES (DOOTS) DUFOUR, Dir., *P.O. Box 13327, Austin, 78711.* Tel: 512-476-4888.

Knights of Columbus—Rev. Msgr. EDWARD RABROKER, Moderator, *P.O. Box 608, Granger, 76530.* Tel: 512-859-2223.

Lifeline—THERESA WARE, Dir., *2026 Guadalupe St., Austin, 78705.* Tel: 512-477-1092.

Catholic Adult Formation Office—Sr. MARY LOU BARBA, M.C.D.P., Dir., *1625 Rutherford Ln., Austin, 78754.* Tel: 512-873-7771; Fax: 512-873-8338.

Mission Council—Rev. LOUIS PAVLICEK, Chm., *St. Luke's, 2807 Oakdale, Temple, 76502.* Tel: 254-773-4541; Fax: 254-774-7044.

Natural Family Planning—Co-Dirs.: RANDY MCCASLIN; NANCY MCCASLIN, *2026 Guadalupe St., Austin, 78705.* Tel: 512-474-2757.

Office of Hispanic Ministry—Rev. ALBERT RUIZ, *2903 E. Rancier Ave., Kileen, 76543-3522.* Tel: 254-634-7878.

Parish Social Ministries—CHRIS ATTAL, Coord., *2811 E. Second, Austin, 78702.* Tel: 512-323-4921; Fax: 512-323-4929.

Pastoral Care—Rev. RICHARD TIJERINA, *203 E. 10th St., Austin, 78701.* Tel: 512-476-6182.

Propagation of the Faith—Bro. THEO FLYNN, C.S.C., *3001 S. Congress Ave., Austin, 78704.* Tel: 512-442-4534.

Religious Education Office—Sr. MARY LOU BARBA, M.C.D.P., Dir., *1625 Rutherford Ln., Austin, 78754.* Tel: 512-873-7771; Fax: 512-873-8338.

Respect Life—ANN BIERSCHENK, *1803 Chincoteague, Round Rock, 78681.* Tel: 512-255-8435.

Rural Life—Rev. Msgr. EDWARD RABROKER, *P.O. Box 608, Granger, 76530.* Tel: 512-859-2223.

Serra Clubs—Rev. WALTER CARR, Chap.-Austin; LEROY C. BOWER, Pres., *8600 Green Valley, Austin, 78759.* Tel: 512-345-3515; 926-6734 (Office).

Special Collections—LEANN POWERS, Dir., *P.O. Box 13327, Austin, 78711.* Tel: 512-476-4888; Fax: 512-469-9537.

Stewardship—LEANN POWERS, Dir., *P.O. Box 13327, Austin, 78711-3327.* Tel: 512-476-4888; Fax: 512-476-5341.

Synod Implementation Office—PAT STANKUS, Dir., *Cedarbrake Renewal Center, P.O. Box 58, Belton, 76513-0058.* Tel: 254-780-2436; Fax: 254-780-2684.

Vicar for Religious—Sr. MARIE ANDRE WALSH, I.H.M., *3001 S. Congress Ave., Austin, 78704.* Tel: 512-448-8617.

Vocations—Rev. PATRICK ZUREK, Dir., *101 Westlake Dr., Austin, 78746.* Tel: 512-328-3220. LYNN JOHNSON, Sec. Tel: 512-873-7771.

Worship Office & Liturgical Commission—Sr. LOIS PAHA, O.P., Dir., *1625 Rutherford Ln., Austin, 78754.* Tel: 512-873-7771; Fax: 512-873-8338.

Miscellaneous

Charitable Trusts—

Father Bernard C. Goertz Scholarship Trust Fund—Sacred Heart Church, Rte. 1, Box 108, Bastrop, 78602.

John J. Kearns Memorial Charitable Trust Fund—P.O. Box 5040, Waco, 78708.

Clerical Endowment Fund—Rev. Msgr. HARRY MAZURKIEWICZ, *Sacred Heart Church, P.O. Box 548, LaGrange, 78945.* Tel: 409-968-3430.

Sts. Cyril & Methodius School Endowment—Rev. Msgr. EDWARD RABROKER, *Sts. Cyril & Methodius, P.O. Box 201, Granger, 76530.*

Clergy Medical and Retirement Trust of the Diocese of Austin and the Diocese of Austin Pension Plan Committee—Most Rev. JOHN E. MCCARTHY, Chm., Diocesan Presbyteral Council.

Seton Fund of the Daughters of Charity of St. Vincent De Paul—ALLAN SHIVERS, JR., Chm., *1201 W. 38th St., Austin, 78705.*

St. Joseph's Foundation of Bryan—MILTON L. DARE, Exec., *2801 Franciscan Dr., Bryan, 77802.* Tel: 409-774-4087.

St. Jude Foundation, Inc.—1306 N. Park, Brenham, 77833.

CLERGY, PARISHES, MISSIONS AND PAROCHIAL SCHOOLS

CITY OF AUSTIN
(Travis County)

1—ST. MARY'S CATHEDRAL (1852), Very Rev. David M. Leibham, Rector. Pastoral Assocs.: Rev. Jerry A. Smith; Rev. Msgr. Edward C. Matocha, P.A., Rector Emeritus; Rev. Larry Stehling; Deacon Willie Cortez.
Res., 203 E. 10th St., 78701. Tel: 512-476-6182; Fax: 512-476-8799.
School—Tel: 512-476-1480; Fax: 512-476-9922. Cecilia Abbott, Prin.
Lay Teachers 16; Students 205.
Catechesis/Religious Programs—Tel: 512-476-4801; Fax: 512-476-8799. Mary Cortez, D.R.E.
Students 247.

2—ST. ALBERT THE GREAT (1987), Rev. Albert A. Palermo; Deacons Jesse Ramsey; Patrick Kennedy.
Office: 12041 Bittern Hollow, 78758. Tel: 512-837-7825; Fax: 512-834-2377.
Res., 1104 Huntridge Cir., 78758. Tel: 512-339-1104. [CEM]
Catechesis/Religious Programs—Students 350.

3—CRISTO REY (1950) (Hispanic), Rev. Lawrence Mattingly, O.F.M.Conv.; Bro. Kerry Guillory, O.F.M.Conv.; Deacons Lupe Medrano; John Ojeda.
Res., 2110 E. 2nd St., 78702. Tel: 512-474-6376; Fax: 512-474-8417.
Catechesis/Religious Programs—Tel: 512-477-1099. Sr. Irene Tapia, F.M.A., D.R.E.
Students 820.

4—EMMAUS CATHOLIC CHURCH (1963), Rev. Msgr. Richard McCabe.
Res., 2203 Lakeway Blvd., 78734. Tel: 512-261-5958; Fax: 512-261-7099. [CEM]
Catechesis/Religious Programs—Students 228.

5—HOLY CROSS (1936) (African American), Rev. Isidore Ndagizimana.
Res., 1610 E. 11th St., 78702. Tel: 512-472-3741; Fax: 512-472-3783.
Catechesis/Religious Programs—D.R.E.: Karen Cobb; Germaine Ewing.
Students 75.

6—HOLY VIETNAMESE MARTYRS (1990) (Vietnamese), Rev. Joe Van Anh Nguyen.
Res., 1107 E. Yager Ln., 78753. Tel: 512-834-8483.
Catechesis/Religious Programs—Tel: 512-836-6632.
Students 216.

7—OUR LADY OF GUADALUPE (1907) (Hispanic), Rev. William Elliott, O.M.I. In res., Deacons Salvador Hernandez; Mario Renteria.
Res., 1206 E. 9th St., 78702. Tel: 512-478-7955; Fax: 512-478-8377.
Catechesis/Religious Programs—Students 132.

8—NUESTRA SENORA DE DOLORES (1952) (Hispanic), Rev. John S. Korcsmar, C.S.C.
Res., 1111 Montopolis Dr., 78741. Tel: 512-385-4333; Fax: 512-385-6116.
Catechesis/Religious Programs—Sr. Rose Moreno, D.R.E.
Students 425.
Convent—Tel: 512-385-5090. Hijas De La Misericordia
Sisters 5.

9—SACRED HEART (1958), Revs. Robert Becker; Edward Maddox; Deacons Roger Behr; James Fuller; Bill Vela; Rob Embry. In res., Rev. Robert Bradley, S.J.
Res., 5909 Reicher Dr., 78723. Tel: 512-926-2552; Fax: 512-926-5138.
School—Tel: 512-926-0687. Sr. Mary Jean Olsovsky, Prin.
Sisters of St. Dominic 1; Lay Teachers 13; Students 218.
Catechesis/Religious Programs—Tel: 512-926-2116. Angelica Mishoe, D.R.E.
Students 495.
Convent—5911 Reicher Dr., 78723. Tel: 512-926-0687.

10—SANTA BARBARA (1991) (Hispanic), Rev. Bernard C. Goertz; Mr. Joe Arellano, Admin.
Mailing Address: 13713 FM 969, 78724. Tel: 512-276-7718.

11—ST. AUSTIN'S (1908), Revs. Patrick Johnson, C.S.P.; Stephen Connor, C.S.P.; Thomas Clerkin, C.S.P. Pastoral Assocs.: Barbara Budde; Michael Flahive; Sr. Sharon Groetsh, D.C. In res., Revs. Bernard Campbell, C.S.P.; Patrick E. Hensy, C.S.P.; Robert Michele, C.S.P.; Edward Philip O'Hern, C.S.P.
Res., 2026 Guadalupe St., 78705. Tel: 512-477-9471; Fax: 512-477-9430.
School—1911 San Antonio St., 78705. Tel: 512-577-3751; Fax: 512-477-3079. Paula Harris, Prin.
Lay Teachers 21; Students 230.
Catechesis/Religious Programs—Cheryle Procell, D.R.E.
Students 185.

12—ST. CATHERINE OF SIENA (1979), Rev. Oliver F. Johnson; Deacons W. J. Ham; Jim Berg.
Church—4800 Convict Hill Rd., 78749. Tel: 512-892-2420; Fax: 512-892-0488.
Res., 4916 Flaming Oak, 78749. Tel: 512-892-1799.
Catechesis/Religious Programs—Tel: 512-892-2426. Maria Marek, D.R.E.
Students 1,302.

13—ST. IGNATIUS MARTYR (1937), Revs. Barry Cabell, C.S.C.; Harold G. Zink, C.S.C.; Jeffrey Allison, C.S.C.; Deacons James T. Graham; Patrick Murray. In res., Rev. John T. Payne, C.S.C.
Res., 2309 Euclid Ave., 78704. Tel: 512-442-3602; Fax: 512-442-3529.
School—Tel: 512-442-8547. Mr. Rob Lewis, Prin.
Lay Teachers 14; Students 250.
Catechesis/Religious Programs—Tel: 512-442-8586. D.R.E.: Kathy Cole; Sr. Judith Hallock, C.S.C.; Sr. Denise Hackett, C.S.C.; Sr. Agnes Murray, I.H.M.
Students 295.

14—ST. JOHN NEUMANN (1984), Revs. Patrick J. Zurek; Harry Dean, Jr.; Deacons Douglas Morris; D. Mark Hamlet.
Office: 101 Westlake Dr., 78746. Tel: 512-328-3220; Fax: 512-328-3226.
Res., 105 Reveille Rd., 78746. Tel: 512-328-6544.
Catechesis/Religious Programs—102 Westlake Dr., 78746. Tel: 512-328-8856; Fax: 512-328-3226.
Students 705.

15—ST. JOHN VIANNEY, Rev. Sam Hose.
Res., 3201 Sunrise, 78864. Tel: 512-218-1183.

16—ST. JULIA (1957), Rev. Msgr. Lonnie C. Reyes.
Res., 3010 Lyons Rd., 78702. Tel: 512-926-4186; Fax: 512-926-8821.
Catechesis/Religious Programs—Tel: 512-928-3381. Ms. Hope Cardenas, D.R.E.
Students 425.

17—ST. LOUIS (1952), Revs. Larry Covington; Le-Minh Pham; Gregory Perez; Ronnie Jenkins. In res., Rev. David Jaeger.
Res., 7601 Burnet Rd., 78757. Tel: 512-454-0384; Fax: 512-454-2010.
School—Tel: 512-454-0384, Ext. 242. Marsha Solana, Prin.
Sisters 1; Lay Teachers 29; Students 459.
Catechesis/Religious Programs—Tel: 512-454-0384, Ext. 225. D.R.E.: Betty Danner, Childhood Ministries; Rene Biediger, Youth Ministries; Charles Balsam, Adult Ministries.
Students 687.

18—ST. MARGARET OF SCOTLAND (1984), Revs. Rodger Hall (Italy); Joseph H. Frazer, Pastor Emeritus.
Mailing Address: P.O. Box 13081, 78711. Tel: 512-444-7587.

19—ST. PAUL'S (1989) (Hispanic), Rev. Paul F. McCallum.
Res., 10000 David Moore Rd., 78748. Tel: 512-280-4460; Fax: 512-280-7219.
Catechesis/Religious Programs—Tel: 512-280-5777; Fax: 512-280-7219. Joyce Gerold, D.R.E.
Students 614.

20—ST. PETER THE APOSTLE (1962), Rev. Msgr. Fred Bomar.
Res., P.O. Box 17575, 4600 E. Ben White Blvd., 78760. Tel: 512-442-0655.
Catechesis/Religious Programs—Tel: 512-444-7477.

Students 209.

21—St. Theresa (1968), Rev. Msgr. Edward F. Jordan; Deacons Clarence Hansen; Ray James.
Res., 4311 Small Dr., 78731. Tel: 512-451-5121; Fax: 512-453-6824.
School—(Grades PreK-6). Tel: 512-451-7105; Fax: 512-451-8808. William S. Davidson, Prin.
Lay Teachers 16; Students 244.
Catechesis/Religious Programs—Tel: 512-451-2940; Fax: 512-453-6824. Rosemary Edwards, D.R.E.
Students 764.

22—St. Thomas More (1978), Revs. Elmer E. Holtman; Keith Koehl; Deacons Peter Schwab; Thomas Mallinger.
Office: 10205 Ranch Rd., 620 N., 78726. Tel: 512-258-1161; Fax: 512-258-8812. [CEM]
Catechesis/Religious Programs—Mary Osborn, D.R.E.
Students 1,161.

23—St. Thomas More Chapel (1958), Chancery Building: 1600 N. Congress Ave., 78701. Tel: 512-476-4888.

24—St. Vincent de Paul (1995), Rev. Daniel E. Garcia; Deacon Allen Desorcie.
Res., 13007 Partridge Bend, 78729. Tel: 512-918-8356; Fax: 512-918-0598. [CEM]
Catechesis/Religious Programs—Students 195.

25—San Francisco (1941) (Hispanic), Rev. James R. Martin, C.S.C.
Res., 9110 Hwy. 183 S., 78747. Tel: 512-243-1404; Fax: 512-243-2995.
Catechesis/Religious Programs—Tel: 512-243-1899. Sr. Jacinta Amengual, F.H.M., D.R.E.
Students 358.

26—San Jose (1939) (Hispanic), Revs. Kirby D. Garner; Jairo Lopez; Deacons John Rivera; Enrique Saenz; Alfredo Vasquez.
Res., 2435 Oak Crest, 78704. Tel: 512-444-7587; Fax: 512-443-1212.
Catechesis/Religious Programs—Tel: 512-444-4664. Anna Singleton, D.R.E.
Students 1,000.

OUTSIDE CITY OF AUSTIN

Andice, Williamson Co., Santa Rosa (1937), Rev. Walter F. Carr.
Mailing Address: c/o St. Helen Catholic Church, 2700 E. University Ave., Georgetown, 78626-9803. Tel: 817-793-2047.

Bastrop, Bastrop Co., Ascension (1911), Rev. Edward J. Dokupil.
Res., P.O. Drawer W, 78602. Tel: 512-321-2452.
Catechesis/Religious Programs—Tel: 512-321-5511. Laura Wymer, D.R.E.
Students 355.

Belton, Bell Co., Christ the King (1969), Rev. Rock I. Vaz; Deacon William Shoemake.
Res., 310 E. 24th Ave., 76513. Tel: 254-939-0806; 939-6109 (Rectory).
Catechesis/Religious Programs—Students 300.

Betram, Burnet Co., Holy Cross (1941) (Hispanic). Attended by Our Mother of Sorrows, Burnet. Rev. Joseph DeVliegher, C.S.C.; Deacon Joe Ruiz.
Mailing Address: P.O. Box 94, 78605. Tel: 512-756-4410.
Catechesis/Religious Programs—Students 90.

Blanco, Blanco Co., St. Ferdinand's (1940), Rev. James Harnan, M.S.C.
Res., Rte. 1, Box 1, 78606. Tel: 210-833-5227. [CEM]
Catechesis/Religious Programs—Tel: 210-833-5227. Mrs. Shirley Cole, D.R.E.
Students 80.
Missions—Johnson City, Blanco Co., Good Shepherd, P.O. Box 528, Johnson City, 78636. Tel: 210-868-0370; Twin Sisters, Blanco Co., Our Lady Help of Christians, 78606.

Bremond, Robertson Co., St. Mary's (1879), Rev. Jozef Musiol.
Res., Rte. 1, Box 58, 76629. Tel: 254-746-7789; Fax: 254-746-7280. [CEM]
Catechesis/Religious Programs—Tel: 254-746-7789.
Students 158.

Brenham, Washington Co., St. Mary of the Immaculate Conception (1870), Rev. Msgr. Ralph A. Brennan; Deacon Bill Januszewski.
Res., 701 Church St., 77833. Tel: 409-836-4441; Fax: 409-836-9383. [CEM]
Catechesis/Religious Programs—Tel: 409-830-8331.
Students 517.
Mission—Old Washington, Washington Co., Blessed Virgin Mary, (1849) 77833. Fax: 409-836-9389.
Mailing Address: c/o St. Mary's of the Immaculate Conception, 701 Church St., 77833.

Bryan, Brazos Co., St. Joseph's (1873), Rev. John McCaffrey; Deacons Switzer Deason; Ray Sis; Gilbert Wilson; Abraham Orozco; Gary Nelson; Luis Doriocourt.
Res., 600 E. 26th St., 77803. Tel: 409-822-2721; Fax: 409-779-3120. [CEM 2]
School—Tel: 409-822-6641. Mr. Tim Luza, Prin.; Mr. Mark Reinberg, Asst. Prin.
Lay Teachers 33; Students 424.
Catechesis/Religious Programs—Tel: 409-823-5568. Becky Luza, D.R.E.
Students 602.

St. Anthony's (1896) (Italian), Rev. Steven Kana.
Res., 306 S. Parker, 77803. Tel: 409-823-8145; Fax: 409-823-6001. [JC]
Mission—Caldwell, San Salvador.
Catechesis/Religious Programs—Tel: 409-822-3700.
Students 514.

Santa Teresa's (1940), Rev. Victor G. Robles; Deacon Louis Garcia.
Res., 1212 Lucky, 77803. Tel: 409-822-2932; Fax: 409-822-6957.
Catechesis/Religious Programs—Tel: 409-822-5557. Nickie Rodriguez, D.R.E.
Students 500.

Buda, Hays Co., Santa Cruz (1941) (Hispanic), Rev. Richard Teall, C.S.C.
Res., P.O. Box 187, 78610. Tel: 512-295-2034.
Catechesis/Religious Programs—Tel: 512-295-4818. Cathryn Green, D.R.E.
Students 200.

Burnet, Burnet Co., Our Mother of Sorrows (1941), Rev. Joseph DeVliegher, C.S.C.; Deacon Eugene Montag.
Res., 507 Buchanan Dr., 78611-2304. Tel: 512-756-4410.
Catechesis/Religious Programs—Tel: 512-756-2323.
Students 175.
Mission—Bertram, Burnet Co., Holy Cross, P.O. Box 90, Bertram, 78611. Tel: 512-355-2972. Deacon Jose Ruiz.

Caldwell, Burleson Co., St. Mary's (1895) (Hispanic), Rev. Dimitrij Colankin; Deacon John Young.
Res., 509 N. Thomas, 77836. Tel: 409-567-3667. [CEM]
Catechesis/Religious Programs—Students 240.

Calvert, Robertson Co., St. Mary (1876) (Hispanic). Attended by St. Mary's Church, Hearne. Rev. Gregory McLaughlin.
Mailing Address: 402 W. First St., Hearne, 77859.
Res., 505 Logan St., 77837. Tel: 409-279-2233; Fax: 409-279-9606. [CEM]

Cameron, Milam Co., St. Monica's (1883), Rev. Thomas J. Hanus; Deacon Juan Garza.
Res., P.O. Box 673, 76520. Tel: 254-697-2107; Fax: 254-697-3334. [CEM]
Church—306 S. Nolan, 76520.
Catechesis/Religious Programs—Tel: 254-697-4544. Martha Bibler, D.R.E.
Students 300.

Cedar Park, Williamson Co., St. Margaret Mary (1942), Rev. William Benish.
Res., P.O. Box 2410, 78630-2410. Tel: 512-259-3126; Fax: 512-259-9658.
Catechesis/Religious Programs—Theresa Robertson, D.R.E.
Students 366.

Chappell Hill, Washington Co., St. Stanislaus (1889) (Polish), Rev. Eugene Sheherd.
Res., P.O. Box 179, 77426. Tel: 409-836-3030; Fax: 409-836-7170. [CEM]
Catechesis/Religious Programs—Diane Curry, D.R.E.
Students 82.

China Spring, McLennan Co., St. Philip (1996). (Mission Parish). Deacon Joseph Weynand, Pastoral Admin.
Res., P.O. Box 430, 76633. Tel: 254-836-4321.

College Station, Brazos Co., St. Mary's (1926), Revs. Michael J. Sis; David A. Konderla; Deacon Bill Scott, Jr.
Res., 103 Nagle St., 77840. Tel: 409-846-5717; Fax: 409-846-4493.

St. Thomas Aquinas (1982), Rev. Dean E. Wilhelm. In res., Rev. Msgr. John C. Malinowski.
Res., 2541 East By-Pass, 77845. Tel: 409-696-3284; 693-6994 (Office); Fax: 409-693-0284.
Catechesis/Religious Programs—Tel: 409-693-7551. Becky Slovak, D.R.E.
Students 560.

Copperas Cove, Coryell Co., Holy Family (1963), Rev. William H. Donahue, C.S.C. In res., Rev. Michael Cerrone, III (SAV) Chaplain, U.S.A.
Res., 1001 Georgetown Rd., 76522. Tel: 254-547-3735. [JC]
Catechesis/Religious Programs—Tel: 254-542-7626. Leslie Noel, D.R.E.
Students 484.

Cyclone, Bell Co., St. Joseph's (1902) (Czech-German), Rev. Charles Davis.
Mailing Address: 20120 FM 485, Burlington, 76519. Tel: 817-985-2280.
Res., Farm Rd. 485, Tel: 817-985-2280. [CEM 2]
Catechesis/Religious Programs—1201 S. St. Joseph Rd. #400, Burlington, 76519. Tel: 817-985-2257.
Students 48.
Mission—Marak, Milam Co., Ss. Cyril & Methodius, FM 485, Burlington, 76519. Tel: 817-985-2280.

Dime Box, Lee Co., St. Joseph's (1902), Rev. Msgr. Emilian Foltyn.
Res., Rte. 1, Box 5A, 77853. Tel: 409-884-3100. [CEM]
Mission—Lexington, Lee Co., Holy Family, (1990) 77853.

Dripping Springs, Hays Co., St. Martin de Porres (1974), Rev. James L. Evans.
Mailing Address: P.O. Box 1062, 78620. Tel: 512-858-5667.
Catechesis/Religious Programs—Mary Carder, D.R.E.
Students 205.

Elgin, Bastrop Co., Sacred Heart (1908), Rev. John G. Boiko; Deacon Larry Dunne.
Res., 302 W. 11th St., 78621. Tel: 512-281-3536. [JC]
Catechesis/Religious Programs—Tel: 512-285-9543. Paula Bramlett, D.R.E.
Students 315.

Elk, McLennon Co., St. Joseph's (1925). Attended by St. Martin, Tours.
Mailing Address: Rte. 2, Box 209-A, West, 76691.
Res., 301 St. Martins Church Rd., West, 76691. Tel: 254-822-1145. [CEM]
Catechesis/Religious Programs—Mary Mann, D.R.E.
Students 70.

Fayetteville, Fayette Co., St. John's (1872) (Czech), Rev. Msgr. Benedict J. Mazurkiewicz.
Res., P.O. Box 57, 78940. Tel: 409-378-2277. [CEM]
Catechesis/Religious Programs—Sr. Euphrosine Honc, D.R.E.
Students 140.
Convent—Tel: 409-378-2275. Sisters of Divine Providence
Missions—Hostyn Hill, Fayette Co., St. Mary's, 78940.; Warrenton, Fayette Co., St. Martin's, 78940.

Frenstat, Burleson Co., Holy Rosary (1888). Attended by St. Ann's, Somerville. Rev. Joel D. McNeil.
Mailing Address: P.O. Box 99, Somerville, 77879. Tel: 409-596-1966; Fax: 409-596-2857. [CEM]

Gatesville, Coryell Co., Our Lady of Lourdes (1946), Rev. Hilario Guajardo; Deacon Victor Beltran.
Res., 1108 W. Main St., 76528-1123. Tel: 254-865-6710.
Catechesis/Religious Programs—Deborah Grmela, D.R.E.
Students 100.

Georgetown, Williamson Co., St. Helen's (1932), Rev. Msgr. Louis J. Wozniak; Rev. Walter F. Carr; Deacons Roger Collins; Juan C. Gonzalez, Jr.; Victor Droll.
Res., 2700 E. University Ave., 78626. Tel: 512-863-3041; Fax: 512-863-8558.
Catechesis/Religious Programs—Tel: 512-863-0799. Maria Kaesberg, D.R.E.
Students 650.
Mission—Andice, Santa Rosa.

Giddings, Lee Co., St. Margaret (1944) (German-Hispanic), Rev. Raphael J. Clancy; Deacon Edward J. Hoefling.
Res., 500 S. Grimes, 78942. Tel: 409-542-3380. [JC]
Catechesis/Religious Programs—Students 200.
Mission—Pin Oak, Bastrop Co., St. Mary's, 78942.

Goldthwaite, Mills Co., St. Peter's (1885). Attended by St. Mary's, San Saba. Rev. Earl M. Hedberg; Deacon Richard Menchara.
Res., P.O. Box 352, 76844. Tel: 915-648-3732. [JC]
Catechesis/Religious Programs—Tel: 915-938-5441. Tani Menchara, D.R.E.
Students 32.

Granger, Williamson Co., SS. Cyril and Methodius (1891) (Czech), Rev. Msgr. Edward Rabroker.
Res., 300 W. Davilla, P.O. Box 608, 76530. Tel: 512-859-2223. [CEM 2]
School—Tel: 512-859-2927. Jim Byfield, Prin.
Lay Teachers 9; Students 93.
Catechesis/Religious Programs—Tel: 512-859-2224. Cara Finn, D.R.E.
Students 250.

Hamilton, Hamilton Co., St. Thomas (1965), Deacon James L. Gallagher, Admin.
Res., 905 N. Nicholson Ave., Rte. 1, Box 305, 76531. Tel: 817-386-5513. [JC]

Harker Heights, Bell Co., St. Paul Chong Hasang

(1986), Rev. Richard O'Rourke, M.S.C. (Ireland).
Mailing Address: P.O. Box 2414, 76548.
Res., 1000 E. FM Rd. 2410, 76548. Tel: 254-698-4110; 698-4338; Fax: 254-698-4608.
Catechesis/Religious Programs—Ms. Olga Touchet, D.R.E.
Students 92.

Hearne, Robertson Co., St. Francis Assisi,
Res., 9896 Edge Cut Off Rd., 77859. Tel: 409-589-2806. Deacon Luis Dariocourt, Pastoral Admin.
St. Mary's (1872) (Italian & Mexican-American), Rev. Gregory McLaughlin.
Res., 402 W. First St., 77859. Tel: 409-279-2233; Fax: 409-279-9606. [CEM]
Catechesis/Religious Programs—Tel: 409-279-2259. Ada Sifuentes, D.R.E.
Students 152.
Mission—Calvert, Robertson Co., St. Mary, 505 Logan St., Calvert, 77837.

Horseshoe Bay, Burnet Co, St. Paul the Apostle (1982), Rev. Robert T. Scott, C.S.P.
Res., P.O. Box 8019, 78657. Tel: 830-598-8342.
Catechesis/Religious Programs—Students 55.

Hostyn Hill, Fayette Co., St. Mary's (1855) (Czech). Attended by St. John's, Fayetteville.
Mailing Address: P.O. Box 57, Fayetteville, 78940. Tel: 409-378-2277. [CEM]

Jarrell, Williamson Co., Holy Trinity (1889) (Czech & German), Rev. Msgr. Arthur Michalka.
Res., 8626 FM 1105, 76537. Tel: 512-863-3020. [CEM]
Catechesis/Religious Programs—Susan Klepac, D.R.E.
Students 104.
Mission—Salado, St. Stephen.

Killeen, Bell Co., St. Joseph (1954), Revs. Walter J. Matus; Albert Ruiz; Deacons Lyman Fansler; George Shieldes. In res., Rev. Charles E. Van Winkle, C.S.C.
Res., 2903 E. Rancier Ave., 76543. Tel: 254-634-7878; 634-7844; Fax: 254-634-1224.
School—(Grades PreK-5). Tel: 254-634-7272.
Lay Teachers 9; Students 125.
Catechesis/Religious Programs—Tel: 254-634-7878.
Students 327.

Kingsland, Llano Co., St. Charles Borromeo (1965), Rev. Joseph Mitrano, C.S.B.; Deacon Dr. George Lillard.
Mailing Address: P.O. Box 1748, 78639.
Res., 1927 Hwy. 1431, 78639. Tel: 915-388-3742.
Mission—Sunrise Beach, Burnet Co., Our Lady of the Lake, 233 Deer Dr., Sunrise Beach, 78643. Tel: 512-598-8342.

Kovar, Bastrop Co., Sts. Peter and Paul (1909). Attended by St. Paul's, Smithville. Rev. Henry Heese.
Res., 204 Mills St., Smithville, 78957. Tel: 512-237-2179. [CEM 2]

Kyle, Hays Co., St. Anthony Marie De Claret (1909) (Hispanic), Rev. Howard Goertz; Deacons Richard Duecker; John Peca; John Lawrence; Joe Flores.
Res., 801 N. Burleson St., P.O. Box 268, 78640. Tel: 512-268-5312; 268-5311 (Office).
Catechesis/Religious Programs—Tel: 512-268-5311; Fax: 512-268-5311.
Students 550.

Lago Vista, Travis Co., St. Mary, Our Lady of the Lake (1970), Rev. Msgr. Joseph J. Schmitt.
Res., 6502 Avenida Ann, 78645. Tel: 512-267-1336; Fax: 512-267-2649.
Catechesis/Religious Programs—Tel: 512-267-2644.
Students 87.

La Grange, Fayette Co., Sacred Heart of Jesus (1886), Rev. Msgr. Harry C. Mazurkiewicz.
Res., Box 548, 78945. Tel: 409-968-3430; Fax: 409-968-5740. [JC]
School—Tel: 409-968-3223. Elmer Faykus, Prin.
Lay Teachers 17; Students 192.
Catechesis/Religious Programs—Sr. Elizabeth Agnes Gabriel, C.V.I., D.R.E.
Students 182.

Lampasas, Lampasas Co., St. Mary's (1885), Rev. Msgr. William C. Kinlough; Deacons Carlos Jasso; Weldon J. Bowling. In res., Rev. Msgr. John D. Frizelle.
Res., P.O. Box 866, 76550-0866. Tel: 512-556-5544; Fax: 512-556-4618.
Catechesis/Religious Programs—Tel: 512-556-6203. Sr. Mary Szabo, D.R.E.
Students 124.
Mission—Lometa, Lampasas Co., Good Shepherd Catholic Church, (1927) 500 W. Main St., Lometa, 76853.

Latium, Washington Co., Sacred Heart (1872) (Polish & Czech). Attended by St. Mary's, Brenham.
701 Church St., Brenham, 77833. Tel: 409-836-4441. [CEM]

Leander, Williamson Co., St. Yoo Peter Catholic Church, Rev. San Yil Lee.
Res., P.O. Box 1476, 78646. Tel: 512-259-3463.

Lexington, Lee Co., Holy Family (1990). Mission of St. Joseph, Dime Box. Rev. Msgr. Emilian Foltyn.
Res., Rte. 1, Box 5A, Dime Box, 77853. Tel: 409-884-3100.

Llano, Llano Co., Holy Trinity (1890). Attended by St. Joseph's Church, Mason. Rev. Karel Fink.
Mailing Address: P.O. Box 673, 78643. Tel: 915-247-4481. [JC]
Catechesis/Religious Programs—Tel: 915-247-4544. Susan Hagar, D.R.E.
Students 70.
Mission—Mason, Box 1572, Mason, 76856.

Lockhart, Caldwell Co., St. Mary's (1887), Rev. Adam Martinez; Deacons Guadalupe Aguilar; William Long; William Haywood.
Res., 205 W. Pecan, 78644. Tel: 512-398-4649; 376-3634; Fax: 512-398-2285. [CEM]
Catechesis/Religious Programs—Tel: 512-398-3506. Eva Mendez, D.R.E.
Students 495.

Lometa, Lampasas Co., Good Shepherd (1927). Attended by St. Mary's, Lampasas. Rev. Msgr. William C. Kinlough. In res., Rev. Msgr. John D. Frizelle.
Mailing Address: P.O. Box 866, Lampasas, 76550-0866. Tel: 512-556-5544; Fax: 512-556-4618.
500 W. Main St., 76853.

Lott, Falls Co., Sacred Heart (1906), Rev. E. Peter Royal.
Res., P.O. Box 371, Marlin, 76661. Tel: 254-883-2016. [CEM]

Luling, Caldwell Co., St. John the Evangelist (1879), Rev. Jesse Euresti.
Res., 500 E. Travis St., 78648. Tel: 830-875-5354; Fax: 830-875-3533. [CEM]
Catechesis/Religious Programs—Tel: 830-875-3901. Sr. Mary Frances Bartsch, O.L.V.M., D.R.E.
Students 230.

Manor, Travis Co., St. Joseph's (1876) (Hispanic), Rev. Robert Mahoney.
Mailing Address: P.O. Box 389, 78653. Tel: 512-272-4004. [JC]
Catechesis/Religious Programs—Students 108.

Marak, Milam Co., SS. Cyril and Methodius (1903) (Czech). Attended from St. Joseph's, Cyclone.
20120 FM 485, Burlington, 76519. Tel: 254-985-2280.
Catechesis/Religious Programs—Students 51.

Marble Falls, Burnet Co., St. John the Evangelist (1961), Rev. Edwin J. Kadzielawski, C.S.C.
Church—105 Hwy. 1431 E., 78654. Tel: 210-693-5134.
Catechesis/Religious Programs—Students 50.

Marlin, Falls Co., St. Joseph's (1876), Rev. E. Peter Royal; Deacon Julian Tyboroski.
Res., Box 371, 76661. Tel: 817-883-2016; Fax: 817-883-2099.
Catechesis/Religious Programs—Marjorie Kasner, D.R.E.
Students 213.
Mission—Lott, Falls Co., Sacred Heart, Lott, 76656.

Martindale, Caldwell Co., Immaculate Heart of Mary (1908). Attended by St. John the Evangelist, San Marcos. Rev. Henry Luna, C.M.F.
Mailing Address: P.O. Box 117, 78655. Tel: 512-357-6573.
Catechesis/Religious Programs—Tel: 512-357-9076. Gloria P. Gonzales, D.R.E.
Students 169.

Mason, Mason Co., St. Joseph's (1873) (Hispanic), Rev. Fawaz Ayoub.
Res., P.O. Box 1572, 76856. Tel: 915-347-6932.
Catechesis/Religious Programs—Aida Dominguez, D.R.E.
Students 120.
Mission—Llano, Holy Trinity Church.

McGregor, McLennan Co., St. Eugene (1958) (Hispanic), Rev. George C. George.
Res., 207 N. Johnson Dr., 76657. Tel: 254-840-3174.
Catechesis/Religious Programs—Tel: 254-666-0021.
Students 113.
Mission—Moody, McLennan Co., Our Lady of San Juan, 207 N. Johnson Dr., 76657. Tel: 254-853-9011.

Mexia, Limestone Co., St. Mary's (1886), Rev. Scott Mikkelson.
Mailing Address: 506 E. Sumpter, 76667. [JC]
Res., 606 N. Bonham, 76667. Tel: 254-562-3619.
Catechesis/Religious Programs—Students 155.

Moody, McLennan Co., Our Lady of San Juan (1991) (Hispanic). Attended by Mission of St. Eugene, McGregor. Rev. George C. George.
207 N. Johnson Dr., McGregor, 76657. Tel: 254-840-3174.
Catechesis/Religious Programs—Tel: 254-853-9011.
Students 43.

Old Washington-on-the Brazos, Washington Co., Blessed Virgin Mary (1849) (African American). Attended by St. Mary's Church, Brenham. Rev. Msgr. Ralph Brennan; Rev. Leonard Cornelius, O.F.M.; Deacon Raymond Sis.
701 Church St., Brenham, 77833. Tel: 409-836-4441; Fax: 409-836-9383. [CEM]

Pflugerville, Travis Co., St. Elizabeth (1932), Revs. Tom Frank; Kevin Rai; Deacons Roy Hubbard; Marc Washburne.
Mailing Address: P.O. Box 524, 78691-0524. Tel: 512-251-9838; Fax: 512-251-9868.
Res., 304 S. 8th St., Tel: 512-251-9866.
Catechesis/Religious Programs—Tel: 512-251-9842.
Students 622.

Pin Oak, Bastrop Co., St. Mary's (1866) (German). Attended by St. Margaret's, Giddings.
500 S. Grimes, Giddings, 78942. Tel: 409-542-3380. [CEM]

Rockdale, Milam Co., St. Joseph's (1880), Revs. Victor Mathias; Giles Amarasekera (Sri Lanka).
Church—P.O. Box 548, 76567. Tel: 512-446-2049; Fax: 512-446-0411.
Res., 521 E. Davilla St., 76567. Tel: 512-446-2196.
Catechesis/Religious Programs—Kathy Kucera, D.R.E.
Students 211.

Rockne, Bastrop Co., Sacred Heart (1876), Rev. Msgr. Clyde Holtman; Deacon Roger Muehr.
Res., Rte. 1, Box 108, Bastrop, 78602. Tel: 512-321-7991. [CEM]
Catechesis/Religious Programs—Jeanease Friske, D.R.E.
Students 200.
Mission—String Prairie, Bastrop Co., Assumption of the Blessed Virgin Mary, Tel: 512-839-4580. [CEM]

Rogers, Bell Co., St. Matthew (1991), Rev. Louis Paulicek; Deacon Juan Garza, Admin.
Mailing Address: P.O. Box 366, 76569.
103 E. Gulf St., 76569. Tel: 817-642-3450.

Rosebud, Falls Co., St. Ann's (1915), Rev. Thaddeus Tabak, S.D.S. (Poland).
Res., P.O. Drawer 85, Burlington, 76519. Tel: 254-869-2525. [CEM]
Catechesis/Religious Programs—Tel: 254-583-4624.
Students 117.
Mission—Burlington, Milam Co., St. Michael's, (1879) P.O. Box 85, Burlington, 76519.

Round Rock, Williamson Co., St. William's (1956), Revs. Don Loftin; Andrew Gunn; Richard Hudson; Beverly Collin, Pastoral Assoc.; Deacons Concho Castillo; Juan Gonzalez, Jr.; Jim Moat. In res., Bro. Luke M. Baldwin, M.M.
Office: 1000 McNeil Rd., 78681. Tel: 512-255-4473; Fax: 512-255-8126.
Res., 1700 St. William's St., 78681. Tel: 512-255-3825.
Catechesis/Religious Programs—Tel: 512-255-9118.
Students 1,050.

Salado, Bell Co., St. Stephen's (1989), Deacon John Petter, Pastoral Admin.
Mailing Address: P.O. Box 662, 76571. Tel: 254-947-8037.
Res., 601 FM 2268, 76751.
Catechesis/Religious Programs—Tel: 254-947-0114. Robert Michalewicz, D.R.E.
Students 67.

San Marcos, Hays Co., St. John the Evangelist (1883), Revs. Brian Culley, C.M.F.; Henry Luna, C.M.F.; Paul Keller, C.M.F.; Daryl Olds, C.M.F. Pastoral Assocs.: Alba Ippolito, Youth Min.; Sr. Maria de Jesus Medina, M.C.M.; Deacons Lalo Duran; Domingo Vargas; Louis Endris. In res., Rev. Art Gramaje, C.M.F., Campus Min.
Res., 624 E. Hopkins, 78666. Tel: 512-353-8969; Fax: 512-396-7522.
Catechesis/Religious Programs—Tel: 512-353-5065. Sr. Adelina Esquivel, M.C.M., D.R.E.
Students 997.
Convent—964 Field St., 78666. Tel: 512-396-5333.
Missions—San Marcos, Hays Co., Guadalupe Chapel, Corner of Roosevelt & Churchill, 78666.; Uhland, Hays Co., St. Michael's, 80 S. Old Spanish Tr., Uhland, 78640. Tel: 512-398-7475. Deacon Lalo Duran, Pastoral Coord.; Martindale, Caldwell Co., Immaculate Heart of Mary, P.O. Box 117, Martindale, 78655. Tel: 512-357-6573.

San Saba, San Saba Co., St. Mary's (1967) (Hispanic), Rev. Earl M. Hedberg; Deacon Richard Menchaca.
Church—P.O. Box 415, 76877. Tel: 915-372-3679.
Catechesis/Religious Programs—Tel: 915-372-5441. Tani Menchaca, D.R.E.

Students 75.
Mission—Lampass Co., Izoro. [JC]

Satin, Satin Falls Co., Santa Rita Shrine (1921) (Hispanic). Attended by St. Francis, Waco.
301 Jefferson Ave., Waco, 76701. Tel: 817-752-8434; Fax: 817-752-2415.

Smithville, Bastrop Co., St. Paul the Apostle (1896), Rev. Henry Heese; Deacon Cleofas Cruz.
Res., 204 Mills St., 78957. Tel: 512-237-2179.
Catechesis/Religious Programs—Students 144.

Somerville, Burleson Co., St. Ann's (1954), Rev. Joel D. McNeil.
Res., P.O. Box 99, 77879. Tel: 409-596-1966; Fax: 409-596-2857.
Catechesis/Religious Programs—Tel: 409-596-1494. Sr. M. John, D.R.E.
Students 70.
Mission—Frenstat, Burleson Co., Holy Rosary, 77879.

Stony Point, Travis Co., Blessed Juan Diego (1987). Attended by St. Anthony, Kyle. Rev. Howard Goertz; Deacon Richard Duecker, Pastoral Admin.
Mailing Address: 200 Janzet Dr., Kyle, 78640. Tel: 512-243-1404.
Res., No. 22 & 43 Stoney Point Dr., Del Valle, 78617. Tel: 512-312-0357.

String Prairie, Bastrop Co., St. Mary's of the Assumption (1876) (German). Attended by Sacred Heart, Rockne. Rev. Msgr. Clyde Holtman.
Rte. 1, Box 108, Bastrop, 78602. Tel: 512-839-4580. [CEM]

Taylor, Williamson Co., St. Mary's (1877), Rev. Lonnie A. Urban.
Res., 408 Washburn St., 76574. Tel: 512-352-2175; Fax: 512-365-1431. [CEM]
School—Tel: 512-352-2313. Sr. Carita Ulm, O.P., Prin.
Sisters 2; Lay Teachers 19; Students 216.
Catechesis/Religious Programs—Tel: 512-352-2133. Mrs. Belinda Ozuna, D.R.E.
Students 354.
Convent—317 E. 4th St., 76574. Tel: 512-352-2144.

Our Lady of Guadalupe (1914) (Hispanic), Rev. Pedro Garcia; Deacon Gumisindo Gonzales.
Res., 113 Dickey St., 76574. Tel: 512-365-2380; Fax: 512-365-1733. [CEM]
Catechesis/Religious Programs—Students 273.

Temple, Bell Co., St. Mary's (1883), Rev. Steven Nesrsta; Deacon Don Burleson. In res., Rev. Victor Mathias.
Res., 1018 S. 7th St., 76504. Tel: 254-773-4541; Fax: 254-774-7044. [JC]
School—Tel: 254-778-8141; Fax: 254-778-1396. Loris Edwards, Prin.
Lay Teachers 19; Students 206.
Catechesis/Religious Programs—Tel: 254-773-1980. Barbara Burleson, D.R.E.
Students 445.
Rectory—1004 S. 7th St., 76504. Tel: 254-773-3238.

St. Luke's (1969), Revs. Louis Paulicek; Steven Ryan; Deacon Jerome J. Klement.
Res., 2807 Oakdale, 76502. Tel: 254-773-1561; Fax: 254-773-4623. [JC]
Catechesis/Religious Programs—Tel: 254-773-2330; Fax: 254-773-2643.
Students 383.

Our Lady of Guadalupe (1952) (Hispanic), Rev. Ricardo Aguilar.
Res., 708 S. 6th St., 76504. Tel: 254-773-6779; Fax: 254-773-5469.
Catechesis/Religious Programs—Students 350.

Tours, McLennan Co., St. Martin (1870) (German-Czech), Rev. Isidore Rozycki.
Res., 301 St. Martin's Church Rd., West, 76691-2135. Tel: 254-822-1145. [CEM]
Catechesis/Religious Programs—Tel: 254-822-1026. Dorothy Middleton, D.R.E.
Students 192.
Mission—Elk, McLennon Co., St. Joseph, 76691.

Uhland, Hays Co., St. Michael's (1924). Attended by St. John's, San Marcos. Rev. Brian Culley, C.M.F.; Deacon Lalo Duran, Pastoral Coord.
Mailing Address: 624 E. Hopkins St., San Marcos, 78666. Tel: 512-353-8969.
Res., 80 Old Spanish Tr., 78640. Tel: 512-398-7475. [JC]
Catechesis/Religious Programs—Mrs. Trina Alvarez, D.R.E.
Students 60.

Waco, McLennan Co.,

1—Sacred Heart, (1957) (Spanish), Rev. Lawrence Soler, T.O.R.
Res., 2621 Bagby Ave., 76711. Tel: 254-756-2656.
Catechesis/Religious Programs—Tel: 254-756-2390.
Students 400.

2—St. Francis on the Brazos, (1924) (Hispanic), Revs. Anthony P. Ferrer, T.O.R.; Anselmo Mondragon, T.O.R.; Deacon Jessie Garza.
Res., 301 Jefferson Ave., 76701. Tel: 254-752-8434; Fax: 254-752-2415. [JC]
School—Tel: 254-753-5565; Fax: 254-753-6816. Sr. Barbara Herrera, Prin.
Sisters 4; Lay Teachers 5; Students 140.
Nursery & Kindergarten—612 N. 3rd St., 76701.
Catechesis/Religious Programs—Tel: 254-752-1159.
Students 610.
Convent—612 N. 3rd St., 76701. Tel: 254-753-5565.
Mission—Satin, Satin Falls Co., Santa Rita.

3—St. Jerome, (1982), Rev. William C. Brooks.
Res., 9820 Chapel Rd., 76712. Tel: 254-666-2120; Fax: 254-666-7722.
Catechesis/Religious Programs—Tel: 254-666-3555; Fax: 254-666-2120. D.R.E.: Nancy Coker; Pam Kosarek.
Students 580.

4—St. John the Baptist, (1953) (African American), Deacons Alton Hithe, Pastoral Admin.; Joseph A. Weynand.
Res., 1312 Dallas St., P.O. Box 585, 76704-0585. Tel: 254-753-6742.
Catechesis/Religious Programs—Students 981.
Mission—Waco.

5—St. Joseph, (Bellmead) (1950), Rev. Timothy V. Vaverek; Deacon Benedict Cepak.
Res., 1011 Boston St., 76705. Tel: 254-799-2531.
Catechesis/Religious Programs—Tel: 254-799-6646. Brenda Fetsch, D.R.E.
Students 200.

6—St. Louis, (1964), Rev. Msgr. Mark Deering. In res., Rev. Robert L. Kincl,., J.C.L., S.T.L.
Res., 2001 N. 25th St., P.O. Box 5040, 76708. Tel: 254-754-1221.
School—Tel: 254-754-2041. John Vasek, Prin.
Lay Teachers 22; Students 349.
Catechesis/Religious Programs—Sally Rue, D.R.E.
Students 132.

7—St. Mary of the Assumption, (1870), Revs. Angelo Bertini; Martin Rabbitte; Deacon Sidney Prewitt.
Res., 1401 Washington Ave., 76701. Tel: 254-753-0146; Fax: 254-753-5100. [JC]
School—Tel: 254-754-1622; Fax: 254-756-6365. Sr. M. Kenneth Regan, C.S.C., Prin.
Sisters 1; Lay Teachers 14; Students 130.
Catechesis/Religious Programs—Tel: 254-756-0548. Sr. Virginia Dunker, D.C., D.R.E.
Students 90.
Convent—224 N. 14th St., 76701. Tel: 254-756-0548.

West, McLennan Co., Assumption (1892) (Czech), Revs. Edward Karasek; Melvin Dornak.
Res., P.O. Box 276, 76691. Tel: 254-826-3705; Fax: 254-826-5497. [CEM]
School—Tel: 254-826-5991; Fax: 254-826-5996. Joe Gough, Prin.
Lay Teachers 10; Students 153.
Catechesis/Religious Programs—D.R.E.: Mrs. Pam Urbanovsky; Mrs. Charlotte Klaus; Mrs. Barbara Kolar.
Students 370.

Westphalia, Falls Co., Visitation (1883), Rev. Reinhold Schmitt, C.M.M.
Res., Rte. 2, Box 53A, Lott, 76656. Tel: 254-584-4983. [CEM]
Catechesis/Religious Programs—Tel: 254-584-4407. Edna Spivey, D.R.E.
Students 132.

Wimberley, Hays Co., St. Mary (1956), Rev. Everett Trebtoske; Deacon John C. Maher.
Res., 14711 Ranch Rd. 12, 78676. Tel: 512-847-9181 (Church); Fax: 512-847-5573. [CEM]
Catechesis/Religious Programs—Diane Whitten, D.R.E.
Students 93.

Chaplains of Public Institutions

Austin. *Brackenridge Hospital.* Rev. Oliver Weerakkody.
St. David's Hospital. 2010 Guadalupe, 78705. Tel: 512-477-9471. Rev. Robert Michele, C.S.P.
School for the Blind. 7601 Burnet Rd., 78757. Tel: 512-454-0384. Rev. Larry Covington.
School for the Deaf. Served by St. Ignatius Catholic Church. 2309 Euclid St., 78704. Tel: 512-442-3602.
State Hospital. 4110 Guadalupe, 78751. Tel: 512-419-2573. Sr. Ruth Steiner, S.M.I.C.
State School. 2010 Guadalupe, 78705. Tel: 512-477-9471. Rev. Patrick Johnson, C.S.P.

Bastrop. *Federal Correctional Institute.* P.O. Box 730, 78602. Rev. Emmett N. Faber (LC).

Gatesville. *State School for Boys.* P.O. Box 665, 76528. Deacon James Gallagher, Chap.

Giddings. *State School.* P.O. Box 600, 78942. Tel: 409-542-3686. Rev. Peter McCabe.

Marlin. *V.A. Hospital.* P.O. Box 371, 76661. Rev. E. Peter Royal.

Mexia. *State School.* 606 N. Bonham, 76667. Tel: 817-562-3619. Rev. Scott Mikkelson.

Temple. *V.A. Hospital.* 1901 S. First St., 76501. Rev. Harry Bilski.

Waco. *V.A. Hospital.* Memorial Dr., 76703. Rev. Thomas J. Niemira.

Special Assignments:
Reverend Monsignors—
Fruge, Donald J. (GAL), Finance Officer
Matocha, Edward C., Vicar General
Reverend Fathers—
Goertz, Bernard C., Rte. 2, Box 129, Cedar Creek, TX 78612
Goertz, Victor, Cedarbrake Renewal Center, P.O. Box 58, Belton, TX 76513

On Duty Outside the Diocese:
Reverend Monsignors—
Chatham, Donald, #12 the Lindens, 222 Kew Rd., Richmond, Surrey TW93LL England
Elmer, Charles, North American College, Casa Maria, Via dell' Umilta, 30, Rome, 00187 Italy
Reverend Fathers—
Chalupa, Fred, Diocese of Galveston-Houston, P.O. Box 907, Houston, TX 77001
Garcia, Pedro, Parroquia de San Isidro Labrador, Hidalgo 204, Apdo. 24, Arteaga, Coahuila C.P. 25350 Mexico
Herald, Robert P., Texas Department of Corrections, Office of the Catholic Chaplain, Ellis Unit I, Rte. 6, Huntsville, TX 77343
Mahoney, Bernard, 1722 Chippendale, Houston, TX 77108
Mulvey, Michael, Scuoia Sarcerdotale, via S. Francesco 4, Vivaio, C.P. 72, Incisa Valdarno (F1) 50064 Italy
Strieder, Leon, St. Mary's Seminary, 9845 Memorial Dr., Houston, TX 77024
Willemsen, Andrew J., Eindhovenseweg 32, 5524 AR Steensel, Netherlands

---

Military Chaplains:
Reverend Fathers—
Moss, Donald G., Naval Chaplain's School, Mailing Address: Code PO 705, NAVAIR WPNSTA, 521 Ninth St., Port Mugo, CA 93042

Absent on Sick Leave:
Reverend Monsignors—
Miller, Frank, Rte. 2, Box 46-E, Abbott, TX 76621

Retired:
Reverend Monsignors—
Frizelle, John D.
Fuchs, Robert A., Rte. 2, Box 48A, Rosebud, TX 76570
Fuchs, Sylvester, Lost Prairie Villa, 9901 FM Rd. 2086, Temple, TX 76501-3528
Stram, Gideon, Rte. 1, Box 138-N, Jarrell, TX 76537. Tel: 512-746-2028
Tydlacka, George, 874 Burleson-Manor Rd., Manor, TX 78653
Widacki, Roman, 400 Austin Ave., #1102, Waco, TX 76703
Reverend Fathers—
Collins, Robert, 3003 Maplelawn Cir., Austin, TX 78723
Conrad, Stanley, Hunterwood Cottage #109, Londonderry, Waco, TX 76712. Tel: 254-751-7687
Guttenberger, Xavier, Duval Oaks Guest Home, 5310 Duval Rd. #44, Austin, TX 78727. Tel: 512-418-8228
Hand, Chester, Jr., 400 Austin Ave., Waco, TX 76703
Tzanakas, George M., 4701 Staggerbrush, #115, Austin, TX 78749. Tel: 512-892-8293

Permanent Deacons:
Adam, Klaus, Ft. Hood Cath. Comm., Killeen
Aguilar, Guadalupe, St. Mary's, Lockhart
Barkley, Roy, St. Joseph's, Manor
Behr, Roger L., Sacred Heart, Austin
Beltran, Victor, Hughes Unit, Gatesville
Berg, James R., St. Catherine of Siena, Austin
Bowling, Weldon, St. Mary's, Lampasas
Burleson, Don, St. Mary's, Temple
Castillo, Concepcion, St. Williams, Round Rock
Cepak, Benny, St. Joseph's, Bellmead
Cochran, Lee
Collins, Roger, St. Helen's, Georgetown
Cortez, Willie, Our Lady's Youth Center, Austin; St. Mary's, Austin
Crochet, Larry, St. Charles Borromeo, Kingsland
Crowley, Joe, Our Lady's, Maronite, Austin
Cruz, Cleofas, Sts. Peter and Paul, Smithville
Deason, Switzer, St. Joseph's, Bryan
Desorcie, Allen, St. Vincent de Paul, Austin
Doriocourt, Luis, St. Joseph, Bryan
Droll, Victor, St. Helen's, Georgetown

Duecker, Richard, Fr. Joel Atwood, Stoney Point
Dufour, E. Generes, Diocesan Prison Ministry
Dunne, Larry, Sacred Heart, Elgin
Duran, Everardo S., St. Michael's, Uhland
Elliott, Gregg, St. Francis Hospital, Tulsa, OK
Embry, Rob, Sacred Heart, Austin
Endris, Lou, St. John the Evangelist, San Marcos
Fansler, Lyman C., St. Joseph's, Killeen
Flores, Joe, St. Anthony's, Kyle
Foreman, Boyce A., Lakeway, Austin
Fuller, James, Sacred Heart, Austin
Gallagher, James, St. Thomas, Hamilton
Garcia, Louis, Santa Teresa, Bryan
Garza, Jessie, St. Francis of the Brazos, Waco
Garza, Juan, St. Matthew's, Rogers
Gonzales, Gumisindo, St. John's, Rochester, MN
Gonzalez, John, St. William, Round Rock
Graham, James, St. Ignatius Martyr, Austin
Ham, W. J., St. Catherine of Siena, Austin
Hamlet, Mark, St. John Neumann, Austin
Hansen, Clarence, St. Theresa's, Austin
Haywood, Daryl, St. Mary's, Lockhart
Hernandez, Salvador, Our Lady of Guadalupe, Austin
Hithe, Alton, St. John's, Waco
Hoefling, Ed, St. Margaret, Giddings
Hubbard, Roy, St. Elizabeth's, Pflugerville
Jacobs, James A., (Retired)
James, Ray, St. Theresa's, Austin
Januszewski, Bill, St. Mary's, Brenham
Jasso, Carlos, St. Mary's, Lampasas
Joseph, George, San Jose, Austin
Kennedy, Pat, St. Albert, Austin
Kim, Peter, St. Mary's, Austin
Klement, Jerome, St. Luke's, Temple
Krotzer, Philip, St. Martin de Porres, Dripping Springs
Larner, Richard, St. Paul's, Austin
Lawrence, John, St. Anthony's, Kyle
Lilliard, George, St. Charles, Kingsland
Long, Bill, St. Mary's, Lockhart
Maher, John, St. Mary's, Wimberly
Mallinger, Thomas, St. Thomas More, Austin
Martinez, Jesse, Apache Shores, Austin
Medrano, Guadalupe, Cristo Rey, Austin
Menchaca, Richard, St. Mary's, San Saba
Moat, Jim, San Isidro Labrador, Arteaga, Mexico
Montag, Eugene J., Our Mother of Sorrows, Burnet
Montalvo, Manuel, San Jisidro Labrador, Arteaga, Coahuila, Mexico
Morris, Douglas, St. John Neumann, Austin
Muehr, Roger, Sacred Heart, Rockne
Murray, Patrick, St. Ignatius, Austin
Murrell, Jack, Good Shepherd, Johnson City
Nelson, Gary, St. Joseph's, Bryan
Nira, Oswaldo, St. Peter the Apostle, Austin
Ojeda, Johnny, Blessed Juan Diego, Stoney Point
Orozco, Abraham
Peca, John M., St. Anthony's, Kyle
Petter, John, St. Stephen's, Salado
Pfuntner, Jordan, St. Mary's, Waco
Potter, Joseph, St. Eugene, McGregor
Prewitt, Sidney, St. Mary's, Waco
Ramsey, Jesse, St. Albert the Great, Austin
Renteria, Mario, Our Lady of Guadalupe, Austin
Reyna, Frank, St. Francis of Assisi, Frisco
Reynolds, Joseph, St. Anne's, Somerville
Rivera, John, San Jose, Austin
Ruiz, Joe, Holy Cross, Bertram
Saenz, Enrique, San Jose, Austin
Schwab, Peter, St. Thomas More, Austin
Scott, Bill, St. Mary's, College Station
Shieldes, George, St. Joseph's, Killeen
Shoemaker, William, Christ the King, Belton
Sis, Ray, St. Joseph's, Bryan
Smetana, Bill, Visitation, Westphalia
Solarzano, Eraclio, St. John the Evangelist, Marble Falls
Terry, Frank, St. Martin de Porres, Dripping Springs
Tyborowski, Julian, St. Joseph's, Marlin
Vargas, Domingo, St. John's, San Marcos
Vasquez, Alfredo, San Jose, Austin
Vela, William, Sacred Heart, Austin
Washburne, Marc, St. Elizabeth, Pflugerville
Weilert, Otto, Diocesan Pastoral Center
Weynand, Joe, St. John's, Waco
Wilson, Gilbert, St. Joseph's, Bryan
Young, John, St. Mary's, Caldwell

INSTITUTIONS LOCATED IN THE DIOCESE

[A] COLLEGES AND UNIVERSITIES

AUSTIN. *St. Edward's University*, (1881) 3001 S. Congress Ave., 78704. Tel: 512-448-8400
For a complete listing, refer to the Colleges and Universities section.

[B] HIGH SCHOOL, DIOCESAN

WACO. *Reicher Catholic High School*, 2102 N. 23rd St., 76708. Rev. Leo A. Baysinger, S.D.B., Prin. Priests 1; Sisters 3; Lay Teachers 18; Students 206.

[C] HIGH SCHOOLS, PRIVATE

AUSTIN. *St. Michaels's Catholic Academy*, 3000 Barton Creek Blvd., 78735. Tel: 512-328-2323. Mr. John (Jack) T. Kennedy, II, Prin. Schoenstatt Sisters of Mary 1; Lay Teachers 38; Students 364.

TEMPLE. *Holy Trinity Catholic High School*, P.O. Box 3723, 76503-3723. Tel: 254-771-0787. Mr. Jim Anderson, Prin.

[D] ELEMENTARY SCHOOL, PRIVATE

AUSTIN. *Dominican Academy*. (Grades K-3), 12475 Trail Driver, 78737. Tel: 512-288-4266. Sr. Leona Castle, O.P.; Sr. Benita Kelly, O.P. Sisters 2; Lay Teachers 2; Students 36.

[E] MATERNITY AND ADOPTION PROGRAM

AUSTIN. *Marywood Children & Family Services*, 510 W. 26th St., 78705. Tel: 512-472-9251; Fax: 512-472-4829. Total in Residence 38; Staff 21. Capacity 35.

[F] GENERAL HOSPITALS

AUSTIN. *Seton East Community Health Center*, 2811 E. Second St., 78702. Tel: 512-323-4930
For a complete listing, refer to the Hospitals section.
Seton Medical Center, 1201 W. 38th St., 78705. Tel: 512-323-1000
For a complete listing, refer to the Hospitals section.
Seton Northwest Hospital, 11113 Research Blvd., 78759. Tel: 512-795-1000.
E-mail: choke@dcnhs-wc.edu
For a complete listing, refer to the Hospitals section.
Seton South Community Health Center, 3706 S. First St., 78704. Tel: 512-323-4940
For a complete listing, refer to the Hospitals section.

BRENHAM. *Trinity Community Medical Center of Brenham*, 700 Medical Pkwy., 77833. Tel: 409-836-6173
For a complete listing, refer to the Hospitals section.

BRYAN. *Burleson Lease Corp. Inc./dba Burleson St. Joseph Health Center*, 2801 Franciscan Dr., 77802. Tel: 409-776-2464.
E-mail: info@mail.st-joseph.org
Web site: http://www.st-joseph.org
For a complete listing, refer to the Hospitals section.
St. Joseph Regional Health Center, 2801 Franciscan Dr., 77802. Tel: 409-776-3777.
E-mail: info@mail.st-joseph.org
Web site: http://www.st-joseph.org
For a complete listing, refer to the Hospitals section.
St. Joseph Services Corp., 2801 Franciscan Dr., 77802. Tel: 409-776-3777.
E-mail: info@mail.st-joseph.org
Web site: http://www.st-joseph.org
For a complete listing, refer to the Hospitals section.

WACO. *Providence Health Center*, 6901 Medical Pkwy., P.O. Box 2589, 76702-2589. Tel: 254-751-4764
For a complete listing, refer to the Hospitals section.

[G] SPECIAL HOSPITAL

WACO. *DePaul Center*, 301 Londonderry Dr., 76712. Tel: 254-776-5970; 1-800-777-5043
For a complete listing, refer to the Special Care Facilities section.

[H] MONASTERIES AND RESIDENCES OF PRIESTS AND BROTHERS

AUSTIN. *Brother Andre House*, 2113 Brackenridge St., 78704. Tel: 512-462-3540; Fax: 512-416-1216. Bro. Thomas G. Krieter, C.S.C.
Brothers of the Congregation of Holy Cross. Brother John Baptist Province Center,
St. Edward's University, No. 1046, 3001 S. Congress, 78704. Tel: 512-442-7856; Fax: 512-444-3133. Bros. Richard Critz, C.S.C., Prov. Supr.; Stephen Walsh, C.S.C., Asst. Provincial; Harold Ehlinger, C.S.C., Steward; John McLaughlin, C.S.C., Sec.; Stanley Culotta, C.S.C., Councilor; Richard Daly, C.S.C., Councilor; William Nick, C.S.C., Councilor; Johnny Juno, C.S.C., Asst. Steward; Mel Keil, C.S.C., Asst. Steward; Carl Smith, C.S.C., Admin. Asst. Total in province 125.
Brothers of the Congregation of the Holy Cross, c/o St. Edward's University, 3001 S. Congress Ave., Box 1041, 78704. Tel: 512-443-3732. Revs. John Collet, O.M.I.; William Davis, O.M.I.; Emmanuel Kawanguzi, St. Joseph Hall.
Congregation of Holy Cross - Southern Province, Provincial Office, 2111 Brackenridge St., 78704. Tel: 512-443-3886; Fax: 512-416-1216. Revs. John R. Birkmeyer, C.S.C., (Retired); Jeremiah R. Buttomer, C.S.C., (Retired); Leonard J. Collins, C.S.C., On Sabbatical; John S. Korcsmar, C.S.C., Prov.; Paul B. Rankin, C.S.C., (Retired); Joseph W. Rehage, C.S.C., (Retired); Charles E. Van Winkle, C.S.C.; Allen L. Cormier, C.S.C., (Retired); Leon J. Boarman, C.S.C., (Retired); Bro. Thomas G. Krieter, C.S.C., Prov. Steward.
Dominican Fathers, 2502 Comburg Castle Way, 78748-5258. Tel: 512-282-3908; Fax: 512-280-9011.
E-mail: chief2@swbell.net
Revs. James A. McDonough, O.P., Supr.; Neal Wise, O.P. Tel: 512-448-8455; Gerardo Guerra-Mayaudon, O.P. Tel: 512-292-3381, 6008 Club Terrace, 78741. Tel: 512-385-1719. Rev. Ralph Rogawski, O.P., 3001 S. Congress, 78704. Tel: 512-442-4534. Rev. Eduardo Gabriel, O.P.
Marist Brothers of the School, 2408 Manor, #104, 78722. Bro. Robert W. Warren, F.M.S.
Moreau House, St. Edward University #1069, 3001 S. Congress, 78704. Tel: 512-448-8595. Bros. Lawrence Atkinson, C.S.C., Dir.; James Kane, C.S.C.; Howard Metz, C.S.C.
St. Joseph Hall, St. Edward University, 3001 S. Congress Ave., 78704. Tel: 512-442-4534; Fax: 512-442-0589. Bro. Edwin Reggio, C.S.C., Supr. In res. Revs. Joseph W. Rehage, C.S.C.; John Mary Vianney Makanda (Uganda); Eduardo Gabriel, O.P.; Leon J. Boarman, C.S.C.; John W. Lubbers, C.S.C. Total in Residence 30; Brothers 25.
Steiner Lodge Retreat, 3117 Westlake Dr., 78746. Tel: 512-328-0459. Rev. Harold W. Essling, C.S.C.

BLANCO. *Missionaries of the Sacred Heart, M.S.C.* (Irish Providence), Rte. 1, Box 1, 78606. Rev. James Harnan, M.S.C.

BRENHAM. *Order of Friars Minor*, St. Francis Friary, 9539 FM 2193, 77833. Tel: 409-830-1554.
E-mail: lencorn@phoenix.net
Rev. Leonard Cornelius, O.F.M. Total in Residence 1.

TEMPLE. *Jesuit Fathers and Brothers*, St. Luke Church, 2807 Oakdale Dr., 76502. Revs. Steven P. Ryan, S.J.; Gerard Steckler, S.J.

WACO. *Salesians of Don Bosco*, Reicher High School, 2102 N. 23rd St., 76708. Tel: 817-752-8349. Rev. Leo A. Baysinger, S.D.B.

[I] CONVENTS AND RESIDENCES FOR SISTERS

AUSTIN. *Adrian Dominican Sisters*, 1943 Dapplegrey Ln., 78727-4590. Tel: 512-834-9620.
E-mail: loispaha@juno.com
Daughters of Charity of St. Vincent De Paul, 1018 W. 31st St., 78705. Tel: 512-453-9655. Sisters 11. 5803 Fairlane Dr., 78757. Tel: 512-452-8980. Sisters 4. Other Address: 3404 Medical Pkwy., 78705. Tel: 512-323-4906. Sisters 4.
Daughters of Mary Help of Christians (Salesian Sisters of St. John Bosco), St. Mary Mazzarello Convent, 747 Cherico, 78702. Tel: 512-385-9122.
E-mail: fmasuoau@ix.netcom.com
Sr. Irene Tapia, F.M.A.; Sr. Jane Jasso, F.M.A.; Sr. Angelita Guzman, F.M.A. Sisters 3.
Dominican Sisters of Houston, 5911 Reicher Dr., 78723. Tel: 512-926-0687. Sr. Mary Jean Olsovsky, 12507 A Traildriver, 78737. Tel: 512-288-5313. Sr. Leona Castle, O.P.; Sr. Benita Kelly, O.P., 12505 B Traildriver, 78737. Tel: 512-301-3911. Sr. Carol Wagner, O.P.; Sr. Steven Anne, O.P.
Franciscan Sisters Daughters of Mercy (Hermanas Franciscanas Hijas de la Misericordia), Dolores Convent, 1111 Montopolis Dr., 78741. Tel: 512-385-5090. Sisters 5. Other Address, 612 N. 3rd St., Waco, 76701. Tel: 817-753-6816. Sisters 4.
Missionary Cathechists of Divine Providence, 1943 Dapplegrey Ln., 78727. Tel: 512-837-7562; 873-7771. Sr. Mary Lou Barba, M.C.D.P., 2301-A Metcalf St., 78741. Tel: 512-448-2430; 444-7477. Sr. Maria Guadalupe Castaneda, M.C.D.P.
Missionary Sisters of the Immaculate Conception of the Mother of God, 4211-B Shoalwood, 78756. Tel: 512-451-2890. Sisters 2.
Secular Institute of Schoenstatt Sisters of Mary, 12022 Ladrido Ln., 78727-6034. Tel: 512-837-4467. Total in Residence 3.
Sinsinawa Dominican Sisters, 11700 Metric Blvd #903, 78758-3215. Tel: 512-836-6424. Sr. Sigrid Simlik, O.P., 6008 Club Terr., 78741. Tel: 512-385-1719. Sr. Helen Raycraft, O.P.; Sr. Guadalupe Soria, O.P. Sisters 3.
Sisters of Notre Dame de Namur, 3111 Parker Ln. #256, 78741. Tel: 512-462-9342.
E-mail: donnaj@admin.stedwards.edu
Sr. Donna M. Jurick, S.N.D.deN., 1615 Redwood Dr., Harker Heights, 76543. Tel: 817-690-1518. Sr. Margaret Hunt, S.N.D.deN.; Sr. Estelle Kessling, S.N.D.deN. Sisters 3.
Sisters of St. Francis of Dubuque, 1943 Dapplegrey Ln., 78727-4590. Tel: 512-834-9793.
Sisters of the Holy Cross, La Casa Convent, 2213 Euclid Ave., 78704. Tel: 512-441-6693.
Sisters of the Holy Cross, Our Lady of Victory Convent, 2215 Euclid Ave., 78704. Tel: 512-441-2927. Sisters 3. Loretto Convent, 2301 East Side Dr., 78704-5214. Tel: 512-441-3850. Sisters 3. Other

Address: 2213 Euclid Ave., 78704-5125. Tel: 512-441-6693.
Rebekah Baines Johnson Center, 21 Waller St., 78702.
Sisters of the Holy Cross, Loretto Convent, 2301 East Side Dr., 78704. Tel: 512-441-3850. Sisters 3.
Sisters, Servants of the Immaculate Heart of Mary, 3300 Parker Ln., #134, 78741. Tel: 512-447-1335; Fax: 512-448-8492. Sr. Marie Andre Walsh, I.H.M., Contact Person, 3311 Parker Ln., #235, 78741. Tel: 512-326-8239. 3001 S. Congress, #1030, 78704. Tel: 512-442-5295. 1508 South Port #229, 78704. Tel: 512-442-1124. 5508 N. Hwy 317, Belton, 76513. Tel: 254-780-1739. 3702 Sierra Blanca, Temple, 76502. Tel: 254-771-1048.

BRENHAM. *Monastery of St. Clare*, 9300 Hwy. 105, 77833. Tel: 409-836-2444; Fax: 409-836-9652.
E-mail: chandler@phoenix.net
Rev. Leonard Cornelius, O.F.M., Chap. Sisters 8. Res., Rte. 2, Box 280, 77833. Tel: 409-830-1554. Sr. Mary Angela Chandler, O.S.C., Abbess.
Sisters of St. Francis of Our Lady of Lourdes (O.S.F.), Trinity Medical Center, 700 Medical Pkwy., 77833. Tel: 512-836-9481. Sisters 3.

BRYAN. *Sisters of St. Francis of Our Lady of Lourdes*, 2801 Franciscan Dr., 77802. Tel: 409-776-2381.
E-mail: info@mail.st-joseph.org
Web site: http://www.st-joseph.org
Sisters 7.

CEDAR CREEK. *Sisters of Divine Providence*, P.O. Box 558, 78612-0558. Tel: 512-471-0541. Sisters 4.

FAYETTEVILLE. *Sisters of Divine Providence*, St. John's Convent, 209 E. Bell, 78940. Tel: 409-378-2275.

LA GRANGE. *Sisters of the Incarnate Word and Blessed Sacrament*, Sacred Heart Convent, 580 Pearl St., 78945. Tel: 409-968-6574.

LAMPASAS. *Sisters of St. John Bosco*, St. Mary Convent, Box 864, 76550. Tel: 512-556-6203. Total in Residence 2.

LULING. *Our Lady of Victory Missionary Sisters*, 500 E. Travis, 78648. Tel: 512-875-5354.

SAN MARCOS. *Cordi-Marian Sisters*, 964 Field St., St. Anthony Claret Mission House, 78666. Tel: 512-396-5333. Sisters 2.

SOMERVILLE. *Missionary Ecumenical*, P.O. Box 367, 77879. Tel: 409-595-1494. Total in Residence 3.

TAYLOR. *Dominican Sisters of Houston*, St. Mary Convent, 317 E. Fourth St., 76574. Tel: 512-352-2144. Sisters 2.
Sisters of St. John Bosco, St. John's Convent, 1101 Symes, 76574. Tel: 512-352-2802.

WACO. *Congregation of the Sisters of the Incarnate Word, C.C.V.I.*, P.O. Box 2589, 76702-2589. Sr. Rosemary Burke, C.C.V.I.
Daughters of Charity of St. Vincent De Paul, 2416 Colcord, 76707. Tel: 254-753-3817. Sisters 4. 213 Bonham Dr., 76643. Tel: 254-666-0611. Sisters 3.
Franciscan Sisters Daughters of Mercy. (Franciscanas Hijas de la Misericordia), 612 N. Third St., 76701. Tel: 817-753-5565. Sisters 4.
Sisters of Charity of the Incarnate Word, 717 Cardinal, 76712. Tel: 254-776-2707; Fax: 254-754-0133. Sr. Stephen Guiry, C.C.V.I.
Sisters of the Holy Cross, St. Mary's Convent, 224 N. 14th St., 76701. Tel: 254-756-0548.

[J] HOMES FOR THE AGED

WACO. *The Regis Retirement Home and St. Elizabeth Nursing Home*, 400 Austin Ave., P.O. Box 1909, 76703. Tel: 254-756-5441; Fax: 254-754-0133
For a complete listing, refer to the Special Care Facilities section.

[K] MISSION CENTERS

SOMERVILLE. *St. Ann Mission Center*, P.O. Box 367, 77879. Missionary Ecumenical. Sr. M. John DellaMorte, M.E., Supr. Kindergarten Students 25; Total Staff 3.

WACO. *St. Francis Mission Center*, 612 N. Third St., 76701. Tel: 817-753-5565. Franciscan Sisters Daughters of Mercy. Sr. Catherine Vallespir, F.H.M., Catechetical, Kindergarten & Nursery; Sr. Barbara Herrera, F.H.M., Supr. Total Staff 11. Sisters 4.

[L] RENEWAL CENTERS

BELTON. *Cedarbrake Renewal Center*, P.O. Box 58, 76513-0058. Tel: 254-780-2436; Fax: 254-780-2684.
E-mail: Cedarbrake@aol.com
Sr. Jean Burbo, I.H.M., Dir. Total in Residence 3; Total Staff 9.

[M] NEWMAN APOSTOLATE

AUSTIN. *University Catholic Center*, 2010 University Ave., 78705. Tel: 512-476-7351; Fax: 512-476-7377.
E-mail: catholic@utcatholic.org
Web site: http://www.utexas.edu/students/univcath
Serving the Catholic community at the University of Texas. Rev. Patrick E. Hensy, C.S.P., Dir. Campus Ministers: Rev. Bernard Campbell, C.S.P.; Bro. Robert Warren, F.M.S.; Dana Campbell, L.M.S.W., Admin.

BRENHAM. *Blinn College Catholic Student Union*, Blinn College, 77833. For Catholic students attending Blinn Jr. College. Rev. Msgr. Ralph A. Brennan; Mr. Daniel Schiller, Sponsor. Tel: 409-830-4417; Deacon William Januszewski, Campus Minister. Tel: 409-836-9329.

COLLEGE STATION. *St. Mary's Catholic Center*, 103 Nagle St., 77840. Tel: 409-846-5717.
E-mail: info@aggiecatholic.org
Web site: http://www.aggiecatholic.org
Campus ministry at Texas A & M University. Revs. Michael J. Sis; David A. Konderla; Deacon Bill Scott, Jr. Total in Residence 2; Total Staff 10.

SAN MARCOS. *Catholic Student Center*, 100 Concho St., 78666. Tel: 512-392-5925; Fax: 512-392-5922. Catholic Students attending Southwest Texas State University. Rev. Art Gramaje, C.M.F.

WACO. *Catholic Student Center at Baylor University*, 821 Speight Ave., P.O. Box 6060, 76706-6060. Tel: 254-757-0636.
E-mail: baylor-catholic@juno.com
For Catholic students attending Baylor University. Mr. Mervyn S. Pacheco, Dir., 4319 Cedar Mountain Dr., 76708. Tel: 254-757-0465.

[N] MISCELLANEOUS

AUSTIN. *Brothers of Holy Cross, South-West Province, Charitable Trust*, 3001 S. Congress Ave., #1046, 78704. Tel: 512-442-7856; Fax: 512-444-3133. Trustees: Bros. Richard Daly, C.S.C.; Harold Ehlinger, C.S.C., Chm.; Ralph Kuder, C.S.C.; William Nick, C.S.C.
Catholic Archives of Texas, N. Congress & W. 16th St., P.O. Box 13124, 78711-3124. Tel: 512-476-6296; Fax: 512-476-3715. Kinga L. Perzynska, Archivist; Susan Eason, Archives Asst. Historical collection of the Church in the Southwest and Texas from 1519.
Catholic Family Fraternal of Texas. KJZT, P.O. Box 1884, 78767-1844. Tel: 512-444-9586. Mrs. Geraldine Nekuza, Pres.; Loretta Shal, Vice Pres.
Catholic Southwest, 1625 Rutherford Ln., Bldg. D, 78754-5105. Patrick Foley, Ph.D., Editor; Jesus F. de la Teja, Ph.D., Mng. Editor.
Children's Hospital Foundation of Austin, 601 E. 15th St., 78701-1996. Tel: 512-324-8420; Fax: 512-324-8435.
E-mail: st-romain@dcnhs-ws.edu
Ms. Martha St. Romain, Contact Person.
Juan Diego Missionary Society, Inc., P.O. Box 67, 78762. Elias and Christina Limon, Dirs.
Ladies of Charity, 510 W. 26th St., 78705. Affiliated with the Ladies of Charity of the United States of America (LCSUA). Other Addresses: P.O. Drawer W, Bastrop, 78602. 104 Shannon Ln., Georgetown, 78628. 1005A S. Ann Blvd., Harker Heights, 76548. 2203 Lakeway Blvd., 78734. P.O. Box 23323, Waco, 76702-3302. Thrift stores are operated by the Ladies of Charity Associations in Austin, Bastrop, Harker Heights, Lakeway and Waco.
National Christ Child Society, 503 Vale St., 78746. Merlie Morales, Contact Person.
North Central Catholic School Corp., 13729 Research Blvd., #610-147, 78750. Tel: 512-219-8914.
E-mail: mara@bga.com
Web site: http://members.aol.com/nccschool/index.html
Mr. Gary Beam, Pres.
Our Lady's Family Center, 1815 E. Sixth St., P.O. Box 6453, 78762. Tel: 512-322-0632.
E-mail: ourlady@austinfreenet.com
Deacon Willie J. Cortez, Dir. Patients Assisted 200; Total Staff 2.
Road to Emmaus (Catholic Home for Girls of all Faiths), P.O. Box 9961, 78766. Tel: 512-502-0765. Joe & Dee Benante, Founders; Teresa Lin Nira, Dir.
The Seton Cove - A Spirituality Center, 3708 Crawford St., 78731. Total Staff 6.
Society of St. Vincent de Paul, 6503 Wolfcreek Pass, 78749-1825. Tel: 512-288-3370; Fax: 512-288-1926. Sr. Mary William Sullivan, Spiritual Advisor; Raymond DuPont, Pres.; Frederick L. Gale, Vice Pres.; Jeannine DuPont, Treasurer; Mary Johnson, Secretary; Bobby L. Sherry, Dir.
Southwest Austin Catholic School, Inc. dba St. Gabriel's Catholic School, 7800 MoPac, Ste. 310, 78759. Tel: 512-346-6097. Dr. C. Leonard Dolce, Chm.
Texas Catholic Conference, 1625 Rutherford Ln., Bldg. D, 78754-5105. Tel: 512-339-9882. Bro. Richard Daly, C.S.C., Exec. Dir.
Texas Catholic Historical Society, c/o Texas Catholic Conference,1625 Rutherford Ln. Bldg. D, 78704-5105. Roy Barkley, Ph.D., Pres.
Texas Conference of Catholic Health Facilities, 1625 Rutherford Ln., Bldg. D, 78754-5105. Tel: 512-339-1157; Fax: 512-339-8670. Rev. Msgr. William L. Broussard, Exec. Dir.
VESS, Volunteers for Educational and Social Services, 1625 Rutherford Ln., Bldg. D, 78754-5105. Tel: 512-339-7123; 1-800-771-5677.
Web site: vess.org
Michael G. Guerra, Dir.

LAGRANGE. *Catholic Union of Texas*, KJT, P.O. Box 297, 78945. Tel: 409-968-5877; Fax: 409-968-5823. Elo J. Goerig, Pres. KJT NEWS, official publication.

RELIGIOUS INSTITUTES OF MEN REPRESENTED IN THE DIOCESE

For further details refer to the corresponding bracketed number in the Religious Institutes of Men or Women section.

[0170]—*Basilian Fathers.* (Galveston-Houston, TX).—C.S.B.
[0600]—*Brothers of the Congregation of Holy Cross.* (Southwest Province).—C.S.C.
[0360]—*Claretian Missionaries.* (South Pasadena, CA).—C.M.F.
[0750]—*Congregation of Marian Hill Missionaries.* (Dearborn Heights, MI).—C.M.M.
[0480]—*Conventual Franciscans.* (Mt. Francis, IN).—O.F.M.Conv.
[0520]—*Franciscan Friars.* (Cincinnati Prov.).—O.F.M.
[0690]—*Jesuit Fathers and Brothers.* (Los Gatos, CA; Detroit, MI).—S.J.
[0770]—*Marist Brothers of the School.* (Bayonne, NJ).—F.M.S.
[0780]—*Marist Fathers.* (Washington, DC).—S.M.
[1110]—*Missionaries of the Sacred Heart.* (Irish Prov.).—M.S.C.
[0910]—*Oblates of Mary Immaculate.* (San Antonio, TX).—O.M.I.
[0430]—*Order of Preachers-Dominicans.* (New Orleans, LA).—O.P.
[1030]—*Paulist Fathers.* (Scarsdale, NY).—C.S.P.
[0610]—*Priests of the Congregation of Holy Cross.* (Southern Prov.).—C.S.C.
[1190]—*Salesians of Don Bosco.* (San Francisco Prov.).—S.D.B.
[1200]—*Society of the Divine Savior.* (Milwaukee, WI).—S.D.S.
[0560]—*Third Order Regular of Saint Francis.* (Waco, TX).—T.O.R.

RELIGIOUS INSTITUTES OF WOMEN REPRESENTED IN THE DIOCESE

[2190]—*Congregation of the Incarnate Word and Blessed Sacrament.* (Houston, TX).—C.V.I.
[0470]—*Congregation of the Sisters of Charity of the Incarnate Word.* (Houston, Texas).—C.C.V.I.
[0460]—*Congregation of the Sisters of Charity of the Incarnate Word.* (San Antonio, TX).—C.C.V.I.
[1920]—*Congregation of the Sisters of the Holy Cross.* (Notre Dame, IN).—C.S.C.
[]—*Cordi-Marian Sisters.* (San Antonio, TX).—M.C.M.
[0760]—*Daughters of Charity of St. Vincent de Paul.* (St. Louis, MO).—D.C.
[0850]—*Daughters of Mary Help of Christian.* (San Antonio, TX).—F.M.A.
[1070-13]—*Dominican Sisters.* (Adrian, MI).—O.P.
[1070-19]—*Dominican Sisters.* (Houston, TX).—O.P.
[1070-03]—*Dominican Sisters.* (Sinsinawa, WI).—O.P.
[1235]—*Franciscan Sisters Daughters of Our Lady of Mercy (Franciscanas Hijas de la Misericordia).* (U.S. delegation: Waco, TX).—F.H.M.
[2690]—*Missionary Catechists of Divine Providence.* (San Antonio, TX).—M.C.D.P.
[]—*Missionary Ecumenical.* (Rome, Italy).—M.E.
[2760]—*Missionary Sisters of the Immaculate Conception of the Mother of God.* (Paterson, NJ).—S.M.I.C.
[3760]—*Order of St. Clare.* (Brenham, TX).—O.S.C.
[3130]—*Our Lady of Victory Missionary Sisters.* (Huntington, IN).—O.L.V.M.
[2970]—*School Sisters of Notre Dame.* (St. Louis, MO).—S.S.N.D.
[]—*Secular Institute of Schoenstatt Sisters of Mary.* (Southern Prov., Rockport, TX).—I.S.S.M.
[1010]—*Sisters of Divine Providence.* (San Antonio, TX).—C.D.P.
[3000]—*Sisters of Notre Dame de Namur.* (Cincinnati, OH).—S.N.D.deN.
[1530]—*Sisters of St. Francis of the Congregation of Our Lady of Lourdes.* (Sylvania, OH).—O.S.F.
[1570]—*Sisters of St. Francis of the Holy Family.* (Dubuque, IA).—O.S.F.
[]—*Sisters of St. John Bosco.* (Taylor, TX).—S.J.B.
[2150]—*Sisters, Servants of the Immaculate Heart of Mary.* (Monroe, MI).—I.H.M.

NECROLOGY

† Gillgannon, Patrick, (Retired). —Died Sept. 11, 1997.
† Herledan, John F., (Retired). —Died Sept. 17, 1997.
† Lazek, Aleck, (Retired). —Died Aug. 16, 1997.

Diocese of Baker

(Dioecesis Bakeriensis)

Most Reverend

THOMAS J. CONNOLLY, D.D., J.C.D.

Bishop of Baker; ordained April 8, 1947; appointed May 4, 1971; consecrated June 30, 1971. *Res., P.O. Box 5999, Bend, OR, 97708.*

ESTABLISHED JUNE 19, 1903.

Square Miles 66,826.

Comprises the counties of Baker, Crook, Deschutes, Gilliam, Grant, Harney, Hood River, Jefferson, Klamath, Lake, Malheur, Morrow, Sherman, Umatilla, Union, Wallowa, Wasco and Wheeler in the State of Oregon.

For legal titles of parishes and diocesan institutions, consult the Chancery Office.

Diocesan Pastoral Office: P.O. Box 5999, Bend, OR, 97708. Tel.: 541-388-4004; Fax: 541-388-2566.

E-mail address: kentpunt@bendnet.com

STATISTICAL OVERVIEW

Personnel	
Bishop	1
Priests: Diocesan Active in Diocese	22
Priests: Active Outside Diocese	3
Priests: Diocesan in Foreign Missions	1
Priests: Retired, Sick or Absent	13
Number of Diocesan Priests	39
Religious Priests in Diocese	8
Extern Priests in Diocese	2
Ordinations:	
Diocesan Priests	1
Transitional Deacons	1
Permanent Deacons in Diocese	5
Total Sisters	34
Parishes	
Parishes	35
With Resident Pastor:	
Resident Diocesan Priests	22
Resident Religious Priests	6
Without Resident Pastor:	
Administered by Priests	7
Missions	29
Professional Ministry Personnel:	
Sisters	7
Lay Ministers	19
Welfare	
Catholic Hospitals	4
Total Assisted	231,609
Homes for the Aged	1
Total Assisted	130
Day Care and Extended Day Care Centers	3
Total Assisted	270
Educational	
Diocesan Students in Other Seminaries	5
Total Seminarians	5
Elementary Schools, Diocesan and Parish	3
Total Students	589
Catechesis/Religious Education:	
High School Students	926
Elementary Students	2,492
Total Students Under Catholic Instruction	4,012
Teachers in the Diocese:	
Sisters	4
Lay Teachers	42
Vital Statistics	
Receptions into the Church:	
Infant Baptism Totals	985
Adult Baptism Totals	146
Received into Full Communion	142
First Communions	766
Confirmations	348
Marriages:	
Catholic	151
Interfaith	102
Total Marriages	253
Deaths	275
Total Catholic Population	34,811
Total Population	413,900

Former Bishops—Rt. Rev. CHARLES J. O'REILLY, D.D., ord. June 29, 1890; appt. June 24, 1903; cons. Bishop of Baker City, Aug. 25, 1903; transferred to the See of Lincoln March 20, 1918; died Feb. 4, 1923.—Most Rev. LEO F. FAHEY, D.D., ord. May 29, 1926; appt. Titular Bishop of Ipsus and Coadjutor "cum jure successionis" March 13, 1948; cons. May 26, 1948; died March 31, 1950.—Most Rev. JOSEPH F. MCGRATH, D.D., assistant at the Pontifical Throne, Bishop of Baker City; ord. Dec. 21, 1895; appt. Dec. 21, 1918; cons. March 25, 1919; died April 12, 1950.—Most Rev. FRANCIS P. LEIPZIG, D.D., ord. April 14, 1920; appt. Bishop of Baker July 18, 1950; cons. Sept. 12, 1950; retired May 4, 1971; died Jan. 17, 1981.

Vicar General—Rev. Msgr. MATTHEW M. CROTTY, J.C.D.

Vicar of Canonical Affairs—Rev. W. THOMAS FAUCHER, J.C.L.

Chancellor and Secretary to the Bishop—MARY ANN DAVIS.

Diocesan Pastoral Office—Mailing Address: P.O. Box 5999, Bend, 97708. Tel: 541-388-4004; Fax: 541-388-2566. *911 S.E. Armour, Bend, 97702.*

Receptionist and Secretary—VIRGINIA MOHR.

Diocesan Tribunal—Tel: 541-388-4010.

Judicial Vicar and Chief Judge—Very Rev. W. THOMAS FAUCHER, J.C.L.

Judge—Rev. Msgr. MATTHEW M. CROTTY, J.C.D.

Defender of the Bond and Promoter of Justice—Rev. LEO F. WECKERLE, J.C.L.; Rev. MATTHEW PU, J.C.D.

Coordinator and Notary—DOLORES FRIBERG.

Council of Priests and Diocesan Consultors—Most Rev. THOMAS J. CONNOLLY, Pres., Ex Officio; Rev. JOSEPH KELBEL, Chm.; Revs. DENNIS J. STRACHOTA; CHARLES V. DREISBACH; JAMES RADLOFF; RICHARD O. FISCHER; ROBERT GREINER; W. THOMAS FAUCHER; Rev. Msgr. MATTHEW M. CROTTY, V.G.

Priestly Life and Ministry—Revs. RICHARD O. FISCHER; LEO F. WECKERLE; CHARLES V. DREISBACH.

Deans—Central: Rev. ROBERT SIMARD; Eastern: Rev. RAYMOND JARBOE; Northern: Rev. DENNIS STRACHOTA; Southern: Rev. CHARLES V. DREISBACH; Western: Rev. JOSEPH A. KELBEL.

Diocesan Offices and Directors

Board of Education—Most Rev. THOMAS J. CONNOLLY; Revs. RONALD E. MAAG; MARTIN HAGGINS, O.F.M.Cap.; W. RAYMOND JARBOE, Principals of Schools and Representatives from each Parish School Board.

Building Committee—Rev. Msgr. MATTHEW M. CROTTY; Revs. ROBERT E. SIMARD; RONALD E. MAAG.

Campus Ministry Apostolate—Rev. W. RAYMOND JARBOE, *829 S.W. Second Ave., Ontario, 97914.* Tel: 541-889-8469.

Catholic Services—MARGUERITE REED, *P.O. Box 563, Baker City, 97814.* Tel: 541-523-2902.

Church Property, Administration of—Most Rev. THOMAS J. CONNOLLY, D.D., Pres.; Rev. Msgr. MATTHEW M. CROTTY, Sec.; JOSEPH LA CASSE, Realtor.

DeSales Program of Adult Education—Direct Inq to: Tel: 800-488-0488. Direct Orders to: *St. An Messenger Press, 1615 Republic St., Cincinnati, OH, 45210.* Fax: 513-241-1197.

Diocesan Attorney—Vacant.

Diocesan Development Office—KENT PUNTENNEY, Dir., *P.O. Box 5999, Bend, 97708.* Tel: 541-388-4004.

Diocesan Finance Minister—MARY ANN DAVIS, Pastoral Office; KENT PUNTENNEY, Accountant.

Diocesan Financial Board—Rev. CHARLES V. DREISBACH; JAMES V. HURLEY; DAVID F. LINDLEY; JOSEPH LACASSE.

Diocesan Pastoral Council—BOB ASHLEY, Chm.; Most Rev. THOMAS J. CONNOLLY, Pres.; TONY BOCCHI, Vice Pres.; ROBERT ILOSKY, Treas. and Exec. Sec. Delegates from each Congregation of Sisters; delegates from each parish; and ex officio members.

Diocesan Superintendent of Schools—Sr. MARY CATHERINE PERKINS, O.P., *P.O. Box 5999, Bend, 97708.* Tel: 541-385-1865.

Director of Campaign for Human Development—Rev. RONALD E. MAAG, *St. Peter Church, P.O. Box 41, The Dalles, 97058.* Tel: 541-296-2026.

Director of Catholic Hospitals—Rev. TODD UNGER, *P.O. Box 786, Madras, 97741.* Tel: 541-475-2936.

Friends of the Catholic University of America—Rev. Msgr. WILLIAM S. STONE, *2633 S.W. Obsidian, No. 52, Redmond, 97756.* Tel: 541-548-6123.

Health and Retirement Board—Most Rev. THOMAS J. CONNOLLY, D.D., Pres.; Rev. Msgr. WILLIAM S. STONE, Chm.; Rev. TODD UNGER, Sec.-Treas.; Revs. FRANKLIN BUCKMAN; RAYMOND HOPP; CHARLES V. DREISBACH; Rev. Msgr. BERNARD A. KEATING.

Office of Worship and Spirituality—Rev. RAYMOND JARBOE, *829 S.W. 2nd Ave., Ontario, 97914.* Tel: 541-889-8469.

Natural Family Planning—PATRICIA PUNTENNEY, Dir., *P.O. Box 5999, Bend, 97708.* Tel: 541-383-8928; 388-4004.

Office of Faith Development and Ministry—Most Rev. THOMAS J. CONNOLLY, D.D., J.C.D., Chm. Directors: KEVIN SAUNDERS; DIANE SAUNDERS, *P.O. Box 9250, Bend, 97708. 911 S.E. Armour, Bend, 97702.* Tel: 541-388-3991.

Adult Education—Sr. M. CATHERINE PERKINS, O.P., Dir. Tel: 541-385-1865.

Office of Hispanic Ministry—Sr. MARIE VIANNEY BILGRIEN, Dir., *P.O. Box 823, Madras, 97741.* Tel: 541-475-2564.

Priests' Continuing Education Committee—Most Rev. THOMAS J. CONNOLLY; Revs. DENNIS J. STRACHOTA, Chm.; ROBERT GREINER; ROBERT C. IRWIN; JOSEPH KELBEL; RAYMOND JARBOE.

R.C.I.A. Office—Rev. DENNIS STRACHOTA, Dir., *800 S.E. Court Ave., Pendleton, 97801.* Tel: 541-276-3615.

Respect for Life Committee—KENT PUNTENNEY, Dir.

Diocesan Scout Director—TED YAROSH, *5160 S. Etna St., Klamath Falls, 97603.* Tel: 541-882-4611.

Vocations—Rev. RONALD E. MAAG, *St. Peter Church, P.O. Box 41, The Dalles, 97058.* Tel: 541-296-2026.

CLERGY, PARISHES, MISSIONS AND PAROCHIAL SCHOOLS

BAKER CITY
(County of Baker)

1—CATHEDRAL OF ST. FRANCIS DE SALES (1871), Rev. James P. Logan, Rector. Pastoral Assocs.: Carole Watt; Michelle Curtis; Mary Margaret Hansen; Lisa Ward, Parish Coord.
Res., 2235 First St., 97814. Tel: 541-523-4521; 523-6244. [CEM]
Catechesis/Religious Programs—Tamara Skidmore, D.R.E.
Students 110.
Missions—Halfway, St. Therese; Unity, St. Joseph's; North Powder, St. Anthony.

OUTSIDE BAKER CITY

Arlington, Gilliam Co., St. Francis (1931), Rev. Richard O. Fischer.
Mailing Address: P.O. Box 485, Condon, 97823. Tel: 541-384-5271.

Bend, Deschutes Co., St. Francis of Assisi (1904), Revs. Martin Haggins, O.F.M.Cap.; Michael Walsh, O.F.M.Cap.; Fintan Whelan, O.F.M.Cap.; Brian McKenna, O.F.M.Cap.; Sr. Patricia Rayburn, O.S.F., Pastoral Assoc.; Deacon Bob Walling; Franke Lanigan, Parish Admin.
Res., 409 N.W. Franklin, 97701. Tel: 541-382-3631; Fax: 541-385-8879.
School—(Grades PreK-8) 720 Bond St., 97701. Tel: 541-382-4701; Fax: 541-382-4701. Sr. Kathleen Cordes, S.H.C.J., Prin.
Lay Teachers 20; Students 243.
Day Care—.
Students 50.
Catechesis/Religious Programs—Tel: 541-382-3731. Sheila O'Connell-Rousell, D.R.E.
Students 280.

Burns, Harney Co., Holy Family (1899), Rev. Matthew C. Pu, Admin.
Res., 685 N. Fairview Ave., 97720. Tel: 541-573-2613; Fax: 541-573-3166.
Catechesis/Religious Programs—620 N. Egan Ave., 97720. Tel: 541-573-1147. Mary Lemos, D.R.E.
Students 155.
Missions—Drewsey, Our Lady of Loretto; Crane, St. Thomas.

Chiloquin, Klamath Co., Our Lady of Mt. Carmel (1927), Rev. Ronald J. Warren.
Res., 503 W. Chocktoot, P.O. Box 396, 97624. Tel: 541-783-2411.
Catechesis/Religious Programs—Students 24.
Mission—Bly, St. James the Apostle.

Condon, Gilliam Co., St. John's (1925), Rev. Richard O. Fischer.
Res., P.O. Box 485, 97823. Tel: 541-384-5271.
Catechesis/Religious Programs—Students 32.
Mission—Fossil, St. Catherine.

Dufur, Wasco Co., St. Alphonsus (1911), Rev. Anselm Fister, O.S.B., Admin.
Res., P.O. Box 395, 97021. Tel: 541-467-2580.
Mission—Maupin, St. Mary's.

Elgin, Union Co., St. Mary (1966). Attended by Our Lady of the Valley, La Grande. Deacon Joseph Garlitz.
Res., P.O. Box 97, 97827. Tel: 541-437-8101.
Catechesis/Religious Programs—Sharon Woody, D.R.E.
Students 20.

Enterprise, Wallowa Co., St. Katherine's (1923), Rev. Richard Saksons, O. Praem.
Res., 301 E. Garfield St., P.O. Box 370, 97828. Tel: 541-426-3043; Fax: 541-426-5975.
Parish Office: Tel: 541-426-4008.
Catechesis/Religious Programs—Vonnie Pottenger, D.R.E.
Students 90.
Mission—Wallowa, St. Pius X.

Heppner, Morrow Co., St. Patrick's (1887), Rev. Gerald W. Condon.
Res., 525 Gale St., P.O. Box 633, 97836. Tel: 541-676-9462.
Catechesis/Religious Programs—D.R.E.: Mike Armato; Kim Armato.
Students 48.

Hermiston, Umatilla Co., Our Lady of Angels (1910), Revs. Juan Turula, S.J.; George Nazareth; Kay Edwards, Parish Admin.
Res., 565 Hermiston Ave., 97838. Tel: 541-567-5812; Fax: 541-564-0933.
Catechesis/Religious Programs—Tel: 541-567-3825. Kay Stull, D.R.E.
Students 243.
Mission—Boardman, Our Lady of Guadalupe.

Hood River, Hood River Co., Immaculate Conception (1906), Revs. Joseph Kelbel; James F. Stephens; Lou DeSitter, Pastoral Assoc.
Res., 1501 Belmont Ave., P.O. Box 693, 97031. Tel: 541-386-3373; Fax: 541-386-1451. [CEM]
Catechesis/Religious Programs—Tel: 541-386-2527. D.R.E.: Maria Ramirez; Angie Bedell.
Students 270.

Ione, Morrow Co., St. William, Rev. Gerald W. Condon.
Mailing Address: P.O. Box 633, Heppner, 97836. Tel: 541-676-9462.
Church—110 Main St., 97843.
Catechesis/Religious Programs—Jeri Mc Elligott, D.R.E.
Students 28.

John Day, Grant Co., St. Elizabeth's (1939), Rev. Robert Van Sickler.
Res., 111 S.W. 2nd St., P.O. Box 189, 97845. Tel: 541-575-1459.
Catechesis/Religious Programs—Mary Ann Vidourek, D.R.E.
Students 17.
Missions—Monument, St. Ann; Seneca, St. Charles; Longcreek, St. Katherine.

Jordan Valley, Malheur Co., St. Bernard's (1915), Rev. Lawrence Kearney, Admin.
Res., P.O. Box 186, 97910. Tel: 541-586-2266.
Catechesis/Religious Programs—Lily Garrard, D.R.E.
Students 16.
Mission—Arock, Holy Family, Arock Rd., 97902.

Klamath Falls, Klamath Co., Sacred Heart (1904), Rev. Charles V. Dreisbach; Deacon P. Kenneth Morton, Pastoral Assoc.
Res., 815 High St., 97601. Tel: 541-884-4566; Fax: 541-882-0472.
Catechesis/Religious Programs—Tel: 541-882-4864. Vicki Bauer, D.R.E.
Students 200.

St. Pius Xth (1957), Rev. Franklin J. Buckman (ORG) Admin. Pastoral Ministers: Karen Marie Bickett; Carol Wilson.
Res., 4880 Bristol Ave., 97603. Tel: 541-884-4242. [CEM]
Catechesis/Religious Programs—Tel: 541-882-7593. Deacon James R. Roy, D.R.E.
Students 209.

La Grande, Union Co., Our Lady of the Valley (1914). (Under the title of the Immaculate Conception). Rev. Louis Henry Albrecht; Margaret Irish, Admin. Asst.
Parish Office: 1002 L Ave., 97850. Tel: 541-963-7341.
Res., 1101 4th St., 97850. Tel: 541-963-0006.
Catechesis/Religious Programs—Charlene Storoe, D.R.E.
Students 124.

La Pine, Deschutes Co., Holy Redeemer (1983), Rev. James A. Radloff.
Res., P.O. Box 299, 97739. Tel: 541-536-3571; Fax: 541-536-5647.
Catechesis/Religious Programs—Students 40.
Missions—Gilchrist, Our Lady of the Snows; Christmas Valley, Holy Family.
Station—Sun River.

Lakeview, Lake Co., St. Patrick's (1912), Rev. Raymond Hopp.
Res., 12 G St. N., P.O. Drawer 29, 97630. Tel: 541-947-2741; Fax: 541-947-2756.
Catechesis/Religious Programs—185 S. G St., Tel: 541-947-3875.
Students 128.
Missions—Adel, St. Richard; Plush, St. Thomas; Paisley, St. John the Apostle.

Madras, Jefferson Co., St. Patrick's (1955), Rev. Todd J. Unger.
Res., 341 S.W. J St., P.O. Box 786, 97741. Tel: 541-475-2936; Fax: 541-475-2444.
Catechesis/Religious Programs—Tel: 541-475-2444. D.R.E.: Barbara Manning; Elouise Kirsch.
Students 229.
Mission—Warm Springs, Jefferson Co., Blessed Kateri Tekakwitha. (Indian Reservation) P.O. Box 764, Warm Springs, 97761. Tel: 541-553-1235. Sr. Pauline Igoe, O.P., Dir. Native American Affairs.

Merrill, Klamath Co., St. Augustine (1939). Unassigned.
Res., 905 E. Front St., P.O. Box 340, 97633. Tel: 541-798-5823.
Catechesis/Religious Programs—Tricia Plass, D.R.E.
Students 125.
Mission—Bonanza, St. Frances Cabrini, Tel: 541-545-6602.
Catechesis/Religious Programs—Students 22.

Milton Freewater, Umatilla Co., St. Francis of Assisi (1940), Rev. C. H. Gillen, Admin.
Res., 925 Vining, 97862. Tel: 541-938-5436.
Catechesis/Religious Programs—Students 34.
Mission—Athena, Sacred Heart, 5th St. & College St., Athena, 97813.

Nyssa, Malheur Co., St. Bridget of Kildare (1951), Rev. Robert M. Greiner.
Res., 504 Locust, 97913-3235. Tel: 541-372-3133.
Catechesis/Religious Programs—Students 100.
Mission—Adrian, Our Lady of Guadalupe. 2nd St. & Owyhee St.

Ontario, Malheur Co., Blessed Sacrament (1911), Rev. W. Raymond Jarboe. Pastoral Assocs.: Sr. Mary Ellen Robinson S.N.J.M.; Mrs. Francis A. Schaffer.
Res., 829 S.W. Second Ave., 97914-2695. Tel: 541-889-8469; Fax: 541-889-8483.
School—Saint Peter, (Grades K-8) 98 S.W. Ninth St., 97914. Tel: 541-889-7363; Fax: 541-889-2852. Sr. Linda Riggers, S.N.J.M., Prin.
Lay Teachers 9; Students 130.
Catechesis/Religious Programs—Tel: 541-889-8404. D.R.E.: Maria Reed; Tim Cables.
Students 195.
Mission—Huntington, St. Joachim, 455 Lincoln Ave., Huntington, 97907. [CEM]

Pendleton, Umatilla Co., St. Andrew's Indian Mission (1847), Rev. Michael J. Fitzpatrick, S.J. Pastoral Assocs.: Faydeena Luke; Josephine Lavadour.
Res., 48022 St. Andrews Rd., 97801. Tel: 541-276-6155. [CEM]
Catechesis/Religious Programs—Tel: 541-276-0767. Lillian Moses, D.R.E.
Students 38.

St. Mary's (1902), Revs. Dennis Strachota; Robert C. Irwin.
Res., 800 S.E. Court Ave., 97801. Tel: 541-276-3615; Fax: 541-276-7484. [CEM]
Catechesis/Religious Programs—Tel: 541-276-6163. Mrs. Darlene Ledbetter, D.R.E.
Students 273.

Pilot Rock, Umatilla Co., St. Helen (1930). Attended by St. Mary's, Pendleton.
Res., 740 S.W. Birch, P.O. Box V, 97868. Tel: 541-443-3151.
Catechesis/Religious Programs—Students 38.

Prineville, Crook Co., St. Joseph's (1943), Rev. Robert E. Simard.
Res., 150 E. First, P.O. Box 338, 97754. Tel: 541-447-6475.
Catechesis/Religious Programs—200 E. First St., P.O. Box 721, 97754. Tel: 541-447-1227. D.R.E.: Krista Lucas; Denise Vargas; Lisa Elmore.
Students 71.

Redmond, Deschutes Co., St. Thomas (1941), Rev. Leo F. Weckerle.
Res., 526 S. 12th, P.O. Box 247, 97756. Tel: 541-923-3390; Fax: 541-548-6630.
Catechesis/Religious Programs—535 S. 11th St., 97756. Tel: 541-923-0597. Mary Lehnertz, D.R.E.
Students 190.

Sisters, Deschutes Co., St. Edward (1984), Rev. W. Thomas Faucher.
Res., 68817 Trinity Way, P.O. Box 489, 97759-0489. Tel: 541-549-0751 (Rectory); 549-9391 (Office); Fax: 541-549-9391.
Catechesis/Religious Programs—Diane Saunders, D.R.E.
Students 65.

The Dalles, Wasco Co., St. Peter's (1848), Rev. Ronald E. Maag.
Res., 1222 W. 10th St., P.O. Box 41, 97058. Tel: 541-296-2026; Fax: 541-296-8634. [CEM]
School—St. Mary, (Grades PreK-7) 1112 Cherry Heights Rd., Tel: 541-296-6004; Fax: 541-296-5834. Stephanie Ritchie, Prin.
Lay Teachers 13; Students 216.
Catechesis/Religious Programs—1111 W. 10th, P.O. Box 41, 97058. Tel: 541-296-3610; Fax: 541-296-5835. Allen Zaugg, D.R.E.
Students 40.

Union, Union Co., Sacred Heart (1905). Attended by Our Lady of the Valley, La Grande.
Church—340 S. 10th St., P.O. Box 473, 97883. Tel: 541-562-6285.
Catechesis/Religious Programs—Willard Bertrand, D.R.E.
Students 10.

Vale, Malheur Co., St. Patrick's (1946), Rev. Lawrence C. Bower.
Res., P.O. Box J, 97918. Tel: 541-473-3906.

Catechesis/Religious Programs—Tel: 541-473-3848. D.R.E.: Audrey Erstrom; Jim Arritola.
Students 65.
Mission—Juntura, St. Charles.
Station—Harper, St. John the Beloved.

Wasco, Sherman Co., St. Mary's (1954), Rev. Anselm Fister, O.S.B.
Res., 807 Barnett St., P.O. Box 14, 97065. Tel: 541-442-5496.
Catechesis/Religious Programs—D.R.E.: Sandy MacNab; Mary Anne MacNab.
Students 26.
Missions—Antelope, St. Mary's; Grass Valley, St. John the Baptist.

Chaplains of Public Institutions

PENDLETON. *Eastern Oregon Correctional Institution.* Vacant.
Eastern Oregon State Hospital. Vacant. St. Mary, 800 S.E. Court, 97801.

Special Assignment:
Reverend Monsignors—
Crotty, Matthew M., Vicar Gen., 1011 S.E. 15th, #31, Bend, OR 97702

On Duty Outside the Diocese:
Reverend Fathers—
Hickie, J. Noel, Sacred Heart General Hospital, 1305 Willagillespie Rd., Eugene, OR 97401
Kiely, Cornelius, Iglesia La Immaculada Concepcion, Puerto Lopez, Manabi, Ecuador
Miles, Michael, Holy Transformation Monastery, P.O. Box 217, Redwood Valley, CA 95470
Reeves, Joseph, 12223 N.W. Cornell Rd., Apt. 306, Portland, OR 97229

Absent on Leave:
Reverend Fathers—
Holmes, Dennis
Kirby, Larry Joseph

Retired:
Reverend Monsignors—
Beard, Raymond, P.O. Box 57, Athena, OR 97813
Keating, Bernard A., P.O. Box 861, Redmond, OR 97756
Phelan, John F., 26 Cedarwood Ave., Laughboy, Co. Kilkenney, Ireland
Stone, William S., 2633 S.W. Obsidian, #52, Redmond, OR 97756
Reverend Fathers—
Collins, Timothy, Pendleton House, Avondale House, Kilrush Rd., Ennis, Co. Clare, Ireland
Conway, Richard J., 950 Pomona, #166, The Dalles, OR 97058
Cribbin, Austin J., 220 Newcastle Rd., Klamath Falls, OR 97601
Fisher, A. J., 1200 W. Dimond #14105, Anchorage, AK 99515
Quigley, Martin J., 3564 E. 2nd, Sp. 73, The Dalles, OR 97058
Scanlon, Thomas R., P.O. Box 695, The Dalles, OR 97058

INSTITUTIONS LOCATED IN THE DIOCESE

[A] GENERAL HOSPITALS

BAKER CITY. *St. Elizabeth Health Services, Inc.*, 3325 Pocahontas Rd., 97814. Tel: 541-523-6461 (Hospital); 523-4452 (Nursing Care); Fax: 541-523-1794
For a complete listing, refer to the Hospitals section.

BEND. *St. Charles Medical Center*, 2500 N.E. Neff Rd., 97701. Tel: 541-382-4321; Fax: 541-388-7723
For a complete listing, refer to the Hospitals section.

ONTARIO. *The Dominican Sisters of Ontario, Inc. dba Holy Rosary Medical Center*, 351 S.W. Ninth St., 97914. Tel: 541-881-7000; Fax: 541-881-7184
For a complete listing, refer to the Hospitals section.

PENDLETON. *St. Anthony Hospital*, 1601 S.E. Court Ave., 97801. Tel: 541-276-5121.
E-mail: kuhl@chiwest.com
For a complete listing, refer to the Hospitals section.

[B] CONVENTS AND RESIDENCES FOR SISTERS

BAKER CITY. *St. Clare Convent*, 3030 A St., 97814. Tel: 541-523-6770. Sisters 2.

LA PINE. *Solitary Hermitesses.* (Hermit Colony), P.O. Box 657, 97739. Members 2.

[C] MISCELLANEOUS

BEND. *Saint Vincent de Paul Society - District Council of Central Oregon*, P.O. Box 1011, 97709. Tel: 541-389-3325. Wes Colbo, Pres.; Judy Mackel, Exec. Dir. Tel: 541-389-5117.
Bend Social Services Conference. Tel: 541-389-6643.

THE DALLES. *Saint Vincent de Paul Society - The Dalles Conference*, 315 W. 3rd St., 97058. Tel: 541-298-7837. David Lutgens, Chm.

LA PINE. *La Pine Conference*, P.O. Box 1008, 97739. Tel: 541-536-1956. Arlene Mura, Pres.

PRINEVILLE. *Saint Vincent de Paul Society - Prineville Conference*, 990 S.E. 2nd St., 97754. Tel: 541-447-4565. John Stolitz, Pres.

REDMOND. *Saint Vincent de Paul Society - Redmond Conference*, 1114 S.W. Evergreen, 97756. Tel: 541-923-5264. Yvonne Light, Pres.

RELIGIOUS INSTITUTES OF MEN REPRESENTED IN THE DIOCESE

For futher details refer to the corresponding bracketed number in the Religious Institutes of Men or Women section.

[0200]—*Benedictine Monks.* (Benet Hills, CA).—O.S.B.
[0900]—*Canons Regular of Premontre, England.*—O. Praem.
[0470]—*The Capuchin Friars.*—O.F.M.Cap.
[0690]—*Jesuit Fathers and Brothers.* (California, Oregon Provs.).—S.J.
[0430]—*Order of Preachers (Dominicans).*—O.P.

RELIGIOUS INSTITUTES OF WOMEN REPRESENTED IN THE DIOCESE

[1070-25]—*Dominican Sisters of Kenosha, WI.*—O.P.
[1070-03]—*Dominican Sisters of Sinsinawa, WI.*—O.P.
[1070-20]—*Dominican Sisters of St. Thomas Aquinas.*—O.P.
[2470]—*Maryknoll Sisters of St. Dominic.*—M.M.
[2970]—*School Sisters of Notre Dame.*—S.S.N.D.
[3000]—*Sisters of Notre Dame de Namur.*—S.N.D.deN.
[1630]—*Sisters of St. Francis of Penance and Christian Charity.*—O.S.F.
[1650]—*Sisters of St. Francis of Philadelphia.*—O.S.F.
[3830]—*Sisters of St. Joseph.*—C.S.J.
[3960]—*Sisters of St. Mary of Oregon.*—S.S.M.O.
[1990]—*Sisters of the Holy Names of Jesus and Mary.*—S.N.J.M.
[4060]—*Society of the Holy Child Jesus.*—S.H.C.J.

NECROLOGY

† Baumgartner, John, (Retired). —Died Feb. 9, 1997.

Archdiocese of Baltimore

(Archidioecesis Baltimorensis)

His Eminence

WILLIAM CARDINAL KEELER, D.D. J.C.D.

Archbishop of Baltimore; ordained July 17, 1955; appointed Titular Bishop of Ulcinium and Auxiliary Bishop of Harrisburg July 24, 1979; ordained Bishop September 21, 1979; appointed Bishop of Harrisburg November 10, 1983; installed January 4, 1984; appointed Archbishop of Baltimore April 6, 1989; installed as Fourteenth Archbishop of Baltimore May 23, 1989; created Cardinal Priest November 26, 1994. *Office: 320 Cathedral St., Baltimore, MD, 21201.* Tel.: 410-547-5437.

Most Reverend

WILLIAM DONALD BORDERS, D.D.

Retired Archbishop of Baltimore; ordained May 18, 1940; appointed Bishop of Orlando May 2, 1968; consecrated June 14, 1968; appointed Archbishop of Baltimore March 25, 1974; installed June 26, 1974; retired April 6, 1989. *Office: 320 Cathedral St., Baltimore, MD, 21201.* Tel.: 410-547-5439.

Most Reverend

P. FRANCIS MURPHY, D.D., V.G.

Auxiliary Bishop of Baltimore, Western Vicar and Titular Bishop of Tacarata; ordained December 20, 1958; ordained Bishop February 29, 1976. *Office: 320 Cathedral St., Baltimore, MD, 21201.* Tel.: 410-547-5447; Fax: 410-727-5432.

Most Reverend

WILLIAM C. NEWMAN, D.D., V.G.

Auxiliary Bishop of Baltimore, Eastern Vicar and Titular Bishop of Numluli; ordained May 29, 1954; ordained Bishop July 2, 1984. *Office: 320 Cathedral St., Baltimore, MD, 21201.* Tel.: 410-547-5438. *Res., 5300 N. Charles St., Baltimore, MD.*

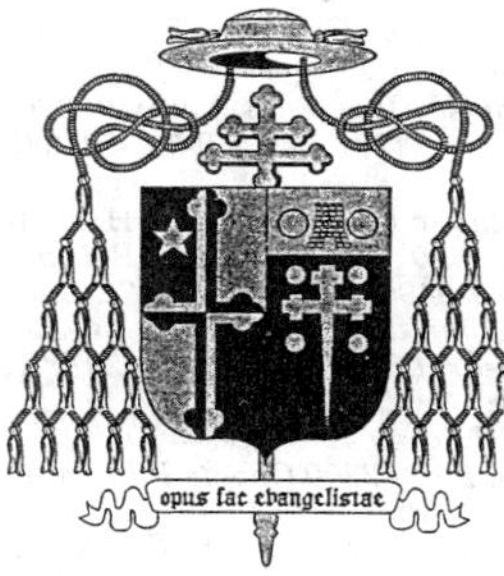

Chancery Office: 320 Cathedral St., Baltimore, MD, 21201. Tel.: 410-547-5446.

Web site address: http://www.archbalt.org

E-mail address: facts@archbalt.org

Most Reverend

GORDON D. BENNETT, S.J.

Auxiliary Bishop of Baltimore and Titular Bishop of Nesqually; ordained June 14, 1975; ordained Bishop March 3, 1998. *Office: 320 Cathedral St., Baltimore, MD, 21201.*

ESTABLISHED A DIOCESE NOVEMBER 6, 1789; ESTABLISHED AN ARCHDIOCESE APRIL 8, 1808.

Square Miles 4,801.

Comprises the City of Baltimore and Allegany, Anne Arundel, Baltimore, Carroll, Frederick, Garrett, Harford, Howard and Washington Counties.

By a Decree of the Sacred Congregation of the Propaganda, July 19, 1858, approved by His Holiness, Pius IX, July 25, 1858, "Prerogative of Place" was conferred on the Archdiocese of Baltimore. By the explicit words of said decree of the Holy See, the Archbishop of Baltimore takes precedence over all Archbishops of the United States (not Cardinals) in Councils, gatherings and meetings of whatever kind of the Hierarchy (in concillis, coetibus et comitiis quibuscumque) regardless of the seniority of other Archbishops in promotion or ordination. Decree signed by Cardinal Barnabo, August 15, 1858.

For legal titles of parishes and archdiocesan institutions, consult the Chancery Office.

STATISTICAL OVERVIEW

Personnel	
Cardinal	1
Retired Archbishops	1
Auxiliary Bishops	2
Priests: Diocesan Active in Diocese	207
Priests: Active Outside Diocese	14
Priests: Retired, Sick or Absent	71
Number of Diocesan Priests	292
Religious Priests in Diocese	250
Extern Priests in Diocese	6
Ordinations:	
Religious Priests	2
Transitional Deacons	6
Permanent Deacons in Diocese	175
Total Brothers	73
Total Sisters	1,362
Parishes	
Parishes	155
With Resident Pastor:	
Resident Diocesan Priests	111
Resident Religious Priests	27
Without Resident Pastor:	
Administered by Priests	12
Administered by Women Religious	5
Missions	7
Pastoral Centers	3
New Parishes Created	2
Closed Parishes	3
Professional Ministry Personnel:	
Brothers	7
Sisters	69
Lay Ministers	169
Welfare	
Catholic Hospitals	5
Total Assisted	1,079,584
Homes for the Aged	18
Total Assisted	1,769
Residential Care of Children	3
Total Assisted	612
Day Care and Extended Day Care Centers	9
Total Assisted	2,048
Specialized Homes	6
Total Assisted	1,548
Special Centers for Social Services	29
Total Assisted	895,862
Residential Care of Disabled	4
Total Assisted	379
Educational	
Seminaries, Diocesan	2
Students from This Diocese	25
Students from Other Diocese	202
Diocesan Students in Other Seminaries	12
Total Seminarians	37
Colleges and Universities	3
Total Students	11,150
High Schools, Diocesan and Parish	9
Total Students	3,588
High Schools, Private	13
Total Students	7,236
Elementary Schools, Diocesan and Parish	67
Total Students	22,915
Elementary Schools, Private	6
Total Students	2,051
Non-residential Schools for the Disabled	5
Total Students	336
Catechesis/Religious Education:	
High School Students	4,499
Elementary Students	32,905
Total Students Under Catholic Instruction	84,717
Teachers in the Diocese:	
Priests	67
Scholastics	3
Brothers	26
Sisters	156
Lay Teachers	2,615
Vital Statistics	
Receptions into the Church:	
Infant Baptism Totals	8,475
Adult Baptism Totals	659
Received into Full Communion	1,237
First Communions	8,280
Confirmations	5,716
Marriages:	
Catholic	1,601
Interfaith	1,089
Total Marriages	2,690
Deaths	5,188
Total Catholic Population	487,499
Total Population	2,845,181

Former Bishops—Most Rev. JOHN CARROLL, D.D., cons. August 15, 1790; Archbishop, April 8, 1808; died Dec. 3, 1815.—Most Rev. LEONARD NEALE, D.D., cons. Coadjutor, Dec. 7, 1800; acceded Dec. 3, 1815; died June 18, 1817.—Most Rev. AMBROSE MARECHAL, S.S., D.D., cons. Dec. 14, 1817; died Jan. 29, 1828.—Most Rev. JAMES WHITFIELD, D.D., cons. May 25, 1828; died Oct. 19, 1834.—Most Rev. SAMUEL ECCLESTON, S.S., D.D., cons. Sept. 14, 1834; died April 22, 1851.—Most Rev. FRANCIS PATRICK KENRICK, D.D., cons. June 6, 1830; Coadjutor Bishop of Philadelphia; promoted to Aug. 19, 1851; died July 8, 1863.—Most Rev. MARTIN JOHN SPALDING, D.D., cons. Sept. 10, 1848; Coadjutor Bishop of Louisville; promoted to May 6, 1864; died Feb. 7, 1872.—Most Rev. JAMES ROOSEVELT BAYLEY, D.D., cons. Oct. 30, 1853; Bishop of Newark; promoted to July 30, 1872; died Oct. 3, 1877.—His Eminence JAMES CARDINAL GIBBONS, cons. Vicar Apostolic of North Carolina, Aug. 16, 1868; transferred to See of Richmond, July 30, 1872; promoted to See of Baltimore, Oct. 3, 1877; created Cardinal Priest of S. Maria in Trastevere, June 7, 1886; died March 24, 1921.—Most Rev. MICHAEL J. CURLEY, D.D., cons. Bishop of St. Augustine, June 30, 1914; promoted to Aug. 10, 1921; died May 16, 1947.—Most Rev. FRANCIS P. KEOUGH, D.D., cons. Bishop of Providence, May 22, 1934; promoted to Nov. 29, 1947; died Dec. 8, 1961.—His Eminence LAWRENCE CARDINAL SHEHAN, cons. Auxiliary Bishop of Baltimore, Dec. 12, 1945; transferred to Diocese of Bridgeport, Aug. 25, 1953; appt. Coadjutor Archbishop of Baltimore, July 10, 1961; acceded Dec. 8, 1961; created

Cardinal Priest of S. Clemente, Feb. 22, 1965; retired March 25, 1974; died Aug. 26, 1984.—Most Rev. WILLIAM DONALD BORDERS, D.D., appt. Bishop of Orlando, May 2, 1968; cons. June 14, 1968; promoted to March 25, 1974; installed June 26, 1974; retired April 6, 1989.

Vicars General—Most Rev. P. FRANCIS MURPHY, D.D., V.G.; Most Rev. WILLIAM C. NEWMAN, D.D., V.G.; Rev. Msgr. W. FRANCIS MALOOLY, V.G.

Archbishop, Office of the—Rev. JOHN B. WARD, Sec. to the Cardinal. Tel: 410-547-5303., *320 Cathedral St., Baltimore, 21201.* Tel: 410-547-5437; Fax: 410-727-8234.

Chancery Office—320 Cathedral St., Baltimore, 21201. Tel: 410-547-5446; Fax: 410-727-8234. Office Hours: Mon.-Fri. 9-5; Closed holidays.

Chancellor—Rev. Msgr. W. FRANCIS MALOOLY, V.G.; Rev. Msgr. JEREMIAH F. KENNEY, Vice Chancellor; Rev. JOHN B. WARD, Asst. Chancellor.

Consultors—Most Rev. P. FRANCIS MURPHY; Most Rev. WILLIAM C. NEWMAN; Rev. Msgr. PAUL G. COOK; Rev. Msgr. ROBERT ARMSTRONG; Rev. Msgr. W. FRANCIS MALOOLY; Rev. Msgr. JAMES MCGOVERN; Rev. Msgr. GEORGE MOELLER; Rev. Msgr. G. MICHAEL SCHLEUPNER; Rev. Msgr. EDWARD F. STAUB; Rev. Msgr. VICTOR GALEONE; Rev. Msgr. ARTHUR VALENZANO.

Eastern Vicar, Office of the—Most Rev. WILLIAM C. NEWMAN, D.D., V.G., Vicar; Sr. EDITHANN KANE, S.N.D., Admin. Asst., *320 Cathedral St., Baltimore, 21201.* Tel: 410-547-5438; Fax: 410-727-5432.

Ecclesiastical Court in Equity—

Chief Judge and Moderator—Rev. Msgr. JEREMIAH F. KENNEY, J.V.

Judges in Equity—Honorables WILSON K. BARNES; J. HAROLD GRADY; JAMES A. PERROTT; ROBERT A. WATTS.

Interdiocesan Tribunal of Appeals of the Province of Baltimore—320 Cathedral St., Baltimore, 21201. Tel: 410-576-6924.

Judicial Vicar—Rev. Msgr. JEREMIAH F. KENNEY, J.V.

Interdiocesan Judges—Rev. Msgr. JOHN P. HANNAN; Rev. Msgr. CHARLES A. KELLY; Rev. Msgr. JOSEPH REBMAN; Rev. Msgr. PAUL J. SCHIERSE; Rev. Msgr. THOMAS F. SHREVE; Revs. FREDERICK P. ANNIE; WILLIAM J. DALE; EMIL DOBOSZ; FREDERICK J. FEUSAHRENS; GEORGE J. GRIFFIN; CHRISTIAN J. HAYDINGER; MARK R. LANE; JOHN S. LEDFORD; MARTIN MCGUILL; CHRISTOPHER P. MOORE; WILLIAM J. NOLTE; EUGENE S. OSTROWSKI; Revs. RICHARD A. REISSMANN; JOHN E. RIDGELL; J. ANTHONY WARNER; EUGENE J. WEBER; Deacon ROBERT GRAHAM.

Defenders of the Bond—Rt. Rev. BENEDICT MCDERMOTT, O.S.B.; Revs. CHARLES DILLINGHAM; ROBERT S. EMBILE; JAMES F. KAUFFMAN; RICHARD T. MOONEY; ANTHONY P. ROBERTS, S.J.; GILBERT J. SEITZ, JR.; JOHN B. WARD; GERALD T. WEYMES.

Notaries—Rev. CHRISTIAN T. CONNELLY; JOANNE D'SURNEY; BETTY I. HICKMAN; JOANN KUBASKO; BARBARA A. LEE; JEANNETTE LINDNER.

Metropolitan Tribunal—320 Cathedral St., Baltimore, 21201. Tel: 410-576-6920.

Cardinal's Delegate for Tribunal Canonical Administration—Rev. Msgr. JEREMIAH F. KENNEY, J.V.

Judicial Vicar—Rev. Msgr. G. MICHAEL SCHLEUPNER.

Adjutant Judicial Vicar—Rev. WILLIAM A. COLLINS.

Judges—Revs. JAMES A. BRENNAN, S.S.; MICHAEL J. CARRION; JAMES J. DITILLO, S.J.; THOMAS J. GOLUEKE; Deacons RAY BRITT; HARRY ST. A. O'NEILL.

Defenders of the Bond—Rev. Msgr. ROBERT A. ARMSTRONG; Rev. WILLIAM Q. SIMMS; LUCY LEE.

Promoter of Justice—Rev. Msgr. JOHN H. MCCALL.

Advocates and Procurators—Revs. BERNARD BAK; MICHAEL J. CALLAGHAN; PATRICK CARRION; E. JOSEPH COTE; RICHARD E. CRAMBLITT; MARTIN E. FEILD; WILLIAM FOLEY; JAMES HANNON; ROBERT HARTNETT; C. LOU MARTIN; EDWARD MILLER; KEVIN MUELLER; G. EUGENE NICKOL; MITCHELL ROZANSKI; RICHARD W. WOY; Deacons JOHN ABELL; ALPHONSE C. BANKARD; NICHOLAS FEURER; PATRICK GOLES; HERMAN GRABENSTEIN; JOHN MCKENNA; ROBERT LEHR; JOHN MARTELLE; WILLIAM NAIRN; STANLEY G. PIET; GERALD RAIBLE; JOHN J. RAFTER; FRANK RONGIONE; WALTER SHIPLEY; DANIEL STRETMATER; FREDDY WENDT; Sr. KATHERINE BELL, R.S.M.; Sr. REGINA BURGAN, S.S.N.D.; Sr. AGNESINE CONNORS, S.S.N.D.; Sr. MARIETTA CULHANE, O.S.F.; Sr. CAROL CZYZEWSKI, F.S.S.J.; Sr. FRANCES DEMARCO, R.S.M.; Sr. JOAN BASTRESS, I.H.M.; Sr. SUSAN ENGEL, M.H.S.H.; Sr. JOYCE HOLDEN, M.H.S.H.; Sr. ELIZABETH KANE, O.S.F.; Sr. PATRICIA MCALPIN, O.S.F.; Sr. JOAN MINELLA, S.S.N.D.; Sr. NANCY STILES, S.U.S.C.; MARY JOYCE BLESSING; C. DOUG KENNEY; ROBERT NICHOLSON; JOHN SAUER; JOHN KUTZ.

Notaries—PATRICIA FREUND; CHRISTINA MAKOWIECKI.

Receptionist—CLARA JULIAO.

Urban Vicar, Office of the—Rev. Msgr. ARTHUR W. BASTRESS, Interim Delegate for the Urban Vicariate, *320 Cathedral St., Baltimore, 21201.* Tel: 410-547-5452; Fax: 410-727-5432.

Western Vicar, Office of the—Most Rev. P. FRANCIS MURPHY, D.D., V.G., Vicar; Sr. DOLORES TODD, S.S.N.D., *320 Cathedral St., Baltimore, 21201.* Tel: 410-547-5447; Fax: 410-727-5432.

Archdiocesan Offices and Directors

African American Ministries, Archdiocesan Office of—THERESE WILSON FAVORS, Dir., *320 Cathedral St., Baltimore, 21201.* Tel: 410-625-8472; Fax: 410-727-5432.

Apostleship of Prayer—Rev. WILLIAM M. J. DRISCOLL, S.J., Dir., *Loyola College, 4501 N. Charles St., Baltimore, 21210.* Tel: 410-323-1010.

Archdiocesan Directory—PATTI MEDINGER, Editor, *320 Cathedral St., Baltimore, 21201.* Tel: 410-547-5324. Official directory of the Archdiocese of Baltimore. Published annually by *The Catholic Review.* 25 dollars per copy.

Archdiocesan Gay-Lesbian Outreach (AGLO)—Rev. JOSEPH HUGHES, Coord., *2034 Park Ave., Baltimore, 21217.* Tel: 410-728-2638.

Archdiocesan Pastoral Council—(See Pastoral Council Archdiocesan).

Archives-Archivist—Rev. PAUL THOMAS, *320 Cathedral St., Baltimore, 21201.* Tel: 410-547-5443 (By appointment).

Associated Catholic Charities, Inc.—HAROLD A. SMITH, Exec. Dir., *320 Cathedral St., Baltimore, 21201.* Tel: 410-547-5495; Fax: 410-752-7260.

Division of Community Services—ANGELO BOER, Dir., *320 Cathedral St., Baltimore, 21201.* Tel: 410-547-5540; Fax: 410-752-2714.

Division of Children's Services—

** FACETS, Inc.—2200 Choate Rd., Fallston, 21047.*

Basic and Transition Services—

Anna's House—P.O. Box 88, Bel Air, 21014. Tel: 410-638-1479; Fax: 410-638-1753.

Christopher Place Academy—709 E. Eager St., Baltimore, 21202. Tel: 410-576-0066; Fax: 410-576-0914.

Holden Hall—761 W. Hamburg St., Baltimore, 21230. Tel: 410-347-9830.

Information and Referral—19 W. Franklin St., Baltimore, 21201. Tel: 410-659-4020.

My Sister's Place—123 W. Mulberry St., Baltimore, 21201. Tel: 410-727-3523; Fax: 410-727-1611.

My Sister's Place Lodge—111 W. Mulberry St., Baltimore, 21201. Tel: 410-528-9002.

Our Daily Bread—411 Cathedral St., Baltimore, 21201. Tel: 410-659-4000; Fax: 410-659-4059.

Sarah's House—2013 20th St., Fort Meade, 20755. Tel: 410-551-7722; Fax: 410-551-7279.

Family Support Programs—

Auburne Center—610 Aldershot Rd., Baltimore, 21229. Tel: 410-744-8961.

Central Maryland Catholic Charities—16840 S. Seton Ave., Emmitsburg, 21727. Tel: 301-447-6740; Fax: 301-447-6325.

Domestic and International Adoption Services—19 W. Franklin St., Baltimore, 21201. Tel: 410-659-4050; Fax: 410-659-4060.

Up-County Family Support Center—303 W. Lincoln Ave., Emmitsburg, 21727. Tel: 301-447-2810; Fax: 301-447-6325.

Villa Louise Family Resource Center—900 S. Caton Ave., Baltimore, 21229. Tel: 410-368-2060.

Western Maryland Office—915 Bishop Walsh Rd., Cumberland, 21502. Tel: 301-777-8685.

Community Outreach Programs—

Hispanic Apostolate—430 S. Broadway, Baltimore, 21231. Tel: 410-522-2668; Fax: 410-675-1451.

Immigration Legal Services—430 S. Broadway, Baltimore, 21231. Tel: 410-534-8015; Fax: 410-675-1451.

Project SERVE—320 Cathedral St., Baltimore, 21201. Tel: 410-547-5540; Fax: 410-752-2714.

SHARE—808 Barkwood Ct., Linthicum, 21090. Tel: 410-636-9615; Fax: 410-636-9629.

Social Concerns—19 W. Franklin St., Baltimore, 21201. Tel: 410-659-4039; Fax: 410-659-4059.

Division of Housing Services—DALE MCARDLE, Dir., *320 Cathedral St., Baltimore, 21201.* Tel: 410-547-5544; Fax: 410-576-0987.

Division of Seniorlife Services—3320 Benson Ave., Baltimore, 21227. Tel: 410-646-6501. S. REBECCA GALLOWAY, Dir. To provide a range of residential and community services throughout the Archdiocese for both independent and frail elderly individuals, their families, parishes and organizations of older persons. To manage, direct or supervise the following programs:

Answers for the Aging—3320 Benson Ave., Baltimore, 21227. Tel: 410-646-0100. LORETTA AYDSIMPSON, Program Admin. Free information and referral service for seniors, their families and caregivers provides answers about community, health and housing services.

Social Casework for the Aging—430 South Broadway, Baltimore, 21231. Tel: 410-732-5000. WANDA WILSON, Program Admin. Information and assistance, counseling of elderly and their families, individual advocacy and case management services for the aged in the community, including adult protective services for those at risk of abuse, neglect or exploitation.

The Joseph Center—430 South Broadway, Baltimore, 21231. Tel: 410-732-5000. BARBARA PEARCE, Dir. Multipurpose center designated as focal point of services for the elderly residents (age 60 and over) of Southeast Baltimore. Social, educational, recreational, health and nutritional services are offered.

Senior Center Plus—430 South Broadway, Baltimore, 21231. Tel: 410-732-5000. BETTY KUTRIK, Coord. Provides opportunities for the frail elderly to take part in senior center activities, to develop friendships and to feel productive. The program, which includes breakfast and lunch and van transportation throughout Baltimore City, is available five days a week at a modest price.

Congregate Housing Services—430 South Broadway, Baltimore, 21231. Tel: 410-732-5000. WANDA WILSON, Program Admin. Provides meals, homemaker services, personal care and case management to eligible residents of Basilica Place, DePaul House, Village Oaks, Kirkwood House, St. Luke's Place, Memorial Apartments, St. Joachim House, Trinity House.

St. Croix House—105 E. West St., Baltimore, 21230. Tel: 410-625-5885. KATHERINE WHITE, Mgr. Group home for 10 individuals in South Baltimore. Twenty-four hour supervision is provided.

Hosanna House—2829 Lodge Farm Rd., Baltimore, 21219. Tel: 410-388-9030. SHARON SHARP, Mgr. Group home for 15 individuals in eastern Baltimore County. Twenty-four hour supervision is provided.

Emmanuel Homes—5013 Cloudburst Hill, Columbia, 21044. Tel: 410-995-5057. MELINDA MEUSHAW, Mgr. Three small group homes, each housing four residents, located in Columbia, Howard County.

St. Joachim House—3310 Benson Ave., Baltimore, 21227. Tel: 410-644-8269. PHYLLIS SEWELL, Mgr. On the campus of The Jenkins Community, offers 90 one-bedroom apartments. Services: pastoral care, convenience store, beauty salon/barber shop, Eating Together program, handicapped units, emergency call system, shuttle bus to St. Agnes HealthCare, bathing suite, community room, laundry facilities, computer center.

DePaul House—3300 Benson Ave., Baltimore, 21227. Tel: 410-644-8484. KRISTEN KINKOPF, Admin. Senior Living On the campus of The Jenkins Community, offers 109 one- and two-bedroom apartments. Services: pastoral care, library, convenience store, beauty salon/barber shop, Eating Together program, handicapped units, emergency call system, shuttle bus to St. Agnes HealthCare, community room, laundry facilities, computer center.

St. Ann Adult Day Services—3320 Benson Ave., Baltimore, 21227. Tel: 410-646-0320. KATE SIMONS, Dir. Licensed medical, adult day care provides a variety of health and social services in a protective group setting. Transportation available.

St. Elizabeth Rehabilitation and Nursing Center (formerly Jenkins Memorial Nursing Home)—3320 Benson Ave., Baltimore, 21227. Tel: 410-644-7100. PATRICIA SUPIK,162-bed skilled care nursing facility. Described more fully under Health Care Institutions.

St. Agnes ContinuCare—900 Caton Ave., Baltimore, 21229. Tel: 410-368-2725. DONNA YORKSTON, Admin. A transitional care unit for those needing rehabilitative or medical care following an acute hospital stay.

Boy Scouts—(See Catholic Youth Activities).

Campaign For Human Development, Archdiocese of Baltimore, Inc.—Rev. Msgr. WILLIAM F. BURKE, Dir., *320 Cathedral St., Baltimore, 21201.* Tel: 410-235-5136; 547-5446.

Campus Ministry (Newman Apostolate)—Rev. ROBERT E. ALBRIGHT, Dir., *7909 York Rd., Baltimore 21204.* Tel: 410-828-0622; Fax: 410-828-4825.

The Cathedral Foundation, Inc.—His Eminence WILLIAM H. KEELER, D.D., J.C.D., Pres. JAMES CURRAN, Vice Pres. Publishers of *The Catholic Review, Official Archdiocesan Directory, Catholic International* and *Cathedral Foundation Press. P.O. Box 777, Baltimore, 21203.* Tel: 410-547-5380.

Catholic Center Operations, Div. of—LOUIS WILLETT, Facilities Mgr., *320 Cathedral St., Baltimore, 21201.* Tel: 410-547-5312; Fax: 410-783-5993.

Catholic Charity Fund, Inc.—320 Cathedral St., Baltimore, 21201.

Catholic Education Ministries, Department of—RONALD J. VALENTI, Ph.D., Sec., *320 Cathedral St., Baltimore, 21201.* Tel: 410-547-5383; Fax: 410-547-5566.

Catholic Relief Services—MARY D'AMBROGI, Archdiocesan Dir., *320 Cathedral St., Baltimore, 21201.* Tel: 410-547-5548.

"The Catholic Review"—His Eminence WILLIAM H. KEELER, D.D., J.C.D., Publisher; DANIEL L. MEDINGER, Assoc. Publisher/Editor; CHRISTOPHER GAUL, Mng. Editor, *320 Cathedral St., P.O. Box 777, Baltimore, 21203.* Tel: 410-547-5380. Newspaper of the Archdiocese of Baltimore. Established 1913. Published every Wednesday by the Cathedral Foundation, Inc.

Catholic Schools Division—Dr. RONALD J. VALENTI, Supt., *320 Cathedral St., Catholic Center, Baltimore, 21201.* Tel: 410-547-5384; Fax: 410-547-5566.

Catholic Students Mission Crusade—See Propagation of the Faith.

Cemeteries, Office of—4300 Old Frederick Rd., Baltimore, 21229. Tel: 410-566-7770; Fax: 410-566-0709.

Censor Librorum—Rev. Msgr. CARROLL E. SATTERFIELD, S.T.D., *363 Homeland Southway, Apt. 1-A, Baltimore, 21212.* Tel: 410-433-6517.

Commission for Ecumenical and Inter-Religious Affairs—Rev. RICHARD H. TILLMAN, Chm., *10431 Twin Rivers Rd., Columbia, 21044.* Tel: 410-964-1425; Fax: 410-730-9253.

Controller, Division of the—PAUL J. AYD, C.P.A., Controller, *320 Cathedral St., Baltimore, 21201.* Tel: 410-547-5300; Fax: 410-332-8233.

Facilities Management, Division of—LOUIS F. BAIRD, Dir. LOUIS WILLETT, Facilities Mgr. ROBERT CLANCY, Facilities Specialist III, *320 Cathedral St., Baltimore, 21201.* Tel: 410-547-5366.

Family Life, Office of—320 Cathedral St., Baltimore, 21201. Tel: 410-547-5422; Fax: 410-347-7896.

Financial Administration, Board of—Rev. Msgr. G. MICHAEL SCHLEUPNER, Chm., *320 Cathedral St., Baltimore, 21201.*

Fiscal Services—PAUL J. AYD, Dir. & Controller, *320 Cathedral St., Baltimore, 21201.* Tel: 410-547-5300; Fax: 410-332-8233.

Fund Development, Department of—THOMAS J. SONNI, Exec. Dir. GEORGE E. REED, III, Sr. Devel. Officer; JANIS M. PECK, Devel. Assoc. LYNN BOERI, DP Spec. ELEANOR CONYERS, Gift Processing Clerk, *320 Cathedral St., Baltimore, 21201.* Tel: 410-547-5356.

Holy Childhood Association—Rev. Msgr. VICTOR GALEONE, Dir., *320 Cathedral St., Baltimore, 21201.*

Human Resources, Department of—SHEILA A. KELLY, S.P.H.R., Sec., *320 Cathedral St., Baltimore, 21201.* Tel: 410-547-5556; Fax: 410-234-2953.

Human Resource Services, Division of—MICHELLY B. MERRICK, P.H.R., Dir., *320 Cathedral St., Baltimore, 21201.* Tel: 410-547-5448; Fax: 410-234-2953.

Information Systems, Division of—JAMES B. TUCKER, Dir., *320 Cathedral St., Baltimore, 21201.* Tel: 410-547-5309; Fax: 410-332-8233.

Insurance, Division of—PETRA PHELPS, Dir., *320 Cathedral St., Baltimore, 21201.* Tel: 410-547-5551; Fax: 410-783-5993.

Insurance Committee—WILLIAM FRANEY, Chm. PETRA PHELPS, Sec., *320 Cathedral St., Baltimore, 21201.* Tel: 410-547-5317.

Lay Employees Retirement Board—JAYNE MCGEEHAN, Chm. PETRA PHELPS, Sec., *320 Cathedral St., Baltimore, 21201.* Tel: 410-547-5317.

League of the Little Flower—Rev. Msgr. PAUL G. COOK, Dir., *320 Cathedral St., Baltimore, 21201.* Tel: 410-547-5361.

Archdiocesan Office of Renew—WILLIAM H. JOHNSTON, *320 Cathedral St., Baltimore, 21201.* Tel: 410-547-5404; Fax: 410-347-7896.

Leadership Development, Division of—JAMES J. DEBOY, Dir., *320 Cathedral St., Baltimore, 21201.* Tel: 410-547-5419; Fax: 410-234-2953.

Management Services, Department of—Rev. Msgr. G. MICHAEL SCHLEUPNER, Sec., *320 Cathedral St., Baltimore, 21201.* Tel: 410-547-5587; Fax: 410-332-8233.

Maryland Catholic Conference—RICHARD J. DOWLING, ESQ., Exec. Dir., *188 Duke of Gloucester St., Annapolis, 21401.* Tel: 410-269-1155 (Bal.); 301-261-1979 (Wash.); Fax: 410-269-1790.

Pastoral Personnel Services, Division of—Revs. RICHARD WOY, Dir. J. BRUCE JARBOE, Assoc. Dir.; Ms. MARTHA SHETLER, Admin. Asst. VERONICA CAVANAUGH, Sec., *320 Cathedral St., Baltimore, 21201.* Tel: 410-547-5427; Fax: 410-234-2953.

Pastoral Council, Archdiocesan—320 Cathedral St., Baltimore, 21201. Tel: 410-547-5455.

Permanent Deacon Formation Program—Rev. RICHARD WOY, Dir., *320 Cathedral St., Baltimore, 21201.* Tel: 410-547-5557.

Planning and Council Services, Division of—Sr. ROSALIE MURPHY, S.N.D., Dir. JOSEPH C. BASKERVILLE, Archdiocesan Information Coord. JENNIFER N. SIEGMUND, Admin. Asst. Tel: 410-547-5455; Fax: 410-783-5993.

Priests Council—Rev. Msgr. ROBERT PASSARELLI; Rev. Msgr. ARTHUR VALENZANO; Revs. LLOYD AIKEN; WILLIAM AU; THOMAS BONDERENKO; PAUL BYRNES; DOMENIC CIERI; JAMES CONN, S.J.; DONALD FEST, S.S.J.; GERARD FRANCIK; DONALD GRZYMSKI, O.F.M.Conv.; PASCHAL MORLINO, O.S.B.; RICHARD PARKS; KEVIN SCHENNING; ALFRED E. SMITH; WILLIAM WATTERS, S.J., *320 Cathedral St., Baltimore, 21201.* Tel: 410-547-5455.

Ex-Officio—His Eminence WILLIAM H. KEELER, D.D., J.C.D.; Most Rev. P. FRANCIS MURPHY; Most Rev. WILLIAM C. NEWMAN; Rev. Msgr. ROBERT ARMSTRONG; Rev. Msgr. ARTHUR W. BASTRESS; Rev. Msgr. PAUL COOK; Rev. Msgr. G. MICHAEL SCHLEUPNER; Rev. Msgr. W. FRANCIS MALOOLY; Rev. Msgr. EDWARD STAUB; Rev. Msgr. JAMES O. MCGOVERN; Rev. Msgr. VICTOR GALEONE; Rev. Msgr. GEORGE B. MOELLER.

Priest Personnel Board—Rev. Msgr. VICTOR GALEONE, Chm.; Rev. Msgr. ARTHUR VALENZANO, Vice Chm.; Rev. Msgr. JOHN MCCALL; Rev. Msgr. JOSEPH LUCA; Rev. Msgr. JAMES MCGOVERN; Rev. Msgr. ROBERT PASSARELLI; Revs. WILLIAM AU; RICHARD BOZZELLI; WILLIAM FRANKIN; WAYNE FUNK; MITCHELL ROZANSKI.

Propagation of the Faith, Home and Foreign Mission Society—His Eminence WILLIAM H. KEELER, D.D., J.C.D., Gen. Dir.; Rev. Msgr. VICTOR GALEONE, Dir., *320 Cathedral St., Baltimore, 21201.* Tel: 410-576-6926; Fax: 410-576-6932.

Communications Office—320 Cathedral St., Baltimore, 21201. Tel: 410-547-5379; Fax: 410-625-8480. KRISTIN FOSTER, Communications Assoc.

Religious Education, Division of—CAROL A. AUGUSTINE, Interim Dir., *320 Cathedral St., Baltimore, 21201.* Tel: 410-547-5403; Fax: 410-347-7896.

Senior Priests Retirement Board—Rev. Msgr. JAMES MCGOVERN, Chm. PETRA PHELPS, Sec., *320 Cathedral St., Baltimore, 21201.* Tel: 410-547-5317.

Urban Affairs, Archdiocesan Office—320 Cathedral St., Baltimore, 21201. Tel: 410-547-5486; Fax: 410-727-5432.

St. Vincent de Paul Society—Baltimore Council: His Eminence WILLIAM H. KEELER, D.D., Honorary Pres.; Rev. Msgr. JEREMIAH F. KENNEY, Spiritual Dir. BARBARA H. MEDCALF, Pres. JOHN J. SCHIAVONE, Exec. Dir., *320 Cathedral St., Baltimore, 21201.* Tel: 410-547-5377.

Vocation Office—Rev. JAMES BARKER, Dir. Tel: 410-547-5426; Fax: 410-234-2953.

Youth and Young Ministry, Office of—MARK PACIONE, Dir., *320 Cathedral St., Baltimore, 21201.* Tel: 410-547-5372; Fax: 410-625-8481.

CLERGY, PARISHES, MISSIONS AND PAROCHIAL SCHOOLS

METROPOLITAN BALTIMORE
(Baltimore City and Baltimore County)

1—CATHEDRAL OF MARY OUR QUEEN (1954), Rev. Msgr. Robert A. Armstrong, Rector; Revs. Thomas Ryan; Lawrence Waudby. In res., Most Rev. William C. Newman, D.D.; Rev. Joseph F. Breighner.
Res., 5300 N. Charles St., 21210-2023. Tel: 410-433-8800; Fax: 410-433-4909.
School—111 Amberly Way, 21210. Tel: 410-433-6204; Fax: 410-433-7678. Sr. Eileen Weisman, S.S.N.D., Prin.
Lay Teachers 26; Students 440.
Catechesis/Religious Programs—115 Amberly Way, 21210. Tel: 410-435-1921.
Students 291.
Parish & Family Ministry—115 Amberly Way, 21210. Tel: 410-532-5269. Mrs. Sharon Buono, Dir.

2—BASILICA OF THE NATIONAL SHRINE OF THE ASSUMPTION OF THE BLESSED VIRGIN MARY (1806). (Co-Cathedral). Corporate Title: The Trustees of the Catholic Cathedral Church of Baltimore (The Basilica); Basilica of the Assumption Historic Trust, Inc. Established for the Preservation of the Basilica as a National Landmark of American Architecture. Cathedral & Mulberry St. Rev. Msgr. James V. Hobbs, Rector; Deacon Robert Oliver.
The Cardinal's Residence: 408 N. Charles St., 21201. Tel: 410-727-3566; Fax: 410-539-0407. His Eminence William Keeler, D.D., J.C.D.; Rev. Msgr. James V. Hobbs, Rector.; Parish Office: 408 N. Charles St., 21201. Tel: 410-727-3565.

3—ST. AGNES (Catonsville) (1852), Rev. Msgr. Francis W. Fortenbaugh, Pastor Emeritus; Rev. Msgr. Victor B. Galeone; Rev. William M. Mannion. In res., Rev. John Abrahams.
Res., 5422 Old Frederick Rd., 21229. Tel: 410-744-2900; Fax: 410-744-8304. [CEM]
School—603 St. Agnes Ln., 21229. Tel: 410-747-4070; Fax: 410-747-0138. Sr. Anne Mary Smith, I.H.M., Prin.
Sisters of the Immaculate Heart of Mary 5; Lay Teachers 21; Students 499.
Catechesis/Religious Programs—Tel: 410-747-9073. Sr. Patricia Anne Huesman, S.S.N.D., D.R.E.
Students 195.

4—THE NEW ALL SAINTS (1912) (African American), Rev. Donald A. Sterling; Deacons Paul D. Shelton; Malcolm Thompson.
Res., 4408 Liberty Heights Ave., 21207. Tel: 410-542-0445; Fax: 410-542-8852.
School—(Grades 4-8) 3510 Eldorado Ave., 21207. Tel: 410-664-9433; Fax: 410-664-9434. Dr. Phyllis Douglass, Prin.
Lay Teachers 8; Students 150.

5—ST. ALPHONSUS (1845) (Lithuanian), Revs. Thomas Bauernfeind, S.T.L.,J.C.L., Rector; John P. Barbernitz, Pastor Emeritus.
Res., 114 W. Saratoga St., 21201. Tel: 410-685-6090; Fax: 410-244-1670.
School—125 W. Saratoga St., 21201. Tel: 410-837-7310; Fax: 410-837-6948.
Lay Teachers 13; Students 200.

6—ST. AMBROSE (1907), Pastoral Ministry: Rev. John Pfannenstiel, O.F.M.Cap.; Deacon Watson Fulton.
Res., 4502 Park Heights Ave., 21215. Tel: 410-367-9918; Fax: 410-542-6056.
School—4506 Park Heights Ave., 21215. Tel: 410-664-2373; Fax: 410-664-0857. Ms. Joanne Rojas, Prin.
Lay Teachers 21; Students 310.
Outreach Center—3445 Park Heights Ave., 21215. Tel: 410-225-0870. Sr. Charmaine Krohe, S.S.N.D., Dir.

7—ST. ANDREW. Closed 1974. Parish records available at the Chancery. Tel: 410-547-5446.

8—ST. ANN (1873) (African American). Merged with St. Wenceslaus, Baltimore.
Res., 528 E. 22nd St., 21218. Tel: 410-235-8169; Fax: 410-675-5746. Deacon James E. Bee; Sr. Jeanne Barasha, S.S.N.D., Pastoral Admin.

9—ANNUNCIATION (1968), Rev. William P. Foley; Sr. Susan Engel, M.H.S.H., Pastoral Assoc.; Deacon Frederick Schoennagel, Jr.
Res., 5212 McCormick Ave., 21206. Tel: 410-866-4020; Fax: 410-866-2754.
Catechesis/Religious Programs—Tel: 410-866-4706. Mrs. Marylou Hare, D.R.E.
Students 194.

10—ST. ANTHONY OF PADUA (1884). Merged with Most Precious Blood. Revs. C. Lou Martin; Salvatore J. Livigni; David B. Kruse.
Res., 4414 Frankford Ave., 21206. Tel: 410-488-0400; Fax: 410-488-0032.
School—4410 Frankford Ave., 21206. Tel: 410-488-4848; Fax: 410-325-3766. Mrs. Mary Jo Hutson, Prin.
Lay Teachers 24; Students 367.

11—ASCENSION (Halethorpe) (1913), Rev. Manuel R. Roman; Rev. Msgr. Gerard W. Spraker, Pastor Emeritus; Revs. Conan H. Timoney, C.P.; Basil Stockmeyer, C.P.; Sr. Mary Catherine Lewandowski, O.S.F., Pastoral Assoc.
Res., 4603 Poplar Ave., 21227. Tel: 410-242-2292; Fax: 410-242-6807.
School—(Grades PreK-8). Tel: 410-242-2020. Ms. Rita Ann Swift, M.S., Prin.
Sisters 1; Lay Teachers 13; Students 214.
Catechesis/Religious Programs—Students 220.

12—ST. ATHANASIUS (1891) (Polish), Rev. Timothy B. Klunk.
Res., 4708 Prudence St., Curtis Bay, 21226. Tel: 410-355-5740; Fax: 410-355-8122.

13—ST. AUGUSTINE (Elkridge) (1844), Rev. Gerard J. Bowen. In res., Rev. Msgr. Chester J. Mieczchowski.
Res., 5976 Old Washington Rd., Elkridge, 21075. Tel: 410-796-1520; Fax: 410-796-8172. [CEM]
School—5990 Old Washington Rd., Elkridge, 21075. Tel: 410-796-3040. Sr. Rita Dorn, S.S.N.D, Prin.
School Sisters of Notre Dame 4; Lay Teachers 9; Students 260.
Catechesis/Religious Programs—Tel: 410-796-8150.
Students 325.

14—ST. BARNABAS. Closed 1931. Parish records available at St. Pius V Church. Tel: 410-523-1930.

15—ST. BENEDICT (1893), Rt. Rev. Paschal A. Morlino, O.S.B. Pastoral Assocs.: Sr. Mary Anna Wilkes, S.S.N.D.; Sr. Beatrice Wise, D.C. In res., Revs. Michael McKay, O.S.B.; Robert A. Reed.
Res., 2612 Wilkens Ave., 21223. Tel: 410-947-4988; Fax: 410-947-6009.

16—ST. BERNARD (Korean). Closed. For parish records prior to 1989 contact the chancery office. For parish records past 1989 contact Holy Korean Martyrs, Baltimore.

17—ST. BERNARDINE (1928) (African American), Rev. Edward M. Miller; Deacons Phillip W. Harcum; Charles Knight.
Res., 3812 Edmondson Ave., 21229. Tel: 410-362-8664; Fax: 410-945-0459.
School—3601 Old Frederick Rd., 21229. Tel: 410-624-5088. Joseph Campbell, Prin.
Lay Teachers 12; Students 292.
Catechesis/Religious Programs—Tel: 410-362-8978.
Students 234.

18—BLESSED SACRAMENT CHURCH (1911), Rev. P. Edward Kenny, Jr.; Sr. Marie Mack, S.S.N.D., Pastoral Admin.
Res., 4103 Old York Rd., 21218. Tel: 410-323-0424; Fax: 410-323-4478. [CEM]

19—ST. BRIGID (1854), Rev. Joseph G. Bochenek.
Res., 911 S. Ellwood Ave., 21224. Tel: 410-563-1717; Fax: 410-563-1776.
School—Bishop John Newmann. See separate listing.

20—ST. CASIMIR (1902), Revs. Ross Syracuse, O.F.M.Conv.; Vincent Gluc, O.F.M.Conv.; Timothy Zientek, O.F.M.Conv. In res., Rev. Timothy Kulbicki, O.F.M.Conv.
Res., 2736 O'Donnell St., 21224. Tel: 410-276-1981; Fax: 410-732-7436.
School—Father Kolbe Interparochial School. See separate listing. Tel: 410-342-2681.

21—ST. CECILIA (1902) (African American). (Twinned with Immaculate Conception, Baltimore.). Revs. Sylvester Peterka, C.M.; Eugene Sheridan, C.M.; Deacon Thomas A. Wilson, Sr.; Mr. John A. Gaither, Jr., Dir. Evangelization.
Res., 3300 Clifton Ave., 21216. Tel: 410-624-3600; Fax: 410-945-0157.

22—ST. CHARLES BORROMEO (Pikesville) (1848), Rev. E. Joseph Cote; Deacon Raymond Bullinger; Sr. M. Martha Geipe, S.S.N.D., Pastoral Min.; Sr. Marylita Friia, S.S.N.D., D.R.E.
Res., 101 Church Ln., 21208. Tel: 410-486-5400; Fax: 410-486-5421. [CEM]

23—CHRIST THE KING (Dundalk) (1957), Rev. Richard P. Wojciechowski.
Res., 335 Sollers Point Rd., 21222. Tel: 410-288-3629; Fax: 410-285-1126.

24—ST. CLARE (Essex) (1956), Revs. Michael W. Carrion; Dale M. Picarella; Deacon Fred Miller.
Res., 714 Myrth Ave., 21221-4898. Tel: 410-687-6011; Fax: 410-687-3054.
School—Tel: 410-687-7787; Fax: 410-687-2715. Mrs. Dorothy Williams, Prin.
Sisters 3; Lay Teachers 16; Students 259.
Catechesis/Religious Programs—Tel: 410-686-7693.
Students 231.

25—ST. CLEMENT (Lansdowne) (1891), Revs. Steven P. Girard; Joseph A. Kenney, Pastor Emeritus; Deacons Norman E. Colson; John I. McKenna; Hugh H. Mills; Thomas J. Yannuzzi.
Res., 2700 Washington Ave., 21227. Tel: 410-242-1025; Fax: 410-536-0636.
School—Tel: 410-242-3432. Mrs. Mary Garmer, Headmistress.
Lay Teachers 9; Students 180.
Catechesis/Religious Programs—139 First Ave., 21227. Tel: 410-242-2230.
Students 167.

26—ST. CLEMENT MARY HOFBAUER (Rosedale) (1925), Revs. Richard Florek, O.F.M.Conv.; Justin Ratajczak, O.F.M.Conv.; Santo Cricchio, O.F.M.Conv.; Deacons Nicholas Feurer, Pastoral Min.; Walter Shipley; Francis Zeiler.
Res., 1220 Chesaco Ave., 21237. Tel: 410-686-6188; Fax: 410-686-6198.
School—Tel: 410-686-3316. Sr. Michael Kathleen, O.S.F., Prin.
Sisters of St. Francis of Philadelphia 2; Lay Teachers 24; Students 443.
Catechesis/Religious Programs—Tel: 410-391-5028. Sr. Maura Walsh, M.H.S.H., Directress.
Students 171.

27—CORPUS CHRISTI (1881), Sr. Jane Coyle, M.M.S., Pastoral Dir.; Sr. Marge Schnellinger, M.M., Pastoral Assoc.; Deacon Frank Hodges.
Res., 110 W. Lafayette Ave., 21217. Tel: 410-523-4161; Fax: 410-523-5745.

28—ST. DOMINIC (1906), Revs. George Loskarn; Matthew Smith.
Res., 5310 Harford Rd., 21214. Tel: 410-426-0354; Fax: 410-444-6963.
School—5304 Harford Rd., 21214. Tel: 410-426-0797; Fax: 410-426-3190. Patricia Larkin, Prin.
Lay Teachers 15; Students 263.

29—ST. EDWARD (1880), Rev. Maurice J. Blackwell; Deacons Earl Smith; Joseph Neale; Carl A. Anderson.
Res., 901 Poplar Grove St., 21216. Tel: 410-362-2000.

30—ST. ELIZABETH OF HUNGARY (1895), Rev. Christopher P. Moore.
Mailing Address & Office: 2 N. Belnord Ave., 21224. Tel: 410-675-8260; Fax: 410-558-0028.
Res., 2638 E. Baltimore St., 21224. Tel: 410-675-7771.
School—35 N. Lakewood Ave., 21224. Tel: 410-276-6344. Ms. Mary Catherine Marshall, Prin.
Lay Teachers 15; Students 220.

31—FOURTEEN HOLY MARTYRS. Closed 1964. Parish records available at St. Martin Church. Tel: 410-947-1242.

32—ST. FRANCIS OF ASSISI (1927), Rev. Msgr. William F. Burke; Rev. Joseph Bonadio, S.S.; Sr. Katherine Bell, R.S.M., Pastoral Assoc.
Res., 3615 Harford Rd., 21218. Tel: 410-235-5136; 235-1371; Fax: 410-467-9503.
School—3617 Harford Rd., 21218. Tel: 410-467-1683.
Sisters of St. Joseph 1; School Sisters of Notre Dame 1; Lay Teachers 21; Students 340.
Catechesis/Religious Programs—Students 65.

33—ST. FRANCIS XAVIER (1793) (African American), Rev. William L. Norvel, S.S.J.; Deacons Russell Matthews; Charles Mercer; Walton Smith. In res., Revs. Joseph C. Verrett, S.S.J.; A. O. Nwachukwu-Udaku, S.S.J.
Res., 1501 E. Oliver St., 21213. Tel: 410-727-3103; 3104; Fax: 410-625-9587.
Catechesis/Religious Programs—Students 150.

34—ST. GABRIEL, Rev. Thomas L. Phillips.
Parish Office: 6950 Dogwood Rd., 21244. Tel: 410-944-2106; Fax: 410-944-7409.
School—John Paul Regional School. See separate listing.

35—ST. GREGORY THE GREAT (1883) (African American), Rev. Damien Nalepa.
Res., 1507 N. Smallwood St., 21216. Tel: 410-669-1233; Fax: 410-669-1385.
Church—1542 Gilmor St., 21217. Tel: 410-523-0061; Fax: 410-669-1385.

36—HOLY CROSS (1858) (German), Rev. Mitchell T. Rozanski. In res., Rev. Msgr. John L. Reinsfelder.
Res., 110 E. West St., 21230. Tel: 410-752-8498; Fax: 410-752-2703. [CEM]
School—Catholic Community School of South Baltimore. See separate listing. Tel: 410-685-6155; Fax: 410-685-0692.

37—HOLY KOREAN MARTYRS, Rev. Joseph Y. Kim.
Res., 5801 Security Blvd., 21207. Tel: 410-265-8767; Fax: 410-265-8885.

38—HOLY ROSARY (1887) (Polish), Revs. Ronald Pytel; Tomasz Kozub, S.Ch. In res., Revs. Francis Okroy, S.Ch.; Paul Henry.
Res., 408 S. Chester St., 21231. Tel: 410-732-3960. [CEM]

39—ST. IGNATIUS (1856), Revs. William J. Watters, S.J.; Francis P. Ernst, S.J.
Res., 740 N. Calvert St., 21202. Tel: 410-727-3848; Fax: 410-727-1573.
Church—Jesuit Community of St. Ignatius Parish, 102 E. Madison St., 21202. Tel: 410-727-3848.
St. Ignatius Social Services Self-Help—Tel: 410-625-4509. Rev. Robert J. Braunreuther, S.J., Dir.

40—IMMACULATE CONCEPTION (1850) (African American). (Twinned with St. Cecilia, Baltimore.). Revs. Sylvester Peterka, C.M.; Eugene Sheridan, C.M.; Bro. William Stover, C.M.; Mr. John A. Gaither, Jr., Dir. Evangelization.
Res., 1512 Druid Hill Ave., 21217. Tel: 410-523-0809; Fax: 410-945-0157.

41—IMMACULATE CONCEPTION (Towson) (1883), Rev. Msgr. Edward J. Lynch; Revs. Charles L. Lafferty; Raymond L. Harris, Jr.; James D. Proffit. In res., Rev. Msgr. Jeremiah F. Kenney; Deacon John C. Giramling.
Res., 200 Ware Ave., 21204. Tel: 410-823-6175; Fax: 410-823-3936. [CEM]
School—(Grades PreK-8). Tel: 410-337-5222. Mrs. Marie Ann Cote, Prin.
Sisters of St. Francis 2; Lay Teachers 31; Students 532.
High School—Towson Catholic, 114 Ware Ave., 21204. Tel: 410-823-8400; Fax: 410-823-8404. Mr. Michael Lynch, Prin.
Lay Teachers 20; Students 193.
Catechesis/Religious Programs—School of Religion, 701 Baltimore Ave., 21204. Tel: 410-821-8287. Ms. Lisa E. Padian, Dir.
Students 206.
Convent—112 Ware Ave., 21204. Tel: 410-823-3470. Sisters of St. Francis

42—IMMACULATE HEART OF MARY (Baynesville) (1948), Revs. Joseph McManus; Michael J. Jendrek; Deacons Jack Martin; Ken Pivec; Charles Hiebler. In res., Rev. John Ward.
Res., 8501 Loch Raven Blvd., 21286. Tel: 410-668-7935; Fax: 410-661-6560.
School—Tel: 410-668-8466; Fax: 410-668-6171. Mrs. Wilma Short, Prin.
Sisters of Mercy 2; Lay Teachers 25; Students 487.
Catechesis/Religious Programs—Tel: 410-661-3820; Fax: 410-661-3838.
Students 187.

43—ST. ISAAC JOGUES (1968), Rev. H. Martin Hammond; Rev. Msgr. James J. Cronin, Pastor Emeritus; Rev. M. Shawn Mahon; Deacons James R. Kent; Arthur L. Micozzi; James Westwater.
Church Office—9215 Old Harford Rd., 21234. Tel: 410-661-4888; Fax: 410-882-1484.
Res., 9400 Old Harford Rd., 21234. Tel: 410-661-4883.
Catechesis/Religious Programs—Tel: 410-665-2561.
Students 704.

44—ST. JAMES AND ST. JOHN. Closed 1986. Parish records available at the Chancery. Tel: 410-547-5446.
School—Queen of Peace Elementary Cluster. See separate listing.

45—ST. JOHN GERMAN CATHOLIC CHURCH. Closed 1841. Original records, stored at The Catholic Center, are available to researchers on microfilm at the Maryland State Archives in Annapolis.

46—ST. JOHN THE EVANGELIST. Closed 1966. Parish records available at the Chancery. Tel: 410-547-5446.

47—ST. JOSEPH. Closed 1962. Parish records available at Holy Cross Rectory. Tel: 410-752-8498.

48—ST. JEROME (1887), Revs. John D. Harvey; Kevin Thompson, O.F.M.Conv.; Deacon Gerald Anthony Roberts. Pastoral Assocs.: Sr. Joan Bastress, I.H.M.; Sr. Teresa Ann Walsh, D.C.; Ann Wagner.
Res., 775 W. Hamburg St., 21230. Tel: 410-727-0430; Fax: 410-727-0432.
School & Social Hall—765 W. Hamburg St., 21230. Tel: 410-539-2429.

49—ST. JOSEPH (Fullerton) (1850) (German), Rev. Msgr. George B. Moeller; Revs. Simon Obeng-Kyeremeh; Paul Sparklin; Stephen R. Sutton; Deacons William DeAngelis; Vincent Perticone; Charles Baynes; William Albaugh.
Res., 8420 Belair Rd., 21236. Tel: 410-256-1630; Fax: 410-529-2990. [CEM]
School—Tel: 410-256-8026; Fax: 410-529-7234. Mrs. Joyce Thaler, Prin.
Sisters of St. Francis of Philadelphia 2; Lay Teachers 28; Students 516.
Catechesis/Religious Programs—Tel: 410-256-8235.
Students 846.

50—ST. JOSEPH PASSIONIST MONASTERY PARISH (1868), Rev. Gregory Paul, C.P., Admin.
Res., 251 S. Morley St., 21229. Tel: 410-566-0877; Fax: 410-233-4974.

51—ST. JUDE SHRINE (1873) (Italian), Revs. Frank S. Donio, S.A.C.; Flavian Bonifazi, S.A.C.
Res., 308 N. Paca St., P.O. Box 2437, 21203. Tel: 410-685-6026; 685-3497; Fax: 410-244-5728.
St. Jude Shrine Corp.—Tel: 410-685-6026.

52—ST. KATHARINE OF SIENNA. Closed 1986. Parish records available at St. Wenceslaus Church. Tel: 410-675-7304.

53—ST. LAWRENCE (1962). Merged with The Shrine of Our Lady of Perpetual Help, Baltimore, to form Woodlawn Catholic Parish, Baltimore.

54—ST. LEO (1881) (Italian), Rev. Michael Salerno, S.A.C.
Res., 227 S. Exeter St., 21202. Tel: 410-675-7275; Fax: 410-675-8291.
School—Father Kolbe Interparochial. See separate listing.

55—LITTLE FLOWER, SHRINE OF (1926), Rev. Michael J. Orchik; Deacon Henry L. Siarkowski; Bro. John J. Brady, F.S.C.
Res., 2854 Brendan Ave., 21213. Tel: 410-483-1700; Fax: 410-488-6482.
School—(Grades PreK-8). Tel: 410-488-1483. Mr. Richard G. Gatto, Prin.
Sisters of St. Francis of Philadelphia 2; Lay Teachers 12; Students 251.

56—ST. LUKE (Edgemere) (1888), Rev. Joseph S. Lizor, Jr.
Res., 7517 N. Point Rd., 21219-1499. Tel: 410-477-5200; Fax: 410-477-5996.
School—Our Lady of Hope/St. Luke's School, 8003 N. Boundary Rd., 21222. Tel: 410-288-2793; Fax: 410-282-9361.

57—ST. MARK (Cantonsville) (1888), Rev. Ross A. LaPorta; Rev. Msgr. Henry F. Zerhusen; Rev. Ronald Zoubek; Sr. Kathleen Martin, M.H.S.H., Pastoral Assoc.

Res., 27 Melvin Ave., 21228. Tel: 410-744-6560; Fax: 410-747-3182.
School—Tel: 410-747-6613; Fax: 410-747-3188. Sr. Raymond Lorenzen, S.S.N.D., Prin.
Lay Teachers 30; Students 575.
Catechesis/Religious Programs—Tel: 410-788-6211.
Students 409.

58—ST. MARTIN (1865), Revs. John D. Harvey, O.F.M.Cap.; Kevin Thompson, O.F.M.Cap. Pastoral Assocs.: Sr. Teresa Ann Walsh, D.C.; Sr. Joan Bastress, I.H.M.; Sr. Eleanor Casey, D.C.; Ann Wagner.
Res., 31 N. Fulton Ave., 21223. Tel: 410-947-1242; Fax: 410-542-6056.

59—ST. MARY OF THE ASSUMPTION (1849), Rev. P. Edward Kenny, Jr.; Deacon Miguel Sainz. In res., Deacon Rochus Vu Dinh Hoat.
Res., 5502 York Rd., 21212. Tel: 410-435-5900; Fax: 410-435-1287. [CEM]
School—Tel: 410-435-5850. Ms. Denise Wallace, Prin.
Lay Teachers 18; Students 235.

60—ST. MARY, STAR OF THE SEA (1868), Rev. Mitchell T. Rozanski.
Res., 1419 Riverside Ave., 21230. Tel: 410-685-2255; Fax: 410-752-2703.
School—Catholic Community School of South Baltimore. See separate listing. Tel: 410-685-6155; Fax: 410-685-0692.
Catechesis/Religious Programs—Students 204.
Convent—1410 Riverside Ave., 21230. Tel: 410-752-4344. Sisters of St. Joseph

61—ST. MATTHEW (1949), Rev. Joseph L. Muth.
Res., 5401 Loch Raven Blvd., 21239. Tel: 410-433-2300; Fax: 410-433-5263.
School—Cardinal Shehan School. See separate listing. Tel: 410-433-2775; Fax: 410-323-6131.

62—ST. MICHAEL (Broadway) (1852) (Hispanic). Merged with St. Patrick. Revs. John P. Lavin, C.SS.R., Supr.; Andrew Carr, C.SS.R.; Deacons Rafael Villagaray; Pablo Osorio; Richard Novak.
Res., 7 S. Wolfe St., 21231. Tel: 410-276-1646; Fax: 410-522-0789.
School—Bishop John Neuman School. See separate listing.

63—ST. MICHAEL (Overlea) (1914), Revs. Christopher M. Carney; John F. Lesnick; J. James Purvey. In res., Rev. James M. Barker.
Res., 2 Willow Ave., 21206. Tel: 410-665-4200; Fax: 410-665-4024.
School—Tel: 410-668-8797; Fax: 410-668-8797. Sr. Patricia Shea, S.S.N.D., Prin.
Lay Teachers 23; Students 440.
Catechesis/Religious Programs—Tel: 410-882-8120.
Students 243.

64—ST. MILDRED CHURCH. Closed 1967. Parish records available at Our Lady of Hope Rectory. Tel: 410-284-6600.

65—ST. MONICA. Closed 1959. Parish records available at the Chancery. Tel: 410-547-5446.

66—MOST PRECIOUS BLOOD, COMMUNITY OF (1948). (Twinned with St. Anthony of Padua, Baltimore.). Revs. C. Lou Martin; Salvatore J. Livigni, S.S.N.D.; David B. Kruse.
Office: 4414 Frankford Ave., 21206. Tel: 410-488-0400; Fax: 410-488-0032. [CEM]

67—OUR LADY OF THE ANGELS CATHOLIC COMMUNITY (Catonsville) (1993), Rev. Leo J. Larrivee, S.S.; Sr. Eileen McFadden, S.S.N.D. Pastoral Assocs.: Sr. Laurentilla Back, S.S.N.D.; Sr. Victoria Kessler, S.S.N.D.
Mailing Address: 711 Maiden Choice Ln., Catonsville, 21228. Tel: 410-247-4779; Fax: 410-737-8826.

68—OUR LADY OF FATIMA (1951), Revs. Henry E. Sattler, C.SS.R.; Lawrence E. Lover, C.SS.R.; Richard K. Poetzel, C.SS.R.; Sr. Juliana Hau, M.H.S.H., Pastoral Assoc.; Deacon Alphonse Bankard, III; Bro. DeSales Zimpfer, C.SS.R., Pastoral Asst. Missionaries: Rev. Gerard Chylko, C.SS.R.
Res., 6420 E. Pratt St., 21224. Tel: 410-633-9393; Fax: 410-631-7239.
School—Tel: 410-633-5882.
School Sisters of Notre Dame 4; Lay Teachers 11; Students 288.
Catechesis/Religious Programs—Tel: 410-633-6256.
Students 135.

69—OUR LADY OF GOOD COUNSEL (1889), Rev. David G. Smith.
Office: 1532 E. Fort Ave., 21230. Tel: 410-752-0205; Fax: 410-576-0929.
School—Catholic Community School of South Baltimore. See separate listing.

70—OUR LADY OF HOPE, Rev. Msgr. Thomas J. Tewes; Revs. Andrew Aaron; Charles H. Young, Jr., Pastor Emeritus; Paul G. Witthauer; Samuel V. Young, Jr.
Res., 1727 Lynch Rd., 21222. Tel: 410-284-6600; Fax: 410-282-9361.
School—(Grades PreK-18) 8003 N. Boundary Rd., 21222. Tel: 410-288-2793.
School Sisters of Notre Dame 3; Lay Teachers 21; Students 335.
Catechesis/Religious Programs—8003 N. Boundary Rd., Tel: 410-282-3120; Fax: 410-282-9361.
Students 350.

71—OUR LADY OF LOURDES. Closed 1995. Parish records available at The New All Saints Church. Tel: 410-542-0445.

72—OUR LADY OF MOUNT CARMEL (Middle River) (1887), Revs. Robert L. Hartnett; Kevin Mueller; Sr. Betty Kane, O.S.F., Pastoral Assoc.
Res., 1704 Old Eastern Ave., 21221. Tel: 410-686-4972; Fax: 410-574-8785.
School—1702 Old Eastern Ave., 21221. Tel: 410-686-0859; Fax: 410-686-4916. Mrs. Kathleen Sipes, Prin.
Sisters of St. Francis of Philadelphia 2; Lay Teachers 28; Students 464.
High School—1706 Old Eastern Ave., 21221. Tel: 410-686-1023. Mrs. Kathleen Sipes, Prin.
Lay Teachers 22; Students 208.
Catechesis/Religious Programs—Tel: 410-686-9016; Fax: 410-574-8785.
Students 676.

73—OUR LADY OF PERPETUAL HELP (1936). Merged with St. Lawrence, Baltimore, to form Woodlawn Catholic Parish, Baltimore.

74—OUR LADY OF POMPEI (1924), Rev. Louis Esposito; Deacon Thom Kuhl.
Res., 3600 Claremont St., 21224. Tel: 410-675-7790; Fax: 410-563-9067.
School—201 S. Conkling St., 21224. Tel: 410-276-6534; Fax: 410-276-6915. Ms. Angela Rebbert, Prin.
Lay Teachers 10; Students 192.
High School—Tel: 410-276-4503. Mr. Christopher Russo, Prin.
Priests 1; Lay Teachers 7; Students 109.

75—OUR LADY OF SORROWS. Closed 1935. Parish records available at Holy Cross Rectory. Tel: 410-752-8498.

76—OUR LADY, QUEEN OF PEACE (1953), Revs. Thomas A. Hagendorf, O.Praem.; Salvatore H. Cuccia, O.Praem.; Deacon George Jenkins.
Res., 10003 Bird River Rd., 21220. Tel: 410-686-3085; Fax: 410-687-1916.
School—10001 Bird River Rd., 21220. Tel: 410-687-8513; Fax: 410-687-1916. Ms. Cynthia Stewart, Prin.; Mr. Richard Brotzman, Asst. Prin.
Lay Teachers 24; Students 219.
Catechesis/Religious Programs—Students 197.

77—OUR LADY OF VICTORY (Arbutus) (1952), Revs. William F. Franken; John Kelmartin, Pastor Emeritus; Deacon William Jauquet.
Res., 4414 Wilkens Ave., 21229. Tel: 410-242-0131; Fax: 410-242-6963.
School—Tel: 410-242-3688; Fax: 410-242-8867. Thomas E. Riddle, Prin.; Deborah Reese, Asst. Prin.
Sisters 3; Lay Teachers 21; Students 501.

78—ST. PATRICK (Broadway) (1792). Twinned with St. Michael (Wolfe St.) 1995. Rev. John P. Lavin, C.SS.R., Supr.
Res., 7 S. Wolfe St., 21231. Tel: 410-276-1646; Fax: 410-522-0789.

79—ST. PAUL'S CATHOLIC CHURCH. Closed. Parish records available at St. Francis Xavier. Tel: 410-727-3103.

80—ST. PETER THE APOSTLE (1842), Revs. John D. Harvey, O.F.M.Cap.; Kevin Thompson, O.F.M.Cap. Pastoral Assocs.: Sr. Joan Bastress, I.H.M.; Sr. Eleanor Casey, D.C.; Sr. Teresa Walsh, D.C.; Ann Wagner.
Res., 848 Hollins St., 21201. Tel: 410-685-5044; Fax: 410-727-0431.

81—ST. PETER CLAVER (1888) (African American), Most Rev. Roger J. Caesar, S.S.J.; Rev. Henry Harper, S.S.J.
Res., 1546 N. Fremont Ave., 21217. Tel: 410-669-0512; Fax: 410-383-8227.
School—Father Charles A. Hall Lower School, (Grades K-3) Carey St., 21217. Tel: 410-225-7555.
Sisters 1; Lay Teachers 7; Students 167.
Convent—1526 N. Fremont Ave., 21217. Tel: 410-383-1288.

82—SS. PHILIP AND JAMES (1897), Rev. William A. Au.
Res., 2801 N. Charles St., 21218. Tel: 410-235-2294; Fax: 410-243-5262.

83—ST. PIUS V (1878) (African American), Rev. John C. Crotty, S.S.J.; Deacon Clifford Lonesome.
Res., 521 N. Schroeder St., 21223. Tel: 410-523-1930; Fax: 410-523-8164.

84—ST. PIUS X (1958), Revs. Thomas J. Golueke; Louis M. Reitz, S.S.; Ms. Ann LaRocque, Pastoral Assoc.; Mrs. Pat Howlett, Parish Admin.
Res., 6428 York Rd., 21212. Tel: 410-377-7440; Fax: 410-377-2651.
School—6432 York Rd., 21212. Tel: 410-377-9738. Martha Pierorazio, Prin.; Geri Morrison, Asst. Prin.
School Sisters of Notre Dame 2; Lay Teachers 25; Students 452.
Catechesis/Religious Programs—Tel: 410-377-0722. Mrs. Pinky Howard, D.R.E.
Students 292.

85—ST. RITA (1922), Rev. William J. Remmel, S.D.S.
Res., 2903 Dunleer Rd., 21222. Tel: 410-284-0388; Fax: 410-284-3998.
School—2905 Dunleer Rd., 21222. Tel: 410-284-3580. Sr. Mary Mark Carnes, I.H.M., Prin.
Sisters of the Immaculate Heart of Mary 2; Lay Teachers 12; Students 190.
Catechesis/Religious Programs—Tel: 410-284-7355.
Students 184.

86—ST. ROSE OF LIMA (1913), Rev. Joseph M. O'Meara; Sr. Kathleen White, O.S.B., Pastoral Assoc.
Res., 3803 4th St., 21225. Tel: 410-355-8515; 8516; Fax: 410-355-1938.
School—Tel: 410-355-1050; Fax: 410-355-2804. Madeline Hobik, Prin.
Lay Teachers 16; Students 230.
Catechesis/Religious Programs—Students 225.

87—SACRED HEART OF JESUS (1873), Revs. Thomas B. Loftus, C.SS.R.; Joseph Freund, C.SS.R.; William Harbison, C.SS.R.; Deacon Leo Nuedling. In res., Revs. Gerard Kurek; John Farrell, C.SS.R.; Henry V. Sattler; Bro. Raphael Rock, C.SS.R.
Res., 600 S. Conkling St., 21224-4294. Tel: 410-342-4336; Fax: 410-522-2022. [CEM]
School—Bishop John Neumann School. See separate listing. Tel: 410-675-6271.
Missions—Baltimore, Baltimore Co., Holy Redeemer Chapel, 800 S. Oldham St., 21224. Tel: 410-342-0151; Baltimore, Baltimore Co., St. Gerard's Chapel, Cardiff & Gusryan St., 21224. Tel: 410-633-9515.

88—SACRED HEART OF MARY (1925), Revs. Richard E. Parks; Leo Warczynski, Pastor Emeritus. In res., Rev. Charles R. Klein; Deacon Albert Chesnavage, (Retired).
Res., 6736 Youngstown Ave., 21222-1097. Tel: 410-633-2828; Fax: 410-633-0349. [CEM]
School—6726 Youngstown Ave., 21222-1098. Tel: 410-633-7040. Sr. M. Philomena, C.S.F.N., Prin.
Sisters of Holy Family of Nazareth 4; Lay Teachers 18; Students 267.
Convent—Tel: 410-633-3355; Fax: 410-633-2318.
Catechesis/Religious Programs—Students 97.

89—SHRINE OF THE SACRED HEART (Mt. Washington) (1867), Rev. Richard E. Cramblitt; Sr. Mary Margaret Savage, S.S.J., Pastoral Assoc. In res., Rev. Msgr. G. Michael Schleupner.
Res., 1701 Regent Rd., 21209. Tel: 410-466-6884; 6885; Fax: 410-664-0523.
School—5800 Smith Ave., 21209. Tel: 410-542-7406; Fax: 410-664-1463. John Moran, Prin.
Lay Teachers 16; Students 223.
Catechesis/Religious Programs—Tel: 410-466-6884, Ext. 15.
Students 138.

90—ST. STANISLAUS KOSTKA (1880) (Polish), Revs. Ross Syracuse, O.F.M.Conv.; William Viola, O.F.M.Conv. In res., Revs. Andrew Kasak, O.F.M.Conv.; Matthew Kotkowski, O.F.M.Conv.; Bro. Roland Warner, O.F.M.Conv.
Res., 700 S. Ann St., 21231. Tel: 410-276-2849. [CEM]
School—Father Kolbe Interparochial. See separate listing.

91—ST. THOMAS AQUINAS (1867), Rev. James Farmer; Sr. Alice Joseph Rohe, O.S.F., Pastoral Assoc. In res., Revs. George Restrepo, S.J.; Blair Raum; William Simms.
Res., 1008 W. 37th St., 21211. Tel: 410-366-4488.
School—Community School of the Holy Spirit, (Grades Pre K-7) 3710 Roland Ave., 21211. Tel: 410-889-4618.
School Sisters of Notre Dame 3; Lay Teachers 8; Students 212.
Catechesis/Religious Programs—Fax: 410-366-8352. Susan Sousa, D.R.E.
Students 153.

92—ST. THOMAS MORE (1961), Rev. John P. Cunningham; Deacon Michael P. McCoy. Pastoral Assocs.: Sr. Mary Small, S.S.J.; Deacon James L. Mann, Jr. In res., Rev. Msgr. W. Francis Malooly.
Parish Center & Mailing Address—6806 McClean Blvd., 21234. Tel: 410-444-6500; Fax: 410-444-6502.
School—Cardinal Shehan School. See separate listing.

93—ST. URSULA (Parkville) (1937), Rev. Msgr. A. Thomas Baumgartner; Rev. Msgr. Myles McGowan, Pastor Emeritus; Revs. Gerald Hynes, C.P.; Robert C. Jones, C.SS.R.; Paul Holthaus; Sr. Anne Mooney, S.S.N.D., Pastoral Min.; Deacons Robert Keenan;

Frank Rongione, Sr.; Harry St. A. O'Neil, (Oakcrest Village Retirement Center).
Res., 8801 Harford Rd., 21234. Tel: 410-665-2111; Fax: 410-665-0758.
School—8900 Harford Rd., 21234. Tel: 410-665-3533; Fax: 410-661-1620. Sr. Joan Kelly, S.N.D., Prin.
Sisters of Notre Dame de Namur 1; Benedictine 1; Lay Teachers 38; Students 746.
Catechesis/Religious Programs—Tel: 410-655-4106.
Students 438.

94—St. Veronica (1945) (African American), Rev. Donald M. Fest, S.S.J.; Deacons Jhan Harris; Williard Pinkney, Jr.; Alexander Smith.
Res., 806 Cherry Hill Rd., 21225. Tel: 410-355-7466; Fax: 410-355-7741.

95—St. Vincent de Paul (1840), Rev. Richard T. Lawrence. In res., Rev. Charles J. Canterna.
Res., 120 N. Front St., 21202. Tel: 410-962-5078; Fax: 410-962-8427. [CEM]
St. Vincent de Paul Church Historic Trust, Inc.—.
Jonestown Planning Council, Inc.—.

96—St. Wenceslaus (1870), Revs. Michael Sergi, C.SS.R.; John McLaughlin, C.SS.R.; Patrick Magnier, C.SS.R.; Scott Bailey, C.SS.R.; Bros. Vincent Hoerner, C.SS.R.; Martin de Porres Smith, C.SS.R. In res., Rev. George Deimel, C.SS.R.
Res., 2111 Ashland Ave., 21205. Tel: 410-675-7304; Fax: 410-675-5746.
School—Queen of Peace Elementary Cluster. See separate listing.
Father George A. Wichland Center—Redemptorist Food Center, 901 E. Eager St. at Valley St., 21202. Tel: 410-625-0553. Rev. John McLoughlin, C.Ss.R., Dir.; Mrs. Deborah Barnes, Program Dir.

97—St. William of York (1914), Rev. Martin H. Demek; Deacons Donald Miller; Daniel Spytkowski.
Res., 600 Cooks Ln., 21229. Tel: 410-566-2140; Fax: 410-362-5475.
School—Tel: 410-945-1442.
Lay Teachers 19; Students 207.

98—Woodlawn Catholic Parish, Rev. Thomas L. Phillips.
Res., 6950 Dogwood Rd., 21244-2697. Tel: 410-944-2106; Fax: 410-944-7409.
School—John Paul Regional Catholic School. See Elementary Schools, Regional and Community in the Institution Section.

OUTSIDE METROPOLITAN BALTIMORE

Aberdeen, Harford Co., St. Joan of Arc (1920), Rev. Kevin T. Schenning; Deacons William Vaughan; George LeFevre; Daniel Kopczyk. In res., Rev. Msgr. James J. Cronin.
Office: 222 S. Law St., 21001. Tel: 410-272-4535; 575-6909; Fax: 410-272-9025.
Res., 257 S. Law St., 21001.
School—Tel: 410-272-1387; Fax: 410-272-1959. Ms. Jane Towery, Prin.
Lay Teachers 19; Students 246.
Catechesis/Religious Programs—Tel: 410-272-6944. Sr. Regina DeAngelis, D.R.E.
Students 246.

Abingdon, Harford Co., St. Francis de Sales (1866), Deacon Richard Stine. In res., Rev. Gilbert Seitz.
Res., 1450 Abingdon Rd., 21009. Tel: 410-676-5119; 679-4555; Fax: 410-676-7520. [CEM]
Catechesis/Religious Programs—Tel: 410-676-3354.
Students 587.

Annapolis, Anne Arundel Co., St. Andrew by the Bay (Cape St. Claire) (1981), Revs. Jay O'Connor; James Kiesel; Deacons R. Paul Woofter; James C. Monaghan, Jr.
Parish Center—701 College Pkwy., 21401. Tel: 410-974-4366; Fax: 410-974-4339.
Catechesis/Religious Programs—Students 705.

St. Mary (1853), Revs. Thomas Siconolfi, C.SS.R.; John Sodomora, C.SS.R.; Eric Hoog, C.SS.R.; John G. Tizio, C.SS.R.; Deacons John L. Wilson; Leroy S. Moore; Anthony F. Norcio. In res., Revs. Bernard Baumgartner, C.SS.R.; Francis X. Murphy, C.SS.R.; Henry O'Meara, C.SS.R. Missionaries: Revs. Patrick Flynn, C.SS.R.; E. Patrick Lynch, C.SS.R.
Res., 109 Duke of Gloucester St., 21401. Tel: 410-263-2397; 269-6092; Fax: 410-263-3027. [CEM]
School—111 Duke of Gloucester St., 21401. Tel: 410-263-2869; Fax: 410-269-6513.
School Sisters of Notre Dame 1; Lay Teachers 39; Students 907.
High School—113 Duke of Gloucester St., 21401. Tel: 410-263-3294; Fax: 410-269-7843.
School Sisters of Notre Dame 3; Lay Teachers 32; Students 540.
Catechesis/Religious Programs—Tel: 410-268-5834; Fax: 410-263-7381.
Students 634.
Convent—4 Shipwright St., 21401. Tel: 410-269-0568.
School Sisters of Notre Dame 5.

Bel Air, Harford Co., St. Margaret (1905), Revs. Francis X. Callahan; Jeffrey Dauses; Thomas R. Malia; Deacons Paul Ciesla; Patrick Goles; J. Donald MacKnew.
Res., 141 Hickory Ave., 21014. Tel: 410-879-2670; Fax: 410-879-2518.
School—205 Hickory Ave., 21014. Tel: 410-879-1113. Ms. Amelia Mike, Prin.
Lay Teachers 29; Students 553.
Catechesis/Religious Programs—Tel: 410-838-4224.
Students 1,300.
Mission—Bel AIr, St. Mary Magdalen, 1716 Churchville Rd., 21015.

Bradshaw, Baltimore Co., St. Stephen (1863), Revs. Lawrence F. Kolson; John A. Messina; Deacons Gilbert Hartlieb; Robert Schott; Frank R. Laws. In res., Rev. John J. Kandathinkara, V.C. (India).
Res., 8030 Bradshaw Rd., 21021. Tel: 410-592-7071; Fax: 410-592-6803. [CEM]
School—8028 Bradshaw Rd., 21021. Tel: 410-592-7617; Fax: 410-592-7330. Mrs. Helena K. Scher, Prin.
Lay Teachers 18; Students 305.
Catechesis/Religious Programs—Tel: 410-592-8666. Sr. Angela DeFontes, O.S.F., D.R.E.
Students 475.

Brunswick, Frederick Co., St. Francis of Assisi (1895), Rev. Lawrence Gesy.
Res., 113 First Ave., 21716. Tel: 301-834-9185; Fax: 301-834-4162. [CEM]
Mission—Petersville, Frederick Co., St. Mary's.

Buckeystown, Frederick Co., St. Joseph-on-Carrollton Manor (1811), Rev. Lawrence K. Frazier; Deacon Robert M. Balderas.
Mailing Address: P.O. Box 33, 21717. Tel: 301-663-0907; Fax: 301-663-6525.
Res., 5843 Manor Woods Rd., Frederick, 21703. [CEM]
Catechesis/Religious Programs—Tel: 301-663-0907, Ext. 104.
Students 292.

Clarksville, Howard Co., St. Louis (1855), Rev. Msgr. Joseph L. Luca; Rev. Richard Bozzell; Sr. Louann Sciubba, S.N.D., Pastoral Assoc.; Deacons Daniel Stretmater; Verdan Wiedel; Lawrence Teixeira.
Res., 21029. Tel: 410-531-6040; Fax: 410-531-6191. [CEM]
School—Tel: 410-531-6664. Mrs. Terry Weiss, Prin.
Sisters 1; Lay Teachers 35; Students 466.
Catechesis/Religious Programs—Tel: 410-531-6688. D.R.E.: Mrs. Gloria Sauter; Mrs. Rhonda Milauskas.
Students 1361.

Cockeysville, Baltimore Co., St. Joseph (1852), Rev. Msgr. Paul G. Cook; Revs. Bernard Bak; John Jicha; Deacon Edward Sulivan. Pastoral Assocs.: Sr. Rose Linder, S.S.N.D.; Sr. Judith Zeiler, M.H.S.H.
Res., 101 Church Ln., 21030. Tel: 410-666-1619; Fax: 410-628-2956. [CEM]
School—Tel: 410-666-0393; Fax: 410-628-6814. Sr. Anne O'Donnell, R.S.M., Prin.
Lay Teachers 21; Students 447.
Catechesis/Religious Programs—40 Church Ln., 21030. Tel: 410-666-8840.
Students 664.

Columbia, Howard Co., St. John the Evangelist (1967), Revs. Richard H. Tillman; William L. Viola; Deacons George Martin; George McAndrews.
Res., 21044.
Interfaith Centers—(Wilde Lake) 10431 Twin Rivers Rd., 21044. Tel: 410-964-1425; Fax: 410-730-9253.
(Oakland Mills) 5885 Robert Oliver Pl., 21045. Tel: 410-964-1434; Fax: 410-740-9323.
Catechesis/Religious Programs—Students 864.

Cresaptown, Allegany Co., St. Ambrose (1886), Rev. Robert E. McCreary, O.F.M.Cap.; Ms. Margaret Gaughan, Pastoral Assoc.
Res., P.O. Box 5130, 21505-5130. Tel: 301-729-2790; Fax: 301-729-2436. [CEM]
Catechesis/Religious Programs—Students 190.

Crofton, Anne Arundel Co., St. Elizabeth Ann Seton (1976), Rev. Edward C. Connelly; Sr. Joan Bunty, O.S.F., Pastoral Assoc.; Deacon Frederick Seibold.
Office: 1800 Seton Dr., 21114. Tel: 410-721-5770; Fax: 410-721-5508. [CEM]
Catechesis/Religious Programs—Tel: 410-721-5774.
Students 614.
School—Arthur Slade Regional Catholic School. See separate listing.

Cumberland, Allegany Co., St. Mary (1900) (Italian), Rev. Milton A. Hipsley; Bro. James T. Kirkpatrick, F.S.C., Pastoral Assoc.; Deacon David A. Conley.
Res., 300 E. Oldtown Rd., 21502. Tel: 301-777-2990; Fax: 301-777-1108. [CEM]
School—St. John Neumann, (Grades K-5). See separate listing.
High School—Bishop Walsl, (Grades 6-12).

St. Patrick (1790) (Irish), Rev. Thomas R. Bevan; Deacons Gerald A. Raible; Paul H. Dignan, Sr.; Loren Mooney; Francis L. Werner, Jr.
Res., 201 N. Centre St., 21502. Tel: 301-777-1750; Fax: 301-777-2669. [CEM]
School—St. John Neumann. See separate listing. Tel: 301-724-4055.

SS. Peter and Paul (1848) (German), Revs. Vance Pastorius, O.F.M.Cap.; Vernon Busch, O.F.M.Cap.; Michael P. Masich, O.F.M.Cap.; Deacon Herman Grabenstein.
Res., 109 N. Small Wood St., 21502-2992. Tel: 301-777-3131; Fax: 301-759-3568. [CEM]
School—St. John Neumann. See separate listing. Tel: 301-724-4055; Fax: 301-724-4827.

Davidsonville, Anne Arundel Co., Holy Family (1929), Rev. Joseph F. Barr; Deacon Robert Graham.
Res., P.O. Box 130, 21035-0130. Tel: 410-269-0586; 261-7399; Fax: 410-798-5315.
Catechesis/Religious Programs—Tel: 410-798-5680.
Students 467.

Edgewater, Anne Arundel Co., Our Lady of Perpetual Help (1976), Rev. Frank J. Brauer.
Res., 515 Loch Haven Rd., 21037. Tel: 410-956-2883; 798-5161; Fax: 410-798-0076; 269-5553.
Catechesis/Religious Programs—Mary Ellen Fisher, D.R.E.
Students 342.

Edgewood, Harford Co., Prince of Peace (1977), Rev. Stephen D. Gosnell.
Res., 1902 Hawthorne Rd., 21040. Tel: 410-679-5912.

Ellicott City, Howard Co., Our Lady of Perpetual Help (1892), Revs. Richard E. Smith; Isaac Karoor; Deacon Raymond Crawford; Sr. Mary McFadden, S.N.D., Pastoral Assoc.
Res., 4795 Ilchester Rd., 21043. Tel: 410-747-4334; Fax: 410-747-4399. [CEM]
School—Tel: 410-744-4251; Fax: 410-788-5210.
Xaverian Brother 1; Lay Teachers 12; Students 261.
Catechesis/Religious Programs—Tel: 410-747-0131; Fax: 410-788-8905.
Students 1,016.

Resurrection (1974), Revs. James O. McGovern; Donald J. Parson; Raymond D. Martin. Pastoral Assocs.: Deacon Ray Britt; Martha Bode; Donald S. Henderson; Linda M. Keedy; Amy McClain. In res., Rev. J. Bryan Hehir.
Office: 3175 Paulskirk Dr., 21042. Tel: 410-461-9111; Fax: 410-203-9419.
School—Resurrection/St. Paul, Tel: 410-465-8746; Fax: 410-461-8621. Sr. Joan Elias, G.N.S.H., Prin.
Lay Teachers 23; Students 336.
Catechesis/Religious Programs—Tel: 410-461-9111, Ext. 221.
Students 1,002.

St. Paul (1838), Rev. Thomas J. Donaghy.
Res., 3755 St. Paul St., 21043. Tel: 410-465-1670; Fax: 410-313-8851. [CEM]
Catechesis/Religious Programs—Tel: 410-465-0622.
Students 182.

Emmitsburg, Frederick Co., St. Anthony Shrine (1805), Rev. Leo R. Tittler; Sr. Carol C. Czyzewski, F.S.S.J., Pastoral Assoc., Tel: 301-271-7300; Sr. Mary Jan Nasiadka, F.S.S.J., Pastoral Admin., Tel: 301-271-7300.
Office—16150 St. Anthony Rd., 21727. Tel: 301-447-2367; Fax: 301-447-6318.

St. Joseph (1793), Revs. Michael J. Kennedy, C.M.; William P. Goff, C.M.; Charles E. Jacobs, C.M.; Joseph R. Wright, C.M. In res., Rev. Louis B. Storms, C.M.
Res., 47 DePaul St., 21727. Tel: 301-447-2326; Fax: 301-447-3579. [CEM 2]

Fallston, Harford Co., St. Mark (1887), Rev. Edward B. Hemler; Deacons T. Russell Gibson; Charles Hicks.
Res., 812 Reckord Rd., 21047. Tel: 410-879-9110; 877-9750; Fax: 410-877-0576.
Catechesis/Religious Programs—Tel: 410-879-1706; 877-1692.
Students 626.

Frederick, Frederick Co., St. John the Evangelist (1763), Revs. Wayne G. Funk; J. Kevin Farmer; Paul P. Iaia, Senior Priest; Deacons Daniel C. Roff; James F. Casey; John L. Manley; J. Michael Zusi.
Res., 116 E. Second St., 21701. Tel: 301-662-8288; Fax: 301-698-1832. [CEM]
School—St. John Regional Catholic School. See separate listing. Tel: 301-662-6722.
Catechesis/Religious Programs—Tel: 410-662-8495.
Students 883.

Frostburg, Allegany Co., St. Michael (1850), Rev. Paul

A. Byrnes; Deacons Bertrand O. Michael; Lou Concordia.
Res., 44 E. Main St., P.O. Box 402, 21532. Tel: 301-689-6767; Fax: 301-689-6411. [CEM]
School—Tel: 301-689-2155.
Lay Teachers 12; Students 138.
Catechesis/Religious Programs—Tel: 301-689-2898.
Students 160.

Fulton, Howard Co., St. Francis of Assisi (1988), Rev. Dennis P. Diehl.
Office: 11305 Rte. 216, 20759. Tel: 410-792-0470; Fax: 410-792-0472.
Res., 10681 Glen Hannah Dr., Laurel, 20723. Tel: 410-880-3068.
Catechesis/Religious Programs—Students 391.

Glen Burnie, Anne Arundel Co., Crucifixion, Church of the, Rev. Brendan T. Carr; Sr. Marlene Cunningham, S.N.D., Pastoral Assoc.
Rectory: 100 Scott Ave., 21060. Tel: 410-768-4880; Fax: 410-768-5025.

Church of the Good Shepherd (1972), Revs. John L. Kelly; Joseph V. Messer, (Retired).
Res., 1451 Furnace Ave., 21060. Tel: 410-761-4607; Fax: 410-761-6019.
School—Arthur Slade Regional Catholic School. See separate listing. Tel: 410-766-7130; Fax: 410-787-0594.
Catechesis/Religious Programs—Students 101.

Holy Trinity (1931), Revs. G. Eugene Nickol; Sam Young; Deacons LeRoy Beimel; John Boscoe; Edward Gardner; Robert Herzog.
Res., 7436 Baltimore-Annapolis Blvd., 21061. Tel: 410-766-1213.
Parish Center—126 Dorsey Rd., 21061. Tel: 410-766-5070; Fax: 410-760-6738.
School—Arthur Slade Regional Catholic School. See separate listing.
Catechesis/Religious Programs—Tel: 410-766-5070; Fax: 410-760-6738. Joseph Goggin, D.R.E.
Students 725.

Glyndon, Baltimore Co., Sacred Heart (1873), Revs. Lloyd E. Aiken; John T. Wielebski; Christopher J. Whatley; James J. Ditillo, S.J.; Deacon James A. Ryan.
Res., 65 Sacred Heart Ln., 21071. Tel: 410-833-1696; Fax: 410-833-2676.
School—Tel: 410-833-0857; Fax: 410-833-0914. Anne H. Price, Interim Prin.; Patricia E. Balcerzak, Interim Asst. Prin.
Lay Teachers 46; Students 660.
Catechesis/Religious Programs—Tel: 410-833-8515.
Students 700.

Grantsville, Northern Garrett Co., St. Ann (1976), Deacon Robert Lilly; Sr. Joan Minella, S.S.N.D., Pastoral Life Dir.
Res., 12814 New Germany Rd., 21536. Tel: 301-895-5877; Fax: 301-895-4353.

Hagerstown, Washington Co., St. Ann (1966), Revs. Edward W. Manalis; Andrew Mohl; Deacons William Nairn; Richard Kunkel.
Res., 1010 Oak Hill Ave., 21742. Tel: 301-791-2727; Fax: 301-733-6218.
Church—1525 Oak Hill Ave., 21742. Tel: 301-733-0410; Fax: 301-733-6218.
Catechesis/Religious Programs—Tel: 301-733-0411.
Students 470.

St. Joseph, Half Way (1951). Unassigned.
Res., 17628 Virginia Ave., 21740. Tel: 301-797-9435; 797-9445; Fax: 301-797-2490.

St. Mary (1790), Rev. George A. Limmer; Rev. Msgr. Robert S. Passarelli, Pastor Emeritus; Rev. John N. Fullen.
Res., 224 W. Washington St., 21740. Tel: 301-739-0390; Fax: 301-739-7082.
School—Tel: 301-733-1184; Fax: 301-745-4997.
School Sisters of Notre Dame 3; Lay Teachers 15; Students 281.
Catechesis/Religious Programs—Tel: 301-790-2444.
Students 208.
Mission—Boonsboro, Washington Co., St. James, c/o 224 W. Washington St., 21740. Tel: 410-432-2887.

Hancock, Washington Co., St. Peter's (1834), Rev. George W. Glick.
Res., 16 E. High St., 21750. Tel: 301-678-6339; Fax: 301-678-7578. [CEM]
Mission—Little Orleans, Allegany Co., St. Patrick's, (1860) 12517 St Patrick Rd. S.E., Little Orleans, 21766. [CEM]
Mailing Address: 16 E. High St., 21750.

Havre de Grace, Harford Co., St. Patrick's (1847), Rev. Frank C. McFadden.
Res., 615 Congress Ave., 21078. Tel: 410-939-2525; 575-6741; Fax: 410-575-6490. [CEM]
Catechesis/Religious Programs—Tel: 410-939-2547.
Students 154.

Hickory, Harford Co., St. Ignatius (1792), Rev. Kenneth Farabaugh; Deacons Robert Lehr; Ralph Trautwein; Sr. Marjorie Gallagher, S.N.D., Pastoral Assoc.
Res., 533 E. Jarrettsville Rd., Forest Hill, 21050. Tel: 410-879-1926; Fax: 410-879-1352. [CEM]
Catechesis/Religious Programs—Tel: 410-879-9390.
Students 1,023.

Hunt Valley, Baltimore Co., St. Francis Xavier (1988), Rev. Msgr. Thomas J. Donellan.
Mailing Address: Ste. LL1, Exec. Plaza I, 11350 McCormick Rd., 21031. Tel: 410-785-0356; Fax: 410-785-1628.
Res., Hampton House, Apt. 515, 204 E. Joppa Rd., Towson, 21286. Tel: 410-938-8860.

Hydes, Baltimore Co., St. John the Evangelist (1822), Revs. Martin R. Strempeck; Charles M. Wible; Deacon J. Donald Murray.
Res., 13305 Long Green Pike, 21082. Tel: 410-592-6206; Fax: 410-817-4432. [CEM]
School—Tel: 410-592-9585, Ext. 120; Fax: 410-817-4548. Mrs. Genevieve Delcher, Prin.
School Sisters of Notre Dame 2; Lay Teachers 27; Students 355.
Catechesis/Religious Programs—Tel: 410-592-6206, Ext. 107. Ms. M. Theresa Konitzer, D.R.E.
Students 774.

Jessup, Anne Arundel Co., St. Lawrence (1866), Rev. William J. Axe, O.SS.T. In res., Rev. Stanley W. DeBoe, O.SS.T.
Res., 7669 Clark Rd., Hanover, 21076. Tel: 410-799-1970; Fax: 410-799-4425. [CEM]
Catechesis/Religious Programs—St. Lawrence School of Religion, P.O. Box 1188, 20794. Tel: 410-799-7790.
Students 129.

Joppa, Harford Co., Church of the Holy Spirit (1963), Rev. Joseph C. Simmons.
Res., 540 Joppa Farm Rd., 21085. Tel: 410-679-2191.
Office: Tel: 410-679-0377; Fax: 410-679-2874.
Catechesis/Religious Programs—Students 205.

Laurel, Anne Arundel Co., Resurrection of Our Lord (1968), Rev. Joseph F. Kitko; Deacon John N. Parrish; Sr. Ann E. Hartnett, S.S.N.D., Pastoral Assoc.
Res., 8402 Brock Bridge Rd., 20724. Tel: 410-792-7982; Fax: 410-792-8337.
Catechesis/Religious Programs—Students 216.

Libertytown, Frederick Co., St. Peter (1821), Rev. John Dietzenbach; Deacons Michael Misulia; James Wright.
Res., 9201 A Church St., Box 278, 21762. Tel: 301-898-5111; 898-9069; Fax: 301-898-4011. [CEM]
Catechesis/Religious Programs—Tel: 301-898-0783; Fax: 301-898-5111.
Students 650.

Linthicum Heights, Anne Arundel Co., St. Philip Neri (1964), Rev. Msgr. Francis X. Zorbach; Rev. John L. Lippold; Deacon Robert Keeley.
Res., 6405 S. Orchard Rd., 21090-2628. Tel: 410-859-0571; Fax: 410-859-5047.
School—6401 Orchard Rd., 21090. Tel: 410-859-1212. Teresa Baker, Prin.
Lay Teachers 25; Students 558.
Catechesis/Religious Programs—Tel: 410-859-0249.
Students 353.

Lonaconing, Allegany Co., St. Mary of the Annunciation (1865), Sr. Marietta Culhane, O.S.F., Pastoral Life Dir.
Res., 16102 St. Mary Ter., 21539. Tel: 301-463-2514; Fax: 301-463-6729. [CEM]

Manchester, Carroll Co., St. Bartholomew (1865), Rev. Michael J. Roach.
Res., 2940 Park Ave., P.O. Box 448, 21102-0448. Tel: 410-239-8207; Fax: 410-239-3216. [CEM]
Parish Center—3071 Park Ave., 21102. Tel: 410-239-8881.
Catechesis/Religious Programs—Students 442.

Middletown, Frederick Co., Holy Family Catholic Community (1986), Rev. John Charles Moore; Deacon P. Gregory Rausch.
Res., 3240 Old National Pike, 21769. Tel: 301-371-3239.
Church—7321 Burkittsville Rd., 21769. Tel: 301-473-4800; Fax: 301-371-6810.
Catechesis/Religious Programs—Students 387.

Midland, Allegany Co., St. Joseph (1891) (Irish), Sr. Joan Maenner, Pastoral Life Dir.
Mailing Address: P.O. Box 1, 21542. Tel: 301-777-7060; Fax: 301-463-6729. [CEM]

Millersville, Anne Arundel Co., Our Lady of the Fields (1902), Revs. John J. Auer; Thomas Gills; Deacons James L. Awalt; Anthony Grillo; Dennis Hayden; Edward Stoops; Albert Kosla; G. William Walker.
Res., 1069 Cecil Ave., 21108. Tel: 410-923-3133; 987-1551; Fax: 410-987-9723. [CEM]
School—Arthur Slade Regional Catholic School. See separate listing.
Catechesis/Religious Programs—Tel: 410-923-2195.
Students 623.

Mount Savage, Allegany Co., St. Patrick (1863), Deacon Robert Lilly; Sr. Joan Minella, S.S.N.D., Pastoral Life Dir.
Mailing Address: P.O. Box 577, 21545. Tel: 301-264-3521; Fax: 301-264-3603. [CEM]
Shipping Address:—15706 Church St., 21545.

Oakland, Garrett Co., St. Peter the Apostle (1852), Rev. F. Richard Spencer; Deacon James L. Comfort, Sr.
Res., 208 S. Fourth St., P.O. Box 186, 21550. Tel: 301-334-2202; Fax: 301-334-9006.
Mission—Kitzmiller, Garrett Co., Immaculate Conception, P.O. Box 186, 21550.

Odenton, Anne Arundel Co., St. Joseph (1924), Revs. John B. Harrison, C.SS.R.; Francis A. Poux, C.SS.R.; Modesto Martinez Navarro, T.C. (Hispanic); Guillermo Casa Ferrer, T.C. (Hispanic); Deacon Richard C. Swann.
Mailing Address: P.O. Box 172, 21113-0172.
Res., 1283 Odenton Rd., 21113. Tel: 410-551-9238; Fax: 410-674-4761.
School—Arthur Slade Regional Catholic School. See separate listing. Tel: 410-766-7130; Fax: 410-787-0594.
Catechesis/Religious Programs—Students 426.

Owensville, Anne Arundel Co., Our Lady of Sorrows (1866), Rev. Mark Logue.
Res., 101 Owensville Rd., West River, 20778. Tel: 410-867-2059 (Local); 269-6803 (Baltimore); Fax: 410-867-8276. [CEM]

Parkton, Baltimore Co., Our Lady of Grace (1974), Rev. Msgr. Nicholas P. Amato.
Res., 425 Everett Rd., P.O. Box 517, Monkton, 21111. Tel: 410-329-2102.
Parish Center—18310 Middletown Rd., P.O. Box 360, 21120. Tel: 410-329-6826.
Catechesis/Religious Programs—Students 473.

Pasadena, Anne Arundel Co., St. Jane Frances de Chantal (Riviera Beach) (1946), Revs. F. Dennis Tinder; Robert A. DiMattei; James Reusing; Deacon Fred Wendt.
Res., 8499 Virginia Ave., 21122. Tel: 410-255-4646; Fax: 410-437-5191.
School—Tel: 410-255-4750. Ronald Burinsky, Prin.
School Sisters of Notre Dame 3; Lay Teachers 23; Students 566.
Catechesis/Religious Programs—Tel: 410-437-4727.
Students 600.

Our Lady of the Chesapeake (1979), Rev. Brian M. Rafferty.
Church—8325 Ventnor Rd., 21122. Tel: 410-255-3677; Fax: 410-437-7527.
Catechesis/Religious Programs—Tel: 410-255-3677; Fax: 410-437-7527.
Students 200.

Poplar Springs, Howard Co., St. Michael (1879), Rev. Michael Ruane; Deacons William Fallon; Gary Fulmer.
Res., 1200 St. Michael's Rd., Mt. Airy P.O., 21771. Tel: 410-489-4211; 442-2845; Fax: 410-442-1486 (Call first). [CEM]
Parish Center—Tel: 410-489-7667; 442-1717; 442-1486; Fax: 410-442-1486 (Call first).
Catechesis/Religious Programs—Tel: 410-489-2979.
Students 559.

Pylesville, Harford Co., St. Mary (1855), Rev. A. Henry Kunkel, III; Deacons Simon Driesen; John R. Simpson.
Res., 1021 St. Mary's Rd., 21132. Tel: 410-452-5166; 879-4015; Fax: 410-452-8493. [CEM]
Catechesis/Religious Programs—Tel: 410-838-7471.
Students 476.

Randallstown, Baltimore Co., Holy Family (1876), Revs. Edward J. Bayer; Walter J. McGovern, Senior Priest; William A. Collins; John J. Lombardi; Deacon Richard W. Montalto, Pastoral Assoc. & Admin.
Res., 9533 Liberty Rd., 21133. Tel: 410-521-3883; Fax: 410-922-3804. [CEM]
Office: Tel: 410-922-3800; Fax: 410-922-3804.
School—Tel: 410-922-3677; Fax: 410-521-9764. Helen Roby, Prin.
Sisters 1; Lay Teachers 16; Students 219.
Catechesis/Religious Programs—9531 Liberty Rd., 21133. Tel: 410-922-2805.
Students 132.

Severn, Anne Arundel Co., St. Bernadette (1969), Rev. Domenic L. Cieri.
Res., 801 Stevenson Rd., 21144. Tel: 410-969-2783; Fax: 410-969-2789.

School—Arthur Slade Regional Catholic School. See separate listing. Tel: 410-766-7130; Fax: 410-787-0594.
Catechesis/Religious Programs—Tel: 410-969-2786.
Students 324.

Severna Park, Anne Arundel Co., St. John the Evangelist (1959), Rev. Msgr. Edward F. Staub; Revs. Joseph J. Cosgrove; Richard B. Hilgartner, Jr.; Deacons John Naughton, (Retired); Dean Lopata.
Res., 689 Ritchie Hwy., S.E., 21146. Tel: 410-647-4884; Fax: 410-544-3047.
School—Tel: 410-647-2283; Fax: 410-431-5438. Sr. Linda Larsen, S.S.J., Prin.
Sisters of St. Joseph, Chestnut Hill 4; Lay Teachers 38; Students 600.
Catechesis/Religious Programs—Tel: 410-647-4892.
Students 748.
Convent—Tel: 410-647-2041.

Sykesville, Carroll Co., St. Joseph (1868), Revs. Patrick J. Tonry, S.M.; Paul A. Reich, S.M.; Terence P. Weik, S.M.; Thomas J. French, S.M.
Office: 915 Liberty Rd., Eldersburg, 21784. Tel: 410-795-7838; Fax: 410-795-7516.
Res., 7620 Mellor Ave., P.O. Box 384, 21784. Tel: 410-795-2722. [CEM]
Catechesis/Religious Programs—Students 1,070.

Taneytown, Carroll Co., St. Joseph (1797), Revs. Martin Eugene Feild; Paul F. Dolan, Pastor Emeritus; Deacons Darrell W. Smith; Stanley Wise.
Res., 44 Frederick St., 21787. Tel: 410-756-2500; Fax: 410-756-1260. [CEM]
Catechesis/Religious Programs—Tel: 410-876-8108.
Students 131.

Thurmont, Frederick Co., Our Lady of Mount Carmel (1856), Rev. Leo R. Tittler; Sr. Carol C. Czyzewski, F.S.S.J., Pastoral Assoc., Tel: 301-271-7300; Sr. Mary Jan Nasiadka, F.S.S.J., Pastoral Min., Tel: 301-271-7300.
Office—16150 St. Anthony Rd., Emmitsburg, 21727. Tel: 301-447-2367; Fax: 301-447-3618.

Timonium, Baltimore Co., Church of the Nativity (1968), Rev. Michael J. White; Rev. Msgr. Charles F. Meisel, Pastor Emeritus.
Office: 20 E. Ridgely Rd., 21093. Tel: 410-252-6080; Fax: 410-252-2657.
Res., Tel: 410-252-0345.
Catechesis/Religious Programs—Kathleen P. Mclhinney, D.R.E.
Students 526.

Urbana, Frederick Co., St. Ignatius Loyola (1879), Rev. Thomas Polk.
Res., 3523 Urbana Pike, Frederick, 21704. Tel: 301-865-5783; Fax: 301-695-0259.
Office: 3523 Urbana Pike, 21701. Tel: 301-695-8845; Fax: 301-695-0259.
Church—R.R. 80, Fingerboard Rd.
Catechesis/Religious Programs—Tel: 301-695-8879.
Students 194.

Walkersville, Frederick Co., St. Timothy (1980), Rev. Richard J. Murphy.
Res., 200 Glade Blvd., 21793. Tel: 301-845-8028; Fax: 301-845-0332.
Catechesis/Religious Programs—Tel: 301-845-8025.
Students 257.

Westernport, Allegany Co., St. Peter (1851), Rev. James W. Hannon.
Res., 127 Church St., 21562. Tel: 301-359-3055; Fax: 301-359-0657. [CEM]
School—Lay Teachers 4; Students 69.
Mission—Barton, St. Gabriel.

Westminster, Carroll Co., St. John (1789), Rev. Msgr. Arthur Valenzano; Revs. John DoBranski; Robert E. Morey; Deacons John Coster; Robert Malinowski.
Res., 43 Monroe St., 21157. Tel: 410-848-4744; 876-2248; Fax: 410-857-1519. [CEM]
School—Tel: 410-848-7455.
Lay Teachers 19; Students 425.
Catechesis/Religious Programs—Tel: 410-848-8443.
Students 1,435.

Williamsport, Washington Co., St. Augustine (1854), Rev. Alfred E. Smith; Deacon Andrew Komarinski.
Res., 32 E. Potomac St., 21795. Tel: 301-223-7959; Fax: 301-223-9506. [CEM]
Mission—Clear Spring, Washington Co., St. Michael.

Woodstock, Baltimore Co., St. Alphonsus Rodriguez (1869), Rev. Joseph R. Lerch, S.J.
Res., 10800 Old Court Rd., 21163. Tel: 410-461-5267; Fax: 410-750-7286. [CEM]
Catechesis/Religious Programs—Students 191.

Chaplains of Public Institutions

BALTIMORE. *Baltimore City Correctional Center, Baltimore Pre-Release Unit*. Deacon Bob Malinowski.
Baltimore City Jail. Rev. Damien Nalepa, Chap.
Baltimore City Jail, Women's Detention Center. Sr. Margaret Costello, S.S.J., Chap.
Carroll County Detention Center. John Shetler, Lay Coord.
Charles H. Hickey School. Deacon Russell Matthews, Chap.
Church Hospital. Covered on rotating basis by St. Casimir, St. Elizabeth, St. Michael (Wolfe St.), Sacred Heart of Jesus, St. Brigid, St. Wenceslaus, Holy Rosary and St. Stanislaus parish staff.
Dismas House. Rev. Joseph R. Wenderoth, Chap.
Francis Scott Key Medical Center. Staffed by Our Lady of Fatima Parish.
Franklin Square Hospital. Rev. E. Gerard Huesman; Deacons Nicholas F. Feurer; Daniel R. Kopczyk; Walter Shipley.
Greater Baltimore Medical Center. Rev. Salvatore J. Livigni.
Harbor Hospital. Covered on rotating basis by Holy Cross, St. Mary Star of the Sea, Our Lady of Good Counsel, St. Veronica, St. Rose and St. Athanasius parish staff.
Johns Hopkins Medical Institutions. Rev. Alphonse G. Rose.
Maryland Correctional Adjustment Center. Rev. Charles J. Canterna, Chap.
Maryland Penitentiary. Deacon Bob Malinowski.
Rosewood State Hospital. Vacant.
Spring Grove Center Hospital. Rev. F. Philip Vogel, S.D.S.
University of Maryland Hospital. Revs. Lawrence Schulmeister, O.F.M.; William H. O'Brien.
Veterans Hospital, Baltimore. Rev. Conan H. Timoney, C.P., Chap.
Veterans Hospital, Fort Howard. Rev. Conan H. Timoney, C.P., Chap.

CROWNSVILLE. *Crownsville Hospital Center*. Staffed by St. Mary's Parish, Annapolis.

HAGERSTOWN. *Maryland Correctional Institution*. Sr. Dolores Chepiga, S.S.J.
Maryland Correctional Training Center. Sr. Dolores Chepiga, S.S.J.
Roxbury Correctional Institution. Sr. Dolores Chepiga, S.S.J.

JESSUP. *Brockbridge Pre-Release Unit*. Jim Sanders, Lay Coord.
Maryland Correctional Institution. Mary Dunn, Lay Coord.
Maryland Correctional Institution for Women. Jim Sanders, Lay Coord.
Maryland House of Correction & Annex. Rev. Jeffrey Carlsen, Chap.
Patuxent Institute. Sr. Beatrice Marriotti.
Perkins Hospital. Sr. Beatrice Marriotti.

SYKESVILLE. *Springfield Hospital Center*. Rev. Stanley Janaites, Chap.; Deacon George C. Wachter, Chap.
Sykesville Laundry Facility. Bryan Masterson, Lay Coord.; Richard Horwitt, Lay Coord.

Special Assignment:
Reverend Monsignors—
Kenney, Jeremiah F., Tribunal, 320 Cathedral St., Baltimore, MD 21201
Malooly, Francis W., Chancellor, 320 Cathedral St., Baltimore, MD 21201
Schleupner, G. Michael, Sec., Dept. of Mgmt. Svcs.
Reverend Fathers—
Abrahams, John, Chap., Perry Point VA Medical Center
Albright, Robert E., Campus Ministry, Towson, MD 21204
Barker, James, Vocation Dir., 320 Cathedral St., Baltimore, MD 21201
Bergquist, Patrick, Missionary Work, Fairbanks, AK
Bonderenko, Thomas, Admin. Shelter & Food Programs, A.C.C.
Breighner, Joseph F., Special Ministry
Byrne, Glenn, St. Anthony Church, Allston, MA 02134
Canterna, Charles J., Chap., Baltimore City Jail & Maryland Penitentiary
Carey, David M., Special Ministry
Carlsen, Jeffrey, Chap., Maryland House of Correction & Annex
Carrion, Patrick, Interim Pastoral Admin.
Chase, Raymond, Gallagher Center
Collins, William A., Tribunal, 320 Cathedral St., Baltimore, MD 21201
Collopy, John C., Dir. Senior & Retired Priests
Delclos, John L., 320 Cathedral St., Baltimore, MD 21201
Francik, Gerard, Chap., Mt. St. Mary's College, Emmitsburg
Hawkins, Robert, Chap., St. Martin Home for Aged
Hendricks, Edward S., Campus Minister, Frostburg, MD
Janaites, Stanley, Chap., Springfield Hospital
Jarboe, J. Bruce, Assoc. Dir., Pastoral Personnel Serv.
Johnson, Lawrence M., Chap., Cardinal Sheehan Center
Lobert, Richard C., Teaching
Lupico, Samuel J., Chap., St. Joseph Hospital, Baltimore
Madden, Denis J., Neareast Welfare, NY
Martin, Joseph C., S.S., 103 Foxridge Dr., Havre de Grace, MD 21078
Raum, Blair, Dir., Project Rachel
Riepe, Charles K., Chap., John Hopkins Univ., Newman Apostolate, Baltimore, MD
Rose, Alphonse G., Chap., John Hopkins Hospital, Baltimore, MD
Simms, William, Archdiocesan Tribunal, 320 Cathedral St., Baltimore, MD 21201
Snouffer, Philip T., Div. of Information Systems, 320 Cathedral St., Baltimore, MD 21201
Spillane, Michael, Washington, DC
Thomas, Paul, Archdiocesan Archivist
Ward, John B., Asst. Chancellor
Wenderoth, Joseph
Woy, Richard, Dir., Pastoral Personnel Svcs.

On Duty Outside the Archdiocese:
Reverend Fathers—
Hisky, William G., Perrypoint V.A. Medical Ctr., 5288 E. Pulaski Hwy., Perryville, MD 21903
Hoffman, David, Immaculate Heart Hermitage, Big Sur, CA
Obrimski, Paul G.
Warman, William C.

Military Chaplains:
Reverend Fathers—
Carter, John T., U.S.N.
Cummings, Carl
Fitzgerald, John L., CHC, U.S.N.
Wilson, Stuart T., U.S.N., 840 17th St., Apt. 402, San Diego, CA 92101
Zeller, Leonard H., U.S.A.F.

Absent on Leave:
Reverend Monsignors—
Kinsella, John
Reverend Fathers—
Cooper, Craig D.
Cox, Brian
DePetris, Joseph J.
Dowdy, James H.
Hart, J. Joseph, Jr.
Hirt, William
Le Fevre, Francis J.
Losemann, Heinrich J., Jr.
Maskell, A. Joseph
Rouse, Charles
Toohey, Jerome
Wade, Michael J.

Awaiting Assignment:
Reverend Fathers—
O'Brien, William

Retired:
Reverend Monsignors—
Bozel, Robert A., St. Elizabeth Hall M-201, 2300 Dulaney Valley Rd., Timonium, MD 21093
Bradley, Joseph P., 116 W. University Pkwy., Apt. 710, Baltimore, MD 21210
Broderick, Gerard W., St. John Hall, Long Crandon, 2300 Dulaney Valley Rd., Timonium, MD 21093
Cronin, James J., St. Joan of Arc, 257 S. Law St., Aberdeen, MD 21001
Fortenbaugh, Francis W., St. Agnes Rectory, 5422 Old Frederick Rd., Baltimore, MD 21228
Kenny, Simon E., St. John Hall, Long Crandon, 2300 Dulaney Valley Rd., Timonium, MD 21093
McGowan, Myles, 3 Baratra Ct., Apt. 204, Timonium, MD 21093
Meisel, Charles F., St. Elizabeth Hall, Apt. W 301, 2300 Dulaney Valley Rd., Timonium, MD 21093
Mieczkowski, Chester J., St. Augustine Rectory, 5976 Old Washington Rd., Elkridge, MD 21227
Passarelli, Robert S., 27 First St., Frostburg, MD 21532
Phillips, Hugh J., Mount St. Mary's College, Emmitsburg, MD 21727
Reinsfelder, John L., Holy Cross Rectory, 110 E. West St., Baltimore, MD 21230
Satterfield, Carroll E., 363 Homeland Southway, Apt. 1, Baltimore, MD 21212
Sauerwein, Anthony L., St. John Hall, Long Crandon, 2300 Dulaney Valley Rd., Timonium, MD 21093
Schwalenberg, Martin, 8465 Meadow Ln., Riviera Beach, MD 21122
Spraker, Gerard W., St. Martin Home, 601 Maiden Choice Ln., Baltimore, MD 21228

Reverend Fathers—
Altmann, George, 32 Carrolls Tract Rd., Fairfield, PA 17320
Barbernitz, John P., P.O. Box 248, Orrville, AL 36767
Bowling, Frederick T., Keswick Multi-Care Center, 700 40th St., Baltimore, MD 21211
Boyle, Howard, Anchorage Tower #301, 2515 Boston St., Baltimore, MD 21224
Buettner, George, 600 Light St., Apt. 351, Baltimore, MD 21230
Byrd, Thomas J., Mount St. Mary's Seminary, Emmitsburg, MD 21727
Carney, John, College Lanes Apts., #801-J, Salisbury, MD 21801
Coady, Edward L., 1221 First St., 8A, Jacksonville Beach, FL 32250-6446
Collopy, John C., St. John Hall, Long Crandon, 2300 Dulaney Valley Rd., Timonium, MD 21093
Coyne, Patrick J., St. Croix House, 106 E. West St., Baltimore, MD 21230
Dolan, Paul F., St. John Hall, Long Crandon, 2300 Dulaney Valley Rd., Timonium, MD 21093
Fannon, Thomas J., St. Elizabeth Hall F210, 2300 Dulaney Valley Rd., Timonium, MD 21093
FitzGerald, William, St. Brigid Rectory, 2 North Belnord Ave., Baltimore, MD 21224
Gallagher, Joseph J., 3838 Roland Ave., #1302, Baltimore, MD 21211
Gies, Norman J., 2453 Brazilia Dr., Apt. 21, Clearwater, FL 21163
Hill, Edward T., U.S.N., 4614 Eugene Ave., Baltimore, MD 21206
Hoat, Rochus Vu Dinh, St. Mary Rectory, 5502 York Rd., Baltimore, MD 21212
Hopkins, Robert, 941 Bishop Walsh Rd., Cumberland, MD 21502
Hughes, Joseph B., 2034 Park Ave., Baltimore, MD 21217
Kaczkowski, Leon, Stella Maris Hospice, 2300 Dulaney Valley Rd., Timonium, MD 21093
Kaiser, Joseph A., St. John Hall, Long Crandon, 2300 Dulaney Valley Rd., Timonium, MD 21093
Kelmartin, John J., 9050 Waltham Woods Rd., Apt. C, Baltimore, MD 21234
Kenney, Joseph A., Stella Maris Hospice, 2300 Dulaney Valley Rd., Timonium, MD 21093
Klein, Charles R., Sacred Heart of Mary, 6736 Youngstown Ave., Baltimore, MD 21222
Krach, Joseph W., 805 Union Ave., Baltimore, MD 21211
La Porta, Gerald, 4136 Fairway Dr., Little River, SC 29566
Messer, Joseph V., Good Shepherd Rectory, 1451 Furnace Ave., Glen Burnie, MD 21061
Moody, William, 86 Mt. Pleasant St., Frostburg, MD 21532
Muller, Kennard, St. Elizabeth, 2 N. Belnoro Ave., Baltimore, MD 21224
Muller, Myles, St. Elizabeth Hall M101, 2300 Dulaney Valley Rd., Timonium, MD 21093
Paulits, Walter J., 7853 Americana Circle, Apt. 102, Glen burnie, MD 21061
Peterson, Casimir M., 3601 Greenway, Apt. 704, Baltimore, MD 21218
Pugevicues, Casimir A., Pal. Jorge Matulaicio 2.3, 2056 Vilnius, Lithuania
Quinn, Charles H., St. John Hall, Long Crandon, 2300 Dulaney Valley Rd., Timonium, MD 21093
Reed, Robert A., St. Benedict Rectory, 2612 Wilkens Ave., Baltimore, MD 21223
Sargus, Edward T., Lawn Acres, 420 S. 57 St., Hollywood, FL 33023
Shaum, David, Mount St. Mary's College, P.O. Box 246, Emmitsburg, MD 21727
Stroup, Edmund F., 36 E. Drumbred Rd., Villas, NJ 08251
Warczynski, Leon, 3316 Beverly Rd., Baltimore, MD 21214
West, Gerald, Franciscan Sisters of Baltimore Generalate, 3725 Ellerslie Ave., Baltimore, MD 21218
Wisniewski, Theodore, 5709 Magie St., Baltimore, MD 21225

Permanent Deacons:
Abell, John H., Jr., Our Lady of Sorrows, Owensville
Albaugh, William S., St. Joseph, Fullerton
Anderson, Carl A., St. Edward, Baltimore
Antczak, George, St. Thomas Aquinas, Baltimore
Awalt, James L., Our Lady of the Fields, Millersville
Bankard, Alphonse, Our Lady of Fatima, Baltimore
Baranoski, Melvin L., (Retired)
Baynes, Charles A., St. Joseph, Fullerton
Bee, James E., St. Ann, Baltimore
Beimel, Leory W., Holy Trinity, Glen Burnie
Berg, James R., San Antonio, TX
Bisser, John, Leave of Absence
Boscoe, John, Holy Trinity, Glen Burnie
Briscoe, John, St. Peter Claver
Britt, Ray, Resurrection, Ellicott City
Bullinger, Raymond A., St. Charles, Pikesville
Carpenter, Harry G., (Retired)
Casey, J. Faherty, St. John, Frederick
Chesnavage, Albert W., Sacred Heart of Mary, Baltimore
Ciesla, Paul R., St. Margaret, Bel Air
Clyde, Harry, Leave of Absence
Codd, John J., Sr., St. Lawrence, Baltimore
Colson, Norman E., (Retired)
Comfort, James L., Sr., St. Peter the Apostle, Oakland
Concordia, Louis, St. Michael, Frostburg
Conley, David, St. Mary, Cumberland
Cook, Charles E., (Retired)
Coster, John E., St. John, Westminster
Crawford, Raymond C., Our Lady of Perpetual Help, Ilchester
Davis, Henry, St. Michael, Overlea
DeAngelis, William J., St. Joseph, Fullerton
Derouaux, Bert, (Retired)
Dignan, Paul H., St. Patrick, Cumberland
Driesen, Simon, St. Mary, Pylesville
Evans, George T., St. Rita, Baltimore
Fallon, William L., St. Michael, Poplar Springs
Feurer, Nicholas E., St. Clement and Franklin Square Hospital, Rosedale
Fitzpatrick, T. Kelly, Unassigned
Fulmer, Gary Lee, St. Michael, Poplar Springs
Fulton, Watson, Jr., St. Ambrose, Baltimore
Gardner, Edward L., Sr., Holy Trinity, Glen Burnie
Gibson, T. Russell, (Retired)
Goles, Patrick J., St. Margaret, Bel Air
Grabenstein, Herman J., SS. Peter & Paul, Cumberland
Graham, Robert L., Holy Family, Davidsonville
Gramling, John C., Immaculate Conception, Towson
Grape, William F., (Retired)
Grillo, Anthony, Our Lady of the Fields, Millersville
Gross, Theodore C., (Retired)
Hacker, Robert, Church Home and Hospital, Baltimore
Harcum, Philip W., St. Bernardine, Baltimore
Harris, Jhan M., St. Veronica, Baltimore
Hartlieb, Gilbert J., St. Stephen, Bradshaw
Hayden, Dennis L., Our Lady of the Fields, Millersville
Hicks, Charles, St. Mark, Fallston
Hiebler, Charles H., Jr., Immaculate Heart of Mary, Baltimore
Hodges, Frank P., Corpus Christi, Baltimore
Jakowski, Chester J., SS. Philip & James, Baltimore
Jauquet, William, Our Lady of Victory, Baltimore
Jenkins, George, Our Lady Queen of Peace, Baltimore
Jensen, Joseph E., Unassigned
Johe, Richard, (Retired)
Kalb, John L., Jr., (Retired)
Keating, Joseph J., (Retired)
Keeley, Robert L., St. Philip Neri, Linthicum Heights
Keenan, Robert G., St. Ursula, Baltimore
Kempf, William J., Jr., Unassigned
Kent, James R., Sr., St. Isaac Jogues, Baltimore
Knight, Charles, St. Bernardine, Baltimore
Komarinski, Andrew, (Retired)
Kopczyk, Daniel R., St. Joan of Arc, Aberdeen
Kosla, Albert F., Our Lady of the Fields, Millersville
Kruger, Charles R., Jr., Holy Rosary, Baltimore
Krysiak, Joseph C., St. Anthony Padua and Most Precious Blood, Baltimore
Kucharczyk, John, Holy Rosary, Baltimore
Kuhl, Thomas, Our Lady of Pompei, Baltimore
Kunkel, Richard, St. Ann, Hagerstown
Lambert, Francis E., Out of State
Landers, Joseph T., St. Anthony, Baltimore
Langbehn, Eugene, St. Francis of Assisi, Fulton
Latrick, Donald P., Holy Family Ukrainian Catholic Church
Laws, Francis R., St. Stephen, Bradshaw
LeFevre, George F., (Retired)
Lehr, Robert I., St. Ignatius, Hickory
Lonesome, Clifford, St. Pius V, Baltimore
Lopata, Dean M., St. John, Severna Park
Lynne, Robert O., SS. Philip and James, Baltimore
MacKnew, J. Donald, St. Margaret, Bel Air
Malinowski, Robert, St. John, Westminster
Manley, John L., St. Timothy, Walkersville
Mann, James L., Sr., St. Thomas More, Baltimore
Mann, Paul T., St. Gabriel, Woodlawn
Maranto, Anthony S., St. Dominic, Baltimore
Martelle, John T., St. Rita and Church Hospital, Dundalk
Martin, George W., St. John, Columbia
Martin, John, Immaculate Heart of Mary, Baltimore
Matthews, Russell, St. Francis Xavier and Maryland Training School for Boys, Baltimore
Matthews, Wayne, Unassigned
McAndrews, George F., St. John, Columbia
McCoy, Michael, St. Thomas More, Baltimore
McKenna, John I., St. Clement, Lansdowne
Mercer, Charles S., St. Francis Xavier, Baltimore
Michael, Bertrand O., St. Michael, Frostburg
Micozzi, Arthur L., St. Isaac Jogues, Baltimore
Miller, Donald, St. William of York, Baltimore
Miller, Eugene, Jr., Unassigned
Miller, Ferdinand G., St. Clare, Essex
Mills, Hugh, Jr., St. Clement, Lansdowne
Misulia, Michael, St. Peter, Libertytown
Monaghan, James, St. Andrew by the Bay, Cape St. Claire
Montalto, Richard W., Holy Family, Randallstown
Mooney, Loren, St. Patrick, Cumberland
Moore, LeRoy S., St. Mary, Annapolis
Moritz, Francis X., (Retired)
Morris, Richard F., St. Elizabeth of Hungary, Baltimore
Murphy, Lawrence, Resurrection, Laurel
Murray, Donald, St. John the Evangelist, Hydes
Nairn, William P., St. Ann, Hagerstown
Naughton, John F., (Retired)
Neale, Joseph L., St. Edward, Baltimore
Norcio, Anthony F., St. Mary, Annapolis
Novak, Richard D., St. Patrick and Church Home Hospital, Baltimore
Nuedling, Leo, Sacred Heart of Jesus, Baltimore
O'Neill, Harry St. A., St. Ursula, Baltimore
Oliver, Robert W., Basilica of the Assumption, Baltimore
Osorio-Carmona, Pablo E., Spanish Ministry
Parrish, John N., Church of Resurrection, Laurel
Perticone, Vincent, Jr., St. Joseph, Fullerton
Piet, Stanley G., (Retired)
Pinkney, Willard A., Jr., St. Veronica, Baltimore
Pivec, J. Kenneth, Immaculate Heart of Mary, Baltimore
Provenza, Vincent, (Retired)
Rafter, John J., Jr., St. John, Hydes
Raible, Gerald A., St. Patrick, Cumberland
Rausch, Paul G., Holy Family, Middletown
Reinsfelder, Edward, Unassigned
Resh, Michael K., Leave of Absence
Roberts, Gerald A., Univ. of Maryland Hospital and St. Jerome, Baltimore
Roff, Daniel, St. John the Evangelist, Frederick
Rongione, Frank, St. Ursula, Baltimore
Rose, Alan, Prison Ministry
Roy, Americus M., (Retired)
Ryan, James A., Sacred Heart,Glyndon
Sainz, Miguel E., St. Mary and Spanish Apostolate, Govans
Schoennagel, Frederick, Annunciation, Baltimore
Schott, Robert G., St. Stephen, Bradshaw
Schultz, Joseph L., St. Anthony, Baltimore
Seibold, Frederick, St. Elizabeth Ann Seton, Crofton
Shelton, Paul D., All Saints, Baltimore
Shipley, Walter R., Jr., (Retired)
Siarkowski, Henry L., Shrine of the Little Flower, Baltimore
Simpson, John R., St. Mary, Pylesville
Smith, Alexander, St. Veronica, Baltimore
Smith, Darrell, St. Joseph, Taneytown
Smith, Earl A., St. Edward, Baltimore
Smith, Walton, St. Francis Xavier, Baltimore
Spytkowski, Daniel, St. William of York, Baltimore
Stine, Richard J., St. Francis de Sales, Abingdon
Stoops, Edward, Our Lady of the Fields, Millersville
Stretmater, Daniel, Jr., St. Louis, Clarksville
Sullivan, Edward C., St. Joseph, Cockeysville
Swann, C. Richard, (Retired)
Swanson, James V., Unassigned
Szuchnicki, Alexander P., (Retired)
Teixeira, Lawrence, St. Louis, Clarksville
Thompson, Malcolm, All Saints, Baltimore
Trautwein, Ralph, St. Ignatius, Hickory
Vassie, Frederick, Unassigned
Vaughan, William E., (Retired)
Villagaray, Rafael F., Hispanic Ministry
Wachter, George C., Springfield Hospital Center, Sykesville
Walker, George W., Jr., Our Lady of the Fields, Millersville
Wendt, Fred, St. Jane Frances de Chantal, Riviera Beach
Werner, Francis L., St. Patrick, Cumberland
Westwater, James, St. Isaac Jogues, Baltimore
Wiedel, Verdaw P., St. Louis, Clarksville
Wilson, John L., St. Mary, Annapolis
Wilson, Thomas A., St. Cecilia, Baltimore
Wise, Stanley L., St. Joseph, Taneytown
Woofter, R. Paul, St. Andrew by the Bay, Cape St. Claire
Wright, James, Hospice of Frederick Co.
Yannuzzi, Thomas J., St. Clement, Lansdowne
Yorkshire, Thomas X., St. Gregory, Baltimore

Zeiler, Francis, St. Clement, Rosedale

INSTITUTIONS LOCATED IN THE ARCHDIOCESE

[A] SEMINARIES, ARCHDIOCESAN

BALTIMORE. *St. Mary's Seminary and University*, 5400 Roland Ave., 21210. Tel: 410-864-4000; Fax: 410-864-4278. Legal Title: *St. Mary's Seminary and University*. His Eminence William Cardinal Keeler, D.D., J.C.D., Archbishop of Baltimore, Chancellor, Chm. Board of Trustees.
Officers of the Administration: Revs. Robert F. Leavitt, S.S., S.T.D., Pres.-Rector; Roger E. McGrath, S.S., Ph.D., Vice Rector; James J. Conn, S.J., J.D., J.C.D., Dean, School of Theology; John W. Bowen, S.S., Alumni News Editor; Richard G. Childs, M.B.A., Vice Pres. for Admin. & Finance; Michael J. Gorman, Ph.D., Dean, Ecumenical Institute of Theology; Rev. Timothy Kulbicki, O.F.M.Conv., H.E.D., Dir. Field Education; Mrs. Christa R. Klein, Ph.D., Dean, Center for Continuing Formation; Mrs. Kathleen P. Mignini, Business Mgr.; Mrs. Susan A. Lemmon, Registrar, School of Theology & Ecumenical Institute of Theology; Ms. Priscilla Y. Gordon, M.A., Financial Aid Officer; Mr. David P. Siemsen, M.L.S., Dir., Library Svcs.; Mrs. Elizabeth L. Visconage, B.S., Dir., Institutional Advancement.
Faculty: Revs. Michael L. Barre, S.S., S.T.L., Ph.D.; Thomas J. Burke, O.SS.T., S.T.M.; E. Michael Camilli, M.S.C., S.T.B., S.T.L.; James J. Conn, S.J., M.A., M.Div., J.C.D., J.D; Michael J. Gorman, M.Div., Ph.D.; Mrs. Tina Lamberti, M.Ed.; Patricia A. Lamoureux, Ph.D.; Revs. Philip S. Keane, S.S., S.T.D.; Robert F. Leavitt, S.S., S.T.D.; Patrick J. Madden, M.A., M.Div., Ph.D.; John J. Markey, O.P., M.Div., Ph.D.; Roger E. McGrath, S.T.L., Ph.D.; David M. O'Leary, M.Ed., S.T.L.; Anthony R. Perez, S.S., M.Div., S.T.D.; Daniel M. Ruff, S.J., M.A., M.Div., S.T.M.; Charles J.T. Talar, M.A., Ph.D., S.T.D.; Mr. David P. Siemsen, M.L.S.
Adjunct Academic Faculty: Mr. Peter Culman, B.A.; Ms. Sylvia P. Moore, B.S.; Mr. Kenneth D. Hines, M.A., S.T.B., Ph.L.; Mrs. Mary E. Hines, M.A., Ph.D.; Revs. Peter A. Lyons, T.O.R., S.T.L., Ph.D.; William W. Rich, M.A., M.Div.; Ross A. Shecterle, S.T.L., M.S.; David D. Thayer, S.S., S.T.M., S.T.L., Ph.D.; Thomas R. Ulshafer, S.S., S.T.L., Ph.D; Stephen J. Vicchio, Ph.D. Diocesan Seminarians 71; Diocesan Seminarians on Pastoral Leave 4; Others Studying 6; Priests 18; Lay Teachers 8.
Ecumenical Institute of Theology, 5400 Roland Ave., 21210. Tel: 410-864-4200. Michael J. Gorman, M.Div., Ph.D. Students 219.

EMMITSBURG. *Mount St. Mary's Seminary*, 21727-7797. Tel: 301-447-5295; Fax: 301-447-5636.
Web site: semweb@msmary.edu
Legal Title: *An integral part of corporation known as Mount St. Mary's College and Seminary.*
Administration: His Eminence William Cardinal Keeler, Chancellor and Chm. of Seminary Committee; Very Rev. Kevin C. Rhoades, S.T.L., J.C.L. (HBG), Rector; Revs. J. Daniel Mindling, O.F.M.Cap., S.T.D., Academic Dean; Lee W. Gross, M.Div. (ARL), Dean of Students; Edward M. Gaffney, O.P., S.T.B., Dir. Spiritual Formation; Sr. Paula Jean Miller, F.S.E., S.T.D., Coord. Pastoral Field Educ.; Mrs. Rosemary S. Mick, Admin. Asst. to Rector, (Admissions, Formation, Finance).
Full Time Faculty: Very Rev. Kevin C. Rhoades, S.T.L., J.C.L. (HBG); Revs. J. Michael Beers, Ph.D., S.S.L. (ALN); Edward M. Gaffney, O.P., S.T.B.; Lee W. Gross, M.Div. (ARL); Donald F. Haggerty, S.T.D. (NY); Frederick M. Jelly, O.P., S.T.D., S.T.Lr., (Sabbatical); J. Daniel Mindling, O.F.M.Cap., S.T.D.; Leonard G. Obloy, S.S.L. (CLV); David Pietropaoli, S.T.D, (BAL); Robert V. Zylla, O.S.C., S.T.L.; Sr. Joan Gormley, Ph.D.; Sr. Paula Jean Miller, F.S.E., S.T.D.; Mr. Richard A. Nicholas, Ph.D.; Dr. Pamela Jackson, Ph.D.
Part Time Faculty: Revs. Jame J. Conn, S.J., J.D., J.C.D.; Michael J. Roach, M.A. (BAL); Dr. Herbert W. Stroup, Ph.D.; Sr. Ann Miriam Gallagher, R.S.M., Ph.D.; Dr. Carol L. Houghton, S.T.D., J.C.D.; Dr. Herbert W. Stroup, Ph.D. Priests 12; Sisters 3; Lay Teachers 4; Lay Administrators 1; Support Staff 2; Total Staff 22; Diocesan Seminarians 194; Religious Seminarians 1; Others 6; Total Enrollment 201.

[B] COLLEGES AND UNIVERSITIES

BALTIMORE. *College of Notre Dame of Maryland*, 4701 N. Charles St., 21210. Tel: 410-435-0100
For a complete listing, refer to the Colleges and Universities section.

**Loyola College*, 4501 N. Charles St., 21210. Tel: 410-617-2000.
Web site: www.loyola.edu
For a complete listing, refer to the Colleges and Universities section.

EMMITSBURG. *Mount Saint Mary's College*, (1808), 21727. Tel: 301-447-6122
For a complete listing, refer to the Colleges and Universities section.

[C] HIGH SCHOOLS, PRIVATE

BALTIMORE. *Archbishop Curley High School*, 3701 Sinclair Ln., 21213. Tel: 410-485-5000; Fax: 410-483-2545.
E-mail: dgrzymski@curley.loyola.edu
Administered by Order of Friars Minor Conventual, St. Anthony of Padua Province (USA). Revs. Donald Grzymski, O.F.M.Conv., Pres. & Guardian; Michael Heine, O.F.M.Conv.; Thomas E. Walsh, O.F.M.Conv., Vicar; Ignatius M. Piatek, O.F.M.Conv.; Michael Martin, O.F.M.Conv., Prin.; Conrad Miller, O.F.M.Conv.; Bro. Christian Katusz, O.F.M.Conv.; Friars Pedro DeOliveira, O.F.M.Conv.; Gary Johnson, O.F.M.Conv. Priests 6; Brothers 1; Friars 2; Lay Teachers 38; Students 584; Total Staff 63.

Calvert Hall College, 8102 La Salle Rd., 21286. Tel: 410-825-4266.
Conducted by the Brothers of the Christian Schools (F.S.C.). Bros. Kevin Strong, F.S.C., Pres.; Kevin Stanton, F.S.C., Prin.; Mr. Louis Heidrick, Asst. Prin. Academic Affairs; Mr. Charles Stembler, Asst. Prin. Student Affairs. Brothers 14; Sisters 1; Lay Teachers 69; Students 1,101.

Cardinal Gibbons School for Boys (1962). (Grades 6-12), 3225 Wilkens Ave., 21229-4286. Tel: 410-644-1770.
E-mail: cardgib@connectinc.com
Mr. Gary T. Meyerl, Prin. Lay Teachers 21; Students 240.

The Catholic High School of Baltimore, 2800 Edison Hwy., 21213. Tel: 410-732-6200.
E-mail: chsb@ix.netcom.com
Web site: www.tchs.pvt.k12.md.us
Sisters of St. Francis of Philadelphia. Sisters 10; Lay Teachers 30; Students 427; Total Staff 58.

Institute of Notre Dame (1847), 901 Aisquith St., 21202. Tel: 410-522-7800. Legal Title: *Institute of Notre Dame, Inc.* Mary Fitzgerald, S.S.N.D., Prin. Sisters 9; Lay Teachers 25; Lay Employees 47; Counselors 2; Students 457.

Loyola High School, P.O. Box 6819, 21285-6819. Tel: 410-823-0601. Revs. James F. McAndrews, S.J., Pres.; J. Gregory Quinn, S.J., Rector; Joseph M. Alminde, S.J.; Michael J. Kuchera, S.J.; Henry Erhart, S.J.; Lloyd D. George, S.J.; D. Bradley Murray, S.J.; Robert B. Cullen, S.J.; Bros. Joseph M. Bonello, S.J., Minister; Darrell J. Burns, S.J., Chap.; Dr. Donald Urbancic, Headmaster; Mr. John T. Butler. Priests 7; Brothers 1; Scholastics 3; Lay Teachers 74; Students 935.

Mercy High School, 1300 E. Northern Pkwy., 21239. Tel: 410-433-8880.
E-mail: mercyhs@charm.net
Sisters of Mercy of the Americas. Sr. Carol E. Wheeler, R.S.M., Prin. Sisters 6; Lay Teachers 40; Students 478; Total Staff 79.

Mount de Sales Academy, 700 Academy Rd., 21228. Tel: 410-744-8498. Sr. Helen Marie Glaser, O.P., Headmistress. Sisters 6; Lay Teachers 32; Students 368.

Mt. St. Joseph College High School, 4403 Frederick Ave., 21229. Tel: 410-644-3300. Xaverian Brothers. Mr. Charles L. Reiter, Ph.D., Pres.; Mr. Barry J. Fitzpatrick, Prin. Priests 1; Brothers 3; Lay Teachers 72; Students 1,080; Total Staff 111.

St. Frances Academy. (Coed), 501 E. Chase St., 21202. Tel: 410-539-5794; Fax: 410-685-2650. Oblate Sisters of Providence. Sr. John Francis Schilling, O.S.P., Pres. & Prin.; Bro. Brian Henderson, F.S.C., Asst. Prin.; Mrs. Judy Treadwell, Dir. Guidance; Mr. Freddie Lee, Dean of Students. Brothers 3; Sisters 6; Lay Teachers 19; Students 254.

The Seton Keough High School, 1201 Caton Ave., 21227-1092. Tel: 410-646-4444. Sr. Marie Danielle Amspacher, S.S.N.D., Pres.; Donna M. Stadler, Prin.; Sr. Margaret Juskelis, S.S.N.D., Asst. Prin. (Academics); Portia Boston, Asst. Prin. & Dean of Students. Sisters 8; Lay Teachers 41; Students 488.

BEL AIR. *The John Carroll School*, 703 Churchville Rd., 21014. Tel: 410-879-2480; Fax: 410-836-8514. Mrs. Carol R. Goldbeck, Prin.; Mrs. Marellen Mayers, Campus Min. Priests 1; Sisters of St. Joseph Chestnut Hill 8; Lay Teachers 50; Students 735; Total Staff 105.

BROOKLANDVILLE. *Maryvale Preparatory School*. (Grades 6-12). (Girls), 21022. Tel: 410-252-3366. Sr. Shawn Marie Maguire, S.N.D., Prin. Sisters of Notre Dame de Namur 2; Lay Teachers 32; Students 290; Total Staff 50.

CUMBERLAND. *Bishop Walsh Middle-High School*. (Grades 6-12), 700 Bishop Walsh Rd., 21502. Tel: 301-724-5360.
E-mail: spartans@miworld.net
Web site: www.miworld.net/bishopwalsh/
Brothers of the Christian Schools, School Sisters of Notre Dame, Ursuline Sisters of Louisville. Bro. Kevin Dalmasse, F.S.C., Prin. Brothers 8; Sisters 2; Lay Teachers 23; Students 312.

FREDERICK. *St. John's Literary Institution at Prospect Hall* (1841). (Grades 9-12). (Coed), 889 Butterfly Ln., 21703. Tel: 301-662-4210.
E-mail: sjph@pop.erols.com
Mr. Thomas J. Peri, Headmaster; Mr. Thomas Farrell, Prin. of Academic Affairs. Priests 1; Lay Teachers 27; Students 245; Total Staff 37.

HAGERSTOWN. *St. Maria Goretti High School*. (Coed), 1535 Oak Hill Ave., 21742. Tel: 301-739-4266; Fax: 301-739-4261.
E-mail: goretti@goretti.org
Web site: goretti.org
Mr. Anthony M. Durso, Prin. Lay Teachers 20; Students 235; Total Staff 29.

SEVERN. *Archbishop Spalding High School*, 8080 New Cut Rd., 21144. Tel: 410-969-9105. Barbara H. Schwitzer, Prin.; Rev. Michael Callaghan, Chap. Priests 1; Lay Teachers 58; Students 876.

TOWSON. *Notre Dame Preparatory School*. (Grades 6-12), 815 Hampton Ln., 21286. Tel: 410-825-6202. Legal Title: *Notre Dame Preparatory School, Inc.* Sr. Christine Mulcahy, S.S.N.D., Headmistress. Sisters 7; Lay Teachers 75; Students 635; Total Staff 103.

[D] ELEMENTARY SCHOOLS, PRIVATE

ELLICOTT CITY. *Trinity School*, 4985 Ilchester Rd., P.O. Box 299, 21041. Tel: 410-744-1524; Fax: 410-744-3617. Sr. Catherine Phelps, Prin. Sisters of Notre Dame de Namur 3; Lay Teachers 24; Students 387.

EMMITSBURG. *Mother Seton School*, 100 Creamery Rd., 21727. Tel: 301-447-3161.
E-mail: msschool@aol.com
Sr. Mary Catherine Conway, Prin. Daughters of Charity of St. Vincent de Paul 4; Sisters 1; Lay Teachers 16; Students 371.

FREDERICK. *Academy of the Visitation*, 200 E. 2nd St., 21701. Tel: 301-662-3322; 662-2814. Dr. Bernadette Emerson, Prin. Sisters of the Visitation 5; Lay Teachers 20; Students 170.

WOODSTOCK. *Woodmont Academy*. (Grades K-8), 10817 Davis Ave., 21163. Tel: 410-203-0619; Fax: 410-465-9162.
E-mail: kslaser@aol.com
Mr. Keith Laser, Prin. Lay Teachers 11; Students 112.

[E] ELEMENTARY SCHOOLS, REGIONAL AND COMMUNITY

BALTIMORE. *Bishop John Neumann School*. (Grades PreK-8), 3500 Foster Ave., 21224. Tel: 410-675-6271; Fax: 410-327-1543.
E-mail: principal@bjnschool.com
Web site: www.bjnschool.com
Miss Katherine Davis, Prin. Lay Teachers 19; Students 250; Total Staff 19.

Cardinal Shehan School, 5407 Loch Raven Blvd., 21239. Tel: 410-433-2775.
E-mail: peacecss@aol.com
Serving the St. Matthew and St. Thomas More Parishes. Sr. Mary Vandergeest, O.S.F., Prin. Lay Teachers 30; Sisters 3; Total Staff 33; Students 428.

Catholic Community School of South Baltimore. (Grades PreK-8), 300 E.Gittings St., 21230. Tel: 410-685-6155; Fax: 410-685-0692. Sr. Josephann Wagoner, S.S.N.D., Prin. Sisters 2; Lay Teachers 11; Students 200. Res. Sisters of St. Joseph, 1410 Riverside Ave., 21230-4695. Tel: 410-752-4344.
Consolidation of the following parishes: Holy Cross; Our Lady of Good Counsel; St. Mary, Star of the Sea.

Father Kolbe Interparochial School, 1035 S. Kenwood Ave., 21224. Tel: 410-342-2681.
Serving the parishes of St. Casimir, St. Leo and St. Stanislaus. Sr. Barbara Ann Brzeczko, F.S.S.J., Prin. Franciscan Sisters of St. Joseph 1; Lay Teachers 10; Students 224.

Holy Spirit, 932 Gorsuch Ave., 21218. Tel: 410-889-0679. Schools Sisters of Notre Dame 2; Lay Teachers 12; Students 218.

John Paul Regional Catholic School, Inc. (Grades 1-8), 6946 Dogwood Rd., 21244. Tel: 410-944-0367. Ms. Mary Frey, Prin., (Grades PreK-K), 5801 Security Blvd., 21207. Tel: 410-265-7454. Mrs. Joann Callahan, Dir. Lay Teachers 28; Students 390.

Mother Seton Academy, 724 S. Ann St., 21231. Tel: 410-563-2833. Sr. Mary Bader, D.C., Prin. Innovative Middle School for Inner City Youth. Sisters 8; Brothers 2; Lay Teachers 1; Lay Volunteers 2; Students 63.

Queen of Peace Elementary Cluster, St. James and St. John School. (Grades PreK-5), 1012 Somerset St.,

21202. Tel: 410-342-3222. Ms. Lauanah King-Cassell, Prin. Sisters 1; Lay Teachers 10; Students 260.

St. Katherine of Sienna School, 1201 N. Rose St., 21213. Tel: 410-327-4738. Mr. Kevin Parson, Prin. Lay Teachers 10; Students 240.

St. Ignatius Loyola Academy, 740 N. Calvert St., 21202. Tel: 410-539-8268; Fax: 410-783-0793. Revs. William J. Watters, S.J., Pres.; Robert J. Braunreuther, S.J., Chap. Middle School for underprivileged boys. Lay Teachers 8; Students 64.

CUMBERLAND. *St. John Neumann School*. (Grades K-5), Fayette St. & Smallwood St., 21502. Tel: 301-724-4055.
E-mail: stjohnneuman@miworld.net
Sr. Kathleen F. Jancuk, S.S.N.D., Prin. Sisters 2; Lay Teachers 16; Students 330.
Bishop Walsh Middle-High School. (See listing under High Schools, Private).

FREDERICK. *St. John Regional Catholic School*. (Grades K-8), 114 E. Second St., 21701. Tel: 301-662-6722.
E-mail: sjrcs@frednet.com
Ms. Lee Jeffrey, Interim Prin. Lay Teachers 22; Students 515.

GLEN BURNIE. *Arthur Slade Regional Catholic School*, 120 Dorsey Rd., 21061. Tel: 410-766-7130.
E-mail: janicecm@umd5.umd.edu
Serving Glen Burnie, Millersville, Odenton, Crofton and Severn Parishes. Mrs. Janice McIntosh, Prin. Lay Teachers 37; Students 884.

[F] SPECIAL EDUCATION

BALTIMORE. *St. Elizabeth School*, 801 Argonne Dr., 21218. Tel: 410-889-5054. Christine Manlove, Ed.D., Prin. Franciscan Sisters of Baltimore 3; Lay Teachers 26; Lay Staff 103; Aides 48; Children 128.

St. Peter's Adult Learning Center, 13 S. Poppleton St., 21201. Tel: 410-685-7340.
E-mail: klnrsm@erols.com
Program for developmentally disabled persons. Sr. Katherine Nueslein, R.S.M., Dir. Sisters 1; Lay Teachers 5; Students 26.

TIMONIUM. *Villa Maria School*. (Main Campus), 2300 Dulaney Valley Rd., 21093. Tel: 410-252-6343; Fax: 410-560-1347. Jackie Donowitz, Dir. Education. Nonpublic (Level V and VI) special education for children with emotional disabilities, ages 6-13. Lay Teachers 22; Teacher Aides 20; Children 112.

Villa Maria School at St. Vincent's, 2600 Pot Spring Rd., 21093. Tel: 410-252-3725; Fax: 410-561-8109. Lay Teachers 7; Teacher Aides 9; Children 35.

Villa Maria School at Seton Keough, 1201 S. Caton Ave., Baltimore, 21227. Tel: 410-644-3792; Fax: 410-644-3796. Lay Teachers 6; Teacher Aides 2; Children 35.

[G] CHILD CARE CENTERS

BALTIMORE. *Good Shepherd Center*, 4100 Maple Ave., 21227. Tel: 410-247-2770. Legal Titles: *House of the Good Shepherd.*; *Sisters of the Good Shepherd, A Corporation*. Sr. Mary Rosaria Baxter, R.G.S., Admin.; Sr. Mary Catherine Massei, R.G.S., Supr.
Residential psychiatric treatment for adolescent girls. Sisters 7; Capacity 105; Residents 79; Total Assisted 192; Total Staff 212.

Mount Providence Child Development Center, 701 Gun Rd., 21227. Tel: 410-247-0449. Oblate Sisters of Providence. Sr. Mary Concetta Melton, O.S.P., Dir. Sisters 2; Students 80; Total Assisted 9; Total Staff 13.

St. Frances Outreach Center, 1026 Brentwood Ave., 21202. Tel: 410-539-1903. Sr. Brenda Motte, O.S.P., Dir. Total Assisted 30 Families; Total Staff 3.

St. Veronica's Headstart Center, 2920 Joseph Ave., 21225. Tel: 410-354-0220. Sr. Loretta Rosendale, S.S.N.D., Dir. Children (3-4) 358.

Sisters Servants of Mary Immaculate Day Nursery & Convent, 100-104 S. Patterson Park Ave., 21231. Tel: 410-276-2630. Sr. Grazyna Rybus, Supr. Total Assisted 75.

Villa Louise Family Resource Center, St. Agnes Hospital, DePaul Bldg., 900 Caton Ave., 21229. Tel: 410-368-2060. Bon Secours Hospital, 2000 W. Baltimore St. Tel: 410-362-3168. Ms. Ellen Warnock-Eckhart, Div. Dir., ACC. Total Staff 9; Total Assisted 200.

CUMBERLAND. *Neumann Early Childhood Center, Inc.*, 209 N. Centre St., 21502. Tel: 301-777-1166. Mrs. G. Louise Elliott, Dir. Total Assisted 144; Total Staff 12.

TIMONIUM. *Francis X. Gallagher Services*, 2520 Pot Spring Rd., 21093. Tel: 410-252-4005. Mark J. Schulz, Admin.
Residential, day habilitation and medical day programs for the developmentally disabled. Priests 1; Residential Capacity 194; Day Capacity 245; Total Assisted 185; Total Staff 34.

St. Vincent's Center, 2600 Pot Spring Rd., 21093. Tel: 410-252-4000; Fax: 410-561-8109. John D. Rusinko, Dir. Children's Continuum of ACC; Mary Maffezzoli, Admin. Residential Treatment Center for children, ages 18 mos.-12 years that are emotionally disturbed, abused, & neglected. Residents 70.

Villa Maria Treatment Center, 2300 Dulaney Valley Rd., 21093. Tel: 410-252-4700; Fax: 410-252-3040. Mark Greenberg, Admin.; Rev. Raymond Chase, Chap.
We operate a full continuum of 11 different mental health and special education programs for children and their families. Children 500; Total Staff 320.

[H] GENERAL HOSPITALS

BALTIMORE. *Bon Secours Baltimore Health Corporation, Inc.*, 2000 W. Baltimore St., 21223. Tel: 410-362-3000.
E-mail: bobknott@bshsi.com
For a complete listing, refer to the Hospitals section.

Mercy Medical Center, Inc., 301 St. Paul Pl., 21202. Tel: 410-332-9000; Fax: 410-962-1303
For a complete listing, refer to the Hospitals section.

St. Agnes HealthCare, Inc., 900 Caton Ave., 21229-5299. Tel: 410-368-6000.
E-mail: info@stagnes.org
Web site: www.stagnes.org
For a complete listing, refer to the Hospitals section.

St. Joseph Medical Center, Inc., 7620 York Rd., 21204. Tel: 410-337-1109; Fax: 410-337-1024
For a complete listing, refer to the Hospitals section.

CUMBERLAND. *Sacred Heart Hospital of the Western Maryland Health System*, 900 Seton Dr., 21502. Tel: 301-759-4200
For a complete listing, refer to the Hospitals section.

[I] NURSING HOMES (SKILLED) AND REHABILITATION CENTERS

BALTIMORE. *Dismas House East*, 1415 N. Caroline St., 21213. Tel: 410-539-2520
For a complete listing, refer to the Special Care Facilities section.

Dismas House West, 105 S. Mount St., P.O. Box 4435, 21223. Tel: 410-566-9400; Fax: 410-233-1622
For a complete listing, refer to the Special Care Facilities section.

St. Elizabeth Rehabilitation and Nursing Center, 3320 Benson Ave., 21227-1088. Tel: 410-644-7100; Fax: 410-644-2154
For a complete listing, refer to the Special Care Facilities section.

ELLICOTT CITY. *St. Agnes Nursing and Rehabilitation Center*, 3000 N. Ridge Rd., 21043. Tel: 410-461-7577; Fax: 410-461-6695
For a complete listing, refer to the Special Care Facilities section.

[J] HOMES FOR AGED

BALTIMORE. *St. Charles Villa*, 603 Maiden Choice Ln., 21228. Tel: 410-747-1211
For a complete listing, refer to the Special Care Facilities section.

St. Joseph's Nursing Home, 1222 Tugwell Dr., 21228. Tel: 410-747-0026; Fax: 410-747-0386
For a complete listing, refer to the Special Care Facilities section.

St. Martin's Home for Aged, Little Sisters of the Poor, 601 Maiden Choice Ln., 21228. Tel: 410-744-9367
For a complete listing, refer to the Special Care Facilities section.

TIMONIUM. *Stella Maris Operating Corporation*, 2300 Dulaney Valley Rd., 21093. Tel: 410-252-4500; Fax: 410-560-9675
For a complete listing, refer to the Special Care Facilities section.

[K] SOCIAL SERVICES

BALTIMORE, MD. *Franciscan Center*, 2212 Maryland Ave., 21218. Tel: 410-467-5340. Franciscan Sisters of Baltimore. Sr. Kathleen DeLancey, Dir. Total Assisted 150,000; Total Staff 18.

Mount Providence Reading Center, 701 Gun Rd., 21227. Tel: 410-247-0448, 242-8500. Oblate Sisters of Providence. Sr. M. Constance Fenwick, O.S.P., Dir. Students 150; Total Assisted 150; Total Staff 10.

Trinitarian Counseling Services, Inc., 8400 Park Heights Ave. P.O. Box 5719, 21282. Tel: 410-476-5764. Rev. Thomas J. Burke, O.SS.T., Dir. Total Assisted 197; Total Staff 2.

EMMITSBURG, MD. *Seton Center, Inc.*, 16840 S. Seton Ave., 21727. Tel: 301-447-6102; Fax: 301-447-1748.
E-mail: seton@clark.net
Social Service; Outreach; Thrift Shop. Daughters of Charity. Sr. Gloria Gilman, D.C., Admin. Total Assisted 19,862; Total Staff 9.

PASADENA, MD. *Mary's Center*, P.O. Box 1804, 21123-1804. Tel: 410-761-8082. Pregnancy Support Services. Anne Fitzsimmons, Dir. Total Assisted 756; Total Staff 29.

[L] RETREAT HOUSES FOR MEN, WOMEN AND YOUTH

BALTIMORE. *Holy Trinity Spiritual Center*, 8400 Park Heights Ave., P.O. Box 5719, 21282. Tel: 410-486-5171.
E-mail: provtreas@aol.com
Rev. Timothy Murphy, O.SS.T., Guest Master Spirituality Center. Total Assisted 1,128; Total Staff 3; Total in Residence 7.

St. Mary's Spiritual Center, 600 N. Paca St., 21201-1995. Tel: 410-728-6464. Rev. John E. McMurry, S.S., Dir. Total Staff 11.

ADAMSTOWN. *Christian Brothers Spiritual Center*, 2535 Buckeystown Pike, P.O. Box 29, 21710. Tel: 301-874-5180; Fax: 301-874-3757. Bro. Richard W. Breese, F.S.C., Admin. Brothers 3.

CATONSVILLE. *Our Lady of Guadalupe Renewal Center*, 10 Sharonwood Ct., 21228. Tel: 410-788-8821. Spiritual Life and Renewal Programs for Religious and Laity. Sr. Anne Colette Potthast, S.N.D., Dir. Total in Residence 2; Total Staff 2; Pastoral Team 12.

EMMITSBURG. *Seton Retreat Center*, 333 S. Seton Ave., 21727. Tel: 301-447-3121, Ext. 4544; Fax: 301-447-6038. Daughters of Charity. Sr. Irene Kraus, D.C., Dir.; Joan Little, Retreat Coord.

MARRIOTTSVILLE. *Bon Secours Spiritual Center*, 21104-1301. Tel: 410-442-1320; Fax: 410-442-8219. Sisters of Bon Secours. Sr. Carol J. Marozzi, S.S.J., Dir. Total Staff 23.

SPARKS. *Msgr. Clare J. O'Dwyer Retreat House*, 15523 York Rd., 21152. Tel: 410-472-2400. Revs. John E. O'Brien, Dir.; John J. Thornsberry. Total Staff 15.

[M] MONASTERIES AND RESIDENCES OF PRIESTS AND BROTHERS

BALTIMORE. *Ferdinand Wheeler Jesuit Community*, 3048 Guilford Ave., 21218. Tel: 410-338-1296. Revs. Mark F. Horak, S.J., Supr.; James R. Stormes, S.J.; Theodore E.A. Brady, S.J.; James R. Conroy, S.J.; Francis R. Carmody, S.J.; Charles P. Costello, S.J.; Thomas P. Gaunt, S.J.; Bro. James Horan, S.J. Priests 7; Brothers 1.

Holy Trinity Monastery, Prov. Admin. & Spiritual Center, 8400 Upper Park Heights Ave., P.O. Box 5742, 21282. Tel: 410-486-5171; Fax: 410-486-0614.
E-mail: provtreas.@aol.com
Office, 8400 Upper Park Heights Ave., P.O. Box 5719, 21282-0742. Tel: 410-486-5764. In res. Revs. John Dorn, O.SS.T., Min. Prov.; Charles J. Flood, O.SS.T., Min. Conventual, Prov. Sec. & Treas.; Timothy Murphy, O.SS.T., Dir. Spiritual Center; Edward Wagner, O.S.S.T., Chap.; Bros. Eric Beardsley, O.SS.T.; Christopher Doyle, O.SS.T.; Daniel Montemarano, O.SS.T. Priests 4; Brothers 3.
Assigned But Serving Elsewhere: Revs. Luke Mennella, O.SS.T., General Council, The Trinitarians, Via Massimi, 114C, Rome, Italy, 00136; Joseph C. Gidaro, O.SS.T., St. Brigid Church, 119 Ave. B, NY, NY 10009; Aaron M. Dowdell, O.SS.T., St. Brigid Church, 119 Ave. B, NY, NY 10009; Jose T. Narlaly, O.SS.T., P.B. No. 2911 Third Main Rd., Jayanagar East Byrasandra, Bangalore 560 011; Damon Geiger, O.SS.T., St. Ann Church, 802 Rifle Camp Rd., West Paterson, NJ 07424; Eric T. Burdt, O.SS.T., Christian Brothers High School, 5900 Walnut Grove Rd., Memphis, TN, 38120-2104. Rev. David Colella, O.SS.T., St. Clare Church, 321 Calumet St., Dallas, TX, 75211. Rev. Italo Gasbarri, O.SS.T., C10 General Curia, via Massimi, 114C, Rome, Italy, 00136. Rev. Donald Hayden, O.SS.T., SS. Cyril & Methodius Church, 125 Half Hollow Rd., Deer Park, NY, 11729-1288. Rev. Armand Iavarone, O.SS.T., St. Joseph's Church, 333 Sneden Pl. W., Spring Valley, NY, 10977-3943. Rev. Weston J. Lamb, O.SS.T., 1258 Sunset Blvd., No. 2-D, Jesup, GA, 31545. Rev. J. Edward Owens, O.SS.T., St. John's Seminary, 5012 Seminary Rd., Camarillo, CA, 93012-2598. Rev. Carl Pfeiffer, O.SS.T., 1109 Cedar Oaks Ln., Harker Heights, TX, 76548. Rev. August Pinci, O.SS.T., The Trinitarians, Via Massimi, 114C, Rome, Italy, 00136. Rev. Alberto Edgardo Rodrigues, O.SS.T., Holy Name of Jesus Church, 345 S. Military Trail, West Palm Beach, FL, 33415-2807. Bro. Ervin J. Wegscheid, O.SS.T., 213 Argonaut, #146, El Paso, TX, 79912-6052. The Trinitarian Community, 8636 Trail View Dr., Ellicott City, 21043. In res. Revs. Thomas J. Burke, O.SS.T.; Damian Anuszewski, O.SS.T.; William J. Moorman, O.SS.T., The Trinitarian Community, 8612 Laverne Dr., Adelphi, 20783. In res. Revs. Claude Gravel, O.SS.T., Christ the King Church, 3423 Rojo, Corpus Christi, TX 78415-4544; Lawrence C. Hernandez, O.SS.T.; William Sullivan, O.SS.T.

Redeemer House, 1401 Battery Ave., 21230-4603. Tel: 410-576-9565. In res. Bros. Richard J. Micka, Prog. Dir.; David Nash, Treas. Brothers 2; Total Staff 2.

Immaculate Heart of Mary Friary, 4220 Erdman Ave., 21213. Tel: 410-485-5511; Fax: 410-483-2545. Residence of Franciscan Friars, O.F.M.Conv., conducting Archbishop Curley High School. Rev. Conrad Miller, O.F.M.Conv.; Bro. Christian Katusz, O.F.M.Conv., Procurator; Revs. Michael Martin, O.F.M.Conv.; Michael Heine, O.F.M.Conv.; Ignatius

M. Piatek, O.F.M.Conv.; Donald Grzymski, O.F.M.Conv., Pres. & Guardian; Thomas Walsh, O.F.M.Conv., Vicar; Friars Pedro DeOliveira, O.F.M.Conv.; Gary Johnson, O.F.M.Conv. Priests 6; Brothers 1; Friars 2; Total Staff 1.

Jesuit Community of Loyola College, Inc., Loyola College, 4501 N. Charles St., 21210-2699. Tel: 410-617-2318. Revs. Patrick F. Earl, S.J., Rector; Ronald J. Anton, S.J.; Charles Borges, S.J.; Timothy B. Brown, S.J.; John L. Brunett, S.J.; Edwin H. Convey, S.J.; William M. Davish, S.J.; Michael D. French, S.J.; C. Kevin Gillespie, S.J.; Edgar B. Graham, S.J.; John H. Gray, S.J.; Frank R. Haig, S.J.; Francis G. Hilton, S.J.; Robert K. Judge, S.J.; Joseph M. Kennedy, S.J.; William K. McGroarty, S.J.; Francis G. McManamin, S.J.; Francis J. Nash, S.J.; Harold E. Ridley, S.J.; Joseph S. Rossi, S.J.; Peter F. Ryan, S.J.; James F. Salmon, S.J.; William J. Sneck, S.J.; Joseph A. Sobierajski, S.J.; Paul Sun; Lawrence Yom, S.J. Total in Residence 27.

Jesuit Fathers and Brothers Maryland Provincial Curia, 5704 Roland Ave., 21210. Tel: 410-532-1400; Fax: 410-532-1419. Legal Title: *Corporation of the Roman Catholic Clergymen*. Very Rev. James R. Stormes, S.J.; Revs. James A. Casciotti, S.J., Supr., Exec. Sec.; J. Donald Freeze, Treas.; John P. McGinty, S.J., Min.; Thomas P. Gaunt, S.J., Asst. for Formation and Studies; David G. Allen, S.J.; Vincent C. Curtin, S.J.; James H. Donahoe, S.J.; Thomas R. Fitzgerald, S.J.; Hugh A. Kennedy, S.J., Asst. Sec.; Francis X. Knott, S.J.; Liborio J. LaMartina, S.J., Res. Archivist; William F. Lamm, S.J., Asst. Treas. & Asst. Sec.; Thomas P. Martin, S.J., Asst. Treas.; Francis X. Metzbower, S.J.; Clement J. Petrik, S.J., Asst. for Pastoral Ministries; Francis R. Carmody, S.J., Dir. Jesuit Seminary and Mission Bureau. Total in Residence 14. Military Chaplains: Revs. E. Paul Betowski, S.J., White Sands Missile Range, NM; Paul J. Shaughnessy, S.J., USS Enterprise CVN 65, FPO AE 09543-2810, Attn: RMD.

Priests of the Province Serving Abroad: Rev. George V. Coyne, S.J., Specola Vaticana, Vatican City State, Italy. Revs. John S. Dear, S.J.; William P. Ryan, S.J., Peter Faber Residence, 28 Brookvale Ave., Belfast BT14 6BW, Northern Ireland. Rev. Philip J. Rosato, S.J., Collegio S. Roberto Bellarmino, Via de Seminario 120, Rome, Italy, 00186. Rev. J. Allan Loftus, S.J., 200 Shakespeare Dr. #1001, Waterloo, Canada, N2L 6C1. Rev. Jerome M. Halls, S.J., Pont Univ. Greg, Piazza della Pilotta 4, Rome, Italy, 00187. Rev. Thomas M. McCoog, S.J., 114 Mount St., London, United Kingdom, W1Y 6A4. Rev. Daniel R. Sweeney, S.J., St. Edmund's College, Cambridge CB3 0BN, England. Rev. Jon J. O'Brien, S.J., North American College, Via del Gianicolo, Vatican City State, Italy, 00128. Rev. John J. Cecero, S.J., 1414 Whitney Ave., Apt. E-3, Hamden, CT, 06517-2444. Rev. Bernard J. Dooley, S.J., 302-A Sea Oats Dr., Juno Beach, FL, 33408. Rev. Bernard G. Filmyer, S.J., 9784 Guisante Ter., San Diego, CA, 92124. Rev. Gerald J. McGlone, S.J., 1607 Cable St., San Diego, CA, 92107-3313. Rev. Joseph C. Sands, S.J., 66 Witherspoon St. #176, Princeton, NJ, 08542. Rev. George B. Wilson, S.J., 5824 Rhode Island Ave. No. 2, Cincinatti, OH, 45237. Rev. Eugene J. Barber, S.J., Resid. S. Pedro Claver, Casilla 2006, Arica, Chile. Rev. John K. Bingham, S.J., Manresa-Novitiate, Darjeeling Dt, Kalimpong, 734 301 West Bengal, India. Rev. Bernard J. Boyle, S.J., Colegio San Luis, Baquedano 855, Casilla 591, Antofagasta, Chile. Rev. Pablo Castro, S.J., Regis College, 105 Madison Ave., Toronto, ON, M5R 2S3 CD. Rev. William J. Currie, S.J., SJ House, Kioicho 7-1, Chiyoda-ku, Tokyo (102), Japan. Rev. Edgar J. Debany, S.J., P.O. Box 1054, Cape Coast, Ghana. Rev. James M. Desjardins, S.J., P.O. Box "Inigo", 630051 Novosibirsk, Russia. Rev. Edward C.A. Dougherty, S.J., Jesuit House of Studies, 4 Baron Rd., Merrivale, Natal 3291, Republic of South Af. Rev. John F. Guidera, S.J., De Nobili School, F R I PO, Dhanbad 828 108, India. Rev. George C. Hartley, S.J., Haus St. Benedikt, St. Benedikt Str. 3, D-97072, Wurzburg, Germany. Rev. George A. Hess, S.J., Xavier Institute of Management, Bhubaneswar 751 013, India. Rev. F. Scott Howell, S.J., SJ House, Kioicho 7-1, Chiyoda-ku, Tokyo (102), Japan. Rev. Gerard S. Barry, S.J., SJ House, Kioicho 7-1, Chiyoda-ku, Tokyo (102), Japan. Rev. Joseph A. Bittner, S.J., Jesuit Retreat House, P.O. Box 29, 8700 Malaybalay, Bukidnon, PI. Rev. Edward J. Brady, S.J., St. Paul's Major Seminary, P.O. Box 1466, Khartoum, Sudan. Rev. Robert F. Currie, S.J., Apartado A-90, Managua 11, Nicaragua. Rev. Angelo D'Agostino, S.J., Loyola House, Box 21399, Nairobi, Kenya. Rev. John J. Deeney, S.J., Claver Bhavan, Amda PO, West Singbhum Dt. 833 101, India. Rev. Carl L. Dincher, S.J., Jesu Bhavan, Old Purulia Rd., Mango, Jamshedpur, 831 012 Bihar, India. Rev. Thomas M. Gavin, S.J., Casa Ejercicios, Casilla 1, Padre Hurtado, Chile. Rev. Robert E. Hamm, S.J., P.O. Box 854, Benin City, Edo State, Nigeria. Rev. John F. Henry, S.J., Resid. S. Pedro Claver, Casilla 2006, Arica, Chile. Rev. Frederick A. Homann, S.J., R.C. Mission, P.O Box 397, Northwest Territories, Canada, XOA OHO. Rev. Richard A. Kenna, S.J., Loyola Hall, PB 153, Jamshedpur, Bihar 831 001, India. Rev. Sigmund J. Laschenski, S.J., Xavier H, 143 Phahonyothin Rd., Victory Monument, Bangkok 10400, Thailand. Rev. John J. Mawhinney, S.J., Iglesia del Carmen, 04102 Santa Tecla, El Salvador, C A. Rev. Edward H. Nash, S.J., St. Xavier's High School, P B 10, Lupungutu, Chaibasa 833 201, India, 833 201. Rev. George W. Quickley, S.J., P.O. Box 579, Benin City, Edo State, Nigeria. Rev. Eugene M. Rooney, S.J., Colegio San Mateo Communidad, Casilla 18-0, Osorno, Chile. Rev. Dominic J. Totaro, S.J., P.O. Box 854, Benin City, Edo State, Nigeria. Rev. Charles E. Wolf, S.J., Loyola House of Studies, P.O. Box 4082, Manila, PI, 1099. Rev. Michael J. Lynch, S.J., Xavier Retreat House, 27 Peak Rd., Cheung Chau, N.T., Hong Kong. Rev. Edward H. McGrath, S.J., Human Life Centre, Vivekananda Marg, Balasore 756 001, India. Rev. John J. Nissel, S.J., Immaculate Heart College, Toso 4-22-1, Kagoshima 890, Japan. Rev. James D. Redington, S.J., Arrupe College, P.O. Box MP 320, Mt. Pleasant, Harare, Zimbabwe. Rev. John W. Swope, S.J., CIDE, Casilla 13608, Santiago 1, Chile. Rev. Eugene A. Welch, S.J., Loyola Hall, P B 153, Jamshedpur, Bihar 831 001, India.

Priests of the Province Serving Elsewhere: Rev. Willy DeCraemer, S.J., Park Towne W. 1808, 2200 Benjamin Franklin Pkwy., Philadelphia, PA, 19130. Rev. Francis X.D. Reese, S.J., 730 Silver Mill Rd., Apt. 2, Marshall, NC, 28753. Rev. Joseph F. Monaghan, S.J., St. Joseph's Hospital, 1600 W. Girard Ave., Philadelphia, PA, 19130. Rev. David L. Ungerleider, S.J., P.O. Box 438210, San Ysidro, CA, 92143-8210.

On Leave: Revs. Joseph F. Curran, S.J.; Daniel C. Doherty, S.J.; Michael J. Maruca, S.J.; Andrew J. Novotney, S.J.; Francis X. Winters, S.J.

Marianist Community, 738 S. Beechfield Ave., 21229. Tel: 410-242-5159. Rev. Paul A. Reich, S.M., Dir.; Bros. Charles J. Johnson, S.M., Dir.; Francis P. Mullan, S.M. Priests 1; Brothers 2; Total in Residence 3; Total Staff 3.

Pallottine Center for Apostolic Causes, 512 W. Saratoga St., 21201. Tel: 410-685-3063; Fax: 410-234-1459. Promotional Center for St. Jude Shrine. Legal Title: *St. Jude Shrine-Pallottine Missions; Pallottine Center for Apostolic Causes, Inc.* Rev. Peter T. Sticco, S.A.C., Dir.

St. Charles Villa, 603 Maiden Choice Ln., 21228. Tel: 410-747-1211. Home for Retired Sulpicians conducted by the Little Sisters of the Poor. Revs. William T. O'Keeffe, S.S. (CLV), Dir. & Supr.; Raymond F. Hesler, S.S. (ALB), Assoc. Dir.; Lawrence A. Bender, S.S. (WDC); John W. Bowen, S.S. (BAL); James H. Brennan, S.S. (BAL); Frederick V. Chudzinski, S.S (TOL); Charles P. Dillon, S.S. (TOL); Claude H. Dukehart, S.S. (BAL); Vincent M. Eaton, S.S. (RIC); James J. Healy, S.S. (MAN); William J. Lee, S.S. (CLV); John F. Mattingly, S.S.; William S. Morris, S.S. (NY); William A. Thielemann, S.S. (WIL); John A. Ward, S.S. (DET); J. Paul Welch, S.S. (SEA); Joseph L. White, S.S. (BAL). Priests 17; Total Staff 10.

St. Joseph Society of the Sacred Heart House of Central Administration, 1130 N. Calvert St., 21202. Tel: 410-727-3386; Fax: 410-385-2331. Very Revs. Robert M. Kearns, S.S.J., Supr. Gen.; Edward J. Chiffriller, S.S.J., Vicar Gen.; Roger J. Caesar, S.S.J., Consultor Gen.; Edward J. Mullowney, S.S.J., Treas. & Rector; Revs. Peter E. Hogan, S.S.J., Archivist; Peter J. Kenney, S.S.J., Historian and Asst. Archivist; Joseph L. Waters, S.S.J., Historian; Mrs. Bernice Jones, Asst. Archivist; Revs. Edward J. Gartner, S.S.J.; Eugene P. McManus, S.S.J., Dir. Public Rels.; Joseph J. McKinley, S.S.J., Treas. Office; Earle A. Newman, S.S.J.; Joseph C. Verrett, S.S.J., Editor, The Josephite Harvest; Robert E. McCall, S.S.J., Dir. Josephite Evangelization; John F. Byrne, S.S.J., Asst. to Admin. Priests 14. Retired: Revs. John J. Conlon, S.S.J.; N. Wilfrid DesRosiers, S.S.J.; Francis H. Fallon, S.S.J.; Dominic A. Marchese, S.S.J.; Ralph R. Ransom, S.S.J.; Joseph R. Murphy, S.S.J.; Paul A. Ortner, S.S.J.; Joseph J. Rimshaw, S.S.J.; W. Dayton Salisbury, S.S.J.; James P. Schappert, S.S.J.

St. Joseph's Manor. (Josephite Fathers and Brothers), 911 W. Lake Ave., 21210. Tel: 410-323-3829. Rectors: Very Rev. Matthew J. O'Rourke, S.S.J.; Revs. John C. Crotty, S.S.J.; Daniel H. Cassidy, S.S.J.; James F. Didas, S.S.J.; Thomas J. Fitzgerald, S.S.J.; Bartholomew F. Hines, S.S.J.; Martin F. Kenney, S.S.J.; Rupert A. MacDonald, S.S.J.; Robert E. McCall, S.S.J.; Eugene J. McKenna, S.S.J.; Robert J. O'Connell, S.S.J.; John J. Rawlins, S.S.J.; Calvin F. Sinclair, S.S.J.; Bro. Andrew Hogya, S.S.J. Priests 13; Brothers 1.

St. Joseph's Passionist Community, 251 S. Morley St., 21229. Tel: 410-566-3750; Fax: 410-233-4974. Congregation of the Most Holy Cross and Passion of Our Lord Jesus Christ. Revs. Basil Stockmeyer, C.P.; Simon Wood, C.P.; Eustace McDonald, C.P.; Kenneth Walsh, C.P.; Daniel Free, C.P.; Gregory Paul, C.P. Priests 6.

Society of Mary (Marianists). (Province of New York), Marianist Provincial House, 4301 Roland Ave., 21210-2793. Tel: 410-366-1300; Fax: 410-889-5743. Rev. George J. Cerniglia, S.M., Asst. Prov.; Bros. Stephen M. Glodek, S.M., Prov.; Howard L. Hughes, S.M.; Frank O'Donnell, S.M., Dir. Education. Priests 1; Brothers 3; Total in Residence 80.

Sulpician Provincial House. (Associated Sulpicians of the United States), 5408 Roland Ave., 21210. Tel: 410-323-5070; Fax: 410-433-6524.
E-mail: 104032.330@compuserve.com
Very Rev. Ronald D. Witherup, S.S., U.S. Prov. of the Society of St. Sulpice; Revs. Thomas R. Ulshafer, S.S., Prov. Sec.; Melvin C. Blanchette, S.S., Dir. Formation and Personnel Svcs. & Dir. Discernment, Admissions; Multicultural Studies and Programs; Louis M. Reitz, S.S., Prov. Treas.; Mr. Joseph M. Reynolds, Exec. Asst. to Prov., Operations Mgr.

Members and Candidates on Individual Assignments: Rev. Joseph J. Bonadio, S.S., St. Francis of Assisi Church, 3615 Harford Rd., 21218-3196. Rev. Gerald L. Brown, S.S., Sabbatical, 1610 Milvia St., Apt. 1, Berkeley, CA, 94709. Revs. Vincent D. Bui; Cornelius Hankomoone, Emmaus Spirituality Center, P.O. Box 320084 Woodlands, Lusaka, Zambia, 157101. Rev. William E. Hartgen, S.S., 634 E. St., N.E., Washington, DC, 20002. Rev. Joseph C. Martin, S.S., 4006 York Dr., Havre De Grace, 21078-2100. Rev. Robert P. Waznak, S.S., 5 Buttercharm Ct., Silver Spring, 20905-5738. Rev. John J. Kselman, S.S., 7 Kirkland Rd., Cambridge, MA, 02138-3012. Rev. Addison G. Wright, S.S., 24 Killian Ave., Trumbull, CT, 06611-4118. Rev. Thomas Doyle, S.S., 1248 Brentwood Pointe, Brentwood, TN, 37027-2945. Rev. Edward J. Frazer, S.S., St. Dominic's Major Seminary, P.O. Box 320-191 Woodlands, Lusaka, Zambia, Central Africa, 157101. Rev. J. Michael Strange, S.S., St. Augustine's Major Seminary, P.O. Box 81011, Kabwe, Zambia, Central Africa, 157101. Rev. Cale J. Crowley, S.S., Rector, Emmaus Spirituality Center, P.O. Box 32-0084 Woodlands, Lusaka, Zambia, Central Africa, 157101. Rev. John L. Bitterman, S.S., Emmaus Spirituality Center, P.O. Box 32-0084, Woodlands, Lusaka, Zambia, Central Africa, 157101. Rev. Gerald V. Lardner, S.S., Emmaus Spirituality Center, P.O. Box 32-0084, Woodlands, Lusaka, Zambia, Central Africa, 157101. Rev. M. Stephen Barrett, S.S., 10910 Olde Woods Way, Columbia, 21044. Rev. Martin Duc Tran, Casa Santa Maria dell'Umilta, Via dell'Umilta 30, Rome, Italy, 00187. Rev. David Mellott, S.S., Studies in Europe, Sulpician Provincial House, 5408 Roland Ave., 21210. Rev. Ronald S. Ochylski, S.S., Calle Canillas 40, #1 Drcha., Madrid, Spain, 28002.

Xaverian Brothers Generalate, 4409 Frederick Ave., 21229. Tel: 410-644-0034. Bros. Matthew Burke, C.F.X., Supr. Gen.; Cornelius Hubbuch, C.F.X., Dir. Staff Formation, Vicar Gen.; Lawrence Harvey, C.F.X., Dir. Xaverian Sponsored Schools.

Legal Titles and Schools Sponsored: Xaverian Brothers USA, Inc.; St. Mary's-Ryken High School, Inc.; Our Lady of Good Counsel High School, Inc.; St. Xavier High School, Inc.; Xaverian High School, Inc.; Holy Family High School, Inc.; Mt. St. Joseph High School, Inc.; Xaverian Brothers Auxiliary; St. Michael's High School Alumni Association; Nazareth Regional High School, Inc.; St. John's Preparatory School, Inc.; St. John's High School, Inc.; Xaverian Brothers High School, Inc.; Malden Catholic High School, Inc.; Xavier High School, Inc.; Isidore Chantable Trust; American Northeastern Province of the Xaverian Brothers, Inc. Brothers 15.

ADAMSTOWN. *Christian Brothers Provincialate*, P.O. Box 29, 21710. Tel: 301-874-5188; Fax: 301-847-5674.
E-mail: fscl845@ix.netcom.com
Web site: delasallebrothers.org
Legal Title: *Christian Brothers of Frederick, Inc.* Brothers of the Christians Schools, Baltimore Province. Bros. Benedict Oliver, F.S.C., Prov.; Timothy J. Froelich, F.S.C., Dir. Finance; Robert I. Schieler, F.S.C., Asst. Prov.; Martin J. Fahey, F.S.C., Admin. Asst. Brothers 4; Total in Residence 210; Total Staff 7.

ANNAPOLIS. *Saint Mary Rectory*, 109 Duke of Gloucester St., 21401. Tel: 410-263-2396.
Web site: www.stmaryschurch.org
Residence of the Redemptorist Fathers and Brothers. Very Rev. Thomas Siconolfi, C.SS.R., Pastor; Revs. Eric Hoog, C.SS.R.; John Sodomora, C.SS.R.;

John G. Tizio, C.SS.R. In res. Revs. Bernard Baumgartner, C.SS.R.; Patrick Flynn, C.SS.R.; E. Patrick Lynch, C.SS.R.; Henry O'Meara, C.SS.R.; Francis X. Murphy, C.SS.R. Total in Residence 9.

CUMBERLAND. *SS. Peter and Paul Friary*, 109 N. Smallwood St., 21502. Tel: 301-777-3131; 301-777-3137. Legal Title: *Province of St. Augustine of the Capuchin Order*. Revs. Vance Pastorius, O.F.M.Cap., Guardian and Pastor; Vernon Busch, O.F.M.Cap., Vicar & Assoc. Pastor; Reginald Russo, O.F.M.Cap., Pastor, St. Ambrose, Cresaptown; Bro. Michael Masich, O.F.M.Cap. Priests 3; Brothers 1.

ELLICOTT CITY. *Friary of St. Joseph Cupertino*, 12290 Folly Quarter Rd., 21042-1499. Tel: 410-988-9822. Companions of St. Anthony. Tel: 410-988-9833. Secular Franciscans. Tel: 410-988-9855. Conventual Franciscan Friars. Revs. Gregory Moore, O.F.M.Conv., Guardian; James Elliot, O.F.M.Conv., Vicar; Bart Karwacki, O.F.M.Conv.; Rick Deptula, O.F.M.Conv.; Jude Winkler, O.F.M.Conv.; Romuald Meograssi, O.F.M.Conv.; Francis Lombardo, O.F.M.Conv.; Bros. Thaddeus Grzankowski, O.F.M.Conv.; Daniel Geary, O.F.M.Conv.

Order of Friars Minor Conventual, 12300 Folly Quarter Rd., 21042-1419. Tel: 410-531-9200; Fax: 410-531-4881. Very Revs. Mark L. Curesky, O.F.M.Conv., Min. Prov.; Gregory Moore, O.F.M.Conv., Vicar Prov.; Revs. Robert Twele, O.F.M.Conv., Sec. & Treas.; Martin Kobos, O.F.M.Conv., Dir. Devel. (Franciscan Devel. Office); Bro. Brian Newbigging, O.F.M.Conv.

On Assignment Outside the U.S.A.: Very Rev. Joachin Giermek, O.F.M.Conv., Asst. General; Revs. Martin Breski, O.F.M.Conv.; Matteo Luo, O.F.M.Conv.; Bro. Joseph Wood, O.F.M.Conv., Curia Generale dei Frati Minori Conventualli, Piazza Ss. Apostoli 51, Rome, Italy, 00187. Rev. George Maslar, O.F.M.Conv., Piazza Inferiore di S Francesco, 06082 Assisi Santuario (PG), Assisi, Italy. Rev. Donald Kos, O.F.M.Conv., Convento S. Antonio Baccelli, 56, Via del Serafico, 1, Rome, Italy, 00153. Rev. Bernard Przewozny, O.F.M.Conv., Seraphicum, Via del Serafico, 1, Rome, Italy, 00142. Rev. Jerome Lukaszewski, O.F.M.Conv., St. Mary's Catholic Church, 16-8 Furuta-cho, Naze-shi 894, Japan. Rev. Ronald Roll, O.F.M.Conv., Parroquia Santa Ana Central America, Campamento, Olancho, Honduras. Rev. Vincent Lachendro, O.F.M.Conv., San Augustin Parish/Village Metro Manila, Novaliches Post Office, P.O. Box 186, Paranaque, Phillipines. Rev. Dominic Slemba, O.F.M.Conv., St. Francis of Assisi Friary West Africa, P.O. Box 238, Saltpond, Ghana. Rev. Giles Zakowicz, O.F.M.Conv., St. Francis of Assisi Friary West Africa, P.O. Box 238, Saltpond, Ghana. Rev. Paul Marut, O.F.M.Conv., P.O. Box 3, Achimota, Accra, Ghana, West Africa. Rev. Nicholas Swiatek, O.F.M. Conv., St. Mary's Catholic Church, 16-8 Furuta-cho, Naze-shi 894, Japan. Bro. Mitchell Sawicki, O.F.M.Conv., St. Bonaventure Friary, P.O. Box 3, Achimota, Accra, Ghana, West Africa. Rev. Henry Karwel, O.F.M.Conv., St. Mary's Parish, 60 South St., Ware, MA, 01082-1619. Rev. Daniel Pietrzak, O.F.M.Conv., St. Joseph Cupertino Friary, 10 Dimar Ct., Dingley, Victoria, Australia, 3172.

Individual Assignment Within the U.S.A.: Rev. Thomas Gwozdz, O.F.M.Conv., (Retired), Pope John Paul II Center, 33 Lincoln Ave., Danbury, CT, 06810. Rev. Felician Plichta, O.F.M.Conv., Corpus Christi Rectory, 324 Quaker Meeting House Rd., East Sandwich, MA, 02537-0384. Rev. Roger M. Haas, O.F.M.Conv., Christ the King Seminary, P.O. Box 607, East Aurora, NY, 14052-0607. Rev. Paul Duzinski, O.F.M.Conv., Sts. Mary and Joseph Home, 4291 Richmond Rd. - #102, Cleveland, OH, 44122-6103. Rev. Clement Jarnot, O.F.M.Conv., St. Mary of Czetochova Parish, 79 S. Main St., Middletown, CT, 06457-3606. Rev. Luke Dyjak, O.F.M.Conv., (Retired), Little Sisters of the Poor, 2100 S. Western Ave., San Pedro, CA, 97032. Rev. Patrick Rolak, O.F.M.Conv., (Retired), Sacred Heart Home, 4520 Ransom Rd., Clarence, NY, 14031. Rev. Ronald Sermak, O.F.M.Conv., Chaplain's Office, 5286 South Park Ave., Hamburg, NY, 14075-1596. Rev. John Bambol, O.F.M.Conv., (Retired), Mater Dolorosa Friary, 71 Maple St., Holyoke, MA, 01040-4698. Total in Residence 195.

St. Joseph Cupertino Friary, Friars Minor Conventual of St. Francis of Assisi, 12290 Folly Quarter Rd., 21042-1499. Tel: 410-988-9822.

Corporate Title: Franciscan Fathers Minor Conventuals of MD, Inc. Secular Franciscans. Tel: 410-988-9855. Revs. Gregory Moore, O.F.M.Conv., Guardian & Vicar Prov.; Bart Karwacki, O.F.M.Conv., Spiritual Asst. for Secular Franciscan Order; James Elliott, O.F.M.Conv., Vicar; Rick Deptula, O.F.M.Conv.; Francis Lombardo, O.F.M.Conv.; Ted Grzankowski, O.F.M.Conv.; Romuald Meograssi, O.F.M.Conv.; Jude Winkler, O.F.M.Conv.; Bro. Daniel Geary, O.F.M.Conv.

EMMITSBURG. *Vincentian House*, P.O. Box 376, 21726. Tel: 301-447-2326; Fax: 301-447-3579. Revs. Joseph R. Wright, C.M., Supr.; Michael J. Kennedy, C.M., Admin.; William P. Goff, C.M.; Louis B. Storms, C.M., Asst. Supr.; Walter J. Menig, C.M., Chap.; Charles E. Jacobs, C.M., Assoc. Pastor. Priests 6.

[N] CONVENTS AND RESIDENCES FOR SISTERS

BALTIMORE. *Carmelite Monastery*, 1318 Dulaney Valley Rd., 21286-1399. Tel: 410-823-7415. Discalced Carmelite Nuns. Sr. Veronica Emmick, Prioress. Professed Sisters 15; Postulants 1.

Chesapeake Province of the Sisters of Notre Dame de Namur, Provincial Offices, 305 Cable St., 21210-2511. Tel: 410-243-1993; Fax: 410-243-2279.
E-mail: armcnally@igc.apc.org
Legal Title: *Chesapeake Province of the Sisters of Notre Dame de Namur, Inc.*
Administrative Team: Sr. Agnes Rose McNally, S.N.D.deN.; Sr. Mary Margaret Pignone, S.N.D-.deN. Sisters in Province 80; Sisters in Diocese 32.

Daughters of Charity, 900 Caton Ave., 21229. Total in Residence 14.

Franciscan Sisters of Baltimore-General Motherhouse and Novitiate, 3725 Ellerslie Ave., 21218. Tel: 410-235-0139; Fax: 410-243-2569. Legal Titles: *Franciscan Sisters of Baltimore City; Declaration of Trust of the Franciscan Sisters of Baltimore, Inc.* Sr. Ritamary Tan, O.S.F., Gen. Supr.; Rev. Gerald West, Chap. Sisters 50.

Little Sisters of Jesus-Regional Residence, 400 N. Streeper St., 21224. Tel: 327-7863.
E-mail: littlesisters@juno.com
Sr. Cathy Wright, Regl. Supr. Sisters 4.

Little Sisters of the Poor-Provincial Residence, 601 Maiden Choice Ln., 21228-3698. Tel: 410-744-9367. Sr. Mary Bernard Du St. Esprit, L.S.P., Prov.; Sr. Marguerite, L.S.P., Supr.; Rev. Robert Hawkins. Sisters 21; Total Assisted 107; Total Staff 127.

Maria Health Care Center, Inc., 6401 N. Charles St., 21212. Tel: 410-377-7774.

Mission Helper Center, 1001 W. Joppa Rd., 21204-3787. Tel: 410-823-8585; Fax: 410-825-6355. Sr. Catharine Dages, Pres.; Sr. Carol Ann Gray, Gen. Treas.; Sr. Natalie DeLuca, Asst.; Sr. Mary Louise Zaworski, Mgr. Sisters 31; Sisters in Diocese 55; Total Staff 17.

Mission Helpers of the Sacred Heart-Our Lady of Pompei Convent, 225 S. Conkling St., 21224. Tel: 410-675-6034. Sisters 3.

Missionaries of Charity, Gift of Hope Convent, 818 N. Collington Ave., 21205. Tel: 410-732-6056. Sr. M. Pietra, M.C., Supr. Sisters 4; Total Assisted 277; Total Staff 8.

Our Lady of Mt. Providence Convent-Motherhouse, 701 Gun Rd., 21227. Tel: 410-242-8500; Fax: 410-242-4963. Oblate Sisters of Providence. Sisters in the Motherhouse 73; Sisters in the Diocese 80; Total in Residence 121; Total Assisted 60; Total Staff 39.
Attended by Sulpician Fathers and Josephite Fathers.

The School Sisters of Notre Dame in the City of Baltimore (Baltimore Prov.), 6401 N. Charles St., 21212. Tel: 410-377-7774. Sr. Jane Burke, S.S.N.D., Prov. Leader; Rev. David M. Carey, Chap. Sisters 100; Novices 1; Sisters in Province 417; Sisters in Diocese 304.

Sisters of Mercy, P.O. Box 11448, 21239. Tel: 410-435-4400.
E-mail: mercycntr@aol.com
Sisters of Mercy of the Americas, Baltimore Regional Community. Sr. Margaret Beatty, R.S.M., Pres. Sisters in Community 242; Sisters in Diocese 120.

Sisters of St. Francis of Philadelphia. Congregational Office - Our Lady of Angels Convent, 609 S. Convent Rd., Aston, PA, 19014. Tel: 215-459-4125, 610-459-0772. Convents in the Diocese: Shrine of the Little Flower Convent, 2851 Kentucky Ave., 21213. Tel: 410-483-3484. Our Lady of Mt. Carmel Convent, 1706 Eastern Ave., 21221. Tel: 410-687-5335. St. Clement Convent, 1212 Chesaco Ave., 21237. Tel: 410-687-4433. St. Elizabeth Convent, 128 N. Linwood Ave., 21224. Tel: 410-675-1301. St. Joseph Convent, 8418 Belair Rd., 21236. Tel: 410-256-8596. St. Joseph Medical Center, 7620 York Rd., 21204. Tel: 410-337-1100. St. Peter Claver Convent, 1526 N. Fremont Ave., 21217. Tel: 410-383-1288. St. Stephen Convent, 8020 Bradshaw Rd., P.O. Box 62, Bradshaw, 21021-0062. Tel: 410-592-9433. Immaculate Conception Convent, 112 Ware Ave., Towson, 21204. Tel: 410-823-3470. Bethany House, 2618 Erdman Ave., 21213. Tel: 410-235-4767. St. Joseph Convent, Box 1, Midland, 21542. Tel: 301-463-2248. Franciscan Residence, 2602 Fleet St., 21224. Tel: 410-276-5099. St. Anthony Convent, 4500 Frankford Ave., 21206. Tel: 410-488-0054. St. Anthony Convent Annex, 4500 Frankford Ave., 21206. Tel: 410-488-0162. Sisters of St. Francis, 34 Acorn Cir. #202, 21286. Tel: 410-832-1858. Sisters of St. Francis, 806D Cinnamon Ridge Pl., Cockeysville, 21030. Tel: 410-683-1427. Sisters of St. Francis, 3675 College Ave., Ellicott, 21043. Tel: 410-418-8823. Sisters of St. Francis, 11 Peroba Ct., 21234. Tel: 410-882-3212. St. Mark Convent, 800 Old Fallston Rd., Fallston, 21047. Tel: 410-879-3702. Genesis House, 9 Skidmore Ct., Towson, 21204. Tel: 410-296-8071. Sisters of St. Francis, 10336 "K" Malcolm Cir., Cockeysville, 21030. Tel: 410-683-9459. Total in Residence 128.

Sisters of the Good Shepherd, 4100 Maple Ave., 21227-4099. Tel: 410-247-2770. Sr. Mary Catherine Massei, R.G.S., Supr. Sisters 16.

Sisters of the Good Shepherd-St. Joseph Residence, 4100 Maple Ave., 21227. Tel: 410-247-3898; 247-2770, Ext. 232; Fax: 410-242-5890. Infirmary and Retirement Center for Washington Province. Sisters 25.

Sisters of the Holy Cross, Holy Cross Place, 3813 Edmondson Ave., 21229. Tel: 410-566-8978. Sisters 1.

Sisters Servants of Mary Immaculate, Inc. Convent and Novitiate. 1220 Tugwell Dr., 21228. Tel: 410-747-1353; Fax: 410-747-0386. Sr. Bernadetta Kozyra, Prov.; Rev. Joseph Sielski, M.I.C., Chap., Sisters Servants of Mary Immaculate Day Nursery & Convent, 100-104 S. Patterson Park Ave., 21231. Tel: 410-276-2630. Sr. Grazyna Rybus, Supr. Sisters 14; Total Assisted 60; Total in Residence 25; Total Staff 12.

The Villa, 6806 Bellona Ave., 21212-1299. Tel: 410-377-2450; Fax: 410-377-2501. Mrs. Martha Coleman, Admin. Convent for Retired Sisters of Mercy and Mission Helpers of the Sacred Heart. Legal Title: *Joint Retirement Convent, Inc.-The Villa*. Sisters 70.

EMMITSBURG. *Daughters of Charity of St. Vincent de Paul, Emmitsburg Province*, 21727. Tel: 301-447-3121. (St. Joseph's Provincial House). Legal Title: *Sisters of Charity of St. Joseph's, Emmitsburg, MD.* Sr. Virginia Ann Brooks, D.C., Prov. Sisters at Provincial House 47; Sisters in Diocese 176; Sisters in Province 286.

Villa St. Michael-St. Joseph's Provincial House, 333 S. Seton Ave., 21727-9299. Tel: 301-447-3121. Home of Daughters of Charity of St. Vincent de Paul. Sr. Mary Sheehan, D.C., Admin. Sisters 100.

FREDERICK. *Visitation Monastery of Frederick, MD*, 200 E. Second St., 21701. Tel: 301-662-3322. Mother Marguerite Therese Leary, V.H.M., Supr. Cloistered Community with Apostolate of Teaching (Grades PreK-8). Sisters 6.

LUTHERVILLE. *Emmanuel Monastery*, 2229 W. Joppa Rd., 21093. Tel: 410-821-5792. Benedictine Sisters of Baltimore.
Ministering in Education, Pastoral Ministry, Retreats and Spiritual Direction, Social Services, Justice Ministry, Hospital Ministry, and Business Admin. Sisters 14.

MARRIOTTSVILLE. *Sisters of Bon Secours, C.B.S., Provincial House*, 21104. Tel: 410-442-1333; Fax: 410-442-1394. Sr. Anne Marie Mack, Pres. Retired Sisters 12; Total in Residence 46; Total Staff 53.

STEVENSON. *Maryland Province Center*, 1531 Greenspring Valley Rd., 21153. Tel: 410-486-5599.
E-mail: sndmd@aol.com
Maryland Province of the Sisters of Notre Dame de Namur. Legal Titles: *Baltimore Province of the Sisters of Notre Dame de Namur, Inc.; Trinity School, Inc.; Maryvale Preparatory School, Inc.; Academy of Notre Dame de Namur, Inc.; Sisters of Notre Dame de Namur, Maryland Province, Charitable Trust.*
Additional Projects Sponsored: Maryland Province Center of Stevenson, MD; Villa Julie at Seven Oaks of Stevenson, MD; Julie Billiart Residence of Washington, DC; Notre Dame Educ. Center at Trinity College, Washington, DC.
Additional Projects Co-Sponsored: The Development Office, a joint project of the Maryland Chesapeake & Notre Dame Base Communities Provinces; Directors: Srs. Alice Gillen, Catharine Lafferty, Ann Patricia May, Elizabeth Lebano. Sr. Bernadette Glodek, Prov. Moderator; Sr. Jeanne McGlone, Prov. Leadership; Sr. Patricia Loome, Prov. Leadership. Sisters in Province 154; Sisters in Diocese 62; Total Staff 13.

Villa Julie at Seven Oaks (Maryland Province), 1531 Greenspring Valley Rd., 21153. Tel: 410-486-6946.
E-mail: sndmo@aol.com
Assisted Living Home for Sisters of Notre Dame and Staff Residence. Sisters 25.

St. Catherine Nursing Home, 331 S. Seton Ave., Emmitsburg, 21727. Tel: 301-447-3121. Sisters of Notre Dame 7.

Stella Maris, 2300 Dulaney Valley Rd., Baltimore, 21204. Tel: 410-461-6695. Sisters of Notre Dame 3.

TIMONIUM. *Sisters of the Visitation-Stella Maris Hospice*, 2300 Dulaney Valley Rd., 21093. Tel: 410-252-9598. Legal Title: *Visitation Monasteries, Inc.* Total in Residence 11.

[O] NEWMAN CENTERS

BALTIMORE. *Archdiocesan Office-Newman Center,* 7909 York Rd., 21204. Tel: 410-828-0622.
E-mail: albright@towson.edu
Rev. Robert E. Albright, Archdiocesan Dir. Total in Residence 3; Total Staff 5.
Johns Hopkins University, Newman House, 2941 N. Charles St., 21218. Tel: 410-243-7066. Rev. Charles K. Riepe.
Morgan State University, St. Matthew Church, 5401 Loch Raven Blvd., 21239. Tel: 410-433-2300.
Towson University, Newman Center, 7909 York Rd., 21204. Tel: 410-828-0622. Rev. Robert E. Albright, Dir.
University of Maryland-Baltimore County, 5401 Wilkens Ave., 21228. Tel: 410-828-0622.
Hood College, St. John Church, Rosemont Ave., Frederick, 21701. Tel: 301-662-8288.
Frostburg State University, Osborne Center, 130 S. Broadway, Frostburg, 21532. Tel: 301-689-5041. Rev. Edward S. Hendricks.
Western Maryland College. Contact St. John Church, Westminster, 21157. Tel: 410-848-4744.

[P] FOUNDATIONS, FUNDS AND TRUSTS

BALTIMORE. *Bon Secours Baltimore Health Corp., Inc.,* 2000 W. Baltimore St., 21223. Tel: 410-362-3000.
Bon Secours Housing, Inc.
Bon Secours Housing II, Inc.
Bon Secours Facilities, Inc.
Bon Secours of Maryland Foundation, Inc.
Unity Properties, Inc.
The Urban Medical Institute Foundation, Inc.
Chancery Office. For further information contact the Secretary of Management Services. Also see Miscellaneous Section for additional listings. 320 Cathedral St., 21201. Tel: 410-547-5444.
Archbishop of Baltimore Annual Appeal Trust.
Archdiocesan Health Plan Trust Fund Agreement.
**Backbone Housing, Inc.*
Basilica of the Assumption Historic Trust, Inc.
The Bethany Community, Inc.
Catholic Charities of Central Maryland, Inc.
The Catholic Housing, Inc.
Cemetery Continuing Care Trust. St. Patrick's Havre de Grace, Cemetery Continuing Care Trust; Holy Cross Cemetery Continuing Care Trust; St. Joseph, Fullerton, Cemetery-Continuing Care Trust Agreement; St. Mary of the Assumption, Govans, Cemetery Continuing Care Trust; St. Mary's, Pylesville Cemetery, Continuing Care Trust.
The Children's Fund, Inc.
Christian Brothers Community Support Charitable Trust.
Corpus Christi Jenkins Memorial Trust, Inc.
Dart, Inc.
Friends of Villa Maria, Inc.
Franciscan Sisters of Baltimore, Inc., Trust.
The Gallagher Family Fund, 320 Cathedral St., 21201.
G S Health, Inc.
G S Health Endowment, Inc.
**G S Housing, Inc.*
G S Properties, Inc.
Gallagher Services Auxiliary, Inc.
Jenkins Apartments, Inc.
Jenkins Housing, Inc.
John Carroll Foundation of the Roman Catholic Archdiocese of Baltimore.
John Paul II Regional School, Inc.
St. Joseph's Texas, School Endowment Trust.
Marian House, Inc.
The Marion Burk Knott Scholarship Fund, Educational Trust.
Maryvale Educational Fund, Inc.
Mercy Primary Care Group, Inc.
The National Black Catholic Congress, Inc.
Neumann Early Childhood Center, Inc.
Our Lady of Good Counsel Historic Trust, Inc.
Pallottine Charitable, Educational and Apostolic Ministry Trust.
Prime E.A.P., Inc.
St. Agnes Clinical Practice Group, Inc.
St. Francis Housing Corporation.
St. Gregory the Great Housing Committee, Inc.
St. Agnes Hospital Foundation, Inc.
St. Augustine School Education Endowment Trust.
St. Jane Frances Educational Endowment Trust.
St. Jerome Housing Corporation, Inc.
St. John Neuwmann Regional School, Inc.
St. Jude Shrine Corporation.
St. Mark's Parish School Endowment Trust.
St. Martha's Housing, Inc.
St. Mary's Housing, Inc.
St. Peter's Cemetery Restoration Fund, Inc.
St. Peter's, Westernport, School Endowment Trust.
St. Pius V Housing Committee, Inc.
St. Vincent's Child Care Center, Inc.
St. Vincent De Paul Historic Trust, Inc.
Sacred Heart Community Health Services, Inc.
Sacred Heart Foundation, Inc.
Sacred Heart Hospital of the Sisters of Charity, Inc.
The SS. Peter & Paul Parish Endowment Trust.
School Sisters of Notre Dame in the City of Baltimore Charitable Trust, Inc.
The Seton Keough High School Endowment Trust.
Seton Regional Foundation, Inc.
Seton Regional Health System, Inc.
Sisters of Notre Dame de Namur Charitable Trusts.
Sisters of Notre Dame de Namur, Maryland Province, Charitable Trust.
Women's Auxiliary Board.
Mercy Medical Center Malpractice Self-Insurance Trust, 301 St. Paul Pl., 21202.
Pallotine Charitable, Educational and Apostolic Ministry Trust, 512 W. Saratoga St., 21201.
St. Augustine School Education Endowment Trust, 5976 Old Washington Rd., 21227.
The Seton Keough High School Endowment Trust, 1201 Caton Ave., 21227.

CUMBERLAND. *The SS. Peter & Paul Parish Endowment Trust,* 125 Fayette St., 21502. Tel: 301-777-3131.

MARRIOTTSVILLE. *Bon Secours Health System, Inc.,* 1505 Marriottsville Rd., 21104. Tel: 410-442-5511. Sr. Patricia A. Eck, C.B.S., Chm. & Board of Directors; Christopher M. Carney, CEO & Pres.
Bon Secours, Inc., 1525 Marriottsville Rd., 21104. Tel: 410-442-1333.
Bon Secours Providers, Inc.

PASADENA. *St. Jane Francis Educational Endowment Trust,* 8499 Virginia Ave., 21122.

[Q] MISCELLANEOUS

BALTIMORE. *Alhambra, International Order of,* Supreme Headquarters, 4200 Leeds Ave., 21229. Nonprofit organization dedicated to assisting the developmentally disabled.
Apostles in the Marketplace (A.I.M.), 320 Cathedral St., 21201.
Apostleship of the Sea (Baltimore), 3048 Guilford Ave., 21218. Tel: 410-338-1296.
Christian hospitality services at an ecumenical Seafarers' Center; the Baltimore International Seafarer's Center. Bro. Jim Horan, S.J., Port Chap.
Bon Secours Community Health Services, Inc., 2000 W. Baltimore St., 21223. Tel: 410-362-3148.
**Cardijn Associates, Inc.,* 1806 Lancaster St., 21231. Tel: 410-563-3190. Ms. Nancy Lee Conrad, Sec.
Carmelite Communities Assoc., 1318 Dulaney Valley Rd., 21286-1399. Total in Residence 170.
The Caroline Center, 900 Somerset St., 21202. Tel: 410-563-1303. Legal Title: *The Caroline Freiss Center, Inc.* Sr. Kathleen Feeley, S.S.N.D., Dir. Total Assisted 120; Total Staff 10. Employment counseling center for women.
Cathedral Library, 5200 N. Charles St., 21210. Tel: 410-433-6769. Elizabeth Howard, Library Chm. Staffed by the Catholic Evidence League.
Catholic Alumni Club, P.O. Box 22305, 21203-2305.
Catholic Community at Relay, 5025 Cedar Ave., 21227. Tel: 410-247-4033. Rev. Nwaka Chris Egbulem, O.P. Total Staff 2.
Catholic Deaf of Baltimore, 2744 Pelham Ave., 21213. Tel: 410-483-2563. Thelma Breighnor, Pres.
Catholic Evidence League, 5200 N. Charles St., 21210.
Catholic Fraternity. Incorporated 1910. 951 Rosedale Ave., 21237. Tel: 410-687-8787.
Catholic Relief Services, U.S.C.C. World Headquarters, 209 W. Fayette St., 21201. Tel: 410-625-2220; Fax: 410-685-1635. Kenneth Hackett, Exec. Dir.
Catholic War Veterans, Inc., 519 Orkney Rd., 21212. Tel: 410-433-5161. Rev. Conan H. Timoney, C.P., State Chap.; John A. Jarosinski, Commander; Jean Jarosinski, Auxiliary Pres.
Cursillo Movement. Rev. Edward J. Bayer, Spiritual Dir. Tel: 410-922-3800; Deacon Albert Kosla, Spiritual Dir., 1311 St. Stephen's Church Rd., Churchville, 21032. Tel: 410-721-2612. Sr. Virginie Fish, O.S.P., Spiritual Dir., 701 Gun Rd., 21227. Tel: 410-242-8500. Sherry Rhoades, Lay Dir., 916 Bernadette Rd., Forest Hill, 21050. Tel: 410-879-2543.
Division of Leadership Development, 320 Cathedral St., 21201.
Efharisto Studio, Inc., 5130 N. Franklintown Rd., 21207-6598. Tel: 410-448-1711; Fax: 410-448-3259. Sr. Stephana Toomey, O.P., Pres.
Services to advance the Roman Catholic religion by charitable, religious, and educational efforts in pursuing a nonprofit ministry of preaching by developing colorful worship areas and art forms to communicate visual meditations and services for the liturgy.
Food for Thought, Inc., 1625 E. Baltimore, 21231. Tel: 410-563-0081. Sr. Mary Ann Hartnett, S.S.N.D., Dir. Tutorial program for children & adult literacy.
Francis House, Inc., 2226 Maryland Ave., 21218-5625. Tel: 410-235-2588; Fax: 410-243-6125.
E-mail: pmcalpin@aol.com
Sr. Patricia McAlpin, O.S.F., Director. Total in Residence 3; Total Staff 2.
Holy Name Society (Union), P.O. Box 12032, 21281. Rev. Msgr. Jeremiah Kenney, Archdiocesan Dir.
House of Mercy, Inc., P.O. Box 11448, 21239. Tel: 410-435-4400. Sr. Margaret Downing, R.S.M., Dir.
Ignatian Lay Volunteer Corps, 108 E. Madison St., 21202. Tel: 410-752-4686. Rev. James R. Conroy, S.J., Exec. Dir. Co-Directors: Rev. Charles P. Costello, S.J.; Barbara Castellano.
International Federation of Catholic Alumnae, Maryland Chapter, 1409 Union Ave., 21211-1906. Tel: 410-235-0406. Ruth Ruggiero, R.S.M., Governor. Total Staff 116. Benefits & other fund raising activities are held to accumulate funds which are rewarded to members catholic schools in the archdiocese, for scholarships & financial assistance to students.
Jesuit Educational Association of Maryland, Inc., 5704 Roland Ave., 21210. Tel: 410-532-1400; Fax: 410-532-1419. Rev. Allen P. Novotny, S.J., Pres.
Jesuit Jamshedpur Mission Society, Inc., 14 W. Cold Spring Ln., #116, 21210-2631. Tel: 410-433-1782. Rev. Joseph M. Kennedy, S.J., Dir. Total Staff 1.
Jesuit Mission Bureau, Maryland Province, Inc., 14 W. Cold Spring Ln., #116, 21210. Tel: 410-435-7090. Revs. Francis R. Carmody, S.J., Pres. & Treas.; Richard J. Colgan, S.J., Asst. Sec.
Jesuit Seminary Guild, Maryland Province, Inc., 14 W. Cold Spring Ln., #116, 21210. Tel: 410-435-7090. Revs. Francis R. Carmody, S.J., Pres. & Treas.; Richard J. Colgan, S.J., Asst. Sec.
Johns Hopkins Hospital Apostolate. Revs. Alphonse G. Rose; Theodore M. Wisniewski.
Chaplain's Office, Johns Hopkins Medical Center, 600 N. Wolfe St., 21287-4170. Tel: 410-955-5842; Fax: 410-550-6765.
Ladies of Charity, 4050 Wilkens Ave., 21229. Rev. Msgr. Victor B. Galeone, Spiritual Dir.; Rosemary Cornelius, Pres.
Legion of Mary. 3229 Birchmede Dr., Ellicott City, 21042. Tel: 410-465-1355. Rev. Patrick Magnier, C.SS.R., Spiritual Dir.; Mr. Jim Saboe, Pres.
Baltimore Regional Senatus, principal council for states of Maryland, Delaware, West Virginia, Virginia, North Carolina and District of Columbia.
Marianist Conference, 4301 Roland Ave., 21210. Tel: 410-366-1300.
E-mail: georgejcer@aol.com
Rev. George J. Cerniglia, S.M., Pres.
Maryland Catholic Health Care Consortium, Inc., Holy Cross Hospital of Silver Spring, Inc., 1500 Forest Glen Rd., 20910.
Mercy Home Health Services, Inc., 102 E. Pleasant St., 21202. Tel: 410-332-9784. Sr. Ann Laidlaw, M.P.H., R.N., Dir.
Mission Helper Productions, Inc. (video production studio), 1001 W. Joppa Rd., 21204-3787. Tel: 410-823-8585, Ext. 240. Sr. Anne Guinan, M.H.S.H., Contact Person.
Mother Seton House on Paca Street, Inc., 600 N. Paca St., 21201. Tel: 410-523-3443.
The Mount Saint Agnes Theological Center for Women, Inc., 5707 Smith Ave., 21209. Tel: 410-466-6039. Sr. Mary Aquin O'Neill, R.S.M., Dir.
Parish Social Ministry Outreach, 1512 Druid Hill Ave., 21217. Tel: 410-523-3256.
Immaculate Conception Parish, Baltimore. Sr. Genevieve Noonan, D.C., Staff.
Radio Mass of Baltimore, Inc., St. Ignatius Church, 740 N. Calvert St., 21202. Tel: 410-539-7812. Rev. William J. Watters, S.J., Dir.
Mass is broadcast every Sunday morning from St. Ignatius Church at 9:30 A.M., WBAL, 1090 AM Radio Dial.
St. Agnes Clinical Practice Group, Inc. (inactive at this time), 900 S. Caton Ave., 21229. Tel: 410-368-6000. Robert E. Pezzoli, Pres.
SS. Matthew and Thomas More Religious Education and Youth Ministry Center, Inc., 6806 McClean Blvd., 21234. Tel: 410-444-4563.
Serra Club Vocation Center, 320 Cathedral St., 21201. Tel: 410-547-5431. Rev. James Barker, Chap.
Veteran Mission Crusade, Archdiocesan, 4415 Asbury Ave., 21206. Tel: 410-485-5575.
Vietnamese Catholic Community at Baltimore (VCCAB), 8515 Philadelphia Rd., 21237. Tel: 410-780-3149. Rev. John the Baptist Thong, Chap.
The Young Christian Workers, Inc., P.O. Box 6052, 21231-0052. Tel: 410-563-3281.

CUMBERLAND. *Catholic Education Ministries of Western Maryland.* Bishop Walsh Middle/High School, 700 Bishop Walsh Rd., 21502. Tel: 301-777-9082; Fax: 301-722-6114.
E-mail: catholicwmd@mindspring.com
Web site: www.mindspring.com
Margaret Meyers, Area Coord.

DUNKIRK. *Family of the Americas Foundation, Inc.,* P.O. Box 1170, 20754-1170. Tel: 301-627-3346; 800-443-3395; Fax: 301-627-0847.
E-mail: family@upbeat.com

ELLICOTT CITY. *Christlife, Inc.,* 12290-A Folly Quarter Rd., 21042. Tel: 410-531-7701; Fax: 410-531-7702.

E-mail: dave@christlife.org
Mr. Dave Nodar, Pres.

Conventual Franciscan Friars, St. Anthony of Padua Province USA, 12300 Folly Quarter Rd., 21042. Tel: 410-531-9200; Fax: 410-531-4881. Legal Title: *Order of Friars Minor Conventual, St. Anthony of Padua Province, U.S.A., Inc.; Franciscan Minor Conventuals of Maryland, Inc. of Ellicott City, MD.; The Franciscan Fathers, Minor Conventuals, of St. Stanislaus Church of Baltimore City, Inc.; Franciscan Friars, St. Anthony of Padua Province, Education Fund, Inc.; Franciscan Friars, St. Anthony of Padua Province, Fund for the Aged and Infirm Friars, Inc.; St. Francis of Assisi Community, Inc., Companions of St. Anthony; St. Stanislaus Cemetery, Inc.* Total in Residence 195.

EMMITSBURG. *National Shrine of St. Elizabeth Ann Seton*, 333 S. Seton Ave., 21727. Tel: 301-447-6606.
E-mail: setonshrine@fwp.net
Web site: www.setonshrine.org
Sr. Cecilia Rose, D.C., Admin.

JOPPA. *Catholic Daughters of the Americas*, 748 Shore Dr., 21085-4552. Tel: 410-679-6867. Rev. Alphonse G. Rose, State Chap.; Most Rev. William Newman, Clergy Consultant; Mrs. Lucretia Coates, State Regent.

LANSDOWNE.
**Coursey Station Apartments, Inc.*, 200 First Ave., 21227. Tel: 410-242-6167. Beverly Britton, Mgr.

LINTHICUM. *Daughters of Charity National Health System East, Inc.*, 891 Elkridge Landing Rd., Ste. 400, 21090-1025. Tel: 410-850-9000; Fax: 410-859-3459. James E. Small, Regional Exec.

MARRIOTTSVILLE. *Bon Secours Health System, Inc.*, 1505 Marriottsville Rd., 21104. Tel: 410-442-5511. Sr. Patricia A. Eck, C.B.S., Chm., Board of Directors; Christopher M. Carney, CEO & Pres.

PASADENA. *Reparation Society of the Immaculate Heart of Mary*, 8006 Caliburn Ct., 21122-6348. Rev. Casimir M. Peterson, S.T.L., J.C.D., Dir. Volunteers 3; Total in Residence 1.

PIKESVILLE. *St. Charles House, Inc.*, 11 Church Ln., 21208. Tel: 410-484-6125. Beverly Britton, Mgr.

SILVER SPRING. *Christian Life Community Regional Information Center*, 201 E. Wayne Ave., 20901. Tel: 301-495-2969; Fax: 301-495-7318.
Web site: www.world.std.com/uclcusa
Mr. Fred C. Leone, Regl. Rep.

TIMONIUM. *St. Thomas More Society of Maryland.* The local branch of the National Society of Catholic Lawyers. Administrative Office, Box 4764, 21093. Tel: 410-252-7916. Anthony R. Mignini, Esq., Pres.

UPPER MARLBORO. *Knights of Columbus*, 9305 Southmoor Ct., 20772. Tel: 301-856-2158. Rev. James A. Finan, State Chap.; John J. Glynn, State Deputy.

WESTMINSTER. *Dominican Pastoral Counseling Center*, 187 E. Main St., 21157. Tel: 410-876-8315. Sr. Dolores A. Pfeiffer, O.P., M.A., M.S., Dir. Total Assisted 260 (Counseling Hrs.); Total Staff 1.

RELIGIOUS INSTITUTES OF MEN REPRESENTED IN THE ARCHDIOCESE

For further details refer to the corresponding bracketed number in the Religious Institutes of Men or Women Section.

[0200]—*Benedictine Monks (Latrobe, PA).*—O.S.B.
[1350]—*Brothers of St. Francis Xavier.*—C.F.X.
[0330]—*Brothers of the Christian Schools.* (Baltimore Prov.).—F.S.C.
[0470]—*The Capuchin Friars.* (Prov. of St. Augustine).—O.F.M.Cap.
[1330]—*Congregation of the Mission.* (Eastern Prov.).—C.M.
[1000]—*Congregation of the Passion.* (Prov. of St. Paul of the Cross).—C.P.
[0480]—*Conventual Franciscans.* (Buffalo, NY).—O.F.M.Conv.
[]—*Crosier Fathers.*—O.S.C.
[0690]—*Jesuit Fathers and Brothers.* (Maryland Prov.).—S.J.
[]—*Norbertine Fathers.* (Immaculate Conception Priory, DE).—O.Praem.
[1310]—*Order of the Most Holy Trinity, Immaculate Heart of Mary Province.*—O.SS.T.
[1070]—*Redemptorist Fathers.* (Baltimore Prov.).—C.SS.R.
[0700]—*St. Joseph's Society of the Sacred Heart.*—S.S.J.
[1260]—*Society of Christ.*—S.Ch.
[0760]—*Society of Mary.*—S.M.
[0990]—*Society of the Catholic Apostolate.* (Immaculate Conception Prov.).—S.A.C.
[1200]—*Society of the Divine Saviour.*—S.D.S.
[1290]—*Society of the Priests of St. Sulpice.*—S.S.
[]—*Sulpicians.*—S.S.

RELIGIOUS INSTITUTES OF WOMEN REPRESENTED IN THE ARCHDIOCESE

[0230]—*Benedictine Sisters of Pontifical Jurisdiction.* (Baltimore).—O.S.B.
[0270]—*Congregation of Bon Secours.*—C.B.S.
[1920]—*Congregation of the Sisters of the Holy Cross.*—C.S.C.
[0760]—*Daughters of Charity of St. Vincent de Paul.*—D.C.
[0420]—*Discalced Carmelite Nuns.*—O.C.D.
[1070-03]—*Dominican Sisters.*—O.P.
[1070-07]—*Dominican Sisters.*—O.P.
[1070-13]—*Dominican Sisters.*—O.P.
[1200]—*Franciscan Sisters of Baltimore.*—O.S.F.
[1470]—*Franciscan Sisters of St. Joseph.*—F.S.S.J.
[1840]—*Grey Nuns of the Sacred Heart.* (Pennsylvania).—G.N.S.H.
[2575]—*Institute of the Sisters of the Mercy of the Americas.*—R.S.M.
[2330]—*Little Sisters of Jesus.*
[2340]—*Little Sisters of the Poor.*—L.S.P.
[2470]—*Maryknoll Sisters.* (New York).—M.M.
[2490]—*Medical Missionary Sisters.* (Pennsylvania).—M.M.S.
[2720]—*Mission Helpers of the Sacred Heart.*—M.H.S.H.
[2710]—*Missionaries of Charity.* (New York).—M.C.
[3040]—*Oblate Sisters of Providence.*—O.S.P.
[]—*Religious of the Cenacle.* (New York).—R.C.
[2070]—*Religious of the Holy Union of the Sacred Hearts.*—S.U.S.C.
[3465]—*Religious of the Sacred Heart of Mary.* (New York).—R.S.H.M.
[2970]—*School Sisters of Notre Dame.*—S.S.N.D.
[0640]—*Sisters of Charity.* (Halifax).—S.C.
[0990]—*Sisters of Divine Providence.*—C.D.P.
[3000]—*Sisters of Notre Dame de Namur.*—S.N.D.deN.
[1650]—*Sisters of St. Francis of Philadelphia.*—O.S.F.
[]—*Sisters of St. Francis of Rochester.* (Minnesota).—O.S.F.
[3830]—*Sisters of St. Joseph.*—C.S.J.
[1030]—*Sisters of the Divine Savior.*—S.D.S.
[1830]—*Sisters of the Good Shepherd.* (Washington Prov.).—R.G.S.
[1970]—*Sisters of the Holy Family of Nazareth.*—C.S.F.N.
[3610]—*Sisters Servants of Mary Immaculate.*—S.S.M.I.
[2150]—*Sisters, Servants of the Immaculate Heart of Mary.*—I.H.M.
[2160]—*Sisters, Servants of the Immaculate Heart of Mary.*—I.H.M.
[4120]—*Ursuline Nuns, of the Congregation of Kentucky.*—O.S.U.
[4190]—*Visitation Nuns.*—V.H.M.

ARCHDIOCESAN CEMETERIES

BALTIMORE. *New Cathedral.*

NECROLOGY

† Begley, Patrick, (Retired). —Died May 30, 1997.
† Echle, Rev. Msgr. Edward V., (Retired). —Died May 16, 1997.
† Harding, Bernard, (Retired). —Died Sept. 13, 1997.
† Hiltz, Peter M., (Retired). —Died Dec. 5, 1996.
† Linn, Rev. Msgr. Francis J., (Retired). —Died Dec. 16, 1996.
† McCall, Rev. Msgr. John H., Fallston, MD, St. Mark. —Died May 19, 1997.
† Melycher, Stephen D., (Retired). —Died Jan. 20, 1997.
† Riggie, Kloman F., Hagerstown, MD, St. Joseph. —Died Dec. 2, 1996.
† Scarff, Rev. Msgr. Stanley J., (Retired). —Died March 6, 1997.
† Taylor, Rev. Msgr. E. Melville, (Retired). —Died May 19, 1997.
† Tierney, John J., (Retired). —Died June 20, 1997.

Diocese of Baton Rouge

(Dioecesis Rubribaculensis)

Most Reverend

ALFRED C. HUGHES, S.T.D.

Bishop of Baton Rouge; ordained December 15, 1957; appointed Auxiliary Bishop of Boston and Titular Bishop of Massimiana in Bizacena July 21, 1981; ordained Bishop September 14, 1981; promoted to Baton Rouge September 7, 1993; installed Fourth Bishop of Baton Rouge November 4, 1993. *Res., P.O. Box 2028, Baton Rouge, LA, 70821-2028.* Tel.: 504-387-0561; Fax: 504-336-8789.

Chancery Office: Catholic Life Center, 1800 S. Acadian Thruway, P.O. Box 2028, Baton Rouge, LA, 70821-2028. Tel.: 504-387-0561; Fax: 504-336-8789.

Web site address: http://www.diobr.org

E-mail address: chancery@diobr.org

ESTABLISHED JULY 20, 1961.

Square Miles 5,513.

Comprises the civil parishes (counties) of Ascension, Assumption, East Baton Rouge, West Baton Rouge, Iberville, Pointe Coupee, East Feliciana, West Feliciana, St. Helena, Tangipahoa, Livingston and St. James in the State of Louisiana.

For legal titles of parishes and diocesan institutions, consult the Chancery Office.

STATISTICAL OVERVIEW

Personnel	
Bishop	1
Priests: Diocesan Active in Diocese	67
Priests: Active Outside Diocese	4
Priests: Retired, Sick or Absent	17
Number of Diocesan Priests	88
Religious Priests in Diocese	45
Extern Priests in Diocese	11
Ordinations:	
Diocesan Priests	1
Religious Priests	1
Transitional Deacons	1
Permanent Deacons in Diocese	28
Total Brothers	11
Total Sisters	120
Parishes	
Parishes	70
With Resident Pastor:	
Resident Diocesan Priests	55
Resident Religious Priests	10
Without Resident Pastor:	
Administered by Priests	4
Administered by Lay People	1
Professional Ministry Personnel:	
Sisters	20
Lay Ministers	68
Welfare	
Catholic Hospitals	1
Total Assisted	230,000
Homes for the Aged	5
Total Assisted	661
Specialized Homes	4
Total Assisted	1,159
Special Centers for Social Services	6
Total Assisted	101,784
Educational	
Diocesan Students in Other Seminaries	10
Total Seminarians	10
Colleges and Universities	1
Total Students	961
High Schools, Diocesan and Parish	6
Total Students	2,589
High Schools, Private	2
Total Students	1,542
Elementary Schools, Diocesan and Parish	26
Total Students	12,391
Catechesis/Religious Education:	
High School Students	5,882
Elementary Students	10,628
Total Students Under Catholic Instruction	34,003
Teachers in the Diocese:	
Priests	1
Brothers	1
Sisters	25
Lay Teachers	877
Vital Statistics	
Receptions into the Church:	
Infant Baptism Totals	2,870
Adult Baptism Totals	192
Received into Full Communion	359
First Communions	2,901
Confirmations	2,384
Marriages:	
Catholic	800
Interfaith	406
Total Marriages	1,206
Deaths	1,649
Total Catholic Population	209,182
Total Population	763,545

Former Bishops—Most Rev. ROBERT E. TRACY, D.D., LL.D., appt. Titular Bishop of Sergentza and Auxiliary of Lafayette March 18, 1959; cons. May 19, 1959; appt. first Bishop of Baton Rouge Aug. 10, 1961; retired March 21, 1974; died April 4, 1980.—Most Rev. JOSEPH V. SULLIVAN, S.T.D., appt. Titular Bishop of Tagamuta and Auxiliary to the Bishop of Kansas City-St. Joseph March 3, 1967; cons. April 3, 1967; appt. Second Bishop of Baton Rouge August 5, 1974; died September 4, 1982.—Most Rev. STANLEY JOSEPH OTT, S.T.D., appt. Titular Bishop of Nicives and Auxiliary Bishop of New Orleans May 24, 1976; cons. June 29, 1976; appt. Third Bishop of Baton Rouge January 18, 1983; died November 28, 1992.

Vicar General & Moderator of the Curia—Very Rev. JOHN CARVILLE, S.T.D., V.G.

Chancery Office—Catholic Life Center, 1800 S. Acadian Thruway, P.O. Box 2028, Baton Rouge, 70821-2028. Tel: 504-387-0561; Fax: 504-336-8789. Office Hours: Mon.-Fri. 8:30-4:30.

Chancellor—Rev. Msgr. ROBERT H. BERGGREEN, M.Ed.

Vice-Chancellors—Very Rev. PAUL D. COUNCE, J.C.L., M.C.L.; Rev. MARTIN A. HERNANDEZ, J.C.L., M.C.L.

Diocesan Tribunal—Catholic Life Center, 1800 S. Acadian Thruway, P.O. Box 1087, Baton Rouge, 70821-1087. Tel: 504-387-0561; Fax: 504-336-8789.

Judicial Vicar—Very Rev. PAUL D. COUNCE, J.C.L., M.C.L.

Promotor of Justice—Very Rev. VINCENT J. DUFRESNE, S.T.L., J.C.L., V.F.

Judges—Rev. Msgr. WILLIAM L. GREENE; Rev. Msgr. GERALD M. LEFEBVRE, V.F.; Revs. FRANK M. UTER; MICHAEL J. MORONEY; DEAN J. MARTIN, J.C.L.

Defenders of the Bond—Very Rev. VINCENT J. DUFRESNE, S.T.L., J.C.L., V.F.; Revs. THAN N. VU, S.T.L.; SHELTON J. FABRE; DANIEL P. LEMOINE; GERARD R. MARTIN.

Notaries—Mrs. JO ZGANJAR; PATRICIA F. SONIAT.

College of Consultors—Very Rev. JOHN CARVILLE, S.T.D., V.G.; Rev. Msgr. ROBERT H. BERGGREEN; Revs. MICHAEL J. MORONEY; GERARD F. YOUNG; HENRY C. VAVASSEUR; SHELTON J. FABRE.

Diocesan Pro-Vicar—

Pro-Vicar for Women Religious—Sr. DIANNE HEINRICH, C.D.P.

Diocesan Corporation (The Roman Catholic Church of the Diocese of Baton Rouge)—Most Rev. ALFRED C. HUGHES, S.T.D.; Very Rev. JOHN CARVILLE, S.T.D., V.G., Vice Pres.; Rev. Msgr. ROBERT H. BERGGREEN, M.Ed., Sec.; Mr. J. ERROL GAUTREAU, Treas.

Diocesan Offices and Directors

Apostleship of Prayer—Rev. Msgr. JOHN A. WEBER, *5445 Government St., #105, Baton Rouge, 70806-6003.* Tel: 504-925-9431; Fax: 504-928-3284.

Apostolate to the Deaf—Mr. WILLIAM G. DUGAS, Dir., *2585 Brightside Ln., Baton Rouge, 70820-3504.* Tel: 504-766-9320; 769-0223; Fax: 504-766-9320.

Archives—Mrs. UNA DAIGRE, Archivist, *P.O. Box 2028, Baton Rouge, 70821-2028.* Tel: 504-387-0561.

Black Catholics—Rev. SHELTON J. FABRE, *P.O. Box 8, Grosse Tete, 70740-0008.* Tel: 504-648-2420.

Campus Ministry—Rev. PATRICK J. MASCARELLA, *P.O. Box 25131, Baton Rouge, 70894-5131.* Tel: 504-383-1574; Fax: 504-344-1920.

Catholic Charismatic Renewal Office—Rev. HENRY W. GAUTREAU, *2121 N. Sherwood Forest Dr., Baton Rouge, 70815-1998.* Tel: 504-275-7280; Fax: 504-275-5845.

Catholic Community Services—Ms. DEBORAH A. ROE, M.S.W., Exec. Dir., Office: *1800 S. Acadian Thruway, P.O. Box 1668, Baton Rouge, 70821-1668.* Tel: 504-336-8770; Fax: 504-336-8745.

Catholic Social Services Dept.—Ms. JANICE SAPP, M.S.W., *4884 Constitution Ave., Suite 1-B, Baton Rouge, 70808-3326.* Tel: 504-927-4930; Fax: 504-927-9246.

Social Responsibility Dept.—Ms. PEGGY STUART.

Family Life Dept.—Dr. TOM C. ABEL, Dir., Office: *1800 S. Acadian Thruway, P.O. Box 1668, Baton Rouge, 70821-1668.* Tel: 504-336-8770; 387-0561; Fax: 504-336-8745.

Cemeteries—Rev. FRANK M. UTER, *P.O. Drawer 1501, Gramercy, 70052-1501.* Tel: 504-869-5324; Fax: 504-869-5325.

Ecumenical Affairs—Rev. MICHAEL J. MORONEY, *445 Marquette Ave., Baton Rouge, 70806-4497.* Tel: 504-926-1883; Fax: 504-923-0448.

Communications—Deacon ROBERT FURLOW, *P.O. Box*

2028, Baton Rouge, 70821-2028. Tel: 504-387-0561; 383-0880; Fax: 504-383-0924.

Continuing Formation for the Clergy—Rev. PATRICK J. MASCARELLA, Dir., *P.O. Box 25131, Baton Rouge, 70894-5131.* Tel: 504-383-1574; Fax: 504-344-1920.

Development—Mr. MARK J. BLANCHARD, Dir., *P.O. Box 2028, Baton Rouge, 70821-2028.* Tel: 504-336-8790; Fax: 504-336-8710.

Finance—Mr. J. ERROL GAUTREAU, Sec. for Finance/ Fiscal Officer, *P.O. Box 2028, Baton Rouge, 70821-2028.* Tel: 504-387-0561; Fax: 504-336-8789.

Christian Formation—Mrs. BETTY BOURGEOIS, *P.O. Box 2028, Baton Rouge, 70821-2028.* Tel: 504-336-8760; Fax: 504-336-8765.

Hispanic Apostolate—Sr. LEAH COUVILLION, S.S.N.D., Dir.; Deacon JOSE RAMON RIOS, Chap., *2585 Brightside Ln., Baton Rouge, 70820-3504.* Tel: 504-766-9320; Fax: 504-766-8973.

Newspaper "The Catholic Commentator"—Mrs. LAURA G. DEAVERS, Exec. Editor and Gen. Mgr., Office: *Catholic Life Center, 1800 S. Acadian Thruway, Baton Rouge, 70821-1668., Mailing Address: P.O. Drawer 14746, Baton Rouge, 70898-4746.* Tel: 504-387-0983; Fax: 504-336-8710.

Permanent Diaconate Office—Deacon ALBERT R. ELLIS, JR., Dir., *7808 St. George Dr., Baton Rouge, 70809-4699.* Tel: 504-293-2212; Fax: 504-291-8063.

Presbyteral Council—Rev. Msgr. ROBERT H. BERGGREEN; Rev. JULES A. BRUNET; Very Rev. JOHN CARVILLE, S.T.D., V.G.; Revs. DEAN J. MARTIN, J.C.L.; ROBERT F. STINE; Very Rev. PAUL D. COUNCE, J.C.L.; Revs. SHELTON J. FABRE; MICHAEL J. MORONEY; HUNG V. NGUYEN; MICHAEL J. SCHATZLE, C.SS.R.; N. JOHN NUTTER; MANSUETO P. PALANG, S.V.D.; ROBERT U. PERRY, O.P.; MARIANO J. RIZZUTO, S.M.; HENRY C. VAVASSEUR; TIMOTHY J. KERNER, C.SS.R.; GERARD F. YOUNG.

Propagation of the Faith and Association of Holy Childhood—Rev. N. JOHN NUTTER, Dir., *P.O. Box 2028, Baton Rouge, 70821-2028.* Tel: 504-387-0561; Fax: 504-336-8789.

Religious Education—Ms. CAROLE OBROKTA, *P.O. Box 2028, Baton Rouge, 70821-2028.* Tel: 504-336-8730; Fax: 504-336-8731.

Catholic Schools—Sr. MARY MICHAELINE GREEN, O.P., Supt. Asst. Supts.: Dr. JUDY H. ARMSTRONG, Ph.D.; Mrs. THAIS T. JOHNSON, *P.O. Box 2028, Baton Rouge, 70821-2028.* Tel: 504-336-8735; Fax: 504-336-8711.

Scouting—Rev. DUANE L. BREAUX, Chap., *P.O. Box 190, Pierre Part, 70339-0190.* Tel: 504-252-6008; Fax: 504-252-8011.

Separated and Divorced—Rev. FRED YOUNGS, Dir., *5657 Thomas Rd., Baton Rouge, 70811-7356.* Tel: 504-775-8850; Fax: 504-775-7072.

Serra Clubs—Rev. M. JEFFREY BAYHI, Spiritual Advisor, *P.O. Box 2028, Baton Rouge, 70821-2028.* Tel: 504-336-8778; Fax: 504-336-8710.

Society of St. Vincent De Paul—Rev. MICHAEL A. MICELI, Spiritual Advisor, *P.O. Box 127, Baton Rouge, 70821-0127.* Tel: 504-383-7837.

Vietnamese Apostolate—Rev. HUNG VIET NGUYEN, I.C.M., Dir., *2580 Tecumseh St., Baton Rouge, 70805-7999.* Tel: 504-357-4787; Fax: 504-355-9794.

Vocations—Rev. M. JEFFREY BAYHI, Dir.; Sr. DIANNE HEINRICH, C.D.P., Assoc. Dir., *P.O. Box 2028, Baton Rouge, 70821-2028.* Tel: 504-336-8778; Fax: 504-336-8710.

Women, Council of Catholic—Vacant.

Worship, Office of—Rev. THOMAS C. RANZINO, Dir., *P.O. Box 2028, Baton Rouge, 70821-2028.* Tel: 504-387-0561; Fax: 504-336-8789.

Youth Ministry—Mr. CHARLES JUMONVILLE, Dir., *P.O. Box 2028, Baton Rouge, 70821-2028.* Tel: 504-336-8751; Fax: 504-336-8765.

CLERGY, PARISHES, MISSIONS AND PAROCHIAL SCHOOLS

CITY OF BATON ROUGE
(East Baton Rouge Parish)

1—ST. JOSEPH CATHEDRAL (1792), Rev. Gerard F. Young; Deacons Robert Furlow; James Wax. In res., Edgar J. Tiblier, S.J.
Res., 412 North St., 70802-5416. Tel: 504-387-5928; Fax: 504-387-5929.

2—ST. AGNES (1917), Rev. Msgr. Robert H. Berggreen. In res., Revs. M. Jeffrey Bayhi; J. Daniel Walsh, C.S.C.
Res., 749 East Blvd., 70802-6398. Tel: 504-383-4127; Fax: 504-383-4154.

3—ST. ALOYSIUS (1955), Revs. Gerald H. Burns; Paul A. McDuffie (CHR).
Mailing Address: 2025 Stuart Ave., 70808-3998. Tel: 504-343-6657; Fax: 504-344-6847.
School—Tel: 504-383-3871; Fax: 504-383-4500. Mr. John L. Bennett, Prin.
Daughters of Jesus 3; Lay Teachers 45; Students 866.

4—ST. ANTHONY OF PADUA (1920), Rev. Hung Viet Nguyen, I.C.M. (Vietnam).
Res., 2580 Tecumseh St., 70805-7999. Tel: 504-357-4800; Fax: 504-355-9794.

5—ST. CHARLES BORROMEO (1964), Rev. Chris M. Haydel; Deacon Brent Duplessis.
Res., 3852 E. Brookstown Dr., 70805-4791. Tel: 504-356-2527; Fax: 504-356-2528.

6—CHRIST THE KING (1980), Revs. Patrick J. Mascarella; Garland T. Belsome.
Mailing Address: P.O. Box 25131, 70894-5131.
Res., Highland Rd. & Dalrymple Dr., 70894. Tel: 504-344-8595; 383-1574; Fax: 504-344-1920.

7—ST. FRANCIS DE SALES PARISH (1979). (Center for Hearing Impaired). Mr. William G. Dugas, Exec. Dir.; Rev. Paul Cabrita, S.M., Chap.
Res., 2585 Brightside Dr., 70820-3504. Tel: 504-766-9320; 769-0223 (Voice/TDD); Fax: 504-766-9320.

8—ST. FRANCIS XAVIER (1918), Revs. Michael K. Saah-Buckman, S.S.J.; Francis J. Schroeder, S.S.J.
Res., 1143 S. 11th St., 70802-4997. Tel: 504-383-3479; Fax: 504-343-4259.
School—(Grades PreK-8). Tel: 504-387-6639. Mrs. Lorina Turner, Prin.
Sisters of the Holy Family 2; Lay Teachers 14; Students 302.

9—ST. GEORGE (1908), Revs. Thomas C. Ranzino; Rubin Reynolds Paliathayil; Deacons Albert R. Ellis; Guy E. Decker.
Office: 7808 St. George Dr., 70809-4699. Tel: 504-293-2212; Fax: 504-291-8063. [CEM]
School—7880 St. George Dr., 70809-4699. Tel: 504-293-1298. Mrs. Ann Bertsch, Prin.
Lay Teachers 35; Students 801.

10—ST. GERARD MAJELLA (1944), Rev. Timothy Kerner, C.SS.R. In res., Rev. Henry F. Porten, C.SS.R.
Res., 3808 Gerard St., 70805-2834. Tel: 504-355-2553; Fax: 504-356-7472.
School—3655 St. Gerard Ave., 70805-2898. Tel: 504-355-1437. Mr. Lee Faucette, Prin.
Lay Teachers 20; Students 287.

11—IMMACULATE CONCEPTION (1958), Rev. Hilton L. Rivet, S.J. In res., Rev. Francis R. Brou, S.J.
Res., 1565 Curtis St., 70807-4906. Tel: 504-775-7067; Fax: 504-775-0775.

12—ST. JEAN VIANNEY (1975), Very Rev. Donald V. Blanchard, V.F.; Rev. Keun-Soo Lee, Ph.D.; Deacon Thomas M. Robinson.
Res., 16166 S. Harrell's Ferry Rd., 70816-3199. Tel: 504-753-7950; Fax: 504-753-7965.
School—(Grades K-8) 16266 S. Harrell's Ferry Rd., 70816-3103. Tel: 504-751-1831; Fax: 504-752-8774. Mr. Mike Lucia, Prin.
Lay Teachers 23; Students 454.
Preschool—Tel: 504-752-5356. Ms. Kathy Simoneaux, Dir.
Lay Teachers 17; Students 131.

13—ST. JUDE THE APOSTLE (1966), Revs. David E. Allen; Michael A. Miceli.
Res., 9150 Highland Rd., 70810-4096. Tel: 504-766-2431; Fax: 504-766-0722.
School—(Grades PreK-8). Tel: 504-769-2344; Fax: 504-769-3290. Mrs. Joy Wagener, Prin.
Lay Teachers 31; Students 663.

14—ST. LOUIS, KING OF FRANCE (1966), Very Rev. Maynard E. Hurst, V.F.; Rev. Henry W. Gautreau.
Res., 2121 N. Sherwood Forest Dr., 70815-1998. Tel: 504-275-7280; Fax: 504-275-5845.
School—(Grades K-8) 2311 N. Sherwood Forest Dr., 70815-1997. Tel: 504-273-3932; Fax: 504-273-3978. Mrs. Karen Weilbacher, Prin.
Lay Teachers 32; Students 505.
Early Learning Center—Tel: 504-272-6438; Fax: 504-275-5845. Diane Blouin, Dir.
Lay Teachers 9; Students 100.

15—MOST BLESSED SACRAMENT (1979), Revs. Michael J. Collins; Mariano Cassar (Malta).
Res., 7853 Broker Ave., 70817-6002. Tel: 504-752-6230; Fax: 504-756-5014.
School—(Grades K-8). Tel: 504-751-0273; Fax: 504-753-7259.
Lay Teachers 26; Students 560.

16—OUR LADY OF MERCY (1947), Revs. Michael J. Moroney; Charles Landry, C.Ss.R.; Victor G. Messina; Deacon Eugene Allen.
Office: 445 Marquette Ave., 70806-4497. Tel: 504-926-1883; Fax: 504-923-0448.
Res., 450 Marquette Ave., 70806-4497. Tel: 504-927-7106.
School—400 Marquette Ave., 70806-4498. Tel: 504-924-1054; Fax: 504-923-2201. Mrs. Carolyn Guidry, Prin.
Lay Teachers 38; Students 798.

17—ST. PATRICK (1974), Rev. Than N. Vu, S.T.L.; Deacon J. Peter Walsh.
Res., 12424 Brogdon Ln., 70816-4801. Tel: 504-753-5750; Fax: 504-756-9636.

18—ST. PAUL THE APOSTLE (1960), Rev. Joseph I. Guidry, S.V.D.
Res., 3912 Gus Young Ave., 70802-1727. Tel: 504-383-2537.

19—ST. PIUS X (1963), Rev. Jon C. Koehler.
Res., 6380 Hooper Rd., 70811-2499. Tel: 504-357-5935; Fax: 504-357-6005.

20—SACRED HEART OF JESUS (1928), Rev. Kenneth A. Smith. In res., Rev. Msgr. Donald J. Songy; Rev. Francis V. Ferrier, S.J.
Res., 2250 Main St., 70802-3198. Tel: 504-387-6671; Fax: 504-387-6672.
School—Tel: 504-383-7481; Fax: 504-383-1810. Sr. Patricia Sullivan, C.S.J., Prin.
Sisters of St. Joseph 5; Lay Teachers 27; Students 498.

21—ST. THOMAS MORE (1959), Very Rev. John Carville, S.T.D., V.G.; Rev. Gerard R. Martin. Pastoral Assocs: Sr. Jane Louise Arbour, C.S.J.; Sr. Dianne Heinrich, C.D.P.; Deacon Clayton Hollier, Ph.D.
Office: 11441 Goodwood Blvd., 70815-6299. Tel: 504-275-3940; Fax: 504-275-1407.
School—Tel: 504-275-2820; Fax: 504-275-0376. Mr. Steve Ketcham, Prin.
Lay Teachers 50; Students 1,054.
Preschool—Tel: 504-272-3477; Fax: 504-272-0468. Ms. Angie Ducote, Dir.
Lay Teachers 15; Students 134.

OUTSIDE THE CITY OF BATON ROUGE

Albany, Livingston Parish, St. Margaret Queen of Scotland (1910), Rev. Msgr. Leo Guillot; Deacon Warren Fortenberry.
Res., P.O. Box 100, 70711-0100. Tel: 504-567-3573; Fax: 504-567-2031. [CEM]

Amite, Tangipahoa Parish, St. Helena (1868), Rev. N. John Nutter.
Res., P.O. Box 685, 70422-0685. Tel: 504-748-9057; Fax: 504-748-9094.

Baker, East Baton Rouge Parish, St. Isidore the Farmer (1958), Rev. Fred Youngs; Deacon Bruno Rizzo. In res., Rev. David A. Vavasseur.
Res., 5657 Thomas Rd., Baton Rouge, 70811-7356. Tel: 504-775-8850 (Office); Fax: 504-775-7072.
School—Tel: 504-775-3336; Fax: 504-775-3351.
Lay Teachers 20; Students 476.

Bayou Pigeon, Iberville Parish, St. Joan of Arc (1965), Rev. Joseph M. Camilleri.
Res., 39315 Hwy. 75, Plaquemine, 70764-9629. Tel: 504-545-8213; Fax: 504-545-2456.

Belle Rose, Assumption Parish, St. Jules (1912), Rev. Mansueto P. Palang.
Res., P.O. Box 38, 70341-0038. Tel: 504-473-8569; Fax: 504-473-2950. [CEM 2]

Brusly, West Baton Rouge Parish, St. John the Baptist (1835), Rev. Eric V. Gyan.
Res., P.O. Box 248, 70719-0248. Tel: 504-749-2189; 687-8363; Fax: 504-749-1921.

Convent, St. James Parish, St. Michael the Archangel (1812), Rev. Mariano J. Rizzuto, S.M.; Deacon Alfred Adams, Sr. In res., Revs. Albert Hebert, S.M.; Paul Cabrita, S.M.
Res., P.O. Box 65, 70723-0065. Tel: 504-562-3211; Fax: 504-562-3211. [CEM 2]

Darrow, Ascension Parish, St. Anthony of Padua (1962), Very Rev. James Martone, V.F.
Res., P.O. Box 151, 70725-0151. Tel: 504-473-9327; Fax: 504-473-0927.

Denham Springs, Livingston Parish, Immaculate Conception (1960), Revs. Cleo J. Milano, S.T.L.; David R. Johnson (PIT).
Mailing Address: P.O. Box 1609, 70727-1609.
Res., 865 Hatchell Ln., 70726. Tel: 504-665-5359; Fax: 504-665-4422.

Donaldsonville, Ascension Parish, Ascension of Our Lord Jesus Christ (1772), Rev. Randy M. Cuevas, S.T.L. In res., Rev. Joseph Goss, O.P.
Res., P.O. Box 508, 70346-0508. Tel: 504-473-3176; Fax: 504-473-3256. [CEM]
St. Catherine of Siena (1924), Rev. Walter A. Cerbin, S.S.J.
Res., P.O. Box 428, 70346-0428. Tel: 504-473-8350; Fax: 504-473-9978.
St. Francis of Assisi (1884), Rev. Michael A. Galea.
Res., 818 W. Tenth St., 70346-9191. Tel: 504-473-8302; Fax: 504-474-0348. [CEM]

French Settlement, Livingston Parish, St. Joseph (1849), Rev. James A. Kinkead; Deacon James A. Little.
Res., 15710 Louisiana Hwy. 16, 70733-9802. Tel: 504-698-3110. [CEM]

Gonzales, Ascension Parish, St. Theresa of Avila (1918), Revs. Philip F. Spano; Gregory J. Daigle.
Res., 1022 N. Burnside Ave., 70737-2551. Tel:

504-647-6588; Fax: 504-647-2223.
School—212 E. New River St., 70737-2499. Tel: 504-647-2803; Fax: 504-647-7814. Mr. Jay L. Sullivan, Prin.
Sisters 4; Lay Teachers 26; Students 594.

St. Mark (1973), Rev. Herculan F.X. DeMaria, O.F.M.Cap.
Res., 42021 Hwy. 621, 70737-9354. Tel: 504-647-8461; Fax: 504-647-5125.

Gramercy, St. James Parish, Most Sacred Heart of Jesus (1961), Rev. Frank M. Uter.
Res., P.O. Box 1501, 70052-1501. Tel: 504-869-5324; Fax: 504-869-5325.

Greenwell Springs, East Baton Rouge Parish, St. Alphonsus Liguori (1962), Revs. Thomas P. Duhe; Stephen J. Hymel; Deacon J. Phillip BeJeaux.
Res., 14040 Greenwell Springs Rd., 70739-3302. Tel: 504-261-4650; Fax: 504-261-5650.
School—Tel: 504-261-5299; Fax: 504-261-2769. Sr. Mary Esther Hulin, C.S.J., Prin.
Lay Teachers 33; Students 683.

Grosse Tete, Iberville Parish, St. Joseph (1904), Rev. Shelton J. Fabre.
Res., P.O. Box 8, 70740-0008. Tel: 504-648-2420; Fax: 504-648-2506.

Hammond, Tangipahoa Parish, Holy Ghost (1902), Revs. Robert U. Perry, O.P.; Justin R. Kauchak, O.P.; Deacon Wallace Gainey, Jr. In res., Rev. Gerald D. Coverdale, O.P.
Res., P.O. Box 1797, 70404-1797. Tel: 504-345-3360; Fax: 504-542-4191.
School—506 N. Magnolia St., 70401-2598. Tel: 504-345-0977; Fax: 504-542-6545. Mr. Thomas W. O'Neill, Jr., Prin.
Lay Teachers 35; Students 674.

Independence, Tangipahoa Parish, Mater Dolorosa (1908), Rev. Dean J. Martin, J.C.L.; Deacon Bennett Flattman.
Res., P.O. Box 349, 70443-0349. Tel: 504-878-9639; Fax: 504-878-6260.
School—P.O. Box 380, 70443-0380. Tel: 504-878-4295; Fax: 504-878-4888. Mrs. Lorraine Brennan, Prin.
Lay Teachers 11; Students 200.

Labadieville, Assumption Parish, St. Philomena (1847), Very Rev. Vincent J. Dufresne, S.T.L., J.C.L., V.F.
Res., P.O. Box 11, 70372-0011. Tel: 504-526-4247; Fax: 504-526-4128. [CEM]
School—120 Convent St., 70732-9760. Tel: 504-526-8508; Fax: 504-526-4128. Mr. Roland J. Cheramie, Prin.
Lay Teachers 11; Students 195.

Lakeland, Pointe Coupee Parish, Immaculate Conception (1859), Very Rev. Matthew P. Lorrain, V.F.
Res., P.O. Box 158, 70752-0158. Tel: 504-627-5124; Fax: 504-627-5125. [CEM 2]

Livonia, Pointe Coupee Parish, St. Frances Xavier Cabrini (1955), Rev. Joseph Thai-Doan Nguyen.
Res., P.O. Box 128, 70755-0128. Tel: 504-637-2396; Fax: 504-637-2390.

Maringouin, Iberville Parish, Immaculate Heart of Mary (1964), Rev. Shelton J. Fabre.
Res., 11140 Hwy. 77, 70757-9703. Tel: 504-625-2438; Fax: 504-625-3513. [CEM]

Maurepas, Livingston Parish, St. Stephen Martyr (1964), Rev. Msgr. Gerald M. Lefebvre, V.F.
Res., 22494 Hwy. 22, 70449-5309. Tel: 504-695-6310; Fax: 504-695-6039.

Morganza, Pointe Coupee Parish, St. Ann (1729), Rev. Louis T. Oubre.
Res., P.O. Box 128, 70759-0128. Tel: 504-694-3781; Fax: 504-694-3711. [CEM 2]

Napoleonville, Assumption Parish, St. Anne (1874), Rev. Caye A. Nelson.
Res., P.O. Box 99, 70390-0090. Tel: 504-369-6656; Fax: 504-369-9718. [CEM 2]

St. Benedict the Moor, Rev. Joseph C. Rodney, S.S.J.
Res., P.O. Box 218, 70390-0218. Tel: 504-369-7225; Fax: 504-369-2772. [CEM 2]

New Roads, Pointe Coupee Parish, St. Augustine (1923), Rev. Raymond A. Woodka, S.S.J. In res., Rev. Philip Tarallo, S.S.J.; Deacon Norman Christophe.
Res., P.O. Box 548, 70760-0548. Tel: 504-638-7553.

St. Mary of False River (1865), Rev. Michael J. Schatzle, C.S.S.R. In res., Rev. J. Joel LeBauve.
Res., 348 W. Main St., 70760-3587. Tel: 504-638-9665; Fax: 504-638-6346. [CEM 2]

Paincourtville, Assumption Parish, St. Elizabeth (1840), Rev. Juan Ramon Vega (San Salvador).
Mailing Address: P.O. Box 1, 70391-0001.
Res., 6057 St. Elizabeth St., 70391. Tel: 504-369-7398; Fax: 504-369-9892. [CEM]

Paulina, St. James Parish, St. Joseph (1900), Rev. Frank M. Uter.
Res., P.O. Box 129, 70763-0129. Tel: 504-869-5751; Fax: 504-869-4166. [CEM]

Pierre Part, Assumption Parish, St. Joseph the Worker (1858), Rev. Duane L. Breaux.
Res., P.O. Box 190, 70339-0190. Tel: 504-252-6008; Fax: 504-252-8011. [CEM 2]

Plaquemine, Iberville Parish, St. Clement of Rome (1964), Revs. Jerome A. Dugas; Michael Jung, O.S.B.; Sr. Cecile Poitras, S.S.J., Pastoral Assoc.
Res., 58725 St. Clement Ave., 70764-3535. Tel: 504-687-3337; 687-1227; 336-9584; Fax: 504-687-3658.

St. John the Evangelist (1850), Rev. Eugene R. Engels.
Office: 57805 Main St., Suite C, 70764-2531.
Res., 57810 Plaquemine St., 70764-2538. Tel: 504-687-2402; Fax: 504-687-1587. [CEM]

Plattenville, Assumption Parish, Assumption of the Blessed Virgin Mary (1793), Rev. Caye A. Nelson.
Mailing Address: P.O. Box 99, Napoleonville, 70390-0099. Tel: 504-369-6656; Fax: 504-369-9718. [CEM]

Ponchatoula, Tangipahoa Parish, St. Joseph (1875), Rev. Richard R. Archer, O.P.; Deacons Milton Schanzbach; Larry Melancon.
Res., P.O. Box 368, 70454-0368. Tel: 504-386-3749; Fax: 504-386-4188. [CEM]
School—(Grades K-8) 175 N. Eighth St., 70454-3306. Tel: 504-386-6421. Mrs. Sherlyne Meissner, Prin.
Lay Teachers 15; Students 255.

Port Allen, West Baton Rouge Parish, Holy Family (1920), Rev. Henry C. Vavasseur.
Res., P.O. Box 290, 70767-0290. Tel: 504-383-1838; Fax: 504-383-1839.
School—(Grades K-8) 335 N. Jefferson Ave., 70767-2798. Tel: 504-344-4100; Fax: 504-344-1928. Sr. Joel Miller, M.S.C., Prin.
Marianites of Holy Cross 1; Lay Teachers 23; Students 494.
Preschool—415 N. Jefferson Ave., 70767-2727. Tel: 504-343-6541. Ms. Diane Harkins, Dir.
Lay Teachers 5; Students 58.

Prairieville, Ascension Parish, St. John the Evangelist (1919), Revs. Martin A. Hernandez, J.C.L., M.C.L.; Adrian C. Pe're'; Deacon Reese Wiggins.
Res., 15208 Hwy. 73, 70769-3507. Tel: 504-673-8307; Fax: 504-673-8680.

St. Amant, Ascension Parish, Holy Rosary (1905), Revs. Robert F. Stine; Gregory J. Daigle; Sr. Mary John Hotard, C.S.J., Pastoral Assoc.
Res., 44450 Hwy. 429, 70774-4597. Tel: 504-647-5321; Fax: 504-647-5322. [CEM 2]

St. Francisville, West Feliciana Parish, Our Lady of Mount Carmel (1874), Rev. Msgr. William L. Greene.
Res., P.O. Box 67, 70775-0067. Tel: 504-635-3630; Fax: 504-383-5219.
Chapel—Angola State Penitentiary, Tel: 504-655-4411, Ext. 2028.

St. Gabriel, Iberville Parish, St. Gabriel (1769), Rev. Robert G. Marcell; Deacon Vernon J. Melancon.
Res., 3625 Hwy. 75, 70776-9411. Tel: 504-642-8441; Fax: 504-642-8491.

St. James, St. James Parish, St. James (1757), Rev. Howard B. Hall; Deacon Henry Zeringue.
Res., 6613 Hwy. 18, 70086-9054. Tel: 504-265-4210; Fax: 504-265-4210. [CEM]

Sorrento, Ascension Parish, St. Anne (1963), Very Rev. James Martone, V.F.; Deacon Jerry Braud.
Res., P.O. Box 9, 70778-0009. Tel: 504-675-8126; Fax: 504-675-6150.

Tickfaw, Tangipahoa Parish, Our Lady of Pompeii (1973), Rev. Ceslaus R. Prazan, O.P.
Res., P.O. Box 276, 70466-0276. Tel: 504-345-8957; Fax: 504-542-1585.

Vacherie, St. James Parish, Our Lady of Peace (1864), Rev. Clarence J. Waguespack.
Res., 13281 Hwy. 644, 70090-9716. Tel: 504-265-3953; Fax: 504-265-2507. [CEM]

St. Philip (1873), Rev. David M. Chauvin; Deacon Francis Waguespack.
Res., 1175 Hwy. 18, 70090-9527. Tel: 504-265-4085; Fax: 504-265-9348. [CEM]

White Castle, Iberville Parish, Our Lady of Prompt Succor (1899), Rev. Jules A. Brunet.
Res., P.O. Box 249, 70788-0249. Tel: 504-545-3635; Fax: 504-545-8615. [CEM 2]
School—32625 Bowie St., 70788-2698. Tel: 504-545-3302; Fax: 504-545-8615. Mrs. Brenda Fremin, Prin.
Lay Teachers 10; Students 132.

Zachary, East Baton Rouge Parish, St. John the Baptist (1964), Rev. Kenneth W. Laird.
Res., 4727 McHugh Dr., 70791-3935. Tel: 504-654-5778; Fax: 504-654-5796.

Chaplains of Public Institutions

BATON ROUGE. *Baton Rouge General Medical Center* P.O. Box 3611, 70821-3611. Tel: 504-387-7000. Rev. Michael Jung, O.S.B., Chap.

Dixon Correctional Institute. Deacon J. Phillip BeJeaux, Chap.

Earl K. Long Hospital. Rev. Daniel P. Lemoine, Res., 445 Marquette Ave., 70806-4497. Tel: 504-382-7729.

Jetson Correctional Institution For Youth. Deacon J. Peter Walsh, Chap.

Nursing Homes not under Catholic auspices. Rev. Peter D. Crifasi, Chap., Res., 6824 Ozark St., 70805-6248. Tel: 504-336-8708; 357-9562. Rev. David A. Vavasseur, Res., 5657 Thomas Rd., 70811-7356. Tel: 504-775-0978.

ANGOLA. *Louisiana State Penitentiary*. St. Augustine Chapel. Rev. J. Joel Labauve, Mailing Address: Mailing Address: P.O. Box 428, 70712-0428. Tel: 504-655-4411; 655-3243.

CARVILLE. *National Hansen's Disease Center* Gillis Long Memorial Hospital. Rev. Reynolds Garland, O.F.M., Chap., 5445 Point Clair Rd., 70721-9607. Tel: 504-642-5533.

JACKSON. *East Feliciana Chronic Disease Hospital and Rehabilitation Center*. Rev. J. Daniel Walsh, C.S.C., Chap., P.O. Box 438, 70748-0438.

ST. GABRIEL. *Hunt Correctional Institute*. Deacon Guy E. Decker, Mailing Address: P.O. Box 174, 70776-0174. Tel: 504-642-3306.

LA Correctional Institute For Women. Deacon Joseph Mamou, Chap.

Special Assignment:
Reverend Fathers—
Counce, Paul D., J.C.L., M.C.L., Diocesan Tribunal, P.O. Box 1087, Baton Rouge, LA 70821-1087. Tel: 504-337-0561; 383-4370; Fax: 504-336-8789
Herbert, Ray, S.C., 855 Hearthstone Dr., Baton Rouge, LA 70806-5599. Tel: 504-383-0381
McCue, Will, S.C., 855 Hearthstone Dr., Baton Rouge, LA 70806-5599. Tel: 504-383-0381
Seynaeve, Jaak, M.Afr., S.T.D., 2187 Olive St., Baton Rouge, LA 70806-6621. Tel: 504-336-9867
Walsh, Miles D., S.T.L., North American College, Vatican City, 00120 Rome. Tel: 011-39-6-684-9384-7; Fax: 011-39-6-686-7561

On Duty Outside the Diocese:
Reverend Fathers—
Landry, Clyde B., 911-A Country Club Dr., Rio Rancho, NM 87124. Tel: 505-892-9853
Smolley, Robert J., St. Basil Seminary, 195 Glenbrook Rd., Stamford, CT 06902-3099. Tel: 203-324-4578; Fax: 203-357-7681

On Leave:
Reverend Fathers—
DeBenedetto, David J.
Maggio, J. Mark

Military Chaplains:
Reverend Fathers—
Rodriguez, Aloysius M.

Retired:
Reverend Monsignors—
Frey, Andrew F., P.O. Box 2458, Bay St. Louis, MS 39521-2458. Tel: 601-467-4382; Fax: 601-466-6477
Songy, Donald J., 2250 Main St., Baton Rouge, LA 70802-3198. Tel: 504-387-6671; Fax: 504-387-6672
Weber, John A., 5445 Government St., #105, Baton Rouge, LA 70806-6003. Tel: 504-925-9431; Fax: 504-928-3284
Reverend Fathers—
Caballero, Lloyd C., 24546 Louand Dr., Lacombe, LA 70445-9801. Tel: 504-626-7765; Fax: 504-626-7765
Clement, James P., 655 North St., #1404, Baton Rouge, LA 70802-5421. Tel: 504-343-5637; Fax: 504-383-0850
Faschan, Matthew, 9108 LA Hwy. 19, Slaughter, LA 70777-9801
Hewson, William J., 24546 Louand Dr., Lacombe, LA 70445-9801. Tel: 504-626-7765; Fax: 504-626-7765
Ibanez, Rodolfo, Domingo Sautu, 15, Murguia, Alava 01130, Spain
Kersey, Walter L., 609 Pierview Way, Oceanside, CA 92054-2861. Tel: 619-966-0515
McDonald, A. John, 333 Lee Dr., #134, Baton Rouge, LA 70808-4974. Tel: 504-767-8237
Rocheleau, Raymond, 338 W. University Blvd., Tucson, AZ 85705-1084
Ruiz, Adolfo, Hurtado de Amezaga, 22 1, 48008 Bilbao, Vizcaya, Spain
Termini, Mario, 38860 LA Hwy. 75, Plaquemine, LA 70764-7729. Tel: 504-545-8213

Permanent Deacons:
Adams, Alfred P., St. Michael the Archangel, Convent

Allen, Eugene F., Our Lady of Mercy Church, Baton Rouge
BeJeaux, J. Phillip, St. Alphonsus Liguori Church, Greenwell Springs
Braud, Jerry W., St. Anne Church, Sorrento
Bustillo, Carlos, (Retired)
Christophe, Norman (OKL), St. Mary of False River and St. Augustine, New Roads
Decker, Guy E., Hunt Correctional Institute, St. Gabriel
Duplessis, W. Brent, St. Charles Borromeo, Baton Rouge
Ellis, Albert R., Jr., St. George Church, Baton Rouge; Diocesan Permanent Diaconate Office
Flattmann, Bennett W., Mater Dolorosa Church, Independence
Fortenberry, Warren D., St. Margaret, Albany
Furlow, Robert E., Jr., Diocesan Communications Office and St. Joseph Cathedral, Baton Rouge
Gainey, Wallace L., Jr., Holy Ghost, Hammond
Hollier, Clayton A., St. Thomas More Church, Baton Rouge
Lacoste, Ronald J., On Leave
Little, James A., St. Joseph Church, French Settlement
Mamou, Joseph (NO), Chap., LA Correctional Institute For Women
Melancon, Larry, St. Joseph Church, Ponchatoula
Melancon, Vernon J., St. Gabriel Church, St. Gabriel
Rios, Jose Ramon (CAM), Chap., Hispanic Ministry
Rizzo, Bruno, St. Isidore the Farmer Church, Baker
Robinson, Thomas H., St. Jean Vianney Church, Baton Rouge
Schanzbach, Dr. Milton, St. Joseph Church, Ponchatoula
Waguespack, Francis, Jr., St. Philip Church, Vacherie
Walsh, J. Peter, St. Patrick Church, Baton Rouge
Wax, James E., St. Joseph Cathedral, Baton Rouge
Wiggins, Reese, St. John the Evangelist, Prairieville
Zeringue, Henry J., St. James Church, St. James

INSTITUTIONS LOCATED IN THE DIOCESE

[A] COLLEGES AND UNIVERSITIES

BATON ROUGE. *Our Lady of the Lake College*, 5345 Brittany Dr., 70808-4398. Tel: 504-768-1710; Fax: 504-768-1726.
Web site: www.ololcollege.cc.la.us
For a complete listing, refer to the Colleges and Universities section.

[B] DIOCESAN HIGH SCHOOLS, INTERPAROCHIAL

BATON ROUGE. *Bishop Joseph V. Sullivan Diocesan Regional Catholic High School.*
E-mail: boycebs.doc@aol.com
Mailing Address: P.O. Box 86110, 70879-6110. 17521 Monitor Ave., 70817-2640. Mr. Joseph M. Scimeca, Prin. Sisters 1; Lay Teachers 56; Students 747.
Redemptorist High School, 4000 St. Gerard Ave., 70805-2999. Tel: 504-357-0936; Fax: 504-357-4555.
E-mail: diobr11@connectinc.com
Mr. John C. Fabre, Prin. Lay Teachers 50; Students 678.
Serving parishes in Baton Rouge, Baker, Brusly, Denham Springs, Greenwell Springs, Lakeland, New Roads, Gonzales, Port Allen, St. Gabriel, Zachary, Plaquemine, Maringouin, Prairieville and Clinton.

DONALDSONVILLE. *Ascension Catholic Interparochial High School*, 311 St. Vincent St., 70346-2697. Mr. Larry Dugas, Prin. Lay Teachers 18; Students 200.
Serving parishes in Donaldsonville, St. James, Belle Rose, Vacherie, White Castle, Darrow, Gonzales, Convent, Paincourtville and Plattenville.

NEW ROADS. *Catholic High School of Pointe Coupee*, 504 Fourth St., 70760-3499. Tel: 504-638-3469.
E-mail: diobr28@connectinc.com
Mr. Kirk J. Guidry, Prin. Lay Teachers 26; Students 419.
Serving parishes in Lakeland, Livonia, Morganza, New Roads and Maringouin.

PLAQUEMINE. *St. John Interparochial High School*, 24250 Regina St., 70764-3598. Tel: 504-687-3056; Fax: 504-687-3658.
E-mail: diobr26@connectinc.com
Mrs. Ruth Larpenteur, Admin.; Mr. Walter Lemoine, Prin. Lay Teachers 15; Students 193.
Serving parishes in Plaquemine, Brusly, Port Allen, Grosse Tete and White Castle.

TANGIPAHOA. *St. Thomas Aquinas Regional Catholic High School*, 14520 Voss Dr., 70401-9801. Tel: 504-542-7662; Fax: 504-542-4010.
E-mail: stthomas@i-55.com
Web site: www.i-55.com/falcon.
Dominican Sisters, Springfield, IL. Sr. Philip Neri Crawford, O.P., Prin. Sisters 2; Lay Teachers 26; Students 307.

[C] HIGH SCHOOLS, PRIVATE

BATON ROUGE. *Catholic High School*, 855 Hearthstone Dr., 70806-5599. Tel: 504-383-0397; Fax: 504-383-0381.
E-mail: cathigh@communique.net
Dr. Gregory Brandao, Prin. Brothers of the Sacred Heart 5; Lay Teachers 59; Boys 814.
St. Joseph's Academy, 3015 Broussard St., 70808-1198. Tel: 504-383-7207; Fax: 504-344-5714. Sr. Judith Brun, C.S.J., Prin. Sisters of St. Joseph 4; Lay Teachers 61; Girls 731.

[D] DIOCESAN ELEMENTARY SCHOOLS, INTERPAROCHIAL

DONALDSONVILLE. *Ascension Catholic Interparochial School*, 311 St. Vincent St., 70346-3499. Tel: 504-473-9227. Mr. Larry Dugas, Admin. Lay Teachers 20; Students 362.
Serving parishes in Donaldsonville, St. James, Belle Rose, Vacherie, White Castle, Darrow, Gonzales, Convent, Paulina, Paincourtville, and Plattenville.

NEW ROADS. *Catholic Elementary School of Pointe Coupee*, 304 Napoleon St., 70760-3527. Tel: 504-638-9313; Fax: 504-638-6471.
E-mail: diobr28@connectinc.com
Dr. Jacqueline C. Lewis, Prin. Sisters of St. Joseph 1; Lay Teachers 21; Students 504.
Serving parishes in Lakeland, Livonia, Morganza, New Roads and Maringouin.

PAINCOURTVILLE. *St. Elizabeth Interparochial.* (Grades PreK-8), P.O. Drawer M, 70391-0420. Tel: 504-369-7402. Mr. Richard N. Prejeant, Prin. Lay Teachers 10; Students 210.
Serving parishes in Belle Rose, Bertrandville, Napoleonville, Paincourtville, Pierre Part and Plattenville.

PAULINA. *St. Peter Chanel Interparochial School*, P.O. Box 159, 70763-0159. Tel: 504-869-5778; Fax: 504-869-8131. Cassie D. Bourgeois, Prin. Lay Teachers 23; Students 350.
Serving parishes in Paulina, Gramercy, Convent, Vacherie and St. James.

PLAQUEMINE. *St. John Interparochial Elementary / Middle School*, 58645 St. Clement Ave., 70764-3599. Ruth H. Larpenteur, Prin. Lay Teachers 26; Students 559.
Serving parishes in Plaquemine, Brusly, Grosse Tete, White Castle, Baton Rouge, Belle Rose, St. Gabriel, Maringouin, Bayou Pigeon, Port Allen, Gonzales and Paincourtville.

[E] SCHOOL, EXCEPTIONAL CHILDREN

BATON ROUGE. *Department of Special Education.* Guardian Angels Center (7-14 yrs.) and Redemptorist Center (15-21 yrs.). P.O. Box 2028, 70821-2028. Tel: 504-383-3066.
E-mail: diobrsped@connectinc.com
Mrs. Gail Campo, Admin. Housed on St. Gerard Elementary Campus and at Redemptorist High School. Teachers 6; Speech Therapist 1; Students 47.

[F] GENERAL HOSPITALS

BATON ROUGE. *Our Lady of the Lake Regional Medical Center*, 5000 Hennessy Blvd., 70808-4398. Tel: 504-765-6565; Fax: 504-766-5645
For a complete listing, refer to the Hospitals section.

[G] HOMES AND SPECIAL CARE FACILITIES

BATON ROUGE. *Assisi Homes, Inc., of Our Lady of the Lake Medical Center*, 5000 Hennessy Blvd., 70808-4398. Tel: 504-765-6565
For a complete listing, refer to the Special Care Facilities section.
Ollie Steele Burden Manor, 4250 Essen Ln., 70809-2196. Tel: 504-926-0091; Fax: 504-926-4937
For a complete listing, refer to the Special Care Facilities section.

[H] MONASTERIES AND RESIDENCES OF PRIESTS OR BROTHERS

BATON ROUGE. *Brothers of the Sacred Heart*, 855 Hearthstone Dr., 70806-5599. Tel: 504-383-7117. Bro. Francis David, S.C., Dir. Brothers 8.
Franciscan Residence, 4155 Essen Ln. #4, 70809-2115. Tel: 504-924-3836. Revs. Marcellus Moorman, O.F.M.; Anthony Walter, O.F.M.
Incarnation Consecratio Mission. (Vietnamese Assoc.), 2305 Choctaw Dr., 70805-7999. Tel: 504-357-1204. Revs. Hung Viet Nguyen, I.C.M., Dir.; Joseph Lien To, I.C.M.; Dominic Khoai Nguyen, I.C.M.; Martin Thanh Nguyen, I.C.M.; Thomas Tranh Dinh, I.C.M.
The Redemptorist Education and Formation, P.O. Box 53900, 70892-3900. Tel: 504-355-2600; Fax: 504-355-6200. Rev. Robert A. Ruhnke, C.SS.R.
Redemptorist Vice Province. Mailing Address: P.O. Box 53900, 70892-3900. Tel: 504-355-2600; Fax: 504-355-6200. Very Rev. Monroe G. Perrier, C.Ss.R., Vice Prov.; Revs. Samuel C. Maranto, C.Ss.R., Vice Prov. Consultor, Local Supr. & Archivist; Joseph F. Pellettieri, C.Ss.R., Vice Prov. Treas.; Bros. Steven E. Fruge, C.Ss.R., Admin. Asst.; Clement J. Furno, C.Ss.R., Asst. Archivist & Librarian. In res. Rev. Eugene J. Staub, C.Ss.R. Priests 5.
Priests of Vice Province in Residences not listed elsewhere: Revs. Carl A. Schindler, C.Ss.R., Chap., U.S. Army Reserve; John C. Vargas, C.Ss.R., Redemptorist Generalate, Rome; Robert O. Curry, C.Ss.R.

[I] CONVENTS AND RESIDENCES FOR SISTERS

BATON ROUGE. *Baton Rouge / Southwest Regional Office*, P.O. Box 65105, 70896-5105. Tel: 504-383-3475. Sr. Carolyn Brady, C.S.J., Development Dir.
Maryville Novitiate and Provincial House, 4200 Essen Lane, 70809-2196. North American Province, 4200 Essen Ln., 70809-2196. Tel: 504-927-7481; 926-1627. Sr. Brendan Mary Ronayne, O.S.F., Prov. Supr.; Sr. Helen Cahill, O.S.F., Formation Dir. Temporary Professed 2; Final Vows 16.
St. Joseph Convent, 3080 Kleinert Ave., 70806-6899. Tel: 504-344-1517.
E-mail: stjosephsbr@juno.com
Sr. Ursula Harelson, C.S.J., Local Coord. Sisters of St. Joseph 14.

TICKFAW. *Our Lady Queen Contemplative Monastery*, 50352 Antioch Rd., 70466-9747. Tel: 504-345-2630. Benedictine Nuns. Very Rev. Mary Herbert Walsh, O.S.B., Prioress; Revs. Marion C. Walsh, O.S.B. (IND), Chap.; Frederick P. Walsh, O.S.B. (IND), (Retired); Joachim E. Walsh, O.S.B. (IND), (Retired). Nuns 7.

[J] RETREAT HOUSES

BATON ROUGE. *Bishop Robert E. Tracy Center.* Mailing Address: P.O. Box 2028, 70821-2028. Tel: 504-336-8750. 3300 Hundred Oaks Ave., 70808-1599. Mr. Charles Jumonville, Admin.

CONVENT. *Manresa, House of Retreats*, Office, P.O. Box 89, 70723-0089. Tel: 504-562-3596; 800-782-9431; Fax: 504-562-3147. Revs. A. Patrick Phillips, S.J., Dir.; Thomas J. Cronin, S.J., Asst. Dir.; Anthony Ostini, S.J., Asst. Dir.; Hacker J. Fagot, S.J., Asst. Dir.; Edward J. Romagosa, S.J., Asst. Dir.

PONCHATOULA. *Rosaryville / Spirit Life Center*, 39003 Rosaryville Rd., 70454-9580. Tel: 504-294-5039; 800-627-9183; Fax: 504-294-3510. Sr. M. Edmund Gibson, O.P., Dir.; Rev. William J. Aldridge, O.P., Chap. Dominican Sisters 3.

[K] CAMPUS MINISTRY

BATON ROUGE. *Christ the King Parish and Catholic Student Center*, Louisiana State University, P.O. Box 25131, 70894-5131. Tel: 504-344-8595; 504-383-1574; Fax: 504-344-1920. Revs. Patrick J. Mascarella; Garland T. Belsome, Highland Rd. & Dalrymple Dr., 70894. Total Catholic Students 14,500.
Martin Luther King, Jr. Student Center, St. Joseph Chapel, Southern University, 586 Harding Blvd., 70807-5301. Tel: 504-775-8691; 775-1301; Fax: 504-775-7067. Rev. Francis R. Brou, S.J., Chap.-Dir. Total Catholic Students 3,270.

HAMMOND. *St. Albert the Great Catholic Center*, 409 W. Dakota St., 70401-2517. Tel: 504-345-7206; Fax: 504-345-7223. Serving Southeastern Louisiana University. Rev. Sean O. Sheehy, Ed.D., Dir. Total Students 15,400.

[L] MISCELLANEOUS

BATON ROUGE. *Bishop Stanley J. Ott Shelter.* Mailing Address: P.O. Box 127, 70821-0127. Tel: 504-383-7837. Mr. Michael Acaldo, Exec. Dir.
Catholic-Presbyterian Apts., Inc., 655 North St., 70802-5420. Tel: 504-383-5551.
E-mail: flash@intersurf.com
Mr. Gordon D. McDowell, Exec. Dir.
FMOL Health Systems, Inc., 4200 Essen Ln., 70809-2196. Tel: 504-923-2701; 926-0708. Mr. John J. Finan, Jr., Pres.
Joseph Homes, Incorporated, P.O. Box 1668, 70821-1668. Tel: 504-387-0561; Fax: 504-336-8789. Ms. Deborah Roe, M.S.W., Contact Person.
Life America, Inc., 646 College Hill Dr., 70808. Dr. John S. Baker, Jr., Pres.
MAGNIFICAT-Baton Rouge Chapter, 4307 Lake Lawrence Cir., 70816-4423. Tel: 504-291-2550. A Ministry to Catholic Women. Mrs. Carol Dazzio, Coord.

Myriam's House, Inc., 1141 W. Chimes St., 70802-8532. Tel: 504-334-0662. Sr. Lydia Champagne, C.S.J., Pres.; Mrs. Myria Andre-Martin, Admin. Sisters of St. Joseph. Facility for homeless women, providing temporary housing, assistance with job placement and other needed services.

Queen of Peace Home and Soup Kitchen, 749 East Blvd., 70802-6399. Tel: 504-383-4127; 383-8367. Missionaries of Charity.

St. Michael's Home. (Vietnamese Assoc.), 2305 Choctaw Dr., 70805-7999. Rev. Hung Viet Nguyen, I.C.M., Dir. Tel: 504-357-1204.

St. Vincent DePaul Dining Room. Mailing Address: P.O. Box 127, 70821-0127. Tel: 504-383-7439. Mr. Michael J. Acaldo, Exec. Dir.

St. Vincent DePaul Store. Mailing Address: P.O. Box 127, 70821-0127. Tel: 504-356-5158. Mr. Al St. Pierre, Mgr. Tel: 504-356-5158; Mr. Michael J. Acaldo, Exec. Dir. Tel: 504-383-7837.

**Sisters of St. Joseph - St. Paul Center*, 3920 Gus Young Ave., 70802-1727. Tel: 504-344-8590. Sr. Kathleen Bahlinger, C.S.J., Dir.

**St. Vincent DePaul Community Pharmacy, Inc.* Mailing Address: P.O. Box 127, 70821-0127. Tel: 504-383-7450. Mr. Michael J. Acaldo, Exec. Dir.

U.S. Federation of Sisters of St. Joseph, 1841 Glenmore Ave., 70808. Tel: 504-927-0273; Fax: 504-927-2735. Sr. Phyllis Manda, C.S.J., Exec. Dir.

Unwed Mothers Home, 715 East Blvd., 70802-6399. Tel: 504-343-2138. Missionaries of Charity.

[M] FOUNDATIONS, FUNDS AND TRUSTS

BATON ROUGE. *Baton Rouge Chancery Office*. Mailing Address: P.O. Box 2028, 70821-2028. 1800 S. Acadian Thruway, 70808-1698. Tel: 504-387-0561; Fax: 504-336-8789.

Ascension Catholic Interparochial School Endowment Fund, Donaldsonville.

Bishop Stanley J. Ott Works of Mercy Trust.

Diocese of Baton Rouge Clergy Retirement Plan.

Diocese of Baton Rouge Lay Retirement Plan.

Diocese of Baton Rouge Trust Fund.

Nim Pecquet Holy Family School Foundation.

Our Lady of Perpetual Help Trust.

Pamphile and Mabyn Donaldson Trust for St. Louis King of France Church.

Pointe Coupee Catholic Interparochial School Endowment Fund, New Roads.

Sacred Heart Parish Endowment Fund.

St. Aloysius School Endowment Fund.

St. Joseph Cathedral Cemetery Fund.

St. Joseph Cathedral Trust.

St. Theresa of Avila Catholic School Educational Foundation, Gonzales.

St. Thomas More School Endowment Trust.

Sherri Lyn Shaffer Trust for St. Thomas More Church.

Veritas Foundation, Hammond.

Vocational Development Fund of the Brothers of the Sacred Heart, Inc., 720 Hearthstone Dr., 70806-5599. Tel: 504-338-0034; Fax: 504-336-0505. Bro. Will McCue, S.C., Pres.

CHS Foundation, 855 Hearthstone Dr., 70806-5599. Tel: 504-389-0978; Fax: 504-389-0983. Bro. Aquin Gauthier, S.C., Pres.

Our Lady of the Lake Foundation, 5000 Hennessy Blvd., 70808-9907. Tel: 504-765-5000.

RELIGIOUS INSTITUTES OF MEN REPRESENTED IN THE DIOCESE

For further details refer to the corresponding bracketed number in the Religious Institutes of Men or Women section.

[0200]—*Benedictine Monks.* (St. Meinrad Archabbey).—O.S.B.

[0200]—*Benedictine Monks.* (St. Joseph Abbey, St. Benedict, LA).—O.S.B.

[1100]—*Brothers of the Sacred Heart.* (New Orleans Prov.).—S.C.

[0470]—*The Capuchin Friars.*—O.F.M.Cap.

[1070]—*Congregation of the Most Holy Redeemer-Redemptorists.* (New Orleans Vice Prov.).—C.Ss.R.

[0520]—*Franciscan Friars.* (Prov. of St. John the Baptist).—O.F.M.

[0850]—*Missionaries of Africa.*—M.Afr.

[0430]—*Order of Preachers-Dominicans.* (Prov. of St. Martin de Porres).—O.P.

[0610]—*Priests of the Congregation of Holy Cross.* (Southern Prov.).—C.S.C.

[0700]—*St. Joseph's Society of the Sacred Heart-Josephites.*—S.S.J.

[0690]—*Society of Jesus.* (New Orleans Prov.).—S.J.

[0760]—*Society of Mary-Marists.* (American Prov.).—S.M.

[0420]—*Society of the Divine Word.* (Southern Prov.).—S.V.D.

RELIGIOUS INSTITUTES OF WOMEN REPRESENTED IN THE DIOCESE

[0233]—*Benedictine Nuns.*—O.S.B.

[0760]—*Daughters of Charity of St. Vincent de Paul.* (West Central Prov.).—D.C.

[0840]—*Daughters of Jesus.*—F.I.

[1070-08]—*Dominican Sisters.*—O.P.

[1070-10]—*Dominican Sisters.*—O.P.

[1140]—*Eucharistic Missionaries of St. Dominic.*

[1380]—*Franciscan Missionaries of Our Lady.*—O.S.F.

[2410]—*Marianites of Holy Cross.*—M.S.C.

[2710]—*Missionaries of Charity.*—M.C.

[1070-03]—*Sinsinawa Dominican Congregation of the Most Holy Rosary.*—O.P.

[0500]—*Sisters of Charity of Nazareth.* (Southern Region).—S.C.N.

[0430]—*Sisters of Charity of the Blessed Virgin Mary.*—B.V.M.

[0990]—*Sisters of Divine Providence.*—C.D.P.

[2570]—*Sisters of Mercy of Philadelphia.*—R.S.M.

[2630]—*Sisters of Mercy of the Holy Cross.*—S.C.S.C.

[3880]—*Sisters of St. Joseph of Medaille.*—C.S.J.

[3830-16]—*Sisters of St. Joseph of Springfield, Mont Marie.*—S.S.J.

[1950]—*Sisters of the Holy Family.*—S.S.F.

[2940]—*Sisters of the Most Holy Sacrament.*—M.H.S.

[4070]—*Society of the Sacred Heart.*—R.S.C.J.

NECROLOGY

† Braud, Edmond P., (Retired). —Died March 10, 1997.

† Brou, Hubert J., Baton Rouge, LA, St. Aloysius. —Died March 24, 1997.

† Merino, Zenon R., (Retired). —Died July 25, 1997.

† Sanchez, Rev. Msgr. Carlos, (Retired). —Died Feb. 7, 1997.

Diocese of Beaumont

(Dioecesis Bellomontensis)

Most Reverend

JOSEPH A. GALANTE, D.D., J.C.D.

Bishop of Beaumont; ordained May 16, 1964; appointed Titular Bishop of Equilum and Auxiliary Bishop of San Antonio October 13, 1992; consecrated December 11, 1992; appointed Bishop of Beaumont April 5, 1994; installed May 9, 1994. *Res., 6550 Lexington, Apt. 259, Beaumont, TX, 77706.* Tel.: 409-860-9410. All official communications should be addressed to the Pastoral Office: *P.O. Box 3948, Beaumont, TX, 77704-3948.* Tel.: 409-838-0451.

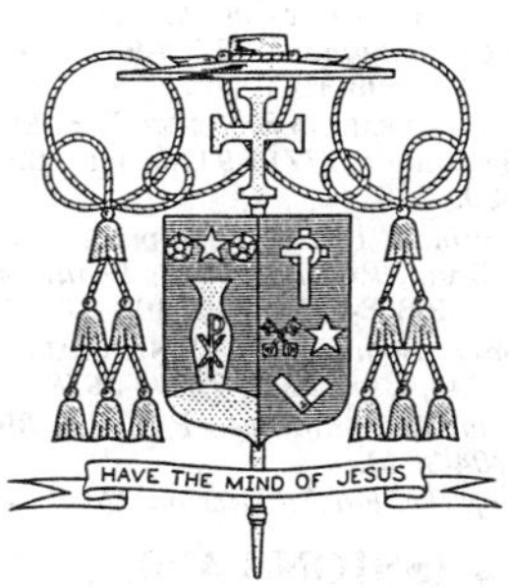

ESTABLISHED SEPTEMBER 29, 1966.

Square Miles 7,878.

Comprises the counties of Chambers, Hardin, Jasper, Jefferson, Liberty, Newton, Orange, Polk and Tyler.

For legal titles of parishes and diocesan institutions, consult the Diocesan Pastoral Office.

Diocesan Pastoral Office: 703 Archie St., P.O. Box 3948, Beaumont, TX, 77704-3948. Tel.: 409-838-0451; Fax: 409-838-4511.

E-mail address: chancery@dioceseofbmt.org

STATISTICAL OVERVIEW

Personnel	
Bishop	1
Priests: Diocesan Active in Diocese	37
Priests: Active Outside Diocese	5
Priests: Retired, Sick or Absent	7
Number of Diocesan Priests	49
Religious Priests in Diocese	23
Extern Priests in Diocese	3
Ordinations:	
Diocesan Priests	3
Permanent Deacons in Diocese	31
Total Brothers	3
Total Sisters	61
Parishes	
Parishes	44
With Resident Pastor:	
Resident Diocesan Priests	28
Resident Religious Priests	16
Without Resident Pastor:	
Missions	9
Pastoral Centers	2
Professional Ministry Personnel:	
Brothers	1
Sisters	38
Lay Ministers	26
Welfare	
Catholic Hospitals	3
Total Assisted	373,063
Specialized Homes	1
Total Assisted	12
Special Centers for Social Services	2
Total Assisted	51,955
Educational	
Diocesan Students in Other Seminaries	10
Total Seminarians	10
High Schools, Diocesan and Parish	1
Total Students	678
Elementary Schools, Diocesan and Parish	7
Total Students	1,913
Catechesis/Religious Education:	
High School Students	1,565
Elementary Students	6,107
Total Students Under Catholic Instruction	10,273
Teachers in the Diocese:	
Priests	1
Brothers	2
Sisters	23
Lay Teachers	198
Vital Statistics	
Receptions into the Church:	
Infant Baptism Totals	1,233
Adult Baptism Totals	143
Received into Full Communion	203
First Communions	1,415
Confirmations	983
Marriages:	
Catholic	236
Interfaith	141
Total Marriages	377
Deaths	792
Total Catholic Population	86,598
Total Population	574,240

Former Bishops—Most Rev. VINCENT M. HARRIS, D.D., ord. March 19, 1938; appt. Bishop of Beaumont, July 4, 1966; cons. Sept. 28, 1966; installed as First Bishop of Beaumont, Sept. 29, 1966; appt. Titular Bishop of Rotaria and Coadjutor with right of succession to the Bishop of Austin, TX, April 21, 1971; succeeded to as Second Bishop of Austin, November 16, 1971; died March 31, 1988.—Most Rev. WARREN L. BOUDREAUX, J.C.D., D.D., ord. May 30, 1942; appt. Titular Bishop of Calynda and Auxiliary Bishop of Lafayette, LA, May 19, 1962; cons. July 25, 1962; appt. second Bishop of Beaumont, June 4, 1971; installed August 25, 1971; appt. first Bishop of Houma-Thibodaux, March 2, 1977; installed as first Bishop of Houma-Thibodaux, June 5, 1977; died Oct. 6, 1997.—Most Rev. BERNARD J. GANTER, D.D., ord. May 22, 1952; appt. first Bishop of Tulsa, Dec. 19, 1972; cons. and installed, Feb. 7, 1973; appt. third Bishop of Beaumont, Oct. 3, 1977; installed Dec. 13, 1977; died Oct. 9, 1993.

Diocesan Pastoral Office—703 Archie St., P.O. Box 3948, Beaumont, 77704-3948. Tel: 409-838-0451; Fax: 409-838-4511. Office Hours: 8:30-5.

Vicar General & Moderator of the Curia—Rev. Msgr. MICHAEL A. JAMAIL, J.C.D., Ed.D., *P.O. Box 3948, Beaumont, 77704-3948.* Tel: 409-838-0451; 835-9902 (Res.); Fax: 409-838-4511.

Episcopal Vicars—Central Vicariate: Rev. Msgr. FRANCIS H. BURLTON, *Our Lady of the Assumption, 4445 Ave. A, Beaumont, 77705.* Eastern Vicariate: Very Rev. FRANCIS X. CONROY, *St. Francis of Assisi, 4300 Meeks Dr., Orange, 77632.* Northern Vicariate: Very Rev. RONALD B. FOSHAGE, M.S., *St. Michael, P.O. Box 239, Jasper, 75951.* Southern Vicariate: Very Rev. DON GOLASINSKI, *Immaculate Conception Church, P.O. Box 967, Groves, 77619.* Western Vicariate: Very Rev. JOSEPH L. STRATMAN, JR., *Our Lady of Sorrows Church, P.O. Box 38, China, 77613-0038.*

Consultors, Diocesan College of—Rev. Msgr. M. N. ENDERLE; Rev. Msgr. MICHAEL A. JAMAIL; Revs. DAN MALAIN, Chm. RONALD FOSHAGE, M.S.; FRANCIS CONROY; T. R. BLANCO, O.S.A.; BENNIE J. PATILLO; FRANK PADUCH; AUGUST PUCAR; WILLIAM MANGER; RODNEY ARMSTRONG, S.S.J.; P. JOSEPH DALEO; LUONG QUANG TRAN, J.C.L.

Chancellor—Sr. ESTHER DUNEGAN, I.W.B.S., J.C.L., *Diocesan Pastoral Office, P.O. Box 3948, Beaumont, 77704-3948.* Tel: 409-838-0451; Fax: 409-838-4511. Mrs. JO FRANCES MANUEL, Bishop's Sec.; Mrs. GAIL HERNANDEZ, Admin. Sec.

Chief Financial Officer/Controller—RUSSELL J. CHIMENO, C.P.A., *Diocesan Pastoral Office, P.O. Box 3948, Beaumont, 77704-3948.* Tel: 409-838-0451; Fax: 409-838-4511.

Tribunal—703 Archie St., P.O. Box 3948, Beaumont, 77704-3948. Tel: 409-838-0451; Fax: 409-838-4511.

Judicial Vicar—Rev. LUONG QUANG TRAN, M.A., J.C.L.

Diocesan Judges—Rev. LUONG QUANG TRAN, M.A., J.C.L., Judicial Vicar; Rev. Msgr. KENNETH R. GREIG, M.Th.; Rev. Msgr. SIDNEY J. MARCEAUX, J.C.D.; Revs. ART MORGAN, J.C.L.; BENNIE PATILLO, M.Ed.; Sr. ESTHER DUNEGAN, I.W.B.S., J.C.L.; Sr. ROSEMARY SMITH, S.C., J.C.D.

Promotor of Justice—Rev. Msgr. FRANCIS H. BURLTON, S.T.L.

Defenders of Bond—Rev. Msgr. MICHAEL A. JAMAIL, J.C.D., Ed.D., V.G.; Rev. SINCLAIR OUBRE, S.T.B., J.C.L. (Cand.).

Advocate—Rev. JOSEPH KHANH HO, S.T.L., J.C.L. (Cand.).

Psychologists for the Tribunal—RAY COXE, Ph.D.; Rev. Msgr. MICHAEL A. JAMAIL, J.C.D., Ed.D.; Mr. PATRICK BRADY, M.A., C.H.

Secretary-Notary—MARILYN PRICE; Sr. BARBARA ANNE OSTERHAUS, C.V.I.

Diocesan Officers and Directors

Apostleship of the Sea—Beaumont Port: Rev. SINCLAIR OUBRE, *3503 Gulfway Dr., Port Arthur, 77642.*

African-American Catholic Commission, Diocesan—WILLIAM JAMES CARTER, Chm., *5298 15th St., Port Arthur, 77642.*

Boy Scouts—Rev. MICHAEL BALUYOT, *St. Jude Thaddeus Church, 6825 Gladys, Beaumont, 77706-3239.*

Building Commission, Diocesan—Rev. S. J. CULOTTA, Chm., *5075 Bigner Rd., Beaumont, 77708.*

Campus Ministry—TOMMY CHATLOSH, Dir. GINA DECUIR, Sec. & Coord. Campus Activities, *P.O. Box 10095, Beaumont, 77710.* Tel: 409-835-3972.

Catholic Charities—Sr. CATHERINE PARENT, C.D.P., Dir., *Mailing Address: P.O. Box 829, Beaumont, 77704-0829. 1410 North St., Beaumont, 77704-0829.* Tel: 409-835-7118; Fax: 409-832-0145.

Catholic Clerical Student Fund—P.O. Box 3948, Beaumont, 77704.

Office of Lifelong Catholic Education—Dr. LORRAINE S. DELUCA, Dir., *P.O. Box 3948, Beaumont, 77704-3948.* Tel: 409-838-0451; Fax: 409-838-4511.

Office of Catholic Schools—Sr. CAROL SHIVELY, O.S.U., Supt., *P.O. Box 3948, Beaumont, 77704-3948.* Tel:

409-838-0451; Fax: 409-838-4511.

Catholic Daughters of America—DEEDE COVINGTON, *9920 N. Major Dr., Beaumont, 77713-9316.* Tel: 409-899-5617; Fax: 409-899-3161.

Catholic Women, Council of—Rev. Msgr. GEORGE F. RABROKER, Moderator, *Our Lady of Assumption Church, 4445 Ave. A, Beaumont, 77705.*

Charismatic Prayer Renewal—Rev. WILLIAM MANGER, Group Liaison, *St. Anne Church, P.O. Box 3429, Beaumont, 77704-3429.*

Communication, Information & Diocesan Press—Rev. JAMES VANDERHOLT, Exec. Dir., *1019 Colorado, Beaumont, 77705.* Tel: 409-832-3944; Fax: 409-832-4129., *P.O. Box 3948, Beaumont, 77704-3948.*

Continuing Education of Religious and Clergy, Office of—Rev. JAMES VANDERHOLT, Dir., *P.O. Box 3948, Beaumont, 77704-3948.* Tel: 409-832-3944.

Diaconate, Permanent Diaconate—Rev. JEREMIAH MCGRATH, Vicar, *St. Anthony Cathedral, P.O. Box 3309, Beaumont, 77704-3309.* Tel: 409-833-6433; Fax: 409-833-6688. Deacon JOSEPH SCHEURICH, Dir., *310 Summerwood St., Beaumont, 77706.* Tel: 409-892-6990; Fax: 409-896-5230.

Diocesan Development & Stewardship, Office of—ANNE STEINMAN, C.P.A., Dir., *P.O. Box 3948, Beaumont, 77704.* Tel: 409-838-0451; Fax: 409-838-4511.

Hispanic Ministry, Diocesan Office of—Sr. PILAR DALMAU, A.C.J., *P.O. Box 3948, Beaumont, 77704-3948.* Tel: 409-838-0451; Fax: 409-838-4511.

Holy Childhood—Ms. ANNE STEINMAN, *P.O. Box 3948, Beaumont, 77704-3948.* Tel: 409-838-0451; Fax: 409-838-4511.

Master of Ceremonies, Diocesan—Rev. PATRICK A. TURNER.

Office of African American Ministry—Mrs. JOSIE CURTIS, Dir., *P.O. Box 3948, Beaumont, 77704-3948.* Tel: 409-838-0451; Fax: 409-838-4511.

Office of Worship; Liturgical Commission; R.C.I.A. Commission—Rev. PATRICK A. TURNER, Dir., *9920 N. Major Dr., Beaumont, 77713-9316.* Tel: 409-899-3427; Fax: 409-899-3161.

Diocesan Choir—ROSALIND SANCHEZ, Dir., *9920 N. Major Dr., Beaumont, 77713-9316.* Tel: 409-899-3427; Fax: 409-899-3161.

Diocese of Beaumont Pension Committee—JOE BROUSSARD, IV, Chm., *P.O. Box 3948, Beaumont, 77704-3948.* Tel: 409-838-0451; Fax: 409-838-4511.

Priests' Personnel Board—Rev. DON GOLASINSKI, Chm., *P.O. Box 3948, Beaumont, 77704-3948.*

Priests' Retirement Committee—*P.O. Box 3948, Beaumont, 77704-3948.*

Propagation of the Faith; Mission Coop.—Ms. ANNE STEINMAN, *P.O. Box 3948, Beaumont, 77704-3948.* Tel: 409-838-0451; Fax: 409-838-4511.

Family Life Office & Respect Life Liaison—Mr. RON GOUGENHEIM, Dir., *P.O. Box 3948, Beaumont, 77704-3948.* Tel: 409-838-0451; Fax: 409-838-4511.

Parish Social Ministry, Office of—Sr. MARY BORDELON, C.D.P., Dir., *1410 North St., Beaumont, 77701.* Tel: 409-835-7118; Fax: 409-832-0145.

School Board, Diocesan—GRACIE SLOVAK, Pres., *P.O. Box 3948, Beaumont, 77704.*

Seminary Director—Rev. Msgr. MICHAEL A. JAMAIL, V.G., *P.O. Box 3948, Beaumont, 77704-3948.* Tel: 409-838-0451; Fax: 409-838-4511.

Synod Office—Sr. MARILYN VOLLMER, S.S.M., Dir., *P.O. Box 3948, Beaumont, 77704-3948.* Tel: 409-838-0451; Fax: 409-838-4511.

Vocations—Rev. Msgr. JOHN DISTEFANO, Dir., *P.O. Box 10095 L.U.S., Beaumont, 77710.* Tel: 409-835-5037.

Women Religious, Vicar For—Sr. JULIE MARIE GRIEG, O.P., Vicar, *9920 N. Major Dr., Beaumont, 77713.* Tel: 409-899-5617; Fax: 409-899-3161.

Youth Ministry, Catholic—TOMMY CHATLOSH, Dir., *P.O. Box 10095 L.U.S., Beaumont, 77710.* Tel: 409-835-3972.

CLERGY, PARISHES, MISSIONS AND PAROCHIAL SCHOOLS

CITY OF BEAUMONT
(Jefferson County)

1—ST. ANTHONY CATHEDRAL (1879), Rev. Jeremiah McGrath; Deacon Harry Davis. In res., Rev. Luong Quane Tran.
Res., 700 Jefferson St., P.O. Box 3309, 77704-3309. Tel: 409-833-6433; Fax: 409-835-5656.
School—Holy Cross Brothers 2; Sisters 2; Lay Teachers 16; Students 263.

2—ST. ANNE (1937), Rev. William Manger; Deacon Joseph Scheurich. In res., Rev. Msgr. Michael Jamail.
Res., Calder Ave. & 11th, P.O. Box 3429, 77704-3429. Tel: 409-832-9963; Fax: 409-832-9964.
School—(Formerly St. Anne Tri-Parish School). Lay Teachers 45; Students 666.

3—BLESSED SACRAMENT (1915) (African American), Rev. Rodney J. Armstrong, S.S.J. In res., Rev. Dan Bastianelli, S.S.J.
Res., 780 Porter St., 77701-7198. Tel: 409-833-6089; Fax: 409-833-6091.

4—CRISTO REY (1951) (Hispanic), Rev. Luis Urriza, O.S.A.; Deacon George Rincon.
Res., 767 Ave. A, 77701. Tel: 409-835-7788; Fax: 409-835-7788.

5—ST. JOSEPH (1905) (Italian-Vietnamese), Rev. Khanh Ho.
Res., 1115 Orange St., 77701-4392. Tel: 409-835-5662; Fax: 409-832-7717.

6—OUR LADY OF THE ASSUMPTION (1951), Rev. Msgr. Francis H. Burlton. In res., Rev. Msgr. George F. Rabroker.
Res., 4445 Ave. A, 77705-4998. Tel: 409-835-5343; Fax: 409-835-5344.

7—OUR MOTHER OF MERCY (1937) (African American), Revs. Ray Bomberger, S.S.J.; John Raphael, S.S.J. In res., Rev. Henry Offer, S.S.J.
Res., 3390 Sarah St., 77705-3098. Tel: 409-842-5533; Fax: 409-842-4710.
School—Sisters 3; Lay Teachers 8; Students 105.
Convent—3380 Sarah St., Tel: 409-842-2940. Sisters of the Holy Spirit and Mary Immaculate & Handmaids of the Holy Child Jesus

8—ST. PIUS X (1954), Rev. Msgr. Salvador J. Culotta; Rev. John Colbert; Deacon Robert Gros.
Res., 5075 Bigner Rd. at East Lucas, 77708-5299. Tel: 409-892-3316; Fax: 409-892-8916.

9—ST. JUDE THADDEUS (1978), Rev. Msgr. Richard DeStefano; Rev. Michael Noel Baluyot; Deacon Dow Wynn.
Res., 6825 Gladys, 77706-3239. Tel: 409-866-5088; Fax: 409-866-1866.

OUTSIDE THE CITY OF BEAUMONT

Ames, Liberty Co., Our Mother of Mercy (1903) (African American), Rev. Raphael Asika, M.S.P., Admin.
Res., R.R. 2, Box 264, Liberty, 77575-9610. Tel: 409-336-3004; Fax: 409-336-3004. [CEM]

Anahuac, Chambers Co., Our Lady of Light (1938), Rev. Louis J. Villarreal, O.M.I.; Deacon E. R. LeBlanc.
Res., Rte. 2, Box 1-F, 77514-9001. Tel: 409-267-3158; Fax: 409-267-3158.

Bridge City, Orange Co., St. Henry (1948), Rev. James McClintock; Deacon Hazen Kenney.
Mailing Address: P.O.Box 427, 77611-0427.
Res., 475 W. Round Bunch Rd., 77611-2448. Tel: 409-735-2422; Fax: 409-738-2158.

Buna, Jasper Co., St. Francis of Assisi Mission (1968), Rev. Charles Sellars, O.M.I., Admin.
Mailing Address: P.O. Box 1688, 77612-1688. Tel: 409-994-3456; Fax: 409-994-2923.

Cheek, Jefferson Co., St. Martin de Porres Mission (1972), Rev. Clement Iglesias, Admin.
Mailing Address: 9894 Gilbert, Beaumont, 77705. Tel: 409-794-2548.

China, Jefferson Co., Our Lady of Sorrows (1918), Rev. Joseph Stratman.
Res., P.O. Box 38, 77613-0038. Tel: 409-752-3571; Fax: 409-752-5134. [CEM]

Cleveland, Liberty Co., St. Mary (1950), Rev. Angelo Scolozzi, M.C.III.O.
Res., P.O. Box 816, 77328-0816. Tel: 281-592-2985; Fax: 281-592-7247.

Corrigan, Polk Co., St. Martin de Porres Mission (1971), Rev. Roger Thibodeaux; Deacon Rudy Cockburn.
Res., 1200 Asia Rd., 75939-9766. Tel: 409-398-2807 (Parish Center).

Eastgate, Liberty Co., St. Anne Mission (1918), Rev. Thomas Phelan, M.S.W., Admin.
Mailing Address: P.O. Box 640, Dayton, 77535-0640. Tel: 409-258-5735; Fax: 409-258-7220.

Dayton, Liberty Co., St. Joseph the Worker (1945), Rev. Thomas E. Phelan, M.S.W.; Deacon Wilbert Wycliff.
Res., P.O. Box 640, 77535-0640. Tel: 409-258-5735; Fax: 409-258-7220. [CEM]

Fannett, Jefferson Co., St. Mary (1964), Rev. Clement M. Iglesias.
Res., 9894 Gilbert Rd., Beaumont, 77705-9696. Tel: 409-794-2548; Fax: 409-794-3411.

Groves, Jefferson Co., Immaculate Conception (1928), Rev. Donald J. Golasinski.
Res., 6248 Washington, P.O. Box 967, 77619-0967. Tel: 409-962-0255; Fax: 409-963-3464.
St. Peter the Apostle (1972), Rev. Msgr. Kenneth R. Greig. In res., Rev. Msgr. M.N. Enderle.
Res., 2049 Taft Ave., 77619-4953. Tel: 409-962-8365; Fax: 409-962-8365.

Jasper, Jasper Co., St. Michael (1951), Rev. Ronald Foshage, M.S.; Deacon David Luther.
Res., P.O. Box 239, 75951-0239. Tel: 409-384-2447; Fax: 409-384-2447.
Station—Toledo Village.

Kirbyville, Jasper Co., Our Lady of La Salette Mission (1948), Rev. Ronald Foshage, M.S., Admin.
Mailing Address: P.O. Box 239, Jasper, 75951-0239. Tel: 409-384-2447; Fax: 409-384-2447.

Kountze, Hardin Co., Holy Spirit Mission (1986), Rev. Paul E. Sumler.
Res., Hwy. 326, P.O. Box 1454, 77625-1454. Tel: 409-246-4457 (Office); Fax: 409-246-4623.

Liberty, Liberty Co., Immaculate Conception (1756), Revs. August Pucar; Joseph Malayampuram, C.M.I.; Deacon Luther Wells.
Res., 411 Milam, 77575-4730. Tel: 409-336-3318; Fax: 409-336-7268. [CEM]

Livingston, Polk Co., St. Joseph (1970), Rev. Roger Thibodeaux; Deacon Rudy Cockburn.
Res., P.O. Box 930, 77351-0930. Tel: 409-967-4657; 967-8385 (Church).

Lumberton, Hardin Co., Infant Jesus (1948), Rev. Paul E. Sumler.
Res., Box 8126, LRS, 77657-0126. Tel: 409-755-1734; Fax: 409-755-2833.

Mauriceville, Orange Co., St. Maurice (1966), Rev. Delphyn J. Meeks.
Res., P.O. Box 940, 77626-0940. Tel: 409-745-4060; Fax: 409-745-4272.

Mont Belvieu, Chambers Co., Holy Trinity Mission, Rev. Louis Villareal, O.M.I., Admin.
Mailing Address: Rte. 2, Box 1-F, Anahuac, TX 77514-9001. Tel: 409-267-3158; Fax: 409-267-3158.

Nederland, Jefferson Co., St. Charles Borromeo (1923), Revs. Dan Malain; Andrew Robert Moore; Deacons Vernon Drummond; Dallas Broussard.
Res., 211 Hardy Ave., 77627-7399. Tel: 409-722-3413; Fax: 409-722-2020.

Orange, Orange Co., St. Mary (1880), Rev. Msgr. P. Joseph Daleo; Deacons Melvin Payne; Eddie Blankenstein.
Res., 912 W. Cherry St., 77630-5017. Tel: 409-883-2883; Fax: 409-883-3547. [CEM]
School—2600 Bob Hall Rd., 77630-2418. Tel: 409-883-8913.
Sisters 2; Lay Teachers 28; Students 400.
St. Therese (1924) (African American), Rev. Henry McKay, M.S.; Deacon Julian Richard.
Res., 1409 N. Sixth St., 77630-3927. Tel: 409-883-3783; Fax: 409-883-4918.
St. Francis of Assisi (1978), Rev. Francis X. Conroy; Deacons Harvey Dubois; Stronnie McBride.
Church—4300 Meeks Dr., 77632-4508. Tel: 409-883-9153; Fax: 409-883-9154.

Orangefield, Orange Co., St. Helen (1938), Rev. Patrick Turner; Deacons Morris Smith; Glen Hebert.
Res., 8105 FM 1442, Orange, 77630. Tel: 409-735-2200 (Office); Fax: 409-735-7786.

Port Arthur, Jefferson Co.,

1—OUR LADY OF GUADALUPE, (1927) (Hispanic), Rev. Telesforo R. Blanco, O.S.A.; Deacon Roy Garcia.
Res., 3648 S. Sgt. Lucian Adams Dr., 77642-6100. Tel: 409-962-6777; Fax: 409-963-0669.

2—QUEEN OF VIETNAM, (1977) (Vietnamese), Revs. Michael Mai Tran, C.M.C.; Martin Tran Van Ban, C.M.C.
Res., 801 Ninth Ave., 77642-3329. Tel: 409-983-7676; Fax: 409-982-1212.
Convent—1148 Ninth Ave., 77642. Tel: 409-985-5102.
Dominican Sisters 5.

3—SACRED HEART, (1915) (African American), Rev. Larry Leduff-Gutierrez, S.S.J.
Res., 920 Washington Ave., 77640-4923. Tel: 409-985-5104; Fax: 409-985-5104.

4—ST. CATHERINE OF SIENA, (1954), Rev. Joseph J. Romero; Deacon Jim Gard.
Res., 3706 Woodrow Dr., 77642-2320. Tel: 409-962-5715; Fax: 409-962-4775. [CEM]
School—Dominican Sisters 2; Lay Teachers 25; Students 282.

5—ST. JAMES, Revs. James Vanderholt; Socorro do Rosario. In res., Rev. Msgr. Martin Bordages; Rev. Sinclair Oubre.
Res., 3503 Gulfway Dr., 77642-3693. Tel: 409-985-8865; Fax: 409-985-3847.

6—ST. JOHN, (1951) (African American), Rev. Louis Delarue; Deacon W. B. Goudeau, Jr.
Res., 620 53rd St., 77640-2351. Tel: 409-985-8010; Fax: 409-833-6091.

7—ST. JOSEPH, (1951), Rev. D. Stephen McCrate.
Res., 4600 Procter St., 77642-1365. Tel: 409-982-6409; Fax: 409-983-5383.

8—ST. MARY, (1903) (African American), Rev. George Kalapurra, C.M.I.; Deacon Roy Cormier, Sr.

Office: 545 Savannah Ave., 77640-6026. Tel: 409-985-9661; Fax: 409-985-9691.

9—St. Therese the Little Flower of Jesus, (1928), Rev. Antony Moozhihzhy, C.M.I.; Deacon Jimmy Bourgeois.
Res., 6412 Garnet Ave., 77640-1308. Tel: 409-736-1536; Fax: 409-736-1537.

Port Neches, Jefferson Co., St. Elizabeth (1922), Rev. Bennie J. Patillo.
Res., 2006 Nall St., 77651-3714. Tel: 409-727-8874; Fax: 409-727-8875.

Raywood, Liberty Co., Sacred Heart (1952) (African American), Rev. Raphael Asika, M.S.P., Admin.
Res., P.O. Box 429, 77582. Tel: 409-587-4631. [CEM]

Sabine Pass, Jefferson Co., St. Paul Mission (1955), Rev. James Vanderholt, Admin.
Mailing Address: 3503 Gulfway Dr., Port Arthur, 77642-3693. Tel: 409-985-8865.

Sam Rayburn, Jasper Co., St. Raymond Mission (1970), Rev. Ronald Foshage, M.S., Admin.
Mailing Address: P.O. Box 239, Jasper, 75951-0239. Tel: 409-384-2447.

Silsbee, Hardin Co., St. Mark the Evangelist (1940), Rev. Charles Sellars, O.M.I.; Deacon Nolen Landry.
Res., 905 N. Ninth St., 77656. Tel: 409-385-4498; 385-5631; Fax: 409-385-6882.

Sour Lake, Hardin Co., Our Lady of Victory (1906), Rev. Frank Paduch, Admin.
Res., 442 Barkley St., P.O. Box 1359, 77659. Tel: 409-287-3287; Fax: 409-287-3287.

Vidor, Orange Co., Our Lady of Lourdes (1938), Rev. Severiano Fernandez, O.S.A.
Res., 1600 N. Main, 77662. Tel: 409-769-2865; Fax: 409-769-2865.

Winnie, Chambers Co., St. Louis (1947), Revs. John Hughes; Michael Hinken, S.O.L.T.
Res., Rte. 1, Box 354, 77665-9711. Tel: 409-296-4200; Fax: 409-296-9715.

Woodville, Tyler Co., Our Lady of the Pines (1950), Rev. Roger Thibodeaux; Deacon Paul Rachal.
Res., P.O. Box 2029, 75979-2029. Tel: 409-283-5367; Fax: 409-283-5367.
Station—Wildwood

Chaplains of Public Institutions

Beaumont. *Baptist Hospital*. Rev. William Richardson, S.S.J.
Columbia Beaumont Hospital. Rev. William Richardson, S.S.J.

Port Arthur. *Convalescent Home Ministry*. Rev. James Engle, 5100 4th St., 77642. Tel: 409-982-3556.

Prisons

Beaumont. *Federal Correctional Complex-Penitentiary*. Rev. Robert K. Spencer (WCH).
Larry Gist State Jail. Deacon Harry Davis, Chap.
Mark Stiles Unit, TDCJ. Deacon Alfred J. O'Brien, Chap.

Dayton. *Plane State Jail*. Ms. Glory Siller, Chap.

Livingston. *Terrell Unit*. Deacon John Stanley, Chap.

Special Assignment:
Reverend Fathers—
Badeaux, Kevin, North American College, Rome

On Duty Outside the Diocese:
Reverend Fathers—
DeFrancisco, Joseph, St. Ambrose Univ., Davenport, IA

Military Chaplains:
Reverend Monsignors—
Marceaux, Sidney J., Chap. Col., U.S.A., CMA451, Noc273, APO, AE 09708
Reverend Fathers—
Beck, Robert P., Chap. Capt., U.S.A.F., PSC 94, Box 3044, APO, AE 09824

Absent On Leave:
Reverend Fathers—
Deeter, Timothy
Gouthier, Nolan
Leger, Steven
Sumler, Kevin

Retired:
Reverend Monsignors—
Bordages, Martin
DiStefano, John
Enderle, Martin N.
Fee, Paul A.
O'Connell, Patrick
Rabroker, George F.
Reverend Fathers—
Montondon, Walter, Chap. Col.
Mudd, Earl

Permanent Deacons:
Blankenstein, Ed, St. Mary, Orange
Bourgeois, Jimmy, St. Therese, Little Flower, Port Arthur
Broussard, Dallas, St. Charles, Nederland
Cockburn, Rudy, St. Martin de Porres, Corrigan
Cormier, Roy, Sr., St. Mary, Port Arthur
Davis, Harry, St. Anthony Cathedral & Larry Gist State Jail, TDCJ, Beaumont
Drummond, Vernon, St. Charles Borromeo, Nederland
Dubois, Harvey, St. Francis, Orange
Garcia, Roy, Our Lady of Guadalupe, Port Arthur
Gard, Jim, St. Catherine of Siena, Port Arthur
Goudeau, W. B., Jr., St. John, Port Arthur
Gros, Robert, St. Pius X, Beaumont
Hebert, Glen, St. Helen, Orangefield
Kenny, Hazen, St. Henry, Bridge City
Landry, Nolen, St. Mark the Evangelist, Silsbee
LeBlanc, E. R., Holy Trinity Mission, Mont Belvieu; Our Lady of Light, Anahuac
Luther, David, St. Michael, Jasper
McBride, Stronnie, St. Francis of Assisi and Southeast Texas Hospice, Orange
McKinney, Tom (GAL), TDCJ, Huntsville
O'Brien, Alfred J., Mark Stiles Unit, TDCJ, Beaumont
Payne, Melvin, St. Mary, Orange
Rachal, Paul, Our Lady of the Pines, Woodville
Richard, Julian, St. Therese, Orange
Rincon, George, Cristo Rey, Beaumont
Scheurich, Joseph, St. Anne and Dir. of Permanent Diaconate, Beaumont
Smith, Morris, St. Helen, Orangefield
Stanley, John, TDCJ, Terrell Unit, Livingston
Wells, Luther, Immaculate Conception, Liberty
Wycliff, Wilbert, St. Joseph the Worker, Dayton
Wynn, Dow, St. Jude Thaddeus, Beaumont

INSTITUTIONS LOCATED IN THE DIOCESE

[A] HIGH SCHOOLS, DIOCESAN

Beaumont. *Monsignor Kelly Catholic High School*, 5950 Kelly Dr., 77707. Tel: 409-866-2351. Mr. Michael J. Collins, Prin.; Rev. Martin Lester Nelson. Sisters 3; Lay Teachers 65; Students 678.

[B] ELEMENTARY SCHOOLS, DIOCESAN

Beaumont. *Our Lady of the Assumption School*, 1345 Woodrow, 77705. Tel: 409-835-2651; Fax: 409-838-0398. Dominican Sisters 3; Lay Teachers 12; Students 141.

Port Arthur. *Sr. Thea Bowman Academy*. (Formerly Central Catholic Parochial School), 4604 Procter St., 77642. Tel: 409-982-4140. Sr. Ann Middlebrooks, S.E.C., Prin. Dominican Sisters 1; Lay Teachers 4; Students 56.

[C] GENERAL HOSPITALS

Beaumont. *St. Elizabeth Hospital of Beaumont*, 2830 Calder Ave., P.O. Box 5405, 77726-5405. Tel: 409-892-7171
For a complete listing, refer to the Hospitals section.

Jasper. *Jasper Memorial Hospital*, 1275 Hancock Dr., 75951
For a complete listing, refer to the Hospitals section.

Port Arthur. *St. Mary Hospital*, 3600 Gates Blvd., P.O. Box 3696, 77643. Tel: 409-985-7431; Fax: 409-985-9404
For a complete listing, refer to the Hospitals section.

[D] MONASTERIES AND RESIDENCES OF PRIESTS AND BROTHERS

Beaumont. *Holy Cross Brothers Residence*, 2520 Liberty, 77702-1912. Tel: 409-835-1699.

[E] NEWMAN CENTERS

Beaumont. *Lamar University-Catholic Student Center*, 1010 E. Virginia, P.O. Box 10095, 77710. Tel: 409-835-3972. Mr. Tommy Chatlosh, Dir.; Gina DeCuir, Sec. & Coord. of Campus Activities.

[F] RETREAT CENTERS

Beaumont. *Holy Family Retreat Center*, 9920 N. Major Dr., 77713-9316. Tel: 409-899-5617; Fax: 409-899-3161. Sr. Julie Greig, O.P., M.A., Dir.; Sr. Carletta LaCour, O.P., B.A., Asst. Dir.

[G] MISCELLANEOUS

Beaumont. *Assumption School Foundation*, 1345 Woodrow, 77705. Mr. Heath Burns, Prin.
Diocese of Beaumont School Foundation, Inc., P.O. Box 3948, 77704-3948. Sr. Carol Shively, O.S.U., Sec. & Treas.
The Garth House, 1895 McFaddin, 77701-1622. Tel: 409-838-9084. Lanis McWilliams, Dir. The Mickey Mehaffy Children's Advocacy Program.
Monsignor Kelly Catholic High School Foundation, Inc., 5950 Kelly Dr., 77707. Camille Mouton, Dir.
Primary Care Clinic, P.O. Box 5405, 77726-5405.
Rev. Herman Vincent Scholarship Fund. 211 Hardy, Nederland, 77627. Rev. Dan Malain, Admin.
St. Anne's Catholic School Foundation, 375 N. 11th St., 77702.
St. Anthony Cathedral School Foundation, 850 Forsythe St., 77701-2890. Sr. Ann Middlebrooks, S.E.C., Prin.
St. Thomas More Society of Southeast Texas, P.O. Box 467, 77704. Mr. John Johnson, Pres.; Rev. Luong Quang Tran, Chap.

Orange. *The Hamlet*, P.O. Box 626, 77631-0626. A residential facility for persons with AIDS and other terminal illnesses. Pat Bowman, Dir.
St. Mary School Foundation, 912 Cherry, 77630.

Port Arthur. *Hospitality Center, Inc.*, 3959 Gulfway Dr., 77642. Tel: 409-982-4842. Jim O'Brien, Dir.
St. Catherine School Foundation, 3840 Woodrow Dr., 77642.
St. Mary Hospital Foundation of Port Arthur, P.O. Box 3696, 77643. Brenda Drago, Exec. Dir.

RELIGIOUS INSTITUTES OF MEN REPRESENTED IN THE DIOCESE

For further details refer to the corresponding bracketed number in the Religious Institutes of Men or Women section.

[0140]—*The Augustinians*. (Prov. of Castile, Spain).—O.S.A.
[0600]—*Brothers of the Congregation of Holy Cross*. (Southwest Prov.).—C.S.C.
[0275]—*Carmelites of Mary Immaculate*. (India).—C.M.I.
[]—*Congregation of the Mother Coredemptrix*. (Missouri).—C.M.C.
[]—*Missionaries of Charity, Third Order*.—M.C.III.O.
[0720]—*The Missionaries of Our Lady of La Salette*. (Prov. of Mary Queen).—M.S.
[]—*Missionaries of St. Paul*.—M.S.P.
[0910]—*Oblates of Mary Immaculate*. (Southern Prov.).—O.M.I.
[0700]—*St. Joseph's Society of the Sacred Heart*. (Baltimore).—S.S.J.
[0975]—*Society of Our Lady of the Most Holy Trinity*. (Texas).—S.O.L.T.

RELIGIOUS INSTITUTES OF WOMEN REPRESENTED IN THE DIOCESE

[1010]—*Congregation of Divine Providence*. (San Antonio).—C.D.P.
[2190]—*Congregation of the Incarnate Word and Blessed Sacrament*. (Houston, TX).—C.V.I.
[2200]—*Congregation of the Incarnate Word and Blessed Sacrament*. (Victoria).—I.W.B.S.
[0470]—*Congregation of the Sisters of Charity of the Incarnate Word*. (Houston, TX).—C.C.V.I.
[1070-03]—*Dominican Sisters*.—O.P.
[1070-19]—*Dominican Sisters*.—O.P.
[1140]—*Eucharistic Missionaries of St. Dominic*. (New Orleans).—O.P.
[]—*Handmaids of the Holy Child Jesus*.—H.H.C.J.
[1870]—*The Handmaids of the Sacred Heart of Jesus*. (U.S. Prov.).—A.C.J.
[]—*Sisters of the Eucharistic Covenant*.—S.E.C.
[2050]—*Sisters of the Holy Spirit and Mary Immaculate*.—S.H.Sp.
[2205]—*Sisters of the Incarnate Word and Blessed Sacrament*. (Corpus Christi).—I.W.B.S.
[4100]—*Sisters of the Sorrowful Mother*. (U.S./Caribbean Prov.).—S.S.M.
[4120]—*Ursuline Nuns of the Congregation of Paris*. (St. Martin, OH).—O.S.U.
[]—*Vietnamese Dominican Sisters*. (Houston).—O.P.

NECROLOGY

† Enderle, Rev. Msgr. Marvin F., Orange, TX, St. Mary. —Died Jan. 16, 1997.
† Hanafin, William, (Retired). —Died Dec. 27, 1996.

Diocese of Belleville

(Dioecesis Bellevillensis)

Most Reverend

WILTON D. GREGORY, S.L.D.

Bishop of Belleville; ordained May 9, 1973; appointed Auxiliary Bishop of Chicago and Titular Bishop of Oliva October 31, 1983; consecrated December 13, 1983; appointed Bishop of Belleville December 29, 1993; installed February 10, 1994. *Mailing Address: Chancery Office, 222 S. Third St., Belleville, IL, 62220.* Tel.: 618-277-8181.

ERECTED JANUARY 7, 1887.

Square Miles 11,678.

Comprises Illinois south of the northern limits of the counties of St. Clair, Clinton, Marion, Clay, Richland and Lawrence.

For legal titles of parishes and diocesan institutions, consult the Chancery Office.

Chancery Office: 222 S. Third St., Belleville, IL, 62220-1985. Tel.: 618-277-8181; 397-1279; Fax: 618-277-0387.

STATISTICAL OVERVIEW

Personnel	
Bishop	1
Priests: Diocesan Active in Diocese	97
Priests: Active Outside Diocese	6
Priests: Retired, Sick or Absent	45
Number of Diocesan Priests	148
Religious Priests in Diocese	38
Extern Priests in Diocese	2
Ordinations:	
Diocesan Priests	1
Transitional Deacons	1
Permanent Deacons	14
Permanent Deacons in Diocese	40
Total Brothers	10
Total Sisters	265
Parishes	
Parishes	131
With Resident Pastor:	
Resident Diocesan Priests	90
Resident Religious Priests	3
Without Resident Pastor:	
Administered by Priests	33
Administered by Permanent Deacons	2
Administered by Lay People	3
Missions	1
Welfare	
Catholic Hospitals	7
Total Assisted	407,412
Homes for the Aged	4
Total Assisted	376
Day Care and Extended Day Care Centers	4
Total Assisted	566
Specialized Homes	1
Total Assisted	182
Special Centers for Social Services	3
Total Assisted	41,975
Educational	
Diocesan Students in Other Seminaries	10
Total Seminarians	10
High Schools, Diocesan and Parish	3
Total Students	1,651
Elementary Schools, Diocesan and Parish	38
Total Students	7,552
Catechesis/Religious Education:	
High School Students	1,875
Elementary Students	8,423
Total Students Under Catholic Instruction	19,511
Teachers in the Diocese:	
Sisters	15
Lay Teachers	391
Vital Statistics	
Receptions into the Church:	
Infant Baptism Totals	1,711
Adult Baptism Totals	274
Received into Full Communion	207
First Communions	1,698
Confirmations	1,817
Marriages:	
Catholic	382
Interfaith	331
Total Marriages	713
Deaths	1,355
Total Catholic Population	113,051
Total Population	855,645

Former Bishops—Most Rev. JOHN JANSSEN, D.D., ord. Nov. 19, 1858; cons. April 25, 1888; died July 2, 1913.—Most Rev. HENRY J. ALTHOFF, D.D., ord. July 26, 1902; appt. Dec. 4, 1913; cons. Feb. 24, 1914; died July 3, 1947.—Most Rev. ALBERT R. ZUROWESTE, D.D., ord. June 8, 1924; appt. Nov. 29, 1947; cons. Jan. 29, 1948; retired Sept. 3, 1976; died March 28, 1987.—Most Rev. WILLIAM M. COSGROVE, D.D., ord. Dec. 18, 1943; Auxiliary Bishop of Cleveland June 19, 1968; cons. Sept. 3, 1968; appt. Bishop of Belleville Sept. 3, 1976; installed Oct. 28, 1976; retired May 19, 1981; died Dec. 11, 1992.—Most Rev. JOHN N. WURM, S.T.D., Ph.D., ord. April 3, 1954; Auxiliary Bishop of St. Louis June 25, 1976; cons. Aug. 17, 1976; appt. Bishop of Belleville Sept. 19, 1981; installed Nov. 4, 1981; died April 27, 1984.—Most Rev. JAMES P. KELEHER, S.T.D., M.Ed., ord. April 12, 1958; appt. Bishop of Belleville Oct. 23, 1984; cons. Dec. 11, 1984; transferred to Kansas City, KS Sept. 8, 1993.

Diocese of Belleville Chancery Office—222 S. Third St., Belleville, 62220-1985. Tel: 618-277-8181; 397-1279; Fax: 618-277-0387.

Diocesan Pastoral Center—2620 Lebanon Ave., Belleville, 62221. Tel: 618-235-9601; Fax: 618-235-7416.

Vicar General—Very Rev. JAMES E. MARGASON, J.C.L., M.Div.

Moderator of the Curia—Very Rev. JAMES E. MARGASON, J.C.L., M.Div., V.G.

Chancellor—Rev. KENNETH J. YORK, J.C.L.

Vice-Chancellor—DAVID R. SPOTANSKI.

Secretary to the Bishop—Sr. JOYCE ANN BERKEL, S.S.N.D.

Chief Fiscal Officer—PHILIP W. BUETTNER.

Archivist—Sr. MARY KENAN WOLF, S.S.N.D., *220 W. Lincoln St., Belleville, 62220.* Tel: 618-234-3157.

Diocesan Tribunal—Diocesan Pastoral Center, 2620 Lebanon Ave., Belleville, 62221. Tel: 618-235-9601. Address all rogatory commissions to the Chancellor at the Chancery Office.

Judicial Vicar—Rev. EDWARD F. SCHAEFER, J.C.L.

Adjutant Judicial Vicar—Rev. PAUL R. WIENHOFF, J.C.L.

Judges—Revs. PAUL R. WIENHOFF, J.C.L.; EDWARD F. SCHAEFER, J.C.L.; Rev. Msgr. HARRY J. JEROME, J.C.L., S.T.L.

Promotor Justitiae—Rev. KENNETH J. YORK, J.C.L.

Defensores Vinculi—Rev. EDWARD J. STOKES, S.J., J.C.D.

Advocates—Revs. JOHN T. MYLER; DONALD W. EICHENSEER.

Notaries—RENEE QUIRIN; JACQUELINE MATT.

Diocesan Consultors—Very Rev. JAMES E. MARGASON, J.C.L., M.Div., V.G.; Revs. THEODORE J. BAUMANN; JAMES A. BLAZINE; VINCENT A. HASELHORST; WILLIAM J. HITPAS; JAMES M. NALL; PATRICK N. PETER; CARL E. SCHERRER; EUGENE H. WOJCIK.

Diocesan Deans—Very Rev. JAMES A. BLAZINE, V.F., Belleville Deanery; Very Rev. JAMES T. LONG, V.F., East St. Louis Deanery; Very Rev. MELVIN B. VANDELOO, V.F., East Deanery; Very Rev. THEODORE J. BAUMANN, V.F., North Central Deanery; Very Rev. DENNIS R. SCHAEFER, V.F., West Deanery; Vacant; South Deanery.

Diocesan Finance Council—JEFF RENNER, Chm.; Very Rev. JAMES E. MARGASON, J.C.L., M.Div., V.G.; PHILIP W. BUETTNER; J. ROY DEE, III; JACK GUNDLACH; VERNON KOVARIK; IRENE KRUSE; Revs. THOMAS MILLER; STEPHEN RUDOLPHI; Sr. JAN RENZ, A.S.C.; JACKIE SETTLES; JOHN SMITH; JAY TEBBE.

Building Commission, Chancery Office—Rev. JEROME D. HARTLEIN, Chm. WILLIAM JOHNSON.

Campaign for Human Development—Rev. J. CLYDE GROGAN, Dir., *771 Vogel Pl., East St. Louis, 62205.* Tel: 618-874-5025.

Catholic Social Service—PETER CERNEKA, III, Dir., Office: *617 S. Belt W., Belleville, 62220.* Tel: 618-277-9200. Branch Offices: *214 S. University, Carbondale, 62901.* Tel: 618-351-0743. *1 Doctor's Park Rd., Ste. H, Mt. Vernon, 62864.* Tel: 618-244-0344. *120 W. Fifth St., P.O. Box 23, Mt. Carmel, 62863.* Tel: 618-263-3863, *509 N. Second St., Breese, 62230.* Tel: 618-526-2267.

Catholic Urban Programs—JOSEPH P. HUBBARD, Co-ord., *771 Vogel Pl., East St. Louis, 62205.* Tel: 618-398-5616.

Holy Angels Shelter—1410 N. 37th St., East St. Louis, 62205. Tel: 618-874-4079. PATRICIA LEWIS, Dir.

Griffin Center—2630 Lincoln Ave., East St. Louis, 62204. Tel: 618-874-2500. Sr. JULIA HUISKAMP, D.C., Dir.

Griffin Center Sites:—De Shields Center: *1235 McCasland, East St. Louis, 62201.* Tel: 618-874-0637. Roosevelt Center: *400 Bunkum Rd., East St. Louis, 62204.* Tel: 618-271-9859. ORR-Weathers Center: *1400 Missouri Ave., D-1 Bldg., East St. Louis, 62201.* Tel: 618-875-0535.

Family Center—705 Summit, East St. Louis, 62201. Tel: 618-875-7295. Sr. CAROL LEHMKUHL, O.P.

St. Regis Center After School Program—3500 Market St., East St. Louis, 62207. GLENDA DREW, Dir., After School Prog.

C.Y.O.—COLETTE KENNETT, Dir.; Rev. BERNARD C. GOEDDE, JR., Spiritual Moderator; JAMES KEIM, Athletic Dir., *Diocesan Pastoral Center.*

Cemeteries—Rev. Msgr. LEONARD A. BAUER, Dir., *Chancery Office.*

Clergymen's Aid Society—Very Rev. THEODORE J. BAUMANN, V.F., Pres., *Box 176, Bartelso, 62218.* Tel: 618-765-2162.

Conciliation and Arbitration Board—THOMAS E. PRICE, Chm., *740 Market St., Mt. Carmel, 62863.* Tel: 618-263-6591.

Council of Women Religious—Sr. HELEN MOORE, A.S.C., Pres., *1036 Rutledge, Belleville, 62221.* Tel: 618-235-5486.

Diocesan Development Office—MARTIN LIEFELD, *Chancery Office.*

Diocesan Liturgical Commission—Rev. EDWARD F. SCHAEFER, J.C.L., *Diocesan Pastoral Center.*

Diocesan Outreach Apostolate—Serving Alexander and Pulaski Counties. Daystar Community Program, *909 Washington Ave., Cairo, 62914.* Tel: 618-734-0178. Sr. CHRISTINE STYKA, P.H.J.C., Dir., *Res., Mary Katherine Convent, 725 22nd St., Cairo, 62914.* Tel: 618-734-0778.

Diaconate, Office of Permanent—Rev. JOHN L. VENEGONI, Vicar of Deacons, *Diocesan Pastoral Center.*

Diocesan Council of Catholic Women—Rev. ALBERT L. JEROME, Diocesan Moderator, *Box 332, Nashville, 62263.* Tel: 618-327-3232. JOSEPHINE FITCH, Pres., *Diocesan Pastoral Center.*

Ecumenical and Interreligious Affairs—Rev. JAMES R. DOUGHERTY, Dir., *133 N. Elm St., Centralia, 62801.* Tel: 618-532-6291.

Formation of Priests—Rev. JAMES R. DEITERS, Chm., *205 W. Third St., O'Fallon, 62269.* Tel: 618-632-3562.

Office of Education—THOMAS H. POSNANSKI, Dir., *Diocesan Pastoral Center.*

Department of Elementary Education—Sr. PATRICIA DELANEY, S.S.N.D., Dir.

Religious Education and Catechesis—MARK MARKULY, Assoc. Dir.

Diocesan Board of Education—MARTHA O'MALLEY, Pres., *44 Glenview Dr., Belleville, 62203.*

Guatemala Mission Society—VIRGINIA KOCH, Chm., *One Park Ln., Centralia, 62801.* Tel: 618-532-6291.

Hispanic Ministry—Carbondale Area: Rev. FEDERICO HIGUERA, *1101 Centennial St., Box 237, Cobden, 62920.* Tel: 618-893-2276. Fairmont City Area: Sr. ROSALIE GUTIERREZ, P.H.J.C., *2728 N. 42nd St., Fairmont City, 62201.* Tel: 618-271-0360.

Holy Childhood Association—Rev. KENNETH J. YORK, Dir., *Chancery.*

Hospitals—Rev. DENNIS F. VOSS, Delegate, *St. Elizabeth Hospital, 211 S. 3rd St., Belleville, 62220.* Tel: 618-234-2120.

Insurance Commission—PHILIP W. BUETTNER, Dir., *Chancery Office.*

Catholic Mutual Group—WILLIAM P. JOHNSON, Claims/Risk Mgr., *Diocesan Pastoral Center.* Tel: 618-233-1090.

Ministry Formation—IRENE DILL, Dir., *Diocesan Pastoral Center.*

Natural Family Planning—*Catholic Social Services, 617 S. Belt W., Belleville, 62220-2414.* Tel: 618-277-9200.

Newman Center—JOHN SCARANO, Diocesan Dir. & Campus Min., *715 S. Washington St., Carbondale, 62901.* Tel: 618-529-3311. Revs. CECIL PICKERT, O.Carm., Campus Min. EDWARD LINTON, O.S.B.

Newman Auxiliary—JOYCE WOLF, Pres., *110 Becky Dr., Waterloo, 62298.* Tel: 618-939-8978.

Newspaper, "The Messenger"—RAPHAEL H. MIDDEKE, Mng. Editor, *Diocesan Pastoral Center.*

Ondessonk, Camp—Diocese of Belleville, Department of Outdoor Education: PATRICK R. HIGGINS, Exec. Dir., *Ozark, 62972.* Tel: 618-695-2489; Fax: 618-695-3593.

Priest Personnel Board—Very Rev. THEODORE J. BAUMANN, V.F., Chm., *Chancery Office.*

Priests Organizations—

Confraternity of Catholic Clergy—Vacant.

Southern Illinois Association of Priests—Co-Chm:: Revs. WALTER M. BARR; GEORGE A. MAUCK, *1171 Jefferson, Carlyle, 62231.* Tel: 618-594-2225.

Pro-Life Office—ANN POLKA, Chm., *Diocesan Pastoral Center.*

Propagation of the Faith—Rev. KENNETH J. YORK, J.C.L., Dir., *Chancery.*

Office for Professional Fitness Review—MARGIE MENSEN, L.C.S.W.- M.S.W., Admin., *220 W. Lincoln St., #407, Belleville, 62220.* Tel: 618-236-1812.

Rural Life Conference—Rev. JOSEPH A. LAWLER, Dir., *R.R. 3-Piopolis, McLeansboro, 62859.* Tel: 618-648-2490.

St. Vincent DePaul Society—RAY BERKEL, Admin., *3718 State St., East St. Louis, 62205.* Tel: 618-397-3113.

Sick and Aged (Ministry)—Rev. EUGENE J. NEFF, Dir., *Diocesan Pastoral Center.* Tel: 618-235-9991.

Vocation Office—Rev. EUGENE H. WOJCIK, Dir., *Diocesan Pastoral Center.*

Worship, Office of—DENISE ANDERSON, *Diocesan Pastoral Center.*

CLERGY, PARISHES, MISSIONS AND PAROCHIAL SCHOOLS

CITY OF BELLEVILLE
(St. Clair County)

1—CATHEDRAL OF ST. PETER, Revs. James A. Buerster, Rector; John C. Iffert; Deacons Robert Becker; Joseph Stock; Donald Deitz; Robert Lippert. In res., Rev. Edward J. Stokes, S.J.
Res., 200 W. Harrison, 62220. Tel: 618-234-1166. [CEM]
School—Cathedral School, 200 S. Second St., 62220. Tel: 618-233-6414. Sr. Deanne Stratmann, S.S.N.D., Prin.
School Sisters of Notre Dame 3; Lay Teachers 21; Students 346.
Catechesis/Religious Programs—D.R.E.: Sr. Theresa Markus, S.S.N.D.; Mrs. Cathy Becker.
Students 160.
Convent—300 S. Second St., 62220. Tel: 618-233-3580.

2—BLESSED SACRAMENT, Rev. Marvin C. Volk, Pastor; Deacon Douglas Boyer.
Res., 8707 W. Main St., 62223. Tel: 618-397-2287; Fax: 618-397-2269.
School—8801 W. Main St., 62223. Tel: 618-397-1111; Fax: 618-397-8431. Ms. Claire Hatch, Prin.
School Sisters of Notre Dame 1; Lay Teachers 12; Students 195.
Catechesis/Religious Programs—Students 76.
Convent—8901 W. Main St., 62233. Tel: 618-397-0039.

3—OUR LADY QUEEN OF PEACE, Rev. John W. McEvilly.
Res., 5923 N. Belt W., 62223. Tel: 618-234-6196; Fax: 618-234-6217.
School—5915 N. Belt W., 62223. Tel: 618-234-1206. Mrs. Jane Spreng, Prin.
Lay Teachers 19; Students 331.
Catechesis/Religious Programs—Students 45.

4—ST. AUGUSTINE OF CANTERBURY, Rev. Andrew J. Knopik.
Res., 1910 W. Belle, 62226. Tel: 618-233-3813.
School—1900 Canterbury Dr., 62223. Tel: 618-234-4958. Dr. Kay Bennett, Prin.
Lay Teachers 18; Students 230.
Catechesis/Religious Programs—Students 69.

5—ST. HENRY, Rev. Bernard L. Voss. In res., Rev. James S. Orumpakkat, C.M.I.
Res., 5315 W. Main St., 62223. Tel: 618-233-2423; Fax: 618-233-9879.
School—5303 W. Main St., 62223. Tel: 618-234-6061; Fax: 618-234-6801. Mr. Ronald Karcher, Prin.
Lay Teachers 8; Students 129.

6—ST. LUKE, Rev. James E. Margason, V.G., J.C.L.; Sr. Grace Marie Mueller, S.S.N.D., Pastoral Assoc., Tel: 618-236-1839; Deacons Peter Cerneka; Robert Lanter.
Res., 301 N. Church St., 62220. Tel: 618-236-1124.
Catechesis/Religious Programs—Students 86.

7—ST. MARY, Very Rev. James A. Blazine, V.F.
Res., 1706 W. Main St., 62226. Tel: 618-233-2391; Fax: 618-233-9201.
School—1722 W. Main St., 62226. Tel: 618-234-2476; Fax: 618-234-7736.
Lay Teachers 9; Students 221.
Catechesis/Religious Programs—Sr. Mary Catherine Clark, A.S.C., D.R.E.
Students 119.

8—ST. TERESA OF THE CHILD JESUS. (Little Flower). Revs. Donald W. Eichenseer; Robert D. Gore.
Res., 1201 Lebanon Ave., 62221. Tel: 618-233-3500; Fax: 618-233-9703.
School—1108 Lebanon Ave., 62221. Tel: 618-235-4066; Fax: 618-235-7930. Mr. Leo Hodapp, Prin.
Lay Teachers 20; Students 364.
Catechesis/Religious Programs—Students 132.

9—CHAPEL OF ST. JOHN CHILDREN'S HOME. Unassigned. Mailing Address: Chancery Office, 222 S. Third St., 62220. Tel: 618-277-8181. [CEM]
Rev. Msgr. James E. Margason, J.C.L.
Convent—Tel: 618-277-9699. Sisters, Poor Handmaids of Jesus Christ.

OUTSIDE THE CITY OF BELLEVILLE

Albers, Clinton Co., St. Bernard, Rev. Leo S. Reinhardt.
Res., 62215. Tel: 618-248-5112. [CEM]
Catechesis/Religious Programs—Mrs. Norma Jansen, D.R.E.
Students 134.

Anna, Union Co., St. Mary, Rev. Thomas W. Miller; Sr. Joan Backes, S.S.N.D., Pastoral Assoc. & D.R.E.
Res., 402 Freeman, 62906. Tel: 618-833-5835; 833-3131.
Catechesis/Religious Programs—Tel: 618-833-3131.
Students 145.

Ava, Jackson Co., St. Elizabeth, Rev. Leo J. Hayes.
Res., 606 W. George St., P.O. Box 157, 62907. Tel: 618-426-3321.

Aviston, Clinton Co., St. Francis of Assisi, Rev. Daniel L. Friedman; Deacons Gerald E. Stockman; Charles Litteken.
Res., 251 S. Clinton, Box 93, 62216. Tel: 618-228-7219; Fax: 618-228-7320. [CEM]
Catechesis/Religious Programs—Tel: 618-228-7245.
Students 220.

Bartelso, Clinton Co., St. Cecilia, Very Rev. Theodore J. Baumann, V.F.
Res., 304 S. Washington St., P.O. Box 176, 62218. Tel: 618-765-2162; Fax: 618-765-2264.
Catechesis/Religious Programs—Fax: 618-765-2163. Sr. Mary Benedict Hayden, A.S.C., D.R.E.
Students 200.

Beaver Prairie, Clinton Co., St. Felicitas. Attended by Marydale. Barbara McQuade, Pastoral Life Coord. Mailing Address: 13322 Church Rd., Carlyle, 62231. Tel: 618-594-3266. [CEM]
Catechesis/Religious Programs—Students 53.

Beckemeyer, Clinton Co., St. Anthony, Very Rev. Richard J. Weidert, Pastor; Rev. James A. Voelker.
Res., P.O. Box 305, 62219. Tel: 618-227-8236. [CEM]
Catechesis/Religious Programs—Students 73.

Benton, Franklin Co., St. Joseph, Rev. Donald J. Lenzini.
Res., 506 W. Main, 62812. Tel: 618-438-9941. [CEM]
Catechesis/Religious Programs—Tel: 618-439-6493.
Students 54.

Breese, Clinton Co., St. Augustine, Rev. Melvin B. Haas; Deacon Paul Bruening.
Res., 525 S. Third St., P.O. Box 67, 62230. Tel: 618-526-4362.
Catechesis/Religious Programs—Students 33.

St. Dominic, Rev. Patrick N. Peter.
Res., 480 N. Second St., 62230. Tel: 618-526-7746; Fax: 618-526-7755. [CEM]
Catechesis/Religious Programs—Mrs. Rill Anthony, D.R.E.
Students 117.

Bridgeport, Lawrence Co., Immaculate Conception. Attended by St. Lawrence, Lawrenceville.
1006 Collins, Lawrenceville, 62439. Tel: 618-943-5255. [CEM]

Cahokia, St. Clair Co., Holy Family, Rev. John T. Myler, D.Min.
Res., 116 Church St., 62206. Tel: 618-337-4548; Fax: 618-332-1699. [CEM 3]
School—Tel: 618-337-2880. Vincent Schmidt, Prin.
Lay Teachers 9; Students 206.

St. Catherine Laboure, Rev. John W. Frerker.
Res., 913 Rome Ln., 62206. Tel: 618-337-4173; Fax: 618-337-1231.
School—1820 Jerome Ln., 62208. Tel: 618-337-4448; Fax: 618-337-1231.
Lay Teachers 9; Students 145.
Day Care—1826 Jerome Ln., 62208. Tel: 618-337-3555.

Cairo, Alexander Co., St. Patrick, Rev. Jerome D. Fortenberry, C.M.
Res., 312 Ninth St., 62914. Tel: 618-734-2061. [CEM]
School—St. Joseph, Tel: 618-734-4182. Louis Fortenberry, Prin.
98105.

Carbondale, Jackson Co., St. Francis Xavier, Rev. Carl E. Scherrer. In res., Rev. Peter Amponsah; Deacon Richard Prien.
Res., 303 S. Poplar St., 62901. Tel: 618-457-4556; Fax: 618-457-7368.
Catechesis/Religious Programs—Toni Intravaia, D.R.E.
Students 215.

Carlyle, Clinton Co., St. Mary. (Immaculate Conception). Rev. George A. Mauck.
Res., 12th St. & Jefferson St., Box 179, 62231. Tel: 618-594-2225; Fax: 618-594-4638. [CEM]
Catechesis/Religious Programs—Tel: 618-594-2284. Sr. Mary Dietz, S.S.N.D., D.R.E.
Students 246.

Carmi, White Co., St. Polycarp, Rev. Stephen A. Rudolphi.
Res., 209 S. Fourth St., P.O. Box 56, 62821. Tel: 618-382-7732. [CEM]
Catechesis/Religious Programs—Students 50.

Carterville, Williamson Co., Church of the Holy Spirit. Attended by Our Lady of Mount Carmel, Herrin.

316 W. Monroe St., Herrin, 62948. Tel: 618-942-3114; Fax: 618-988-1375.
Catechesis/Religious Programs—Tel: 618-985-6929.
Students 66.

Caseyville, St. Clair Co., St. Stephen, Rev. Thomas D. Flach; Deacon William DeWolf.
Res., 901 S. Main St., P.O. Box 458, 62232. Tel: 618-397-0666; Fax: 618-397-4430.

Centralia, Marion Co., St. Mary, Rev. James R. Dougherty.
Res., 424 E. Broadway, 62801. Tel: 618-532-6291; Fax: 618-532-4758. [CEM]
Church Office: 424 E. Broadway, 62801.
School—Tel: 618-532-3473. Mrs. Jeanette Shaw, Prin.
Lay Teachers 8; Students 138.
Catechesis/Religious Programs—Mrs. Dolores Sanders, D.R.E.
Students 90.

Centreville, St. Clair Co., Immaculate Conception, Rev. Elmar Mauer, O.M.I.; Bro. Edward Driggins, O.M.I., Pastoral Assoc.
Res., 6210 Church Rd., 62207. Tel: 618-337-5682; 337-7493; Fax: 618-337-7493. [CEM]

Chester, Randolph Co., St. Mary Help of Christians, Very Rev. Dennis R. Schaefer, V.F.
Res., 911 Swanwick St., 62233. Tel: 618-826-2444. [CEM]
School—Tel: 618-826-3120; Fax: 618-826-3486. Alecia Poetker, Prin.
Sisters 1; Lay Teachers 11; Students 150.
Catechesis/Religious Programs—Tel: 618-826-2526. Sr. Catherine Schmiz, A.S.C., D.R.E.
Students 44.

Christopher, Franklin Co., St. Andrew, Rev. Walter M. Barr.
Res., 412 E. Washington St., 62822. Tel: 618-724-4114. [CEM]
Catechesis/Religious Programs—Elaine Polbinski, D.R.E.
Students 77.

Cobden, Union Co., St. Joseph, Rev. Federico Higuera; Deacon Patrick Patterson.
Res., 101 Centennial St., P.O. Box 237, 62920. Tel: 618-893-2276. [CEM]
Catechesis/Religious Programs—Tel: 618-893-2368.
Students 72.

Columbia, Monroe Co., Immaculate Conception of the B.V.M., Rev. Stephen J. Humphrey; Sr. Lorraine DeFebbo, O.S.F., Pastoral Assoc.; Deacons John DuPrey; Linus Horcher.
Res., 117 E. Madison, 62236. Tel: 618-281-5105. [CEM]
School—Tel: 618-281-5353. Michael Kish, Prin.
Lay Teachers 18; Students 371.
Catechesis/Religious Programs—Students 140.

Coulterville, Randolph Co., St. Anthony. Attended by St. Anthony, Lively Grove. Rev. D. Steven Witte.
6101 St. Anthony Church Rd., Oakdale, 62268. Tel: 618-824-6271.

Dahlgren, Hamilton Co., St. John Nepomucene. Attended by St. Clement, McLeansboro. Rev. E. Alan Ruppert.
7th & Main Sts, P.O. Box 220, 62828. Tel: 618-736-2879; 643-3552. [CEM]
Res., 103 N. Hancock, McLeansboro, 62859.
Catechesis/Religious Programs—Rita Rapp, D.R.E.
Students 59.

Damiansville, Clinton Co., St. Damian. Attended by St. Bernard, Albers. Rev. Leo S. Reinhardt, Pastor.
Res., One W. Main St., 62215. Tel: 618-248-5134. [CEM]
Catechesis/Religious Programs—Students 91.

Dubois, Washington Co., St. Charles Borromeo, Rev. Daniel J. Jurek.
Res., P.O. Box 6, 62831. Tel: 618-787-2781. [CEM]
School—Tel: 618-787-2722. Mrs. Charlotte Pestka, Prin.
Lay Teachers 5; Students 37.

Dupo, St. Clair Co., Sacred Heart of Jesus, Rev. Paul R. Wienhoff.
Res., 100 S. 3rd St., 62239. Tel: 618-286-3224.
Catechesis/Religious Programs—Tel: 618-286-4373.
Students 42.

Du Quoin, Perry Co., Sacred Heart of Jesus, Rev. Richard L. Daly.
Res., 17 N. Walnut St., 62832. Tel: 618-542-3423. [CEM]
School—Tel: 618-542-2335; Fax: 618-542-2329. William Daters, Prin.
Lay Teachers 8; Students 86.
Catechesis/Religious Programs—Students 33.

East St. Louis, St. Clair Co.,

1—Immaculate Conception, (Lithuanian), Rev. Kenneth J. York, Admin.
1509 Baugh Ave., 62205. Tel: 618-874-0162.

2—St. John Francis Regis. Attended by St. Patrick, East St. Louis.
Tel: 618-874-5025.

3—St. Joseph, Revs. Robert J. Luchi, S.J.; Robert L. Sullivan, S.J.
Res., 408 Columbia Pl., 62205. Tel: 618-274-0655.
Catechesis/Religious Programs—Nicole Younge, D.R.E.
Students 27.

4—St. Patrick, Rev. James Clyde Grogan; Deacon John Coates. In res., Rev. James A. Voelker.
Res., 771 Vogel Pl., 62205. Tel: 618-874-5025; Fax: 618-274-4659. [CEM]
Catechesis/Religious Programs—Students 31.

5—St. Philip, Rev. James A. Voelker, Pastor.
Res., 771 Vogel Pl., 62205. Tel: 618-271-6168. [CEM]
Church—8313 Church Ln., 62203. Tel: 618-397-1860.

Eldorado, Saline Co., St. Mary, Rev. Donald E. Abell.
Res., 1158 N. 2nd St., 62930. Tel: 618-273-6947; Fax: 618-273-3147. [CEM]
Catechesis/Religious Programs—Students 90.

Elizabethtown, Hardin Co., St. Joseph. Attended by St. Rose of Lima, Metropolis. Rev. Joseph L. Trapp, Admin.
Res., 185E 350N. Rd., Rte. 1, P.O. Box 140, 62931-9711. Tel: 618-285-3332. [CEM]
Catechesis/Religious Programs—Tel: 618-287-8847.
Students 35.

Ellis Grove, Randolph Co., Divine Maternity of the B.V.M., Deacon Omer E. DuBois.
Res., 7362 Shawneetown Trail, 62241. Tel: 618-859-3541.

Enfield, White Co., St. Patrick. Attended by St. Polycarp, Carmi. Rev. Stephen A. Rudolphi, Admin.
Church—Rte. 2, 62835. Tel: 618-963-2013. [CEM]

Equality, Gallatin Co., St. Joseph. Attended by St. Joseph, Ridgway. Rev. Mark D. Stec.
Mailing Address: P.O. Box 99, 62934. Tel: 618-276-4252.
Res., P.O. Box 190, Ridgway, 62979. Tel: 618-272-7059. [CEM]

Evansville, Randolph Co., St. Boniface, Rev. Joseph C. Rascher; Sr. Diane Marie Turner, S.S.N.D., Pastoral Assoc.
Res., 1003 Olive St., 62242. Tel: 618-853-4453; Fax: 618-853-4453. [CEM]
Catechesis/Religious Programs—Students 33.

Fairfield, Wayne Co., St. Edward, Rev. Gerald R. Hechenberger.
Res., 300 N.W. 5th St., 62837. Tel: 618-847-7931.
Catechesis/Religious Programs—Jean Hadfield, D.R.E.
Students 36.

Fairmont City, St. Clair Co., Holy Rosary, Rev. David M. Wilke, Pastor.
Res., 2716 N. 42nd St., 62201. Tel: 618-274-3486; Fax: 618-274-1814.
School—Tel: 618-271-8600. Mrs. Shirley Kurre, Prin.
Lay Teachers 6; Students 107.

Fairview Heights, St. Clair Co., Our Lady of the Assumption, Rev. James H. Jansen; Deacons Dennis C. Rickert; Thomas Underwood.
Res., 9950 Bunkum Rd., 62208. Tel: 618-397-0121.
Catechesis/Religious Programs—Students 196.

St. Albert the Great, Very Rev. James T. Long, V.F.; Deacon Thomas Underwood.
Res., 15 E. Lincoln Hwy., 62208. Tel: 618-632-5334; Fax: 618-632-0903.
School—Tel: 618-632-4937. Sr. Mary Jane Nowakowski, O.S.F., Prin.
Sisters 4; Lay Teachers 11; Students 235.
Catechesis/Religious Programs—Tel: 618-632-8577. Robert Bigham, D.R.E.
Students 198.

Fayetteville, St. Clair Co., St. Pancratius, Very Rev. James A. Blazine, V.F.; Deacon George Munie.
Res., 2213 N. 2nd St., 62258. Tel: 618-677-2717. [CEM]

Flora, Clay Co., St. Stephen, Rev. Hyacinth Mazuchowski.
Res., 812 N. Main St., 62839. Tel: 618-662-6261. [CEM]
Catechesis/Religious Programs—Tel: 618-662-8121.
Students 75.

Freeburg, St. Clair Co., St. Joseph, Rev. Henry J. Fischer.
Res., 9 N. Alton St., 62243. Tel: 618-539-3209. [CEM]
School—Tel: 618-539-3930. Sr. Cynthia Weber, S.S.N.D., Prin.
Sisters 2; Lay Teachers 8; Students 150.
Catechesis/Religious Programs—Tel: 618-539-3209.
Students 139.

Germantown, Clinton Co., St. Boniface, Rev. Vincent A. Haselhorst.
Res., 402 Munster St., Box 280, 62245. Tel: 618-523-4271. [CEM]
Catechesis/Religious Programs—Students 260.

Grand Chain, Pulaski Co., St. Catherine. Attended by Immaculate Conception-St. Mary, Mound City. Sr. Nancy Flamm, S.S.N.D., Pastoral Assoc.
517 N. Walnut St., Box 67, Mound City, 62963. Tel: 618-748-9113; Fax: 618-748-9639. [CEM]

Harrisburg, Saline Co., St. Mary, Rev. John E. Stallings; Margaret Bickett, Pastoral Assoc.
Res., 2000 W. Poplar St., 62946. Tel: 618-253-7408; Fax: 618-252-7874. [CEM]
Catechesis/Religious Programs—Tel: 618-252-7874.
Students 61.

Hecker, Monroe Co., St. Augustine of Canterbury, Rev. Ralph L. Haas.
Res., P.O. Box 126, 62248. Tel: 618-473-2217; Fax: 618-473-9141. [CEM]

Herrin, Williamson Co., Our Lady of Mount Carmel, Revs. Kenneth J. Schaefer; Steven F. Poole.
Res., 316 W. Monroe St., 62948. Tel: 618-942-3114; Fax: 618-988-1375. [CEM]
School—Tel: 618-942-4484. Mr. Terry Hughes, Prin.
Lay Teachers 13; Students 265.
Catechesis/Religious Programs—Students 50.

Johnston City, Williamson Co., St. Paul, Rev. Msgr. Paulin J. Dobkowski.
Res., 1103 Washington St., 62951. Tel: 618-983-5073.
Oratory— Students 50.

Kaskaskia, Randolph Co., Immaculate Conception. (Independent Mission).
Mailing Address:St. Mary's, MO 63673.

Kinmundy, Marion Co., St. Elizabeth Ann Seton. Attended by St. Theresa of Avila, Salem.
719 Markland St., Salem, 62881. Tel: 618-548-0899.

Lawrenceville, Lawrence Co., St. Lawrence, Rev. Charles Durkin, Admin.
Res., 1006 Collins, 62439. Tel: 618-943-5255; Fax: 618-943-3147. [JC]
Catechesis/Religious Programs—Students 60.

Lebanon, St. Clair Co., St. Joseph, Revs. James E. Margason; Eugene J. Neff; Mrs. Brenda Pehle, Parish Life Coord.
Res., 901 N. Alton St., 62254. Tel: 618-537-2575. [CEM]
Catechesis/Religious Programs—Students 52.

Lively Grove, Washington Co., St. Anthony, Rev. D. Steven Witte.
Res., 6101 St. Anthony Church Rd., Oakdale, 62268. Tel: 618-824-6271; Fax: 618-824-6200. [CEM]
Catechesis/Religious Programs—Tel: 618-824-6271.
Students 68.

Madonnaville, Monroe Co., Immaculate Conception. Attended by St. Mary, Valmeyer.
101 S. Meyer St., Valmeyer, 62295.; Tel: 618-939-6618; 935-2247.

Marion, Williamson Co., St. Joseph, Rev. Richard G. Mohr.
Res., 600 N. Russell St., P.O. Box 1679, 62959. Tel: 618-993-3194; Fax: 618-997-9391.
Catechesis/Religious Programs—Tel: 618-997-9046. Sr. Anastasia Wehner, S.S.N.D., D.R.E.
Students 232.

Marydale, Clinton Co., St. Teresa of Avila, Mrs. Esther Noreen Berns, Pastoral Life Coord.
18021 Marydale Rd., Carlyle, 62231. Tel: 618-594-3266.
Catechesis/Religious Programs—Tel: 618-594-4298. Deacon John Hempen, D.R.E.
Students 98.

Mascoutah, St. Clair Co., Holy Childhood of Jesus, Rev. Jerome D. Hartlein.
Res., 104 N. Independence St., P.O. Box 160, 62258. Tel: 618-566-2958. [CEM]
School—Tel: 618-566-2922. Diana Roberts, Prin.
Sisters 1; Lay Teachers 16; Students 218.
Catechesis/Religious Programs—Tel: 618-566-2922. Sr. Frances McDonagh, O.S.U., D.R.E.
Students 134.

McLeansboro, Hamilton Co., St. Clement, Rev. E. Alan Ruppert.
Res., 103 N. Hancock, 62859. Tel: 618-643-3552. [CEM]
Catechesis/Religious Programs—Tel: 618-643-3628. D.R.E.: Robin Hylton; Kathy Smith.
Students 79.

Metropolis, Massac Co., St. Rose of Lima, Rev. Joseph L. Trapp.

Res., 315 E. Third St., 62960-2229. Tel: 618-524-9006.
Catechesis/Religious Programs—Office:, 405 E. Third St., 62960. Tel: 618-524-8202. Marjorie J. Hawes, D.R.E.
Students 48.

Millstadt, St. Clair Co., St. James, Rev. Bernard C. Goedde, Jr.; Deacon Ronald Karcher.
Res., 405 W. Madison St., 62260. Tel: 618-476-3513. [CEM]
School—Tel: 618-476-3510. Sr. Barbara Hudock, A.S.C., Prin.
Sisters 3; Lay Teachers 7; Students 186.
Catechesis/Religious Programs—Students 115.

Modoc, Randolph Co., St. Leo. Attended by St. Patrick, Ruma. Rev. John J. Joyce, Admin.
Res., #1 Pioneer Ln., Red Bud, 62278. Tel: 618-282-3176. [CEM]

Mound City, Pulaski Co., Church of the Immaculate Conception-St. Mary, Rev. William P. McGhee; Sr. Nancy Flamm, S.S.N.D., Pastoral Assoc.
Res., 517 N. Walnut St., Box 67, 62963. Tel: 618-748-9113; Fax: 618-748-9639. [CEM]

Mount Carmel, Wabash Co., St. Mary, Rev. William J. Rowe; Deacon Charles Speaks.
Res., 125 W. Fifth St., 62863. Tel: 618-262-5337; Fax: 618-262-5333. [CEM]
School—Tel: 618-263-3183; Fax: 618-263-3596.
Lay Teachers 12; Students 193.
Catechesis/Religious Programs—Students 71.

Mount Vernon, Jefferson Co., St. Mary, Very Rev. Melvin B. Vandeloo, V.F.
Res., 115 N. 14th St., 62864. Tel: 618-244-1559; Fax: 618-242-5365. [CEM]
School—Tel: 618-242-5353; Fax: 618-242-5365. Sr. Susan Cunningham, Prin.
Lay Teachers 8; Students 109.
Catechesis/Religious Programs—Students 245.

Murphysboro, Jackson Co., St. Andrew, Rev. Gary P. Gummersheimer; Deacons Michael Dougherty; Joseph Teaff.
Res., 724 Mulberry St., 62966. Tel: 618-687-2012; Fax: 618-687-2012. [CEM]
School—Tel: 618-687-2013; Fax: 618-684-4969. Marilyn Johnson, Prin.
Lay Teachers 12; Students 187.
Catechesis/Religious Programs—Tel: 618-684-6364. Mrs. Patti Wagnitz, D.R.E.
Students 130.

Nashville, Washington Co., St. Ann, Rev. Albert L. Jerome.
Res., 631 S. Mill St., 62263. Tel: 618-327-3232; Fax: 618-327-3232. [CEM]
School—Tel: 618-327-8741. Laurie Klostermann, Prin.
Lay Teachers 8; Students 102.
Catechesis/Religious Programs—Tel: 618-327-3232.
Students 89.
Convent—695 S. Mill St., 62263. Tel: 618-327-3771.

New Athens, St. Clair Co., St. Agatha, Rev. David M. Darin.
Res., 205 S. Market St., 62264. Tel: 618-475-2331; Fax: 618-475-3472.
School—Tel: 618-475-2170. Sr. Annette M. Kaba, O.S.F., Prin.
Lay Teachers 4; Students 67.
Catechesis/Religious Programs—Students 90.

New Baden, Clinton Co., St. George, Rev. Thomas M. Barrett.
Res., 200 N. 3rd St., 62265. Tel: 618-588-4323. [CEM]
Catechesis/Religious Programs—Tel: 618-588-3504.
Students 245.

O'Fallon, St. Clair Co., St. Clare, Rev. James E. Deiters; Deacon Robert Lippert.
Res., 205 W. 3rd St., 62269. Tel: 618-632-3562; Fax: 618-632-9036. [CEM]
School—214 W. 3rd St., 62269. Tel: 618-632-6327; Fax: 618-632-5587.
Lay Teachers 24; Students 437.
Catechesis/Religious Programs—Tel: 618-632-4281. Mrs. Betty Cloughley, D.R.E.
Students 300.

St. Nicholas, Rev. William J. Hitpas; Deacon Richard H. Olson.
Res., 900 N. Smiley, 62269. Tel: 618-632-1797; Fax: 618-632-7703.
Church—625 St. Nicholas Dr., 62269.
Catechesis/Religious Programs—Tel: 618-632-1007. Barbara Furdek, D.R.E.
Students 204.

Okawville, Washington Co., St. Barbara, Rev. Msgr. Angelo J. Lombardo.
Res., 305 N. Front St., 62271. Tel: 618-243-6236. [CEM]
Catechesis/Religious Programs—Tel: 618-243-6236.
Students 93.

Olney, Richland Co., St. Joseph, Rev. Jerry E. Wirth.
Res., 215 S. Elliott St., 62450. Tel: 618-392-8181; Fax: 618-395-8500. [CEM]
School—Tel: 618-395-8500; Fax: 618-395-8500. Carol Steinman, Prin.
Lay Teachers 13; Students 214.
Catechesis/Religious Programs—Students 63.

Paderborn, St. Clair Co., St. Michael, Rev. Joseph D. Hansmann.
Res., 4576 Buss Branch Rd., Waterloo, 62298. Tel: 618-473-2798. [CEM]
Catechesis/Religious Programs—Tel: 618-473-2915. Jackie Billings, D.R.E.
Students 79.

Pinckneyville, Perry Co., St. Bruno, Rev. John L. Venegoni.
Res., 204 N. Gordon Ave., P.O. Box 205, 62274. Tel: 618-357-5510; Fax: 618-357-6050. [CEM]
School—Tel: 618-357-8276; Fax: 618-357-6425. Mrs. Sandra Bray, Prin.
Sisters 2; Lay Teachers 8; Students 146.
Catechesis/Religious Programs—Marcia Hagene, D.R.E.
Students 75.

Piopolis, Hamilton Co., St. John the Baptist, Rev. Joseph A. Lawler.
Res., Rte. 3, P.O. Box 170, McLeansboro, 62859. Tel: 618-648-2490. [CEM]
Catechesis/Religious Programs—Jewell Wilson, D.R.E.
Students 63.

Pond Settlement, Gallatin Co., St. Patrick. Attended by St. Mary, Shawneetown.
P.O. Box 579, Shawneetown, 62984. Tel: 618-269-3318.

Posen, Washington Co., Our Lady of Perpetual Help. Attended by St. Mary Magdalen, Todd's Mill. Rev. James R. Van Oss.
Res., 19824 Posen Rd., Nashville, 62263. Tel: 618-327-3556. [CEM]

Prairie du Rocher, Randolph Co., St. Joseph, Rev. Albert E. Kreher.
Res., 802 Middle St., 62277. Tel: 618-284-3314. [CEM]
Catechesis/Religious Programs—Students 52.

Raddle, Jackson Co., St. Ann. Attended by St. Elizabeth, Ava.
606 W. George St., P.O. Box 157, Ava, 62907. Tel: 618-426-3321.

Radom, Washington Co., St. Michael, Rev. Jerome H. Hibner.
Res., 52 S. Third St., 62876. Tel: 618-485-2265. [CEM]
School—Tel: 618-485-6461. Mrs. Mary Czerniejewski, Prin.
Lay Teachers 5; Students 66.
Catechesis/Religious Programs—Students 66.

Red Bud, Randolph Co., St. John the Baptist, Rev. Thomas Stout.
Res., 515 Locust St., 62278. Tel: 618-282-3222. [CEM]
School—Tel: 618-282-3215. Sr. Louise O'Connor, S.S.N.D., Prin.
School Sisters of Notre Dame 2; Lay Teachers 8; Students 206.
Catechesis/Religious Programs—Students 70.

Renault, Monroe Co., Our Lady of Good Counsel, Rev. Roger R. Karban, Admin.
Res., P.O. Box 98, 62279. Tel: 618-458-7710; Fax: 618-458-7710. [CEM]

Ridgway, Gallatin Co., St. Joseph, Rev. Mark D. Stec.
Res., P.O. Box 190, 62979. Tel: 618-272-7059; Fax: 618-272-5400. [CEM]
Catechesis/Religious Programs—Tel: 618-272-7455.
Students 130.

Royalton, Franklin Co., St. Aloysius, Rev. Peter Hsu.
Res., Pecan St., P.O. Box 100, 62983. Tel: 618-984-2146. [CEM]
Catechesis/Religious Programs—Students 6.

Ruma, Randolph Co., St. Patrick, Rev. John J. Joyce, Admin.
Res., #1 Pioneer Ln., Red Bud, 62278. Tel: 618-282-3176. [CEM]
Catechesis/Religious Programs—Students 22.

St. Francisville, Lawrence Co., St. Francis Xavier. Attended by St. Lawrence.
1006 Collins St., Lawrenceville, 62439. Tel: 618-943-5255. [CEM]

St. Libory, St. Clair Co., St. Liborius, Rev. Jose Ancheril; Deacon Andrew Lintken.
Res., P.O. Box 331, 62282. Tel: 618-768-4921; Fax: 618-768-4207. [CEM]
Catechesis/Religious Programs—Tel: 618-768-4992. Donna Dressler, D.R.E.
Students 115.

St. Rose, Clinton Co., St. Rose, Rev. Edward F. Schaefer.
Res., 18010 St. Rose Rd., 62230-2506. Tel: 618-526-4118; Fax: 618-526-0004. [CEM]
Catechesis/Religious Programs—Tel: 618-526-4886. Sr. Justina Schaefer, A.S.C., D.R.E.
Students 307.

St. Sebastian, Wabash Co., St. Sebastian. Attended by St. Edward, Fairfield.
300 N.W. Fifth St., Fairfield, 62837. Tel: 618-847-7931. [CEM]

Salem, Marion Co., St. Theresa of Avila, Rev. Jon O'Guinn. In res., 812 W. Main St., 62881. Tel: 618-548-0899 [CEM]
School—Tel: 618-548-3492. Sr. Ruth Chausse, S.S.N.D., Prin.
School Sisters of Notre Dame 1; Lay Teachers 6; Students 83.
Catechesis/Religious Programs—Students 86.

Sandoval, Marion Co., St. Lawrence, Rev. Charles W. Tuttle.
Church—311 W.M St., P.O. Box 278, 62882. Tel: 618-247-3300. [CEM]
Res., P.O. Box 189, Breese, 62230. Tel: 618-594-2131.
Catechesis/Religious Programs—Students 56.

Scheller, Jefferson Co., St. Barbara. Attended by St. Michael, Radom.
Res., 62883. Tel: 618-279-7207.

Sesser, Franklin Co., St. Mary, Rev. Louis A. Koehr.
Res., 100 N. Poplar St.; P.O. Box 568, 62884. Tel: 618-625-5053.
Catechesis/Religious Programs—Students 31.

Shawneetown, Gallatin Co., St. Mary, Rev. Henry Ray Engelhart.
Res., P.O. Box 579, 62984. Tel: 618-269-3318. [CEM]
Catechesis/Religious Programs—Students 47.

Shiloh, St. Clair Co., Corpus Christi, Rev. Gerald C. Miriani.
Res., 206 Rasp St., O'Fallon, 62269. Tel: 618-632-5631.
Catechesis/Religious Programs—Tel: 618-632-7614.
Students 67.

Smithton, St. Clair Co., St. John the Baptist, Rev. Kenneth J. York, J.C.L.
Res., 10 S. Lincoln St., 62285-1614. Tel: 618-234-2068; Fax: 618-234-0179. [CEM]
School—Tel: 618-233-0581. Stephen Boyer, Prin.
Lay Teachers 8; Students 114.

Sparta, Randolph Co., Our Lady of Lourdes, Rev. William F. Rensing; Deacon J. Richard Downen.
Res., 611 W. Broadway, 62286. Tel: 618-443-2811.
Catechesis/Religious Programs—Tel: 618-443-2878. Lila Lehnherr, D.R.E.
Students 142.

Stonefort, Williamson Co., St. Francis de Sales. Attended by St. Paul, Vienna.
2020 State Rte. 146E., Vienna, 62995. Tel: 618-658-4501.

Stringtown, Richland Co., St. Joseph. Attended by Holy Cross, Wendelin.
6342 N. Stringtown Rd., Olney, 62450. Tel: 618-392-6711; Fax: 618-395-8500. [CEM]
Catechesis/Religious Programs—Tel: 618-395-2862. Barbara Ochs, D.R.E.
Students 71.

Tamaroa, Perry Co., Immaculate Conception. Attended by St. Charles Borromeo, Dubois. Rev. Daniel J. Jurek.
Res., R.R. 2, Box 91, 62888. Tel: 618-496-5867.
Catechesis/Religious Programs—Tel: 618-496-3200.
Students 44.

Tipton, Monroe Co., St. Patrick, Rev. Eugene J. Wojcik.
Res., 5675 LL Rd., Waterloo, 62298. Tel: 618-458-6875. [CEM]

Todd's Mill, Perry Co., St. Mary Magdalen, Rev. James R. Van Oss.
Res., R.R. 3, Box 145, Nashville, 62263. Tel: 618-336-5414. [CEM]

Trenton, Clinton Co., St. Mary, Rev. Robert B. Flannery; Sr. Angela J. Schrage, A.S.C., Pastoral Assoc. & D.R.E.; Deacon John P. Dilley.
Res., 215 W. Kentucky St., 62293. Tel: 618-224-9335; Fax: 618-224-9346. [CEM]
Catechesis/Religious Programs—Students 185.

Ullin, Pulaski Co., Our Lady of Fatima. Attended by St. Mary, Mound City. Sr. Nancy Flamm, S.S.N.D., Pastoral Assoc.
517 N. Walnut St., Box 67, Mound City, 62963. Tel: 618-748-9113; Fax: 618-748-9639. [CEM]

Valmeyer, Monroe Co., Seven Dolors of the B.V.M., Rev. Edwin H. Hustedde.
Res., 101 Meyer Dr., P.O. Box 206, 62295. Tel: 618-939-6618; 935-2247.
Catechesis/Religious Programs—Tel: 618-935-2521. Mrs. Cary L. Sondag, D.R.E.

Students 65.

Vienna, Johnson Co., St. Paul, Rev. Edward Balestrieri, Admin.
Res., 2020 State Rte. 146E., 62995. Tel: 618-658-4501.
Catechesis/Religious Programs—Students 46.

Walsh, Randolph Co., St. Pius. Attended by St. Boniface, Evansville. Sr. Diane Marie Turner, S.S.N.D., Pastoral Assoc.
7679 Walsh Rd., P.O. Box 32, 62297. Tel: 618-853-4404.
Catechesis/Religious Programs—Students 33.

Washington Park, St. Clair Co., St. Martin of Tours, Rev. James A. Yoelker.
Res., 771 Vogel Pl., East St. Louis, 62205. Tel: 618-874-0713; 271-6168.
Church—1340 N. 58th St., 62204.

Waterloo, Monroe Co., SS. Peter and Paul, Rev. Francis L. Seyer.
Res., 204 W. Mill St., 62298. Tel: 618-939-6426; Fax: 618-939-5606. [CEM]
School—Tel: 618-939-7217. Mrs. Ruth Rosenhauer, Prin.
Lay Teachers 21; Students 361.
Catechesis/Religious Programs—Lucille Ohms, D.R.E.
Students 240.

Wendelin, Clay Co., Holy Cross, Rev. David L. Braun.
Res., P.O. Star Rte., Newton, 62448. Tel: 618-752-5671. [CEM]
Catechesis/Religious Programs—Students 202.

West Frankfort, Franklin Co., St. John the Baptist, Rev. Brian Barker.
Res., 703 E. Main St., 62896. Tel: 618-932-2828. [CEM]
School—Tel: 618-937-2017. Sr. Lucia Pinski, O.S.F., Prin.
Franciscan Sisters of Our Lady of Perpetual Help 2; Lay Teachers 6; Students 94.
Catechesis/Religious Programs—Kathy Heim, D.R.E.
Students 21.

Willisville, Perry Co., St. Joseph. Attended by St. Elizabeth, Ava.
606 George St., P.O. Box 157, Ava, 62907. Tel: 618-426-3321. [CEM]
Catechesis/Religious Programs—Students 28.

Zeigler, Franklin Co., Sacred Heart. Attended by St. Aloysius, Royalton.
Pecan St., P.O. Box 100, Royalton, 62983. Tel: 618-984-2146.
Catechesis/Religious Programs—Students 11.

Sacramental Records Located In Chancery Archives:

1—St. John's Orphanage, Belleville.
2—Holy Angels Church, East St. Louis.
3—Sacred Heart Church, East St. Louis.
4—St. Adalbert Church, East St. Louis.
5—SS. Cyril and Methodius Church, East St. Louis.
6—St. Elizabeth Church, East St. Louis.
7—St. Henry Church, East St. Louis.
8—St. Mary Church, East St. Louis.
9—St. Thomas Church, Millstadt.
10—St. Augustine Church, East St. Louis.
11—St. Joseph Church, Wetaug.

Chaplains of Correctional Institutions and State Hospitals

Anna. *Anna State Hospital*. Attended from St. Mary Church, Anna. Thomas W. Miller, Chap., Tel: 618-833-5835.

Centralia. *Centralia Correctional Center.* P.O. Box 1266, 62801. Rev. George A. Mauck.

Chester. *Chester Mental Health Center.* P.O. Box 31, 62233. Tel: 618-826-4571. 310 N. Main St., Hecker, 62248. Tel: 618-473-2217. Rev. Ralph L. Haas, Chap.

Harrisburg. *Illinois Youth Center*. Vacant. P.O. Box 300, 62946.

Ina. *Big Muddy River Correctional Center.* 62846. Rev. Donald J. Lenzini, Contact, Tel: 618-438-9941.

Marion. *Federal Maximum Security Prison.* P.O. Box 2000, 62959. Deacon Pat Patterson, Chap., Tel: 618-964-1441.
Veterans Hospital. Attended from St. Joseph, Marion. Vacant.

Menard. *Menard Correctional Center.* P.O. Box 711, 62259. Rev. Leo J. Hayes, Chap., Tel: 618-826-5071.

Vienna. *Dixon Springs Work Camp*. 62995. Rev. Thomas W. Miller, Contact.
Shawnee Correctional Center. Box 400, 62995. Rev. Thomas W. Miller, Chap.
Vienna Correctional Center. Attended from Anna. Rev. Thomas W. Miller, Chap., Tel: 618-833-5835.

Military Chaplains:
Reverend Fathers—
Gegotek, Tadeusz, U.S.N.
Voelker, David A., U.S.A.F.

Special Assignment:
Reverend Fathers—
Geller, Charles H., Fort Stockton, TX
Nall, James M., Rome, IL
Schultze, C. Ray, Las Vegas, NV
Thoonkuzhy, Joseph, Kansas City, KS

Leave of Absence:
Reverend Monsignors—
Schwaegel, Joseph R.
Reverend Fathers—
Chlopecki, Robert J.
Crook, David G.
Harbaugh, Paul E.
Kownacki, Raymond F.
Linnemann, Eugene C.
O'Shea, Robert J.
Peterson, Louis P.
Sebescak, Gary
Unverferth, Steven R.
Vonnahmen, Robert J.

Retired:
Reverend Monsignors—
Driscoll, Maurice F., 228 River Bend Dr., Mobile, AL 36605-3198
Drone, Raphael E., Ch. Col. U.S.A.F., 5723 Worchester Dr., Montgomery, AL 36116
Dunn, Meinrad M., Hincke Residence for Priests, 2620 Lebanon Ave., Belleville, IL 62221
Fellner, John V., Breese Nursing Home, 1155 N. 1st St., Breese, IL 62230
Kuhl, Urban B., Hincke Residence for Priests, 2620 Lebanon Ave., Belleville, IL 62221
McCormick, James R., Hincke Residence for Priests, 2620 Lebanon Ave., Belleville, IL 62221
Nebel, Charles A., Hincke Residence for Priests, 2620 Lebanon Ave., Belleville, IL 62221
Reverend Fathers—
Arentsen, Edwin F., Sense Residence, 2620 Lebanon Ave., Belleville, IL 62221
Arnold, J. Ralph, Hincke Residence for Priests, 2620 Lebanon Ave., Belleville, IL 62221
Bertsche, Conrad J., 6451 Fairlynn Blvd., Yorba Linda, CA 92686
Brandmeyer, William H., 126 Pullen Blvd., Centralia, IL 62801
Braun, Dean E., 101 E. Randolph, Pinckneyville, IL 62274
Dollar, Robert J., 222 S. Third St., Belleville, IL 62220
Feldmann, Jerome W., 14210 Old U.S. Rte. 50, Carlyle, IL, 62231
Gasiunas, John, Shore Plaza Bldg., Apt. 215, 1893 Shore Dr., South Pasadena, FL 33707
Hays, Joseph C., Sense Residence, 2620 Lebanon Ave., Belleville, IL 62221
Hentschel, Cletus B., 5315 W. Main St., Belleville, IL 62223
Iffert, Wilbert J., 147 Juniper Dr., Oak Grove Terrace, Mount Vernon, IL 62864
Kastner, Edwin H., 222 S. Third St., Belleville, IL 62220
Kopff, Herbert C., 4419 Taft, St. Louis, MO 63116
Kribs, Charles R., Jefferson Town Homes, 2686 Elkhill Dr., St. Louis, MO 63125
Lopardo, Vito R., Hincke Residence for Priests, 2620 Lebanon Ave., Belleville, IL 62221
MacPherson, Walter E., 222 S. Third St., Belleville, IL 62220
Malec, Raymond S., Hincke Residence for Priests, 2620 Lebanon Ave., Belleville, IL 62221
Maughan, Michael, S.M.A., Hincke Residence for Priests, 2620 Lebanon Ave., Belleville, IL 62221
Meskenas, Vincent A., St. Isidore Church, 222 Clark Ave., Yuba City, CA 95991
Misho, Lloyd P., Sense Residence, 2620 Lebanon Ave., Belleville, IL 62221
Mueller, Joseph P., Hincke Residence for Priests, 2620 Lebanon Ave., Belleville, IL 62221
Perjak, Edmond J., 210 Pelham Rd., Pier 1, Apt. 108-B, Fort Walton Beach, FL 32547
Podrasky, Michael P., 1500 Hardy St., Eldorado, IL 62930
Ratermann, Jerome B., 303 Hillcrest Dr., Belleville, IL 62286-1203
Reeb, Edward J., 1427 Evergreen Ln., Columbia, IL 62236
Ruggles, John J., P.O. Box 271, Okawville, IL 62271
Stauder, Paul W., Hincke Residence for Priests, 2620 Lebanon Ave., Belleville, IL 62221

Permanent Deacons:
Becker, Robert H.
Boyer, Douglas
Bruening, Paul
Cerneka, Peter
Coates, John
DeWolf, William
Dietz, Donald
Dilley, John P.
Dougherty, Michael
Downen, J. Richard
DuBois, Omer E.
Duff, James P., On Sick Leave
DuPrey, John L.
Gasawski, Julius S., (Retired)
Gillan, Garth J., Leave of Absence
Hauptmann, Carl J., (Retired)
Hempen, John
Horcher, Linus H.
Igel, Joseph H., (Retired)
Karcher, Ronald
Kirchgraber, Robert B., (Retired)
Kronenberger, Ken, (Retired)
Lanter, Robert
Lintker, Andrew
Lippert, Robert
Litteken, Charles
Munie, George J.
Olson, Richard H.
Patterson, Pat
Prien, Richard K.
Rickert, Dennis
Speaks, Charles
Stock, Joseph E.
Stockmann, Gerald E.
Teaff, Joseph
Theis, Francis D., Leave of Absence
Underwood, Thomas
Weilbacher, L. Arthur, Jr., (Retired)

INSTITUTIONS LOCATED IN THE DIOCESE

[A] HIGH SCHOOLS, DIOCESAN

Belleville. *Althoff Catholic High School*, 5401 W. Main St., 62223. Tel: 618-235-1100. Sr. Jan Renz, A.S.C., Prin. Priests 2; Sisters 2; Lay Teachers 50; Students 767.

Breese. *Mater Dei High School*, 900 N. Mater Dei Dr., 62230. Tel: 618-526-7216. Central Catholic High School for Clinton Co. Curt L. Winter, Prin.; Sr. Virginia Kampwerth, P.H.J.C., Asst. Prin., Academics; Dennis Litteken, Asst. Prin., Student Affairs; Rev. Charles W. Tuttle. Priests 1; Sisters 3; Lay Teachers 41; Students 556.

Waterloo. *Gibault Catholic High School*, 501 Columbia Ave., 62298. Tel: 618-939-3883.
E-mail: gboffice@hte.net.
Mr. Daniel J. Brueggeman, Prin.; Revs. Edwin H. Hustedde, Dir. of Devel.; Roger R. Karban. Priests 2; Adorers of the Blood of Christ 1; Lay Teachers 23; Students 328.

[B] ELEMENTARY SCHOOLS

Breese. *All Saints Academy.* (Grades PreK-8), 295 N. Clinton St., 62230. Tel: 618-526-4323. Consolidated schools of Saint Augustine, Saint Dominic parishes, Breese, IL, and St. Anthony Parish, Beckemeyer, IL. Alice Gardner, Prin.; Kelly Koishor, Asst. Prin. Sisters 1; Lay Teachers 25; Students 500.

East St. Louis. *Sister Thea Bowman Catholic School*, 8213 Church Ln., 62203. Tel: 618-397-0316. Mr. Richard Williams, Prin.; Cynthia Rivera, Asst. Prin. Sisters 3; Lay Teachers 12; Students 280.

Fairview Heights. *Elizabeth Ann Seton Catholic School*, 9940 Bunkum Rd., 62208. Tel: 618-398-3011.
E-mail: belveseton@connectinc.com
Consolidated schools of St. Stephen Parish, Caseyville, IL, and Our Lady of the Assumption Parish, Fairview Heights, IL. Sr. Patricia Gravemann, S.S.N.D., Prin. Sisters 2; Lay Teachers 10; Students 212.

[C] DAY CARE CENTERS

Belleville. *Don Bosco Home Children's Center*, 300 N. Church St., 62220. Tel: 618-277-7055. Michele Dain, Dir. Administrative Office, 305 N. Charles St., 62220.
St. Henry Day Care Center, 5301 W. Main St., 62223. Tel: 618-233-3454. Coordinators: Judy Shovlin; Linda Moyer. Children 107.
St. John Children's Home, 2620 Lebanon Ave., 62221. Very Rev. James E. Margason, V.G., Chancery Office, 222 S. Third St., 62220. Tel: 618-277-8181.
St. John Day Care Center, 2620 Lebanon Ave., 62221. Tel: 618-235-6717. Pamela Buettner, Dir. Lay Women 11; Children 80.

EAST ST. LOUIS. *Catholic Day Care Center*, 617 Summit Ave., 62201. Tel: 618-874-7178. Nursery and Kindergarten. Conducted by the Cordi-Marian Sisters. Sr. Gema Juarez, M.C.M., Dir.; Sr. Henrietta Torres, M.C.M., Supr., 2417 Ridge Ave., 62205. Tel: 618-875-1447. Sisters 3; Lay Teachers 14; Children 100.

[D] GENERAL HOSPITALS

BELLEVILLE. *St. Elizabeth Hospital*, 211 S. Third St., 62222. Tel: 618-234-2120; Fax: 618-234-4391
For a complete listing, refer to the Hospitals section.

BREESE. *St. Joseph Hospital*, 9515 Holy Cross Ln., 62230. Tel: 618-526-4511
For a complete listing, refer to the Hospitals section.

CENTRALIA. *St. Mary's Hospital*, 400 N. Pleasant Ave., 62801. Tel: 618-532-6731
For a complete listing, refer to the Hospitals section.

EAST ST. LOUIS. *St. Mary's Hospital*, 129 N. 8th St., 62201. Tel: 618-274-1900
For a complete listing, refer to the Hospitals section.

MOUNT VERNON. *Good Samaritan Regional Health Center*, 605 N. 12th St., 62864. Tel: 618-242-4600
For a complete listing, refer to the Hospitals section.

MURPHYSBORO. *St. Joseph Memorial Hospital*, 2 S. Hospital Dr., 62966. Tel: 618-684-3156
For a complete listing, refer to the Hospitals section.

RED BUD. *St. Clement Health Services*, One St. Clement Blvd., 62278. Tel: 618-282-3831; Fax: 618-282-6101
For a complete listing, refer to the Hospitals section.

[E] HOMES FOR SENIOR CITIZENS

BELLEVILLE. *Charles and Bertha Hincke Residence for Priests and Sense Residence*, 2620 Lebanon Ave., 62221. Tel: 618-234-5722
For a complete listing, refer to the Special Care Facilities section.

Meredith Memorial Home, 16 S. Illinois St., 62220. Tel: 618-233-8780; Fax: 618-233-9602
For a complete listing, refer to the Special Care Facilities section.

Our Lady of the Snows Apartment Community Retirement Home, 726 Community Dr., 62223. Tel: 618-397-6700
For a complete listing, refer to the Special Care Facilities section.

RED BUD. *Maria Care*, 350 W. South First St., 62278. Tel: 618-282-3891
For a complete listing, refer to the Special Care Facilities section.

[F] MONASTERIES AND RESIDENCES OF PRIESTS AND BROTHERS

BELLEVILLE. *Missionary Oblates of Mary Immaculate - St. Henry's Oblate Residence*, 200 N. 60th St., 62223. Tel: 618-233-2991. Revs. Michael S. Deis, O.M.I., Supr. Oblate Community; Ronald Carignan, O.M.I.; Andrew G. Chalkey, O.M.I.; William Clark, O.M.I.; Rene DuFour, O.M.I.; John Ettensohn, O.M.I.; Vincent Fitzgerald, O.M.I.; Urban Figge; Eugene Glaub, O.M.I.; Joseph Knoeber, O.M.I.; Robert Morin, O.M.I.; James E. Taylor, O.M.I.; James J. Wynne, O.M.I.; Bros. David Schell, O.M.I.; Paul Hoemeke, O.M.I.; Francis Sullivan, O.M.I. Priests 12; Brothers 3.

Shrine of Our Lady of the Snows, 442 S. DeMazenod Dr., 62223. Tel: 618-397-6700. Missionary Oblates of Mary Immaculate. Revs. Louis Studer, O.M.I., Dir.; Clarence Zachman, O.M.I., Supr.; Leo Figge, O.M.I.; Floyd B. Boeckman, O.M.I.; Gary Gallagher, O.M.I.; Gabriel Biondolillo, O.M.I.; Zygmunt Dzierzek, O.M.I.; Boniface Wittenbrink, O.M.I.; Robert Braun, O.M.I.; Robert Eimer, O.M.I.; Bro. Lorenzo Williams.

[G] CONVENTS AND RESIDENCES FOR SISTERS

BELLEVILLE. *Hospital Sisters of St. Francis*, 1036 Rutledge Dr., 62221. Tel: 618-235-5486. Sisters 4.

Hospital Sisters of St. Francis, 1000 Royal Heights Rd., Apt. 58, 62223. Tel: 618-233-1687. Sisters 2.

Motherhouse and Novitiate of Ursuline Sisters of Belleville, 1026 N. Douglas Ave., 62220-4198. Tel: 618-235-3444. Sr. Dorothy Helbling, O.S.U., Community Leader. Total Membership of Congregation 18.

Poor Clare Monastery of Our Lady of Mercy, 300 N. 60th St., 62223. Tel: 618-235-4407. Mother Mary Therese, P.C.C., Abbess; Rev. James S. Orumpakkat, C.M.I., Chap. Tel: 618-233-6378. Sisters 8.

CAIRO. *Mary Katherine Convent, Poor Handmaids of Jesus Christ*, 725 22nd St., 62914. Tel: 618-734-0778. Sisters 4.

EAST ST. LOUIS. *St. Mary Convent, Poor Handmaids of Jesus Christ*, 5727 Warren St., 62204. Tel: 618-875-7570. Sisters 2.

MOUNT VERNON. *Franciscan Sisters of Mary Convent*, 4235 Lincolnshire Dr., #3-C, 62864-2164. Tel: 618-244-3091.

RUMA. *Province Center, Adorers of the Blood of Christ, Province of Ruma*, 2 Pioneer Ln., 62278. Tel: 618-282-3848.
E-mail: rumacent@atc.net
Sr. Margaret Mary Kopish, A.S.C., Prov. Supr.; Sr. Ann Frances Gross, A.S.C., Local Admin.; Rev. John J. Joyce, Chap. Sisters 81; Total Membership of the Province 205.

[H] RETREAT HOUSES

BELLEVILLE. *Retreat and Renewal Center*, 700 N. 66th St., 62223-3949. Tel: 618-397-0584; Fax: 618-397-5123. Rev. Robert Aaron, O.M.I.; Bro. William Johnson, O.M.I., Team Moderator; Revs. James Donovan, O.M.I.; Roger Schoenhofen, O.M.I.; David Kraus, O.M.I.; Bro. Victor Capek, O.M.I.

[I] NEWMAN CENTERS

CARBONDALE. *The Newman Center*, Southern Illinois University, 715 S. Washington, 62901. Tel: 618-529-3311.
E-mail: jscarano@siu.edu
Web site: http:/www.siu.edu/~newman
Mr. John Scarano, Diocesan Dir.; Rev. Cecil Pickert, O.Carm., Campus Min.

[J] MISCELLANEOUS LISTINGS

BELLEVILLE. *Althoff Catholic High School Educational Endowment Trust*, 5401 W. Main St., 62223. Tel: 618-235-1100. Sr. Jan Renz, A.S.C., Contact Person.

Ancient Order of Hibernians. 1303 Edgewood Dr., Fairview Heights, 62208. Tel: 618-397-6494. Charles Herr, Pres.

Ancient Order of Hibernians (LAOH). 9773 Holy Cross Rd., Fairview Heights, 62208. Tel: 618-397-0451. Betty Martz, Pres.

Catholic Committee on Scouting of the Diocese of Belleville. 19824 Posen Rd., Nashville, 62263. Tel: 618-336-5414. Rev. James R. Van Oss, Chap.

Catholic Daughters of the Americas. 429 S. Elm St., Centralia, 62801. Tel: 618-532-8352. Miss Mercedes Campbell, Diocesan Chm.

Catholic Knights and Ladies of Illinois, P.O.Box 327, 62222. Tel: 618-233-0286.

Catholic War Veterans, Hincke Residence for Priests, 2620 Lebanon Ave., 62221. Tel: 618-257-1584. Rev. Msgr. Urban B. Kuhl, Chap.

Cursillos in Christianity. Belleville Diocese, 1105 Olive St., 62220. Tel: 618-234-2515. Nick Lang, Lay Dir.

Engaged Encounter, 221 S. 17th St., 62223. Tel: 618-277-1652. Gerry Bach, Coord.; Ann Bach, Coord.

Health Care Endowment Fund of the Reverend Oblate Fathers, 726 Community Dr., 62223. Tel: 618-397-6700.
Oblate Fathers and Trustees. D. Robert McCardle, Admin. & Contact Person. Legal Title: *Health Care Endowment Fund of the Reverend Oblate Fathers at the Shrine of Our Lady of the Snows.*

Missionary Association of Mary Immaculate-Missionary Oblates of Mary Immaculate. Serving the missions of the Missionary Oblates, the National Shrine of Our Lady of the Snows, and the Tekakwitha Indian Missions. 9480 N. De Mazenod Dr., 62223-1160. Tel: 618-398-4848. Rev. Louis B. Studer, O.M.I., Dir.; Mr. William J. Nixon, Exec. Dir.; Mr. William P. O'Connor, Planned Giving Dir. Planned Giving Associates: Revs. Floyd B. Boeckman, O.M.I.; James E. Taylor, O.M.I.; Mrs. Rosalee Cavataio; Mr. Dennis Kempf.

Oblate Preaching Team, 200 N. 60th St., 62223. Tel: 618-233-2991. Specializing in Parish Missions. Revs. John Ettensohn, O.M.I., Dir.; Robert Morin, O.M.I.; Lon Konold, O.M.I.; Deacon Thomas Underwood.

Our Lady of the Snows Layman's Association, 442 DeMazenod Dr., 62223. Tel: 618-397-6700. Mr. Dennis Bielke, Pres.; Rev. Louis B. Studer, O.M.I., Spiritual Mod.

Radio Information Service for Blind and Print Handicapped, 9541 Church Circle Dr., 62223. Tel: 618-397-6700, Ext. 2221; Fax: 618-398-6549. Closed Circuit Radio for the blind and print handicapped. Mr. Joseph E. Kasperek, Exec. Dir.

St. Francis Thrift Shop, 800 E. Main St., 62220. Tel: 618-233-6998. Mrs. Catherine Heap, Mgr.

Scott Air Force Base, Scott AFB Chapel, 375 AW/HC, 320 J St., Bldg. 1620, 62225-5256. Tel: 618-256-3303. Revs. John R. Mulnix, C.P., Col., Senior Catholic Chap.; Robert S. Hochreiter, Major, Chap.; Donald T. Burnet, Lt. Col., Chap.

Secular Franciscan Order, 200 W. Harrison, 62220. Tel: 618-234-1166. St. Peter Fraternity.

Serra Club of St. Clair County, P.O. Box 23017, Dutch Hallow Sta., 62223. Tel: 618-234-2773. Chaplains: Rev. Msgr. Leonard A. Bauer, 16 S. Illinois St., 62220. Rev. Bernard L. Voss, 5315 W. Main St., 62223. Tel: 618-233-2423.

TEC (Teens Encounter Christ), 2620 Lebanon Ave., 62221.

Victorious Missionaries, 442 S. DeMazenod Dr., 62223. Tel: 618-397-6700 (Voice/TDD), Ext. 2281. Spiritual Support Network for people with disabilities. Bro. Francis Sullivan, O.M.I., Natl. Dir.

Western Catholic Union, Br. No. 59, 405 Southgate, 62223. Tel: 618-277-2892. Mr. Marion Mueth, Pres.

Worldwide Marriage Encounter, 8116 Circle Dr., 62223. Tel: 618-398-1614. Executive Couple: Dave & Carol Daly.

BREESE. *Daughters of Isabella*. Precious Blood Circle #718, 248 W. Elm, Aviston, 62216. Tel: 618-228-7372. Miss Amelia Wesselmann, Diocesan Chairperson.

CARLYLE. *Carlyle Priest Center*. Contact the Chancery, Tel: 618-277-8181. R.R. 3, 62231.

DAHLGREN. *Couple to Couple League*. 4934 Itaska, St. Louis, MO, 63109. Tel: 314-481-1908. John & Vicki Wiese, 338 Amy Dr., O'Fallon, 62269. Tel: 618-624-0902. Mike & Denise Terneus, Public Rels.

EAST ST. LOUIS. *St. Mary Hospital of East St. Louis, Illinois Volunteers*, 129 N. 8th St., 62201. Tel: 618-274-1900. Richard Mark, Pres. & CEO.

St. Mary's Hospital Health Foundation, 129 N. 8th St., 62201.
E-mail: ascott@ancilla.org

O'FALLON. *ASC Health Services*, 6 Eagle Center, Ste. 4, 62269. Tel: 618-632-1284. Sr. Mary Louise Degenhart, A.S.C., Exec. Dir.

RED BUD. *Senior Adorers*, 2 Pioneer Ln., 62278. Tel: 618-282-3848. Sr. Irene McGrath, A.S.C., Pres.

RUMA. *World Apostolate of Fatima, The Blue Army, U.S.A.*, 105 W. Mill St., 62278. Tel: 618-282-4108. Rev. John Myler, Spiritual Advisor. Tel: 618-337-4548; Mr. Roger Mathews, Pres.

INCORPORATED CEMETERIES

BELLEVILLE. *Green Mount Catholic Cemetery of the Cathedral Congregation of Belleville.*

BREESE. *St. Dominic Roman Catholic Cemetery of Breese.*

EAST ST. LOUIS. *Holy Cross Cemetery of St. Henry Roman Catholic Church of East St. Louis.*

Mount Carmel Cemetery of St. Patrick Roman Catholic Church.

FAIRVIEW HEIGHTS. *St. Adalbert Association (An Illinois Religious Corporation).*

O'FALLON. *Mount Calvary Cemetery of St. Clare Roman Catholic Congregation.*

VILLA RIDGE. *Calvary Cemetery of St. Patrick Roman Catholic Church of Cairo.*

NECROLOGY

† Baggio, John A., West Frankfort, IL, St. John the Baptist. —Died June 1, 1997.

† Bungay, Eugene L., (Retired). —Died Feb. 1, 1997.

† Sullivan, Rev. Msgr. Bernard O., (Retired). —Died Feb. 24, 1997.

Diocese of Biloxi

(Dioecesis Biloxiiensis)

Most Reverend

JOSEPH LAWSON HOWZE, D.D.

Bishop of Biloxi; ordained May 7, 1959; appointed Titular Bishop of Maxita and Auxiliary of Natchez-Jackson November 8, 1972; ordained Bishop January 28, 1973; appointed Bishop of Biloxi March 1, 1977; installed June 6, 1977. *Mailing Address: P.O. Box 1189, Biloxi, MS, 39533.*

Legal Title: "Catholic Diocese of Biloxi".

ESTABLISHED MARCH 1, 1977.

Square Miles 9,653.

Comprises 17 counties in southern Mississippi: Jackson, Harrison, Hancock, George, Stone, Pearl River, Greene, Perry, Forrest, Lamar, Marion, Walthall, Wayne, Jones, Covington, Jefferson Davis and Lawrence.

For legal titles of parishes and diocesan institutions, consult the Chancery Office.

Chancery Office: 120 Reynoir St., P.O. Box 1189, Biloxi, MS, 39533. Tel.: 601-374-0222; Fax: 601-435-7949.

STATISTICAL OVERVIEW

Personnel	
Bishop	1
Priests: Diocesan Active in Diocese	41
Priests: Active Outside Diocese	1
Priests: Diocesan in Foreign Missions	1
Priests: Retired, Sick or Absent	15
Number of Diocesan Priests	58
Religious Priests in Diocese	27
Extern Priests in Diocese	11
Ordinations:	
Diocesan Priests	2
Permanent Deacons in Diocese	21
Total Brothers	34
Total Sisters	38
Parishes	
Parishes	44
With Resident Pastor:	
Resident Diocesan Priests	35
Resident Religious Priests	7
Without Resident Pastor:	
Administered by Priests	2
Missions	14
Professional Ministry Personnel:	
Brothers	1
Sisters	12
Lay Ministers	8
Welfare	
Homes for the Aged	7
Total Assisted	636
Special Centers for Social Services	6
Total Assisted	101,377
Other Institutions	1
Total Assisted	3,000
Educational	
Diocesan Students in Other Seminaries	6
Total Seminarians	6
High Schools, Diocesan and Parish	4
Total Students	1,232
High Schools, Private	1
Total Students	548
Elementary Schools, Diocesan and Parish	14
Total Students	3,226
Catechesis/Religious Education:	
High School Students	2,174
Elementary Students	4,294
Total Students Under Catholic Instruction	11,480
Teachers in the Diocese:	
Brothers	7
Sisters	19
Lay Teachers	325
Vital Statistics	
Receptions into the Church:	
Infant Baptism Totals	794
Adult Baptism Totals	406
Received into Full Communion	216
First Communions	1,214
Confirmations	631
Marriages:	
Catholic	246
Interfaith	182
Total Marriages	428
Deaths	655
Total Catholic Population	65,524
Total Population	715,740

Office of the Bishop—120 Reynoir St., P.O. Box 1189, Biloxi, 39533. Tel: 228-374-0220.

Vicar General—Rev. Msgr. ANDREW MURRAY, J.C.L., *120 Reynoir St., P.O. Box 1189, Biloxi, 39533.* Tel: 228-374-0222.

Chancery Office—120 Reynoir St., P.O. Box 1189, Biloxi, 39533. Tel: 228-374-0222; Fax: 228-435-7949. Office Hours: Mon.-Fri. 8:30-5 All Offices are at this address unless otherwise noted.

Chancellor—Rev. Msgr. ANDREW MURRAY, J.C.L. Tel: 228-374-0222.

Vice Chancellor—Rev. JOHN R. MCGRATH, J.C.L. Tel: 228-374-0226.

Office for Planning and Development—Deacon ROBERTO JIMENEZ, Dir. Tel: 228-374-2009.

Marriage Tribunal—

Judicial Vicar—Rev. JOHN R. MCGRATH, J.C.L. Tel: 228-374-0226.

Director of the Tribunal—Mr. RICK I. CONASON, J.C.L.

Promotor of Justice—Rev. Msgr. JAMES J. HANNON, J.C.D.

Defenders of the Bond—Rev. Msgr. RONALD P. HERZOG; Rev. Msgr. JAMES P. MCGOUGH, J.C.D.; Rev. THOMAS CONWAY; Deacon JACK HUNTER; Deacon GEORGE SORENSEN.

Pro-Synodal Judges—Rev. Msgr. JAMES J. HANNON, J.C.D.; Rev. Msgr. JAMES P. MCGOUGH, J.C.D.; Rev. JAMES B. TAYLOR.

Advocates—Revs. LOUIS LOHAN; PATRICK MOCKLER.

Canonical Ecclesiastical Notary—Mrs. CLAIRE D. JONES.

Deans—West Coast Deanery: Rev. Msgr. RONALD P. HERZOG; Central Coast Deanery: Rev. Msgr. JAMES P. MCGOUGH, J.C.D.; East Central Coast Deanery: Rev. Msgr. JAMES M. RUSSELL; East Coast Deanery: Rev. GERARD M. CLEARY; Northern Deanery: Rev. THOMAS CONWAY.

Diocesan Attorney—KEVIN J. NECAISE, *P.O. Box 636, Gulfport, 39502.* Tel: 228-864-4345.

Department of Administration and Finance

Comptroller—DANIEL R. BLAKE; MARJORIE GILL, Chief Accountant. Tel: 228-374-0224.

Diocesan Risk Management for Property and Medical—Mr. A. J. SCARDINO, Contact Person. Tel: 228-374-0222; 452-3014.

Catholic Foundation of the Diocese of Biloxi, Inc.—Deacon ROBERTO JIMENEZ, Exec. Dir. Tel: 228-374-2009.

Mission Office—Rev. Msgr. JAMES M. RUSSELL. Tel: 228-374-1717. Rev. Msgr. ANDREW MURRAY. Tel: 228-374-0222.

Department of Communications—

"Gulf Pine Catholic Newspaper"—Rev. Msgr. JAMES M. RUSSELL, Dir. SHIRLEY HENDERSON, Editor. Tel: 228-374-8318.

Radio & Television—SHIRLEY HENDERSON. Tel: 228-374-8318.

Department of Education—

Office of Superintendent of Catholic Schools—Sr. JOANNE COZZI, D.C. Tel: 228-374-0440; 374-0229., *Res., 314 Jim Money Rd., Biloxi, 39531.* Tel: 228-388-8912.

Office of Resource Center—Sr. JOANNE COZZI, D.C., Dir.; Sr. ROSEMARY EICH, C.H.M., Coord. Tel: 228-374-0440.

Office of Special Education—Sr. JOANNE COZZI, D.C.

Office of Religious Education—Sr. JANE WALKER, O.P., Dir., *Res., 164 E. Beach Blvd., Apt. 201, Gulfport, 39507.* Tel: 228-863-6263.

Office of Youth Ministry—BRAGG MOORE, Dir. Tel: 228-436-6046.

Catholic Boy Scouts—ERNEST J. FALGO, JR., *3511 Magnolia St., Pascagoula, 39567.* Tel: 228-762-8174.

Campus Ministry—Rev. MICHAEL TRACEY, Dir., *3117 W. Fourth St., Hattiesburg, 39401.* Tel: 601-264-5192.

Priests' Continuing Education and Retreat Programs—Rev. GREGORY M. BARRAS, Dir., *8343 Woolmarket Rd., Biloxi, 39532.* Tel: 601-392-7500.

Ecumenical & Interreligious Affairs—Sr. JANE WALKER, O.P., Contact Person. Tel: 228-374-0229.

Liturgy, Office of—Rev. Msgr. RONALD P. HERZOG, Dir., *P.O. Box 548, Pass Christian, 39571.* Tel: 228-452-4686.

Renew 2000—MICHAEL B. FABIAN, Dir. Tel: 228-374-8317.

Department of Social and Community Services—120 Reynoir St., P.O. Box 1457, Biloxi, 39533. Tel: 228-374-8316. All offices at this address unless otherwise noted. Legal Title: Catholic Social and Community Services, Inc. Sr. REBECCA RUTKOWSKI, A.C.S.W., Exec. Dir.

Hattiesburg Regional Office—208 S. 25th Ave., Hattiesburg, 39401. Tel: 601-545-1616. VICKI TAYLOR, L.M.S.W., Dir. POLLY SUMRALL, Office Mgr.

Pascagoula Regional Office—3512 Magnolia St., Pascagoula, 39567-3113. Tel: 228-769-8283; 769-8151.

Council of the St. Vincent de Paul Society—Dr. PETER PAVLOV, Pres. Tel: 228-875-5230.

Counseling Services—DENNIS CENAC, L.S.W.

Adoption Services—BRENDA STILES, L.S.W., *2204 24th Ave., Gulfport.* Tel: 228-864-7917.

Emergency Assistance—DELANE KRAUSE; DIANNE

PURSER, *870 Nativity Dr., Biloxi, 39533.* Tel: 228-432-0045; 800-851-3702. JANNIE GREENE FUNCHESS, *208 S. 25th Ave., Hattiesburg, 39401.* Tel: 601-545-1616.

Morning Star Pregnancy Care Center—(Unplanned pregnancy services); NANCY LOFTUS, Maternity Caseworker; ANN RIVERA, Office Mgr., *2204 24th Ave., Gulfport.* Tel: 228-864-4221; 800-570-LOVE.

Respect Life Office—BETH RILEY, Dir. Tel: 228-374-8316.

12 Baskets Food Bank—SHIRLEY HEGGINS, Dir. Tel: 228-374-6884.

Refugee Resettlement—Mrs. MAGDA LELEAUX, Dir., *870 Nativity Dr., Biloxi, 39530.* Tel: 228-374-6507.

Family Life Office—Tel: 228-374-8316.

Catholic Charities Housing Association of Biloxi, Inc.

Santa Maria Retirement Apartments; Villa Maria Retirement Apartments—Most Rev. JOSEPH L. HOWZE, D.D., Pres. Tel: 228-374-0220. Sr. REBECCA RUTKOWSKI, A.C.S.W., Contact Person. Tel: 228-374-8316.

Samaritan Housing, Inc.—Most Rev. JOSEPH L. HOWZE, D.D., Pres. Tel: 228-374-0220. Sr. REBECCA RUTKOWSKI, A.C.S.W., Contact Person. Tel: 228-374-8316.

Notre Dame de la Mer, Inc.—Most Rev. JOSEPH L. HOWZE, D.D., Pres. Tel: 228-374-0220. Sr. REBECCA RUTKOWSKI, A.C.S.W. Tel: 228-374-8316.

Gabriel Manor, Inc.—Most Rev. JOSEPH L. HOWZE, D.D., Pres. Tel: 228-374-0220. Sr. REBECCA RUTKOWSKI, A.C.S.W. Tel: 228-374-8316.

Caritas Manor, Inc.—Most Rev. JOSEPH L. HOWZE, D.D., Pres. Tel: 228-374-0220. Sr. REBECCA RUTKOWSKI, A.C.S.W. Tel: 228-374-8316.

Carlow Manor—Most Rev. JOSEPH L. HOWZE, D.D., Pres. Tel: 228-374-0220. Sr. REBECCA RUTKOWSKI, A.C.S.W. Tel: 228-374-8316.

Gabriel Manor II, Inc.—Most Rev. JOSEPH L. HOWZE, D.D., Pres. Tel: 228-374-8316. Sr. REBECCA RUTKOWSKI, A.C.S.W. Tel: 228-374-8316.

Apostleship of the Sea—Deacon CHARLES L. WALKER; HAROLD SEAMEN, JR.

Vietnamese Apostolate—Rev. DOMINIC PHAN, *St. Michael Church, P.O. Box 523, Biloxi, 39533.* Tel: 228-435-5578.

Prison Apostolate—Deacon VICTOR BAGLIONI, Dir. Tel: 228-475-5437. Jackson County Jails: Deacon THOMAS MILLER; HARRISON COUNTY JAILS: Tel: 228-388-5467. South Mississippi Correctional Facility: Rev. CHARLES C. VENUS, JR.

Diocesan Boards and Committees—

Association of Priests (Diocese of Biloxi and Jackson)—Most Rev. JOSEPH L. HOWZE, D.D., Bishop of Biloxi & Co-Chm.; Most Rev. WILLIAM R. HOUCK, Bishop of Jackson & Co-Chm.; Rev. Msgr. NOEL FOLEY, Pres.; Rev. Msgr. RONALD HERZOG, Sec. & Treas. Trustees: Rev. Msgr. MICHAEL THORNTON; Revs. THOMAS CONWAY; KENT BOWLDS; THOMAS MCGING.

Building and Real Estate Committee—Rev. Msgr. FRANCIS FARRELL, Chm.; LEONARD COLLINS; EDWARD CRAIG; WILLIAM H. CRAIG; H. F. FOUNTAIN, JR.; GERALD HOPKINS; GERALD PORCHE; MARK SEYMOUR; BOB SLAUGHTER.

Catholic Foundation-Diocese of Biloxi—Most Rev. JOSEPH L. HOWZE, D.D., Pres.; Rev. Msgr. ANDREW MURRAY, Vice Pres.; Deacon ROBERTO JIMENEZ, Exec. Dir.; Dr. HARRY SCHMIDT, JR., Chm.; CHARLES HEWES; JOSEPH HUDSON; TED LONGO; DAVID LORD; ALFRED PARKER; MICHAEL PELA; ROBERT TUCEI.

Catholic Housing Board—Most Rev. JOSEPH L. HOWZE, D.D., Pres.; Sr. REBECCA RUTKOWSKI, A.C.S.W., Chm.; Rev. Msgr. ANDREW MURRAY; Rev. BERNARD FARRELL; DANIEL R. BLAKE; SALVADOR DOMINO; MICHAEL FOX; GERALD HOPKINS.

Council of Religious—Sr. JANE WALKER, O.P., Pres., *P.O. Box 1189, Biloxi, 39533.* Tel: 228-374-0229.

Diocesan Counsultors—Rev. Msgr. RONALD P. HERZOG; Rev. Msgr. JAMES P. MCGOUGH, J.C.D.; Rev. Msgr. ANDREW MURRAY; Rev. Msgr. JAMES M. RUSSELL; Revs. THOMAS CONWAY; GERARD M. CLEARY.

Finance Council—Most Rev. JOSEPH L. HOWZE, D.D.; WILLIAM PENEGUY, Chm.; Rev. Msgr. FRANCIS FARRELL; Rev. Msgr. ANDREW MURRAY; RAYMOND HUDACHEK; JOSEPH P. HUDSON; DAVID L. LORD; STEVE MONTAGNET; JOHN P. MYERS; A. J.M. OUSTALET, JR.; DAVID A. TRUETEL.

Insurance Committee—Most Rev. JOSEPH L. HOWZE, D.D.; Dr. LANNY ACOSTA; Sr. JOANNE COZZI, D.C.; Rev. Msgr. RONALD P. HERZOG; Sr. MARY JO MIKE, O.S.F.; Dr. MATTHEW F. MCNULTY, JR., Sc.D.; Sr. REBECCA RUTKOWSKI, A.C.S.W.; STEVE MONTAGNET; Rev. Msgr. ANDREW MURRAY. Advisors: DANIEL R. BLAKE; A. J. SCARDINO, JR.

Mission Board—Most Rev. JOSEPH L. HOWZE, D.D.; Rev. Msgr. ANDREW MURRAY; Rev. Msgr. JAMES M. RUSSELL.

Personnel Board—Rev. Msgr. FRANCIS FARRELL; Rev. Msgr. JOSEPH MERCIER; Rev. Msgr. ANDREW MURRAY; Rev. Msgr. JAMES M. RUSSELL; Rev. KENNETH RAMON-LANDRY.

Presbyteral Council—Most Rev. JOSEPH L. HOWZE, D.D., Pres.; Revs. DENNIS CARVER; GERARD M. CLEARY; BERNARD FARRELL; Rev. Msgr. RONALD P. HERZOG; Rev. WILLIAM KELLY, S.V.D.; Revs. LOUIS LOHAN; ANTONE LYNCH; Rev. Msgr. JAMES P. MCGOUGH, J.C.D.; Revs. JOHN MCGRATH; THOMAS CONWAY; CUTHBERT O'CONNELL; Rev. Msgr. ANDREW MURRAY; Rev. KENNETH RAMON-LANDRY; Rev. Msgr. JAMES M. RUSSELL; Rev. ROBERT SULLIVAN, S.S.J.

Vocations Committee—Most Rev. JOSEPH L. HOWZE, D.D.; Rev. Msgr. JOSEPH MERCIER; Revs. I. ANTHONY ARGUELLES; LOUIS LOHAN; GREGORY M. BARRAS.

Miscellaneous Apostolates—

Campaign for Human Development—Rev. IVAN J. WEIS, Dir., *27074 St. Matthew Church Rd., Perkinson, 39573.*

Catholic Relief Services—Sr. REBECCA RUTKOWSKI, A.C.S.W., *P.O. Box 1457, Biloxi, 39533.*

Catholic University, Friends of—Rev. Msgr. ANDREW MURRAY, *P.O. Box 1189, Biloxi, 39533.*

Charismatic Renewal—Rev. GEORGE KITCHIN, Dir., *4900 Riley Rd., Ocean Springs, 39564.*

Cursillo and Retreats—Rev. DENNIS CARVER, *14595 Vidalia Rd., Pass Christian, 39571.* Tel: 228-255-7560.

Deaf and Disabled, Office of the—RODNEY W. WOODS, Ph.D., Dir., *de l'Epee Deaf Center, Inc., 1450 North St., Gulfport, 39507., Mailing Address: P.O. Box 6918, Gulfport, 39506-6918.* Tel: 228-897-2280 (Voice-TDD); Fax: 228-897-2462.

Latin American Apostolate—Mission-Saltillo, Mexico, co-sponsored with Diocese of Jackson. Rev. Msgr. MICHAEL THORNTON, *Suc. "A" Apdo. 509, Saltillo, Coah., Mexico, C.P., 25000.*

Legion of Mary—Deacon VICTOR A. BAGLIONI, *3855 Riverpine Dr., Moss Point, 39563.*

Permanent Diaconate Program—Deacon MARTIN FINNEGAN, Dir., *5713 Belle Fontaine Dr., Ocean Springs, 39564.* Assoc. Directors: Deacons VICTOR BAGLIONI, (Formation); THOMAS LEBLANC, (Continuing Education & Formation).

Pontifical Association of the Holy Childhood—Rev. Msgr. JAMES M. RUSSELL, Dir., *P.O. Box 367, Biloxi, 39533.*

Propagation of the Faith—Rev. Msgr. JAMES M. RUSSELL, Dir., *P.O. Box 367, Biloxi, 39533.*

Vocations—Rev. Msgr. JAMES M. RUSSELL, Dir., *P.O. Box 367, Biloxi, 39533.* Tel: 228-374-1717.

CLERGY, PARISHES, MISSIONS AND PAROCHIAL SCHOOLS

CITY OF BILOXI
(Harrison County)

1—CATHEDRAL OF THE NATIVITY OF THE BLESSED VIRGIN MARY (1843), Rev. Msgr. James M. Russell, Rector; Rev. Michael E. Snyder; Deacons Rene J. Moniot; Ray DeRosier; Sr. Mary Riordan, R.S.M., Pastoral Assoc. & D.R.E.
Res., 870 Howard Ave., P.O. Box 367, 39533. Tel: 228-374-1717; Fax: 228-374-1773.
School—(Grades K-6). Tel: 228-432-2269. Sr. Mary Jo Mike, O.S.F., Prin.
Nativity 1; Lay Teachers 19; Students 296.
Catechesis/Religious Programs—Students 222.

2—OUR LADY OF FATIMA (1957), Rev. Msgr. Francis Farrell.
Res., 2090 Pass Rd., 39531. Tel: 228-388-3887; Fax: 228-388-7980.
School—(Grades PreK-6) 320 Jim Money Rd., 39531. Tel: 228-388-3609. Sr. Mary Ann Peltier, M.S.C., Prin.
Lay Teachers 16; Students 226.
Catechesis/Religious Programs—Tel: 228-388-5737. Sr. Lynda Rink, D.R.E.
Students 150.

3—OUR MOTHER OF SORROWS (1914) (African American), Rev. Peter O. Quinn (JKS).
Res., 803 Division St., 39530. Tel: 228-436-6503.

4—SACRED HEART (1921), Rev. Patrick M. McDermott. In res., Rev. Denis Harlow; Rev. Msgr. Andrew Murray.
Res., 10446 Le Moyne Blvd., 39532. Tel: 228-392-4526.
School—(Grades PreK-6). Tel: 228-392-4180. Sr. Joan Landry, R.S.M., Prin.
Sisters of Mercy 4; Lay Teachers 8; Students 185.
Catechesis/Religious Programs—Tel: 228-392-4180. Sr. Julia Marie Burke, R.S.M., D.R.E.
Students 462.

5—ST. JOHN (1922), Rev. I. Anthony Arguelles.
Res., 724 Bradford St., 39530. Tel: 228-374-0116; 0117.
Catechesis/Religious Programs—Tel: 228-374-1717.
Students 53.

6—ST. LOUIS (1957), Rev. I. Anthony Arguelles. In res., Rev. Msgr. Kevin Bambrick.
Res., 425 Division St., 39530. Tel: 228-432-7735.

7—ST. MARY (1973), Rev. Greg Barras.
Res., 8343 Woolmarket Rd., 39532. Tel: 228-392-7500; Fax: 228-392-1999.
Catechesis/Religious Programs—Tel: 228-392-1999.
Students 160.

8—ST. MICHAEL (1917), Revs. Patrick O'Shaughnessy; Dominic Phan, Dir. Vietnamese Apostolate.
Res., 177 First St., P.O. Box 523, 39533. Tel: 228-435-5578; Fax: 228-435-5579.

OUTSIDE THE CITY OF BILOXI

Bassfield, Jefferson Davis Co., St. Peter (1904) (Irish), Rev. Cuthbert O'Connell; Deacon Robert Everard.
Res., P.O. Box 10, 39421. Tel: 601-943-5104. [CEM 2][JC 2]
Catechesis/Religious Programs—Tel: 601-943-6259. Mrs. Mary E. Coulter, D.R.E.
Students 119.
Missions—Carson, Jefferson Davis Co., St. Elizabeth; Prentiss, Jefferson Davis Co., St. Mary's.

Bay St. Louis, Hancock Co., Our Lady of the Gulf (1847), Revs. Peter F. Mockler (Ireland); Anthony Doan Tran (Vietnamese). In res., Rev. John T. O'Brien, (Retired).
Res., 228 S. Beach Blvd., P.O. Box 208, 39520-0208. Tel: 228-467-6509; Fax: 228-467-6509. [CEM]
School—Bay St. Louis Catholic Elementary, (Grades PreK-6). Tel: 228-467-5158. Mrs. Myrna Jordan, Prin.
Lay Teachers 18; Students 355.
High School—Tel: 228-467-7048. Sr. Donella Hartman, Prin.
Sisters 3; Lay Teachers 18; Students 235.
Catechesis/Religious Programs—Students 275.

St. Rose De Lima (1926) (African American), Rev. A. Francis Theriault, S.V.D.
Res., 301 S. Necaise Ave., 39520. Tel: 228-467-7347.
Catechesis/Religious Programs—Tel: 228-466-2769. Mrs. Joan Thomas, D.R.E.
Students 91.

Clermont Harbor, Hancock Co., St. Ann (1915), Rev. John J. Kelly.
Res., 5858 Lower Bay Rd., P.O. Box 1037, Lakeshore, 39558-1037. Tel: 228-467-4746.
Catechesis/Religious Programs—Anna Medley, D.R.E.
Students 122.
Mission—Lakeshore, Hancock Co., St. John.

Columbia, Marion Co., Most Holy Trinity (1959), Rev. Tommy Conway.
Res., 1429 N. Park Ave., 39429. Tel: 601-736-3136.
Catechesis/Religious Programs—Tel: 601-736-8787. D.R.E.: Sharon Rogers, (Holy Trinity); Betty Smet, (St. Paul the Apostle).
Students 84.
Mission—Tylertown, Walthall Co., St. Paul the Apostle, 702 Union Rd., Tylertown, 39667. Tel: 228-876-6422.

DeLisle, Harrison Co., The Catholic Church in DeLisle (1874), Rev. Walter O'Donnell, S.T.; Bro. Senan Gallagher, S.T., Pastoral Assoc.; Deacon Regis Brennan.
Res., 25220 St. Stephen Rd., 39571. Tel: 228-255-1294; Fax: 228-255-7479.
Catechesis/Religious Programs—Students 323.
Missions—Dubuisson, Harrison Co., St. Ann, Vidalia Rd., 39571.; Rotten Bayou, Harrison Co., St. William, Edwin Ladner Rd., 39571.

Gautier, Jackson Co., St. Mary (1968), Rev. Patrick Hayes; Deacon Patrick Houghton.
Res., 809 De La Pointe Rd., P.O. Box 151, 39553. Tel: 228-497-2364.
Catechesis/Religious Programs—Bonnie Bond, D.R.E.
Students 134.

Gulfport, Harrison Co.,

1—ST. ANN, (1939), Rev. Fintan J. Kilmurray.
Res., 23529 Hwy. 53, 39503. Tel: 228-832-2560.
Catechesis/Religious Programs—Tel: 228-831-9452. Robert Earl Lizana, D.R.E.
Students 21.
Mission—Delmas Dedeaux, Harrison Co., Our Lady of Chartres.

2—ST. JAMES, (1898), Rev. Msgr. James P. McGough; Rev. Todd Dominick Fullam; Deacon John R. Henderson.
Res., 366 Cowan Rd., P.O. Box 7267, 39506. Tel: 228-896-6059; Fax: 228-896-6095. [CEM]
School—(Grades PreK-6). Tel: 228-896-6631; Fax:

228-896-6638. Sr. Rita Murray, R.S.M., Prin. Sisters of Mercy (Ennis, Ireland) 4; Lay Teachers 11; Students 218.
Catechesis/Religious Programs—Tel: 228-896-4579. Mr. Robert Russo, D.R.E.
Students 233.

3—St. John the Evangelist, (1900), Rev. Thomas White. In res., Rev. Clement Kovacsik, S.T.
Res., 2414 17th St., P.O. Box 970, 39501. Tel: 228-864-2272; Fax: 228-864-2273.
School—(Grades PreK-6). Tel: 228-863-1606; Fax: 228-863-9677. Patty Zupko, Prin.
Presentation Sisters 1; Lay Teachers 27; Students 298.
High School—Tel: 228-863-8343; Fax: 228-864-2788. Lanny Acosta, Prin.
Lay Teachers 31; Students 430.
Catechesis/Religious Programs—D.R.E.: Sr. Lelia O'Sullivan; Kimberly Goodson.
Students 45.

4—St. Joseph Catholic Church, (Northwood Hills) (1966), Rev. Antone J. Lynch; Deacon Jack Hunter.
Res., 12290 DePew Rd., 39503. Tel: 228-832-3244; 832-1166; Fax: 228-832-1166.
Catechesis/Religious Programs—Mrs. Bernice Engel, D.R.E.
Students 100.

5—St. Therese, (1932) (African American), Rev. John J. O'Rourke, S.S.J.
Res., 3521 19th St., 39501. Tel: 228-863-0624.
Catechesis/Religious Programs—Tel: 228-863-7719. Judy Lombard Whitfield, D.R.E.
Students 106.

Hattiesburg, Forrest Co., Holy Rosary (1949) (African American), Rev. William Vollor.
Res., 900 Dabbs St., 39401. Tel: 601-584-6528; Fax: 601-584-9533.

Sacred Heart (1900), Rev. George Murphy.
Res., 313 Walnut St., P.O. Box 1027, 39401. Tel: 601-583-9404; Fax: 601-583-9486.
School—(Grades PreK-7). Tel: 601-583-8683; Fax: 601-582-2470. Sr. Sharon Friedrich, M.S.C., Prin. Sisters 1; Lay Teachers 8; Students 208.
Catechesis/Religious Programs—Tel: 601-583-9404. Sr. Mary Anne Poeschl, R.S.M., D.R.E.
Students 302.

St. Thomas Aquinas (1968). (University of Southern Mississippi-Student Parish). Rev. Michael J. Tracey.
Res., 3117 W. Fourth St., 39401. Tel: 601-264-5192; Fax: 601-264-0834.
Catechesis/Religious Programs—Tel: 601-261-9627. Mary Coghlan, D.R.E.
Students 141.
Station—Danforth Chapel, U.S.M. (University of Southern Mississippi-Student Parish). Sr. Annette Seymour, R.S.M., Campus Min.

Kiln, Hancock Co., Annunciation (1869), Rev. Henry McInerney; Deacon Lucien Moragas.
Res., P.O. Box 97, 39556. Tel: 228-255-1800; Fax: 228-255-1800.
Catechesis/Religious Programs—Tel: 228-255-1869. Ms. Jean Bruneau, D.R.E.
Students 162.

Laurel, Jones Co., Immaculate Conception (1887), Rev. Kenneth Ramon-Landry; Mrs. Suzie Middleton, Youth Min.
Res., 833 W. Sixth St., 39440. Tel: 601-426-3473.
School—(Grades PreK-6). Tel: 601-428-0129; Fax: 601-428-2056. Sr. Jacqueline Tarrant, R.S.M., Prin. Religious 1; Lay Teachers 12; Students 167.
Catechesis/Religious Programs—Tel: 601-426-3473.
Students 111.
Convent—610 N. Eighth Ave., 39440. Tel: 601-426-2610.

Long Beach, Harrison Co., St. Thomas the Apostle (1903), Rev. Louis Lohan; Sr. Mary Anne O'Brien, Pastoral Assoc.; Deacon Bob Jones.
Res., 720 E. Beach Blvd., 39560. Tel: 228-863-1610; Fax: 228-868-6068.
School—(Grades PreK-6). Tel: 228-863-6876. Mrs. J. B. Pike, Prin.
Lay Teachers 8; Students 168.
Catechesis/Religious Programs—Tel: 228-868-3774. Sr. Consilio Buckley, D.R.E.
Students 520.

Lumberton, Lamar Co., Our Lady of Perpetual Help (1922), Rev. Clark Bearden; Mrs. Katie Murphy, Pastoral Assoc.
Res., 379 W. Seneca Rd., 39455-9519. Tel: 601-796-3051 (Office); 769-3053 (Rectory). [CEM]
Catechesis/Religious Programs—Students 88.
Mission—Poplarville, Pearl River Co., St. Joseph, P.O. Box 202, Poplarville, 39470. Tel: 601-795-4471.

Moss Point, Jackson Co., St. Joseph (1950), Rev. Dominick Fullum; Deacons Victor A. Baglioni; Emery E. Elder.
Res., 4114 First St., P.O. Box 8549, 39562-8549. Tel: 228-475-0777; Fax: 228-475-3672.
Catechesis/Religious Programs—D.R.E.: Mrs. Triss Elder, (St. Joseph), Tel: 228-475-3449; Mrs. Rhonda Boudreaux, (St. Ann), Tel: 228-588-6736.
Students 129.
Mission—Hurley, Jackson Co., St. Ann, P.O. Box 8549, 39562-8549.

Ocean Springs, Jackson Co., St. Alphonsus (1860), Revs. Bernard Farrell; Gary Michael Nance; Deacon Thomas Miller.
Res., 502 Jackson Ave., 39564. Tel: 228-875-5419.
School—(Grades PreK-6). Tel: 228-875-5329; Fax: 228-875-3458. Sherrie McAllister, Prin.
Lay Teachers 21; Students 321.
Catechesis/Religious Programs—Tel: 228-872-2652. Sr. Eileen Lowney, D.R.E.
Students 375.

St. Elizabeth Ann Seton (1975), Rev. George Kitchin; Deacon Tom Le Blanc, Pastoral Assoc.
Res., 4900 Riley Rd., 39564. Tel: 228-875-0654.
Catechesis/Religious Programs—Deacon Martin Finnegan, D.R.E.
Students 210.

Pascagoula, Jackson Co., Our Lady of Victories (1855), Rev. Gerard Cleary.
Res., 510 Convent St., P.O. Box 368, 39568. Tel: 228-762-1653.
Catechesis/Religious Programs—Tel: 228-762-1227. Michele Hill, D.R.E.
Students 95.

Sacred Heart (1963), Rev. Michael Kelleher; Sr. Audrey Mae Kihnemann, S.S.N.D., Pastoral Assoc.; Deacon Warren Goff. In res., Rev. James B. Taylor, (Retired).
Mailing Address: P.O. Box 2190, 39569. Tel: 228-762-1837.
Res., 3702 Quinn Dr., 39581. Tel: 228-762-1837.
School—Resurrection School-Elementary, (Grades PreK-5) 3704 Quinn Dr., 39581-2356. Tel: 228-762-7207; Fax: 228-762-0611. Jean Pisors, Prin.
Lay Teachers 14; Students 290.
Catechesis/Religious Programs—Tel: 228-762-3764. Mrs. Kathleen Parker, D.R.E.
Students 88.

St. Peter the Apostle (1907) (African American), Rev. Robert Sullivan, S.S.J.
Res., 1715 Telephone Rd., P.O. Box 876, 39567. Tel: 228-762-1759; Fax: 228-762-1759.
School—(Grades K-6). Tel: 228-762-3766. Sr. Bernadette McNamara, S.H.Sp., Prin.
Servants of the Holy Spirit 3; Lay Teachers 8; Students 89.
Catechesis/Religious Programs—Tel: 228-762-1759. Mrs. Edna Fields, D.R.E.
Students 137.

Pass Christian, Harrison Co., Our Mother of Mercy (1911) (African American), Revs. Batholomew Enslow, S.S.J.; John Osom, M.S.P.
Res., 222 E. Railroad Ave., 39571. Tel: 228-452-4514; Fax: 228-452-4514. [JC]
Catechesis/Religious Programs—Tel: 228-452-7711.
Students 106.
Convent—251 Saucier Ave., P.O. Box 157, 39571.

Sacred Heart (Dedeaux) (1967), Rev. Dennis Carver; Deacon Roberto Jiminez.
Res., 14595 Vidalia Rd., 39571. Tel: 228-255-7453; Fax: 228-255-7560.
Catechesis/Religious Programs—Students 157.
Station—Cursillo Center, Tel: 228-255-7560.
Students 160.

St. Paul (Dedeaux) (1847), Rev. Msgr. Ronald P. Herzog; Deacon George Sorensen, (Retired).
Res., 140 E. Beach Blvd., P.O. Box 548, 39571. Tel: 228-452-4686; Fax: 228-452-5488. [CEM]
School—(Grades PreK-6). Tel: 228-452-7359. Mrs. Myrna Bourgeois, Prin.
; Lay Teachers 17; Students 163.
Catechesis/Religious Programs—Students 48.

Pearlington, Hancock Co., St. Joseph (1939), Rev. Dominic Cangemi, S.T., Ph.D.
Mailing Address: P.O. Box 39, 39572. Tel: 228-533-7968. [JC]

Picayune, Pearl River Co., St. Charles Borromeo (1950), Rev. John Noone.
Res., 321 Juniper St., 39466. Tel: 601-798-4779; Fax: 601-798-4779.
Catechesis/Religious Programs—Dorothy Ducote, D.R.E.
Students 270.

Pineville, Harrison Co., Our Lady of Lourdes (Pass Christian) (1973), Rev. Robert M. Shay, S.T.
Mailing Address: P.O. Box 508, Pass Christian, 39571. Tel: 228-452-7132.
Res., 22342 Evangeline Rd., Pass Christian, 39571. Tel: 228-452-7132.

Vancleave, Jackson Co., Catholic Church of the Holy Spirit (1980), Rev. John McGrath.
Res., P.O. Box 5032, 39564. Tel: 228-826-4256.
Catechesis/Religious Programs—Students 181.
Mission—Latimer, Jackson Co., Christ the King, 10601 Daisy Vestry, Latimer, 39565. Tel: 228-392-0340.

Waveland, Hancock Co., St. Clare (1919), Rev. Noel Fannon.
Res., 236 S. Beach Blvd., P.O. Box 500, 39576. Tel: 228-467-9275.
School—Ms. Harriet Bellone, Prin. Lay Teachers 8; Students 180.
Catechesis/Religious Programs—Mrs. Andrew Scafidi, D.R.E.
Students 150.

Waynesboro, Wayne Co., St. Bernadette (1977), Rev. Ken Ramon Landry.
Res., 401 Mississippi Dr., 39367. Tel: 601-735-9420. [JC]
Catechesis/Religious Programs—Students 14.
Mission—Leakesville, Holy Trinity.

White Cypress, Hancock Co., St. Matthew the Apostle (1982), Rev. Ivan Weis.
Res., 27074 St. Matthew Church Rd., Perkinston, 39573. Tel: 228-255-7720.
Catechesis/Religious Programs—Students 180.

Wiggins, Stone Co., St. Francis Xavier (1961), Rev. Patrick J. Mockler.
Res., 1200 Hwy. 26 E., P.O. Box 566, 39577. Tel: 601-928-2182; Fax: 601-928-2182.
Church—Tel: 601-947-9756.
Catechesis/Religious Programs—Students 85.
Mission—Lucedale, George Co., St. Lucy, CB6308, Lucedale, 39452. Tel: 601-947-9968. Deacon Caruba L. Merrill.
Station—Perkinston Junior College.

Chaplains of Public Institutions

Biloxi. *Biloxi Regional Hospital, Gulf Coast Community Hospital*. Rev. Denis Harlow.
Keesler Airforce Base. Revs. Richard Munsell, Maj.; Paul Stewart, Capt.; Arthur Lee, Capt.
V.A. Center. Revs. Frank Popeleski; Joseph Dilettuso.

Columbia. *Industrial and Training School*. Rev. Thomas Conway.

Gulfport. *Naval Const. Bn. Center*. Rev. Jerry Kienzle, Cdr.
U.S. Naval Home. Rev. Clement Kovascik, S.T.
V.A. Hospital. Revs. Frank Popeleski; Joseph Dilettuso.

Hattiesburg. *University of Southern Mississippi*. Rev. Michael J. Tracey.

Leakesville. *South Mississippi Correctional Institution*. Rev. Charles C. Venus, Jr.

Special Assignment:
Reverend Fathers—
Dilettuso, Joseph, Veterans Affairs Hospital, Biloxi, MS 39531

Military Chaplains:
Reverend Fathers—
Higginbotham, Robert, U.S.A.F.

Retired:
Reverend Monsignors—
Bambrick, Kevin
Hannon, James J.
Johnson, Gregory
Mercier, Joseph
Reverend Fathers—
Filipich, Nicholas
Izral, John
Kavanagh, Morgan
Kozak, Remigius A.
O'Brien, John
Scott, Francis
Taylor, James B.

Permanent Deacons:
Baglioni, Victor A., St. Joseph, Moss Point
DesRosier, Raymond, Nativity B.V.M. Cathedral, Biloxi
Elder, Emery, St. Joseph, Moss Point
Everard, Robert, St. Peter, Bassfield
Finnegan, Martin, St. Elizabeth Seton, Ocean Springs
Gaule, Harold, St. Charles Borromeo, Picayune
Goff, Warren P., Sr., Sacred Heart, Pascagoula
Henderson, John R., St. James, Gulfport
Houghton, Patrick, St. Mary, Gautier
Hunter, Jack, St. Joseph, Gulfport
Jimenez, Roberto, Sacred Heart, Pass Christian
Jones, Bob, St. Thomas, Long Beach
LeBlanc, Tom, St. Elizabeth Seton, Ocean Springs
Merrill, Caruba L., St. Lucy, Lucedale
Miller, Thomas M., St. Alphonsus, Ocean Springs
Moniot, Rene Joseph, Nativity of the Blessed Virgin Mary, Biloxi

Moragas, Lucien F., Jr., Annunciation, Kiln
Sorensen, George, St. Paul, Pass Christian
Stockert, Al, Catholic Church of the Holy Spirit, Vancleave
Walker, Charles L., St. John the Evangelist, Gulfport

INSTITUTIONS LOCATED IN THE DIOCESE

[A] SEMINARIES, RELIGIOUS OR SCHOLASTICATES

BAY ST. LOUIS. *St. Augustine's*, 199 Seminary Dr., 39520. Tel: 228-467-6414; Fax: 228-466-4393. The Society of the Divine Word. Retreat Center. Tel: 228-467-9837. Very Rev. Michael Sucharski, S.V.D., Rector; Bro. Richard Chambers, S.V.D., Fin. Admin.; Rev. William Kelley, S.V.D., Retreat Dir., Media Production Center. Tel: 228-467-1097. Rev. James Pawlicki, S.V.D., Dir. Media Production Center. In res. Revs. John Kersten, S.V.D.; William Kelley, S.V.D.; Arthur Winters, S.V.D.; Robert Kelly, S.V.D.; James Pawlicki, S.V.D.; Stephen Schuler, S.V.D.; William Halvey, S.V.D.; John LaBauve, S.V.D.; Thaddeus Boucrees, S.V.D.; Pete Smits, S.V.D. Priests 11. Bros. Joachim Brignac, S.V.D.; Paul Lengyel, S.V.D.; Lawrence Morton, S.V.D.; James Heeb, S.V.D.; Richard Chambers, S.V.D.; Michael Decker, S.V.D. Brothers 6.

[B] HIGH SCHOOLS, INTERPAROCHIAL

BILOXI. *Mercy Cross Inter-Parochial High School.* (Grades 7-12). (Coed; includes junior high school), 390 Crusader Dr., 39530. Tel: 228-374-4145; Fax: 228-374-8119. Martha Watjus, Ed.D., Prin. Lay Teachers 28; Students 360.

BAY ST. LOUIS. *Our Lady's Academy.* (Grades 7-12). (Girls), 222 S. Beach Blvd., 39520-4320. Tel: 228-467-7048; Fax: 228-467-1666.
E-mail: OLASTAFF@datasync.com
Web site: http:www:datasynd.com/~ola
Sr. Mary Donella Hartman, R.S.M., Prin. Sisters of Mercy 3; Lay Teachers 18; Students 235.

GULFPORT. *St. John Inter-Parochial High School.* (Coed), 620 Pass Rd., 39501-6494. Tel: 228-863-8141; Fax: 228-864-2788. Dr. Lanny J. Acosta, Prin. Lay Teachers 29; Students 450.

PASCAGOULA. *Resurrection School-Jr. / Sr. School.* (Coed), P.O. Box 1267, Watts & Magnolia, 39568. Sr. Richard Marie Burke, S.S.N.D., Prin. Religious 2; Lay Teachers 18; Students 198.

[C] HIGH SCHOOLS AND ELEMENTARY SCHOOLS, DIOCESAN

BAY ST. LOUIS. *St. Stanislaus College*, P.O. Box 8001, 39521-8001. Tel: 228-467-9057; Fax: 288-466-2972.
E-mail: ssc@datasync.com
Web site: http://wwwsync.com/~ssc
Boys boarding and day school, secondary and elementary. Brothers of the Sacred Heart. Bros. Donnan Berry, S.C., Pres.; Ronald Talbot, S.C., Prin.; Noel Lemmon, S.C., Dir. Admissions. Brothers 26; Lay Teachers 43; Students 580.

[D] HOUSING FOR THE ELDERLY

BILOXI. *Gabriel Manor*, 2321 Atkinson Rd., 39531. Tel: 228-388-1013; Fax: 228-388-1176
For a complete listing, refer to the Special Care Facilities section.

Santa Maria Retirement Apartments, 674 Beach, 39530. Tel: 228-432-1289; Fax: 228-435-0380.
E-mail: santa.maria.del.mar@worldnet.attnet
For a complete listing, refer to the Special Care Facilities section.

BAY ST. LOUIS. *Notre Dame de la Mer Retirement Apartments*, 292 Hwy. 90, 39520. Tel: 228-467-2885; Fax: 228-466-6300
For a complete listing, refer to the Special Care Facilities section.

GULFPORT. *Carlow Manor*, 15195 Barbara Dr., 39503. Tel: 228-539-0707; Fax: 228-539-0704
For a complete listing, refer to the Special Care Facilities section.

OCEAN SPRINGS. *Samaritan House*, 642 Jackson Ave., 39564. Tel: 228-875-1087; Fax: 228-872-9500
For a complete listing, refer to the Special Care Facilities section.

Villa Maria Retirement Apartments, 921 Porter Ave., 39564. Tel: 228-875-8811; Fax: 228-875-8889
For a complete listing, refer to the Special Care Facilities section.

PETAL. *Caritas Manor*, 145 W. 10th Ave., 39465. Tel: 601-545-7744; Fax: 601-545-7740
For a complete listing, refer to the Special Care Facilities section.

[E] MONASTERIES AND RESIDENCES OF PRIESTS AND BROTHERS

BILOXI. *St. John Neumann Residence*, 1044 Beach Blvd., 39530. Tel: 228-374-1800. Redemptorists. Revs. Matthew J. Kerschen, C.Ss.R., Supr.; Albert Babin, C.Ss.R.; Warren Drinkwater, C.Ss.R.; Joseph Elworthy, C.Ss.R.; John A. Hensgen, C.Ss.R.; Edward C. Cosgrove, C.Ss.R.; Earl Toups, C.Ss.R.; Joseph Armshaw, C.Ss.R.

BAY ST. LOUIS. *Media Production Center "In A Word"*, 199 Seminary Dr., 39520. Tel: 228-467-1097; Fax: 228-466-4393.
E-mail: editor@inaword.com
Web site: http:www.inaword.com
Rev. James Pawlicki, S.V.D., Dir. & Editor.

Saint Stanislaus Community, 304 S. Beach Blvd., P.O. Box 8001, 39521-8001. Tel: 228-466-3419; 466-3411.
E-mail: bros@datasync.com
Brothers of the Sacred Heart. Bro. Xavier Werneth, S.C., Dir. Total in Residence 21.

Southern Province of St. Augustine - Provincial Residence, 201 Ruella Ave., 39520. Tel: 228-467-4322; Fax: 228-466-5618. Society of the Divine Word. Very Rev. Clifton Labbe, S.V.D., Prov.; Rev. Thomas James, S.V.D., Prov.; Bro. Richard Chambers, S.V.D., Treas.

Province Development Office. Tel: 228-467-3815. Rev. Robert Kelly, S.V.D., Dir.

Retreats. Tel: 228-467-9837. Rev. William Kelley, S.V.D. Priests 51; Brothers 9; Parishes 23; Mission Stations 3; Elementary Schools 5.

WAVELAND. *Brothers of the Sacred Heart*, 126 Bienville St., 39576. Tel: 228-463-0282. Bro. Adrian Gaudin, S.C., Dir. Total in Residence 4.

[F] CONVENTS AND RESIDENCES FOR SISTERS

BILOXI. *Congregation of Humility of Mary*, 126 Reynoir St., Apt. No. 2, 39530. Sr. Rose Mary Eich, C.H.M.

Our Lady of Fatima Convent, 314 Jim Money Rd., 39531. Tel: 228-388-8912. Marianite of Holy Cross 1; Sisters of the Living Word 1; Daughter of Charity 1; Total Staff 3.

Sisters of Mercy Convent, 11454 Spring Ln., 39532. Tel: 228-392-2575. Sr. M. Aimee Starks, R.S.M., Contact Person. Religious Sisters of Mercy of the Americas 5.

GULFPORT. *Eucharistic Missionaries of St. Dominic*, 164 E. Beach Blvd., Apt. 201, 39507. Tel: 228-863-6263. Other Address: Seashore Manor, 1450 Beach Blvd., Apt. 221, Biloxi, 39530. Tel: 228-432-8698. Sr. Catherine Marie Drawe, O.P., Pres.

Sisters of Mercy - St. James Convent, 366 Cowan Rd., 39507. Tel: 228-896-3277. Sisters of Mercy of the Americas. Sr. Susan Carr, R.S.M.; Sr. Anna Quinlan, R.S.M.; Sr. Eileen Lowney, R.S.M. Sisters of Mercy (Ireland) 2. Other Addresses: 15 Lafayette Pl., 39507. Tel: 228-896-5598. Sr. Rita Murray, R.S.M.; Sr. Rose Fennesy, R.S.M.; Sr. Kathleen Byrne, R.S.M. Sisters 3. 2805 Oakridge Cir., 39507. Tel: 228-896-6302. Sr. Mary Riordan, R.S.M.; Sr. Kathleen Curtin, R.S.M.; Sr. Therese O'Connor, R.S.M.; Sr. Teresa McNamara, R.S.M. Sisters 4.

HATTIESBURG. *Sisters For Christian Community*, #4 North Ln., 39402. Tel: 601-264-9307.

LONG BEACH. *Congregation of the Holy Rosary.* (Vietnamese), 5122 N. Gates Ave., 39560. Tel: 228-863-3045. Sisters 4; Aspirants 15.

Presentation Convent, 18091 Commission Rd., 39560. Tel: 228-864-8418. Union of the Sisters of the Presentation of the Blessed Virgin Mary.

PASCAGOULA. *Emmaus Community*, 5507 LeMans Cir., 39581. Tel: 228-762-8401. School Sisters of Notre Dame 2.

St. Peter the Apostle Convent, 1703 Telephone Rd., 39567. Sisters of the Holy Spirit and Mary Immaculate Consensus Community Sisters 3; Total Staff 10; Total in Residence 3.

WAVELAND. *St. Clare Convent*, 234 S. Beach Blvd., 39576. Tel: 228-467-7071.

[G] NEWMAN CENTERS

HATTIESBURG. *University of Southern Mississippi*, St. Thomas Aquinas Chapel, 3117 W. Fourth St., 39401. Rev. Michael J. Tracey, Chap.

LAUREL. *c/o Immaculate Conception Church*, 833 W. Sixth St., 39440. Rev. Kenneth Ramon-Landry, Chap.

[H] MISCELLANEOUS

BILOXI. *Gabriel Manor II, Inc.*, c/o The Catholic Diocese of Biloxi, P.O. Box 1189, 39533. Tel: 228-374-8316; 374-0220. Most Rev. Joseph Lawson Howze, D.D., Pres.; Sr. Rebecca Rutkowski, A.C.S.W., Contact Person.

Magnificat - Mississippi Gulf Coast Chapter, 154 Azalea Dr., 39530. Tel: 228-374-5685. Mrs. Wilhelmine "Billie" Marie Biasi, Contact Person.

BAY ST. LOUIS. *SSC Progression Corporation*, 304 S. Beach Blvd., 39520. Tel: 228-466-3401. Patricia A. Modenbach, Pres.

Camp Stanislaus. Tel: 228-466-3418. Bro. Lee Barker, Pres.

RELIGIOUS INSTITUTES OF MEN REPRESENTED IN THE DIOCESE

For further details refer to the corresponding bracketed number in the Religious Institutes of Men or Women section.

[1100]—*Brothers of the Sacred Heart.*—S.C.
[1330]—*Congregation of the Mission (Southern Prov.).*—C.M.
[0840]—*Missionary Servants of the Most Holy Trinity.*—S.T.
[1070]—*Redemptorist Fathers.*—C.Ss.R.
[0700]—*St. Joseph's Society of the Sacred Heart.*—S.S.J.
[0420]—*Society of the Divine Word.*—S.V.D.

RELIGIOUS INSTITUTES OF WOMEN REPRESENTED IN THE DIOCESE

[2100]—*Congregation of the Humility of Mary.*—C.H.M.
[2410]—*Congregation of the Marianites of Holy Cross.*—M.S.C.
[1920]—*Congregation of the Sisters of the Holy Cross.*—C.S.C.
[0760]—*Daughters of Charity of St. Vincent de Paul.*—D.C.
[]—*Daughters of Our Lady of the Holy Rosary.*—F.M.S.R.
[1070-11]—*Dominican Sisters.*—O.P.
[1140]—*Eucharistic Missionaries of St. Dominic.*—O.P.
[2575]—*Institute of the Sisters of Mercy of the Americas.*—R.S.M.
[2790]—*Missionary Servants of the Most Blessed Trinity.*—M.S.B.T.
[3530]—*Missionary Sisters Servants of the Holy Spirit.*—S.Sp.S.
[3280]—*Presentation of the Blessed Virgin Mary Sisters.*—P.B.V.M.
[3450]—*Religious of Jesus-Mary.*—R.J.M.
[2970]—*School Sisters of Notre Dame.*—S.S.N.D.
[]—*Sisters for Christian Community.*—S.F.C.C.
[0430]—*Sisters of Charity of the Blessed Virgin Mary.*—B.V.M.
[2560]—*Sisters of Mercy (Killaloe).*
[1510]—*Sisters of St. Francis.*—O.S.F.
[2040]—*Sisters of the Holy Spirit.*—S.H.S.
[2350]—*Sisters of the Living Word.*—S.L.W.
[2940]—*Sisters of the Most Holy Sacrament.*—M.H.S.

NECROLOGY

(No Deaths)

Diocese of Birmingham

(Dioecesis Birminghamiensis)

Most Reverend

DAVID E. FOLEY, D.D.

Bishop of Birmingham; ordained May 26, 1956; appointed Titular Bishop of Ottaba and Auxiliary Bishop of Richmond May 3, 1986; consecrated June 27, 1986; appointed Bishop of Birmingham 1994; installed May 13, 1994.

Chancery Office: St. Thomas Catholic Life Center, P.O. Box 12047, Birmingham, AL, 35202-2047. Tel.: 205-838-8322; Fax: 205-836-1910.

E-mail address: Chancery@bhmdiocese.org

ESTABLISHED JUNE 28, 1969.

Square Miles 28,091.

Comprises the Counties of North Alabama in an irregular line between the Counties (west to east) of Sumter and Choctaw and following the base of the following Counties: Marengo, Perry, Chilton, Coosa, Tallapoosa and Chambers or comprising the Counties of: Bibb, Blount, Calhoun, Chambers, Cherokee, Chilton, Clay, Clebourne, Colbert, Coosa, Cullman, DeKalb, Etowah, Fayette, Franklin, Greene, Hale, Jackson, Jefferson, Lamar, Lauderdale, Lawrence, Limestone, Madison, Marengo, Marion, Marshall, Morgan, Perry, Pickens, Randolph, St. Clair, Shelby, Sumter, Talladega, Tallapoosa, Tuscaloosa, Walker and Winston.

Legal Title: *The Catholic Bishop of Birmingham in Alabama, a Corporation Sole.*

For legal titles of institutions, consult the Chancery Office.

STATISTICAL OVERVIEW

Personnel	
Bishop	1
Abbots	1
Retired Abbots	3
Priests: Diocesan Active in Diocese	53
Priests: Active Outside Diocese	3
Priests: Diocesan in Foreign Missions	2
Priests: Retired, Sick or Absent	15
Number of Diocesan Priests	73
Religious Priests in Diocese	44
Ordinations:	
Diocesan Priests	1
Permanent Deacons in Diocese	25
Total Brothers	22
Total Sisters	172
Parishes	
Parishes	60
With Resident Pastor:	
Resident Diocesan Priests	40
Resident Religious Priests	14
Without Resident Pastor:	
Administered by Permanent Deacons	2
Administered by Women Religious	2
Administered by Lay People	2
Missions	16
Closed Parishes	1
Professional Ministry Personnel:	
Brothers	3
Sisters	23
Lay Ministers	59
Welfare	
Catholic Hospitals	1
Total Assisted	122,764
Health Care Centers	1
Total Assisted	880,527
Special Centers for Social Services	14
Total Assisted	66,964
Educational	
Diocesan Students in Other Seminaries	12
Students Religious	2
Total Seminarians	14
High Schools, Diocesan and Parish	4
Total Students	1,416
High Schools, Private	1
Total Students	111
Elementary Schools, Diocesan and Parish	19
Total Students	5,045
Elementary Schools, Private	1
Total Students	195
Non-residential Schools for the Disabled	1
Total Students	143
Catechesis/Religious Education:	
High School Students	1,766
Elementary Students	5,548
Total Students Under Catholic Instruction	14,238
Teachers in the Diocese:	
Priests	4
Brothers	2
Sisters	11
Lay Teachers	325
Vital Statistics	
Receptions into the Church:	
Infant Baptism Totals	1,336
Adult Baptism Totals	213
Received into Full Communion	445
First Communions	1,265
Confirmations	1,003
Marriages:	
Catholic	171
Interfaith	286
Total Marriages	457
Deaths	480
Total Catholic Population	71,958
Total Population	2,644,644

Former Bishops—Most Rev. JOSEPH G. VATH, ord. June 7, 1941; appt. Auxiliary Bishop of Mobile-Birmingham March 25, 1966; cons. May 26, 1966; transferred to the Diocese of Birmingham Dec. 9, 1969; died July 14, 1987.—Most Rev. RAYMOND J. BOLAND, D.D., ord. June 16, 1957; appt. Bishop of Birmingham Feb. 2, 1988; cons. March 25, 1988; transferred to Kansas City-St. Joseph Sept. 9, 1993.—Most Rev. DAVID E. FOLEY, D.D., ord. May 26, 1956; appt. Titular Bishop of Ottaba and Auxiliary Bishop of Richmond, May 3, 1986; cons. June 27, 1986; appt. Bishop of Birmingham in Alabama, March 22, 1994; installed May 13, 1994.

Chancery Office—P.O. Box 12047, Birmingham, 35202-2047. St. Thomas Center, *8131 Fourth Ave. S., Birmingham, 35206.* Tel: 205-838-8322; Fax: 205-836-1910. Address all Diocesan Correspondence to the above Post Office Box unless otherwise indicated. Telephones listed below.

Office of the Bishop—Tel: 205-838-8318. PEGGY SELIG, Sec.

Chancellor—Sr. MARY FRANCES LOFTIN, D.C. Tel: 205-833-0175. GERRY NABORS, Sec.

Priests' Council—Most Rev. DAVID E. FOLEY, D.D., Pres.; Rev. PHILIP O'KENNEDY, Moderator. Tel: 205-882-1844. Members: Rev. Msgr. MICHAEL SEXTON, V.G.; Revs. GREGORY BITTNER; EDWIN DILL, S.T. Tel: 334-289-2767. KEVIN COOKE; JOSEPH CULOTTA; RAYMOND DUNMYER; JOHN FALLON; TIMOTHY J. HILL. Tel: 205-785-9625. VERNON HUGUELY. Tel: 205-328-7729. THOMAS KELLY; RAYMOND MURRIN; FRANK MUSCOLINO; JOHN OWEN; PAUL ROHLING.

Diocesan College of Consultors—Rev. Msgr. MICHAEL SEXTON, V.G.; Revs. GREGORY BITTNER; JOSEPH CULOTTA; RAYMOND DUNMYER; BRIAN EGAN; JOHN FALLON; FRANK MUSCOLINO; PAUL ROHLING.

Diocesan College of Vicars—Rev. Msgr. MICHAEL SEXTON, Vicar General-Vicar for Northwest Deanery. Tel: 205-764-3303. Revs. GREGORY BITTNER, Judicial Vicar. Tel: 205-838-8307. PAUL ROHLING, Vicar for Clergy. Tel: 205-871-1153. FRANK MUSCOLINO, Vicar for Ecumenism. Tel: 205-933-2500. BRIAN EGAN, Vicar for Admin. Tel: 205-838-8309. WILLIAM LUCAS, Vicar for Vocations. Tel: 205-435-3238. JOHN IGOE, Vicar for West Birmingham Deanery. Tel: 205-838-8305. PATRICK SULLIVAN, Vicar for Central Birmingham Deanery. Tel: 205-822-4480. EUGENE O'CONNOR, Vicar for East Birmingham Deanery. Tel: 205-833-0334. LOUIS GIARDINO, Vicar for Northeast Deanery. Tel: 205-881-4781. JOHN FALLON, Vicar for Southwest Deanery. Tel: 205-553-9733. RICHARD DONOHOE, Vicar for Southeast Deanery. Tel: 205-237-3011.

Diocesan Pastoral Council—Most Rev. DAVID E. FOLEY, D.D., Pres.; Sr. MARY FRANCES LOFTIN, D.C., Moderator Members include lay representatives of the Diocesan Deaneries, four Vicars for Deaneries, four religious and a staff representative.

Diocesan Finance Council—Most Rev. DAVID E. FOLEY, D.D., Pres.; Rev. BRIAN EGAN, Vicar for Admin. THOMAS CURTIN, Chm. Members: Rev. GREGORY BITTNER; GREG CLARK; JOHN DEWITT, C.P.A.; J. ROBERT DOODY; RAY G. DYER, JR., C.P.A.; MICHAEL L. PATTERSON; MARY ELLEN PETERS; ANDREW RUCKS; PAT RUMORE; YOLANDA N. SULLIVAN, C.P.A.; Sr. MARY FRANCES LOFTIN, Ex Officio. Staff Members: MICHAEL TORTORICE, Finance Officer.

Tribunal—Rev. GREGORY T. BITTNER, J.C.L., Judicial Vicar. Tel: 205-838-8307; 838-8320. CYWILLA FABIJANIC, Sec.-Notary-Case Mgt. Trial Advocates: Revs. TIMOTHY BURNS; KEVIN COOKE.

Judges—Sr. MARILYN VASSALLO, C.S.J., J.C.L.; Revs. RICHARD DONOHOE; LOUIS GIARDINO.

Defenders of the Bond—Revs. BRIAN EGAN; PAUL ROHLING; KEVIN HAMMON, O.F.M.Conv. Please address all Rogatory Commissions to the Office of the Tribunal, *St. Thomas Center.* Tel: 205-838-8307.

Catholic Social Services—Sr. ELAINE SEBERA, R.S.M., Board Pres. Tel: 205-761-6344.

Catholic Family Services—TOM COOK, D.S.W., Dir., *2164 11th Ave. S., Birmingham, 35205.* Tel: 205-324-6561.

Catholic Family Services Offices—LAURA DINWIDDLE, Dir., *1010 Church St., Huntsville, 35804.* Tel: 205-536-0073. TOM COOK, D.S.W., Supvr., *733 37th St. E., Tuscaloosa, 35405.* Tel: 205-553-9045.

Catholic Centers of Concern—Birmingham; Anniston;

Gadsden; Hamilton; Huntsville; Eutaw; Winfield; Sulligent; Fayette.
Apostolate to the Aged—AL GERMANN, *369 Midwood Ave., Birmingham, 35228.* Tel: 205-923-7108.
Engaged Encounter—PAM DIPIAZZA; ANTHONY DIPIAZZA, *1932 Crossvine Rd., Birmingham, 35244.* Tel: 205-987-0977.
Natural Family Planning—HAROLD GRAY; CATHY GRAY, *613 Bienville Ln., Birmingham, 35213.* Tel: 205-879-2042.
Department of Education—FRANK X. SAVAGE, Dir., Catholic Education & Lifelong Learning.
Catholic Schools Office—Sr. M. LEANNE WELCH, P.B.V.M., Supt. Tel: 205-838-8303.
Religious Education Office—Bro. HENRY WERNER, F.S.C., Dir. Tel: 205-838-8312.
Apostolate with Mentally Retarded Persons—Rev. PATRICK CULLEN; Sr. MARY VERNON GENTLE, R.S.M., *The Nazareth House, 2120 Third Ave. N., Birmingham, 35202.* Tel: 205-251-1279 (Voice or TDD).
Catholic Youth Ministry—LAURIE DELGATTO, Dir. Tel: 205-838-8301.
Campus Ministry—Rev. RAYMOND DUNMYER, Dir., *St. Francis University Parish, 811 Fifth Ave., Tuscaloosa, 35401.* Tel: 205-758-5672.
Catholic Scouting—LAURIE DELGATTO, Dir. Tel: 205-838-8301.
Toy Bowl Association—MICHAEL CAMMARATA, Dir., *222 73rd St., N., Birmingham.* Tel: 205-838-2112.
Board of Education—JOHN KEARNEY, Chm. Tel: 205-942-1100 (Office); 979-4928 (Res.).
Finance Office and Administration—
Diocesan Finance Officer—MICHAEL TORTORICE. Tel: 205-833-0173.
Diocesan Development and Annual Catholic Charities Appeal, Campaign for Human Development, and *Catholic Relief Services*—Rev. BRIAN EGAN, Dir. Tel: 205-838-8309.
Office of Pastoral Services—
Beginning Experience—HELEN BOWERS. Tel: 205-802-6216; 969-8509 (Voice Mail).
Children's Beginning Experience—JEANNETTE CAMPISI, *c/o St. Peter Church, 2061 Patton Chapel Rd., Bham, 35216.* Tel: 205-822-4480.
Cursillo Program—Directors: DICK SWEENEY; JANE SWEENEY. Tel: 205-987-8038.
Hispanic Ministries—BRENDA BULLOCK, Dir. Tel: 205-838-8306.
Lay Ministries Program—Sr. MARIE LEONARD, O.S.B., Dir. Tel: 205-838-8300.
Marriage Encounter—DEL FISHER; NANCY FISHER. Tel: 205-556-6471.
Office of Black Ministry—OLIVIA HILL, Dir. Tel: 205-838-8313.
Pro-Life Activities—Rev. JOHN IGOE, Dir. Tel: 205-838-8305.
Propagation of the Faith and Holy Childhood—Rev. RAYMOND MURRIN, Dir. RUTH CARMELLO, Asst. Dir. Tel: 205-838-8306.
Serra Club of Birmingham—MICHAEL RENDA, Pres. Tel: 205-987-8038.
Vocations Office—Rev. WILLIAM LUCAS, Dir. Tel: 205-435-3238.
"One Voice"—Diocesan weekly; Rev. JOHN IGOE, Editor. Tel: 205-838-8305. MARY ALICE CROCKETT, Editorial Asst. SAMUEL A. CIULLA, Advertising; ANN LANZI, Circulation, *The Birmingham Catholic Press, Inc., P.O. Box 10822, Birmingham, 35202.* Tel: 205-838-8305; Fax: 205-838-8319.
Council of Religious—Sr. ROSE SEVENICH, O.S.F., Chm., *420A Elder Oaks Way, Birmingham, 35209.* Tel: 205-870-1791.
Diocesan Council of Catholic Women—FRANCES WIDEMAN, Pres., *106 Lockerbie Cir., Birmingham, 35223.* Tel: 205-428-9559.
Priests' Retirement Fund—Rev. JOSEPH UNDERWOOD, Chm., *6520 Court K, Birmingham, 35228.* Tel: 205-925-8239.
RENEW 2000—Sr. MADELINE CONTORNO, O.S.B., Coord.; Mrs. ARLENE DEL BUENO, Sec., *P.O. Box 12047, Birmingham, 35202-2047.* Tel: 205-838-8323; Fax: 205-836-1910.

CLERGY, PARISHES, MISSIONS AND PAROCHIAL SCHOOLS

CITY OF BIRMINGHAM
(Jefferson County)

1—ST. PAUL'S CATHEDRAL (1871), Rev. Patrick P. Cullen; Deacon Hugh O'Brien. In res., Most Rev. David E. Foley, D.D.; Rev. Desmond Regan.
Mailing Address: P.O. Box 10044, 35202. Tel: 205-251-1279; Fax: 205-251-1284.
Res., 2120 Third Ave. N., 35203.
School—Tel: 205-251-9345. Gladys J. McGee, Prin. Lay Teachers 17; Students 211.

2—ST. ANTHONY'S (1900). Closed. For inquiries for parish records contact St. Paul Cathedral, Birmingham.

3—ST. BARNABAS (1908), Rev. Eugene O'Connor.
Mailing Address: P.O. Box 610304, 35261.
Res., 7921 First Ave. N., 35206. Tel: 205-833-0334; 833-5695.
School—7901 First Ave. N., 35206. Tel: 205-836-5385; Fax: 205-833-0272. Tillie S. Barnhill, Prin. Lay Teachers 11; Students 225.
Mailing Address: P.O. Box 610347, 35261.
Catechesis/Religious Programs—Tel: 205-836-4567. Rosemary Gagliano, D.R.E.
Students 50.

4—ST. BERNARD'S (Inglenook) (1928). Closed. For inquiries for parish records contact St. Paul Cathedral, Birmingham.

5—BLESSED SACRAMENT (1910), Rev. Matthew F. Brennan. In res., Rev. Charles V. Cross.
Res., 1460 Pearson Ave., S.W., P.O. Box 110006, 35211. Tel: 205-785-9840.

6—ST. FRANCIS XAVIER (1953), Revs. Paul Rohling; Andrew Sullivan; Sr. Jane Bishop, O.S.B., Pastoral Min.; Deacon George Mickwee. In res., Bro. Henry Werner, F.S.C.
Res., P.O. Box 130669, 35213. Tel: 205-871-1153; Fax: 205-871-9831.
School—Tel: 205-871-1687. Sr. Judith Dianne McGowan, R.S.M., Prin.
Sisters 1; Lay Teachers 15; Students 221.
Catechesis/Religious Programs—Sr. Therese Francis Walker, M.S.B.T., D.R.E.
Students 268.

7—HOLY FAMILY (1938) (African American), Revs. Robert Crossmeyer, C.P.; Thaddeus Tamm, C.P.; E. John Hilgert, C.P.; Deacon Benjamin Jett.
Res., 1910 19th St., 35218. Tel: 205-780-3440; Fax: 205-780-5272.
School—1916 19th St., Ensley, 35218. Tel: 205-785-5858; Fax: 205-785-2666. Sr. M. DePorres Collier, C.S.S.F., Prin.
Sisters 2; Lay Teachers 14; Students 300.
Catechesis/Religious Programs—Students 490.
Mission—Fairfield, Jefferson Co., St. Mary's, 6101 Dr. Martin Luther King Dr., 35064. Tel: 205-923-0202.

8—HOLY ROSARY (Gate City) (1889), Revs. James Naughton, S.D.B.; Peter V. Malloy, S.D.B.; Anthony D'Angelo, S.D.B.; Bro. Charles Todel, S.D.B.
Mailing Address: P.O. Box 321576, 35232. Tel: 205-595-0652; Fax: 205-595-3091.
Res., 7414 Georgia Rd. S., 35212.

9—ST. JOHN BOSCO (1973), Rev. James Naughton, S.D.B. In res., Rev. Sean Rooney, S.D.B.
Mailing Address: P.O. Box 321576, 35232. Tel: 205-595-1009; Fax: 205-595-3091.
Res., 5224 First Ave., N., 35212.

10—ST. JOSEPH'S (1921) (Italian), Rev. John T. Igoe; Deacon Al Germann.
Res., 3020 Avenue K, 35218. Tel: 205-781-4612.
School—Tel: 205-787-9711; Fax: 205-787-9839.
Convent—1100-31st St., 35218. Tel: 205-787-1517.

11—KOREAN CATHOLIC COMMUNITY, ST. LUKE HWANG (1995) (Korean), Rev. John Sung Kyu Kim.
Res., 460 Park Ter., 35226. Tel: 205-823-6511; Fax: 205-324-0001.

12—ST. MARGARET'S. Closed. 1986. For inquiries for parish records contact Blessed Sacrament Parish, Birmingham.

13—ST. MARK'S (1904), Rev. Raymond Murrin, Admin.
Res., Tel: 205-674-1426.

14—OUR LADY OF FATIMA (1905), Rev. Paul Oberg, S.S.J.; Deacons Andrew Andrews; Willie Moore.
Res., 708 First St., S., 35205. Tel: 205-322-1205.
School—630 First St. S., 35205. Tel: 205-251-8395. Sr. M. Ann Christine, S.N.D., Prin.
Sisters of Notre Dame of Covington, KY 4; Lay Teachers 9; Students 150.
Catechesis/Religious Programs—Tel: 205-251-8395. Sr. Mary Carleta, S.N.D., D.R.E.
Students 92.

15—OUR LADY OF LOURDES (1959), Rev. Andrew Kennedy.
Res., 980 Huffman Rd., 35215.
Office: Tel: 205-836-2274; Fax: 205-836-5436.
Catechesis/Religious Programs—Robin Barron, D.R.E.
Students 288.

16—OUR LADY OF SORROWS (1887), Revs. Martin M. Muller; Sean Merino. In res., Rev. Paschal A. Ferlisi, O.S.B.
Mailing Address: P.O. Box 59447, 35259. Tel: 205-871-8121; Fax: 205-871-8180.
Res., (Homewood) 1728 Oxmoor Rd., 35209.
School—Tel: 205-879-3237; Fax: 205-879-9332. Mrs. Deborah White, Prin.
Lay Teachers 29; Students 455.
Catechesis/Religious Programs—Tel: 205-871-1431. D.R.E.: Patricia Higuera; Barbara Bess.
Students 435.

17—OUR LADY OF THE VALLEY (1974), Rev. Michael MacMahon.
Res., 5514 Double Oak Ln., 35242. Tel: 205-991-6288; Fax: 205-991-5181.
Church—Tel: 205-991-5488; Fax: 205-991-5181.
School—Tel: 205-991-5692; Fax: 205-991-1251. Mrs. Sandra Roden, Prin.
Lay Teachers 34; Students 424.
Catechesis/Religious Programs—Tel: 205-991-5489; Fax: 205-991-5181. Phyllis Schifanella, D.R.E.
Students 406.

18—OUR LADY QUEEN OF THE UNIVERSE (1955), Rev. Vernon Huguley.
Res., 961 Center St., N., 35204. Tel: 205-328-7729; Fax: 205-328-7703.
Mission—Collegeville, Jefferson Co., Sacred Heart.

19—ST. PATRICK'S (1983), Rev. Raymond J. Murrin; Sr. Maura Sampson, P.B.V.M., Pastoral Min. & D.R.E.; Deacon Daniel Whitaker.
Res., 301 Shamrock Tr., Adamsville, 35005. Tel: 205-674-1426; Fax: 205-798-5330. Sr. Maura Sampson, P.B.V.M. Tel: 205-787-1517.
Church—Tel: 205-798-5326.
Catechesis/Religious Programs—Tel: 205-798-5326; Fax: 205-798-5330.
Students 133.
Family Life Center—Tel: 205-798-0372.

20—ST. PETER THE APOSTLE (1962), Revs. Patrick J. Sullivan; Robert J. Sullivan; Sr. Virginia Rohling, O.S.B., Pastoral Assoc.; Deacon Dr. Sam Anzalone.
Res., 2061 Patton Chapel Rd., 35216. Tel: 205-822-4480; Fax: 205-822-4534.
Catechesis/Religious Programs—Tel: 205-823-6324; Fax: 205-822-4534. Dr. Rebecca Sullivan.
Students 525.

21—PRINCE OF PEACE (1984), Rev. Jerry Deasy; Deacons Frank Iovino; John Ferguson.
Mailing Address: P.O. Box 26209, 35226.
Church—4600 Moss Creek Blvd., Hoover, 35226. Tel: 205-822-9125; Fax: 205-822-9127.
Res., 614 Valley St., 35226. Tel: 205-979-7776.
Catechesis/Religious Programs—Tel: 205-822-9125; Fax: 205-822-9127. Kathleen Dunne, D.R.E.
Students 420.

22—SACRED HEART (1955), Rev. Vernon Huguley.
Church—3401 27th Ct. N., 35207. Tel: 205-252-8909.

23—ST. STANISLAUS (1914), Rev. Timothy Hill.
Mailing Address: 904 Indiana St., 35224. Tel: 205-785-9625.

24—ST. STEPHEN UNIVERSITY PARISH (1990), Rev. Frank J. Muscolino. Pastoral Assoc.: Sr. Mary Ann O'Brien, D.C.; Sr. Jacqueline DeBone.
Res., 1515 12th Ave. S., 35205. Tel: 205-933-2500; Fax: 205-939-1500.

25—ST. THERESA'S. Closed. For inquiries for parish records contact St. Paul's Cathedral, Birmingham.

OUTSIDE THE CITY OF BIRMINGHAM

Alexander City, Tallapoosa Co., St. John the Apostle (1948), Rev. Robert J. Stone, C.M.
Res., 454 N. Central St., 35010. Tel: 205-234-3631; Fax: 205-234-3789.
Catechesis/Religious Programs—Tel: 205-329-2592. Martha Rodriguez, D.R.E.
Students 65.

Anniston, Calhoun Co., Sacred Heart of Jesus (1886), Rev. Richard E. Donohoe; Deacon William Taffee.
Res., 3005 Woodbridge Dr., 36207. Tel: 205-237-3011; Fax: 205-237-2615.
School—1821 McCall Dr., 36207. Tel: 205-237-4231. Ms. Robin Woolsey, Prin.
Lay Teachers 10; Students 180.
Catechesis/Religious Programs—Tel: 205-237-3011; Fax: 205-237-2615. Mary Zielinski, D.R.E.
Students 93.
All Saints. Unassigned. Contact Ms. Naurrese Phillips 205-237-0128.
Res., 1104 W. 15th St., 36204. Tel: 205-237-9230.

Ashland, St. Mark's Catholic Community, Rev. Robert Stone, C.M. Tel: 205-234-3631.
Mailing Address: P.O. Box 295, 36251.
Res., 454 N. Central Ave., Alexander City, 35010.
Mrs. Rosanne Gaither, Community Coord.; Res., 35450 Hwy. 775, 36251. Tel: 205-354-2923; Fax: 205-354-4237.

Athens, Limestone Co., St. Paul's (1959), Rev. Joseph C. Allen.
Mailing Address: P.O. Box 998, 35612.
Res., 1900 Hwy. 72 W., 35611. Tel: 205-232-4191.
Catechesis/Religious Programs—Tel: 205-232-4191. Mrs. Sharon Prohaska, D.R.E.
Students 159.

Bessemer, Jefferson Co., St. Aloysius Church (1886), Rev. Liam Sullivan.

Mailing Address: P.O. Box 1570, 35021.
Res., 204 Westwood Dr., 35022. Tel: 205-424-2984.
School—Tel: 205-425-0045; Fax: 205-425-0046. Mrs. Lisa Corona, Prin.
Lay Teachers 12; Students 208.
Catechesis/Religious Programs—Tel: 205-425-3448. Mrs. Donna Duchock, D.R.E.
Students 65.

St. Francis of Assisi (1940) (African American), Rev. Noel Danielewicz, O.F.M.Conv.; Bro. John Obara, O.F.M.Conv.
Res., 2400 Seventh Ave. N., 35020. Tel: 205-425-0984; Fax: 205-428-4758.
School—2410 Seventh Ave. N., 35020. Tel: 205-428-1684; Fax: 205-428-1684. Sr. Maria Dina, M.C., Prin.
Consolata Missionary Sister 1; Franciscan Friars 2; Lay Teachers 8; Students 125.

Cullman, Cullman Co., Sacred Heart (1877) (German), Revs. Kevin D. McGrath, O.S.B.; Leo J. Carter, O.S.B.; Deacon William Roberson.
Res., 217 Second St. S.E., P.O. Box 1085, 35056. Tel: 205-734-3730; Fax: 205-734-3476. [CEM]
School—Tel: 205-734-4563; Fax: 205-734-5882. Sr. Tonette Sperando, O.S.B., Prin.
Order of St. Benedict 2; Lay Teachers 4; Students 223.
Catechesis/Religious Programs—Tel: 205-734-3730; Fax: 205-734-3476. Mary Merritt, D.R.E.
Students 95.
Mission—Hanceville, Cullman Co., St. Boniface, P.O. Box 1085, 35056. Tel: 205-734-3730; Fax: 205-734-3476. [CEM] Rev. Leo J. Carter, O.S.B.

Decatur, Morgan Co., St. Ann's (1870), Rev. Joseph Culotta; Sr. Janet Marie Flemming, O.S.B., Pastoral Assoc.
Res., 250 Johnston St. S.E., 35601. Tel: 205-353-2667; Fax: 205-353-8994. [JC]
School—Tel: 205-353-6543. Sr. Lois Justen, O.S.F., Prin.
Lay Teachers 11; Students 235.
Catechesis/Religious Programs—Tel: 205-353-2667; Fax: 205-353-8994. Barbara Romei, D.R.E.
Students 210.
Mission—Hartselle, Morgan Co., Holy Family, P.O. Box 783, Hartselle, 35640. Tel: 205-773-5701.

Demopolis, Marengo Co., St. Leo (1936), Rev. Edwin Dill, S.T.
Res., 307 Main Ave., P.O. Box 937, 36732. Tel: 334-289-2767; Fax: 334-289-0544.
Mission—Greensboro, Hale Co., Our Lady of Lourdes.

Eutaw, Greene Co., St. Mary (1948) (African American). Administered by West Alabama Mission. Rev. David Buchanan, Dir.
Res., 733 37th St., E., Tuscaloosa, 35405. Tel: 205-553-2200.

Fairfield, Jefferson Co., St. Mary (1943), Rev. E. John Hilgert, C.P.
Res., 1910 19th St., Birmingham, 35218. Tel: 205-780-3440; Fax: 205-785-2666.
Church—6101 Dr. Martin Luther King Dr., 35064. Tel: 205-923-0202.
School—6124 Myron Massey Blvd., 35064. Tel: 205-923-5161; Fax: 205-923-5166. Mary Collins, Prin.
Lay Teachers 15; Students 230.

Florence, Lauderdale Co., St. Joseph's (1898), Rev. Msgr. Michael Sexton, V.G.
Res., 1111 E. College St., 35630. Tel: 205-764-3303, 767-9069 (Rectory); Fax: 205-718-0208.
School—Tel: 205-766-1923; 766-1955; Fax: 205-718-0208. Susan B. Halfman, Prin.
Lay Teachers 18; Students 231.
Catechesis/Religious Programs—Tel: 205-760-9171. Marylu Torrison, D.R.E.
Students 140.

St. Michael (1873), Rt. Rev. Victor J. Clark, O.S.B.
Res., 2751 County Rd. 30, 35634. Tel: 205-764-1885. [CEM]
Catechesis/Religious Programs—D.R.E.: Karen Holden, (High School); Ron Smith, (Elementary).
Students 39.

Gadsden, Etowah Co., St. James (1912), Rev. Kevin Cooke.
Mailing Address: P.O. Box 38, 35902.
Res., 225 Carleen St., 35901. Tel: 205-546-2975; Fax: 205-546-2930.
Church—622 Chestnut St., 35901. Tel: 205-546-2975; Fax: 205-546-2930.
School—Tel: 205-546-0132. Sr. M. Cecilia MacDermott, O.S.B., Prin.
Lay Teachers 15; Students 165.
Catechesis/Religious Programs—Judy Ritter, D.R.E.
Students 126.
Mission—Fort Payne, DeKalb Co., Our Lady of the Valley, P.O. Box 1446, Fort Payne, 35967. Tel: 205-845-4774; Fax: 205-845-4708.

St. Martin de Porres. Closed. For inquiries for parish records contact St. James, Gadsden.

Gardendale, Jefferson Co., St. Elizabeth Ann Seton (1976), Rev. Ray W. Keiser.
Mailing Address: 334 Main St., P.O. Box 1027, 35071. Tel: 205-631-9398.
Res., 105 Powell Dr., P.O. Box 1027, 35071. Tel: 205-631-8582. [CEM]
Catechesis/Religious Programs—Sam Dunne, D.R.E.
Students 103.
Mission—Warrior, Jefferson Co., St. Henry, 211 5th St., Warrior, 35180. Tel: 205-647-7738.

Guntersville, Marshall Co., St. William's (1952), Rev. Thomas M. Kelly.
Res., 929 Gunter Ave., 35976. Tel: 205-582-4964; 582-4245 (Office).
Catechesis/Religious Programs—Ms. Darice Perreault, D.R.E.
Students 100.

Huntsville, Madison Co.,

1—Good Shepherd, (1981), Rev. Philip N. O'Kennedy; Sr. Deborah Kennedy, R.S.M., Pastoral Assoc.; Deacons Ron Puent; Helmut Sassenfeld.
Res., P.O. Box 4447, 35815-4447. Tel: 205-882-1844; Fax: 205-882-1841.
Catechesis/Religious Programs—Tel: 205-822-1844. Katherine Maxwell, D.R.E.
Students 506.

2—St. Mary of the Visitation, (1861), Revs. William M. Kelly, S.D.S.; Dominic Giles, S.D.S.
Res., 222 N. Jefferson St., 35801. Tel: 205-536-6349; Fax: 205-536-6349.
Catechesis/Religious Programs—Tel: 205-536-6760. Mrs. Evelyn Jaap, D.R.E.
Students 68.

3—St. Joseph's, (1952), Revs. Gregory Coulthard, S.D.S.; Thomas Perrin, S.D.S.
Res., 2300 Beasley Ave., N.W., 35816. Tel: 205-534-8459; Fax: 205-534-8450.
School—Holy Family School, 205-538-5221. Ms. Susan McGraw, Prin.
Sisters of the Divine Savior 3; Lay Teachers 17; Students 267.
Catechesis/Religious Programs—Tel: 205-534-1310. Carmen Amato, D.R.E.
Students 170.

4—Holy Spirit, (1965), Revs. Louis Giardino; James Thomas Ackerman, Jr.; Deacons Lee Roy Hoekenschnieder, Sr.; Gerald Motherway; Bro. Benedict Stoegbauer, S.D.S.
Res., 625 Airport Rd., 35802. Tel: 205-881-4781; Fax: 205-880-6389.
School—Tel: 205-881-4852; Fax: 205-881-4904. Mr. James Bell, Prin.
Lay Teachers 23; Students 353.
Catechesis/Religious Programs—Tel: 205-881-0345. Mrs. Carolyn Brunty, D.R.E.
Students 382.

5—Our Lady Queen of the Universe, (1965), Rev. Timothy L. Burns.
Mailing Address: P.O. Box 3268, 35810.
Res., 3701 Grizzard, 35810. Tel: 205-852-0788; Fax: 205-852-0788.
Church—2421 Shady Lane Dr., N.W., 35810.
Catechesis/Religious Programs—Susan Turner, D.R.E.
Students 148.

Jacksonville, Calhoun Co., St. Charles (1964), Rev. William Lucas.
Church—308 Seventh St. N.E., 36265. Tel: 205-435-3238; Fax: 205-435-4942.
Res., 400 Seventh St. N.E., 36265. Tel: 205-435-1307.
Catechesis/Religious Programs—Marcia Anzur, D.R.E.
Students 109.
Mission—Piedmont, Calhoun Co., St. Joachim, 308 7th St. N.E., 36265.

Jasper, Walker Co., St. Cecilia (1964), Rev. Albert Fisher.
Res., P.O. Box 3638, 35502. Tel: 205-384-4800.
Catechesis/Religious Programs—Tel: 205-384-4800. Rosemary Jones, D.R.E.
Students 81.
Mission—Haleyville, Winston Co., Our Lady of Guadalupe, P.O. Box 3638, 35502. Tel: 205-486-9691, 487-2331. Sr. Catherine Concannon, S.S.N.D., Pastoral Min.

Lanett, Chambers Co., Holy Family (1915), Rev. Martin McGeough, C.M.
Res., 705 N. Third Ave., 36863-0325. Tel: 334-644-4405; Fax: 334-644-4405.
Catechesis/Religious Programs—Deacon Donald Canonica, D.R.E.
Students 45.
Mission—Roanoke, Randolph Co., Immaculate Conception, Tel: 205-863-4418.

Leeds, Jefferson Co., St. Theresa's (1951), Rev. Peter T. MacCarthy.
Res., P.O. Box 525, 35094. Tel: 205-699-8534. [CEM]

Lineville, Randolph Co., The Vincentian Mission of East Central Alabama (1995), Rev. Francis W. Sacks, C.M., Dir.
Mailing Address: P.O. Box 38, 36266-0038. Tel: 205-396-6168; Fax: 205-396-0806.

Livingston, Sumter Co., St. Francis of Assisi (1972). Administered by West Alabama Missions. Rev. David Buchanan, Dir.
Mailing Address: 733 37th St., E., Tuscaloosa, 35405.
Res., Hwy. 28 E., 35470. Tel: 205-652-7742.

Madison, Madison Co., St. John the Baptist (1973), Rev. Patrick Murphy; Deacons Dan Laurita; Darrell Diem; Terry Thompson, Pastoral Asst. & D.R.E.
Res., 1055 Hughes Rd., 35758. Tel: 205-722-0130; Fax: 205-722-0303.
School—1057 Hughes Rd., 35758. Tel: 205-722-0772; Fax: 205-722-0151. Tommy Bridges, Prin.
Lay Teachers 12; Students 224.
Catechesis/Religious Programs—Tel: 205-722-8590.
Students 700.

Marion, Perry Co., Marion Military Institute, Rev. Charles McNeice, S.S.E.
Res., Washington St., 36756. Tel: 334-874-8931.

Montevallo, Shelby Co., St. Thomas the Apostle (1951), Rev. Raymond J. Remke; Sr. Pat Hinton, O.S.F., Pastoral Assoc.
Res. & Mailing Address: 80 St. Thomas Way, 35115. Tel: 205-663-3936; Fax: 205-663-3929.
Catechesis/Religious Programs—Students 217.
Mission—Clanton, Chilton Co., Church of the Resurrection, P.O. Box 735, Clanton, 35046. Tel: 205-755-5498; Fax: 205-755-0715. Sr. Veronica Ryan, O.S.B., Pastoral Coord.

Moulton, Lawrence Co., Resurrection Catholic Chapel (1993), Deacon Bob Laremore, Pastoral Coord.
Res., 7363 Alabama Hwy. 33, 35650. Tel: 205-292-3333.

Oneonta, Blount Co., Corpus Christi (1983), Deacon Al Girodo, Pastoral Admin.
Church—Rte. 3, P.O. Box 751, 35121. Tel: 205-625-6078. [CEM]

Pell City, St. Clair Co., Our Lady of the Lake (1969), Rev. Gregory T. Bittner.
Mailing Address: Hwy. 231 S., P.O. Box 388, 35125.
Res., 117 Ingram Lane, Cropwell, 35054. Tel: 205-525-4711; 525-5161 (Church); Fax: 205-991-6312.
Catechesis/Religious Programs—Students 42.

Russellville, Franklin Co., Good Shepherd Church (1973), Rev. Robert A. Dalton; Miss Lynne Wrocklage, Pastoral Assoc.
Res., 1700 N. Jackson Ave., P.O. Box 630, 35653. Tel: 205-332-4861. [JC]
Catechesis/Religious Programs—Students 60.

Scottsboro, Jackson Co., St. Jude (1971), Rev. Camillus W. Blazak; Deacon Jerome P. Raispis.
Res., P.O. Box 971, 35768. Tel: 205-259-2520.
Catechesis/Religious Programs—Tel: 205-574-6156. Barbara Altonji, D.R.E.
Students 66.

Sylacauga, Talladega Co., St. Jude (1947), Sr. Rose Mae Rausch, O.S.F., Pastoral Admin.
Res., 306 W. Bay St., P.O. Box 111, 35150. Tel: 205-245-7741. [JC]
Catechesis/Religious Programs—Students 42.
Mission—Childersburg, Holy Name of Jesus, 4th St., N.W., 35044.

Talladega, Talladega Co., St. Francis of Assisi (1951), Rev. Henry A. McDaid.
Res., 722 S. East St., P.O. Box 1142, 35160. Tel: 205-362-5372; Fax: 205-362-5372.
Catechesis/Religious Programs—Students 51.

Trussville, Jefferson Co., Holy Infant of Prague (1941), Rev. Patrick O'Donoghue. Pastoral Ministers: Sr. Marie Carolyn Cutcliff, R.S.M., D.R.E.; Mrs. Terry Pruet; Deacon Ed Pruet. In res., Rev. John Owens.
Res., 215 Hewitt St., P.O. Box 43, 35173. Tel: 205-655-2541; Fax: 205-661-9231.
Catechesis/Religious Programs—Tel: 205-655-3002.
Students 286.

Tuscaloosa, Tuscaloosa Co., Holy Spirit (1961), Revs. John Fallon; David Buchanan, Dir. West Alabama Missions.
Res., 733 37th St. E., 35405. Tel: 205-553-9733; Fax: 205-554-0136.
School—711 37th St., 35405. Tel: 205-553-9630; Fax: 205-553-8880. Ana MacCrone, Prin.
Lay Teachers 34; Students 617.
Catechesis/Religious Programs—Students 145.
Missions—Tuscaloosa, Tuscaloosa Co., St. John, c/o Rev. David Buchanan at Holy Spirit, 8th & Lurleen Wallace Blvd., 35401. Tel: 205-553-9733; Reform, Dickens Co., St. Robert. Administered by West Alabama Mission. c/o Rev. David Buchanan at Holy

Spirit, Hwy. 17 S., Reform, 35481. Tel: 205-375-8141.

St. Francis of Assisi University Parish (1929), Revs. Raymond A. Dunmyer; Donald Dietz, O.M.I.; Ms. Molly Campbell, Campus Co-Min.
Res., 811 Fifth Ave., 35401. Tel: 205-758-5672; Fax: 205-758-5673.
Catechesis/Religious Programs—Nancy Woodbury, D.R.E.
Students 140.

Tuscumbia, Colbert Co., Our Lady of the Shoals (1869), Rev. Patrick J. Tierney.
Res., 200 N.E. Commons, 35674. Tel: 205-383-7207; 381-2699; Fax: 205-383-7883. [CEM]
Church—200 N. East Commons, 35674. Tel: 205-383-7207.
Catechesis/Religious Programs—Carolyn Wilson, D.R.E.
Students 98.

Winfield, Marion Co., Holy Spirit (1965), Rev. Gerald Peterson, Glmy. Pastoral Ministers: Tel: 205-487-2331. Sr. Catherine Concannon, S.S.N.D.; Sr. Mary Burke, S.S.N.D.
Res., 154 Meadowbrook Ave., Rte. 2, Box 277, 35594. Tel: 205-487-4307.
Catechesis/Religious Programs—Students 35.
Mission—Fayette, Fayette Co., Holy Family, 423 19th St. N.W., Fayette, 35555. Tel: 205-932-6242.

On Duty Outside the Diocese:
Reverend Monsignors—
Marino, Joseph, Secretariat of State, Second Section, Vatican City, Rome, EVR 120 Italy. Tel: 39-6-698-831 (Office); 39-6-688-973 (Home)
Reverend Fathers—
Appel, George, Caixa Postal 1103, Belem Para, Brazil, 66-017-970 South America
Klauck, Michael, c/o Sister Mangala Missionaries of Charity, 727 N.W. 17th St., Miami, FL 33136
Reynolds, Jeffrie S., P.O. Box 51, Perry Point, MD 21902. Tel: 410-642-2411, Ext. 5601

Absent on Leave:
Reverend Fathers—
Cairns, Thomas
Summitt, James A.
Ventura, John

Retired:
Reverend Fathers—
Bordenca, Charles, P.O. Box 933, Fairhope, AL 36533. Tel: 334-990-9860 (Office)
DeFazio, Crescenzio, 7404 Colony Park Dr., Birmingham, AL 35243. Tel: 205-967-0563
Donnelly, Paul J., 112 Fairway Blvd., Apt. 206, Panama City, FL 32407. Tel: 904-234-0659
Finneran, Michael, 6224 Lake Lugano, Jacksonville, FL 32256
Inkel, Roland, St. Bernard Abbey, 1600 St. Bernard Dr. S.E., Cullman, AL 35055. Tel: 205-734-8291
Kula, Joseph, St. John Vianney Villa, 1464 Green Trails Dr., Naperville, IL 60540-83. Tel: 630-548-3953 (Office)
Mulvaney, James J., 1321 Santa Maria, Lady Lake, FL 32159. Tel: 904-750-4284
O'Connor, Thomas, O.S.B., St. Bernard Abbey, 1600 St. Bernard Dr. S.E., Cullman, AL 35055. Tel: 205-734-8291
O'Sullivan, Robert, 1500 S.W. 66th Ave., Boca Raton, FL 33428. Tel: 407-488-6147
Owen, John J., P.O. Box 259, Trussville, AL 35173. Tel: 205-655-9092
Regan, Desmond, Cathedral of St. Paul, P.O. Box 10044, Birmingham, AL 35202. Tel: 205-324-0237 (Private)
Sheehan, J. Peter, 653 S.E. Lakeview Dr., Sebring, FL 33870. Tel: 813-471-0378
Thorsen, Henry, 700 Connell Dr., Pensacola, FL 32507. Tel: 904-469-0919
Underwood, Joseph, 6520 Court K, Birmingham, AL 35228. Tel: 205-925-8329
White, Michael J., 4616 Lake Valley Dr., Birmingham, AL 35244. Tel: 205-733-8328

Permanent Deacons:
Andrews, Andy, Our Lady of Fatima, Birmingham
Anzalone, Sam, St. Peter the Apostle, Birmingham
Canonica, Donald, Holy Family, Lanett
Diem, Darrell, St. John the Baptist, Madison
Ferguson, John, Prince of Peace, Birmingham
Germann, Aloysius A., St. Joseph, Birmingham
Girodo, Albert, Admin., Corpus Christi Church, Oneonta
Hoekenschnieder, Lee Roy, Holy Spirit, Huntsville
Iovino, Frank, Prince of Peace, Birmingham
Jett, Benjamin, Holy Family, Birmingham
Joly, Walter Jerome, On Leave
Kelly, Alfred, (Retired)
Laremore, Robert, Glen Mary Ministries, Moulton
Laurita, Dan, St. John the Baptist, Madison
Mickwee, George, St. Francis Xavier, Birmingham
Moore, William, Our Lady of Fatima, Birmingham
Motherway, Gerald, Holy Spirit, Huntsville
O'Brien, Hugh A., Cathedral of St. Paul, Birmingham
Pruett, Ed, Holy Infant of Prague, Trussville
Puent, Ron, Good Shepherd, Huntsville
Raispis, Jerome P., St. Jude, Scottsboro
Ritchey, Seraphim, St. George the Great Martyr
Roberson, William, Sacred Heart, Cullman
Sassenfeld, Helmut, Good Shepherd, Huntsville
Taffee, William Francis, Jr., Sacred Heart of Jesus, Anniston
Whitaker, Dan, St. Patrick, Adamsville; St. Cecilia, Jasper
Zieverink, Edward Walter, Jr., Cathedral of St. Paul, Birmingham

INSTITUTIONS LOCATED IN THE DIOCESE

[A] HIGH SCHOOLS, DIOCESAN

BIRMINGHAM. *John Carroll High School*, 300 Lakeshore Pkwy., P.O. Box 19907, 35219. Tel: 205-940-2400; Fax: 205-940-2400.
E-mail: LWFisher@usit.net
Mr. Lee W. Fisher, Prin.; Revs. Sean Merino; Andrew Sullivan; Robert J. Sullivan; Peter V. Malloy, S.D.B. Priests 4; Sisters 1; Lay Teachers 62; Students 943.

HUNTSVILLE. *Catholic High School*, 4810 Bradford Dr., 35805. Tel: 205-430-1760; Fax: 205-430-1766.
E-mail: ahession@chs.prk12.al.us
Ms. Alice I. Hession, Prin. Priests 1; Lay Teachers 10; Students 80.

TUSCALOOSA. *Holy Spirit High School*, 601 37th St., E., 35405. Tel: 205-553-5606; Fax: 205-556-7103.
E-mail: hspirit@no.com
Mr. Michael Burke, Prin. Lay Teachers 22; Students 208.

[B] HIGH SCHOOLS, PRIVATE

BIRMINGHAM. *Holy Family High School*, 2001 19th St., 35218. Tel: 205-787-9937.
E-mail: deporres@aol.com
Passionist Community of Chicago, IL. Mrs. Phyllis Jones, Prin. Sisters 1; Lay Teachers 14; Deacons 1; Students 185.

CULLMAN. *St. Bernard Preparatory School, Inc.*, 101 St. Bernard Dr., 35055. Tel: 205-739-6682; Fax: 205-734-2925.
E-mail: sbprep@hiwaay.net
Web site: www.sbabbeyprep.org
Revs. Marcus J. Voss, O.S.B., Pres.; Joel W. Martin, O.S.B., Headmaster. Priests 1; Sisters 2; Brothers 2; Lay Teachers 15; Students 111.

[C] ELEMENTARY SCHOOLS, PRIVATE

BIRMINGHAM. *St. Rose of Lima Academy*. (Grades K-8), 1401 S. 22nd St., 35219. Tel: 205-933-0549; Fax: 205-933-0501; 933-8847. Sr. Mary George, O.P., Prin. Dominican Sisters of Nashville, TN. Sisters 6; Lay Teachers 14; Students 195.

[D] GENERAL HOSPITALS

BIRMINGHAM. *St. Vincent's Hospital*, P.O. Box 12407, 35202-2407. Tel: 205-939-7000.
E-mail: apurdy@stv.org
Web site: www.stv.inter.net
For a complete listing, refer to the Hospitals section.
Seton Health Corporation of North Alabama, P.O. Box 12407, 35202-2407. Tel: 205-939-8600
For a complete listing, refer to the Hospitals section.

[E] MONASTERIES AND RESIDENCES OF PRIESTS AND BROTHERS

BIRMINGHAM. *Franciscan Missionaries of the Eternal Word, A Public Association of the Christian Faithful*, 5821 Old Leeds Rd., 35210. Tel: 205-956-6455. Revs. Joseph M. Wolfe, M.F.V.A., Father Guardian; John Mary Klobuchar, M.F.V.A.; Augustine Mary Hedderman, M.F.V.A. Professed 16 (3 Priests; 13 Brothers); Novices 4; Total in Residence 20.

CULLMAN. *St. Bernard Abbey*. (Corporate Title: Benedictine Society of Alabama, Inc.), 1600 St. Bernard Dr., 35055. Tel: 205-734-8291; Fax: 205-734-2925. Rt. Revs. Cletus D. Meagher, O.S.B., Abbot; Victor J. Clark, O.S.B., Retired Abbot; Hilary B. Dreaper, O.S.B., Retired Abbot; Gregory J. Roettger, O.S.B., J.U.D., Retired Abbot; Very Rev. Thomas J. O'Connor, O.S.B., Prior; Revs. Eric D. Guthrie, O.S.B.; Thomas J. Schnurr, O.S.B.; Paul G. Koehler, O.S.B.; Mark C. Mages, O.S.B.; Michael T. Morgan, O.S.B.; George J. Salem, O.S.B.; Charles J. Reiner, O.S.B.; Bernard J. Patterson, O.S.B.; Leo J. Carter, O.S.B.; Roger R.S. Lott, O.S.B.; Edward P. Markley, O.S.B.; Ignatius B. Kane, O.S.B.; Howard R. Moussier, O.S.B.; Marcus J. Voss, O.S.B.; Paschal A. Ferlisi, O.S.B.; Kevin D. McGrath, O.S.B.; Jose Ramon Mascareno, O.S.B.; M. Lawrence Bouchea, O.S.B.; Joel W. Martin, O.S.B. Total Priests of Abbey 24; Brothers 12.

[F] CONVENTS AND RESIDENCES OF SISTERS

BIRMINGHAM. *Our Lady of the Angels Monastery, Inc.*, 5817 Old Leeds Rd., 35210. Tel: 205-956-5987; Fax: 205-271-2927. Mother M. Angelica, P.C.P.A., Abbess & Pres. Poor Clare Nuns of Perpetual Adoration. Sisters 32; Novices 3; Postulants 2; 50 Members of the Lay Missionaries of the Eternal Word. Properties owned or sponsored: Eternal Word Television Network, Inc. (EWTN); WEWN Shortwave Network; EWTN Online Services (Internet Web Site) and EWTN Religious Catalog, Inc. Legal Titles: *Eternal Word Television Network, Inc. (EWTN).*; *WEWN Shortwave Network and AM/FM Radio.*; *EWTN Religious Catalog, Inc.*; *EWTN Catholic Publisher*. Global television, radio, and book apostolates.
Sister Servants of the Eternal Word, A Public Association of the Christian Faithful, 3721 Belmont Rd., 35210. Tel: 205-951-2486. Mother Mary Gabriel, Supr. Sisters in Residence 8.

CULLMAN. *Sacred Heart Monastery*, P.O. Box 488, 35056. Tel: 205-734-4622; 734-2199. Sr. Treva Heinberg, O.S.B., Prioress. Benedictine Sisters. Professed Sisters 63.

[G] DIOCESAN SOCIAL SERVICE

BIRMINGHAM. *Catholic Center of Concern*. (Div. of Catholic Charities), 712 Fourth Ct., W., 35204. Tel: 205-786-4388. Richard Turcotte, Ph.D., Dir.; Sr. Cecilia Clara Zamboni, M.C. Total Staff 5; Total Assisted 32,000. Consolata Missionary Sisters.
Catholic Family Services, 2164 11th Ave., S., 35205. Tel: 205-324-6561; Fax: 205-323-0475. Thomas Cook, Dir. Total Staff 6; Total Assisted 1,073.

ANNISTON. *All Saints Interfaith Center of Concern*, 1029 W. 15th St., 36201. Tel: 205-236-7793. Sr. Mary Roy, D.H.S., Dir. Tel: 205-238-1365. Total Staff 1; Total Assisted 17,500.

EUTAW. *Consolata Apostolate*, 331 Boligee St., P.O. Box 538, 35462. Tel: 205-372-3497. Sr. Zelita M. Bragagnolo, M.C., Dir. Total Staff 3; Total Assisted 1,858.

FAYETTE. *Christian Center of Concern*. Mailing Address: P.O. Box 466, 35555. 631 First St., N.W., 35555. Tel: 205-932-3218. Shelia Hunt, Dir. Staff 10; Total Assisted 2,602.

GADSDEN. *Catholic Center of Concern*, P.O. Box 94, 35902. J. A., Heiberger, Acting Dir. Total Assisted 5,000.

HAMILTON. *Christian Center of Concern*, P.O. Box 973, 35570. Tel: 205-921-3470. Sonja Leonelli, Dir. Total Assisted 233.

HUNTSVILLE. *Catholic Center of Concern*, 1010 Church St., N.W., P.O. Box 745, 35804. Tel: 205-536-0041. Cindy M. Whalen, L.B.S.W., Dir. Total Assisted 2,915.
Catholic Family Services, 1010 Church St., N.W., P.O. Box 745, 35804. Tel: 205-536-0073; Fax: 205-534-3141. Laura Dinwiddie, Dir. Total Served 603.

SULLIGENT. *Christian Center of Concern*, P.O. Box 1154, 35584. Tel: 205-698-7197. Martha Richards, Dir. Staff 4; Total Assisted 249.

TUSCALOOSA. *Catholic Family Services*, 733 37th St., E., 35405. Tel: 205-553-9046. Ms. Debbie Renfroe, L.C.S.W., P.I.P. Total Serviced 356.

WINFIELD. *Christian Center of Concern*, 197 State Hwy. 253, 35594. Tel: 205-487-6230. Marie Weeks, Dir. Total Assisted 1,465.

[H] CAMPUS MINISTRY

BIRMINGHAM. *St. Stephen University Parish*, Catholic Campus Center, 1515 12th Ave. S., 35205. Tel: 205-933-2500. Rev. Frank J. Muscolino.

FLORENCE. *University of North Alabama*, St. Joseph's Church, 1111 E. College St., 35630. Tel: 205-764-3303. Rev. Msgr. Michael Sexton.

JACKSONVILLE. *Jacksonville State University*, St. Charles Church, 308 Seventh St., N.E., 36265. Tel: 205-435-3238. Rev. William Lucas. Total Staff 2; Total in Program 25.

MONTEVALLO. *University of Montevallo*, St. Thomas the Apostle Catholic Campus Ministry, 80 St. Thomas Way, 35115. Tel: 205-665-7379. Rev. Raymond J. Remke.

TALLADEGA. *Talladega College Catholic Campus Ministry*, St. Francis of Assisi, P.O. Box 1142, 35160. Rev. Henry A. McDaid.

TUSCALOOSA. *Diocesan Campus Ministry Office*, St. Francis University Parish, 811 Fifth Ave., 35401. Tel: 205-758-5672.
E-mail: cathst@valvm.va.edu
Rev. Raymond A. Dunmyer, Dir. Total Staff 1; Total

in Residence 1.

University of Alabama in Tuscaloosa, St. Francis University Parish, 811 Fifth Ave., 35401. Tel: 205-758-5672.
E-mail: cathst@valva.va.edu
Campus Ministers: Revs. Raymond A. Dunmyer; Donald Dietz, O.M.I.; Ms. Molly Campbell. Total Staff 3; Total in Residence 2.

[I] MISCELLANEOUS LISTINGS

BIRMINGHAM. *Agape Institute of St. Teresa of Jesus,* 3528 Deerfield Dr., 35226. Bob and Rita Tevebaugh, Co-Founders; Rev. Paul Rohling, Mod. Members 28.

Catholic Horizons, Inc., 2828 Crestwood Blvd., 35210. Tel: 205-956-1053; 1-888-266-5701; Fax: 205-956-1950. Sue M. Dominick, Advisory Board Pres. Diocesan book, gift, & information center.

Catholic Housing of Birmingham, Inc., P.O. Box 12047, 35202. Tel: 205-838-8309. 8131 Fourth Ave., S., 35206. Albert H. Rohling, Pres.

Congregation of the Passion: Holy Family Community, Inc. (House of Religious Men), 1910 19th St., Ensley, 35218. Tel: 205-780-3440. Corporation for Holy Family Church, and Holy Family Elementary, Birmingham, and St. Mary's Church, Fairfield, St. Mary Elementary, Fairfield.

Contemplative Outreach Birmingham. Sacred Heart Monastery, P.O. Box 488, Cullman, 35056. Tel: 205-734-4622. Sr. Mary McGehee, O.S.B., Coord.; Aloysius Golden, Area Contact Person. Tel: 205-592-3930.

Holy Family Educational Foundation, 1910 19th St., 35218. Tel: 205-780-3440.

Holy Name of Jesus Hospital Trust. (Senior Citizen Housing), c/o Regions Bank, P.O. Box 10247, 35202. Tel: 205-326-7219; Fax: 205-326-7052. Sidney O. Roebuck, Jr., Trustee, Vice Pres. & Senior Trust Officer, First Alabama Bank. Total Assisted 109.

John Carroll Catholic Education Foundation, Inc., 300 Lakeshore Pkwy., 35209.
E-mail: lwfisher@usit.net

Magnificat: Mary, Woman of Faith Chapter, 1341 Forest Ridge Ct., 35226. Tel: 205-941-0144.

Our Lady of Sorrows Educational School Foundation, 1728 Oxmoor Rd., 35209. Tel: 205-871-8121.

Our Lady of the Valley Educational Foundation, 5514 Double Oak Ln., 35242. Tel: 205-991-5488; Fax: 205-991-5181.

St. Barnabas Regional School Educational Foundation, 7921 First Ave. N., 35206. Tel: 205-833-0334.
E-mail: kleeman975@aol.com

St. Francis Xavier Catholic School Education Foundation, P.O. Box 130669, 35213. Tel: 205-871-1153. Sr. Judith Dianne McGowan, R.S.M., Prin. & Contact Person.

St. Paul Cathedral School Education Foundation, P.O. Box 370104, 35237. Tel: 205-251-9345; Fax: 205-251-9668.

St. Peter's Endowment Foundation, 2061 Patton Chapel Rd., 35216.

Villa Maria, 500 82nd St., S., 35206. Tel: 205-836-7839. Violet Ashworth, Mgr. Total Staff 7; Total in Residence 65.

ANNISTON. *Gertrude C. Luther, M.D. Charitable Trust,* 1821 McCall Dr., 36207. Tel: 205-237-4231.

Sacred Heart of Jesus Charitable Trust, 1821 McCall Dr., 36207. Tel: 205-237-4231.

BESSEMER. *St. Aloysius Educational Foundation,* P.O. Box 1570, 35021. Total Assisted Monthly 183.

CULLMAN. *Benedictine Manor Retirement Home, Inc.,* 200 Janeway Dr., 35055. Tel: 205-739-2853. Sr. Bertha True, O.S.B., Dir. Sisters 2; Resident Capacity 40-50.

Benedictine Spirituality and Conference Center, P.O. Box 488, 35056. Tel: 205-734-8302.
E-mail: shmon@hiwaay.net
Sr. Eleanor Harrison, O.S.B., Dir. Beds 72; Total Staff 5.

DECATUR. *St. Ann's Educational Foundation,* 240 Johnson St. S.E., 35601. Sr. Lois Justen, O.S.F.

FLORENCE. *St. Joseph School Foundation, Florence,* 115 Plum St., 35630.

GADSDEN. *St. James Educational Foundation,* 700 Albert Rains Blvd., 35901. Total Staff 1.

HUNTSVILLE. *Holy Family Regional School Foundation,* 2300 Beasley Ave., 35816-4004. Total Staff 23; Total Assisted 260.

Holy Spirit Regional School Foundation, 625 Airport Rd., 35802. Tel: 205-881-4781.

Society of St. Vincent de Paul, P.O. Box 16070, 35802.

MADISON. *St. John's Educational Foundation,* 1055 Hughes Rd., 35758. Tel: 205-722-0130. Rev. Patrick J. Murphy, Contact Person.

TUSCALOOSA. *Holy Spirit School of Tuscaloosa Endowment Foundation,* 711 37th St., E., 35405.

RELIGIOUS INSTITUTES OF MEN REPRESENTED IN THE DIOCESE

For further details refer to the corresponding bracketed number in the Religious Institutes of Men or Women section.

[0200]—*Benedictine Monks.*—O.S.B.
[1350]—*Brothers of St. Francis Xavier.*—C.F.X.
[0330]—*Brothers of the Christian Schools.*—F.S.C.
[1330]—*Congregation of the Mission.* (Eastern Prov.).—C.M.
[1000]—*Congregation of the Passion.*—C.P.
[0480]—*Conventual Franciscans.* (Prov. of St. Anthony of Padua).—O.F.M.Conv.
[]—*Franciscan Missionaries of the Eternal Word.*—M.F.V.A.
[0570]—*Glenmary Home Missioners.* (Cincinnati, OH).
[0840]—*Missionary Servants of the Most Holy Trinity.*—S.T.
[0700]—*St. Joseph's Society of the Sacred Heart.* (Baltimore, MD).—S.S.J.
[1190]—*Salesians of Don Bosco.*—S.D.B.
[1200]—*Society of the Divine Savior.*—S.D.S.

RELIGIOUS INSTITUTES OF WOMEN REPRESENTED IN THE DIOCESE

[0230]—*Benedictine Sisters of Pontifical Jurisdiction.*—O.S.B.
[0720]—*Consolata Missionary Sisters.*—M.C.
[0760]—*Daughters of Charity of St. Vincent de Paul.*—D.C.
[0820]—*Daughters of the Holy Spirit.*—D.H.S.
[1070-03]—*Dominican Sisters.* (Adrian, MI).—O.P.
[1070-07]—*Dominican Sisters.* (Nashville, TN).—O.P.
[1070-13]—*Dominican Sisters.* (Sinsinawa, WI).—O.P.
[1170]—*Felician Sisters.*—C.S.S.F.
[1310]—*Franciscan Sisters.* (Little Falls, MN).—O.S.F.
[2790]—*Missionary Servants of the Most Blessed Trinity.*—M.S.B.T.
[3210]—*Poor Clares of Perpetual Adoration.*—P.C.P.A.
[0850]—*Salisian Sisters, Daughters of Mary, Help of Christians (Salisian Sisters).*—F.M.A.
[2970]—*School Sisters of Notre Dame.*—S.S.N.D.
[]—*Sister Servants of the Eternal Word.*—S.S.E.W.
[2575]—*Sisters of Mercy of the Americas.*—R.S.M.
[2990]—*Sisters of Notre Dame.*—S.N.D.
[3000]—*Sisters of Notre Dame de Namur.*—S.N.D.deN.
[1705]—*The Sisters of St. Francis of Assisi.*—O.S.F.
[1650]—*Sisters of St. Francis of Philadelphia.*—O.S.F.
[3840]—*Sisters of St. Joseph of Carondelet.*—C.S.J.
[1030]—*Sisters of the Divine Savior.*—S.D.S.
[3320]—*Sisters of the Presentation of the B.V.M.*—P.B.V.M.
[4048]—*Society of Sisters Faithful Companions of Jesus.*—F.C.J.
[4190]—*Visitation Nuns.*—V.H.M.

NECROLOGY

† Bauler, Robert John, (Retired). —Died June 26, 1997.

Diocese of Bismarck

(Dioecesis Bismarckiensis)

Most Reverend

PAUL A. ZIPFEL, D.D.

Bishop of Bismarck; ordained March 18, 1961; appointed Titular Bishop of Walla Walla and Auxiliary Bishop of St. Louis May 16, 1989; consecrated June 29, 1989; appointed Bishop of Bismarck December 31, 1996; installed February 20, 1997.

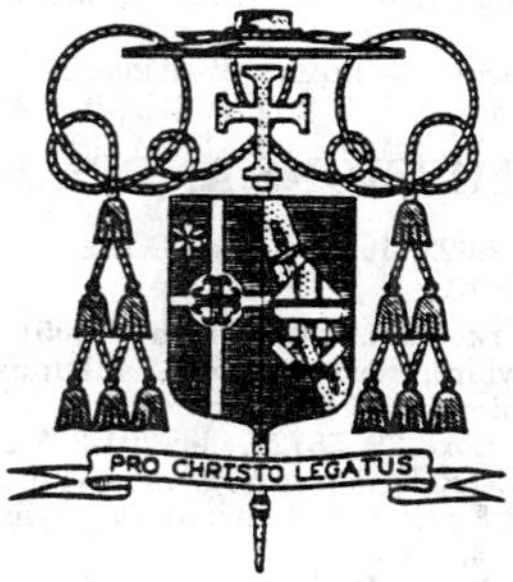

ESTABLISHED DECEMBER 31, 1909.

Square Miles 34,268.

Comprises the Counties of Adams, Billings, Bowman, Burke, Burleigh, Divide, Dunn, Emmons, Golden Valley, Grant, Hettinger, McKenzie, McLean, Mercer, Morton, Mountrail, Oliver, Renville, Sioux, Slope, Stark, Ward and Williams in the State of North Dakota.

For legal titles of parishes and diocesan institutions, consult the Chancery Office.

Chancery Office: 420 Raymond St., Box 1575, Bismarck, ND, 58502-1575. Tel.: 701-223-1347; Fax: 701-223-3693.

STATISTICAL OVERVIEW

Personnel	
Bishop	1
Abbots	1
Retired Abbots	2
Priests: Diocesan Active in Diocese	49
Priests: Active Outside Diocese	5
Priests: Retired, Sick or Absent	14
Number of Diocesan Priests	68
Religious Priests in Diocese	28
Extern Priests in Diocese	5
Ordinations:	
Diocesan Priests	2
Transitional Deacons	2
Permanent Deacons	3
Permanent Deacons in Diocese	54
Total Brothers	27
Total Sisters	162
Parishes	
Parishes	65
With Resident Pastor:	
Resident Diocesan Priests	46
Resident Religious Priests	7
Without Resident Pastor:	
Administered by Priests	11
Administered by Permanent Deacons	1
Missions	39
Closed Parishes	1
Professional Ministry Personnel:	
Brothers	1
Sisters	13
Lay Ministers	24
Welfare	
Catholic Hospitals	6
Total Assisted	283,790
Homes for the Aged	4
Total Assisted	476
Specialized Homes	1
Total Assisted	170
Other Institutions	1
Total Assisted	7
Educational	
Diocesan Students in Other Seminaries	21
Students Religious	1
Total Seminarians	22
Colleges and Universities	1
Total Students	2,016
High Schools, Diocesan and Parish	3
Total Students	1,230
Elementary Schools, Diocesan and Parish	14
Total Students	1,950
Catechesis/Religious Education:	
High School Students	3,094
Elementary Students	7,694
Total Students Under Catholic Instruction	16,006
Teachers in the Diocese:	
Priests	6
Brothers	1
Sisters	10
Lay Teachers	182
Vital Statistics	
Receptions into the Church:	
Infant Baptism Totals	1,208
Adult Baptism Totals	98
Received into Full Communion	151
First Communions	1,435
Confirmations	1,376
Marriages:	
Catholic	281
Interfaith	159
Total Marriages	440
Deaths	697
Total Catholic Population	66,956
Total Population	253,552

Former Bishops—Most Rev. VINCENT DE PAUL WEHRLE, O.S.B., D.D., appt. Bishop of Bismarck, April 9, 1910; cons. May 19, 1910; retired Dec. 11, 1939; named Titular Bishop of Teos by Pope Pius XII; died Nov. 2, 1941.—Most Rev. VINCENT J. RYAN, D.D., LL.D., appt. March 19, 1940; cons. May 28, 1940; died Nov. 10, 1951.—Most Rev. LAMBERT A. HOCH, D.D., L.L.D., appt. Jan. 23, 1952; cons. March 25, 1952; transferred to Diocese of Sioux Falls, Dec. 5, 1956; died June 27, 1990.—Most Rev. HILARY B. HACKER, D.D., appt. Bishop, Dec. 29, 1956; retired June 28, 1982; died Nov. 6, 1990.—Most Rev. JOHN F. KINNEY, D.D., J.C.D., appt. June 28, 1982 Episcopal Ord. Jan. 25, 1977; installed Aug. 23, 1982; transferred to Diocese of St. Cloud, July 6, 1995.

Vicar General—Rev. THOMAS E. KRAMER.

Chancery Office—420 Raymond St., Box 1575, Bismarck, 58502-1575. Tel: 701-223-1347; Fax: 701-223-3693.

Chancellor—Sr. JOANNE GRAHAM, O.S.B., J.C.L.

Center for Pastoral Ministry Office—520 N. Washington St., P.O. Box 1137, Bismarck, 58502-1137. Tel: 701-222-3035.

Diocesan Tribunal—520 N. Washington St., P.O. Box 1137, Bismarck, 58502-1137. Tel: 701-222-3035.

Judicial Vicar—Rev. DAVID L. ZIMMER, J.C.L.

Defensor Vinculi—Revs. LEONARD A. ECKROTH; GENE LINDEMANN, J.C.L.

Pro-Synodal Judges—Revs. THEODORE F. GUSTIN; GEORGE A. DUKART; ROBERT H. KIPPLEY; MARVIN J. KLEMMER; BRUCE D. KREBS; THOMAS E. KRAMER; MICHAEL T. KRANK; ALBERT R. LEARY; EDWIN P. WEHNER; GERALD RUELLE, O.S.B.; Rev. Msgr. GERALD J. WALSH.

Procurator/Advocates—ROSE BALL; RUTH MOERICKE.

Notary—TAMMY J. MUNSON.

Presbyteral Council—Revs. THOMAS E. KRAMER; DAVID ZIMMER; BRUCE D. KREBS; THOMAS J. RICHTER, Sec.; CHRIS B. WALTER; EDWARD F. KORTE; EDWIN P. WEHNER, Chm.; JOHN G. GUTHRIE; Rt. Rev. PATRICK MOORE, O.S.B.

Diocesan Corporate Board—Most Rev. PAUL A. ZIPFEL, Pres.; Revs. THOMAS E. KRAMER, Vice Pres. PAUL D. BECKER; JAMES B. BRAATEN; Sr. JOANNE GRAHAM, O.S.B., J.C.L., Sec.

Diocesan Finance Council—Most Rev. PAUL A. ZIPFEL; Revs. THOMAS E. KRAMER, Chm.; JAMES B. BRAATEN; PAUL D. BECKER; Mr. WILLIAM HETH; RICHARD F. WHITE; ERNEST B. BORR; MIKE SCHWINDT; MARVIN HEINERT; JEFFRY TESCHER; Sr. JOANNE GRAHAM, O.S.B., J.C.L.; RON SCHATZ.

Due Process Service—Sr. JOANNE GRAHAM, O.S.B., J.C.L.

Pastoral Council—Vacant.

Diocesan Offices and Directors

Archives—KENNETH SMALL, *Box 1137, Bismarck, 58502-1137.* Tel: 701-222-3035.

Boy Scouts—KEN ROETHLER, Chm., *1210 N. 18th St., Bismarck, 58501.*

Campaign For Human Development—Sr. JOANNE GRAHAM, O.S.B., J.C.L., Dir., *P.O. Box 1575, Bismarck, 58502-1575.* Tel: 701-223-1347.

Catholic Family Service—ROGER SCHWINGHAMMER, Exec. Dir., *2537 University Dr. S., Fargo, 58103.* Tel: 701-235-4457., Other Locations: *1223 S. 12th, Bismarck, 58504.* Tel: 701-255-1793., *400-22nd Ave., N.W., Minot, 58701.* Tel: 701-852-2854.

Catholic Relief—Sr. JOANNE GRAHAM, O.S.B., J.C.L., Dir., *P.O. Box 1575, Bismarck, 58502-1575.* Tel: 701-223-1347.

Office of Vocations—Rev. Msgr. GERALD J. WALSH, Dir.; Rev. DENNIS SCHAFER, Asst. Dir., *P.O. Box 1137, Bismarck, 58502-1137.* Tel: 701-222-3035.

Vicar for Presbyters—Rev. Msgr. GERALD J. WALSH, *P.O. Box 1137, Bismarck, 58502-1137.* Tel: 701-222-3035.

Office of Worship—Rev. GENE LINDEMANN, *Box 1137, Bismarck, 58501.* Tel: 701-222-3035.

Continuing Education for Clergy—Rev. CASIMIRS PALUCK, *P.O. Box 1137, Bismarck, 58502-1137.* Tel: 701-222-3035.

Ecumenism—Rev. MARVIN J. KLEMMER, *1902 S. Third St., Bismarck, 58504.* Tel: 701-223-3606.

Health Care Commission—Sr. JOANNE GRAHAM, O.S.B., J.C.L., *P.O. Box 1575, Bismarck, 58502-1575.* Tel: 701-223-1347.

Holy Childhood—Sr. JOANNE GRAHAM, O.S.B., J.C.L., Dir., *P.O. Box 1575, Bismarck, 58502-1575.* Tel: 701-223-1347.

Newspaper—"Dakota Catholic Action", MARGE GROSZ, Editor, *P.O. Box 1137, Bismarck, 58502-1137.* Tel: 701-222-3035.

North Dakota Catholic Conference—CHRISTOPHER DODSON, *227 W. Broadway, Ste. 2, Bismarck, 58501.* Tel: 701-223-2519; Fax: 701-223-6075.

Pastoral Planning—Sr. JOANNE GRAHAM, O.S.B., J.C.L.,

Dir., *P.O. Box 1137, Bismarck, 58502-1137.* Tel: 701-223-1347.

Permanent Diaconate Office—Rev. THEODORE F. GUSTIN, Vicar for Deacons; Deacons STEPHEN B. MAYS, Dir. ALVIN W. SCHWINDT, Dir., Formation Prog. Permanent Diaconate, *P.O. Box 1137, Bismarck, 58502-1137.* Tel: 701-222-3035.

Priests' Benefit Association—Most Rev. PAUL A. ZIPFEL, Pres.; Revs. WILLIAM J. FAHNLANDER; JAMES B. BRAATEN, Vice Chm. DAVID MORMAN; WILLIAM RUSHFORD; PAUL L. CERVINSKI; HENRY W. SCHNEIDER.

Priests' Personnel Board—Rev. ALBERT R. LEARY, Chm.; Rev. Msgr. GERALD J. WALSH; Revs. DENNIS R. SCHAFER; BRUCE D. KREBS; NORMAN J. DUKART.

Propagation of the Faith—Sr. JOANNE GRAHAM, O.S.B., J.C.L., *P.O. Box 1575, Bismarck, 58502-1575.* Tel: 701-223-1347.

Communications Office—Rev. JOHN J. OWENS, *P.O. Box 1137, Bismarck, 58502-1137.* Tel: 701-222-3035; Fax: 701-673-3178.

Office of Catechesis—Sr. KATHLEEN ATKINSON, O.S.B., *Box 1137, Bismarck, 58502-1137.* Tel: 701-222-3035.

Pro-Life—Rev. JOHN J. OWENS, *P.O. Box 1137, Bismarck, 58502-1137.* Tel: 701-222-3035; Fax: 701-673-3178.

Office of Education—ROMAN WEILER, Dir., *P.O. Box 1137, Bismarck, 58502-1137.* Tel: 701-222-3035.

Social Concerns—ANNETTA SUTTON, Dir., *Box 1137, Bismarck, 58502-1137.* Tel: 701-222-3035.

Stewardship and Resource Development Office—RONALD SCHATZ, Dir., *Box 1137, Bismarck, 58502-1137.* Tel: 701-222-3035.

Directors for Office of Religious—Rev. DANIEL MALONEY, O.S.B., *Annunciation Priory, 7520 University Dr., Bismarck, 58504-9653.* Tel: 701-255-1520. Sr. JOANNE GRAHAM, O.S.B., J.C.L., *P.O. Box 1575, Bismarck, 58502-1575.* Tel: 701-223-1347.

Youth Ministry—KENNETH H. ROSHAU, Dir., *Box 1137, Bismarck, 58502-1137.* Tel: 701-222-3035.

Search Program—KENNETH H. ROSHAU, *Box 1137, Bismarck, 58502-1137.* Tel: 701-222-3035.

CLERGY, PARISHES, MISSIONS AND PAROCHIAL SCHOOLS

CITY OF BISMARCK
(Burleigh County)

1—CATHEDRAL OF THE HOLY SPIRIT (1947), Revs. Thomas E. Kramer; Thomas J. Richter; Deacons Wilfred Wolf; Ralph von Reuden.
Res., 519 Raymond St., 58501. Tel: 701-223-1033; Fax: 701-223-1438. [JC]
School—Tel: 701-223-5484. Elizabeth Gross, Prin.
Sisters of St. Benedict 2; Lay Teachers 17; Students 262.
Catechesis/Religious Programs—Tel: 701-222-2259. Helen Poling, D.R.E.
Students 274.

2—ASCENSION (1974), Rev. Marvin J. Klemmer; Deacons John Lamontagne; Ray Grabar; Al Schwindt; Larry Dorrheim.
Res., 1905 S. Third St., 58504. Tel: 701-223-3606; Fax: 701-223-5783. [JC]
Catechesis/Religious Programs—Tel: 701-258-5692. Marie Krous-Gabel, D.R.E.
Students 747.

3—CORPUS CHRISTI (1964), Rev. Stephen R. Zastoupil; Sr. Ivo Schoch, Pastoral Assoc.; Deacons Lynn Clancy; Harry M. Deichert; Joseph J. Mathern; Rex McDowell; LeRoy M. Kuss; James V. Ressler; Robert Schuller; John Tharaldsen; Duane J. Koble, Admin.
Res., 1936 N. Second St., 58501. Tel: 701-255-4620; Fax: 701-255-4616. [JC]
Catechesis/Religious Programs—Tel: 701-255-3104. D.R.E.: Patricia Clark; Mary Kay Vetter; Patrick Hall.
Students 978.

4—ST. ANNE (1957), Revs. Edwin P. Wehner; Kuriakose Nediakala, M.C.B.S. (India); Betty E. Greff, Pastoral Assoc.; Alice Maher, Parish Admin.; Deacons Alvin Schmitz; Kasper Greff; Wayne Jundt.
Res., 1321 Braman Ave., 58501. Tel: 701-223-1549.
School—(Grades PreK-8). Tel: 701-223-3373. Mrs. Darlene Reinarts, Prin.
Lay Teachers 12; Students 220.
Catechesis/Religious Programs—Tel: 701-224-0847. Mrs. Frances I. Roehrich, D.R.E.
Students 498.

5—ST. MARY (1877), Rev. Charles A. Heidt; Steve Braus, Admin.; Sr. Patricia Schap, O.S.B., Pastoral Min.; Sr. Colette Wolfe, O.S.B., Pastorial Min.; Deacons Kenneth Klein, Patorial Min.; Morris Martin; Tony Dworshak.
Res., 806 E. Broadway, 58501. Tel: 701-223-5562; Fax: 701-250-9918. [JC]
School—Tel: 701-223-0225. Gwyn Marlack-Tschosik, Prin.
Lay Teachers 13; Students 201.
Catechesis/Religious Programs—Students 100.

OUTSIDE THE CITY OF BISMARCK

Beach, Golden Valley Co., St. John the Baptist (1909), Rev. David G. Morman; Deacons Samuel Larson; Donald Nistler; James Wosepka.
Res., Box 337, 58621. Tel: 701-872-4153; Fax: 701-872-4695. [CEM 2]
Catechesis/Religious Programs—Carla Steffen, D.R.E.
Students 195.
Mission—Golva, Golden Valley Co., St. Mary, P.O. Box 337, 58621. [CEM 3]

Belfield, Stark Co., St. Bernard (1910), Rev. John G. Guthrie.
Res., P.O. Box 38, 58622. Tel: 701-575-4295. [CEM]
Catechesis/Religious Programs—Tel: 701-575-4099. D.R.E.: Diane Procive; Pam Evoniuk, (Elementary); Jolynn Roller, (High School).
Students 198.
Mission—Medora, Billings Co., St. Mary, Box 11, Medora, 58645. Tel: 701-623-4450.

Beulah, Mercer Co., St. Joseph (1915) (German-Russian), Revs. Edwin Volk; James E. Reardon.
Res., P.O. Box 146, 58523. Tel: 701-873-5397; Fax: 701-873-5614. [CEM]
Catechesis/Religious Programs—Tel: 701-873-5006; 873-5622. Julie Knodel, D.R.E.
Students 301.

Bowbells, Burke Co., St. Joseph (1905) (German-Scandinavian), Rev. George Uralikunnel (India); Deacon Edmund Morgel.
Res., P.O. Box 339, 58721. Tel: 701-377-2611.
Catechesis/Religious Programs—Tel: 701-377-2766. D.R.E.: Clarice Corey; Mary Hawbaker.
Students 24.
Mission—Portal, Burke Co., St. John the Baptist, Portal, 58772. Tel: 701-926-4621. [CEM]

Bowman, Bowman Co., St. Charles (1910), Rev. Charles Zins.
Res., 58623. Tel: 701-523-5292. [CEM]
Catechesis/Religious Programs—Tel: 701-523-5415. Faye Burke, D.R.E. (Grades 1-12).
Students 129.
Missions—Rhame, Bowman Co., St. Mel, P.O. Box 709, 58623. Tel: 701-523-5292; Marmarth, Slope Co., Immaculate Heart of Mary, P.O. Box 709, 58623.

Burlington, Ward Co., St. Francis of Assisi. Closed. For inquiries for parish records contact the Chancery. (Quasi-Parish).

Carson, Grant Co., St. Theresa the Child Jesus (1920), Rev. Kenneth G. Phillips.
Res., 421 Court St., Flasher, 58535-7216. Tel: 701-597-3570; 597-3228. [JC]
Catechesis/Religious Programs—Tel: 701-597-3228.
Students 55.

Center, Oliver Co., St. Martin (1916), Rev. Austin A. Vetter.
Res., P.O. Box 2766, 58530. Tel: 701-794-3329. [CEM][JC 2]
Catechesis/Religious Programs—Tel: 201-794-3191. D.R.E.: Judith McNulty; Alice Henderscheid.
Students 127.

Crosby, Divide Co., St. Patrick (1917), Rev. Ed Korte.
Res., P.O. Box 89, 58730. Tel: 701-965-6537. [CEM 3][JC 2]
Catechesis/Religious Programs—Students 84.
Mission—Noonan, Divide Co., St. Luke, 304 Main St., Noonan, 58765.

Crown Butte, Morton Co., St. Vincent (1896), Deacon Robert Olson; Loretta Olson, Pastoral Assoc. & D.R.E.
Mailing Address: 3180 36th St., Mandan, 58554.
Res., 1703 1/2 N.E. Second, Mandan, 58554. Tel: 701-663-2544. [CEM]
Catechesis/Religious Programs—Students 14.

Dickinson, Stark Co.,

1—QUEEN OF PEACE CHURCH, (1973), Rev. Jerome G. Kautzman.
Office: 725 12th St. W., 58601-3516. Tel: 701-225-2134; 225-2991 (Res.). [JC]
Catechesis/Religious Programs—Tel: 701-225-9894. Dickie Jo Boespflug, D.R.E.
Students 212.

2—ST. JOSEPH, (1902) (German-Russian), Rev. C. Robert Kavaney; Deacon Ralph Stockert.
Res., 240 E. Broadway, 58601. Tel: 701-225-2222.
School—Tel: 701-225-6162.
Sisters 1; Lay Teachers 7; Students 82.
Catechesis/Religious Programs—Marlene Reisenauer, D.R.E.
Students 211.

3—ST. PATRICK, (1885), Rev. George A. Dukart; Sr. Stephanie Dolyniuk, O.S.B., Pastoral Assoc.; Deacons Joe Kappel; Anton Wanner.
Res., 229 Third Ave. W., 58601. Tel: 701-225-2012; Fax: 701-225-2012.
School—Tel: 701-225-8094. Sr. Richarde Marie Wolf, S.S.N.D., Prin.
Sisters 2; Lay Teachers 10; Students 170.
Catechesis/Religious Programs—Tel: 701-225-8831. Mary Agostini, D.R.E.
Students 109.

4—ST. PIUS. Closed. For inquiries for parish records contact the Chancery.

5—ST. WENCESLAUS, (1912), Revs. Peter L. Kramer; John Mathai Assariparambil; Deacons Eugene F. Morman; Raymond Jilek.
Res., 525 Third St. E., 58601. Tel: 701-225-3972.
School—Tel: 701-225-9463. Sr. Mary Elizabeth Muscha, Prin.
Lay Teachers 9; Students 185.
Catechesis/Religious Programs—Tel: 701-225-4973. Gini Zent, D.R.E.
Students 305.

Flasher, Morton Co., St. Lawrence (1912), Rev. Kenneth G. Phillips.
Res., 421 Court St., 58535-7216. Tel: 701-597-3570. [CEM]
Catechesis/Religious Programs—Tel: 701-597-3228.
Students 116.

Fort Yates, Sioux Co., St. Peter - Catholic Indian Mission (1878). (Standing Rock Indian Reservation). Revs. Casimir A. Paluck; Leonard Savel Koul.
Res., P.O. Box 394, 58538. Tel: 701-854-3473; Fax: 701-854-3474. [CEM]
School—St. Bernard Mission School, Tel: 701-854-7413. Sr. Julie Brandt, S.S.N.D., Prin.
Sisters 5; Lay Teachers 3; Students 103.
Catechesis/Religious Programs—Sr. Irene Dohmen, S.S.N.D., D.R.E.
Students 55.
Missions—Cannon Ball, Sioux Co., St. Elizabeth, P.O. Box 394, 58538. [CEM]
Porcupine, Sioux Co., St. James. [CEM]

Foxholm, Ward Co., St. Mary, Rev. Paul D. Becker.
Res., 17901 128th Ave. N.W., 58718-9643. Tel: 701-852-8575. [CEM]
Catechesis/Religious Programs—Tel: 701-468-5648.
Students 122.
Mission—Berthold, Ward Co., St. Ann, Berthold, 58718. Tel: 701-453-3660.

Garrison, McLean Co., St. Nicholas (1905), Rev. Hugo L. Blotsky, O.S.B.
Res., 235 Second St. N.E., P.O. Box 870, 58540. Tel: 701-463-2327; Fax: 701-463-2323. [CEM]
Catechesis/Religious Programs—Tel: 701-337-2296. Jane Krausert, D.R.E.
Students 145.
Mission—Max, McClean Co., Immaculate Conception, P.O. Box 295, Max, 58759.

Glenburn, Renville Co., St. Philomena (1948) (German-Scandinavian), Rev. Jacob Konath.
Res., 302 Raymond St., Box 68, 58740. Tel: 701-362-7571; Fax: 701-362-7571. [CEM]
Catechesis/Religious Programs—Tel: 701-362-7437. Dianne Henson, D.R.E.
Students 45.
Mission—Lansford, Bottineau Co., St. John, Rte. 2, Box 3, Lansford, 58750. Tel: 701-784-5421.

Glen Ullin, Morton Co., Sacred Heart of Jesus (1883) (German-Russian), Rev. Claude Seeberger, O.S.B.
Res., Box 609, 58631. Tel: 701-348-3518. [CEM 2]
Catechesis/Religious Programs—Tel: 701-348-3527. Mrs. Kathy Schirado, D.R.E.
Students 141.
Mission—Glen Ullin, Grant Co., St. Joseph, 58631-0609.

Grenora, Williams Co., St. Boniface, Rev. Raymond A. Aydt.
Church—P.O. Box 37, 58845. Tel: 701-694-3743.
Res., 118 Fifth St., W., Williston, 58801. Tel: 701-572-6732. [JC]
Catechesis/Religious Programs—Peggy Degele, D.R.E.
Students 18.

Hague, Emmons Co., St. Mary (1890) (German-Russian), Rev. Leonard A. Eckroth.
Church—P.O. Box 156, 58542. Tel: 701-336-7119.
Res., Box 322, Strasburg, 58573. Tel: 701-336-2603; 336-7172. [CEM 2]
Catechesis/Religious Programs—Tel: 701-336-7102. Sr. Rose Schwab, S.S.N.D., D.R.E.
Students 24.

Halliday, Dunn Co., St. Paul (1952). (Quasi-Parish). Rev. Gerald Ruelle, O.S.B.

Res., P.O. Box 299, Killdeer, 58640. Tel: 701-764-5357. [CEM][JC]
Catechesis/Religious Programs—Tel: 701-938-4504. D.R.E.: Vickie Clarys; Deacon Edward J. Ziman; Herman Dukart.
Students 57.

Hazelton, Emmons Co., St. Paul (1905), Revs. Jeffrey A. Zwack; Berchmans Konnully (India); Deacon Kenneth Wolbaum.
Res., P.O. Box 758, Linton, 58552. Tel: 701-254-4588.
Catechesis/Religious Programs—Tel: 701-782-6281. Charlotte Beastrom, D.R.E.
Students 71.
Mission—Braddock, Emmons Co., St. Katherine, P.O. Box 758, Linton, 58552. [CEM 2]

Hazen, Mercer Co., St. Martin (1914), Rev. James E. Reardon.
Res., P.O. Box 387, 58545. Tel: 701-748-2121. [CEM]
Catechesis/Religious Programs—D.R.E.: Peg Rahn; LuAnn Woeste.
Students 217.

Hebron, Morton Co., St. Ann (1906) (German), Rev. Francis dos Remedios, O.S.B.
Res., P.O. Box 12, 58638. Tel: 701-878-4658. [CEM 3]
Catechesis/Religious Programs—Harvey Tibor, D.R.E.
Students 92.
Mission—Haymarsh, Morton Co., St. Clement, P.O. Box 12, 58638.

Hettinger, Adams Co., Holy Trinity (1916) (German), Rev. Bruce Krebs.
Res., 405 3rd St. N., 58639. Tel: 701-567-2772; Fax: 701-567-2772. [JC]
Catechesis/Religious Programs—Grace Meier, D.R.E.
Students 91.
Missions—Reeder, Adams Co., Sacred Heart, 405-3rd St. N., 58639. Tel: 701-853-2920; Scranton, Bowman Co., Sacred Heart, 405-3rd St. N., 58639. Tel: 701-275-8778.

Kenmare, Ward Co., St. Agnes (1901), Rev. Kenneth Wald, Admin.
Res., P.O. Box 488, 58746. Tel: 701-385-4311. [CEM]
Catechesis/Religious Programs—Tel: 701-386-2403. Evan and Deb Zeltinger, D.R.E.
Students 98.
Mission—Donnybrook, Ward Co., St. Anthony, Donnybrook, 58734. [CEM]

Killdeer, Dunn Co., St. Joseph (1917), Rev. Gerald Ruelle, O.S.B.; Deacon Edward J. Ziman.
Res., P.O. Box 299, 58640. Tel: 701-764-5357. [CEM][JC 2]
Catechesis/Religious Programs—Tel: 701-548-8068. Candice Benz, D.R.E.
Students 119.

Lefor, Stark Co., St. Elizabeth (1898), Rev. Lawrence L. Wagner, O.S.B.
Res., 18401 168th Ave. S.E., 58641-5010. Tel: 701-225-3375. [CEM][JC 3]
Catechesis/Religious Programs—Rev. Lawrence L. Wagner, O.S.B., D.R.E.
Students 9.
Mission—Gladstone, Stark Co., St. Thomas the Apostle, 58641-5010.

Linton, Emmons Co., St. Anthony (1909), Revs. Jeffrey A. Zwack; Berchmans Konnully (India); Deacon Martin Schumacher.
Res., Box 758, 58552. Tel: 701-254-4588. [CEM]
Catechesis/Religious Programs—Tel: 701-254-4646. Diane Wangler, D.R.E.
Students 187.

Mandan, Morton Co., Christ the King (1957), Rev. Albert R. Leary; Deacons Ward Johnson; Emil Riehl.
Res., 505-10th Ave., N.W., 58554-2599. Tel: 701-663-8842; Fax: 701-667-1730. [CEM]
School—Tel: 701-663-6200; Fax: 701-667-1730. Rev. Albert R. Leary, Prin.
Lay Teachers 13; Students 130.
Catechesis/Religious Programs—Julie Schatz, D.R.E.
Students 196.

St. Joseph (1881), Rev. Robert E. Feeney; Deacon Peter Hoffman.
Res., 108 Third St. N.E., P.O. Box 603, 58554. Tel: 701-663-9562; Fax: 701-663-0183. [CEM]
School—(Grades K-6). Tel: 701-663-9563.
Lay Teachers 10; Students 118.
Catechesis/Religious Programs—D.R.E.: Al Shreve, (Grades K-8); Randy Frohlich, (Confirmation Dir.).
Students 214.

Spirit of Life (1978), Rev. Cyprian T. Meier; Deacon David Vaughn.
Mailing Address: Box 247, 58554.
Res., 801 First St. S.E., 58554. Tel: 701-663-1660; Fax: 701-667-2021.
Catechesis/Religious Programs—Jim Fritzhuspen, D.R.E.
Students 348.

Mandaree, Dunn Co., St. Anthony (Native American), Rev. Stephen Kranz, O.S.B.; Bro. Bernard Vogel, O.S.B., Pastoral Assoc.
Res., Fr. Berthold Reservation, HCO 2, Box 27, 58757. Tel: 701-759-3412. [CEM]
Catechesis/Religious Programs—Students 229.
Missions—Twin Buttes, Dunn Co., St. Joseph, 58757.; White Shield, McLean Co., Sacred Heart, 58757.

Menoken, Burleigh Co., St. Hildegard (1949), Rev. John J. Owens.
Res., 17200 Hwy. 10, 58558-9604. Tel: 701-673-3177; Fax: 701-673-3178.
Catechesis/Religious Programs—Janice Aberle, D.R.E.
Students 70.
Mission—Driscoll, Burleigh Co., St. Anthony, 17200 Hwy. 10, 58558-9604. [JC]

Minot, Ward Co.,

1—Minot Air Force Base Chapel, (1954), Rev. Anthony C. Williams.
Res., 5 BW/HC, 230 Missile Ave., 58505-5003. Tel: 701-723-2456; Fax: 701-723-3052.
Catechesis/Religious Programs—Students 219.

2—Our Lady of Grace, (1959), Revs. Robert H. Kippley; Wayne V. Sattler.
Res., 715 16th Ave., S.W., 58701. Tel: 701-839-6834; Fax: 701-838-5929.
Catechesis/Religious Programs—D.R.E.: Darlene Demars, (Grades K-6); Joan Aftem, (Grades 7-12).
Students 410.

3—St. John the Apostle, (1961), Rev. Henry W. Schneider; Deacon M. Stephen Mays.
Res., 109-25th St. N.W., 58701. Tel: 701-839-7076. [JC]
Catechesis/Religious Programs—Tel: 701-839-4076. Mrs. Winston Black, D.R.E.
Students 286.

4—St. Leo, (1886) (German), Rev. Chris B. Walter.
Res., 305 First St. S.E., 58701. Tel: 701-838-1026. [CEM]
Catechesis/Religious Programs—Tel: 701-838-1026. Rosie Workman, D.R.E.
Students 175.

5—St. Theresa, the Little Flower, (1954), Rev. Paul L. Cervinski.
Res., 800 University Ave., W., 58703. Tel: 701-838-1520; Fax: 701-839-8567. [JC]
School—See separate listing under Institutions Located in the Diocese. Tel: 701-839-5882.
Catechesis/Religious Programs—D.R.E.: Sr. Angela Korte, O.S.F., Pastoral Assoc.; Mary Wolf.
Students 125.

Mohall, Renville Co., St. Jerome (1906), Rev. James B. Braaten.
Res., 307 E. Main St., 58761. Tel: 701-756-6601. [CEM]
Catechesis/Religious Programs—Students 106.
Mission—Sherwood, Renville Co., St. James, Mohall, 58761. Tel: 701-756-6601.

Mott, Hettinger Co., St. Vincent de Paul (1907), Rev. Dennis R. Schafer; Deacon Ervin Schneider.
Res., 408 Iowa Ave., 58646. Tel: 701-824-2651. [CEM]
School—Tel: 701-824-2521.
Lay Teachers 4; Students 29.
Catechesis/Religious Programs—Mary Jo Fries, D.R.E.
Students 110.
Mission—New Leipzig, Grant Co., St. John the Baptist, New Leipzig, 58562.

New England, Hettinger Co., St. Mary (1910), Rev. Patrick A. Schumacher, S.T.L.
Res., 437 Main Ave., P.O. Box 369, 58647. Tel: 701-579-4312; Fax: 701-579-4874.
Catechesis/Religious Programs—Theresa Jacobs, D.R.E.
Students 139.
Mission—Regent, Hettinger Co., St. Henry's, P.O. Box 155, Regent, 58650. Tel: 701-563-4595.

New Hradec, Dunn Co., SS. Peter and Paul (1898) (Czech), Rev. Wilfrid J. Splonskowski, O.S.B.
Res., Box 35-B, Dickinson, 58601-9304. Tel: 701-225-2644. [CEM]
Catechesis/Religious Programs—Students 40.
Mission—Gladstone, Dunn Co., St. Philip, P.O. Box 72, Gladstone, 58630. [CEM]

New Salem, Morton Co., St. Pius V (1912), Rev. David L. Zimmer.
Res., P.O. Box C, 58563. Tel: 701-843-7144. [CEM]
Catechesis/Religious Programs—Tel: 701-843-7061. Mary Lou Klemisch, D.R.E.
Students 166.
Mission—Almont, Morton Co., St. Mary, Queen of Peace, Almont, 58520.

New Town, Mountrail Co., St. Anthony (1954), Rev. John P. O'Leary.
Res., P.O. Box 715, 58763. Tel: 701-627-4423. [CEM 4][JC]
Catechesis/Religious Programs—D.R.E.: Sr. Anna Rose, O.S.B.; Julie Herbal.
Students 108.

Parshall, Mountrail Co., St. Bridget (1917), Rev. Thomas P. Sullivan.
Res., 12 First St., N.E., Box 519, 58770-0519. Tel: 701-862-3484. [JC 3]
Catechesis/Religious Programs—Claudia Schneider, D.R.E.
Students 36.
Missions—Plaza, Mountrail Co., Sacred Heart, 58770-0519.; Makoti, Ward Co., St. Elizabeth, 58770-0519.

Raleigh, Grant Co., St. Gertrude (1913), Rev. Kenneth G. Phillips.
Res., 421 Court St., Flasher, 58535-7216. Tel: 701-597-3570. [CEM]
Catechesis/Religious Programs—Tel: 701-597-3228.
Students 34.

Regent, Hettinger Co., St. Henry (1913), Rev. Patrick A. Schumacher.
Res., P.O. Box 155, 58650-0155. Tel: 701-563-4595. [JC]
Catechesis/Religious Programs—Tel: 701-563-4543. D.R.E.: Karen Kouba; Cindy Krauter.
Students 74.

Richardton, Stark Co., St. Mary (1895), Rev. Brian Wangler, O.S.B.
Res., P.O. Box A, 58652. Tel: 701-974-3569. [CEM]
School—Tel: 701-974-3674. Deborah Bohn, Prin.
Lay Teachers 5; Students 59.
Catechesis/Religious Programs—Marilyn Metz, D.R.E. (Grades K-11).
Students 110.
Mission—Richardton, Stark Co., St. Stephen, Box A, 58652. Tel: 701-974-3332.

St. Anthony, Morton Co., St. Anthony (1897) (German-Russian), Rev. Gene E. Lindemann, J.C.L.
Res., P.O. Box 45, 58566. Tel: 701-445-7373. [CEM]
Catechesis/Religious Programs—Students 92.
Mission—Huff, Morton Co., St. Martin, 58566-0045. Tel: 701-445-7373.

St. Michael, Emmons Co., St. Michael's. Closed. For inquiries for parish records contact the Chancery.

Selfridge, Sioux Co., St. Philomena (1919) (German-Russian), Rev. Casimir A. Paluck.
Res., Box 85, 58568. Tel: 701-854-3473; Fax: 701-854-3474. [CEM]
Mailing Address: P.O. Box 394, Ft. Yates, 58538.
Catechesis/Religious Programs—David Volk, D.R.E.
Students 46.
Mission—Solen, Sioux Co., Sacred Heart, 58568.

South Heart, Stark Co., St. Mary (1923), Rev. John G. Guthrie.
Res., P.O. Box 189, 58655. Tel: 701-677-5886. [CEM]
Catechesis/Religious Programs—Students 97.

Stanley, Mountrail Co., Queen of the Most Holy Rosary (1908), Rev. Vincent Chembakassery.
Res., P.O. Box 159, 58784. Tel: 701-628-2323. [JC]
Catechesis/Religious Programs—Betty Leith, D.R.E.
Students 89.
Mission—Powers Lake, Burke Co., St. James, 8334 Hwy. 50, Powers Lake, 58773. Tel: 701-464-5771. [JC]

Strasburg, Emmons Co., Sts. Peter and Paul (1889) (German-Russian), Rev. Leonard A. Eckroth.
Res., Box 322, 58573. Tel: 701-336-2603; 336-7172. [CEM]
Catechesis/Religious Programs—Tel: 701-336-7102. Sr. Rose Schwab, S.S.N.D., D.R.E.
Students 142.
Mission—Rural Linton, Emmons Co., St. Michael's, P.O. Box 322, 58573-0322.

Tioga, Williams Co., St. Thomas (1914), Rev. Thomas Dignan.
Res., P.O. Box 667, 58852. Tel: 701-664-2445. [CEM][JC]
Catechesis/Religious Programs—Students 75.
Mission—Ray, Williams Co., St. Michael, Ray, 58849. Tel: 701-568-2252.

Underwood, McLean Co., St. Bonaventure (1913), Rev. James W. Ryan.
Res., P.O. Box 700, 58576. Tel: 701-442-5229.
Catechesis/Religious Programs—Tel: 701-442-3412.
Students 99.
Mission—Turtle Lake, McLean Co., St. Catherine, Main St., Turtle Lake, 58575. Tel: 701-488-9289. [CEM][JC]

Watford City, McKenzie Co., Epiphany (1915), Rev. John M. Pfeifer.
Res., P.O. Box 670, 58854. Tel: 701-842-3505.
Catechesis/Religious Programs—Tel: 701-842-3791. Kathy Johnson, D.R.E.

Students 143.

Missions—Alexander, McKenzie Co., Our Lady of Consolation, R.R. 1, Box 58, Alexander, 58831. Tel: 701-586-3720; Grassy Butte, McKenzie Co., St. Peter Canisius, 58854.

Williston, Williams Co., St. Joseph (1901), Revs. Norman J. Dukart; Thomas Pittappilly (India).

Res., 124 Sixth St. W., P.O. Box K, 58802. Tel: 701-572-6731. [JC]

School—Tel: 701-572-6384. Pamela Lambert, Prin. Lay Teachers 14; Students 136.

Catechesis/Religious Programs—Tel: 701-572-0201. Ida Kirchmeier, D.R.E.

Students 489.

Mission—Trenton, Williams Co., St. John the Baptist, P.O. Box K, 58802. Tel: 701-572-6731.

Wilton, McLean Co., Sacred Heart (1908), Rev. Theodore F. Gustin.

Res., P.O. Box 128, 58579. Tel: 701-734-6384. [JC]

Catechesis/Religious Programs—Tel: 701-734-8136. Debbie Smith, D.R.E.

Students 186.

Missions—Washburn, McLean Co., St. Edwin, P.O.Box 65, Washburn, 58577. Tel: 701-462-3340; Wing, Burleigh Co., St. Ignatius, P.O. Box 128, Wilton, 58477.

INDIAN MISSIONS

Fort Berthold Reservation, Sacred Heart Indian Mission. (Ree, Gros Venture and Mandan).

Res., St. Anthony, R.R. 12, Box 27, Mandaree, 58701. Tel: 701-759-3412. Rev. Stephen Kranz, O.S.B.

Chaplains of Public Institutions

BISMARCK. *Bismarck State College* Schafer St., 58501. Tel: 701-224-5400. Deacon John Lamontagne, Chap.

North Dakota State Penitentiary 2905 Winnipeg Dr., 58501. Tel: 701-258-7566. Deacon John Tharaldsen.

North Dakota Youth Correctional Center 215 E. Arbor, Apt. 308C, 58504. Tel: 701-224-1302. Deacon Morris E. Martin.

Special Assignment:

Reverend Monsignors—

Walsh, Gerald J., P.O. Box 1137, Bismarck, ND 58502-1137

On Duty Outside the Diocese:

Reverend Fathers—

Allen, Joseph A., Diocese of Fargo, ND

Deichert, Joseph, 16 SOW/HC, 210 Cody Ave., Hurlburt Field, FL 32544-5306

Hill, Donald, Chap., Army National Guard, Washington, DC

Kuss, Allen R., Dir., U.S. Navy, Religious Ministeries Center, McRD ERR, P.O. Box 19601, Parris Island, SC 29905

Wehner, Eugene C., O.C.D., Franciscan Friars, 5345 S. University Ave., Chicago, IL 60615

Graduate Studies:

Reverend Fathers—

Brown, Phillip J., North American College, Rome

Retired:

Reverend Fathers—

Adkins, Joseph H., 1409 2nd Ave. S.W., Minot, ND 58701

Backes, Charles H., 1020 N. 26th St., Bismarck, ND 58501

Backes, Hugo G., 1050 N. 28th St., Bismarck, ND 58501-3193

Bova, Eugene R., 360 Pinon Rd., Bailey, CO 80421

Brydl, Ladislaus C., 1020 N. 26th St., Bismarck, ND 58501

Cook, Blaine, Emmaus Place, 1020 N. 26th St., Bismarck, ND 58501

Fahnlander, William J., Emmaus Place, 1020 N. 26th St., Bismarck, ND 58501

Frank, Eugene G., Mission Nursing Home, 3401 Medicine Lake Blvd. E., Plymouth, MN 55441

Krank, Michael T., P.O. Box 745, Dickinson, ND 58602

Kuhn, John H., 1020 N. 26th St., Bismarck, ND 58501

Rushford, William A., 1020 N. 26th St., Bismarck, ND 58501

Schumacher, Jacob J., Emmaus Place, 1020 N. 26th St., Bismarck, ND 58501

Spain, P. Arnold, 2881 B Warwick Loop, Bismarck, ND 58504

Williams, Robert A., 2669 5th Ave. W., #9, Dickinson, ND 58601

Permanent Deacons:

Barone, Daniel, St. Anthony, New Town

Berg, Melvin J., (Retired)

Brannan, Steve M., Queen of Peace, Dickinson

Clancy, Lynn, Corpus Christi, Bismarck

Cunningham, Patrick M., Little Flower, Minot

Dean, Dennis L., St. John, Lansford

Deichert, Harry M., Corpus Christi, Bismarck

Dorrheim, Larry L., Ascension, Bismarck

DuKart, Herman, St. Joseph, Killdeer

Dworshak, Anton T., St. Mary, Bismarck

Grabar, Ray A., Ascension, Bismarck

Greff, Kasper N., St. Anne, Bismarck

Harmon, Steve M., Bismarck

Hibl, Albert W., (Retired)

Hoffman, Peter, St. Joseph, Mandan

Jilek, Raymond, St. Wenceslaus, Dickinson

Johnson, Ed J., Sr., Rolla, ND

Johnson, Ward A., Christ the King, Mandan

Jundt, Wayne M., St. Anne, Bismarck

Kappel, Joseph, St. Patrick, Dickinson

Kilzer, Werner J., (Retired)

Klein, Kenneth M., St. Mary, Bismarck

Knopik, Martin, (Retired)

Kordonowy, Leonard J., Ukranian Church of St. Demetrius, Fairfield

Kuss, Leroy M., Corpus Christi, Bismarck

Lamontagne, John H., Ascension, Bismarck

Larson, Samuel, St. John the Baptist, Beach

Martin, Morris E., St. Mary, Bismarck

Mathern, Joseph J., Corpus Christi, Bismarck

Mays, Stephen B., St. John, Minot

McDowall, Rexford R., Corpus Christi, Bismarck

Morgel, Edmund D., St. John the Baptist, Portal

Morman, Eugene F., St. Wenceslaus, Dickinson

Nistler, Donald R., St. Mary, Golva

Nistler, James A., Kenya, East Africa

Olson, Robert C., St. Vincent De Paul, Crown Butte

Piasecki, Stanley T., Diocese of Cheyenne, WY

Ressler, James V., Corpus Christi, Bismarck

Riehl, Emil J., Christ the King, Mandan

Schmitz, Alvin R., St. Anne, Bismarck

Schneider, Ervin H., St. Vincent de Paul, Mott

Schuller, Robert P., Corpus Christi, Bismarck

Schumacher, Martin, St. Anthony, Linton

Schwindt, Alvin W., Ascension, Bismarck

Stockert, Ralph F., St. Joseph, Dickinson

Streitz, Steven F., Our Lady of Grace, Minot

Tharaldsen, John, Corpus Christi, Bismarck

Vaughn, David L., Spirit of Life, Mandan

Von Ruden, Ralph, Cathedral of the Holy Spirit, Bismarck

Wanner, Anton, Jr., St. Patrick, Dickinson

Wolbaum, Kenneth J., St. Katherine, Braddock

Wolf, Wilfred P., Cathedral of the Holy Spirit, Bismarck

Wosepka, James, St. John the Baptist, Beach

Ziman, Edward J., St. Joseph, Killdeer; St. Paul, Halliday

INSTITUTIONS LOCATED IN THE DIOCESE

[A] SEMINARIES, RELIGIOUS OR SCHOLASTICATES

RICHARDTON. *Assumption Abbey*, P.O. Box A, 58652. Tel: 701-974-3315; Fax: 701-974-3317. Rt. Revs. Patrick Moore, O.S.B., Abbot; Lawrence Wagner, O.S.B., Retired Abbot; Robert West, O.S.B., Retired Abbot; Very Rev. Valerian Odermann, O.S.B., Prior; Revs. Thomas Wordekemper, O.S.B., Subprior; David Wolf, O.S.B., Business Mgr.; Florian Fairbanks, O.S.B.; Eugene Hornstein, O.S.B.; Claude Seeberger, O.S.B.; Gerald Ruelle, O.S.B.; Wilfrid J. Splonskowski, O.S.B.; Raymond Dietlein, O.S.B.; Richard Wilhelmi, O.S.B.; John Odermann, O.S.B. (FAR); Stephen Kranz, O.S.B.; Damian Dietlein, O.S.B. (IND); Raphael Stovik, O.S.B.; Sebastian Schmidt, O.S.B., (Overseas); Denis Fournier, O.S.B.; Francis Wehri, O.S.B., (Overseas); Terrence Kardong, O.S.B.; Victor Feser, O.S.B.; Odo Muggli, O.S.B.; Daniel Maloney, O.S.B.; Brian Wangler, O.S.B.; Philip Vanderlin, O.S.B., (Overseas); Francis dos Remedios, O.S.B.; Carlos Suarez, O.S.B., (Overseas); Julian Nix, O.S.B.; Hugo L. Blotsky, O.S.B.; Efraim Villegas, O.S.B., (Overseas); Boniface Muggli, O.S.B.; Gonzalo Blanco, O.S.B., (Overseas). Priests 33; Brothers 26; Seminarians 3.

[B] COLLEGES AND UNIVERSITIES

BISMARCK. *University of Mary*, 7500 University Dr., 58504-9652. Tel: 701-255-7500.

E-mail: marauder@umary.edu

Web site: http://www.umary.edu

For a complete listing, refer to the Colleges and Universities section.

[C] HIGH SCHOOLS, INTERPAROCHIAL AND PARISH

BISMARCK. *St. Mary Central High School*, 1025 N. Second St., 58501. Tel: 701-223-4113.

E-mail: smchs@btigate.com

Web site: www.smchs.org

Les Kramer, Supt.; Cheryl Kalberer, Prin. Priests 2; Sisters 2; Lay Teachers 30; Students 449.

DICKINSON. *Trinity High School*, 810 Empire Rd., P.O. Box 1177, 58602-1177. Tel: 701-225-6081. Steve M. Brannan, Supt. Lay Teachers 23; Students 365.

MINOT. *Bishop Ryan High School*, 316 11th Ave. N.W., 58701. Tel: 701-852-4004. Don Bunce, Supt.; Patrick McNally, Prin. Priests 1; Lay Teachers 25; Students 416.

[D] GENERAL HOSPITALS

BISMARCK. *St. Alexius Medical Center*, P.O. Box 5510, 58502. Tel: 701-224-7000; Fax: 701-224-7284

For a complete listing, refer to the Hospitals section.

DICKINSON. *St. Joseph's Hospital and Health Center*, 30 W. Seventh St., 58601. Tel: 701-225-7271

For a complete listing, refer to the Hospitals section.

GARRISON. *Garrison Memorial Hospital*, P.O. Box 39, 58540. Tel: 701-463-2275

For a complete listing, refer to the Hospitals section.

*KENMARE. *Kenmare Community Hospital*, P.O. Box 697, 58746. Tel: 701-385-4296

For a complete listing, refer to the Hospitals section.

MINOT. *St. Joseph's Hospital dba UniMed Medical Center*, Attn: Administration, P.O. Box 5001, 58702. Tel: 701-857-2000; Fax: 701-839-8947

For a complete listing, refer to the Hospitals section.

UniMed Medical Center Foundation, 407 3rd St., S.E., 58701. Tel: 701-857-2070

For a complete listing, refer to the Hospitals section.

WILLISTON. *Mercy Hospital*, 1301 15th Ave. W., 58801. Tel: 701-774-7400; Fax: 701-774-7409

For a complete listing, refer to the Hospitals section.

Mercy Medical Center - Affiliate of Catholic Health Initiatives, 1301 15th Ave., W., 58801. Tel: 701-774-7401

For a complete listing, refer to the Hospitals section.

Mercy Medical Foundation, 1301 15th Ave., W., 58801. Tel: 701-774-7404

For a complete listing, refer to the Hospitals section.

Mercy Recovery Center, 1301 15th Ave. W., 58801. Tel: 701-774-7409; Fax: 701-774-7479

For a complete listing, refer to the Hospitals section.

[E] SPECIAL CARE FACILITIES

DICKINSON. *St. Benedict's Health Center*, 851 Fourth Ave. E., 58601. Tel: 701-225-5138; Fax: 701-225-3947. Operated by Benedictine Living Communities, Inc. Kevin A. Greff, Admin. Bed Capacity 175; Total Staff 230; Total Assisted 175.

GARRISON. *Benedictine Living Center of Garrison fka Garrison Nursing Center*, Eastern Acres, P.O. Box 219, 58540. Tel: 701-463-2226; Fax: 701-463-2650. Operated by Benedictine Health System Long Term Care, Inc. Mark Seibold, Admin. Bed Capacity 71; Total Staff 78; Total Assisted 71.

[F] PROTECTIVE INSTITUTIONS

SENTINEL BUTTE. *Home On The Range*, 16351 I-94, 58654-9500. Tel: 701-872-3745; Fax: 701-872-3748

For a complete listing, refer to the Special Care Facilities section.

[G] HOMES FOR AGED

BISMARCK. *Emmaus Place*, 1020 N. 26th St., 58501. Tel: 701-258-2618

For a complete listing, refer to the Special Care Facilities section.

Marillac Manor, 1016 N. 28th St., 58501. Tel: 701-258-8702; Fax: 701-223-3127

For a complete listing, refer to the Special Care Facilities section.

St. Vincent's Care Center, 1021 N. 26 St., 58501-3199. Tel: 701-223-6888

For a complete listing, refer to the Special Care Facilities section.

[H] CONVENTS AND RESIDENCES FOR SISTERS

BISMARCK. *Annunciation Priory*, 7520 University Dr., 58504-9653. Tel: 701-255-1520. Sr. Susan Berger, O.S.B., Prioress; Rev. Daniel Maloney, O.S.B., Res. Chap. Motherhouse and Novitiate of the Benedictine Sisters, B.M.V. Professed Sisters 97.

RICHARDTON. *Sacred Heart Monastery*, P.O. Box 364, 58652. Tel: 701-974-2121.

E-mail: sacheart@richardton.ctctel.com

Web site: www.rc.net/bismarck/shm

Sr. Paula Larson, O.S.B., Prioress. Motherhouse

and Novitiate of the Sisters of the Order of St. Benedict. Professed Sisters 40.

[I] NEWMAN CENTERS

DICKINSON. *Catholic Student Center*, 238 Eighth Ave., W., 58601. Tel: 701-225-6210. Louise A. Oleson, Dir. Total Staff 1.

MINOT. *Catholic Student Center*, 409 University Ave., N.W., 58703-2212. Tel: 701-838-2815. Louise A. Oleson, Dir. Total Staff 1.

[J] MISCELLANEOUS

DICKINSON. *Subiaco Manor*, 2441 10th Ave., W., 58601. Tel: 701225-4220.
E-mail: sister_renee@eagle.dsu.nodak.edu
Sponsored by the Benedictine Sisters of Sacred Heart Monastery in Richardton. Sr. Renee Branigan, O.S.B., Res. Mgr. Total Staff 3; Total in Residence 12.

MINOT. *Minot Catholic Schools Corporation*, 316 11th Ave., N.W., 58703-2299. Tel: 701-852-4004; Fax: 701-839-4651. Don Bunce, Supt. Total Staff 3; Total Assisted 5,600.

Bishop Ryan High School, 316 11th Ave., N.W., 58703-2299. Tel: 701-852-4004; Fax: 701-839-4651. Patrick McNally, Prin. Priests 1; Lay Teachers 25; Students 416.

Little Flower School, 800 University Ave., W., 58703. Tel: 701-839-5882; Fax: 701-839-8567. Diane Zander, Prin. Lay Teachers 10; Students 136.

St. Leo's School, 305 First St., S.E., 58701. Tel: 701-838-2597. Kevin Harmon, Prin. Lay Teachers 12; Students 188.

RICHARDTON. *Sacred Heart Benedictine Foundation*, P.O. Box 364, 58652-0364.
E-mail: sacheart@richardton.etctel.com
Web site: http://www.rc.net/bismarck/shm

RELIGIOUS INSTITUTES OF MEN REPRESENTED IN THE DIOCESE

For further details refer to the corresponding bracketed number in the Religious Institutes of Men or Women section.

[0200]—*Benedictine Monks*. (Richardton, ND) .—O.S.B.

[]—*Missionary Congregation of the Blessed Sacrament*. (Kerala, India).—M.C.B.S.

[1200]—*Society of the Divine Savior*. (Milwaukee, WI).—S.D.S.

RELIGIOUS INSTITUTES OF WOMEN REPRESENTED IN THE DIOCESE

[0230]—*Benedictine Sisters of Pontifical Jurisdiction*. (Bismarck; Richardton, ND; Watertown, SD; Yankton, SD; Duluth, MN).—O.S.B.

[2970]—*School Sisters of Notre Dame*. (Mankato Prov.).—S.S.N.D.

[0990]—*Sisters of Divine Providence*. (Allison Park, PA).—C.D.P.

[]—*Sisters of Mary of the Presentation*. (Valley City, ND).—SMP.

[2630]—*Sisters of Mercy of the Holy Cross*. (Merrill, WI).—S.C.S.C.

[2475]—*Sisters of Mercy of the Union*. (Omaha, NE).—R.S.M.

[1630]—*Sisters of St. Francis of Penance and Christian Charity*. (Denver, CO).—O.S.F.

[]—*Sisters of St. Francis of the Holy Family*. (Dubuque, IA).—OSF.

[3320]—*Sisters of the Presentation of the Blessed Virgin Mary*. (Fargo, ND; Aberdeen, SD).—P.B.V.M.

NECROLOGY

† Flavin, Daniel, (Retired). —Died April 8, 1997.

Diocese of Boise

(Dioecesis Xylopolitana)

Most Reverend

TOD DAVID BROWN

Bishop of Boise; ordained May 1, 1963; appointed December 27, 1988; Episcopal Ordination April 3, 1989. *Res., 303 Federal Way, Boise, ID, 83705-5925.*

ESTABLISHED AS A VICARIATE-APOSTOLIC MARCH 3, 1868.

ERECTED A DIOCESE BY HIS HOLINESS POPE LEO XIII, AUGUST 26, 1893.

Square Miles 83,557.

Legal Title: "Roman Catholic Diocese of Boise."

Comprises the State of Idaho, with a Total Population of 1,218,000.

For legal titles of parishes and diocesan institutions, consult the Chancery Office.

Chancery Office: 303 Federal Way, Boise, ID, 83705-5925. Tel.: 208-342-1311; Fax: 208-342-0224.

E-mail address: jbowen@rcdb.org

STATISTICAL OVERVIEW

Personnel	
Bishop	1
Priests: Diocesan Active in Diocese	60
Priests: Active Outside Diocese	7
Priests: Retired, Sick or Absent	29
Number of Diocesan Priests	96
Religious Priests in Diocese	18
Extern Priests in Diocese	3
Ordinations:	
Diocesan Priests	1
Permanent Deacons in Diocese	29
Total Brothers	9
Total Sisters	106
Parishes	
Parishes	63
With Resident Pastor:	
Resident Diocesan Priests	50
Resident Religious Priests	5
Without Resident Pastor:	
Administered by Priests	7
Administered by Women Religious	1
Missions	32
Pastoral Centers	17
Closed Parishes	10
Professional Ministry Personnel:	
Brothers	3
Sisters	10
Lay Ministers	33
Welfare	
Catholic Hospitals	5
Total Assisted	586,031
Day Care and Extended Day Care Centers	4
Total Assisted	138
Special Centers for Social Services	13
Total Assisted	62,771
Educational	
Diocesan Students in Other Seminaries	15
Total Seminarians	15
High Schools, Diocesan and Parish	1
Total Students	738
Elementary Schools, Diocesan and Parish	13
Total Students	2,477
Catechesis/Religious Education:	
High School Students	3,124
Elementary Students	7,064
Total Students Under Catholic Instruction	13,418
Teachers in the Diocese:	
Sisters	3
Lay Teachers	166
Vital Statistics	
Receptions into the Church:	
Infant Baptism Totals	2,487
Adult Baptism Totals	237
Received into Full Communion	197
First Communions	1,898
Confirmations	1,065
Marriages:	
Catholic	345
Interfaith	352
Total Marriages	697
Deaths	786
Total Catholic Population	120,000
Total Population	1,218,000

Former Bishops—Rt. Rev. LOUIS LOOTENS, D.D., appt. first Vicar-Apostolic of Idaho, March 3, 1868; cons. Bishop of Castabala, Aug. 9, 1868; resigned July 16, 1876; died Jan. 13, 1898.—Rt. Rev. ALPHONSE JOSEPH GLORIEUX, D.D., appt. second Vicar-Apostolic of Idaho, Feb. 27, 1885; cons. Titular Bishop of Apolonia, April 19, 1885; appt. first Bishop of the Diocese of Boise, Aug. 26, 1893; died Aug. 25, 1917.—Rt. Rev. DANIEL MARY GORMAN, D.D. LL.D., cons. May 1, 1918; died June 9, 1927.—Most Rev. EDWARD JOSEPH KELLY, D.D., cons. March 6, 1928; died April 21, 1956.—Most Rev. JAMES J. BYRNE, D.D., S.T.D., ord. June 3, 1933; appt. Titular Bishop of Etenna and Auxiliary of St. Paul, July 2, 1947; cons. July 2, 1947; transferred to Boise June 16, 1956; appt. Archbishop of Dubuque, March 19, 1962; retired Aug. 23, 1983; died Aug. 2, 1996.—Most Rev. SYLVESTER WILLIAM TREINEN, D.D., ord. June 11, 1946; appt. May 19, 1962; cons. July 25, 1962; retired Aug. 17, 1988; died Sept. 30, 1996.

Vicar General / Moderator of the Curia—Rev. Msgr. DENNIS G. FALK, V.G.

Vicar for Religious—Rev. Msgr. DENNIS G. FALK, V.G.

Vicar for Administration—Rev. Msgr. DENNIS G. FALK, V.G.

Office of Multi-Cultural / Ethnic Ministry—Deacon GERMAN A. TORO, Dir., *303 Federal Way, Boise, 83705-5925.* Tel: 208-342-1311.

Chancery Office—*303 Federal Way, Boise, 83705-5925.* Tel: 208-342-1311; Fax: 208-342-0224.

Chancellor—Deacon JAMES BOWEN.

Notary—LODICE GRANT.

Diocesan Tribunal—*303 Federal Way, Boise, 83705-5925.* Tel: 208-344-1344; Fax: 208-342-0224. (Direct all correspondence here.).

Director—Dr. DIANE L. BARR, J.C.D.

Judicial Vicar—Very Rev. JOSEPH F. MCDONALD, III, J.C.L.

Vice Judicial Vicar—Rev. GERALD J. FUNKE.

Promotor of Justice—Dr. DIANE L. BARR.

Notaries—Rev. Msgr. DENNIS G. FALK, V.G.; Deacon JAMES E. BOWEN; Dr. DIANE L. BARR; RUTH GRAFF; LISA WILLIAMS; THERESA WEBSTER.

Judges—Revs. JOHN W. MORGAN; WILLIAM C. CROWLEY; WILLIAM DOHMAN; SIMEON VAN DE VOORD, O.S.B.; SEAN CAULFIELD; Very Rev. JOSEPH MCDONALD, III, J.C.L.; Revs. GERALD FUNKE; HENRY CARMONA; GEORGE KING; Rev. Msgr. RAYMOND PEPLINSKI.

Defenders of the Bond—Dr. DIANE L. BARR; Sr. BERNICE WESSELS, O.S.B.; Rev. ANDREW SCHUMACHER.

Consultors—Rev. Msgr. DENNIS G. FALK; Very Revs. GERALD DYE, V.F.; WILLIAM CROWLEY, V.F.; ROGER LACHANCE, V.F.; ANDREW SCHUMACHER, V.U.; JOHN MORGAN, V.F.; TIMOTHY O'TOOLE, V.F.; Revs. JOHN KOELSCH; ALFRED PUCCINELLI, S.M.; JOSEPH SCHMIDT; MICHAEL ST. MARIE; ENRIQUE TERRIQUEZ.

Deans—Very Rev. ROGER LACHANCE, V.F., Northern Deanery; Very Rev. WILLIAM CROWLEY, V.F., North Central Deanery; Very Rev. GERALD DYE, V.F., Western Deanery; Very Rev. ANDREW SCHUMACHER, V.U., West Central Deanery; Very Rev. JOHN MORGAN, V.F., Southern Deanery; Very Rev. TIMOTHY O'TOOLE, V.F., Eastern Deanery.

Presbyteral Council—Rev. Msgr. DENNIS G. FALK; Very Revs. GERALD DYE, V.F.; ROGER LACHANCE, V.F.; WILLIAM CROWLEY, V.F.; ANDREW SCHUMACHER, V.U.; JOHN MORGAN, V.F.; TIMOTHY O'TOOLE, V.F.; Revs. JOHN KOELSCH; ALFRED PUCCINELLI, S.M.; JOSEPH SCHMIDT; MICHAEL ST. MARIE; ENRIQUE TERRIQUEZ.

Priest Personnel Commission—Most Rev. TOD D. BROWN; Rev. Msgr. DENNIS G. FALK, V.G.; Revs. WILLIAM GOULD; JOHN KOELSCH; RICHARD HALDANE; JOSEPH MUHA; CARLOS PEREZ; MERLYN SPRUTE; STEVE RUKAVINA.

Finance Council—Most Rev. TOD D. BROWN; Rev. Msgr. DENNIS G. FALK, V.G., Chm.; JAMES BRUCE; LARRY HELLHAKE; Rev. Msgr. RAYMOND PEPLINSKI, P.A.; STANLEY WELSH; JAMES BRUCE; SUSAN COPPLE; T. STEVE JOYCE; RANDY STEINER, Finance Office Consultant.

Building Committee—Deacon JAMES BOWEN; CHARLES HUMMEL; MARILYN SCANLAN; DAVID DAVIES.

Priest Retirement Committee—Rev. Msgr. DENNIS G. FALK, V.G.; Revs. JOHN KOELSCH; ROBB KELLER; DONALD RIFFLE; JOHN MORGAN; DENNIS WASSMUTH; RICHARD HALDANE, *303 Federal Way, Boise, 83705.* Tel: 208-342-1311.

Diocesan Offices and Directors

Apostleship of Prayer—Vacant.

Bureau of Information—*"Idaho Catholic Register", 303 Federal Way, Boise, 83705-5925.*

Campaign for Human Development—Deacon JAMES E. BOWEN, *303 Federal Way, Boise, 83705-5925.*

Catholic Communications Center—Vacant.

Catholic Relief Services—Rev. Msgr. DENNIS G. FALK, V.G., *303 Federal Way, Boise, 83705-5925.*

Catholic Scouts—Rev. ROGER LACHANCE, Chap., *St. Pius X, 625 E. Haycraft, Coeur d'Alene, 83814.* Tel: 208-765-5108.

Catholic Daughters of the Americas—BONNIE MCDOWELL, State Regent, *1146 N. 15th St., Coeur d'Alene, 83814.* Tel: 208-664-4888.

Catholic Elementary Schools—Dr. ROBERT FONTAINE,

Supt., *303 Federal Way, Boise, 83705-5925.*

Catholic Hospitals—Rev. MARK R. SCHMACHER, *St. Augustine's Catholic Center, Box 3457 University Sta., Moscow, 83843.* Tel: 208-882-4613.

Catholic Liturgical Commission—Most Rev. TOD D. BROWN; JOHN ANNEN; MARCIA BECKMAN; DELINDA FEHRINGER; LARRY HARRISON; Bro. ERNEST MORASCI, S.M.; MARY HERSLEY; Deacon RALPH PIERCE; Sr. CECILE MARIE UHLORN, O.S.B.; Sr. JENNIFER HORNER, O.S.B.; Rev. LEN MACMILLAN, *303 Federal Way, Boise, 83705.* Tel: 208-342-1311.

Censor Librorum—Rev. ANDREW SCHUMACHER, *2612 W. State St., Boise, 83702.*

Charismatic Renewal—Rev. ROBB KELLER, *152 7th Ave. E., Twin Falls, 83301.*

Priest Retirement Plan—Direct Inquiries to the Chancery, *303 Federal Way, Boise, 83705.*

Cursillo Movement—Rev. JOHN KOELSCH, Spiritual Dir., *P.O. Box 5127, Boise, 83705.* Rev. MAURICIO MEDINA, Hispanic Dir., *584 W. Sexton, Blackfoot, 83221.*

Development/Stewardship Office—Rev. DONALD J. RIFFLE.

Ecumenical Commission—Rev. JOHN KOELSCH, *P.O. Box 5127, Boise, 83705.*

Education Ministries Office—Dr. ROBERT FONTAINE, Dir. ANN WHITWOOD, Administrative Asst., *303 Federal Way, Boise, 83705.* Tel: 208-342-1311.

Supt. of Schools—Dr. ROBERT FONTAINE.

Children's Catechesis,—Sr. CLARISSA GOECKNER, O.S.B.

Youth Ministry—DIANE LIND.

Adult Education—Sr. ARLENE ELLIS, S.S.C.

Resource Center—CAROL MEADOWS.

Eucharistic League—Rev. Msgr. DENNIS G. FALK, V.G.

Family Life—Vacant.

Finance Officer—RANDY STEINER.

Idaho Council of Catholic Women—RITA RIENER, Pres., *P.O. Box 537, Cottonwood, 83522.*

Knights of Columbus—ROGER A. GRAEFE, State Deputy, *421 N. Beaken St., Twin Falls, 83301.* Rev. ROBB KELLER, State Chap.

Legislative Liaison—TIMOTHY BRENNAN.

Campus Ministry—Sr. DAVID HARTSE, O.S.U., *1915 University Dr., Boise, 83706.*

Newspaper—"Idaho Catholic Register"; Most Rev. TOD BROWN, Publisher; COLETTE COWMAN, Exec. Editor; LEONARD GEORGE, Advertising/Business/Circulation; BARBARA HAMILTON, Artist/Library/Production, *303 Federal Way, Boise, 83705.* Tel: 208-342-1311.

Deacons, Director—Deacon RICHARD BONNEY, *11 Stanford, Pocatello, 83201.* Tel: 208-233-4661.

Deacon Council President—Deacon RALPH FLAGER, *5152 Burlington Dr., Boise, 83704.* Tel: 208-375-2459.

Deacon Formation Director—Sr. GRAYCE ROSS, S.N.J.M., *4450 N. Five Mile Rd., Boise, 83713.* Tel: 208-376-5787.

Prison Ministry—ALFREDO CORTEZ, *P.O. Box 413, Parma, 83660.* Tel: 208-722-7545.

Propagation of Faith—Rev. Msgr. DENNIS G. FALK, V.G., *303 Federal Way, Boise, 83705.*

Respect Life Program—Deacon RALPH FLAGER, Dir., *5152 Burlington Dr., Boise, 83704.* Tel: 208-375-2459.

St. Vincent de Paul Society—Rev. ANDREW SCHUMACHER, Diocesan Spiritual Dir., *2612 W. State St., Boise, 83702.* Tel: 208-344-2597. Deacon JAMES E. BOWEN, Diocesan Dir., *303 Federal Way, Boise, 83705.* Tel: 208-342-1311.

Vocations—Rev. RONALD COOK, Dir., *P.O. Box 626, Buhl, 83316.* Tel: 208-543-5136.

CLERGY, PARISHES, MISSIONS AND PAROCHIAL SCHOOLS

CITY OF BOISE
(Ada County)

1—CATHEDRAL OF ST. JOHN THE EVANGELIST, Revs. Donald J. Riffle; Simeon Van De Voord, O.S.B.; Deacons Ken Hiner; Richard Henning.
Res., 804 N. 9th St., 83702. Tel: 208-342-3511; 3512.
School—St. Joseph's School. Mrs. Kathleen Giles, Prin.
Lay Teachers 17; Students 301.
Catechesis/Religious Programs—Linda Bratnober, D.R.E.
Students 274.

2—ST. MARK'S, Revs. John F. Donoghue; Marcellus Fernandez; Deacons Ralph Pierce; James Bowen.
Res., 7503 Northview St., 83704. Tel: 208-375-6651; Fax: 208-375-3211.
School—Dan Maloney, Prin. Lay Teachers 12; Students 242.
Catechesis/Religious Programs—Students 574.

3—ST. MARY'S, Rev. Andrew J. Schumacher; Sr. Angela Uhlhorn, O.S.B., Pastoral Assoc.
Res., 2612 W. State St., 83702. Tel: 208-344-2597; Fax: 208-344-9337.
School—2620 W. State St., 83702. Tel: 208-342-7476; Fax: 208-345-5154. Marcia Beckman, Prin.
Lay Teachers 11; Students 240.
Catechesis/Religious Programs—Terry Jung, D.R.E.
Students 228.

4—OUR LADY OF THE ROSARY, Revs. Dennis Wassmuth; Morse Later; Deacon Michael Dessert.
Res., 1500 E. Wright, 83706. Tel: 208-343-9041.
Catechesis/Religious Programs—Rosie Skoro, D.R.E.
Students 310.
Chapel—Idaho City, St. Joseph's.

5—RISEN CHRIST CATHOLIC COMMUNITY, Rev. Joseph da Silva; Deacon Michael Eisenbeiss.
Res., 11511 W. Lake Hazel Rd., 83709. Tel: 208-362-6584; Fax: 208-362-9545.
Catechesis/Religious Programs—Students 222.

6—SACRED HEART, Rev. John W. Koelsch; Deacons Alan Shaber; James Kelly. Office: P.O. Box 5127, 83705-0127. Fax: 208-344-8312.
Res., 3902 Camas St., 83705. Tel: 208-344-8311.
School—3901 Cassia St., 83705. Tel: 208-344-9738. John Loffer, Prin.
Sisters 1; Lay Teachers 13; Students 249.
Catechesis/Religious Programs—Deborah Fischer, D.R.E.
Students 118.

7—ST. PAUL'S. Closed. See Our Lady of the Rosary, Boise for details.

OUTSIDE THE CITY OF BOISE

Aberdeen, Bingham Co., Blessed Sacrament, Rev. B. Ernest Anderson.
Res., Hwy. 39 & S. 4th W., P.O. Drawer C, 83210. Tel: 208-397-4028.
Catechesis/Religious Programs—Aren Schanh, D.R.E.
Students 100.

American Falls, Power Co., St. Mary, Rev. B. Ernest Anderson.
Mailing Address: P.O. Box 117, 83211. Tel: 208-226-5217.
Catechesis/Religious Programs—Kathy Barkdull, D.R.E.
Students 132.

Arco, Butte Co., St. Ann's. See St. Charles, Salmon for details.

Blackfoot, Bingham Co., St. Bernard's, Rev. Mauricio Medina, Admin.
Res., 584 W. Sexton St., 83221. Tel: 208-785-1935; Fax: 208-785-1935.
Catechesis/Religious Programs—Sharon Cathrae, D.R.E.
Students 165.
Station—Pingree, St. John's.

Bonners Ferry, Boundary Co., St. Ann's, Rev. Gordon Taylor.
Res., El Paso & Lincoln, P.O. Box 58, 83805. Tel: 208-267-2852; Fax: 208-267-5612.
Catechesis/Religious Programs—Anette Stuurmans, D.R.E.
Students 67.

Buhl, Twin Falls Co., Immaculate Conception, Rev. Ronald Cook.
Res., 1701 Poplar, Box 626, 83316. Tel: 208-543-5136; Fax: 208-543-5714.
Catechesis/Religious Programs—Christine Welch, D.R.E.
Students 133.
Station—Hagerman, St. Catherine's.

Burley, Cassia Co., St. Theresa, Rev. Juan Maria Garatea.
Res., 1550 Oakley, Box 1223, 83318. Tel: 208-678-5453; Fax: 208-678-5479.
Catechesis/Religious Programs—Dorothy Gagnon, D.R.E.
Students 180.

Caldwell, Canyon Co., St. Mary, Revs. Enrique Terriquez; Leslie Paul Kish.
Office: 616 Dearborn, P.O. Box 399, 83606. Tel: 208-459-3653; Fax: 208-459-3653.
Catechesis/Religious Programs—Students 459.
Chapel—Marsing, Good Shepherd.

Chubbuck, Bannock Co., St. Paul's, Rev. James E. Rodenspiel.
Res., 831 Todd St., Box 5367, 83202. Tel: 208-237-7167; Fax: 208-237-2724.
Church—820 W. Chubbuck, 83202.
Catechesis/Religious Programs—Theresa Owen, D.R.E.
Students 73.
Station—Blessed Kateri Tekakwitha Chapel, Sheepskin Rd., Fort Hall, 83203.

Coeur D'Alene, Kootenai Co., St. Pius X, Rev. Roger LaChance; Deacon Gary McSwain.
Office: 625 E. Haycraft, 83715.
Res., 2804 N. 6th St., 83715. Tel: 208-765-5108; Fax: 208-664-5325.
Catechesis/Religious Programs—D.R.E.: Sr. Roberta Lamanna, S.N.J.M.; Sr. Rosemary Thielman, S.N.J.M.
Students 410.

St. Thomas, Revs. Richard Quinn, C.SS.R.; George Rassley, C.SS.R.; Robert Simon, C.SS.R.; George Dawson, C.SS.R.; Bro. Dennis Lee, C.SS.R., Pastoral Assoc.
Res., 919 Indiana Ave., 83814. Tel: 208-664-9259.
Catechesis/Religious Programs—Carol White, D.R.E.
Students 123.

Cottonwood, Idaho Co., St. Mary's, Rev. Joseph Muha.
Mailing Address: P.O. Box 425, 83522-0425. Tel: 208-962-3214; Fax: 208-962-5477.
Res., 503 Garrett St., 83522. Tel: 208-962-3111.
Catechesis/Religious Programs—Mary Jane Arnzen, D.R.E.
Students 190.
Chapel—Keuterville, Holy Cross.

Council, Adams Co., St. Jude Chapel. See St. Agnes, Weiser for details.

DeSmet, Benewah Co., Sacred Heart, Revs. Thomas Connolly, S.J.; Joseph L. Obersinner, S.J.; Sr. Dolores Ellwart, S.P., Pastoral Assoc.
Res., Box 306, 83824. Tel: 208-274-5871; Fax: 208-274-3015.
Stations—Plummer, Our Lady of Perpetual Help; Worley, St. Michael's.

Eagle, Ada Co., St. Matthew, Rev. Timothy Ritchey; Deacon Ralph Flager.
Res., 500 N. Eagle Rd., P.O. Box 296, 83616. Tel: 208-939-6801; Fax: 208-939-1045.
Catechesis/Religious Programs—Mike & Debbie Lee, D.R.E.
Students 225.
Chapel—Horshoe Bend, Our Lady Queen Of Angels.

Emmett, Gem Co., Sacred Heart, Rev. David Riffle.
Res., 211 E. First, 83617. Tel: 208-365-4320; Fax: 208-365-0754.
Catechesis/Religious Programs—Students 122.
Station—Garden Valley, St. Jude.

Ferdinand, Idaho Co., Assumption, Rev. Canisius Hayes, S.T., Admin.
Mailing Address: P.O. Box 112, 83526. Tel: 208-962-5220; Fax: 208-962-3726.
Catechesis/Religious Programs—Mary Jane Arnzen, D.R.E.
Students 54.

Garden Valley, Boise Co., St. Jude's. See Sacred Heart, Emmett for details.

Genesee, Latah Co., St. Mary Station. See St. Mary's, Moscow for details. In res., Rev. Robert Finucane.
Res., 138 N. Jackson, P.O. Box 36, 83832. Tel: 208-285-1218.
Catechesis/Religious Programs—Connie Esser, D.R.E.
Students 37.

Glenns Ferry, Elmore Co., Our Lady of Limerick Station. See Our Lady of Good Counsel, Mountain Home for details. In res., Rev. Eugene Esch, O.S.B.
Res., 113 W. Arthur St., Box 216, 83623. Tel: 208-366-7721.
Catechesis/Religious Programs—Dixie Black, D.R.E.
Students 100.

Gooding, Gooding Co., St. Elizabeth's, Rev. Michael St. Marie.
Res., 1515 California St., Box 147, 83330. Tel: 208-934-5634; Fax: 208-934-5634.
Catechesis/Religious Programs—Jane Woodland, D.R.E.
Students 120.
Station—Wendell, St. Anthony's.

Grandview, Owyhee Co., St. Henry Chapel. See Our Lady of Good Counsel, Mountain Home for details.

Grangeville, Idaho Co., SS. Peter and Paul, Rev. William Dohman, J.C.L.
Res., 318 S. B St., 83530. Tel: 208-983-0403; Fax: 208-983-1152.
School—Tel: 208-983-2182. Elizabeth Kuszlejko, Prin.
Sisters 1; Lay Teachers 3; Students 61.
Catechesis/Religious Programs—Students 65.
Station—Nez Perce, Holy Trinity.

Greencreek, Idaho Co., St. Anthony's, Rev. Canisius Hayes, S.T., Admin.
Res., Rte. 1, Box 90, 83533. Tel: 208-962-3565; Fax: 208-962-3726.
Catechesis/Religious Programs—Mary Jane Arnzen, D.R.E.
Students 78.

Hagerman, Gooding Co., St. Catherine's. See Immaculate Conception, Buhl for details.

Hailey, Blaine Co., St. Charles Borromeo, Revs. John W. Morgan, Admin.; Thomas F. Keller; Deacon Bill Mallory, (Retired).
Res., 311 S. 1st. Ave. E, Box 789, 83333. Tel: 208-788-3024; Fax: 208-788-0726.
Catechesis/Religious Programs—Students 99.
Chapel—Fairfield, Immaculate Conception.

Homedale, Owyhee Co., St. Hubert, Rev. Oscar Jaramillo.
Res., 115 E. Owyhee St., Box 186, 83628. Tel: 208-337-3153.
Catechesis/Religious Programs—Lynne Tiddens, D.R.E.
Students 165.
Chapel—Silver City, Our Lady of Tears.

Horseshoe Bend, Boise Co., Our Lady Queen of Angels Chapel. See St. Matthew's, Eagle for details.

Idaho City, Boise Co., St. Joseph's Chapel. See Our Lady of the Rosary, Boise for details. Rev. Morse A. Later, Admin.
Res., 7225 Cascade Dr., Boise, 83704. Tel: 208-376-1940.

Idaho Falls, Bonneville Co., Holy Rosary, Revs. Gerald J. Funke; Calvin Blankinship, Jr.; Deacon Richard Kelso.
Res., 228 Ninth St., Box 50899, 83405. Tel: 208-522-4366; Fax: 208-523-3827.
Office: 145 Ninth St., 83404.
School—161 Ninth St., 83404. Tel: 208-522-7781.
Lay Teachers 10; Students 241. Head Teachers: Rebecca Banko; Karen Hague.
Catechesis/Religious Programs—Denise Echiverri, D.R.E.
Students 740.
Stations—Roberts, St Anthony's; Mud Lake, St. Ann's.

Christ the King, Rev. Timothy L. O'Toole; Deacon James Goettsche.
Res., 1690 E. 17th St., 83404. Tel: 208-529-8170; Fax: 208-528-9164.
Catechesis/Religious Programs—Susan Clark, D.R.E.
Students 198.
Chapel—Shelley, Our Lady of Guadalupe.

Jerome, Jerome Co., St. Jerome's, Rev. Jesus Camacho; Deacon William Last.
Res., 216 2nd Ave. E., Box 169, 83338. Tel: 208-324-8794.
Catechesis/Religious Programs—Theresa May, D.R.E.
Students 230.

Kamiah, Lewis Co., St. Catherine's of Siena, Rev. George L. King.
Res., 407 7th St., Box 685, 83536. Tel: 208-935-2130; Fax: 208-935-2984.
Catechesis/Religious Programs—Students 34.

Kellogg, Shoshone Co., St. Rita's, Rev. Mel Sprute; Deacon Walt Jackson.
Res., 27 Kellogg Ave., 83837-2626. Tel: 208-784-7361.

Keuterville, Idaho Co., Holy Cross. Merged with St. Mary's, Cottonwood.

Lapwai, Nez Perce Co., Sacred Heart Station. See Our Lady of Lourdes, Lewiston for details.

Leadore, Lemhi Co., St. Joseph's Chapel. See St. Charles, Salmon for details.

Lewiston, Nez Perce Co., St. Stanislaus, Rev. Sean Caulfield; Sr. Margie Schmidt, O.S.B., Pastoral Assoc.
Res., 633 5th Ave., 83501. Tel: 208-743-7331; Fax: 208-746-7134.
School—Tri-Parish School. Marcia Ney, Prin.
Sisters 1; Lay Teachers 6; Students 171.
Catechesis/Religious Programs—Students 78.

Our Lady of Lourdes, Rev. James R. Wilson.
Church & Res.—2015 13th Ave., 83501. Tel: 208-743-3238; 743-6101 (Church); Fax: 208-743-5301.
Catechesis/Religious Programs—Students 160.
Station—Lapwai, Sacred Heart.

St. James, Rev. William C. Crowley.
Office: 1519 Ripon Ave., 83501. Tel: 208-743-8231; Fax: 208-798-8407.
Catechesis/Religious Programs—Students 135.

McCall, Valley Co., Our Lady of the Lake, Rev. Donald D. Fraser; Deacon William Petzak.
Res., 501 Cross Rd., Box 821, 83638. Tel: 208-634-5474.
Station—Cascade, St. John the Baptist.
Chapel—Riggins, St. Jerome's.

Meridian, Ada Co., Holy Spirit, Rev. Timothy M. Ritchey; Deacon Ralph Flager.
Res., 828 W. Cherry Ln., Box 708, 83680. Tel: 208-888-1182; Fax: 208-884-1800.
Catechesis/Religious Programs—Gina Welsh, D.R.E.
Students 281.

Moscow, Latah Co., St. Mary's, Rev. Joseph F. Schmidt.
Res., 618 E. First St., Box 9106, 83843. Tel: 208-882-4813; Fax: 208-883-0608.
School—412 N. Monroe, 83843. Tel: 208-882-2121.
Sr. Margaret Johnson, O.S.U., Prin.
Lay Teachers 11; Students 186.
Kindergarten & Preschool, St. Rose—Owned by the Ursuline Nuns, affiliated with St. Mary's School. 412 N. Howard, 83843. Tel: 208-882-4014.
Catechesis/Religious Programs—Students 203.
Station—Genessee, St. Mary's.

St. Augustine's. (Catholic Center). Rev. Mark R. Schumacher; Deacon Verne Geidl.
Res., 628 Deakin St., Box 3457 University Sta., 83843. Tel: 208-882-4613.
Station—Potlatch, St. Mary's.

Mountain Home Air Force Base, Elmore Co., St. Mary's, Rev. Eugene H. Schnipke, C.PP.S.
Res., 366 Wing/HC, 420 Gunfighter Ave., 83648. Tel: 208-828-6417; Fax: 208-828-4570.

Mountain Home, Elmore Co., Our Lady of Good Counsel, Rev. Raul R. Covarrubias.
Res., 115 N. 4th St. E., Box 310, 83647. Tel: 208-587-3046; Fax: 208-587-6373.
Catechesis/Religious Programs—Barbara Faneuf, D.R.E.
Students 268.
Stations—Bruneau, St. Bridget; Glenn's Ferry, Our Lady of Limerick.
Chapel—Grandview, St. Henry's.

Nampa, Canyon Co., St. Paul's, Revs. Alfred H. Puccinelli, S.M.; Paul Mathews, S.M.; Bros. Ernie Morasci, S.M.; Joseph Grima, S.M.
Res., 1515 8th St. S., 83651. Tel: 208-466-7031; Fax: 208-467-6485.
School—Tel: 208-467-3601. Thomas Antonoplos, Prin.
Sisters 1; Lay Teachers 9; Students 226.
Catechesis/Religious Programs—Students 202.
Station—Melba, St. Joseph.
Chapels—Nampa, Our Lady of Guadalupe.; Oreana, Queen of Heaven.

Our Lady of Guadalupe Chapel. See St. Paul's, Nampa for details. In res., Rev. Carlos Perez.
Res., 1203 Seventh St. N., 83687. Tel: 208-467-6798; 467-5438; Fax: 208-467-6798.
Catechesis/Religious Programs—Hortencia Lemus, D.R.E.
Students 90.

New Plymouth, Payette Co., St. Aloysius, Rev. Gerald B. Dye; Sr. Mary Louise Deroin, C.S.C., Pastoral Assoc.
Res., 217 W. Elm, P.O. Box 377, 83655. Tel: 208-278-5802; Fax: 208-642-1099.
Catechesis/Religious Programs—Students 65.

Nezperce, Lewis Co., Holy Trinity. See SS. Peter and Paul, Grangeville for details. In res., Rev. Kenneth Arnzen.
Res., 506 Willow St., Box 65, 83543. Tel: 208-937-2300.
Catechesis/Religious Programs—Students 67.

Oreana, Owyhee Co., Queen of Heaven Chapel. See St. Paul's, Nampa for details.

Orofino, Clearwater Co., St. Theresa's, Rev. George L. King.
Res., 446 Brown Ave., Box 1169, 83544. Tel: 208-476-5121.
Catechesis/Religious Programs—Students 42.
Chapel—Pierce, Our Lady of Woodland.

Parma, Canyon Co., Sacred Hearts of Jesus and Mary, Rev. Oscar Jaramillo, Admin.
Mailing Address: P.O. Box 777, 83660.
Res., 101 E. Owyhee St., P.O. Box 186, Homedale, 83628. Tel: 208-337-3153.
Catechesis/Religious Programs—Students 88.

Payette, Payette Co., Holy Family, Rev. Gerald B. Dye, Admin.; Sr. Mary Louise Deroin, C.S.C., Pastoral Assoc.
Res., 1212 First Ave. S., P.O. Box 818, 83661. Tel: 208-642-2261.
Catechesis/Religious Programs—Students 34.

Pocatello, Bannock Co., St. Joseph's, Rev. Steven Rukavina.
Res., 455 N. Hays, P.O. Box 757, 83204. Tel: 208-232-1470; Fax: 208-232-0586.
Catechesis/Religious Programs—Kathryn Brokaw, D.R.E.
Students 85.

St. Anthony's, Rev. Xavier Aresseril; Deacon Mel Hardy.
Res., 524 N. 7th Ave., Box 4188, 83205. Tel: 208-232-1196; Fax: 208-234-1624.
School—540 N. 7th Ave., 83205. Tel: 208-232-5763. Linda Creighton, Prin.
Lay Teachers 8; Students 162.
Catechesis/Religious Programs—Ann Hysell, D.R.E.
Students 224.

St. John's Community, Very Rev. Joseph F. McDonald, III; Deacon Richard Bonney.
Res., 920 E. Lovejoy St., I.S.U., Box 8129, 83209. Tel: 208-233-0880; Fax: 208-233-5745.

Post Falls, Kootenai Co., St. George's, Rev. William R. Gould.
Res., 2004 N. William St., Box 10, 83854-0010. Tel: 208-773-4715; Fax: 208-777-1549.
Catechesis/Religious Programs—Valerie Clapper, D.R.E.
Students 180.

Potlatch, Latah Co., St. Mary's Station. See St. Augustine's, Moscow for details.

Priest River, Bonner Co., St. Catherine's, Rev. Dennis Day; Sr. Jane Kelly, S.N.J.M., Admin.
Res., 206 Summit Blvd., Box 445, 83856. Tel: 208-448-2127.
Catechesis/Religious Programs—Students 24.
Station—Priest Lake, St. Blanche.

Rathdrum, Kootenai Co., St. Stanislaus, Rev. Michael S. Scarcello.
Res., W. 3500 Scarcello Rd., 83858. Tel: 208-687-0788.
Catechesis/Religious Programs—D.R.E.: Mr. Paul Franz; Mrs. Beth Franz.
Students 80.
Station—Spirit Lake, St. Joseph's.

Rupert, Minidoka Co., St. Nicholas, Rev. Henry Carmona; Deacon Pete Rodriquez.
Res., 802 F St., Box 115, 83350. Tel: 208-436-3781.
School—P.O. Box 26, 83350. Tel: 208-436-6320.
Rev. Henry Carmona, Acting Prin.
Lay Teachers 5; Students 144.
Catechesis/Religious Programs—Students 206.

St. Anthony, Fremont Co., Mary Immaculate, Rev. Paul H. Wander.
Res., 328 W. First N., Box 527, 83445. Tel: 208-624-7459.
Catechesis/Religious Programs—Mrs. Jeanne Fischer, D.R.E.
Students 90.
Stations—Rexburg, St. Patrick's; Driggs, Good Shepherd; Island Park, Chapel of the Pines.

Saint Maries, Benewah Co., St. Mary's, Rev. William Taylor.
Res., 921 Jefferson St., Box 335, 83861. Tel: 208-245-2977.
Catechesis/Religious Programs—Kelly Pugh, D.R.E.
Students 108.
Station—Harrison, Our Lady of Perpetual Help.

Salmon, Lemhi Co., St. Charles, Revs. Richard S. Haldane; Anthony DiLoreto; Peter Bourne.
Res., 505 Hope Ave., 83467. Tel: 208-756-2432; Fax: 208-756-2432.
Catechesis/Religious Programs—Mary Vander Schaaf, D.R.E.
Students 137.
Stations—Arco, St. Ann; Challis, St. Louise; Mackay, St. Barbara.
Chapel—Leadore, St. Joseph.

Sandpoint, Bonner Co., St. Joseph's, Rev. Dennis C. Day; Deacon Ralph Arndt, (Retired).
Res., 621 Oak St., P.O. Box 279, 83864-0279. Tel: 208-263-3720; Fax: 208-265-4974.
Catechesis/Religious Programs—Irene Sundquist, D.R.E.
Students 158.
Chapel—Clark Fork, Sacred Heart.

Shoshone, Lincoln Co., St. Peter's, Rev. Michael St. Marie; Deacon Dee Aslett.
Res., 215 W. B St., Box 336, 83352. Tel: 208-886-2002; 934-5634; Fax: 208-886-2030.
Catechesis/Religious Programs—Students 19.

Soda Springs, Caribou Co., St. Mary's, Rev. John Worster.
Res., 99 W. Center, 83276. Tel: 208-547-3200.
Stations—Montpelier, Blessed Sacrament; Malad City, St. Paul's; Preston, St. Peter's; Lava Hot Springs, Our Lady of Lourdes.

Sun Valley, Blaine Co., Our Lady of the Snows, Rev. John W. Morgan.
Res., Sun Valley Rd., Box 1650, 83353. Tel: 208-622-3432; Fax: 208-622-4348.
Catechesis/Religious Programs—Students 97.

Twin Falls, Twin Falls Co., St. Edward's, Rev. Robb Keller; Deacons John McKinley; Lloyd LeClair; Robert Sass.
Res., 152 7th Ave., E., 83301-6319. Tel: 208-733-3907; Fax: 208-733-3935.
School—Tel: 208-734-3872. Margaret Peck, Prin.
Lay Teachers 8; Students 175.
Catechesis/Religious Programs—Jean Thompson, D.R.E.
Students 275.

Our Lady of Guadalupe, Rev. Thomas J. Loucks.
Res., 630 Falls Ave., 83301-3300. Tel: 208-734-2327; 734-4145; Fax: 208-734-4145.

Wallace, Shoshone Co., St. Alphonsus, Rev. Mel Sprute, Admin.; Deacon Walt Jackson.
Res., 214 Pine St., Box 970, 83873. Tel: 208-752-3551.
Chapel—Mullan, St. Michael's.

Weiser, Washington Co., St. Agnes, Revs. Jairo Restrepo; Nondier Zuleta; Deacon Francis Wander.

Res., 214 E. Liberty, P.O. Box 87, 83672. Tel: 208-549-0088; Fax: 208-549-1080.
Catechesis/Religious Programs—Students 220.
Station—Cambridge, Holy Rosary.
Chapel—Council, St. Jude the Apostle.

Wendell, Gooding Co., St. Anthony's. See St. Elizabeth's, Gooding for details.

Chaplains of Public Institutions

BOISE. *Chateau de Boise Retirement Center* 7250 Poplar St., 83704. Tel: 208-372-0257. Rev. Patrick Russell.
Elks Rehabilitation. Attended by St. John Cathedral, 804 N. 9th St., Boise, ID, 83702. Tel: 208-342-3511. Vacant. 204 Fort Pl., 83702.
St. Luke's Medical Center. Attended by St. John Cathedral, 804 N. 9th St., Boise, ID, 83702. Tel: 208-342-3511. Vacant. 190 E. Bannock, 83712.
VA Hospital. Attended by St. John Cathedral, 804 N. 9th St., Boise, ID, 83702. Tel: 208-342-3511. Vacant. 5th St. & Fort St., 83401.

COTTONWOOD. *Monastery of St. Gertrude* HC 3 Box 121, 83522. Tel: 208-962-3224. Rev. Norbert Lemke, S.J.

On Special Assignment:
Reverend Monsignors—
Falk, Dennis G., Vicar Gen. & Moderator of the Curia

On Duty Outside the Diocese:
Reverend Fathers—
Dennis, Patrick, FCI Tucson, 8901 S. Wilmot Rd., Tucson, AZ 85706
Dolan, Raymond, Box 217, M.H. Station, Staten Island, NY 10303
Faucher, W. Thomas, St. Edward's, 68817 Trinity Way, P.O. Box 489, Sisters, OR 97759
Legerski, John, 200 O'Connor Dr., San Jose, CA 95128
Pu, Matthew C., Holy Family, 685 N. Fairview, Burns, OR 97720
Segatta, Bruno, Gonzaga in Florence, Piazza Antinori No. 3, Florence, Italy
Stravinskas, Peter, 42 Fairview, Mt. Pocono, PA 18344

Graduate Studies:
Reverend Fathers—
MacMillan, Leonard
Wekerle, Ronald

Leave of Absence:
Reverend Fathers—
Davia, Liam
Harlow, Francis

Retired:
Reverend Monsignors—
Hallissey, James T., Galena Ct., Box 370, Mountain Home, ID 83647
Hughes, Nicholas V., Rosemount, Kilkenny, Co. Johnston, Ireland
Peplinski, Raymond J., P.A., 322 S. Manville St., Boise, ID 83705
Simmons, Donald W., 2612 E. 44th St., Spokane, WA 99223
Reverend Fathers—
Carroll, William, 569 Fairview Dr., Hamilton, MT 59840
Daws, Dominic, 215 W. Heyburn Ave., Twin Falls, ID 83301
Dodds, Perry W., P.O. Box 264, Twin Falls, ID 83303
Dodgson, William, 2852 N. Rosedale, Boise, ID 83704
Dulberg, Albert V., Box 943, Post Falls, ID 83854
Gebhardt, Joseph M., 3060 S.E. Stark St., Portland, OR 97214
Grant, Robert H., 80 Andover St., Andover, MA 01810
Hebert, Francis, Rte. 2, Box 2018, Heppner, OR 97836
Hughes, Martin F., Rosemount, Kilkenny, Co. Johnston, Ireland
Later, Morse A., 7225 Cascade Dr., Boise, ID 83704
Lustig, Victor Joseph, Rte. 1, Box 109A, Cottonwood, ID 83522
McGoldrick, John T., 106 N. 12th St., #4C, Payette, ID 83661
McNeill, Malachy, 6 Dublin Rd., Drogheda, Co. Louth, Ireland
O'Donovan, Timothy John, Box 266, Hope, ID 83836
O'Sullivan, John, 700 E. Fairview, #116, Meridian, ID 83642
Peterson, Francis A., 107 20th Ave. S., Nampa, ID 83651
Riffle, Douglas H., P.O. Box 456, Meridian, ID 83642
Shimmaly, Edward E., P.O. Box 148, Eagle, ID 83616
Shinnick, James F., 1520 N. Fillmore, Jerome, ID 83338
Spegele, Michael A., P.O Box 23, Keuterville, ID 83538
Steinhoff, Henry, P.O. Box 626, Eureka, MT 59917
Waldmann, Robert J., P.O. Box 112, Ferdinand, ID 83526

Permanent Deacons:
Arndt, Ralph, (Retired)
Aslett, Devon H., St. Peter, Shoshone
Bonney, Richard James, II, St. John's, Pocatello
Bowen, James E., St. Mark, Boise
Dessert, Michael, Our Lady of the Rosary, Boise
Eisenbeiss, Michael, Risen Christ Catholic Community, Boise
Flager, Ralph, St. Matthew, Eagle
Geidl, Verne, St. Augustine Catholic Center, Moscow
Goettsche, James, Christ the King, Idaho Falls
Hardy, Melvin, St. Anthony's, Pocatello
Henning, Richard, St. John Cathedral, Boise
Hiner, Kenneth, St. John Cathedral, Boise
Jackson, Walter, St. Alphonsus, Wallace
Kelly, James, Sacred Heart, Boise
Kelso, Richard, Holy Rosary, Idaho Falls
Kreilcamp, Ben, (Retired)
Last, William, St. Jerome, Jerome
Le Clair, Lloyd, St. Edward, Twin Falls
Mallory, William, (Medical Leave of Absence)
McKinley, John D., Jr., St. Edward, Twin Falls
McSwain, Gary, St. Pius X, Coeur d'Alene
Petzak, William, Our Lady of the Lake, McCall
Pierce, Ralph, St. Mark, Boise
Rodriguez, Pete, St. Nicholas, Rupert
Sass, Robert, St. Edward, Twin Falls
Shaber, Alan, Sacred Heart, Boise
Solbrig, Charles W., Christ the King, Idaho Falls
Toro, German, St. Paul, Nampa
Wander, Francis, St. Agnes, Weiser

INSTITUTIONS LOCATED IN THE DIOCESE

[A] HIGH SCHOOLS, INTER-PAROCHIAL

BOISE. *Bishop Kelly High School*, 7009 Franklin Rd., 83709-0998. Tel: 208-375-6010; Fax: 208-375-3626. Dr. David Lachiondo, Prin. Lay Teachers 48; Students 738.

COEUR D'ALENE. *Holy Family Catholic School of Coeur d'Alene*, 406 N. Tenth, 83814. Tel: 208-765-4327; Fax: 208-664-2903. Tom Feldhausen, Prin. Lay Teachers 5; Students 79.

[B] GENERAL HOSPITALS

BOISE. *St. Alphonsus Regional Medical Center, Inc.*, 1055 N. Curtis Rd., 83706. Tel: 208-378-2121
For a complete listing, refer to the Hospitals section.

COTTONWOOD. *St. Mary's Hospital*, 83522. Tel: 208-962-3251; Fax: 208-962-3722
For a complete listing, refer to the Hospitals section.

JEROME. *St. Benedict Family Medical Center*, 709 N. Lincoln, 83338. Tel: 208-324-4301
For a complete listing, refer to the Hospitals section.

LEWISTON. *St. Joseph Regional Medical Center*, 415 6th St., P.O. Box 816, 83501. Tel: 208-743-2511
For a complete listing, refer to the Hospitals section.

NAMPA. *Mercy Medical Center*, 1512 12th Avenue Rd., 83686. Tel: 208-467-1171
For a complete listing, refer to the Hospitals section.

[C] MONASTERIES AND RESIDENCES OF PRIESTS AND BROTHERS

JEROME. *Ascension Priory*, 541 East, 100 South, 83338. Tel: 208-324-2377. Order of St. Benedict. Revs. Boniface Lautz, O.S.B., Prior; Meinrad Schallberger, O.S.B., Subprior; Jude Anderson, O.S.B.; Andrew Baumgartner, O.S.B.; Hugh Feiss, O.S.B.; Joel Kehoe, O.S.B.; Eugene Esch, O.S.B.; Simeon VanDeVoord, O.S.B.; Bros. Sylvester Sonnen, O.S.B.; Tobiah Urrutia, O.S.B.; Kevin McMullen, O.S.B.; Inigo Echanove, O.S.B.

LEMHI. *Hermitage of St. Joseph*, Box 37, 83465. Hermits of Mt. Carmel. Rev. Peter Bourne, H.M.C., Prior; Bro. Maurice Mansfield, H.M.C.

[D] CONVENTS AND RESIDENCES OF SISTERS

BOISE. *St. Alphonsus Regional Medical Center Convent-Sisters of Holy Cross*, 2480 N. Westminster Ln., 83704. Tel: 208-367-2121. 8650 W. Rifleman St., Apt. D104, 83704. Tel: 208-323-0019. 217 W. Elm St., P.O. Box 377, New Plymouth, 83655. Tel: 208-278-5802. Legal Title: *Sisters of the Holy Cross, Inc.* Sisters 5.

COTTONWOOD. *Monastery of St. Gertrude, Motherhouse and Novitiate*, HC3 Box 121, 83522-9408. Tel: 208-962-3224; Fax: 208-962-7212. Sr. Mary Kay Henry, O.S.B., Prioress; Sr. Corinne Forsman, O.S.B., Subprioress. Sisters of St. Benedict 85.

MESA. *Marymount Hermitage, Inc., Hermit Sisters of Mary*, 2150 Hermitage Ln., 83643-5005. Tel: 208-256-4354 (msg. only). Sr. Rebecca Mary Bonnell, H.S.M., Supr.; Rev. Charles Prass, O.M.I., Chap. Sisters 2.

[E] RETREAT HOUSES

BOISE. *Nazareth*, 4450 N. Five Mile Rd., 83713-2709. Tel: 208-375-2932; Fax: 208-376-5787. Sr. Grayce E. Ross, S.N.J.M., Exec. Dir. Board of Directors: Mr. James Ballantyne; Mr. Cornelius O'Keefe; Mrs. Greta Pate; Rev. Joseph DaSilva.

[F] CAMPUS MINISTRY

BOISE. *Boise State University, St. Paul's Catholic Center*, 1915 University Dr., 83706. Tel: 208-343-2128. Sr. David Hartse, O.S.U., Dir.

CALDWELL. *Albertson's College of Idaho*, c/o St. Mary, 616 Dearborn, Box 399, 83606. Rev. Enrique Terriquez.

COEUR D'ALENE. *North Idaho College*, St Pius X, 625 E. Haycraft, 83815. Tel: 208-765-5108. Rev. Roger LaChance.

LEWISTON. *Lewis and Clark State College*, St. Stanislaus, 633 5th Ave., 83501. Tel: 208-743-7331. Rev. Sean Caulfield.

MOSCOW. *University of Idaho, St. Augustine Catholic Center*, 628 Deakin, Box 3457, University Sta., 83843-1911. Tel: 208-882-4613. Rev. Mark R. Schumacher.

POCATELLO. *Idaho State University, St. John's Community*, 920 E. Lovejoy, I.S.U. Box 8129, 83209. Tel: 208-233-0880; Fax: 208-233-5745. Rev. Joseph F. McDonald, III, Campus Min.

TWIN FALLS. *College of Southern Idaho*. Attended by Our Lady of Guadalupe, Twin Falls. 630 Falls Ave., 83301-3300. Tel: 208-734-2327. Rev. Thomas J. Loucks.

[G] MISCELLANEOUS

BOISE. *St. Vincent de Paul Society*. St. Francis of Assisi Conference. 6464 W. State St., 83703. Tel: 208-853-4921; Fax: 208-853-4935. Charles Nilles, Exec. Dir.
St. Vincent de Paul Society. St. John's Conference. 3717 Ticonderoga, 83706. Tel: 208-344-0702. Margo Henning, Pres.
St. Vincent de Paul Society. Risen Christ Conference. 11945 W. Combes Park Dr., 83713. Tel: 208-378-7449. Henry Krewer, Pres.

BLACKFOOT. *St. Vincent de Paul Thrift Store*. St. Bernard Conference. 206 S. Spruce, 83221. Tel: 208-785-0353; 785-0423. Margene Belnap, Pres.

CALDWELL. *Society of St. Vincent de Paul*. St. Vincent de Paul of Canyon County Conference. 3719 E. Cleveland Blvd., 83605. Tel: 208-454-2132. Jerry Phillips, Store Mgr.

CLARKSTON, WA. *Lewis and Clark District Council of St. Vincent de Paul*. St. Stanislaus Conference. 604 2nd St., 99403. Tel: 208-746-7860. 3138 5th St., Lewiston, ID, 83501. Tel: 208-746-7860. Collen Stevens, Pres.; Kathie McConnell, Store Mgr.

COEUR D'ALENE. *Redemptorist Fathers*, 919 Indiana Ave., 83814.
St. Vincent de Paul Store. St. Thomas Conference. 108 E. Walnut, 83814. Tel: 208-664-3095; Fax: 208-664-1772. Lynn Peterson, Exec. Dir.

IDAHO FALLS. *St. Vincent de Paul Society of Idaho Falls*, 184 First St., 83404. Tel: 208-528-9979. Jack Crane, Mgr.

KELLOGG. *Society of St. Vincent de Paul*. St. Rita Conference. 104 E. Riverside, 83837. Tel: 208-783-5551. Jim Koskimaki, Conference Pres.; Terry Davis, Mgr.

MERIDIAN. *St. Vincent Thrift Store*, 213 E. First St., 83642. Tel: 208-888-9101. Charles Nilles, Exec. Dir.

MOUNTAIN HOME. *St. Vincent de Paul Society*. Our Lady of Good Counsel Conference. 115 N. 4th East St., 83647. Tel: 208-587-3046. Monique Drauszewski, Pres.

NAMPA. *Mercy Housing Idaho, Inc.*, 1512 12th Avenue Rd., 83686. Tel: 208-463-5858; Fax: 208-463-5859. Mary W. Pridmore, Vice Pres. of Regl. Devel.
Mercy Properties II, Inc.
Mercy Affordable Housing, Inc.
Mercy Housing Idaho Properties, Inc.
Mercy Twin Falls, Inc.
Mercy Moscow, Inc., 1512 12th Avenue Rd., 83686.

Tel: 208-463-5858; Fax: 208-463-5859. Mary Pridmore, Vice Pres. of Regl. Devel.

Mercy Southeast Idaho, Inc., 1512 12th Avenue Rd., 83686. Tel: 208-463-5858; Fax: 208-463-5859.

POCATELLO. *Port Neuf Valley (St. Vincent de Paul)*, P.O. Box 2553, 83206-2553. Tel: 208-233-2555. Marla Wilson, Store Mgr.

TWIN FALLS. *St. Michael Conference (St. Vincent de Paul)*, 244 Main Ave. S., 83301. Tel: 208-734-9143. Mary Nutting, Pres.; Rick Mesaros, Store Mgr.

RELIGIOUS INSTITUTES OF MEN REPRESENTED IN THE DIOCESE

For further details refer to the corresponding bracketed number in the Religious Institutes of Men or Women section.

[0200]—*Benedictine Monks.* (Oregon).—O.S.B.

[0690]—*Jesuit Fathers.* (Oregon Prov.).—S.J.

[]—*Missionary Oblates.*—O.M.I.

[0840]—*Missionary Servants of the Most Holy Trinity.*—S.T.

[1070]—*Redemptorist Fathers.* (Oakland Prov.).—C.SS.R.

[0760]—*Society of Mary.* (San Francisco Western Prov.).—S.M.

RELIGIOUS INSTITUTES OF WOMEN REPRESENTED IN THE DIOCESE

[0230]—*Benedictine Sisters of Pontifical Jurisdiction.*—O.S.B.

[1920]—*Congregation of the Sisters of the Holy Cross.*—C.S.C.

[1780]—*Congregation of the Sisters of the Third Order of St. Francis of Perpetual Adoration.*—F.S.P.A.

[1070-21]—*Dominican Sisters.*—O.P.

[]—*Hermit Sisters of Mary.*—H.S.M.

[1250]—*Institute of the Franciscan Sisters of the Eucharist.*—F.S.E.

[2575]—*Institute of the Sisters of Mercy of the Americas.*—R.S.M.

[3340]—*Sisters of Providence.*—S.P.

[3830]—*Sisters of St. Joseph.*—C.S.J.

[1990]—*Sisters of the Holy Names.*—S.N.J.M.

[]—*Society of Sisters of the Church.*—S.S.C.

[4110]—*Ursuline Nuns.* (Western Prov.).—O.S.U.

NECROLOGY

(No Deaths)

Archdiocese of Boston

(Archidioecesis Bostoniensis)

His Eminence

BERNARD CARDINAL LAW, D.D.

Archbishop of Boston; ordained May 21, 1961; appointed Bishop of Springfield-Cape Girardeau October 22, 1973; ordained Bishop December 5, 1973; promoted Boston January 24, 1984; installed March 23, 1984; Created Cardinal Priest, May 25, 1985. *Res., 2101 Commonwealth Ave., Boston, MA, 02135.*

Chancery Office: 2121 Commonwealth Ave., Brighton, MA, 02135. Tel.: 617-254-0100; Fax: 617-783-4564.

Web site address: http://www.rcab.org

Most Reverend

WILLIAM FRANCIS MURPHY, D.D., S.T.D.

Auxiliary Bishop of Boston and Titular Bishop of Saia Maior; ordained December 16, 1964; ordained Bishop December 27, 1995. *Office: 2121 Commonwealth Ave., Boston, MA, 02135-3193.* Tel.: 617-254-0100; Fax: 617-783-2947. *Res., St. John Rectory, 9 Glen Rd., Wellesley, MA, 02181-1600.*

Most Reverend

JOHN RICHARD McNAMARA, D.D.

Auxiliary Bishop of Boston and Titular Bishop of Risinium; ordained January 10, 1952; ordained Bishop May 21, 1992. *Office and Residence: 70 Lawrence St., Lowell, MA, 01852-2697.* Tel.: 978-459-4082; Fax: 978-452-5584.

Most Reverend

JOHN PATRICK BOLES, D.D., ED.D.

Auxiliary Bishop of Boston and Titular Bishop of Nova Sparsa; ordained February 2, 1955; ordained Bishop May 21, 1992. *Office: 307 Bowdoin St., Boston, MA, 02122-2245.* Tel.: 617-436-3113; Fax: 617-436-7619. *Res., St. Gregory Rectory, 2223 Dorchester Ave., Boston, MA, 02124-5671.*

Most Reverend

JOHN BRENDAN McCORMACK, D.D., M.S.W.

Auxiliary Bishop of Boston and Titular Bishop of Cerbali; ordained February 2, 1960; ordained Bishop December 27, 1995. *Office: 236 Pleasant St., Weymouth, MA, 02190-2599.* Tel.: 781-337-4413; Fax: 781-337-3625. *Res., St. Francis Xavier Rectory, 261 Pleasant St., Weymouth, MA, 02190-2598.*

Most Reverend

FRANCIS XAVIER IRWIN, D.D., A.C.S.W.

Auxiliary Bishop of Boston and Titular Bishop of Ubaza; ordained February 2, 1960; ordained Bishop September 17, 1996. *Office and Residence: 2 Gardener St., Peabody, MA, 01960-1896.* Tel.: 978-531-1013; Fax: 978-531-5312.

Most Reverend

EMILIO SIMEON ALLUE, S.D.B., D.D., PH.D.

Auxiliary Bishop of Boston and Titular Bishop of Croe; ordained December 22, 1996; ordained Bishop September 17, 1996. *Office: 558 South Ave., Weston, MA, 02193-2699.* Tel.: 781-647-4179; Fax: 781-894-4262. *Res., St. Stephen Rectory, 21 Concord St., Framingham, MA, 01702-6700.*

Most Reverend

LAWRENCE JOSEPH RILEY, D.D., S.T.D.

Auxiliary Bishop Emeritus of Boston and Titular Bishop of Daimlaig; ordained September 21, 1940; ordained Bishop February 2, 1972. *Office and Residence: Most Precious Blood Rectory, 43 Maple St., Boston, MA, 02136-2738.* Tel.: 617-364-9500; Fax: 617-364-2590.

ERECTED APRIL 8, 1808; CREATED AN ARCHBISHOPRIC 1875.

Square Miles 2,465.

Comprises the Counties of Essex, Middlesex, Suffolk, Norfolk and Plymouth in the State of Massachusetts, the towns of Mattapoisett, Marion and Wareham excepted.

For legal titles of parishes and archdiocesan institutions, consult the Chancery Office.

STATISTICAL OVERVIEW

Personnel	
Cardinal	1
Auxiliary Bishops	6
Retired Bishops	1
Abbots	1
Priests: Diocesan Active in Diocese	618
Priests: Active Outside Diocese	73
Priests: Retired, Sick or Absent	280
Number of Diocesan Priests	971
Religious Priests in Diocese	874
Ordinations:	
Diocesan Priests	9
Permanent Deacons in Diocese	187
Total Brothers	178
Total Sisters	2,873
Parishes	
Parishes	388
With Resident Pastor:	
Resident Diocesan Priests	348
Resident Religious Priests	32
Without Resident Pastor:	
Administered by Priests	8
New Parishes Created	1
Closed Parishes	7
Professional Ministry Personnel:	
Sisters	78
Lay Ministers	47
Welfare	
Catholic Hospitals	10
Total Assisted	846,384
Health Care Centers	2
Total Assisted	253
Homes for the Aged	11
Total Assisted	2,619
Residential Care of Children	1
Total Assisted	441
Day Care and Extended Day Care Centers	10
Total Assisted	1,862
Specialized Homes	18
Total Assisted	1,308
Special Centers for Social Services	46
Total Assisted	155,824
Residential Care of Disabled	9
Total Assisted	219
Other Institutions	3
Total Assisted	23,560
Educational	
Seminaries, Diocesan	3
Students from This Diocese	54
Students from Other Diocese	115
Seminaries, Religious	4
Total Seminarians	54
Colleges and Universities	9
Total Students	20,351
High Schools, Diocesan and Parish	17
Total Students	5,739
High Schools, Private	19
Total Students	9,010
Elementary Schools, Diocesan and Parish	119
Total Students	36,316
Elementary Schools, Private	11
Total Students	3,560
Catechesis/Religious Education:	
High School Students	28,563
Elementary Students	125,551
Total Students Under Catholic Instruction	229,144
Teachers in the Diocese:	
Priests	14
Brothers	35
Sisters	301
Lay Teachers	2,734
Vital Statistics	
Receptions into the Church:	
Infant Baptism Totals	29,282
Adult Baptism Totals	478
Received into Full Communion	350
First Communions	23,721
Confirmations	15,734
Marriages:	
Catholic	6,957
Interfaith	1,939
Total Marriages	8,896
Deaths	18,847
Total Catholic Population	2,002,322
Total Population	3,764,400

Former Bishops—Most Rev. JOHN LEFEVRE DE CHEVERUS, ord. Dec. 18, 1790; appt. first Bishop of Boston, Apr. 8, 1808; cons. Nov. 1, 1810; transferred to Montauban, Jan. 15, 1823, thence to Bordeaux, Oct. 2, 1826; appt. Cardinal Archbishop of Bordeaux, Oct. 2, 1826; died July 19, 1836.—Most Rev. BENEDICT J. FENWICK, S.J., ord. June 11, 1808; appt. second Bishop of Boston, May 10, 1825; cons. Nov. 1, 1825; died Aug. 11, 1846.—Most Rev. JOHN BERNARD FITZPATRICK, ord. June 13, 1840; appt. Titular Bishop of Callipolis and Coadjutor of Boston, Nov. 21, 1843; cons. March 24, 1844; appt. third Bishop of Boston, Aug. 11, 1846; died Feb. 13, 1866.—Most Rev. JOHN JOSEPH WILLIAMS, D.D., ord. May 17, 1845; appt. Titular Bishop of Tripolis and Coadjutor of Boston, Jan. 8, 1866; appt. fourth Bishop of Boston, March 11, 1866; created first Archbishop of Boston, Feb. 12, 1875; died Aug. 30, 1907.—His Eminence WILLIAM CARDINAL O'CONNELL, ord. June 7, 1884; appt. third Bishop of Portland, Maine, Feb. 8, 1901; cons. May 19, 1901; appt. Titular Archbishop of Constantia and Coadjutor with right of succession to the Archbishop of Boston, Feb. 8, 1906; appt. fifth Bishop and second Archbishop of Boston, April 30, 1907; created Cardinal, Nov. 27, 1911; died April 22, 1944.—His Eminence RICHARD CARDINAL CUSHING, ord. May

26, 1921; appt. Titular Bishop of Mela and Auxiliary of Boston, June 10, 1939; cons. June 29, 1939; appt. sixth Bishop and third Archbishop of Boston, Sept. 25, 1944; created and proclaimed Cardinal Priest under the title of St. Susanna in the Consistory of December 15, 1958; died Nov. 2, 1970.—His Eminence Humberto Cardinal Medeiros, ord. June 15, 1946; appt. second Bishop of Brownsville, April 14, 1966; cons. June 9, 1966; appt. seventh Bishop and fourth Archbishop of Boston, Sept. 8, 1970; created and proclaimed Cardinal Priest under the title of St. Susanna in the Consistory of March 5, 1973; died Sept. 17, 1983.

Regional Bishops—Central Region: Most Rev. John P. Boles, D.D., Ed.D., Bishop's Office: *307 Bowdoin St., Dorchester, 02122-2245.* Tel: 617-436-3113; Fax: 617-436-7619. South Region: Most Rev. John B. McCormack, D.D., M.S.W., Bishop's Office: *236 Pleasant St., Weymouth, 02190-2599.* Tel: 781-337-4413; Fax: 781-337-3625. Merrimack Region: Most Rev. John R. McNamara, D.D., Bishop's Office: *70 Lawrence St., Lowell, 01852-2697.* Tel: 978-459-4082; Fax: 978-452-5584. West Region: Most Rev. Emilio S. Allue, D.D., S.T.B., S.T.L., Ph.D., Bishop's Office: *558 South Ave., Weston, 02193.* Tel: 781-647-4179; Fax: 781-894-4262. North Region: Most Rev. Francis X. Irwin, D.D., A.S.C.W., Bishop's Office: *2 Gardener St., Peabody, 01960-1896.* Tel: 978-531-1013; Fax: 978-531-5312.

Vicars General—Most Rev. John R. McNamara, D.D.; Most Rev. John P. Boles, D.D.; Most Rev. John B. McCormack, D.D.; Most Rev. Francis X. Irwin; Most Rev. Emilio S. Allue, S.D.B.; Most Rev. William F. Murphy.

Vicars—CENTRAL REGION: Very Rev. Charles J. Bourque, V.F., Vicariate I, *Our Lady of Lourdes Rectory, Jamaica Plain.* Tel: 617-524-0434. Very Rev. John F. Cullotty, V.F., Vicariate II, *St. Brigid Rectory, 841 E. Broadway, Boston, 02127-2397.* Tel: 617-268-2122. Very Rev. Albert J. Sallese, V.F., Vicariate III, *Sacred Heart Rectory, East Boston.* Tel: 617-567-5776. Very Rev. Peter J. Casey, V.F., Vicariate IV, *St. Ann Rectory, Somerville.* Tel: 617-625-1904. *SOUTH REGION: Very Rev.* Joseph F. Manning, V.F., Brockton Vicariate, *Our Lady of Lourdes Rectory, Brockton.* Tel: 508-586-4715. Very Rev. James L. McCune, V.F., Norwood Vicariate, *St. John Rectory, 700 Washington St., Canton, 02021.* Tel: 781-828-0090. Very Rev. John Mark Hannon, V.F., Plymouth Vicariate, *St. Joseph the Worker Rectory, Hanson.* Tel: 781-293-3581. Very Rev. Daniel M. Graham, V.F., Quincy Vicariate, *St. Joseph Rectory, Quincy.* Tel: 617-472-6321. Very Rev. James J. Rafferty, V.F., Weymouth Vicariate, *St. Paul Rectory, Hingham.* Tel: 781-749-0587. *WEST REGION: Very Rev.* Francis V. Strahan, V.F., Framingham Vicariate, *St. Bridget Rectory, Framingham.* Tel: 508-875-5959. Very Rev. Robert D. Tyrrell, V.F., Marlboro Vicariate, *St. Julia Rectory, Weston.* Tel: 781-899-2611. Very Rev. Joseph G. Lind, V.F., Natick Vicariate, *St. Paul Rectory, Wellesley.* Tel: 781-235-1060. Very Rev. Robert Fichtner, V.F., Newton Vicariate, *St. Patrick Rectory, Watertown.* Tel: 617-926-9680. *MERRIMACK REGION: Vacant, Concord Vicariate; Very Rev.* Mark S. Sheehan, V.F., Chelmsford Vicariate, *St. Michael Rectory, Bedford.* Tel: 781-275-6318. Very Rev. Emile Guilmette, S.M., V.F., Haverhill Vicariate, *St. Joseph Rectory, Haverhill.* Tel: 978-372-7721. Very Rev. George F. Carlson, V.F., Lawrence Vicariate, *St. Patrick Rectory, Lawrence.* Tel: 978-683-9416. Very Rev. John W. Hanley, O.M.I., V.F., Lowell Vicariate, *St. Marie Parish, 75 Chamberlain St., Lowell, 01852-5523.* Tel: 978-453-2134. *NORTH REGION: Very Rev.* John E. Farrell, V.F., Gloucester Vicariate, *Our Lady of the Assumption Rectory, Lynnfield.* Tel: 781-598-4313. Very Rev. Francis E. Daley, V.F., Medford Vicariate, *St. James the Apostle Rectory, Arlington.* Tel: 781-643-0636. Very Rev. Paul F. Garrity, V.F., Salem Vicariate, *St. Mary Parish, 8 S. Common St., Lynn, 01902-4489.* Tel: 781-598-4907. Very Rev. Vincent P. Mellone, V.F., Stoneham Vicariate, *St. Barbara Rectory, Woburn.* Tel: 781-933-4130.

Presbyteral Council—His Eminence Bernard Cardinal Law, Pres.; Rev. Richard G. Lennon, Moderator. Members: Most Rev. Lawrence J. Riley; Most Rev. John R. McNamara; Most Rev. John P. Boles; Most Rev. John B. McCormack; Most Rev. William F. Murphy; Most Rev. Francis X. Irwin; Most Rev. Emilio S. Allue, S.D.B.; Rev. Msgr. Robert P. Deeley; Rev. Msgr. Francis D. Kelly; Rev. Msgr. Timothy J. Moran; Revs. Andrew R. Albert, S.M.; Francisco Anzoategui, S.X.; Robert M. Blaney; Robert J. Bouffier, S.M.; Ephrem Vu Kiem Cung, C.M.C.; Peter V. Conley; Albert J. Contons; Arthur J. Driscoll; George P. Evans; John E. Farrell; Gerald J. Fitzgerald; Edward P. Geary; Peter G. Gori, O.S.A.; James J. Harrington; Michael J. Kallock, C.S.P.; John F. Leonard; James D. Lyons; Richard J. Malone; John F. Mulloy; Frederick J. Murphy; James Nibler, O.M.V.; James O'Brien, S.S.C.; Edward M. O'Flaherty, S.J.; John J. Philbin; Paul A. Phinn; Primo Piscitello, O.F.M.; Joseph K. Raeke; Joseph M. Rossi; John E. Sassani; Kevin M. Sepe; John P. Spencer, S.J.; Eugene P. Sullivan; Vincent P. Von Euw; Leo Wetzel, O.M.I.

Archdiocesan College of Consultors—Most Rev. Lawrence J. Riley; Most Rev. John R. McNamara; Most Rev. John P. Boles; Most Rev. John B. McCormack; Most Rev. William F. Murphy; Most Rev. Francis X. Irwin; Most Rev. Emilio S. Allue, S.D.B.; Revs. Peter G. Gori, O.S.A., J.C.D.; John F. Leonard; John F. Mulloy.

Finance Council—His Eminence Bernard Cardinal Law, Pres. Members: Most. Rev. William F. Murphy; Ms. Regina E. Caines; Mr. John Cunningham; Mr. Thomas J. Flatley, Sr.; Sr. Therese Higgins, C.S.J.; Mr. John A. Kaneb; Mr. Peter S. Lynch; Mr. William F. McCall; Mr. Robert J. Morrissey; Mr. Giles Mosher, Jr.; Mr. John A. McNiece; Mr. Gerald T. Reilly; Mrs. Michael A. Valerio; Mr. Francis M. Ward.

Archdiocesan Pastoral Council—His Eminence Bernard Cardinal Law, Pres. Ex officio: Most. Rev. William F. Murphy; Most Rev. John R. McNamara; Most Rev. John P. Boles; Most Rev. John B. McCormack; Most Rev. Francis X. Irwin; Most Rev. Emilio S. Allue, S.D.B.; Most Rev. Lawrence J. Riley; Rev. Msgr. Francis D. Kelly; Rev. Msgr. Timothy J. Moran; Rev. John E. Sassani; Mr. Gerald T. Reilly. Appointed: Very Rev. Charles Bourque; Sr. Rita Brereton, S.S.N.D.; Sr. Nancy Rowen, S.N.D.; Deacons Charles Cornell; Paul Markey; Bro. Edward Keefe, C.F.X.; Rev. Msgr. Robert Deeley; Rev. Msgr. Paul McInerny; Revs. Russell W. Best; Richard F. Clancy; Joseph Cogo, C.S.; John Connolly; William D. Coughlin; Michael S. Foster; William M. Helmick; Deacon Eugene Stenstrom; Sr. Mary Anne Doyle, C.S.J.; Sr. Linda James, F.S.P.; Ms. Mary Beth Begley; Ms. Ellin Carroll; Ms. Johanna Chao; Mrs. Anne Shine Cimini; Ms. Roseli DaSilva; Mrs. Cecelia Doherty; Mrs. Eunice Fallon; Mrs. Margaret Fortes; Mrs. Catherine Hirst; Mrs. Suzanne Lagasse; Mrs. Mary MacLean; Ms. Gisela Morales-Barreto; Miss Susan Murphy; Ms. Winifred Murphy; Ms. Sharon Mutrie; Ms. Maureen Rocks; Ms. Janice Rogers; Mrs. Carolyn Ryan; Ms. Eleanor Wernig; Mr. Kevin Delehanty; Mr. Joseph DiNardo; Mr. George Fischer; Mr. John J. Geary; Mr. James J. Healey; Mr. William Hobbib; Mr. Irving Kane; Mr. Phil LaFond; Mr. David R. MacKay; Mr. Stephen Mahoney; Mr. James F. McArdle; Mr. Andrew O'Brien; Mr. Laurence Quigley; Mr. John M. Riley; Mr. Paul E. Robinson; Mr. Paul D. Snyder; Mr. Michael Spillane.

Vicar General and Moderator of the Curia—Most Rev. William F. Murphy, S.T.D., *2121 Commonwealth Ave., Brighton, 02135.* Tel: 617-254-0100; Fax: 617-783-2947.

Assistant to the Moderator of the Curia for Administrative Affairs—Rev. Thomas J. Daly.

Assistant to the Moderator of the Curia for Canonical Affairs—Rev. Richard G. Lennon.

Office of Development—Robert X. Chandler, *2121 Commonwealth Ave., Brighton, 02135.* Tel: 617-254-0100; Fax: 617-783-6366.

Office of Planning and Research—Rev. Robert McMillan, S.J., *2121 Commonwealth Ave., Brighton, 02135.* Tel: 617-254-0100; Fax: 617-783-2947.

Office of Propagation of the Faith—Rev. Msgr. Andrew F. Connell, *49 Franklin St., Boston, 02110.* Tel: 617-542-1776; Fax: 617-542-1778.

Office of Holy Childhood Association—Rev. Msgr. Andrew F. Connell, *49 Franklin St., Boston, 02110.* Tel: 617-542-1771; Fax: 617-542-1778.

Society of St. Peter the Apostle—Rev. Msgr. Andrew F. Connell, *49 Franklin St., Boston, 02110.* Tel: 617-542-1771; Fax: 617-542-1778.

Synod Office—Rev. Thomas J. Daly, Exec. Dir., *2121 Commonwealth Ave., Brighton, 02135.* Tel: 617-254-0100.

Cabinet Secretaries

Secretary for Pastoral Services—Rev. Paul B. O'Brien, *2121 Commonwealth Ave., Brighton, 02135.* Tel: 617-254-0100; Fax: 617-783-2947.

Secretary for Education—Rev. Richard J. Malone, *One Lake St., Brighton, 02135.* Tel: 617-254-4425; Fax: 617-782-0213.

Secretary for Community Relations—John B. Walsh, *2121 Commonwealth Ave., Brighton, 02135.* Tel: 617-254-0100; Fax: 617-782-8358.

Secretary for Social Services—Dr. Joseph Doolin, *49 Franklin St., Boston, 02110.* Tel: 617-482-5440; Fax: 617-451-0337.

Secretary for Health Care Services—Michael F. Collins, M.D., *736 Cambridge St., Brighton, 02135-2997.* Tel: 617-789-2500; Fax: 617-789-2124.

Secretary for Ministerial Personnel—Rev. Paul E. Miceli, *2121 Commonwealth Ave., Brighton, 02135.* Tel: 617-254-0100; Fax: 617-783-2947.

Delegate for Religious—Sr. Roberta Marie Brown, C.S.J., *2121 Commonwealth Ave., Boston, 02135-3173.* Tel: 617-254-0100; Fax: 617-783-2947.

Secretary for Central Services—Gerald T. Reilly, C.P.A., *2121 Commonwealth Ave., Brighton, 02135;* Fax: 617-783-4564.

Chancery Office—2121 Commonwealth Ave., Brighton, 02135. Tel: 617-254-0100; Fax: 617-783-4564. Office Hours: Mon.-Fri. 9-5.

Chancellor—Gerald T. Reilly.

Archivist—Robert Johnson-Lally. Tel: 617-254-0100; Fax: 617-783-5642.

Secretaries to the Cardinal and Master of Ceremonies—Rev. Msgr. Paul B. McInerny; Rev. John J. Connolly.

Metropolitan Tribunal—One Lake St., Brighton, 02135. Tel: 617-746-5900; Fax: 617-783-2423. Office Hours: Mon.-Fri. 9-5.

Judicial Vicar—Rev. Msgr. Robert P. Deeley, J.C.D.

Associate Judicial Vicar—Rev. Michael S. Foster, J.C.D.

Promotor of Justice—Rev. Richard G. Cunningham, J.C.D.

Defender of the Bond—Rev. James G. Burke, J.C.L.

Secretary to the Tribunal—Joanne M. Curry, M.A.

Diocesan Judges—Revs. David P. Bailey, J.C.L.; James G. Burke, J.C.L.; Rodney J. Copp, J.C.L.; Richard G. Cunningham, J.C.D.; Rev. Msgr. Robert P. Deeley, J.C.D.; Rev. Michael S. Foster, J.C.D.; Rev. Msgr. Paul B. McInerny, J.C.L.; Rev. James A. O'Donohoe, J.C.D.; Sr. Margaret L. Sullivan, C.S.J., J.C.L.

Judge Auditor—Rev. James W. DeAdder, S.T.D., Ph.D., J.D.

Court Advocates—Rev. Peter G. Gori, O.S.A., J.C.D.

Advocates—Revs. Joseph A. Antonellis; James J. Barry; Robert Braunreuther, S.J.; Michael J. Bova Conti; John E. Buckley; Richard A. Buntel; James M. Carroll; Peter J. Casey; Dismas Centrella, O.F.M.; Henry G. Chambers; William D. Coughlin; John A. Dooher; Paul J. Finegan; Paul R. E. Francis, J.C.B., S.T.D.; Michael Harkins; George G. Hogan; Francis H. Kelley; Thomas A. Kopp; James F. Lanergan; Victor C. Lavoie; John F. Leonard; Antonio Medeiros; Brian F. Manning; Leonard T. McGrath; Dennis J. Nason; Peter J. O'Hara, A.C.S.W.; James E. O'Leary; Leonard F. O'Malley; Gerald J. Osterman; Peter F. Quinn; Thomas J. Reilly; Frank J. Silva; Martin J. Walsh; Thomas J. Walsh; Robert A. Ward.

Psychological Consultants—Family Counseling & Guidance Centers, Inc., Neil J. Cronin, L.I.C.S.W., Clinical Dir. Joseph Doherty, Ed.D.; Charles J. Ferro, M.Ed.; Margaret L. Hager, L.I.C.S.W.; Thomas F. Higgins, Ed.D.; Charles H. Hogan, Psy.D.; Francis J. Kelly, L.I.C.S.W., M.S.W.; Helen O'Meara, L.I.C.S.W.; Claire O'Rourke; Michael St. Clair, M.A., Ph.D.; Joseph Liftik, Ph.D.; Thomas H. Kelley, Ph.D.; Kernan T. Manion, M.D.; Paul McCormick, M.Div., Ph.D.; A. Eugene Newman, Ph.D.; Daniel J. Quinn, L.I.C.S.W.

Ecclesiastical Notary—Laura M. Cellucci; M. Connie Murphy.

Provincial Tribunal

Tribunal of Boston Province-Regional Matrimonial Appeal Court—2121 Commonwealth Ave., Brighton, 02135. Tel: 617-254-2772; Fax: 617-562-1104.

Judicial Vicar—Rev. David P. Bailey, J.C.L.

Associate Judicial Vicars and Defenders of the Bond—Most Rev. Bernard J. Flanagan, S.T.L., J.C.D.; Rev. Msgr. Donald J. Gilbert, Jr.; Rev. Henry G. Bowen, S.T.L., J.C.D.; Rev. Msgr. Robert P. Deeley, J.C.D.; Revs. Jay T. Maddock, J.C.L.; Paul F. Stefanko, J.C.L.

Promoter of Justice—Rev. Henry G. Bowen, S.T.L., J.C.D.

Judges—(Boston); Revs. David P. Bailey, J.C.L.; Dennis J. Burns, J.C.D.; Rev. Msgr. Robert P. Deeley, J.C.D.; Rev. Michael S. Foster, J.C.D.; Rev. Msgr. Paul B. McInerny, J.C.L.; Revs. James A. O'Donohoe, J.C.D., (Burlington): Revs. Gerald W. Bombardier, M.A., J.C.L.; Walter D. Miller, J.C.D., (Fall River): Rev. Msgr. Thomas J. Harrington; Revs. Gerard Hebert, J.C.L.; Mark R. Hession, J.C.L.; Thomas E. McGlynn, J.C.L.; Rev. Jay T. Maddock, J.C.L., (Manchester): Rev. Msgr. Raymond O. Blair, S.T.L., J.C.D.; Rev. Msgr. Norman P. Bolduc, J.C.L.; Rev. Msgr. Paul L. Bouchard, S.T.L., M.A., J.C.L.; Revs. Francis L. Demers, O.M.I., J.C.D.; Rev. Msgr. Donald J. Gilbert, J.C.L.; Sr. Louise Tessier, P.M., J.C.L.; Rev. Michael A. Henchal, J.C.L., (Portland): Rev. Msgr. Raymond F. Begin, J.C.D.; Rev. Msgr. Vincent A. Tatarczuk, S.T.L., J.C.D.; Revs. Joseph J. Koury, S.J., J.C.D.; Mark P. Nolette,

J.C.L.; PAUL F. STEFANKO, J.C.L.; Sr. CLAUDIA BARBRE, R.S.M., J.C.L.; Sr. RITA-MAE BISSONNETTE, R.S.R., J.C.L.; Sr. ANN KEEVAN, C.S.J., J.C.D.; GEORGE G. PAVLOFF, J.C.D., (Springfield): Rev. Msgr. JOHN F. HARRINGTON, J.C.L.; Rev. Msgr. JOSEPH I. JOHNSON, J.C.D.; Rev. Msgr. ROGER VIAU, J.C.D.; Revs. HENRY KARWEL, O.F.M.Conv., J.C.L.; DANIEL P. LISTON, J.C.L.; JOHN P. MCDONAGH, J.C.L.; JOHN J. SHEA, S.T.L., J.C.D.; JOHN L. SULLIVAN, J.C.L.; ROBERT W. THRASHER, J.C.D., (Worchester): Most Rev. BERNARD J. FLANAGAN, S.T.L., J.C.D.; Revs. HENRY G. BOWEN, S.T.L., J.C.D.; BRIAN R. CORMIER, J.C.L.; PAUL T. O'CONNELL, J.C.D.; F. STEPHEN PEDONE.

Seminaries—

Pope John XXIII National Seminary—Rev. Msgr. FRANCIS D. KELLY, S.T.D., Rector, *558 South St., Weston, 02193.* Tel: 781-899-5500; Fax: 781-899-9057.

St. John's Seminary School of Theology—Rev. Msgr. TIMOTHY J. MORAN, S.T.D., Rector, *Lake St., Brighton, 02135.* Tel: 617-254-2610; Fax: 617-787-2336.

St. John's Seminary College of Liberal Arts—Rev. ROBERT W. FLAGG, S.T.L., Dean, *197 Foster St., Brighton, 02135.* Tel: 617-254-2610; Fax: 617-787-2336.

Continuing Education and Spiritual Enrichment of Priests—Rev. JOHN E. MACINNIS, *5 Lake St., Brighton, 02135.* Tel: 617-254-2610.

Pastoral Services

Pastoral Services—Rev. PAUL B. O'BRIEN, Cabinet Sec., *2121 Commonwealth Ave., Brighton, 02135.* Tel: 617-254-0100; Fax: 617-783-2947.

Black Catholics, Office for—MEYER CHAMBERS, *2121 Commonwealth Ave., Brighton, 02135.* Tel: 617-254-0100; Fax: 617-783-5642.

Charismatic Renewal—DAVID THORP, *20 Pond St., Waltham, 02154.* Tel: 781-891-3592; Fax: 781-891-3593.

Cursillo—Rev. ROBERT W. FLAGG, *St. John's Seminary, 127 Lake St., Brighton, 02135.* Tel: 617-254-2610.

Deaf Apostolate—Rev. MICHAEL J. MEDAS, *2121 Commonwealth Ave., Boston, 02135.* Tel: 617-254-0100.

Ethnic Apostolates—Rev. JOSEPH COGO, C.S., Coord., *Sacred Heart Parish, 12 North Square, Boston, 02113.* Tel: 617-523-5638. Sr. PEGGY LOFTUS, S.N.D.; Sr. CHARLOTTE KANE, S.N.D., *2121 Commonwealth Ave., Brighton, 02135.* Tel: 617-254-0100; Fax: 617-783-5642.

Asian Indian Apostolate—Rev. THOMAS D'SOUZA. Tel: 617-631-3443.

Brazilian Apostolate—Rev. ROBERT BOUFFIER, S.M. Tel: 617-354-5008.

Cambodian Apostolate—Rev. ANTHONY GIANG NGUYEN. Tel: 617-889-2774. Sr. PEGGY CUMMINS, S.N.D. Tel: 508-454-7663.

Cameroon Apostolate—Sr. MARILYN GIGNAC. Tel: 508-458-8862.

Cape Verdean Apostolate—Rev. PIO GOTTIN, O.F.M.Cap. Tel: 617-445-7645.

Chinese Apostolate (Mandarin)—Rev. DENIS R. COMO, S.J. Tel: 617-482-2949.

Croatian Apostolate—JOYCE GALANTIC. Tel: 617-484-2619.

Ethiopian/Eritrean Apostolate—Rev. HABTAMARIAN KETEMA. Tel: 617-289-1234.

Laotion Apostolate—Sr. EILEEN BURNS, S.N.D. Tel: 508-599-7750.

Filipino Apostolate—Rev. JOHN COSS, F.M.S.I. Tel: 508-879-6711.

French Apostolate—*Office for Ethnic Apostolates.* Tel: 617-254-0100.

Ghanaian Apostolate—Rev. PETER AYOROGO. Tel: 617-325-1404.

German Apostolate—Rev. FREDERICK J. MURPHY. Tel: 617-542-5682.

Haitian Apostolate—Rev. JOHN MORIN, O.M.I. Tel: 617-298-0080.

Hmong Apostolate—PAULE VERDET. Tel: 617-965-2499.

Irish Apostolate—Rev. DANIEL FINN. Tel: 617-288-2367.

Italian Apostolate—Rev. PRIMO PISCITELLO, O.F.M. Tel: 617-523-2110.

Japanese Apostolate—Sr. FEDRE TANNO, P.D.D.M. Tel: 617-482-0978.

Khmhu Laotian Apostolate—Rev. JOHN FAGAN, S.J. Tel: 617-445-1524.

Korean Apostolate—Rev. PAUL RI. Tel: 617-899-9947. Dr. KYU KIM. Tel: 508-835-6947.

Liberian Apostolate—Rev. JAMES CALLAHAN, S.M.A. Tel: 617-329-4774.

Lithuanian Apostolate—Rev. ALBERT CONTONS. Tel: 617-268-0353.

Nigerian Apostolate—Rev. GERALD OSTERMAN. Tel: 617-442-1431.

Polish Apostolate—Rev. Msgr. STANISLAUS SYPEK. Tel: 617-361-0565.

Portuguese Apostolate—Rev. JOSE S. FERREIRA. Tel: 617-547-5593.

Rwanda Apostolate—Rev. BASILE BAZINE. Tel: 617-229-6884.

Ugandan Apostolate—Dr. ALOYSIUS LUGIRA. Tel: 617-729-9245.

Vietnamese Apostolate—Rev. EPHREM VU KIEM CUNG, C.M.C. Tel: 617-265-2479.

Zaire Apostolate—Rev. BASILE BAZINE. Tel: 617-229-6884.

Family Life Apostolate—MARY ALICE BREINLINGER, *2121 Commonwealth Ave., Brighton, 02135.* Tel: 617-783-2451; Fax: 617-783-5642.

Health Care Ministry, Office for—KELLY L. DUNN, *St. Elizabeth's Hospital, 736 Cambridge St., Brighton, 02135.* Tel: 617-789-2456; Fax: 617-789-2573.

Hispanic Apostolate, Office for the—Rev. JAMES F. GAUDREAU, Dir., *2121 Commonwealth Ave., Brighton, 02135-3193.* Tel: 617-746-5816; Fax: 617-783-5642.

Holy Name Society—Rev. JOHN MCLAUGHLIN, *25 Arlington St., Somerville, 02145.* Tel: 617-625-0029.

Juvenile Court Chaplain—Rev. JAMES F. FRATUS, *601 Broadway, Chelsea, 02150.* Tel: 617-889-2774.

League of Catholic Women—Rev. MARTIN CONNOR, Spiritual Dir., *St. John's Seminary, 127 Lake St., Brighton, 02135.* Tel: 617-254-2610; Fax: 617-783-2336.

Legion of Mary—Rev. ALFRED PUCCINI, *12 Thacher St., Malden, 02148.* Tel: 781-322-6142.

Liturgical Commission—Rev. SEAN M. MCCARTHY, Chm. Tel: 617-769-2522.

Marian Devotions Coordinator—Rev. WILLIAM R. CARROLL, *24 Medford St., Arlington, 02174.* Tel: 781-648-0220; Fax: 781-643-8955.

Pilgrimages, Coordinator of—Rev. WALTER H. CUENIN, *573 Washington St., Newton, 02158.* Tel: 617-527-7560; Fax: 617-527-1338.

Prison Ministry Office—Deacon WALTER J. MILES, JR., Dir., *253 Watertown St., Newton, 02158.* Tel: 617-244-7544.

Seaport of Boston—Waterfront Chapel, Rev. PHILIP LAPLANTE, S.M., *27 Isabella St., Boston, 02116.* Tel: 617-482-5495; Fax: 617-268-8100.

Spiritual Development, Office of—Rev. JOHN E. SASSANI, *2121 Commonwealth Ave., Brighton, 02135.* Tel: 617-254-1040; Fax: 617-254-6469.

Worship, Office for—Rev. JAMES F. FIELD, *2121 Commonwealth Ave., Brighton, 02135.* Tel: 617-746-5880; Fax: 617-787-8144.

Young Adult Ministry, Office for—JAMES J. BREEN, *2121 Commonwealth Ave., Brighton, 02135.* Tel: 617-254-0100; 783-4505; Fax: 617-783-5642.

Youth Ministry, Office for—Rev. THOMAS A. DUNNE, S.D.B., *139 Crescent St., Quincy, 02169.* Tel: 617-472-0333; Fax: 617-479-6298.

Education

Education—Rev. RICHARD J. MALONE, Cabinet Sec., *One Lake St., Brighton, 02135-3800.* Tel: 617-782-0690; Fax: 617-782-0213.

Campus Ministry—Sr. KATHLEEN CROWLEY, S.C.H., Dir., *68 St. Stephen St., Boston, 02115.* Tel: 617-266-2635; Fax: 617-266-6148.

Office of Religious Education—Rev. RICHARD J. MALONE, Dir., *One Lake St., Brighton, 02135.* Tel: 617-254-4425; Fax: 617-782-0213.

Catholic School Office—Sr. ANN DOMINIC ROACH, O.P., Supt., Schools, *2200 Dorchester Ave., Boston, 02124-5607.* Tel: 617-298-6555; Fax: 617-298-6622.

Social Services

Social Services—Dr. JOSEPH DOOLIN, Ph.D., Cabinet Sec., *49 Franklin St., Boston, 02110.* Tel: 617-482-5440; Fax: 617-451-0337.

Catholic Charitable Bureau of the Archdiocese of Boston, Inc.—Dr. JOSEPH DOOLIN, *49 Franklin St., Boston, 02110.* Tel: 617-482-5440; Fax: 617-482-2429.

Catholic Relief Services—Dr. JOSEPH DOOLIN, *49 Franklin St., Boston, 02110.* Tel: 617-482-5440; Fax: 617-482-2429.

Life Resources, Inc.—ROBERT M. TURILLO, *199 State St., 5th Fl., Boston, 02109.* Tel: 617-227-8766.

Office of AIDS Ministry—Sr. ZITA FLEMING, C.S.J., *49 Franklin St., Boston, 02110.* Tel: 617-482-5440; Fax: 617-482-2429.

Office of Pro-Life Activities—BARBARA THORP, *159 Washington St., Brighton, 02135.* Tel: 617-783-5410; Fax: 617-787-7797.

Society of St. Vincent de Paul—ALBERT CROCKER, Coord., *1280 Washington St., Boston, 02118.* Tel: 617-542-0883.

Nazareth, Inc.—JOAN KILDAY PULEO, *19 St. Joseph St., Jamaica Plain, 02130.* Tel: 617-522-4040.

St. Ann's Home, Inc.—Dr. PATRICK T. VILLANI, *100A Haverhill St., Methuen, 01844.* Tel: 978-682-5276.

Health Care Services

Caritas Christi Health Care System—MICHAEL F. COLLINS, M.D., Pres./C.E.O., *736 Cambridge St., Brighton, 02135-2997.* Tel: 617-789-2500; Fax: 617-789-2124. - Holy Family Hospital, Inc., Methuen - St. Elizabeth's Medical Center, Brighton - St. John of God Hospital, Brighton - Good Samaritan Hospice, Inc., Brighton - Good Samaritan Medical Center, Inc., Brockton & Stoughton - Caritas Christi Support Services, Inc., Boston - Holy Family Hospital Foundation, Inc., Methuen - Valley Regional Health System, Inc., Methuen - Valley Regional Support Services, Inc., Methuen - Metropolitan Boston Dialysis Center, Waltham Archdiocesan Liaison with all other Catholic Hospitals in the Archdiocese - The Carney Hospital, Boston - Franciscan Children's Hospital & Rehabilitation Center, Boston - Sancta Maria Hospital, Cambridge - Youville Hospital, Cambridge - Bethany Hospital, Framingham - Saints Memorial Medical Center, Inc., Lowell.

Nurses, Archdiocesan Council of—Rev. J. JOSEPH KIERCE, *35 Virginia St., Dorchester, 02125.* Tel: 617-436-2777.

Community Relations

Community Relations—JOHN B. WALSH, Cabinet Sec. Tel: 617-254-0100; Fax: 617-562-1104.

Labor Guild—Rev. EDWARD F. BOYLE, S.J., Dir., *883 Hancock St., Quincy, 02170.* Tel: 617-786-1822; Fax: 617-472-2486.

Planning Office for Urban Affairs—Rev. MICHAEL F. GRODEN, Dir., *185 Devonshire St., Boston, 02110.* Tel: 617-350-8885; Fax: 617-350-8889.

Boston Catholic Directory—Rev. PETER V. CONLEY, Editor; Rev. ROBERT M. O'GRADY, Asst. to the Editor, *49 Franklin St., Boston, 02110.* Tel: 617-542-8393; Fax: 617-542-9547.

Campaign for Human Development—Rev. WILLIAM F. JOY, *St. Angela Parish, 1548 Blue Hill Ave., Boston, 02126.* Tel: 617-298-0080; Fax: 617-298-2388.

Office of Communications—JOHN WALSH, Dir., *2121 Commonwealth Ave., Brighton, 02135-2947.* Tel: 617-254-0100; Fax: 617-562-1104.

Ecumenical and Interreligious Affairs—Rev. EDWARD M. O'FLAHERTY, S.J., Dir., *2121 Commonwealth Ave., Brighton, 02135.* Tel: 617-254-0100; Fax: 617-562-1104.

Liasion for Catholic-Jewish Relations—Rev. JOHN P. MCGINTY, *St. Theresa of Avila Parish, 10 St. Theresa St., Boston, 02132.* Tel: 617-325-1300; Fax: 617-325-0380.

Mass Catholic Conference—GERALD D'AVOLIO, Exec. Dir., *49 Franklin St., Boston, 02110-1304.* Tel: 617-574-0771; Fax: 617-574-9227.

The Pilot—Revs. PETER V. CONLEY, Editor in Chief; ROBERT M. O'GRADY, Asst. to the Editor, *49 Franklin St., Boston, 02110-1381.* Tel: 617-482-4316; Fax: 617-482-5647.

Radio Apostolate—Vacant.

Office of Social Justice—Rev. WILLIAM P. JOY, Dir., *St. Angela Parish, 1548 Blue Hill Ave., Boston, 02126.* Tel: 617-298-0080; Fax: 617-298-2388.

TV Apostolate—Rev. FRANCIS T. MCFARLAND, *55 Chapel St., P.O. Box 9109, Newton, 02158-9109.* Tel: 617-965-0050; Fax: 617-965-6587. *Boston Catholic Television Center, Inc.*

Ministerial Personnel

Ministerial Personnel—Revs. PAUL E. MICELI, Cabinet Sec. WILLIAM F. MURPHY, Delegate to the Archbishop. Co-Delegates: Sr. RITA MCCARTHY, C.S.J.; Rev. JOHN A. DOOHER. Tel: 617-254-0100; Fax: 617-783-2947.

Clergy Personnel Office—Revs. JAMES J. MCCARTHY; RICHARD W. FITZGERALD, *One Lake St., Brighton, 02135.* Tel: 617-254-2085; Fax: 617-254-8407.

Delegate for Religious—Sr. ROBERTA MARIE BROWN, C.S.J., *2121 Commonwealth Ave., Brighton, 02135.* Tel: 617-254-0100; Fax: 617-783-2947.

Office of Pastoral Ministries—BARBARA A. SHINE, Dir.; Sr. DOROTHEA MASURET, C.S.J., *One Lake St., Brighton, 02135.* Tel: 617-782-6675; Fax: 617-254-8407.

Pastoral Support for Priests—Rev. EDWARD M. O'FLAHERTY, S.J., *5 Lake St., Brighton, 02135.* Tel: 617-254-2610.

Office of Senior Priests—Rev. Msgr. JAMES E. TIERNEY, Dir.; Rev. BERNARD J. LANE, Assoc. Dir., *Regina Cleri, 60 Wm. Cardinal O'Connell Way, Boston, 02114.* Tel: 617-523-1861; Fax: 617-720-0585.

Permanent Diaconate Program—Deacon DONOGHUE, Dir.; Rev. JOSE CORRAL, S.J., Assoc. Dir. for Hispanic Deacons; Sr. CLARE O'KEEFE, S.C.H., Asst. Dir., *774 Boylston St., Chestnut Hill, 02167.* Tel: 617-730-8477; Fax: 617-783-3330.

Priests Recovery Program—Rev. ROBERT P. BEALE, Dir., *287 Highland St., Milton, 02186.* Tel: 617-696-0593.

Regina Cleri, Inc.—Rev. Msgr. JAMES E. TIERNEY, *60 Wm. Cardinal O'Connell Way, Boston, 02114.* Tel: 617-523-1861; Fax: 617-720-0585.

Society of St. James the Apostle—Rev. GABRIEL TROY,

24 Clark St., Boston, 02109. Tel: 617-742-4715; Fax: 617-723-7389.
Vocation Information Center—Revs. ROBERT W. FLAGG; ROBERT M. BLANEY, *127 Lake St., Brighton, 02135.* Tel: 617-254-2610; Fax: 617-787-2336.
Sisters Senate—Sr. MARY RITA GRADY, C.S.J., *72 Cresent Ave., Newton, 02159.* Tel: 617-630-9057.
Lay Volunteer Program—PATRICK MARCHAN, *Pallotti Center, 159 Washington St., Brighton, 02135.* Tel: 617-783-3924.

Central Services - Chancery

Central Services—GERALD T. REILLY, C.P.A., Cabinet Sec. & Chancellor. Tel: 617-254-0100; Fax: 617-783-4564.
Cemeteries—REGIS FLAHERTY, *175 Broadway, Malden, 02148.* Tel: 781-322-6300; Fax: 781-332-3801.
Office for Volunteers—Mrs. ANN LALLY, *2121 Commonwealth Ave., Brighton, 02135.* Tel: 617-254-0100; Fax: 617-783-4564.

CLERGY, PARISHES, MISSIONS AND PAROCHIAL SCHOOLS

BOSTON
(Suffolk County)

1—CATHEDRAL OF THE HOLY CROSS (1788), Revs. Frederick J. Murphy, Rector; Terence J. Moran; Rev. Msgr. William H. Roche; Deacons Luis Casillas; Andres Rosa; Sr. M. Celeste Burgos, M.H.S.H., Pastoral Assoc. In res., Bro. Steven B. Wang, F.M.S.
Res., 75 Union Park St., 02118. Tel: 617-542-5682; Fax: 617-542-5926.
School—Tel: 617-422-0042.
Sisters 3; Lay Teachers 7; Students 191.

2—ST. ADALBERT (1913) (Polish), Rev. Msgr. Stanislaus T. Sypek. In res., Rev. Thaddeus A. Saja.
Res., 1450 River St., Hyde Park, 02136-2150. Tel: 617-361-0565; Fax: 617-361-0565.

3—ALL SAINTS (1894). Closed. Parochial records at St. Joseph Parish, Roxbury.

4—ST. AMBROSE (1914), Rev. Vincent P. Von Euw. In res., Revs. J. Joseph Kierce; John Raymaker, C.I.C.M.
Res., 240 Adams St., Dorchester, 02122-1380. Tel: 617-265-5302; Fax: 617-265-0886.
School—Tel: 617-825-9400.
Sisters 5; Lay Teachers 9; Students 250.

5—ST. ANDREW (1918), Rev. Richard J. Mehm.
Res., 40 Walk Hill St., Forest Hills, 02130-4196. Tel: 617-522-1222; Fax: 617-522-0489.
School—Tel: 617-524-7733.
Sisters 6; Lay Teachers 3; Students 226.

6—ST. ANGELA (1907), Revs. William Joy; John Morin, O.M.I. Pastoral Assocs.: Sr. Maria Charles Norton, C.S.J.; Sr. Paula Coelho, S.U.S.C.
Res., 1548 Blue Hill Ave., Mattapan, 02126. Tel: 617-298-0080; Fax: 617-298-2388.
School—Tel: 617-296-1161.
Lay Teachers 7; Students 222.

7—ST. ANN (1945), Rev. Paul E. Kilroy. Pastoral Assocs.: Sr. Rosemary Mulvihill, R.S.M.; Sr. Mary Walsh, S.U.
Tel: 617-266-2635.

8—ST. ANN (1889), Revs. Walter F. Keymont; John E. Sheridan. In res., Rev. Joseph Hennessey.
Res., 243 Neponset Ave., Dorchester, 02122-3239. Tel: 617-825-6180; Fax: 617-825-7869.
School—Tel: 617-825-6262.
Religious 5; Lay Teachers 12; Students 328.

9—ST. ANNE (1919), Rev. William F. Joyce.
Res., 79 W. Milton St., Readville, 02136-1929. Tel: 617-361-3443; Fax: 617-361-6690.
School—Tel: 617-361-3563.
Lay Teachers 11; Students 225; Religious 1.

10—ANNUNCIATION CATHEDRAL (1908) (Melkite), Rt. Rev. Edward G. Kakaty, Rector; Rev. John Ghavy; Deacon Paul Lawler.
Res., 7 V.F.W. Pkwy., Roslindale, 02131-1098. Tel: 617-323-5242; Fax: 617-325-2662.

11—ST. ANTHONY (1896), Revs. Daniel P. Hegarty; Robert Bouffier, S.M.; Glen F. Byrne; Bro. Michael Galvin, S.M.
Res., 43 Holton St., Allston, 02134-1397. Tel: 617-782-0775; Fax: 617-782-2008.
School—Tel: 617-782-7170.
Lay Teachers 8; Students 119.

12—ST. AUGUSTINE (1868), Revs. Thomas J. McDonnell; James H. Lane.
Res., 9 F St., South Boston, 02127-2898. Tel: 617-268-1230; Fax: 617-269-2233.
School—Tel: 617-269-2233.
Sisters 2; Lay Teachers 9; Students 249.

13—OUR LADY OF PERPETUAL HELP (1868), Very Rev. John J. Hennessy, C.SS.R.; Revs. Vincent J. Kelly, C.SS.R.; Lawrence J. Buckley, C.SS.R.; John Devin, C.SS.R.; John Furey, C.SS.R.; Joseph Adamec, C.SS.R.; Joseph E. Manton, C.SS.R.; Edward McDonough, C.SS.R.; John E. Doherty, C.SS.R.; Philip Cabasino, C.SS.R.; George C. Gardner, C.SS.R.; John Ryan, C.SS.R.; George W. Drew, C.SS.R.; Paul Henderson, C.SS.R.; Richard S. Moran, C.SS.R.
Res., 1545 Tremont St., Roxbury, 02120-2996. Tel: 617-445-2600; Fax: 617-445-1857.
School—(Grades 1-6). Tel: 617-442-2660.
Sisters 4; Lay Teachers 3; Students 152.

14—BLESSED SACRAMENT (1891), Rev. Michael F. McLellan; Deacons Luciano Herrera; Jesus Quites.
Res., 365 Centre St., Jamaica Plain, 02130-1240. Tel: 617-522-0650; Fax: 617-983-1407.
School—Tel: 617-522-1870.
Sisters 2; Lay Teachers 7; Students 198.

15—ST. BRENDAN (1929), Revs. Ronald D. Coyne; Stephen S. Josoma; Deacon James B. Little. In res., Rev. Timothy Linchan.
Res., 15 Rita Rd., Dorchester, 02124. Tel: 617-436-0310; Fax: 617-436-1386.
School—Tel: 617-282-3388.
Sisters 2; Lay Teachers 9; Students 245.

16—ST. BRIGID (1908), Revs. John P. Culloty; Joseph S. McCarthy. In res., Rev. Richard Clancy.
Res., 841 E. Broadway, South Boston, 02127-2397. Tel: 617-268-2122; Fax: 617-268-2666.
School—Tel: 617-268-2326.
Sisters 2; Lay Teachers 7; Students 275.

17—ST. CATHERINE OF SIENA (1887), Rev. James H. DiPerri.
Res., 49 Vine St., Charlestown, 02129. Tel: 617-242-1750; Fax: 617-242-1899.
School—Tel: 617-242-0169.
Lay Teachers 8; Students 161.

18—ST. CECILIA (1888), Rev. Michael F. Groden. In res., Revs. Thomas Grenham, S.P.S.; Peter Walsh, C.S.C.; Wilson Mudha Maina.
Res., 30 St. Cecilia St., 02115-3132. Tel: 617-536-4548; Fax: 617-536-1781.

19—ST. CHRISTOPHER (1956), Rev. George A. Carrigg, Admin.
Res., 263 Mt. Vernon St., Dorchester, 02125-3182. Tel: 617-436-7273; Fax: 617-436-7273.

20—CHRIST THE KING (1940) (Ukrainian), Rev. Jaroslav Nalysnyk.
Res., 146 Forest Hills St., Jamaica Plain, 02130. Tel: 617-522-9720; Fax: 617-983-0309.

21—ST. COLUMBKILLE (1871), Revs. Richard J. Shmaruk; James J. O'Rourke; Deacon Eddy Montes. In res., Rev. Carney E. Gavin.
Res., 321 Market St., Brighton, 02135-2199. Tel: 617-782-5126; 782-5774; Fax: 617-782-7283.
School—Tel: 617-254-3110.
Sisters 2; Lay Teachers 6; Students 200.

22—ST. FRANCIS DE SALES-ST. PHILIP (1867), Rev. Thomas F. Clark, S.J. Pastoral Assocs.: Sr. Mary Hart, R.G.S.; Mr. James Atkins; Mr. Tipp Harris. In res., Rev. Robert G. McMillan, S.J.
Res., One Warwick St., Roxbury, 02120-2415. Tel: 617-445-8915; Fax: 617-445-6522.

23—ST. FRANCIS DE SALES (1859), Rev. Daniel J. Mahoney. In res., Rev. John J. Walsh, S.J.
Res., 303 Bunker Hill St., Charlestown, 02129-1826. Tel: 617-242-0147; Fax: 617-242-3026.

24—ST. GABRIEL (1934), Rev. Justinian Manning, C.P. In res., Rev. Brendan Breen, C.P.
Res., 139 Washington St., Brighton, 02135-4325. Tel: 617-254-6582; Fax: 617-783-1766.

25—GATE OF HEAVEN (1862), Revs. Alexander J. Keenan; Anthony J. Medairos; A. Paul White; Deacon Richard C. Martin, Sr.
Res., 606 E. 4th St., South Boston, 02127-3092. Tel: 617-268-3344; Fax: 617-269-4299.
School—Tel: 617-268-8431.
Sisters 3; Lay Teachers 17; Students 483.

26—ST. GREGORY (1863), Revs. Paul T. Ryan; James M. Larner; John F. O'Donnell. In res., Most Rev. John P. Boles.
Res., 2223 Dorchester Ave., Dorchester, 02124. Tel: 617-298-2460; Fax: 617-298-9232.
School—Tel: 617-296-1210.
Sisters 2; Lay Teachers 8; Students 495.

27—HOLY FAMILY (1995), Rev. William C. Francis; Deacon Francisco Guerrios; Sr. Rita Brereton, S.S.N.D., Pastoral Assoc. In res., Rev. Jose C. Corral, S.J.
Mailing Address: One Lingard St., Dorchester, 02125-2732. Tel: 617-445-9553; Fax: 617-445-2417.
School—516 Columbia Rd., Dorchester, 02125. Tel: 617-825-3883.

28—HOLY NAME (1927), Revs. Paul Rouse; William F. Murphy; Richard J. Malone; John A. Currie.
Res., 1689 Centre St., West Roxbury, 02132-1292. Tel: 617-325-4865; Fax: 617-327-6122.
School—Tel: 617-325-9338.
Sisters 10; Lay Teachers 19; Students 639.

29—HOLY TRINITY (1844) (German), Rev. Hugh H. O'Regan, Admin.
Res., 140 Shawmut Ave., 02118-2227. Tel: 617-426-6142; Fax: 617-426-6142.

30—IMMACULATE CONCEPTION CHURCH (1858). (Jesuit Urban Center). Revs. Charles B. Connolly, S.J.; James M. Shaughnessy, S.J.; Sr. Jeanette Normandin, S.S.A., Pastoral Assoc.
Res., 775 Harrison Ave., 02118. Tel: 617-536-8440; Fax: 617-536-2142.

31—ST. JAMES THE GREATER (1854), Revs. Hugh H. O'Regan; Daniel J. McCarthy, SS.CC.; Robert Pollis. In res., Rev. Joseph J. Baggetta.
Mailing Address: Box 1538, 02205-1538. Tel: 617-542-5044; 542-8489; Fax: 617-542-2708.
Res., 135 Harrison Ave., 02111.

32—ST. JOHN-ST. HUGH (1901), Rev. Gerald J. Osterman. In res., Rev. Anthony Oyeyipo.
Church—517 Blue Hill Ave., Roxbury, 02121.
Res., 26 Lawrence Ave., Dorchester, 02121. Tel: 617-442-1431; Fax: 617-442-2965.

33—ST. JOHN BAPTIST (1921) (Portuguese), Very Rev. Albert J. Sallese, V.F., Admin.
Res., 303 Paris St., East Boston, 02128. Tel: 617-567-5776; Fax: 617-567-3042.

34—ST. JOHN CHRYSOSTOM (1952), Revs. Paul A. Phinn; Charles B. Flaherty, S.S.C.; Sr. Maureen Taaffe, S.C.N., Pastoral Assoc.
Res., 4740 Washington St., West Roxbury, 02132-2199. Tel: 617-323-4410; Fax: 617-323-0423.

35—ST. JOSEPH (1862), Rev. Gerald L. Bucke. In res., Rev. Philip E. McGaugh.
Res., 68 Cardinal O'Connell Way, 02114. Tel: 617-523-4342; Fax: 617-523-8459.

36—ST. JOSEPH (1845), Revs. Walter J. Waldron; Russell W.M. Best, Jr. Pastoral Assocs.: Sr. Gerard Ndagano, I.H.M.R.; Sr. Marie Mullane, R.C.
Res., 85 Regent St., Roxbury, 02119-1990. Tel: 617-442-0900; Fax: 617-442-0900.
School—18 Hulbert St., Roxbury, 02119. Tel: 617-442-2675.
Lay Teachers 9; Students 159; Religious 1.

37—ST. JOSEPH-ST. LAZARUS (1891), Rev. Richard P. McLaughlin.
Res., 59 Ashley St., East Boston, 02128. Tel: 617-569-0406; Fax: 617-569-8212.

38—ST. JOSEPH (1938), Revs. William H. McLaughlin; John M. Toomey.
Res., 21 Chapel Rd., Hyde Park, 02136. Tel: 617-361-1314; Fax: 617-364-7129.

39—ST. KEVIN (1945). Closed. Merged with St. Paul to form Holy Family Parish, Dorchester.

40—ST. LAZARUS (1892). See St. Joseph Parish, now known as St. Joseph-St. Lazarus.

41—ST. LEO (1902), Rev. Leandre Jeannot; Deacon Aubert Lauture.
Res., 177 Harvard St., Box 307, Dorchester, 02124-0307. Tel: 617-436-1445; Fax: 617-436-1445.

42—ST. LEONARD OF PORT MAURICE (1873) (Italian), Revs. Michael Nappo, O.F.M.; Richard Passeri, O.F.M.; Dismas Centrella, O.F.M.; Bro. Charles Trebino, O.F.M.
Res., 14 N. Bennet St., 02113. Tel: 617-523-2110; Fax: 617-367-0456.
Chapel—St. Mary, 150 Endicott St., 02113.

43—ST. MARGARET (1893), Revs. Nicholas Ciccone; Joseph C. O'Brien; Raymond P. Benoit; Sr. Catherine Therese Barrett, S.C.H., Pastoral Assoc.
Res., 800 Columbia Rd., Dorchester, 02125-1750. Tel: 617-436-2190; Fax: 617-282-5428.
School—Tel: 617-282-5621.
Sisters of Charity 8; Lay Teachers 9; Students 316.
High School—Msgr. Ryan Memorial High School, Tel: 617-282-2818.
Sisters 7; Lay Teachers 1; Girls 227.

44—ST. MARK (1905), Revs. Daniel J. Finn; Robert T. Kickham. In res., Revs. John J. Jennings; Timothy J. O'Sullivan.
Res., 20 Roseland St., Dorchester, 02124. Tel: 617-825-2852; Fax: 617-825-0514.
School—Tel: 617-282-2577.
Sisters 7; Lay Teachers 15; Students 512.

45—ST. MARY. See St. Leonard of Port Maurice for details.

46—ST. MARY (1828), Rev. James B. Canniff. In res., Rev. Paul E. McCarthy.
Res., One Monument Sq., Charlestown, 02129-3499. Tel: 617-242-4664; Fax: 617-242-0016.

47—ST. MARY OF THE ANGELS (1904), Rev. John E. Fagan, S.J.
Res., 377 Walnut Ave., Roxbury, 02119. Tel: 617-445-1524; Fax: 617-442-6455.

48—ST. MARY, STAR OF THE SEA (1864), Rev. Robert R. Kennedy.

Res., 63 Moore St., East Boston, 02128-1547. Tel: 617-567-0056; Fax: 617-569-8440.
School—Tel: 617-567-6609.
Lay Teachers 10; Students 266.

49—St. Matthew (1900), Rev. Leandre Jeannot. Pastoral Assocs.: Michael Bolivar; Immacula Bernard.
Res., 33 Stanton St., Dorchester, 02124-3716. Tel: 617-436-3590; Fax: 617-822-0407.
School—Tel: 617-825-7955.
Sisters 2; Lay Teachers 10; Students 247.

50—St. Monica (1907), Rev. Thomas J. McDonnell.
Res., 70 Devine Way, South Boston, 02127-3536. Tel: 617-269-6760; Fax: 617-269-3654.

51—Most Holy Redeemer (1844), Rev. Robert F. Hennessey; Deacon Antonio M. Perea.
Res., St. Agnes Building, 65 London St., East Boston, 02128-1924. Tel: 617-567-3227; Fax: 617-569-6950. Member Central Catholic School of East Boston.

52—Most Precious Blood (1880), Revs. Peter P. Nolan, C.S.Sp.; James B. Clark. In res., Rev. Msgr. John D. Day; Most Rev. Lawrence J. Riley.
Res., 43 Maple St., Hyde Park, 02136-2738. Tel: 617-364-9500; Fax: 617-364-2590.
School—Tel: 617-361-2162.
Sisters 2; Lay Teachers 6; Students 187.

53—Our Lady of the Assumption (1869), Revs. Adelard J. Gagnon; Giuseppe Vescera, C.P.
Res., 404 Sumner St., East Boston, 02128. Tel: 617-567-1223; Fax: 617-561-6319. Member East Boston Central Catholic School Consortium.

54—Our Lady of The Cedars of Lebanon (1893) (Maronite), Chorbishop Joseph F. Lahoud; Deacon Nicholas Nashawaty.
Res., 61 Rockwood St., Jamaica Plain, 02130. Tel: 617-522-0225; Fax: 617-522-0194.

55—Our Lady of Czestochowa (1893) (Polish), Revs. Andrew Sujka, O.F.M.Conv.; Jan Hernik, O.F.M.Conv. In res., Revs. Stephen Majewski, O.F.M.Conv.; Germain Kopaczynski, O.F.M. Conv.
Res., 655 Dorchester Ave., South Boston, 02127-3551. Tel: 617-268-4355; Fax: 617-268-4599.
School—Tel: 617-268-3766.
Felician Sisters 3; Lay Teachers 6; Students 202.
Convent—666 Dorchester Ave., 02127.

56—Our Lady of Lourdes (1908), Very Rev. Charles J. Bourque, V.F.; Deacon Leonard F. De Coste. In res., Rev. Michael F. McLellan.
Res., 46 Brookside Ave., Jamaica Plain, 02130-2370. Tel: 617-524-0434; Fax: 617-524-1888.
School—Tel: 617-524-6136.
Sisters 3; Lay Teachers 8; Students 220.

57—Our Lady of Mt. Carmel (1905) (Italian), Revs. Francis de Sales Paolo, O.F.M.; Kenneth Garofalo, O.F.M.; Aubert Marie Picardi, O.F.M. In res., Rev. Donald D'Ippolito, O.F.M.; Bro. Stephen Colangelo, O.F.M.
Res., 128 Gove St., East Boston, 02128. Tel: 617-567-3215; Fax: 617-569-0552. Member East Boston Central Catholic School.

58—Our Lady of the Presentation (1909), Rev. William F. Salmon. In res., Rev. Joseph K. Coleman.
Res., 676 Washington St., Brighton, 02135-1612. Tel: 617-782-6260; 6261; Fax: 617-782-3303.
School—Tel: 617-782-8670.
Sisters 1; Lay Teachers 9; Students 226.

59—Our Lady of Victories (1880) (French), Revs. Andrew R. Albert, S.M.; Armand Robicheau, S.M.; Armand Thibault, S.M.; Kenneth Thibodeau, S.M.; Albert DiIanni, S.M.; Lucien Chasse, S.M.; Philip Laplante, S.M.; Huberti Akhwesso, S.M.; Joseph Hinderlang, S.M.; Bros. Gregory Theriault, S.M.; Jude Roy, S.M.; Roland Bernier, S.M.
Res., 27 Isabella St., 02117. Tel: 617-426-4448; Fax: 617-482-1570.

60—St. Patrick (1836), Revs. Walter J. Waldron; Russell W. Best; Terence J. Moran. Pastoral Assocs.: Sr. Mary Andreas, S.B.S.; Sr. Immaculada Silva, F.I.C.; Sr. M. Matthias Gallagher, S.B.S.; Sr. Mary Hurley, S.B.S.; Sr. Maria Macedo, F.I.C.; Sr. Mary Thomasine Twomey, M.S.B.T.; Sr. Luisa Vasconcelos, F.I.C.; Sr. Domingas Baptista, F.I.C.; Revs. Pio Gottin, O.F.M.Cap.; Paolino Pina, O.F.M.Cap.; Bernardo Vaschetto, O.F.M.Cap.
Res., 10 Magazine St., Roxbury, 02119-2797. Tel: 617-445-7645; Fax: 617-445-6166.
School—Tel: 617-427-3881.
Sisters 2; Lay Teachers 14; Students 349.

61—St. Paul (1907). Closed. Merged with St. Kevin to form Holy Family Parish, Dorchester.

62—St. Peter (1872), Revs. John L. Doyle; Andrew Nguyen, C.M.C.; Hilary Nguyen Haikhana; Mark Doan Quang Bean, C.M.C.; Deacon Jesus Ortiz; Sr. Sally McLaughlin, S.C.H., Pastoral Assoc.; Sr. Glenna Connors, S.C.H., Pastoral Assoc.
Res., 309 Bowdoin St., Dorchester, 02122-1834. Tel: 617-265-1132; Fax: 617-265-0463.
School—Tel: 617-282-8573.
Sisters 3; Lay Teachers 5; Students 210.

63—St. Peter (1904) (Lithuanian), Rev. Albert J. Contons.
Res., 50 Orton-Marotta Way, South Boston, 02127-2006. Tel: 617-268-0353; Fax: 617-268-2588.
School—Tel: 617-268-0750.
Sisters 3; Lay Teachers 8; Students 260.

64—SS. Peter and Paul (1844). Closed. See St. Vincent de Paul, South Boston.

65—St. Philip. Closed. See St. Francis de Sales-St. Philip, Roxbury.

66—St. Richard. Closed. Parochial records at St. Joseph's Parish, Roxbury.

67—Sacred Heart (1888) (Italian), Rev. Joseph A. Cogo, C.S. In res., Revs. Mario Tardivo, C.S.; Peter Bortolazzo, C.S.; Deacon Mario Lopriore.
Res., 12 North Sq., 02113-2498. Tel: 617-523-5638; Fax: 617-227-4552.
School—St. John's School, Tel: 617-227-3143.
Lay Teachers 11; Students 171.

68—Sacred Heart (1873), Very Rev. Albert J. Sallese, V.F.; Rev. Thomas J. Stanton.
Res., 303 Paris St., East Boston, 02128-3063. Tel: 617-567-5776; Fax: 617-567-3042.
School—Member East Boston Catholic School Consortium.
Sisters 1; Brothers 3; Lay Teachers 8; Students 229.

69—Sacred Heart (1893), Revs. Francis H. Kelley; John J. Mendicoa; John J. Graham; Sr. Virginia Bobrowsky, S.S.N.D., Pastoral Assoc. In res., Revs. Peter Arroygo; Luis Duque.
Res., 169 Cummins Hwy., Roslindale, 02131-3739. Tel: 617-325-3322; Fax: 617-325-2145.
School—Tel: 617-323-2500.
Sisters 2; Lay Teachers 15; Students 464.

70—St. Stephen (1843), Revs. Gabriel Troy; Milton Eggerling; Patrick J. Cleary.
Res., 24 Clark St., 02109. Tel: 617-523-1230; Fax: 617-723-7389.

71—St. Theresa (1895), Revs. William M. Helmick; John P. McGinty; Michael W. MacEwen. In res., Revs. Raymond F. Helmick, S.J.; Robert E. Reed.
Res., 10 St. Theresa Ave., West Roxbury, 02132-3499. Tel: 617-325-1300; Fax: 617-325-0380.
School—Tel: 617-323-1050.
Sisters 2; Lay Teachers 20; Students 589.

72—St. Thomas Aquinas (1869), Rev. John E. Thomas. In res., Sr. Jeanne Marie Gribaudo, C.S.J.
Res., 97 South St., Jamaica Plain, 02130-3899. Tel: 617-524-0240; Fax: 617-524-1840.

73—St. Vincent de Paul (1872), Rev. Richard F. Cannon. In res., Rev. Msgr. Andrew F. Connell; Sr. Catherine Panetta, S.N.D., Pastoral Assoc.
Res., 55 W. Broadway, South Boston, 02127. Tel: 617-268-0710; Fax: 617-268-1277.

74—St. William (1909), Revs. Daniel J. Riley; Kenneth C. Overbeck; Joseph Chinh Nguyen; Deacon Stanley Pugsley.
Res., 1048 Dorchester Ave., Dorchester, 02125-1750. Tel: 617-265-0100; Fax: 617-265-5464.
School—Tel: 617-265-7110.
Lay Teachers 9; Students 193.

OUTSIDE THE CITY OF BOSTON

Abington, Plymouth Co., St. Bridget (1863), Revs. Allan L.W. Butler; Louis R. Palmieri; Michael J. Regan; Deacon Thomas H. Hanlon; Sr. Jane Sellmayer, S.U.S.C., Pastoral Assoc.
Res., 455 Plymouth St., 02351-1841. Tel: 781-878-0900; Fax: 781-878-6566.
School—Tel: 617-878-8482.
Lay Teachers 11; Students 249.

St. Nicholas (1964), Revs. Joseph L. Welsh; Robert B. Costello.
Res., 127 N. Quincy St., 02351-1073. Tel: 781-857-2461; 2462; Fax: 781-857-2923.

Acton, Middlesex Co., St. Elizabeth of Hungary (1945), Revs. Robert J. Boyle; James J. Daley; Edmond L Parker; Peggy Lauzon, Pastoral Assoc.; Deacons Alexander J. Patrick; Eugene Counihan; Howard P. Hardin.
Res., 89 Arlington St., 01720. Tel: 978-263-4305; Fax: 978-263-9014.

Amesbury, Essex Co., St. Joseph (1866), In res., Rev. John D. Silk.
Res., 9 Sparhawk St., 01913. Tel: 978-388-0160.

Sacred Heart (1903) (French), Team Ministry: Revs. Robert E. Casey; Thomas J. Buckley; Deacon Richard R. Bowley.
Res., 9 Sparhawk St., 01913. Tel: 978-388-0330; Fax: 978-388-1451.

Andover, Essex Co., St. Augustine (1866), Revs. Alfred J. Ellis, O.S.A.; Richard L. Foley, O.S.A.; Terence Highland, O.S.A.; Deacon John J. Capomaccio. In res., Revs. Fritz J. Cerullo, O.S.A.; George R. Morgan, O.S.A.
Res., 43 Essex St., 01810-3779. Tel: 978-475-0050; Fax: 978-475-3078. [CEM]
School—Tel: 508-475-2414.
Sisters 2; Lay Teachers 21; Students 405.
Mission—Ballardville, St. Joseph's, (1881).

St. Robert Bellarmine (1961), Revs. Arthur J. Driscoll; Francis C. O'Hare; Deacon Thomas Raymond; Mrs. Betty Pendergast, Pastoral Assoc.
Res., 198 Haggetts Pond Rd., 01810. Tel: 978-683-8922; Fax: 978-689-8878.

Arlington, Middlesex Co.,

1—St. Agnes, (1872), Revs. Brian M. Flatley; William R. Carroll; Charles E. Herlihy; Sr. Margaret Lowell, C.S.J., Pastoral Assoc.; Deacon Francis A. Mendoza.
Res. 24 Medford St., 02174. Tel: 781-648-0220; Fax: 781-643-7883.
School—Tel: 617-643-9031.
Religious 1; Lay Teachers 20; Students 426.
High School—Tel: 617-646-7770; Fax: 617-648-8345.
Religious 5; Lay Teachers 24; Students 628.

2—St. Camillus, (1950), Rev. James E. O'Leary.
Res., 1175 Concord Tpke., 02174-7298. Tel: 781-643-3132; Fax: 781-643-8228.

3—St. James the Apostle, (1914), Very Rev. Francis E. Daley, V.F. In res., Revs. Kenneth F. McAskill; Robert F. McAuliffe.
Res., 22 Appleton St., 02174-5900. Tel: 781-643-0636; Fax: 781-643-7488.

4—St. Jerome, (1934), Rev. James L. Publicover.
Res., 201 Lake St., 02174-0298. Tel: 781-648-2506; Fax: 781-648-2126.

Ashland, Middlesex Co., St. Cecilia (1885), Revs. Paul F. Mulligan; Carlos C. Kim. In res., Rev. Darius Sleszynski.
Res., 54 Esty St., 01721-2126. Tel: 508-881-1107; Fax: 508-881-8606.

Avon, Norfolk Co., St. Michael (1908), Rev. John W. McElroy.
Res., 87 N. Main St., 02322-1286. Tel: 508-586-7210; Fax: 508-586-7211.

Ayer, Middlesex Co., St. Mary (1858), Rev. Richard Gosselin.
Res., 31 Shirley St., 01432-1295. Tel: 978-772-2414; Fax: 978-772-0727.

Bedford, Middlesex Co., St. Michael (1931), Very Rev. Mark S. Sheehan, V.F.; Revs. Henry W. Gagnon; William P. Smith. In res., Rev. Joseph P. Robinson.
Res., 90 Concord Rd., 01730-1596. Tel: 781-275-6318; Fax: 781-271-9879.

Bellingham, Norfolk Co., Assumption (1927), Deacon Bertrand H. Guerin. In res., Rev. Daniel J. Gilmartin.
Res., 370 Pulaski Blvd., 02019. Tel: 508-883-8226; Fax: 508-883-1713.

St. Blaise (1962), Rev. James H. Connolly; Phyllis Calvey, Pastoral Assoc.
Res., 1158 S. Main St., 02019-1597. Tel: 508-966-1258; Fax: 508-966-0310.

St. Brendan (1945), Rev. David J. Mullen.
Res., 384 Hartford Ave., 02019. Tel: 508-966-0260; Fax: 508-966-4404.

Belmont, Middlesex Co., St. Joseph (1900), Revs. William C. Burckhart; Timothy A. Harrison. In res., Rev. Richard R. Santerre.
Res., 345 Waverley St., 02178-2418. Tel: 617-484-0279; Fax: 617-489-5445.

St. Luke (1919), Rev. Msgr. Roger J. Brady; Sr. Ernestine Quealy, C.S.J., Pastoral Assoc.
Res., 132 Lexington St., 02178-1239. Tel: 617-484-1996; Fax: 617-484-7831.

Our Lady of Mercy (1926), Rev. James J. McGowan.
Res., 15 Lawndale St., 02178-3451. Tel: 617-489-1160; Fax: 617-489-9682.

Beverly, Essex Co., St. John the Evangelist (1955), Revs. George J. Butera; Joseph Keville; Sr. Agnes Therrien, S.S.C.H., Pastoral Assoc.; Deacon Tomas Sanchez.
Res., 552 Cabot St., 01915. Tel: 978-922-5542; Fax: 978-921-4563.
School—Tel: 508-922-0048.
Sisters 1; Lay Teachers 8; Students 157.

St. Mary Star of the Sea (1870), Rev. Charles J. Hughes; Deacon Joseph Kasenenko. Pastoral Assocs.: Sr. Marian Patrice, S.N.D.; Sr. Bernadette Mary, S.N.D.
Res., 253 Cabot St., 01915-4597. Tel: 978-922-0113; Fax: 978-922-8501.
School—Tel: 508-927-3259.
Sisters 4; Lay Teachers 6; Students 212.

St. Margaret (1905), Revs. James L. Fahey; Cyril J. Conroy; Sr. Elizabeth O'Connor, S.N.D., Pastoral Assoc.
Res., 672 Hale St., 01915-2119. Tel: 978-927-0069; Fax: 978-927-8359.

Billerica, Middlesex Co., St. Andrew (1868), Rev. Michael J. Parise. In res., Rev. Francis L. Gallagher.

Res., 45 Talbot Ave., 01862-1414. Tel: 978-663-3624; Fax: 978-670-1433.
St. Mary (1937), Revs. Edward M. McMahon; Lawrence J. O'Toole, S.J.; Deacon Allan R. Shanahan.
Res., 796 Boston Rd., 01821. Tel: 978-663-2215; Fax: 978-663-0127.
St. Theresa of Lisieux (1945), Revs. Eugene D. Tully; Mark J. Coiro; John J. McCormick; Deacon Thomas F. Mullins.
Res., 80 Concord Rd., 01821. Tel: 978-663-8816; Fax: 978-663-0577.

Braintree, Norfolk Co., St. Clare (1959), Revs. Paul S. Shugrue; Brian M. Clary; Deacon John J. McDonough.
Res., 1244 Liberty St., 02184-8299. Tel: 781-848-7480; Fax: 781-356-8380.
St. Francis of Assisi (1903), Revs. Richard P. Crowley; William H. Mullin. In res., Revs. Charles I. Sheehy; Daniel J. Crowley.
Res., 856 Washington St., 02184-6464. Tel: 781-843-1332; Fax: 781-848-0976.
School—Tel: 617-848-0842.
Lay Teachers 8; Students 193.
St. Thomas More (1938), Revs. Cornelius J. Mullaney; Joseph M. Rossi. In res., Rev. John M. Capuci.
Res., 8 Hawthorn Rd., Box 330, 02184-0330. Tel: 781-843-1980; Fax: 781-843-7110.

Bridgewater, Plymouth Co., St. Thomas Aquinas (1853), Revs. Lawrence J. Drennan; Michael J. Guarino; Edward J. McLaughlin.
Res., 103 Center St., 02324-1397. Tel: 508-697-9528; Fax: 508-279-1859.

Brockton, Plymouth Co.,

1—St. Casimir, (1898) (Lithuanian), Rev. John P. Prusaitis.
Res., 21 Sawtell Ave., 02402. Tel: 508-586-2226; Fax: 508-559-2761.
School—Tel: 508-587-7367.
Sisters 1; Lay Teachers 5; Students 176.

2—St. Colman of Cloyne, (1910), Revs. John E. Schatzel; James A. Flavin.
Res., 42 Wendell Ave., 02402-3191. Tel: 508-586-1575; Fax: 508-586-9393.

3—St. Edward, (1897), Revs. Robert N. Kelleher; John F. Reardon; Sr. Mary Lou McCarthy, C.S.J., Pastoral Assoc.
Res., 71 E. Main St., 02401-2461. Tel: 508-586-6491; Fax: 508-587-1796.
School—Tel: 508-583-6231.
Lay Teachers 9; Students 238.

4—St. Margaret, (1902), Revs. Joseph F. Donovan; Thomas D. Reynolds; William J. McConnell.
Res., Box 3025, 917 Montello St., 02404-6657. Tel: 508-586-1295; Fax: 508-586-8443.

5—Our Lady of Lourdes, (1931), Very Rev. Joseph H. Manning, V.F.; Rev. David C. Murphy. In res., Rev. Francis G. Goss.
Res., 439 West St., 02401-4899. Tel: 508-586-4715; Fax: 508-584-6257.

6—Our Lady of Ostrobrama, (1914) (Polish), Rev. Msgr. John B. Missa.
Res., 696 N. Main St., 02401-2444. Tel: 508-586-4270; Fax: 508-586-7507.

7—St. Patrick, (1856), Revs. Francis J. Cloherty; Joseph A. Gaudet; Sr. Jane Elizabeth O'Connell, S.C.N., Pastoral Assoc. In res., Rev. Msgr. Paul L. Moritz.
Res., 335 Main St., 02401-5396. Tel: 508-586-4840; Fax: 508-941-0639.

8—Sacred Heart, (1891) (French), Revs. Thomas A. Kopp; Jean Marx Pierre-Louis.
Res., 235 Court St., 02402-4698. Tel: 508-586-1740; Fax: 508-584-8553.
School—Tel: 508-588-4481.
Sisters 3; Lay Teachers 6; Students 228.

9—St. Theresa, (Maronite), Rev. Anthony Weiler, Admin.
Mailing Address: Box 2567, 02405. Tel: 508-586-1428; Fax: 508-587-8139.
Res., 10 Lebanon St., 02401.

Brookline, Norfolk Co.,

1—St. Aidan, (1911), Rev. Leonard A. Coppenrath. In res., Rev. James H. Coffey.
Res., 158 Pleasant St., 02146-3149. Tel: 617-277-0799; Fax: 617-277-3922.

2—Infant Jesus, (1938), Rev. Peter V. Conley, Admin.
Res., 6 Woodcliff Rd., 02167-3719. Tel: 617-469-0234; Fax: 617-469-0234.

3—St. Lawrence, (1898), Rev. Paul B. O'Brien, Admin.; Deacon John J. Mannion. In res., Rev. Nathan Munsch, O.S.B.
Res., 774 Boylston St., 02167-2501. Tel: 617-566-3131; Fax: 617-738-3330.

4—St. Mary of the Assumption, (1852), Revs. Jack Ahern; Joseph T. MacCarthy; Deacon Richard F. Radford, Jr. In res., Revs. Richard G. Lennon; Michael Burns.
Res., 5 Linden Pl., 02146-7311. Tel: 617-734-0444; Fax: 617-734-3001.
School—Tel: 617-566-7184.
Sisters 1; Lay Teachers 10; Students 185.

Burlington, Middlesex Co., St. Margaret (1945), Revs. John R. Crispo; John E. Buckley. In res., Rev. Basile Bazina.
Res., 111 Winn St., 01803-3124. Tel: 781-272-3111; Fax: 781-272-9204.
St. Malachy (1964), Rev. Leonard F. O'Malley; Deacon B. Richard McLaughlin; Mr. Ken Meltz, Pastoral Assoc. In res., Rev. John O'Brien, C.P.
Res., 99 Bedford St., 01803. Tel: 781-272-5111; Fax: 781-270-9407.

Cambridge, Middlesex Co.,

1—St. Anthony, (1902) (Portuguese), Revs. Jose S. Ferreira; Walter A. Carreiro.
Res., 400 Cardinal Medeiros Ave., 02141. Tel: 617-547-5593; Fax: 617-547-1505.

2—Blessed Sacrament, (1905), Rev. Paul W. Hurley.
Res., 189 Pearl St., 02139-4087. Tel: 617-547-1669; Fax: 617-547-3220.

3—St. Francis of Assisi, (1917) (Italian), Revs. Norbert DeAmato, O.F.M.; Lucius Annese, O.F.M.; Zdravko Kujundzija.
Res., 42 Sciarappa St., 02141-1204. Tel: 617-876-6754; Fax: 617-876-6753.

4—St. Hedwig, (1907) (Polish). Closed. For inquiries for parish records contact the Chancery.

5—Holy Cross, (1920) (Armenian), Rev. Rafael Andonian, C.M.Vd.
Res., 200 Lexington St., Belmont, 02178. Tel: 617-489-2280; Fax: 617-489-2280.

6—Immaculate Conception, (1910) (Lithuanian), Rev. Simeon W. Saulenas. In res., Rev. Clement Kasinskas, C.P.
Res., 432 Windsor St., 02141-1343. Tel: 617-547-1623; Fax: 617-547-0336.

7—Immaculate Conception, (1926), Rev. Arthur F. Wright; Sr. Phyllis O'Callagahn, C.S.J., Pastoral Assoc. In res., Rev. W. James Nyhan.
Res., 45 Alewife Brook Pkwy., 02140-1098. Tel: 617-547-3456; Fax: 617-354-8052.

8—St. John the Evangelist, (1893), Revs. Charles E. Collins; William J. Minigan.
Res., 2254 Massachusetts Ave., 02140-1891. Tel: 617-547-4880; Fax: 617-441-8028.
School—Tel: 617-876-3589. Miss Marian Burns, Prin.
Lay Teachers 10; Students 198.

9—St. Mary of the Annunciation, (1867), Revs. John D. Crowley; Alfred Monsalue. In res., Rev. Andres G. Nino, O.S.A.; Sr. Edna Molloy, S.N.D., Pastoral Assoc.
Res., 134 Norfolk St., 02139-1805. Tel: 617-547-0120; Fax: 617-547-0232.

10—Our Lady of Pity, (1892) (French), Revs. Ronald A. Lajoie, S.M.; Jean Paul Souvenir, S.M. Pastoral Assocs.: Sr. Irene Menard, S.U.S.C.; Sr. Claire LaRoche, S.U.S.C. In res., Revs. Anthony Charest, S.M.; Guy Cyr, S.M.; Deacon Alfred Geneus.
Res., 35 Middlesex St., 02140. Tel: 617-547-2037; Fax: 617-547-3037.

11—St. Patrick, (1908). Closed. For sacramental records contact Sacred Heart of Jesus, Cambridge.

12—St. Paul, (1875), Rev. Msgr. Dennis F. Sheehan; Rev. James W. Savage. In res., Rev. George S. Salzmann, O.S.F.S.
Res., 29 Mt. Auburn St., 02138. Tel: 617-491-8400; Fax: 617-354-7092.
School—Tel: 617-868-8658.
Sisters 2; Lay Teachers 4; Students 49.

13—St. Peter, (1848), Rev. William D. Walsh. In res., Rev. Richard Powers.
Res., 31 Buckingham St., 02138-2297. Tel: 617-547-4235; Fax: 617-547-1525.
School—Tel: 617-547-0101.
Sisters 5; Lay Teachers 7; Students 201.

14—Sacred Heart of Jesus, (1842), Rev. John P. Tackney. In res., Revs. David G. Bonfiglio; Paul W. Miceli.
Res., 49 Sixth St., 02141-1594. Tel: 617-547-0399; Fax: 617-441-8648.

Canton, Norfolk Co., St. Gerard Majella (1960), Revs. Bernard P. McLaughlin; Paul F. Curran; Sr. Christiana Cronin, C.S.J.
Res., 1860 Washington St., 02021-1642. Tel: 781-828-3420; Fax: 781-828-2520.
St. John the Evangelist (1861), Very Rev. James L. McCune, V.F.; Rev. Raymond P. Kiley; Deacon Edward M. Quigley.
Res., 700 Washington St., 02021-3036. Tel: 781-828-0090; Fax: 781-828-2480.
School—Tel: 617-828-2130.
Sisters 1; Lay Teachers 11; Students 256.

Carlisle, Middlesex Co., St. Irene (1960), Rev. Thomas P. Donohoe; Donald M. Nicholson, Pastoral Assoc. In res., Rev. Terence Langley, S.C.J.; Deacon Dean Bulpett.
Res., 187 East St., 01741. Tel: 978-369-3940; Fax: 978-287-1440.

Carver, Plymouth Co., Our Lady of Lourdes (1950), Rev. Edward L. Gallagher; Sr. Elizabeth Brabazon, C.S.J., Pastoral Assoc.
Res., 192 Center St., 02355-0068. Tel: 508-866-4491; Fax: 508-866-5588.
Box 68, 02355-0068.

Chelmsford, Middlesex Co., St. John the Evangelist (1893), Revs. Richard J. Craig; John W. Gentleman; Deacon Joseph A. Donnelly; Joyce Wholey, Pastoral Assoc.
Res., 115 Middlesex St., 01863-2037. Tel: 978-251-8571; Fax: 978-251-7873.
St. Mary (1931), Revs. Leo E. Martel; Paul J. Finegan; Michael J. Harkins; Deacon Robert W. Dzuris.
Res., 25 North Rd., 01824-2767. Tel: 978-256-2374; Fax: 978-256-0122.

Chelsea, Suffolk Co.,

1—Our Lady of the Assumption, (1907) (French), Rev. James F. Fratus, Admin.
Res., 601 Broadway, 02150. Tel: 617-889-2045; Fax: 617-889-2854.
School—Tel: 617-884-5194.
Lay Teachers 9; Students 151.

2—St. Rose of Lima, (1849), Revs. James F. Fratus; Francis X. Mawn; Robert J. Carr; Anthony Giang Nguyen; Andrew An, C.M.C.; Deacon An Ros. Pastoral Assocs.: Sr. Sergia M.S.H.J.; Sr. Digna, M.S.H.J.; Sr. Josepha M.S.H.J.
Res., 601 Broadway, 02150-2998. Tel: 617-889-2774; Fax: 617-889-2854.
School—Tel: 617-884-2626.
Sisters 8; Lay Teachers 10; Students 423.

3—St. Stanislaus, (1905) (Polish), Rev. Andrezj Grelak.
Res., 163 Chestnut St., 02150. Tel: 617-889-0261; Fax: 617-889-2967.

4—Our Lady of Grace (1913), Revs. James J. Barry; Gerald J. Fitzgerald; Sr. Ann Kelly, S.N.D.; Deacon Leo A. Martin, Pastoral Assoc.
Res., 59 Nichols St., 02150. Tel: 617-884-0030; Fax: 617-884-0957.
School—Tel: 617-387-8034.
Lay Teachers 7; Students 147.

Cohasset, Norfolk Co., St. Anthony (1873), Rev. John R. Mulvehill; Deacon Joseph A. Cancua.
Res., 129 S. Main St., 02025-2006. Tel: 781-383-0219; Fax: 781-383-2988.

Concord, Middlesex Co., St. Bernard (1863), Rev. John A. Murray; Deacon Alfred Murphy.
Res., 70 Monument Sq., 01742. Tel: 978-369-3778; Fax: 978-371-3346.
Our Lady Help of Christians (1907), Rev. Austin H. Fleming; Deacon Charles Clough.
Res., 1004 Main St., 01742-2937. Tel: 978-369-2810; Fax: 978-371-0853.

Danvers, Essex Co., St. Mary of the Annunciation (1871), Revs. Gerard L. Dorgan; William M. Walsh; Richard F. Ahearn.
Res., 24 Conant St., 01923-2988. Tel: 978-774-0340; Fax: 978-774-9407.
St. Richard (1963), Revs. Charles J. Higgins; Edward Doughty; Deacon David Shrader.
Res., 90 Forest St., 01923. Tel: 978-774-7575; Fax: 978-774-9543.
St. Alphonsus (1917), Rev. Robert W. Kirchmeyer; Robert Tufts, Pastoral Assoc. In res., Rev. Edward D. Cowhig.
Res., 488 Elliott St., Beverly, 01915-2399. Tel: 978-922-1240; Fax: 978-922-8614.

Dedham, Norfolk Co., St. Mary (1866), Revs. John J. Dooher; Christopher J. Hickey. In res., Revs. Edward J. Banks, S.J.; John H. Curley.
Res., 420 High St., 02026-2892. Tel: 781-326-0550; Fax: 781-326-1809.
St. Susanna (1960), Rev. Terence P. Curley; Deacon Frank Winn. In res., Rev. Kenneth Gandolfo.
Res., 262 Needham St., 02026-0033. Tel: 781-329-9575; Fax: 781-329-5966.

Dover, Norfolk Co., Most Precious Blood (1959), Rev. Joseph P. Fratic.
Res., 30 Center St., Box 33, 02030-0033. Tel: 508-785-0305; Fax: 508-785-0432.

Dracut, Middlesex Co., St. Francis (1963), Rev. Brian P. Kiely.
Res., 110 Percy St., 01826. Tel: 978-452-6611; Fax: 978-452-0772.
St. Mary of the Assumption (1909), Rev. Lucien H. Loiselle. In res., Rev. Arnold E. Kelly.
Res., 1868 Lakeview Ave., 01826. Tel: 978-957-3214; Fax: 978-957-7883.
St. Therese (1927) (French), Revs. Lawrence J. Chane; Paul T. Clifford.
Res., 1340 Lakeview Ave., 01826-3499. Tel: 978-957-0322; Fax: 978-957-5266.

Duxbury, Plymouth Co., Holy Family (1945), Rev. Msgr. William F. Glynn; Rev. Joseph F. Mozer; Deacon Arthur J. Keefe.
Church—601 Tremont St., 02332-4450. Tel: 781-934-5055; Fax: 781-934-5796.

East Bridgewater, Plymouth Co., St. John (1902), Rev. John W. Corcoran; Deacons Leo J. Donoghue; Lee A. Beatrice; Brendan Fitzgerald, Pastoral Assoc.
Res., 210 Central St., 02333-1998. Tel: 508-378-4207; Fax: 508-378-7317.

Essex, Essex Co., St. John the Baptist (1931), Rev. Thomas W. Buckley.
Res., 52 Main St., 01929. Tel: 978-768-6284; Fax: 978-768-2533.

Everett, Middlesex Co.,

1—St. Anthony, (1927) (Italian), Rev. Camillo Lando, C.S.; Deacon Thomas W. Marchant.
Res., 38 Oakes St., 02149. Tel: 617-387-0310; Fax: 617-387-1229.
School—Tel: 617-389-2448.
Sisters 2; Lay Teachers 8; Students 213.

2—Immaculate Conception, (1885), Revs. Edmond J. Sviokla; Joseph L. Crehan, S.S.C.; Keith LeBlanc.
Res., 489 Broadway, 02149. Tel: 617-389-5660; 5661; Fax: 617-389-2456.
School—Tel: 617-387-8304.
Sisters 3; Lay Teachers 9; Students 270.

3—St. Joseph, (1912), Rev. Philip J. DesRosiers.
Res., 195 Bucknam St., 02149-1297. Tel: 617-387-3343; Fax: 617-389-4733.

4—St. Therese, (1927), Rev. Msgr. William J. Forster; Rev. Roger C. Cormier.
Res., 20 Gledhill Ave., 02149-4605. Tel: 617-389-0412; Fax: 617-387-0052.

Foxboro, Norfolk Co., St. Mary (1859), Revs. Thomas J. Reilly; Stephen J. Madden; Ms. Lenore Danesco, Pastoral Assoc. In res., Rev. John J. Hever.
Res., 83 Central St., 02035. Tel: 508-543-7726; Fax: 508-543-7728.

Framingham, Middlesex Co.,

1—St. Bridget, (1878), Very Rev. Francis V. Strahan, V.F.; Rev. Michael A. Hobson; Mrs. Elizabeth Mingolelli, Pastoral Assoc.
Res., 15 Wheeler Ave., 01702-2902. Tel: 508-875-5959; Fax: 508-875-1270.
School—Tel: 508-875-0181.
Lay Teachers 14; Students 242.

2—St. George, (Saxonville) (1847), Revs. Francis E. O'Brien; Albert C. Hughes; Sr. Ann Marie McAndrews, S.N.D., Pastoral Assoc.; Deacon Neil F. Lacey.
Res., 74 School St., 01701. Tel: 508-877-5130; Fax: 508-877-3080.

3—St. Jeremiah, (1958), Rev. William J. O'Connor.
Res., 41 Brook St., 01701-3996. Tel: 508-877-1428; Fax: 508-788-1592.

4—St. Stephen, (1883), Revs. Albert H. Stankard; George F. Emerson; Sr. Beverly Good, Pastoral Assoc.; Deacons Guy Spiri; Pedro Torres. In res., Most Rev. Emilio S. Allue.
Res., 221 Concord St., 01702. Tel: 508-875-4788; Fax: 508-875-2577.

5—St. Tarcisius, (1907) (Italian), Revs. Joseph A. Scopa, C.S.; Roque R. Pattussi, C.S.
Res., 35 Cedar St., 01702-6950. Tel: 508-875-8623; Fax: 508-875-6358.
School—Tel: 508-872-8188.

Franklin, Norfolk Co., St. Mary (1877), Revs. Thomas J. Walsh; D. George Spagnolia; David F. Ziomek. In res., Rev. Francis W. Beksha.
Res., Church Sq., 02038-1896. Tel: 508-528-0020; Fax: 508-528-0020.

Georgetown, Essex Co., St. Mary (1870), Rev. Frederick J. Collins. In res., Rev. Gerald B. Horgan.
Res., 94 Andover St., Box 396, 01833. Tel: 978-352-2024; Fax: 978-352-5513.

Gloucester, Essex Co.,

1—St. Ann, (1855), Revs. Frederick Guthrie; James J. O'Driscoll; Deacon Richard Gindel.
Res., 60 Prospect St., 01930. Tel: 978-283-0054; Fax: 978-283-5313.
School—Tel: 508-283-3455.
Sisters 3; Lay Teachers 6; Students 185.
Mission—Magnolia, St. Joseph's Chapel.

2—Our Lady of Good Voyage, (1889) (Portuguese), Rev. Eugene L. Alves.
Res., 142 Prospect St., 01930-3797. Tel: 978-283-1490; Fax: 978-283-0787.

3—St. Peter, (1928), Revs. Thomas J. Fleming; Richard G. Johnson.
Res., One Brightside Ave., 01930-3299. Tel: 508-283-0874; Fax: 508-283-8223.
Chapel—Eastern Point, St. Anthony-by-the-Sea.

4—Sacred Heart, (1946), Rev. Myron F. Bullock.
Res., 5 High St., 01930-1113. Tel: 978-283-4457; Fax: 978-281-7279.

Groton, Middlesex Co., St. James (1945), Revs. John T. Atwater; Stirling MacDonald; Ella Kingsley, Pastoral Assoc.
Res., 29 Old Orchard Rd., Box 186, 01472-0186. Tel: 978-448-5513; Fax: 978-448-9308.

Sacred Heart (1907), Rev. John T. Atwater; Ella Kingsley, Pastoral Assoc.
Res., 271 Main St., Box 259, 01450. Tel: 978-448-6633; Fax: 978-448-2732.

Groveland, Essex Co., St. Patrick (1946), Rev. Robert H. Gosselin.
Res., 728 Salem St., 01834. Tel: 978-372-6044; Fax: 978-374-9006.

Halifax, Plymouth Co., Our Lady of the Lake (1945), Revs. Paul G. McPartland; Charles D. Logue.
Res., 580 Monponsett St., Box 35, 02338-0035. Tel: 781-293-7971; Fax: 781-293-7969.

Hamilton, Essex Co., St. Paul (1922), Rev. Louis D. Bourgeois.
Res., 50 Union St., 01982-2118. Tel: 978-468-2337; Fax: 978-468-6538.

Hanover, Plymouth Co., St. Mary of the Sacred Heart (1907), Revs. Henry F. Doherty; Bruce G. Flanagan. In res., Rev. John P. Mahoney.
Res., 392 Hanover St., 02339-2215. Tel: 781-826-4303; Fax: 781-826-5203.

Hanson, Plymouth Co., St. Joseph the Worker (1956), Very Rev. John Mark Hannon, V.F.; Rev. Paul Kevin Hurley.
Res., One Maquan St., 02341-0714. Tel: 781-293-3581; Fax: 781-294-1052.

Haverhill, Essex Co.,

1—St. George, (1961), Rev. James M. Broderick.
Res., 440 Washington St., 01832-5243. Tel: 978-374-8853; Fax: 978-469-0790.

2—St. James, (1859), Revs. Frederick R. McGowan; Edward L. King; Robert D. Smith; Charles J. Higgins.
Res., 6 Cottage St., 01830-4999. Tel: 978-372-8537; Fax: 978-373-1505.

3—St. John the Baptist, (1955), Rev. Frederick E. Sweeney.
Res., 110 Lincoln Ave., 01830. Tel: 978-372-2780; Fax: 978-469-0947.

4—St. Joseph, (1876) (French), Revs. Emile Guilmette, S.M.; Julian Rondeau, S.M.; Robert Graham, S.M.; Bro. Leonard Haley, S.M., Pastoral Assoc.
Res., 120 Bellevue Ave., 01832. Tel: 978-372-7721; Fax: 978-372-2085.
School—Tel: 508-521-4256.
Sisters 3; Lay Teachers 13; Students 279.

5—St. Michael, (1910) (Polish), Rev. Stanley Wlodyka, O.F.M.Conv.
Res., 71 High St., 01832-5496. Tel: 978-372-0023; Fax: 978-521-0544.

6—St. Rita, (1932), Rev. James M. Carroll; Sr. Mildred Malone, C.S.J., Pastoral Assoc.
Res., 61 Temple St., 01832-5499. Tel: 978-372-2513; Fax: 978-374-2477.

7—Sacred Hearts, (1908), Revs. Marc A. Piche; James T. Kelly; Deacon Robert J. Gaudreau.
Res., 48 Chestnut St., 01835-7446. Tel: 978-373-1281; Fax: 978-374-3043.
School—Tel: 508-372-5451.
Sisters 1; Lay Teachers 9; Students 247.

Hingham, Plymouth Co., St. Paul (1871), Revs. James F. Rafferty; Albert M. Faretra; Joseph D. Flynn; Deacons John W. McHugh; John B. Halloran, Jr.; Timothy A. Lawless; Sr. Eleanor Ballantine, S.C., Pastoral Assoc.
Res., 147 North St., 02043-7894. Tel: 781-749-0587; Fax: 781-749-8053.
School—18 Fearing Rd., 02043. Tel: 781-749-2407.
Lay Teachers 9; Students 253; Religious 1.

Resurrection of Our Lord and Saviour Jesus Christ (1957), Rev. Arthur M. Calter; Deacon Charles E. Sullivan. In res., Rev. Robert C. Bryson.
Res., 1057 Main St., 02043-1497. Tel: 781-749-3577; Fax: 781-740-0689.

Holbrook, Norfolk Co., St. Joseph (1887), Revs. Joseph K. Raeke; John J. Stagnaro.
Res., 153 S. Franklin St., 02343. Tel: 781-767-0605; Fax: 781-767-2563.
School—143 S. Franklin St., 02343. Tel: 781-767-1544.
Sisters 2; Lay Teachers 14; Students 290.

Holliston, Middlesex Co., St. Mary (1870), Revs. William J. Haley; Mark A. Mahoney; Deacons Martin Breinlinger; Philip Caruso.
Res., 8 Church St., 01746-1741. Tel: 508-429-4427; Fax: 508-429-3324.

Hopkinton, Middlesex Co., St. John the Evangelist (1866), Revs. James F. Degnan; Joseph Diem.
Res., 25 Main St., 01748. Tel: 508-435-3313; Fax: 508-435-5651.

Hudson, Middlesex Co., Christ the King (1927), Rev. Leo R. Mahoney.
Res., 12 Florence St., 01749-2098. Tel: 781-562-7662; Fax: 781-562-9762.

St. Michael (1870), Revs. Thomas M. Curran; Robert W. Conole; Antonio L Andrade.
Res., 20 High St., 01749-2391. Tel: 978-562-2552; Fax: 978-568-1761.
School—Tel: 978-562-2917.
Lay Teachers 8; Students 119.
High School—Hudson Catholic, Tel: 978-562-6701.

Hull, Plymouth Co., St. Mary of the Assumption (1938), Revs. William G. Williams; Joseph M. White; Deacon Edward L. Doyle.
Res., 58 Nantasket Ave., 02045. Tel: 781-925-0680; Fax: 781-925-0685.

Ipswich, Essex Co.,

1—Our Lady of Hope, (1997), Rev. Lawrence J. Wetterholm.
Res., One Pineswamp Rd., 01938-2909. Tel: 978-356-3944; Fax: 978-356-9592.

2—St. Joseph, (1889). Closed. For inquiries for parish records contact Our Lady of Hope, Ipswich.

3—Sacred Heart, (1908) (Polish). Closed. For inquiries for parish records contact Our Lady of Hope, Ipswich.

4—St. Stanislaus, (1910) (French). Closed. For inquiries for parish records contact Our Lady of Hope, Ipswich.

Kingston, Plymouth Co., St. Joseph (1908), Rev. Frederick J. Ryan; Deacon William Nagle.
Res., 268 Main St., 02364-1922. Tel: 781-585-6679; Fax: 781-585-7104.

Lakeville, Plymouth Co., Saints Martha and Mary (1958), Rev. Daniel F. Moran. In res., Rev. Thomas J. Mooney.
Res., 354 Bedford St., 02347-2107. Tel: 508-947-2107; Fax: 508-947-6543.

Lawrence, Essex Co.,

1—St. Anne. Closed. For sacramental records contact Sacred Heart, Lawrence.

2—St. Anthony, (1903) (Maronite), Rev. Msgr. James T. Khoury (SAM); Deacon Allen Ramey; Subdeacon Abraham Abdulla.
Res., 145 Amesbury St., 01841-3400. Tel: 978-685-7233.

3—Asuncion de la Virgen Maria, (1993) (Spanish), Rev. Vincent E. Daily. Pastoral Assocs.: Sr. Jeanette Gaudet, M.F.I.C.; Sr. Terentia Hynes, M.F.I.C.; Sr. Marguerite Kelly, M.F.I.C.; Deacons Orlando Martinez; Domingo Naveo.
Res., 216 Lawrence St., 01841-1715. Tel: 978-683-1069; Fax: 978-686-4677.

4—St. Augustine, (1935), Rev. Peter G. Gori, O.S.A.; Sr. Monica Madden, S.N.D., Pastoral Assoc.; Deacon Edward J. Grimley.
Res., 124 Ames St., 01841. Tel: 978-686-0727; Fax: 978-686-1988.
School—Tel: 978-682-9761.
Sisters of Notre Dame de Namur 1; Lay Teachers 9; Students 226.

5—St. Francis, (1903) (Lithuanian), Rev. Richard J. Brady.
Res., 94 Bradford St., 01840-1003. Tel: 978-687-7356; Fax: 978-687-6480.

6—Holy Rosary, (1904) (Italian), Revs. Dennis M. McGowan, O.S.A.; Thomas J. Casey, O.S.A.
Res., 35 Essex St., 01840-1797. Tel: 978-685-1711; Fax: 978-687-9047.

7—Holy Trinity, (1905) (Polish), Revs. Conrad Salach, O.F.M.Conv.; Stanley Sobiech, O.F.M.Conv.; Valerian Czywil, O.F.M.Conv.
Res., 30 Trinity St., 01841. Tel: 978-688-7226; Fax: 978-681-5356.
School—Tel: 978-686-3007.
Sisters 2; Lay Teachers 7; Students 231.

8—St. Joseph, (1902) (Melkite), Rev. Youssef A. Youssef, B.S.O.; Deacons Bryan McNeill; John MacMillan.
Res., 241 Hampshire St., 01841. Tel: 978-682-8152; Fax: 978-685-0275.

9—St. Mary Immaculate Conception, (1848), Revs. William F. Waters, O.S.A.; Frank Barr, O.S.A.; Arthur G. O'Rourke, O.S.A.; Jorge A. Reyes, O.S.A.; Deacons Steven Murphy; John D. Harrison; Diego Rodriguez; Carlos Urbina, Pastoral Assoc.
Res., 300 Haverhill St., 01840-3698. Tel: 978-685-1111; Fax: 978-686-5555.
School—Tel: 978-685-2091.
Sisters 2; Lay Teachers 8; Students 171.

10—St. Patrick, (1872), Very Rev. George F. Carlson, V.F.; Revs. Kenneth N. German; James P. Seymour; Lawrence J. Doyle; Sr. Mary O'Connor, S.S.N.D., Pastoral Assoc.; Deacon Paul V. Specht.
Res., 118 S. Broadway, 01843-1427. Tel: 978-683-9416; Fax: 978-681-5808.
School—101 Parker St., 01843. Tel: 978-683-5822.
Sisters 6; Lay Teachers 11; Students 440.

11—SS. Peter and Paul, (1907) (Portuguese), Rev.

Albert A. Sylvia; Deacon Richard A. Rocha.
Res., 125 Chestnut St., 01841-3844. Tel: 978-681-9080; Fax: 978-687-4112.

12—SACRED HEART, (1905) (French), Revs. Gerard A. Demers, S.M.; Raymond Fournier, S.M.; Laurence Ross, S.M.; Clifton W. Moors, S.M.; Deacon Gerard E. Gagne.
Res., 321 S. Broadway, 01843-2691. Tel: 978-686-7921; Fax: 978-686-5687.
School—Tel: 978-682-8935.
Sisters 1; Lay Teachers 13; Students 289.

Lexington, Middlesex Co., St. Brigid (1931), Revs. Eugene P. Curtin; David P. O'Donnell; Francine Edwards, Pastoral Assoc.; Deacon William H. Wildes. In res., Rev. Msgr. Robert P. Deeley.
Res., 2001 Massachusetts Ave., 02173. Tel: 781-862-0335; Fax: 781-862-1409.
Sacred Heart (1931), Revs. Arnold F. Coletti; Patrick Tarrant; Deacon Anthony Rizzuto.
Res., 21 Follen Rd., 02173-5921. Tel: 781-862-4646; Fax: 781-863-5614.

Lincoln, Middlesex Co., St. Joseph (1945), Rev. John G. Kiley.
Res., 142 Lincoln Rd., Box 234, 01773-0234. Tel: 781-259-8364; Fax: 781-259-3332.

Littleton, Middlesex Co., St. Anne (1945), Rev. James G. Burke.
Res., 75 King St., Box 2246, 01460-3246. Tel: 978-486-4100; Fax: 978-952-6303.

Lowell, Middlesex Co.,

1—ST. ANTHONY, (1901) (Portuguese), Revs. Francis M. Glynn; Pedro J. Damazio. In res., Rev. Antonio Medeiros.
Res., 893 Central St., 01852-3407. Tel: 978-452-1506; Fax: 978-458-9662.

2—HOLY TRINITY, (1904) (Polish), Rev. Stanislaus Kempa.
Res., 340 High St., 01852. Tel: 978-452-2564; Fax: 978-452-4679.
School—St. Stanislaus, Tel: 978-453-2360.
Sisters 2; Lay Teachers 6; Students 224.

3—IMMACULATE CONCEPTION, (1869), Revs. John J. Lyons, O.M.I.; Francis Ouelette, O.M.I.; John F. McHugh, O.M.I.; Patrick J. Hollywood, O.M.I.; Donald O'Brien, O.M.I.; Bro. James S. Lucas, O.M.I.
Res., 3 Fayette St., 01852-1298. Tel: 978-458-1474; Fax: 978-446-0790.
School—Tel: 978-454-5339.
Sisters 1; Lay Teachers 8; Students 175.

4—SAINT JEANNE D'ARC, (1922), Revs. Roger E. Lamoureux, O.M.I.; Donald Lozier, O.M.I.; Anatole Lessard, O.M.I.; Paul Beauregard, O.M.I.
Res., 129 Fourth Ave., 01854-2904. Tel: 978-458-6316; Fax: 978-970-2299.
School—Tel: 978-453-4114.
Sisters 2; Lay Teachers 18; Students 466.

5—ST. JEAN BAPTISTE. Closed. For sacramental records contact St. Louis de France, Lowell.

6—ST. JOSEPH, (1908) (Lithuanian), Rev. Leonard T. McGrath; Sr. Claire Couillard, S.A.S.V.
Res., 151 Rogers St., 01852. Tel: 978-452-5992; Fax: 978-446-0249.

7—ST. LOUIS DE FRANCE, (1904) (French), Team Ministry: Revs. Leonard E. Pelletier, Mod.; John E. Gallagher; Deacon Gerard J. Hardy.
Res., 221 W. Sixth St., 01850. Tel: 978-454-0496; Fax: 978-446-7992.
School—Tel: 978-458-7594.
Sisters 5; Lay Teachers 6; Students 275.

8—ST. MARGARET, (1910), Revs. Joseph A. Ruggeri; John F. Walsh; Deacon Barry Lloyd.
Res., 374 Stevens St., 01851-3695. Tel: 978-454-5143; Fax: 978-458-8472. [CEM]
School—Tel: 978-453-8491.
Sisters 1; Lay Teachers 19; Students 430.

9—ST. MARIE, (1931) (French), Revs. John Hanley, O.M.I.; Norman Parent, O.M.I.; Deacon Daniel A. Dunn.
Res., 80 Chamberlain St., 01852-5523. Tel: 978-453-2134; Fax: 978-446-0324.

10—ST. MICHAEL, (1883), Revs. Albert L. Capone; Mario Orrigo; Deacon John S. McGrail; Mary T. Carleton, Pastoral Assoc.
Res., 543 Bridge St., 01850. Tel: 978-459-0713; Fax: 978-453-1123.
School—Lay Teachers 9; Students 260.

11—NOTRE DAME DE LOURDES, (1908) (French), Rev. James P. Robichaud, O.M.I. Pastoral Assocs.: Carmen Coughlan; Jeanne C. Pinard.
Res., 101 Smith St., 01851-2698. Tel: 978-459-2339; Fax: 978-446-0838.

12—NUESTRA SENORA DEL CARMEN, (1990), Revs. James Loiacono, O.M.I.; Terrence E. O'Connell, O.M.I.; Dwight C. Hoeberechts, O.M.I. In res., Rev. George Protopapas, O.M.I.
Res., 725 Merrimack St., 01854-3978. Tel: 978-459-7829; Fax: 978-446-0442.

13—ST. PATRICK, (1831), Revs. Arthur M. Coyle; Anthony Giang Nguyen; Deacon Peter An Ros.
Res., 282 Suffolk St., 01854-4297. Tel: 978-459-0561; Fax: 978-446-0266.
School—Tel: 978-458-4232.
Sisters 2; Lay Teachers 8; Students 231.

14—ST. PETER, (1841). Closed. For inquiries for parish records contact Sacred Heart, Lowell.

15—ST. RITA, (1910), Revs. Daniel M. Magni; Paul R. Soper.
Res., 158 Mammoth Rd., 01854. Tel: 978-452-4812; Fax: 978-459-8969.

16—SACRED HEART, (1884), Very Rev. John W. Hanley, O.M.I., V.F.; Revs. Leo Wetzel, O.M.I.; Gerald R. Forkin, O.M.I.; Sr. Joan Gregoire, S.N.D. In res., Rev. Gerald Forkin, O.M.I.
Res., 159 Moore St., 01852-5099. Tel: 978-453-3962; Fax: 978-454-3466.
School—Tel: 978-453-4751.
Sisters 1; Lay Teachers 8; Students 255.

Lynn, Essex Co.,

1—HOLY FAMILY, (1922) (Italian), Rev. Gregory J. Mercurio, Admin.
Res., 26 Bessom St., 01902-1205. Tel: 781-599-7200; Fax: 781-599-7201.

2—ST. JEAN BAPTISTE, (1886) (French). Closed. For inquiries for parish records contact Our Lady of Hope, Ipswich.

3—ST. JOSEPH, (1874), Revs. James E. Gaudreau; Joseph T. Canavan; Ignacio Berrio.
Res., 40 Green St., 01902-2999. Tel: 781-599-7040; Fax: 781-598-7439.
Convent—.Sisters of St. Joseph 2.

4—ST. MARY, (1862), Very Rev. Paul V. Garrity, V.F.; Revs. Michael M. Ferraro; Lamartine Petit-Monsieur; Timothy Kearney; Sr. Eileen Burns, S.N.D., Pastoral Assoc.; Deacon Timothy F. Dempsey.
Res., 8 S. Common St., 01902-4489. Tel: 781-598-4907; Fax: 781-599-2088.
High School—Tel: 781-595-7885.
Lay Teachers 16; Students 291.

5—ST. MICHAEL, (1906) (Polish), Rev. Kazimierz Zastawny.
Res., 567 Summer St., 01905-2011. Tel: 781-593-4584; Fax: 781-599-7547.

6—ST. PATRICK, (1906). Closed. For inquiries for parish records contact Our Lady of Hope, Ipswich.

7—ST. PIUS FIFTH, (1912), Team Ministry: Revs. Edward T. Malone; John F. Carmichael; Scott Euvrad; Deacon Edward Elibero. In res., Rev. Msgr. Peter F. Hart.
Res., 215 Maple St., 01904-2799. Tel: 781-595-7487; Fax: 781-595-7270.
School—Tel: 781-593-8292.
Sisters 2; Lay Teachers 8; Students 540.

8—SACRED HEART, (1894), Revs. Jerome F. Gillespie; Oscar J. Pratt; Deacon John Hardy.
Res., 571 Boston St., 01905-2160. Tel: 781-593-8047; Fax: 781-599-4040.
School—Tel: 781-592-7581.
Sisters 1; Lay Teachers 8; Students 261.

Lynnfield, Essex Co., Our Lady of the Assumption (1937), Very Rev. John E. Farrell, V.F.; Rev. Kevin J. O'Leary.
Res., 17 Grove St., 01940-1446. Tel: 781-598-4313; Fax: 781-598-0055.
School—Sisters 1; Lay Teachers 16; Students 457.
St. Maria Goretti (1960), Rev. J. Michael Lawlor.
Res., 112 Chestnut St., 01940. Tel: 781-334-2367; Fax: 781-334-9819.

Malden, Middlesex Co.,

1—IMMACULATE CONCEPTION, (1854), Revs. Frank J. Silva; John M. Sullivan; Henry T. Ronan; Peter J. Murphy. Pastoral Assocs.: Sr. Laetitia Campbell, O.P.; Sr. Julienn E. Sullivan, S.N.D.
Res., 10 Fellsway E., 02148. Tel: 781-324-4941; Fax: 781-397-8571.
School—Tel: 781-322-0129.
Sisters 3; Lay Teachers 14; Students 426.

2—ST. JOSEPH, (1902), Revs. John A. Daley; Richard T. Bakker, S.M.A.
Res., 790 Salem St., 02148. Tel: 781-324-0402; Fax: 781-324-1790.

3—SACRED HEARTS, (1890), Revs. Daniel J. Hickey; Francis E. Sullivan.
Res., 297 Main St., 02148. Tel: 781-324-0728; Fax: 781-324-2714.
School—Tel: 781-324-6584.
Sisters 2; Lay Teachers 17; Students 463.

4—ST. PETER, (1972) (Italian), Rev. Alfred V. Puccini. In res., Rev. John U. Paris.
Res., 12 Thacher St., 02148. Tel: 781-322-6142; Fax: 781-321-6169.

Manchester by the Sea, Essex Co., Sacred Heart (1905), Rev. James J. Harrington.
Res., 62 School St., 01944. Tel: 978-526-1263; Fax: 978-526-4335.

Marblehead, Essex Co., Our Lady, Star of the Sea (1859), Revs. Dennis J. Burns; Joseph R. Foster.
Res., 85 Atlantic Ave., 01945-3036. Tel: 781-631-0086; Fax: 781-631-5668.

Marlboro, Middlesex Co.,

1—ST. ANN, (1921) (Italian), Rev. G. Michael Bercik, O.F.M.; Bro. Damien Johnson, O.F.M.
Res., 466 Lincoln St., 01752-3036. Tel: 508-485-1968; Fax: 508-481-7255.

2—IMMACULATE CONCEPTION, (1854), Revs. Paul J. McLaughlin; J. Garret Thompson; Deacon Douglas Peltak. In res., Rev. Geraldo Ildeo Franco.
Res., 17 Washington Ct., 01752. Tel: 508-485-0016; Fax: 508-480-9644.
School—Tel: 508-460-3400.
Lay Teachers 14; Students 257.

3—ST. MARY, (1870) (French), Revs. Laurier J. Martineau; Lionel P. Ouellette.
Res., 26 Broad St., 01752-4098. Tel: 508-485-0390; Fax: 508-480-9835.

4—ST. MATTHIAS, (1963), Rev. John R. Lizio; Deacon Robert I. Hoaglund.
Res., 409 Hemenway St., 01752-6710. Tel: 508-460-9255; Fax: 508-480-8801.

Marshfield, Plymouth Co., St. Ann by the Sea (1945), Revs. Edward T. Serena; Stephen M. Healy.
Res., 591 Ocean St. P.O. Box 2607, 02065-2607. Tel: 781-834-4953; Fax: 781-834-7472.
St. Christine (1945), Revs. Francis A. Regan; Vincent P. Doolan. Pastoral Assocs.: Mary Doolan; Barbara MacRae.
Res., Rte. 3A, Box 274, 02051-0274. Tel: 781-834-6003; Fax: 781-834-0671.
Mission—Humarock, St. Theresa's.
Our Lady of the Assumption (1949), Rev. Donald P. Clifford.
Res., 40 Canal St., Box 368, 02041-0368. Tel: 781-834-6252; Fax: 781-834-5694.

Maynard, Middlesex Co., St. Bridget (1881), Revs. Kenneth Quinn; Michael A.J. Alfano; Deacon John Pepi.
Res., One Percival St., 01754-1699. Tel: 978-897-2171; Fax: 978-897-5358.
St. Casimir (1912) (Polish), Rev. Louis S. Bilicky.
Res., 253 Main St., 01754. Tel: 978-897-2403; Fax: 978-897-1258.

Medfield, Norfolk Co., St. Edward the Confessor (1892), Rev. Leroy E. Owens; Sr. Mary Jane Sullivan, R.S.C.J., Pastoral Assoc.
Res., 133 Spring St., Box 336, 02052-0003. Tel: 508-359-2633; Fax: 508-359-1846.

Medford, Middlesex Co.,

1—ST. FRANCIS OF ASSISI, (1921), Revs. Joseph F. Scorzello; Paul Coughlin; Sr. Mary Ridge, S.N.D., Pastoral Assoc.; Deacon Henry A. Mariani.
Res., 441 Fellsway W., 02155. Tel: 781-396-3400; Fax: 781-396-3254.
School—Tel: 781-395-9170.
Sisters 4; Lay Teachers 12; Students 347.

2—ST. JAMES, (1919), Rev. Paul R. Franz; Deacon Arthur F. Rogers, Jr.
Res., 779 Fellsway, 02155-4953. Tel: 781-396-0025; Fax: 781-396-2161.

3—ST. JOSEPH, (1883), Team Ministry: Revs. Robert J. Fountain; Patrick J. McLaughlin; Sr. Jane Houlihan, S.C., Pastoral Assoc.; Deacon Robert Amerault. In res., Rev. Francis T. McFarland.
Res., 114 High St., 02155-3882. Tel: 781-396-3860; Fax: 781-391-2919.
School—Tel: 781-396-3636.
Sisters 5; Lay Teachers 14; Students 342.

4—ST. RAPHAEL, (1905), Revs. Dennis T. Nason; Mark G. Derrane. In res., Rev. Charles T. Duggan, Senior Priest.
Mailing Address: 512 High St., 02155-6722.
Res., 38 Boston Ave., 02155-6722. Tel: 781-488-5444; Fax: 781-483-3375.
School—Sisters of St. Joseph 2; Lay Teachers 11; Students 283.

5—SACRED HEART, (1937), Rev. Robert J. Doherty. In res., Rev. Anthony J. Vasaturo.
Res., 51 Winthrop St., 02155-5324. Tel: 781-396-2232; Fax: 781-396-3731.

Medway, Norfolk Co., St. Joseph (1885), Rev. William M. MacKenzie.
Res., 2 Barber St., Box 557, 02053-0557. Tel: 508-533-6500; Fax: 508-533-1236.

Melrose, Middlesex Co., Incarnation (1958), Team Ministry: Revs. David F. Delaney; Lawrence E. Pratt; Deacon John W. Wise.
Res., 429 Upham St., 02176-3233. Tel: 781-662-8844; Fax: 781-662-6653.
St. Mary of the Annunciation (1894), Rev. John J. Ronaghan; Rev. Msgr. Alfonso G. Palladino; Revs. David P. Callahan; Bernard J. Shea, S.J.

Res., 46 Myrtle St., 02176-3898. Tel: 781-665-0152; Fax: 781-665-2750.
School—4 Myrtle St., 02176. Tel: 781-665-5037.
Lay Teachers 10; Students 198.

Merrimac, Essex Co., Nativity (1891). Unassigned.
Res., 4 Green St., 01860. Tel: 978-346-8604; Fax: 978-346-9970.

Methuen, Essex Co.,

1—ST. LUCY, (1958), Revs. Angelo P. Loscocco; Thomas E. Keyes; Deacon Leonard B. Albis.
Res., 254 Merrimack St., 01844. Tel: 978-686-3311; Fax: 978-686-5343.

2—ST. MONICA, (1917), Revs. Richard P. Little; David A. Keene.
Res., 231 Broadway, 01844-3067. Tel: 978-683-1193; Fax: 978-686-0249.
School—Tel: 978-686-1801.
Sisters 4; Lay Teachers 12; Students 522.

3—OUR LADY OF MOUNT CARMEL, (1937), Revs. Andre Gosselin, S.M.; John Meade, S.M.; Roland Lacasse, S.M.
Res., 78 Union St., 01844-3699. Tel: 978-682-9160; Fax: 978-725-6099.
School—Tel: 978-688-3040.
Sisters 1; Lay Teachers 9; Students 221.

4—ST. THERESA, (1936) (French), Revs. George Szal, S.M.; Leo Bourdeau, S.M. In res., Rev. Irenee DuPerry, S.M.
Res., 22 Plymouth St., 01844-4299. Tel: 978-686-3984; Fax: 978-686-8300.

Middleboro, Plymouth Co., Sacred Heart (1885), Rev. Ronald G. Calhoun; Mrs. Nan Bouche, Pastoral Assoc. In res., Rev. John J. Philbin.
Res., 340 Center St., 02346-2102. Tel: 508-947-0444; Fax: 508-947-2364.

Middleton, Essex Co., St. Agnes (1945), Rev. Jon C. Martin; Deacon John M. Bresnahan; Janine Bowes, Pastoral Assoc.
Res., 22 Boston St., 01949-2199. Tel: 978-774-1958; Fax: 978-774-1964.

Millis, Norfolk Co., St. Thomas the Apostle (1937), Rev. Henry C. Chambers.
Res., 111 Exchange St., 02054-9998. Tel: 508-376-2621; Fax: 508-376-4308.

Milton, Norfolk Co.,

1—ST. AGATHA, (1922), Rev. Robert J. Bowers; Sr. Rita MacDonald, S.C., Pastoral Assoc.; Deacon Daniel F. Sullivan. In res., Rev. Charles E. Anadore, Senior Priest.
Res., 432 Adams St., 02186-4399. Tel: 617-698-2439; Fax: 617-698-1517.
School—Tel: 617-696-3548.
Sisters 2; Lay Teachers 15; Students 377.

2—ST. ELIZABETH, (1946), Revs. Gilbert S. Phinn; William R. Coen; Sr. Regina Harrington, C.S.J., Pastoral Assoc.; Deacon Joseph MacDonald.
Res., 350 Reedsdale Rd., 02186. Tel: 617-696-6688; Fax: 617-698-4864.

3—ST. MARY OF THE HILLS, (1931), Rev. Thomas C. Foley; Deacon John P. Connor, Jr.
Res., 29 St. Mary's Rd., 02186-2024. Tel: 617-696-0120; Fax: 617-696-7044.
School—Tel: 617-698-2464.
Sisters 2; Lay Teachers 14; Students 307.

4—ST. PIUS TENTH, (1954), Rev. David M. Burke.
Res., 865 Brush Hill Rd., 02186-1299. Tel: 617-333-0401; Fax: 617-333-0191.

Nahant, Essex Co., St. Thomas Aquinas (1902), Rev. Henry H. Cunney.
Res., 248 Nahant Rd., 01908. Tel: 781-581-0023; Fax: 781-598-8860.

Natick, Middlesex Co., St. Linus (1950), Rev. J. Robert Giggi.
Res., 119 Hartford St., 01760-2497. Tel: 508-653-5505; Fax: 508-655-4577.

St. Patrick (1856), Rev. Daniel F. Twomey; Denise Perreault, Pastoral Assoc.
Res., 44 E. Central St., 01760-4639. Tel: 508-653-1093; Fax: 508-650-2922.

Sacred Heart (1891), Rev. Thomas F. Murray. In res., Rev. William J. Donlon, Senior Priest.
Res., 19 Eliot St., 01760-6092. Tel: 508-653-5113; Fax: 508-653-3051.

Needham, Norfolk Co., St. Bartholomew (1952), Revs. Francis D. Garrity; Henry J. Meade.
Res., 1180 Greendale Ave., 02192-4700. Tel: 781-444-3434; Fax: 781-449-7550.

St. Joseph (1917), Revs. James J. Haddad; John W. Delaney; Deacon William J. McCarty. In res., Rev. Msgr. Francis J. McGann.
Res., 1382 Highland Ave., 02192-2694. Tel: 781-444-0245; Fax: 781-444-7713.
School—Tel: 781-444-4459.
Sisters 1; Lay Teachers 18; Students 411.

Newburyport, Essex Co., Immaculate Conception (1848), Revs. Robert L. Connors; Kevin P. Horrigan; John J. Jusseaume; Sr. Ellen Julie Flanagan, S.N.D., Pastoral Assoc.; Deacon Milton E. Connelly, Jr.
Res., 7 Court St., 01950-2502. Tel: 978-462-2724; Fax: 978-463-6989.
School—Tel: 978-465-7780.
Sisters 2; Lay Teachers 7; Students 198.
Mission—Plum Island, St. James.

St. Louis de Gonzague (1902) (French), Rev. Robert L. Connors; Deborah Bartlett, Pastoral Assoc.
Mailing Address: 17 Federal St., 01950-2899.

Newton, Middlesex Co.,

1—ST. BERNARD, (1876), Revs. Gerard D. Barry; Stephen J. Malloy; Daniel O'Connell; Sr. Diane Valerio, O.S.F., Pastoral Assoc. In res., Rev. Francis M. Conroy.
Res., 1529 Washington St., 02165-4419. Tel: 617-244-0608; Fax: 617-332-4951.

2—CORPUS CHRISTI, (1922), Rev. Joseph F. McGlone; Sr. Anne Marie Ralph, S.N.D., Pastoral Assoc. In res., Rev. Vincent H. Poirier.
Res., 45 Ash St., 02166. Tel: 617-244-9110; Fax: 617-558-7515.

3—ST. IGNATIUS, (1926), Revs. Robert F. VerEecke, S.J.; James F. Morgan, S.J.; Joseph E. O'Connor, S.J.; James A. Benson, S.J.; James Mattaliano, S.J.
Res., 28 Commonwealth Ave., 02167-3849. Tel: 617-332-1104; Fax: 617-244-0488.

4—ST. JOHN THE EVANGELIST, (1911). Closed. For inquiries for parish records contact Our Lady of Hope, Ipswich.

5—MARY IMMACULATE OF LOURDES, (1870), Rev. Stephen E. Koen. In res., Revs. James Fitzmaurice, O.F.M.; David G. Roberts.
Res., 270 Elliot St., 02164-203. Tel: 617-244-0558; Fax: 617-965-4815.

6—OUR LADY HELP OF CHRISTIANS, (1878), Rev. Walter H. Cuenin; Deacon Robert Johnson. Pastoral Assocs.: Mr. Thomas Leahy; Marie Labollita; Mary Ellen Cocks. In res., Revs. Paul E. Kilroy; Kevin Spicer, C.S.C.; Peter Wolf.
Res., 573 Washington St., 02158-1494. Tel: 617-527-7560; Fax: 617-527-1338.
High School—Trinity Catholic High School Inter-parish, Tel: 617-244-1841.
Sisters 2; Lay Teachers 10; Students 152.

7—ST. PHILIP NERI, (1934), Rev. Charles J. McCoy. In res., Rev. Paul Ri.
Res., 1518 Beacon St., 02168-1530. Tel: 617-244-0590; Fax: 617-558-7522.

8—SACRED HEART, (1890), Rev. John J. Connelly; Sr. Ellen Pomphret, C.S.J., Pastoral Assoc.
Res., 1321 Centre St., 02159-2496. Tel: 617-969-2248; Fax: 617-965-7515.

Norfolk, Norfolk Co., St. Jude (1949), Rev. Robert M. Connor.
Res., 86 Main St., Box 305, 02056-0305. Tel: 508-528-0170; Fax: 508-528-1470.

North Andover, Essex Co., St. Michael (1900), Revs. Paul T. Keyes; George C. Hogan; Michael C Randone.
Res., 196 Main St., 01845-2598. Tel: 978-686-4050; Fax: 978-606-5408.
School—Tel: 978-686-1862.
Sisters 8; Lay Teachers 8; Students 153.

North Reading, Middlesex Co., St. Theresa (1945), Revs. Thomas M. Gillespie; Paul L. Ring; Deacon Alfred Balestracci; Paula Frew, Pastoral Assoc.
Res., 63 Winter St., 01864-2264. Tel: 978-664-3412; Fax: 978-276-0034.

Norwell, Plymouth Co., St. Helen (1950), Rev. Richard J. Smith.
Res., 383 Washington St., 02061-2009. Tel: 781-659-2993; Fax: 781-659-7861.

Norwood, Norfolk Co.,

1—ST. CATHERINE OF SIENA, (1890), Revs. Arthur A. Brown; Emile R. Boutin; James P. Braley; Sr. Frances Sears, C.S.J., Pastoral Assoc.
Res., 547 Washington St., 02062-0547. Tel: 781-762-6080; Fax: 781-256-9312.
School—Tel: 781-769-5354.
Sisters 1; Lay Teachers 20; Students 472.

2—ST. GEORGE, (1912) (Lithuanian), Rev. William L. Wolkovich.
Res., 36 St. George Ave., 02062-4420. Tel: 781-762-0979; Fax: 781-762-6389.

3—ST. PETER, (1918) (Polish). Closed. For inquiries for parish records contact Our Lady of Hope, Ipswich.

4—ST. TIMOTHY, (1963), Revs. Richard J. Butler; Sean M. McCarthy; Francis E. O'Brien. In res., Rev. James A. Field.
Res., 650 Nichols St., 02062. Tel: 781-769-2522; Fax: 781-769-9362.

Peabody, Essex Co.,

1—ST. ADELAIDE, (1962), Revs. Robert H. Blute; John C. Chaisson; Deacons Anthony Juliano; Gerald Kaelin.
Res., 17 Bow St., 01960-3427. Tel: 978-535-1985; Fax: 978-535-4845.

2—ST. ANN, (1937), Rev. Wallace E. Blackwood; Deacon Martin J. Walsh.
Res., 136 Lynn St., 01960-6432. Tel: 978-531-1480; Fax: 978-531-6683.

3—ST. JOHN THE BAPTIST, (1874), Rev. Msgr. John P. McDonough; Revs. Robert M. Blaney; Francisco J. Anzoategui, S.X.; Rev. Msgr. Francis G. O'Sullivan; Rev. Clifton M. Thuma; Sr. Nancy Rowen, S.N.D., Pastoral Assoc.
Res., 17 Chestnut St., 01960-5480. Tel: 978-531-0002; Fax: 978-531-5199.
School—Tel: 978-531-0444.
Sisters 5; Lay Teachers 5; Students 578.

4—ST. JOSEPH, (1927). Closed. For inquiries for parish records contact Our Lady of Hope, Ipswich.

5—OUR LADY OF FATIMA, (1965), Rev. John Mendonca; Sr. Ellen Dabrieo, S.N.D., Pastoral Assoc.
Res., 35 Newcastle Rd., 01960. Tel: 978-532-0272; Fax: 978-977-2991.

Pembroke, Plymouth Co., St. Thecla (1964), Revs. Robert J. Sullivan; James E. Robertson.
Res., 145 Washington St., 02358-0587. Tel: 781-826-9786; Fax: 781-826-3484.

Pepperell, Middlesex Co., St. Joseph (1870), Rev. Robert J. Butler; Sr. Roberta Rzeznik, S.N.D., Pastoral Assoc.
Res., 28 Tarbell St., Box 1486, 01463-3486. Tel: 978-433-5737; Fax: 978-433-9566.

Plainville, Norfolk Co., St. Martha (1953), Rev. Vincent R. Maffei.
Res., 227 South St., Box 1745, 02762-1745. Tel: 508-699-8543; Fax: 508-699-6677.

Plymouth, Plymouth Co.,

1—BLESSED KATERI TEKAKWITHA, (1982), Rev. William T. Kremmell; Deacon Edward F. Creutz.
Res., 126 S. Meadow Rd., 02360-4740. Tel: 508-747-1568; Fax: 508-747-0616.

2—ST. BONAVENTURE, (1950), Revs. Robert J. Deehan; Edward F. Doughty; Deacon Charles H. Bower.
Res., 807 State Rd., Box 996, 02345-0996. Tel: 508-224-3636; Fax: 508-224-5889.
Mission—White Horse Beach, St. Catherine's Chapel.

3—ST. MARY, (1915), Revs. Francis A. O'Hara; James F. Lanergan.
Res., 313 Court St., 02360-4336. Tel: 508-746-0426; Fax: 508-747-5886.

4—ST. PETER, (1876), Revs. Paul F. Bailey; John J. Shea.
Res., 81 Court St., 02360-3886. Tel: 508-746-0663; Fax: 508-747-1071.

Quincy, Norfolk Co.,

1—ST. ANN, (1922), Revs. Thomas F. Keane; Gerard V. Dever; Garrett J. Barry.
Res., 757 Hancock St., 02170-2761. Tel: 617-479-5400; Fax: 617-479-0955.
School—St. Ann's Rd., 02170. Tel: 617-471-9071.
Sisters 4; Lay Teachers 8; Students 176.

2—ST. BONIFACE, (1956), Rev. Michael J. Kearney; Deacon John R. Menz.
Res., 26 Shed St., 02169-5923. Tel: 617-479-9200; Fax: 617-479-5766.

3—ST. JOHN THE BAPTIST, (1863), Revs. Peter F. Quinn; Richard S. Moran, C.SS.R.; Gerard Petringa; Deacon Joseph A. Papile. In res., Revs. Theodore L. Fortier, A.A.; William R. McCarthy.
Res., 21 Gay St., 02169-6602. Tel: 617-773-1021; Fax: 617-773-5608.

4—ST. JOSEPH, (1917), Revs. Daniel M. Graham; Robert J. Monagle; Deacon John F. Jennette.
Res., 556 Washington St., 02169-7216. Tel: 617-472-6321; Fax: 617-471-8849.
School—Tel: 617-773-8080.
Sisters 3; Lay Teachers 9; Students 234.

5—ST. MARY, (1840), Revs. Ronald L. Bourgault; John M. Rowan.
Res., 115 Crescent St., 02169. Tel: 617-773-0120; Fax: 617-786-9199.
School—Tel: 617-773-5237.
Lay Teachers 10; Students 226.

6—MOST BLESSED SACRAMENT, (1915), Revs. William J. English; John P. Carroll; Deacon Paul G. Markey; Maureen C. Simons, Pastoral Assoc.
Res., 1000 Sea St., 02169. Tel: 617-773-0233; Fax: 617-471-7143.

7—OUR LADY OF GOOD COUNSEL, (1938), Rev. James F. Curtin; Sr. Barbara Higgins, S.C., Pastoral Assoc.
Res., 227 Sea St., 02169-2537. Tel: 617-472-1408; Fax: 617-847-3958.

8—SACRED HEART, (1903), Revs. John W. O'Brien; David P. White; Deacon John D. Salenius. In res., Rev. James F. Hawker.
Res., 386 Hancock St., 02171-2414. Tel: 617-328-8666; Fax: 617-773-2522.
School—Tel: 617-328-3830.
Sisters 5; Lay Teachers 16; Students 479.

9—STAR OF THE SEA, (1945), Rev. Charles R. McGahey.

Res., 107 Bellevue Rd., 02171. Tel: 617-328-0866; Fax: 617-328-8457.

Randolph, Norfolk Co., St. Bernadette (1937), Revs. Richard C. Conway; Joseph Slyva; Deacon John J. Ego.
Res., 1026 N. Main St., 02368-3099. Tel: 781-963-1327; Fax: 781-963-0198.

St. Mary (1851), Revs. Richard L. Harrington; Kevin M. Sepe; Deacon James Eames.
Res., 211 N. Main St., 02368. Tel: 781-963-4141; Fax: 781-963-0884.

Reading, Middlesex Co., St. Agnes (1904), Revs. Arthur C. Flynn; Thomas J. Powers; Carol A. Gaudette, Pastoral Assoc.
Res., 186 Woburn St., 01867-3599. Tel: 617-944-0490; Fax: 617-944-4409.

St. Athanasius (1961), Revs. Thomas D. Conway; Richard T. Conway; Sr. Jean Delaney, O.P., Pastoral Assoc.
Res., 306 Haverhill St., 01867-1898. Tel: 781-944-0330; Fax: 781-944-1266.

Revere, Suffolk Co.,

1—St. Anthony of Padua, (1906) (Italian), Revs. F. Dominic Menna; Anthony J. Rebeiro; Mark De Angelis; Deacon Joseph Belmonte.
Res., 250 Revere St., 02151-4618. Tel: 781-289-1234; Fax: 781-284-7123.

2—Immaculate Conception, (1888), Revs. Joseph A. Antonellis; Ronald A. Barker; Deacon Francis M. Gaffney.
Res., 22 Lowe St., 02151-3125. Tel: 781-289-0735; Fax: 781-286-1124.
School—Tel: 781-284-0519.
Sisters 3; Lay Teachers 6; Students 269.

3—St. John Vianney, (1950), Rev. Francis B. Leonard.
Res., 7 Harrington Ave., 02151. Tel: 781-289-5268; Fax: 781-289-1950.

4—St. Mary of the Assumption, (1947), Rev. William L. Butler.
Res., 670 Washington Ave., 02151. Tel: 781-284-5252; Fax: 781-284-5801.

5—Our Lady of Lourdes, (1905), Rev. Vincent J. Gianni.
Res., One Endicott Ave., 02151. Tel: 781-284-0234; Fax: 781-284-0235.

6—St. Theresa, (1937), Rev. Edward J. Gaudette.
Res., 500 Revere St., 02151-1536. Tel: 781-289-2404; Fax: 781-286-9256.

Rochester, Plymouth Co., St. Rose of Lima, Rev. John P. Lyons.
Res., 282 Vaughan Hill Rd., Box 40, 02770-0040. Tel: 508-763-2244; Fax: 508-763-9877.

Rockland, Plymouth Co., Holy Family (1882), Revs. James F. Hickey; John J. Walsh, S.J.; Sr. Ann Conway, C.S.J., Pastoral Assoc. In res., Rev. Henry F. Barry, Senior Priest.
Res., 403 Union St., 02370-1799. Tel: 781-878-0160; Fax: 781-871-6389.
School—Tel: 781-878-1154.
Religious 3; Lay Teachers 14; Students 315.

Rockport, Essex Co., St. Joachim (1870), Rev. Ronald J. Gariboldi; Deacon William F.X. Kane.
Res., 9 Broadway Ave., 01966. Tel: 978-546-6756; Fax: 978-546-2272.

Rowley, Essex Co., St. Mary (1945), Rev. James D. Lyons; Deacon Daniel E. McCarthy.
Res., Main St., 01969-0737. Tel: 978-948-3344; Fax: 978-948-3356.

Salem, Essex Co.,

1—St. Anne, (1901) (French), Rev. George J. Dufour; Deacon Lewis Warren.
Res., 292 Jefferson Ave., 01970-2895. Tel: 978-744-1930; Fax: 978-745-1190.

2—Immaculate Conception, (1826), Revs. Daniel J. Doyle; Timothy J. Murphy.
Res., 15 Hawthorne Blvd., 01970-3709. Tel: 978-745-6303; Fax: 978-744-4382.

3—St. James, (1850), Revs. John F. Leonard; Francis J. Ritchie. In res., Rev. Maurice V. Connolly; Deacon George L'Italien.
Res., 161 Federal St., 01970-3297. Tel: 978-745-9060; Fax: 978-745-4229.

4—St. John the Baptist, (1903) (Polish), Rev. Stanley Parsieniczyk (Poland).
Res., 28 St. Peter St., 01970. Tel: 978-744-1278; Fax: 978-744-2093.

5—St. John the Baptist, (1918) (Ukrainian), Rev. James Morris.
Res., Bridge and Lemon St., Box 208, 01970-0208. Tel: 978-745-3151; Fax: 978-745-3151.

6—St. Joseph, (1873) (French), Revs. Lawrence J. Rondeau; James D. Foley; Deacon Norman P. LaPointe.
Res., 135 Lafayette St., 01970-5099. Tel: 978-744-0095; Fax: 978-744-3312.
School—Tel: 978-744-4773.
Sisters 4; Lay Teachers 6; Students 232.

7—St. Mary, (1918) (Italian), Rev. Edward M. Keohan, Admin.
Res., 56 Margin St., 01970. Tel: 978-744-0631; Fax: 978-744-4620.

8—St. Thomas the Apostle, (1927), Revs. Daniel J. Sheehan; Francis H. Delaney; Deacon John M. Barton.
Res., One Margin St., Peabody, 01960-1999. Tel: 978-531-0224; Fax: 978-531-6517.

Salisbury, Essex Co., Star of the Sea (1947), Rev. Thomas B. Morgan.
Res., 18 Beach Rd., 01950-2007. Tel: 978-465-3334; Fax: 978-465-5524.

Saugus, Essex Co., Blessed Sacrament (1917), Revs. John F. Mulloy; Gerald J. Foley; Paul Flammia; Sr. Mary O'Rourke, C.S.J., Pastoral Assoc.
Res., 14 Summer St., 01906-2139. Tel: 781-233-2497; Fax: 781-231-5569.

St. Margaret (1949), Rev. George E. Morin.
Res., 431 Lincoln Ave., 01906-3917. Tel: 781-233-1040; Fax: 781-233-7135.

Scituate, Plymouth Co., St. Frances Xavier Cabrini (1960), Rev. Paul V. MacDonald.
Res., 78 Mann Hill Rd., 02066-2117. Tel: 781-545-4585; Fax: 781-545-4249.

St. Mary of the Nativity (1921), Rev. Msgr. Eugene P. McNamara; Rev. Michael J. Doyle; Deacon C. Michael Hickey.
Res., One Kent St., 02066-4215. Tel: 781-545-3335; Fax: 781-545-6538.

Sharon, Norfolk Co., Our Lady of Sorrows (1906), Rev. Robert W. Bullock; Deacon Michael Iwanowicz.
Res., 59 Cottage St., 02067-2132. Tel: 781-784-2265; Fax: 781-784-2540.

Sherborn, Middlesex Co., St. Theresa (1945), Rev. David P. Bailey.
Res., 24 S. Main St., Box 176, 01770. Tel: 508-653-6253; Fax: 508-651-1318.

Shirley, Middlesex Co., St. Anthony (1905), Rev. Edmond Derosier; Deacon Raymond Gagnon.
Res., 12 Phoenix St., Box 595, 01464-0595. Tel: 978-425-4588; Fax: 978-425-2033.

Somerville, Middlesex Co.,

1—St. Ann, (1881), Very Rev. Peter J. Casey, V.F.; Rev. Steven Poitras; Deacon Lawrence J. Bloom; Sr. Margaret Stinson, C.S.J., Pastoral Assoc. In res., Rev. John Sawicki, C.S.S.P.
Res., 399 Medford St., 02145-3899. Tel: 617-625-1904; Fax: 617-625-7043.
School—Tel: 617-625-1108.
Sisters 4; Lay Teachers 6; Students 235.

2—St. Anthony, (1915) (Italian), Revs. Vincent Monaco, C.S.; Marcos daSilva, C.S.
Res., 12 Properzi Way, 02143-3226. Tel: 617-625-4530; Fax: 617-625-2457.
School—Tel: 617-623-0995.
Sisters 5; Lay Teachers 5; Students 204.

3—St. Benedict, (1911), Revs. John E. McLaughlin; David A. Doucet; Joachim Martinez, S.J.
Res., 25 Arlington St., 02145-3342. Tel: 617-625-0029; Fax: 617-666-5944.
School—Tel: 617-628-7775.
Sisters 5; Lay Teachers 4; Students 196.

4—St. Catherine of Genoa, (1891), Revs. Brian F. Manning; Robert W. Murray; Robert A. Ward; Sr. Mary Nagle, C.S.J., Pastoral Assoc.
Res., 179 Summer St., 02143-2596. Tel: 617-666-2087; Fax: 617-666-5470.
School—Tel: 617-666-9116.
Sisters 2; Lay Teachers 9; Students 225.

5—St. Clement, (1912), Revs. Dennis A. Dever; John E. McLaughlin; Michael Oruche (Nigeria); Deacon Andrew Goldy.
Res., 71 Warner St., 02144-1399. Tel: 617-625-0122; Fax: 617-628-7767.
School—Tel: 617-625-3459.
Sisters of St. Joseph 2; Lay Teachers 17; Students 421.
High School—Sisters 2; Lay Teachers 3; Students 196.

6—Patronage of St. Joseph, (1869), Revs. Henry J. Jennings; Stephen Brennick. In res., Revs. John P. Kelly, Senior Priest; Thomas P. Halleran, S.V.D.
Res., 264 Washington St., 02143-3313. Tel: 617-666-4140; Fax: 617-628-0557.

7—St. Polycarp, (1927), Rev. Robert M. Doyle; Timothy McGonigle, Pastoral Assoc.
Res., 100 Temple St., 02145. Tel: 617-625-3322; Fax: 617-625-3322.

Stoneham, Middlesex Co., St. Patrick (1868), Revs. William T. Schmidt; Scott B. Hendricks; Mark J. Riley. Pastoral Assocs.: Sr. Neonilla Barrett, C.S.J.; Sr. Marylou A. Cassidy, C.S.J.; Deacons John R. Turner; Cyril T. O'Neil.
Res., 9 Pomeworth St., 02180-2025. Tel: 781-438-0960; Fax: 781-438-6809.
School—Tel: 781-438-2593.
Lay Teachers 10; Students 223.

Stoughton, Norfolk Co., Immaculate Conception (1872), Revs. Joseph P. McDermott; Joseph K. Fagan; Aristide D. Arude; Deacon Francis X. Heffernan.
Res., 122 Canton St., 02072-2271. Tel: 781-344-2073; Fax: 781-344-2979.

St. James (1962), Rev. John E. Kelly. In res., Deacon Joseph G. Arsenault.
Res., 560 Page St., 02072. Tel: 781-344-9121; Fax: 781-341-9323.

Our Lady of the Rosary (1958), Rev. Maurice J. O'Connor; Deacon Eugene V. Stenstrom.
Res., 39 South St., 02072-3705. Tel: 781-341-6110; Fax: 781-344-3306.

Stow, Middlesex Co., St. Isidore (1961), Rev. Robert P. Soucy; Deacon Charles A. Cornell; Shirley Ormsby, Pastoral Assoc.
Res., 429 Great Rd., Box 279, 01775-1101. Tel: 978-897-2710; Fax: 978-461-0577.

Sudbury, Middlesex Co., St. Anselm (1963), Rev. Very James Bertelli.
Res., 100 Landham Rd., 01776-0916. Tel: 978-443-8981; Fax: 978-443-7032.

Our Lady of Fatima (1955), Rev. Michael J. Bova Conte; Sr. Brenda Forry, C.S.J., Pastoral Assoc.; Deacon Walter J. Miles.
Res., 160 Concord Rd., Box 916, 01776-0916. Tel: 978-443-2647; Fax: 978-443-6264.

Swampscott, Essex Co., St. John the Evangelist (1907), Rev. Joseph T. Sheehy.
Res., 174 Humphrey St., 01907-2512. Tel: 781-593-2544; Fax: 781-593-3616.

Tewksbury, Middlesex Co., St. William (1935), Revs. William O'Donnell, O.M.I.; Martin Walsh, O.M.I.; Deacon William Emerson. In res., Rev. Edward Lowney, O.M.I.
Mailing Address: 1268 Main St., 01876.
Res., 1351 Main St., 01876-2098. Tel: 978-851-7331; Fax: 978-858-0544.

Topsfield, Essex Co., St. Rose of Lima (1945), Rev. Richard A. Driscoll; Deacon Ronald Gagne.
Res., 17 Prospect St., Box 258, 01983-0458. Tel: 978-887-5505; Fax: 978-887-8201.

Townsend, Middlesex Co., St. John (1945), Rev. Clyde H. Chetwynde.
Res., One School St., Box 533, 01469-0523. Tel: 978-597-2291; Fax: 978-597-3401.

Tyngsboro, Middlesex Co., St. Mary Magdalen (1959), Rev. Ronald L. St. Pierre; Deacon Everett F. Penney, Jr.
Res., 93 Lakeview Ave., Box 100, 01879. Tel: 978-649-7315; Fax: 978-649-3796.

Wakefield, Middlesex Co., St. Florence (1947), Rev. H. Joseph Murphy.
Res., 49 Butler Ave., 01880-5125. Tel: 781-245-2711; Fax: 781-245-4512.

St. Joseph (1854), Revs. Michael J. Steele; Lawrence J. Burns, M.M.; David J. Barnes.
Res., 173 Albion St., 01880-3296. Tel: 781-245-5770; Fax: 781-246-2423.
School—Tel: 781-245-2081.
Sisters 1; Lay Teachers 7; Students 167.

Most Blessed Sacrament (1931), Revs. William D. Coughlin; Thomas P. MacLeod; Deacon Robert Hackett.
Res., 11 Grove St., 01880-4222. Tel: 781-245-2080; Fax: 781-245-7981.

Walpole, Norfolk Co., Blessed Sacrament (1874), Revs. Timothy J. Kelleher; Joseph D. Flynn; Christopher J. Kirwan, Jr.; Christopher G. Perillo; Sr. Anne O'Brien, C.S.J., Pastoral Assoc.
Res., 10 Diamond St., 02081-3408. Tel: 508-668-4700; Fax: 508-668-3554.
School—Tel: 508-668-2336.
Sisters 3; Lay Teachers 17; Students 433.

St. Mary (1931). Unassigned.
Res., 176 Washington St., Box 131, 02032-0131. Tel: 508-668-4974; Fax: 508-668-3083.

Waltham, Middlesex Co.,

1—St. Charles Borromeo, (1909), Rev. Rodney J. Copp; Deacon James C. Callahan.
Res., 51 Hall St., 02154-5217. Tel: 781-893-0330; Fax: 781-893-2060.

2—St. Joseph, (1894) (French), Rev. Roger N. Jacques; Deacon Albert J. Aucoin.
Res., 519 Main St., 02154-5524. Tel: 781-893-3185; Fax: 781-893-9681.

3—St. Jude, (1949), Rev. Robert J. Waldron; Deacon Alfred E. Santosuosso.
Res., 147 Main St., 02154-6622. Tel: 781-893-3100; Fax: 781-893-6635.
School—Tel: 781-899-3644.
Sisters 2; Lay Teachers 8; Students 199.

4—St. Mary, (1839), Revs. Wendell Verrill; Lawrence E. Novello; Henry M. Adeyanju; Deacons Francisco Alicea; Teodoro Camacho. In res., Rev. David C. Michael.
Res., 133 School St., 02154. Tel: 781-891-1730; Fax: 781-642-0604.

5—OUR LADY, COMFORTER OF THE AFFLICTED, (1930), Revs. Joseph F. Byrne; Kenneth A. LeBlanc; Deacon William E. MacKenzie.
Res., 857 Trapelo Rd., 02154. Tel: 781-894-3481; Fax: 781-894-0021.
School—Tel: 781-899-0353.
Lay Teachers 8; Students 180.

6—SACRED HEART, (1922), Rev. Gregory J. Hoppough, C.S.S.
Res., 311 River St., 02154. Tel: 781-899-0469; Fax: 781-899-0081.

Watertown, Middlesex Co., St. Patrick (1847), Very Rev. Robert C. Fichtner, V.F.; Rev. Thomas P. Kelly; Deacon Leo F. LaBrache.
Res., 25 Chestnut St., 02172-2337. Tel: 617-926-9680; Fax: 617-926-3715.
Sacred Heart (1893), Revs. Paul H. McEntee; Joseph L. Curran; Sr. Estellyn Ganley, C.S.J., Pastoral Assoc. In res., Rev. Robert M. O'Grady.
Res., 770 Mt. Auburn St., 02172-1567. Tel: 617-924-9110; Fax: 617-926-3341.
St. Theresa of the Child Jesus (1927), Rev. John J. Nichols.
Res., 248 School St., 02172-1495. Tel: 617-924-3222; Fax: 617-923-0380.

Wayland, Middlesex Co., St. Ann (1945), Rev. Patrick J. Kelly.
Res., 124 Cochituate Rd., 01778-2610. Tel: 508-358-2985; Fax: 508-358-3415.
St. Zepherin (Cochituate Village) (1889), Rev. Paul W. Berube; Sr. Theresa Regan, S.C., Pastoral Assoc.
Res., 99 Main St., 01778-4936. Tel: 508-653-8013; Fax: 508-655-6948.

Wellesley, Norfolk Co., St. James the Great (1950), Revs. George D. Vertzelis; James F. Power.
Res., 900 Worcester St., 02181. Tel: 781-237-1160; Fax: 781-237-0497.
St. John the Evangelist (1890), Revs. Thomas F. Powers; Bryan Mahoney; Sr. Evelyn Ronan, S.N.D., Pastoral Assoc. In res., Most Rev. William F. Murphy.
Res., 9 Glen Rd., 02181. Tel: 781-235-0045; Fax: 781-235-6990.
School—Tel: 781-235-0300.
Sisters 2; Lay Teachers 5; Students 187.
St. Paul (1922), Very Rev. Joseph G. Lind, V.F.; Rev. Bryan K. Parrish. In res., Rev. Richard J. Fitzgerald.
Res., 502 Washington St., 02181-5907. Tel: 781-235-1060; Fax: 781-235-4620.
School—Tel: 781-235-1510.
Sisters 3; Lay Teachers 7; Students 134.

West Bridgewater, Plymouth Co., St. Ann (1938), Rev. Edward C. McDonagh.
Res., 103 N. Main St., Box 427, 02379-0427. Tel: 508-586-4880; Fax: 508-588-0239.

Westford, Middlesex Co., St. Catherine of Alexandria (1922), Revs. Daniel F. Cronin; Robert E. Bergeron; William M. Sullivan.
Res., 107 N. Main St., 01886-1219. Tel: 978-692-6353; Fax: 978-392-0644.

West Newbury, Essex Co., St. Ann (1945), Rev. Laurence E. Kelley.
Res., 46 Maple St., Box 237, 01985. Tel: 978-363-2303; Fax: 978-363-2046.

Weston, Middlesex Co., St. Julia (1919), Rev. Robert D. Tyrell; Susan Bayard, Pastoral Assoc.
Res., 374 Boston Post Rd., 02193. Tel: 781-899-2611; Fax: 781-899-8046.

Westwood, Norfolk Co., St. Margaret Mary (1931), Rev. T. Joseph Moynihan; Deacons Joseph Holderried; Joseph M. Messina.
Res., 845 High St., Box 386, 02090-0386. Tel: 781-326-1071; Fax: 781-329-1879.
St. Denis (1949), Rev. Frederick J. Murray; Deacons Joseph L. Delaney; Joseph I. Crowley, Jr.
Res., 157 Washington St., 02090-1336. Tel: 781-326-5858; Fax: 781-326-1232.

Weymouth, Norfolk Co.,

1—ST. ALBERT THE GREAT, (1950), Rev. Laurence Borges; Sr. Catherine O'Brien, S.N.D. In res., Rev. Msgr. Robert J. Powers.
Res., 1130 Washington St., 02189-1997. Tel: 781-337-8778; Fax: 781-335-5850.

2—ST. FRANCIS XAVIER, (1851), Revs. Eugene P. Sullivan; Stephen M. Boyle; Deacon Joseph Vitello. In res., Revs. John B. McCormack; Charles J. Murphy.
Res., 261 Pleasant St., 02190-2507. Tel: 781-337-2171; Fax: 781-331-4192.
School—Pleasant St., 02190. Tel: 781-335-6868.
Religious 2; Lay Teachers 5; Students 172.

3—IMMACULATE CONCEPTION, (1879), Revs. Peter T. Martocchio; Thomas C. Healy. Pastoral Assocs.: Mrs. Mary Fox; Sr. Florita Rodman, C.D.P.; Deacon Josep T. Nickley.
Res., 1199 Commercial St., 02189. Tel: 781-337-0380; Fax: 781-340-3979.

4—ST. JEROME, (1928), Revs. Thomas F. Wyndham; Gerard J. Pineau.
Res., 632 Bridge St., 02191-1845. Tel: 781-335-2038; Fax: 781-340-7165.
School—Tel: 781-335-1235.
Sisters 1; Lay Teachers 9; Students 234.

5—SACRED HEART, (1871), Rev. Brian J. McHugh; Deacon Henry Welch.
Res., 55 Commercial St., 02188-2604. Tel: 781-337-6333.
School—Tel: 781-335-6010.
Sisters 2; Lay Teachers 7; Students 165.

Whitman, Plymouth Co., Holy Ghost (1897), Rev. Henry P. Boivin; Deacon Gerald F. Ryan.
Res., 518 Washington St., 02382. Tel: 781-447-4421; Fax: 781-447-1375.

Wilmington, Middlesex Co., St. Dorothy (1954), Revs. Rickard J. O'Donovan; Donald Abbott.
Res., 11 Harnden St., 01887-3519. Tel: 978-658-3550; Fax: 978-658-2006.
St. Thomas of Villanova (1919), Revs. Robert M. Browne; Edward F. Sherry; Paul Merullo, Pastoral Assoc.
Res., 126 Middlesex Ave., Box 397, 01887-2723. Tel: 978-658-4665; Fax: 978-658-4670.

Winchester, Middlesex Co., St. Eulalia (1966), Revs. Victor Lavoie; James L. Laughlin; Sr. Rose Marie Lipke, C.D.P, Pastoral Assoc.
Res., 50 Ridge St., 01890. Tel: 781-729-8220; Fax: 781-729-0919.
Immaculate Conception (1931), Rev. Thomas J. Naughton.
Res., 1004 Main St., 01890-1929. Tel: 781-729-1858; Fax: 781-721-5329.
St. Mary (1876), Revs. Richard C. Messina; Paul G. Kelley; Thomas S. Foley; Mr. Salvatore Caraviello, Pastoral Assoc.
Res., 158 Washington St., 01890. Tel: 781-729-0055; Fax: 781-721-6542.
School—Lay Teachers 7; Students 144.

Winthrop, Suffolk Co., Holy Rosary (1953), Rev. Thomas DiLorenzo, Admin.
Res., 993 Shirley St., 02152-2535. Tel: 617-846-1210; Fax: 617-539-4402.
St. John the Evangelist (1907), Revs. Paul Sullivan; Gerald Perno; Sr. Jane Iannaccone, S.P., Pastoral Assoc.
Res., 320 Winthrop St., 02152. Tel: 617-846-7400; Fax: 617-539-0627.

Woburn, Middlesex Co.,

1—ST. ANTHONY, (1945), Revs. Leo X. Lynch; Hubert E. Desmond.
Res., 80 Elm St., 01801-1855. Tel: 781-933-1323; Fax: 781-937-3233.

2—ST. BARBARA, (1954), Very Rev. Vincent P. Mellone, V.F.; Revs. Thomas C. Boudreau; Edward G. Carroll; Deacon William E. Kerns.
Res., 138 Cambridge Rd., 01801-4772. Tel: 781-933-4130; Fax: 781-932-2536.

3—ST. CHARLES, (1862), Revs. Timothy J. Shea; Wayne Belschner; Joseph F. Donahue, S.V.D.
Res., 280 Main St., 01801-3294. Tel: 781-933-0300; Fax: 781-932-7581.
School—Tel: 781-935-4635.
Lay Teachers 19; Students 315.

4—ST. JOSEPH, (1906), Rev. Harold E. LeBlanc.
Res., 22 Central St., 01801. Tel: 781-938-0473; Fax: 781-938-7818.

Wrentham, Norfolk Co., St. Mary (1928), Rev. John G. Connolly; Deacon Kenneth W. Oles. In res., Rev. John E. Fernz.
Res., 130 South St., Box 326, 02093-0326. Tel: 508-384-3373; Fax: 508-384-5747.

Chaplains of Public Institutions

BOSTON. *Health Care Ministry* Our Lady Hall, St. Elizabeth Medical Center, 736 Cambridge St., 02135-2997. Tel: 617-789-2457; Fax: 617-789-2573. Ms. Kelly L. Dunn, Dir.

NEWTON. *Office of Prison Ministry* 251 Watertown St., 02158. Tel: 617-244-7544; Fax: 617-244-7891.

Hospitals

BOSTON. *Arbour Hospital.* Attended by Our Lady of Lourdes, Jamaica Plain. 49 Robinwood Ave., 02130. Tel: 617-522-4400.
Beth Israel Deaconess Medical Center, East Campus (Beth Israel). 330 Brookline Ave., 02215. Tel: 617-667-4205. Rev. John R. Carroll.
Beth Israel Deaconess Medical Center, West Campus (Deaconess). One Deaconess Rd., 02215. Tel: 617-632-8103. Rev. Paul Bolduc.
Boston Medical Center.
University Campus, One Medical Center Pl., 02118-2393. Tel: 617-638-6851. Rev. Raymond Benoit,
Boston City Campus, 818 Harrison Ave., 02118. Tel: 617-534-7560. Sr. Claire Hayes, C.D.P.; Carmela D'Elia.
Brigham and Women's Hospital. 75 Francis St., 02115-6195. Tel: 617-732-7480; Fax: 617-232-2746. Revs. George P. Winchester, S.J.; Francis T. Zlotkowski, C.S.C.
Children's Hospital. 300 Longwood Ave., 02115. Tel: 617-355-7729. Rev. Donald Kelpinski, O.M.V.; Deacon Joseph I. Crowley; Sr. Carlotta Gilarde, C.S.J.
Dana Farber Cancer Institute. 44 Binney St., 02115. Tel: 617-732-3000. Rev. John E. Doherty, C.SS.R. Tel: 617-732-3000.
Hebrew Rehabilitation Center. Attended by Sacred Heart, Roslindale. 1200 Centre St., 02131. Tel: 617-325-8000.
Jewish Memorial Hospital. Attended by St. Joseph, Roxbury. 59 Townsend St., 02119. Tel: 617-442-8760.
Massachusetts General Hospital. 32 Fruit St., 02114. Tel: 617-726-2222; Fax: 617-724-3401. Revs. Philip E. McGaugh; Felix Ojimba; Sr. Sheila Hammond, R.S.C.J.
Metro West Medical Center.
Framingham Campus, 115 Lincoln St., Framingham, 01701-9167. Tel: 508-383-1007. Rev. Robert Champagne, S.M.; Sr. Ursula Tisdall, O.S.F.,
Leonard Morse Campus, Attended by St. Patrick, Natick. 67 Union St., Natick, 01760. Tel: 508-650-7331.
New England Medical Center. 750 Washington St., 02111. Tel: 617-636-7500. Revs. Daniel J. McCarthy, SS.CC. Tel: 617-965-5000; Dac Tat Tran, O.F.M.; James M. Shaughnessy, S.J.; Sr. Claire Walsh, M.H.S.H., Dir.; Amy Edmonds.
St. Elizabeth's Medical Center. Revs. Phillip M. Conroy; Robert Labrie; Thomas Grenham; Sr. Catherine O'Connor, C.S.B.; Sr. Ivan Cadigan, C.S.J.; Sr. Nora O'Connell, S.N.D.; Sr. MaryAnn Gallagher, O.S.F.; Deacon Patrick Guerrini; Dr. Fran Bogle; Ann Cody; Edna Lizotte, St. Margaret's Center: Martha Sullivan.
Shriners Burn Institute. Attended by St. Joseph, Boston. 51 Blossom St., 02114. Tel: 617-722-3000.
Spaulding Rehabilitation Hospital. 125 Nashua St., 02114-1198. Tel: 617-720-6400; Fax: 617-720-6960. Rev. William Doyle, S.J.; Sr. Mary Samson, S.H.C.J.
Veterans Administration Hospital.
Bedford, 200 Spring Rd., Bedford, 01730. Tel: 781-275-7500. Revs. Joseph P. Robinson; Philip A. Cabasino, C.SS.R.; Ronald Lawson; Aidan J. Walsh; Deacon John W. Watson,
Brockton-West Roxbury, 940 Belmont St., Brockton, 02402. Tel: 508-583-4500, Ext. 1125. Revs. Henry P. Nichols; Avelino R. Garcia,
Jamaica Plain, 150 S. Huntington Ave., Jamaica Plain, 02130. Tel: 617-232-9500. Revs. Phillip Salois; Roger A. Sinclair.

ARLINGTON. *Medical Center at Symmes.* Attended by St. Agnes, Arlington. Hospital Rd., 02174. Tel: 781-646-1500.

AYER. *Deaconess-Nashoba Hospital.* Attended by St. Mary, Ayer. 200 Groton St., 01432. Tel: 978-772-0200.

BELMONT. *Fernald Developmental Center.* Box 150, 02178. Tel: 781-894-3600, Ext. 2117. Rev. William T. Leonard; Deacon Eugene Counihan.
McLean Hospital. Attended by St. Luke, Belmont. 115 Mill St., 02178. Tel: 617-855-2000.

BEVERLY. *Beverly Hospital.* Herrick St., 01915. Tel: 978-922-3000, Ext. 2790. Sr. Bernadette Mary McGrath, S.N.D.; John Carley Tel: 508-922-3000.

BRAINTREE. *Braintree Hospital.* Attended by St. Francis of Assisi, Braintree. 250 Pond St., 02184. Tel: 781-848-5353.
Massachusetts Respiratory Hospital. Attended by St. Clare, Braintree. 2001 Washington St., 02185. Tel: 781-843-0690.

BRIGHTON. *Franciscan Children's Hospital.* 30 Warren St., 02135. Tel: 617-254-3800. Sr. Helen Mary McGonagle, C.S.J.; Sr. Doris McShane, F.M.M.
St. John of God Hospital. 296 Allston St., 02146. Tel: 617-277-5750. Rev. Joseph Coleman; Sr. Alicia Brennan, D.C.
Vencor Hospital Boston. 1515 Commonwealth Ave., 02135. Tel: 617-254-1100. Rev. William J. Mulligan, S.J.

BROCKTON. *Brockton Hospital.* 680 Centre St., 02402. Tel: 508-941-7000, Ext. 2550. Deacon John Connor.
Good Samaritan Medical Center. 235 N. Pearl St., 02401. Tel: 508-427-2376. Rev. Richard Visbisky; Sr. Margaret Crowley, S.C.N.; Sr. George Powell, C.J.C.; Sr. Helen Carpinelli, S.U.S.C.

BROOKLINE. *Bournewood Hospital.* Attended by Infant Jesus, Brookline. 300 South St., 02146. Tel: 617-469-0300.

BURLINGTON. *Lahey Hitchcock Medical Center.* 41 Mall Rd., 01805. Tel: 781-744-8800. Rev. Clif Moors, S.M.; William W. Houghton; Kathleen Rice.

CAMBRIDGE. *Cambridge Hospital.* Attended by St. Mary, Cambridge. 1493 Cambridge St., 02139. Tel: 617-498-1000.
Mount Auburn Hospital. 330 Mt. Auburn St., 02238. Tel: 617-499-5665, Ext. 4669. Rev. Peter Grover, O.M.V.; Patricia Huff.

Youville Lifecare, Inc. 1575 Cambridge St., 02138-4398. Tel: 617-876-4344, Ext. 2601. Revs. Jennifer Casstevens; William J. Mulligan, S.J.; Patricia Kennedy; Elizabeth Walsh.

CANTON. *Massachusetts Hospital School.* Attended by St. Gerard Majella, Canton. Randolph St., 02121. Tel: 781-828-2440.

CHELSEA. *Quigley Memorial Hospital.* 91 Crest Ave., 02150. Tel: 617-884-5660. Rev. Lawrence F. Sullivan.

CONCORD. *Emerson Hospital.* Rte. 2 ORNAC, P.O. Box 9120, 01742-9120. Tel: 978-287-3015. Virginia Allen.

DORCHESTER. *Daughters of Charity National Health System - Boston, Inc.* (Formerly The Carney Hospital) 2100 Dorchester Ave., 02124-5666. Tel: 617-296-4000; Fax: 617-296-9513. Rev. Lucien A. Sawyer, O.M.I.; Sr. Paula Tinlin, S.N.D.; Sr. Lillian McDonald, C.S.J.; Jean Marchant.

EVERETT. *Whidden Memorial Hospital.* Attended by Our Lady of Grace, Chelsea. 103 Garland St., 02149. Tel: 617-389-6270.

GLOUCESTER. *Addison Gilbert Hospital.* Attended by St. Ann, Gloucester. 298 Washington St., 01930. Tel: 978-283-4000.

HAVERHILL. *Hale/Haverhill Municipal Hospital.* Attended by St. John the Baptist, Haverhill. 140 Lincoln Ave., 01830. Tel: 978-374-2000.

Whittier Rehabilitation Hospital. Attended by St. Joseph, Haverhill. 76 Summer St., 01830. Tel: 978-372-8000.

JAMAICA PLAIN. *Faulkner Hospital.* 1153 Centre St., 02130. Tel: 617-522-5800. Deacon Leonard F. DeCoste.

Lemuel Shattuck Hospital. 170 Morton St., 02130. Tel: 617-522-8110. Rev. Leonard J. Tighe.

LAWRENCE. *Lawrence General Hospital.* One General St., 01842. Tel: 978-683-4000, Ext. 2349. Maureen LaBelle.

LOWELL. *Lowell General Hospital.* 295 Varnum Ave., 01854. Tel: 978-937-6000. Sr. Eileen Auger, C.S.C.

St. Joseph Health Care Center. 200 Pawtuckett St., 01854. Tel: 978-446-1791; Fax: 978-458-9903. Martha Byron.

Saints Memorial Medical Center. Hospital Dr. (Box 30), 01852. Tel: 978-458-1411. Revs. John J. Hogan, O.M.I.; Francis X. Gorham, O.M.I.; Romeo J. Murphy, O.M.I.; Sr. Doris Brouillette, S.C.O.; Sr. Rina Brunetti, P.M.; Patricia Hardy.

LYNN. *Atlanticare Medical Center.* 500 Lynnfield St., 01904. Tel: 781-581-9200. Deacon Lawrence R. McManus Tel: 617-598-5100.

MALDEN. *Malden Hospital.* Hospital Rd., 02148-3591. Tel: 781-322-7560, Ext. 5629. Sr. Agnes Melly, C.S.J.

MARLBOROUGH. *Marlborough Hospital.* Attended by St. Mary, Marlborough. 57 Union St., 01752. Tel: 508-485-1121.

MEDFIELD. *Medfield State Hospital.* 45 Hospital Rd., 02052-2406. Tel: 508-359-7312, Ext. 4371. Rev. John J. Hever.

MEDFORD. *Lawrence Memorial Hospital of Medford.* 170 Governor's Ave., 02155. Tel: 781-396-9250. Rosemary Burke.

MELROSE. *Melrose-Wakefield Hospital.* 585 Lebannon St., 02176. Tel: 781-979-3000. Sr. Eunice Condrick, C.S.J.

METHUEN. *Holy Family Hospital, Inc.* 70 East St., 01844. Tel: 978-687-0151, Ext. 2005. Rev. John T. Crabb, S.J.; Anne Duquette.

MIDDLEBOROUGH. *Cranberry Specialty Hospital.* Attended by Sacred Heart, Middleborough. 52 Oak St., 02346. Tel: 508-947-6000.

MILTON. *Milton Hospital.* 92 Highland St., 02186. Tel: 617-696-4600, Ext. 1801. Judith LoGerfo.

NEEDHAM. *Deaconess-Glover Hospital.* Attended by St. Joseph, Needham. 148 Chestnut St., 02192. Tel: 781-444-5600.

NEWBURYPORT. *Anna Jacques Hospital.* Attended by Immaculate Conception, Newburyport. Highland Ave., 01950. Tel: 978-462-6601.

NEWTON. *Newton-Wellesley Hospital.* 2014 Washington St., 02162. Tel: 617-243-6634. Ann Lomuto.

NORFOLK. *Southwood Community Hospital.* Attended by St. Jude, Norfolk. 111 Dedham St., 02056. Tel: 508-668-0385.

NORWOOD. *Norwood Hospital.* 800 Washington St., 02062. Tel: 781-769-4000, Ext. 2012. Sr. Barbara Lavin, O.P.

PEABODY. *THC-Boston.* Attended by St. John the Baptist, Peabody. 15 King St., 01960. Tel: 978-531-2900.

PLYMOUTH. *Jordan Hospital.* Attended by St. Peter, Plymouth. 275 Sandwich St., 02360. Tel: 508-830-2005.

QUINCY. *Quincy Hospital.* 114 Whitwell St., 02169. Tel: 617-773-6100, Ext. 5501. Rev. Theodore Fortier, A.A.

ROXBURY. *New England Baptist Hospital.* 91 Parker Hill Ave., 02120. Tel: 617-754-5160. Rev. Joseph O'Brien.

SALEM. *North Shore Medical Center.* 57 Highland Ave., 01970. Tel: 978-741-0631 (P.C. Dept.); 741-1215, Ext. 7698. Rev. Edward M. Keohan; Jane Korins.

SOMERVILLE. *Somerville Hospital.* 230 Highland Ave., 02143. Tel: 617-666-4400. Deacon John F. Cabral.

SOUTH WEYMOUTH. *South Shore Hospital.* 55 Frogg Rd., 02190. Tel: 781-340-8589; 340-8612. Rev. Daniel Crowley; Mary T. O'Connor.

STONEHAM. *Boston Regional Medical Center.* Attended by St. Patrick, Stoneham. 5 Woodland Rd., 02180. Tel: 781-665-1740.

STOUGHTON. *New England Sinai Hospital.* 150 York St., 02072. Tel: 781-344-0600, Ext. 302; Fax: 781-344-3226. Rev. Msgr. William Granville; Sr. Ellen Reilly, S.N.D.

TEWKSBURY. *Tewksbury Hospital.* East St., 01876. Tel: 978-851-7321, Ext. 288. Rev. Edward Lowney, O.M.I.

WALTHAM. *Deaconess-Waltham Hospital.* Hope Ave., 02154. Tel: 781-647-6573. Elinor Quill.

Middlesex County Hospital. Attended by Our Lady, Comforter of the Afflicted, Waltham. 775 Trapelo Rd., 02154. Tel: 781-894-4600.

WESTWOOD. *Westwood Lodge Hospital.* Attended by St. Margaret Mary, Westwood. 45 Clapboard St., 02090. Tel: 781-762-7764.

WINCHESTER. *Winchester Hospital.* 41 Highland Ave., 01890. Tel: 781-729-9000. Sr. Geraldine DeFilippo, R.C.E.

WOBURN. *New England Rehabilitation Hospital.* Attended by St. Barbara, Woburn. Two Rehabilitation Way, 01801. Tel: 617-636-7500.

WRENTHAM. *Wrentham State School.* Box 144, 02093. Tel: 508-384-3114. Rev. John Fernz.

Prisons

BRIDGEWATER. *Bridgewater State Hospital & Treatment Center.* 12 Administration Rd., 02324. Tel: 617-727-7672. Rev. James F. Lanergan.

Massachusetts Boot Camp. 12 Administration Rd., 02324. Tel: 617-727-7672. Deacon John W. McHugh.

Old Colony Correction Center. One Administration Rd., 02324. Tel: 617-727-3400. Deacon John W. McHugh.

Southeastern Correctional Center. 12 Administration Rd., 02324. Tel: 617-727-7672. Deacon Charles H. Bower.

CARVER. *MCI-Plymouth.* Myles Standish State Forest, Box 207, 02355. Tel: 617-727-8938. Deacon John W. McHugh.

CONCORD. *MCI-Concord.* 965 Elm St., Box 00, 01742. Tel: 617-727-1950. Rev. Thomas Forry.

Northeast Correctional Center. Barretts Mill Rd., 01742. Tel: 617-727-0288. Deacon Robert P. Amerault.

FRAMINGHAM. *MCI-Framingham.* 99 Loring St., 01701. Tel: 617-727-5056. Sr. Maureen Clark, C.S.J.

South Middlesex Correctional Center. 135 Western Ave., Box 850, 01701. Tel: 617-727-5676. Sr. Maureen Clark, C.S.J.

JAMAICA PLAIN. *Shattuck Hospital Correctional Unit.* 180 Morton St., 02130. Tel: 617-727-5203. Rev.. Leonard J. Tighe.

MATTAPAN. *Metropolitan Youth Service Center.* 591 Morton St., 02126. Tel: 617-288-9100. Rev. Joseph J. Baggetta.

NORFOLK. *Baystate Correctional Facility.* 28 Clark St., Box 73, 02056. Tel: 617-727-8474. Deacon John J. Mannion.

MCI-Norfolk. Two Clark St., Box 43, 02056. Tel: 617-727-1480. Rev. Robert Rivard, F.M.S.I.; Sr. Kathleen Denevan, O.S.F.; Deacon Gerald Rooney; Ms. Ruth Raichle.

Pondville Correctional Center. Box 146, 02056. Tel: 617-727-5203. Ms. Elizabeth Slaney, Catholic Coord.

ROSLINDALE. *Judge John J. Connelly Youth Center.* 450 Cantebury St., 02131. Tel: 617-288-9100. Rev. Joseph J. Baggetta.

SHIRLEY. *MCI-Shirley.* Medium & Minimum Facilities, P.O. Box 1218, 01464. Tel: 978-792-7760. Rev. John Kilmartin, F.D.P.; Deacon Carroll H. Taylor.

SOUTH WALPOLE. *MCI-Cedar Junction.* Rte. 1A, Box 100, 02071. Tel: 617-727-1686. Deacon John Mannion.

County Facilities

BOSTON. *Nashua Street Jail.* 200 Nashua St., 02114. Tel: 617-635-1100. Rev. John J. Mullen, S.J.

Suffolk County House of Correction at South Bay. 20 Brandston St., 02118. Tel: 617-635-1000. Bro. George T. Williams, S.J.

BILERICA. *Middlesex County House of Correction.* Treble Pond Rd., 01821. Tel: 617-494-4375. Rev. Msgr. Francis S. Rossiter; Deacon Harold E. Killam.

CAMBRIDGE. *Middlesex County Jail.* 40 Thorndike St., 02146. Tel: 617-494-4375. Rev. Msgr. Francis S. Rossiter; Deacon Harold E. Killam.

DEDHAM. *Norfolk County House of Correction.* 200 West St., 02026. Tel: 617-696-0593. Rev. Robert P. Beale.

MIDDLETON. *Essex County Correctional Facility.* 20 Manning Ave., 01949. Tel: 978-750-1900, Ext. 503. Rev. Jon C. Martin; Mr. Jack McCauley, Catholic Coord.

NEWTON. *Guild of Our Lady of Ransom.* 251 Watertown St., 02158. Tel: 617-244-7544; Fax: 617-244-7891.

PLYMOUTH. *Plymouth County Correctional Facility.* (Vacant). 26 Long Pond Rd., 02360. Tel: 508-830-6200.

On Duty Outside the Archdiocese:
(For further information contact Tel: 617-254-2085.)
Reverend Monsignors—
Abruzzese, John A.
Edyvean, Walter J.
Fay, William P.
Reverend Fathers—
Berthold, George C.
Brown, Francis E.
Carrigg, William J.
Donahue, Richard T.
Driscoll, Joseph J.
Flanagan, James H.
Foley, James J.
Galvin, John P.
Hawker, James F.
Hehir, J. Bryan
Kelley, Edward J.
Kramer, George C.
McMahon, Gerard T.
McNeil, John R.
Moran, James F.
O'Brien, Richard M.
O'Leary, David M.
Oliveira, Joel D.
Picardi, John M.
Regan, John J.
Ronan, James J.
Sullivan, Brendan J.

Military & VA Chaplains:
(For further information contact Tel: 617-254-2085.)
Reverend Fathers—
Bourke, Charles E.
Butler, Timothy A.
Condon, Edwin D.
Crowley, Francis J.
Cuddy, William F.
Deeley, Kevin J.
Devine, William J.
Donohoe, Stephen S.
Girardin, Peter T.
Kennedy, William M.
Linehan, Stephen J.
Nichols, Henry P.
Pucciarelli, George W.
Raux, Redmond
Robinson, Joseph P.
Rock, Stephen B.
Russo, Lawrence J.

Graduate Studies:
(For further information contact Tel: 617-254-2085.)
Reverend Fathers—
Blaney, Robert M.
O'Connell, Mark
Russell, Paul F.
Zukas, Stephen P.

Society of St. James the Apostle:
(For further information contact Tel: 617-742-4715.)
Reverend Fathers—
Domurat, Thomas S.
Fairbairn, Frank E.
Flynn, George R.
Grimes, John J.
Kirke, Eugene K.
Martin, Joseph I.
McCarthy, Jeremiah J.
O'Meara, Gerard J.
O'Sullivan, Raymond S.
Oates, Thomas F.
Pashby, John J.
Pearsall, William T.
Stanley, Charles R.
Sullivan, John L.
Thomas, Robert W.
Troy, Gabriel
Tynan, Desmond A.

Emergency Response Group:
(For further information contact Tel: 617-254-2085.)
Reverend Fathers—
Charest, Edmund P.
Darcy, James F.
Keane, John F.
McQuade, Richard E.
Smyth, Joseph P.
Swencki, John T.

Awaiting Assignment:
(For further information contact Tel: 617-254-2085.)
Reverend Fathers—
Bogusz, Joseph C.
Buntel, Richard A.
Casey, Richard L.
Cavanaugh, Daniel J.
Delay, Donald R.
Donahue, Daniel J.
Driscoll, Nicholas J.
Fallon, John F.
Flaherty, Daniel E.
Gale, Robert
German, Kenneth N.
Hickey, Gerald J.
Jezowski, Anthony C.
Keefe, Dennis A.
Kelley, Arnold E.
Manning, Paul F.
Mason, Albert M.
McCabe, Edward D.
McManus, Paul G.
McNamara, Michael J.
Murphy, David C.
O'Hara, Peter J.
Purdy, Robert M.
Tivnan, Paul J.
Uftring, Richard A.
Whelan, Thomas J.

Absent on Leave:
(For further information contact Tel: 617-254-2085.)
Reverend Fathers—
Borowski, Douglas V.
Bouton, Thomas F.
Crowley, Kevin J.
Gomes, Ronald A.
Kearns, John P.
Montague, James A.
Novello, Lawrence E.
Schiavone, Christopher F.
Walsh, Martin J.

Health Leave:
(For further information contact Tel: 617-254-2085.)
Reverend Fathers—
Balcom, Gary E.
Butler, James P.
Conte, Denis A.
DiFruscio, John A.
Fay, Robert D.
Fraser, Gerald C.
Frost, Peter J.
Hession, James J.
Higgins, Michael J.
Kinsella, Charles R.
Mahan, Paul J.
Matte, Richard O.
Meskell, David B.
Morris, John S.
Morrisette, Robert H.
Motherway, Thomas F.
Mullin, Jay M.
Paquin, Ronald H.
Rosenkranz, George J.
Santerre, Richard R.
Scanlan, William J.

Permanent Disability:
(For further information contact Tel: 617-254-2085.)
Reverend Fathers—
Barrett, Robert E.
Bowab, Michael L.
Brennan, James F.
Dolan, Patrick J.
Driscoll, Walter L.
Finn, Alfred E.
Foley, John T.
Jansonis, Alphonse B.
Lawson, Harold F.
McGrade, Kevin M.
O'Hearn, Paul V.
Reardon, Arthur L.
Regan, Michael J.
Rothwell, Joseph T.
Sullivan, James L.
Tolland, Cyril E.
Tourigney, Ernest E.
Weber, Charles P.

Retired:
(For further information contact Tel: 617-523-1861.)
Most Rev.—
Riley, Lawrence J.
Reverend Monsignors—
Abucewicz, John A.
Alves, Joseph T.
Broderick, John A.
Carroll, John P.
Collins, Russell J.
Day, John D.
Finnegan, Thomas J.
Granville, William A.
Hart, Peter F.
Kearney, Philip J.
Keilty, John P.
Keohane, Mark H.
Lawler, John F.
Low, Albert W.
McCarthy, Charles W.
McGann, Francis J.
McManus, Paul J.
Moritz, Paul L.
Novello, Russell R.
O'Sullivan, Francis G.
Palladino, Alfonso G.
Roche, William H.
Rossiter, Francis S.
Sennott, Robert J.
Shea, William B.
Sheehan, John J.
Sullivan, Timothy E.
Reverend Fathers—
Abracinskas, Albert C.
Anadore, Charles E.
Anderson, William R.
Aubut, Charles E.
Baltrushunas, Anthony P.
Barrett, Daniel J.
Barry, Henry F.
Beksha, Francis W.
Bernatonis, John F.
Berube, John J.
Bonfilgio, David G.
Boucher, Clarence R.
Boyle, Robert J.
Brennan, Gerard M.
Brudzynski, Peter F.
Bryson, Robert C.
Buchette, Anthony J.
Buckley, Frederick J.
Buckley, John K.
Burke, Leonard J.
Burns, John F.
Campbell, William W.
Carr, John F.
Carr, Mark V.
Casey, Walter E.
Cedrone, Laurence C.
Cintolo, Antonio A.
Clifford, Donald G.
Coen, William R.
Coffey, James H.
Collins, Joseph I.
Commane, William J.
Connick, Alfred J.
Connolly, Maurice V.
Connor, John E.
Conroy, Cyril J.
Cormier, Leo G.
Cowhig, Edward D.
Creighton, Gerard E.
Daley, Joseph D.
Daly, James J.
Daniele, Anthony J.
DeAdder, James W.
Delaney, Francis H.
Dempsy, Thomas F.
Donelin, John M.
Donlon, William J.
Donovan, John L.
Doocey, Michael F.
Doonan, John A.
Downey, Joseph J.
Doyle, Lawrence J.
Dufour, Louis C.
Duggan, Charles T.
Duquette, Delphis O.
Fallon, John J.
Finnegan, John T.
Flynn, John H.
Flynn, Robert G.
Foley, John E.
Foley, John I.
Francis, Paul R.
Gallager, Edward L.
Gallagher, Francis L.
Geoghan, John J.
Gillis, Edward F.
Gilmartin, Daniel J.
Goss, Francis G.
Goulet, Raymond O.
Grant, Frederick A.
Greaney, Francis M.
Guarcello, Russell V.
Guerette, William J.
Guiney, John E.
Hane, Howard S.
Hanlon, John R.
Hart, James P.
Hogan, Cornelius J.
Horgan, Gerald B.
Janiunas, Albin F.
Jennings, John J.
Johnson, Harold J.
Johnson, Richard G.
Joyal, Rene J
Jusseaume, John E.
Keeley, John A.
Kelley, Paul G.
Kelly, John P.
Kenneally, William F.
Kierce, J. Joseph
Lambert, Raymond P.
Langley, Joseph W.
Laraia, Joseph P.
Laurano, Anthony J.
Lawler, John T.
Leonard, Clyde A.
Logue, Charles D.
Lombard, Samuel J.
Lucey, William F.
Lucid, Vincent F.
Lukas, Joseph S.
Lynch, Daniel G.
MacDonald, Sterling B.
Maguire, John J.
Mahoney, James F.
Mahoney, John P.
Mansfield, John L.
Masciarelli, Rudolph
McAskill, Kenneth F.
McAuliffe, Robert J.
McCarthy, William R.
McConville, Philip G.J.
McDonald, James T.
McGann, Gerard J.
McManus, Frederick R.
McNulty, Joseph P.
Meade, Henry J.
Meade, Maurice P.
Medeiros, Antonio S.
Meffan, Robert V.
Mooney, Thomas J.
Morgan, William H.
Moriarty, Thomas W.
Mosley, Francis J.
Mottau, Robert S.
Mowatt, John J.
Moynihan, Paul V.
Mulkern, John F.
Murphy, Kenneth B.
Murphy, Lawrence F.
Naguszewski, Edward B.
Navien, Thomas A.
Noonan, William J.
O'Brien, Frederick W.
O'Connor, William B.
O'Hare, Francis C.
O'Leary, Adrian P.
O'Leary, Arthur P.
O'Sullivan, Eugene M.
Ouelette, Lionel P.
Palmieri, John A.
Pearsall, Ernest P.
Perron, Richard J.
Philbin, John J.
Pied, Wilfred L.
Piscitelli, Vincent J.
Pollis, Robert G.
Powers, Richard J.
Ready, Francis P.
Reilly, Joseph L.
Riley, James H.
Riordan, Daniel F.
Rogers, James M.
Ronan, Henry T.
Ryan, Joseph E.
Rynne, Paul P.
Saja, Thaddeus A.
Saunders, John A.
Shakalis, Peter A.
Shanley, Paul R.
Sheehy, Charles I.
Silk, John D.
Silva, John F.
Slejzer, Ferdinand E.
Stocklosa, J. Walter
Sullivan, Francis P.
Sullivan, Michael D.
Sullivan, Paul V.
Sullivan, William P.
Svirskas, Joseph J.
Toland, Paul L.
Vasaturo, Anthony J.
Veneto, Joseph P.
Wasnewski, Richard P.
White, John J.
Whittier, James E.
Williams, George J.
Zuromskis, John D.

Permanent Deacons:
Alicea, Francisco, St. Mary, Waltham
Amerault, Robert P., St. Joseph, Medford
Arsenault, Joseph G., Awaiting Assignment
Aucoin, Albert J., (Retired)
Balestracci, Alfred, St. Theresa, North Reading
Barton, John M., St. Thomas, Peabody
Beatrice, Lee A., St. John, East Bridgewater
Belmonte, Joseph A., St. Anthony, Revere
Bloom, Laurence J., St. Ann, Somerville
Bower, Charles H., St. Bonaventure, Manomet
Bowley, Richard R., Sacred Heart, Amesbury
Breinlinger, Martin, St. Mary's, Holliston
Bresnahan, John M., St. Agnes, Middleton
Bulpett, Dean C., St. Irene, Carlisle
Cabral, John F., Somerville Hospital
Callahan, James C., St. Charles Borromeo, Waltham
Camacho, Teodoro, St. Mary, Waltham
Canoua, Joseph A., St. Anthony, Cohasset
Capomaccio, John J., Sick Leave
Caruso, Philip M., St. Mary, Holliston
Casillas, Luis, Cathedral of the Holy Cross, Boston
Chevarley, Joseph W., (Retired)
Chisholm, Finley H., St. Joseph, Lynn
Clough, Charles I., Our Lady Help of Christians, Concord
Connelly, Milton E., Jr., Immaculate Conception, Newburyport
Connor, John P., Chap., Brockton Hospital, St. Mary of the Hills, Milton
Cordeau, Richard W., St. Jean Baptiste, Lynn
Cornell, Charles A., St. Isidore, Stowe
Counihan, Eugene A., St. Elizabeth, Acton & Fernald School, Waltham
Creutz, Edward F., Blessed Kateri Tekakwitha, Plymouth
Crosby, Herbert W., (Retired)
Crowley, Joseph I, Jr., Children's Hospital, Boston
Crump, James M., Awaiting Assignment
D'Ambrosio, Francis A., M.D., (Retired)
Dacey, Dennis J., Sick Leave
DeCoste, Leonard F., Our Lady of Lourdes, Jamaica Plain
Delaney, Joseph L., St. Denis, Westwood
Dempsey, Timothy F., St. Mary, Lynn
Diotalevi, Augustus J., St. Tarcisius, Framingham
Donnelly, Joseph A., St. John, Chelmsford
Donoghue, Leo J., Dir., Office of Permanent Deaconate, St. John the Evangelist, East Bridgewater
Doyle, Edward L., St. Mary of the Assumption, Hull
Dunn, Daniel A., St. Marie, Lowell
Dzuris, Robert W., St. Mary, Chelmsford
Eames, James H., St. Mary, Randolph
Egan, Thomas F., St. Brendan, Dorchester
Ego, John J., St. Bernadette, Randolph
Elibero, Edward P., St. Pius V, Lynn
Farguheson, Wood Rowe, St. Joseph, Salem
Fenton, Jack H., St. Agnes, Reading
Gaffney, Francis M., Immaculate Conception, Revere
Gagne, Gerard E., Sacred Heart, Lawrence
Gagne, Ronald D., St. Rose of Lima, Topsfield
Gagnon, Raymond A., St. Anthony, Shirley
Gardyna, Henry A., Sick Leave
Gaudreau, Robert J., Sacred Hearts, Haverhill
Geneus, Alfred J., Our Lady of Pity, Cambridge
Gindel, Richard W., St. Ann, Gloucester
Goldy, Andrew J., St. Clement, Somerville
Grimley, Edward J., St. Augustine, Lawrence
Guerin, Bertrand H., Assumption, Bellingham
Guerrini, Patrick E., St. Elizabeth's Medical Center, Brighton
Guerrios, Francisco, Holy Family, Dorchester
Guillet, Andre
Hackett, Robert T., Most Blessed Sacrament, Wakefield
Halloran, John B., St. Paul, Hingham
Hanlon, Thomas H., St. Bridget, Abington & MCI-Bridgewater
Hardcastle, Philip P., St. Charles, Woburn
Hardin, Howard P., St. Elizabeth of Hungary, Acton
Hardy, Gerard J., St. Louis de France, Lowell
Hardy, John W., Sacred Heart, Lynn
Harrison, John D., St. Mary-Immaculate Conception, Lawrence
Heffernan, Francis X., Immaculate Conception, Stoughton
Herrera, Luciano, Blessed Sacrament, Jamaica Plain
Hickey, Charles M., St. Jerome, Weymouth
Hoaglund, Robert, St. Matthias, Marlboro
Holderried, Joseph E., St. Margaret Mary, Westwood
Iwanowicz, Michael A., Our Lady of Sorrows, Sharon
James, William H., St. Paul, Hamilton
Jennette, John F., St. Joseph, Quincy
Johnson, Robert N., Our Lady Help of Christians, Newton
Juliano, Anthony J., St. Adelaide, Peabody
Kaelin, Gerard J., St. Adelaide, Peabody
Kane, William F.X., St. Joachim, Rockport
Kasenenko, Joseph S., St. Mary Star of the Sea, Beverly
Keefe, Arthur J., Holy Family, Duxbury
Kerns, William E., St. Barbara, Woburn
Killam, Harold E., Prison Ministry
King, Clifford D., St. Thomas, Wilmington
Kramich, Robert A., Unassigned
L'Italien, George G., St. James, Salem
LaBrache, Leo F., St. Patrick, Watertown
Lacey, Neil F., St. George, Framingham
LaFargue, John L., St. Joseph, Holbrook
LaPointe, Norman P., St. Joseph, Salem
Lauture, Aubert, St. Leo, Dorchester
Lawless, Timothy, St. Paul, Hingham
LePage, Donald E., (Retired)
Leslie, Charles O., Holy Name, West Roxbury
Little, James B., St. Brendan, Dorchester
Lloyd, Barry V., St. Margaret, Lowell
LoPriore, Mario, Sacred Heart, Boston
MacDonald, Joseph P., St. Elizabeth, Milton
Machicado, Hernan, (Retired)
MacKenzie, William E., Our Lady Comforter of the Afflicted, Waltham
Mandoza, Francis A., St. Agnes, Arlington
Mannion, John J., St. Lawrence, Brookline & MCI-Cedar Junction, Walpole
Marchant, Thomas W., St. Anthony, Everett
Mariani, Henry A., St. Francis of Assisi, Medford
Markey, Paul G., Most Blessed Sacrament, Quincy
Martin, Leo A., Our Lady of Grace, Chelsea
Martin, Richard C., Sr., Gate of Heaven, South Boston
Martinez, Orlando, Asuncion de la Virgen Maria, Lawrence
McCarthy, Daniel E., St. Mary, Rowley
McCarthy, John P., (Retired)
McCarty, William J., St. Joseph, Needham
McDavitt, Thomas S., Regl. Bishop's Office (South)
McDonough, John J., St. Clare, Braintree
McGrail, John S., St. Michael, Lowell
McHugh, John W., Chap., MCI-Bridgewater, St. Paul, Hingham
McLaughlin, Richard B., St. Malachy, Burlington
McManus, Lawrence R., St. Joseph, Lynn
Menz, John R., St. Boniface, Quincy
Messina, Joseph M., St. Margaret Mary, Westwood
Miles, Walter J., Jr., Coord., Office of Prison Ministry, Our Lady of Fatima, Sudbury
Mills, Chester P., Unassigned
Montes, Edward M., St. Columbkille, Brighton
Morey, Russell W., St. Catherine, Westford
Mullins, Thomas F., St. Theresa, Billerica
Murphy, Alfred I., St. Bernard, Concord
Murphy, Steven J., St. Mary-Immaculate Conception, Lawrence
Nagle, William V., St. Joseph, Kingston
Nashawaty, Nicholas, Our Lady of Cedars of Lebanon, Jamaica Plain
Naveo, Jose, Asuncion de la Virgen Maria, Lawrence
Nickley, Joseph T., Jr., Immaculate Conception, Weymouth
O'Neil, Cyril T., St. Patrick, Stoneham
Oles, Kenneth W., St. Mary, Wrentham
Ortiz, Jesus M., St. Peter, Dorchester
Papile, Joseph A., St. John the Baptist, Quincy
Patrick, Alexander J., Jr., St. Elizabeth of Hungary, Acton
Peltak, Douglas P., Immaculate Conception, Marlboro
Penney, Edward F., Jr., St. Mary Magdalene, Tyngsboro
Pepe, John W., St. Bridget, Maynard
Perea, Antonio M., Most Holy Redeemer, East Boston
Pugsley, Stanley G., St. William, Dorchester
Quigley, Edward M., (Retired)
Quiles, Jesus, Blessed Sacrament, Jamaica Plain
Radford, Richard F., Jr., St. Mary, Brookline
Ramey, Allan A., St. Anthony, Lawrence
Ramrath, Joseph R., St. Anselm, Sudbury
Rivera, Louis, St. Rose, Chelsea
Rivera, Valentin, St. John, Peabody
Rizzuto, Anthony P., Sacred Heart, Lexington
Rocha, Richard H., SS. Peter & Paul, Lawrence
Rodriguez, Diego N., St. Mary-Immaculate Conception, Lawrence
Rogers, Arthur F., Jr., St. James, Medford
Rooney, Gerard P., (Retired)
Ros, Peter An, St. Patrick, Lowell
Rosa, Andres, Cathedral of the Holy Cross, Boston
Ryan, Gerald P., Holy Ghost, Whitman
Ryan, John G., (Retired)
Salenius, John D., Sacred Heart, Quincy
Sanchez, Tomas E., St. John the Evangelist, Beverly
Santosuosso, Alfred E., St. Jude, Waltham
Shanahan, Allan R., St. Mary, Billerica
Shrader, David J., St. Richard, Danvers
Sicuso, Anthony C., Absent on Leave
Specht, Paul V., St. Patrick, Lawrence
Spiri, Guy J., St. Stephen, Framingham
Stenstrom, Eugene, Our Lady of the Rosary, Stoughton
Sullivan, Charles E., Resurrection, Hingham
Sullivan, Daniel F., St. Agatha, Milton
Taylor, Carroll H., Prison Ministry
Torres, Pedro Luis, St. Stephen, Framingham
Turner, J. Robert, St. Patrick, Stoneham
Valeri, Frank A., St. Peter, Malden
Vitello, Joseph V., St. Francis Xavier, Weymouth
Walsh, Martin J., St. Ann, Peabody
Warren, Lewis F., St. Anne, Salem
Watson, John W., Jr., VA Medical Center, Bedford
Welch, Henry M., Unassigned
Werner, Robert M., Unassigned
Whipple, John E., Our Lady Star of the Sea, Marblehead
Wildes, William H., (Retired)
Wise, John W., Incarnation, Melrose
Yanikoski, Florian F., (Retired)

INSTITUTIONS LOCATED IN THE ARCHDIOCESE

[A] SEMINARIES, ARCHDIOCESAN

BOSTON. *St. John's Seminary*. College of Liberal Arts, 197 Foster St., Brighton, 02135. Tel: 617-254-2610. Rev. Robert W. Flagg, M.Div., M.S., S.T.L., Dean of College & Admissions; John J. Clabeaux, Ph.D., Academic Dean; Revs. Thomas F. Nestor, Ph.D., Dean of Students; George P. Evans, S.T.D., Spiritual Formation; Richard M. Erikson, Ph.D., Pastoral Formation; Mark L. Noonan, Ph.D.; Thomas T. Howard, Ph.D.; Deborah DeChiara-Quenzer, Ph.D.; Jeffrey Hause, Ph.D.; Tracey Stark, Ph.D. Priests 5; Lay Teachers 5; Students 37.

St. John's Seminary School of Theology. 127 Lake St., Brighton, 02135. Tel: 617-254-2610. Rev. Msgr. Timothy J. Moran, J.C.L., S.T.D., Rector; Revs. Martin P. Connor, S.T.L.; Laurence W. McGrath, M.S., M.A.; John L. Sullivan, S.S.L.; Walter J. Woods, S.T.D.; Robert E. Sullivan, Ph.D.; George P. Evans, M.Div., S.T.D.; Stephen E. Salocks, S.S.L.; Richard G. Cunningham, J.C.D.; Robin C. Ryan, C.P., Ph.D.; John P. McGinty, S.T.D.; John E. MacInnis, S.T.D.; Paul E. Ritt, S.T.D.; Thomas E. Nestor, Ph.D.; William B. Palardy, Ph.D.

WESTON. *Pope John XXIII National Seminary*, 558 South Ave., 02193. Tel: 781-899-5500; Fax: 781-899-9057. Rev. Msgr. Francis D. Kelly, S.T.L., Ph.D., Rector & Pres.; Revs. Paul P. Gilmartin, S.J., S.T.L., S.T.D.; James W. De Adder, Ph.D., S.T.D.; Alfred McBride, O.Praem., Ph.D.; Charles J. Healey, S.J., S.T.L., S.T.D.; James Massa, Ph.D., Coord.; Paul M. Parker, M.A., S.T.L.; Peter Uglietto, S.T.D.; Pius Murray, C.S.S., S.S.L.; Sr. Rose Clarisse Gadoury, S.S.A., M.A., M.Div.; Leonard Maluf, S.T.D. A Major National Seminary open to men over thirty studying for the diocesan and religious priesthood. Students 77.

[B] SEMINARIES, RELIGIOUS OR SCHOLASTICATES

BOSTON. *Oblate Provincialate*, 2 Ipswich St., 02215-3607. Tel: 617-536-7471; 536-4141; Fax: 617-536-7016.
E-mail: omvusaprov@aol.com
Web site: http://www.omv.org
St. Ignatius Province of the Oblates of the Virgin Mary, Inc. Revs. Timothy Gallagher, O.M.V., Prov.; William Brown, O.M.V., Prov. Treas.; Bro. Luigi Falbo, O.M.V., Asst. Treas. Priests of the Province on Special Assignment:
Philippines: Revs. Thomas Haake, O.M.V.; John Lyons, O.M.V.
Italy: Revs. Vincenzo Antolini, O.M.V.; Roberto Jakanovich, O.M.V.
U.S.A.: Revs. Mark Avila, O.M.V.; Frank Cinque, O.M.V.; Thomas Cinque, O.M.V.; Placido Ferracino, O.M.V.; John Ferrara, O.M.V.; Stephen McAndrew, O.M.V.; Bruce Williamson, O.M.V.

Our Lady of Grace Seminary, 1105 Boylston St., 02215-3660. Tel: 617-266-5999; Fax: 617-247-7576.
E-mail: petergrover@juno.com
Web site: http://www.omv.org
St. Ignatius Province of the Oblates of the Virgin Mary, Inc. Revs. Peter P. Gojuk, O.M.V., Rector; David M. Beauregard, O.M.V., Dean of Students. Formation Staff: Revs. Thomas Carzon, O.M.V.; Peter Grover, O.M.V.; Bro. David Guza, O.M.V. Students 12.

BRIGHTON. *Oblate Seminary Residence*, 62 Kirkwood Rd., 02135-5157. Tel: 617-787-0008. Bro. Richard Cote, O.M.I., Dir.

CAMBRIDGE. *Weston Jesuit School of Theology*, 3 Phillips Pl., 02138. Tel: 617-492-1960.
E-mail: rmanning@wjst.edu
Revs. Robert E. Manning, S.J., Pres.; Randall Sacks, S.J., Acting Dean. Legal Title: *Weston College Corporation*. Priests 16; Sisters 3; Brothers 1; Lay Teachers 10; Students 212.

DANVERS. *Xavier Center*. House of Formation. 21 Spring St., 01923. Tel: 508-777-1326. American Northeastern Province of the Brothers of St. Francis Xavier (Xaverian Brothers). Bro. John D. Hamilton, C.F.X., Dir. Brothers Professed 3.

FRAMINGHAM. *Sylva Maria*, 567 Salem End Rd., 01701. Tel: 508-879-7667; Fax: 508-879-6711; 879-2541. Motherhouse and Novitiate of the Sons of Mary Missionary Society. Revs. John Murphy, F.M.S.I.; John Coss, F.M.S.I.; Henry Cicale, F.M.S.I.; Robert Rivard, F.M.S.I.; Joseph Saulnier, F.M.S.I.; Henry Branagan, F.M.S.I.; John Wallace, F.M.S.I. Priests 7; Brothers 5.

HAVERHILL. *Sons of Divine Providence School for Exceptional Boys* (Bradford), Groveland Rd., P.O. Box 205, 01835. Tel: 508-373-0461. Rev. Gino Marchesani, F.D.P.

[C] COLLEGES AND UNIVERSITIES

BOSTON. *Emmanuel College*, 400 The Fenway, 02115. Tel: 617-277-9340; 735-9825
For a complete listing, refer to the Colleges and Universities section.

*CHESTNUT HILL. *Boston College*, 02167. Tel: 617-552-8000.
Web site: http://www.bc.edu
For a complete listing, refer to the Colleges and Universities section.

NORTH ANDOVER. *Merrimack College*, 01845. Tel: 978-837-5000
For a complete listing, refer to the Colleges and Universities section.

WESTON. *Regis College*, Wellesley St., 02193. Tel: 617-893-1820
For a complete listing, refer to the Colleges and Universities section.

[D] HIGH SCHOOLS, DIOCESAN

BOSTON. *Cathedral High School*, 74 Union Park St., 02118. Tel: 617-542-2325. Mary Kay Brady, Prin. Brothers 1; Sisters 6; Lay Teachers 20; Students 274.

St. Clare High School, 190 Cummins Hwy., 02131. Tel: 617-323-0966.
E-mail: stclare@stclare.mec.edu
Web site: http://www.stclare.mec.edu
Donna L. Fiori, Ph.D., Prin. Sisters 8; Lay Teachers 13; Students 205.

BRAINTREE. *Archbishop Williams' High School*, 80 Independence Ave., 02184. Tel: 617-843-3636. Mary Ellen Barnes, Prin.; Rev. John M. Capuci, Chap. Priests 1; Sisters 4; Lay Teachers 37; Students 574.

BRIGHTON. *Archdiocesan Central High Schools, Inc.*, 2121 Commonwealth Ave., 02135. His Eminence Bernard Cardinal Law; Most Rev. John P. Boles; Rev. Robert J. Boyle; Paul R. Gauron, Esq.; Dorothy H. Jodice, Sec. Educ.; Sr. Ann Dominic Roach, O.P.; Sr. Blaithin Sullivan, C.S.J.

BROCKTON. *Cardinal Spellman High School*, 738 Court St., 02402. Tel: 508-583-6875; Fax: 508-580-1977.
E-mail: ARBOSHO58@connectinc.com
Sisters of St. Joseph. Sr. Thomasine Knowlton, C.S.J., Prin. Priests 1; Sisters 7; Lay Teachers 34; Students 475.

CAMBRIDGE. *Matignon High School*, One Matignon Rd., 02140. Tel: 617-876-1212. Mr. Gary R. LeFave, Prin.; Ms. Kathleen Fraser, Asst. Prin.; Rev. James Nyhan, Chap. College Preparatory. Religious 3; Lay Teachers 38; Students 600.

North Cambridge Catholic High School, 40 Norris St., 02140. Tel: 617-876-6068. Sr. Ellen Powers, C.S.J., Prin. Sisters 5; Lay Teachers 12; Students 180.

EVERETT. *Pope John XXIII Central High School*, 888 Broadway, 02149. Tel: 617-389-0240. Sr. Kristin Hokanson, S.N.D., Prin. Sisters 4; Lay Teachers 22; Students 400.

FRAMINGHAM. *Marian High School*, 273 Union Ave., 01702. Tel: 508-875-7646; Fax: 508-875-0838.
E-mail: ARBOSH78@connectinc.com
Bro. Paul R. Alves, SS.CC., Prin. Brothers 1; Sisters 3; Lay Teachers 21; Students 284.

LAWRENCE. *Notre Dame Education Center*. (Adults), 301 Haverhill St., P.O. Box 1012, 01842-9998. Tel: 978-682-6441; Fax: 978-974-8940.
E-mail: sndmemurph@aol.com
Sisters of Notre Dame de Namur. Sr. Mary Murphy, S.N.D.deN., Dir. Sisters 15; Adults 500; Total Staff 24.

PEABODY. *Bishop Fenwick High School*, 99 Margin St., 01960. Tel: 508-531-8200; Fax: 508-532-9053.
Web site: http://www.fenwick.org
Robert McNamara, Prin.; Rev. John V. Sutton, Chap. Religious 7; Brothers 1; Lay Teachers 53; Students 880.

[E] HIGH SCHOOLS, PRIVATE

BOSTON. *Boston College High School & Jesuit Community*. 150 Morrissey Blvd., Dorchester, 02125. Tel: 617-436-3900; Fax: 617-282-7503.
E-mail: pusaterisj@bchigh.edu
Web site: http://www.bchigh.edu./
Revs. Joseph R. Fahey, S.J., Pres. Tel: 617-436-3900; Philip A. Pusateri, S.J., Rector. Tel: 617-929-9413; Joseph T. Bennett, S.J. Tel: 617-929-9482; Edward F. Boyle, S.J. Tel: 617-929-9483; James P. Carr, S.J. Tel: 617-929-9429; William J. Hamilton, S.J. Tel: 617-929-9478; John J. Hanwell, S.J. Tel: 617-929-9442; Philip K. Harrigan, S.J. Tel: 617-929-9493; James J. Hosie, S.J. Tel: 617-929-9488; Daniel C. Lewis, S.J. Tel: 617-929-9456; Thomas J.C. Kelly, S.J. Tel: 617-929-9438; John L. Mahoney, S.J. Tel: 617-929-9433; Joaquin Martinez-Mari, S.J. (Bolivia). Tel: 617-929-9463; Perard C. Monestime, S.J. Tel: 617-929-9424; James W. O'Neil, S.J. Tel: 617-929-9452; Francis J. O'Neill, S.J. Tel: 617-929-9494; Joseph P. O'Neill, S.J. Tel: 617-929-9425; Clement L. Pelletier, S.J. Tel: 617-929-9430; Ignatius F. Pennisi, S.J. Tel: 617-929-9430; George A. Duffy, S.J. Tel: 617-929-9441; Robert M. Hanlon, S.J.; Peter D. Hickey, S.J. Tel: 617-929-9495; Stephen F. Dawber, S.J. Tel: 617-929-9423; Joseph R. Laughlin, S.J. Tel: 617-929-9470; Jose C. Corral, S.J. (Castilla); John Joseph Walsh, S.J. Tel: 617-929-9462; Bros. Cornelius C. Murphy, S.J. Tel: 617-929-9414; Donald J. Murray, S.J. Tel: 617-436-3900; Pedro O. Carrasquillo, S.J., Scholastic. Tel: 617-929-9427. Religious 29; Lay Teachers 69; Students 1,160. Jesuit Community. Tel: 617-929-9423; Fax: 617-929-9459.

Catholic Memorial High School and Lower School. (Grades 7-12). 235 Baker St., West Roxbury, 02132-4395. Tel: 617-323-7333; Fax: 617-325-0888. Congregation of Christian Brothers. Bro. John B. Flaherty, C.F.C., Pres.; Mr. Luke Nawrocki, Prin.; Rev. Robert J. Cordery, Chap. Priests 1; Brothers 8; Lay Teachers 43; Boys 650.

Don Bosco Preparatory School, 300 Tremont St., 02116. Tel: 617-426-9457.
E-mail: DIRECTOR@DBPboston.org
Web site: http://www.DBPboston.org
Rev. Richard J. McCormick, S.D.B., Dir.; Mr. Robert D. Gillis, Headmaster; Revs. Richard Alejunas, Vice Dir. & Coord. Youth Min.; Angelo Bongiorno, S.D.B.; James Mulloy, S.D.B.; Thomas Dunne, S.D.B.; Emil Fardellone, S.D.B. In res. Bros. William Hanna; Frank Tilton. Priests 6; Brothers 2; Lay Teachers 22; Boys 210.

Savio Preparatory High School. 145 Byron St., East Boston, 02128. Tel: 617-567-2710. Mr. Edward Minor, Exec. Dir.; Dr. Richard K. Chrystal, Prin. A college preparatory school. Lay Teachers 23; Students 336.

BRIGHTON. *Mt. St. Joseph Academy*, 617 Cambridge St., 02135. Tel: 617-254-8383 (School Office); 783-4747 (Guidance Office). Sponsored by Sisters of St. Joseph of Boston. Sr. Mary L. Murphy, C.S.J., Prin. Sisters 4; Lay Teachers 17; Girls 300.

DANVERS. *St. John's Preparatory School*, 01923. Tel: 978-774-1050; Fax: 978-774-5069.
E-mail: wdrinan@stjohnsprep.org
Web site: http://www.stjohnsprep.org
Day Students. Bro. William Drinan, C.F.X., Headmaster. Brothers 6; Lay Teachers 72; Boys 1,029.

DEDHAM. *Ursuline Academy*. (Grades 7-12), 85 Lowder St., 02026-4299. Tel: 781-326-6161. Sr. Mercedes Videira, O.S.U., Prin. Operated by Ursuline Convent. Ursuline Nuns. College Prep School for Girls. Sisters 8; Lay Teachers 37; Girls 350.

HINGHAM. *Notre Dame Academy*, 1073 Main St., 02043. Tel: 617-749-5930; 749-4727. Sr. Barbara A. Barry, S.N.D., Prin. Total Staff 70; Girls 550.

KINGSTON. *Sacred Heart High School*, 399 Bishops Hwy., 02364. Tel: 617-585-7511. Mrs. Susan Krastin, Prin. Asst. Prins.: Mr. John F. Enos; Dr. Thomas Gorsuch, Ph.D. Religious 9; Lay Teachers 35; Students 558.

LAWRENCE. *Central Catholic High School of Lawrence, Inc.*, 300 Hampshire St., 01841. Tel: 508-682-0260. Bro. Richard J. Carey, F.M.S., Prin. Conducted by the Marist Brothers of the Schools. Religious 8; Lay Teachers 46; Boys 870.

LOWELL. *Lowell Catholic High School, Inc.*, 530 Stevens St., 01851. Tel: 508-452-1794.
E-mail: ed2000@tiac.com
Mr. Edward J. Quinn, Prin. Sisters 2; Lay Teachers 16; Students 270.

MALDEN. *Malden Catholic High School*, 99 Crystal St., 02148. Tel: 617-322-3098; Fax: 617-397-0573.
E-mail: arbosh121@connectinc.com
Web site: http://www.maldencatholic.com
Xaverian Brothers. Bro. Richard Cook, C.F.X., Headmaster. Brothers 4; Lay Teachers 30; Boys 540.

METHUEN. *Presentation of Mary Academy*, 209 Lawrence St., 01844. Tel: 978-682-9391; Fax: 978-975-3595.
E-mail: pma@pmamethuen.org
Web site: http://www.pmamethuen.org
Sisters of the Presentation of Mary. Sr. Rose Marie Dupre, Prin. Sisters 9; Lay Teachers 15; Total Staff 37; Girls 247.

MILTON. *Fontbonne Academy*, 930 Brook Rd., 02186. Tel: 617-696-3241. Sr. Marilyn McGoldrick, Pres. Sisters of St. Joseph 6; Lay Teachers 31; Students 532.

NEEDHAM. *St. Sebastian's Country Day School, Inc.* (Grades 7-12), 1191 Greendale Ave., 02192. Tel: 617-449-5200; Fax: 617-449-5630. Mr. William L. Burke, III, Headmaster; Revs. John F. Arens; John U. Paris. Priests 2; Lay Teachers 45; Boys 320.

NEWTON. *Country Day School of the Sacred Heart*. (Grades 5-12), 785 Centre St., 02158. Tel: 617-244-4246. Sr. Barbara Rogers, R.S.C.J., Prin. Legal Title: *Boston Academy of the Sacred Heart*. Religious of the Sacred Heart 1; Lay Teachers 30; Girls 212.

Mount Alvernia High School, 790 Centre St., 02158. Tel: 617-964-5643 (Convent); 969-2260 (School). Missionary Franciscan Sisters of the Immaculate Conception. Sr. Suzanne Fondini, O.S.F., Prin. Sisters 12; Lay Teachers 18; Girls 240.

READING. *Austin Preparatory School*, 101 Willow St., 01867. Tel: 617-944-4900. Paul J. Moran, Headmaster; Revs. John D. Harrington (England); Kenneth Healey, S.M.; James Morris. Priests 3; Sisters 1; Brothers 1; Lay Teachers 35; Students 564.

TYNGSBORO. *Academy of Notre Dame*, 01879. Tel: 508-649-7611.
Web site: http://www.netiplus.com/users/notredame/nda.htm
Sr. Maureen Marr, S.N.D., Prin. Sisters of Notre Dame de Namur 3; Faculty 28; Girls 248.

WAKEFIELD. *Our Lady of Nazareth Academy*, 14 Winship Dr., 01880. Tel: 617-245-5210. Sisters of Charity of Nazareth. Mrs. Molly Kelley, Prin. Lay Teachers 18; Girls 178.

WESTWOOD. *Xaverian Brothers High School*, 800 Clapboardtree St., 02090. Tel: 617-326-6392. Xaverian Brothers. Bro. Daniel Skala, C.F.X., Headmaster. Brothers 4; Lay Teachers 52; Boys 750.

[F] ELEMENTARY SCHOOLS, DIOCESAN

DANVERS. *St. Mary of the Annunciation School*, 14 Otis St., 01923. Tel: 508-774-0307.
E-mail: ARBOSEO72@connectinc.com
Mrs. Constance Morency, M.Ed., Prin. (Grades K-8 & Extended Day Care). Sisters of Notre Dame de Namur 1; Lay Teachers 29; Students 548.

[G] MONTESSORI SCHOOLS

HAVERHILL. *The Merrimack Montessori School*, 55 Saltonstall Rd., 01830. Tel: 508-374-6103. Juliet Nagle, Prin. (For boys and girls aged 3-5). Lay Teachers 8; Students 115.

MARLBORO. *The St. Anne Montessori School*, 720 Boston Post Rd., 01752. Tel: 508-485-3791. Sr. Doreen Scott, S.S.A., Dir. (For boys and girls aged 3-5). Religious 1; Lay Teachers 2; Students 72.

NEWTON. *Walnut Park Montessori School*, 47 Walnut Park, 02158. Tel: 617-969-9208. Sr. Mary Ann Connolly, S.C., Prin. Religious 5; Lay Teachers 5; Students 145.

WENHAM. *Notre Dame Children's Class*, 74 Grapevine Rd., 01984. Tel: 508-468-1340. Sr. Barbara Beauchamp, S.N.D., Dir.; Sr. Susan Raymo, S.N.D., Co-Dir. Religious 2; Lay Teachers 4; Primary Class 28; Preschool Students 50.

[H] ELEMENTARY SCHOOLS, PRIVATE

BOSTON. *Lt. Joseph P. Kennedy, Jr., Memorial School*. (Under the patronage of Our Lady of Czestochowa.). 17 Hale St., Hyde Park, 02136. Tel: 617-364-4975; 361-1726. Bernardine Sisters of the Third Order of St. Francis of Mass., Inc. Sr. Joanne Helen Grejdus, O.S.F., Prin.; Sr. M. Theresine Jablonski, O.S.F., Clerk-Treas. Sisters 6; Lay Teachers 6; Students 245.

Nativity Preparatory School. (Grades 5-8). 30 Raynor Cir., Roxbury, 02120. Tel: 617-442-1993. Legal Title: *Nativity-Boston, Inc.* Revs. Alfred J. Hicks, S.J., Prin.; William J. Cullen, S.J. A Jesuit Middle School. Priests 3; Lay Teachers 13; Boys 60.

BRAINTREE. *St. Coletta Day School, Inc.*, 85 Washington St., 02184. Tel: 617-848-6250; Fax: 617-848-0640. Day School for multiply handicapped, developmentally delayed children, ages 4-22 years. Legal Title: *Braintree St. Coletta Day School*. Sisters of St. Francis of Assisi 2; Lay Teachers 33; Students 69.

DORCHESTER. *Mother Caroline Academy*. (Grades 5-8), 35 Bird St., 02125. Tel: 617-288-3300.
E-mail: info@mothercaroline.org
Web site: http://www.mothercaroline.org
School Sisters of Notre Dame. Sr. Mary Dooley, S.S.N.D., Exec. Dir.; Sr. Frances Butler, S.S.N.D., Prin. Legal Title: *Mother Caroline Academy for*

Girls, Inc. Students 60; Sisters 3; Lay Teachers 10.

GLOUCESTER. *St. Mel Independent Day School*, 12 Edgemoor Rd., 01930. Tel: 508-283-1700.
E-mail: ABOSE123082@connectinc.com
Principals: Sr. Catherine Mary Albright, O.P.; Maureen J. Kelleher. Sisters 3; Lay Teachers 7; Students 84.

GROTON. *Country Day School of the Holy Union*, 14 Main St., Box 993, 01450. Tel: 978-448-5646; Fax: 978-448-2392.
E-mail: ARBOSE083@connectinc.com
Sr. Lucille Guay, S.U.S.C., Prin. Sisters of the Holy Union 2; Lay Teachers 8; Students 224.

HANOVER. *Cardinal Cushing School and Training Center, Inc.*, 400 Washington St., 02339. Tel: 617-826-6371. Dr. Henry W. Perrin, Jr., Dir. Sisters 6; Lay Staff 253; Students 146.

KINGSTON. *Sacred Heart Elementary School*. (Day School), 329 Bishops Hwy., 02364. Tel: 617-585-2114. Sr. Jeanne Morris, C.D.P., Prin. (Grades 1-6). Sisters of Divine Providence 8; Lay Teachers 17; Students 444.

Sacred Heart Pre-Primary School, 363 Bishops Hwy., 02364-2035. Tel: 781-585-3545. Sr. Angela Provost, C.D.P., Dir. Religious 1; Lay Teachers 4; Students 62.

LOWELL. *Franco-American Private School*, 357 Pawtucket St., 01854. Tel: 508-458-0308.
E-mail: ARBOSE105@connectinc.com
Sr. Lorraine Richard, S.C.Q., Prin. Religious 4; Lay Teachers 21; Students 384.

MARLBORO. *Our Lady Preschool Learning Center*, 197 Pleasant St., 01752. Tel: 617-481-0654. Sr. Debra Bow, S.S.Ch., Dir. Religious 2; Students 80 (ages 3-5).

MILTON. *Jeanne d'Arc Convent*, 55 Parkwood Dr., 02186. Tel: 617-698-8265; 698-8266. Religious of Christian Education. Sisters 7.

NEWTON. *Jackson School Elementary*. (Grades 1-6), 200 Jackson Rd., 02158-1428. Tel: 617-969-1537; Fax: 617-244-8596.
E-mail: jaccsj@aol.com
Mrs. Susan G. Niden, Prin. Sisters 9; Lay Teachers 16; Students 240.

Mount Alvernia Academy. (Grades N-6). 20 Manet Rd., Chestnut Hill, 02167. Tel: 617-527-7540; Fax: 617-527-7995.
E-mail: ARBOSE142@connectinc.com
Missionary Franciscan Sisters 7; Lay Teachers 29; Students 310. Convent School. Tel: 617-527-7540. Sr. Irene Laurence, O.S.F., Prin. Convent. Tel: 617-244-3696.

TYNGSBORO. *Academy of Notre Dame at Tyngsboro*, 180 Middlesex Rd., 01879. Tel: 508-649-7611.
E-mail: ARBOSE165@connectinc.com
Sr. Marcia Billings, S.N.D., Prin. Sisters of Notre Dame de Namur 3; Lay Teachers 25; Students 454.

[I] SPECIAL SCHOOLS

BOSTON. *Emmanuel House Kindergarten*, 11 Newcomb St., 02118. Tel: 617-445-2037; Fax: 617-445-2479. Community Based Agency of Catholic Charitable Bureau of Archdiocese of Boston, Inc. Sr. Kristine Koba, S.A., Dir. Franciscan Sisters of the Atonement 4; Lay Teachers 4; Students 44.

Laboure College, Inc., 2120 Dorchester Ave., 02124. Tel: 617-296-8300; Fax: 617-296-7947.
Web site: http://www.labourecollege.org
Sr. Clarisse Correia, D.C., Pres. Two year college for nursing and allied health. Member of Caritas Christi Health Care System. Priests 1; Sisters 5; Lay Teachers 70; Students 450.

METHUEN. *St. Ann's Home Special Needs School*, 100 A. Haverhill St., 01844. Patrick Villani, Ph.D., Exec. Dir. Lay Teachers 35; Residential Students 150; Day Students 80.

MILTON. *Aquinas College at Milton*. Degree-Granting Programs. 303 Adams St., 02186-4296. Tel: 617-696-3100. Dr. Mary Huegel, Pres. Sisters 6; Students 255.

NEWTON. *Aquinas College at Newton*, 15 Walnut Park, 02158. Tel: 617-969-4400. Sisters of St. Joseph. Mary Huegel, Acting Pres. A Two Year College. Students 160.

PEABODY. *Holy Childhood Nursery & Kindergarten*, 5 Wheatland St., 01960. Tel: 508-531-4733. Sr. Bernadette Zaccardi, Supr.; Sr. M. Joan Melei, O.Carm., Co-Dir. Sisters 5; Lay Teachers 5; Students 93.

RANDOLPH. *The Boston School Serving Deaf & Aphasic Children*, 800 N. Main St., 02368. Tel: 617-963-8150. Sr. Bernadette Kenney, C.S.J., Exec. Dir. Sisters of St. Joseph. Lay Teachers 14; Students 68.

SWAMPSCOTT. *Marian Court College*, Little's Point Rd., 01907. Tel: 617-595-6768; Fax: 617-595-3560. Sr. Joanne Bibeau, R.S.M., Pres. Sisters 5; Lay Staff 44; Students 225.

WATERTOWN. *Rosary Academy Learning Center*, 2 Rosary Dr., 02172. Tel: 617-923-1935.
E-mail: ROSARY1@erols.com
Preschool & Day Care. Sr. Rosaire Hickey, O.P., Dir. Sisters of St. Dominic (St. Catherine, KY). Sisters 3; Lay Teachers 7; Students 70.

[J] CATHOLIC CHARITIES

BOSTON. *Catholic Charitable Bureau of the Archdiocese of Boston, Inc.*, Central Office, 49 Franklin St., 02110. Tel: 617-482-5440; Fax: 617-451-0337. Dr. Joseph Doolin, Pres. Multi-Service Agency. Total Clients served 144,828.

[K] FAMILY COUNSELING AND GUIDANCE CENTERS

BOSTON. *Family Counseling and Guidance Centers*. A Division of Catholic Charities. Admin. Headquarters, 49 Franklin St., 02110. Tel: 617-482-4355. Mr. Jack E. Mazzotti, III, M.A, Clinic Admin.
Local Clinics:
Metropolitan Boston, 49 Franklin St., 02110. Tel: 617-542-0903.
South Shore Braintree, 40 Independence Ave., Braintree, 02184. Tel: 617-848-7840.
West Area-Framingham, 350 Worcester Rd., Framingham, 01701. Tel: 508-875-0648.
North Shore-Danvers, 6 State Rd., Danvers, 01923. Tel: 508-774-6820.
Plymouth County-Marshfield, 475 School, Marshfield, 02050. Tel: 617-837-1133.

QUINCY. *The Good Shepherd: Maria Droste Services*, 1354 Hancock St., Suite 209, 02169. Tel: 617-471-5686. Sr. Joanne Westwater, Exec. Dir. Legal Title: *Madonna Hall*. Total Staff 4; Volunteers 20; Total Assisted 350.

[L] SOCIETY OF ST. VINCENT DE PAUL

BOSTON. *Society of St. Vincent DePaul, Central Office*, 1280 Washington St., 02118. Tel: 617-542-0883. Mr. Albert N. Crocker, Exec. Dir.

[M] CHILD CARE AGENCIES

BOSTON. *The Laboure Center/Catholic Charities*, 371 & 376 W. Fourth St., 02127. Tel: 617-268-9670. Daughters of Charity of St. Vincent de Paul. Sr. Maryadele Robinson, D.C., Dir., Laboure Center; Mrs. Margaret Kelly, Dir. Early Childhood Services (includes Infant-Toddler, Preschool, Child Care, Special Needs). Sisters 1; Lay Teachers 12; Students 80.

JAMAICA PLAIN. *Nazareth Day Care*, 19 St. Joseph St., 02130. Tel: 617-522-4040. Sr. Theresa Marie O'Leary, L.I.C.S.W., Pres. Legal Title: *Nazareth*. Capacity 89; Total Staff 22.

METHUEN. *St. Ann's Home, Inc.*, 100A Haverhill St., 01844. Tel: 508-682-5276. Patrick T. Villani, Ph.D., Dir.; Mrs. Sharon Cutter, Business Mgr. School. Children 135. Residential Treatment Center: Children 85. Total in Residence 85; Total Staff 180.

ROXBURY. *Nazareth Residence for Mothers and Children*, 91 Regent St., 02119. Tel: 617-541-0100. Sr. Theresa Marie O'Leary, L.I.C.S.W., Pres. Home for mothers and children who are HIV positive. Capacity 8-10 Families; Total Staff 10.

[N] SETTLEMENT HOUSES

BOSTON. *Chinese Catholic Pastoral Center*, 78 Tyler St., 02111-1831. Tel: 617-482-2949. Total Assisted 70; Total Staff 2.

El Centro Del Cardenal/Catholic Charities, 76 Union Park St., 02118. Tel: 617-542-9292; Fax: 617-542-6912. Ms. Elisabeth Zweig-Snippe.

Emmanuel House/Catholic Charities - Community Social Service Center, 11 Newcomb St., 02118. Tel: 617-445-2037; Fax: 617-445-2479. Sr. Kristine Koba, S.A., Exec. Dir. Community Based Agency of Catholic Charitable Bureau of Archdiocese of Boston, Inc. Various Adult Programs-Multi-Service. Franciscan Sisters of the Atonement 4; Total Assisted 2,377; Total Staff 8.

Haitian Multi-Service Center/Catholic Charitable Bureau of Boston. 12 Bicknell St., Dorchester, 02121. Tel: 617-436-2848. Mr. Jean Marc Jean-Baptiste, Dir. Education and Outreach, Day Care, Counseling and Advocacy.

Salesian Boys & Girls Club. (Central Unit), 189 Paris St., 02128. Tel: 617-567-0508.
E-mail: sbgclub@juno.com
(Orient Heights Unit), 145-150 Bryon St. Salesians of St. John Bosco. Revs. Mark Hyde, S.D.B., Rector; Michael Conway, S.D.B., Exec. Dir.; Richard Cressman, S.D.B.; Jack Janko, S.D.B., Ph.D., Club Admin. & Psychologist; Terence O'Donnell, S.D.B., Comm. Admin.; Bros. John Robert Metell, S.D.B., Program Dir.; George Sheehan, S.D.B.
In Formation: Bros. Donald Caldwell, S.D.B.; Lucien Pierre, S.D.B. Total Assisted 3,000; Total Staff 20.

HULL. *Children's Vacation House/Catholic Charities*, 138 Edgewater Rd., 02045. Tel: 617-925-0710. Conducted by the Catholic Charitable Bureau of Boston. Children 300.

[O] GUIDANCE CENTERS

BOSTON. *Life Resources, Inc.*, 199 State St., Fifth Floor, 02109; Fax: 617-523-1747. Mr. William J. Chiaradonna, L.I.C.S.W., B.C.D., Pres. Tel: 617-227-8766. Total in Residence 252; Total Staff 157; Total Assisted 359.

St. Mary's Women and Infants Center, 90 Cushing Ave., 02125. Tel: 617-436-8600. For pregnant & parenting women & their children. Caritas Christi. Joyce Murphy, Pres. & CEO. Patients assisted annually 250; Total Staff 60.

BROCKTON. *Phaneuf Center*, 104 Market St., 02401. Tel: 508-584-0500. Coed emergency shelter for 9 adolescents.

Phaneuf Out-Patient, 792 N. Main St., 02401. Tel: 508-588-2882. Drug and Alcohol outpatient counseling for all ages.

LAKEVILLE. *Bishop Joseph John Ruocco House*, 22 Highland Rd., 02347. Tel: 508-947-2823. Mr. Stephen Folino, Dir. Long term residential group home for 17 male adolescents. To provide comprehensive life skill services to residents and their families.

LITTLETON. *Life Resources/Alpha-Omega*, Four Omega Way, P.O. Box 922, 01460. Tel: 508-486-8919; Fax: 508-486-3990. A long term residence for 17 adolescent boys. John C. Comeau, Prog. Dir.

[P] INFORMATION - CONFERENCE CENTERS

BOSTON. *Archdiocesan Information Center*, Boston Catholic Directory, 49 Franklin St., 02110. Tel: 617-542-8393. Rev. Peter V. Conley, Editor. Assistants to the Editor: Rev. Robert M. O'Grady; Sr. Mary Ellen Sweney, S.N.D.; Sr. Theresa Cunningham, S.N.D.; Mrs. Anita Sweet.

Paulist Center, 5 Park St., 02108. Tel: 617-742-4460. Revs. Stanley F. MacNevin, C.S.P., Supr.; Joseph T. Griffin, C.S.P.; Walter J. Sullivan, C.S.P.; Thomas J. Holanhaw, C.S.P.; Harold J. Foye, C.S.P.; Robert J. Sadowski, C.S.P.; Francis M. Sweeney, C.S.P.; John P. Campbell, C.S.P.; Michael J. Kallock, C.S.P.; Edward J. McDonald, C.S.P.; Charles E. Cunniff, C.S.P.; Richard J. Colgan, C.S.P. Total in Residence 12; Total Staff 4.

ANDOVER. *Franciscan Center*, 475 River Rd., 01810. Tel: 508-851-3391. Order of Friars Minor. Rev. John D. Bavaro, O.F.M., Dir.; Guardian, Retreat Team. Retreat Team: Revs. Roland Petinge, O.F.M., Vicar; John C. DiMauro, O.F.M.; Robert J. Caprio, O.F.M.; Bro. Gabriel Aceto, O.F.M.; Sr. Lorraine Pianka, S.S.N.D.; Mrs. Mildred Sheehan, Sec.; Jerrie Lou Buffo; Eileen Bowes; Margaret McCarthy; Joanna Howorth. Total in Residence 7; Total Staff 11.

BROCKTON. *Chapel of Our Savior-Catholic Pastoral and Information Center*, 475 Westgate Dr., 02401-1819. Tel: 508-583-8357. Revs. Boniface Riedmann, S.A.; Joseph DiMauro, S.A., Acting Dir.; Malcolm Martin, S.A.; Bro. Louis Marek, S.A. Priests 3; Brothers 1.

PEABODY. *Catholic Information Center*, North Shore Shopping Center, 01960. Tel: 508-531-6145. Revs. Ferdinand T. Schaefer, O.Carm., Dir.; Kilian Healy, O.Carm.; Alan N. Crowley, O.Carm.; Peter Thomas Sherry, O.Carm.; Lambert Zulkie, O.Carm.; Bro. Damien Chong, O.Carm. Priests 8; Brothers 2.

[Q] GENERAL HOSPITALS

BOSTON. *Daughters of Charity National Health System - Boston, Inc.*, 2100 Dorchester Ave., 02124. Tel: 617-296-4000
For a complete listing, refer to the Hospitals section.

BRIGHTON. *St. Elizabeth's Hospital of Boston*, 736 Cambridge St., 02135. Tel: 617-789-3000
For a complete listing, refer to the Hospitals section.

BROCKTON. *Good Samaritan Medical Center*, 235 N. Pearl St., 02401. Tel: 508-427-3000; 427-3151
For a complete listing, refer to the Hospitals section.

LOWELL. *Saints Memorial Health System, Inc.* P.O. Box 30, 01852. Tel: 508-458-1411; Fax: 508-458-8369.
For a complete listing, refer to the Hospitals section.

METHUEN. *Holy Family Hospital and Medical Center*, 70 East St., 01844-4597. Tel: 978-687-0151.
Web site: http://www.holyfamilyhosp.org
For a complete listing, refer to the Hospitals section.

[R] SPECIAL HOSPITALS

BOSTON. *Franciscan Children's Hospital and Rehabilitation Center* 30 Warren St. Brighton, 02135. Tel: 617-254-3800.
For a complete listing, refer to the Special Care Facilities section.

BRIGHTON. *St. John of God Hospital*, 296 Allston St., 02146. Tel: 617-277-5750
For a complete listing, refer to the Special Care Facilities section.

*CAMBRIDGE. *Youville Hospital & Rehabilitation Center, Inc.*, 1575 Cambridge St., 02138-4398. Tel: 617-876-4344
For a complete listing, refer to the Special Care Facilities section.

[S] SOCIAL SERVICES

BOSTON. *The Laboure Center/Catholic Charities*, 371 &

376 W. Fourth St., 02127. Tel: 617-268-9670. Sr. Maryadele Robinson, D.C., Dir. Certified Home Health Services, Elderly Social Services, Early Childhood Services, Adult Day Health Program, Substance Abuse and Mental Health Counseling, Family Intervention Services, Emergency Assistance, Afterschool Programs, and Support Groups. Daughters of Charity of St. Vincent de Paul 5.

DORCHESTER. *Little Sisters of the Assumption, Family Health Service, Inc.* (Project Hope), 45 Magnolia St., 02125. Tel: 617-442-1880; Fax: 617-442-1356. A community based shelter for homeless families offering food pantry, education, child care and social services. Total Assisted 1,776; Staff 35; Sisters 3.

LEXINGTON. *Grey Nuns Adult Day Health Center, Inc.*, 10 Pelham Rd., 02173. Sr. Dorothy Cooper, S.G.M., Prov. Supvr.

[T] PROTECTIVE INSTITUTIONS

BOSTON. *St. Mary's Women and Infants Center* 90 Cushing Ave. Dorchester, 02125.
For a complete listing, refer to the Special Care Facilities section.

[U] HOMES FOR AGED-RESIDENTS & NURSING

BOSTON. *Don Orione Nursing Home* 111 Orient Ave. East Boston, 02128. Tel: 617-569-2100.
For a complete listing, refer to the Special Care Facilities section.

Marian Manor, (1954) 130 Dorchester St. South Boston, 02127. Tel: 617-268-3333.
For a complete listing, refer to the Special Care Facilities section.

St. Joseph Nursing Care Center 321 Centre St. Dorchester, 02122. Tel: 617-825-6320; Fax: 617-825-7410.
For a complete listing, refer to the Special Care Facilities section.

BROCKTON. *St. Joseph Manor Nursing & Extended Care Facility*, 215 Thatcher St., 02402-3999. Tel: 508-583-5834; Fax: 508-583-8551
For a complete listing, refer to the Special Care Facilities section.

*CAMBRIDGE. *Youville Healthcare Center, Inc.*, 1575 Cambridge St., 02138-4398. Tel: 617-876-4344
For a complete listing, refer to the Special Care Facilities section.

FRAMINGHAM. *Carmel Terrace*, 933 Central St., 01701. Tel: 508-788-8000
For a complete listing, refer to the Special Care Facilities section.

St. Patrick's Manor, Inc., 863 Central St., 01701. Tel: 508-879-8000; Fax: 508-626-1604
For a complete listing, refer to the Special Care Facilities section.

*LAWRENCE. *M.I. Adult Day Health Center, Inc.*, 189 Maple St., 01841. Tel: 508-682-7575
For a complete listing, refer to the Special Care Facilities section.

M.I. Nursing-Restorative Center, Inc., 172 Lawrence St., 01841. Tel: 508-685-6321
For a complete listing, refer to the Special Care Facilities section.

M.I. Residential Community II, Inc., 191 Maple St., 01841. Tel: 508-682-7575
For a complete listing, refer to the Special Care Facilities section.

M.I. Residential Community III, Inc., 193 Maple St., 01841. Tel: 508-682-7575
For a complete listing, refer to the Special Care Facilities section.

M.I. Residential Community, Inc., 189 Maple St., 01841. Tel: 508-682-7575
For a complete listing, refer to the Special Care Facilities section.

**M.I. Transportation, Inc.*, 189 Maple St., 01841. Tel: 508-682-7575
For a complete listing, refer to the Special Care Facilities section.

LOWELL. *D'Youville Manor*, 981 Varnum Ave., 01854. Tel: 508-454-5681
For a complete listing, refer to the Special Care Facilities section.

MARLBORO. *Marie Esther Health Center, Inc.*, 720 Boston Post Rd., 01752. Tel: 508-485-3791
For a complete listing, refer to the Special Care Facilities section.

SOMERVILLE. *Jeanne Jugan Pavilion*, 190 Highland Ave., 02143
For a complete listing, refer to the Special Care Facilities section.

Jeanne Jugan Residence, 186 Highland Ave., 02143. Tel: 617-776-4420; Fax: 617-623-0707
For a complete listing, refer to the Special Care Facilities section.

WALTHAM. *Maristhill Nursing & Rehabilitation Center*, 66 Newton St., 02154. Tel: 781-893-0240; Fax: 781-894-6330
For a complete listing, refer to the Special Care Facilities section.

[V] PERSONAL PRELATURES

CAMBRIDGE. *Opus Dei, Prelature of the Holy Cross and Opus Dei*, 25 Follen St., 02138. Tel: 617-354-3204.
Web site: http://www.opusdei.org
Rev. John C. Agnew.

CHESTNUT HILL. *Opus Dei*, 481 Hammond St., 02167. Tel: 617-738-7348.
Web site: http://www.opusdei.org
Revs. David Cavanagh; Richard W. Rieman; Alvaro Silva; Raphael Caamano; Timothy J. Uhen.

[W] MONASTERIES AND RESIDENCES OF PRIESTS AND BROTHERS

BOSTON. *Arrupe House*, 35 Creighton St., 02130. Tel: 617-524-9328. Revs. James A. Gillon, S.J., Supr. & Novice Dir.; Walter M. Abbott, S.J.; Francis H. Belcher, S.J. Priests 3; Novices 9.

Divine Word Missionaries, 184 Beacon St., 02116. Tel: 617-267-5143; Fax: 617-267-0726. Divine Word Missionaries. Revs. Donald P. Mulrenan, S.V.D., Supr. & Mission Dir.; Joseph Connolly, S.V.D., Asst. Mission Dir. In res. Revs. William Kane, S.V.D.; Donald Skerry, S.V.D.; Bro. Noel Tecson, S.V.D.

Jesuit Urban Center & Immaculate Conception Community, 775 Harrison Ave., 02118-2311. Tel: 617-536-8440; Fax: 617-536-2142.
E-mail: jucboston@aol.com
Revs. David I. Donovan, S.J., Supr.; Charles B. Connolly, S.J., Minister and Treas.; Denis R. Como, S.J.; John R. d'Anjou, S.J.; Jon D. Fuller, S.J.; Thomas J. Gallagher, S.J.; James M. Shaughnessy, S.J.; Simon E. Smith, S.J.; George P. Winchester, S.J.

Little Brothers of St. Francis, 785-789 Parker St., 02120. Tel: 617-442-2556. Bro. James Curran, L.B.S.F., Guardian. Regional Fraternity and Novitiate. Legal Title: *Little Brothers of St. Francis Franciscan Fraternity of Peace and Love.* Brothers 3; Novices 1; Postulants 2.

Loyola House, 300 Newbury St., 02115. Tel: 617-267-1008.
E-mail: loybos@aol.com
The Society of Jesus. Revs. Joseph J. Bruce, S.J.; Thomas F. Clark, S.J.; Herbert J. Cleary, S.J.; John T. Crabb, S.J.; Charles G. Crowley, S.J.; William J. Cullen, S.J.; William F. Doyle, S.J.; John E. Fagan, S.J.; William G. Guindon, S.J.; Robert F. Hoey, S.J.; Norman H. Houle, S.J.; William J. Larkin, S.J.; Paul T. Lucey, S.J.; Robert G. McMillan, S.J.; George S. Mahan, S.J.; Edward J. Murawski, S.J.; William J. Raftery, S.J., Supr.; Joseph A. Riel, S.J.; James T. Sheehan, S.J.; S. Jin-yeul Song, S.J.; Alfred O. Winshman, S.J.; Bros. John Wu Po-Jeh, S.J.; Paul J. Geysen, S.J.; James J. Moran, S.J.; Austin J. Burns, S.J. Priests 21; Brothers 3; Scholastics 1; Total in Residence 25; Total Staff 5.

Marist Fathers and Brothers Provincial House, 27 Isabella St., 02116-5216. Tel: 617-426-5297; 426-4448; Fax: 617-482-1570. Very Rev. Kenneth Thibodeau, S.M., Prov.; Rev. Albert DiIanni, S.M., Vicar Prov.
Priests of the Province Not Listed Elsewhere: Rev. William Foley, S.M., (Retired Army Chaplain-Leave of Absence), 31 Fillmore Ct., Satellite Beach, FL, 32937. Rev. Armand Thibault, S.M., 27 Isabella St., 02116-5216. Rev. Robert Poirier, S.M., Rocky Creek Village, 8629 Quartz St., #208, Tampa, FL, 33615-1434. Rev. Faustino Cruz, S.M., 28 Colborne Rd., Apt. 14, Brighton, 02135. Rev. Joseph Hindelang, S.M., 27 Isabella St., 02116-5216. Rev. Gerard Timmerman, S.M., 4 Christine Ave., Stoneham, 02180-3093.

Marist Fathers Lourdes Residence, 698 Beacon St., 02215. Tel: 617-262-2271. Revs. Gerard Caron, S.M., Dir.; Michael Pavlick, S.M.; Paul H. Pepin, S.M.; J. Armand Robichaud, S.M. Priests 4.

Marist Fathers of Our Lady of Victories (Boston Prov.), 27 Isabella St., 02116. Tel: 617-426-4448. Revs. Andrew R. Albert, S.M.; Kenneth Thibodeau, S.M.; Lucien Chasse, S.M.; Joseph Hindelang, S.M.; Albert DiIanni, S.M.; Philip Laplante, S.M.; Armand Robichaud, S.M.; Armand Thibault, S.M.; Bros. Roland Bernier, S.M.; Jude Roy, S.M.; Gregory Theriault, S.M. Priests 8; Brothers 3; Sisters 5.

Ministry of the Word. Revs. Philip O'Shea, O.F.M.; John Anglin, O.F.M.; James Fitzmaurice, O.F.M.; Bro. Robert Frazzetta, O.F.M.

Paulist Fathers Residence, 5 Park St., 02108-4897. Tel: 617-742-4460.
E-mail: stancsp@aol.com
Revs. Stanley F. MacNevin, C.S.P., Supr.; John P. Campbell, C.S.P.; Charles E. Cunniff, C.S.P.; Harold J. Foye, C.S.P.; Joseph T. Griffin, C.S.P.; Paul A. Reynolds, C.S.P.; Michael J. Kallock, C.S.P., Dir.; Richard Colgan, C.S.P.; Edward J. McDonald, C.S.P.; Robert J. Sadowski, C.S.P.; Walter J. Sullivan, C.S.P.; Francis M. Sweeney, C.S.P. Total in Residence 12; Total Staff 3.

St. Christopher Friary, 18 N. Bennet St., Box 230, 02113. Tel: 617-742-4190. Revs. Primo P. Piscitello, O.F.M., Guardian; Francis DeSales Paolo, O.F.M.; Regis Gallo, O.F.M.; Friars Michael Ciryak, O.F.M.; Michael DellaPenna, O.F.M.; Vit Fiala, O.F.M.; Michael MacInnis, O.F.M.; Richard Martignetti, O.F.M.; Christopher Meyers, O.F.M.; Juniper O'Connor, O.F.M.; Edwin Paniagua, O.F.M.; Lawrence Parent, O.F.M.; Thomas Washburn, O.F.M.; James Welch, O.F.M. Priests 4; Brothers 11.

The Society of Jesus of New England-Provincial Offices, 771 Harrison Ave., 02118-2311. Tel: 617-266-7233; Fax: 617-536-8074.
E-mail: wjk@world.std.com
Revs. Robert J. Levens, S.J., Prov.; John P. Murray, S.J., Socius to Prov., Asst. for Secondary Education & Liason for Formation; Ronald Anderson, S.J., Asst. for Higher Education; Thomas J. Gibbons, S.J., Asst. for Prov. Finances; William C. Russell, S.J., Asst. for Development & Vocation Dir.; Thomas H. Schneider, S.J., Liason for Intl. Ministries; James F. Walsh, S.J., Liason for Social Ministries; Deacon William R. Campbell, Liason for Pastoral Ministries.
Priests of Province on Special Assignment: Revs. Albert A. Agresti, S.J.; George S. Albert, S.J.; Brian E. Albino, S.J.; Joseph A. Appleyard, S.J.; Robert J. Araujo, S.J.; Edward J. Banks, S.J.; John J. Begley, S.J.; Aram J. Berard, S.J.; Richard D. Bertrand, S.J.; B. Jeffrey Blangiardi, S.J.; Stephen J. Bonian, S.J.; James M. Bowler, S.J.; Richard P. Boyle, S.J.; Robert J. Braunreuther, S.J.; James F. Bresnahan, S.J.; Scott N. Brodeur, S.J.; Joseph J. Bruce, S.J.; Robert R. Burke, S.J.; Gregory C. Chisholm, S.J.; Thomas F. Clark, S.J.; Michael J. Connolly, S.J.; Joseph D. Devlin, S.J.; Michael J. Doody, S.J.; Robert R. Dorin, S.J.; Robert F. Drinan, S.J.; Raymond V. Dunn, S.J.; John E. Fagan, S.J.; Michael A. Fahey, S.J.; Peter J. Fennessy, S.J.; Gerald F. Finnegan, S.J.; James J. Fleming, S.J.; John F. Foley, S.J.; William B. Foley, S.J.; Anthony J. Forte, S.J.; Francois Gick, S.J.; Robert G. Gilroy, S.J.; Julio Giulietti, S.J.; Donald F. Grady, S.J.; William J. Hamilton, S.J.; John B. Handrahan, S.J.; Robert M. Hanlon, S.J.; Paul F. Harman, S.J.; Charles J. Healey, S.J.; Daniel P. Jamros, S.J.; John J. Karwin, S.J.; James M. Keegan, S.J.; Charles F. Kelley, S.J.; William J. Kennedy, S.J.; Philip S. Kiley, S.J.; Michael J. Kossak, S.J.; James F. Lafontaine, S.J.; Robert E. Lindsay, S.J.; Kenneth G. Loftus, S.J.; Daniel J. Lusch, S.J.; Frederic A. Maples, S.J.; Richard B. McCafferty, S.J.; Martin F. McCarthy, S.J.; Michael C. McFarland, S.J.; Peter R. McGrath, S.J.; Frederick G. McLeod, S.J.; Francis J. McManus, S.J.; Robert G. McMillan, S.J.; Ronald A. Mercier, S.J.; John J. Moriarty, S.J.; Francis J. Moy, S.J.; John J. Mullen, S.J.; Joseph E. Mullen, S.J.; John F. Mullin, S.J.; George R. Murphy, S.J.; Frederick J. O'Brien, S.J.; Thomas P. O'Malley, S.J.; Francis J. O'Neill, S.J.; Lawrence J. O'Toole, S.J.; Arthur H. Pare, S.J.; Robert V. Paskey, S.J.; Ernest F. Passero, S.J.; Anthony R. Picariello, S.J.; James F.X. Pratt, S.J.; Robert F. Regan, S.J.; Richard W. Rousseau, S.J.; Gregory R. Roy, S.J.; Solomon I. Sara, S.J.; Francis X. Sarjeant, S.J.; Thomas J. Savage, S.J.; Joseph J. Schad, S.J.; Andrew J. Scopp, S.J.; James M. Shea, S.J.; James F. Sheehan, S.J.; John F.X. Sheehan, S.J.; Myles N. Sheehan, S.J.; Thomas J. Sheehan, S.J.; Edward J. Small, S.J.; Walter J. Smith, S.J.; Paul M. Sullivan, S.J.; Robert J. Sullivan, S.J.; John E. Surette, S.J.; Paul J. Tabor, S.J.; Robert F. Taft, S.J.; David O. Travers, S.J.; James F. Walsh, S.J.; John Joseph Walsh, S.J.; Terrance G. Walsh, S.J.; Ronald E. Wozniak, S.J.; Walter J. Young, S.J.
Chaplains: Revs. Robert L. Keane, S.J.; Lawrence C. Smith, S.J., Res. Ignatius House, 771 Harrison Ave, 02118-2311. Revs. John P. Murray, S.J.; Thomas J. Gibbons, S.J.; Alfred J. Hicks, S.J.; Walter J. Kane, S.J.; Paul C. Kenney, S.J.; Robert J. Levens, S.J.; James G. Stinson, S.J.; Bros. Edward P. Babinski, S.J.; H. Francis Cluff, S.J.; James P. McDavitt, S.J. Priests 7; Brothers 3.

The Society of St. James the Apostle, Inc., 24 Clark St., 02109. Tel: 617-742-4715. Revs. Gabriel Troy, Dir.; Patrick J. Cleary (England); Milton Eggerling (OAK).
Founded by His Eminence Richard Cardinal Cushing, in 1958 to recruit Priest volunteers for South America. See American Foreign Missions Section for Diocesan Priests serving in Latin America.

ANDOVER. *St. Francis Friary*, 459 River Rd., 01810. Tel: 508-851-3391. Revs. Roland Petinge, O.F.M., Vicar, Retreat Team; John D. Bavaro, O.F.M., Dir., Guardian, Retreat Team; John C. DiMauro, O.F.M., Retreat Team; Robert J. Caprio, O.F.M., Retreat Team; Dennis Wheatley, O.F.M.; Bro. Gabriel Aceto, O.F.M. Total in Residence 7; Total Staff 11.

BRIGHTON. *Assumptionist Center*, 330 Market St., 02135. Tel: 617-783-0400. Very Rev. John L. Franck, A.A., Prov. Supr.; Bro. Stephen Goguen, A.A., Prov. Treas., Supr.; Revs. Ernest Fortin, A.A.; Joseph Richard, A.A.; Richard E. Richards, A.A.; Yvon Dubois, A.A.;

George Tavard, A.A.
Assumption Guild, Inc.: Bro. Stephen Goguen, A.A., Dir.
Attached to Province: Rev. Gregory Boisvert, A.A., Our Lady of Fatima Church, 860 Louisville Rd., Alcoa, TN, 37701. Rev. Theodore L. Fortier, A.A., St. John, 21 Gay St., Quincy, 02169. Rev. Anselm Morrison, A.A., Immaculate Conception, 98 Summer St., Portsmouth, NH, 03801. Rev. John Martin, A.A., 229 W. 14th St., New York, NY, 10011.
Serving Abroad: Rev. Claude Grenache, A.A., Parroquia Emperatriz de America, Mercaderes 99, 03900 Mexico D.F., Mexico. Rev. Norman Meiklejohn, A.A., P.O. Box 57, Moscow, Russia, 121248. Rev. Gary Perron, A.A., Parroquia Emperatriz de America, Mercaderes 99, 03900 Mexico D.F., Mexico. Rev. Camillus Thibault, A.A., Parroquia de la Emperatriz, Mercaderes 99, Mexico D.F., Mexico. Rev. Roger Tougas, A.A., Montmartre Canadien, 1676 Chemin, St. Louis, Quebec, QUE GIS 165, Canada. Rev. Robert Fortin, A.A., St. Peter in Gallicantu, P.O. Box 31653, 91316 Jerusalem, Israel. Rev. Leo Brassard, A.A., 836-24 Naebang Dong, Sogu, Korea, 502-250. Revs. Luc Martel, A.A.; Richard Brunelle, A.A., Assumptionist Community, P.O. Box 58488, Nairobi, Kenya.
Special Situations: Rev. John Martin, A.A.; Edward Pepka, A.A.

Carmelite Monastery, 166 Foster St., 02135-3902. Tel: 617-787-5056; Fax: 617-783-1396. Discalced Carmelite Friars. Revs. Giles Dzuban, O.C.D.; Emmanuel Sullivan, O.C.D.; Anthony Haglof, O.C.D.; Vincent Bowes, O.C.D.; Paul Trementozzi, O.C.D.; Lawrence F. Sullivan, O.C.D.; Albert Bourke, O.C.D.; Michael Dodd, O.C.D.; Salvatore Sciurba, O.C.D.; Stephen-Joseph Ross, O.C.D.; Benedict Bishop, O.C.D. Priests 11; Brothers 1; Total in Residence 14.

St. Bonaventure Friary, Franciscan Friars, 284 Foster St., 02135. Tel: 617-254-2447.
E-mail: sbonfriary@aol.com
Revs. Primo P. Piscitello, O.F.M., Guardian; Valerian Faugno, O.F.M., Vicar, Proc., FMU Prom.
In Formation: Bros. Michael Ciryak, O.F.M.; Michael Della Penna, O.F.M.; Vit Fiala, O.F.M.; Michael MacInnis, O.F.M.; Lawrence Parent, O.F.M.; Thomas Washburn, O.F.M. Priests 2.

St. Gabriel's Passionist Community, 139 Washington St., 02135-4235. Tel: 617-254-6582; 254-8512. The Congregation of the Passion (The Passionists). Rev. Justinian Manning, C.P., Supr. Pastor. In res. Revs. Brendan Breen, C.P.; Marcellus White, C.P.; Daniel Hunt, C.P.; Clement Kasinskas, C.P. Priests 5.

St. Gabriel's Residence, 201 Washington St., 02135. Tel: 617-787-0859. The Congregation of the Passion (The Passionists). Revs. Canisius W. Hazlett, C.P.; Daniel J. Hunt, C.P.; Marcellus R. White, C.P. Priests 3.

BROCKTON. *Chapel of Our Saviour*, 475 Westgate Dr., 02401-1819. Tel: 508-583-8357. Franciscan Friars of the Atonement. Revs. Boniface Riedmann, S.A.; Joseph Di Mauro, S.A., Acting Dir.; Malcolm Martin, S.A.; Bro. Louis Marek, S.A. Priests 3; Brothers 1.

CAMBRIDGE. *Faber House*, 42 Kirkland St., 02138. Tel: 617-497-5564. Revs. Thomas Brodie, O.P. (Ireland); Kevin F. Burke, S.J. (Missouri); Kenneth J. Hughes, S.J. (New England); Robert Kaslyn, S.J. (New York); G. Thomas Krettek, S.J. (Wisconsin); Timothy R. Lannon, S.J. (Wisconsin), House Coord.; William L. Mulligan, S.J. (New England); Christopher Pedley, S.J. (Great Britain); William Russel, S.J. (New England); Hae-Wuk Ryu, S.J. (Korea); Thomas H. Schneider, S.J. (New England); Augustine Tsang, S.J. (California); Bros. Thomas Williams, S.J. (Maryland); Christopher Daignault, S.S.E., Scholastics; Mark Torres, S.J. (California). Residence for Jesuit Priests and Scholastics.

Our Lady of Mercy Marist Novitiate, 15 Notre Dame Ave., 02140-2598. Tel: 617-354-6214. Revs. Philip Parent, S.M., Novice Dir.; Michael McElhinny, S.M., Novice Dir. Novices 3.

Weston Jesuit Community, 20 Sumner Rd., 02138. Tel: 617-547-3742. Rev. John J. O'Donnell, S.J., Rector.
Residences of Priests: Rev. Richard J. Clifford, S.J., 7 Kirkland Rd., 02138. Tel: 617-661-4155. Rev. Edward Glynn, S.J., Claver House, 7 Kirkland Rd., 01238. Tel: 617-661-4155. Rev. William Ibach, S.J., 15 Hawthorn St., 02138. Tel: 617-497-0164. Rev. Frank J. Devine, S.J., 15 Hawthorn St., 02138. Tel: 617-497-6621. Rev. Peter E. Fink, S.J., 6 Sumner Rd., 02138. Tel: 617-547-5310. Rev. Daniel J. Harrington, S.J., 12 Linnaean St., 02138. Tel: 617-547-0931. Rev. Stanley B. Marrow, S.J., 3 Phillips Pl., 02138. Tel: 617-492-1960. Rev. Thomas Massaro, S.J., Xavier House, 80 Lexington Ave., 02138. Tel: 617-491-0864. Rev. James Keenan, S.J., 10 Martin St., 02138. Tel: 617-491-2155. Rev. John W. O'Malley, S.J., 10 Martin St., 02138. Tel: 617-491-2155. Rev. John R. Sachs, S.J., 6 Sumner Rd., 02136. Tel: 617-547-5310. Rev. Edward V. Vacek, S.J., 40 Kirkland St., 02138. Tel: 617-868-6568. Rev. Roger D. Haight, S.J., 7 Kirkland Rd., 02138. Tel: 617-661-4155. Rev. Robert Kaslyn, S.J., 42 Kirkland St., 02138. Tel: 617-497-5564. Rev. William Mulligan, S.S., Faber House, 42 Kirkland St., 02138. Tel: 617-497-5564. Rev. Kenneth J. Hughes, S.J., 42 Kirkland St., 02138. Tel: 617-497-5565. Rev. Kevin F. Burke, S.J., 42 Kirkland St., 02138. Tel: 617-497-5564. Rev. George L. Drury, S.J., 40 Kirkland St., 02138. Tel: 617-497-5564. Rev. Robert E. Manning, S.J., 7 Kirkland Rd., 02138. Rev. William C. Russell, S.J., 42 Kirkland St., 02138. Priests 42; Brothers 3; Scholastics 48.

CHESTNUT HILL. *The Jesuit Community at Boston College*, 02167. Tel: 617-552-8200.
Web site: http://fmwww.bc.edu/sj/
Very Rev. Frank R. Herrmann, S.J., Rector; Revs. James M. Collins, S.J., Admin. & Treas. & Asst. Rector; Francis J. Nicholson, S.J., Asst. Rector; Edward M. O'Flaherty, S.J., Asst. Rector; R. Bentley Anderson, S.J. (New Orleans); Ronald Anderson, S.J.; Joseph A. Appleyard, S.J.; Felipe Bacalso, S.J. (Philippines/China); J. Robert Barth, S.J. (New York); James W. Bernauer, S.J. (New York); Stanley J. Bezuszka, S.J.; Richard Blake, S.J. (NY); Jeyarah Boniface, S.J. (India); Thomas Brennan, S.J. (Wisconsin); Michael Buckley, S.J. (California); Edward R. Callahan, S.J.; John F. Caulfield, S.J.; Richard T. Cleary, S.J.; Francis X. Clooney, S.J. (New York); John J.L. Collins, S.J.; Walter Conlan, S.J. (BAH); Joseph J. Connor, S.J.; J. Daniel Daly, S.J. (Missouri); Robert J. Daly, S.J.; Neil F. Decker, S.J.; John F. Devane, S.J.; Terrence P. Devino, S.J.; John A. Dinneen, S.J. (New York); Charles F. Donovan, S.J.; Joseph P. Duffy, S.J.; William Dych, S.J. (Maryland); Theodore Dziak, S.J.; Harvey D. Egan, S.J.; Frederick Enman, S.J.; Wellington Fernando, S.J. (India); Robert Farrell, S.J.; Joseph F. X. Flanagan, S.J.; Thomas F. Fleming, S.J.; David H. Gill, S.J.; Paul P. Gilmartin, S.J.; Joseph A. Glavin, S.J.; Howard Gray, S.J. (Detroit); Gary Gurtler, S.J. (New York); Edward J. Hanrahan, S.J.; Charles J. Healey, S.J.; Raymond G. Helmick, S.J.; David Hollenbach, S.J. (Maryland); John W. Howard, S.J.; John Izzo, S.J. (California); T. Frank Kennedy, S.J.; Peter Kim Se Mang, S.J. (Indonesia); Kevin Kersten, S.J. (Korea); Geoffrey King, S.J. (Australia); William Leahy, S.J. (Wisconsin); William J. Larkin, S.J.; William J. Leonard, S.J.; Francis Liuima, S.J. (Lithuania); Daniel J. Lusch, S.J.; Martin MacDonnell, S.J.; Arthur A. MacGillivray, S.J.; Francis C. Mackin, S.J.; Donald A. MacMillan, S.J.; Arthur R. Madigan, S.J. (New York); James B. Malley, S.J.; Paulin Manwelo, S.J. (Central Africa); Douglas Marcouiller, S.J. (Missouri); James Mattaliano, S.J.; Richard A. McGowan, S.J. (Maryland); William McInnes, S.J.; John P. McIntyre, S.J.; William W. Meissner, S.J. (New York); Paul McNellis, S.J. (NY); Paul A. Messer, S.J.; Daryl Miranda, S.J. (CSU); Francis P. Molloy, S.J.; J. Donald Monan, S.J. (New York), Pres.; James F. Morgan, S.J.; Franco Mormando, S.J.; Bruce Morrill, S.J.; Frederick L. Moriarty, S.J.; John F. Mullin, S.J.; Paul A. Nash, S.J.; William B. Neenan, S.J. (Wisconsin); Edward H. Nowlan, S.J.; Gerard C. O'Brien, S.J.; James C. O'Brien, S.J.; Joseph O'Keefe, S.J.; Virgilio Oliveira e.Costa, S.J. (Portugal); Cyril Opeil, S.J. (Maryland); John Paris, S.J.; Frank J. Parker, S.J.; Donald J. Plocke, S.J.; Joseph F. Quane, S.J.; William J. Richardson, S.J. (New York); Herminio Rico, S.J. (Portugal); James W. Ring, S.J.; Jesse Rodriguez, S.J. (New Orleans); Patrick J. Ryan, S.J.; John Savard, S.J.; Magdi Seif, S.J. (Egypt); Joop Schopman, S.J. (Netherlands); Arul Sivan, S.J. (Madurai); James W. Skehan, S.J.; John Spencer, S.J.; Francis A. Sullivan, S.J.; William Sullivan, S.J. (Wisconsin); Francis W. Sweeney, S.J.; Ronald K. Tacelli, S.J.; Felix F. Talbot, S.J.; Charles B. Toomey, S.J.; Benedict Triatmoko, S.J. (Indonesia); Joao J. Vila-Cha, S.J. (Portugal/Lusitania); Andrea Vicini, S.J. (Italy); Francis W. Vye, S.J.; Gerard Walmsley, S.J. (Great Britain); John R. Willis, S.J.; James A. Woods, S.J.; Dennis J. Yesalonia, S.J.; Michael Zampelli, S.J. (Maryland).

COHASSET. *Bellarmine House*, 150 Howard Gleason Rd., 02025. Tel: 617-383-0723. Rev. James M. Collins, S.J., Admin. (Summer Res. for Jesuits of New England Prov.).

DANVERS. *Xavier Center*, 21 Spring St., 01923. Tel: 508-777-1326. American Northeastern Province of The Brothers of St. Francis Xavier (Xaverian Brothers). Bro. John D. Hamilton, C.F.X., Dir. of Formation, House of Formation. Brothers Professed 3.

DEDHAM. *African Mission House*. Society of African Missions, Inc. 269-337 Common St., 02026-4030. Tel: 617-326-3288; 326-4670.
E-mail: smausa-d@ix.netcom.com
Web site: http://www.smafathers.org
Revs. Thomas E. Hayden, S.M.A.; Paul W. Alrutz, S.M.A.; James F. Callahan, S.M.A.; Francis B. Gillis, S.M.A.; James B. Hill, S.M.A.; Michael J. Rooney, S.M.A.; John P. Sweeney, S.M.A.; Michael J. Feeley, S.M.A.; James C. Hickey, S.M.A.; Francis S. Hynes, S.M.A. Priests 10.

DOVER. *St. Stephen Priory*, 20 Glen St., Box 370, 02030. Tel: 508-785-0124; Fax: 508-785-1020. Revs. Walter C. Wagner, O.P., Prior; John E. Allard, O.P.; E. Henry Gallagher, O.P.; Bruce A. Williams, O.P.; Richard A. Fleck, O.P.; John Stephen Fitzhenry, O.P.; Stephen D. Ryan, O.P.; Bro. Patrick Foley, O.P. Spiritual Life Center and Retreat Center. Priests 7; Religious Brothers 1.

DUXBURY. *Society of the Divine Word*, 121 Parks St., P.O. Box M, 02331. Tel: 617-585-2460. Revs. Edward Dudink, S.V.D.; John J. Bergin, S.V.D.; Edward Tuohy, S.V.D.; Robert Mallonee, S.V.D.; Robert Jones, S.V.D., Rector; Patrick Wenrick, S.V.D. Priests 6.

EAST WALPOLE. *Maryknoll Department of Development*, 80 Emerson Rd., 02032-1349. Tel: 508-668-6831.
E-mail: mklboston@igc.org
Revs. Fernand L. Gosselin, M.M.; Alfred Keane, M.M.; Gerald E. Kelly, M.M., Dir.

HINGHAM. *Glastonbury Abbey*, 16 Hull St., 02043. Tel: 617-749-2155; Fax: 617-749-6236.
E-mail: office@glastonburyabbey.org
Web site: http://www.glastonburyabbey.org
Rt. Revs. Nicholas J. Morcone, O.S.B., Abbot; Edward C. Campbell, O.S.B., Retired Abbot; Very Rev. Timothy J. Joyce, Prior; Revs. Andrew M. Quillen; Paul J. Evich, O.S.B.; Gerald T. Leibenguth, O.S.B.; Richard J. Bourgeois, O.S.B.; Thomas J. O'Connor; Roger Nolette; Bros. David K. Coakley, O.S.B.; James Crowley, O.S.B.; Daniel F. Walters, O.S.B. Priests 9; Brothers 3. Retreat Center. Benedictine Monks. Capacity 29. Lincoln School Apartments for the Elderly.

HOLLISTON. *Xaverian Missionaries*, Mission Education Center, 101 Summer St., P.O. Box 5857, 01746-5857. Tel: 508-429-2144. Revs. Robert S. Maloney, S.X., Supr.; Dominic Calarco, S.X.; Tony Lalli, S.X.; Ivan Marchesin, S.X.; Aniello Salicone, S.X. Priests 5.

IPSWICH. *Missionaries of Our Lady of LaSalette Corp.* National Shrine of Our Lady of LaSalette. Formation Res., 251 Topsfield Rd., 01938-1195. Tel: 508-356-3151.

LAWRENCE. *Marist Brothers Residence*, 12 Sheridan St., 01841. Tel: 508-682-1163. Bros. William Lambert, F.M.S., Dir.; C. Vincent Dinnean, F.M.S.; Ernest Beland, F.M.S.; Richard Carey, F.M.S. Brothers 4.

LOWELL. *Missionary Oblates of Mary Immaculate*, 27 Kirk St., 01852. Tel: 508-937-9594. Andre Garin Retirement Residence. Bro. Charles Gilbert, Dir. Tel: 508-441-1245; Revs. Roland Couture, Asst. Dir.; Lionel Desjardins; George Dupont; Marcel Bolduc; Bro. Josephe Gagne.

Missionary Oblates of Mary Immaculate. St. Eugene House, 285 Andover St., 01852. Tel: 978-441-0649; Fax: 978-454-0677. Revs. Charles Breault, O.M.I.; Herve Gagnon, O.M.I.; Lucien Richard, O.M.I.; Francis Demers, O.M.I., Preaching Team; Bevil Bramwell, O.M.I. Total in Residence 5.

Missionary Oblates of Mary Immaculate. Administration Office, 60 Wyman St., 01852. Tel: 978-458-9912; Fax: 978-458-7274. Revs. Charles Breault, O.M.I., Prov. Treas.; Herve Gagnon, O.M.I., Asst. Treas. Total Staff 2.

LYNN. *Franciscan Community (Province of Immaculate Conception)*, 38 Michigan Ave., 01902. Tel: 617-592-7396; Fax: 617-593-8805. Revs. Alfonse Ferreira, O.F.M., Procurator & Guardian; Bede Ferrara, O.F.M.

"The Listening Place", 36 Michigan Ave., 01902. Rev. Alfonse Ferreira, O.F.M., Dir.; Sr. Jane Hogan, O.S.F., Assoc. Dir.

MILTON. *Oblate Residence (St. Joseph House)*, 65 Fr. Carney Dr., 02186-4206. Tel: 617-698-6785; Fax: 617-698-7621. Congregation of the Oblates of the Virgin Mary. Revs. Timothy Gallagher, O.M.V.; D. Clifford Graham, O.M.V.; Donald Kelpinski, O.M.V.; David Kueter, O.M.V.; Robert Lowry, O.M.V.; James Nibler, O.M.V.; Gerald Wright, O.M.V.; Bro. Joseph O'Connor, O.M.V. Priests 7; Brothers 1.

Xaverian Brothers, 704 Brush Hill Rd., 02186. Tel: 617-333-0970.
E-mail: edkeefecfx@aol.com
Bros. Alois O'Toole, C.F.X.; John Dagwell, C.F.X.; Edward Keefe, C.F.X.; Sebastian Barresi, C.F.X. Brothers 4; Total in Residence 5.

NATICK. *Annunciation Friary*, 29 Purington Ave., 01760.

QUINCY. *St. Columban's Foreign Mission Society*, 310 Adams St., 02169. Tel: 472-1494. Rev. John S. Roche, S.S.C., P.O. Box 227, Humarock, 02047. Rev. Edward A. Roberts, S.S.C., 20 Frisbie Rd., Marshfield, 02050. Rev. James O'Brien, Supr., 310 Adams St., 02169. Rev. Michael Breen, S.S.C., 310 Adams St., 02169. Rev. Charles B. Flaherty, S.S.C., St. John Chrystostom, 4750 Washington St., West Roxbury, 02132. Rev. Michael F. Cody, S.S.C., 310

Adams St., 02169. Rev. George V. Herrgott, S.S.C., 78 Tyler St., Boston, 02111. Rev. Joseph L. Crehan, S.S.C., Immaculate Conception, 487 Broadway, Everett, 02149. Rev. Francis J. Keaney, S.S.C. (Philippines), 22 Border St., Winchester, 01890. Rev. Paul O'Malley, S.S.C., Presentation Apts., #54, 309 Church St., Clinton, 01510. Priests 8.

SOMERVILLE. *Brotherhood of Hope*, 194 Summer St., 02143-2525. Tel: 617-623-9592; Fax: 617-625-1837. E-mail: bh-hope@juno.com
Total in Residence 16.

TEWKSBURY. *Oblate Fathers-Oblate World/Missionary Association of Mary Immaculate*, 486 Chandler St., Box 680, 01876. Rev. Thomas J. Reddy, O.M.I., Editor & Prov. Dir.

Oblate Fathers-Office of the Provincial Treasurer, 486 Chandler St., Box 419, 01876; Fax: 508-858-3661. Rev. Patrick J. Hollywood, O.M.I., Prov. Treas. Legal Title: *Society of Oblate Fathers for Missions Among the Poor.*

WALTHAM. *Stigmatine Fathers & Brothers Provincial House*, 554 Lexington St., 02154. Tel: 617-894-7713. Very Rev. Robert S. White, C.S.S., Prov. Supr.; Revs. Anthony Corigliano, C.S.S.; Charles Dolan, C.S.S. (Thailand); Donald Toner, C.S.S.; Richard Woodarek, C.S.S. (Thailand); John Ford, C.S.S. (Brazil); Carmen Russo, C.S.S.

Stigmatine House. Bertoni Hall, 554 Lexington, 02154. Tel: 617-899-6525. Revs. David F. Gallagher, C.S.S.; Francis L. Keefe, C.S.S.; Pius C.W. Murray, C.S.S.; Anthony Penna, C.S.S.; Donald Higgins, C.S.S.; Nicholas Spagnolo, C.S.S.

WESTON. *Campion Center*, 319 Concord Rd., 02193. Tel: 617-894-0751; Fax: 617-894-5864. Revs. Ronald J. Amiot, S.J., Rector; Edward J. Banks, S.J.; David G. Boulton, S.J.; John F. Broderick, S.J.; Harry J. Cain, S.J.; Joseph H. Casey, S.J.; Ned H. Cassem, S.J.; Lawrence E. Corcoran, S.J.; John J. Diskin, S.J.; Robert G. Doherty, S.J.; Thomas P. Donovan, S.J.; Robert T. Ferrick, S.J.; John F. Foley, S.J.; Gabriel Ghirlando, S.J. (Malta); Francis J. Griffin, S.J.; Joseph I. Holland, S.J.; Philip S. Kiley, S.J.; Robert E. Maguire, S.J.; John J. Mandile, S.J.; James P. McCaffrey, S.J.; Paul T. McCarty, S.J.; John J. McGrath, S.J.; John J. Mullen, S.J.; George B. Murray, S.J.; Lawrence J. O'Toole, S.J.; Anthony R. Picariello, S.J.; William J. Sheehan, S.J.; Thomas J. Spillane, S.J.; Patrick A. Sullivan, S.J.; John J. Tucker, S.J.; Wilfred J. Vigeant, S.J.; E. Corbett Walsh, S.J.; James P. Walsh, S.J.; Harry A. Williamson, S.J.; Bros. Vincent M. Brennan, S.J.; Edward L. Niziolek, S.J.; Italo A. Parnoff, S.J. Legal Title: *Campion Residence & Renewal Center, Inc.* Priests 76; Brothers 7.

Campion Health Center, Inc., 319 Concord Rd., 02193. Tel: 617-894-0751. Revs. William J. Raftery, S.J., Rector; Frederick J. Adelmann, S.J.; George F. Barry, S.J.; James H. Barry, S.J.; Richard M. Brackett, S.J.; Eugene C. Brissette, S.J.; Henry J. Butler, S.J.; Maurice L. Buttimer, S.J.; Francis F. Callahan, S.J.; Richard J. Coakley, S.J.; Joseph J. Connor, S.J.; Hubert F. Cunniff, S.J.; Ralph B. Delaney, S.J.; Joseph A. Devenny, S.J.; William J. Duffy, S.J.; Peter T. Farrelly, S.J.; Joseph G. Fennell, S.J.; Francis J. Gilday, S.J.; Frederick A. Harkins, S.J.; Henry A. Jurewich, S.J.; Gerald A. Kinsella, S.J.; Laurence C. Langguth, S.J.; Joseph A. Martus, S.J.; George V. McCabe, S.J.; Raymond E. McCluskey, S.J.; Thomas F. McDermott, S.J.; Nicholas J. McNeil, S.J.; James L. Monks, S.J.; William F. O'Connor, S.J.; Richard F. Olson, S.J.; Francis J. Osborne, S.J.; Joseph A. Paquet, S.J.; Michael G. Pierce, S.J.; William J. Power, S.J.; James E. Powers, S.J.; Joseph F. Quane, S.J.; Martin E. Ryan, S.J.; Daniel J. Shine, S.J.; Laurence J. Skelly, S.J.; John W. Sullivan, S.J.; John J. Walsh, S.J.; William H. Weeks, S.J.; Bros. Robert J. Clifford, S.J.; Joseph A. Garneau, S.J.; Edgar J. LeBlanc, S.J.; Anthony A. Somers, S.J.

[X] CONVENTS AND RESIDENCES FOR SISTERS

BOSTON. *Cardinal's Residence*. 2101 Commonwealth Ave., Brighton, 02135. Tel: 617-782-2101; Fax: 617-782-8358. Sisters of St. Joan of Arc of Quebec 4.

Columban Sisters. 73 Mapleton St., Brighton, 02135. Tel: 617-782-5683. Sr. Ruth Duckert, Regl. Coord. Professed Sisters 5. Legal Title: *Missionary Sisters of Saint Columban.*

Daughters of St. Paul Inc. 50 St. Paul's Ave., Jamaica Plain, 02130. Tel: 617-522-8911.
Web site: http://www.pauline.org
Prov. Community 6; Perpetually Professed Sisters 54; Temporary Professed 10; Novices 6; Initial Formation 6. Legal Title: *Daughters of St. Paul, Inc. Novitiate, Juniorate, Provincialate Headquarters, and Technical Apostolate Center for U.S.*

Pauline Book & Media Center, 885 Providence Hwy., Dedham, 02026. Tel: 617-326-5385.

Franciscan Missionary Sisters for Africa. (USA Headquarters and only house.). Serving in Uganda, Kenya, Zambia, Ethiopia, Zimbabwe, And South Africa. Completely a Missionary congregation. 172 Foster St., Box 35095, Brighton, 02135. Tel: 617-254-4343; Fax: 617-787-8007. Sisters 7.

Franciscan Monastery of St. Clare, The, 920 Centre St., 02130. Tel: 617-524-1760. Franciscan Poor Clare Nuns.
Solemn Vows. Cloistered Solemnly Professed 24; Extern Sisters 2.

Immaculate Conception Convent. 120 Orient Ave., East Boston, 02128. Tel: 617-569-2100; Fax: 617-569-2061. Little Missionary Sisters of Charity. Sr. Mary D'Loreto, Contact. Sisters 3.

Little Sisters of the Assumption Convent. 65 Magnolia St., Dorchester, 02125. Tel: 617-442-9411; Fax: 617-442-2590. Legal Title: *Little Sisters of the Assumption Family Health Services, Inc., dba Project Hope, Co-Opportunity, Inc.* 45 Magnolia St., Dorchester, 02125. Tel: 617-442-1880. Sisters 5.

Monastery of Discalced Carmelites. 61 Mt. Pleasant Ave., Roxbury, 02119. Tel: 617-442-1411.
E-mail: bostoncarmel@juno.com
Cloistered. Sr. Mary Teresa, O.C.D., Prioress. Professed 8.

Motherhouse of the Sisters of St. Joseph of Boston. 637 Cambridge St., Brighton, 02135. Tel: 617-746-2020.
E-mail: boscsj@aol.com
Sr. Kathleen McCluskey, C.S.J., Pres. Sisters 80.

Sacred Heart Convent. Mission Helpers of the Sacred Heart. Legal Title: *Institute of Mission Helpers*. 286 Shawmut Ave., 02118-1613. Tel: 617-542-1143. Sisters 2.

St. Theresa House. 50 Brown Ave., Roslindale, 02131. Tel: 617-323-4644. Sr. Mary. Little Missionaries (A Pious Society) 1; Sisters 1; Lay Associates 12.

Sister Disciples of the Divine Master, Convent and Eucharistic Center, 43 West St., 02111. Tel: 482-0978; 423-2629. Sr. M. Lucille Van Hoogmoed, P.D.D.M., Supr. Sisters 10.

Sisters of Notre Dame de Namur (Boston Province Offices). Mailing Address: 351 Broadway, Everett, 02149-3425.
E-mail: bosprovctr@aol.com
Legal Title: *The Boston Province of the Sisters of Notre Dame de Namur, Inc.*

Sisters of the Good Shepherd. 35 Tyndale St., Roslindale, 02131. Tel: 617-469-2492. Sisters 3.

ANDOVER. *Monastery of St. Clare*, 460 River Rd., 01810-4260. Tel: 978-851-6743. Poor Clare Nuns. Sr. Therese Lacroix, O.S.C., Abbess. Cloistered Solemnly Professed 12; Extern Perpetually Professed 2.

BRADFORD. *Sacred Hearts Convent*, 48 S. Chestnut St., 10835. Tel: 508-521-6867. Sr. Marie Gerarda Lirette, Supr. Servants of the Immaculate Heart of Mary. Good Shepherd Sisters of Quebec 5.

BROCKTON. *Our Lady of Sorrows Convent*, 261 Thatcher St., 02402-3997. Tel: 508-588-5070. Sr. Mary Valliere, C.J.C., Supr. Gen. Poor Sisters of Jesus Crucified and the Sorrowful Mother. Sisters 53.

CAMBRIDGE. *Franciscan Missionaries of Mary*, 16 Lancaster St., 02140. Tel: 617-868-8036. Sr. Mary Petrosky, F.M.M., Prov., 3305 Wallace Ave., Bronx, NY, 10467-6599. Sr. Thesesa Conway, F.M.M.; Sr. Maeda Sumiko, F.M.M.; Sr. Doris McShane, F.M.M.; Sr. Anne Richards, F.M.M.; Sr. Margarida Tavares, F.M.M.; Sr. Patricia Murphy, F.M.M.; Sr. Elizabeth A. Conyers, F.M.M.; Sr. Pauline Williams, F.M.M., Coord.; Sr. Carol Flaherty, F.M.M.

Sancta Maria Convent, 799 Concord Ave., 02238. Tel: 617-868-2200, Ext. 2950.

CHELSEA. *Don Guanella Center, Inc., Daughters of St. Mary of Providence*, 37 Nichols St., 02150. Tel: 617-889-0179. Sr. Arlene Riccio, D.S.M.P., Dir. of Center, Family Support Respite for Developmentally Handicapped Ladies (Ages 10-65). Families 90; Total Staff 22. Sisters 2.

DANVERS. *Discalced Carmelite Monastery*, 15 Mt. Carmel Rd., 01923-3796. Tel: 978-774-3008. Mother Michael of Christ the King, O.C.D., Prioress. Professed Nuns 15; Novices 1; Postulants 1.

DEDHAM. *Ursuline Convent*, 65 Lowder St., 02026-4205. Tel: 617-326-3158. Sr. Dorothy Doyle, O.S.U., Prioress. Sisters 15.

Ursuline Provincialate, 45 Lowder St., 02026-4200. Tel: 617-326-6219.
E-mail: provosu@aol.com
Sr. Dorothy Doyle, O.S.U., Prov. Ursulines of the Roman Union, Northeastern Province 60.

EAST BOSTON. *Little Missionary Sisters of Charity, Immaculate Conception Convent*, 120 Orient Ave., 02128. Tel: 617-569-2100; Fax: 617-569-2061. Sr. Mary D'Loreto, Contact, Mailing Address: Little Missionary Sisters of Charity, Inc., 120 Orient Ave., 02128. Sisters 3.

EVERETT. *Pope John XXIII Convent*, 888 Broadway, 02149. Sr. Marjarita, Coord. Sisters 3.

FRAMINGHAM. *Fontbonne Hall*, 85 Bethany Rd., 01702. Tel: 508-879-1295. Sr. Maureen Doherty, C.S.J., Admin.; Sr. Rena Foley, C.S.J., Pastoral Min.; Rev. Henry Bourgeois, C.S.C., Chap. Professed Sisters 82.

GROTON. *Sisters of the Holy Union Provincial House*, Main St., Box 993, 01450. Tel: 978-448-6049. Sr. Alice Arsenault, S.U.S.C., Prov. Supr. Sisters 7.

IPSWICH. *Sisters of Notre Dame de Namur (Provincial Residence)*, 30 Jeffrey's Neck Rd., 01938-1310. Tel: 978-356-4381; Fax: 978-356-9759.
E-mail: prvncoff@aol.com
Sr. Therese Julie Fitzmaurice, S.N.D., Prov. Admin. Legal Title: *Notre Dame Training School, Inc.* Sisters 84; Total Staff 15.

Sisters of Notre Dame de Namur Generalate Office, 30 Jeffrey's Neck Rd., 01938. Tel: 978-356-2159; Fax: 978-356-1034.
E-mail: juanamcc@aol.com

Casa Generalizia di Suore di Nostra Signora di Namur. (Generalate), Via Raffaello Sardiello, 20, Rome, Italy, 00165. Tel: 39-6-6641-8704; Fax: 39-6-6641-8709. Sr. Ellen Gielty, S.N.D.deN., Gen. Mod.

KINGSTON. *Provincial Residence, Sisters of Divine Providence*, Our Lady of Divine Providence Province, 363 Bishops Hwy., 02364. Tel: 617-585-7707.
E-mail: itpcn129@ibm.net
Sr. Claudia Ward, C.D.P., Prov.

LEXINGTON. *Congregation of Armenian Catholic Sisters of Immaculate Conception, Inc.*, 6 Eliot Rd., 02173. Tel: 617-863-5962. Sr. Veronica Achikian. Sisters 3.

Grey Nuns Provincial Offices, 10 Pelham Rd., 02173-5799. Tel: 781-862-4700; Fax: 781-861-9641. Headquarters (U.S.A. Province) of the Sisters of Charity of Montreal. "Grey Nuns". General Administration, 138 Rue Saint-Pierre, Montreal, Canada, PQ H2Y 2L7. Sr. June Ketterer, S.G.M., Prov. Supr.; Rev. Robert P. Deeley, Chap. Sisters 2.

LOWELL. *Convent of the Holy Union Retirement Home*, 142 Chestnut St., 01852. Tel: 508-458-8862; 458-8835; Fax: 508-970-3780. Sisters of the Holy Union. Sr. Pauline LaRoche, S.U.S.C.; Sr. Marilyn Gignac, S.U.S.C. Sisters 31.

Notre Dame Development Fund, Inc., 88 11th St., 01850. Tel: 508-970-0531. Sr. Janice Waters, S.N.D., Co-Dir.; Mrs. Claire Lawlor, Devel. Dir.

St. Joseph Provincial House, 975 Varnum Ave., 01854. Tel: 978-453-4993. Sisters of Charity of Ottawa (Grey Nuns of the Cross). Sr. Gabrielle Jean, S.C.O., Prov. Supr. Sisters 27.

LYNN. *Sisters of St. Chretienne*, 30 Basset St., 01902. Tel: 781-593-1014. Sr. Lisette Michaud, S.S.Ch. Sisters 4.

MARLBORO. *Sisters of St. Anne, Provincialate*, 720 Boston Post Rd., 01752. Tel: 508-481-4934; Fax: 508-481-4934.
E-mail: smjacques@hotmail.com
Headquarters of American Province. Sisters 157.

Community of the Sisters of Saint Anne. St. Anne Convent, 720 Boston Post Rd., E., 01752. Tel: 508-485-3791. Sisters 75.

Sisters of Ste. Chretienne, 197 Pleasant St., 01752-1169. Tel: 508-485-0740. Sr. Lorraine Michaud, S.S.Ch., Local Coord. House of Retirement. Sisters 34.

Sisters of Ste. Chretienne, 207 Pleasant St., 01752-1169. Sr. Yvette Campbell, S.S.Ch., Local Coord. Sisters 6.

Sisters of the Good Shepherd. 406 Hemenway St., 01752. Tel: 508-485-0970. Superiors: Sr. Lillian Masse, R.G.S. Sisters 31.

METHUEN. *Our Lady of Mount Carmel Convent*, 82 Union St., 01844. Tel: 508-682-4833. Sr. Fernande Marquis, Supr. Servants of the Immaculate Heart of Mary. Good Shepherd Sisters of Quebec 5.

Provincial House, 209 Lawrence St., 01844. Tel: 508-687-1369; Fax: 978-975-1998.
E-mail: prov@netway.com
Sr. Helene Bissonnette, Prov. Supr. Presentation of Mary. Sisters 163.

MIDDLEBORO. *Sacred Heart Convent*, 40 Oak St., 02346. Tel: 508-947-4333. Daughters of the Charity of the Sacred Heart of Jesus, F.C.S.C.J.

MILTON. *Franciscan Sisters of the Immaculate Conception, St. Mary of the Hills*, 260 Brook Rd., 02186. Sr. Rita Murray, O.S.F., Supr. School. St. Mary of the Hills. (Grades K-8).

Religious of Christian Education, Inc., Provincial Office, 55 Parkwood Dr., 02186. Tel: 617-698-8265. Sr. Martha Brigham, R.C.E., Prov.

NEWTON. *Franciscan Sisters of the Immaculate Conception, St. Francis Community*, 790 Centre St., 02158; Fax: 617-964-6338. Sisters 7.

Immaculate Conception Provincialate, 790 Centre St., 02158. Tel: 617-527-1004; Fax: 617-527-2528.
E-mail: usaprov@world.std.com
Missionary Franciscan Sisters of the Immaculate Conception. Sr. M. Michele Craig, M.F.I.C. Total in Residence 5; Total Staff 3.

Mt. Alvernia Convent, 790 Centre St., 02158-2529. Tel: 617-969-4766; Fax: 617-527-2528. Sisters 38.

PLAINVILLE. *Jesus and Mary Mission Center*, 92 School St., 02762-2033. Tel: 508-699-4427; Fax: 508-643-4179. Sr. Michelle Authier, R.J.M., Admin. Total in Residence 15.

QUINCY. *Sisters of Charity (Halifax)*. (Boston Branch Office), 26 Phipps St., 02169. Tel: 617-773-6085; Fax: 617-472-7179. Sr. Esther Plefka, Congregational Councillor. Tel: 617-773-6076.

Sisters of Charity of Nazareth Regional House, 169 Fenno St., 02170. Tel: 617-479-4909. Sr. Gwen McMahon, S.C.N., Regional. Legal Title: *Nazareth Literary and Benevolent Institution*.

SALEM. *St. Chretienne Convent*, 12 Pope St., 01970. Tel: 508-744-1228. Sisters 3.

SOMERVILLE. *Medical Missionaries of Mary, Inc.*, Somerville House, 179 Highland Ave., 02143. Tel: 617-666-3223. Congregation of the Medical Missionaries of Mary Motherhouse, Beechgrove, Drogheda, Ireland. Professed Sisters 7.

WALTHAM. *Marist Missionary Sisters*. Legal Title: *Missionary Sisters of the Society of Mary, Inc., S.M.S.M.* Provincial Offices, 349 Grove St., 02154. Tel: 617-893-0149. Sr. Rosalie Warpeha, S.M.S.M., Prov., Residence for Senior Sisters, 62 Newton St. Tel: 617-893-3960. Sisters 33.
Other Local Communities: 60 Newton St., 02154. Tel: 617-899-1837. Sisters 4. 21 Beech St., Belmont, 02178. Tel: 617-489-3587. Sisters 5. 4 Craig St., Framingham, 02107. Tel: 617-877-7371. Sisters 2. 357 Grove St., 02154. Tel: 617-899-3839. Sisters 7. 20 Bartlett Ave., Arlington, 02174. Tel: 617-648-4341. Sisters 6. 94 Irene St., Lawrence, 01841. Sisters 2. 193 Maple St., #6E, Lawrence, 01841. Sisters 2.

WATERTOWN. *Rosary Manor*, One Rosary Dr., 02172. Tel: 617-924-1717. Sr. Mary Esther Owens, O.P., Coord. Total in Residence 40; Total Staff 2.

WAYLAND. *Emmanuel House*, Sisters of St. Anne, 17 Forty Acres Dr., 01778. Tel: 508-358-4033. Sisters 7.

WELLESLEY. *Elizabeth Seton Residence, Inc.*, 125 Oakland St., 02181; Fax: 617-431-2589. 84 bed Skilled Nursing & Rehab Facility. Medicare-Medicaid Certified. Accredited by Joint Commission on Accreditation of Healthcare Organizations (JCAHO). Sr. Blanche LaRose, S.C., Admin. Sisters of Charity of St. Vincent de Paul, Halifax, Nova Scotia, Canada.

Mount Saint Vincent Assisted Living, Inc., 125 Oakland St., 02181. Tel: 617-237-2161; Fax: 617-431-2589. Sr. Lillian Conroy, Dir.

WRENTHAM. *Mount St. Mary's Abbey*, 300 Arnold St., 02093. Tel: 508-528-1282.
Web site: http://www.msmabbey.org
Legal Title: *The Cistercians of the Strict Observance in Massachusetts, Inc.* The Cistercian Nuns of the Strict Observance (Trappistines). Mother M. Agnes Day, O.C.S.O., Abbess. Professed Sisters 52.

St. Chretienne Provincialate, 297 Arnold St., 02093-1798. Tel: 508-384-8066; 384-7841; Fax: 508-384-3170.
E-mail: ssch@pop.tiac.net
Sisters of St. Chretienne. Sr. Suzanne Beaudoin, S.S.Ch. Sisters 5; Total in Residence 5.

[Y] RETREAT HOUSES

ANDOVER. *Franciscan Center - Retreat House*, 459 River Rd., 01810. Tel: 508-851-3391. Order of Friars Minor. Revs. John D. Bavaro, O.F.M., Dir.; Guardian, Retreat Team; Roland Petinge, O.F.M., Vicar, Retreat Team; John C. DiMauro, O.F.M., Retreat Team; Robert J. Caprio, O.F.M., Retreat Team; Sr. Lorraine Pianka, S.S.N.D.; Bro. Gabriel Aceto, O.F.M.; Mrs. Mildred Sheehan, Sec. Youth Ministry: Eileen Bowes; Joanna Howorth. Total in Residence 7; Total Staff 11.

BILLERICA. *St. Thecla's Retreat House*, 77 Dudley Rd., 01821. Tel: 508-667-5580. Mailing Address: c/o 50 St. Paul Ave., Boston, 02130. Daughters of St. Paul.

BRADFORD. *Don Orione Center*, Old Groveland Rd., P.O. Box 205, 01835. Tel: 508-373-0461. Rev. Gino Marchesani, F.D.P., Dir.

COHASSET. *Retreat Center*, 339 Jerusalem Rd., 02025. Tel: 617-383-6029; 383-6024. Sisters of St. Joseph 3.

DEDHAM. *Boston Cenacle Society*, 25 Avery St., 02026-2804. Tel: 617-326-1393. Sisters of the Congregation of Our Lady of the Retreat in the Cenacle. Sr. Helen Harber, R.C., Contact Person; Sr. Marian Hahm, R.C., Prov. Liaison. Professed Sisters 13.

DOVER. *St. Stephen Priory Spiritual Life Center*, 20 Glen St., Box 370, 02030-0370. Tel: 508-785-0124; Fax: 508-785-1020. Revs. Walter C. Wagner, O.P., Prior; Richard A. Fleck, O.P., Subprior. Co-Directors of Retreat & Renewal: Rev. John E. Allard, O.P.; Sr. Maureen Casey, S.N.D. Dominican Priests 7; Religious Brother 1; Total in Residence 8.

DUXBURY. *Miramar Retreat Center*, 121 Parks St., P.O. Box M, 02331. Tel: 617-585-2460. Rev. Robert M. Jones, Rector. Total in Residence 6; Total Staff 16.

FRAMINGHAM CENTRE. *The Marist House*, 518 Pleasant St., 01701. Tel: 508-879-1620. Revs. Raymond J. Arsenault, S.M., Supr.; Peter D'Ambrosia, S.M., Retreat Dir.; Fernard J. Gallant, S.M.; James Strasz, S.M.; Robert E. Champagne, S.M.; Dolor Ginchereau, S.M.; Henry Rancourt, S.M.; Raymond Boulanger, S.M. Total in Residence 10; Total Staff 5.

GLOUCESTER. *Eastern Point Retreat House*, Gonzaga Hall, 37 Niles Pond Rd., 01930. Tel: 978-283-0013.
E-mail: wgdsj@aol.com
Revs. William G. Devine, S.J., Supr. & Dir.; John B. Kerdiejus, S.J.; Joseph B. McHugh, S.J.; Richard H. Roos, S.J.; Bro. William J. Spokesfield, S.J.; Sr. Nancy Y. Sheridan, S.A.S.V. Priests 4; Brothers 1; Sisters 1.

IPSWICH. *LaSalette Retreat House at Newman Hall*, 251 Topsfield Rd., 01938. Tel: 508-356-3151. Revs. Hector O. LaChapelle, M.S., Dir.; Phil M. Negley, M.S., Dir. Shrine Ministries; Ms. Tensi Boylan, Admin. Asst.

Sacred Heart Retreat Center, Rte. 1A, P.O. Box 567, 01938. Tel: 508-356-3838. Salesians of St. John Bosco. Revs. Gerard Pellegrino, S.D.B., Retreat Dir.; Paul Bedard, S.D.B.; Joseph Doran, S.D.B.; Hector Poulin, S.D.B.; Bro. Peter Bersezio, S.D.B. Priests 4; Lay Brothers 1; Total in Residence 5; Total Staff 7.

SCITUATE. *Foyer of Charity*, 74 Hollett St., 02066. Tel: 781-545-1080. Rev. Matthew Bradley, Dir. Total in Residence 2; Total Staff 6.

WALTHAM. *Espousal Retreat House and Conference Center*, 554 Lexington St., 02154. Tel: 617-647-0033. Stigmatine Fathers and Brothers. Weekend and Weekly Retreats, Days-Evenings of Recollection. Rev. Robert Masciocchi, C.S.S. Total in Residence 1; Total Staff 5.

WESTON. *Campion Renewal Center*, 319 Concord Rd., 02193. Tel: 617-894-3199. Revs. Joseph F. McHugh, S.J., Dir; Ronald J. Amiot, Rector; Robert G. Dougherty, S.J.; John F. Foley, S.J.; William J. Sheehan, S.J., Dir.; James P. Walsh, S.J., Staff. Total in Residence 6; Total Staff 8.

[Z] RETIREMENT RESIDENCES FOR PRIESTS AND BROTHERS

BOSTON. *Regina Cleri, Inc.*, 60 William Cardinal O'Connell Way, 02114. Tel: 617-523-1861. Rev. Msgr. James E. Tierney, Dir. Residence for Retired Archdiocesan Priests. Priests 41; Sisters 2.

Saint Anthony Residence, 103 Arch St., 02110-1102. Tel: 617-542-6454; 6455; Fax: 617-542-6659.
(For Retired Franciscan Friars). Revs. Robert Lynch, O.F.M.; David Fleming, O.F.M.; Lawrence Kidder, O.F.M.; Amadeus Burke, O.F.M.; Gordon A. Murphy, O.F.M.; Cormac Dungan, O.F.M.; Fabian Joyce, O.F.M.; Martin L. McCormack, O.F.M.; Cornelius F. Kelly, O.F.M.; Urban A. Cain, O.F.M.; Francis B. Carroll, O.F.M.; Kenan Morris, O.F.M.; Bro. Frank Waywood, O.F.M., Vicar; Rev. Remy A. Goudreau, O.F.M.; Bro. Albert Aldrich, O.F.M., Vicar. Total in Residence 15.

LAWRENCE. *Marist Brothers*, 26 Leeds Ter., 01843. Tel: 508-686-7411. Bros. Kenneth Hogan, F.M.S.; Eugene Birmingham, F.M.S.; Joseph DiBenedetto, F.M.S.; Richard La Rose, F.M.S.; Jerry Dowsky, F.M.S. Brothers 5.

TEWKSBURY. *Immaculate Heart of Mary Novitiate-Infirmary*, 486 Chandler St., P.O. Box 419, 01876. Tel: 508-851-7258. Revs. F. William Denzel, O.M.I.; William J. Kirwin, O.M.I.; Patrick M. Linehan, O.M.I.; Patrick J. Hollywood, O.M.I., Supr.; Salvatore Costa, O.M.I.; Robert F. Kilroy, O.M.I.; Francis D. Flanagan, O.M.I.; Thomas D. Manning, O.M.I.; Francis P. McCartin, O.M.I.; Joseph O. Stack, O.M.I.; Thomas F. Walsh, O.M.I.; Thomas J. Reddy, O.M.I.; Francis X. McCarron, O.M.I.; Joseph C. Wild, O.M.I.; George P. Buckley, O.M.I.; George Waggett, O.M.I.; Joseph A. Ryan, O.M.I.; Patrick F. Healy, O.M.I.; William Keohane, O.M.I.; John Tracy, O.M.I.; Francis Campbell, O.M.I.; Joseph Murphy, O.M.I.; Bros. Earl Wetzel, O.M.I.; Patrick O'Neil; Francis Linehan. Priests 23; Brothers 3.

WALTHAM. *Stigmatine Fathers and Brothers*, St. Joseph's Hall, 554 Lexington St., 02154. Tel: 617-647-0005; 0006. Revs. Richard Ahern, C.S.S. Tel: 617-894-7125; James Cunningham, C.S.S., Chap. Waltham Hospital; Rocco Leotilo, C.S.S.; Paul Merrill, C.S.S.; Ettore Canzano, C.S.S.; Charles Egan, C.S.S.; Gerald Goggin, C.S.S.; Henry Linse, C.S.S.; Robert Masciocchi, C.S.S.; Carlo Bevilacqua, C.S.S.; Vito Cannizzo, C.S.S.; Charles Grady, C.S.S.; Anthony Parcheski, C.S.S.; Dominic Ruscetta, C.S.S.; Camillo Santini, C.S.S.; James Shea, C.S.S.; Joseph Welch, C.S.S.; Samuel Fayad, C.S.S.; Bros. John E. Fowler, C.S.S.; David L. Gallagher, C.S.S.; Daniel Egan, C.S.S.; Richard Spencer, C.S.S. Priests 18; Brothers 4.

[AA] RESIDENCES FOR MEN AND WOMEN

BOSTON. *Our Lady of the Way Residence*. 60-80 Pond St., Jamaica Plain, 02130. Tel: 617-524-1640. Oblate Sisters of the Most Holy Redeemer. Residence young women. (students, workers, travelers). Sisters 3; Residents 25.

Our Lady's Guild House - Residence for Women, 20 Charlesgate W., 02215. Tel: 617-536-3000. Andrea Beall, Admin. Daughters of Mary of the Immaculate Conception 2; Residents 126.

St. Helena House, 89 Union Park St., 02118. Tel: 617-426-2922; Fax: 617-542-3460. Seniors, low income & disabled persons. Kay Gillespie, Property Mgr. Residents 89.

[BB] PUBLIC ORATORIES AND CHAPELS

BOSTON. *Chapel of Our Lady of Lourdes*, 698 Beacon St., 02215. Tel: 617-536-2761. Marist Fathers. Marist Fathers Residence. Tel: 617-262-2271. Revs. Gerard Caron, S.M., Dir.; Michael Pavlick, S.M.; Paul H. Pepin, S.M.; J. Armand Robichaud, S.M. Priests 4.

Chapel of the Holy Spirit, Paulist Center, 5 Park St., 02108. Tel: 617-742-4460. Paulist Fathers. Revs. Michael J. Kallock, C.S.P., Dir.; Richard J. Colgan, C.S.P.

Madonna Queen Shrine. 111 Orient Ave., East Boston, 02128. Tel: 617-569-2100; Fax: 617-569-8701.
E-mail: MQNSUSA@aol.com
Don Orione Fathers. Rev. John Kilmartin, F.D.P., Rector.

Our Lady of Good Voyage Chapel, 65 Northern Ave., 02110. Tel: 617-268-0710. Revs. John A. Dooher, Admin.; Philip La Plante, S.M., Chap. to Seaport, Sts. Peter & Paul Rectory, 02127.

St. Anthony Shrine, 100 Arch St., P.O. Box 2278, 02107-2278. Tel: 617-542-6440; Fax: 617-542-4225. Revs. Kevin J. Mullen, O.F.M., Guardian & Rector; Brice A. Leavins, O.F.M., Vice Rector; Vincent Carroll, O.F.M.; Kevin J. Daly, O.F.M.; Stephen Doyle, O.F.M.; Aidan Duffy, O.F.M.; Michael Feeney, O.F.M.; Lawrence D. Ford, O.F.M.; Fergus Healey, O.F.M.; Wilfrid Hept, O.F.M.; Hugh Hines, O.F.M.; John P. Hogan, O.F.M.; Philip Lavere, O.F.M.; Patrick Leary, O.F.M.; Raymond Mann, O.F.M.; Gerald T. McCaffrey, O.F.M.; Myron McCormick, O.F.M.; Donan McGovern, O.F.M; Emeric Meier, O.F.M.; Carmel Miotke, O.F.M.; Gerald R. Mudd, O.F.M.; Samuel O'Connor, O.F.M.; Zachary O'Friel, O.F.M.; Colin O'Rourke, O.F.M.; Cyril Seaman, O.F.M.; Flavian Tobin, O.F.M.; Dac Tran, O.F.M.; John R. Ullrich, O.F.M.; Alexander Wyse, O.F.M.; Francis R. Yazawa, O.F.M. Priests 30; Brothers 13.

St. Clement's Archdiocesan Eucharistic Shrine, 1105 Boylston St., 02215-3660. Tel: 617-266-5999; Fax: 617-247-7576. St. Ignatius Province of the Oblates of the Virgin Mary. Rev. Peter Grover, O.M.V., Dir. of Shrine. Priests 1.

St. Francis Chapel, Prudential Center Plaza, 800 Boylston St., #21, 02199. Tel: 617-437-7117. St. Ignatius Province of the Oblates of the Virgin Mary. Revs. James Nibler, O.M.V., Dir.; Thomas Carzon, O.M.V.; Robert Lowrey, O.M.V.; Gerald Wright, O.M.V.; Bro. Joseph O'Connor, O.M.V. Priests 4; Brothers 1.

St. Thomas More Chapel, 49 Franklin St., 02110. Tel: 617-482-4324. Rev. Msgr. Andrew F. Connell, K.J.

BROCKTON. *Chapel of Our Saviour*, 475 Westgate Dr., 02401-1819. Tel: 508-583-8357. Revs. Malcolm Martin, S.A.; Boniface Riedmann, S.A.; Joseph Di Mauro, S.A., Acting Dir.; Bro. Louis Marek, S.A. Priests 3; Brothers 1.

EAST BOSTON. *Our Lady of the Airways Chapel*, Logan Airport, 02128. Tel: 617-567-2800; Fax: 617-569-6950. Rev. Robert F. Hennessey, Res. Most Holy Redeemer Rectory, 65 London St., Boston, 02128. Tel: 617-567-3227.

HOLLISTON. *Our Lady of Fatima Shrine*, 101 Summer St., P.O. Box 5857, 01746-5857. Tel: 508-429-2144. Xaverian Missionaries. Rev. Tony Lalli, S.X., Dir.

IPSWICH. *National Shrine of Our Lady of La Salette*, 251 Topsfield Rd., 01938-1195. Tel: 508-356-3151. Rev. John R. Dolan, M.S., Dir. Total in Residence 4; Total Staff 9.

PEABODY. *St. Theresa Carmelite Chapel*, North Shore Shopping Center, 01960. Tel: 508-531-6145. Revs. Ferdinand T. Schaefer, O.Carm., Supr. & Dir.; Kilian Healy, O.Carm., Supr.; Alan N. Crowley, O.Carm.; Peter Thomas Sherry, O.Carm.; Lambert Zulkie, O.Carm.; Bro. Damien Chong, O.Carm. Priests 5.

[CC] CAMPUS MINISTRY

BOSTON. *Emmanuel College Campus Ministry*, 400 The Fenway, 02115. Tel: 617-735-9777. Sr. Patricia McSharry, S.N.D.

Newman House Catholic Center at Boston University, 211 Bay State Rd., 02215. Tel: 617-353-3632.
E-mail: frchuck@bu.edu or lamarche@bu.edu
Web site: http://www.bu.edu/CATHOLIC
Rev. Charles E. Cunniff, C.S.P.; Dr. Jane M. LaMarche, D.Min.

St. Ann's University Parish. Catholic Student Center,

68 St. Stephen St., 02115. Tel: 617-266-2635; Fax: 617-266-9015.
E-mail: stann@lynx.neu.edu
(Serving Northeastern University and the Fenway Colleges). Rev. Paul E. Kilroy, Campus Min., Northeastern Univ. Pastoral Assocs. - Campus Ministers: Sr. Rosemary Mulvihill, R.S.M., Northeastern Univ.; Sr. Mary Walsh, S.U., Emerson College.

BRIDGEWATER. *Bridgewater State College Catholic Center*, 122 Park Ave., 02324. Tel: 508-697-1346. Campus Ministers: Rev. John F. Denning, C.S.C.; Sr. Mary Ellen Dow, S.N.D.

CAMBRIDGE. *Harvard-Radcliffe Catholic Student Center*, 20 Arrow St., 02138. Tel: 617-868-6585. Revs. J. Bryan Hehir; George S. Salzmann, O.S.F.S.; Jacqueline L. Landry; Joan Travers.

Massachusetts Institute of Technology Catholic Community, 40 Massachusetts Ave., W-11, 02139. Tel: 617-253-2981.
E-mail: catholic@mit.edu
Web site: http://web.mit.edu/tcc/www
Rev. Paul A. Reynolds, C.S.P.; Ms. Susan Troy. Total Staff 2.

CHESTNUT HILL. *Boston College University Chaplaincy*, McElroy 215, 02167. Tel: 617-552-3475. Rev. Richard T. Cleary, S.J. Total in Residence 3; Total Staff 9.

DORCHESTER. *University of Massachusetts at Boston Campus Ministry*, Harbor Campus, 02125. Tel: 617-287-5839. Rev. Richard F. Chancy; Mrs. Aldona Lingertat.

FRAMINGHAM. *Framingham State College Campus Ministry*, 100 State St., 01701. Tel: 508-626-4610.
E-mail: vpoirier@wellesley.edu
Rev. Vincent H. Poirier.

LOWELL. *The Catholic Center U Mass, Lowell*, 52 Colonial Ave., 01854. Tel: 508-454-0151.
E-mail: soperp@woods.uml.edu or gradyc@woods.uml.edu
Web site: http://www.uml.edu
Rev. Paul R. Soper; Ms. Cheryl Grady. Total in Residence 6; Total Staff 3.

MEDFORD. *Tufts University Catholic Center*, 58 Winthrop St., 02155. Tel: 617-391-7272. Rev. Michael J. Hunt, C.S.P.

MILTON. *Aquinas College at Milton Campus Ministry*, 303 Adams St., 02186. Tel: 617-696-3100. Sr. Helen Callahan, C.S.J.

NEWTON. *Aquinas College at Newton Campus Ministry*, 15 Walnut Park, 02158. Tel: 617-969-4400. Peggy Lindwall, Campus Min. Total Assisted 50; Total Staff 2.

NORTH ANDOVER. *Merrimack College Campus Ministry Center*, 303 Gildea Hall, 01845. Tel: 508-837-5450. Sr. Elaine Polcari, S.S.N.D., Dir. Campus Ministers: Revs. Joseph L. Farrell, O.S.A.; Scott C. Ness, O.S.A.

SALEM. *Salem State College, Catholic Campus Ministry*, 352 Lafayette St., 01970. Tel: 508-741-6074.
E-mail: kathleen.crowley@clipper.salem.mass.edu
Rev. Scott Euvrard; Sr. Kathleen Crowley, S.C.; Ms. Eileen Snow.

WALTHAM. *Bentley College Campus Ministry*, 175 Forest St., 02154-4705. Tel: 617-891-2194. Sr. Peggy Nichols, C.S.J., Dir. Campus Min.

Brandeis University Campus Ministry, M.S. U5, 02154. Tel: 617-736-3574. Rev. David C. Michael.

WELLESLEY. *Babson College Campus Ministry*, 9 Glen Rd., 02181. Tel: 617-235-1200. Sr. Frances Sheehey, O.S.F., Campus Coord.

Wellesley College Campus Ministry, 02181. Tel: 781-283-2688.
E-mail: vpoirier@wellesley.edu
Rev. Vincent H. Poirier.

WESTON. *Regis College Office of Campus Ministry*, 235 Wellesley St., 02193. Tel: 781-768-7027; 7028; 7029. Mildred Crowley, Dir.; Joan Collupy, Campus Min.

[DD] FOUNDATIONS, FUNDS & TRUSTS

BOSTON. *The Archdiocese of Boston Self-Insurance Group, Inc.* 2121 Commonwealth Ave., Brighton, 02135.

Chancery Office. 2121 Commonwealth Ave., Brighton, 02135. Tel: 617-254-0100. Also see Miscellaneous Section for additional listings.

The Cardinal Medeiros Trust.

Cardinal Cushing General Hospital Foundation, Brockton.

The Carney Hospital Foundation, Inc. (Formerly The New Caritas Christi Hospital, Inc.), 2100 Dorchester Ave., 02124. Tel: 617-296-1788. J. Barry Driscoll, Pres.; Paul J. Kingston, Vice Pres.; Daniel J. McDevitt, Sec.; William F. Henderson, Exec. Dir.

**Catholic Schools Foundation, Inc.* (Formerly St. Anthony's Scholarship Fund, Inc.).

Clergy Benefit Trust. Most Rev. William F. Murphy, Sec.

Clergy Fund Society.

Clergy Medical-Hospitalization Trust.

Clergy Retirement-Disability Trust.

Family Counseling Endowment Fund, Inc., One Bromfield St., 02108. Tel: 617-482-4355.

Marist Capital Trust Fund. c/o Financial Admin., The Missionary Sisters of the Society of Mary, Inc., 349 Grove St., Waltham, 02154. Tel: 617-893-0149. Sr. Virginia Fornasa, S.M.S.M., Trustee; John E. McCormack.

Metropolitan Boston Dialysis Center, Inc., 125 Technology Dr., Bldg. 1, Ste. 5, Waltham, 02154. Tel: 617-893-8544.

Mission Promotion..Missionary Sisters of the Society of Mary. c/o Mission Promoter, 13 Pelham Rd., Lexington, 02173. Tel: 617-861-6116.

Roman Catholic Archdiocese of Boston Health Benefit Trust. Mr. David W. Smith, Admin.

Roman Catholic Archdiocese of Boston Insurance Trust. Benefit Office. Mr. David W. Smith, Admin.

Roman Catholic Archdiocese of Boston Pension Trust. Benefit Office. Mr. David W. Smith, Admin.

Roman Catholic Archdiocese of Boston Long Term Disability Trust. Mr. David W. Smith, Admin.

Roman Catholic Archdiocese of Boston Common Investment Fund.

Roman Catholic Archdiocese of Boston Fixed Income Investment Fund.

St. Charles Borromeo Educational Foundation, Inc.

Sacred Heart Trust Fund, c/o Society of Jesus, Trustee, 761 Harrison Ave., 02118. Tel: 617-536-5604. Bro. H. Francis Cluff, S.J.

St. Elizabeth's Hospital Foundation, Inc., 159 Washington St., Brighton, 02135.

Holy Family Hospital Foundation, Inc.

Catholic Foundation of the Archdiocese of Boston, 2121 Commonwealth Ave., Brighton, 02135. Mr. John A. McNeice, Jr., Pres.

The Xaverian Brothers Northeastern Community Support Charitable Trust Fund, 704 Brush Hill Rd., Milton, 02186.

Benefit Trust for Non-Incardinated Priests. Legal Title: *Benefit Trust for Non-Incardinated Priest Duly Assigned for Service in the Archdiocese of Boston.*

BRIGHTON. *Clergy Assistance Trust*, 2121 Commonwealth Ave., 02135.

FRAMINGHAM. *Senior Religious Trust Fund of Marist Fathers of Boston*, 518 Pleasant St., 01701-2898.

HANOVER. *St. Coletta's of Massachusetts, Inc.*, 405 Washington St., 02339. Tel: 617-826-6371.
Web site: http://www.coletta.org
Mr. Paul J. Hudson, Pres. & CEO.

IPSWICH. *Blin Charitable Trust*, 30 Jeffrey's Neck Rd., 01938; Fax: 978-356-9759.
E-mail: PRVNOFF@aol.com
Sisters of Notre Dame de Namur.

LOWELL. *Saints Memorial Medical Center Foundation*, P.O. Box 367, 01853-0367. Tel: 508-934-8334; Fax: 508-934-8252.
E-mail: 102246.272@compuserve.com
Thom Clark, Pres. & CEO; Kevin E. Coughlin, Vice Pres.

METHUEN. *Holy Family Hospital Foundation, Inc.*, 70 East St., 01844-4597. Tel: 508-687-0151. Mrs. Noreen V. Mallen, Ex. Dir.

NEEDHAM. *St. Joseph's Parish School Fund, Inc., Needham*, 1382 Highland Ave., 02192. Mr. James S. DiStasio, Treas.

TEWKSBURY. *The Society of Oblate Fathers Continuing Support Fund*, c/o the Society of Oblate Fathers for Missions Among the Poor, 486 Chandler St., 01876; Fax: 508-858-3661. Rev. William Sheehan, O.M.I., Prov.

The Society of Oblate Fathers for Missions Among the Poor Formation Charitable Trust, 486 Chandler St., P.O. Box 419, 01876; Fax: 508-858-3661. Rev. William Sheehan, O.M.I., Prov.

[EE] LIFE RESOURCES

BRAINTREE.

**Pilgrim Center for Boys*, 140 Adams St., P.O. Box 850907, 02185-0907. Tel: 617-848-5510. Students 24.

[FF] MISCELLANEOUS

BOSTON. *Caritas Christi - A Catholic Health Care System.* 736 Cambridge St., Brighton, 02135. Tel: 617-789-2500. Michael F. Collins, M.D., Pres. & CEO.

Caritas Christi Support Services, Inc.

C.C. Medical Associates, Inc.

Caritas Christi Diagnostic Support Services, Inc.

St. Elizabeth's Realty Corporation.

Metropolitan Boston Dialysis Center.

Good Samaritan Hospice.

The Catholic Lawyers Guild of the Archdiocese of Boston, Inc., One Union St., 02108. Tel: 617-523-2640. Hon. Joseph R. Nolan, Pres.

Catholic Social Services, Inc., 49 Franklin St., 02110. Tel: 617-482-5440; Fax: 617-451-0337. Joseph Doolin, Ph.D., Pres. & CEO.

Equestrian Order of the Holy Sepulchre of Jerusalem. Northeastern Lieutenancy, 12 Kenilworth Rd., Milton, 02186. Mr. George T. Ryan, KGCHS Lt.; Dennis J. Looney, Jr., KC HS Chancellor.

League of Catholic Women of the Archdiocese of Boston. 127 Lake St., Brighton, 02135. Tel: 617-254-2610. Mrs. Joseph Cullinan, Pres.; Rev. Martin P. Connor, Spiritual Dir.

Lourdes Bureau, 698 Beacon St., 02215. Tel: 617-536-2761. Marist Fathers. Official Representatives in America for the Shrine of Lourdes, France.

Medaille Corporation, 637 Cambridge St., 02135. Tel: 617-746-2020. Sr. Kathleen McCluskey, C.S.J., Pres.; Sr. Frances Wool, C.S.J., Treas.

MI Management, Inc. Covenant Health Systems. 172 Lawrence St., Lawrence, 01841. Tel: 978-685-6321; Fax: 978-975-0050. Barbara E. Grant, Pres. & CEO.

Ministry of Evangelization and Catechesis, 286 Shawmut Ave., 02118-1613. Tel: 617-542-1143. Legal Title: *Institute of Mission Helpers.* Mission Helpers of the Sacred Heart. Sr. Joanne Frey, M.H.S.H., Local Coord. & Contact Person.

National Catholic Group Purchasing Association, Inc. 580 Washington St., Newton, 02158. Tel: 617-965-4343; Fax: 617-965-5430. Mr. Richard J. Wasilauskas, Pres.

Pine Street Inn, 444 Harrison Ave., 02118. Tel: 617-482-4944. Shelter for homeless men and women. Erik Payne Butler, Pres.

Pope John Center, 159 Washington St., 02135. Tel: 617-787-1900; Fax: 617-787-4900.
E-mail: postmaster@pjcenter.org
Web site: http://www.pjcenter.org
John M. Haas, Ph.D., S.T.L., Pres.; Rev. Germain Kopaczynski, O.F.M.Conv., Ph.D., S.T.D., Dir. Education; Peter J. Cataldo, Ph.D., Dir. of Research; Edward J. Furton, M.A., Ph.D., Dir. Publications; Joseph W. Ford, Dir. Public Relations; Rev. Albert S. Moraczewski, O.P., Ph.D., Pres. Emeritus, Distinguished Scholar in Residence; Thomas E. Gannoe, Systems Dir.; Donald J. Powers, Dir. Finance.

Propagation of the Faith and Holy Childhood Association & Society of St. Peter the Apostle, 49 Franklin St., 02110. Tel: 617-542-1776; Fax: 617-542-1778. Rev. Msgr. Andrew F. Connell, K.J., Dir.

St. Francis Charities, 2121 Commonwealth Ave., 02135.

Spiritearth, Inc., 771 Harrison Ave., 02118-2311. Tel: 617-266-7233. Total in Residence 2.

BRAINTREE. *Our Lady of Kazan Russian Greek Catholic Mission.* Byzantine Slavonic Rite. Records at St. Peter & Paul Rectory, Braintree.

St. Peter & Paul Rectory, 55 W. Broadway, South Boston, 02127. Tel: 617-268-8100. Rev. John A. Dooher.

The Cambridge Center for the Study of Faith and Culture, Inc., 2101 Commonwealth Ave., Brighton, 02135. Tel: 617-782-2544. Sr. Madonna Murphy, C.S.C., Pres.

St. Vincent Pallotti Center for Apostolic Development of Boston, Inc., 159 Washington St., Brighton, 02135. Tel: 617-783-3924; Fax: 617-787-7797. Ms. Carolyn C. Thompson, Dir.

BRIGHTON.

**Women Affirming Life, Inc.*, P.O. Box 35532, 02135. Tel: 617-254-2277; Fax: 617-254-2299. Marianne Luthin, Exec. Dir.

CAMBRIDGE. *Notre Dame Mission Volunteer Corporation*, 203 Erie St., 02134.
E-mail: ndamercrps@aol.com
Branch Office: 403 Markland Ave., Baltimore, MD, 21212. Tel: 410-532-6864.

Sancta Maria Nursing Facility, 799 Concord Ave., 02138. Tel: 617-868-2200. Daughters of Mary of the Immaculate Conception. Sr. Mary Mark, D.M., Admin. In-Patients/Residents 141; Bed Capacity 141; Sisters 3.

**The Youville House, Inc.*, 1575 Cambridge St., 02138-4398. Tel: 617-876-4344. Mr. T. Richard Quigley, Pres. & CEO; Ms. Marsha V. Whelan, Vice Pres. Mission Integration. Chaplains: Revs. William L. Mulligan, S.J.; Jennifer Casstevens; Ms. Patricia Kennedy, Dir. of Pastoral Care Services; Ms. Elizabeth Walsh.
Member of Youville Lifecare, Inc. Priests 1; Sisters of Charity (Grey Nuns) 3; Assisted Living Units 95.

**Youville Lifecare, Inc.*, 1575 Cambridge St., 02138-4398. Tel: 617-876-4344. Mr. T. Richard Quigley, Pres. & CEO; Ms. Marsha V. Whelan, Vice Pres. Mission Integration.
Member of Covenant Health Systems, Lexington, MA. Total Staff 237.

DEDHAM. *St. Pauline Book and Media*, 885 Providence Hwy., Rte. 1, 02026. Tel: 781-326-5385.
E-mail: jspdedham@aol.com
Pious Society, Daughters of St. Paul (Missionary Sisters of the Media of Social Communication).

FRAMINGHAM. *Bethany Health Care Center, Inc.*, 97 Bethany Rd., 01701. Tel: 508-872-6750; Fax: 508-875-5425. Skilled Nursing Facility and Health Clinic. Congregation of Sisters of St. Joseph of Boston. Rev. Francis J. O'Neil, S.J., Chap. Bed Capacity 101.

Bethany Hill School, Inc., 89 Bethany Rd., 01701. Legal Title: *Bethany Health Care Center, Inc.*

IPSWICH. *Cuvilly Arts and Earth Center, Inc.*, 10 Jeffrey Neck Rd., 01938. Tel: 508-356-4288. Sr. Catherine Owens, S.N.D., Pres. Total Assisted 85; Total Staff 7.

LEXINGTON. *Covenant Health Systems, Inc.*, 420 Bedford St., 02173. Tel: 781-862-1634.
Web site: http://www.covenanths.com
David R. Lincoln, Pres. & CEO. Member organizations: Youville Lifecare, Cambridge, MA; St. Joseph Healthcare, Nashua, NH; Sisters of Charity Health Care, Lewiston, ME; Mary Immaculate Health/Care Services, Lawrence, MA; Maristhill Nursing Home, Waltham, MA; St. Joseph Manor Health Care, Brockton, MA; Fanny Allen Corp., Colchester, VT. Affiliate organizations: Sancta Maria Nursing Facility, Cambridge, MA; Optima Healthcare, Manchester, NH.

LOWELL. *Oblate Ministry Development Service*, 27 Kirk St., P.O. Box 1401, 01853-1401. Tel: 508-459-1637. Rev. Adhemar Deveau, O.M.I. Legal Title: *Oblate Ministry Development Service.*

Pro Maria Committee, 22 Second Ave., 01854-2808. Tel: 978508-453-5281. Miss Doris M. Poisson, Sec.

MALDEN. *Xaverian Brothers Province Development Office.* (Corporate Title: American Northeastern Province of Xaverian Brothers, Inc. and Working Boy's Home), 99 Crystal St., 02148-5994. Tel: 617-324-8099. Bro. Edward Rice, C.F.X.

METHUEN. *Holy Family Hospital Men's Guild*, 70 East St., 01844-4597. Tel: 508-687-0151, Ext. 2304.

Valley Regional Health System, Inc., 70 East St., 01844-4597. Tel: 508-687-0151.
Holy Family Hospital, Inc.
Holy Family Hospital Auxiliary.
Valley Regional Support Services, Inc.

NEWTON. *Focolare Movement*, Women's Branch, 189 Jackson Rd., 02158-1427. Tel: 617-965-4879. Total in Residence 5.

The Ministry Development Center for Women Religious, Inc., 15 Walnut Park, Rm. 208, 02158. Tel: 617-964-3230; Fax: 617-796-7933. Sr. Peggy Nichols, C.S.J., Exec. Dir. Total Assisted 300.

RELIGIOUS INSTITUTES OF MEN REPRESENTED IN THE ARCHDIOCESE

For further details refer to the corresponding bracketed number in the Religious Institutes of Men or Women section.

[0130]—*Assumptionists.*—A.A.
[1040]—*The Augustinians.* (Villanova, PA).—O.S.A.
[0200]—*Benedictine Monks.*—O.S.B.
[1350]—*Brothers of St. Francis Xavier.*—C.F.X.
[0330]—*Brothers of the Christian Schools.* (Long Island, New England Provs.).—F.S.C.
[0470]—*The Capuchin Friars.* (Prov. of Mary).—O.F.M.Cap.
[0270]—*Carmelite Fathers & Brothers.* (Prov. of Most Pure Heart of Mary).—O.Carm.
[0310]—*Congregation of Christian Brothers.* (Eastern Prov.).—C.F.C.
[1210]—*Congregation of the Missionaries of St. Charles.*—C.S.
[1000]—*Congregation of the Passion.* (St. Paul of the Cross Prov.).—C.P.
[1140]—*Congregation of the Sacred Hearts of Jesus and Mary.*—SS.CC.
[0480]—*Conventual Franciscans.* (Buffalo, NY).—O.F.M.Conv.
[0260]—*Discalced Carmelite Friars.*—O.C.D.
[0520]—*Franciscan Friars.* (Assumption of B.V.M., Holy Name, Immaculate Conception Provs.).—O.F.M.
[0530]—*Franciscan Friars of the Atonement.*—S.A.
[0670]—*Hospitaller Brothers of St. John of God.*—O.H.
[0690]—*Jesuit Fathers and Brother.* (New England Prov.).—S.J.
[0770]—*The Marist Brothers.* (Poughkeepsie, NJ).—F.M.S.
[0780]—*Marist Fathers.* (Boston Prov.).—S.M.
[0800]—*Maryknoll.*—M.M.
[]—*Mekhitarist Fathers.*—C.M.Vd.
[0720]—*The Missionaries of Our Lady of La Salette.* (Eastern Prov.).—M.S.
[0910]—*Oblates of Mary Immaculate.* (Eastern, St. John the Baptist Provs.).—O.M.I.
[0430]—*Order of Preachers-Dominicans.* (Prov. of St. Joseph).—O.P.
[1030]—*Paulist Fathers.*—C.S.P.
[0610]—*Priests of the Congregation of Holy Cross.* (Eastern Prov.).—C.S.C.
[1070]—*Redemptorist Fathers.* (Baltimore Prov.).—C.SS.R.
[1190]—*Salesians of Don Bosco.* (Prov. of St. Philip).—S.D.B.
[0110]—*Society of African Missions.*—S.M.A.
[0420]—*Society of Divine Word.* (Sacred Heart Prov.).—S.V.D.
[0850]—*Society of Missionaries of Africa.*—M.Afr.
[0370]—*Society of St. Columban.* (American Region).—S.S.C.
[0410]—*Sons of Divine Providence.*—F.D.P.
[1270]—*Sons of Mary Missionary Society.*—F.M.S.I.
[1280]—*Stigmatine Fathers and Brothers.* (Rome, Italy).—C.S.S.
[1360]—*Xaverian Missionary Fathers.*—S.X.

RELIGIOUS INSTITUTES OF WOMEN REPRESENTED IN THE ARCHDIOCESE

[0330]—*Carmelite Sisters for the Aged and Infirm.*—O.Carm.
[0670]—*Cistercian Nuns of the Strict Observance.*—O.C.S.O.
[0270]—*Congregation of Bon Secours.*—C.B.S.
[3110]—*Congregation of Our lady of the Retreat in the Cenacle.*—R.C.
[]—*Congregation of the Armenian Catholic Sisters of the Immaculate Conception, Inc.*.
[1920]—*Congregation of the Sisters of the Holy Cross.*—C.S.C.
[0760]—*Daughters of Charity of St. Vincent de Paul.*—D.C.
[0860]—*Daughters of Mary of the Immaculate Conception.*—C.M.
[0420]—*Discalced Carmelite Nuns.*—O.C.D.
[1070-01]—*Dominican Sisters.*—O.P.
[1070-03]—*Dominican Sisters.*—O.P.
[1070-13]—*Dominican Sisters.*—O.P.
[1170]—*Felician Sisters.*—C.S.S.F.
[1370]—*Franciscan Missionaries of Mary.*—F.M.M.
[1320]—*Franciscan Missionary Sisters for Africa.* (Co. Louth, Ireland).—O.S.F.
[1180]—*Franciscan Sisters of Allegany, New York.*—O.S.F.
[1470]—*Franciscan Sisters of St. Joseph.*—F.S.S.J.
[1840]—*Grey Nuns of the Sacred Heart.*—G.N.S.H.
[0410]—*Institute of the Sisters of Our Lady of Mt. Carmel.*—O.Carm.
[2290]—*Little Missionary Sisters of Charity.*—L.M.S.C.
[2310]—*Little Sisters of the Assumption.*—L.S.A.
[2320]—*Little Sisters of the Holy Family.*—P.S.S.F.
[2340]—*Little Sisters of the Poor.*—L.S.P.
[2420]—*Marist Missionary Sisters-Missionary Sisters of the Society of Mary.*—S.M.S.M.
[2470]—*Maryknoll Sisters of St. Dominic.*—M.M.
[2480]—*Medical Missionaries of Mary.*—M.M.M.
[1360]—*Missionary Franciscan Sisters of the Immaculate Conception.*—O.S.F.
[2790]—*Missionary Servants of the Most Blessed Trinity.*—M.S.B.T.
[2880]—*Missionary Sisters of St. Columban.*—S.S.C.
[2800]—*Missionary Sisters of the Most Sacred Heart of Jesus of Hiltrup.*—M.S.C.
[3030]—*Oblates of the Most Holy Redeemer.*—O.SS.R.
[3760]—*Order of St. Clare.*—O.S.C.
[0950]—*Pious Society Daughters of St. Paul.*—D.S.P.
[3240]—*Poor Sisters of Jesus Crucified and the Sorrowful Mother.*—C.J.C.
[3410]—*Religious of Christian Education.*—R.C.E.
[2070]—*Religious of the Holy Union of the Sacred Hearts.*—S.U.S.C.
[2970]—*School Sisters of Notre Dame.*—S.S.N.D.
[3550]—*Servants of the Immaculate Heart of Mary.*—S.C.I.M.
[0980]—*Sisters Disciples of the Divine Master.*—P.D.D.M.
[0490]—*Sisters of Charity of Montreal-Grey Nuns.*—S.G.M.
[0500]—*Sisters of Charity of Nazareth.*—S.C.N.
[0560]—*Sisters of Charity of Quebec-Grey Nuns.*—S.C.Q.
[0590]—*Sisters of Charity of Saint Elizabeth, Convent Station.*—S.C.
[0640]—*Sisters of Charity of St. Vincent de Paul, Halifax.*—S.C.
[0540]—*Sisters of Charity, At Ottawa-Grey Nuns of the Cross.*—S.C.O.
[0990]—*Sisters of Divine Providence.*—C.D.P.
[2580]—*Sisters of Mercy of the Union in the United States of America.*—R.S.M.
[3000]—*Sisters of Notre Dame de Namur.*—S.N.D.deN.
[3360]—*Sisters of Providence of Saint Mary-Of-The-Woods, Indiana.*—S.P.
[3950]—*Sisters of Saint Mary of Namur.*—S.S.M.N.
[3720]—*Sisters of St. Anne.*—S.S.A.
[3750]—*Sisters of St. Chretienne.*—S.S.Ch.
[1650]—*Sisters of St. Francis of Philadelphia.*—O.S.F.
[3830]—*Sisters of St. Joseph.*—C.S.J.
[3815]—*Sisters of Ste. Jeanne D'Arc.*—S.J.A.
[0150]—*Sisters of the Assumption B.V.*—S.A.S.V.
[1830]—*Sisters of the Good Shepherd.*—R.G.S.
[3310]—*Sisters of the Presentation of Mary.*—P.M.
[1490]—*Sisters of the Third Franciscan Order.*—O.S.F.
[1705]—*Sisters of the Third Order of St. Francis of Assisi.*—O.S.F.
[4060]—*Society of the Holy Child Jesus.*—S.H.C.J.
[4070]—*Society of the Sacred Heart.*—R.S.C.J.
[4110]—*Ursuline Nuns.* (Eastern Prov.).—O.S.U.

ARCHDIOCESAN CEMETERIES

BOSTON. *Diocesan Office.* 175 Broadway, Malden, 02148. Mr. D. F. Kenney, Dir.
ARLINGTON. *St. Paul.*
BEVERLY. *St. Mary.*
CAMBRIDGE. *North Cambridge Catholic.*
CHARLESTOWN. *St. Francis de Sales.*
HAVERHILL. *St. James, St. Joseph & St. Patrick.*
LOWELL. *St. Patrick.*
LYNN. *St. Mary, St. Joseph & St. Jean Baptiste.*
MALDEN. *Holy Cross & St. Mary.*
MARBLEHEAD. *Star of the Sea.*
SALEM. *St. Mary.*
SAXONVILLE. *St. George.*
STONEHAM. *St. Patrick.*
WALTHAM. *Calvary.*
WATERTOWN. *Mount Auburn & St. Patrick.*
WOBURN. *Calvary.*

NECROLOGY

† Beauvais, Leon F., Boston, MA, Sacred Heart. —Died March 23, 1997.
† Bergeron, Arthur I., (Retired). —Died Oct. 25, 1996.
† Boyle, James Leo, (Retired). —Died Nov. 25, 1996.
† Buckley, Robert G., Methuen, MA, St. Monica. —Died June 20, 1997.
† Connors, Francis P., (Retired). —Died Oct. 7, 1996.
† Dacier, Gerard A., (Retired). —Died June 18, 1997.
† Edwards, John G., (Retired). —Died Sept. 3, 1997.
† Foley, John J., (Retired). —Died Jan. 22, 1996.
† Hyland, Rev. Msgr. Charles H., (Retired). —Died Dec. 22, 1996.
† Kerivan, William C., (Permanent Disability). —Died Dec. 3, 1996.
† Linehan, William J., (Retired). —Died Oct. 3, 1997.
† McAndrews, Walter J., (Retired). —Died June 14, 1997.
† McNeill, Rev. Msgr. Robert W., Kingston, MA, St. Joseph. —Died Dec. 15, 1996.
† Minigan, Frederick J., (Retired). —Died July 27, 1997.
† O'Brien, Robert E., Boston, MA, St. Andrew. —Died Dec. 28, 1996.
† Roche, Allan E., (Retired). —Died Aug. 10, 1997.
† Segadelli, Joseph D., (Retired). —Died Feb. 28, 1997.
† Wilson, Joseph C., Billerica, MA, St. Andrew. —Died Feb. 17, 1997.

Diocese of Bridgeport

(Dioecesis Bridgeportensis)

Most Reverend

EDWARD M. EGAN, J.C.D., D.D.

Bishop of Bridgeport; ordained December 15, 1957; appointed Titular Bishop of Allegheny and Auxiliary Bishop of New York April 1, 1985; consecrated May 22, 1985; appointed Bishop of Bridgeport November 8, 1988; installed December 14, 1988. *Office: The Catholic Center, 238 Jewett Ave., Bridgeport, CT, 06606-2892.* Tel.: 203-372-4301.

Chancery: The Catholic Center, 238 Jewett Ave., Bridgeport, CT, 06606-2892. Tel.: 203-372-4301; Fax: 203-371-8698.

ESTABLISHED AUGUST 6, 1953.

Square Miles 633.

Corporate Title: *The Bridgeport Roman Catholic Diocesan Corporation.*

Comprises all of Fairfield County in the State of Connecticut.

For legal titles of parishes and diocesan institutions, consult the Chancery at The Catholic Center.

STATISTICAL OVERVIEW

Personnel	
Bishop	1
Priests: Diocesan Active in Diocese	191
Priests: Active Outside Diocese	16
Priests: Diocesan in Foreign Missions	2
Priests: Retired, Sick or Absent	53
Number of Diocesan Priests	262
Religious Priests in Diocese	76
Extern Priests in Diocese	7
Ordinations:	
Diocesan Priests	7
Transitional Deacons	5
Permanent Deacons in Diocese	77
Total Brothers	2
Total Sisters	522
Parishes	
Parishes	88
With Resident Pastor:	
Resident Diocesan Priests	84
Resident Religious Priests	4
Without Resident Pastor:	
Missions	2
Professional Ministry Personnel:	
Brothers	1
Sisters	48
Lay Ministers	76
Welfare	
Catholic Hospitals	2
Total Assisted	200,000
Homes for the Aged	4
Total Assisted	829
Day Care and Extended Day Care Centers	21
Total Assisted	373
Specialized Homes	21
Total Assisted	63
Special Centers for Social Services	20
Total Assisted	14,271
Other Institutions	2
Total Assisted	21
Educational	
Seminaries, Diocesan	1
Students from This Diocese	16
Diocesan Students in Other Seminaries	16
Total Seminarians	32
Colleges and Universities	3
Total Students	10,905
High Schools, Diocesan and Parish	5
Total Students	2,476
High Schools, Private	3
Total Students	1,013
Elementary Schools, Diocesan and Parish	33
Total Students	10,854
Elementary Schools, Private	2
Total Students	422
Catechesis/Religious Education:	
High School Students	2,907
Elementary Students	27,068
Total Students Under Catholic Instruction	55,677
Teachers in the Diocese:	
Priests	18
Brothers	1
Sisters	44
Lay Teachers	717
Vital Statistics	
Receptions into the Church:	
Infant Baptism Totals	6,160
Adult Baptism Totals	173
Received into Full Communion	128
First Communions	5,186
Confirmations	3,886
Marriages:	
Catholic	1,869
Interfaith	404
Total Marriages	2,273
Deaths	3,616
Total Catholic Population	360,918
Total Population	833,761

Former Bishops—His Eminence LAWRENCE J. CARDINAL SHEHAN, D.D., ord. Dec. 23, 1922; cons. Dec. 12, 1945 as Auxiliary Bishop of Baltimore; installed as first Bishop of Bridgeport, Dec. 1, 1953; transferred to Archdiocese of Baltimore, July 10, 1961; created Cardinal, Feb. 22, 1965; died Aug. 26, 1984.—Most Rev. WALTER W. CURTIS, S.T.D., ord. Dec. 8, 1937; appt. Auxiliary Bishop of Newark and Titular Bishop of Bisica in Tunis; cons. Sept. 24, 1957; appt. Bishop of Bridgeport, Sept. 23, 1961; installed Nov. 20, 1961; retired June 28, 1988; died Oct. 18, 1997.

Vicars General—Rev. Msgr. WILLIAM J. SCHEYD, P.A.; Rev. Msgr. THOMAS J. DRISCOLL, V.G., *238 Jewett Ave., Bridgeport, 06606-2892.*

Chancery—The Catholic Center, 238 Jewett Ave., Bridgeport, 06606-2892. Tel: 203-372-4301; Fax: 203-371-8698. Office Hours: Sept.-June Mon.-Fri. 9-5; July-Aug. 9-4.

Chancellor—Rev. Msgr. THOMAS J. DRISCOLL, V.G., *Catholic Center, 238 Jewett Ave., Bridgeport, 06606-2892.* Tel: 203-372-4301.

Vice Chancellor & Secretary to the Bishop—Rev. MICHAEL K. JONES.

Assistant to the Chancellor for Special Projects—Rev. Msgr. STEPHEN M. DIGIOVANNI.

Episcopal Vicar for Clergy and Religious—Rev. Msgr. LAURENCE R. BRONKIEWICZ, S.T.D.

Episcopal Vicar for Hispanics—Rev. Msgr. ANICETO VILLAMIDE.

Finance Officer—BERNARD E. REIDY, M.B.A., K.C.S.G.

Judicial Vicar—Rev. Msgr. JERALD A. DOYLE, Ph.D., J.C.D.

Diocesan Tribunal—The Catholic Center, 238 Jewett Ave., Bridgeport, 06606-2892. Tel: 203-372-4301.

Judges—Rev. Msgr. WILLIAM A. GENUARIO, P.A., J.C.D.; Rev. Msgr. THOMAS J. DRISCOLL, V.G.; Rev. Msgr. JEAN C. TETREAULT; Rev. Msgr. J. JAMES CUNEO, J.C.D.; Rev. Msgr. GEORGE D. BIRGE; Rev. MICHAEL A. BOCCACCIO; Rev. Msgr. JOHN B. HOSSAN; Rev. Canon ALBERT W. WATTS, J.C.L.; Revs. JOSEPH K. PARAMPATH, J.C.D.; ALBERT W. MCGOLDRICK, J.C.L.; MICHAEL R. MOYNIHAN, J.C.L.

Defenders of the Bond—Revs. RICHARD F. FUTIE, J.C.D.; WILLIAM F. VERRILLI; PAUL D. GRIFFIN.

Notaries—MARY A. MOLLOY; MARIE PECYLAK.

Promotor of Justice—Rev. G. FRANTZ DESRUISSEAUX, J.C.L.

Diocesan General Counsel—MICHAEL T. DOLAN, ESQ.

Diocesan Censors—Rev. Msgr. THOMAS J. DRISCOLL, V.G.; Rev. CHRISTOPHER J. WALSH, Ph.D.

Diocesan Consultors—Rev. Msgr. LAURENCE R. BRONKIEWICZ; Rev. Msgr. THOMAS J. DRISCOLL, V.G.; Rev. Msgr. JOSEPH D. POTTER; Rev. Msgr. BERNARD S. SCANLON; Rev. Msgr. JOHN C. SANDERS; Rev. Msgr. WILLIAM J. SCHEYD, P.A., V.G.; Rev. Msgr. EDWARD R. SURWILO; Rev. Msgr. ANICETO VILLAMIDE; Rev. Msgr. KEVIN W. WALLIN; Rev. Msgr. JERALD A. DOYLE; Rev. MICHAEL C. PALMER.

Presbyteral Council—Most Rev. EDWARD M. EGAN, Chm.; Rev. Msgr. LAURENCE R. BRONKIEWICZ; Rev. Msgr. JERALD A. DOYLE; Rev. Msgr. WILLIAM J. SCHEYD, P.A., V.G., Vice Chm.; Rev. Msgr. BERNARD S. SCANLON; Rev. Msgr. MARTIN P. RYAN; Rev. Msgr. ANICETO VILLAMIDE; Rev. Msgr. KEVIN W. WALLIN; Rev. Msgr. THOMAS J. DRISCOLL, V.G.; Rev. Msgr. NICHOLAS V. GRIECO; Rev. Msgr. BLASE M. GINTOLI; Rev. MATTHEW BERNELLI; Rev. Msgr. EDWIN F. BURKE; Rev. Msgr. GEORGE D. BIRGE; Revs. MICHAEL F. DOGALI; ERNEST T. ESPOSITO; FRANCIS T. HOFFMAN; WILLIAM KENNEDY, S.J.; DAVID C. LEOPOLD; WILLIAM R. MOYNIHAN; WALTER C. ORLONSKI; ROBERT G. POHLEY; JOSEPH A. PRINCE; MICHAEL K. JONES; ANDREW G. VARGA; ROBERT E. WEISS; INNOCENT C. KURKOWSKI, O.F.M.Conv.

Pastoral Council—Most Rev. EDWARD EGAN, J.C.D.; Rev. Msgr. WILLIAM J. SCHEYD, P.A., V.G.; Rev. G. FRANTZ DESRUISSEAUX; Rev. Msgr. ANICETO VILLAMIDE; Deacons DANIEL J. IANNIELLO; JOHN J. MORANSKI; Mr. TIMOTHY DEVINE; Sr. CHRISTINE KILEY, A.S.C.J.; Sr. MADELINE MCADAM, S.N.D.; THOMAS MULLIGAN, JR., ESQ.; ROBERT SALVESTRINI; HELEN F. CARROLL; NANCY DOLAN; Dr. ROMELEE A. HOWARD, K.S.G.; EILEEN HOWARD; Mrs. ROLAND J. WILSON, JR.; ISRAEL CORTES; MARY LOUISE SAMEDO; FRANK J. CARROLL; STEFAN GAWEL; MARIE WALSH; NICHOLAS PAVIA; ANNE CHATLOS; EMILIO ALICEA; ADRIANA MOLINA; Rev. MICHAEL K. JONES.

Finance Council—Most Rev. EDWARD M. EGAN; Rev. Msgr. WILLIAM J. SCHEYD, P.A., V.G.; Rev. Msgr. THOMAS J. DRISCOLL, V.G.; Mr. DIGBY W. BARRIOS; EDWARD P. LYONS; WILLIAM G. MALONEY, K.M.,

K.H.S., K.C.S.G.; DONALD T. STUDLEY, C.P.A.; BERNARD E. REIDY, M.B.A., K.C.S.G.; GEORGE TAYLOR; WILLIAM TOTTON.

Parochial Examiners—Rev. Msgr. LOUIS A. DEPROFIO; Rev. Msgr. JOHN E. GILMARTIN; Rev. Msgr. JOSEPH D. POTTER; Rev. Msgr. JOHN F. JAZOWSKI; Rev. Msgr. BARTHOLOMEW J. LAURELLO; Rev. MICHAEL C. PALMER; Rev. Msgr. JOSEPH A. SULLIVAN; Rev. Msgr. ANICETO VILLAMIDE.

Territorial Vicars—Vicariate I (Stamford, Darien, Glenbrook, Greenwich, Byram, Riverside): Rev. ROBERT G. POHLEY, Vicar, *Sacred Heart Rectory, 37 Schuyler Ave., Stamford, 06902.* Tel: 203-324-9544. Vicariate II (Norwalk, New Canaan, Wilton, Weston, Westport): Rev. Msgr. EDWIN T. BURKE, Vicar, *St. Ladislaus Rectory, 25 Cliff St., South Norwalk, 06856.* Tel: 203-866-1867. Vicariate III (Fairfield, Easton, West Bridgeport): Rev. Msgr. BLASE M. GINTOLI, Vicar, *Assumption Rectory, 545 Stratfield Rd., Fairfield, 06432.* Tel: 203-333-9065. Vicariate IV (East Bridgeport, Stratford, Trumbull, Monroe, Shelton): Rev. ROBERT E. WEISS, Vicar, *St. Joseph Rectory, 50 Fairmont Pl., Shelton, 06484.* Tel: 203-924-8611. Vicariate V (Bethel, Brookfield, Danbury, Georgetown, Newtown, New Fairfield, Redding, Ridgefield, Sherman): Rev. Msgr. MARTIN P. RYAN, *St. Edward Rectory, 3 Macbean Dr., P.O. Box 8866, New Fairfield, 06812.* Tel: 203-746-2200.

Ministry for Clergy and Religious—Rev. Msgr. LAURENCE R. BRONKIEWICZ, S.T.D., Episcopal Vicar & Dir. Clergy Personnel; Rev. ERNEST T. ESPOSITO, Asst. Vicar for Religious.

The Catholic Center—238 Jewett Ave., Bridgeport, 06606. Tel: 203-372-4301.

Finance Office—Business Office; BERNARD E. REIDY, M.B.A., K.C.S.G., Finance Officer; JOSEPH E. TANGREDI, JR., Controller; JOHN P. ROONEY, Dir., Parish Accounting and Finance, *The Catholic Center, 238 Jewett Ave., Bridgeport, 06606-2892.* Tel: 203-372-4301.

Members of the Clergy Personnel Committee—Rev. Msgr. STANLEY B. ROUSSEAU, Chm.; Rev. KEVIN T. ROYAL; Rev. Msgr. PETER P. DORA.

Office for the Continuing Education of Clergy—Rev. ERNEST T. ESPOSITO, Dir.

Office of Vocations—Rev. KEVIN T. ROYAL, Dir., *St. John Fisher Residence, 894 Newfield Ave., Stamford, 06905.* Tel: 203-322-5331.

Office of the Permanent Diaconate—Deacons ANTHONY J. DETJE, Dir., Formation; RICHARD STENBERG, Dir., Continuing Education; Rev. Msgr. LAURENCE R. BRONKIEWICZ, S.T.D., Spiritual Dir., Formation, *The Catholic Center, 238 Jewett Ave., Bridgeport, 06606-2892.* Tel: 203-372-4301.

Office for Ecumenical and Interreligious Affairs—Rev. Msgr. ALAN F. DETSCHER, S.L.D., Dir., *St. Catherine of Siena Rectory, 4 Riverside, 06878.* Tel: 203-637-3661.

Office of Liturgy—Vacant, *The Catholic Center, 238 Jewett Ave., Bridgeport, 06606-2892.* Tel: 203-372-4301.

Diocesan Commission on the Liturgy—Rev. ANDREW G. VARGA, D.Min., Chm., *Res., St. Luke, 84 Long Lots Rd., Westport, 06880-3917.*

Pastoral Planning—Rev. Msgr. THOMAS J. DRISCOLL, V.G., *238 Jewett Ave., Bridgeport, 06606-2892.* Tel: 203-372-4301.

Catechesis, Office for—Dr. JOAN M. KELLY, Dir., *The Catholic Center, 238 Jewett Ave., Bridgeport, 06606-2892.* Tel: 203-372-4301.
Catechist Formation—OLIVE S. GREENE, Asst. Dir.
Special Services—K. JANE KRESSER, Asst. Dir.
Catechumenate—ELIZABETH GIGLIO, Asst. Dir.
Youth Services—JOHN P. CAMPBELL, Asst. Dir.
Catholic Scouts—Deacon JOSEPH MELITA, Dir.

Office for Education—ARMAND R. FABBRI, Dir. & Supt., Schools; Sr. JOHN VIANNEY ZULLO, S.S.N.D., Asst. Dir., Elementary Education, *238 Jewett Ave., Bridgeport, 06606-2892.* Tel: 203-372-4301. WILLIAM J. ADAMS, Coord., Federal-State Programs, *238 Jewett Ave., Bridgeport, 06606.* Tel: 203-576-7944.

Special Education—Sr. ELEACE KING, I.H.M., Ed.D., Dir., *The Catholic Center, 238 Jewett Ave., Bridgeport, 06606-2892.* Tel: 203-372-4301, Ext. 330. THERESA DEPASCALE, Coord., Ministry to the Deaf. Tel: 203-372-4782 (TTY).

Apostolate for the Deaf—Rev. PETER A. DEMARCO, Moderator, *St. Teresa Rectory, 5302 Main St., Trumbull, 06611.* Tel: 203-261-3672; 459-0484 (TTY).

Catholic Charities of Fairfield County, Inc.—BRIAN A. CRONIN, A.C.S.W., C.I.S.W., Exec. Dir. BENEDICT P. MAZATOS, Comptroller, *Catholic Center, 238 Jewett Ave., Bridgeport, 06606-2892.* Tel: 203-372-4301, Ext. 379; 564; Fax: 203-372-5045.

Diocesan Offices and Directors

Ethnic and Cultural Services—Deacon JOSEPH J. FARLEY, Sec., *238 Jewett Ave., Bridgeport, 06606-2892.* Tel: 203-372-4301.

Aging, Diocesan Task Force—EDIE CASSIDY, Chm., *238 Jewett Ave., Bridgeport, 06606-2892.* Tel: 203-372-4301.

Archives—Rev. Msgr. JOHN V. HORGAN, Archivist, *238 Jewett Ave., Bridgeport, 06606-2892.* Tel: 203-372-4301.

African Americans, Apostolate of—Rev. Msgr. JOHN C. SANDERS, Dir., *St. Mary Rectory, 669 West Ave., Norwalk, 06850.* Tel: 203-866-5546.

Catholic Lawyers—Rev. Msgr. J. JAMES CUNEO, J.C.D., Spiritual Moderator; JAMES J. RUANE, ESQ., Coord., St. Thomas More Society of Fairfield Co., *238 Jewett Ave., Bridgeport, 06606-2892.* Tel: 203-372-4301.

Catholic Physicians Guild—Dr. THOMAS G. FLYNN, Coord., *39 Old Studio Rd., New Canaan, 06840.* Tel: 203-966-1959.

Catholic Women, Council of—Rev. MICHAEL R. MOYNIHAN, Diocesan Dir., *St. Michaels Rectory, 469 N. St., Greenwich, 06083.* Tel: 203-869-5421. Mrs. HELEN F. CARROLL, Diocesan Pres., *1216 Noble Ave., Bridgeport, 06608.* Tel: 203-335-7468. District Spiritual Directors: Revs. ERNEST T. ESPOSITO, (Bridgeport): MARTIN S. IGOE, (Greenwich): Rev. Msgr. EDWIN F. BURKE, (Norwalk): Rev. ROBERT G. POHLEY, (Stamford):

Cemeteries—BERNARD E. REIDY, M.B.A., K.C.S.G., Dir., *238 Jewett Ave., Bridgeport, 06606-2892.* Tel: 203-372-4301. LAWRENCE W. ARSZYLA, Mgr., *238 Jewett Ave., Bridgeport, 06606-2892.* Tel: 203-372-4301.

Charismatic Renewal—BETTY ANN CASARETTI, *238 Jewett Ave., Bridgeport, 06606-2892.* Tel: 203-372-4301.

Communications—Rev. CHRISTOPHER J. WALSH, Ph.D., Dir., *238 Jewett Ave., Bridgeport, 06606-2892.* Tel: 203-372-4301., *Res., St. John Fisher Residence, 894 Newfield Ave., Stamford, 06905.* Tel: 203-322-5331. Rev. MARK CONNOLLY, Diocesan Dir., Radio & Television, *10 Millbrook Rd. West, Stamford, 06902.* Tel: 203-348-7114.

Connecticut Catholic Conference—Dr. MARIE HILLIARD, Exec. Dir., *134 Farmington Ave., Hartford, 06105.* Tel: 203-524-7882.

Cursillos of Fairfield County, Inc.—Rev. PAUL F. MERRY, Advisor for English Language, *Blessed Sacrament Church, 275 Union Ave., Bridgeport, 06607.* Tel: 203-333-1202. Rev. Msgr. ANICETO VILLAMIDE, Advisor for Spanish Language, *St. Peter Rectory, 695 Colorado Ave., Bridgeport, 06605.* Tel: 203-366-5611.

Deaf, Apostolate for—Rev. PETER A. DEMARCO, Moderator, *Res., St. Teresa Rectory, 5301 Main St., Trumbull, 06611.* Tel: 203-261-3676; 459-0484 (TTY).

Development, Office of—JOHN G. BYRNE, Dir. Planned Giving; Rev. Msgr. KEVIN W. WALLIN, Dir. Inner City Foundation; Mr. THOMAS M. SWEENEY, Dir., Annual Bishop's Appeal, *238 Jewett Ave., Bridgeport, 06606-2892.* Tel: 203-372-4301.

Fairfield Foundation of the Diocese of Bridgeport, Inc.—MICHELLE JONES DELMHORST, Pres. JOHN CROFFY, Exec. Dir., *238 Jewett Ave., Bridgeport, 06606-2892.* Tel: 203-372-4301.

Inner-City Foundation for Charity and Education—Rev. Msgr. KEVIN W. WALLIN, Exec. Dir., *238 Jewett Ave., Bridgeport, 06606-2892.* Tel: 203-372-4301.

Catholic Ministry for the Elderly—Rev. DAVID H. KRAHEL, Chap. (Greenwich, Darien, Stamford), *Our Lady Star of the Sea Rectory, 1200 Shippan Ave., Stamford, 06902.* Tel: 203-357-7956.

Hispanic Apostolate, Episcopal Vicar for—Rev. Msgr. ANICETO VILLAMIDE, Vicar, *The Catholic Center, 238 Jewett Ave., Bridgeport, 06606-2892.* Tel: 203-372-4301.

Insurance Office—JOSEPH G. BURTON, Claims & Risk Mgr., *Catholic Mutual Group, 238 Jewett Ave., Bridgeport, 06606.* Tel: 203-371-8471.

Nurses, Council of Catholic—Rev. STEPHEN J. GLEESON, Dir., *St. Stephen's Rectory, 6949 Main St., Trumbull, 06611.* Tel: 203-268-6217; Fax: 203-268-9861.

Official Newspapers—"The Fairfield County Catholic", (Monthly), Rev. CHRISTOPHER J. WALSH, Ph.D., Editor, *238 Jewett Ave., Bridgeport, 06606.* Tel: 203-372-4301., *"The Catholic Transcript"*, (Weekly), *785 Asylum Ave., Hartford, 06105.* Tel: 203-527-1175.

Pilgrimages, Office of Diocesan—Rev. Msgr. WILLIAM J. LOUGHLIN, *St. Thomas Rectory, 1719 Post Rd., Fairfield, 06430.* Tel: 203-255-1097.

Pontifical Association of the Holy Childhood—Rev. ROBERT J. MATY, Dir. ELIZABETH SAULNIER, Coord. for Schools; R.E. Programs, *The Catholic Center, 238 Jewett Ave., Bridgeport, 06606-2892.* Tel: 203-372-4301.

Portuguese-Speaking People, Apostolate for—Rev. Msgr. CONSTANTINO R. CALDAS, Dir., *429 Huntington Rd., Bridgeport, 06608.* Tel: 203-333-7575.

Propagation of the Faith—Rev. ROBERT J. MATY, Dir., *The Catholic Center, 238 Jewett Ave., Bridgeport, 06606-2892.* Tel: 203-372-4301.

Boy Scouts and Girl Scouts—Deacon JOSEPH MELITA, Dir., *Catholic Center, 238 Jewett Ave., Bridgeport, 06606-2982.* Tel: 203-372-4301. Rev. STEPHEN J. BALINT, *Res., St. Ladislaus Rectory, 25 Cliff St., South Norwalk, 06854.* Tel: 203-866-1867.

Retired Priests—Rev. Msgr. BERNARD S. SCANLON, Dir., *Queen of the Clergy Residence, 128 Strawberry Hill Ave., Stamford, 06904.* Tel: 203-353-2250.

CLERGY, PARISHES, MISSIONS AND PAROCHIAL SCHOOLS

CITY OF BRIDGEPORT
(Fairfield County)

1—ST. AUGUSTINE CATHEDRAL (1842), Rev. Msgr. Stanley B. Rousseau. In res., Revs. John Punnakunnel; Donald L. Kloster; Alphonsus Tran Van Dong; Sr. Antoinette Mongkolrutana, S.L.C., Vietnamese Pastoral Assoc., Tel: 203-333-0837; Deacon Timothy Sullivan.
Res., 359 Washington Ave., 06604. Tel: 203-368-6777; Fax: 203-368-6386.
School—See separate listing under Elementary Schools, Regional in the Institution section.
Catechesis/Religious Programs—Students 250.

2—ST. AMBROSE (1928), Revs. Dennis G. Bludnicki; John Paul Long. In res., Rev. Nello A. Barachini, C.M.; Deacon James Volpe.
Res., 1596 Boston Ave., 06610. Tel: 203-333-1336; Fax: 203-330-9085.
School—See separate listing under Elementary Schools, Regional in the Institution section.
Stations—Bishop Curtis Homes, Tel: 203-366-4333; Success Park.

3—ST. ANDREW (1961), Revs. J. Barry Furey; Joseph J. Saba; Deacons Roland Blier; Edward Hendricks.
Res., 435 Anton St., 06606. Tel: 203-374-6171; Fax: 203-374-6172.
School—See separate listing under Elementary Schools, Regional in the Institution section.
Catechesis/Religious Programs—Mrs. Jeanne Bisson, D.R.E.
Students 323.

4—ST. ANN'S (1922), Revs. Joseph J. Malloy; Norman J. Guilbert, Jr.; Sr. Phyllis Campoli, Pastoral Assoc. & Prin.; Deacon John J. Moranski.
Res., 481 Brewster St., 06605. Tel: 203-368-1607; Fax: 203-368-0859.
School—See separate listing under Elementary Schools, Regional in the Institution section.
Catechesis/Religious Programs—Tel: 203-334-5856.
Students 25.

5—ST. ANTHONY OF PADUA. Merged with St. Peter, Bridgeport. See separate listing.

6—BLESSED SACRAMENT (1917), Rev. Paul F. Merry; Deacon Ricardo Martinez.
Mailing Address: 254 Wilmot Ave., 06607. Tel: 203-333-1202.
Res., 275 Union Ave., 06607.

7—ST. CHARLES (1902), Rev. Msgr. Joseph D. Potter; Revs. Gustavo Adolfo Falla; Marcel St. Jean; Sr. Antoinette Mongkolrutana, S.L.C., Laotian Pastoral Assoc., Tel: 203-333-0837.
Res., 391 Ogden St., 06608. Tel: 203-333-2147; Fax: 203-330-8316.
Catechesis/Religious Programs—Tel: 203-576-1629. Sr. Ann Moles, S.S.N.D., D.R.E.
Students 537.

8—SS. CYRIL AND METHODIUS (1907) (Slovak), Rev. Msgr. Joseph W. Pekar.
Res., 79 Church St., 06608. Tel: 203-333-7003.

9—ST. GEORGE'S (1907), Rev. Jose Rebaque, S.A.C., Admin., Tel: 203-579-1653.
Res., 443 Park Ave., 06604. Tel: 203-335-1797.

10—HOLY ROSARY (1903) (Italian), Rev. Guido G. Montanaro; Deacon Daniel Ianniello. In res., Rev. Robert J. Maty.
Res., 365 E. Washington Ave., 06608. Tel: 203-334-2447; Fax: 203-335-5334.

11—ST. JOHN NEPOMUCENE. Closed. For inquiries for parish records contact Holy Name of Jesus, Stratford.

12—ST. JOSEPH'S. Closed. May 23, 1988. For inquiries for parish records contact the Catholic Center.

13—ST. MARY'S (1857), Revs. Matthew Bernelli; Joseph J. Karcsinski.
Res., 25 Sherman St., 06608. Tel: 203-334-8811; Fax: 203-334-8574.

14—ST. MICHAEL THE ARCHANGEL (1989) (Polish), Revs. James Smyka, O.F.M.Conv.; Stefan Morawski, O.F.M.Conv. In res., Revs. Chester Kicia, O.F.M.Conv.; Marcel Sokalski; Edwin Agonis, O.F.M.Conv.

Res., 310 Pulaski St., 06608. Tel: 203-334-1822; Fax: 203-696-0078.

15—OUR LADY OF FATIMA (1962) (Portugese), Rev. Msgr. Constantino R. Caldas; Rev. Joseph De Brito Alves (Portugal); Deacon Gabriel A. Pereira.
Res., 429 Huntington Rd., 06608. Tel: 203-333-7575.
Catechesis/Religious Programs—Students 332.

16—OUR LADY OF GOOD COUNSEL (1955), Rev. Martin J. Nikodem. In res., Rev. Msgr. Gregory M. Smith.
Res., 163 Ortega Ave., 06606. Tel: 203-372-3533.
Catechesis/Religious Programs—Virginia Mora, D.R.E.
Students 35.

17—ST. PATRICK CHURCH (1889), Rev. Msgr. Andrew G. Marus; Rev. Michael J. Bachman; Sr. Eleanore Studwell, Pastoral Assoc. In res., Rev. Eugene R. Szantyr; Deacon William J. Bissenden.
Res. and Business Office: 170 Thompson St., 06604. Tel: 203-335-0106.
Church—851 North Ave., 06606. Tel: 203-367-4679.
Catechesis/Religious Programs—Sandra Mihalek, D.R.E.
Students 105.
Stations—Connecticut State Correctional Institution.; St. Vincent Medical Center, Tel: 203-576-6000; Barnett Multi Health Facility, Tel: 203-336-0232.

18—ST. PETER'S (1900) (Spanish), Rev. Msgr. Aniceto Villamide; Deacon Domingo Reveron. In res., Rev. Msgr. Stephen M. DiGiovanni; Rev. Jose Rebaque, S.A.C.
Res., 695 Colorado Ave., 06605. Tel: 203-366-5611; Fax: 203-335-1924.
School—See separate listing under Elementary Schools, Regional in the Institution section.
Catechesis/Religious Programs—Tel: 203-334-5681. Sr. Mirta Cruz, D.R.E.
Students 250.

19—ST. RAPHAEL'S (1925) (Italian), Revs. Carducci S. D'Amico; Grazioso Artuso; Deacon Joseph Melita. In res., Rev. Michael A. D'Elia.
Res., 162 Oak St., 06604. Tel: 203-333-3161; Fax: 203-368-1727.
School—See separate listing under Elementary Schools, Regional in the Institution section.
Catechesis/Religious Programs—Students 338.
Convent—671 Oak St., 06604. Tel: 203-535-9817.
Chapel—St. Margaret's, 2539 Park Ave., 06604.

OUTSIDE THE CITY OF BRIDGEPORT

Bethel, Fairfield Co., St. Mary's (1996), Rev. Msgr. Edward B. Karl; Revs. Richard J. Gemza; Francis T. Hoffmann; Deacon Robert Becker.
Office: 237 Greenwood Ave., P.O. Box 289, 06801. Tel: 203-744-5777; Fax: 203-744-3740. [CEM]
Church—24 Dodgingtown Rd., 06801.
School—See separate listing under Elementary Schools, Regional in the Institution section.
Catechesis/Religious Programs—Tel: 203-743-4557. Mary Amend, D.R.E.
Students 938.
Convent—Tel: 203-743-6985.

Brookfield, Fairfield Co., St. Joseph's (1941), Rev. Russell A. Augustine; Deacons William Shaughnessy; Richard Kovacs; Anthony Detje.
Res., 159 Whisconier Rd., P.O. Box 5072, 06804. Tel: 203-775-1035; Fax: 203-775-1684.
School—See separate listing under Elementary Schools, Regional in the Institution section.
Catechesis/Religious Programs—Tel: 203-775-5806.
Students 560.

St. Marguerite Bourgeoys (1982), Revs. Albert D. Audette; James J. Cole; Brian P. Gannon; Deacon Louis F. Howe.
Res., 138 Candlewood Lake Rd., 06804. Tel: 203-775-5117; Fax: 203-775-9254.
Catechesis/Religious Programs—Tel: 203-775-2644.
Students 225.

Danbury, Fairfield Co.,

1—ST. GREGORY'S, (1960), Revs. Angelo S. Arrando; John Stronkowski; Raymond M. Scherba; Deacons Robert Blankschen; William D. Murphy; Daniel N. Myott; Donald J. Naiman.
Res., 85 Great Plain Rd., 06811. Tel: 203-797-0222; Fax: 203-743-5464.
School—See separate listing under Elementary Schools, Regional in the Institution section.
Catechesis/Religious Programs—Tel: 203-743-5168. Mrs. Frances Britt, D.R.E.
Students 503.

2—IMMACULATE HEART OF MARY, (1980) (Portuguese), Rev. Antonio Carvalho de Azevedo, Admin.; Deacon Jose Rodrigues Cabral.
Res., 149 Deer Hill Ave., 06811. Tel: 203-797-1821; Fax: 203-743-9146.
Catechesis/Religious Programs—Students 168.

3—OUR LADY OF GUADALUPE, (Spanish), Rev. Frederick L. Saviano.
Res., 29 Golden Hill Rd., 06811-4629. Tel: 203-743-1021; Fax: 203-798-8143.

4—ST. JOSEPH'S, (1905), Revs. James D. Grosso; John F. Pikulski, Ph.D.; Cyprian P. LaPastina; Deacon David Vaughn. In res., Rev. Joseph V. Rossitto.
Res., 8 Robinson Ave., 06810. Tel: 203-748-8177; Fax: 203-748-2010.
School—See separate listing under Elementary Schools, Regional in the Institution section.
Catechesis/Religious Programs—Tel: 203-743-7754.
Students 327.

5—ST. PETER'S, (1851), Rev. Msgr. Kevin W. Wallin; Revs. Corey V. Piccinino; Jonas V. DeMoraes (Brazil); Douglas J. Tufaro; Gregg D. Mecca.
Res., 104 Main St., 06810. Tel: 203-743-2707; Fax: 203-794-1928.
School—See separate listing under Elementary Schools, Regional in the Institution section.
Catechesis/Religious Programs—Tel: 203-743-1048; Fax: 203-797-9471. Margaret M. Curran, D.R.E.
Students 260.

6—SACRED HEART, (1925) (Polish), Revs. Maurice Piszczatowski, O.F.M.Conv.; Gerald Waterman, O.F.M.Conv.; Deacon John F. Esterheld. In res., Rev. Robert Schlageter, O.F.M.Conv., Campus Min. West Connecticut Univ.; Bro. Joseph Colarossi.
Res., 12 Cottage St., 06810. Tel: 203-748-9029; Fax: 203-748-9168.
School—See separate listing under Elementary Schools, Regional in the Institution section.
Catechesis/Religious Programs—Students 86.
Convent—46 Stone St., 06810. Tel: 203-743-6406.

Darien, Fairfield Co., St. John (1895), Revs. Michael Jude Fay; Joseph Cervero; Deacon William K. Rowe. In res., Rev. Msgr. Joseph J. Kohut.
Res., 1986 Post Rd., 06820. Tel: 203-655-1145; Fax: 203-655-1048.
Catechesis/Religious Programs—Tel: 203-655-8020. John Cunningham, D.R.E.
Students 425.

St. Thomas More (1966), Rev. Msgr. Edward J. Howley; Rev. William F. Verrilli; Sr. Madeline McAdam, S.N.D., Pastoral Assoc.; Deacon Joseph Rowan.
Res., 384 Middlesex Rd., 06820. Tel: 203-655-3303; Fax: 203-655-8901.
Catechesis/Religious Programs—374 Middlesex Rd., 06820. Tel: 203-655-3077. Mrs. Zita O'Brian, D.R.E. Lay Teachers 70; Students 700.
Convent—370 Middlesex Rd., 06820. Tel: 203-655-3580.
Sisters of Notre Dame de Namur 4.

Easton, Fairfield Co., Notre Dame of Easton (1956), Revs. Robert J. Hyl; Albert W. McGoldrick; Deacons Harold J. Lynch; Gerald F. Sabol.
Res., 640 Morehouse Rd., 06612. Tel: 203-268-5838.
Church—655 Morehouse Rd., 06612. Tel: 203-261-5596.
Catechesis/Religious Programs—Students 358.

Fairfield, Fairfield Co.,

1—ST. ANTHONY OF PADUA, (1927) (Polish), Revs. Innocent Kurkowski, O.F.M.Conv.; Berard Dudek, O.F.M.Conv.
Res., 149 S. Pine Creek Rd., 06430. Tel: 203-259-0358; Fax: 203-259-0358.

2—ASSUMPTION, (1922), Rev. Msgr. Blase M. Gintoli; Revs. John P. Baran; Ernest T. Esposito; Deacons George I. Saulnier; Donald J. Ross, Jr.
Res., 545 Stratfield Rd., 06430. Tel: 203-333-9065; Fax: 203-333-2562.
School—See separate listing under Elementary Schools, Regional in the Institution section.
Catechesis/Religious Programs—Frank Macari, D.R.E.
Students 400.
Convent—605 Stratfield Rd., 06432. Tel: 203-336-3419.

3—ST. EMERY'S, (1932) (Hungarian). (United with St. Stephen's of Bridgeport). Revs. Robert Nemeth, O.F.M.; Emeric Szlezak, O.F.M.
Res., 838 King's Hwy., 06432. Tel: 203-334-0312; Fax: 203-579-9423.
Convent—105 Biro St., 06432. Tel: 203-334-3913.
Congregation of Notre Dame 3.

4—HOLY CROSS, (Slovenian), Revs. Louis M. Dytkowski, Admin.; Milan Dimic, S.D.B., Pastoral Assoc.; Deacon Kevin Moore.
Res., 750 Tahmore Dr., 06430. Tel: 203-372-4595; Fax: 203-372-4668.
Catechesis/Religious Programs—Tel: 203-373-0466.
Students 156.

5—HOLY FAMILY, (1938), Revs. William D. Donovan; Peter J. Towsley; Mr. Gerald Cryan, Pastoral Min.
Res., 700 Old Stratfield Rd., 06430. Tel: 203-336-1835; Fax: 203-336-0342.
School—See separate listing under Elementary Schools, Regional in the Institution section.
Catechesis/Religious Programs—Sr. Monica Leonard, C.N.D., D.R.E.
Students 250.
Convent—70 Laurel St., 06432. Tel: 203-333-3423.

6—ST. PIUS X, (1955), Rev. Msgr. Edward J. Scull; Rev. George Sankoorikal; Deacon Richard Stenberg.
Res., 834 Brookside Dr., 06430. Tel: 203-255-6134; Fax: 203-255-5232.
Catechesis/Religious Programs—Tel: 203-259-4800.
Students 464.

7—ST. THOMAS AQUINAS, (1876), Revs. Victor T. Martin; Paul D. Griffin; Michael K. Jones; William J. Loughlin.
Res., 1719 Post Rd., 06430. Tel: 203-255-1097; Fax: 203-256-8177. [CEM]
School—See separate listing under Elementary Schools, Regional in the Institution section.
Catechesis/Religious Programs—Tel: 203-255-1984. Sr. Catherine Jemapete, S.S.N.D., D.R.E.
Students 412.

Georgetown, Fairfield Co., Sacred Heart (1881), Revs. M. Joseph Joaquin; Mark E. Grimes.
Res., 30 Church St., Box 388, 06829. Tel: 203-544-8345; Fax: 203-544-1246.
Catechesis/Religious Programs—Tel: 203-544-8423.
Students 225.

Greenwich, Fairfield Co.,

1—ST. MARY'S, (1874), Rev. Msgr. Frank C. Wissel, D.Min.; Revs. Francis J. Moy, S.J.; Michael F. Dogali; German Martinez, O.S.B., (Spain) Hispanic Ministry; Sr. Michael Marie Fitzpatrick, S.S.N.D., Pastoral Assoc.; Deacon Matthew T. Ashe.
Res., 178 Greenwich Ave., 06830. Tel: 203-869-9393; Fax: 203-869-1032.
Catechesis/Religious Programs—Tel: 203-869-9250; Fax: 203-625-4760. Sr. Patricia Wachter, S.S.N.D., D.R.E.
Students 350.

2—ST. MICHAEL THE ARCHANGEL, (1963) (Korean), Revs. Michael Robert Moynihan; William J. Kennedy, S.J.; Mark Connolly.
Res., 469 North St., 06830. Tel: 203-869-5421; Fax: 203-869-0169.
Catechesis/Religious Programs—Tel: 203-661-3088. Sr. Celine M. Flynn, S.S.N.D., D.R.E.
Students 385.
Mission—Greenwich, Fairfield Co., St. Timothy's, 1034 North St., 06830.

3—ST. PAUL'S, (1902), Revs. Joseph A. Sullivan; Roger F. McDonough.
Res., 84 Sherwood Ave., 06831. Tel: 203-531-8741.
Catechesis/Religious Programs—Tel: 203-531-4265. Sr. Margaret Hoban, D.R.E.
Students 195.

4—ST. ROCH, (1938) (Italian), Rev. Nicholas J. Calabro.
Res., 10 St. Roch Ave., 06830. Tel: 203-869-4176; Fax: 203-618-0341.
Catechesis/Religious Programs—Harry Florentine, D.R.E.
Students 212.

5—ST. AGNES, (1963), Rev. Stephen J. DeLuca.
Res., 247 Stanwich Rd., 06830. Tel: 203-869-5396; Fax: 203-625-0596.
Catechesis/Religious Programs—Mrs. Linda Nardone, D.R.E.
Students 40.

6—SACRED HEART, (1990), Rev. Martin S. Igoe.
Res., 95 Henry St., 06830. Tel: 203-531-8730; Fax: 203-531-8794.
Catechesis/Religious Programs—Tel: 203-531-4772. Sr. Elizabeth Telford, S.A., D.R.E.
Students 19.

Huntington, Fairfield Co., St. Lawrence (1955), Rev. Msgr. Joseph M. Fitzgerald; Revs. Robert J. Crofut; Nicholas A. Cirillo; Deacons James A. Brown; Joseph Filingeri; F. Robert Dwyer.
Res., 505 Shelton Ave., Shelton, 06484. Tel: 203-929-5355; Fax: 203-929-8939.
School—See separate listing under Elementary Schools, Regional in the Institution section.
Catechesis/Religious Programs—Tel: 203-929-8421. Mrs. Barbara Pekar, D.R.E.
Students 850.

Monroe, Fairfield Co., St. Jude (1973), Rev. Msgr. John B. Sabia.
Res., 707 Monroe Tpke., 06468. Tel: 203-261-6404; Fax: 203-261-7507.
School—See separate listing under Elementary Schools, Regional in the Institution section.
Catechesis/Religious Programs—Tel: 203-261-6788. Mrs. Jean Paul, D.R.E.
Students 1,024.

New Canaan, Fairfield Co., St. Aloysius (1896), Rev. Msgr. J. Peter Cullen; Revs. Dariusz J. Zielonka;

Robert J. Valentine; Deacon John H. Tugman.
Res., 40 Maple St., 06840. Tel: 203-966-0020; Fax: 203-972-7691.
School—See separate listing under Elementary Schools, Regional in the Institution section.
Catechesis/Religious Programs—30 Maple St., 06840. Tel: 203-966-4555.
Students 800.

New Fairfield, Fairfield Co., St. Edward the Confessor (1954), Rev. Msgr. Martin P. Ryan; Revs. Bose Raja Selvaraj; John Castaldo; Deacons Paul Pilkington; Henry Hein.
Res., P.O. Box 8866, 06812. Tel: 203-746-2200; Fax: 203-746-4856.
Catechesis/Religious Programs—Tel: 203-746-4270. Ms. Joan Marschall, D.R.E.
Students 1,219.

Newtown, Fairfield Co., St. Rose of Lima (1859), Revs. George D. Birge; Lawrence A. Larson. In res., Rev. Msgr. Jean C. Tetreault; Deacon Kenneth P. Stroud.
Res., 46 Church Hill Rd., 06470. Tel: 203-426-2572; Fax: 203-426-6222. [CEM]
School—See separate listing under Elementary Schools, Regional in the Institution section.
Catechesis/Religious Programs—Tel: 203-426-2333. Alice Kohler, D.R.E.
Students 1,087.

Norwalk, Fairfield Co.,

1—St. Jerome, (1960), Revs. David W. Blanchfield; Joseph Palacino.
Church—23 Half Mile Rd., 06851. Tel: 203-847-5349; Fax: 203-846-0238.
Catechesis/Religious Programs—Tel: 203-846-2111.
Students 415.

2—St. Joseph's, (South Norwalk) (1895), Revs. David W. Howell; Gilbert P. D'Souza. In res., Rev. G. Frantz Desruisseaux; Deacon William O. Murphy.
Res., 85 S. Main St., P.O. Box 443, 06856. Tel: 203-838-4171; Fax: 203-899-0007.
Catechesis/Religious Programs—Tel: 203-866-1225. Deacon William O. Murphy, D.R.E.
Students 390.
Convent—14 Chestnut St., 06854. Tel: 203-866-9452.

3—St. Ladislaus, (1907) (Hungarian), Rev. Msgr. Edwin F. Burke. In res., Rev. Stephen J. Balint.
Res., 25 Cliff St., 06854. Tel: 203-866-1867; Fax: 203-866-7830.

4—St. Mary's, (1848), Rev. Alfred J. Bietighofer; Rev. Msgr. John C. Sanders.
Res., 669 West Ave., 06850. Tel: 203-866-5546; Fax: 203-866-0464.
Catechesis/Religious Programs—Tel: 203-866-7429. Mrs. Deborah Ruffin, D.R.E.
Students 145.

5—St. Matthew, (1957), Revs. Walter C. Orlowski; Gregory J. Huminski; Deacon David M. Sochacki.
Res., 216 Scribner Ave., 06854. Tel: 203-838-3788; Fax: 203-838-9185.
Catechesis/Religious Programs—Tel: 203-838-0231. Kathleen B. Sochacki, D.R.E.
Students 515.

6—St. Philip, (1964), Revs. Michael A. Boccaccio; Albert G. Pinciaro, III.
Res., One Fr. Conlon Pl., 06851. Tel: 203-847-4549 (Office); Fax: 203-847-4148.
Catechesis/Religious Programs—Tel: 203-847-4286. Sr. Mary Ann McPartland, C.N.D., D.R.E.
Students 355.
Convent—23 France St., 06851. Tel: 203-847-1478.

7—St. Thomas the Apostle, (1935), Rev. Msgr. William J. Scheyd, P.A., V.G.; Revs. Michael F. Flynn; Richard Daniel Murphy.
Res., 203 East Ave., 06855. Tel: 203-866-3141; Fax: 203-866-1219.
Good Counsel's Malta House—5 Prowitt St., 06855.
Catechesis/Religious Programs—Tel: 203-866-1189. Mrs. Patricia Braccio, D.R.E.
Students 553.

Redding, Fairfield Co., St. Patrick (1879), Rev. John B. Hossan; Deacon William C. Timmel.
Res., 169 Black Rock Tpke., P.O. Box 119, Redding Ridge, 06876. Tel: 203-938-2253; Fax: 203-938-3396.
Catechesis/Religious Programs—Tel: 203-938-2963. Barbara L. Clarke, D.R.E.
Students 196.

Ridgefield, Fairfield Co., St. Elizabeth Seton (1978), Rev. Joseph A. Prince; Deacons Bart Mauceri; Terence Grant.
Res., 520 Ridgebury Rd., 06877. Tel: 203-438-7292; Fax: 203-438-0600.
Catechesis/Religious Programs—Tel: 203-438-9707; Fax: 203-438-0600. Andrea Kennedy, D.R.E.
Students 700.

St. Mary's, Fairfield Co, (1882), Revs. Robert P. Morrissey; Roy N. Henderson; Edward Small, S.J.; Leszek Szymaszek; Deacon Norman Roos.
Res., 183 High Ridge Ave., 06877. Tel: 203-438-6538; Fax: 203-438-4406. [CEM]
School—See separate listing under Elementary Schools, Regional in the Institution Section.
Catechesis/Religious Programs—Tel: 203-438-7335. Sr. Joan Brennan, D.R.E.
Students 1,200.

Riverside, Fairfield Co., St. Catherine of Siena (1913), Rev. Msgr. William A. Genuario, P.A.; Rev. Msgr. Alan F. Detscher; Revs. Robert A. Loftus; William F. Platt; Deacons Renato Berzolla; Robert Henrey; Vincent Heidenreich.
Res., 4 Riverside Ave., 06878. Tel: 203-637-3661; Fax: 203-637-8934.
Catechesis/Religious Programs—13 Riverside Ave., 06878. Tel: 203-637-4213; Fax: 203-637-2089. Barbara Glynn, D.R.E.
Students 49.

Shelton, Fairfield Co., St. Joseph's (1906), Revs. Robert E. Weiss; Paul G. Murphy; George F. O'Neill; Deacon David Munson.
Res., 50 Fairmont Pl., 06484. Tel: 203-924-8611; Fax: 203-924-9446.
School—See separate listing under Elementary Schools, Regional in the Institution section.
Catechesis/Religious Programs—430 Coram Ave., 06484. Tel: 203-924-9677. Mrs. Patricia Heller, D.R.E.
Students 460.
Convent—420 Coram Ave., 06484. Tel: 203-924-1545. Sisters of St. Joseph Chambery

St. Margaret Mary (1963), Rev. Msgr. Thomas J. Whalen; Deacon Matthew Skurat.
Res., 380 Long Hill Ave., 06484. Tel: 203-924-4929; Fax: 203-924-4929.
Catechesis/Religious Programs—Tel: 203-924-2679. Mrs. Carol D'Amico, D.R.E.
Students 297.

Sherman, Fairfield Co., Holy Trinity (1985), Rev. David J. Riley.
Res., Rte. 37 & 39, P.O. Box 97, 06784. Tel: 860-354-1414; Fax: 860-355-9439.
Catechesis/Religious Programs—Tel: 203-354-1498. Ms. Ginny Verhoff, D.R.E.
Students 180.

Stamford, Fairfield Co.,

1—St. Benedict's, (1930) (Slovak), Rev. Vincent J. Veich.
Res., One St. Benedict Cir., 06902. Tel: 203-327-7250; Fax: 203-327-7251.

2—St. Bridget, (1963), Rev. Gill C. Babeu.
Res., 278 Strawberry Hill Ave., 06902. Tel: 203-324-2910; Fax: 203-363-0135.
Catechesis/Religious Programs—Tel: 203-357-8157. Mrs. Rose Stearns, D.R.E.
Students 97.

3—St. Cecilia's, (1926), Rev. Msgr. Roger J. Watts; Rev. William G. Carey.
Res., 1184 Newfield Ave., 06905. Tel: 203-322-1562; Fax: 203-968-1550.
School—See separate listing under Elementary Schools, Regional in the Institution section.

4—St. Clement's, (1928), Revs. Andre R. Dube; David W. Franklin; Deacon Paul E. Tupper.
Res., 535 Fairfield Ave., 06902. Tel: 203-348-4206; Fax: 203-316-8131.
Catechesis/Religious Programs—Students 108.

5—St. Gabriel, (1963), Rev. Robert A. Uzzilio; Deacon Larry Buzzeo. In res., Rev. Brian M. Gray.
Res., 914 Newfield Ave., 06905. Tel: 203-322-7426; Fax: 203-968-6266.
School—See separate listing under Elementary Schools, Regional in the Institution section.
Catechesis/Religious Programs—Tel: 203-329-1978. Sr. Ann Marie Stileckis, C.N.D., D.R.E.
Students 216.

6—Holy Name of Jesus, (1903) (Polish), Revs. Sherman W. Gray, Jr.; Stanley Staniszewski, C.M.
Res., 4 Pulaski St., 06902. Tel: 203-323-4967; Fax: 203-323-6403.
Catechesis/Religious Programs—Tel: 203-359-3618; Fax: 203-323-4546. Sr. Theresa Kovacs, S.M.M.I., D.R.E.
Students 110.

7—Holy Spirit, (1962), Rev. Msgr. Normand A. Methe.
Res., 403 Scofieldtown Rd., 06903. Tel: 203-322-3722; Fax: 203-322-0543.
School—See separate listing under Elementary Schools, Regional in the Institution section.
Catechesis/Religious Programs—Tel: 203-357-1094. Linda Dunn, D.R.E.
Students 163.

8—St. John's, (1847), Revs. William A. Nagle; Kevin P. Fitzpatrick.
Res., 279 Atlantic St., 06901. Tel: 203-324-1553; Fax: 203-359-2660.
Catechesis/Religious Programs—Tel: 203-359-2052. Sr. Frances C.S.J., D.R.E.
Students 239.

9—St. Leo's, (1960), Rev. Msgr. Benedict F. Tighe; Rev. Thomas P. Thorne; Deacons Joseph J. Farley; Ralph Hammock.
Res., 24 Roxbury Rd., 06902. Tel: 203-322-1669; 329-8884; Fax: 203-461-9761.
Catechesis/Religious Programs—Tel: 203-348-0052. Mrs. Florence Gambino, D.R.E.
Students 450.

10—St. Mary's, (1907), Revs. Richard F. Futie; Carlos Rodrigues; Paul B. Lalic; Dario Gomez.
Res., 566 Elm St., 06902. Tel: 203-324-7321; Fax: 203-323-9407.
Catechesis/Religious Programs—Sr. Theresa Kovacs, D.R.E.
Students 251.

11—St. Maurice, (1935), Revs. Gerald T. Devore; Bernard A. Keefe.
Res., 358 Glenbrook Rd., 06906-2198. Tel: 203-324-3434; Fax: 203-964-8023.
Catechesis/Religious Programs—Tel: 203-348-8768; Fax: 203-964-8023. Margaret Borders, D.R.E.
Students 198.

12—Our Lady of Montserrat, (1984) (Spanish), Rev. Matthew R. Mauriello, Admin.; Deacon Ramon Isidro.
Res., 93 Hope St., 06906. Tel: 203-323-7379; Fax: 203-323-0798.
Catechesis/Religious Programs—Students 550.

13—Our Lady Star of the Sea, (1964), Rev. Msgr. Edward R. Surwilo; Deacons Edward R. Kovacs; John Mann. In res., Rev. David H. Krahel.
Res., 1200 Shippan Ave., 06902. Tel: 203-324-4634; Fax: 203-348-9963.
School—See separate listing under Elementary Schools, Regional in the Institution section.
Convent—1216 Shippan Ave., 06902. Tel: 203-359-1127.

14—Sacred Heart, (1920) (Italian), Revs. Robert G. Pohley; Alfred F. Pecaric; Robert J. Post, Ph.D.; Rufin Kuveikis, O.F.M.Cap.; Deacons Louis F. Howe; Fred Harrity.
Res., 37 Schuyler Ave., 06902. Tel: 203-324-9544; Fax: 203-324-9202.
School—See separate listing under Elementary Schools, Regional in the Institution section.
Catechesis/Religious Programs—Students 195.
Convent—21 Schuyler Ave., 06902. Tel: 203-323-3524.

Stratford, Fairfield Co.,

1—Holy Name of Jesus, (1923) (Slovak), Rev. Msgr. Peter P. Dora; Rev. Msgr. James J. Cuneo; Rev. Michael L. Dunn; Deacon Thomas Freibott.
Res., 1950 Barnum Ave., 06497. Tel: 203-375-5815; Fax: 203-375-5954.
School—See separate listing under Elementary Schools, Regional in the Institution section.
Catechesis/Religious Programs—Students 360.
Convent—2 Mary Ave., 06497. Tel: 203-378-1203.

2—St. James, (1886), Revs. Thomas F. Lynch; Lawrence J. Carroll; Daniel Kennelly; Darius J. Zielonka; Michael Patrick Lyons; Deacon John Barton.
Res., 2110 Main St., 06497. Tel: 203-375-5887; Fax: 203-378-1562.
School—See separate listing under Elementary Schools, Regional in the Institution section.
Catechesis/Religious Programs—Kathleen Donnelly, D.R.E.
Students 664.

3—St. Mark's, (1960), Rev. Msgr. Lawrence J. McMahon; Rev. Stanley N. Koziol; Deacons T. Emmet Murray; F. Paul Kurmay; Andrew Dzujna.
Res., 500 Wigwam Ln., 06497. Tel: 203-377-0444; Fax: 203-378-7913.
School—See separate listing under Elementary Schools, Regional in the Institution section.
Catechesis/Religious Programs—Tel: 203-377-3158. Helen E. Bendyk, D.R.E.
Students 1,040.

4—Our Lady of Grace, (1954), Rev. Msgr. William F. Schultz. In res., Rev. Msgr. Jerald A. Doyle; Rev. Thomas D. Nicastro.
Res., 497 Second Hill Ln., 06497. Tel: 203-377-0928.
Parish Center—375 Second Hill Ln., 06497. Tel: 203-375-2005.
Catechesis/Religious Programs—Tel: 203-375-5168. Susan Czaplicki, D.R.E.
Students 265.

5—Our Lady of Peace, (1948), Rev. Msgr. John E. Gilmartin. In res., Rev. Msgr. Thomas J. Driscoll.
Res., 230 Park Blvd., Lordship, 06497. Tel: 203-377-4863; Fax: 203-378-5253.
Catechesis/Religious Programs—Tel: 203-378-3053. Ms. Sandra Klunn, D.R.E.
Students 159.

Trumbull, Fairfield Co.,

1—Christ the King, (1962), Revs. Bernard M. Dolan; Lawrence F. Carew.
Res., 4700 Madison Ave., 06611. Tel: 203-268-8695.

Catechesis/Religious Programs—Tel: 203-261-2583.
Students 380.

2—St. Catherine of Siena, Rev. Msgr. Richard J. Shea; Revs. Michael J. Madden; Robert D. Karpinski.
Res., 200 Shelton Rd., 06611. Tel: 203-377-3133; Fax: 203-377-1023.
School—See separate listing under Elementary Schools, Regional in the Institution section. Tel: 203-375-1847; Fax: 203-378-3935.
Convent—19 Rosemond Ter., 06611. Tel: 203-261-3848.

3—St. Stephen, (1953), Rev. Stephen J. Gleeson; Deacons Gary Carpenter; Donald Brunetto; Michael Wolfer. In res., Rev. Edward A. Colohan.
Res., 6948 Main St., 06611. Tel: 203-268-6217; Fax: 203-268-9861.
Catechesis/Religious Programs—Tel: 203-268-6860. Sr. Beth McGlynn, S.S.N.D., D.R.E.
Students 522.

4—St. Theresa's, (1934), Rev. Msgr. Louis A. DeProfio; Revs. Walter J. Seekamp; Peter A. DeMarco; Sr. Joan Flynn, R.S.M., Dir. Pastoral Min.; Deacon H. Paul Herman. In res., Rev. William F. Sangiovanni.
Res., 5301 Main St., 06611. Tel: 203-261-3676; Fax: 203-268-8723.
School—See separate listing under Elementary Schools, Regional in the Institution section.
Catechesis/Religious Programs—19 Rosemond Ter., 06611. Tel: 203-261-4706. Mrs. Earline C. Sullivan, C.S.F.N., D.R.E.
Students 753.
Convent—Tel: 203-261-3848.
School Sisters of Notre Dame 8.

Weston, Fairfield Co., St. Francis of Assisi (1955), Rev. Msgr. Nicholas V. Grieco. In res., Rev. Joseph K. Parampath.
Res., 35 Norfield Rd, P.O. Box 1025, 06883. Tel: 203-227-1341; Fax: 203-226-1154.
Catechesis/Religious Programs—Tel: 203-226-9474.
Students 375.

Westport, Fairfield Co., Assumption (1876), Revs. Frank C. McGrath; David C. Leopold; Deacons Eugene P. Kamper; John S. Fay. In res., Rev. Msgr. Laurence R. Bronkiewicz.
Res., 98 Riverside Ave., 06880. Tel: 203-227-5161; Fax: 203-227-1206. [CEM]
Catechesis/Religious Programs—Tel: 203-226-5448. Carol Lynn Brown, D.R.E.
Students 297.

St. Luke (1957), Revs. Andrew G. Varga; Samuel V. Scott; Deacon Brian Kelly.
Res., 84 Long Lots Rd., 06880. Tel: 203-227-7245; Fax: 203-226-8063.
Catechesis/Religious Programs—Tel: 203-226-0729; Fax: 203-226-8063. Jane Ferreira, D.R.E.
Students 748.

Wilton, Fairfield Co., Our Lady of Fatima (1953), Revs. Michael C. Palmer; John Kallattil; James Breen; Deacon Thomas K. Seith.
Res., 229 Danbury Rd., 06897. Tel: 203-762-3928; Fax: 203-834-1261.
School—See separate listing under Elementary Schools, Regional in the Institution section.
Catechesis/Religious Programs—Tel: 203-762-9080; Fax: 203-831-1261. Mrs. Kathleen Rooney, D.R.E.
Students 935.

Chaplains of Public Institutions

Bridgeport. *Bridgeport Community Correctional Facility,* 1106 North Ave., 06604. Tel: 203-579-6131. Deacon Carl M. Vecca Tel: 203-582-6477.
Bridgeport Health Care, 600 Bond St., 06610. Tel: 203-384-6400. Rev. Michael A. D'Elia.
Bridgeport Hospital, 267 Grant St., 06610. Tel: 203-384-3311. Revs. Eugene R. Szantyr, Assoc. Chap.; Nello A. Barachini.

Danbury. *Danbury Area Mental Health Authority,* 64 West St., 06810. Tel: 203-778-1640, Ext. 247. Rev. Arthur E. Norton, Assoc. Chap.
Danbury Hospital, 24 Hospital Ave., 06810. Tel: 203-797-7000. Rev. John F. Pikulski.
Federal Correctional Institution, 06811. Tel: 203-743-6471. Rev. James A. McDevitt, Chaplain; Sr. Anne Marie Raftery, O.S.F., Dir. of Pastoral Care.

Greenwich. *Greenwich Hospital,* 06830. Tel: 203-863-3000. Rev. James McIntyre, O.F.M.Cap.

Norwalk. *Norwalk Hospital,* 06856. Tel: 203-852-2000. Rev. Rufin Kuveikis, O.F.M.Cap.

Stamford. *Stamford Hospital,* 06902. Tel: 203-325-7584. Rev. Brian M. Gray.

On Duty Outside the Diocese:
Reverend Monsignors—
Cusack, Andrew T., Dir. National Institute for Clergy Formation, Seton Hall University, 400 S. Orange Ave., South Orange, NJ 07079
Green, Thomas J., Catholic University of America, Department of Canon Law, Washington, DC 20017
Millea, William V., Via della Nocetta 63, Rome, 00164 Italy
Reverend Fathers—
Barrett, M. Stephen, S.S., 10910 Olde Woods Way, Columbia, Maryland 21044
Holbrook, Harold M., Padres De Santiago Apostol, Casilla 1021, Oruro, Bolivia
Lincon, J. Bruce, St. Pius X, 5620 Gollihar Rd., Corpus Christi, TX 78412
Mitchell, John C., P.O. Box 701, Carmel, NY 10072
Posluszny, Francis, Parroquia San Juan Apostal, APTO 735, Chiclayo, Peru
Smolko, John F., Catholic University of America, 9808 Dale Dr., Upper Marlboro, MD 20870
Talar, Charles J.T., St. Mary Seminary & University, 5400 Roland Rd., Baltimore, MD 21210
Terentieff, Robert J., Mount St. Mary College, Emmitsburg, MD 21727
Tracy, David W., University of Chicago, The Divinity School, 5521 S. University, Chicago, IL 60637

Graduate Studies:
Reverend Fathers—
Check, Paul N., North American College, Vatican City State, Rome 00120 Italy
Guglielmi, Donald A., Pontifical University of St. Thomas Aquinas, Rome
Powers, Thomas W., North American College, Vatican City State, Rome 00120 Italy

---

Military Chaplains:
Reverend Fathers—
Carey, William F., U.S. Army
Gay, James A., U.S. Navy
Thompson, William D., U.S. Air Force

Awaiting Assignment:
Reverend Fathers—
Rodriguez, Bernardo C.

Leave of Absence:
Reverend Monsignors—
Smith, Gregory M.
Stubbs, Charles W.
Reverend Fathers—
Ahearn, Kieran T.
Biondino, Joseph P.
Carr, Charles T.
Federici, Martin J.
Moore, Joseph P.
Yocis, David A.

Retired:
Reverend Monsignors—
Botton, Pierre A.
Caldas, Constantino R.
Campagnone, Francis A.
Foley, Daniel J.
Guinan, Thomas P.
Hale, Harry L.
Halloran, Edward D.
Henahan, Thomas F.
Horgan, John V.
Kohut, Joseph J.
Laurello, Bartholomew J.
Lengen, James G.
Pranckus, Francis J.
Scanlon, Bernard S.
Tetreault, Jean C.
Reverend Fathers—
Brady, Philip W.
Coleman, W. Philip
Coyne, Edwin J.
Dennehy, Martin J.
Dennis, James J.
Dunn, Richard R.
Fernandez, Jose A.
Fonseca, John
Gregori, Emidio O.
Grise, J. Clifford
Hitchcock, Martin B.
Hribsek, Aloysius J.
Jazowski, John F.
Knurek, Dennis A.
Maglione, Joseph J.
Medinski, Francis J.
Monahan, Richard J.
Morrissey, Philip T.
Odie, John P.
Onze, Robert E.
Polinsky, John R.
Rarus, Boleslaus J.
Rossitto, Joseph V.
Suwinski, Leo S.
Usenza, Robert J.

Permanent Deacons:
Ashe, Matthew, St. Mary, Greenwich
Barton, Jack, St. James, Stratford
Becker, Robert, St. Mary, Bethel
Berzolla, Renato L., St. Catherine, Riverside
Bissenden, William J., St. Patrick, Bridgeport
Blankschen, Robert, St. Gregory, Danbury
Blier, Roland, St. Andrew, Bridgeport
Brown, James, St. Lawrence, Huntington
Brunetto, Donald W., St. Stephen, Trumbull
Buzzeo, Michael L., St. Gabriel, Stamford
Cabral, Jose R., Immaculate Heart of Mary, Danbury
Calabrese, Robert P., St. Anthony Maronite, Danbury
Carpenter, Gary E., St. Stephen, Trumbull
Chiappetta, Frank, St. Philip, Norwalk
Detje, Anthony, St. Edward the Confessor, New Fairfield
Dwyer, F. Robert, St. Joseph, Shelton
Dzujna, Andrew W., St. Mark, Stratford
Esterheld, John, Sacred Heart, Danbury
Farley, Joseph J., St. Leo, Stamford
Fay, John S., Assumption, Westport
Filingeri, Joseph, St. Lawrence, Huntington
Freibott, Thomas, Holy Name, Stratford
Garcia, Santos, Florida
Grant, Terence J., St. Elizabeth Seton, Ridgefield
Hammock, Ralph, St. Leo, Stamford
Harrity, Frederick A., Sacred Heart, Stamford
Heidenreich, Vincent, St. Catherine, Riverside
Hein, Henry R., St. Edward, New Fairfield
Hendricks, Edward R., St. Andrew, Bridgeport
Henrey, Robert, St. Catherine of Siena, Riverside
Herman, H. Paul, St. Teresa, Trumbull
Howe, Louis F., Sacred Heart, Stamford
Ianniello, Daniel, Holy Rosary, Bridgeport
Isidro, Ramon, Our Lady of Montserrat, Stamford
Kamper, Eugene P., Assumption, Westport
Kelly, Brian J., St. Luke, Westport
Kovacs, Edward, Our Lady Star of the Sea, Stamford
Kovacs, Richard, St. Joseph, Brookfield
Kurmay, Paul, St. Mark, Stratford
Lynch, Harold, Notre Dame, Easton
Mann, John J., Our Lady Star of the Sea, Stamford
Martinez, Ricardo, Blessed Sacrament, Bridgeport
Mauceri, Bartholomew, St. Elizabeth Seton, Ridgefield
Melita, Joseph, St. Raphael, Bridgeport
Moore, Kevin, Holy Cross, Fairfield
Moranski, John J., St. Ann, Bridgeport
Munson, David D., St. Joseph, Shelton
Murphy, William D., St. Gregory the Great, Danbury
Murphy, William O., St. Joseph, Norwalk
Murray, Emmet, St. Mark, Stratford
Myott, Daniel N., St. Gregory the Great, Danbury
Naiman, Donald, St. Gregory, Danbury
Nelson, Thomas E., Marguerite Bourgeoys, Brookfield
Pereira, Gabriel, Our Lady of Fatima, Bridgeport
Pilkington, Paul, St. Edward, New Fairfield
Reilly, Paul, St. Philip, Norwalk
Reveron, Domingo, St. Peter, Bridgeport
Ross, Donald J., Assumption, Fairfield
Ross, Norman, St. Mary, Ridgefield
Rowan, Joseph L., St. Thomas More, Darien
Rowe, William K., St. John, Darien
Sabol, Gerald, Notre Dame, Easton
Saulnier, George, Assumption, Fairfield
Saymon, Richard F., Leave of Absence
Seith, Thomas K., Our Lady of Fatima, Wilton
Shaughnessy, William, St. Joseph, Brookfield
Skurat, Matthew, St. Margaret Mary, Shelton
Sochacki, David, St. Matthew, Norwalk
Stenberg, S. Richard, St. Pius X, Fairfield
Stroud, Kenneth, St. Rose, Newtown
Sullivan, Timothy, St. Augustine Cathedral, Bridgeport
Timmel, William C., St. Patrick, Redding
Tugman, John H., St. Aloysius, New Canaan
Tupper, Paul, St. Clement, Stamford
Vaughn, David J., St. Joseph, Danbury
Volpe, James, St. Ambrose, Bridgeport
Wolfer, Michael K., St. Stephen, Trumbull

INSTITUTIONS LOCATED IN THE DIOCESE

[A] COLLEGES AND UNIVERSITIES

BRIDGEPORT. *St. Vincent's College*, 2800 Main St., 06606. Tel: 203-576-5235.
E-mail: svcadmin@snet.net
For a complete listing, refer to the Colleges and Universities section.

*FAIRFIELD. *Fairfield University*, 1073 N. Benson Rd., 06430-5195. Tel: 203-254-4000; Fax: 203-254-4007.
Web site: www.fairfield.edu
For a complete listing, refer to the Colleges and Universities section.

**Sacred Heart University*, 5151 Park Ave., 06432-1000. Tel: 203-371-7999.
E-mail: QUINNM@sacredheart.edu
Web site: sacredheart.edu
For a complete listing, refer to the Colleges and Universities section.

[B] SPECIAL SCHOOLS, DIOCESAN

BRIDGEPORT. *Queen of Saints, The Catholic Center*, 238 Jewett Ave., 06606. Tel: 203-372-4301, Ext. 217. School of Religion and Spirituality and Retreat Facility.

[C] HIGH SCHOOLS, DIOCESAN

BRIDGEPORT. *Kolbe-Cathedral High School*, 33 Calhoun Pl., 06604. Tel: 203-335-2554. Mrs. Jo Anne Jakab, Prin.; Ms. Carol A. Jones, Asst. Prin.; Revs. Marcel Sokalski, O.F.M.Conv.; James J. Midgley, Spiritual Dir. Priests 2; Lay Teachers 20; Administrators 2; Students 290. Kolbe Teen Health Center. Mrs. JoAnne Jakab, Dir.

DANBURY. *Immaculate High School*, 73 Southern Blvd., 06810. Tel: 203-744-1510.
E-mail: imacula@mail1.NAI.NET
Web site: http://W3.NAI.NE/~IMMACULA/
Dr. Joseph Gerics, Prin.; Mr. Richard T. Stoops, Asst. Prin.; Rev. Corey V. Piccinino, Spiritual Dir. Priests 3; Sisters 1; Lay Teachers 27; Students 370.

FAIRFIELD. *Notre Dame Catholic High School*, 220 Jefferson St., 06432. Tel: 203-372-6521; Fax: 203-374-0387.
E-mail: info@notredame.org
Web site: www.notredame.org
Rev. William F. Sangiovanni, Prin.; Mr. Carl Philipp, Asst. Prin.; Rev. Michael L. Dunn, Spiritual Dir. Priests 2; Sisters of Notre Dame de Namur 2; Lay Teachers 40; Students 670.

STAMFORD. *Trinity Catholic High School*. (Formerly Stamford Catholic High School), 926 Newfield Ave., 09605. Tel: 203-322-3401; Fax: 203-322-5330.
E-mail: TCHS1@JUNO.COM
Sr. Ritamary Schulz, A.S.C.J., Prin.; Robert D'Aquila, Asst. Prin.; Sr. Christine Kiley, A.S.C.J., Asst. Prin.; Rev. William F. Verrilli, Spiritual Dir.; Mr. Michael Roper, Dir. Guidance; Mr. Tracy Nichols, Athletic Dir.; Mrs. Susan Dougherty, Dir. Devel. & Alumni Rels.; Mrs. Mary D'Aquila, Volunteer Coord. Priests 1; Sisters 3; Lay Teachers 30; Students 465. Records for Central Catholic High School, Norwich, and St. Mary's High School, Greenwich, located at Trinity.

TRUMBULL. *St. Joseph High School*, 2320 Huntington Tpke., 06611-5099. Tel: 203-378-9378; Fax: 203-378-7306.
E-mail: stjosephs@snet.net
Mr. Richard A. Bishop, Prin.; Rev. Robert D. Karpinski, Prin. Student Affairs; Mrs. Joan M. Caliendo, Asst. Prin. for Academic Affairs; Mrs. Susan L. Unger, Dir. of Guidance; Rev. Robert D. Karpinski, Spiritual Dir.; Mr. Vito M. Montelli, Dir. Athletics; Mr. Norman DeTullio, Alumni Relations; Ms. Lee Thompson, Coord. for Student Activities; Mr. Thomas Roach, Dean of Students; Mrs. Margaret Marino, Admissions Coord.; Sr. Marie E. Iannuccillo, Dir. of Campus Min.; Mrs. Laurene Collins, Registrar; Mrs. Doreen Rafferty, Bunsar. Priests 1; Sisters 3; Lay Teachers 44; Students 706.

[D] HIGH SCHOOLS, PRIVATE

FAIRFIELD. *Fairfield College Preparatory School*, N. Benson Rd., 06430. Tel: 203-254-4000; Fax: 203-254-4108.
Web site: www.prep.fairfield.edu
A preparatory day school for boys, established in 1942. Society of Jesus of New England. Very Rev. Aloysius P. Kelley, S.J., Pres. Fairfield University; Revs. Michael Boughton, S.J., Pres.; Donald M. Barry, S.J.; Richard G. Cipolla; William J. Eagan, S.J.; George A. Gallarelli, S.J.; Walter R. Pelletier, S.J.; Ronald V. Perry, S.J.; Lawrence D. Ryan, S.J.; Martin G. Shaughnessy, S.J.; Paul A. Zahonski, S.J. Priests 11; Lay Teachers 37; Students 777.

GREENWICH. *Convent of the Sacred Heart, Religious of the Sacred Heart*, 1177 King St., 06831. Tel: 203-531-6500; Fax: 203-531-5206. Sr. Joan Magnetti, R.S.C.J., Headmistress.
Day School for girls (Grades PreK-12). Students 511.

STAMFORD. *Sacred Heart Academy*, 200 Strawberry Hill Ave., 06902-2589. Tel: 203-323-3173.
E-mail: sacred.heart.academy@snet.net
Sisters of St. Joseph. Sr. Jeanne Paulella, C.S.J., Prin. Sisters 3; Lay Teachers 17; Students 100.

[E] ELEMENTARY SCHOOLS, REGIONAL

BRIDGEPORT. *Catholic Elementary Schools-Region X*, The Catholic Center, 238 Jewett Ave., 06606. Tel: 203-372-4301, Ext. 233. Mr. Richard Christensen, Business Mgr.
St. Ambrose. (Grades PreK-8), 461 Mill Hill Ave., 06610. Tel: 203-368-2835; Fax: 203-366-0599. Mrs. Susan Gulyas, Prin.; Sr. Richard Mary Peters, I.H.M., Supr. Servants of the Immaculate of Mary 4; Lay Teachers 10; Students 346. St. Andrew. (Grades K-8), 395 Anton St., 06606. Tel: 203-372-4819; Fax: 203-373-0641. Mr. Michael Fettig, Prin. Lay Teachers 10; Students 238. St. Ann. (Grades PreK-8), 521 Brewster St., 06605. Tel: 203-334-5856; Fax: 203-333-8263. Sr. Phyllis Campoli, C.S.J., Prin. Daughters of the Holy Spirit 1; Lay Teachers 10; Students 239. St. Augustine Cathedral. (Grades PreK-8), 63 Pequonnock St., 06604. Tel: 203-367-5896; Fax: 203-333-6694. Mrs. Barbara A. Coscio, Prin. Lay Teachers 11; Students 235. St. Peter. (Grades K-8), 659 Beechwood Ave., 06605. Tel: 203-333-2048; Fax: 203-333-2878. Miss Suzanna Zello, Prin. Sisters 2; Lay Teachers 8; Students 241. St. Raphael. (Grades PreK-8), 324 Frank St., 06604. Tel: 203-333-6818; Fax: 203-336-9205. Sr. Kathleen Mary Coonan, A.S.C.J., Prin. Apostles of the Sacred Heart 2; Lay Teachers 13; Students 328.

DANBURY. *Catholic Elementary Schools-Region IX and XI*, St. Gregory, 3 Tammany Tr., 06811. Tel: 203-744-6248.
Region XI. St. Mary. (Grades K-8), 24 Dodgingtown Rd., Bethel, 06801. Tel: 203-744-2922; Fax: 203-798-8803. Sr. Anne McCarthy, S.S.N.D., Prin. Religious 1; Lay Teachers 9; Students 226.
Region XI. St. Joseph. (Grades K-8), Rte. 133, Brookfield, 06804. Tel: 203-775-2774; Fax: 203-775-5810. Mrs. Barbara Blank, Prin. Lay Teachers 10; Students 238.
Region IX. Sacred Heart. (Grades K-8), 17 Cottage St., 06810. Tel: 203-792-6194. Sr. M. Benilda Nadolski, F.S.S.J., Prin. Franciscan Sisters of St. Joseph 2; Lay Teachers 8; Students 214.
Region IX. St. Gregory the Great. (Grades K-8), 85 Great Plains Rd., 06811. Tel: 203-748-1217. Sr. Mary John O'Rourke, O.S.U., Prin. Lay Teachers 10; Students 326.
Region IX. St. Joseph. (Grades K-8), 370 Main St., 06810. Tel: 203-748-6615. Mrs. Sharon Quish, Prin. Lay Teachers 15; Students 325.
Region IX. St. Peter. (Grades PreK-8), 98 Main St., 06810. Tel: 203-748-2895. Mrs. Josephine P. Ferry, Prin. Sisters of Mercy 3; Lay Teachers 12; Students 300.
Region XI. St. Rose. (Grades K-8), 40 Church Hill Rd., Newtown, 06470. Tel: 203-426-5102; Fax: 203-426-5374. Mrs. Donna DeLuca, Prin. Lay Teachers 13; Students 234.

FAIRFIELD. *Catholic Elementary Schools-Region V*, Fairfield/Easton Regional Catholic School, Inc., 118 Ruane St., 06430. Tel: 203-259-6735. Mrs. Jean Correa, Business Mgr., Holy Family. (Grades PreK-8), Edison Ave., 06430. Tel: 203-367-5409; Fax: 203-335-7317. Mrs. Mary McCormack. Lay Teachers 15; Students 302. Our Lady of the Assumption. (Grades PreK-8), 605 Stratfield Rd., 06432. Tel: 203-334-6271; Fax: 203-334-1374. Ms. Gerri Desio, Prin. Sisters of St. Dominic of Newburgh 1; Lay Teachers 17; Students 371. St. Thomas Aquinas. (Grades PreK-8), 118 Ruane St., 06430. Tel: 203-255-0556; Fax: 203-256-0860. Mr. Francis F. Daily, Prin. Lay Teachers 20; Students 480.

GREENWICH. *Catholic Elementary Schools-Region I*, Greenwich Catholic School, 471 North St., 06830. Tel: 203-869-4000; Fax: 203-869-3405.
E-mail: GREENCATH@aol.com
Web site: http://members.aol.com/greencath/gindex.htm
Mrs. Mary Flume, Business Mgr., Greenwich Catholic School. (Grades PreK-8), 471 North St., 06830. Tel: 203-869-4000. Mrs. Genevieve Madonna, Prin. Lay Teachers 30; Students 458.

NORWALK. *Catholic Elementary Schools-Region III*, All Saints Catholic School, 139 W. Rocks Rd., 06851. Tel: 203-847-3881; Fax: 203-847-3884. Mrs. Jean Nichols, Business Mgr., All Saints Catholic Elementary School. (Grades DayCare-8), 139 W. Rocks Rd., 06851. Tel: 203-847-3881. Sr. Catherine Sheehy, R.S.M., Prin. Lay Teachers 51; Sisters 3; Students 844.

SHELTON. *Catholic Elementary Schools-Region VIII*, St. Lawrence Rectory, 505 Shelton Ave., 06484. Tel: 203-926-8495. Mrs. Joanne Simpson, Business Mgr., St. Joseph. (Grades PreK-8), 430 Coram Ave., 06484. Tel: 203-924-4669. Sr. Ethel MacIlvain, C.S.J., Prin. Sisters of St. Joseph of Chambery 1; Lay Teachers 13; Students 398. St. Lawrence. (Grades PreK-8), 503 Shelton Ave., Huntington, 06484. Tel: 203-929-4422; Fax: 203-929-3669. Mrs. Kathleen Gosart, Prin. Sisters 1; Lay Teachers 11; Students 300.

STAMFORD. *Catholic Elementary Schools-Region II*, Catholic Regional School System, Inc., 926 Newfield Ave., P.O. Box 3127, 06905-0127. Tel: 203-968-2795. Mrs. Kathleen K. Carty, Business Mgr., St. Aloysius. (Grades K-8), 33 South Ave., New Canaan, 06840. Tel: 203-966-0786; Fax: 203-972-6960. Bro. James Timoney, C.F.C., Prin. Lay Teachers 10; Students 186. Holy Spirit. (Grades PreK-5), 403 Scofieldtown Rd., 06903. Tel: 203-329-1623; Fax: 203-595-0858. Sr. Marie Vianney Gallagher, S.S.N.D., Prin. Lay Teachers 7; Students 177. Our Lady Star of the Sea. (Grades PreK-5), 1170 Shippan Ave., 06902. Tel: 203-348-1155; Fax: 203-324-6150. Mrs. Gail Ryan, Prin. Ursuline Sisters 1; Lay Teachers 6; Students 139. Sacred Heart. (Grades PreK-8), One Schuyler Ave., 06902. Tel: 203-323-4844; Fax: 203-359-9859. Sr. Pietrina Mazzola, M.P.F., Prin. Religious Teachers Filippini 1; Lay Teachers 9; Students 190. St. Cecilia. (Grades PreK-5), 1186 Newfield Ave., 06905. Tel: 203-322-6505; Fax: 203-322-6835. Mrs. Joann Borchetta, Prin. Sisters 1; Lay Teachers 14; Students 335. St. Gabriel. (Grades 6-8), 948 Newfield Ave., 06905. Tel: 203-322-7383; Fax: 203-322-4435. Mr. Peter Borchetta, Prin. Lay Teachers 16; Students 283.

STRATFORD. *Catholic Elementary Schools-Region VI*, Stratford Catholic Regional School, St. James Campus, One Monument Pl., 06497. Tel: 203-380-1990; Fax: 203-380-0749.
E-mail: stjames.school.01@snet.net
Mrs. Natalia Zamachaj, Business Mgr., St. James. (Grades K-8), One Monument Pl., 06497. Tel: 203-375-5994; Fax: 203-380-0749. Mrs. Carolyn S. Potts, Prin.; Sr. Gloria Marie Kascak, S.S.C.M., Asst. Prin. Lay Teachers 31; Students 498. St. Mark. (Grades K-8), 500 Wigwam Ln., 06497. Tel: 203-375-4291; Fax: 203-386-1955. Mr. Phillip T. Adzima, Prin. Lay Teachers 10; Students 293.

TRUMBULL. *Catholic Elementary Schools-Region VII*, St. Catherine of Siena, 190 Shelton Rd., 06611. Tel: 203-375-1947; Fax: 203-378-3935. Mr. Ray LaLuna, Business Mgr., St. Jude. (Grades PreK-8), 707 Monroe Tpke., Monroe, 06468. Tel: 203-261-3619; Fax: 203-261-7507. Sr. Dorothy Anne Novak, C.S.F.N., Prin. Sisters of the Holy Family of Nazareth 1; Lay Teachers 9; Students 290. St. Catherine of Siena. (Grades PreK-8), 190 Shelton Rd., 06611. Tel: 203-375-1947; Fax: 203-378-3935. Sr. Anne Marie Dorff, S.S.N.D., Prin. Lay Teachers 10; Students 308. St. Theresa. (Grades PreK-8), 55 Rosemond Ter., 06611. Tel: 203-268-3236. Mr. William M. Reynolds, Prin. Sisters 1; Lay Teachers 12; Students 308.

WILTON. *Catholic Elementary Schools-Region IV*, Our Lady of Fatima School, 225 Danbury Rd., 06897. Tel: 203-762-8100.
Web site: www.wiltonCT.com/Fatima/
Mrs. Mary Gardiner, Business Mgr., Our Lady of Fatima. (Grades PreK-8), 225 Danbury Rd., 06897. Tel: 203-762-8100; Fax: 203-834-1261. Mrs. Mary Ann Bozzuti, Prin. Lay Teachers 14; Students 270. Saint Mary's. (Grades K-1), 183 High Ridge Ave., Ridgefield, 06877. Tel: 203-438-6538; Fax: 203-438-4406. Miss Jeannine Hangac, Prin. Lay Teachers 3; Students 27.

[F] ELEMENTARY SCHOOLS, PRIVATE

GREENWICH. *Convent of the Sacred Heart*, 1177 King St., 06831. Tel: 203-531-6500; Fax: 203-531-5206.
E-mail: sacredheart@cshgreenwich.org
Sr. Joan Magnetti, R.S.C.J., Headmistress. Students 511.

STAMFORD. *Villa Maria Education Center*, 161 Sky Meadow Dr., 06903. Tel: 203-322-5886; Fax: 203-322-0228. Bernardine Sisters. School for Children with Learning Disabilities. Sr. Carol Ann, O.S.F., Exec. Dir.; Sr. Marie, O.S.F., Education Dir. Students 60.

[G] CATHOLIC CHARITIES

BRIDGEPORT. *Catholic Charities of Fairfield County*, Catholic Center, 238 Jewett Ave., 06606-2892. Tel: 203-372-4301, Ext. 379; 564; Fax: 203-372-5045.
E-mail: info@cathcharitiesffldcty.com
Web site: http://www.cathcharitiesffldcty.com
Brian A. Cronin, A.C.S.W., L.C.S.W., Exec. Dir.; Benedict P. Mazotas, Controller.
Adoption Program. China Identified Adoptions, Traditional Adoptions and Home Studies. 238 Jewett Ave., 06606. Tel: 203-372-4301 ext. 370. Anne Steers, Dir.
Catholic Family Services, Bridgeport, 238 Jewett Ave., 06606. Tel: 203-372-4301, Ext. 348. Michael

Tintrup, A.C.S.W., L.C.S.W., District Exec. Dir.
Catholic Family Services, Danbury, 30 Main St., Suite 503, Danbury, 06810. Tel: 203-743-4412. Edward S. Laskowski, A.C.S.W., L.C.S.W., District Exec. Dir.
Catholic Family Services, Norwalk, 7 Chapel St., P.O. Box 2025, Norwalk, 06852. Tel: 203-838-2316. Susan Williams, L.C.S.W., District Exec. Dir.
Catholic Family Services, Stamford, 30 Myano Ln., Stamford, 06902. Tel: 203-323-1105. Joan Pollack, A.C.S.W., L.C.S.W., District Exec. Dir.
Catholic Family Services Outreach Offices: 1986 Post Rd., Darien, 06820. Tel: 203-655-2169. 387 Main St., Ridgefield, 06877. Tel: 203-431-8170. 452 Howe Ave., Shelton, 06484. Tel: 203-924-9604. 80 Ferry Blvd., Stratford, 06497. Tel: 203-375-9553. 44 Old Ridgefield Rd., Wilton, 06897. Tel: 203-834-2076. Day Care Programs, 208 East Ave., Norwalk, 06855. Tel: 203-831-8200; Fax: 203-855-0637. Susan Williams, L.C.S.W., Interim Dir.
Houses of Hospitality:
New Covenant House of Hospitality (Yerwood Center), 90 Fairfield Ave., Stamford, 06904. Tel: 203-964-8228. Deacon Frank Chiappetta, Dir.
Thomas Merton Center, 43 Madison Ave., 06604. Tel: 203-367-9036. Mary Ann Furlong, R.N., Dir.
Family Life Ministry. Please call Rev. Ernest T. Esposito, Exec. Dir., Tel: 203-372-4301, Ext. 314, for the following programs: Ministry to Widows; Bereavement; Job Transition; Post-Abortion Support; Divorced and Separated; Marriage Profile; Marriage Preparation; Marriage Enrichment; and Family Enrichment. Diocesan Office, 238 Jewett Ave., 06606-2892. Tel: 203-372-4301, Ext. 320. Rev. Ernest T. Esposito, D.Min., Dir.
Family Life / Respect Life Catholic Center, 238 Jewett Ave., 06606-2892. Tel: 203-372-4301, Ext. 314.
Gary Crooks / St. Stephen's Emergency Food Center, 301 Bostwick Ave., 06605. Tel: 203-384-6904. Community Mental Health Support Services. Donna Tenney, M.P.A., Dir.
Mental Health Outreach: Danbury, Barrett House, 235 White St., Danbury, 06810. Tel: 203-794-0819. Sandy Harris, Dir. Case Management Program, 233 White St., Danbury, 06810. Tel: 203-748-0848. Sandy Cole, Supervisor; Donna Tenney, Dir.
Thresholds. (Shelter for Women & Children), 5 Harmony St., Danbury, 06810. Tel: 203-792-8609. Claudia Fields, Program Dir.
Nutrition and Aging Services, 30 Myano Ln., Stamford, 06902. Tel: 203-324-6175. Cindy Phelps, Dir.
Senior Citizen Outreach, 233 White St., Danbury, 06810. Tel: 203-743-4412. Mrs. Clare Hipp, B.A., Program Coord.
Social Action-Campaign for Human Needs, Catholic Relief Services.
Social Concern Ministries, Catholic Center, 238 Jewett Ave., 06606-2892. Tel: 203-372-4301, Ext. 386.
Social Issues Advocacy. Edie Cassidy, Dir. Health, Aging Issues. Tel: 203-372-4301, Ext. 394.
St. Joseph Residence for Mother and Child, 96 Catherine St., 06604. Tel: 203-366-0443. Laurene Tucciarone, Dir.
St. Joseph Center for Poor and Needy, Inc., 238 Jewett Ave., 06606. Tel: 203-372-4301 ext. 564. Brian A. Cronin, Exec. Dir.

[H] DAY NURSERIES

BRIDGEPORT. *Daughters of Charity of the Most Precious Blood Day Nursery*, 1490 North Ave., 06604. Tel: 203-334-7000. Sr. Theresa Tremblay, Dir.
STAMFORD. *Our Lady of Grace Day Nursery*, 635 Glenbrook Rd., 06906. Little Workers of the Sacred Hearts. Sr. Lillian Cairo, P.O.S.C., Supr.
Stepping Stones Preschool, Inc., Sacred Heart Academy, 200 Strawberry Hill Ave., 06902. Tel: 203-323-3173. Sisters of Saint Joseph.

[I] GENERAL HOSPITALS

BRIDGEPORT. *St. Vincent's Development Corporation*, 2800 Main St., 06606. Tel: 203-576-5459
For a complete listing, refer to the Hospitals section.
St. Vincent's Health Services Corporation, 2800 Main St., 06606. Tel: 203-576-5455
For a complete listing, refer to the Hospitals section.
St. Vincent's Medical Center, 2800 Main St., 06606. Tel: 203-576-6000
For a complete listing, refer to the Hospitals section.
St. Vincent's Medical Center Foundation, 2800 Main St., 06606. Tel: 203-576-5451
For a complete listing, refer to the Hospitals section.
STAMFORD. *St. Joseph Medical Center* 128 Strawberry Hill Ave., 06904-1222. Tel: 203-353-2001.
For a complete listing, refer to the Hospitals section.
St. Joseph Medical Center Foundation, Inc., 128 Strawberry Hill Ave., 06904
For a complete listing, refer to the Hospitals section.

[J] SPECIAL HOSPITALS

BRIDGEPORT. *Bridgeport Diocesan Health Care Corporation*, 238 Jewett Ave., 06606. Tel: 203-372-4301
For a complete listing, refer to the Special Care Facilities section.
The Pope John Paul II Foundation, Inc., 238 Jewett Ave., 06606
For a complete listing, refer to the Special Care Facilities section.
St. Camillus Home Foundation, Inc., 238 Jewett Ave., 06606 Fax: 203-353-0550
For a complete listing, refer to the Special Care Facilities section.
DANBURY. *The Pope John Paul II Center for Health Care, Inc.*, 33 Lincoln Ave., 06810. Tel: 203-797-9300; Fax: 203-790-4645
For a complete listing, refer to the Special Care Facilities section.
STAMFORD. *St. Camillus Health Center*, 494 Elm St., 06902. Tel: 203-353-0550; Fax: 203-325-0200
For a complete listing, refer to the Special Care Facilities section.

[K] HOMES FOR AGED

BRIDGEPORT. *Augustana Homes Bishop Curtis Homes - Danbury*, 238 Jewett Ave., 06606
For a complete listing, refer to the Special Care Facilities section.
Augustana Homes / Bishop Curtis Homes, 525 Palisade Ave., 06610. Tel: 203-366-4333; Fax: 203-576-6790
For a complete listing, refer to the Special Care Facilities section.
Augustana Homes / Bishop Curtis Homes, 280 Jewett Ave., 06606. Tel: 203-374-5346
For a complete listing, refer to the Special Care Facilities section.
Augustana Homes / Bishop Curtis Homes - East Bridgeport, 238 Jewett Ave., 06606. Tel: 203-372-4301; Fax: 203-371-8698
For a complete listing, refer to the Special Care Facilities section.
Roncalli Apartments, 430 Grant St., 06610. Tel: 203-384-9984
For a complete listing, refer to the Special Care Facilities section.
BETHEL. *Augustana Homes / Bishop Curtis Homes*, Simeon Rd., 06801. Tel: 203-743-2508
For a complete listing, refer to the Special Care Facilities section.
FAIRFIELD. *Augustana Homes / Bishop Curtis Homes*, 1677 Post Rd., 06430
For a complete listing, refer to the Special Care Facilities section.
RIVERSIDE. *Augustana Homes of Greenwich / Bishop Curtis Homes*, 1040 E. Putnam Ave., 06878
For a complete listing, refer to the Special Care Facilities section.
STAMFORD. *Augustana Homes / Bishop Curtis Homes - Glenbrook*, 352 Glenbrook Rd., 06902. Tel: 203-576-0823
For a complete listing, refer to the Special Care Facilities section.
TRUMBULL. *Carmel Ridge*, 6454 Main St., 06611. Tel: 203-261-2229
For a complete listing, refer to the Special Care Facilities section.
St. Joseph's Housing Corporation, Teresian Towers & Carmel Ridge Estates, 6448 Main St., 06611. Tel: 203-261-2229
For a complete listing, refer to the Special Care Facilities section.
St. Joseph's Manor, 6448 Main St., 06611. Tel: 203-268-6204; Fax: 203-268-5271
For a complete listing, refer to the Special Care Facilities section.

[L] CONVALESCENT HOMES

NORWALK. *Notre Dame Convalescent Home*, 76 W. Rocks Rd., 06851. Tel: 203-847-5893
For a complete listing, refer to the Special Care Facilities section.

[M] SOCIAL PROGRAMS

BRIDGEPORT. *Social Issues Advocate-Parish Social Concerns*, 238 Jewett Ave., 06606. Tel: 203-372-4301. Brian A. Cronin, Campaign for Human Development; Edith Cassidy, Social Concerns Dir.

[N] MONASTIC FOUNDATIONS

WEST REDDING. *The Benedictine Grange*, 06896. Tel: 203-938-3689. Rev. John B. Giuliani, Dir.

[O] RESIDENCES OF PRIESTS AND BROTHERS

BRIDGEPORT. *Provincial Offices of the Priests and Brothers of Holy Cross, Eastern Province*. (Province of Our Lady of Holy Cross), 835 Clinton Ave., 06604. Tel: 203-367-7252; Fax: 203-366-7886.
E-mail: HUGH@UNIBIZ.NET
Web site: www.stonehill.Edu.HolyCross
Revs. Hugh W. Cleary, C.S.C., Prov.; Wilfred J. Raymond, Asst. Prov.; Leo Polselli, C.S.C., Treas., Holy Cross Novitiate, Marigreen Pines, Cascade, CO.
Educational Institutions: King's College, Wilkes-Barre, PA, 18711. Stonehill College, North Easton, MA, 02356. Holy Cross Brothers, Prov., New Rochelle, NY. Rev. Robert E. de Leon, C.S.C, St. Vincent's Medical Center, 06606. Revs. Thaddeus S. Swertz, C.S.C; Robert J. Malone, C.S.C., Mount St. John's School, Deep River, 06417-0415. Rev. Francis T. Zlotkowski, C.S.C, Brigham & Womens' Hospital, Boston, MA, 02115. Legal Title: *Congregation of Holy Cross - Eastern Province, Inc.*
FAIRFIELD. *The Fairfield Jesuit Community-Fairfield University*, 06430-5195. Tel: 203-256-1650.
E-mail: TTOOHTG@FairT.Fairfield.EDU
Revs. Charles H. Allen, S.J.; Francis R. Allen, S.J.; Donald M. Barry, S.J.; James R. Blaetter, S.J.; John V. Borgo, S.J.; Michael Boughton, S.J.; Gerhard H. Bowering, S.J. (Germany); Vincent M. Burns, S.J.; Albert A. Cardoni, S.J.; William F. Carr, S.J.; Paul E. Carrier, S.J.; Richard D. Costello, S.J.; Joseph D. Devlin, S.J.; Anthony J. Eiardi, S.J.; John W. Elder, S.J.; George A. Gallarelli, S.J.; Andrew J. Garavel, S.J.; Gregg Grovenburg, S.J.; G. Simon Harak, S.J.; Kenneth J. Jorgensen, S.J.; Aloysius P. Kelley, S.J.; William J. Kennedy, S.J.; Johannes B. Hari Kustanto, S.J. (Indonesia); Victor F. Leeber, S.J.; Francis W. Lewis, S.J.; Donald D. Lynch, S.J.; Joseph F. MacDonnell, S.J.; James J. Mayzik, S.J.; Francis J. Moy, S.J.; Henry J. Murphy, S.J.; Thomas A. Murphy, S.J.; Renato Oliveros, S.J.; W. Laurence O'Neil, S.J.; Mark J. Burke, S.J.; John J. Cecero, S.J.; William J. Eagan, S.J.; Walter R. Pelletier, S.J.; Ronald V. Perry, S.J.; Francis T. Hannafey, S.J.; Francis J. McManus, S.J.; G. Paul Peterson, S.J.; Albert F. Reddy, S.J.; Thomas J. Regan, S.J.; Joseph L. Ryan, S.J.; Laurence D. Ryan, S.J.; James P. Scull, S.J.; Martin G. Shaughnessy, S.J.; Edward J. Small, S.J.; Robert N. Sproule, S.J.; Richard J. Stanley, S.J.; Christopher W. Steck, S.J.; Timothy E. Toohig, S.J., Rector; Maurice Wong, S.J.
STAMFORD. *Our Lady Queen of the Clergy Home*. Home for Retired Priests. 128 Strawberry Hill Ave., 06904. Rev. Msgr. Bernard S. Scanlon; Rev. Msgr. James G. Lengen; His Eminence Ignatius Cardinal Kung; Rev. Msgr. John V. Horgan; Rev. Msgr. Edward D. Halloran; Revs. John P. Odie; John R. Polinsky.
St. John Fisher Seminary Residence, 894 Newfield Ave., 06905. Tel: 203-322-5331; Fax: 203-461-9876. Revs. Kevin T. Royal, S.T.L., Rector; Christopher J. Walsh, Ph.D., Spiritual Dir.; Rev. Msgr. James C. Turro, S.T.L., S.S.L., A.M., Ph.D., Confessor.

[P] CONVENTS AND RESIDENCES FOR SISTERS

BRIDGEPORT. *Convent of Mary Immaculate, Missionary Sisters of the Blessed Sacrament and Mary Immaculate*. Prov. Headquarters. 1111 Wordin Ave., 06605. Tel: 203-334-5681. Sr. Presentacion Zabala, Provincial. Sisters 6. Assisting the Apostolate to Spanish-Speaking People.
Daughters of Charity of the Most Precious Blood Convent, 1482 North Ave., 06604. Tel: 203-334-7000.
Holy Spirit Convent, Daughters of the Holy Spirit, 50 Pequonnock St., 06604. Tel: 203-334-6926.
Staffing & ministry work in public health.
Sisters of the Company of the Savior, 820 Clinton Ave., 06604. Tel: 203-368-1875. Spanish-Speaking Apostolate. Mother Constanza Lopez, Supr.
GREENWICH. *Sacred Heart Convent*, 38 Gold St., 06830. Tel: 203-531-8547. Franciscan Sisters of the Atonement 4.
MONROE. *Provincial House, Immaculate Heart of Mary Province, Sisters of the Holy Family of Nazareth, C.S.F.N.*, 1428 Monroe Tpke., 06468. Tel: 203-268-7646. Sr. M. Janice Kobierowski, C.S.F.N., Prov. Supr.; Rev. Raymond Petrucci, Chap. Professed 67.
NORWALK. *Regional House of Sisters of St. Thomas of Villanova*, 76 W. Rocks Rd., 06851. Tel: 203-847-2885. Mother Edmond, S.S.T.V., Supr. Notre Dame Convalescent Home; Rev. Albert W. Watts, Chap. Professed 5.
RIDGEFIELD. *Provincial House, Congregation de Notre Dame*, 223 W. Mountain Rd., 06877. Tel: 203-438-5282; Fax: 203-438-3150. Sr. Anne Leonard, C.N.D., Prov. Supr.; Sr. Alyn Larson, C.N.D., Supr., Local Community. Tel: 203-438-3115; Rev. Michael J. McCarthy, Chap.
STAMFORD. *Heart of Mary Convent (Residence for Bernardine Sisters)*, 163 Sky Meadow Dr., 06903. Tel: 203-322-5920. Sr. M. Dymphna Zakowski, O.S.F., Admin. Tel: 203-322-8721. Bernardine Sisters 12.
Villa Maria Education Center. Tel: 203-322-5886. School for children with learning disabilities (Grades 1-8). Sr. Carol Ann Nawracaj, O.S.F., Prin.
Monastery of St. Clare, 1954 Long Ridge Rd., 06903-3232. Tel: 203-329-2252.

E-mail: stamfdmsc@aol.com
Web site: http://www.geocities.com/heartland/hills/8054
Sr. Mary Michael Biosseau, O.S.C., Abbess.
Our Lady of Grace Convent, 635 Glenbrook Rd., 06906. Tel: 203-348-5531. Motherhouse and Novitiate of Little Workers of Sacred Hearts. Sr. Lillian Cairo, P.O.S.C., Supr.
Sisters Minor of Mary Immaculate, Holy Name of Jesus Convent, 305 Washington Blvd., 06902. Sr. Anna Raszkowska, S.S.M.I., Local Supr. Sisters 5.
St. Francis Villa Custody House, Immaculate Conception Custody, 138 Brushy Hill Rd., Danbury, 06810. Sr. Theresa Marie Kovacs, S.M.M.I., Custodian, Local Supr. and V.G. Sisters 3.
Villa Divino Amore Convent, Little Workers of the Sacred Hearts of Jesus & Mary, 117 Hope St., 06906. Tel: 203-324-2449. Sr. Giacinta Scaramuzzo, P.O.S.C., Supr.

WILTON. *Lourdes Health Care Center*, 345 Belden Hill Rd., 06897. Tel: 203-762-3318, Ext. 361. Rev. Victor Chaupetta, M.S., Res. Chap.
School Sisters of Notre Dame Motherhouse (Northeastern Province), 345 Belden Hill Rd., 06897. Tel: 203-762-3318.
Web site: http://www.SSND.ORG
Sr. Marie Jeannette Blatz, Prov. Supr.; Rev. Victor W. Chaupetta, M.S. Tel: 203-762-3318. Priests 1; Professed 148.

[Q] SECULAR INSTITUTES

BRIDGEPORT. *The Society of Our Lady of the Way*, 584 Capitol Ave., Apt. 6, 06606. A secular institute for women. Miss Margaret Gould, Unit Dir.; Rev. Timothy Curtin, S.J.

[R] FOUNDATIONS, TRUSTS AND FUNDS

BRIDGEPORT. *Fairfield Foundation of the Diocese of Bridgeport, Inc.*, 238 Jewett Ave., 06606-2892. Tel: 203-372-4301; Fax: 203-371-8698. Mrs. Michele H. Jones Delmhorst, Pres.; Mr. John Croffy, Exec. Dir.
Inner-City Foundation for Charity & Education, 238 Jewett Ave., 06606-2892. Tel: 203-372-4301. Rev. Msgr. Kevin W. Wallin, Exec. Dir.

[S] GUEST HOUSES

DARIEN. *Convent of St. Birgitta*, 06820. Tel: 203-655-1068.
E-mail: vikingsborg.retreathouse@juno.com
Sr. M. Sabina Kavanadi, O.SS.S., Supr.; Rev. Richard G. Cipolla, Chap.

[T] HOUSES OF STUDIES

BRIDGEPORT. *St. Peter's Parish, St. Maximillian Kolbe House of Studies*, 535 Colorado Ave., 06605. Tel: 203-335-4992. Rev. Msgr. Francis C. Wissel, Dir.; Ms. Carmen Serrano, Supr.

[U] RETREAT HOUSES

BRIDGEPORT. *The Urban Center of St. Charles Parish*, 1279 E. Main St., 06608. Tel: 203-366-4190. Luis Baeza, House Manager; Rev. Msgr. Joseph D. Potter, Consultant; Sr. Ann Moles, S.S.N.D., Consultants.

NORTH STAMFORD. *Villa Maria Retreat House*, 159 Sky Meadow Dr., 06903. Tel: 203-322-0107. Retreat house for men & women. Sr. Maria J. Riedel, O.S.F., Co-Dir.; Sr. Josandra Ciucci, O.S.F., Co-Dir.; Sr. Joanne Slanga, O.S.F., Retreat Team, Spiritual Direction, Directed Retreats, MBTI Reiki Master; Sr. Bernadine Grego, O.S.F., Retreat Team, Reiki Practicioner, Enneagram; Sr. Patricia Jamison, C.N.D., Program Dev. Dir., Spiritual Direction; Sr. Peggy Riordan, R.S.M., Program Dev. Dir., Spiritual Director, Reiki Practitioner; Rev. Msgr. John F. Jazowski, Chap. Bernardine Franciscan Sisters 8.

[V] NEWMAN CENTERS

FAIRFIELD. *Newman Centers - Campus Ministry*, 06432-1000. Dr. Margaret A. Palliser, Dir. of Campus Ministry. Campus Ministers: Rev. Thomas M. McLernon; Ms. Patricia Leonard-Pasley.
Sacred Heart University (Fairfield), 5151 Park Ave., 06430-1000. Tel: 203-371-7840. Rev. Robert Schlageter, O.F.M.Conv., Dir. Campus Ministry.
Western Connecticut State University (Danbury), P.O. Box 706, Danbury, 06813. Tel: 203-837-9225.
Fairfield University (Fairfield), N. Benson Rd., Bridgeport, 06430. Tel: 203-255-4511. Revs. Paul E. Carrier, S.J.; Joseph J. Shad, S.J., Asst. Chap.; Richard J. Stanley, S.J., Asst. Chaplain; Mr. Robert W. Canter, S.J., Asst. Chaplain.

[W] MISCELLANEOUS LISTINGS

BRIDGEPORT. *Blessed Brother Andre Charitable Trust*, 835 Clinton Ave., 06604.
E-mail: Hugh@unibiz.net
Cardinal Shehan Center, Inc., 1494 Main St., 06604. Tel: 203-336-4468. Mr. Terry O'Connor, Exec. Dir.
Caroline House, Inc., 574 Stillman St., 06608.
The Diocesan Cemetery Care Fund, Inc., 238 Jewett Ave, 06606.
Faith in the Future Fund, Inc., 238 Jewett Ave., 06606.
Hispanic Social Ministries of Fairfield County, Inc., 238 Jewett Ave., 06606-9990. Rev. Msgr. Aniceto Villamide, Contact Person.
Needle Fund, Inc., 238 Jewett Ave., 06606.
The Queen's Daughters, c/o Sr. Therese, D.H.S., 50 Pequonnock St., 06604. Miss Mary Keating, Pres. Sponsoring agency for Holy Spirit Convent. Care of the sick and poor in their homes by Daughters of the Holy Spirit.

FAIRFIELD. *The Institute for Religious Education and Pastoral Studies (REAPS)*, Sacred Heart University, 5151 Park Ave., 06432-1000. Tel: 203-371-7843; 371-7867; Fax: 203-374-9968.
E-mail: REAPS@sacredheart.edu
Dr. Donna Dodge, Interim Dir.; Mrs. Carole Akers, M.A., Asst. to the Dir.; Deacon Daniel Ianniello, Dir. of Devel. & Grants; Mrs. Patricia Maurer, Coord. Admissions/Retention; Mrs. Catherine Brewer, Admin. Sec.

GREENWICH. *Clemons Productions, Inc.* (In association with That's The Spirit Productions, Inc.), P.O. Box 7466, 06836; Fax: 203-316-9396.
Web site: http://www.spirituality.org
Rev. Mark Connolly, Pres. Tel: 203-316-9394, Spirituality For Today.

RIDGEFIELD. *The St. Mary's Endowment Trust*, 183 High Ridge Ave., 06877.

SHELTON. *Fr. McKenna St. Vincent de Paul Shoppe*, P.O. Box 271, 06484-0271. Tel: 203-924-4817. Rev. Robert G. Pohley, Chap.; Barbara Samor, Dir.; Sandie Bailie, Asst. Dir.

STAMFORD. *Stamford Catholic Library*, 566 Elm St., 06902. Tel: 203-348-4422. Mr. Nicholas Cognetta, Pres.; Rev. Robert G. Pohley, Chap.; Mary Louise Flowers, Contact Person.

WILTON. *St. Benedict Guild*, Cannondale Depot, 06897. Tel: 203-762-3633. Mary Anne McFadden, Co-Mgr.

RELIGIOUS INSTITUTES OF MEN REPRESENTED IN THE DIOCESE

For further details refer to the corresponding bracketed number in the Religious Institutes of Men or Women section.

[0200]—*Benedictine Monks*.—O.S.B.
[0470]—*The Capuchin Friars*. (Prov. of St. Mary).—O.F.M.Cap.
[0270]—*Carmelite Fathers & Brothers*. (St. Elias Prov. New York).—O.Carm.
[0480]—*Conventual Franciscans*. (St. Anthony of Padua Prov.).—O.F.M.Conv.
[0490]—*Franciscan Brothers of Brooklyn*.—O.S.F.
[0520]—*Franciscan Friars*. (Commissariat of St. Stephen).—O.F.M.
[0650]—*Holy Ghost Fathers*. (Irish Prov.).—C.S.Sp.
[0690]—*Jesuit Fathers and Brothers*. (New England Prov.).—S.J.
[0870]—*Montfort Missionaries*. (Haitian Prov.).—S.M.M.
[0610]—*Priests of the Congregation of Holy Cross*. (Prov. of Our Lady of Holy Cross).—C.S.C.

RELIGIOUS INSTITUTES OF WOMEN REPRESENTED IN THE DIOCESE

[0130]—*Apostles of the Sacred Heart of Jesus*.—A.S.C.J.
[1810]—*Bernardine Sisters of the Third Order of St. Francis*.—O.S.F.
[0280]—*Brigittine Sisters*.—O.SS.S.
[0330]—*Carmelite Sisters for the Aged and Infirm*.—O.Carm.
[0710]—*Company of the Savior*.—C.S.
[4030]—*Congregation of Sisters of St. Thomas of Villanova*.—S.S.T.V.
[0760]—*Daughters of Charity of St. Vincent de Paul*.—D.C.
[0740]—*Daughters of Charity of the Most Precious Blood*.
[0790]—*Daughters of Divine Charity*.—F.D.C.
[0820]—*Daughters of the Holy Spirit*.—D.H.S.
[0960]—*Daughters of Wisdom*.—D.W.
[1070]—*Dominican Sisters*.—O.P.
[1470]—*Franciscan Sisters of St. Joseph*.—F.S.S.J.
[1190]—*Franciscan Sisters of the Atonement*.—S.A.
[2575]—*Institute of the Sisters of Mercy of the Americas*.—R.S.M.
[2345]—*Little Workers of the Sacred Hearts of Jesus & Mary*.—P.O.S.C.
[2780]—*Missionary Sisters of the Most Blessed Sacrament*. (Spain).—M.SS.S.
[3430]—*Religious Teachers Filippini*.—M.P.F.
[2970]—*School Sisters of Notre Dame*.—S.S.N.D.
[]—*Sisters Minor of the Mary Immaculate*.—S.M.M.I.
[0590]—*Sisters of Charity of Saint Elizabeth, Convent Station*.—S.C.
[0620]—*Sisters of Charity of St. Louis*.—S.C.S.L.
[2990]—*Sisters of Notre Dame*.—S.N.D.
[3000]—*Sisters of Notre Dame de Namur*.—S.N.D.deN.
[3780]—*Sisters of Saints Cyril and Methodius*.—SS.C.M.
[3850]—*Sisters of St. Joseph of Chambery*.
[2980]—*Sisters of the Congregation de Notre Dame*.—C.N.D.
[1970]—*Sisters of the Holy Family of Nazareth*.—C.S.F.N.
[3480]—*Sisters of the Resurrection*. (Eastern Prov.).—C.R.
[2160]—*Sisters, Servants of the Immaculate Heart of Mary*.—I.H.M.
[4070]—*Society of the Sacred Heart*.—R.S.C.J.
[4130]—*Ursuline Sisters of the Congregation of Tildonk, Belgium*.—O.S.U.

DIOCESAN CEMETERIES

BRIDGEPORT. *St. Michael's*, 2205 Stratford Ave., 06497. Tel: 203-378-0404.

DANBURY. *St. Peter's*, Lake Ave. Exit, 06810. Tel: 203-743-9626.

GREENWICH. *Putnam*, 35 Parsonage Rd., 06830. Tel: 203-869-4828.
St. Mary's, 399 North St., 06830. Tel: 203-869-7026.

NEWTOWN. *Resurrection*, c/o St. Peter Cemetery, Lake Ave. Exit, 06810. Tel: 203-743-9626.

NORWALK. *St. John's & St. Mary's*, 223 Richards Ave., 06850. Tel: 203-838-4271.

STAMFORD. *Queen of Peace*, c/o St. John Cemetery, 25 Camp Ave., 06820. Tel: 203-322-0455.
St. John's, 25 Camp Ave., 06820. Tel: 203-322-0455.

TRUMBULL. *Gate of Heaven*, c/o St. Michael's, 2205 Stratford Ave., 06497. Tel: 203-378-0404.

WESTPORT. *Assumption Green Farms*, Kings Hwy., c/o St. John Cemetery, 223 Richards Ave., 06850. Tel: 203-838-4271.

NECROLOGY

✠ Curtis, Most Rev. Walter William, Bishop Emeritus. —Died Oct. 18, 1997.
† Conroy, Rev. Msgr. Walter Richard, Newton, CT, Saint Rose of Lima. —Died July 17, 1997.
† Sienkiewicz, Rev. Msgr. Alfred Joseph, Stamford, CT, Holy Spirit. —Died Dec. 1, 1996.

Diocese of Brooklyn

(Dioecesis Bruklyniensis)

Most Reverend

THOMAS V. DAILY, D.D.

Sixth Bishop of Brooklyn; ordained January 10, 1952; appointed Auxiliary to the Archbishop of Boston and Titular Bishop of Bladia December 31, 1974; consecrated February 11, 1975; appointed First Bishop of Palm Beach July 17, 1984; appointed Sixth Bishop of Brooklyn February 20, 1990; took possession April 16, 1990; installed April 18, 1990. *Mailing Address: 75 Greene Ave., P.O. Box C, Brooklyn, NY, 11202.*

Most Reverend

JOSEPH M. SULLIVAN, M.S.W., M.P.A., V.E.

Tenth Auxiliary to the Bishop of Brooklyn; ordained June 2, 1956; appointed Titular Bishop of Suliana October 7, 1980; episcopal ordination November 24, 1980. *Mailing Address: 378 Clermont Ave., Brooklyn, NY, 11238.*

Most Reverend

RENE A. VALERO, M.S.W.

Eleventh Auxiliary to the Bishop of Brooklyn; priestly ordination June 2, 1956; appointed Titular Bishop of Vicus Turris October 7, 1980; episcopal ordination November 24, 1980. *Res., 34-43 93rd St., Jackson Heights, NY, 11372.*

Most Reverend

IGNATIUS A. CATANELLO, PH.D.

Twelfth Auxiliary to the Bishop of Brooklyn; ordained May 28, 1966; appointed Titular Bishop of Deulto June 28, 1994; episcopal ordination August 22, 1994. *Res., 175-20 74th Ave., Flushing, NY, 11366.*

Most Reverend

GERALD M. BARBARITO, D.D., J.C.L.

Thirteenth Auxiliary to the Bishop of Brooklyn; ordained January 31, 1976; appointed Titular Bishop of Gisipa June 28, 1994; episcopal ordination August 22, 1994. *Mailing Address: 1956 Batchelder St., Brooklyn, NY, 11229.*

ESTABLISHED JULY 29, 1853.

Square Miles 179.25.

Comprises Kings and Queens Counties in the State of New York.

For legal titles of parishes and diocesan institutions, consult the Chancery Office.

Chancery Office: 75 Greene Ave., P.O. Box C, Brooklyn, NY, 11202. Tel.: 718-399-5990; Fax: 718-399-5934.

STATISTICAL OVERVIEW

Personnel	
Bishop	1
Auxiliary Bishops	4
Priests: Diocesan Active in Diocese	445
Priests: Active Outside Diocese	51
Priests: Diocesan in Foreign Missions	2
Priests: Retired, Sick or Absent	187
Number of Diocesan Priests	685
Religious Priests in Diocese	206
Extern Priests in Diocese	44
Ordinations:	
Diocesan Priests	9
Transitional Deacons	5
Permanent Deacons in Diocese	146
Total Brothers	188
Total Sisters	1,321
Parishes	
Parishes	222
With Resident Pastor:	
Resident Diocesan Priests	196
Resident Religious Priests	23
Without Resident Pastor:	
Administered by Priests	3
Professional Ministry Personnel:	
Brothers	9
Sisters	130
Lay Ministers	165
Welfare	
Catholic Hospitals	4
Total Assisted	1,033,371
Health Care Centers	17
Total Assisted	509,521
Homes for the Aged	6
Total Assisted	1,200
Residential Care of Children	18
Total Assisted	7,340
Day Care and Extended Day Care Centers	20
Total Assisted	2,100
Specialized Homes	35
Total Assisted	13,419
Special Centers for Social Services	90
Total Assisted	71,074
Residential Care of Disabled	75
Total Assisted	2,714
Other Institutions	17
Total Assisted	2,229
Educational	
Seminaries, Diocesan	1
Students from This Diocese	14
Students from Other Diocese	7
Diocesan Students in Other Seminaries	24
Seminaries, Religious	2
Students Religious	16
Total Seminarians	54
Colleges and Universities	3
Total Students	18,970
High Schools, Diocesan and Parish	4
Total Students	2,013
High Schools, Private	18
Total Students	15,990
Elementary Schools, Diocesan and Parish	155
Total Students	55,048
Elementary Schools, Private	3
Total Students	478
Non-residential Schools for the Disabled	1
Total Students	103
Catechesis/Religious Education:	
High School Students	9,850
Elementary Students	49,250
Total Students Under Catholic Instruction	151,756
Teachers in the Diocese:	
Priests	6
Brothers	78
Sisters	268
Lay Teachers	3,290
Vital Statistics	
Receptions into the Church:	
Infant Baptism Totals	22,457
Adult Baptism Totals	928
Received into Full Communion	1,165
First Communions	15,759
Confirmations	11,383
Marriages:	
Catholic	4,199
Interfaith	484
Total Marriages	4,683
Deaths	12,018
Total Catholic Population	1,615,117
Total Population	4,254,609

Former Bishops—Rt. Rev. JOHN LOUGHLIN, D.D., First Bishop of Brooklyn; ord. Oct. 18, 1840; cons. Oct. 30, 1853; died Dec. 28, 1891.—Rt. Rev. CHARLES E. MCDONNELL, D.D., Second Bishop of Brooklyn; ord. May 19, 1878; cons. April 25, 1892; died Aug. 8, 1921.—Most Rev. THOMAS E. MOLLOY, D.D., Third Bishop of Brooklyn; ord. Sept. 19, 1908; cons. Second Auxiliary Bishop of Brooklyn, Oct. 3, 1920; appt. Bishop of Brooklyn, Nov. 21, 1921; installed Feb. 15, 1922; died Nov. 26, 1956.—Most Rev. BRYAN J. MCENTEGART, D.D., LL.D., Fourth Bishop of Brooklyn; ord. September 8, 1917; appt. Bishop of Ogdensburg, June 5, 1943; cons. August 3, 1943; appt. Rector of the Catholic University of America, Washington, DC, June 26, 1953; appt. Titular Bishop of Aradi, Aug. 19, 1953; appt. Bishop of Brooklyn, April 16, 1957; installed June 13, 1957; retired and appt. Titular Archbishop of Gabii, July 17, 1968; died Sept. 30, 1968.—Most Rev. FRANCIS J. MUGAVERO, D.D., Fifth Bishop of Brooklyn; ord. May 18, 1940; Bishop of Brooklyn; appt. July 15, 1968; cons. Sept. 12, 1968; installed Sept. 12, 1968; retired Feb. 20, 1990; died July 12, 1991.

Central Offices—75 Greene Ave., Brooklyn, 11238. Mailing Address: P.O. Box C, Brooklyn, 11202-3604. Tel: 718-399-5900. Office Hours: Mon.-Fri. 9-4:30.

Vicar General—Rev. Msgr. OTTO L. GARCIA, J.C.D., V.G., *75 Greene Ave., P.O. Box C, Brooklyn, 11202.* Tel: 718-399-5900.

Regional Bishop of Brooklyn West and Episcopal Vicar for Human Services—Most Rev. JOSEPH M. SULLIVAN, M.S.W., M.P.A., V.E., *191 Joralemon St., Brooklyn, 11201.* Tel: 718-722-6000.

Regional Bishop of Queens North and Episcopal Vicar for Elderly and Racial Concerns—Most Rev. RENE A. VALERO, M.S.W., V.E., *7200 Douglaston Pkwy., Douglaston, 11362.* Tel: 718-229-8001, Ext. 710; 700.

Regional Bishop of Queens South and Episcopal Vicar for Evangelization and Spiritual Development—Most Rev. IGNATIUS A. CANTANELLO, Ph.D., V.E., *St. John's University, St. John's Hall, Rm. 103, 8000 Utipia Pkwy., Jamaica, 11439.* Tel: 718-990-6161, Ext. 5490.

Regional Bishop of Brooklyn East and Episcopal Vicar for Ministry—Most Rev. GERALD M. BARBARITO, D.D., J.C.L., V.E., *1956 Batchelder St., Brooklyn, 11229.* Tel: 718-339-4639; Fax: 718-339-4587.

Episcopal Vicars-Territorial—Brooklyn West: Rev. Msgr. RAYMOND F. CHAPPETTO, V.E., *St. Agatha, 702 48th St., Brooklyn, 11220.* Tel: 718-436-1080. Brooklyn East: Very Rev. JOHN E. MAHONEY, V.E., *St. Thomas Aquinas, 1550 Hendrickson St., Brooklyn, 11234.* Tel: 718-253-4404. Queens South: Rev. Msgr. DENIS M. HERRON, V.E., *Our Lady of Lourdes, 92-96 220th St., Queens Village, 11428.* Tel: 718-479-5111. Queens North: Very Rev. EDWARD A. RYAN, V.E., *Mary's Nativity, 46-02 Parson's Blvd., Flushing, 11355.* Tel: 718-359-5996.

Episcopal Vicar for Temporalities—Rev. Msgr. JOHN J. BRACKEN, *310 Prospect Park West, Brooklyn, 11215.* Tel: 718-965-7300; Fax: 718-965-7314.

Finance Office—Rev. Msgr. JOHN J. BRACKEN, Dir.; Mr. THOMAS GALLIGAN, Admin.; Rev. Msgr. AUSTIN BENNETT, Consultant. Tel: 718-399-5900; Fax: 718-399-5966.

Pension Office—Rev. THOMAS V. DOYLE, Admin. ANNMARIE FAHEY, Mgr. Tel: 718-399-5920; Fax: 718-399-5917.

Parish Services Corp.—FLORENCE C. FLYNN, Mgr., *The Chancery, 75 Greene Ave., Brooklyn, 11202.* Tel: 718-399-5900; Fax: 718-399-5942.

Development Office—Rev. Msgr. JOHN J. BRACKEN, Dir. Tel: 718-229-8001, Ext. 310; Fax: 718-225-4808.

Medical Insurance Office—VINNI C. LOPRESTI, Program Mgr. Tel: 718-229-8001, Ext. 115; Fax: 718-631-4606.

Building and Property Administration—Rev. WILLIAM KRLIS, Dir. Tel: 718-229-8001, Ext. 300; Fax: 718-229-1324.

The Brooklyn & Queens Asbestos Management Corp.—JAMES A. O'BRIEN, Exec. Dir. Tel: 718-229-8001, Ext. 320; Fax: 718-279-0264.

Institutional Services—Rev. MICHAEL HARDIMAN, Exec. Dir. ROBERT RYMERS, Dir. of Operations, *The Immaculate Conception Center, 7200 Douglaston Pkwy., Douglaston, 11362.* Tel: 718-229-8001, Ext. 8290; Fax: 718-279-3004.

Episcopal Vicar for Education—Rev. Msgr. GUY J. PUGLISI, *6025 Sixth Ave., Brooklyn, 11202.* Tel: 718-492-1800; Fax: 718-439-0784.

Chancery Office—*75 Greene Ave., P.O. Box C., Brooklyn, 11202.* Tel: 718-399-5990; Fax: 718-399-5934.

Chancellor—Rev. Msgr. OTTO L. GARCIA, J.C.D., V.G.

Vice-Chancellors—Rev. ANDREW J. VACCARI, J.C.L.; Sr. JANE SCANLON, C.N.D., M.Div.

Diocesan Archivist—JOSEPH W. COEN, C.A., Mailing Address: *7200 Douglaston Pky., Douglaston, 11362.* Tel: 718-229-8001, Ext. 475.

Censors of Books—Rev. PETER I. VACCARI, S.T.L., *75 Greene Ave., P.O. Box C, Brooklyn, 11202.*

Secretary to the Diocesan Bishop—Rev. RALPH J. MARESCA, M.Div. Tel: 718-399-5970; Fax: 718-399-5975.

Masters of Ceremonies to Bishops—*Bishop Daily*—Rev. RALPH J. MARESCA, M.Div. *Bishop Sullivan*—Revs. STEVEN J. AGUGGIA; JOSEPH R. GIBINO; MICHAEL J. HARDIMAN; MICHAEL A. CARRANO. *Bishop Valero*—Revs. JOHN F. BROGAN; JOHN COSTELLO; THOMAS V. DOYLE; WILLIAM A. MCLAUGHLIN. *Bishop Catanello*—Revs. THOMAS G. CASERTA; JOSEPH T. HOLCOMB; GREGORY C. WIELUNSKI; ANDREW J. VACCARI. *Bishop Barbarito*—Revs. JOHN J. O'CONNOR; CHRISTOPHER J. TURCZANY; JOSEPH R. GRIMALDI; BRIAN P. DOWD.

Tribunal—*7200 Douglaston Pkwy., Douglaston, 11362.* Tel: 718-229-8131; Fax: 718-631-1339.

Officialis-Judicial Vicar—Rev. Msgr. EDWARD B. SCHARFENBERGER, S.T.L., J.C.L., J.D.

Vice Officiales-Associate Judicial Vicars—Revs. THOMAS CHENG, J.C.D., M.A.; GREGORY C. WIELUNSKI, J.C.D.; JOSEPH R. GRIMALDI, J.C.L.; HUGO BEDOYA, S.T.L., J.C.D.

Defenders of the Marriage Bond—Revs. JOHN J. BROWN, S.T.L., J.C.L.; ROBERT J. YOUNG, J.C.L.

Promoter of Justice—Rev. Msgr. WILLIAM A. VARVARO, P.A., S.T.D., J.C.D.

Attorneys and Counselors at Canon Law—Sr. M. JOSITA WALSH, R.S.M., M.A.; MARIA CHRISTINA PRINCE, M.A.; Sr. MARY PARRY, O.P., M.A.; Revs. JOHN D. CAPILLO, M.Div.; RUSS MACARANES, J.C.D.; THOMAS MACHALSKI, M.Div.; EDWARD G. BROPHY, M.Div.; Sr. JEANNE MONAHAN, O.P., Ph.D.; Deacon JEROME KREBS.

Senior Priests, Episcopal Delegate for—Rev. JEFFREY T. DILLON, *7200 Douglaston Pkwy., Douglaston, 11362.* Tel: 718-229-8001, Ext. 411.

Religious, Episcopal Delegate for—Sr. JANE SCANLON, C.N.D., *75 Greene Ave., P.O. Box C, Brooklyn, 11202.* Tel: 718-399-5900.

Cemeteries—Rev. MICHAEL J. REID, Dir., *80-01 Metropolitan Ave., Middle Village, 11379.* Tel: 718-894-4888.

Education, Offices—(See Institutions Located in the Diocese for details).

Family Life Office—Rev. JOHN COSTELLO, S.T.L., Dir. ('89); Deacon LEON F. MILLER, Asst. Dir. for Hispanics, *7200 Douglaston Pkwy., Douglaston, 11362.* Tel: 718-229-8001, Ext. 342.

Liturgical Office—Rev. JOHN C. TOSI, Exec. Sec., *75 Greene Ave., P.O. Box C, Brooklyn, 11202.* Tel: 718-399-5980; Fax: 718-399-5930.

Mediation and Arbitration, Board of—Rev. Msgr. EDWARD J. BREEN, Exec. Sec., *Mailing Address: P.O. Box C, Brooklyn, 11202.*

Ministerial Development Program—Most Rev. GERALD M. BARBARITO, D.D., J.C.L., V.E., Dir., Newly Ordained & Ministry to Priests Programs, *1956 Batchelder St., Brooklyn, 11229.* Tel: 718-339-4639; Fax: 718-339-4587.

Newspaper "The Tablet"—Vacant, Assoc. Publisher; ED WILKINSON, Editor, *653 Hicks St., Brooklyn, 11231.* Tel: 718-858-3838.

Permanent Diaconate Program—Rev. Msgr. EDWARD V. WETTERER, Dir.; Deacon SALVATORE V. LICATA, Exec. Sec., *75 Greene Ave., P.O. Box C, Brooklyn, 11202.* Tel: 718-399-5900.

Office of Clergy Personnel—Rev. JOHN J. BROWN, Dir., *75 Greene Ave., P.O. Box C, Brooklyn, 11202.* Tel: 718-399-5941; Fax: 718-399-7194.

Assignment Board—Rev. JOHN J. BROWN, Chm.; Rev. Msgr. RAYMOND F. CHAPPETTO; Rev. Msgr. DENIS M. HERRON; Very Rev. JOHN E. MAHONEY; Very Rev. EDWARD A. RYAN; Revs. FERNANDO FERRARESE; SEAN G. OGLE.

Personnel Board (Clergy)—Rev. JOHN J. BROWN, Chm.; Very Rev. EDWARD A. RYAN; Revs. STEVEN A. FERRARI; MICHAEL C. GRIBBON.

Propagation of the Faith—Rev. Msgr. JOHN J. CONDON, Dir., Office: *191 Joralemon St., P.O. Box 200, Brooklyn, 11202.* Tel: 718-875-4375.

Holy Childhood, Pontifical Association—Rev. Msgr. JOHN J. CONDON, Dir., *191 Joralemon St., P.O. Box 200, Brooklyn, 11202.*

Public Information Office—FRANK DEROSA, Dir., *75 Greene Ave., P.O. Box C, Brooklyn, 11202.* Tel: 718-399-5955; Fax: 718-399-5957.

Retirement Board (Priests)—Most Rev. RENE A. VALERO, M.S.W., V.E., Chm., *Mailing Address: 7200 Douglaston Pkwy., Douglaston, 11362.* Members: Rev. Msgr. AUSTIN P. BENNETT; Rev. Msgr. JOHN J. ANTONCIC; Rev. Msgr. MARTIN P. BANNAN; Rev. Msgr. OCTAVIO CISNEROS; Rev. Msgr. GEORGE T. DEAS; Rev. Msgr. GEORGE V. FOGARTY; Rev. Msgr. PETER V. KAIN; Revs. THOMAS F. BROSNAN; JOHN J. BROWN; JEFFREY T. DILLON; MICHAEL M. GREENE; PAUL V. JERVIS; MARCELLO J. LATONA; LEWIS H. MAYNARD; Mrs. PAT BRENNAN, R.N.; ANN C. CARROLL.

Vocations, Office of—Rev. MICHAEL G. TEDONE, Dir.; Sr. REGINA WILSON, I.H.M., Assoc. Dir., *75 Greene Ave., P.O. Box C, Brooklyn, 11202.* Tel: 718-399-5900.

Consultative Bodies

Presbyteral Council—Rev. Msgr. JOHN C. ANTONCIC, Exec. Sec.; Most Rev. JOSEPH M. SULLIVAN, M.S.W., M.P.A., V.E.; Most. Rev. RENE A. VALERO, M.S.W., V.E.; Most Rev. IGNATIUS A. CATANELLO, Ph.D., V.E.; Most Rev. GERALD M. BARBARITO, D.D., J.C.L., V.E.; Rev. Msgr. OTTO L. GARCIA, V.G.; Rev. Msgr. JOSEPH G. KONRAD, J.C.D.; Rev. Msgr. JOHN STRYNKOWSKI; Rev. Msgr. ED SCHARFENBERGER; Rev. Msgr. WILLIAM A. VARVARO; Very Rev. DENIS M. HERRON; Revs. THOMAS AHEARN; JOHN BROWN; WILLIAM HOPPE; THADDEUS KAZANECKI; JAMES KING; KEVIN MCBRIEN; EDWARD MAURER; JAMES O'BRIEN; ARTHUR PURCELL; VICTOR ULTO; PATRICK WEST, *75 Greene Ave., P.O. Box C, Brooklyn, 11202.*

Diocesan Budget Committee—Rev. Msgr. JOHN J. BRACKEN, Chm.

Subcommittee for Assisted Schools and Parishes—Rev. THOMAS V. DOYLE.

Subcommittee for Agencies—Rev. Msgr. JOHN J. BRACKEN.

Subcommittee for Parishes—Rev. Msgr. RAYMOND W. KUTNER.

Subcommittee for Schools—Sr. KAREN LADEMANN, O.P.

Diocesan Consultors—Rev. Msgr. OTTO L. GARCIA, J.C.D., V.G., Sec.; Most Rev. JOSEPH M. SULLIVAN, M.S.W., M.P.A., V.E.; Most Rev. RENE A. VALERO, M.S.W., V.E.; Most Rev. IGNATIUS A. CATANELLO, Ph.D., V.E.; Most Rev. GERALD M. BARBARITO, D.D., J.C.L., V.E.; Rev. Msgr. JAMES P. KING, P.A., V.G.; Rev. Msgr. KEVIN B. NOONE; Rev. Msgr. WILLIAM A. VARVARO; Revs. JOSEPH T. HOLCOMB; SEAN G. OGLE, M.Div., *75 Greene Ave., P.O. Box C, Brooklyn, 11202.*

Diocesan Pastoral Council—NORMA JEAN DEMBINSKI, Pres.; Rev. DANIEL S. MURPHY, Liaison Officer, *6713 Ridge Blvd., Brooklyn, 11220.*

Brothers' Senate—Bro. LAWRENCE SEWARD, S.C., *71-06 31st Ave., East Elmhurst, 11370.* Tel: 718-898-9600.

Commissions and Offices for Pastoral Services

Alcoholism Committee—Rev. Msgr. KIERAN MARTIN, Chm., *1550 Hendrickson St., Brooklyn, 11234.* Tel: 718-951-7302; Fax: 718-951-7233.

Art and Architecture Commission—Revs. JOHN C. TOSI, Exec. Sec. THOMAS G. PETTEI; VITO BUONANNO; THOMAS V. DOYLE; Sr. MARY JANE KELLY, O.P., Chm., Office: *75 Greene Ave., P.O. Box C, Brooklyn, 11202.*

Black Ministry, Office of—MADELINE ANDERSON, Exec. Dir., *666 Essex St., Brooklyn, 11238.* Tel: 718-257-2570; Fax: 718-272-5412.

Hispanic Ministry, Office of—Rev. JOHN F. BROGAN, Dir., *7200 Douglaston Pkwy., Douglaston, 11362.* Tel: 718-229-8001, Ext. 741.

Catholic Consultation Center—Rev. MICHAEL R. PARISI, Ph.D., Dir. Counselors: Rev. THOMAS M. HAGGERTY, C.S.W.; JUSTINE JOHNSON, B.S.N., M.S.; ROY INTERNICOLA, M.S.; VINCENT FOLEY, Ph.D., Staff Psychologist, *7200 Douglaston Pkwy., Douglaston, 11362.* Tel: 718-279-1700.

Catholic Charities—Most Rev. JOSEPH M. SULLIVAN, Episcopal Vicar, Human Svcs. and Sec., Bishop for Charities, *191 Joralemon St., Brooklyn, 11201.* Tel: 718-722-6000; Fax: 718-643-0522. (See Institutions located in the Diocese for details).

Catholic Migration and Refugee Office—(See Institutions located in the Diocese for details).

Catholic Migration Services, Inc.—Rev. RONALD T. MARINO, Dir. Tel: 718-236-3000.

Diocesan Institute of Languages—Rev. MICHAEL J. HARDIMAN, Dir., *7200 Douglaston Pkwy., Douglaston, 11362.* Tel: 718-229-8001.

Chaplains and Uniformed Services, Official—Police Department: Rev. Msgr. JOHN P. MCCULLAGH; Fire Department: Rev. JOHN DELENDICK; Sanitation Department: Rev. VINCENT J. TERMINE; BMT Holy Name Society: Rev. Msgr. WILLIAM J. FLOOD.

Diocesan Building Commission—Revs. WILLIAM F. KRLIS, Chm. VINCENT M. DALY; JAMES J. MUELLER, S.T.L.; Rev. Msgr. KEVIN B. NOONE; Rev. GARY P. ROGERS; FRANK GALLIGAN, Consultant, Mailing Address: *7200 Douglaston Pkwy., Douglaston, 11362.*

Diocesan Real Estate Board—Rev. Msgr. RAYMOND W. KUTNER, Chm.; Revs. JOSEPH D. COLBERT; JOHN DELENDICK; WILLIAM F. KRLIS; Mr. JOHN TYNAN, Mailing Address: *34-43 93rd St., Jackson Heights, 11372.*

Diocesan Food Service—Mr. JAMES AUSTIN, Dir., *7200 Douglaston Pkwy., Douglaston, 11362.* Tel: 718-229-8001, Ext. 100.

Ecumenical and Interreligious Affairs, Diocesan Commission for—Rev. GUY MASSIE, M.Div., Exec. Sec.

Committee for Eastern Orthodox-Catholic Relations—Prof. THOMAS E. BIRD, Chm.

Committee for Christian Relations—Rev. Msgr. MICHAEL J. CANTLEY, S.T.D., Chm.

Committee for Catholic-Jewish Relations—Rev. GUY MASSIE, M.Div.

Catholic Muslim-Dialogue—Rev. MICHAEL LYNCH, S.T.L., Chm.

Evangelization Commission—Members: JUNE BAKER; Dr. THOMAS BIRD; Rev. ROBERT BLAUVELT; Rev. JOHN BROGAN; JOSEPHINE CACHIA; Rev. Msgr. MICHAEL J. CANTLEY; Rev. Msgr. OCTAVIO CISNEROS; Sr. PATRICIA CONROY; Rev. JOHN COSTELLO; Rev. JOSEPH DIELE; Sr. BERNADETTE DOWNES; ROBERT FALLON; Rev. Msgr. EUGENE FELDHAUS; Rev. JOSEPH MALAGRECA; Sr. PATRICIA O'BRIEN; RON RIZZUTO; Rev. GUY SANSARICG; Rev. Msgr. EDWARD SCHARFENBERGER; Rev. Msgr. ANTHONY SHERMAN; Rev. JOHN TOSI; MARY WING. Office of Religious Education: Rev. MICHAEL CARRANO; Rev. JOSEPH GIBINO; Sr. ALICE MICHAEL; JOAN SOKOLL; Sr. EILEEN SWEENEY,Episcopal Liaison: Most Rev. IGNATIUS A. CATANELLO, Auxiliary Bishop of Brooklyn; JOAN SNOW, Chair; Rev. DENNIS MCAULIFFE, Ph.D., Exec. Sec. Tel: 718-492-1800.

Home School Association—Rev. Msgr. THOMAS A. GRAHAM. Tel: 718-525-9099.

Liturgical Commission—Rev. Msgr. EDWARD J. BREEN; Very Rev. JOHN E. MAHONEY, V.E.; Revs. JOHN F. BROGAN; JOSEPH R. GIBINO; MARTIN F. KIRBY; EDWARD L. MAURER; Sr. MARY JANE KELLY, O.P.; Sr. MARY ALICE PIIL, C.S.J.; Sr. JULIE UPTON, R.S.M.; Mrs. JOAN SNOW; BRIAN ZUAR; Rev. JOHN C. TOSI, Exec. Sec., Office: *75 Greene Ave., P.O. Box C, Brooklyn, 11202.* Tel: 718-399-5980.

Music Commission—BRIAN ZUAR; Revs. PETER D. GILLEN; SEAN G. OGLE; JOHN C. TOSI, Exec. Sec.; Mrs. JOSEPHINE SANGES; EDWARD BURKARD; STEVEN R. GIUSTO; CHARLES MALLIA; MERRY A. NADDEO, Ed.D.; JOSEPH B. SMITH; Mr. EMMANUEL BOLOGNA; TERESA BRYANT; ROBERT ZAPPULLA; Dr. FRANK RETZEL, Mailing Address: *7200 Douglaston Pkwy., Douglaston, 11362.* Tel: 718-229-8001.

Pastoral Care of the Sick Office—(See Institutions located in the Diocese for details).

Pastoral Communications, Office of—Rev. Msgr. MICHAEL J. DEMPSEY, Dir., *1712 10th Ave., Brooklyn, 11215.* Tel: 718-499-9705. Legal Title: *Trans Video Communications, Inc.*

Pastoral Institute, Continuing Education of Priests—Rev. MARTIN F. KIRBY, S.S.L., Dir., General Course and Special Programs, *7200 Douglaston Pkwy., Douglaston, 11362.* Tel: 718-631-4267.

Prison Ministries Office—(See Listing Under Catholic Charities).

Religious Education, Office of—Evangelization and Catholic Formation: JOAN M. SNOW, Diocesan Dir.; Sr. EILEEN SWEENEY, O.S.F., Dir. Elementary Religious Educ. JOAN R. SOKOLL, Dir. Rel. Educ., Elementary; Rev. MICHAEL A. CORRANO, Dir. Youth Min. & Adolescent Catechesis/Dir. College Campus Min.; Sr. ALICE MICHAEL, Dir. Rel. Educ., Cultural & Ethnic Groups/Coord. R.C.I.A.; Rev. JOSEPH R. GIBINO, Dir. Adult Rel. Educ.; Rev. DENNIS MCAULIFFE, Ph.D., Coord. Evangelization.

Respect Life Office—EVELYN AQUILA, Dir., *75 Greene Ave., P.O. Box C, Brooklyn, 11202.* Tel: 718-399-5900.

Synod, Office of the—Rev. CORNELIUS H. MAHONEY, Dir., Mailing Address: *7200 Douglaston Pkwy., Douglaston, 11362.* Tel: 718-229-8001, Ext. 736; Fax: 718-428-4574.

Apostolic Organizations

Catholic Youth Organization, Diocesan—MICHAEL ABERNETHY, Dir., *191 Joralemon St., Brooklyn, 11201.* Tel: 718-596-5500, Ext. 234. JUDY AGEE, Queens Co. Dir. Tel: 718-779-1600.

Charismatic Groups, Catholic—

Charismatic Renewal (English-speaking) of the Diocese of Brooklyn—JOSEPHINE CACHIA, Dir. JOSEPHINE MCNALLY, Sec., *240 Jay St., Brooklyn, 11201.* Tel: 718-260-9111; Fax: 718-260-9121.

Renouveau Charismatique of the Diocese of Brooklyn—(serving the Haitian Charismatics of the Diocese); Rev. Msgr. JOSEPH MALAGRECA, Dir., *218-26 105th Ave., Queens Village, 11429.* Tel: 718-465-0124; Fax: 718-479-3548.

Renovacion Carismatica of the Diocese of Brooklyn—(serving the Hispanic Charismatics of the Diocese); Rev. Msgr. JOSEPH MALAGRECA, Dir., *218-26 105th Ave., Queens Village, 11429.* Tel: 718-465-0124; Fax: 718-479-3548.

Confraternity of the Guard of Honor and Confraternity of the Holy Hour—Rev. Msgr. THOMAS F. CRIBBIN, Dir., *St. Joseph's Residence, 256 Clinton Ave., Brooklyn, 11205.*

Confraternity of the Precious Blood—Rev. Msgr. JOSEPH K. PARKS, Dir., *5300 Fort Hamilton Pkwy., Brooklyn, 11219.* Tel: 718-436-1120.

Guilds—

Accountants—Rev. Msgr. WALTER C. MURPHY, Dir.

Catholic Cemetery Guild—Rev. MICHAEL J. REID, Moderator.

Lawyers—Rev. EDWARD B. SCHARFENBERGER, S.T.L., J.C.L., J.D., Kings Co.: Rev. Msgr. THOMAS F. DONOVAN, Queens Co.:

Pharmacists—Rev. Msgr. ALFRED A. VARRIALE, Dir.

Physicians—Rev. Msgr. JOSEPH C. KONRAD, J.C.D., Kings Co. Chapter Moderator.

Teachers—Rev. Msgr. THOMAS F. NOONAN, M.S., Dir.

Holy Name Society—Rev. RAYMOND MCKIERNAN, Moderator.

Marriage Encounter—Coords.: BOB NOBBS; MELINDA NOBBS. Tel: 718-805-7232.

National Council of Catholic Women—CLAIRE DUNNE, Pres.; Rev. Msgr. LAWRENCE J. MCALISTER, Spiritual Dir., *35-60 158th St., Flushing, 11358.*

Legion of Mary—Rev. Msgr. VINCENT F. FULLAM, Dir.; Rev. Msgr. JOSEPH ROSA, Spanish Curia; Deacon JEAN BAPTISTE BOURSIQUOT, Haitian Curia; Revs. JOSEPH AMN, Korean Curia; ALFRED WEINLICH, Flushing Curia; CHARLES REPOLE, O.F.M.Cap., N.W. Queens Curia; JOSEPH MARRIN, C.SS.R., Bay Ridge Curia, *82-00 35th Ave., Jackson Heights, 11372.* Tel: 718-429-2333.

Nocturnal Adoration Society—Rev. Msgr. JOHN F. WILSON, *245 Prospect Park W., Brooklyn, 11215.*

Priests' Eucharistic League—Rev. Msgr. JOHN F. WILSON, *245 Prospect Park W., Brooklyn, 11215.*

Sodality Union—Vacant.

St. John's Priests Relief Society—Rev. Msgr. GEORGE M. SCHUSTER, Pres.; Rev. Msgr. WILLIAM A. VARVARO, Recording Sec.; Rev. Msgr. WILLIAM FLOOD, 1st Vice Pres.; Rev. RAYMOND STAFFORD, 2nd Vice Pres. and Acting Treas.; Rev. MATTHEW W. SHERIDAN, Fin. Sec., *66-05 79th Rd., Middle Village, 11379.* Tel: 718-326-1911.

CLERGY, PARISHES, MISSIONS AND PAROCHIAL SCHOOLS

CITY OF NEW YORK
BOROUGH OF BROOKLYN

1—THE CATHEDRAL-BASILICA OF ST. JAMES (Jay St. at Tillary), Rev. Msgr. John C. Tosi. In res., Rev. Msgr. Otto L. Garcia, J.C.D.; Rev. Joseph R. Gibino.
Res., 250 Cathedral Pl., 11201. Tel: 718-852-4002; Fax: 718-852-9452.

2—ST. AGATHA'S, Rev. Msgr. Paul R. Sanchez; Rev. Lewis H. Maynard; Sr. Ann Heavey, R.S.M., Pastoral Assoc.; Deacons George M. Tokarcsik; Juan R. Vargas. In res., Very Rev. Msgr. Raymond F. Chappetto, V.E.
Res., 702 48th St., 11220. Tel: 718-436-1080; Fax: 718-436-8870.
School—736 48th St., 11220. Tel: 718-435-3137; Fax: 718-437-7505. Sr. Mary Davies, O.P., Prin.
Sisters of Mercy 3; Lay Teachers 8; Students 282.
Catechesis/Religious Programs—Tel: 718-438-4512. Peggy Horgan, D.R.E.
Students 310.

3—ST. AGNES, Revs. John Delendick; George Manchapilly, C.M.I. (India); Deacon Aurelio Pagan. In res., Rev. Msgr. Guy J. Puglisi.
Res., 417 Sackett St., 11231. Tel: 718-625-1717; Fax: 718-625-1929.

4—ALL SAINTS, Rev. Donald J. Kenna.
Res., 115 Throop Ave., 11206. Tel: 718-388-1951; Fax: 718-388-7712.
School—113 Throop Ave., 11206. Tel: 718-782-0569. Ms. Maureen Friss, Prin.
Lay Teachers 9; Students 158.

5—ST. ALPHONSUS. Merged 1976. Records at St. Anthony of Padua-St. Alphonsus.

6—ST. AMBROSE. Merged 1978. Records at Our Lady of Monserrate-St. Ambrose.

7—ST. ANDREW THE APOSTLE, Rev. Daniel S. Murphy; Deacons Gregory Dixon; William Wander.
Res., 6713 Ridge Blvd., 11220. Tel: 718-680-1010; Fax: 718-680-3160.
Catechesis/Religious Programs—6725 Ridge Blvd., 11220. Tel: 718-630-5856; Fax: 718-630-5856.
Students 170.

8—ST. ANN-ST. GEORGE, Rev. Joseph Diele; Mr. Richard Carter, Pastoral Assoc.
Res., 207 York St., 11201. Tel: 718-625-0794; Fax: 718-625-4986.

9—ANNUNCIATION OF THE BLESSED VIRGIN MARY, Rev. Vytautas A. Palubinskas. In res., Rev. Daniel Jankevicius.
Res., 259 N. Fifth St., 11211. Tel: 718-387-2111; Fax: 718-782-4459.

10—ST. ANSELM'S, Rev. Msgr. Michael J. Phillips; Revs. Charles McLaughlin; James King; Joseph Vu; Deacon Thomas Davis. In res., Rev. Herbert A. Travis.
Res., 356 82nd St., 11209. Tel: 718-238-2900; Fax: 718-238-2902.
School—357 83rd St., 11209. Sr. Eileen Mary McMahon, S.S.N.D., Prin.
Sisters of Notre Dame 3; Lay Teachers 26; Students 680.
Catechesis/Religious Programs—Sr. Anne Bernadette, M.S.B.T., D.R.E.
Students 215.
Missionary Cenacle—351 83rd St., 11209. Tel: 718-836-0957. Sr. Regina Corde, O.P., Pastoral Ministry, Tel: 718-836-0780; Sr. Mary Gilmore, O.P., Dir. of Spirituality.
Missionary Servants of the Most Blessed Trinity 3.

11—ST. ANTHONY OF PADUA-ST. ALPHONSUS, Revs. John H. Reilly; William A. McLaughlin; Bro. Richard O'Brien, C.S.C. In res., Rev. Msgr. Anthony F. Passarella, Pastor Emeritus.
Res., 862 Manhattan Ave., 11222. Tel: 718-383-3339; Fax: 718-383-6958.
School—725 Leonard St., 11222. Tel: 718-383-5860; Fax: 718-389-5953. Sr. Ann Franklin, C.S.J., Prin.
Lay Teachers 18; Students 291.
Catechesis/Religious Programs—Tel: 718-383-6935. Rose Accetta, Prin.
Students 300.

12—ASSUMPTION OF THE BLESSED VIRGIN MARY, Rev. Msgr. Joseph A. Funaro. In res., Rev. Msgr. Thomas F. Cribbin; Revs. John J. Cremins; Michael A. Carrano.
Res., 64 Middagh St., 11201. Tel: 718-625-1161; Fax: 718-625-7223.

13—ST. ATHANASIUS, Revs. Fernando A. Ferrarese, M.Div.; John J. O'Connor, S.L.L.; Thaddeus J. Kazanecki, C.O. In res., Rev. Dennis McAuliffe, Ph.D.
Res., 2154 61st St., 11204. Tel: 718-236-0124; Fax: 718-236-4960.
School—6120 Bay Pkwy., 11204. Tel: 718-236-4791. Sr. Elizabeth Schroeder, C.S.J., Prin.
Lay Teachers 15; Students 280.
Catechesis/Religious Programs—Tel: 718-331-8811; Fax: 718-331-2582. Mrs. Marilyn Trabulsi, D.R.E.
Students 383.
Convent—2201 62nd St., 11204. Tel: 718-236-2680.

14—ST. AUGUSTINE, Revs. Robert J. Whelan; James G. Hannan; Deacon Joseph Bichotte. In res., Revs. Robert Freuh; Agnelo Pinto.
Res., 116 Sixth Ave., 11217. Tel: 718-783-3132; Fax: 718-638-4669.

15—ST. BARBARA, Rev. Msgr. John J. Powis; Rev. James Krische. In res., Rev. Peter A. Mahoney.
Res., 138 Bleecker St., 11221. Tel: 718-452-3660; Fax: 718-452-1279.

16—ST. BENEDICT'S. Closed. For inquiries for parish records contact the Chancery.

17—ST. BERNARD. Closed. For inquiries for parish records contact the Chancery.

18—ST. BERNADETTE, Revs. Robert J. Romano, M.Div.; Eugene P. Coyle; Ralph E. Barile. In res., Rev. Msgr. Cosmo G. Saporito, Pastor Emeritus; Rev. Msgr. Santi J. Privitera, Pastor Emeritus; Revs. David J. Dettmer; Joseph K. Dolan.
Res., 8201 13th Ave., 11228. Tel: 718-837-3400; Fax: 718-236-5883.
School—1313 83rd St., 11228. Tel: 718-236-1560.
Religious Teachers Filippini 3; Lay Teachers 12; Students 308.

19—ST. BERNARD'S, Rev. Vincent J. Gallo; Deacon Frank J. D'Accordo. In res., Rev. Msgr. Thomas C. Clancey, Pastor Emeritus.
Res., 2055 E. 69th St., 11234. Tel: 718-763-5533; Fax: 718-763-0224.
School—2030 E. 69th St., 11234. Tel: 718-241-6040; Fax: 718-241-7258. Linda Mele, Prin.
Lay Teachers 17; Students 322.
Catechesis/Religious Programs—Tel: 718-444-4674.
Students 311.

20—ST. BLAISE. Merged with St. Francis of Assisi in 1980. Records at St. Francis of Assisi-St. Blaise.

21—BLESSED SACRAMENT, Revs. Thomas F. Brosnan; James F. Fitzpatrick. In res., Rev. Msgr. Raymond Rau; Rev. Anselm E. Onuoha (Nigeria).
Res., 198 Euclid Ave., 11208. Tel: 718-827-1200; Fax: 718-827-2422.
School—187 Euclid Ave., 11208. Tel: 718-235-4863. Catherine Marlowe, Prin.
Lay Teachers 12; Students 315.
Catechesis/Religious Programs—Tel: 718-277-3231. Sr. Catherine Thornton, O.P., D.R.E.
Students 500.

22—ST. BONIFACE, Very Rev. Dennis M. Corrado, C.O., Pastor & Provost, Brooklyn Oratory; Rev. Mark Lane, C.O., D.R.E. In res., Rev. Terence Gleason, C.O.; Bros. James Simon, C.O.; Joel Warden, C.O.
Res., 109 Willoughby St., 11201. Tel: 718-875-2096; Fax: 718-875-4678.

23—ST. BRENDAN'S, Rev. Msgr. James B. McMahon; Rev. Richard E. Long.
Res., 1525 E. 12th St., 11230. Tel: 718-339-2828; Fax: 718-339-5951.

24—ST. BRIGID, Rev. Msgr. James J. Kelly; Rev. Vincente Sanchez; Deacon Philip J. Ehresmann. In res., Rev. John H. Wilkinson.
Res., 409 Linden St., 11237. Tel: 718-821-1690; Fax: 718-386-4302.
School—438 Grove St. E., 11237. Tel: 718-821-1477. Francine Guastello, Prin.
Sisters 1; Lay Teachers 10; Students 280.
Catechesis/Religious Programs—Tel: 718-821-6401. Sr. Patricia Neary, O.P., D.R.E.
Students 910.

25—ST. CASIMIR (Polish). Merged with Our Lady of Czestochowa in 1980. Records at Our Lady of Czestochowa-St. Casimir.

26—ST. CATHARINE OF ALEXANDRIA, Revs. John S. Wtulich; Robert M. Powers.
Res., 1119 41st St., 11218. Tel: 718-436-5917; Fax: 718-871-5140.
School—1053 41st St., 11219. Tel: 718-436-9721; Fax: 718-853-3347.
Sisters, Religious Sisters of the Sacred Heart of Mary 1; Lay Teachers 9; Students 285.
Catechesis/Religious Programs—Tel: 718-438-2613. Sr. Rosalind Picciano, C.S.J., D.R.E.
Students 396.

27—ST. CATHERINE OF GENOA, Rev. Gerald Dumont; Deacon Louis Guastella.
Res., 520 Linden Blvd., 11203. Tel: 718-282-7162; Fax: 718-282-5568.
School—870 Albany Ave., 11203. Tel: 718-284-1050; Fax: 718-284-3461.
Lay Teachers 19; Students 404. Co-Principals: Patricia Maio; Mary Blanchard.

28—ST. CECILIA, Revs. Kevin J. O'Donoghue; Richard W. Conlon; Deacons Nicholas J. Mazza; Carlos Valderama. In res., Rev. Joseph F. Buckley.
Res., 84 Herbert St., 11222. Tel: 718-389-0010; Fax: 718-389-5090.
School—Tel: 718-389-3161. Sr. Miriam Daniels, C.S.J., Prin.
Sisters 4; Lay Teachers 20; Students 479.

Catechesis/Religious Programs—1-15 Monitor St., 11222. Tel: 718-389-2546. Bro. Philip Zeller, F.S.C., D.R.E.
Students 141.

29—ST. CHARLES BORROMEO, Rev. Charles A. Kraus; Rev. Msgr. Charles E. Diviney, Pastor Emeritus; Rev. Thaddeus A. Grzelak; Bro. Becket Ryan, O.S.F.; Deacon John Flannery.
Res., 21 Sidney Pl., 11201. Tel: 718-625-1177; Fax: 718-624-1627.
School—23 Sidney Pl., 11201. Tel: 718-596-1362; Fax: 718-875-9471. Sr. Eileen McGuire, C.S.J., Prin.
Sisters of St. Joseph 1; Lay Teachers 13; Students 206.
Catechesis/Religious Programs—Students 70.

30—ST. COLUMBA, Revs. Edward J. Kiernan; Anthony C. Casey; Sr. Emily Masse, O.P., Pastoral Assoc.; Deacon Lawrence Coyle. In res., Rev. James P. Collins.
Res., 2245 Kimball St., 11234. Tel: 718-338-6265; Fax: 718-377-6440.
Catechesis/Religious Programs—Tel: 718-253-8840. Nancy Azzaro, D.R.E.
Students 229.

31—ST. COLUMBKILLE. Closed. Parochial records are at SS. Cyril and Methodius. Became Mission in 1939.

32—SS. CYRIL AND METHODIUS (Polish), Revs. Joseph Mietelski, C.M.; Stephen J. Minkiel, C.M.; Tadeusz Maciejewski, C.M.
Res., 119 Eagle St., 11222. Tel: 718-389-4424; Fax: 718-389-4191.
School—96 Dupont St., 11222. Tel: 718-389-4926. Sisters of the Holy Family of Nazareth 1; Lay Teachers 9; Students 142.

33—ST. DOMINIC, Revs. Arthur Minichello; Italo Barozzi; Sr. Margaret Cavanagh, O.P., Pastoral Min.; Deacons Carlo V. Mellace; Dante Colandrea.
Res., 2001 Bay Ridge Pkwy., 11204. Tel: 718-259-4636; 4637; 4638; Fax: 718-259-3066.
Catechesis/Religious Programs—Sr. Mary Jane Rolston, O.P., D.R.E., Tel: 718-259-6383.
Students 690.

34—ST. EDMUND'S, Rev. Msgr. Thomas F. Noonan; Revs. Brian P. Dowd, Chap., Denis Maloney Institute; Joseph A. Cestaro.
Res., 2460 Ocean Ave., 11229. Tel: 718-743-0102; Fax: 718-891-7834.
School—1902 Avenue T, 11229. Tel: 718-648-9229. Patricia O'Connor, Prin.
Lay Teachers 18; Students 375.
High School—Denis Maloney Institute, 2474 Ocean Ave., 11229. Tel: 718-743-6100; Fax: 718-743-5243. Mr. John Lorenzetti, Prin.
Sisters 2; Lay Teachers 30; Students 506. Chaplains: Revs. Steven Aggugia; John J. O'Connor.
Catechesis/Religious Programs—Tel: 718-743-8107. Marie Graham, D.R.E.
Students 255.

35—ST. EDWARD. Merged with St. Michael Archangel in 1942. Parochial records are at St. Michael-St. Edward, 108 St. Edwards St., 11205.

36—ST. EPHREM'S, Rev. Msgr. Peter V. Kain; Revs. Edward R. Stewart; Robert A. Moore, (Retired); Joseph Giordano, C.I.C.M.; Deacons Charles C. DiTargiani; Wilfred Malone; Wilfred Horne.
Res., 929 75th St., 11228. Tel: 718-833-1010; Fax: 718-921-5232.
School—Tel: 718-833-1440; Fax: 718-745-5301. Sr. Nora Ashe, C.S.J., Prin.
Sisters, Servants of the Immaculate Heart of Mary 4; Lay Teachers 17; Students 368.
Catechesis/Religious Programs—Tel: 718-745-7486. Diane Mosconi, D.R.E.
Students 311.
Convent—935 75th St., 11228. Tel: 718-833-1555.

37—EPIPHANY, Rev. Msgr. Matthew F. Foley; Deacon Angel Baez.
Res., 96 S. Ninth St., 11211. Tel: 718-387-6328; Fax: 718-387-2449.
Catechesis/Religious Programs—Students 90.
Arriba Juntos—Forward Together, Inc. Center—96 S. Ninth St., 11211. Tel: 718-384-2121.

38—ST. FINBAR'S, Rev. Msgr. Anthony S. Danna; Rev. Luke Wei; Deacon Giovanni Rizzo. In res., Revs. Nicholas Polichnowski, T.O.R.; Boban Zecharia.
Res., 138 Bay 20th St., 11214. Tel: 718-236-3312; Fax: 718-236-3750.
School—1825 Bath Ave., 11214. Tel: 718-256-0818. Sr. Mary Hyacinth, C.S.A.C., Prin.
Sisters of the Catholic Apostolate 4; Lay Teachers 13; Students 220.
Catechesis/Religious Programs—Tel: 718-837-3935. Sr. Ann Joachim, C.S.A.C., D.R.E.
Students 380.

39—ST. FORTUNATA, Revs. Freddy Cintron; Charles F. Harth, Pastor Emeritus; Deacon Edward Aigbojie. In res., Rev. Msgr. James W. Ryan, Pastor Emeritus.
Res., 2609 Linden Blvd., 11208. Tel: 718-647-2632; Fax: 718-647-1321.
School—Linden Blvd., 11208. Tel: 718-647-6440; Fax: 718-647-2166. Miss Marian J. Siconolfi, Prin.
Lay Teachers 12; Students 282.
Catechesis/Religious Programs—Rev. Freddy Cintron, D.R.E.
Students 215.

40—FOURTEEN HOLY MARTYRS. Merged with St. Martin of Tours in 1976. Records at St. Martin of Tours-Fourteen Holy Martyrs.

41—ST. FRANCES CABRINI, Rev. Emilio J. Salerno.
Res., 35 Bay 11th St., 11228. Tel: 718-236-9165; Fax: 718-331-8139.
School—21 Bay 11th St., 11228. Tel: 718-232-6700. Sr. Martin Marie Doran, O.P., Prin.
Sisters of St. Dominic 2; Lay Teachers 8; Students 324.
Catechesis/Religious Programs—Tel: 718-232-4228. Eileen Maguire, D.R.E.
Students 338.

42—ST. FRANCES CABRINI CHAPEL. Closed. For inquiries for parish records contact the Chancery.

43—ST. FRANCES DE CHANTAL, Revs. Arthur D. Purcell; Jose George (India); Andriej Lukianiuk. In res., Revs. Michael J. Hunt, Pastor Emeritus; Benedict Barszcz, S.A.C. (Poland).
Res., 1273 58th St., 11219. Tel: 718-436-6407; Fax: 718-854-2761.
Catechesis/Religious Programs—Lay Teachers 18; Students 320.

44—ST. FRANCIS IN THE FIELDS. Closed. For inquiries for parish records contact the Chancery.

45—ST. FRANCIS OF ASSISI-ST. BLAISE, Revs. Gerard G. Pelletier, S.M.; Omer St. Onge, S.M.; Roger Bourgea, S.M.
Res., Tel: 718-756-2015; Fax: 718-756-1773.
Church—1081 Nostrand Ave., 11225.
School—Tel: 718-778-1300. Sr. Theresa Scanlon, C.S.J., Prin.
Sisters 4; Lay Teachers 14; Students 454.
Catechesis/Religious Programs—Tel: 718-778-1302. Mrs. Gilbert Verna, D.R.E.
Students 300.

46—ST. FRANCIS OF PAOLA (Italian), Rev. Andrew R. Varano.
Res., 219 Conselyea St., 11211. Tel: 718-387-0256; Fax: 718-387-6344.
Catechesis/Religious Programs—Students 85.

47—ST. FRANCIS XAVIER, Revs. Edward P. Doran; Stephen Placa; Deacons John Franca; James Ramos. In res., Rev. Paul W. Farin.
Res., 225 Sixth Ave., 11215. Tel: 718-638-1880; Fax: 718-638-2839.
School—763 President St., 11215. Tel: 718-857-2559. Sr. Kathleen Sullivan, C.S.J., Prin.
Sisters of St. Joseph 3; Lay Teachers 15; Students 520.
Catechesis/Religious Programs—Tel: 718-857-2903. Sr. Helene Conway, D.R.E.
Students 195.

48—ST. GABRIEL THE ARCHANGEL, Rev. Carlos Walker (Argentina). In res., Rev. Eduardo Coll (Argentina).
Res., 749 Linwood St., 11208. Tel: 718-257-0612; Fax: 718-257-6076.
Catechesis/Religious Programs—666 Essex St., 11208. Tel: 718-649-0450.
Students 228.

49—ST. GEORGE. Merged with St. Ann in 1986. Records at St. Ann-St. George.

50—GOOD SHEPHERD, Rev. Msgr. Thomas F. Brady; Revs. Richard M. Lewkiewicz; James K. Cunningham. In res., Rev. Msgr. Robert E. Welsh, Pastor Emeritus; Rev. Garvey G. Meade.
Res., 1950 Batchelder St., 11229. Tel: 718-998-2800; Fax: 718-382-5428.
School—1943 Brown St., 11229. Tel: 718-339-2745. Mr. Anthony Paparelli, Prin.
Sisters of St. Dominic 1; Lay Teachers 22; Students 523.
Catechesis/Religious Programs—Tel: 718-375-0899; Fax: 718-645-4513.
Students 460.

51—ST. GREGORY THE GREAT, Rev. Gary P. Rogers; Deacons Roy N. George; Andres De Leon, Jr.
Res., 224 Brooklyn Ave., 11213-2505. Tel: 718-773-0100; Fax: 718-773-4198.
School—991 St. Johns Pl., 11213-2532. Tel: 718-774-3330; Fax: 718-774-3332.
Lay Teachers 15; Students 300.
Catechesis/Religious Programs—Tel: 718-773-0100. Julia Bramwell, D.R.E.
Students 175.

52—GUARDIAN ANGEL, Rev. Msgr. Perfecto Vazquez; Rev. John Prakasam (India); Deacon Anthony J. Russo.
Res., 2978 Ocean Pkwy., 11235. Tel: 718-266-1561; Fax: 718-372-1603.
Catechesis/Religious Programs—Tel: 718-372-1967. Ariene Ambert, D.R.E.
Students 226.

53—HOLY CROSS, Rev. Msgr. Rollin J. Darbouze.
Res., 2530 Church Ave., 11226. Tel: 718-469-5900; Fax: 718-469-5901.
School—Tel: 718-282-1710. Sr. Angela Patrice Murray, C.S.J., Prin.
Sisters of St. Joseph 2; Lay Teachers 13; Students 240.
Catechesis/Religious Programs—Tel: 718-941-5066.
Students 470.

54—HOLY FAMILY, Rev. Thomas E. Fox; Deacon Hector Montalvo. In res., Revs. Anankwah Danquah (Ghana); Leo Nitural.
Res., 205 14th St., 11215. Tel: 718-768-0736; Fax: 718-832-2879.
Catechesis/Religious Programs—Students 160.

55—HOLY FAMILY, Revs. John A. McShane; Paul Vazhapilly; Edward R. Kane. In res., Rev. Michael J. Lynch.
Res., 9719 Flatlands Ave., 11236. Tel: 718-257-4423; Fax: 718-257-4806.
School—216 Conklin Ave., 11236. Tel: 718-257-2954. Mary Lou Reitz, Prin.
Lay Teachers 15; Students 301.
Catechesis/Religious Programs—Tel: 718-257-8016; Fax: 718-257-4806. Elizabeth Mathew, D.R.E.
Students 340.

56—HOLY FAMILY (Slovak), Rev. Sebastian Kochuparackal, C.M.I. (India).
Res., 21 Nassau Ave., 11222. Tel: 718-388-5145.

57—HOLY INNOCENTS, Revs. Joseph J. Weber; Alfred R. Guthrie; Jean-Miguel Auguste; Deacon Antoine Felix. In res., Rev. Robert B. Hume, Pastor Emeritus.
Res., 279 E. 17th St., 11226. Tel: 718-469-9500; Fax: 718-941-4931.
School—249 E. 17th St., 11226. Tel: 718-282-5294. Sr. Mary Immaculate, R.S.M., Prin.
Sisters of Mercy 2; Lay Teachers 13; Students 307.
Catechesis/Religious Programs—Tel: 718-469-8159.
Students 420.

58—HOLY NAME, Revs. Dennis J. Farrell; Raymond McKiernan; Matthew Manalel; Benjamin Gomes; Deacon Abel Torres. In res., Rev. Msgr. John F. Wilson, Pastor Emeritus.
Res., 245 Prospect Park W., 11215. Tel: 718-768-3071; Fax: 718-369-2039.
School—241 Prospect Park W., 11215. Tel: 718-768-7629. Robert Hughes, Prin. & D.R.E.
Sisters of St. Joseph 1; Lay Teachers 17; Students 224.
Catechesis/Religious Programs—243 Prospect Park W., 11215. Tel: 718-768-3007; Fax: 718-369-2039.
Students 170.

59—HOLY ROSARY, Rev. William Smith.
Res., 141 Chauncey St., 11233. Tel: 718-493-8001; Fax: 718-493-8002.
School—Tel: 718-493-8471; Fax: 718-483-8471. Sr. Kathleen Appier, Prin.; Sr. Cheryl Hillig, Vice Prin.
Sisters 2; Lay Teachers 13; Students 350.

60—HOLY SPIRIT, Revs. Jerome T. Jecewiz; David Bertolotti; Deacon Wilfredo Hernandez.
Res., 1712 45th St., 11204. Tel: 718-436-5565; Fax: 718-436-5586.
School—1668 46th St., 11204. Tel: 718-633-3959.
Sisters of St. Joseph 2; Lay Teachers 7; Students 160.
Convent—1679 47th St., 11204.

61—MOST HOLY TRINITY, Revs. Russell Governale, O.F.M.Conv.; Timothy Dore, O.F.M.Conv.; Bro. Vincent Vivian, O.F.M.Conv., Pastoral Assoc. In res., Rev. Joseph Kerwin, O.F.M.Conv.
Res., 138 Montrose Ave., 11206. Tel: 718-384-0215; Fax: 718-384-3030.
School—140 Montrose Ave., 11206. Tel: 718-384-1101. Sr. Joseph Maureen Zick, O.P., Prin.

62—ST. IGNATIUS, Revs. John R. Hyatt, S.J.; Steven Pugliese, S.J.; Alfredo S. Quevedo, S.J.; Donald C. Maldari, S.J.; Deacons Berthal Beaubrun; Jean-Baptiste Boursiquot.
Res., 1101 Carroll St., 11225. Tel: 718-774-2102; Fax: 718-774-5821.
Catechesis/Religious Programs—Students 170.

63—IMMACULATE CONCEPTION OF THE BLESSED VIRGIN MARY, Revs. Robert P. Morales, Admin.; Dagoberto Noguera (Colombia).
Res., 72 Maujer St., 11206. Tel: 718-384-0765; Fax: 718-384-2898.
Catechesis/Religious Programs—Students 140.

64—IMMACULATE HEART OF MARY, Revs. Patrick J. McNelis; John E. Capillo. In res., Rev. Edward T. O'Connor, Pastor Emeritus.
Res., 2805 Ft. Hamilton Pkwy., 11218. Tel: 718-871-1310; Fax: 718-633-1866.
School—3002 Ft. Hamilton Pkwy., 11218. Tel: 718-438-7873. Sr. Theresa Sweeney, Prin.

Sisters 2; Lay Teachers 14; Students 267.
Catechesis/Religious Programs—Joyce Checkett, D.R.E., Tel: 718-854-7326.
Students 260.

65—ST. JEROME'S, Revs. Guy Sansaricq; Antonius P. Gopaul; C. Thevenin; Deacons Anthony Arthur; Magloire Marcel.
Res., 2900 Newkirk Ave., 11226. Tel: 718-462-0223; Fax: 718-462-7753.
School—465 E. 29th St., 11226. Tel: 718-462-0211; Fax: 718-462-1828.
Sisters of Mercy 2; Lay Teachers 16; Students 360.
Principals: Ms. Linda Mele; Mrs. Satti Marchan.
Catechesis/Religious Programs—Paul Norman, D.R.E.
Students 310.

66—ST. JOHN THE BAPTIST, Revs. Stephen M. Grozio, C.M.; Joseph V. Agostino, C.M.; John P. Timlin, C.M., Supr. In res., Rev. Thomas S. Krafinski, C.M.; Bro. Joseph Tauraso, C.M.
Res., 75 Lewis Ave., 11206. Tel: 718-455-6864; Fax: 718-452-3738.
School—82 Lewis Ave., 11206. Tel: 718-453-1000; Fax: 718-453-1000. Sr. Mary Jane Raeihle, C.S.J., Prin.
Sisters 2; Lay Teachers 20; Students 509.
Catechesis/Religious Programs—Sr. Patricia Evanick, D.C., D.R.E.
Students 170.

67—ST. JOHN CANTIUS, Rev. John A. Gurrieri; Deacon Rafael Marte. Pastoral Assocs.: Sr. Mary Alice MacKenzie, S.C.; Sr. Rita Rompre, C.N.D. In res., Rev. Msgr. Walter C. Galuszka, Pastor Emeritus; Rev. James Sweeney.
Res., 479 New Jersey Ave., 11207. Tel: 718-342-2679; Fax: 718-342-4878.
School—Tel: 718-385-7494. Mrs. Margaret Otunba, Prin.
Lay Teachers 10; Students 236.
Catechesis/Religious Programs—Students 355.

68—ST. JOHN THE EVANGELIST, Rev. Joseph Nugent.
Res., 250 21st St., 11215. Tel: 718-768-3751; Fax: 718-768-4689.

69—ST. JOHN'S CHAPEL. Closed. For inquiries for parish records contact the Chancery.

70—ST. JOSEPH'S, Rev. Robert Vitaglione; Sr. Genevieve Delaney, Pastoral Assoc.
Res., 856 Pacific St., 11238. Tel: 718-783-4500.
Catechesis/Religious Programs—Students 135.

71—ST. JOSEPH PATRON OF THE UNIVERSAL CHURCH. (Scalabrini Fathers). Revs. Gianni Agostinelli, C.S.; Vincenzo Ronchi, C.S.; Jairo Alfonso, C.S.
Res., 185 Suydam St., 11221. Tel: 718-386-0175; Fax: 718-821-1726.
School—St. Frances Cabrini, 181 Suydam St., 11221. Tel: 718-386-9277. Miss Maria Crifasi, Prin.
Lay Teachers 11; Students 220.

72—SHRINE CHURCH OF ST. JUDE, Revs. Mateo J. Rizzo; Frank Caggiano; Deacon Arthur J. Cuccia.
Res., 1677 Canarsie Rd., 11236. Tel: 718-763-6300; Fax: 718-531-9655.
School—1696 Canarsie Rd., 11236. Tel: 718-241-5533.
Sisters 1; Lay Teachers 15; Students 320.
Catechesis/Religious Programs—Mr. Ronald Rizzuto, D.R.E.
Students 200.
Convent—(Amityville) 2195 Canarsie Rd., 11236.
Sisters of St. Dominic

73—ST. LAURENCE, Rev. Steven A. Ferrari; Sr. Theresa Agliardi, R.S.M., Pastoral Assoc.
Res., 1020 Van Siclen Ave., 11207. Tel: 718-649-0545; Fax: 718-649-1606.
Catechesis/Religious Programs—Tel: 718-927-3310. Sr. Mary Jareth, D.R.E.
Students 248.
Convent—990 Van Siclen Ave., 11207. Tel: 718-272-2875.
Sisters of Mercy, Brooklyn 3.

74—ST. LEONARD OF PORT MAURICE. Closed 1978. Records at St. Joseph, Patron of the Universal Church.

75—ST. LOUIS. Closed. Became a Mission of St. Lucy in 1939. Parochial records are at St. Lucy-St. Patrick's, 285 Willoughby Ave., 11205. Tel: 718-622-8748; Fax: 718-622-6330.

76—ST. LUCY-ST. PATRICK, Rev. Francis Shannon; Cristiana Perez, Pastoral Assoc.; Deacon Jose Ramos.
Res., 285 Willoughby Ave., 11205. Tel: 718-622-8748; Fax: 718-622-6330.
Catechesis/Religious Programs—Students 175.

77—ST. MALACHY'S, Revs. Raymond J. Kelly; Maximo Leoz; Remedios Guerrero, M.A., Pastoral Assoc. In res., Rev. Joseph W. Denzer.
Res., 207 Hendrix St., 11207. Tel: 718-647-5900.
Catechesis/Religious Programs—Tel: 718-235-3562. Remedios Guerrero, M.A., D.R.E.
Students 332.

78—ST. MARGARET MARY, Rev. Walter A. Mitchell.
Res., 215 Exeter St., Manhattan Beach, 11235. Tel: 718-743-1824; Fax: 718-743-0232.

79—ST. MARK'S, Rev. Msgr. Gerard J. Arella; Rev. Cyril J. Doody. Pastoral Assocs.: Sr. Gloria Lepere, O.P.; Deacon Mark Seliga. In res., Rev. Joseph P. Quigley.
Res., 2609 E. 19th St., 11235. Tel: 718-891-3100; Fax: 718-891-9677.
Church—Ocean Ave. & Avenue Z, 11235.
School—2602 E. 19th St., 11235. Tel: 718-332-9604; Fax: 718-891-9677. Sr. Catherine Roche, O.P., Prin.
Sisters of St. Dominic 3; Lay Teachers 11; Students 294.
Catechesis/Religious Programs—Tel: 718-769-6311. Mr. Kevin McCutchan, D.R.E.
Students 375.

80—ST. MARTIN OF TOURS-FOURTEEN HOLY MARTYRS, Rev. Joseph M. Hoffman. In res., Rev. John F. Brogan.
Res., 1288 Hancock St., 11221. Tel: 718-443-8484; Fax: 718-443-2968.
School—See St. Elizabeth Seton under Consolidated Elementary Schools in the Institutions located in the Diocese. Tel: 718-386-4050.
Catechesis/Religious Programs—Sr. Mary Tully, D.R.E.
Students 215.

81—ST. MARY MOTHER OF JESUS, Rev. Msgr. Rocco D. Villani; Revs. Gregory A. Stankus; Angelo A. Venuti.
Res., 2326 84th St., 11214. Tel: 718-372-4000; Fax: 718-372-4002.
School—8401 23rd Ave., 11214. Sr. Thomasine Stagnitta, C.S.J., Prin.
Sisters of St. Joseph 7; Lay Teachers 22; Students 565.
Catechesis/Religious Programs—Tel: 718-449-8263. Sr. Patricia Conroy, R.S.M., D.R.E.
Students 400.

82—ST. MARY OF THE ANGELS (Lithuanian). Closed 1981. Records at Annunciation Parish, Brooklyn.

83—MARY QUEEN OF HEAVEN, Revs. Martin Kull; John A. Burns, Pastor Emeritus; Eugene J. Stoklie; John Mendonca; Deacons Charles J. Smith; John Joseph Murphy.
Res., 1395 E. 56th St., 11234. Tel: 718-763-2330; Fax: 718-763-6592.
School—1326 E. 57th St., 11234. Tel: 718-763-2360.
Sisters 1; Lay Teachers 15; Students 215.
Catechesis/Religious Programs—Tel: 718-763-2590.
Students 515.

84—ST. MARY, STAR OF THE SEA, Revs. Thomas J. O'Rourke; Robert S. Lawsine; Francis X. Nelson.
Res., 467 Court St., 11231. Tel: 718-625-2270; Fax: 718-624-9017.

85—ST. MATTHEW'S, Rev. Edward J. Smith; Deacons Florencio Cruz; Dennis A. DaCosta; Herve Desdunes.
Res., 1123 Eastern Pkwy., 11213. Tel: 718-774-6747; Fax: 718-953-4895.
Catechesis/Religious Programs—Sr. Christine Scherer, D.W., D.R.E.
Students 850.
Social Action Coord.—Sr. Dolores Augustine, P.V.M.I.

86—ST. MICHAEL'S, Revs. Michael J. Brennan; Ricardo Raveneau. In res., Rev. Youssef Bochra Nasri.
Res., 352 42nd St., 11232. Tel: 718-768-6065; Fax: 718-768-3336.
School—4222 Fourth Ave., 11232. Tel: 718-768-3582. Sr. Margaret M. Ford, C.S.J., Prin.
Sisters of St. Joseph 1; Lay Teachers 8; Students 240.
Catechesis/Religious Programs—Sr. Helene Jakubowski, R.S.M., D.R.E.
Students 206.

87—ST. MICHAEL'S, Rev. Philip F. Bohan, O.F.M.Cap.; Deacon Leon Miller; Jose Arturo Gonzalez, Pastoral Assoc. In res., Revs. Raphael Iannone, O.F.M.Cap., Supr.; William Hugo, O.F.M.Cap.
Parish Address—284 Warwick St., 11207. Tel: 718-647-1818; Fax: 718-647-2384.
Res., St. Michael Friary, 225 Jerome St., 11207. Tel: 718-827-6990.
School—Tel: 718-277-6766.
Catechesis/Religious Programs—Tel: 718-647-1818.
Students 224.

88—ST. MICHAEL ARCHANGEL AND ST. EDWARD, Revs. John A. Thompson; James A. Hughes.
Res., 108 St. Edward's St., 11205. Tel: 718-625-3017; Fax: 718-625-2536.

89—NATIVITY OF OUR BLESSED LORD. Merged with St. Peter Claver in 1973. Records at St. Peter Claver Church.

90—ST. NICHOLAS, Rev. Pedro Nel Ossa.
Res., 26 Olive St., 11211. Tel: 718-388-1420; Fax: 718-388-9516.
School—287 Powers St., 11211. Tel: 718-388-7992. Sr. Joan Losson, O.P., Prin.
Sisters of St. Dominic 4; Lay Teachers 10; Students 220.
Convent—312 De Voe St., 11211.

91—OUR LADY OF ANGELS, Rev. Msgr. James M. Cavanagh; Revs. Kenneth J. Calder; John G. Hauser; Deacon Michael J. Troy. In res., Rev. Thomas F. Kelly.
Res., 7320 Fourth Ave., 11209. Tel: 718-836-7200; Fax: 718-238-2466.
School—Tel: 718-238-5045. Mrs. Dorothy La Mere, Prin.
Lay Teachers 17; Students 291.
Catechesis/Religious Programs—Tel: 718-748-6553. Sr. Lucille Aliperti, C.S.J., D.R.E.
Students 373.

92—OUR LADY OF CHARITY, Rev. Edward J. Smith, Admin.
Res., 1669 Dean St., 11213. Tel: 718-774-5100; Fax: 718-778-3335.
Catechesis/Religious Programs—Fax: 718-778-3338. Ethel Ando-Menson, D.R.E.
Students 60.

93—OUR LADY OF CONSOLATION (Polish), Revs. Wlodzimierz R. Las, S.D.S. (Poland); Tadeusz Majcher, S.D.S. (Poland); Wieslaw P. Strzadala, S.D.S. (Poland).
Res., 184 Metropolitan Ave., 11211. Tel: 718-388-1942; Fax: 718-388-8993.

94—OUR LADY OF CZESTOCHOWA-ST. CASIMIR (Polish), Revs. Peter W. Zendzian; Stephen J. Jozwicki; Witold Mroziewski.
Res., 183 25th St., 11232. Tel: 718-768-5724; Fax: 718-768-4996.
Catechesis/Religious Programs—Students 160.

95—OUR LADY OF GOOD COUNSEL, Rev. James Bukofsky.
Res., 915 Putnam Ave., 11221. Tel: 718-443-7211; Fax: 718-443-0121.
Catechesis/Religious Programs—Ms. Christine Rahner, D.R.E.
Students 158.

96—OUR LADY OF GRACE, Revs. Dominick F. Cutrone; Barry W. Frazzitta; James L. Tighe; Sr. Jane Talbot, Pastoral Min.
Res., 430 Avenue W, 11223. Tel: 718-627-2020; Fax: 718-336-8033.
School—385 Avenue W, 11223. Tel: 718-375-2081; Fax: 718-376-7685. Mrs. Monica Crowley, Prin.
Lay Teachers 14; Students 310.
Catechesis/Religious Programs—Tel: 718-375-0404; Fax: 718-376-7685. Linda Nacinovich, D.R.E.
Students 310.

97—OUR LADY OF GUADALUPE, Rev. Msgr. Kevin B. Noone; Rev. John C. Miller; Sr. Ann Elizabeth, O.P, Pastoral Assoc.
Res., 7201 Fifteenth Ave., 11228. Tel: 718-236-8300; Fax: 718-236-8119.
School—1518 73rd St., 11228. Tel: 718-331-2070. Sr. Lora Bannon, O.P., Prin.
Sisters of St. Dominic 3; Sisters of St. Joseph 1; Lay Teachers 21; Students 661.
Catechesis/Religious Programs—Tel: 718-331-4003. Mrs. Suzanne O'Connor, D.R.E.
Students 350.

98—OUR LADY HELP OF CHRISTIANS, Revs. Anthony M. Rucando; Joseph D. Pasciuto. In res., Rev. Guy Massie.
Res., 1315 E. 28th St., 11210. Tel: 718-338-5242; Fax: 718-258-5341.
School—1340 E. 29th St., 11210. Tel: 718-377-1800; Fax: 718-377-6374. Ms. Joanne Aldorisio, Prin.
Lay Teachers 12; Students 155.
Catechesis/Religious Programs—Tel: 718-377-6932; Fax: 718-258-5341. Stephen Rzonca, D.R.E.
Students 120.

99—OUR LADY OF LORETO, Rev. Msgr. James A. Hunt, Admin.; Rev. Fredi A. Rosales.
Res., 124 Sackman St., 11233. Tel: 718-385-3740; Fax: 718-385-3446.

100—OUR LADY OF LOURDES, Rev. Frank Capellupo.
Res., 11 DeSales Pl., 11207. Tel: 718-452-2260; Fax: 718-452-6828.
School—2-12 Aberdeen St., 11207. Tel: 718-455-0037.
Lay Teachers 10; Students 190.

101—OUR LADY OF MERCY, Rev. James H. Sweeney.
Res., 680 Mother Gaston Blvd., 11212. Tel: 718-346-3166; Fax: 718-346-5776.
Catechesis/Religious Programs—Sr. Bernadette Sassone, D.W., D.R.E.
Students 306.

102—OUR LADY OF MERCY. Closed 1908. Second church at Schermerhorn & Bond closed April, Debevoise Place & DeKalb Ave. For inquiries for parish records contact the chancery.

103—OUR LADY OF MIRACLES, Revs. Thomas F. Leach; Steven J. Aguggia. In res., Revs. Gennaro M.

Simonetti, Pastor Emeritus; Giovanna Piccioli, Pastoral Outreach.
Res., 757 E. 86th St., 11236. Tel: 718-257-2400; Fax: 718-257-4634.
School—Tel: 718-649-0271; Fax: 718-649-3113. Sr. Anna Desiderio, C.S.J., Prin.
Sisters 2; Lay Teachers 10; Students 298.
Catechesis/Religious Programs—Sr. Carmel Ann Sperti, D.R.E., Tel: 718-649-1006.
Students 300.

104—OUR LADY OF MONSERRATE-ST. AMBROSE, Rev. Francis Shannon.
Res., 134 Vernon Ave., 11206. Tel: 718-388-5196; Fax: 718-388-5153.
Catechesis/Religious Programs—Mrs. Justina Velqzquez, D.R.E.
Students 180.

105—SHRINE OF OUR LADY OF MOUNT CARMEL (Italian), Rev. Msgr. David L. Cassato; Rev. Carmelo Gagliardi, O.F.M.Cap. Pastoral Assocs.: Giuditta Coccia, O.A., Italian Apostolate; John S. Fruner.
Res., 275 N. Eighth St., 11211. Tel: 718-384-0223; Fax: 718-384-5838.
School—Mt. Carmel Academy, 10 Withers St., 11211. Tel: 718-782-1110. Sr. Helen Gulczynski, C.S.J., Prin.
Catechesis/Religious Programs—Students 135.

106—OUR LADY OF PEACE (Italian), Revs. Roderick A. Crispo, O.F.M.; Bruno Ciardiello, O.F.M.
Res., 522 Carroll St., 11215. Tel: 718-624-5122; Fax: 718-852-6149.
Convent—209 First St., 11215. Tel: 718-624-6720; Fax: 718-852-6149. Hermanas Franciscanas de la Immaculada

107—OUR LADY OF PERPETUAL HELP BASILICA, Very Rev. Kevin Moley, C.SS.R., Pastor & Rector; Revs. Norman S. Bennett, C.SS.R.; Joseph Buono, C.SS.R.; Edward Byrne, C.SS.R.; Martin Crowe, C.SS.R.; Edward Dunne, C.SS.R.; Sylvester E. Feeley, C.SS.R.; Thomas F. Hickey, C.SS.R.; Joseph A. Keenan, C.SS.R.; Francis P. McElroy, C.SS.R.; John McGuire, C.SS.R.; Thomas J. McLellan, C.SS.R.; Thomas Maceda, C.SS.R.; Thomas J. Maher, C.SS.R.; Joseph Marron, C.SS.R.; John J. Travers, C.SS.R. Pastoral Assocs.: Sr. Bernard Loretto, C.S.J.; Sr. Noraleen Murphy, C.S.J.; Deacons Abdon Mejia (Peru); Eduviges Lopez; Jesus Soto. In res., Most Rev. Ronald Connors, C.SS.R., (Retired).
Res., 526-59th St., 11220. Tel: 718-492-9200; Fax: 718-439-8528.
School—Tel: 718-492-8067; Fax: 718-439-8081. Sr. Madeline Therese DiCarlo, C.S.J., Prin.
Sisters 6; Lay Teachers 13; Students 323.
High School—Tel: 718-492-5800; Fax: 718-492-2588. Sr. Mary Febronia, C.S.J., Prin.
Sisters 9; Lay Teachers 16; Students 212.
Catechesis/Religious Programs—584 60th St., 11220. Tel: 718-492-4019.
Students 410.

108—OUR LADY OF THE PRESENTATION, Rev. Msgr. James A. Hunt; Rev. Fredi A. Rosales; Sr. Margaret Nnamene, D.D.L., Assoc.; Deacon Jaime Landron.
Res., 1661 St. Marks Ave., 11233. Tel: 718-345-2604; Fax: 718-345-4639.

109—OUR LADY OF REFUGE, Revs. Andrew L. Struzzieri; Augustin Almy.
Res., 2020 Foster Ave., 11210. Tel: 718-434-2090; Fax: 718-859-7411.
School—1087 Ocean Ave., 11230. Tel: 718-434-4117. Sr. Karen Lademan, O.P., Prin.
Sisters of St. Dominic 2; Lay Teachers 21; Students 472.

110—OUR LADY OF THE ROSARY OF POMPEII, Revs. Peter Sticco, S.A.C.; Anthony Lorento, S.A.C.; Deacon William Sharkey.
Res., 225 Siegel St., 11206. Tel: 718-497-0614; Fax: 718-366-3236.

111—OUR LADY OF SOLACE, Rev. Albert Bellantonio; Deacon Dan J. Marley.
Res., 2866 W. 17th St., 11224. Tel: 718-266-1612; Fax: 718-946-3651.
School—2865 W. 19th St., 11224. Tel: 718-372-0997. Mr. Robert P. Thomas, Prin.
Lay Teachers 13; Students 228.
Catechesis/Religious Programs—Mr. Nelson Caraballo, D.R.E.
Students 274.

112—OUR LADY OF SORROWS. Merged with St. Leonard in 1942. Parochial records are at St. Joseph Patron of the Universal Church.

113—OUR LADY OF VICTORY, Revs. Martin J. Carter, S.A.; Martan Madison, S.A.
Res., 583 Throop Ave., 11216-2496. Tel: 718-574-5772; Fax: 718-919-2265.
Catechesis/Religious Programs—Students 100.

114—ST. PATRICK'S. Merged with St. Lucy's in 1974. Records at St. Lucy-St. Patrick's.

115—ST. PATRICK, Rev. Msgr. Fursey O'Toole; Rev. Msgr. Martin J. Bannon; Revs. Thomas Anastasio; Jamie J. Gigantiello; Sr. Jeanne Elaine, Pastoral Assoc. In res., Rev. Msgr. Joseph K. Parks, Pastor Emeritus; Deacon Charles Postler.
Res., 9511 Fourth Ave., 11209. Tel: 718-238-2600; Fax: 718-238-1508.
School—401 97th St., 11209. Tel: 718-833-0124; Fax: 718-238-6840. Mrs. Mary T. Biers, Prin.
Lay Teachers 20; Students 302.
Catechesis/Religious Programs—Miss Michelle Reid, D.R.E., Tel: 718-238-2600.
Students 302.

116—ST. PETER-ST. PAUL-OUR LADY OF PILAR, Revs. Gabriel D. Real, C.M., (Spain) Supr.; Robin E. Rodriguez, C.M., Pastoral Assoc. In res., Rev. Jorge Comas, C.M.
Res., 234 Congress St., 11201. Tel: 718-624-3425; Fax: 718-834-0380.
Catechesis/Religious Programs—Tel: 718-797-9262. Rev. Robin E. Rodriguez, C.M.
Lay Teachers 10; Students 123.

117—ST. PETER CLAVER, Rev. Patrick J. West.
Res., 29 Claver Pl., 11238. Tel: 718-622-4647; Fax: 718-622-3304.
Catechesis/Religious Programs—Mrs. Glencora Smith, Coord.
Students 52.

118—SS. PETER AND PAUL'S, Rev. Msgr. Agustin Ruiz.
Res., 71 S. Third St., 11211. Tel: 718-388-9576; Fax: 718-388-4735.
School—Tel: 718-388-1041. Sr. Teresa Chesnavage, Prin.
Lay Teachers 10; Students 224.
Catechesis/Religious Programs—Sr. Maria Monserrat.
Students 181.

119—MOST PRECIOUS BLOOD, Rev. Joseph Rosa.
Res., 70 Bay 47th St., 11214. Tel: 718-372-8022; Fax: 718-996-6575.
School—133-157 27th Ave., 11214. Tel: 718-373-7343.
Sisters 4; Lay Teachers 6; Students 250.
Catechesis/Religious Programs—Natalie Coangelo, D.R.E.
Students 202.

120—QUEEN OF ALL SAINTS, Rev. Victor A. Ulto. In res., Revs. John J. Brown; Joseph T. Holcomb.
Res., 300 Vanderbilt Ave., 11205. Tel: 718-638-7625; 7626; Fax: 718-638-7393.
School—Lafayette & Vanderbilt Ave., 11205. Tel: 718-857-3114; Fax: 718-857-0632. Theresa Attianese, Prin.
Sisters 1; Lay Teachers 12; Students 220.
Catechesis/Religious Programs—Lay Teachers 13; Students 140.

121—REGINA PACIS VOTIVE SHRINE. Attended by St. Rosalia, 65 St. & 12th Ave.
1230 65th St., 11219. Tel: 718-236-0909; Fax: 718-236-5357.

122—RESURRECTION, Rev. Msgr. Francis J. Fahy; Rev. Msgr. Raymond R. Shevlin, Pastor Emeritus; Revs. Jerome J. Schmidt, Senior Priest (Retired); James T. O'Brien.
Res., 2329 Gerrittsen Ave., 11229. Tel: 718-743-7234; 7235.
School—2335 Gerrittsen Ave., 11229. Tel: 718-332-9806; Fax: 718-743-0152. Mrs. Susan Cappiello, Prin.
Sisters 1; Lay Teachers 10; Students 288.
Catechesis/Religious Programs—Tel: 718-891-0888; Fax: 718-743-0152. Mrs. Angela Parente, D.R.E.
Students 375.

123—RESURRECTION CATHOLIC COPTIC CHAPEL, Rev. Youssef Bochra Nasri, (Coptic Catholic Patriarchate).
Mailing Address: 352 42nd St., 11232. Tel: 718-965-0422.
Church—328 14th St., 11215. Tel: 718-499-6946.

124—ST. RITA'S, Rev. Msgr. John T. Peyton; Deacons Ronald Ronacher; Ernst Paul.
Res., 275 Shepherd Ave., 11208. Tel: 718-647-4910; Fax: 718-827-2767.
School—280 Shepherd Ave., 11208. Tel: 718-647-6040. William Geasor, Prin.
Sisters 2; Lay Teachers 18; Students 525.
Catechesis/Religious Programs—Mrs. Annemarie Ronacher, D.R.E.
Students 386.

125—ST. ROCCO'S, Rev. Faustino Cordero. In res., Rev. George Ebejer.
Res., 216 27th St., 11232. Tel: 718-768-9798; Fax: 718-768-7742.
Catechesis/Religious Programs—Elsie De Jesus.
Students 144.

126—ST. ROSALIA-REGINA PACIS, Rev. Msgr. Dino M. Zeni; Revs. John Maduri; Edward A. Cassar; Deacon Joseph Cafiero. In res., Rev. Ronald T. Marino.
Res., 1230 65th St., 11219. Tel: 718-236-0909; Fax: 718-236-5357.
Center Regina Center, Inc.—1258 65th St., 11219. Tel: 718-232-4340.
School—1201 66th St., 11219. Tel: 718-236-8150. Mr. Vincent Tannacore, Prin.
Lay Teachers 15; Students 208.
Catechesis/Religious Programs—Tel: 718-331-5465. Mr. Vincent Tannacore, Dir.
Students 519.
Mission—Brooklyn, Regina Pacis Votive Shrine.

127—ST. ROSE OF LIMA, Revs. Joseph P. Byrns; Thomas B. Nohilly.
Res., 269 Parkville Ave., 11230. Tel: 718-434-8040; Fax: 718-421-4223.
School—259 Parkville Ave., 11230. Tel: 718-434-1739.
Sisters of St. Joseph 3; Lay Teachers 11; Students 211.
Catechesis/Religious Programs—Students 140.

128—SACRED HEART, Rev. Msgr. Walter C. Murphy; Sr. Eileen Neary, R.S.M., Pastoral Assoc. & D.R.E.
Res., 41 Adelphi St., 11205. Tel: 718-625-5115; Fax: 718-625-2918.

129—SACRED HEART CHAPEL. Closed. 1996. For inquiries for parish records contact the Chancery.

130—SACRED HEART MISSION. Closed. 1942. For inquiries for parish records contact the Chancery.

131—SACRED HEARTS OF JESUS AND MARY AND ST. STEPHEN, Rev. Anthony J. Acciarito; Sr. Barbara Leonardo, M.S.C., Pastoral Assoc. In res., Revs. Charles J. Mariani; Vincent La Rocca; Charles Nichols.
Res., 108 Carroll St., 11231. Tel: 718-596-7750; Fax: 718-260-9233.
School—Tel: 718-625-2267.
Lay Teachers 10; Students 146.
Chapel—St. Frances Cabrini Chapel, Degraw St., 11231.
Day Care Center—56 Strong Pl., 11231. Tel: 718-624-2993.

132—ST. SAVIOUR, Rev. Msgr. Joseph P. Nagle; Rev. Darrell A. Da Costa; Deacon William Williamsen; Sr. Patricia Hanley, O.P.
Res., 611 Eighth Ave., 11215. Tel: 718-768-4055; 768-7983; Fax: 718-768-4872.
School—701 Eighth Ave., 11215. Tel: 718-768-8000. Mr. James Flanagan, Prin.
Lay Teachers 23; Students 451.
High School—588 Sixth St., 11215. Tel: 718-768-4406; Fax: 718-369-2688. Sr. Valeria Belanger, S.S.N.D., Prin.
Students 275.
Catechesis/Religious Programs—Tel: 718-768-4980; Fax: 718-768-4980.
Students 65.

133—SS. SIMON AND JUDE, Revs. Edward A. Floretta; Christopher Pliauplis; Paul Vazhapilly.
Res., 185 Van Sicklen St., 11223. Tel: 718-375-9600; Fax: 718-375-6642.
School—Tel: 718-449-1857.
Lay Teachers 13; Students 196.
Catechesis/Religious Programs—Tel: 718-372-0733.
Students 425.

134—ST. STANISLAUS KOSTKA, Revs. Roman Gorowski, C.M.; Stanislaw Miekina, C.M.; Joseph Lachowski, C.M.; Edmund Gutowski, C.M.; Joseph Wisniewski, C.M.; Bogdan Konarzewski, C.M.; Jan Urbaniak, C.M.
Res., 607 Humboldt St., 11222. Tel: 718-388-0170; Fax: 718-384-5290.
School—10 Newel St., 11222. Tel: 718-383-1970; Fax: 718-384-5290. Sr. M. Marita Ruppe, Prin.
Priests 7; Sisters of the Holy Family of Nazareth 6; Lay Teachers 19; Students 429.
Catechesis/Religious Programs—Tel: 718-388-0170.
Students 328.

135—ST. STANISLAUS MARTYR. Merged with Holy Family (14th St.) in 1979. Records at Holy Family, 14th St., between Sixth and Seventh Aves.

136—ST. STEPHEN. Merged with Sacred Hearts in 1941. Parochial records are at Sacred Hearts-St. Stephen Church, Carroll St.

137—ST. SYLVESTER, Revs. Thomas M. Haggerty; Raymond C. Gruhn. In res., Rev. Charles P. Vogel.
Res., 416 Grant Ave., 11208. Tel: 718-647-1995; Fax: 718-348-4035.
School—396 Grant Ave., 11208. Tel: 718-235-4729. Carmen Padin, Prin.
Lay Teachers 11; Students 257.
Catechesis/Religious Programs—Tel: 718-647-6810. Sr. Elizabeth Folles, D.R.E.
Students 257.

138—ST. TERESA OF AVILA, Rev. Philip Pizzo.
Res., 563 Sterling Pl., 11238. Tel: 718-622-6500; Fax: 718-622-2234.
School—Tel: 718-638-5884; Fax: 718-638-0893. Dr. Kenneth J. Cottrell, Ed.D., Prin.

Lay Teachers 13; Students 275.
Catechesis/Religious Programs—Students 135.

139—St. Therese of Lisieux. (The Little Flower). Revs. Roger Pierre, Co-Pastor; Joseph Pelligrin, Co-Pastor; William M. Hoppe; Deacon Mauclair Simon.
Res., 1281 Troy Ave., 11203. Tel: 718-451-1500; Fax: 718-451-1502.
School—4410 Avenue D, 11203. Tel: 718-629-9330; Fax: 718-451-1671. Sr. Paulette Pollina, R.S.M., Prin.
Sisters of Mercy 3; Lay Teachers 20; Students 374.
Catechesis/Religious Programs—Tel: 718-451-1671. Frances McCormick, D.R.E.
Students 202.

140—St. Thomas Aquinas, Revs. James Sidoti, O.Carm.; Stanislaus Lewinski.
Res., 249 Ninth St., 11215. Tel: 718-768-9471; Fax: 718-965-4022.
School—211 Eighth St., 11215. Tel: 718-768-9007.
Sisters 1; Lay Teachers 10; Students 238.
Catechesis/Religious Programs—Tel: 718-768-9219. Sr. Mary Parry, O.P., D.R.E.
Students 182.

141—St. Thomas Aquinas, Rev. Msgr. Brian F. Callahan; Revs. Thomas J. Lyons; Edward M. Kachurka; Deacon James Kennedy. In res., Very Rev. John E. Mahoney, V.E.; Rev. Msgr. Kieran J. Martin; Sr. Carole Fitzpatrick, C.S.J.
Res., 1550 Hendrickson St., 11234. Tel: 718-253-4404; Fax: 718-951-7573.
School—1501 Hendrickson St., 11234. Tel: 718-377-0442; Fax: 718-377-0442. Sr. M. Alice Traynor, O.S.U., Prin.
Lay Teachers 18; Students 388.
Catechesis/Religious Programs—Tel: 718-338-3542. Rev. Joseph G. Fonti, D.R.E.
Students 479.

142—Transfiguration, Rev. Msgr. Bryan J. Karvelis; Deacon German Martinez.
Res., 263 Marcy Ave., 11211. Tel: 718-388-8773; Fax: 718-387-8774.
School—Tel: 718-388-1120. Sr. Mary Anne Ricioppo, Prin.
Sisters 1; Lay Teachers 8; Students 239.
Catechesis/Religious Programs—Students 200.
Southside Mission for Social Services—280 Marcy Ave., 11211. Tel: 718-388-3784. Sr. Kathryn Walsh, Dir.

143—St. Vincent de Paul, Rev. Richard J. McCormack. In res., Rev. Msgr. John P. McCullagh; Rev. Justo Beltran (Philippines).
Res., 167 N. Sixth St., 11211. Tel: 718-388-4218.
School—Mrs. Mary Capalb, Prin. Religious 1; Lay Teachers 9; Students 155.
Catechesis/Religious Programs—Students 17.

144—St. Vincent Ferrer, Revs. Coman V. Brady; Raymond J. Dundon, Pastor Emeritus; Anthony P. Mullen, C.S.Sp. (Ireland); Mrs. Mary Anne Muller, Pastoral Assoc.
Res., 1603 Brooklyn Ave., 11210-3495. Tel: 718-859-0041; Fax: 718-859-9032.
Church—E. 37th St. & Glenwood Rd., 11210.
School—Tel: 718-859-3505. Ms. Jean Guy, Prin.
Lay Teachers 13; Students 328.
Catechesis/Religious Programs—Mary Anne Muller, D.R.E.
Students 320.

145—Visitation of the Blessed Virgin Mary, Rev. Msgr. John E. Waldron.
Res., 98 Richards St., 11231. Tel: 718-624-1572; Fax: 718-722-7748.
Catechesis/Religious Programs—Sr. Marjorie McHugh, R.S.M., D.R.E.
Students 166.

BOROUGH AND COUNTY OF QUEENS

146—St. Adalbert, Revs. Timothy Pasek, O.F.M.Conv., Guardian; Gerard Maciejewski, O.F.M.Conv.; Paul Miskiewicz, O.F.M.Conv.; Edwin Mendez, O.F.M.Conv.; Bro. Hugh Dymski, O.F.M.Conv.
Res., 52-29 83rd St., Elmhurst, 11373. Tel: 718-639-0212; Fax: 718-651-1705.
School—52-17 83rd St., Elmhurst, 11373. Tel: 718-424-2376.
Sisters 2; Lay Teachers 18; Students 399.
Catechesis/Religious Programs—Tel: 718-446-8622. Mary Hellman, D.R.E.
Students 115.
Office for Pastoral Care of the Sick—Tel: 718-429-2005.

147—St. Aloysius, Revs. Eugene F. McGovern; Luke Pham Anh Du; Anthony V. Dell'Anno; Deacon Fabio Flaim; Sr. Noemi Valdes, S.M.R., Min. to Homebound.
Res., 382 Onderdonk Ave., Ridgewood, 11385. Tel: 718-821-0231; Fax: 718-628-7304.
School—360 Seneca Ave., Ridgewood, 11385. Tel: 718-821-7384. Sr. Naomi Varrone, O.P., Prin.
Sisters of St. Dominic 2; Lay Teachers 11; Students 254.
Catechesis/Religious Programs—Tel: 718-417-6327. Blanche Ciangiulli, D.R.E.
Students 96.
Pastoral Care Office—Tel: 718-963-7687.

148—American Martyrs, Revs. John F. Keppler; John J. Murray. In res., Rev. Anthony S. Ercolano.
Res., 79-43 Bell Blvd., Bayside, 11364. Tel: 718-464-4582; Fax: 718-464-5488.
School—216-15 Peck Ave., Bayside, 11364. Tel: 718-776-3779. Sr. Maureen Coyne, O.P., Prin.
Religious 1; Lay Teachers 12; Students 270.
Catechesis/Religious Programs—Mrs. Roberta VanBuskirk, D.R.E.
Students 250.

149—St. Anastasia, Rev. Msgr. Michael J. Cantley; Revs. John J. Gribbon; George J. Lutjen; Francis J. Mann.
Res., 45-14 245th St., Douglaston, 11362. Tel: 718-631-4454; Fax: 718-631-1774.
School—45-11 245th St., Douglaston, 11362. Tel: 718-631-3153. Mrs. JoAnn Dolan, Prin.
Lay Teachers 19; Students 306.
Catechesis/Religious Programs—Tel: 718-225-5191. Florence Rose, D.R.E.
Students 350.

150—St. Andrew Avellino, Rev. Msgr. James P. Grace, S.T.L.; Revs. Matthew J. Diamond; Gerard T. Walker; Wilfred Dewan, C.S.P. In res., Rev. Msgr. Lawrence J. McAlister, Pastor Emeritus; Rev. John J. Costello, S.T.L.
Res., 35-60 158th St., Flushing, 11358. Tel: 718-359-0417; Fax: 718-539-2830.
School—35-50 158th St., Flushing, 11358. Tel: 718-359-7887; Fax: 718-359-2295.
Lay Teachers 20; Students 336.
Catechesis/Religious Programs—Tel: 718-445-7012; Fax: 718-539-2830.
Students 270.

151—St. Ann's, Revs. George A. Pfundstein; Joseph N. Grisaitis; Anthony Sikandar.
Res., 142-30 58th Ave., Flushing, 11355. Tel: 718-886-3890; Fax: 718-358-4964.
School—142-25 58th Rd., Flushing, 11355. Tel: 718-463-1238. Mrs. Elizabeth Vecchio, Prin.
Sisters 2; Lay Teachers 16; Students 398.
Catechesis/Religious Programs—Tel: 718-359-8019; Fax: 718-358-4964. Sr. Joan Hackett, C.S.J., D.R.E.
Students 150.

152—St. Anthony of Padua, Revs. James J. Mueller; Thomas Muthukattil (India); Deacon J. Edward Joesten.
Res., 133-25 128th St., South Ozone Park, 11420. Tel: 718-843-7410; 843-3356; Fax: 718-659-1478.
School—125-18 Rockaway Blvd., South Ozone Park, 11420. Tel: 718-641-0212; Fax: 718-641-8079. Sr. Julia Mary, S.S.N.D., Prin.
School Sisters of Notre Dame 2; Sisters of Mercy 1; Lay Teachers 11; Students 421.
Catechesis/Religious Programs—Tel: 718-848-1127. Marcella Slobodzian, D.R.E.
Students 100.

153—Ascension, Revs. Vito Buonanno; Daniel G. Keohane. In res., Rev. Msgr. Charles A. Bleilevens, Pastor Emeritus; Revs. Wisdom Akalefu; Peter Chidi Osuagwu.
Res., 86-13 55th Ave., Elmhurst, 11373. Tel: 718-335-2626; Fax: 718-335-4181.
School—86-37 53rd Ave., Elmhurst, 11373. Tel: 718-335-9755.
Sisters 3; Lay Teachers 10; Students 310.
Catechesis/Religious Programs—Sr. Barbara Ann Haran, C.S.J., D.R.E.
Students 80.
Convent—53-04 Seabury St., Elmhurst, 11373. Tel: 718-446-8352. Sisters of St. Joseph

154—St. Bartholomew's, Rev. Msgr. James E. Gotimer; Revs. Frank A. Black; Francisco Walker; Eugene Soriano (Philippines).
Res., 43-22 Ithaca St., Elmhurst, 11373. Tel: 718-424-5400; Fax: 718-899-5257.
School—44-15 Judge St., Elmhurst, 11373. Tel: 718-446-7575.
Sisters of St. Dominic 4; Sisters of St. Frances 2; Lay Teachers 32; Students 725.
Catechesis/Religious Programs—Tel: 718-898-0096. James Thompson, D.R.E.
Students 650.

155—St. Benedict Joseph Labre, Rev. Msgr. John H. O'Brien; Rev. Kevin P. Cavalluzzi; Deacon Angel R. Rivera. In res., Rev. John J. Jurgensen; Rev. Msgr. John J. Condon.
Res., 94-40 118th St., Richmond Hill, 11419. Tel: 718-849-4048; Fax: 718-856-0732.
School—94-25 117th St., Richmond Hill, 11419. Tel: 718-441-6674; Fax: 718-441-4367.
Sisters 3; Lay Teachers 18; Students 534.
Convent—94-24 118th St., Richmond Hill, 11419. Tel: 718-849-5571.

156—St. Benedict, the Moor, Rev. Paul C. Palmiotto.
Res., 171-17 110th Ave., Jamaica, 11433. Tel: 718-526-4018.
Catechesis/Religious Programs—Caroll Forbes, D.R.E.
Students 20.

157—Blessed Sacrament, Rev. Msgr. Raymond W. Kutner; Revs. Jesus Cuadros; Patrick G. Burns; Deacon Roberto J. Pouso. In res., Most Rev. Rene A. Valero.
Res., 34-43 93rd St., Jackson Heights, 11372. Tel: 718-639-3888; Fax: 718-478-5536.
School—34-20 94th St., Jackson Heights, 11372. Tel: 718-446-4449; Fax: 718-446-5366.
Grey Nuns of the Sacred Heart 5; Lay Teachers 18; Students 434.

158—Blessed Virgin Mary, Help of Christians, Revs. Donald M. Berran; Christopher Lee Coleman; Deacon Kevin Ryan. In res., Rev. Thomas M. Catania.
Res., 70-31 48th Ave., Woodside, 11377. Tel: 718-672-4848; Fax: 718-457-4055.
School—70-20 47th Ave., Woodside, 11377. Maureen Cliffora, Prin.
Lay Teachers 14; Students 251.
Catechesis/Religious Programs—Tel: 718-672-4784; Fax: 718-651-0445. Sheila Smith Gonzalez, D.R.E.
Students 204.

159—St. Bonaventure's, Rev. Paul Palmiotto; Deacon Harry Coleman.
Res., 114-58 170th St., Jamaica, 11434. Tel: 718-526-0040; Fax: 718-526-4825.
Catechesis/Religious Programs—Students 85.

160—St. Camillus, Revs. James M. Dunne; Alfred LoPinto.
Res., 99-15 Rockaway Beach Blvd., Rockaway Beach, 11694. Tel: 718-634-8229; Fax: 718-634-8353.
School—185 Beach & 99th St., Rockaway Beach, 11694. Tel: 718-634-5260; 634-8353. Sr. Francis Bernadette, Prin.
Sisters of St. Joseph 2; Lay Teachers 10; Students 200.
Catechesis/Religious Programs—Tel: 718-474-3101. Sr. St. Claude, D.R.E.
Students 135.

161—St. Catherine of Sienna, Rev. John J. Amann; Deacons James Burrell; Luis Taylor.
Res., 118-22 Riverton St., St. Albans, 11412. Tel: 718-528-1220; Fax: 718-528-7907.
School—Tel: 718-528-1857. Sr. Barbara Kradick, O.P., Prin.
Lay Teachers 17; Students 467.
Catechesis/Religious Programs—Sr. Mary Tropeano, C.S.J., D.R.E.
Students 107.

162—Christ the King, Rev. George F. Zatarga; Deacons Winston M. Mayers; John P. Coffey.
Res., 145-39 Farmers Blvd., Springfield Gardens, 11434. Tel: 718-528-6010; Fax: 718-949-3255.
Catechesis/Religious Programs—Deacon John D. Coffey, D.R.E.
Students 143.

163—St. Clare, Rev. Msgr. James Cooney; Revs. Edward G. Brophy; Louis Uzoh. In res., Rev. William F. Sweeney.
Res., 137-35 Brookville Blvd., Rosedale, 11422. Tel: 718-341-1018; Fax: 718-276-2001.
School—137-25 Brookville Blvd., Rosedale, 11422. Tel: 718-528-7174; 276-2001. Mr. Anthony Danile, Prin.
Lay Teachers 20; Students 525.
Catechesis/Religious Programs—Tel: 718-527-6153. Richard Pipchinski, D.R.E.
Students 130.

164—St. Clement Pope, Rev. Edward J. Brenkert; Deacon Robert Nero.
Res., 141-11 123rd Ave., Jamaica, 11436. Tel: 718-529-0273; Fax: 718-529-3089.
School—Tel: 718-659-9011. Sr. Ave Regina Laffey, Prin.
Religious 2; Lay Teachers 14; Students 360.
Catechesis/Religious Programs—Students 127.

165—Corpus Christi, Rev. Msgr. Richard F. Dunn; Rev. George Berrios (Venezuela); Deacon John O'Neill. In res., Rev. James Frost.
Res., 31-30 61st St., Woodside, 11377. Tel: 718-278-8114; Fax: 718-278-3619.
School—31-29 60th St., Woodside, 11377. Tel: 718-721-2484. Lucetta Darragh, Prin.
Lay Teachers 13; Students 270.
Catechesis/Religious Programs—Tel: 718-721-2484.
Students 146.

166—St. Elizabeth's, Revs. John A. Thompson; Michael S. Melendez; Sr. Charlene Kay, O.P., Parish Min. In res., Rev. Thomas D. Dolan.

Res., 94-20 85th St., Ozone Park, 11416. Tel: 718-296-4900; Fax: 718-296-1140.
School—Tel: 718-641-6990; Fax: 718-323-5010. Sr. Francis Marie Sheridan, R.S.M., Prin.
Lay Teachers 12; Students 350.
Catechesis/Religious Programs—Tel: 718-738-3294. Sr. Patricia Anglin, O.P., D.R.E.
Students 127.

167—ST. FIDELIS, Revs. James E. Devlin; Ronald M. D'Antonio; Sr. Helen Muhlbauer, O.P., Pastoral Min.; Sr. Angela DiPaola, A.O.; Deacon Theodore J. Van de Van. In res., Pastor Emeriti: Rev. Peter J. Seeger; Rev. Msgr. William J. Osborne.
Res., 123-06 14th Ave., College Point, 11356. Tel: 718-445-6164; Fax: 718-445-1623.
School—124-06 14th Ave., College Point, 11356. Tel: 718-539-2628. Sr. Joan Martin, O.P., Prin.
Sisters of St. Dominic 3; Lay Teachers 20; Students 501.
Catechesis/Religious Programs—Tel: 718-359-1249. Joan Colombo, D.R.E.
Students 420.

168—ST. FRANCIS OF ASSISI, Rev. Leonard F. Badia, Ph.D.; Deacons John Sucich; Savior Hili. In res., Rev. Msgr. Thomas P. Campbell, Pastoral Emeritus.
Res., 21-17 45 St., Long Island City, 11105. Tel: 718-728-7801; Fax: 718-728-7853.
School—21-18 46th St., Astoria, 11105. Tel: 718-726-9405. Barbara McArdle, Prin.
Lay Teachers 20; Students 340.
Catechesis/Religious Programs—Tel: 718-278-0259.
Students 250.

169—ST. FRANCIS DE SALES, Rev. Msgr. Martin T. Geraghty; Rev. Louis J. DeGaetano; Deacon Robert Hitter.
Res., 129-16 Rockaway Beach Blvd., Belle Harbor, 11694. Tel: 718-634-6464; Fax: 718-634-0716.
School—216 Beach & 130th St., Belle Harbor, 11694. Tel: 718-634-2775; Fax: 718-634-6673. Sr. Patricia Chelius, C.S.J., Prin.
Sisters of St. Joseph 4; Lay Teachers 17; Students 607.
Catechesis/Religious Programs—Tel: 718-945-6911. Sr. Margaret Murphy, C.S.J., D.R.E.
Students 348.

170—ST. GABRIEL, Rev. Robert F. Barclay. In res., Revs. Celestine Anyanwu (Nigeria); Robert Titone.
Res., 26-26 98th St., East Elmhurst, 11369. Tel: 718-639-0474; Fax: 718-639-2810.
School—26-25 97th St., East Elmhurst, 11369. Tel: 718-426-7170; Fax: 718-426-1741. Bro. Edward Shields, F.S.C., Prin.
Sisters 2; Brothers 1; Lay Teachers 13; Students 380.
Catechesis/Religious Programs—Tel: 718-426-9577.
Students 95.

171—ST. GENEVIEVE, Rev. John Cullinane.
Res., 6 Beach 178 St., Rockaway Point, 11697. Tel: 718-634-7276; Fax: 718-318-7905.
Catechesis/Religious Programs—Students 49.

172—ST. GERARD MAJELLA, Rev. Msgr. James F. Spengler; Deacon Guillermo Gomez. In res., Rev. Msgr. Eugene A. Feldhaus, Senior Priest.
Res., 188-16 91st Ave., Hollis, 11423. Tel: 718-468-6565; Fax: 718-468-3136.
School—Tel: 718-468-1166.
Sisters 1; Lay Teachers 11; Students 325.

173—ST. GERTRUDE, Rev. Brendan W. Downing; Sr. Patricia DeMarco, O.P., Pastoral Assoc.; Deacon Alfred L. Whelan.
Res., 336 Beach 38th St., Far Rockaway, 11691. Tel: 718-327-5673; Fax: 718-471-6405.

174—ST. GREGORY THE GREAT, Revs. Joseph L. Cunningham, S.T.L.; Kevin F. McBrien, S.T.L.
Res., 242-20 88th Ave., Bellerose, 11426. Tel: 718-347-3707; Fax: 718-343-0926.
School—244-44 87th Ave., Bellerose, 11426. Tel: 718-343-5053; Fax: 718-347-1142. Sr. Mary Arline Hornidge, O.P., Prin.
Sisters 3; Lay Teachers 24; Students 514.
Catechesis/Religious Programs—Tel: 718-347-0525. Regina Joyce, D.R.E.
Students 350.
Convent—88-19 Cross Island Pkwy., Bellerose, 11426.

175—ST. HELEN, Rev. Msgr. Joseph C. Pfeiffer; Revs. Richard Bretone; Francis J. Hughes; Sr. Hannah Marie Cox, P.B.V.M., Pastoral Assoc.; Deacon Anthony Cusumano.
Res., 157-10 83 St., Howard Beach, 11414. Tel: 718-738-1616; Fax: 718-835-5144.
School—83-09 157th Ave., Howard Beach, 11414. Tel: 718-835-4155.
Religious 2; Lay Teachers 14; Students 387.
Catechesis/Religious Programs—Tel: 718-835-6216.
Students 455.

176—HOLY CHILD JESUS, Rev. Msgr. John J. Antoncic; Revs. John J. Boylan; William F. Krlis; Deacons Sal Licata; Dean Tully.
Res., 111-11 86th Ave., Richmond Hill, 11418. Tel: 718-847-1860; Fax: 718-847-2696.
School—112-02 86th Ave., Richmond Hill, 11418. Tel: 718-849-3988.
Sisters of St. Joseph 2; Lay Teachers 20; Students 415.
Catechesis/Religious Programs—Tel: 718-849-8560. Sr. Catherine Bernadette, M.S.B.T., D.R.E.
Students 360.
Missionary Cenacle—8622 112th St., Richmond Hill, 11418. Missionary Servants of the Most Blessed Trinity.

177—HOLY CROSS (Polish), Rev. Msgr. John J. Strynkowski, S.T.D.; Revs. Andrzej Kurowski, S.A.C. (Poland); Ryszard Koper (Poland); Thomas C. Machalski; Rev. Msgr. Edward A. Fus, Pastor Emeritus.
Res., 61-21 56th Rd., Maspeth, 11378-2498. Tel: 718-894-1387; Fax: 718-416-9245.
School—56-01 61st St., Maspeth, 11378-2499. Tel: 718-894-2356. Sr. Rose Thelma Meckowski, C.S.F.N., Prin.
Sisters 1; Lay Teachers 9; Students 287.

178—HOLY FAMILY, Rev. Msgr. Joseph L. Stafford; Revs. Louis D. Aufiero, Pastoral Assoc.; Thaddeus Abraham (India). In res., Rev. Edward M. Keane; Most Rev. Ignatius Catanello, D.D.
Res., 175-20 74th Ave., Flushing, 11366. Tel: 718-969-2448; Fax: 718-591-6166.
School—75th Ave. & 175th St., Flushing, 11366. Tel: 718-969-2124. Sr. Matthew Mary Gay, C.S.J., Prin.
Sisters of St. Joseph 5; Lay Teachers 17; Students 403.
Catechesis/Religious Programs—Tel: 718-591-6438. Barbara Makolin, D.R.E.
Students 330.

179—HOLY TRINITY, Revs. Marcello J. Latona; Joseph A. Pfaff, D.R.E.; James F. Fraser. In res., Rev. James E. Sullivan, Senior Priest.
Res., 14-51 143rd St., Whitestone, 11357. Tel: 718-746-7730; Fax: 718-767-1368.
School—Tel: 718-746-1479; Fax: 718-746-4793. Eleanor Menna, Prin.
Lay Teachers 11; Students 198.
Catechesis/Religious Programs—Students 140.

180—IMMACULATE CONCEPTION, Revs. Thomas Joyce, C.P.; Jack Douglas, C.P.; Theophane Cooney, C.P.
Res., 86-45 Edgerton Blvd., Jamaica, 11432. Tel: 718-739-0880; Fax: 718-657-0543.
School—179-14 Dalny Rd., Jamaica, 11432. Tel: 718-739-5933. Dr. Charlene Jaffie, Prin.
Sisters of St. Joseph 6; Lay Teachers 19; Students 420.
Catechesis/Religious Programs—86-16 Midland Pkwy., Jamaica, 11432. Tel: 718-291-3080. Sr. Elizabeth Gildea, C.S.J., D.R.E.
Students 287.

181—IMMACULATE CONCEPTION, Rev. Msgr. Charles P. Boccio. In res., Revs. James D. Gajere (Nigeria); Leo V. Rosero (Philippines).
Res., 21-47 29th St., Long Island City, 11105. Tel: 718-728-1613; Fax: 718-956-9229.
School—21-63 29th St., Long Island City, 11105. Tel: 718-728-1969. Sr. Jeanne Stegmann, S.U.S.C., Prin.
Sisters 2; Lay Teachers 19; Students 415.
Catechesis/Religious Programs—Tel: 718-956-4494. Marylyn Crum, D.R.E.
Students 345.
Convent—21-60 31st St., Long Island City, 11105. Fax: 718-959-9229.

182—INCARNATION, Rev. Msgr. John F. Casey; Rev. Robert J. Armato; Deacons Thomas F. Rogers; Francois Innocent. In res., Rev. Msgr. Edward J. Nolan, Pastor Emeritus.
Res., 89-43 Francis Lewis Blvd., Queens Village, 11427. Tel: 718-465-8534; Fax: 718-465-3834.
School—89-15 Francis Lewis Blvd., Queens Village, 11427. Tel: 718-465-5066; Fax: 718-464-4128. Sr. Ellen Patrice, Prin.
Sisters of St. Dominic (Amityville) 7; Lay Teachers 16; Students 510.
Catechesis/Religious Programs—Tel: 718-776-8956. Sr. Kathleen Thomas, O.P., D.R.E.
Students 180.

183—SS. JOACHIM AND ANNE, Rev. Msgr. Joseph P. Malagreca; Rev. John W. Byrnes.
Res., 218-26 105 Ave., Queens Village, 11429. Tel: 718-465-0124; Fax: 718-479-3548.
School—218-19 105th Ave., Queens Village, 11429. Tel: 718-465-2230. Linda Freebes, Prin.
Sisters of Notre Dame de Namur 1; Lay Teachers 20; Students 565.
Catechesis/Religious Programs—Teresa Rosero, D.R.E.
Students 351.
Convent—St. Boniface 621 Elmont Rd., Elmont, 11003.

184—ST. JOAN OF ARC, Rev. John A. McGuirl; Rev. Msgr. James F. Donegan, Pastor Emeritus; Revs. Timothy J. Hirten; Stephen Valdazo; Alexander G. Abugel.
Res., 82-00 35th Ave., Jackson Heights, 11372. Tel: 718-429-2333; Fax: 718-672-5881.
School—35-27 82nd St., Jackson Heights, 11372. Tel: 718-639-9020; Fax: 718-639-5428. Linda C. Kelly, Prin.
Grey Nuns of the Sacred Heart 1; Lay Teachers 24; Students 579.
Catechesis/Religious Programs—Tel: 718-478-5593.
Students 461.

185—ST. JOHN VIANNEY, Rev. Carlos Valencia; Deacon John McGreevey.
Res., 140-10 34th Ave., Flushing, 11354. Tel: 718-762-7920; Fax: 718-460-8032.
Catechesis/Religious Programs—Tel: 718-961-5092. Eileen Nesi, D.R.E.
Students 170.

186—ST. JOSAPHAT (Polish), Rev. Francis P. Bien. In res., Rev. Martin J. Sullivan.
Res., 34-32 210th St., Bayside, 11361. Tel: 718-229-1663; Fax: 718-229-8018.

187—ST. JOSEPH (Polish), Revs. Krzysztof Bugno, S.D.S. (Poland); Andrzej Waszczenko, S.D.S. (Poland).
Res., 108-43 Sutphin Blvd., Jamaica, 11435. Tel: 718-739-4781; Fax: 718-658-5447.

188—ST. JOSEPH, Revs. George J. Ryan; Michael J. McGee; Anthony J. Sansone; Deacon Felipe J. Alvarez.
Res., 43-19 30th Ave., Long Island City, 11103. Tel: 718-278-1611; Fax: 718-956-3589.
School—28-46 44th St., Long Island City, 11103. Tel: 718-728-0724; Fax: 718-728-8372.
Sisters of St. Dominic 3; Lay Teachers 29; Students 560.
Catechesis/Religious Programs—Tel: 718-545-7338.
Students 425.

189—ST. KEVIN, Rev. James T. Smith; Rev. Msgr. George V. Fogarty, Pastor Emeritus; Revs. John P. Maloney; Charles B. Kehoe. In res., Revs. Michael Parlsi; Paul A. Wood.
Res., 45-21 194 St., Flushing, 11358. Tel: 718-357-8888; Fax: 718-357-3671.
School—45-50 195th St., Flushing, 11358. Tel: 718-357-8110; Fax: 718-357-2519.
Sisters of Mercy (Dallas, PA) 3; Lay Teachers 23; Students 495.
Catechesis/Religious Programs—Tel: 718-357-5317. Mrs. Laura Stroligo, D.R.E.
Students 265.

190—ST. LEO, Revs. Charles P. Keeney; Thomas Ahern; Sr. Joan S. Dawber, S.C., Pastoral Assoc.; Deacon Rafael Diaz.
Res., 104-05 49th Ave., Corona, 11368. Tel: 718-592-7569; Fax: 718-271-6726.
School—104-19 49th Ave., Corona, 11368. Tel: 718-592-7050.
Lay Teachers 19; Students 396.
Catechesis/Religious Programs—Tel: 718-699-8565.
Students 270.
Mission—Brooklyn, Queens Co., Our Lady of Mount Carmel, 103-56 52nd Ave., Corona, 11368. Tel: 718-592-7569.

191—ST. LUKE, Rev. Msgr. Nicholas J. Capua; Revs. Joaquin S. Longres; Joseph F. Wilson; Deacon Harry A. Svebel. In res., Rev. Msgr. James W. Asip; Rev. John J. McVernon.
Res., 16-34 Clintonville St., Whitestone, 11357. Tel: 718-746-8102; Fax: 718-746-3589.
School—16-01 150th Pl., Whitestone, 11357. Tel: 718-746-3833. Jean Howlett, Prin.
Sisters of St. Dominic 3; Lay Teachers 18; Students 324.
Catechesis/Religious Programs—Tel: 718-746-3409. Theresa Mulgrew Agrusa, D.R.E.
Students 500.

192—ST. MARGARET, Rev. Msgr. William A. Varvaro; Revs. Brian M. Keller; Christopher Marcynski; Deacon Vincent F. DeBiase. In res., Revs. Gregory Wielunski; William R. Dulaney; Joseph F. Daly.
Res., 66-05 79th Pl., Middle Village, 11379. Tel: 718-326-1911; Fax: 718-326-1883.
School—66-10 80th St., Middle Village, 11379. Tel: 718-326-0922. Sr. Bridget Olwell, O.S.U., Prin.
Sisters of St. Dominic 4; Lay Teachers 19; Students 503.
Catechesis/Religious Programs—Margaret Walter, D.R.E.
Students 468.

193—ST. MARGARET MARY, Rev. Edmund P. Brady; Sr. Maryann McHugh, C.S.J., Pastoral Assoc.

Res., 9-18 27th Ave., Long Island City, 11102. Tel: 718-721-9020; Fax: 718-278-0998.
Catechesis/Religious Programs—Sr. Judy Fay, C.S.J., D.R.E.
Students 125.

194—St. Mary, Rev. Raymond F. Schmidt.
Res., 10-08 49th Ave., Long Island City, 11101. Tel: 718-786-0705; Fax: 718-482-7115.
Catechesis/Religious Programs—Students 28.

195—St. Mary Gate of Heaven, Revs. Matthew J. Considine, S.M.M.; Bernard Brault, S.M.M.; James Brady, S.M.M.; Bros. Paul Llorens, S.M.M.; Richard Politte, S.M.M.; Deacons Thomas Heaphy; Richard Gilligan.
Res., 101-25 104th St., Ozone Park, 11416. Tel: 718-847-5957; Fax: 718-846-6489.
School—104-06 101st Ave., Ozone Park, 11416. Tel: 718-846-0689. Patrick Scannell, Prin.
Sisters 2; Lay Teachers 25; Students 608.
Catechesis/Religious Programs—Tel: 718-849-9329. Sr. Kathy Hickey, C.S.J., D.R.E.
Students 285.

196—St. Mary Magdalene, Rev. John Maloney; Deacon Lee C. Williams; Sr. Marian Jagiello, S.C.; Sr. Christine Mulready, C.S.J.
Res., 218-12 136th Ave., Springfield Gardens, 11413. Tel: 718-949-4311; Fax: 718-528-7208.

197—Mary's Nativity, Rev. Msgr. Edward J. Bottino; Rev. Gary Sommermeyer. In res., Revs. Edward A. Ryan, V.E.; Joseph F. Wiseman.
Res., 46-02 Parsons Blvd., Flushing, 11355. Tel: 718-359-5996; Fax: 718-939-6737.
School—146-28 Jasmine Ave., Flushing, 11355. Tel: 718-359-1800. Mrs. Eileen Burke Ogoff, Prin.
Sisters of St. Joseph 7; Lay Teachers 9; Students 262.
Catechesis/Religious Programs—Tel: 718-353-5961. Donna Marie Sticco, D.R.E.
Students 300.

198—St. Mary Star of the Sea, Revs. Sean G. Ogle; Anthony M. Hernandez; Rev. Msgr. James J. McKenna, Pastor Emeritus.
Res., 1920 New Haven Ave., Far Rockaway, 11691. Tel: 718-327-1133; Fax: 718-327-3276.
School—595 Beach 19th St., Far Rockaway, 11691. Tel: 718-327-2242. Miss Angela Brucia, Prin.
Priests 3; Lay Teachers 14; Students 337.
Catechesis/Religious Programs—1920 New Haven Ave., Far Rockaway, 11691. Sr. Ann Reyes, O.P., D.R.E.
Students 353.

199—St. Matthias, Rev. Msgr. Anthony F. Sherman; Revs. James J.M. Reynolds; Richard J. Beuther; Deacons Gerard Steffens; John Sands. In res., Rev. Msgr. Joseph G. Konrad.
Res., 58-15 Catalpa Ave., Ridgewood, 11385. Tel: 718-821-6447; 6448; 6449; Fax: 718-821-6876.
School—58-25 Catalpa Ave., Ridgewood, 11385. Tel: 718-381-8003; Fax: 718-381-5319. Sr. Serafine Della Croce, S.S.N.D., Prin.
Sisters of Notre Dame 6; Lay Teachers 10; Students 329.
Catechesis/Religious Programs—Tel: 718-386-1077. Mrs. Carol E. Powell, D.R.E.
Students 400.

200—St. Mel, Rev. George R. Cowan; Rev. Msgr. James P. King, Senior Priest; Rev. James S. Musumeci.
Res., 28-20 154th St., Flushing, 11354. Tel: 718-886-0201; 886-0881; Fax: 718-886-0882.
School—154-24 26th Ave., Flushing, 11354. Tel: 718-539-8211. Sr. Mary Spencer, O.P., Prin.
Sisters 5; Lay Teachers 17; Students 460.
Catechesis/Religious Programs—Tel: 718-461-9840. Marie Hayes, D.R.E.
Students 265.

201—St. Michael, Rev. Msgr. Edward V. Wetterer; Revs. Jose R. Aldegunde; Kaleem Umrahn; Deacon Elias Yepes.
Res., 136-76 41st Ave., Flushing, 11355. Tel: 718-961-0295; 961-0182; Fax: 718-961-1403.
School—136-58 41st Ave., Flushing, 11355. Tel: 718-961-0246. Sr. Miriam Blake, C.S.J., Prin.
Sisters of St. Joseph 3; Lay Teachers 19; Students 460.
Catechesis/Religious Programs—Tel: 718-961-0312. Mrs. Zilia Hirsch, Coord.
Students 371.

202—St. Monica (Jamaican). Closed. For inquiries for parish records contact the Chancery.

203—Most Precious Blood, Rev. Raymond W. Stafford; Rev. Msgr. George T. Voiland, (Retired); Revs. Michael J. McHugh; Anton Bozanic (Yugoslavia); Vincent F. Miceli. In res., Rev. Andrew Niccoli (Yugoslavia) (Retired).
Res., 32-23 36th St., Long Island City, 11106. Tel: 718-278-3337.
School—32-52 37th St., Long Island City, 11103. Tel: 718-278-4081. Mr. Anthony Biscione, Prin.
Sisters of St. Joseph 4; Lay Teachers 26; Students 610.
Catechesis/Religious Programs—Tel: 718-721-9850; Fax: 718-278-3089.
Students 255.
Convent—36-16 36th St., Long Island City, 11106.

204—Nativity of the Blessed Virgin Mary, Rev. Msgr. Robert J. Thelen; Revs. Angelo B. Pezzullo; Frank W. Spacek; Deacon Andrew A. Marchello. In res., Rev. Msgr. Dominick J. Adessa, P.E., Senior Priest.
Res., 101-41 91st St., Ozone Park, 11416. Tel: 718-845-3691; Fax: 718-845-8978.
School—101-60 92nd St., Ozone Park, 11416. Tel: 718-845-3074. Sr. Marguerite Torre, O.S.U., Prin.
Sisters 1; Lay Teachers 13; Students 404.
Catechesis/Religious Programs—101-38 92nd St., Ozone Park, 11416. Tel: 718-845-1524. Michael Rosa, D.R.E.
Students 400.

205—St. Nicholas of Tolentine, Revs. Robert J. McConnin; Kevin J. Sweeney; Ambrose Ejeu (Nigeria); Deacon Lionel Knight. In res., Rev. Msgr. Thomas M. O'Brien, P.E.
Res., 150-75 Goethals Ave., Jamaica, 11432. Tel: 718-969-3226; Fax: 718-380-0345.
School—80-22 Parsons Blvd., Jamaica, 11432. Tel: 718-380-1900; Fax: 718-591-6977. Sr. Elizabeth McNeelan, S.C., Prin.
Sisters of St. Dominic 1; Lay Teachers 21; Students 531.
Catechesis/Religious Programs—Tel: 718-591-6536. Sr. Agnes Moylan, O.P., D.R.E.
Students 190.

206—Our Lady of the Angelus, Rev. Msgr. John R. Dwyer; Rev. Gabriel Lee; Deacon Edwin Cancel. In res., Rev. Msgr. William T. Hickey, Pastoral Emeritus; Rev. Rafael R. Macaranas (Philippines).
Res., 63-63 98th St., Rego Park, 11374. Tel: 718-897-4444; Fax: 718-897-1453.
School—Tel: 718-896-7220. Ms. Mary Ann Rys, Prin.
Sisters 2; Lay Teachers 12; Students 262.
Catechesis/Religious Programs—Tel: 718-896-4388; Fax: 718-897-1453. Sr. Jo Ann Schwarz, D.R.E.
Students 300.

207—Our Lady of the Blessed Sacrament, Rev. Msgr. Vincent A. Keane; Revs. William J. Rueger; Heebong B. Nam.
Res., 34-24 203rd St., Bayside, 11361. Tel: 718-229-5929; Fax: 718-229-5929.
School—34-45 202nd St., Bayside, 11361. Tel: 718-229-4434; Fax: 718-229-5820.
Sisters 1; Lay Teachers 29; Students 496.
Catechesis/Religious Programs—Tel: 718-229-6179. Mary Mullaney, D.R.E.
Students 248.

208—Our Lady of the Cenacle, Rev. Msgr. Cornelius T. Kneafsey; Revs. Peter De Sanctis; Pablo Sans. In res., Revs. James P. Bradley; Mathew Kulapurath, Hospital Chap.
Res., 136-06 87th Ave., Richmond Hill, 11418. Tel: 718-291-2540; Fax: 718-291-6211.
School—Tel: 718-657-6690. Katherine Massell, Prin.
Sisters of Charity (Halifax) 2; Lay Teachers 16; Students 421.
Catechesis/Religious Programs—Sr. Florence Symes, C.S.J., D.R.E.
Sisters 2; Lay Teachers 22; Students 310.

209—Our Lady of China Chapel, Rev. Thomas Sung, C.S.J.B. (Taiwan).
Res., 54-09 92nd St., Elmhurst, 11373. Tel: 718-699-1929; Fax: 718-271-3215.
School—Tel: 718-699-1929.
Catechesis/Religious Programs—Fax: 718-371-3215.
Students 870.
Chinese School—Ming Yuan Chinese School, Tel: 718-271-3944. See Monasteries and Residences for Priests and Brothers for the Religious Community.

210—Our Lady of Fatima, Rev. Msgr. Edward J. Breen; Revs. Eugene F. Donnelly; James Zona. In res., Revs. Patrick J. Frawley; Francis J. Passenant.
Res., 25-02 80th St., Jackson Heights, 11370. Tel: 718-899-2801; Fax: 718-429-6404.
School—25-38 80th St., Jackson Heights, 11370. Tel: 718-429-7031; Fax: 718-899-2811. Mrs. Cassie Zelic, Prin.
Lay Teachers 29; Students 730.
Catechesis/Religious Programs—Tel: 718-457-3457.
Students 219.
Convent—25-56 80th St., Jackson Heights, 11370. Tel: 718-446-7097.

211—Our Lady of Grace, Rev. Msgr. William Flood; Deacon Joseph Campisi. In res., Rev. Francis J. Labita; Rev. Msgr. Francis J. Evans, Pastor Emeritus.
Res., 100-05 159th Ave., Howard Beach, 11414. Tel: 718-843-6218; Fax: 718-738-8208.
School—158-12 101st St., Howard Beach, 11414. Tel: 718-848-7440; Fax: 718-641-3464. Patricia Slattery, Prin.
Ursuline Sisters 1; Lay Teachers 14; Students 430.
Catechesis/Religious Programs—Tel: 718-835-2765. Sr. Ann Martha, O.P., D.R.E.
Sisters 1; Students 200.

212—Our Lady of Hope, Rev. Msgr. Nicholas W. Sivillo; Rev. Gaetano J. Sbordone. In res., Rev. Joseph R. Grimaldi, M.Div.; Rev. Msgr. Anthony J. Barretta; Deacon Robert F. Lavanco.
Res., 61-27 71st St., Middle Village, 11379. Tel: 718-429-5438; Fax: 718-429-2764.
School—Tel: 718-458-3535; Fax: 718-458-9031.
Sisters 5; Lay Teachers 26; Students 744.
Catechesis/Religious Programs—Tel: 718-335-8394.
Students 235.

213—Our Lady of Lourdes, Rev. Msgr. Robert J. Pawson; Rev. Donald Kavanagh; Deacon Warren Winkler. In res., Revs. Denis Herron, V.E.; John A. McNeill.
Res., 92-96 220th St., Queens Village, 11428. Tel: 718-479-5111; Fax: 718-479-0826.
School—92-80 220th St., Queens Village, 11428. Tel: 718-464-1480; Fax: 718-740-4091. Sr. Josephine Barbiere, C.S.J., Prin.
Lay Teachers 24; Students 484.
Catechesis/Religious Programs—Tel: 718-740-4090. Joanne Russo, D.R.E.
Students 313.

214—Our Lady of Mercy, Rev. Msgr. Gerald J. Langelier; Rev. William A. With; Deacon Edward Smolinski. In res., Rev. Msgr. Edward B. Scharfenberger.
Res., 70-01 Kessel St., Forest Hills, 11375. Tel: 718-268-6143; Fax: 718-544-3764.
School—70-25 Kessel St., Forest Hills, 11375. Tel: 718-793-2086.
Sisters Servants of the Immaculate Heart of Mary 6; Lay Teachers 13; Students 299.

215—Our Lady of the Miraculous Medal, Rev. Msgr. George M. Schuster; Revs. Marc Swartvagher; William A. Smith; Marc Caliwan (Philippines); Deacon Jerome Krebs. In res., Revs. William T. Davis; Andrew J. Vaccari.
Res., 62-81 60th Pl., Ridgewood, 11385. Tel: 718-366-3360; Fax: 718-456-0564.
School—Bleecker & 61st St., Ridgewood, 11385. Tel: 718-821-2221. Ms. Margaret A. Baxter, Prin.
Lay Teachers 14; Students 264.
Catechesis/Religious Programs—Tel: 718-456-3275. Mary Macchiaroli, D.R.E.
Students 342.

216—Our Lady of Mount Carmel, Revs. Frank Lynch; Joseph Pham; Anthony Raso. In res., Revs. Edmund P. Brady; Raymond P. Roden.
Res., 23-25 Newtown Ave., Long Island City, 11102. Tel: 718-278-1834; Fax: 718-278-0998.
School—25-15 Newtown Ave., Long Island City, 11102. Tel: 718-728-8376. Ms. Angela Fazio, Prin.
Lay Teachers 12; Students 360.
Catechesis/Religious Programs—Tel: 718-545-7987.
Students 150.

217—Our Lady of Perpetual Help, Revs. Edward W. Richards; John G. Garkowski; John Ugochukwu. In res., Rev. James T. Devine.
Res., 111-50 115th St., South Ozone Park, 11420. Tel: 718-843-1212; Fax: 718-843-3554.
School—111-10 115th St., South Ozone Park, 11420. Tel: 718-843-4184; Fax: 718-323-2333. Sr. Maria Rypkema, Prin.
Lay Teachers 20; Students 510.
Catechesis/Religious Programs—Tel: 718-641-6165. Thomas Columbia, D.R.E.
Students 220.

218—Our Lady, Queen of Martyrs, Rev. Msgr. Thomas J. Gradilone; Revs. Daniel Weiscopf; Thomas P. Murtagh; Deacon Thomas McCarthy. In res., Rev. Msgr. Michael J. Dempsey.
Res., 110-06 Queens Blvd., Forest Hills, 11375. Tel: 718-268-6251.
School—Sisters 2; Lay Teachers 12; Students 325.
Convent—109-04 72 Rd., Forest Hills, 11375.

219—Our Lady of the Skies Chapel, Rev. James T. Devine, Admin.
Church—Kennedy International Airport, International Arrivals Bldg., Second Floor, Jamaica, 11430. Tel: 718-656-5348; Fax: 718-656-8162.

220—Our Lady of the Snows, Revs. James C. Tugwood; Casper Furnari; George J. Stack; Deacon Henry J. Smith.
Res., 258-15 80th Ave., Floral Park, 11004. Tel: 718-347-6070; Fax: 718-343-3221.
School—79-33 258th St., Floral Park, 11004. Tel: 718-343-1346; Fax: 718-343-7303. Sr. Roberta Oberle, Prin.
Sisters of St. Joseph 2; Lay Teachers 16; Students 510.

Catechesis/Religious Programs—Tel: 718-347-3511.
Students 480.

221—OUR LADY OF SORROWS, Revs. Thomas J. Healy; Lawrence Gellel, S.J.; Manuel Ros; Deacon Orlando Pascal. In res., Rev. Constantine V. Pesaresi, Pastor Emeritus.
Res., 104-11 37th Ave., Corona, 11368. Tel: 718-424-7554; Fax: 718-424-4910.
School—35-33 104th St., Corona, 11368. Tel: 718-426-5517. Sr. Katherine Hanrahan, C.S.J., Prin.
Sisters of St. Joseph 2; Lay Teachers 19; Students 397.
Catechesis/Religious Programs—Tel: 718-651-5682. Deacon Elias Yepes, D.R.E.
Lay Teachers 55; Students 1,010.

222—ST. PANCRAS, Rev. Joseph D. Colbert.
Res., 72-22 68th St., Glendale, 11385. Tel: 718-821-2323; Fax: 718-417-8021.
School—Myrtle Ave. & 68th St., Glendale, 11385. Tel: 718-821-6721. Sr. Jane Creighton, O.P., Prin.
Lay Teachers 18; Students 381.
Catechesis/Religious Programs—Tel: 718-479-0590. Mary E. McIntyre, D.R.E.
Students 420.

223—ST. PASCAL BAYLON, Rev. Msgr. Robert R. McCourt. Pastoral Assocs.: Sr. Mary Walsh, C.S.J.; Sr. Susan Smolinsky, S.C. In res., Rev. John W. Maloney.
Res., 112-43 198th St., St. Albans, 11412. Tel: 718-468-3511; Fax: 718-479-2303.
Catechesis/Religious Programs—Fax: 718-479-2403.
Students 130.

224—ST. PATRICK, Rev. Robert M. Robinson, Admin. In res., Rev. Jean-Pierre Ruiz, S.T.D.
Res., 39-38 29th St., Long Island City, 11101. Tel: 718-729-6060; Fax: 718-729-1276.
Catechesis/Religious Programs—Tel: 718-937-1239. Sr. Flora Marinelli, C.S.J., D.R.E.
Students 125.

225—ST. PAUL THE APOSTLE, Revs. Paul W. Jervis; Joaquin Suran (Argentina). In res., Rev. Jose Sanchez (Philippines).
Res., 98-16 55 Ave., Corona, 11368. Tel: 718-271-1100; Fax: 718-760-3496.

226—ST. PAUL CHONG HA-SANG ROMAN CATHOLIC CHAPEL (Korean Apostolate), Revs. Insungt Kim; Sung Wo Park; Deacon Paul M. Chin. In res., Bro. Thomas Burns, C.S.C.
Office: 32-15 Parsons Blvd., Flushing, 11354. Tel: 718-321-7676; Fax: 718-321-7005.
Catechesis/Religious Programs—D.R.E.: Sr. Bonifacio Ro, O.S.B.; Sr. Bona Lee, O.S.B.; Dr. Chang Dong Keun.
Students 450.
Convent—32-15 Parsons Blvd., Flushing, 11354. Olivetan Benedictine Sisters
St. Augustine Yu Chin-gil Chapel: 2115 61st St., Brooklyn, 11204.; Korean Martyrs Chapel: 35-20 Greenpoint Ave., Long Island City, 11101. Rev. Benedict Ku (Korea).

227—ST. PIUS V, Rev. Richard J. Ahlemeyer; Deacon James Grace.
Res., 106-12 Liverpool St., Jamaica, 11435. Tel: 718-739-3731; Fax: 718-739-7086.
Catechesis/Religious Programs—Students 200.

228—ST. PIUS X, Rev. Msgr. Thomas A. Graham; Revs. James F. Marron; Joachim Fernando (Sri Lanka). In res., Rev. Denis M. Dore, (Retired).
Res., 148-10 249th St., Rosedale, 11422. Tel: 718-525-9099; Fax: 718-276-2467.
School—147-65 249th St., Rosedale, 11422. Tel: 718-525-7171. John Toomey, Prin.
Religious of the Sacred Heart of Mary 1; Lay Teachers 9; Students 266.
Catechesis/Religious Programs—Marianne Gratto, D.R.E.
Students 175.

229—PRESENTATION OF THE BLESSED VIRGIN MARY, Rev. Michael M. Greene; Rev. Msgr. Thomas O'Brien, P.E.; Rev. Stephen Lynch. In res., Rev. Richard J. Ahlemeyer.
Res., 88-19 Parsons Blvd., Jamaica, 11432. Tel: 718-739-0241; Fax: 718-739-2753.
Providence House III—159-23 89th Ave., Jamaica, 11432. Tel: 718-739-1348.
School—Tel: 718-739-2003; Fax: 718-526-8152. Sr. Judith Flanagan, O.P., Prin.
Lay Teachers 14; Students 320.
Catechesis/Religious Programs—Tel: 718-526-4152.
Students 352.

230—QUEEN OF ANGELS, Revs. Matthew W. Sheridan; George M. Hernandez; Deacon Juan Calvo.
Res., 44-04 Skillman Ave., Long Island City, 11104. Tel: 718-392-0011; 0012; Fax: 718-472-2625.
School—41-12 44th St., Long Island City, 11104. Tel: 718-786-2990. Sr. Adrienne Runiewicz, R.S.M., Prin.
Sisters of Mercy 1; Lay Teachers 12; Students 240.
Catechesis/Religious Programs—Tel: 718-937-5174.
Students 200.

231—QUEEN OF PEACE, Rev. Ralph J. Caputo. In res., Pastor Emeriti: Rev. Msgr. Celsus Collini; Rev. John C. Reilly.
Res., 141-36 77th Ave., Flushing, 11367. Tel: 718-380-5031; Fax: 718-969-2025.
School—141-25 77th Rd., Flushing, 11367. Tel: 718-969-3640; Fax: 718-969-5640. Mrs. Louise McNamara, Prin.
Lay Teachers 10; Students 350.
Convent—Tel: 718-380-4293. Sisters of St. Dominic

232—ST. RAPHAEL, Rev. Thomas G. Pettei.
Res., 35-20 Greenpoint Ave., Long Island City, 11101. Tel: 718-729-8957; Fax: 718-729-5238.
School—48-25 37th St., Long Island City, 11101. Tel: 718-784-0482. Sr. Maureen Ahlemeyer, P.B.V.M., Prin.
Sisters of the Presentation 2; Lay Teachers 13; Students 300.
Catechesis/Religious Programs—Students 80.

233—RESURRECTION-ASCENSION, Rev. Msgr. Joseph P. Bynon; Revs. Salvatore Amato; Robert W. Blauvelt. In res., Rev. Msgr. John J. Bracken.
Res., 61-11 85th St., Rego Park, 11374. Tel: 718-424-5212; Fax: 718-639-8679.
School—85-25 61st Rd., Rego Park, 11374. Tel: 718-426-4963. Sr. Margaret Sweeney, C.S.J., Prin.
Sisters 2; Lay Teachers 17; Students 380.
Catechesis/Religious Programs—Tel: 718-533-7898.
Students 125.

234—ST. RITA, Rev. John P. Harrington; Deacon Vincent Parisi. In res., Rev. Michael G. Tedone.
Res., 36-25 11th St., Long Island City, 11106. Tel: 718-361-1884; Fax: 718-472-9362; 786-4573.
School—36-14 12th St., Long Island City, 11106. Tel: 718-729-1594. Mrs. Anne Schaefer, Prin.
Lay Teachers 11; Students 141.
Catechesis/Religious Programs—Students 120.

235—ST. ROBERT BELLARMINE, Rev. Msgr. John B. Lavin; Revs. Christopher J. Turczany; Abraham P. Mathew.
Res., 56-15 213th St., Bayside, 11364. Tel: 718-229-6465; Fax: 718-229-8126.
School—56-10 214th St., Bayside, 11364. Tel: 718-225-3181. Sr. Mary Ann Carotenuto, C.S.J., Prin.
Sisters of St. Joseph 6; Lay Teachers 18; Students 495.
Catechesis/Religious Programs—Students 204.

236—ST. ROSE OF LIMA, Revs. Peter D. Gillen; Francis J. McGee; Francisco J. Ares.
Res., 130 Beach 84th St., Rockaway Beach, 11693. Tel: 718-634-7394; Fax: 718-474-7489.
School—154 Beach 84th St., Rockaway Beach, 11693. Tel: 718-474-7079; Fax: 718-634-0524. Mrs. Theresa Andersen, Prin.
Sisters 2; Lay Teachers 12; Students 275.
Catechesis/Religious Programs—Tel: 718-945-4850. Ms. Antoinette Camarda, D.R.E.
Students 120.

237—SACRED HEART OF JESUS, Rev. Msgr. Thomas F. Donovan; Revs. Kenneth J. Hand; Noel Moynihan; Sr. Kathleen Masterson, Pastoral Min. In res., Rev. Coleman Costello.
Res., 215-35 38th Ave., Bayside, 11361. Tel: 718-428-2200; Fax: 718-428-5840.
School—216-33 38th Ave., Bayside, 11361. Tel: 718-631-4804. Dennis J. Farrell, Prin.
Lay Teachers 25; Students 525.
Catechesis/Religious Programs—Tel: 718-631-1307. Mrs. Georgette Lyons, D.R.E.
Students 250.

238—SACRED HEART, Revs. Michael C. Gribbon; Jean-Augustin Francois; Felix Akpabio (Nigeria); Caleb A. Buchanan; Sr. Margaret Mary Igoe, O.P., Pastoral Assoc.; Sr. Carmelle Nerette; Deacons Paul Dorsinville; Roy Dudley. In res., Rev. Joseph M. Nolan.
Res., 115-58 222 St., Cambria Heights, 11411. Tel: 718-528-0577; Fax: 718-341-0253.
School—115-50 221st St., Cambria Heights, 11411. Tel: 718-527-0123.
Lay Teachers 24; Students 386.
Catechesis/Religious Programs—Elizabeth Wright, D.R.E.
Students 120.

239—SACRED HEART, Revs. John J. Fullum; James Stapleton, C.S.P.; Deacons John P. Dennehy; Arthur A. Candreva. In res., Rev. Msgr. John F. Hartmann; Rev. Romano Zanon.
Res., 83-17 78th Ave., East Glendale, 11385. Tel: 718-821-6434; Fax: 718-497-2881.
School—84-05 78th Ave., East Glendale, 11385. Tel: 718-456-6636.
Sisters of St. Dominic 1; Lay Teachers 11; Students 361.
Catechesis/Religious Programs—Tel: 718-386-5616.
Students 311.

240—ST. SEBASTIAN, Rev. Msgr. D. Joseph Finnerty; Revs. Kenneth J. Grande; Christopher Cashman; Sabino Estrada; Deacon Stephen Damato.
Res., 39-63 57th St., Woodside, 11377. Tel: 718-429-4442; Fax: 718-429-7581.
School—39-68 58th St., Woodside, 11377. Sr. Kathleen Michael, S.C.H., Prin.
Sisters of Charity (Halifax) 2; Lay Teachers 19; Students 462.
Catechesis/Religious Programs—39-66 58th St., Woodside, 11377. Tel: 718-899-3341. Sr. Dolores Ryan, C.S.J., D.R.E.
Students 498.

241—ST. STANISLAUS BISHOP AND MARTYR, Revs. James J. Meszaros; Andrzej Gorczyca; Francis C. Romanowski, Pastor Emeritus.
Res., 88-10 102nd Ave., Ozone Park, 11416. Tel: 718-845-6206; Fax: 718-843-6408.
School—90-01 101st Ave., Ozone Park, 11416. Tel: 718-845-3188. Sr. Francis Marie, C.S.F.N., Prin.
Sisters of the Holy Family of Nazareth 1; Lay Teachers 8; Students 200.
Catechesis/Religious Programs—Students 130.

242—ST. STANISLAUS KOSTKA, Revs. Michael J. Walsh, S.T.D.; Edward L. Maurer; Joseph Palackal, C.M.I (India).
Res., 57-15 61st St., Maspeth, 11378. Tel: 718-326-2185; Fax: 718-416-2108.
School—61-17 Grand Ave., Maspeth, 11378. Tel: 718-326-1815.
Lay Teachers 18; Students 300.
Catechesis/Religious Programs—Students 180.

243—ST. TERESA, Rev. Msgr. Lawrence E. Hinch; Revs. Colm Campbell (Ireland); Adnel Burgos. In res., Rev. Hugo Bedoya, C.M. (Colombia).
Res., 50-20 45th St., Woodside, 11377. Tel: 718-784-2123; Fax: 718-706-6797.
School—50-15 44th St., Woodside, 11377. Tel: 718-784-0178; Fax: 718-784-3288. Martin C. Abruzzo, Prin.
Lay Teachers 11; Students 248.
Catechesis/Religious Programs—Tel: 718-937-4819.
Students 350.

244—ST. TERESA OF AVILA, Revs. Vincent M. Daly; Richard Hoare; Deacon Ramon Smith.
Res., 109-26 130th St., South Ozone Park, 11420. Tel: 718-529-3587; Fax: 718-529-0324.
School—Tel: 718-641-1316. Ms. Loretta Rybacki, Prin.
Lay Teachers 12; Students 285.
Catechesis/Religious Programs—Tel: 718-641-5710. Elaine L'Etoile, D.R.E.
Students 225.

245—ST. THOMAS APOSTLE, Rev. Msgr. Joseph A. Martusciello; Revs. Felice J. De Laura; Jude Awalaka (Nigeria).
Res., 87-19 88th Ave., Woodhaven, 11421. Tel: 718-847-1353; Fax: 718-849-3776.
School—87-49 87th St., Woodhaven, 11421.
Sisters 1; Lay Teachers 11; Students 342.
Catechesis/Religious Programs—Tel: 718-441-8409. Jean Tuohy, D.R.E.
Students 366.

246—ST. THOMAS MORE-ST. EDMUND, Rev. Msgr. Michael J. Connelly; Revs. Hugh A. Byrne; Michael A. Perry; Sr. Mary Beata Gerrity, R.S.M., Pastoral Min.; Deacons Bernard M. Deschier; Richard G. Lee.
Res., 204-25 Rockaway Point Blvd., Rockaway Point, 11697. Tel: 718-634-6357; Fax: 718-634-7900.

247—TRANSFIGURATION (Lithuanian), Rev. James T. Rooney. In res., Rev. Msgr. Francis J. Bulovas, Pastor Emeritus.
Res., 64-14 Clinton Ave., Maspeth, 11378. Tel: 718-326-2236; Fax: 718-326-2249.

248—ST. VIRGILIUS (Noel Rd.), Rev. Charles H. White.
Res., 210 Noel Rd., Broad Channel, 11693-1091. Tel: 718-634-5680; Fax: 718-474-1538.
School—Tel: 718-634-6237; Fax: 718-634-2325. Martha A. Accordino, Prin.
Lay Teachers 9; Students 158.
Catechesis/Religious Programs—Students 60.

Chaplains of Public Institutions

BROOKLYN. *Brookdale Hospital Medical Center*. Vacant.
Brooklyn Correctional Facility. Vacant.
The Brooklyn Hospital. Rev. Joseph Diele.
Brooklyn House of Detention. Rev. Walter Mitchell.
Coney Island Hospital. Rev. Joseph P. Quigley.
Downstate Medical Center. Sr. Karen O'Neil, C.S.J.
Kings County Hospital Center. Rev. Lucien Charlot.
Kingsboro Psychiatric Center. Rev. Robert Frueh.
Long Island College Hospital. Vacant.
Lutheran Medical Center. Vacant.

Maimonides Medical Center of Brooklyn. Sr. Mary Catherine Murphy, R.S.H.M.
Methodist Hospital. Sr. Therese Marie Camardella, C.S.J.
Veterans Administration Medical Center. Rev. Thomas Mullen.
Victory Memorial Hospital. Bro. Lewis Morrow, C.S.C.
Woodhull Medical & Mental Health Center. Rev. Justo Beltran Regado; Sr. Claudia Paredes.
Wyckoff Heights Hospital. Rev. Remigio.
QUEENS. *Bedford Hills Correctional Facility*. Sr. Elaine Roulet, C.S.J., Family Liaison & Dir. Children's Center.
Creedmoor Psychiatric Center. Revs. Paul Chenot, C.P.; August J. Iantosca.
Elmhurst General Hospital. Rev. Alan Briceland, S.J.
Flushing Hospital and Medical Center. Sr. Florence Dippold, C.S.J.
Jamaica Hospital - Trump Pavilion. Rev. Matthew Kulapurath, C.M.I.
Long Island Jewish Hospital. Sr. Benedicta Dega, F.S.S.J.
N.Y. Hospital Medical Center of Queens. Vacant.
Peninsula Hospital Center. Sr. Joanne Feulner, C.S.J.
Queens Hospital Center—Pastoral Care Office. Rev. Jose Cadusale (Philippines).
Queens House of Detention. Rev. John H. Wilkinson.
Queensboro Correctional Facility. Deacon Frank DeTucci.
Veterans Affairs Extended Care Center, St. Albans, NY. Revs. Joseph Gleeson; James T. Devine.
Western Queens Community Hospital. Sr. Frances Casteran, C.S.J.

Special Assignment:
Reverend Monsignors—
Reilly, Philip J., Chap., Monastery of the Precious Blood, 5400 Ft. Hamilton Pkwy., Brooklyn, NY 11219
Reverend Fathers—
Mahoney, Cornelius H., Office of the Synod, 7200 Douglaston Pkwy., Douglaston, NY 11362-1997
Maresca, Ralph J., Sec. to the Diocesan Bishop, 75 Greene Ave., P.O. Box C, Brooklyn, NY 11202
Massie, Guy A., Brooklyn College Newman Club, Our Lady Help of Christians, 1315 E. 28th St., Brooklyn, NY 11210
Parisi, Michael R., Catholic Consultation Center, 7200 Douglaston Pkwy., Rm. # 213, Douglaston, NY 11362
Reid, Michael R., Diocesan Dir., Catholic Cemeteries, Catholic Cemeteries, 137-35 Brookville Blvd., Rosedale, NY 11422
Tedone, Michael G., Dir. of Vocations, St. Rita, 36-26 11th St., Long Island City, NY 11106

Military Chaplains:
Reverend Monsignors—
Gilhooley, John P., (Retired), 1260 Stevens Ave., Arbutus, MD 21227
Reverend Fathers—
Boyd, James A., Chap. Dept., Naval Air Sta., Barbers Point, HI 96862-5050
Ceriello, Joseph A., NAB Chapel, Naval Amphibious Base, Little Creek, Norfolk, VA 23521
Dillon, James P., 1834 Tara Dr., Prattville, AL 36060
Leibold, James C., Office of the Base Chap., MCB, Camp 5.D. Butler, Butler, FPO AP 96373-5001
Leone, James M., 126 Laurelton Dr., P.O. Box 426, Mastic Beach, NY 11951
Mulkerin, Terrence J., Chaplain's Office, USCG Reserve Training Center, Yorktown, VA 23690-9761
Teahan, Timothy J., HHC 8th SPT GRP, CMR 426 Box 563, APO AE 09613
Vella, Joseph C., 1297B Redwood Dr., Grand Forks AFB, ND 58204

Released from Diocesan Assignment:
Reverend Monsignors—
Ecker, Robert J., 300 Second St., Coronado, CA 92118
LaRocca, Vincent R., 108 Carroll St., Brooklyn, NY 11231
Maksymowicz, John H., Apostolic Nunciature, 3339 Massachusetts Ave., N.W., Washington, DC 20008
Sarno, Robert J., Congregation for the Causes of Saints, Vatican City State 00120
White, Leo J., St. George's Cathedral House, Westminster Bridge Rd., London SE1 7HY, England
Reverend Fathers—
Bordeleau, Normand G.
Brennan, Edward C.
Catania, Thomas M., B.V.M. Help of Christians, 70-31 48th Ave., Woodside, NY 11377
Cremins, John J., Assumption, 64 Middagh St., Brooklyn, NY 11201
Curran, Michael J., Casa Santa Maria, Villa Dell' Umilta, '30, 00187 Rome, Italy
D'Albro, Thomas G., 62A Widmer Rd., Wappingers Falls, NY 12590
Diffley, Patrick J., 283 Paulette Dr., Newport News, VA 23602
Dunne, Richard J., Dept. of Veterans Affairs, P.O. Box 5474, Hampton, VA 23667
Finley, James F., Kath. Amerikanische Gemeinde, Huttenweig, 46, 14195 Berlin, Germany
Folchetti, John T., Christian Brothers Academy, 850 Newman Springs Rd., Lincroft, NJ 07738
Heffernan, James F., Chap., Veterans Admin. Medical Center, Northport, NY 11768
Heffernan, Thomas A., Northwest Covenant Medical Center, Denville, NJ 07834
Himes, Michael J., Department of Theology, Boston College, Chestnut Hill, MA 02167-3806
Johnston, John F., Oratory Prep School, One Beverly Rd., Summit, NJ 07901
Lanahan, William F., 215 N. Power Rd., Mesa, AZ 85205
Lauder, Robert E., Cathedral Residence, 7200 Douglaston Pkwy., Douglaston, NY 11362
Longo, Robert M., O.F.M.Cap., Capuchin Franciscans, Our Lady of Guadalupe Friary, 319 36th St., P.O. Box 809, Union City, NJ 07087
LoPinto, Alfred P., 1450 N. D St., San Bernardino, CA 92405
Mariano, John M., 1620 S. Ocean Blvd. (9N), Pompano Beach, FL 33062
Matonti, Charles, 175-20 Wexford Ter., Jamaica, NY 11432
McNicholas, Edward J., Bishop Mugavero Residence, 7200 Douglaston Pkwy., P.O. Box 630433, Little Neck, NY 11363-0433
McVernon, John J., 16-34 Clintonville St., Whitestone, NY 11357
Mulqueen, Joseph C., Apostolic Nunciature, 3339 Massachusetts Ave., N.W., Washington, DC 20008-3687
Nadine, Jerome E., St. Elizabeth Ann Seton Church, 18-11 Pueblo Vista Dr., Las Vegas, NV 89128
Passenant, Francis J., Our Lady of Fatima Church, 25-02 80th St., Jackson Heights, NY 11370
Paterno, Salvatore D., St. Mary, 42 Goshen Ave., Washingtonville, NY 10992
Penta, Leo J., Am Hegewinkel, 5B, D-14169 Berlin, Germany
Pomilio, Matthew J., 175-20 Wexford Ter., Jamaica, NY 11432
Ruiz, Jean-Pierre, S.T.D., St. Patrick Rectory, 39-38 29th St., Long Island City, NY 11101
Schuck, Joseph J., 1011 State Hwy. 7, Unadilla, NY 13847-9771
Sears, William J., 1745 Padre Ln., Englewood, FL 34223
Smith, LeRoy J., Red Cottage, Chatham Center, NY 12184
Steinhauser, Kenneth B., Belmont Abbey College, Belmont, NC 28012
Steinhauser, Michael G., Toronto School of Theology, 47 Queen's Park, Crescent Park, Toronto, Ontario M55 2CS Canada
Tivenan, John J., Mercy Medical Center, 1512 12th Ave. Rd., Nampa, ID 83686
Trombetta, Paul N., 219 Old Oak Bucket Rd., Scituate, MA 02066
Upson, Michael G., Immaculate Conception Church, 445 Frederick Douglas St., Rochester, NY 14608
Vaccari, Peter I., Immaculate Conception Seminary, W. Neck Rd.-Lloyd Harbor, Huntington, NY 11743
Vendetti, Michael A., 94-26 Sutter Ave., Ozone Park, NY 11417
Wulinski, Stanley F., 1701 N.E. 42nd St., Beacon Heights, FL 33064
Zaccagnigno, Raffaele, Rome, Italy

Graduate Studies:
Reverend Fathers—
Caccavale, Charles, Casa Santa Maria, 00187 Rome, Italy
Fonti, Joseph, Casa Santa Maria, 00187 Rome, Italy

Absent on Sick Leave:
Reverend Monsignors—
Demski, Arthur A.
Reverend Fathers—
Denzer, Joseph W.
Early, William F.
Esposito, Joseph J.
Failla, Anthony
Flynn, Francis J.
Grant, Matthew M.
Mangini, Charles M.
Newell, John J.
O'Brien, David G.
Prochaski, Adam F.
Sabatos, Daniel C.
Wildgruber, Francis C.

Absent on Leave:
Reverend Monsignors—
Manzo, Francis J.
Reverend Fathers—
Barbetta, Philip
Beliveau, Richard
Boyle, Victor J.
Brown, Charles L.
Ferraro, Romano J.
Ferro, Robert A.
Higuero, Francisco J.
Kozma, Raymond M.
Lazar, John E.
Liona, Kenneth J.
Mason, Edward J.
Merolla, George R.
Miller, Joseph A.
Morris, James J.
Morrow, Thomas O.
Peyton, Thomas
Piro, Gerald J.
Ryan, Barry
Sexton, Patrick D.
Visich, Eduard C.
Walsh, John F.
Wood, Paul F.

Retired:
Reverend Monsignors—
Adessa, Dominick J., 555 Albany Ave., Amityville, NY 11701
Asip, James W., 16-34 Clintonville St., Whitestone, NY 11357
Barretta, Anthony J., 61-27 71st St., Middle Village, NY 11379
Bednartz, August C., Cathedral Prep Seminary, 56-25 92nd St., Elmhurst, NY 11373
Bennett, Austin P., 75 Greene Ave., P.O. Box C, Brooklyn, NY 11202
Bleilevens, Charles A., 86-13 55th Ave., Elmhurst, NY 11373-4394
Brugli, Angelo F., Msgr. Fitzpatrick Pavilion, 152-11 89th Ave., Jamaica, NY 11421
Bulovas, Francis J., 64 Clinton Ave., Brooklyn, NY
Burke, William F., Bishop Mugavero Residence, 7200 Douglaston Pkwy., P.O. Box 433, Little Neck, NY 11363-0433
Burns, John A., 1395 E. 56th St., Brooklyn, NY 11234
Campbell, Thomas P., 21-17 45th St., Long Island City, NY 11105
Clancy, Thomas C., 2055 E. 69th St., Brooklyn, NY 11234
Collini, Celsus O., 141-36 77th Ave., Kew Gardens Hills, NY 11367
Cosgrove, Henry P., Bishop Mugavero Residence, 7200 Douglaston Pkwy., P.O. Box 433, Little Neck, NY 11363-0433
Cribbin, Thomas F., 256 Clinton Ave., Brooklyn, NY 11205
D'Anca, Achille, 274 Beachway Dr., Palm Coast, FL 32137
Deas, George T., Bishop Mugavero Residence, 7200 Douglaston Pkwy., P.O. Box 630433, Little Neck, NY 11363-0433
Diviney, Charles E., 21 Sidney Pl., Brooklyn, NY 11201
Donegan, James F., St. Joan of Arc, 82-00 35th Ave., Jackson Heights, NY 11372
Evans, Francis J., 100-05 159th Ave., Howard Beach, NY 11414
Fagan, John T., Little Flower Children's Services, N. Wading River Rd., Wading River, NY 11792
Feldhaus, Eugene A., 188-16 91st Ave., Hollis, NY 11423
Fitzpatrick, Franklin E., 91-18 86th Ave., Woodhaven, NY 11421
Flanagan, Thomas J., P.O. Box 804, Beatrice Ct., Hampton Bays, NY 11946
Florido, Raphael A., 9719 Flatlands Ave., Brooklyn, NY 11236
Fogarty, George V., Bishop Mugavero Residence, 7200 Douglaston Pkwy., P.O. Box 433, Little Neck, NY 11363-0433
Fus, Edward A., 43 Highpoint Dr., Kunkletown, PA 18058
Galuszka, Walter C., 479 New Jersey Ave., Brooklyn, NY 11207
Haggarty, James J., St. Pius, 1100 Woodside Rd., Redwood City, CA 94061
Haggerty, James J., St. Saviour, 611 Eighth Ave., Brooklyn, NY 11215
Hendel, Thomas W., 94-40 118th St., Richmond Hill, NY 11419
Jolley, Edward W., Bishop Mugavero Residence, 7200 Douglaston Pkwy., P.O. Box 433, Little Neck, NY 11363-0433
Kean, John J., 1281 Troy Ave., Brooklyn, NY 11203
King, James P., 28-20 154th St., Flushing, NY 11354

Konrad, Joseph G., 5815 Catalpa Ave., Ridgewood, NY 11385
Landi, Andrew P., St. Stephen, 142 E. 29th St., New York, NY 10016
Martin, Kieran J., 1550 Hendrickson St., Brooklyn, NY 11234
McAlister, Lawrence J., 638 Rathbun Ave., Staten Island, NY 10312-2613
McKenna, James J., St. Mary Star of the Sea, 1920 New Haven Ave., Far Rockaway, NY 11691
Mooney, George A., 66-01 80th St., Middle Village, NY 11379
Mulhall, Francis X., Bishop Mugavero Residence, 7200 Douglaston Pkwy., Box 433, Little Neck, NY 11363-0433
Nolan, Edward J., 89-43 Francis Lewis Blvd., Queens Village, NY 11427
Osborne, William J., 9-41 120 St., College Point, NY 11356
Parks, Joseph K., St. Patrick, 9511 Fourth Ave., Brooklyn, NY 11209
Passarella, Anthony F., 862 Manhattan Ave., Brooklyn, NY 11222
Piombini, Mario G., Holy Family Home, 1740 84th St., Brooklyn, NY 11214
Privitera, Santi J., Sts. Joachim and Ann Residence, 2720 Surf Ave., Brooklyn, NY 11224
Rau, Raymond F., 1302 Lantana St., Corpus Christi, TX 78407
Rodgers, William J., Queen of Peace Residence, 110-30 221st St., Queens Village, NY 11429
Ryan, James W., 2609 Linden Blvd., Brooklyn, NY 11208
Sapporito, Cosmo G., St. Bernadette, 8201 13th Ave., Brooklyn, NY 11228
Shevlin, Raymond R., 2325 Gerritsen Ave., Brooklyn, NY 11229
Voiland, George T., 32-23 36th St., Long Island City, NY 11106
Welsh, Robert E., 199 River Rd., Nissequoque, NY 11780
Wilson, John F., 245 Prospect Park W., Brooklyn, NY 11215

Reverend Fathers—
Abrams, John L., Bishop Mugavero Residence, 7200 Douglaston Pkwy., P.O. Box 630433, Little Neck, NY 11363-0433
Angles, Sebastian, 2601 Muscatello St., Orlando, FL 32821
Baltrucki, Leon S., 19 Wright St., Gardner, MA 01440
Bartruff, Louis B., Bishop Mugavero Residence, 7200 Douglaston Pkwy., P.O. Box 433, Little Neck, NY 11363-0433
Bihler, Joseph J., Queen of Peace Residence, 110-30 221st St., Queens Village, NY 11429
Blaeser, Alfred A., 1088 Lloyd St., Franklin Square, NY 11010
Borzaga, Rinaldo, Manhattan College, Riverdale, NY 10471
Brevetti, Adrian, Via Vicinale, DellaMachia #9, Rocca Di Papa, Rome, 00040 Italy
Brown, Vincent A., 63-63 98th St., Rego Park, NY 11374
Buckley, Joseph F., St. Cecilia, 84 Herbert St., Brooklyn, NY 11222
Buetow, Harold A., Bishop Mugavero Residence, 7200 Douglaston Pkwy., P.O. Box 433, Little Neck, NY 11363-0433
Byrnes, Francis J., P.O. Box 784, Welaka, FL 32193
Byrnes, John W., 218-26 105th Ave., Queens Village, NY 11429
Calderwood, Vincent T., 38 Duncan Dr., Morganville, NJ 07751
Conroy, Edward G., 98-10 103rd Ave., Ozone Park, NY 11417
Cronin, John F., Bishop Mugavero Residence, 7200 Douglaston Pkwy., P.O. Box 433, Little Neck, NY 11363-0433
Culkin, Harry W., Bishop Mugavero Residence, 7200 Douglaston Pkwy., P.O. Box 630433, Little Neck, NY 11363-0433
Cushing, Charles B., 46-41 217th St., Bayside, NY 11361
D'Amato, James J., 1550 Hendrickson St., Brooklyn, NY 11234
Daly, Joseph F., 66-05 79th Pl., Middle Village, NY 11379
Davis, William J., 62-81 60th Pl., Ridgewood, NY 11385
Dennen, Gerard F., P.O. Box 2143, Pinehurst, NC 28374
Dolan, Thomas D., 94-20 85th St., Ozone Park, NY 11416
Donnelly, Eugene F., 25-02 80th St., Jackson Heights, NY 11370
Dore, Denis, 148-10 249 St., Rosedale, NY 11422
Dundon, Raymond J., St. Vincent Ferrer, 1603 Brooklyn Ave., Brooklyn, NY 11210
Duran, Ernesto, Santa Beatriz 269, Apt. 503, Santiago 9, Chile S.A.
Ebejer, George, 216 27th St., Brooklyn, NY 11232
Flynn, Francis J., 1550 Hendrickson St., Brooklyn, NY 11234
Forsyth, George W., 2 Pheasant Ln., Lloyd Harbor, NY 11743
Franco, Salvator, 15 Park W., New Hyde Park, NY 11040
Giuliano, Louis A., 52-10 NW 53rd. Ave., Cocoanut Creek, FL 33073
Grillo, Anthony, Bishop Mugavero Residence, 7200 Douglaston Pkwy., P.O. Box 433, Little Neck, NY 11363-0433
Harth, Charles F., 2609 Linden Blvd., Brooklyn, NY 11208
Heerey, John J., P.O. Box 207, Interlachen, FL 32148
Hickey, William T., 63-63 98th St., Rego Park, NY 11374
Hogan, Edward P., 130 Oceanside, Rockaway Pt., NY 11697
Hughes, John F., Queen of Peace Residence, 110-30 221st St., Queens Village, NY 11429
Hume, Robert B., Holy Innocents, 279 E. 17th St., Brooklyn, NY 11226
Hunt, Michael J., Mugavero Geriatric Center, 155 Dean St., Brooklyn, NY 11217
Jozwicki, Stephen J., 183 25th St., Brooklyn, NY 11232
Jurgensen, John W., 94-40 118th St., Richmond Hill, NY 11419
Kakizaki, John T., 99-15 Rockaway Beach Blvd., Rockaway Park, NY 11694
Keane, Edward M., 175-20 74th Ave., Flushing, NY 11366
Keane, Joseph P., Two Pinetop Dr., Shirley, NY 11967
Kelly, Thomas F., 7320 Fourth Ave., Brooklyn, NY 11209
Kenny, Albert N., 273 78th St., Brooklyn, NY 11209
Kenny, Michael J., 17 Old Rte. 9W, Fort Montgomery, NY 10922
Kirrane, James A., St. Anthony of Padua, 20 Cheshire Pl., Box 308, E. Northport, NY 11731
Klohr, Paul McC., Queen of Peace Residence, 110-30 221st St., Queens Village, NY 11429
Labita, Francis J., 100-05 159th St., Howard Beach, NY 11414
Lang, Henry A., 56-15 213th St., Bayside Hills, NY 11364
LoGatto, Rosario J., 2334 Sunset Dr., Escondido, CA 92025
Maceli, Anthony J., 6908 Stonesthrow Cir. N., St. Petersburg, FL 33710
Malleck, Joseph L., 24 Steven St., Plainview, NY 11803
Mankowski, Edmund A., R.R. 2, Box 319 Locust Dr. & Noyack Rd., Sag Harbor, NY 11963
Mannion, Thomas F., 415 Gauntlatt, P.O. Box 33, Gold Beach, OR 97444
Mariani, Charles J., 108 Carroll St., Brooklyn, NY 11231
McCarren, William J., 8000 Roma N.E., Albuquerque, NM 87108
McDermott, James P., 1600 N. Ocean Blvd., Apt. 408, Pompano Beach, FL 33062
McElroy, Herbert, Holy Family Home, 1740 84th St., Brooklyn, NY 11214
McGee, Francis J., 130 Beach 84th St., Rockaway Beach, NY 11693
McGuirk, Raymond A., 279 E. 17th St., Brooklyn, NY 11226
McLoughlin, William J., Bishop Mugavero Residence, 7200 Douglaston Pkwy., P.O. Box 630433, Little Neck, NY 11363-0433
McNeill, John A., Our Lady of Lourdes, 92-96 220th St., Queens Village, NY 11428
Milde, Robert F., Bishop Mugavero Residence, 7200 Douglaston Pkwy., P.O. Box 433, Little Neck, NY 11363-0433
Moore, Robert A., 929 Bay Ridge Pkwy., Brooklyn, NY 11228
Morgan, Raymond J., Bishop Mugavero Residence, 7200 Douglaston Pkwy., P.O. Box 433 7, Little Neck, NY 11363-0433
Mueller, Anthony E., 204-25 Rockaway Point Blvd., Rockaway Point, NY 11697
Mullen, Joseph A., 555 Albany Ave., Amityville, NY 11701
Mulqueen, John C., 344 Avondale Dr., Shirley, NY 11967
Niccoli, Andrew, 32-23 36th St., Long Island City, NY 11106
Nichols, Charles P., Sacred Hearts of Jesus & Mary - St. Steven, 108 Carroll St., Brooklyn, NY 11231
Nolan, Joseph M., 115-58 222nd St., Cambria Heights, NY 11411
O'Brien, Thomas, 150-75 Goethals Ave., Jamaica, NY 11432
O'Connor, Edward T., 6255 S.E. Charleston Pl., Hobe Sound, FL 33455
O'Leary, William A., 215 Beach 216th St., Breezy Point, NY 11697
O'Sullivan, John J., 22 Woods Ln., Southampton, NY 11968
Oravecz, John F., Bishop Mugavero Residence, 7200 Douglaston Pkwy., P.O. Box 433, Little Neck, NY 11363-0433
Pakalniskis, John L., Bishop Mugavero Residence, 7200 Douglaston Pkwy., P.O. Box 433, Little Neck, NY 11363-0433
Pesaresi, Constantine V., Our Lady of Sorrows, 104-11 37th Ave., Corona, NY 11368
Pikturna, Vytautas, 2800 Ocean Dr. B 6D, Riviera Beach, FL 33404
Powers, Anthony F., 124 Beaver Dr., Mastic Beach, NY 11951
Pullo, Francis S., Bishop Mugavero Residence, 7200 Douglaston Pkwy., P.O. Box 433, Little Neck, NY 11363-0433
Pupin, Vito A., Mugavero Geriatric Center, 155 Dean St., Brooklyn, NY 11217
Raila, Stanislaus, Bishop Mugavero Residence, 7200 Douglaston Pkwy., P.O. Box 433, Little Neck, NY 11363-0433
Rau, Raymond F., 198 Euclid Ave., Brooklyn, NY 11208
Reilly, John C., 141-36 77 Ave., Kew Gardens Hills, NY 11367
Rizzi, Salvatore, 126 Pond Rd., Woodbury, NY 11797
Romanowski, Francis C., St. Stanislaus, Bishop & Martyr, 88-10 102nd Ave., Ozone Park, NY 11416
Schmidt, Jerome J., 2325 Gerritson Ave., Brooklyn, NY 11229
Schwind, Donald F., 182 Monitor St., Brooklyn, NY 11222
Seeger, Francis J., P.O. Box 6678, Flushing, NY 11365
Seeger, Peter J., 123-06 14th Ave., College Point, NY 11356
Simonetti, Gennaro M., Our Lady of Miracles, 757 E. 86 St., Brooklyn, NY 11236
Stonebridge, John H., 83-17 78th Ave., East Glendale, NY 11385
Sullivan, James E., Most Holy Trinity, 14-51 143rd St., Whitestone, NY 11357
Suran, Joachim, 98-16 55th Ave., Corona, NY 11368-3015
Termine, Vincent J., 3736 Bayview Ave., Brooklyn, NY 11224
Travis, Herbert A., St. Anselm, 356 82nd St., Brooklyn, NY 11209
Tully, James J., 24 Brookway Dr., Greensboro, NC 27410
Vivona, Anthony, 922 E. 96th St., Brooklyn, NY 11236-2304
Vogel, Charles P., 416 Grant Ave., Brooklyn, NY 11208
Walsh, Michael J., 80 John St., Staten Island, NY 10302
Wang, Barnabas, Bishop Mugavero Residence, 7200 Douglaston Pkwy., Douglaston, NY 11362
Weinlich, Alfred J., St. Luke, 16-34 Clintonville St., Whitestone, NY 11357
Wiseman, Joseph, 48-02 Parsons Blvd., Flushing, NY 11355
Witterholt, Herbert M., 42-41 201 St., Bayside, NY 11361
Yonson, Wenceslaus, 279 E. 17 St., Brooklyn, NY 11226
Young, Robert J., Bishop Mugavero Residence, 7200 Douglaston Pkwy, P.O. Box 630433, Little Neck, NY 11363-0433

Permanent Deacons:
Aigbojie, Edward A., St. Fortunata, Brooklyn
Almodovar, Ismael, Diocese of Orlando
Alvarez, Felipe J., St. Joseph, Long Island City
Arcand, Dennis A., Diocese of Savannah
Aris, Anthony J., Inactive
Arthur, Anthony H., St. Jerome, Brooklyn
Baez, Angel, Epiphany, Brooklyn
Beaubrun, Berthal, St. Ignatius, Brooklyn
Bichotte, Joseph, St. Augustine, Brooklyn
Boursiquot, Jean B., St. Ignatius, Brooklyn
Burrell, James, St. Catherine of Siena, St. Alban
Caceres, Ycelso, Inactive
Cafiero, Joseph D., St. Rosalia, Brooklyn
Cajiao, Henry, Diocese of St. Petersburg
Calvo, Juan, Queen of Angels, Long Island City
Campisi, Joseph, Our Lady Grace, Howard Beach
Cancel, Edwin, Our Lady of the Angelus, Rego Park
Candreva, Arthur, Sacred Heart, Glendale
Cardona, Ramon, Diocese of Mayaguez, PR
Cederroth, Charles J., Diocese of Trenton
Chin, Paul M., St. Paul Chong Ha-Sang Chapel, Flushing
Coffey, John P., Christ the King, Springfield Gardens
Colandrea, Dante, St. Dominic, Brooklyn
Coleman, Harry J., St. Bonaventure, Jamaica

Colon, Rafael, St. Augustine, Brooklyn
Coyle, Lawrence J., St. Columba, Brooklyn
Coyle, Richard J., Unassigned
Cruz, Florencio, St. Matthew, Brooklyn
Cruz, Rafael, Archdiocese of Miami
Cuccia, Arthur J., St. Jude
Cusumano, Anthony P., St. Helen, Howard Beach
D'Accordo, Frank J., Saint Bernard, Brooklyn
Da Costa, Dennis A., St. Matthew, Brooklyn
Damato, Stephen T., St. Sebastian, Woodside
Davis, Thomas G., St. Anselm, Brooklyn
De Cola, Joseph P., Diocese of Palm Beach
De Tucci, Frank A., Catholic Charities Office for Prison Ministry
DeBiase, Vincent F., St. Margaret, Middle Village
DeLeon, Andres, St. Gregory the Great, Brooklyn
Dennehy, John P., St. Anastasia, Douglaston
Desdunes, Herve, St. Matthew, Brooklyn
Devaney, Thomas J., Immaculate Heart of Mary, Brooklyn
Diaz, Rafael A., St. Leo, Corona
DiTargiani, Charles C., St. Ephrem, Brooklyn
Dixon, Gregory D., St. Andrew the Apostle, Brooklyn
Dorsinville, Paul C., Sacred Heart, Cambria Heights
Dudley, Roy A., Sacred Heart, Cambria Heights
Earley, George G., Diocese of Rockville Centre
Ehresmann, Philip J., St. Brigid, Brooklyn
Felix, Antoine, Holy Innocents, Brooklyn
Flaim, Fabio, St. Aloysius, Ridgewood
Flannery, John A., St. Charles Borromeo, Brooklyn
Fogerty, James P., Diocese of Rockville Centre
Franca, John J., St. Francis Xavier, Brooklyn
Francis, John J., Unassigned
Francois, Joseph K., Our Lady of the Presentation, Brooklyn
Fugelsang, Louis, Inactive
Gannon, John J., Unassigned
Garamella, Robert, Diocese of Rockville Centre
George, Roy N., St. Gregory the Great, Brooklyn
Germain, Moliere, St. Vincent Ferrer, Brooklyn
Giglio, John P., Unassigned
Gilligan, Richard J., St. Mary Gate of Heaven, Ozone Park
Gomez, Guillermo D., St. Gerard Majella, Hollis
Gonzalez, Rafael, Diocese of Orlando
Grace, James T., St. Pius V, Jamaica
Guastella, Louis J., St. Catherine of Genoa, Brooklyn
Heaphy, Thomas F., St. Mary Gate of Heaven, Ozone Park
Heinrich, Joseph, Office of Disabled Persons, Catholic Charities
Hernandez, Rafael, Diocese of Orlando
Hernandez, Wilfredo, Holy Spirit, Brooklyn
Hili, Saviour, St. Francis of Assisi, Long Island City
Hitter, Robert A., St. Francis de Sales, Belle Harbor
Horne, Wilfred N., Archdiocese for the Military Services, USA
Huckemeyer, Edward J., On Personal Leave
Innocent, Francois, Incarnation, Brooklyn
Joesten, F. Edward, St. Anthony of Padua, South Ozone Park
Johnson, Stanley D., Unassigned
Kennedy, James F., St. Thomas Aquinas, Brooklyn
Knight, Lionel A., St. Nicholas of Tolentine, Jamaica
Krebs, Jerome H., Our Lady Miraculous Medal, Brooklyn
Landron, Jaime, Our Lady of the Presentation, Brooklyn
Lavanco, Robert F., Our Lady of Hope, Middle Village
Lee, Richard G., St. Thomas More-St. Edmund, Rockaway Point
Licata, Salvatore V., Exec. Sec. Permanent Diaconate Office
Lima, Ramon, Unassigned
Lopez, Eduvigis, Our Lady of Perpetual Help, Brooklyn
Lopez, Hiram, Archdiocese of New York
Maldonado, Andres, Diocese of Ponce, PR
Malone, William F., St. Ephrem, Brooklyn
Marcel, Magloire, St. Jerome, Brooklyn
Marchello, Andrew A., Nativity of the Blessed Virgin Mary, Queens
Marley, Daniel J., Our Lady of Solace, Brooklyn
Marte, Rafael, St. John Cantius, Brooklyn
Martinez, German, Transfiguration, Brooklyn
Mayers, Winston M., Christ the King, Springfield Gardens
Mazza, Nicholas, St. Cecilia, Brooklyn
McCarthy, Thomas R., Our Lady Queen of Martyrs, Forest Hills
McGreevey, John F., St. John Vianney, Brooklyn
McGuire, Joseph P., St. Brendan, Brooklyn
Mejia, Abdon, Our Lady of Perpetual Help, South Ozone Park
Mellace, Carlo V., St. Dominic, Brooklyn
Miller, Leon F., St. Michael, East New York
Montalvo, Hector, Holy Family, Brooklyn
Morales, Julio A., Diocese of Orlando
Mulroy, Martin B., Unassigned
Murphy, John J., Mary Queen of Heaven, Brooklyn
Nero, Robert V., (Retired)
O'Neill, John P., Corpus Christi, Woodside
Occhiuto, Joseph J., Inactive
Ortiz, Sergio, Unassigned
Pagan, Aurelio, St. Agnes, Brooklyn
Parisi, Vincent, St. Rita, Long Island City
Pascal, Orlando, Our Lady of Sorrows, Corona
Paul, Ernst, St. Rita, Brooklyn
Postler, Charles A., St. Patrick, Brooklyn
Pouso, Roberto J., Blessed Sacrament, Jackson Heights
Proce, Horatio A., Inactive
Ramirez, Manuel, Diocese of Scranton
Ramos, James, St. Francis Xavier, Brooklyn
Ramos, Jose A., St. Lucy-St. Patrick, Brooklyn
Ramos, Pedro, Diocese of Caguas, PR
Rivera, Angel R., St. Benedict Joseph Labre, Richmond Hill
Rivera, Hector R., Archdiocese of San Juan, PR
Rizzo, Giovanni A., St. Finbar, Brooklyn
Roberts, Lionel V., Unassigned
Rogers, Thomas F., Incarnation, Queens Village
Ronacher, Ronald M., St. Rita, Brooklyn
Rosati, Frank J., Catholic Charities, Pastoral Care of the Sick
Ruiz, Jose D., Diocese of Ponce, PR
Russo, Anthony J., (Retired)
Ryan, Kevin F., Blessed Virgin Mary Help of Christians, Queens
Sands, John E., St. Matthias, Ridgewood
Sawney, Ira, Florida
Sclafani, Leonard A., St. Paul Center, Long Island City
Seliga, Mark A., St. Mark, Brooklyn
Simon, Mauclair, St. Therese of Lisieux, Brooklyn
Sinisi, Henry C., On Leave
Smith, Charles J., Mary Queen of Heaven, Brooklyn
Smith, Henry J., Our Lady of the Snows, North Floral Park
Smith, Ramon, St. Teresa of Avila, S. Ozone Park
Smolinski, Chester, (Retired)
Smolinski, Edward A., Our Lady of Mercy, Forest Hills
Soto, Jesus, Our Lady of Perpetual Help, Brooklyn
Steffens, Gerard K., St. Matthias, Ridgewood
Sucich, John R., St. Francis of Assisi, Long Island City
Svebel, Harry A., St. Luke, Whitestone
Taylor, Luis C., St. Catherine of Sienna, St. Alban
Tierney, John A., Diocese of Albany
Tokarcsik, George M., St. Agatha, Brooklyn
Torres, Abel, Holy Name, Brooklyn
Troy, Michael J., Our Lady of Angels, Brooklyn
Tully, Dean T., Holy Child Jesus, Richmond Hill
Valderrana, Carlos, St. Cecilia, Brooklyn
Valle Valle, Esteban, Archdiocese of San Juan, PR
Van de Ven, Theodore J., St. Fidelis, College Point
Van Wassenhove, Raymond J., Diocese of Peoria
Vargas, Juan R., St. Agatha, Brooklyn
Vermilyea, Richard, Unassigned
Waldron, Martin T., St. Mary Star of the Sea, Far Rockaway
Wander, William H., St. Andrew the Apostle, Brooklyn
Whelan, Alfred L., St. Gertrude, Far Rockaway
Williams, Lee C., St. Mary Magdalene, Springfield Gardens
Williamsen, William, St. Saviour, Brooklyn
Winkler, Warren A., Our Lady of Lourdes, Queens Village
Yepes, Elias H., St. Michael, Flushing

INSTITUTIONS LOCATED IN THE DIOCESE

[A] PASTORAL CENTERS

DOUGLASTON. *Immaculate Conception Pastoral Center*, 7200 Douglaston Pkwy., 11362-1997. Tel: 718-229-8001; Fax: 718-229-2658. Rev. Michael J. Hardiman, Dir.; Mr. Thomas D. Flynn, Asst. Dir. Controller; Mr. Gerard King, Asst. Dir. Plant Svcs. & Maintenance; Mr. James Austin, Asst. Dir. Dining Svcs.; Mr. Charles C. Lindner, Librarian; Mr. Brian Zuar, Performing Arts.

Offices Located at the Center include Cathedral Residence; Bishop Mugavero Residence; The Tribunal; Office of the Synod Institutional Svcs.; Bldg. & Property Office; Pastoral Institute; Regl. Bishop of Queens-N.; Office of the Archivist; Office of the Diocesan Dir. of Music; Hispanic Ministry; Diocesan Devel.; Futures in Educ.; and Brooklyn-Queens Environmental Mgmt. Corp.: Catholic Consultation Center, Family Life Ministry, Institute of Languages and Cultures, and Francis X. McDermott Religious Studies Library.

[B] SEMINARIES, DIOCESAN

DOUGLASTON. *Cathedral Residence of the Immaculate Conception*, 7200 Douglaston Pkwy., 11362. Tel: 718-229-8001. Residence for college level and post college level candidates for Priesthood. Rev. Msgr. Octavio Cisneros, M.Div., Rector; Revs. Conrad R. Dietz, Ph.D., Academic Dean, Philosophy Prof.; Thomas G. Caserta, M.A., M.Div., D.Min., Spiritual Dir.; Dennis D. Klein, Ph.D., Philosophy Prof. In res. Revs. Martin F. Kirby, M.A.; Robert E. Lauder, Ph.D.; Cornelius H. Mahoney, M.Div. Priests 4; Lay Teachers 3; Seminarians 23.

ELMHURST. *Cathedral Preparatory Seminary of the Immaculate Conception*, 56-25 92nd St., 11373. Tel: 718-592-6800. Rev. Msgr. Richard E. Marchese, Rector & Prin.; Revs. William R. Dulaney, Vice Rector; Joseph Calise, Asst. Prin. Devel.; Fred Marano, Spiritual Dir. In res. Rev. Sofronio LoFranco. Priests 4; Brothers 1; Sisters 2; Lay Teachers 14; Seminarians 203.

[C] SEMINARIES, RELIGIOUS

WHITESTONE. *St. Alphonsus Formation Residence*, 22-04 Parsons Blvd., 11357-3440. Tel: 718-321-1096; Fax: 718-321-1246.
E-mail: psousacssr@aol.com
Very Rev. Peter E. Sousa, C.SS.R., Rector/Dir. of Formation; Revs. Paul J. Borowski, C.SS.R., Asst. Dir.; Edmund Faliskie, C.SS.R., Vocation Dir.; James J. Toulas, C.SS.R.; Bro. Darrell Cevasco, C.SS.R. Priests 4; Brothers 1; Students 13.

[D] COLLEGES AND UNIVERSITIES

*BROOKLYN. *St. Francis College*, 180 Remsen St., 11201. Tel: 718-489-5200
For a complete listing, refer to the Colleges and Universities section.

**St. Joseph's College*, 245 Clinton Ave., 11205. Tel: 718-636-6800
For a complete listing, refer to the Colleges and Universities section.

JAMAICA. *St. John's University*, 8000 Utopia Pkwy., 11439. Tel: 718-990-6161; Fax: 718-990-5886.
Web site: http://www.stjohns.edu
For a complete listing, refer to the Colleges and Universities section.

STATEN ISLAND. *St. John's University, Staten Island Campus*, 300 Howard Ave., 10301. Tel: 718-390-4545; Fax: 718-816-4520.
Web site: http://www.stjohns.edu
For a complete listing, refer to the Colleges and Universities section.

[E] CATHOLIC EDUCATION OFFICES

BROOKLYN. *Office of Religious Education: Evangelization and Catholic Formation*, 6025 6th Ave., 11220. Tel: 718-492-1800.
E-mail: Dirre6025@aol.com
Web site: http:www.bkevanreled.org
Mrs. Joan M. Snow, Diocesan Dir.; Sr. Eileen Sweeney, Dir. of Elementary Rel. Educ.; Joan R. Sokoll, Dir. Elementary Rel. Educ.; Rev. Michael A. Carrano, Dir. Youth Ministry & Adolescent Catechesis, & Dir. College Campus Ministry; Sr. Alice Michael, S.U.S.C., Dir. Rel. Educ. for Cultural and Ethnic Groups & Coord. RCIA; Rev. Joseph R. Gibino, Ph.D., Dir. of Adult Rel. Educ.

Diocesan Evangelization Commission. Most Rev. Ignatius A. Catanello, Episcopal Liason; Joan M. Snow, Chair; Rev. Dennis McAuliff, Exec. Sec.

Campus Ministers and Ministry Centers. Revs. Guy Massie, Brooklyn College; Paul Farin, Pratt Institute; Paul Wood, Queens College; Bros. John Reidy, C.F.C., Kingsboro Community College; Thomas Grady, O.S.F., St. Francis College; Sr. Margaret Smith, C.I.J., Long Island University; Sr. Alice Danaher, O.P., Queensboro Community College.
Legal Titles & Corporations: Newman Apostolate, Inc.

Office of the Superintendent of Schools, 6025 Sixth Ave., 11220. Tel: 718-492-1800; Fax: 718-439-0784.
E-mail: dobsuptsch@connectinc.com
Rev. Msgr. Guy J. Puglisi, Supt. of Schools; Mr. Robert A. Annucci, Deputy Supt. - Dir. Personnel; Mrs. Patricia Kelly-Stiles, Assoc. Supt. Prin. Personnel; Mrs. Mary Santos, Assoc. Supt. Prog. Mgmt.; Bro. Lawrence Boyle, O.S.F., Dist. Supt. - Brooklyn East Schools; Mr. Thomas Chadzutko, Dist. Supt. - Brooklyn West Schools; Sr. Ruth Cunningham, C.S.J., Dist. Supt. - Queens North Schools; Sr. Jane Ellis, I.H.M., Dist. Supt. - Queens South Schools; Sr. Sheila Conley, S.C., Assoc. Supt. Curriculum; Sr. Margaret Schmit, O.P., Asst. Dir. Personnel & Office Mgr.; Miss June Stuart, Admin. Asst. Personnel; Mr. William E. Slow, Assoc. Supt., Special Ed.; Mr. Gilbert Ortiz, Exec. Dir. Prog. for the Devel. of Human Potential.

Diocese of Brooklyn Education Offices. Legal Titles

& Corporations: Department of Education, Diocese of Brooklyn; Henry M. Hald High School Association; Saint John's Preparatory School, Brooklyn.

[F] HIGH SCHOOLS, DIOCESAN

BROOKLYN. *Bishop Loughlin Memorial High School*, 357 Clermont Ave., 11238. Tel: 718-857-2700; Fax: 718-398-4227.
(Coed).
Legal Corp.: Henry M. Hald Assoc. Rev. Patrick West, Chap. Brothers of the Christian Schools 7; Priests 1; Sisters 1; Lay Teachers 53; Students 925.

[G] HIGH SCHOOLS, PRIVATE

BROOKLYN. *Bishop Ford Central Catholic High School*, 500 19th St., 11215. Tel: 718-965-6400.
(Coed). Mr. James G. Mullaney, Pres.; Mr. Rocco V. Grella, Asst. Prin. Sisters 1; Lay Teachers 36; Students 864.

Bishop Kearney, 2202 60th St., 11204-2599. Tel: 718-236-6363; Fax: 718-236-7784.
(Girls). Sr. Joan McAvoy, C.S.J., Prin.; Rev. James P. Collins, M.Div., Chap. Priests 2; Sisters of St. Joseph (Brentwood Community) 25; Sisters 1; Lay Teachers 53; Students 1,060.

Catherine McAuley, 710 E. 37th St., 11203. Tel: 718-462-7282; Fax: 718-462-7284.
(Girls). Sr. Peggy Lake, R.S.M., Prin.; Rev. John W. Maloney, Spiritual Dir. Sisters of Mercy 7; Lay Teachers 21; Students 300.

Fontbonne Hall, 9901 Shore Rd., 11209. Tel: 718-748-2244.
(Girls). Sr. Anne P. Clancy, C.S.J., Prin. Sisters of St. Joseph (Brentwood Community) 6; Lay Teachers 29; Students 516.

Nazareth Regional, 475 E. 57th St., 11203. Tel: 718-763-1100.
(Coed). Dr. Robert Muccigrosso, Ph.D., Prin. Sisters 1; Lay Teachers 30; Students 585.

St. Joseph, 80 Willoughby St., 11201. Tel: 718-624-3618; Fax: 718-723-3477.
(Girls). Sr. Eugenia Calabrese, C.S.J., Prin. Sisters of St. Joseph (Brentwood Community) 20; Lay Teachers 18; Students 300.

Xaverian, 7100 Shore Rd., 11209. Tel: 718-836-7100; Fax: 718-836-7114.
(Boys). Mr. Salvatore Ferrera, Pres.; Dr. Joseph Marino, Prin.; Mr. Vincent Torti, Dir. Admissions & Devel.; Mr. George Donnelly, Asst. Prin. Academics; Mr. Robert Maroney, Asst. Prin. Staff Devel.; Mr. Thomas Burns, Asst. Prin. Attendance & Building; Mr. Kevin McCormack, Asst. Prin. Discipline; Mr. Sigfried Heiles, Dir. of Alumni Affairs; Rev. David J. Dettmer, Chap. Priests 1; Xaverian Brothers 10; Lay Teachers 85; Students 1,350.

Queens

ASTORIA. *St. John Preparatory School*, 21-21 Crescent St., 11105-3398. Tel: 718-721-7200.
(Coed). Mr. William A. Higgins, Prin.; Rev. Raymond P. Roden, Spiritual Dir. Priests 2; Sisters 8; Lay Teachers 72; Students 1,380.

BRIARWOOD. *Archbishop Molloy*, 83-53 Manton St., 11435. Tel: 718-441-2100.
(Boys). Bro. Richard Van Houten, F.M.S., Prin. Brothers 22; Sisters 2; Lay Teachers 51; Students 1,450.

COLLEGE POINT. *St. Agnes Academic*, 13-20 124 St., 11356-1814. Tel: 718-353-6276; Fax: 718-353-6068.
(Girls). Sr. Marguerite Warren, Prin. Sisters of St. Dominic (Amityville) 18; Lay Teachers 22; Students 440.

EAST ELMHURST. *Monsignor McClancy*, 71-06 31st Ave., 11370. Tel: 718-898-3800.
(Boys). Bro. Joseph Rocco, S.C., Prin. Brothers 11; Sisters 2; Lay Teachers 30; Boys 700.

FLUSHING. *Holy Cross High School*, 26-20 Francis Lewis Blvd., 11358. Tel: 718-886-7250.
E-mail: hchs@panix.com
Web site: http://www.panix.com/~hchs
(Boys). Bro. Stephen LaMendola, C.S.C., Pres.; Mr. Joseph Giannuzzi, Prin. Brothers of Holy Cross 6; Sisters 1; Lay Teachers 46; Students 965.

FRESH MEADOWS. *St. Francis Preparatory School*, 6100 Francis Lewis Blvd., 11365. Tel: 718-423-8810.
(Coed). Bro. Leonard Conway, O.S.F., Prin.; Rev. William Sweeney, Chap. Priests 1; Franciscan Brothers 15; Sisters 24; Lay Teachers 110; Students 2,850.

JAMAICA. *Dominican Commercial*, 161-06 89th Ave., 11432. Tel: 718-739-2060.
(Girls). Sisters of St. Dominic (Amityville) 15; Lay Teachers/Staff 17; Students 300.

JAMAICA ESTATES. *The Mary Louis Academy (College Preparatory)*, 176-21 Wexford Ter., 11432. Tel: 718-297-2120.
(Girls). Sr. Kathleen McKinney, C.S.J., Prin. Priests 1; Sisters of St. Joseph (Brentwood Community) 30; Sisters of St. Dominic (Amityville) 1; Sisters of Mercy (Brooklyn) 1; Lay Teachers 62; Students 908.

MIDDLE VILLAGE. *Christ the King*, 6802 Metropolitan Ave., 11379. Tel: 718-366-7400.
(Coed). Daughters of Wisdom. Mr. Hugh Kirwan, Prin.; Rev. Anthony S. Ercolano, Chap. Priests 1; Sisters 5; Lay Teachers 88; Students 1,815.

ROCKAWAY PARK. *Stella Maris*, Beach 112th St., 11694. Tel: 718-634-4994.
(Girls). Miss Geri Martinez, Prin. Sisters of St. Joseph (Brentwood) 8; Lay Teachers 42; Students 469.

Maura Clarke Coed Jr. High Program. (Grades 7-8). Mr. Joseph Zoltowski, Dir.

[H] HIGH SCHOOLS PAROCHIAL

BROOKLYN. *Denis Maloney Institute/St. Edmund Preparatory High School*, 2474 Ocean Ave., 11229. Tel: 718-743-6100; Fax: 718-743-5243.
E-mail: dobsephs@connect.com
(Coed). Mr. John P. Lorenzetti, Prin.; Sr. Barbara Doyle, C.S.J., Asst. Prin. Sisters 2; Lay Teachers 31; Students 575.

Our Lady of Perpetual Help, 550-59th St., 11220. Tel: 718-492-5800; 492-2588.
(Girls). Sr. Mary Febronia, C.S.J., Prin.; Ms. Patricia Conley, Asst. Prin. Priests 1; Sisters 9; Lay Teachers 16; Students 220.

St. Saviour, 588 6th St., 11215. Tel: 718-768-4406; Fax: 718-369-2688.
(Girls). Sr. Valeria Belanger, S.S.N.D., Prin.; Mrs. Margaret Bernstein, Asst. Prin. School Sisters of Notre Dame 6; Lay Teachers 23; Students 275.

[I] SPECIAL SCHOOLS

BROOKLYN. *Robert F. Kennedy Incentive Program*, 2635 Linden Blvd., 11208-4992. Tel: 718-235-0744.
(Coed). Bro. Adrian Fannon, O.S.F., Prin. Brothers 1; Lay Teachers 2; Students 66.

St. Francis de Sales School for the Deaf, 260 Eastern Pkwy., 11225. Tel: 718-636-4573; Fax: 718-636-4577.
E-mail: sfdssd@earthlink.net
Infant through Elementary Grades. Edward McCormack, M.A., Supt. Sisters 6; Lay Teachers 55; Students 180.

SPRINGFIELD GARDENS. *Martin de Porres School*, 136-25 218th St., 11413-2226. Tel: 718-525-3414. Specialized day school for emotionally disturbed children, ages 7-21. Brothers 2; Sisters 1; Staff 50; Capacity 156.

[J] ELEMENTARY SCHOOLS PRIVATE

BROOKLYN. *St. Agnes Seminary*, 2221 Avenue R, 11229. Tel: 718-376-2756; Fax: 718-376-8834.
E-mail: dobsc103@connectinc.com
Sr. Grace Eidt, C.S.J., Prin. Sisters of St. Joseph 2; School Sisters of Notre Dame 1; Lay Teachers 14; Students 179.

St. Angela Hall Academy, 290 Washington Ave., 11205. Tel: 718-622-6919. Sr. Mary Sivillo, C.S.J., Prin. Under supervision of Sisters of St. Joseph. Sisters 1; Lay Teachers 9; Students 125.

Visitation Academy, 8902 Ridge Blvd., 11209. Tel: 718-680-9452; Fax: 718-680-4441. Sr. Marie Anatrella, Supr. Sisters of the Visitation 8; Lay Teachers 18; Girls 180.

[K] CONSOLIDATED ELEMENTARY SCHOOLS (REGIONAL)

BROOKLYN. *St. Elizabeth Seton*, 751 Knickerbocker Ave., 11221. Tel: 718-386-4050.
E-mail: dobsc123@connectinc.com
Consolidated from Fourteen Holy Martyrs and St. Martin of Tours. Sr. Mary Tully, C.S.J., Prin. Sisters 3; Lay Teachers 12; Students 395.

St. Frances Cabrini, 181 Suydam St., 11221. Tel: 718-386-9277. Maria Crifasi, Prin. Lay Teachers 10; Students 211.

St. Michael, 237 Jerome St., 11207. Tel: 718-277-6766. Sr. Margaret Merritt, O.P., Prin. Sisters 1; Lay Teachers 16; Students 372.

[L] CATHOLIC CHARITIES

BROOKLYN. *Catholic Charities*, Central Office, 191 Joralemon St., 11201. Tel: 718-722-6000; Fax: 718-722-6096. Most Revs. Thomas V. Daily, D.D., Corp. Member; Joseph M. Sullivan, D.D., M.S., M.P.A., Exec. Vice Pres. & Episcopal Vicar for Human Svcs.; Mr. Thomas A. DeStefano, M.S.W., Exec. Dir.; Mr. Antonio M. Blanco, C.S.W., Assoc. Exec. Dir.; Rev. Msgr. Thomas F. Cribbin, Assoc. Exec. Dir.; Carlo de Rege, M.U.P., Assoc. Exec. Dir.; Robert Siebel, M.S.W., Assoc. Exec. Dir.; Emmie Glynn Ryan, Esq., Dir. Legal Affairs; Sr. Frances Picone, R.S.M., Regl. Admin. Brooklyn East; Sr. Ellen Patricia Finn, O.P., Regl. Admin. Brooklyn West; Robert Marquez, Regl. Admin. Queens North; Robert Mundy, Regl. Admin. Queens South; Rev. Msgr. Joseph Funaro, Special Asst. to Exec. Dir.; Sr. Lorna Colin, C.S.J., Special Asst. to Exec. Dir.; Sr. Kathleen Newell, B.V.M., Special Asst. to Exec. Dir.; Joan M. Murphy, M.A., C.F.R.E., Dir. Public Affairs; Stephanie Raneri, M.A., Dir. Govt. Rels. & Public Policy; Mary O'Reilly, Assoc. Dir. Family Svcs.; Fran Kimmor, Assoc. Dir. Residential Svcs.; Rev. Peter Mahoney, Assoc. Dir. Evaluation; Lisa Rosen, Dir. Quality Assurance; Barbara Conley, M.S.W., Dir. Child Care; Sr. Bernadette Downes, C.I.J., Research & Devel. & Pastoral Svcs.; Sharon Fox, M.S.W., Assoc. Dir. Training; John Tynan, M.U.P., Dir. Housing; Gayle DeRienzis, M.S.W., Assoc. Dir. Targeted Svcs.; Rev. Msgr. Howard B. Basler, M.A., Dir. Social Action & Campaign for Human Devel.; Rosalyn Ferguson, M.S.W., Employee Assistance Prog.; Robert Driscoll, Dir. Employee Rels.; Marie Meyer, Dir. Financial Affairs; Kenneth Haag, Dir. Financial Svcs., B.F.F.Y.; Frank Paterno, Dir. Computer Svcs.; Margaret Keaveney, Coord. Public Rels.
Aging Services:

Golden Age Clubs, 191 Joralemon St., 11201. Tel: 718-722-6022.
Human Services:

Center for Pregnant Women, 191 Joralemon St., 11201. Tel: 718-722-6200.
Family Centers:

Brooklyn West, 191 Joralemon St., 11201. Tel: 718-722-6002.

Brooklyn East, 2341 Coney Island Ave., 11235. Tel: 718-998-7321.

Queens North, 70-11 48th Ave., Woodside, 11377. Tel: 718-899-8493.

Queens South, 90-39 189th St., Hollis, 11423. Tel: 718-217-1238.
Services For Disabled Persons:

Deafness Services, 191 Joralemon St., 11201. Tel: 718-722-6214.
Comprehensive Human Services:

Builders for the Family and Youth of the Diocese of Brooklyn, Inc. Most Rev. Joseph M. Sullivan, Pres.; Mr. Thomas A. De Stefano, Vice Pres. Operations; Mr. Antonio M. Blanco, Vice Pres. Svcs.; Mr. Kenneth Haag, Exec. Sec.
B.F.F.Y. - Administration: Regional Office - Brooklyn West, 191 Joralemon St., 11201. Tel: 718-722-6050. Regional Office - Brooklyn East, 2341 Coney Island Ave., 11235. Tel: 718-788-8422. Regional Office - Queens South, 90-39 189th St., Hollis, 11423. Tel: 718-217-1440. Regional Office - Queens North, 70-11 48th Ave., Woodside, 11377. Tel: 718-899-8487.
Aging Services:

Alzheimers Adult Day Care, 157-16- 65th Ave., Flushing, 11357. Tel: 718-358-3541.

Bayside Senior Center, 221-15 Horace Harding Expwy., Bayside, 11364. Tel: 718-225-1144.

Bayside Senior Services, 45-50 195th St., Flushing, 11358. Tel: 718-357-4903.

Bensonhurst Senior Services Center, 1867 Bath Ave., 11241. Tel: 718-236-3205.

Catherine Sheridan Senior Center, 35-24 83rd St., Jackson Heights, 11372. Tel: 718-458-4600.

Narrows Senior Services Center, 7907 New Utrecht Ave., 11214. Tel: 718-256-1166.

Ozone Park Senior Center, 103-12 101st Ave., Ozone Park, 11420. Tel: 718-847-2100.

Peter J. Della Monica Center for Seniors, 23-56 Broadway, Astoria, 11106. Tel: 718-626-1500.

Richmond Hill Senior Center, 123-08 Jamaica Ave., Richmond Hill, 11418. Tel: 718-846-2511.

Sheepshead Bay Senior Services, 1215 Avenue O, 11230. Tel: 718-375-3377.

Southwest Queens Senior Services, 87-04 88th Ave., Woodhaven, 11421. Tel: 718-847-9200.

St. Charles Jubilee Center, 55 Pierrepont St., 11201. Tel: 718-855-0326.

St. Louis Senior Center, 230 Kingston Ave., 11213. Tel: 718-771-7945.

St. Mary's Senior Center, 10-15 49th Ave., Long Island City, 11101. Tel: 718-729-2688.

Steinway Senior Center, 20-43 Steinway St., Astoria, 11105. Tel: 718-728-8472.

Wakefield Senior Center, 135-45 Lefferts Blvd., South Ozone Park, 11420. Tel: 718-641-0454.

Woodhaven Senior Center, 61-20 Woodside Ave., Woodhaven, 11421. Tel: 718-849-4187.

Woodside Senior Assistance Center, 70-11 48th Ave., Woodside, 11377. Tel: 718-799-1234.
B.F.F.Y. - Child Care & Head Start Programs:

Coney Island Child Care Center, 2757 W. 33rd St., 11224. Tel: 718-946-8759.

Farragut Child Care Center, 32 Navy St., 11201. Tel: 718-875-7555.

J. Di Marco Child Care Center, 36-49 11th St., Long Island City, 11106. Tel: 718-786-1166.

J.F. Kennedy Child Care Center, 103-15 Farragut Rd., 11236. Tel: 718-272-8751.

John Oravecz Child Care Center, 25 Nassau Ave., 11222. Tel: 718-782-2727.

R.F. Kennedy Child Care Center, 741 Flushing Ave., 11206. Tel: 718-782-0766.

Vincent J. Caristo Child Care Center, 5901 13th

Ave., 11219. Tel: 718-853-8300.
De Paul Head Start, 71 Lincoln Pl., 11215. Tel: 718-622-2060.
Madeline Jones Head Start, 3415 Neptune Ave., 11224. Tel: 718-266-5987.
Padre Kennedy Head Start, 288 Berry St., 11211. Tel: 718-387-3679.
St. Barbara's Head Start, 139 Menahan St., 11221. Tel: 718-443-9800.
St. Joseph's Head Start, 300 Vernon Ave., 11206. Tel: 718-455-5900.
St. Margaret Mary Head Start, 9-16 27th Ave., Long Island City, 11102. Tel: 718-721-8065.
Therese Cervini Head Start, 35-34 105th St., Corona, 11368. Tel: 718-478-7786.
St. Malachy Child Development Center, 220 Hendricks St., 11207. Tel: 718-277-0625.
St. Malachy Head Start, 220 Hendricks St., 11207. Tel: 718-277-0625.
B.F.F.Y. - Human Services:
Compeer, 165-15 88th Ave., Jamaica, 11432. Tel: 718-291-4848.
F.A.N. Program, 89-56 162nd St., Jamaica, 11432. Tel: 718-523-2220.
B.F.F.Y. - Mental Health Services:
Bethlehem CSS, 157 Graham Ave., 11211. Tel: 718-963-3958.
Brooklyn Community Living, 2000 Flatbush Ave., 11234. Tel: 718-253-1366.
Corona - Elmhurst Clinic, 37-22 82 St., Jackson Heights, 11372. Tel: 718-779-1600.
Corona Elmhurst Community Support Systems, 37-22 82nd St. & 37-66 72nd St., Jackson Heights, 11372. Tel: 718-779-2803.
Flatbush Addiction Treatment Center, 1457-69 Flatbush Ave., 11234. Tel: 718-951-9009.
Flatlands Guidance Clinic, 2000 Flatbush Ave., 11234. Tel: 718-377-5755.
Glendale Child Guidance Center, 67-29 Myrtle Ave., Glendale, 11385. Tel: 718-456-7001.
Human Outreach Mobile Exc., 492-94 Pacific St., 11201. Tel: 718-875-5015.
Queens Homeless Outreach, 165-15 88th Ave., Jamaica, 11432. Tel: 718-297-4848.
Innovation Club, 80-45 Winchester Blvd., Queens Village, 11427. Tel: 718-468-4700.
Jamaica CSS - Cont. Treatment, 165-15 88th Ave., Jamaica, 11432. Tel: 718-291-4848.
Jamaica CSS - Whitman Home, 160-11 89th Ave., Jamaica, 11432. Tel: 718-291-7173.
Mobile Crisis Psych. Team, 327 Beach 19th St., Far Rockaway, 11694. Tel: 718-337-6800.
On-Site School Project, 67-13 Myrtle Ave., Glendale, 11385. Tel: 718-456-7001.
Partnership of Hope, 715 Dean St., 11238. Tel: 718-398-0409.
Queen Community Living Program, 35-24 83rd St., Jackson Heights, 11372. Tel: 718-639-0700.
Rockaway CSS - Central Manor, 1509 Central Ave., Far Rockaway, 11691. Tel: 718-471-7545.
Rockaway CSS - Surfside Manor, 95-04 Rockaway Beach Blvd., Rockaway Park. Tel: 718-471-7545.
Rockaway CSS - Screening Team, 13-19 Beach Channel Dr., Far Rockaway, 11691. Tel: 718-471-7586.
Rockaway Community Life Skills (Freedom Village), 13-29 Beach Channel Dr., Far Rockaway, 11691. Tel: 718-471-7545.
Rockaway Community Life Skills - Cont. Treatment, 13-19 Beach Channel Dr., Far Rockaway, 11691. Tel: 718-337-6850.
Rockaway Mental Health Services, 13-19 Beach Channel Dr., Far Rockaway, 11691. Tel: 718-337-6800.
Rose House (RCCA), 80-45 Winchester Blvd., Queens Village, 11427. Tel: 718-468-4700.
The Open Door, 2000 Flatbush Ave., 11234. Tel: 718-377-7757.
Woodside Senior Assistance Center, 61-20 Woodside Ave., Woodside, 11377. Tel: 718-799-1234.
Monica House, 161-01 89th Ave., Jamaica, 11432. Tel: 718-657-9027.
B.F.F.Y. - Prevention of Foster Care:
Coney Island Family Resource Center, 2201 Neptune Ave., 11224. Tel: 718-372-6400.
Family Support Center of East New York, 2635 Linden Blvd., 11208. Tel: 718-827-5700.
Jamaica Family & Youth Center, 120-09 141st. St., South Ozone Park, 11432. Tel: 718-738-2500.
B.F.F.Y. - Services for Disabled Persons:
Peter J. Connelly Residence, 15 Willow St., 11201. Tel: 718-625-5590.
Adessa House, 101-38 92 St., Ozone Park, 11416. Tel: 718-848-1940.
Alhambra Day Treatment Center, 11-29 Catherine St., 11211. Tel: 718-388-5900.
Caldwell House, 121-01 116th Ave., South Ozone Park, 11420. Tel: 718-845-1200.
Carmel Residence, 275 N. Eighth St., 11211. Tel: 718-388-6109.
Cribbin House, 218-20 104th Ave., Queens Village, 11429. Tel: 718-776-4190.
Dawson Manor, 94-17 84th St., Ozone Park, 11416. Tel: 718-296-1172.
Donald Savio Residence, 104-22 48th Ave., Corona, 11368. Tel: 718-699-7800.
Fitzpatrick Residence, 240 McKinley Ave., 11208. Tel: 718-647-7070.
Garfield Manor, 305 Garfield Pl., 11215. Tel: 718-622-2100.
Golden Residence, 225 Brooklyn Ave., 11213. Tel: 718-953-4444.
Graci Residence, 132-14 90th St., Ozone Park, 11416. Tel: 718-848-1970.
Helen Owen Carey Residence, 174 Java St., 11222. Tel: 718-383-2451.
McLees House, 112-16 200th St., St. Albans, 11412. Tel: 718-217-0285.
Mugavero Manor, 145-16 Farmers Blvd., Springfield Gardens, 11434. Tel: 718-217-0285.
Mulrooney Manor, 479 E. 29th St., 11226. Tel: 718-287-7553.
Senior F.U.N., 415 Bleeker St., 1121. Tel: 718-417-5316.
Sterling Residence, 152 Sterling St., 11225. Tel: 718-282-8045.
Straus Residence, 3730 Shore Pkwy., 11233. Tel: 718-769-8836.
Supportive Living Apartments, 243 Prospect Park W., 11215. Tel: 718-788-8422.
The Francis De Falco Dental Clinic, 11-29 Catherine St., 11211. Tel: 718-384-0303.
B.F.F.Y. - Services for Persons Living with AIDS:
Circle of Hope, 2341 Coney Island, 11235. Tel: 718-788-8422.
B.F.F.Y. - Youth Services:
N.E. Queens Young Parents, 41-06 163rd St., Flushing, 11358. Tel: 718-217-1238.
N.Q. Parenting Partnership, 70-11 48th Ave., Woodside, 11377. Tel: 718-899-8487.
Project Bridge, 144 Bleeker St., 11221. Tel: 718-455-4649.
Rainbow Workshops for Youth, 144 Bleeker St., 11221. Tel: 718-455-4649.
St. Mary's Youth Center, 10-08 49th Ave., Long Island City, 11101. Tel: 718-899-8487.
Project Reach Out - Youth In Rockaway, 336 Beach 38th St., Far Rockaway, 11691. Tel: 718-217-1238.
Work Experience Program, 191 Joralemon St., 11201. Tel: 718-596-5500.
Housing Development and Management Services:
Progress of Peoples Development Corporation. John Tynan, M.U.P., Dir.
Progress of Peoples Managment Corporation. Maureen McKeown, Dir., Housing Svcs.; Terri Mejillones, Assoc. Dir. Fiscal Svcs.
Housing Corporations:
Bellerose Senior Housing, HDFC, Inc., 191 Joralemon St., 11201.
Bethlehem Community HDFC, Inc., 191 Joralemon St., 11201.
Bishop Boardman Apartments, HDFC, Inc., 191 Joralemon St., 11201.
Bishop Francis J. Mugavero, HDFC, Inc., 191 Joralemon St., 11201.
Sr. Lucian Apartments, HDFC, Inc., 191 Joralemon St., 11201.
Caring Communities Associates, HDFC, Inc., 191 Joralemon St., 11201.
Mary Star of the Sea Apartments, HFDC, Inc., 191 Joralemon St., 11201.
Pope John Paul II, HDFC, Inc., 191 Joralemon St., 11201.
Pierrepont House for the Elderly, Inc., 191 Joralemon St., 11201.
Queens Rehab, 191 Joralemon St., 11201.
St. Brendans Apartments, HDFC, Inc., 191 Joralemon St., 11201.
Msgr. John O'Brien Apts., HDFC, Inc., 191 Joralemon St., 11201.
Msgr. Mullaney Apartments, 191 Joralemon St., 11201.
Long Island City Senior House, 191 Joralemon St., 11201.
Families Together, 191 Joralemon St., 11201.
Parkville, HDFC, 191 Joralemon St., 11201.
Holy Spirit/Rego Park, 191 Joralemon St., 11201.
Msgr. Joseph F. Stedman, HDFC, Inc., 191 Joralemon St., 11201.
161-01 89th Avenue Corp., 191 Joralemon St., 11201.
Our Lady of Fatima Apts., HDFC, Inc., 191 Joralemon St., 11201.
David Minkin Residence, HDFC, Inc., 191 Joralemon St., 11201.
Emmaus of the Diocese of Brooklyn, Inc., 191 Joralemon St., 11201.
St. Pius V, HDFC, Inc., 191 Joralemon St., 11201.
Youth Development and Recreation:
Catholic Youth Organization of the Diocese of Brooklyn, Inc., 191 Joralemon St., 11201. Tel: 718-596-5500.
Nursing Home:
Ss. Joachim & Anne Residence, 2720 Surf Ave., 11224. Tel: 718-714-4800.
Home Care for the Sick:
Care at Home for the Diocese of Brooklyn, Inc., 6910 Fifth Ave., 11209. Tel: 718-238-4700.
Residences for Women:
Providence House, Inc., P.O. Box 210529, 11221. Tel: 718-455-0197. Sr. Marie Leniham, C.S.J., Exec. Dir., Providence House 1, 2518 Church Ave., 11226. Providence House 2, 172 Bainbridge St., 11233. Providence House 3, 159-23 89th Ave., Jamaica, 11432. Providence House 4, 89 Sickles Ave., New Rochelle, 10801. Providence House, 87 Sickles Ave., New Rochelle, 10801. Providence House 5, 396 Lincoln Rd., 11225. Providence House 6, 2876 W. 17 St., 11224.
Community Centers:
Dr. White Community Center, 200 Gold St., 11201. Tel: 718-875-8801.
Bhrags, Inc., 1212 E. New York Ave., 11212. Tel: 718-778-5484. Sr. Rosemary McKenna, D.W., Exec. Dir.
Haitian Center, 1063 Winthrop St., 11212. Tel: 718-778-5485. Edouard Louis, Dir.
Other Affiliated Agencies:
Anthonian Hall, Inc. Thomas A. De Stefano, Treas.; Most Rev. Joseph M. Sullivan, Treas.; Rev. Msgr. Thomas F. Cribbin, Sec.
Catholic Guild for the Blind, Diocese of Brooklyn, Inc. Rev. Msgr. Thomas F. Cribbin.
Ecclesial Consultants, Inc., 191 Joralemon St., 11201. Tel: 718-596-5500.
A management service for Church agencies and organizations. Directors: Most Rev. Joseph M. Sullivan; Rev. Msgr. Emmet Fagan (RVC); Rev. Msgr. Charles J. Fahey (RVC).
Ferrini Welfare League, 98-21 101 Ave., Ozone Park, 11416. Tel: 718-845-0539.
Flowers With Care, Diocese of Brooklyn, Inc., 23-40 Astoria Blvd., Astoria, 11102. Tel: 718-726-9790.
Italian Board of Guardians, 7808 18 Ave., 11214. Tel: 718-232-4242. Rev. Anthony J. Failla, Mod.; Ms. Elise Wunder, Exec. Dir.; Mrs. Beatrice Rizzo, Exec. Sec.
Mary's Hall, Inc. Most Rev. Joseph M. Sullivan, Pres.
Society of St. Vincent de Paul in Diocese of Brooklyn, Central Office, 191 Joralemon St., 11201. Tel: 718-625-1400. Most Rev. Thomas V. Daily, D.D., Spiritual Advisor; Rev. Msgr. James W. Asip, Assoc. Spiritual Advisor; Mr. Joseph Martino, Pres., District Council of Kings, 191 Joralemon St., 11201. Tel: 718-625-1400. Rev. Raymond J. Kelly, S.T.L., Spiritual Advisor; Mr. Frank Mauro, Pres., District Council of Queens, 191 Joralemon St., 11201. Tel: 718-625-1400. Rev. Msgr. James W. Asip, Spiritual Advisor; Mr. Vito Buccaria, Pres.
Catholic Guild for the Blind, Diocese of Brooklyn, Inc. Rev. Msgr. Thomas F. Cribbin.
Bread & Life Soup Kitchen, 75 Lewis Ave., 11206. Tel: 718-574-0058. Rev. James J. Maher, C.M., Pres.

[M] NURSING SERVICES

BROOKLYN. *Nursing Sisters Home Visiting Service, Inc.*, Corporate Office, 310 Prospect Park W., 11215. Tel: 516-683-1370. Sr. Mary Nadine Casey, C.I.J., Pres.; Sr. Agnes Stumpf, C.I.J., Exec. Dir., Nursing Service Offices, Kings County, 310 Prospect Park W., 11215. Tel: 718-965-7339. Mrs. Elise Mattia, Supvr.

[N] HOSPITALS

JAMAICA. *Catholic Medical Center of Brooklyn & Queens*, 88-25 153rd St., 11432. Tel: 718-558-6900
For a complete listing, refer to the Hospitals section.

[O] CHILD CARE AGENCIES

BROOKLYN. *The Angel Guardian Homes*, 6301 12th Ave., 11219. Tel: 718-232-1500; Fax: 718-232-0331. Ms. Sheila N. Pelan, Exec. Dir. Sisters 5; Children in Care 750.
Foster Boarding Home and Adoption Services, 372 Clinton Ave., 11238. Tel: 718-638-7424. Adoption Service and Residence for Mother-Baby.
Preventive Programs, Fort Greene, 430 Myrtle Ave., 11205. Tel: 718-624-2100.
Family Support Center, 57 Willoughby St., 11201. Tel: 718-855-7778.
Catholic Child Care Society of the Diocese of Brooklyn, 540 Atlantic Ave., 11217. Tel: 718-797-6080; Fax: 718-797-6092. John J. Bennett, Jr., Pres.; Cecilia Rivera Healy, C.S.W., Exec. Dir.
Good Shepherd Services, 441 Fourth Ave., 11215. Tel: 718-788-0666. Sr. Paulette LoMonaco, R.G.S., Exec. Dir. Provides a comprehensive range of neighborhood family services to individuals & youth from the South Brooklyn community. Services include educational support, employment, counseling & crisis intervention, literacy, skills training & advocacy

services to children & families as well as foster care & adoption & residences for teenagers.

HeartShare Human Services of New York, Roman Catholic Diocese of Brooklyn, 191 Joralemon St., 11201. Tel: 718-330-0600; Fax: 718-522-4506. E-mail: Heartshare@aol.com Web site: www.heartshare.com William R. Guarinello, M.S., Pres. & CEO. Foster Boarding Home Program, Adoption Program, Family Service Centers. Programs for Developmentally Disabled: Group Homes, Supportive Apartments, Preschool Program (Early Childhood Centers), Respite/ Recreation Program, Day Treatment/Day Habilitation Programs, Services for People with HIV/AIDS, School-Based Beacon Program, Youth Services, Traditional Preschool Program.

HeartShare Human Services - Clinton Residence, 217 Clinton Ave., 11205. Tel: 718-638-2625.

HeartShare Human Services - Clermont Residence, 26 Clermont Ave., 11205. Tel: 718-834-9317.

HeartShare Human Services - Msgr. Thomas G. Hagerty Residence, 128 Montrose Ave., 11206. Tel: 718-387-3595.

HeartShare Human Services - Dr. Catherine White Residence, 175 Metropolitan Ave., 11211. Tel: 718-782-9104.

HeartShare Human Services - Rocco Anthony Torre Residence, 1966 54th St., 11204. Tel: 718-259-4432.

HeartShare Human Services - Antonetta Ferraro Residence, 603 Beach 19 St., Far Rockaway, 11691. Tel: 718-327-9000.

HeartShare Human Services - Thomas J. Cuite Residence, 50-36 45th St., Woodside, 11377. Tel: 718-786-3113.

HeartShare Human Services - 35th Avenue Residence, 172-07 35th Ave., Flushing, 11358. Tel: 718-961-7673.

HeartShare Human Services - Doonan-Drake Residence, 300 E. 18th St., 11226. Tel: 718-469-5000.

HeartShare Human Services - Hart Street Residence, 689 Hart St., 11221. Tel: 718-919-7477.

HeartShare Human Services - James and Kathleen Buckley Residence, 977-979 E. 92nd St., 11236. Tel: 718-272-1441.

HeartShare Human Services - Frances Aiello Day Treatment Center, 163 MacDonough St., 11206. Tel: 718-443-5071.

HeartShare Human Services - Eileen and William Lavin Day Treatment Center, 545 Broadway, 11206. Tel: 718-388-1665.

HeartShare Human Services - John and Lillian Sharkey, Sr. Residence, 60-12 56th St., Maspeth, 11378. Tel: 718-417-6846.

HeartShare Human Services - Harry Hoffman Day Treatment Center, 62-10 Northern Blvd., Woodside, 11377. Tel: 718-899-2752.

HeartShare Human Services - Matilda Raffa Cuomo First Step Early Childhood Center, 115-15 101st Ave., Richmond Hill, 11419. Tel: 718-441-5333.

HeartShare Human Services - Lefferts/Liberty Kiwanis First Step Early Childhood Center, 82-12 151st Ave., Howard Beach, 11414. Tel: 718-848-0300.

HeartShare Human Services - Dolly and Frank Russo Sr. First Step Early Childhood Center, 118-01/03 101 Ave., Richmond Hill, 11419. Tel: 718-805-7117.

HeartShare Human Services - Red Hook Family Services, 732 Henry St., 11231. Tel: 718-858-8387.

HeartShare Human Services - Residential Housing Program, 221 Smith St., 11201. Tel: 718-596-3391.

HeartShare Human Services - South Brooklyn Family Services, 213 Smith St., 11201. Tel: 718-596-3391.

HeartShare Human Services - East Brooklyn Family Services, 3005 Glenwood Rd., 11210. Tel: 718-434-7900.

HeartShare Human Services - Bensonhurst Family Services, 138 Bay 20th St., 11214. Tel: 718-234-1717.

HeartShare Human Services - Beacon & Family Services Program at P.S. 288 Surfside Family Services, 2950 W. 25 St., 11224. Tel: 718-714-0103.

HeartShare Human Services - Community Follow-up Program, 2882 W. 15 St., 11224. Tel: 718-372-0580.

HeartShare Human Services - Bay Ridge Early Childhood Center, 7002 Fourth Ave., 11209. Tel: 718-238-4637.

HeartShare Human Services - Adult Day Habilitation Program, 61-58 Springfield Blvd., Bayside, 11364. Tel: 718-281-0480. Total Assisted 10,291.

HeartShare Human Services - Rita Short Hegarty Residence, 296 Columbia St., 11201. Tel: 718-246-9114.

HeartShare Human Services - Family Support Services Program, 186 Joralemon St., 10th Floor, 11201. Tel: 718-330-1813.

HeartShare Human Services - Supportive Apartment Program, 186 Joralemon St., 9th Floor, 11201. Tel: 718-330-1596.

HeartShare Human Services - Adult Day Habilitation Program, 50 Ct. St., 9th Floor, 11201. Tel: 718-330-2202.

HeartShare Human Services - Foster Care/Adoption Services (Brooklyn Office), 191 Joralemon St., 11201. Tel: 718-330-0600.

HeartShare Human Services - Foster Care/Adoption Services (Queens Office), 90-26 161st St., Jamaica, 11432. Tel: 718-739-5000.

HeartShare Human Services - First Step Early Childhood Evaluation Center, 162-30 Cross Bay Blvd., Howard Beach, 11414. Tel: 718-323-2877.

Little Flower Children's Services, 186 Remsen St., 11201. Tel: 718-260-8840. Rev. Msgr. John T. Fagan, M.S.W., Exec. Vice Pres.; Mary G. Ryder, Exec. Dir.; Sr. Agnese Palczynski, C.S.F.N., Supr. Foster Care, Adoption & Post Adoption Services, Services for Adult MR/DD clients; Residential Treatment Center, U.F.S.D., & Family Day Care at Wading River, NY; Teen Mothers & Infants in Foster Homes.

Mercy Home for Children, 310 Prospect Park W., 11215. Tel: 718-965-7342. Sr. Catherine Crumlish. Under the sponsorship of the Sisters of Mercy. Six Intermediate Care Facilities (Residences) for adolescents & adults who are severely developmentally disabled: Visitation Residence; Harold Warren Residence; M. Vincent Haire Residence; Littlejohn Residence; Santulli Residence; Kevin Keating Residence. Sisters 10; Staff 176; Residents 72.

St. Francis Home for Boys, 132 Eagle St., 11222. Tel: 718-383-9870. Rev. Benedict J. Groeschel, C.F.R., Exec. Dir.; Mr. Joseph Campo, Dir. Residents 5.

St. Joseph Services for Children and Families, 540 Atlantic Ave., 11217. Tel: 718-858-8700. Cecilia Rivera Healy, C.S.W., Exec. Dir. Sisters of Charity of Mount St. Vincent, NY. Programs: Foster Boarding Homes, Group Homes, 24 Hour Emergency Foster Boarding Homes, Adoption Services, Williamsburgh Family Services, Bushwick Family Services, S.T.A.R.S. (Specialized Treatment & AIDS Related Services), Mother/Child Residential Program.

St. Vincent's Services, Inc. (Formerly St. Vincent's Home for Boys and St. Vincent's Hall, Inc.), 66 Boerum Pl., 11201. Tel: 718-522-3700; Fax: 718-875-8536. Rev. Msgr. Robert M. Harris, M.S.W., M.Phil, M.A., Pres. & CEO. Services include: Foster Boarding Homes, Group Homes, Adoption Services, Pediatric AIDS Program, Refugee Assistance Program, Enhanced Independent Living Program, Mental Health Services OutPatient Service, & Residences for the Developmentally Disabled. Sisters 6; Priests 2; Children 1,300.

ROCKAWAY PARK. *St. John's for Boys*, 144-Beach 111 St., 11694. Tel: 718-945-2800. Bro. Thomas N. Trager, S.M., Exec. Dir. Conducted by the Brothers of Society of Mary (Marianists). Residential care for adolescent boys. Diagnostic Reception Centers, Non-Secure Detention/Independent Living Program. Brothers 8; Residents 100.

SEA CLIFF. *St. Christopher-Ottilie*, Park and Downing Aves., 11579. Tel: 516-671-1253; 718-895-8670; Fax: 516-671-2899. Mr. Robert J. McMahon, Exec. Dir.; Mary Hall, Dir. of Intake and Placement. Residential Treatment Center for the profoundly & severely mentally retarded, Intermediate Care Facilities, Group Homes for Adolescent Teenage Boys and Girls, Teen Mother-Child Residence Program, Homeless Program for Teenage Boys, Preventive Programs (3), EFBH Network, Unaccompanied Vietnamese Program, Supervised Independent Living Apartments, Therapeutic Foster Boarding Homes, Residential Treatment Facility, Article 81 School. Regular Foster Care Program for Mentally Retarded Individuals, Crisis Respite, Home & Community Based Waiver Services, Madonna Heights Services. Children 2,650.

[P] GROUP HOMES FOR RETARDED CHILDREN

SPRINGFIELD GARDENS. *Martin De Porres Group Homes*, 136-25 218th St., 11413

For a complete listing, refer to the Special Care Facilities section.

[Q] SUMMER CAMPS AND DAY CAMPS

BROOKLYN. *Bishop McDonnell Camp*, c/o Society of St. Vincent De Paul, 191 Joralemon St., 11201. Tel: 718-625-1400. Joseph E. Collins, Dir. Day Outings for Senior Citizen Groups, Handicapped & Children from poor areas. Sponsored by the Society of St. Vincent de Paul Brooklyn Diocese.

CENTERPORT. *Camp Alvernia*, Prospect Rd., P.O. Box 301, 11721. Tel: 516-261-5730.

Under the supervision of the Franciscan Brothers.

[R] RESIDENCES FOR THE AGED

BROOKLYN. *Bishop Francis J. Mugavero Center for Geriatric Care, Inc.*, 155 Dean St., 11217. Tel: 718-694-6700

For a complete listing, refer to the Special Care Facilities section.

Holy Family Home, 1740 84th St., 11214. Tel: 718-232-3666

For a complete listing, refer to the Special Care Facilities section.

SS. Joachim & Anne Residence, Inc., 2720 Surf Ave., 11224. Tel: 718-714-4800

For a complete listing, refer to the Special Care Facilities section.

BAYSIDE. *Ozanam Hall of Queens Nursing Home, Inc.*, 42-41 201st St., 11361. Tel: 718-423-2000

For a complete listing, refer to the Special Care Facilities section.

JAMAICA. *Msgr. James H. Fitzpatrick Pavilion for Skilled Nursing Care*, 152-11 89th Ave., 11432. Tel: 718-558-2800

For a complete listing, refer to the Special Care Facilities section.

QUEENS VILLAGE. *Queen of Peace Residence*, 110-30 221st St., 11429. Tel: 718-464-1800

For a complete listing, refer to the Special Care Facilities section.

[S] SETTLEMENT ASSOCIATIONS

GLENDALE. *Kolping Center*, 65-04 Myrtle Ave., 11385. Tel: 718-456-7727. Ms. Louise G. Conte, Pres. Legal Title: *Catholic Kolping Society (Katholischer Gesellen Verein) of Brooklyn, Inc.*

[T] CATHOLIC MIGRATION AND REFUGEE OFFICES

BROOKLYN. *Catholic Migration & Refugee Office, Catholic Migration Services, Inc.*, 1258 65th St., 11219. Tel: 718-236-3000; Fax: 718-256-9707. Rev. Ronald T. Marino, Dir. Apostolate Coordinators.

Brazilian Apostolate. Rev. Amarilho Checon, Coord.

Chinese Apostolate-Queens. Rev. Thomas Sung.

Chinese Apostolate-Brooklyn. Rev. John Tan.

Croation Apostolate. Rev. Anton Bozanic, Coord.

Filipino Apostolate. Rev. Eugene Soriano, Coord.

Haitian Apostolate. Rev. Guy Sansaricq, Coord.

Hispanic Ministry Office. Rev. John F. Brogan.

Indian Apostolate. Rev. Paul Vazhapilly, Coord.

Indonesian Apostolate. Rev. Alex Soesilo Wijoyo, S.J., Coord.

Irish Apostolate. Rev. Colm Campbell, Coord.

Italian Apostolate. Rev. John Costello, Coord.

Korean Apostolate. Rev. Ronald Marino, Temporary Coord.

Knanaya Indian Apostolate. Rev. Joseph Saurimakel, Coord.

Nigerian Apostolate. Rev. Louis Uzoh.

Pakistan Apostolate. Rev. Anthony Sikander.

Portuguese Apostolate.

Polish Apostolate. Rev. Peter W. Zendzian, Coord.

Rumanian Apostolate.

Russian Apostolate. Rev. John Soles.

Vietnamese Apostolate. Rev. Luke Pham Anh Du, Coord.

West Indian Apostolate. Rev. Martin J. Carter, S.A., Coord.

Resources, Inc., 1258 65th St., 11219. Tel: 718-236-3000; Fax: 718-256-9707. Rev. Ronald T. Marino, Dir.

Catholic Immigrant Ministries, Inc., 1258 65th St., 11219. Rev. Ronald T. Marino, Dir.

Apostleship of the Sea. Stella Maris Center, 45 DeGraw St., 11231. Tel: 718-834-1234.

[U] MONASTERIES AND RESIDENCES OF PRIESTS AND BROTHERS

BROOKLYN. *Carmelites of Mary Immaculate, Inc.*, 21 Nassau Ave., 11222. Tel: 718-388-5145. Rev. Sebastian Kochuparackal, C.M.I. (India), Supr. & Regl. Coord.

Christian Brothers Residence, 367 Clermont Ave., 11238. Bros. Peter Bonventre, F.S.C.; James Brennan, F.S.C.; David Carroll, F.S.C.; Raphael Cecchini, F.S.C.; Richard Grieco, F.S.C.; Charles Guglielmo, F.S.C.; William Kemmerer, F.S.C.; John McMahon, F.S.C.; Frederick Del Antonio, F.S.C.; Philip Zeller, F.S.C., Dir. Brothers 11.

Curial Residence, 378 Clermont Ave., 11238. Tel: 718-638-0697. Most Rev. Joseph M. Sullivan, M.S.W., D.D.; Rev. Msgr. Austin P. Bennett, J.C.D.; Rev. Thomas Doyle.

Little Brothers of the Gospel, 554 Hart St., 11221. Bros. Rick Dixon; Jay McGowan; Giorgio Gonella.

Oratory of Saint Philip Neri, Congregation Pontifical Rite, 109 Willoughby St., 11201. Tel: 718-875-2096; Fax: 718-875-4678. Very Rev. Dennis M. Corrado, C.O., Provost; Bros. James Simon, C.O.; Joel Warden, C.O.; Revs. Terence P. Gleeson, C.O.; Mark J. Lane, C.O. Priests 3; Brothers 2; Full Member Triennial Seminarian 1.

Our Lady of Good Counsel Residence, 7509 Shore Rd., 11209. Tel: 718-833-1900; Fax: 718-630-5666. Provincial Residence for Redemptorist Fathers and Brothers. Very Rev. George J. Keaveney, C.SS.R., Prov. Supr.; Revs. Patrick F. Woods, C.SS.R., Prov. Vicar; Albert R. Schreiber, C.SS.R., Sec. of Prov.; Francis J. O'Rourke, C.SS.R., Prov. Consultor; Francis P. Nelson, C.SS.R., Procurator; Gerard J. Knapp, C.SS.R., Asst. Procurator; Carl W. Hoegerl, C.SS.R.,

Prov. Archivist. Priests 6; Brothers 1.

St. Casimir's Monastery, Printing Plant and Cultural Center, 361 Highland Blvd., 11207. Tel: 718-235-5962. Franciscan Fathers of the Lithuanian Province of St. Casimir. Most Rev. Paul Baltakis, O.F.M.; Rev. Francis Giedgaudas, O.F.M., Dir. Printery & Supr. Priests 1; Brothers 1.

St. Francis Monastery-Generalate Offices of Franciscan Brothers, 135 Remsen St., 11201-4212. Tel: 718-858-8217. Bros. Kevin Smith, O.S.F., Supr. Gen.; James McVeigh, O.S.F., Vocation Dir.; Joseph Moloney, O.S.F., 1st Councillor; Edward Wesley, O.S.F., 2nd Councillor; Robert Smith, O.S.F., 3rd Councillor; Gabriel O'Brien, O.S.F., 4th Councillor; Timothy Walsh, O.S.F., Bus. Mgr.; Edwin Gill, O.S.F., Treas. Gen. Brothers 108.

St. John the Baptist Rectory, 75 Lewis Ave., 11206. Tel: 718-455-6864. Revs. Stephen M. Grozio, C.M., Pastor; Thomas S. Krafinski, C.M.; Joseph V. Agostino, C.M.; John P. Timlin, Supr.; Bro. Joseph Tauraso, C.M.

St. Joseph's Priest Residence, 256 Clinton Ave., 11205. Tel: 718-783-4989. Rev. Msgr. Thomas F. Cribbin; Rev. Msgr. Howard B. Basler, S.T.B., M.A.; Rev. Msgr. Martin Bannan, B.A., M.S.W.; Rev. Robert Frueh, M.S.

St. Michael's Friary, 225 Jerome St., 11207. Tel: 718-827-6990. Revs. Philip Bohan, O.F.M.Cap., Pastor; Raphael Iannone, O.F.M.Cap., Supr. & Co-Dir. of Capuchin Postulancy Prog.; William Hugo, O.F.M.Cap., Friary Vicar & Co-Dir. of Capuchin Postulancy Prog. In res. Gavin Reilly, O.F.M.Cap., Parochial Asst. Priests 4; Postulants 5.

DOUGLASTON. *Bishop Mugavero Residence*, 7200 Douglaston Pkwy., 11362. Tel: 718-229-8001; Fax: 718-229-2658. Rev. Jeffry T. Dillon, Dir. In res. Rev. Msgr. George T. Deas; Rev. Msgr. Francis X. Mulhall; Rev. Msgr. George V. Fogarty; Rev. Msgr. Edward W. Jolley; Rev. Msgr. James L. Tahaney; Revs. Louis B. Bartruff; Harold A. Buetow; Harry M. Culkin; John F. Cronin; Raymond J. Morgan; John F. Oravecz; John L. Pakalniskis; Francis S. Pullo; Stanislaus Raila; Robert Young; Barnabas Wang; Robert F. Milde; John L. Abrama; Anthony Grillo; Anthony Luis; William J. McLoughlin; Edward J. McNicholas.

Institutional Services Residence, 7200 Douglaston Pkwy., 11362-1997. Tel: 718-229-8290; Fax: 718-279-3004. Rev. Michael J. Hardiman, Exec. Dir.; Mr. Robert Rymers, Dir. Oper.; Mr. Thomas D. Flynn, Controller; Mr. Frederick Publisi, Dir. Purchasing.

ELMHURST. *Congregation of St. John the Baptist of China*, 55-21 92nd St., 11373. Tel: 718-592-5981; Fax: 718-271-3215. Revs. Thomas Sung, C.S.J.B. (Taiwan), Prior; Dehua Zhang, C.S.J.B.; Bro. Silvester Liang, C.S.J.B. Priests 6; Brothers 12.

FOREST HILLS. *Augustinian Fathers-Province of Castile, Spain*, 111-41 77th Ave., 11375. Tel: 718-575-3546. Rev. Manuel J. Rodriguez, O.S.A.

JAMAICA. *Immaculate Conception Monastery*, 86-45 Edgerton Blvd., 11432. Tel: 718-739-6502; Fax: 718-657-0578. Very Rev. Justin Kerber, C.P., Rector; Revs. Stanislaus Wasek, C.P., Vice Rector; Giles Ahrens, C.P.; Lawrence Bellew, C.P., Chap.; Jerome Bracken, C.P.; Albert Catanzaro, C.P.; Paul Chenot, C.P., Chap.; Theophane Cooney, C.P., Asst. Pastor; Paul Joseph Fullam, C.P.; Mario Gallipoli, C.P.; Bernardine Grande, C.P.; Thomas Griffiths, C.P.; Joseph D. Guzinski, C.P.; Colman Haggerty, C.P.; Arnold Horner, C.P.; Ernest Hotz, C.P.; Thomas Joyce, C.P., Pastor; Owen Lally, C.P.; Dominic Papa, C.P., Dir., Preaching Office; Albert Pellicane, C.P., Chap.; John Chrysostom Ryan, C.P.; Theodore Walsh, C.P.; Nicholas Zitz, C.P.; Neil Davin, C.P.; John Douglas, C.P.; John R. Mescall, C.P.; John P. Moore, C.P.; Kenan Peters, C.P.; Claudio Piccinini, C.P.; James Price, C.P., Vocation Dir.; Lawrence Rywalt, C.P.; Robin Ryan, C.P., Retreat Dir.; Cletus Dawson, C.P.; Angelo Iacovone, C.P.; Henry Kavanagh, C.P.; Neil Tiedemann, C.P.; James O'Shea, C.P.; Bros. Vincent Basile, C.P., Econome; Philip Maggiulli, C.P.; Kenneth Pughe, C.P.; Angelo Sena, C.P.; Paul J. Morgan, C.P.; Anselm Catalucci, C.P. Priests 37; Brothers 6. Marist Brothers of Ulster County, 83-53 Manton St., 11435-1697.

Parsons Manor, 88-25 153rd St., 11432. Tel: 718-558-2000. Revs. John L. Kiernan; Daniel J. Sheehan; Romano J. Ferraro; Jose Cadusale (Philippines); James P. Sweeney.

Saint Charles House of Studies, 168-41 84th Ave., 11432. Tel: 718-526-3917. Rev. Mariano Cisco, C.S., Rector.

St. Vincent's House, 84-15 Kendrick Pl., 11432. Tel: 718-262-8265. Vincentian Fathers. Revs. James O. Kiernan, C.M.; Joseph V. Daly, C.M., Supr.; Joseph P. Foley, C.M.; John B. Freund, C.M.; Donald J. Harrington, C.M.; James J. Maher, C.M.; John McKenna, C.M.; Bernard M. Tracey, C.M.; Robert R. Vignola, C.M.; Thomas A. Casella, C.M.; Dennis Holtschneider, C.M.

Vincentian Residence, St. John's University, 8000 Utopia Pkwy., 11439. Tel: 718-990-6744. Revs. Michael J. Carroll, C.M., Supr.; Peter J. Albano, C.M.; Michael J. Callahan; Thomas V. Concagh, C.M.; Stephen J. Denig, C.M.; James Dorr, C.M.; Peter D. Goldbach, C.M.; Richard J. Kehoe; James Kelly, C.M.; John McDonnell, C.M.; James A. Morris; Michael F. Mullen, C.M.; John B. Murray, C.M.; David M. O'Connell, C.M.; Joseph M. O'Donnell, C.M.; Martin Peterson, C.M.; Thomas Prior, C.M.; Kenneth F. Slattery, C.M.; Daniel J. Sullivan, C.M.; Robert J. Swain; Michael D. Whalen, C.M.; Bro. Carmen V. Ciardullo, C.M.

JAMAICA ESTATES. *Paulist Fathers - Generalate*, 86-11 Midland Pkwy., 11432. Tel: 718-291-5995.

KEW GARDENS. *St. Columbans Foreign Mission Society*, 118-32 80 Rd., 11415. Tel: 718-847-3700; Fax: 718-847-3702. Revs. Patrick Meehan, S.S.C.; James D. Dwyer, S.S.C.; Gerard A. Markey, S.S.C. Priests 3.

LONG ISLAND CITY. *Holy Ghost Fathers of Ireland*, 48-49 37th St., 11101. Tel: 718-729-5273; Fax: 718-729-6949. Very Rev. Vincent O'Connell, C.S.Sp., Prov. Delegate; Revs. Michael J. McCarthy, C.S.Sp.; Patrick Holohan, C.S.Sp.; James Delaney, C.S.Sp.

OZONE PARK. *Montfort Missionaries Provincialate - for Nation Community*, 101-18 104th St., 11416. Tel: 718-849-5885; 849-1684 (Nation); 849-0071 (Vocations). Revs. Gerald J. Fitzsimmons, S.M.M., Prov. Supr.; Matthew J. Considine, S.M.M., Prov. Treas.; James Brady, S.M.M., Formation Dir.; Roy Tvrdik, S.M.M., Vocation Dir.; Frank Setzer, S.M.M., (Retired). Priests 4.

Priests of Province Serving Abroad: Revs. Everett Brown, S.M.M.; Peter D'Abele, S.M.M., Chontales, Nicaragua; John Breslin, S.M.M., Dominican Republic; William J. Considine, S.M.M., Superior General, Rome, Italy.

QUEENS VILLAGE. *DePaul Residence*, 80-14 217th St., 11427. Revs. Richard J. Devine, C.M.; Stephen C. Bicsko, C.M.; Michael J. Cummins, C.M.; John D. McElynn, C.M.

SOUTH OZONE PARK. *Sacred Heart Provincialate*. (NY Province), 141-11 123 Ave., 11436-1426. Tel: 718-322-3309; Fax: 718-529-6004.
E-mail: bro_rocco@prodigy.net
Bro. Joseph Rocco, S.C., Prov. Brothers 3.

SPRINGFIELD GARDENS. *Martin De Porres Brothers Community*, 136-01 219th St., 11413. Tel: 718-978-7155; Fax: 718-525-0982.

[V] CONVENTS AND RESIDENCES FOR SISTERS

BROOKLYN. *Congregation of the Infant Jesus*, 310 Prospect Park W., 11215. Tel: 718-965-7300. Sr. Mary Louise Kelly, C.I.J., Pres. Nursing Sisters of the Sick Poor-Congregation of the Infant Jesus. Sisters 76.

Discalced Carmelite Nuns, 745 St. John's Pl., 11216.

Franciscan Sisters of the Poor, Congregational Office, 133 Remsen St., 11201. Tel: 718-643-1919; Fax: 718-643-9710. Sr. Jeanne M. Glisky, S.F.P.

Missionaries of Charity, Contemplative Our Lady of Lourdes Convent, 34 Aberdeen St., 11207. Tel: 718-443-2868. Sr. M. Maria, M.C., Supr. Sisters 6.

Monastery of the Sisters Adorers of the Precious Blood, 54th St. and Ft. Hamilton Pkwy., 11219. Sr. Mary Mediatrix; Rev. Msgr. Joseph K. Parks, Dir. Confraternity of the Precious Blood; Rev. Msgr. Philip J. Reilly, Chap. Sisters 17.

Monastery of the Visitation, 8902 Ridge Blvd., 11209. Tel: 718-745-5151; Fax: 718-680-4441. Marie Anatrella, Supr. Professed Sisters 22.

Motherhouse and Convent of the Sisters of Mercy of the Americas, Brooklyn Regional Community, 273 Willoughby Ave., 11205. Tel: 718-622-5840. Sr. Camille D'Arienzo, R.S.M., Pres. Sisters 29.

Sisters of the Good Shepherd, 348 Ninth St., 11215. Tel: 718-499-9212. Sisters 2. 420 E. 5th St., 11218. Tel: 718-851-4844. Provincial Office, 82-31 Dancaster Pl., Jamaica, 11432.

JAMAICA. *Provincialate of the Sisters of the Good Shepherd*, 82-31 Doncaster Pl., 11432. Tel: 718-380-3270; Fax: 718-591-9376. Legal Title: *Sisters of the Good Shepherd, Province of New York*. Sr. Helene Hayes, R.G.S.; Margaret Miley, Prov. Sec. Sisters 3.

Ursuline Provincial Administration Office, Glengarda, 81-15 Utopia Pkwy., 11432. Tel: 718-591-0681; Fax: 718-969-4275. Sr. Catherine Talia, O.S.U., Prov. Supr.

QUEENS VILLAGE. *Little Sisters of the Poor*, Provincial Residence, 110-30 221st St., 11429. Tel: 718-464-1800. Mother Genevieve Regina, L.S.P., Prov. Sisters 173; Fraternity Jeanne Jugan 3.

St. Ann's Novitiate, Little Sisters of the Poor, 110-39 Springfield Blvd., P.O. Box 280356, 11428. Tel: 718-464-4920; Fax: 718-479-3126. Sr. Mary Richard, L.S.P., Supr. & Mistress of Novices; Rev. Msgr. Thomas C. Clancy, Chap. Sisters 7; Novices 10; Postulants 5.

REGO PARK. *Blessed Trinity Missionary Cenacle*, 85-10 61 Rd., 11374. Tel: 718-424-7563. Parish Social Ministry, Ministry to the Handicapped, Elderly, Bereaved and Homebound. Missionary Servants of the Most Blessed Trinity 3.

RIDGEWOOD. *Convent of the Sisters of Mary Reparatrix*, 62-67 60 Pl., 11385. Tel: 718-456-4242: 386-1107 (Altar Bread Department); Fax: 718-386-1107. Sr. Patricia Mullen, S.M.R., Supr. Sisters 7.

ROCKAWAY PARK. *Stella Maris Convent, Sisters of St. Joseph*, 11694-2497. Sisters 15.

[W] EVANGELIZATION AND RENEWAL CENTERS

BROOKLYN. *Centro Evangelizacion San Vicente de Paul*, 118 Congress St., 11201. Tel: 718-624-5670. Revs. Jose Barcelo, C.M. (Spain), Dir. & Dir. of Cursillo Movement; Balduino Martinez, C.M. (Spain), Dir. of Jornada Movement.

ASTORIA. *St. Paul Center*, 21-35 Crescent St., 11105. Tel: 718-932-0752. Rev. Joseph T. Holcomb, Dir. Staff: Mrs. Carolyn Conides; Mr. Phil Crivelli; Mrs. Carmela Crivelli; Deacon Len Sclafani; Ms. Maureen Powers, Sec. Center for Lay Spirituality; American Cursillo in English; Christian Awakening.

FLUSHING. *Cenacle Center for Spiritual Renewal*, 154-27 Horace Harding Expwy., 11367. Tel: 718-463-2073. Sr. Mary F. Walsh, R.C., Contact Person.

JAMAICA. *Bishop Molloy Retreat House for Laymen*, 86-45 Edgerton Blvd., 11432. Tel: 718-739-1229. Passionist Fathers. Rev. Robin Ryan, C.P., Retreat Dir. Associates: Revs. John Patrick Moore, C.P.; Lawrence Ryalt, C.P.; Sr. Sabyna Schmitz, R.S.H.M.

[X] SECULAR INSTITUTES

BROOKLYN. *The Institute of Apostolic Oblates*, 730 E. 87th St., 11236. Tel: 718-649-0324; Fax: 718-272-5012. Giovanna Piccioli, Local Mod.

[Y] MISCELLANEOUS LISTINGS

BROOKLYN. *Bay Webster Corporation, Inc.*, 143 Bay 20th St., 11214. Mailing Address: 214 W. Maple Ave., Merchantville, NJ, 08109. Very Rev. Peter T. Sticco, S.A.C., Pres.

Clermont Residence, 26 Clermont Ave., 11205. Tel: 718-834-9317; Fax: 718-834-9364. Miss Sharon Bewry, Res. Mgr. Residence for Developmentally Disabled Adults.

En El, Inc., 75 Greene Ave., 11238.

Good Shepherd Volunteers, Saint Germaines Services, 235 Prospect Park W., 11215. Tel: 718-768-8452. Sr. Maureen McGowan, R.G.S., Dir.

Jornada Movement, 118 Congress St., 11201. Tel: 718-624-5670. Rev. Balduino Martinez, C.M. (Spain), Dir.

Latvian Roman Catholic Mission. (Our Lady of Aglona Center), 361 Highland Blvd., 11207. Rev. Msgr. Leons Varna, S.T.D., Dir.

Mercy Montessori School, 1397 Brooklyn Ave., 11203. Tel: 718-469-2834. Sr. Mary Harvey, R.S.M., Dir.

National Center of the Haitian Apostolate, 455 E. 29th St., 11226. Tel: 718-856-3323. Rev. Guy Sansaricq, Exec. Dir.

Neighbors Together, 160 Thomas S. Boyland St., P.O. Box 330-562, 11233. Tel: 718-498-7256. Anne Kohler, Exec. Dir. Services for the Poor. Soup Kitchen and Social Services Advocacy.

New Horizons Adult Education Program, Inc., St. John's Center, 75 Lewis Ave., 11206. Tel: 718-455-1166; 455-1033; Fax: 718-452-3047. Sr. Ann Spencer, D.C., Exec. Dir.

Pro Sanctity Movement, 730 E. 87th St., 11236. Tel: 718-649-0324; Fax: 718-272-5012. Ms. Gloria Florez, Co-Dir.; Mrs. Liz Shellman, Co-Dir.; Rev. John J. Costello, Spiritual Advisor.

The Roman Catholic Pontifical Lay Association Memores Domini, 181 Senator St., 11220. Tel: 718-833-3992; Fax: 718-833-7374.

Men's House, 181 Senator St., 11220. Tel: 718-833-3992. Angelo Sala, Head of the House.

Women's House, 1122 71 St., 11228. Tel: 718-745-3649. Elvira Parravicini, Head of the House.

St. James Cathedral Foundation, Inc., 250 Cathedral Pl., 11201. Tel: 718-852-4002. Rev. Msgr. John C. Tosi, Sec.

St. John's Bread & Life Program, Inc. (Soup Kitchen, Employment Counseling, HIV/AIDS Support Group/ Food Pantry, Counseling, Referrals and Advocacy), 75 Lewis Ave., 11206. Tel: 718-574-0058. Mr. Hossein Saadat, M.S.A., Exec. Dir.; Sr. Bernadette Szyhczak, D.C., Soup Kitchen Coord.

**The Maura Clarke Ita Ford Center*, 138 Bleeker St., 11221. Tel: 718-452-0167; Fax: 718-452-5173. Sr. Mary Burns, S.C., Co-Dir.; Sr. Mary Dowd, O.S.U., Co-Dir.

ASTORIA. *Flowers With Care Youth Services, Diocese of Brooklyn, Inc.*, 23-40 Astoria Blvd., 11102. Tel: 718-726-9790. Paula Beltrone, Exec. Dir.

BAYSIDE. *Oznam Geriatric Foundation*, 42-41 201 St., 11361.

BRENTWOOD. *Congregation of the Sisters of St. Joseph*,

Charitable Trust, Brentwood Rd., 11717-5587. Sr. Joan Larkin, Treas.

DOUGLASTON. *Brooklyn-Queens Environmental Management Corporation*, Immaculate Conception Center, 7200 Douglaston Pkwy., 11362. Tel: 718-229-8001. James A. O'Brien. Legal Title: *Brooklyn-Queens Environmental Management Corporation of the Roman Catholic Diocese of Brooklyn.*

Society of the Immaculate Conception of Brooklyn. (Missionary Society), 7200 Douglaston Pkwy., 11362. Tel: 718-229-8001, Ext. 743. Rev. John J. Brogan, Exec. Dir.

JAMAICA. *Mary Immaculate, Inc.*, 88-25 153rd St., 11432. Tel: 718-558-6900.

Vincentian Service Corps.-East Inc., Saint John's University - SVH 102, 11439. Tel: 718-990-6266; Fax: 718-990-8939. A program for laywomen and men willing to commit to one year of service to the poor. Rev. Paul K. Cavanaugh, C.M., Dir.

QUEENS. *Focolare Movement.* Queens Office, 6359 83rd St., Middle Village, 11379. Tel: 718-898-2611.

ROCKVILLE CENTRE.

**Women Helping Women*, 255 Merrick Rd., 11570.

RELIGIOUS INSTITUTES OF MEN REPRESENTED IN THE DIOCESE

For further details refer to the corresponding bracketed number in the Religious Institutes of Men or Women section.

[0140]—*The Augustinians.*—O.S.A.
[1350]—*Brothers of St. Francis Xavier.* (Sacred Heart Prov.).—C.F.X.
[0330]—*Brothers of the Christian Schools.*—F.S.C.
[0600]—*Brothers of the Congregation of Holy Cross.*—C.S.C.
[1100]—*Brothers of the Sacred Heart.*—S.C.
[0470]—*The Capuchin Friars.* (Prov. of St. Mary).—O.F.M.Cap.
[0270]—*Carmelite Fathers & Brothers.* (St. Elias Prov.).—O.Carm.
[1330]—*Congregation of the Mission.* (Eastern, New England, Spanish Provs.).—C.M.
[1210]—*Congregation of the Missionaries of St. Charles.*—C.S.
[1000]—*Congregation of the Passion.* (Prov. of St. Paul of the Cross).—C.P.
[0480]—*Conventual Franciscans.* (Polish Prov.).—O.F.M.Conv.
[0490]—*Franciscan Brothers of Brooklyn.*—O.S.F.
[0520]—*Franciscan Friars.* (Immaculate Conception Prov.; Lithuanian Vicariate).—O.F.M.
[0650]—*Holy Ghost Fathers.*—C.S.Sp.
[0690]—*Jesuit Fathers and Brothers.* (New York Prov.).—S.J.
[0770]—*The Marist Brothers.*—F.M.S.
[0780]—*The Marist Fathers.*—S.M.
[0870]—*Montfort Missionaries.*—S.M.M.
[0950]—*Oratorians.* (Brooklyn).—C.O.
[0610]—*Priests of the Congregation of Holy Cross.* (Eastern Prov.).—C.S.C.
[1070]—*The Redemptorists.*—C.SS.R.
[0760]—*Society of Mary (Marianists).* (New York Prov.).—S.M.
[0370]—*Society of St. Columban.*—S.S.C.
[0990]—*Society of the Catholic Apostolate.*—S.A.C.
[1200]—*Society of the Divine Savior.*—S.D.S.

RELIGIOUS INSTITUTES OF WOMEN REPRESENTED IN THE DIOCESE

[]—*Altagracia Sisters.* (Dominican Republic).
[0340]—*Carmelite Sisters of Charity.*—C.Ch.
[0330]—*Carmelite Sisters of the Aged and Infirm.*—O.Carm.
[2980]—*Congregation of Notre Dame.*—C.N.D.
[2950]—*Congregation of Notre Dame de Sion.*—N.D.S.
[]—*Congregation of Olivetan Benedictine Sisters.* (Korea).
[]—*Congregation of Our Lady of Sion.*
[3110]—*Congregation of Our Lady of the Retreat in the Cenacle.*—R.C.
[2230]—*Congregation of the Infant Jesus.*—C.I.J.
[0760]—*Daughters of Charity of St. Vincent de Paul.*—D.C.
[0960]—*Daughters of Wisdom.*—D.W.
[0420]—*Discalced Carmelite Nuns.*—O.C.D.
[1070-01]—*Dominican Sisters.*—O.P.
[1070-02]—*Dominican Sisters.*—O.P.
[1070-05]—*Dominican Sisters.*—O.P.
[1070-06]—*Dominican Sisters.*—O.P.
[1070-11]—*Dominican Sisters.*—O.P.
[1400]—*Franciscan Missionary Sisters of the Sacred Heart.*—F.M.S.C.
[1180]—*Franciscan Sisters of Allegany, NY.*—O.S.F.
[1425]—*Franciscan Sisters of Peace.*—F.S.P.
[1420]—*Franciscan Sisters of Ringwood.*—F.S.R.
[1470]—*Franciscan Sisters of St. Joseph.*—F.S.S.J.
[1190]—*Franciscan Sisters of the Atonement.*—S.A.
[]—*Franciscan Sisters of the Immaculate (Honduras).*—H.F.I.
[1440]—*Franciscan Sisters of the Poor.*—S.F.P.
[1840]—*Grey Nuns of the Sacred Heart.*—G.N.S.H.
[]—*Little Sisters of the Gospel.* (France).—L.S.G.
[2340]—*Little Sisters of the Poor.*—L.S.P.
[2420]—*Marist Missionary Sisters (Missionary Sisters of the Society of Mary) Inc.*—S.M.S.M.
[2470]—*Marknoll Sisters of St Dominic.*—M.M.
[2710]—*Missionaries of Charity.*—M.C.
[2860]—*Missionaries of the Sacred Heart.*—M.S.C.
[1360]—*Missionary Franciscan Sisters of the Immaculate Conception.*—O.S.F.
[2790]—*Missionary Servants of the Most Blessed Trinity.*—M.S.B.T.
[3160]—*Parish Visitors of Mary Immaculate.*—P.V.M.I.
[2070]—*Religious of the Holy Union of the Sacred Hearts.*—S.U.S.C.
[3465]—*Religious of the Sacred Heart of Mary.*—R.S.H.M.
[3430]—*Religious Teachers Filippini.*—M.P.F.
[2970]—*School Sisters of Notre Dame.* (Wilton, CT; Baltimore, MD).—S.S.N.D.
[0110]—*Sisters Adorers of the Precious Blood.*—A.P.B.
[0650]—*Sisters of Charity of St. Vincent de Paul of New York.*—S.C.
[0640]—*Sisters of Charity of St. Vincent de Paul, Halifax.*—S.C.
[0430]—*Sisters of Charity of the Blessed Virgin Mary.*—B.V.M.
[1000]—*Sisters of Divine Providence of Kentucky.*—C.D.P.
[2575]—*Sisters of Mercy of the Americas.* (Brooklyn, NY; Dallas, TX).—R.S.M.
[3000]—*Sisters of Notre Dame de Namur.*—S.N.D.deN.
[2670]—*Sisters of Our Lady of Mercy.*—S.O.L.M.
[3820]—*Sisters of St. John the Baptist.*—C.S.J.B.
[3830-05]—*Sisters of St. Joseph.*—C.S.J.
[3140]—*Sisters of the Catholic Apostolate-Pallottine.*—C.S.A.C.
[3180]—*Sisters of the Cross and Passion.*—C.P.
[1830]—*Sisters of the Good Shepherd.*—R.G.S.
[1970]—*Sisters of the Holy Family of Nazareth.* (Immaculate Heart of Mary Prov.).—C.S.F.N.
[3320]—*Sisters of the Presentation of the B.V.M.*. (Newburgh).—P.B.V.M.
[2160]—*Sisters, Servants of the Immaculate Heart of Mary.*—I.H.M.
[2460]—*Society of Mary Reparatrix.*—S.M.R.
[4070]—*Society of the Sacred Heart.*—R.S.C.J.
[4130]—*Ursuline Sisters of the Congregation of Tildonk, Belgium.*—O.S.U.
[4190]—*Visitation Nuns.*—V.H.M.

DIOCESAN CEMETERIES

BROOKLYN. *Holy Cross*, Brooklyn & Tilden Ave., 11203. Rev. Msgr. Anthony J. Barretta, Chap.

FARMINGDALE. *Resurrection*, Conklin St., 11735. Tel: 516-249-8700.

St. Charles, Conklin St., 11735. Tel: 516-249-8700. Rev. Msgr. August C. Bednartz, Chap.

FLUSHING. *Mount St. Mary*, 172-00 Booth Memorial Ave., 11365. Tel: 718-353-1560. Rev. Romano Zanon, Chap.

MIDDLE VILLAGE. *St. John's.* Administration Offices for the Diocesan Cemeteries. 80-01 Metropolitan Ave., 11379. Tel: 718-894-4888. Rev. Ralph Guarracino, Chap.

PARISH CEMETERIES

AMITYVILLE. *Most Holy Trinity.* Most Holy Trinity Parish, Brooklyn.

Trinity. Most Holy Trinity Parish, Brooklyn.

ROCKAWAY. *St. Mary Star of the Sea*, Rockaway Blvd., 11691. Tel: 718-894-4888.

NECROLOGY

(No Deaths)

Diocese of Brownsville

(Dioecesis Brownsvillensis)

Most Reverend

RAYMUNDO J. PENA, D.D.

Bishop of Brownsville; ordained May 25, 1957; appointed Titular Bishop of Trisipa and Auxiliary of San Antonio October 16, 1976; consecrated December 13, 1976; appointed Bishop of El Paso April 29, 1980; installed June 18, 1980; appointed Bishop of Brownsville May 23, 1995; installed August 6, 1995. *Mailing Address: P.O. Box 2279, Brownsville, TX, 78522-2279.*

Most Reverend

JOHN J. FITZPATRICK, D.D.

Retired Bishop of Brownsville; ordained December 13, 1942; appointed Auxiliary of Miami June 24, 1968; consecrated August 28, 1968; appointed Bishop of Brownsville April 27, 1971; installed May 27, 1971; retired November 30, 1991. *Mailing Address: P.O. Box 2279, Brownsville, TX, 78522-2279.*

ESTABLISHED JULY 10, 1965.

Square Miles 4,226.

Comprises the four Counties of Cameron, Hidalgo, Starr and Willacy in the State of Texas.

For legal titles of parishes and diocesan institutions, consult the Catholic Pastoral Center.

Catholic Pastoral Center: 1910 E. Elizabeth St., P.O. Box 2279, Brownsville, TX, 78522-2279. Tel.: 956-542-2501; Fax: 956-542-6751.

E-mail address: cathdioc@aol.com

STATISTICAL OVERVIEW

Personnel	
Bishop	1
Retired Bishops	1
Priests: Diocesan Active in Diocese	36
Priests: Active Outside Diocese	4
Priests: Diocesan in Foreign Missions	2
Priests: Retired, Sick or Absent	15
Number of Diocesan Priests	57
Religious Priests in Diocese	47
Extern Priests in Diocese	7
Ordinations:	
Religious Priests	1
Permanent Deacons in Diocese	83
Total Brothers	16
Total Sisters	127
Parishes	
Parishes	63
With Resident Pastor:	
Resident Diocesan Priests	24
Resident Religious Priests	27
Without Resident Pastor:	
Administered by Priests	1
Administered by Pastoral Teams, etc.	11
Missions	46
Pastoral Centers	1
Professional Ministry Personnel:	
Brothers	4
Sisters	24
Lay Ministers	121
Welfare	
Health Care Centers	2
Total Assisted	265
Homes for the Aged	2
Total Assisted	1,550
Day Care and Extended Day Care Centers	1
Total Assisted	81
Specialized Homes	1
Total Assisted	482
Special Centers for Social Services	4
Total Assisted	28,135
Other Institutions	2
Total Assisted	1,975
Educational	
Diocesan Students in Other Seminaries	8
Total Seminarians	8
High Schools, Private	1
Total Students	669
Elementary Schools, Diocesan and Parish	6
Total Students	2,035
Elementary Schools, Private	2
Total Students	552
Catechesis/Religious Education:	
High School Students	7,066
Elementary Students	24,725
Total Students Under Catholic Instruction	35,055
Teachers in the Diocese:	
Brothers	3
Sisters	20
Lay Teachers	215
Vital Statistics	
Receptions into the Church:	
Infant Baptism Totals	5,607
Adult Baptism Totals	2,615
Received into Full Communion	486
First Communions	6,346
Confirmations	2,468
Marriages:	
Catholic	1,388
Interfaith	105
Total Marriages	1,493
Deaths	2,407
Total Catholic Population	748,326
Total Population	923,859

Former Prelates—Rt. Rev. DOMINIC MANUCY, Titular Bishop of Delma and Vicar Apostolic of Brownsville; cons. Dec. 8, 1874; transferred to Mobile, March 9, 1884 reappointed to Vicariate Apostolic of Brownsville, Feb. 1, 1885; died Dec. 4, 1885.—Rt. Rev. PETER VERDAGUER, Titular Bishop of Aulon and Vicar Apostolic of Brownsville; cons. Nov. 9, 1890; died Oct. 26, 1911.—Rt. Rev. CLAUDE JAILLET, O.P., Administrator of Vicariate Apostolic of Brownsville, 1911-1913.

Former Bishops—Most Rev. ADOLPH MARX, D.D., J.C.D., First Bishop of Brownsville; ord. May 2, 1940; appt. Titular Bishop of Citrus and Auxiliary Bishop of Corpus Christi, July 6, 1956; cons. Oct. 9, 1956; appt. first Bishop of Brownsville, July 19, 1965; installed Sept. 2, 1965; died in Cologne, Germany Nov. 1, 1965.—His Eminence HUMBERTO CARDINAL MEDEIROS, D.D., second Bishop of Brownsville; appt. April 14, 1966; cons. June 9, 1966; installed Bishop of Brownsville, June 29, 1966; appt. Archbishop of Boston, Sept. 8, 1970; installed Archbishop of Boston, Oct. 7, 1970; created Cardinal, March 5, 1973; died Sept. 17, 1983.—Most Rev. JOHN J. FITZPATRICK, third Bishop of Brownsville; ord. Dec 13, 1942; appt. Auxiliary Bishop of Miami, June 24, 1968; cons. Aug. 28, 1968; appt. Bishop of Brownsville, April 27, 1971; installed May 27, 1971; retired Nov. 30, 1991.—Most Rev. ENRIQUE SAN PEDRO, S.J., S.T.D., S.S.L., fourth Bishop of Brownsville; ord. March 18, 1957; appt. Auxiliary Bishop of Galveston-Houston April 1, 1986; cons. June 29, 1986; appt. Coadjutor of Brownsville, August 13, 1991; installed Sept. 26, 1991; succeeded to the See, Nov. 30, 1991; died July 17, 1994.

Catholic Pastoral Center—P.O. Box 2279, Brownsville, 78522-2279. Tel: 956-542-2501; Fax: 956-542-6751.

Vicar General—Rev. Msgr. PATRICK J. DOHERTY, V.G.

Vicar Episcopal for Evangelization—Rev. JUAN NICOLAU.

Moderators of the Curia—Lower Valley: Rev. IVAN M. ROVIRA; Upper Valley: Rev. ARMANDO ESCOBEDO.

Bishop's Administrative Assistant—Rev. EDUARDO ORTEGA.

Chancellor—Rev. EDUARDO ORTEGA.

Vice-Chancellor—CLARA M. MARTINEZ.

Presbyteral Council—Rev. Msgr. PATRICK J. DOHERTY, V.G., Commissioner for Parish Needs; Revs. CRAIG CAROLAN, Commissioner for Justice and Peace; F. ROBERT DAVOLA, Commissioner for Vocations/Seminarians; HERMAN J. DEFLER, M.S.F., Commissioner for Administration; EDUARDO ORTEGA, Sec., Notary & Commissioner for Worship and Liturgy; ARMANDO ESCOBEDO, Commissioner for Permanent Deacons and Lay Ministry; GERALD W. FRANK, Commissioner for Marriage and Family Life; JUAN VICTOR HEREDIA, Commissioner for Social Services;

GUSTAVO BARRERA, Commissioner for Evangelization; JUAN NICOLAU, Commissioner for Priestly Life and Ministry; IVAN M. ROVIRA, Commissioner for Education and Formation; PATRICK K. SEITZ, Commissioner for the Diocesan Shrine; ROY LEE SNIPES, O.M.I., Commissioner for Youth and Young Adult Ministry.

Diocesan College of Consultors—Rev. Msgr. PATRICK J. DOHERTY; Revs. F. ROBERT DAVOLA; ARMANDO ESCOBEDO; JUAN VICTOR HEREDIA; IVAN M. ROVIRA; ROY LEE SNIPES, O.M.I.

Deans—Rev. GUSTAVO BARRERA, Brownsville Deanery; Rev. LAWRENCE J. KLEIN, Harlingen Deanery; Rev. FRANCISCO CASTILLO, Weslaco Deanery; Rev. AGOSTINHO S. PACHECO, McAllen Deanery; Rev. ROBERT E. MAHER, Mission Deanery; Rev. IGNACIO LUNA, Rio Grande City Deanery.

Parish Priests' Consultors & Priests' Personnel Board—Revs. F. ROBERT DAVOLA; RUBEN M. DELGADO; GEORGE E. HARRIS; GREGORY M. KUCZMANSKI.

Diocesan Liturgist/Bishop's Master of Ceremonies—Rev. EDUARDO ORTEGA.

Diocesan Tribunal—*P.O. Box 2279, Brownsville, 78522-2279.* Tel: 956-550-1512; Fax: 956-542-6751.

Pro-Judicial Vicar—Rev. HERMAN J. DEFLER, M.S.F.

Promoter of Justice—Rev. GUSTAVO BARRERA.

Director of the Tribunal/Notary—SYLVIA W. GARCIA.

Defenders of the Bond—Revs. GUSTAVO BARRERA; F. ROBERT DAVOLA; RICHARD J. MACDONALD, S.C.J.

Judges—Most. Rev. JOHN J. FITZPATRICK; Revs. MICHAEL ANNUNZIATO, SS.CC.; THOMAS G. KULLECK.

Procurator/Advocate—Sr. MARY DOLORES DOYLE, C.C.V.I.

Comptroller—ANITA A. RODRIGUEZ, *P.O. Box 2279, Brownsville, 78522-2279.* Tel: 956-550-1534; Fax: 956-542-6751.

Accountant—Mrs. SOCORRO PADILLA.

Parish Accounting Services—MARY GUAJARDO.

Insurance and Pension Plans—JUDY PLATA.

Diocesan Finance Council—NOBLE ALLEN; ALONZO CANTU; CHARLES ELLARD; MATT GORGES; JOSE A. HINOJOSA; GRACIELA GUTIERREZ; MICHAEL POWERS.

Diocesan Offices and Directors

Computer Specialist—JESSE CANDANOZA, *1910 E. Elizabeth St., Brownsville, 78520., P.O. Box 2279, Brownsville, 78522-2279.* Tel: 956-542-2501; Fax: 956-542-6751.

Human Resources Office—BENJAMIN SANDOVAL, *P.O. Box 2279, Brownsville, 78522-2279.* Tel: 956-550-1541; Fax: 956-542-6751.

Ministry Resource Center—Sr. MAUREEN CROSBY, S.S.D., Audio/Visual; Sr. SUSAN KLEIN, O.P., Library Resource, *727 E. Bowie, P.O. Box 547, Alamo, 78516-0547.* Tel: 956-787-8571; Fax: 956-787-5778.

Vicar for Religious—Rev. F. ROBERT DAVOLA, *1119 Francisco Ave., Mission, 78572.* Tel: 956-585-2701; Fax: 956-581-4801.

Office of Youth Ministry—LINDA MEYER, Coord., *727 E. Bowie, P.O. Box 547, Alamo, 78516-0547.* Tel: 956-787-8571; Fax: 956-787-5778.

Building & Property Manager—ELADIO CUELLAR, JR., *400 N. Nebraska, P.O. Box 2714, San Juan, 78589.* Tel: 956-782-1728; Fax: 956-787-2908.

Director of Seminarians—Rev. IVAN M. ROVIRA, *P.O. Box 2279, Brownsville, 78522-2279.* Tel: 956-550-1547; Fax: 956-542-6751.

Director of Communications—Rev. PEDRO BRISENO, *KMBH-TV60, 1701 Tennessee Ave., P.O. Box 2147, Harlingen, 78551.* Tel: 956-421-4111; Fax: 956-421-4150.

Superintendent of Catholic Schools—Sr. MARCELLA EWERS, D.C., *727 E. Bowie, P.O. Box 547, Alamo, 78516-0547.* Tel: 956-787-8571; Fax: 956-787-5778.

Office of Permanent Deacons—Sr. CECILIA CASAS, R.S.M., *727 E. Bowie, P.O. Box 547, Alamo, 78516-0547.* Tel: 956-787-8571; Fax: 956-787-5778.

Young Adult Ministry—Sr. GLORIA ANN FIEDLER, C.D.P., *1850 Ridgely Rd., Brownsville, 78520.* Tel: 956-542-3942. See Campus Ministry for more listings.

Encuentro Matrimonial—ALFONSO GONZALEZ; MINERVA GONZALEZ, *RR 3, Box 6095, Harlingen, 78550.* Tel: 956-546-1982.

Engaged Encounter—GEORGE GANDARA; ANA GANDARA, *1524 S. 14th St., Edinburg, 78539.* Tel: 956-318-1035.

Boy Scouts—Rev. CRAIG CAROLAN, Chap., *412 S. "C" St., Harlingen, 78550.* Tel: 956-423-0855.

Marriage Encounter—JAVIER ROCHA; ESTHER ROCHA, *Rte. 1, Box 8, Magnum Rd., Mission, 78572.* Tel: 956-580-9010.

Movimiento Familiar Cristiano—ALFONSO SALAZAR; ELVIA SALAZAR, *P.O. Box 772, Port Isabel, 78578.* Tel: 956-943-2958. JOSE FUENTES; REYES FUENTES, *Rte. 6, Box 250, Weslaco, 78596.* Tel: 956-968-8330.

Catholic Foundation of the Rio Grande Valley—ROY DE LEON; RICHARD WALKER; LUIS CORTINAS; RAY COCOZZA; MS. GRACIELA GUTIERREZ; Rev. IVAN M. ROVIRA, Ex-Officio (Education Commission); ANITA RODRIGUEZ, Staff, *P.O. Box 2279, Brownsville, 78522-2279.* Tel: 956-542-2501; Fax: 956-542-6751.

Building Committee—JOSE A. CHANIN; BRIAN CROWEL; OSCAR FALCON; CESAR R. PEREZ; MICHAEL E. VOURCOUS. Staff:: ELADIO CUELLAR, JR.; GEORGE MENDOZA, *400 N. Nebraska, P.O. Box 747, San Juan, 78589.* Tel: 956-782-1728; Fax: 956-782-0418.

Catholic Social Services Office—TELMA LONGORIA, *400 N. Nebraska, P.O. Box 128, San Juan, 78589.* Tel: 956-702-4088. (See separate listing for branch offices and extended services).

Campaign for Human Development—HERNAN GONZALEZ, *P.O. Box 2279, Brownsville, 78522.* Tel: 956-542-2501; Fax: 956-542-6751.

Office of Evangelization—Rev. JUAN NICOLAU, V.E., Dir., *400 N. Nebraska, San Juan, 78589.* Tel: 956-787-0033; Fax: 956-787-2908.

Office of Family Life—Mrs. LYDIA PESINA, *P.O. Box 547, Alamo, 78516.* Tel: 956-787-8571; Fax: 956-787-5778.

Santuario de Nuestra Senora de San Juan del Valle—Board of Directors—Revs. RICHARD ALANIZ; FERNANDO MANCIAS; JORGE MEDINA. Ex-Officios: Most Rev. RAYMUNDO J. PENA; Rev. PATRICK K. SEITZ, (Commission for the Shrine); BENITO MARTINEZ, Consultant; Rev. JUAN NICOLAU, Rector. Associates: Revs. CARLOS GARZA; RICARDO AYALA, III, *P.O. Box 2279, Brownsville, 78522-2279.* Tel: 956-550-1510; Fax: 956-542-6751.

Housing Board—ANITA A. RODRIGUEZ; ANA ZAMARRIPA, Mgr., *El Rosario Homes, P.O. Box 971, Mission, 78572.* Tel: 956-585-5051., *La Merced Homes, P.O. Box 806, Mercedes, 78570.* Tel: 956-565-2622.

Jail Ministry—Cameron County Jail and Bayview Detention Center, Sr. JULIANA GARCIA, M.J., *1850 Ridgely Rd., Brownsville, 78520.* Tel: 956-541-0220. Hidalgo County Jail, Deacon JOSE SOLIS, *315 E. Peter St., Edinburg, 78539.* Tel: 956-383-4324. Starr County Jail, Deacon RODOLFO C. SALINAS, *304 North East St., Rio Grande City, 78582.* Tel: 956-487-3112. Willacy County Jail; AURORA PEDRAZA, *945 E. Harris St., Raymondville, 78580.* Tel: 956-689-3798.

Office of Catechesis—Sr. MARIA LUISA PENA, M.D-.P.V.M., *P.O. Box 547, Alamo, 78516.* Tel: 956-787-8571; Fax: 956-787-5778.

Diocesan Offices—

Archives—CLARA M. MARTINEZ, *P.O. Box 2279, Brownsville, 78522-2279.* Tel: 956-550-1531; Fax: 956-542-6751.

Attorney—DAVID C. GARZA, *P.O. Box 2025, Brownsville, 78520.* Tel: 956-541-4914; Fax: 956-542-7403.

Catholic Lawyers Guild—Mr. FIDENCIO GUERRA, JR., *P.O. Box 4227, McAllen, 78501.* Tel: 956-682-1465.

Holy Childhood Association—Sr. MARCELLA EWERS, D.C., *P.O. Box 547, Alamo, 78516.* Tel: 956-787-8571; Fax: 956-787-5778.

Natural Family Planning—Mrs. WILLY KOPECKY, *1012 W. Third, Weslaco, 78596.* Tel: 956-969-3079.

Propagation of the Faith—Rev. Msgr. PATRICK J. DOHERTY, V.G., *P.O. Box 2279, Brownsville, 78522-2279.* Tel: 956-550-1526.

Serra Club International—Brownsville: ROLANDO RAMIREZ, *1905 W. Madison, Brownsville, 78520.* Tel: 956-541-1453. Rev. GUSTAVO BARRERA, Chap., *1914 Barnard Rd., Brownsville, 78520.* Tel: 956-546-3800. McAllen: LEONEL BARRERA, JR., *117 W. Camellia, McAllen, 78501.* Tel: 956-687-4922. Rev. IVAN M. ROVIRA, Chap., *P.O. Box 2279, Brownsville, 78522-2279.* Tel: 956-550-1547. Rio Grande City: ANTONIO E. GARCIA, Pres., *2016 Heron, McAllen, 78504.* Tel: 956-618-3626.

Office of Public & Governmental Relations—PAMELA DOWNING, *1910 E. Elizabeth St., Brownsville, 78520., P.O. Box 2279, Brownsville, 78522-2279.* Tel: 956-550-1541; Fax: 956-542-6751.

Office of Vocations—Rev. IVAN M. ROVIRA; Sr. NINFA GARZA, M.J., *P.O. Box 2279, Brownsville, 78522-2279.* Tel: 956-550-1547; Fax: 956-542-6751.

Office of Stewardship & Development—HERNAN GONZALEZ, Stewardship; JESUS SALINAS, Development, *P.O. Box 2279, Brownsville, 78522-2279.* Tel: 956-550-1543; Fax: 956-542-6751.

Pro-Life Activities—Rev. MATTHEW KREMPEL, O.F.M., *P.O. Box 216, Progreso, 78596.* Tel: 956-565-6856.

R.C.I.A.—Rev. LAWRENCE J. KLEIN, *P.O. Box 116, La Feria, 78579.* Tel: 956-797-2666.

Knights of Columbus—Rev. Msgr. PATRICK J. DOHERTY, V.G., *P.O. Box 2279, Brownsville, 78522-2279.* Tel: 956-550-1526; Fax: 956-542-6751.

Ministry & Adult Education—GRACE MACKINNON, *1910 E. Elizabeth St., Brownsville, 78520., P.O. Box 2279, Brownsville, 78522-2279.* Tel: 956-542-2501; Fax: 956-542-6751.

Casa de San Jose-House of Studies—Rev. JAMES P. FISCHLER, C.I.C.M., Dir. Spiritual Directors: Revs. GEORGE HARRIS; JUAN VICTOR HEREDIA; PATRICK K. SEITZ, *Rte. 8, Box 684-F, Brownsville, 78520.* Tel: 956-546-2688; 546-3397.

CLERGY, PARISHES, MISSIONS AND PAROCHIAL SCHOOLS

CITY OF BROWNSVILLE
(Cameron County)

1—IMMACULATE CONCEPTION CATHEDRAL (1849), Revs. Pasquale Lanese, O.M.I.; Charles Moran, O.M.I.; Deacons John Kinch; Arturo Rodriguez.
Res., 1218 E. Jefferson St., P.O. Box 311, 78522. Tel: 956-546-3178; Fax: 956-546-1284.
Missions—Brownsville, Cameron Co., St. Thomas, 155 E. Jefferson St., 78520; Brownsville, Cameron Co., Sacred Heart, 602 E. Elizabeth St., 78520.
Chapel—La Muralla, D St., 78520.

2—CHRIST THE KING (1953), Rev. Alfonso M. Guevara; Deacon Felipe Trevino.
2255 Southmost Rd., 78521. Tel: 956-546-1982; Fax: 956-546-7120.
Mission—Brownsville, Cameron Co., Blessed Juan Diego de Guadalupe, Valle Escondido, 78521.

3—CHURCH OF THE GOOD SHEPHERD (1968), Rev. Horacio Chavarria; Deacon Paul McArdle.
Res., 2645 Tulipan, 78521. Tel: 956-542-5142; Fax: 956-542-5278.

4—HOLY FAMILY (1966), Rev. John A. O'Malley; Deacon Alejandro Flores.
Res., 2308 E. Tyler, 78520. Tel: 956-546-6975; Fax: 956-546-4883.

5—OUR LADY OF GOOD COUNSEL (1966), Pastoral Team: Rev. Msgr. Patrick J. Doherty, V.G., Moderator; Rev. Jose M. Villalon; Deacons Enrique Saldana; Alvino C. Olvera.
1055 Military Hwy., 78520. Tel: 956-541-8341; Fax: 956-548-0229.
Mission—San Pedro, San Pedro.

6—OUR LADY OF GUADALUPE (1928), Pastoral Team: Rev. Msgr. Patrick J. Doherty, V.G., Moderator; Rev. Jose M. Villalon; Deacons Jose Guerra; Ramon Leal.
Res., 1200 E. Lincoln St., 78521. Tel: 956-542-4823; Fax: 956-542-5944.

7—ST. EUGENE DE MAZENOD (1996), Rev. Harry Schuckenbrock, O.M.I.; Bro. John Lasseigne, O.M.I.; Deacon Bruno Cedillo.
Res., 5409 Austin Rd., 78251. Tel: 956-831-9923.
Chapel—Kopernick Shores, St. Michael Archangel.

8—ST. JOSEPH (1953), Revs. John G. Castro, O.M.I.; Jan Rademaker, O.M.I.; Deacon Frank Galvan.
Res., 555 W. St. Francis St., 78520. Tel: 956-542-2709; Fax: 956-546-5162.

9—ST. LUKE (1974), Rev. Juan Victor Heredia; Deacons Francisco Garza; Juan Pablo Navarro.
Res., 2800 Rockwell Dr., 78521. Tel: 956-541-1480; 541-4973; Fax: 956-542-8043.
School—2850 Price Rd., 78521. Tel: 956-544-7982; Fax: 956-544-4874. Dr. Christina Saavedra, Prin.
Lay Teachers 17; Students 252.

10—SAINT MARY, MOTHER OF THE CHURCH (1967), Rev. Gustavo Barrera; Deacons Gilbert Borja; Roberto Cano; Heriberto Solis; Heriberto Trevino. In res., Most Rev. John J. Fitzpatrick, (Retired).
Res., 1914 Barnard Rd., 78520-8247. Tel: 956-546-3800; Fax: 956-546-1589.
School—1300 Los Ebanos Blvd., 78520. Tel: 956-546-1805; Fax: 956-546-0787. Mr. Juan Barreda, Prin.
Religious 3; Lay Teachers 28; Students 603.

11—SAN FELIPE DE JESUS (1996), Rev. Michael Seifert, S.M.; Bro. Albert Phillipp, F.M.S., Pastoral Assoc.
P.O. Box 8093, 78526-8093.
Res., 2215 Avenida Rancho Viejo, 78521. Tel: 956-982-2007.

OUTSIDE THE CITY OF BROWNSVILLE

Alamo, Hidalgo Co., Resurrection (1926). (Formerly St. Joseph/Our Lady of Fatima). Rev. Louis L. Brum; Deacon Jesus P. Galvan.
Res., 834 E. Citrus St., P.O. Box 1159, 78516. Tel: 956-787-2963; Fax: 956-787-6788.

Alton, Hidalgo Co., San Martin de Porres (1967), Rev. Anselme Malonda, C.I.C.M.; Bro. Charles Phukuta Khonde, C.I.C.M.
Res., Five Miles N. Conway W., P.O. Box 9023, Mission, 78572. Tel: 956-585-8001; Fax: 956-585-0715.

Donna, Hidalgo Co., St. Joseph (1928), Revs. Philip Sosa, M.S.F.; Herman J. Defler, M.S.F.
Res., 306 S. D Salinas Blvd., 78537. Tel: 956-464-3331; Fax: 956-464-6808.
Mission—Colonia Nueva, Christ the King.

Edcouch, Hidalgo Co., St. Theresa of the Infant Jesus (1948), Rev. Gregory M. Kuczmanski; Deacon Alvin H. Gerbermann.
Res., 200 P. Salazar, P.O. Box 307, 78538. Tel: 956-262-1347.
Mission—La Villa, Our Lady of Guadalupe.

Edinburg, Hidalgo Co., Holy Family (1967), Rev. Esteban Hernandez, M.S.F.; Deacons Inocencio Diaz; Ruben Lopez.
Res., 1302 E. Champion, 78539-4864. Tel: 956-383-5472; 383-4593; Fax: 956-383-5034.
Sacred Heart (1927), Revs. Michael Annunziato, SS.CC.; Richard Czerwien, SS.CC.; Deacons Jose Solis; Oscar Cuevas; Gilberto Lopez.
Res., 215 N. 16th Ave., 78539. Tel: 956-383-3253.
Mission—Lull, Capilla de San Jose.
St. Joseph (1948), Rev. Robert E. Maher; Deacons Silvestre Garcia; Irineo Gonzalez, Jr.
Res., 122 W. Fay St., 78539. Tel: 956-383-3728; Fax: 956-383-8630.
School—119 W. Fay St., 78539. Tel: 956-383-3957. Mr. Edward LoPresto, Prin.
Religious 2; Lay Teachers 22; Students 187.

Elsa, Hidalgo Co., Sacred Heart (1948), Rev. Emmanuel Bialoncik, O.F.M.; Deacon Hugo de la Cruz.
Res., 1100 N. Broadway, P.O. Box 6, 78543. Tel: 956-262-1406; Fax: 956-262-4265.
Mission—Monte Alto, Hidalgo Co., Christ the King, Holy Cross Catechetical Center, Mile 15, Monte Alto, 78538.

Escobares, Starr Co., Sacred Heart (1967), Pastoral Team: Revs. Ignacio Luna; Lee DaCosta; Lionel Lopez; Marcelo Tobar.
Res., P.O. Box 1180, Roma, 78584. Tel: 956-849-1741; Fax: 956-849-4589.
Missions—Rosita, Santa Rosa de Lima; El Sauz, Our Lady of Guadalupe.

Grulla, Starr Co., Holy Family (1967), Pastoral Team: Revs. Ignacio Luna, Moderator; Lee DaCosta; Lionel Lopez; Marcelo Tobar; Deacon Rodolfo C. Salinas.
Res., P.O. Box 67, 78548. Tel: 956-487-3365.
Mission—Cristo Rey, La Victoria.

Harlingen, Cameron Co.,

1—Our Lady of the Assumption, (1958), Pastoral Team: Revs. Craig Carolan, Moderator; Pedro Briseno; Heberto M. Diaz, Jr.; Deacon Ignacio Gonzales.
1313 W. Buchanan St., 78550. Tel: 956-423-4670; Fax: 956-423-5970.
Mission—San Felipe, Austin Co., Rangerville Rd., San Felipe, 77473.

2—Immaculate Heart of Mary, (1927), Pastoral Team: Revs. Craig Carolan, Moderator; Pedro Briseno; Heberto M. Diaz; Terence L. Fowler; Jerome Felion, (Retired); Deacon Abel Castillo.
Res., 412 S. C St., 78550. Tel: 956-423-0855; Fax: 956-421-1071.

3—Queen of Peace, (1967), Rev. Matthias Shanley, SS.CC.; Deacon Juan Valenzuela.
Res., 1509 New Combes Hwy., 78550. Tel: 956-423-6341; Fax: 956-423-2864.

4—St. Anthony, (1940), Rev. Thomas L. Pincelli; Deacon Julio Flores, Jr.
Res., 209 S. 10th, 78550. Tel: 956-428-6111; Fax: 956-428-4276.
School—1015 E. Harrison St., 78550. Tel: 956-423-2486. Ms. Johna Hays, Prin.
Lay Teachers 14; Students 238.
Mission—Le Moyne Chapel.

Hidalgo, Hidalgo Co., Sacred Heart (1967), Rev. Joseph Bukase, C.I.C.M.
Res., 308 E. Camelia St., P.O. Box 742, 78557. Tel: 956-843-2463.

La Feria, Cameron Co., St. Francis Xavier (1930), Rev. Lawrence J. Klein.
Res., 500 S. Canal St., P.O. Box 116, 78559. Tel: 956-797-2666; Fax: 956-797-3387.

La Joya, Hidalgo Co., Our Lady, Queen of Angels (1960), Revs. Michael Montoya, C.I.C.M.; Plutarco Belanggoy, C.I.C.M.; Deacons Alberto Chapa; Lucio Flores.
Res., P.O. Drawer D, 78560. Tel: 956-585-5223; Fax: 956-585-4878.
Missions—Abram, St. Mary Magdalene; Penitas, St. Anthony; Los Ebanos, St. Michael; Sullivan City, St. William.

Los Fresnos, Cameron Co., St. Cecilia (1964), Rev. George E. Harris; Deacons Augusto Chapa, Jr.; Andres Munoz.
Res., 606 W. Ocean Blvd., P.O. Box 39, 78566. Tel: 956-233-5619.
Mission—Olmito, Our Heavenly Father.

Lyford, Willacy Co., Prince of Peace (1967), Revs. Richard J. MacDonald, S.C.J.; David Jackson, S.C.J.
Res., 1100 Park Ave., P.O. Box 460, 78569. Tel: 956-347-3580; Fax: 956-347-3649.
Missions—Santa Monica, Santa Monica; Sebastian, Willacy Co., St. Martin, Box 247, Sebastian, 78594.

McAllen, Hidalgo Co.,

1—Our Lady of Perpetual Help, (1967), Rev. Francisco Acosta; Deacon Rene Villalon, Sr., S.F.O.
Res., 2209 Kendlewood Ave., 78501. Tel: 956-682-4238.

2—Our Lady of Sorrows, (1941), Rev. Agostinho S. Pacheco; Deacons John Schwarz; Israel Sagrado.
Res., 1108 Hackberry St., 78501-4304. Tel: 956-686-0251; Fax: 956-686-0322.
School—1100 Gumwood, 78501. Tel: 956-686-3651; Fax: 956-686-0324. Mrs. Jeanne L. Bruton, Prin. & Dir. of Day Care.
Lay Teachers 29; Students 592.
Day Care—.

3—Sacred Heart, (1917), Revs. James Pfeifer, O.M.I.; Henry Janssen, O.M.I.; Deacon Eduardo Reyna.
Res., 306 S. 15th St., P.O. Box 370, 78505-0370. Tel: 956-686-7711.

4—St. Joseph the Worker, (1967), Revs. Bart A. Flaat, C.I.C.M.; Albert Lelo-Luemba, C.I.C.M.; Bro. Faustin Boleli, C.I.C.M.; Deacons Alejandro Gamboa; Salvador Rojas.
Res., 2315 Ithaca St., 78501. Tel: 956-682-1351; Fax: 956-971-9480.

5—Holy Spirit, (1981), Rev. Gerald W. Frank; Deacons Lorenzo Contreras, Jr.; Carlos S. Trevino. In res., Rev. Thomas Kulleck.
Res., 2201 Martin Ave., 78504. Tel: 956-631-5295; Fax: 956-631-5460.
Preschool & Day Care Center—Tel: 956-682-6562. Mrs. Toni F. Espinoza, Dir.

McCook, Hidalgo Co., Immaculate Conception (1950), Rev. Thomas Kulleck.
Rte. 3, Box 188-E, Edinburg, 78539. Tel: 956-842-3663.

Mercedes, Hidalgo Co., Our Lady of Mercy (1909), Pastoral Team: Revs. Armando Escobedo; Wenceslao Mendoza; Deacon Juan Trevino.
Res., 322 S. Vermont Ave., P.O. Box 805, 78570. Tel: 956-565-1141.
Sacred Heart Church (1969),
Pastoral Team: Revs. Armando Escobedo; Wenceslao Mendoza; Deacon Roberto Cantu.
Res., 920 Anacuitas, 78570. Tel: 956-565-0271.

Mission, Hidalgo Co.,

1—Our Lady of Guadalupe, (1899), Revs. Roy Lee Snipes, O.M.I.; Norman Racette, O.M.I.; Timothy Paulsen, O.M.I.; Deacon Ricardo Ayala, Jr.
Res., 620 Dunlap St., P.O. Box 1047, 78572-1047. Tel: 956-585-2623. [CEM]

2—Our Lady of the Holy Rosary, (1968), Rev. Vicente Azcoiti.
Res., 923 Matamoros St., P.O. Box 1439, 78572. Tel: 956-581-2193.
Missions—Madero, Our Lady of Lourdes; Granjeno, Our Lady of Fatima.

3—Our Lady of St. John of the Fields, (1967), Revs. Ricardo Garcia; Anton Hestasusilo, C.I.C.M.; Deacons Daniel Zamora; Peter Requenez.
Res., 1052 Washington St., 78572. Tel: 956-585-2325; Fax: 956-585-8179.

4—St. Paul, (1915), Rev. F. Robert DaVola; Deacons Ismael Garcia; Robert Ledesma.
Res., 1119 Francisco Ave., 78572. Tel: 956-585-2701; Fax: 956-581-4801.

Pharr, Hidalgo Co., St. Anne, Mother of Mary (1973), Rev. Gerry Shanley, SS.CC.; Deacon Jose R. Castro.
Res., 710 E. Lucas, 78577. Tel: 956-787-8122.
St. Jude Thaddeus (1951), Very Rev. Leo Francis Daniels, C.O.; Rev. Jose Encarnacion Losoya, C.O.; Bro. Mario Alberto Aviles, C.O.
Res., 505 S. Ironwood, P.O. Drawer J, 78577-1210. Tel: 956-781-2489; Fax: 956-783-4614.
School—Oratory Academy, P.O. Drawer ii, 78577. Tel: 956-781-3056; Fax: 956-702-3047. Mrs. G. Yvonne Perez, Dir.
Priests 1; Lay Teachers 24; Students 315.
Mission—Las Milpas, Nuestro Senor del Sagrado Corazon, Tel: 956-787-3554.
St. Margaret Mary (1927), Rev. James Brown; Deacon Pedro F. Sanchez.
Res., 122 W. Hawk Ave., 78577. Tel: 956-787-8563.

Port Isabel, Cameron Co., Our Lady Star of the Sea (1927), Revs. Joseph J. O'Brien, O.M.I.; Jack Franko, O.M.I.
Res., 705 S. Longoria St., Box 6504, 78578. Tel: 956-943-1297; Fax: 956-943-1907.

Progreso, Hidalgo Co., Holy Spirit (1969), Rev. Matthew Krempel, O.F.M.
Res., P.O. Box 216, 78579. Tel: 956-565-6856; Fax: 956-565-6856.
Missions—Santa Maria, St. Margaret Ann; Bluetown, Cristo Rey.

Ranchito, Cameron Co., St. Ignatius (1967), Pastoral Team: Revs. Patrick J. Doherty, V.G.; Jose M. Villalon, Jr.; Deacon Salvador G. Saldivar.
Rte. 10, Box 159, San Benito, 78586. Tel: 956-399-2022.
Missions—La Paloma, Our Lady of Lourdes; Las Rucias, Sacred Heart.

Raymondville, Willacy Co., Our Lady of Guadalupe (1927), Revs. Richard J. MacDonald, S.C.J.; Steve Pujdak, S.C.J.; Gregory M. Speck, S.C.J.; Deacon Juan Francisco Gonzalez.
Res., 693 N. Third St., 78580. Tel: 956-689-2408; Fax: 956-689-3583.
Missions—La Sara, St. Patrick; Hargill, St. Frances Xavier Cabrini.
St. Anthony (1907), Rev. Edward E. Day.
Res., 464 S. First St., 78580. Tel: 956-689-3380.
Mission—San Perlita, Sacred Heart.

Rio Grande City, Starr Co., Immaculate Conception (1880), Pastoral Team: Revs. Ignacio Luna; Lee DaCosta; Lionel Lopez; Marcelo Tobar.
Res., P.O. Box 1, 101 E. Third St., 78582. Tel: 956-487-2317; Fax: 956-487-8246. [CEM]
School—305 N. Britton Ave., 78582. Tel: 956-487-2558; Fax: 956-487-1033. Sr. Helen Rottier, C.S.J., Prin.
Religious 1; Lay Teachers 12; Students 163.
Missions—La Puerta, St. Paul; Los Garcias Ranch, Sacred Heart. Deacon Benito Saenz.

Rio Hondo, Cameron Co., St. Helen (1943), Rev. Terrence Gorski, O.F.M.; Deacon Genaro Ibarra.
Res., 228 Huisache, P.O. Box 451, 78583. Tel: 956-748-2327.
Mission—Lozano, St. Vincent de Paul.

Roma, Starr Co., Our Lady of Refuge (1853), Rev. Hugo Van den Bussche, O.M.I.
Res., P.O. Box 156, 78584. Tel: 956-849-1455; Fax: 956-849-2257.
Missions—Falcon Heights, Holy Trinity; Salineno, St. Joseph; Los Saenz, Holy Family; Fronton, Lamb of God.

San Benito, Cameron Co., Our Lady, Queen of the Universe (1960), Rev. Jorge A. Gonzalez. In res., Rev. Norbert J. Deddens.
Res., 121 Garrison Dr., 78586. Tel: 956-399-2865; Fax: 956-399-2045.
Mission—San Benito, St. Joseph, 1001 W. Hwy. 77, 78586.
St. Benedict (1912), Rev. Richard Guerra, O.M.I.; Deacons Manuel Sanchez; Margarito Briones.
Res., 351 S. Bowie, P.O. Box 950, 78586. Tel: 956-399-2353.
St. Theresa (1954), Rev. Patrick K. Seitz; Deacon Benito Flores.
Res., 1300 Combes St., P.O. Box 1830, 78586. Tel: 956-399-3247; Fax: 956-399-3247.

San Carlos, Hidalgo Co., St. Joseph the Worker (1970), Rev. Samuel Arizpe; Deacon Hector Perez.
Res., Rte. 1, Box 202-E, Edinburg, 78539-9801. Tel: 956-383-5880.
Missions—San Manuel, St. Anne; Faysville, St. Theresa.

San Isidro, Starr Co., St. Isidore (1964), Pastoral Team: Revs. Ignacio Luna; Lee DaCosta; Lionel Lopez; Marcelo Tobar.
Rte. 1, Box 2, 78588. Tel: 956-481-3392.

San Juan, Hidalgo Co., Santuario de Nuestra Senora de San Juan del Valle, Pastoral Team: Revs. Juan Nicolau, Rector; Carlos Garza; Ricardo Ayala, III.
Res., 400 N. Nebraska, 78589. Tel: 956-787-0033.
St. John the Baptist (1949), Rev. Richard J. Sheehan, O.M.I.; Deacons Agapito L. Cantu; Julio Castilleja.
216 W. First St., P.O. Box 1196, 78589. Tel: 956-783-1196.
Mission—Lopezville, Immaculate Conception.

Santa Rosa, Cameron Co., St. Mary (1967), Rev. Alfredo Garcia, SS.CC.
Res., 101 San Antonio Ave., P.O. Box 365, 78593. Tel: 956-636-1211.

Weslaco, Hidalgo Co., St. Joan of Arc (1929), Rev. Francisco Castillo; Deacons Jesus Aguayo; Francisco Caballero.
Res., 109 S. Illinois Ave., 78596. Tel: 956-968-3670; Fax: 956-968-1872.
San Martin de Porres (1967), Rev. Ruben Delgado; Deacons Abraham Cardosa; Juan Delgado; Jose G. Garza.
Res., 901 N. Texas Blvd., 78596. Tel: 956-968-2691; Fax: 956-968-1473.
Missions—Weslaco, St. Jude Chapel; Expressway Heights, Nuestra Senora de Guadalupe.
St. Pius X (1955), Rev. William Zapalac, O.M.I.; Deacon Jose Oscar Perez.
Res., 600 S. Oklahoma Ave., 78596. Tel: 956-968-7471; Fax: 956-969-3040.

Chaplains of Public Institutions

Brownsville. *Brownsville Medical Center,* 1040 W. Jefferson St., 78520. Tel: 956-544-1426, Ext. 26. Dr. Ethel Winchester-Didsbury, Chap.; Deacon Frank Galvan, Chap. Asst.

Cameron County Jail. Sr. Juliana Garcia, M.J., Chap., Mailing Address: 1850 Ridgely Rd., 78521. Tel: 956-541-0220.
Columbia Valley Regional Medical Center, One Ted Hunt Blvd., 78521. Tel: 956-831-9611. Dr. Ethel Winchester-Didsbury, Chap.; Deacon Frank Galvan, Chap. Asst.

EDINBURG. *Edinburg Hospital,* 333 W. Freddy Gonzalez Dr., 78539. Tel: 956-383-6211; 585-0019. Sr. Gloria Morales, M.J., Mailing Address: 610 Delia St., 78539. Tel: 956-383-6056.
Hidalgo County Jail. Deacon Jose Solis, Chap., Mailing Address: 315 E. Peter St., 78539. Tel: 956-383-4324.

HARLINGEN. *Valley Baptist Medical Center,* 2101 Pease St., 78550. Tel: 956-421-1194. Rev. Frank Clancy, S.C.J., Chap.; Sr. Therese Rodriguez, O.P., Chap.

LOS FRESNOS. *Bayview Detention Center,* Buena Vista Rd., 78577. Tel: 956-541-0220. Sr. Juliana Garcia, M.J., Chap.

MCALLEN. *McAllen Medical Center,* 701 S. Main St., 78501. Tel: 956-632-4177; 686-3912. Rev. Willy Verboomen, C.I.C.M., Chap.
Rio Grande Regional Hospital, 101 E. Ridge Rd., 78501. Tel: 956-632-6616. Sr. Helen Roper, S.S.N.D., Chap.

MISSION. *Mission Hospital,* 900 S. Bryan Rd., 78572. Tel: 956-580-9000. Sr. Gloria Morales, M.J., Chap., Mailing Address: 610 Delia St., Edinburg, 78539. Tel: 956-383-6056.

RIO GRANDE CITY. *Starr County Jail.* Deacon R. C. Salinas, Chap., Mailing Address: 304 N. East, 78582. Tel: 956-487-3112.

WESLACO. *Knapp Memorial Medical Center,* P.O. Box 1895, 78596. Tel: 956-969-5258; 973-1968. Sr. Dominga Mosqueda, S.F.C.C., Chap.

Graduate Studies:
Reverend Fathers—
Piette, Gilbert M., Houston, TX

On Assignment Outside the Diocese:
Reverend Fathers—
Garza, Amador, St. Meinrad Seminary, St. Meinrad, IN 47577-1030
McDonnell, Patrick J., Our Lady of Sorrows, 3816 E. State St., Mercerville, NJ 08619
Mestas, Leonard J., St. Joseph the Worker Church, 10816 Mount View Ave., Loma Linda, CA 92354

On Leave:
Reverend Fathers—
Correa, Adrian R.
Fowler, Terrence

Absent:
Reverend Fathers—
Acosta, Humberto J.
Anderson, Ronald C.
Ellerbrock, Timothy
Farias, Jorge
Mireles, Richard
Zuber, Marti G.

Retired:
Reverend Fathers—
Diaz, Robert, P.O. Box 2279, Brownsville, TX 78520-2279
Gomez, Frank, 6803 N. Navarro, Apt. 4, Victoria, TX 77904. Tel: 956-578-2376
Lambert, John C., 2212 Betty Blvd., Edinburg, TX 78539. Tel: 956-383-4037
Mateos, Tomas, R.R. 15, Box 7747, Mission, TX 78572. Tel: 956-584-8883
Ortiz, Benedicto, 2735 E. 31st St., Brownsville, TX 78521. Tel: 956-546-6790
Smith, Peter J., P.O. Box 570, Rhineback, NY 12572
Sweeney, Robert L., P.O. Box 994, San Juan, TX 78589. Tel: 956-782-4371

Permanent Deacons:
Aguayo, Jesus, St. Joan of Arc, Weslaco
Aiken, Bruce, (Retired)
Ayala, Ricardo, Jr., Our Lady of Guadalupe, Mission
Barrera, Ernesto, On Leave
Borja, Gilberto, St. Mary, Mother of the Church, Brownsville
Briones, Margarito, St. Benedict, San Benito
Caballero, Francisco, St. Joan of Arc, Weslaco
Cano, Roberto, St. Mary, Mother of the Church, Brownsville
Cantu, Agapito L., St. John the Baptist, San Juan
Cantu, Roberto, Sacred Heart, Mercedes
Cardosa, Abraham, San Martin de Porres, Weslaco
Casas, Noe, Inactive
Castilleja, Julio, St. John the Baptist, San Juan
Castillo, Abel, Immaculate Heart of Mary, Harlingen
Castro, Jose R., St. Anne, Mother of Mary, Pharr
Cedillo, Bruno, St. Eugene de Mazenod, Brownsville
Chapa, Alberto X., Our Lady, Queen of Angels, La Joya
Chapa, Augusto, Jr., St. Cecilia, Los Fresnos
Contreras, Lorenzo, Jr., Holy Spirit, McAllen
Crixell, Alfred V., Coord., On Leave
Cuevas, Oscar, Sacred Heart, Edinburg
de la Cruz, Hugo, Sacred Heart, Elsa
Delgado, Juan, San Martin de Porres, Weslaco
Diaz, Inocencio, Holy Family, Edinburg
Eklund, Bruce, Albuquerque, NM
Flores, Alejandro, Holy Family, Brownsville
Flores, Benito, St. Theresa, San Benito
Flores, Julio, Jr., St. Anthony, Harlingen
Flores, Lucio, Our Lady, Queen of Angels, La Joya
Galvan, Frank, St. Joseph, Brownsville
Galvan, Jesus P., Resurrection, Alamo
Gamboa, Alejandro, St. Joseph the Worker, McAllen
Garcia, Ismael, St. Paul, Mission
Garcia, Silvestre, St. Joseph, Edinburg
Garza, Francisco, St. Luke, Brownsville
Garza, Jose G., San Martin de Porres, Weslaco
Gerbermann, Alvin H., St. Theresa of the Infant Jesus, Edcouch
Gonzales, Ignacio R., Our Lady of Assumption, Harlingen
Gonzalez, Irineo, Jr., St. Joseph, Edinburg
Gonzalez, Juan F., Our Lady of Guadalupe, Raymondville
Gonzalez, Leopoldo, Inactive
Grimaldo, Jose N., Inactive
Guerra, Jose, Our Lady of Guadalupe, Brownsville
Ibarra, Genaro, St. Helen, Rio Hondo
Jurado, Mariano, St. Theresa Mission, Faysville
Kinch, John, Immaculate Conception Cathedral, Brownsville
Leal, Ramon G., Our Lady of Guadalupe, Brownsville
Ledesma, Robert, St. Paul, Mission
Lopez, Albert C., On Leave
Lopez, Gilberto, Sacred Heart, Edinburg
Lopez, Ruben, Holy Family, Edinburg
McArdle, Paul, Good Shepherd, Brownsville
Munoz, Andres, Our Heavenly Father Mission, Olmito
Navarro, Juan Pablo, St. Luke, Brownsville
Oden, Luis, Inactive
Olvera, Alvino C., Our Lady of Good Counsel, Brownsville
Ovalle, Eduardo, Sr., St. Joseph, Donna
Perez, Hector, St. Joseph the Worker, San Carlos
Perez, Jose Oscar, St. Pius X, Weslaco
Requenez, Peter, Our Lady of St. John of the Fields, Mission
Reyes, Jesus H., Our Lady of Assumption, Harlington
Reyna, Eduardo, Sacred Heart, McAllen
Rodriguez, Arturo, Immaculate Conception Cathedral, Brownsville
Rojas, Salvador, St. Joseph the Worker, McAllen
Rousset, Louis, Inactive
Saenz, Benito, Jr., Our Lady of Peace, La Casita & St. Paul, La Puerta
Sagredo, Israel, Our Lady Of Sorrows, McAllen
Saldana, Enrique, Our Lady of Good Counsel, Brownsville
Saldivar, Salvador G., St. Ignatius, Ranchito
Salinas, Rodolfo C., Holy Family, Grulla
Sanchez, Manuel, St. Benedict, San Benito
Sanchez, Pedro F., St. Margaret Mary, Pharr
Schwarz, John, Our Lady of Sorrows, McAllen
Solis, Heriberto, St. Mary, Mother of the Church, Brownsville
Solis, Jose, Sacred Heart, Edinburg
Trevino, Carlos S., Holy Spirit, McAllen
Trevino, Felipe, Christ the King, Brownsville
Trevino, Heriberto, St. Mary, Mother of the Church, Brownsville
Trevino, Juan, Our Lady of Mercy, Mercedes
Valenzuela, Juan, Queen of Peace, Harlingen
Villalon, Rene, Sr., S.F.O., Our Lady of Perpetual Help, McAllen
Villarreal, Arturo, (Retired)
Webre, Alfred L., Jr., (Retired)
Zamora, Daniel, Our Lady of St. John of the Fields, Mission

INSTITUTIONS LOCATED IN THE DIOCESE

[A] HIGH SCHOOLS, PRIVATE

BROWNSVILLE. *St. Joseph Academy.* (Grades 7-12), 101 St. Joseph Dr., 78520. Tel: 956-542-3581. Bro. John Venturella, F.M.S., Prin. Marist Brothers, Esopus Province. Religious 10; Lay Teachers 48; Students 669.

[B] ELEMENTARY SCHOOLS, PRIVATE

BROWNSVILLE. *Incarnate Word Academy Elementary and Middle School.* (Convent Academy of the Incarnate Word), 244 Resaca Blvd., 78520. Tel: 956-546-4486. Sisters of the Incarnate Word and Blessed Sacrament. Sr. Teresita Rodriguez, I.W.B.S., Prin. (Elementary); Miss Christina Moreno, Prin. (Middle). Religious 6; Lay Teachers 18; Students 237.

PHARR. *Oratory Academy,* P.O. Drawer ii, 78577. Tel: 956-781-3056. Mrs. G. Yvonne Perez, Dir. Religious 1; Lay Teachers 24; Students 315.

[C] CATHOLIC SOCIAL SERVICES

BROWNSVILLE. *Bayview Detention Center Ministry,* 1850 Ridgely Rd., 78520. Tel: 956-541-0220. Sr. Juliana Garcia, S.J., Chap.
Catholic Charities, P.O. Box 2279, 78522. Tel: 956-542-2501. Legal Title: *Catholic Charities of the Diocese of Brownsville, a Texas Non-Profit Corporation.* Most Rev. Raymundo J. Pena, Chm.
Catholic Social Services Branch Office, 1850 Ridgely Rd., 78520. Tel: 956-541-0220. Sr. Norma Pimentel, M.J., Family Counselor; Telma Longoria, Dir. Tel: 956-702-4088; FAX:956-702-4042.

SAN JUAN. *Catholic Social Services Office,* 400 N. Nebraska, P.O. Box 128, 78589. Tel: 956-702-4088; Fax: 956-702-4042. Telma Longoria, Dir.; Deacon Ricardo Ayala, Jr., Family Counseling.

[D] HOMES FOR THE AGED

BROWNSVILLE. *Mother of Perpetual Help Nursing Home, Inc.,* 519 A East Madison St., 78520. Tel: 956-546-6745; Fax: 956-546-0711
For a complete listing, refer to the Special Care Facilities section.

SAN JUAN. *San Juan Home Health and Hospice,* 300 N. Nebraska, P.O. Box 2359, 78589. Tel: 956-782-0333; Fax: 956-782-0335
For a complete listing, refer to the Special Care Facilities section.
San Juan Nursing Home, 300 N. Nebraska, P.O. Box 1238, 78589. Tel: 956-787-1771; Fax: 956-787-8091
For a complete listing, refer to the Special Care Facilities section.

[E] RESIDENCES FOR PRIESTS AND BROTHERS

BROWNSVILLE. *El Rancho Grande Apartments,* 1225 Central Blvd., #903, 78520. Tel: 956-542-4744. Rev. Edward W. Wichmann (PBL).
Marist Brothers of the Schools, Champagnat Hall, 105 St. Joseph Dr., 78520. Tel: 956-546-3038. Brothers 2.
Marist Brothers, St. Joseph Academy, 101 St. Joseph Dr., 78520. Tel: 956-546-2608. Brothers 6.

HARLINGEN. *Priests of the Sacred Heart,* 144 W. Spencer Ct., 78550. Tel: 956-428-8344. Rev. Frank Clancy, S.C.J.

PHARR. *Oratory of St. Philip Neri, of Pontifical Right,* P.O. Box ii, 78577-1235. Tel: 956-843-8217; Fax: 956-843-2946. Very Rev. Leo Francis Daniels, C.O., Provost; Revs. Jose Encarnacion Losoya, C.O., Sec. & Treas.; David Garcia, C.O.; Bro. Mario Alberto Aviles, C.O.

RAYMONDVILLE. *Sacred Heart Fathers,* Rte. 2, Box 788, 78580. Tel: 956-689-6428. Priests 4; Brothers 1.

SAN BENITO. *Our Lady of Tenderness Fraternity, Inc.* (El Ranchito), Rte. 10, Box 159, 78586. Tel: 956-399-2552. In res. Bro. David Lopez, O.S.F.

[F] CONVENTS AND RESIDENCES FOR SISTERS

BROWNSVILLE. *Dominican Sisters of Charity of the Presentation,* 934 W. St. Charles St., 78520. Tel: 956-542-7225. Sisters 3.
Missionaries of Jesus, 1501 W. Adams, 78520. Tel: 956-542-2180. Sisters 7; Novices 1.
School Sisters of Notre Dame, 600 Lakeside Blvd., Apt. 6AA, 78520. Tel: 956-548-0056. Sisters 2.
Sisters of Charity of the Incarnate Word (San Antonio). Mailing Address: P.O. Box 2279, 78522-2279. Lakeside Apts., 600 Lakeside Blvd., Apt. 5E, 78520. Tel: 956-548-1963.
Sisters of the Incarnate Word and Blessed Sacrament, 535 W. St. Charles St., 78520. Tel: 956-544-2542; 546-8298. Sisters 3.

ALAMO. *Missionary Sisters of the Immaculate Heart of Mary,* Rte. 2, Box 133A, 78516. Tel: 956-702-0524. Sisters 3.
Sisters of St. Joseph of Lyon, P.O. Box 1201, 78516. Tel: 956-781-3994.

EDINBURG. *Sisters of St. Joseph of Carondelet,* 502 E. Kuhn St., 78539. Tel: 956-383-6870.

HARLINGEN. *Franciscan Sisters of Mary,* 3401 Business 83, #85, 78552-3517. Tel: 956-423-9447.
Sisters of the Incarnate Word and Blessed Sacrement, 502 E. Polk St., 78550. Tel: 956-428-3567.

LA FERIA. *Congregation of Notre Dame of Montreal,* 208

W. Cypress St., P.O. Box 1476, 78559-1116. Tel: 956-797-2774.

MCALLEN. *Maryknoll Sisters of St. Dominic, Inc.*, 700 Jackson Ave., #161, 78501. Tel: 956-682-3112. Sisters 2.

Missionary Sisters of the Immaculate Heart of Mary, 816 S. 27th St., 78501-7750. Tel: 956-631-0208. Sisters 2.

School Sisters of Notre Dame, 700 W. Jackson Ave., #151, 78501. Tel: 956-682-2482. Sisters 2.

Sisters of Mercy of the Americas. (St. Louis), 1400 N. 16th St., Apt. 111, 78501-4460. Tel: 956-687-2620.

Sisters of Mercy of the Americas. (St. Louis), Rte. 4, Box 1680, 78504-9802. Tel: 956-686-6047. Sisters 2.

MISSION. *Misioneras Catequistas de los Pobres*, 615 Dunlap, 78572. Tel: 956-585-1376. Sisters 2.

Misioneras Eucaristicas Franciscanas, 2207 Washington St., 78572. Tel: 956-581-3741. Sisters 3.

Sisters of St. Joseph of Carondelet, 1711 W. Gastel Cir., 78572-3037. Tel: 956-585-4870. Sisters 2.

PHARR. *Congregation of Divine Providence*, Rte. 2, Box 228-A, 78577. Tel: 956-682-3990.

Missionary Catechists of Divine Providence, 1501 W. Kelly, #367, 78577. Tel: 956-702-0453. Sisters 4.

Sisters of Mercy of the Americas. (St. Louis), 6900 Mars Ln., 78577. Tel: 956-781-5208.

PORT ISABEL. *Sisters of St. Francis*, 705 Manautau St., P.O. Box 6504, 78578. Tel: 956-943-2136.

PROGRESO. *Sisters of St. Dorothy*, P.O. Box 536, 78579. Tel: 956-565-9430. Sisters 2.

RAYMONDVILLE. *Sisters of Mercy of the Americas.* (St. Louis), 693 N. Third St., 78580. Tel: 956-689-3151.

Sisters of the Holy Cross, Casa de la Luz, 317 S. King St., 78580-2307. Tel: 956-689-3059. Sisters 3.

RIO GRANDE CITY. *Benedictine Sisters of the Good Shepherd*, Rte. 1, Box 3401, 78582. Tel: 956-486-2680. Sisters 3.

Sisters of St. Benedict, 107 S. Valle, 78582. Tel: 956-487-7927. Sisters 3.

SAN BENITO. *Missionary Sisters of the Immaculate Heart of Mary*, 1221 Combes St., 78586. Tel: 956-399-8122. Sisters 2.

Sisters of St. Francis of Penance and Charity, R.R. 1, Box 65C, 78586. Tel: 956-399-4394.

SAN JUAN. *Sisters of the Sacred Heart of Jesus*, P.O. Box 464, 78589-0464. Tel: 956-702-1967. Sisters 3.

WESLACO. *Sisters of St. Francis*, Siesta Village, Box 332, 78596. Tel: 956-968-0471. Sisters 2.

[G] RETREAT HOUSES

SAN JUAN. *San Juan Diocesan Retreat Center*, P.O. Box 747, 78589. Tel: 956-787-0033.

[H] CAMPUS MINISTRY

BROWNSVILLE. *Young Adult Ministry / University of Texas at Brownsville-Texas Southmost College*, 1850 Ridgely Rd., 78520. Tel: 956-542-3942. Sr. Gloria Ann Fiedler, C.D.P.; Hilda Escandon.

EDINBURG. *University of Texas Pan American Campus at Edinburg*, 1615 W. Kuhn St., 78539. Tel: 956-383-0133. Sr. Gloria Ann Fiedler, C.D.P.

[I] MISCELLANEOUS

BROWNSVILLE. *Bishop Enrique San Pedro, S.J. Ozanam Center*, 656 N. Minnesota Ave., 78521. Tel: 956-831-6331. Alejandro Fuentes, Dir.

Society of St. Vincent De Paul District Council, 1158 E. Jefferson St., 78520. Tel: 956-541-1755; Fax: 956-541-2374. Joan Cortinas, District Pres.

Villa Maria Language Institute, 224 Resaca Blvd., 78520. Tel: 956-546-7196. Sr. Mary Lelia Aguilar, I.W.B.S., Dir.

HARLINGEN. *KMBH-TV 60 / KHID-FM 88.1 / KMBH-FM 88.9*, P.O. Box 2147, 78551. Tel: 956-421-4111; Fax: 956-421-4150. Revs. Pedro Briseno, Admin. Supvr.; Pedro Briseno, Dir.

Board of Directors: Mary Rose Cardenas; Very Rev. Leo Francis Daniels, C.O.; Rick Diaz; Noe Gonzalez, Judge; Rogelio Rotello Rios.

Ex-Officios: Revs. Gustave Barrera, (Commission for Evangelization); Eduardo Ortega, Chancellor.

Consultants: Pamela Downing; Sonia Perez.

MCALLEN. *Comfort House / Casa del Conseulo*, 617 Dallas Ave., 78501. Tel: 956-687-7367; Fax: 956-630-6423. Sr. Marian Strohmeyer, R.S.M., Admin. & Dir. Bed Capacity 10. AIDS Education & Outreach.

Secular Franciscan Order, Fraternity of Our Lady of Guadalupe, 3600 N. 23rd, Ste. 205, 78501. Tel: 956-687-6816. Rev. Tomas Mateos, S.F.O., Asst. Spiritual Dir.; Paula Cortez, Min. Prefect; Maria Celia Solis, Vice Min. Prefect; Rafael Solis, Sec. & Treas.; Sr. Teresita L. MacLang, S.F.O., Formator.

MERCEDES. *La Merced Charitable Trust*, 413 S. Virginia, P.O. Box 806, 78570. Tel: 956-565-2622.

Housing Board: Mrs. Anita A. Rodriguez, Staff; Mrs. Ana Zamarripa, Res. Mgr.

MISSION. *Cursillos* (San Juan), 1100 Elm St., 78572. Tel: 956-585-1337. Epitacio Flores, Contact Person.

El Rosario Charitable Trust, 119 Retama, P.O. Box 971, 78572. Tel: 956-585-5051.

SAN JUAN. *Virgen de San Juan del Valle Shrine*, P.O. Box 747, 78589. Tel: 956-787-0033; Fax: 956-787-2908. Rev. Juan Nicolau, Rector. Associates: Revs. Carlos Garza; Ricardo Ayala, III.

San Juan Retreat Center. Tel: 956-787-0033.

San Juan Pilgrim House / Hotel. Tel: 956-787-0033, Ext. 249.

Religious Gift & Book Store. Tel: 956-787-0033, Ext. 332.

San Juan Print Shop. Tel: 956-787-0033, Ext. 350.

RELIGIOUS INSTITUTES OF MEN REPRESENTED IN THE DIOCESE

For further details refer to the corresponding bracketed number in the Religious Institutes of Men or Women section.

[0630]—*Congregation of the Missionaries of the Holy Family*.—M.S.F.

[1130]—*Congregation of the Priests of the Sacred Heart*.—S.C.J.

[1140]—*Fathers of the Sacred Hearts*.—SS.CC.

[0410]—*Franciscans-Assumption BVM Province*.—O.F.M.

[0770]—*The Marist Brothers*.—F.M.S.

[0780]—*Marist Priests and Brothers of the Society of Mary*.—S.M.

[0860]—*Missionhurst Congregation of the Immaculate Heart of Mary*.—C.I.C.M.

[0910]—*Oblates of Mary Immaculate*.—O.M.I.

[0950]—*Oratorians of St. Philip Neri*.—C.O.

RELIGIOUS INSTITUTES OF WOMEN REPRESENTED IN THE DIOCESE

[]—*Adorers of the Blood of Christ*.

[]—*Benedictine Sisters of Crookston, Minnesota*.—O.S.B.

[]—*Benedictine Sisters of the Good Shepherd (Monastery)*.—O.S.B.

[]—*Congregation of Divine Providence (Helotes)*.—C.D.P.

[]—*Congregation of Notre Dame*.—C.N.D.

[0470]—*Congregation of the Sisters of Charity of the Incarnate Word, Houston, Texas*.—C.C.V.I.

[1920]—*Congregation of the Sisters of the Holy Cross*.—C.S.C.

[0760]—*Daughters of Charity of St. Vincent de Paul*.—D.C.

[]—*Dominican Sisters of Grand Rapids, Michigan*.—O.P.

[]—*Dominican Sisters of Sinsinawa, WI*.—O.P.

[]—*Dominican Sisters of St. Catherine of Kentucky*.—O.P.

[1070-09]—*Dominican Sisters of St. Dominic*. (Racine, WI).—O.P.

[1070-05]—*Dominican Sisters of the Presentation*.—O.P.

[1200]—*Franciscan Sisters of Baltimore*.—O.S.F.

[1310]—*Franciscan Sisters of Little Falls, Minnesota*.—O.S.F.

[1415]—*Franciscan Sisters of Mary*.—F.S.M.

[2470]—*Maryknoll Sisters of St. Dominic, Inc.*.—M.M.

[1150]—*Misioneras Eucaristicas Franciscanas*.—M.E.F.

[2690]—*Missionary Catechists of Divine Providence*.—M.C.D.P.

[]—*Missionary Sisters of Jesus*.—M.J.

[2750]—*Missionary Sisters of the Immaculate Heart of Mary*.—I.C.M.

[]—*Missionary Sisters of the Society of Mary*.—S.M.S.M.

[]—*Missioneras Catequistas de los Pobres*.—M.C.P.

[2420]—*Missionary Sisters of the Society of Mary*.—S.M.S.M.

[2970]—*School Sisters of Notre Dame*. (Prov. of Dallas).—S.S.N.D.

[]—*School Sisters of Notre Dame*. (Mankato Prov.).—S.S.N.D.

[]—*Sisters for a Christian Community*.—S.F.C.C.

[0440]—*Sisters of Charity of Cincinnati, Ohio*.—S.C.

[0480]—*Sisters of Charity of Leavenworth, Kansas*.—S.C.L.

[0460]—*Sisters of Charity of the Incarnate Word*. (San Antonio, TX).—C.C.V.I.

[]—*Sisters of Christian Charity*.—S.C.C.

[]—*Sisters of Divine Providence*. (Pennsylvania).—C.D.P.

[1010]—*Sisters of Divine Providence of St. Louis*.—C.D.P.

[2575]—*Sisters of Mercy of the Americas*. (St. Louis, MO; Cincinnati, OH).—R.S.M.

[3790]—*Sisters of St. Dorothy*.—S.S.D.

[1720]—*Sisters of St. Francis of Our Lady of Lourdes*.—O.S.F.

[1760]—*Sisters of St. Francis of Penance and Charity*.—O.S.F.

[3840]—*Sisters of St. Joseph of Carondelet*. (St. Paul & St. Louis Provs.).—C.S.J.

[]—*Sisters of St. Joseph of Lyon*.

[2980]—*Sisters of the Congregation of Notre Dame of Montreal*.—C.N.D.

[2050]—*Sisters of the Holy Spirit and Mary Immaculate*.—S.H.Sp.

[2200]—*Sisters of the Incarnate Word and Blessed Sacrament*.—I.W.B.S.

[]—*Sisters of the Living Word*.—S.L.W.

[3320]—*Sisters of the Presentation of the Blessed Virgin Mary*.—P.B.V.M.

[3670]—*Sisters of the Sacred Heart of Jesus*.—S.S.C.J.

[]—*Ursuline Sisters*.—O.S.U.

NECROLOGY

(No Deaths)

Diocese of Buffalo

(Dioecesis Buffalensis)

Most Reverend

HENRY J. MANSELL, D.D.

Bishop of Buffalo; ordained December 19, 1962; appointed Titular Bishop of Marazane and Auxiliary of New York November 24, 1992; ordained January 6, 1993; appointed to Buffalo April 18, 1995; installed June 12, 1995. *Res., 77 Oakland Pl., Buffalo, NY, 14222-2041.*

Chancery Office: 795 Main St., Buffalo, NY, 14203. Tel.: 716-847-5500; Fax: 716-847-5557.

Web site address: http://www.buffalodiocese.org

E-mail address: dob@servtech.com

Most Reverend

EDWARD D. HEAD, D.D.

Bishop Emeritus of Buffalo; ordained January 27, 1945; appointed Titular Bishop of Ardstratha and Auxiliary of New York January 27, 1970; consecrated March 19, 1970; appointed to Buffalo January 17, 1973; installed March 19, 1973; retired June 12, 1995. *Res., 795 Main St., Buffalo, NY, 14203-1250.*

Most Reverend

BERNARD J. McLAUGHLIN, D.D., V.G.

Retired Auxiliary Bishop of Buffalo; Titular Bishop of Mottola; ordained December 21, 1935; appointed December 28, 1968; consecrated January 6, 1969; retired January 15, 1988. *Res., 204 Knoche Rd., Tonawanda, NY, 14150.*

Most Reverend

EDWARD M. GROSZ, D.D.

Auxiliary Bishop of Buffalo; Titular Bishop of Morosbisdo; ordained May 29, 1971; appointed November 22, 1989; consecrated February 2, 1990. *Res., St. Stanislaus Kostka Rectory, 2437 Niagara St., Niagara Falls, NY, 14303-1925.*

ESTABLISHED APRIL 23, 1847.

Incorporated under the laws of the State of New York October 30th, 1897. Re-incorporated by special act passed April 5, 1951, Chapter 568 of the laws of 1951. Corporate Title: *The Diocese of Buffalo, N.Y.*

Square Miles 6,357.

Comprises the Counties of Erie, Niagara, Genesee, Orleans, Chautauqua, Wyoming, Cattaraugus and Allegany in the State of New York.

For legal titles of parishes and diocesan institutions, consult the Chancery Office.

STATISTICAL OVERVIEW

Personnel	
Bishop	1
Auxiliary Bishops	1
Retired Bishops	2
Priests: Diocesan Active in Diocese	325
Priests: Active Outside Diocese	11
Priests: Diocesan in Foreign Missions	1
Priests: Retired, Sick or Absent	111
Number of Diocesan Priests	448
Religious Priests in Diocese	199
Extern Priests in Diocese	6
Ordinations:	
Diocesan Priests	6
Transitional Deacons	1
Permanent Deacons	6
Permanent Deacons in Diocese	88
Total Brothers	47
Total Sisters	1,472
Parishes	
Parishes	266
With Resident Pastor:	
Resident Diocesan Priests	215
Resident Religious Priests	15
Without Resident Pastor:	
Administered by Priests	35
Administered by Women Religious	1
Missions	10
Welfare	
Catholic Hospitals	7
Total Assisted	989,424
Homes for the Aged	16
Total Assisted	1,702
Day Care and Extended Day Care Centers	2
Total Assisted	203
Specialized Homes	3
Total Assisted	337
Special Centers for Social Services	4
Total Assisted	2,756
Educational	
Seminaries, Diocesan	2
Students from This Diocese	9
Students from Other Diocese	15
Diocesan Students in Other Seminaries	9
Total Seminarians	18
Colleges and Universities	7
Total Students	14,765
High Schools, Private	17
Total Students	6,046
Elementary Schools, Diocesan and Parish	88
Total Students	22,864
Elementary Schools, Private	6
Total Students	1,743
Catechesis/Religious Education:	
High School Students	12,741
Elementary Students	40,459
Total Students Under Catholic Instruction	98,636
Teachers in the Diocese:	
Priests	22
Brothers	6
Sisters	140
Lay Teachers	1,818
Vital Statistics	
Receptions into the Church:	
Infant Baptism Totals	8,140
Adult Baptism Totals	219
Received into Full Communion	521
First Communions	8,314
Confirmations	6,051
Marriages:	
Catholic	2,234
Interfaith	809
Total Marriages	3,043
Deaths	7,299
Total Catholic Population	749,655
Total Population	1,603,544

Former Bishops—Rt. Rev. JOHN TIMON, D.D., C.M., cons. Oct. 17, 1847; died April 16, 1867.—Rt. Rev. STEPHEN V. RYAN, D.D., C.M., cons. Nov. 8, 1868; died April 10, 1896.—Rt. Rev. JAMES EDWARD QUIGLEY, D.D., cons. Bishop of Buffalo, Feb. 24, 1897; promoted to the Archdiocese of Chicago, Feb. 19, 1903; died July 10, 1915.—Rt. Rev. CHARLES HENRY COLTON, D.D., cons. Aug. 24, 1903; died May 9, 1915.—His Eminence DENIS CARDINAL DOUGHERTY, D.D., cons. Bishop of Nueva Segovia, June 14, 1903; transferred to the Diocese of Jaro, April 19, 1908; transferred to the Diocese of Buffalo, Dec. 6, 1915; promoted to Archdiocese of Philadelphia, May 1, 1918; created Cardinal, March 7, 1921; died May 31, 1951.—Most Rev. WILLIAM TURNER, D.D., cons. March 30, 1919; died July 10, 1936.—Most Rev. JOHN A. DUFFY, D.D., cons. Bishop of Syracuse, June 29, 1933; transferred to the Diocese of Buffalo, April 14, 1937; died Sept. 27, 1944.—His Eminence JOHN CARDINAL O'HARA, C.S.C., ord. Sept. 9, 1916; appt. Military Delegate of the Armed Forces and Titular Bishop of Mylasa, Dec. 11, 1939; cons. Jan. 15, 1940; transferred to Buffalo, March 10, 1945; installed May 8, 1945; promoted to the Archdiocese of Philadelphia, Nov. 23, 1951; created Cardinal, Dec. 15, 1958; died Aug. 28, 1960.—Most Rev. JOSEPH A. BURKE, D.D., cons. Titular Bishop of Vita and Auxiliary, June 29, 1943; promoted to the See, Feb. 9, 1952; died Oct. 16, 1962.—Most Rev. JAMES A. McNULTY, D.D., cons. Oct. 7, 1947; Titular Bishop of Methone and Auxiliary Bishop of Newark, NJ; appt. Bishop of Paterson, NJ April 9, 1953; transferred to Buffalo, Feb. 12, 1963; died Sept. 4, 1972.—Most Rev. EDWARD D. HEAD, D.D., ord. Jan. 27, 1945; appt. Titular Bishop of Ardstratha and Auxiliary of New York, Jan. 27, 1970; cons. March 19, 1970; appt. Bishop of Buffalo, Jan. 17, 1973; installed March 19, 1973; retired June 12, 1995.

Vicars General—Most Rev. EDWARD M. GROSZ, D.D.; Rev. Msgr. ROBERT J. CUNNINGHAM, P.A., J.C.L.

Chancery Office—795 Main St., Buffalo, 14203. Tel: 716-847-5500; Fax: 716-847-5557. Office Hours: Mon.-Fri. 9-4:30.

Chancellor—Rev. Msgr. ROBERT J. CUNNINGHAM, P.A., J.C.L., V.G.

Vice Chancellor—Rev. PAUL A. LITWIN, J.C.L.

Secretary to Ordinary and Vice Chancellor—Rev. DAVID G. LIPUMA.

Diocesan Tribunal—795 Main St., Buffalo, 14203. Tel: 716-847-8769; Fax: 716-847-8772. Send all rogatory commissions to the Tribunal.

Judicial Vicar—Rev. SALVATORE MANGANELLO, S.T.L., J.C.L.

Adjunct Judicial Vicar—Rev. PAUL P. SABO.

Defenders of the Bond—Revs. FRANCIS T. NOWAK; EDWARD R. CZARNECKI; FRANCIS X. MAZUR; GREGORY M. FAULHAUBER; DENNIS A. FRONCZAK; DONALD E. LEVAN, J.C.L.; ROBERT E. ZAPFEL, S.T.D.; DAVID A. ZWIFKA, J.C.L.

Advocates—Deacons DANIEL E. BRICK; MICHAEL P. MCKEATING; Revs. RICHARD DIGIULIO; ROBERT W. VOGT.

Auditor—Sr. MARY HARTLEY, S.S.M.N.

Promotor of Justice—Rev. Msgr. JEROME W. SULLIVAN, J.C.D.

Judges—Revs. JAMES M. AUGUSTYN; VINCENT J. BECKER; WALLACE T. BORUCKI; PAUL R. BOSSI; Rev. Msgr. ANTHONY J. CALIGIURI; Rev. Msgr. ROBERT J. CUNNINGHAM, J.C.L., V.G.; Revs. CHESTER S. FRYSIAK; JOHN R. GAGLIONE; Rev. Msgr. WILLIAM J. GALLAGHER; Rev. FRED D. INGALLS; Sr. JOLENE JASINSKI, C.S.S.F., J.C.L.; Revs. JEROME E. KOPEC, J.C.L.; DONALD E. LEVAN, J.C.L.; PAUL A. LITWIN, J.C.L.; Rev. Msgr. JOHN W. MADSEN; Sr. SANDRA MAKOWSKI, J.C.L.; Revs. SALVATORE MANGANELLO, J.C.L.; BERNARD OLSZEWSKI, O.F.M.Conv., J.C.D.; HENRY A. ORSZULAK; PAUL P. SABO; Rev. Msgr. DAVID S. SLUBECKY, S.T.L., J.C.L.; Rev. Msgr. GEORGE B. YIENGST; Rev. DAVID A. ZWIFKA.

Notaries—Sr. AGNITA BROWN; LUCILLE BUCZEK; ROBIN COLVIN.

Consultors, College of—Most Rev. EDWARD M. GROSZ, D.D.; Rev. Msgr. ROBERT J. CUNNINGHAM, P.A., J.C.L., V.G.; Rev. RODERICK M. BROWN, O.P.; Rev. Msgr. RICHARD M. CAHILL; Rev. Msgr. GERALD L. GREEN; Rev. JEROME E. KOPEC; Rev. Msgr. JOHN W. MADSEN; Rev. LOUIS P. TROTTA, C.M.

Council of Priests—Most Rev. HENRY J. MANSELL, D.D., Pres.; Most Rev. EDWARD M. GROSZ, D.D.; Rev. Msgr. ROBERT J. CUNNINGHAM, P.A., J.C.L., V.G.; Revs. JOSEPH BAYNE, O.F.M.Conv.; RODERICK M. BROWN, O.P.; Rev. Msgr. RICHARD M. CAHILL; Rev. Msgr. ALBERT W. CLODY; Rev. Msgr. JOHN J. CONNIFF; Revs. GREGORY J. DOBSON; JOSEPH G. FIFAGROWICZ; Rev. Msgr. GERARD L. GREEN; Rev. Msgr. HENRY J. GUGINO; Revs. A. MARK ILLIG; JEROME E. KOPEC; JOHN J. LEISING; MICHAEL P. MCNICHOLL; Rev. Msgr. JOHN W. MADSEN; Revs. ROBERT A. MARTIN; ROBERT M. MOCK; Rev. Msgr. ROBERT E. MURPHY; Revs. SEBASTIAN C. PIERRO; JOSEPH F. POWER, O.S.F.; RICHARD A. REINA; Rev. Msgr. EDWARD J. SCANLAN; Revs. RICHARD W. SIEPKA; BERNARD C. STASZAK; PAUL W. STELLER; JEROME J. STELMACH; PAUL F. STENGEL; WALTER J. SZCZESNY; LOUIS P. TROTTA, C.M.; MICHAEL G. UEBLER; ROBERT W. VOGT; Rev. Msgr. JAMES E. WALL; Rev. MARK J. WOLSKI; Rev. Msgr. RUPERT A. WRIGHT; Rev. RICHARD E. ZAJAC.

Vicariates—

Vicars—Rev. PAUL R. BOSSI, Northwest Buffalo; Rev. RODERICK M. BROWN, O.P., Central Buffalo; Rev. Msgr. MATTHEW S. KOPACZ, Southeast Buffalo; Rev. Msgr. RUPERT A. WRIGHT, Northern Erie; Rev. Msgr. DAVID S. SLUBECKY, Eastern Erie; Rev. Msgr. ROBERT C. WURTZ, Western Erie; Rev. DENNIS G. WOLF, Allegany; Rev. LAWRENCE M. MILBY, Northern Cattaraugus; Rev. GREGORY J. DOBSON, Southern Cattaraugus; Rev. PATRICK H. ELIS, Northern Chautauqua; Rev. Msgr. ANTOINE P. ATTEA, Southern Chautauqua; Rev. Msgr. LEO F. MCCARTHY, Genesee; Rev. Msgr. DONALD R. WANGLER, Eastern Niagara; Most Rev. EDWARD M. GROSZ, Western Niagara; Rev. RICHARD A. CSIZMAR, Orleans; Rev. RICHARD W. BLAZEJEWSKI, Wyoming.

The Diocese of Buffalo, N.Y.—A corporation under the laws of the State of New York. Most Rev. HENRY J. MANSELL, D.D., Pres.; Most Rev. EDWARD M. GROSZ, D.D., Vice Pres.; Rev. Msgr. ROBERT J. CUNNINGHAM, J.C.L., Sec.

Diocesan Offices and Directors

All offices are located at: *795 Main St., Buffalo, 14203.* Tel: 716-847-8700; Fax: 716-847-5557. (Unless otherwise noted)

Apostleship of Prayer—Rev. Msgr. WALTER O. KERN, Dir., *5337 Genesee St., Bowmansville, 14026.*

Apostleship of the Sea—Rev. Msgr. JOHN I. DUCETTE, Dir., *Res., 565 E. Park Dr., Tonawanda, 14150.*

Archives—Rev. Msgr. WALTER O. KERN, Dir. Tel: 716-847-5500.

Bishop's Committee for Christian Home and Family—Rev. Msgr. FRED R. VOORHES, Moderator. Tel: 716-847-2210.

Boy Scouts—Rev. JOHN E. KELLY, Chap. Tel: 716-847-8789. VINCENT J. HARMON, Lay Dir., *99 Clark St., Tonawanda, 15150.* Tel: 716-693-7558.

Buildings and Properties—MICHAEL SULLIVAN. Tel: 716-847-8750.

Camping—Rev. GARY J. BAGLEY. Tel: 716-847-8789.

Catholic Alumni Club—ROBERT A. LIPOME, Pres.; Rev. RICHARD W. BLAZEJEWSKI, Chap., *P.O. Box 87, Kenmore, 14223.*

Catholic Charities—Rev. Msgr. HENRY J. GUGINO, Dir., *525 Washington St., Buffalo, 14203.* Rev. JOSEPH J. SICARI, Assoc. Dir. Tel: 716-856-4494; Fax: 716-856-2005.

Catholic Charities Appeal—Rev. Msgr. HENRY J. GUGINO, Dir., Office: *525 Washington St., Buffalo, 14203.* Tel: 716-856-4494.

Catholic Communications of Western New York, Inc.—CLAIRE RUNG, Senior Producer. Tel: 716-847-8719.

Catholic Relief Services—Rev. Msgr. HENRY J. GUGINO, Dir., *525 Washington St., Buffalo, 14203.* Tel: 716-856-4494.

Church Ministry, Office of—Mrs. KATHLEEN B. HEFFERN, Coord. Tel: 716-847-5531.

Council of Catholic Men—Rev. Msgr. WILLIAM A. SCHWINGER, Moderator, *50 Franklin St., Buffalo, 14202.* Tel: 716-852-6040.

Council of Catholic Women—Rev. Msgr. JAMES E. WALL, Moderator, *6892 Lake Shore, P.O. Box 816, Derby, 14047.*

Cemeteries—CARMEN COLAO, Dir., *Mt. Olivet Cemetery, 4000 Elmwood Ave., Kenmore.* Tel: 716-873-6500.

Censors—Board of Diocesan Censors of Books and Vigilance for the Faith—Rev. Msgr. SAMUEL J. FAIOLA, S.T.D.; Rev. Msgr. THOMAS E. CRANE, S.S.L.

Charismatic Renewal Program—Rev. RICHARD S. DIGIULIO, Dir.

Christian Life Communities (Sodalities)—Rev. JOHN D. GARVEY, S.J., Diocesan Dir., *2001 Main St., Buffalo, 14208.* Tel: 716-883-7000.

Central City Apostolate—Rev. RODERICK BROWN, O.P., Vicar.

Clergy Personnel Board—Rev. PAUL W. STELLER, Coord. Tel: 716-847-5537. Rev. Msgr. WILLIAM G. STANTON; Rev. Msgr. RICHARD M. CAHILL; Rev. Msgr. FRANCIS G. WELDGEN; Revs. EUGENE P. ULRICH; CHARLES E. SLIZ; RICHARD E. ZAJAC.

Commission on Women in Church and Society—ESTHER RAE, Chm., *215 Lamarck Dr., Snyder, 14226.* Tel: 716-839-0797.

Communication—Rev. Msgr. DAVID M. LEE, Dir. Tel: 716-847-8719.

Diocesan Directory—Mrs. ROMANA REGER.

Public Relations, Assistant Director of Communications—MICHELLE MOORE.

Assistant Director of Communications for Radio—GREGG PRINCE.

Coordinator of Telecommunications—LISA STUTZ.

Computer Services (Diocesan)—JAMES C. KAVANAGH, Dir. Tel: 716-847-5500.

Continuing Education for Clergy—Co-Directors: Rev. Msgr. JAMES E. WALL; Rev. RICHARD W. SIEPKA, *Christ the King Seminary, P.O. Box 607, East Aurora, 14052.* Tel: 716-652-8900.

Cursillo Movement—ROBERT HELLER, Lay Coord.

Deaf—Rev. CONRAD P. STACHOWIAK, Chap., *425 Penora St., Depew, 14043-3721.* Tel: 716-683-3038.

Due Process—Rev. SALVATORE MANGANELLO, J.C.L., Chm., Catholic Center. Tel: 716-847-8769.

Ecumenism—(Ecumenical Liaison Committee); Revs. RICHARD E. ZAJAC; THOMAS D. DOYLE; JAMES C. CROGLIO; A. MARK ILLIG; JACOB C. LEDWON; BRENDA EASLEY-WEBB; Rev. DAVID A. ZWIFKA; Sr. DIANE LOUTTIT, D.C.; Rev. FRANCIS X. MAZUR, Ecumenical Officer.

Catholic Education (Superintendent of)—Bro. ROBERT R. BIMONTE, F.S.C., *795 Main St., Buffalo, 14203-1250.* Tel: 716-847-5501; Fax: 716-847-5593. Mrs. JUDITH M. MACDONALD, Diocesan Dir. Schools; Miss DENISE MCKENZIE, Diocesan Dir. Religious Education; Sr. M. CHRISTELLE SAWICKI, C.S.S.F., Assoc. Dir. Schools; Mrs. MARY LOU SCHULZ, Assoc. Dir. Religious Education; Mrs. MARY ELLEN O'NEIL, Dir. Curriculum & Technology; Sr. JULIE UHRICH, O.S.F., Regl. Dir. Religious Education in Allegany & Southern Cattaraugus Counties. Tel: 716-968-5776. Sr. M. CYNTHIA KILIAN, C.S.S.F., Regl. Dir. Religious Education in Chautauqua, Genesee & Northern Cattaraugus Counties, *Fredonia.* Tel: 716-679-4175., *Batavia.* Tel: 716-343-3104. Sr. MARIE PARES, O.S.F., Dir. Athletics & Physical Education; Mr. BRUCE EVERT, Dir. Finance; Mr. THOMAS E. PETERS, Dir. Govt. Programs; Sr. M. EVARISTA GOLEN, F.S.S.J., School Psychologist; Mrs. SALLY DAVIS, Dir. Food Serv.; Mrs. SUE HILL, Senior Accountant for Diocesan Education; Mrs. TINA TABERSKI, Office Mgr.

Evangelization Commission—Rev. DANIEL J. PALYS, Chm., *5271 Clinton St., Elma, 14059.* Tel: 716-668-4017.

Family Life—Rev. Msgr. FRED R. VOORHES, Dir. Tel: 716-847-2210.

Finance Office—JOHN R. O'BRIEN. Tel: 716-847-5500.

Guild for the Blind, Inc.—Rev. Msgr. HENRY J. GUGINO, Chap., Office: *525 Washington St., Buffalo.* Tel: 716-856-4494.

Health Care Apostolate—Rev. Msgr. HENRY J. GUGINO, Bishop's Rep., *525 Washington St., Buffalo, 14203.* Tel: 716-856-4494.

Holy Childhood (Pontifical) Association—Rev. Msgr. HAROLD WAGNER, Dir. Tel: 716-847-8773.

Holy Name Society—Rev. Msgr. FRANCIS B. JUCHNOWSKI, Moderator. Tel: 716-847-2202.

Hospital Chaplains—Rev. RICHARD H. AUGUSTYN, Dir. Hospital Ministry, *100 High St., Buffalo, 14203.* Tel: 716-859-5600.

Human Resources—PAUL C. EBERHARDT, Dir. Tel: 716-847-8376.

Legion of Mary—Rev. DAVID W. BIALKOWSKI, Moderator. Tel: 716-847-5545.

Liturgical Commission—Mrs. JUDITH WAGGONER, Dir. Office of Worship & Catechumenate. Tel: 716-847-5545. KAREN PODD, Pres.; Rev. RONALD B. MIERZWA, Vice Pres.

Newman Club Chaplains—Rev. PAUL W. STELLER, *Vicar Campus Ministry and Newman Club Centers, 6325 Main St., Williamsville, 14221.* Tel: 716-632-8898.

Newspaper—*"The Western New York Catholic"*; Rev. Msgr. DAVID M. LEE, Editor-in-Chief. Tel: 716-847-8719. Sr. M. FRANCIS GANGLOFF, O.S.F., Managing Editor. Tel: 716-849-8719.

Pamphlet Society (Catholic) of Buffalo, Inc.—Rev. Msgr. WALTER O. KERN, Dir., *120 Old Maryvale Dr., Cheektowaga, 14225.* Tel: 716-833-6617.

Pastoral Council—Rev. Msgr. WILLIAM J. MCDONNELL, Pres., *885 Sweet Home Rd., Buffalo, 14226.* Tel: 716-835-8905.

Peace and Justice (Diocesan Commission)—Rev. Msgr. JAMES G. KELLY.

Permanent Diaconate—Deacon PAUL F. WEISENBERGER, Dir.; Deacon THADDEUS V. PIJACKI, Dir. Formation. Tel: 716-847-5543.

Priests, Vicar for—Rev. Msgr. JAMES E. WALL.

Pro-Life Activities—JUDITH A. GORMAN, Coord. Tel: 716-847-2205.

Propagation of the Faith—Rev. Msgr. HAROLD WAGNER. Tel: 716-847-8711.

Purchasing (Diocesan)—Mr. PETER M. MCKEE. Tel: 716-847-8700.

Research and Planning—Sr. REGINA MURPHY, S.S.M.N. Tel: 716-847-5539.

St. Peter Claver Youth Program, Inc.—HOSIE ARNOLD, Exec. Dir., *185 Lang Ave., Buffalo, 14215.* Tel: 716-893-4651.

St. Vincent de Paul Society—Rev. Msgr. HENRY J. GUGINO, Spiritual Moderator, *1298 Main St., Buffalo, 14209.* Tel: 716-882-3360; Fax: 716-882-3556.

Spanish Speaking Apostolate—AMADOR LOPEZ, Dir.

Worship, Office of—Mrs. JUDITH WAGGONER, Dir.

Vicar for Religious—Sr. MARY DOLORES COOK, O.S.F.; Rev. JAMES J. RUDDICK, S.J., Assoc. Dir. Tel: 718-847-5529.

Vocations—Rev. ROBERT A. WOZNIAK, Dir. Tel: 716-847-5535.

Diocesan Youth Council—Rev. GARY J. BAGLEY, Dir. Tel: 716-847-8789.

Young Adult Ministry—PATRICIA BUBAR. Tel: 716-847-8788.

Dunkirk-Fredonia Youth Ministry—GAIL HASSETT, Dir., *54 Holmes Pl., Fredonia, 14063.* Tel: 716-679-7172.

CLERGY, PARISHES, MISSIONS AND PAROCHIAL SCHOOLS

CITY OF BUFFALO
(Erie County)

1—ST. JOSEPH'S CATHEDRAL (1851), Rev. Msgr. James F. Campbell, Rector. In res., Rev. Msgr. William A. Schwinger.
Res., 50 Franklin St., 14202. Tel: 716-854-5855; Fax: 716-854-5861.
School—Catholic Academy of West Buffalo Regional School. See separate listing under Regional and Consolidated Elementary Schools in the Institutions located in the Diocese.

2—ST. ADALBERT'S BASILICA (1886) (Polish), Rev. Thaddeus Nicholas Bocianowski.
Res., 212 Stanislaus St., 14212. Tel: 716-895-8091. [CEM]

3—ST. AGATHA (1921), Rev. James W. Fliss.
Res., 54 Alamo Pl., 14220. Tel: 716-822-2668.
School—Tel: 716-824-4510. Ms. Dolores Oakes, Prin.
Lay Teachers 13; Students 180.

4—ST. AGNES (1883), Rev. Guy F. Siracuse.
Res., 194 Ludington St., 14206. Tel: 716-893-0509.
School—Tel: 716-892-1441. Sr. Ann Helene Koenig, O.S.F., Prin.
Lay Teachers 15; Students 250.
Catechesis/Religious Programs—Mrs. Donna Weber, D.R.E.
Students 135.
Catholic Charities—Tel: 716-893-6418. Sr. Rose Therese Di Gregorio, O.S.F., TLCIM Project Dir.

5—ALL SAINTS (1911), Rev. Msgr. Albert W. Clody; Sr. Patrice Yarborough, S.S.M.N., Pastoral Assoc. In

res., Rev. Msgr. Francis V. Engler.
Res., 127 Chadduck Ave., 14207-1531. Tel: 716-875-8183; Fax: 716-875-6597.
School—Tel: 716-875-4174. Mrs. Cynthia Jacobs, Prin.
Sisters 2; Lay Teachers 20; Students 335.
Catechesis/Religious Programs—Nancy Schorb, D.R.E.
Students 168.

6—ST. AMBROSE (1930), Rev. Msgr. William G. Stanton; Rev. R.B. Michael Oliver; Sr. Martha Mary Whelan, R.S.M.
Res., 65 Ridgewood Rd., 14220. Tel: 716-822-5962; Fax: 716-822-0966.
School—Tel: 716-824-6360. June F. Neuner, Prin.
Sisters 2; Lay Teachers 20; Students 427.
Catechesis/Religious Programs—Tel: 716-826-4125. Sr. Pauline Petruzzella, R.S.M., D.R.E.
Students 352.

7—ST. ANN (1858), Revs. James L. Pierce, S.J.; John Heigl, M.Afr.; Sr. Marie Davis, O.S.F., Pastoral Assoc. In res., Revs. John Heigl, M.Afr.; William E. Frankhauser, S.J.
Office: 491 Emslie St., 14212. Tel: 716-852-3316.
Res., 501 Emslie St., 14212. Tel: 716-854-3742; Fax: 716-854-4131.
School—Catholic Central Regional School. See separate listing under Regional and Consolidated Elementary Schools in the Institutions located in the Diocese.

8—ANNUNCIATION (1885), Rev. James G. Judge.
Res., 18 Greenwood Pl., 14213. Tel: 716-885-2469.
Church—Lafayette Ave. & Grant St., 14213.
School—Catholic Academy of West Buffalo Regional School. See separate listing under Regional and Consolidated Elementary Schools in the Institutions located in the Diocese. Tel: 716-886-5384.
Catechesis/Religious Programs—Students 146.
Convent—257 Lafayette Ave., 14213. Tel: 716-885-6252. Sisters of St. Mary of Namur

9—ST. ANTHONY OF PADUA (1891) (Italian), Rev. Secondo Casarotto, C.S.
Res., 160 Court St., 14202. Tel: 716-854-2563.
School—Catholic Academy of West Buffalo Regional School. See separate listing under Regional and Consolidated Elementary Schools in the Institutions located in the Diocese.

10—ASSUMPTION (1888) (Polish), Rev. Richard Jedrzejewski.
Res., 435 Amherst St., 14207. Tel: 716-875-7626.
School—Our Lady of Black Rock Consolidated, 16 Germain St., 14207. Tel: 716-873-7497.
Felician Sisters 2; Students 173.

11—ST. BARTHOLOMEW. Closed 1993. Merged with Blessed Trinity Church. Records at the Catholic Center, 795 Main St., Buffalo, 14203.

12—ST. BENEDICT THE MOOR. Closed. For inquiries for parish records contact the Chancery.

13—ST. BERNARD (1906), Rev. Msgr. Francis B. Juchnowski; Revs. Francis J. Chmielewski; Donald J. Lutz.
Res., 414 S. Ogden, 14206. Tel: 716-822-8856; Fax: 716-822-8856.
School—Tel: 716-822-8057.
Congregation of Sisters of St. Felix 3; Lay Teachers 16; Students 335.

14—BLESSED SACRAMENT (1887), Rev. Paul R. Bossi; Sr. Mary Ann Mundy, S.S.M.N., Pastoral Assoc. In res., Rev. Salvatore Manganello.
Res., 330 Linwood Ave., 14209-1689. Tel: 716-884-0053; Fax: 716-884-2279.
School—Catholic Academy of West Buffalo Regional School. See separate listing under Regional and Consolidated Elementary Schools in the Institutions located in the Diocese. Tel: 716-885-6111.
Catechesis/Religious Programs—James J. Kennedy, D.R.E.
Students 80.

15—BLESSED TRINITY (1906), Rev. George L. Reger.
Res., 317 Leroy Ave., 14214. Tel: 716-833-0301; Fax: 716-834-4711.
School—Catholic Central Regional School. See separate listing under Regional and Consolidated Elementary Schools in the Institutions located in the Diocese.

16—ST. BONIFACE. Closed. For inquiries for parish records contact the Chancery.

17—ST. BRIGID. Merged with St. Columba. For inquiries for parish records contact SS. Columba & Brigid.

18—ST. CASIMIR (Polish), Rev. Msgr. Matthew S. Kopacz; Rev. James T. Bartnik. In res., Rev. Msgr. Eugene V. Marcinkiewicz.
Res., 160 Cable St., 14206. Tel: 716-824-9589.

19—SS. COLUMBA & BRIGID (1888), Rev. Roderick M. Brown, O.P., Admin.
Res., 418 N. Division St., 14204. Tel: 716-852-3331; Fax: 716-852-3331.
School—Catholic Central Regional School. See separate listing under Regional and Consolidated Elementary Schools in the Institutions located in the Diocese.

20—CORONATION OF THE BLESSED VIRGIN MARY (1950), Rev. Norman P. McTigue, Admin.
Res., 348 Dewitt St., 14213. Tel: 716-882-2650.
School—Our Lady of Black Rock School. See separate listing under Regional and Consolidated Elementary Schools in the Institutions located in the Diocese.
Catechesis/Religious Programs—Tel: 716-882-6360. Frank Antonucci, D.R.E.
Students 89.

21—CORPUS CHRISTI (Polish). (St. Anthony's Convent). Revs. Karl Kolodziejski, O.F.M.Conv.; Anthony M. Konieczny, O.F.M.Conv., Pastor Emeritus; Gregory Kwapisz, O.F.M.Conv.; Roman Siola, O.F.M.Conv.; Joseph Trawinski, O.F.M.Conv. In res., Rev. Valentine Rajter, O.F.M.Conv.
Res., 199 Clark St., 14212-1407. Tel: 716-896-1050.

22—ST. ELIZABETH OF HUNGARY (1906) (Hungarian), Rev. John Skrapits.
Res., 986 Grant St., 14207. Tel: 716-875-6586.
Convent—89 Military Rd., 14207. Tel: 716-876-2168.
Sisters of the Divine Redeemer 3.

23—ST. FLORIAN (1917), Rev. Msgr. Edward F. Synowiak; Rev. Jan Pasiewala, S.A.C.
Res., 567 Hertel Ave., 14207. Tel: 716-875-3246.
School—Our Lady of Black Rock Consolidated School. See separate listing under Regional and Consolidated Elementary Schools in the Institutions located in the Diocese.

24—ST. FRANCIS OF ASSISI (1909), Rev. Msgr. Michael E. DelVecchio; Sr. Grace Cascia, S.S.J., Pastoral Assoc.
Res., 118 Schiller St., 14206. Tel: 716-895-6813.

25—ST. FRANCIS XAVIER (1849) (German). Attended by St. John the Baptist, Buffalo. Rev. George J. Stephan; Sr. Leandra Kosmoski, S.S.J., Pastoral Assoc.
Res., 157 East St., 14207. Tel: 716-873-1911. [CEM]
School—Our Lady of Black Rock Consolidated School. See separate listing under Regional and Consolidated Elementary Schools in the Institutions located in the Diocese. Tel: 716-873-7497.
Catechesis/Religious Programs—Students 38.

26—ST. GERARD (1902) (German), Rev. Francis X. Mazur.
Res., 1190 E. Delavan Ave., 14215. Tel: 716-895-5761; Fax: 716-895-6311.
Catechesis/Religious Programs—Tel: 716-895-3751. Debra Stafford, D.R.E.
Students 66.

27—HOLY ANGELS (1852), Revs. Anthony Rigoli, O.M.I.; Martin J. McMahon, O.M.I.; Louis Longen, O.M.I.; Randy Oswald, O.M.I.; Sr. Mary Courts, G.N.S.H., Pastoral Assoc. In res., Revs. Eugene Tremblay, O.M.I.; Stephen Vasek, O.M.I.; George Kirwin, O.M.I.; Daniel F. O'Leary, O.M.I., Dean of Studies, Niagara Univ.; Bro. Richard Schultz, O.M.I.
Res., 348 Porter Ave., 14201. Tel: 716-885-3767.
School—Catholic Academy of West Buffalo Regional School. See separate listing under Regional and Consolidated Elementary Schools in the Institutions located in the Diocese. Tel: 716-885-6111; Fax: 716-882-8211.
Catechesis/Religious Programs—Sr. Mary Courts, G.N.S.H., D.R.E.
Students 100.

28—HOLY APOSTLES SS. PETER AND PAUL (1909) (Polish), Rev. Ronald A. Bagienski.
Res., 660 Smith St., 14210. Tel: 716-854-8971.
Catechesis/Religious Programs—Tel: 716-856-5790.
Students 180.

29—HOLY CROSS (1914), Rev. Dennis W. Mende.
Res., 345 Seventh St., 14201. Tel: 716-847-6930; Fax: 716-847-6934.
School—Catholic Academy of West Buffalo Regional School. See separate listing under Regional and Consolidated Elementary Schools in the Institutions located in the Diocese. Tel: 716-885-6111; Fax: 716-885-6452.
Catechesis/Religious Programs—D.R.E.: Marangely Gonzalez; Sr. Olivia Ortiz, C.S.S.F.
Students 58.

30—HOLY FAMILY (1902) (Irish), Rev. William R. Bigelow.
Res., 1885 S. Park Ave., 14220. Tel: 716-822-0308.
School—Tel: 716-826-6017.
Sisters of Mercy 3; Lay Teachers 15; Students 309.

31—HOLY NAME OF JESUS (1887), Rev. Robert J. Hora, Admin.
Res., 1947 Bailey Ave., 14211. Tel: 716-892-8056; Fax: 716-892-0836.

32—HOLY SPIRIT (1910), Rev. Msgr. Charles T. Griffin; Rev. Paul D. Seil.
Res., 91 Dakota Ave., 14216. Tel: 716-875-8102.
School—85 Dakota Ave., 14216. Tel: 716-875-9478. Miss Karen Adamski, Prin.
Lay Teachers 10; Students 149.

33—IMMACULATE CONCEPTION (1849), Rev. Antonio L. Rodriguez.
Res., 144 Edward St., 14201. Tel: 716-886-5627.
School—Catholic Academy of West Buffalo Regional School. See separate listing under Regional and Consolidated Elementary Schools in the Institutions located in the Diocese. Tel: 716-885-6111.
Catechesis/Religious Programs—D.R.E.: Maria Orta; Kim Vargas.
Students 44.

34—IMMACULATE HEART OF MARY (1946), Rev. Richard H. Augustyn, Admin.
Res., 381 Edison St., 14215. Tel: 716-894-6953.

35—ST. JAMES (1916), Revs. Robert L. Gebhard, Admin.; Peter Nami, O.M.I.; Sr. Katherine Bogner, S.S.M.N., Pastoral Assoc.; Deacon Dennis Kapsiak.
Res., 10 Hastings Ave., 14215. Tel: 716-834-5601.
Convent—36 Davidson St., 14215. Tel: 716-836-7835.

36—ST. JOACHIM. Closed. For inquiries for parish records contact the Chancery.

37—ST. JOHN THE BAPTIST (1867). Attended by St. Francis Xavier, Buffalo. Rev. George J. Stephan.
Res., 60 Hertel Ave., 14207-2595. Tel: 716-875-4390.
Parish Center—410 East St., 14207. Tel: 716-873-8660.
School—Our Lady of Black Rock Consolidated School. See separate listing under Regional and Consolidated Elementary Schools in the Institutions located in the Diocese.

38—ST. JOHN THE EVANGELIST (1906), Rev. Mark J. Wolski; Sr. Catherine McGady, G.N.S.H., Pastoral Assoc.
Res., 2315 Seneca St., 14210. Tel: 716-822-2315.

39—ST. JOHN KANTY (Polish), Rev. Anthony Lutostanski. In res., Rev. Msgr. Joseph P. Waclawski; Rev. Boniface D. Ferens.
Res., 101 Swinburne St., 14212. Tel: 716-893-0412; Fax: 716-893-9864.

40—ST. JOSEPH (1850), Rev. Jacob C. Ledwon; Sr. Jeremy Midura, Pastoral Assoc.; Deacon Thaddeus V. Pijacki.
Res., 3269 Main St., 14214. Tel: 716-833-0298; Fax: 716-833-7339.
School—3275 Main St., 14214. Tel: 716-835-7395.
Sisters of St. Joseph 1; Sisters of St. Mary of Namur 2; Sisters of St. Francis of Penance and Christian Charity 2; Lay Teachers 12; Students 249.
Catechesis/Religious Programs—Tel: 716-837-2971.
Students 181.

41—ST. LAWRENCE (1929), Rev. Richard A. Reina; Sr. Jolene Ellis, O.S.F., Pastoral Assoc.; Deacon Paul Weisenburger. In res., Rev. Norbert F. Orsolits.
Res., 1520 E. Delavan Ave., 14215. Tel: 716-892-2471; Fax: 716-892-2478.
School—Kolbe Catholic Regional School. See St. John Gualbert, Cheektowaga for details. Tel: 716-895-3127.
Catechesis/Religious Programs—Tel: 716-896-0047. Sr. Joanne Fogarty, O.S.F., D.R.E.
Students 120.

42—ST. LOUIS (1829), Rev. Msgr. Robert A. Mack.
Res., 35 Edward St., 14202. Tel: 716-852-6040; Fax: 716-853-9225.
School—Catholic Academy of West Buffalo Regional School. See separate listing under Regional and Consolidated Elementary Schools in the Institutions located in the Diocese.

43—ST. LUKE (Polish). Closed. For inquiries for parish records contact the Chancery.

44—ST. MARGARET (1916), Rev. Msgr. James G. Kelly; Rev. Joseph F. Moreno; Deacon Alex Molnar.
Res., 1395 Hertel Ave., 14216. Tel: 716-876-5318; Fax: 716-875-9068.
School—Tel: 716-876-8885.
Sisters of St. Joseph 1; Lay Teachers 13; Students 194.
Catechesis/Religious Programs—Tel: 716-876-6122.
Students 208.

45—ST. MARK (1908), Rev. Msgr. Francis Braun.
Res., 401 Woodward Ave., 14214. Tel: 716-836-1600.
School—Tel: 716-836-1191.
Sisters of St. Joseph 2; Lay Teachers 15; Students 300.
Convent—223 Summit Ave., 14214. Tel: 716-837-9055.

46—ST. MARTIN (1926), Revs. Vincent J. Becker; Samuel J. Venne. In res., Rev. Thomas N. Shepherd.

Res., 1140 Abbott Rd., 14220. Tel: 716-823-7077; Fax: 716-823-4197.
School—Tel: 716-824-0726; 0727; Fax: 716-824-0727. Sr. M. Roberta, R.S.M., Prin.
Lay Teachers 24; Students 395.
Catechesis/Religious Programs—Barbara Kramer, D.R.E.
Students 130.

47—St. Mary of Sorrows (1872), Sr. Mary Augusta Kaiser, S.S.J., Parish Life Coord.; Sr. Jean Marie Zirnheld, S.S.J., Pastoral Assoc.; Deacon Jimmie L. Boyd, Sr.
Church & Offices—333 Guilford St., 14211. Tel: 716-892-4115.
School—Catholic Central Regional School. See separate listing under Regional and Consolidated Elementary Schools in the Institutions located in the Diocese.
Convent—20 Rich St., 14211. Tel: 716-892-4116; Fax: 716-896-5332. Sisters of St. Joseph.

48—St. Matthew. Closed. For inquiries for parish records contact St. Martin de Porres.

49—St. Martin de Porres (1993) (African American), Rev. Roderick M. Brown, O.P.; Deacon Ronald Walker; Sr. Philip Marie.
Office: 80 Durham Ave., 14215. Tel: 716-892-0528.
Res., 26 Wyoming Ave., 14215. Tel: 716-893-6079.
School—Catholic Central Regional School. See Regional and Consolidated Elementary Schools under Institutions Located in the Diocese.

50—St. Michael (1851), Revs. Patrick T. Sullivan, S.J.; Robert J. Boyle, S.J.; Edward L. Guth, S.J.; Thomas D. McMahon, S.J.; John G. Sturm, S.J.; Joseph R. Spellerberg, S.J.; H. James Roleke, S.J. In res., Rev. Richard J. Zanoni, S.J.
Res., 651 Washington St., 14203. Tel: 716-854-6726; Fax: 716-854-4616.
School—Catholic Academy of West Buffalo Regional School. See separate listing under Regional and Consolidated Elementary Schools in the Institutions located in the Diocese. Tel: 716-885-6111; 886-5384.

51—St. Monica. Closed. For inquiries for parish records contact the Chancery.

52—The Nativity of the Blessed Virgin (1898), Rev. Angelo M. Chimera; Deacon Caesar Zymanek.
Res., 20 Herkimer St., 14213. Tel: 716-885-1344; Fax: 716-885-2385.
School—Catholic Academy of West Buffalo Regional School. See separate listing under Regional and Consolidated Elementary Schools in the Institutions located in the Diocese. Tel: 716-885-6111.
Catechesis/Religious Programs—Tel: 716-885-4017. Mr. Leonard Rizzo, D.R.E.
Students 80.

53—Our Lady of Loretto (1940), Rev. Ronald A. Lord; Deacon Roberto Miranda.
Res., 172 15th St., 14213. Tel: 716-885-7573; Fax: 716-885-0739.
School—Catholic Academy of West Buffalo Regional School. See separate listing under Regional and Consolidated Elementary Schools in the Institutions located in the Diocese.
Catechesis/Religious Programs—Elise McDowell, D.R.E.
Students 95.

54—Our Lady of Lourdes. Closed. For inquiries for parish records contact the Chancery.

55—Our Lady of Perpetual Help, Rev. Dennis G. Riter.
Res., 115 O'Connell Ave., 14204. Tel: 716-852-2671.

56—Precious Blood (1899) (Polish), Rev. Msgr. Ronald P. Sciera.
Res., 140 Lewis St., 14206. Tel: 716-854-4623.

57—Queen of the Most Holy Rosary (Polish). Closed. For inquiries for parish records contact the Chancery.

58—Queen of Peace (1920) (Polish), Rev. Msgr. Chester S. Frysiak, Admin.
Res., 1955 Genesee St., 14211. Tel: 716-892-5646; Fax: 716-892-5647.

59—SS. Rita & Patrick (1854), Revs. Ronald Pecci, O.F.M.; Paul Osborne, O.F.M.; Bro. Maurice V. Swartout, O.F.M., Pastoral Assoc. In res., Revs. David Blake, O.F.M.; Robert Struzynski, O.F.M.; Bros. Timothy S. Dauenhauser, O.F.M.; Michael Oberst, O.F.M.
Res., St. Patrick Friary, 102 Seymour St., 14210. Tel: 716-856-5790; Fax: 716-856-4019.

60—St. Rose of Lima (1926), Revs. Theodore C. Rog; Francis J. Zmozynski.
Res., 500 Parker Ave., 14216. Tel: 716-834-6688.
School—201 Winston Rd., 14216. Tel: 716-833-4100.
Grey Nuns of the Sacred Heart 1; Lay Teachers 16; Students 220.
Catechesis/Religious Programs—Tel: 716-833-4130. Mrs. Amy Vossen Vukelic, D.R.E.
Students 195.

61—St. Stanislaus (1873) (Polish), Rev. Msgr. John R. Gabalski, P.A.
Res., 123 Townsend St., 14212. Tel: 716-854-5511. [CEM]
School—Tel: 716-854-1803.
Felician Sisters 4; Lay Teachers 10; Students 94.

62—St. Stephen (1875). (Formerly Shrine of St. Jude). Rev. Robert A. Stolinski.
Res., 193 Elk St., 14210-1499.

63—St. Teresa (1897), Rev. Msgr. S. Theodore Berg. In res., Rev. Msgr. Richard C. Crumlish.
Res., 1974 Seneca St., 14210. Tel: 716-822-0608.
School—Tel: 716-822-4546.
Sisters 2; Lay Teachers 13; Students 340.
Catechesis/Religious Programs—Students 170.

64—St. Thomas Aquinas (1920), Rev. Arthur J. Smith. In res., Rev. Msgr. Eugene E. O'Loughlin.
Res., 450 Abbott Rd., 14220-1796. Tel: 716-822-1250; Fax: 716-822-2594.
School—20 Athol St., 14220-1796. Tel: 716-824-5046; Fax: 716-824-2539.
Sisters 1; Lay Teachers 25; Students 441.

65—Transfiguration (Polish). Closed. For inquiries for parish records contact the Chancery.

66—St. Valentine, Rev. Dennis G. Riter.
Res., 522 S. Park Ave., 14204. Tel: 716-854-7193.

67—St. Vincent de Paul. Closed. For inquiries for parish records contact the Chancery.

68—The Visitation of the B.V.M. (1898), Rev. Paul P. Sabo.
Res., 1040 Lovejoy St., 14206. Tel: 716-892-2289.

OUTSIDE THE CITY OF BUFFALO

Akron, Erie Co., St. Teresa of Avila (1859), Rev. Msgr. Robert J. Williamson.
Res., 5771 Buell St., P.O. Box 168, 14001. Tel: 716-542-9103. [CEM]
Catechesis/Religious Programs—Tel: 716-542-9717. Sr. Mary Ruth Warejko, C.S.S.F., D.R.E.
Students 236.

Albion, Orleans Co., St. Mary Assumption (1891) (Polish), Rev. Richard A. Csizmar; Deacon James L. Collichio.
Res., 47 Brown St., 14411. Tel: 716-589-4243; 589-5162.
St. Joseph (1852), Revs. Richard A. Csizmar; Peter J. Karalus; Deacon James L. Collichio.
Res., 106 S. Main St., 14411. Tel: 716-589-4243.
Catechesis/Religious Programs—Tel: 716-589-4492. D.R.E.: Sally Rytlewski; Carla Nellist.
Students 350.

Alden, Erie Co., St. John the Baptist (1850) (German), Revs. Fred D. Ingalls; Ivan Skenderovic; Deacon Richard J. Mahaney.
Res., 2021 Sandridge Rd., 14004. Tel: 716-937-6959. [CEM]
School—Tel: 716-937-9483; Fax: 716-937-9483. Mary Jane Liszewski, Prin.
Lay Teachers 17; Students 173.
Catechesis/Religious Programs—Tel: 716-937-3448. Mary Weisenburger, D.R.E.
Students 449.

Allegany, Cattaraugus Co., St. Bonaventure (1854), Revs. Bernardine Kessing, O.F.M.; Aquinas Reding, O.F.M.
Res., 95 E. Main St., 14706. Tel: 716-373-1330; Fax: 716-373-4220.
School—Southern Tier Catholic Regional School. See separate listing under Regional and Consolidated Elementary Schools in the Institutions located in the Diocese. Tel: 716-372-2891.
Catechesis/Religious Programs—Tel: 716-373-0430. Mrs. Margaret Duch, D.R.E.
Students 273.
Mission—Vandalia, Cattaraugus Co., St. John the Baptist. S. Nine Mile Rd.

Almond, Allegany Co., SS. Brendan and Jude (1992), Rev. Eugene P. Ulrich. Pastoral Assocs.: Susan Fowler; Robert Donius.
Res., 14804. Tel: 607-276-5304; Fax: 607-587-9411.
Church—11 S. Main St., Box G, 14804.

Amherst, Erie Co., St. Leo (1953), Rev. Msgr. William J. McDonnell; Revs. Karl E. Loeb; John E. Kelly.
Res., 885 Sweet Home Rd., Buffalo, 14226. Tel: 716-835-8905; Fax: 716-835-8997.
School—Tel: 716-832-6340. Mr. George J. Drescher, Prin.
Sisters of Third Order of St. Francis 1; Lay Teachers 10; Students 194; Preschool Students 81.
Catechesis/Religious Programs—Tel: 716-833-8359. Sr. Judith Beiswanger, O.S.F., D.R.E.
Students 438.

Andover, Allegany Co., Blessed Sacrament (1855), Rev. Fred G. Fingerle.
Res., One Church St., Box 761, 14806-0761. Tel: 607-478-8885. [CEM]

Angelica, Allegany Co., Sacred Heart (1848), Rev. John E. Kelly.
Res., 5 Milton St., Belmont, 14813-1119. Tel: 716-268-7272; Fax: 716-268-7272.
Church—Park Cir., 14709.

Angola, Erie Co., Most Precious Blood, Revs. Bernard U. Nowak; James A. Staebell. In res., Rev. Msgr. Gerald J. Kreuzer.
Res., 22 Prospect St., 14006. Tel: 716-549-0420. [CEM]
School—17 Prospect St., 14006. Tel: 716-549-1818. Franciscan Sisters of St. Joseph 3; Lay Teachers 7; Students 160.

Arcade, Wyoming Co., SS. Peter and Paul (1907), Rev. Michael G. Uebler.
Res., 417 Main St., 14009-1195. Tel: 716-492-5330. [CEM]
Catechesis/Religious Programs—Students 159.

Athol Springs, Erie Co., St. Francis of Assisi (1929), Revs. Steven G. Frenier, O.F.M.Conv.; Michael Englert, O.F.M.Conv.; Sharon Kabel, Pastoral Assoc.
Res., S-4263 St. Francis Dr., 14010. Tel: 716-627-2710; Fax: 716-627-5263.
School—Tel: 716-627-2841. Sr. Mary Anne Siwak, F.S.S.J., Prin.
Franciscan Sisters of St. Joseph 1; Lay Teachers 10; Students 61.
Catechesis/Religious Programs—Tel: 716-627-3357. Annette Breen, D.R.E.
Students 411.

Attica, Wyoming Co., St. Vincent de Paul (1857), Rev. Stanley R. Chwalinski.
Res., 50 East Ave., 14011. Tel: 716-591-1228; Fax: 716-591-1614. [CEM]
School—Genesee-Wyoming Catholic Central Consolidated School. See separate listing under Regional and Consolidated Elementary Schools in the Institutions located in the Diocese. Tel: 716-591-2515; Fax: 716-741-9762.
Catechesis/Religious Programs—Students 236.

Barker, Niagara Co., St. Patrick (1856), Rev. James F. Hassett.
Res., 14012. Tel: 716-795-3331; Fax: 716-795-3919.
Catechesis/Religious Programs—Students 181.

Batavia, Genesee Co.,

1—St. Anthony, (1908) (Italian), Rev. Joseph S. Spatorico.
Res., 122 Liberty St., 14020. Tel: 716-343-0914; Fax: 716-344-8376.
School—Tel: 716-343-5561.
Sisters of Mercy 2; Lay Teachers 13; Students 125.
Catechesis/Religious Programs—Students 245.

2—St. Joseph, (1849), Rev. Msgr. Leo F. McCarthy; Deacon John Stone. In res., Revs. Robert A. Martin; Matthias W. Kibuka.
Res., 303 E. Main St., 14020. Tel: 716-343-5800; Fax: 716-345-9525. [CEM]
School—Tel: 716-343-6154. Samuel Zalacca, Prin.
Lay Teachers 15; Students 278; Preschool Students 52.
Catechesis/Religious Programs—Samuel Zalacca, D.R.E.
Students 295.
Mission—South Byron, Genesee Co., St. Michael, (1892). Rev. Msgr. Leo F. McCarthy.

3—St. Mary, (1906), Revs. Donald W. Becker; Ivan R. Trujillo.
Res., 18 Ellicott St., 14020. Tel: 716-343-5400; Fax: 716-344-0213.
School—Tel: 716-343-6866.
Lay Teachers 8; Students 153.
Catechesis/Religious Programs—40 Woodrow Rd., 14020.
Students 160.
Mission—St. Pius X. Closed. For inquiries for Sacramental Records contact St. Mary, Batavia.

4—Sacred Heart, (1904) (Polish), Rev. Eugene S. Slomba.
Res., 15 Sumner St., 14020. Tel: 716-343-1796; Fax: 716-344-3752.

Belfast, Allegany Co., St. Patrick (1859), Rev. Francis J. Jann.
Res., 31 E. Hughes St., 14711. Tel: 716-365-2115. [CEM]

Belmont, Allegany Co., St. Mary (1861), Rev. John E. Kelly.
Res., 5 Milton St., 14813. Tel: 716-268-7272; Fax: 716-268-7272.
Mission—Scio, Allegany Co., St. Joseph. [CEM]

Bemus Point, Chautauqua Co., Our Lady of Lourdes (1948), Rev. John L. Kuhlmann.
Res., 42 Main St., P.O. Box 500, 14712. Tel: 716-386-2400; Fax: 716-386-2400.

Bennington Center, Wyoming Co., Sacred Heart of Jesus (1872) (Polish), Rev. Joseph A. Fiore.
Res., 1230 Clinton St., Attica, 14011. Tel: 716-591-0176; Fax: 716-591-4818. [CEM]
School—Genesee-Wyoming Catholic Central Consolidated School. See separate listing under Regional and Consolidated Elementary Schools in the

Institutions located in the Diocese. Tel: 716-591-2515; Fax: 716-591-1614.
Catechesis/Religious Programs—Tel: 716-591-0205. Mrs. Wendy Murray, D.R.E.
Students 103.

Bergen, Genesee Co., St. Brigid (1861), Rev. Richard J. Keppeler.
Res., P.O. Box 219, 14416. Tel: 716-494-1110. [CEM]
Catechesis/Religious Programs—Students 190.

Blasdell, Erie Co., Our Mother of Good Counsel (1905), Revs. Lawrence E. Burns; Edward R. Czarnecki.
Res., 3688 S. Park Ave., 14219. Tel: 716-822-2630.
School—15 Oakwood Ave., 14219. Tel: 716-823-6286. Mrs. Bonnie Ryan, Prin.
Sisters of St. Joseph 1; Lay Teachers 14; Students 186.
Catechesis/Religious Programs—Cheryl McNerney, D.R.E.
Students 350.

Bliss, Wyoming Co., St. Joseph (1907), Rev. Edward E. Muerder.
Res., St. Nicholas Rectory, Rte. 98, North Java, 14113. Tel: 716-535-7457.
Church—P.O. Box 80, 14024. Tel: 716-322-8866.

Blossom, Erie Co., St. Gabriel (1925), Revs. Daniel J. Palys; Perry A. Ciambella; Arthur J. Mattulke; Ann Bauman, Pastoral Assoc.
Res., 5271 Clinton St., P.O. Elma, 14059-7617. Tel: 716-668-4017; Fax: 716-656-0616.
Catechesis/Religious Programs—Tel: 716-668-2070. Rose Andrews, D.R.E.
Students 1,070.

Bolivar, Allegany Co., St. Mary (1903), Rev. Robert J. Schober; Deacon Don Radlinski.
Res., Sacred Heart, 43 Maple Ave., Portville, 14770. Tel: 716-933-6394. [CEM]
Church—111 Wellsville St., 14715. Tel: 716-928-1024.

Boston, Erie Co., St. John the Baptist (1869), Rev. Msgr. Paul F. Stengel.
Res., 14025. Tel: 716-941-3549. [CEM]
Catechesis/Religious Programs—Tel: 716-941-6363.
Students 290.

Bowmansville, Erie Co., Sacred Heart (1920), Rev. Msgr. Walter O. Kern; Rev. Msgr. Arnold J. Schneider.
Res., 5337 Genesee St., 14026-1098. Tel: 716-683-2375. [CEM]
School—SS. Peter & Paul Consolidated School. See separate listing under Regional and Consolidated Elementary Schools in the Institutions located in the Diocese. Tel: 716-683-8049.

Brant, Erie Co., Our Lady of Mt. Carmel (1906), Rev. James E. Fitzgerald.
Res., 10708 Brant-Angola Rd., P.O. Box 225, 14027-0225. Tel: 716-549-2418; Fax: 716-549-7740. [CEM]

Brocton, Chautauqua Co., St. Patrick (1922), Rev. Robert G. Beiter.
Res., 12 Central Ave., P.O. Box P, 14716-0675. Tel: 716-792-4125; Fax: 716-792-4772.
School—Northern Chautauqua Catholic Regional School. See separate listing under Regional and Consolidated Elementary Schools in the Institutions located in the Diocese.
Catechesis/Religious Programs—Diana Giambra, D.R.E.
Students 120.

Canaseraga, Allegany Co., St. Mary (1855), Rev. Robert M. Mock.
Mailing Address: P.O. Box 404, Portageville, 14536-0404.
Res., 7 North St., Box 234, 14822. Tel: 607-545-8943; Fax: 716-468-2126. [CEM]

Cassadaga, Chautauqua Co., Immaculate Conception, Rev. Patrick H. Elis.
Res., 14718. Tel: 716-595-3141.

Cattaraugus, Cattaraugus Co., St. Mary's (1863), Rev. Wallace T. Borucki.
Res., 36 Washington St., 14719. Tel: 716-257-9351.
Convent—65 South St., 14719. Tel: 716-257-9781. Missionary Sisters of the Divine Child

Cheektowaga, Erie Co.,

1—St. Aloysius Gonzaga, (1940), Rev. Msgr. Peter J. Popadick; Deacon Melvin Carroll.
Res., 157 Cleveland Dr., Buffalo, 14215. Tel: 716-833-1715.
School—Tel: 716-836-4549. Sr. Marilyn Ann Dudek, C.S.S.F., Prin.
Sisters of St. Felix of Cantalice 3; Lay Teachers 22; Students 302.

2—Infant of Prague, (1946), Rev. Msgr. Angelo M. Caligiuri; Rev. Richard A. Massar; Deacon Alan A. Meister. In res., Rev. Patrick Zengierski.
Res., 921 Cleveland Dr., 14225. Tel: 716-634-3660; Fax: 716-634-3661.
School—Tel: 716-632-5482; 632-5539. Robert L. Figuerca, Prin.
Sisters 3; Lay Teachers 27; Students 320.
Catechesis/Religious Programs—Sr. M. Antonita Sikorski, C.S.S.F., D.R.E.
Students 360.

3—St. John Gualbert, (1917) (Polish), Revs. Daniel A. Pokornowski; David W. Bialkowski; Deacon Franklyn C. Steffen.
Res., 83 Gualbert Ave., 14211. Tel: 716-892-5746; Fax: 716-897-3906.
School—Kolbe Catholic, Tel: 716-895-3127. Sr. Lori-ette Tokasz, Prin.
Felician Sisters 1; Lay Teachers 16; Students 239.
Catechesis/Religious Programs—Tel: 716-897-2619. Mrs. Karen Pszczolkowski, D.R.E.
Students 104.

4—St. Josaphat, (1906) (Polish), Rev. Charles E. Slisz. In res., Revs. Bernard T. Sokolowski; Robert A. Wozniak.
Res., 20 Peoria Ave., 14206. Tel: 716-893-1086; Fax: 716-893-1099.
School—Tel: 716-893-6448. Sr. Mary Thomas Frys, C.S.S.F., Prin.
Felician Sisters 1; Lay Teachers 13; Students 190.
Catechesis/Religious Programs—Tel: 716-896-5007. Maryanne Mann, D.R.E.
Students 205.

5—Most Holy Redeemer, (1913), Rev. F. Norman Sullivan. In res., Rev. Francis D. Sullivan, O.F.M.
Res., 25 Avery Pl., 14225. Tel: 716-895-7589.
School—Kolbe Catholic. See St. John Gualbert, Cheektowaga.
Catechesis/Religious Programs—Kenneth Nieves, D.R.E.
Students 55.

6—Mother of Divine Grace, (1946), Rev. Msgr. S. Paul Ayoub.
Res., 120 Old Maryvale Dr., 14225. Tel: 716-834-8488; Fax: 716-834-0335.
Catechesis/Religious Programs—Tel: 716-834-8533.
Students 160.

7—Our Lady Help of Christians, (1890). National Historic Society. Rev. Msgr. Paul R. Letourneau; Rev. Martin L. Pavlock.
Res., 4125 Union Rd., 14225. Tel: 716-634-3420; 634-3428; Fax: 716-634-3464. [CEM]
School—Tel: 716-632-4199; Fax: 716-632-4298.
Lay Teachers 15; Students 139; Preschool 78.
Catechesis/Religious Programs—Tel: 716-632-3532. Nancy Roscoe, D.R.E.
Students 382.

8—Our Lady of Czestochowa, (1922) (Polish American), Rev. Harry F. Szczesniak. In res., Rev. James H. Kasprzyk.
Res., 23 Willowlawn Pkwy., Buffalo, 14206. Tel: 716-822-5590.
School—Tel: 716-824-2225.
Lay Teachers 14; Students 125.

9—St. Philip the Apostle, (1967), Revs. Joseph H. Penkaus; James B. Cunningham; Deacon Dennis W. Kapsiak. In res., Rev. Msgr. Anthony J. Jasinski, Pastor Emeritus.
Res., 950 Losson Rd., 14227. Tel: 716-668-8370; Fax: 716-668-3824.
Catechesis/Religious Programs—Tel: 716-668-3344. Madeline Fuller, D.R.E.
Students 805.

10—Queen of Martyrs, (1946), Rev. Msgr. Max M. Kozminski; Rev. Walter Grabowski. In res., Rev. John J. Sardina.
Res., 180 George Urban Blvd., Buffalo, 14225-3095. Tel: 716-892-1746; Fax: 716-892-3005.
School—Tel: 716-895-6280. Sr. Diane Marie, C.S.S.F., Prin.
Felician Sisters 2; Lay Teachers 11; Students 134.
Catechesis/Religious Programs—Tel: 716-895-2162. Kathy Seibold, D.R.E.
Students 262.

11—Resurrection, (1944), Rev. Walter L. Matuszak; Rev. Msgr. George E. Maj, S.A.C.
Res., 130 Como Park Blvd., 14227. Tel: 716-683-3712; Fax: 716-683-3712.
School—Tel: 716-683-8785; Fax: 716-683-8785. Sr. M. Christinnete Lojewski, Prin.
Sisters 1; Lay Teachers 10; Students 105.
Catechesis/Religious Programs—Tel: 716-683-3422.
Students 178.

Cherry Creek, Chautauqua Co., St. Elizabeth. Closed. For inquiries for parish records contact the Chancery.

Clarence, Erie Co., Our Lady of Peace (1922), Rev. Msgr. Richard L. Wetter. In res., Rev. Abraham Pulikoottil.
Res., 10950 Main St., 14031. Tel: 716-759-8554; Fax: 716-759-8537.
Catechesis/Religious Programs—Students 491.

Clarence Center, Erie Co., St. Augustine (1949), Rev. Edward H. Schroeder; Deacon Norman Foster.
Res., 8700 Goodrich Rd., 14032. Tel: 716-741-2258.
Catechesis/Religious Programs—Rosey Frost, D.R.E.
Students 262.

Colden, Erie Co., Our Lady of the Sacred Heart (1912), Rev. Richard C. Coveny.
Res., 8428 Heath Rd., 14033. Tel: 716-941-5817.

Collins Center, Erie Co., St. Frances Cabrini (1955), Rev. Lawrence P. Damian.
Res., 13940 Sisson Hwy., P.O. 332, 14035. Tel: 716-532-9431.

Corfu, Genesee Co., St. Francis of Assisi, Rev. Robert E. Waters.
Res., 14036. Tel: 716-599-4933.
Mission—Crittenden, St. Patrick.

Cuba, Allegany Co., Our Lady of Angels (1850), Rev. Jerome M. Dissek.
Res., 50 South St., 14727. Tel: 716-968-2885; Fax: 716-968-0123. [CEM]
School—Southern Tier Catholic Regional School. See separate listing under Regional and Consolidated Elementary Schools in the Institutions located in the Diocese.
Catechesis/Religious Programs—Students 160.
Mission—Friendship, Sacred Heart.

Darien Center, Genesee Co., Our Lady of Good Counsel, Rev. Joseph A. Fiore. In res., Rev. Roy T. Herberger.
Res., 14040. Tel: 716-547-3547. [CEM]
School—Genesee-Wyoming Catholic Central Consolidated School. See separate listing under Regional and Consolidated Elementary Schools in the Institutions located in the Diocese.

Dayton, Cattaraugus Co., St. Paul of the Cross. Closed. For inquiries for parish records contact St. John Fisher, South Dayton.

Delevan, Cattaraugus Co., Blessed Sacrament (1947), Rev. Raymond F. Uschold.
Res., 10 N. Main St., P.O. Box 188, 14042. Tel: 716-492-2383.
Catechesis/Religious Programs—Kathleen Morris, D.R.E.
Students 131.

Depew, Erie Co.,

1—St. Augustine, (1909) (Polish), Rev. Conrad P. Stachowiak; Rev. Msgr. Henry J. Stachewicz, Pastor Emeritus.
Res., 425 Penora St., 14043. Tel: 716-683-3038. [CEM]

2—St. Barnabas, (1960), Rev. Msgr. John W. Madsen; Rev. Joseph E. Vatter; Deacon Thaddeus P. May. In res., Rev. Donald L. Measer.
Res., 2049 George Urban Blvd., 14043. Tel: 716-685-2350; Fax: 716-685-8679.
School—Tel: 716-684-1444. Sr. M. Rosa Mystica, O.S.F., Prin.
Sisters 1; Lay Teachers 15; Students 193.
Catechesis/Religious Programs—2099 George Urban Blvd., 14043. Tel: 716-685-2000. Patricia Manderscheid, D.R.E.
Students 400.

3—St. James, (1897), Rev. David J. Borowiak. In res., Rev. Henry M. Borowiak.
Res., 496 Terrace Blvd., 14043. Tel: 716-683-2746; Fax: 716-683-3121.
School—500 Terrace Blvd., 14043. Tel: 716-683-0050. Sr. Mary Georgette, Prin.
Sisters 2; Lay Teachers 17; Students 170.
Catechesis/Religious Programs—Kermy Haraszko, D.R.E.
Students 240.
Convent—55 Westfield Ave., 14043. Tel: 716-683-6653. Felician Nuns

4—SS. Peter and Paul, (1896) (Polish), Rev. Stanley F. Nowak.
Res., 86 Burlington Ave., 14043. Tel: 716-683-1645.
School—SS. Peter & Paul Consolidated School. See separate listing under Regional and Consolidated Elementary Schools in the Institutions located in the Diocese. Tel: 716-683-8049.
Catechesis/Religious Programs—Barbara Schmitt, D.R.E.
Students 180.

5—Our Lady of the Blessed Sacrament, (1965), Revs. Louis S. Dolinic; Daniel F. Fiebelkorn. In res., Rev. Msgr. Dino J. Lorenzetti.
Res., 10 French Rd., 14043. Tel: 716-684-6342; Fax: 716-684-1853.
School—20 French Rd., 14043. Tel: 716-685-2544; Fax: 716-685-9103.
Felician Sisters 1; Lay Teachers 12; Students 256.
Catechesis/Religious Programs—Tel: 716-684-2546.
Students 649.

Dunkirk, Chautauqua Co.,

1—St. Hedwig, (1902) (Polish), Rev. Joseph J. Janaczek.

Res., 324 Townsend St., 14048. Tel: 716-366-1615. [CEM]
School—Northern Chautauqua Catholic Regional School. See separate listing under Regional and Consolidated Elementary Schools in the Institutions located in the Diocese.

2—HOLY TRINITY, (1908) (Italian), Rev. Sebastian C. Pierro.
Res., 1032 Central Ave., 14048. Tel: 716-366-2306; Fax: 716-366-2309. [CEM]
School—Northern Chautauqua Catholic Regional School. See separate listing under Regional and Consolidated Elementary Schools in the Institutions located in the Diocese. Tel: 716-366-0630.
Catechesis/Religious Programs—Tel: 716-366-0499. Ruth Wilson, D.R.E.
Students 240.

3—ST. HYACINTH, (1875) (Polish American), Rev. Richard M. Poblocki; Deacon Daniel Mackowiak.
Res., 295 Lakeshore Dr., E., 14048. Tel: 716-366-7266; Fax: 716-363-0031. [CEM]
School—Tel: 716-366-1950.
Felician Sisters 3; Lay Teachers 7; Students 168.

4—ST. ELIZABETH ANN SETON, (1975), Rev. Thomas J. Wopperer; Deacons Thomas Nadeau; Moises N. Cruz; Jose J. Ruiz.
Res., 328 Washington Ave., 14048. Tel: 716-366-1750; Fax: 716-366-4398. [CEM]
School—Northern Chautauqua Catholic Regional School. See separate listing under Regional and Consolidated Elementary Schools in the Institutions located in the Diocese. Tel: 716-366-0630.
Catechesis/Religious Programs—Tel: 716-366-2827. Samuel Mancuso, D.R.E.
Students 350.

East Arcade, Wyoming Co., St. Mary's (1846), Rev. Michael G. Uebler.
Rectory & Mailing Address—6785 E. Arcade Rd., Arcade, 14009. Tel: 716-492-2282.
Res., 417 Main St., Arcade, 14009. Tel: 716-492-5330.

East Aurora, Erie Co., Immaculate Conception (1901), Rev. Msgr. Kevin T. O'Neill.
Res., 520 Oakwood Ave., 14052. Tel: 716-652-6400; Fax: 716-652-7168. [CEM]
School—510 Oakwood Ave., 14052. Tel: 716-652-5855. Susan K. Gregg, Prin.
Lay Teachers 15; Students 223.
Catechesis/Religious Programs—Tel: 716-655-0067. Rosemary A. Sacilowski, D.R.E.
Students 707.

East Bethany, Genesee Co., Immaculate Conception, Rev. Thomas L. Kemp.
Res., 5865 Ellicott St., 14054. Tel: 716-343-4537.
Catechesis/Religious Programs—Students 125.

East Eden, Erie Co., St. Mary (1835) (German-Polish), Rev. James A. Grimmer.
Res., 8175 E. Eden Rd., 14057. Tel: 716-992-4237. [CEM]
Catechesis/Religious Programs—Tel: 716-992-3123. Dorothy Zydel, D.R.E.
Students 186.

East Otto, Cattaraugus Co., St. Isidore (1957), Rev. Wallace T. Borucki.
Res., 36 Washington St., Cattaraugus, 14719. Tel: 716-257-9351.

East Pembroke, Genesee Co., Holy Name of Mary (1868), Rev. David J. Scheider, Admin.
Res., P.O. Box 219, 14056. Tel: 716-762-9006.

Eden, Erie Co., Immaculate Conception (1908), Rev. David J. Peter; Deacon Richard H. Kelsey; Sr. Phyllis Fuest, O.S.F., Pastoral Assoc. In res., Rev. Francis Parella, S.S.P.
Res., 8791 S. Main St., 14057. Tel: 716-992-3933.
School—8783 S. Main St., 14057. Tel: 716-992-3508; Fax: 716-992-2243. Mr. James Lowe, Prin.
Lay Teachers 16; Students 130.
Catechesis/Religious Programs—Sharon Reed, D.R.E.
Students 352.

St. Mary of Immaculate Conception (1858), Rev. Lawrence P. Damian.
Res., (New Oregon) 5107 Langford Rd., 14057. Tel: 716-337-2291. [CEM]

Eggertsville, Erie Co., St. Benedict (1920), Rev. Msgr. John M. Ryan; Rev. Patrick T. O'Keefe.
Res., 1317 Eggert Rd., 14226. Tel: 716-834-1041; Fax: 716-835-5949.
School—Tel: 716-835-2518. Sr. Aline Henderson, Prin.
Sisters of St. Francis of Penance and Christian Charity 4; Lay Teachers 22; Students 387.
Catechesis/Religious Programs—Tel: 716-836-6444. Sr. Virginia Judge, O.S.P., D.R.E.
Students 377.

Elba, Genesee Co., Our Lady of Fatima, Rev. Robert A. Martin, Admin.
Res., 65 S. Main St., P.O. Box 185, 14058-0185. Tel: 716-757-6891.

Ellicottville, Cattaraugus Co., Holy Name of Mary (1850), Rev. Ronald B. Mierzwa.
Res., P.O. Box 543, 14731. Tel: 716-699-2592. [CEM]
Catechesis/Religious Programs—Students 156.

Elma, Erie Co., Annunciation of the Blessed Virgin Mary (1906), Revs. Emil P. Swiatek; Robert W. Wood; Deacon Joseph Mercurio.
Res., 7580 Clinton St., 14059. Tel: 716-683-5254; Fax: 716-685-2401. [CEM]
School—Tel: 716-681-1327.
Sisters 1; Lay Teachers 20; Students 194; Preschool Students 53.
Catechesis/Religious Programs—Tel: 716-683-5515.
Students 610.

Falconer, Chautauqua Co., Our Lady of Loreto (1912) (Italian), Rev. Carlton J. Westfield.
Res., 309 W. Everett St., 14733. Tel: 716-665-4253.
Catechesis/Religious Programs—Tel: 716-665-3764. D.R.E.: Beverly Smeragliuolo; Kathy Nicastro.
Students 135.

Farnham, Erie Co., St. Anthony's (1904), Rev. Gary R. Kibler.
Res., 421 Commercial St., 14061. Tel: 716-549-1159; Fax: 716-549-7722. [CEM]
Catechesis/Religious Programs—Fax: 716-549-7742. Kathleen Brachmann, D.R.E.
Students 243.

Fillmore, Allegany Co., St. Patrick (1881), Rev. Francis P. Kowalewski.
Res., 14735. Tel: 716-567-2282. [CEM]

Forestville, Chautauqua Co., St. Rose of Lima (1850), Rev. Gerald P. Sheehan.
Res., 2773 Main Rd., Sheridan, 14135. Tel: 716-679-4951.

Franklinville, Cattaraugus Co., St. Philomena (1906), Rev. Michael D. O'Hara.
Res., 26 N. Plymouth Ave., 14737. Tel: 716-676-3629.
Catechesis/Religious Programs—Tel: 716-676-2123. Kathy Berry, D.R.E.
Students 68.

Fredonia, Chautauqua Co., St. Anthony (1905) (Italian), Rev. Daniel P. Walsh; Deacons Moises Cruz; Donald Shultz.
Res., 42 Orchard St., 14063. Tel: 716-679-4050; 674-4046 (Office).
School—Northern Chautauqua Catholic Regional School. See separate listing under Regional and Consolidated Elementary Schools in the Institutions located in the Diocese. Tel: 716-366-0630.
Catechesis/Religious Programs—Tel: 716-674-1268. Mrs. Barbara O'Connell, D.R.E.
Students 310.

St. Joseph (1899), Rev. James C. O'Connor; Deacon Matthew A. Podniesinski.
Res., 145 E. Main St., 14063. Tel: 716-679-4116; Fax: 716-679-1352 (1-5 P.M.).
School—Northern Chautauqua Catholic Regional School. See separate listing under Regional and Consolidated Elementary Schools in the Institutions located in the Diocese. Tel: 716-366-0630.
Catechesis/Religious Programs—Tel: 716-672-2647.
Students 200.

French Creek, Chautauqua Co., St. Matthias, Rev. Bernard C. Staszak.
Res., 1762 French Creek Mina Rd., Clymer, 14724-0660. Tel: 716-355-8891. [CEM]
Mission—Panama, Our Lady of the Snows, Box 236, Panama, 14767.

Frewsburg, Chautauqua Co., Our Lady of Victory (1950), Rev. Carlton J. Westfield.
Res., 14738. Tel: 716-569-4725.
Catechesis/Religious Programs—D.R.E.: Beverly Smeragliuolo; Kathy Nicastro.
Students 61.

Friendship, Allegany Co., Sacred Heart (1912), Rev. Jerome M. Dissek.
Res., 81 W. Main St., 14739. Tel: 716-973-2871. [CEM]

Gasport, Niagara Co., St. Mary (1968), Rev. Msgr. James E. Streng; Rev. Joseph P. Badding; Deacon Victor P. Crimi.
Res., 8110 West Ave., 14067. Tel: 716-772-7803.
Catechesis/Religious Programs—Deborah Brown, D.R.E.
Students 142.

Getzville, Erie Co., St. Pius X (1958), Rev. Msgr. George B. Yiengst; Rev. Raymond R. Russell; Deacon Brian Walkowiak.
Res., 1700 N. French Rd., P.O. Box 162, 14068-0162. Tel: 716-688-9143; Fax: 716-688-5417.
Catechesis/Religious Programs—Tel: 716-688-5417.
Students 682.

Gowanda, Erie Co., St. Joseph (1900), Rev. Lawrence M. Milby.
Res., 26 Erie Ave., 14070. Tel: 716-532-5100; 532-4096. [CEM]
School—Tel: 716-532-2520. Sr. Frances Clare Perry, O.S.F., Prin.
Sisters of St. Francis of Penance and Christian Charity 1; Lay Teachers 9; Students 113.

Grand Island, Erie Co., St. Stephen (1862), Rev. Msgr. Richard M. Cahill; Revs. Dennis A. Fronczak; Francis Johnson; Deacon John A. Polizzi.
Res., 2100 Baseline Rd., 14072. Tel: 716-773-7647; Fax: 716-773-5792. [CEM]
School—2080 Baseline Rd., 14072. Tel: 716-773-4347. Sr. Christina Marie Luczynski, C.S.S.F., Prin.
Felician Sisters 2; Lay Teachers 21; Students 274.
Catechesis/Religious Programs—Tel: 716-773-2002. D.R.E.: Angela Diebold; Donna Wilson.
Students 880.

Hamburg, Erie Co., SS. Peter and Paul (1844), Rev. Msgr. Gerard L. Green; Rev. Msgr. Stanley A. Ropelski; Rev. Walter J. Szczesny; Deacon Lawrence D. Eschbach.
Res., 66 E. Main St., 14075. Tel: 716-649-2765; Fax: 716-649-5218. [CEM]
School—68 E. Main St., 14075. Tel: 716-649-7030. Kathleen Walters, Prin.
Lay Teachers 23; Students 314.
Catechesis/Religious Programs—Tel: 716-649-0231. D.R.E.: Mary Ann Senchyne; Sr. Eileen Steen, R.S.M.
Students 1,022.

St. Mary of the Lake (1948), Rev. Msgr. W. Jerome Sullivan.
Res., S-4737 Lake Shore Rd., 14075. Tel: 716-627-3123; Fax: 716-627-7062.
School—Tel: 716-627-7700. Mrs. Elaine Poleto, Prin.
Franciscan Sisters of St. Joseph 2; Lay Teachers 18; Students 199.
Catechesis/Religious Programs—Tel: 716-627-7150. Ms. Mary Margaret Joyce, D.R.E.
Students 405.

Harris Hill, Erie Co., Nativity of the Blessed Virgin Mary (1954), Rev. Msgr. Raymond F. Paa; Revs. Daniel J. Fawls; Daniel A. Young; Deacon Frank R. Krahling.
Res., 4375 Harris Hill Rd., Williamsville, 14221. Tel: 716-632-8838; Fax: 716-632-7898.
School—Tel: 716-633-7441. Mrs. Cherie M. Ansuini, Prin.
Lay Teachers 16; Students 200.
Catechesis/Religious Programs—8550 Main St., Williamsville, 14221. Tel: 716-634-3130. Mrs. Mary Ann Hoag, D.R.E.
Students 736.

Hinsdale, Cattaraugus Co., St. Helen (1947), Rev. Barry J. Allaire, Admin.
Res., 3826 Main St., P.O. Box 248, 14743-0248. Tel: 716-557-8841.
School—Southern Tier Catholic Regional School. See separate listing under Regional and Consolidated Elementary Schools in the Institutions located in the Diocese.

Holland, Erie Co., St. Joseph (1890), Rev. Msgr. Mecislaus S. Wendzikowski.
Res., 46 N. Main St., 14080-0006. Tel: 716-537-9434. [CEM 2]
Catechesis/Religious Programs—D.R.E.: Mrs. Theresa Leach Tel: 716-537-9868; Mrs. Joyce Faust Tel: 716-537-9778.
Students 289.

Holley, Orleans Co., St. Mary (1866), Rev. Joseph F. Kozlowski.
Res., 11 S. Main St., 14470-1107. Tel: 716-638-6718; Fax: 716-638-3210. [CEM]
Catechesis/Religious Programs—Tel: 716-638-6027. Jean M. Mullins, D.R.E.
Students 176.
Mission—Hulberton, Orleans Co., St. Rocco, 14470.

Humphrey, Cattaraugus Co., St. Pacificus, Mission of St. Bonaventure University Friary (1855), Rev. J. Gregory Brennan, O.F.M.
Res., St. Bonaventure University, St. Bonaventure, 14778. Tel: 716-375-2545; Fax: 716-375-2625. [CEM]

Jamestown, Chautauqua Co., St. James (1915) (Italian), Rev. Msgr. Antoine Attea; Rev. Patrick O. Fernandes.
Res., 27 Allen St., 14701. Tel: 716-487-0125; Fax: 716-661-3677. [CEM]
Catechesis/Religious Programs—Tel: 716-664-4237. Anne Gordon, D.R.E.
Students 388.

St. John (1939), Rev. Donald S. Fafinski.
Res., 270 Newton Ave., 14701. Tel: 716-664-4556; Fax: 716-483-2108.
Parish Center: Tel: 716-484-1875.
Catechesis/Religious Programs—Students 90.

St. Peter and Paul (1854), Rev. John J. Mitka.
Res., 508 Cherry St., 14701. Tel: 716-664-5703;

Fax: 716-664-5288. [CEM]
School—1135 N. Main St., 14701. Tel: 716-483-3245; Fax: 716-484-8492.
Sisters 1; Lay Teachers 22; Students 275.
Catechesis/Religious Programs—Tel: 716-484-8958.
Students 295.

Java Center, Wyoming Co., St. Patrick, Rev. Edward E. Muerder.
Res., 14082. Tel: 716-457-9532.
School—Genesee-Wyoming Catholic Central Consolidated School. See separate listing under Regional and Consolidated Elementary Schools in the Institutions located in the Diocese.
Catechesis/Religious Programs—Mary Gentner, D.R.E.
Students 118.

Kendall, Orleans Co., St. Mark (1984), Rev. Joseph F. Kozlowski. In res., Rev. Elmer A. McNamara (ROC).
Res., 11 S. Main St., Holley, 14470-1107. Tel: 716-638-6718; Fax: 716-638-3210.
Catechesis/Religious Programs—Tel: 716-659-8631. Sr. Mary Anne Rapp, O.S.F., D.R.E.
Students 127.

Kenmore, Erie Co.,

1—St. Andrew, (1944), Rev. Msgr. Richard A. Graeber; Revs. Eric L. Sikora; Jeffrey M. Sturmer. In res., Rev. Vincent J. Ferraro, Chap.
Res., 1525 Sheridan Dr., 14217. Tel: 716-873-6716; Fax: 716-873-2214.
School—Tel: 716-877-0422.
Felician Sisters 2; Lay Teachers 42; Students 638.
Catechesis/Religious Programs—Beth Lenegan, D.R.E.
Students 890.

2—Blessed Sacrament, Rev. Msgr. Robert K. Golombek; Rev. Adolph M. Kowalozyk.
Res., 263 Claremont Ave., 14223. Tel: 716-834-4282.
School—Felician Sisters 3; Lay Teachers 13; Students 208.

3—St. John the Baptist, (1836), Rev. Msgr. Kenneth M. Menge; Revs. Thomas J. McCarthy; Michael H. Burzynski; Deacon Bernard M. Thomann. In res., Rev. Edward C. Metzger, O.F.M.
Res., 1085 Englewood Ave., 14223. Tel: 716-873-1122; Fax: 716-873-3305. [CEM]
School—Englewood & Belmont, 14223. Tel: 716-877-6401; Fax: 716-877-9139. Marilynn Camp, Prin.
Lay Teachers 48; Students 668.
Catechesis/Religious Programs—Tel: 716-877-0474. Catherine Salzman, D.R.E.
Students 418.

4—St. Paul, (1897), Revs. Paul M. Nogaro; Frederick Hinton; Richard E. Sowinski; William J. Quinlivan.
Res., 33 Victoria Blvd., 14217. Tel: 716-875-2730; Fax: 716-877-3475.
School—Tel: 716-877-6308; Fax: 716-877-3874. Louise Lopardi, Prin.
Lay Teachers 28; Students 470.
Catechesis/Religious Programs—Tel: 716-873-9429.
Students 700.

Knapp Creek, Cattaraugus Co., Sacred Heart, Mission of Allegany. Closed. For sacramental records contact St. Mary of the Angels, Olean.

Lackawanna, Erie Co.,

1—Basilica of Our Lady of Victory, (1854). (National Shrine). Rev. Msgr. Robert C. Wurtz, P.A.; Rev. Msgr. John H. Bugman; Rev. Msgr. Robert E. Murphy; Revs. Joseph Klos; Matthew J. Zirnheld; Deacon Thomas M. Forcucci.
Res., 767 Ridge Rd., 14218. Tel: 716-828-9444; Fax: 716-828-9429.
School—Tel: 716-828-9434. Sr. Ellen O'Keefe, Prin.
Sisters 6; Lay Teachers 19; Students 425.
Catechesis/Religious Programs—Tel: 716-828-9437. Sheila Flynn, D.R.E.
Students 125.

2—St. Anthony, (1917) (Italian), Revs. Peter J. Drilling; Frank E. Barone.
Res., 306 Ingham Ave., 14218. Tel: 716-823-0782.

3—Assumption, (1918) (Hungarian), Rev. Kalman Miskolczy, Sch.P., Admin.
Church—80 Steelawanna Ave., 14218. Tel: 716-822-9828.

4—St. Barbara, (1903) (Polish), Rev. Lawrence F. Cobel.
Res., 551 Ridge Rd., 14218. Tel: 716-822-3470; Fax: 716-822-2412.

5—St. Hyacinth, (1911) (Polish), Rev. Henry A. Orszulak, Admin.
Res., 253 Ridge Rd., 14218. Tel: 716-823-0845.

6—St. Michael the Archangel, (1921) (Polish), Rev. James M. Augustyn.
Res., 144 Warsaw St., 14218. Tel: 716-826-0880.
Catechesis/Religious Programs—Tel: 716-822-8526. Sr. Mary Sidonia Luczak, C.S.S.F., D.R.E.
Students 120.

7—Our Lady of Bistrica, (1917) (Croatian), Revs. Christopher Coric, O.F.M.Conv. (Croatia); Zarco Mula, O.F.M.Conv. (Croatia). In res., Rev. Msgr. Stephen F. Lackovic (Croatia).
Res., 1619 Abbott Rd., 14218. Tel: 716-822-0818; Fax: 716-822-0818.
Coordinator for Croatian Conventual Franciscans—.

8—Queen of All Saints, (1949), Rev. Thomas P. Taton, Admin.
Res., 206 Ridge Rd., 14218. Tel: 716-824-8797.
Catechesis/Religious Programs—Cynthia Lopez, D.R.E.
Students 105.

Lake View, Erie Co., Our Lady of Perpetual Help (1922), Rev. Msgr. John W. Zeitler; Sr. Sharon Erickson, R.S.M.
Res., 2052 Lake View Ave., 14085. Tel: 716-627-2910; Fax: 716-627-7972.
School—Southtowns Catholic Consolidated School. See separate listing under Regional and Consolidated Elementary Schools in the Institutions located in the Diocese. Tel: 716-627-5011.
Catechesis/Religious Programs—Tel: 716-627-9397. Mrs. Barbara Manley, D.R.E.
Students 394.

Lakewood, Chautauqua Co., Sacred Heart (1912), Rev. Msgr. Joseph M. Dowdell.
Res., 380 E. Fairmount Ave., 14750-2197. Tel: 716-763-2815; Fax: 716-763-5646.
Catechesis/Religious Programs—Marilyn Wozneak, Pastoral Assoc. & D.R.E.
Students 345.

Lancaster, Erie Co., St. Mary of the Assumption (1850), Rev. Msgr. Frederick D. Leising; Revs. Berard Pulikoottil; David R. Glassmire. In res., Rev. Msgr. Paschal Acquaria, (Retired).
Res., 14086-2094. Tel: 716-683-6445; Fax: 716-684-8446. [CEM]
School—Tel: 716-683-2112; Fax: 716-683-2134. Sr. Barbara Jean Wajda, O.S.F., Prin.
Sisters of Third Order of St. Francis 3; Lay Teachers 19; Students 351.
Catechesis/Religious Programs—Tel: 716-683-8564. Mrs. Elaine Driscoll, D.R.E.
Students 676.

Our Lady of Pompeii (1909), Rev. Jay W. McGinnis; Deacon John Klein. In res., Rev. John P. Mack.
Res., 158 Laverack Ave., 14086. Tel: 716-683-6522; Fax: 716-685-8066.
School—(Grades PreK-8). Tel: 716-684-4664. Mrs. Christine M. Schierer, Prin.
Sisters 4; Lay Teachers 14; Students 275.
Catechesis/Religious Programs—D.R.E.: Antoinette Duran, (Elementary); Joseph Blatz, (High School).
Students 545.

Langford, Erie Co., St. Martin (1851), Rev. Lawrence P. Damian.
Res., 10893 Sisson Hwy. (Langford), North Collins, 14111. Tel: 716-337-2686. [CEM]

Le Roy, Genesee Co., St. Joseph (Italian), Rev. Msgr. Emil P. Zupa.
Res., 27 Lake St., 14482. Tel: 716-768-6600.
Catechesis/Religious Programs—Students 100.

St. Peter (1849), Rev. Robert W. Wardenski.
Res., 44 Lake St., Leroy, 14482. Tel: 716-768-6543. [CEM]
School—Tel: 716-768-7390. Mrs. Barbara McVean, Prin.
Lay Teachers 7; Students 148.
Catechesis/Religious Programs—Students 166.
Mission—Lime Rock, Genesee Co., St. Anthony.

Lewiston, Niagara Co., Holy Family (1953) (Tuscarora Indian Nation), Rev. Ubaldo M. Fior, C.R.S.P.
Res., 1023 Swan Rd., Youngstown, 14174-9797. Tel: 716-754-7489. [JC]

St. Peter (1851), Rev. Msgr. Anthony J. Caligiuri, P.A. In res., Rev. Slavomir Siok, S.A.C.
Res., 620 Center St., 14092. Tel: 716-754-4118; Fax: 716-754-4118.
School—Tel: 716-754-4470; Fax: 716-754-0167. Sr. Mary Donald Mruk, Prin.
Franciscan Sisters of St. Joseph 2; Lay Teachers 16; Students 299.
Catechesis/Religious Programs—Tel: 716-754-2812.
Students 321.
Convent—421 Plain St., 14092. Tel: 716-754-4761.

Limestone, Cattaraugus Co., St. Patrick (1875), Rev. Jerome J. Stelmach.
Res., 16 Church St., 14753. Tel: 716-925-8596. [CEM]

Little Valley, Cattaraugus Co., St. Mary (1874), Revs. Wallace T. Borucki; Joseph K. Lowry, Jr., Pastor Emeritus.
Mailing Address: 36 Washington St., Cattaraugus, 14719. Tel: 716-257-9351.

Lockport, Niagara Co.,

1—St. Anthony, (1928), Rev. Louis F. Della Neve.
Res., 9 Bristol Ave., 14094. Tel: 716-434-5025.
School—Lockport Catholic Consolidated School. See separate listing under Regional and Consolidated Elementary Schools in the Institutions located in the Diocese.
Catechesis/Religious Programs—D.R.E.: Patricia Riexenger; Kathleen D'Agostino.
Students 131.

2—St. John the Baptist, (1834), Rev. Msgr. Donald L. Wangler; Revs. Joseph C. Dumphrey, O.S.F.S.; Robert J. Orlowski.
Res., 168 Chestnut St., 14094. Tel: 716-433-8118; Fax: 716-433-3562.
School—Lockport Catholic Consolidated School. See separate listing under Regional and Consolidated Elementary Schools in the Institutions located in the Diocese. Tel: 716-433-6422; Fax: 716-434-4002.
Catechesis/Religious Programs—Tel: 716-434-2492. Sr. Mary Helen, F.M.D.C., D.R.E.
Students 900.
Convent—159 Chestnut St., 14094. Tel: 716-434-8303.

3—St. Joseph, (1912) (Italian), Rev. Nicholas A. Rossello.
Res., 391 Market St., 14094. Tel: 716-433-5792.
School—Lockport Catholic Consolidated School. See separate listing under Regional and Consolidated Elementary Schools in the Institutions located in the Diocese. Tel: 716-433-6422.
Catechesis/Religious Programs—Tel: 716-433-3194. Mrs. Marea Eggert, D.R.E.
Students 128.

4—St. Mary, (1859) (German), Rev. Msgr. Michael J. Yunk.
Res., 5 Saxton St., 14094. Tel: 716-434-6316.
School—DeSales Catholic School. See separate listing under Regional and Consolidated Elementary Schools in the Institutions located in the Diocese. Tel: 716-433-6222.
Catechesis/Religious Programs—Tel: 716-433-0340.
Students 160.

5—St. Patrick, (1864) (Irish), Rev. Francis Schimscheiner, O.S.F.S. In res., Revs. Gerald Bartko, O.S.F.S.; Joseph C. Dumphrey, O.S.F.S.
Res., 76 Church St., 14094. Tel: 716-433-3707. [CEM]
School—See separate listing for DeSales Catholic School, Lockport, under Regional and Consolidated Elementary Schools in the Institutions located in the Diocese.
Catechesis/Religious Programs—Tel: 716-433-6672. Sr. Rene Ruberto, S.S.M.N., D.R.E.
Students 197.
Convent—138 N. Transit St., 14094. Tel: 716-433-9193.

Lyndonville, Orleans Co., St. Joseph (1962), Revs. Joseph G. Fifagrowicz; Albert J. Bosack.
Res., 38 Lake Ave., P.O. Box 308, 14098. Tel: 716-765-9722.

Machias, Cattaraugus Co., Holy Family (1948), Rev. Raymond F. Uschold.
Res., 10 N. Main St., P.O. Box 188, Delevan, 14042. Tel: 716-492-2383.

Mayville, Chautauqua Co., St. Mary (1925), Rev. Raymond A.J. Donohue.
Res., 24 E. Chautauqua St., Box 148, 14757. Tel: 716-753-2332; Fax: 716-753-3836.

Medina, Orleans Co., St. Mary (1840), Rev. Msgr. Paul J. Whitney; Deacon Nelson Darroch.
Res., 211 Eagle St., 14103. Tel: 716-798-0112. [CEM]
Catechesis/Religious Programs—Tel: 716-798-5399. Marguerite J. Moriarty, D.R.E.
Students 237.

Sacred Heart (1910), Rev. Joseph G. Fifagrowicz.
Res., 208 Ann St., 14103. Tel: 716-798-0356. [CEM]

Middleport, Niagara Co., St. Stephen (1854), Rev. Joseph P. Badding; Rev. Msgr. James E. Streng.
Res., 19 Vernon St., 14105-1321. Tel: 716-735-9433. [CEM]
Catechesis/Religious Programs—Tel: 716-735-7008.
Students 195.

Newfane, Niagara Co., St. Bridget (1859), Rev. John J. Leising.
Res., 3455 Ewings Rd., Box 87, 14108-0087. Tel: 716-778-9822. [CEM]
Catechesis/Religious Programs—Carol Piech, D.R.E.
Students 219.

Niagara Falls, Niagara Co.,

1—St. Charles, (1970), Rev. Joseph C. Carlo.
Res., 5604 Lindbergh Ave., 14304. Tel: 716-283-7602.

2—St. George, (1915) (Lithuanian), Rev. Seweryn J.

Koszyk, S.A.C.
Res., 1910 Falls St., 14303. Tel: 716-282-4587.

3—HOLY TRINITY, (1902) (Polish), Most Rev. Edward M. Grosz, D.D., V.G.
Res., 1419 Falls St., 14303. Tel: 716-284-6628; Fax: 716-282-2297. [CEM]

4—ST. JOHN DE LA SALLE, (1907), Rev. Jerome E. Kopec; Rev. Msgr. Robert J. Hogan, Pastor Emeritus; Deacon David P. Slish, Pastoral Assoc.
Res., 8469 Buffalo Ave., 14304. Tel: 716-283-2238.
School—Tel: 716-283-3031.
Lay Teachers 14; Students 180.

5—ST. JOSEPH, (1903) (Italian), Rev. Msgr. Richard S. Amico; Sr. Francis Marie Vallone, F.M.D.C., Pastoral Assoc.
Res., 1413 Pine Ave., 14301. Tel: 716-282-1379; Fax: 716-285-3704. [CEM]
School—625 Tronolone Pl., 14301. Tel: 716-282-8144.
Franciscan Sisters of Allegany 1; Lay Teachers 21; Students 230.
Catechesis/Religious Programs—Students 154.

6—ST. LEO, (1957), Rev. David G. Griffin.
Res., 2748 Military Rd., 14304. Tel: 716-297-3690.
Catechesis/Religious Programs—Tel: 716-297-5010.
Students 300.

7—ST. MARY OF THE CATARACT, Rev. Msgr. William J. Stillwell. In res., Revs. Mark M. Friel, Chap., Memorial Medical Center; Francis Gross, O.S.F.S.; Bro. Francis Murray, O.S.F.S.
Res., 259 Fourth St., 14303. Tel: 716-282-0059; Fax: 716-282-3372.

8—OUR LADY OF LEBANON, (1914) (Lebanese), Rev. Henry M. Bradbury, C.M.
Res., 1120 Niagara St., 14303. Tel: 716-282-0729.

9—OUR LADY OF MOUNT CARMEL, (1949), Rev. Duane R. Klizek. In res., Rev. Robert S. Hughson.
Res., 2486 Grand Ave., 14301. Tel: 716-282-5546; Fax: 716-282-6395.
School—2499 Independence Ave., 14301. Tel: 716-282-0645.
Lay Teachers 12; Students 244.
Catechesis/Religious Programs—Students 186.

10—OUR LADY OF THE ROSARY, (1906), Rev. John R. Gaglione.
Res., 339 22nd St., 14303. Tel: 716-282-0264; Fax: 716-282-0264.

11—PRINCE OF PEACE, (1943), Revs. William C. McGarry; Stewart M. Lindsay, O.S.F.S. In res., Rev. Salvatore J. Cusimano.
Res., 1040 Cayuga Dr., 14304. Tel: 716-283-2715.
School—(Grades PreK-6). Tel: 716-283-1455. Sr. Mary Asarese, S.S.M.N., Prin.
Sisters 2; Students 288.
Catechesis/Religious Programs—Tel: 716-283-0569.
Students 251.

12—SACRED HEART, (1854), Revs. James J. Kasinski; Richard Strassberger, Senior Assoc.
Res., 1917 11th St., 14305. Tel: 716-282-1749.
School—Tel: 716-282-8484. Sr. Mary Walz, S.S.J., Prin.
Sisters of St. Joseph 1; Lay Teachers 10; Students 140.
Catechesis/Religious Programs—Patricia McCarthy, D.R.E.
Students 100.

13—ST. STANISLAUS KOSTKA, (1917) (Polish), Most Rev. Edward M. Grosz, D.D., V.G. In res., Rev. Msgr. Edward J. Scanlan.
Res., 2437 Niagara St., 14303. Tel: 716-285-3604; Fax: 716-282-2297.

14—ST. TERESA OF THE INFANT JESUS, (1930), Rev. Msgr. Leonard E. Biniszkiewicz.
Res., 3840 Macklem Ave., 14305. Tel: 716-282-5583; Fax: 716-282-0453.
Catechesis/Religious Programs—Tel: 716-282-0795. Catherine Halliday, D.R.E.
Students 218.

North Collins, Erie Co., Holy Spirit (1958), Rev. Msgr. Daniel J. Szostak.
Res., 2017 Halley Rd., 14111. Tel: 716-337-2544. [CEM 2]
Catechesis/Religious Programs—Tel: 716-337-3803. Sr. Julia Witkowski, D.R.E.
Students 166.

North Evans, Erie Co., St. Vincent (1914), Revs. William R. Tuyn; Brian M. Hatrick; Deacon John Setera.
Res., 2050 S. Creek Rd., 14112. Tel: 716-627-3382. [CEM]
School—Southtowns Catholic Consolidated School. See separate listing under Regional and Consolidated Elementary Schools in the Institutions located in the Diocese. Tel: 716-627-5011; Fax: 716-627-2455.
Catechesis/Religious Programs—Tel: 716-627-7673. Ann Kirkpatrick, D.R.E.
Students 433.

North Java, Wyoming Co., St. Nicholas, Rev. Edward E. Muerder.
Res., 14113. Tel: 716-535-7457. [CEM]
School—Genesee-Wyoming Catholic Central Consolidated School. See separate listing under Regional and Consolidated Elementary Schools in the Institutions located in the Diocese.

North Tonawanda, Niagara Co.,

1—ASCENSION, (1887), Rev. Gary Szczepankiewicz.
Res., 168 Robinson St., 14120. Tel: 716-693-1211; Fax: 716-693-1263.
School—North Tonawanda Consolidated Catholic School. See separate listing under Regional and Consolidated Elementary Schools in the Institutions located in the Diocese. Tel: 716-693-2828; Fax: 716-693-0169.
Catechesis/Religious Programs—Tel: 716-694-3754. Mrs. Jeanne Wantz, D.R.E.
Students 339.

2—ST. ALBERT THE GREAT, (1960), Rev. Msgr. Edward T. Fisher; Deacon Daniel E. Brick; Mr. Gary Copeland, Pastoral Assoc. In res., Rev. Duane G. Fimbel.
Res., 1520 Kingston Ave., 14120. Tel: 716-694-0540.
Catechesis/Religious Programs—Tel: 716-694-4540.
Students 743.

3—ST. JOSEPH, (1947) (Polish), Rev. Msgr. Thomas E. Crane.
Res., 1451 Payne Ave., 14120. Tel: 716-693-2791; Fax: 716-743-1405.
School—North Tonawanda Catholic Consolidated School. See separate listing under Regional and Consolidated Elementary Schools in the Institutions located in the Diocese. Tel: 716-693-4769.
Catechesis/Religious Programs—Tel: 716-693-0421. Mrs. Lorraine Schintzius, D.R.E.
Students 560.

4—OUR LADY OF CZESTOCHOWA, (1903) (Polish), Revs. Dennis F. Fronckowiak; Michael R. Kopczynski.
Res., 64 Center Ave., 14120. Tel: 716-693-3822; Fax: 716-693-3882.
School—North Tonawanda Catholic Consolidated School. See separate listing under Regional and Consolidated Elementary Schools in the Institutions located in the Diocese. Tel: 716-694-3644; Fax: 716-693-0169.
Catechesis/Religious Programs—Tel: 716-693-3855.
Students 169.
Convent—Tel: 716-692-0276.

Oakfield, Genesee Co., St. Cecilia (1907), Rev. Thomas D. Doyle.
Res., 56 Maple Ave., 14125. Tel: 716-948-5344; Fax: 716-948-8239. [CEM]
Catechesis/Religious Programs—Students 166.
Mission—Wheatville, Genesee Co., St. Patrick.

Olcott, Niagara Co., St. Charles Borromeo (1912), Rev. James F. Hassett. In res., Rev. Eugene L. Wagner, Pastor Emeritus.
Res., 5969 Washington St., 14126. Tel: 716-778-7592; 795-3331 (Church).

Olean, Cattaraugus Co., St. John (1896) (Irish-Italian), Rev. Msgr. William O. Wangler.
Res., 931 N. Union St., 14760. Tel: 716-372-5313; Fax: 716-373-0919.
School—Southern Tier Catholic Regional School. See separate listing under Regional and Consolidated Elementary Schools in the Institutions located in the Diocese. Tel: 716-372-2891; Fax: 716-373-1175.
Catechesis/Religious Programs—Tel: 716-372-6633.
Students 210.

St. Mary of the Angels (1876), Rev. Gregory J. Dobson.
Res., 202 S. Union St., 14760. Tel: 716-372-4841; Fax: 716-372-5905.
School—Southern Tier Catholic Regional School. See separate listing under Regional and Consolidated Elementary Schools in the Institutions located in the Diocese.

Transfiguration (1912) (Polish), Rev. Jerome J. Stelmach.
Res., 1102 Walnut St., 14760. Tel: 716-372-5430; Fax: 716-373-4719.
School—Southern Tier Catholic Regional School. See separate listing under Regional and Consolidated Elementary Schools in the Institutions located in the Diocese.

Orchard Park, Erie Co.,

1—NATIVITY, (1908), Rev. Msgr. Thomas J. Beasley; Revs. Joseph A. Gullo; Joseph D. Porpigilia. In res., Rev. Msgr. H. Gil Weil.
Res., 26 Thorn Ave., 14127. Tel: 716-662-9339; Fax: 716-662-2195. [CEM]
School—Tel: 716-662-7572. Ruth Frost, Prin.
Sisters of St. Francis of Penance and Christian Charity 1; Lay Teachers 28; Students 360.
Catechesis/Religious Programs—Tel: 716-662-2169. Mary Ann Pietrzak, D.R.E.
Students 942.

2—ST. BERNADETTE, (1957), Rev. Msgr. Richard T. Nugent; Revs. Raymond J. McNicholas, S.S.C.; Ronald P. Sajdak.
Res., 5930 S. Abbott Rd., 14127-4516. Tel: 716-649-3090; Fax: 716-649-0211.
School—Tel: 716-649-3369. Sr. Diane Swanson, Prin.
Lay Teachers 18; Students 200.
Catechesis/Religious Programs—Tel: 716-648-1720. Joan Ersing, D.R.E.
Students 847.

3—OUR LADY OF THE SACRED HEART, (1920), Rev. Msgr. Paul J.E. Burkard; Revs. Joseph D. Wolf; Mieczyslaw F. Nycz.
Res., 3148 Abbott Rd., 14127. Tel: 716-824-2935; Fax: 716-827-7643.
School—3144 Abbott Rd., 14127. Tel: 716-824-8208. Sr. Monica Riordan, R.S.M., Prin.
Sisters of Mercy 4; Lay Teachers 34; Students 650.
Catechesis/Religious Programs—Tel: 716-824-8209. Paula White, D.R.E.
Students 749.

4—ST. JOHN VIANNEY, (1958), Rev. Msgr. William J. Gallagher.
Res., 2950 Southwestern Blvd., 14127. Tel: 716-674-9133; Fax: 716-674-9134.
School—Tel: 716-674-9232.
Lay Teachers 15; Students 133.
Catechesis/Religious Programs—Tel: 716-674-9145. Sharon Kirsch, D.R.E.
Students 463.

Pavilion, Genesee Co., St. Mary (1870), Rev. Daniel A. Young.
Res., 14525. Tel: 716-584-3280. [CEM]
Catechesis/Religious Programs—Odette McClurg, D.R.E.
Students 180.

Pendleton, Niagara Co., Good Shepherd (1847), Rev. Msgr. Paul J. Belzer.
Res., 5442 Tonawanda Creek Rd., North Tonawanda, 14120-9699. Tel: 716-625-8594. [CEM]
Catechesis/Religious Programs—Tel: 716-625-8817. Elizabeth McDermott, D.R.E.
Students 228.

Perry, Wyoming Co., St. Joseph (1879) (Italian), Rev. Richard W. Blazejewski.
Res., 8 Park St., 14530. Tel: 716-237-2625. [CEM]

St. Stanislaus Kostka (1910) (Polish), Rev. Richard J. Blazejewski.
Res., 8 Park St., 14530. Tel: 716-237-3869. [CEM]

Perrysburg, Cattaraugus Co., St. Joan of Arc (1950). All Records are kept at St. John Fisher, South Dayton. Rev. John S. Kwiecien.
Office: St. John Fisher Church, South Dayton, 14138. Tel: 716-988-5568.
Res., P.O. Box 222, 14129-0222. Tel: 716-532-4556.

Portageville, Wyoming Co., Assumption B.V.M. (1849), Rev. Robert M. Mock.
Res., P.O. Box 404, 14536. Tel: 716-468-2643; Fax: 716-468-2126. [CEM]

Portville, Cattaraugus Co., Sacred Heart (1909), Rev. Robert J. Schober.
Res., 14770. Tel: 716-933-6394.
School—Southern Tier Catholic Regional School. See separate listing under Regional and Consolidated Elementary Schools in the Institutions located in the Diocese.

Randolph, Cattaraugus Co., St. Patrick (1853), Rev. Msgr. Leon M. Neu.
Res., 189 Main St., 14772. Tel: 716-358-2991. [CEM]
Catechesis/Religious Programs—Students 116.

Ransomville, Niagara Co., Immaculate Conception (1891), Revs. Herold M. Nuwer; Salvatore J. Piazza, (Retired).
Res., 4671 Townline Rd., Rte. 429, 14131-9799. Tel: 716-731-4822.
Catechesis/Religious Programs—Mrs. Judith A. Kirkpatrick, D.R.E.
Students 448.

Rushford, Allegany Co., St. Mark (1948), Rev. Francis J. Jann, Admin.
Res., 14777. Tel: 716-437-5332.

Salamanca, Cattaraugus Co., Holy Cross (1893) (Polish), Rev. Constantine Kwiatkowski.
Res., 284 Broad St., 14779. Tel: 716-945-4966. [JC]

St. Patrick (1868), Rev. Michael P. Juran.
Res., 101 River St., 14779. Tel: 716-945-5522. [CEM]

Sardinia, Erie Co., St. Jude (1953), Rev. Richard A. Jesionowski, Temp. Admin.
Res., 12820 Genesee Rd., 14134-0267. Tel: 716-496-7535.

Sheldon, Wyoming Co., St. Cecilia (1848), Rev. Donald C. Weber; Deacon Daniel Molik.
Res., Strykersville, 14145. Tel: 716-457-9437. [CEM 2]
School—Genesee-Wyoming Catholic Central Consolidated School. See separate listing under Regional and Consolidated Elementary Schools in the Institutions located in the Diocese. Tel: 716-591-2515.

Sheridan, Chautauqua Co., St. John Bosco (1949), Rev. Gerald P. Sheehan.
Res., Box 3, 14135. Tel: 716-679-4951.

Sherman, Chautauqua Co., St. Isaac Jogues (1947), Rev. Raymond A.J. Donohue.
Res., 24 E. Chautanqua St., Box 148, Mayville, 14757. Tel: 716-753-2332; Fax: 716-753-3836.

Silver Creek, Chautauqua Co., Our Lady of Mt. Carmel (1882), Rev. Msgr. Richard J. Gill.
Res., 165 Central Ave., 14136. Tel: 716-934-2233; Fax: 716-934-6216. [CEM]
School—Northern Chautauqua Catholic Regional School. See separate listing under Regional and Consolidated Elementary Schools in the Institutions located in the Diocese. Tel: 716-366-0630.
Catechesis/Religious Programs—Tel: 716-934-4891.
Students 225.

Silver Springs, Wyoming Co., St. Mary, Rev. Bart Lipiec; Deacon John Kelly.
Res., 23 Church St., Box 305, 14550. Tel: 716-493-5265. [CEM]

Sinclairville, Chautauqua Co., St. John the Evangelist, Rev. Patrick H. Elis.
Res., 14782. Tel: 716-962-3781.

Sloan, Erie Co., St. Andrew (1915) (Polish), Rev. Robert D. Moss.
Res., 34 Francis St., 14212. Tel: 716-892-0425; Fax: 716-892-0425.
School—14212. Tel: 716-896-2566.
Felician Sisters 2; Lay Teachers 16; Students 141.
Catechesis/Religious Programs—Students 167.

Snyder, Erie Co., Christ the King (1926), Rev. Msgr. James J. Lichtenthal; Rev. David A. Bellittiere.
Res., 30 Lamarck Dr., 14226. Tel: 716-839-1430; Fax: 716-839-1433.
School—Tel: 716-839-0473; Fax: 716-839-0473.
Franciscan Sisters of Allegany 1; Lay Teachers 18; Students 252.
Catechesis/Religious Programs—Tel: 716-839-0946.
Students 564.

South Dayton, Cattaraugus Co., St. John Fisher (1946), Rev. John S. Kwiecien.
Mailing Address: P.O. Box 242, 14138. Tel: 716-988-5568.
Res., Perrysburg, 14129. Tel: 716-532-4556.

Springbrook, Erie Co., St. Vincent (1850), Rev. James A. Walter.
Res., 14140. Tel: 716-652-3972; Fax: 716-652-3972. [CEM]
School—Tel: 716-652-8697. Ms. Jane Hibschweiler, Prin.
Sisters of the Third Order of St. Francis 2; Lay Teachers 9; Students 170.
Catechesis/Religious Programs—Tel: 716-652-7242. Marjory Moretta, D.R.E.
Students 280.

Springville, Erie Co., St. Aloysius (1853), Rev. Charles J. Zadora.
Res., 190 Franklin St., 14141-1199. Tel: 716-592-2701; Fax: 716-592-4347. [CEM]
School—Tel: 716-592-7002. Sr. Marie McTarnaghan, Prin.
Sisters of Third Order of St. Francis 2; Lay Teachers 16; Students 210.
Catechesis/Religious Programs—Tel: 716-592-4869. Ms. Sharon Stachowiak, D.R.E.
Students 339.

Strykersville, Wyoming Co., St. Mary, Queen of the Rosary (1885), Rev. Michael P. McNicholl.
Res., 3854 Main St., 14145. Tel: 716-457-3021; 457-3222; Fax: 716-457-1310. [CEM]
Catechesis/Religious Programs—Ms. Sharon Lowery, D.R.E.
Students 170.

Swormville, Erie Co., St. Mary (1849), Rev. Robert M. Yetter; Deacon Howard J. Edbauer, Jr.
Res., 6919 Transit Rd., Box 460, 14146. Tel: 716-688-9380; Fax: 716-688-6173. [CEM]
School—Tel: 716-689-8424.
Sisters of the Third Order of St. Francis 2; Lay Teachers 15; Students 199.
Catechesis/Religious Programs—Tel: 716-688-0599.
Students 850.

Tonawanda, Erie Co.,

1—St. Amelia, (1953), Rev. Msgr. Thomas F. Maloney; Revs. Leon J. Biernat; Michael J. Parker; Sr. Rita Claire, S.S.M.N., Pastoral Assoc.; Deacon Richard W. Parker. In res., Rev. Msgr. John L. McHugh, Pastor Emeritus.
Res., 210 St. Amelia Dr., 14150. Tel: 716-836-0011; Fax: 716-832-5439.
School—Tel: 716-836-2230; Fax: 716-832-9700. James Mule, Prin.
Lay Teachers 27; Students 432.
Catechesis/Religious Programs—Tel: 716-833-8647. Elaine Dankowski, D.R.E.
Students 857.

2—St. Christopher, (1928), Rev. Msgr. Francis G. Weldgen; Rev. Edward F. Jost, Jr.; Deacon Francis A. Zwack.
Res., 2660 Niagara Falls Blvd., 14150. Tel: 716-692-2660; Fax: 716-693-5639.
School—Tel: 716-693-5604.
Lay Teachers 31; Students 501.
Catechesis/Religious Programs—Tel: 716-694-4310.
Students 860.

3—St. Edmund, (1965), Rev. Msgr. Onofrio R. Smiroldo; Deacon Robert Bauer.
Res., 530 Ellicott Creek Rd., 14150. Tel: 716-694-5656; Fax: 716-694-5902.
School—Tel: 716-694-5900.
Felician Sisters 1; Lay Teachers 9; Students 144.
Catechesis/Religious Programs—Students 250.

4—St. Francis of Assisi, (1858), Revs. Robert W. Vogt; James M. Monaco; Deacon Paul Schnettler.
Res., 73 Adam St., 14150. Tel: 716-693-1150; Fax: 716-693-2025. [CEM]
School—Tel: 716-692-7886.
Lay Teachers 17; Students 209.
Catechesis/Religious Programs—Students 422.

5—St. Timothy, (1960), Rev. Msgr. John I. Ducette; Deacon Gordon J. Steinagle. In res., Rev. Msgr. John Kempczynski.
Res., 565 E. Park Dr., 14150. Tel: 716-875-9430.
Catechesis/Religious Programs—Students 170.

Vandalia, Cattaraugus Co., St. John the Baptist, Rev. Bernadine Kessing, O.F.M.
Res., St. Bonaventure, 14778. Tel: 716-375-2531.
School—Sourthern Tier Catholic Regional School. See separate listing under Regional and Consolidated Elementary Schools in the Institutions located in the Diocese.

Varysburg, Wyoming Co., St. Joseph (1910) (German), Rev. Msgr. Joseph A. Boruszewski.
Res., 14167. Tel: 716-535-7342. [CEM]
School—Genesee-Wyoming Catholic Central Consolidated School. See separate listing under Regional and Consolidated Elementary Schools in the Institutions located in the Diocese.

Warsaw, Wyoming Co., St. Michael (1858), Rev. Bart Lipiec; Deacon John J. Kelly.
Res., 171 N. Main St., 14569. Tel: 716-786-2400. [CEM]
School—(Grades PreK-6) 16 North St., 14569. Tel: 716-786-8561. Don Felix, Prin.
Lay Teachers 6; Students 75.
Catechesis/Religious Programs—Students 70.

Wellsville, Allegany Co., Immaculate Conception (1850) (Irish-German), Rev. Dennis G. Wolf.
Res., 6 Maple Ave., 14895. Tel: 716-593-4834; Fax: 716-593-7167. [CEM]
School—(Grades PreK-8) 24 Maple Ave., 14895. Tel: 716-593-5840; Fax: 716-593-5846. Sr. Alice Roach, Prin.
Sisters of Mercy 2; Lay Teachers 13; Students 160.
Catechesis/Religious Programs—Tel: 716-593-1862. D.R.E.: Mrs. Carol Gardner, (Grades 9-11); Sr. Margaret M. Gleason, (Grades PreK-8).
Students 127.

West Falls, Erie Co., St. George (Jewettville) (1942), Rev. Albert M. Hansen.
Res., 74 Old Glenwood Rd., 14170. Tel: 716-652-3153.
Catechesis/Religious Programs—Tel: 716-652-0126.
Students 155.

Westfield, Chautauqua Co., St. James (1860), Rev. Daniel A. Lapinski.
Res., 15 Union St., 14787-1494. Tel: 716-326-2816; Fax: 716-326-4863. [CEM]
Catechesis/Religious Programs—Tel: 716-326-2338; Fax: 716-326-2732. D.R.E.: Mrs. Cecilia Filipkowski; Mr. Robert Ducato.
Students 109.
Mission—Ripley, Chautauqua Co., St. Thomas More, 66 E. Main St., Ripley, 14775. Tel: 716-736-5200.

West Seneca, Erie Co.,

1—St. Bonaventure, (1918), Revs. Benoit J. Drapeau, C.J.M., Supr.; Ronald M. Bagley, C.J.M., Dir.; J. Gregory Sampson, C.J.M.
Total in Residence 3; Total Staff 5.
Res., 36 Flohr Ave., 14224. Tel: 716-823-1090; Fax: 716-825-4376.
School—2784 Seneca St., 14224. Tel: 716-822-7260; Fax: 716-822-7296.
Lay Teachers 14; Students 158.
Catechesis/Religious Programs—Tel: 716-825-5053. Mrs. Lynn Lipczynski, D.R.E.
Students 382.

2—St. Catherine of Siena, (1967), Rev. Pascal D. Ipolito; Deacon Joseph M. Barr; Suzanne M. Buttino, Pastoral Assoc.
Res., 4928 Seneca St., 14224. Tel: 716-675-0531; Fax: 716-675-1530.
Catechesis/Religious Programs—Students 261.

3—Fourteen Holy Helpers, (1864) (German-Polish), Rev. Msgr. David S. Slubecky; Rev. Dennis J. Mancuso.
Res., 1345 Indian Church Rd., Buffalo, 14224. Tel: 716-674-2374; Fax: 716-675-4864. [CEM]
School—Tel: 716-674-1670. Ms. Susan Jagosh, Prin.
Lay Teachers 19; Students 344.
Catechesis/Religious Programs—Tel: 716-674-2180.
Students 402.

4—St. William, (1926), Rev. James L. Breitnauer; Joan Morreal, Pastoral Assoc. & D.R.E.
Res., Arcade St., 14224. Tel: 716-822-5449; Fax: 716-822-5457.
School—Affiliated with St. Bonaventure and Fourteen Holy Helpers. Tel: 716-822-7260; Fax: 716-822-7296.
Catechesis/Religious Programs—Tel: 716-822-1531.
Students 200.

5—Queen of Heaven, (1955), Revs. Thomas J. Quinlivan; Peter J. Cronin, S.S.C.
Res., 4220 Seneca St., 14224. Tel: 716-674-3468; Fax: 716-674-3475.
School—839 Mill Rd., 14224. Tel: 716-674-5206. Mrs. Judith Talbot, Prin.
Lay Teachers 23; Students 352.
Catechesis/Religious Programs—Tel: 716-675-3714. D.R.E.: Sr. Catherine Taberski, S.S.M.N.; Dorothy Flynn.
Students 635.

West Valley, Cattaraugus Co., St. John the Baptist (1904), Rev. Carl L. Kuehmeier.
Res., 5381 Depot St., P.O. Box 315, 14171-0315. Tel: 716-942-3259. [CEM]
Catechesis/Religious Programs—Janet Vant, D.R.E.
Students 110.

Whitesville, Allegany Co., St. John of the Cross (1949), Rev. Fred G. Fingerle.
Res., One Church St., Box 761, Andover, 14806. Tel: 607-478-8885.
Church—540 Main St., Box 137, 14897.

Williamsville, Erie Co., St. Gregory the Great (1958), Rev. Msgr. Rupert A. Wright; Revs. James R. Bastien; Joseph S. Rogliano; James D. Ciupek.
Res., 100 St. Gregory Ct., 14221. Tel: 716-688-5678; 5679; Fax: 716-688-2315.
School—250 St. Gregory Ct., 14221. Tel: 716-688-5323; Fax: 716-688-6629. Mrs. Patricia Boyd, Prin.
Sisters 1; Lay Teachers 37; Students 630.
Catechesis/Religious Programs—Tel: 716-688-5760; Fax: 716-639-8251. Mrs. Joan Rischmiller, D.R.E.
Students 1,770.

SS. Peter and Paul (1836), Rev. Msgr. David M. Gallivan; Revs. Alfons M. Osiander; Robert J. Schober; Mrs. Linda Downey, Pastoral Assoc.
Res., 5480 Main St., 14221. Tel: 716-632-2559; Fax: 716-626-0971. [CEM 2]
School—Tel: 716-632-6146. Mrs. Marianne Maines, Prin.
Lay Teachers 16; Students 303.
Catechesis/Religious Programs—Tel: 716-632-2678. Ms. Susan Golebiewski, D.R.E.
Students 831.

Wilson, Niagara Co., Our Lady of the Rosary (1920), Rev. John J. Leising.
Res., 359 Lake St., Box 116, 14172-0116. Tel: 716-751-6459.
Catechesis/Religious Programs—D.R.E.: Mrs. Barbara Mosher; Mrs. Kathleen Higgins.
Students 124.

Woodlawn, Erie Co., Our Lady of Grace (1940), Rev. John F. Kasprzak.
Res., S. 3319 Lake Shore Rd., 14219. Tel: 716-822-0607.
Catechesis/Religious Programs—BettyLou Regueira, D.R.E.
Students 140.

Youngstown, Niagara Co., St. Bernard's (1946), Rev. Msgr. J. Thomas Moran.
Res., 218 Hinman St., 14174. Tel: 716-745-7460. [CEM]
Catechesis/Religious Programs—Blanche Sylvester, D.R.E.
Students 278.

Chaplains of Public Institutions

BUFFALO. *Buffalo General Hospital*. Revs. Douglas F. Faraci; Norbert F. Orsolits; Richard H. Augustyn.
Buffalo Psychiatric Center, 400 Forest Ave., 14213. Rev. Norman P. McTigue.
Children's Hospital. Vacant.
Columbus Hospital. Attended by Oblates from Holy Angels.
Erie County Medical Center. Rev. Robert A. Stolinski.
Millard Fillmore Hospital. Vacant.
Roswell Park Memorial Institute. Rev. Douglas F. Faraci.
Sheehan Memorial Emergency Hospital. Vacant.
Veterans Hospital. Rev. Francis J. Chmielewski, 414 S. Ogden St., 14206. Tel: 716-822-8856.

ALBION. *Albion Correctional Facility*. Rev. Eugene S. Slomba Tel: 716-343-1796.

ALDEN. *Erie County Correctional Facility*. Rev. Robert Moreno, 11580 Walden Ave., 14004. Tel: 716-937-5693.

AMHERST. *Millard Fillmore Suburban Hospital*. Rev. Joseph W. Bertha.

ATTICA. *Attica Correctional Facility*. Rev. John Kilian.

BATAVIA. *Veterans Hospital*. Rev. John P. Bernard.

DUNKIRK. *Brooks Memorial Hospital*. Deacon Matthew A. Podnieskinski, Chap.

HELMUTH. *Collins Correctional Facility*. Vacant.

JAMESTOWN. *Jamestown Women's Christian Association Hospital*. Rev. John L. Kuhlmann, Chap., 42 Main St., P.O. Box 500, Bemus Point, 14172-0500. Tel: 716-386-2400.

NIAGARA FALLS. *Niagara Falls Memorial Medical Centers*. Rev. Mark M. Friel.

NORTH TONAWANDA. *DeGraff Memorial Hospital,* 1520 Kingston Ave., 14120. Tel: 716-694-4500. Rev. Duane G. Fimbel.
Orleans Correction Facility. Rev. Thomas D. Doyle, 50 Maple Ave., Oakfield, 14125. Tel: 716-386-2400.

PERRYSBURG. *J. N. Adam Memorial Hospital*. St. Aloysius Chapel. Deacon Robert A. Bauer.
Wende Correctional Facility. Rev. Frank Barone.

WEST SENECA. *Development Center*. Carol Ann Corey.
Wyoming Correctional Facility. Vacant.

On Duty Outside the Diocese:
Reverend Monsignors—
Kraus, Theodore W., 521 Boden Way, Oakland, CA 94610-3609
Reverend Fathers—
Blesnuk, Donald J., Casilla 313, Linares, Chile
Conoscenti, Frederick M., 605 Grove St., D4, Clifton, NJ 07013
Enright, James C., Auburn Correctional Facility, 135 State St., Auburn, NY 13021
Krysa, Czeslaw M., SS. Cyril & Methodius Seminary, Orchard Lake, MI 48033
Nielsen, Kenneth M., SS. Peter & Paul Church, 55 W. Broadway, Boston, MA 02127
Sheedy, Edward J., Wadhams Hall Seminary, Ogdensburg, NY 13669
Wild, Robert A., Madonna House, Combermere, Ontario, Canada
Zapfel, Robert E., S.T.D., Congregation for Catholic Education, 00120 Vatican City State

---

Military Chaplains:
Reverend Fathers—
Koester, Timothy J., HQ BTN, HQ USMC, Henderson Hall, Arlington, VA 22214-5001
Rappl, Joseph P., 2411 Scots Pine Crossing, Durham, NC 27713-6221
Zuffoletto, Michael P., U.S. Navy, 3747 Bengal Rd., Gulf Breeze, FL 32561

Absent on Leave:
Reverend Fathers—
Biesinger, Robert J.
Gresock, Thomas G.
Maryanski, Fabian J.
Swartz, Michael R.
Tuchols, Franklin J.

Retired:
Reverend Monsignors—
Acquavia, Paschal L., St. Mary of the Assumption, St. Mary Hill, Lancaster, NY 14086-2094
Brennan, George J., 4 Lockwood Ln., Orchard Park, NY 14127
Bugman, John H., Our Lady of Victory, 767 Ridge Rd., Lackawanna, NY 14218
Caine, Martin J., 4000 Ridgeline Dr., Austin, TX 78731
Connelly, James N., O'Hara Residence, 69 O'Hara Rd., Tonawanda, NY 14150
Conniff, John J., 1088 Delaware Ave., Buffalo, NY 14209
Coughlin, Joseph F., Queen of Heaven Rectory, 4220 Seneca St., West Seneca, NY 14224
Cronin, Paul T., Sheehan Residence, 330 Linwood Ave., Buffalo, NY 14209
Crumlish, Richard C., 1974 Seneca St., Buffalo, NY 14210
Duggan, John M., 127 Keil St., North Tonawanda, NY 14120
Englehardt, Herbert G., 43 Circle End Dr., West Seneca, NY 14224
Engler, Francis V., All Saints, 127 Chadduck Ave., Buffalo, NY 14207-1531
Faiola, Samuel J., 72B Lexington Ct., Lockport, NY 14094
Gernatt, David A., 11742 Markham Rd., Gowanda, NY 14070
Hammerl, Leo E., O'Hara Residence, 69 O'Hara Rd., Tonawanda, NY 14783-0224
Hogan, Robert J., St. John de LaSalle, 8469 Buffalo Ave., Niagara Falls, NY 14304-4396
Jasinski, Anthony J., 950 Losson Rd., South Cheektowaga, NY 14227
Joseph, Joseph D., 10537 Oldro Hill Rd., Steamburg, NY 14783-0224
Juenker, Paul R., O'Hara Residence, 69 O'Hara Rd., Tonawanda, NY 14150
Kazmierczak, Edward L., 32 Gregory Dr., West Seneca, NY 14224
Kempczynski, John, St. Timothy Rectory, 565 E. Park Dr., Tonawanda, NY 14150
Klein, Stanley H., Chap. Col., 11 Philip Dr., Buffalo, NY 14227
Krajewski, Walter M., Brookview Condominiums, 1108-22 Indian Church Rd., W., Seneca, NY 14224
Kreuzer, Gerald J., Most Precious Blood Rectory, 22 Prospect St., Angola, NY 14006
Lackovic, Stephen F., Our Lady of Bistrica, 1619 Abbott Rd., Lackawanna, NY 14218
LaRusch, Alton J., 132 E. Main St., Hamburg, NY 14075
Lombardo, Samuel L., 129 Laverack Ave., Lancaster, NY 14086
Lorenzetti, Dino J., 10 French Rd., Depew, NY 14043
Marcinkiewicz, Eugene V., St. Casimir Rectory, 160 Cable St., Buffalo, NY 14206
McHugh, John L., St. Amelia Rectory, 210 St. Amelia Dr., Tonawanda, NY 14150
Meloch, Chester A., 12 Christian Dr., Cheektowaga, NY 14225
Murphy, Robert E., Our Lady of Victory Basilica, 767 Ridge Rd., Lackawanna, NY 14218
Myszka, Daniel J., 391 Bristol St., Buffalo, NY 14206-3721
O'Loughlin, Eugene E., St. Thomas Aquinas Rectory, 450 Abbott Rd., Buffalo, NY 14220-1796
Radon, Eugene M., Coronation of BVM, 348 Dewitt St., Buffalo, NY 14213
Ronald, Roy K., 200 Boncroft Dr., West Seneca, NY 14224
Scanlan, Edward J., 2437 Niagara St., Niagara Falls, NY 14303-1925
Schneider, Arnold J., 5337 Genesee St., Bowmansville, NY 14026-1034
Schwab, Robert C., 2164 N.E. 36th St., Apt. 49, Lighthouse Point, FL 33064-7555
Schwinger, William A., 50 Franklin St., Buffalo, NY 14202
Skupien, Francis M., 46 Mill St., Middleport, NY 14105-1018
Skupien, Joseph F., P.O. Box 287, North Boston, NY 14110
Sobierajski, Edward J., O'Hara Residence, 69 O'Hara Rd., Tonawanda, NY 14150
Sorci, Francis P., 34 Loch Lee, Williamsville, NY 14221
Stachewicz, Henry J., 103 Kokomo, Depew, NY 14043-3705
Streng, James E., P.O. Box 167, Crittenden, NY 14038
Sutherland, William J., 4350 McCullough St., Port Charlotte, FL 33948-9490
Swiatkowski, Francis M., O'Hara Residence, 69 O'Hara Rd., Tonawanda, NY 14150
Szabo, Julius J., O'Hara Residence, 69 O'Hara Rd., Tonawanda, NY 14150
Trevett, Cyril I., Our Lady of Mercy Generalate, S. 5245 Murphy Rd., Orchard Park, NY 14127
Waclawski, Joseph P., 101 Swinburne St., Buffalo, NY 14212-9864
Walker, Edward J., 31 Stevenson St., Buffalo, NY 14220
Zak, Casimir A., O'Hara Residence, 69 O'Hara Rd., Tonawanda, NY 14150
Reverend Fathers—
Bohn, Raymond G., Sheehan Residence, 330 Linwood Ave., Buffalo, NY 14209
Borowiak, Henry M., St. James Rectory, 496 Terrace Blvd., Depew, NY 14043
Bosack, Albert J., St. Joseph Rectory, 38 Lake Ave., Box 308, Lydonville, NY 14098
Coppola, Paul R., Rte. 3, Box 221 P, Interlachen, FL 32148
Cusimano, Salvatore J., Prince of Peace Rectory, 1040 Cayuga Rd., Niagara Falls, NY 14304
Czechowicz, Bernard J., Oceans Clover Leaf North, Four Oceans West Blvd., 206-C, Daytona Beach, FL 32118
Daley, James M., Quaker Towne Apartments, 150 Countryside Ln., Orchard Park, NY 14127
Dawidziak, Stanley J., 6796 Woodland Dr., Hamburg, NY 14075-6523
Federico, Ralph P., 83 Wilderness Park, Clarendon, PA 16313-9747
Fitzgerald, Donald J., Box 3100, Bonita Springs, FL 33959
Flynn, James P., Trocaire Place, 427 E. Main St., Batavia, NY 14020
Fox, John J., P.O. Box 852, Amherst, NY 14226
Gagliardo, Anthony F., P.O. Box 7184, Colorado Springs, CO 80933-7184
Gimbrone, Richard J., 157 Pennsylvania Ave., Buffalo, NY 14201
Gonter, Louis J., 9980 S.E. 161st Pl., Summerfield, FL 34491
Haran, James E., 81 South St., Cattaraugus, NY 14719
Hennessey, John P., 1955 Eleventh St., S.W., Largo, FL 33778-1118
Hogan, Francis T., 2792 N. Breeze Rd., Melbourne, FL 32935
Hughes, Donald R., McAuley Residence, 2950 Elmwood Ave., Kenmore, NY 14217
Kasprzyk, James H., Our Lady of Czestochowa, 23 Willowlawn Pkwy., Buffalo, NY 14206
Kaukus, Edwin J., 245 Richmond Ave., Buffalo, NY 14222
Klos, Walter, Albertine Home, 1501 Hoffman St., Hammond, IN 46327
Kuntz, Aloysius G., Sheehan Residence, 330 Linwood Ave., Buffalo, NY 14209
Kwolek, Joseph, 580 Doat St., Buffalo, NY 14211
Lex, Henry V., Sheehan Residence, 330 Linwood Ave., Buffalo, NY 14209
Lowry, Joseph K., Jr., 124 Division St., Salamanca, NY 14779
Martlock, Loville N., Our Lady of Good Counsel Rectory, 10675 Allegany Rd., Darien Center, NY 14040
McGrath, James R., 536 St. Lawrence Ave., Buffalo, NY 14216
Measer, Donald L., 2049 George Urban Blvd., Depew, NY 14043
Meegan, William H., 62 Eagan Dr., Lackawanna, NY 14218
Miller, Francis N., Our Lady of Victory Hospital, 55 Melroy St., Lackawanna, NY 14218
Naber, John T., P.O. Box 868, Buffalo, NY 14205-0868
O'Shea, John T., 3178 Merchant Rd., Warsaw, NY 14565
Paa, Joseph F., 21 Foxwood Row, Depew, NY 14043
Piazza, Salvatore J., 4671 Townline Rd. (Rte.429), Ransomville, NY 14131-9740
Priester, Robert E., Father Baker Manor, 6400 Powers Rd., Orchard Park, NY 14301
Pulikoottil, Abroham, 297 Collins Ave., West Seneca, NY 14224
Roche, Christopher J., Sheehan Residence, 330 Linwood Ave., Buffalo, NY 14209
Roche, David V., Sheehan Residence, 330 Linwood Ave., Buffalo, NY 14209
Selzler, Norbert E., 5020 Carpenter Rd., Hamburg, NY 14075
Shepherd, Thomas N., 1140 Abbot Rd., Buffalo, NY 14220
Snyder, Clatus E., 101 Century Rd., Buffalo, NY 14215
Sokolowski, Bernard T., St. Josaphat Rectory, 20 Peoria Ave., Cheektowaga, NY 14206
Staebell, James E., 12428 Barone Dr., Silver Creek, NY 14136-1204
Strassberger, H. Richard, 1917 11th St., Niagara Falls, NY 14305
Tomiak, Walter L., St. Elizabeth Home, 5539 Broadway, Lancaster, NY 14086
Vallone, Louis A., 7931 Villa Nova Dr., Boca Raton, FL 33433
Wagner, Eugene L., St. Charles Borromeo, 5969 Washington St., Olcott, NY 14126
Ward, William G., 33 Jack Rd., Williamsville, NY 14221
Werth, Charles M., 108 Wellington Ct., Buffalo, NY 14221-6750
Wright, Vincent L., 10848 Bowen Rd., Attica, NY 14011
Zancan, Robert D., P.O. Box 61, Morse Mill, MO 63066-0061

Permanent Deacons:
Barr, Joseph M.
Bauer, Robert A.
Boyd, Jimmie L., Sr.

Brick, Daniel E.
Bringenberg, Thomas B.
Burke, John H.
Burns, Robert E.
Burns, William R.
Calby, Edward T.
Carmody, Paul F.
Carroll, Melvin W.
Collichio, James L.
Crimi, Victor
Cruz, Moises C.
Dains, Ronald
Darroch, Nelson
Edbauer, Howard J., Jr.
Eschbach, Lawrence D.
Farstad, Dan K.
Forcucci, Thomas M.
Fortuna, Chester J., M.D.
Foster, Norman E.
Fox, Albert F.
Friedman, Heinz H.
Fudala, Walter N.
Gainey, John C.
Gill, Joseph J.
Griesbaum, Charles J., Jr.
Hart, Thomas J.
Jerome, David R.
Kane, Joseph P.
Kapsiak, Dennis W.
Kelly, John J.
Kelsey, Richard H.
Klein, George L.
Klein, John P.
Kopczynski, Michael R.
Krahling, Francis R.
Lankes, George A.
Licata, Thomas G.
Mackowiak, Daniel H.
Mahaney, Richard J.
Maloney, Timothy
Marino, Benjamin
Markowski, Lawrence
May, Thaddeus P.
McGuire, Daniel G.
McKeating, Michael P.
Meister, Alan A.
Menke, Richard A.
Mercurio, Joseph P.
Miranda, Roberto G.
Molik, Daniel J.
Molnar, Alexander
Moses, Robert J.
O'Connell, Edward G.
Parker, Richard W.
Penksa, Daniel M.
Pijacki, Thaddeus V.
Podniesnski, Matthew A.
Polizzi, Frank S.
Polizzi, John A.
Prince, James A.
Radlinski, Donald
Ramos, Carlos W.
Ruiz, Jose J.
Santana, Reinaldo
Schnettler, Paul J.
Schultz, Thomas E.
Setera, John T.
Shaunhnessey, Frank J.
Shultz, Donald W., Sr.
Slish, David P.
Stahl, Raymond H.
Steffen, Franklyn C.
Steinagle, Gordon J.
Stone, John G.
Suffoletto, Albert D.
Thomann, Bernard M.
Walders, Peter J.
Walek, Edward S.
Walker, Ronald
Walkowiak, Brian C.
Weisenburger, Paul F.
Wetter, Donald A.
Wick, John G.
Willis, William W.
Zwack, Francis A.
Zymanek, Caesar F.

INSTITUTIONS LOCATED IN THE DIOCESE

[A] SEMINARIES

BUFFALO. *Pope John II Residence*, 217 Winston Rd., 14216. Tel: 716-836-5526. Rev. Joseph C. Gatto, Acting Dir. Students 7; Priests 1; Total Staff 1.

EAST AURORA. *Christ the King Seminary*. Graduate School of Theology, 711 Knox Rd., P.O. Box 607, 14052. Tel: 716-652-8900.
E-mail: cksdia@gentech-online.com
Interdiocesan Theologate. Owned and operated by the Diocese of Buffalo. Seminarians are assigned by the Bishop of any diocese for preparation for ordination to Priesthood. Administration and Faculty: Revs. Richard W. Siepka, M.A., S.T.L., Pres. Rector; Joseph C. Gatto, S.T.D., Vice Rector; Sr. Judith M. Kubicki, Ph.D., Academic Dean; Nancy J. Balbick, M.S.W., C.S.W., M.A.T., Asst. to the Academic Dean; Mrs. Nancy Ehlers, Treas.; Mr. Joseph Roos, Dir. of Institutional Advancement; Mr. Michael Murphy, Dir. of Facilities; Rev. Bonaventure F. Hayes, O.F.M., M.A., S.T.L, M.L.S., Dir. Library. Faculty: Revs. Charles R. Amico, Ph.D., S.T.D.; Richard Cassidy, Ph.D.; Charles O'Connor, O.F.M., S.T.D.; Gabriel Scarfia, O.F.M., S.T.D.; Gregory Faulhaber, S.T.D.; Roger M. Haas, O.F.M. Conv., Ph.D.; Sr. Charlene Nowak, C.S.S.F., M.A.; Rev. Thomas Sheehan, O.F.M.; Sr. M. Tiburtia, Gorecki, F.S.S.J., M.L.S., Librarian; Rev. Peter Drilling, Th.D.; Dr. Susan Roll, Ph.D.; Rev. David Zwifka, M.A., J.C.D. Formation Faculty: Revs. Joseph Gatto; Gregory Faulhaber, S.T.D. Adjunct Faculty: Revs. Alfons M. Osiander; Paul W. Steller; Sr. Jean Thompson, O.S.F. Priests 12; Sisters 3; Lay Staff 17; Students 141; Total Staff 34.

[B] SEMINARIES, RELIGIOUS

YOUNGSTOWN. *The National Shrine Basilica of Our Lady of Fatima*, 1023 Swan Rd., 14174. Tel: 716-754-7489; Fax: 716-754-9130. Very Rev. Julio M. Ciavaglia, C.R.S.P.; Rev. Paul M. Keeling, C.R.S.P., Assoc. Dir.

St. Anthony M. Zaccaria Seminary, The Barbabite Fathers, Inc. 1023 Swann Rd., 14174. Tel: 716-754-7489; Fax: 716-754-9130.
E-mail: ourladfati@aol.com
Web site: http://www.catholic-church.org/barnabites
Revs. Paul M. Keeling, C.R.S.P.; Julio M. Ciavaglia, C.R.S.P., Shrine Dir., Prov. Supr., & Comm. Supr.; Ubaldo M. Fior, C.R.S.P.; Joseph M. Gariolo, C.R.S.P.; Luciano M. Visconti, C.R.S.P. Priests 5; Students 2; Total Staff 28.

[C] COLLEGES AND UNIVERSITIES

BUFFALO. *Canisius College*, 2001 Main St., 14208-1098. Tel: 716-883-7000; Fax: 716-888-2525.
E-mail: cookev@canisius.edu
Web site: http://www.canisius.edu
For a complete listing, refer to the Colleges and Universities section.

**D'Youville College*, 320 Porter Ave., 14201. Tel: 716-881-3200; Fax: 716-881-7780.
E-mail: bordercb@dyc.edu
Web site: www.dyc.edu
For a complete listing, refer to the Colleges and Universities section.

Trocaire College, 360 Choate Ave., 14220. Tel: 716-826-1200.
Web site: www.trocaire.edu
For a complete listing, refer to the Colleges and Universities section.

Villa Maria College of Buffalo, 240 Pine Ridge Rd., 14225-3999. Tel: 716-896-0700; Fax: 716-896-0705.
Web site: www.villa.edu
For a complete listing, refer to the Colleges and Universities section.

HAMBURG. *Hilbert College*, 5200 S. Park Ave., 14075. Tel: 716-649-7900
For a complete listing, refer to the Colleges and Universities section.

NIAGARA UNIVERSITY. *Niagara University*, Lewiston Rd., 14109-2015. Tel: 716-285-1212; Fax: 716-286-8355.
E-mail: jbm@niagara.edu
Web site: www.niagara.edu
For a complete listing, refer to the Colleges and Universities section.

ST. BONAVENTURE. *St. Bonaventure University*, 14778. Tel: 716-375-2000; Fax: 716-375-2055.
E-mail: fstorms@sbu.edu
Web site: http://www.sbu.edu
For a complete listing, refer to the Colleges and Universities section.

[D] HIGH SCHOOLS, PRIVATE

BUFFALO. *Bishop Timon-St. Jude High School*, 601 McKinley Pkwy., 14220. Tel: 716-826-3610. Owned and operated by Bishop Timon Board of Trustees. Mr. Thomas J. Sullivan, Prin. Franciscans 2; Lay Teachers 30; Students 370; Total Staff 40.

Canisius High School, 1180 Delaware Ave., 14209. Tel: 716-882-0466; Fax: 716-883-1870.
E-mail: president@canisiushs.buffalo.ny.us
Web site: www.canisiushs.buffalo.ny.us
Society of Jesus. Revs. Charles F. Kelley, S.J., Pres.; John J. Mattimore, S.J., Prin.; Louis T. Garaventa, S.J.; Joseph J. Kamiensky, S.J.; James R. Van Dyke, S.J.; Ronald W. Sams, S.J.; Richard J. Zanoni, S.J.; Eugene A. Zimpfer, S.J.; Robert Reiser, S.J.; Bro. James T. Dennehy, S.J.; Mr. David McCallum, S.J. Priests 9; Brothers 1; Scholastic 1; Lay Teachers 50; Students 707; Total Staff 81.

Holy Angels' Academy, 24 Shoshone Dr., 14214-1097. Tel: 716-834-7120. Jo Anne Grippi, Prin. Priests 1; Grey Nuns of the Sacred Heart 7; Lay Teachers 25; Religious 2; Students 250; Total Staff 36.

Mt. Mercy Academy, 88 Red Jacket Pkwy., 14220. Tel: 716-825-8796. Sisters of Mercy. Ms. Kathleen V. Collins, Prin. Students 491; Total Staff 68.

Nardin Academy High School, 135 Cleveland Ave., 14222. Tel: 716-881-6262; Fax: 716-881-4190. Miss Barbara Rapier, D.H.M., Pres.; Rev. Jeffrey M. Sturmer, Chap. Lay Teachers 48; Girls 437.

St. Joseph's Collegiate Institute, 845 Kenmore Ave., 14223. Tel: 716-874-4024; Fax: 716-874-4956.
E-mail: brotomsjci@msn.com
Web site: http://www.catholic.org/desalle/1.2.1.2.6.htm/
Brothers of the Christian Schools. (De La Salle Christian Brothers). Rev. James Croglio, Chap. of School and Brothers' Community; Bros. Thomas Lackey, F.S.C., Prin.; Edward Martin, F.S.C., Community Dir. Priests 1; Brothers 6; Lay Teachers 50; Students 779; Total Staff 57.

Turner Carroll High School, 185 Lang Ave., 14215. Tel: 716-896-4911; Fax: 716-896-4947.
E-mail: turnerchs@aol.com
Owned and operated by Turner/Carroll Board of Trustees. Sisters 1; Lay Teachers 15; Students 145; Total Staff 32.

Villa Maria Academy, 600 Doat St., 14211. Tel: 716-894-0398; Fax: 716-894-0468. Felician Sisters. Sr. Mary Kevin Szeluga, Prin. Sisters 16; Lay Teachers 20; Students 180; Total Staff 36.

ATHOL SPRINGS. *St. Francis High School*, 4129 Lake Shore Rd., 14010-0185. Tel: 716-627-1200; Fax: 716-627-4610. St. Anthony Province of the Order of Friars Minor Conventual. Revs. Robert Augustine Twele, OFM Conv., Prin.; Brad Heckathorne, OFM Conv., Asst. Prin.; Joseph Benicewicz, OFM Conv., Asst. Prin.; Aurelian W. Brzezniak, OFM Conv.; Charles Jagodzinski, OFM Conv.; Mark David Skura, OFM Conv.; Mark Thomas Booth, OFM Conv.; Felix Bracikowski, OFM Conv.; Bernard Olszewski, OFM Conv.; Roger Haas, OFM Conv.; Adrian Gallagher, OFM Conv.; Bro. Lawrence LaFlame, OFM Conv. Priests 9; Brothers 1; Sisters 3; Lay Teachers 37; Total Staff 49; Students 575.

BATAVIA. *Notre Dame High School of Batavia*, 73 Union St., 14020. Tel: 716-343-2783; Fax: 716-343-7323.
E-mail: notredme@iinc.com
Web site: www.5a.ndhs.com
Owned and operated by Notre Dame Board of Trustees. Mr. Frank C. Ferrando, Pres. & Prin.; Mr. Lance Bennett, Asst. Prin.; Rev. Robert A. Martin. Priests 1; Lay Teachers 20; Students 218; Total Staff 40.

HAMBURG. *Immaculata Academy*, 5138 S. Park Ave., 14075. Tel: 716-649-6161. Franciscan Sisters of St. Joseph. Sr. M. Paulette Tirone, Prin. Sisters 5; Lay Teachers 14; Students 165; Total Staff 29.

KENMORE. *Mt. St. Mary Academy*, 3756 Delaware Ave., 14217. Tel: 716-877-1358. Sisters of St. Mary of Namur. Mrs. Joan M. Spencer, Prin. Sisters 1; Lay Teachers 26; Girls 225; Day Care Center 130.

LANCASTER. *St. Mary's High School*, 142 Laverack Ave., 14086. Tel: 716-683-4824; Fax: 716-683-4996. Owned and operated by St. Mary's Board of Trustees. Mr. Lewiston Manuel, Prin.; Revs. Michael G. Uebler; John P. Mack. Priests 1; Sisters 1; Lay Teachers 30; Students 349; Total Staff 32.

NIAGARA FALLS. *Niagara Catholic Junior-Senior School*, 520-66th St., 14304. Tel: 716-774-8000.
E-mail: nchs@conject
Owned and operated by Niagara Catholic Board of Trustees. Ronald K. Buggs, Pres.; Ms. Patricia Menkiena, Prin.; Mr. Marc Graff, Assoc. Prin.; Revs. Robert S. Hughson; Gerald L. Bartko, O.S.F.S. Priests 2; Lay Teachers 32; Students 400.

OLEAN. *Archbishop Walsh High School*, 208 N. 24th St., 14760-1985. Tel: 716-372-8122. Owned and operated by Archbishop Walsh Board of Trustees. Ms. Mary Jane Telford, Prin.; Rev. Barry J. Allaire. Priests 1; Lay Teachers 12; Students 94; Total Staff 24.

TONAWANDA. *Cardinal O'Hara High School*, 39 O'Hara Rd., 14150. Tel: 716-695-2600. Timothy J. Sember, Prin. Sisters 4; Lay Teachers 30; Students 325. Owned and operated by Cardinal O'Hara Board of Trustees. Convent, 9 O'Hara Rd., 14150. Tel: 716-694-2370. Felician Sisters. Franciscan Missionary Sisters of the Divine Child.

[E] ELEMENTARY SCHOOLS, PRIVATE

BUFFALO. *Mount St. Joseph Academy*. Elementary Division: 2064 Main St., 14208. Tel: 716-883-1515. Mr. Theodore A. Callisto, Prin. Sisters 4; Lay Teachers 28; Students 320.

Nardin Academy, 135 Cleveland Ave., 14222. Tel: 716-881-6262. (Montessori-Grade 12).

LEWISTON. *Sacred Heart Villa School*. (Grades PreK-6),

5269 Lewiston Rd., 14092. Tel: 716-284-8273; Fax: 716-284-8273. Sr. Elizabeth Domin, S.S.H.J., Prin. Sisters 6; Lay Teachers 2; Students 117; Total Staff 12.

[F] ELEMENTARY SCHOOLS, SPECIAL

BUFFALO. *Cantalician Center for Learning, Inc.*, 3233 Main St., 14214. Tel: 716-833-5353. Program for the disabled: Infant, Toddler and Preschool; Elementary and Secondary. Workshop for adult individuals with disabilities, day treatment-lite program, & day habilitation for retired, disabled adults. Group homes/I.R.A. for adult individuals with disabilities. Sr. Patricia Tomasik, C.S.S.F., Exec. Dir.; Rev. Msgr. Harold Wagner, Chap. Priests 1; Brothers 1; Sisters 4; Laystaff 257; Students 474; Total Staff 263.

[G] REGIONAL AND CONSOLIDATED ELEMENTARY SCHOOLS

BUFFALO. *Catholic Academy of West Buffalo.* Delaware Campus: (Grades 3-8), 1069 Delaware Ave., 14209. Tel: 716-885-6111. Lafayette Campus: (Grades PreK-2), 279 Lafayette Ave., 14213. Tel: 716-886-5384. Miss Louise M. Myszka, Supervising Prin.; Sr. Gail Glenn, S.S.J., Bldg. Prin. (Delaware Campus); Mrs. Geraldine Kizielewicz, Bldg. Prin., (Lafayette Campus).
Sponsoring parishes: Annunciation, St. Anthony, Blessed Sacrament, Holy Angels, Holy Cross, Immaculate Conception, St. Joseph's Cathedral, St. Louis, St. Michael, Nativity, Our Lady of Loretto. Sisters 2; Lay Teachers 29; Students 447; Total Staff 32.

Catholic Central School. (Grades K-8), 476 Emslie St., 14212. Sr. Roberta Fulton, S.M.N.N., Prin.
Sponsoring parishes: St. Ann, Blessed Trinity, SS. Columba & Brigid, St. Mary of Sorrows, & St. Martin de Porres. Sisters 7; Lay Teachers 17; Students 302; Total Staff 27.

Our Lady of Black Rock, 16 Germain St., 14207. Tel: 716-873-7497. Sr. Mary Francianne Zielezinski, C.S.S.F., Prin.
Sponsoring parishes: Assumption, St. Florian, St. Francis Xavier, Coronation, St. Elizabeth, St. John the Baptist. Sisters 3; Lay Teachers 13; Students 173; Total Staff 16.

ATTICA. *Genesee-Wyoming Catholic Central Consolidated School*, 72 East Ave., 14011. Tel: 716-591-2515. William F. Schofield, Prin.
Sponsoring parishes: Attica, St. Vincent; Bennington Center, Sacred Heart; Darien Center, Our Lady of Good Counsel; Java Center, St. Patrick; North Java, St. Nicholas; Sheldon, St. Cecelia; Varysburg, St. Joseph; Warsaw, St. Michael. Lay Teachers 15; Students 160.

CHEEKTOWAGA. *Kolbe Catholic Regional School*, 120 Alexander Ave., 14211. Sr. M. Loriette, C.S.S.F., Prin.
Sponsoring Parishes: St. Lawrence, Holy Name, St. Gerard, St. John Kanty, St. John Gualbert, Most Holy Redeemer. Lay Teachers 16; Students 232; Total Staff 17.

DEPEW. *SS. Peter & Paul Catholic School*, 52 Burlington Ave., 14043. Tel: 716-683-8049.
Sponsoring parishes: SS. Peter & Paul, Depew; Sacred Heart, Bowmansville. Sisters 1; Lay Teachers 14; Students 230; Total Staff 15.

DUNKIRK. *Northern Chautauqua Catholic*, 336 Washington Ave., 14048. Tel: 716-366-0630. Kathy Y. Moser, Prin.
Sponsoring parishes: Brocton, St. Patrick; Dunkirk: St. Elizabeth Ann Seton, St. Hedwig, Holy Trinity; Fredonia: St. Anthony, St. Joseph Newman Center; Silver Creek: Our Lady of Mt. Carmel; Cassadaga: Immaculate Conception; Sinclairville: St. John the Evangelist; Westfield: St. James Major; Ripley: St. Thomas More; Sheridan: St. John Bosco; Forestville: St. Rose of Lima. Lay Teachers 14; Students 193; Total Staff 22.

LAKE VIEW. *Southtowns Catholic*, 2052 Lakeview Rd., Box 86, 14085. Tel: 716-627-5011; Fax: 716-627-5335. Sr. M. Diane Miller, C.S.S.F., Prin.
Sponsoring parishes: St. Vincent de Paul, North Evans; Our Lady of Perpetual Help, Lake View. Sisters 3; Lay Teachers 23; Students 262; Total Staff 26.

LOCKPORT. *DeSales Catholic School*, 6914 Chestnut School, 14094. Tel: 716-433-6422. Sr. Roberta Thoen, S.S.M.N. Sisters 2; Lay Teachers 33; Students 580; Total Staff 35.

NORTH TONAWANDA. *North Tonawanda Catholic.* Ascension Campus: (Grades 6-8), 75 Keil St., 14120. Tel: 716-693-2828. Sr. Rosemarie Kutsko, C.S.S.F., Supervising Prin., OLC Campus: (Grades PreK-2), 57 Center Ave., 14120. Tel: 716-694-3644. St. Joseph Campus: (Grades 3-5), 1469 Payne Ave., 14120. Tel: 716-693-4769.
Sponsoring parishes: Ascension, Our Lady of Czestochowa, St. Albert the Great and St. Joseph. Sisters 3; Lay Teachers 23; Students 278; Total Staff 26.

OLEAN. *Southern Tier Catholic*, 205 W. Henley St., 14760. Tel: 716-372-2891. Mr. Lawrence D. Ford, Sr., Prin.
Sponsoring parishes: Allegany, St. Bonaventure; Cuba, Our Lady of the Angels; Hinsdale, St. Helen; Portville, Sacred Heart; Olean, St. Mary of the Angels, St. John, Transfiguration; Vandalia, St. John the Baptist. Lay Teachers 18; Students 209; Total Staff 25.

[H] CATHOLIC CHARITIES

BUFFALO. *The Catholic Charities of the Diocese of Buffalo*, 525 Washington St., 14203. Tel: 716-856-4494. Rev. Msgr. Henry J. Gugino, Diocesan Dir.
Central Office: All Offices, Directors, and Supervisors are located at 525 Washington St., Buffalo, NY 14203, unless otherwise indicated.
Finance Dept. Theodore S. Lesinski, Comptroller. Tel: 716-856-4494; James P. Hayes, Dir. Devel. Tel: 716-856-4494; Mrs. Margaret Connors, Admin. Asst.
Catholic Charities Manpower Services. Rev. Msgr. Henry J. Gugino, Exec. Dir. Tel: 716-856-4494; Mr. Dennis Walczyk, Dir. Programs & Svcs. Tel: 716-856-4494.
Central Intake. Mrs. Kathryn Heavey, Supvr.
Parish Social Work Program, 188 Oakmont Ave., 14215. Tel: 716-835-6894. Jesselyn Garcia, Supvr.
Black Rock/Riverside Office, 819 Tonawanda St., 14207. Tel: 716-877-4716.
West Side Family Counseling Center, 412 Niagara St., 14201. Tel: 716-854-3622.
Lackawanna Family Counseling Center, 33-37 Wilkesbarre Ave., Lackawanna, 14218. Tel: 716-822-6877.
Preventative Services & Batterer's Intervention Program, 1581 Bailey Ave., 14212. Tel: 716-896-6390. Diane Greenaway, Coord. Legal Title: *Preventative Services and Batterer's Intervention Program, and Therapeutic Supervised Visitation Program.*
School Intervention Service, 3370 Delaware Ave., Kenmore, 14217. Tel: 716-877-8822. Adele Wawrzynek, Supvr., 9 E. Union, P.O. Box 94, Hamburg, 14075. Tel: 716-648-6515. Sharon Herlehy, Supvr., 3719 Union Rd., Ste. 214, Cheektowaga, 14225. Tel: 716-681-7394. Sara Murphy, Supvr., 4498 Main St., Amherst, 14226. Tel: 716-839-4066. Maria Picone, Supvr.
Department of Manpower & Educational Services, 33 Main St., P.O. Box 33, Bowmansville, 14026. Tel: 716-685-3400. Michael Talluto, Dir.
Day Care Services. Tel: 716-856-4494.
Diocesan Resettlement Division, 73 Edward St., 14203. Tel: 716-842-6816. Ann Brittain, Supvr.
Youth Careers Program, 33 Main St., P.O. Box 33, Bowmansville, 14026. Tel: 716-685-3400.
Department of Parish Based Social Services. Tel: 716-856-4494. Sr. Mary Anne Weldon, R.S.M., Dir.
Parish Outreach Program.
Office of Pastoral Ministry With Handicapped Persons. Tel: 716-856-4494. Sr. Rose Mary Cauley, G.N.S.H., Supvr.
South Chautauqua Elderly Project, 116 Aldren Ave., Jamestown, 14701. Tel: 716-665-4374. Claire Trubits, Supvr.
Department of District Services. Tel: 716-856-4494. Mr. Leonard J. Haefner, Dir.
Adoptions, Child Care Division, and Young Parents Program. Miss Mary M. Horrigan, Supvr.
Batavia, 113-119 Main St., Batavia, 14020. Tel: 716-343-0614. Mrs. Margaret Meyer, Supvr.
Dunkirk, 173 Lakeshore Dr. E., Dunkirk, 14048. Tel: 716-366-3533. Randy Hulbert, Supvr. Dunkirk & Jamestown.
Jamestown, 413 N. Main St., Jamestown, 14701. Tel: 716-484-9188.
Niagara Falls, 345 Third St., Ste. 515, Niagara Falls, 14303. Tel: 716-282-2351. Kathleen Hall, Supvr.
Olean, 520 W. State St., P.O. Box 554, Olean, 14140. Tel: 716-372-0101. Mrs. Kim Moricca, Supvr.
Women, Infants & Children (W.I.C.) of Niagara County, 237 Fourth St., Niagara Falls, 14303. Tel: 716-285-0975. Mrs. Claudia Weber, Coord.
Catholic Charities Satellite Offices: Blackrock-Riverside: 819 Tonawanda St., 14207. Tel: 716-877-4716. East Side: 1581 Bailey Ave., 14212. Tel: 716-896-6390. Grider St.: 359 Grider St., 14215. Tel: 716-895-7715. Oakmont Ave.: 188 Oakmont Ave., 14215. Tel: 716-835-6894. Perry St.: 488 Perry St., 14204. Tel: 716-856-4456. South Buffalo: 2315 Seneca St., 14210. Tel: 716-821-1929. Albion: 243 S. Main St., Albion, 14411. Tel: 716-589-7477. Amherst: 4498 Main St., Amherst, 14226. Tel: 716-839-4066. Cheektowaga: 3719 Union Rd., Cheektowaga, 14225. Tel: 716-681-7394. Hamburg: 9 E. Union St., 14075. Tel: 716-648-6515. Kenmore: 3370 Delaware Ave., Kenmore, 14217. Tel: 716-877-8822. Lockport: 39 East Ave., Lockport, 14094. Tel: 716-433-0246. North Tonawanda: 74 Webster St., North Tonawanda, 14120. Tel: 716-692-1440. Southtowns Office: 34 Barnstead Dr., Springville, 14141. Tel: 716-592-3420. Warsaw: 2-10 W. Buffalo St., Warsaw, 14569. Tel: 716-786-3440. Wellsville: 25 E. Pearl St., Wellsville, 14895. Tel: 716-595-2015. West Seneca: 4105 Seneca St., West Seneca, 14224. Tel: 716-675-3785.
Catholic Charities Appeal, 525 Washington St., 14203. Tel: 716-856-4494. Rev. Msgr. Henry J. Gugino, Diocesan Dir.; Rev. Joseph J. Sicari, Assoc. Dir.
Department of Clinical Services. Christopher J. Pino, Ph.D., Dir.
Marriage Counseling Center, 4498 Main St., 14226. Tel: 716-839-4066. David Catalano, Supvr.
St. Joseph's Day Training Center, 930 Fillmore Ave., 14211. Tel: 716-896-6038. Marsha Sladeski, Ph.D., Supvr.
Developmental Disabilities/Family Support Program, 359 Grider St., 14215. Tel: 716-895-7715. Maryruth Morris, R.N.
Diocesan Counseling Service for Clergy and Religious, 16 Columbus St., Cheektowaga, 14227. Tel: 716-894-2743. Sr. Anne Marie Jablonicky, C.S.S.F., Dir.
Chemical Dependency Program, Substance Abuse Prevention & Counseling Program. Tel: 716-835-9745. Judith Vogtli, Ph.D., Dir.
Geriatrics Outreach Treatment Team, 359 Grider St., 14215. Tel: 716-895-7715. Suzanna Mattingly, Supvr.
Department of Services to the Aging. Tel: 716-856-4494. Ms. Mary Jo Giambelluca, Dir.
Home Care Services. Deborah Alberth, R.N., Supvr.
Family Focus Program, 30 Rich St., 14211. Tel: 716-896-8262. Kathleen Pharris, Supvr.
Senior Day Center, 30 Rich St., 14211. Tel: 716-896-6388. Mrs. Kathleen Pharris, Dir.
Housing and Supportive Services. Tel: 716-856-4494. Mrs. Marie Bakowski, Supvr.; Deborah Alberth, R.N., Supvr.
Foster Grandparents Program, 525 Washington St., 14203. Tel: 716-856-4494. Dorothy Turchiarelli, Supvr.
Friendly Phones, 525 Washington St., 14203. Tel: 718-856-4494. Dorothy Turchiarelli, Supvr.
Department of Institutional Services to Aging, 525 Washington St., 14203. Tel: 716-856-4494. Carol Kennedy, R.N., Dir.
Volunteer Agencies:
Catholic Guild for the Blind. Tel: 716-856-4494. Sr. Rosemary Cauley, Prog. Dir.
Guild of St. Apollonia. Tel: 716-856-4494. Rev. Msgr. Henry J. Gugino, Spiritual Dir.
Ladies of Charity, 1122 Broadway, 14212. Tel: 716-895-4001. Rev. Msgr. Henry J. Gugino; Mrs. Eileen Nowak, Prog. Dir.
Society of St. Vincent de Paul, 1298 Main St., 14209. Tel: 716-852-7415. Rev. Msgr. Henry J. Gugino, Spiritual Dir.; Mr. Mark S. Zirnheld, Dir.
Delta Development Low Income Housing Development & Management, 525 Washington St., 14203. Tel: 716-856-4494. Janet Meiselman, Supvr. Total Assisted 211; Total Staff 39.
St. Clare Apartments Housing Development, c/o Catholic Charities, 525 Washington St., 14203. Rev. Msgr. Henry J. Gugino.

[I] ORPHANAGES AND INFANT HOMES

BUFFALO. *German Roman Catholic Orphan Home*, 795 Main St., 14203
For a complete listing, refer to the Special Care Facilities section.

[J] PROTECTIVE INSTITUTES

BUFFALO. *The Franciscan Center, Inc.*, 1910 Seneca St., 14210-1842. Tel: 716-822-8017; Fax: 716-822-8537
For a complete listing, refer to the Special Care Facilities section.

LACKAWANNA. *Baker Victory Services*, 780 Ridge Rd., 14218. Tel: 716-828-9500; 888-287-1160
For a complete listing, refer to the Special Care Facilities section.

[K] GENERAL HOSPITALS

BUFFALO. *McAuley Mercy Corporation*, 515 Abbott Rd., 14220. Tel: 716-828-2750
For a complete listing, refer to the Hospitals section.
Mercy Health System of Western New York Marian Professional Center, 515 Abbott Rd., Ste. 508, 14220. Tel: 716-828-2750.
For a complete listing, refer to the Hospitals section.
Mercy Hospital, 565 Abbott Rd., 14220. Tel: 716-826-7000.
E-mail: mercyhosp@aol.com
For a complete listing, refer to the Hospitals section.
Sisters Hospital Foundation, Inc., 2130 Main St., 14214. Tel: 716-862-2533
For a complete listing, refer to the Hospitals section.
Sisters of Charity Hospital of Buffalo, NY, 2157 Main St., 14214. Tel: 716-862-1000; Fax: 716-862-1899.
E-mail: mdougher@sisters-buffalo.org
Web site: http://www.sisters-buffalo.org81
For a complete listing, refer to the Hospitals section.

BATAVIA. *St. Jerome Hospital*, 16 Bank St., 14020. Tel: 716-343-3131
For a complete listing, refer to the Hospitals section.

CHEEKTOWAGA. *McAuley-Seton Home Care*, 14 Appletree Business Park, 14227. Tel: 716-685-4870
For a complete listing, refer to the Hospitals section.
St. Joseph Hospital, 2605 Harlem Rd., 14225-4097. Tel: 716-891-2400; Fax: 716-891-2616
For a complete listing, refer to the Hospitals section.

KENMORE. *Kenmore Mercy Foundation Inc.*, 2950 Elmwood Ave., 14217. Tel: 716-879-6204
For a complete listing, refer to the Hospitals section.
Kenmore Mercy Hospital, 2950 Elmwood Ave., 14217. Tel: 716-447-6100; Fax: 716-447-6090
For a complete listing, refer to the Hospitals section.

LACKAWANNA. *Our Lady of Victory Hospital*, 55 Melroy at Ridge Rd., 14218. Tel: 716-825-8000; Fax: 716-825-4681
For a complete listing, refer to the Hospitals section.
Our Lady of Victory Hospital Auxiliary, 55 Melroy Ave., 14218. Tel: 716-825-8000; Fax: 716-825-4583
For a complete listing, refer to the Hospitals section.

LEWISTON. *Mount St. Mary's Hospital of Niagara Falls*, 5300 Military Rd., 14092-1997. Tel: 716-297-4800
For a complete listing, refer to the Hospitals section.

LOCKPORT. *Niagara Homemaker Services, dba Mercy Home Care of Western New York*, 111 Main St., 14094. Tel: 716-434-2388
For a complete listing, refer to the Hospitals section.

[L] HEALTH CARE FACILITIES

BUFFALO. *St. Francis Geriatric and Healthcare Services, Inc.*, 2787 Main St., 14214. Tel: 716-837-4200; Fax: 716-837-4218
For a complete listing, refer to the Special Care Facilities section.

[M] HOMES FOR AGED

BUFFALO. *Nazareth Nursing Home*, 291 North St., 14201. Tel: 716-881-2323
For a complete listing, refer to the Special Care Facilities section.

BATAVIA. *St. Luke Manor*, 17 Wiard St., 14020. Tel: 716-343-8806
For a complete listing, refer to the Special Care Facilities section.

CLARENCE. *Brothers of Mercy Housing Co., Inc.*, 10500 Bergtold Rd., 14031. Tel: 716-795-2122
For a complete listing, refer to the Special Care Facilities section.
Brothers of Mercy Nursing & Rehabilitation Center, 10570 Bergtold Rd., 14031. Tel: 716-759-6985
For a complete listing, refer to the Special Care Facilities section.
Brothers of Mercy Sacred Heart Home, Inc., 4520 Ransom Rd., 14031. Tel: 716-759-2644
For a complete listing, refer to the Special Care Facilities section.

DUNKIRK. *St. Vincent's Home for the Aged*, 319 Washington Ave., 14048. Tel: 716-366-2066; Fax: 716-366-0545
For a complete listing, refer to the Special Care Facilities section.

KENMORE. *KMH Homes, Inc.* Administrative Offices, 2950 Elmwood Ave., 14217.
For a complete listing, refer to the Special Care Facilities section.

LANCASTER. *St. Elizabeth's Home*, 5539 Broadway, 14086. Tel: 716-683-5150; Fax: 716-683-4049
For a complete listing, refer to the Special Care Facilities section.

LOCKPORT. *St. Clare Manor*, 543 Locust St., 14094 Fax: 716-434-5900
For a complete listing, refer to the Special Care Facilities section.

NIAGARA FALLS. *Mount St. Mary's LTC Facility, Inc.*, 2600 Main St., 14305.
E-mail: jlomeo@aol.com
For a complete listing, refer to the Special Care Facilities section.
St. Mary's Manor, 515 Sixth St., 14301. Tel: 716-285-3236
For a complete listing, refer to the Special Care Facilities section.

OLEAN. *St. Joseph Manor*, 2211 W. State St., 14760 Fax: 716-373-4375
For a complete listing, refer to the Special Care Facilities section.

ORCHARD PARK. *W.N.Y. Catholic LongTerm Care, Inc. dba Father Baker Manor*, 6400 Powers Rd., 14127. Tel: 716-667-0001; Fax: 716-667-0028.
E-mail: ronz2977@aol.com
For a complete listing, refer to the Special Care Facilities section.

SILVER CREEK. *St. Columbans on the Lake, Home for the Aged*, 2546 Lake Rd., 14136. Tel: 716-934-4515
For a complete listing, refer to the Special Care Facilities section.

WILLIAMSVILLE. *Holy Family Home*, 410 Mill St., 14221. Tel: 716-634-5400
For a complete listing, refer to the Special Care Facilities section.
St. Francis Home of Williamsville, 147 Reist St., 14221. Tel: 716-633-5400; Fax: 716-663-6404
For a complete listing, refer to the Special Care Facilities section.

[N] DAY CARE CENTERS

BUFFALO. *Guardian Angel Day Care Center*, 1193 Delaware Ave., 14209. Dana M. Cassiano, Admin. Lay Staff 15; Children 72; Total Staff 15.
Holy Innocents Day Care Center, 30 Rich St., 14211. Tel: 716-896-6386. Mrs. Ann Marie Zaccarine, Dir. Day care for children age 6 weeks to 12 yrs. Total Staff 19.

[O] MONASTERIES AND RESIDENCES OF PRIESTS AND BROTHERS

BUFFALO. *Bishop's Residence*, 77 Oakland Pl., 14222. Most Rev. Henry J. Mansell, D.D.; Rev. Msgr. Robert J. Cunningham; Revs. David G. LiPuma; Paul A. Litwin.
Canisius Jesuit Community, 2001 Main St., 14208. Tel: 716-883-7000.
E-mail: higgins@canisius.edu
Web site: http://www.canisius.edu
Legal Title: *The Jesuits of Canisius College, Inc.* Revs. James P. Higgins, S.J., Rector; Richard J. Hoar, S.J., Min.; William C. Carroll, S.J.; Bro. Thomas J. Casey, S.J.; Revs. Joseph F. Burke, S.J.; J. Peter Conroy, S.J.; Vincent M. Cooke, S.J.; Bro. James T. Dennehy, S.J.; Revs. James L. Dugan, S.J.; Paul J. Dugan, S.J.; Adelmo P. Dunghe, S.J.; Edward T. Dunn, S.J.; Benjamin Fiore, S.J.; Thomas E. Fleming, S.J.; Richard H. Galligan, S.J.; Louis T. Garaventa, S.J.; John J. Garvey, S.J.; Robert A. Haus, S.J.; Steven Hawkes-Teeples, S.J.; Daniel P. Jamros, S.J.; Ladislaus F. Juhasz, S.J. (Hungary); Joseph J. Kamiensky, S.J.; Charles F. Kelley, S.J.; Mark G. Kriz, S.J.; Daniel P. Liderbach, S.J.; Patrick J. Lynch, S.J.; John J. Mattimore, S.J.; David C. McCallum, S.J.; Paul J. McCarthy, S.J.; Martin X. Moleski, S.J.; Paul W. Nochelski, S.J.; Thomas A. O'Connor, S.J.; Michael H. Pastizzo, S.J.; Robert E. Reiser, S.J.; Frederick J. Reisert, S.J.; James J. Ruddick, S.J.; Ronald W. Sams, S.J.; Brendan T. Scott, S.J.; Edward P. Sullivan, S.J.; Michael F. Tunney, S.J.; James R. Van Dyke, S.J.; Eugene A. Zimpfer, S.J.; Daniel J. Lusch, S.J., Elmwood 4, 4845 Transit Rd., 14043. Total in Residence 42; Total Staff 15.
Maryknoll House, 71 Jewett Pkwy., 14214-2396. Tel: 716-834-6065.
E-mail: mklbuf@igc.org
Revs. Douglas May, M.M., Dir.; Joseph Turowski, M.M. Total in Residence 2; Total Staff 2.
Sheehan Residence for Priests, 330 Linwood Ave., 14209-1689. Tel: 716-884-0053; Fax: 716-884-2279. Residence for retired priests. Revs. Robert J. Biesinger; Raymond G. Bohn; Rev. Msgr. Paul T. Cronin; Revs. Aloysius G. Kuntz; Henry V. Lex; Christopher J. Roche; David V. Roche.

ATHOL SPRINGS. *Father Justin Rosary Hour Radio Apostolate*, St. Anthony of Padua Friary, 4190 St. Francis Dr., 14010. Tel: 716-627-3861; Fax: 716-627-4059.
E-mail: Rosaryhr@localnet.com
Web site: http://www.cam.org/~darek/rosary.hour
Revs. Marion M. Tolczyk, O.F.M.Conv., Guardian & Dir.; Lucian Krolikowski, O.F.M.Conv.; Eligius Kozak, O.F.M.Conv. (Poland); Wladek Mezyk, O.F.M.Conv. (Poland); Jacek Macki, O.F.M.Conv. Staff to the Rosary Apostolate: Sr. Mary Angelica Bielski, C.S.S.F., Executive Secretary; Sr. Mary Rosette Kubisty, C.S.S.F.
St. Francis of Assisi Friary, 4129 Lake Shore Rd., 14010-0185. Tel: 716-627-5762; Fax: 716-627-4610. Faculty Residence for St. Francis High School. Revs. Aurelian W. Brzezniak, O.F.M.Conv.; Bernard Olszewski, O.F.M.Conv.; Charles Jagodzinski, O.F.M.Conv.; Felix Bracikowski, O.F.M.Conv.; Mark David Skura, O.F.M.Conv., Guardian; Joseph Benicewicz, O.F.M.Conv., Prin.; Roger Haas, O.F.M.Conv.; Brad Heckathorne, O.F.M.Conv.; Adrian Gallagher, O.F.M.Conv.; Friar Michael Laskey; Bros. Lawrence LaFlame, O.F.M.Conv.; Paschal Kolodziej, O.F.M.Conv., Vicar. Priests 9; Brothers 2; Friars 1; Total in Residence 12.

CLARENCE. *Provincial Motherhouse of Brothers of Mercy*, 4520 Ransom Rd., 14031. Tel: 716-759-8341. Legal Title: *Brothers of Mercy, Inc.* Bro. Jude Holzfoerster, F.M.M., Prov.; Rev. John J. Sardina, Chap. Brothers 14; In Formation 4.

DERBY. *Piarist Fathers*, 6472 Lake Shore Rd., Box 786, 14047. Tel: 716-947-4412. Revs. Alphonse Vercek, Sch.P.; Kalman Miskolczy, Sch.P., Supr.; Nicholas Vitez Fodor, Sch.P. Total in Residence 3; Total Staff 2.
Society of St. Paul. Mailing Address: Box 757, 14047. Tel: 716-947-5407; Fax: 716-947-5407. Very Rev. Matthew Roehrig, S.S.P., Prov. Supr.

LEROY. *Order of the BVM of Mercy/Mercedarian Friars*, Mercygrove, 7758 E. Main Rd., 14482-9701. Tel: 716-768-7110; Fax: 716-768-4803. United States headquarters for the community. Pre-novitiate and Novitiate formation community. Very Rev. Jerome P. Laubacker, O.de.M., Vicar Prov. & Local Supr.; Revs. Eugene Costa, O.de.M., Novice Master; Michael Rock, O.de.M., Retreat Dir. & Devel. Office; Wayne C. Genereux, O.de.M., Vocation Dir. & Master of Postulants. Total in Community: Professed Religious 4; Novices 6; Postulants 4.
St. Raymond Nonnatus Novitiate. Order of the BVM of Mercy. Mercygrove, 7758 E. Main Rd., 14482-9701. Tel: 716-768-7110. Rev. Eugene Costa, O.de.M., Novice Master. Novices 6.

NIAGARA FALLS. *Catholic Worker Center*, 931 Niagara Ave., 14305. Tel: 716-282-8683. Jim Serafin, Exec. Dir.

NIAGARA UNIVERSITY. *Vincentian Community at Niagara University*, Meade Hall, 14109-2209. Tel: 716-286-8110; Fax: 716-286-8766.
E-mail: meade@niagara.edu
Revs. John A. Kettelberger, C.M., Supr.; Joseph G. Hubbert, C.M., Asst.; Bro. Augustine D. Towey, C.M., Sub-Asst.; Revs. Patrick S.L. Flanagan, C.M., Procurator; John C. Bowes, C.M.; Kevin G. Creagh, C.M.; Peter A. Fitzgerald, C.M.; Paul L. Golden, C.M.; William L. Green, C.M.; Thomas P. Mallaghan, C.M.; Thomas P. McGourty, C.M.; Daniel F. O'Leary, O.M.I.; Vincent J. O'Malley, C.M.; Francis X. Prior, C.M.; Martin J. Sleasman, C.M.; John J. Trainor, C.M.; Louis P. Trotta, C.M.; Michael J. Tumulty, C.M.; Bros. Stephen J. Kennedy, C.M.; Martin J. Schneider, C.M.

NORTH TONAWANDA. *Society of the Catholic Apostolate.* Infant Jesus Delegature, 3452 Niagara Falls Blvd., P.O. Box 563, 14120-0563. Tel: 716-694-4313. Revs. Anthony Zemula, S.A.C., Supr. & Prov. Delegate; Francis A. Cegielka, S.A.C., Shrine Dir.; Jan B. Posiewala, S.A.C.; Andrzej Kurowski, S.A.C.; Seweryn J. Koszyk, S.A.C.; Benedict Barszcz, S.A.C.; Slavomir Siok, S.A.C.; George Poltorak, S.A.C. Chaplains, VA Hospital: Rev. Ignatius Curzydlo, S.A.C.; Rev. Msgr. George C. Maj, S.A.C.

ST. BONAVENTURE. *St. Bonaventure Friary*, 14778. Tel: 716-375-2000; Fax: 716-375-2424.
Web site: http://www.sbu.edu
Bro. Anthony J. LoGalbo, O.F.M., Vicar; Revs. Jack Zibert, O.F.M., Guardian; Giles F. Bello, O.F.M.; Michael Blastic, O.F.M.Conv.; David D. Blake, O.F.M.; Thomas Blow, O.F.M.; J. Gregory Brennan, O.F.M.; Anthony M. Carrozzo, O.F.M.; Mathias F. Doyle; Regis A. Duffy, O.F.M.; Richard C. Flaherty, O.F.M.; Gedeon Gal, O.F.M.; Xavier J. Seubert, O.F.M.; Francis Storms, O.F.M., Treas.; Peter Schneible, O.F.M.; Robert Stewart, O.F.M.; Alphonsus A. Trabold, O.F.M.; Allen Weber, O.F.M.; Gervase White, O.F.M.; Robert H. White, O.F.M.; Allan Wolter, O.F.M.; Bros. Thomas Cole, O.F.M.; David Haack, O.F.M.; Michael W. Montgomery, O.F.M.; Adrian A. Riester, O.F.M.; Julian Riester, O.F.M.; Basil J. Valente, O.F.M. Fathers 20; Brothers 7.

TONAWANDA. *O'Hara Residence*, 69 O'Hara Rd., 14150-6227. Tel: 716-743-0037. Rev. Msgr. James N. Connelly; Rev. Msgr. Leo E. Hammerl; Rev. Msgr. Paul R. Juenker, P.A.; Rev. Msgr. Edward J. Sobierajski; Rev. Msgr. Francis M. Swiatkowski; Rev. Msgr. Julius J. Szabo; Rev. Msgr. Casimir A. Zak. Total in Residence 7; Total Staff 3.

WEST SENECA. *St. Bonaventure*, 36 Flohr Ave., 14224-1818. Tel: 716-823-1090. Revs. Benoit J. Drapeau, C.J.M., Pastor, Supr.; Ronald M. Bagley, C.J.M., Dir. St. John Eudes Center; J. Gregory Sampson, C.J.M. Total in Residence 3; Total Staff 5.

[P] CONVENTS AND RESIDENCES FOR SISTERS

BUFFALO. *Congregation of the Sisters of St. Joseph Generalate.*
E-mail: Buffssj@aol.com
Administrative Offices, 23 Agassiz Cir., 14214. Tel: 716-838-4400. Total in Residence 80; Total Staff 22; Professed Sisters 156.
Discalced Carmelite Monastery of St. Teresa of the Child Jesus (1920), 75 Carmel Rd., 14214. Tel: 716-837-6499. Mother Miriam of Jesus, O.C.D., Prioress. Cloistered Professed Sisters 15; Extern Professed Sisters 3; Novices 1; Postulants 3.
Holy Name Province - Provincial Motherhouse.
Sisters of St. Francis of Holy Name Province, Inc., 4421 Lower River Rd., Stella Niagara, 14144. Tel: 716-754-4312. Sr. Mary McCarrick, O.S.F., Prov. Min.
Center of Renewal, Inc., 4421 Lower River Rd., Stella Niagara, 14144. Tel: 716-754-4312. Sr. Mary McCarrick, O.S.F., Prov. Min.
Francis Center, Inc., 4421 Lower Rd., Stella Niagara, 14144. Tel: 716-754-4312. Sr. Mary McCarrick, O.S.F., Prov. Min.
Stella Niagara Education Park, Inc., 4421 Lower

River Rd., Stella Niagara, 14144. Tel: 716-754-4312. Sr. Mary McCarrick, O.S.F., Prov. Min.
The Stella Niagara Education Park Endowment Foundation, 4421 Lower River Rd., Stella Niagara, 14144. Tel: 716-754-4312. Sr. Mary McCarrick, O.S.F., Prov. Min.
The Sisters of St. Francis Retirement Fund, 4421 Lower River Rd., Stella Niagara, 14144. Tel: 716-754-4312. Sr. Mary McCarrick, O.S.F., Prov. Min.
The Providence Fund, 4421 Lower River Rd., Stella Niagara, 14144. Tel: 716-754-4312. Sr. Mary McCarrick, O.S.F., Prov. Min.
Buffalo Academy of the Sacred Heart, Inc., 3860 Main St., 14226. Tel: 716-754-4312. Sr. Mary McCarrick, O.S.F., Prov. Min.
Immaculate Heart of Mary Provincial House and Convent. Villa Maria, 600 Doat St., 14211. Tel: 716-892-4141; Fax: 716-892-4177. Sr. Mary Raymond Kasprzak, C.S.S.F., Prov. Min.; Revs. Donald E. Levan, Provincial House Chap.; Joseph Kwolek, Infirmary and Residence Chap. Felician Sisters 312.
Monastery of Our Lady of the Rosary, 335 Doat St., 14211-2199. Tel: 716-892-0066; Fax: 716-892-8846. Mother Rose of St. Mary, O.P., Prioress; Rev. Jacob Restrick, O.P., Chap./Contemplative Dominican Nuns. Legal Title: ***Dominican Nuns of the Perpetual Rosary, Buffalo, NY.*** Professed Nuns 30; Postulants 4.
Mount Mercy Convent, 625 Abbott Rd., 14220. Tel: 716-826-6192. Total in Residence 26.
St. Mary's Convent, 138 Wesley St., 14214. Tel: 716-837-5816. Sisters of St. Mary of Namur. Professed Sisters 4.
Sisters of Social Service District Residence, 440 Linwood Ave., 14209. Tel: 716-883-0112.
E-mail: sss@pcom.net
Sr. Angela Homoki-Szabo, S.S.S., District Moderator. Sisters 9.
Other Convents: Generalate Res. and Novitiate, 296 Summit Ave., 14214. Tel: 716-834-0197. Sr. Anne Lehner, S.S.S., Gen. Moderator. Sisters 5. Scholastica House, 210 Winston Rd., 14216. Tel: 716-833-7412. Sisters 3; Sisters Living Alone 2; Sisters in Other Religious Retirement Homes 1.
Sisters of St. Mary, 250 Bryant St., 14222. Tel: 716-884-8221; Fax: 716-884-2950. Provincial House of the Sisters of St. Mary of Namur. Sr. Maureen Quinn, S.S.M.N., Prov. Supr.; Sr. Barbara Riter, S.S.M.N., Prov. Councillor. Professed Sisters 111.

ALLEGANY. *St. Elizabeth's Motherhouse*, 14706. Tel: 716-373-0200; Fax: 716-372-5774. Motherhouse of the Franciscan Sisters of Allegany. Sr. Margaret Mary Kimmins, O.S.F., Gen. Min.; Sr. Marigene Kennedy, O.S.F., Local Min. Sisters 96; Total Staff 15.

BELMONT. *Immaculate Conception Convent*, 5173 State Rte. 244, 14813. Franciscan Missionary Sisters of the Divine Child. Conducts catechetical centers in 7 villages. Sr. Rosemary Benson, Supr. Sisters 2.

CLARENCE. *Sisters of St. Joseph*. Clarence Residence, 4975 Strickler Rd., 14031. Tel: 716-759-6893. Coordinators: Sr. Marian Schwenk, S.S.J.; Sr. Marie Denise Heineman, S.S.J. Total in Residence 48; Total Staff 17.

DELEVAN. *Franciscan Sisters of Allegany, New York-Blessed Sacrament Mission Center*, 8 N. Main St., 14042. Tel: 716-492-2266. Conducted by Franciscan Sisters of Allegany. Services Region 21. Sr. Mary Richard Burke, O.S.F., Chaplaincy Svc.; Sr. Veronica Mary Louis, Field Mgr. Mission Society; Sr. Ellen Michael Schafer, O.S.F., Dir. Oleon Southern Tier Catechetical Office.

DERBY. *Sisters of St. Mary of Namur*, 7110 Lake Shore Rd., 14047. Tel: 716-947-4061. Sr. Bernadette Capolla; Sr. Genevieve Kenney; Sr. Mary R. Thompson. Sisters 3.

HAMBURG. *Immaculate Conception Convent*, 5286 S. Park Ave., 14075; Fax: 716-649-5958. Motherhouse of the Franciscan Sisters of St. Joseph. Sr. M. Andrea Ciszewski, F.S.S.J., Gen. Min.; Rev. Ronald Sermak, O.F.M.Conv., Chap. Sisters 126.
North American Union of the Sisters of Our Lady of Charity, 3800 Howard Rd., 14075. Tel: 716-648-4988. Legal Title: *Sisters of Our Lady of Charity of the Refuge, Inc.* Sr. Rosemary Toth, Local Supr.; Sr. Ellen Patrick Stapleton, Business Mgr. Sisters 24.

LACKAWANNA. *Sisters of Charity of St. Vincent de Paul of Zagreb, Croatia*, 211 W. Elmview Ave., 14218. Tel: 716-825-1461. Sr. Stella, Supr. Sisters 2.

LEWISTON. *Sisters of the Sacred Heart of Jesus (S.S.H.J.)*, Sacred Heart School & Convent, 5269 Lewiston Rd., 14092. Tel: 716-284-8273. Sr. M. Terenzia Giudice, S.S.H.J., Supr. Sisters 8.

LOCKPORT. *St. Joseph's Convent - Sisters of St. Mary of Namur*, 104 Garden St., 10494. Tel: 716-433-3966.
E-mail: MASSMN@juno.com
Sisters of St. Mary of Namur. Professed Sisters 3; Total in Residence 3.

ORCHARD PARK. *Sisters of Mercy of the Buffalo Diocese Retirement Corp.*, 5245 Murphy Rd., 14127. Tel: 716-662-9836; 662-5120; Fax: 716-662-9766.
E-mail: mercybuf@buffnet.net
Sr. Peggy Gorman, R.S.M., Pres.
Sisters of Mercy-Regional Community Offices, 5245 Murphy Rd., 14127. Tel: 716-662-9836; 662-5120; Fax: 716-662-9766.
E-mail: mercybuf@buffnet.net
Sisters of Mercy. Sr. Peggy Gorman, R.S.M., Pres.; Rev. Msgr. Cyril I. Trevett, Chap. Sisters Professed 196; Candidates 4.

SILVER CREEK. *Missionary Sisters of St. Columbans, St. Columban's on the Lake*, 14136. Rev. John C. Healy, S.S.C., Chap. Professed Sisters 12.

WEST SENECA. *Sisters of Charity of St. Vincent de Paul of Zagreb, Croatia*, 171 Knox Ave., 14224. Tel: 716-825-5859; 822-6841. Sr. Marija Mirna Matic, Supr. Professed Sisters 23. Legal Title: *Sisters of Charity of St. Vincent de Paul of Zagreb, Croatia - U.S.A. Delegacy Headquarters.*

WILLIAMSVILLE. *Franciscan Missionary Sisters of the Divine Child, Inc.*, 6380 Main St., 14221. Tel: 716-632-3144. Sr. Margaret C. Krantz, Min. Gen.; Sr. Marianne Ferguson, Asst. Supr., Vicar. Sisters 32.
Private Kindergarten - Divine Child Kindergarten, 6380 Main St., 14221. Sr. Renee Kopacz, F.M.D.C., Prin.; Rev. Gary J. Bagley, Community Chap.
Sisters of St. Francis of the Third Order Regular, St. Mary of the Angels, P.O. Box 275, 14231-0275. Tel: 716-632-2155; Fax: 716-632-0339. Motherhouse of the Sisters of St. Francis of the Third Order Regular. Sr. Patricia Burkard, Gen. Min.; Rev. Msgr. Fred R. Voorhes, Chap. Sisters 137.

[Q] RETREAT HOUSES

DERBY. *St. Columban's Center*, 6892 Lake Shore Rd., P.O. Box 816, 14047-0816. Tel: 716-947-4708; Fax: 716-947-5759. Rev. Msgr. James E. Wall, Dir.; Sr. Mary Leah Krauth, O.S.F., Assoc. Dir.; Sr. Mary Catherine Cummins, O.S.U., Assoc. Dir.; Rev. John J. Mergenhagen, Assoc. Dir. Total in Residence 4; Total Staff 22.

LEROY. *St. Peter Nolasco Spiritual Center*, Mercygrove, 7770 E. Main Rd., 14482-9701. Tel: 716-768-7110; 768-6408. Offering directed or private retreats. Facility available for overnight programs. Rev. Michael R. Rock, O.de.M., Dir.

WEST CLARKSVILLE. *Mount Irenaeus, Franciscan Mountain Retreat & Holy Peace Friary*, P.O. Box 100, 14786. Tel: 716-973-2470. Order of Friars Minor Holy Name Province. Revs. Daniel Riley, O.F.M., Pres. & Guardian; Daniel Hurley, O.F.M.; James Falduti, O.F.M.; Bro. Joseph Kotula, O.F.M.; Rev. Louis McCormick, O.F.M. Total in Residence 5.

[R] CAMPUS MINISTRY AND NEWMAN CENTERS

WILLIAMSVILLE. *Campus Ministry*, 6325 Main St., 14221. Tel: 716-632-8898. Rev. Paul W. Steller, Episcopal, Vicar of Campus Ministry.
Canisius College. Campus Ministry Office, 2001 Main St., Buffalo, 14208. Tel: 716-888-2420. Sr. Marlene Butler, G.N.S.H., Dir. Assoc. Campus Ministers: Revs. Richard R. Galligan, S.J.; Thomas A. O'Connor, S.J.; Mark G. Kriz, S.J.; Sr. Patricia Brady, S.S.M.N.; Mr. J. Joseph Volkenbeurg.
Daemen College. Campus Ministry Office, 4380 Main St., Buffalo, 14226. Tel: 716-839-3600. Ms. Joanne Stiller, Dir.; Rev. A. Mark Illig.
D'Youville College. 320 Porter Ave., Buffalo, 14201. Tel: 716-881-7693. Bro. James Sarach, T.O.R., Dir.; Rev. Anthony Rigoli, O.M.I.
Erie Community College. City Campus, 121 Ellicott St., Buffalo, 14203. Tel: 716-842-2770. Sr. Ruth Marie Penksa, G.N.S.H., Dir. Campus Ministry, North Campus, Newman Center, 6325 Main St., 14221. Tel: 716-632-8898. Rev. Paul W. Steller, Dir.; Carol Kwadrans, Sec., South Campus, Newman Center, 4196 Abbott Rd., Orchard Park, 14127. Tel: 716-648-5400; 649-6186. Rev. Msgr. David M. Lee, Dir.
Medaille College. Campus Ministry, 18 Agassiz Cir., Buffalo, 14214.
Niagara University, Lewiston Rd., Niagara University, 14109. Tel: 716-285-1212. Revs. Patrick Flanagan, C.M.; Kevin Creagh, C.M.; Ms. Mary Beth Coates, Dir.; Mr. Thomas Hughes.
State University College at Buffalo. Newman Center, 1219 Elmwood Ave., Buffalo, 14222. Tel: 716-882-1080. Rev. Msgr. John C. Weimer, Dir. Assoc. Directors: Sr. Charlene Fontana, S.S.J.; Susan Spadinger; Dorothy Gardiner, Sec.
State University of New York at Buffalo (Main St. South Campus), St. Joseph's University Parish, 3269 Main St., Buffalo, 14214. Tel: 716-833-0298. Rev. Jacob C. Ledwon, Dir.; Mr. Matthew Smith.
Trocaire College, 110 Red Jacket Pkwy., Buffalo, 14220. Tel: 716-826-1200. Ms. Nicole Pollard, Dir.
Villa Maria College, 240 Pine Ridge Rd., Buffalo, 14225. Tel: 716-896-0700. Mr. Frank Antonnucci.
St. Jude's Chapel at Alfred University & Alfred State College, Box 1154, Lower College Dr., Alfred, 14802. Tel: 607-587-9411. Rev. Eugene P. Ulrich, Dir.; Robert Donius; Sue Fowler.
State University of New York at Buffalo (North Campus) Newman Center, UB Commons-Ste. 209, Amherst, 14228. Rev. Msgr. J. Patrick Keleher, Dir.; Anne Tupper.
Genesee Community, One College Rd., Batavia, 14020.
State University College at Fredonia, 222 Temple St., Fredonia, 14063. Tel: 716-679-4686. Rev. James Vacco, O.F.M., Dir.; Karen M. Cave, Sec.
Hilbert College. Campus Ministry Office, 5200 S. Park Ave., Hamburg, 14075. Tel: 716-649-7900. Rev. Bernard Olszewski, O.F.M.Conv., Dir.; Ms. Sheila Dunphy.
St. Bonaventure University, St. Bonaventure, 14778. Tel: 716-375-2000. Revs. Daniel Hurley, O.F.M.; James Falduti, O.F.M.; Daniel Riley, O.F.M.; Bro. Thomas Cole, O.F.M.; Sr. M. Kathryn Dougherty, O.S.F., Dir.; Ms. Tina Denena; Ms. Christine Ryder.

[S] CAMPS AND COMMUNITY CENTERS

ALLEGANY STATE PARK. *Camp Turner*. Office, 795 Main St., Buffalo, 14203. (Coed). Rev. Gary J. Bagley.

ANGOLA. *St. Vincent de Paul Camp*. Office, 72 E. Huron St., Buffalo, 14203. (Camp for needy boys and girls). Rev. Msgr. John J. Conniff, Spiritual Dir.

[T] MISCELLANEOUS

BUFFALO. *158 Chenango Street Housing Development Fund Company, Inc.*, 525 Washington St., 14203.
50-60 Kosciuzko Street Housing Development Fund Company, Inc., 525 Washington St., 14203.
Catholic Charities of Buffalo, NY, Foundation, Inc., 525 Washington St., 14203.
Catholic Communications of Western New York, Inc., 795 Main St., 14203.
Catholic Union Store, 795 Main St., 14203. Tel: 716-847-8715; Fax: 716-847-8702. Peter M. McKee, Dir.
Federation of Catholic School Parents, Diocese of Buffalo, NY, 795 Main St., 14203. Tel: 716-847-5501. Barbara B. Ashcroft, Pres.
The Foundation of the Roman Catholic Diocese of Buffalo, NY, Inc., 795 Main St., 14203-1250.
Franciscan Mystery Players, Inc., 102 Seymour St., 14210.
Good Counsel Apartments, 525 Washington St., 14203. Housing for handicapped & elderly of low income. Rev. Msgr. John J. Conniff, Pres.; Rev. Msgr. Robert J. Cunningham; Rev. Msgr. Henry J. Gugino, Sec. & Treas. Total in Residence 39; Total Staff 4.
Hope of Buffalo, Inc., 335 Grider St., 14215. Tel: 716-892-8224.
E-mail: Kayhope@aol.com
Rev. Roy T. Herberger; Sr. Karen Klimczak, Dir. Total in Residence 10; Total Staff 1.
Immaculate Heart of Mary Home for Children, Inc., 600 Doat St., 14211.
Kolping Catholic Young Men's Association of Buffalo, NY dba Kolping Society of Buffalo, 29 Delphi Dr., 14227. Tel: 716-668-0120. Ludwig Haberle, Jr., Pres.; Rev. Msgr. Paul R. Letourneau, Mod.
La Casa Del Tainos Housing Development Fund Company, Inc., 525 Washington St., 14203. Rev. Msgr. Henry J. Gugino, Dir.
Mercy Health System of Western New York. Marian Professional Center, 515 Abbott Rd., Ste. 508, 14220.
Monsignor Adamski Village Housing Development Fund Company, Inc., 123 Townsend St., 14212. Rev. Msgr. Robert J. Cunningham, Pres.
Monsignor Adamski Village, Inc., 123 Townsend St., 14212. Rev. Msgr. John R. Gabalski. Facility for elderly and handicapped persons of low income.
Monsignor Carr Institute, 76 W. Humboldt Pkwy., 14214. Tel: 716-835-9745. Field Agency of Catholic Charities for Psychiatric and Psychological, Substance Abuse and Developmental Disabilities Plus Special Needs Services. Christopher J. Pino, Ph.D., Dir. Total Assisted 22,656; Total Staff 38.
Monsignor Kirby Apartments Housing Development Fund Company, Inc., 525 Washington St., 14203. Tel: 716-853-4424, Ext. 3095. Rev. Msgr. Henry J. Gugino, Contact Person. Total in Residence 39; Total Staff 2.
Mother of Divine Grace Housing Development Fund Company, Inc., 3233 Main St., 14214. Tel: 716-833-5353. Purpose: To provide housing for persons of low income, particularly handicapped mentally retarded and developmentally disabled adults. Sr. Mary Patricia Tomasik, Exec. Dir. Total in Residence 10; Total Staff 10.
Nativity Housing Development Fund Company, Inc., 3233 Main St., 14214. Tel: 716-833-5353. Purpose: To provide housing for persons of low income, particularly handicapped mentally retarded and developmentally disabled adults. Sr. Mary Patricia Tomasik, Exec. Dir. Total in Residence 11; Total Staff 10.
Our Lady of Peace Housing Development Fund Company, Inc., 3323 Main St., 14214.

St. Francis Respite Program, Inc.
St. Rita's Home for Children, Inc., 600 Doat St., 14211.
St. Timothy's Park Villa Housing Development Fund Company, Inc., 525 Washington St., 14203. Tel: 716-853-4424, Ext. 3095. Rev. Msgr. Henry J. Gugino, Contact Person. Total in Residence 49; Total Staff 3.
Salesian Studios, 152 Plymouth St., 14201-1214. Tel: 716-886-6597. Thomas Ribits.
Santa Maria Towers, Office, 525 Washington St., 14203. Housing for handicapped and elderly of low income.
Monsignor Gambino Tower, Ltd. Most Rev. Edward D. Head, Pres.
Timon Towers Housing Development Fund Company, Inc., 525 Washington St., 14203. Rev. Msgr. John J. Conniff, Pres. Low income housing for the handicapped and elderly. Total Staff 6.

AMHERST. *St. Andrew Kim Roman Catholic Church Society of Amherst, NY, Diocese of Buffalo.* 795 Main St., 14203-1250. Tel: 716-847-5529. Rev. James J. Ruddick, S.J.

BOWMANSVILLE. *International Institute of the Heart of Jesus.* North American Office (IIHJ-NAO), 5337 Genesee St., 14026. Tel: 716-683-2375. Rev. Msgr. Walter O. Kern.

LACKAWANNA. *Our Lady of Victory Homes of Charity.* (Formerly Baker Hall, Our Lady of Victory Infant Home, St. Joseph Orphanage and St. John's Protectory), 780 Ridge Rd., 14218. Tel: 716-828-9648.
E-mail: olv@buffnet.net
Web site: www.OurLadyofVictory.org
Rev. Msgr. Robert C. Wurtz, Exec. Vice Pres. & Treas.
(Formerly Association of Our Lady of Victory). Legal Titles: *Our Lady of Victory Homes of Charity.*; *Society for the Protection of Destitute Roman Catholic Children at Buffalo, NY.*; *Father Baker's.* Includes the following Institutions: Baker Victory Services 716-828-9500 or 1-888-287-9500 or 1-888-287-1160 (Formerly Baker Hall, Our Lady of Victory Infant Home, St. Joseph Orphanage and St. John's Protectory). Total Assisted 2,500; Total Staff 900.
Western New York Catholic Healthcare Corporation, Our Lady of Victory Hospital, 55 Melroy Ave., 14218.

NEW YORK. *St. Bonaventure Lake House West Bank Perimeter Road at Kinzua South Valley, N.Y.*, 126 W. 32nd St., 10001-3202.

NIAGARA UNIVERSITY. *Our Lady of Angels Association.* Marian House, 14109-1918. Tel: 716-286-8150; Fax: 716-286-8155.
E-mail: wobrien@niagara.edu
Web site: www.niagara.edu/olaa/
Rev. William J. O'Brien, C.M., Dir. Development Office for the Congregation of the Mission, Eastern Province. Total Staff 11.

NORTH TONAWANDA. *Shrine of the Infant Jesus.* Administered by the Pallottine Fathers. 3452 Niagara Falls Blvd., P.O. Box 563, 14120-0563.

STELLA NIAGARA. *DeSales Resource Center*, 4421 Lower River Rd., 14144-1001. Rev. Joseph Power, O.S.F.S., Dir.; Joanne Kinney, Administrative Asst.; Marilyn Marrone, Business Mgr.

WEST SENECA. *Victorious Missionaries*, 791 Seneca Creek Rd., 14224. Tel: 716-675-5891. Deacon William W. Willis, Spiritual Dir. A spiritual and social movement for the handicapped and chronically ill.

WILLIAMSVILLE. *400 Mill Street, Inc.* (Formerly Mount St. Mary's Hospital of Niagara Falls), 400 Mill St., P.O. Box 275, 14231.
Annabachmann, Inc. (Formerly St. Francis Geriatric & Healthcare Services, Inc.), 400 Mill St., P.O. Box 275, 14231.

RELIGIOUS INSTITUTES OF MEN REPRESENTED IN THE DIOCESE

For further details refer to the corresponding bracketed number in the Religious Institutes of Men or Women section.

[0810]—*Brothers of Mercy.*—F.M.M.
[0330]—*Brothers of the Christian Schools.* (New York Prov.).—F.S.C.
[0160]—*Clerics Regular of St. Paul.*—C.R.S.P.
[0450]—*Congregation of Jesus and Mary.*—C.J.M.
[1330]—*Congregation of the Mission.* (Eastern Prov.).—C.M.
[0390]—*Consolata Missionaries.*—I.M.C.
[0480]—*Conventual Franciscans.* (St. Anthony of Padua).—O.F.M.Conv.
[0520]—*Franciscan Friars.* (Holy Name Prov.).—O.F.M.
[0690]—*Jesuit Fathers and Brothers.* (New York Prov.).—S.J.
[0800]—*Maryknoll.* (Buffalo).—M.M.
[1210]—*Missionaries of St. Charles-Scalabrinians.*—C.S.
[0910]—*Oblates of Mary Immaculate.* (Eastern Prov.).—O.M.I.
[0920]—*Oblates of St. Francis De Sales.*—O.S.F.S.
[0970]—*Order of Our Lady of Mercy.* (Le Roy).—O.deM.
[0430]—*Order of Preachers-Dominicans.* (Provs. of St. Joseph; St. Albert the Great).—O.P.
[1020]—*Pauline Fathers and Brothers.* (Derby).—S.S.P.
[1040]—*Piarist Fathers.*—Sch.P.
[0370]—*Society of St. Columban.*—S.S.C.
[0990]—*Society of the Catholic Apostolate.* (Christ the King Prov.).—S.A.C.

RELIGIOUS INSTITUTES OF WOMEN REPRESENTED IN THE DIOCESE

[0760]—*Daughters of Charity of St. Vincent de Paul.*—D.C.
[0810]—*Daughters of the Heart of Mary.*—D.H.M.
[0420]—*Discalced Carmelite Nuns.*—O.C.D.
[1060]—*Dominican Contemplative Sisters.*—O.P.
[1170]—*Felician Sisters.*—C.S.S.F.
[1340]—*Franciscan Missionary Sisters of the Divine Child.*—F.M.D.C.
[1180]—*Franciscan Sisters of Allegany, New York.*—O.S.F.
[1470]—*Franciscan Sisters of St. Joseph.*—F.S.S.J.
[1280]—*Franciscan Sisters of the Immaculate Conception.*—O.S.F.
[1840]—*Grey Nuns of the Sacred Heart.*—G.N.S.H.
[2575]—*Institute of the Sisters of Mercy of the Americas.*—R.S.M.
[2830]—*Missionary Sisters of Our Lady of Mercy.*—M.O.M.
[2880]—*Missionary Sisters of St. Columban.*—S.S.C.
[3040]—*Oblate Sisters of Providence.*—O.S.P.
[0630]—*Sisters of Charity of St. Vincent de Paul.*—S.V.Z.
[]—*Sisters of Christ the King.*—S.C.K.
[3070]—*Sisters of Our Lady of Charity.*—N.A.U.-O.L.C.
[3950]—*Sisters of Saint Mary of Namur.*—S.S.M.N.
[4090]—*Sisters of Social Service.*—S.S.S.
[1630]—*Sisters of St. Francis of Penance and Christian Charity.*—O.S.F.
[1800]—*Sisters of St. Francis of the Third Order Regular.* (Williamsville, NY).—O.S.F.
[3830]—*Sisters of St. Joseph.*—C.S.J.
[1020]—*Sisters of the Divine Redeemer.*—S.D.R.
[]—*Sisters of the Sacred Heart of Jesus.*—S.S.H.J.
[1720]—*Sisters of the Third Order Regular of St. Francis of the Congregation of Our Lady of Lourdes.*—O.S.F.

DIOCESAN CEMETERIES

CHEEKTOWAGA. *Holy Sepulchre.*
GRAND ISLAND. *Assumption.*
KENMORE. *Mount Olivet*, 4000 Elmwood Ave., 14217. Tel: 716-873-6500.
LACKAWANNA. *Holy Cross.*
LOCKPORT. *Queen of Heaven.*
NIAGARA FALLS. *Gate of Heaven.*

NECROLOGY

† Bednar, Merrick J., Tonawanda, NY, St. Francis of Assisi. —Died May 12, 1997.
† Bilotta, Anthony J., (Retired). —Died Aug. 17, 1997.
† Conlin, Robert P., Pavilion, NY, St. Mary. —Died Dec. 9, 1997.
† Hall, Francis J., (Retired). —Died Feb. 13, 1997.
† Krupa, Rev. Msgr. Francis A., (Retired). —Died June 8, 1997.
† McCarthy, John P., (Retired). —Died Oct. 11, 1997.
† Ormsby, Rev. Msgr. Basil A., (Retired). —Died June 14, 1997.
† Setlock, Rev. Msgr. William A., (Retired). —Died Feb. 25, 1997.
† Sweeny, Robert S., (Retired). —Died May 5, 1997.
† Woods, Rev. Msgr. Patrick J., Arcade, NY, SS. Peter and Paul. —Died Feb. 14, 1997.

Diocese of Burlington

(Dioecesis Burlingtonensis)

Most Reverend

KENNETH A. ANGELL, D.D.

Bishop of Burlington; ordained May 26, 1956; appointed Auxiliary Bishop of Providence August 9, 1974; consecrated October 7, 1974; transferred to Bishop of Burlington October 6, 1992; installed November 9, 1992. *Mailing Address: 351 North Ave., P.O. Box 526, Burlington, VT, 05402-0526; Fax: 802-658-0436.*

ESTABLISHED JULY 29, 1853.

Square Miles 9,135.

Comprises the State of Vermont.

For legal titles of parishes and diocesan institutions, consult the Chancery Office.

Chancery Office: 351 North Ave., P.O. Box 526, Burlington, VT, 05402-0526. Tel.: 802-658-6110; Fax: 802-658-0436.

STATISTICAL OVERVIEW

Personnel	
Bishop	1
Priests: Diocesan Active in Diocese	89
Priests: Active Outside Diocese	4
Priests: Retired, Sick or Absent	47
Number of Diocesan Priests	140
Religious Priests in Diocese	48
Extern Priests in Diocese	2
Ordinations:	
Permanent Deacons	38
Permanent Deacons in Diocese	38
Total Brothers	21
Total Sisters	254
Parishes	
Parishes	99
With Resident Pastor:	
Resident Diocesan Priests	79
Resident Religious Priests	14
Without Resident Pastor:	
Administered by Priests	6
Missions	39
Pastoral Centers	1
Professional Ministry Personnel:	
Sisters	15
Lay Ministers	20
Welfare	
Homes for the Aged	4
Total Assisted	152
Residential Care of Children	1
Total Assisted	30
Special Centers for Social Services	1
Total Assisted	4,971
Other Institutions	1
Total Assisted	11,838
Educational	
Diocesan Students in Other Seminaries	10
Students Religious	4
Total Seminarians	14
Colleges and Universities	3
Total Students	4,005
High Schools, Diocesan and Parish	2
Total Students	734
Elementary Schools, Diocesan and Parish	9
Total Students	1,816
Elementary Schools, Private	2
Total Students	560
Catechesis/Religious Education:	
High School Students	1,118
Elementary Students	5,846
Total Students Under Catholic Instruction	14,093
Teachers in the Diocese:	
Priests	1
Brothers	1
Sisters	21
Lay Teachers	211
Vital Statistics	
Receptions into the Church:	
Infant Baptism Totals	1,878
Adult Baptism Totals	82
Received into Full Communion	136
First Communions	1,942
Confirmations	1,233
Marriages:	
Catholic	480
Interfaith	269
Total Marriages	749
Deaths	1,662
Total Catholic Population	147,624
Total Population	588,654

Former Bishops—Rt. Rev. LOUIS DE GOESBRIAND, D.D., cons. Oct. 30, 1853; died Nov. 3, 1899.—Rt. Rev. JOHN S. MICHAUD, D.D., cons. June 29, 1892; died Dec. 22, 1908.—Most Rev. JOSEPH J. RICE, D.D., cons. April 14, 1910; died April 1, 1938.—Most Rev. MATTHEW F. BRADY, D.D., cons. Oct. 26, 1938; transferred to Manchester, NH, Nov. 11, 1944; died Sept. 20, 1959.—Most Rev. EDWARD F. RYAN, D.D., cons. Jan. 3, 1945; died Nov. 3, 1956.—Most Rev. ROBERT F. JOYCE, D.D., cons. Auxiliary Bishop Oct. 28, 1954; installed Diocesan Bishop Feb. 26, 1957; retired Jan. 25, 1972; died Sept. 2, 1990.—Most Rev. JOHN ALOYSIUS MARSHALL, D.D., elected Bishop of Burlington November 30, 1971; ord. and installed January 25, 1972; transferred to Springfield, MA, Dec. 27, 1991; died July 3, 1994.

Vicar General and Moderator of the Curia—Rev. Msgr. JOHN R. MCSWEENEY, V.G., J.C.L.

Vicar General—Rev. WENDALL H. SEARLES, V.G.

Chancery Office—351 North Ave., P.O. Box 526, Burlington, 05402-0526. Tel: 802-658-6110; Fax: 802-658-0436. Office Hours: Mon.-Fri. 9-12 & 1-5.

Finance Office—Mr. KEVIN J. HEFFERNAN, C.P.A., Finance Officer, *351 North Ave., P.O. Box 526, Burlington, 05402-0526.* Tel: 802-658-6110; Fax: 802-658-0436.

Episcopal Vicar for Administration—Rev. JAY C. HASKIN, M.Ch.A.

Episcopal Vicar for Lay Apostolates—Rev. Msgr. W. JOHN FRADET.

Chancellor—Rev. JAY C. HASKIN, M.Ch.A.

Secretary to the Most Reverend Bishop and Vice Chancellor—Rev. WALTER D. MILLER, J.C.D., *351 North Ave., P.O. Box 526, Burlington, 05402-0526.* Tel: 802-658-6110.

Office of the Tribunal—351 North Ave., P.O. Box 526, Burlington, 05402-0526. Tel: 802-658-6110; Fax: 802-658-4118.

Judicial Vicar—Rev. WALTER D. MILLER, M.Div., J.C.D.

Adjutant Judicial Vicar—Rev. GERALD W. BOMBARDIER, M.A., J.C.L.

Judges—Rev. Msgr. JOHN R. MCSWEENEY, V.G., J.C.L.; Revs. THOMAS V. MATTISON, M.Div., J.C.L., M.C.L.; WILLIAM D. CORCORAN, J.C.L.

Promoter of Justice—Rev. BERNARD F. DEPEAUX, J.C.L.

Defenders of the Bond—Revs. ROGER L. CHARBONNEAU; MICHEL J. ST. PIERRE; ROBERT B. WHALEN.

Advocates—Revs. JOHN G. FELTZ; RAYMOND A. GIROUX; PETER A. ROUTHIER.

Auditor—ANNE AICHER.

Notaries—Mrs. SHIRLEY J. MEACHAM; Mrs. JANE B. KELLNER; Mrs. ELSA M. WHEEL.

Diocesan Administrative Board—Most Rev. KENNETH A. ANGELL, D.D., Chm.; Rev. Msgr. JOHN R. MCSWEENEY, V.G., J.C.L.; Rev. WENDELL H. SEARLES, V.G.; Rev. Msgr. W. JOHN FRADET; Sr. MARY BOISELLE, R.S.M.; Rev. JAY C. HASKIN, Sec.

Diocesan Consultors—Rev. Msgr. JOHN R. MCSWEENEY, V.G., J.C.L.; Rev. Msgr. PAUL M. BRESNEHAN; Revs. JAY C. HASKIN; WENDELL H. SEARLES, V.G.; REID C. MAYO; MICHAEL W. DEFORGE; JOHN W. HAMILTON.

Deans—Revs. RICHARD A. FOWLER; BERNARD E. GAUDREAU; JOHN W. HAMILTON; JULIEN J. LAFLAMME; PIERRE A. LAVALLEE; RICHARD G. LAVALLEY; JOSEPH A. LIVELY; JAMES J. MCSHANE; STEPHEN J. NICHOLS; MAURICE J. ROY; RICHARD W. TINNEY; DONAL WARD.

Diocesan Offices and Directors

Alcohol Advisory Committee—Rev. RAYMOND A. GIROUX, Chm., *St. John Vianney Rectory, 160 Hinesburg Rd., South Burlington, 05403.* Tel: 802-864-4166.

Apostolate for the Deaf—Rev. PETER Y. WILLIAMS, *351 North Ave., P.O. Box 526, Burlington, 05402-0526.* Tel: 802-658-6110.

Apostolate for the Handicapped—Mrs. LINDA PREVITI, Coord., *Office of Catholic Formation, Special Needs Ministry, 351 North Ave., P.O. Box 526, Burlington, 05402-0526.* Tel: 802-658-6110.

Bishop's Commission on Women—Ms. DIANE FOSTER, Chm., *351 North Ave., P.O. Box 526, Burlington, 05402-0526.* Tel: 802-658-6110.

Bishop's Fund Office—Rev. WENDELL H. SEARLES, Exec. Dir., *351 North Ave., P.O. Box 526, Burlington, 05402-0526.* Tel: 802-658-6110.

Boy Scouts—Rev. YVON J. ROYER, *St. Joseph Rectory, 85 Elmwood Ave., Burlington, 05401.* Tel: 802-863-2388.

Building Commission—Rev. PETER A. ROUTHIER, Chm., *Chancery Office, 351 North Ave., P.O. Box 526, Burlington, 05402-0526.* Tel: 802-658-6110.

Vermont Catholic Charities Inc.—Rev. ROLAND J. RIVARD, Dir., *Central Office, 351 North Ave., P.O. Box 526, Burlington, 05402-0526.* Tel: 802-658-6110; Fax: 802-860-0451. Mrs. MARY M. MCNAMARA, A.C.S.W., Supvr. Professional Svcs., *351 North Ave., P.O. Box 526, Burlington, 05402-0526.* Tel: 802-658-6110., Rutland Office: *24 1/2 Center St., Rutland, 05701.* Tel: 802-773-3379.

Campaign for Human Development—Rev. ROLAND J. RIVARD, Dir., *351 North Ave., P.O. Box 526, Burlington, 05402-0526.* Tel: 802-658-6110.

Catholic Daughters of The Americas—Rev. PATRICK J. FORMAN, *St. Paul Rectory, Eastern Ave., Barton,*

05822. Tel: 802-525-3711.

Catholic Relief Services—Rev. ROLAND J. RIVARD, *351 North Ave., P.O. Box 526, Burlington, 05402-0526.* Tel: 802-658-6110.

Catholic Women, Vermont Council of—Rev. GEORGE H. DUPUIS, Diocesan Moderator, *St. Margaret Mary Rectory, Main St., Arlington, 05250.* Tel: 802-375-2849. Mrs. THERESA BIASUZZI, Pres.

Censor Librorum—Rev. MICHEL J. ST-PIERRE, *351 North Ave., P.O. Box 526, Burlington, 05402-0526.* Tel: 802-658-6110.

Charismatic Renewal—Rev. FORREST W. ROUELLE, *St. Mary Star of the Sea Rectory, 5 Clermont Ter., Newport, 05855.* Tel: 802-334-5066.

Chief Administrator for Catholic Formation—Sr. MARIANNE READ, R.S.M., M.Ed., C.A.E.S.

Continuing Education for Clergy—Rev. BERNARD E. GAUDREAU, Dir., *Blessed Sacrament Rectory, Mountain Rd., P.O. Box 27, Stowe, 05672.* Tel: 802-253-7536.

Diocesan Archives—WILLIAM GOSS, *351 North Ave., P.O. Box 526, Burlington, 05402-0526.* Tel: 802-658-6110.

Diocesan Coordinator of the Vietnamese Ministry—Rev. FRANCIS M. HOLLAND, *8 Cedar, Glen North, 05403.* Tel: 802-864-0297.

Office of Development & Stewardship—LORRAINE CLARKE, Dir., *351 North Ave., P.O. Box 526, Burlington, 05402-0526.* Tel: 802-658-6110.

Office of Communications—GLORIA J. GIBSON, Dir., *351 North Ave., P.O. Box 526, Burlington, 05402-0526.* Tel: 802-658-6110.

Daughters of Isabella—Rev. JOHN M. MILANESE, Chap., *Sts. Donatian & Rogatian Rectory, 25 South Pleasant St., Randolph, 05060.* Tel: 802-728-3227.

Diocesan Cemeteries—ROBERT DELARICHELIERE, Chm. DONALD MCKENZIE, Supvr., *Resurrection Park, South Burlington, 05403.* Tel: 802-862-1530., *St. Joseph's Cemetery, Burlington, 05401.*

Diocesan Finance Council—Ex-Officio Members: Most Rev. KENNETH A. ANGELL; Rev. WENDELL H. SEARLES, V.G.; KEVIN J. HEFFERNAN, Finance Officer & Chm. Board Members: Sr. MARY I. GRANT, R.S.M.; JAMES STROUSE; CAROL MARKEY; JOHN KELLY.

Diocesan Insurance Office—PETER WELLS, Dir., *351 North Ave., P.O. Box 526, Burlington, 05402-0526.* Tel: 802-658-6110.

Diocesan Pastoral Planning—Rev. WENDELL H. SEARLES, V.G., Dir., *351 North Ave., P.O. Box 526, Burlington, 05402-0526.* Tel: 802-658-6110.

Ecumenical Commission—JAMES G. CASE, *R.F.D., Box 80, Richmond, 05477.* Tel: 802-482-2420.

Education, Board of—Ms. MADELEINE ROY, *P.O. Box 338, Barton, 05822.*

Evangelization—Rev. JOSEPH T. SULLIVAN, Dir., *351 North Ave., P.O. Box 526, Burlington, 05402-0526.* Tel: 802-658-6110.

Office of Family Life / Respect Life Office—RUTH CHARLESWORTH, Dir., *351 North Ave., P.O. Box 526, Burlington, 05402-0526.* Tel: 802-658-6110.

Finance Office—KEVIN J. HEFFERNAN, C.P.A., Finance Officer, *351 North Ave., P.O. Box 526, Burlington, 05402-0526.* Tel: 802-658-6110.

Liturgical Commission—Rev. ROBERT C. RICHARDSON, Chm., *St. Anne Rectory, P.O. Box 1098, Middletown Springs, 05757.* Tel: 802-235-2156; Fax: 802-235-2820.

Director of Liturgical Formation—Rev. ROBERT C. RICHARDSON, Dir., *St. Anne Rectory, P.O. Box 1098, Middletown Springs, 05757.* Tel: 802-235-2156; Fax: 802-235-2820.

Diocesan Coordinator for Health Affairs—Rev. LEOPOLD J. BILODEAU, *Fletcher Allen Health Care, 111 Colchester Ave., Burlington, 05401.* Tel: 802-656-2345.

Holy Childhood Association—Rev. THOMAS V. MATTISON, Dir., *351 North Ave., P.O. Box 526, Burlington, 05402-0526.* Tel: 802-658-6110.

House of Discernment—Revs. MICHAEL W. DEFORGE, Dir.; PETER Y. WILLIAMS, *The Catholic Center at UVM, 390 South Prospect St., Burlington, 05401.* Tel: 802-862-8403; Fax: 802-865-9480.

Knights of Columbus—Rev. JOHN C. LEDOUX, *State Chaplain, 16 Clover Dr. 9-C, Essex Junction, 05452.* Tel: 802-879-0623.

Leap—Rev. MICHAEL P. CRONOGUE, S.S.E., *St. Michael's College, Winooski Park, Colchester, 05439.* Tel: 802-654-2386.

Marriage Encounter, Vermont—DAVID ERKSON; JENNIE ERKSON, *R.R. 1, Box 462, Jericho Rd., Richmond, 05477.* Tel: 802-434-4218.

Diocesan Master of Ceremonies—Rev. WALTER D. MILLER, J.C.D., *351 North Ave., P.O. Box 526, Burlington, 05402-0526.* Tel: 802-658-6110; Fax: 802-658-0436.

Office of Ministerial Formation—Rev. BERNARD E. GAUDREAU, Dir., *Blessed Sacrament Rectory, Mountain Rd., P.O. Box 27, Stowe, 05672.* Tel: 802-253-7536; Fax: 802-253-4445.

National Catholic Conference for Interracial Justice—Rev. WALTER D. MILLER, J.C.D., Diocesan Coord., *351 North Ave., P.O. Box 526, Burlington, 05402-0526.* Tel: 802-658-6110; Fax: 802-658-0436.

National Shrine of the Immaculate Conception, Washington—Rev. ROGER L. CHARBONNEAU, *Holy Cross Rectory, 47 Church Rd., Colchester, 05446.* Tel: 802-863-3002.

Office of Catholic Formation—Deacon IVAN HAWK, Dir. Coordinators: CHRISTOPHER FOUNTAIN; TERESA MIELE.

Office of Pastoral Planning—Rev. WENDELL H. SEARLES, Dir., *351 North Ave., P.O. Box 526, Burlington, 05402-0526.* Tel: 802-658-6110; Fax: 802-658-0436.

Office of Worship—Rev. ROBERT C. RICHARDSON, Dir., *St. Anne Rectory, P.O. Box 1098, Middletown Springs, 05757.* Tel: 802-235-2156; Fax: 802-235-2820.

Permanent Diaconate—Rev. BERNARD E. GAUDREAU, Dir., *Blessed Sacrament Rectory, Mountain Rd., P.O. Box 27, Stowe, 05672.* Tel: 802-253-7536; Fax: 802-253-4445.

Diocesan Presbyteral Council—Members Ex-Officio: Most Rev. KENNETH A. ANGELL; Rev. Msgr. JOHN R. MCSWEENEY, V.G., J.C.L.; Revs. WENDELL H. SEARLES, V.G.; JAY C. HASKIN; MICHAEL W. DEFORGE; BERNARD E. GAUDREAU. Elected Members: Revs. PIERRE A. LAVALLEE; ALBERT G. BALTZ; GEORGE H. DUPUIS; DENIS R. BRETON; MAURICE J. ROY; REID C. MAYO; JOHN W. HAMILTON; JAMES J. MCSHANE; WILLIAM P. GIROUX; STEPHEN J. NICHOLS; ROLAND J. RIVARD; LEOPOLD J. BILODEAU; FRANCIS M. HOLLAND; BERNARD W. BOURGEOIS.

Press, (Diocesan)—Diocesan Media Board: HENRY DELBIANCO, Chm. Newspaper: "The Vermont Catholic Tribune"; Most Rev. KENNETH A. ANGELL, Publisher; Rev. RAYMOND A. GIROUX, Assoc. to the Publisher; PAT GORE, Editor, Editorial and Business Office: *351 North Ave., P.O. Box 526, Burlington, 05402-0526.* Tel: 802-658-6110; Fax: 802-658-0436.

Priests' Benefit Fund—Rev. FRANCIS R. PRIVE, Chm., *351 North Ave., P.O. Box 526, Burlington, 05402-0526.* Tel: 802-658-6110.

Prison Ministry—Deacon STEPHEN RATTE, *351 North Ave., P.O. Box 526, Burlington, 05402-0526.* Tel: 802-658-6110.

Pro-Life—RUTH CHARLESWORTH, Dir., *351 North Ave., P.O. Box 526, Burlington, 05402-0526.* Tel: 802-658-6110; Fax: 802-860-0451.

Propagation of the Faith—Rev. THOMAS V. MATTISON, Dir., *351 North Ave., P.O. Box 526, Burlington, 05402-0526.* Tel: 802-658-6110.

Rural Life—Deacon JEAN LOUIS RAINVILLE, *Box 122G, R.F.D., Gore Rd., Highgate Center, 05459.*

Office of Catholic Schools—Sr. MARIANNE READ, R.S.M., M.Ed., C.A.E.S., Supt. of Schools, *351 North Ave., P.O. Box 526, Burlington, 05402-0526.* Tel: 802-658-6110; Fax: 802-658-0436.

Secular Franciscans—Rev. RICHARD A. FOWLER, *St. Anthony Rectory, Church St., Box 63, Bethel, 05032.* Tel: 802-234-9916.

Senate of Sisters—Sr. MARY POLWORTH, S.S.J., *Sisters of St. Joseph Convent, 131 Convent Ave., Rutland, 05701.* Tel: 802-775-5133.

Liaison for Religious—Vacant.

Vermont Cursillo Secretariat—HELENE LOUX, Pres., *P.O. Box 48, North Troy, 05859.* Tel: 802-988-2983.

Vocations and Seminarians—Rev. MICHAEL W. DEFORGE, Dir., *The Catholic Center at UVM, 390 South Prospect St., Burlington, 05401.* Tel: 802-862-8403; Fax: 802-865-9480.

CLERGY, PARISHES, MISSIONS AND PAROCHIAL SCHOOLS

CITY OF BURLINGTON
(Chittenden County)

1—CATHEDRAL OF THE IMMACULATE CONCEPTION (1830), Rev. Thomas J. Ball, Rector.
Res., 20 Pine St., 05401. Tel: 802-658-4333.

2—ST. ANTHONY'S (1903), Rev. Msgr. W. John Fradet, Admin.; Deacon Louis Meunier. In res., Revs. Michel J. St. Pierre; Roland J. Rivard.
Res., 305 Flynn Ave., 05401. Tel: 802-864-0478.

3—CHRIST THE KING (1940), Rev. Msgr. W. John Fradet.
Res., 136 Locust St., 05401-4849. Tel: 802-862-5784.
School—Tel: 802-862-6696.
Sisters 3; Lay Teachers 22; Students 246.

4—ST. JOSEPH'S (1850), Revs. Pierre A. Lavallee; Yvon J. Royer.
Res., 85 Elmwood Ave., 05401. Tel: 802-863-2388; Fax: 802-863-2380. [CEM]
School—Tel: 802-864-5623; Fax: 802-860-2627.
Lay Teachers 14; Students 172.

5—ST. MARK'S (1940), Rev. Msgr. John R. McSweeney, V.G., J.C.L.; Rev. Paul C. Houde.
Res., 1251 North Ave., 05401. Tel: 802-864-7686; Fax: 802-651-9391.

OUTSIDE THE CITY OF BURLINGTON

Alburg, Grand Isle Co., St. Amadeus (1886), Rev. Maurice U. Boucher, S.S.E.
Res., 05440. Tel: 802-796-3481; Fax: 802-928-3305. [CEM]
Mission—Isle LaMotte, Grand Isle Co., St. Joseph, P.O. Box 65, Isle LaMotte, 05463. [CEM]
Chapel—Isle La Motte, St. Anne's Shrine, P.O. Box 280, 05463. Tel: 802-928-3362; Fax: 802-928-3305.

Arlington, Bennington Co., St. Margaret Mary (1946), Rev. George H. Dupuis; Deacon Peter Putis.
Res., Main St., Box 36, 05250-0036. Tel: 802-375-2849. [CEM]

Barre, Washington Co., St. Monica (1892), Revs. Peter A. Routhier; Bernard W. Bourgeois; Deacons Fernand Rivard; David Bisson.
Res., 79 Summer St., 05641. Tel: 802-479-3253; Fax: 802-479-3154.
School—Tel: 802-476-5015.
Lay Teachers 14; Students 172.
Convent—73 Summer St., 05641. Tel: 802-476-6514.

Barton, Orleans Co., Conversion of St. Paul (1893), Rev. Patrick J. Forman, Admin.
Res., Eastern Ave., P.O. Box 319, 05822. Tel: 802-525-3711. [CEM]
School—Tel: 802-525-6578.
Lay Teachers 6; Students 60.
Mission—East Albany, Orleans Co., St. John of the Cross. [CEM]

Bellows Falls, Windham Co., St. Charles (1871), Rev. James J. McShane.
Res., 31 Cherry Hill, 05101. Tel: 802-463-3128; Fax: 802-463-8179. [CEM]
Sacred Heart (1909), Rev. Felix J. Reczek, O.F.M., Admin.; Deacon John Blicharz.
Res., 39 Green St., 05101. Tel: 802-463-4110. [CEM]

Bennington, Bennington Co., Sacred Heart/St. Francis de Sales (1995), Revs. Laurence M. Olszewski, C.S.C.; William H. Kelley, C.S.C.; Deacon Eugene M. Krawczyk Tel: 802-442-7979.
Parish Office: 238 W. Main St., 05201. Tel: 802-442-3141; Fax: 802-442-3142.
School—Sacred Heart School, 307 School St., 05201. Tel: 802-442-2446; Fax: 802-442-3584. Mr. David B. Estes, Prin.
Lay Teachers 11; Students 189.
Mission—North Pownal, Our Lady of Lourdes.
Station—Vermont Veterans Home, Tel: 802-442-6353.

Bethel, Windsor Co., St. Anthony (1950), Rev. Richard A. Fowler.
Res., P.O. Box 63, Church St., 05032. Tel: 802-234-9916.
Missions—Pittsfield, Rutland Co., St. Denis; Rochester, Windsor Co., St. Elizabeth; South Royalton, Windsor Co., St. Matthew.

Bradford, Orange Co., Our Lady of Perpetual Help (1945), Rev. Philip R. Lamothe; Deacon Kelly Fitzpatrick.
Res., Box 314, 05033. Tel: 802-222-5268.
Missions—Norwich, Windsor Co., St. Francis of Assisi; Wells River, Orange Co., St. Eugene; South Strafford, Orange Co., Our Lady of Light.

Brandon, Rutland Co., St. Mary's (1867), Rev. Douglas W. Hawkins, C.S.C.
Res., 38 Carver St., 05733. Tel: 802-247-6351. [CEM]
Mission—Leicester, Addison Co., St. Agnes.

Brattleboro, Windham Co., St. Michael (1855), Revs. J.H. Normand Nadeau; Bruce Michael Wood (AMA).
Res., 20 Walnut St., 05301. Tel: 802-257-5101, 254-5229. [CEM]
School—Mr. Frank J. Vara, Prin. Lay Teachers 9; Students 233.
Convent—27 Grove St., 05301. Tel: 802-254-9431.

Bristol, Addison Co., St. Ambrose (1893), Rev. Albert G. Baltz.
Res., 11 School St., 05443. Tel: 802-453-2488. [CEM]

Cambridge, Lamoille Co., St. Mary (1964), Rev. John J. Arnott (PIT) Admin.
Res., P.O. Box 129, 05444. Tel: 802-644-5073; Fax: 802-644-2546.
Mission—Johnson, Lamoille Co., St. John the Apostle.

Canaan, Essex Co., Assumption of the Blessed Virgin Mary (1950), Rev. John B. Loughnane, Jr (MAN).

Res., P.O. Box 176, Beecher Falls, 05902. Tel: 603-246-8829; Fax: 603-246-7169. [CEM]

Castleton, Rutland Co., St. John the Baptist (1899), Rev. J. Charles Durham.
Res., P.O. Box 128, 05735. Tel: 802-468-5706; Fax: 802-468-5299.

Charlotte, Chittenden Co., Our Lady of Mount Carmel (1858), Rev. Gerald Ragis.
Res., P.O. Box 158, Spear St., 05445. Tel: 802-425-2637. [CEM]

Chester, Windsor Co., St. Joseph (1946), Rev. Paul E. Sackevich; Deacon Eugene Allen, Jr.
Res., P.O. Box 40, 05143. Tel: 802-875-2610.
Mission—Proctorsville, Windsor Co., Holy Name of Mary.
Station—Londonderry, St. Joseph.

Chittenden, Rutland Co., St. Robert (1965), Rev. Adam J. Krempa.
Res., c/o Rev. Adam J. Krempa, Immaculate Heart of Mary, 18 Lincoln Ave., Rutland, 05701. Tel: 802-747-7088.

Colchester, Chittenden Co., Holy Cross (1950), Rev. Roger L. Charbonneau.
Res., 47 Church Rd., 05446. Tel: 802-863-3002; Fax: 802-862-5687. [CEM]

Our Lady of Grace (1966), Rev. Brian E. Mead; Deacon William Glinka.
Res., 76 Main St., 05446. Tel: 802-878-5987; Fax: 802-878-9308.

Derby Line, Orleans Co., St. Edward (1946), Rev. Ernest Passero, S.J.; Deacon John P.E. Gratton.
Res., 24 Main St., 05830. Tel: 802-873-3522. [CEM]
Mission—West Charleston, Orleans Co., St. Benedict Labre.

East Dorset, Bennington Co., St. Jerome (1868), Rev. Michael A. Demasi, Admin.
Res., 05253. Tel: 802-362-2320. [CEM]
Mission—Danby, Rutland Co., Holy Trinity.

Enosburg Falls, Franklin Co., St. John the Baptist (1874), Rev. Gerard P. Leclerc.
Res., P.O. Box 563, 05450. Tel: 802-933-4464; Fax: 802-933-8940. [CEM]

Essex Center, Chittenden Co., St. Pius X (1957), Rev. William P. Giroux.
Res., 20 Jericho Rd., Essex Junction, 05452-2707. Tel: 802-878-5997.

Essex Junction, Chittenden Co., Holy Family (1893), Rev. Charles P. Davignon.
Res., 4 Prospect St., 05452. Tel: 802-878-5331. [CEM]

St. Lawrence, Martyr (1966), Rev. Paul F. St. James.
Res., 158 West St., 05452. Tel: 802-878-8271; Fax: 802-879-8687.

Fairfax, Franklin Co., St. Luke (1943), Rev. John G. Feltz; Deacon Stephen Ratte.
Res., 17 Huntsville Rd., P.O. Box 7, 05454. Tel: 802-849-6205; Fax: 802-849-6078. [CEM]
Mission—Georgia, Franklin Co., Ascension.

Fairfield, Franklin Co., St. Patrick (1858), Rev. Thomas V. Mattison, Admin.; Deacon James Rock.
Res., 05455. Tel: 802-827-3203. [CEM]
Mission—East Fairfield, Franklin Co., St. Anthony-St. George.

Fair Haven, Rutland Co., Our Lady of Seven Dolors (1866), Rev. Raymond G. Maloney.
Res., 10 Washington St., 05743. Tel: 802-265-3135. [CEM]
Mission—West Castleton, Rutland Co., St. Matthew of Avalon.

Gilman, Essex Co., St. Theresa (1939), Rev. Joseph A. Lively, Admin.; Deacon William J. Brown, III.
Res., Commercial Ave., Box 119, 05904. Tel: 802-892-5380.
Mission—Lunenburg, Essex Co., St. Leo.

Graniteville, Washington Co., St. Sylvester (1899), Rev. William S. Chant.
Res., 217 Church Hill Rd., 05654. Tel: 802-476-3913. [CEM]
Mission—Williamstown, Orange Co., St. Edward.

Greensboro Bend, Orleans Co., St. Michael (1954), Rev. Michael E. Augustinowitz, Admin.
Mailing Address: c/o St. Norbert Parish, P.O. Box 496, Hardwick, 05843. [CEM]
Res., 05842. Tel: 802-533-2377. [CEM]
Mission—Craftsbury, Orleans Co., Our Lady of Fatima, (1951).

Hardwick, Caledonia Co., St. Norbert (1911), Rev. Michael E. Augustinowitz.
Mailing Address: P.O. Box 496, 05843.
Res., 15 S. Main St., 05843. Tel: 802-472-5544. [CEM]

Highgate Center, Franklin Co., St. Louis (1886), Rev. Charles H. Ranges, S.S.E.; Deacon Jean-Louis Rainville.
Mailing Address: P.O. Box 78, 05459. Tel: 802-868-4517; Fax: 802-868-4262.
Res., 65 Canada St., Swanton, 05488. Tel: 802-862-4502. [CEM 2]

Hinesburg, Chittenden Co., St. Jude the Apostle (1946), Rev. William D. Corcoran.
Res., P.O. Box 69, 05461-0069. Tel: 802-482-2290; Fax: 802-482-5263.

Hyde Park, Lamoille Co., St. Teresa (1872), Rev. Denis R. Breton, Admin.
Res., c/o Holy Cross Rectory, P.O. Box 339, Morrisville, 05661.
Church—05655. Tel: 802-888-3318.
Mission—Eden, Lamoille Co., St. Gabriel.

Island Pond, Essex Co., St. James the Greater (1871), Rev. James H. Mattison.
Res., P.O. Box 407, 05846. Tel: 802-723-4312. [CEM]
Mission—Norton, Essex Co., St. Bernard.

Ludlow, Windsor Co., Annunciation (1885), Rev. James A. Lawrence.
Res., 7 Depot St., 05149. Tel: 802-228-3451.

Lyndonville, Caledonia Co., St. Elizabeth (1891), Rev. Thomas L. Mosher; Deacon Alfred Toborg.
Res., 7 East St., P.O. Box 141, 05851-0141. Tel: 802-626-5267; Fax: 802-626-3324. [CEM]
Mission—Danville, Caledonia Co., Our Lady Queen of Peace, P.O. Box 141, Lyndonville 05851-0141.

Manchester Center, Bennington Co., Conversion of St. Paul (1896), Rev. Julien J. LaFlamme.
Res., Bonnet St., R.R. 2, Box 2830, 05255. Tel: 802-362-1380.

Middlebury, Addison Co., Assumption of the Blessed Virgin Mary (1855), Rev. John J. McDermott, Admin.
Res., 19 College St., 05753. Tel: 802-388-2943. [CEM]
Mission—Bridport, Addison Co., St. Bernadette.

Middletown Springs, Rutland Co., St. Anne (1963), Rev. Robert C. Richardson; Deacon Richard Perkins.
Res., 05757. Tel: 802-235-2156; Fax: 802-235-2820.
Missions—West Pawlet, Rutland Co., St. Frances Cabrini; Wells, Rutland Co., St. Paul.

Milton, Chittenden Co., St. Ann (1866), Rev. Donald J. Roy; Deacon Roger Lauziere.
Res., P.O. Box 1, 05468. Tel: 802-893-2487. [CEM]

Montgomery Center, Franklin Co., St. Isidore (1890). Attended by All Saints, Richford.
152 Main St., Richford, 05476. Tel: 802-848-7741. [CEM]

Montpelier, Washington Co., St. Augustine (1850), Revs. William R. Beaudin; Charles R. Danielson; Deacons Regis Cummings; Daniel Pudvah.
Res., 16 Barre St., 05602. Tel: 802-223-5285; Fax: 802-223-3621. [CEM]
School—St. Michael School, 46 Barre St., 05602. Tel: 802-223-6430.
Sisters 2; Lay Teachers 8; Students 130.
Mission—Marshfield, Washington Co., North American Martyrs, (1963) Marshfield, 05658.

Morrisville, Lamoille Co., Holy Cross (1946), Rev. Denis R. Breton; Deacon Thomas Cooney.
Res., Brooklyn St., P.O. Box 339, 05661. Tel: 803-888-3318.

Newport, Orleans Co., St. Mary Star of the Sea (1873), Rev. Forrest W. Rouelle.
Res., 5 Clermont Ter., 05855. Tel: 802-334-5066; Fax: 802-334-5067. [CEM]

North Bennington, Bennington Co., St. John the Baptist (1885), Rev. Robert J. Baffa.
Res., 05257. Tel: 802-447-7504. [CEM]

Northfield, Washington Co., St. John the Evangelist (1865), Rev. Kevin E. Rooney.
Res., 23 Vine St., 05663. Tel: 802-485-8313. [CEM]

North Troy, Orleans Co., St. Vincent de Paul (1939), Rev. George A. Paulin.
Res., Pleasant St., 05859. Tel: 802-988-2608. [CEM]

Orleans, Orleans Co., St. Theresa of Child Jesus (1942), Rev. Thomas A. Bransfield, Admin.
Res., 5 Willoughby Ave., 05860. Tel: 802-754-6049. [CEM]
Mission—Irasburg, Orleans Co., St. John Vianney. [CEM]

Orwell, Addison Co., St. Paul (1886), Rev. Robert J. McKnight.
Res., P.O. Box 41, 05760. Tel: 802-948-2951. [CEM]
Mission—Shoreham, Addison Co., St. Geneviere.

Pittsford, Rutland Co., St. Alphonsus Liguori (1893), Rev. Joseph E. Romano.
Res., R.R. 2, Box 2114, 05763. Tel: 802-483-2301; Fax: 802-483-2136. [CEM]

Poultney, Rutland Co., St. Raphael (1894), Rev. Joseph M. Vignoe.
Res., Main St., 05764. Tel: 802-287-5703. [CEM]

Proctor, Rutland Co., St. Dominic (1888), Rev. Msgr. Paul M. Bresnehan.
Res., 45 South St., 05765. Tel: 802-459-2221. [CEM]

Putney, Windham Co., Our Lady of Mercy (1931), Revs. John T. Scully, S.S.E.; Frederick E. McLachlan, S.S.E.; Deacon Robert Degnon.
Res., Old Depot Rd., 05346. Tel: 802-387-5861.
Missions—Saxtons River, Windham Co., St. Edmund of Canterbury; Stratton Mountain, Windham Co., Chapel of the Snows; Townshend, Windham Co., Our Lady of the Valley; Wardsboro, Windham Co., Our Lady of Hope.

Randolph, Orange Co., SS. Donatian and Rogatian (1903), Rev. John M. Milanese; Deacon Paul Lissandrello.
Res., 25 S. Pleasant St., 05060. Tel: 802-728-3227. [CEM]

Readsboro, Bennington Co., St. Joachim (1895), Rev. James E. Beauregard.
Res., 36 Tunnel St., 05350-9738. Tel: 802-423-5267.
Mission—Stamford, Bennington Co., St. John Bosco.

Richford, Franklin Co., All Saints (1899), Rev. Francis C. Eksterowicz; Deacons Clifford Chagnon; Jon Ramey.
Res., 152 Main St., 05476. Tel: 802-848-7741. [CEM]
Mission—East Berkshire, Franklin Co., Our Lady of Lourdes.

Richmond, Chittenden Co., Our Lady of the Holy Rosary (1860), Rev. Ronald H. Benoit.
Res., P.O. Box 243, 05477. Tel: 802-434-2521. [CEM 2]

Rutland, Rutland Co., Christ the King (1907), Revs. Reid C. Mayo; Lance W. Harlow.
Res., 66 S. Main St., 05701. Tel: 802-773-6820; Fax: 802-773-6820, Ext. 136.
School—Sisters 3; Lay Teachers 22; Students 246.

Immaculate Heart of Mary (1869), Rev. Richard W. Tinney. In res., Rev. Adam J. Krempa.
Res., 18 Lincoln Ave., 05701. Tel: 802-775-0846. [CEM]

St. Peter (1855), Revs. Wilfred Andre Houle; John J. Herbert. In res., Rev. John A. Guischard, (Retired).
Res., 134 Convent Ave., 05701. Tel: 802-775-1994; Fax: 802-775-0178. [CEM]

St. Albans, Franklin Co., Holy Angels (1872), Rev. Maurice J. Roy.
Res., 246 Lake St., 05478. Tel: 802-524-2585. [CEM]

Immaculate Conception (1847), Rev. Leonidas B. Laroche; Deacon John Rixon.
Res., 45 Fairfield St., 05478. Tel: 802-527-7775. [CEM]

St. Albans Bay, Our Lady of the Lake. Closed. For inquiries for parish records contact the Chancery.

St. Johnsbury, Caledonia Co., St. John the Evangelist (1896), Rev. Joseph A. Lively; Deacons Bruce Burk; Raymond Desilets; Bernier Mayo.
Res., 2 Winter St., 05819. Tel: 802-748-8129. [CEM]

Shelburne, Chittenden Co., St. Catherine of Siena (1906), Rev. John W. Hamilton.
Res., Church St., P.O. Box 70, 05482. Tel: 802-985-2373. [CEM]

Sheldon Springs, Franklin Co., St. Anthony (1906), Rev. Bernard J. Bechard, S.S.E.
Res., Mill St., P.O. Box 97, 05485-0097. Tel: 802-933-8921; Fax: 802-933-8921. [CEM]
Mission—Franklin, Franklin Co., St. Mary.

Sherburne, Rutland Co., Our Lady of the Mountains (1979), Rev. Adam J. Krempa.
Res., c/o Rev. Adam J. Krempa, Immaculate Heart of Mary, 18 Lincoln Ave., Rutland, 05701. Tel: 802-747-7088.

South Burlington, Chittenden Co., St. John Vianney (1940), Rev. Raymond A. Giroux; Deacons Joseph Lane; Anthony Previti.
Res., 160 Hinesburg Rd., 05403. Tel: 802-864-4166; Fax: 802-863-6065.

South Hero, Grand Isle Co., St. Rose of Lima (1895), Rev. Philip J. Branon.
Res., 501 Rte. 2, 05486. Tel: 802-372-4092; Fax: 802-372-4770.
Missions—Grand Isle, Grand Isle Co., St. Joseph, 185 Rte. 2, 05458. Tel: 802-372-5627; North Hero, Grand Isle Co., St. Benedict Joseph Labre.

Springfield, Windsor Co., Maternity of the Blessed Virgin Mary (1901), Rev. James M. Shea.
Res., 40 Summer St., 05156. Tel: 802-885-3400; 885-2250. [CEM]

Stowe, Lamoille Co., Blessed Sacrament (1954), Rev. Bernard E. Gaudreau.
Res., Mountain Rd., P.O. Box 27, 05672. Tel: 802-253-7536; Fax: 802-253-4445.

Swanton, Franklin Co., Nativity of the Blessed Virgin Mary (1854), Rev. Charles H. Ranges, S.S.E., Admin.

Res., 65 Canada St., 05488. Tel: 802-868-4517; Fax: 802-868-4262. [CEM]

Troy, Orleans Co., Sacred Heart of Jesus (1931), Rev. Stephen J. Nichols.
Res., 05868. Tel: 802-744-2239. [CEM]
Mission—Lowell, Orleans Co., St. Ignatius Loyola.

Underhill Center, Chittenden Co., St. Thomas (1856), Rev. Francis R. Prive.
Res., P.O. Box 3, 05490-0003. Tel: 802-899-4632; Fax: 802-899-4770. [CEM 3]

Vergennes, Addison Co., St. Peter (1881), Rev. Donal Ward.
Res., 85 S. Maple St., P.O. Box 324, 05491. Tel: 802-877-2367; Fax: 802-877-1063. [CEM]

Waitsfield, Washington Co., Our Lady of the Snows (1964), Rev. Donald E. Ritchie, Admin.
Mailing Address: c/o 109 S. Main St., Waterbury, 05676. Tel: 802-244-7734.
Mission—Moretown, Washington Co., St. Patrick.

Wallingford, Rutland Co., St. Patrick (1910), Rev. Joseph M. Quinn, C.S.C.
Res., 30 N. Main St., 05773. Tel: 802-446-2161. [CEM]
Mission—Mount Holly, Rutland Co., St. Mary.

Washington, Orange Co., St. Cecilia (1961), Rev. William P. Morgan.
Res., P.O. Box 204, 05675. Tel: 802-883-2285.
Mission—East Barre, Orange Co., Mother Cabrini.

Waterbury, Washington Co., St. Andrew (1869), Rev. Donald E. Ritchie.
Res., 109 S. Main St., 05676. Tel: 802-244-7734. [CEM]

West Rutland, Rutland Co., St. Bridget (1857), Rev. Raymond D. Walsh.
Res., One Church St., 05777-0087. Tel: 802-438-2490. [CEM 2]
St. Stanislaus Kostka (1904), Rev. Frank S. Warzocha.
Res., 9 Barnes St., 05777. Tel: 802-438-5671. [CEM]

White River Junction, Windsor Co., St. Anthony (1869), Revs. Ronald Saunders, S.M.; Adrien O. Pelletier, S.M.; Deacon John P. Guarino.
Res., One Church St., 05001. Tel: 802-295-2225; Fax: 802-296-6008. [CEM]
Convent—7 Church St., 05001. Tel: 802-295-7176.
Station—White River Junction, Veterans Administration Hospital, Tel: 802-295-9363.

Williston, Chittenden Co., Immaculate Heart of Mary (1951), Rev. Donald J. Ravey.
Res., P.O. Box 1047, 05495. Tel: 802-878-4513.

Wilmington, Windham Co., Our Lady of Fatima (1959), Rev. Joseph H. Tate, C.S.C.; Deacon Paul Mello.
Res., P.O. Box 188, 05363. Tel: 802-464-7329.

Windsor, Windsor Co., St. Francis of Assisi (1886), Rev. Paul Belhumeur, M.S.
Res., 30 Union St., P.O. Box 46, 05089. Tel: 802-674-2157; 674-2156. [CEM]

Winooski, Chittenden Co., St. Francis Xavier (1868), Rev. Richard G. LaValley; Deacons Norman Langlois; John F. Place.
Res., St. Peter St., 05404. Tel: 802-655-2290; Fax: 802-655-3036. [CEM]
School—Tel: 802-655-2600.
Sisters 3; Lay Teachers 12; Students 260.
Convent—Tel: 802-655-2395; Fax: 802-655-3888.
St. Vincent de Paul Center—Tel: 802-655-3006.
Daycare—Tel: 802-655-4660.
St. Stephen (1882), Rev. Gerald W. Bombardier. In res., Rev. Jay C. Haskin.
Res., 115 Barlow St., 05404. Tel: 802-655-0318; Fax: 802-658-4118. [CEM]

Woodstock, Windsor Co., Our Lady of the Snows (1894), Rev. William P. Gallagher.
Res., 7 South St., 05091. Tel: 802-457-2322; Fax: 802-457-5805.

Chaplains of Public Institutions

BURLINGTON. *Fletcher Allen Health Care*, 05401. Tel: 802-656-2770. Revs. Leopold J. Bilodeau; Francis E. Connors; Sr. Monica Rock, R.H.S.J., Pastoral Assoc.

WATERBURY. *State Hospital*. Rev. Louis R. Logue.

WHITE RIVER JUNCTION. *Veterans Administration Hospital*. Rev. Adrien O. Pelletier, S.M.

On Duty Outside the Diocese:
Reverend Fathers—
Daley, Daniel P., St. Mary, 307 N. Church St., Bloomfield, NM 87413
Dowd, Barry G., Mary Queen of the Universe Shrine, 8300 Vineland Ave., Orlando, FL 32821

Military Chaplains:
Reverend Fathers—
Soutiere, Ronald, USN

Other Residence:
Reverend Fathers—
Bruder, John W., O.C.S.O., R.R. 1, Box 143, West Danville, VT 05873-9801

Retired:
Reverend Monsignors—
Adams, Raymond A., 9 Cascadnac Ave., Essex Junction, VT 05452
Buckley, Edwin T., 22 Wellesley Grove, 630 Hinesburg Rd., South Burlington, VT 05403
Flanagan, Francis B., 59 Meadow St., Rutland, VT 05701
Foster, Edward C., The Waterford, 3333 University Blvd., Kensington, MD 20895
Gelineau, Edward J., St. Joseph's Home, 243 N. Prospect St., Burlington, VT 05401
Powers, Robert J., St. Albert Rectory, 1130 Washington St., Weymouth, MA 02189
Reverend Fathers—
Beary, Thomas J., St. Joseph's Home, 243 N. Prospect St., Burlington, VT 05401
Brackett, Anthony H., 9854 Wildginger Dr., S.W., Fort Myers, FL 33919
Brochu, Gerard H., P.O. Box 7223, Statesville, NC 28687
Couture, Bernard G., Box 202, East Barre, VT 05639
Demasi, Michael A., St. Jerome, East Dorset, VT 05253
Dennigan, Patrick J., P.O. Box 931, North Adams, MA 01247
Depeaux, Bernard F., P.O. Box 4000, Shelburne, VT 05482
Dufault, Omer L., St. Joseph's Home, 243 N. Prospect St., Burlington, VT 05401
Duquette, Lucien G., 6 Roland Ct., Winooski, VT 05404
Falvella, Richard J., Crystal Haven Rd., Bomoseen, VT 05732
Foley, James F., Burlington Health & Rehab Center, 300 Pearl St., Burlington, VT 05401
Guischard, John A., St. Peter Rectory, 134 Convent Ave., Rutland, VT 05701
Hackett, John P., 59 Upper Welden St., Apt. 15, St. Albans, VT 05478
Hart, Edward J., St. Joseph's Home, 243 N. Prospect St., Burlington, VT 05401
Holland, Francis M., 8 Cedar Glen N., South Burlington, VT 05403
Kennedy, David G., 4580 N. Kolb Rd., Tucson, AZ 85715-6103
Kenney, John B., 8 Hullcrest Ln., Shelburne, VT 05482. Tel: 802-985-2333
Lagor, Joseph J., Box 28, Sharon, VT 05065
Laliberte, William F., 113 Robbins St., Rutland, VT 05701
Lapan, Robert, St. Joseph's Home, 243 N. Prospect St., Burlington, VT 05401. Tel: 802-862-2036
Laplante, Jean-Paul, 64 N. Elm St., St. Albans, VT 05478
Lawlor, Brendan W., 695 Americana Dr., Apt. 17, Annapolis, MD 21403
Ledoux, John C., 16 Clover Dr., 9-C, Essex Junction, VT 05452
Moore, Edward F., 86 Westview Heights Dr., Stowe, VT 05672-4361. Tel: 802-253-5085
Mulligan, William R., 20 N. 28th Ave., Longport, NJ 08403
Murtagh, George O., 2640 N.E. 52nd Ct., #42, Silver Springs, FL 34488-9402
Pagliuca, Joseph P., Villaggio S. Berardo, No. 16, Pescina, Province L'Aguila, 67057 Italy
Pray, Joseph N, P.O. Box 85, Castleton, VT 05735
Provost, Raymond C., Birchwood Terrace Healthcare, 43 Starr Farm Rd., Burlington, VT 05401
Rousseau, Peter A., D10, Stonehedge Dr., South Burlington, VT 05403
Sullivan, Joseph T., P.O. Box 421, St. Albans Bay, VT 05481. Tel: 802-527-0272
Von Fauer, Stephen C., Mary Theotokos Center, P.O. Box 88, West Burke, VT 05871

Permanent Deacons:
Allen, Eugene, Jr., St. Joseph, Chester
Bisson, David A., St. Monica, Barre
Blicharz, John F., Sacred Heart, Bellow Falls
Brown, William, III, St. Theresa, Gilman
Burk, Bruce, St. John, St. Johnsbury
Chagnon, Clifford, All Saints, Richford
Cooney, Thomas, On Leave
Cummings, Regis E., St. Augustine, Montpelier
Degnon, Robert F, Our Lady of Hope, West Wardsboro
Desilets, Raymond J., St. John, St. Johnsbury
Fitzpatrick, Kelly, Our Lady of Perpetual Help, Bradford
Glinka, William, Our Lady of Grace, Colchester
Gratton, John, St. Benedict, West Charleston
Guarino, John P., St. Anthony, White River Junction
Hawk, Ivan, Holy Cross, Colchester
Herrick, Eugene, St. Mark, Burlington
Krawczyk, Eugene, Sacred Heart-St. Francis de Sales, Bennington
Lane, Joseph W., Sr., St. John Vianney, South Burlington
Langlois, Norman S., St. Francis Xavier, Winooski
Lauziere, Roger J., St. Ann, Milton
Lissandrello, Paul, Sts. Donatian and Rogatian, Randolph
Mayo, Bernier L., St. John, St. Johnsbury
Mello, Paul, Our Lady of Fatima, Wilmington
Meunier, Louis A., St. Anthony, Burlington
Nadeau, Thomas, On Duty Outside the Diocese
Perkins, Richard, St. Francis Cabrini, West Pawlet
Place, John F., St. Francis Xavier, Winooski
Previti, Anthony, St. John Vianney, South Burlington
Pudvah, Daniel, St. Augustine, Montpelier
Putis, Peter, St. Margaret Mary, Arlington
Rainville, John L., St. Louis, Highgate Center
Ramey, Jon, St. Isidore, Montgomery Center
Ratte, Stephen J., St. Luke, Fairfax
Rivard, Fernand R., St. Monica, Barre
Rixon, John, St. Mary, St. Albans
Rock, James E., St. Patrick, Fairfield
Toborg, Alfred, St. Elizabeth, Lyndonville
Vincelette, Alan, St. Amadeus, Alburg

INSTITUTIONS LOCATED IN THE DIOCESE

[A] COLLEGES AND UNIVERSITIES

BURLINGTON. *Trinity College of Vermont*, President's Office, 208 Colchester Ave., 05401. Tel: 802-658-0337
For a complete listing, refer to the Colleges and Universities section.

COLCHESTER. *St. Michael's College*, Winooski Park, 05439. Tel: 802-654-2211; Fax: 802-654-2701.
E-mail: mcormier@smcvt.edu
Web site: www.smcvt.edu
For a complete listing, refer to the Colleges and Universities section.

RUTLAND. *College of St. Joseph in Vermont*, 71 Clement Rd., 05701-3899. Tel: 802-773-5900
For a complete listing, refer to the Colleges and Universities section.

[B] CENTRAL HIGH SCHOOLS, DIOCESAN AND PAROCHIAL

RUTLAND. *Mt. St. Joseph Academy*, 127 Convent Ave., 05701. Tel: 802-775-0151. Sisters of St. Joseph. Sr. Shirley A. Davis, S.S.J., Pres.; Mrs. Loretta A. Canales, Prin.; Kathryn Sheridan, Guidance Dir.; Mr. Hurley Cavacas, Dean of Students. Priests 1; Sisters 2; Lay Teachers 20; Students 218.

SOUTH BURLINGTON. *Rice Memorial High School*, 99 Proctor Ave., 05403. Tel: 802-862-6521.
E-mail: rice@ricehs.k12.vt.us
Web site: www.together.net/~ricemhs/ricemhs.htm
Bro. Roger Lemoyne, S.C., Prin.; Mrs. Andrea Torello, Guidance Dir. Sisters 3; Brothers 2; Lay Teachers 35; Students 516.

[C] ELEMENTARY SCHOOLS, PAROCHIAL

BURLINGTON. *Christ The King*. (Grades PreK-8), 136 Locust St., 05401. Tel: 802-862-6696.
E-mail: cksburl@aol.com
Mr. James Provost, Prin. Sisters 3; Lay Teachers 22; Students 246.
Mater Christi School, 50 Mansfield Ave., 05401. Tel: 802-658-3992. Sr. Laura Della Santa, R.S.M., Prin. Sisters 5; Lay Teachers 25; Students 410.
St. Joseph. (Grades PreK-8), 20 Allen St., 05401. Tel: 802-864-5623; Fax: 802-860-2627. Evelyn Rogerson, Prin. Sisters 1; Lay Teachers 13; Students 208.

BARRE. *St. Monica's*. (Grades PreK-8), 73 Summer St., 05641. Tel: 802-476-5015. Mrs. Betty Foley, Prin. Lay Teachers 14; Students 172.

BARTON. *St. Paul's*. (Grades K-8), Eastern Ave., 05822. Tel: 802-525-6578.
E-mail: stpaul@together.net
Mrs. Jane Williams, Prin. Lay Teachers 6; Students 60.

BENNINGTON. *Sacred Heart*. (Grades K-6), 307 School St., 05201. Tel: 802-442-2446; Fax: 802-442-3584.
E-mail: destes@sover.net
Web site: www.rc.net/burlington/
Mr. David Estes, Prin. Lay Teachers 10; Students 189.

BRATTLEBORO. *St. Michael's*. (Grades PreK-6), 23 Walnut St., 05301. Tel: 802-254-5666. Mr. Frank J. Vara, Prin. Lay Teachers 17; Students 138.

MONTPELIER. *St. Michael's School.* (Grades K-6), 46 Barre St., 05602. Tel: 802-223-6430. Sr. Nancy Mencel, S.N.D., Prin. Sisters 2; Lay Teachers 8; Students 130.

NEWPORT. *Sacred Heart Schools, Inc.* (Grades K-8), P.O. Box 930, 05855. Tel: 802-334-8185; 334-7803 (Bus. Office). Mrs. Nancy Croteau, Prin. Lay Teachers 10; Students 150.

RUTLAND. *Christ the King.* (Grades PreK-8), 60 S. Main St., 05701. Tel: 802-773-6820, Ext. 17. Mr. Jeffrey G. Johnson, Prin. Sisters 2; Lay Teachers 24; Students 418.

WINOOSKI. *St. Francis Xavier.* (Grades PreK-8), St. Peter St., 05404. Tel: 802-655-2600. Mr. Roderick Marcotte, Prin. Sisters 3; Lay Teachers 12; Students 260.

[D] HOMES FOR AGED

BURLINGTON. *St. Joseph's Home for Aged,* 243 N. Prospect St., 05401. Tel: 802-864-0264
For a complete listing, refer to the Special Care Facilities section.

DERBY LINE. *Michaud Memorial Manor,* 05830. Tel: 802-873-3152
For a complete listing, refer to the Special Care Facilities section.

RUTLAND. *Loretto Home for Aged,* 05701. Tel: 802-773-8840
For a complete listing, refer to the Special Care Facilities section.
St. Joseph Assisted Living Residence/Kervick Home, 131 Convent Ave., 05701. Tel: 802-775-5133
For a complete listing, refer to the Special Care Facilities section.

[E] MONASTERIES AND RESIDENCES OF PRIESTS AND BROTHERS

BURLINGTON. *Brothers of the Sacred Heart.* 190 White St., South Burlington, 05403. Tel: 802-658-6624. Bros. Damian Goudreau, S.C., Dir.; Roger Lemoyne, S.C.; Richard Labbe, S.C. Brothers 3.

ARLINGTON. *Carthusian Foundation, Charterhouse of the Transfiguration,* R.R. 2, Box 2411, 05250. Revs. Andre Poisson, O.Cart. (France), Prior; Francois Rheault, O.Cart. (Canada); Lorenzo Maria Tolentino de la Rosa, Jr., O.Cart. (Philippines), Vicar, Novice Master of Brothers; Mary Joseph Kim, O.Cart (Korea), Novice Master of Cloister Monks; Mary Paul Chapeau, O.Cart. (France), Antiquior. Carthusian Foundation, Association Fraternelle Romande. Choir Monks: Solemn Professed 6; Temporary Professed 3; Novices 2; Converse Brothers: Solemn Professed 4; Temporary Professed 2; Perpetual Donates 2.

COLCHESTER. *Society of St. Edmund.* (Edmundite Generalate), 270 Winooski Park, 05439. Tel: 802-654-3400.
Central Offices, Society of Saint Edmund. Revs. Joseph L. Hart, S.S.E., Supr. Gen.; James R. Coombs, S.S.E.; Eymard Galligan, S.S.E.; Edward J. Dubriske, S.S.E. (Venezuela); Howard J. Muehlberger, S.S.E. (Venezuela); Philippe Simonnet, S.S.E. (France); Bro. Christopher Daignault, S.S.E.
Society of St. Edmund. (Edmundite Community at St. Michael's College), 05439. Tel: 802-654-2000. Revs. Marcel Rainville, S.S.E., Supr.; Richard N. Berube, S.S.E.; Paul E. Couture, S.S.E.; Michael P. Cronogue, S.S.E.; Brian J. Cummings, S.S.E.; Lorenzo D'Agostino, S.S.E.; Raymond J. Doherty, S.S.E.; Joseph M. McLaughlin, S.S.E.; Robert J. Sheehey, S.S.E.; John A. Stankiewicz, S.S.E.; Romeo A. Trahan, S.S.E.; Richard L. VanderWeel, S.S.E.; Bros. Anthony Krutch, S.S.E.; Daniel H. Manzano, S.S.E.

WESTON. *Priory of Benedictine Monks,* 58 Priory Hill Rd., 05161. Tel: 802-824-5409. Very Rev. John Hammond, O.S.B., Prior; Revs. Richard Iaquinto, O.S.B., Asst. Prior; Peter Claude Anctil, O.S.B.; Robert J. Kiernan, O.S.B.; Mark Ronald Nicolosi, O.S.B. Priests 5; Brothers 10.

[F] CONVENTS AND RESIDENCES OF SISTERS

BURLINGTON. *Mount St. Mary Convent,* 100 Mansfield Ave., 05401. Tel: 802-863-6835.
E-mail: clairebouchard@hotmail
Motherhouse and Novitiate of Sisters of Mercy. Sr. Jeannine Mercure, R.S.M., Pres. In res. Rev. Wendell H. Searles, Chap.
Institute for Spiritual Development, 208 Colchester Ave., 05401. Tel: 802-658-0339, Ext. 410. Sisters 89.

BARTON. *St. Paul's Convent,* HC 63, Box 7, 05822-0007. Tel: 802-525-3178.

COLCHESTER. *Religious Hospitallers of St. Joseph,* 101 College Pkwy., 05446. Tel: 802-655-1160.
E-mail: rhfa@juno.com
Sr. Rita Vallee, R.H.S.J., Supr. Sisters 16.

NEWPORT. *Sacred Heart Convent,* P.O. Box 375, 05855. Tel: 802-334-7058. Sisters 10.

RUTLAND. *Sisters of St. Joseph Society, Inc.,* 131 Convent Ave., 05701. Tel: 802-775-5133. Administrative Offices, 129 Convent Ave., 05701. Tel: 802-775-0665.
Other Residences: St. Francis Residence, 11 Clement Rd., 05701.
Guest Houses: Avila Hall, 7 Clement Rd., 05701. Marion Hall, 9 Clement Rd., 05701. St. Joseph, 333 Elm St., Bennington, 05201. Fontbonne Hall, 13 Clement Rd., 05701. Sisters 51.

WESTFIELD. *Monastery of the Immaculate Heart of Mary,* H.C.R. #13, Box 11, 05874. Tel: 802-744-6525. Benedictine Cloistered Nuns, Congregation of Solesmes. Rev. Mother Marguerite Derome, O.S.B., Prioress; Rev. Dom Guy-Marie Oury, O.S.B., Res. Chap., Monk of Solesmes, France. Professed Nuns 14.

WINOOSKI. *Missionary Sisters of Our Lady of Africa (M.S.O.L.A.),* 47 W. Spring St., 05404. Tel: 802-655-4003. Sr. Nora Indelicato, Supr. Sisters 16.
Our Lady of Providence Convent, 47 W. Spring St., 05404. Tel: 802-655-2395. Sr. Lorraine Boyer, S.P., Supr. Sisters 27.

[G] SUMMER CAMPS

BURLINGTON. *Camp Holy Cross, Inc.,* 351 North Ave., 05401. Summer Camp for Boys. Day Camp for Boys and Girls. Diocesan institution under direction of Board of Trustees. Capacity 100.
Camp Tara, Catholic Charities Central Office, 351 North Ave., 05401. Tel: 802-658-6110. Summer camp for underprivileged Vermont children. Diocesan institution under direction of Vermont Catholic Charities. Capacity 222.

[H] NEWMAN CENTERS

BURLINGTON. *University of Vermont-The Catholic Center at UVM,* 390 S. Prospect St., 05401. Tel: 802-862-8403; Fax: 802-865-9480.
E-mail: cathuvm@together.net
Web site: www.uvm.edu/~catholic/
Chaplains: Revs. Michael W. DeForge; Peter Y. Williams.
Castleton State College, St. John Rectory, P.O. Box 128, Castleton, 05735. Rev. J. Charles Durham, Chap.
Goddard College, Plainfield, 05667.
Green Mountain College, St. Raphael Rectory, Main St., Poultney, 05764. Rev. Joseph M. Vignoe, Chap.
Johnson State College (Johnson). Attended by St. Mary, Cambridge. P.O. Box 129, Cambridge, 05444. Rev. John J. Arnott (PIT), Chap.
Lyndon State College, Lyndon Center, 05850. Rev. Thomas Mosher, Chap., St. Elizabeth Church, P.O. Box 141, Lyndonville, 05851.
Middlebury College, St. Mary Rectory, 19 College St., Middlebury, 05753. Rev. John McDermott, Chap.
Norwich Newman Apostolate, Norwich University, Northfield, 05663. Chaplains: Rev. Michael W. DeForge, The Catholic Center at UVM, 390 S. Prospect St., 05401. Rev. Richard G. LaValley, St. Francis Xavier Rectory, St. Peter St., Winooski, 05404.
Vermont Technical College, Sts. Donatian and Rogatian Rectory, 25 S. Pleasant St., Randolph, 05060.

[I] MISCELLANEOUS

BURLINGTON. *Institute for Spiritual Development,* 208 Colchester Ave., 05401. Tel: 802-658-0337, Ext. 410; Fax: 802-658-5446. Sr. Claire Boissy, R.S.M., Admin. Dir.

BENSON. *Lumen Christi Retreat House,* 05731. Tel: 802-537-4531. Reservations for retreat call Tel: 802-658-0337, Ext. 410.

COLCHESTER. *Fanny Allen Hospital,* 101 College Pkwy., 05446. Tel: 802-656-2345. Fanny Allen Hospital has the oversight responsibility to assure that the Fletcher Allen Health Care Corporation does not conduct actions on the Fanny Allen Campus that conflicts with the teachings, traditions, Canons or other laws of the Roman Catholic Church or the Constitutions and Directives of the Religious Hospitallers of St. Joseph.

ISLE LA MOTTE. *St. Anne's Shrine,* 05463. Tel: 802-928-3362; Fax: 802-928-3305. Conducted by Fathers of Society of St. Edmund. Rev. Maurice U. Boucher, S.S.E.
Open May 15-Oct. 15.

RANDOLPH. *Opus Dei,* Wynnview Center, R.D. 1, 05060. Tel: 802-728-5414; Fax: 802-728-3334.
Legal Names: Opus Dei; The Work of God.

WEST BRATTLEBORO. *Neringa, Inc.,* RFD 4, Box 155, 05301.

RELIGIOUS INSTITUTES OF MEN REPRESENTED IN THE DIOCESE

For further details refer to the corresponding bracketed number in the Religious Institutes of Men or Women section.

[0200]—*Benedictine Monks.*—O.S.B.
[1100]—*Brothers of the Sacred Heart.* (New England Prov.).—S.C.
[0300]—*Cistercian Order of the Strict Observance (Trappists).*—O.C.S.O.
[0520]—*Franciscan Friars.*—O.F.M.
[0690]—*Jesuit Fathers and Brothers.*—S.J.
[0780]—*Marist Fathers.*—S.M.
[0720]—*The Missionaries of Our Lady of La Salette.* (Prov. of the Immaculate Heart of Mary).—M.S.
[0280]—*Order of Carthusians.*—O.Cart.
[0610]—*Priests of the Congregation of Holy Cross.* (Eastern Prov.).—C.S.C.
[0440]—*Society of Saint Edmund.*—S.S.E.

RELIGIOUS INSTITUTES OF WOMEN REPRESENTED IN THE DIOCESE

[0170]—*Benedictine Cloistered Nuns of the Congregation of Solesmes.*—O.S.B.
[0750]—*Daughters of the Charity of the Sacred Heart of Jesus.*—F.C.S.C.J.
[0820]—*Daughters of the Holy Spirit.*—D.H.S.
[0960]—*Daughters of Wisdom.*—D.W.
[1070]—*Dominican Sisters.*—O.P.
[1190]—*Franciscan Sisters of the Atonement.*—S.A.
[]—*Missionary Sisters of Our Lady of Africa.*—M.S.O.L.A.
[3440]—*Religious Hospitallers of Saint Joseph.*—R.H.S.J.
[1930]—*Sisters of Holy Cross.*—C.S.C.
[2550]—*Sisters of Mercy.*—R.S.M.
[3000]—*Sisters of Notre Dame de Namur.*—S.N.D.deN.
[3340]—*Sisters of Providence.*—S.P.
[3830-01]—*Sisters of St. Joseph (Boston, MA).*—C.S.J.
[3830-07]—*Sisters of St. Joseph (Burlington, VT).*—S.S.J.
[4130]—*Ursuline Sisters of the Congregation of Tildonk, Belgium.*—O.S.U.

DIOCESAN CEMETERIES

BURLINGTON. *St. Joseph's Cemetery,* 05401.
SOUTH BURLINGTON. *Resurrection Park Cemetery,* 05403.

NECROLOGY

† Gagnon, John L., (Retired). —Died Nov. 13, 1996.
† Messier, Bernard H., Barre, VT, St. Monica. —Died Dec. 28, 1996.

Diocese of Camden

(Dioecesis Camdensis)

Most Reverend

JAMES T. McHUGH, S.T.D.

Bishop of Camden; ordained May 25, 1957; appointed Titular Bishop of Morosbisdo and Auxiliary Bishop of Newark November 20, 1987; consecrated January 25, 1988; appointed Bishop of Camden May 13, 1989; installed June 20, 1989. *Res., Marywood, P.O. Box 577, 1600 Peter Cheeseman Rd., Blackwood, NJ, 08012. Office: Camden Diocesan Center, P.O. Box 709, Camden, NJ, 08101-0709.*

Most Reverend

JAMES L. SCHAD, D.D.

Retired Auxiliary Bishop of Camden; appointed Titular Bishop of Panatoria October 18, 1966; consecrated December 8, 1966; retired January 26, 1993. *Res., Neumann House, St. Mary's Home, Ste. 102, 1730 Kresson Rd., Cherry Hill, NJ, 08003.*

The Chancery: Camden Diocesan Center, 1845 Haddon Ave., P.O. Box 709, Camden, NJ, 08101-0709. Tel.: 609-756-7900; Fax: 609-963-2655.

Legal Corporate Title: "The Diocese of Camden, New Jersey."

ESTABLISHED DECEMBER 9, 1937.

Square Miles 2,691.

Comprises six Counties in the State of New Jersey—viz., Atlantic, Camden, Cape May, Cumberland, Gloucester and Salem.

For legal titles of parishes and diocesan institutions, consult the Chancery Office.

STATISTICAL OVERVIEW

Personnel	
Bishop	1
Retired Bishops	1
Priests: Diocesan Active in Diocese	221
Priests: Active Outside Diocese	29
Priests: Diocesan in Foreign Missions	7
Priests: Retired, Sick or Absent	65
Number of Diocesan Priests	322
Religious Priests in Diocese	48
Extern Priests in Diocese	16
Ordinations:	
Diocesan Priests	3
Permanent Deacons	31
Permanent Deacons in Diocese	125
Total Brothers	15
Total Sisters	375
Parishes	
Parishes	125
With Resident Pastor:	
Resident Diocesan Priests	120
Resident Religious Priests	5
Without Resident Pastor:	
Missions	7
Pastoral Centers	24
Professional Ministry Personnel:	
Brothers	3
Sisters	40
Lay Ministers	32
Welfare	
Catholic Hospitals	1
Total Assisted	228,155
Health Care Centers	4
Total Assisted	11,164
Homes for the Aged	5
Total Assisted	1,012
Day Care and Extended Day Care Centers	1
Total Assisted	60
Specialized Homes	1
Total Assisted	1,000
Special Centers for Social Services	12
Total Assisted	8,731
Other Institutions	23
Total Assisted	250,282
Educational	
Diocesan Students in Other Seminaries	24
Total Seminarians	24
High Schools, Diocesan and Parish	8
Total Students	4,625
High Schools, Private	3
Total Students	1,169
Elementary Schools, Diocesan and Parish	61
Total Students	18,157
Non-residential Schools for the Disabled	1
Total Students	616
Catechesis/Religious Education:	
High School Students	400
Elementary Students	33,830
Total Students Under Catholic Instruction	58,821
Teachers in the Diocese:	
Priests	17
Brothers	4
Sisters	128
Lay Teachers	1,109
Vital Statistics	
Receptions into the Church:	
Infant Baptism Totals	6,980
Adult Baptism Totals	571
Received into Full Communion	432
First Communions	6,840
Confirmations	5,388
Marriages:	
Catholic	1,376
Interfaith	551
Total Marriages	1,927
Total Catholic Population	415,717
Total Population	1,287,805

Former Bishops—Most Rev. BARTHOLOMEW J. EUSTACE, S.T.D., First Bishop of Camden; cons. March 25, 1938; died Dec. 11, 1956.—Most Rev. JUSTIN J. McCARTHY, S.T.D., LL.D., Second Bishop of Camden; cons. June 17, 1954; appt. to Camden, Jan. 27, 1957; died Dec. 26, 1959.—Most Rev. CELESTINE J. DAMIANO, D.D., Third Bishop of Camden; cons. Feb. 11, 1953; transferred to Camden, Jan. 24, 1960, with the personal title of Archbishop; died Oct. 2, 1967.—Most Rev. GEORGE H. GUILFOYLE, D.D., J.D., ord. March 25, 1944; appt. Titular Bishop of Marazanae and Auxiliary Bishop of New York, Oct. 17, 1964; cons. Fourth Bishop of Camden, Nov. 30, 1964; appt. Jan. 2, 1968; installed March 4, 1968; retired May 22, 1989; died June 11, 1991.

Chancery:

Camden Diocesan Center—1845 Haddon Ave., P.O. Box 709, Camden, 08101-0709. Tel: 609-756-7900; Fax: 609-963-2655. Address all official business to this office.

The Diocese of Camden—A corporation under the laws of the State of New Jersey.

Officers—Most Rev. JAMES T. McHUGH, S.T.D., Pres.; Rev. Msgr. DAVID F. BUDNEY, V.G., Vice Pres.; Rev. Msgr. JOSEPH W. POKUSA, J.C.D., Sec.

Diocesan Bishop—Most Rev. JAMES T. McHUGH, S.T.D. Tel: 609-756-7913.

Retired Auxiliary Bishop—Most Rev. JAMES L. SCHAD, D.D.

Vicar General—Rev. Msgr. DAVID F. BUDNEY, V.G. Tel: 609-756-7906.

Judicial Vicar—Rev. Msgr. LEONARD G. SCOTT, J.C.D. Tel: 609-756-7972.

Chancellor and Episcopal Vicar for Canonical Affairs—Rev. Msgr. JOSEPH W. POKUSA, J.C.D. Tel: 609-756-7916.

Secretariat—Rev. JAMES F. CHECCHIO, Sec. to Bishop McHugh and Vice Chancellor. Tel: 609-756-7907.

Assistant Chancellor—Rev. MICHAEL ORSI, Ed.D.

Episcopal Vicars:

City of Camden—Rev. Msgr. ROBERT T. McDERMOTT, V.E., *St. Joseph Pro-Cathedral, 2907 Federal St., Camden, 08105.* Tel: 609-964-2776.

Clergy—Rev. Msgr. JAMES P. McINTYRE, V.E. Tel: 609-756-7915.

Communications and Community Relations—Rev. Msgr. CHARLES J. GIGLIO, V.E., Ph.D. Tel: 609-756-7926.

Pastoral Services—Rev. Msgr. THOMAS J. McINTYRE, V.E. Tel: 609-756-7908. Rev. MICHAEL P. ORSI, Asst. Vicar. Tel: 609-756-7957.

Vicars:

Health Affairs—Rev. HARRY J. JORDON, Acting Vicar, *St. Mary, 426 Monmouth St., Gloucester, 08030.* Tel: 609-456-0052.

For Religious—Rev. Msgr. EDWARD F. MULLEN, *St. Augustine, 1310 Ocean Ave., Ocean City, 08226-3295.* Tel: 609-399-0648.

For Clergy—Rev. Msgr. JAMES P. WELSH, *St. Pius X, 344*

Kresson Rd., Cherry Hill, 08034. Tel: 609-429-1330.
Deaneries and Vicars Forane—
Atlantic Deanery—Rev. Msgr. MICHAEL J. COYNE, V.F., *St. Elizabeth Ann Seton, 591 New Jersey Ave., Absecon, 08201-2424.* Tel: 609-641-1480.
Cape May Deanery—Rev. Msgr. WILLIAM QUINN, V.F., *St. Ann, 2900 Pacific Ave., Wildwood, 08260-4943.* Tel: 609-522-5583.
Camden City Deanery—Rev. Msgr. ROBERT T. MCDERMOTT, V.E., *St. Joseph Pro-Cathedral, 2907 Federal St., Camden, 08105-2229.* Tel: 609-964-2776.
Camden North Deanery—Rev. Msgr. JAMES R. TRACY, Ph.D., V.F., *St. Peter Celestine, 402 Kings Hwy. N., Cherry Hill, 08034-1091.* Tel: 609-667-2440.
Camden South Deanery—Rev. Msgr. EDWARD J. KORDA, V.F., *St. Gregory, 340 Evesham Ave., Magnolia, 08049-1098.* Tel: 609-784-4090.
Camden West Deanery—Rev. Msgr. JOSEPH C. DOWNING, V.F., *St. Stephen, 6306 Browning Rd., Pennsauken, 08109-1549.* Tel: 609-662-9338.
Central Deanery—Rev. JOHN F. BOURKE, V.F., *Our Lady of Mount Carmel, 178 W. White Horse Pike, Berlin, 08009-2023.* Tel: 609-767-2563.
Cumberland Deanery—Rev. Msgr. JOSEPH G. STOERLEIN, P.A., V.F., *Sacred Heart, 1010 E. Landis Ave., Vineland, 08360-4096.* Tel: 609-691-0420.
Gloucester Deanery—Rev. JAMES P. CURRAN, V.F., *Our Lady of Lourdes, 500 Greentree Rd., Glassboro, 08028-1427.* Tel: 609-881-0909.
Southwest Deanery—Rev. Msgr. ROCCO A. CONTINILLO, V.F., *Corpus Christi, 369 Georgetown Rd., Carneys Point, 08069-2598.* Tel: 609-299-3833.

Diocesan Tribunal:
Tel: 609-756-7972.
Judicial Vicar—Rev. Msgr. LEONARD G. SCOTT, J.C.D. Tel: 609-756-7972; Fax: 609-756-0113.
Adjutant Judicial Vicars—Rev. EDWARD J. LIPINSKI; Rev. Msgr. PATRICK J. MADDEN.
Judges—Rev. Msgr. EDWARD D. ALLEYNE; Rev. Msgr. BERNARD P. HEWITT, V.F.; Rev. Msgr. JOHN R. LUBICKY; Rev. Msgr. EDWARD F. MULLEN; Rev. Msgr. THOMAS F. SHARKEY, J.C.D.; Revs. FRANCIS P. GAFFNEY; JOSEPH A. SALERNO.
Notaries—ROSE MCFADDEN; ROSEMARY MANZO; ALICE PEDERSEN; JOAN WHITELOCK.
Promoter of Justice—Rev. Msgr. EUGENE J. FITZSIMMONS, J.C.D., *St. Michael, 313 Memorial Ave., Gibbstown, 08027.* Tel: 609-423-0007.
Presbyteral Council—Most Rev. JAMES T. MCHUGH, S.T.D., Chm. Officers: Revs. DANIEL M. SHERMAN, Pres.; CADMUS D. MAZZARELLA, Vice Pres.; ROBERT E. HUGHES, Sec. Representatives by Age: Revs. CHARLES P. BARTH; PATRICK S. CHIARILLI; JOHN J. VIGNONE. Representatives by Geography: Revs. RONALD S. FALOTICO; THOMAS B. FITZSIMMONS; WILLIAM P. GRAHAM; ROBERT E. HUGHES; MICHAEL J. MATVEENKO. Representatives by Ministry: Revs. FRANCIS X. HUDSON; HARRY J. JORDON; STEPHEN LAROSA, O.S.A.; ROBERT C. PALSEY; DANIEL A. SHERMAN. Members by Appointment: Rev. Msgr. EDWARD D. ALLEYNE; Rev. Msgr. ROCCO A. CONTINILLO, V.F.; Rev. Msgr. JOSEPH C. DOWNING, V.F.; Rev. Msgr. J. GERALD GALLAGHER; Rev. Msgr. JOSEPH P. HERRON, V.E.; Rev. Msgr. EDWARD L. KORDA, V.F.; Rev. Msgr. ROBERT T. MCDERMOTT, V.E.; Rev. Msgr. VICTOR S. MURO; Rev. Msgr. CIARAN P. O'MEARAIN; Rev. Msgr. WILLIAM QUINN, V.F.; Rev. Msgr. JAMES R. TRACY; Revs. JOHN F. BOURKE, V.F.; LARRY BOYLE, V.F.; JAMES P. CURRAN, V.F.; JOHN T. FREY; CADMUS D. MAZZARELLA; RUSSELL L. ROCK. Ex-Officio Members: Most Rev. JAMES L. SCHAD, D.D.; Rev. Msgr. DAVID F. BUDNEY, V.G.; Rev. Msgr. JOSEPH W. POKUSA, J.C.D. Permanent Observers: Rev. Msgr. CHARLES J. GIGLIO, V.E.; Rev. Msgr. JAMES P. MCINTYRE, V.E.; Rev. Msgr. THOMAS J. MCINTYRE, V.E.; Rev. Msgr. LEONARD G. SCOTT.
College of Consultors—Most Rev. JAMES L. SCHAD, D.D.; Rev. Msgr. DAVID F. BUDNEY, V.G.; Rev. Msgr. RICHARD J. CALLAHAN; Rev. Msgr. ROCCO A. CONTINILLO, V.F.; Rev. Msgr. MICHAEL J. COYNE, V.F.; Rev. Msgr. J. GERALD GALLAGHER; Rev. Msgr. JOSEPH P. HERRON, V.E.; Rev. Msgr. THOMAS J. MCINTYRE, V.E.; Rev. Msgr. CIARAN P. O'MEARAIN; Rev. Msgr. WILLIAM QUINN, V.F.; Rev. Msgr. PATRICK M. TIERNEY; Rev. RUSSELL L. ROCK.
Diocesan Pastoral Council—Most Rev. JAMES T. MCHUGH, S.T.D., Chm. Executive Committee: Rev. Msgr. CIARIAN O'MEARAIN; Sr. ALBERTINE CONWAY, S.S.J.; Mr. EDWARD G. BARRY; Miss GERTRUDE EVANS; Mrs. ANN MARIE GAVIN; Mrs. JEANNE LORGE; Mr. VINCENT PREMONE; Mrs. CAROLE SMITH; Mrs. KATHI TERRY; Mrs. HELEN YECCO.
Sisters' Council—Sr. MARIANNE MCCANN, M.P.F., Pres., *Paul VI Convent, Hopkins Rd., Haddon Twp., 08033.* Tel: 609-854-3678.
Diocesan Finance Council—Most Rev. JAMES T. MCHUGH, S.T.D.; Rev. Msgr. DAVID F. BUDNEY, V.G.; Rev. Msgr. CHARLES J. BARTH; Rev. Msgr. J. GERALD GALLAGHER; Rev. Msgr. JOSEPH P. HERRON; Rev. Msgr. JOSEPH W. POKUSA; Rev. Msgr. WILLIAM QUINN, V.F.; Rev. Msgr. PATRICK M. TIERNEY, V.F.; WILLIAM J. MURRAY; WILLIAM CONWAY.
Finance Council Committee Chairmen—Rev. Msgr. J. GERALD GALLAGHER, Finance; Rev. Msgr. CHARLES J. BARTH, Buildings & Property; Rev. Msgr. DAVID F. BUDNEY, V.G., Investment; Rev. Msgr. PATRICK M. TIERNEY, Insurance; Rev. Msgr. JOSEPH W. POKUSA, Employee Benefits & Compensation.

Diocesan Offices and Directors

The following offices and directors are located at the Camden Diocesan Center unless otherwise indicated.
Camden Diocesan Center—1845 Haddon Ave., P.O. Box 709, Camden, 08101-0709. Tel: 609-756-7900.

Office of the Vicar General

Vicar General—Rev. Msgr. DAVID F. BUDNEY, V.G. Tel: 609-756-7906.

Agencies Reporting to the Vicar General:
Special Committees—Interparochial Cooperation Board; Deposit and Loan Fund; Parish Finance Councils; New Parish Development Committee.
House of Charity—Rev. Msgr. THOMAS A. GUENTHER, Dir. Tel: 609-756-7939.
Stewardship Program—Rev. Msgr. J. GERALD GALLAGHER, *St. Patrick, 64 Cooper St., Woodbury, 08096.* Tel: 609-845-0123.

Reporting to the Chancellor:
Office of Human Resources—Mr. JOHN J. RAFTERY, Dir. Tel: 609-756-7903.

Secretariat for Diocesan & Parish Finances:
Secretary—WILLIAM J. MURRAY. Tel: 609-756-7934.
Accounting Services—Mrs. LISA M. CILIBERTO, C.P.A., Comptroller & Dir. Tel: 609-756-7980.
Department of Finance—
Accounting—Mr. PAUL J. WORTHINGTON.
Department of Health Benefits—JAMES SMITH, Dir. Tel: 609-756-7953; 756-7928.
Department Risk Management—PAUL F. ZAKULEC, Dir. Tel: 609-756-7928.

Secretariat for Diocesan & Parish Operations:
Secretary—ROBERT SPEAKMAN. Tel: 609-756-7935.
Special Projects Coordinator—THOMAS BECHARD. Tel: 609-756-7989.
Department of Buildings—ARTHUR BASCIANO, A.I.A., Diocesan Architect & Dir. JOSEPH COSTANZO, Assoc. Dir. Tel: 609-756-7979.
Department of Cemeteries—ARTHUR HEINTZ, Dir., Mailing Address: *1845 Haddon Ave., P.O. Box 709, Camden, 08101-0709.* Tel: 609-424-8728 (Cherry Hill).
Department of Real Estate—KENNETH MCILVANE, Assoc. Dir. Tel: 609-756-7925.

Vicariate for Clergy Personnel

Vicar—Rev. Msgr. JAMES P. MCINTYRE.
Office of Priest Personnel—Rev. Msgr. JAMES P. MCINTYRE, Dir. Tel: 609-756-7915.
Priests Personnel Board—Rev. WILLIAM P. BRENNAN, Chm., *St. Pius X, 344 Kresson Rd., Cherry Hill, 08034.* Tel: 609-429-1330. Rev. Msgr. EDWARD D. ALLEYNE; Rev. Msgr. JOSEPH P. JOYNES; Revs. LEWIS A. BATTISTI; MICHAEL J. COFFEY; JAMES P. CURRAN, V.F.; NEAL F. DANTE; RONALD S. FALOTICO; DAVID A. GROVER; WILLIAM H. HART; PETER M. JOYCE; ANDREW E. MARTIN; BRIAN E. O'NEILL. Non-Voting Members: Most Rev. JAMES T. MCHUGH; Rev. Msgr. DAVID F. BUDNEY, V.G.; Rev. Msgr. JAMES P. MCINTYRE, V.E.; Rev. Msgr. JOSEPH W. POKUSA; DANIEL M. SHERMAN.
Permanent Diaconate—Rev. FREDERICK G. LINK, Dir. Tel: 609-756-7950.
Vocations Apostolate—Rev. LOUIS A. MARUCCI, Dir.; Sr. DOROTHY ALOISIO, Assoc. Dir.; Rev. JOSEPH T. SZOLACK, Liaison, St. Charles Borromeo Seminary. Tel: 609-756-7966.
Vocation Advisory Board—Rev. Msgr. LAWRENCE P. BOYLE, V.F.; Rev. Msgr. RICHARD J. CALLAHAN; Rev. Msgr. MARTIN J. MANNION; Rev. Msgr. ROBERT T. MCDERMOTT; Rev. Msgr. JAMES P. MCINTYRE; Rev. Msgr. JAMES R. TRACY, Ph.D.; Revs. WILLIAM A. HODGE; LOUIS A. MARUCCI; CADMUS D. MAZZARELLA; Sr. DOROTHY ALOISIO.
Friends of the Sacred Heart—Mr. CHARLES MCGETTIGAN; Rev. Msgr. CHARLES P. BARTH, J.C.D., Chap., *St. Peter, 43 W. Maple Ave., Merchantville, 08109-5141.* Tel: 609-663-1373.
Serra Clubs International—District 15: Mr. CHARLES MCGETTIGAN, Governor; Atlantic City East: Mr. GEORGE WINEBERG, Pres.; Rev. BRENDAN V. SULLIVAN, Chap.; Cape May County: Mr. JOHN PARIS, Pres.; Rev. MARK CAVAGNARO, Chap.; Cumberland County: PHILLIP BORGESE, Pres.; Rev. RAYMOND GORMLEY, Chap.
Continuing Education and Spiritual Formation of Priests—Rev. KENNETH JOHNSTON, Dir. Tel: 609-756-7908.
Liaison with Retired Priests—Rev. HARRY J. JORDAN.
Clergy Health Panel—Rev. Msgr. JAMES P. MCINTYRE, Chm.; Rev. Msgr. JAMES A. CARR; Rev. Msgr. ROBERT T. MCDERMOTT; Revs. LEWIS A. BATTISTI; JOHN T. FREY; Dr. JOSEPH W. SOKOLOWSKI.

Vicariate for Communications and Community Relations

Vicar—Rev. Msgr. CHARLES J. GIGLIO, Ph.D. Tel: 609-756-7926.

Secretariat for Communications:
Newspaper—*"The Catholic Star Herald"*, (Official organ of the Diocese of Camden). A corporation under the laws of NJ.
Trustees and Officers—Most Rev. JAMES T. MCHUGH, S.T.D., Pres. & Treas.; Rev. Msgr. DAVID F. BUDNEY, V.G., Vice Pres.; Rev. Msgr. JOSEPH W. POKUSA, J.C.D., Sec.
Communications—Rev. JAMES F. CHECCHIO, J.C.L., Dir. Tel: 609-756-7907.
Office of Public Relations and Promotion—Ms. SUSAN GIBBS, Dir. Tel: 609-756-7982.
Executive Editor—Rev. Msgr. CHARLES J. GIGLIO, Ph.D. Tel: 609-756-7910.
Managing Editor—CARL D. PETERS. Tel: 609-756-7910.
Editorial and Business Office—1845 Haddon Ave., Camden, 08101. Tel: 609-756-7910.
Diocesan Historian—Rev. Msgr. CHARLES J. GIGLIO, Ph.D. Tel: 609-756-7910.

Secretariat for Community Relations:
Propagation of the Faith; Society of the Holy Childhood; Brazilian Missions—Rev. Msgr. THOMAS A. GUENTHER, Dir. Tel: 609-756-7924.
Ecumenical and Interreligious Affairs—Rev. JOSEPH D. WALLACE, Coord. Tel: 609-756-7982.
Commission on Ecumenical and Interreligious Affairs—Rev. Msgr. EUGENE J. FITZSIMMONS, J.C.D., Chm., *St. Michael's, 313 Memorial Ave., Gibbstown, 08027.* Tel: 609-423-0007.
Pro-Life Office—JOYCE LIVELY, Coord. Tel: 609-756-7992.
Prison Ministry—Vacant.
Hospital Ministry—Vacant.
Community Affairs—Rev. EDWARD J. WALSH, Coord.
Campaign for Human Development—Rev. EDWARD J. WALSH, Dir., *Immaculate Heart of Mary, 201 Cooper St., Woodlynne, 08107.* Tel: 609-962-8610.
Special Collections—Rev. JAMES F. CHECCHIO, J.C.L., Coord. Tel: 609-756-7907.
Catholic Relief Services—Vacant.
Operation Rice Bowl—Vacant.
Jubilate Deo Chorale and Orchestra—Rev. LOUIS A. MARUCCI, Exec. Dir.; Rev. Msgr. CARL J. MARUCCI, Conductor. Tel: 609-756-7966.

Secretariat for Social Services:
Catholic Social Services—*"Catholic Social Services of the Diocese of Camden, NJ"*—A Corporation under the laws of the State of New Jersey.
Trustees and Officers—Most Rev. JAMES T. MCHUGH, S.T.D., Pres.; Rev. Msgr. DAVID F. BUDNEY, V.G., Vice Pres.; Rev. Msgr. JOSEPH W. POKUSA, J.C.D.
Executive Director—PATRICIA D. LANGAN, M.A., M.Ed. Tel: 609-663-9800.
Counseling Services—Rev. EDWARD A. IGLE, A.C.S.W., Clinical Dir., *Catholic Social Services, P.O. Box 737, Newfield, 08344-0737.* Tel: 609-697-0744.
Pregnancy and Adoption Services—ANN GALLAGHER, A.C.S.W., Supvr., *Catholic Social Services, 810 Montrose Ave., Vineland, 08360.* Tel: 609-691-1841.
Project Rachel—(Post-Abortion Counseling and Support)—SYLVIA LOUMEAU, M.S.W., Coord., *P.O. Box 737, Newfield, 08344-0737.* Tel: 609-756-7954. Rev. ANDREW J. BOLCAR, Moderator. Tel: 609-456-4136.
Aids Ministry—Sr. RUTH HARKINS, I.H.M., M.A., *2830 Marlton Pike, Pennsauken, 08105.* Tel: 609-663-0085.
Immigration and Refugee Services—THOMAS B. HENKEL, P.D., *6981 N. Park Dr., Ste. 104W, Pennsauken, 08109.* Tel: 609-317-0202.
Legal Assistance to the Poor—JOHN J. GROGAN, J.D., *Camden Center for Law and Social Justice, Inc., 511 State St., Camden, 08102.* Tel: 609-966-8896.
Ladies of Charity—Rev. JAMES J. DURKIN, Spiritual Dir., *Our Lady of Pompeii, 4680 Dante Ave., Vineland, 08360-6810.* Tel: 609-691-7526. Tel: 609-962-9725. Mrs. KATALINA UYEHARA, *167 N. Mansfield Blvd., Cherry Hill, 08034.* Tel: 609-795-4340.
St. Vincent De Paul Society—Mrs. THELMA REPASS, Pres., *1230 Old Black Horse Pike, Blackwood, 08012.* Tel: 609-227-4684.

Vicariate for Pastoral Services

Vicar—Rev. Msgr. THOMAS J. MCINTYRE. Tel: 609-756-7908.

Assistant to Vicar—Rev. MICHAEL P. ORSI, Ed.D. Tel: 609-756-7908.

Agencies Reporting to the Vicar:

Office for Pastoral Statistics and Data—Rev. DOUGLAS R. TOBIN, Coord. Tel: 609-756-7932.

Office of Black Ministry—Deacon WILLIAM JOHNSON, Chm., *312 Shephars Mill Rd., Bridgeton, 08302.* Tel: 609-455-1821.

Ministry with the Deaf—Rev. BRIAN E. O'NEILL, *St. Mary, 426 Monmouth St., Gloucester, 08030.* Tel: 609-456-0052.

Apostolate to Hispanics—Rev. Msgr. VICTOR S. MURO, Dir., *Spanish Catholic Center, 410 S. 8th St., Vineland, 08360.* Tel: 609-692-8992.

Office of Pastoral Planning and Research—Vacant.

Institute for Religious Studies—Rev. ROBERT J. GREGORIO, Dir., *St. Lucy, 250 S. Pte. 73, Blue Anchor, 08037.* Tel: 609-561-6116.

Secretariat for Education and Religious Formation:

Department of Schools—DAVID T. COGHLAN, Ph.D., Supt. Schools; Sr. STELLA LOTZ, S.S.J., Asst. Supt. Lay Personnel & Govt. Programs; Sr. ANTOINE THERESE LAWLOR, I.H.M., Asst. Supt. Relig. Education; Sr. ST. EUGENE FIORINO, O.S.F., Asst. Supt. Educational Svcs.; Sr. ROSE DIFLURI, I.H.M., Asst. Supt. Educational Programs. Tel: 609-756-7988.

Board of Education—Most Rev. JAMES T. MCHUGH, S.T.D., Chm. HELEN NOTO, Pres.

Special Education—Miss KATHLEEN FLYNN, Dir. Tel: 609-756-7993.

Office of Religious Education—MICHAEL E. STEIER, D.Min., Dir. THERESA H. GERLACH, Asst. Dir. Elementary Rel. Educ.; Mr. DOMINIC LOMBARDI, Asst. Dir. Secondary and Adult Rel. Educ. Tel: 609-756-7987.

Media Resource Center—CONNIE TEESDALE, *St. Pius X Retreat House, P.O. Box 216, Blackwood, 08012.* Tel: 609-228-6881.

Parent-Teacher Association—Rev. JAMES P. CURRAN, Moderator, *Our Lady of Lourdes, 500 Greentree Road, Glassboro, 08028.* Tel: 609-881-0909. Sr. ROSE DIFLURI, I.H.M., Honorary Pres. Tel: 609-756-7988. MAUREEN MCLOONE, Pres., *17 E. Chestnut Ave., Merchantville, 08109.* Tel: 609-665-6271. Mrs. RAE O'NEILL, Vice Pres., *702 N. New St., Clayton, 08312.* Tel: 609-881-7185. Mrs. CAROL BASARA, Sec., *4 Dorset Dr., Cherry Hill, 08003.* Tel: 609-424-3976. Mr. GARY BATTISTINI, Treas., *4 Northfield Plaza, Northfield, 08225.* Tel: 609-646-4880.

Secretariat for Family Life:

Family Life Bureau—Rev. MICHAEL P. ORSI, Ed.D., Dir. Tel: 609-756-7957. Mr. STEVEN BOZZA, Assoc. Dir. Tel: 609-756-7921.

Resource Development—TERRY WARNICK, Assoc. Dir. Tel: 609-756-7964. Parish Family Ministry; Parents of Gays/Lesbians; Collaborative Ministry; Leadership Training; Elizabeth Ministry.

Singles/Single Again; Bereavement Ministry—Sr. KATHLEEN DUFFY, R.S.M., Coord. Tel: 609-756-7942. Grief Mgmt. Support Groups (death, separation, divorce); Affiliate Groups; Enrichment retreats and workshops, Bereavement Ministry Training, Rainbows Program - Rainbows- Elementary Schools, Spectrum - High School, Prism - Parents.

Marriage Preparation—Rev. PAUL D. HARTE, Coord. Tel: 609-756-7965. Pre-Cana, Engaged Encounter, Second Marriages.

Marriage Enrichment—STEVEN BOZZA, Coord. Tel: 609-756-7921. Covenant Love, Infertility support, Diocesan Wedding Anniversary, World Marriage Day, Retrouvaille.

Natural Family Planning—MARY ANN CHEZIK, Ph.D., Coord. Tel: 609-756-7965. Natural Family Planning, Human Sexuality Education, Diocesan Devel. Program for NFP, Chastity Education.

Parenting Programs—BOB LENTO, Consultant. Tel: 609-756-7957. Positive Parenting; The Emerging Adolescent; Self Esteem; Getting Ready for Kindergarten; Sibling Rivalry.

Office of Youth and Young Adult Ministry—JEFFREY CORDNER, Dir. Tel: 609-756-7919. Rev. CADMUS D. MAZZARELLA, Moderator.

Life Teen—TOM HOFACKER, Consultant. Tel: 609-783-2045.

Scouting—Rev. ALBERT E. HARSHAW, Chaplain; EDMUND A. DOMANSKI, Chm. Tel: 609-784-3153.

Young Adult Ministry—Vacant.

Campus Ministry—Rev. CADMUS D. MAZZARELLA. Tel: 609-881-5642.

C.Y.O. Youth and Family Fitness Center—Mr. JOHN MILLER, Dir., *P.O. Box 250, Blackwood, 08012.* Tel: 609-227-1359.

Secretariat for Parish Life:

Secretary—Vacant. Tel: 609-756-7908.

Parish Spiritual Development—Vacant.

St. Pius X Spiritual Life Center—Rev. DAVID E. BEEBE, Dir., *P.O. Box 216, Blackwood, 08012.* Tel: 609-227-1436; Fax: 609-227-2907.

RCIA Implementation—Rev. MICHAEL J. FIELD, Dir. Tel: 609-756-7947., *St. Celestine, 402 Kings Hwy. N., Cherry Hill, 08034.* Tel: 609-667-2440.

RCIA Commission—Rev. Msgr. JAMES R. TRACY, Chm. Members: Revs. JOSEPH ADAMSON; JOHN H. BURTON; WAYNE PATRICK LAVIN; FRED VOLTAGGIO; STANLEY L. WITCOSKIE; Deacon JERRY WILSON; Mr. STEVE BOZZA; Mr. BERNARD GARBOWSKI; Ms. AMY GARCIA; Mrs. KAREN KUDLISS; Dr. DOMINIC LOMBARDI; Ms. JOAN MULLIN; Ms. ALICE POLOCZ.

Office of Worship—Rev. JOHN H. BURTON, Dir. Tel: 609-756-7948.

Diocesan Music Office—JON RANIA, Dir. Tel: 609-756-7900, Ext. 355.

Liturgical Commission—Rev. JOHN BURTON, Chm.; Rev. Msgr. JOSEPH W. POKUSA, J.C.D.; Revs. JAMES F. CHECCHIO; THOMAS B. FITZSIMMONS; DAVID A. GROVER; ROBERT E. HUGHES; THOMAS A. NEWTON; Sr. EMILY MCMULLEN, S.S.J.; Sr. MARIA G. PINO, S.S.J.; Mrs. CARL INNOCENZO; Mrs. JAMES KEOUGH; Ms. KATHLEEN RANDO; Deacon THOMAS O'BRIEN; JON RANIA.

Office of Evangelization—Vacant.

Office of Lay Ministry Development—Vacant.

Office of Parish Council Development—Vacant.

Office of Social Justice—Vacant.

Marian Commission—Rev. WILLIAM A. HODGE, Chm., *St. Nicholas of Tolentine, 1409 Pacific Ave., Atlantic City, 08401.* Tel: 609-344-1040; Fax: 609-344-2471.

Legion of Mary—Rev. WILLIAM A. HODGE, Spiritual Dir. Tel: 609-344-1040; Fax: 609-344-2471.

Holy Name Society—Rev. JEROME C. ROMANOWSKI, Dir., *St. Mary, 256 Old Dutch Mill, P.O. Box M, Malaga, 08328-1796.* Tel: 609-694-2576.

Charismatic Movement—Rev. Msgr. JAMES P. MCINTYRE, Moderator For information contact FRANK IULA, M.D., P.D. Tel: 609-547-4875.

Cursillo—Rev. ALVERO DIAZ, Spiritual Dir. Spanish Cursillo, *St. Isidore, 1655 Magnolia Rd., Vineland, 08360-6536.* Tel: 609-692-8992.

Vicariate for Health Affairs—Rev. HARRY J. JORDON, Acting Vicar; Mr. MARTIN IDLER, Executive Dir.

Long Term Care Facilities—Miss FRANCES DEGORI, Dir., Finances.

Department of Housing—Mr. RUDOLPH G. WEISENBACH, JR., Dir.

St. Luke Catholic Medical Services—Rev. MARK C. AITA, S.J., M.D.

Guadalupe Family Services—

St. John's Prenatal Clinic—Ms. PATRICIA A. CHICO, L.P.N., Coord.

St. Mary Catholic Home—Sr. BEATRIX WIECZOREK, L.S.I.C., L.N.H.A., Admin.

The Manor at St. Mary's—Sr. FRANCIS M. SZYMANSKA, L.S.I.C., Admin.

Mater Dei Nursing Home—Sr. ANNE EBERSOLD, M.S.C., L.N.H.A., Admin.

Our Lady's Residence—Sr. M. AURELIA DAMIANI, H.S.M., L.N.H.A., Admin.

Bishop McCarthy Residence—Sr. LUCY MAROOR, H.S.M., Admin.

CLERGY, PARISHES, MISSIONS AND PAROCHIAL SCHOOLS

CITY OF CAMDEN
(Camden County)

1—IMMACULATE CONCEPTION CATHEDRAL (1864), Rev. Msgr. Charles J. Giglio; Rev. Thomas A. Harkins; Deacons William P. Iannuzzi; William L. Watts. In res., Rev. David J. Klein.
Res., 642 Market St., 08102. Tel: 609-964-1580; Fax: 609-757-0438. [CEM]

2—ST. ANTHONY OF PADUA (1945), Revs. Christopher Posch, O.F.M.; Paul Breslin, O.F.M.; Bro. Christoper Coccia, O.F.M., Admin.; Deacon Felix Miranda
Res., 2818 River Ave., 08105. Tel: 609-963-5884; Fax: 609-635-1286.
School—Tel: 609-966-6791; 966-1616; Fax: 609-966-1616. Mrs. Linda Meehan, Prin.
Sisters of the Third Franciscan Order, Minor Conventuals (Syracuse, NY) 3; Lay Teachers 8; Students 232.
Catechesis/Religious Programs—Students 187.

3—ST. BARTHOLOMEW'S (1940), Rev. Wayne Patrick Lavin.
Res., 751 Kaighns Ave., 08103. Tel: 609-365-0573; Fax: 609-963-3146.
School—St. Bartholomew Parkside School, 1725 Park Blvd., Tel: 609-963-3133; Fax: 609-963-3146. Joan Ciccone, Ph.D., Prin.
Sisters 3; Lay Teachers 7; Students 150.
Convent—Tel: 609-964-0603; Fax: 609-963-3146. Sr. Anna Cox, S.B.S.; Sr. Bernadette Stack, S.B.S.

4—HOLY NAME (1913), Revs. Frank T. Kaminski, S.J.; Donald Ward, S.J.; Sr. Linda Stilling, S.S.N.D., Pastoral Assoc. In res., Revs. Mark C. Aita, S.J., M.D.; Richard G. Malloy, S.J.; Mr. Daniel Joyce, S.J.
Res., 522 State St., 08102-1919. Tel: 609-963-1621; Fax: 609-338-0793.
School—Tel: 609-365-7930; Fax: 609-365-8041. Mrs. Patricia Munyan, Prin.
Sisters 3; Lay Teachers 8; Students 215.
Convent—517 State St., Tel: 609-964-1233. Sisters of St. Joseph (Chestnut Hill) School Sisters of Notre Dame (Baltimore), Tel: 609-488-3540.

5—ST. JOAN OF ARC (1920), Rev. William C. Pierce.
Res., 3107 Alabama Rd., 08104. Tel: 609-962-8642; Fax: 609-962-7123.
School—Tel: 609-962-7226. Miss Mary Beth Holahan, Prin.
Lay Teachers 10; Students 176.

6—ST. JOSEPH'S (1892) (Polish), Rev. Msgr. Edward H. Bucia; Rev. Jacek Stefanski. In res., Rev. Charles J. Becker, S.S., (Retired).
Res., 1010 Liberty St., 08104. Tel: 609-963-1285. [CEM]

7—ST. JOSEPH'S PRO-CATHEDRAL (1893), Rev. Msgr. Robert T. McDermott; Revs. Kenneth P. Hallahan; Joseph An Nguyen; Sr. Margaret Mary Schmiher, O.S.F., Pastoral Min.; Deacon Bienvenido Negron. In res., Rev. Andrew Martin.
Res., 2907 Federal St., 08105. Tel: 609-964-2776; Fax: 609-964-0044.
School—Tel: 609-964-4336. Mrs. Kathleen Shiflet, Prin.
Lay Teachers 10; Students 260.
Nursery School—17 Church St., 08105. Tel: 609-963-0452.
Sisters 2; Children 46. Franciscan Sisters of the Infant Jesus. Sr. Maria DeRosia, F.M.I.J., Supr.

8—OUR LADY OF FATIMA AND MOUNT CARMEL (1953), Revs. Salvatore A. Scuderi, M.SS.CC.; Bruce Bumbarger, M.SS.CC.; Deacon Miguel Rivera; Bro. David Graber, M.SS.CC.
Res., 832 S. 4th St., 08103. Tel: 609-541-7618; Fax: 609-541-2835.

9—SACRED HEART (1885), Revs. Michael Doyle; Charles G. Gonzalez, S.J. In res., Rev. Arthur T. Anderson.
Res., 1739 Ferry Ave., 08104. Tel: 609-966-6700; Fax: 609-756-0102.
School—Fourth & Jaspers Sts., 08104. Tel: 609-963-1341. Mrs. Janet Williams, Prin.
Sisters 1; Lay Teachers 11; Students 253. Records for St. George kept at Sacred Heart, Camden. Records for Sts. Peter and Paul kept at the Cathedral of the Immaculate Conception, Camden. Records for St. John the Baptist kept at St. Joseph Pro-Cathedral, Camden.

OUTSIDE THE CITY OF CAMDEN

Absecon, Atlantic Co., St. Elizabeth Ann Seton (1975), Rev. Msgr. Michael J. Coyne; Rev. Thomas S. Donio; Deacon Joseph Becker.
Res., 591 New Jersey Ave., 08201. Tel: 609-641-1480; Fax: 609-641-7396.
School—Assumption Regional School, Pomona. See separate listing. Tel: 609-652-7134; Fax: 609-965-4149.
Catechesis/Religious Programs—Students 634.

Atco, Camden Co., Assumption (1947), Revs. Howard E. Muhlbaier; Michael Coffey; Deacons Charles McAleer; Charles Smith.
Parish Office: 318 Carl Hasselhan Dr., 08004. Tel: 609-767-0719; Fax: 609-753-7917.
Res., 2131 Cooper Rd., 08004. Tel: 609-767-0848; Fax: 609-753-7917.
School—Tel: 609-767-0569; Fax: 609-753-7917. Mrs. Paula Angiletta, Prin., Tel: 609-767-0569.
Lay Teachers 8; Students 227.
Catechesis/Religious Programs—Tel: 609-767-3414.
Students 537.

Atlantic City, Atlantic Co.,

1—HOLY SPIRIT, (1908), Revs. Eldridge T. Evans; Felipe Moyano (Argentina); Deacon Angel Vega.
Res., 626 Oriental Ave., 08401. Tel: 609-344-6533; Fax: 609-344-2099.

2—ST. MICHAEL'S, (1904) (Italian), Rev. Michael H. D'Amico; Deacon Raymond Ferrario.
Res., 10 N. Mississippi Ave., 08401. Tel: 609-344-8536.

3—ST. MONICA'S, (1925), Rev. J. Overton Jones.
Res., 108 N. Pennsylvania Ave., 08401. Tel: 609-345-1786.

4—ST. NICHOLAS OF TOLENTINE, (1855), Rev. William A. Hodge, Admin. In res., Rev. Donal J. Sheahan, Chap.
Res., 1409 Pacific Ave., 08401. Tel: 609-344-1040;

Fax: 609-344-2471.
5—OUR LADY STAR OF THE SEA, (1894), Revs. Patrick J. Brady; Paul C. Wise; Joseph An Nguyen; Deacons Agatino Garufi; James Tully.
Res., 2651 Atlantic Ave., 08401. Tel: 609-345-1878; Fax: 609-348-0248.
School—Tel: 609-345-0648. Sr. Mary Shamus, R.S.M., Prin. & Supr.
Sisters 7; Lay Teachers 9; Students 336.
Convent—15 N. California Ave., Tel: 609-347-0434. Sisters of Mercy

Audubon, Camden Co., Church of the Holy Maternity (1957), Revs. Michael J. McGilley; Edward J. Lipinski.
Res., 431 W. Nicholson Rd., 08106. Tel: 609-547-0444; Fax: 609-547-0045.
School—Sacred Heart Regional School, Mount Ephraim. See separate listing.

Avalon, Cape May Co., Maris Stella (1961), Rev. Msgr. Patrick M. Tierney.
Res., 5012 Dune Dr., 08202. Tel: 609-967-3746.
School—St. Joseph Regional School, Sea Isle City. See separate listing. Tel: 609-263-4296.

Barrington, Camden Co., St. Francis de Sales (1955), Rev. Francis J. Gramigna; Deacon Michael Harkins. In res., Rev. Msgr. William F. Poyatt; Rev. Robert E. Hughes.
Res., 199 Willmont Ave., 08007. Tel: 609-547-2313; Fax: 609-547-8225.
School—St. Francis de Sales Regional School. See separate listing. Tel: 609-547-7958.
Catechesis/Religious Programs—Students 182.
Convent—424 Browning Rd., Bellmawr, 08031. Tel: 609-931-8973.

Bellmawr, Camden Co., Annunciation (1951), Rev. William F. Ryan. In res., Rev. Edward Lipinski.
Res., 601 W. Browning Rd., 08031. Tel: 609-931-6307; Fax: 609-931-0155.
School—Tel: 609-931-0122; Fax: 609-931-4390. Sr. Marie St. James, I.H.M., Prin.
Sisters 3; Lay Teachers 11; Students 350.
Convent—603 W. Browning Rd., Tel: 609-931-7192. Sisters Servants of Immaculate Heart of Mary

Mary, Mother of the Church (1965), Rev. Francis P. Gaffney. In res., Rev. John J. Byrnes; Deacon Ron Olesienicz.
Res., 20 Braisington Ave., 08031. Tel: 609-931-0204.
School—St. Francis de Sales Regional, Barrington. See separate listing. Tel: 609-547-7958.

Berlin, Camden Co., Our Lady of Mt. Carmel (1903), Revs. John F. Bourke; Edward M. Friel; Deacons Joseph Beebe; Richard F. McCarthy.
Res., 178 W. White Horse Pike, 08009. Tel: 609-767-2563; Fax: 609-767-8791. [CEM]
School—Our Lady of Mt. Carmel Regional School. See separate listing. Tel: 609-767-1751; Fax: 609-767-1293.
Catechesis/Religious Programs—Tel: 609-767-1537; Fax: 609-767-3304.
Students 505.

Blackwood, Camden Co., St. Agnes (1946), Rev. Msgr. Joseph V. DiMauro; Revs. John E. Bruni; Cornelius F. Lambert; Deacons Henry S. Custodio; Phillip Giordano; John Werner. In res., Rev. Msgr. John R. Lubicky, (Retired).
Res., 701 Little Gloucester Rd., 08012. Tel: 609-228-4331; Fax: 609-227-0743.
School—St. Agnes Regional School, Blackwood. See separate listing. Tel: 609-228-7076; Fax: 609-228-7527.
Catechesis/Religious Programs—200 Coles Rd., 08012. Tel: 609-227-0555; Fax: 609-228-4920.
Students 983.

St. Jude's (1961), Rev. Msgr. Thomas J. McIntyre; Rev. Carmel F. Polidano; Deacons William J. Drum; Michael McDonaugh.
Res., 402 S. Black Horse Pike, 08012. Tel: 609-227-0572; Fax: 609-227-1276.
School—St. Jude Regional School, Blackwood. See separate listing. Tel: 609-227-4442.
Catechesis/Religious Programs—Students 475.

Blue Anchor, Camden Co., St. Lucy's (1925), Rev. Robert J. Gregorio. In res., Rev. Albert E. Harshaw.
Res., 250 S. Rte. 73, 08037. Tel: 609-561-6116; Fax: 609-561-9305.
School—St. Joseph Regional School, Hammonton. See separate listing.
Mission—Cedar Brook, Camden Co., Sacred Heart, (1904).

Bridgeton, Cumberland Co., Immaculate Conception (1874), Revs. James P. Rush; Thomas J. Barcellona; Deacons C. J. Achee; Carmen Bischer. In res., Revs. John P. Connor; Robert P. Weber.
Res., 312 N. Pearl St., 08302. Tel: 609-451-0254; Fax: 609-451-7842. [CEM]
School—Immaculate Conception Regional School, Bridgeton. See separate listing. Tel: 609-451-2134.

St. Teresa of Avila, Cumberland, (1961), Rev. Msgr. Stanley E. Kloskowski. In res., Rev. Daniel A. DiNardo.
Res., 46 Central Ave., 08302. Tel: 609-455-2323; Fax: 609-455-7291.
School—Immaculate Conception Regional School, Bridgeton. See separate listing.

Brigantine, Atlantic Co., St. Thomas (1958), Rev. Msgr. Lawrence P. Boyle; Rev. Bernard J. Gannon. In res., Rev. Joseph A. Perreault.
Res., 331 8th St., S., 08203. Tel: 609-266-2123; Fax: 609-266-6416.
School—Tel: 609-266-3154. Sr. M. Annunziata, D.M., Prin.
Sisters 1; Lay Teachers 9; Students 156.
Convent—42nd and Brigantine Ave., Tel: 609-266-3507. St. Philip the Apostle Daughters of Our Lady of Mercy

Brooklawn, Camden Co., St. Maurice's (1955), Rev. Thomas E. Ploude.
Res., 401 Community Rd., 08030. Tel: 609-456-9039.

Cape May, Cape May Co., Our Lady Star of the Sea (1878), Rev. Msgr. Timothy A. Ryan; Rev. Edward W. Garay.
Res., 525 Washington St., 08204. Tel: 609-884-5311; Fax: 609-884-0162. [CEM]
School—Our Lady Star of the Sea Regional School, Cape May. See separate listing. Tel: 609-884-4437; Fax: 609-884-4437.
Chapel—Cape May Point, St. Agnes.

Cape May Court House, Cape May Co., Our Lady of the Angels (1956), Rev. Msgr. Donald D. Velozo. In res., Rev. Max S. Fasciglione.
Res., 106 Mechanic St., P.O. Box 324, 08210. Tel: 609-465-5245.
School—Our Lady Star of the Sea Regional School, Cape May. See separate listing.

Carneys Point, Salem Co., Corpus Christi (1966), Rev. Msgr. Rocco A. Continillo, V.F.
Res., 369 Georgetown Rd., 08069. Tel: 609-299-3833.
School—St. James Regional School, Penns Grove. See separate listing. Tel: 609-299-0397.
Catechesis/Religious Programs—Students 158.

Cedarville, Cumberland Co., St. Michael's (1942), Rev. William James Bleiler.
Res., 367 Main St., P.O. Box 327, 08311. Tel: 609-447-3480.
School—Immaculate Conception Regional School, Bridgeton. See separate listing.
Mission—Port Norris, St. Anthony.
Stations—NJ State Medium Security Prison, Bayside Prison, Tel: 609-785-0040; Laurel Lake, Our Lady of the Lake Chapel; Delmont, Southern State Correctional Facility.

Cherry Hill, Camden Co.,
1—ST. MARY'S, (1961), Revs. John C. Killeen; David A. Grover.
Res., 2001 Springdale Rd., 08003. Tel: 609-424-1454; Fax: 609-424-8270.
School—Holy Rosary Regional School, Cherry Hill. See separate listing.
Catechesis/Religious Programs—Tel: 609-424-2679.
Students 475.
2—HOLY ROSARY, Rev. Michael M. Signiski; Deacon Raymond Radziak. In res., Rev. Msgr. Leonard G. Scott.
Res., 99 Burnt Mill Rd., 08003. Tel: 609-428-2382 (Res.); 609-428-9456 (Office); Fax: 609-428-9152.
School—Tel: 609-428-4855. Mrs. Patricia Connell, Prin.
Lay Teachers 9; Students 170.
Catechesis/Religious Programs—Mrs. Anita D'Imperio, D.R.E.
Students 220.
Convent—Tel: 609-429-1364. Sisters of Saint Joseph
3—ST. PETER CELESTINE, (1961), Rev. Msgr. James R. Tracy; Revs. Michael J. Field; Donald F. Trinkle; William Iannuzzi; Deacons W. Leo McBlain; William Watts.
Res., 402 N. Kings Hwy., 08034. Tel: 609-667-2440; Fax: 609-482-0332.
School—Tel: 609-667-3034; Fax: 609-667-9160. Mrs. Camille Forrest, Prin.
Sisters of St. Joseph (Chestnut Hill, PA) 2; Lay Teachers 23; Students 346; Special Educ. Students 24.
Catechesis/Religious Programs—Tel: 609-667-4250.
Students 486.
4—ST. PIUS X, (1961), Revs. William P. Brennan; Timothy E. Byerley; Deacon Peter J. Powell.
Res., 344 Kresson Rd., 08034. Tel: 609-429-1330; Fax: 609-429-8679.
School—Christ the King Regional School, Haddonfield. See separate listing.
5—ST. THOMAS MORE, (1968), Rev. Msgr. David F. Budney; Rev. Patsy C. Amabile. In res., Rev. William C. Hart.
Res., 1439 Springdale Rd., 08003. Tel: 609-424-3212; Fax: 609-424-2411, Ext. 51.
School—Holy Rosary Regional School, Cherry Hill. See separate listing.
Catechesis/Religious Programs—Students 286.
6—QUEEN OF HEAVEN, (1955), Rev. Msgr. Edward D. Alleyne; Rev. Carlton C. Stoegbauer; Deacons Charles C. Reiss; James H. Rocks. In res., Rev. Thomas H. Jarka.
Res., 700 W. Marlton Pike, 08002. Tel: 609-429-3334; Fax: 609-795-3318.
School—Tel: 609-428-2890; Fax: 609-428-4640. Sr. Marita Regina, I.H.M., Prin.
Sisters 4; Lay Teachers 8; Students 247.
Catechesis/Religious Programs—Students 245.
Convent—Queen of Heaven Convent, 10 Massachusetts Ave., 08002. Tel: 609-428-8818.

Clayton, Gloucester Co., St. Catherine's (1943), Rev. James F. Barry; Deacon Matthew J. Hanrahan. In res., Rev. Cadmus D. Mazzarella.
Res., 49 W. North St., 08312. Tel: 609-881-9155; Fax: 609-881-9166.
Preschool—(Children ages 2 1/2-5). Tel: 609-881-8707. Mrs. Lynne Holscher, Dir.
Students 18.
School—51 W. North St., 08312. Tel: 609-881-0067. Miss Janice Bruni, Prin.
Lay Teachers 9; Students 220.

Collings Lakes, Atlantic Co., Our Lady of the Lakes (1976), Rev. Marjan L. Bober; Deacon Edward Freed.
Res., 19 Malaga Rd., 08094. Tel: 609-561-8313.
School—Notre Dame Regional School, Landisville. See separate listing.

Collingswood, Camden Co., St. John's (1903), Rev. Msgr. Martin J. Mannion; Rev. John C. Muscat; Deacon Frank P. Gargin. In res., Rev. Robert C. Pasley.
Res., 809 Park Ave., 08108. Tel: 609-858-0298.
School—Tel: 609-858-1562. Miss Joan Simpson, Prin.
Lay Teachers 15; Students 237.
Catechesis/Religious Programs—Students 297.

Delair, Camden Co., St. Veronica's (1961), Rev. James T. McCall.
Res., 8329 Holman Ave., 08110. Tel: 609-662-8050.

Deptford, Gloucester Co., St. John Vianney, Rev. Msgr. James J. Rynne. In res., Rev. Kenneth J. Johnston.
Res., 2901 Good Intent Rd., 08096. Tel: 609-227-2623; Fax: 609-228-1823.
School—St. Agnes Regional School, Blackwood. See separate listing.
Catechesis/Religious Programs—Students 203.

Egg Harbor City, Atlantic Co., St. Nicholas (1864), Revs. Calogero N. LaVerde; Ivan Callone, I.M.C.; Deacon Michael H. Guerrieri.
Res., 525 St. Louis Ave., 08215-2224. Tel: 609-965-0350; Fax: 609-804-1313.
School—526 Chicago Ave., Tel: 609-965-2398; Fax: 609-804-1658. Sr. Kathleen Kelly, O.S.F., Prin.
Sisters 1; Lay Teachers 10; Students 150.
Catechesis/Religious Programs—Tel: 609-965-0720.
Students 210.
Convent—526 St. Louis Ave., 08215. Tel: 609-965-0890.

Elmer, Salem Co., St. Ann's (1961), Rev. Anthony L. Minniti; Deacons Edward J. Harkins; Robert Fanelli.
Res., 115 Broad St., 08318. Tel: 609-358-3106.
School—St. Rose Regional School, Newfield. See separate listing.

Franklinville, Gloucester Co., Nativity (1961), Rev. William F. Collins.
Res., P.O. Box 249, 08322. Tel: 609-694-2349; Fax: 609-694-4131.
School—St. Rose Regional School, Newfield. See separate listing.

Gibbsboro, Camden Co., St. Andrew the Apostle (1963), Rev. Msgr. Ciaran P. O'Mearain; Rev. Gerald C. Marable; Deacon Thomas B. Henkel.
Res., 120 United States Ave., 08026. Tel: 609-784-3878; Fax: 609-435-7508.
School—Our Lady of Mt. Carmel Regional School, Berlin. See separate listing.
Catechesis/Religious Programs—Tel: 609-783-0550; Fax: 609-783-7935.
Students 982.

Gibbstown, Gloucester Co., St. Michael's (1940), Rev. Msgr. Eugene J. Fitzsimmons; Rev. Victor J. Jurkowski, O.F.M.Cap.; Deacons James Kiley; Robert Willson.
Res., 313 Memorial Ave., 08027. Tel: 609-423-0007; Fax: 609-423-1445.
Catechesis/Religious Programs—Students 312.

Glassboro, Gloucester Co., St. Bridget's (1887), Revs. Robert V. Smith; Alfred S. Aversa; Deacon Joseph W. Loungo.

Res., 125 Church St., 08028. Tel: 609-881-2753; Fax: 609-881-9697. [CEM]
School—St. Bridget's Regional School, Glassboro. See separate listing. Tel: 609-881-2578; Fax: 609-881-8771.
Catechesis/Religious Programs—Students 269.

Our Lady of Lourdes (1966), Revs. James P. Curran; John D. Bohrer. In res., Rev. Msgr. James J. Gaffney, (Retired).
Res., 500 Greentree Rd., 08028. Tel: 609-881-0909; Fax: 609-881-5457.
School—St. Bridget Regional School, Glassboro. See separate listing.

Gloucester, Camden Co., St. Mary's (1848), Revs. Harry J. Jordan; George C. Seiter; Deacon Frank Crosson. In res., Revs. Brian E. O'Neill; Timothy L. Hubbs.
Res., 426 Monmouth St., 08030. Tel: 609-456-0052; Fax: 609-456-1837. [CEM]
School—Tel: 609-456-0913; Fax: 609-456-7382. Sr. Nora Foley, O.P., Prin.
Dominican Sisters of Hope 2; Lay Teachers 14; Students 376.
Catechesis/Religious Programs—Students 240.

Haddonfield, Camden Co., Christ the King Regional School (1927), Rev. Msgr. Thomas J. Morgan; Rev. Daniel Rocco; Deacon Thomas Hafner. In res., Rev. Paul D. Harte.
Res., 200 Windsor Ave., 08033. Tel: 609-429-1600; Fax: 609-429-2734.
School—Christ the King Regional School, Haddonfield. See separate listing. Tel: 609-429-2084.
Catechesis/Religious Programs—Tel: 609-354-5030.
Students 400.
Convent—168 Hopkins Ave., 08033. Tel: 609-429-3988. Sr. Mary Therese Maher, O.S.F., Local Min.

Haddon Heights, Camden Co., St. Rose's (1896), Rev. Msgr. Richard J. Callahan; Revs. Krzysztof Wtorek; James M. Maggart; Deacon Frank A. Iula, M.D. In res., Rev. Alfred J. Hewett.
Res., 300 Kings Hwy, 08035-1397. Tel: 609-547-0564; Fax: 609-547-7311.
School—Tel: 609-546-6166. Mrs. Kathryn Lange, Prin.
Sisters of St. Dominic (Newburgh, NY) 1; Lay Teachers 16; Students 407.
Catechesis/Religious Programs—Students 522.

Haddon Township, Camden Co., St. Vincent Pallotti (1963), Rev. Msgr. Salvatore J. Adamo; Rev. Msgr. John H. Casey. In res., Rev. Russell L. Rock.
Res., 901 Hopkins Rd., Haddonfield, 08033. Tel: 609-858-1313; 1314; Fax: 609-869-9010.

Hammonton, Atlantic Co., St. Anthony of Padua (1965), Rev. Joseph H. Burns; Deacon Rocco A. Mangino. In res., Rev. John M. Fleming.
Res., P.O. Box 1087, 285 Rte. 206, 08037. Tel: 609-561-3313; Fax: 609-567-7764.
School—St. Joseph Regional School, Hammonton. See separate listing.

St. Joseph's (1886), Revs. Louis Micca, S.A.C.; Michael Parente, S.A.C.; Deacon Ismael Perez Tavarez.
Res., 226 French St., 08037. Tel: 609-561-0180; Fax: 609-561-6808. [CEM]
School—St. Joseph Regional School, Hammonton. See separate listing.

St. Martin de Porres (1962), Rev. John A. DelDuca. In res., Rev. Joseph R. Ferrara; Rev. Msgr. Pasquale M. DiBuono, (Retired).
Res., 129 Park Ave., 08037. Tel: 609-561-4322; Fax: 609-501-4433.
School—St. Joseph Regional School, Hammonton. See separate listing. Tel: 609-561-0689.
Catechesis/Religious Programs—Students 300.

Landisville, Atlantic Co., Our Lady of Victories (1952), Revs. Ernest R. Soprano; Ireneo Lopez-Tovar; Deacon Joseph Perella.
Res., 202 North Blvd., 08326. Tel: 609-697-1450; Fax: 609-697-3874. [CEM]
School—Notre Dame Regional School, Landisville. See separate listing. Tel: 609-697-3456.

Lindenwold, Camden Co., St. Lawrence's (1896), Revs. William P. Graham; Paul A. Olszewski. In res., Rev. Zbigniew J. Jezierski.
Res., 100 South Ave., 08021. Tel: 609-627-2222; 627-7522.
School—Tel: 609-783-0710. Mrs. Patricia Ceralli, Prin.
Lay Teachers 13; Students 240.
Catechesis/Religious Programs—Tel: 609-346-0902.
Students 305.

Linwood, Atlantic Co., Our Lady of Sorrows (1965), Revs. Malcolm C. McLeod, M.SS.CC.; John Perdue, M.SS.CC.
Res., 200 Wilson Ave., 08221. Tel: 609-927-1154.
Catechesis/Religious Programs—Tel: 609-927-0121.
Students 550.

Longport, Atlantic Co., Epiphany (1954), Rev. Msgr. Joseph P. Herron.
Res., 2801 Ventnor Ave., 08403. Tel: 609-822-8940.
School—Blessed Sacrament Regional School, Margate. See separate listing.

Magnolia, Camden Co., St. Gregory's (1955), Rev. Msgr. Edward L. Korda; Rev. A. Robert Cairone; Deacon Leonard P. Carlucci.
Res., Evesham Ave., 08049. Tel: 609-784-4090; Fax: 609-784-6371.
School—Our Lady of Grace Regional School, Somerdale. See separate listing.
Convent—230 E. Evesham Ave., 08049. Tel: 609-784-1576. Sr. Victoria Masterpaul, O.S.F., Local Min.

Malaga, Gloucester Co., St. Mary's (1961), Rev. Jerome C. Romanowski.
Res., Dutch Mill Rd., P.O. Box M, 08328. Tel: 609-694-2576.
School—Notre Dame Regional School, Newfield. See separate listing.

Mantua, Gloucester Co., Incarnation (1956), Revs. Joseph A. Salerno; Thomas A. Newton; Deacon Thomas F. O'Brien.
Res., 234 Shadow Pl., P.O. Box 295, 08051. Tel: 609-468-1314; Fax: 609-468-4886.
School—School St. Margaret Regional School, Woodbury Heights. See separate listing. Tel: 609-845-5200.
Catechesis/Religious Programs—Tel: 609-468-7566.
Students 700.

Margate, Atlantic Co., Blessed Sacrament (1945), Revs. Lewis A. Battisti; Robert F. Walker.
Res., 11 N. Kenyon Ave., 08402. Tel: 609-822-7105; Fax: 609-822-3817.
School—Blessed Sacrament Regional School, Margate. See separate listing. Tel: 609-822-9243.
Convent—14 N. Jerome Ave., 08402. Tel: 609-822-5543. Sr. Kathryn Rush, O.S.F., Local Supr.

Marmora, Cape May Co., The Church of the Resurrection (1975), Revs. Mark R. Cavagnaro; Joseph M. Reilly.
Res., 200 W. Tuckahoe Rd., 08223. Tel: 609-390-0664; Fax: 609-390-7700.
School—St. Augustine Regional School, Ocean City. See separate listing.

Mays Landing, Atlantic Co., St. Vincent de Paul (1906), Revs. John F. Sugrue; Edward J. Maher; Deacon Richard Wigglesworth.
Res., 114 Rte. 50, 08330. Tel: 609-625-2124. [CEM]
School—Tel: 609-625-1565; Fax: 609-625-4703. Miss Linda Pirolli, Prin.
Sisters 1; Lay Teachers 8; Students 226.
Catechesis/Religious Programs—5809 Main St., 08330. Tel: 609-625-1567.
Students 410.
Convent—5807 Main St., 08330. Tel: 609-625-1566. Sisters of St. Joseph of Chestnut Hill Sr. Marie Fenton, S.S.J., Local Coord.
Mission—Dorothy, Atlantic Co., St. Bernard. [CEM]

Merchantville, Camden Co., St. Peter's (1903), Rev. Msgr. Charles P. Barth; Revs. Glenn R. Hartman; Pawel Kryszkiewicz; Deacons Peter J. Gilmartin; Ray Ellis. In res., Rev. Joseph T. Szolack.
Res., 43 W. Maple Ave., 08109. Tel: 609-663-1373; Fax: 609-488-0647.
School—Tel: 609-665-5789; Fax: 609-665-4943. Sr. Alice Ivanyo, M.P.F., Prin.
Lay Teachers 17; Students 489.
Catechesis/Religious Programs—Sheila O'Boyle, D.R.E.
Students 456.

Millville, Cumberland Co., St. Mary Magdalen's (1864), Revs. Anthony J. Manuppella; David V. Minniti.
Res., 621 Dock St., 08332. Tel: 609-825-0021; Fax: 609-825-0073. [CEM]
School—7 W. Powell St., 08332. Tel: 609-825-3600. Armida of the Holy Eucharist M.D.P.V.M., Prin.
Sisters 8; Lay Teachers 9; Students 330.
Convent—3 W. Powell St., 08332. Tel: 609-327-2235. Missionary Daughters of the Holy Eucharist Mother Armida of the Holy Eucharist M.D.P.V.M., Supr.

St. John Bosco (1966), In res., Rev. Francis X. Hudson.
Res., 2 Hillcrest Ave., 08332. Tel: 609-825-1513; Fax: 609-327-7752.
Catechesis/Religious Programs—Students 182.

Minotola, Atlantic Co., St. Michael's (1902), Rev. Donald C. Chiavello.
Res., 504 S. West Ave., 08341-0587. Tel: 609-697-0942.
School—Notre Dame Regional School, Newfield. See separate listing. Tel: 609-697-0155; Fax: 609-697-8540.

Mount Ephraim, Camden Co., Sacred Heart (1939), Revs. Robert J. Dunphy; James O. Dabrowski; Deacon William Norquist.
Res., 11 N. Black Horse Pike, 08059. Tel: 609-931-1441; Fax: 609-931-9433.
School—Sacred Heart Regional School, Mount Ephraim. See separate listing.

Mullica Hill, Gloucester Co., Holy Name of Jesus (1901), Rev. Michael P. Rush; Deacon Sam Nastasi. In res., Rev. Peter M. Saporito.
Res., 17 Earlington Ave., 08062. Tel: 609-478-2294. [CEM]
Catechesis/Religious Programs—Tel: 609-478-9694.
Students 800.

National Park, Gloucester Co., St. Matthew's (1915), Rev. Edward F. Sobolewski; Deacon William J. Rumaker.
Res., 214 Columbia Blvd., 08063. Tel: 609-845-2523; Fax: 609-251-0822.
School—St. Matthew Regional School. See separate listing. Verga, 08093. Tel: 609-845-7203; Fax: 609-853-7711.
Catechesis/Religious Programs—Students 380.
Convent—Hessian Ave., Verga, 08093. Tel: 609-845-7204.

Newfield, Gloucester Co., St. Rose of Lima (1922), Rev. John Joseph Tumosa. In res., Rev. Edward A. Igle.
Res., 104 Catawba Ave., 08344. Tel: 609-697-3232; Fax: 609-697-1455.
School—Notre Dame Regional School, Newfield. See separate listing. Tel: 609-697-0155.

North Cape May, Cape May Co., St. John of God (1966), Revs. Richard L. Forbes, Admin.; Jaromir Michalak.
Res., 680 Town Bank Rd., 08204. Tel: 609-884-1656.
School—St. Raymond Regional School, Villas. See separate listing.

Northfield, Atlantic Co., St. Bernadette (1966), Rev. Msgr. Donald D. Velozo; Rev. Perry A. Cherubini.
Res., 1421 New Rd., 08225. Tel: 609-646-3499; 646-5611; Fax: 609-484-8345.
School—Blessed Sacrament Regional School, Margate. See separate listing.
Catechesis/Religious Programs—Students 409.

Oaklyn, Camden Co., St. Aloysius (1935), Rev. Msgr. Thomas M. Flynn. In res., Rev. Douglas R. Tobin.
Res., 37 W. Haddon Ave., 08107. Tel: 609-858-2848; 854-2352.
School—St. John Regional School, Collingswood. See separate listing.

Ocean City, Cape May Co., St. Augustine's (1894), Rev. Msgr. Edward F. Mullen; Rev. William S. Vandegrift. In res., Rev. Edward D. Lyons.
Res., 1310 Ocean Ave., 08226. Tel: 609-399-0648; Fax: 609-399-0063.
School—St. Augustine Regional School, Ocean City. See separate listing.

St. Frances Cabrini (1966), Rev. Msgr. Patrick A. McCabe.
Res., 114 Atlantic Ave., 08226. Tel: 609-399-4776; Fax: 609-391-9412.
School—St. Augustine Regional School, Ocean City. See separate listing.
Catechesis/Religious Programs—Students 150.

Our Lady of Good Counsel (1961), Rev. Msgr. Andrew Duignan; Deacon James J. Teeney.
Res., 3948 Central Ave., 08226. Tel: 609-399-2085; 398-3654 (Office).
School—St. Augustine Regional School, Ocean City. See separate listing. Tel: 609-399-1435; Fax: 609-399-8675.

Paulsboro, Gloucester Co., St. John's (1904), Rev. William J. Fallon.
Res., 647 Beacon Ave., 08066. Tel: 609-423-0086; Fax: 609-423-0123.
School—712 Mantua Ave., 08066. Tel: 609-423-0099.
Lay Teachers 8; Students 102.
Convent—700 Seventh St., 08066. Tel: 609-423-0723. Sr. Ann Byrnes, R.S.M., Supr.

Pennsauken, Camden Co., St. Cecilia's (1939), Revs. Fred Voltaggio; Anthony DiBardino; Deacon D. Eugene Burns. In res., Rev. James R. Ryan.
Res., 4824 Camden Ave., 08110. Tel: 609-662-2721; Fax: 609-486-2089.
School—Tel: 609-662-0149. Miss Patricia Flannery, Prin.
Lay Teachers 9; Students 185.
Catechesis/Religious Programs—49th & Camden Ave., 08110. Tel: 609-661-9489.
Students 210.

St. Stephen (1961), Rev. Msgr. Joseph C. Downing; Rev. Antoine F. St. Germain; Sr. Barbara Beck, O.S.F.
Res., 6306 Browning Rd., 08109. Tel: 609-662-9338; Fax: 609-662-9339.
School—Tel: 609-662-5935; Fax: 609-662-6128. Sr. Kathleen M. Boyle, S.S.J., Prin.
Sisters of St. Joseph 1; Lay Teachers 12; Students 172.
Catechesis/Religious Programs—Students 189.

Penns Grove, Salem Co., St. James (1901), Rev.

William S. Vandegrift; Deacon Joseph A. Ganci.
Res., 114 State St., 08069. Tel: 609-299-0399; Fax: 609-299-3728.
School—St. James Regional School, Penns Grove. See separate listing. Tel: 609-299-0397.

Pennsville, Salem Co., Queen of the Apostles (1955), Rev. William F. Moore; Deacon Jack Cromer. In res., Rev. Peter J. Osinski.
Res., 391 S. Broadway, 08070. Tel: 609-678-5400; Fax: 609-678-4153.
School—St. Mary Regional School, Salem. See separate listing. Tel: 609-784-4853.
Catechesis/Religious Programs—Students 199.

Pine Hill, Camden Co., St. Edward's (1953), Revs. John P. Ward; Dennis W. Bajkowski.
Res., 500 Erial Rd., 08021. Tel: 609-783-2670; Fax: 609-627-9373.
School—Sr. Bridget Gedji, S.O.L.M., Prin. & Supr. Sisters of Mercy (Rome) 3; Lay Teachers 10; Students 185.
Catechesis/Religious Programs—Tel: 609-783-0293.
Students 600.

Pitman, Gloucester Co., Our Lady Queen of Peace (1949), Rev. Msgr. John F. Cooke.
Res., 161 Pitman Ave., 08071. Tel: 609-589-5673; Fax: 609-589-0102.
School—St. Bridget Regional School, Glassboro. See separate listing.

Pleasantville, Atlantic Co., St. Peter's (1896), Revs. Ronald S. Falotico; Michael Kim; Laserian I. Nwoga. In res., Rev. C. Jeffries Burton, S.J.
Res., 25 W. Verona Ave., 08232. Tel: 609-641-0285; Fax: 609-641-0385.
School—Tel: 609-646-3057. Miss Patricia Ellis, Prin.
Lay Teachers 9; Students 212.

Pomona, Atlantic Co., Assumption (1938), Revs. Joseph P. Rush; Daniel M. Sherman. In res., Rev. Peter F. Finnerty.
Res., 276 W. White Horse Pike, 08240. Tel: 609-965-4021; Fax: 609-965-4149.
School—Assumption Regional School, Pomona. See separate listing.

Rosenhayn, Cumberland Co., St. Mary's, Rev. Joseph A. Salerno. In res., Rev. Sebastian V. Annino.
Res., Morton Ave., P.O. Box 376, 08352-0376. Tel: 609-451-8763. [CEM]
School—Immaculate Conception Regional School, Bridgeton. See separate listing.

Runnemede, Camden Co., St. Maria Goretti (1965), Rev. Msgr. James P. McIntyre; Rev. Joseph J. Adamson.
Res., 321 Orchard Ave., 08078. Tel: 609-933-0037; Fax: 609-933-0036.
School—St. Teresa Regional School, Runnemede. See separate listing.
Catechesis/Religious Programs—Students 187.

St. Teresa of the Infant Jesus (1929), Rev. Msgr. Joseph W. Pokusa, J.C.D.; Rev. John J. Vignone; Deacons A. Kenneth Bandiera; Louis Curcio.
Res., 13 E. Evesham Rd., 08078. Tel: 609-939-1681.
School—St. Teresa Regional School, Runnemede. See separate listing. Tel: 609-939-0333; Fax: 609-939-1204.
Catechesis/Religious Programs—Tel: 609-939-0592.
Students 331.

Salem, Salem Co., St. Mary's (1864), Revs. Richard J. Hadyka; Joseph F. Ganiel.
Res., 25 Oak St., 08079. Tel: 609-935-0288. [CEM]
School—St. Mary Regional School, Salem. See separate listing. Tel: 609-935-0660; Fax: 609-935-7610.

Sea Isle City, Cape May Co., St. Joseph's (1884), Revs. Stephen Carey; John A. Cavagnaro; Deacons Liam C. O'Clisham; Norbert Klimaszewski.
Res., 4308 Landis Ave., 08243. Tel: 609-263-8696.
School—St. Joseph Regional School, Sea Isle City. See separate listing. Tel: 609-263-4296.
Catechesis/Religious Programs—Tel: 609-263-2087.
Students 275.

Sicklerville, Camden Co., St. John Neumann (1977), Revs. Edward B. Rosinski; Brendan J. Meaney; Deacons John Schiavo; Anthony Kijonka.
Res., 234 Sicklerville Rd., Box G, 08081-0438. Tel: 609-728-1060.
Catechesis/Religious Programs—Students 383.

Somerdale, Camden Co., Our Lady of Grace (1954), Rev. Msgr. Dominic J. Bottino; Revs. Michael Heggarty; Henry McBride; Deacon Frank Pepe. In res., Rev. Msgr. J. Francis Flaherty, P.A.
Res., 35 N. White Horse Pike, 08083. Tel: 609-783-2256; Fax: 609-435-1722.
School—Our Lady of Grace Regional School, Somerdale. See separate listing. Tel: 609-784-0372.
Catechesis/Religious Programs—Tel: 609-627-3036.
Students 375.

Somers Point, Atlantic Co., St. Joseph's (1946), Revs. Josef A. Wagenhoffer; Joseph A. Newell, S.J.; Deacons Jerome Wilson; John L. Glasser. In res., Rev. Robert T. Matysik.
Res., 606 Shore Rd., 08244. Tel: 609-927-3568; Fax: 609-653-8707.
School—St. Joseph Regional School. Regionalized with Our Lady of Sorrows Parish, Linwood. Tel: 609-927-2228. Sr. Gloria Schaab, Prin.
Sisters 3; Lay Teachers 11; Students 280.
Catechesis/Religious Programs—Tel: 609-927-3302.
Students 660.
Convent—580 Shore Rd., 08244. Tel: 609-926-9127. Sisters of St. Joseph

Stone Harbor, Cape May Co., St. Paul's (1911), Rev. Eugene J. Kernan.
Res., 9910 Third Ave., 08247. Tel: 609-368-3091; Fax: 609-368-2775.
School—St. Joseph Regional School, Sea Isle City. See separate listing. Tel: 609-263-4296.

Stratford, Camden Co., St. Luke (1961), Revs. Thomas B. Fitzsimmons; John D. Wasilewski; Deacons James D'Angelillio; George R. Liss.
Res., 55 Warwick Rd., 08084. Tel: 609-783-5555; Fax: 609-782-8336.
School—Tel: 609-783-3088; Fax: 609-783-8889. Mrs. Cathleen Sheridan, Prin.
Lay Teachers 12; Students 300.
Special Education—.
Lay Teachers 2; Students 15.
Catechesis/Religious Programs—Students 320.

Swedesboro, Gloucester Co., St. Joseph's (1854), Revs. John F. Bloh; Paul Hao Trinh; Deacon Robert W. Hardy.
Res., 140 N. Broad St., 08085. Tel: 609-467-0037; Fax: 609-467-0038. [CEM]
School—225 Kings Hwy., 08085. Tel: 609-467-1154. Mr. Dennis Reitano, Prin.
Lay Teachers 9; Students 161.

Ventnor, Atlantic Co., St. James (1922), Revs. Brendan V. Sullivan; Herman N. Burger; Deacon James Clair.
Res., 6415 Atlantic Ave., 08406. Tel: 609-822-2176; Fax: 609-487-8137.
School—Tel: 609-822-2234. Sr. Joan Mary Baldridge, O.P., Prin.
Sisters 2; Brothers 1; Lay Teachers 8; Students 265.
Convent—Portland & Atlantic Ave., 08406. Tel: 609-487-8110. Dominican Sisters (Sinsinawa, WI)

Villas, Cape May Co., St. Raymond (1937), Revs. John H. Burton; Anthony Giudice, O.F.M.Cap.
Res., 25 E. Hudson Ave., 08251. Tel: 609-886-5366; Fax: 609-886-9415.
School—St. Raymond Regional School, Villas. See separate listing. Tel: 609-886-2893; Fax: 609-889-8335.
Catechesis/Religious Programs—Tel: 609-886-3663.
Students 229.

Vineland, Cumberland Co.,

1—Our Lady of Pompeii, (1909), Rev. James J. Durkin.
Res., 4680 Dante Ave., 08360. Tel: 609-691-7526; Fax: 609-692-2686. [CEM]
School—St. Mary Regional School, Vineland. See separate listing.

2—Sacred Heart, (1874), Rev. Msgr. Joseph G. Stoerlein, V.F.; Revs. Salvatore L. DeIelse; Raymond P. Gormley; Deacon Robert Andreacchio. In res., Rev. Msgr. Joseph A. von Hartleben.
Res., 1010 Landis Ave., 08360. Tel: 609-691-0420; Fax: 609-691-1516. [CEM]
School—Sacred Heart Regional School, Vineland. See separate listing.

3—St. Francis of Assisi, (1961), Rev. Msgr. Patrick S. Chiarilli; Rev. Hugh J. Bradley. In res., Rev. Msgr. Victor S. Muro.
Res., 23 W. Chestnut Ave., 08360. Tel: 609-691-9181; Fax: 609-794-9029.
School—Tel: 609-691-9184. Mrs. Anita Meale, Prin.
Lay Teachers 15; Students 300.
Catechesis/Religious Programs—Students 218.
Convent—W. Chestnut Ave., 08360. Tel: 609-691-8129. Daughters of Mercy

4—St. Isidore, (1962), Rev. John T. Frey. In res., Revs. Edward P. Sommers; Alvaro Diaz, O.F.M.
Res., 1655 Magnolia Ave., 08361-6598. Tel: 609-691-9077; Fax: 609-692-3305.
School—Sacred Heart Regional School, Vineland. See separate listing. Tel: 609-691-4490; Fax: 609-691-1516.
Catechesis/Religious Programs—Tel: 609-563-0482. Sr. Catherine Kane, O.S.F., D.R.E.
Students 250.

5—St. Mary's, (1887), Revs. Paul P. Onufer; Julian K. Karczewski; Edward F. Namiotka.
Res., 9 S. Union Rd., 08360. Tel: 609-691-9721; Fax: 609-692-5034. [CEM]
School—St. Mary Regional School. See separate listing. Tel: 609-692-8537.
Mission—Richland, Atlantic Co., St. Joseph.

Washington Township, Gloucester Co., St. Charles Borromeo (1965), Rev. Msgr. Joseph F. O'Connell; Rev. John O'Leary; Deacon John R. Gallimore.
Res., 176 Stagecoach Rd., Sicklerville, 08081. Tel: 609-629-0411; Fax: 609-629-0412.
School—St. Jude Regional School, Blackwood. See separate listing.
Catechesis/Religious Programs—Tel: 609-228-5694. Mrs. Mary Ann Exler, D.R.E.
Students 775.

SS. Peter and Paul (1973), Revs. John A. Clarke; Richard J. Regan; Deacons Edward X. Guidotti; Liberato F. Tumulo. In res., Rev. Michael J. Bourke.
Res., Ganttown Rd., P.O. Box 1022, Turnersville, 08012. Tel: 609-589-3366.
School—St. Jude Regional School, Blackwood. See separate listing.

Holy Family (1974), Rev. Msgr. Joseph P. Joynes; Revs. Marcel Tabone; Conleth Eleanya; Deacons Vincent Fausto; George M. Ferland.
Res., 226 Hurffville Rd., Sewell, 08080. Tel: 609-228-1616; Fax: 609-228-6332.
School—St. Jude Regional School, Blackwood. See separate listing. Tel: 609-227-4442; Fax: 609-227-1276.
Catechesis/Religious Programs—Students 1,330.

Waterford, Camden Co., St. Anthony (1966), Rev. Ambrose S. Bryce.
Res., 436 Pennington Ave., 08089. Tel: 609-767-7535.
School—St. Joseph Regional School, Hammonton. See separate listing.

West Collingswood, Camden Co., Transfiguration (1950), Revs. Richard J. Lodge; Nathan I. DeMarco; Deacon William C. Robinson. In res., Rev. Msgr. Thomas A. Guenther.
Res., 445 White Horse Pike, 08107. Tel: 609-854-0364; Fax: 609-869-5129.

Westmont, Camden Co., Holy Saviour (1928), Revs. Terry M. Odien; Edward F. Heintzelman. In res., Rev. Michael P. Orsi.
Res., 50 Emerald Ave., 08108. Tel: 609-854-0022; Fax: 609-854-5741.
School—30 Emerald Ave., 08108. Tel: 609-858-1966. Sr. Janice Novak, Prin.; Sr. Bernarda Ribeiro, Supr.
Sisters, Franciscan Missionaries of the Immaculate Heart of Mary 4; Lay Teachers 7; Students 239.

Westville, Gloucester Co., St. Anne's (1921), Rev. Andrew J. Bolcar; Deacon Anthony C. Como. In res., Rev. Frederick G. Link.
Res., 213 Woodbine Ave., 08093. Tel: 609-456-4136; Fax: 609-742-0619.
School—St. Matthew Regional School, National Park. See separate listing. Tel: 609-845-7203.
Catechesis/Religious Programs—Tel: 609-456-4136.
Students 157.

Westville Grove, Gloucester Co., Most Holy Redeemer (1958), Revs. Neal F. Dante; Piotr Szamocki.
Res., 1219 Delsea Dr., 08093. Tel: 609-848-6779; Fax: 609-848-6208.
School—Tel: 609-848-6826. Mrs. Donna DiPasquale, Prin.; Sr. Hugh Marie Layton, S.S.J., Supr.
Sisters of St. Joseph (Chestnut Hill) 2; Lay Teachers 8; Students 245.
Catechesis/Religious Programs—Tel: 609-384-6070. Sr. Beatrice Ena, M.P.F., D.R.E.
Students 171.

Wildwood, Cape May Co., St. Ann's (1895), Rev. Msgr. William Quinn, V.F.; Rev. Stanley Witcoskie; Deacon Joseph Pierce. In res., Revs. Paul J. Maguire, (Retired); Charles Conaty.
Res., 2900 Pacific Ave., 08260. Tel: 609-522-5583; Fax: 609-522-9375.
School—St. Ann Regional School Regionalized with Assumption Parish, Wildwood Crest, 2901 New Jersey Ave., 08260. Tel: 609-522-2704; Fax: 609-522-5329. Sr. Sheila Murphy, S.S.J., Prin.
Sisters of St. Joseph 3; Lay Teachers 8; Students 331.
Catechesis/Religious Programs—Students 704.
Convent—119 E. Glenwood Ave., 08260. Tel: 609-522-5721. Sr. Marie Scherr, S.S.J., Supr.

Wildwood Crest, Cape May Co., Assumption B.V.M. (1961), Revs. Thomas S. Tracey; James R. Plummer; Deacons Joseph A. Costello; Ralph Catanese. In res., Rev. Msgr. John J. Kelly, (Retired).
Res., 7110 Seaview Ave., 08260. Tel: 609-522-4114; 522-6071. [JC]
School—St. Ann Regional School, Wildwood. See separate listing under St. Ann's Parish.

Williamstown, Gloucester Co., St. Mary's (1906), Revs. Carmen A. Carlone; Peter Joyce; Deacons John J. Leyden; John Kirk; John Kacy.
Res., 32 Carrol Ave., 08094. Tel: 609-629-6142; Fax:

609-875-2097.
School—Tel: 609-629-6190; Fax: 609-728-1437. Miss Judith McBride, Prin.
Lay Teachers 25; Students 518.
Catechesis/Religious Programs—Tel: 609-629-0614.
Students 950.
Convent—640 S. Main St., 08094. Tel: 609-262-1358. St. Joseph Sisters

Woodbine, Cape May Co., St. Casimir's (1939), Rev. Robert Yori.
Res., 304 Clay St., P.O. Box 533, 08270. Tel: 609-861-3771; Fax: 609-861-7112. [CEM]
School—St. Joseph Regional School, Sea Isle City. See separate listing.
Mission—Goshen, Cape May Co., St. Elizabeth, Rte. 47, Goshen, 08218. Tel: 609-861-5218. [CEM]

Woodbury, Gloucester Co., St. Patrick's (1877), Revs. J. Gerald Gallagher; E. Joseph Byerley; Deacons Robert Lorenzo; David Murnane.
Res., 64 Cooper St., 08096. Tel: 609-845-0123; Fax: 609-845-7409.
School—Mrs. Dorice Palumbo, Prin. Lay Teachers 11; Students 250.
Catechesis/Religious Programs—Students 410.

Woodbury Heights, Gloucester Co., St. Margaret's (1961), Rev. Msgr. Felix M. O'Neill; Rev. Joseph D. Wallace; Deacon Robert M. Kenney.
Res., P.O. Box 186, 334 Beech Ave., 08097. Tel: 609-848-0047; Fax: 609-384-8123.
School—St. Margaret Regional School, Woodbury Heights. See separate listing. Tel: 609-845-5200; Fax: 609-845-2405.
Catechesis/Religious Programs—Tel: 609-845-5251.
Students 600.

Woodlynne, Camden Co., Immaculate Heart of Mary (1949), Rev. Edward J. Walsh.
Res., 201 Cooper Ave., 08107. Tel: 609-962-8610.

Woodstown, Salem Co., St. Joseph's (1895), Rev. Stephen F. Cervoni; Deacon Kenneth H. Demarest. In res., Rev. Joseph R. Ferrara.
Res., 51 Broad St., 08098. Tel: 609-769-0004. [CEM]

Chaplains of Public Institutions

ANCORA. *New Jersey State Mental Hospital.* Rev. Albert E. Harshaw, St. Lucy's Church, 250 S. Rte. 73, Blue Anchor, 08037.

DELMONT. *Southern State Correctional Facility.* Tel: 609-785-1300. Rev. Robert P. Weber.

LAKELAND. *Camden County Hospital at Lakeland.* Sr. Mary de Sales Vesey, S.S.J., St. Jude's Church, 402 S. Black Horse Pike, Blackwood, 08012. Tel: 609-227-0572.
St. Joseph's Chapel. Vacant. Camden County Hospital, Blackwood Post Office, 08012.

LEESBURG. *New Jersey State Medium Security Prison,* 08327. Revs. Sean McArdle; Robert P. Weber.

VINELAND. *Vineland State School.* Attended by Sacred Heart Church, Vineland. Tel: 609-691-0420.

WOODBINE. *State Colony.* Rev. Robert Yori, St. Casimir's Church, Tel: 609-861-3771.

On Duty Outside the Diocese:
Reverend Monsignors—
Daiber, Sean J., Brazilian Missions, Central Mailing Address, Paroguia de Sao Jose Rua 107, Setor Sul, Caiza Postal 716, 74,000 Goiania Goias, Brazil S.A.
Marucci, Carl J., The Permanent Observer., Mission of the Holy See to the U.N., 25 E. 39th St., New York, NY 20016-0903. Tel: 212-370-7885
O'Leary, Cornelius, 25098 Jaclyn Ave., Moreno Valley, CA 92387
Reverend Fathers—
Chirico, Peter F., S.S., St. James Cathedral, 804 Ninth Ave., Seattle, WA 98104
Davis, Charles J., RR1, Box 20-1, Woodsville, NH 03785
Gomes, Robert, St. Luke the Evangelist, 2757 Alderman Rd., Palm Harbor, FL 34684. Tel: 813-786-3648
Kocik, Franc W., St. Patrick, Pincourt, Ile Perrot, Province of Quebec, Canada
Kunzman, Richard T., P.O. Box 61, Big Flats, NY 14814
Mannion, Michael, Office of Catholic Ministry, Catholic University of America., 620 Michigan Ave., N.E., Washington, DC 20064-1567
Martin, Vincente Moreno, Venice, Florida
McGrath, Roger E., S.S., St. Mary Seminary and University, 5400 Roland Ave., Baltimore, MD 21210. Tel: 410-323-3200
Norton, Daniel J., Brazilian Missions
Reese, Donald B., Lake Dr., Lake Hauto, Box 40c, RD 1, Nesquehoning, PA 18240
Selleck, John P., St. of Francis of Assisi, 334 Gaskin St., Blountstown, FL 32424-2127
Stout, O. Hugh, Holy Ghost, 2015 Louisiana Ave., New Orleans, LA 70015
Vazquez, Roman, O.F.M.
Wade, Edward C., Our Lady of Perpetual Help, 15 Lebreton St., Ottawa, ON K1R-7H1 Canada. Tel: 613-232-6960; Fax: 613-234-4568

Military Chaplains:
Reverend Fathers—
Betz, James, U.S. Army
McLaughlin, Peter A., U.S. Navy
Newton, John G., U.S. Navy

On Educational Leave of Absence:
Reverend Fathers—
Checchio, James F., North American College, Rome, Italy
Idler, Peter M., Pontifical North American College, Rome, Italy

On Sick Leave:
Reverend Fathers—
Bean, Charles S.
Gerbino, A. Richard
Hardin, Roy
O'Sullivan, James
Pisik, Timothy E.
Shannon, Joseph E.

On Leave of Absence:
Reverend Fathers—
Weaver, Patrick

Retired:
Reverend Monsignors—
Adamo, Salvatore J., 114 James St., Burlington, NJ 08016
Argullo, Michael A., St. Rose of Lima Church, 3 Green St., Haddon Heights, NJ 08035
Beausang, Charles C., 13595 Clara Ln., Port Charlotte, FL 33981
Cannon, Thomas, St. Peter, 359 W. New York Ave., P.O. Box 3700, Deland, FL 32723
Carr, James A., 918 Society Hill, Cherry Hill, NJ 08003
Chmielewski, Joseph, 5 S. Suffolk Ave., Ventnor, NJ 08406
Clark, John J., 644 Pleasure Ave., Ocean City, NJ 08226
Conlon, Joseph E., St. Mary Nursing Home, 1730 Kresson Rd., Cherry Hill, NJ 08003
DiBuono, Pasquale M., St. Martin de Porres, 129 Park Ave., Hammonton, NJ 08037
Flaherty, J. Francis, Our Lady of Grace, 35 N. White Horse Pike, Somerdale, NJ 08083-1796
Gaffney, James J., J.C.D., Our Lady of Lourdes, 500 Green Tree Rd., Glassboro, NJ 08028-1427
Giammarino, Vincent J., St. Mary Nursing Home, 1730 Kresson Rd., Cherry Hill, NJ 08003
Hewitt, Bernard P., Garden Lakes Trailer Park, Lot 144, Eighth Ave., Court House, Cape May, NJ 08210
Hudzik, Leo A., 705 Pilgrim Plaza, North Cape May, NJ 08204
Kelly, John J., Assumption, 710 Seaview Ave., Wildwood Crest, NJ 08260-3826
Kennedy, Edward J., 4901 Harbor Beach Blvd., Apt. P-12, Brigantine, NJ 08203. Tel: 609-266-6244
Leary, Joseph W., 130 N. Railroad, Frockville, PA 17931
Lubicky, John R., St. Agnes, 701 Little Gloucester Rd., Blackwood, NJ 08012-7309
Madden, Patrick J., 401 Washington Mall, Cape May, NJ 08204
McCaffrey, John, 201 N. Flagler Dr. Room 501, West Palm Beach, FL 33401
McDaid, Edward J., Sacred Heart Priests Residence, 200 St. Mary's Dr., Cherry Hill, NJ 08003-2517
O'Connor, Edward J., 46 Asbury Rd., Ocean City, NJ 08226
O'Connor, Paul, 23 N. Wissahickan Ave, Ventnor, NJ 08406
Rigney, Philip, 139 Fairview W., Tequesta, FL 33458
Robertson, Glendon E., 4800 Harper Beach Blvd., #4106, Brigantine, NJ 08203
Seidenburg, Augustine J., 150 W. Cedar Ave., Somers Point, NJ 08244
Sharkey, Thomas H., 3 Catherine Place, Northfield, NJ 08225
Wieckowski, John F., Grand View Apts., 428-C, Crafton Ave., Pitman, NJ 08071
Zegers, James J., P.A., 21 Red Clover Dr., Marmora, NJ 08223
Reverend Fathers—
Barr, Stanley J., 3 South Wissahickon Ave., Ventnor, NJ 08406
Becker, Charles J., S.S., St. Charles Villa, 603 Maiden Choice Ln., Baltimore, MD 21228
Bernard, John P., 4327 Lockport Rd., Elba, NY 14058
Burns, Thomas E., 6713A Monmouth Ave., Ventnor, NJ 08406-2128. Tel: 609-822-7102
Campuzano, J. Eduardo, Puerto del Carmen 4-A, Maspalomas 35100 (Las Palmas), Spain
Carta, Umberto, 23 Pine Ave., Elmtown E, Hammonton, NJ 08037
Darby, Bernard M., 6548 165th St., Flushing, NY 11365
Eckert, William F., 9 Lori Ct., Pittsfield, MA 01201-7145
Hayden, Joseph M., 4747 N. Road 33, Lot 354, Lakeland, FL 33805
Hewett, Alfred J., St. Rose of Lima, 300 Kings Hwy., Haddon Heights, NJ 08035-1397
Kolton, Stanislaus J., P.O. Box 72, Spring Lake, NJ 07762
Kuhl, Charles E.
Maguire, Paul J., St. Ann, 2900 Pacific Ave., Wildwood, NJ 08260-4943
McCormick, George, Dow Rd., RR1 Box 32, Deer Isle, ME 04629
McDonnell, Cyril, 1920 S. Ocean Dr., Apt. 201, Fort Lauderdale, FL 33316
McGarvey, Joseph F., 32 Central Ave., Audubon, NJ 08106-1904
Melvin, James M., Sacred Heart Priests Residence, 200 St. Mary's Dr., Cherry Hill, NJ 08003-2517
Mroczkowski, Leonard A., 1981 Washington Ave., Seaside Heights, NJ 08751
Orsini, Joseph E., 42 W. 50th St., Bayonne, NJ 07002
Pastore, Peter J., 3534 Canter Dr., Las Vegas, NV 89030
Weber, George A., Box 272114, Tampa, FL 33688-2114

Permanent Deacons:
Achee, C. J.
Andreaccho, Robert A.
Bandiera, A. Kenneth
Beebe, Joseph
Bischer, Carmen
Bradley, Patrick
Bucher, Joseph L.
Burns, D. Eugene
Carlucci, Leonard P.
Cassidy, Joseph P.
Clair, John
Como, Anthony C.
Costello, Joseph A.
Cromer, John
Custodio, Henry S.
D'Angelillio, James J.
Demarest, Kenneth H.
Donohue, J. Frank
Drum, William J.
Ellis, Raymond V.
Engel, Frank J.
Fausto, Vincent
Ferland, George M.
Ferrario, Raymond C.
Freed, Edward E.
Gallimore, John R.
Ganci, Joseph A.
Gargin, Frank P.
Garufi, Agatino
Gilmartin, Peter J.
Giordano, Philip
Glasser, John L.
Gonzalez, Carmelo
Guerrieri, Michael H.
Guidotti, Edward
Hafner, Thomas J.
Hagan, William T.
Hanrahan, Matthew J.
Hardy, Robert W.
Harkins, Edward J.
Harkins, Michael J.
Harris, Philip
Henkel, Thomas B.
Hynes, John C.
Iannuzzi, William P.
Iula, Dr. Frank A.
Johnson, Paul F.
Kearney, J. Brian
Kenney, Robert M.
Kijonka, Anthony
Kiley, James
Kulesa, Stanley
Leone, John
Lewis, Alfred W.
Leyden, John J.
Lorenzo, Robert
Lytle, George V.
Majewski, Walter, Jr.
Mangino, Rocco A.
McAleer, Charles
McBlain, Leo

McCarthy, Richard F.
McDonaugh, Michael
McLeer, Eugene L.
Mija, Theodore
Nastasi, Santo
Norquist, William V.
O'Brien, Thomas F.
Olesiewicz, Ronald J.
Pepe, Frank, Jr.
Porowicz, Alfred T.
Quiles, Bernardino
Radziak, Raymond
Raftovich, Robert V.
Ralbusky, Emil A.
Reiss, Dr. Charles C.
Rios, Jose R.
Rivera, Miguel A.
Robinson, William C.
Rocks, James H.
Rumaker, William J.
Seppanen, Henry R.
Tavarez, Ismael Perez
Teeney, James J.
Traxler, Harold G., Jr.
Tully, James
Tumulo, Liberato F.
Valle, Wilfredo
Vargo, Frank T.
Vega, Angel Ramos
Verycken, Edward J.
Watts, William L.
Wigglesworth, Richard
Wilson, Jerome I.

INSTITUTIONS LOCATED IN THE DIOCESE

[A] HIGH SCHOOLS, DIOCESAN

ABSECON. *Holy Spirit High School*, New Rd., 08201. Tel: 609-646-3000; Fax: 609-646-1770. Rev. Joseph A. Perreault, Prin. Sisters of Mercy 3; Priests 1; Lay Teachers 41; Students 902.

CARNEYS POINT. *St. James High School*, 350 Georgetown Rd., 08069. Tel: 609-299-0400. Rev. Peter J. Osinski, Prin. Priests 1; Lay Teachers 17; Students 250.

CHERRY HILL. *Camden Catholic High School*, Rte. 38 and Cuthbert Rd., 08002. Tel: 609-663-2247. Rev. Andrew E. Martin, Prin.; Joan Urello, Vice Prin.; Revs. William C. Hart; Robert C. Pasley. Priests 3; Sisters of Mercy 3; Lay Teachers 35; Students 837.

HADDONFIELD. *Paul VI High School*, 901 Hopkins Rd., Ste. B, 08033. Tel: 609-858-4900. Rev. Russell L. Rock, Prin.; Sr. Marianne McCann, M.P.F., Asst. Prin.; Revs. John J. Byrnes; Timothy Hubbs; Robert E. Hughes. Priests 4; Religious Teachers Filippini 3; Lay Teachers 48; Students 1,100.

HAMMONTON. *St. Joseph*, 133 N. 3rd St., 08037. Tel: 609-561-0689. Mr. James J. Cavalieri, Prin.; Rev. Edward F. Namiotka. Religious Sisters Filippini 2; Lay Teachers 20; Students 343.

[B] HIGH SCHOOLS, PAROCHIAL

GLOUCESTER. *Gloucester Catholic High School*, 333 Ridgeway St., 08030. Tel: 609-456-4400. Rev. Kenneth J. Johnston, Prin. Priests 1; Deacons 1; Dominican Sisters 1; Lay Teachers 36; Students 748.

VINELAND. *Sacred Heart High School*, 21 N. East Ave., 08360. Tel: 609-691-4491. Sr. Clare de Chantal, S.S.J., Prin. 1; Sisters of St. Joseph 2; Lay Teachers 17; Students 260.

WILDWOOD. *Wildwood Catholic High School*, 1500 Central Ave., 08260. Tel: 609-522-7257. Sr. Mary Ellen Ford, S.S.J., Prin.; Richard Turco, Asst. Prin.; Rev. Charles Conaty. Priests 1; Brothers 1; Sisters of St. Joseph 3; Lay Teachers 19; Students 330.

[C] HIGH SCHOOLS, PRIVATE

NEWFIELD. *Our Lady of Mercy Academy*, 1001 Main Rd., 08344. Tel: 609-697-2008. Daughters of Our Lady of Mercy. Sr. Grace Marie, D.M., Prin. Sisters 3; Lay Teachers 9; Students 143.

PENNSAUKEN. *Bishop Eustace Prep School*, 5552 Rte. 70, 08109-4798. Tel: 609-662-2160, ext. 214; 662-0865 (Res.). Society of the Catholic Apostolate, Province of the Immaculate Conception. Revs. Ralph Firneno, S.A.C., Rector & Prin.; Joseph Capella, S.A.C., Chap.; Robert J. Nolan, S.A.C., Faculty; James MacDonald, S.A.C., Province Vocation Dir.; Bro. James Beamesderfer, S.A.C. In res. Rev. Joseph Mungari, S.A.C. Priests 5; Brothers 1; Lay Teachers 52; Students 750.

RICHLAND. *St. Augustine Preparatory School*. (Boys), N. Cedar Ave., 08350. Tel: 609-697-2600. Order of St. Augustine, Province of St. Thomas of Villanova. Revs. Paul W. Galetto, O.S.A.; Stephen J. La Rosa, O.S.A., Pres.; Cherubin Kerr, O.S.A.; Ronald Hamaday, O.S.A.; James Cassidy, O.S.A.; Bros. Frank Cucinotta, O.S.A.; David Graber, M.SS.CC. Priests 5; Brothers 2; Lay Teachers 16; Students 268.

[D] ELEMENTARY SCHOOLS, PRIVATE

CAMDEN. *San Miguel School, Inc.* (Grades 6), 836 S. 4th St., 08103. Tel: 609-342-6707; Fax: 609-342-6708. Bro. William Johnson, F.S.C., Prin. Students 15.

[E] REGIONAL SCHOOLS, ELEMENTARY

BARRINGTON. *St. Francis de Sales*, West Gloucester Pike, 08007. Tel: 609-547-7958.
E-mail: sfdsale@erols.com
Web site: www.erols.com\sfdsale
Sr. Catherine Mulcahy, F.D.N.S.C., Supr. & Prin. Daughters of Our Lady of the Sacred Heart 6; Lay Teachers 9; Students 296. Serving St. Francis de Sales, Barrington and Mary, Mother of the Church, Bellmawr.

BERLIN. *Our Lady of Mt. Carmel*, One Maple Ave., 08009. Tel: 609-767-2115. Sr. M. Agnes, R.S.M., Prin.; Sr. Annette Tobin. Sisters of Mercy (American Province) 6; Lay Teachers 12; Students 298. Serving Our Lady of Mt. Carmel, Berlin and St. Andrew, Gibbsboro.

BLACKWOOD. *St. Agnes*, 117 W. Church St., 08012. Tel: 609-228-7076. Mr. John T. Cafagna, Prin. Lay Teachers 10; Students 260. Serving St. Agnes, Blackwood; St. John Vianney, Deptford.

St. Jude, 400 S. Black Horse Pike, 08012. Tel: 609-227-4442. Sr. Paula Marie Randow, O.S.F., Prin.; Sr. Janice Novak, F.M.I.H.M., Supr. Franciscan Sisters 3; Lay Teachers 23; Students 475. Serving St. Jude, Blackwood; SS. Peter & Paul, St. Charles Borromeo, & Holy Family, Washington Township.

BRIDGETON. *Immaculate Conception Regional School*, 398 N. Pearl St., 08302. Tel: 609-451-2134. Mrs. Kathleen Bischer, Prin. Lay Teachers 10; Students 172. Serving Immaculate Conception, St. Teresa of Avila, Bridgeton; St. Michael, Cedarville; St. Mary, Rosenhayn.

CAPE MAY. *Our Lady, Star of the Sea*, 520 Lafayette St., 08204. Tel: 609-884-4437. Ms. Barbara Byrne, Prin. Sisters of St. Joseph 1; Lay Teachers 13; Students 246. Serving Our Lady, Star of the Sea, Cape May; Our Lady of the Angels, Cape May Court House.

COLLINGSWOOD. *St. John*, 100 Lees Ave., 08108. Tel: 609-858-1562. Miss Joan Simpson, Prin. Lay Teachers 10; Students 238. Serving St. John, Collingswood; St. Aloysius, Oaklyn.

GLASSBORO. *St. Bridget Regional School*, W. High St., 08028. Tel: 609-881-2578. Sr. Lisa Marie, C.S.S.F., Prin. Felician Sisters 2; Lay Teachers 14; Students 299. Serving St. Bridget, Our Lady of Lourdes, Glassboro; Our Lady, Queen of Peace, Pitman.

HADDONFIELD. *Christ the King Regional School*, 168 Hopkins Ave., 08033. Tel: 609-429-2084. Miss Jane M. McErlane, Prin. Franciscan Sisters of Allegany 1; Lay Teachers 17; Students 304. Serving Christ the King, Haddonfield; St. Pius X, Cherry Hill.

HAMMONTON. *St. Joseph*, 133 N. 3rd St., 08037. Tel: 609-561-5980. Sr. Barbara Ranere, M.P.F., Prin. Religious Teachers Filippini 5; Lay Teachers 12; Students 310. Serving St. Joseph, St. Martin de Porres, St. Anthony of Padua, Hammonton; St. Anthony, Waterford; St. Lucy, Blue Anchor; Sacred Heart Mission, Cedar Brook.

MARGATE. *Blessed Sacrament*, 14 N. Jerome St., 08402. Tel: 609-822-9243. Sr. Rosaline Walters, O.S.F., Prin. Sisters of St. Francis of Syracuse, NY. Lay Teachers 9; Students 203. Serving Blessed Sacrament, Margate; St. Bernadette, Northfield; Epiphany, Longport.

MOUNT EPHRAIM. *Sacred Heart School*, W. Buckingham Ave., 08059. Tel: 609-931-5498. Ms. Rosemarie DelCorio, Prin. Lay Teachers 10; Students 175. Serving Sacred Heart, Mt. Ephraim; Holy Maternity, Audubon.

NEWFIELD. *Notre Dame Regional School*, 108 Church St., 08344. Tel: 609-697-0155, (Newfield) (Grades 1-4); 609-697-3456, (Grades 5-8); (Landisville).
E-mail: ndrsnj@aol.com
Mrs. Mary Brogan, Prin. Lay Teachers 15; Students 300. Serving Our Lady of Victories, Landisville; St. Michael, Minotola; Our Lady of the Lakes, Collings Lakes; St. Rose, Newfield; St. Mary, Malaga; Nativity, Franklinville; St. Ann, Elmer.

OCEAN CITY. *St. Augustine*, 1337 Asbury Ave., 08226-3299. Tel: 609-399-1435; Fax: 609-399-8675. Sr. de Paul Juliano, O.S.F. Sisters of St. Francis 1; Lay Teachers 9; Students 260. Serving St. Augustine, St. Frances Cabrini, Our Lady of Good Counsel, Ocean City; Resurrection, Marmora.

PENNS GROVE. *St. James*, 56 Beach Ave., 08069. Tel: 609-299-0397. Mrs. Claire Whittaker; Rev. Peter M. Saporito, Acting Prin. Lay Teachers 11; Students 180. Serving St. James, Penns Grove; Corpus Christi, Carneys Point; St. Joseph, Woodstown.

POMONA. *Assumption*, White Horse Pike, 08240. Tel: 609-652-7134. Mr. Joseph S. Mancuso, Prin. Lay Teachers 10; Students 205. Serving Assumption, Pomona; St. Elizabeth Ann Seton, Absecon.

RUNNEMEDE. *St. Teresa*, 18 Ardmore Rd., 08078. Tel: 609-939-0333. Sr. Margaret M. Langer, I.H.M., Supr. & Prin. Sisters Servants of the Immaculate Heart of Mary 7; Lay Teachers 9; Students 299. Serving St. Teresa, St. Maria Goretti, Runnemede.

SALEM. *St. Mary*, 31 Oak St., 08079. Tel: 609-935-0660. Sr. Marian, C.S.J.P., Prin. Sisters of St. Joseph of Peace 2; Lay Teachers 8; Students 145. Serving St. Mary, Salem; Queen of Apostles, Pennsville.

SEA ISLE CITY. *St. Joseph*, 132 44th St., 08243. Tel: 609-263-4296. Sr. Rosalie Pronsati, R.S.M., Prin.; Sr. Patricia Tomlin, S.S.J., D.R.E. Sisters of Mercy (Merion, PA) 1; Lay Teachers 12; Students 265. Serving St. Joseph, Sea Isle City; Maris Stella, Avalon; St. Casimir, Woodbine; St. Paul, Stone Harbor.

SOMERDALE. *Our Lady of Grace School*, 105 N. White Horse Pike, 08083. Tel: 609-784-0372; Fax: 609-784-5496. Sr. Patricia O'Donnell, I.H.M., Prin.; Sr. Helen Marie Gates, I.H.M., Supr. Sisters Servants of Immaculate Heart of Mary 3; Lay Teachers 17; Students 374. Serving Our Lady of Grace, Somerdale; St. Gregory, Magnolia.

VERGA. *St. Matthew*, 08093. Tel: 609-845-7203; Fax: 609-853-7711. Sr. Maria Liber, Prin. Little Servant Sisters of the Immaculate Conception 4; Lay Teachers 8; Students 220. Serving St. Matthew, National Park; St. Anne, Westville.

VILLAS. *St. Raymond*, 25 E. Ocean Ave., 08251. Tel: 609-886-2893. Sr. Ellen M. Giardino, Supr. & Prin. Servants of the Immaculate Heart of Mary 9; Lay Teachers 9; Students 194. Serving St. Raymond, Villas; St. John of God, North Cape May.

VINELAND. *Sacred Heart*, 922 E. Landis Ave., 08360. Tel: 609-691-4490. Sr. Bernadette Mary Leahy, S.S.J., Prin.; Sr. Inez Patricia, S.S.J., Supr. Sisters of St. Joseph 3; Lay Teachers 16; Students 462. Serving Sacred Heart, St. Isidore, Spanish Catholic Center, Vineland.

St. Mary, 8 S. Union Rd., 08360. Tel: 609-692-8537.
E-mail: stmarys@us.com
Web site: www.cambel.com/stmarys
Sr. M. Bernardine, D.M., Prin. Daughters of Our Lady of Mercy 2; Lay Teachers 12; Students 303. Serving St. Mary; St. Joseph Mission, Richland; Our Lady of Pompeii, East Vineland.

WOODBURY HEIGHTS. *St. Margaret*, 745 Third St., 08097. Tel: 609-845-5200. Sr. Lorraine Klein, F.M.I.J., Prin.; Sr. Rosaria Sillitti, F.M.I.J., Supr. Sisters 4; Lay Teachers 10; Students 497. Serving St. Margaret, Woodbury Heights; Incarnation, Mantua.

[F] SCHOOLS FOR SPECIAL CHILDREN

WESTVILLE GROVE. *Archbishop Damiano School / St. John of God Community Services*.
E-mail: ads@jersey.net
1145 Delsea Dr., 08093-9489. Tel: 609-848-4700. Ms. Muncie Buckalew, Exec. Dir. Brothers 4; Sisters 2; Lay Teachers 76; Students 600; Total Staff 178.

[G] CATHOLIC FOUNDATIONS

CAMDEN. *The Frank J. and Rosina W. Suttill Catholic Foundation*, 1845 Haddon Ave., P.O. Box 709, 08101. Rev. Msgr. Joseph P. Herron, Sec.

The Tuition Assistance Fund, Inc., 1845 Haddon Ave., P.O. Box 709, 08100. Rev. Msgr. Thomas J. McIntyre, Sec.

OCEAN CITY. *The Sharkey Family Charitable Trust*. Our Lady of Good Counsel, 3948 Central Ave., 08226. Rev. Msgr. Thomas H. Sharkey, Trustee.

[H] GENERAL HOSPITALS

CAMDEN. *Our Lady of Lourdes Medical Center, Inc.* 1600 Haddon Ave., 08103. Tel: 609-757-3500.
For a complete listing, refer to the Hospitals section.

[I] NURSING HOMES

CHERRY HILL. *St. Mary's Nursing Home*, 210 St. Mary's Dr., 08003. Tel: 609-424-9521; Fax: 609-424-5143
For a complete listing, refer to the Special Care Facilities section.

NEWFIELD. *Mater Dei Nursing Home*, 176 Rte. 40, 08344. Tel: 609-358-2061
For a complete listing, refer to the Special Care Facilities section.

PLEASANTVILLE. *Our Lady's Residence*, 1100 Clematis Ave., 08232
For a complete listing, refer to the Special Care Facilities section.

VINELAND. *Bishop McCarthy Residence*, 1045 E. Chestnut Ave., 08360
For a complete listing, refer to the Special Care Facilities section.

[J] VISITING NURSES

CAPE MAY. *Holy Redeemer Rehabilitation Center*, 1261

Rte. 9 S., Ste. 1, Cape May Court House, 08210. Tel: 609-465-3866. Carol Frankenfield, P.T., Chief Therapist.

MAYS LANDING. *Atlantic Co. Office*, 701 Rte. 50, 08330. Tel: 609-625-220; 800-788-3029. Jennifer Savon, R.N., Admin.

SWAINTON. *Holy Redeemer Visiting Nurse Agency, Inc.* Subsidiary of Holy Redeemer Health System, Inc. 1801 Rte. 9 N., 08210. Tel: 609-465-2082; 800-745-4693; Fax: 609-463-0196. Sponsored by Sisters of the Holy Redeemer, C.S.R. Mr. Jerold S. Cohen, R.N., Pres.

[K] HOUSING FOR AGED

CAPE MAY. *Victorian Towers Associates*, 608 Washington St., 08204. Tel: 609-884-5883
For a complete listing, refer to the Special Care Facilities section.

CHERRY HILL. *The Manor at St. Mary's*, 220 St. Mary's Dr., 08003
For a complete listing, refer to the Special Care Facilities section.

Marian Residence, 1000 Cropwell Rd., 08003. Tel: 609-424-1131
For a complete listing, refer to the Special Care Facilities section.

Village Apartments of Cherry Hill, NJ, Inc., 212 Lourdes Ct., 08003. Tel: 609-424-7913
For a complete listing, refer to the Special Care Facilities section.

[L] CHILD CARE CENTERS

CAMDEN. *St. Joseph's Nursery School*, 17 Church St., P.O. Box 1443, 08105. Tel: 609-963-0452; 365-4653 (Convent); Fax: 609-963-0103. Sr. Maria DiRosa, Prin.; Sr. Angela D'Alessandro, Supr. Franciscan Missionary Sisters of the Infant Jesus 2.

[M] MONASTERIES AND RESIDENCES OF PRIESTS AND BROTHERS

CAMDEN. *Dominican Sisters of the Perpetual Rosary Chaplain's Residence*, 1500 Haddon Ave., 08103. Tel: 609-365-4427. Rev. Raymond M. McCabe, O.P. In res. Rev. Anthony I. Cataudo, O.P.

BLACKWOOD. *Bishop's Residence.* Marywood, 1600 Peter Cheeseman Rd., P.O. Box 577, 08012. In res. Most Rev. James T. McHugh, S.T.D.; Rev. James Checchio.

CHERRY HILL. *Neumann House, Village of St. Mary*, 250 St. Mary's Dr., 08003.

Vianney Villa, 1730 Kresson Rd., 08003. Tel: 609-424-2035. Rev. William D. Titmas, Dir. In res. Rev. Msgr. Joseph W. Devlin; Revs. Charles S. Bean; A. Richard Gerbino; James O'Sullivan.

LINWOOD. *Villa Pieta.* Missionaries of the Sacred Hearts of Jesus & Mary. 2249 Shore Rd., 08221. Tel: 609-927-5600. Revs. Roque Longo, M.SS.CC.; Anthony Patrizio, M.SS.CC., Rector & Delegate; Leonard Carrieri, M.SS.CC.; Robert McDade, M.SS.CC.; Bro. Sigfried Troche, M.SS.CC.

MARGATE. *Franciscan Friars' Vacation Home.* Holy Name Province. 118 S. Mansfield Ave., 08402. Tel: 609-822-9552. Rev. Joel Munzing, O.F.M., Curator. Total Staff 1.

OCEAN CITY. *Augustinian Friars Summer Home.* St. Rita of Cascia Cottage, 823 5th St., 08226. Tel: 609-398-1299.

Ocean Rest Summer School and Retreat House, 31st and Central Ave., 08226. Brothers of Christian Schools Summer Home and Retreat House. Bro. James F. Rieck, F.S.C., Dir. Tel: 609-399-6480, Mailing Address: LaSalle College High School, 8605 Cheltenham Ave., Wyndmoor, PA, 19038. Tel: 215-233-2911.

PITTSGROVE. *Villa St. Joseph*, 9 Harding Hwy., 08318. Tel: 609-358-2841. Oblates of St. Francis de Sales. Revs. John P. Connolly, O.S.F.S., Supr.; Joseph A. Connolly, O.S.F.S.; Nicholas C. DiIenno, O.S.F.S.; J. Stuart Dooling, O.S.F.S.; Thomas W. Kelly, O.S.F.S.; John M. McDevitt, O.S.F.S.; Edmund F. O'Rourke, O.S.F.S.; Joseph P. Schaefer, O.S.F.S.; Joseph A. Travers, O.S.F.S.; Bro. Eugene J. Rehrman, O.S.F.S. Total in Residence 11; Total Staff 3.

WESTVILLE GROVE. *Hospitaller Order of St. John of God*, 532 Delsea Dr., 08093. Tel: 609-848-4700. Bros. Bernard Farrell, O.H., Supr.; Derek O'Connell, O.H., Dir. Vocations. Brothers 4.

[N] CONVENTS AND RESIDENCES FOR SISTERS

CAMDEN. *Monastery of the Dominican Nuns of the Perpetual Rosary*, 1500 Haddon Ave., 08103. Mother Mary of the Immaculate Heart, O.P., Prioress; Rev. Raymond M. McCabe, O.P., Chap. Sisters 7.

ATLANTIC CITY. *St. John's Retreat House and Rest Home*, 128 S. Dover Ave., 08401. Little Servant Sisters of the Immaculate Conception. Sr. Xavier Czachor, L.S.I.C., Supvr. Sisters 4.

CHERRY HILL. *Franciscan Missionary Sisters of the Infant Jesus.* U.S. Province and Novitiate, 1215 Kresson Rd., 08003. Tel: 609-428-7930; Fax: 609-428-7930. Sr. Chiara Lilia Ferrario, F.M.I.J., Delegate Supr. Sisters 4.

Little Servant Sisters of the Immaculate Conception. Provincialate and Novitiate. 1000 Cropwell Rd., 08003. Tel: 609-424-1962. Mother M. Leonarda, L.S.I.C., Prov.; Rev. Julian S. Rozycki, O.P., Chap. Professed Sisters 20; Novices 1.

Queen of Heaven Convent, 10 Massachusetts Ave., 08002. Tel: 609-428-8818. Sr. Loretta B. Achuff, I.H.M., Supr. Sisters Servants of the Immaculate Heart of Mary 4.

HADDONFIELD. *St. Mary of the Angels Convent*, 134 Kings Hwy. W., 08033. Tel: 609-428-0824. Franciscan Sisters of Allegany. Sr. Poverello Wells, O.S.F., Local Min. & Admin. Sisters 11.

MAPLE SHADE. *Emmaus Community*, Ryan's Run East Apts. #2312, 1330 Old Kings Hwy., 08052. Tel: 609-235-7739.
E-mail: mariepac@juno.com
School Sisters of Notre Dame 2.

NEWFIELD. *Villa Rossello.* Provincial House and Novitiate of Daughters of Our Lady of Mercy. 1009 Main Rd., 08344. Tel: 609-697-2983; Fax: 609-697-8595.
E-mail: dmnewfield@juno.com
Sr. Grace Marie, D.M., Prov. Sisters 26.

PLEASANTVILLE. *Hospitaler Sisters of Mercy Novitiate*, 915 S. Main St., 08232. Sr. Ann Maria K. Mathew, Supr. Total in Residence 2.

SEA ISLE CITY. *The Sisters of St. Francis of Philadelphia*, 55th & Landis Ave., 08243. Mailing Address: Our Lady of Angels Convent 19014, 609 S. Convent Rd., Aston, PA.

STONE HARBOR. *Villa Maria by the Sea.* Retreat House, 08247. Sisters, Servants of the Immaculate Heart of Mary (Immaculata, PA).

SWAINTON. *Sisters of the Holy Redeemer.* Our Lady of Peace Convent, 8 Brooks Ave., 08210. Tel: 609-465-3549. Total in Residence 3.

VENTNOR. *The Benedictine Sisters of Elizabeth, NJ*, 114 S. Troy Ave., 08406.
E-mail: bensisnj@aol.com

Convent of Mary the Ocean Star, 112 S. Dorset Ave., 08406. Tel: 609-823-3977. Sisters of Charity of St. Vincent De Paul (Mt. St. Vincent, NY).

Holy Family, Seaside Convent, 110 S. Dorset Ave., 08406. Sisters of St. Dominic (Blauvelt, NY). Sr. Jane McDermott, O.P.

McAuley House, 102 S. Derby Pl., 08406. Sisters of Mercy (Baltimore Regl. Community).

Mercy By-the-Sea, 114 S. Portland Ave., 08406. Sisters of Mercy (Plainfield - Watchung).

Mercy Villa, 104 S. Derby Pl., 08406. Sisters of Mercy (Prov. of New York).

St. Joseph House by the Sea, 107 S. Derby Ave., 08406. Tel: 609-823-1159. Franciscan Sisters of Peace. 317 Charleston E., Wildwood Crest, 08260. Tel: 609-523-1167.

VINELAND. *Bishop McCarthy Residence Convent*, 1045 E. Chestnut Ave., 08360. Sr. Eletta Felli, Supr. Hospitaler Sisters of Mercy 5.

[O] RETREAT HOUSES

BLACKWOOD. *St. Pius X Spiritual Life Center.* St. Pius X Retreat House, Peter Cheeseman Rd., Box 216, 08012. Tel: 609-227-1436; Fax: 609-227-2907. Rev. David E. Beebe, Dir.; Bro. Nicholas Crosby, S.D.S. In res. Revs. Joseph M. Messina; Louis A. Marucci.

[P] APOSTOLIC CENTERS

CAPE MAY POINT. *Marianist Family Retreat Center*, 417 Yale Ave., Box 502, 08212-0456. Tel: 609-884-3829. Rev. Richard V. Kuhn, S.M.; Bros. Albert Koch, S.M.; Raymond McQuade, S.M., Local Community Dir.; Walter Oberster, S.M.; Edward Underdorfer, S.M. Exec. Co-Directors: Terrence Siple; Vesta Siple.

VINELAND. *Spanish Catholic Center*, 410 S. 8th St., 08360. Tel: 609-692-8992. Rev. Victor S. Muro, Dir., 23 W. Chestnut Ave., 08360. Rev. Alvaro Diaz, St. Isidore, 1655 Magnolia Rd., 08360.

[Q] LOCAL OFFICES OF CATHOLIC SOCIAL SERVICES

CAMDEN. *Catholic Social Services*, 1035 Mechanic St., 08104. Tel: 609-964-2133. Ms. Cereida Medina, Dir.

St. John the Baptist Pre-Natal Clinic, 6th St. & Erie St., 08102. Tel: 609-757-9540. Patricia A. Chico, L.P.N., B.A., Admin.

ATLANTIC CITY. *Catholic Social Services*, 9 N. Georgia Ave., 08401. Tel: 609-345-3448. Sr. Grace Nolan, R.S.M., Coord.

CAPE MAY. *Catholic Social Services Senior Center.* Victorian Towers, 608 Washington St., 08204. Tel: 609-884-5624. Sr. Terese Elizabeth Cunningham, S.S.J., Dir.

GIBBSTOWN. *Catholic Social Services, Camden/Gloucester Regional Counseling Center*, 320 Memorial Ave., 08027. Tel: 609-224-0945. Ms. Mary Nicoletto, Dir. Total Assisted 2,853; Total Staff 12.

NEWFIELD. *Catholic Social Services Regional Counseling Center*, P.O. Box 737, 08344. Tel: 609-697-0744. Rev. Frank X. Hudson, L.C.S.W., C.A.D.C., Dir. Total Assisted 2,139; Total Staff 3.

PENNSAUKEN. *Catholic Social Services Family Center*, 2830 Marlton Pike, 08105. Tel: 609-663-9800; Fax: 609-663-0253. Miss Patricia Langan, M.A., M.Ed., Exec. Dir. Total Assisted 1,493; Total Staff 4.

PLEASANTVILLE. *Catholic Social Services.* Cape Atlantic Counseling Center, 21 W. Verona Ave., 08232. Tel: 609-383-0909. Mr. Michael Murphy, L.C.S.W., Dir.

RIO GRANDE. *Catholic Social Services Family Center.* Cape May County Office. Village Shoppes, 1304 Rte. 47 S., 08242. Tel: 609-886-2662. Eileen Henderson, Coord.

SALEM. *Catholic Social Services.* Salem County Office: 21 W. Main St., Penns Grove, 08069. Tel: 609-299-1296. An Emergency Services Agency.

VINELAND. *Catholic Social Services of Vineland*, 810 Montrose St., 08360. Tel: 609-691-1841. Mr. John Desparrois, Coord.

WOODBURY. *Catholic Social Services, Gloucester County Office*, 8 Green Ave., 08096. Tel: 609-845-9200. Mr. Robert S. Skrzot, Coord.

[R] NEWMAN CENTERS

CAMDEN. *Camden Diocesan Center*, 1845 Haddon Ave., 08101. Tel: 609-756-7900.

Rutgers College of South Jersey, 406 Penn St., 08102. Rev. Thomas A. Newton.

GLASSBORO. *Rowan University.* Rev. Cadmus D. Mazzarella, Newman Center, Rte. 322 & Bowe Blvd., 08028.

MAYS LANDING. *Atlantic Community College*, 08330. Rev. C. Jeffries Burton, S.J., St. Peter, 25 W. Verona Ave., Pleasantville, 08232. Tel: 609-641-0285.

POMONA. *Richard Stockton College of New Jersey*, Jim Leeds Rd., 08240. Rev. C. Jeffries Burton, S.J.

[S] MEDICAL CLINICS

CAMDEN. *Saint Luke's Catholic Medical Services, Inc.*, 511 State St., 08102. Tel: 609-365-4642
For a complete listing, refer to the Hospitals section.

[T] LEGAL SERVICES

CAMDEN. *Camden Center for Law and Social Justice, Inc.*, 509 State St., 08102. Tel: 609-966-8896; Fax: 609-541-8826.
E-mail: jjgrogan@crab.rutgas.edu
John J. Grogan, Esq. Total Assisted 800; Total Staff 3.

[U] FOOD CENTERS

CAMDEN. *The Cathedral Soup Kitchen, Inc.*, 642 Market St., 08102. Tel: 609-964-1580. Total Assisted 56,000; Total Staff 4.

[V] MISCELLANEOUS

CAMDEN. *Guadalupe Family Services*, 511 State St., 08102.

NORTH CAPE MAY. *Christ Child Society, Cape May County Chapter*, P.O. Box 882, 08204.

RELIGIOUS INSTITUTES OF MEN REPRESENTED IN THE DIOCESE

For further details refer to the corresponding bracketed number in the Religious Institutes of Men or Women section.

[0140]—*The Augustinians.* (Vice Prov. of Our Lady of Good Counsel, Villanova, PA).—O.S.A.
[0330]—*Brothers of the Christian Schools.*—F.S.C.
[0480]—*Conventual Franciscans.* (Syracuse, NY).—O.F.M.Conv.
[0520]—*Franciscan Friars.* (Prov. of the Most Holy Name of Jesus).—O.F.M.
[0670]—*Hospitaller Brothers of St. John of God.*—O.H.
[0690]—*Jesuit Fathers and Brothers.*—S.J.
[1120]—*Missionaries of the Sacred Hearts of Jesus and Mary.*—M.SS.CC.
[0920]—*Oblates of St. Francis De Sales.* (Wilmington-Philadelphia).—O.S.F.S.
[0430]—*Order of Preachers-Dominicans.* (St. Joseph Prov., New York).—O.P.
[0760]—*Society of Mary.*—S.M.
[0990]—*Society of the Catholic Apostolate.*—S.A.C.
[1200]—*Society of the Divine Savior.*—S.D.S.
[0560]—*Third Order Regular of Saint Francis.*—T.O.R.

RELIGIOUS INSTITUTES OF WOMEN REPRESENTED IN THE DIOCESE

[0230]—*Benedictine Sisters of Pontifical Jurisdiction.* (Newark, NJ).—O.S.B.
[2410]—*Congregation of the Marianites of Holy Cross.*—M.S.C.
[0850]—*Daughters of Mary Help of Christians.* (Paterson).—F.M.A.
[0900]—*Daughters of Our Lady of the Sacred Heart.*—F.D.N.S.C.

[1050]—*Dominican Contemplative Nuns.*—O.P.
[1070-03]—*Dominican Sisters.*—O.P.
[1070-06]—*Dominican Sisters.*—O.P.
[1070-13]—*Dominican Sisters.*—O.P.
[1070-15]—*Dominican Sisters.*—O.P.
[1170]—*Felician Sisters.* (Immaculate Conception Prov., Lodi, NJ).—C.S.S.F.
[1400]—*Franciscan Missionary Sisters of the Sacred Heart.*—F.M.S.C.
[1180]—*Franciscan Sisters of Allegany, New York.*—O.S.F.
[1190]—*Franciscan Sisters of the Atonement.*—S.A.
[2575]—*Institute of the Sisters of Mercy of the Americas.* (Merion, PA; Baltimore, MD).—R.S.M.
[2300]—*Little Servant Sisters of the Immaculate Conception.*—L.S.I.C.
[]—*Missionary Daughters of the Most Pure Virgin Mary.*—M.D.P.V.M.
[2790]—*Missionary Servants of the Most Blessed Trinity.*—M.S.B.T.
[3430]—*Religious Teachers Filippini.* (Morristown, NJ).—M.P.F.
[2970]—*School Sisters of Notre Dame.* (Baltimore Prov.).—S.S.N.D.
[0650]—*Sisters of Charity of St. Vincent de Paul, of New York.*—S.C.
[2517]—*Sisters of Mercy.*
[2670]—*Sisters of Our Lady of Mercy.*—S.O.L.M.
[3893]—*Sisters of Saint Joseph of Chestnut Hill, Philadelphia.*—S.S.J.
[1650]—*Sisters of St. Francis of Philadelphia.*—O.S.F.
[3890]—*Sisters of St. Joseph of Peace.*—C.S.J.P.
[0260]—*Sisters of the Blessed Sacrament for Indians and Colored People.*—S.B.S.
[2000]—*Sisters of the Holy Redeemer.*—C.S.R.
[1490]—*Sisters of the Third Franciscan Order.*—O.S.F.
[2170]—*Sisters, Servants of the Immaculate Heart of Mary.*—I.H.M.

NECROLOGY

† Cannon, William B., (Retired). —Died Feb. 1, 1998.
† DeMarco, Nathan I., West Collingswood, NJ, Transfiguration. —Died Dec. 13, 1997.
† McLaughlin, Francis J., Barrington, NJ, St. Francis de Sales. —Died Oct. 7, 1997.
† Zegers, Rev. Msgr. James J., (Retired). —Died June 14, 1997.

Diocese of Charleston

(Dioecesis Carolopolitana)

Most Reverend

DAVID B. THOMPSON, D.D., J.C.L.

Bishop of Charleston; ordained May 27, 1950; appointed Coadjutor Bishop of Charleston April 22, 1989; ordained May 24, 1989; succeeded to Bishop of Charleston February 22, 1990. *Res., 114 Broad St., Charleston, SC, 29401. Office: 119 Broad St., Charleston, SC, 29401. Mailing Address: P.O. Box 818, Charleston, SC, 29402.* Tel.: 843-723-3488; Fax: 843-724-6387.

ESTABLISHED JULY 11, 1820.

Square Miles 31,055.

Comprises the State of South Carolina.

For legal titles of parishes and diocesan institutions, consult the Chancery Office.

Chancery Office: 119 Broad St., P.O. Box 818, Charleston, SC, 29402. Tel.: 843-723-3488; Fax: 843-724-6387.

Web site address: http://www.catholic-doc.org

E-mail address: sam@catholic-doc.org

STATISTICAL OVERVIEW

Personnel	
Bishop	1
Abbots	1
Retired Abbots	1
Priests: Diocesan Active in Diocese	67
Priests: Active Outside Diocese	6
Priests: Diocesan in Foreign Missions	1
Priests: Retired, Sick or Absent	24
Number of Diocesan Priests	98
Religious Priests in Diocese	33
Extern Priests in Diocese	6
Ordinations:	
Diocesan Priests	4
Permanent Deacons in Diocese	64
Total Brothers	28
Total Sisters	162
Parishes	
Parishes	84
With Resident Pastor:	
Resident Diocesan Priests	57
Resident Religious Priests	13
Without Resident Pastor:	
Administered by Priests	4
Administered by Permanent Deacons	5
Administered by Professed Men Religious	1
Administered by Women Religious	3
Administered by Pastoral Teams, etc.	1
Missions	27
Pastoral Centers	11
Professional Ministry Personnel:	
Brothers	7
Sisters	26
Lay Ministers	39
Welfare	
Catholic Hospitals	3
Total Assisted	399,254
Health Care Centers	1
Total Assisted	327
Homes for the Aged	1
Total Assisted	17
Special Centers for Social Services	7
Total Assisted	102,880
Educational	
Diocesan Students in Other Seminaries	11
Total Seminarians	11
High Schools, Diocesan and Parish	2
Total Students	1,291
Elementary Schools, Diocesan and Parish	25
Total Students	6,448
Catechesis/Religious Education:	
High School Students	2,057
Elementary Students	9,928
Total Students Under Catholic Instruction	19,735
Teachers in the Diocese:	
Priests	2
Sisters	14
Lay Teachers	407
Vital Statistics	
Receptions into the Church:	
Infant Baptism Totals	1,991
Adult Baptism Totals	244
Received into Full Communion	392
First Communions	2,304
Confirmations	1,878
Marriages:	
Catholic	323
Interfaith	346
Total Marriages	669
Deaths	783
Total Catholic Population	116,726
Total Population	3,699,000

Former Bishops—Rt. Rev. JOHN ENGLAND, D.D., first Bishop; cons. Sept. 21, 1820; died April 11, 1842.—Rt. Rev. WILLIAM CLANCY, D.D., cons. Dec. 21, 1834, Coadjutor made Vicar-Apostolic of British Guiana, April 12, 1837; died June 19, 1847.—Rt. Rev. IGNATIUS A. REYNOLDS, D.D., second Bishop; cons. March 19, 1844; died March 6, 1855.—Rt. Rev. PATRICK N. LYNCH, D.D., third Bishop; cons. March 14, 1858; died Feb. 26, 1882.—Rt. Rev. HENRY P. NORTHROP, D.D., fourth Bishop; cons. Titular-Bishop of Rosalia and Vicar-Apostolic of North Carolina, Jan. 8, 1882; transferred to Charleston, by brief dated Jan. 27, 1883; died June 7, 1916.—Rt. Rev. WILLIAM T. RUSSELL, D.D., fifth Bishop; cons. March 15, 1917; died March 18, 1927.—Most Rev. EMMET M. WALSH D.D., cons. Sept. 8, 1927; transferred to Youngstown, Ohio, as Coadjutor Bishop, Sept. 8, 1949.—Most Rev. JOHN J. RUSSELL, D.D., cons. March 14, 1950; transferred to Bishop of Richmond, July 10, 1958.—Most Rev. PAUL J. HALLINAN, D.D., cons. Oct. 28, 1958; transferred to Archbishop of Atlanta, Feb. 21, 1962.—Most Rev. FRANCIS F. REH, S.T.L., J.C.D., cons. June 29, 1962; appt. Titular Bishop of Macriana in Mauretania and Rector of North American College, Rome, Italy, Sept. 5, 1964; transferred to Saginaw, Dec. 18, 1968; installed Feb. 26, 1969; retired April 29, 1980.—Most Rev. ERNEST L. UNTERKOEFLER, D.D., J.C.D., S.T.L., Bishop of Charleston; ord. May 18, 1944; appt. Titular Bishop of Latopolis and Auxiliary Bishop of Richmond, Dec. 13, 1961; cons. Feb. 22, 1962; appt. Bishop of Charleston, Dec. 12, 1964; resigned Feb. 22, 1990; died Jan. 4, 1993.

Vicar General—Rev. Msgr. SAM R. MIGLARESE, V.G.

Chancery Office—119 Broad St., P.O. Box 818, Charleston, 29402. Tel: 843-723-3488; Fax: 843-724-6387.

Chancellor for Administration—CLEO E. CANTEY.

Archivist—SUSAN L. KING. Tel: 843-724-8372.

Office of Finance—DENNIS F. ATWOOD, Chief Financial Officer; BERNADETTE M. WORSHAM, Controller, *1662 Ingram Rd., Charleston, 29407.* Tel: 843-769-4480; Fax: 843-769-2179.

Diocesan Curia—Rev. Msgr. SAM R. MIGLARESE, V.G., Moderator; Rev. Msgr. JAMES A. CARTER, Vicar for Clergy; Rev. Msgr. LEIGH A. LEHOCKY, V.F., Vicar for Ecumenical Affairs & Pastoral Organizations; Rev. Msgr. CHARLES H. ROWLAND, Vicar for Judicial Affairs; Sr. SUSAN SCHORSTEN, H.M., Dir., Catholic Charities & Diocesan Social Ministry; Dr. GAY G. ROWZIE, Dir., Christian Formation/Education; DENNIS F. ATWOOD, Chief Financial Officer; SANDY FERENCZ, Dir., Stewardship & Devel. MARY M. JEFFCOAT, Dir., Office of Communications & Information; JAY E. LEVAN, Dir. Planning & Synod Implementation.

Diocesan Tribunal—114 Rear Broad St., P.O. Box 818, Charleston, 29402. Tel: 843-724-8363; Fax: 843-724-6366.

Vicar Judicial—Rev. Msgr. CHARLES H. ROWLAND, J.C.L.

Adjutant Vicar Judicial—Rev. THOMAS X. HOFMANN, J.C.L.

Director of the Tribunal—MARY M. SMIRCIC.

Judges—Rev. Msgr. CHARLES H. ROWLAND, J.C.L.; Rev. Msgr. ROBERT J. KELLY; Rev. Msgr. LAWRENCE B. MCINERNY, J.C.L.; Rev. Msgr. SAM R. MIGLARESE, V.G.; Rev. Msgr. JOSEPH R. ROTH; Revs. THOMAS X. HOFMANN, J.C.L.; JOSEPH J. MAHER; H. GREGORY WEST, J.C.L.

Defenders of the Bond—Rev. Msgr. THOMAS R. DUFFY; Rev. Msgr. EDWARD D. LOFTON; Revs. J. SCOTT NEWMAN, J.C.L.

Promotor of Justice—Rev. DENNIS B. WILLEY.

Advocates—Sr. AGNES ASSISI, O.S.F.; ERNEST M. COMAR; JOANNE M. COMAR; CLARA S. DUNN; FRANK MODICA; NANCY L. ROWLAND; MARY M. SMIRCIC; SUZANNE A. TIERNEY.

Notaries—ELIZABETH S. BECKER; CLEO E. CANTEY.

College of Consultors—Rev. Msgr. SAM R. MIGLARESE, V.G.; Rev. Msgr. JAMES A. CARTER; Rev. Msgr. THOMAS R. DUFFY, V.F.; Rev. Msgr. ROBERT J. KELLY; Rev. Msgr. E. CHRISTOPHER LATHEM, V.F.; Rev. Msgr. LEIGH A. LEHOCKY, V.F.; Rev. Msgr. CHARLES H. ROWLAND; Rev. MICHAEL F. MCCAFFERTY; Very Rev. JOSEPH A. WAHL C.O.; Revs. PETER CLARKE; THOMAS A. EVATT; PAUL M. WILLIAMS, O.F.M.

Deans—Rev. Msgr. E. CHRISTOPHER LATHEM, V.F., Coastal Deanery; Rev. Msgr. LEIGH A. LEHOCKY, V.F., Midlands Deanery; Rev. Msgr. THOMAS R. DUFFY, V.F., Pee Dee Deanery; Very Rev. CHESTER M. MOCZYDLOWSKI, V.F., Piedmont Deanery.

Diocesan Finance Committee—Rev. Msgr. Sam R. Miglarese, V.G., Chm., *P.O. Box 818, Charleston, 29402.* Tel: 843-723-3488.

Presbyteral Council—Most Rev. David B. Thompson; Rev. Msgr. Sam R. Miglarese, V.G., Facilitator; Rev. Msgr. James A. Carter; Rev. Msgr. Thomas R. Duffy, V.F.; Rev. Msgr. Robert J. Kelly; Rev. Msgr. E. Christopher Lathem, V.F.; Rev. Msgr. Leigh A. Lehocky, V.F.; Rev. Msgr. Charles H. Rowland; Very Revs. Chester M. Moczydlowski, V.F.; Joseph A. Wahl, C.O.; Revs. Peter Clarke; Thomas A. Evatt; Richard D. Harris; Joseph F. Hanley, Jr.; Timothy M. Lijewski; Jerome F. Schwab; Paul M. Williams, O.F.M.; Sr. Bridget Sullivan, O.L.M., Sec.

Bishop's Missionary Support Committee—Rev. Msgr. Robert J. Kelly, *P.O. Box 1257, Folly Beach, 29439.* Tel: 843-588-2336.

Building Committee—Rev. Msgr. James A. Carter, Chm., *P.O. Box 724, Mt. Pleasant, 29465.* Tel: 843-884-5587.

Catholic Charities—Sr. Susan Schorsten, H.M., Dir., *1662 Ingram Rd., Charleston, 29407.* Tel: 843-769-4466.

Catholic Women, Council of—Rev. William F. Pentis, C.O., Moderator, *P.O. Box 11586, Rock Hill, 29731.* Tel: 803-327-2097.

Cemeteries—Dennis F. Atwood, Dir., *1662 Ingram Rd., Charleston, 29407.* Tel: 843-769-4480.

Charismatic Renewals and Prayer Groups—Joseph Balazs, Diocesan Liaison, *114 Horseshoe Cove, Sumter, 29150.* Tel: 803-773-1160.

Commission for Divine Worship and Sacraments—William N. Schlitt, Chm., *120 Broad St., Charleston, 29401.* Tel: 843-724-8395.

Christian Formation/Education—Dr. Gay G. Rowzie, Sec., Education & Evangelization; Lawrence Olesksiak, M.S., Asst. Supt. of Schools; Paul D. Schroeder, M.T.S., Dir., Catechesis, Initiation & Evangelization; Gerald C. White, M.A., Dir., Youth & Young Adult Ministry, *1662 Ingram Rd., Charleston, 29407.* Tel: 843-769-2160. Ann Penick, M.A., L.P.C., Coord., *Campus Ministry, 120 Broad St., Charleston, 29407.* Tel: 843-965-4997.

Holy Childhood Association—Rev. Msgr. Robert J. Kelly, Dir., *P.O. Box 1257, Folly Beach, 49439.* Tel: 843-588-2336.

Marian Programs—Rev. D. Anthony Droze, Moderator, *111 Hampton Ave., Greenville, 29601.* Tel: 864-271-8422.

Master of Episcopal Ceremonies—Diocesan- Rev. H. Gregory West, J.C.L., *P.O. Box 487, Hardeeville, 29927.* Tel: 843-784-2943. Episcopal- Rev. Dennis B. Willey, *120 Broad St., Charleston, 29401.* Tel: 843-724-8395.

Office of Prayer & Worship—Rt. Rev. Francis Kline, O.C.S.O., *P.O. Box 818, Charleston, 29402.* Tel: 843-724-6364.

Newspaper—*"The New Catholic Miscellany"*, Jordan B. McMorrough, Editor, *P.O. Box 818, Charleston, 29402.* Tel: 843-724-8375; Fax: 843-724-8368

Propagation of the Faith—Rev. Msgr. Robert J. Kelly, Dir., *P.O. Box 1257, Folly Beach, 29439.* Tel: 843-588-2336.

Office of Communications & Information—Mary M. Jeffcoat, Dir., *P.O. Box 818, Charleston, 29402.* Tel: 843-724-8375; Fax: 843-724-8368.

Vocations—Rev. Henry T. Barron, *1662 Ingram Rd., Charleston, 29407.* Tel: 843-769-2184; 795-3821.

Bishop's Missionary League—*P.O. Box 818, Charleston, 29402.* Tel: 843-723-3488.

Cursillo Movement—Rev. Charles J. Snopek, Spiritual Dir., *Waverly-Shell Rd., Rte. 3, Box 455, Pawley's Island, 29585.* Tel: 843-237-3428.

Permanent Diaconate—Rev. Msgr. Joseph R. Roth, Dir., *503 37th Ave. N., Myrtle Beach, 29577.* Tel: 843-448-5930.

Campaign for Human Development—Sr. Susan Schorsten, H.M., Chm., *1662 Ingram Rd., Charleston, 29407.* Tel: 843-769-4466.

Office of Stewardship & Development—Sandy Ferencz, Dir., *P.O. Box 818, Charleston, 29402.* Tel: 843-724-6369.

Personnel Committee—Rev. Msgr. James A. Carter, Chm.; Rev. Msgr. Thomas R. Duffy, V.F.; Rev. Msgr. E. Christopher Lathem, V.F.; Rev. Msgr. Leigh A. Lehocky, V.F.; Rev. Msgr. Joseph R. Roth; Very Rev. Chester M. Moczydlowski, V.F.; Rev. Henry T. Barron; Sr. Bernadine Jax, O.S.F.; Mr. John Carroll.

Priests' Retirement—Rev. Msgr. Sam R. Miglarese, V.G., Dir., *P.O. Box 818, Charleston, 29402.* Tel: 843-723-3488.

Scouting Programs—Sam E. Hanvey, *P.O. Box 639, Charleston, 29402.* Tel: 843-577-2600.

Office of Planning and Synod Implementation—Jay E. LeVan, Dir., *P.O. Box 818, Charleston, 29402.* Tel: 843-724-8366; Fax: 843-965-4990.

Vietnamese Ministry—Rev. Vincent The' Quang Nguyen, *111 Hampton Ave., Greenville, 29601.* Tel: 803-271-8422.

Vicar for African American Catholics—Rev. Paul M. Williams, O.F.M., *307 Gower St., Greenville, 29611.* Tel: 803-233-7717.

Vicar for Ecumenism—Rev. Msgr. Leigh A. Lehocky, V.F., *P.O. Box 1896, Columbia, 29202.* Tel: 803-779-0036.

Office for Hispanics—Sr. Susan Schorsten, H.M., *1662 Ingram Rd., Charleston, 29407.* Tel: 843-769-4466.

Society of St. Vincent de Paul—Eleanor Serra, Dioc. Council Pres., *155 Hermitage Rd., Lexington, 29072.* Tel: 803-359-6643.

Office of Black Catholic Ministry—Catherine Fleming Bruce, Coord., *P.O. Box 5734, Columbia, 29250.* Tel: 803-933-9007.

CLERGY, PARISHES, MISSIONS AND PAROCHIAL SCHOOLS

GREATER CHARLESTON
(Charleston County)

1—Cathedral of St. John the Baptist, Rev. Msgr. Sam R. Miglarese, V.G.; Rev. Dennis B. Willey.
Mailing Address: Cathedral Center, 120 Broad St., 29401. Tel: 843-724-8395; Fax: 843-724-6386.
Res., 105 Queen St., 29401.
School—Charleston Catholic School. See Sacred Heart for details.

2—St. Mary's, Rev. Msgr. John A. Simonin.
Res., 89 Hasell St., 29401. Tel: 843-722-7696; Fax: 843-577-5036. [CEM]

3—St. Patrick's, Rev. Richard D. Harris.
Res., 125 St. Philip St., P.O. Box 20726, 29413. Tel: 843-723-6066; Fax: 843-853-8114. [CEM]
School—Charleston Catholic School. See Sacred Heart for details.

4—Sacred Heart, Rev. Michael J. Davino.
Res., 888 King St., 29403-4139. Tel: 843-722-7018; Fax: 843-577-4055.
School—Charleston Catholic School, Tel: 843-577-4495; Fax: 843-577-6662. Sr. Carol Ann Kleindinst, S.S.M.N., Prin.
Lay Teachers 17; Students 226.

5—Our Lady of Mercy, Rev. Richard D. Harris; Sr. Maigread Conway, O.S.F., Pastoral Admin.
Res., 77 America St., 29403. Tel: 843-723-5129.

6—St. John's, Bros. Edward E. Bergeron, C.F.C., Pastoral Admin.; William P. Cronin, C.F.C., Pastoral Admin.; Leonard A. Quinn, C.F.C.
Res., 3921 St. John's Ave., North Charleston, 29405-7158. Tel: 843-744-6201.
School—Tel: 843-744-3901; Fax: 843-744-3689. Mrs. Harriet M. Condon, Prin.
Lay Teachers 15; Students 137.

7—Blessed Sacrament, Rev. Joseph F. Hanley.
Res., 5 St. Teresa Dr., 29407. Tel: 843-556-0801; Fax: 843-556-2851.
School—7 St. Teresa Dr., 27407. Tel: 843-766-2128. Sr. Linda Marie Bolinski, SS.C.M., Prin.
Lay Teachers 29; Students 472.
Convent—O Moore Dr., 29407. Tel: 843-766-5120.

8—St. Peter's. Closed. For inquiries for parish records contact St. Patrick, P.O. Box 20726, Charleston, SC 29413.

9—Divine Redeemer, Berkeley Co., Rev. J. Scott Newman, J.C.L.
Office: 1106 Fort Dr., Hanahan, 29406. Tel: 843-553-0340; Fax: 843-553-0346.
Res., 1022 Recess Rd., Hanahan, 29406. Tel: 843-572-3532.
School—1104 Fort Dr., Hanahan, 29406. Tel: 843-553-1521; Fax: 843-553-7109. Dr. Edward F. Droge, Jr., Prin.
Lay Teachers 15; Students 264.

10—Stella Maris, Rev. Msgr. Lawrence B. McInerny.
Res., 1204 Middle St., P.O. Box 280, Sullivan's Island, 29482. Tel: 843-883-3108 (Office); 883-9158 (Rectory); Fax: 843-883-3160.

11—Church of the Nativity, Rev. Henry T. Barron. In res., Rev. Joseph G. Maher.
Office & Mailing Address: 1061 Folly Rd., 29412. Tel: 843-795-3821; Fax: 843-795-2714.
Res., 1129 Pittsford Cir., 29412. Tel: 843-795-5525; Fax: 843-795-2714.
School—Tel: 843-795-3975. Mrs. Margaret Neises, Prin.
Sisters of SS. Cyril and Methodius 1; Lay Teachers 22; Students 331.
Mission—Folly Beach, Charleston Co., Our Lady of Good Counsel, 56 Center St., P.O. Box 1257, Folly Beach, 29439. Tel: 843-588-6384. Rev. Msgr. Robert J. Kelly.

12—St. Joseph, Rev. Gabriel J. Smith.
Office & Mailing Address: 1695 Wallenberg Blvd., 29407. Tel: 843-556-4611; Fax: 843-556-4612.
Res., 1549 Montclair St., 29407.

13—St. Joseph's. Closed. For inquiries for parish records contact St. Joseph, 1695 Wallenberg Blvd., Charleston, SC 29407.

14—St. Thomas The Apostle, Rev. Arturo O. Dalupang.
Res., 6650 Dorchester Rd., Charleston Heights, 29418. Tel: 843-552-9045; 552-2223; Fax: 843-552-9077.

15—Church of the Holy Spirit, Rev. James Parker.
Res., 2545 Bohicket Rd., Johns Island, 29455. Tel: 843-559-0353. [CEM]

16—Christ the Divine Teacher, Rev. Michael J. Davino.
Mailing Address: MSC 58, The Citadel, 171 Moultrie St., 29409. Tel: 843-953-7692; 722-7018 (Res.); Fax: 843-953-4811 (Res.).

17—Christ Our King, Rev. Msgr. James A. Carter; Rev. James N. Dubrouillet.
Res., 1122 Russell Dr., P.O. Box 724, Mount Pleasant, 29465. Tel: 843-884-5587; Fax: 843-884-7086.
School—Christ Our King-Stella Maris School, 1183 Russell Dr., Mount Pleasant, 29464. Tel: 843-884-4721; Fax: 843-971-9666. Sr. Stella Maris Craven, O.L.M., Prin.
Sisters 1; Lay Teachers 37; Students 683.

OUTSIDE OF THE CITY OF CHARLESTON

Abbeville, Abbeville Co., Sacred Heart, Sr. Joan Kobe, D.W., Pastoral Admin.
Res., 230 N. Main St. at Pinckney St., P.O. Box 812, 29620. Tel: 864-459-5150.
Mission—McCormick, McCormick Co., Good Shepherd, P.O. Box 1468, McCormick, 29835. Tel: 864-465-3615. Sr. Joan Kobe, D.W., Pastoral Admin.
Station—Abbeville, McCormick Correction Institution.

Aiken, Aiken Co., St. Mary, Help of Christians, Revs. Thomas A. Evatt; Edward W. Fitzgerald.
Res., 219 York St. S.E., P.O. Box 438, 29802. Tel: 803-649-4777; Fax: 803-642-6421. [CEM]
School—Tel: 803-649-2171; Fax: 803-643-0092. Mr. D. Keith Darr, Prin.
Sisters of Charity of Our Lady of Mercy 1; Lay Teachers 30; Students 327.

St. Gerard's, Rev. Thomas M. Gillin, S.J.
Res., 640 Edrie St. N.E., 29801. Tel: 803-649-3030.
School—Merged with St. Mary's School.

Anderson, Anderson Co., St. Joseph's, Rev. Thomas D. Timlin.
Office: 1303 McLees Rd., 29622. Tel: 864-225-5341; Fax: 864-224-0538.
Res., 1107 McLees Rd., P.O. Box 1013, 29622. Tel: 864-224-4415.
Church—1200 Cornelia Rd., 29621.
School—1200 Cornelia Rd., 29621. Tel: 864-225-2143. Mrs. Marilyn Butterfoss, Prin.
Lay Teachers 9; Students 160.

St. Mary of the Angels, Rev. David L. Hyman, O.F.M. In res., Rev. Thomas F. Vigliotta, O.F.M.
Res., 1821 White St., P.O. Box 3, 29622. Tel: 864-226-8621; Fax: 864-226-2536.

Batesburg, Lexington Co., St. John of the Cross, Rev. Filemon Juya (Garagoa) Admin.
Res., 320 W. Columbia Ave., P.O. Box 438, 29006. Tel: 803-532-1208.

Beaufort, Beaufort Co., St. Peter's, Rev. Ronald R. Cellini (PIT).
Res., 70 Lady's Island Dr., 29902. Tel: 843-522-9555; Fax: 843-522-0667. [CEM]
School—Tel: 843-522-2163. Mr. William Gabrielson, Prin.
Lay Teachers 18; Students 186.
Mission—Saint Helena Island, Beaufort Co., Holy Cross.

Bluffton, Beaufort Co., St. Andrew's, Rev. H. Gregory West, J.C.L.
Res., 232 Pinckney Colony Rd., 29910. Tel: 843-757-2986; Fax: 843-757-2986.
Office & Mailing: 220 Pinckney Colony Rd., 29910. [CEM]
Mission—Hardeeville, Jasper Co., St. Anthony's, P.O. Box 497, Hardeeville, 29927.

Camden, Kershaw Co., Our Lady of Perpetual Help, Rev. John P. Coffey.
Res., 1709 Lyttleton St., 29020. Tel: 803-432-6131; Fax: 803-432-3440.

Chapin, Lexington Co., Our Lady of the Lake, Rev.

Andrew J. Vollkommer.
Mailing Address: 195 Amicks Ferry Rd., P.O. Box 631, 29036. Tel: 803-345-3962; Fax: 803-345-8933.
Res., 2 Oak Stand Ct., Irmo, 29063. Tel: 803-781-8767.

Cheraw, Chesterfield Co., St. Peter's, Rev. Patrick E. Cooper.
Res., 602 Market St., P.O. Box 905, 29520. Tel: 843-537-7351.
Missions—Bennettsville, Marlboro Co., St. Denis; Pageland, Chesterfield Co., St. Ernest.

Chester, Chester Co., St. Joseph's, Rev. Thomas F. Morrison; Deacon Jon E. Dwyer, Pastoral Admin.
Res., 110 West End, P.O. Box 869, 29706. Tel: 803-377-4695.

Clemson, Pickens Co., St. Andrew, Revs. Johns J. Kenny, C.S.P.; Gerard J. Aylward, C.S.P.; Augustus S. McGuire, C.S.P.; James M. Brucz, C.S.P.
Res., 123 Folger St., P.O. Box 112, 29633. Tel: 864-654-2711; 654-1757; Fax: 864-654-2950.
Missions—Seneca, Oconee Co., St. Paul the Apostle; Walhalla, Oconee Co., St. Francis of Assisi.
Station—Clemson, Clemson University.

Columbia, Richland Co.,

1—St. Peter's, Rev. Msgr. Leigh A. Lehocky.
Mailing Address: P.O. Box 1896, 29202.
Res., 2125 Raven Tr., West Columbia, 29169.
Church—1529 Assembly St., 29201. Tel: 803-779-0036; Fax: 803-799-2438. [CEM 3]
School—Tel: 803-252-8285. Mrs. Madeline McMillion, Prin.
Lay Teachers 15; Students 187.
Station—Columbia, South Carolina State Hospital.

2—St. Joseph, Rev. Msgr. Charles H. Rowland; Rev. Jeffrey A. Kendall.
Office: 3512 Devine St., 29205. Tel: 803-254-7646; Fax: 803-799-7607.
Res., 3451 Blossom St., 29205. Tel: 803-540-1910.
Church—3600 Devine St., 29205.
School—3700 Devine St., 29205. Tel: 803-254-6736; Fax: 803-540-1913. Sr. Christina Murphy, S.N.D., Prin.
Ursuline Nuns of the Congregation of Paris 3; Lay Teachers 24; Students 300.
Mission—Winnsboro, Fairfield Co., St. Theresa. Rev. Timothy M. Lijewski.
Res., 1610 Greene St., 29201. Tel: 803-799-5870.

3—Saint Martin de Porres, Rev. James L. LeBlanc, Admin.
Res., 2229 Hampton St., P.O. Box 4187, 29240. Tel: 803-254-6862; Fax: 803-779-4720.
School—Tel: 803-254-6862. Mrs. Sandra Leatherwood, Prin.
Lay Teachers 14; Students 144.
Station—Columbia, Correctional Institutions in the Greater Columbia Area.

4—Our Lady of the Hills, Rev. Robert H. Fix.
Mailing Address: & Religious Education Center: 2700 Ashland Rd., 29210. Tel: 803-772-7400; Fax: 803-798-8030.
Res., 120 Marydale Ln., 29210. Tel: 803-772-6692.

5—St. John Neumann, Rev. Frederick F. Masad.
Res., 2816 Bancroff Rd., P.O. Box 23689, 29224. Tel: 803-788-1274; 788-0811 (Office); Fax: 803-788-1501 (Office).
Church—100 Polo Rd., 29223. Tel: 803-788-1478.
School—721 Polo Rd., 29223. Tel: 803-788-1367; Fax: 803-788-7330. Dr. Margaret Adams, Prin.
Lay Teachers 31; Students 354.
Station—Blythewood Catholic Community, 313 Seton Hall Dr., 29223. Tel: 803-736-4876. Sr. Clare Reinert, S.S.N.D., Pastoral Admin.

6—Good Shepherd, Rev. William D. Ladkau.
Mailing Address: P.O. Box 1298, 29202.
Res., 1625 Granby Rd., Cayce, 29033. Tel: 803-791-4596; 765-1334 (Office); Fax: 803-765-2208.

Conway, Horry Co., St. James, Rev. Frederick LaBrecque.
Church & Office: 1071 Academy Dr., 29526. Tel: 843-347-5168; Fax: 843-347-1212.
Res., 181 Long Ave., 29526. Tel: 843-248-7148.
Mission—Loris, Horry Co., Church of the Resurrection, 1929 Business Hwy. 9E, Loris, 29569. Tel: 843-756-6168.

Dillon, Dillon Co., St. Louis, Sr. Bernadine Jax, O.S.F., Pastoral Admin.
Res., 607 N. Fourth Ave., 29536. Tel: 843-744-9401.
Mission—Marion, Marion Co., Infant Jesus.

Edgefield, Edgefield Co., St. Mary's, Rev. Robert W. Ninedorf.
Res., 302 Jeter St., P.O. Box 386, 29824. Tel: 803-637-6248; Fax: 803-637-6248. [CEM]
Church—305 Buncombe St., 29824.

Florence, Florence Co., St. Anthony's All Souls Memorial, Revs. Basil P. Congro; William A. Maley.
Res., 2536 W. Hoffmeyer Rd., P.O. Box 5327, 29502. Tel: 843-665-5853; 662-5674; Fax: 843-662-4800.
School—Tel: 843-662-1910. Mr. Frank J. Cottone, Prin.
Priests 1; Lay Teachers 22; Students 290.

St. Ann, Rev. Michael T. Corrigan (GAL).
Res., 113 S. Kemp St., 29501. Tel: 843-662-1736; Fax: 843-662-1736.
Convent—Tel: 843-662-6360.
Sisters of St. Mary of Namur 3.

Gaffney, Cherokee Co., Sacred Heart, Rev. Gary S. Linsky.
Res., 407 Grace St., 29340. Tel: 864-489-9453.

Garden City, Horry Co., St. Michael, Rev. Msgr. Thomas R. Duffy; Rev. Mathew Alapatt, M.S.F.S. (India).
Mailing Address: P.O. Box 14357, Surfside Beach, 29587.
Res., 574 Cypress Ave., 29576. Tel: 843-651-3737; Fax: 843-651-6316.

Georgetown, Georgetown Co., St. Mary's. (Our Lady of Ransom). Rev. Steven L. Brovey.
Office: 317 Broad St., P.O. Box 766, 29442. Tel: 843-546-7416; Fax: 843-546-7003.
Res., 810 Highmark St., 29442.
Missions—Andrews, Georgetown Co., St. Leo the Great; McClellanville, Charleston Co., McClellanville Mission.

St. Cyprian, Rev. Steven L. Brovey; Sr. Kathleen Driscoll, D.C., Pastoral Admin.
Center & Mailing Address: 1905 Front St., P.O. Box 2037, 29442. Tel: 843-546-1470; Fax: 843-527-2139.

Gloverville, Aiken Co., Our Lady of the Valley, Rev. John L. Lawlor, C.M.; Deacon Robert J. Waters, Pastoral Admin.
Mailing Address: P.O. Box 419, 29828. Tel: 803-593-2241; Fax: 803-593-2241.
Res., 2429 Augusta Rd., 29828. Tel: 803-593-2241.
Parish Community Center—Tel: 803-593-2241.
Convent—Horsecreek Valley Convent, P.O. Box 358, 29828. Tel: 803-593-9862.
Daughters of Charity 5.

Goose Creek, Berkeley Co., Immaculate Conception, Rev. Frank Palmieri, C.R.M.
Res., 510 St. James Ave., 29445. Tel: 843-553-1386; 572-1270; Fax: 843-572-3129.

Greenville, Greenville Co., St. Mary's, Rev. Msgr. Charles J. Baum, Pastor Emeritus; Revs. D. Anthony Droze; Antonio M. Londono, S.P.; Charles J. McPadden, M.M. In res., Rev. Vincent The' Quang Nguyen.
Mailing Address: 111 Hampton Ave., 29601. Tel: 864-271-8422; Fax: 864-370-9880.
Res., 338 W. Washington St., 29601. Fax: 864-235-2868.
School—101 Hampton Ave., 29601. Tel: 864-271-3870. Sr. Veronica Janas, O.L.M., Prin.
Sisters of Charity of Our Lady of Mercy 1; Lay Teachers 17; Students 304.

Our Lady of the Rosary, Rev. Charles J. Day.
Res., 3710 Augusta Rd., P.O. Box 8396, 29604. Tel: 864-422-1648; Fax: 864-277-5969.
School—Tel: 864-277-5350; Fax: 864-277-7745. Mr. Paul Herr, Prin.
Lay Teachers 16; Students 204.

St. Anthony of Padua, Rev. Paul M. Williams, O.F.M. In res., Rev. Francis A. Gorman, O.F.M., (Retired).
Res., 307 Gower St., 29611. Tel: 864-233-7717; Fax: 864-233-2852.
School—309 Gower St., 29611. Tel: 864-271-0167; Fax: 864-271-2936. Sr. Catherine Noecker, O.S.F., Prin.
Sisters of St. Francis of Williamsville 3; Lay Teachers 8; Students 128.

Greenwood, Greenwood Co., Our Lady of Lourdes, Rev. Hayden J. Vaverek.
Office: 110 E. Laurel Ave., 29649. Tel: 864-223-8410; Fax: 864-223-4039.
Res., 120 Colonial Dr., 29649. Tel: 864-223-3003.

Greer, Greenville Co., Blessed Trinity, Rev. Nicholas R. Bayard.
Res., 111 Becky Don Dr., Apt. 9, 29651. Tel: 864-879-3812; Fax: 864-879-4225.
Church—901 River Rd., P.O. Box 1371, 29652. Tel: 864-879-4225.

Hartsville, Darlington Co., St. Mary the Virgin Mother, Rev. Gerald J. Ryfinski.
Res., 115 Church St., P.O. Box 1378, 29551. Tel: 843-332-6664; 332-3136; Fax: 843-332-6664.
Mission—Darlington, Darlington Co., St. Joseph the Worker.

St. Joseph's. Closed. For inquiries for parish records contact St. Mary's, P.O. Box 1378, Hartsville, SC 29550.

Hilton Head Island, Beaufort Co., Holy Family, Rev. Edmund M. McCaffrey.
Res., 24 Pope Ave., P.O. Box 5397, 29938. Tel: 843-785-2895; 785-2876; Fax: 843-842-7494.

St. Francis By the Sea, Revs. Michael F. McCafferty,.; Donald F. Grady, S.J.
Res., 45 Beach City Rd., P.O. Box 22239, 29925. Tel: 843-681-6350; Fax: 843-689-5502.
School—P.O. Box 1482, 29925. Tel: 843-681-6501. Dr. Kathleen Sutcliffe, Prin.
Lay Teachers 5; Students 93.

Joanna, Laurens Co., St. Boniface, Rev. James M. Crowley, O.M.I.
Res., 403 Main St., P.O. Box 188, 29351. Tel: 864-697-6745.
Station—Joanna, Whitten Center.

Kingstree, Williamsburg Co., St. Ann's, Deacon John P. Kiely, Pastoral Admin.
Res., 300 Ashton Ave., 29556. Tel: 843-354-7798.
Center—906 Thorne Ave., 29556. Tel: 843-354-9415.
Convent—908 Thorne Ave., 29556. Tel: 843-354-9415.
Felician Sisters 2.

Lake City, Florence Co., St. Philip's, Deacon John P. Kiely, Pastoral Admin.
Res., 146 Anderson St., P.O. Box 399, 29560. Tel: 843-394-8343.
Mission—Johnsonville, Florence Co., St. Patrick.

Lancaster, Lancaster Co., St. Catherine's, Rev. Thomas F. Morrison.
Res., 720 W. Meeting St., P.O. Box 814, 29720. Tel: 803-283-3362; Fax: 803-283-3363.
Mission—Great Falls, Chester Co., St. Michael.

Lexington, Lexington Co., Corpus Christi, Rev. Jerome F. Schwab.
Res., 2350 Augusta Hwy., 29072. Tel: 803-359-4391; Fax: 803-359-8885.

Mauldin, Greenville Co., St. Elizabeth Ann Seton, Rev. Howard L. Coughlin.
Mailing Address: & Office: P.O. Box 672, 29662-0672. Tel: 864-963-3959; 963-8428; Fax: 864-967-9726.
Res., 115 Ivy Dr., Simpsonville, 29680-6124. Tel: 864-967-3125.

Moncks Corner, Berkeley Co., St. Philip Benizi, Rev. Thomas X. Hofmann.
Res., 1404 Old Hwy. 52 S., 29461. Tel: 843-761-3777.
Mission—Bonneau, Berkeley Co., Our Lady of Peace, 224 Murry Ferry Rd., Bonneau, 29431.

Murphy Village, Edgefield Co., St. Edward, Rev. Peter Clarke.
Res., 1370 Edgefield Rd., P.O. Box 6340, North Augusta, 29861. Tel: 803-279-1837; Fax: 803-279-1837.

Myrtle Beach, Horry Co., St. Andrew's, Rev. Msgr. Joseph R. Roth; Rev. Paul A. McDuffie.
Parish Center—512 36th Ave. N., 29577. Tel: 843-448-5930; Fax: 843-448-3947.
Res., 503 37th Ave. N., 29577. Tel: 843-448-5930; Fax: 843-448-3947.
School—3601 N. Kings Hwy., 29577. Tel: 843-448-6062. Mrs. Mary H. Halasz, Prin.
Sisters 1; Lay Teachers 16; Students 260.

Newberry, Newberry Co., St. Mark, Rev. James M. Crowley, O.M.I.
Res., 928 Boundary St., 29108. Tel: 803-276-6446; Fax: 803-276-0856.

North Augusta, Aiken Co., Our Lady of Peace, Revs. C. Alexander McDonald; Luis Augusto Soler (Tunja).
Res., 856 Old Edgefield Rd., P.O. Box 6605, 29861-6605. Tel: 803-279-0315; Fax: 803-279-5247.
School—Tel: 803-279-8396. Mrs. Kathleen Morton, Prin.
Lay Teachers 23; Students 224.

North Myrtle Beach, Horry Co., Our Lady Star of the Sea, Rev. George F. Moynihan.
Office: 1100 Eighth Ave. N., 29582. Tel: 843-249-2356; Fax: 843-249-8514.
Res., 1105 Golf View Dr., 29582. Tel: 843-249-8049.

Orangeburg, Orangeburg Co., Holy Trinity, Rev. Michael J. Polewczak (ALB).
Res., 2161 Griffith Dr., N.W. P.O. Box 1207, 29116. Tel: 803-534-8177; Fax: 803-535-0012.
School—2202 Riverbank Dr. N.W., 29118. Tel: 803-534-0461. Mrs. Doris Trezevant, Prin.
Lay Teachers 10; Students 86.
Brothers Residence—1710 Amelia St., N.E., 29115. Tel: 803-534-2302.
Xaverian Brothers (St. Joseph Prov.) 4.
Missions—Allendale, Barnwell Co., St. Mary; Barnwell, Barnwell Co., St. Andrew the Apostle, c/o Rev. Louis J.P. Kennedy, P.O. Box 604, Barnwell, 29812. Tel: 803-259-7593; Blackville, Barnwell Co., Sacred Heart; Springfield, Orangeburg Co., St. Theresa.
Station—Orangeburg, Santee.

Christ the King. Closed. For inquiries for parish records contact Holy Trinity, 351 Amelia St. N.E., P.O. Box 1207, Orangeburg, SC 29115. Tel: 803-534-8177.

Pawleys Island, Georgetown Co., Precious Blood of Christ, Rev. Charles J. Snopek.
Res., 100 Arcadia Rd., 29585.
Office: 1633 Waverly Rd., 29585. Tel: 843-237-3428; Fax: 843-237-2293.

Pickens, Pickens Co., Holy Cross, Rev. Francis J. Travis.

Res., 416 John St., P.O. Box 855, 29671. Tel: 864-878-0574.
Church—558-560 Hampton St., 29671. Tel: 864-878-3820; Fax: 864-878-0028.
Mission—Easley, Anderson Co., St. Luke, Tel: 864-269-6891.

Ridgeland, Jasper Co., St. Anthony's, Rev. Michael J. Hussey, O.M.I.
Res., U.S. Hwy. 17, P.O. Box 548, 29936. Tel: 843-726-3606; 943-4019.
Mission—Hampton, Hampton Co., St. Mary.

Rock Hill, York Co., St. Anne's, Rev. William F. Pentis, C.O.
Office & Mailing Address: 1694 Bird St., 29730. Tel: 803-329-2662; Fax: 803-329-2190.
Res., 434 Charlotte Ave., 29731. Tel: 803-327-3236.
School—Tel: 803-324-4814; Fax: 803-324-4281. Mr. Frederick J. McKay, Jr., Prin.
Lay Teachers 20; Students 344.
Mission—Fort Mill, York Co., St. Philip Neri, P.O. Box 3413, Fort Mill, 29715. Tel: 803-328-2620. Rev. John P. Giuliani, C.O., Admin.

St. Mary's, Bro. David Boone, C.O., Pastoral Admin.; Sr. Francis K. Saring, M.S.B.T., Pastoral Admin.
Office—Bannon Hall, 902 Crawford Rd., P.O. Box 11982, 29731. Tel: 803-329-1008; Fax: 803-329-1008.
Convent—Missionary Servants of the Most Blessed Trinity. 915 Crawford Rd., 29730. Tel: 803-327-7450. St. Mary's Missionary Cenacle.
Saint Martin de Porres Recreation Center—911 Crawford Rd., 29730.

Simpsonville, Greenville Co., St. Mary Magdalene, Rev. Herbert K. Conner, S.J.
Res., 107 Wickersham Dr., 29681. Tel: 864-234-5323.
Church & Office: 2252 Woodruff Rd., 29681. Tel: 864-288-4884; Fax: 864-297-5804.

Spartanburg, Spartanburg Co., St. Paul the Apostle, Rev. Michael R. DeAntonio.
Res., 161 N. Dean St., 29302. Tel: 864-582-0674; Fax: 864-582-0716.
School—Tel: 864-582-6645; Fax: 864-582-1225. Mrs. Ann Marie Sullivan, Prin.
Lay Teachers 16; Students 223.

St. Joseph's, Rev. Michael R. DeAntonio.
Office: 450 Duncan St., P.O. Box 5091, 29304. Tel: 864-582-1870.
Res., 161 N. Dean St., 29302. Tel: 864-582-0674.

Jesus Our Risen Savior, Rev. Eugene A. Leonard.
Res., 2565 Reidville Rd., P.O. Box 17059, 29301. Tel: 864-576-1164; 576-0726.

Summerton, Clarendon Co., St. Mary's, Rev. Raymond E. DuMouchel; Deacon Charles M. Walsh, Pastoral Admin.
Res., 10 N. Cantey St., P.O. Box 960, 29148. Tel: 803-485-2925; Fax: 803-473-5111.
Mission—Holly Hill, Orangeburg Co., St. Ann, 8309 Old State Rd., Holly Hill, 29059. Tel: 803-496-7636. Rev. Raymond E. DuMouchel.

Summerville, Dorchester Co., St. John the Beloved, Rev. Msgr. E. Christopher Lathem; Rev. Duane T. Riplog.
Res., 28 Sumter Ave., 29483. Tel: 843-873-0631; Fax: 843-873-0654.
School—Summerville Regional Catholic School, (Grades K-8) 226 Black Oak Blvd., 29483. Tel: 843-873-9310; Fax: 843-873-5709. Ms. Carole Anne White, Prin.
Sisters 1; Lay Teachers 23; Students 385.

St. Theresa the Little Flower, Rev. Msgr. Edward D. Lofton.
Res., 11001 Dorchester Rd., 29485. Tel: 843-875-5002; 875-3609; Fax: 843-875-4884.
Station—Summerville, MacDougall Correction Center.

Sumter, Sumter Co., St. Anne's, Revs. David J. Sharrock, C.SS.R.; Alistair J. McKay, C.SS.R.
Res., 216 E. Liberty St., 29150. Tel: 803-773-3524; Fax: 803-778-1644. [CEM]
School—Tel: 803-775-3692. Mr. John Fer, Prin.
Lay Teachers 24; Students 233.

St. Jude, Rev. Michael Varady, C.SS.R.
Res., 611 W. Oakland Ave., P.O. Box 1589, 29150. Tel: 803-773-9244; Fax: 803-775-6913.
Preschool & Tutorial Program—114 S. Purdy St., 29150. Tel: 803-775-4895.
Convent—609 W. Oakland Ave., P.O. Box 1197, 29150. Tel: 803-775-3721.
Sisters of St. Mary of Namur 4.

Taylors, Greenville Co., Prince of Peace, Very Rev. Chester M. Moczydlowski; Rev. Santiago A. Mora, C.M.F.
Mailing Address: 1209 Brushy Creek Rd., 29687. Tel: 864-268-4352; Fax: 864-322-2239.
Res., 1201 Brushy Creek Rd., 29687. Tel: 864-244-7799.

Union, Union Co., St. Augustine's, Rev. Gary S. Linsky.
Res., 103 E. South St., P.O. Box 507, 29379. Tel: 864-427-7240.
Mission—Laurens, Laurens Co., Holy Spirit, P.O. Box 864, Laurens, 29360. Tel: 864-984-2880. Sr. Mary Laura Lesniak, S.S.M.N., Pastoral Admin.

Walterboro, Colleton Co., St. Anthony's, Rev. Paul F.X. Seitz.
Res., 925 S. Jefferies Blvd., P.O. Box 933, 29488. Tel: 843-549-5230.
Mission—Ritter, Colleton Co., St. James. [CEM]

St. Joseph's. Closed. For inquiries for parish records contact St. Anthony's, P.O. Box 933, Walterboro, SC 29488.

Ward, Saluda Co., St. William's, Rev. Robert W. Ninedorf; Deacon John P. Klein, Pastoral Admin.
Res., Saluda Hwy. No. 39, 29166. Tel: 864-445-7215; Fax: 864-445-7215. [CEM]
Convent—Tel: 864-445-3302. Daughters of Wisdom

Yonges Island, Charleston Co., St. Mary, Rev. William G. Kinney.
Res., 4255 State Hwy. 165, 29449. Tel: 843-889-8549; Fax: 843-869-0124.
Mission—Edisto Island, Charleston Co., SS. Frederick & Stephen.

York, York Co., Divine Saviour, Rev. Edward P. McDevitt, C.O.
Res., 232 Herndon Ave., P.O. Box 341, 29745. Tel: 803-684-3431; 327-2097; Fax: 803-684-3431.
Mission—Lake Wylie, York Co., All Saints.

Chaplains of Public Institutions

LEXINGTON. *Correctional Institutions in the Greater Columbia Area,* 4214 Grand St., 29203. Tel: 803-786-7177. Mr. Roland L. Thomas.

Special Assignment:
Rev.—
Kennedy, Ernest E., 105 Driftwood, Bonneau, SC 29431

On Duty Outside the Diocese:
Reverend Monsignors—
Gorski, J. Donald, Casa Parroquial, Zorritos-Tumbes, Peru
Reverend Fathers—
Abbott, Donald S., St. Dorothy's Church, 11 Harnden St., Wilmington, MA 01887-3519
Buchanan, J. Scott, North American College, Vatican City State, Rome 00120, Italy
McDuffie, Paul A., Aloysius Gonzaga Church, 2025 Stuart Ave., Baton Rouge, LA 70808-3998
White, Leland J., Theology Dept., St. John's Univ., Grand Central Pkwy. & Utopia Pkwy., Jamaica, NY 11439
Zaratti, Filiberto, Via Di Morena 45, Ciampino, Roma, 00043, Italy

---

Military Chaplains:
Reverend Fathers—
Mintegui, Marc A., U.S. Army
Torm, Agustin, U.S. Army

Absent On Leave:
Reverend Fathers—
Bench, John F.
Bleiler, William C.
Condon, Eugene L.
Dilley, Gary D.
Sorce, John J.
Vinasco, Diego H.

Retired:
Reverend Monsignors—
Aiken, Roy F., P.O. Box 1728, Columbia, SC 29202
Baum, Charles J., 7 S. Memminger St., P.O. Box 2406, Greenville, SC 29602
Hamburger, Donald C., P.O. Box 1051, Columbia, SC 29202
Hopwood, Frederick J.
McManus, J. Fleming, 1809 Mepkin Dr., Charleston, SC 29407
Sterker, Louis F., P.A., P.O. Box 1728, Columbia, SC 29202
Reverend Fathers—
Burke, Henry J., 720 Garden Lake St., Murrells Inlet, SC 29576
Burn, William C., 2107 Westchase Dr., Charleston, SC 29407-8829
Chmely, Edward V., White Oak Manor of York, P.O. Box 629, York, SC 29745
Cilwick, Theodore T., 2225 Ashley River Rd., Apt. 182, Charleston, SC 29414
Mullen, Edward F., 8155 Tydor Dr., Jonesboro, GA 30236
Murphy, Joseph J., 203 Center St., Mount Pleasant, SC 29464
Owens-Howard, Robert J.
Patat, St. John E., 2 Riverdale Dr., Charleston, SC 29407
Powers, Jerome C., 1405 Sarsfield Ave., Camden, SC 29020
Schiller, Davis J., 950 Travelers Blvd., Apt. A-3, Summerville, SC 29485
Suggs, Fred H., Brian Center, 3514 Sidney Rd., Columbia, SC 29210

Permanent Deacons:
Anonie, Joseph A., Immaculate Conception Church, Goose Creek
Biviano, Joseph P., Our Lady of the Lake Church, Chapin
Brown, John H., St. Joseph's Church, Charleston
Cahill, Joseph F., Christ Our King Church, Mount Pleasant
Carmody, Joseph E., St. John the Beloved Church, Summerville
Cassandra, Anthony J., Our Lady of the Rosary Church, Greenville
Cole, Stephen D., St. Peter's Church, Columbia
Conick, John E., On Duty Outside the Diocese
Crocker, Dr. Jack L., Our Lady of the Hills Church, Columbia
Cuomo, Nicholas G., Sacred Heart Church, Charleston
Dashnaw, Donald R. (OG), Divine Redeemer Church, Hanahan
Davis, Thomas E., St. Thomas the Apostle Church, Charleston
DeBlasio, Anthony A. (MET), St. Andrew's Church, Myrtle Beach
Delmonte, Richard (HRT), St.John the Beloved Church, Summerville
Dillard, Henry, St. Anthony's Church, Greenville
DiRusso, Charles R., Our Lady of the Hills Church, Columbia
Dwyer, John E., St. Joseph, Chester
Easterling, Charles M., St. Peter's Church, Columbia
Ellis, Billy, Maj. Gen. (Retired), St. Jude's Church, Sumter
Farina, Frank J., St. Mary's Church, Greenville
Gorman, Chester E., St. Andrew's Church, Myrtle Beach
Grismore, Gerald, Prince of Peace Church, Taylors
Hanvey, Samuel E., Cathedral of St. John the Baptist, Charleston
High, Raymond, Corpus Christi Church, Lexington
Hoffmann, Frederick G., Corpus Christi Church, Lexington
Hyland, James P., St. Anne's Church, Rock Hill
Johnson, James H., St. Ann's Church, Florence
Jones, Dennis N., On Duty Outside the Diocese
Jones, Robert L., On Duty Outside the Diocese
Karandisevsky, John F., St. Mary's Church, Greenville
Kemper, Joseph C., (Retired)
Kiely, John D. (TR), St. Philip the Apostle Church, Lake City
Klein, John P. (NY), St. William's Church, Ward
Kronyak, Robert C. (Pat), St. Ann's Church, Holly Hill
Langford, Walter H., Jr., On leave
Lenny, William P. (DET), St. Elizabeth Ann Seton Church, Mauldin
Lorenzo, Anthony J. (RVC), (Retired), St. Andrew's Church, Myrtle Beach
Mahaffey, Robert L., Jr., St. Paul the Apostle Church, Spartanburg
McDonald, Thomas F., Divine Redeemer Church, Hanahan
Meyer, John P. (PAT), Unassigned
Meyer, Philip M., Stella Maris Church, Sullivan Island
Mirande, August J., Our Lady Star of the Sea Church, North Myrtle Beach
Murtaugh, Richard J., Jr., St. Mary's Church, Greenville
Nazzaro, Joseph J. (NEW), St. Francis by the Sea Church, Hilton Head
O'Connor, Joseph P., St. Andrew's Church, Myrtle Beach
O'Donnell, John D., St. Anthony's Church, Florence
Osbourne, R. Michael, Stella Maris Church, Sullivan's Island
Pecko, Harry C., St. Augustine's Church, Union
Petrusak, Frank T., St. Thomas the Apostle Church, Charleston
Pezanowski, Walter S., Stella Maris Church, Sullivan's Island
Poole, Charles P., Jr., St. Joseph's Church, Columbia
Richardson, David W. (NEW), Holy Spirit Church, Johns Island
Rock, Paul J., On Duty Outside the Diocese
Rush, James J. (NY), Unassigned
Schiekel, Frank W. (ALB), St. Michael's Church, Garden City
Sharkey, Donald F., St. John the Beloved Church, Summerville
Shook, Paul F., St. Joseph Church, Anderson
Sturm, Robert M., Our Risen Savior Church, Spartanburg

Thomas, Roland L., St. Martin de Porres Church, Columbia
Tierney, George, St. Mary's Magdalene Church, Simpsonville
Traxler, Harold Gr. Jr. (CAM), St. Andrew's Church, Clemson
Walsh, Charles Michael (CHI), St. Mary's Church, Summerton
Waters, Robert J., St. Mary Help of Christians Church, Aiken
West, James L., Holy Cross Church, Pickens
Whitford, James E. Sr. (ROC), Immaculate Conception Church, Goose Creek
Williams, Thomas P., Unassigned
Wright, Winston C., St. Anthony's Church, Greenville
Young, James R., St. Mary's Church, Georgetown

INSTITUTIONS LOCATED IN THE DIOCESE

[A] HIGH SCHOOLS, DIOCESAN

CHARLESTON. *Bishop England High School*, 203 Calhoun St., 29401-3522. Tel: 843-723-3637; Fax: 843-724-8389. Rev. Msgr. Lawrence B. McInerny, Rector.
Assoc. Prin.: Mr. Nicholas J. Theos; Mr. David F. Held. Priests 1; Sisters 1; Lay Teachers 53; Students 835.

COLUMBIA. *Cardinal Newman High School*. (Grades 7-12), 4701 Forest Dr., 29206. Tel: 803-782-2814; Fax: 803-782-9314. Mr. Harold J. Bayerl, Prin. Sisters 2; Lay Teachers 36; Students 468.

[B] GENERAL HOSPITALS

CHARLESTON. *Bon Secours-St. Francis Xavier Hospital*, 2095 Henry Tecklenburg Dr., 29414. Tel: 843-402-1000
For a complete listing, refer to the Hospitals section.

DILLON. *Saint Eugene Community Hospital*, 301 E. Jackson St., P.O. Box 1327, 29536-1327. Tel: 843-774-4111; Fax: 843-774-1563
For a complete listing, refer to the Hospitals section.

*GREENVILLE. *Franciscan Health System of South Carolina, Inc.*, One St. Francis Dr., 29601. Tel: 864-255-1000
For a complete listing, refer to the Hospitals section.

[C] HOMES FOR AGED

CHARLESTON. *Carter-May Home*, 1660 Ingram Rd., 29407. Tel: 843-556-8314
For a complete listing, refer to the Special Care Facilities section.

[D] MONASTERIES AND RESIDENCES OF PRIESTS AND BROTHERS

MONCKS CORNER. *Mepkin Abbey*. (Trappist Monks), 1098 Mepkin Abbey Rd., 29461. Tel: 843-761-8509; Fax: 843-761-6719. Rt. Revs. Francis Kline, O.C.S.O.; Christian Aidan Carr, O.C.S.O., (Retired); Revs. Benjamin Clark, O.C.S.O.; Leonard A. Cunningham, O.C.S.O.; Aelred Hagan, O.C.S.O., Novice Dir.; Guerric Frederick A. Heckel (RIC); Richard G. McGuire, O.C.S.O.; Edward T. Morley, O.C.S.O.; Bro. Stephen Petronek, O.C.S.O., Prior; Revs. Malachy Wall, O.C.S.O.; Feliciano Manalili, O.C.S.O. (Philippines); Bro. Stan Gumula, O.S.C.O., Bus. Mgr. Professed Monks 26; Priests 10; Novices 1; Number in Community 27.

ROCK HILL. *Oratory of St. Philip Neri, Congregation of the Oratory of Pontifical Rite*, 434 Charlotte Ave., Box 11586, 29730. Tel: 803-327-2097. Very Rev. Joseph A. Wahl, C.O., S.T.D., Provost; Revs. William F. Pentis, C.O., First Deputy, Vicar & Sec.; David D. Valtierra, C.O., Deputy; Bros. David Boone, C.O., Treas.; Joseph Guyon, C.O., Sec.; Revs. Robert S. Dell, C.O.; John P. Giuliani, C.O.; Edward P. McDevitt, C.O.; James Moran, C.O.; Paul C. Proodian, C.O.; Halbert Weidner, C.O., Ph.D.; Clarence Edward Jones, C.O. Fathers 10; Brothers 5; Scholastics 1.

[E] CONVENTS AND RESIDENCES FOR SISTERS

CHARLESTON. *Convent of the Franciscan Sister*, 5 Riverside Dr., 29403. Tel: 843-722-2335. Sr. M. Maigread, Coord. Sisters of the Third Order Regular of St. Francis of the Congregation of Our Lady of Lourdes 2.
Daughters of St. Paul Convent, 243 King St., 29401. Tel: 843-577-0175; Fax: 843-577-9833. Sr. Christine Virginia Orfeo, F.S.P., Local Supr. Sisters 3.
May Forest, Generaltae and Motherhouse of the Sisters of Charity of Our Lady of Mercy, 424 Ft. Johnson Rd., 29412. Tel: 843-795-6083; Fax: 843-795-6083, Ext. 15. Mailing Address: P.O. Box 12410, 29422. Sr. Anne Francis Campbell, O.L.M., Gen. Supr. Tel: 803-795-2866. Professed Sisters in Community 32.
St. Katharine Convent, 34 Wentworth St., 29401. Tel: 843-723-0053. Sr. Elsa Maria Lopez, O.S.P., Coord. Oblate Sisters of Providence 2.
Sisters of Bon Secours Convent, 878 Friendly Cir., 29414. Tel: 843-763-2336. Sisters 2.
Sisters of St. Mary Convent, 28 Riverside Dr., 29403. Tel: 843-722-4198. Sisters 2.

COLUMBIA. *Dominican House*, 3605 Hanson Ave., 29204. Tel: 803-738-0890. Sisters 2.
Ursuline Convent, 1607 Edgehill Rd., 29204. Tel: 803-782-3121. Sr. Maria Lovett., O.S.U., Local Supr. Ursline Nuns of the Congregation of Paris (Louisville, KY) 2.

CONWAY. *St. Joseph's Convent*, 1210 Main St., 29526. Tel: 843-248-3564.

DILLON. *Franciscan Sisters of Mary*, 803 N. 6th Ave., 29536. Tel: 843-774-7008. Franciscan Sisters of Mary 2.

GREENVILLE. *Monastery of St. Clare*, 1916 N. Pleasantburg Dr., 29609-4080. Tel: 864-244-4514. Franciscan Poor Clare Nuns. Sr. Rucia Rauton, O.S.C., Abbess. Cloistered Nuns in Solemn Vows 17; Postulants 1; Extern in Perpetual Vows 1.

RIDGEVILLE. *Sisters of St. Dominic*. (Givhans), 2151 Hwy. 61, 29472-6454. Tel: 843-875-4817. Sisters of St. Dominic (Adrian, MI) 2.

ROCK HILL. *Franciscan Sisters of Mary*, 1545 Cameron Dr., 29730-3203. Tel: 803-366-5969.

ST. HELENA ISLAND. *Franciscan Center*, 85 Mattis Rd., U.S. Hwy. 21, P.O. Box 682, 29920. Tel: 843-838-3924. Sisters of St. Francis of Philadelphia, Glen Riddle-Aston, PA 2.

[F] CATHOLIC CHARITIES

CHARLESTON. *Catholic Charities of the Diocese of Charleston*, 1662 Ingram Rd., 29407. Tel: 843-769-4466; Fax: 803-769-2179. Sr. Susan Schorsten, H.M., Dir., Coastal Regional Office, 1662 Ingram Rd., 29407. Tel: 843-769-2244. Sr. Pat Keating, O.P., Regl. Coord., Midlands Regional Office, 1012 Taylor St., P.O. Box 7245, Columbia, 29202-7245. Tel: 803-254-9776. Mrs. Peggy Sookikian, Regl. Coord., Pee Dee Regional Office, 1071 Academy Dr., Conway, 29526. Tel: 843-347-5157. Mrs. Diane Bullard, Regl. Coord., Piedmont Regional Office, 111 Hampton Ave., P.O. Box 216, Greenville, 29602-0216; Fax: 864-370-9880. Sr. Margie Hosch, O.S.F., Regl. Coord.
Echo House-Inner City Apostolate, 1911 Hackemann Ave., 29405. Tel: 843-554-7319. Sr. Maigread Conway, O.S.F., Dir.
Neighborhood House-Inner City Apostolate, 77 America St., 29403. Tel: 843-723-5129. Sr. Maigread Conway, O.S.F., Dir.

[G] NEWMAN CENTERS

CHARLESTON. *The Catholic Campus Ministry of the College of Charleston; Medical University of South Carolina*, c/o 120 Broad St., 29401. Tel: 843-965-4997. Ms. Ann Penick, Campus Min.
Charleston Southern University. Mailing Address: c/o 28 Sumter Ave., Summerville, 29483. Tel: 843-873-0631. Rev. Msgr. E. Christopher Lathem.
The Citadel, MSC 58, The Citadel, 171 Moultrie St., 29409. Tel: 843-953-7692; 722-7018; Fax: 843-953-4811. Rev. Michael J. Davino.

AIKEN. *University of South Carolina, Aiken Extension Newman Center*, P.O. Box 438, 29802. Tel: 803-649-4777. Rev. Edward W. Fitzgerald.

ANDERSON. *Anderson College Newman Center*, P.O. Box 1013, 29622. Tel: 864-225-5341. Deacon Paul F. Shook.

BEAUFORT. *University of South Carolina, Beaufort Extension Newman Center*, 70 Lady's Island Dr., 29902. Tel: 843-522-9555. Rev. Ronald R. Cellini (PIT).

CLEMSON. *Clemson University, Southern Wesleyan University*, 209 Sloan St., P.O. Box 112, 29633. Tel: 864-654-7804; 654-1757; 654-9670. Rev. James M. Brucz, C.S.P. Legal Title: *Clemson University - Catholic Campus Ministry at St. Andrew's Church and the Catholic Student Association.*

CLINTON. *Presbyterian College Newman Center*, c/o 928 Boundry St., Newberry, 29108. Tel: 803-276-6446. Rev. James M. Crowley.

COLUMBIA. *Allen University, Benedict College Newman Center*, c/o St. Martin de Porres Church, 2229 Hampton St., P.O. Box 4187, 29240. Tel: 803-254-6862.
University of South Carolina, St. Thomas More Center, 1610 Greene St., 29201. Tel: 803-799-5870; Fax: 803-765-0800. Rev. Timothy M. Lijewski.

CONWAY. *Coastal Carolina University*, P.O. Box 1754, 29526.

DUE WEST. *Erskine College Newman Center*. P.O. Box 812, Abbeville, 29620. Tel: 864-459-5150. Sr. Joan Kobe, D.W.

FLORENCE. *Francis Marion University Newman Center*, 113 S. Kemp St., 29501. Tel: 843-662-1736. Rev. Michael T. Corrigan (GAL).

GAFFNEY. *Limestone College Newman Center*, 407 Grace St., 29340. Tel: 864-489-9453. Rev. Gary S. Linsky.

GREENVILLE. *Furman University Newman Center*, 307 Gower St., 29611. Tel: 864-233-7717; Fax: 864-233-2852. Rev. Paul M. Williams.

GREENWOOD. *Lander College Newman Center*, Office, 110 E. Laurel Ave., 29649. Tel: 864-223-8410. Rev. Hayden J. Vaverek.

HARTSVILLE. *Coker College Newman Center*, 115 Church St., P.O. Box 1378, 29550. Tel: 843-332-6664; 332-3136. Rev. Gerald J. Ryfinski.

NEWBERRY. *Newberry College Newman Center*, 928 Boundry St., 29108. Tel: 803-276-6446. Rev. James M. Crowley.

ORANGEBURG. *South Carolina State University Newman Center & Claflin College*, 1710 Amelia St., N.E., 29115. Tel: 803-534-2302. Bro. Jim Connolly, C.F.X., Campus Minister.

ROCK HILL. *Winthrop University, York Co. Tech Center Newman Center*, 434 Charlotte Ave., Box 11586, 29731. Tel: 803-327-2097. Rev. David D. Valtierra, C.O.

SPARTANBURG. *Converse College, Wofford College, Spartanburg Methodist College Newman Center*, 161 N. Dean St., 29302. Tel: 864-582-0674. Rev. Michael R. DeAntonio.
Wofford College, 429 N. Church St., 29303-3668.

SUMTER. *Morris College*, P.O. Box 1589, 29150. Tel: 803-773-9244. Rev. Michael Varady, C.SS.R.

[H] RETREAT CENTERS

EDISTO BEACH. *Sea of Peace House of Prayer*, 802 Jungle Rd., 29438. Tel: 843-869-0513.

KINGSTREE. *Springbank Christian Center-Dominican Retreat House*, Rte. 2, Box 180, 29556. Tel: 843-382-3426.

[I] MISCELLANEOUS

CHARLESTON. *Ladies of Charity of Sacred Heart Church*, 888 King St., 29403-4138. Tel: 843-722-7018.
Pauline Books & Media, 243 King St., 29401. Tel: 843-577-0175; Fax: 843-577-9833. Daughters of St. Paul.
The Sisters of Charity of Our Lady of Mercy Charitable Trust, 424 Ft. Johnson Rd., P.O. Box 12410, 29422. Tel: 843-795-2866; Fax: 843-795-6083, Ext. 15.

COLUMBIA. *CSA Providence Ministries*, P.O. Box 2786, 29202-2786. Tel: 1-888-223-1886; Fax: 216-696-2204.
Sisters of Charity Foundation of South Carolina, 2601 Laurel St., Ste. 250, 29204. Tel: 803-254-0230; Fax: 803-749-0444.

JOHNS ISLAND. *Our Lady of Mercy Community Outreach Services, Inc.*, 1684 Brownswood Rd., 29455. Tel: 843-559-4109. P.O. Box 607, 29457.
Sponsored by Sisters of Charity of Our Lady of Mercy.

MYRTLE BEACH. *Mercy Hospice Foundation of Horry County*, P.O. Box 1409, 29578. Tel: 843-347-2282; 236-2282. Member of SSM Health Care.

RELIGIOUS INSTITUTES OF MEN REPRESENTED IN THE DIOCESE

For further details refer to the corresponding bracketed number in the Religious Institutes of Men or Women section.

[0100]—*Adorno Fathers.*—C.R.M.
[1350]—*Brothers of St. Francis Xavier.* (St. Joseph Prov.).—C.F.X.
[0350]—*Cistercians Order of the Strict Observance-Trappist.*—O.C.S.O. [1330]—Congregation of the Mission. (Eastern Prov.).—C.M.
[0360]—*Claretian Missionaries.* (Eastern Prov.).—C.M.F.
[0520]—*Franciscan Friars.* (Prov. of the Most Holy Name).—O.F.M.
[0690]—*Jesuit Fathers and Brothers.* (New Orleans; New England Provs.).—S.J.
[0800]—*Maryknoll.*—M.M.
[0910]—*Oblates of Mary Immaculate.* (Eastern American Prov.).—O.M.I.
[0950]—*Oratorians.*—C.O.
[1030]—*Paulist Fathers.*—C.S.P.
[1070]—*Redemptorist Fathers.* (Richmond Vice Prov.).—C.SS.R.

RELIGIOUS INSTITUTES OF WOMEN REPRESENTED IN THE DIOCESE

[0270]—*Congregation of Bon Secours.*—C.B.S.
[1000]—*Congregation of Divine Providence.* (KY).—C.D.P.
[1730]—*Congregation of the Sisters of the Third Order of St. Francis.* (Oldenburg, IN).—O.S.F.

[0760]—*Daughters of Charity of St. Vincent de Paul.*—D.C.
[0960]—*Daughters of Wisdom.* (American Prov.).—D.W.
[1070-03]—*Dominican Sisters.* (Sinsinawa, WI).—O.P.
[1070-11]—*Dominican Sisters.* (Sparkill, NY).—O.P.
[1070-13]—*Dominican Sisters.* (Adrian, MI).—O.P.
[1070-04]—*Dominican Sisters.* (San Rafael, CA).—O.P.
[1170]—*Felician Sisters.*—C.S.S.F.
[1310]—*Franciscan Sisters of Little Fall.* (Minnesota).—O.S.F.
[1415]—*Franciscan Sisters of Mary.*—F.S.M.
[1425]—*Franciscan Sisters of Peace.*—F.S.P.
[1440]—*Franciscan Sisters of the Poor.*—S.F.P.
[1360]—*Missionary Franciscan Sisters of the Immaculate Conception.*—M.F.I.C.
[2790]—*Missionary Servants of the Most Blessed Trinity.*—M.S.B.T.
[3040]—*Oblate Sisters of Providence.*—O.S.P.
[3760]—*Order of St. Clare.*—O.S.C.
[0950]—*Pious Daughters of St. Paul.*—F.S.P.
[2970]—*School Sisters of Notre Dame.*—S.S.N.D.
[1680]—*School Sisters of St. Francis.* (Milwaukee).—O.S.F.
[0500]—*Sisters of Charity of Nazareth.*—S.C.N.
[0510]—*Sisters of Charity of Our Lady of Mercy.*—O.L.M.
[0580]—*Sisters of Charity of St. Augustine.*—C.S.A.
[2575]—*Sisters of Mercy of the Americas.* (Belmont, NC; Dallas, PA;).—R.S.M.
[3000]—*Sisters of Notre Dame de Namur.* (Baltimore; Boston).—S.N.D.deN.
[3950]—*Sisters of Saint Mary of Namur.*—S.S.M.N.
[3780]—*Sisters of Saints Cyril and Methodius.*—SS.C.M.
[1540]—*Sisters of St. Francis.* (Clinton, IA).—O.S.F.
[1650]—*Sisters of St. Francis of Philadelphia.*—O.S.F.
[1800]—*Sisters of St. Francis of the Third Order Regular.* (Williamsville, New York).—O.S.F.
[3840]—*Sisters of St. Joseph of Carondelet.* (Prov. of St. Louis).—C.S.J.
[2110]—*Sisters of the Humility of Mary.*—H.M.
[1720]—*Sisters of the Third Order of St. Francis of the Congregation of Our Lady of Lourdes.* (Rochester).—O.S.F.
[1890]—*Society of Helpers.*—H.H.S.
[4120-03]—*Ursuline Nuns, of the Congregation of Paris.*—O.S.U.

DIOCESAN CEMETERIES

CHARLESTON. *St. Lawrence and Holy Cross,* 1662 Ingram Rd., 29407. Tel: 803-769-4480. Mr. Dennis F. Atwood, Dir.

NECROLOGY

† Berberich, Peter Kurt, (Retired). —Died Jan. 20, 1997.

† Faase, Albert Anthony, (Retired). —Died April 11, 1997.

Diocese of Charlotte

(Dioecesis Carolinana)

Most Reverend

WILLIAM G. CURLIN, D.D.

Bishop of Charlotte; ordained May 25, 1957; appointed Auxiliary Bishop of Washington November 2, 1988; consecrated December 20, 1988; appointed Bishop of Charlotte February 22, 1994; installed April 13, 1994. *Res., 1521 Dilworth Rd., Charlotte, NC, 28203.* Tel.: 704-376-4337; Fax: 704-375-7359.

Most Reverend

MICHAEL J. BEGLEY, D.D.

Retired Bishop of Charlotte; ordained May 26, 1934; appointed November 30, 1971; consecrated First Bishop of Charlotte January 12, 1972; resigned 1984. *Mailing Address: 1315 Greensboro Rd., High Point, NC, 27260.*

ESTABLISHED JANUARY 12, 1972.

Square Miles 20,470.

Comprises the Counties of Alexander, Alleghany, Anson, Ashe, Avery, Buncombe, Burke, Cabarrus, Caldwell, Catawba, Cherokee, Clay, Cleveland, Davidson, Davie, Forsyth, Gaston, Graham, Guilford, Haywood, Henderson, Iredell, Jackson, Lincoln, Macon, Madison, McDowell, Mecklenberg, Mitchell, Montgomery, Polk, Randolph, Richmond, Rockingham, Rowan, Rutherford, Stanley, Stokes, Surry, Swain, Transylvania, Union, Watauga, Wilkes, Yadkin and Yancey in the State of North Carolina.

For legal titles of parishes and diocesan institutions, consult the Chancery.

Chancery: P.O. Box 36776, Charlotte, NC, 28236. Tel.: 704-370-6299; Fax: 704-370-3378.

STATISTICAL OVERVIEW

Personnel	
Bishop	1
Retired Bishops	1
Abbots	1
Retired Abbots	1
Priests: Diocesan Active in Diocese	56
Priests: Active Outside Diocese	5
Priests: Retired, Sick or Absent	21
Number of Diocesan Priests	82
Religious Priests in Diocese	55
Extern Priests in Diocese	6
Ordinations:	
Diocesan Priests	2
Permanent Deacons in Diocese	63
Total Brothers	1
Total Sisters	182
Parishes	
Parishes	66
With Resident Pastor:	
Resident Diocesan Priests	44
Resident Religious Priests	20
Without Resident Pastor:	
Administered by Women Religious	2
Missions	24
Pastoral Centers	4
Professional Ministry Personnel:	
Brothers	1
Sisters	16
Lay Ministers	92
Welfare	
Catholic Hospitals	1
Total Assisted	69,157
Health Care Centers	8
Total Assisted	142,685
Homes for the Aged	1
Total Assisted	122
Day Care and Extended Day Care Centers	4
Total Assisted	381
Specialized Homes	2
Total Assisted	83
Residential Care of Disabled	1
Total Assisted	65
Other Institutions	1
Total Assisted	70
Educational	
Diocesan Students in Other Seminaries	28
Total Seminarians	28
Colleges and Universities	2
Total Students	902
High Schools, Diocesan and Parish	2
Total Students	1,159
Elementary Schools, Diocesan and Parish	15
Total Students	5,708
Catechesis/Religious Education:	
High School Students	3,936
Elementary Students	12,080
Total Students Under Catholic Instruction	23,813
Teachers in the Diocese:	
Priests	2
Sisters	7
Lay Teachers	372
Vital Statistics	
Receptions into the Church:	
Infant Baptism Totals	2,865
Adult Baptism Totals	298
Received into Full Communion	452
First Communions	2,579
Confirmations	1,936
Marriages:	
Catholic	338
Interfaith	432
Total Marriages	770
Deaths	622
Total Catholic Population	116,539
Total Population	3,784,559

Former Bishops—Most Rev. MICHAEL J. BEGLEY, ord. May 26, 1934; appt. Nov. 30, 1971; cons. first Bishop of Charlotte Jan. 12, 1972; resigned 1984.—Most Rev. JOHN F. DONOGHUE, ord. June 4, 1955; appt. Nov. 6, 1984; cons. Dec. 18, 1984; appt. Archbishop of Atlanta June 22, 1993; cons. Aug. 19, 1993.

Vicar General In Curia—Very Rev. MAURICIO W. WEST, *P.O. Box 36776, Charlotte, 28236.* Tel: 704-370-6299.

Chancery—*P.O. Box 36776, Charlotte, 28236.* Tel: 704-370-6299; Fax: 704-370-3379.

Chancellor—Very Rev. MAURICIO W. WEST, *P.O. Box 36776, Charlotte, 28236.* Tel: 704-370-6299; 370-3326.

Vice Chancellor—Deacon CURTISS P. TODD, *P.O. Box 36776, Charlotte, 28236.* Tel: 704-370-3339.

Secretary to the Bishop—Rev. ANTHONY J. MARCACCIO, *P.O. Box 36776, Charlotte, 28236.* Tel: 704-370-3316; Fax: 704-370-3379.

Fiscal Manager—WILLIAM G. WELDON, C.P.A., *P.O. Box 36776, Charlotte, 28236.* Tel: 704-370-3313.

Controller—TRACY HILDRETH, *P.O. Box 36776, Charlotte, 28236.* Tel: 704-370-3312.

Diocesan Properties—Deacon GUY A. PICHE, Dir., *P.O. Box 36776, Charlotte, 28236.* Tel: 704-370-3304.

Employee Benefits—TERRI WILHELM, Coord., *P.O. Box 36776, Charlotte, 28236.* Tel: 704-370-3338.

Diocesan Tribunal—*1123 S. Church St., Charlotte, 28203.* Tel: 704-370-3343.

Judicial Vicar—Rev. PETER J. JUGIS, J.C.D.; MARY L. HILDRETH, Dir., *1123 S. Church St., Charlotte, 28203.*

Diocesan Consultors—Very. Rev. MAURICIO W. WEST, V.G.; Rev. Msgr. JOSEPH S. SHOWFETY; Rev. Msgr. RICHARD ALLEN; Revs. JAMES DEVEREUX; PETER J. JUGIS; M. JOSEPH KELLEHER.

Vicar for Education—Rev. JAMES HAWKER (BO), *1123 S. Church St., Charlotte, 28203.* Tel: 704-370-3210; Fax: 704-370-3291.

Vicars—Asheville: Very Rev. JOHN SCHNEIDER V.F.; Boone: Very Rev. ROLAND HAUTZ, Glmy.; Charlotte: Very Rev. EDWARD J. SHERIDAN, V.F.; Gastonia: Vacant; Greensboro: Very Rev. JAMES P. O'NEILL, O.S.F.S., V.F.; Hickory: Very Rev. WILBUR N. THOMAS, V.F.; Albemarle: Very Rev. THOMAS P. CLEMENTS, V.F.; Smoky Mountains: Very Rev. JAMES P. CAHILL, V.F.; Winston-Salem: Very Rev. JOSEPH M. KELLEHER, V.F.

Vicar for Priests—Vacant.

Diocesan Offices and Directors

Apostleship of Prayer—Rev. EUGENE MCCREESH, S.J., *St. Peter Church, 507 S. Tryon St., Charlotte, 28202.* Tel: 704-332-2901.

Archives—JOHANNA MIMS, Dir., *1123 S. Church St., Charlotte, 28203.* Tel: 704-370-3215; Fax: 704-370-3378.

Boy Scouts—Deacon JAMES R. JOHNSON, *St. Charles Borromeo Church, 714 W. Union St., Morganton, 28655.* Tel: 704-437-3221; 437-3461.

Campus Ministry—Ms. COLLEEN MCDERMOTT, Dir., *1123 S. Church St., Charlotte, 28203.* Tel: 704-370-3212; Fax: 704-370-3378.

Communications—JOANN KEANE, Dir., *1123 S. Church St., Charlotte, 28203.* Tel: 704-370-3336; Fax: 704-370-3382.

Office of Faith Formation—Dr. CRIS VILLAPANDO, Dir., *1123 S. Church St., Charlotte, 28203.* Tel: 704-370-3246; Fax: 704-370-3378.
Campaign for Human Development—Dr. BARNEY OFFERMAN, Dir., *1123 S. Church St., Charlotte, 28203.* Tel: 704-370-3234; Fax: 704-370-3288.
Justice and Peace—JOANNE FRAZER, Dir., *1123 S. Church St., Charlotte, 28203.* Tel: 704-370-3225; Fax: 704-370-3288.
Youth Ministry—PAUL KOTLOWSKI, *1123 S. Church St., Charlotte, 28203.* Tel: 704-370-3211.
Charismatic Renewal Services—Vacant, *1123 S. Church St., Charlotte, 28203.* Tel: 704-370-6299.
Cursillo—Rev. Msgr. ANTHONY KOVACIC, Dir.
Development—JAMES K. KELLEY, Dir. BARBARA ROHRMAN, Assoc. Dir., *1123 S. Church St., Charlotte, 28203.* Tel: 704-370-3301; 3302; Fax: 704-370-3378.
Evangelization—Rev. EDWARD VILKAUSKAS, C.S.Sp., Dir., *1123 S. Church St., Charlotte, 28203.* Tel: 704-370-3214; Fax: 704-370-3378.
Foundation of the Roman Catholic Diocese of Charlotte, Inc., The—JAMES KELLEY, Exec. Dir., *1123 S. Church St., Charlotte, 28203.* Tel: 704-370-3301.
Hispanic Ministry—Rev. VINCENT H. FINNERTY, C.M., Diocesan Dir., *Centro Catolico Hispano, 2117 Shenandoah Ave., Charlotte, 28205-6021.* Tel: 704-335-1281; 527-6745.
Holy Childhood Association—Rev. Msgr. ANTHONY KOVACIC, Dir., *1123 S. Church St., Charlotte, 28203.* Tel: 704-370-6299; Fax: 704-370-3378.
Home Missions—Rev. Msgr. ANTHONY KOVACIC, *1123 S. Church St., Charlotte, 28203.* Tel: 704-370-6299; Fax: 704-370-3378.
Human Resources—CURTISS P. TODD, Dir. TERRI WILHELM, Assoc., *1123 S. Church St., Charlotte, 28203.* Tel: 704-370-3338; 3339; Fax: 704-370-3378.
Korean Catholic Cultural Center—Rev. JAE YEONG (CHOI), Dir., *7101 Robinson Church Rd., Charlotte, 28215.* Tel: 704-531-8417.
Lay Ministry—Sr. M. TIMOTHY WARREN, R.S.M., Dir., *1123 S. Church St., Charlotte, 28203.* Tel: 704-370-3213; Fax: 704-370-3378.
African-American Ministry—Deacon CURTISS P. TODD, Coord., *1123 S. Church St., Charlotte, 28203.* Tel: 704-370-3339.
Media Resource Center & Telecommunications—LORETTA WNETRZAK, Acting Dir., *1123 S. Church St., Charlotte, 28203.* Tel: 704-370-3242.
Cathedral Publishing Corporation—Mailing Address: P.O. Box 37267, Charlotte, 28237. Tel: 704-370-6299. *1123 S. Church St., Charlotte, 28203.* Tel: 704-370-3336.
Newspaper: "Catholic News & Herald"—MICHAEL KROKOS, Editor, *P.O. Box 37267, Charlotte, 28237.* Tel: 704-370-3330; Fax: 704-370-3382.
Permanent Diaconate—Very Rev. MAURICIO W. WEST, V.G., *P.O. Box 36776, Charlotte, 28236.* Tel: 704-370-6299; Fax: 704-370-3379.
Planning—GEORGE COBB, Dir., *1123 S. Church St., Charlotte, 28203.* Tel: 704-370-3328; Fax: 704-370-3378.
Propagation of the Faith—Rev. Msgr. ANTHONY KOVACIC, *1123 S. Church St., Charlotte, 28203.* Tel: 704-370-6299; Fax: 704-370-3378.
St. Vincent de Paul—ELIZABETH THURBEE, A.C.S.W., *1123 S. Church St., Charlotte, 28203.*
School—MICHAEL F. SKUBE, Ed.D., Supt. of Schools, *1123 S. Church St., Charlotte, 28203.* Tel: 704-370-3271; Fax: 704-370-3291.

Mecklenburg Area Catholic Schools—1123 S. Church St., Charlotte, 28203. Tel: 704-370-3270; Fax: 704-370-3291.

Presbyteral Council—Most Rev. WILLIAM G. CURLIN, D.D.; Very Rev. MAURICIO W. WEST, V.G.; Rev. Msgr. RICHARD ALLEN; Rev. Msgr. JOSEPH S. SHOWFETY; Revs. RICHARD BELLOW, O.F.M.Conv.; FRANCIS T. CANCRO; JAMES DEVEREUX, S.J.; PAUL Q. GARY; PETER J. JUGIS; JOSEPH KELLEHER; BERNARD A. MANLEY; ANTHONY MARCACCIO; KIERAN NIELSON, O.S.B.; FRANCIS J. O'ROURKE; JAMES W. O'NEILL, O.S.F.S.; JOHN W. SCHNEIDER; WILBUR N. THOMAS; EDWARD VILKAUSKAS, C.S.Sp., *1123 S. Church St., Charlotte, 28203.*

Social Services—ELIZABETH THURBEE, A.C.S.W., Diocesan Dir., *1123 S. Church St., Charlotte, 28203.* Tel: 704-370-3228.

Vietnamese Apostolate—c/o St. Ann Church, 3635 Park Rd., Charlotte, 28209. Tel: 704-529-0553. Rev. TAN VAN LE, Chap.

Vocations—Rev. ERIC HOUSEKNECHT, Dir., *P.O. Box 1359, Maggie Valley, 28751.* Tel: 704-926-0106; Fax: 704-926-0855.

Worship—Rev. ANTHONY MARCACCIO, *1123 S. Church St., Charlotte, 28203.* Tel: 704-370-3316; Fax: 704-370-3379.

CLERGY, PARISHES, MISSIONS AND PAROCHIAL SCHOOLS

CITY OF CHARLOTTE
(Mecklenburg County)

1—ST. PATRICK CATHEDRAL. (Phelan Memorial). Revs. Paul Q. Gary; Walter Ray Williams; Deacon Nicholas Fadero.
Res., 1621 Dilworth Rd., E., 28203. Tel: 704-334-2283; Fax: 704-377-6403.
Catechesis/Religious Programs—Students 137.

2—OUR LADY OF THE ASSUMPTION, Rev. Francis J. Gillespie, S.J.; Deacons Stephen J. Horai; Peter Duca.
Res., 4207 Shamrock Dr., 28215. Tel: 704-535-9965; 535-9970; Fax: 704-535-3621.
Catechesis/Religious Programs—Michael S. Hjellming, C.R.E., Tel: 704-535-3310.
Students 275.

3—OUR LADY OF CONSOLATION, Revs. Cecil W. Tice; Damion J. Lynch; Deacon Curtiss P. Todd.
Res., 1224 Dearborn Ave., 28206-2491. Tel: 704-375-4339; Fax: 704-375-8039.
Catechesis/Religious Programs—Tel: 704-344-0821.
Students 109.

4—ST. ANN, Rev. Msgr. Richard F. Allen; Revs. John D. Hanic; Tan Van Le. In res., Rev. James Hawker (BO).
Church—3635 Park Rd., 28209. Tel: 704-523-4641; Fax: 704-527-8671.
Res., 632 Hillside Ave., 28209.
Catechesis/Religious Programs—Tel: 704-523-0122; Fax: 704-523-0122.
Students 175.
Convent—3452 Willow Oak Rd., 28209. Tel: 704-523-0331.

5—ST. GABRIEL, Very Rev. Édward J. Sheridan; Rev. Richard Bellow; Deacons Bernard Wenning; Fred Dobens; Robert Gettlefinger.
Res., 3016 Providence Rd., 28211. Tel: 704-364-5431; Fax: 704-362-5049.
Catechesis/Religious Programs—Susan Krasniewski, D.R.E., Tel: 704-366-2738.
Students 936.

6—ST. JOHN NEUMANN, Rev. Anthony Marcaccio, Admin.; Deacons Neil Chirico; Joseph Mack.
Res., 8451 Idlewild Rd., 28227. Tel: 704-536-6520; Fax: 704-536-3147.
Catechesis/Religious Programs—Tel: 704-535-4197.
Students 669.

7—ST LUKE, Rev. Joseph V. Mulligan.
Res., 13700 Lawyers Rd., 28227. Tel: 704-545-1224; Fax: 704-545-7288.
Catechesis/Religious Programs—Tel: 704-545-0065.
Students 281.

8—ST. MATTHEW, Revs. Edmund Walker, O.F.M. Cap.; Stephen Hoyt, O.F.M. Cap.; Robert Yurgel, O.F.M. Cap.; Sr. Jeanne Marie Kienast, R.S.M., Pastoral Assoc.; Deacons James Hamrlik; Keith Kolodziej.
Office: 8015 Ballantyne Commons Pkwy., 28277. Tel: 704-543-7677; Fax: 704-542-7244.
Res., 5725 Providence Rd., W., 28277. Tel: 704-846-6311; Fax: 704-846-6311.
Catechesis/Religious Programs—Tel: 704-541-8362; Fax: 704-542-7244.
Students 1510.

9—ST. PETER, Revs. James A. Devereux, S.J.; Eugene P. McCreesh, S.J. In res., Rev. Robert J. Paquet, S.J.
Res., 507 S. Tryon St., 28202. Tel: 704-372-6808; Fax: 704-358-0050.
Catechesis/Religious Programs—Tel: 704-332-2901; Fax: 704-358-0050.
Students 95.

10—ST. THOMAS AQUINAS, Revs. Ignatius Zampino, O.F.M.Cap.; Martin Schratz, O.F.M.Cap.; Deacon Carl Macero; Miriam Picconi, Pastoral Coord.
Res., 1400 Suther Rd., 28213. Tel: 704-549-1607; Fax: 704-549-1614.
Catechesis/Religious Programs—Sr. Carol L. Bennett, O.S.F., D.R.E.
Students 1,300.

11—ST. VINCENT DE PAUL, Rev. Msgr. William N. Pharr; Rev. Richard N. Hanson; Deacon Gerald P. Hickey.
Res., 6828 Old Reid Rd., 28210. Tel: 704-554-7088; Fax: 704-554-0490.
Catechesis/Religious Programs—Tel: 704-554-1622; Fax: 704-554-0490. Joan Mahony, D.R.E.
Students 214.

OUTSIDE THE CITY OF CHARLOTTE

Albemarle, Stanly Co., Our Lady of the Annunciation, Rev. Joseph Ayathupadam.
Res., 416 N. Second St., 28001. Tel: 704-982-2910.
Catechesis/Religious Programs—Barbara Newkirk, D.R.E.
Students 108.
Mission—Biscoe, Montgomery Co., Our Lady of the Americas, 105 Hyde St., P.O. Box 1187, Biscoe, 27209. Tel: 910-428-3051. Rev. Mark Lawlor, Admin.

Andrews, Cherokee Co., Holy Redeemer, Rev. James J. Wilmes.
Res., 32 Aquone Rd., P.O. Box 698, 28901. Tel: 704-321-4463.
Mission—Robbinsville, Graham Co., Prince of Peace, Rte. #129. S., Robbinsville, 28771.
Catechesis/Religious Programs—Students 12.

Arden, Buncombe Co., St. Barnabas, Very Rev. John W. Schneider; Deacon Arthur J. Kingsley; Neil Mogensen, Pastoral Assoc.
Mailing Address: P.O. Box 38, 28704. Tel: 704-684-6098; Fax: 704-684-6152.
Res., 4 Pointview Ct., 28704. Tel: 704-684-5343.
Catechesis/Religious Programs—Miss Sheryl Peyton, D.R.E.
Students 375.

Asheboro, Randolph Co., St. Joseph, Rev. Joseph W. Mack.
Res., 512 W. Wainman Ave., 27203. Tel: 910-629-0221.
Catechesis/Religious Programs—Students 175.

Asheville, Buncombe Co., Basilica of St. Lawrence, Rev. Msgr. John J. McSweeney; Rev. J. Arturo DeAguilar.
Res., 97 Haywood St., 28801. Tel: 704-252-6042; Fax: 704-254-0414.
Catechesis/Religious Programs—Mrs. Karen Ascik, D.R.E.
Students 151.
St. Eugene, Rev. Francis T. Cancro; Deacons Joseph Vandermeer, Pastoral Assoc.; Lou Rinkus, Prison Ministry.
Office: One Culvern St., 28814.
Mailing Address: P.O. Box 8160, 28814. Tel: 704-254-5193; Fax: 704-254-5797.
Catechesis/Religious Programs—Ms. Vicki Fedor, D.R.E.
Students 345.
St. Joan of Arc, Rev. C. Morris Boyd.
Res., 919 Haywood Rd., 28806. Tel: 704-252-3151.
Catechesis/Religious Programs—Mary Ann Poli, D.R.E.
Students 120.

Belmont, Gaston Co., Queen of the Apostles, Rev. Richard P. Hokanson; Deacon Guy Piche.
Church—503 N. Main St., 28012. Tel: 704-825-5277; Fax: 704-825-1413.
Res., 2121 Ferncliff Ln., 28012. Tel: 704-825-9600.
Catechesis/Religious Programs—Students 162.
Mission—Spencer Mountain, St. Helen.

Boone, Watauga Co., St. Elizabeth, Rev. Conrad Hoover.
Office: 259 Pilgrim's Way, 28607. Tel: 704-264-8338; 264-6347; Fax: 704-262-3721.
Res., 199 Highland Ave., Apt. 1, 28607. Tel: 704-264-4503.
Catechesis/Religious Programs—Carol Brown, D.R.E.
Students 175.
Mission—Blowing Rock, Epiphany, 163 Galax Ln., 28607. Tel: 704-275-0908.

Brevard, Transylvania Co., Sacred Heart, Rev. Carl Del Giudice.
Res., 4 Fortune Cove, 28712. Tel: 704-883-9572; Fax: 704-884-2535.
Catechesis/Religious Programs—Tel: 704-884-2535.
Students 108.
Mission—Sapphire Valley, Transylvania Co., St. Jude, P.O. Box 543, Highlands, 28741. Tel: 704-526-2418.

Bryson City, Swain Co., St. Joseph, Rev. Thomas E. Field, Glmy.
Res., P.O. Box 727, 28713. Tel: 704-488-6766.
Catechesis/Religious Programs—Students 30.
Mission—Cherokee, Our Lady of Guadalupe.

Clemmons, Forsyth Co., Holy Family, Revs. Francis J. O'Rourke; Fidel Melo; Deacons Gerard Schumacher; Michael Langsdorf.
Res., 2890 Knobb Hill Dr., P.O. Box 130, 27012. Tel: 910-766-1882; Fax: 910-766-8133.
Catechesis/Religious Programs—Tel: 910-766-8189. Marcy Boyer, D.F.F.; Mary Langsdorf, Coord., Youth Ministry.
Students 585.
Mission—Yadkinville, Yadkin Co., Cristo Rey Catholic Hispanic Center of Yadkin Valley, U.S. Hwy. 601 & Hoot Rd., P.O. Box 788, Yadkinville, 27055. Tel: 910-463-5533. Sr. Andrea Inkrott, O.S.F., Coord.; Sr. Linda Scheckelhoff, O.S.F.

Concord, Cabarrus Co., St. James, Revs. Daniel J.

Carboy, C.SS.R.; Francis Sands, C.SS.R.; Karl Aschmann, C.SS.R.; Deacon J. Daniel Carl.
Mailing Address: P.O. Box 123, 28026. Tel: 704-786-9131; Fax: 704-786-5412.
Res., 251 Union St., N., 28025.
Catechesis/Religious Programs—D.R.E.: Cecelia Rouse; Janice Wellman, (St. Joseph Mission). Students 595.
Mission—Kannapolis, St. Joseph, 108 St. Joseph St., P.O. Box 220, Kannapolis, 28082. Tel: 704-932-4607.

Eden, Rockingham Co., St. Joseph of the Hills, Sr. Bernadette McNamara, R.S.M., Parochial Admin.; Deacon Gerald W. Potkay.
Res., 316 Boone Rd., 27288. Tel: 910-623-2661.
Catechesis/Religious Programs—Students 62.

Forest City, Rutherford Co., Immaculate Conception, Rev. Gabriel Meehan; Deacon Andrew Cilone.
Res., 1024 W. Main St., 28043. Tel: 704-245-4017.
Catechesis/Religious Programs—Students 95.

Franklin, Macon Co., St. Francis of Assisi, Revs. Richard T. McCue; Robert M. Collins.
Res., 299 Maple St., 28734. Tel: 704-524-2289.
Catechesis/Religious Programs—Tel: 704-369-8131. D.R.E.: Sharon Edwards; Ron Brahmer. Students 85.
Mission—Highlands, Macon Co., Our Lady of the Mountains, P.O. Box 2729, Highlands, 28741. Tel: 704-526-2418.

Gastonia, Gaston County, St. Michael, Rev. George M. Kloster.
Res., 708 St. Michael's Ln., 28052. Tel: 704-853-8808.
Church—Tel: 704-867-6212; Fax: 704-867-6379.
School—Tel: 704-865-4382.
Lay Teachers 14; Students 246.
Catechesis/Religious Programs—Tel: 704-865-5537.
Students 325.

Greensboro, Guilford Co.,

1—Our Lady of Grace. (Ethel Clay Price Memorial). Revs. Mark Lamprich, M.I.C.; Waldek Ziolkowski, M.I.C. (Poland); Deacons Timothy Rohan; Paul Teich.
Res., 2205 W. Market St., 27403. Tel: 910-274-6520; 275-5376; Fax: 910-274-7326.
School—Tel: 910-275-1522. Roberta Hutchcraft, Prin.
Lay Teachers 27; Students 463.
Catechesis/Religious Programs—James D. McCullough, D.R.E.
Students 289.

2—St. Benedict, Rev. Msgr. Joseph S. Showfety; Deacon Philip Killian.
Res., 109 W. Smith St., 27401. Tel: 910-272-0303.
Catechesis/Religious Programs—Students 14.

3—St. Mary, Revs. Robert J. Prior, C.M.; Michael M. Nguyen, C.M.; Deacon Vincent Shaw. In res., Rev. Vincent H. Finnerty, C.M.
Mailing Address: P.O. Box 21012, 27420.
Res., 812 Duke St., 27401. Tel: 910-272-8650; Fax: 910-274-5396.
Social Ministry Office—Tel: 910-275-8377.
St. Vincent de Paul Office—Tel: 910-272-0336.
Catechesis/Religious Programs—Students 130.

4—St. Paul the Apostle, Very Rev. James W. O'Neill, O.S.F.S.; Revs. Tony Gilborges; John A. Gilvey, O.S.F.S.; Deacons Gordon L. Forester; William Shaw.
Res., 2715 Horsepen Creek Rd., 27410. Tel: 910-294-6160; 294-4696 (Office); Fax: 910-294-6149.
Catechesis/Religious Programs—Students 920.

5—St. Pius X, Rev. Francis T. Connolly; Sr. Phyllis Tierney, S.S.J., M.S.W., Pastoral Assoc. In res., Rev. Louis Canino, O.F.M.
Office: 2210 N. Elm St., 27408. Tel: 910-272-4681; 272-8598; Fax: 910-274-8112.
School—Tel: 910-273-9865; Fax: 910-273-0199. Mrs. Sue Geraghty, Prin.
Lay Teachers 20; Students 374.
Catechesis/Religious Programs—Students 155.
Convent—19-A Fountain Manor Dr., 27405. Tel: 910-275-5915; Fax: 910-275-5915.
Daughters of Charity 2.
Franciscan Center—233 N. Greene St., 27401. Tel: 910-273-2554.
Catholic Campus Connection (Thea House)—1009 Bluford St., 27401. Tel: 910-272-5868.

Hamlet, Richmond Co., St. James, Rev. William Morris Evans.
Mailing Address: P.O. Box 1208, 28345. Tel: 910-582-0207; 582-8776 (Rectory).
Catechesis/Religious Programs—Ann Peters, D.R.E. Students 47.

Hendersonville, Henderson Co., Immaculate Conception, Revs. John C. Aurilia, O.F.M.Cap.; Alfonso Pagliara, O.F.M.Cap.
Parish Office: 229 Sixth Ave., W., 28739-4305. Tel: 704-693-6901; Fax: 704-697-1656.
Res., 717 Buncombe St., 28791-3609. Tel: 704-692-0550.
School—Immaculata, 711 Buncombe St., 28739. Tel: 704-693-3277. Mr. James Erdman, Prin.
Lay Teachers 18; Students 201.
Catechesis/Religious Programs—Tel: 704-697-7420. Deacon William Pivarnik, D.R.E.
Students 127.

Hickory, Catawba Co., St. Aloysius, Very Rev. Wilbur N. Thomas; Deacons Joseph E. Garavaglia; Hugo L. May; Thomas A. Rasmussen. In res., Rev. William H. Tanguay (RI).
Res., 902 Second St., N.E., 28601. Tel: 704-327-2341; Fax: 704-327-3376.
Catechesis/Religious Programs—Sr. Mary Norman Woodend, C.L.H.C., D.R.E.
Students 538.

High Point, Guilford Co., Immaculate Heart of Mary, Revs. Joseph C. Zuschmidt, O.S.F.S.; James M. Turner, O.S.F.S.; Deacons Thomas Kak; Joseph T. Smith.
Res., 512 Montlieu Ave., 27262. Tel: 910-884-5212; Fax: 910-884-1849.
School—Tel: 910-887-2613; Fax: 910-884-1849. Frank McGrail, Prin.
Lay Teachers 16; Students 260.
Catechesis/Religious Programs—Tel: 910-885-5210. Sr. Mary Sheehan, S.M.G., D.R.E.
Students 279.
Christ the King, Rev. Philip Kollithanath.
Res., 1505 Kivett Dr., 27260. Tel: 910-884-0244; Fax: 910-887-1200.

Huntersville, Mecklenburg Co., St. Mark, Rev. Msgr. Joseph A. Kerin.
Res., 15415 Ranson Rd., 28078. Tel: 704-948-0231; Fax: 704-948-0231.
Catechesis/Religious Programs—Tel: 704-895-8470.
Students 560.

Jefferson, Ashe Co., St. Francis of Assisi, Very Rev. Roland Hautz, Glmy.
Mailing Address: P.O. Box 1, 28640. Tel: 910-246-9151.
Res., Tel: 910-246-5925; Fax: 910-246-5925.
Catechesis/Religious Programs—Students 94.
Mission—Sparta, Alleghany Co., St. Frances of Rome, P.O. Box 367, Sparta, 28675. Tel: 910-372-8846.

Kernersville, Forsyth Co., Holy Cross, Revs. Joseph E. Tustin, O.S.F.S.; Gerardo R. Clarke, O.S.F.S.
Res., 616 S. Cherry St., 27284. Tel: 910-996-5109; Fax: 910-996-5115.
Child Developmental Center—Tel: 910-996-5144; Fax: 910-996-5115. Maria Rosato, Dir.
Catechesis/Religious Programs—Tel: 910-996-5109; Fax: 910-996-5115. Louise Hiatt, D.R.E.
Students 180.

Lenoir, Caldwell Co., St. Francis of Assisi, Rev. Michael Buttner; Deacon Ronald Caplette.
Res., 1025 College Ave., S.W., 28645-5433. Tel: 704-754-5281; Fax: 704-754-5281.
Catechesis/Religious Programs—Students 129.
Mission—Taylorsville, Alexander Co., Holy Trinity, Hwy. 90 W., 655 W. Main Ave., Taylorsville, 28681. Tel: 704-632-8009. In res., Rev. Joseph Waters.

Lexington, Davidson Co., Our Lady of the Rosary, Very Rev. M. Joseph Kelleher; Deacon Edward Morovich.
Res., 619 S. Main St., 27292. Tel: 910-248-2463.
Catechesis/Religious Programs—Students 87.

Lincolnton, Lincoln Co., St. Dorothy, Rev. Richard B. Farwell.
Res., 148 St. Dorothy Ln., 28092. Tel: 704-735-5575; Fax: 704-735-5890.
Catechesis/Religious Programs—Students 100.

Maggie Valley, Haywood Co., St. Margaret, Rev. Eric Houseknecht, Admin. In res., Rev. Gregory J. Littleton.
Mailing Address: P.O. Box 1359, 28751. Tel: 704-926-0106; Fax: 704-926-0855.
Res., 37 Murphy Dr., 28751. Tel: 704-926-0025.
Mission—Cherokee, Our Lady of Gaudalupe, Lambert Branch Rd., Cherokee, 28719.

Mars Hill, Madison Co., St. Andrew the Apostle, Rev. Edward M. Ifkovits, S.J.
Mailing Address: P.O. Box 1406, 28754-1406. Tel: 704-689-3719; 649-2781.
Res. & Church—149 Brook St., 28754.
Missions—Burnsville, Yancey Co., Sacred Heart, P.O. Box 1406, Mars Hill, 28754-1406.; Hot Springs, Madison Co., Chapel of the Redeemer. Jesuit House of Prayer. P.O. Box 7, Hot Springs, 28743. Tel: 704-622-7366. Revs. Vincent Alagia, S.J.; Joseph J. McGovern, S.J.
Catechesis/Religious Programs—Students 31.

Mocksville, Davie Co., St. Francis of Assisi, Sr. Carmelita Hagan, R.S.M., Parochial Admin.
Mailing Address: P.O. Box 642, 27028. Tel: 704-634-2973; Fax: 704-634-2973.
Church—862 Yadkinville Rd., 27028.
Catechesis/Religious Programs—Students 61.

Monroe, Union Co., Our Lady of Lourdes, Revs. Edward J. Vilkauskas, C.S.Sp.; Vincent J. Donovan, C.S.Sp.
Res., 725 Deese St., 28112. Tel: 704-289-2773; Fax: 704-283-7210.
Catechesis/Religious Programs—Tel: 704-289-2773; Fax: 704-283-7210.
Students 309.
Mission—Wadesboro, Sacred Heart, 205 Rutherford St., P.O. Box 1123, Wadesboro, 28710.

Mooresville, Iredell Co., St. Therese, Revs. Robert D. Wiesenbaugh, S.J.; James V. Keogh, S.J.; William J. Lynch, S.J.; Deacon John Sims.
Res., 217 Brawley School Rd., 28115-9103. Tel: 704-664-3992; Fax: 704-660-6321.
Mission—Denver, Lincoln Co., Holy Spirit, 537 N. Hwy. 16, Denver, 28037-9235. Tel: 704-483-6448. Rev. James Collins, Admin.
Catechesis/Religious Programs—Students 274.

Morganton, Burke Co., St. Charles Borromeo, Rev. Kenneth L. Whittington; Deacon James R. Johnson.
Res., 714 W. Union St., 28655. Tel: 704-437-3108;704-437-6262.
Catechesis/Religious Programs—Terri Martino, D.R.E.
Students 190.
Mission—Marion, McDowell Co., Our Lady of the Angels. Rev. Jerome Aung Shwe (Burma).

Mt. Airy, Surry Co., Holy Angels, Rev. Thomas D. Stott.
Res., 1208 N. Main St., 27030. Tel: 910-786-8147; Fax: 910-786-8147.
Mission—Dobson, Sacred Heart.
Catechesis/Religious Programs—Mrs. Gloria Bunn, D.R.E.
Students 67.

Murphy, Cherokee Co., St. William, Rev. Edmund D. Kirsch; Deacon Anthony Marini.
Res., 109 Andrews Rd., P.O. Box 546, 28906. Tel: 704-837-2000.
Mission—Hayesville, Clay Co., Immaculate Heart of Mary.
Catechesis/Religious Programs—Students 44.

Newton, Catawba Co., St. Joseph, Rev. Gordon Pillon, Admin.; Deacon Harold Markle.
Church—720 W. 13th St., 28658-3899. Tel: 704-464-9207.
Holy Family Parish Center—Tel: 704-465-2878.
Catechesis/Religious Programs—Tel: 704-465-2878.
Students 135.

North Wilkesboro, Wilkes Co., St. John Baptist de LaSalle, Rev. Francis M. Cintula; Deacon Frank Aversa.
Res., 275 C.C. Wright School Rd., 28659. Tel: 910-838-5562.
Catechesis/Religious Programs—Students 94.
Mission—Elkin, Surry Co., St. Stephen, 101 Hawthorne, Elkin, 28621. Tel: 910-835-3007.

Reidsville, Rockingham Co., Holy Infant, Rev. John T. Putnam, Jr., Admin.
Res., 1042 Freeway Dr., P.O. Box 1197, 27323. Tel: 910-342-1448.
Catechesis/Religious Programs—Students 100.

Salisbury, Rowan Co., Sacred Heart, Very Rev. Thomas P. Clements; Deacon Patrick Vallandingham.
Res., 128 N. Fulton St., 28144. Tel: 704-633-0591; Fax: 704-647-0126.
School—Tel: 704-633-2841. Mrs. Kathleen Miller, Prin.
Lay Teachers 22; Students 258.
Convent—425 W. Council St., 28144. Tel: 704-636-4070; Fax: 704-636-2564. Sisters of Mercy
Catechesis/Religious Programs—Tel: 704-638-0172.
Students 189.

Shelby, Cleveland Co., St. Mary's, Rev. Carl E. Kaltreider.
Res., 818 McGowan Rd., 28150. Tel: 704-484-3241.
Mission—Kings Mountain, Cleveland Co., Christ the King, 714 Stone St., Kings Mountain, 28086. Tel: 704-739-3214.
Catechesis/Religious Programs—D.R.E.: Ron Maskarinec; Ann Marie Bridges.
Students 144.

Spruce Pine, Mitchell Co., St. Lucien, Rev. Aloysius J. D'Silva.
Res., 503 Summit St., P.O. Box 688, 28777. Tel: 704-765-2224.
Mission—Linville, Avery Co., St. Bernadette, P.O. Box 1252, Linville, 28646. Tel: 704-898-6900.
Catechesis/Religious Programs—Students 47.

Statesville, Iredell Co., St. Philip the Apostle, Rev. Peter L. Fitzgibbons; Deacon Charles Brantley. In res., Rev. James M. Byer.
Mailing Address: P.O. Box 882, 28687-0882. Tel: 704-873-8641.
Office: Tel: 704-872-2579; Fax: 704-872-2579.

Res., 525 Camden Dr., 28677.
Catechesis/Religious Programs—Tel: 704-872-2579; Fax: 704-872-2579.
Students 199.

Swannanoa, Buncombe Co., St. Margaret Mary, Rev. Andrew J. Latsko.
Res., 102 Andrews Pl., Box 99, 28778. Tel: 704-686-3243; Fax: 704-686-3243.
Catechesis/Religious Programs—Students 65.

Sylva, Jackson Co., St. Mary, Very Rev. James P. Cahill; Deacon Jerry Herbers.
Res., 22 Bartlett St., 28779. Tel: 704-586-9496.
Catechesis/Religious Programs—Tel: 704-586-9496.
Students 100.

Thomasville, Davidson Co., Our Lady of the Highways, Rev. Thomas J. Fitzpatrick, O.S.F.S.; Deacons Wayne Adams; Ron Steinkamp.
Res., 943 Ball Park Rd., 27360. Tel: 910-475-2732; Fax: 910-476-3337.
Catechesis/Religious Programs—Tel: 910-475-2732; Fax: 910-476-3337.
Students 141.

Tryon, Polk Co., St. John the Baptist, Rev. Lawrence W. Heiney (HBG); Deacon Bruce H. Haslett.
Mailing Address: P.O. Box 1597, 28782.
Res., 600 Laurel Ave., 28782. Tel: 704-859-9574; Fax: 704-859-5932.
Catechesis/Religious Programs—Students 61.

Waynesville, Haywood Co., St. John the Evangelist, Rev. Raymond B. Hourihan.
Res., 234 Church St., 28786. Tel: 704-456-6707; Fax: 704-456-6707.
Catechesis/Religious Programs—Tel: 704-456-7450.
Students 60.
Mission—Canton, Haywood Co., Immaculate Conception.

Winston-Salem, Forsyth Co., Our Lady of Mercy, Rev. Conall McHugh, O.F.M.Conv. In res., Revs. Joseph Madden, O.F.M.Conv.; Edgar Holden, O.F.M.Conv.; George Sullivan, O.F.M.Conv.; Deacons Joseph Schumacher; Pedro Herran.
Res., 1910 S. Main St., 27127. Tel: 910-724-6806; Fax: 910-768-8292.
School—Tel: 910-722-7204; Fax: 910-725-2294. Sandra McMonagle, Prin.
Sisters of St. Joseph 2; Lay Teachers 16; Students 270.
Convent—1922 S. Main St., 27127. Tel: 910-727-0925.
Mission—Winston-Salem, Forsyth Co., Our Lady of Fatima, 211 W. 3rd St., Winston-Salem, 27101. Tel: 910-723-8238.
Catechesis/Religious Programs—Tel: 910-722-7001; Fax: 910-722-0465.
Students 185.

St. Benedict the Moor, Rev. Lawrence J. Hunt, S.J.
Res., 1625 E. Twelfth St., 27101. Tel: 910-725-9200; Fax: 910-777-1062.
Mission—King, Stokes Co., Good Shepherd, P.O. Box 1149, King, 27021.
Catechesis/Religious Programs—Students 117.

St. Leo's, Revs. James K. Solari; John J. Tuller; Deacons Dennis O'Madigan; Robert DeSautels; Thomas O'Connell.
Res., 406 Springdale Ave., 27104. Tel: 910-724-5314.
Church—335 Springdale Ave., 27104. Tel: 910-724-0561; Fax: 910-724-7036.
School—333 Springdale Ave., 27104. Tel: 910-748-8252; Fax: 910-748-9005.
Sisters of St. Joseph 2; Lay Teachers 18; Students 285.
Catechesis/Religious Programs—Students 410.
Convent—1975 Georgia Ave., 27104. Tel: 910-723-3639.

Special Assignment:
Reverend Fathers—
Hoover, John P.
Marcaccio, Anthony J., Sec. to Bishop
West, Mauricio W., Vicar Gen. & Chancellor

On Duty Outside the Diocese:
Reverend Fathers—
Farrell, William, Diocese of Ogdensburg, NY
Marecki, Ronald A., Diocese of Rochester, NY
Pagel, John M., Diocese of San Antonio, TX
Tarasi, Carlo D., Diocese of Trenton, NJ
Valentine, Joseph R., Fraternity of St. Peter
Wilderotter, Paul C., Diocese of Charleston, SC

Military Chaplains:
Reverend Fathers—
Fitzgibbons, Peter L., U.S. Army
Klepacki, Michael S., U.S. Navy

Absent On Leave:
Reverend Fathers—
Baker, Donald P.
Bradley, John Paul
Kuhn, Dennis R.
Orlando, Samuel
Williamson, Thomas

Retired:
Reverend Monsignors—
Burke, Thomas P., 207 Eagle St., Belmont, NC 28012
Duncan, Arthur L., Maryfield Nursing Home, 1315 Greensboro Rd., High Point, NC 27260
Kelaher, Felix R., 7401 Ashfield Ct., Charlotte, NC 28226
Roueche, John F., St. Joseph of the Pines Hospital, 590 Central Ave., Southern Pines, NC 28387
Reverend Fathers—
Berg, Ramon A., 2500 Morgan Mill Rd., Brevard, NC 28712
Erb, Vincent I., 1001 Easton Rd., Apt. 615, Willow Grove, PA 19090
Gavigan, P. Patrick, 2945 Reynolda Rd., Room 217, Winston-Salem, NC 27106
Kimbrough, Conrad
Lash, Joseph J., 3078 W. 136th St., Cleveland, OH 44111. Tel: 216-476-9610
Manley, Bernard A., 420 Lakeshore Dr., Asheville, NC 28804
McCarthy, Joseph L., Sardis Nursing Home, 5151 Sardis Rd., Charlotte, NC 28270
Morse, Guy E., Teresian House, 200 Washington Ave. Ext., Albany, NY 12203-5394
O'Doherty, Edward, Tubbercurry, Co. Sligo, Eire Ireland
Reese, Charles T., 800 Bay Dr., No. 25, Niceville, FL 32578
Sullivan, D. Edward
Walsh, Thomas R., 12 N. 6th St., Allegany, NY 14706

Permanent Deacons:
Adams, Wayne, Our Lady of the Highways, Thomasville
Aversa, Frank, St. John, N. Wilkesboro
Brantley, Charles, St. Philip the Apostle, Statesville
Burke, John, Sacred Heart, Brevard
Caplette, Ronald, St. Francis of Assisi, Lenoir
Carl, Daniel, St. James, Concord
Chirico, Neil, St. John Neumann, Charlotte
Cilone, Andrew, Immaculate Conception, Forest City
DeSauntels, Charles, St. Leo, Winston-Salem
Dobens, Frederick, St. Gabriel, Charlotte
Dotson, Robert, St. John, Waynesville
Duca, Peter, Our Lady of the Assumption, Charlotte
Fadero, Nick, St. Patrick, Charlotte
Forester, Gordon L., St. Paul the Apostle, Greensboro
Garavaglia, Joseph E., St. Aloysius, Hickory
Gettlefinger, Robert, St. Gabriel, Charlotte
Hamrlik, James, St. Matthew, Charlotte
Haslett, Bruce, St. John the Baptizer, Tryon
Herbers, Jerome, St. Mary, Sylva
Herran, Pedro, Our Lady of Mercy, Winston-Salem
Hickey, Gerald P., St. Vincent, Charlotte
Horai, Stephen J., Our Lady of the Assumption, Charlotte
Johnson, James R., St. Charles, Morganton
Kak, Thomas, Immaculate Heart of Mary, High Point
Killian, Philip, Jr., St. Benedict, Greensboro
Kingsley, Arthur, St. Barnabas, Arden
Kolodziej, Keith, St. Matthew, Charlotte
Langsdorf, Michael, Holy Family, Clemmons
Macero, Carl, St. Thomas Aquinas, Charlotte
Mack, Joseph H., Jr., St. John Neumann, Charlotte
Manning, Franklin L., Sr., Christ the King, High Point
Marini, Anthony, St. William, Murphy
Markle, Harold, St. Joseph, Newton
May, Hugo L., (Retired)
Medina, Carlos, Hispanic Center, Charlotte
Morovich, Edward, (Retired)
O'Connell, Thomas, St. Leo, Winston-Salem
O'Madigan, Dennis T., St. Leo, Winston-Salem
Pais, Louis, St. Gabriel, Charlotte
Piche, Guy, Queen of Apostles, Belmont
Pivarnik, William, Immaculate Conception, Hendersonville
Potkay, Gerald, St. Joseph of the Hills, Eden
Rasmussen, Thomas, St. Aloysius, Hickory
Renuart, Albert, Immaculate Conception, Hendersonville
Rinkus, Louis, (Retired)
Rodriguez, Edwin, Hispanic Center, Charlotte
Rohan, Timothy, Our Lady of Grace, Greensboro
Schumacher, Gerard, Holy Family, Clemmons
Schumacher, Joseph N., Our Lady of Mercy, Winston-Salem
Shaw, Vincent, Jr., St. Mary, Greensboro
Shaw, William, St. Paul the Apostle, Greensboro
Sims, John, St. Therese, Mooresville
Smith, Joseph T., Immaculate Heart of Mary, High Point
Steinkamp, Ronald, Our Lady of the Highways, Thomasville
Szalony, George, St. Luke, Charlotte
Teich, Paul, Our Lady of Grace, Greensboro
Todd, Curtiss, Our Lady of Consolation, Charlotte
Torres, Rafael, Hispanic Center, Charlotte
Vallandingham, Patrick, Sacred Heart, Salisbury
Vandermeer, Jos A., St. Eugene, Asheville
Weisenhorn, John, St. Michael, Gastonia
Wenning, Bernard, St. Gabriel, Charlotte

INSTITUTIONS LOCATED IN THE DIOCESE

[A] COLLEGES AND UNIVERSITIES

*BELMONT. *Belmont Abbey College*, 100 Belmont-Mount Holly Rd., 28012-2795. Tel: 704-825-6700; Fax: 704-825-6670.
E-mail: schup@crusader.bac.edu
Web site: bac.edu
For a complete listing, refer to the Colleges and Universities section.

Sacred Heart College, 100 Mercy Dr., 28012. Tel: 704-829-5110; Fax: 704-829-5137
For a complete listing, refer to the Colleges and Universities section.

[B] HIGH SCHOOLS

WINSTON-SALEM. *Bishop McGuinness Memorial High School*, 1730 Link Rd., 27103. Tel: 910-725-4247; Fax: 910-725-6669. George L. Repass, M.Ed., Prin. Sisters of St. Joseph 1; Deacons 1; Lay Teachers 28; Students 360.

[C] ELEMENTARY SCHOOLS, INTER-PAROCHIAL

ASHEVILLE. *Asheville Catholic School*, 12 Culvern St., 28804. Tel: 704-252-7896; Fax: 704-252-5708. Judith E. Cavallo, Prin. Lay Teachers 14; Students 246.

[D] REGIONAL SCHOOLS

CHARLOTTE. *Mecklenburg Area Catholic Schools (M.A.C.S.).* Education Foundation, Inc., 1123 S. Church St., 28203. Tel: 704-370-3303; Fax: 704-370-3378. David Mancos, Business Mgr.

Charlotte Catholic High School (Bishop Hafey Memorial), 7702 Matthews-Mint Hill Rd., 28226. Tel: 704-543-1127; Fax: 704-543-1217. Sr. Paulette Williams, R.S.M., Prin.; Rev. Stephen Hoyt, O.F.M. Cap., Chap. Priests 1; Sisters 1; Lay Teachers 57; Students 808.

Charlotte Catholic High School Athletic Association.

Charlotte Catholic High School Alumni Association.

Charlotte Catholic High School Home School Association.

Holy Trinity Middle School, 3100 Park Rd., 28209. Tel: 704-527-7822; Fax: 704-525-7288. Gerald A. Healy, Prin. Lay Teachers 49; Students 854.

All Saints Catholic School, 7100 Endhaven Ln., 28277. Tel: 704-544-2070. Mrs. Betsy Denoyer, Prin. Lay Teachers 41; Students 594.

Our Lady of the Assumption School, 4225 Shamrock Dr., 28215. Tel: 704-531-0067. Mrs. Patricia Murphy, Prin. Lay Teachers 25; Students 288.

St. Ann School, 600 Hillside Ave., 28209. Tel: 704-525-4938. Sr. Helene Nagle, S.S.J., Prin. Lay Teachers 23; Students 323.

St. Gabriel School, 3028 Providence Rd., 28211. Tel: 704-366-2409. Deacon Fred Dobens, Prin. Lay Teachers 31; Students 533.

St. Patrick School, 1125 Buchanan St., 28203. Tel: 704-333-3174. Mrs. Janice Ritter, Prin. Lay Teachers 24; Students 382.

[E] GENERAL HOSPITALS

CHARLOTTE. *Selwyn Life Center at Mercy*, 1921 Vail Ave., 28207. Tel: 704-379-5005
For a complete listing, refer to the Hospitals section.

ASHEVILLE. *St. Joseph's Health Services Corporation*, 345 Biltmore Ave., 28801
For a complete listing, refer to the Hospitals section.

St. Joseph's Hospital, 428 Biltmore Ave., 28801. Tel: 704-255-3100
For a complete listing, refer to the Hospitals section.

St. Joseph's Urgent Care, Inc., 345 Biltmore Ave., 28801. Tel: 704-258-6569
For a complete listing, refer to the Hospitals section.

[F] SPECIAL CARE FACILITIES

*BELMONT. *Holy Angels, Inc.*, 6600 Wilkinson Blvd., P.O. Box 710, 28012. Tel: 704-825-4161; Fax: 704-825-0553
For a complete listing, refer to the Special Care Facilities section.

[G] CATHOLIC SOCIAL SERVICES

CHARLOTTE. *Catholic Social Services of the Diocese of Charlotte, Inc.*
The Catholic Center, 1123 S. Church St., 28203. Tel: 704-377-6871. Elizabeth K. Thurbee, A.C.S.W., Diocesan Dir.
Area Offices:
Asheville-Smoky Mountain Vicariates, 35 Orange St., Asheville, 28801. Tel: 704-255-0146. Sr. Marie Frechette, M.S.B.T., A.C.S.W., Dir.
Albemarle-Charlotte-Gastonia Vicariates, 1123 S. Church St., 28203. Tel: 704-377-6871. Geri King, M.S.W., Dir.
Boone-Greensboro-Hickory-Winston-Salem Vicariates. P.O. Box 10962, Winston-Salem, 27108. 621 W. Second St., Winston-Salem, 27101. Tel: 910-727-0705. David W. Harold, A.C.S.W., Dir.
Catholic Social Services Refugee Office, 1123 S. Church St., 28203. Tel: 704-377-6871. Cira Ponce, Dir.
Special Ministries:
Adoption. Contact the Domestic Adoption Unit at CSS offices. Tel: 704-255-0146, Asheville; Tel: 910-727-0505, Winston-Salem; Tel: 704-377-6871, Charlotte. Tel: 704-343-9954, Charlotte.
Adoption International, Asheville. Tel: 704-255-0146; 888-990-4199. Carol Meyerriecks, M.S.W.
CRISM. Catholic Retirees Invited to Special Ministries, Contact Diocesan Office. Suzanne Bach, Contact Person. Tel: 704-377-6871.
Disaster. Contact the Office of Special Ministries., Winston-Salem. Tel: 910-922-3628. Gerard Carter, Contact Person.
Engaged Encounter. Contact Diocesan Office. Tel: 704-377-6871. Marlo Wallace, Contact Person; Carl & Mary Shultz, Chm.
Family Life. Contact the Office of Special Ministries., Winston-Salem. Gerard Carter, Dir. Tel: 910-922-3628.
Hand to Hand. Contact Winston-Salem Office., Winston-Salem. Tel: 910-727-0705. Connie McVey, Contact Person.
Hispanic/Migrant Outreach. Contact Asheville, Winston-Salem, or Charlotte Offices. Tel: 704-255-0146 (Asheville); 910-727-0705 (Winston-Salem); 704-377-6871.
Host Homes. Contact Winston-Salem Office., Winston-Salem. Tel: 910-727-0705. Mable Stevenson, Contact Person.
Natural Family Planning. Contact the Diocesan Office. Tel: 704-377-6871. Gerard Carter, Contact Person.
Prison Ministry. Contact Diocesan Office. Tel: 704-377-6871. Mr. Bill Matevie, Contact Person.
Problem Pregnancy. Contact the pregnancy support worker at any of the CSS offices. Tel: 704-377-6871 (Charlotte); 255-0146 (Asheville); 910-727-0705 (Winston-Salem).
Respect Life. Contact the Diocesan Office. Tel: 704-377-6871. Maggi Nadol, Contact Person.
Retrouvaille. Contact Diocesan Office. Tel: 704-377-6871. Deacon Nick Fadero, Contact Person.
Widowed-Separated-Divorced. Contact the Diocesan Office. Tel: 704-377-6871. Suzanne Bach, Contact Person.

HAMPTONVILLE. *Well of Mercy*, 181 Mercy Ln., 27020. Tel: 704-539-5449; Fax: 704-539-5449. Co-Directors: Sr. Brigid McCarthy, R.S.M.; Sr. Donna Marie Vaillancourt, R.S.M. Retreats and psycho-spiritual development programs.

[H] HOME HEALTH CARE

HAYESVILLE. *Good Shepherd Home Health & Hospice Agency, Inc.*, P.O. Box 465, 28904. Tel: 704-389-6311; Fax: 704-389-9584
For a complete listing, refer to the Special Care Facilities section.

*ROSMAN. *Frances Warde Health Service*, Star Rte. 1, Box 581, 28772. Tel: 704-884-7990; Fax: 704-966-9609
For a complete listing, refer to the Special Care Facilities section.

[I] NURSING HOMES

HIGH POINT. *Maryfield Nursing Home*, 1315 Greensboro Rd., 27260. Tel: 910-886-2444; Fax: 910-886-4036
For a complete listing, refer to the Special Care Facilities section.

[J] MONASTERIES AND RESIDENCES OF PRIESTS AND BROTHERS

CHARLOTTE. *Jesuit Community*, 507 S. Tryon St., 28202. Tel: 704-372-6808. Legal Title: *Jesuit Community in Western North Carolina.* Revs. James A. Devereux, S.J., Supr.; Vincent P. Alagia, S.J.; Francis J. Gillespie, S.J.; George R. Hohman, S.J.; Lawrence J. Hunt, S.J.; Edward M. Ifkovits, S.J.; James P. Keogh, S.J.; William J. Lynch, S.J.; Eugene P. McCreesh, S.J.; Joseph J. McGovern, S.J.; Robert J. Paquet, S.J.; Francis X.D. Reese, S.J.; Robert D. Weisenbaugh, S.J.

BELMONT. *Belmont Abbey*, 100 Belmont-Mount Holly Rd., 28012-2795. Tel: 704-825-6675. Legal Title: *Southern Benedictine Society of North Carolina, Inc.* Rt. Revs. Oscar C. Burnett, O.S.B.; Walter A. Coggin, O.S.B., Ph.D., D.D., (Retired), Abbot-Nullius; Very Revs. Christopher A. Kirchgessner, O.S.B., Prior; David G. Brown, O.S.B., Sub-Prior; Revs. Bernard L. Rosswog, O.S.B., S.T.D.; Anselm G. Biggs, O.S.B., Ph.D.; Raymond J. Geyer, O.S.B.; Matthew T. McSorley, O.S.B.; John A. Oetgen, O.S.B.; Kenneth A. Geyer, O.S.B.; David R. Kessinger, O.S.B.; Kieran A. Neilson, O.S.B.; Francis P. Forster, O.S.B.; Arthur J. Pendleton, O.S.B.; Lawrence R. Willis, O.S.B.; W. Frederick George, O.S.B.; Paschal M. Baumstein, O.S.B., Custos Archivorum; Placid D. Solari, O.S.B., S.T.D. Abbots 2; Monk Priests of Abbey 16; Priests in Residence 16; Brothers 2.

GREENSBORO. *Franciscan Friary*, 614 Kimberly Dr., 27408-5198. Tel: 910-379-7568. Rev. Louis Canino, O.F.M., Dir.

[K] CONVENTS AND RESIDENCES FOR SISTERS

CHARLOTTE. *Blessed Trinity Missionary Cenacle*, 801 Bromley Rd., 28207. Tel: 704-377-3254. Social work. Sisters 2.
Coolock House, 2328 Red Barn Ln., 28210. Tel: 704-554-1967. Parish and health care. Sisters of Mercy of the Americas 2.
Missionaries of Charity, 236 S. Torrence St., 28204. Tel: 704-334-8685. Ministry for poor. Sisters 4.
Sisters of St. Francis Convent, 4516 Randolph Rd., Apt. 87, 28211. Tel: 704-364-1361. Sisters 2.
Sisters' Residence, Carmel House, 3035 Carmel Rd., 28226. Tel: 704-552-2899; Fax: 704-552-2899. Administration, nursing education & bookkeeping. Sisters 2; Candidates 1.

ASHEVILLE. *St. Joseph Hospital Convent*, 428 Biltmore Ave., 28801. Tel: 704-255-6674; 255-3100 (Hospital). Sisters 7; Health Care 5.

BELMONT. *Sisters of Mercy of North Carolina, Inc.*, Sacred Heart Convent, 100 Mercy Dr., 28012-2738. Tel: 704-829-5100; Fax: 704-829-5137.
Web site: www.AsaSystems.com/mercy
Motherhouse and Novitiate of Sisters of Mercy of the Americas, Regional Community of North Carolina. Sr. Mary Rosalind Picot, R.S.M., Pres.; Sr. Mary Andrew Ray, R.S.M., Motherhouse Coord. Sisters in Motherhouse 45; Professed Sisters in Community 135. Connected with the Motherhouse are Holy Angels, Inc., the McAuley Center, House of Mercy, Inc., and Catherine's House, Inc.

CHEROKEE. *Our Lady of Guadalupe Convent*, P.O. Box 202, 28719. Tel: 704-497-2029. Sisters of St. Francis (Tiffin, OH) 2. Pastoral work.

MAGGIE VALLEY. *Living Waters Convent*, 103 Living Waters Ln., 28751. Tel: 704-926-9393. Sisters 3. Retreat work.

ROSMAN. *Sisters Residence*, Star Rte. 1, Box 581, 28772. Tel: 704-884-7990; 884-9528; 883-2789; Fax: 704-966-9609. Sisters 4. Health service.

VALE. *Maryvale Motherhouse*, 2522 June Bug Rd., 28168. Tel: 704-276-2626. Mother Mary Louis, Foundress and Supr. Congregation of Our Lady Help of the Clergy, (Maryvale Sisters). Sisters 5. Parish ministry, day-care center, spiritual/retreat center, religious education and pastoral ministry.

[L] CAMPUS MINISTRY CENTERS

CHARLOTTE. *Diocesan Office of Campus Ministry.* Colleen McDermott, Dir., Res., 1123 S. Church St., 28203. Tel: 704-377-6871; Fax: 704-358-1208.
University of North Carolina-Charlotte, ORA, 9201 University City Blvd., UNC-Charlotte, 28223-0001. Tel: 704-547-4069; 394-8308. Barbara L. Neff-Hutchinson, Catholic Campus Min.
Belmont Abbey College, Belmont, 28012. Tel: 704-829-7196; 825-6697. Dr. Elizabeth Sechler, Dir. Campus Ministry; Rev. Kieran Neilson, O.S.B., Chap.
Appalachian State University, 232 Faculty St., Boone, 28607. Tel: 704-264-7067; Fax: 704-262-3721.
Catholic Campus Ministry: Mr. Ed Alton.
Western Carolina University, Catholic Student Center, P.O. Box 364, Cullowhee, 28723-0364. Tel: 704-293-9374; 586-8068. Gloria Schweizer, Catholic Campus Min.
Davidson College. (Davidson), 217 Brawley School Rd., P.O. Box 1364, Mooresville, 28115-1364. Tel: 704-664-3992. Rev. Robert Weisenbaugh, S.J., Catholic Campus Min.
NC Agricultural and Technical State University & Bennett College, 1009 Bluford St., Greensboro, 27401. Tel: 910-272-5868; 545-1468. Alberta Hairston.
University of North Carolina-Greensboro, Greensboro College & Guilford College, 1331 W. Friendly Ave., Greensboro, 27403. Tel: 910-334-5548; 691-0592. Rev. John A. Gilvey, O.S.F.S.
Wake Forest University and Winston-Salem University, P.O. Box 7204, Reynolda Station, Winston-Salem, 27109. Tel: 910-759-5018; 727-7590.
Salem College and N.C. School of the Arts, P.O. Box 10548, Chaplain's Office, Salem College, Winston-Salem, 27108. Tel: 910-758-5962. Rev. Jude DeAngelo, O.F.M.Conv.; Shawn Adams, Catholic Campus Min.

[M] RETREAT CENTERS

HOT SPRINGS.
**Jesuit House of Prayer*, P.O. Box 7, 28743. Tel: 704-622-7366. Revs. Vincent P. Alagia, S.J., Dir.; Joseph J. McGovern, S.J. Directed, private individual retreats and small group retreats for men and women, as well as ecumenical. Overnight hostel for Appalachian hikers.

[N] REFLECTION CENTERS

BELMONT. *The McAuley Center*, Center for Adult Religious Education Sacred Heart Convent, 28012. Tel: 704-829-5113. Sr. Mary Hugh Mauldin, Dir.

MAGGIE VALLEY. *Living Waters Catholic Reflection Center*, 103 Living Waters Ln., 28751. Tel: 704-926-3833. Sr. Jane Schmenk, O.S.F., Dir.; Sr. Jean Linder, O.S.F.; Sr. Francine Sartor, O.S.F. Retreats, days of recollection, and continuing education.

[O] HISPANIC MINISTRY

CHARLOTTE. *Centro Catolico Hispano*, 2117 Shenandoah Ave., 28205-6021. Tel: 704-335-1281. Rev. Vincent H. Finnerty, C.M., Diocesan Dir. of Hispanic Ministry; Deacon Carlos Medina.

[P] CONFERENCE CENTERS

HICKORY. *Catholic Conference Center*, 1551 Trinity Lane, 28602-9247. Tel: 704-327-7441; Fax: 704-327-0872. Deacon Guy A. Piche, Dir.

[Q] MISCELLANEOUS

CHARLOTTE.
**Room at the Inn, Inc.*, 3737 Weona Ave., 28209. Mailing Address: P.O. Box 30544, 28230-0544. Tel: 704-525-4673. Rev. Conrad L. Kimbrough, Pres.; Albert Hodges, Exec. Dir. A long-term residence for single pregnant women, with or without previous children.
Sisters of Mercy of North Carolina Foundation, Inc., 2115 Rexford Rd., Suite 401, 28211. Tel: 704-366-0087. Sr. Mary Jerome Spradley, R.S.M., Pres.

ASHEVILLE. *St. Joseph Addictions Recovery Program*, 129 Biltmore Ave., 28801. Tel: 704-254-2700.

BELMONT.
**Catherine's House*, 402 Mercy Dr., P.O. Box 1633, 28012. Tel: 704-825-9599; Fax: 704-829-5137. Sr. Mary Barbara Sullivan, R.S.M., CEO. Transitional housing for women and women with children, who are homeless.
House of Mercy, Inc., 701 Mercy Dr., 28012. Tel: 704-825-4711; Fax: 704-825-9976. Mailing Address: P.O. Box 808, 28012. Provides a home for persons living with AIDS in the advanced stages who have no other housing alternative in an 11 county region. Stan Patterson, Pres. & CEO. Beds 6.
Sisters of Mercy of North Carolina, Inc., 101 Mercy Dr., 28012. Tel: 704-829-5260; Fax: 704-829-5267.
E-mail: ncsrsmercy@aol.com
Web site: www.AsAsystems.com/mercy
Sr. M. Rosalind Picot, R.S.M., Pres.

GREENSBORO. *Society of St. Vincent De Paul*, 1414 Gorrell St., 27401. Tel: 910-272-0336.

RELIGIOUS INSTITUTES OF MEN REPRESENTED IN THE DIOCESE

For further details refer to the corresponding bracketed number in the Religious Institutes of Men or Women section.

[0200]—*Benedictine Monks.* (Belmont, NC).—O.S.B.
[0470]—*The Capuchin Friars Province of the Stigmata.*—O.F.M.Cap.
[]—*Carmelites of Mary Immaculate.* (India).—C.M.I.
[0740]—*Congregation of Marians of the Immaculate Conception.*—M.I.C.
[1330]—*Congregation of the Mission.* (Eastern Prov.).—C.M.
[0480]—*Conventual Franciscans.* (Union City, NJ).—O.F.M.Conv.
[0520]—*Franciscan Friars.* (New York, NY).—O.F.M.
[0570]—*Glenmary Home Missioners.*—Glmy.
[0650]—*Holy Ghost Fathers.* (Bethel Park, PA).—C.S.Sp.

[0690]—*Jesuit Fathers and Brother.* (Maryland Prov.; Milwaukee, WI).—S.J.
[0920]—*Oblates of St. Francis De Sales.* (Wilmington-Philadelphia).—O.S.F.S.
[1070]—*Redemptorist Fathers.* (Baltimore Prov.).—C.SS.R.

RELIGIOUS INSTITUTES OF WOMEN REPRESENTED IN THE DIOCESE

[3080]—*Congregation of Our Lady, Help of the Clergy.*—C.L.H.C.
[1920]—*Congregation of the Sisters of the Holy Cross.*—C.S.C.
[0760]—*Daughters of Charity of St. Vincent de Paul.*—D.C.
[2710]—*Missionaries of Charity.*—M.C.
[2790]—*Missionary Servants of the Most Blessed Trinity.*—M.S.B.T.
[3640]—*Poor Servants of the Mother of God.*—S.M.G.
[0590]—*Sisters of Charity of Saint Elizabeth, Convent Station.*—S.C.
[0650]—*Sisters of Charity of St. Vincent de Paul, of New York.*—S.C.
[2570]—*Sisters of Mercy.* (Belmont, NC; Watchung, NJ).—R.S.M.
[2580]—*Sisters of Mercy of the Union in the United States of America.* (Dallas, TX; Detroit, MI; Cincinnati, OH).—R.S.M.
[3000]—*Sisters of Notre Dame de Namur.*—S.N.D.deN.
[3893]—*Sisters of Saint Joseph of Chestnut Hill, Philadelphia.*—S.S.J.
[1570]—*Sisters of St. Francis of the Holy Family.*—O.S.F.
[1760]—*Sisters of the Third Order of St. Francis of Penance and Charity.*—O.S.F.
[4060]—*Society of the Holy Child Jesus.* (Drexel Hill).—S.H.C.J.

NECROLOGY

† Murray, John J., Morganton, NC, St. Charles Borromeo. —Died Sept. 29, 1997.

† Wellein, Rev. Msgr. William G., (Retired). —Died Oct. 2, 1997.

Diocese of Cheyenne

(Dioecesis Cheyennensis)

Most Reverend

JOSEPH HART, D.D.

Bishop of Cheyenne; ordained May 1, 1956; appointed July 1, 1976; appointed Titular Bishop of Timida Regia; episcopal ordination August 31, 1976; installed June 12, 1978. *Res., Box 468, Cheyenne, WY, 82003.*

ESTABLISHED AUGUST 2, 1887.

Square Miles 97,548.

Comprises the State of Wyoming and Yellowstone National Park.

For legal titles of parishes and diocesan institutions, consult the Chancery Office.

Chancery Office: 2121 Capitol Ave., Box 426, Cheyenne, WY, 82003-0426. Tel.: 307-638-1530; Fax: 307-637-7936.

E-mail address: cheycathbish@worldnet.att.net

STATISTICAL OVERVIEW

Personnel	
Bishop	1
Priests: Diocesan Active in Diocese	38
Priests: Active Outside Diocese	2
Priests: Retired, Sick or Absent	11
Number of Diocesan Priests	51
Religious Priests in Diocese	9
Extern Priests in Diocese	2
Permanent Deacons in Diocese	8
Total Brothers	1
Total Sisters	31
Parishes	
Parishes	36
With Resident Pastor:	
Resident Diocesan Priests	30
Resident Religious Priests	5
Without Resident Pastor:	
Administered by Priests	1
Missions	42
Professional Ministry Personnel:	
Sisters	15
Lay Ministers	46
Welfare	
Homes for the Aged	2
Total Assisted	94
Day Care and Extended Day Care Centers	5
Total Assisted	250
Specialized Homes	1
Total Assisted	100
Special Centers for Social Services	10
Total Assisted	10,933
Educational	
Diocesan Students in Other Seminaries	5
Total Seminarians	5
Elementary Schools, Diocesan and Parish	7
Total Students	1,263
Catechesis/Religious Education:	
High School Students	1,639
Elementary Students	5,853
Total Students Under Catholic Instruction	8,760
Teachers in the Diocese:	
Priests	2
Scholastics	1
Sisters	2
Lay Teachers	94
Vital Statistics	
Receptions into the Church:	
Infant Baptism Totals	995
Adult Baptism Totals	168
Received into Full Communion	286
First Communions	1,083
Confirmations	915
Marriages:	
Catholic	149
Interfaith	166
Total Marriages	315
Deaths	567
Total Catholic Population	48,911
Total Population	481,400

Former Bishops—Rt. Rev. MAURICE F. BURKE, D.D., cons. Oct. 28, 1887; transferred to the See of St. Joseph, MO, June 19, 1893; died March 17, 1923.—Rt. Rev. THOMAS M. LENIHAN, D.D., cons. Feb. 24, 1897; died Dec. 15, 1901.—Most Rev. JAMES J. KEANE, D.D., cons. Bishop of Cheyenne Oct. 28, 1902; raised to the archiepiscopal dignity and transferred to Archdiocese of Dubuque, Aug. 11, 1911; died Aug. 2, 1929.—Most Rev. PATRICK A. MCGOVERN, D.D., LL.D., ord. Aug. 18, 1895 assistant at the Pontifical Throne; appt. Jan. 19, 1912; cons. April 11, 1912; died Nov. 8, 1951.—Most Rev. HUBERT M. NEWELL, D.D., LL.D., ord. June 15, 1930; appt. Coadjutor Aug. 2, 1947; cons. Sept. 24, 1947; succeeded to the See Nov. 8, 1951; retired Jan. 3, 1978; died Sept. 8, 1987.

Chancery Office—2121 Capitol Ave., P.O. Box 426, Cheyenne, 82003-0426. Tel: 307-638-1530; Fax: 307-637-7936.

Catholic Ministries Office—623 S. Wolcott, Casper, 82601. Tel: 307-237-2723; Fax: 307-235-9157.

Vicar-General / Moderator of the Curia—Very Rev. EUGENE SULLIVAN, V.G., *P.O. Box 2024, Sheridan, 82801.* Tel: 307-674-7441; 672-2848; Fax: 307-674-9187.

Chancellor—CAROL DELOIS, *P.O. Box 426, Cheyenne, 82003-0426.* Tel: 307-638-1530; Fax: 307-637-7936.

Vice-Chancellors—Revs. CARL A. BEAVERS; VERNON CLARK, M.C.L., J.C.L.; Very Revs. MICHAEL CARR; CHARLES F. TAYLOR, J.C.D.

College of Consultors—Very Rev. EUGENE SULLIVAN, V.G.; Revs. THOMAS E. CRONKLETON, JR., J.C.L.; AUGUST KOEUNE; GARY RUZICKA; JOHN SAVIO; GERALD A. SULLIVAN.

Council of Priests—Most Rev. JOSEPH HART, D.D.; Very Rev. EUGENE SULLIVAN, V.G., Ex Officio; Revs. AUGUST KOEUNE, Chm.; CARL GALLINGER, Vice-Chm. THOMAS E. CRONKLETON, JR., J.C.L.; ANDREW DUNCAN; WILLIAM ESPENSHADE; Rev. Msgr. LAWRENCE ETCHINGHAM; Revs. CLIFF JACOBSON; GARY RUZICKA; JOHN SAVIO; GERALD A. SULLIVAN; Very Rev. CHARLES TAYLOR; Rev. CHARLES VELASQUEZ.

Episcopal Vicar for Priestly Life and Ministry—Rev. GARY RUZICKA, *P.O. Box 50397, Casper, 82605-0397.* Tel: 307-235-5535; Fax: 307-237-7244.

Vicars Forane—Very Rev. JOHN MURRAY, Casper Deanery; Very Rev. MICHAEL CARR, Cheyenne Deanery; Very Rev. CHARLES F. TAYLOR, Rock Springs Deanery; Very Rev. EUGENE SULLIVAN, V.G., Sheridan Deanery; Very Rev. RONALD STOLCIS, Thermopolis Deanery.

Director of Diocesan Programs—FINN MCCARTHY, *623 S. Wolcott, Casper, 82601.* Tel: 307-237-2723; Fax: 307-235-9157.

Finance Officer—JAMES S. VANCE, *P.O. Box 426, Cheyenne, 82003-0426.* Tel: 307-638-1530; Fax: 307-637-7936.

Finance Council—Most Rev. JOSEPH HART, D.D.; Ex Officios, Voting: Very Rev. EUGENE SULLIVAN, V.G.; Rev. GARY RUZICKA; MICHAEL SULLIVAN; EDWARD F. MURRAY. Ex Officios, Non-Voting: Revs. THOMAS E. CRONKLETON, JR.; THOMAS OGG; JAMES S. VANCE; FINN MCCARTHY; JAMES FAULKNER. Appointed: HOWARD BAKER, Chm.; PATTY BERRY; WILLIAM DOWNES; RODNEY KINSKEY; ORION LORENZI; JOHN OSTLUND; FRANK ROTELLINI; Rev. JOHN SAVIO; JANE SCHNAUBER.

Tribunal Office—All marriage correspondence is to be directed to: *The Tribunal Office: P.O. Box 426, Cheyenne, 82003-0426.* Tel: 307-638-1530; 800-788-4606; Fax: 307-637-7936.

Judicial Vicar—Rev. THOMAS E. CRONKLETON, JR., J.C.L., J.C.D. (Cand.).

Director of the Tribunal—DARLENE FLYNN.

Auditors—DARLENE FLYNN; CONNIE KASSAHN.

Administrative Assistant / Ecclesiastical Notary—CONNIE KASSAHN.

Bookkeeper / Clerk / Ecclesiastical Notary—LESLIE CONNAGHAN.

Promoter of Justice—Very Rev. CHARLES F. TAYLOR, J.C.D.

Judges—Very. Rev. MICHAEL CARR; Revs. GERALD F. CHLEBORAD, J.C.L.; THOMAS E. CRONKLETON, JR., J.C.L.; DAVID ALAN ZWIFKA, J.C.L.

Defenders of the Bond—Revs. VERNON F. CLARK, M.C.L., J.C.L.; WILLIAM T. ESPENSHADE; THOMAS G. OGG; SAMUEL HAYES; GERALD A. SULLIVAN; RICHARD R. RYAN, J.C.D.; Very Rev. CHARLES F. TAYLOR, J.C.D.; Deacon LEE PICO.

Advocates—SUSAN SIMON; BONNIE BAUMBERGER.

Diocesan Administrative Offices and Boards

Catholic Social Services of Wyoming, Inc.—BETSY GROOM, M.S.W., Dir., *P.O. Box 1026, Cheyenne, 82003-1026.* Tel: 307-638-1530; Fax: 307-637-7936. Board of Directors: Most Rev. JOSEPH HART, D.D.; Very Rev. EUGENE SULLIVAN, V.G.; PAUL NOVAK, Chm. Board of Trustees: Rev. GERALD A. SULLIVAN; MARY SHARP, Vice-Chm. ELIZABETH GROOM, M.S.W., Dir. HELEN CHADEY; HENRY CHADEY; JAN COBB; DICK DESOMBER; JO DESOMBER; JIM ZANCANELLA; LILLIAN ZANCANELLA, Sec.

Education Office—Deacon ED MCCARTHY, Dir.; Sr. MARY SUTTON, Media Consultant, *623 S. Wolcott, Casper, 82601.* Tel: 307-237-2723; Fax: 307-235-9157.

Education Office Board—Most Rev. JOSEPH HART, D.D.; Deacon ED MCCARTHY, Supt. Education; Revs. ANDREW DUNCAN; ROBERT G. LYNCH, S.J.; RAY RODRIGUEZ; Sr. MARY SUTTON, Media Consultant; Sr. RUTH ELLERT, O.L.V.M.; Sr. MARY SCHAEFER, C.S.J.; Sr. ELIZABETH SKALICKY, S.C.L.; ANDREA CHOJNACKY, (Glenrock); APRIL CRAMER, (Lander); MARY ANN CUMMINS, (Buffalo); DONNA DUNCAN, (Torrington); PAM EVANOFF, (Rock Springs); JANE JOHNSON, (Gillette); SUSIE PALMER, (Jackson); SUE SANDEEN, (Laramie); PAT MCCARTHY, Family Life Dir.; JIM ZIERDEN, Youth Dir.

Family Services Office—PAT MCCARTHY, Dir., *623 S. Wolcott, Casper, 82601.* Tel: 307-237-2723; Fax: 307-235-9157.

Family Services Board—Most Rev. JOSEPH HART, D.D.; Very Rev. EUGENE SULLIVAN, V.G.; Rev. RAY ROGRIGUEZ; MARY ANN DURAN; RUTHIE HALVORSEN; LINDA HURLESS; CHARLIE LUX; FRANK MCGINTY; DICK MILLS; PAT MILLS; RALPH SPECHT; CAROL SPECHT; BETSY VIGNERI; BRAD ZETTL; JENNIFER ZETTL; BYRON ZUEHLSDORFF; TRACY ZUEHLSDORFF.

Lay Ministry Office—Deacon ED MCCARTHY, Dir., *623 S. Wolcott, Casper, 82601.* Tel: 307-237-2723; Fax: 307-235-9157.

Lay Ministry Formation Board—Most Rev. JOSEPH HART, D.D.; Deacon ED MCCARTHY, Dir.; Rev. Msgr. JAMES O'NEILL; Revs. AUGUST KOEUNE; THOMAS OGG; Dr. MARY BURKE; Dr. TOM BURKE; ALISON MCNULTY; DAVID MCNULTY; THERESA WYBURN.

Newspaper "Wyoming Catholic Register"—published by the Catholic Press Society of Wyoming. SCOTT FARRIS, Editor, *P.O. Box 1308, Cheyenne, 82003-1308.* Street Address: *2121 Capitol Ave., Cheyenne, 82003-1308.* Tel: 307-638-1530; Fax: 307-637-7936.

Newspaper, Wyoming Catholic Register Board—Most Rev. JOSEPH HART, D.D.; SCOTT FARRIS, Editor; Rev. Msgr. JAMES O'NEILL; Rev. WILLIAM ESPENSHADE; JOAN BARRON; GLORIA CARLSON; HELEN FITCH; SALVADOR MANZANARES.

Planned Giving Office—FINN MCCARTHY, Dir., *623 S. Wolcott, Casper, 82601.* Tel: 307-237-2723; Fax: 307-235-9157.

Vocation Office—Rev. CARL GALLINGER, Dir., *1800 E. Grand Ave., Laramie, 82070.* Tel: 307-745-5461; Fax: 307-742-0521.

Youth Office—JIM ZIERDEN, Dir. ELIZABETH LOVELETT, Asst. Dir., *623 S. Wolcott, Casper, 82601.* Tel: 307-237-2723; Fax: 307-235-9257.

Youth Ministry Board—Revs. CARL GALLINGER; DREW DUNCAN; CLIFF JACOBSON; RAY RODRIGUEZ; Mr. BEN CAROTTA; JOHN CHICK; MONICA ELSINGER; JOAN KASTNER; LIZ LOVELETT; JIM SCALIA; CHRIS TRUJILLO; JIM ZIERDEN.

Other Diocesan Boards, Councils and Programs

Diocesan Trustees, Board of Directors—Most Rev. JOSEPH HART, D.D.; Very Rev. EUGENE SULLIVAN, V.G.; Rev. GARY RUZICKA; MICHAEL SULLIVAN; EDWARD F. MURRAY, JR.

Apostolate for Evangelization—Rev. RAY MOSS, *617 S. 4th St., Laramie, 82070.* Tel: 307-745-3115.

Bishop's Annual Campaign, "Bishop's Appeal"—JAMES S. VANCE, *P.O. Box 426, Cheyenne, 82003.* Tel: 307-638-1530; Fax: 307-637-7936. FINN MCCARTHY, *623 S. Wolcott, Casper, 82601.* Tel: 307-237-2723; Fax: 307-235-9157.

Boy and Girl Scouts—Rev. THOMAS KADERA, *Holy Rosary Church, P.O. Box 1047, Lander, 82520.* Tel: 307-332-4952.

Building Commission—Most Rev. JOSEPH HART, D.D.; ROGER BAALMAN, Chm.; Very Rev. EUGENE SULLIVAN, V.G.; Revs. GERALD F. CHLEBORAD; PHILIP COLIBRARO; MICHAEL HELLMAN; JOHN SAVIO; Mr. CLINTON BLACK; VIRGIL SLOUGH; JAMES S. VANCE, Sec.

Catholic Relief Services—BETSY GROOM, M.S.W., *P.O. Box 426, Cheyenne, 82003.* Tel: 307-638-1530.

Catholic Telecommunications—Deacon JOHN ALOISIO, *St. Margaret's School, 220 N. 7th E., Riverton, 82501.* Tel: 307-856-5922; Fax: 307-857-5892.

Catholic University, Friends of—Very Rev. CHARLES F. TAYLOR, *P.O. Box 311, Kemmerer, 83101-0311.* Tel: 307-877-4573.

Confraternity of Christian Doctrine—Deacon ED MCCARTHY, Dir., *623 S. Wolcott, Casper, 82601.* Tel: 307-237-2723.

Council of Religious—Sr. THERESE STEINER, S.C.L.; Sr. BRIDGID RYAN, S.O.L.W.

Cursillo Board—Rev. WILLIAM ESPENSHADE; PENNY VILLALVA, Pres. LLOYD HEARNS; VIRGINIA SPINDLER; MARY BONOGOFSKY.

Diaconate Program, Permanent—Rev. GARY RUZICKA, *P.O. Box 50397, Casper, 82605-0397.* Tel: 307-235-5535; Fax: 307-237-7244.

Diaconate Board—Most Rev. JOSEPH HART, D.D.; Revs. CARL GALLINGER, Bishop's Delegate; GARY RUZICKA, Dir. Deacons; THOMAS OGG; Very Rev. RONALD STOLCIS; Deacons JOHN ALOISIO; JOSEPH KRISTUFEK.

Ecumenism Commission—Revs. JOSEPH DALEY, Chm. GERALD F. CHLEBORAD.

Endowment Funds and Trusts—

Catholic Schools Endowment Fund, Seminarian Education Endowment—JAMES S. VANCE, *P.O. Box 426, Cheyenne, 82003.* Tel: 307-638-1530.

Knights of Columbus Charitable Trust for Seminarian Education and Priests' Retirement—FINN MCCARTHY, *623 S. Wolcott, Casper, 82601.* Tel: 307-237-2723.

St. Mary's School Foundation—Rev. CARL A. BEAVERS, *P.O. Box 1268, Cheyenne, 82003.* Tel: 307-635-9261.

Family Services Divisions—PAT MCCARTHY, Dir.

Beginning Experience for Divorced or Widowed—VIKKI EPPERSON; JESS THIEL, *P.O. Box 9953, Casper, 82609.* Tel: 307-234-2551; 237-6013.

Divorced / Separated / Widowed Ministry—LINDA HURLESS. Tel: 307-265-3509.

Engaged Encounter—JAN MARTIN; STEVE MARTIN, *1340 Nottingham Dr., Casper, 82609.* Tel: 307-577-3009.

Marriage Encounter—DEBBIE ROBBINS; STEVE ROBBINS, *1103 Overdale, Gillette, 82718.* Tel: 307-686-7471.

Marriage Preparation—PAT MCCARTHY.

Natural Family Planning—PAT MCCARTHY.

Rainbows for All God's Children—AMY ROJO, *121 S. Connor, Sheridan, 82801.* Tel: 307-674-7301.

Respect Life Catholic Pro-Life Ministry—PAT MCCARTHY.

Retrouvaille, Ministry for Hurting Marriages—PAT MCCARTHY.

Holy Child Pontifical Association—Deacon ED MCCARTHY, Dir., *623 S. Wolcott, Casper, 82601.* Tel: 307-237-2723.

Housing—Rev. CARL A. BEAVERS, *P.O. Box 1268, Cheyenne, 82003-1268.* Tel: 307-635-9261., *St. Anthony Manor, 211 E. Sixth, Casper, 82601.* Tel: 307-237-0843., *Holy Trinity Manor, 2516 E. 18th St., Cheyenne, 82001.* Tel: 307-778-8850.

Information Office—SCOTT FARRIS, *P.O. Box 1308, Cheyenne, 82003-1308.* Tel: 307-638-1530; Fax: 307-637-7936.

Liturgical Commission—Most Rev. JOSEPH HART, D.D.; Revs. GARY RUZICKA, Exec. Sec. GERALD F. CHLEBORAD; THOMAS CRONKLETON, JR.; MICHAEL HELLMAN; BETTY MCCARTHY; BRENDA WILKING.

Pastoral Council—Most Rev. JOSEPH HART, D.D., Chm.; CYNTHIA JOHNSON, Vice-Chm.; Very Rev. EUGENE SULLIVAN, V.G., Ex Officio; CAROL DELOIS, Chancellor; FINN MCCARTHY, Exec. Sec., *623 S. Wolcott, Casper, 82601.* Tel: 307-237-2723. JAMES S. VANCE, Finance Officer. Casper Deanery: Very Rev. JOHN MURRAY; WILLIAM COUGHLIN; DOLLY MEEHAN; MARILYN CRULL. Cheyenne Deanery: Rev. RAY RODRIGUEZ; SANDY GADDIS; CHARLES GARCIA; JOSEPH NIES; MICHAEL MCNAMEE. Rock Springs Deanery: Rev. AUGUST KOEUNE; JAN HOTCHKIN; PHILANN LUX; DOTTIE PASENELLI. Sheridan Deanery: Rev. RICHARD MACLELLAN; SHIRLEY GENEREAUX; BLASE GILTNER; RAY O'LEARY. Thermopolis Deanery: Vacant. Clergy Rep. CYNTHIA CONNOR; JIM HEISER; CYNTHIA JOHNSON; APRIL PENDLETON. Religious: Sr. RITA DOWNEY, O.S.B.; Sr. RUTH ANN HEHN, S.C.L., Recording Sec.; Sr. LETITIA LENHERR, S.C.L.; Rev. CHARLES VELASQUEZ, Hispanic Rep. MARY ANN WHITEMAN, Native American Rep.

Priests' Eucharistic League—Very Rev. EUGENE SULLIVAN, V.G., *P.O. Box 2024, Sheridan, 82801-2024.*

Priests' Personnel Board—Most Rev. JOSEPH HART, D.D., Chm.; Very Revs. MICHAEL CARR; CHARLES F. TAYLOR, J.C.D.; Revs. WILLIAM ESPENSHADE; SAMUEL HAYES.

Propagation of the Faith—Deacon JOHN ALOISIO, *220 N. 7th E., Riverton, 82501.* Tel: 307-856-5922.

Rural Life Conference—Rev. SAM HAYES, *P.O. Box 992, Jackson, 83001.* Tel: 307-733-2516.

St. Joseph's Society for Sick and Retired Priests (Clergy Mutual Benefit Society)—Most Rev. JOSEPH HART, D.D.; Rev. THOMAS OGG, Pres.; Rev. Msgr. LAWRENCE ETCHINGHAM; Very Revs. RONALD STOLCIS; CHARLES F. TAYLOR, J.C.D.; Revs. THOMAS E. CRONKLETON, JR., J.C.L.; KEVIN KOCH; GERALD A. SULLIVAN; Mr. LEO RILEY, Admin.

Spanish-Speaking Apostolate Board—Most Rev. JOSEPH HART, D.D.; Rev. CHARLES VELAZQUEZ, Chap., *1009 9th St., Wheatland, 82201.* Tel: 307-322-2070.

CLERGY, PARISHES, MISSIONS AND PAROCHIAL SCHOOLS

CITY OF CHEYENNE
(Laramie County)

1—ST. MARY'S CATHEDRAL (1868), Revs. Carl A. Beavers; Rory Schiffbauer; Roy Rodriguez; Deacon Lee Pico. In res., Rev. Joseph E. Moroney.
Mailing Address: P.O. Box 1268, 82003-1268. Tel: 307-635-9261; Fax: 307-637-7936. [CEM]
School—Tel: 307-638-9268; Fax: 307-635-2347. Gilbert Sanchez, Prin.
Lay Teachers 21; Students 352.
Catechesis / Religious Programs—Tel: 307-637-4009; 635-9261; Fax: 307-637-7936. D.R.E.: Charlotte Hommel, (Grades PreK-8); Cathy Mohatt, (Grades 9-12).
Students 615.
Convent—716 E. 21st St., 82001. Tel: 307-638-6005. Sisters 2.

2—HOLY TRINITY (1957), Rev. Gerald A. Sullivan. In res., Rev. Msgr. William Delaney, (Retired); Rev. Msgr. Lawrence Etchingham, (Retired); Rev. James Doudican, (Retired).
Res., 1836 Hot Springs Ave., P.O. Box 5720, 82003-5720. Tel: 307-632-5872; 637-7150; Fax: 307-637-7150.
Catechesis / Religious Programs—Tel: 307-632-4482. D.R.E.: Martha Thein; Terri Mercer.
Sisters of Charity of Leavenworth 1; Students 212.

3—ST. JOSEPH'S (1929) (Hispanic), Rev. Michael Carr.
Mailing Address: P.O. Box 1141, 82003-1141. Tel: 307-634-4625; Fax: 307-635-4700.
Office: 314 E. Sixth St., 82007.
Res., 515 House, 82007. Tel: 307-634-4625; Fax: 307-635-4700. [CEM]
Church—300 E. 6th St., 82007.
Catechesis / Religious Programs—Brad Armitage, D.R.E.
Students 292.

OUTSIDE CITY OF CHEYENNE

Buffalo, Johnson Co., St. John the Baptist (1885) (Basque), Rev. Vernon F. Clark.
Res., 532 N. Lobban, 82834. Tel: 307-684-7268; Fax: 307-684-5490.
Catechesis / Religious Programs—Tel: 307-684-7217. Mary Ann Cummins, D.R.E.
Students 180.
Missions—Clearmont, Johnson Co., St. Mary, 82834.; Kaycee, Johnson Co., St. Hubert, 82834.

Casper, Natrona Co., St. Anthony of Padua (1903), Rev. Msgr. James O'Neill; Rev. Clifford Jacobson; Deacon Don Stewart.
Office: 604 S. Center, 82601. Tel: 307-266-2666; Fax: 307-266-4127.
School—218 E. Seventh, 82601. Tel: 307-234-2873; Fax: 307-235-4946. Mrs. Mary Kozola, Prin.
Sisters 1; Lay Teachers 18; Students 267.
Catechesis / Religious Programs—Ruthie Halvorsen, D.R.E.
Students 391.
Mission—Midwest, Natrona Co., St. Francis Mission, Midwest, 82643.

Our Lady of Fatima (1954), Revs. Philip Colibraro; Daniel Colibraro, (Retired); Deacon Ed McCarthy.
Res., 1401 CY Ave., 82604. Tel: 307-265-5586; Fax: 307-266-2958.
Catechesis / Religious Programs—Tel: 307-234-3971; Fax: 307-266-2958. D.R.E.: Teresa Sears; Donna Macklin.
Students 114.

Saint Patrick's (1963), Rev. Gary J. Ruzicka; Deacon Russ Humphreys.
Res., 425 S. Illinois, Box 50397, 82605-0397. Tel: 307-235-5535; 266-2495; Fax: 307-237-7244.
Catechesis / Religious Programs—Tel: 307-265-4881. D.R.E.: Marilyn Crull; Ellen Klym; Mary Lou Stoecklin.
Students 338.

Cody, Park Co., St. Anthony (1942), Rev. Joseph A. Daley.
Res., 1333 Monument Dr., 82414-3406. Tel: 307-587-3388; Fax: 307-587-3383.
Catechesis / Religious Programs—Tel: 307-587-2567. Audrey Hall, D.R.E.
Students 276.
Missions—Yellowstone National Park, Park Co. Sunday Masses at Old Faithful, Lake Lodge, Canyon Lodge, and Grant Village in summer only. 82414.; Meeteetsee, Park Co., St. Theresa, 82414.

Douglas, Converse Co., St. James (1907), Very Rev. John E. Murray.
Res., 243 S. Fifth St., P.O. Box 1500, 82633-1500. Tel: 307-358-2338. [JC]
Catechesis / Religious Programs—Tel: 307-358-5540. Rita Magee, D.R.E.
Students 155.
Mission—Glendo, Platte Co., Our Lady of Lourdes, 423 A St., Glendo, 82213. Tel: 307-358-2338.

Evanston, Uinta Co., St. Mary Magdalen (1878), Rev. August Koeune.

Mailing Address: Box 163, 82931-0163. Tel: 307-789-2189; Fax: 307-789-307-789-2788.
Catechesis/Religious Programs—Tel: 307-789-9046; Fax: 307-789-9480. Dottie Pasenelli, D.R.E. Students 200.
Mission—Fort Bridger, Uinta Co., St. Helen, P.O. Box 183, Fort Bridger, 82933. Tel: 307-782-6190.
Catechesis/Religious Programs—Tel: 307-787-6590. Bonnie La Fond, D.R.E.
Students 70.

Gillette, Campbell Co., St. Matthew's (1926), Revs. Thomas Ogg; Andrew Duncan; Deacon Stanley Piasecki, Pastoral Assoc.
Res., 900 Butler Spaeth Rd., 82716. Tel: 307-682-3319; Fax: 307-682-6386.
Catechesis/Religious Programs—Tel: 307-682-5321. Jane Johnson, D.R.E.
Students 757.
Missions—Wright, Campbell Co., Blessed Sacrament, 624 Wright Blvd., Wright, 82732. Tel: 307-464-0809; Moorcroft, Crook Co., St. Patrick, 216 N. Belle Fourche, Moorcroft, 82721. Tel: 307-756-9478.

Glenrock, Converse Co., St. Louis (1920), Rev. Ralph H. Talkin, S.J.
Mailing Address: P.O. Box 27, 82637-0027. Tel: 307-436-9529. [JC]
Catechesis/Religious Programs—Tel: 307-436-5769. Andrea Chojnacky, D.R.E.
Students 60.

Green River, Sweetwater Co., Immaculate Conception (1884), Rev. Michael P. Hellman.
Mailing Address: P.O. Box 70, 82935-0128. Tel: 307-875-2441.
Catechesis/Religious Programs—Tel: 307-875-2184. Peggy Hyslope, D.R.E.
Students 262.

Greybull, Big Horn Co., Sacred Heart (1919), Rev. Peter Johnson.
Mailing Address: P.O. Box 231, 82426-0231. Tel: 307-765-2438.
Catechesis/Religious Programs—Esther Lindsey, D.R.E.
Students 53.
Mission—Basin, Big Horn Co., St. Philip.

Guernsey, Platte Co., St. Anthony's (1969), Rev. Robert H. Cousineau, S.J.
Res., P.O. Box 430, 82214-0430. Tel: 307-836-2586.
Catechesis/Religious Programs—Tel: 307-836-2051. Kari Gerhold, D.R.E.
Students 45.

Jackson, Teton Co., Our Lady of the Mountains (1955), Rev. Sam Hayes; Deacon Robert Miller.
Mailing Address: P.O. Box 992, 83001-0992. Tel: 307-733-2516; Fax: 307-739-1478.
Catechesis/Religious Programs—Tel: 307-733-6391. Susie Palmer, D.R.E.
Students 135.
Mission—Afton, Lincoln Co., Holy Family.
Chapel—Moran, Sacred Heart.

Kemmerer, Lincoln Co., St. Patrick's (1901), Rev. Charles F. Taylor.
Mailing Address: Box 311, 83101-0311. Tel: 307-877-4573; Fax: 307-877-4079.
Catechesis/Religious Programs—Tel: 307-877-4079.
Students 84.
Missions—Cokeville, Lincoln Co., St. Dominic; La Barge, Lincoln Co., La Barge Catholic Community Center.

Lander, Fremont Co., Holy Rosary (1882), Revs. Thomas R. Kadera; Robert K.C. Siu (HON).
Res., 163 Leedy Rd., P.O. Box 1047, 82520-0503. Tel: 307-332-4952; Fax: 307-332-9332.
Catechesis/Religious Programs—Tel: 307-332-4803. Sr. Delores Herbeck, D.R.E.
Students 172.
Missions—Hudson, Freemont Co., Ascension; Jeffrey City, Freemont Co., St. Brendan.

Laramie, Albany Co., St. Laurence O'Toole (1872), Rev. Ray Moss.
Mailing Address: 617 S. Fourth St., 82070-1045. Tel: 307-745-3115; Fax: 307-745-3131. [CEM]
School—(Grades K-6). Tel: 307-742-6363; Fax: 307-745-3131.
Sisters 2; Lay Teachers 6; Students 125.
Catechesis/Religious Programs—D.R.E.: Sr. Elizabeth Skalicky, (Grades PreK-6); Marge Carlson, (Grades 7-12).
Students 135.
Convent—420 Kearney St., 82070. Tel: 307-745-9278.

St. Paul's Newman Center (1957), Revs. Roger W. Schmit, O.S.B.; Carl J. Gallinger; Sr. Mary Frost, S.D.S., Pastoral Assoc.; Joseph A. Zenk, Campus Min.
Office & Mailing Address: 1800 E. Grand Ave., 82070-4316. Tel: 307-745-5461; Fax: 307-745-0521.
Res., 1819 E. Garfield, 82070-4338.
Catechesis/Religious Programs—Students 105.

Lovell, Big Horn Co., St. Joseph's (1979), Rev. Peter Johnson.
Res., 100 Wyoming St., P.O. Box 185, 82431-0185. Tel: 307-548-2282.
Church—1141 Shoshone Ave., 82431.
Catechesis/Religious Programs—Rochelle Haupster, D.R.E.
Students 70.

Lusk, Niobrara Co., St. Leo's (1911), Rev. Evan P. Shea.
Res., 900 W. Fifth St., Box 959, 82225-0959. Tel: 307-334-2702; Fax: 307-334-3161.
Catechesis/Religious Programs—Tel: 307-334-3096. Connie Sampers, D.R.E.
Students 38.

Newcastle, Weston Co., Corpus Christi (1890), Rev. Richard H. MacLellan; Sr. Frances Schaf, O.S.U., Ministries Coord.
Res., 19 W. Winthrop, 82701. Tel: 307-746-4219; Fax: 307-746-9909.
Catechesis/Religious Programs—Students 183.
Missions—Sundance, Crook Co., St. Paul, P.O. Box 28, Sundance, 82729. Tel: 307-283-2382; Upton, Weston Co., St. Anthony, P.O. Box 177, Upton, 82730. Tel: 307-468-2236; Hulett, Crook Co., St. Matthew's, 26 Hunter, Hulett, 82720.

Pine Bluffs, Laramie Co., St. Paul's (1913), Rev. Thomas E. Cronkleton, Jr.
Res., P.O. Box 97, 82082-0097. Tel: 307-245-3761.
Catechesis/Religious Programs—Tel: 307-246-3255. Carleen Graves, D.R.E.
Students 87.
Missions—Albin, Laramie Co., St. Joseph; Carpenter, Laramie Co., St. Peter.

Pinedale, Sublette Co., Our Lady of Peace (1940), Rev. Robert G. Lynch, S.J.
Mailing Address: P.O. Box 70, 82941-0070. Tel: 307-367-2359.
Catechesis/Religious Programs—Tel: 307-367-2802. Bernie Majhanovich, D.R.E.
Students 70.
Missions—Big Piney, Sublette Co., St. Anne, Box 742, Big Piney, 83113. Tel: 307-276-3227; Eden, Sweetwater Co., St. Christopher, Eden, 82926.

Powell, Park Co., St. Barbara (1910), Rev. John A. Wright.
Res., 115 E. Third, P.O. Box 818, 82435-0818. Tel: 307-754-2480.
Catechesis/Religious Programs—Tel: 307-754-3361. Pokey Heny, D.R.E.
Students 115.
Mission—Clark, Park Co., Our Lady of the Valley, P.O. Box 818, 82435. Tel: 307-754-2480.

Rawlins, Carbon Co., St. Joseph's (1867), Rev. Malcolm Reid.
Mailing Address: P.O. Box 68, 82301-0068. Tel: 307-324-4631.
Catechesis/Religious Programs—Tel: 307-324-4033. Catherine Faber, D.R.E.
Students 234.
Mission—Baggs, Carbon Co., Our Lady of the Sage, P.O. Box 26, Baggs, 82321. Tel: 307-383-2695.

Riverton, Fremont Co., St. Margaret's (1908), Revs. William T. Espenshade; Jan J. Santich, O.S.B., Pastoral Assoc.; Frits J. Braakhuis, C.M.
Res., 622 E. Park, P.O. Box 888, 82501-0888. Tel: 307-856-3757; Fax: 307-856-8533.
School—(Grades PreK-5). Tel: 307-856-5922; Fax: 307-857-5892. Deacon John Aloisio, Prin.
Lay Teachers 15; Students 120.
Catechesis/Religious Programs—Tel: 307-856-3757; Fax: 307-856-8533. Marlene Aloisio, D.R.E.
Students 178.
Missions—Shoshoni, Fremont Co., St. Joseph, 211 Wyoming St., Shoshoni, 82649. Tel: 307-876-2760; Dubois, Fremont Co., Our Lady of the Woods, 4 S. Riverton St., P.O. Box 1134, Dubois, 82513. Tel: 307-455-2533; Kinnear, Fremont Co., St. Edward, Kinnear Rectory, 11350 US Hwy. 26, P.O. Box 34, Kinnear, 82516. Tel: 307-856-5502.

Rock Springs, Sweetwater Co., Our Lady of Sorrows (1887). Consolidated with Sts. Cyril & Methodius Church, Rock Springs. Revs. John Savio; Bruce Clapham; Thomas Sheridan.
Res., 633 Bridger Ave., P.O. Box 6038, 82901. Tel: 307-362-2611.
School—Rock Springs Catholic School. (Bi-parish). Tel: 307-362-6077. Mr. Mark Sawtelle, Prin.
Lay Teachers 10; Students 168.
Catechesis/Religious Programs—Tel: 307-382-4911. Dean and Elaine Menardi, D.R.E.
Students 426.
Missions—Superior, Sweetwater Co., St. Vivian; Wamsutter, Sweetwater Co., Catholic Community.

SS. Cyril and Methodius (1910). Consolidated with Our Lady of Sorrows Church, Rock Springs.

Our Lady of Sorrows/Sts. Cyril & Methodius, Revs. John Savio; Bruce Clapham; Thomas Sheridan.
Office: P.O. Box 6038, 82901. Tel: 307-362-2611; Fax: 307-382-4911.
Rectory—633 Bridger Ave., 82901. Tel: 307-362-3493.
Catechesis/Religious Programs—Tel: 307-382-4911. Dean & Elaine Melardi, D.R.E.
Students 400.
Missions—Superior, St. Vivian; Wamsutter, St. Anthony.

Saratoga, Carbon Co., St. Ann's (1960), Rev. Gerald Chleborad.
Mailing Address: P.O. Box 667, 82331-0667. Tel: 307-326-5461; Fax: 307-326-5461.
Catechesis/Religious Programs—Tel: 307-327-5722. D.R.E.: Cathy Lynch; Ginger Miller.
Students 50.
Missions—Hanna, Carbon Co., St. Joseph, P.O. Box 782, Hanna, 82327.; Medicine Bow, Carbon Co., St. Malachy, P.O. Box 223, Medicine Bow, 82329.

St. Stephens, Fremont Co., St. Stephen's (1884) (Native American). Indian Mission for the Shoshone and Arapahoe Indians. St. Stephen's Indian Mission, Inc. Revs. Eugene Zimmerman, S.J.; Daniel J. Gannon, S.J.; David G. Matzko, S.J.
Mailing Address: Box 250, 82524-0250. Tel: 307-856-5937; Fax: 307-856-6797.
Catechesis/Religious Programs—Tel: 307-856-7806.
Students 120.
Missions—Ethete, Fremont Co., St. Joseph, Box 8358, Ethete, 82520. Tel: 307-332-4415; Fort Washakie, Fremont Co., Blessed Sacrament, Box 307, Fort Washakie, 82514-0307. Tel: 307-332-2252.

Sheridan, Sheridan Co., Holy Name (1885), Very Rev. Eugene P. Sullivan; Rev. James A. Schumacher; Deacon Joe Kristufek.
Mailing Address: Box 2024, 82801-2024. Tel: 307-674-7441; Fax: 307-674-9187.
School—121 S. Connor, 82801. Tel: 307-672-2021; Fax: 307-672-2021. Mrs. Patricia Morgan, Prin.
Sisters of Charity (Leavenworth) 2; Lay Teachers 13; Students 186.
Catechesis/Religious Programs—Tel: 307-672-7455. Cel Hope, D.R.E.
Students 214.
Missions—Story, Sheridan Co., Our Lady of the Pines, P.O. Box 2024, 82801. Tel: 307-674-7441; Ranchester, Sheridan Co., St. Edmund, P.O. Box 197, Ranchester, 82839. Tel: 307-655-2357.

Thermopolis, Hot Springs Co., St. Francis (1906), Rev. William A. Caspers.
Mailing Address: P.O. Box 272, 82443-0272. Tel: 307-864-2674.
Catechesis/Religious Programs—Tel: 307-864-2674. Madonna McIntosh, D.R.E.
Students 37.

Torrington, Goshen Co., St. Rose (1906), Rev. Kevin A. Koch.
Res., 605 E. 22nd Ave., 82240. Tel: 307-532-5556; Fax: 307-534-2329.
Catechesis/Religious Programs—Tel: 307-532-5880. D.R.E.: Cindy Haught; Donna Duncan.
Students 229.

Wheatland, Platte Co., St. Patrick's (1891), Rev. Charles J. Velasquez.
Res., 1009 Ninth St., 82201. Tel: 307-322-2070; Fax: 307-322-2386.
Catechesis/Religious Programs—Tel: 307-322-4213.
Students 95.
Mission—Chugwater, Platte Co., St. Theresa, 1009 9th St., 82201. Tel: 307-322-2070.

Worland, Washakie Co., St. Mary Magdalen (1949), Very Rev. Ronald A. Stolcis; Sr. Dorothy Henscheid, S.C.L., Pastoral Assoc.
Mailing Address: Box 901, 82401-0901. Tel: 307-347-2820; Fax: 307-347-2450.
Shipping Address: 1099 Charles Ave., 82401.
Catechesis/Religious Programs—Tel: 307-347-6441.
Students 106.

Chaplains of Public Institutions

CHEYENNE. *U.S. Veterans Administration Hospital 1*, 90 MW/HC, F.E. Warren AFB, 82005. Revs. Dennis Hanley Tel: 307-775-2451; 772-3434; Carl A. Beavers, Chap., Tel: 800-788-4606; 638-1530.

EVANSTON. *Wyoming State Hospital*. Vacant.

RAWLINS. *Wyoming State Penitentiary*. Mailing Address: P.O. Box 468, 82301-0068. Tel: 307-324-4631. Rev. Malcolm Reid.

SHERIDAN. *U.S. Veterans Administration Hospital*. Mailing Address: Box 4013, 82801-4013. Tel: 307-672-3473, Ext. 263. Rev. John Norton, O.P.

In Residence:
Reverend Fathers—
Robinson, John, O.S.B.
Siu, Robert K.C., Holy Rosary Church, P.O. Box

1047, Lander, WY 82520-1047

On Duty Outside the Diocese:
Reverend Fathers—
Jablonowski, Anthony, C.M.M.I., St. Theresa Parish, P.O. Box 435, Patagonia, AZ 85624
Wendel, Fred, Immaculate Heart of Mary, 2855 Briarcliff Rd., N.E., Atlanta, GA 30329

Retired:
Reverend Monsignors—
Carroll, Daniel, 639 Ave. H, #157, Powell, WY 82435. Tel: 307-754-9746
Delaney, William, P.O. Box 5720, Cheyenne, WY 82003-5720
Etchingham, Lawrence, P.O. Box 5720, Cheyenne, WY 82003
Godley, James, Ballyheige, Kerry Ireland
Reverend Fathers—
Colibraro, Daniel, 1401 CY Ave., Casper, WY 82604-3511
Doudican, James, P.O. Box 5720, Cheyenne, WY 82003
Fahey, Thomas C., O.F.M., Chap., Victory Noll Sisters, 1900 W. Park Dr., Box 109, Huntington, IN 46750
Fraher, Joseph P., Church of St. Mary Magdalen, 2771 Zenobia St., Denver, CO 80212
Gianola, William, 3954 Quail Ln. N., Chattanooga, TN 37415
Moroney, Joseph E., 100 W. 21st St., Cheyenne, WY 82001
Prado, Cletus, 802 N. 29th St., Phoenix, AZ 85008

Permanent Deacons:
Aloisio, John, St. Margaret's Catholic School, Riverton
Humphreys, Russ, St. Patrick's Church, Casper
Kristufek, Joseph, Holy Name Church, Sheridan
McCarthy, Ed, Our Lady of Fatima, Casper
Miller, Robert, Our Lady of the Mountains, Jackson
Piasecki, Stanley, St. Matthew, Gillette
Pico, Lee, St. Mary's Cathedral, Cheyenne
Stewart, Don, St. Anthony's Church, Casper

INSTITUTIONS LOCATED IN THE DIOCESE

[A] PROTECTIVE INSTITUTIONS

TORRINGTON. *St. Joseph's Children's Home*, Box 1117, 82240-1117. Tel: 307-532-4197; Fax: 307-532-8405.
E-mail: stjch@prairieweb.com
For a complete listing, refer to the Special Care Facilities section.

[B] HOUSING FOR THE ELDERLY (LOW INCOME)

CHEYENNE. *Holy Trinity Manor*, 2516 E. 18th St., 82001. Tel: 307-778-8850
For a complete listing, refer to the Special Care Facilities section.

CASPER. *St. Anthony Manor*, 211 E. Sixth St., 82601. Tel: 307-237-0843
For a complete listing, refer to the Special Care Facilities section.

[C] MONASTERIES AND RESIDENCES FOR PRIESTS AND BROTHERS

ST. STEPHENS. *St. Stephens Mission - Jesuit Community*, Box 250, 82524. Tel: 307-865-5937.
E-mail: dmatzko@wyoming.com
Revs. Eugene Zimmerman, S.J.; Daniel J. Gannon, S.J.; David Matzko, S.J.

[D] CONVENTS AND RESIDENCES FOR SISTERS

DAYTON. *Benedictine Sisters of Perpetual Adoration*, San Benito Monastery, P.O. Box 510, 82836-0520. Tel: 307-655-9013.
Web site: http://www.icon-stl.net/~congbspa/index/html
Sr. M. Hope Rodenborn, Supr. Sisters 5.

[E] CAMPUS MINISTRY

CASPER. *Casper Community College*, St. Francis Newman Center, 1732 S. Elm St., 82601. Tel: 307-577-1421.
E-mail: bzettl@coffey.com
Total Staff 2.
Attended by St. Anthony of Padua, Casper.

LARAMIE. *University of Wyoming*, St. Paul's Newman Center, University Catholic Parish, 1800 E. Grand Ave., 82070-4316. Tel: 307-745-5461.
E-mail: newman@lariat.org
Web site: www.newmancenter.org
Rev. Roger W. Schmit, O.S.B. Total Staff 9.

POWELL. *NorthWest College*, John Henry Newman Center, 674 N. Absaroka, 82435. Tel: 307-754-7063.
Rev. John Wright, Chap. & Dir.; Jennifer Martinez, Asst. Dir.
Attended by St. Barbara, Powell.

[F] MISCELLANEOUS LISTINGS

CHEYENNE. *St. Mary's Goods Bookstore*, 2417 Central Ave., 82001. Tel: 307-635-4228. Zula Samuelson, Mgr. Total Staff 8; Total Assisted 150.

CASPER.
**Holy Cross Food Center, Inc.*, 1030 N. Lincoln, 82601. Tel: 307-577-1041. Operated by Holy Cross Brothers. Bro. Francis Kjeldgaard, C.S.C., Dir. Total Staff 22; Total Assisted 10,022.
**Mother Seton Housing, Inc.*, 906 N. Beach St., 82601. Tel: 307-577-8026. Emergency/Transitional Housing for Homeless Women and Children/Homeless Men and Children. Terri A. Gregory, Exec. Dir., Shelter, 324 E. H St., 82601. Tel: 307-234-1119. Total Assisted 60-65 families per year; Individuals 417.

ROCK SPRINGS. *Rock Springs Catholic School Foundation*, P.O. Box 6038, 82901-0038. Rev. John Savio.

ST. STEPHENS. *St. Stephens Indian Mission Foundation* (1974), P.O. Box 278, 82524-0278. Tel: 307-856-6797.
E-mail: dmatzkd@wyoming.com
Rev. Eugene Zimmerman, S.J., Dir.

RELIGIOUS INSTITUTES OF MEN REPRESENTED IN THE DIOCESE

For further details refer to the corresponding bracketed number in the Religious Institutes of Men or Women section.

[0200]—*Benedictine Monks.*—O.S.B.
[0600]—*Brothers of the Congregation of Holy Cross.* (South-West Prov.).—C.S.C.
[0275]—*Carmelites of Mary Immaculate.*—C.M.M.I.
[1330]—*Congregation of the Mission.*—C.M.
[0690]—*Jesuit Fathers and Brothers Jesus.*—S.J.
[0430]—*Order of Preachers (Dominicans).*—O.P.

RELIGIOUS INSTITUTES OF WOMEN REPRESENTED IN THE DIOCESE

[0230]—*Benedictine Sisters of Pontifical Jurisdiction.*—O.S.B.
[1070-03]—*Dominican Sisters.*—O.P.
[3130]—*Our Lady of Victory Missionary Sisters.*—O.L.V.M.
[]—*Religious Sisters of Mercy.*—R.S.M.
[1680]—*School Sisters of St. Francis.* (Milwaukee, WI).—O.S.F.
[0480]—*Sisters of Charity of Leavenworth, Kansas.*—S.C.L.
[0430]—*Sisters of Charity of the Blessed Virgin Mary.*—B.V.M.
[2360]—*Sisters of Loretto At the Foot of the Cross.*—S.L.
[1650]—*Sisters of St. Francis of Philadelphia.*—O.S.F.
[3830]—*Sisters of St. Joseph.*—C.S.J.
[1030]—*Sisters of the Divine Savior.*—S.D.S.
[4120-03]—*Ursuline Nuns, of the Congregation of Paris.*—O.S.U.

DIOCESAN CEMETERIES

CHEYENNE. *Olivet Cemetery.*

NECROLOGY

† Ornelas, Angel, Laramie, WY, St. Lawrence O'Toole. —Died March 19, 1997.

Archdiocese of Chicago

(Archidioecesis Chicagiensis)

Most Reverend

ALFRED L. ABRAMOWICZ

Retired Auxiliary Bishop of Chicago; ordained May 1, 1943; appointed Auxiliary Bishop of Chicago and Titular Bishop of Paestum on May 8, 1968; consecrated June 13, 1968; retired January 24, 1995. *Res., 6101 S. 75th Ave., Summit-Argo, IL, 60501.*

Most Reverend

TIMOTHY J. LYNE

Retired Auxiliary Bishop of Chicago; ordained May 1, 1943; appointed Auxiliary Bishop of Chicago and Titular Bishop of Vamalla October 31, 1983; consecrated December 13, 1983; retired January 24, 1995. *Res., 730 N. Wabash, Chicago, IL, 60611.*

Most Reverend

THAD J. JAKUBOWSKI

Auxiliary Bishop of Chicago; ordained May 3, 1950; appointed Auxiliary Bishop of Chicago and Titular Bishop of Plestia February 16, 1988; consecrated April 11, 1988. *Res., 6002 W. Berteau Ave., Chicago, IL, 60634-1630.* Tel.: 312-202-7720.

Most Reverend

JOHN R. GORMAN

Auxiliary Bishop of Chicago and Titular Bishop of Catula; ordained May 1, 1952; appointed February 16, 1988; consecrated April 11, 1988. *Res., 2330 W. 118th St., Chicago, IL, 60643.*

Most Reverend

RAYMOND E. GOEDERT

Auxiliary Bishop of Chicago; ordained May 1, 1952; appointed Auxiliary Bishop of Chicago and Titular Bishop of Tamazeni July 8, 1991; consecrated August 29, 1991. *Res., 1555 N. State Pkwy., Chicago, IL, 60610.*

His Eminence

FRANCIS CARDINAL GEORGE, O.M.I., PH.D., S.T.D.

Archbishop of Chicago; Profession of Perpetual Vows September 8, 1961; ordained December 21, 1963; appointed Bishop of Yakima July 10, 1990; Episcopal Ordination and Installation September 21, 1990; appointed Archbishop of Portland in Oregon April 30, 1996; installed May 27, 1996; appointed Archbishop of Chicago April 8, 1997; installed May 7, 1997; created Cardinal Priest February 21, 1998. *Res., 1555 N. State Pkwy., Chicago, IL, 60610.*

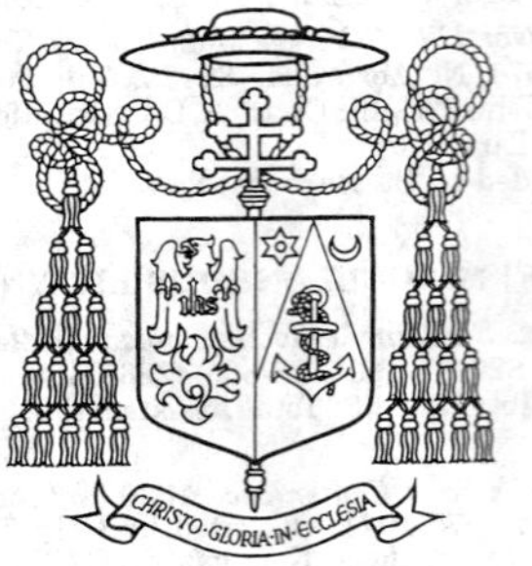

The Pastoral Center: P.O. Box 1979, Chicago, IL, 60690. Tel.: 312-751-7999 ext. 8200.

Web site address: http://www.archdiocese-chgo.org

Most Reverend

EDWIN M. CONWAY

Auxiliary Bishop of Chicago; ordained May 3, 1960; appointed Auxiliary Bishop of Chicago and Titular Bishop of Auguro January 24, 1995; consecrated March 20, 1995. *Res., 126 N. Desplaines, Chicago, IL, 60661.*

Most Reverend

GERALD F. KICANAS

Auxiliary Bishop of Chicago; ordained April 27, 1967; appointed Auxiliary Bishop of Chicago and Titular Bishop of Bela January 24, 1995; consecrated March 20, 1995. *Res., 200 N. Milwaukee Ave., Libertyville, IL, 60048.*

Most Reverend

GEORGE V. MURRY, S.J.

Auxiliary Bishop of Chicago; ordained 1979; appointed Auxiliary Bishop of Chicago and Titular Bishop of Fuerteventura January 24, 1995; consecrated March 20, 1995. *Mailing Address: P.O. Box 733, South Holland, IL, 60473-0733.*

Most Reverend

JOHN R. MANZ

Auxiliary Bishop of Chicago; ordained May 12, 1971; appointed Auxiliary Bishop of Chicago and Titular Bishop of Mulia January 23, 1996; consecrated March 5, 1996. *Mailing Address: 1820 S. Leavitt St., Chicago, IL, 60608.*

ESTABLISHED NOVEMBER 28, 1843; CREATED 1880.

Square Miles 1,411.

Comprises the Counties of Cook and Lake in the State of Illinois.

Legal Title: The Catholic Bishop of Chicago, a Corporation Sole.

For legal titles of institutions, consult The Pastoral Center.

STATISTICAL OVERVIEW

Personnel	
Cardinal	1
Auxiliary Bishops	7
Retired Bishops	2
Priests: Diocesan Active in Diocese	595
Priests: Active Outside Diocese	29
Priests: Diocesan in Foreign Missions	6
Priests: Retired, Sick or Absent	311
Number of Diocesan Priests	941
Religious Priests in Diocese	811
Extern Priests in Diocese	75
Ordinations:	
Diocesan Priests	7
Religious Priests	8
Transitional Deacons	12
Permanent Deacons	30
Permanent Deacons in Diocese	599
Total Brothers	366
Total Sisters	3,263
Parishes	
Parishes	378
With Resident Pastor:	
Resident Diocesan Priests	313
Resident Religious Priests	53
Without Resident Pastor:	
Administered by Priests	9
Administered by Women Religious	2
Administered by Lay People	1
Missions	11
Pastoral Centers	8
Professional Ministry Personnel:	
Brothers	15
Sisters	191
Lay Ministers	483
Welfare	
Catholic Hospitals	19
Total Assisted	2,799,947
Health Care Centers	1
Total Assisted	4,500
Homes for the Aged	30
Total Assisted	6,000
Day Care and Extended Day Care Centers	11
Total Assisted	2,100
Specialized Homes	20
Total Assisted	11,000
Special Centers for Social Services	45
Total Assisted	98,000
Residential Care of Disabled	9
Total Assisted	1,300
Other Institutions	50
Total Assisted	347,000
Educational	
Seminaries, Diocesan	3
Students from This Diocese	324
Students from Other Diocese	147
Diocesan Students in Other Seminaries	4
Seminaries, Religious	1
Students Religious	85
Total Seminarians	413
Colleges and Universities	6
Total Students	40,814
High Schools, Diocesan and Parish	8
Total Students	2,501
High Schools, Private	39
Total Students	30,303
Elementary Schools, Diocesan and Parish	273
Total Students	100,566
Elementary Schools, Private	1
Total Students	357
Non-residential Schools for the Disabled	7
Total Students	600
Catechesis/Religious Education:	
High School Students	8,793
Elementary Students	97,405
Total Students Under Catholic Instruction	281,752
Teachers in the Diocese:	
Priests	49
Scholastics	5
Brothers	72
Sisters	334
Lay Teachers	5,816
Vital Statistics	
Receptions into the Church:	
Infant Baptism Totals	39,134
Adult Baptism Totals	1,982
Received into Full Communion	1,914
First Communions	29,417
Confirmations	19,917
Marriages:	
Catholic	8,467
Interfaith	2,097
Total Marriages	10,564
Deaths	18,580
Total Catholic Population	2,349,000
Total Population	5,729,000

Former Bishops—Rt. Rev. WILLIAM QUARTER, D.D., cons. March 10, 1844; died April 10, 1848.—Rt. Rev. JAMES O. VAN DE VELDE, D.D., cons. Feb. 11, 1849; transferred to Natchez, July 29, 1853; died Nov. 13, 1855.—Rt. Rev. ANTHONY O'REGAN, D.D., cons. July 25, 1854; resigned 1858; died Nov., 1866.—Rt. Rev. JAMES DUGGAN, D.D., cons. Bishop of Antigone, and Coadjutor to the Archbishop of St. Louis, May 1, 1857; transferred to Chicago, Jan. 21, 1859; hospitalized, 1869; died March 27, 1899.—Rt. Rev. THOMAS FOLEY, D.D., Coadjutor-Bishop and Administrator of the diocese; cons. Bishop of Pergamus, Feb. 27, 1870; died Feb. 19, 1879.—Most Rev. PATRICK A. FEEHAN, D.D., First Archbishop of Chicago; cons. Bishop of Nashville, Nov. 1, 1865; promoted to Chicago, Sept. 10, 1880; died July 12, 1902.—Most Rev. JAMES EDWARD QUIGLEY, D.D., Archbishop of Chicago; ord. April 12, 1879; cons. Bishop of Buffalo, Feb. 24, 1897; promoted to Archbishop of Chicago, Jan. 8, 1903; died July 10, 1915.—His Eminence GEORGE CARDINAL MUNDELEIN, Archbishop of Chicago; ord. June 8, 1895; cons. Titular Bishop of Loryma and Auxiliary Bishop of Brooklyn, Sept. 21, 1909; promoted to the See of Chicago, Dec. 9, 1915; created Cardinal Priest, March 24, 1924; died Oct. 2, 1939.—His Eminence SAMUEL CARDINAL STRITCH, Archbishop of Chicago; ord. May 21, 1910; appt. Bishop of Toledo, Aug. 10, 1921; promoted to Archbishop of Milwaukee, Aug. 26, 1930; transferred to Archbishop of Chicago, Dec. 27, 1939; created Cardinal Priest Feb. 18, 1946; elevated to the Roman Curia, Sacred Congregation for the Propagation of the Faith, March 1, 1958; died in Rome, May 27, 1958.—His Eminence ALBERT CARDINAL MEYER, Archbishop of Chicago; ord. July 11, 1926; appt. Bishop of Superior, Feb. 18, 1946; promoted to Archbishop of Milwaukee, July 21, 1953; transferred to Archbishop of Chicago, Sept. 19, 1958; created Cardinal Priest, Dec. 14, 1959; died April 9, 1965.—His Eminence JOHN CARDINAL CODY, Archbishop of Chicago; ord. Dec. 8, 1931; appt. Auxiliary Bishop of St. Louis, May 14, 1947; cons. July 2, 1947; promoted to Coadjutor of St. Joseph, Jan. 27, 1954; transferred to Kansas City-St. Joseph, Aug. 29, 1956; promoted to Coadjutor Archbishop of New Orleans, Aug. 14, 1961; acceded the See of New Orleans, Nov. 8, 1964; transferred to the Archdiocese of Chicago, June 16, 1965; created Cardinal Priest in the Consistory, June 26, 1967; died April 25, 1982.—His Eminence JOSEPH CARDINAL BERNARDIN, Archbishop of Chicago; ord. April 26, 1952; appt. Auxiliary Bishop of Atlanta, March 9, 1966; cons. April 26, 1966; appt. Archbishop of Cincinnati, Nov. 21, 1972; appt. Archbishop of Chicago, July 10, 1982; installed Aug. 25, 1982; created Cardinal Priest, Feb. 2, 1983; died Nov. 14, 1996.

Vicar General—Most Rev. RAYMOND E. GOEDERT.

Episcopal Vicars—Most Rev. GERALD KICANAS, Vicariate I (Deaneries A, B); Most Rev. EDWIN M. CONWAY, Vicariate II (Deaneries A, B, C, D, E, F); Most Rev. JOHN R. MANZ, Vicariate III (Deaneries A, B, C, D, E); Most Rev. THAD J. JAKUBOWSKI, Vicariate IV (Deaneries A, B, C); Most Rev. JOHN L. GORMAN, Vicariate V (Deaneries A, B, C, D, E); Most Rev. GEORGE V. MURRY, S.J., Vicariate VI (Deaneries A, B, C, D).

Deans—Revs. FARRELL KANE, Deanery I-A; JOHN J. HURLEY, Deanery I-B; EDWARD HOOVER, Deanery II-A; LAWRENCE F. MADDOCK, Deanery II-B; ROBERT J. HEIDENREICH, Deanery II-C; JOHN R. HOFFMAN, Deanery II-D; RONALD N. KALAS, Deanery II-E; MICHAEL A. WULSCH, Deanery II-F; THOMAS A. TIVY, Deanery III-A; MICHAEL DANEK, C.R., Deanery III-B; ANTHONY M. TALARICO, Deanery III-C; LAWRENCE M. CHOATE, O.S.M., Deanery III-D; JAMES T. KACZOROWSKI, Deanery III-E; DANIEL G. MAYALL, Deanery IV-A; FRANCIS C. JENKS, Deanery IV-B; JOHN C. ROSEMEYER, Deanery IV-C; ROBERT J. ROLL, Deanery V-A; STANLEY G. RATAJ, Deanery V-B Midway-East-California Corridor; MARCEL J. PASCIAK, Deanery V-B Midway-West; PATRICK M. LYONS, Deanery V-C; PAUL C. BURAK, Deanery V-D; EDWARD F. UPTON, Deanery V-E; JAMES J. MARTIN, Deanery VI-A; LAWRENCE M. DURIS, Deanery VI-B; THOMAS FRANZMAN, Deanery VI-C; THOMAS E. CIMA, Deanery VI-D.

College of Consultors—Revs. JEREMIAH M. BOLAND; GINO DALPIAZ, C.S.; THOMAS M. DORE; LAWRENCE F. HANLEY; JOHN H. HARVEY; FRANCIS C. JENKS; JAMES T. KACZOROWSKI; J. CLETUS KILEY; JOHN A. KUZINSKAS; PATRICK J. POLLARD; DONALD SENIOR, O.P.; MICHAEL A. WULSCH; THOMAS J. PAPROCKI, Sec.

Presbyteral Council—Revs. JEREMIAH M. BOLAND, Chm.; JOHN M. COLLINS, Vice Chm.; RONALD J. MASS, Sec.; CURTIS A. LAMBERT, Treas.

Finance Council—Vice Chairmen: Rev. R. PETER BOWMAN; Mr. FRANK W. CONSIDINE; Mr. JAMES M. DENNY; Rev. KEVIN J. SPIESS. Members: Miss EILEEN T. CORCORAN; Mr. JOHN W. CROGHAN; Most Rev. RAYMOND E. GOEDERT; Mr. WILLIAM M. GOODYEAR; Mr. DONALD GOSS; Sr. LOIS GRAVER, R.S.M.; Rev. RICHARD M. HOMA; Mr. MITCHELL KOBELINSKI; Hon. GEORGE N. LEIGHTON; Mr. WILLIAM A. MCINTOSH; Mr. ANDREW J. MCKENNA, SR.; Mr. HENRY MENDOZA; Mr. R. MICHAEL MURRAY, JR.; Mr. OLIVER NICKLIN; Mr. THOMAS H. QUINN; Mr. PHILIP P. ROONEY; Rev. GEORGE L. SCHOPP; Mr. EDMUND A. STEPHAN; Mr. JEROME VAN GORKOM; Mr. FIDELIS N. UMEH; Mr. ARTHUR R. VELASQUEZ; Rev. THOMAS F. VENTURA; Mrs. PATRICIA A. WEIR.

Pastoral Council—DAVID SHERMAN, Chm.; ANN SUPPLITT, Exec. Sec. Tel: 312-751-5357.

Consejo Pastoral Hispano Arquidiocesano—Co-Chm.: TERESA HERNANDEZ; GLADYS MELENDEZ. Tel: 312-782-2163; 847-455-7472. Sr. DOMINGA ZAPATA, S.H., Exec. Dir. Tel: 312-751-8343. Most Rev. JOHN G. MANZ, Archbishop's Delegate. Tel: 312-243-4655.

Provincial Offices

The Catholic Conference Of Illinois—Mr. DOUGLAS DELANEY, Exec. Dir., *500 N. Clark St., Chicago, 60610-4202.* Tel: 312-467-4375.

Provincial Court of Appeals—Revs. ROBERT L. KEALY, S.T.L., J.D., J.C.D., Judicial Vicar; JOHN P. LUCAS, Adjutant Judicial Vicar; Ms. JANE HALPIN, Chief Notary, *20 N. Wacker Dr., Ste. 3420, Chicago, 60606.* Tel: 312-553-4080; 800-572-7835 (In Illinois); Fax: 312-553-4085.

Archdiocesan Offices

All Archdiocesan Departments can be contacted through *The Pastoral Center, 155 E. Superior St., Chicago, IL 60611.* (Street & Package Delivery Address). Address all mail to: *P.O. Box 1979, Chicago, IL 60690.* Tel: 312-751-7999, Ext. 8200. unless otherwise indicated.

Office of the Archbishop—Rev. JOHN J. MCDONNELL, Sec. to the Archbishop. Tel: 312-751-7999, Ext. 8219. Sr. ANITA BAIRD, D.H.M., Exec. Asst. to the Archbishop. Tel: 312-751-7999, Ext. 8236. Rev. ALPHONSE P. SPILLY, C.PP.S., Spec. Asst. to the Archbishop. Tel: 312-751-7999, Ext. 8299.

The Chancery—See Office of the Chancellor.

The Metropolitan Tribunal—See Office of the Chancellor.

Research Theologian for the Curia & Consul for Policy Development—Rev. MICHAEL D. PLACE, S.T.D. Tel: 312-751-7999, Ext. 8354.

Senior Administrators Serving the Archbishop

Vicar General—Most Rev. RAYMOND E. GOEDERT. Tel: 312-751-7999, Ext. 8271.

Moderator of the Curia—Rev. R. PETER BOWMAN. Tel: 312-751-7999, Ext. 5250.

Executive Assistant to the Archbishop—Sr. ANITA BAIRD, D.H.M. Tel: 312-751-7999, Ext. 8236.

Secretary to the Archbishop—Rev. JOHN J. MCDONNELL. Tel: 312-751-7999, Ext. 8219.

Vicar General

Vicar General—Most Rev. RAYMOND E. GOEDERT. Tel: 312-751-7999, Ext. 8271.

Office of Research & Planning—Rev. DAVID E. BALDWIN. Tel: 312-751-7999, Ext. 8345.

Office of Ethnic Ministries—Rev. JOHN P. BOIVIN. Tel: 312-751-7999, Ext. 8308.

Moderator of the Curia

Moderator of the Curia—Rev. R. PETER BOWMAN. Tel: 312-751-7999, Ext. 5250.

Department Directors—Rev. RAYMOND BAUMHART, S.J., Evangelization & Christian Life; JOHN F. BENWARE, Financial Svcs.; Most Rev. EDWIN M. CONWAY, Human Svcs.; DANIEL CONWAY, Stewardship & Devel.; Rev. DONALD J. NEVINS, Ministry Formation; Dr. CAROL FOWLER, Personnel Svcs.; JAMES W. VODAK, Communications & Public Rels.

Legal Services—JOHN C. O'MALLEY, Dir. Tel: 312-751-7999, Ext. 5379.

Research & Planning—Rev. DAVID E. BALDWIN, Dir. Tel: 312-751-7999, Ext. 8345. Assoc. Dirs. of Planning: Mr. TONY M. FIDANZO. Tel: 312-751-7999, Ext. 5283. Mr. CHARLES A. HOLLAND, JR. Tel: 312-751-7999, Ext. 5370. Ms. CONSTANCE O'BRIEN. Tel: 312-751-7999, Ext. 5371. DAVID F. SCHWARTZ, Assoc. Dir., Research. Tel: 312-751-7999, Ext. 8344. Rev. ROBERT L. EBROM, Research Asst. Tel: 312-751-7999, Ext. 5338.

Office of the Chancellor

The Chancery—Fax: 312-751-5381.

Chancellor—Rev. THOMAS J. PAPROCKI, S.T.L., J.D., J.C.D. Tel: 312-751-7999, Ext. 8220.

Vice-Chancellors—Revs. RICHARD B. SAUDIS; EMMETT J. GAVIN, O.Carm. Tel: 312-751-7999, Ext. 8207.

Associate Chancellor—Rev. ROBERT GEISINGER, S.J., J.C.D. Tel: 312-751-7999, Ext. 8211.

Assistant to the Chancellor—Rev. JEFFREY S. GROB. Tel: 312-751-7999, Ext. 8213.

Assistant Chancellor for Archives and Records—JOHN J. TREANOR, *711 W. Monroe St., Chicago, 60606.* Tel: 312-831-0711.

Metropolitan Tribunal—

Judicial Vicar—Rev. PATRICK R. LAGGES, J.C.D. Tel: 312-751-7999, Ext. 8250.

Adjutant Judicial Vicar—Rev. DANIEL A. SMILANIC, J.C.D. Tel: 312-751-7999, Ext. 8206.

Applications Coordinator—GLENDA MCFADDEN. Tel: 312-751-7999, Ext. 8523.

Promoter of Justice—Rev. WILLIAM WOESTMAN, O.M.I.

Judges—Rev. MICHAEL A. HACK, J.C.D.; Sr. JOYCE HOBEN, S.N.D.; Revs. STANLEY DREWNIAK; ROBERT GEISINGER, S.J., J.C.D.; MICHAEL KURZ, J.C.L.; PATRICK R. LAGGES, J.C.D.; DAVID J. MULVIHILL, J.C.D.; DANIEL SMILANIC, J.C.D.; Sr. CARMEN GONZALEZ, C.D.P., J.C.L.; Revs. DAVID M. HYNOUS, O.P.; MARK SIMPSON, J.C.L.; MICHAEL BRADLEY, J.C.L.

Defenders of the Bond—Rev. JOHN A. ROLEK, B.A.; Sr. THERESE GUERIN SULLIVAN, S.P.

Delegate of the Archbishop for Privilege Cases—Rev. JOHN A. ROLEK, B.A.

Advocates—Revs. JOHN GRIFFITHS; JOSEPH MOL; Deacon STEFAN STANCZAK.

Auditors—Rev. ALEC WOLFF; Ms. MONICA MAURIC; Ms. SUSAN MILLER; Sr. NATALIA COMPOS-SOLIS, R.S.C.J.; Rev. JOHN C. HERGENROTHER.

Office of Conciliation—RALPH BONACCORSI, Exec. Dir. Tel: 312-751-8291.

Office of Professional Fitness Review—Ms. BERNADETTE CONNOLLY, Admin., *One E. Superior St., Ste. 504, Chicago, 60611.* Tel: 312-751-5205; 800-994-6200.

Office of Professional Responsibility—RALPH BONACCORSI, Dir.; MYRA FLORES, Admin. Asst., *676 N. St. Clair, Ste. 2240, Chicago, 60611.* Tel: 312-751-8256.

Department of Communications and Public Relations

Department of Communications and Public Relations—JAMES W. VODAK. Tel: 312-751-8289; Fax: 312-751-5306.

Communications, Office of—MARY MCDONOUGH, Communications Mgr. Tel: 312-751-8227; Fax: 312-751-5306.

Catholic Information Service—BECKY SUTTON, Dir. Tel: 312-751-7999, Ext. 8204.

Office of Radio & TV—JOE LOUGHLIN, Dir. Tel: 312-751-7999, Ext. 8277.

Consultant—THOMAS DEMINT. Tel: 312-751-8264.

New World Publications—THOMAS H. SHERIDAN, Gen. Mgr.; MARY CLAIRE GART, Editor Pro Tem, *1144 W. Jackson, Chicago, 60607.* Tel: 312-243-1300.

Media Chaplain—Rev. JOHN J. WALL, Dir., *718 W. Adams, Chicago, 60606.* Tel: 312-782-6171.

Department of Stewardship and Development

Department of Stewardship and Development—DAN CONWAY. Tel: 312-563-5737.

Development, Archdiocesan—RAYMOND P. COUGHLIN, Dir. Tel: 312-563-5737. MICHAEL J. GLEASON, Assoc. Dir., *225 S. Aberdeen Ave., Chicago, 60067.* Tel: 312-563-5740.

Annual Catholic Appeal—JOAN B. PATTERSON-TURK. Tel: 312-563-5735.

Planned Giving/Annuities—Mr. RICHARD S. GOODE, Devel. Assoc. MABLE MCKNUCKLES, Admin. Asst. Tel: 312-563-5726.

Stewardship/Parish Development—DAN CHORNEY, Dir. Tel: 312-563-5738.

Seminary Development-Archbishop Quigley Preparatory Seminary—Mr. THOMAS LECLAIR. Tel: 312-787-9343., *St. Joseph Seminary,* MARIE COMPOSTO. Tel: 773-631-1017., *St. Mary of the Lake, Mundelein;* Mr. TIMOTHY DOCKERY. Tel: 847-566-6401.

Donor Research—PATRICIA MCNICHOLAS. Tel: 312-563-5736.

Big Shoulders Fund—JUDITH SILEKIS. Tel: 312-751-8337.

Department of Financial Services

Director—JOHN F. BENWARE. Tel: 312-751-8218.

Facilities Services and Construction—C. GREGORY VEITH, Mgr. Tel: 312-751-8342.

Controller's Operations—JAMES C. ROJEK, Mgr. Tel: 312-751-5277.

Accounting—MARK COSENTINO, Mgr. Tel: 312-751-5266.

Office Services—PHIL WAGNER, Mgr. Tel: 312-751-8246.

Management Information Services (MIS)—Mr. GANG CHEN, Mgr. Tel: 312-751-5349.

Insurance—MATTHEW KAMINSKI, Mgr. Tel: 312-751-8295.
Real Estate—Ms. MAUREEN O'BRIEN, Mgr. Tel: 312-751-8221.
Vicariate Administrative Consultants (VACS)—
Vicariate Adminstrative Manager—TAFFIE IWANICKI. Tel: 312-751-5312.
Vicariate I—MARY P. HALL. Tel: 312-751-5322. Vicariate Office: Tel: 847-549-0165.
Vicariate II—GENE MYERS. Tel: 312-751-5321. Vicariate Office: Tel: 773-763-1661.
Vicariate III—DENNIS ROBAK. Tel: 312-751-5323. Vicariate Office: Tel: 312-243-1135.
Vicariate IV—PATRICIA POMYKALSKI. Tel: 312-751-5312. Vicariate Office: Tel: 773-202-7722.
Vicariate V—TOM BARTHOLOMEW. Tel: 312-751-5318. Vicariate Office: Tel: 773-779-9165.
Vicariate VI—JASON BERTRAND. Tel: 708-333-6132. Vicariate Office: Tel: 312-493-2993.
Catholic Cemeteries—Rev. PATRICK J. POLLARD, Dir. DONALD MASSARO, Exec. Dir.; Rev. Msgr. FRANCIS J. MCELLIGOTT, Consultant, *1400 S. Wolf Rd., Hillside, 60162*. Tel: 708-449-6100; Fax: 708-449-3419.

Department of Evangelization and Christian Life

Director—Rev. RAYMOND BAUMHART S.J., Dir. Tel: 312-751-8346.
Archdiocesan Council of Catholic Women (ACCW)—CLARICE BROWN, Pres.; Rev. STAN JANKOWSKI, O.F.M., Dir. Tel: 312-751-8325.
Catholic Charismatic Renewal Center of Chicago (CCRCC)—Revs. PATRICK J. HENRY, Archbishop's Liaison; RICHARD T. SIMON, Liaison for Hispanics, *12905 S. Division St., Blue Island, 60406*. Tel: 708-371-2727.
Catholic Missions Office—
Propagation of the Faith—Co-Dirs.: Rev. JOHN J. GRACE; Sr. ANN CAROL KAUFENBERG, S.S.N.D., *225 S. Aberdeen Ave., Chicago, 60607*. Tel: 312-563-5750.
Holy Childhood Association—Co-Dirs.: Rev. JOHN J. GRACE; Sr. ANN CAROL KAUFENBERG, S.S.N.D., *225 S. Aberdeen Ave., Chicago, 60607*. Tel: 312-563-5750.
Partnership in Mission Archdiocese of Chicago/Diocese of Chilpancingo-Chilapa-Catholic Missions Office—225 S. Aberdeen Ave., Chicago, 60607. Tel: 312-563-5750.
Catholic Youth Office—Revs. JOHN P. SMYTH, Dir.; DAVID RYAN, Asst. Exec. Dir., *1658 W. Grand Ave., Chicago, 60622*. Tel: 312-733-7405.
Chaplaincies—
The Catholic Ministry at Chicago O'Hare International Airport—Rev. JOHN A. JAMNICKY, Chap.; Deacon JAMES O'MALLEY, Assoc. Chap., *P.O. Box 66353, Chicago, 60666-0353*. Tel: 773-686-2636.
Airport, Midway—Rev. GEORGE P. MCKENNA, Chap. Tel: 773-767-0500.
Firefighters/Paramedics—Rev. THOMAS A. MULCRONE, Chap., *1140 W. Jackson Blvd., Chicago, 60607*. Tel: 312-738-9246.
Police—Rev. THOMAS R. NANGLE, Chap., *1140 W. Jackson Blvd., Chicago, 60607*. Tel: 312-738-7588.
Seafarers—Rev. JAMES P. KEATING, Chap., *10201 S. Ewing, Chicago, 60617*. Tel: 773-734-1383.
Cursillo Movement, Chicago Catholic Office of—Vacant, *2226 N. Hoyne Ave., Chicago, 60647*. Tel: 773-486-5101; Fax: 773-486-5111.
Ecumenism and Interreligious Affairs, Office for—Sr. JOAN MCGUIRE, O.P., Dir. Tel: 312-751-7999, Ext. 5325. Sr. MARY ELLEN COOMBE, N.D.S., Assoc Dir. Tel: 312-751-5325. Dr. JON NILSON, Asst. Dir. Tel: 773-508-2347. Adjunct Staff: Rev. LEONARD DUBI; Deacon EDMUND GRONKIEWICZ; Revs. HENRY KRICEK; ANDREW LUCZAK; Mr. J. MICHAEL THOMPSON; Rev. RAYMOND WEBB.
Ethnic Ministries, Office for—Rev. JOHN P. BOIVIN, Dir.; Mrs. SHEILA ADAMS, African-American Consultant; Mrs. TERESITA L. NUVAL, Asian-American Consultant; Mrs. KRYSTYNA ZAMBRZYCKI, European-American Consultant; Sr. DOMINGA ZAPATA, S.H., Hispanic-American Consultant. Tel: 312-751-8301; Fax: 312-751-5313. Rev. JERZY ZIEBA, C.R., Polish Liaison.
Vicariate Hispanic Coordinators—
Vicariate I—GRACIELA CONTRERAS, O.S.A., *200 N. Milwaukee Ave., Ste. 212, Libertyville, 60048*. Tel: 847-549-0164.
Vicariate II—JORGE RIVERA, *1651 W. Diversey, Chicago, 60614*. Tel: 773-388-8675.
Vicariate III—ROBERTO RIVAS, *1840 S. Leavitt, Chicago, 60608*. Tel: 312-432-9804; 432-9805.
Vicariate IV—Ms. MODESTA MARTINEZ, *912 Dolores Dr., Bensenville, 60106*. Tel: 630-238-1593.
Vicariate V—Ms. OLGA TORRES, *2330 W. 118th St., Chicago, 60643*. Tel: 773-779-9324.
Vicariate VI—Ms. CLEMENCIA PADILLA, *16160 Seton Rd., South Holland, 60473*. Tel: 708-339-5044.
Ministry Missions or Centers—
American Indian Apostolate—Sr. ANTOINETTE HARRIS, Dir., *Anawin Center, 4545 N. Broadway, Ste. 258, Chicago, 60640*. Tel: 773-561-6155.
Angel Guardian Croatian Catholic Mission—Rev. NICHOLAS DUGANDZIC, O.P., Dir., *6346 N. Ridge Ave., Chicago, 60660*. Tel: 773-262-0535.
Chinese Catholic Mission (St. Therese Chinese Mission)—Vacant, *218 W. Alexander, Chicago, 60616*. Tel: 312-842-6777.
Haitian Catholic Center—Vacant, *Our Lady of Peace, 7851 S. Jeffrey, Chicago, 60649*. Tel: 773-768-0105.
Holy Trinity Polish Mission—Rev. WLADYSLAW GOWIN, S.Ch., Dir., *1118 N. Noble, Chicago, 60622*. Tel: 773-489-4140.
Indochinese Catholic Center—Rev. PHIEN T. NGUYEN, Acting Dir., *4827 N. Kenmore, Chicago, 60640*. Tel: 773-784-1932.
Italian Catholic Apostolate—Rev. ERMETE NAZZANI, C.S., Dir., *1621 N. 39th Ave., Stone Park, 60165*. Tel: 708-345-3842.
Knanya Catholic Mission—Rev. SIMON EDADTHIPARAMBIL, Dir., *3834 N. Spaulding, Chicago, 60618*. Tel: 773-509-9147.
Korean Catholic Mission of Chicago—Rev. JOHN SMITH, S.S.C., Dir., *4115 N. Kedvale, Chicago, 60641*. Tel: 773-283-3979.
Blessed George Matulaitis Lithuanian Catholic Mission—Rev. ALGIRDAS PALIOKAS, S.J., Dir., *14915 127th St., Unit 101, Lemont, 60439*. Tel: 630-257-5613.
St. Paul Chong Hasang Korean Catholic Mission—Rev. THOMAS KIM, Dir., *675 Dursey Ln., Des Plaines, 60016*. Tel: 847-699-6334; Fax: 847-966-1029.
Sacred Heart Mission House—Rev. LESZEK BALCZEWSKI, S.J., Supr., *4105 N. Avers Ave., Chicago, 60618*. Tel: 773-588-7476.
Slovenian Catholic Mission—Rev. DAVID SRUMPF, Dir., *14246 Main St., P.O. Box 608, Lemont, 60439*. Tel: 630-257-2068.
Slovak Catholic Mission—Rev. EDWARD SLOSARCIK, Dir., *5900 W. 147th St., Oak Forest, 60452*. Tel: 708-535-1090.
Syro-Malabar Catholic Mission—Rev. JOS KANDATHIKUDY, Dir., *Mar Thoma Shleeha Center, 5000 St. Charles Rd., Bellwood, 60104*. Tel: 708-544-7250.
Syro-Malankara Catholic Center—Rev. ZACHARIAS NANTHIYATTU, O.I.C., Dir., *1634 W. Gregory St., Chicago, 60640. 1208 Ashland Ave., Evanston, 60202*. Tel: 773-907-2092.
Family Ministries—Mr. FRANCIS P. HANNIGAN, Dir. Tel: 312-751-8351. ALICIA RIVERA, Assoc. Dir. Tel: 312-751-8240.
Cana Conference—Mr. FRANCIS P. HANNIGAN, Contact. Tel: 312-751-8340.
Hispanic Family Ministries—ALICIA RIVERA, Contact. Tel: 312-751-8240.
Natural Family Planning—SHARON DAUSMAN, Contact. Tel: 312-751-8351.
Phoenix Ministry—For Separated, Divorced and Remarried. Beginning Experience, Single Parenting. ELSIE MANNIX, Contact. Tel: 312-751-8353.
Widowed, Ministry to the—RITA ANTON, Coord. Tel: 312-751-8351.
Food Service Professionals, Archdiocese—Mr. RON HUNTER, Dir., *5150 Northwest Hwy., Chicago, 60638*. Tel: 773-385-5100.
Ministry in Higher Education—JAN SLATTERY, Dir., *700 S. Morgan, Chicago, 60607*. Tel: 312-829-0670.
Office of Catholic Education—ELAINE M. SCHUSTER, Ph.D., Supt. Tel: 312-751-5200.
Divine Worship, Office for—Mrs. SHEILA MCLAUGHLIN, Dir.; Sr. MARILYN BARNETT, C.S.J., Assoc. Dir.; Ms. MARY BETH KUNDE-ANDERSON, Dir. Liturgical Music; Ms. KATHLEEN SULLIVAN-STEWART, Prog. Coord. & L.I.C. Dir.; Mr. JOSE CASTILLO, Coord. Hispanic Programs; Ms. DENISE LAGIGLIA, Asst. Prog. Dir.; Rev. PHILIP HARRIGAN, Dir., Environment & Art; Liturgy Training Publications (LTP); Mr. GABE HUCK, Dir., *1800 N. Hermitage Ave., Chicago, 60622*. Tel: 773-486-5153 (ODW); 486-8970 (LTP); Fax: 773-486-7094.
Office of Religious Education—Dr. CAROL EIPERS, Dir.; Dr. JACQUELYNNE POKORNY, Asst. Dir., *1025 W. Fry St., Chicago, 60622*. Tel: 312-243-3700; Fax: 312-243-3801.
Parish Pastoral Councils—Ms. RITA KATTNER, Dir. Tel: 312-751-8364.
Christ Renews His Parish—Ms. RITA KATTNER, Dir. Tel: 312-751-8364.
Office for the Ministry of Peace & Justice—Co-Dirs.: Mr. JAMES LUND; Dr. MARY HEIDKAMP. Tel: 312-751-7999, Ext. 8390, 8367, 4333, 5383.
Catholic Relief Services/International Affairs—Mr. JAMES LUND, Dir. Tel: 312-751-5383.
Campaign for Human Development—Dr. MARY HEIDKAMP, Dir. Tel: 312-751-5333.
Parish Sharing Program—Mr. JAMES LUND, Dir. Tel: 312-751-7999, Ext. 8390.
Prison Ministry/Kolbe House—Rev. LAWRENCE J. CRAIG, Dir., *2434 S. California, Chicago, 60608*. Tel: 773-247-0700.
Respect Life/Pro-Life Activities—Ms. MARY A. HALLAN, Dir. Tel: 312-751-5355; Fax: 312-787-1554.
Project Rachel—155 E. Superior St., Chicago, 60611. Tel: 312-337-1962.
Special Religious Education (SPRED)—Rev. JAMES H. MCCARTHY, Dir., *2956 S. Lowe, Chicago, 60616*. Tel: 312-842-1039; Fax: 312-842-4449. Sr. MARY THERESE HARRINGTON, S.H.; Sr. SUSANNE GALLAGHER, S.P.
Young Adult Ministry/Singles—Rev. JOHN C. CUSICK, Dir.; Ms. KATHERINE F. DEVRIES, Assoc. Dir., *711 W. Monroe St., Chicago, 60661*. Tel: 312-466-9473.
Lay Groups and Organizations—
Archdiocesan Council of Catholic Men—Rev. JOHN C. CUSICK, *711 W. Monroe St., Chicago, 60661*. Tel: 312-466-9473.
Christian Family Movement—Rev. R. PETER BOWMAN, Chap., *155 E. Superior St., Chicago, 60611*. Chicago Federation Chaircouple: MARY LOU GORMAN; PHIL GORMAN, *900 E. Wilmette Rd., #122, Palatine, 60067*. Tel: 847-202-1032. Area Chaircouple: JIM QUINLAN; BONNIE QUINLAN, *20 Sarah's Grove, Schaumburg, 60193*. Tel: 630-529-2575.
Knights of Columbus—Tel: 312-751-7999, Ext. 5377.
Legion of Mary—Rev. CHARLES LENAGHAN, S.J., Spiritual Dir., *St. Philomena Parish*. Tel: 773-489-1100.
Marriage Encounter—Rev. EDMUND J. SCHREIBER, Spiritual Dir. Tel: 708-445-0971.
Naim (Widowers & Widows)—Rev. GEORGE A. SLOMINSKI, Chap., *721 N. LaSalle, Chicago, 60610*. Tel: 312-944-1286.

Department of Human Services

Director—Most Rev. EDWIN M. CONWAY, D.D., *126 N. Desplaines St., Chicago, 60661*. Tel: 312-655-7031.
Catholic Charities of Chicago—Rev. MICHAEL M. BOLAND, Admin.; Mr. JIMMY LAGO, Exec. Dir.; Rev. CHARLES T. RUBEY, Dir., Programs. Assoc. Admins.: Revs. RICHARD E. BULWITH; FRANCIS A. CIMARRUSTI; ROGER J. COUGHLIN; DANIEL M. HOLIHAN; DANIEL C. JANKOWSKI; JAMES M. RAY, *126 N. Desplaines St., Chicago, 60661-2357*. Tel: 312-655-7000. (Refer to Catholic Charities section under the Institutions located in the Archdiocese for further listings.).
Catholic Office of the Deaf—Rev. JOSEPH A. MULCRONE, Dir.; Ms. NANCY HUBER, Religious Education Dir., *721 N. LaSalle, Chicago, 60610*. Tel: 312-655-7899.
Apostolate of the Handicapped—Rev. CHARLES F. KELLY, Moderator, *5330 S. Nashville, Chicago, 60638*. Tel: 312-586-1223.
Health/Hospital Affairs—Tel: 312-655-7040.
Mercy Home for Boys and Girls—Rev. JAMES J. CLOSE, Pres.; Rev. SCOTT DONAHUE, Assoc. Pres., *1140 W. Jackson, Chicago, 60607*. Tel: 312-738-7560; Fax: 312-738-0484.
Office for Persons with Disabilities—Rev. MICHAEL SOLAZZO, *6300 N. Ridge, Chicago, 60660*. Tel: 773-973-6300.

Department of Ministry Formations

Director—Rev. DONALD J. NEVINS, *St. Francis of Assisi, 813 W. Roosevelt, Chicago, 60608*. Tel: 312-850-1448.
University of St. Mary of the Lake—
Mundelein Seminary—Revs. JOHN F. CANARY, Rector; JOHN G. LODGE, Academic Dean; BARTHOLOMEW S. WINTERS, Dean of Formation, *Mundelein, 60060*. Tel: 847-566-6401.
Center for Development in Ministry (CDM)—Rev. JOSEPH C. GEDERS, C.M., Dir.; Dr. JUAN LORENZO HINOJOSA, Dir., Hillenbrand Institute. Educational Associates: Sr. JOYE GROS, O.P.; Revs. WILLIAM J. STENZEL; GEORGE SCHOPP, *University of St. Mary of the Lake, Mundelein, 60060*. Tel: 847-566-8290; Fax: 847-566-7971.
St. Joseph Seminary at Loyola University—Rev. JAMES PRESTA, Rector, *6551 N. Sheridan Rd., Chicago, 60626*. Tel: 773-973-9700.
Archbishop Quigley Preparatory Seminary—Rev. MICHAEL G. FOLEY, Rector-Pres., *103 E. Chestnut, Chicago, 60611*. Tel: 312-787-9343.
Vocation Office—Rev. JOHN G. KLEIN, Dir.; Sr. JUDITH ANNE HAASE, O.P., Coord. Tel: 312-787-9343.
Amate House/Young Adult Volunteer Program—Mrs. CHRISTINA R. ZAKER, Dir., *2601 N. Sayre Ave., Chicago, 60635*. Tel: 773-745-0002; 800-383-2038.
Cardinal Stritch Retreat House—Revs. LOUIS J. CAMELI, Dir. EDMUND J. SIEDLECKI, Admin., *P.O. Box 455, Mundelein, 60060*. Tel: 847-566-6060; Fax: 847-566-6082.
Casa Jesus—Rev. MICHAEL T. HERMAN, Dir.; Ms. KAREN HERMAN DEMURO, Project Mgr., *1335 W. Harrison St., Chicago, 60607*. Tel: 773-243-7400.
Lay Ministry Programs—GRAZIANO MARCHESCHI, Dir.,

1025 Columbian, Oak Park, 60302-1327. Tel: 708-383-3727; Fax: 708-383-4509.

Diaconate Permanent—*1025 Columbia Ave., Oak Park, 60302.* Tel: 708-383-9200. Rev. EDWARD P. SALMON, Vicar/Diaconate Community; THOMAS MCGOREY, Assoc. Dir., Personnel; CHARLES O'DONNELL, Assoc. Dir., Formation.

Instituto De Liderazgo Pastoral (Hispanic Programs for Lay Ministry and Permanent Diaconate).—Mr. ENRIQUE ALONSO, Dir. Assoc. Directors: Mrs. ANA M. RIVAS; Mrs. REBECCA VILANUEVA, *1025 Columbian Ave., Oak Park, 60302.* Tel: 708-383-7948; Fax: 708-383-4509.

Department of Personnel Services

Director—Dr. CAROL FOWLER. Tel: 312-751-8349.

Employee Services—FRED VAN DEN HENDE, Mgr. Tel: 312-751-5352.

Lay Pastoral Ministry, Office for—Mrs. LUCILLE M. MERLIHAN, Dir. ALICE ALTIVEROS-LADAO, Coord. Placement. Tel: 312-751-5262; 751-5284 (Job Hotline); Fax: 312-751-5281.

Vicar for Priests—Revs. DANIEL P. COUGHLIN; LAWRENCE P. MCBRADY, Vicar for Priests, *645 N. Michigan Ave., Ste. 543, Chicago, 60611.* Tel: 312-642-1837. Rev. ANDREW J. MCDONAGH, Asst. to Vicar for Priests, *6939 N. Hiawatha, Chicago, 60646.* Tel: 312-631-2428.

Vicar for Senior Priests—Most Rev. TIMOTHY J. LYNE, Vicar. Asst. Vicars: Rev. Msgr. FRANCIS MCELLIGOTT, Asst. Vicar; Revs. DONALD J. AHEARN; JOHN A. KUZINSKAS. Tel: 312-787-8040.

Religious, Office for—Sr. JOAN MCGLINCHEY, M.S.C., Dir.; Sr. MARGARET COLEMAN, Retirement Collection. Tel: 312-751-8333.

Vicar for Diaconate Community—Rev. EDWARD P. SALMON, *1025 Columbian Ave., Oak Park, 60302.* Tel: 708-383-9200.

Priests' Retirement and Mutual Aid Association (PRMAA)—Rev. DONALD J. AHEARN, Chm., *7142 N. Osceola, Chicago, 60631.* Tel: 773-631-4127.

Priests' Placement Board—Rev. JEREMIAH BOLAND, Exec. Dir. Tel: 312-751-5270; Fax: 312-751-5281.

Commission on the Mission and Life of the Diocesan Priest—Rev. DANIEL P. COUGHLIN, Chm., *645 N. Michigan Ave., Ste. 543, Chicago, 60611.* Tel: 312-642-1837.

Parish Staffing Team—Rev. R. PETER BOWMAN, Chm. Tel: 312-751-5250.

Office of Ministeral Evaluation—MARY YUNGER, Dir. Tel: 312-751-5265; Fax: 312-751-5281.

Miscellaneous Archdiocesan Agencies

Apostleship of Prayer—Rev. Msgr. JAMES C. HARDIMAN, Dir., *4126 W. 99th St., Oak Lawn, 60453.* Tel: 708-425-8732.

Pilgrimage and Shrine Apostolate—Rev. DAVID J. BYRNE, Dir., *P.O.Box 557816, Chicago, 60655.* Tel: 708-499-3283; Fax: 708-422-8699.

Millennium Committee—Rev. WAYNE PRIST, Chm. ALEJANDRO CASTILLO, Dir., *6820 N. Sauganash Ave., Chicago, 60646.* Tel: 773-736-6060; Fax: 773-736-6099.

CLERGY, PARISHES, MISSIONS AND PAROCHIAL SCHOOLS

CITY OF CHICAGO
(Cook County)

1—CATHEDRAL OF THE HOLY NAME, Revs. Robert E. McLaughlin, Rector and Pastor of Parish; William J. Sheridan; John Boivin. Pastoral Ministers: Ms. Cathleen Mika; Mrs. Ann Klocke; Deacon Michael McCloskey; Sr. Roberta Popara, O.P., Coord. of Ministry; Mr. Matthew Walsh, Dir. Music; Mrs. Rosalie V. Clifford, Business Mgr.; Mrs. Cathy Fannon, Parish Sec.; Sr. Michaeleen Gibbons, B.V.M., Financial Admin.; Dr. Alice Carney, D.R.E. In res., Most Rev. Timothy J. Lyne, Pastor Emeritus & Auxiliary Bishop of Chicago (Retired); Rev. Msgr. John J. Egan; Revs. Robert J. Wielosinski; Michael M. Boland; William J. Moriarity; James P. Roache; Thomas J. Paprocki; Eugene F. Durkin, (Retired).
Rectory: 730 N. Wabash Ave., 60611. Tel: 312-787-8040; Fax: 312-787-9113.
Archbishop's Residence—1555 N. State Pkwy., 60610. Most Rev. Raymond E. Goedert, Auxiliary Bishop & Vicar General; Rev. John J. McDonnell, Sec. to the Archbishop.
School—Frances Xavier Warde School, 751 N. State St., 60611. Tel: 312-466-0700; Fax: 312-337-7180. Sr. Mary Ellen Caron, R.S.M., Prin.
Religious 1; Lay Teachers 34; Students 536.
Convents—750 N. Wabash Ave., 60611. Tel: 312-664-1462. Sisters of Charity of the Blessed Virgin Mary; 740 N. Wabash Ave., 60611. Tel: 312-787-8040; Fax: 312-787-9113. Little Sisters of the Holy Family

2—ST. ADALBERT, Revs. James Kaczorowski; Alejandro Garrido.
Res., 1650 W. 17th St., 60608. Tel: 312-226-0340.

3—ST. ADRIAN, Rev. Theodore L. Ostrowski.
Res., 7000 S. Fairfield Ave., 60629. Tel: 773-434-3223.
Church—70th and S. Washtenaw Ave., 60619.
School—Sisters of the Institute of the Blessed Virgin Mary (Ladies of Loretto) 4; Lay Teachers 9; Students 260.
Convent—7020 S. Washtenaw Ave., 60629.

4—ST. AGATHA, Revs. Michael T. Ivers; Matthew S. Eyerman; Sr. Jo Mary Davis, S.N.D., Pastoral Assoc.; Deacon Roy Warren.
Res., 3147 W. Douglas Blvd., 60623. Tel: 773-522-3050; Fax: 773-522-3842.
School—Campus No. One—Our Lady of the Westside Catholic School. Serving the following parishes: St. Agatha, Precious Blood and Presentation. Totals represent all three campuses. Tel: 773-762-1809.
Sisters 6; Lay Teachers 23; Students 609.
Convent—3143 W. Douglas Blvd., 60623. Tel: 773-762-7969.

5—ST. AGNES OF BOHEMIA, Revs. John G. Klein; Francis T. Pribyl, Pastor Emeritus; Mark Bartosic; Timothy J. O'Malley. Pastoral Assocs.: Sr. Irma Fuentes; Sr. Norma Celis; Sr. Yolanda Gil; Deacons Jose Luis Mendoza; Angel Favila.
Res., 2651 S. Central Park Ave., 60623. Tel: 773-522-0142; Fax: 773-522-0172.
School—2643 S. Central Park Ave., 60623. Tel: 773-522-0143.
Sisters 3; Lay Teachers 19; Students 630.
Convent—2658 S. Central Park Ave., 60623. Misioneras de San Pio X

6—ST. AILBE, Rev. John S. Breslin; Deacon Bruce T. McElrath; Mrs. Marie C. Davis, Pastoral Assoc.
Res., 9015 S. Harper Ave., 60619. Tel: 773-374-2345; Fax: 773-374-7096.
School—9137 S. Harper Ave., 60619. Tel: 773-734-1386; Fax: 773-734-1440. Sr. Kathryn Hartnett, Prin.
Sisters of St. Dominic (Adrian, MI) 1; Lay Teachers 15; Students 320.

7—ALL SAINTS-ST. ANTHONY, Rev. Raymond P. Devereux; Deacons Peter Liberti; Martin Mackert; Duke Vemich.
Res., 518 W. 28th Pl., 60616. Tel: 312-842-2744; Fax: 312-842-2791.
School—Participant in Bridgeport Catholic Academy. See separate listing for Consolidated Elementary Schools.

8—ST. ALOYSIUS, Revs. Michael S. Michelini; Moises M. Marin; Deacons Santiago Rodriguez; Jose Gonzalez; Adolph Lopez; Dennis Ramos. In res., Rev. Sebastian Ugochukwu.
Res., 2300 W. Le Moyne St., 60622. Tel: 773-278-4808; Fax: 773-278-4898.

9—ST. ALPHONSUS (German), Revs. Joseph Morin, C.Ss.R.; Joseph Dorcey, C.Ss.R.; Deacons Joseph Riffner; Raul Mendieta. In res., Revs. John Dowd, C.Ss.R.; Walter George, C.Ss.R.; Bernard Guenther, C.Ss.R.; Peter Schavitz, C.Ss.R.; James Nugent, C.Ss.R.; Matthew Kessler, C.Ss.R.
Res., 1429 W. Wellington Ave., 60657. Tel: 773-525-0709.
Co-Redemptorist Association Office—Tel: 773-472-8509. Rev. John Andree, C.Ss.R.
School—School Sisters of Notre Dame 2; Lay Teachers 12; Students 280.
Convent—1456 Oakdale Ave., 60657.

10—ST. AMBROSE, Rev. David A. Jones.
Res., 1012 E. 47th St., 60653. Tel: 773-624-3695; Fax: 773-624-3697.
School—1014 E. 47th St., 60653-3698. Tel: 773-373-7311.
Lay Teachers 10; Students 163.

11—ST. ANDREW, Rev. John W. Parker; Rev. Msgr. John S. Quinn, Pastor Emeritus; Rev. Joseph Thai Nguyen. In res., Rev. Philip X. Guerin, (Retired).
Res., 3546 N. Paulina St., 60657. Tel: 773-525-3016; Fax: 773-248-2709.
School—1710 W. Addison, 60613. Tel: 773-248-2500.
Lay Teachers 18; Students 370.

12—ST. ANGELA, Rev. Dennis S. Riley; Rev. Msgr. Edward M. Pellicore, Pastor Emeritus; Sr. Joseph Ellen Keitzer, S.P., Pastoral Assoc.; Deacon Jose Uroza.
Res., 5758 W. Potomac Ave., 60651. Tel: 773-379-7700.
School—Sisters 4; Lay Teachers 16; Students 525.
Convent—1325 N. Menard Ave., 60651.

13—ANGEL GUARDIAN CROATIAN CATHOLIC MISSION. (Independent Mission). In res., Rev. Harvey Blaschko, O.P.
Res., 6346 N. Ridge, 60660. Tel: 773-262-0535; Fax: 773-262-4603.

14—ST. ANN, Rev. John J. Keehan; Deacons Rodrigo Silva; Bricio Lopez. In res., Rev. Louis J. Zake.
Res., 1840 S. Leavitt St., 60608. Tel: 312-733-7486.
School—2211 W. 18th Pl., 60608. Sr. Michael Marie Franzak, Prin.
Lay Teachers 7; Students 324.

15—ANNUNCIATA, Revs. George Luznicky, O.S.M.; Mark M. Dennehy, O.S.M., Pastor Emeritus; Marco Antonio Elias, O.S.M.; Bro. Brian Fitzkpatrick, O.S.M., Pastoral Assoc.; Sr. Judene Studer, S.S.N.D., D.R.E.; Mr. Mike Schnabel, Business Mgr. In res., Rev. Conrad M. Borntrager, O.S.M.
Res., 11128 S. Avenue G, 60617. Tel: 773-221-1040; Fax: 773-221-1556.
School—Lay Teachers 13; Students 325.

16—ST. ANSELM, Rev. William Hegarty; Bros. Jim Fisher, S.V.D., Pastoral Assoc.; Darcy Litzenberger, S.V.D.
Res., 6045 S. Michigan Ave., 60637. Tel: 773-493-5959; Fax: 773-363-1887.

17—ST. ANTHONY (Italian), Revs. Charles LaVerde, C.S.; Peter Corbellini, C.S.; Deacon Edward Ryan.
Res., 11530 S. Prairie Ave., 60628. Tel: 773-468-1200; Fax: 773-468-3570.
School—Lay Teachers 11; Students 155.

18—ASSUMPTION OF THE BLESSED VIRGIN MARY, Rev. Paul M. Cullen, O.S.M. In res., Revs. Anthony M. O'Connell, O.S.M.; John M. Pawlikowski, O.S.M.; David M. Brown, O.S.M.; John M. Dowd, O.S.M.
Res., 323 W. Illinois St., 60610. Tel: 312-644-0036; Fax: 312-644-1838.

19—ASSUMPTION OF THE B.V.M./ST. CATHERINE OF GENOA, Rev. Robert C. Behnke; Deacon Tommy West.
Res., 640 W. 118th St., 60628. Tel: 773-785-6600.
School—11756 S. Lowe, 60628. Catherine M. Valek, Prin.
Lay Teachers 10; Students 202.

20—ASSUMPTION, Revs. Lawrence J. Craig; David A. Kelly, C.PP.S.
Res., 2434 S. California Ave., 60608. Tel: 773-247-6644; Fax: 773-247-0569.
Convent—2831 W. 24th St. Blvd., 60623. Tel: 773-247-3560.
Kolbe House—Catholic Prison Ministry. Tel: 773-247-0070. Rev. Lawrence J. Craig, Dir.

21—ST. BARBARA, Rev. Michael T. Yakaitis; Deacon Andrew Brongiel.
Res., 2859 S. Throop St., 60608. Tel: 312-842-7979; Fax: 312-842-7978.
School—2867 S. Throop St., 60608. Tel: 312-326-6243.
Sisters of St. Joseph of the Third Order of St. Francis (Chicago, IL) 1; Lay Teachers 11; Students 257.
High School—Tel: 312-842-0042.
Sisters of St. Joseph of the Third Order of St. Francis (Chicago, IL) 2; Lay Teachers 12; Students 170.

22—ST. BARNABAS, Revs. Raymond J. Tillrock; Kenneth J. Fleck; Coletta Hogan, Pastoral Assoc.; Deacons James Temple; William Sullivan; James L. Conway.
Res., 10134 S. Longwood Dr., 60643. Tel: 773-779-1166; Fax: 773-445-9671.
School—10121 S. Longwood Dr., 60643. Tel: 773-445-7711.
Dominican Sisters (Sinsinawa, WI) 1; Lay Teachers 27; Students 624.

23—ST. BARTHOLOMEW, Revs. George F. Cerny; Casimir J. Kozien, (Retired); J. Edward Duggan, (Retired); J. Lester Mollohan, (Retired). Lay Ministers: Mr. Robert Puhala; Ms. Nancy Hoppe.
Res., 4949 W. Patterson Ave., 60641. Tel: 773-286-7871; Fax: 773-286-4808.
School—4941 W. Patterson Ave., 60641. Tel: 773-282-9373; Fax: 773-282-4757.
Sisters 1; Lay Teachers 24; Students 463.
Convent—Tel: 773-545-2119; Fax: 773-282-4757.

24—ST. BASIL/VISITATION, Revs. Brian G. Walker, O.P.; Thomas Jackson, O.P.; Deacon Roosevelt Jones.
Res., 843 W. Garfield Blvd., 60621. Tel: 773-846-3570; Fax: 773-925-7091.
Schools—St. Basil School, 1824 W. Garfield Blvd., 60609. Tel: 773-778-4448; Fax: 773-925-7091.
Sisters of the Living Word 1; Lay Teachers 10; Students 160; Visitation School, 900 W. Garfield Blvd., 60609.
Dominican Sisters (Sinsinawa, WI) 3; Lay Teachers 15; Students 353.

25—ST. BEDE THE VENERABLE, Revs. Jeremiah C. Duggan; Francis G. Scanlan; Marion Soprych; Deacons Donald Kotwas; James F. Delaney.

Res., 8200 S. Kostner Ave., 60652. Tel: 773-582-9100; Fax: 773-582-0026.
School—4420 W. 83rd St., 60652. Tel: 773-582-8800.
Lay Teachers 44; Students 1,100.

26—ST. BENEDICT, Revs. Robert A. Heidenreich; Dennis B. O'Neill; Jason A. Malave; Peter Heidenrich; Deacon Robert Jacob.
Res., 2215 W. Irving Park Rd., 60618. Tel: 773-588-6484; Fax: 773-588-4927.
School—3920 N. Leavitt St., 60618. Tel: 773-463-6797.
Lay Teachers 25; Students 434.
High School—Priests 1; Sisters 8; Lay Teachers 30; Students 647.

27—ST. BENEDICT THE AFRICAN (WEST), Revs. James J. Martin; John L. Harvey; Deacon Louis Constanopolis; Sr. Joann Sambs, Pastoral Assoc.
Worship Site—7033 S. Honore, 60636.
Office—6012 S. Laflin St., 60636. Tel: 773-476-4831; Fax: 773-925-1010.
School—Academy of St. Benedict the African.
Total Students for 3 Sites 840.
Honore Site—7033 S. Honore St., 60636. Tel: 773-476-2258.
Laflin Site—6020 S. Laflin St., 60636. Tel: 773-776-3316.
Stewart Site—6547 S. Stewart St., 60636. Tel: 773-994-6100.

28—ST. BENEDICT THE AFRICAN (EAST), Rev. David E. Baldwin; Sr. Mary Pokorny, Pastoral Assoc.
340 W. 66th St., 60621. Tel: 773-873-4464; Fax: 773-925-1010.
School—Academy of St. Benedict the African.
Total Students for 3 Sites 800.
Stewart Site—6547 S. Stewart, 60621. Tel: 773-944-6100.

29—BLESSED SACRAMENT, Revs. Richard A. Boever, C.Ss.R.; William Bueche, C.Ss.R.; Bros. Eugene Patin, C.Ss.R.; Paul Jorns, C.Ss.R.; Deacon Juan Sierra. In res., Rev. John Phelps, C.Ss.R.
Res., 2153 S. Millard Ave., 60623. Tel: 773-521-5595; Fax: 773-521-6076.
School—2130 S. Central Park Ave., 60623.
Lay Teachers 11; Students 265.
Convents—2128 S. Central Park Ave., 60623. Dominican Sisters (Sinsinawa, WI); 2135 S. Central Park Ave., 60623. Sisters of Charity of the Blessed Virgin

30—ST. BONAVENTURE, Rev. James P. Heneghan; Deacons Emiliano Rodriguez; Tito Roman; Jose Alvarez. In res., Revs. Richard E. Bulwith; Joseph Moffat, C.S.B.; Louis J. Cameli.
Res., 1641 W. Diversey Pkwy., 60614. Tel: 773-281-6588; Fax: 773-281-1051.

31—ST. BRIDE, Rev. Robert J. Kyfes.
Res., 7811 S. Coles Ave., 60649. Tel: 773-731-8822.
School—7760 South Shore Dr., 60649. Tel: 773-721-5459.
Sisters of Institute of the B.V.M. 4; Lay Teachers 8; Students 260.

32—ST. BRONISLAVA, Revs. Michael J. Bonner, S.V.D., Admin.; Frank Drzaic, S.V.D., Pastoral Assoc.
Res., 8708 S. Colfax Ave., 60617. Tel: 773-734-0776; Fax: 773-734-1426.

33—ST. BRUNO, Revs. Joseph P. Grembla; Ernest Ciemiega; Edmund S. Szlanga, Pastor Emeritus; Idzi Stacherczak; Deacon Sal Villa.
Res., 4751 S. Harding Ave., 60632. Tel: 773-523-3467; Fax: 773-523-4253.
School—Tel: 773-847-0697; Fax: 773-847-1620.
Lay Teachers 13; Students 271.

34—ST. CAJETAN, Revs. William Maloney; Kevin Sheahan. Pastoral Assocs.: Sr. Annette Kelley, O.P.; Sr. Margaret Mary, C.S.F.N.; Deacon Don Newhall.
Res., 11234 S. Artesian Ave., 60655. Tel: 773-238-4100.
School—2447 W. 112th St., 60655. Tel: 773-233-8844.
Lay Teachers 28; Students 565.

35—ST. CALLISTUS (Italian). Closed. Merged with Notre Dame. For inquiries for parish records contact Notre Dame.

36—ST. CAMILLUS, Rev. Norman M. Czajka. In res., Revs. Stanley Drewniak; Waclaw Jamroz, S.D.S.
Res., 5426 S. Lockwood Ave., 60638. Tel: 773-767-8183; Fax: 773-284-3812.
School—5432 S. Lockwood Ave., 60638.
Sisters of the Holy Family of Nazareth 6; Lay Teachers 8; Students 250.

37—CHRIST THE KING, Revs. Joseph W. Seitz; Thomas J. Raftery, (Retired); Deacons Larry Antonsen; William Hurley; Terry Childers.
Res., 9235 S. Hamilton Ave., 60620. Tel: 773-238-4877; Fax: 773-238-4963.
School—9240 S. Hoyne Ave., 60620. Tel: 773-779-3329.
Lay Teachers 23; Students 336.

38—CHRIST THE REDEEMER BYZANTINE BIELARUSIAN, Rev. John McDonnell, Admin.
Res., 3107 W. Fullerton Ave., 60647. Tel: 773-342-7373.

39—ST. CHRISTINA, Revs. Martin E. O'Donovan; Patrick J. Henry; Christopher E. Gustafson; Deacon Thomas Ryan.
Res., 11005 S. Homan Ave., 60655. Tel: 773-779-7181; Fax: 773-238-2942.
School—Tel: 773-445-2969; Fax: 773-445-0444.
Dominican Sisters (Springfield, IL) 2; Lay Teachers 27; Students 660.
Convent—11033 S. Christiana, 60655.

40—ST. CLARE OF MONTEFALCO, Revs. Anthony B. Pizzo, O.S.A.; John E. Flynn, O.S.A. In res., Revs. Daniel J. Hartigan, O.S.A.; Gerrardo M. Garcia, O.S.A., (Retired).
Res., 5443 S. Washtenaw Ave., 60632. Tel: 773-436-4422; Fax: 773-476-1888.
School—5450 S. Talman Ave., 60632. Tel: 773-434-2427. Iris Foley, Prin.
Religious 3; Lay Teachers 8; Students 186.

41—ST. CLEMENT, Revs. Thomas E. Hickey; John W. McGivern, Assoc.; Sr. Diane Boutet, O.P., Pastoral Assoc. In res., Rev. Daniel P. Coughlin.
Res., 642 W. Deming Pl., 60614. Tel: 773-281-0371; Fax: 773-281-2509.
School—2524 N. Orchard St., 60614. Tel: 773-348-8212; Fax: 773-348-4712.
Lay Teachers 17; Students 301.

42—ST. CLOTILDE, Rev. Michael G. Meany. In res., Rev. Giancarlo Ghezzi, P.I.M.E.
Res., 8430 Calumet Ave., 60619. Tel: 773-874-1022; Fax: 773-874-1736.
School—321 E. 84th St., 60619. Tel: 773-488-4214. Mr. Joseph Cailles, Prin.
Lay Teachers 8; Students 145.

43—ST. COLUMBA, Revs. Kilian M. Knittel; Henry A. Olejniczak, Pastor Emeritus.
Res., 13323 S. Green Bay Ave., 60633. Tel: 773-646-2660; Fax: 773-646-6821.
School—Tel: 773-646-0751; Fax: 773-646-0640.
School Sisters of Notre Dame 1; Lay Teachers 7; Students 180.

44—ST. COLUMBANUS, Rev. Philip E. Cyscon; Deacons William McKinnis; George Borka.
Res., 331 E. 71st St., 60619. Tel: 773-224-1022.
School—7120 S. Calumet, 60619.
Lay Teachers 16; Students 350.

45—ST. CONSTANCE, Revs. Thomas R. Rzepiela; Martin R. Borowczyk, Pastor Emeritus; Andrew Izyk; Philip J. Grib, S.J.; Sr. Marie Ellen Sullivan, Pastoral Assoc.; Deacons Ted Lisowski; James Schlitz; George Gniech; Edward Lukaszewski.
Res., 5843 W. Strong St., 60630. Tel: 773-545-8581; Fax: 773-545-0227.
School—5841 W. Strong St., 60630. Tel: 773-283-2311.
Lay Teachers 17; Students 260.

46—ST. CORNELIUS, Revs. Edwin D. Pacocha; Erwin J. Friedl; Marion A. Matlak, Pastor Emeritus; Deacon Carl D. Olson. In res., Rev. Robert S. Brodfuehrer, (Retired).
Res., 5205 N. Lieb Ave., 60630. Tel: 773-283-5222.
School—Tel: 773-283-2192; Fax: 773-283-1377.
Lay Teachers 19; Students 376.

47—CORPUS CHRISTI, Revs. Christian Reuter, O.F.M.; Michael Perry, O.F.M.; Howard A. Tuite.
Res., Corpus Christi Friary, 4920 King Dr., 60615. Tel: 773-285-7720.

48—ST. DANIEL THE PROPHET, Revs. Lawrence J. Malcolm; John M. Cassidy; Peter Gacki; Charles F. Kelly, Pastor Emeritus; Sr. Eileen Tierney, C.N.D., Pastoral Assoc.; Deacons Albert Malec; Chester Golab.
Res., 5330 S. Nashville Ave., 60638. Tel: 773-586-1223; Fax: 773-586-1238.
School—5337 S. Natoma Ave., 60638.
Lay Teachers 29; Students 675.

49—ST. DAVID. Closed. For inquiries for parish records contact the Chancery.

50—ST. DENIS, Revs. Lawrence R. Dowling; Patrick J. Pollard; Dennis Stafford; Sr. Norine Burns, O.P., Pastoral Assoc.; Deacons Thomas Ewers; Thomas Solon; Sr. Mary Anne Yanz, O.P., D.R.E.
Res., 8301 S. St. Louis Ave., 60652. Tel: 773-434-3313; Fax: 773-776-3922.
School—8332 S. St. Louis Ave., 60652. Sr. Elizabeth Lynch, O.P., Prin.
Sisters 2; Lay Teachers 17; Students 349.

51—ST. DOROTHY, Revs. Kenneth J. Fischer; David Kusi (Ghana).
Res., 450 E. 78th St., 60619. Tel: 773-651-7000; Fax: 773-651-0969.
School—7740 S. Eberhart Ave., 60619.
Sisters of the Presentation of the Blessed Virgin Mary 1; Lay Teachers 17; Students 480.

52—ST. EDWARD, Revs. John M. Murphy; John J. Donohue, Pastor Emeritus; Joseph C. Taylor, Assoc.; Edward A. Carlson, Assoc.
Res., 4350 W. Sunnyside Ave., 60630-4147. Tel: 773-545-6496; Fax: 773-545-1136.
School—4343 W. Sunnyside Ave., 60630-4147. Tel: 773-736-9133; Fax: 773-736-9280.
Dominican Sisters (Springfield, IL) 5; Lay Teachers 23; Students 576.

53—ST. ELIZABETH, Revs. Donald J. Ehr, S.V.D.; George Kintiba, S.V.D.; Bros. Thomas Joseph, S.V.D.; Gary Burr, S.V.D.
Res., 50 E. 41st St., 60653. Tel: 773-268-1518; Fax: 773-373-8640.
School—4052 S. Wabash, 60653. Tel: 773-548-4100; Fax: 773-548-8641.
Sisters 5; Lay Teachers 18; Students 445.

54—EPIPHANY, Rev. Peter B. McQuinn, Admin.; Rev. Msgr. John M. Hayes, Pastor Emeritus.
Res., 2524 S. Keeler Ave., 60623. Tel: 773-521-1112.
School—4225 W. 25th St., 60623. Sr. Leona Bruck, O.P., Prin.; Sr. Berta Lopez, M.H.S.P.X., D.R.E.
Sisters 3; Lay Teachers 13; Students 245.

55—ST. ETHELREDA, Rev. James F. Nallen.
Res., 8754 S. Paulina St., 60620. Tel: 773-238-6118; Fax: 773-238-6059.
School—8734 S. Paulina St., 60620. Tel: 773-238-1757.
Lay Teachers 14; Students 328.

56—ST. EUGENE, Revs. James J. O'Brien; Francis W. Shaunessy, Pastor Emeritus; Frank L. Schouten; Deacons Gerard Kwasegroch; Edward O'Leary. In res., Rev. George J. Helfrich, (Retired).
Res., 7958 W. Foster Ave., 60656-1698. Tel: 773-775-6659; Fax: 773-775-2832.
School—7930 W. Foster Ave., 60656. Tel: 773-763-2235; Fax: 773-763-2775.
Sisters of Charity B.V.M. 1; Lay Teachers 32; Students 586.

57—ST. FELICITAS, Revs. John T. Boyle; Thomas S. Boyle, Pastor Emeritus; Deacons James Hubbard; Ralph Shaw.
Res., 1526 E. 84th St., 60619. Tel: 773-734-2300; Fax: 773-731-5381.
School—1521 E. 83rd Pl., 60652. Tel: 773-721-0858.
Lay Teachers 10; Students 250.

58—ST. FERDINAND, Revs. David J. Cortesi; Maxim Lasrado, O.C.D.; Walter Juszczak, C.Ss.R.; Walter J. Takuski; William M. Holbrook; Mr. Daniel P. Costigan, Pastoral Assoc.; Deacon Irwin Hotcaveg. In res., Rev. Joseph Kromenaker.
Res., 5900 W. Barry Ave., 60634. Tel: 773-622-5900; Fax: 773-622-5903.
School—3131 N. Mason Ave., 60634. Tel: 773-622-3022. Mrs. Marilyn Hilberg, Prin.
Lay Teachers 34; Students 638.

59—ST. FIDELIS, Sr. Leonette Kaluzny, S.Sp.S., Pastoral Coord.; Rev. Francis A. Cimmarrusti; Deacons Roberto Figueroa; Jaimie Rios.
Res., 1406 N. Washtenaw Ave., 60622. Tel: 773-486-8700; Fax: 773-486-8944.

60—FIVE HOLY MARTYRS, Rev. Andrew P. Wypych; Most Rev. Alfred L. Abramowicz, D.D., Pastor Emeritus; Revs. Edmund J. Siedlecki, Pastor Emeritus; Leonard M. Kruzel; Franciszek Florczyk (Poland); Deacon Richard Wieczorek. In res., Rev. John Latka (Poland).
Res., 2905 W. Pope John Paul II Dr., 60632. Tel: 773-254-3636; Fax: 773-254-3609.
Bishop's Residence—6101 S. 75th Ave., Argo, 60501.
School—4325 S. Richmond St., 60632. Tel: 773-523-6161.
Franciscan Sisters of Chicago 2; Lay Teachers 10; Students 310.

61—ST. FLORIAN, Rev. Casimir M. Szatkowski, Admin. In res., Rev. Wojciech Warmuz, O.Cist.
Res., 13145 S. Houston Ave., 60633. Tel: 773-646-4877; Fax: 773-646-5965.
School—Lay Teachers 12; Students 230.

62—ST. FRANCIS OF ASSISI (Spanish Speaking Parish), Revs. Donald J. Nevins; Arturo J. Perez; Deacons Zeferino Ochoa; Manuel Rodriguez; Arturo Velasco.
Res., 813 W. Roosevelt Rd., 60608. Tel: 312-226-7575.

63—ST. FRANCIS OF ASSISI/OUR LADY OF THE ANGELS, Revs. Nicholas R. Desmond; Wojiech Kwiecen; Deacon Salvador Sanchez.
Res., 932 N. Kostner, 60651. Tel: 773-235-3132; Fax: 773-486-7726.
School—3814 W. Iowa St., 60651.
Lay Teachers 10; Students 191.

64—ST. FRANCIS BORGIA, Revs. Daniel G. Mayall; Robert S. Brodfuehrer, Pastor Emeritus; Joseph A. Mulcrone; Joseph T. Noonan; Martin R. Borowczyk.
Res., 8033 W. Addison St., 60634. Tel: 773-625-1118; Fax: 773-625-1110.
School—Tel: 773-589-1000.
Sisters 1; Lay Teachers 21; Students 547.
Convent—3521 N. Panama St., 60634.

65—ST. FRANCIS DE SALES, Rev. James P. Keating; Deacon Joseph Pastirik. In res., Rev. Ildephonse

Skorup, O.F.M.
Res., 10201 S. Ewing Ave., 60617. Tel: 773-734-1383; Fax: 773-734-3022.

66—ST. GABRIEL, Rev. John P. McNalis.
Res., 4522 S. Wallace St., 60609. Tel: 773-268-9595; Fax: 773-268-9586.
Church—45th St. and Lowe Ave., 60609.
School—4500 S. Wallace St., 60609. Tel: 773-268-6636; Fax: 773-268-2501.
Lay Teachers 14; Students 279.

67—ST. GALL, Revs. David P. Dowdle; William Wilkosz; John J. Dowling, O.S.A.; Deacons Michael Slajchert; Albert Herrera.
Res., 5511 S. Sawyer Ave., 60629. Tel: 773-737-3113; Fax: 773-737-0272.
School—5515 S. Sawyer Ave., 60629.
Lay Teachers 15; Students 292.

68—ST. GELASIUS, Rev. Peter McGarry, O.Carm.; Deacon James Morgan. In res., Revs. Martin Curtis, O.Carm.; Terrence Pfender, O.Carm.; John Benedict, O.Carm.; Samuel Citero, O.Carm.
Res., 6415 S. Woodlawn Ave., 60637. Tel: 773-363-6500; Fax: 773-363-3279.
School—Lay Teachers 10; Students 287.

69—ST. GENEVIEVE, Revs. Leoncio S. Santiago; Thomas F. Maher, Pastor Emeritus; Rev. Msgr. Thomas J. Mohan, Pastor Emeritus; Rev. Sergio Romo; Sr. Jean Michael Rafferty, S.P., Pastoral Assoc.; Deacon Benito Centeno.
Res., 4835 W. Altgeld St., 60639. Tel: 773-237-3011; Fax: 773-237-3043.
School—4854 W. Montana St., 60639. Tel: 773-237-7131; Fax: 773-237-7265.
Lay Teachers 11; Students 242.

70—ST. GEORGE (Slovenian), Rev. Raphael A. Sesek, O.F.M.
Res., 9546 S. Ewing Ave., 60617. Tel: 773-734-0554.

71—ST. GERTRUDE, Rev. William G. Kenneally; Mr. Peter Buttitta, Pastoral Assoc.
Res., 1420 W. Granville Ave., 60660. Tel: 773-764-3621; Fax: 773-761-4164.
School—Northside Catholic Academy, 6216 N. Glenwood Ave., 60660.
Sisters 1; Lay Teachers 17; Students 333.

72—GOOD SHEPHERD, Rev. Donald J. Lund.
Res., 2719 S. Kolin Ave., 60623. Tel: 773-762-2322.
School—2733 S. Kolin Ave., 60623.
Lay Teachers 11; Students 254.

73—ST. GREGORY, Revs. John W. Clemens; Alberto Rojas; Sr. Barbara Quinn, S.N.D.deN., Pastoral Assoc. In res., Rev. Zacharias Nanthiyattu, O.I.C.
Res., 1634 W. Gregory St., 60640. Tel: 773-561-3546.
School—Northside Catholic Academy, Tel: 773-907-2094.
Lay Teachers 17; Students 300.
High School—1677 W. Bryn Mawr Ave., 60660. Tel: 773-907-2100.
Lay Teachers 30; Students 350.

74—ST. HEDWIG, Revs. Michael E. Danek, C.R.; Casimir V. Polinski, C.R.; Gary Hogan, C.R. In res., Revs. Walter Wilczek, C.R.; Eugene Szarek, C.R.; Bro. Ed Howe, C.R.; Deacons Gilberto Cintron; Salomon Villegas.
Res., 2226 N. Hoyne Ave., 60647. Tel: 773-486-1660.

75—ST. HELEN, Rev. Bronislaus Chmiel.
Res., 2315 W. Augusta Blvd., 60622. Tel: 773-235-3575; Fax: 773-235-3576.
School—2347 W. Augusta Blvd., 60622.
Lay Teachers 15; Students 263.

76—ST. HELENA, Rev. Thomas J. Kaminski; Sr. Mary Leroy Rowland, S.S.N.D., Pastoral Assoc.
Res., 10121 S. Parnell Ave., 60628. Tel: 773-779-2243; Fax: 773-779-2749.
School—10115 S. Parnell Ave., 60628.
Sisters 1; Lay Teachers 9; Students 215.

77—ST. HENRY, Rev. Edward A. Harasim; Deacon Frank G. Duffy.
Res., 6335 N. Hoyne Ave., 60659. Tel: 773-764-7413; Fax: 773-764-5994.
School—Northside Catholic Academy, 6325 N. Hoyne, 60659. Tel: 773-274-5227; Fax: 773-274-2157.
Convent—1956 W. Devon, 60660.

78—ST. HILARY, Revs. Robert G. Darow; Matt A. Bednarz, Pastor Emeritus; Deacons Edmund Tryba; Donald Wehling.
Res., 5600 N. Fairfield Ave., 60659. Tel: 773-561-3474; Fax: 773-561-6409.
School—5614 N. Fairfield Ave., 60659. Tel: 773-561-5885.
Lay Teachers 17; Students 405.

79—HOLY ANGELS, Revs. John W. Calicott; Robert J. Miller; Paul B. Smith (ALX); Deacons Jasper Roy; Dexter Watson.
Res., 607 E. Oakwood Blvd., 60653. Tel: 773-624-5375.
School—545 E. Oakwood Blvd., 60653.
Priests 1; Sisters 18; Lay Teachers 30; Students 1,300.

80—HOLY CROSS/IMMACULATE HEART OF MARY, Revs. Peter Rodriguez, C.M.F.; Tom Joyce, C.M.F.; Miguel Estrada, C.M.F.; John Cirone, C.M.F.; Bruce Wellems, C.M.F.; Milton Alvsarez, C.M.F.
Res., 4557 S. Wood St., 60609. Tel: 773-376-3900; Fax: 773-376-8929.

81—HOLY FAMILY, Rev. Donald J. Nevins; Deacon Rudolph Kotleba.
Res., 1019 S. May St., 60607. Tel: 312-226-7575; Fax: 312-226-6283.

82—HOLY INNOCENTS, Revs. Richard J. Klajbor; Antoni Bradlo, C.Ss.R.
Res., 743 N. Armour St., 60622. Tel: 312-666-3675; Fax: 312-666-0714.
School—1444-56 W. Superior St., 60622.
Felician Sisters (Chicago, IL) 5; Lay Teachers 11; Students 240.

83—HOLY NAME OF MARY, Revs. James F. Flynn; Anthony J. Vader, Pastor Emeritus; Deacon Richard Boyd.
Res., 11159 S. Loomis St., 60643. Tel: 773-238-6800; Fax: 773-445-1248.
School—1421 W. 112th St., 60643. Tel: 773-445-3277.
Oblate Sisters of Providence 3; Lay Teachers 7; Students 155.
Mission—Chicago, Cook Co., Sacred Heart, 11652 S. Church St., 60643.

84—HOLY ROSARY, Rev. Richard C. Creagh. In res., Rev. Ronald L. Kondziolka.
Res., 351 E. 113th St., 60628. Tel: 773-568-4455; Fax: 773-568-4456.

85—HOLY ROSARY, Rev. Anthony M. Talarico; Deacons Jose Colon, (Retired); Martin Hare, (Retired); Jorge Rozo.
Res., 612 N. Western Ave., 60612. Tel: 773-278-4820; Fax: 773-278-3770.

86—HOLY TRINITY (Croatian), Rev. Charles W. Dahm, O.P., Admin.
Res., 1850 S. Throop St., 60608. Tel: 312-226-2736.
Catechesis/Religious Programs—1840 S. Throop St., 60608.
Priests 1; Sisters of St. Francis of Christ the King 3.

87—HOLY TRINITY MISSION (Polish), Revs. Wladyslaw Gowin, S.Chr.; Jacek Walkiewicz, S.Chr.
Res., 1118 N. Noble St., 60622. Tel: 773-489-4140; Fax: 773-489-5918.

88—ST. HYACINTH, Revs. Michael Osuch, C.R.; Francis Rog, C.R.; Andrzej Lewandowski, C.R.; Jerzy Zieba, C.R.; Wieslaw Janowski, C.R.; Deacons Fred Girjatowicz; Stefan Stanczak. In res., Rev. Joseph Wise, C.R.
Res., 3636 W. Wolfram St., 60618. Tel: 773-342-3636; Fax: 773-342-3638.
School—3640 W. Wolfram St., 60618.
Sisters of the Holy Family of Nazareth (Des Plaines) 3; Lay Teachers 21; Students 309.

89—ST. IGNATIUS, Revs. Robert I. Grib, S.J.; Paul J. Clifford, S.J.; Patrick J. McAteer, S.J. In res., Rev. Robert J. Geisinger, S.J.
Res., 6559 N. Glenwood Ave., 60626. Tel: 773-764-5936; Fax: 773-764-4360.

90—IMMACULATE CONCEPTION OF THE BLESSED VIRGIN MARY, Rev. Patrick J. Lee. In res., Rev. Lawrence J. McBrady.
Res., 1431 N. North Park Ave., 60610. Tel: 773-944-1230; Fax: 773-944-0673.

91—IMMACULATE CONCEPTION, Revs. Michael J. Hoolahan, C.P.; Eric Meyer, C.P.; Peter Berendt, C.P.
Res., 7211 W. Talcott Ave., 60631. Tel: 773-775-3833.
School—7263 W. Talcott Ave., 60631.
Sisters 2; Lay Teachers 38; Students 673.

92—IMMACULATE CONCEPTION (Lithuanian), Rev. Anthony C. Puchenski; Rev. Msgr. Damasus A. Mozeris, Pastor Emeritus; Revs. Edward J. Maxa; Fabian V. Kireilis.
Res., 2745 W. 44th St., 60632-1999. Tel: 773-523-1402.
School—4426 S. Fairfield Ave., 60632.
Sisters of St. Casimir 3; Lay Teachers 8; Students 248.

93—IMMACULATE CONCEPTION OF THE BLESSED VIRGIN MARY, Rev. Michael P. Enright.
Parish Office and Rectory: 2944 E. 88th St., 60627. Tel: 773-768-2100; Fax: 773-221-9121.
Church—88th & Commercial Ave., 60617.

94—IMMACULATE HEART OF MARY, Revs. James F. Blazek; Norbert J. Zawistanowicz, Pastor Emeritus; Joseph Thanugundla; Deacon John Kearney. In res., Revs. Simon Edathiparampil; Robert Onofrey, C.PP.S.
Res., 3834 N. Spaulding Ave., 60618. Tel: 773-478-1157; Fax: 773-478-6044.
School—3820 N. Spaulding Ave., 60618.
Lay Teachers 18; Students 403.
Convent—3817 N. Christiana Ave., 60618.

95—IMMACULATE HEART OF MARY VICARIATE. See Holy Cross, Wood St.

96—SAINT ITA, Revs. Laurence F. Maddock; Robert G. Casey; Vinh Ha; Deacon Frank Gaughan.
Res., 1220 West Catalpa Ave., 60640. Tel: 773-561-5343; Fax: 773-561-5609.
School—Northside Catholic Academy, 5525 N. Magnolia Ave., 60640.
Sisters 2; Lay Teachers 11; Students 230.

97—ST. JAMES, Revs. Thomas M. Frayne; Jamels James (India).
Res., 2942 S. Wabash Ave., 60616. Tel: 312-842-1919; Fax: 312-842-3612.
School—2920 S. Wabash Ave., 60616.
Sisters 2; Lay Teachers 12; Students 270.

98—ST. JAMES, Revs. Joseph R. Szabelski; John L. Wodniak, Pastor Emeritus; Joseph Weligala. In res., Rev. Joseph Lee.
Res., 5730 W. Fullerton Ave., 60639. Tel: 773-237-1474.
School—2456 N. Mango Ave., 60639. Tel: 773-237-0549.
Felician Sisters (Chicago, IL) 4; Lay Teachers 7; Students 290.

99—ST. JANE DE CHANTAL, Rev. Thomas E. Srenn; Sr. Jan Brynda, O.P., Pastoral Assoc.; Deacon Ron Morowczynski. In res., Rev. Edmund S. Szlanga.
Res., 5252 S. Austin Ave., 60638. Tel: 773-767-2411; Fax: 773-767-2769.
School—5201 S. McVicker Ave., 60638.
Lay Teachers 13; Students 276.

100—ST. JEROME, Revs. Harold A. Bonin; Juan Sanchez; Deacons Fritz Jean-Pierre; Sigifredo Hernandez; Victor LaCoursiere; Robert Murphy; Raymond Ward. In res., Rev. William P. Grogan.
Res., 1709 W. Lunt Ave., 60626. Tel: 773-262-3170; Fax: 773-262-2834.

101—ST. JEROME (Croatian), Revs. Jozo Grubisic, O.F.M.; Mark Kozina, O.F.M.
Res., 2823 S. Princeton Ave., 60616. Tel: 312-842-1871; Fax: 312-842-6427.
School—2813 S. Princeton Ave., 60616.
Sisters Adorers of the Blood of Christ 3; Lay Teachers 8; Students 169.

102—ST. JOACHIM, Rev. Frank M. Sasso.
Res., 700 E. 91st St., 60619. Tel: 773-488-4488; Fax: 773-994-8945.

103—ST. JOHN THE BAPTIST (Slovak). Closed. For inquiries for parish records contact the Chancery.

104—ST. JOHN DE LA SALLE, Rev. Oliver Jennings.
Res., 10205 King Dr., 60628. Tel: 773-785-2022.
School—Tel: 773-785-2331. Sharon Dale, Prin.
Lay Teachers 10; Students 256.

105—ST. JOHN BERCHMANS, Revs. William B. Gubbins; Michael G. Foley; Deacons Virgilio Bonifazi; Jorge Cabrera; Guillermo Mendizabal; Marcial Herrera.
Res., 2517 W. Logan Blvd., 60647. Tel: 773-486-4300.
School—2509 W. Logan Blvd., 60647. Tel: 773-486-1334; Fax: 773-486-1782.
Dominican Sisters (St. Catherine, KY) 1; Lay Teachers 24; Students 435.

106—ST. JOHN BOSCO, Revs. Eugene W. Gratkowski, Admin.; Salvatore J. Ognibene, Pastor Emeritus; Deacons Wilfredo Perez; Pedro Soto; Ronald Swiatek; Ron Weiner.
Res., 2250 N. McVicker Ave., 60639. Tel: 773-622-4620; Fax: 773-622-5040.

107—ST. JOHN CANTIUS (Polish), Revs. C. Frank Phillips, C.R.; Edwin Karlowicz, C.R.
Res., 825 N. Carpenter St., 60622. Tel: 312-243-7373; Fax: 312-666-4653.

108—ST. JOHN FISHER, Rev. Thomas J. Purtell; Rev. Msgr. Francis J. McElligott, Pastor Emeritus; Rev. Thomas P. May; Deacons Sidney Mench; Raymond Reilly; Clayton Kort.
Res., 10234 S. Washtenaw Ave., 60655. Tel: 773-445-6565; Fax: 773-445-1644.
School—10200 S. Washtenaw Ave., 60642. Tel: 773-445-4737.
Sisters of St. Joseph (LaGrange, IL) 2; Lay Teachers 46; Students 775.

109—ST. JOSAPHAT, Revs. Dominic J. Grassi; Daniel R. Whiteside.
Res., 2311 N. Southport Ave., 60614. Tel: 773-327-8955; Fax: 773-327-2047.
School—2245 N. Southport Ave., 60614.
Lay Teachers 16; Students 296.

110—ST. JOSEPH, Rev. Sebastian C. Lewis, O.S.B.
Res., 1107 N. Orleans St., 60610. Tel: 312-787-7174; Fax: 312-787-9825.
School—Sisters 1; Lay Teachers 9; Students 210.

111—ST. JOSEPH, Revs. Anthony Cirignani, O.F.M.; Arturo Ocampo, O.F.M.; Bro. Mark Zapczynski, O.F.M.

Res., 4821 S. Hermitage Ave., 60609. Tel: 773-254-2366.
School—4800 S. Paulina St., 60609. Tel: 773-927-8312.
Sisters 5; Lay Teachers 15; Students 365.
High School—4831 S. Hermitage Ave., 60609.
Felician Sisters 3; Lay Teachers 20; Students 250.
Convent—4818 S. Paulina St., 60609.
Shrine—Shrine of St. Joseph.

112—St. Juliana, Revs. Philip J. Dressler; Donald J. Ahearn, Pastor Emeritus; Roger J. Caplis; Ms. Pam Francisco, Pastoral Assoc.; Deacons Michael Finnegan; Robert Ryan; Edward Dolan; Louis Wojtowicz.
Res., 7142 N. Osceola Ave., 60631. Tel: 773-631-4127; Fax: 773-631-4150.
School—7400 W. Touhy, 60648.
Lay Teachers 39; Religious 2; Students 723.

113—St. Kevin, Rev. Alfredo Gundrum, O.F.M.Cap.
Res., 10509 S. Torrence Ave., 60617. Tel: 773-721-2563.

114—St. Kilian, Revs. William E. Vanecko; John W. Shirey, (Retired).
Res., 8725 S. May St., 60620. Tel: 773-651-4000.

115—St. Ladislaus, Revs. Stephen F. Kanonik; William J. Lisowski, Pastor Emeritus; Walter J. Zmija, Pastor Emeritus; Peter Kreis (Poland); Marek Jurzyk (Poland).
Res., 5345 W. Roscoe St., 60641. Tel: 773-725-2300.
School—3330 N. Lockwood Ave., 60641. Tel: 773-545-5600.
Sisters of the Holy Family of Nazareth (Des Plaines, IL) 3; Lay Teachers 15; Students 358.

116—St. Laurence, Rev. Gerald K. O'Reilly; Deacons Willie Cooper; Roy Lilly.
Res., 7140 S. Dorchester Ave., 60619. Tel: 773-493-1118.

117—St. Leo The Great, Rev. Michael J. Furlan; Deacons Dorsey Chappell; Mervin O. Johnson. In res., Rev. Paschal Atomori.
Res., 7747 S. Emerald Ave., 60620. Tel: 773-846-6146.
School—7746 S. Emerald Ave., 60620. Tel: 773-483-2335.
Lay Teachers 11; Students 250.

118—Santa Lucia-Santa Maria Incoronata, Rev. Nicholas A. Marro, C.S.
Res., 3022 S. Wells St., 60616. Tel: 312-842-6115; Fax: 312-842-0103.
School—3017 S. Wells St., 60616. Geraldine Maratea, Prin.
Lay Teachers 11; Students 229.

119—St. Malachy, Rev. Ralph E. Starus.
Res., 2248 W. Washington Blvd., 60612. Tel: 312-733-1068.
School—2252 W. Washington Blvd., 60612.
Sisters 6; Brothers 2; Lay Teachers 10; Students 250.

120—St. Margaret of Scotland, Revs. Daniel J. Mallette; Robert A. Sheridan. In res., Rev. Claude Souffrant, S.J. (Haiti).
Res., 9837 S. Throop St., 60643. Tel: 773-779-5151; Fax: 773-779-6198.
School—9833 S. Throop St., 60643. Tel: 773-238-1088; Fax: 773-238-1033.
School Sisters of Notre Dame 3; Lay Teachers 15; Students 320.

121—St. Margaret Mary, Revs. Mark B. Sorvillo; John J. O'Shea, (Retired); Deacon Thomas Stanton. In res., Revs. Oliver Nwachukwu; William T. Corcoran.
Res., 2324 W. Chase Ave., 60645. Tel: 773-764-0615; Fax: 773-764-0641.
School—Tel: 773-764-0641.
Lay Teachers 21; Students 455.

122—Santa Maria Addolorata, Revs. Louis Gandolfi, C.S.; Alex Peloso, C.S., Pastor Emeritus; Miguel Alvarez, C.S.; Deacons Arthur DeLuna; Luis Perez.
Res., 528 N. Ada St., 60622. Tel: 312-421-3122.
School—1337 W. Ohio St., 60622. Tel: 312-421-5482.
Joliet Franciscan 1; Sisters of the Holy Family of Nazareth 1; Lay Teachers 8; Students 219.

123—St. Mark, Rev. Domingo Hurtado-Badillo; Deacons Jorg Gutierrez; Abraham Rosa; Andrew Matuga; Ignacio Ortega; Antonio Villalobos; Mel Maldonado.
Res., 1048 N. Campbell Ave., 60622. Tel: 773-342-1516; Fax: 773-342-1372.
School—2510 W. Cortez St., 60622. Tel: 773-486-0430.
Sisters of Providence 3; Religious 1; Lay Teachers 9; Students 270.

124—St. Martin De Porres, Revs. Austin MacAdam, M.Afr.; Abdon Gamulani, M.Afr. (Malawi, Central Africa); Julien Cormier, M.Afr.
Res., 5112 W. Washington Blvd., 60644. Tel: 773-287-0206.
Schools—Resurrection, 5072 W. Jackson Blvd., 60661.
Sisters 4; Lay Teachers 17; Students 530; St. Thomas Aquinas, 116 N. LeClaire, 60644.
Lay Teachers 11; Students 310.

125—Old St. Mary, Revs. James W. Donovan, C.S.P.; Charles J. Brunick, C.S.P.; Richard C. Sparks, C.S.P. In res., Rev. James O'Gara, C.S.P.; Deacon Timothy Donovan.
Res., 21 E. Van Buren St., 60605. Tel: 312-922-3444; Fax: 312-922-3447.

126—St. Mary, Rev. Joseph T. Cook; Deacons John Amberg; Thomas Duffner.
Res., 310 E. 137th St., 60827. Tel: 773-568-1611; Fax: 773-568-6268.
School—Our Lady of the Gardens, 13300 S. Langley Ave., 60627. Tel: 773-568-4099.
Sisters 4; Lay Teachers 9.
Daughters of Charity.

127—St. Mary of the Angels, Revs. Hilary F. Mahaney; John P. Debicki. In res., Rev. Charles M. Ferrer.
Res., 1850 N. Hermitage Ave., 60622. Tel: 773-278-2644; Fax: 773-278-8904.
School—1810 N. Hermitage Ave., 60622.
Sisters of the Resurrection (Chicago, IL) 1; Lay Teachers 14; Students 240.

128—St. Mary of the Lake, Most Rev. Edwin M. Conway, Episcopal Vicar & Resident; Revs. Robert G. Mair; Eduardo Pinzon, S.J.; Deacon Paul Spalla, Pastoral Assoc. In res., Rev. Daniel J. Collins.
Res., 4200 N. Sheridan Rd., 60613. Tel: 773-472-3711.
School—1026 W. Buena Ave., 60613. Tel: 773-281-0018.
Lay Teachers 12; Students 225.

129—St. Mary Magdalene, Revs. Philip Howard, C.S.Sp.; Egbert J. Figaro, C.S.Sp.
Res., 8426 S. Marquette Ave., 60617. Tel: 773-768-1700; Fax: 773-734-8518.

130—St. Mary of Perpetual Help, Rev. Donald J. Mulsoff.
Res., 1039 W. 32nd St., 60608. Tel: 773-927-6646; Fax: 773-523-4565.
School—Participant in Bridgeport Catholic Academy. See separate listing under Consolidated Elementary Schools in the Institutions section.

131—St. Mary, Star of the Sea, Revs. Michael J. Adams; Ralph H. Zwirn; Robert A. Kilbridge, O.P.; Deacons Jesse Navarro; Gregory Serratore.
Res., 6435 S. Kilbourn Ave., 60629. Tel: 773-767-1246.
School—6424 S. Kenneth Ave., 60629.
Lay Teachers 32; Students 860.

132—St. Mary of the Woods, Revs. Gregory Sakwoicz; Leo Mahon, Pastor Emeritus; Andrew J. McDonagh, Pastor Emeritus; Deacon William Mages. In res., Rev. Thomas F. Maher.
Res., 7033 N. Moselle Ave., 60646. Tel: 773-763-0206; Fax: 773-763-4968.
School—Religious 1; Lay Teachers 26; Students 481.

133—Maternity of the Blessed Virgin Mary, Rev. Thomas Pelton; Deacons Jose R. Vazquez; Benito Velasco; Milton Rodriguez.
Res., 3647 W. North Ave., 60647. Tel: 773-772-9401; Fax: 773-772-7454.
School—1537 N. Lawndale Ave., 60651. Tel: 773-227-1140.
Sisters of Providence of Saint Mary-of-the-Woods, IN 2; Lay Teachers 14; Students 285.

134—St. Matthias, Revs. Miguel B. Alcantara; Thomas J. McHugh, Pastor Emeritus; Deacons John Fay; Andres Pecson; D.J. Shinkle. In res., Revs. Francis A. Cimarrusti; Romarico Eugenio (Philippines).
Res., 2310 W. Ainslie St., 60625. Tel: 773-561-6020.
School—4910 N. Claremont Ave., 60625.
Sisters 7; Lay Teachers 15; Students 387.

135—St. Maurice, Rev. Thomas Enneking; Sr. Marie Paryse, S.S.S.F., Pastoral Coord.; Deacon Dismas Fernandez.
Res., 3615 S. Hoyne Ave., 60609. Tel: 773-847-3357.
School—McKinley Park Catholic, 3625 S. Hoyne Ave., 60609.
Students 286.

136—St. Michael, Very Revs. James Keena, C.SS.R.; Edward Wilhelm, C.SS.R.; Kenneth Sedlak, C.SS.R. In res., Revs. Milton Girse, C.SS.R.; Albert Castellino, C.SS.R.; Francis Novak, C.SS.R.; John Andree, C.SS.R.; John Schmidt, C.SS.R.
Res., 1633 N. Cleveland Ave., 60614. Tel: 312-642-2498; Fax: 312-642-9283.
Perpetual Help Confraternity Office—Tel: 312-642-9399. Bro. Patrick Considine, C.SS.R.

137—St. Michael Archangel (Italian), Rev. Vincent Gennardo, C.S.
Res., 2325 W. 24th Pl., 60608. Tel: 773-847-2727; Fax: 773-847-7618.
School—2315 W. 24th Pl., 60608. Tel: 773-847-9070; Fax: 773-847-7618.
Missionary Sisters of St. Charles 4; Lay Teachers 6; Students 206.

138—St. Michael, Revs. Thomas R. Franzman; Joseph G. Nowak, Pastor Emeritus; Deacon Albin J. Wegner, Jr. In res., Rev. Daniel P. Borlick, C.M.
Res., 8237 South Shore Dr., 60617. Tel: 773-734-4921; Fax: 773-734-8723.
School—8231 South Shore Dr., 60617. Tel: 773-221-0212. Sr. Judine Hilbing, O.P., Prin.
Presentation of the Blessed Virgin Mary 1; Lay Teachers 12; Students 311.

139—St. Michael the Archangel (Slovak), Rev. John E. Tilford.
Res., 4821 S. Damen Ave., 60609. Tel: 773-523-1248.

140—St. Monica, Revs. Michael A. Wulsch; John T. Beyenka, Pastor Emeritus; David R. Straub; Sr. Kathleen Maloney, O.S.B., Pastoral Assoc. In res., Rev. Michaelsami Arockiam.
Office—5136 N. Nottingham Ave., 60656. Tel: 773-763-1661; Fax: 773-763-4917.
Res., 5135 N. Mont Clare Ave., 60656.
School—Tel: 773-631-7880; Fax: 773-631-3266.
Sisters 1; Lay Teachers 20; Students 437.

141—Nativity of the Blessed Virgin Mary, Revs. Michael T. Yakaitis, S.T.D.; John A. Kuzinskas, Pastor Emeritus; Anthony J. Zakarauskas, Pastor Emeritus; Vaclovas Zakarauskas, (Retired); Vito E. Mikolaitis, (Retired); Francis J. Kelpsas, (Retired).
Res., 6812 S. Washtenaw Ave., 60629. Tel: 773-776-4600; Fax: 773-776-0677.
School—6820 S. Washtenaw Ave., 60629. Tel: 773-476-0571.
Sisters of St. Casimir 3; Lay Teachers 8; Students 186.
Convent—6804 S. Washentaw Ave., 60629.

142—Nativity of Our Lord, Revs. James P. Kehoe; Edward P. O'Brien, Pastor Emeritus; Michael Flynn, O.Carm., Resident; Deacon Francis Henry.
Res., 653 W. 37th St., 60609. Tel: 773-927-6263.
School—Participant in Bridgeport Catholic Academy. See separate listing under Consolidated Elementary Schools in the Institutions section.

143—St. Nicholas of Tolentine, Revs. Stanley G. Rataj; Edward J. Brzozowski, Pastor Emeritus; Francis P. Cassidy; William Zimmer.
Res., 3721 W. 62nd St., 60629. Tel: 773-735-1121; Fax: 773-735-1135.
School—3743 W. 62nd St., 60629.
Lay Teachers 24; Students 503.

144—Notre Dame, Revs. Steven M. Lanza, Admin.; Michael T. Herman. In res., Most Rev. John R. Manz, Auxiliary Bishop of Chicago; Rev. Thomas Mulcrone, Chap. Chicago Fire Dept.; Deacons Candelario Rodriguez; Joseph Siranovic.
Res., 1335 W. Harrison St., 60607-3318. Tel: 312-243-7400; Fax: 312-243-7614.

145—Our Lady of Fatima, Revs. Anthony A. Englert; Pierre J. Barr, Pastor Emeritus; Raymond J. Gerrity, Pastor Emeritus; Richard J. Vogt, S.J.; Deacon Candido Torres.
Res., 2751 W. 38th Pl., 60632. Tel: 773-927-2421.
School—2744 W. Pershing Rd., 60632.
Lay Teachers 12; Students 325.

146—Our Lady Gate of Heaven, Rev. Kevin Covert, O.F.M.Cap. In res., Bro. Vincent L. Reyes, O.F.M.Cap.
Res., 2338 E. 99th St., 60617. Tel: 773-375-3059; Fax: 773-375-3091.

147—Our Lady of Good Counsel, Revs. James M. Hyland; Richard J. O'Donnell, Pastor Emeritus.
Res., 3528 S. Hermitage Ave., 60609. Tel: 773-523-3917.
School—McKinley Park Catholic. (Merged with St. Maurice & SS. Peter & Paul). 3540 S. Hermitage Ave., 60609.
Lay Teachers 6; Students 158.

148—Our Lady of Grace, Revs. Thomas A. Tivy; Stanley J. Rokicinski, Pastor Emeritus; Esequiel Sanchez; Sr. Florence Norton, S.P., Pastoral Assoc.; Deacons Russell Drinan; Enrique Alonso; James Kwasigroch; Gregorio Lugo; Carlos Nazario. In res., Rev. Lawrence E. Gorski.
Res., 2455 N. Hamlin Ave., 60647. Tel: 773-772-5900.
School—2446 N. Ridgeway Ave., 60647.
Dominican Sisters (Springfield, IL) 6; Lay Teachers 12; Students 286.

149—Our Lady of Guadalupe, Revs. Daniel Drinan, C.M.F.; Michael Fernandez, C.M.F.; Mark J. Brummel, C.M.F.; John-Marie Lemrise, C.M.F.; George Morgan, C.M.F.; Richard White, C.M.F.; Deacons Margarito Alvarez; Raul Nunez; Juan Valdivia.
Res., 3200 E. 91st, 60617. Tel: 773-768-0793.
School—Lay Teachers 12; Students 297.
Shrine—National Shrine of St. Jude. (Claretian Missionaries).

150—Our Lady Help of Christians, Rev. Kenneth M. Brigham.

Res., 832 N. Leclaire Ave., 60651. Tel: 773-287-0244.
School—847 N. Leamington, 60651. Tel: 773-626-5700.
Lay Teachers 10; Students 189.

151—OUR LADY OF LOURDES, Rev. Curtis Lambert; Deacons Roy Henry; John Klemanovic; Miguel Valle. In res., Revs. Carlos Liagas, S.J.; Manuel Duterte (Philippines).
Res., 4640 N. Ashland Ave., 60640. Tel: 773-561-2141; Fax: 773-561-9853.
School—4641 N. Ashland Ave., 60640. Mrs. Anne Balzanto, Prin.
Lay Teachers 15; Students 225.

152—OUR LADY OF LOURDES, Rev. Ramon Dompke, C.SS.R.; Sr. Caritas Wehrman, S.S.N.D., Pastoral Assoc.
Res., 1444 S. Keeler Ave., 60623. Tel: 773-762-5700; Fax: 773-762-5960.
School—Blessed Sacrament/Our Lady of Lourdes, Central Park and Cermak, 60623. Tel: 773-277-8575.
Students 250.

153—OUR LADY OF MERCY, Rev. Donald J. Headley. Pastoral Assocs.: Ms. Theresita Davila; Mr. Walter Fircowycz; Deacons Manuel R. Del llano; Roberto Rivas. In res., Revs. Patrick R. Lagges; Mathew Azhakatch, O.C.D.
Res., 4432 N. Troy St., 60625. Tel: 773-588-2620.
School—4416 N. Troy, 60625. Debbie Sullivan, Prin.
Lay Teachers 23; Students 307.

154—OUR LADY, MOTHER OF THE CHURCH, Rev. Daniel R. Fallon. Pastor Emeriti: Revs. Joseph F. Ognibene; Peter F. Hayes.
Res., 8747 W. Lawrence Ave., 60656. Tel: 773-625-3369; Fax: 773-625-0226.

155—OUR LADY OF MOUNT CARMEL, Revs. Thomas I. Healy; Frank J. Latzko; Deacon Edmund Gronkiewicz. In res., Rev. Peter Snieg.
Res., 690 W. Belmont Ave., 60657. Tel: 773-525-0453; Fax: 773-525-9438.
School—708 W. Belmont Ave., 60657. Tel: 773-525-8779.
Lay Teachers 19; Students 335.

156—OUR LADY OF PEACE, Rev. Lawrence M. Duris; Deacon John Hill; Dr. Sloan T. Letman, Pastoral Coord.
Res., 7851 S. Jeffrey Ave., 60649. Tel: 773-768-0105; Fax: 773-721-3835.
School—Lay Teachers 11; Students 220.

157—OUR LADY OF POMPEII. Closed. For inquiries for parish records contact the Chancery.

158—OUR LADY OF THE SNOWS, Rev. James A. Mezydlo. In res., Rev. Dennis A. Ziomek.
Res., 4858 S. Leamington Ave., 60638. Tel: 773-582-2266.
School—4810 S. Leamington Ave., 60638. Tel: 773-735-4810.
Lay Teachers 11; Students 220.

159—OUR LADY OF SORROWS, BASILICA OF, Rev. Joseph M. Chamblain, O.S.M., Admin.; Deacon Joseph Lewis.
Res., 3121 W. Jackson Blvd., 60612. Tel: 773-638-5800; Fax: 773-638-3036.
School—3141 W. Jackson Blvd., 60612. Tel: 773-638-5010.
Lay Teachers 9; Students 180.

160—OUR LADY OF TEPEYAC, Revs. James W. Miller; Mark J. Krylowicz; Sr. Carol Ann Berte, O.S.F., Pastoral Assoc.; Deacons Ramon Echeverria; Vincente Limon.
Res., 2226 S. Whipple St., 60623. Tel: 773-521-8400; Fax: 773-927-1610.
School—2235 S. Albany, 60623.
Lay Teachers 9; Students 165.
High School—2228 S. Whipple St., 60623.
Felician Sisters 2; Sisters of the Resurrection (Chicago) 1; Lay Teachers 12; Students 195.

161—OUR LADY OF VICTORY, Revs. Daniel P. McCarthy; Gary J. Lewanski; Deacons Robert Leck; Rudolph Schoewe; Dennis Ranke. In res., Revs. Norbert J. Zawistanowicz, (Retired); Edward M. Mikolajczyk; Denis Carneiro.
Res., 5212 W. Agatite Ave., 60630. Tel: 773-286-2950; Fax: 773-286-8579.
School—4434 N. Laramie, 60630. Tel: 773-283-2229; Fax: 773-283-0842.
School Sisters of St. Francis 1; Lay Teachers 30; Students 511.
Convent—5240 W. Agatite Ave., 60630.
School Sisters of St. Francis 5.

162—OUR LADY OF AGLONA (Latvian), (Independent Mission), Revs. Boleslaus Baginskis, M.I.C.; Victor Civzelis, M.I.C.
Res., 2541 W. Wabansia, 60647. Tel: 773-276-9566.

163—ST. PANCRATIUS, Revs. Andrew P. Wypych; Walter Stefanski, Pastor Emeritus.
Res., 4025 S. Sacramento Ave., 60632. Tel: 773-523-5666; Fax: 773-523-5666.
School—2940 W. 40th Pl., 60632.
Franciscan Sisters of Chicago 2; Lay Teachers 9; Students 200.

164—ST. PASCAL, Revs. Gary M. Miller; Tirso S. Villaverde; Edmund J. Fitzpatrick, Liturigal Assistance; Deacons Eugene Dorgan; Thomas Stubstad; Ms. Catherine Crino, Pastoral Assoc.
Res., 3935 N. Melvina Ave., 60634. Tel: 773-725-7641; Fax: 773-725-9368.
School—6143 W. Irving Park Rd., 60634. Tel: 773-736-8806.
Lay Teachers 25; Students 543.
Convent-Senior Center—3954 N. Meade Ave., 60634. Tel: 773-545-9453.

165—ST. PATRICK, Revs. John J. Wall; John C. Cusick; Gene F. Smith; Anthony Aravindassery (India).
Res., 700 W. Adams St., 60606. Tel: 312-782-6171.

166—ST. PAUL, Revs. George Ruffolo, C.M.F.; Marco Cardenas, C.M.F.; Wayne Schimmelman, C.M.F.; John Molyneus, C.M.F.
Res., 2127 W. 22nd Pl., 60608. Tel: 773-847-7622; Fax: 773-847-8687.
School—2114 W. 22nd Pl., 60608. Tel: 773-847-6078.
Sisters 3; Lay Teachers 8; Students 275.

167—ST. PETER'S, Revs. Thomas Aldworth; Thomas Fratus, O.F.M.; Wenceslaus Church, O.F.M.
Res., St. Peter's Friary, 110 W. Madison St., 60602. Tel: 312-372-5111; Fax: 312-853-2361.
Priests 21; Brothers 9. (For complete listing see Section [N] Residences of Priests and Brothers.).

168—ST. PETER CANISIUS, Rev. Robert E. Bridge; Deacon Jose Gonzalez. In res., Rev. John T. Hillenbrand.
Res., 5057 W. North Ave., 60639-4565. Tel: 773-637-2075; Fax: 773-889-3929.

169—SS. PETER AND PAUL, Revs. Robert C. Behnke, Admin.; Bruno B. Grinis, Pastor Emeritus.
Res., 12433 S. Halsted St., 60628. Tel: 773-785-1200.

170—SS. PETER AND PAUL, Revs. Robert J. Roll; Joseph F. Mytych, Pastor Emeritus; Michael V. Kalck; Steven Bauer, O.S.C.
Res., 3745 S. Paulina St., 60609. Tel: 773-523-3410; Fax: 773-523-0540.
Convent—1640 W. 38th St., 60608. Tel: 773-523-0916.
Felician Sisters 3; Poor Handmaids of Jesus Christ 2.

171—ST. PHILIP NERI, Revs. Lawrence M. Duris; William H. Sheridan; Deacon Wilmer Hatch.
Res., 2132 E. 72nd St., 60649. Tel: 773-363-1700.
School—2110 E. 72nd St., 60649.
Lay Teachers 13; Students 345.

172—ST. PHILOMENA, Revs. Daniel J. Cassidy; Charles G. Lenaghan, S.J.; Stephen F. Lesniewski; Lys Florival, C.S.Sp.; Deacons Francisco Ramos; Pedro Soto; Israel Valentin; Edwin Martinez; Benjamin Diaz.
Res., 1921 N. Kedvale Ave., 60639. Tel: 773-489-1100.
School—4131 W. Cortland Ave., 60639.
Lay Teachers 10; Students 250.

173—ST. PIUS V, Revs. Charles W. Dahm, O.P.; Matthias R. Mueller, O.P.; Antonio Romero, O.P.
Res., 1914 S. Ashland Ave., 60608. Tel: 312-829-1931; Fax: 312-226-6119.
School—1919 S. Ashland Ave., 60608. Mrs. Nancy Nasko, Prin.
Dominican Sisters 1; Lay Teachers 9; Students 268.
Shrine—Shrine of St. Jude Thaddeus.

174—PRECIOUS BLOOD, Revs. William Mason, O.M.I.; Mark Stroba, O.M.I.; Mr. Sabino Gaytan, Pastoral Assoc. (Hispanic Community); Deacon Mario Avila. In res., Revs. Gregory Cholewa, O.M.I.; Joseph A. Pitts, O.M.I.
Res., 2411 W. Congress Pkwy., 60612. Tel: 312-733-5331.
School—Campus No. Two—Our Lady of the Westside School. See St. Agatha Parish listing for further details.

175—PRESENTATION, Revs. Thomas P. Walsh; Mark Kalema (Uganda); Ms. Latessa Harper, Pastoral Assoc.
Res., 734 S. Springfield Ave., 60624. Tel: 773-533-2820; Fax: 773-638-2803.
School—Campus No. Three—Our Lady of the Westside School. See St. Agatha Parish listing for further details.

176—ST. PRISCILLA, Revs. John J. Cunningham; Darrio L. Boscutti; Albert Tanghal; Deacons Robert Odegard; Fred Spitzerri. In res., Rev. Albert Judy, O.P.
Res., 6949 W. Addison St., 60634. Tel: 773-545-8840; Fax: 773-545-8919.
School—7011 W. Addison St., 60634. Tel: 773-685-3581.
Lay Teachers 24; Students 510.

177—ST. PROCOPIUS, Revs. James G. Gartland, S.J.; Charles W. Niehaus, S.P. In res., Rev. John P. Foley, S.J.
Res., 1641 S. Allport St., 60608. Tel: 312-226-7887.
School—Lay Teachers 10; Students 220.

178—PROVIDENCE OF GOD, Rev. Robert R. Perez; Deacon Max Carrizales.
Res., 717 W. 18th St., 60616. Tel: 312-226-2929; Fax: 312-226-3694.

179—QUEEN OF ALL SAINTS BASILICA, Revs. Wayne F. Prist; H. Robert Clark, Pastor Emeritus; Thomas J. Bradley; Mrs. Charlene Keane, Pastoral Assoc.; Deacons Michael Monnelly; Raymond Ward. In res., Revs. Wayne F. Watts; George Velloorattil.
Res., 6280 N. Sauganash Ave., 60646. Tel: 773-736-6060; Fax: 773-736-6099.
School—Sisters 3; Lay Teachers 28; Students 759.
Convent—6275 N. Ionia Ave., 60646.

180—QUEEN OF ANGELS, Revs. William J. O'Brien; Thomas E. Lamping; Terence M. Keehan; Deacon Donald O'Grady, (Retired).
Res., 2330 W. Sunnyside Ave., 60625. Tel: 773-561-5118; Fax: 773-561-2510.
School—4520 N. Western Ave., 60625. Tel: 773-769-4211; Fax: 773-769-4289.
Lay Teachers 23; Students 411.

181—QUEEN OF THE UNIVERSE, Revs. Lawrence R. McNally; Richard L. Skriba; Michael G. McGovern.
Res., 7114 S. Hamlin Ave., 60629. Tel: 773-582-4662; Fax: 773-581-3313.
School—7130 S. Hamlin Ave., 60629.
Lay Teachers 19; Students 377.

182—ST. RENE GOUPIL, Revs. Peter P. Paurazas; Edward M. Flannery, Pastor Emeritus; Deacon Owen Boehm. In res., Rev. James Sweeney, M.H.M.
Res., 6949 W. 63rd Pl., 60638. Tel: 773-229-8523.
School—6340 S. New England Ave., 60638. Valerio Bellucci, Prin.
Sisters 1; Lay Teachers 13; Students 330.

183—RESURRECTION, Revs. Jesus P. Garza, Admin.; Phillip C. Kiley; Deacons Efrain Ayala; Paul Bovyn; Feliciano Crespo; George Fuller, (Retired); Camilo Vera.
Business Office: 3043 N. Francisco Ave., 60618. Tel: 773-478-9705; Fax: 773-478-1387.
Res., 2840 W. Nelson St., 60618. Tel: 773-478-1441.
School—2845 W. Barry, 60618. Tel: 773-478-9191.
Lay Teachers 12; Students 280.

184—ST. RICHARD, Revs. Jerome S. Siwek; Roger Kutzner; Andrew S. Grzela; Deacons Albert Schroetlin; George Steinhable.
Res., 5032 S. Kostner Ave., 60632. Tel: 773-585-1221; Fax: 773-585-4959.
School—5025 S. Kenneth Ave., 60632. Tel: 773-582-8083.
Lay Teachers 13; Students 292.

185—ST. RITA OF CASCIA, Revs. William E. Lego, O.S.A.; Edward J. Kersten, O.S.A.; Robert F. Dueweke, O.S.A.; Bro. William Wiegel, O.S.A.; Deacon Juan Rodriguez. In res., Rev. John J. Dowling, O.S.A.
Res., 6243 S. Fairfield Ave., 60629. Tel: 773-434-9600; Fax: 773-434-9668.

186—ST. ROBERT BELLARMINE, Rev. Michael A. Goergan; Deacon Edward Swiech. In res., Rev. L. Scott Donahue.
Res., 4646 N. Austin Ave., 60630. Tel: 773-777-2666; Fax: 773-777-2770.
School—6036 W. Eastwood Ave., 60630.
Sisters 6; Lay Teachers 20; Students 402.

187—ST. ROMAN, Rev. Juan J. Huitrado; Deacon Jose Marrero; Sr. Ma del Refugio Gutierrez, D.R.E.
Res., 2311 S. Washtenaw Ave., 60608. Tel: 773-247-6645; Fax: 773-927-1610.

188—ST. SABINA, Rev. Michael L. Pfleger.
Res., 1210 W. 78th Pl., 60620. Tel: 773-483-4300.
School—7801 S. Throop St., 60620.
Dominican Sisters (Sinsinawa, WI) 3; Congregation of Mother of Carmel 4; Lay Teachers 25; Students 514.

189—SACRED HEART (Croatian), Revs. Paul Maslach, O.F.M.; Jago Soce, O.F.M.
Res., 2864 E. 96th St., 60617. Tel: 773-768-1423; Fax: 773-768-3750.
School—2906 E. 96th St., 60617.
School Sisters of St. Francis 3; Lay Teachers 8; Students 220.

190—SACRED HEART MISSION OF HOLY NAME OF MARY, Rev. Anthony J. Vader.
Res., 11652 S. Church St., 60643. Tel: 773-238-6800; 233-3955.

191—ST. SIMON THE APOSTLE, Rev. Francis Q. Kub; Laura L. Zbella, Pastoral Assoc.; Deacon Angelo Cordoba. In res., Rev. Charles J. Kouba, (Retired).
Res., 5157 S. California Ave., 60632. Tel: 773-436-1045; Fax: 773-436-4684.
School—5135 S. California Ave., 60632. Tel: 773-434-5036.
Sisters of SS. Cyril & Methodius 3; Lay Teachers 9;

Students 264.

192—St. Stanislaus, Bishop and Martyr, Revs. Anthony Dziorek, C.R.; Francis Grzechowiak, C.R.; Marion Wroblewski, C.R.; Jacek Praski; Deacons Zygfryd Oborski; Mitchell Szady.
Res., 5352 W. Belden Ave., 60639. Tel: 773-237-5800; Fax: 773-237-7029.
School—2342 N. Lorel Ave., 60639. Tel: 773-622-3342; Fax: 773-622-9160.
Franciscan Sisters of Chicago 2; Lay Teachers 20; Students 400.

193—St. Stanislaus Kostka (Polish, Spanish, English), Revs. Anthony Bus, C.R.; Emil Stec, C.R.; Deacons Nicolas Flores; Miguel Garcia; Juan Ibarra.
Res., 1351 W. Evergreen Ave., 60622. Tel: 773-278-2470; Fax: 773-278-2471.
School—1255 N. Noble St., 60622.
Sisters 2; Lay Teachers 9; Students 197.

194—St. Stephen, Revs. Blase Chemazar, O.F.M.; Callistus F. Langerholz, O.F.M.; Deacon John Vidmar.
Res., 1852 W. 22nd Pl., 60608. Tel: 773-376-4334; Fax: 773-376-3303.

195—St. Stephen, King of Hungary, Rev. Joseph Somos (STL).
Res., 2015 W. Augusta Blvd., 60622. Tel: 773-486-1896; Fax: 773-486-1902.

196—St. Sylvester, Revs. Kevin J. Feeney; Joseph Tito; Deacons Confessor DeJesus; Sigifredo Ortiz; Santos Soto; Francisco Roman; Harry Kowalski.
Res., 2157 N. Humboldt Blvd., 60647. Tel: 773-235-3646; Fax: 773-489-0974.
School—Sisters 3; Lay Teachers 15; Students 351.

197—St. Symphorosa and Seven Sons, Revs. Marcel J. Pasciak; Francis N. Maniola, Pastor Emeritus; Norman J. Trela.
Res., 6135 S. Austin Ave., 60638. Tel: 773-767-1523.
School—6125 S. Austin Ave., 60638.
Benedictine Sisters of Pontifical Jurisdiction 3; Lay Teachers 28; Students 609.

198—St. Tarcissus, Revs. John J. Grace; Leonard J. Felczak, Pastor Emeritus; Thomas F. Baldonieri; Sleeva R. Policetti; Deacon Gregory M. Bzdon. In res., Revs. William T. Hock; Bruno Switalski.
Res., 6020 W. Ardmore Ave., 60646. Tel: 773-763-8228.
School—6040 W. Ardmore Ave., 60646. Tel: 773-763-7080.
Lay Teachers 30; Students 712.

199—St. Teresa, Rev. John R. Hoffman; Deacon Hector Rivera. In res., Rev. R. Peter Bowman.
Res., 1037 W. Armitage Ave., 60614. Tel: 773-528-6650; Fax: 773-871-6766.

200—St. Thaddeus, Rev. John M. Collins; Deacon Jimmie Flewellen.
Res., 9540 S. Harvard Ave., 60628. Tel: 773-568-7077; Fax: 773-928-5447.
School—Lay Teachers 10; Students 265.

201—St. Thecla, Revs. Gerard E. Rogala; Matt A. Bednarz, Pastor Emeritus; Leon J. Rezula; Deacon Eugene Bates. In res., Rev. Adam Galek.
Res., 6725 W. Devon Ave., 60631. Tel: 773-792-3077; Fax: 773-792-3820.
School—6323 N. Newcastle Ave., 60631. Tel: 773-763-3380; Fax: 773-763-6151.
Lay Teachers 10; Students 323.

202—St. Therese of the Infant Jesus. Closed. For inquiries for parish records contact the Chancery. (The Little Flower).

203—St. Therese Catholic Chinese Church, Rev. Raymond P. Devereux, Temporary Admin.
Res., 218 W. Alexander St., 60616. Tel: 312-842-6777.
School—247 W. 23rd St., 60616.
Sisters 1; Lay Teachers 14; Students 240.

204—St. Thomas Apostle, Revs. John A. Farry; Thomas J. Fitzgerald, Pastor Emeritus; Thomas R. Seitz, (Retired); Deacon Robert Monica.
Res., 5472 S. Kimbark Ave., 60615. Tel: 773-324-2626; Fax: 773-753-7415.
School—5467 S. Woodlawn Ave., 60615. Tel: 773-667-1142; Fax: 773-753-7434.
Dominican Sisters (Sinsinawa, WI) 3; Lay Teachers 20; Students 444.

205—St. Thomas of Canterbury, Revs. Richard T. Simon; Trinh Peter Hung (SCL) (Vietnamese Apostolate); Deacons Richard Leigh; Orlando Perez; Duc Nguyen. In res., Rev. Peter T. Nguyen.
Res., 4827 N. Kenmore Ave., 60640. Tel: 773-878-5507.
School—Lay Teachers 11; Students 275.

206—St. Thomas More, Revs. Anthony J. Brankin; Theodore McNulty; John J. Sullivan; John P. Frawley, (Retired); Thomas J. Curley, (Retired).
Res., 2825 W. 81st St., 60652. Tel: 773-436-4444.
School—8130 S. California Ave., 60652. Tel: 773-434-4575; Fax: 773-434-2026.
Dominican Sisters (Sinsinawa, WI) 3; Lay Teachers 17; Students 305.

207—St. Timothy, Revs. Harold B. Murphy; Gilbert A. Carroll, Pastor Emeritus. In res., Rev. Maximus Ssekiwala (Uganda).
Res., 6326 N. Washtenaw Ave., 60659. Tel: 773-262-6600; Fax: 773-262-9214.

208—Transfiguration of Our Lord, Rev. John J. Rudnik. In res., Revs. Kevin Ugomadi; Americo Dalbelo, C.S.S.R.; Ricardo Recera.
Res., 2609 W. Carmen Ave., 60625. Tel: 773-561-7953.
School—5044 N. Rockwell, 60625. Tel: 773-334-0239; Fax: 773-334-0107.
Lay Teachers 10; Students 198.

209—St. Turibius, Revs. Raymond M. Barlog; Michael Bowler; Rev. Msgr. Joseph Mroczkowski, Pastor Emeritus; Rev. Waldemar Dynak. In res., Rev. Stanley J. Rokicinski.
Res., 5646 S. Karlov Ave., 60629. Tel: 773-581-2730.
School—4120 W. 57th St., 60629. Tel: 773-585-5150; Fax: 773-585-5328.
Felician Sisters 4; Lay Teachers 19; Students 470.

210—St. Viator, Revs. William L. Carpenter, C.S.V.; Robert T. Bolser, C.S.V.; C. Gregory Jones, C.S.V.; Bro. Dan Belanger, C.S.V.; Deacon Camillo Vera.
Res., 4170 W. Addison St., 60641. Tel: 773-286-4040; Fax: 773-286-4058.
School—4140 W. Addison St., 60641. Tel: 773-545-2173; Fax: 773-545-1683.
Sisters of St. Joseph of Carondelet (St. Louis, MO) 4; Lay Teachers 28; Students 520.

211—St. Vincent de Paul, Rev. Donald Ours, C.M.
Res., 1010 W. Webster Ave., 60614. Tel: 773-327-1113; Fax: 773-327-2326.

212—St. Walter, Revs. John M. Sevick; Joseph D. Ryan, (Retired); Sr. Margaret Mary Kowalczyk, C.S.F.M., Pastoral Assoc.; Deacons Thomas O'Connell; Daniel Carroll; Donald Niersbach.
Res., 11722 S. Oakley Ave., 60643. Tel: 773-779-1515; Fax: 773-779-0381.
School—11741 S. Western Ave., 60643. Tel: 773-445-8850.
Lay Teachers 9; Students 224.

213—St. Wenceslaus, Rev. Eugene R. Winkowski.
Res., 3400 N. Monticello Ave., 60618. Tel: 773-588-1135.

214—St. William, Revs. William J. Hastings; Henry J. Michalek, Pastor Emeritus; Michael G. Zaniolo; Thomas Hoffman; Deacons Christopher Virruso; Dennis Colgan.
Res., 2600 N. Sayre Ave., 60635. Tel: 773-637-6565; Fax: 773-745-4200.
School—2559 N. Sayre Ave., 60635.
Lay Teachers 25; Students 320.

OUTSIDE THE CITY OF CHICAGO

Alsip, Cook Co., St. Terrence, Revs. William J. Lyons; Patrick J. O'Neill.
Res., 4300 W. 119th Pl., 60803. Tel: 708-597-0970; Fax: 708-597-9118.

Antioch, Lake Co., St. Peter, Revs. Ronald H. Anglim; William J. Costello; Deacons Robert A. Gagnon; Frank M. Colette, (Retired); Paul M. Neurauter; Jeffrey Barton.
Res., 557 W. Lake St., 60002. Tel: 847-395-0274; Fax: 847-395-4553.
School—Lay Teachers 12; Students 288.

Argo, Cook Co., St. Blase, Rev. Norbert J. Waszak; Deacon Antonio Ponce. In res., Most Rev. Alfred L. Abramowicz, D.D.; Rev. Joseph Mytych.
Res., 6101 S. 75th Ave., 60501. Tel: 708-458-0007.

Arlington Heights, Cook Co., St. Edna, Revs. John J. Hurley; Daniel F. Sullivan; Deacons Raymond Graffia, Jr.; Robert Manthie; Vern Valenziano. In res., Rev. Eugene J. Faucher.
Res., 2525 N. Arlington Heights Rd., 60004. Tel: 847-398-3362; Fax: 847-394-5226.

St. James, Revs. William J. Zavaski; William J. Vollmer; Timothy J. Fairman; Sr. Kathleen A. Donohoe, O.S.F., Pastoral Assoc.; Deacons Richard Dinneen; Robert Plantz; Joseph Phillippi; Louis Lekan; John Lyons, (Retired); Armand Ferrani; Matt Hennessy.
Office: 820 N. Arlington Heights Rd., 60004. Tel: 847-253-6305; Fax: 847-253-0269.
School—821 Arlington Heights Rd., 60004.
Lay Teachers 35; Students 939.

Our Lady of the Wayside, Revs. Vincent F. Costello; Ronald C. Lewandowski; John J. Mackin, Pastor Emeritus; Harold T. O'Hara, Pastor Emeritus; Deacons Robert Duffy; Donald Grossnickle; Brendan Foley; Denise Niziolek, Pastoral Assoc.
Res., 432 W. Park St., 60005. Tel: 847-253-5353; Fax: 847-253-7175.
School—Lay Teachers 42; Students 634.

Barrington, Lake Co., St. Anne, Revs. John W. Dewes; Arthur J. Dillon, Pastor Emeritus; James F. Hurlbert; Deacons Richard Baum; Robert C. Brauch; James Condill; Richard Seveska.
Res., 120 N. Ela St., 60010. Tel: 847-382-5300; Fax: 847-382-5363.
School—312 E. Chestnut St., 60010.
School Sisters of St. Francis 6; Lay Teachers 30; Students 625.

Bartlett, Cook Co., St. Peter Damian, Revs. William L. Lupo; Jerome G. Klug, Pastor Emeritus; Deacons David Sattler; Robert Newton.
Res., 109 S. Crest Ave., 60103. Tel: 630-837-5411; Fax: 630-837-9424.

Bellwood, Cook Co., St. Simeon, Revs. John J. McCarville; Mariano L. Vita, Pastor Emeritus. In res., Rev. Joseph Ekpo.
Res., 430 Bohland Ave., 60104. Tel: 708-547-6868.
School—501 Bellwood Ave., 60104. Tel: 708-547-7350.
Lay Teachers 13; Students 200.

Berwyn, Cook Co., St. Leonard, Rev. William J. Curran; Rev. Msgr. John J. Farrell, Pastor Emeritus; Revs. Kenneth S. Laske; Edward G. Corcoran; Deacon Joel Chrastka.
Res., 3318 S. Clarence Ave., 60402. Tel: 708-484-0015; Fax: 708-484-6982.
School—3322 S. Clarence Ave., 60402. Tel: 708-749-3666.
Lay Teachers 19; Students 406.
Convent—6634 W. 34th St., 60402. Sisters of St. Joseph (La Grange, IL)

St. Mary of Celle, Rev. Richard J. Prendergast; Deacon Larry Spohr. In res., Rev. Keith McClellan, O.S.B.
Res., 1428 Wesley Ave., 60402. Tel: 708-788-0876; Fax: 708-788-0242.
School—1448 S. Wesley Ave., 60402. Tel: 708-749-1989.
Lay Teachers 14; Students 192.

St. Odilo, Rev. Peter J. Cyscon. In res., Revs. Richard B. Saudis; Thomas J. Kaveney, (Retired); William P. Fegan.
Res., 2244 S. East Ave., 60402. Tel: 708-484-2161.
School—2301 S. Clarence Ave., 60402. Tel: 708-484-0755. William Donegan, Prin.
Sisters of Charity B.V.M. 2; Lay Teachers 14; Students 299.
National Shrine—Poor Souls.

Blue Island, Cook Co., St. Benedict, Revs. George L. Schopp; Edward P. Connors, Pastor Emeritus; Kevin M. Birmingham; John Bola Atoyebi (Nigeria); Deacons Thomas Grotto; Juan Limon; Ellery Shandro; Jose Zapata.
Res., 2339 York St., 60406. Tel: 708-385-8510; Fax: 708-371-2631.
School—2324 New St., 60406.
School Sisters of Notre Dame 1; Adrian Dominicans 3; Lay Teachers 7; Students 299.
Mission—Robbins, Cook Co., St. Peter Claver, 14125 Claire Blvd., Robbins, 60472. Tel: 708-389-2434.

St. Donatus, Revs. Robert Kleiner, M.C.C.J.; Aldo Pozza, M.C.C.J.; Hugo Riva, M.C.C.J.
Res., 1939 Union St., 60406. Tel: 708-385-2890; Fax: 708-385-4708.

St. Isidore, Revs. Gregory A. Rom; Sylvester W. Dudzinski, Pastor Emeritus; Sr. Patricia Walsh, O.P., Pastoral Assoc.
Res., 1811 W. Burr Oak Ave., 60406. Tel: 708-388-0807.
School—12731 S. Wood St., 60406. Tel: 708-388-6914.
Sisters 1; Lay Teachers 8; Students 163.

Bridgeview, Cook Co., St. Fabian, Revs. Walter J. Turlo; Walter A. Strus; Deacons Kenneth Schoenfeld; Kenneth Zawadzki.
Res., 8300 S. Thomas Ave., 60455. Tel: 708-599-1110; Fax: 708-599-0673.

Brookfield, Cook Co., St. Barbara, Revs. Maurice J. Kissane; Thomas A. Bernas; Sr. Margaret Halligan, C.S.J., Pastoral Assoc.; Deacons John Debnar; Robert Motycka; Gerald Fox. In res., Rev. John Birk (SPK).
Res., 4008 Prairie Ave., 60513. Tel: 708-485-0589.
School—8900 Windemere Ave., 60513.
Sisters 1; Lay Teachers 15; Students 255.

Buffalo Grove, Lake Co., St. Mary, Revs. Kenneth G. Kiepura; Donald J. Duffy, Pastor Emeritus; Thomas A. Bishop; John S. Plotkowski; Deacons I. James Young, M.D.; Dennis Brown; Robert LaCosse; Eugene Kukla; Bruce Peters; Kevin Kanter.
Res., 75 N. Buffalo Grove Rd., 60089. Tel: 847-541-1450; Fax: 847-541-2443. [CEM]
School—50 N. Buffalo Grove Rd., 60089.
Lay Teachers 45; Students 736.

Burbank, Cook Co., St. Albert the Great, Revs. Edward M. Mackowiak; Joseph P. Lynch, Pastor Emeritus; Frank J. Burek; Bruno Janik; Deacon Irvin Bryce.
Res., 5555 W. State Rd., 60459. Tel: 708-423-0321.
School—5535 W. State Rd., 60459. Tel: 708-424-7757.
Dominican Sisters (Adrian, MI) 2; Lay Teachers 22;

Students 400.

Burnham, Cook Co., Mother of God, Rev. Edmund F. Guz.
Res., 14207 S. Green Bay Ave., 60633. Tel: 708-862-8777; Fax: 708-891-1349.

Calumet City, Cook Co., St. Andrew the Apostle, Revs. Martin E. Michniewicz; Michael G. Zaniolo; Deacon Robert Banet.
Res., 768 Lincoln Ave., 60409. Tel: 708-862-4165; Fax: 708-862-4124.
School—331-155th Pl., 60409.
Sisters of the Holy Family of Nazareth (Des Plaines, IL) 2; Lay Teachers 17; Students 277.

Our Lady of Knock, Revs. Donald J. Fenske; Michael L. Zoufal; Sr. Alban Hermes, O.P., Pastoral Assoc.; Deacon Albert Lundy.
Res., 501 163rd St., 60409. Tel: 708-862-3011; Fax: 708-862-9618.
School—497 163rd St., 60409.
Lay Teachers 11; Students 231.

St. Victor, Revs. Thomas E. Cima; Peter Galek; Sr. Clara Chandler, H.M., D.R.E.; Deacons Eugene Cichoracki; Romeo Munoz; Daniel Ragonese; Ronald Schultz.
Res., 553 Hirsch Ave., 60409. Tel: 708-891-8920; Fax: 708-891-8943.
School—Lay Teachers 20; Students 365.

Calumet Park, Cook Co., Seven Holy Founders, Rev. Aldo Pozza, M.C.C.J.
Res., 12400 S. Ada St., 60643. Tel: 708-385-8459.

Chicago Heights, Cook Co., St. Agnes, Rev. John S. Siemanowski; Deacons Thomas Nowack; Raymond Deabel.
Res., 1501 Chicago Rd., 60411. Tel: 708-709-2694; Fax: 708-709-2693.
School—1501 Chicago Rd., 60411.
Sisters of St. Francis of the Perpetual Adoration 2; Lay Teachers 16; Students 290.

St. Kieran, Revs. William A. Eddy; Daniel A. Flens; Deacons Eugene La Belle; William Jablonski; Bernard Halper.
Res., 724 W. 195th St., 60411. Tel: 708-755-0074.
School—700 W. 195th St., 60411.
Lay Teachers 12; Students 250.

St. Paul, Revs. William T. O'Connor; Bernard G. Guirsch, Pastor Emeritus; Deacon Juan Garza.
Res., 206 E. 25th St., 60411. Tel: 708-754-3120; Fax: 708-754-0076.

Chicago Ridge, Cook Co., Our Lady of the Ridge, Rev. Paul Burak; Rev. Msgr. M. Edward Roche, Pastor Emeritus; Rev. Robert J. Keener; Sr. Dominic Krivich, O.S.F., Pastoral Assoc.; Deacon Michael Krapez.
Res., 10811 S. Ridgeland Ave., 60415. Tel: 708-425-3800; Fax: 708-425-2792.
School—10859 S. Ridgeland Ave., 60415. Tel: 708-424-4409.
Franciscan Sisters of Our Lady of Perpetual Help 2; Lay Teachers 11; Students 287.

Cicero, Cook Co.,

1—St. Anthony, Rev. James J. Kastigar; Deacons Alfonso Salgado; Claude Hensley. In res., Rev. Michael J. Bradley.
Res., 1515 S. 50th Ave., 60650. Tel: 708-652-0231; Fax: 708-652-0228.
St. Anthony Center—1506 S. 49th Ct., 60650. Tel: 708-652-0081; 656-7260.

2—St. Frances of Rome, Revs. Mark P. Canavan; Daniel P. Buck.
Res., 1428 S. 59th Ct., 60650. Tel: 708-652-2140; Fax: 708-652-6513.
School—1400 S. Austin Blvd., 60650. Tel: 708-652-2277.
School Sisters of Charity of the Incarnate Word (St. Louis, MO) 1; Lay Teachers 10; Students 200.

3—St. Mary of Czestochowa, (Polish), Rev. Thaddeus Dzieszko.
Res., 3010 S. 48th Ct., 60650. Tel: 708-652-0948.
School—3009 S. 49th Ave., 60650.
Sisters of St. Joseph of the Third Order of St. Francis 3; Lay Teachers 10; Students 221.

4—Mary, Queen of Heaven, Revs. John R. Price; Francis J. Spellman, Pastor Emeritus; Deacons Julio Rosado; Armando Herrera. In res., Rev. Edward N. Coffey.
Res., 5300 W. 24th St., 60804. Tel: 708-863-6608; Fax: 708-863-2349.
School—5314 W. 24th Pl., 60804. Tel: 708-652-6312.
Lay Teachers 10; Students 287.

5—Our Lady of Charity, Rev. Medard P. Laz, Admin. In res., Rev. John A. Rolek.
Res., 3600 57th Ct., 60650. Tel: 708-863-1207.
School—3620 57th Ct., 60650. Tel: 708-652-0262.
Lay Teachers 10; Students 212.
Convent—School Sisters of St. Francis 6.

6—Our Lady of the Mount, Revs. Joseph T. LeVoy; Gary W. Stefanski; Ramiro M. Trejo; Deacons Robert E. Devereux; William Ciston; Antonio Llano.
Res., 2414 S. 61st Ave., 60804. Tel: 708-652-2791; Fax: 708-863-6014.
School—2400 S. 61st Ave., 60804.
Lay Teachers 10; Students 310.

Country Club Hills, Cook Co., St. Emeric, Revs. Paul G. Seaman; John J. Rochford, Pastor Emeritus; Deacons James Detloff; Thomas O'Brien, (Retired).
Res., 4330 W. 180th St., 60478. Tel: 708-798-0757.
School—4300 W. 180th St., 60478.
Lay Teachers 6; Students 99.

Deerfield, Lake Co., Holy Cross, Rev. John M. Thinnes. Pastoral Assocs.: Sr. Dee Peppard, B.V.M.; Anne Schank; Deacons Thomas Bresler; Jerome Kasimatis; Anthony Sabato; Robert Smith. In res., Rev. Jeremiah M. Boland.
Res., 724 Elder Ln., 60015. Tel: 847-945-0430; Fax: 847-945-7651.
School—720 Elder Ln., 60015. Ms. Lorraine Gawlik, Prin.; Mrs. Marilyn Peters Krawczyk, D.R.E.
Lay Teachers 28; Students 440.

Des Plaines, Cook Co.,

1—St. Mary, Revs. Gene Dyer; Paul F. Rosemeyer, Pastor Emeritus; Flavio Gonzalez; Edward J. Barrett.
Res., 794 Pearson St., 60016. Tel: 847-824-8144; Fax: 847-824-3906.
School—Our Lady of Destiny (North Campus), 795 Center St., 60016.
Lay Teachers 7; Students 138.

2—St. Paul Chong Hasang, Cook, Rev. Thomas Kim.
Res., 675 Dursey Ln., 60016. Tel: 847-699-6334; Fax: 847-966-1029.

3—St. Stephen Protomartyr, Revs. Michael A. Olivero; Leonard T. Mezydlo, Pastor Emeritus; Deacon Donald J. Telposky.
1267 Everett Ave., 60018-2398. Tel: 847-824-2026; Fax: 847-824-3842.
School—Our Lady of Destiny (South Campus), 1880 Ash St., 60018-2343. Tel: 847-827-2900.
Lay Teachers 6; Students 130.

4—St. Zachary, Revs. Joseph P. McGinnity; Lawrence F. Springer; Deacons Peter N. Lagges; John J. Smith. In res., Rev. Thomas P. Conley, (Retired).
Res., 567 W. Algonquin Rd., 60016. Tel: 847-956-7020; Fax: 847-956-7313.
School—Sisters 2; Lay Teachers 13; Students 264.

Elk Grove Village, Cook Co., St. Julian Eymard Church, Rev. John F. Dedek.
Res., 601 Biesterfield Rd., 60007. Tel: 847-956-0130; Fax: 847-956-0189.

Queen of the Rosary, Revs. Arthur J. Fagan; Francis J. Cerniglia; John A. Robinson; Deacon Ted Czarnecki. In res., Rev. Robert L. Ebrom.
Res., 750 Elk Grove Blvd., 60007. Tel: 847-437-0403; Fax: 847-981-7192.
School—690 Elk Grove Blvd., 60007.
Lay Teachers 20; Students 370.

Elmwood Park, Cook Co., St. Celestine, Revs. Walter G. DeRoeck; Lawrence J. Sullivan. Pastoral Assocs.: Sr. Jean Schulte, R.S.M.; Deacons James Devine; Michael DeLarco; Gregory Stevens. In res., Rev. Bernard C. White.
Res., 3020 N. 76th Ct., 60707. Tel: 708-453-2555; Fax: 708-462-0560.
School—Lay Teachers 23; Students 606.

Evanston, Cook Co., St. Athanasius, Revs. William D. Mannion; James Heyd; Deacon Richard S. Jay.
Res., 1615 Lincoln St., 60201. Tel: 847-328-1430; Fax: 847-328-1809.
School—2510 Ashland, 60201. Tel: 847-864-2650.
Lay Teachers 25; Students 335.

St. Mary, Rev. Edward F. Hoover; Deacon John Arndt; Christopher M. Murphy, Pastoral Assoc. In res., Rev. Valerian Laini (Africa).
Res., 1012 Lake St., 60201. Tel: 847-864-0333.
Parish Center—Fax: 847-864-0354.
School—Consolidated with St. Nicholas Parish to form Pope John XXIII School. See St. Nicholas for further details.

St. Nicholas, Rev. Robert H. Oldershaw. In res., Rev. James R. Halstead, O.S.A.
Res., 806 Ridge Ave., 60202. Tel: 847-864-1185; Fax: 847-864-7810.
School—Consolidated with St. Mary Parish to form Pope John XXIII School. 1120 Washington, 60202. Tel: 847-475-5678. Mrs. Lucine Mastalerz, Prin.
Lay Teachers 20; Students 327.

Evergreen Park, Cook Co., St. Bernadette, Rev. David J. Byrne. In res., Revs. Alfredo J. Salera; Bernard Blasich.
Res., 9343 Francisco Ave., 60642. Tel: 708-422-8995; Fax: 708-422-8699.
School—9311 S. Francisco Ave., 60642. Tel: 708-422-6429.
Dominican Sisters (Springfield, IL) 2; Lay Teachers 19; Students 372.

Most Holy Redeemer, Revs. Richard J. Dempsey; Charles Ezerskis; Anthony L. Markus. In res., Rev. Albert R. Adamich, (Retired).
Res., 9525 S. Lawndale Ave., 60642. Tel: 708-425-5354.
School—3650 W. 96th St., 60642.
Sisters of the Holy Cross (South Bend, IN) 2; Lay Teachers 17; Students 492.

Queen of Martyrs, Revs. Patrick M. Lyons; William P. Murphy, Pastor Emeritus; Rev. Msgr. John J. Doyle; Deacon Charles Tipperrenter.
Res., 10233 S. Central Park, 60805-3799. Tel: 708-423-8110; Fax: 708-423-7372.
School—3550 W. 103rd St., 60805.
Lay Teachers 32; Students 688.

Flossmoor, Cook Co., Infant Jesus of Prague, Revs. Michael A. Hack; William J. Flaherty, Pastor Emeritus; Joseph D. Ryan, Pastor Emeritus; Richard L. Hills, Pastor Emeritus; Thomas Winnikates; Deacon George Brooks. In res., Rev. Matthias H. Hoffman.
Res., 1131 Douglas Ave., 60422. Tel: 708-799-5400.
School—1101 Douglas Ave., 60422.
Lay Teachers 22; Students 514.

Forest Park, Cook Co., St. Bernardine, Revs. Patrick M. Tucker; William J. Quinlan, Pastor Emeritus; Phillip F. Cioffi; Deacons Timothy Rehor; John Walters. In res., Rev. Francis J. Grady, S.S.C.
Res., 7246 Harrison St., 60130. Tel: 708-366-0839.
School—815 Elgin Ave., 60130.
Lay Teachers 16; Students 260.
Convent—816 Marengo Ave., 60130.

Franklin Park, Cook Co., St. Gertrude, Revs. Alfred P. Corbo; Ramon Perez; Deacons Robert Murphy; Sebastian Rivera; Lorenzo Chaidez. In res., Revs. William T. Hock, Pastor Emeritus; Edmund J. Schreiber.
Res., 9613 Schiller Blvd., 60131. Tel: 847-455-1100; Fax: 847-455-1209.

Glenview, Cook Co., St. Catherine Laboure, Revs. James P. Murphy; Joseph J. O'Brien; Deacons Ray Gavin; Michael Bretz; Frank Beil.
Res., 3535 Thornwood Ln., 60025. Tel: 847-729-1414.
School—3425 Thornwood Ln., 60025.
Sisters 1; Lay Teachers 16; Students 212.

Our Lady of Perpetual Help, Revs. John E. Flavin; Marc W. Reszel; Richard J. Jakubik; Deacons James Revord; Alan Sedivy.
Res., 1775 Grove St., 60025. Tel: 847-729-1525; Fax: 847-724-7025.
School—1123 Church St., 60025.
School Sisters of St. Francis 4; Lay Teachers 74; Students 1010.

Glenwood, Cook Co., St. John, Revs. John R. Kauzlarich; Stanley C. Limanowski, Pastor Emeritus.
Res., 301 S. Cottage Grove Ave., 60425. Tel: 708-758-5098.

Grayslake, Lake Co., St. Gilbert, Revs. Robert W. Beaven; Thomas Refermat; Deacons Chester Kozuchowski; Henry Iwan; Jeffrey Newman; Chris Monoello; Richard Globis.
Res., 301 E. Belvidere Rd., 60030. Tel: 847-223-4731.
School—251 E. Belvidere Rd., 60030. Tel: 847-223-8600.
Sisters of the Holy Family of Nazareth 2; Lay Teachers 24; Students 575.

Gurnee, Lake Co., St. Paul the Apostle, Revs. Farrell J. Kane, O.Carm.; Philip Nessinger, O.Carm.; Deacon Michael Penich.
Res., 6401 Gages Lake Rd., 60031. Tel: 847-918-0600; Fax: 847-918-0640.

Hanover Park, Cook Co., St. Ansgar, Revs. John W. Tapper; Jerome F. Riordan, Pastor Emeritus; Deacons Louis Barone; Nick Tereza; Robert Ziomek; Clemente Petricca; Oscar Monterroso; Jose Garcia; Ronald Weber.
Res., 2040 Laurel Ave., 60103. Tel: 630-837-5553; Fax: 630-837-9847.

Harvey, Cook Co., Ascension-St. Susanna, Rev. Joseph W. Altman; Deacons Thomas R. Carvlin; Henry Burke, Jr.
Res., 15234 Myrtle Ave., 60426. Tel: 708-333-0931; Fax: 708-333-3281.
School—Mary of Nazareth, 15727 S. Emerald Ave., 60426.
Sisters of the Holy Family of Nazareth 4; Lay Teachers 5; Students 201.

St. John the Baptist (Polish), Revs. Edward Romanski (Poland) Admin.; Clarence J. Juchcinski, Pastor Emeritus; Michael Wasiel, (Retired).
Res., 15746 Union Ave., 60426. Tel: 708-333-0184; Fax: 708-333-0861.
School—15727 Emerald Ave., 60426.
Sisters of the Holy Family of Nazareth (Des Plaines, IL) 3; Lay Teachers 8; Students 178.

Harwood Heights, Norridge, Cook Co., St. Rosalie, Revs. John C. Cain; Richard J. Ehrens; Deacon Joseph E. Bishop, Pastoral Assoc.
Res., 4401 N. Oak Park Ave., Harwood Heights-Norridge, 60656. Tel: 708-867-8817.

Hazel Crest, Cook Co., St. Anne, Rev. Leonard A. Dubi; Sr. Joan Klega, S.P., Pastoral Assoc.; Deacons John Leonas, (Retired); Theodore Perez; Herman Benthey; Steven Moore.
Res., 16802 S. Lincoln St., 60429. Tel: 708-335-3221; Fax: 708-335-1953.
School—16801 Dixie Hwy., 60429. Tel: 708-335-2288.
Lay Teachers 10; Students 263.
Early Learning Center—16777 Dixie Hwy., 60429. Tel: 708-335-4831.

Hickory Hills, Cook Co., St. Patricia, Revs. Gerald F. Mulcahy; Norbert A. Chapell, Pastor Emeritus; Michael E. Flynn; Joseph C. Mol; Deacons Charles Keegan; Norbert Weitendorf.
Res., 9050 S. 86th Ave., 60457. Tel: 708-598-5222; Fax: 708-598-5280.
School—9000 S. 86th Ave., 60457.
Sisters of the Holy Family of Nazareth (Des Plaines, IL) 4; Lay Teachers 17; Students 500.

Highland Park, Lake Co., Immaculate Conception, Revs. Robert L. Kealy; John E. O'Brien, Pastor Emeritus; Alec J. Wolff; Deacons Louis Vignocchi; William L. Moorman.
Res., 770 W. Deerfield Rd., 60035. Tel: 847-433-0130; Fax: 847-433-0669.

Highwood, Lake Co., St. James, Rev. James O'Malley; Deacons Bruno Pagliai; James Gallagher.
Res., 134 North Ave., 60040. Tel: 847-433-1494.
School—140 North Ave., 60040.
Lay Teachers 15; Students 206.

Hillside, Cook Co., St. Domitilla, Revs. Frank M. Falco, O.S.M.; Vincent M. O'Shea, O.S.M.; Deacons Angelo Marotto; Kenneth Bell. In res., Revs. Michael M. Guimon, O.S.M.; Christopher Krymski, O.S.M.; Bro. Bonfilius McGovern, O.S.M.
Res., 4940 Washington St., 60162. Tel: 708-449-8430; Fax: 708-449-2009.
School—601 Hillside Ave., 60162.
Sisters 4; Lay Teachers 10; Students 298.

Hoffman Estates, Cook Co., St. Hubert, Rev. Eugene J. Nowak; Deacon James Knippen. In res., Rev. Richard M. Zboroswki.
Res., 729 Grand Canyon St., 60194. Tel: 847-885-7700; Fax: 847-885-4631.
School—Lay Teachers 42; Students 822.

Hometown, Cook Co., Our Lady of Loretto, Revs. William A. Burke; John J. Mackin, (Retired); Sr. Kathryn McDonald, B.V.M., Pastoral Assoc.; Deacon Thomas Meehan.
Res., 8925 S. Kostner Ave., 60456. Tel: 708-424-7471; Fax: 708-424-7588.
School—Lay Teachers 13; Students 246.

Homewood, Cook Co., St. Joseph, Revs. James M. Sayers; Robert A. Stepek; Deacons Jack O'Leary; George Maddock.
Res., 17951 Dixie Hwy., 60430. Tel: 708-798-0622; Fax: 708-798-6137.
School—17949 Dixie Hwy., 60430.
Dominican Sisters (Adrian, MI) 1; Lay Teachers 17; Students 239.

Ingleside, Lake Co., St. Bede, Revs. John F. Krebs; Robert J. Fitzpatrick, Pastor Emeritus; John E. Hefferan; Deacons John McMahon; Edward Quackenbush.
Res., 36455 N. Wilson Rd., 60041. Tel: 847-587-2251; Fax: 847-973-1765.
School—36399 N. Wilson Rd., 60041.
Lay Teachers 13; Students 243.

Inverness, Cook Co., Holy Family, Revs. Patrick J. Brennan; George J. Kane, (Retired); Deacons Andrew Repak; Robert Anstiss.
Res., 2515 W. Palatine Rd., 60067. Tel: 847-359-0042; Fax: 847-359-0639.

La Grange, Cook Co., St. Cletus, Revs. Raymond F. Klees; Charles Gallagher, Pastor Emeritus; Tim Fiala; Deacon Walter Klimke, (Retired).
Res., 600 W. 55th St., 60525. Tel: 708-352-6209; Fax: 708-352-0707.
School—700 W. 55th St., 60525. Tel: 708-352-4820.
Lay Teachers 25; Students 417.

St. Francis Xavier, Revs. William J. Stenzel; Pierce J. Joyce, Pastor Emeritus; Michael J. Shanahan; Lawrence M. Lisowski.
Res., 124 N. Spring Ave., 60525. Tel: 708-352-0168; Fax: 708-352-4904.
School—145 N. Waiola Ave., 60525. Tel: 708-352-2175.
Lay Teachers 35; Students 549.

La Grange Park, Cook Co., St. Louise de Marillac, Revs. Fred W. Tomzik; Cletus J. Lynch, Pastor Emeritus; Michael J. Wanda; Deacons Michael McLynn; Dennis Huslig; David Kowalski; James Grevenites.
Res., 1144 Harrison Ave., 60526. Tel: 708-352-7388; Fax: 708-352-0714.
School—Lay Teachers 20; Students 250.
Youth Ministry—1125 Harrison Ave., 60526.

Lake Forest, Lake Co., St. Mary, Revs. George J. Rassas; Michael F. McMahon; James D. Brett, Pastor Emeritus; Deacons James L. Kenney; Joseph G. Krakora. Pastoral Assocs.: Joan O'Keefe; Patricia Moran.
Res., 175 E. Illinois Rd., 60045. Tel: 847-234-0205; Fax: 847-234-9860.
School—185 E. Illinois Rd., 60045. Tel: 847-234-0371; Fax: 847-234-9593.
Lay Teachers 36; Students 660.

St. Patrick, Rev. William J. McNulty.
Res., 991 S. Waukegan Rd., 60045. Tel: 847-234-1401; Fax: 847-234-1433.

Lake Villa, Lake Co., Prince of Peace, Revs. Richard M. Yanos; Richard W. Fassbinder, Pastor Emeritus; James F. Ouletta; Deacons Timothy Leonard; Leonard Milender.
Res., 135 S. Milwaukee Ave., 60046. Tel: 847-356-7915; Fax: 847-265-1678.
School—Lay Teachers 12; Students 225.

Lake Zurich, Lake Co., St. Francis de Sales, Revs. Ronald J. Gollatz; James E. Schmaus; James Swarthout.
Res., 277 E. Main St., 60047. Tel: 847-438-6622; Fax: 847-438-6638.
School—11 S. Buesching Rd., 60047.
Lay Teachers 25; Students 540.

Lansing, Cook Co., St. Ann, Revs. Michael A. Gabriel; Joseph P. Allen. Pastoral Assocs.: Deacons Richard Mauch, (Retired); John Rowe; D. Todd Williamson; Joseph T. Ceh.
Parish Office: 3010 Ridge Rd., 60438.
Res., 3026 Ridge Rd., 60438. Tel: 708-895-6700; Fax: 708-895-6877.
School—3014 Ridge Rd., 60438. Tel: 708-895-1661.
Lay Teachers 24; Students 549.

Lemont, Cook Co.,

1—St. Alphonsus, Revs. Kevin J. Spiess; Julian G. Grinis, Pastor Emeritus.
Res., 215 E. Logan, 60439. Tel: 630-257-2414; Fax: 630-257-2476.
School—St. Alphonsus-St. Patrick Consolidated, (Grades K-8) Admin. Office: 205 Cass St., 60439. Tel: 708-257-2380.
Sisters 4; Lay Teachers 9; Students 260.

2—Blessed Jurgis Matulaitis, Rev. Algirdas Paliokas, S.J.
Res., Lithuanian Catholic Mission, 14915 - 127th St., Unit 101, 60439. Tel: 708-257-5613.

3—SS. Cyril and Methodius, Revs. Victor J. Sivore; Richard M. Jozwiak, Pastor Emeritus; Peter Nowacki, O.P.; Deacons Norbert Lesnieski; Gilbert Ende.
Res., 608 Sobieski St., 60439. Tel: 630-257-2776; Fax: 630-257-9372.
School—607 Sobieski St., 60439. Tel: 630-257-6488; Fax: 630-257-6465.
Lay Teachers 14; Students 458.

4—St. James at Sag Bridge, Revs. Edwin V. Bohula; George F. Aschenbrenner, Pastor Emeritus; James P. Davitt, Pastor Emeritus.
Res., 106th Archer Rd., 60439. Tel: 708-257-7000; Fax: 708-257-7912. [CEM]

5—St. Patrick, Revs. Richard J. Shannon; John J. McCaig, Pastor Emeritus.
Res., 200 Illinois St., 60439. Tel: 630-257-6134; Fax: 630-257-0401.
School—St. Alphonsus-St. Patrick Consolidated, (Grades PreK-8) Admin. Office: 205 Cass St., 60439. Tel: 630-257-2380.
Lay Teachers 9; Students 255.

Libertyville, Lake Co., St. Joseph, Revs. John E. Hennessey; Ronald H. Folger; Deacons Dennis I. Mudd; Dennis J. Dunn; Robert E. Matthews. In res., Rev. Victor J. Ivers.
Res., 121 E. Maple Ave., 60048. Tel: 847-362-2073; Fax: 847-362-6821.
School—221 Park Pl., 60048. Tel: 847-362-0730.
Lay Teachers 31; Students 566.

Lyons, Cook Co., St. Hugh, Revs. Thomas A. Moran; James W. Keating, Pastor Emeritus; James F. Galivan.
Res., 7939 W. 43rd St., 60534. Tel: 708-447-3108; Fax: 708-447-9870.
School—4315 Joliet Ave., 60534.
Lay Teachers 13; Students 159.
Catechesis/Religious Programs—Tel: 708-447-5711.
Students 93.

Markham, Cook Co., St. Gerard Majella, Rev. Michael J. Nallen, Admin.
Res., 3536 W. 161st St., 60426. Tel: 708-331-8400.

Matteson, Cook Co., St. Lawrence O'Toole, Revs. James P. Finno; Andrew J. Santos, III; Danilo C. Soriano; Deacons Timothy Keating; Wayne Morton; Gerald Savercool; Ronald Zanardo.
Res., 4101 St. Lawrence Ave., 60443. Tel: 708-748-6090; Fax: 708-748-4055.
School—Lay Teachers 24; Students 519.

Maywood, Cook Co., St. Eulalia, Rev. James V. Quinlan; Rev. Msgr. William J. Quinn, Pastor Emeritus; Deacons Ben Bacchi; Giulio Camerini; George Lambert. In res., Rev. Robert A. Bacchi.
Res., 1851 S. 9th Ave., 60153. Tel: 708-343-6120.
School—815 Lexington St., 60153.
Sisters 4; Lay Teachers 10; Students 340.

St. James, Rev. Herbert J. Meyr; Sr. Jane McCarthy, O.S.F., Pastoral Assoc.; Deacons Antonio Maney; Roman Revering; Norberto Ojeda.
Res., 305 S. 6th Ave., 60153. Tel: 708-343-5210; Fax: 708-343-9317.

Melrose Park, Cook Co., St. Charles Borromeo, Rev. Claire Antonio Orso, C.S.; Deacon Dominic Marella.
Res., 1637 N. 37th Ave., 60160. Tel: 708-343-7646; Fax: 708-343-3527.

Our Lady of Mount Carmel (Italian), Revs. Richard Zanotti, C.S.; Vincent Cutrara, C.S.; Deacon Rafael Donates.
Res., 1101 N. 23rd Ave., 60160. Tel: 708-344-4140.
School—1102 N. 22nd Ave., 60160. Tel: 708-343-7030. Bro. Charles Muscat, C.S., D.R.E.
Lay Teachers 10; Students 239.

Sacred Heart, Revs. Cosmo F. Militello; Edward J. Kniewel, Pastor Emeritus; Richard J. Kozak; Deacons Raymond Behrendt; Victor Colucci; John Hendricks.
Res., 819 N. 16th Ave., 60160. Tel: 708-344-0757; Fax: 708-344-5906.
School—1503 W. Rice St., 60160.
Sisters of the Third Order of St. Francis of the Holy Family 1; Lay Teachers 20; Students 301.

Midlothian, Cook Co., St. Christopher, Revs. William E. Killeen; Terrence M. Johnson; Deacons Joseph Brady; Charles Yucuis.
Res., 14641 S. Keeler Ave., 60445. Tel: 708-388-8190; Fax: 708-388-0072.
School—14611 S. Keeler Ave., 60445. Tel: 708-385-8776.
Sisters 2; Lay Teachers 22; Students 511.

Morton Grove, Cook Co., St. Martha, Revs. Robert J. Burnell; Eugene J. Faucher, Pastor Emeritus; Deacon Peter Meehan.
Res., 8523 Georgiana Ave., 60053. Tel: 847-965-0262; Fax: 847-965-2535.
School—Lay Teachers 14; Students 160.
Catechesis/Religious Programs—Tel: 847-965-8062. Sr. M. Constance Kuczwara, C.S.F., D.R.E.
Students 250.

Mt. Prospect, Cook Co.,

1—St. Cecilia, Revs. Daniel J. Brady; Raymond A. Pavis, Pastor Emeritus; Elzear Gehlen, S.V.D.
Res., 700 S. Meier Rd., 60056. Tel: 847-437-6208; Fax: 847-437-6209.

2—St. Emily, Revs. Robert L. Tuzik; John A. McLoraine, Pastor Emeritus; Denis Condon; Sr. Joanne Marie Schuts, S.S.C.M., Pastoral Assoc.; Deacons James Sanford; Bill DiCanio.
Res., 101 N. Horner Ln., 60056. Tel: 847-824-5049; Fax: 847-297-0358.
School—1400 E. Central Rd., 60056. Tel: 847-296-3490.
Sisters of the Holy Family of Nazareth 4; Lay Teachers 29; Students 618.

3—St. Raymond de Penafort, Revs. Bernard J. Pietrzak; William J. Buhrfeind, Pastor Emeritus; Steven Dombrowski; Charles J. Skach; Deacons Thomas Corcoran; Thomas Lambert; William Reinert; John Lorbach.
Res., 311 S. Ioka St., Box 509, 60056. Tel: 847-253-2444; Fax: 847-253-0023.
School—300 S. Elmhurst Rd., 60056. Tel: 847-253-8555.
Lay Teachers 33; Students 611.

4—St. Thomas a Becket, Revs. John W. Roller; Ralph R. Mollan, Pastor Emeritus; Catherine Weiland Sims, Pastoral Assoc.
Res., 1321 Burning Bush Ln., 60056. Tel: 847-827-9220; Fax: 847-827-0370.

Mundelein, Lake Co., Santa Maria Del Popolo, Revs. James W. Kinn; William J. Shields, (Retired); Hal Mysliwiec; Deacons John Simmons; Bill Dunn; Dave Auld; William Sands.
Res., 116 N. Lake St., 60060. Tel: 847-949-8300; Fax: 847-949-2339.
School—126 N. Lake St., 60060. Tel: 847-949-2335; Fax: 847-949-9721.
Lay Teachers 18; Students 411.
Convent—133 N. Lincoln Ave., 60060.

St. Mary (Fremont Center), Revs. Ronald J. Lewinski; James E. Morrissey, Pastor Emeritus; Deacon Robert A. Poletto.
Res., 22333 W. Erhart Rd., 60060. Tel: 847-223-0010; Fax: 847-223-5960.
School—Franciscan Sisters of the Sacred Heart 2; Lay Teachers 8; Students 220.

Niles, Cook Co., St. Isaac Jogues, Revs. Edward Fialkowski; George Koeune; Deacons Frederick W. Ray; Robert C. O'Keefe.
Res., 8149 Golf Rd., 60714. Tel: 847-967-1060; Fax:

847-967-1070.

St. John Brebeuf, Revs. Robert S. Banzin; Andrew A. Barzyk; David F. Mannelli; Deacons John Perkowitz; Thomas Paluch.
Res., 8307 N. Harlem Ave., 60714. Tel: 847-966-8145.
School—8301 Harlem Ave., 60714.
Sisters 2; Lay Teachers 20; Students 433.

Our Lady of Ransom, Revs. John R. Hall; James J. Donovan; Robert C. Rizzo; Deacons Robert Crandall; Daniel Collins; Charles O'Donnell.
Ministry Center: 8624 W. Normal, 60714. Tel: 847-823-2550; Fax: 847-823-4291.
School—8350 N. Greenwood, 60714.
Felician Sisters 3; Lay Teachers 24; Students 480.

Norridge, Cook Co., Divine Savior, Revs. Stephen J. Tebes; William A. Schackmuth, Pastor Emeritus; Ronald R. Turcich, O.S.A (PEO); Deacons Gus Jeffery; William Lehman; Ronald Gronek.
Res., 7740 W. Montrose, 60634. Tel: 708-456-9000.
School—7750 W. Montrose, 60634-1098.
Sisters 6; Lay Teachers 8; Students 205.

Northbrook, Cook Co., St. Norbert, Revs. Richard J. Mueller; Robert J. Lutz, Pastor Emeritus; Richard J. Valker; Mr. Daniel P. Costigan, Pastoral Assoc.
Res., 1809 Walters Ave., 60062. Tel: 847-272-7090; Fax: 847-272-7771.
School—1817 Elm St., 60062. Tel: 847-272-0051. Sr. Ann Busch, S.S.S.F., Prin.
Sisters of St. Casimir 2; Lay Teachers 22; Students 315.

Our Lady of the Brook, Revs. Richard E. Sztorc; Robert G. Herne, Pastor Emeritus; Kenneth F. Tabor.
Res., 3700 W. Dundee Rd., 60062. Tel: 847-272-5686; Fax: 847-498-0899.

North Chicago, Lake Co., Queen of Peace, Rev. James E. Merold; Deacons Michael Boucha; Gary Munda; Dean Hermann.
Res., 910 14th St., 60064. Tel: 847-473-4079; Fax: 847-473-4143.

Northfield, Cook Co., St. Philip the Apostle, Rev. Laurence J. Dunn. In res., Rev. Stephen E. Grunow.
Res., 1962 Old Willow Rd., 60093. Tel: 847-446-8383; Fax: 847-446-8338.
School—1980 Old Willow Rd., 60093.
Lay Teachers 14; Students 115.

Northlake, Cook Co., St. John Baptist Vianney, Cure of Ars, Revs. Charles V. Fanelli; Raymond J. Morrison, Pastor Emeritus; Deacons William Ruppert; John Zurawski. In res., Revs. Joseph S. Thomas, (Retired); Salvador Simoni; Devasahayam Gudime (India).
Res., 46 N. Wolf Rd., 60164. Tel: 708-562-0500; Fax: 708-562-1824.
School—Lay Teachers 18; Students 240.

North Riverside, Cook Co., Mater Christi, Rev. M. Cyril Nemecek; Deacon Richard Gordus.
Res., 2431 S. 10th Ave., 60546. Tel: 708-442-5611.
School—2400 S. 10th Ave., 60546.
Lay Teachers 10; Students 156.

Oak Forest, Cook Co., St. Damian, Rev. James L. Cullinan; Rev. Msgr. Martin J. O'Day, Pastor Emeritus; Revs. Michael P. Knotek; Francis Kaucky; Deacons Michael Kush; Patrick O'Donnell, (Retired); Len Steinbeigle; Thomas Hipelius; William Stearns.
Res., 5220 W. 155th St., 60452. Tel: 708-687-1370; Fax: 708-687-1377.
School—5300 W. 155th St., 60452. Barbara Wesolowski, Prin.
Lay Teachers 32; Students 764.

Oak Lawn, Cook Co.,

1—St. Catherine of Alexandria, Revs. William J. Lion; John R. Dolehide, O.P.; Daniel F. Jarosewic; George P. McKenna, Pastor Emeritus; Deacons James Hughes, (Retired); James Crane.
Res., 4100 W. 107th St., 60453. Tel: 708-425-2850; Fax: 708-425-2313.
School—10621 S. Kedvale Ave., 60453.
Lay Teachers 19; Students 545.

2—St. Gerald, Revs. Richard J. LoBianco; William J. White, Pastor Emeritus; Rev. Msgr. William J. McNichols, Pastor Emeritus; Rev. Martin T. Marren. In res., Revs. William J. Buhrfeind, (Retired); Robert E. Dovick, (Retired).
Res., 9349 S. Central Ave., 60453. Tel: 708-422-0234; Fax: 708-422-0822.
School—9320 S. 55th Ct., 60453.
Sisters of St. Francis (Clinton, IA) 2; Lay Teachers 22; Students 479.

3—St. Germaine, Revs. William E. Malloy; Edward S. Stockus; William O. Goedert, Pastor Emeritus; Mark J. Walter; Deacons John Flanagan; Donald Daum; John L. Malone.
Res., 4240 W. 98th St., 60453. Tel: 708-636-5060; Fax: 708-636-8007.
School—9735 S. Kolin, 60453.
Sisters of the Presentation of the B.V.M. 1; Lay Teachers 18; Students 390.

4—St. Linus, Rev. Joseph E. Auer; Rev. Msgr. John I. Cardiff, Pastor Emeritus; Rev. Charles Balskus; Deacons Richard Feltes; Edward Gadomski; James Reinhart.
Res., 10300 S. Lawler Ave., 60453. Tel: 708-422-2400; Fax: 708-422-2707.
School—10331 Linus Ln., 60453.
Felician Sisters 5; Lay Teachers 25; Students 550.

5—St. Louis de Montfort, Rev. William J. Quinn; Deacons Michael Karnoski; Michael Sharwarko; William Sullivan.
Res., 8808 S. Ridgeland, 60453. Tel: 708-599-5300; Fax: 708-599-2678.
School—Lay Teachers 10; Students 283.

Oak Park, Cook Co.,

1—Ascension, Revs. Francis C. Jenks; John Moulder. In res., Rev. Harold B. Stanger.
Res., 815 S. East Ave., 60304. Tel: 708-848-2703; Fax: 708-848-2773.
School—601 Van Buren, 60304.
Lay Teachers 25; Students 429.

2—St. Catherine of Siena-St. Lucy, Revs. John R. Lynch; John J. Carolan, Pastor Emeritus; Sr. Patricia Lucas, D.H.M., Pastoral Assoc.; Deacon Bruce Bardford.
Res., 38 N. Austin Blvd., 60302. Tel: 708-386-8077; Fax: 708-386-7755.
School—27 Washington Blvd., 60302. Tel: 708-386-5286; Fax: 708-386-7328.
Sisters of Mercy 2; Lay Teachers 12; Students 400.

3—St. Edmund, Rev. Joseph B. Ruiz; Deacon Edward P. DeLorenzo. In res., Revs. John P. Lucas; Edward C. Dufficy. Pastoral Assocs.: Deacon Edward P. DeLorenzo; Sr. Madeleva Deegan, R.S.M.
Res., 188 S. Oak Park Ave., 60302. Tel: 708-848-4417; Fax: 708-848-0049.
School—200 S. Oak Park Ave., 60302.
Lay Teachers 17; Students 240.

4—St. Giles, Revs. Thomas M. Dore; Thomas J. Campana; Leroy Wickowski; Deacons Loretto J. Madonia; Gerald Zych. In res., Rev. Edward M. Salmon.
Res., 1045 Columbian Ave., 60302. Tel: 708-383-3430; Fax: 708-383-8644.
School—1030 Columbian Ave., 60302.
Lay Teachers 26; Students 480.

Orland Hills, Cook Co., St. Elizabeth Seton, Revs. William T. O'Mara; Ronald A. Hicks; Brian Ardagh.
Res., 9300 W. 167th St., 60477. Tel: 708-403-0101; Fax: 708-403-0105.

Orland Park, Cook Co., St. Francis of Assisi, Revs. Edward F. Upton; Michael J. Weidman.
Res., 15050 S. Wolf Rd., 60462. Tel: 708-460-0042; Fax: 708-460-0136.

St. Michael, Revs. Edward J. McLaughlin; Kurt Boras; Louis J. Tylka; Sr. Marietta Umlor, C.S.C., Pastoral Assoc.; Deacons Michael McDonough; Thomas Bartholomew; Tony Cocco. In res., Rev. Reynaldo B. Treyes.
Res., 14327 Highland Ave., 60462. Tel: 708-349-0903; Fax: 708-349-6015.
School—14355 Highland Ave., 60462.
Sisters 1; Lay Teachers 29; Students 849.

Our Lady of the Woods, Revs. Michael W. O'Connell; William J. Finnegan, Pastor Emeritus; Thomas Libera; Deacons John Benware; Daniel Welter.
Res., 10731 W. 131st St., 60462. Tel: 708-361-4754; Fax: 708-361-5965.

Palatine, Cook Co., St. Theresa, Revs. John P. McNamara; Charles M. Schlax; Deacons Stephen Norys; John Conick; Frank Gildea; Richard Pizzato; Lou Riccio; Jeffrey Shaw.
Res., 455 N. Benton, 60067. Tel: 847-705-2080; Fax: 847-202-8941.
Church—465 N. Benton, 60067.
Ministry Center: 455 N. Benton, 60067. Tel: 847-359-2846.
School—445 N. Benton, 60067. Tel: 847-359-1820.
Lay Teachers 40; Students 780.

Mision Juan Diego, Revs. Edward J. Maloney; Raphael Orozco, Pastor Emeritus.
Res., 36 W. Wilson St., 60067. Tel: 847-202-1028.

St. Thomas of Villanova, Revs. Raymond A. Yadron; James J. Rowley, Pastor Emeritus; Joseph M. Jackson; Deacons Edward Kaczmarek; Kevin Leo; Thomas Maloney; Ray Braski, (Retired); Thomas Dunne; James Zdeb; Richard Willer.
Office: 1152 E. Anderson Dr., 60067. Tel: 847-358-6999; Fax: 847-934-4919.
School—1141 E. Anderson Dr., 60067.
Lay Teachers 14; Students 310.

Palos Heights, Cook Co., Incarnation, Revs. Ronald J. Mass; Robert E. Dovick, Pastor Emeritus; William B. Lynch, Pastor Emeritus; Richard J. Martin; Deacons John Seitz; James Langwell.
Res., 5757 W. 127th St., 60463. Tel: 708-597-3180.
School—Felician Sisters 3; Lay Teachers 11; Students 315.

St. Alexander, Revs. Edward J. Cronin; Thomas M. McKiernan; Mr. Harry Leddy, Pastoral Assoc.
Res., 7025 W. 126th St., 60463. Tel: 708-448-4861; Fax: 708-448-0039.
School—126th St. at 71st Ave., 60463.
Sisters of Providence of Saint Mary-of-the-Woods, IN 2; Lay Teachers 25; Students 464.

Palos Hills, Cook Co., Sacred Heart, Revs. Robert F. McGinnity; Michael J. Walsh; Deacon William Barker. In res., Rev. Robert G. Herne.
Res., 8245 W. 111th St., 60465. Tel: 708-974-3336; Fax: 708-974-3556.

Park Forest, Cook Co., St. Irenaeus, Revs. Daniel J. O'Sullivan; Francis A. Garrity, Pastor Emeritus.
Res., 78 Cherry St., 60466. Tel: 708-748-6891.

Park Ridge, Cook Co., Mary, Seat of Wisdom, Revs. Ronald N. Kalas; Michael F. Conroy, S.P.S.; Theodore Stone; Deacon Michael Ruffner. In res., Rev. James Michaletz, C.S.V.
Res., 920 Granville Ave., 60068. Tel: 847-825-3153; Fax: 847-825-3484.
School—1352 S. Cumberland, 60068.
Sisters 1; Lay Teachers 23; Students 650.

St. Paul of the Cross, Revs. Carl Morello; Joseph J. Kinane, Pastor Emeritus; Kenneth A. Budzikowski; Robert C. Rizzo; Deacon Aloysius J. Memmel. In res., Rev. Daniel A. Smilanic.
Res., 320 S. Washington St., 60068. Tel: 847-825-7605; Fax: 847-825-5186.
School—Sisters 1; Lay Teachers 25; Students 530.

Posen, Cook Co., St. Stanislaus Bishop and Martyr, Rev. David B. Krolczyk; Deacons Joseph Wilczynski; Daniel Dutkiewicz.
Res., 14414 McKinley Ave., 60469. Tel: 708-597-4910.
School—14418 McKinley Ave., 60469.
Lay Teachers 10; Students 250.

Prospect Heights, Cook Co., St. Alphonsus Liguori, Revs. Robert P. Heinz; Richard J. Maginot, Pastor Emeritus; Raymond A. Dunne, S.J.; Deacon Norbert Ciesil.
Res., 411 N. Wheeling Rd., 60070. Tel: 847-255-7452; Fax: 847-255-7520.
School—Sisters 1; Lay Teachers 20; Students 341.

Riverdale, Cook Co., Queen of Apostles, Revs. Daniel M. Tomich; John F. Gorman, Pastor Emeritus; Sr. Dorothy Wolsiffer, S.P., Pastoral Assoc.; Deacon Gerald Hahn.
Res., 207 W. 145th St., 60627. Tel: 708-849-4901.
School—14419 S. Atlantic, 60627.
Lay Teachers 10; Students 295.

River Forest, Cook Co., St. Luke, Revs. A. Paul Reicher; Richard Milek; Deacons Terry Norton; John O'Neill; Thomas Coffey; Paul Faherty.
Res., 528 Lathrop Ave., 60305. Tel: 708-771-8250; Fax: 708-771-8809.
School—519 Ashland Ave., 60305.
Lay Teachers 26; Students 434.

St. Vincent Ferrer Priory, Revs. John G. McGreevy, O.P.; Thomas Saucier, O.P.; Robert J. Botthof, O.P. In res., Revs. James B. Kelly, O.P.; Thomas C. Donlan, O.P.; Giles Klapperich, O.P.; Vincent I. Zarlenga, O.P.; John J. O'Malley, O.P.; Harold D. Ostidek, O.P.; Louis S. Morrone, O.P.; Bro. Scott Steinkerchner, O.P.
Res., 1530 Jackson Ave., 60305. Tel: 708-366-7090; Fax: 708-366-7092.
Church—Lathrop and North Aves., 60305.
School—1515 Lathrop Ave., 60305.
Dominican Sisters 2; Lay Teachers 17; Students 380.

River Grove, Cook Co., St. Cyprian, Revs. Ronald E. Navoy; Thomas M. Powers, Pastor Emeritus; Waldemar Kilian; Deacon James Platt.
Res., 2601 Clinton St., 60171. Tel: 708-453-4800; Fax: 708-453-6141.
School—2565 Clinton St., 60171.
Religious 4; Lay Teachers 9; Students 186.

Riverside, Cook Co., St. Mary, Revs. Gerald T. Gunderson; Leon R. Wagner, Pastor Emeritus; Thomas R. Kasputis; Sr. Margaret Sannasardo, B.V.M., Pastoral Assoc.
Res., 126 Herrick Rd., 60546. Tel: 708-447-1020; Fax: 708-447-3309.
School—97 Herrick Rd., 60546.
Sisters 5; Lay Teachers 21; Students 410.

Rolling Meadows, Cook Co., St. Colette, Revs. Michael P. Ahlstrom; Michael A. Nacius; Deacons John Connor; John Gallagher. In res., Rev. Joseph F. Ognibene, (Retired).
Res., 3900 S. Meadow Dr., 60008. Tel: 847-394-8100; Fax: 847-394-8102.
School—Lay Teachers 16; Students 288.

Rosemont-Des Plaines, Cook Co., Our Lady of Hope, Rev. Thomas E. Schwab.
Res., 9711 W. Devon Ave., Rosemont, 60018. Tel: 847-825-HOPE (4673).

Round Lake, Lake Co., St. Joseph, Rev. Raymond F. Skriba; Deacons John Brooks; Theodore Kuntz. In

res., Rev. Robert J. Fitzpatrick, (Retired).
Res., 114 N. Lincoln Ave., 60073. Tel: 847-546-3449.
School—Lay Teachers 16; Students 403.

Sauk Village, Cook Co., St. James, Rev. Thomas P. Conde; Deacons Thomas McCarthy; Thomas Schroeder. In res., Rev. Paul E. Schwartz, (Retired).
Res., 22244 S. Torrence Ave., 60411-5144. Tel: 708-757-2170; Fax: 708-757-2176.
School—22410 S. Torrence Ave., 60411-5144. Tel: 708-757-2175.
Sisters of Providence (Terre Haute, IN) 2; Lay Teachers 8; Students 208.
Convent—21903 Orion St., 60411. Tel: 708-757-2179.

Schaumburg, Cook Co., St. Marcelline, Revs. Warren J. McCarthy, Pastor Emeritus; Charles J. Dietmer, Pastor Emeritus; Peter M. Yangas; Deacons Edward Boggio; Joe Garcia; Richard Flam.
Res., 822 Springinsguth, 60193. Tel: 847-524-4429; Fax: 847-524-4597.

Church of the Holy Spirit, Revs. William Tkachuk; George J. Kane, Pastor Emeritus; Deacons Raymond Doud; Lowell Taylor; Timothy Kryszak, Sr.; Luis Trevino.
Res., 1451 W. Bode Rd., 60194. Tel: 847-882-7580; Fax: 847-882-1845.

St. Matthew, Revs. Joseph M. Wilk; Edward J. Hughes, Pastor Emeritus; Kenneth R. Bratko, C.R.; Deacons Thomas Halt; William Reisen; Thomas Duszynski; Stanley Kozloski; John Koziol.
Res., 1001 E. Schaumburg Rd., 60194. Tel: 847-891-1220; Fax: 847-891-2575.

Schiller Park, Cook Co., St. Beatrice, Rev. John J. Bresnahan.
Res., 4157 Atlantic Ave., 60176. Tel: 847-678-0138; Fax: 847-678-3974.
School—Religious 2; Lay Teachers 10; Students 255.

St. Maria Goretti, Rev. Thomas C. McNeff.
Res., 3929 N. Wehrman Ave., 60176. Tel: 847-678-3988.
School—Lay Teachers 12; Students 257.

Skokie, Cook Co., St. Joan of Arc, Rev. James L. Barrett. Pastor Emeriti: Revs. James F. Moriarty; John J. McMahon. In res., Rev. Matthew D. McDonald.
Res., 9248 N. Lawndale Ave., Evanston, 60203. Tel: 847-673-0409; Fax: 847-673-9626.
School—Lay Teachers 18; Students 240.

St. Lambert, Revs. Andrew E. Luczak; James J. Murtaugh, Pastor Emeritus; William P. Welsh.
Res., 8148 Karlov Ave., 60076. Tel: 847-673-5090; Fax: 847-677-5135.
School—Sisters 1; Lay Teachers 15; Students 183.

St. Peter, Revs. Edward D. Grace; Kenneth P. Klose, Pastor Emeritus; Leo F. Carton, (Retired); Henry C. Kricek; James D. Beath; Deacons James Wills; William D. Miller. In res., Rev. Thomas A. Baima.
Res., 8116 Niles Center Rd., 60077. Tel: 847-673-1492; Fax: 847-673-6979.
School—8140 Niles Center Rd., 60077. Tel: 847-673-0918; Fax: 847-673-6469.
School Sisters of St. Francis 1; Lay Teachers 21; Students 283.

South Holland, Cook Co., St. Jude the Apostle, Revs. Thomas S. Cabala; John J. Powers, Pastor Emeritus; Victor Miranda (India); Deacons Herbert Drazba; Arthur Nylen.
Res., 880 E. 154th St., 60473. Tel: 708-333-3550; Fax: 708-339-3336.
School—900 E. 154th St., 60473.
Sisters 2; Lay Teachers 22; Students 487.

Holy Ghost, Revs. Joseph R. Bennett; Richard J. Feller, Pastor Emeritus.
Res., 700 E. 170th St., 60473. Tel: 708-333-7011; Fax: 708-333-7020.
School—Lay Teachers 14; Students 300.

Stickney, Cook Co., St. Pius X, Revs. Thomas E. Unz; Thomas P. Conley, Pastor Emeritus; Deacon Marvin Kocar. In res., Rev. James F. Moriarty.
Res., 4314 S. Oak Park Ave., 60402. Tel: 708-484-7951; Fax: 708-749-8515.

Streamwood, Cook Co., St. John the Evangelist, Revs. Robert F. Tonelli; Fred C. Pesek; John M. Kyle, Pastor Emeritus; Deacons Earl Dahl; Louis Farinella; James Furey; Robert DeFiore; James Nimietz; Ronald Lino; Charles Moran; Michael Nugent.
Res., 427 Cedarcrest Dr., 60107. Tel: 630-837-6500; Fax: 630-483-3153.
School—Lay Teachers 9; Students 241.

Summit, Cook Co., St. Joseph, Revs. Thaddeus J. Bojczuk; Henry Pozdol, Pastor Emeritus; Gerald C. Kroeger, O.P.; Deacons Ben Michalowski; Peter Manning.
Res., 7240 W. 57th St., 60501. Tel: 708-458-0501.
School—5641 S. 73rd Ave., 60501. Tel: 708-458-2927.
Sisters 1; Lay Teachers 9; Students 252.

Tinley Park, Cook Co., St. George, Revs. Donald C. Cahill; Gerald Walsh; Marek Grzela; Deacons Richard Kristinat; Paul Gilbert; Dominick Dattoli; Joseph Stalcup; John Ficker; Joseph Chausse.
Res., 6707 W. 175th St., 60477. Tel: 708-532-2243; Fax: 708-532-2055.
School—6700 W. 176th St., 60477.
Mantellate Sisters 1; Lay Teachers 23; Students 535.

Saint Julie Billiart, Revs. Richard M. Homa; Robert M. Duffy, (Retired); James Curry; Deacons Joseph Callahan; Richard Miska; Michael Kiley.
Res., 7399 W. 159th St., 60477. Tel: 708-429-6767; Fax: 708-429-6788.

Vernon Hills, Lake Co., St. Mary of Vernon, Rev. John P. Finnegan; Deacons Mark R. Zwolski; Dante D. Virgilio; James Wogan.
Res., 236A U.S. Hwy. 45, Indian Creek, 60061. Tel: 847-362-1005; Fax: 847-362-6375.

Volo, Lake Co., St. Peter, Rev. James P. Doyle.
Res., 27551 Volo Village Rd., 60073. Tel: 815-385-5496.

Wadsworth, Lake Co., St. Patrick, Revs. Patrick G. Cecil; George J. Dyer, Pastor Emeritus; Paul B. McDermott (PEO); Deacons John Richardson; Louis Abboud; Phillip Fragassi; Edward Tomkowiak; David Egan.
Res., 15000 Wadsworth Rd., 60083. Tel: 847-244-4161; Fax: 847-336-0630.
School—Marcella Bosnak, Prin. Lay Teachers 19; Students 570.

Wauconda, Lake Co., Transfiguration, Revs. Thomas M. Enright; Robert G. Aguirre; Byron G. Maher, Pastor Emeritus; Deacons Stephen Cenek; Marion Omiatek; John Zimmerman. Pastoral Assocs.: Marilyn Omiatek; Dee Zimmerman.
Res., 318 Bangs St., 60084. Tel: 847-526-2400; Fax: 847-526-2961.
School—Lay Teachers 16; Students 323.

Waukegan, Lake Co.,

1—St. Anastasia, Revs. Terrence A. McCarthy; Edward S. Maraczewski, Pastor Emeritus; Aloysius Funtila, C.I.C.M.
Res., 624 Douglas Ave., 60085. Tel: 847-623-2875; Fax: 847-623-4882.
School—Lay Teachers 18; Students 439.

2—St. Bartholomew. Merged with St. Joseph. See Holy Family for details.

3—St. Dismas, Revs. John M. Ryan; Paul J. Cull, Pastor Emeritus; Deacons Anthony Sacramento; Paul Telle. In res., Revs. Regis Kleene, S.D.S.; Edward E. Lisowski.
Res., 2600 Sunset Ave., 60087. Tel: 847-623-5050.

4—Holy Family, Revs. Gary M. Graf; William O'Connell, Pastor Emeritus; Deacons Edward Scarbalis; Angel Velazquez; Eusebio Moreno. In res., Revs. Thomas W. McQuaid; Michael Boehm.
Res., 501 S. Utica St., P.O. Box 440, 60085. Tel: 847-623-2655.
School—Participant in Lake Shore Catholic Academy. 515 S. Utica St., 60085.

5—St. Joseph. Merged with St. Bartholomew. See Holy Family listing for details.

6—Immaculate Conception B.V.M., Rev. Frank W. Plotka.
Res., 508 Grand Ave., 60085. Tel: 847-336-3684; Fax: 847-336-9040.
School—Lay Teachers 16; Students 303.

Westchester, Cook Co., Divine Infant, Revs. Gerald P. Joyce; William M. Henkel, Pastor Emeritus; Dean F. Semmer.
Res., 1601 Newcastle Ave., 60154. Tel: 708-865-8071.
School—Lay Teachers 15; Students 310.
Convent— Institute of the Blessed Virgin Mary (I.B.V.M.)

Divine Providence, Revs. John C. Rosemeyer; Joseph J. Wojcik; Sr. Kay Buechele, O.P., Pastoral Assoc.; Deacon Frank DeVita.
Res., 2550 S. Mayfair Ave., 60154. Tel: 708-562-3364; Fax: 708-562-3134.
School—2500 S. Mayfair Ave., 60154. Tel: 708-562-2258.
Sisters of Divine Providence (Normandy, MO) 2; Lay Teachers 14; Students 215.

Western Springs, Cook Co., St. John of the Cross, Revs. Richard P. Hynes; Joseph F. McDonnell, Pastor Emeritus; William J. Martin; Edward J. Fealey; Sr. Jeanne Bonneau, C.N.D., Pastoral Assoc.; Deacons William Engler; Thomas McGorey; Joseph Pepitone.
Res., 5005 Wolf Rd., 60558. Tel: 708-246-4404; Fax: 708-246-4566.
School—705 51st St., 60558. Tel: 708-246-4454; Fax: 708-246-9010.
Sisters 1; Lay Teachers 38; Students 800.
Convent—5103 Caroline Ave., 60558. Tel: 708-246-0014.

Wheeling, Cook Co., St. Joseph the Worker, Rev. Frederick L. Brandstrader; Deacon Perry Duderstadt. In res., Rev. John C. Massion.
Res., 181 W. Dundee Rd., 60090. Tel: 847-537-2740; Fax: 847-537-7914.

Wilmette, Cook Co., St. Francis Xavier, Revs. Edward F. Harnett; George W. Klein. Pastoral Assocs.: Sr. Joyce Shanabarger, O.S.F.; Deacon Michael Cavanaugh; Patty Jane Pelton. In res., Rev. Michael D. Place.
Office: 524 Ninth St., 60091. Tel: 847-256-4250; Fax: 847-256-4254.
Res., 912 Linden Ave., 60091.
School—808 Linden Ave., 60091. Tel: 847-256-0644. Sr. Mary K. O'Brien, B.V.M., Prin.
Sisters 1; Lay Teachers 26; Students 447.

St. Joseph, Rev. Francis J. Kane; Rev. Msgr. Charles N. Meter, Pastor Emeritus; Rev. John Szmyd; Ms. Dana McKenna, Pastoral Assoc.
Res., 1747 Lake Ave., 60091. Tel: 847-251-0771; Fax: 847-251-5715.

Winnetka, Cook Co., SS. Faith, Hope and Charity, Rev. Thomas F. Ventura; Rev. Msgr. Eugene F. Lyons, Pastor Emeritus; Rev. Jeffrey Grob; Deacons Terrence Levins; Roger Mullaney. In res., Rev. William Flaherty.
Res., 191 Linden St., 60093. Tel: 847-446-7646; Fax: 847-446-7630.
School—180 Ridge Ave., 60093. Tel: 847-446-0031.
Sisters 1; Lay Teachers 24; Students 359.

Sacred Heart, Revs. Robert E. Ferrigan; Thomas J. Raftery, Pastor Emeritus; Mark Simpson; Deacons D. J. Shinkle; Michael McNulty; John Fay.
Res., 905 Burr Ave., 60093. Tel: 847-446-0856; Fax: 847-501-5311.
School—1095 Gage St., 60093.
Lay Teachers 18; Students 210.
Parish Center—1077 Tower Rd., 60093. Tel: 847-446-0856.

Zion-Beach Park, Lake Co., Our Lady of Humility, Revs. David J. Mulvihill; John E. Hayes, Pastor Emeritus; Sr. Mary O'Connell, S.H.C.J., Pastoral Assoc.; Deacons Philip Horne; Max Jinkens; Michael Mercure.
Res., 10655 Wadsworth Rd., 60099. Tel: 847-872-8778; Fax: 847-872-8780.
School—10601 Wadsworth Rd., 60099. Ms. Deborah Poturalski, Prin.
Lay Teachers 13; Students 255.

Syro-Malabar Rite

Chicago, Cook Co., Knanite Syro-Malabar Catholic Mission of the Archdiocese of Chicago, Rev. Simon Edathiparampil, Dir.
Res., Immaculate Heart of Mary, 3834 N. Spaulding, 60618. Tel: 773-509-9147; Fax: 773-478-1844.

Northlake, Cook Co., Syro-Malabar Catholic Mission of the Archdiocese of Chicago, Rev. Joseph Kandathiduky, Dir.
Center Mar Thoma Shleeha Church: 5000 St. Charles Rd., Bellwood, 60104. Tel: 708-544-7250; Fax: 708-544-5890.

Malankara Rite

Chicago, Cook Co., Syro-Malankara Catholic Mission of the Archdiocese of Chicago,
Divine Liturgy at: 1208 Ashland St., Evanston, 60202. Tel: 708-475-4093. Rev. Zacharias Nanthiyattu, O.I.C., Dir.

Chaplains of Public Institutions

Chicago. *Chicago O'Hare International Airport,* P.O. Box 66353, 60666. Rev. John A. Jamnicky.
Cook County Hospital. Revs. George A. Wallenhorst, S.J.; William O. Madden, S.J.; John Pennington, S.J.; Deacon James Davis; Sr. Marie Louise Julk, S.Sp.S.
Hines V.A. Hospital. Revs. John G. Birk (SPK); Bruno H. Kowalkowski, O.P.
V.A. Lakeside Medical Center. Rev. Robert J. Borre (MAD).

Oak Forest. *Oak Forest Hospital.* Revs. Melchior Toczek, O.F.M.; Victorian Haladus, O.F.M.; Michael Windolph, O.F.M.; Adam Wolf, O.F.M.; Bro. Innocent Gill, O.F.M.

On Duty Outside the Archdiocese:
Reverend Monsignors—
Sarauskas, R. George, Office to Aid Central/Eastern Europe Catholic Church, 3211 4th St. N.E., Washington, DC 20017-1194
Trisco, Robert F., Curley Hall, Catholic University of America, Washington, DC 20064
Reverend Fathers—
Barnum, Martin, Sacred Heart School of Theology, 7335 S. Hwy. 100, P.O. Box 429, Hales Corners, WI 53130-0429
Brankin, Patrick M., St. Theresa Church, P.O. Box 297, Collinsville, OK 74021-0297
Broccolo, Gerard T., 1011 S. Valentia St., #135, Denver, CO 80231

Clements, George H., 1101 14th St. N.W., #630, Washington, DC 20005
Dempsey, Robert J., Editor, L'Osservatore Romano, Villa Stritch, Via della Nocetta, 63, 00164 Rome, Italy
Filipetto, Silvano, Via Roma #224, 0038 Spina (VE), Italy
Hotchkin, John F., Bishops' Commission for Ecumenical Affairs, 3211 Fourth St. N.E., Washington, DC 20017-1194
Keusal, Eugene L., St. Theresa Church, 25 W. Lipoa St., Kihei, HI 96753
Kiley, J. Cletus, Staff House, 4001 14th St., N.E., Washington, DC 20017
Lorenz, Matthais E., 5531 E. Lake Dr., Lisle, IL 60532
Martinek, John B., Our Lady of the Snows Parish, P.O. Box 89, Nulato, AK 99765
Pollard, John E., Office of the Catechism, National Conference for Catholic Bishops, 3211 4th St. N.E., Washington, DC 20017
Rugen, Patrick J., St. Mary University, Campus Box 1431, 700 Terrace Heights, Winona, MI 55987-1399

Military Chaplains:
Reverend Monsignors—
Dobes, George E., 3370 S. Second St., Arlington, VA 22204-1709
Reverend Fathers—
Baldwin, John F., CAPT, CHC, USN, Office of the Chap., Naval Postgraduate School, University Cir., Rm. 126, Monterey, CA 93943-5009
Ball, David, USN, 109 Northport Pl., Northport, MI 46970
Falkenthal, Thomas W., Group Chaplain's Office, 2nd FSSG, PSC Box 20002, Camp Lejeune, NC 28542-0002
Joslyn, James W., PSC 824, Box 2640, FPO, AE 09627-1000
Kastigar, John J., Military Chap., U.S.A.F., 1774 Lexington Dr., Sierra Vista, AZ 85635
Kloak, David G., Office of the Chap., Naval Air Station, Alameda, CA 94501
Murray, John W., Chaplain, V.A. Palo Alto Health Care System (125), 3801 Miranda Ave., Palo Alto, CA 94304
Simpson, Brian L., 6B Kamakami Pl., Honolulu, HI 96818
Stake, Ronald P., P.O. Box 42221, Port Hueneme, CA 93404-5421

Graduate Studies:
Reverend Fathers—
Ford, David R., 1709 Shattuck Ave., 118, Berkeley, CA 94709
Griffiths, John M., Casa Santa Maria, Via dell' Umilta 30, 00187 Rome, Italy
Lyle, Dennis J., Casa Santa Maria, Via dell' Umilta 30, 00187 Rome, Italy
Mulvihill, John E., Casa Santa Maria, Via dell' Umilta 30, 00187 Rome, Italy

Missionary Work:
Reverend Fathers—
Cleary, Philip C., Nuestros Pequenos Hermanos, Apartado Postal, 333, 62000 Cuernavaca, Morelos, Mexico
Colleran, James A., Archdiocesan Mission Team, St. James the Apostle, Diocese of Chilpancingo-Chilapa, Santiago Apbstol, Quachultanango, 39250
Cowell, Raymond, Parroquia Nuestra Senoria de Fatima, El Pari Casilla 919, Santa Cruz, Bolivia
Foley, Matthew, Mission of St. James the Apostle, Santiago Apostal, Quechultenango Guerrero, Mexico
Hays, Kevin W., Sociedad Misionera de Santiago Apostol, Apartado 18-1025 Miraflores, Lima 18, Peru
Rochford, E. Michael, Society of St. James, 2455 N. Hamlin Ave., Chicago, IL 60647

Other Assignments:
Reverend Fathers—
Becker, Charles P., 24955 N. Hwy. 12, Lake Zurich, IL 60047
Coleman, Robert P., 1921 N. Kedvale Ave., Chicago, IL 60639
Colomb, Jackson, 1421 Oak Ave., Evanston, IL 60201
Curran, John W., 17951 Dixie Hwy., Homewood, IL 60630
Curtis, Joseph C., 10655 Wadsworth Rd., Beach Park/Zion, IL 60099
Danowski, Daniel G., 4170 N. Marine Dr., #5G, Chicago, IL 60613
Dearhammer, John W., 3615 S. Hoyne Ave., Chicago, IL 60609
Durkin, Charles T., 163 Vandera, Robertsville, MO 63072
Egan, Gerard P., Loyola University, 820 N. Michigan, Chicago, IL 60611
Gilligan, Michael J., American Catholic Press, 16160 S. Seton Dr., South Holland, IL 60473
Gleeson, Edward D., P.O. Box 653, Oak Lawn, IL 60454
Grace, James N., 8116 Niles Center Rd., Skokie, IL 60077
Greeley, Andrew M., N.O.R.C., 1155 E. 60th St., Chicago, IL 60637
Hannigan, John T., 611 E. Clark, Litchfield, IL 62056
Hergenrother, John C., 1144 Harrison, LaGrange Park, IL 60526
Hurley, John W., 1315 S. 50th Ct., 1st Rear, Cicero, IL 60650
Koys, Thomas R., 8200 S. Kostner Ave., Chicago, IL 60652
LaChance, Charles P., 810 W. Montrose Ave., Chicago, IL 60613
Leja, Casimir, 646 N. Michigan Ave., Ste. 543, Chicago, IL 60611
Lisowski, Brian A., 9525 S. Lawndale Ave., Evergreen Park, IL 60805
Maday, Norbert J., P.O. Box 455, Mundelein, IL 60060
Malone, William P., 2226 S. Whipple, Chicago, IL 60623
McCarthy, James H., Special Religious Ed. Div., 2953 S. Lowe, Chicago, IL 60616
McGlinn, Robert J., Cristo Rey Parish, 800 Wisconsin Ave., Racine, WI 53403
McKenna, Edward J., 2944 E. 88th St., Chicago, IL 60617-3242
Michet, John M., 4522 S. Wallace, Chicago, IL 60609
Motycka, Robert R., 14327 Highland Ave., Orland Park, IL 60462
Nangle, Thomas R., Police Chaplaincy, 1140 W. Jackson, Chicago, IL 60607
Nicola, John J., P.O. Box 1505, Pinehurst, NC 28374
O'Keefe, Millard, 2525 59th St., Wood Ridge, IL 60517-1114
Perkins, Robert S., 151 Sanchez St., San Francisco, CA 94114
Pokladowski, Gregory S., 1430 Hale St., Vallejo, CA 94591-4134
Ray, James M., P.O. Box 455, Mundelein, IL 60060
Ruge, Kenneth C., P.O. Box 455, Mundelein, IL 60060
Shields, James P., 116 N. Lake St., Mundelein, IL 60060
Solazzo, Michael J., Misericordia-North, 6300 N. Ridge Ave., Chicago, IL 60660
Steiner, Daniel R., 10233 S. Central Park, Evergreen Park, IL 60805
Strand, Ralph S., P.O. Box 455, Mundelein, IL 60060
Swade, Thomas J., 2058 N. Clark St., Chicago, IL 60614
Vitro, Thomas J., P.O. Box 932, Lake Geneva, WI 53147
Wurst, Wayne H., Vianney House, 918 W. 33rd St., Chicago, IL 60608

Retired:
Reverend Monsignors—
Bergin, Clifford E., 1245 W. Norwood, Chicago, IL 60660
Cardiff, John I., St. Linus, 10300 S. Lawler Ave., Oak Lawn, IL 60453
Carroll, Donald M., 7260 W. Peterson, Chicago, IL 60631
Chess, Edwin R., 11812 Song Dr., San Antonio, TX 78216
Egan, John J., 730 N. Wabash, Chicago, IL 60611
Farrell, John J., St. Andrew Home, 7000 N. Newark, Niles, IL 60714
Hardiman, James C., 4126 W. 99th St., Oak Lawn, IL 60453
Hayes, John M., 2524 S. Keeler, Chicago, IL 60623
Higgins, George C., Curley Hall 220, Catholic University of America, Washington, DC 20064
Koenig, Harry C., Addolorata Villa, 555 McHenry Rd., Wheeling, IL 60090
Lyons, Eugene F., Addolorata Villa, 555 McHenry Rd., Wheeling, IL 60090
McDermott, Ignatius D., The McDermott Foundation, 932 W. Washington St., Chicago, IL 60607
McElligott, Francis J., St. John Fisher, 10234 S. Washtenaw, Chicago, IL 60642
McNichols, William J., Holy Family Villa, 123rd & Will Cook Rd., Lemont, IL 60439
Meter, Charles N., 1747 Lake Ave., Wilmette, IL 60091
Mohan, Thomas J., Addolorata Villa, 559 McHenry Rd., Wheeling, IL 60090
Mozeris, Damasus A., Immaculate Conception, 2745 W. 44th St., Chicago, IL 60632
Mroczkowski, Joseph J., 1501 Hoffman St., Hammond, IN 46327
O'Day, Martin J., 13240 W. Circle Dr., No. 305, Crestwood, IL 60445
Pellicore, Edward M., 1801 35th St., Apt. 1421, Oak Brook, IL 60521
Quinn, John S., St. Andrew, 3546 N. Paulina St., Chicago, IL 60657
Quinn, William J., St. Eulalia, 1851 S. 9th Ave., Maywood, IL 60153
Roche, M. Edward, 10811 S. Ridgeland, Chicago Ridge, IL 60415
Stanek, Wenceslaus, St. Benedict's Home, 6930 W. Touhy Ave., Niles, IL 60714
Reverend Fathers—
Adamich, Albert R., Most Holy Redeemer, 9525 S. Lawndale Ave., Evergreen Park, IL 60042
Ahearn, Donald J., St. Juliana, 7142 N. Osceola, Chicago, IL 60631
Ahern, John J., 765 Busse Hwy., Apt. #1C, Park Ridge, IL 60068-2455
Ahern, John J., 6804 Joliet Rd., Indian Head Park, IL 60525
Aschenbrenner, George F., 1598 Main St., Lemont, IL 60439
Ballweber, Eugene L., 2302 Julie S.W., Albuquerque, NM 87105
Barr, Pierre J., 3825 S. California Ave., Chicago, IL 60633
Barron, Edward M., 1515 E. 154th St., #130, Dolton, IL 60419
Bednarz, Matt A., 5600 N. Fairfield, Chicago, IL 60659-4817
Beyenka, John T., Addolorata Villa, 555 McHenry Rd., Wheeling, IL 60090
Boreczky, John V., 35 Rosada Dr., Bravard, NC 28712
Borowczyk, Martin R., St. Francis Borgia, 8033 W. Addison, Chicago, IL 60634
Boyle, Thomas S., One Cambridge Ct., Michigan City, IN 46360
Braun, David F., P.O. Box 745, Sublette, IL 61637
Brett, James D., P.O. Box 268, Delevan, WI 53115
Brodfuehrer, Robert S., 5205 N. Lieb, Chicago, IL 60630-1433
Brzozowski, Edward J., 13356 Buffalo Ave., Chicago, IL 60633
Buhrfeind, William J., St. Gerald, 9349 S. Central, Oak Lawn, IL 60453
Bull, Albert D., 13047 W. Ballad Dr., Sun City West, AZ 85375-1812
Burns, Eugene P., 797 Waverly Rd., LaPorte, IN 46350
Bykowski, Norbert H., 1318 Millstream Dr., McHenry, IL 60050
Carolan, John J., St. Juliana, 7142 N. Osceola Ave., Chicago, IL 60631
Carroll, Gilbert A., St. Timothy, 6326 N. Washtenaw, Chicago, IL 60659
Carton, Leo F., 8116 Niles Center Rd., Skokie, IL 60077
Cerniglia, Francis J., Queen of the Rosary, 750 Elk Grove Blvd., Elk Grove, IL 60007-4298
Chapell, Norbert A., 7737 Golf View Dr., Palos Heights, IL 60463
Chen, Anthony K., 3929 Wehrman, Schiller Park, IL 60176
Chisek, Anthony S., 1 Thornwood Mall, Apt. 1002, University Park, IL 60466
Clark, H. Robert, Queen of All Saints Basilica, 6280 N. Sauganash Ave., Chicago, IL 60646
Coffey, Edward N., 5300 W. 24th St., Cicero, IL 60650
Conley, Thomas P., St. Zachary, 567 N. Algonquin Rd., Des Plaines, IL 60016
Connors, Edward P., 2339 York St., Blue Island, IL 60406
Coughlin, Roger J., 721 N. LaSalle St., Chicago, IL 60610
Crosby, John M., 7933 Golf Dr., Apt. #1B, Palos Heights, IL 60463
Cross, Robert A., c/o James and Mary Catherine Meeks, 700 Ashland, River Forest, IL 60305
Cull, Paul J., 920 Vost Dr., Apt. #212, Gurnee, IL 60031
Cullen, George H., St. Benedict Home for the Aged, 6930 W. Touhy, Niles, IL 60714
Curley, Thomas J., 2825 W. 81st St., Chicago, IL 60652
Davitt, James P., St. James, 106 Archer Rd., Lemont, IL 60439
Devine, William J., P.O. Box 53, Worth, IL 60482
Diemer, Charles J., 35801 W. Cook Ave., Antioch, IL 60002
Dilla, Francis E., P.O. Box 88, New Carlisle, IN 46552
Dillon, Arthur J., P.O. Box 125, Powers Lake, WI 53159
Dolciamore, John V., Mundelein Seminary of the University of St. Mary of the Lake, Mundelein, IL 60060
Donohue, John J., 2400 Archbury Ln., Park Ridge, IL 60068

Dovick, Robert F., 9349 S. Central Ave., Oak Lawn, IL 60453
Downes, Thomas J., 2630 Sierra Dr., Colorado Springs, CO 80917
Dudzinski, Sylvester W., Mother Theresa Home, 1270 Franciscan Dr., #114, Lemont, IL 60437
Dufficy, Edward C., St. Edmund, 188 S. Oak Park Ave., Oak Park, IL 60302
Duffy, Donald J., 75 N. Buffalo Grove Rd., Buffalo Grove, IL 60089
Duffy, Robert M., 7399 W. 159th St., Tinley Park, IL 60477
Duggan, J. Edward, St. Bartholomew, 4949 W. Patterson Ave., Chicago, IL 60641
Durkin, Eugene F., Holy Name Cathedral, 730 N. Wabash Ave., Chicago, IL 60611
Dyer, George J., St. Patrick, 15000 Wadsworth Rd., Wadsworth, IL 60083
Enright, John P., 1801 W. 35th St., #1217, Oakbrook, IL 60521
Fassbinder, Richard W., 135 S. Milwaukee Ave., Lake Villa, IL 60046
Faucher, Eugene J., St. Edna, 2525 N. Arlington Hts. Rd., Arlington Heights, IL 60004
Felczak, Leonard J., 4325 S. Spaulding, Chicago, IL 60632
Feller, Richard J., 1201 Bonita Dr., Park Ridge, IL 60068-5017
Festle, Robert H., 5046 N. Ashland Ave., Chicago, IL 60640
Finnegan, William J., Our Lady of the Woods, 10731 W. 131st St., Orland Park, IL 60462
Fisher, Frederick J., Little Company of Mary, Health Facility, 7520 S. 421, San Pierre, IN 46374
Fitzgerald, Edward P., Mercy Hospital and Medical Center, Stevenson Expwy. at King Dr., Chicago, IL 60616
Fitzgerald, Thomas J., 5472 S. Kimbark, Chicago, IL 60615
Fitzpatrick, Edmund J., St. Pascal, 3935 N. Melvina Ave., Chicago, IL 60634
Fitzpatrick, Robert J., St. Joseph, 114 N. Lincoln Ave., Round Lake, IL 60073
Flaherty, William J., 191 Linden St., Winnetka, IL 60093-3832
Flannery, Edward M., 21 Spinning Wheel Dr., Hinsdale, IL 60521
Fraser, Gerald D., 900 Center St., #2F, Des Plaines, IL 60016-6562
Frawley, John P., 2825 W. 81st St., Chicago, IL 60652-2722
Gallagher, Charles G., St. Cletus, 600 W. 55th St., La Grange, IL 60525
Garrity, Francis A., 78 Cherry St., Park Forest, IL 60466
Gerrity, Raymond J., 917 S. 8th Ave., #2, LaGrange, IL 60525
Giese, Vincent J., P.O. Box 772, Rensselaer, IN 47978
Goedert, William O., St. Germaine, 2330 W. 118th St., Chicago, IL 60643-4710
Gorman, John F., Resurrection Nursing Pavilion, 1001 N. Greenwood, Park Ridge, IL 60068
Gorman, Lawrence J., c/o Mr. & Mrs. Henry Lenz, 7706 Sequoia Dr., Palos Heights, IL 60463
Graff, J. Austin, 1141 Iroquois, Apt. 215, Naperville, IL 60540
Grinis, Bruno B., 12433 S. Halsted St., Chicago, IL 60628
Grinis, Julian G., Box 108, Oak Lawn, IL 60453
Gruchot, Stanley J., 7000 Newark, Chicago, IL 60643
Guerin, Philip X., 3546 N. Paulina St., Chicago, IL 60657
Guirsch, Bernard G., 206 E. 25th St., Chicago Heights, IL 60411
Gunia, Edward S., 850 Front St., Lisle, IL 60532
Hanley, Lawrence F., 7112 Concord Ln., Fox Lake, IL 60020
Hanlon, Thomas C., 8536 W. Berwyn, Chicago, IL 60656
Hayes, John E., Rte. 1, Box 4E, Dakota, MN 55925
Hayes, Peter F., 4623 N. Chester, No. 207-W, Chicago, IL 60656
Helfrich, George J., 7958 W. Foster Ave., Chicago, IL 60656
Henkel, William M., Mother Teresa Home, 1260 Franciscan Dr., Room #127, Lemont, IL 60438
Herne, Robert G., Sacred Heart Parish, 8245 W. 111th St., Palos Hills, IL 60465
Hills, Richard L., St. Benedict Home, 6930 W. Touhy Ave., Niles, IL 60714
Hock, William T., St. Tarcissus Parish, 6020 W. Ardmore, Chicago, IL 60646
Hoffman, Matthias H., 1131 Douglas Ave., Flossmoor, IL 60422
Hosty, Thomas J., 8419 Bailey Rd., Darien, IL 60561
Hughes, Edward J., 1001 E. Schaumburg Rd., Schaumburg, IL 60194
Huske, Leonard G., 14619 S. Keystone, Midlothian, IL 60445
Ivers, Victor J., St. Joseph, 121 E. Maple Ave., Libertyville, IL 60048-2283
Janiak, Anthony J., St. Benedict Home, 6930 W. Touhy Ave., Niles, IL 60714
Jarzynski, Edward M., St. Benedict's Home for the Aged, 6930 W. Touhy, Niles, IL 60714
Jasinski, Raymond J., 211 E. 27th St., Kearney, NE 68847
Joyce, Pierce J., 124 N. Spring Ave., La Grange, IL 60525
Jozwiak, Richard M., 385 N. Edinburgh, Frankfort, IL 60423
Juchcinski, Clarence J., 16001 Lowe Ave., Harvey, IL 60426
Kane, George J., 1700 Cambourne, Schaumburg, IL 60194
Kash, Robert J., 21 S. Spring Ave., Unit A, LeGrange, IL 50525-2272
Kaveney, Thomas J., St. Odilo, 2244 S. East Ave., Berwyn, IL 60402
Keating, James W., 7939 W. 43rd St., Lyons, IL 60534
Kelly, Charles F., St. Daniel the Prophet, 5330 S. Nashville Ave., Chicago, IL 60638
Kelly, William J., c/o Jones, 3332 S. 59th Ave., Cicero, IL 60650
Kelpsas, Francis J., Nativity B.V.M., 6812 S. Washtenaw St., Chicago, IL 60629
Kinane, Joseph J., St. Paul of the Cross, 320 S. Washington St., Park Ridge, IL 60068
Kireilis, Fabian P., Immaculate Conception, 2745 W. 44th St., Chicago, IL 60632
Kirkilas, Michael, 6666 20th Ave., N.E., St. Petersburg, FL 33710
Kleiber, Kenneth R., 15202 N. 40th St., #223-2, Phoenix, AZ 85032-4652
Klose, Kenneth P., St. Benedict Home, 6930 W. Touhy Ave., Niles, IL 60714
Klug, Jerome G., 26166 W. Mattalina Ct., Ingleside, IL 60041
Kniewel, Edward J., 2600 N. Nordica, Chicago, IL 60635
Kouba, Charles J., 5157 S. California, Chicago, IL 60632
Kozien, Casimir J., 4949 W. Patterson Ave., Chicago, IL 60641
Kuzinskas, John A., 12375 McCarthy Rd., Lemont, IL 60438
Kyle, John M., 7000 N. Newark, No. 516, Niles, IL 60648
Lambert, Rollins E., 10112 Menaul N.E. #L-23, Albuquerque, NM 87112
Limanowski, Stanley C., 100 Mutiny Ln., Apt. #104, Merritt Island, FL 32952-2521
Lisowski, William J., 15714 Old Orchard Ct., Orland Park, IL 60462
Lutz, Robert J., St. Norbert, 1809 Walters Ave., Northbrook, IL 60062
Lynch, Cletus J., 1010 American Eagle Blvd., #609, Sun City Center, FL 33573
Lynch, Joseph P., 14130 Green Valley Dr., Orland Park, IL 60462
Lynch, William B., 5727 W. 127th St., Palos Heights, IL 60463
Lyons, James W., 520 Donovan St., Woodstock, IL 60098
Lyons, Leo J., 14226 - 84th Ave., Orland Park, IL 60462
Mackin, John J., 8925 S. Kostner, Hometown, IL 60456
Maginot, Richard J., St. Alphonsus Liguori, 411 N. Wheeling Rd., Prospect Heights, IL 60070
Maher, Byron G., 416 E. Jefferson, Burlington, WI 53105
Maher, Thomas F., St. Mary-of-the-Woods, 7033 N. Moselle Ave., Chicago, IL 60646
Makaras, Joseph V., c/o Ms. Irene Tumas, 817 S. Theodore St., Appleton, WI 54915
Makuch, Thaddeus J., 3020 S. 48th Ct., Cicero, IL 60650
Maniola, Francis N., 6135 S. Austin, Chicago, IL 60638
Maraczewski, Edward S., 1516 E. Lowden, Mt. Prospect, IL 60056
Marszalek, Paul B., 15103 Quail Hollow Dr., Unit #601, Orland Park, IL 60462
Matlak, Marion A., 7264 W. Peterson Ave., C-218, Chicago, IL 60631-3624
McCaig, John J., St. Patrick, 200 Illinois St., Lemont, IL 60439
McDonagh, Andrew J., 6939 N. Hiawatha, Chicago, IL 60646
McDonald, Matthew D., 9248 N. Lawndale, P.O., Evanston, IL 60203
McDonnell, Joseph F., 17 W. 706 Butterfield Rd., Oakbrook Terrace, IL 60181
McGrath, John F., 10726 S. Sacramento, Chicago, IL 60655
McHugh, Thomas J., St. Matthias Parish, 2310 W. Ainslie, Chicago, IL 60625
McKenna, George P., Bayport Apartments, 9820 S. Pulaski Rd., Oak Lawn, IL 60453
McLaughlin, Charles J., Box 2308 R.F.D., Long Grove, IL 60047
McLoraine, John A., 790 McCormick Dr., Lake Forest, IL 60045
McMahon, John J., 2535 Lake Ave., Wilmette, IL 60092
Meyer, Charles R., Mundelein Seminary, University of St. Mary-of-the-Lake, Mundelein, IL 60060
Mezydlo, Leonard T., St. Stephen Protomartyr Parish, 1267 Everett St., Des Plaines, IL 60018
Michalek, Henry J., 7264 W. Peterson Ave., C-605, Chicago, IL 60631
Mikolaitis, Vito E., 6812 S. Washtenaw, Chicago, IL 60629
Millea, Thomas V., 4342 N. Lieb, Chicago, IL 60630
Mollan, Ralph R., 1321 Burning Bush Ln., Mt. Prospect, IL 60056
Mollohan, James L., 4949 W. Patterson, Chicago, IL 60641
Morgan, Edward J., 119 Evergreen Dr., Frankfort, IL 60423
Moriarty, James F., St. Pius X, 4314 S. Oak Park, Stickney, IL 60402
Morris, John J., 2214 S.W. 29th Ter. No. 33, Topeka, KS 66611-1956
Morrison, Raymond J., St. Andrew Home for the Aged, 7000 N. Newark, Niles, IL 60714
Morrissey, James E., Maryhaven West, 1700 E. Lake St., Glenview, IL 60025
Murphy, William P., Queen of Martyrs, 10233 S. Central Pk., Evergreen Park, IL 60642
Murtaugh, James J., 400 E. Randolph, #3107, Chicago, IL 60602
Mytych, Joseph F., 6101 S. 75th Ave., Argo, IL 60501
Nikliborc, Francis U., Resurrection Nursing Pavilion, 1001 N. Greenwood Ave., Park Ridge, IL 60068
Norkett, Edward J., 26 S. Central, Highwood, IL 60040
Novak, Robert J., 2960 N. Lake Shore Dr., Apt. 1209, Chicago, IL 60657
Nowak, Joseph G., 8237 S. Shore Dr., Chicago, IL 60617
O'Brien, Edward P., Bethlehem Woods #1147, 1571 W. Ogden Ave., LaGrange Park, IL 60525
O'Brien, John E., 12329 First Ct., Kenosha, WI 53140
O'Connell, William M., 2310 Greentree Ct., Lindenhurst, IL 60046
O'Connor, James T., Our Lady of the Mount, 2414 S. 61st Ave., Cicero, IL 60804-2698
O'Donnell, Richard J., 3528 S. Hermitage, Chicago, IL 60609
O'Hara, Harold T., 170 N.W. 27th St., Pompano Beach, FL 33064
O'Shea, John J., 2324 W. Chase Ave., Chicago, IL 60645
Ognibene, Joseph F., St. Colette, 3900 S. Meadow Dr., Rolling Meadows, IL 60008
Ognibene, Salvatore J., St. Mary of Providence Home, 4200 N. Austin, Chicago, IL 60634
Olejniczak, Henry A., 15704 Lake Hills Ct., Orland Park, IL 60462
Orozco, Raphael R., P.O. Box 1006, Palatine, IL 60068
Pastick, Joseph A., 4939 Floramar Terr., #608, New Port Richey, FL 34652-3310
Pavis, Raymond A., P.O. Box 12, Powers Lake, WI 53159
Peng, John B., 3420 N. Kolmar, Chicago, IL 60641
Powers, John J., St. Jude the Apostle, 880 E. 154th St., South Holland, IL 60473
Powers, Thomas M., St. Cyprian Parish, 2601 Clinton St., River Grove, 60171
Pozdol, Henry, 7240 W. 57th St., Summit, IL 60501
Pribyl, Francis T., 2651 S. Central Park, Chicago, IL 60623
Quinlan, William J., June- November, Our Lady of the Wayside, 432 W. Park St., Arlington Heights, IL 60005
Raftery, Thomas J., Christ the King, 9235 S. Hamilton, Chicago, IL 60620
Riordan, Jerome F., 7114 Hawthorne Ln., Hanover Park, IL 60102
Rochford, John J., 18102 S. 66th Ct., #401, Tinley Park, IL 60477
Rokicinski, Stanley J., 5646 S. Karlov, Chicago, IL 60629
Rooney, William J., Curley Hall, Catholic University of America, Washington, DC 20064
Rosemeyer, Paul F., St. Theresa, 467 Benton, Palatine, IL 60067
Rowley, James J., 1138 E. Anderson Dr., Palatine, IL 60067
Rudcki, Stanley R., 7712 W. Oak Ridge Ct., #2B, Palos Heights, IL 60463

Ryan, Joseph D., 11722 S. Oakley, Chicago, IL 60643
Schackmuth, William A., 4041 W. 97th St., Oak Lawn, IL 60453
Schreiber, Edmund J., 9613 Schiller Blvd., Franklin Park, IL 60131
Schroeder, Richard F., 7216 Oxford Cir., Fox Lake, IL 60020
Schwartz, Paul E., St. James, 22244 S. Torrence Ave., Sauk Village, IL 60411-5144
Seitz, Thomas R., St. Thomas the Apostle, 5472 S. Kimbark, Chicago, IL 60615
Shannon, Robert J., Mercy Hospital, Stevenson Expy. at King Dr., Chicago, IL 60616
Shaunessy, Francis W., P.O. Box 528, Powers Lake, WI 53159
Sheridan, Robert A., St. Margaret of Scotland, 9837 S. Throop St., Chicago, IL 60643
Shields, James P., 116 N. Lake St., Mundelein, IL 60060
Shields, William J., 116 N. Lake St., Mundelein, IL 60060
Shirey, John W., 8725 S. May, Chicago, IL 60620
Siedlecki, Edmund J., Cardinal Stritch House, 1000 E. Maple, P.O. Box 455, Mundelein, IL 60060
Skach, Charles J., P.O. Box 509, Mt. Prospect, IL 60056
Skriba, Richard L., 1130 S. Michigan Ave., #3209, Chicago, IL 60605
Skupien, Edward D., St. Andrew Home for the Aged, 7000 N. Newark, Niles, IL 60714
Slominski, George A., St. Andrew Home for the Aged, 6930 W. Touhy, Niles, IL 60714
Slosarcik, Edward A., 13950 Main St., Lemont, IL 60439
Somerville, Walter F., 7574 E. Camine de Querabi, Tuscon, AZ 85715
Spellman, Francis J., St. Benedict's Home for the Aged, 6930 W. Touhy, Niles, IL 60714
Stefanski, Walter, 29 E. McEldowney St., Chicago Heights, IL 60411
Stoga, Stanley C., 8200 S. Kostner, Chicago, IL 60652
Sullivan, C. Otis, St. Benedict Home, 6930 W. Touhy Ave., Niles, IL 60714
Sullivan, Daniel J., 3217 W. 184th St., Homewood, IL 60430
Szatkowski, Casimir M., 8030 S. Pulaski, Chicago, IL 60652
Szlanga, Edmund S., St. Jane de Chantal, 5252 S. Austin Ave., Chicago, IL 60638
Taylor, Joseph C., 4350 W. Sunnyside Ave., Chicago, IL 60630
Tessmer, Richard A., 800 W. Biesterfield Rd., Elk Grove Village, IL 60007
Tlapa, Richard J., 6350 S. Taft Ave., Merrillville, IN 46410
Troy, Henry A., c/o Mr. Edward L. Troy, 9727 Lindgren Ave., Sun City, AZ 85373
Ubowski, Chester, Resurrection Hospital, 7435 W. Talcott, Chicago, IL 60631
Ulatowski, Donald F., 2839 County Z, Adams, WI 53910
Vader, Anthony J., 11652 S. Church St., Chicago, IL 60643
Velutis, John, 11129 S. Homan, Chicago, IL 60655
Vita, Mariano L., 1809 E. 31st St., La Grange Park, IL 60525
Wagner, Leon R., 2435 Seabrook Island Rd., John Island, SC 29455
Wasiel, Michael J., 546 E. 155th St., Harvey, IL 60426
Weber, Gerard P., 4316 Lanai Rd., Encino, CA 91436
White, Bernard C., St. Henry, 6335 North Hoyne, Chicago, IL 60659
White, William J., St. Gerald, 9349 S. Central Ave., Oak Lawn, IL 60453
Windle, John J., 459 Homestead, La Grange Park, IL 60525
Winters, Martin N., Benedictine Monastery of Our Lady of Sorrows, 5800 W. 147th St., Oak Forest, IL 60452
Wodniak, John L., 5730 W. Fullerton, Chicago, IL 60639
Wojcik, Richard J., Mundelein Seminary of the Univerisity of St. Mary-of-the-Lake, Mundelein, 60060
Wozny, William J., 1318 S. 61st Ave., Cicero, IL 60650
Zakarauskas, Anthony J., 6812 S. Washtenaw, Chicago, IL 60629
Zakarauskas, Vaclovas, 6812 S. Washtenaw, Chicago, IL 60629
Zawistanowicz, Norbert J., Our Lady of Victory Parish, 5212 W. Agatite Ave., Chicago, IL 60630
Zmija, Walter J., 5345 W. Roscoe, Chicago, IL 60641

Permanent Deacons:
Abboud, Louis, St. Patrick, Wadsworth
Allen, Leslie, Jr., St. Sabina, Chicago
Allen, Warren, (Retired)
Alonso, Enrique, Our Lady of Grace, Chicago
Alvarez, Jose, St. Bonaventure, Chicago
Alvarez, Margarito, Our Lady of Guadalupe, Chicago
Amberg, John, St. Mary of the Assumption, Chicago
Antiss, Robert S., Holy Family, Inverness
Antonsen, Larry, Christ the King, Chicago
Arndt, John, St. Mary, Evanston
Auld, David D., Santa Maria del Popolo, Mundelein
Avila, Mario, Precious Blood, Chicago
Ayala, Efrain, Resurrection, Chicago
Bacchi, Benedict, St. Eulalia, Maywood
Banet, Robert, St. Andrew the Apostle, Calumet City
Barker, William, Sacred Heart, Palos Hills
Barone, Louis, St. Ansgar, Hanover Park
Bartholomew, Thomas, St. Michael, Orland Park
Barton, Jeffrey, St. Peter, Antioch
Bates, Eugene, St. Thecla, Chicago
Baum, Richard, St. Anne, Barrington
Behrendt, Raymond J., Sacred Heart, Melrose Park
Beil, Frank, St. Catherine Laboure, Glenview
Belanger, James, (Retired)
Bell, Kenneth, (Retired), St. Domitilla, Hillside
Benthey, Herman, St. Anne, Hazel Crest
Benware, John, Our Lady of the Woods, Orland Park
Bergquist, Bernard, St. Tarcissus, Chicago
Bishop, Joseph, St. Rosalie, Harwood Heights
Blais, Emile, St. Mary of the Angels
Boehm, Owen, St. Rene, Chicago
Boggio, Edward, St. Marcelline, Schaumburg
Bohannon, Morris E., (Retired), St. Clotilde, Chicago
Boivin, Edward, Catholic Charities
Bonifazi, Virgilio, St. John Berchmans, Chicago
Borha, George, St. Columbanus, Chicago
Boucha, Michael, Queen of Peace, North Chicago
Bovyn, Paul, Resurrection, Chicago
Braddock, J. Michael
Bradford, Bruce, St. Catherine of Siena/St. Lucy, Oak Park
Brady, Joseph, St. Christopher, Midlothian
Braski, Ray, (Retired), St. Thomas of Villanova, Palatine
Brauch, Robert, St. Anne, Barrington
Bresler, Thomas, Holy Cross, Deerfield
Bretz, Michael, St. Catherine Laboure, Glenview
Brongiel, Andrew, St. Barbara, Chicago
Brooks, George, Infant Jesus of Prague, Flossmoor
Brooks, John, (Retired), St. Joseph, Round Lake
Brown, Dennis G., St. Mary, Buffalo Grove
Bryce, Irvin, St. Albert the Great, Burbank
Brzoski, Chester, (Retired), St. Nicholas of Tolentine, Chicago
Burke, Henry, Ascension/St. Susanna, Harvey
Burns, James, St. Donatus, Blue Island
Bustos, Gregorio, St. Clare of Montefalco, Chicago
Bzdon, Gregory M., St. Tarcissus, Chicago
Cabrera, Jorge, St. John Berchmans, Chicago
Callahan, Joseph, St. Julie Billiart, Tinley Park
Camerini, Guilio, St. Eulalia, Maywood
Carrizales, Maximiliano, Providence of God, Chicago
Carroll, Daniel, St. Walter, Chicago
Carvlin, Thomas, Ascension/St. Susanna, Harvey
Cascino, Joseph, Jr., St. Mary of the Woods, Chicago
Castanon, Toribio, Holy Cross-Immaculate Heart of Mary, Chicago
Cavanaugh, Michael, St. Francis Xavier, Wilmette
Cenek, Stephen, Transfiguration, Wauconda
Centeno, Benito, St. Genevieve, Chicago
Cesario, Carmen, Our Lady, Mother of the Church
Chaldez, Lorenzo, St. Gertrude, Franklin Park
Chappel, Dorsey, St. Leo the Great, Chicago
Chausse, Joseph, St. George, Tinley Park
Chavez, Abraham, St. Simeon, Bellwood
Chavez, Raul, Immaculate Conception, Waukegan
Childers, Terry D., Christ the King, Chicago
Chrastka, Joel, St. Leonard, Berwyn
Cichoracki, Eugene L., St. Victor, Calumet City
Ciesil, Norbert, St. Alphonsus, Prospect Heights
Cintron, Gilberto, St. Hedwig, Chicago
Ciston, William, Our Lady of the Mount, Cicero
Cnota, Robert F., St. Francis Borgia, Chicago
Cocco, Anthony, St. Michael, Orland Park
Coffey, Thomas W., St. Luke, River Forest
Colgan, Dennis L., St. William, Chicago
Collins, Dan, Our Lady of Ransom, Niles
Colucci, Victor, Sacred Heart, Melrose Park
Condill, James, St. Anne, Barrington
Conick, John, (Retired), St. Theresa, Palatine
Connor, John, St. Colette, Rolling Meadows
Constanopolis, Louis, St. Benedict the African (West), Chicago
Conway, James, St. Barnabas, Chicago
Cooper, Willie, St. Laurence, Chicago
Corcoran, Thomas, St. Raymond de Penafort, Mount Prospect
Cordesman, Ellsworth, (Retired), St. James, Highwood
Cordoba, Angelo, St. Simon the Apostle, Chicago
Crandall, Robert, (Retired), Our Lady of Ransom, Niles
Crane, Walter James, St. Catherine of Alexandria, Oak Lawn
Crespo, Feliciano, Resurrection, Chicago
Czarnecki, Thaddeus, Queen of the Rosary, Elk Grove Village
Dahl, Earl, St. John the Evangelist, Streamwood
Dahn, James, St. Alphonsus Ligouri, Prospect Heights
Dattoli, Dominick, St. George, Tinley Park
Daum, Donald, St. Germaine, Oak Lawn
Davis, James, St. Martin de Porres, Chicago
Deabel, Raymond, St. James Hospital, Chicago Heights
Debnar, John, St. Barbara, Brookfield
DeFiore, Robert, St. John the Evangelist, Streamwood
DeJesus, Confesor, St. Sylvester, Chicago
Del Llano, Manuel, Our Lady of Mercy, Chicago
Delaney, James, St. Bede the Venerable, Chicago
DeLarco, Michael, St. Celestine, Elmwood Park
DeLorenzo, Edward, St. Edmund, Oak Park
DeLuna, Arthur, Sta. Maria Addolorata, Chicago
DeRose, Ronald, Kolbe House, Chicago
Detloff, James, St. Emeric, Country Club Hills
Devereux, Robert, Our Lady of the Mount, Cicero
Devine, James, St. Celestine, Elmwood Park
DeVita, Frank, Divine Providence, Westchester
Diaz, Benjamin, St. Philomena, Chicago
Diaz, Raymundo De Leon, St. Blase, Argo
DiCanio, Vito W., St. Emily, Mt. Prospect
Dienberg, Clifford, St. Vincent Ferrer, River Forest
Dinneen, Richard, St. James, Arlington Heights
Disparte, Philip, Alexian Brothers Hospital, Elk Grove Village
DiVirgilio, Dante, St. Mary of Vernon, Indian Creek
Dolan, Edward, St. Juliana, Chicago
Donates, Rafael, Our Lady of Mt. Carmel, Melrose Park
Donovan, Timothy, Old St. Mary's, Chicago
Dorgan, Eugene J., St. Pascal, Chicago
Doud, Raymond, Church of the Holy Spirit, Schaumburg
Downs, Sylvester, (Retired), St. Joachim, Chicago
Drazba, Herbert, St. Jude the Apostle, South Holland
Drinan, Russell, Our Lady of Grace, Chicago
Duderstadt, Peery, St. Joseph the Worker, Wheeling
Duffner, Thomas, St. Mary of the Assumption, Chicago
Duffy, Frank, St. Henry, Chicago
Duffy, Robert, Our Lady of the Wayside, Arlington Heights
Dulen, John, (Retired), St. John Brebeur, Niles
Dunn, Dennis, St. Joseph, Libertyville
Dunn, William F., Jr., Santa Maria del Popolo, Mundelein
Dunne, Thomas, St. Thomas of Villanova, Palatine
Duszynski, Thomas, St. Matthew, Schaumburg
Dutkiewicz, Daniel, St. Stanislaus, Bishop & Martyr, Posen
Dwyer, James T., (Retired), Church of the Holy Spirit, Schaumburg
Echevarria, Ramon, Our Lady of Tepeyac, Chicago
Egan, David, Immaculate Conception, Waukegan
Ende, Gilbert, SS. Cyril & Methodius, Lemont
Engler, William, St. John of the Cross, Western Springs
Ernst, James, Our Lady of Hope, Rosemont
Estrada, Vincente, Immaculate Conception, Chicago
Ewers, Thomas, St. Denis, Chicago
Faherty, Paul, St. Luke, River Forest
Farinella, Louis A., St. John the Evangelist, Streamwood
Favila, Angel, St. Agnes of Bohemia, Chicago
Fay, John, Sacred Heart, Winnetka
Feltes, Richard, St. Linus, Oak Lawn
Fernandez, Dismas, St. Maurice, Chicago
Ferrini, Armand, St. James, Arlington Heights
Ficker, John, St. George, Tinley Park
Figueroa, Roberto, St. Fidelis, Chicago
Finnegan, Michael, St. Juliana, Chicago
Flam, Richard, St. Marcelline, Schaumburg
Flanagan, John, St. Germaine, Oak Lawn
Flewellen, James, St. Thaddeus, Chicago
Flores, Nicolas, St. Stanislaus Kostka, Chicago
Flores, Roman, St. Gertrude, Franklin Park
Foley, Brendan, Our Lady of the Wayside, Arlington Heights

Forey, James P., St. John the Evangelist, Streamwood
Fox, Gerald, St. Barbara, Brookfield
Fragassi, Phillip, St. Patrick, Wadsworth
Fronczek, Casimir, St. Francis Borgia Deaf Center, Chicago
Fuller, George, (Retired), Resurrection, Chicago
Gadomski, Edward, St. Linus, Oak Lawn
Gagnon, Robert, St. Peter, Antioch
Gallagher, James, St. James, Highwood
Gallagher, John, St. Colette, Rolling Meadows
Ganschow, Howard W., II, St. Mary, Buffalo Grove
Garcia, Jose, St. Marcelline, Schaumburg
Garcia, Miguel, St. Stanislaus Kostka, Chicago
Garstki, Edwin, Office of the Vicar for the Diaconate
Garza, Juan L., St. Paul, Chicago Heights
Gaspari, Alfred V., St. Colette, Rolling Meadows
Gaughan, Francis, St. Ita, Chicago
Gavin, Raymond, St. Catherine Laboure, Glenview
Gembara, Emil, St. Alexander, Palos Heights
Gilbert, Paul, St. George, Tinley Park
Gildea, Francis, St. Theresa, Palatine
Globis, Richard J., St. Gilbert, Grayslake
Gniech, George, St. Constance, Chicago
Golab, Chester J., St. Daniel the Prophet, Chicago
Gonzales, Jose, St. Aloysius, Chicago
Gonzalez, Jose M., St. Peter Canisius, Chicago
Gordus, Richard, Mater Christi, North Riverside
Graffia, Raymond, St. Edna, Arlington Heights
Green, Richard, St. Turibius, Chicago
Grevenites, James, St. Louise de Marillace, LaGrange Park
Gronek, Ronald, Divine Savior, Norridge
Grossnickle, Donald R., Our Lady of the Wayside, Arlington Heights
Gutierrez, Jorge, St. Mark, Chicago
Hahn, Gerald E., Queen of Apostles, Riverdale
Halper, Bernard, (Retired), St. Kieran, Chicago Heights
Halt, Thomas, St. Matthew, Schaumburg
Hankett, Richard G., Queen of Angels, Chicago
Hare, Martin, (Retired), Holy Rosary, Chicago
Harrington, John, Kolbe House
Harris, Wallace, St. Dorothy, Chicago
Hart, Vernon, Seven Holy Founders, Calumet Park
Hatch, Wilmer, (Retired), St. Philip Neri, Chicago
Helmer, Everett, (Retired), St. Germaine, Oak Lawn
Hempen, Harold, St. Irenaeus, Park Forest
Hennessy, Matthew, St. James, Arlington Heights
Henricks, John, Sacred Heart, Melrose Park
Henry, Francis, Nativity of Our Lord, Chicago
Henry, Roy, Our Lady of Lourdes, Chicago
Hensley, Claude, St. Anthony, Cicero
Hermann, Dean, Queen of Peace, North Chicago
Hernandez, Armando, St. Michael, Chicago
Hernandez, Sigifredo, St. Jerome, Chicago
Herrera, Albert, St. Gall, Chicago
Herrera, Armando, Mary Queen of Heaven, Chicago
Herrera, Marcial, St. John Berchmans, Chicago
Hill, John, (Retired), Our Lady of Peace, Chicago
Hinch, Ralph, St. Francis Borgia Deaf Center, Chicago
Hipelius, Thomas, St. Damian, Oak Forest
Hjelmgren, Bob, St. John Vianney, Northlake
Hogan, Ralph, (Retired), St. Mary of Vernon, Mundelein
Horne, Philip G., Our Lady of Humility, Zion
Hotcaveg, Irwin E., St. Ferdinand, Chicago
Howard, Samuel E., Infant Jesus of Prague, Flossmoor
Hubbard, James, St. Felicitas, Chicago
Huber, Charles, St. Francis Borgia, Chicago
Hughes, James, (Retired), St. Catherine of Alexandria, Oak Lawn
Hurley, William, Christ the King, Chicago
Huslig, Dennis, St. Louise de Marillac, La Grange Park
Ibarra, Juan, St. Stanislaus Kostka, Chicago
Iwan, Henry, St. Gilbert, Grayslake
Jablonski, Robert, St. Bartholomew, Chicago
Jablonski, William, St. Kiernan, Chicago Heights
Jacob, Robert, St. Benedict, Chicago
Jay, Richard, St. Athanasius, Evanston
Jean-Pierre, Fritz, St. Jerome, Chicago
Jeffrey, August, Divine Savior, Norridge
Jenney, Kenneth, Jr., Immaculate Heart of Mary, Chicago
Jinkens, Max R., Our Lady of Humility, Zion
Johnson, Mervin, St. Leo the Great, Chicago
Jones, Roosevelt, St. Anselm, Chicago
Kaczmarek, Edward, St. Thomas of Villanova, Palatine
Kalivoda, Bill, Addolorata Villa, Wheeling
Kancler, Lawrence, Unassigned
Kanter, Kevin, St. Mary, Buffalo Grove
Karnoski, Michael, St. Louis de Montfort, Oak Lawn
Kasimatis, Jerome, Holy Cross, Deerfield
Kearney, John, Immaculate Heart of Mary, Chicago
Keating, Timothy, St. Lawrence O'Toole, Matteson
Keegan, Charles, St. Patricia, Hickory Hills
Kenney, James, St. Mary, Lake Forest
Kiley, Michael E., St. Julie Billart, Tinley Park
Klemanovic, John, Our Lady of Lourdes, Chicago
Klimcke, Walter, (Retired), St. Cletus, LaGrange
Knippen, James, (Retired), St. Hubert, Hoffman Esttes
Kocar, Marvin, St. Pius X, Stickney
Kort, Clayton, St. John Fisher, Chicago
Kotleba, Rudolf, Holy Family/St. Francis Assisi, Chicago
Kotwas, Donald, St. Bede the Venerable, Chicago
Kowalski, David J., St. Louise de Marillac, LaGrange Park
Koziol, John, St. Matthew, Schaumburg
Kozloski, Stanley, St. Matthew, Schaumburg
Kozuchowski, Chester, St. Gilbert, Grayslake
Krakora, Joseph, St. Mary, Lake Forest
Krapez, Michael, Our Lady of the Ridge, Chicago Ridge
Kristinat, Richard L., St. George, Tinley Park
Kryszak, Timothy, Holy Spirit, Schaumburg
Kukla, Eugene, St. Mary, Buffalo Grove
Kush, Michael, St. Damian, Oak Forest
Kwasegroch, Gerald, St. Eugene, Chicago
Kwasigroch, James, Our Lady of Grace, Chicago
La Belle, Eugene, St. Kieran, Chicago Heights
LaCosse, Robert, St. James, Arlington Heights
LaCoursiere, Victor, St. Jerome, Chicago
Lagges, Peter, St. Zachary, Des Plaines
Lambert, George, St. Eulalia, Maywood
Lambert, Thomas, St. Raymond, Mt. Prospect
Langwell, James E., Incarnation, Palos Heights
Leck, Robert, Our Lady of Victory, Chicago
Lehman, William B., Divine Savior, Norridge
Lekan, Louis, St. James, Arlington Heights
Leo, Kevin, St. Thomas of Villanova, Palatine
Leonard, Timothy, Prince of Peace, Lake Villa
Leonas, John, (Retired), St. Anne, Hazel Crest
Lesnieski, Norbert, SS. Cyril & Methodius, Lemont
Levins, Terrence, SS. Faith, Hope & Charity, Winnetka
Lewis, Joseph, Our Lady of Sorrows, Chicago
Liberti, Peter, All Saints-St. Anthony, Chicago
Lilly, Leroy, St. Laurence, Chicago
Limon, Juan, St. Benedict, Blue Island
Limon, Vincente, Our Lady of Tepeyac, Chicago
Lino, Ronald, St. John the Evangelist, Streamwood
Lisowski, Thaddeus, St. Constance, Chicago
Llano, Antonio, Our Lady of the Mount, Cicero
Llorens, Anthony, St. Martin de Porres, Chicago
Lopez, Adolf, St. Aloysius, Chicago
Lopez, Bricio, University of Illinois Hospitals
Lorbach, John, St. Raymond de Penafort, Mt. Prospect
Lugo, Gregorio, Our Lady of Grace, Chicago
Lukaszewski, Edward, St. Constance, Chicago
Lundy, Albert, Our Lady of Knock, Calumet City
Lyons, John, (Retired), St. James, Arlington Heights
Mackert, Martin, All Saints-St. Anthony, Chicago
Maddock, George, St. Joseph, Homewood
Madonia, Loretto, St. Giles, Oak Park
Mages, William, St. Mary of the Woods, Chicago
Maldonado, Meliquides, St. Mark, Chicago
Malec, Albert, St. Daniel the Prophet, Chicago
Mally, Joseph, St. Adalbert, Chicago
Malone, Jack, St. Germaine, Oak Lawn
Maloney, Thomas J., St. Thomas of Villanova, Palatine
Maney, Antonio, St. James, Maywood
Manning, Peter, St. Joseph, Summit
Manthie, Robert, St. Edna, Arlington Heights
Marella, Dominic, St. Charles Borromeo, Melrose Park
Marotto, Angelo, St. Domitilla, Hillside
Marquez, J. Frank, (Retired), St. Pascal, Chicago
Marrero, Jose, St. Roman, Chicago
Martinez, Francisco, St. Philomena, Chicago
Mason, Frederick, Catholic Youth Organization
Matthews, Robert, St. Joseph, Libertyville
Mauch, Richard, (Retired), St. Ann, Lansing
Maune, William, St. Irenaeus, Park Forest
Maurer, William, Infant Jesus of Prague, Flossmoor
McCarthy, Thomas, St. James, Sauk Village
McCloskey, Michael, Holy Name Cathedral, Chicago
McDonough, Michael, St. Michael, Orland Park
McElrath, Bruce, St. Ailbe, Chicago
McGorey, Thomas, St. John of the Cross, Western Springs
McKinnis, William, St. Columbanus, Chicago
McLynn, Michael, St. Louis de Marillac, La Grange Park
McMahon, John, St. Bede, Ingleside
McNulty, Michael, Sacred Heart, Winnetka
Meehan, Peter, St. Martha, Morton Grove
Meehan, Thomas, Our Lady of Loretto, Hometown
Mele, John, Special Ministry
Melkovitz, Emil, (Retired), St. Francis Borgia, Chicago
Memmel, Aloysius, St. Paul of the Cross, Park Ridge
Mench, Sidney, (Retired), St. John Fisher, Chicago
Mendez, Genaro, Holy Rosary, Chicago
Mendieta, Raul, St. Alphonsus, Chicago
Mendizabal, Guillermo, St. John Berchmans, Chicago
Mendoza, Jose Luis, St. Agnes of Bohemia, Chicago
Mercure, Michael, Our Lady of Humility, Zion-Beach Park
Metallo, Arthur, St. Francis Hospital, Evanston
Michalowski, Benedict, St. Joseph, Summit
Milender, Leonard, Prince of Peace, Lake Villa
Miller, William, St. Peter, Skokie
Miska, Richard, St. Julie Billiart, Tinley Park
Mondello, Christopher, St. Gilbert, Grayslake
Mongan, Martin, St. Bernadette, Evergreen Park
Monica, Robert, St. Thomas the Apostle, Chicago
Monnelly, Michael, Queen of All Saints, Chicago
Monterroso, Oscar, St. Ansgar, Hanover Park
Moore, Steven, St. Anne, Hazel Crest
Moorman, William, Immaculate Conception, Highland Park
Morales, Juan, St. Anthony, Cicero
Moran, Charles, St. John the Evangelist, Streamwood
Moreno, Eusebio, Holy Family, Waukegan
Morgan, James, St. Gelasius, Chicago
Morowczynski, Romuald, St. Jane de Chantal, Chicago
Morton, Wayne, St. Lawrence O'Toole, Matteson
Motycka, Robert, St. Barbara, Brookfield
Mudd, Dennis, Sr., St. Joseph, Libertyville
Mujica, Ines, (Retired)
Mullaney, Roger, SS. Faith, Hope & Charity, Winnetka
Munda, Gary, Sr., Queen of Peace, North Chicago
Munoz, Romeo, St. Victor, Calumet City
Murphy, Robert, St. Gertrude, Franklin Park
Murphy, Robert, St. Jerome, Chicago
Murray, Michael, (Retired), Our Lady of the Brook, Northbrook
Navarro, Anthonio, St. Mark, Chicago
Navarro, Jesse, St. Mary, Star of the Sea, Chicago
Nazario, Carlos, Our Lady of Grace, Chicago
Negron, Julio A., Queen of Peace, North Chicago
Neurauter, Paul, St. Peter, Antioch
Newhall, Redondo, St. Cajetan, Chicago
Newman, Jeffrey, St. Gilbert, Grayslake
Newton, Robert, St. Peter Damian, Bartlett
Nguyen, Duc Van, St. Thomas of Canterbury, Chicago
Niersbach, Donald, St. Walter, Chicago
Nieves, Bienvenido, St. Josaphat, Chicago
Nimietz, James, St. John the Evangelist, Streamwood
Nolan, John, St. Celestine, Elmwood Park
Norton, Terrence, St. Luke, River Forest
Norys, Stephen, St. Theresa, Palatine
Nowak, Thomas, St. Agnes, Chicago Heights
Nugent, J Michael, St. John the Evangelist, Streamwood
Nunez, Raul, Our Lady of Guadalupe, Chicago
Nylen, Arthur A., St. Jude the Apostle, South Holland
O'Brien, Thomas, (Retired), St. Emeric, Country Club Hills
O'Connell, Thomas, St. Walter, Chicago
O'Donnell, Charles, Our Lady of Ransom, Niles
O'Donnell, Patrick, (Retired), St. Damian, Oak Forest
O'Grady, Donald A., (Retired), Queen of Angels, Chicago
O'Keefe, Robert C., St. Isaac Jogues, Niles
O'Leary, Edward, St. Eugene, Chicago
O'Leary, John A., St. Joseph, Homewood
O'Malley, James, O'Hare Airport Chapel, Chicago
O'Neill, John, St. Luke, River Forest
Oborski, Zygfryd, St. Stanislaus Bishop & Martyr, Chicago
Ochoa, Zeferino, Holy Family/St. Francis of Assisi, Chicago
Odegard, Robert, St. Priscilla, Chicago
Ojeda, Norberto, St. James, Maywood
Olson, Carl, St. Cornelius, Chicago
Omiatek, Marion, Transfiguration, Wauconda
Ontiveros, Philip, St. Marcelline, Schaumburg
Ortego, Ignacio, St. Mark, Chicago
Ortiz, Sigifredo, St. Sylvester, Chicago
Pagliai, Bruno, St. James, Highwood
Paluch, Thomas M., St. John Brebeuf, Niles
Panek, Joseph, Office of the Vicar for Diaconate
Pastirik, Joseph, St. Francis de Sales, Chicago
Penich, Michael, Jr., St. Paul the Apostle, Gurnee
Pepitone, Joe, St. John of the Cross, Western Springs
Perez, Alphonse M., Assumption, Chicago
Perez, Carlos, St. Joseph, Chicago

Perez, Luis, Santa Maria Addolorata, Chicago
Perez, Miguel, St. Pius V., Chicago
Perez, Orlando, St. Thomas of Canterbury, Chicago
Perez, Teodoro, St. Anne, Hazel Crest
Perez, Wilfredo, St. John Bosco, Chicago
Perkowitz, John, St. John Brebeuf, Niles
Peters, Bruce, St. Mary, Buffalo Grove
Peterson, George A., (Retired)
Petricca, Clemente, St. Ansgar, Hanover Park
Phillippi, Joseph, St. James, Arlington Heights
Pineda, Javier, St. Adrian, Chicago
Pineiro, Ismael, St. Simeon, Bellwood
Pizzato, Richard, St. Theresa, Palatine
Plantz, Robert, St. James, Arlington Heights
Platt, James, St. Cyprian, River Grove
Poletto, Robert, St. Mary, Fremont Center, Mundelein
Ponce, Antonio, St. Blase, Argo
Quackenbush, Edward, St. Bede, Ingleside
Quinn, Eugene, Holy Ghost, South Holland
Ragonese, Dan, St. Victor, Calumet City
Ramirez, Jorge V., Our Lady of Good Counsel, Chicago
Ramos, Dennis, St. Aloysius, Chicago
Ramos, Francisco, St. Philomena, Chicago
Ranke, Dennis, Our Lady of Victory, Chicago
Ray, Frederick W., St. Isaac Jogues, Niles
Rehor, Timothy, St. Bernardine, Forest Park
Reilly, Raymond, St. John Fisher, Chicago
Reinert, William, St. Raymond de Penafort, Mount Prospect
Reinhart, James, St. Linus, Oak Lawn
Reisen, William, St. Matthew, Schaumburg
Renk, Dennis, St. Joseph, Chicago
Revering, Roman, St. James, Maywood
Revord, James, Our Lady of Perpetual Help, Glenview
Riccio, Louis, Charismatic Renewal, St. Theresa, Palatine
Richardson, John, St. Patrick, Wadsworth
Richardson, Leonard M., St. Sabina, Chicago
Riffner, Joseph, St. Alphonsus, Chicago
Riner, Edwin, Unassigned
Rios, Jamie, St. Fidelis, Chicago
Rivas, Roberto, Our Lady of Mercy, Chicago
Rivera, Hector, St. Teresa of Avila, Chicago
Rivera, Sebastian, St. Gertrude, Franklin Park
Rodriguez, Antonio, Resurrection, Chicago
Rodriguez, Candelario, Notre Dame, Chicago
Rodriguez, Emiliano, St. Bonaventure, Chicago
Rodriguez, Juan, St. Rita of Cascia, Chicago
Rodriguez, Manuel, St. Francis of Assisi, Chicago
Rodriguez, Milton, Maternity of B.V.M., Chicago
Rodriguez, Santiago, St. Aloysius, Chicago
Rodriguez, Uriol, Resurrection, Chicago
Roman, Francisco, St. Sylvester, Chicago
Roman, Tito, St. Bonaventure, Chicago
Romano, Michael, Columbus Hospital, Chicago
Rosa, Abraham, St. Mark, Chicago
Rosado, Julio, Mary, Queen of Heaven, Cicero
Rowe, John, St. Ann, Lansing
Roy, Jasper, Holy Angels, Chicago
Rozo, Jorge, Holy Rosary, Chicago
Ruffner, R. Michael, Mary, Seat of Wisdom, Park Ridge
Ruppert, William, St. John Vianney, Northlake
Ryan, Edward, St. Anthony, Chicago
Ryan, Robert E., Sr., St. Juliana, Chicago
Ryan, Thomas, St. Christina, Chicago
Sabato, Anthony, Holy Cross, Deerfield
Sacramento, Anthony, St. Dismas, Waukegan
Salgado, Alfonso, St. Anthony, Cicero
Sanchez, Sabino, St. Francis and Our Lady of the Angels, Chicago
Sanchez, Salvador, St. Francis of Assisi/Our Lady of the Angels, Chicago
Sands, William, Sta. Maria Del Popolo, Mundelein
Sanford, James, St. Emily, Mount Prospect
Sanzone, Michael J., Immaculate Conception, Waukegan
Sassetti, Robert C., St. Vincent Ferrer, River Forest
Sattler, David, St. Peter Damien, Bartlett
Savercool, Gerald, St. Lawrence O'Toole, Matteson
Scarbalis, Edward, Holy Family, Waukegan
Schiltz, James, St. Constance, Chicago
Schoenfeld, Kenneth, St. Fabian, Bridgeview
Schoewe, Rudolph, Our Lady of Victory, Chicago
Schroeder, Thomas, St. James, Sauk Village
Schroetlin, Albert, St. Richard, Chicago
Schultz, Ronald, St. Victor, Calumet City
Sedivy, Alan, Our Lady of Perpetual Help, Glenview
Seitz, John, Incarnation, Palos Heights
Serratore, Gregory, St. Mary Star of Sea, Chicago
Seveska, Richard, St. Anne, Barrington
Shandro, Ellery, St. Benedict, Blue Island
Sharwarko, Michael, St. Louis de Monfort, Oak Lawn
Shaw, Jeffrey L., St. Theresa, Palatine
Shinkle, Derald, Sacred Heart, Winnetka
Silva, Rodrigo, St. Ann, Chicago
Simmons, John, Santa Maria del Popolo, Mundelein
Siranovic, Joseph, Notre Dame de Chicago, Chicago
Slajchert, Michael, St. Gall, Chicago
Smith, John J., St. Zachary, Des Plaines
Smith, Robert S., Jr., Holy Cross, Deerfield
Solon, Thomas, St. Denis, Chicago
Soto, Pedro, St. John Bosco, Chicago
Soto, Santos, St. Sylvester, Chicago
Spalla, Paul, St. Mary-of-the-Lake, Chicago
Spitizzeri, Fred, St. Priscilla, Chicago
Spohr, Lawrence, St. Mary of Celle, Berwyn
Stalcup, Joseph, Sr., St. George, Tinley Park
Stanczak, Stefan, St. Hyacinth, Chicago
Stearns, William, St. Damian, Oak Forest
Steinbeigle, Francis, St. Damian, Oak Forest
Stevens, Gregory, St. Celestine, Elmwood Park
Stubstad, Thomas, St. Pascal, Chicago
Sullivan, William, St. Barnabas, Chicago
Sullivan, William, St. Louis de Montfort, Oak Lawn
Sutton, Daniel, St. Helena of the Cross, Chicago
Swiatek, Ronald, St. John Bosco, Chicago
Swiech, Edward, St. Robert Bellarmine, Chicago
Szady, Mitchell, St. Stanislaus B & M, Chicago
Taylor, Lowell, (Retired), Church of the Holy Spirit, Schaumburg
Telle, Paul, St. Dismas, Waukegan
Telposky, Donald, St. Stephen, Des Plaines
Temple, James, St. Barnabas, Chicago
Tereza, Nick, St. Ansgar, Hanover Park
Tipperreiter, Charles, Queen of Martyrs, Evergreen Park
Tomkowiak, Edward, St. Patrick, Wadsworth
Torres, Candido, Our Lady of Fatima, Chicago
Trakszelis, Jerome, St. Vincent Ferror, River Forest
Trevino, Luis, Church of the Holy Spirit, Schaumburg
Troy, Daniel J., Holy Ghost, South Holland
Tryba, Edmund, (Retired), St. Hilary, Chicago
Uroza, Jose, St. Angela, Chicago
Valadez, Abundio, St. Benedict, Chicago
Valdivia, Juan, Our Lady of Guadalupe, Chicago
Valentin, Israel, St. Philomena, Chicago
Valenziano, Vern, St. Edna, Arlington Heights
Valle, Miguel Angel, Our Lady of Lourdes, Chicago
Vazquez, Jose, Maternity B.V.M., Chicago
Velasco, Arturo, St. Francis of Assisi, Chicago
Velasco, Benito, Maternity B.V.M., Chicago
Velazquez, Angel, Holy Family, Waukegan
Vemich, Duke, All Saints-St. Anthony, Chicago
Vera, Camilo, St. Viator, Chicago
Vidmar, John, St. Stephen, Chicago
Vignocchi, Louis, Immaculate Conception, Highland Park
Villa, Salvatore, St. Bruno, Chicago
Villalobos, Antonio, St. Mark, Chicago
Villalpando, Adam, St. Peter Canisius, Chicago
Villasenor, Faustino, St. Stanislaus Kostka, Chicago
Villegas, Salomon, St. Hedwig, Chicago
Virruso, Christopher, Our Lady, Mother of the Church, Chicago
Walters, John, St. Bernardine, Forest Park
Ward, Raymond, Queen of All Saints, Chicago
Ward, Raymond E., St. Jerome, Chicago
Warfield, Richard, Chap. Police Dept., Chicago
Warren, Roy, St. Agatha, Chicago
Watson, Dexter, Holy Angels, Chicago
Weber, Ronald J., St. Ansgar, Hanover Park
Wegner, Albin J., Jr., St. Michael, Chicago
Wehling, Donald, St. Hilary, Chicago
Weiner, Ronald, St. John Bosco, Chicago
Weitendorf, Norbert, St. Patricia, Hickory Hills
Welter, Daniel, Our Lady of the Woods, Orland Park
West, Tommy, Assumption/St. Catherine of Genoa, Chicago
White, Philip, Mercy Mission, Chicago
Wieczorek, Richard, Five Holy Martyrs, Chicago
Wilczynski, Joseph, St. Stanislaus B & M, Posen
Willer, Richard, St. Thomas of Villanova, Palatine
Williams, Rufus, (Retired), St. Benedict the African, Chicago
Wills, James, St. Peter, Skokie
Winblad, Joseph, Unassigned
Wogan, James, St. Mary of Vernon, Indian Creek
Wojtowicz, Louis M., St. Juliana, Chicago
Young, Irving, St. Mary, Buffalo Grove
Yucuis, Charles, St. Christopher, Midlothian
Zanardo, Ronald, St. Lawrence O'Toole, Matteson
Zawadzki, Kenneth, St. Fabian, Bridgeview
Zdeb, James, St. Thomas of Villanova, Palatine
Zeller, John, St. Marcelline, Schaumburg
Zimmerman, Edward, Our Lady of the Snows, Chicago
Zimmermann, John, Transfiguration, Wauconda
Ziomek, Robert, St. Ansgar, Hanover Park
Zurawski, John, St. John Vianney, Northlake
Zwolski, Mark, St. Mary of Vernon, Mundelein
Zych, Gerald, St. Giles, Oak Park

INSTITUTIONS LOCATED IN THE ARCHDIOCESE

[A] SEMINARIES, ARCHDIOCESAN

CHICAGO. *Archbishop Quigley Preparatory Seminary*, 103 E. Chestnut St., 60611. Tel: 312-787-9343. Revs. Michael G. Foley, Rector & Pres.; Wayne F. Watts; Peter Snieg; Edward M. Mikolajczyk, Dean of Students; Louis J. Zake; Dennis A. Ziomek; Edward B. Panek, Dean of Formation. Priests 7; Lay Teachers 18; Students 219.

Institute of Vocation Awareness, 103 E. Chestnut St., 60611. Tel: 312-787-9343. Rev. Harold B. Stanger.

A Vocation Out-Reach Program for the Archdiocese of Chicago.

St. Joseph Seminary, The Seminary College at Loyola University, 6551 N. Sheridan Rd., 60626. Tel: 773-973-9700; Fax: 773-973-9718. Administration: Revs. James Presta, M. Div., S.T.L., Rector-Pres.; John J. Clair, M.Div., Vice Pres.; William M. Frigo, O.F.M.Cap., M.S.W., Instructor; Thomas J. Hurley, B.A., M.Div., Dir. Recruitment; Henry C. Kricek, M.A., S.T.L., Academic Dean, Philosophy Instructor; Daniel J. McCormack, B.A., M.Div., M.A. (Cand.), Dir. Liturgy; Dr. Dennis M. Composoto, Ph.D., M.Ed., Comptroller & Dir. Finanical Aid, Political Science Lecturer; Mr. Michael D. Martino, M.A., Dir. of Pre-College Prog.; Mr. Patrick McCarthy, B.S., Assoc. Dir. of Recruitment; Mrs. Marie Composto, Dir. Seminary Devel.; Ms. Yuvanka Juarez, B.A., Financial Aid Admin.; Ms. Theresa Rooney, Dir. of Community Relations; Mr. John A. Houlihan, M.A., M.S., J.D., Computer Science Dir.; Mrs. Maria DeJesus Lemus, B.A., M.A. (Cand.), Registrar; Mr. Marco A. Lopez, M.T.S., Dir. Pastoral Formation, Lecturer.

MUNDELEIN. *University of St. Mary of the Lake-Mundelein Seminary*, 60060. Tel: 847-566-6401; Fax: 847-566-7330. Resident Faculty: Very Rev. John F. Canary, Rector, Pres.; Revs. Bartholomew S. Winters, M. Div., M.A.S., S.T.D.; John G. Lodge, M.Div., M.A., S.T.L., S.S.L., S.T.D., Academic Dean; Leo D. Lefebure, Ph.D., Dean of Canonically Recognized Faculty; Sr. Linda Sevcik, S.M., S.T.L., Dir. Field Ed.; Revs. Raymond J. Webb, Ph.D., Dir. Newly Ordained Program; John H. Barkemeyer, Dir. Vocations; August J. Belauskas, Ph.D. (Cand.), Admissions Dir.; Patrick J. Boyle, S.J., Ph.D.; Sr. Sara Butler, M.S.B.T., Ph.D.; Sr. Dorothy Folliard, O.P., Ph.D., M.A.R.S.; Sr. Veronica Mendez, R.C.D., M.T.S.; Revs. Victor Alvarez, S.S.P., B.A.; Robert E. Barron, S.T.D. (Cand.); Kenneth Davis, O.F.M.Conv., B.A., M.A., D.Min.; John Dearhammer, B.A., M.Div.; John V. Dolciamore, J.C.L.; Brian J. Fischer, S.L.D. (Cand.); Stephen Giorono, S.T., B.A., M.A.; Lawrence R. Hennessey, Ph.D.; Leo D. Lefebure, Ph.D.; Jerome E. Listecki, J.C.D., J.D., S.T.D.; Charles R. Meyer, S.T.D., Prof. Emeritus; James P. McIlhone, Ph.D.; Patrick O'Malley, M.A., S.T.L.; Steven Patte, B.A.; Martin Zielinski, Ph.D.; Joseph Mol, Canonical Recorder; Arlene Michna, Mus. B., Mus. M.; Revs. B. James Murphy, M.Div. (JOL); David P. Pavlik, M.A., M. Div.; Robert L. Schoenstene, S.S.L. (JOL); Daniel S. Siwek, S.T.L.; Paul H. Wachdorf, M.C.Sp.; Richard J. Wojcik, M.C.G., Prof. Emeritus; Dennis M. Zalecki; Mr. Herman Peterson, M.S., M.T.S., Librarian; Rev. Anthony M. O'Connell, O.S.M., Psy.D., Non-Resident. Priests 31; Sisters 4; Lay Teachers 2; Students 192.

Convent. Sr. Consuelo Vazquez, Supr. Oblate Sisters of Jesus the Priest 8.

[B] SEMINARIES, RELIGIOUS OR SCHOLASTICATES

CHICAGO. *The Catholic Theological Union at Chicago*, 5401 S. Cornell Ave., 60615. Tel: 773-324-8000. Major Seminary. Serving the following: Franciscans, Servites, Passionists, Augustinians, Norbertines, Society of the Divine Word, Missionaries of the Precious Blood, Claretians, Crosier Fathers, Holy Ghost Fathers, Sacred Heart Missionaries, Viatorians, Comboni Missionaries, Franciscans Capuchins, Sacred Heart Fathers and Brothers, Ukrainian Catholic Diocese, Congregation of the Blessed Sacrament, Columban Missionaries, Redemptorist Fathers, Oblates of Mary Immaculate, Xaverian Missionaries, Maryknoll Missionaries, Conventual Franciscans, Oratorians, Scalabrinians, Discalced Carmelites, Vincentians. Revs. Donald Senior, C.P., S.T.D., Pres.; Gary Riebe-Estrella, S.V.D., S.T.D., Vice Pres. & Academic Dean; Ms. Bernice Frederick, M.A.P.S., Vice Pres. Admin. & Finance; Ms. Virginia A. Piecuch, M.Div., Dean of Students & C.T.U. Community Svcs.; Dr. Emily R. John, Ph.D.,

Dir. Institutional Advancement; Rev. Kenneth O'Malley, C.P., Ph.D., Dir. Library; Ms. Priscilla Sporrong, M.B.A., Dir., Public Rels.; Rev. Kevin Madigan, P.H.D., Dir. M.A. Prog.; Sr. Eleanor Holland, I.B.V.M., M.A., Dir. Continuing Educ. Prog.; Revs. Genska Depaul, O.F.M., M.T.S., Admin.; Gerald Persha, M.M., Ph.D., S.T.D., Dir. M.Div. Prog. Faculty: Dr. Herbert Anderson, Ph.D.; Dr. Claude-Marie Barbour, S.T.D.; Sr. Dianne Bergant, C.S.A., Ph.D., Dir. D.Min. Prog.; Revs. Stephen B. Bevans, S.V.D., Ph.D.; Timothy A. Lenchak, S.V.D.; Sr. Barbara Bowe, R.S.C.J., Th.D.; Sr. Jeanette Lucinio, S.P., Dir. M.A.P.S. Prog. & Dir. Field Educ.; Sr. Eleanor Doidge, L.O.B., D.Min.; Dr. Kevin Madigan, Ph.D.; Revs. Edward Foley, O.F.M.Cap., Ph.D., M.Mus.; Archimedes Fornasari, M.C.C.J., Ph.D.; Richard Fragomeni, Ph.D.; Mark R. Francis, C.S.V., S.L.D.; Dr. Mary Frolich, Ph.D.; Sr. Marianne Race, C.S.J., M.A., Dir. Israel Study Programs; Revs. Anthony Gittins, C.S.Sp., Ph.D.; Zachary Hayes, O.F.M., Dr.Th.; Leslie J. Hoppe, O.F.M., Ph.D.; John M. Kaserow, M.M., Ph.D.; John E. Linnan, C.S.V., S.T.D.; Eugene A. LaVerdiere, S.S.S., Ph.D.; Thomas Nairn, O.F.M., Ph.D.; James C. Okoye, C.S.Sp.; Sr. Carolyn Osiek, R.S.C.J., Th.D.; Revs. Gilbert Ostdiek, O.F.M., S.T.D., Dir. M.Div. Prog.; John M. Pawlikowski, O.S.M., Ph.D.; Rabbi Hayim Goren Perelmuter, D.H.L.; Sr. Jamie Phelps, O.P., Ph.D.; Sr. Barbara Reid, O.P., Ph.D.; Revs. Gary Riebe-Estrella, S.V.D., Ph.D., S.T.D.; Robert Schreiter, C.PP.S., Th.D., Dir. Bernardin Center; Roger P. Schroeder, S.V.D., D.Miss.; Donald Senior, C.P., S.T.D.; Paul Wadell, C.P., Ph.D.; Mr. Bruce Lescher, Ph.D. Priests 23; Sisters 9; Lay Teachers 3; Non-Catholic Clergy 3; Students 348.

TECHNY. *Divine Word Residence.* (Formerly Divine Word Seminary-St. Mary's Mission House), P.O. Box 6000, 60082-6000. Tel: 847-272-2700; Fax: 847-272-2873. Legal Title: *Divine Word Techny Community Corporation.* Revs. Kazimerz Garbacz, S.V.D., Rector; James Bergin, S.V.D.; Michael J. Bonner, S.V.D.; Edward Borkowski, S.V.D.; James Braband, S.V.D.; Walter Bracken, S.V.D.; Emil Cernaj, S.V.D.; Thomas Commons, S.V.D.; Joseph Connors, S.V.D.; Paul Connors, S.V.D.; John Donaghey, S.V.D.; Francis Drzaic, S.V.D.; Leo Dusheck, S.V.D.; John Fu, S.V.D.; Gerald Garry, S.V.D.; Gilbert Gawlik, S.V.D.; Elzear Gehlen, S.V.D.; Thomas Griffith, S.V.D.; Walter Hafner, S.V.D.; Gerard Hofstee, S.V.D.; Leo Hotze, S.V.D.; Francis Hughes, S.V.D.; Henry Jungbluth, S.V.D.; Francis J. Kamp, S.V.D.; John Koster, S.V.D.; Francis Kowalski, S.V.D.; Anthony Krajci, S.V.D.; Thomas A. Krosnicki, S.V.D.; Joseph LeBeau, S.V.D.; Paschal LoBianco, S.V.D.; Louis Luzbetak, S.V.D.; Andrew Masters, S.V.D.; Wilbert Morman, S.V.D.; Robert Myers, S.V.D.; Edward Norton, S.V.D.; Chester Nowicki, S.V.D.; Edward Peklo, S.V.D.; Lawrence Poetz, S.V.D.; Raymond Quetchenbach, S.V.D.; Claire Risse, S.V.D.; Charles Roesslein, S.V.D.; Frederick Rudolph, S.V.D.; Charles Schoderbek, S.V.D.; Eugene Stoll; John Swift, S.V.D.; Lawrence Thornton, S.V.D.; Stanley Uroda, S.V.D.; John Vogelgesang, S.V.D.; Bros. John Carlucci, S.V.D.; Douglas Edmonds, S.V.D.; Rene Gawlik, S.V.D.; George Haegele, S.V.D.; Rudolph Heckel, S.V.D.; Jude Heeks, S.V.D.; James Hunt, S.V.D.; Clement Meyer, S.V.D.; David Noonan, S.V.D.; Joachim Oros, S.V.D.; Stephen Pardy, S.V.D.; Gerard Pashia, S.V.D.; Pius Resch, S.V.D.; James Ryan, S.V.D.; Cyril Schroeder, S.V.D.; Alois Terendy, S.V.D.; Joseph Urban, S.V.D.; Kenneth Valois, S.V.D.; Edwin Wirth, S.V.D.; Matthew Zemel, S.V.D.

Divine Word Theologate. Major Seminary of the Chicago Province. 5342 S. University Ave., Chicago, 60615. Tel: 773-288-2777; Fax: 773-288-6307. Rev. Mark Weber, S.V.D., Rector. Staff: Revs. Roger S. Arnold, S.V.D.; Stephen Bevens, S.V.D.; Timothy A. Lenchak, S.V.D.; Gary Riebe-Estrella, S.V.D.; Roger P. Schroeder, S.V.D.; Derek Simons, S.V.D.; Higinio M. Yescas, S.V.D.

[C] COLLEGES AND UNIVERSITIES

CHICAGO. *De Paul University,* One E. Jackson Blvd., 60604. Tel: 312-362-8000
For a complete listing, refer to the Colleges and Universities section.

Jesuit Community at Loyola University of Chicago, Jesuit Residence, 6525 N. Sheridan Rd., 60626. Tel: 773-508-8800; Fax: 773-508-2098
For a complete listing, refer to the Colleges and Universities section.

Loyola University-Chicago, 6525 N. Sheridan Rd., 60626. Tel: 773-274-3000
For a complete listing, refer to the Colleges and Universities section.

Saint Xavier University, 3700 West 103rd St., 60655. Tel: 773-298-3000
For a complete listing, refer to the Colleges and Universities section.

Vincentian Community at DePaul University, 2233 N. Kenmore Ave., 60614. Tel: 312-880-2968
For a complete listing, refer to the Colleges and Universities section.

LAKE FOREST. *Barat College,* 700 Westleigh Rd., 60045. Tel: 708-234-3000
For a complete listing, refer to the Colleges and Universities section.

RIVER FOREST. *Dominican University (Formerly Rosary College),* 7900 W. Division St., 60305. Tel: 708-366-2490
For a complete listing, refer to the Colleges and Universities section.

[D] HIGH SCHOOLS, PRIVATE

CHICAGO. *Academy of Our Lady,* 1309 W. 95th St., 60643. Tel: 312-445-2300. Legal Title: *Academy of Our Lady.* A Day School (Girls). School Sisters of Notre Dame. Mrs. Trudy L. Hunter, Prin. Sisters 1; Lay Teachers 18; Students 308.

Brother Rice High School, 10001 S. Pulaski Rd., 60655-3356. Tel: 773-779-3410. Congregation of Christian Brothers. Bro. Daniel J. Casey, C.F.C., Prin. Brothers 14; Lay Teachers 17; Students 1,366.

Cristo Rey Jesuit High School, Inc., 1851 W. Cermak Rd., 60608. Tel: 773-523-6800. Rev. John P. Foley, S.J., Pres.; Sr. Judith Murphy, O.S.B., Prin. Priests 1; Sisters 1; Brothers 1; Lay Teachers 20; Students 200.

Cristo Rey Work/Study Program, Inc., 1851 W. Cermak Rd., 60608. Tel: 773-523-6800. Preston Kendall, Dir.

De La Salle High School, 3455 S. Wabash Ave., 60616. Tel: 312-842-7355. Legal Title: *De La Salle Institute.* Brothers of the Christian Schools. Bro. Michael Quirk, F.S.C., Pres.; Dr. James M. Gay, Prin. Brothers 6; Sisters 1; Lay Teachers 55; Students 975.

Good Counsel High School, Inc., 3900 Peterson Ave., 60659. Tel: 773-478-3655. Legal Title: *Good Counsel High School, Inc.* Day School. Sr. Beatrice Knipple, C.S.S.F., Prin. Sisters 12; Lay Teachers 55; Students 628.

Gordon Technical High School, 3633 N. California Ave., 60618. Tel: 773-539-3600. Rev. Joseph Glab, C.R., Pres.; Mr. Casimir Kozlik, Prin.; Revs. Marion Gienko, C.R.; Edward J. Jaskula, C.R.; Stephen Juda, C.R.; Thomas Kubik, C.R.; Joseph Malczyk, C.R.; Chester Norkiewicz, C.R.; Aloysius M. Orzechowski, C.R.; Paul Sims, C.R., Supr.; John Stephen, C.R.; Donald Zinn, C.R. Priests 10; Brothers 1; Lay Teachers 49; Students 850.

**Hales Franciscan High School, Inc.,* 4930 Cottage Grove Ave., 60615. Tel: 773-285-8400. Mr. Timothy King, Pres.; Mr. Thomas Calhoun, V.P. of Academic Affairs; Revs. John Paul Cafiero, O.F.M., Dir. Campus Ministry; Phil D. Hogan, O.F.M., Coord. Student Activities & Spec. Programs; David Rodriguez, O.F.M., Guardian; Fine Arts & Theology Chair; Gary Bernhardt, O.F.M.; Arturo O'Campo, O.F.M.; Paul Pare, O.F.M. Priests 6; Brothers 2; Lay Teachers 20; Students 350.

Holy Spirit Friary. Revs. Charles E. Payne, O.F.M., Ph.D.; Thomas Nairn, O.F.M.; Salvador Valdez, O.F.M.

Holy Trinity High School, 1443 W. Division St., 60622. Tel: 312-278-4212. Brothers of Holy Cross. Bro. Philip R. Smith, C.S.C. Priests 1; Brothers 6; Sisters 5; Lay Teachers 28; Students 420.

Josephinum High School, 1501 N. Oakley Blvd., 60622. Tel: 773-276-1261. Legal Title: *Josephinum High School, Inc.* Fully accredited high school. Lay Teachers 21; Girls 240.

Leo High School, 7901 S. Sangamon, 60620. Tel: 312-224-9600. Mr. Robert W. Foster, Prin. Boys 200.

Lourdes High School, 4034 W. 56th St., 60629. Tel: 773-581-2555; Fax: 773-581-9358. Sisters of St. Joseph, Third Order of St. Francis. Ms. Mary Iannucilli, Prin. Sisters 7; Lay Teachers 35; Students 535.

Madonna High School, 4055 W. Belmont, 60641. Tel: 312-282-2552. Franciscan Sisters of Chicago. Sr. Carol Marie Schommer, O.S.F., Prin. Priests 1; Sisters 6; Lay Teachers 22; Students 325.

Maria High School. (Formerly St. Casimir Academy), 6727 S. California Ave., 60629. Tel: 312-925-8686; Fax: 312-925-8885. Sisters of St. Casimir. Local Coordinators: Sr. M. Georgine; Sr. Helene Chernesky; Sr. M. Reginald; Sr. Margaret Zalot, S.S.C., Pres.; Mrs. Barbara McKee, Prin. Sisters 14; Lay Teachers 59; Students 820.

Marist High School, 4200 W. 115th St., 60655-4397. Tel: 773-881-6360. Marist Brothers. Tel: 773-881-5300. Bro. John Cummings, F.M.S. Brothers 14; Sisters 2; Lay Teachers 69; Students 1,330.

Mother McAuley Liberal Arts High School, 3737 W. 99th St., 60655. Tel: 773-881-6500. Sisters of Mercy. Sr. Rose Wiorek, R.S.M. Sisters 11; Lay Teachers 108; Students 1,995.

Mt. Carmel High School, 6410 S. Dante Ave., 60637. Tel: 773-324-1020; Fax: 773-324-9235. Res., 6401 S. Harper Ave., 60638. Carmelite Fathers. Revs. Benjamin Aguilar, O.Carm.; Carl J. Markelz, O.Carm., Prin.; John Knoernschild, O.Carm.; Daniel Carroll, O.Carm.; Glen Snow, O.Carm.; Leander Troy, O.Carm.; George L. O'Keefe, O.Carm.; Bro. Timothy Sklopan, O.Carm., Prior. Priests 8; Brothers 1; Lay Teachers 40; Students 770.

Notre Dame High School, 3000 N. Mango Ave., 60634. Tel: 773-622-9494. Sisters of Notre Dame de Namur. Sr. Mary Bridget Murphy, Pres.; Mrs. Judy Schutter, Prin. Sisters 4; Lay Teachers 45; Girls 625.

Resurrection High School, 7500 W. Talcott Ave., 60631. Tel: 773-775-6616; Fax: 773-775-0611. Sisters of the Resurrection. Ms. Therese M. Fenney, Prin. Sisters 4; Lay Teachers 51; Girls 940.

St. Francis de Sales High School, 10155 S. Ewing Ave., 60617. Tel: 312-773-7272. Mr. Walter Schultz, Prin. Sisters 1; Priests 1; Lay Teachers 30; Students 500.

St. Ignatius College Prep, 1076 W. Roosevelt Rd., 60608-1594. Tel: 312-421-5900; Fax: 312-829-5846. Rev. Donald F. Rowe, S.J., Pres.; Dr. James Lalley, Prin.; Revs. Joseph T. Brennan, S.J.; George R. Menke, S.J.; Robert C. Thul, S.J.; Gerald C. Walling, S.J. Priests 5; Sisters 2; Lay Teachers 93; Students 1,269.

St. Ignatius Jesuit Community, 1025 W. Taylor, 60607. Tel: 312-829-2297; Fax: 312-829-9552. Revs. Joseph T. Brennan, S.J.; James C.L. Arimond, S.J., Rector; John P. Coakley, S.J.; James J. Creighton, S.J.; Francis J. Daly, S.J.; John M. Dennis, S.J.; Phillip J. Grib, S.J.; John H. Lane, S.J.; William O. Madden, S.J.; Richard J. O'Brien, S.J.; Bradley M. Schaeffer, S.J.; Robert C. Thul, S.J.; Richard J. Vogt, S.J.; James F. Vorwoldt, S.J.; Bros. Anthony R. Kreutzjans, S.J.; Robert W. Schneider, S.J.; David Garcia, S.J.

St. Patrick High School, 5900 W. Belmont Ave., 60634. Tel: 773-282-8844; Fax: 773-282-2361. Legal Title: *St. Patrick High School.* Brothers of the Christian Schools. Bro. Konrad Diebold, F.S.C., Pres.; Dr. Joseph Schmidt, Prin.; Mr. Charles Schmidt, Asst. Prin. Brothers 4; Lay Teachers 56; Students 904.

St. Rita High School. (See separate listing for residence information), 7740 S. Western Ave., 60620. Tel: 773-925-6600. Rev. Michael J. O'Connor, O.S.A., Pres.; Mr. Joseph F. Bamberger, Prin.; Rev. Edward Andrews, O.S.A., Prior. Priests 8; Sisters 1; Lay Teachers 41; Students 738.

St. Scholastica Academy, 7416 N. Ridge Blvd., 60645. Tel: 773-764-5715. Sr. Judith Zonsius, O.S.B., Prin. Sisters 9; Lay Teachers 29; Students 291.

Convent, 7430 N. Ridge Blvd., 60645.

Weber High School, 5252 W. Palmer St., 60639-3098. Tel: 312-637-7500. Faculty Res., 2250 N. Latrobe Ave., 60639. Tel: 312-622-0477. Conducted by the Fathers and Brothers of the Congregation of the Resurrection. Very Rev. John Nowak, C.R., Prov. Supr.; Revs. Fred Ciesla, C.R.; Jerome Andracki, C.R.; Steve Bartczyszyn, C.R.; Richard P. Balazs, C.R.; Joseph Przysucha, C.R.; Adolph Istok, C.R.; Bros. Edward Jaszkowski, C.R.; William Hallas, C.R.; Revs. Joseph Korabik, C.R.; Frank Majewicz, C.R.; Charles Mrowinski, C.R.; Dennis Sanders, C.R.; Jerome Twarog, C.R., Supr. Priests 3; Brothers 1; Sisters 2; Lay Teachers 27; Students 400.

Weber Endowment Fund, 5252 W. Palmer, 60639. Ms. Linda Forestor, Contact Person.

ARLINGTON HEIGHTS. *St. Viator High School,* 1213 E. Oakton St., 60004. Tel: 708-392-4050; Fax: 708-392-4101. Clerics of St. Viator. Revs. Charles G. Bolser, C.S.V., Pres.; George G. Harris, C.S.V.; Arnold E. Perham, C.S.V.; John E. VanWiel, C.S.V.; Bros. Robert Ruhl, C.S.V.; Brian Cooper, C.S.V.; Michael Rice, C.S.V. Priests 4; Brothers 3; Lay Teachers 53; Students 813.

BURBANK. *Queen of Peace High School.* (Girls). 7659 S. Linder Ave., 60459. Tel: 708-458-7600. Ms. Patricia Nolan Fitzgerald, Prin. Sisters 5; Lay Teachers 77; Students 1,265.

St. Laurence High School, Inc., 5556 W. 77th St., 60459. Tel: 708-458-6900. Congregation of Christian Brothers. Mr. Thomas J. Ondrla, Prin. Priests 1; Brothers 10; Lay Teachers 47; Students 935.

CHICAGO HEIGHTS. *Marian Catholic High School,* 700 Ashland Ave., 60411. Tel: 708-755-7565; Fax: 708-755-0042. Dominican Sisters (Springfield, IL). Sr. M. Paul McCaughey, O.P., Prin. Sisters 16; Lay Teachers 71; Students 1,533.

LAGRANGE PARK. *Nazareth Academy,* 1209 W. Ogden Ave., 60526. Tel: 708-354-0061; Fax: 708-354-0109. Sisters of St. Joseph. Sr. Jacqueline Schmitz, C.S.J., Prin. Sisters 8; Lay Teachers 40; Students 779.

LAKE FOREST. *Woodlands Academy of the Sacred Heart,* 760 E. Westleigh Rd., 60045-3298. Tel: 708-234-4300. Religious of Sacred Heart. Sr. Claude Demoustier, R.S.C.J., Headmistress. Sisters 1; Lay Teachers 29; Students 185.

LEMONT. *Mt. Assisi Academy,* 13860 Main St., 60439. Tel: 630-257-7844; Fax: 630-257-6362. Sisters of St.

Francis of Christ the King. Sr. Mary Francis Werner, O.S.F. Sisters 9; Lay Teachers 34; Students 380.

MUNDELEIN. *Carmel High School*, One Carmel Pkwy., 60060. Tel: 847-566-3000; Fax: 847-566-8465. Sr. Mary Frances McLaughlin, Pres.; Rev. Robert Carroll, O.Carm., Prin. Priests 2; Sisters 4; Brothers 1; Lay Teachers 71; Students 1,285.

NILES. *Notre Dame High School*. (Boys), 7655 Dempster St., 60648. Tel: 708-965-2900; Fax: 708-965-2975. Revs. Kenneth Molinaro, C.S.C., Prin.; Jerome Esper, C.S.C.; Mr. Robert Schmiege, Dir. Devel.; Mr. Steven Zeier, Asst. Prin. Academics; Mr. Michael Hennessey, Asst. Prin. Student Life; Mr. James Boylan, Dean of Men; Bro. Patrick Lynch, C.S.C., Finance Officer; Mrs. Donna Cassidy, Dir. Guidance; Mr. Michael Hennessey, Dir. Athletics; Revs. William Brinker, C.S.C., (Retired); Jerome Esper, C.S.C.; Christopher A. Kuhn, C.S.C.; Norbert Hess, C.S.C., (Retired); Randall Rentner, C.S.C.; Bro. Patrick Lynch, C.S.C. Priests 6; Retired Priests 2; Brothers 1; Sisters 2; Lay Teachers 41; Students 660.

OAK PARK. *Fenwick High School*, 505 Washington Blvd., 60302. Tel: 708-386-0127. Dominican Order. Revs. Daniel C. Davis, O.P., Pres.; William J. Bernacki, O.P.; Malachy R. Dooley, O.P.; Joseph Ekpo; John M. Gambro, O.P.; Harold Ostdiek, O.P.; Joseph I. Hren, O.P.; Paul Whittington, O.P.; Bros. Gabriel J. Dault, O.P.; Scott Steinkerchner, O.P.; Sr. Mary Nugent, O.P.; Sr. Louise J. Brogacz, O.P. Priests 8; Brothers 2; Sisters 2; Lay Teachers 66; Students 1,120.

RIVER FOREST. *Trinity High School*, 7574 W. Division St., 60305. Tel: 708-771-8383. Dominican Sisters (Sinsinawa, WI). Sr. Michelle Germanson, O.P., Pres.; Sr. Jeanne Bessette, O.S.F., Prin. Sisters 5; Lay Teachers 40; Students 491.

RIVER GROVE. *Holy Cross High School*, 3000-80th, 60171. Tel: 708-456-5110. Brothers of Holy Cross. Bros. Douglas Roach, C.S.C., Pres.; Donald Fleischhacker, C.S.C., Dir.; Rev. Bernard Kennedy, O.F.M., Dir. Campus Ministry. Priests 1; Brothers 10; Lay Teachers 32; Students 500.

Mother Theodore Guerin High School, 8001 Belmont Ave., 60171. Tel: 312-625-3278; Fax: 708-453-6296. Sisters of Providence. Sr. Cathy Campbell, S.P., Pres.; Sr. Ann Welch, R.S.M. Sisters 4; Lay Teachers 59; Students 740.

SOUTH HOLLAND. *Seton Academy*, 16100 Seton Rd., 60473-1899. Tel: 708-333-6300. Sisters 1; Lay Teachers 24; Students 400.

WESTCHESTER. *Immaculate Heart of Mary High School*, 10900 W. Cermak Rd., 60154. Tel: 708-562-3115. Sisters, Servants of the Immaculate Heart of Mary. Catherine A. Karl, Ph.D., Prin. Sisters 3; Lay Teachers 36; Students 545.

St. Joseph High School, 1840 Mayfair, 60154-4299. Tel: 708-562-4433. Brothers of the Christian Schools. Mr. Charles J. Lynch, Jr., Pres.; Mr. David L. Hotek, Prin.; Mr. Thomas Reif, Asst. Prin. Brothers 3; Lay Teachers 47; Students 562.

WILMETTE. *Loyola Academy*, 1100 N. Laramie Ave., 60091. Tel: 708-256-1100; Fax: 708-251-4031. Revs. Theodore G. Munz, S.J., Pres.; Norman E. Harland, S.J., Rector; Terrence A. Baum, S.J., Headmaster; Mr. William A. Graf, Athletic Dir.; Mr. John E. Hoerster, Dir. Admissions; Dr. Lorraine Ozar, Academic Dean; Mr. Kenneth Maziarka, Dean of Students; Mr. John P. Brady, Business Mgr.; Revs. Raymond A. Dunne, S.J,; Robert G. Humbert, S.J.; Steven F. Hurd, S.J.; Paul J. Faulstich, S.J.; John J. Foley, S.J.; Bro. James W. Small, S.J.; Rev. Robert A. Ytsen, S.J Priests 9; Sisters 3; Brothers 1; Lay Teachers 165; Students 2,000.

Regina Dominican High School, 701 Locust Rd., 60091. Tel: 847-256-7660; Fax: 847-256-3726. Sisters of St. Dominic (Adrian, MI). Sr. Carol Fleming, O.P., Pres.; Sr. Diane O'Donnell, B.V.M. Sisters 10; Lay Teachers 36; Students 452.

[E] ELEMENTARY SCHOOLS, PRIVATE

CHICAGO. *Sacred Heart Schools (Academy of the Sacred Heart for Girls, Hardey Prep. for Boys)*. (Grades K-8), 6250 N. Sheridan Rd., 60660-1799. Tel: 773-262-4446. Religious of the Sacred Heart. Sr. Susan Maxwell, R.S.C.J., Dir. Schools; Mrs. Janet Underwood, Head of Schools. Sisters 5; Lay Teachers 37; Students 358.

[F] CONSOLIDATED ELEMENTARY SCHOOLS

CHICAGO. *Bridgeport Catholic Academy*, Admin. Office, 1040 W. 32nd Pl., 60608. Tel: 312-376-0142. Nona Barrientos, Prin.
Serving the following parishes: All Saints-St. Anthony (518 W. 28th Pl.); St. Mary of Perpetual Help (1039 W. 32nd St.); Nativity of Our Lord (653 W. 37th St.). Lay Teachers 24; Students 400.

[G] CATHOLIC CHARITIES

CHICAGO. *Catholic Charities of the Archdiocese of Chicago-Archdiocesan Offices*, 126 N. Desplaines St., 60661. Tel: 312-655-7000. Administers charitable activities of the Archdiocese. Rev. Michael M. Boland, Admin.; Mr. Jimmy M. Lago, Exec. Dir.; Rev. Charles T. Rubey, Dir.-Programs. Assoc. Admins.: Revs. Roger J. Coughlin; Richard E. Bulwith; Daniel C. Jankowski; Daniel M. Holihan; James M. Ray; Francis A. Cimarrusti; Charles T. Rubey; Most Rev. Edwin M. Conway, Consultant.

Dept. of Development. Tel: 312-655-7289. Michelle A. Arnold, Dir.

Dept. of Communications. Tel: 312-655-7024. Mr. William J. Sullivan, Jr., Dir.

Office of Board Relations and Major Events. Tel: 312-655-7768. Mr. Brian Wiley, Dir.

Financial Services, 721 N. LaSalle, 60610. Ms. Cynthia Smetana, Dir. of Finance.

Division of Family and Parish Support Services. Tel: 312-655-7136. Ms. Ellen E. Gorney, Div. Mgr.

Central Information and Referral Services. Tel: 312-655-7700. Ms. Kathleen Donahue, Dept. Dir.

Emergency Assistance Program, 121 W. Superior St., 60610. Tel: 312-655-7500. Ms. Christene Dykes, Program Dir.

Northwest Suburban Family Shelter, 1911 Rohlwing Rd., Ste. E, Rolling Meadows, 60008. Tel: 312-655-7700.

Dept. of Family and Aging Services. Tel: 312-655-7153. Ms. Veronica Glodowski, Dept. Dir.

Archdiocesan AIDS Ministry Office. Tel: 312-655-7294. Mrs. Marianne Zelewsky, Dir.

Specialized Mental Health Services Network. Tel: 312-655-7298.

Holbrook Center for Counseling and Psychotherapy, 721 N. LaSalle, 60610. Tel: 312-655-7550. Ms. Dorothy Auw, Dept. Dir.

Community Family Service Center, 2189 W. Bowler, 60612. Tel: 312-733-5661. Ms. Sigrid Brooks, Prog. Dir.

Immigration & Naturalization Services and Refuge Resettlement Program, 126 N. Desplaines St., 60661. Tel: 312-655-7359. Mr. J. Zeferino Ochoa, Dept. Dir.

LOSS (Loving Outreach to Survivors of Suicide). Tel: 312-655-7283. Ms. Laina Lurito, Prog. Dir.

Joseph Cardinal Bernardin Family Shelter Program, 126 N. Desplaines St., 60661. Tel: 312-655-7268. Ms. Mildred Lincoln, Dept. Dir.

Assumption B.V.M. Family Shelter, 12242 S. Parnell, 60628.

St. Francis de Paula Hospitality House, 7811 S. Ellis, 60619.

St. Sylvester Family Shelter, 2915 W. Palmer St., 60647.

St. Susanna Family Shelter, 14926 S. Honore, Harvey, 60426.

Sousa Transitional Shelter, 7000 S. Aberdeen, 60621. Tel: 773-874-4000. Ms. Darlene Rivers, Supr. Tel: 312-874-4400.

Cooke's Manor Transitional Housing For Men, 124 N. Sangamon, 60607. Tel: 312-997-2756. Rev. Richard E. Bulwith, Dept. Dir.

Pioneer House, 3909 N. Bell, 60618.

Forever Free-Women's Wholistic Recovery Home, 4539 S. Wells St., 60609. Tel: 773-548-9500. Ms. Josephine Abi-Rached, Prog. Dir.

Forever Free Phase II-Transitional Housing For Women, 7021 S. May St., 60621. Tel: 312-224-3232. Ms. Josephine Abi-Rached, Prog. Dir.

Society of St. Vincent De Paul of Chicago, 645 W. Randolph St., 60661. Tel: 312-655-7181. Mrs. Claudia Pieske, Pres.; Rev. Thomas A. Grace, C.M., Exec. Dir.; Mr. William Dolan, Budget Dir.; Mrs. Marge Walsh, Dir. Store Warehouse Oper.; Revs. Michael M. Boland, Spiritual Advisor; Michael L. Zoufal, Asst. Spiritual Advisor; Mr. Patrick Gaughen, Pres. District Council I; Ms. Mary Van Wazer, Pres. District Council III; Mr. William Stein, Pres. District Council IV; Mr. Ben Gallardo, Pres. District Council VII; Mr. John Hovorka, Pres. District Council VIII; Mr. Richard Kress, Pres. District Council IX; Mrs. John Rosenthal, Pres. District Council X; Ms. Rose Reynaud, Pres. District Council XI; Ms. Nicki Blank, Pres. District Council XII; Mr. Richard Kress, Regional Coord.; Ms. Janet Deckenbach, Regional Coord.; Mrs. Kathy Keith, Youth Coord.; Mr. Thomas Van Wazer, Disaster Chm. & Regl. Coord.; Mrs. Mary Van Wazer, Elder Care Coord.; Mr. Edward Bara, Sr., Ozanam Cause Coord.; Deacon John Perkowitz, Funding & Twinning Coord.- Asst. to Pres.; Mr. Karl Gawlas, Treas.; Mr. Ed Stachon, Vice Pres.; Mrs. Barbara Collins, ADC Sec.

St. Stanislaus Kostka Soup Kitchen, 1351 W. Evergreen, 60622. Tel: 773-278-2470. Sr. Ann Schaffer, Dir.

Cara Program, 126 N. DesPlaines, 60610. Tel: 312-655-7153. Veronica Glodowski, Prog. Dir.

Lake County Services. Joseph Cardinal Bernardin Center for Lake County Services, 671 S. Lewis Ave., Waukegan, 60085. Tel: 847-782-4000. Ms. Mary Clare Jakes, Assoc. Div. Mgr., Community Casework Services, 671 S. Lewis Ave., Waukegan, 60085. Tel: 847-782-4131. Ms. Maureen Murphy, Prog. Dir.

Samaritan House, 601 Tenth St., North Chicago, 60064. Ms. Susan Villarreac.

Consumer Credit Counseling Services. Joseph Cardinal Bernardin Center for Lake County Services, 671 S. Lewis Ave., Waukegan, 60085. Tel: 847-249-0000. Ms. Charlene Foster, Supr.

Regional Services Dept., 1911 Rohlwing Rd., Ste. E, Rolling Meadows, 60008. Tel: 847-870-0560. Rita Wiley, Regl. Svcs. Representative, Cicero: West Suburban Services, 1400 S. Austin Blvd., Cicero, 60804. Tel: 708-222-1491. Susanne A. Dillon, Regl. Svcs. Representative, Calumet Park: South Suburban Services, 12420 S. Ada, Calumet Park, 60643. Tel: 708-388-0743. Sr. Ruth Platte, Regl. Svcs. Representative, Chicago Services Regional Offices, 7020 S. Aberdeen St., 60621. Tel: 773-488-8208. Arlene Jackson-Ervin, Regl. Svcs. Representative, Chicago Services Regional Office, 721 N. LaSalle, 60610. Tel: 312-655-7403. Betty Siuba, Regl. Svcs. Representative, Southwest Suburban Services, 10661 Roberts Rd., Palos Hills, 60465. Tel: 708-430-0428. Cosina Dean, Regl. Svcs. Representative, North Suburban Services, 1700 E. Lake St., Room 207, Glenview, 60025. Tel: 847-657-0946. Stephen O'Brien-Combs, Assoc. Div. Mgr., Physician Referral Service, 1911 Rohlwing Rd., Ste. E, Rolling Meadows, 60008. Tel: 847-870-0202. Ms. Karen Kordisch, Prog. Dir.

Division of Non-Residential Services for Children and Youth for Cook and Lake Counties, 641 W. Lake St., Ste. 306, 60661. Tel: 312-655-7097. Mr. Everett T. Petlicki, Div. Mgr.; Mr. Jadonal Ford, Sr. Assoc. Div. Mgr. Tel: 312-655-7100.

Child Protective Services, 901 W. Jackson, 60607. Tel: 312-382-2521. 671 S. Lewis Ave., Waukegan, 60085. Tel: 847-782-4000.

Family Based Services, 916 N. Western Ave., 60622. Tel: 312-655-7601. Patricia Green, Dept. Dir.

Maternity/Adoption Services, 651 W. Lake St., 60661. Tel: 312-655-7076. Miss Ann Abrams, Dept. Dir.

Madonna/Saint Joseph Center, 1114 W. Grace St., 60613. Tel: 773-472-3343. Ms. Sally Heyneman, Prog. Admin.

Roseland Adolescent Parent Project, 10809 S. State St., 60628. Tel: 773-995-1737. Velma Brown-Walker, Dept. Dir.

Children & Adolescent Parent Program, 721 N. La Salle, 60610. Tel: 312-655-7848. Sandra Braine, Dept. Dir.

Teen Parent Initative Program, 3040 W. Walnut St., 60612. Tel: 773-826-0506. Ms. Catarina Williamson, Supvr.; Ms. Sandra Braine, Program Dir.

Arts of Living-Core Program, 721 N. La Salle, 60610. Tel: 312-655-7388. Ms. Patricia Canessa, Dept. Dir.

Relative Family Care Services, 901 W. Jackson, 60607. Tel: 312-655-7646. Ms. Sylvia Flory, Assoc. Div. Mgr.

Traditional and Specialized Foster Care Services, 651 W. Lake St., 60661. Tel: 312-655-7250. Mr. George Thibeault, Assoc. Div. Mgr.

Div. of Residential Child-Adult Care Services. Tel: 312-655-7289.

Division of Community Development Services, 721 N. La Salle, 60610. Tel: 312-655-7474. Mr. Walter H. Ousley, Div. Mgr.; Ms. Michele Bianchi, Assoc. Div. Mgr. Tel: 312-655-7538; Mr. Dennis McSwain, Assoc. Div. Mgr. Tel: 312-655-7482; Mr. Richard Klemundt, Assoc. Div. Mgr. Tel: 312-655-7568.

Addiction Consultation and Educational Services, 721 N. La Salle, 60610. Tel: 312-655-7450. Ms. Mary Ellen Flynn, Prog. Dir.

Central States Institute for Addiction, 120 W. Huron St., 60610. Tel: 312-655-7540. Mr. Anthony Rizzato, Dept. Dir.

Disruptive Behavior Intervention. Tel: 312-655-7474. Bro. William Tomes, Consultant.

El Centro De La Causa, 731 W. 17th St., 60616. Tel: 312-243-8508. Mr. Felip (Phil) Ayala, Dept. Dir.

Respond Now, 1439 Emerald Ave., P.O. Box 215, 60411. Tel: 708-755-4357. Mr. Dennis Condon, Prog. Dir.

Keen Ager News, 721 N. La Salle, 60610. Tel: 312-655-7425. Ms. Yolanda Roman, Editor.

Mother and Child Food and Nurtition Program (MAC), 721 N. La Salle, 60610. Tel: 312-655-7484. Mr. Aldo Pedrosa, Dir.

Roseland Center, 11013 S. Indiana Ave., 60628.

Westside Center, 1017 N. Cicero Ave., 60651.

WIC Food Centers Program, 721 N. La Salle St., 60610. Tel: 312-655-7480. Mr. Phil Parson, Dir.
WIC Food Centers: 907 N. Larrabee, Chicago, IL 60610; 2907 S. Wabash Ave., Chicago, IL 60616; 416 E. 43rd St., Chicago, IL 60653; 5060 S. State St., Chicago, IL 60609; 6202 S. Halsted St., Chicago, IL 60621; 2310 W. Roosevelt Rd., Chicago,

IL 60608; 5332 S. Western, Chicago, IL 60609; 3110 W. Armitage, Chicago, IL 60647; WIC Warehouse: 4500 W. Chicago Ave., Chicago, IL 60651; 1643 W. Cermak Rd., Chicago, IL 60608; 1734 W. Chicago Ave., Chicago, IL 60622; 3932 W. Madison St., Chicago, IL 60624; 4622 W. Diversey, Chicago, IL 60639; 11255 S. Michigan, Chicago, IL 60628; 1802 E. 71st St., Chicago, IL 60649; and at 5125 W. Chicago, Chicago, IL 60651, a mentoring program with APEC.

Garfield Alternative High School, 220 W. 45th Pl., 60609. Tel: 773-924-0543. Mr. Oyemola Kale, Prog. Dir.

Employment and Training Program, 721 N. LaSalle, 60610. Tel: 312-655-8490. Ms. Christine L. Tamani, Prog. Dir.

Day Care Services. Tel: 312-655-7875. Ms. Ethel Barnes, Dept. Dir.

Head Start Services. Tel: 312-655-7896. Mr. Neil Myrie, Dept. Dir.

Day Care Services, 2822 W. Jackson Blvd., 60612. Tel: 312-722-7440. Sr. Yvonne Thranow, D.C., Consultant.

Division of Senior Social Services, 721 N. La Salle Dr., 60610. Tel: 312-655-7572. Wendy S. Thomas, Div. Mgr.

Northeast/Northwest Chicago Case Management Services, 5801 N. Pulaski, Bldg. A, 60646. Tel: 773-583-9224. Sarah Cohen, Dept. Dir.

South Suburban Senior Services and Senior Activity Center, 15300 S. Lexington, Harvey, 60426. Tel: 708-596-2222. Gwen Westley, Dept. Dir.

Lake County Senior Case Management Services, 116 N. Lincoln, Round Lake, 60073. Tel: 847-546-5733. Jan Ahlgrin, Dept. Dir.

Congregate Senior Housing, Maplehurst, 2312 Elisha, Zion, 60099. Tel: 847-872-7527. Frank Phillps, Dept. Dir.

Lake County Senior Community Services & Nutrition Program Site, 414 S. Lewis Ave., Waukegan, 60085. Tel: 847-662-0085. Frank Phillips, Dept. Dir., Antioch Area Center, 817 Holbeck St., Antioch, 60002. Tel: 847-395-7120. Mr. Paul Howard, Ctr. Dir., Ela Township Area Center, 95 E. Main St., Lake Zurich, 60047. Tel: 847-438-0303. Mr. Rusty Miller, Ctr. Dir., Libertyville Civic Center, 135 W. Church St., Libertyville, 60048. Tel: 847-367-8210. Ms. Lois Pacente, Ctr. Dir.

Lake County Nutrition Programs for Seniors. Round Lake Senior Center, 814 Hart Rd., Round Lake, 60073. Tel: 847-546-0056. Fox Lake Community Senior Center, 79 E. Keystone, Fox Lake, 60020. Tel: 847-587-3335.

Northwest Suburban Senior Services, 306 W. Park St., Arlington Heights, 60005. Tel: 847-253-5500. Ms. Cindy Gunderson, Prog. Dir.

Cook County Senior Community Services, 6414 S. Halsted, 60621. Tel: 773-994-8923. Ms. Barbara Carlo, Dept. Dir.

De Sales Senior Center, 10160 Ave. J, 60617. Tel: 773-768-2850. Ms. Carole Kozak, Prog. Dir.

Ada S. Niles Senior Center and Adult Day Care Services, 6412-14 S. Halsted St., 60621. Tel: 773-874-2400. Ms. Denise King, Senior Ctr. Dir.; Ms. Norma Nalls, Day Care Senior Center Supvr.

Senior Aides Employment Program. Tel: 773-874-2400. Mr. Victor Dodd, Supr.

St. Joseph Center, 7240 W. 57th St., Summit, 60501. Tel: 708-458-0501. Mr. Henry Lambke, Ctr. Dir.

Catholic Home Care, Inc., 721 N. La Salle St., 60610. Tel: 312-655-7415. Ms. Anne Demke, R.N., Dept. Dir.

Division of Senior Residential Services and Catholic Charities Housing Development Corporation, 721 N. LaSalle St., 60610. Tel: 312-655-7490; 655-7975; Fax: 312-944-1550. William G. D'Arcy, Div. Mgr. Assoc. Div. Mgrs.: Lawrence Brozek; Brian Gillen; Mary Grondin.

Villa Scalabrini, Inc. A Real Estate Corporation.

Under Development: Bernardin Manor, Lawrence Manor, Ozanam Manor, St. Ailbe Senior Apts., St. Ailbe Housing for Physically Disabled, St. Sabina Senior Suites.

Senior Residences:

Cortland Manor Retirement Home, 1900 N. Karlov, 60639. Tel: 773-235-3670. Maureen Scholle, Admin.

Hayes Manor, 1211 W. Marquette Rd., 60636. Tel: 773-873-7400. Delores Davis, Admin.

Matthew Manor, 271 N. Albany Ave., 60612. Tel: 773-533-0001. Margaret Bridgmon, Admin.

Roseland Manor, 11717 S. State St., 60628. Tel: 773-995-9000. Shirley Caldwell, Admin.

St. Brendan Apts., 6717 S. Elizabeth St., 60636. Tel: 773-846-8600. Sylvia Moore, Admin.

St. Theodore Apts., 6209 S. Paulina St., 60636. Tel: 773-776-0200. Sylvia Moore, Admin.

Tolton Manor, 6345 S. Stewart, 60621. Tel: 773-783-7800. Lee Cole, Admin.

Frances Manor, 1270 E. Golf Rd., DesPlaines, 60016. Tel: 847-390-1270. Elaine Layden, Admin.

Maryhaven, Inc., 1700 E. Lake Ave., Glenview, 60025. Tel: 847-729-1300. Paul Asselin, Admin.

Bethlehem Woods Retirement and Assisted Living Center, 1571 W. Ogden Ave., LaGrange Park, 60526. Tel: 708-579-3663. Deborah Anderson, Admin.

Holy Family Villa, 12375 McCarthy Rd., Lemont, 60439. Tel: 630-257-2334. Roberta Magurany, Admin.

St. Andrew Home, 7000 N. Newark Ave., Niles, 60714. Tel: 847-647-8332. Judy Pitzele, Admin.

St. Benedict Home, 6930 W. Touhy Ave., Niles, 60714. Tel: 847-647-0003. Mary Grondin, Acting Admin.

Casa San Carlo, 420 N. Wolf Rd., Northlake, 60164. Tel: 708-562-4300. Barbara Paccione, Admin.

Villa Scalabrini, 480 N. Wolf Rd., Northlake, 60164. Tel: 708-562-0040. Sally Myers, Admin.

Human Resources. Tel: 312-655-7115. Ms. Violet Sabo, Dir.

Facilities Operations. Tel: 312-655-7104. Mr. Richard Whalen, Dept. Dir.

Governmental Relations, 721 N. La Salle, 60610. Tel: 312-655-7314. Ms. Laurie Barretto, Dept. Dir.

Research and Planning Services, 721 N. La Salle, 60610. Tel: 312-655-7492. Ms. Jean Welter, Dept. Dir.

Mission of the Holy Cross, 126 N. Deplaines St., 60606. Tel: 312-655-7460. Rev. Michael M. Boland.

[H] RESIDENTIAL CHILD-YOUTH CARE

CHICAGO. *Mission of Our Lady of Mercy-Mercy Home for Boys and Girls*, 1140 W. Jackson Blvd., 60607. Tel: 312-738-7560. Revs. James J. Close, Pres. & CEO; L. Scott Donahue, Assoc. Pres.; Maureen Meter, Chief Admin. Officer; Theresa Gossman, Exec. Vice Pres. Youth Prog.; Mark Mroz, Exec. Vice Pres. Communications; Mark Teresi, Exec. Vice Pres. Devel.; Sr. Mary Hrovat, O.P., Asst. to Pres.; Rob Gaskill, The Mission Press. Staff 63; Full Time Religious 5; Youths 221.

DES PLAINES. *Maryville Academy*, 1150 N. River Rd., 60016. Tel: 708-824-6126. Legal Title: *Maryville Academy*. Rev. John P. Smyth, Exec. Dir. Students 273.

[I] DAY NURSERIES, SETTLEMENTS AND SOCIAL CENTERS

CHICAGO. *Cordi-Marian Center*, 1100 S. May St., 60607. Tel: 312-666-3787. Cordi-Marian Missionary Sisters. Sr. M. Theresa Alonso, M.C.M., Supr. Sisters 7; People under care 1,095; Day Care capacity 349.

Marillac Social Center, 2822 W. Jackson Blvd., 60612. Tel: 773-722-7440. Sr. Yvonne Thranow, D.C., Exec. Dir. Day care for children ages 2 1/2 to 12 years; Recreation programs for ages 6 to 25 years; emergency assistance food and clothing for poor families; day shelter for the homeless; child abuse and neglect treatment; counselling services; programs for pregnant & parenting teens and their babies; home bound elderly; services for teenage mothers. Day Care capacity 422.

**Port Ministries*. A Franciscan outreach of the Assumption of the Blessed Virgin Mary Province, Pulaski, WI. Soup Kitchen, food pantry, overnight shelters (men, women & family), GED, ESL, family services, mobile soup kitchen, neighborhood gym. 5013 S. Hermitage Ave., 60609. Tel: 773-778-5955. Rev. Augustin Milon, O.F.M., Founder & Pres. Total Staff 30; Total Assisted 6,000.

Resurrection Day Care Center, 1849 N. Hermitage Ave., 60622. Tel: 773-384-7142. Sisters of the Resurrection. Sr. M. Paulette Pieta, C.R., Supr. and Admin. Sisters 5; Daily Attendance 30 Children.

St. Rose Center, 4911 S. Hoyne, 60609. Tel: 773-436-1433. Sr. Theresa Tamburo, D.S.M.P., Admin. Day training program for mentally impaired adults. Sisters 2; Developmental Instructors 2; Devlopmental Trainers 3; Work Activity Director 1; Capacity 50.

St. Vincent de Paul Center, 2145 N. Halsted St., 60614. Tel: 312-943-6776. Sr. Cathrine Mary Norris, D.C., Admin. Day care for children 4 mos. to 11 yrs.; family social services; therapeutic program for child abuse referred families. Daughters of Charity 5; Capacity 421. Provides youth and adult recreational and athletic programs for ages 18 years through adult. Individual registration 468. Provides case management, counseling and emergency relief for senior citizens. Provides intergenerational living quarters for 15 seniors (low income) and 5 young adults. Individual registration 175.

**San Miguel Center, Inc.* Operated by DeLaSalle Christian Brothers and Secular Franciscans. Free Catholic Middle School for at risk youth; Adult education (ESL, GED & Job Training); after school and evening youth programs, ages 11-21; emergency assistance with food, clothing and housing. 1949 W. 48th St., 60609. Tel: 773-890-0233. Officers: Gene Downes, Officer; Sandra Downes; Bros. Gordon Hannon, F.S.C.; Ed Siderewicz, F.S.C. Total Staff 12; Total Assisted 500.

[J] HOSPITALS

CHICAGO. *Columbus Hospital*, 2520 N. Lakeview Ave., 60614

For a complete listing, refer to the Hospitals section.

Holy Cross Hospital, 2701 W. 68th St., 60629. Tel: 312-471-8000

For a complete listing, refer to the Hospitals section.

Mercy Hospital and Medical Center, 2525 S. Michigan Ave Stevenson Expwy. at King Dr., 60616. Tel: 312-567-2100; Fax: 312-567-6575.

For a complete listing, refer to the Hospitals section.

**Our Lady of the Resurrection Medical Center*, 5645 W. Addison, 60634. Tel: 773-282-7000

For a complete listing, refer to the Hospitals section.

Resurrection Medical Center, 7435 Talcott Ave., 60631. Tel: 773-774-8000

For a complete listing, refer to the Hospitals section.

St. Anthony Hospital, 2875 W. 19th St., 60623. Tel: 773-521-1710

For a complete listing, refer to the Hospitals section.

St. Bernard Hospital & Health Care Center, 326 W. 64th St., 60621. Tel: 773-962-3900

For a complete listing, refer to the Hospitals section.

St. Elizabeth's Hospital, 1431 N. Claremont Ave., 60622. Tel: 773-278-2000

For a complete listing, refer to the Hospitals section.

St. Joseph Hospital, 2900 N. Lake Shore Dr., 60657. Tel: 773-665-3000

For a complete listing, refer to the Hospitals section.

St. Mary of Nazareth Hospital Center, 2233 W. Division, 60622. Tel: 312-770-2000

For a complete listing, refer to the Hospitals section.

BLUE ISLAND. *St. Francis Hospital and Health Center*, 12935 S. Gregory St., 60406. Tel: 708-597-2000

For a complete listing, refer to the Hospitals section.

CHICAGO HEIGHTS. *Alverno Lakeside Corporation*, 1423 Chicago Rd., 60411

For a complete listing, refer to the Hospitals section.

St. James Hospital and Health Centers, 1423 Chicago Rd., 60411. Tel: 708-756-1000

For a complete listing, refer to the Hospitals section.

CRESTWOOD. *St. Francis Family Health Center*, 13755 Cicero Ave., 60445

For a complete listing, refer to the Hospitals section.

DES PLAINES. *Holy Family Medical Center*, 100 N. River Rd., 60016. Tel: 847-297-1800; Fax: 847-297-1863

For a complete listing, refer to the Hospitals section.

DOLTON. *St. Francis Family Health Center*, 13826 S. Lincoln Ave., 60419

For a complete listing, refer to the Hospitals section.

ELK GROVE VILLAGE. *Alexian Brothers Medical Center, Inc.*, 800 Biesterfield Rd., 60007-3397. Tel: 847-437-5500

For a complete listing, refer to the Hospitals section.

EVANSTON. *Saint Francis Hospital of Evanston*, 355 Ridge Ave., 60202. Tel: 847-316-4000

For a complete listing, refer to the Hospitals section.

EVERGREEN PARK. *Little Company of Mary Hospital and Health Care Centers*, 2800 W. 95th St., 60805. Tel: 708-422-6200; Fax: 708-425-9369

For a complete listing, refer to the Hospitals section.

MAYWOOD. *Foster G. McGaw Hospital of Loyola University of Chicago*, 2160 S. First Ave., 60153. Tel: 708-216-9056

For a complete listing, refer to the Hospitals section.

OAK PARK. *Oak Park Hospital*, 520 S. Maple Ave., 60304. Tel: 708-383-9300

For a complete listing, refer to the Hospitals section.

TINLEY PARK. *St. Francis Family Health Center*, 17148 S. Harlem Ave., 60477

For a complete listing, refer to the Hospitals section.

WAUKEGAN. *Saint Therese Medical Center*, 2615 Washington St., 60085. Tel: 847-249-3900

For a complete listing, refer to the Hospitals section.

WORTH. *St. Francis Family Health Center*, 11415 S. Harlem Ave., 60482

For a complete listing, refer to the Hospitals section.

[K] HEALTH CARE CENTERS

CHICAGO. *St. Basil Health Service - Free People's Clinic*, 1850 W. Garfield, 60609. Tel: 773-436-4758

For a complete listing, refer to the Hospitals section.

[L] PROTECTIVE INSTITUTIONS

CHICAGO. *Big Sisters*, 721 N. LaSalle St., Room 434, 60610. Tel: 312-751-0111

For a complete listing, refer to the Special Care Facilities section.

**Dehon House*, 6451 N. Greenview, 60626. Tel: 773-465-1526; Fax: 773-465-9422

For a complete listing, refer to the Special Care Facilities section.

House of the Good Shepherd, 1114 W. Grace St., 60613. Tel: 773-935-3434; Fax: 773-935-3523

For a complete listing, refer to the Special Care Facilities section.

Misericordia Home South, 2916 W. 47th St., 60632. Tel: 773-254-9595

For a complete listing, refer to the Special Care Facilities section.

Misericordia/Heart of Mercy Center, 6300 N. Ridge, 60660. Tel: 773-973-6300
For a complete listing, refer to the Special Care Facilities section.

St. Joseph's Carondelet Child Center, 739 E. 35th St., 60616. Tel: 773-624-7443; Fax: 773-624-7676
For a complete listing, refer to the Special Care Facilities section.

St. Mary of Providence, 4200 N. Austin Ave., 60634. Tel: 773-545-8300; Fax: 773-545-8035
For a complete listing, refer to the Special Care Facilities section.

BARTLETT. *Bartlett Learning Center*, 801 W. Bartlett Rd., 60103. Tel: 630-289-4221
For a complete listing, refer to the Special Care Facilities section.

LAKE ZURICH. *Mt. St. Joseph Home*, 24955 North Hwy. 12, 60047. Tel: 847-438-5050; Fax: 847-438-1561
For a complete listing, refer to the Special Care Facilities section.

OAK PARK. *Ephpheta Center and Hearing Conservation Service*, 119 S. Harvey Ave., 60302
For a complete listing, refer to the Special Care Facilities section.

PALOS PARK. *St. Coletta's of Illinois*, 123rd and Wolf Rd., 60464. Tel: 708-448-6520
For a complete listing, refer to the Special Care Facilities section.

[M] SENIOR CARE INSTITUTIONS

CHICAGO. *Cortland Manor Retirement Home*, 1900 N. Karlov, 60639. Tel: 773-235-3670
For a complete listing, refer to the Special Care Facilities section.

Jugan Terrace, 2300 N. Racine, 60614. Tel: 773-935-9600; Fax: 773-935-4291
For a complete listing, refer to the Special Care Facilities section.

Little Sisters of the Poor Center for the Aging, 2325 N. Lakewood Ave., 60614. Tel: 773-935-9600; Fax: 773-935-9614
For a complete listing, refer to the Special Care Facilities section.

Resurrection Retirement Community, 7262 W. Peterson Ave., 60631. Tel: 773-792-7930
For a complete listing, refer to the Special Care Facilities section.

St. Joseph Home of Chicago, Inc., 2650 N. Ridgeway Ave., 60647. Tel: 773-235-8600; Fax: 773-235-2933
For a complete listing, refer to the Special Care Facilities section.

DES PLAINES. *Holy Family Health Center*, 2380 Dempster, 60016. Tel: 847-296-3335
For a complete listing, refer to the Special Care Facilities section.

Nazarethville, 300 N. River Rd., 60016. Tel: 847-297-5900
For a complete listing, refer to the Special Care Facilities section.

GLENVIEW. *Maryhaven Inc.*, 1700 East Lake Ave., 60025. Tel: 847-729-1300; Fax: 847-729-9202
For a complete listing, refer to the Special Care Facilities section.

HOMEWOOD. *Mercy Health Care and Rehabilitation Center*, 19000 S. Halsted St., 60430. Tel: 708-957-9200; Fax: 708-799-4787
For a complete listing, refer to the Special Care Facilities section.

JUSTICE. *Rosary Hill Home*, 9000 W. 81st St., 60458. Tel: 708-458-3040
For a complete listing, refer to the Special Care Facilities section.

LEMONT. *Alvernia Manor*, 13950 Main St., 60439. Tel: 708-257-7721
For a complete listing, refer to the Special Care Facilities section.

Holy Family Villa, 12375 McCarthy Rd., 60439
For a complete listing, refer to the Special Care Facilities section.

Mother Theresa Home, 1270 Franciscan Dr., 60439. Tel: 708-257-5801; Fax: 708-257-1328
For a complete listing, refer to the Special Care Facilities section.

NILES. *St. Andrew Home for the Aged*, 7000 N. Newark Ave., 60714-4497. Tel: 847-647-8332
For a complete listing, refer to the Special Care Facilities section.

St. Benedict Home for the Aged, 6930 W. Touhy Ave., 60714. Tel: 847-647-0003
For a complete listing, refer to the Special Care Facilities section.

NORTHLAKE. *Villa Scalabrini Home for the Aged*, 480 N. Wolf Rd., 60164-1667. Tel: 708-562-0040
For a complete listing, refer to the Special Care Facilities section.

OLYMPIA FIELDS. *Mercy Residence at Tolentine Center*, 20300 Governors Hwy., 60461. Tel: 708-748-9500; Fax: 708-481-2090
For a complete listing, refer to the Special Care Facilities section.

PALATINE. *St. Joseph's Home for the Elderly*, 80 W. Northwest Hwy., 60067. Tel: 847-358-5700; Fax: 847-358-5763
For a complete listing, refer to the Special Care Facilities section.

PARK RIDGE. *Resurrection Nursing and Rehabilitation Center*, 1001 N. Greenwood, 60068. Tel: 708-692-5600; Fax: 708-692-2305
For a complete listing, refer to the Special Care Facilities section.

WHEELING. *Addolorata Villa*, 555 McHenry Rd., 60090. Tel: 847-537-2900; Fax: 847-215-5805
For a complete listing, refer to the Special Care Facilities section.

[N] MONASTERIES AND RESIDENCES OF PRIESTS AND BROTHERS

CHICAGO. *Brandsma House*, 1036 W. Loyola Ave., #3, 60626-5233. Tel: 773-761-5139. Revs. Eamon R. Carroll, O.Carm.; Aloysius A. Sieracki, O.Carm.

Carmelite Fathers Residence, 4747 S. Dorchester Ave., 60615. Tel: 773-268-9745. Revs. Emmett Gavin, O.Carm.; Daniel O'Neill, O.Carm.; Bro. Timothy Sklopan, O.Carm.

Carmelite Priory of St. Cyril, 6401 S. Harper Ave., 60637. Tel: 312-684-0112; Fax: 312-684-0113. Bro. Timothy Sklopan, O.Carm., Prior & Prin.; Revs. Jerry Williams, O.Carm.; Leander Troy, O.Carm., (Retired); Daniel Carroll, O.Carm.; George L. O'Keefe, O.Carm., (Retired); Glen Snow, O.Carm. Residing here are all the priests who teach at Mt. Carmel High School. Revs. Carl Markelz, O.Carm., Prin.; John Knoerschild, O.Carm.

Chicago Province of the Society of Jesus-Provincial Office, 2050 N. Clark St., 60614. Tel: 773-975-6363; Fax: 773-975-0230. Very Rev. Richard J. Bauman, S.J., Prov.; Revs. Richard H. McGurn, S.J., Exec. Asst. & Asst. Formation; Gerald P. Grace, S.J., Asst. Intl. Apostolates, Jesuit Intl. Missions, & Social Ministries; James A. Stoeger, S.J., Asst. Secondary Education & Pastoral Ministries; James P. Gschwend, S.J., Asst. for Continuing Ed. & Asst. for Jesuits in Diaspora; John F. Costello, S.J., Asst. for Devel. & Communications; Paul V. Robb, S.J., Asst. Treas.; Daniel L. Flaherty, S.J., Asst. for Business & Finance; William O. Madden, S.J., Asst. Records & Res.; Brian G. Paulson, S.J., Asst. for Vocation Promotion.
Jesuits Serving Abroad: Rev. Kevin E. Gallagher, S.J., Interprovince Liaison, Apdo 10226, Lima 1, Peru. Revs. Robert E. Beckman, S.J. (Peru); Fred F. Bergewisch, S.J. (Peru); Kevin H. Flaherty, S.J. (Peru); Daniel F. Hartnett, S.J. (Peru); Jeffrey L. Klaiber, S.J. (Peru); Lewis C. Murtaugh, S.J. (Peru); John R. Crocker, S.J. (Jerusalem); John R. Sima, S.J. (Peru); Henry T. Chamberlain, S.J. (Rome); James M. O'Leary, S.J. (Peru); John D. Baggarly, S.J. (Rome); Paul V. Mankowski, S.J. (Rome); Mark W. Andrews, S.J. (DET); Joseph H. Boel, S.J. (DET); Robert J. Ochs, S.J. (OAK); Charles A. Hofmann, S.J. (SFR); Denis A. Dirscherl, S.J. (BAL); Bradley W. Schaeffer, S.J. (WDC); Thomas W. Florek, S.J. (NY).
Residing elsewhere in the U.S.: Revs. Richard J. Bautch, S.J., Notre Dame, IN; Francis P. O'Donnell, S.J., Albuquerque, NM.

Clark Street Jesuit Residence, 2050 N. Clark St., 60614. Tel: 773-975-6900. Bro. Donald J. Butler, S.J.; Revs. Charles J. Brannen, S.J.; James F. Bresnahan, S.J.; John F. Costello, S.J.; Michael E. Dorrler, S.J.; Gerald P. Grace, S.J.; James P. Gschwend, S.J.; George A. Lane, S.J.; Richard H. McGurn, S.J.; John F. Pennington, S.J.; Edward W. Schmidt, S.J.; Peter G. Sharkey, S.J. Priests 7.

Woodlawn Jesuit Community, 5554 S. Woodlawn Ave., 60637. Tel: 773-667-1395. Revs. Philip J. Chmielewski, S.J., Supr.; Robert E. Finn, S.J.; Michael N. Madubuko, S.J.; James M. McCann, S.J.; Paul R. Mueller, S.J.; Pablo Mora Mendoza, S.J.; Paul V. Robb, S.J.

Claretian Missionaries, St. Jude League, Inc., 205 W. Monroe, 60606. Tel: 312-236-7782; Fax: 312-236-7230.
Editorial Offices: "U.S. Catholic" and other Claretian newsletters; U.S. Catholic Bookstore. Directors: Revs. Mark J. Brummel, C.M.F.; Theodore Salvatore Cirone, C.M.F.; Robert Fath, C.M.F., Asst. Dir.

Columban Fathers Mission Center, 6449 N. Magnolia Ave., 60626. Tel: 773-274-9111; Fax: 773-274-9053. Revs. Thomas P. Reynolds, S.S.C.; Thomas G. Glennon, S.S.C.; Sean Conneely, S.S.C.

Columban Fathers Theologate, 5722 S. Drexel, 60637. Tel: 312-955-5044. Rev. Mark Mengel, S.S.C., Rector. Priests 1; Columbian Seminarians 2; Lay Missionaries in formation 7.

Comboni Missionaries Theologate (M.C.C.J.), Verona Fathers, 5512 Hyde Park Blvd., 60637. Tel: 312-667-8920. Revs. Lorenzo Diaz, M.C.C.J. (Spain); Mussie Abraham, M.C.C.J. (Eritrea). Theology students 20.

Congregation of Alexian Brothers-Alexian Brothers Novitiate, 6007 N. Kenmore Ave., 60660-2953. Tel: 773-275-9300; Fax: 773-275-9373. Bro. John Howard, C.F.A., Dir. Novices. Professed Brothers 2; Novices 7.

Congregation of Christian Brothers, Brother Rice Community, 10001 S. Pulaski Rd., 60642. Tel: 773-445-5048. Bros. Eugene O. Carty, C.F.C.; Daniel Casey, C.F.C., Prin.; Thomas J. Collins, C.F.C., Community Leader; Edmund V. Corrigan, C.F.C.; Austin D. Devane, C.F.C.; Charles E. Joyce, C.F.C.; James A. Houlihan, C.F.C.; Peter J. Martin, C.F.C.; John B. Moore, C.F.C.; Patrick B. Martin, C.F.C.; John Toole, C.F.C.; James B. Sloan, C.F.C.; Ross E. Willatz, C.F.C.; Patrick T. Varilla, C.F.C.; Frank S. Verre, C.F.C.; John S. O'Keefe, C.F.C.; Francis R. Finch, C.F.C.; William F. Kramer, C.F.C.; William L. McInerney, C.F.C. Brothers 18.

Congregation of Marian Fathers of the Immaculate Conception, 6336 S. Kilbourn Ave., 60629. Tel: 773-582-8191 (Provincial Office); 767-1687 (Religious House); Fax: 773-582-8961 (Provincial Office). Very Rev. Donald Petraitis, M.I.C., Prov.; Revs. Victor Rimselis, M.I.C., Councillor I; Timothy Roth, M.I.C., Councillor II; Boniface Vaisnoras, M.I.C., Councillor III; Bro. Donald Schaefer, M.I.C., Councillor IV & Prov. Treas.; Revs. Vytautas Bagdanavicius, M.I.C.; Jonas Duoba, M.I.C., Sec.; John Jancius, M.I.C.; Anthony Miciunas, M.I.C.; Bros. Matthew Pulauskas, M.I.C.; Vincent Zvingilas, M.I.C. Priests 4; Brothers 3.

Conventual Franciscans of St. Bonaventure Province, 6107 N. Kenmore Ave., 60660. Tel: 773-274-7681; Fax: 773-274-9751. Very Revs. Anthony Labedis, O.F.M.Conv., Prov.; Justin Kusibab, O.F.M.Conv., Vicar Prov.; Bro. Thomas Surmann, O.F.M.Conv., Treas.; Rev. Joseph Kruszynski, O.F.M.Conv., Guardian. In res. Bro. George Searles, O.F.M.Conv.
Assigned but serving elsewhere: Rev. Francis Kiley, O.F.M.Conv., Vianney Renewal Center, Eime Rd., P.O. Box 130, Dittmer, MO, 63023.
Friars of the Province Serving Abroad: Revs. John Calgaro, O.F.M.Conv. (Mexico); Abraham Crisostomo, O.F.M.Conv. (Mexico); Bro. Paschal Metzger, O.F.M.Conv. (Mexico).

The Conventual Franciscans of Saint Bonaventure Province Corporation. Legal Title: *The Conventual Franciscans of Saint Bonaventure Province Charitable Continuing Care Trust Fund.*

Franciscan Friars Educational Corporation.

St. Hedwig Cemetery and Mausoleum Corporation. Legal Title: *Franciscan Friars Retirement Corporation.*

Croatian Dominican Fathers, 6346 N. Ridge, 60660. Tel: 773-262-0535. Revs. Nicholas Dugandzic, O.P., Chap., Croatian Catholic Mission; Harvey Blaschko, O.P., Asst. Chap.

Croatian Franciscan Custody of the Holy Family, 4848 S. Ellis Ave., 60615. Tel: 773-373-3463. Revs. Slavko Soldo, Custos; Jerome Kucan, O.F.M.; Mark Kozina, O.F.M.; Ljubo Krasic, O.F.M.; Timothy Majic, O.F.M.; Dionizije Lasic, O.F.M.; Vjekoslav Bambir, O.F.M.; Doiminik Coric; Miron Lasic; Kvirin Vasilj, O.F.M.

Crosier Community of Chicago, 5401 S. Cornell Ave., 60615. Tel: 773-684-6975. Revs. Stephan Bauer, O.S.C.; Thomas Enneking, O.S.C.; Bros. Michael McNeil, O.S.C.; David Donnay, O.S.C.

Daneo Hall. (Passionist Retirement Wing), 7233 W. Talcott Ave., 60631. Tel: 312-631-5179. Revs. Finan Storey, C.P.; Ralph Brisk, C.P. Priests 2.

Divine Word Theologate, 5342 S. University, 60615. Tel: 312-288-2777; Fax: 312-288-6307. Very Rev. Roger P. Schroeder, S.V.D.; Revs. Mark E. Weber, S.V.D., Rector; Timothy A. Lenchak, S.V.D., Vice-Rector; Roger S. Arnold, S.V.D., Dir. Formation; Gary L. Riebe-Estrella, S.V.D.; Stephen B. Bevans, S.V.D.; Thomas Kovattiyil, S.V.D.; Derek Simons, S.V.D.; Mark Schramm, S.V.D.; Joseph Arul, S.V.D.; Reinaldo Zbrun, S.V.D.; Dariusz Gabraciak, S.V.D.; Norbert Betan, S.V.D.; Higinio M. Yescas, S.V.D. Priests 14; Students 32.

Dominican Community, 1914 S. Ashland Ave., 60608. Tel: 312-829-0074. Revs. Charles W. Dahm, O.P.; Matthias R. Mueller, O.P.

Dominicans (Provincial Office), St. Pius V. Priory, 1909 S. Ashland Ave., 60608. Tel: 312-226-0074. Provincial Office. Tel: 312-666-3244; Fax: 312-829-8471. Legal Title: *Dominicans, Province of St. Albert the Great, U.S.A. (Central Dominican Province).* Provincial Staff: Very Revs. Edward M. Ruane, O.P., Prior Prov.; David F. Wright, O.P., Socius & Vicar Prov.; Gerald L. Stookey, O.P., Vicar Prov.; Revs. Benjamin J. Russell, O.P., Dir. Mission Advancement & Society Vocational Support; Dennis R. Zusy, O.P., Regent Studies; Michael A. Winkels, O.P., Economic Admin.; Very Revs. David F. Wright, O.P., Prov. Archivist; Louis S. Morrone, O.P., Dir. Vocations; Revs. Bede R. Jagoe, O.P., Dir. St. Dominic Mission & Shrine of St. Jude Thaddeus;

Michael A. Winkels, O.P., Dir. Dominican Conference Center; Charles W. Dahm, O.P., Promoter of Social Justice; Steven F. Kuhlmann, O.P., Dir. Dominican Social Action Fund; Regis R. Hovald, O.P., Prov. Rep. to Dominican Laity; Vincent I. Zarlenga, O.P., Dir., Fra Angelico Art Foundation.

St. Pius V Priory. Very Revs. Edward M. Ruane, O.P., Prior Prov.; David F. Wright, O.P., Socius & Vicar Prov.; Gerald L. Stookey, O.P., Vicar, Prov.; Anthony E. Romero, O.P., Prior; Revs. Patrick M.J. Clancy, O.P.; David L. Delich, O.P.; Richard de Ranitz, O.P.; Kevin R. Fane, O.P.; Michael A. Garcia, O.P.; Robert A. Goedert, O.P.; Bruno H. Kowalkowski, O.P.; Thomas A. Morrison, O.P.; Benjamin J. Rusell, O.P.; David J. Staszak, O.P.; Paul DePorres Whittington, O.P.; Paul J. Wierenga, O.P.; Deacon J. Reid Perkins-Buzo, O.P.; Bros. Paul T. Leahy, O.P.; Gerald Pidcock, O.P.

Assigned but Serving Elsewhere: Revs. Roderick M. Brown, O.P.; Vincent W. Bryce, O.P.; Gerard B. Cleator, O.P.; Paul H. Colloton, O.P.; Francis R. Crowe, O.P.; John R. Dolehide, O.P.; Francis X. Dyer, O.P.; John C. Fabian, O.P.; Rapael A. Fabish, O.P.; James M. Karepin, O.P.; Thomas L. Kearney, O.P.; Gerald C. Kroeger, O.P.; Daniel W. Morrissey, O.P.; Frank M. Nouza, O.P.; Robert F. Pieper, O.P.; Matthew D. Powell, O.P. (PRO); Ceslaus R. Prazan, O.P.; Richard J. Woods, O.P.; Bros. Benedict G. Baer, O.P.; Michael F. McGreal, O.P.; Joachim M. Thiel, O.P.

Priests of the Province Serving Abroad: Revs. James Q. Barnett, O.P., Honduras; Gerard B. Cleator, O.P., Mexico; Eric deWasseige, O.P., Bolivia; Thomas P. Lynch, O.P., Bolivia; Joseph P. Kenny, O.P., Nigeria; John J. Meany, O.P., Jerusalem; Thomas K. McDermott, O.P., Nigeria; Peter Otillio, O.P., Nigeria; Justus M. Pokrzewinski, O.P., Nigeria; Edward H. Riley, O.P., Nigeria; Lewis M. Shea, O.P., Kenya; James A. Spahn, O.P., Bolivia; Benedict T. Viviano, O.P., Switzerland; Ambrose P. Windbacher, O.P., Nigeria; Bro. Stephen D. Lucas, O.P., Nigeria. Legal Titles: *Spirituality Today Journal, Inc.; Shrine of St. Jude Thaddeus; Society for Vocational Support, Inc.; St. Dominic Mission Society; Dominican Social Action Fund; Dominican Laity; Fra Angelico Art Foundation.*

Edith Stein House of Studies, 5401 S. Cornell Ave., 60615. Tel: 312-572-6943; 324-8000 Ext. 384 (Office); Fax: 312-572-6594. Legal Title: *Edith Stein House of Studies of the Order of Discalced Carmelite Friars.* Revs. Bonaventure Lussier, O.C.D., Rector; Marc Foley, O.C.D., Sub-Rector; Kevin Culligan, O.C.D. Friars: Alan Meyer, O.C.D.; Steven Schmirler, O.C.D.; Mark DeVelis, O.C.D.; Joseph Girouard, O.C.D.; Donald Brick, O.C.D. Priests 3; Students 5.

Franciscan House of Studies, 6107 N. Kenmore Ave., 60660. Tel: 312-764-8811. A Formation House of Conventual Franciscan Friars.

The Holy Evangelists Friary. Order of Friars Minor. 4513 N. Ashland Ave., 60650-5401. Revs. Lawrence Jagdfeld; Robert Pawell; Eulogio Roselada. Priests 3.

Holy Name Friary, Assumption BVM Province, 5103 S. Ellis Ave., 60615. Tel: 312-947-9147. Revs. John E. Wojtowicz, O.F.M., Local Supr. & Franciscan Pilgrimage Asst. Dir.; Leslie J. Hoppe, O.F.M., Prof. Catholic Theological Union; Stanley Janowski, O.F.M., Dir. ACCW & Friary Vicar; Anthony Chojnacki, O.F.M., Friary Staff; Lawrence Janowski, O.F.M., Faculty, Wright College; Bros. Neal Kaminski, O.F.M., Prov. Preaching Staff; Bros. Brian Maloney, O.F.M., Mercy Home Staff; William Olendick, O.F.M., Student CTU.

Immaculate Conception Monastery, 5700 N. Harlem Ave., 60631. Tel: 773-631-1686; Fax: 773-631-8059. Revs. James Thoman, C.P., Supr.; Myron Gohmann, C.P.; Luke Connolly, Dir., Passionist Missions Appeals; Finan Storey, C.P.; Christopher Gibson, C.P.; Frederick Sucher, C.P.; John Cyril Jablonovsky, C.P.; Louis Doherty, C.P.; Michael J. Hoolahan, C.P., Pastor, Immaculate Conception Parish; Lawrence Browning, C.P.; Paul I. Bechtold, C.P.; Roger Mercurio, C.P., Prov. Archivist; Rian Clancy, C.P.; John T. Render, C.P., Dir. Passionist Resource Center; Leon Grantz, C.P., Chap., Our Lady of the Resurrection Hospital; Francis X. Keenan, C.P., Chap., Lutheran General Hospital; Brian Mahedy, C.P.; John F. Kobler, C.P.; Ralph Brisk, C.P.; Eric Meyer, C.P.; Michael J. Stengel, C.P.; Kenny Lynch, C.P.; Peter Berendt, C.P.; John B. Pechulis, C.P.; Bros. Peter Fitzpatrick, C.F.X.; Raymond Sanchez, C.P., Chap. Cook Co. Jail; Joseph Stadtfeld, C.P. Priests 24; Brothers 3. Legal Title: *Congregation of the Passion: Immaculate Conception Community.*

Korean Catholic Center, 4115 N. Kedvale, 60641. Tel: 773-283-3979. Rev. John Smith, S.S.C., Dir.

Lithuanian American Jesuits. (Della Strada Residence and Lithuanian Youth Center), 2345 W. 56th St., 60636. Tel: 773-737-8400; Fax: 773-737-0486. Legal Title: *Jesuit Fathers of Della Strada.* Revs. Antanas V. Saulaitis, S.J., Supr.; Jonas Kidykas, S.J., Minister; Kazimieras Raudeliunas, S.J., Treas. Members of the Community: Revs. Vaclovas Gutauskas, S.J.; Bruno Markaitis, S.J.; Juozas Vaisnys, S.J., Editor of, Letters to Lithuanians; Algirdas Paliokas, S.J., Chap. Dir.

Blessed Jurgis Matulaitis Mission, 14911 E. 127th St., Lemont, 60439. Tel: 630-257-5613. Bros. Jurgis Janeliunas, S.J.; Petras Kleinotas, S.J. Priests 7; Brothers 2.

Lithuanian Youth Center, 5620 S. Claremont Ave., 60636. Tel: 773-778-7500.

Marist Brothers, 1016 W. Polk St., 60607. Tel: 312-491-9301. Bro. John Murray, F.M.S.

Marist Brothers, Monastery Community, 4200 W. 115th St., 60655. Tel: 773-881-6380. Bros. Patrick Magee, Dir.; M. Oswald Ouellette; Clement Legare; Philip McEnaney; Brice Byzynski; Julian Roy; Thomas Kelly; Richard Sharpe; Paul Forgues; Fabian Mayor; Gerard Brown; Richard Grenier.

Marist Brothers, St. Ann Residence, 10114 S. Leavitt, 60643. Tel: 773-239-4116. Bros. Timothy Brady, Dir.; Vito Aresto, Dir.; Louis Richard; Hugh Turley; Henry Hammer.

Maryknoll Fathers & Brothers, 3600 S. Seeley Ave., 60609. Tel: 773-927-9257. Legal Title: *The Catholic Foreign Mission Society of America.* Revs. Peter C. Brien, M.M., Dir.; Edward O. Custer, M.M.; John R. Heisse, M.M.; John C. Moynihan, M.M.; Bro. Anthony Lopez, M.M.

Miguel Pro Jesuit Community, 1611 S. Allport St., 60608. Tel: 312-226-6496; Fax: 312-226-2915. Revs. John P. Foley, S.J., Local Supr.; James G. Gartland, S.J.; Charles W. Niehaus, S.J.; Louis Busemeyer, S.J.; Bro. David L. Henderson, S.J.

Missionaries of Africa, St. Martin de Porres, 5112 W. Washington, 60644. Tel: 312-287-0206. Revs. Austin MacAdam, M.Afr. (Canada); Abdon Gamulani, M.Afr. (Malawi, Central Africa); Julien Cormier, M.Afr. (Canada). Priests 3.

Monastery of the Holy Cross, 3111 S. Aberdeen St., 60608-6503. Tel: 773-927-7424; Fax: 773-927-5734. Benedictine Monks Subiaco Congregation of the Order of St. Benedict. Revs. Thomas A. Baxter, O.S.B., Prior; Patrick D. Creeden, O.S.B.; Edward J. Glanzmann, O.S.B.

The Oblate House of Theology, 5535 S. Kenwood Ave., 60637. Tel: 773-493-3590; Fax: 773-493-6239. Revs. James Allen, O.M.I., Supr.; Philip Singarayar, O.M.I., Assoc. Scholastics 7.

Passionist Community-CTU, 5401 S. Cornell Ave., 60615. Tel: 773-324-2704. Revs. Kenneth O'Malley, C.P., Supr.; Alfred Pooler, C.P., Dir.-Students; James Barry, C.P.; Robert Carbonneau, C.P.; Isaiah Murphy, O.S.B.; Leo O'Boyle, C.P.; Paul Fatt Lean Saw, F.M.S.; Donald Senior, C.P. Priests 5; Scholastics 1; Brothers 2. Legal Title: *Congregation of the Passion: St. Vincent Strambi Community.*

Passionist Provincial Office, 5700 N. Harlem Ave., 60631. Tel: 773-631-6336; Fax: 773-631-8059. Very Rev. Michael Joseph Stengel, C.P., Prov.; Revs. Michael Higgins, C.P., Asst. Prov.; Blaise Czaja, C.P., Consultor; Clemente Barron, C.P., Consultor; James Thoman, C.P., Consultor.

Special Assignment: Most Rev. Paul M. Boyle, C.P., Apostolic Vicar of Mandeville, P.O. Box 8, Mandeville, Jamaica, West Indies. Rev. Jerome G. Stowell, C.P., 50 Cedar Bluff Dr., #8, Lake St. Louis, MO, 63367. Rev. Richard Johnson, C.P., 2412 Linda Ave., Key West, FL, 33040-5100. Rev. John Gabriel R. Mulnix, C.P., 204 E. Losey St., Scott AFB, 62225. Rev. Robert Coward, C.P., Curia Generalizia Dei Passionist, Piazza SS. Giovanni e Paolo 13, Rome, Italy, 00184. Rev. Arhtur Carrillo, C.P., Curia Generalizia Dei Passionisti, Piazza SS. Giovanni e Paolo 13, Rome, Italy, 00184. Rev. Joseph Vanleeuwen, C.P., Ashram J.X.P., Pallichal Rd. - Palluruthy, Cochin 682-006, India. Rev. Thomas M. Newbold, C.P., Sisters of Mercy Motherhouse, 535 Sacramento St., Auburn, CA, 95603. Bro. John Monzyk, C.P., Prof., St. Francis Xavier Rectory, 303 S. Poplar St., Carbondale, 62901. Rev. Faustinus Moran, C.P., 5900 Delhi Rd., Mount St. Joseph, OH, 45051. Rev. Joseph Moons, C.P., Regl. Vicar, Passionist Community, Carmelaramn P.O., Bangalore, India, 560-035. Rev. Warren Womack, C.P., Katolska Forsamlingen, Parkgatan 14, Box 413, Gothenburg, Sweden, 401 26.

Stauros U.S.A. Sr. Ardis Cloutier, O.S.F., Exec. Dir., Catholic Theological Union at Chicago, 5401 S. Cornell Ave., 60615. Tel: 773-324-8000.

Passionist Missions of India, 5700 N. Harlem Ave., 60631. Tel: 773-631-6336. Rev. Walter Kaelin, C.P., Procurator.

Congregation of the Passion. Mother of Good Counsel Community, 5700 N. Harlem Ave., 60634. Tel: 773-631-1686.

Passionist Missions, Inc., 5700 N. Harlem Ave., 60636. Tel: 773-631-1686. Mr. Edward Scholl, Dir.; Rev. Luke Connolly, C.P., Mission Appeals.

Passionist Lay Missioners, 5700 N. Harlem Ave., 60636. Tel: 773-631-6336. Anne Avellone, Dir. Legal Title: *Congregation of the Passion (Holy Cross Province).*

Premonstratensian Fathers and Brothers (Norbertines), 4841 S. Woodlawn Ave., 60615. Tel: 773-548-8020. Holy Spirit House of Studies. Revs. Brian Prunty, O.Praem., Supr.; Alan D. Scheible, O.Praem.; Dane Radecki, O.Praem.; Paul Therly, O.Praem.; Bro. Terrence Lauerman, O.Praem.; Revs. Jay Fostner, O.Praem.; James Stein, O.Praem.; Jeremy Tobin, O.Praem. Priests 4; Norbertine seminarians attending Catholic Theological Union 1.

Priests of the Sacred Heart. (House of Studies), 4840 S. Woodlawn Ave., 60615-1920. Tel: 773-373-2739. Rev. Michael Burke, S.C.J., Dir. Priests 4; Scholastics 3. Rev. Robert W. Bossie, S.C.J., 4946 N. Sheridan, Apt. 222, 60640. Tel: 773-275-9516. Rev. Michael McMillen, S.C.J., 6227 N. Magnolia, #2, 60660. Tel: 773-743-7247. Brothers 1.

Provincial Office of the Congregation of the Resurrection, 2250 N. Latrobe Ave., 60639. Tel: 773-637-0999. Very Rev. John H. Nowak, C.R., Prov.; Rev. C. Frank Phillips, C.R., Vocation Dir. Tel: 312-243-7373.

Priests serving abroad: Very Rev. Norbert W. Raszeja, C.R., Via San Sebastianello 11 00187, Rome, Italy. Tel: 011-39-6-679-5908. Revs. James Gibson, C.R.; Casimir Tadla, C.R.; Gerald Watt, C.R., Our Lady of Guadalupe House Mission, APDO 1512, 68000 Oaxaca, Oaxaca, Mexico. Tel: 011-52-951-507-56. Rev. Glen Baptiste, C.R., Stella Maria Catholic Church, P.O. Box G378, St. George's, Bermuda GE BX. Tel: 441-297-0512. Revs. Stephen Glab, C.R.; Gregory Helminski, C.R., Resurrection Center Retreat House, Woodstock, 60098. Rev. Dennis Sanders, C.R., Weber High School, 60639.

Redemptorist Theology Residence, 1027 E. Hyde Park Blvd., 60615-2807. Tel: 773-363-2094. Revs. Harry A. Grile, C.SS.R., Supr. & Formation Dir.; Gilbert A. Enderle, C.SS.R., Formation Dir.; Bros. Joseph The Pham, C.SS.R.; Tuan Anh Pham, C.SS.R.; Eugene Harrison, C.SS.R.; Lamar Partin, C.SS.R.; Martin Pham, C.SS.R.; Chuong Van Cao, C.SS.R.; Steven J. Myl, C.SS.R.; Charles A. Wehrley, Jr., C.SS.R.; Steven N. Wilson, C.SS.R. Priests 2; Students 9.

Redemptorists: Revs. William Cleary, C.Ss.R.; William Peterson, C.Ss.R.; Robert Wirth, C.Ss.R.; John Willett, C.Ss.R.; Bro. Daniel Hall, C.Ss.R., P.O. Box 29585 Secretariat, Bodija, Ibadan, Oyo State, Nigeria. Rev. William Fitzgerald, C.Ss.R., C.P. 400, Juazerio, Babia, Brazil, 48900. Rev. Harold Thiel, C.Ss.R., T. Chang Phuek A. Muang, 88 Chotana Rd., Chaing Mai, Thailand, 50300.

Serving Elsewhere, Not Listed: Rev. John McPhee, C.Ss.R., 61847 Glenview Terrace, Washington, MI, 49084. Rev. Thomas Franciscus, C.Ss.R., The Tribunal, 1550 N. Fresno St., Fresno, CA, 93703-3788. Rev. T. William Coyle, C.Ss.R., 608 Broadway, Fargo, ND, 58102. Rev. Pascal Dreici, C.Ss.R., 1035 E. Walthen, Fresno, CA, 93710. Rev. Ricardo Elford, C.Ss.R., P.O. Box 574, Cortaro, AZ, 85652. Rev. Joseph Nuttmann, C.Ss.R., P.O. Box 235, Carlin, NV, 89822. Rev. Richard Strass, C.Ss.R., P.O. Box 207, Seward, Alphonsus, 99664.

Sacred Heart Mission House, 4105 N. Avers Ave., 60618. Tel: 773-588-7476; Fax: 773-588-6517. Legal Title: *The Polish Messenger of The Sacred Heart, Inc.* Revs. Leslaw Balczewski, S.J., Supr.; Stefan Filipowicz, S.J., Editor, The Messenger of The Sacred Heart in Polish language; Stanislaw Gron, S.J.; Jerzy Sermak, S.J.; Bro. Edward Jawor, S.J. Priests 4; Brothers 1.

Jan Beyzym Society, Inc. (Polish Jesuit Foreign Missions), 4105 N. Avers Ave., 60618. Tel: 773-588-7476. Rev. Leslaw Balczewski, S.J.

St. Clare Friary, 3407 S. Archer Ave., 60608-6817. Tel: 773-890-1238; Fax: 773-890-0484. Rev. Mark Joseph Costello, O.F.M.Cap., Local Min.; Friars Robert Thorn, O.F.M.Cap.; Jozef Timmers, O.F.M.Cap.; David Heffron, O.F.M.Cap.; Mark Carrico, O.F.M.Cap.; Robert Roemer, O.F.M.Cap.

St. John Stone Friary, 1165 E. 54th Pl., 60615. Tel: 773-684-6510. Revs. Wes Benak, O.S.A., Prior; James Thompson, O.S.A., Dir. Formation; Michael Slattery, O.S.A., Treas.; R. William Sullivan, O.S.A.

St. Joseph Interprovincial Post-Novitiate Formation House. (A Franciscan House of the Sacred Heart) Province, 5495 S. Hyde Park Blvd., 60615. Tel: 773-363-0072; Fax: 773-363-0076. Revs. Tod Laverty, O.F.M., Formation Staff; Gino Correa, O.F.M., Guardian & Formation Staff; Arthur Anderson, O.F.M., Formation Staff; Zachary Hayes, O.F.M., Professor CTU; Gil Ostdiek, O.F.M., Professor CTU; David Dodge, O.F.M. Professed 15.

St. Mary Magdalene Friary, 8425 S. Saginaw Ave., 60617. Tel: 312-374-1590. Franciscan House of Formation (St. John the Baptist Province, Cincinnati, OH). Bro. Tim Sucher, O.F.M., Local Guardian & Formation Dir.; Rev. Tod Laverty, O.F.M.; Bros. Edward Gura, O.F.M.; Francis Williams, O.F.M.;

Brian Maloney, O.F.M. Priests 1; Brothers 4; Temporary Professed Clerics 2; Temporary Professed Brothers 1.

St. Patrick's Missionary Society, 1347 W. Granville Ave., 60660. Tel: 773-973-3737. Revs. Karl Langsdorf, Supr.; Sean Cullen.

St. Peter's Friary, 110 W. Madison St., 60602-4196. Tel: 312-372-5111. Order of Friars Minor. Revs. Thomas Aldworth; Elric Sampson; Boniface Baum; Jerome Baum; Bro. John Bush; Revs. Vincent Callahan; Wenceslaus Church; Michael Clarahan; Bro. Sammy Danna; Revs. Barnabas DieKemper; Kenan Dulzer; Thomas Ess; Charles Faso; Bro. James Finn; Revs. Tarsicius Fischer; Thomas Fratus; Francis Jerome Gray; Bro. Patrick Hanrahan; Revs. Robert Hutmacher; Robert Karris; Bros. Clarence Klingert; Thomas Krull; Rev. Paul Lachance; Bro. William Lanning; Revs. Clement Leahy; George Musial; Fred Radtke; Bill Rooney, O.F.M.; Bros. Terrence Santiapillai, O.F.M.; Raymond Shuhert; Rev. Joseph Windolph.

St. Rita Monastery, 7740 S. Western Ave., 60620-5867. Tel: 773-476-3879. (For information concerning school, see separate listing). Revs. Michael J. O'Connor, O.S.A.; Thomas McCarthy, O.S.A.; John A. Kret; Gerald VanOverbeek, O.S.A.; Edward Andrews, O.S.A., Prior.

Scalabrini House of Theology, 5121 S. University Ave., 60615. Tel: 773-684-5230; 684-4340; Fax: 773-684-5240. Revs. Raniero Alessandrini, C.S., Rector; Mario Lorenzana, Animator; Angelo Moscato, C.S., Spiritual Dir. Priests 3; Students 8.

Servite Friars - Eastern Province, Provincial Center, 3121 W. Jackson Blvd., 60612-2729. Tel: 773-533-0360; Fax: 773-533-8307. Very Rev. Michael M. Guimon, O.S.M., Prior Prov.; Revs. Joseph M. Chamblain, O.S.M., Asst. Prov.; Conrad M. Borntrager, O.S.M., Prov. Councilor; Paul M. Cullen, O.S.M., Prov. Councilor; Paul M. Novak, O.S.M., Prov. Councilor; Bros. Edmund Baran, O.S.M., Prov. Treas.; Michael M. Callary, O.S.M., Prov./Corp. Sec. & Mission Procurator; Revs. Conrad M. Borntrager, O.S.M., Prov. Archivist & Historian; Donald M. Siple, O.S.M., Natl. Vocation Dir. & Natl. Asst. Servite Secular Order.

Monastery of Our Lady of Sorrows, 3121 W. Jackson Blvd., 60612-2729. Tel: 773-638-5800. Bros. Edmund M. Baran, O.S.M.; Robert M. Fandel, O.S.M.; Joseph Fundak, O.S.M.; Dennis Driz, O.S.M.; Kevin O'Byrne, O.S.M.; Revs. Charles M. Brennan, O.S.M.; Walter M. Brennan, O.S.M.; Joseph M. Chamblain, O.S.M.; Lawrence M. Choate, O.S.M.; Donald M. Gantley, O.S.M.; Jerome M. Hurley, O.S.M.; Donald M. Siple, O.S.M.; Robert M. Warsey, O.S.M.

Annunciata Priory, 11128 S. Avenue G, 60617. Tel: 773-221-1043; Fax: 773-221-1556. Bro. Brian M. Fitzpatrick, O.S.M.; Revs. Conrad M. Borntrager, O.S.M.; Mark M. Dennehy, O.S.M.; George M. Luznicky, O.S.M.; Marco Antonio Elias, O.S.M.

Assumption Priory, 323 W. Illinois St., 60610. Tel: 312-644-0392; Fax: 312-644-1838. Revs. David Brown, O.S.M.; Paul M. Cullen, O.S.M.; John M. Dowd, O.S.M.; Anthony M. O'Connell, O.S.M.; John M. Pawlikowski, O.S.M.

St. Bonfilius Priory, 3401 S. Home Ave., Berwyn, 60402-3399. Tel: 708-484-2595; Fax: 708-484-0064. Bros. Michael Callary, O.S.M.; Martin Doherty, O.S.M.; Revs. Bernard M. Barnes, O.S.M.; Thomas M. Heskin, O.S.M.; Paul M. Novak, O.S.M.; Peter M. Rookey, O.S.M.

Servite Development Office, 1439 S. Harlem Ave., Berwyn, 60402. Tel: 708-795-8885; Fax: 708-795-8892.

St. Domitilla Priory, 4940 Washington, Hillside, 60162-1297. Tel: 708-449-8430; Fax: 708-449-2009. Very Rev. Michael M. Guimon, O.S.M.; Revs. Frank M. Falco, O.S.M.; Christopher M. Krymski, O.S.M.; Philip M. McGlynn, O.S.M.; Vincent O'Shea, O.S.M.; Bro. Bonfilius McGovern, O.S.M.

Members of the Province Located Elsewhere in the Archdiocese of Chicago and Other Locations in the U.S.: Revs. Frank M. Calkins, O.S.M., Addolorata Villa, Wheeling IL; Damian M. Charbonneau, O.S.M., Our Lady of Grace Priory, Palm Bay, FL.; Louis M. Cortney, O.S.M., Addolorata Villa, Wheeling, IL; Thomas M. Crotty, O.S.M., St. Catherine of Siena Mission, Kissimmee, FL.; James M. Dore, O.S.M., Our Lady of Grace Priory, Palm Bay, FL; Lawrence Michael Doyle, O.S.M., United States Air Force, Denver, CO; Thomas M. Duff, O.S.M., St. Joseph Husband of Mary Parish, Las Vegas, NV.; Edward M. Edwards, O.S.M., St. Mary Academy, North Plainfield, NJ; Carl M. Feil, O.S.M., Our Lady of Belen Priory, Belen, NM.; John M. Fontana, O.S.M., Seven Holy Founders Priory, Affton, MO; Albert M. Gallegos, O.S.M., Our Lady of Guadalupe Parish, Peralta, NM; David M. Gallegos, O.S.M., Our Lady of Belen Priory, Anaheim, CA; Anthony M. Gaydos, O.S.M., St. Marie du Lac Parish, Ironton, MO; Paul M. Gins, O.S.M., St. Philip Benizi Priory, Fullerton, CA; Thomas M. Greaney, O.S.M., Our Lady of Belen Priory, Belen, NM.; Ignatius M. Kissel, O.S.M., St. Philip Benizi Priory, Fullerton, CA; Damian M. Kobus, O.S.M., St. John Neumann, Yuma, AZ; David M. Kondik, O.S.M., St. Juliana Falconieri Priory, Fullerton, CA; Timothy M. Kremen, O.S.M., Seven Holy Founders Priory, Affton, MO; Augustine M. Kulbis, O.S.M., Christ the King Priory, Milwaukie, OR; Francis M. Martin, O.S.M., Seven Holy Founders Priory, Affton, MO; John J. Martin, O.S.M., Our Lady of Grace Priory, Palm Bay, FL.; Vidal Martinez, O.S.M., St. Catherine of Siena Mission, Kissimmee, FL; George M. O'Connell, O.S.M., Little Sisters of the Poor, Chicago, IL; Michael M. Scanlon, O.S.M., Addolorata Villa, Wheeling, IL; Philip M. Scherer, O.S.M., Mother of Sorrows Convent, Blue Island, IL; Luke M. Stano, O.S.M., St. John Berchmans-St. Juliana, Detroit, MI; John M. Topper, O.S.M., The Sanctuary of Our Sorrowful Mother, Portland, OR; Bros. Joel A. Lechner, O.S.M., Seven Holy Founders Priory, Anaheim, CA; Christopher Moran, O.S.M., Our Lady of Belen Priory, Belen, NM.

Members of the Province Serving Abroad: Revs. Matthew M. Ford, O.S.M., Benburb, Northern Ireland; John M. Huels, O.S.M., Ottawa, Canada; John M. LeMay, O.S.M., Zululand, South Africa; Edwin M. Kinch, O.S.B., Zululand, South Africa; Robert M. Kucera, O.S.M., Zululand, South Africa; Frederick Reiman, O.S.M., Zululand, South Africa; Amideus M. Wickers, O.S.M., Dusseldorf-Nord, Germany; Bro. Andrew M. Motsko, O.S.M., Zululand, South Africa. Priests 55; Brothers 9; Temporary Professed 2.

Viatorian Residence, 1201 W. Belden, 60614. Revs. Thomas F. McMahon, C.S.V.; John E. Linnan, C.S.V.; Mark R. Francis, C.S.V.; Robert M. Egan; Bros. Donald P. Houde, C.S.V.; Leo V. Ryan, C.S.V. Priests 3; Brothers 3.

Vincentian Community, Congregation of the Mission, Midwest Province, 2210-12 N. Racine Ave., 60614. Tel: 773-880-2968. Revs. Thomas Croak, C.M., Supr.; Joseph C. Geders, C.M., Treas.; Robert Lucas, C.M.; Edward Udovic, C.M.; Thomas A. Grace, C.M.; J. Patrick Murphy, C.M.; David Nygren, C.M.; Daniel Theiss, C.M.; William T. Gaughan, C.M.; Paul L. Golden, C.M.; Paul A. Sisul; Bros. Mark Elder, C.M.; Timothy Opferman, C.M.

Xaverian Missionaries (S.X.), 1347 E. Hyde Park Blvd., 60615-2924. Tel: 773-643-5745. Revs. Eugenio Montesi, S.X., Rector; Lino Sgarbossa, S.X.

ARLINGTON HEIGHTS. *Clerics of St. Viator-Provincial Residence*, 1212 E. Euclid St., 60004. Tel: 847-398-1354. Revs. Robert M. Egan, C.S.V., Prov.; Richard A. Rinn, C.S.V., Asst. Prov.; Donald J. Fitzsimmons, C.S.V.; Robert E. Erickson, C.S.V.; Bro. Michael A. Rice, C.S.V. Priests 4; Brothers 1.

Viatorian Mission House, 1212 E. Euclid St., 60004. Tel: 847-255-9292. Clerics of St. Viator. Rev. Richard A. Rinn, C.S.V., Mission Procurator, Dir. of Viatorian Seminary Aid Assn. & Dir. of Pious A.

Viatorian Province Center-Clerics of St. Viator, 1212 E. Euclid St., 60004. Tel: 847-398-1350. Revs. George Auger, C.S.V.; Thomas G. O'Brien, C.S.V.; Thomas L. Sullivan, C.S.V.; William C. Meyer, C.S.V.; Charles L. Maranto, C.S.V.; Thomas P. McCarthy, C.S.V.; Casimir C. Kicmal, C.S.V.; Michael J. O'Brien, C.S.V.; John C. Puisis, C.S.V.; Joseph M. Lofy, C.S.V.; Robert E. Erickson, C.S.V.; Christopher J. Glancy, C.S.V.; Richard A. Rinn, C.S.V.; John A. Toolan, C.S.V.

Priests of the Province Serving Abroad: Revs. Pedro E. Herrera, C.S.V.; Luis E. Lopez, C.S.V.; John A. Pisors, C.S.V.; Albeyro Vanagas, C.S.V., Colegio San Viator, Kilmetro 14, Autopista del Norte, Bogota 2, D.E., Columbia, 54-11-62. Mailing Address: Apartado Aereo 102413, Bogota 10, D.E., Columbia. Bros. Alejandro Adame, C.S.V.; Fredy Santos, C.S.V.; Fernando Nunez, C.S.V.; Carlos Luis Claro, C.S.V.; Carlos Florez, C.S.V.; Felipe Montes, C.S.V.; Rev. Roger C. Drolet, C.S.V., 38 Takan-Tsuen, Pali Hsiang, Taipei, Hsien (249), Taiwan, R.O.C. Military Chaplains: Rev. Daniel Hall, C.S.V., 8600 Glen Myrtle #2816, Norfolk, VA, 23505.

Priests Serving Elsewhere In U.S.A.: Rev. Victor E. Bertrand, North Little Rock, AR. Rev. Joseph B. Tremonti, 240 S. Curtis St., Kankakee, 60901. Tel: 815-932-3001. Revs. Donald W. Huntimer, C.S.V., Tucson, AZ; Thomas G. Kass, C.S.V., Manchester, NH; Alan M. Syslo, C.S.V., Monterey, CA; Robert H. Carey, C.S.V., San Jose, CA.

BLUE ISLAND. *Marist Brothers*, 12212 Irving Ave., 60406. Tel: 708-385-1488. Bro. Sumner Herrick, Dir.

BODIJA, IBADAN, OYO STATE, NIGERIA, P.O. Box 29585 Secretariat. Rev. William Fitzgerald, C.Ss.R., C.P. 400, Juazeiro, Babia, Brazil, 48900. Rev. Harold Thiel, C.Ss.R., 88 Chotana Rd. T. Chang Phuek A. Muang, Chaing Mai, Thailand, 50300. 61847 Glenview Ter., Washington, MI, 49084. Rev. Thomas Fransiscus, C.Ss.R., The Tribunal, 1550 N. Fresno St., Fresno, CA, 93703-3788. Rev. T. William Coyle, C.Ss.R., 608 Broadway, Fargo, ND, 58102. Rev. Pascal Dreici, C.Ss.R., 1035 E. Walthen, Fresno, CA, 93710. Rev. Ricardo Elford, C.Ss.R., P.O. Box 574, Cortaro, AZ, 85652. Rev. Joseph Nuttmann, C.Ss.R.

COUNTRYSIDE. *St. Gratian Friary, Franciscan Friars*, 5536 S. Edgewood Ave., 60525-3426. Tel: 708-482-4546. Revs. James Walton, O.F.M.; Dennis Koopman, O.F.M.; James Hoffman, O.F.M.; Albert Merz, O.F.M.; Ildephonse Skorup, O.F.M.; Kieran Kemner, O.F.M.; Bros. Leon Beranek, O.F.M.; Herbert Rempe, O.F.M. Fathers 6; Brothers 2.

ELK GROVE VILLAGE. *Congregation of Alexian Brothers Immaculate Conception Province, Inc.*, 600 Alexian Way, 60007. Tel: 708-640-7550; Fax: 708-981-5561. Bro. Edward Walsh, C.F.A., Prov. Supr. Provincial Councilors: Bros. Philip Kennedy, C.F.A.; Thomas Keusenkothen, C.F.A.; Lawrence Krueger, C.F.A.; Andrew Thome, C.F.A., Dir.-Vocations/ Community. Brothers 12. Res., 801 Gloucester Dr., 60007. Tel: 708-439-5845.

Brothers of St. Alexius Health and Welfare Fund, Inc.

EVANSTON. *Canisius House*. (Loyola Press Jesuit Authors Residence), 201 Dempster St., 60201-4704. Tel: 847-475-1825; Fax: 847-475-1869. Revs. F. Michael Perko, S.J., Supr.; Joseph F. Downey, S.J.; Daniel L. Flaherty, S.J.; Thomas L. Kenealy, S.J.; Donald J. McGuire, S.J.

GLENVIEW. *The Redemptorists of Glenview, Illinois*. North American Redemptorist Novitiate, Redemptorist Foreign Mission Office and Villa Redeemer Retreat Center, 1111 N. Milwaukee Ave., P.O. Box 6, 60025. Tel: 847-724-0425; Fax: 847-724-8953. Revs. Wilfred Lowery, C.Ss.R., Local Supr. & Dir. Foreign Mission Office; Joseph T. Hurley, C.Ss.R., Novice Dir., Vicar, & 1st Consultor; Henry Novak, C.Ss.R., 2nd Consultor & Treas.; Kevin Fraher, C.Ss.R., Asst. Novice Dir. & Dir. Retreat Center; Bro. Thomas Sanhuber, C.Ss.R.

Redemptorist Denver Province Foreign Mission Office. Rev. Wilfred Lowery, C.Ss.R., Dir., 1111 N. Milwaukee Ave., P.O. Box 6, 60025.

LA GRANGE PARK. *Comboni Mission Center*, 1615 E. 31st St., 60526. Tel: 708-354-1999; Fax: 708-354-2006. Revs. Angelo Biancalana, M.C.C.J., Dir., C. Lay Miss. Prog.; Tom Vermiglio, M.C.C.J., Mission Dir.; Valentino Saoncella, M.C.C.J., Supr.; Sixtus Agostino, M.C.C.J., Lay Miss. Prog. Priests 4.

LEMONT. *The Slovene Franciscan Fathers, Order of Friars Minor, Commissariat of the Holy Cross*, 14246 Main St., P.O. Box 608, 60439. Tel: 630-257-2494; Fax: 630-257-8559. Revs. Blase Chemazar, O.F.M., Pres.; Vendelin Spendov, O.F.M., Guardian; Leonard Bogolin, O.F.M.; Benno Korbic, O.F.M.; Bernardin Susnik, O.F.M.; Fortunat Zorman, O.F.M.; Martin Stepanich, O.F.M.; Athanasius Lovrencic, O.F.M.; David Srumpf, O.F.M.; Bro. Robert Hochevar, O.F.M. Priests 9; Brothers 1.

LIBERTYVILLE. *Marytown, Our Lady of Fatima Friary*, 1600 W. Park Ave., 60048-2593. Tel: 847-367-7800. Community of Conventual Franciscan Friars administering the U.S. National Center of the Militia of the Immaculata Movement (M.I.). Bro. Juniper Kriss, O.F.M.Conv., Vicar; Rev. Patrick Greenough, O.F.M.Conv., Guardian & Prov. Asst., J.I. Editorial Office for Immaculata Magazine & Prow Books.

Conventual Franciscan Friars of Marytown.

Shrine of St. Maximilian Kolbe. Conventual Franciscan Friars 15.

MUNDELEIN. *Carmelite Monastery*, 999 E. McKinley Ave., 60060. Tel: 847-566-4070. Bro. Dominic Saganich, O.Carm., Prior; Revs. John-Benedict Weber, O.Carm.; William J. Harry, O.Carm.; John J. Comerford, O.Carm.; Robert Carroll, O.Carm.; Cletus Sullivan, O.Carm.; Bro. John Sprissler, O.Carm.

OAK FOREST. *St. Roch Friary-Franciscan Fathers*, 4700 W. 159th St., 60452. Tel: 708-687-2035. Chaplains: Revs. Melchior Toczek, O.F.M.; Victorian Haladus, O.F.M., Supr.; Conrad Schneider, O.F.M. In res. Rev. Michael Windolph, O.F.M., Vicar; Bro. Crispin Koeppl, O.F.M. Priests 4; Brothers 1.

OAK PARK. *Claretian Fathers Headquarters of U.S.A. Eastern Province*, 400 N. Euclid, 60302. Tel: 708-848-2076; Fax: 708-848-2069. Very Rev. Theodore Salvatore Cirone, C.M.F., Prov.; Revs. Robert Fath, C.M.F., Supr.; Richard Bartlett, C.M.F.; Thomas Paramo, C.M.F.; Ronald Luka, C.M.F.; James Maloney, C.M.F.; Richard J. Todd, C.M.F.; Walter Mischke, C.M.F.; James Curran, C.M.F.; Bros. Richard Wilga; James Santmiquel Oriols.

Priests serving outside Province: Rev. Donald Lavelle, C.M.F., Dominguez Retreat Renewal Center, 18127 S. Alameda St., Rancho Dominguez, CA, 90220. Revs. Walter Mischke, C.M.F.; Edmundo Andres, C.M.F.; Daniel Vogt, C.M.F., Parroquia San Pedro, El Estor, Izabal, Guatemala, C.A. Rev. Thomas Moran, C.M.F., Parroquia Nuestra Senora del Rosario, Livingston, Izabal, Guatemala, C.A. Rev. Thomas Brummel, C.M.F., Claretian

Theologate, Attakwu P.O. Box 80, Enugu, Enugu State, Nigeria. Priests 42; Scholastics 1; Brothers 4.

Claretian Missionaries Community Support Trust, 400 N. Euclid Ave., 60302. Tel: 708-848-2076. Rev. Theodore Salvatore Cirone, C.M.F., Pres. Vice Presidents: Revs. Mark J. Brummel, C.M.F.; Gregory D. Kenny, C.M.F.; Ronald Stua; Thomas Joyce, C.M.F., Sec.

Dominican Community of St. Martin de Porres, 204 S. Humphrey, 60302. Revs. Michael Winkels, O.P.; Daniel Davis, O.P.; James Marchionda, O.P.; Bro. Gabriel Dault, O.P.

Missionaries of Saint Charles, Provincial Residence, 546 N. East Ave., 60302. Tel: 708-386-4430; Fax: 708-386-4457. Legal Title: *Fathers of St. Charles.* Rev. Livio Stella, C.S., Prov., Scalabrini Development Office, 3800 W. Division, Stone Park, 60165. Tel: 708-345-2626.

Scalabrinians Community Support Corporation, Oak Park.

Scalabrinians Community Formation Corporation, Oak Park.

Italian Cultural Center, 1621 N. 39th Ave., Stone Park, 60165. Tel: 708-345-3842.

OLYMPIA FIELDS. *The Augustinian Provincialate Tolentine Center*, 20300 Governors Hwy., 60461. Tel: 708-748-9500. Very Rev. David L. Brecht, O.S.A., Prior Prov.; Bros. Kenneth D. Mehn, O.S.A., Prov. Sec.; Bruce A. Jendraszak, O.S.A., Prov. Treas. & Dir. Tolentine Ctr.; Mr. Michael Kiley, Acting Dir. Devel.; Revs. G. Jerome Kneis, O.S.A., Personnel Dir. & Asst. Prov.; W. Timothy Cuny, O.S.A., Personnel Dir. & Vocation Dir.; John W. Beretta, O.S.A.; James V. Corrigan, O.S.A.; Robert J. Dodaro, O.S.A.; Edward G. Grace, O.S.A.; Bernard R. Danber, O.S.A.; Bro. Mark Emken, O.S.A.; Revs. Thomas F. Martin, O.S.A.; Karl A. Gersbach, O.S.A.; Donald W. Harkabus, O.S.A.; Richard M. Jacobs, O.S.A.; Martin S. Laird, O.S.A.

Foreign Missionaries assigned to the Provincialate: Revs. Alfred M. Burke, O.S.A.; Charles J. Bodden, O.S.A.; Most Rev. John J. McNabb, O.S.A.; Revs. Richard D. Palmer, O.S.A.; Robert F. Prevost, O.S.A.; Bro. David A. Sharp, O.S.A.; Revs. John P. Tasto, O.S.A.; Daniel T. Turley, O.S.A.; John A. Tyma, O.S.A.

Austin Friary, 20300 Governors Hwy., 60461-1081. Tel: 708-748-9500. Revs. G. Jerome Kines, O.S.A., Prior; Donald J. Bates, O.S.A.; Terry A. Deffenbaugh, O.S.A.; Bros. David W. Adelsbach, O.S.A.; Bruce A. Jendraszak, O.S.A. Priests 3; Brothers 2.

Tolentine Monastery at Tolentine Center, 20300 Governors Hwy., 60461. Tel: 708-748-9500; Fax: 708-481-2090; 748-0018. Very Rev. David L. Brecht, O.S.A., Prior Prov.; Rev. James Friedel, O.S.A., Prior; Bro. Martin Shaw, O.S.A., Sub-Prior; Revs. W. Timothy Cuny, O.S.A., Treas.; John R. Mabarak, O.S.A.; John J. Flaherty, O.S.A.; Edwin R. Kuczynski, O.S.A.; Thomas A. McGowan, O.S.A.; Bros. Anthony Schander, O.S.A.; John Stobba, O.S.A., Sacristan; Angelo Sturn, O.S.A.

Viatorian Residence, 20300 Governors Hwy., Apt. 23, 60461. Rev. John E. Durkee, C.S.V.

RIVER FOREST. *St. Thomas Aquinas Priory*, 7200 Division St., 60305. Tel: 708-771-3030. Very Revs. Peter J. Hereley, O.P., Prior; William J. Bernacki, O.P., Subprior; Revs. Richard R. Farmer, O.P., Business Mgr. & Vicar; Malachy R. Dooley, O.P.; James M. Erwin, O.P.; Hilary J. Freeman, O.P.; John M. Gambro, O.P.; Joseph I. Hren, O.P.; David M. Hynous, O.P.; Bede R. Jagoe, O.P.; Victor S. LaMotte, O.P.; Richard C. LaPata, O.P., Vicar; Jordan A. McGrath, O.P.; Robert J. Miller, O.P.; Quentin E. Moriarty, O.P.; Jerome A. O'Leary, O.P.; James Regan, O.P.; Very Rev. Timothy H. Sparks, O.P. Assigned, but not living at the Priory: Revs. Jordan Aumann, O.P.; Joseph C. Della Penta, O.P.; Robert L. Barry, O.P.; Robert I. Campbell, O.P.; Edward L. Cleary, O.P.; Gilbert J. Graham, O.P.; Jacob Joerger, O.P.; Albert Judy, O.P.; Robert A. Kilbridge, O.P.; Walter T. O'Connell, O.P.; Thomas Aquinas F. O'Meara, O.P.; Robert F. O'Riley, O.P.; David J. Santoro, O.P.; Bros. Terence G. Bullock, O.P., (Assigned, but living elsewhere); Kevin W. Carroll, O.P.; Carlos Griego, O.P.; Regis R. Hovald, O.P.; Michael McGovern, O.P.; John Patrick Mulkeen, O.P.; Reginald W. Neu, O.P. Priests 31; Brothers 7. Legal Subsidiaries and holdings: The Priory Press, theology texts for high schools; "Listening", journal of Religion and Culture; Vestments and Vessels; Dominican Conference Center; Carpentier Art Collection.

American Friends of the Earth Biblique: Rev. Peter J. Hereley, O.P., Pres.

STONE PARK. *Scalabrini Mission Center.* (Formerly Sacred Heart Seminary- Scalabrini Renewal Center), 3800 W. Division St., 60165. Tel: 708-345-8270. Revs. Gino Dalpiaz, C.S., Dir.; Aldo Vendramin, C.S., Dir. Scalabrini Devel. Office; Gina Corradin, C.S., Asst., Mission Center. Priests 2; Brothers 1; Missionary Sisters of St. Charles Borromeo 2.

TECHNY. *Society of the Divine Word, Provincial Headquarter-Chicago Prov.* (Province of Blessed Joseph Freinademetz, S.V.D.), 1985 Waukegan Rd., P.O. Box 6038, 60082-6038. Tel: 847-272-2700; Fax: 847-272-2517. Very Rev. Stanley Uroda, S.V.D., Prov.; Bro. Douglas Edmonds, S.V.D., Vice Prov.; Revs. Thomas Griffith, S.V.D., Treas.; Chester Nowicki, S.V.D., Asst. Treas. Legal Title: *Divine Word Missionaries, Inc.; Divine Word Funds, Inc.; Catholic Universities, Inc.; Blessed Arnold Charitable Trust.* Revs. Thomas A. Krosnicki, S.V.D., Pres.; Francis J. Kamp, S.V.D., Mission Treas.; Walter Bracken, S.V.D., Delegated Supr. For Missionaries on Leave; John Donaghey, S.V.D., Prov. Admin.; James Braband, S.V.D., Sec. of Education/Formation/Recruitment; Bro. Dennis Newton, S.V.D., Vocation Dir.

Blessed Arnold Charitable Trust. Rev. Thomas Griffith, S.V.D., Pres.

S.V.D. Funds, Inc. Revs. Stanley Uroda, S.V.D., Pres.; Thomas Griffith, S.V.D., Treas.; Chester Nowicki, S.V.D., Asst. Treas.; Raymond Quetchenbach, S.V.D., Dir., Charitable Gift Annuities.

Divine Word International, 2001 Waukegan Rd., P.O. Box 176, 60082-0176. Tel: 847-272-1100; Fax: 847-272-9363. Bro. David Noonan, S.V.D., Dir.; Revs. Paul Connors, S.V.D.; Gilbert Gawlik, S.V.D.

House of Religious Men: Divine Word Theologate, 5342 University Ave., Chicago, 60615. Tel: 773-288-2777. Revs. Mark Weber, S.V.D., Rector; Roger S. Arnold, S.V.D.; Phelim Jordan, S.V.D.; Timothy A. Lenchak, S.V.D.; Roger P. Schroeder, S.V.D., Rector; Derek Simons, S.V.D.; Higinlo M. Yescas, S.V.D.

Edward McGuinn House of Studies, 5487 S. Hyde Park, #1N, Chicago, 60615. Tel: 773-643-1518. Revs. Stephan Bevans, S.V.D.; Gary Riebe-Estrella, S.V.D.

Divine Word Novitiate, 1940 Waukegan Rd., 60082-6000. Tel: 847-272-0299. Revs. Edward Peklo, S.V.D., Novice Dir.; James Bergin, S.V.D., Asst. Novice Dir.

Divine Word Residence, 1901 Waukegan Rd., P.O. Box 6000, 60082-6000. Tel: 847-272-2700; Fax: 847-272-2873. Rev. Kazimerz Garbacz, S.V.D., Rector.

Slovak Department, 1985 Waukegan Rd., P.O. Box 6068, 60082-6068. Tel: 847-272-2700. Rev. Emil Cernaj, S.V.D.

Werbisci, 1985 Waukegan Rd., P.O. Box 6024, 60082-6024. Rev. Kazimerz Garbacz, S.V.D.

Mision Verbita, 1002 Jeanette Ave., DesPlaines, 60016. Tel: 847-759-0439. Revs. Crescente de Rivera, S.V.D.; Lloyd Cunningham, S.V.D.; Bro. Douglas Edmonds, S.V.D. Fathers 55; Brothers 21.

WILLOW SPRINGS. *Cistercian Fathers*, Our Lady Mother of the Church, 8121 Archer Rd., 60480. Tel: 708-839-6808. Mailing Address: Box 334, Argo, 60501. Rt. Rev. Hubert Kostrzanski, S.O.Cist., (Retired), Abbot of Szczyrzyc (Poland); Revs. Michael Blicharski, S.O.Cist.; Gregory Szydlowski, S.O.Cist.; Alberic Lipinski, S.O.Cist.; John Muc, S.O.Cist.

Cistercian Priory dependant monastery of the Abbey in Szczyrzyc, Poland (Polish Congregation) est. 1982. Legal Title: *Cistercian Monasteries Auxiliary.* Priests 5.

[O] CONVENTS AND RESIDENCES FOR SISTERS

CHICAGO. *Administrative Center of the Sisters of Mercy of the Americas*, Regional Community of Chicago, 10024 S. Central Park, 60655-3132. Tel: 773-779-6011. Sr. Lucille McKillop, R.S.M., Pres. Sisters 14.

Sisters of Mercy of the Americas, Regional Community of Chicago Charitable Trust.

Benedictine Sisters of Chicago, St. Scholastica Monastery. (Motherhouse), 7430 N. Ridge Blvd., 60645. Sr. Karen Bland, O.S.B., Prioress. Sisters 88.

Comboni Missionary Sisters, 1125 E. 50th St., 60615. Tel: 773-624-1122. Sisters 4.

Daughters of St. Mary of Providence, Provincialate: 4200 N. Austin Ave., 60634. Tel: 773-545-8300. Sr. Bernardine Kauffmann, Prov.

Daughters of St. Paul, 172 N. Michigan, 60601. Tel: 312-346-4228; 346-3240; Fax: 312-346-5415. Sr. Frances Aurelia Obrovac, F.S.P., Supr. Sisters 4.

Little Sisters of Jesus, 1529 S. Sawyer St., 60623. Sisters 3.

Little Sisters of the Poor, The, 2325 N. Lakewood Ave., 60614; Fax: 773-935-9614. Sr. Marcel Joseph, L.S.P., Supr. Legal Title: *Little Sisters of the Poor of Chicago, Inc.* Sisters 13.

Medical Missionaries of Mary, 3410 W. 60th Pl., 60629. Tel: 773-737-3458; Fax: 773-737-4582. Sisters 4.

Missionaries of Charity, 2234 W. Washington Blvd., 60612. Tel: 312-421-0038. Sr. M. Marilyn, M.C.

Missionary Sisters of Christ the King, 1118 N. Noble St., 60622. Tel: 773-489-0714. Irena Gertruda Szymanska, Supr., 5936 W. Barry Ave., 60634-5130. Tel: 773-889-7979. Sr. Weronika E. Ilnicka, Supr. Sisters 9.

Missionary Sisters of the Sacred Heart of Jesus, Cabrini Hall, 428 St. James Pl., 60614.

Other Addresses: 422 W. Deming Pl., 60614. 420 W. Deming Pl., 60614. 9430 Golf Rd., Des Plaines, 60016. 2826 W. Cermak Rd., 60623. Sisters 26.

Mother of Good Counsel Provincialate, 3800 Peterson Ave., 60659. Tel: 773-463-3020. Provincialate of the Felician Sisters, Good Counsel High School, Novitiate, Our Lady of the Angels, St. Ann, Bl. Angela, St. Colette, St. Elizabeth of Hungary. Sr. Mary Barbara Ann Bosch, C.S.S.F., Prov. Min.; Revs. Justin Kusibab, O.F.M.Conv., Chap. Provincialate; Michale Suszynski, O.F.M.Conv., Chap. Our Lady of the Angels Convent. Professed Sisters 275. Our Lady of the Angels, 3800 W. Peterson, 60659.

Queen of the Resurrection House of Prayer, 7430 W. Talcott Ave., 60631. Sr. M. Laurette Winiarski, C.R., Supr. Sisters 20.

Sisters of St. Casimir, Motherhouse and Novitiate, 2601 W. Marquette Rd., 60629-1817. Tel: 773-776-1324; Fax: 773-776-1324. Sr. Marilyn Kuzmickus, S.S.C., Gen. Supr. Sisters 209.

Sisters of the Good Shepherd, 1114 W. Grace St., 60613. Tel: 773-935-3434; Fax: 773-935-3523. Sr. Kathleen Moore, R.G.S., Supr. Sisters 7.

Sisters of the Holy Cross, 7422 N. Harlem, 60631-4409. Tel: 773-774-5449. Sr. Karen Anne Jackson, C.S.C.

Other Residences: 3650 W. 96th St., Evergreen Park, 60805. 15119 Catalina Dr., Orland Park, 60462. 6918 W. 112th Pl., Worth, 60482. Sisters of the Holy Cross 6.

Sisters of the Resurrection Provincial House and Novitiate, 7432 Talcott Ave., 60631. Sr. Virginia Ann Wanzek, C.R., Prov. Supr. Sisters 32. Congregation of the Sisters of the Resurrection, Chicago Province. Legal Title: *Sisters of the Resurrection.*

Attended by Passionist Fathers.

Society of Helpers, 303 W. Barry, 60657. Tel: 773-248-8646; Fax: 773-248-0547. Provincial Office, 3206 S. Aberdeen, 60608. Tel: 773-523-8638; Fax: 773-523-8715. Sr. Mary Therese Harrington, Prov. Professed Sisters 43.

Other residences: 1536 W. Wellington, 60657. 2043 N. Humboldt Blvd., 60647. 2933 N. Sheridan Rd., 60657. 1100 N. Hermitage, 60622. 515 W. Barry, #458, 60657. 1930 N. Kenmore, 60614. 1850 S. Throop St., 60608. 3130 N. Lake Shore Dr., 60657.

Wright Hall-Sisters of Charity B.V.M., 6364 Sheridan Rd., 60660. Tel: 773-761-7550. Professed Sisters B.V.M. 93.

ALSIP. *Hospital Sisters of the Third Order of St. Francis*, 11923 S. Ridgeway, #10, 60658.

ARLINGTON HEIGHTS. *Missionaries of the Sacred Heart of Jesus and Our Lady of Guadalupe M.S.C.Gpe.*, 1212 E. Euclid Ave., 60004. Tel: 847-255-5616.

Sisters of the Living Word, 800 N. Fernandez Ave. B, 60004-5316. Tel: 708-577-5972; Fax: 708-577-5980. Sr. Mary Ann Zrust, S.L.W., Supr. Gen. & Coord. of Spiritual Life. Sisters 80.

BARTLETT. *Immaculata Congretional Home*, 801 W. Bartlett Rd., 60103-4061. Tel: 708-837-3502; Fax: 708-837-0052. Congregational Home of the Sisters of St. Joseph, T.O.S.F. Management Team: Sr. Lydia Bilecki, S.S.J.-T.O.S.F.; Sr. Elaine Haiduk, S.S.J.-T.O.S.F.; Sr. Patricia Schafke, S.S.J.-T.O.S.F. Sisters in Residence 61.

BERWYN. *Poor Handmaids of Jesus Christ*, 1916 S. Clarence Ave., 60402. Tel: 708-749-0125. Sisters 2.

School Sisters of Notre Dame. (Chicago Province), 1431 Euclid Ave., 60402. Tel: 708-749-1380; 749-1381. Sr. Catherine Sarther, S.S.N.D., Prov. Leader. Professed Sisters 160.

BLUE ISLAND. *Franciscan Sisters of Mary*, 12101 Artesian Ave., 60406-1047. Tel: 708-597-2720. Sisters 3.

Mother of Sorrows Convent, 13811 S. Western Ave., 60406. Tel: 708-385-2103. Legal Title: *Mantellate Sisters Servants of Mary.*

Motherhouse of the Servants of Mary. Sr. M. Gabriel Cossa, O.S.M., Prov. Sisters 23.

DES PLAINES. *Monastery of Discalced Carmelities*, River Rd. and Central, 60016. Tel: 847-298-4241. Mother Catherine of the Mother of God, Prioress.

Attended by Holy Cross Fathers.

Provincial House of the Sisters of the Holy Family of Nazareth, 310 N. River Rd., 60016-1211. Tel: 847-298-6760; Fax: 847-803-1941. Sr. M. Lucille Madura, C.S.F.N., Prov. Supr. Professed Sisters 43.

EVERGREEN PARK. *American Province of Little Company of Mary Sisters.* (Little Company of Mary Sisters), 9350 S. California, 60805. Tel: 708-422-0130; Fax: 708-422-2212. Sr. Carol Pacini, Prov. Leader. Total in Community 31.

Charitable Trust: American Province of Little Company of Mary Sisters Charitable Trust.

HIGHWOOD. *Daughters of Divine Love Congregation*, 140 North Ave., St. James Convent, 60040. Tel: 847-432-9003. Sr. Mary Paul Asoegwu, D.D.L., Supr.

HOFFMAN ESTATES. *Poor Handmaids of Jesus Christ, Annunciation Convent*, 1480 Ashley Rd., 60195. Tel: 847-519-1384.

HOMETOWN. *Adrian Dominican Sisters, Upper Midwest Mission Chapter*, 8925 S. Kostner Ave., 60456-1006. Tel: 708-636-8178; Fax: 708-636-0031. Sr. Mary Margaret Mannard, O.P., Chapter Prioress.

Adrian Dominican Sisters, Midwest Dominican Mission Chapter, 8925 S. Kostner Ave., 60456-1006. Tel: 708-636-7566; Fax: 708-636-0031. Sr. Joella Miller, O.P., Chapter Prioress.

JUSTICE. *Immaculate Conception Prov. House and Novitiate of the Dominican Sisters*, 9000 W. 81st St., 60458. Sr. Natalie, O.P., Prov. Sisters 17.

LA GRANGE PARK. *Sisters of St. Joseph of La Grange*, 1515 W. Ogden Ave., 60526. Tel: 708-354-9200; Fax: 708-354-9573. Legal Title: *Bethlehem Woods Retirement Living Center, Nazareth Academy, Sisters of St. Joseph Charitable Trust*. Sr. Carol J. Crepeau, C.S.J., Pres. Sponsored ministries include retirement care co-sponsored with Catholic Charities, secondary education and School on Wheels, an adult literacy program. Total in Community 114.

LAKE VILLA. *Handmaids of the Precious Blood-Priory of the Heart of Mary*, 24140 W. Petite Lake Rd., 60046. Tel: 847-356-7729. Sr. Mel Pierre, H.P.B., Prioress. Sisters 3.

LAKE ZURICH. *Daughters of St. Mary of Providence*, Novitiate: 24955 N. Hwy. 12, 60047. Tel: 847-438-5050. Sr. Caryn Haas, Formation Dir.

LEMONT. *Mount Assisi Convent, Sisters of St. Francis of Christ the King*, 13900 Main St., 60439-9736. Sr. M. Ann Barbara Plavac, O.S.F., Prov. Supr. Sisters 80.

Our Lady of Victory Convent, 14700 Main St., 60439. Tel: 630-257-7776; Fax: 630-257-7887. General Motherhouse and Novitiate of the Franciscan Sisters of Chicago. Legal Title: *Franciscan Sisters of Chicago*. Sr. M. Francis Clare Radke, Gen. Supr. Professed Sisters 76.

MELROSE PARK. *Sisters of St. Charles Borromeo*. Missionary Sisters of St. Charles Borromeo(Scalabrinians), 1414 N. 37th Ave., 60160. Tel: 708-343-2162. Sr. Marciana Zambiasi, M.S.S.C., Prov. Supr. Sisters 63; Residents 13.

Charitable Trust: Sisters of St. Charles Borromeo, Province of Our Lady of Fatima Charitable Trust.

OAK FOREST. *Our Lady of Sorrows Priory, Benedictine Sisters of Pontifical Jurisdiction*, 5900 W. 147th St., 60452. Tel: 708-687-2877. Sr. Irene Sebo, O.S.B., Prioress. In res. Rev. Martin N. Winters. Professed 6.

TECHNY. *Provincial House of the Missionary Sisters Servants of the Holy Spirit*, 2600 Waukegan Rd., P.O. Box 6026, 60082-6026. Tel: 847-272-5930. Sr. Priscilla Burke, Prov. Supr.; Sr. Dolores Marie Kuhl. Professed Sisters 105.

Arnold Janssen Foundation.

WAUKEGAN. *Franciscan Missionaries of Mary*, 726 S. Lincoln St., 60085. Tel: 847-662-8439. Sr. Noreen Murray, F.M.M., Coord. Sisters 4.

WILMETTE. *Maria Immaculata Convent*, 1041 Ridge Rd., 60091-1560. Tel: 847-853-3400; Fax: 847-251-0482. Motherhouse and Novitiate of the Sisters of Christian Charity. Sr. M. Judith Moran, S.C.C., Prov. Supr. Sisters 25.

Sacred Heart Convent, 2221 Elmwood Ave., 60091-1435. Tel: 847-251-3770; Fax: 847-251-3771. A home for aged and infirm Sisters of Christian Charity. Motherhouse in Wilmette, Illinois. Sr. Anna Domeier, S.C.C., Supr. Sisters in Residence 70.

[P] SECULAR INSTITUTES

RIVER FOREST. *Caritas Christi*, P.O. Box 5162, 60305. Legal Title: *Cultural Crossroads, Inc*. An International Secular Institute of Pontifical Rite, which forms and gives to the Church laywomen who according to their callings, talents, and professional skills seek to respond to the love of Christ in their providential environment by following the demands of the Gospel.

[Q] PIOUS UNIONS AND OTHER SOCIETIES

CHICAGO. *Teresian Institute*, 3926 N. Kildare, 60641. Tel: 773-545-2979. C. Fernandez-Aguinaco, Contact Person.

An international association of the faithful of pontifical right, founded in Spain in 1911. Aim: To promote the integration of Christian faith and culture, through the professional activity of its members. They live out their Christian call from within existing temporal structures, seeking to order and illumine them according to the plan of God, in the manner of leaven.

LIBERTYVILLE. *Marytown, U.S. National Center of the Militia of the Immaculata Movement*, Shrine of St. Maximilian Kolbe, 1600 W. Park Ave., 60048-2593. Tel: 847-367-7800.

International Latin name: Militia Immaculatae (M.I.). An association of clergy, religious and laity dedicated to Catholic evangelization, founded 1917 in Rome by St. Maximilian Kolbe. Rev. Patrick Greenough, O.F.M.Conv., Prov. Asst. for M.I.

[R] VISITING AND NURSING OF THE SICK IN THEIR HOMES

CHICAGO. *Catholic Home Care*, 721 N. LaSalle St., 60610. Tel: 312-655-7415

For a complete listing, refer to the Special Care Facilities section.

Catholic Home Care Home Services, 721 N. LaSalle St., 60610. Tel: 312-655-7415

For a complete listing, refer to the Special Care Facilities section.

[S] SOCIETIES, CLUBS AND RESIDENCES

CHICAGO. *Equestrian Order of the Holy Sepulchre of Jerusalem*. (North Central Lieutenancy), 1035 N. Dearborn, 60610. Tel: 312-280-8633; Fax: 312-280-2568. Sir Matthew J. Lamb, K.G.C.H.S., Lieutenant; Sir Thomas J. McCabe, K.C.H.S., Sec.

Kolping Center, 5826 N. Elston, 60646. Tel: 773-792-2190. Rev. Richard J. Ehrens.

The Catholic Kolping Society of Chicago.

[T] RETREAT HOUSES

CHICAGO. *Congregation of Our Lady of the Retreat in the Cenacle*, 513 Fullerton Pkwy., 60614. Tel: 312-528-6300. Sr. Marguerite Gautreau, Prov. Professed Sisters 30.

Focolare Movement-Mariapolis Center, 5001 S. Greenwood Ave., 60615. Tel: 773-285-2746. Daytime Capacity 60; Overnight Capacity 30.

BARRINGTON. *Bellarmine Hall*, Box 268, 60011. Tel: 847-381-1261. Jesuit retreat house for laity, priests, and religious. Revs. Donald J. Hayes, S.J.; Bernard J. Mulhern, S.J.; Bros. William R. Haas, S.J.; George A. Prickril, S.J.

The Jesuit Retreat League of Chicago. Tel: 847-381-1261. Revs. George W. Steenken, S.J.; Robert J. Lab, S.J.; J. Michael Sparough, S.J.; Michael E. Dorrler, S.J.

DES PLAINES. *Cabrini Retreat Center*. (Formerly St. Frances Cabrini Retreat House), 9430 Golf Rd., 60016. Tel: 847-297-6530. Sr. Catherine Garry, M.S.C., Dir. Sisters 3. Retreats for priests, religious, laity & youth. Staffed by Missionary Sisters of the Sacred Heart of Jesus.

GLENVIEW. *Villa Redeemer*, 1111 N. Milwaukee Ave., Box 6, 60025. Tel: 847-724-7804; Fax: 847-724-7816. Retreats for men, women, married and engaged couples and special groups. Conducted by the Redemptorists. Rev. Kevin Fraher, C.Ss.R., Dir. Legal Title: *The Redemptorists of Glenview, IL*.

LEMONT. *St. Mary's Retreat House*, 14230 Main St., P.O. Box 608, 60439. Tel: 630-257-5102. Bro. Robert Hochevar, O.F.M., Acting Dir.

MUNDELEIN. *Cardinal Stritch Retreat House*, 1000 E. Maple, P.O. Box 455, 60060. Tel: 847-566-6060; Fax: 847-566-6082. Rev. Edmund J. Siedlicki, Admin.

Serves the clergy of Chicago and Region VII. Retreatants during year 1,600.

[U] NATIONAL INSTITUTIONS

CHICAGO. *The Catholic Church Extension Society*, Headquarters, 150 S. Wacker Dr., 20th Fl., 60606. Tel: 312-236-7240; Fax: 312-236-5276. Legal Title: *The Catholic Church Extension Society of the United States of America*. Most Rev. Francis E. George, Chancellor; Rev. Msgr. Kenneth J. Velo, Pres.; Mr. Richard A. Ritter, Vice Pres./Treas.; Paul E. Flaherty, Gen. Sec.

**Catholic Guild for the Blind*. Provides devotional services including large print Mass, free tape-lending library, spiritual magazine available in Braille, large print and on audio cassette; programs for Catholic schools; the liturgy of the Hours in large print or audio cassette; the sacramental rites in large print; and large print Bibles. 180 N. Michigan Ave., STE. 1700, 60601-7463. Tel: 312-236-8569; Fax: 312-236-8128. Mr. David M. McGowan, Exec. Dir.

Catholic Kolping Society of America-National Endowment Fund. 1804 Aspen Dr., Mount Prospect, 60056. Tel: 847-824-8768. William B. Mahrenholz, Treas.

Catholic League for Religious Assistance to Poland, Headquarters, 984 N. Milwaukee Ave., 60622-4199. Tel: 773-276-2334. Legal Title: *Catholic League*. Most Rev. Thad J. Jakubowski, D.D., Exec. Dir.; Revs. Thaddeus Dzieszko, Asst. Dir.; Thomas A. Bernas, Treas.

Jan Beyzym Society, Inc., 4105 N. Avers Ave., 60618. Tel: 773-588-7476; Fax: 773-588-6517. Polish Jesuits Foreign Missions.

National Association of Diaconate Directors (NADD), 1337 W. Ohio, 60622. Tel: 312-226-4033; Fax: 312-829-8915. Deacons Maury Reed, Pres.; Peter D'Heilly, Pres. Elect.

National Coalition for Church Vocations, 5420 S. Cornell, 60615. Tel: 312-663-5453; Fax: 312-663-5030. Sr. Diane Poplawski, O.P., Exec. Dir.

National Organization for Continuing Education of Roman Catholic Clergy, Inc., 1337 W. Ohio, 60622. Tel: 312-226-1890; Fax: 312-829-8915. Rev. Francis S. Tebbe, O.F.M., Pres.; Bro. Paul J. Murray, C.F.X., Exec. Dir. Description: A professional organization of those involved in the continuing education-formation of clergy in the Catholic Church. Dioceses and religious communities in the U.S. are full members. Institutions and organizations which are concerned with continuing education-formation of clergy are associate members. Dioceses and provinces outside the U.S. may also be associate members. NOCERCC was founded in 1973 through the efforts of the National Federation of Priests Councils. It is governed by a Board of Directors which involves a president selected by the membership, elected representatives from the 13 NCCB Regions and 2 elected religious representatives. Its services include bi-monthly NewsNotes, Resource publications, an Annual Convention, training for new and experienced directors, regional meetings, consultations and service to regional and interdiocesan programs.

National Religious Vocation Conference, 5420 S. Cornell, 60615. Tel: 312-663-5454; Fax: 312-663-5030. Sr. Catherine Bertrand, S.S.N.D., Exec. Dir.

**Trinity House*. Treatment Center for Clergy and Religious. 3230 S. Lituanica Ave., 60608. Tel: 773-247-7707; Fax: 773-247-1588. Rev. John Keenan, S.S.S., Psy.D., Ph.D., Dir.

**Zambian Rehabilitation Institute*. Organized to raise funds and recruit volunteers in the U.S. to assist in the establishment of an addictions treatmment center for clergy, religious and laity. Initial location of center in Zambia will also serve Eastern and South Africa. 5414 N. Luna Ave., 60630-1310. Tel: 773-792-2380; Fax: 773-792-9093. Mr. Thomas F. Healy, Contact Person.

RIVER FOREST.

**American Friends of the Ecole Biblique*, 7200 W. Division St., 60305-1294. Tel: 708-771-3030; Fax: 708-771-4510. Rev. Peter J. Hereley, O.P., Pres.; Judy Valentine Gerth, Managing Dir. Tel: 847-475-4114. Organized to raise funds in the U.S. to support the work of the Ecole Biblique et Archeologique Francaise de Jerusalem and promote the dissemination of biblical scholarship and archeological research through newsletters, receptions, and seminars with biblical scholars.

Dominican Leadership Conference, 7200 W. Division St., 60305-1294. Tel: 708-771-0909; Fax: 708-771-4510. Sr. Mary Ellen O'Grady, O.P., Exec. Dir. Legal Title: *Dominican Leadership Conference of Dominican Men and Women Religious in the United States of America*.

Conferences:

Parable Conference for Dominican Life and Mission.

Opus: A History of the Order of Preachers in the United States.

TECHNY. *Divine Word Missionaries, Inc., Divine Word Funds, Inc.*, 1835 Waukegan Rd., Box 6099, 60082-6099. Tel: 847-272-7600; Fax: 847-272-8572. Revs. Thomas A. Krosnicki, S.V.D., Pres.; Francis J. Kamp, S.V.D., Treas.

S.V.D., Catholic Universities, Inc., 1835 Waukegan Rd., Box 6099, 60082-6099. Tel: 847-272-7600; Fax: 847-272-8572. Revs. Thomas A. Krosnicki, S.V.D., Pres.; Francis J. Kamp, S.V.D., Treas.

[V] MINISTRY IN HIGHER EDUCATION

CHICAGO. *Ministry in Higher Education*, 700 S. Morgan St., 60607. Tel: 312-829-0670. Ms. Jan Slattery, Dir. Non-Catholic Institutions:

Chicago State University, 95th & Martin Luther King Dr., 60628. Tel: 773-995-3869. Ms. Corrine Grant.

College of Lake County, 19351 W. Washington, Grayslake, 60030. Tel: 847-2236-6601, Ext. 740.

Moraine Valley Community College, P.O. Box 311, Worth, 60482. Tel: 708-974-5221. Mr. William Droel.

Northeastern Illinois University/North Park College, c/o Precious Blood, 2411 W. Congress Pkwy., 60612. Tel: 312-733-5331. Rev. Joseph A. Pitts, O.M.I.

Northwestern University/Kendall College, Sheil Center, 2110 N. Sheridan Rd., Evanston, 60201. Tel: 847-328-4648. Rev. Kenneth C. Simpson, B.S., M.Div., D.Min., Dir.

University of Chicago Calvert House, 5735 S. University Ave., 60637. Tel: 312-288-2311. Rev. Willard F. Jabusch, Ph.D., Dir.

University of Illinois at Chicago - John Paul II Newman Center, 700 S. Morgan St., 60607-3429. Tel: 312-226-1880. Rev. Patrick M. Marshall, Dir.

University of Illinois at the Medical Center, 916 S. Wolcott Ave., 60612. Tel: 312-666-9215. Rev. Patrick M. Marshall.

Triton Community College, Triton Campus Ministry, P.O. Box 803, Maywood, 60153. Tel: 708-456-0300, Ext. 3752. Sr. Christine Myskow, O.S.F.

Illinois Institute of Technology, c/o St. James, 2942

S. Wabash Ave., 60616. Tel: 312-567-3160. Mr. Eric Schwister.
Truman City College, c/o 4827 N. Kenmore Ave., 60640. Tel: 312-784-1932. Rev. Trinh Peter Hung.
Wilbur Wright College, c/o 3020 W. 76th Ct., Elmwood Park, 60707. Tel: 312-481-8874. Sr. Judith Flinn, C.S.J.
Columbia College/Roosevelt University/Art Institute/John Marshall Law School, c/o Old St. Mary's, 21 E. Van Buren St., 60605. Tel: 312-922-3444.
Lake Forest College, c/o St. Mary, 175 E. Illinois St., 60045. Tel: 708-234-0205.
Catholic Institutions:
Barat College, 700 E. Westleigh Rd., Lake Forest, 60045. Tel: 847-234-3000. Ms. Karen Rushen; Sr. Patricia Reiss, R.S.C.J.
De Paul University, Campus Ministry-Stewart Center, 2320 N. Kenmore, 60614. Tel: 773-325-7902. Ms. Cathy Flaherty, Admin. Asst.
De Paul University, Campus Ministry Department, 25 E. Jackson Blvd., 60604. Tel: 312-362-6910. Dr. Robert Ludwig, Dir.
Loyola University of Chicago, University Ministry Dept., 6525 N. Sheridan Rd., 60626. Tel: 312-508-2200. Mr. Lucien Roy, Dir.; Rev. Lawrence Reuter, S.J., Vice Pres. of University Ministry. Tel: 773-508-2089.
Loyola University of Chicago, 820 N. Michigan Ave., 60611. Tel: 312-915-7255. Mr. Lucien Roy, Dir.
Loyola University Medical Center, 2160 S. First Ave., Maywood, 60153. Tel: 708-216-3561. Ms. Maureen Fuechtmann, Dir.
Dominican University, 7900 W. Division St., River Forest, 60305. Tel: 708-266-2490.
St. Xavier University, 3700 W. 103rd St., 60655. Tel: 773-779-3300. Ms. Eileen Doherty.

[W] PERSONAL PRELATURE

CHICAGO. *Midtown Center*, 1825 N. Wood St., 60622. Tel: 773-292-5450; 292-0660. Revs. Charles M. Ferrer; James Socias.
Northview University Center, 7225 N. Greenview Ave., 60626. Tel: 773-465-3468. Revs. Fred Piegl; Claudio Urbano.
Opus Dei. (Prelature of the Holy Cross and Opus Dei), Delegate Vicariate, 5800 N. Keating Ave., 60646. Tel: 773-283-5800. Very Rev. William H. Stetson, Delegate Vicar; Revs. Peter V. Armenio; John R. Meyer.

OAK PARK. *Oak Park Study Center*, 831 S. Euclid Ave., 60304. Tel: 708-383-0928. Revs. Richard L. Schendt; Barry Cole. Legal Title: *The Work of God, Inc.*

[X] MISCELLANEOUS LISTINGS

CHICAGO.
**Aid for Women.* Dedicated to upholding the principles of Humanae Vitae and Evangelium Vitae, the organization maintains a crisis center where any pregnant woman will find help and encouragement to choose life for her unborn child through pregnancy testing, confidential counseling and referral to community resources. 8 S. Michigan Ave., 60603. Tel: 312-621-1100; Fax: 312-621-1972. Ms. Megan Lynch, Dir.
Angel Guardian German Catholic Orphan Society of Chicago, 126 N. Des Plaines St., 60661. Tel: 312-655-7040.
Apostolate of the Handicapped, 721 N. LaSalle, 60610. Tel: 312-655-7188. James Grady, Pres.; Rev. Charles F. Kelly, St. Daniel the Prophet, 5330 S. Nashville, 60638. Active membership 750.
The Aquin Guild, 1025 W. Fry St., 60622. Tel: 312-280-9199. Rev. John W. Clemens, Dir. Provides spiritual direction to Catholics engaged in public and parochial education.
Bonaventure House, Inc., P.O. Box 148187, 60614-8187. Tel: 773-327-9921; Fax: 773-327-9113. Mr. Timothy McCormick, CEO. Congregation of Alexian Brothers, Immaculate Conception Province. Residences for persons with AIDS.
Catholic Chaplaincy at O'Hare. Mailing Address: Chicago O'Hare International Airport, P.O. Box 66353, 60666. Tel: 773-686-2636; Fax: 773-686-0130. Rev. John A. Jamnicky, Chap.; Deacon James O'Malley, Assoc. Chap.
Catholic Conference of Illinois, 500 N. Clark, 60610. Tel: 312-467-4375. 200 Broadway, Springfield, 62701. Tel: 217-528-9200. Mr. Doug Delaney, Exec. Dir.; Ms. Joan McKinney, Assoc. Dir.
Catholic Health Alliance for Metropolitan Chicago, 203 N. Wabash Ave., Suite 1404, 60601. Tel: 312-606-0266; Fax: 312-606-0357. Sr. Tommasina Lanski, M.S.C.
Catholic Health Partners Services. Sponsored by the Daughters of Charity National Health System-East Central, Inc. and the Missionary Sisters of the Sacred Heart of Jesus to operate St. Anthony, Columbus and St. Joseph hospitals. 2913 N. Commonwealth Ave., 60657. Tel: 773-665-3170.
Catholic Office of the Deaf, 721 N. LaSalle, 60610. Tel: 312-655-7899 (Voice); 751-8368 (TDD); Fax: 312-751-0394. Rev. Joseph Mulcrone, Dir.
Catholic Youth, Archdiocese of Chicago, 1658 W. Grand Ave., 60622. Tel: 312-733-7405. Revs. John P. Smyth, Dir.; David Ryan, Dir., Oper. Mgmt.; Joanne Walczynski, Youth Ministry Coord. of Vicariate I; Patrick Pacer, Youth Ministry Coord. of Vicariate II; Jesse Estrade, Youth Ministry Coord. of Vicariate III; Michael Molitor, Youth Ministry Coord. of Vicariate IV; Maria Perez Eraci, Youth Ministry Coord. of Vicariate V; Deacon Frederick Mason, Youth Ministry Coord. of Vicariate VI; Ms. Kimberly Williams, Coord. Athletics; Irene Friend, Coord. of Training & Faith Formation; Arlene Nash, Sec. & Admin. Asst. to TEC, Day of the Spirit, Boy Scouts, Girl Scouts, Campfire; James Eraci, Dir., Archdiocesan Camping Prog. Office Mgr., Special Events, Newsletter (Shout).
**Central American Martyrs Center (Su Casa Catholic Worker Community)*, 5045 S. Laflin, 60609. Tel: 773-376-9263. Sr. Mary Davis, I.H.M.; Monica Sandschafer, Cabrini Vol.; Bro. Denis Murphy, F.S.C.; Dorothy Dvorachek; Ole Nicolaisen; Caludia Thomas; Douglas Pierce.
The Chicago Center for Peace Studies, P.O. Box 909706, 60690. Tel: 312-701-7262. James A. Serritella, Contact Person.
The Chicago Marian Center, 7262 W. Foster Ave., 60656. Tel: 773-774-7700. Kathleen Long, Contact Person.
Claret Center, 5540 S. Everett, 60637. Tel: 312-643-6259. Resources for Counseling and Spiritual Direction. Anne M. Luther, Exec. Dir.
Claretian Associates, Inc. Organization to provide affordable housing and encourage neighborhood improvement in South Chicago. 9108 S. Brandon Ave., 60617. Tel: 773-734-9181. Ms. Donna Drinan, Contact Person.
Claretian Volunteers and Lay Missionaries, 205 W. Monroe St., 60606. Tel: 312-236-7782; Fax: 312-236-7230. Directors: Ms. Becky Morrill; Ms. Michelle Scheidt.
Court of Appeals-Province of Chicago, 20 N. Wacker Dr., Ste. 3420, 60606. Tel: 312-553-4080. The Court of Second Instance in matrimonial cases for the Tribunals of the Province of Chicago. Revs. Robert L. Kealy, S.T.L., J.D., J.C.D., Judicial Vicar; John P. Lucas, S.T.L., J.C.L., Adjutant Judicial Vicar; Ms. Jane Halpin, Chief Notary.
Focolare Movement, P.O. Box 53426, 60653. Tel: 773-285-2746. Women, 5017 S. Greenwood Ave., 60615. Tel: 773-536-7873; Fax: 773-536-5054. Ms. Paola Santostefano, Contact Person, Men, 1112 S. Oak Park Ave., Oak Park, 60304. Tel: 708-848-6576; Fax: 708-848-6950. Mr. William Neu, Contact Person.
Work of Mary founded in Trent, Italy in 1943. International headquarters are in Rome, Italy; national formation center in New York.
Foundation for Adult Catechetical Teaching Aids, 6007 N. Sheridan Rd., Suite 22A, 60660. Tel: 773-334-6774; Fax: 773-334-6806. Rev. Gerard P. Weber, Pres.; Mr. Buckley, Contact Person.
Franciscan Friars Retirement Corporation, 6107 Kenmore Ave., 60660-2797.
Franciscan Outreach Assoc., 1645 W. LeMoyne St., 60622. Tel: 773-278-6724. Bro. Herb Rempe, O.F.M., Exec. Dir.
Owns & operates: Marquard Center and House of Mary & Joseph in Chicago.
Friends of the Metropolitan Andrew Sheptysky Hospital, 126 N. DesPlaines, 60661. Most Rev. Edwin Conway, Pres.
Holy Family Church Inc., 2050 N. Clark St., 60614.
Institute for Spiritual Leadership, Kimbark & 55th St., P.O. Box 53147, 60653-0147. Tel: 773-752-5962; Fax: 773-752-5964. Education Center for Spiritual Direction and Renewal. Sr. Patricia M. Bombard, B.V.M., Exec. Dir.; Sr. Ann McElhatton, R.S.C.J., Pres.
Intercommunity Housing Corporation, 2900 N. Lakeshore Dr., 60657. Tel: 773-665-3129. Janet Bilandic, Exec. Dir.
Jesuit International Missions, Inc., 2050 N. Clark St., 60614. Tel: 312-975-6363. Rev. Gerald P. Grace, S.J.
Kolbe House, 2434 S. California Ave., 60608. Tel: 773-247-0070; Fax: 773-247-0569. Catholic prison ministry. Revs. Lawrence J. Craig, Exec. Dir.; David A. Kelly, C.PP.S.; Sr. Miriam Wilson, O.S.B.; Deacons James Morgan; Ronald DeRose; George Brooks; John Harrington; John Richardson.
Loyola Press, 3441 N. Ashland Ave., 60657. Tel: 773-281-1818. Rev. George A. Lane, S.J., Dir.
Marist Volunteer Program, 4200 W. 115th St., 60655. Tel: 773-881-5300.
Martin de Porres House, 3322 Washington Blvd., 60624. Tel: 773-826-9336. Margaret Brooks, Pres.; Cathryn Peters, Vice Pres.; Claire Cummings, Sec.
Mercy Housing Corporation, 10024 S. Central Park, 60655-3132. Tel: 773-779-6011. Sisters of Mercy of the Americas, Regional Community of Chicago. Sr. Lucille McKillop, R.S.M., Contact Person.
The Midwest Patrons of the Arts in the Vatican Museums, 221 N. LaSalle St., Ste. 1000, 60601. Most Rev. Francis E. George, O.M.I., Chm.; Mr. Edmund M. Burke, Pres.
Mother Cabrini League, 434 W. Deming Pl., 60614. Tel: 773-883-7329. The purpose of the League is to spread devotion to St. Frances Xavier Cabrini. Sr. Philippa Provenzano, M.S.C.; Anna Grenvich.
Mundelein College. Mailing Address: Office of the General Counsel of Loyola University-Chicago, 820 N. Michigan Ave., 60611. Tel: 312-915-6195. 6525 N. Sheridan Rd., 60626. Tel: 773-508-3029. Ms. Deborah L. Holmes, Pres.; Ms. Ellen Kane Munro, Sec.; Ms. Patricia M. Furgat, Vice Pres. & Treas.
The New World, 1144 W. Jackson Blvd., 60607. Tel: 312-243-1300. Publishers of The New World; Chicago Catolico; and the Archdiocesan Directory. Mary Claire Gart, Editor Pro Tem.
Nowe Zycie Association, 7015 W. Diversey Ave., 60707. Tel: 773-637-7312; Fax: 773-637-7430. Mr. Roman Harmata, Contact Person.
Polish Manual Training School for Boys, 126 N. Des Plaines St., 60661. Tel: 312-655-7040.
S.F.V., Inc., 1645 W. LeMoyne St., 60622. Tel: 773-278-6724. Sponsor corporation of St. Francis Village (a retirement village) in Crowley, TX. Rev. J. Michael Ewert, O.F.M., Pres.
St. Hedwig's Industrial School for Girls, 126 N. Des Plaines St., 60661. Tel: 312-655-7040.
St. Joseph Bohemian Orphanage, 126 N. Des Plaines St., 60661. Tel: 312-655-7040.
St. Thomas Aquinas Foundation. (STAF) (St. Albert the Great Prov.), 1909 S. Ashland Ave., 60608-2994. Very Rev. Edward M. Ruane, O.P., Sec. & Treas.
Serra International. U.S./Canada Council, 65 E. Wacker Pl., Ste. 1210, 60601-7203. Tel: 312-782-2163; Fax: 312-782-2358. Mr. Robert Raccuglia, Exec. Dir., Sierra International; Mr. E. V. Verbeke, Exec. Admin., U.S./Canada Council.
Servite Friars-Eastern Province Retirement Trust, 3121 W. Jackson Blvd., 60612. Tel: 773-533-0360.
Servite Friars-Eastern Province, Inc., 3121 W. Jackson Blvd., 60612. Tel: 773-533-0360.
Shelters for the Homeless, Inc., 126 N. Desplaines St., 60606. Tel: 312-655-7666.
**The Institute on Religious Life*, 3051 N. Christiana, 60618. Tel: 773-267-1195; Fax: 773-267-2044. Mailing Address: P.O. Box 41007, 60641. Rev. L. Dudley Day, O.S.A., Assoc. Exec. Dir.
United Stand Family Center, 3731 W. 62nd St., 60629. Tel: 773-585-4499. Dr. Kim Mis, C.S.S.F., Exec. Dir. Staff 45. Education, Prevention, Problem Identification, Consultation, and Intervention with Children and Families.
Villa Guadalupe Senior Services Corporation, 9108 S. Brandon Ave., 60617. Tel: 773-734-9181. Organization to provide affordable housing and related services for Senior Citizens in South Chicago. Marta C. Bukata, Chair.; Carmen Mendoza, Treas.
The Warde Corporation, 10024 S. Central Park, 60655-3132. Tel: 773-779-6011. Sisters of Mercy of the Americas, Regional Community of Chicago. Sr. Lucille McKillop, R.S.M., Contact Person.

BERWYN. *Servants of Mary, Inc.*, 1439 S. Harlem Ave., 60402. Tel: 708-795-8885.

BLUE ISLAND. *St. Francis Health Care Foundation*, 12935 S. Gregory St., 60406. Tel: 708-597-2000. A Member of the SSM Health Care System.

ELK GROVE VILLAGE. *Alexian Brothers Health Management, Inc., (ABHM)*, 600 Alexian Way, 60007; Fax: 708-981-5561. Congregation of Alexian Brothers, Immaculate Conception Province.
**Alexian Brothers Health System Inc., Investment Trust*, 600 Alexian Way, 60007; Fax: 708-981-5561. Congregation of Alexian Brothers, Immaculate Conception Province.
**Alexian Brothers Health System, Inc. Investment Trust*, 600 Alexian Way, 60007.
Alexian Brothers of America, Inc., 600 Alexian Way, 60007; Fax: 708-981-5561. Congregation of Alexian Brothers, Immaculate Conception Province.
**Chicago Catholic Healthcare System, Inc.*, 600 Alexian Way, 60007; Fax: 708-981-5561. Congregation of Alexian Brothers, Immaculate Conception Province.

EVERGREEN PARK. *American Province of Little Company of Mary Sisters Charitable Trust*, 9350 S. California, 60805. Tel: 708-422-0130; Fax: 708-422-2212.
Little Company of Mary Hospital and Health Care Centers, 2800 W. 95th St., 60642.

LAGRANGE PARK. *Sisters of St. Joseph of LaGrange Charitable Trust*, 1515 W. Ogden Ave., 60525. Tel: 708-354-9200; Fax: 708-354-9573.

MUNDELEIN. *Civitas Dei Foundation*, P.O. Box 665, 60060. Tel: 847-382-5853. The Journal is named Chicago Studies. Rev. George J. Dyer.

NORTHLAKE. *Italian Catholic Federation*, 46 N. Wolf Rd., 60164. Tel: 708-562-0500. Rev. Charles V. Fanelli, Chap.
Scalabrini Village, 444 N. Wolf Rd., 60164. Tel: 708-562-4402.

SCHAUMBURG. *Rainbows for All God's Children, Inc.*, 1111 Tower Rd., 60173-4305. Tel: 847-310-1880; Fax: 847-310-0120. Mrs. Suzy Yehl Marta, Founder & Pres.

TECHNY. *Blessed Arnold Religious Charitable Trust*, 1985 Waukegan Rd., 60082. Tel: 847-272-2700; Fax: 847-272-6942. Society of the Divine Word. Rev. Thomas Griffith, S.V.D., Contact Person.

WAUKEGAN. *Lake Shore Catholic Academy*, 510 Tenth St., 60085. Tel: 847-623-4070. Sr. Miriam Patrick Cummings, S.S.N.D., Admin.

WESTCHESTER. *Christian Brothers Counseling Center, Inc.*, 1840 Mayfair Ave., 60154. Tel: 708-562-1260. Sr. M. Jean Keeley, O.P., Ph.D., Dir. Staff Psychologists & Counselors: James Zullo, F.S.C., Ph.D.; Sr. Joan Scanlon, O.P., Ph.D.; Sr. M. Jean Keeley, O.P., Ph.D.; Patricia Campion, Psy.D.; Denise Simmons Giblin, M.S.W., L.C.S.W.; Barbara DeCoursey Roy, M.A.; Joseph Fortunato, Psy.D. (Cand.).

WILMETTE. *Musica Pacis*, Office of the Treasurer, P.O. Box 969, 60091. Tel: 708-624-2559. Revs. Willard F. Jabusch, Pres.; Robert H. Festle, Sec.; Alec J. Wolff, Treas.

[Y] CLOSED INSTITUTIONS

CHICAGO. *Chicago Archdiocesan Archives and Records Center*, 711 West Monroe St., 60661. Tel: 312-831-0711; Fax: 312-831-0610. The following parish, school or institution records may be found at the above address unless otherwise indicated. Notations to sacramental records of closed parishes held by the Archives and Records Center should be directed to the Archives and Records Center and should specify the name of the parish. The location of records periodically changes. Inquiries for records of parishes, schools or institutions not on this list should be directed to the above address.

Academy of St. Benedict the African (May St.).
Academy of the Sacred Heart. Sacred Heart Schools, 6250 N. Sheridan Rd., 60660. Tel: 773-262-4446.
St. Adalbert School, St. Adalbert Parish, 1650 W. 17th St., 60608. Tel: 312-226-0340.
St. Agatha School.
Blessed Agnes Commercial High School, St. Agnes of Bohemia School, 2643 S. Central Park, 60623. Tel: 312-522-0143.
St. Agnes (39th St.).
St. Agnes School (39th & Washtenaw).
Alexine Learning Center School.
All Saints (State St.).
All Saints School (State St.).
All Saints (Wallace St.).
All Saints/St. Anthony School.
St. Aloysius School & Commercial High School.
St. Alphonsus School (Lemont), St. Alphonsus/St. Patrick, 205 Cass St., Lemont, 60439. Tel: 708-257-2380.
St. Alphonsus Commercial High School (Chicago).
Alvernia Conservatory of Music. Unknown.
Alvernia High School.
St. Andrew High School.
St. Andrew Misson (Wadsworth), St. Patrick Parish, 15000 Wadsworth Rd., Wadsworth, 60083. Tel: 708-244-4161.
Angel Guardian Orphanage.
St. Ann (Chicago Heights).
St. Ann School (Chicago Heights).
St. Ann High School (Leavitt St.), St. Ann, 2211 W. 18th Pl., 60608. Tel: 312-829-4153.
St. Ann Hospital, St. Elizabeth Hospital, 1431 N. Claremont Ave., 60622. Tel: 773-278-2000.
St. Anne (Garfield Blvd.).
St. Anne School (Garfield Blvd.).
St. Anne (Waukegan), Immaculate Conception, 508 Grand Ave., Waukegan, 60085. Tel: 708-336-3684.
St. Anne Mission Chapel (Richton), St. Liborius, 71 W. 35th St., Steger, 60475. Tel: 708-754-1363.
Annunciation (Wabansia).
Annunciation School (Wabansia).
St. Anselm School.
St. Anthony of Padua (24th Pl.), All Saints-St. Anthony, 518 W. 28th Pl., 60616. Tel: 312-842-2744.
St. Anthony School (Cicero).
St. Anthony School & Commercial High School (29th St.).
St. Anthony Commercial High School.
Aquinas Catholic High School.
Aquinas Dominican High School.
Ascension (Harvey).
Ascension-St. Susanna (Harvey).
Ascension of Our Lord (Evanston).
Ascension of Our Lord School (Evanston).
Assumption School (24th St.).
Assumption (Marshfield Ave.).
Assumption School (Marshfield Ave.).
Assumption BVM (123rd St.).
Assumption BVM School (123rd St.).
Assumption School (Illinois St.). Unknown.
St. Attracta (Cicero).
St. Attracta School (Cicero).
St. Attracta-St. Valentine.
St. Attracta-St. Valentine School (Cicero).
St. Augustine (S. Laflin).
St. Augustine School & High School.
St. Bartholomew, Holy Family, 501 S. Utica, Waukegan, 60079-0440. Tel: 708-623-2655.
St. Bartholomew School (Waukegan).
St. Basil, St. Basil/Visitation 5443 S. Honore, 60609.
Bellarmine School of Theology-Loyola University of Chicago, Dean of Students of Arts and Sciences, 820 N. Michigan Ave., 60611.
St. Bernard (65th St.).
St. Bernard School.
Bishop Quarter Boarding School for Motherless Boys.
Bishop Quarter Junior Military School.
St. Blase School, St. Joseph School, 5641 S. 73rd St., Summit, 60501. Tel: 708-458-2927.
Blessed Sacrament School.
St. Bonaventure School (Diversey).
St. Boniface (N. Noble).
St. Boniface School (N. Noble).
St. Brendan (Racine).
St. Brendan School (Racine).
St. Bridget.
St. Bridget School & High School.
St. Bronislava School.
Brother Candidates High School (Techny), Divine Word Missionaries, Box 107, East Troy, WI, 53120. Tel: 414-642-3300.
Cabrini Green Alternate High School. Catholic Charities, Division of Services for Children and Youth, 126 N. Des Plaines, 60606. Tel: 312-236-5172, Ext. 429.
St. Callistus Church - Notre Dame Parish, 1335 W. Harrison, 60607.
St. Callistus School.
Cardinal Stritch High School.
Carmel High School. (Boys and Girls), Carmel High School, One Carmel Pkwy., Mundelein, 60060-2499. Tel: 708-566-3000.
St. Carthage (73rd St.).
St. Carthage School.
St. Casimir Academy, Maria High School, 6727 S. California Ave., 60629-1887. Tel: 773-925-8686.
St. Casimir (Chicago Heights).
St. Casimir School (Chicago Heights).
St. Casimir (Whipple St.), Our Lady of Tepeyac, 2226 S. Whipple St., 60623. Tel: 773-521-8400.
St. Casimir School (Whipple St.).
St. Casimir High School, Our Lady of Tepeyac High School, 2228 S. Whipple St., 60623. Tel: 773-522-0023.
St. Catherine Academy.
St. Catherine High School. see Siena High School.
Cathedral High School.
Chrysalis Program.
Corpus Christi School.
St. Catherine of Genoa.
St. Catherine of Genoa School.
St. Catherine of Siena (Oak Park).
Sacramental Records: St. Catherine/St. Lucy Parish, 38 N. Austin Blvd., Oak Park, 60302. Tel: 708-386-8077.
School Records: St. Catherine/St. Lucy School, 27 W. Washington Blvd., Oak Park, 60302. Tel: 708-386-5286.
St. Cecelia (Wells St.).
St. Cecelia School (Wells St.).
St. Charles Borromeo (Hoyne Ave.).
St. Charles Borromeo School (Hoyne Ave.).
St. Charles Borromeo School (Melrose Park).
St. Charles Lwanga (W. Garfield).
St. Charles Lwanga School (W. Garfield).
St. Clara (Woodlawn).
St. Clara School (Woodlawn), St. Gelasius School, 6358 S. Blackstone, 60637. Tel: 312-324-8430.
St. Clara-St. Cyril (S. Woodlawn).
St. Clara-St. Cyril School (Woodlawn), St. Gelasius School, 6358 S. Blackstone, 60637. Tel: 312-324-8430.
St. Clement High School.
St. Columbkille (Paulina).
St. Columbkille School & Commercial High School.
St. Columbkille High School, Mother Guerin High School, 8001 Belmont Ave., River Grove, 60171. Tel: 708-453-6233.
St. Constance High School.
Corpus Christi High School, Hales Franciscan High School, 4930 S. Cottage Grove, 60615. Tel: 312-285-8400.
St. Cyril (Blackstone).
St. Cyril School (Blackstone), St. Gelasius School, 6358 S. Blackstone, 60637. Tel: 312-324-8430.
Ss. Cyril & Methodius Church & School (Walton St.).
Ss. Cyril & Methodius Church & School (Hermitage St.).
St. David School.
St. David Church, All Saints-St. Anthony, 518 W. 28th Pl., 60616. Tel: 312-842-2744.
De Lourdes College (Des Plaines), Holy Family College, Registrar's Office, Grant Ave. & Frankford Ave., Philadelphia, PA, 19114. Tel: 215-637-4851.
DePaul Academy, DePaul University, Registrar's Office, 243 S. Wabash, 60604. Tel: 312-341-8610.
St. Dionysius (Cicero).
St. Dionysius School (Cicero).
St. Dominic (Locust).
St. Dominic School & High School.
St. Donatus School.
St. Elizabeth High School.
St. Emeric Church, St. Stephen King of Hungary, 2015 W. Augusta Blvd., 60622-4947. Tel: 773-486-1896.
Englewood Catholic Academy (Honore St.).
Englewood Catholic Academy (Laflin St.).
Englewood Catholic Academy (May St.).
Englewood Catholic Academy (Princeton St.).
Felician College.
St. Fidelis School (N. Washtenaw).
St. Finbarr Church (14th St.).
St. Finbarr High School and School. Unknown.
St. Florian Mission (52nd & Archer), St. Camillus, 5426 S. Lockwood Ave., 60638. Tel: 312-767-8183.
Ford City Catholic Center.
Fornier Institute, DePaul University, Registrar's Office, 243 S. Wabash, 60604. Tel: 312-341-8610.
St. Frances Xavier Cabrini (Lexinton St.).
St. Frances Xavier Cabrini School (Lexinton St.).
St. Francis de Paula.
St. Frances de Paula School (S. Ellis).
St. Francis de Sales School.
St. Francis of Assisi Church (Kostner Ave.), St. Francis of Assisi/Our Lady of the Angels, 3808 W. Iowa St., 60651. Tel: 773-235-3132.
St. Francis of Assisi School (Roosevelt Rd.).
St. Francis of Assisi School (Kostner Ave.).
St. Francis Xavier (Nelson), Resurrection, 2840 W. Nelson, 60618-7012. Tel: 312-478-9705.
St. Francis Xavier School (Nelson).
St. Gabriel Commercial High School.
St. George (Lituanica Ave.).
St. George School & Commercial High School (Lituanica Ave.).
St. George School (Ewing Ave.).
St. George (Wentworth Ave.).
St. George School (Wentworth Ave.).
St. George High School (Evanston), Christian Brothers Center, 200 De La Salle Dr., Romeoville, 60441. Tel: 312-242-1240.
St. Gerard Majella School (Markham).
St. Gertrude School (Chicago).
St. Gertrude School (Franklin Park).
Good Shepherd Chapel. (Illinois Technical School for Colored Girls).
St. Gregory the Great.
Hardley Preparatory, Sacred Heart Schools, 6250 N. Sheridan Rd., 60660. Tel: 773-262-4446.
Heart of Mary High School.
St. Hedwig Mission, St. John Berchmans, 2517 W. Logan Blvd., 60647. Tel: 312-486-4300.
St. Hedwig Orphanage (Niles).
St. Hedwig School.
St. Henry School.
Holy Child High School (Waukegan), St. Anastasia School, 629 Glen Flora, Waukegan, 60685. Tel: 708-623-8320.
Holy Cross (65th St.).
Holy Cross School (65th St.).
Holy Cross School (Wood St.).
Holy Family (North Chicago).
Holy Family School (North Chicago).
Holy Family School (May St.).
Holy Family Academy (Division St.).
Holy Family Extension High School (Des Plaines), Sisters of Holy Family of Nazareth, Provincial Archives, 353 N. River Rd., Des Plaines, 60016. Tel: 708-298-6760.
Holy Ghost Church & School.
Holy Guardian Angel (Arthington/Cabrini).
Holy Guardian Angel School.
Holy Name Cathedral School.
Holy Rosary Slovak (108th St.).
Holy Rosary Slovak School (108th St.).
Holy Rosary School (113th St.).
Holy Rosary (North Chicago).
Holy Rosary School (North Chicago).
Holy Rosary School (Western Ave.).
Holy Trinity School (Noble St.).
Holy Trinity (Wolcott Ave.).
Holy Trinity School (Wolcott Ave.).
Holy Trinity School (Throop St.).
Holy Trinity School (Taylor St.).
St. Hyacinth Mission (Spaulding), St. Hyacinth Parish, 3636 N. Wolfram, 60618. Tel: 312-342-3636.
St. Ignatius College, St. Ignatius College Prep., 1073 W. Roosevelt Rd., 60608. Tel: 312-421-5900.
St. Ignatius School.
Immaculata High School.
Immaculate Conception School (Aberdeen St.).

Immaculate Conception Commercial High School (Aberdeen St.).
Immaculate Conception-St. Bridget School.
Immaculate Conception (Aberdeen St.).
Immaculate Conception School (Exchange Ave.).
Immaculate Conception School (Highland Park).
Immaculate Conception School (North Park Ave.).
Immaculate Heart of Mary Vicariate (Ashland Ave.), Holy Cross-Immaculate Heart of Mary Parish, 4541 S. Wood St., 60609. Tel: 312-376-3900.
St. Irenaeus School (Park Forest).
St. Isaac Jogues School (Niles).
St. Ita School.
St. Ita High School.
St. James School (Maywood). Illinois Technical School for Colored Girls.
St. James (Fremont Center), St. Mary, 22333 W. Erhart Rd., Mundelein, 60060. Tel: 708-223-0010.
St. Jarlath (Jackson).
St. Jarlath School (Jackson).
St. Jean Baptiste (33rd Pl. & Wood St.).
St. Jerome School.
Jesuit School of Theology. Loyola University of Chicago, Office of the Dean of Graduate School, 820 N. Michigan Ave, 60611.
Jesus, Our Brother School.
St. Joachim School.
St. John Bosco School.
Old St. John (18th St.).
St. John Cantius School.
St. John Chrysostom (Bellwood).
St. John Chrysostom School (Bellwood).
St. John Nepmucene Church & School.
St. John of God Church & School (S. Throop).
St. John the Baptist (50th Pl.).
St. John the Baptist Church (Burley).
St. John the Baptist School (50th Pl.).
St. John the Baptist School (Harvey), Mary of Nazareth School, 15727 S. Emerald, Harvey, 60426. Tel: 708-331-5076.
St. Joseph Commercial Business College.
St. Joseph the Worker School.
St. Joseph High School (Hermitage).
St. Joseph's Institute.
St. Joseph (17th St.).
St. Joseph School (17th St.).
St. Joseph (Saginaw St.).
St. Joseph School (Saginaw St.).
St. Joseph (Chicago Heights).
St. Joseph School (Chicago Heights).
St. Joseph & SS. Joseph & Bartholomew (Waukegan), Holy Family, 501 S. Utica, Waukegan, 60079-0440. Tel: 708-623-2655.
St. Joseph School (Waukegan).
St. Joseph School (Wilmette), St. Joseph Parish, 1747 Lake Ave., Wilmette, 60091. Tel: 708-251-0771.
St. Joseph & St. Anne, Our Lady of Fatima, 2751 W. 38th Pl., 60632-1686. Tel: 312-927-2421.
St. Joseph Mission (13th St.).
St. Joseph Mission School.
St. Joseph Servite Seminary (Elgin-St. Charles), Provincial Archives, Servite Provincial Center, 3121 W. Jackson Blvd., 60612. Tel: 312-533-0360.
St. Joseph's Home for the Friendless, St. Joseph's Corondelet Child Center, 739 E. 35th St., 60616. Tel: 773-624-7443.
St. Josaphat Commercial High School.
St. Justin Martyr (71st St.).
St. Justin Martyr School.
St. Kevin School.
St. Kilian School.
St. Laurence School.
St. Leonard Commercial High School (Berwyn), St. Leonard School, 3322 S. Clarence, Berwyn, 60402. Tel: 708-749-1989.
Lewis Memorial Maternity Hospital.
Little Flower School.
Little Flower High School.
Loretto Academy (Woodlawn).
Loretto Academy & High School (Englewood).
St. Louis de France (117th St.).
St. Louis de France School (117th St.).
St. Louis (Polk St.).
St. Louis Academy (117th Ave.), St. Jude the Apostle Convent, 890 E. 154th St., South Holland, 60473. Tel: 708-333-7595.
Loyola Academy (Chicago).
Loyola Academy (Wilmette), 1100 N. Laramie Ave., Wilmette, 60091. Tel: 847-256-1100.
St. Lucy. Sacramental Records: St. Catherine-St. Lucy, 38 N. Austin Blvd., Oak Park, 60302. Tel: 708-386-8077.
School Records:
St. Lucy School Records.
St. Ludmilla, Our Lady of Tepeyac, 2226 S. Whipple St., 60623. Tel: 773-521-8400.
St. Ludmilla School.
St. Louis de Marillac High School.
St. Malachy High School, St. Malachy School, 2252 W. Washington, 60612. Tel: 312-733-2252.
Mallinckrodt High School.
Marian School. Catholic Charities, Division of Services for Children & Youth, 126 N. Des Plaines, 60606. Tel: 312-236-5172, Ext. 429.
Maria Immaculata Academy.
St. Mark the Evangelist School.
Marquette Institute (Clark St.).
St. Martin (Princeton).
St. Martin de Porres Academy.
St. Martin School & Commerical High School (Princeton).
St. Mary School (Des Plaines).
St. Mary School (Evanston).
St. Mary (Lemont), St Patrick, 200 Illinois St., Lemont, 60439. Tel: 708-257-6134.
St. Mary (Waukegan), Immaculate Conception, 508 Grand Ave., Waukegan, 60085. Tel: 708-336-3684.
St. Mary Alternative High School. (to 1976), Collections University of Illinois at Chicago, University Library, Special Collections, Dawson Technical School and University of Chicago Library, P.O. 8198, 60680. Tel: 312-996-2742.
St. Mary School (Riverside).
St. Mary Alternative High School (Grenshaw). (1976-1979; some to Dawson Technical School), Chicago City-Wide College-Admissions and Records, 226 W. Jackson Blvd., 60606. Tel: 312-368-7159; 312-641-2595, Ext. 2539.
St. Mary Magdalen School.
St. Mary of the Assumption School (137th St.).
St. Mary of Mt. Carmel (Hermitage).
St. Mary of Mt. Carmel School (Hermitage).
St. Mary of Perpetual Help School, Bridgeport Catholic Academy West Campus, 1040 W. 32nd Pl., 60608. Tel: 312-927-1041.
St. Mary of Perpetual Help High School.
St. Mary Mission Seminary (Techny), Catholic Theological Union, 5401 S. Cornell, 60615-5698. Tel: 773-324-8000.
St. Mary Training School, Maryville Academy, 1150 N. River Rd., Des Plaines, 60016. Tel: 708-824-6126.
St. Mary School of Nursing (Des Plaines), Holy Family College, Registrar's Office, Grant Ave. & Frankford Ave., Philadelphia, PA, 19114. Tel: 215-637-4851.
Marywood High School (Evanston), Mother Guerin High School, 8001 Belmont Ave., River Grove, 60171. Tel: 312-625-3278.
Mater Dolorosa Seminary (Hillside). See Servite Seminary.
St. Matthew (Walnut St.).
St. Matthew School (Walnut St.).
St. Maurice School.
St. Mel & St. Mel-Holy Ghost.
St. Mel & St. Mel-Holy Ghost School.
St. Mel High School. (up to 1969), Christian Brothers Center, 200 De La Salle Dr., Romeoville, 60441. Tel: 312-242-1240.
Mendel High School.
Mercy High School.
Mercy Mission High School.
St. Michael School (Cleveland Ave.).
St. Michael Central High School (Cleveland Ave.).
St. Michael (Wabansia).
St. Michael School (Wabansia).
St. Michael the Archangel School.
St. Michael Commercial High School (South Shore Dr.).
Misericordia Hospital. Sacramental Records in registers of St. Agnes, 39th St. Client Records & Adoption Placements: Catholic Charities, 126 N. Des Plaines, 60606. Tel: 312-876-2288; 236-5172, Ext. 330.
Mission of the Holy Ghost (Techny), St. Norbert, 1809 Walters Ave., Northbrook, 60062. Tel: 312-272-7090.
St. Monica (36th St.).
Monastery of Mt. St. Phillip Servite Novitiate. (Granville, WI), Provincial Archives, Servite Provincial Center, 3121 W. Jackson Blvd., 60612. Tel: 312-533-0360.
Montay College.
Mother of God (Waukegan).
Mother of God School (Waukegan).
Mother of Sorrows Grade and High School (Blue Island).
Mount Carmel School (Chicago Heights).
Mundelein High School.
Municipal Tuberculosis Sanitarium. (Sacred Heart Chapel).
Nativity of Our Lord School & Commercial High School, Bridgeport Catholic Academy South Campus, 3700 S. Lowe, 60609. Tel: 312-376-6223.
St. Nicholas School (Evanston).
St. Nicholas (State St.).
St. Nicholas School (State St.).
Niles College.
Notre Dame de Chicago School.
Our Lady of Bethlehem Academy.
Our Lady of Fatima Mission, St. Hyacinth Parish, 3636 N. Wolfram, 60618. Tel: 312-342-3636.
Our Lady of the Garden, St. Mary of the Assumption, 310 E. 137th St., 60627-1896. Tel: 773-568-1611.
Our Lady of Good Counsel (Western Ave.).
Our Lady of Good Counsel School (Western Ave.).
Our Lady of Good Counsel School (Hermitage).
Our Lady of Guadalupe Chapel, Holy Cross-Immaculate Heart of Mary, 4541 S. Wood St., 60609. Tel: 312-376-3900.
Our Lady of Hope School (Des Plaines).
Our Lady of Hungary (93rd St.).
Our Lady of Hungary School (93rd St.).
Our Lady of Lourdes Commercial High School (Keeler).
Our Lady of Lourdes School (Keeler).
Our Lady of Perpetual Help Vicariate (13th St.).
Our Lady of Perpetual Help Vicariate School (13th St.).
Our Lady of Providence Academy. See Providence Academy.
Our Lady of Solace (Sangamon).
Our Lady of Solace School (Sangamon).
Our Lady of the Angels, St. Francis of Assisi/Our Lady of the Angels, 3808 W. Iowa St., 60651. Tel: 773-235-3132.
Our Lady of Angels (Iowa).
Our Lady of the Cross Mission Chapel, St. Margaret Mary, 2324 W. Chase, 60645. Tel: 312-764-0615.
Our Lady of Pompeii School.
Our Lady of Pompeii Church, Our Lady of Pompeii Shrine, 1224 W. Lexington, 60607. Tel: 312-421-3757.
Our Lady of Vilna (23rd St.).
Our Lady of Vilna School (23rd St.), St. Paul School, 2114 W. 22nd Pl., 60608. Tel: 312-847-6078.
St. Patrick Academy (Chicago), McAulay High School, 3737 W. 99th St., 60642. Tel: 312-881-6522.
St. Patrick School. (pre-1967).
St. Patrick School (Lemont), St. Alphonsus-St. Patrick School, 205 Cass St., Lemont, 60439. Tel: 708-257-2380.
St. Patrick (Commercial Ave.).
St. Patrick School (Commercial Ave.).
St. Patrick Academy (Des Plaines), McAulay High School, 3737 W. 99th St., 60642. Tel: 312-881-6522.
St. Patrick High School. (Boys), 5900 W. Belmont, 60634. Tel: 312-282-8844.
St. Patrick High School (Adams St.). (Girls).
St. Paul School (Chicago Heights).
St. Paul High School, Christian Brother Center, 200 De La Salle Dr., Romeoville, 60441. Tel: 312-242-1240.
St. Paul (12th St.).
St. Peter School (Volo), St. Peter, 27551 W. Hwy. 120, Round Lake, 60073. Tel: 708-385-5496.
St. Peter Canisius School.
SS. Peter and Paul (Exchange St.).
SS. Peter and Paul School (Exchange St.).
St. Peter & Paul School (Halsted St.).
Ss. Peter & Paul School (Paulina St.).
SS. Peter & Paul (Libertyville), St. Joseph, 121 E. Maple, Libertyville, 60048. Tel: 708-362-2073.
SS. Peter & Paul High School (Exchange St.), St. Francis de Sales High School, 10155 S. Ewing, 60617. Tel: 312-731-7272.
St. Peter & Paul Church (Central Park Ave.), St. Nicholas (Byzantine Rite), 8103 Columbia Ave., Munster, IN, 46321-1802. Tel: 219-838-9380.
St. Philip Benizi (Maypole St.).
St. Philip Benizi (Oak St.).
St. Philip Benizi School (Oak St.).
St. Philip High School.
St. Philomena Commercial High School, St. Philomena School, 4131 W. Cortland, 60639. Tel: 312-235-0120.
St. Pius V Commercial High School, St. Pius V School, 1919 S. Ashland, 60608. Tel: 312-226-1590.
St. Pius X (Stickney).
Precious Blood School.
Presentation School.
Presentation-Precious Blood Unit School. Our Lady of the West Side Catholic, Precious Blood Campus, 2401 W. Congress, 60612. Tel: 312-421-6157.
St. Procopius School.
St. Procopius High School.
Providence Academy & High School, Mother Guerin High School, 8001 Belmont Ave., River Grove, 60171. Tel: 312-625-3278.
Providence of God School.
Providence-St. Mel High School, 119 S. Central Park Blvd., 60624. Tel: 312-722-4600.
Quigley Preparatory Seminary North.
Quigley Preparatory Seminary South, Archbishop Quigley Preparatory Seminary, 103 E. Chesnut St., 60611. Tel: 321-787-9343.
Quigley Preparatory Seminary. (pre-1961).
St. Raphael (60th St.).
St. Raphael School (60th St.).
Resurrection (Jackson Blvd.).
St. Rita College. St. Rita High School, St. Rita High

School, 7740 S. Western Ave., 60620. Tel: 773-925-6600.
St. Rita of Cascia School.
St. Rocco (Chicago Heights). School Records: see Mt. Carmel School.
St. Roman School.
St. Rosalie School (Harwood Heights).
St. Rose of Lima (W. 48th St.).
St. Rose of Lima School.
Sacred Heart (19th St.).
Sacred Heart School & High School (19th St.).
Sacred Heart (70th St.).
Sacred Heart School & High School (70th St.).
Sacred Heart (Oakley Blvd.).
Sacred Heart School (Oakley Blvd.).
Sacred Heart (Church St.), Sacred Heart Mission, 11652 S. Church St., 60643. Tel: 312-233-3955.
Sacred Heart of Jesus (Honore St.).
Sacred Heart of Jesus School (Honore St.).
Sacred Heart of Jesus High School (Honore St.).
Sacred Heart of Mary High School (Arlington Heights), St. Viator High School, 1213 E. Oakton St., Arlington Heights, 60004. Tel: 708-392-4050.
Sacred Heart Seminary (Melrose Park) (Stone Park), Scalabrini Mission Center, 3800 W. Division St., Stone Park, 60165. Tel: 708-345-8270.
St. Salomea (S. Indiana).
St. Salomea School (S. Indiana).
San Callisto Mission.
San Marcello Mission (Evergreen), Immaculate Conception, 1415 N. North Park, 60610. Tel: 312-944-1230.
Santa Lucia Mission. Sacramental Records: Santa Lucia-Santa Maria Incoranata, 3022 S. Wells, 60616. Tel: 312-842-6115. School Records: Santa Lucia School, 3017 S. Wells, 60616. Tel: 312-326-1839.
Santa Maria Incoranata. Sacramental Records: Santa Lucia-Santa Maria Incoranata, 3022 S. Wells, 60616. Tel: 312-842-6115. School Records: Santa Lucia School, 3017 S. Wells, 60616. Tel: 312-326-1839.
Santa Teresita Vicariate (Palatine), Mision Juan Diego, 35 W. Wood St., Palatine, 60067. Tel: 847-358-6337.
St. Sebastian (W. Wellington).
St. Sebastian School & High School.
Servite Seminary (Hillside), Provincial Archives, Servite Provincial Center, 3121 W. Jackson Blvd., 60612. Tel: 312-533-0360.
Seven Holy Founders School (Calumet Park).
Sheil Institute.
Siena High School, McAuley High School, 3737 W. 99th St., 60642. Tel: 312-881-6522.
St. Stanislaus College, Weber High School, 5252 W. Palmer, 60639. Tel: 312-637-7500.
St. Stanislaus Kostka High School, St. Stanislaus Kostka Elementary, 1255 N. Noble, 60622. Tel: 312-278-4560.
St. Stephen School (22nd Pl.).
St. Stephen Protomartyr School (Des Plaines).
Old St. Stephen (Ohio St.).
Old St. Stephen School (Ohio St.).
St. Susanna (Harvey), Ascension-St. Susanna, 15234 Myrtle, Harvey, 60426-3194. Tel: 708-333-0931.
St. Susanna School (Harvey).
St. Sylvester High School, St. Sylvester School, 3027 W. Palmer, 60647. Tel: 312-772-5222.
St. Theodore (S. Paulina).
St. Theodore School.
St. Teresa of Avila School.
St. Therese of the Infant Jesus Church, St. Sabina, 1210 W. 78th Pl., 60620. Tel: 773-483-4300.
St. Thomas Aquinas (Washington).
St. Thomas Mission (River Forest), St. Luke, 528 Lathrop, River Forest, 60305. Tel: 708-771-8250.
St. Thomas the Apostle High School, St. Thomas the Apostle School, 5467 S. Woodlawn, 60615. Tel: 312-667-1142.
St. Thomas Aquinas School.
St. Timothy School.
Unity Catholic High School.
St. Valentine (Cicero).
St. Valentine School (Cicero).
St. Veronica, Resurrection, 2840 W. Nelson, 60618. Tel: 312-478-9705.
St. Veronica School (Whipple St.).
Villa Nazareth High School (Whipple St.).
St. Vincent de Paul School.
St. Vincent de Paul Academy. (Girls)(Depaul High School & St. Vincent Academy, location of records unknown).
St. Vincent de Paul High School Seminary. St. Mary Seminary, Perryville, MO, 63775. Tel: 314-547-6533.
St. Vincent Orphanage. Client & School Records: Catholic Charities, Division of Services for Children and Youth, 126 N. Des Plaines, 60606. Tel: 312-876-2288; 236-5172, Ext. 330. Sacramental Records: Holy Name Cathedral, 730 N. Wabash, 60611. Tel: 312-787-8040.
St. Vincent Infant Hospital School of Child Care, St. Vincent de Paul Center, 2145 N. Halsted, 60614. Tel: 312-943-6776.
Visitation.
Visitation Academy (Evanston). see Marywood High School.
Visitation High School.
St. Vitus at St. Adalbert Parish, 1650 W. 17th St., 60608. Tel: 312-226-0340.
St. Vitus School.
St. Wenceslaus School (Monticello St.).
St. Wenceslaus Church (DeKoven St.).
St. Willibrord (114th St.).
St. Willibrord School (114th St.).
Willibrord Catholic High School.
St. Willibrord High School.
St. Xaiver Academy, Mother McAuley High School, 3737 W. 99th St., 60655. Tel: 773-881-6500.

RELIGIOUS INSTITUTES OF MEN REPRESENTED IN THE ARCHDIOCESE

For further details refer to the corresponding bracketed number in the Religious Institutes of Men or Women section.

[0120]—*Alexian Brothers.*—C.F.A.
[0140]—*The Augustinians (Mother of Good Counsel).* Chicago.—O.S.A.
[0200]—*Benedictine Monks.*—O.S.B.
[0330]—*Brothers of the Christian Schools.*—F.S.C.
[0600]—*Brothers of the Congregation of Holy Cross.*—C.S.C.
[0900]—*Canons Regular of Premontre.* (U.S. Circary).—O.Praem.
[0400]—*Canons Regular of the Order of the Holy Cross.* (Prov. of St. Odilia, Minneapolis, MN).—O.S.C.
[0470]—*The Capuchin Friars.*—O.F.M.Cap.
[0270]—*Carmelite Fathers & Brothers.* (Most Pure Heart of Mary).—O.Carm.
[0360]—*Claretian Missionaries.*—C.M.F.
[1320]—*Clerics of St. Viator.* (Chicago, IL).—C.S.V.
[0380]—*Comboni Missionaries of the Heart of Jesus-Verona.*—M.C.C.J.
[0310]—*Congregation of Christian Brothers.*—C.F.C.
[0750]—*Congregation of Marianhill Missionaries.*—C.M.M.
[0220]—*Congregation of the Blessed Sacrament.* (Rome, Italy).—S.S.S.
[1330]—*Congregation of the Mission.* (Western Prov.).—C.M.
[1210]—*Congregation of the Missionaries of St. Charles.* (Western Prov.).—C.S.
[1000]—*Congregation of the Passion.* (Western Prov.).—C.P.
[1130]—*Congregation of the Priests of the Sacred Heart.*—S.C.J.
[1080]—*Congregation of the Resurrection.* (Chicago Prov.).—C.R.
[0480]—*Conventual Franciscans.* (St. Bonaventure, Our Lady of Consolation Provs.).—O.F.M.Conv.
[0260]—*Discalced Carmelite Friars.*—O.C.D.
[0520]—*Franciscan Friars.* (Sacred Heart, Assumption of B.V.M. Provs.; Commissariats of the Holy Cross, Holy Family).—O.F.M.
[0650]—*Holy Ghost Fathers.* (Eastern Prov.).—C.SS.P.
[0690]—*Jesuit Fathers and Brothers.* (Chicago, Polish, Lithuanian Provs.).—S.J.
[0740]—*Marian Fathers.*—M.I.C.
[0770]—*The Marist Brothers.*—F.M.S.
[0780]—*Marist Fathers.*—S.M.
[0800]—*Maryknoll.*—M.M.
[0830]—*Mill Hill Missionaries.*—M.H.M.
[0860]—*Missionhurst Congregation of the Immaculate Heart of Mary.*—C.I.C.M.
[0910]—*Oblates of Mary Immaculate.*—O.M.I.
[0430]—*Order of Preachers-Dominicans.*—O.P.
[1030]—*Paulist Fathers.* (New York Prov.).—C.S.P.
[0610]—*Priests of the Congregation of Holy Cross.* (Notre Dame, IN).—C.S.C.
[1070]—*Redemptorist Fathers.* (Denver).—C.SS.R.
[1170]—*St. Patrick Missionary Society.*—S.P.S.
[1220]—*Servants of Charity.*—S.C.
[1240]—*Servites.* (Chicago, IL).—O.S.M.
[1260]—*Society of Christ.*—S.Ch.
[0760]—*Society of Mary.*—S.M.
[0850]—*Society of Missionaries of Africa.*—M.Afr.
[0370]—*Society of St. Columban.*—S.S.C.
[1200]—*Society of the Divine Savior.*—S.D.S.
[0420]—*Society of the Divine Word.*—S.V.D.
[1060]—*Society of the Precious Blood.* (Kansas City Prov.).—C.PP.S.
[1360]—*Xaverian Missionary Fathers.*—S.X.

RELIGIOUS INSTITUTES OF WOMEN REPRESENTED IN THE ARCHDIOCESE

[0100]—*Adorers of the Blood of Christ.*—A.S.C.
[0230]—*Benedictine Sisters of Pontifical Jurisdiction.* (Chicago, IL; Duluth, MN).—O.S.B.
[0690]—*Comboni Missionary Sisters.*—C.M.S.
[3110]—*Congregation of Our Lady of the Retreat in the Cenacle.*—R.C.
[1860]—*Congregation of the Handmaids of the Precious Blood.*—H.P.B.
[2100]—*Congregation of the Humility of Mary.*—C.H.M.
[0460]—*Congregation of the Sisters of Charity of the Incarnate Word.*—C.C.V.I.
[3710]—*Congregation of the Sisters of Saint Agnes.*—C.S.A.
[1920]—*Congregation of the Sisters of the Holy Cross.*—C.S.C.
[1780]—*Congregation of the Sisters of the Third Order of St. Francis of Perpetual Adoration.*—F.S.P.A.
[1710]—*Congregation of the Third Order of St. Francis of Mary Immaculate, Joliet, IL.*—O.S.F.
[1730]—*Congregation of the Third Order of St. Francis, Oldenburg, IN.*—O.S.F.
[0760]—*Daughters of Charity of St. Vincent de Paul.*—D.C.
[0793]—*Daughters of Divine Love.*—D.D.L.
[0940]—*Daughters of St. Mary of Providence.*—D.S.M.P.
[0810]—*Daughters of the Heart of Mary.*—D.H.M.
[0420]—*Discalced Carmelite Nuns.*—O.C.D.
[1070-01]—*Dominican Sisters.*—O.P.
[1070-03]—*Dominican Sisters.*—O.P.
[1070-10]—*Dominican Sisters.*—O.P.
[1070-13]—*Dominican Sisters.*—O.P.
[1070-27]—*Dominican Sisters.*—O.P.
[1170]—*Felician Sisters.*—C.S.S.F.
[1370]—*Franciscan Missionaries of Mary.*—F.M.M.
[1210]—*Franciscan Sisters of Chicago.*—O.S.F.
[1230]—*Franciscan Sisters of Christian Charity.*—O.S.F.
[1310]—*Franciscan Sisters of Little Falls, Minnesota.*—O.S.F.
[1415]—*Franciscan Sisters of Mary.*—F.S.M.
[1430]—*Franciscan Sisters of Our Lady of Perpetual Help.*—O.S.F.
[1450]—*Franciscan Sisters of the Sacred Heart.*—O.S.F.
[1240]—*Franciscan Sisters, Daughters of the Sacred Hearts of Jesus and Mary.*—O.S.F.
[1820]—*Hospital Sisters of the Third Order of St. Francis.*—O.S.F.
[2370]—*Institute of the Blessed Virgin Mary (Loretto Sisters).*—I.B.V.M.
[2330]—*Little Sisters of Jesus.*—L.S.J.
[2320]—*Little Sisters of the Holy Family.*—P.S.S.F.
[2340]—*Little Sisters of the Poor.*—L.S.P.
[3570]—*Mantellate Sisters, Servants of Mary of Blue Island.*—O.S.M.
[2420]—*Marist Missionary Sisters.*—S.M.S.M.
[2430]—*Marist Sisters Congregation of Mary.*—S.M.
[2470]—*Maryknoll Sisters of St. Dominic.*—M.M.
[2480]—*Medical Missionaries of Mary.*—M.M.M.
[2680]—*Misericordia Sisters.*—S.M.
[2710]—*Missionaries of Charity.*—M.C.
[2865]—*Missionaries of the Sacred Heart of Jesus and Our Lady of Guadalupe.*—M.S.C.Gpe.
[2790]—*Missionary Servants of the Most Blessed Trinity.*—M.S.B.T.
[2715]—*Missionary Sisters of Christ the King for Polonia.*—M.S.C.K.
[2900]—*Missionary Sisters of St. Charles Borromeo.*—M.S.S.C.B.
[3990]—*Missionary Sisters of St. Peter Claver.*—S.S.P.C.
[2860]—*Missionary Sisters of the Sacred Heart.*—M.S.C.
[3530]—*Missionary Sisters Servants of the Holy Spirit.*—S.Sp.S.
[3040]—*Oblate Sisters of Providence.*—O.S.P.
[3130]—*Our Lady of Victory Missionary Sisters.*—O.L.V.M.
[0950]—*Pious Society Daughters of St. Paul.*—F.S.P.
[3230]—*Poor Handmaids of Jesus Christ.*—P.H.J.C.
[3440]—*Religious Hospitallers of Saint Joseph.*—R.H.S.J.
[2970]—*School Sisters of Notre Dame.*—S.S.N.D.
[1680]—*School Sisters of St. Francis.*—O.S.F.
[3590]—*Servants of Mary (Servite Sisters).*—O.S.M.
[3520]—*Servants of the Holy Heart of Mary.*—S.S.C.M.
[0440]—*Sisters of Charity of Cincinnati, Ohio.*—S.C.
[0570]—*Sisters of Charity of Seton Hill, Greensburg, Pennsylvania.*—S.C.
[0630]—*Sisters of Charity of St. Vincent de Paul.*—S.V.Z.
[0430]—*Sisters of Charity of the Blessed Virgin Mary.*—B.V.M.

[0660]—*Sisters of Christian Charity.*—S.C.C.
[0990]—*Sisters of Divine Providence.*—C.D.P.
[2360]—*Sisters of Loretto at the Foot of the Cross.*—S.L.
[2575]—*Sisters of Mercy of the Americas.* (Chicago, IL).—R.S.M.
[3000]—*Sisters of Notre Dame de Namur.*—S.N.D.deN.
[3080]—*Sisters of Our Lady Christian Doctrine.*—R.C.D.
[3350]—*Sisters of Providence.*—S.P.
[3360]—*Sisters of Providence of Saint Mary-of-the-Woods, IN.*—S.P.
[1620]—*Sisters of Saint Francis of Millvale, Pennsylvania.*—O.S.F.
[1540]—*Sisters of Saint Francis, Clinton, Iowa.*—O.S.F.
[3780]—*Sisters of Saints Cyril and Methodius.*—SS.C.M.
[3740]—*Sisters of St. Casimir.*—S.S.C.
[1520]—*Sisters of St. Francis of Christ the King.*—O.S.F.
[1640]—*Sisters of St. Francis of Perpetual Adoration.*—O.S.F.
[1570]—*Sisters of St. Francis of the Holy Family.*—O.S.F.
[1800]—*Sisters of St. Francis of the Third Order Regular (Williamsville, New York).*—O.S.F.
[3830-02]—*Sisters of St. Joseph.*—C.S.J.
[3830-15]—*Sisters of St. Joseph.*—C.S.J.
[3840]—*Sisters of St. Joseph of Carondelet.*—C.S.J.
[3930]—*Sisters of St. Joseph of the Third Order of St. Francis.*—S.S.J.-T.O.S.F.
[0260]—*Sisters of the Blessed Sacrament for Indians and Colored People.*—S.B.S.
[2980]—*Sisters of the Congregation de Notre Dame.*—C.N.D.
[1030]—*Sisters of the Divine Savior.*—S.D.S.
[1830]—*Sisters of the Good Shepherd.*—R.G.S.
[1970]—*Sisters of the Holy Family of Nazareth.*—C.S.F.N.
[2110]—*Sisters of the Humility of Mary.*—H.M.
[2140]—*Sisters of the Immaculate Conception of the Blessed Virgin Mary.* (Lithuanian).
[2270]—*Sisters of the Little Company of Mary.*—L.C.M.
[2350]—*Sisters of the Living Word.*—S.L.W.
[3320]—*Sisters of the Presentation of the B.V.M.*—P.B.V.M.
[3480]—*Sisters of the Resurrection.*—C.R.
[1705]—*Sisters of the Third Order of St. Francis of Assisi.*—O.S.F.
[1720]—*Sisters of the Third Order of St. Francis of the Congregation of Our Lady of Lourdes.*—O.S.F.
[2150]—*Sisters, Servants of the Immaculate Heart of Mary.*—I.H.M.
[1890]—*Society of Helpers.*—H.H.S.
[4060]—*Society of the Holy Child Jesus.*—S.H.C.J.
[4070]—*Society of the Sacred Heart.*—R.S.C.J.

ARCHDIOCESAN CEMETERIES

CHICAGO. *Central Office.* Catholic Cemeteries, 1400 S. Wolf Rd., Hillside, 60162-2197. Tel: 708-449-6100; Fax: 708-449-3419. Rev. Patrick J. Pollard, Archdiocesan Dir.; Mr. Donald A. Massaro, Exec. Dir.
Mt. Olivet.
St. Boniface.
St. Casimir.
St. Henry.
CALUMET CITY. *Holy Cross.*
CRESTWOOD. *St. Benedict.*
DES PLAINES. *All Saints.*
EVANSTON. *Calvary.*
EVERGREEN PARK. *St. Mary.*
FOX LAKE. *St. Bede.*
FREMONT CENTER. *St. Mary.*
GLENWOOD. *Assumption.*
HIGHLAND PARK. *St. Mary.*
HILLSIDE. *Mt. Carmel.*
Our Lady of Sorrows.
Queen of Heaven.
JUSTICE. *Resurrection.*
LAKE FOREST. *St. Mary.*
LEMONT. *St. Alphonsus.*
St. James, Sag Bridge.
St. Patrick.
SS. Cyril & Methodius.
LIBERTYVILLE. *Ascension.*
NILES. *Maryhill.*
St. Adalbert.
NORTHBROOK. *Sacred Heart.*
OAK FOREST. *St. Gabriel.*
ORLAND PARK. *St. Michael.*
PALATINE. *St. Michael the Archangel.*
PARK FOREST. *St. Anne.*
RIVER FOREST. *St. Joseph.*
ROSENCRANS. *St. Patrick.*
ROUND LAKE. *St. Joseph.*
SAUK VILLAGE. *St. James.*
SKOKIE. *St. Peter.*
STEGER. *Calvary.*
VOLO. *St. Peter.*
WAUCONDA. *Transfiguration.*
WAUKEGAN. *St. Mary.*
WEST LAKE FOREST. *St. Patrick.*
WILMETTE. *St. Joseph.*
WORTH. *Holy Sepulchre.*

NECROLOGY

† Ackerman, Raymond J., (Retired). —Died Oct. 6, 1997.
† Baseheart, Edward J., (Retired). —Died Jan. 31, 1997.
† Brackin, Rev. Msgr. Francis A., (Retired). —Died Oct. 10, 1997.
† Burns, Robert E., (Retired). —Died Oct. 28, 1997.
† Carroll, Clement D., (Retired). —Died Jan. 11, 1997.
† Carroll, John D., Chap., Veterans Admin. —Died July 28, 1997.
† Coneglio, Andrew F., (Retired). —Died May 1, 1997.
† Cooke, Rev. Msgr. Vincent W., (Retired). —Died May 30, 1997.
† Detloff, Edward X., Chicago, IL, St. Tarcissus. —Died March 6, 1997.
† Fearon, John F., (Retired). —Died Feb. 10, 1997.
† Heffernan, John J., (Retired). —Died June 6, 1997.
† Hosty, Edward M., (Retired). —Died Feb. 24, 1997.
† Kaczorowski, Rev. Msgr. Theodore A., (Retired). —Died Jan. 12, 1996.
† Kelly, Joseph A., (Retired). —Died April 4, 1997.
† Kupinski, Raymond P., (Retired). —Died Dec. 19, 1996.
† Le, John Thang, Berwyn, IL, St. Mary of Celle. —Died Nov. 11, 1997.
† Montalbano, Daniel F., Chicago, IL, Resurrection. —Died May 25, 1997.
† Murtaugh, Daniel J., (Retired). —Died Dec. 30, 1996.
† Myers, Edward F., (Retired). —Died Aug. 20, 1997.
† O'Brien, Hugh V., (Retired). —Died Jan. 21, 1997.
† Pachorek, Joseph, (Retired). —Died Dec. 23, 1996.
† Scheid, Bernard W., (Retired). —Died April 25, 1997.
† Stankevicius, John P., (Retired). —Died April 24, 1997.
† Zukowski, John A., (Retired). —Died May 4, 1997.

Archdiocese of Cincinnati

(Archidioecesis Cincinnatensis)

Most Reverend

DANIEL E. PILARCZYK, S.T.D., PH.D.

Archbishop of Cincinnati; ordained December 20, 1959; appointed Titular Bishop of Hodelm and Auxiliary Bishop of Cincinnati November 12, 1974; consecrated December 20, 1974; appointed Archbishop of Cincinnati November 2, 1982; installed December 20, 1982. *Res., 100 E. Eighth St., Cincinnati, OH, 45202.*

Most Reverend

CARL K. MOEDDEL, M.A., M.DIV., D.D.

Auxiliary Bishop of Cincinnati; ordained August 15, 1962; appointed Titular Bishop of Bistue and Auxiliary Bishop of Cincinnati August 24, 1993. *Res., 100 E. Eighth St., Cincinnati, OH, 45202.*

ERECTED DIOCESE JUNE 19, 1821; ARCHDIOCESE JULY 19, 1850.

Square Miles 8,543.

Comprises that part of the State of Ohio lying south of 40 degrees, 41 minutes, being the 19 Counties south of the northern line of Mercer, Auglaize, and Logan, all west of the eastern line of Logan, Champaign, Clark, Greene, Clinton, Highland and Adams Counties.

For legal titles of parishes and archdiocesan institutions, consult the Chancery Office.

Archdiocesan Offices: 100 E. Eighth St., Cincinnati, OH, 45202. Tel.: 513-421-3131; Fax: 513-421-6225.

Web site address: http://www.archdiocese-cinti.org

STATISTICAL OVERVIEW

Personnel	
Archbishop	1
Auxiliary Bishops	1
Priests: Diocesan Active in Diocese	238
Priests: Active Outside Diocese	12
Priests: Diocesan in Foreign Missions	2
Priests: Retired, Sick or Absent	100
Number of Diocesan Priests	352
Religious Priests in Diocese	246
Extern Priests in Diocese	7
Ordinations:	
Diocesan Priests	4
Transitional Deacons	2
Permanent Deacons in Diocese	126
Total Brothers	182
Total Sisters	1,439
Parishes	
Parishes	235
With Resident Pastor:	
Resident Diocesan Priests	165
Resident Religious Priests	32
Without Resident Pastor:	
Administered by Priests	38
Pastoral Centers	1
Closed Parishes	1
Professional Ministry Personnel:	
Brothers	7
Sisters	54
Lay Ministers	286
Welfare	
Catholic Hospitals	11
Total Assisted	162,504
Health Care Centers	2
Total Assisted	284
Homes for the Aged	11
Total Assisted	1,240
Residential Care of Children	4
Total Assisted	660
Day Care and Extended Day Care Centers	1
Total Assisted	98
Specialized Homes	3
Total Assisted	173
Special Centers for Social Services	6
Total Assisted	95,450
Residential Care of Disabled	1
Total Assisted	17
Other Institutions	5
Total Assisted	900
Educational	
Seminaries, Diocesan	1
Students from This Diocese	25
Students from Other Diocese	1
Diocesan Students in Other Seminaries	6
Total Seminarians	31
Colleges and Universities	4
Total Students	19,329
High Schools, Diocesan and Parish	18
Total Students	12,874
High Schools, Private	4
Total Students	2,842
Elementary Schools, Diocesan and Parish	110
Total Students	39,712
Elementary Schools, Private	2
Total Students	1,025
Catechesis/Religious Education:	
High School Students	5,678
Elementary Students	35,105
Total Students Under Catholic Instruction	116,596
Teachers in the Diocese:	
Priests	11
Brothers	26
Sisters	129
Lay Teachers	3,231
Vital Statistics	
Receptions into the Church:	
Infant Baptism Totals	8,377
Adult Baptism Totals	1,196
Received into Full Communion	910
First Communions	9,399
Confirmations	8,699
Marriages:	
Catholic	1,934
Interfaith	1,414
Total Marriages	3,348
Deaths	4,709
Total Catholic Population	547,000
Total Population	2,927,300

Former Bishops—Rt. Rev. EDWARD FENWICK, O.P., D.D., cons. Jan. 13, 1822; died Sept. 26, 1832.—Most Rev. JOHN BAPTIST PURCELL, D.D., cons. Oct. 13, 1833; appt. Archbishop, July 19, 1850; died July 4, 1883.—Most Rev. WILLIAM HENRY ELDER, D.D., cons. Bishop of Natchez May 3, 1857; appt. Titular Bishop of Avar, and Coadjutor to the Archbishop of Cincinnati *cum jure successionis,* Jan. 30, 1880; succeeded to the See of Cincinnati, July 4, 1883; died Oct. 31, 1904.—Most Rev. HENRY MOELLER, D.D., cons. Bishop of Columbus, Aug. 25, 1900; promoted to Archiepiscopal See of Areopolis and made Coadjutor to the Most Rev. WILLIAM HENRY ELDER *cum jure successionis,* April 27, 1903; appt. Archbishop of Cincinnati, Oct. 31, 1904; died Jan. 5, 1925.—Most Rev. JOHN T. MCNICHOLAS, O.P., S.T.M., cons. Bishop of Duluth, MN Sept. 8, 1918; promoted to Archiepiscopal See of Cincinnati, July 8, 1925; appt. Assistant at the Pontifical Throne, Feb. 18, 1923; died April 22, 1950.—Most Rev. KARL J. ALTER, D.D., cons. Bishop of Toledo, June 17, 1931; appt. Assistant to the Pontifical Throne, May 30, 1950; elevated to Archbishop of Cincinnati, June 21, 1950; retired July 23, 1969; died Aug. 23, 1977.—Most Rev. PAUL F. LEIBOLD, D.D., J.C.D., appt. Titular Bishop of Trebenna and Auxiliary of Cincinnati, April 10, 1958; cons. June 17, 1958; installed as Bishop of Evansville, June 15, 1966; transferred to Archdiocese of Cincinnati, July 23, 1969; installed Oct. 2, 1969; died June 1, 1972.—His Eminence JOSEPH CARDINAL BERNARDIN, D.D., appt. Titular Bishop of Lugura and Auxiliary Bishop of Atlanta, March 9, 1966; cons. April 26, 1966; appt. Archbishop of Cincinnati, Nov. 21, 1972; installed Dec. 19, 1972; appt. Archbishop of Chicago, July 5, 1982; installed Aug. 25, 1982; created Cardinal Priest, Feb. 2, 1983.

Vicar General—Most Rev. CARL K. MOEDDEL.

Archdiocesan Department Directors—ROBERT DAVIS, Dir., Community Svcs.; Sr. KATHRYN ANN CONNELLY, S.C., Dir., Educational Svcs.; Revs. CHRISTOPHER R. ARMSTRONG, Dir., Exec. Svcs.; HOWARD P. PECQUET, Dir., Financial Svcs.; Most Rev. CARL K. MOEDDEL, Dir., Pastoral Svcs.; VINCENT FRASHER, Dir., Personnel Svcs.

Presbyteral Council—Ex Officio Members: Most Rev. DANIEL E. PILARCZYK; Most Rev. CARL K. MOEDDEL. Priest Councilors: Revs. THOMAS BRENBERGER, C.PP.S.; TIM BUNCH; THOMAS DIEHL, S.J.; PATRICK

DUFFY; ROBERT FARRELL; ANTHONY J. GERACI; EDWARD A. HASKAMP; TED KOSSE; FRANCIS G. LAMMEIER; JAMES J. MANNING; JIM MEADE; ROBERT J. MONNIN; FRIDOLIN VOEGELE, O.F.M.

Vicarri Foranei (Deans)—Rev. JAMES A. BRAMLAGE, Cathedral Deanery; Rev. MICHAEL PUCKE, St. Andrew Deanery; Rev. DENNIS J. CAYLOR, St. Francis de Sales Deanery; Rev. JAMES R. COLLINS, St. Lawrence Deanery; Rev. RAYMOND E. LARGER, St. Margaret Mary Deanery; Rev. JEFFREY P. SILVER, Hamilton Deanery; Rev. JOHN P. FISHER, St. Martin Deanery; Rev. Msgr. LAWRENCE K. BRESLIN, Dayton Deanery; Rev. JOHN D. MACQUARRIE, Springfield Deanery; Rev. EUGENE F. VONDERHAAR, Sidney Deanery; Rev. RONALD H. WILKER, St. Mary's Deanery.

Consultors—Most Rev. CARL K. MOEDDEL, Aux. Bishop; Revs. ERWIN J. BERTKE; TIMOTHY S. BUNCH; WILLIAM H. CROSS; ANTHONY J. GERACI; JEFFREY M. KEMPER; TED KOSSE; DONALD G. MCCARTHY; JAMES J. MANNING; JAMES MEADE; ROBERT J. MONNIN; JOHN E. WESSLING.

Archdiocesan Offices

All Archdiocesan Offices and Directors are located at 100 E. Eighth St., Cincinnati, OH 45202. Tel: 513-421-3131; Fax: 513-421-6225, unless otherwise indicated.

Office of the Archbishop—Rev. MALCOLM S. GRAD, Admin. Asst. LINDA CHOUTEAU, Exec. Sec. to the Archbishop; JOAN RANZ, Sec.

Office of Mediation—JOSEPH B. CROWE, Admin. Tel: 513-421-3131, Ext. 408.

Department of Executive Services

Rev. CHRISTOPHER R. ARMSTRONG, Dir.

Chancery—

Chancellor—Rev. CHRISTOPHER R. ARMSTRONG.

Vice Chancellor—Rev. MALCOLM S. GRAD.

Archivist—DON H. BUSKE, (Special Address & Phone No. for Historical Archives Only), *6616 Beechmont Ave., Cincinnati, 45230.* Tel: 513-231-0810.

Censors—Revs. ROBERT J. BUSCHMILLER; EDWARD J. GRATSCH; RALPH J. LAWRENCE; ROBERT L. HAGEDORN; CHRISTOPHER R. ARMSTRONG, J.C.L.

Communications Office—DAN ANDRIACCO, Dir.

Newspaper—"The Catholic Telegraph"—Most Rev. DANIEL E. PILARCZYK, Publisher.

Planning and Research—JEFFRY W. REXHAUSEN, Dir.

Tribunal-Archdiocese of Cincinnati—Tel: 513-421-3145; Fax: 513-723-1035.

Director—Sr. VICTORIA VONDENBERGER, R.S.M., J.C.L.

Judicial Vicar—Rev. EDWIN F. GEARHART, J.C.L.

Adjutant Judicial Vicar—Rev. RAYMOND C. KELLERMAN, J.C.L.

Judges—Deacon MICHAEL A. ASCOLESE; Rev. Msgr. LAWRENCE K. BRESLIN; Revs. CHRISTOPHER R. ARMSTRONG, J.C.L.; MICHAEL D. BEATTY; JAMES A. BRAMLAGE; JOHN L. CAVANAUGH, J.C.D.; DENNIS J. CAYLOR, J.C.L.; R. DANIEL CONLON, J.C.D.; J. RAYMOND FAVRET; DAVID E. FAY; JOHN P. FISCHER; MICHAEL T. FLAHERTY; GERALD R. HAEMMERLE; TIMOTHY S. KALLAHER; RICHARD L. KLUG; EMIL J. LABBE, J.C.D.; FRANCIS G. LAMMEIER; NORMAN W. LANGENBRUNNER; RALPH J. LAWRENCE; WALTER J. MACPHERSON; THOMAS C. NOLKER; ROBERT A. OBERMEYER; EDWARD L. RUDEMILLER; OSCAR H. SEGER; R. MARC SHERLOCK; TERRENCE W. SMITH; PAUL L. STOLZ; LAWRENCE R. STRITTMATTER; RICHARD J. SWEENEY; LARRY P. THARP; FRANCIS W. VOELLMECKE; EUGENE F. VONDERHAAR; JOHN R. WHITE; BARRY M. WINDHOLTZ, J.C.L.; WILLIAM H. WYSONG, J.C.L.

Defenders of the Bond—Revs. HERMAN H. KENNING; THOMAS A. SNODGRASS, J.C.L.; Sr. VICTORIA VONDENBERGER, R.S.M., J.C.L.

Promoter of Justice—Sr. VICTORIA VONDENBERGER, R.S.M., J.C.L.

Assessor—Mrs. ELVA BRUNNER.

Auditors—Ms. CHRISTINE GATELY; Mrs. SUSAN E. JINKENS; Mrs. BETTY L. MEDER; Mrs. KELLY M. TERRY; Mrs. MARY G. WILKIE.

Secretary/Auditor—Mrs. JULIANN BUCHER.

Department of Community Services

ROBERT DAVIS, Dir.

Archdiocesan Office of Catholic Charities—RAYMOND F. EGAN, Dir.

Association of Ladies of Charity—LENDRA WRIGHT, Pres. Tel: 513-421-3131.

Catholic Federation for the Mentally Retarded—DONALD MINK, Pres. Tel: 513-741-9689.

Catholic Social Services of Hamilton—MAUREEN KRAH, Exec. Dir., *140 N. Fifth St., Hamilton, 45011.* Tel: 513-863-6129.

Catholic Social Services of Miami Valley—RONALD A. ECKERLE, Exec. Dir., *922 W. Riverview Dr., Dayton, 45407.* Tel: 513-223-7217.

Catholic Social Services of Southwest Ohio—RAYMOND F. EGAN, Exec. Dir. Tel: 513-241-7745.

Catholic Social Services of Springfield—VINCENT CHASE, Exec. Dir., *641 High St., Springfield, 45505.* Tel: 513-325-8715.

Cemeteries—ROBERT DAVIS, Dir.; IRWIN BENKIN, Asst. Dir., *11000 Montgomery Rd., Cincinnati, 45242.* Tel: 513-489-0300.

Ecumenical and Interfaith Relations—LOUISE BARNES, Program Coord.

St. Vincent de Paul Society—MARK CASELLA, Pres.; Rev. HERMAN KENNING, Spiritual Dir. (See Special Listing: St. Vincent de Paul Society).

Health Affairs—ROBERT DAVIS. Tel: 513-241-7745.

Rural Life Conference—BRIAN HENTIES, *266 Bainbridge St., Dayton, 45402.* Tel: 513-224-3026.

Social Action and World Peace—THOMAS CHOQUETTE, Exec. Dir. *Dayton Office,* BRIAN HENTIES, Assoc. Dir., *266 Bainbridge St., Dayton, 45402.* Tel: 513-224-3026.

Department of Educational Services

Sr. KATHRYN ANN CONNELLY, S.C., Dir.

School Office—Sr. KATHRYN ANN CONNELLY, S.C., Supt., Schools, Dayton North; MICHAEL T. MCCORMICK, Area Supt., *266 Bainbridge St., Dayton, 45402.* Tel: 513-223-5151.

Religious Education Office—KENNETH GLEASON, Archdiocesan Dir. DAVID RILEY, Regional Dir., *226 Bainbridge St., Dayton, 45402.* Tel: 513-223-4075. *Sidney,* JANE PIERRON, Regl. Dir., *401-A S. Main St., Sidney, 45365.* Tel: 513-498-1192.

Department of Financial Services

HOWARD P. PECQUET, Treas. & Dir.

Office of Property Management-Central Services—GARY RAFFEL, Dir.

Office for Financial Development—JOAN SCHROEDER, Dir.

Department of Pastoral Services

Most Rev. CARL K. MOEDDEL, Dir.

Campus Ministry—Dr. JANE STEINHAUSER, Dir., *444 W. Third St., Dayton, 45402.* (See Special Listing: Campus Ministry).

African American Catholic Ministries—GEORGE C. FINDLEY, Dir.

Family Life—MARGARET BLACK, Dir. *Dayton:* MARILYN PORCINO, Assoc. Dir., *266 Bainbridge St., Dayton, 45402.* Tel: 513-222-0227. *Northern Area:* VELMA JEAN BORGERT, *401-A S. Main St., Sidney, 45365.* Tel: 513-492-4449.

Missions—

Pontifical Mission Aid Societies—Most Rev. CARL K. MOEDDEL.

Missions Office—ARCHIE BRUUN, Dir., *100 E. Eighth St., Cincinnati, 45202.*

Pastoral Council Secretariat—Rev. MALCOLM S. GRAD, Exec. Sec.

Hispanic Catholic Ministry, Dayton—Ms. PURISSIMA MIRA, Moderator, *266 Bainbridge St., Dayton, 45402.* Tel: 513-222-1340.

Hispanic Catholic Ministry, Cincinnati—Rev. JOSEPH NELSON, O.F.M., Moderator-Chap., *100 E. Eighth St., Cincinnati, 45202.* Tel: 513-421-3131.

Worship—Rev. LAWRENCE R. TENSI, Dir.

Youth—Mr. SEAN REYNOLDS, Dir., *100 East Eighth St., Cincinnati, 45202.* Tel: 513-421-3131. TIMOTHY E. COLBERT, Reg. Dir.; *Dayton & Northern Area: 266 Bainbridge St., Dayton, 45402.* Tel: 513-223-1001.

Department of Personnel Services

VINCENT FRASHER, Dir.

Office of Religious—Sr. MARY GARKE, C.PP.S., Dir.

Permanent Diaconate Office—Vacant.

Personnel Office for Archdiocesan Administrative Offices—VINCE FRASHER, Dir.

Priestly Formation—Rev. THOMAS P. DI FOLCO, Dir.

Priests' Personnel Director—Most Rev. CARL K. MOEDDEL, Dir.

Vocations Office—Rev. MARK T. WATKINS, Dir.

CLERGY, PARISHES, MISSIONS AND PAROCHIAL SCHOOLS

GREATER CINCINNATI (HAMILTON COUNTY)

1—ST. PETER IN CHAINS CATHEDRAL, Rev. James A. Bramlage. In res., Revs. James M. Willig; Carl J. Geers.
Res., 325 W. Eighth St., 45202. Tel: 513-421-5354; Fax: 513-241-9517.
Church—Eighth & Plum St., 45202.

2—ST. AGNES (Bond Hill), Rev. Thomas DiFolco; Sr. M. Jerome Buchert, O.S.U., Pastoral Admin.
Res., 1619 California Ave., 45237. Tel: 513-242-4747; Fax: 513-242-4748.

3—ALL SAINTS (Kenwood), Rev. J. Dennis Jaspers; Mrs. Jennifer Cmar, Pastoral Assoc.
Res., 8939 Montgomery Rd., 45236. Tel: 513-791-6351; Fax: 513-792-4730.
School—Tel: 513-792-4732; Fax: 513-792-7990. Mrs. Mary E. Stratford, Prin.
Lay Teachers 25; Students 488.
Catechesis/Religious Programs—Tel: 513-791-6351, Ext. 103; Fax: 513-792-4730. Mrs. Tanya Monsour Stager, D.R.E.
Students 736.

4—ST. ALOYSIUS GONZAGA (Bridgetown), Revs. Paul Rehling; Paul L. Friedrichs; Sr. Josetta Boeing, S.C., Pastoral Assoc.
Res., 4366 Bridgetown Rd., 45211. Tel: 513-574-4840; Fax: 513-574-4402.
School—4390 Bridgetown Rd., 45211. Tel: 513-574-4035. Mrs. Bernadine Stone, Prin.
Lay Teachers 14; Students 357.
Catechesis/Religious Programs—Tel: 513-574-4840; Fax: 513-574-4402. Mr. Kevin Hibner, D.R.E.
Students 257.

5—ST. ALOYSIUS-ON-THE-OHIO, Rev. Donald R. Rettig.
Res., 134 Whipple St., 45233. Tel: 513-941-3445; Fax: 513-941-7831.
School—6207 Portage, 45233. Tel: 513-941-7831. Sr. Daria Mitchell, O.F.M., Prin.
Lay Teachers 12; Students 206.
Catechesis/Religious Programs—Tel: 513-941-2797; Fax: 513-941-7831.
Students 45.

6—ST. ALOYSIUS (Elmwood Pl.), Rev. Thomas A. Snodgrass.
Res., 115 W. Seymour Ave., 45216. Tel: 513-821-2971.
Church—314 Township Ave., 45216. Tel: 513-242-5496.

7—ST. ANDREW, Rev. Terence A. Meehan.
3401 Reading Rd., P.O. Box 29064, 45229. Tel: 513-281-7504.

8—ST. ANN (Groesbeck), Revs. William M. Kennedy; Charles Mentrup.
Res., 2900 Galbraith Rd., 45239. Tel: 513-521-8440; Fax: 513-521-8447.
School—2940 W. Galbraith Rd., 45239. Tel: 513-931-3070; Fax: 513-931-3071. Mary E. Henninger, Prin.
Sisters 1; Lay Teachers 21; Students 375.
Catechesis/Religious Programs—Tel: 513-729-2180. Diane C. Ferrier, D.R.E.
Students 275.

9—ANNUNCIATION OF THE BLESSED VIRGIN MARY, Rev. Richard L. Klug. In res., Rev. Edward Trippel.
Res., 3547 Clifton Ave., 45220. Tel: 513-861-1295.
School—3545 Clifton Ave., 45220. Tel: 513-221-1230; Fax: 513-281-8009. Mrs. Lynn Sundermann, Prin.
Lay Teachers 11; Students 220.
Catechesis/Religious Programs—Tel: 513-861-1295.
Students 35.

10—ST. ANTHONY (Madisonville), Rev. Leonard C. Wenke.
Res., 6104 Desmond St., 45227. Tel: 513-271-0920; Fax: 513-271-6630. [CEM]
School—See St. John Vianney Cure of Ars. Tel: 513-271-5510.
Catechesis/Religious Programs—Tel: 513-271-0920. D.R.E.: Rita Balcom, (Youth); Nancy Tunnat, (Adults).
Students 173.

11—ST. ANTONINUS, Revs. Donald G. McCarthy; Lawrence Mick; Deacon William Petrie.
Res., 1500 Linneman Rd., 45238. Tel: 513-922-5400; Fax: 513-451-5871.
School—5425 Julmar Dr., 45238. Tel: 513-922-2500. Mr. James Leisring, Prin.
Lay Teachers 26; Students 608.
Catechesis/Religious Programs—Tel: 513-922-4759. Mr. Robert Schroeder, D.R.E.
Students 63.

12—ASSUMPTION OF THE BLESSED VIRGIN MARY (Walnut Hills), Rev. Thomas Bokenkotter.
Res., 2622 Gilbert Ave., 45206. Tel: 513-961-3242; 271-0016.

13—ASSUMPTION (Mount Healthy), Revs. Francis G. Lammeier; Jeffrey M. Fulmer.
Res., 7711 Joseph St., 45231. Tel: 513-521-7274; Fax: 513-521-3728.
School—1500 McMakin Ave., Mt. Healthy, 45231. Tel: 513-522-0071. William J. Walborn, Prin.
Lay Teachers 18; Students 380.
Catechesis/Religious Programs—Tel: 513-728-4953. Sr. Marietta Sharkey, O.S.F., D.R.E.
Students 85.

14—ST. BARTHOLOMEW, Revs. William F. Krumpe; Robert W. Hasselhoff; Raymond C. Kellerman.

Res., 9375 Winton Rd., 45231. Tel: 513-522-3680; Fax: 513-728-3141.
School—St. Bartholomew Consolidated School. See separate listing.
Catechesis/Religious Programs—Jenny Luchsinger, D.R.E.
Students 129.

15—ST. BERNARD, Revs. James Shappelle; Michael Paraniuk.
Res., 740 Circle Ave., 45232. Tel: 513-541-3732.
Catechesis/Religious Programs—Students 18.

16—ST. BERNARD (Taylor's Creek), Rev. Stanley D. Doerger; Mr. Charles Karst, Pastoral Assoc.
Res., 7130 Harrison Rd., 45247. Tel: 513-353-4207; Fax: 513-353-9600.
School—Tel: 513-353-4224; Fax: 513-353-3598.
Sisters of Notre Dame of Covington, KY 2; Lay Teachers 13; Students 261.

17—ST. BONAVENTURE, Rev. David Reilly; Sr. Joseph Marion Shappelle, S.C., Pastoral Assoc.
Res., 1798 Queen City Ave., 45214. Tel: 513-921-2547; Fax: 513-921-2548.
Chapel—Cincinnati, San Antonio di Padova. (Italian). Tel: 513-921-6411.

18—ST. BONIFACE, Rev. Joseph A. Robinson; Deacon Ted Schmidt.
Res., 1750 Chase Ave., 45223. Tel: 513-541-1563.
School—St. Boniface Consolidated. See separate listing. Tel: 513-541-5122; Fax: 513-541-3939.

19—ST. CATHARINE, Rev. Robert E. Schmitz; Deacon Thomas Gargan. Pastoral Min: Therese Bower Hibdon; Meg Paul.
Res., 2848 Fischer Pl., P.O. Box 111115, 45211. Tel: 513-661-0651; Fax: 513-661-0652.
School—3324 Wunder Ave., 45211. Tel: 513-481-7683; Fax: 513-661-0652. William Schlater, Prin.
Lay Teachers 20; Students 458.
Catechesis/Religious Programs—Tel: 513-481-7977; Fax: 513-661-0652.
Students 50.

20—ST. CECILIA (Oakley), Rev. Elmer W. Smith; Deacon John Slattery. In res., Rev. Robert J. Buschmiller, (Retired).
Res., 3105 Madison Rd., 45209. Tel: 513-871-5757; Fax: 513-533-6066.
School—4115 Taylor Ave., 45209. Tel: 513-533-6060;. Fax: 513-533-6068. Sr. Mary Ellen Matts, R.S.M., Prin.
Sisters 2; Lay Teachers 12; Students 255.
Catechesis/Religious Programs—Barbara Browarsky, D.R.E.
Students 71.
Parish Center—4030 Gilmore Ave., 45209. Tel: 513-553-6067.

21—ST. CHARLES BORROMEO (Carthage), Rev. Thomas A. Snodgrass.
Res., 115 W. Seymour Ave., 45216. Tel: 513-821-2971.

22—ST. CLARE (College Hill), Rev. Dale Peterka; Sr. Mary Luke Prickel, O.S.F., Pastoral Assoc. In res., Rev. Robert J. Hater.
Res., 1443 Cedar Ave., 45224. Tel: 513-541-2100.
School—5800 Salvia Ave., 45224. Tel: 513-541-5751. Mrs. Carol Graler, Prin.
Catechesis/Religious Programs—Students 214.

23—ST. CLEMENT (St. Bernard), Revs. Joseph L. Rigali, O.F.M.; Carl Langenderfer, O.F.M.; Bro. Joel Soldenski, O.F.M., Pastoral Assoc.
Res., St. Clement Friary, 4536 Vine St., 45217. Tel: 513-641-3176; 641-2257 (Friary); Fax: 513-641-2262.
School—4534 Vine St., 45217. Tel: 513-641-2137; Fax: 513-641-0149. Mrs. Helen Romes, Prin.
Sisters 3; Lay Teachers 15; Students 343.
Catechesis/Religious Programs—Tel: 513-641-0147. Colleen Gerke, D.R.E.
Students 45.

24—CORPUS CHRISTI, Revs. Don Holtgrewe, O.F.M.; Fridolin Voegele, O.F.M.; Deacon John Gingras. In res., Revs. Jeremy Harrington, O.F.M.; Thomas Speier, O.F.M.; Connie Leyendecker, Business Mgr.
Res., 2014 Springdale Rd., 45231. Tel: 513-825-0618; Fax: 513-825-0674.
School—St. Bartholomew Consolidated. See separate listing.
Catechesis/Religious Programs—Tel: 513-825-0182. Barbara Conway, D.R.E.
Students 186.

25—ST. DOMINIC (Delhi Hills), Revs. James R. Collins; Gregory J. Konerman.
Res., 4551 Delhi Pike, 45238. Tel: 513-471-7741; Fax: 513-471-0363.
School—371 Pedretti Ave., 45238. Tel: 513-251-1276. Sr. Patrick Ann O'Connor, S.C., Prin.
Sisters 3; Lay Teachers 31; Students 745.
Catechesis/Religious Programs—Students 251.

26—ST. FRANCIS SERAPH, Rev. E. John Stein, O.F.M.; Bros. Josef Anderlohr, O.F.M.; Ronald Bolfeta, O.F.M.
Res., St. Francis Friary, 1615 Vine St., 45210. Tel: 513-721-4700; Fax: 513-421-9672.
School—14 E. Liberty St., 45210. Tel: 513-721-7778; Fax: 513-721-5445. Sr. Janet Linz, O.S.F., Prin.
Brothers 1; Sisters 3; Lay Teachers 10; Students 150.

27—ST. FRANCIS DE SALES, Rev. Edward M. Jach, S.M.; Bro. David Betz, S.M.
Res., 1600 Madison Rd., 45206. Tel: 513-961-1945; Fax: 513-221-4907.
School—Tel: 513-961-1953; Fax: 513-221-4907. Sr. Carol Ann Wenning, R.S.M., Prin.
Brothers 1; Sisters 1; Lay Teachers 10; Students 230.

28—ST. FRANCIS XAVIER, Revs. Robert J. Thiesing, S.J.; Paul A. Huber, S.J.; Donald O. Nastold, S.J.; Frederic G. Middendorf, S.J.; Robert C. O'Connor, S.J.; Sr. Caroline Benken, C.S.J., Pastoral Assoc.
Res., 607 Sycamore St., 45202. Tel: 513-721-4045; Fax: 513-723-0451.

29—ST. GABRIEL (Glendale), Rev. David E. Fay; Sr. Mary Doeker, Pastoral Assoc.; Deacon Herman H. Bryant.
Res., 48 W. Sharon Ave., 45246. Tel: 513-771-4700; Fax: 513-612-4545.
School—St. Gabriel Consolidated School. See separate listing. Tel: 513-771-5220; Fax: 513-771-5133.
Catechesis/Religious Programs—Sr. Charlotte Foppe, R.S.M., D.R.E.
Students 118.

30—ST. GERTRUDE (Madeira), Revs. William A. Holt, O.P., Prior; Clement Burns, O.P., Novice Master; George Schommer, Assoc. In res., Revs. Thomas F. Carroll, O.P., Pastoral Assoc.; Harvey B. Schaller, O.P.; James M. Sullivan, O.P.
Res., 7630 Shawnee Run Rd., 45243. Tel: 513-561-5954; Fax: 513-561-6740.
School—6551 Miami Ave., 45243. Tel: 513-561-8020; Fax: 513-561-7184. Sr. Mary Michael, O.P., Prin.
Dominican Sisters (Nashville, TN) 3; Lay Teachers 15; Students 470.
Catechesis/Religious Programs—Tel: 513-561-8369. Patricia DeVoss, D.R.E.
Students 600.

31—GOOD SHEPHERD (1973), Rev. Thomas R. Axe. Pastoral Assocs.: Sr. Terry Maher, C.PP.S.; Donald S. Kruse; Stephen P. Lindner; Elmer H. Fischesser; Scott Mussari; Patricia Blomer.
Res., 8815 East Kemper Rd., 45249. Tel: 513-489-8815; Fax: 513-489-8521.
Catechesis/Religious Programs—Students 1,105.

32—GUARDIAN ANGELS (Mt. Washington), Revs. Thomas C. Nolker; Barnabas Gillespie, O.S.B.; William L. Schroeder, (Retired); Carl J. Wollering; Deacons Rick Novick; Bill Wakefield; Carole Niemeier, Pastoral Assoc.
Res., 6531 Beechmont Ave., 45230. Tel: 513-231-7440; Fax: 513-624-3145.
School—6539 Beechmont Ave., 45230. Tel: 513-624-3141; Fax: 513-624-3145. Mr. David A. Reker, Prin.
Lay Teachers 44; Students 860.
Catechesis/Religious Programs—Tel: 513-624-3146; Fax: 513-624-3145.
Students 459.

33—HOLY ANGELS, Rev. Msgr. Robert A. Amann; Deacon Philip Wersching. In res., Rev. John R. White.
Res., 2130 Grandin Rd., 45208. Tel: 513-321-3880.

34—HOLY CROSS-IMMACULATA (Mount Adams), Rev. Stanley H. Neiheisel. In res., Rev. Terence A. Meehan.
Res., 30 Guido St., 45202. Tel: 513-721-6544; Fax: 513-721-6177.

35—HOLY FAMILY (Price Hill). Includes the consolidation of Our Lady of Grace and Our Lady of Perpetual Help Parishes. Rev. Mark J. Burger; Deacon Dave Childers.
Res., 814 Hawthorne Ave., 45205. Tel: 513-921-7527; Fax: 513-921-6033.
School—(Grades K-8) 3001 Price Ave., 45205. Tel: 513-921-8483. Sr. Kathleen Ann Murray, S.C., Prin.
Sisters 10; Lay Teachers 2; Students 185.

36—HOLY NAME, Rev. Terence A. Meehan; Sr. Elizabeth Bowyer, S.N.D.deN., Pastoral Admin.
Res., 2448 Auburn Ave., 45219. Tel: 513-721-5608.

37—HOLY TRINITY CHURCH (Norwood) (1994), Revs. Michael L. Bidwell; Edward F. Haskamp.
Res., 2420 Drex Ave., 45212. Tel: 513-366-4400; Fax: 513-366-4404.
School—Holy Trinity School, Tel: 513-366-4406; Fax: 513-366-4420.
Lay Teachers 17; Students 347.
Catechesis/Religious Programs—Tel: 513-366-4400; Fax: 513-366-4404.
Students 30.

38—ST. IGNATIUS LOYOLA (Monfort Heights), Revs. Thomas L. Bolte; John J. Mattscheck; Deacon Luis Riva; Barb Campbell, Business Mgr. In res., Rev. J. Paul Gruber.
Res., 5222 N. Bend Rd., 45247. Tel: 513-661-6565; Fax: 513-389-3241.
School—Tel: 513-389-3242; Fax: 513-389-3255. Timothy Reilly, Prin.
Lay Teachers 26; Students 743.
Catechesis/Religious Programs—Tel: 513-389-3247. Kris Schoettmer, D.R.E.
Students 179.

39—IMMACULATE HEART OF MARY (Forestville), Rev. Jan Kevin Schmidt; Deacons Jim Sonnenberg; Gene Miller.
Res., 7820 Beechmont Ave., 45255. Tel: 513-474-5570; Fax: 513-388-4097.
School—Tel: 513-388-4086; Fax: 513-388-4097. Bro. Edward Kesler, Prin.
Brothers 1; Lay Teachers 29; Students 587.
Catechesis/Religious Programs—Tel: 513-388-4093; Fax: 513-388-4097. D.R.E.: Leisa Anslinger, (Catholic Formation); Patrick Lesher, (Youth Formation).
Students 631.

40—ST. JAMES THE GREATER (White Oak), Revs. Raymond E. Larger; Patrick L. Sloneker; Sr. Joan Roach, O.S.U., Pastoral Assoc.; Deacon Paul J. Kluener.
Res., 3565 Hubble Rd., 45247. Tel: 513-741-5300; Fax: 513-741-5302. [CEM]
School—6111 Cheviot Rd., 45247. Tel: 513-741-5333; Fax: 513-741-5312. John Merritt, Prin.
Lay Teachers 41; Students 1,109.
Catechesis/Religious Programs—Tel: 513-741-5335; Fax: 513-741-5302.
Students 115.

41—ST. JAMES (Wyoming), Rev. Robert B. Buening; Deacon John Cooper. In res., Rev. James E. Ulrich.
Res., 411 Springfield Pk., 45215. Tel: 513-948-1218; Fax: 513-948-1225.
School—Tel: 513-821-9054; Fax: 513-821-9556. Lisa Schaffer, Prin.
Lay Teachers 12; Students 192.
Catechesis/Religious Programs—Tel: 513-948-1212; Fax: 513-948-1225. Mrs. Jeanne Hunt, D.R.E.
Students 261.

42—ST. JEROME, Rev. Carl J. Wollering. In res., Rev. James Peaker.
Church—131 Rohde Ave., 45228.
Res., 5858 Kellogg Ave., 45228. Tel: 513-231-7042.
Catechesis/Religious Programs—Guardian Angels, 6531 Beechmont Ave., 45230. Tel: 513-624-3146.
Students 51.

43—ST. JOHN THE BAPTIST (Dry Ridge), Rev. Charles Bowes.
Res., 5361 Dry Ridge Rd., 45252. Tel: 513-385-8010; Fax: 513-385-8080.
School—5375 Dry Ridge Rd., 45252. Tel: 513-385-7970; Fax: 513-385-5554. Mrs. Sandi Buschmann, Prin.
Sisters 2; Lay Teachers 18; Students 458.
Catechesis/Religious Programs—Tel: 513-385-6239.
Students 125.

44—ST. JOHN THE BAPTIST (Harrison), Revs. Edward J. Shine; Robert A. Marine.
Res., 110 N. Hill St., Harrison, 45030. Tel: 513-367-9086; Fax: 513-367-6864. [CEM]
School—Tel: 513-367-6826.
Sisters 2; Lay Teachers 23; Students 498.
Catechesis/Religious Programs—Tel: 513-367-9878.
Students 500.

45—ST. JOHN THE EVANGELIST, Rev. Thomas Espelage; Jerry Jones, Business Mgr.
Res., 7121 Plainfield Rd., 45236. Tel: 513-791-3238.
School—7131 Plainfield Rd., 45236. Tel: 513-791-6283; Fax: 513-791-6345. Adele Iwanusa, Prin.
Lay Teachers 17; Students 243.
Catechesis/Religious Programs—Chris Schell, D.R.E.
Students 65.

46—ST. JOHN FISHER (Newtown), Rev. Giles H. Pater.
Office: 3227 Church St., 45244. Tel: 513-561-9431; Fax: 513-561-7513.
Res., 3211 Church St., 45244. Tel: 513-271-4904.
Catechesis/Religious Programs—Tel: 513-561-9431.
Students 130.

47—ST. JOHN VIANNEY (Madison Pl.), Revs. Paul J. Edrich; William H. Cross.
Res., 4448 Berwick, 45227. Tel: 513-271-5490.
School—Cure of Ars, Tel: 513-271-5510; Fax: 513-271-0205.
Lay Teachers 9; Students 145.
Catechesis/Religious Programs—Tel: 513-272-6347.
Students 25.

48—ST. JOHN NEUMANN (Springfield Township), Rev. Robert C. Waller. Pastoral Assocs.: Sr. Adria Connors, C.S.C.; Mary Striebich; Deacons Thomas M.

Kiley; John R. Gobbi.
Res., 12191 Mill Rd., 45240. Tel: 513-742-0953; Fax: 513-742-5875.
School—St. Bartholomew Consolidated. See separate listing.
Catechesis/Religious Programs—Tel: 513-742-0953. Mary Lou Tansey, D.R.E.
Students 261.

49—St. Joseph, Rev. Philip O. Seher; Deacon Raphael Simmons.
Res., 745 Ezzard Charles Dr., 45203. Tel: 513-381-4526; Fax: 513-381-0191.
School—Tel: 513-381-2126; Fax: 513-381-6513. Mr. Wilbur Sanford, Prin.
Lay Teachers 13; Students 220.
Catechesis/Religious Programs—Bro. Rey Taylor, C.F.P., D.R.E.
Students 80.

50—St. Joseph (North Bend), Rev. Harry J. Gerdes; Sr. Helen Groeber, S.C.
Res., 25 E. Harrison Ave., 45052. Tel: 513-941-3661; Fax: 513-941-8559.
Catechesis/Religious Programs—Tel: 513-941-0733. Susan K. Rensing, D.R.E.
Students 217.

51—St. Jude the Apostle, Revs. Richard E. Dressman; Gerard Hiland; G.R. Keith Albrecht; Deacon James Sunderman.
Res., 5924 Bridgetown Rd., 45248. Tel: 513-574-1230; Fax: 513-598-2118.
School—5940 Bridgetown Rd., 45248. Tel: 513-598-2100; Fax: 513-598-2118. Joan Axt, Prin.
Lay Teachers 23; Students 467.
Catechesis/Religious Programs—Tel: 513-598-2101.
Students 205.

52—St. Lawrence (Price Hill), Rev. Ralph A. Westerhoff; Sr. Helen Julia Hahn, Pastoral Assoc. In res., Rev. Erwin J. Bertke.
Res., 3680 Warsaw Ave., 45205. Tel: 513-921-0328.
School—1020 Carson Ave., 45205. Tel: 513-921-4996; Fax: 513-921-5108. Mrs. Mary DeBrunner, Prin.
Lay Teachers 16; Students 349.
Catechesis/Religious Programs—Students 418.

53—St. Leo the Great, Rev. Edwin F. Gearhart.
Res., 2573 St. Leo Pl., 45225. Tel: 513-921-0025.
School—St. Boniface Consolidated. See separate listing. Tel: 513-541- 5122.
Catechesis/Religious Programs—Students 36.

54—St. Louis, Revs. Edward B. Stolze; James N. Brichetto, S.J.; Barry M. Windholtz, Res. Assoc.; Sr. Mary William Luxford, O.S.U., Pastoral Assoc.
Res., 29 E. Eighth St., 45202-2086. Tel: 513-421-3157; Fax: 513-333-0579.

55—St. Margaret of Cortona (Madisonville), Rev. Michael T. Flaherty; Deacon William Aufderheide.
Res., 4100 Watterson St., 45227. Tel: 513-271-0856; Fax: 513-271-1513.
School—4100 Simpson Ave., 45227. Tel: 513-271-8288; Fax: 513-272-1740. Sr. Sharon Ann Wiedmar, R.S.M., Prin.
Sisters 1; Lay Teachers 10; Students 170.
Convent—Tel: 513-271-1956. Sisters of Mercy

56—St. Margaret Mary (North College Hill), Revs. John E. Wall; David Lucas; Deacon Raymond S. Burger.
Res., 1830 W. Galbraith Rd., 45239. Tel: 513-521-7387; Fax: 513-521-7388.
School—1820 W. Galbraith Rd., 45239. Tel: 513-521-8619; Fax: 513-521-8620. Ann Heilman, Prin.
Lay Teachers 19; Students 350.
Catechesis/Religious Programs—Tel: 513-729-1551. Al Cuchetti, D.R.E.
Students 3.

57—St. Mark, Rev. Raymond J. Zarate, C.PP.S.
Res., 3500 Montgomery Rd., 45207. Tel: 513-961-0472; Fax: 513-961-0492.
School—1712 Duck Creek Rd., 45207. Tel: 513-751-3257; Fax: 513-751-6652. Mr. Robert A. Veite, Prin.
Lay Teachers 20; Students 240.

58—St. Martin of Tours (Cheviot), Revs. George C. Kunkel; Ronald J. Piepmeyer; Robert Mick; Deacon Howard R. Wiehe.
Res., 3720 St. Martin Pl., 45211. Tel: 513-661-2000; Fax: 513-661-1432.
School—3729 Harding Ave., 45211. Tel: 513-661-7609; Fax: 513-661-8102. Sr. Mary Reinette Kroeger, S.N.D., Prin.
Sisters 2; Lay Teachers 22; Students 540.
Catechesis/Religious Programs—Students 40.

59—St. Martin De Porres (Lincoln Heights), Rev. Thomas P. DiFolco.
Res., 9927 Wayne Ave., 45215. Tel: 513-554-4010.
School—St. Gabriel School. See separate listing. Tel: 513-771-5220.

60—Old St. Mary, Rev. Francis W. Voellmecke.
Res., 123 E. 13th St., 45210. Tel: 513-721-2988.

61—St. Mary (Hyde Park), Rev. David C. Robisch; Deacon John Thamann. Pastoral Assocs.: Mr. Michael Kleshock; Mrs. Judy Wickert; Mrs. Emilty Besl Henry.
Res., 2853 Erie Ave., 45208. Tel: 513-321-1207; Fax: 513-533-5518.
School—2845 Erie Ave., 45208. Tel: 513-321-0703; Fax: 513-533-5518. Jane Welling, Prin.
Lay Teachers 24; Students 538.
Catechesis/Religious Programs—Tel: 513-321-0703; Fax: 513-533-5518.
Students 85.

62—St. Matthias (Forest Park), Revs. William A. Drain; Gerard A. Evers; Deacons Raymond George; Michael Metz.
Res., 1050 W. Kemper Rd., 45240. Tel: 513-851-1930; Fax: 513-589-3850.
Catechesis/Religious Programs—Tel: 513-589-3845; Fax: 513-589-3850.
Students 85.

63—St. Michael, Rev. Mark Burger.
Res., 2110 St. Michael St., 45204. Tel: 513-921-0766.

64—St. Michael (Sharonville), Revs. Michael U. Pucke; James Willig; William J. Frantz, Admin. Assoc.; Michael Gable, Pastoral Assoc.; Brian Bisig, Dir. Music.
11144 Spinner Ave., 45241. Tel: 513-563-6377; Fax: 513-554-3543.
School—Tel: 513-554-3555; Fax: 513-554-3543. Jody Farrell, Prin.
Lay Teachers 21; Students 505.
Catechesis/Religious Programs—Tel: 513-554-3547; Fax: 513-554-3543. Sr. Carol Gaeke, O.P., D.R.E.
Students 287.

65—St. Monica-St. George Parish Newman Center, Revs. Jeffrey Scheeler, O.F.M.; Leonard J. Fecko; Alan Hirt, O.F.M.; Sr. Lucy Zientek, C.D.P., Pastoral Assoc.
Res., 328 W. McMillan St., 45219. Tel: 513-381-6400; Fax: 513-381-2540.
Church—Tel: 513-381-6400.

66—Mother of Christ, Rev. James Shappelle; Sr. Mary Macke, O.S.U., Pastoral Admin.
Church—5301 Winneste Ave., 45232. Tel: 513-242-0164.
Res., 740 Circle Ave., 45232. Tel: 513-541-3732.
Catechesis/Religious Programs—Students 10.

67—Nativity of Our Lord (Pleasant Ridge), Rev. Robert J. Farrell.
Res., 5935 Pandora Ave., 45213. Tel: 513-531-3164; Fax: 513-531-6368.
School—5936 Ridge Ave., 45213. Tel: 513-531-5138; Fax: 513-531-6368. Robert C. Herring, Prin.
Lay Teachers 21; Students 457.
Catechesis/Religious Programs—Students 60.

68—Our Lady of Lourdes (Westwood), Revs. Edward L. Rudemiller; Christopher Lack; Deacon Thomas E. Westerfield. Pastoral Min.: Sr. Ann Mary Lay; Betty Frisz. In res., Revs. Robert R. Wolfer; Paul J. Wolfer.
Res., 2832 Rosebud Dr., 45238. Tel: 513-922-0715; 347-2641 (Res.); Fax: 513-347-2644.
School—5835 Glenway Ave., 45238. Tel: 513-347-2660; Fax: 513-347-2663. Ms. Karen A. Rusche, Prin.
Lay Teachers 28; Students 644.
Catechesis/Religious Programs—Students 190.

69—Our Lady of the Rosary (Greenhills), Rev. Paul A. Bader; Deacon Harry S. Walker.
Res., 17 Farragut Rd., 45218. Tel: 513-825-8626; Fax: 513-825-2783.
School—Tel: 513-825-2336; Fax: 513-825-2783. Mrs. Judy Grubb, Prin.
Lay Teachers 17; Students 260.
Catechesis/Religious Programs—19 Farragut Rd., 45218. Tel: 513-825-2338; Fax: 513-825-2783. Sr. Mary Laura Miceli, S.C., D.R.E.
Students 240.

70—Our Lady of the Sacred Heart (Reading), Rev. Jack W. Wehman; Deacons James Geraci; Robert Glassmeyer.
Res., 169 Siebenthaler Ave., 45215. Tel: 513-733-4950.
School—Tel: 513-733-5225; Fax: 513-733-0186. Ms. Barbara Adelmann, Prin.
Lay Teachers 18; Students 354.
Catechesis/Religious Programs—Students 50.

71—Our Lady of Victory (Delhi Hills), Revs. Patrick P. Duffy; Peter Thomas St. George; Deacons Charles Jenkins; Joseph Schultheis; Ms. Donna Watts, Pastoral Assoc.
Res., 810 Neeb Rd., 45233. Tel: 513-922-4460; Fax: 513-922-5476.
School—808 Neeb Rd., 45233. Tel: 513-347-2072; Fax: 513-922-5476. Mr. Mel Schlomer, Prin.
Lay Teachers 32; Students 710.
Catechesis/Religious Programs—Tel: 513-347-2071; Fax: 513-922-5476. Mary Jo Wolfram, D.R.E.
Students 228.

72—Our Lady of Visitation (Mack), Revs. John E. Wessling; Bernard Weldishofer; Deacon William A. Dehmer; Sr. Gertrude Ann Knipper, C.D.P., Pastoral Assoc.
Res., 3172 South Rd., 45248. Tel: 513-922-2056; Fax: 513-347-2238.
School—3180 South Rd., 45248. Tel: 513-347-2222; Fax: 513-347-2225. Mr. Terry P. Chapman, Prin.
Sisters 1; Lay Teachers 36; Students 858.
Catechesis/Religious Programs—Tel: 513-347-2228; Fax: 513-347-2225. Sr. Mary Tewes, O.S.B., D.R.E.
Students 164.

73—Our Lord, Christ the King (Mt. Lookout), Revs. Robert A. Obermeyer; Anthony Muller.
Res., 3223 Linwood Rd., 45226. Tel: 513-321-4121; Fax: 513-871-3978.
School—Cardinal Pacelli, 927 Ellison, 45226. Tel: 513-321-1048; Fax: 513-871-3978. Fran Moore, Prin.
Lay Teachers 21; Students 457.
Catechesis/Religious Programs—Students 55.

74—Our Mother of Sorrows (Roselawn), Rev. Steven P. Walter; Deacon Michael A. Ascolese.
Res., 7243 Eastlawn Dr., 45237. Tel: 513-731-6480; Fax: 513-731-4640.
School—Tel: 513-731-8838; Fax: 513-731-4640. Paul F. McLaughlin, Prin.
Lay Teachers 12; Students 160.
Catechesis/Religious Programs—Students 170.

75—Sts. Peter and Paul (Reading), Rev. Paul L. Stolz. In res., Rev. Mark T. Watkins.
Res., 417 W. Vine St., Reading, 45215. Tel: 513-554-1010; Fax: 513-554-0190.
School—Tel: 513-554-1311; Fax: 513-554-4667. Mr. Paul D. Mertzman, Prin.
Lay Teachers 7; Students 195.
Catechesis/Religious Programs—Tel: 513-821-7448. Sr. Judith Wessels, S.N.D.de N., D.R.E.
Students 58.

76—St. Pius, Rev. Albert Lauer.
Res., 1814 Dreman Ave., 45223. Tel: 513-541-0211.

77—Resurrection of Our Lord, Rev. Robert E. Keller.
Res., 1744 Iliff Ave., 45205. Tel: 513-471-2700; Fax: 513-471-2703.
School—1740 Iliff Ave., 45205. Tel: 513-471-6600. Thomas F. Miller, Prin.
Sisters 2; Lay Teachers 10; Students 190.
Catechesis/Religious Programs—Students 6.

78—St. Robert Bellarmine, Rev. Richard W. Bollman, S.J.; Lauren McDonough Renneker, Dir. Pastoral Min., Tel: 513-745-3008; Guy M. Vanasse, Dir. Music Min., Tel: 513-745-3270; Michael W. Jarrold-Grapes, Dir. Youth Min., Tel: 513-745-4224.
Res., Xavier University, 3844 Victory Pkwy., 45207. Tel: 513-745-3398; Fax: 513-745-2031.
Catechesis/Religious Programs—Tel: 513-745-3317; Fax: 513-745-2031. Rosemary G. Conrad, D.R.E.
Students 113.

79—St. Rose of Lima, Rev. Lawrence R. Krusling.
Res., 2501 Eastern Ave., 45202. Tel: 513-871-1162.

80—Sacred Heart, Rev. Mario Rauzi, C.S.
Res., 2733 Massachusetts Ave., 45225. Tel: 513-541-4654; Fax: 513-541-4662.
School—Corryville Catholic Elementary School. See separate listing.

81—St. Saviour (Rossmoyne), Rev. Robert W. Goebel; Deacon Jerry Cain.
Res., 4136 Myrtle Ave., 45236. Tel: 513-791-9004; Fax: 513-791-6530.
School—4122 Myrtle Ave., 45236. Tel: 513-791-2734; Fax: 513-791-6530. Jay McNitt, Prin.
Lay Teachers 11; Students 160.
Catechesis/Religious Programs—Students 84.

82—St. Simon the Apostle, Rev. Michael D. Beatty.
Res., 825 Pontius Rd., 45233. Tel: 513-941-3656; Fax: 513-941-2329.
Catechesis/Religious Programs—Tel: 513-941-6173; Fax: 513-941-3656. Carolyn Meyers, D.R.E.
Students 255.

83—St. Stephen, Rev. Ronald J. Averbeck.
Res., 320 Donham Ave., 45226. Tel: 513-871-3373.

84—St. Teresa, Rev. Larry R. Tharp; Deacon Michael Davenport.
Res., 1175 Overlook Ave., 45238. Tel: 513-921-9200; Fax: 513-921-4446.
School—1194 Rulison Ave., 45238. Tel: 513-471-4530. Barbara A. Cooke, Prin.
Sisters 1; Lay Teachers 19; Students 477.
Catechesis/Religious Programs—Tel: 513-471-4530. David L. Donovan, D.R.E.
Students 67.

85—St. Therese, The Little Flower (Mt. Airy), Revs. Thomas M. King; Robert A. Stricker.
Res., 5560 Kirby Ave., 45239. Tel: 513-541-5560; Fax: 513-681-2631.

School—5555 Little Flower Ave., 45239. Tel: 513-542-6787. Mrs. Patricia Kennedy, Prin.
Lay Teachers 24; Students 508.
Catechesis/Religious Programs—Sr. Francis Margaret Maag, C.D.P., D.R.E.
Students 70.

86—St. Vincent Ferrer (Kenwood), Rev. Terence J. Hamilton. In res., Rev. Joseph C. Heskamp, (Retired).
Res., 7754 Montgomery Rd., 45236. Tel: 513-791-9030; Fax: 513-791-7405.
School—Tel: 513-791-6320; Fax: 513-791-7405.
Lay Teachers 15; Students 260.
Catechesis/Religious Programs—Tel: 513-791-6321; Fax: 513-791-7405. Sr. Kaye Lednik, C.S.J., D.R.E.
Students 141.

87—St. Vincent de Paul, Rev. Gary J. Witsken.
Res., 4026 River Rd., 45204. Tel: 513-451-5714.
School—4044 River Rd., 45204. Tel: 513-451-5656. Sr. Miriam Clare Glandorf, S.C., Prin.
Sisters 1; Lay Teachers 5; Students 66.

88—St. Vivian, Rev. John E. Filippine; Mr. Greg Hogg, Pastoral Assoc.; Deacons William R. Michael; Gerald Coomes.
Res., 7600 Winton Rd., 45224. Tel: 513-728-4331; Fax: 513-728-4335.
School—885 Denier Pl., 45224. Tel: 513-522-6858; Fax: 513-728-4335.
Lay Teachers 18; Students 370.
Catechesis/Religious Programs—Tel: 513-728-4333; Fax: 513-728-4335. Christine Siciliano, D.R.E.
Students 91.

89—St. William, Rev. Philip O. Seher; Deacon C. Edward Brockman. Pastoral Min.: Mr. Jerry DiCristoforo; Sr. Claire Foken, S.C. In res., Rev. Msgr. Francis B. Kennedy; Rev. Christopher R. Armstrong.
Res., 4108 W. Eighth St., 45205. Tel: 513-921-0247; Fax: 513-921-2810.
School—4125 St. William Ave., 45205. Tel: 513-471-2989; Fax: 513-471-8226. Elaine Haas, Prin.
Sisters 1; Lay Teachers 25; Students 445.

OUTSIDE THE CITY OF CINCINNATI

Amelia, Clermont Co., St. Bernadette's, Rev. Hans H. Gruenbauer.
Res., 1479 Locust Lake Rd., 45102. Tel: 513-753-5566; Fax: 513-753-5566.
School—1453 Locust Lake Rd., 45102. Tel: 513-753-4744. Mr. Dan Teller, Prin.
Lay Teachers 13; Students 200.
Catechesis/Religious Programs—Tel: 513-753-5566. Kelly Lafferty, D.R.E.
Students 140.

Arnheim, Brown Co., St. Mary, Rev. Dohrman W. Byers.
Res., 6647 Van Buren St., Georgetown, 45121. Tel: 937-446-2555; Fax: 937-446-2554.
Catechesis/Religious Programs—Tel: 937-446-2013.
Students 83.

Batavia, Clermont Co., Holy Trinity, Rev. William R. Stockelman; Deacon James Hennessey.
Res., 140 N. 6th St., 45103. Tel: 513-732-2024.
Catechesis/Religious Programs—Tel: 513-732-2024. Patricia Bruce, D.R.E.
Students 117.

Beavercreek, Greene Co., St. Luke, Rev. William J. Kramer.
Res., 1440 N. Fairfield Rd., 45432. Tel: 937-426-1733; Fax: 937-426-3965.
School—(Grades K-8) 1442 N. Fairfield Rd., 45432. Tel: 937-426-8551; Fax: 937-426-6435. Mrs. Leslie Vondrell, Prin.
Lay Teachers 20; Students 490.
Catechesis/Religious Programs—1444 N. Fairfield Rd., 45432. Tel: 937-426-5656.
Students 479.

Bellefontaine, Logan Co., St. Patrick's, Rev. Henry F. Albietz; Deacon Harold Dipple.
Res., 328 E. Patterson Ave., 43311. Tel: 937-592-1656.
Catechesis/Religious Programs—320 E. Patterson Rd., 43311. Tel: 937-592-6621. Mrs. Barbara Daly, D.R.E.
Students 263.

Bethel, Clermont Co., St. Mary, Rev. Patrick H. Crone.
Res., 3398 S.R. 125, 45106. Tel: 513-734-4041; Fax: 513-734-3588.
Catechesis/Religious Programs—Tel: 513-734-3676; Fax: 513-934-3588. Joan St. Clair, D.R.E.
Students 200.

Blanchester, Clinton Co., Holy Name, Rev. Michael A. Savino.
Res. & Church: 746 S. S.R. 133, 45107. Tel: 937-783-3956; Fax: 937-783-9035.
Catechesis/Religious Programs—Tel: 937-783-2275. Kathy Baxter, D.R.E.
Students 72.

Botkins, Shelby Co., Immaculate Conception, Rev. James J. O'Connor.
Res., 116 N. Mill St., P.O. Box 519, 45306. Tel: 937-693-2561.
Catechesis/Religious Programs—Students 308.

Bradford, Miami Co., Immaculate Conception, Rev. James S. Duell.
Res., 5874 N. Buckneck Rd., R.R. 2, 45308. Tel: 937-448-6220.
Catechesis/Religious Programs—Students 48.

Burkettsville, Mercer Co., St. Bernard, Rev. Albert A. Reed, C.PP.S.
Res., 71 W. Main St., P.O. Box 146, 45310. Tel: 419-375-2333.
St. Henry Catechetical Center—See St. Henry, St. Henry for details. Tel: 419-678-3811.

Camden, Preble Co., St. Mary's, Rev. Francis R. Monnig.
Res., 5304 Jacksonburg Rd., Trenton, 45067. Tel: 513-726-6294.
Church—7721 N. Main St., 45311. Tel: 937-452-3352.

Carthagena, Mercer Co., St. Aloysius, Rev. David A. Hoying, C.PP.S.
Res., 1509 Cranberry Rd., St. Henry, 45883. Tel: 419-925-4776.
Church—State Rte. 274, Celina, 45822.
St. Henry Catechetical Center—For details call Tel: 419-678-3811.

Cassella, Mercer Co., Nativity of the Blessed Virgin Mary, Rev. Frederick Ryder, C.PP.S.
Res., 6524 State Rte. 119, Maria Stein, 45860. Tel: 419-925-4630. [CEM]
Catechesis/Religious Programs—Carolyn Stucke, D.R.E.
Students 117.

Celina, Mercer Co., Immaculate Conception of the Blessed Virgin Mary, Revs. James C. Seibert, C.PP.S.; Richard R. Riedel, C.PP.S. In res., Deacon Thomas Huff.
Res., 229 W. Anthony St., 45822. Tel: 419-586-6648; Fax: 419-586-6649. [CEM]
School—Tel: 419-586-2379; Fax: 419-586-6649. Ms. Kathryn Mescher, Prin.
Sisters of the Precious Blood 1; Lay Teachers 15; Students 246.
Catechesis/Religious Programs—Wayne & Walnut Sts., Tel: 419-586-2370; Fax: 419-586-6649.
Students 534.

Centerville, Montgomery Co., Incarnation, Revs. Thomas A. Kuhn; Daniel J. Meyer. Pastoral Assocs.: Mary Fogler; Tim Niesel; Deacon Robert Zinck.
Res., 55 Williamsburg Ln., 45459. Tel: 937-433-1188; Fax: 937-433-3263.
School—45 Williamsburg Ln., 45459. Tel: 937-433-1051; Fax: 937-433-9796. Cheryl Reichel, Prin.
Lay Teachers 31; Students 700.
Catechesis/Religious Programs—Tel: 937-433-3377; Fax: 937-433-3263.
Students 569.

St. Francis of Assisi (1969), Revs. John B. Turnbull, O.F.M.; Knute Kinross, O.F.M.; Melvin Holtel, O.F.M.; Marilyn Hutler, Parish Sec.; Frances Obringer, Sec. of Rel. Ed.
Res., 6245 Wilmington Pike, 45459. Tel: 937-433-1013; Fax: 937-433-1699.
Catechesis/Religious Programs—Tel: 937-433-0128; Fax: 937-433-1699. D.R.E.: Mary Ellen Singer; Mary Ann Monseur.
Students 624.

Chickasaw, Mercer Co., Most Precious Blood, Rev. John L. Bensman.
Res., Box 26, 35 S. Maple St., 45826-0026. Tel: 419-925-4391. [CEM]
Catechesis/Religious Programs—Margie Ronnebaum, D.R.E.
Students 188.

Coldwater, Mercer Co., Holy Trinity, Revs. Ronald H. Wilker; Frank Amberger.
Res., 116 E. Main St., 45828. Tel: 419-678-4802; Fax: 419-678-4803. [CEM]
Catechesis/Religious Programs—110 N. Second St., 45828. Tel: 419-678-3328. D.R.E.: Helen Vagedes; Catherine Wenning.
Students 1,132.

Covington, Miami Co., St. Teresa, Rev. James S. Duell.
Res., 6925 W. U.S. 36, 45318. Tel: 937-473-2970. [JC]
Catechesis/Religious Programs—Tel: 937-473-2970. Donald Kuether, D.R.E.
Students 74.

Cranberry Prairie, Mercer Co., St. Francis, Rev. David A. Hoying, C.PP.S.
Res., 1509 Cranberry Rd., St. Henry, 45883. Tel: 419-925-4776. [CEM]
St. Henry Catechetical Center—See St. Henry, St. Henry for details. Tel: 419-678-3811.

Dayton, Montgomery Co.,

1—St. Adalbert's, (Polish), Rev. Michael J. Holloran. Office 1511 Valley St., 45404. Tel: 937-228-8782.
Catechesis/Religious Programs—1509 Valley St., 45404. Tel: 937-228-8604. Doreen Matulavitch, D.R.E.
Students 40.

2—St. Agnes, Rev. James R. Schutte; Nympha Clark, Pastoral Admin.
Res., 811 N. Paul L. Dunbar St., 45407. Tel: 937-274-2212; Fax: 937-274-0976.
School—Dayton Catholic Elementary Consolidated. See separate listing. Tel: 937-275-8114.

3—St. Albert the Great, Revs. James J. Manning; Lawrence R. Strittmatter; Sr. Patrice Vales, S.C., Pastoral Assoc.; Deacons Ray Blum; Steve Bermick.
Res., 3033 Far Hills Ave., 45429. Tel: 937-293-1191; Fax: 937-293-1848.
School—Tel: 937-293-9452; Fax: 937-293-1848. Mr. Walt Klimaski, Prin.
Lay Teachers 26; Students 593.
Catechesis/Religious Programs—104 Dorothy Ln., Kettering, 45429. Tel: 937-298-2402; Fax: 937-293-1848.
Students 375.

4—St. Anthony of Padua, Rev. Thomas M. Shearer. In res., Revs. Thomas J. Ballman; Christian A. Rohmiller.
Res., 820 Bowen St., 45410. Tel: 937-253-9132; Fax: 937-253-6658.
School—Tel: 937-253-6251; Fax: 937-253-1541.
Lay Teachers 21; Students 429.

5—Ascension, Revs. David E. Brinkmoeller; Mark Meyer. In res., Rev. Ronald Nuzzi. Pastoral Assocs.: Sr. Florence Seifert, C.PP.S.; Sr. Marie Langhals, C.PP.S.
Res., 2025 Woodman Dr., Kettering, 45420. Tel: 937-253-5171.
School—Tel: 937-245-5411; Fax: 937-254-1105. Sr. Maureen Heavey, R.S.M., Prin.
Sisters 1; Lay Teachers 17; Students 395.
Catechesis/Religious Programs—Tel: 937-254-0622. Mary Ellen Fargey, D.R.E.
Students 268.

6—Assumption, Rev. John E. Krumm; Sr. Mary M. Garascia, Pastoral Admin.
Parish Address: 3805 Kings Hwy., 45406. Tel: 937-275-9042.
School—Dayton Catholic Elementary Consolidated. See separate listing. Tel: 937-275-8144; Fax: 937-275-5737.

7—St. Charles Borromeo, Rev. Msgr. Lawrence K. Breslin; Rev. George Schmitz; Deacon Leonard Baltes.
Res., 4500 Ackerman Rd., 45429. Tel: 937-434-6081; Fax: 937-434-6251.
School—Tel: 937-434-4933. Miss Judy Ellerbrock, Prin.
Sisters 3; Lay Teachers 27; Students 660.
Catechesis/Religious Programs—Students 455.

8—Corpus Christi, Rev. James R. Schutte; Deacon Milton Royer.
Res., 224 Squirrel Rd., 45405. Tel: 937-228-6672; Fax: 937-461-0611.
School—200 Homewood Ave., 45405. Tel: 937-228-3091; Fax: 937-461-0611.
Lay Teachers 13; Students 204.

9—Emmanuel, Revs. Lee Sciarrotta, S.M.; Francis J. Kenney, S.M.; Charles Bergedick, S.M.
Res., 149 Franklin St., 45402. Tel: 937-228-2013.
Catechesis/Religious Programs—Tel: 937-228-5354.
Students 141.

10—St. Helen, Rev. Paul F. DeLuca; Deacons John J. Jachimowicz; Susano Mascorro; Roy Deardorff.
Res., 605 Granville Pl., 45431. Tel: 937-254-6233; Fax: 937-256-6117.
School—Tel: 937-256-1761. Sr. Annette Paveglio, S.C., Prin.
Sisters 5; Lay Teachers 21; Students 438.
Catechesis/Religious Programs—Tel: 937-256-8815. Joan Torres, D.R.E.
Students 147.
Convent—5098 Burkhardt Rd., 45431. Tel: 937-252-7972. Sisters of Notre Dame

11—St. Henry, Revs. Lawrence E. Mierenfeld; Steven L. Shoup; Sr. Joanne Termini, S.C., Pastoral Assoc.; Deacon Alan W. Arber.
Res., 6696 Springboro Rd., 45449. Tel: 937-434-9231; Fax: 937-434-6798.
School—Bishop Leibold Consolidated. See separate listing. Tel: 937-434-9343.
Catechesis/Religious Programs—Tel: 937-433-8220.
Students 395.

12—Holy Angels, Rev. Thomas E. Meyer; Deacon Eldon M. Cotterman; Sr. Ann C. Joseph, S.C., Pastoral Assoc.
Parish Office: 218 K St., 45409. Tel: 937-222-7807;

Fax: 937-222-8167.
Church—Brown & L Sts., 45409.
School—Tel: 937-222-0365. Louise P. Moore, Prin.
Lay Teachers 21; Students 270.
Catechesis/Religious Programs—Tel: 937-222-2641. Karen D. Davis, D.R.E.
Students 300.

13—HOLY CROSS, (Lithuanian), Rev. Michael J. Holloran.
Res., 1924 Leo St., 45404-1997. Tel: 937-228-8902.

14—HOLY FAMILY, Rev. Thomas M. Gaeke; Deacon William Stevenson, Jr. In res., Revs. Edward Haggerty; Ernesto Caro (Mexico).
Res., 140 S. Findlay St., 45403. Tel: 937-253-1109; Fax: 937-253-2172.
School—121 S. Monmouth St., 45403. Tel: 937-253-4859; Fax: 937-253-5552. G. Janell Postawski, Prin.
Sisters 2; Lay Teachers 8; Students 220.
Convent—141 S. Monmouth St., 45403. Tel: 937-252-0101. Sisters of Notre Dame de Namur
Catechesis/Religious Programs—St. Mary Church, 310 Allen St., 45410. Tel: 937-256-5633; Fax: 937-256-7138.
Students 12.

15—HOLY TRINITY, Rev. Walter J. MacPherson; Deacon George Zvonar; Sr. Helen McDermott, S.N.D., Pastoral Asst.; Mary C. Wlodarski, Christian Formation Min.; Judith L. Trick, Business Mgr.
Res., 272 Bainbridge St., 45402. Tel: 937-228-1223; Fax: 937-445-0232.

16—ST. JAMES, Revs. Freddy Washington, C.S.Sp.; George Crocenzi, C.S.Sp.; Francis Tandoh, C.S.Sp.; Deacon Jacob Jerigan.
Res., 719 Edgemont Ave., 45408. Tel: 937-228-7023.
Church—Heck & Cincinnati St., 45408.
School—Dayton Catholic Elementary. See separate listing.
Catechesis/Religious Programs—Anna Burns, D.R.E.
Students 30.

17—ST. JOSEPH, Rev. Louis Osterhage, C.PP.S.
Res., 411 E. Second St., 45402. Tel: 937-228-9272; 228-9522; Fax: 937-228-6144.

18—ST. MARY'S, Rev. Thomas M. Gaeke; Deacon William Saluke.
Res., 310 Allen St., 45410. Tel: 937-256-5633; Fax: 937-256-7138.
Catechesis/Religious Programs—Tel: 937-256-5633; Fax: 937-256-7138. Dr. Robert Obach, D.R.E.
Students 39.

19—OUR LADY OF THE IMMACULATE CONCEPTION, Rev. Timothy S. Kallaher. Pastoral Assocs.: Pauline Everman; Deacons Dan Kraus; Vince Orlando; Art Kronenberger.
Res., 2300 S. Smithville Rd., 45420. Tel: 937-252-9919; Fax: 937-252-0890.
School—Tel: 937-253-8831; Fax: 937-252-8832. Rachelle Cordonnier, Prin.
Sisters 2; Lay Teachers 20; Students 460.
Catechesis/Religious Programs—Students 60.

20—OUR LADY OF MERCY, Rev. John E. Krumm. Pastoral Assocs.: Carolyn Mackenzie; Bill Painter; Kathy Shirley; Deacon Thomas Platfoot.
Res., 220 W. Siebenthaler Ave., 45405. Tel: 937-274-2107; Fax: 937-274-4363.
School—Tel: 937-278-5483. Sr. M. Karen Sammons, S.C., Prin.
Lay Teachers 16; Students 230.
Catechesis/Religious Programs—Students 30.

21—OUR LADY OF THE ROSARY, Rev. Anthony M. Dattilo; Deacon Henry B. Beck.
Res., 22 Notre Dame Ave., 45404. Tel: 937-228-8802.
School—40 Notre Dame Ave., 45404. Tel: 937-222-7231; Fax: 937-222-7393. Genevieve S. Ritzel, Prin.
Lay Teachers 10; Students 215.

22—ST. PETER, (Huber Heights), Revs. Earl Francis Simone; Francis B. Pilliod; Michael T. Mahoney; Deacons Allen K. Miller; Robert Borgerding.
Res., 6161 Chambersburg Rd., 45424. Tel: 937-233-1503; Fax: 937-237-3523.
School—Tel: 937-233-8710; Fax: 937-237-3974. Feliza Poling, Prin.
Lay Teachers 43; Students 936.
Catechesis/Religious Programs—Tel: 937-237-3516; Fax: 937-233-5717. Mrs. Janet Lewis, D.R.E.
Students 464.

23—PRECIOUS BLOOD, Rev. Mark Hoying, C.PP.S.; Deacon Richard Janowiecki. In res., Rev. Angelo P. Anthony, C.PP.S.; Bro. Bernard Barga, C.PP.S.
Res., 4961 Salem Ave., 45416. Tel: 937-276-5954; Fax: 937-276-5955.
School—4870 Denlinger Rd., 45426. Tel: 937-277-2291. Sr. Anne Schulz, C.PP.S., Prin.
Lay Teachers 19; Students 410.
Catechesis/Religious Programs—Tel: 937-277-2454.
Students 270.

24—QUEEN OF APOSTLES, Greene Co., Rev. James Bartlett, S.M., Priest Coord.
Church—4400 Shakertown Rd., 45430-1075. Tel: 937-429-0510; Fax: 937-429-0881.
Catechesis/Religious Programs—Tel: 937-426-0881; Fax: 937-429-0881. Marilyn McCrate, D.R.E.
Students 104.

25—QUEEN OF MARTYRS, (Northridge), Rev. Thomas R. Hopp; Jane Bensman, Pastoral Assoc.
Res., 4144 Cedar Ridge Rd., 45414. Tel: 937-277-2092; Fax: 937-277-2773.
School—Tel: 937-274-5592. Lucianne Lilienthal, Prin.
Sisters 2; Lay Teachers 7; Students 200.
Catechesis/Religious Programs—Tel: 937-277-2092.
Students 35.

26—RESURRECTION OF OUR LORD, Revs. Freddy Washington; Francis Tandoh, C.S.Sp.; Deacon Jacob Jerigan.
Res., 130 Gramont Ave., 45417. Tel: 937-268-6697.
School—Tel: 937-268-6391; Fax: 937-268-9775. Ms. Debra Johnson, Prin.
Lay Teachers 9; Students 247.

27—ST. RITA, Rev. Kenneth R. Baker.
Res., 5401 N. Main St., 45415. Tel: 937-278-5815; Fax: 937-275-3302.
School—Tel: 937-277-8978. Mary Ann Eismann, Prin.
Lay Teachers 16; Students 348.
Catechesis/Religious Programs—Karen Sipos, D.R.E.
Students 105.

28—ST. STEPHEN, (North Dayton), Rev. Anthony M. Dattilo.
Res., 1114 Troy St., 45404. Tel: 937-223-8306.

Eaton, Preble Co., Visitation of the Blessed Virgin Mary, Rev. J. Thomas Fitzsimmons; Deacon Joseph James.
Res., 407 E. Main St., 45320. Tel: 937-456-3380.
Catechesis/Religious Programs—Tel: 937-456-3395. Sharon Stump, D.R.E.
Students 120.

Egypt, Auglaize Co., St. Joseph, Rev. Thomas R. Brenberger, C.PP.S. In res., Rev. Oscar H. Seger.
Res., 02441 SR 364, 45865. Tel: 419-628-2614; Fax: 419-628-2958. [CEM]
Catechesis/Religious Programs—Students 32.

Englewood, Montgomery Co., St. Paul's, Rev. Todd Grogan; Deacon Joseph Subler.
Res., 1000 W. Wenger Rd., 45322. Tel: 937-836-7535; Fax: 937-836-1130.
Catechesis/Religious Programs—Tel: 937-836-2337. Dr. Sandra Chakeres, D.R.E.
Students 585.

Fairborn, Greene Co., Mary Help of Christians, Revs. Joseph R. Raudabaugh; John R. Kummer; Anne Rusen, Pastoral Assoc.; Deacon Max Roadruck.
Res., 954 N. Maple Ave., 45324-5498. Tel: 937-878-8353; Fax: 937-879-8800.
School—934 N. Maple Ave., 45324-5499. Tel: 937-878-9152. Joseph L. Pizza, Prin.
Lay Teachers 18; Students 335.
Catechesis/Religious Programs—1030 N. Maple Ave., 45324. Tel: 937-878-7325. Gloria L. Leigh, D.R.E.
Students 159.

Fairfield, Butler Co., Sacred Heart of Jesus, Rev. Norman Langenbrunner.
Church—400 Nilles Rd., 45014. Tel: 513-829-4383; Fax: 513-858-4211.
Res., 5202 Mississippi Dr., 45014. Tel: 513-863-5318; Fax: 513-863-5318, Ext. [*]51.
School—Tel: 513-858-4215; Fax: 513-858-4218. Joseph Nagle, Prin.
Lay Teachers 19; Students 470.
Catechesis/Religious Programs—Tel: 513-858-4213.
Students 266.

Fayetteville, Brown Co., St. Patrick's, Rev. Jerome J. Gardner.
Mailing Address: P.O. Box 279, 45118. Tel: 513-875-2082.
Res., 130 Stone Alley, Fayettville, 45118.
Catechesis/Religious Programs—Tel: 513-875-2161. Debbie Rosselot, D.R.E.
Students 120.

Felicity, Clermont Co., Our Mother of Good Counsel. Closed. For inquiries for parish records contact the Chancery.

Fort Loramie, Shelby Co., St. Michael's, Revs. Timothy S. Bunch; Aloysius B. Boeke; Deacon Werner Bensman.
Res., 33 Elm St., P.O. Box 7, 45845. Tel: 937-295-2891; Fax: 937-295-3349. [CEM]
Catechesis/Religious Programs—Tel: 937-295-2179; Fax: 937-295-3349. D.R.E.: Marge Rethman; Frank Turner.
Students 597.

Fort Recovery, Mercer Co., Mary Help of Christians, Revs. Paul W. Wohlwend, C.PP.S.; Norbert Loshe, C.PP.S.; Deacon John Parker.
Res., 403 Sharpsburg Rd., 45846. Tel: 419-375-4153. [CEM]
Catechesis/Religious Programs—Tel: 419-375-4153.
Students 372.
St. Peter, Rev. George Kuzara, C.PP.S.
Res., 1477 Philothea Rd., St. Peter, 45846. Tel: 419-375-4344; Fax: 419-375-4030.
Catechesis/Religious Programs—Tel: 419-375-4344. Ginny Gehret, D.R.E.
Students 176.

Franklin, Warren Co., St. Mary's, Rev. Joseph B. Bruening.
Res., 115 S. Main St., 45005. Tel: 513-746-5404.
Catechesis/Religious Programs—Tel: 513-746-1404; Fax: 513-746-1404.
Students 209.

Frenchtown, Darke Co., Holy Family, Rev. Leo A. Hoying.
Res., 14 E. Wood St., Versailles, 45380. Tel: 937-526-4945.
Catechesis/Religious Programs—Students 100.

Fryburg, Auglaize Co., St. John, Rev. Charles F. Lang.
Res., 11319 Van Buren St., Wapokoneta, 45895-8467. Tel: 419-738-6043; Fax: 419-738-4364.
Catechesis/Religious Programs—Tel: 419-738-6043. Richard Westbay, D.R.E.
Students 84.

Georgetown, Brown Co., St. George, Rev. Earl O. Metz.
Res., 109 Elm St., 45121. Tel: 937-378-6829.
Church—507 E. State St.
Catechesis/Religious Programs—Mary Gaskin, D.R.E.
Students 80.

Germantown, Montgomery Co., St. Augustine, Rev. Paul F. Hurst.
Res., 6891 Weaver Rd., 45327. Tel: 937-855-2289.
Catechesis/Religious Programs—Tel: 937-855-2289.
Students 91.

Glynwood, Auglaize Co., St. Patrick, Rev. Charles F. Lang.
Res., 06959 Glynwood Rd., St. Marys, 45885. Tel: 419-738-6308; Fax: 419-738-7113.
Catechesis/Religious Programs—Tel: 419-394-8458. Irene Heilers, D.R.E.
Students 68.

Greenfield, Highland Co., St. Benignus, Rev. Ronald C. Cooper.
Res., 218 S. Second St., 45123. Tel: 937-981-2785. [CEM]
Catechesis/Religious Programs—Jessie Spangler, D.R.E.
Students 59.

Greenville, Darke Co., St. Mary, Rev. Harold W. Kist.
Res., 233 W. 3rd St., 45331. Tel: 937-548-1616.
School—238 W. Third St., 45331. Tel: 937-548-2345; Fax: 937-548-0878.
Lay Teachers 12; Students 147.
Catechesis/Religious Programs—Tel: 937-548-1616. Sr. Elaine Beimesche, C.S.J., D.R.E.
Students 228.

Hamilton, Butler Co.,

1—ST. ANN'S, Rev. Dennis Dettenwanger; Deacon Mark E. Brunner; Pat Miller, Pastoral Min.
Res., 646 Clinton Ave., 45015. Tel: 513-863-4963; Fax: 513-863-2017.
School—3064 Pleasant Ave., 45015. Tel: 513-863-0604. Mrs. Donna L. Weber, Prin.
Sisters 1; Lay Teachers 10; Students 229.
Catechesis/Religious Programs—Tel: 513-863-4963.
Students 44.
Convent—(Oldenburg, IN) 646 Clinton Ave., 45015. Tel: 513-863-1701. Sisters of the Third Order Regular of St. Francis

2—ST. JOSEPH'S, Rev. Dennis Dettenwanger; Deacon James Kowalki, Pastoral Admin.
Res., 171 Washington St., 45011. Tel: 513-863-1424; Fax: 513-863-1468.
School—Tel: 513-863-8758; Fax: 513-863-5253. Gail Kist Kline, Ph.D., Ed., Prin.
Lay Teachers 10; Students 190.
Catechesis/Religious Programs—Students 229.

3—ST. JULIE BILLIART, (1989). (This parish is the successor in interest to St. Mary, St. Stephen and St. Veronica parishes, formerly located in Hamilton, Ohio.). Rev. Jeffrey P. Silver; Deacons James S. McCormick; William B. Renneker.
Church—224 Dayton St., 45011. Tel: 513-863-1040; Fax: 513-863-1132.
School—(Grades K-8) 1206 Shuler Ave., 45011. Tel: 513-867-8477; Fax: 513-867-0139. Mrs. Margaret Hunsberger, Prin.
Lay Teachers 12; Students 233.

4—ST. PETER IN CHAINS, Rev. William H. Schwartz.
Res., 382 Liberty Ave., 45013. Tel: 513-863-3938;

Fax: 513-863-3344.
School—451 Ridgelawn Ave., 45013. Tel: 513-863-0685.
Lay Teachers 20; Students 425.
Catechesis/Religious Programs—Tel: 513-863-3344.
Students 99.

Hillsboro, Highland Co., St. Mary's, Rev. Stanley E. Luehrmann; Miss Carole J. Grady, Pastoral Assoc. & D.R.E.
Res., 212 S. High St., 45133-1445. Tel: 937-393-1742. [CEM]
Catechesis/Religious Programs—Tel: 937-393-4017.
Students 130.

Jamestown, Greene Co., St. Augustine, Rev. William V. Thomas.
Res., 31 S. Chillicothe St., P.O. Box F, South Charleston, 45368-0806. Tel: 937-462-8971.
Catechesis/Religious Programs—D.R.E.: Rita Canty Tel: 937-675-3219; Carmen Montgomery Tel: 937-675-3707.
Students 26.

Lebanon, Warren Co., St. Francis de Sales, Rev. Louis R. Hohlmayer; Deacons Herschel Steward; John Taylor; Ned Ostendorf.
Res., 15 DeSales Ave., 45036. Tel: 513-932-2601.
School—20 DeSales Ave., 45036. Tel: 513-932-6501; Fax: 513-932-9919. Jo Anne Fischesser, Prin.
Lay Teachers 8; Students 214.
Catechesis/Religious Programs—Tel: 513-897-6498.
Students 200.

Loveland, Clermont Co., St. Columban, Rev. Terrance W. Smith; Deacons Joseph Coll; James Miller.
Office: 894 Oakland Rd., 45140. Tel: 513-683-7903; Fax: 513-683-1389.
Res., 855 Oakland Rd., 45140. Tel: 513-677-8084.
School—896 Oakland Rd., 45140. Tel: 513-683-7903; Fax: 513-683-7904. Sr. Mary Suzanne Rose, S.N.D., Prin.
Sisters 2; Lay Teachers 21; Students 542.
Catechesis/Religious Programs—Students 205.
Convent—(Covington, KY) 896 Oakland Rd., 45140. Tel: 513-683-0255. Sisters of Notre Dame

Manchester, Adams Co., St. Mary. (Vicariate). Rev. David Glockner, Glmy.
Res., 612 E. Mulberry St., West Union, 45693. Tel: 937-544-2757.

Maria Stein, Mercer Co., St. John the Baptist, Rev. Emil J. Labbe, C.PP.S.; Deacons Carl Franzer; Omer Bertke.
Res., 8533 State Rte. 119, 45860. Tel: 419-925-4522.
Catechesis/Religious Programs—Tel: 419-925-4442.
Students 290.

Mason, Warren Co., St. Susanna, Rev. Harry J. Meyer; Karen Gottschall, Pastoral Assoc. for Youth; Deacons James A. Merritt; Daniel L. Rader; Gerald L. Barney; Ralph W. Popp, Bus. Mgr.; Rosie Leugers, Pastoral Assoc.
Res., 305 Fourth Ave., 45040. Tel: 513-398-3821; Fax: 513-398-2254.
School—500 Reading Rd., 45040. Tel: 513-398-5826. Kenneth L. Beiser, Prin.
Lay Teachers 16; Students 406.
Catechesis/Religious Programs—Tel: 513-398-1234.
Students 1,095.

McCartyville, Shelby Co., Sacred Heart of Jesus, Rev. Gerald E. Bensman.
Res., 9333 State Rte. 119, Anna, 45302. Tel: 937-394-3823; 419-628-2502; Fax: (Call for fax number).
Catechesis/Religious Programs—Tel: 937-394-3823. Barbara Riethman, D.R.E.
Students 393.

Mechanicsburg, Champaign Co., St. Michael's, Rev. Clarence G. Heis.
Res., 40 Walnut St., 43044. Tel: 513-834-2413.

Miamisburg, Montgomery Co., Our Lady of Good Hope, Rev. Bernard H. Bruening; Deacon Joseph J. Sprinkle.
Res., 6 S. Third St., 45342. Tel: 937-866-1432.
School—Bishop Leibold Consolidated, Dayton. See separate listing. Tel: 937-866-3021.

Middletown, Butler Co., Holy Family. (This parish is the successor in interest to Holy Trinity, St. John the Baptist and St. Mary parishes, formerly located in Middletown, OH). Rev. John R. Civille; Sr. Jean Sora, O.S.F., Pastoral Assoc. In res., Revs. Charles L. Moore, (Retired); Paul L. Gebhardt; Deacons Thomas Coyle; William Krumm.
Office: 201 Clark St., 45042. Tel: 513-422-0602; Fax: 513-424-7416.
School—John XXIII Consolidated, Middletown. See separate listing. Tel: 513-424-0838; Fax: 513-420-8475.
Catechesis/Religious Programs—Tel: 513-422-0602; Fax: 513-424-7416.
Students 160.

Milford, Clermont Co., St. Andrew, Revs. William C. Wagner; P. Del Staigers.
Res., 552 Main St., 45150. Tel: 513-831-3353; Fax: 513-831-6597.
School—St. Andrew-St. Elizabeth Seton, (Grades K-8). Consolidated. 555 Main St., 45150. Tel: 513-831-5277. Donna J. Beebe, Prin.
Lay Teachers 24; Students 602.
Catechesis/Religious Programs—Tel: 513-831-3812; Fax: 513-831-6597. Barbara Aluotto, D.R.E.
Students 152.

Millville, Butler Co., Queen of Peace, Rev. Kenneth J. Schoettmer; Deacon Bill Brunsman.
Res., 2550 Millville Rd., Hamilton, 45013. Tel: 513-863-4344; Fax: 513-863-4364.
School—Tel: 513-863-8705; Fax: 513-863-4310. Kathleen Daulton, Prin.
Lay Teachers 11; Students 301.
Catechesis/Religious Programs—Students 114.

Minster, Auglaize Co., St. Augustine's, Rev. Thomas R. Brenberger, C.PP.S.; Deacon John J. Schmiesing; Bro. Tim Cahill, C.PP.S., Pastoral Assoc.
Res., 48 N. Hanover St., P.O. Box 93, 45865. Tel: 419-628-2614; Fax: 419-628-1078.
Catechesis/Religious Programs—47 N. Lincoln St., P.O. Box 93, 45865. Tel: 419-628-3434. D.R.E.: Jane Boeke; Kathy Sommer.
Students 770.

Monroe, Butler Co., Our Lady of Sorrows, Rev. John Kroeger.
Res., 416 Lebanon St., 45050. Tel: 513-539-8383.
Catechesis/Religious Programs—330 Lebanon St., 45050. Tel: 513-539-8061. Sr. Bridget Cottle, S.C.N., D.R.E.
Students 85.

Montezuma, Mercer Co., Our Lady of Guadalupe, Rev. Carl A. Wise, C.PP.S., Admin.
Res., P.O. Box 69, 45866. Tel: 419-268-2312.
Catechesis/Religious Programs—Tel: 419-268-2312. Carol Niekamp, D.R.E.
Students 193.

Morrow, Warren Co., St. Philip the Apostle, Rev. Joseph C. Allison.
Res., 944 East U.S. 22-3, 45152. Tel: 513-899-3601; Fax: 513-899-3601.
Catechesis/Religious Programs—Tel: 513-899-3785; Fax: 513-899-2079. Sr. Jane Roberts, S.N.D.deN., D.R.E.
Students 170.

Mount Carmel, Clermont Co., St. Veronica, Rev. Dennis J. Caylor; Sr. Therese Beringer, C.S.J., Pastoral Assoc.
Res., 4473 Mt. Carmel-Tobasco Rd., Cincinnati, 45244. Tel: 513-528-1622; Fax: 513-528-1622.
School—Tel: 513-528-0442; Fax: 513-528-0513. Ms. Kay Hohner Stefanics, Prin.
Sisters 3; Lay Teachers 17; Students 469.
Catechesis/Religious Programs—Students 213.

Mount Orab, Brown Co., St. Michael, Rev. Earl O. Metz.
Res., St. George Church, 109 Elm St., Georgetown, 45121. Tel: 937-378-6829.
Church—220 S. High St., 45154.
Catechesis/Religious Programs—Connie Carroll, D.R.E.
Students 54.

Mount Repose, Clermont Co., St. Elizabeth Ann Seton, Rev. Thomas J. Dennemann.
Res., 5890 Buckwheat Rd., Milford, 45150. Tel: 513-575-0119; Fax: 513-575-1078.
School—5900 Buckwheat Rd., Milford, 45150. Tel: 513-375-0093; Fax: 513-575-1078. Ms. Donna Beebe, Prin.
Lay Teachers 25; Students 550.
Preschool—Tel: 513-575-0093. Mrs. Terri Imming, Dir.
Lay Teachers 8; Students 130.
Catechesis/Religious Programs—Students 290.

New Bremen, Auglaize Co., Holy Redeemer, Rev. R. Daniel Conlon.
Res., 120 S. Eastmoor Dr., 45869. Tel: 419-629-2543.
Catechesis/Religious Programs—Students 495.

New Carlisle, Clark Co., Sacred Heart, Rev. John MacQuarrie; Deacon Robert Kozlowski.
Res., 476 N. Scott St., 45344. Tel: 937-845-3121; Fax: 937-846-1223.
Catechesis/Religious Programs—Tel: 937-845-1373; Fax: 937-846-1223. Joan Steinlage, D.R.E.
Students 225.

New Paris, Preble Co., St. John, Rev. J. Thomas Fitzsimmons.
Res., Visitation, 407 E. Main St., Eaton, 45320. Tel: 937-456-3380.
Catechesis/Religious Programs—Students 40.

Newport, Shelby Co., SS. Peter and Paul, Rev. Donald E. Shelander.
Res., 6788 State Rte. 66, Ft. Loramie, 45845. Tel: 937-295-3001.
Catechesis/Religious Programs—Tel: 937-295-2536. Susan Francis, D.R.E.
Students 180.

New Richmond, Clermont Co., St. Peter, Rev. Theodore C. Kosse.
Res., 1192 Bethel-New Richmond Rd., 45157. Tel: 513-553-3267; Fax: 513-553-4321.
Catechesis/Religious Programs—Sr. Patricia Corbett, C.S.J., D.R.E.
Students 157.

New Vienna, Clinton Co., St. Michael, Rev. Ronald C. Cooper.
Res., St. Benignus, 218 S. Second St., Greenfield, 45123. Tel: 937-981-2785.

North Lewisburg, Champaign Co., Immaculate Conception, Rev. Clarence G. Heis.
Res., 40 Walnut St., Mechanicsburg, 43044. Tel: 937-834-2413.

North Star, Darke Co., St. Louis, Rev. James M. Schmitmeyer.
Parish Office: P.O. Box 9, Osgood, 45351. Tel: 419-582-2531; Fax: 419-582-2531. [CEM]
Catechesis/Religious Programs—Linda Wehrkamp, D.R.E.
Students 193.

Osgood, Darke Co., St. Nicholas, Rev. James M. Schmitmeyer.
Office: 128 Church St., P.O. Box 9, 45351. Tel: 419-582-2531; Fax: 419-582-2531.
Catechesis/Religious Programs—Donna Grieshop, D.R.E.
Students 159.

Owensville, Clermont Co., St. Louis, Rev. John R. Wolbert.
Res., 210 N. Broadway, 45160. Tel: 513-732-2218; Fax: 513-732-1748.
School—250 N. Broadway, 45160. Tel: 513-732-0636; Fax: 513-732-1748. Ms. Mary Lottinville, Prin.
Ursuline Sisters 2; Lay Teachers 12; Students 205.
Catechesis/Religious Programs—Tel: 513-732-2580.
Students 59.

Oxford, Butler Co., St. Mary Church and Catholic Campus Ministry (Miami U.), Rev. Terrance L. Schneider; John V. Kruse, Dir. Campus Min.
Res., 111 E. High St., 45056. Tel: 513-523-2153; Fax: 513-523-0559.

Peebles, Adams Co., St. Mary Queen of Heaven. (Vicariate). Rev. David Glockner, Glmy.
Res., Holy Trinity, 612 E. Mulberry St., West Union, 45693. Tel: 513-544-2757.
Catechesis/Religious Programs—Students 38.

Philothea, Mercer Co., St. Mary's, Rev. Louis J. Barga, C.PP.S.
Res., 3821 Philothea Rd., Coldwater, 45828. Tel: 419-678-2795.
Catechesis/Religious Programs—Esther Homan, D.R.E.
Students 106.

Piqua, Miami Co., St. Boniface, Rev. Rick Unwin.
Res., 310 S. Downing St., 45356. Tel: 937-773-1656; Fax: 937-773-2665. Rev. Angelo C. Caserta Tel: 513-778-9526.
School—Piqua Catholic School, Piqua. (Consolidated) See separate listing. Tel: 937-773-3876.
Catechesis/Religious Programs—Tel: 937-773-0710.
Students 135.

St. Mary, Rev. Francis J. Keferl; Joan Dunn, Pastoral Assoc. In res., Rev. Anselm F. Boeke, (Retired).
Res., 528 Broadway, 45356. Tel: 937-773-1327; Fax: 937-773-2313.
School—Piqua Catholic School, Piqua. See separate listing. Tel: 937-773-1564.
Catechesis/Religious Programs—Tel: 937-778-8770. Helen Metzger, D.R.E.
Students 55.

Princeton, Butler Co., St. Maximilian Kolbe (1989), Rev. John Porter. Pastoral Assocs.: Joan Stoltz; Carol Heuser.
Res., 7168 St. Albans Way, Hamilton, 45011. Tel: 513-777-4322; Fax: 513-777-7264.
Church—5720 Hamilton-Mason Rd., Liberty Township, 45011.
School—St. Gabriel Consolidated School. See separate listing.
Catechesis/Religious Programs—Tel: 513-779-3433.
Students 1,080.

Rhine, Shelby Co., St. Lawrence, Rev. James J. O'Connor.
Res., 16053 Botkins Rd., P.O. Box 519, Botkins, 45306. Tel: 937-693-2561.
Catechesis/Religious Programs—Tel: 937-693-2571.
Students 137.

Ripley, Brown Co., St. Michael, Rev. Thomas F. Feldhaus.
Res., 16 N. Fourth St., 45167. Tel: 937-392-1116.
School—Tel: 937-392-4202. Sr. Rosemary Winkeljohann, O.S.U., Prin.
Sisters 1; Lay Teachers 4; Students 55.
Catechesis/Religious Programs—Tel: 937-392-1335. Joseph P. Shadle, D.R.E.
Students 139.

Rockford, Mercer Co., St. Teresa, Rev. Clement B. Alt, C.PP.S.
Res., 213 S. Franklin St., P.O. Box 445, 45882. Tel: 419-363-2633.
Catechesis/Religious Programs—Tel: 419-363-2327. Alice Provci, D.R.E.
Students 78.

Russells Point, Logan Co., St. Mary of the Woods, Rev. Anthony J. Geraci.
Res., P.O. Box 278, 43348. Tel: 937-843-3127; Fax: 937-843-3866.
Catechesis/Religious Programs—Madison Ave., 43348. Tel: 937-843-4227.
Students 136.

Russia, Shelby Co., St. Remy, Rev. Eugene F. Vonderhaar.
Res., 108 E. Main St., P.O. Box 275, 45363. Tel: 937-526-3437; Fax: 937-526-5326.
Catechesis/Religious Programs—Tel: 937-526-3437. Nancy Luthman, D.R.E.
Students 330.

St. Anthony, Mercer Co., St. Anthony, Rev. John Mencsik, C.PP.S.; Deacon Cletus H. Homan.
Res., 471 St. Anthony Rd., Fort Recovery, 45846. Tel: 419-942-1795. [CEM]
Catechesis/Religious Programs—Tel: 419-942-1795.
Students 104.

St. Henry, Mercer Co., St. Henry, Rev. Larry Wyen, C.PP.S.
Res., Box 301, 272 E. Main St., 45883. Tel: 419-678-4118; Fax: 419-678-8285.
Inter-parish Center—162 S. Walnut, 45883. Tel: 419-678-3811.
Catechesis/Religious Programs—Bro. Thomas Bohman, C.PP.S., D.R.E.
Students 715.

St. Joseph, Mercer Co., St. Joseph 1839 (German), Rev. George Kuzara, C.PP.S.
Res., 1477 Philothea Rd., St. Peter, 45846. Tel: 419-375-4344; Fax: 419-375-4030. [CEM]
Church—1689 St. Joe Rd., Fort Recovery, 45846.

Saint Martin, Brown Co., Saint Martin, Rev. Michael A. Savino.
Res., 746 S. State Rte. 133, Blanchester, 45107. Tel: 937-783-3956; Fax: 937-783-9035. [CEM]
Church—20864 State Rte. 251 N., St. Martin, 45118. Tel: 513-875-2790.
Catechesis/Religious Programs—Terry Brinkman, D.R.E.
Students 95.

St. Marys, Auglaize Co., Holy Rosary, Rev. David A. Heinl. In res., Rev. James O. Byrne.
Res., 511 E. Spring St., 45885. Tel: 419-394-5050.
School—Tel: 419-394-5291. Bruce Ludwig, Prin.
Lay Teachers 18; Students 271.
Catechesis/Religious Programs—Tel: 419-394-5291. Connie Bargdill, D.R.E.
Students 243.

St. Paris, Champaign Co., Sacred Heart, Rev. David L. Zink.
Res., 231 Washington Ave., Urbana, 43078-1728. Tel: 937-653-1375.
Catechesis/Religious Programs—Students 45.

St. Rose, Mercer Co., St. Rose, Rev. Frederick Ryder.
Res., 7428 State Rte. 119, Maria Stein, 45860. Tel: 419-925-4775. [CEM]
Catechesis/Religious Programs—Students 100.

St. Sebastian, Mercer Co., St. Sebastian, Rev. John L. Bensman.
Res., Precious Blood Church, 35 S. Maple St., Box 26, Chickasaw, 45826-0026. Tel: 419-925-4391.
Catechesis/Religious Programs—Nancy Broering, D.R.E.
Students 75.

St. Wendelin, Mercer Co., St. Wendelin, Rev. Milton A. Ballor, C.PP.S.
Res., 517 Meiring Rd., Fort Recovery, 45846. Tel: 419-375-2603.
Catechesis/Religious Programs—Students 77.

Sardinia, Brown Co., St. Elizabeth Parish, Rev. Dohrman W. Byers.
Res., 6647 Van Buren St., Georgetown, 45121. Tel: 937-446-2555; Fax: 937-446-2554.
Church—122 N. Main St., 45171.
Catechesis/Religious Programs—Tel: 937-446-2013.
Students 50.

Shandon, Butler Co., St. Aloysius, Rev. William J. Dorrmann; Deacon Lawrence A. Maag.
Res., P.O. Box 95, 45063. Tel: 513-738-1014; Fax: 513-738-2084.
Catechesis/Religious Programs—Tel: 513-738-4641. Joan Mills, D.R.E.
Students 255.

Sharpsburg, Mercer Co., St. Paul, Rev. Milton A. Ballor, C.PP.S.
Res., 517 Meiring Rd., Fort Recovery, 45846. Tel: 419-375-2603.
Catechesis/Religious Programs—Cleopha Link, D.R.E.
Students 246.

Sidney, Shelby Co., Holy Angels, Revs. Glen W. Perin; David L. Zink; Benedict O'Cinnsealaigh; Deacon Philip Myers.
Res., 324 S. Ohio Ave., 45365. Tel: 937-498-2307.
School—Tel: 937-492-9293; Fax: 937-492-8578. Regina Seubert, Prin.
Lay Teachers 20; Students 484.
Catechesis/Religious Programs—Tel: 937-498-0433. Marianne Dunson, D.R.E.
Students 367.

South Charleston, Clark Co., St. Charles Borromeo, Rev. William V. Thomas.
Res., 31 S. Chillicothe St., P.O. Box F, 45368-0806. Tel: 513-462-8971.
Catechesis/Religious Programs—Tel: 937-462-8077. Denise Federle, D.R.E.
Students 47.

Springfield, Clark Co.,

1—St. Bernard, Rev. Donald C. Huebner.
Res., 910 Lagonda Ave., 45503. Tel: 937-322-5243; Fax: 937-322-3788.
School—800 Lagonda Ave, 45503. Tel: 937-324-4551; Fax: 937-322-3788.
Lay Teachers 11; Students 225.
Catechesis/Religious Programs—Tel: 937-324-2870; Fax: 937-322-3788. Sr. Teresa Noser, O.S.F., D.R.E.
Students 118.

2—St. Joseph, Rev. J. Frederick McGuire.
Res., 802 Kenton St., 45505. Tel: 937-323-8483; Fax: 937-323-8471.
School—Holy Trinity Catholic School, Springfield. See separate listing.
Catechesis/Religious Programs—Tel: 937-327-4057. Sr. Angela Jarboe, D.R.E.
Students 84.

3—St. Mary, Rev. David P. Vincent.
Res., 1027 W. High St., 45506-1398. Tel: 937-322-7272; Fax: 937-322-7272.
School—Holy Trinity Catholic School, Springfield. See separate listing. Tel: 937-322-8781.
Catechesis/Religious Programs—Tel: 937-322-7272. Patricia Evans, D.R.E.
Students 38.

4—St. Raphael, Rev. M. Edmund Hussey; Deacon Norman G. Horstmann.
Res., 225 E. High St., 45505. Tel: 937-323-7523.
School—Holy Trinity Catholic School, Springfield. See separate listing.
Catechesis/Religious Programs—Tel: 937-323-7523.
Students 185.

5—St. Teresa of the Child Jesus, Rev. Richard W. Walling.
Res., 137 Floral Ave., 45504. Tel: 937-399-4339; Fax: 937-399-5451.
School—Tel: 937-399-5451. Mrs. Martha Szczesny, Prin.
Lay Teachers 11; Students 245.
Catechesis/Religious Programs—Tel: 937-399-5451.
Students 65.

Stonelick, Clermont Co., St. Philomena, Rev. John R. Wolbert.
Res., 210 N. Broadway, Box 85, Owensville, 45160. Tel: 513-732-2218; Fax: 513-732-1748. [CEM]

Tipp City, Miami Co., St. John the Baptist, Rev. Thomas A. Dorenbusch.
Res., 218 S. Third St., 45371. Tel: 937-667-3419; Fax: 937-667-9267. [CEM]
Catechesis/Religious Programs—Tel: 937-667-6092. Nelda Schwab, D.R.E.
Students 385.

Trenton, Butler Co., Holy Name, Rev. George W. Klein; Deacon William Martin.
Res., 222 Hamilton Ave., 45067. Tel: 513-988-6335. [CEM]
Catechesis/Religious Programs—Tel: 513-988-9348.
Students 90.

Troy, Miami Co., St. Patrick, Revs. Thomas J. Brunner; Charles B. Rohrkemper; Deacon Michael Knight.
Res., 409 E. Main St., 45373. Tel: 937-335-2833; Fax: 937-335-1453.
School—Tel: 937-339-3705. James O'Leary, Prin.
Lay Teachers 8; Students 177.
Catechesis/Religious Programs—409 E. Main St., 45373. Tel: 937-339-5517.
Students 309.

Twenty Mile Stand, Warren Co., St. Margaret of York, Rev. Thomas W. Kreidler; Deacon Raymond Kroger.
Res., 9483 Columbia Rd., Loveland, 45140. Tel: 513-683-7100; Fax: 513-683-7101.
School—Tel: 513-683-9793. Co-Principals: Sr. Mary Ann Trotta, R.S.M.; Sr. Ann Gorman, R.S.M.
Lay Teachers 27; Students 630.
Catechesis/Religious Programs—Tel: 513-583-0536. Mark Spanyer, D.R.E.
Students 401.

Urbana, Champaign Co., St. Mary, Rev. David L. Zink.
Res., 231 Washington Ave., 43078. Tel: 937-653-1375.
School—Tel: 937-653-1370; Fax: 937-653-1376. Mrs. Karen Berkhofer, Prin.
Lay Teachers 10; Students 128.
Catechesis/Religious Programs—Tel: 937-788-2251.
Students 104.

Vandalia, Montgomery Co., St. Christopher, Rev. Robert J. Monnin.
Res., 435 E. National Rd., 45377. Tel: 937-898-3542; Fax: 937-898-1017.
School—(Grades K-8). Tel: 937-898-5104.
Lay Teachers 13; Students 301.
Catechesis/Religious Programs—Tel: 937-788-2251; Fax: 937-898-1017.
Students 395.

Versailles, Darke Co., St. Denis, Rev. Leo A. Hoying.
Res., 14 E. Wood St., 45380. Tel: 937-526-4945. [CEM]
Catechesis/Religious Programs—D.R.E.: Arlene Niekamp; Judy Pierron.
Students 600.

Wapakoneta, Auglaize Co., St. Joseph, Rev. William A. O'Donnell, C.PP.S. In res., Rev. Dennis Chriszt, C.PP.S.
Res., 309 S. Perry St., 45895. Tel: 419-738-2115; Fax: 419-738-4525. [CEM]
School—1101 Lincoln Hwy., 45895. Tel: 419-738-3311; Fax: 419-738-7706.
Lay Teachers 13; Students 236.
Catechesis/Religious Programs—Tel: 419-738-2115; Fax: 419-738-4525.
Students 370.

Waynesville, Warren Co., St. Augustine, Rev. Raymond Kammerer.
Res., 5715 Lytle Rd., 45068. Tel: 513-897-2821.
Catechesis/Religious Programs—Tel: 937-433-7114. Pat Ebright, D.R.E.
Students 164.

West Chester, Butler Co., St. John, Rev. James W. Meade. In res., Rev. J. Raymond Favret.
Res., 9080 Cincinnati-Dayton Rd., 45069. Tel: 513-777-6433; Fax: 513-777-9741.
Catechesis/Religious Programs—Students 464.

West Milton, Miami Co., Transfiguration, Rev. Thomas J. Grilliot; Deacon Robert Huffman.
Res., 972 S. Miami St., 45383. Tel: 937-698-4520.
Catechesis/Religious Programs—Students 220.

West Union, Adams Co., Holy Trinity, Rev. David Glockner, Glmy. In res., Rev. Robert Berson, Glmy.
Res., 612 E. Mulberry St., 45693. Tel: 937-544-2757.
Catechesis/Religious Programs—Students 55.

Williamsburg, Clermont Co., St. Ann, Rev. William R. Stockelman.
Res., 140 N. Sixth St., Batavia, 45103. Tel: 513-732-2024.
Catechesis/Religious Programs—Tel: 513-732-2024. Patricia Bruce, D.R.E.
Students 25.

Wilmington, Clinton Co., St. Columbkille, Rev. R. Marc Sherlock; Deacons Robert G. Baker; Robert E. Meyer.
Res., 73 N. Mulberry St., 45177-2277. Tel: 937-382-2236; Fax: 937-382-0676, Ext. 2.
Catechesis/Religious Programs—Tel: 937-382-1596. Daniel L. Thomas, D.R.E.
Students 253.

Withamsville, Clermont Co., St. Thomas More, Revs. John P. Fischer; Joseph Bruemmer, (Retired); Francis E. Fritz, (Retired); Deacon Michael E. Metz. Pastoral Assocs.: Sr. Kay Garnett; Mr. Michael Thomas.
Res., 800 Ohio Pike, Cincinnati, 45245. Tel: 513-752-2080, Ext. 10 (Office), Ext. 15 (Pastor); Fax: 513-753-2542.
School—788 Ohio Pike, Cincinnati, 45245. Tel: 513-752-2080, Ext. 22; Fax: 513-753-2542. Mr. Michael Kirry, Prin. & D.R.E.
Lay Teachers 12; Students 241.
Catechesis/Religious Programs—Tel: 513-752-2080, Ext. 23; Fax: 513-753-2542.
Students 191.

Xenia, Greene Co., St. Brigid, Rev. Kennneth Schartz.
Res., 258 Purcell Ave., 45385. Tel: 937-372-3193;

Fax: 937-374-3622. [CEM]
School—Tel: 937-372-3222. Sr. Lois Jean Goettke, Prin.
Sisters 1; Lay Teachers 10; Students 241.
Convent—216 Purcell Ave., 45385. Tel: 937-372-0994. Sisters of Charity of Cincinnati, OH
Catechesis/Religious Programs—Tel: 937-372-3222.
Students 125.

Yellow Springs, Greene Co., St. Paul, Rev. Joseph W. Goetz; Deacon Paul E. Richardson.
Res., 308 Phillips St., 45387. Tel: 937-767-7450; Fax: 937-767-7465.
Catechesis/Religious Programs—Students 110.

Closed and Merged Parishes

Greater Cincinnati

1—COMMUNITY OF HOPE. Consolidated with Holy Family Parish.

2—ST. ELIZABETH CHURCH (Norwood). Merged with Holy Trinity Church (Norwood).

3—ST. GEORGE PARISH & NEWMAN CENTER. Closed. For inquiries for parish records contact St. Monica-St. George Newman Center.

4—ST. MATTHEW CHURCH (Norwood). Merged with Holy Trinity Church (Norwood).

5—OUR LADY OF GRACE (Price Hill). Consolidated with Holy Family Parish.

6—OUR LADY OF LORETTO. Merged with St. Margaret of Cortona.

7—OUR LADY OF PERPETUAL HELP (Sedamsville). Consolidated with Holy Family Parish.

8—OUR LADY OF PRESENTATION. Closed. For inquiries for parish records contact St. Leo the Great, Cincinnati.

9—ST. PATRICK (Northside). Merged with St. Boniface, Cincinnati. See listing for details.

10—STS. PETER AND PAUL CHURCH (Norwood). Merged with Holy Trinity Church (Norwood).

11—ST. RICHARD OF CHICHESTER (College Hill). Merged with St. Therese, the Little Flower, Cincinnati. See listing for details.

12—ST. THOMAS AQUINAS. Closed. For inquiries for parish records contact the Chancery.

13—SAN ANTONIO DI PADOVA (Italian). Refer to St. Bonaventure for details.

Blue Creek, Adams Co., St. Joseph. Closed. For inquiries for parish records contact the Chancery.

Dayton, Montgomery Co., Sacred Heart. Closed. For inquiries for parish records contact Emmanuel, Dayton.

Felicity, Clermont Co., Our Mother of Good Counsel. Closed. For inquiries for parish records contact the Chancery.

Hamilton, Butler Co., St. Mary. Merged. Now known as St. Julie Billiart.
St. Stephen. Merged. Now known as St. Julie Billiart.
St. Veronica. Merged. Now known as St. Julie Billiart.

Middletown, Butler Co., Holy Trinity. Merged. Now known as Holy Family.
St. John the Baptist. Merged. Now known as Holy Family.
St. Mary. Merged. Now known as Holy Family.

New Miami, St. Lawrence. Merged. Now known as St. Julie Billiart, Hamilton.

St. Patrick, Shelby Co., St. Patrick. Closed. For inquiries for parish records contact St. Michael, Fort Loramie.

Vera Cruz, Brown Co., Holy Ghost (Vicariate). Closed. For inquiries for parish records contact St. Patrick, Fayetteville. [CEM]

On Special and Diocesan Assignment:
Reverend Fathers—
DeVore, David G., 520 E. Epworth Ave., Cincinnati, OH 45232
Friedrichs, Paul L., 2702 Jefferson Ave., Cincinnati, OH 45219
Grad, Malcolm, Admin. Asst., Archbishop's Office, 100 E. 8th St., Cincinnati, OH 15202
Guntzelman, Louis J., 10709 Adventure Lane, Cincinnati, OH 45242
Lauer, Albert E., 123 E. 13th St., Cincinnati, OH 45210
Mick, Lawrence E., 3103 Observation Trail, Dayton, OH 45449
Nguyen, Huan Tien, 5440 Moeller Ave., Cincinnati, OH 45212
Rivers, Clarence J., 17 Erkenbrecher Ave., Cincinnati, OH 45220
Seger, Oscar H., 782 Osterloh, Minster, OH 45865
Tensi, Lawrence R., Dir. Worship Office, 100 E. Eighth St., Cincinnati, OH 45202

On Duty Outside the Archdiocese:
Reverend Fathers—
Binzer, Joe, Catholic University of America, Divine Word College, 1025 Michigan Ave., N.E., Washington, DC 20017
Conlon, Edward F., St. Andrew R.C. Church, Grenada, West Indies
Kelly, William T., 4015 Yupon St., Houston, TX 47006-4840
Lemkuhl, David A., Maryknoll Assoc. Program, Maryknoll, NY 10545
Pater, Daniel R., Secretariat of State, Nunciature Apostolic Au Carrie, Vatican City, 00120 Italy
Smith, Edward P., North American College, Vatican City State, 00120 Italy
Umberg, Andrew J., Pontifical College Josephinum, College of Liberal Arts, 7625 N. High St., Columbus, OH 43235-1498
Walsh, James J., NCEA, Seminary Dept., 1077 30th St. N.W., Washington, DC 20007-3852
Wenke, Leonard C., 1001 Spring St. #306, Silver Springs, MD 20910

Military Chaplains:
Reverend Fathers—
Breaker, Donald J., CH MAJ, Office of Post Chaplain, Fort Leonard Wood, MO 65473
Janning, Timothy J., CHC USNR, 3800 Parkview Ln. #26C, Irvine, CA 92715
Kaising, John J., CH COL, 3709 S. George Mason Dr. #608E, Falls Church, VA 22041
Leurck, Raymond J., CH LTC, Chief of Chap., 855 Sunset Blvd., Knob Noster, MO 65336-1700
Niemeier, Dennis, CH MAJ, Office of Post Chaplain, Attn: APUR-FW-CH (Niemeier), 1060 Gaffney 5999, Fort Wainwright, AK 99703-5999
Sunberg, David, CMR 475, Box 462, APO, AE 09036
Whalen, Frank J., CH COL, Installation Staff Chap., 3100 Indiana Ave., Fort Campbell, KY 42223-6202

Leave of Absence:
Reverend Fathers—
Albrecht, G.R. Keith

Retired:
Reverend Monsignors—
Evans, Ferdinand A., 850 Ohio Ave., Englewood, FL 34223. Tel: 813-474-2178
Favret, J. Raymond, St. John Church, 9080 Cincinnati-Dayton Rd., Westchester, OH 45069. Tel: 513-777-6433
Franer, William J., 4124 Settle Rd., Apt. A, Cincinnati, OH 45227. Tel: 513-271-9401
Kennedy, Francis B., 4108 W. 8th St., Cincinnati, OH 45205. Tel: 513-921-5767
Klocker, Henry J., 5440 Moeller Ave., Cincinnati, OH 45212. Tel: 513-631-2913
Vogelpohl, Henry J., 977 Bayley Place Dr., Cincinnati, OH 45233. Tel: 513-347-5566
Whalen, Earl L., 972 Bayley Place Dr., Cinncinnati, OH 45233. Tel: 513-347-5638
Reverend Fathers—
Andres, Joseph P., P.O. Box 54458, Cincinnati, OH 45254. Tel: 513-231-0508
Ballman, Thomas J., 820 Bowen St., Dayton, OH 45410. Tel: 513-253-9132
Bastian, Robert J., 1585 N.W. Washington Blvd., Hamilton, OH 45013. Tel: 513-894-7425
Beckman, Joseph F., 6616 Beechmont Ave., Cincinnati, OH 45230. Tel: 513-624-0554
Behler, Donald, 135 Garfield Pl. #514, Cincinnati, OH 45202. Tel: 513-621-1061
Berning, Cornelius C., St. Margaret Hall, 1960 Madison Rd., Cincinnati, OH 45206
Berning, John B., P.O. Box 4023, St. Petersburg, FL 33731
Bertke, Erwin J., 3680 Warsaw Ave., Cincinnati, OH 45205. Tel: 513-921-0328
Birarelli, Carl A., 4000 E. Fletcher Ave., #G203, Tampa, FL 33613. Tel: 813-979-9205
Boeke, Aloysius B., 33 Elm St., Fort Loramie, OH 45845. Tel: 513-295-2891
Boeke, Anselm F., 528 Broadway, Piqua, OH 45356. Tel: 937-773-1327
Bramlage, Vincent J., 148 Thomas Blvd., Hamilton, OH 45013. Tel: 513-894-7426
Braun, Norbert L., Western Hills Retirement, 6210 Cleves Warsaw Ave., Cincinnati, OH 45224. Tel: 513-467-2752
Brennan, Elmer F., 7283 Kingswood Dr., West Chester, OH 45069. Tel: 513-777-7372
Brinkman, Norbert C., 100 Compton Rd., Cincinnati, OH 45215
Broering, Victor F., 9568 Dry Fork Rd., Harrison, OH 45030. Tel: 513-367-0091
Bruemmer, Joseph A., 1477 Pembridge Dr., Cincinnati, OH 45255. Tel: 513-474-7922
Buerger, Francis J., Schroder Manor Retirement Community, 1302 Millville Ave., Hamilton, OH 45103. Tel: 513-844-6486
Burns, John T., 8843 Carrousel Park Cir. #19, Cincinnati, OH 45251. Tel: 513-385-1032
Buschmiller, Robert J., 3105 Madison Rd., Cincinnati, OH 45209. Tel: 513-871-5757
Byrne, James O., 511 Spring St., St. Marys, OH 45885. Tel: 513-394-5050
Calme, Stephen J., 3630 W. Liberty St., Cincinnati, OH 45205. Tel: 513-471-2464
Caserta, Angelo C., P.O. Box 1636, Piqua, OH 45356. Tel: 937-778-9526
Caserta, Charles W., 133 Douglas, Lewisburg, OH 45338. Tel: 937-962-2500
Cavanaugh, John L., 100 Compton Rd., Cincinnati, OH 45215
Coghlan, John C., 8414 Donna Ln., #8, Cincinnati, OH 45236. Tel: 513-891-4261
Conlon, Edward F., St. Andrew Roman Catholic Church, Grenada, West Indies
DeFrancesco, Albert J., 6059 State Rd., Georgetown, OH 45121. Tel: 513-375-4281
Diegelman, Clarence L., St. Charles Seminary, Carthagena, OH 45822. Tel: 513-925-4516
Drapp, Alfred E., 3797 Summit Glen Dr., Dayton, OH 45449
Evans, Ferdinand A., 950 Ohio Ave., Englewood, FL 34223. Tel: 813-474-9096
Evers, Gerard A., 1044 W. Kemper Rd., Cincinnati, OH 45240. Tel: 513-851-1930
Felix, Bernard J., St. Margaret Hall, 1960 Madison Rd., Cincinnati, OH 45206
Francis, A. Edwin, Dorothy Love Retirement Home, 2500 N. Kuther Rd. #110, Sidney, OH 45365. Tel: 937-497-7271
Fritz, Francis E., 150 Gateway Dr., Milford, OH 45150. Tel: 513-831-2542
Frommeyer, James F., Mallard Core, 1410 Mallard Cove Dr., Sharonville, OH 45246
Geers, Carl J., 325 W. 8th St., Cincinnati, OH 45202. Tel: 513-421-5354
Gratsch, Edward J., 6616 Beechmont Ave., Cincinnati, OH 45230. Tel: 513-232-0631
Gruber, J. Paul, 5403 Bluesky Dr., #6, Cincinnati, OH 45247. Tel: 513-598-1424
Gude, George W., West Park Retirement Community, 2950 West Park Dr., Cincinnati, OH 45238
Hagedorn, Robert L., 808 Schiff Ave. #1, Cincinnati, OH 45205. Tel: 513-921-0379
Haskamp, Edward F., 11080 Montgomery, Cincinnati, OH 45249. Tel: 513-469-9157
Henz, Kenneth W., 1805 John Glenn Rd., Dayton, OH 45420. Tel: 937-253-2829
Heskamp, Joseph C., 7754 Montgomery Rd., Cincinnati, OH 45236. Tel: 513-791-9030
Jaekle, Lawrence E., 24 Catalpa, Versailles, OH 45380. Tel: 937-526-5862
Jennings, John P., 1227 Ebenezer Rd., Cincinnati, OH 45238. Tel: 513-941-0932
Keller, Neil J., 836 N. Hill Ln., Cincinnati, OH 45224. Tel: 513-522-5578
Kenning, Herman H., 60 Compton Rd., Cincinnati, OH 45215. Tel: 513-821-1886
Kesting, Philip A., 2497 Eastern Ave., Cincinnati, OH 45202. Tel: 513-221-7011
Kneipp, August J., Leibold Home, 476 Riddle Rd., Cincinnati, OH 45220. Tel: 513-281-2648
Koegel, Victor C., Parkwood Estates, Lot 150, 2900 Gulf to Bay Blvd., Clearwater, FL 34619
Lawrence, Ralph J., 140 Ewing Dr., #C, Fairfield, OH 45014. Tel: 513-939-2363
Lutmer, Joseph H., 4688 Largo Dr., Cincinnati, OH 45236. Tel: 513-793-9937
Massarella, Francis A., 235 W. Orchard Springs Dr., Dayton, OH 45415. Tel: 937-275-4377
Mauntel, Robert J., 19 Mohave Dr., Sardinia, OH 45171. Tel: 513-446-3491
McWilliam, James J., 6616 Beechmont Ave., Cincinnati, OH 45230. Tel: 513-232-5080
Mick, Lawrence, 1500 Linneman Rd., Cincinnati, OH 45238. Tel: 513-922-5400
Mick, Robert, 3720 St. Martin Pl., Cincinnati, OH 45211
Miller, Francis J., 4988 Lord Alfred Ct., Cincinnati, OH 45241-2196. Tel: 513-247-0966
Minic, John F., 968 Sharewood Ct., Kettering, OH 45429. Tel: 937-299-2747
Moore, Charles L., 3917 Central Ave., Middletown, OH 45044. Tel: 513-423-9692
Mueller, Eugene J., 3525 Burke St., Cincinnati, OH 45241. Tel: 513-563-2640
Niehaus, Francis H., P.O. Box 727, Florence, KY 41042
Noll, Donald T., 2734 E. Towers Dr., #518, Cincinnati, OH 45238. Tel: 513-662-2791

Pater, Thomas G., Catholic University of America, Curley Hall, Washington, DC 20064
Peaker, James N., 5858 Kellogg Ave., Cincinnati, OH 45228. Tel: 513-232-6006
Perryman, John E., 138 Heritage Dr., Urbana, OH 43078. Tel: 937-663-5749
Pilliod, Francis B., 8100 Clyo Rd., Centerville, OH 45458. Tel: 937-237-3522
Plagge, Robert J., 6210 Cleves-Warsaw Pike, Cincinnati, OH 45233. Tel: 513-467-2724
Powers, Alfred J., 2344 N. Limestone #1, Springfield, OH 45503. Tel: 937-399-7757
Poynter, Gail A., 6509 Azure Way, West Carrollton, OH 45449. Tel: 513-438-9001
Putnick, Robert J., West Park Community, 2950 West Park Dr., Cincinnati, OH 45238. Tel: 513-922-2836
Ries, Victor F., 6161 Chambersburg Rd., Dayton, OH 45424. Tel: 937-233-1503
Rohrkemper, Charles B., 109 Freedom Ct., Sidney, OH 45365. Tel: 937-492-3010
Sahlfeld, Francis J., 8 Muirfield Ln., Cincinnati, OH 45241-3257. Tel: 513-891-6852
Schetter, Albert E., 1124 Circle Dr., St. Mary's, OH 45885. Tel: 419-394-8672
Schroeder, William L., 7432 Tower View, Cincinnati, OH 45255. Tel: 513-232-3074
Schutte, Robert W., 100 Compton Rd., Cincinnati, OH 45215. Tel: 513-821-8843
Steinbicker, Carl R., 3636 Semloh Ave., Cincinnati, OH 45247. Tel: 513-923-3816
Stricker, Robert A., 5560 Kirby Rd., Cincinnati, OH 45239. Tel: 513-541-5560
Suver, Robert J., 8100 Clyo Rd., Centerville, OH 45458. Tel: 937-434-1312
Thorsen, Robert J., 5002 Lord Alfred Ct., Cincinnati, OH 45241. Tel: 513-469-0921
Trippel, Edward G., 3547 Clifton Ave., Cincinnati, OH 45220. Tel: 513-861-1295
Urbain, Joseph V., 2692 Enterprise Rd., E. #1303, Clearwater, FL 34619. Tel: 813-799-2546
Wiemeyer, Raymond G., 5367 Julmar Dr., Cincinnati, OH 45238. Tel: 513-922-2791
Will, Carl G., 8731 Washington Colony Dr., Centerville, OH 45459. Tel: 937-438-9583
Williams, Edward T., 2731 E. Towers Dr., #410, Cincinnati, OH 45238. Tel: 513-661-2861
Wintermeyer, William P., 1080-A Wittshire Ln., Cincinnati, OH 45255
Wolfer, Paul J., 2832 Rosebud Dr., Cincinnati, OH 45238. Tel: 513-922-0715
Wolfer, Robert R., 2832 Rosebud Dr., Cincinnati, OH 45238. Tel: 513-922-0715
Zugelter, Alvin T., 135 Garfield Dr., Cincinnati, OH 45202. Tel: 513-684-9492

Permanent Deacons:
Arber, Alan W., St. Henry, Dayton
Ascolese, Michael A., Our Mother of Sorrows, Cincinnati
Aufderheide, William, St. Margaret of Cortona, Cincinnati
Baker, Robert, St. Columbkille, Wilmington
Baltes, Leonard W., St. Charles, Kettering
Barney, Gerald L., St. Susanna, Mason
Beck, Henry B., Our Lady of the Rosary, Dayton
Bensman, Werner, SS. Peter & Paul, Newport; St. Michael, Ft. Laramie
Bermick, Stephen C., III, St. Albert the Great, Kettering
Bertke, Omer H., St. John the Baptist, Maria Stein
Blum, Raymond, St. Albert the Great, Dayton
Borgerding, Robert H., St. Peter, Dayton
Brockmann, C. Edward, St. William, Cincinnati
Brodeur, Wilfred J., Unassigned
Brunner, Mark E., St. Ann, Hamilton
Brunsman, Willard, Queen of Peace, Millville
Bryant, Herman, St. Gabriel, Cincinnati
Burger, Raymond S., St. Margaret Mary, Cincinnati
Cain, Jerome J., St. Saviour, Cincinnati
Camele, David G., (Retired)
Cecere, Gregory, Unassigned
Childers, David E., Holy Family, Cincinnati
Coll, Joseph J., St. Columban, Loveland
Coomes, Gerald L., St. Vivian, Cincinnati
Cooper, John H., St. James, Wyoming
Cotterman, Eldon, Holy Angels, Dayton
Couzins, Jerome, Unassigned
Coyle, Thomas J., Holy Family, Middletown
Davenport, Michael D., St. Teresa of Avila, Cincinnati
Dawson, David A., Holy Trinity, West Union
Deardorff, Roy L., St. Helen, Dayton
Dehmer, William A., Our Lady of Visitation, Cincinnati
Dipple, Harold I., St. Patrick, Bellefontaine
Fischesser, Elmer, New Jerusalem Community, Cincinnati
Franzer, Carl C., St. John the Baptist, Maria Stein
Gargan, Thomas, St. Catharine, Cincinnati
George, Raymond W., St. Matthias, Cincinnati
Geraci, James L., Our Lady of the Sacred Heart, Reading
Gingras, John J., Corpus Christi, New Burlington
Glassmeyer, Robert A., Our Lady of the Sacred Heart, Reading
Glynn, John T., Unassigned
Gobbi, John R., St. John Neumann, Cincinnati
Haas, Frederick J., Unassigned
Hennessey, James F., Holy Trinity, Batavia
Homan, Cletus H., St. Anthony, Ft. Recovery
Horstman, Norman G., St. Raphael, Springfield
Huber, Robert, Unassigned
Huff, Thomas, Immaculate Conception, Celina
Huffman, Robert J., Transfiguration, West Milton
Jachimowicz, John J., St. Helen, Dayton
James, Joseph, Visitation, Eaton
Janowiecki, Richard J., Precious Blood, Dayton
Jenkins, Charles J., Our Lady of Victory, Cincinnati
Jernigan, Jacob, Resurrection, Dayton
Keller, David R., St. Clement, Cincinnati
Kelly, George J., (Retired)
Kiley, Thomas M., St. John Neumann, Cincinnati
Kluener, Paul J., St. James, White Oak
Kowalski, James, Unassigned
Kozlowski, Robert R., St. Adalbert, Dayton
Kraus, Daniel E., Immaculate Conception, Dayton
Kroger, Raymond, St. Margaret of York, Twenty Mile Stand
Kronenberger, Arthur, Immaculate Conception, Dayton
Krumm, William T., Holy Family, Middletown
Maag, Lawrence A., St. Aloysius, Shanoon
Martin, William, Holy Name, Trenton
Mascorro, Susano, St. Helen, Dayton
McCormick, James S., St. Julie Billiart, Hamilton
Merritt, James A., Unassigned
Metz, Michael, St. Thomas More, Withamsville
Meyer, Robert E., St. Columbkille, Wilmington
Michael, William R., St. Vivian, Cincinnati
Miller, Allen K., St. Peter, Dayton
Miller, Eugene M., Immaculate Heart of Mary, Cincinnati
Miller, James A., St. Columban, Loveland
Montgomery, Michael, O.F.M., St. Francis of Assisi, Centerville
Murphy, Robert D., St. Maximilian Kolbe, Hamilton
Myers, Philip B., Holy Angels, Sidney
Novick, Rick, Guardian Angels, Cincinnati
Orlando, Vincent, Immaculate Conception, Dayton.
Ostendorf, Edward B., St. Francis de Sales, Lebanon
Parker, John G., Mary, Help of Christians, Fort Recovery
Perry, Robert, Our Lady, Queen of Peace, Wright Patterson Air Force Base
Perryman, Clifton, St. Augustine, Minster
Petrie, William J., St. Antoninus, Cincinnati
Platfoot, Thomas F., Our Lady of Mercy, Dayton
Rader, Daniel L., St. Susanna, Mason
Reeves, Paul S., Unassigned
Rekers, Louis J., St. James, Wyoming
Renneker, William B., St. Julie Billiart, Hamilton
Richardson, Paul E., St. Paul, Yellow Springs
Riva-Saleta, Luis O., St. Ignatius, Cincinnati
Roadruck, Max, Mary Help of Christians, Fairborn
Royer, Milton W., Corpus Christi, Dayton
Runnels, Arthur, St. Charles Borromeo, Carthage; St. Aloysius, Elmwood Place
Saluke, William M., St. Mary, Dayton
Schmidt, Joseph Ted, St. Boniface, Cincinnati
Schmiesing, John J., St. Augustine, Minster
Schneider, Jerry R., Unassigned
Schroeder, Robert J., St. Antoninus, Cincinnati
Schultheis, Joseph R., Our Lady of Victory, Cincinnati
Simmons, Raphael, St. Joseph, Cincinnati
Slattery, John M., St. Cecilia, Cincinnati
Sonnenberg, James J., Immaculate Heart of Mary, Cincinnati
Sprinkle, Joseph, Our Lady of Good Hope, Miamisburg
Stevenson, William, Holy Family, Dayton
Steward, Herschel R., St. Francis De Sales, Lebanon
Subler, Joseph, St. Paul, Englewood
Sunderman, James P., St. Jude the Apostle, Cincinnati
Taylor, John, St. Francis de Sales, Lebanon
Thamann, John D., St. Mary, Cincinnati
Vilaboy, Manuel D., Spanish Community, Cincinnati
Wakefield, W. Bill, Guardian Angels, Cincinnati
Waldbillig, Urban J., Unassigned
Walker, Harry S., Our Lady of the Rosary, Cincinnati
Wallace, Forrest, Unassigned
Weitzel, Paul J., St. Teresa, Springfield
Wersching, J. Phillip, Holy Angels, Cincinnati
Westerfield, Thomas E., Our Lady of Lourdes, Cincinnati
Wiene, Howard R., Unassigned
Woeste, James H., Unassigned
Zinck, Robert C., Jr., Incarnation, Centerville
Zvonar, George J., St. Christopher, Vandalia

INSTITUTIONS LOCATED IN THE ARCHDIOCESE

[A] THE ATHENAEUM OF OHIO

CINCINNATI. *The Athenaeum of Ohio*, Mt. St. Mary's Seminary, 6616 Beechmont Ave., 45230. Tel: 513-231-2223. Most Rev. Daniel E. Pilarczyk, D.D., Archbishop of Cincinnati, Chancellor, Chm. of Bd. of Trustees; Rev. Gerald R. Haemmmerle, M.A.; Dr. Terrance D. Callan, Ph.D., Dean, Athenaeum of Ohio; Mr. Dennis K. Eagan, B.B.A., Bus. Mgr. It was incorporated March 24, 1928 by the State of Ohio and presently has three divisions: Mt. St. Mary's Seminary of the West; the Lay Pastoral Ministry Program and the Special Studies Division.

Lay Pastoral Ministry Program, 6616 Beechmont Ave., 45230. Tel: 513-231-1200. Ms. Mary Sue O'Donnell, M.A.R., Dir.; Ms. Judith Ebbeler, M.A., Assoc. Dir.; Sr. Nancy McMullen, C.PP.S., Program Coord.; Sr. Susan Keferl, S.N.D.deN., M.A., Assoc. Dir.

The St. Gregory Seminary Trust, 100 E. Eighth St., 45202.

[B] SEMINARIES

CINCINNATI. *Mt. St. Mary's Seminary of the West.* (Diocesan), 6616 Beechmont Ave., 45230. Tel: 513-231-2223; Fax: 513-231-3254.
E-mail: ath@mtsm.org
Major seminary for students in Theology. Rev. Gerald R. Haemmerle, M.A., Rector; Dr. Terrance D. Callan, Ph.D., Athenaeum Academic Dean; Revs. Richard A. Marzheuser, S.T.D., Seminary Dean; Raymond P. Aichele, M.R.E., Dir. Formation; Sr. Susan Keferl, S.N.D., M.A., Dir. Field Education Prog.; Rev. Michael A. Savino, M.Div., Dir. of Pastoral Internship; Mr. Michael E. Sweeney, M.A., Registrar; Dennis K. Eagan, B.B.A., Business Mgr.; John Gutting, Ph.D., Dir. Pastoral Counseling Degree. In res. Most Rev. Carl K. Moeddel; Revs. Raymond P. Aichele, M.R.E.; Gerald R. Haemmerle, M.A.; James M. Daprile, M.A.; Jeffrey M. Kemper, Ph.D.; Richard A. Marzheuser, S.T.D.; Timothy P. Schehr, Ph.D.; Michael Seger, S.T.D.; P. Del Staigers, M.A. Non-Resident Faculty: Mr. Terrance Callan, Ph.D.; Mr. Anthony Dicello, M.M.; Sr. Barbara Fiand, Ph.D.; John Gutting, Ph.D.; Sr. Deborah Harmeling, M.S.L.; Sr. Betty Jane Lillie, Ph.D. In res. Revs. Joseph Beckman; Edward J. Gratsch; James J. McWilliam.

CARTHAGENA. *St. Charles*, Society of the Precious Blood, 45822. Tel: 419-925-4516. Revs. William Eilerman, C.PP.S., Dir.; Joseph Anthamatten, C.PP.S.; John Benen, C.PP.S.; Casper Bonifas, C.PP.S.; John Bosch, C.PP.S.; Robert Conway, C.PP.S.; Leonard Fullenkamp, C.PP.S.; Robert Gaertner, C.PP.S.; Benedict D'Angelo, C.PP.S.; Clarence L. Diegelman; Harold Diller, C.PP.S.; William Donohoe, C.PP.S.; Mark Dorenkemper, C.PP.S.; William Dougherty, C.PP.S.; Urban Dumminger, C.PP.S.; Richard Elo, C.PP.S.; Cornelius Fenton, C.PP.S.; Aloys Friedrich, C.PP.S.; Anthony Gamble, C.PP.S.; Leo Gaulrapp, C.PP.S.; Raymond Grevencamp, C.PP.S.; Joseph Hajduch, C.PP.S.; Augustine Hanchak, C.PP.S.; Florian Hartke, C.PP.S.; Ambrose Heimann, C.PP.S.; John Jadgchew, C.PP.S.; Alphonse Jungwirth, C.PP.S.; Edgar Jutte, C.PP.S.; James Kelley, C.PP.S.; Gerold Koller, C.PP.S.; Clement Kuhns, C.PP.S.; Henry Langhals, C.PP.S.; Robert Lechner, C.PP.S.; John Lefko, C.PP.S.; Ambrose R. Lengerich, C.PP.S.; Joseph Lima, C.PP.S.; Carl Longanback, C.PP.S.; Arnold Meiring, C.PP.S.; Bernard Meiring, C.PP.S.; Charles Meyer, C.PP.S.; James Miller, C.PP.S.; Othmar Missler, C.PP.S.; Alfred Naseman, C.PP.S.; Daniel Raible, C.PP.S.; Ambrose Ruschau, C.PP.S.; Vincent Schuster, C.PP.S.; Raymond Seifert, C.PP.S.; Robert Siebeneck, C.PP.S.; Joseph Smolar, C.PP.S.; John Spatt, C.PP.S.; Leonard Sudhoff, C.PP.S.; Anthony Traser, C.PP.S.; Hugh Ulrich, C.PP.S.; William Volk, C.PP.S.; Bro. Gerald Hall, C.PP.S., Treas. Priests 53; Brothers 17; Sisters 4.

[C] NOVITIATES AND HOUSES OF STUDY

CINCINNATI. *Dominican Novitiate*, 7630 Shawnee Run Rd., 45243. Tel: 513-527-3972; Fax: 513-527-3973.
E-mail: burnsop@juno.com
Rev. Joseph Clement Burns, O.P., Novice Master. Novices 7.

St. Anthony Shrine, Francisan Candidacy, St. John the Baptist Province, 5000 Colerain Ave., 45223. Tel: 513-541-2146; Fax: 513-541-9347. Revs. Clyde Young, O.F.M., Vicar; Dennis Bosse, O.F.M., Instructor; Varian Slacke, O.F.M., (Retired); Kenan Freson, O.F.M., Prov. Treas.; Frank Geers, O.F.M., Dir. of Candidates; Bros. Gabriel Balassone, O.F.M.; Vincent Delorenzo, O.F.M., Guardian; Scott Obrecht, O.F.M.; Donald Rewers, O.F.M. Priests 5; Brothers 4; Candidates 1.

DAYTON. *Marianist Novitiate*, 4435 E. Patterson Rd., 45430-1095. Tel: 937-426-5721. Rev. Theodore K. Cassidy, S.M., Dir. Novices; Bro. Steven P. O'Neil, S.M., Asst. Dir. Novices. Priests 2; Brothers 9.

[D] COLLEGES AND UNIVERSITIES

CINCINNATI. *College of Mount St. Joseph*, 5701 Delhi Rd., 45233-1670. Tel: 513-244-4200.
E-mail: greggrady@mail.msj.edu
Web site: www.msj.edu
For a complete listing, refer to the Colleges and Universities section.

Xavier University, 3800 Victory Pkwy. at Dana Ave., 45207. Tel: 513-745-3000
For a complete listing, refer to the Colleges and Universities section.

DAYTON. *The University of Dayton*, (1850) 300 College Park Ave., 45469-1624. Tel: 937-229-1000.
Web site: www.udayton.edu
For a complete listing, refer to the Colleges and Universities section.

SAINT MARTIN. *Chatfield College*, Brown County Ursulines, 20918 State Rte. 251, 45118. Tel: 937-875-3344; Fax: 937-875-3912
For a complete listing, refer to the Colleges and Universities section.

[E] HIGH SCHOOLS, INTER-PAROCHIAL

CINCINNATI. *Elder High School*, 3900 Vincent Ave., 45205-1699. Tel: 513-921-3744.
Web site: www.elderhs.org
Revs. James G. Kiffmeyer; Donald R. Rettig. Priests 2; Lay Teachers 61; Students 1,023.

LaSalle High School, 3091 N. Bend Rd., 45239-7696. Tel: 513-741-3000; Fax: 513-741-2666.
Web site: www.HCCA.ohio.GOU/LASALLE
Mr. John M. Strathern, Prin. Lay Teachers 50; Students 950.

McAuley High School, 6000 Oakwood Ave., 45224. Tel: 513-681-1800.
E-mail: sucher-c@hccai.hcca.ohio.gov
Mrs. Cheryl A. Sucher, Prin.; Mrs. Connie Kampschmidt, Asst. Prin. Sisters of Mercy 2; Lay Teachers 64; Girls 978. Convents, 1768 Cedar Ave. 5925 Oakwood Ave. 5764 Belmont Ave., 45224.

McNicholas High School, 6536 Beechmont Ave., 45230. Tel: 513-231-3500. Sisters of St. Joseph of Medaille (Cincinnati Prov.). Mr. Jerome P. Couzins, Prin. Priests 1; Lay Teachers 59; Students 854.

Moeller High School, 9001 Montgomery Rd., 45242. Tel: 513-791-1680.
E-mail: bbalbach@moeller.org
Web site: www.moeller.org
Mr. Daniel J. Ledford, Prin.; Rev. Michael F. Leshney. Sisters of Mercy 1; Diocesan Priest 1; Brothers 7; Lay Teachers 50; Students 900.

Mother of Mercy High School, 3036 Werk Rd., 45211. Tel: 513-661-2740. Sr. Nancy Merkle, R.S.M., Prin. Priests 1; Sisters of Mercy 2; Lay Teachers 54; Girls 636.

Mt. Notre Dame High School, 711 E. Columbia Ave., 45215. Tel: 513-821-3044; Fax: 513-821-6068. Mrs. Maureen Baldock, Prin. Sisters 4; Lay Teachers 56; Girls 712.

Purcell Marian High School. (Walnut Hills), 2935 Hackberry St., 45206. Tel:.513-751-1230.
Web site: www.rcch.com/pmhs
Janis M. Rich, Prin.; Brenda Pfeiffer, Business Mgr.; Mr. David Campbell, Dir. Ministry. Priests 1; Brothers 3; Sisters 1; Lay Teachers 55; Students 740.

Roger Bacon High School, 4320 Vine St., 45217. Tel: 513-641-1300; Fax: 513-641-0498.
E-mail: bosse_r@hcca.ohio.gov
Web site: www.w3.one.net/~sputnik/spartans
Franciscan Friars of the Cincinnati Province of St. John the Baptist. Revs. Roger Bosse, O.F.M., Prin.; Patrick McCloskey, O.F.M., Chap., Teacher; Dennis Bosse, O.F.M., Student Activity Dir., Teacher; Bros. Christopher Cahill, O.F.M., Computer Network Coordinator; Conrad Rebmann, O.F.M., Community Svcs. Coord. Priests 3; Brothers 2; Sisters 3; Lay Teachers 53; Students 880.

Seton High School. (Price Hill), 3901 Glenway Ave., 45205. Tel: 513-471-2600; Fax: 513-471-0529. Ms. Susan M. Gibbons, Prin.; Ms. Jane Acra, Assoc. Prin. of Academics; Mr. Thomas E. McKiernan, Assoc. Prin.-Treas. Priests 1; Sisters of Charity of Cincinnati 8; Lay Teachers 25; Students 706.

DAYTON. *Archbishop Alter High School*, 940 E. David Rd., 45429. Tel: 937-434-4434. Ms. Katherine Beimesche, Prin. Sisters 2; Lay Teachers 51; Students 746.

Carroll High School, 4524 Linden Ave., 45432. Tel: 513-253-8188. Mr. Joseph R. Sens, Prin. Sisters 2; Lay Teachers 58; Students 1,145.

Chaminade-Julienne High School, 505 S. Ludlow St., 45402. Tel: 937-461-3740.
E-mail: aoccj@connectinc.com
Web site: www.udayton.cdu/cj/
Conducted by the Society of Mary (Marianists) and Sisters of Notre Dame de Namur. Mr. Lorcan Barnes, Pres.; Bro. Edward Brink, S.M., Prin.; Mrs. Patsy Puterbaugh, Asst. Prin. for Student Svcs.; Mrs. Shirley Kuchta, Asst. Prin. for Academics; Mr. Matt Ernst, Dir. Admin. Svcs.; Rev. Christopher Wittman, S.M., Dir. Pastoral Svcs.; Sr. Damienne Grismer, S.N.D.deN. Priests 2; Brothers 3; Sisters 5; Lay Teachers 70; Students 920.

HAMILTON. *Stephen T. Badin High School*, 571 New London Rd., 45013. Tel: 513-863-3993. Ms. Margaret R. Winkeljohn, Prin.; Rev. Jeffrey Fulmer. Priests 1; Lay Teachers 46; Students 774.

MIDDLETOWN. *Bishop Fenwick High School*, 3800 Manchester Rd., 45042. Tel: 513-423-0723; Fax: 513-420-8690.
E-mail: c1_birck@swoca.ohio.gov
Revs. Charles E. Mentrup, Prin.; Paul L. Gebhardt. Priests 2; Deacons 1; Lay Teachers 25; Students 372.

SIDNEY. *Lehman High School*, 2400 St. Mary's Ave., 45365. Tel: 937-498-1161; Fax: 937-492-3911.
E-mail: 1c_001@k.12.woco.ohio.gov
Mr. Michael Barhorst, Prin. Sisters 1; Lay Teachers 26; Students 380.

SPRINGFIELD. *Catholic Central High School*, 1200 E. High St., 45505-1124. Tel: 937-325-9204.
E-mail: tlaengle@cd.pvt.klz.oh.us
Sr. Teresa Marie Laengle, S.C., Prin. Sisters 2; Lay Teachers 26; Students 350.

[F] HIGH SCHOOLS, PRIVATE

CINCINNATI. *St. Ursula Academy High School*, 1339 E. McMillan St., 45206. Tel: 513-961-3410; Fax: 513-961-3856. Francis Romweber, Prin. Lay Teachers 46; Girls 511.

St. Xavier High School, 600 N. Bend Rd., 45224. Tel: 513-761-7600. Mr. David B. Mueller, Prin.; Rev. William L. Verbryke, S.J., Pres.; Mr. William Sandquist, Jr., Asst. Prin.; Revs. John J. Beckman, S.J.; J. Paul O'Brien, S.J.; Edward L. Pigott, S.J., Rector; Francis Daly, S.J., Rector. Priests 4; Sisters 1; Scholastics 3; Lay Teachers 97; Students 1,408.

Summit Country Day School. (Grades PreK-12), 2161 Grandin Rd., 45208-3300. Tel: 513-871-4700; Fax: 513-533-5373. Mr. Edward C. Tyrrell, Headmaster and Pres. Lay Teachers 121; Students 1,028.

Ursuline Academy of Cincinnati. Senior High School. 5535 Pfeiffer Rd., 45242. Tel: 513-791-5791. Ursuline Sisters of Brown Co. Saint Martin, OH. Rev. John E. Wessling; Mrs. Shirley G. Speaks, Exec. Dir. Priests 1; Sisters 4; Lay Teachers 66; Girls 646.

[G] CONSOLIDATED ELEMENTARY SCHOOLS

CINCINNATI. *Corryville Catholic Elementary School*, 108 Calhoun St., 45219. Tel: 513-281-4856. Sr. Marie Smith, S.N.D., Prin. Sisters 5; Lay Teachers 8; Students 178.
Consolidated school serving the parishes of St. George, St. Monica, Holy Name, St. Andrew, Assumption and Sacred Heart.

St. Bartholomew. (Grades K-8), 9375 Winton Rd., 45231. Tel: 513-521-0860.
E-mail: crowe_a@hcca.ohio.gov
Mrs. Anne Crowe, Prin.; Mrs. Sally Hicks, Asst. Prin. Lay Teachers 33; Students 740.
Consolidated school serving the parishes of St. Bartholomew, Corpus Christi and St. John Neumann, Cincinnati.

St. Boniface School, 4305 Pitts Ave., 45223. Tel: 513-541-5122; Fax: 513-541-3939. Sr. Joanne Geis, S.C., Prin. Sisters 2; Lay Teachers 8; Students 220.
Serving the parishes of St. Boniface and St. Leo, Cincinnati.

St. Gabriel. (Grades K-8), 18 W. Sharon Ave., 45246. Tel: 513-771-5220.
E-mail: @hccai.hcca.ohio.gov
Florence Edelmann, Prin. Lay Teachers 17; Students 393.
Consolidated school serving the parishes of St. Gabriel, Glendale; St. John, West Chester; St. Martin de Porres, Lincoln Heights; St. Matthias, Forest Park; St. Maximilian Kolbe, West Chester.

DAYTON. *Bishop Leibold School*. West Campus: (Grades K-3), 24 S. Third St., 45342. Tel: 937-866-3021. East Campus: (Grades 4-8), 6666 Springboro Rd., 45449. Tel: 937-434-9343. Mr. Charles Lanasa, Prin. Lay Teachers 24; Students 535.
Serving the Parishes of St. Henry, Dayton and Our Lady of Good Hope, Miamisburg.

Dayton Catholic Elementary School. (Grades K-8), 3805 King's Hwy., 45406. Tel: 937-275-8114. Mrs. Karyn J. Hecker, Prin. Lay Teachers 12; Students 247.
Serving the parishes of St. Agnes, Assumption and St. James, Dayton.

HAMILTON. *St. Joseph Consolidated School*. (Grades K-8), 925 S. Second St., 45011. Tel: 513-863-8758; Fax: 513-863-5253. Dr. Gail Kist-Kline, Prin. Lay Teachers 11; Students 191.
Serving the parishes of St. Aloysius, Shandon and St. Joseph, Hamilton.

MIDDLETOWN. *John XXIII Elementary School*. (Grades K-5). East Campus: 3907 Central Ave., 45044. Tel: 513-424-0838. North Campus: (Grades 6-8), 3806 Manchester Rd., 45042. Tel: 513-424-1196. Sr. Nancy Krista, S.N.D., Prin. Sisters 2; Lay Teachers 22; Students 473.
Serving the parishes of Holy Family, Middletown and St. Mary, Franklin.

PIQUA. *Piqua Catholic School*. North St. Campus: (Grades 4-8), 503 W. North St., 45356. Tel: 937-773-1564. Downing St. Campus: (Grades K-3), 218 S. Downing St., 45356. Tel: 937-773-3876. Mr. David Skelton, Prin. Lay Teachers 23; Students 480.
Serving the parishes of St. Boniface and St. Mary.

SPRINGFIELD. *Holy Trinity Catholic School*. (Grades K-8), 1035 W. High St., 45506. Tel: 937-322-8781. Sr. Sharon Blank, Prin. Lay Teachers 11; Students 230.
Serving the parishes of St. Joseph, St. Mary and St. Raphael.

[H] ELEMENTARY SCHOOLS, PRIVATE

CINCINNATI. *St. Ursula Villa*. (Grades PreK-8), 3660 Vineyard Pl., 45226. Tel: 513-871-7218. Mr. Paul Loechle. Sisters 2; Lay Teachers 33; Students 505.

Summit Country Day School. (Grades PreK-12), 2161 Grandin Rd., 45208-3300. Tel: 513-871-4700; Fax: 513-533-5373. Edward C. Tyrrell, Headmaster and Pres. Lay Teachers 121; Students 1,028.

[I] CHILD CARE INSTITUTIONS

CINCINNATI. *St. Aloysius Orphanage*, 4721 Reading Rd., 45237. Tel: 513-242-7600; Fax: 513-242-2845
For a complete listing, refer to the Special Care Facilities section.

St. Joseph Infant and Maternity Home dba St. Joseph Home, 10722 Wyscarver Rd., 45241. Tel: 513-563-2520
For a complete listing, refer to the Special Care Facilities section.

St. Joseph Orphanage, 5400 Edalbert, 45239
For a complete listing, refer to the Special Care Facilities section.

[J] SPECIAL SCHOOLS

CINCINNATI. *St. Rita School for the Deaf*, 1720 Glendale-Milford Rd., 45215. Tel: 513-771-7600. Mr. Gregroy R. Ernst, Supt.; Mr. Martin Keller, Prin.; Mr. Peter Keller, Dir. of Student Life; Ms. Mary Ann Stansfield, Dir. Special Svcs.; Rev. William H. Wysong. Sisters of Charity 3; Lay Teachers 35; High School Students 41; Elementary Students 83; Pre-School 36. Residential and day school for deaf and hard of hearing children.

[K] GENERAL HOSPITALS

CINCINNATI. *Franciscan Hospital, Mt. Airy Campus*, 2446 Kipling Ave., 45239. Tel: 513-853-5000
For a complete listing, refer to the Hospitals section.

Franciscan Hospital, Western Hills Campus, 3131 Queen City Ave., 45238. Tel: 513-389-5000
For a complete listing, refer to the Hospitals section.

Good Samaritan Hospital, 375 Dixmyth Ave., 45220. Tel: 513-872-1400; Fax: 513-872-3435
For a complete listing, refer to the Hospitals section.

Mercy Hospital Anderson, 7500 State Rd., 45255. Tel: 513-624-4500
For a complete listing, refer to the Hospitals section.

BATAVIA. *Clermont Mercy Hospital*, 3000 Hospital Dr., 45103. Tel: 513-732-8200
For a complete listing, refer to the Hospitals section.

DAYTON. *Franciscan Medical Center - Dayton Campus*, One Franciscan Way, 45408. Tel: 513-229-6000
For a complete listing, refer to the Hospitals section.

Good Samaritan Hospital, 2222 Philadelphia Dr., 45406. Tel: 937-278-2612
For a complete listing, refer to the Hospitals section.

FAIRFIELD. *Mercy Ambulatory Surgery Center*, 2990 Mack Rd., 45014. Tel: 513-874-6440
For a complete listing, refer to the Hospitals section.

HAMILTON. *Mercy Hospital of Hamilton-Fairfield*, 100 Riverfront Plaza, P.O. Box 418, 45011. Tel: 513-867-6400; Fax: 513-867-9043
For a complete listing, refer to the Hospitals section.

SPRINGFIELD. *Mercy Medical Center*, 1343 N. Fountain Blvd., 45501-1380. Tel: 937-390-5000; Fax: 937-890-5507
For a complete listing, refer to the Hospitals section.

URBANA. *Mercy Memorial Hospital*, 904 Scioto St., 43078. Tel: 937-653-5231
For a complete listing, refer to the Hospitals section.

[L] SENIOR RESIDENCES

CINCINNATI. *Archbishop Leibold Home for the Aged*, 476 Riddle Rd., 45220-2493. Tel: 513-281-8001
For a complete listing, refer to the Special Care Facilities section.

The Franciscan at St. Clare, 100 Compton Rd., 45215. Tel: 513-761-9036
For a complete listing, refer to the Special Care Facilities section.

The Franciscan at West Park, 2950 West Park Dr., 45238. Tel: 513-451-8900
For a complete listing, refer to the Special Care Facilities section.

Mercy St. Theresa Center, 7010 Rowan Hill Dr., Ste. 200, 45227. Tel: 513-271-7010; Fax: 513-527-0181
For a complete listing, refer to the Special Care Facilities section.

St. Margaret Hall, 1960 Madison Rd., 45206-1896. Tel: 513-751-5880; Fax: 513-751-9813
For a complete listing, refer to the Special Care Facilities section.

Sisters of Charity Senior Care Corp., dba Bayley Place, 990 Bayley Place Dr., 45233. Tel: 513-347-5500; Fax: 513-347-5553
For a complete listing, refer to the Special Care Facilities section.

CENTERVILLE. *The Franciscan at St. Leonard*, 8100 Clyo Rd., 45458. Tel: 937-433-0480
For a complete listing, refer to the Special Care Facilities section.

DAYTON. *The Maria Joseph Living Care Center*, 4830 Salem Ave., 45416. Tel: 937-278-2692; Fax: 937-278-9016
For a complete listing, refer to the Special Care Facilities section.

Mercy Siena Woods, 235 W. Orchard Springs Dr., 45415. Tel: 937-278-8211; Fax: 937-278-8046.
E-mail: shayes@erinet.com
For a complete listing, refer to the Special Care Facilities section.

Siena Springs, 6215 N. Main St., 45415. Tel: 937-274-4790
For a complete listing, refer to the Special Care Facilities section.

HAMILTON. *The Franciscan at Schroder*, 1302 Millville Ave., 45013. Tel: 513-867-1300; Fax: 513-867-1415
For a complete listing, refer to the Special Care Facilities section.

SPRINGFIELD. *Oakwood Village Retirement Community*, 1500 Villa Rd., 45503. Tel: 937-390-9000; Fax: 937-390-9333
For a complete listing, refer to the Special Care Facilities section.

URBANA. *Mercy McAuley Center-Mercy Health Systems*, 906 Scioto St., 43078. Tel: 937-653-5432; Fax: 937-652-2072
For a complete listing, refer to the Special Care Facilities section.

[M] MONASTERIES AND RESIDENCES OF PRIESTS AND BROTHERS

CINCINNATI. *The Catholic Foreign Mission Society of America, Inc.*, 104 Elm Ave., Wyoming, 45215. Tel: 513-761-5888.
E-mail: mklcin@igc.apc.org
Maryknoll Fathers. Revs. Robert W. Greene, M.M.; Leslie F. Blowers, M.M., Dir.

Comboni Missionaries (Verona Fathers)-Comboni Mission Center. Houses Comboni Missionaries of the Heart of Jesus, Inc., The Offices of the Province of North America, including the Office of the Provincial. 8108 Beechmont Ave., 45255-3194. Tel: 513-474-4997; Fax: 513-474-0382.
E-mail: combonipn@igc.apc.org
Revs. John Converset, M.C.C.J., Prov. Tel: 513-474-3818; Joseph Bragotti, M.C.C.J., Vice Prov.; Sergio Contran, M.C.C.J., Prov. Treas.; Sr. Rosanne White, O.S.U., Finance Dir.; Revs. Mario Ongaro, M.C.C.J., Personnel Dir.; Paul Donohue, M.C.C.J., Editor Comboni Missions Newsletter & Comboni Press Feature Service; Cindy Browne, Mgr. & Editor, CPN Newsletter; Tim McDowell, Development Dir.; Rev. Kenneth Gerth, M.C.C.J. Priests 4.

Faber Jesuit Community, 790 Clinton Springs Ave., 45229. Tel: 513-961-7700; Fax: 513-569-4582. Revs. Edward W. Carter, S.J.; Robert Dressman, S.J.; Daniel Foley, S.J.; John N. Felten, S.J.; John M. Ferone, S.J.; Robert J. Hagee, S.J.; John P. Heim, S.J., Supr.; Donald O'Shaughnessy, S.J.; Herbert J Raterman, S.J.; Harold Sommer, S.J.; John J. Beckman, S.J.
4105 Hoffman Ave., 45236. Rev. James M. Brichetto, S.J.

St. Louis Rectory, 29 E. 8th St., 45202. Rev. Robert J. Ross, S.J.
2028 Mackoy Ave., 41014. Bros. Donald H. Bengert, S.J.; Robert G. Cardosi, S.J.; John P. Martin, S.J. Priests 14; Brothers 3.

Jesuit Community at St. Xavier High School, Jesuit Community, 7361 View Pl., 45224. Tel: 513-761-5522; Fax: 513-761-0514. Revs. Edward L. Pigott, S.J., Rector; Lester A. Linz, S.J.; Eugene J. Nevins, S.J.; J. Paul O'Brien, S.J.; William L. Verbryke, S.J.

Jesuit Community at Xavier Unversity, Jesuit Community Residence, 3844 Victory Pkwy., 45207. Tel: 513-745-3591. Members of the Jesuit Community (Society of Jesus, S.J.). Revs. Joseph A. Bracken, S.J., Rector; Robert C. Baumiller, S.J.; Richard W. Bollman, S.J.; Louis A. Bonacci, S.J.; Eugene J. Carmichael, S.J.; Matthew Gamber, S.J.; Michael J. Graham, S.J.; James E. Hoff, S.J.; Francis D. Johnson, S.J.; Thomas P. Kennealy, S.J.; William F. King, S.J.; J. Leo Klein, S.J.; John J. LaRocca, S.J.; James McCann, S.J.; Edward T. O'Donnell, S.J.; Robert W. Schmidt, S.J.; Theodore C. Thepe, S.J.; Benjamin J. Urmston, S.J.; George B. Wilson, S.J.; Bro. Jerome J. Pryor, S.J. Priests 18; Brothers 1.

Marianist Community, 2708 Johnstone Pl., 45206-1822. Tel: 513-961-6244. Revs. Daniel Winters, S.M.; Louis Wiesner, S.M. Priests 2; Brothers 6.

Marianist Community, 1600 Madison Rd., 45206-1815. Tel: 513-961-1945. Bros. Lawrence W. Corbin, S.M., Dir.; David K. Betz, S.M.; Giancarlo Bonutti, S.M.; Rev. Edward M. Jack, S.M. Priests 1; Brothers 3.

Marianist Community, 9025 Montgomery Rd., 45242-7711. Tel: 513-793-4777.
E-mail: rflaherty@moeller.org
Web site: www.moeller.org
Bro. Robert M. Flaherty, S.M., Dir.; Rev. Joseph L. Kerr, S.M. Priests 1; Brothers 9.

Marianist Community, 118 Findlay St., Apt. #1, 45210-2402. Tel: 513-369-0388; Fax: 513-369-0408.
Web site: www.geocities.com/heartland/prairie/9125index.htm/
Rev. Michael L. Lisbeth, S.M.; Bros. Robert P. Donovan, S.M., Dir.; J. Mitchell Schweickart, S.M.; Paul Hoffman, S.M. Brothers 3; Priests 1.

Pleasant Street Friary, 1723 Pleasant St., 45210. Tel: 513-621-0599. Friars Daniel J. Anderson, O.F.M.; Jovian C. Weigel, O.F.M.; Jack R. Wintz, O.F.M.; Murray L. Bodo, O.F.M.

St. Ann Friary, 2936 W. Galbraith Rd., 45239. Tel: 513-522-7420.
E-mail: schreckj@aol.com
Revs. Nicholas Lohkamp, O.F.M.; Joseph Rayes, O.F.M.; Joseph Ricchini, O.F.M.; Dominic Wachtel, O.F.M.; Bro. John Schreck, O.F.M.

St. Clare Friary, 5831 Saranac Ave., 45224. Tel: 513-541-5742; Fax: 513-541-5774. Revs. Patrick McCloskey, O.F.M.; James Bok, O.F.M.; Bros. Gene Mayer, O.F.M.; Francisco Meyer, O.F.M.

St. Clement Friary. St. John the Baptist Province. Residence for Faculty of Roger Bacon High School, Pastors of St. Clement Parish and other Friars. 4536 Vine St., 45217. Tel: 513-641-2257; Fax: 513-641-2262. Revs. Joseph L. Rigali, O.F.M., Pastor; Carl J. Langenderfer, O.F.M., Local Min.; Stanley Bir, O.F.M., Prov. Personnel Advisor; Christopher Schneider, O.F.M., Substitute; Vincent A. Dieckman, O.F.M., (Retired); Frank D. Frey, O.F.M.; Fabian Gerstle, O.F.M., (Retired); Warren Zeisler, O.F.M.; Curt C. Lanzrath, O.F.M., Care of Senior Friars; Otto Krische, O.F.M., (Retired); Roger T. Bosse, O.F.M., Prin., Roger Bacon High School; Donnul Suttmann, O.F.M., (Retired); William Reichel, O.F.M., Retreats; Valens J. Waldschmidt, O.F.M., Chap.; Bros. Conrad F. Rebmann, O.F.M., Staff, Roger Bacon High School; Louis Lamping, O.F.M., Treas. & Fraternal Svc.; Louis Zant, O.F.M., Maintenance; Bernard Jennings, O.F.M., Fraternal Svc.; Kenneth Beetz, O.F.M., Maintenance; Joel Soldenski, O.F.M., Sacristan; Didacus Casanave, O.F.M., (Retired); Jerry Jackson, O.F.M., Fraternal Svc.; Joseph Haley, O.F.M., Friars Club Purchaser; Francis Williams, O.F.M., (Retired). Priests 14; Brothers 10.

St. Francis Center, 10290 Mill Rd., 45231. Tel: 513-825-4465 (Friary); 825-9300 (Center). Vocation Office. Tel: 513-825-1082. Archives. Tel: 513-851-1388. St. John the Baptist Province. Revs. Bruno Kremp, O.F.M., Supr. & Admin.; Marcan Hetteberg, O.F.M., Franciscan Archives; Adrian Schneider, O.F.M.; Germain Krizmanich, O.F.M., Drake Hospital; Bro. Linus Border, O.F.M.

St. Francis Seraph Friary. Provincial Headquarters of the Province of St. John the Baptist of the Order of Friars Minor. 1615 Vine St., 45210. Tel: 513-721-4700; Fax: 513-421-9672.
E-mail: secsjb@franciscan.com
Revs. John Stein, O.F.M., Pastor; John Bok, O.F.M., Prov. Min.; Alan Hirt, O.F.M., Vicar Prov.; Kenan Freson, O.F.M., Prov. Treas.; James Bok, O.F.M., Dir. Devel.; John R. Boehman, O.F.M., Office for Senior Friars; Francis S. Tebbe, O.F.M., Dir. Ongoing Formation; Rock Travnikar, O.F.M., Vocation Dir.; Toni Cashnelli, Dir. Communications; Henry Beck, O.F.M., Office of Justice, Peace and Integrity of Creation; Bert Heise, O.F.M., Guardian; Theobald Hattrup, O.F.M., (Retired); Peter Paul James, O.F.M., (Retired); Bros. Scott Obrecht, O.F.M., Dir. Franciscan Mission Office & Missionary Union; Gene Mayer, O.F.M., Prov. Sec.; Josef Anderlohr, O.F.M., Assoc. Pastor, Liturgical Design Consultant, & Vicar; Christopher Cahill, O.F.M., Instructor, Roger Bacon High School; John Carey, O.F.M., Assoc., Mission Office; Dominic Lococo, O.F.M., SAM Sales Rep.; Robert Lucero, O.F.M., SAM Production Mgr.; Kevin Schroeder, O.F.M., SAM Video Dept.; Bill Spond, O.F.M., Porter. Priests 5; Brothers 7.
Priests of the Province Serving Abroad: Rev. James Fehrenbach, O.F.M., Ainmillerstr, 5 Whg. 608, Munchen, Germany, 80801. Rev. Max Langenderfer, O.F.M., Franciscans, P.O. Box 14355. Rev. John Quigley, O.F.M., Curia Generale, Via. S. Maria Mediatrice, 25, 00165. Rev. Daniel Kroger, O.F.M., Our Lady of the Angels Seminary, P.O. Box 191.

St. Gertrude Priory, 7630 Shawnee Run Rd., 45243. Tel: 513-561-5954. Revs. William A. Holt, O.P., Prior & Pastor; Clement Burns, O.P., Novice Master; Thomas F. Carroll, O.P., Assoc.; George Schommer, O.P., Assoc.; James M. Sullivan, O.P., Assoc. In res. Rev. Harvey B. Schaller, O.P.

DAYTON. *Marianist Provincialate.* Cincinnati Province of the Society of Mary (Brothers of Mary, Marianists), 4435 E. Patterson Rd., 45430-1095. Tel: 937-513-429-0794; Fax: 937-513-429-3195. Revs. Joseph H. Lackner, S.M., Asst. Provincial & Asst. for Educ.; Joseph P. Tedesco, S.M., Asst. for Religious Life; Bros. Joseph H. Kamis, S.M., Provincial; Robert J. Metzger, S.M., Asst. for Temporalities & Prov. Treas.; Joseph T. Markel, S.M., Asst. Treas.; Ms. Phyllis J. Lipker, Sec.
Priests of the Province on Special Assignment: Rev. Robert E. Hogan, S.M.; Bro. Bernard J. Ploeger, S.M., Councilor, Casa San Juan, 2107 Davy Crockett, San Antonio, TX, 78238-5109. Rev. Thomas J. Stanley, S.M., Marianist Community, 5000 Monroe St., Hollywood, FL, 33021-7270. Rev. Dennis J. Gatto, S.M., 8120 S.W. 54th Ave., Miami, FL, 33143. Rev. James A. Russell, S.M., Marianist Community, 5131 Jackson St., Hollywood, FL, 33021-7233. Rev. Joseph H. Lackner, S.M., Marianist Seminary, 175 Phelan Ave., San Francisco, CA, 94112-1897. Rev. John L. Bakle, S.M., St. Agatha Rectory, 1860 Northam Rd., Columbus, 43221-3299. Rev. Norbert C. Brockman, S.M., 3033 W. Woodlawn Ave., San Antonio, TX, 78228-4800. Rev. Robert J. Bouffier, S.M., St. Anthony Parish, 43 Holton St., Allston, MA, 02134. Rev. Raymond J. Kacirk, S.M., 25149 Hanover St., Dearborn, MI, 48125-1831. Rev. Edmund L. Rhodes, S.M., Marianist Community, 5000 Monroe St., Hollywood, FL, 33021-7270. Rev. Kenneth J. Sommer, S.M., 5541 Bosworth Pl., Cincinnati, 45212. Rev. James F. Kunes, S.M., 4649 D Country Ln., St. Louis, MO, 63074.
Priests of the Province Serving Overseas: Rev. Michael R. Reaume, S.M., St. Columba, Church Ave., Ballybrack, Ireland.
Priests of the Province Serving in the Missions: Rev. William R. Behringer, S.M., Brother Vincent House, P.O. Box 25156, Nairobi, Kenya. Rev. Robert W. Hertweck, S.M., Marianist Novitiate, P.O. Box 210, Limuru, Kenya. Rev. Martin A. Solma, S.M., Reg. Supr. & Reg. Admin., Marianist Regional House, P.O. Box 50504, Nairobi, Kenya. Rev. Charles J. Stander, S.M., Marianist Novitiate, P.O. Box 210, Limuru, Kenya. Rev. Richard A. Loehrlein, S.M., Chaminade Marianist Community, P.O. Box 100, Karonga, Malawi.

Marianist Community, 100 Chambers St., 45409-2817. Tel: 937-223-7150. Revs. J. Eugene Contadino, S.M.; Joseph H. Lackner, S.M.; Bertrand A. Buby, S.M; Bro. Thomas E. Oldenski, S.M, Dir. Priests 3; Brothers 4.

Marianist Community, 149 Franklin St., 45402-2598. Tel: 937-228-2013. Revs. Lee Sciarrotta, S.M., Dir.; Francis J. Kenney, S.M. Priests 2; Brothers 2.

Marianist Community, Meyer Hall, 4435 East Patterson Rd., 45430-1095. Tel: 937-426-7852; 426-7858. Revs. Richard K. Knuge, S.M.; John D. Mulligan, S.M. (NY); Bro. Thomas A. Payne, S.M., Dir. Priests 2; Brothers 7.

Marianist Community, Novitiate, 4435 E. Patterson Rd., 45430-1095. Tel: 937-426-5721. Revs. Theodore K. Cassidy, S.M. (NY), Dir.; H. James Bartlett, S.M.; Kazuo Louis Ibar Shimizu, S.M. (Japan). Priests 3; Brothers 6.

Marianist Community, 141 Washington St., 45402-2530. Tel: 937-224-9978. Bro. Robert N. Wiethorn, S.M., Dir.; Revs. Charles T. Bergedick, S.M.; John A. McGrath, S.M. (NY); Thomas A. Schroer, S.M.; Christopher T. Wittmann, S.M. Priests 4; Brothers 8.

Marianist Community, 62 Indiana Ave, 45410-2308. Tel: 937-258-3212. Bro. John J. Jansen, S.M., Dir.;

Revs. Norbert C. Burns, S.M.; Cyril Middendorf, S.M. Tel: 513-258-3250. Priests 2; Brothers 4.
Marianist Community, 340 Stonemill Rd., 45409-2543. Tel: 937-285-8611; 285-8612. Revs. Gerald T. Chinchar, S.M.; Christopher W. Conlon, S.M. (NY); Bro. Mark A. Twehues, S.M., Dir. Priests 2; Brothers 2.
Marianist Community, 121 Sawmill Rd., 45409-2524. Tel: 937-222-4928. Revs. Matthew F. Kohmescher, S.M., Dir.; Thomas A. Schoen, S.M. Priests 2; Brothers 3.
Marianist Community, 1903 Trinity Ave., 45409-2445. Tel: 937-293-9744. Bro. Daniel L. Klco, S.M., Dir.; Revs. James F. Fitz, S.M.; James L. Heft, S.M. Priests 2; Brothers 4.
The Marianist Mission, Mount Saint John, 45481-0001. Tel: 513-222-4641. Rev. John D. Mulligan, S.M., Dir., Marianist Community, Alumni Hall, University of Dayton, 45469-0300. Tel: 937-229-4695. Revs. Paul F. Vieson, S.M., Dir.; John J. Kelley, S.M.; Theodore A. Koehler, S.M. (France); Joseph F. Kozar, S.M.; Joseph S. McDonald, S.M.; John S. Putka, S.M.; Johann B.G. Roten, S.M. (Suisse); Thomas A. Thompson, S.M.; Adolf M. Windisch, S.M. Priests 9; Brothers 19.
The Franciscan at St. Leonard, Assisted Living & Nursing Assistance, 8100 Clyo Rd., 45458. Tel: 937-433-0480. Bro. John J. Schneider, S.M., Dir.; Revs. John D. Pawlos, S.M. (NY); Bernard C. Stueve, S.M. Priests 2; Brothers 15.
Marianist Community, 1234 Duckview Ct., 45458. Tel: 937-439-5941. Bro. John J. Schneider, Dir.; Rev. Philip C. Hoelle, S.M. Brothers 3; Priests 1.
Marianist Community, 57 Woodland Ave., 45409-2853. Tel: 937-285-8091. Bro. Philip T. Aaron, S.M., Dir.; Rev. Kenneth A. Templin, S.M. Priests 1; Brothers 2.
Marianist Press. Religious 2; Total Staff 7.
Marianist Network for the Arts. Religious 3; Total Staff 3.
North American Center for Marianist Studies. Religious 2; Total Staff 7.
Marianist Mission. Religious 6; Total Staff 65.
Marianist Voluntary Service Communities. Religious 2; Total Staff 6.
Marianist Environmental Education Center. Religious 2; Total Staff 2.
Provincial House of the Cincinnati Province of the Society of the Precious Blood, 431 East Second St., 45402. Tel: 937-228-9263; Fax: 937-228-6878. Very Rev. Kenneth F. Pleiman, C.PP.S., Prov. Dir.; Bro. Joseph J. Fisher, C.PP.S., Treas. Members of the Provincial Council: Rev. James F. McCabe, C.PP.S., Vice Prov. & Sec., 4106 State Rte. 269, Bellevue, 44811. Rev. Clarence E. Williams, C.PP.S., 1st Councilor, 11430 Morang Dr., Detroit, MI, 48224. Rev. William A. O'Donnell, C.PP.S., 2nd Councilor, 309 S. Perry St., Wapakoneta, 45895. Rev. James C. Seibert, C.PP.S., 3rd Councilor, 229 W. Anthony St., Celina, 45822. Bro. Joseph J. Fisher, C.PP.S., 4th Councilor, 431 E. Second St., 45402. Bro. Benjamin Basile, C.PP.S., 5th Councilor, 2400 New York Ave., Whiting, IN, 46394. Vocation Office, 431 E. 2nd St., 45402-1764. Tel: 937-228-6224; Fax: 937-228-6878. Rev. Angelo P. Anthony, C.PP.S., Vocation Dir.
Military: Rev. Louis L. Schmit, C.PP.S., 110 Forbes Ave., Quarters B, Carlisle, PA, 17013-5001. Rev. Eugene H. Schnipke, C.PP.S., 765 Willow Dr., Mountain Home, AFB ID, 83647. Rev. Kenneth J. Schroeder, C.PP.S., United States Army Garrison, Post Chapel, Bldg. #4419, Fort George, G. Meade, MD, 20755-5065. Rev. John S. Srode, C.PP.S., 49 FW/HC 661 New Mexico Ave., Holloman AFB, NM, 88330-8284.
Priests of the Province Serving Abroad: Rev. Frederick T. Licciardi, C.PP.S., Bergstrasse 3, 8004, Zurich, Switzerland.
Foreign Mission: Rev. Richard L. Beischel, C.PP.S., Casilla 619, Valdivia, Chile. Rev. William J. Beuth, C.PP.S., Apartado 2483, 01901 Guatemala City, Guatemala. Rev. Paul A. Buehler, C.PP.S., Apartado 1983, Lima 100, Peru. Rev. Joseph F. Deardorff, C.PP.S., Apartado 2348, Lima, 100, Peru. Rev. Gerald G. Dreiling, C.PP.S., Apartado 07-0148, Lima 07, Peru. Rev. John F. Falter, C.PP.S., Casilla 619, Valdivia, Chile. Rev. Barry J. Fischer, C.PP.S., Moderator General, Viale Di Porta Ardeatina 66, Rome, Italy, I-00154. Rev. James E. Gaynor, C.PP.S., Apartado 36, La Oroya, Peru. Rev. James W. Bender, C.PP.S., Apartado 36, LaOroya, Peru. Rev. Daniel J. Mangen, C.PP.S., Casilla 194, Purranque, Chile. Rev. Ernest W. Ranly, C.PP.S., Apartado 1983, Lima, 100, Peru. Rev. Donald J. Thieman, C.PP.S., Casilla 176-2, Santiago, Chile.
Returned to U.S.A.:
In Residences Not Listed Elsewhere: Rev. John E. Bolan, C.PP.S., 16359 Emerald Point Dr., Middleburg Hts., 44130. Rev. James K. Grothjan, C.PP.S., 1135 Bayshore Dr., Valparaiso, FL, 32580. Rev. Robert W. Hunt, C.PP.S., P.O. Box 389, Bellevue, 44811. Rev. Howard J. Lesch, C.PP.S., 1115 Coral Dr., Niceville, FL, 32578. Rev. Francis W. McCarthy, C.PP.S., 52411 C.R. 425, Fresno, 43824. Rev. Paul F. Schaaf, C.PP.S., 100 Bluff View Dr., 106C, Belleair Bluffs, FL, 34640. Rev. Emil A. Schuwey, C.PP.S., 1108 Fenley Ave., Louisville, KY, 40222. Rev. Paul Aumen, C.PP.S., 4380 York Rd. #46, New Oxford, PA, 17350. Rev. Robert Onofrey, C.PP.S., 15700 Orlan Dr. #169, Orland Park, IL, 60462.

FAIRFIELD. *Headquarters of Glenmary Home Missioners*, P.O. Box 465618, 45246-5618. 4119 Glenmary Trace, 45014. Tel: 513-874-8900; Fax: 513-874-1690. The Home Missioners of America. Revs. Jerry Dorn, Glmy., Pres.; Will Steinbacher, Glmy., 1st Vice Pres. & Dir. of Education Dept.; Bro. Jack Henn, Glmy., 2nd Vice Pres. & COO. Senior Members: Revs. Edward Haggerty, Glmy.; Del Holmes, Glmy.; Charles Hughes, Glmy.; Patrick O'Donnell, Glmy.; Joseph O'Donnell, Glmy.; John Otterbacher, Glmy.; Raymond Orlett, Glmy.; George Mathis, Glmy.; John McNearney, Glmy.; Joseph Dean, Glmy.; Robert Healy, Glmy.; William Smith, Glmy.; Joseph Gartner, Glmy.; James Kelly, Glmy.; Francisco Schenk, Glmy.; Bob Berson, Glmy.; John Garvey, Glmy.; Bros. Thomas Kelly; Vincent Wilmes; George Sauer; Paul Wilhelm; Bernie Stern; Revs. Peter Richardson, Glmy., Editor of the Glenmary Challenge; August Guppenberger, Glmy., Mission Office; Dominic Duggins, Glmy., Mission Office & Cincinnati House Dir.; Richard Kreimer, Glmy., Mission OFC; Bro. Mike Springer, Glmy., Senior Member Coordinator.
On Special Assignment: Revs. Thomas Meehan, AIDS Ministry, Atlanta, GA; John Rausch, Human Economics Ministry, Berea, KY; Donald Levernier, Glmy., On Loan to Lithuania.

HAMILTON. *St. Francis Friary*, 723 Main St., 45013-2548. Tel: 513-896-5326. Brothers of the Poor of St. Francis. Bros. Eric Lauer, C.F.P.; Howard Parent, C.F.P.

HUNTSVILLE. *St. George Chapel of Marianist Community*, 9636 Lakeshore Dr., E., 43324-9633. Tel: 513-842-4902.
E-mail: govisl@bright.net
Bros. Donald L. Smith, S.M., Dir.; Robert V. Kelly, S.M.; Revs. John F. Mueller, S.M.; Robert J. Hoeper, S.M. Priests 2; Brothers 2.

[N] CONVENTS AND RESIDENCES FOR SISTERS

CINCINNATI. *Central Office of Sisters of St. Joseph of Medaille*, 1821 Summit Rd., Ste. 210, 45237-2819. Tel: 513-761-2888; Fax: 513-761-9957.
E-mail: 10277.2402@compuserve.com
Sr. Lucy Silvio, C.S.J., Pres.; Sr. Maria Hill, C.S.J., Vice Pres. General Councilors: Sr. Joan Hartlaub, C.S.J.; Sr. Janice Miller, C.S.J. Sisters in Archdiocese 22; Total Congregation 199.
Cincinnati Regional Community, Institute of the Sisters of Mercy of the Americas, 2335 Grandview Ave., 45206. Tel: 513-221-1800.
E-mail: mercycin@aol.com
Sr. Marie Hartmann, R.S.M., Pres. Cincinnati Reg. Community; Sr. Wanda Smith, R.S.M., Vocation Dir. Professed Sisters 393; Candidates 1.
Convent of St. Dominic, 916 York St., 45214. Tel: 513-621-5899. Dominican Sisters of Hope 5; Sisters of Saint Francis of Oldenburg, IN 1.
Director of Higher Education, 1768 Cedar Ave., 45224. Tel: 513-681-5328. Sr. Mary Virginia Sullivan, R.S.M., Dir.
Dominican Sisters, 3840 Applegate, Apt. 604, 45211. Tel: 513-481-6691. Sr. Clarita Elder, O.P.; Sr. Laurene Hagman, O.P.; Sr. Vivian Kessler, O.P. Dominican Sisters 3.
Franciscan Monastery of St. Clare (Poor Clares), 868 Finney Trail, 45224-1319. Tel: 513-522-4795. Contemplative Sisters 3; Novices 2.
McAuley Convent, 1768 Cedar Ave., 45224. Tel: 513-681-2100. Sr. Kathleen Marie Noonan, R.S.M., Dir. Sisters of Mercy 46.
Mercy Center, 2335 Grandview Ave., 45206. Tel: 513-221-1800. Sr. Bernice O'Neil, R.S.M., Local Coord. Professed Sisters 8.
Mercy Hall, 2317 Grandview Ave., 45206. Tel: 513-475-6726. Professed Sisters 5.
Provincial House, Health Center of Sisters of Notre Dame de Namur, 701 E. Columbia Ave., 45215. Tel: 513-821-7448. Sr. Claire Foley, S.N.D.deN., Prov. Supr.; Sr. Anne Flanagan, S.N.D.deN., Local Coord.; Sr. Phyllis Angerer, S.N.D.deN., Admin. Sisters 110.
St. Clare Convent, Franciscan Sisters of the Poor, 60 Compton Rd., 45215. Tel: 513-761-9036. Sr. Madeline M. Hill, Community Min.; Rev. Herman H. Kenning, Res. Chap. Sisters 23.
St. Rose Convent, 3952 W. Eighth St., 45205.
E-mail: saintrose@juno.com
Total in Residence 3.
Sisters of Charity of Cincinnati, Ohio, 5900 Delhi Rd., 45051. Tel: 513-347-5201; Fax: 513-347-5228.
Web site: www.nsj.edu/sc
Sr. Mary Ellen Murphy, S.C., Pres. Sisters in Congregation 670; Sisters in Archdiocese 487. Franciscan Fathers, St. John the Baptist Province. Tel: 513-721-4700.
Sisters of Mercy, Administrative Offices, 2335 Grandview Ave, 45206. Institute of the Sisters of Mercy of the Americas 3.
Sisters of the Good Shepherd. (Cincinnati Province), 2849 Fischer Pl., 45211-5915. Tel: 513-661-1833; Fax: 513-661-1216. Sr. Dolores Kalina, Prov.; Sr. Marilyn Atwell, Sec. Sisters 2.
Sisters of the Good Shepherd, 2108 Hatmaker St., 45204-1906. Tel: 513-921-5923.
Ursulines of Cincinnati, 1339 E. McMillan St., 45206. Tel: 513-961-3410; Fax: 513-961-0129. Ursuline Sisters. Sisters 29.
Sisters of this community sponsor one high school, sponsor one elementary school, serve in pastoral ministry, counseling, chaplaincy, elementary education and administration, adult education.

BATAVIA. *Sisters of Mercy*, Clermont, 4315 Elizabeth Dr., 45103. Tel: 513-732-6335.

DAYTON. *Sisters of the Precious Blood Generalate*, 4000 Denlinger Rd., 45426. Tel: 937-837-3302.
E-mail: pdvx17a@prodigy.com
Web site: www.bright.net/~cppsnews
Sr. Joyce Langhals, C.PP.S., Pres.; Sr. Nancy Raley, C.PP.S., Vice Pres. & Councilor; Sr. Judy Kroeger, C.PP.S., Councilor & Sec.; Sr. Joyce Lehman, C.PP.S., Councilor; Sr. Benita Volk, C.PP.S., Councilor; Sr. Barbara Brown, C.PP.S., Treas.
Sisters of the Precious Blood, Salem Heights Convent, 4960 Salem Ave., 45416. Tel: 937-278-8722; Fax: 937-278-8722. Sr. Corinne Staub, O.P., Admin.; Sr. Mary Ellen Andrisin, C.PP.S., Dir. Resident Life; Rev. Joseph Pax, C.PP.S., Chap. Sisters 100.

HAMILTON. *Franciscan at St. Raphael, Inc.*, 233 Dayton St., 45011. Tel: 513-893-1370. Mr. Robert Moore, Exec. Dir. Assist Social Service.

SAINT MARTIN. *Ursuline Convent of the Immaculate Heart of Mary*. (Also known as Ursulines of Brown County), Ursuline Center, 20860 State Rte. 251, 45118-9705. Tel: 513-875-2020; Fax: 513-875-2311. Ursuline Order, Congregation of Paris. Sr. Nacy Vollman, O.S.U., Supr. Sisters 40.

[O] RESIDENCES FOR ADULTS AND YOUTHS

CINCINNATI. *Catholic Residential Services of the Archdiocese of Cincinnati with People with Mental Retardation*, 100 E. Eighth St., 45202. Tel: 513-241-7745; Fax: 513-241-4333. Ms. Christine Hoekzema. Legal Title: *Catholic Residential Services of Archdiocese of Cincinnati with People with Mental Retardation*.
Friars Club, 65 W. McMillan St., 45219. Tel: 513-381-5432. Beth Bowsky, Exec. Dir.; Rev. James M. Bok, O.F.M., Pres., Bd. of Trustees. Residential programs for male teens, residency for men, transitional living for mentally ill, counseling, education for teen school dropouts, youth sports, and community outreach for high risk youth, family resource center, housing & support for homeless families.

[P] RETREAT HOUSES, CONFERENCE AND RENEWAL CENTERS

CINCINNATI. *Friarhurst Retreat Center*, 8136 Wooster Pike, 45227. Tel: 513-561-2270. Revs. Hilarion H. Kistner, O.F.M.; Lambert R. Dannenfelser, O.F.M.; Bro. Stephen Richter, O.F.M.

DAYTON. *Bergamo*, 4400 Shakertown Rd., 45430-1075. Tel: 937-426-2363; Fax: 937-426-1090.
E-mail: bergamo@erinet.com
Mr. Thomas A. Cox, Exec. Dir.; Bro. Joseph Markel, S.M., Chief Financial Officer; Sr. Madeline Columbro, S.N.D., Dir. of Adult Development; Sr. Darlene Denton, O.S.U., Dir. Hospitality Svcs.; Barbara Kozlowski, Dir. of Youth Development; Patricia O'Grady, Dir. of Reservations; Dorothy Clake, Dir. of Food Services.

LOVELAND. *Grailville*, 932 O'Bannonville Rd., 45140. Tel: 513-683-2340; Fax: 513-683-4752. National Center of International Grail Movement. Audrey Sorrento, Program Dir.; Mindy Burger, Sec.

MILFORD. *Milford Spiritual Center*, 5361 S. Milford Rd., 45150-9746. Tel: 513-248-3500; Fax: 513-248-3503. Revs. R. Michael Brophy, S.J., Supr.; Frank M. Oppenheim, S.J.; George W. Traub, S.J.; Thomas J. Diehl, S.J.; Kenneth Overberg, S.J.; Thomas Widner; Bro. Paul F. Mattingly, S.J.; Daniel O. Roche, Exec. Dir. Officers: Sr. Janice Bachman, O.P., Chm.; Mr. Robert Stautberg, S.J., Vice Chm.; William Michael, Sec.

[Q] CAMPUS MINISTRY AND NEWMAN CENTERS

CINCINNATI. *College of Mt. St. Joseph Campus Ministry*, 5701 Delhi Rd., 45233-1670. Tel: 513-244-4245.
E-mail: greg_grady@mail.msj.edu
Web site: www.msj.edu

Sr. Marge Kloos, S.C., Campus Ministry. Tel: 513-244-4245.

University of Cincinnati Newman Center, 328 W. McMillan St., 45219-1224. Tel: 513-381-6400.
E-mail: scheeljj@ucbeh.san.uc.edu
Web site: www.uc.edu/~scheeljj
Revs. Jeffrey Scheeler, O.F.M.; Leonard Fecko; Alan Hirt, O.F.M.; Sr. Lucy Zientek, C.D.P.; Ms. Peggy Hilvers; Ms. Jill Hack.

Xavier University Campus Ministry, 3800 Victory Pkwy., 45207-2411. Tel: 513-745-3567.
E-mail: goetzi@admin.xu.edu
Web site: www.xu.edu/spiritual
Ms. Chris Potter, Dir.; Mr. Tom Sheilbley, Retreat Coord.; Rev. Louis Bonacci, S.J., Coord. Pastoral Ministry in Residence Halls; Mr. Guy Vanasse, Coord. Liturgical Music; Marci Kerscher, Campus Ministry Intern.

DAYTON. *Sinclair Community College Campus Ministry*, 444 W. Third St., 45402. Tel: 513-226-2768.
E-mail: jsteinha@sinclair.edu
Dr. V. Jane Steinhauser, Archdiocesan Dir. of Campus Ministry.

University of Dayton Campus Ministry, 45469; Fax: 937-229-2035.
E-mail: campus-ministry@udayton.edu
Web site: www.udayton.edu/~campmin/
Revs. Gerald T. Chinchar, S.M. Tel: 937-229-2725; Christopher W. Conlon, S.M., Dir. Tel: 937-229-3339; Kenneth Templin, S.M. Tel: 937-229-3570; Sr. Eileen J. Cehyra, F.M.I. Tel: 937-229-3339; Sr. Nancy Bramlage, S.C. Tel: 937-229-2576; Sr. Mary Louise Foley, F.M.I. Tel: 937-229-2093; Sr. Jody O'Neil, S.P. Tel: 937-229-2574; Sr. Kathleen Rossman, O.S.F. Tel: 937-229-3310; Sr. Monica Gundler, S.C. Tel: 937-229-2010; Bros. Philip Aaron, S.M. Tel: 937-229-2575; Thomas Pieper, S.M. Tel: 937-229-2211.

FAIRBORN. *Campus Ministry Center*, 3640 Colonel Glenn Hwy., 45324-2096. Tel: 937-426-1836; Fax: 937-426-3490.
E-mail: crohmill@discover.wright.edu
Rev. Christian A. Rohmiller, Campus Min.; Mr. Alex Abuyuan, Music Min.; Ms. Joan Marquis, Liturgical Min.; Mrs. Constance Newman, Sec.

OXFORD. *Miami University Catholic Campus Ministry*, 111 E. High St., 45056. Tel: 513-523-2153; Fax: 513-523-0559.
E-mail: cathmin@miamiu.muohio.edu
Rev. Terrance L. Schneider; John V. Kruse, Dir. Campus Ministry; Christina M. Flum, D.R.E.

SPRINGFIELD. *Mercy Medical Center, Wittenberg University Campus Ministry*, 1343 N. Fountain Blvd., 45501. Tel: 937-390-5000. Rev. Marvin R. Hackman, Dir. Pastoral Care.

URBANA. *Urbana University Campus Ministry*, 231 Washington Ave., 43078. Tel: 937-653-1375. Rev. David Zink.
Pastoral care available through St. Mary Parish.

WILBERFORCE. *Interfaith Campus Ministry*, 1401 Brush Rd., P.O. Box 386, 45384. Tel: 937-376-9037.

WILMINGTON. *Wilmington College Campus Ministry*, 73 N. Mulberry St., 45177. Tel: 937-382-2236. Rev. R. Marc Sherlock.
Pastoral care available through St. Columbkille Parish.

YELLOW SPRINGS. *Antioch College Campus Ministry*, 308 Phillips St., 45387. Tel: 937-767-7450. Rev. Joseph W. Goetz.
Pastoral care available through St. Paul Parish.

[R] COMMUNITY CENTERS

CINCINNATI. *Franciscan at St. John*, P.O. Box 14368, 45250. A member of the Franciscan Health System of the Ohio Valley, Inc. 121 E. 13th St., 45210. Tel: 513-241-2186. Ms. Marylyn Middendorf, Exec. Dir.; R. Christopher West, Pres.
Provides a full-range of emergency and educational services, encourages self-determination and self-improvement to over 25,000 clients annually.

Mercy Connections, 2540 Woodburn Ave., 45206. Tel: 513-475-6744. Sr. Sarah Marie Sherman, R.S.M., Pres. & Treas.; Sr. Carren Herring, R.S.M., Vice Pres. & Sec.

Program for the Medically Underserved of Cincinnati, 3131 Queen City Ave., 45238. Tel: 513-389-5295. Sr. Kathleen Brogle, R.S.M., M.S.W., Exec. Dir. Annual Participants 2,750.

HAMILTON. *The Franciscan at St. Raphael, Inc.* A member of the Franciscan Health System of the Ohio Valley, Inc. 233 Dayton St., 45011. Tel: 513-893-1370. R. Christopher West, Pres. of FHSOV, Inc.; Robert Moore, Exec. Dir.; Sr. Bonnieen Steinlage, Pearly Gates Program.
Provides food and other emergency services and self sufficiency programs to over 10,000 clients annually.

SPRINGFIELD. *Mercy-St. John's Center*, 100 W. McCreight Ave., 45504. Tel: 937-399-9910. Marianne S. Wildermuth, Admin.
Day care center for adults, skilled & intermediate long term care facility for all ages, Alzheimer's unit, ventilator unit. Total Assisted 50; Total Staff 45.

[S] ST. VINCENT DE PAUL SOCIETY

CINCINNATI. *Archdiocesan Central Council of Cincinnati*, 1125 Bank St., 45214. Tel: 513-562-8841; 8842. Rev. Louis R. Hohlmayer, Spiritual Advisor.
Central Council: Mr. Richard J. Powell, Pres.; Mr. Carl Rayles, Vice Pres.; Mr. Richard Niklas, Sec.; Mr. Marvin E. Doane, Treas.

District Council of Cincinnati and Subordinate Parish Conferences. 1125 Bank St., 45214. Mr. Mark A. Casella, Pres.; Rev. Barry M. Windhotz, Spiritual Advisor.

District Council of Dayton and Subordinate Parish Conferences. 695 Fulmer Dr., Dayton, 45403. Tel: 937-254-0115. Deacon Robert Zink, Spiritual Advisor; Mr. Jack L. Vandegrift, Pres. & Contact; Philip A. Parmley, Treas.

District Council of Hamilton and Subordinate Parish Conferences, 401 N. Washington Blvd., Hamilton, 45013. Tel: 513-863-5091. Mr. Howard Hetterich, Pres.; Mr. James Meyer, Sec.; Mr. Donald Arent, Treas.; Rev. Charles E. Moore, Spiritual Advisor.

District Council of Springfield and Subordinate Parish Conferences, 2425 E. High St., Springfield, 45505. Deacon Norman G. Horstman, Spiritual Advisor; Mr. Melvin Buck, Pres.; Ms. Audrey Farland, Vice Pres.; Mrs. Janice Drake, Sec.; Mr. Richard Hale, Treas.

District Council of Saint Martin and Subordinate Parish Conferences, 6336 Trailridge Ct., Milford, 45140. Tel: 513-683-4166. Patrick White, Pres.; Rev. James N. Peaker, Spiritual Advisor. Tel: 513-232-6006.

St. Vincent de Paul Stores, Inc., 1125 Bank St., 45214. J. Timothy Heile, Dir.

St. Vincent de Paul Stores of Dayton, Ohio, Inc. Tel: 937-222-5555. 945 S. Edwin C. Moses Blvd., Dayton, 45408. Tel: 513-222-5555. Mr. Tony Staub, Dir.

St. Vincent de Paul Store of Springfield, OH, 2425 E. High St., Springfield, 45505.

St. Vincent Hotel, Inc., 212 W. Fifth St., Dayton, 45402. Tel: 937-461-7837. James H. Butler, Dir.

De Paul Industries, 15 S. Sinclair St., Dayton, 45402. Tel: 937-461-7837. Mr. James H. Butler, Dir.

[T] HEALTH CARE SYSTEMS

CINCINNATI. *Catholic Healthcare Partners*, 2335 Grandview Ave., 45206. Tel: 513-221-2736; Fax: 513-559-3835.
Web site: www.health-partners.org
Michael Connelly, Pres. & CEO. 20 acute care hospitals, 9 long-term care facilities, 1 continuing care facility, 7 elderly housing projects. Mercy Health System is co-sponsored by the Sisters of Mercy, Cincinnati Regional Community; Sisters of Mercy, Dallas (PA) Regional Community; Covenant Health System, Sisters of the Humility of Mary. Patients assisted annually 3.5 Million; Residence for Senior Citizens: 399.

Franciscan Health System of the Ohio Valley, 2446 Kipling Ave., 45239. Tel: 513-853-5000. R. Christopher West, Pres.; Sr. Arlene McGowan, Vice Pres. Mission and Support Svcs.; Don Rohling, Dir. of Mission. Sisters 3. Includes Franciscan Hospital-Mt. Airy Campus, Franciscan Hospital- Western Hills Campus; Franciscan at St. Clare; Franciscan at West Park; Franciscan at St. John; Franciscan Home Development; Franciscan at St. Raphael; Franciscan Home Health Services; Franciscan Diabetes Centers; Franciscan Center for Sight; Franciscan Medicenter-Harrison Campus; Franciscan/University of Cincinnati Family Practice Center; Franciscan Rehabilitation Centers; Franciscan Sports Medicine Centers; Franciscan Holistic Health Center; Francisican Workplace Health; Franciscan Senior Network; Franciscan Medical Management Services.

Franciscan Health System of the Ohio Valley (FH-SOV). A member of the Franciscan Health System of Cincinnati, Inc. 2446 Kipling Ave., 45239. Tel: 513-853-5000. James Strieby, C.E.O.; R. Christopher West, Pres.; Sr. Arlene McGowan, Vice Pres., Mission and Support Svcs.; Don Rohling, Dir. of Mission. Sisters 1.

Mercy Health System, Greater Cincinnati Regional, 4340 Glendale-Milford Rd., Ste. 100, 45242. Julia Hanser, Pres. & CEO.

Mercy Shared Services, Inc., 7010 Rowan Hill Dr., 45227. Tel: 513-271-6700.

Sisters of Charity Health Care Systems, Inc., 345 Neeb Rd., 45233. Tel: 513-347-1000. An affiliate of Catholic Health Initiatives.

DAYTON. *Franciscan Health System of the Ohio Valley operations in Dayton, OH*, One Franciscan Way, 45408. Tel: 937-229-6000. Rev. Allen Weimer, Dir. Spiritual Care, Franciscan Medical Center- Dayton Campus; Sr. Karen Hartman, S.F.P., Vice Pres., Mission. Includes Franciscan Medical Center-Dayton Campus; Franciscan at Schroder; Franciscan at St.Leonard; Franciscan Medicenters; St. Elizabeth Hopeland Family Practice Center; St. Elizabeth Family Practice Residency Program; Franciscan Home Health Services; Franciscan Rehabilitation Centers; Franciscan Sports Medicine Centers; Franciscan Senior Network; Franciscan Workplace Health; Franciscan Medical Management Services.

Samaritan Health Partners, 2222 Philadelphia Dr., 45406. Tel: 937-278-2612. Affiliate of Catholic Health Initiative.

SPRINGFIELD. *Mercy Health System - Western Ohio, Sisters of Mercy*, 1 S. Limestone St., P.O. Box 688, 45501-0688. Tel: 513-328-7013. Jerrold A. Maki, Pres. & C.E.O.; Sr. Betty Anne Darch, Senior Vice Pres. Mission Svc.

[U] FOUNDATIONS AND ENDOWMENTS

CINCINNATI. *Community Support Charitable Trust*, 1615 Vine St., 45210. Tel: 513-721-4700; Fax: 513-421-9672. Trustees: Revs. Kenan Freson, O.F.M.; Roger Bosse, O.F.M.; Bart Pax, O.F.M. Legal Title: *Community Support Charitable Trust for the Province of St. John the Baptist of the Order of Friars Minor.*

The Congregation of Our Lady of Charity of the Good Shepherd, Community Support Trust, 2849 Fischer Pl., 45211-5915. Tel: 513-661-1833; Fax: 513-661-1216. Sr. Dolores Kalina, Prov.

Eldercare Foundation, Inc. c/o CHI, 345 Neeb Rd., 45233. Tel: 513-347-1000. Sr. Celestia Koebel, S.C., Pres.; Mitch H. Milfi, Esq., Sec.

Friars Club Foundation, Inc., 1615 Vine St., 45210. Tel: 513-721-4700. Trustees: Mr. Thomas Klinedinst, Jr., Trustee & Pres.; Rev. Kenan Freson, O.F.M., Trustee & Treas.; Mr. John O'Connor, Vice Pres. & Sec.

Good Samaritan Hospital Foundation of Cincinnati, Inc., 375 Dixmyth Ave., 45220-2489. Tel: 513-872-3786.

Mercy Hospital Anderson Foundation, 7500 State Rd., 45255. Tel: 513-624-4910; Fax: 513-624-4858. Helen B. Balush, Vice Pres. A Subsidiary of Mercy Hospital Anderson.

Roger Bacon High School Endowment, 4320 Vine St., 45217. Tel: 513-641-1300. Rev. Roger Bosse, O.F.M.

Seton High School Foundation, 3901 Glenway Ave., 45205. Tel: 513-471-2600; Fax: 513-471-0529. Mr. Thomas E. McKiernan, Chm.; Ms. Susan M. Gibbons, Pres.

Sisters of Charity Foundation, Inc. dba SC Ministry Foundation, 345 Neeb Rd., 45233. Tel: 513-347-1122. Sr. Maryanna Coyles, S.C., Pres.

Sisters of Charity of Cincinnati-Charitable Trust, 5900 Delhi Rd., 45051. Tel: 513-347-5201. A designated trust fund to primarily support older and infirmed members of the congregation. Sr. Mary Ellen Murphy, S.C., Pres.

Sisters of Notre Dame De Namur, Ohio Province, Charitable Trust, 701 E. Columbia Ave., 45215. Tel: 513-761-7636. Sr. Clare Foley, Prov.

The Summit Country Day School Foundation, 2161 Grandin Rd., 45208. Tel: 513-579-6560. Edward C. Tyrrell, Pres.; Thomas Grote, Jr., Chm.; Richard Alder, Sec. & Treas.

Ursulines of Cincinnati, Ohio Charitable Trust, 1339 E. McMillan St., 45206. Tel: 513-961-3410. Sr. Elizabeth Lang, O.S.U.

DAYTON. *Community Support Charitable Trust*, 431 E. Second St., 45402. Tel: 937-228-9263. Trustees: Revs. Albert A. Reed, C.PP.S.; Thomas R. Brenberger, C.PP.S.; Angelo P. Anthony, C.PP.S.; Scott T. Kramer, C.PP.S.; Thomas J. Beischel, C.PP.S.; Bros. Joseph J. Fisher, C.PP.S.; Thomas R. Bohman, C.PP.S.

**Samaritan Health Foundation*, 2222 Philadelphia Dr., 45406. Tel: 937-278-5770; Fax: 937-278-5140. J. Kay Timmons, Pres. Affiliate of Catholic Health Initiatives and Samaritan Health Partners.

FAIRFIELD. *Glenmary Home Missioners Charitable Trust*, 4119 Glenmary Trace, 45014. Tel: 513-874-8900. Rev. Robert C. Berson, Trustee.

[V] MISCELLANEOUS LISTINGS

CINCINNATI. *Apostleship of Prayer*, 607 Sycamore St., 45202. Rev. Paul A. Huber, S.J.

Apostolate to Aid the Dying, 80 Compton Rd., 45215. Tel: 513-761-9036. Sr. M. Cornelia Evans, S.F.P.

Catholic Alumni Club (Cincinnati Chapter), 100 E. 8th St., 45202. Tel: 513-421-3131.

Catholic Charismatic Renewal Liaison, 5924 Bridgetown Rd., 45248. Tel: 513-574-1230. Rev. Richard E. Dressman.

Catholic Cursillo of Cincinnati, 10290 Mill Rd., 45231. Tel: 513-851-9399. Mary Pat Golden, Dir. Tel: 937-435-9367; Bro. Allan Schmitz, O.F.M., Spiritual Advisor. Tel: 513-245-2334.

Cincinnati Catholic Women's Association, 958 Marion Ave., 45229. Tel: 513-961-3566. Mary K. Mairose, Pres.

The Comboni Lay Missionaries Association, 8108 Beechmont Ave., 45255-3194. Tel: 513-474-4997; Fax: 513-474-0382. Rev. Sixtus Agostini, M.C.C.J., Pres.; Sr. Jeanne Oursler, C.S.J., Sec./Treas.

The Comboni Missionaries Auxiliary, Inc., 8108 Beechmont Ave., 45255-3194. Tel: 513-474-4997; Fax: 513-474-0382.
E-mail: combonipn@igc.apc.org
Evelyn Huber, Pres.; Catherine Ewers, Vice Pres.; Terry Kunke, Treas.; Janet Tate, Sec.; Mario Ongaro, M.C.C.J., Spiritual Advisor.

Franciscan Brothers Work Crew, St. Clement Friary, 4536 Vine St., 45217. Tel: 513-641-2257. Bro. Louis P. Zant, O.F.M., Mgr.

Franciscan Central Purchasing, St. Clement Friary, 4536 Vine St., 45217. Tel: 513-641-2257. Bro. Louis Zant, O.F.M., Dir.

Franciscan Home Development, Inc. A member of the Franciscan Health System of the Ohio Valley, 1300 Main St., 45210. Tel: 513-651-6457. R. Christopher West, Pres.; Ms. Stephanie Sweeney, Ex. Dir. Provides housing to over 200 persons in over 171 residential units.

Franciscan Missionary Union, 1615 Vine St., 45210-1297. Tel: 513-721-4700, Ext. 3222. Bro. Scott Obrecht, O.F.M., Exec. Dir.

HIV/AIDS Ministry Team, Archdiocese of Cincinnati, 100 E. Eighth St., 45202. Tel: 513-357-6187. Ms. Kathy Cox, Coord.

Jesuit Development Office, 2245 Gilbert Ave., 45206. Tel: 513-751-6688. Mark J. McLaughlin, Dir.

Legion of Mary, 3105 Madison Rd., 45209. Rev. Elmer W. Smith, Dir.

Living Monuments of Reparation, P.O. Box 29372, 45229. Tel: 513-569-4587. Rev. Herbert J. Raterman, S.J., Dir.

Marian Center of Cincinnati, 5365 Cleves Warsaw, 45238. Tel: 513-922-1250. Mr. Robert E. Hater, Lay Dir.; Rev. Robert J. Plagge, Spiritual Dir.

Ministers of Service, 745 Ezzard Charles, 45203. Tel: 513-381-0630. Mr. Jack D. McWilliams, Dir.

New Jerusalem Community, 745 Derby Ave., 45232. Tel: 513-541-4748; Fax: 513-541-4811. Leadership Council: Elmer Fischesser; Debbie Metz; Jerry Carrico; Tom Frey; Mary Merrill; Carol Metz, Coord. Community Life; William A. Zins, Admin.

North American Ursuline Education Services, 1339 E. McMillan St., 45206. Tel: 513-961-3410, Ext. 417; 937-392-4202. Sr. Rosemary Ninkeljohann, O.S.U., Pres.; Sr. Lois Castillion, O.S.U., Exec. Dir.

Priests Eucharistic League, 5222 N. Bend Rd., 45247. Rev. John J. Mattscheck, Dir.

St. Andrew Kim Korean Catholic Society, 3171 Struble Rd., 45251. Tel: 513-851-3065. Revs. John E. Porter; Leslie F. Blowers, M.M.; Kyung WonAhn.

St. Anthony Messenger, St. Anthony Messenger Press and Franciscan Communications, 1615 Republic St., 45210. Tel: 513-241-5615.
E-mail: st.anthony@americancatholic.org
Web site: www.americancatholic.org
Operated by the St. John the Baptist Province of the Franciscan Friars.

St. Dymphna Ministry, The Lewis Center, State Mental Hospital, P.O. Box 16061, 45216. Tel: 513-641-2257, Ext. 49; 641-4834. Rev. Valens J. Waldschmidt, O.F.M.

St. Francis Bookshop. Conducted by the St. John the Baptist Province of the Franciscan Friars. 1618 Vine St., 45210. Tel: 513-241-7304.
E-mail: st.francis_bookshop@MSN.com

Secular Franciscan Order. Holy Trinity Regional Fraternity, Inc. Founded by St. Francis of Assisi before A.D. 1215. Information concerning the Secular Franciscan Order can be obtained from SFO Office, St. Francis Center, 10290 Mill Rd. St. Francis Center, 10290 Mill Rd., 45231. Roo Potts, Minister, (Beaver Creek, OH); Bette Dries, V-Min., (Louisville, KY); Don Lipps, Sec., (Cincinnati, OH); Ralph Bidelman, Treas., (Cincinnati, OH); Ralph Schluetter, Formation Dir., (Cincinnati, OH).

Stimuli, Inc., 17 Erkenbrecher Ave., 45220-2202. Tel: 513-221-3889; 221-5538. The revitalization of Euro American worship according to the norms of Vatican II, focusing the light of tradition into the warmth of authentic worship, to reach transcendence in worship. Rev. Clarence R.J. Rivers, Ph.D., Pres.

**The Couple to Couple League International*, 4290 Delhi Pk., 45238. Tel: 513-471-2000; Fax: 513-557-2449.
E-mail: ccli@ccli.org
Web site: www.ccli.org
Mailing Address: P.O. Box 111184, 45211. John F. Kippley, Pres.

Vietnamese-Catholic Community, 5440 Moeller Ave., 45212. Tel: 513-531-3307. Rev. Huan Tien Nguyen.

CENTERVILLE. *Catholic Alumni Club (Dayton Chapter)*, 55 Williamsburg Ln., 45459. Tel: 937-433-1188. Rev. Daniel J. Meyer, Chap.

St. Leonard Faith Community, 8100 Clyo Rd., 45458. Tel: 937-435-3626; 433-7224 (Friary). Rev. Msgr. Anthony J. Giannamore, Moderator/Chap.

DAYTON. *Marianist Voluntary Service Communities, MVSC*, P.O. Box 9224, Wright Bros. Branch, 45409. Tel: 937-229-4630; 229-3287; Fax: 937-229-2772.
E-mail: mvsc@saber.udayton.edu
Michelle Cano, Assoc. Dir.; Ms. Laura Libertore, Dir.

MARIA STEIN. *Maria Stein Center Shrine of the Holy Relics*, 2291 St. John Rd., 45860. Tel: 419-925-4532; Fax: 513-925-5413. Sr. Barbara Ann Hoying, C.PP.S., Dir.

RELIGIOUS INSTITUTES OF MEN REPRESENTED IN THE ARCHDIOCESE

For further details refer to the corresponding bracketed number in the Religious Institutes of Men or Women section.

[0460]—*Brothers of the Poor of St. Francis.*—C.F.P.
[0380]—*Comboni Missionaries of the Heart of Jesus (Verona).*—M.C.C.J.
[0520]—*Franciscan Friars.*—O.F.M.
[0570]—*Glenmary Home Missioners.*—Glmy.
[0650]—*Holy Ghost Fathers.* (Eastern Province).—C.S.Sp.
[0690]—*Jesuit Fathers and Brothers.* (Chicago Province).—S.J.
[0800]—*Maryknoll.*—M.M.
[1210]—*Missionaries of St. Charles (Scalabrinians).*—C.S.
[0430]—*Order of Preachers (Dominicans).* (St. Joseph Province).—O.P.
[0760]—*Society of Mary (Marianists).* (Cincinnati Province).—S.M.
[1060]—*Society of the Precious Blood.* (Cincinnati Province).—C.PP.S.

RELIGIOUS INSTITUTES OF WOMEN REPRESENTED IN THE ARCHDIOCESE

[0230]—*Benedictine Sisters of Pontifical Jurisdiction.* (Crookston, MN; Covington, KY).—O.S.B.
[0330]—*Carmelite Sisters for the Aged and Infirm.*—O.Carm.
[0870]—*Congregation of the Daughters of Mary Immaculate (Marianist Sisters).*—F.M.I.
[3710]—*Congregation of the Sisters of Saint Agnes.*—C.S.A.
[1920]—*Congregation of the Sisters of the Holy Cross.*—C.S.C.
[1730]—*Congregation of the Sisters of the Third Order of St. Francis, Oldenburg, IN.*—O.S.F.
[1710]—*Congregation of the Third Order of St. Francis of Mary Immaculate, Joliet, IL.*—O.S.F.
[1070-07]—*Dominican Sisters.* (Adrian, MI).—O.P.
[1070-13]—*Dominican Sisters.* (St. Mary of the Springs, Columbus, OH).—O.P.
[1070-16]—*Dominican Sisters.* (Nashville, TN).—O.P.
[1070-15]—*Dominican Sisters of Hope.*—O.P.
[1440]—*Franciscan Sisters of the Poor.*—S.F.P.
[2340]—*Little Sisters of the Poor.*—L.S.P.
[2470]—*Maryknoll Sisters of St. Dominic.*—M.M.
[2490]—*Medical Mission Sisters.*—M.M.S.
[3760]—*Order of St. Clare-Poor Clares.*—O.S.C.
[3130]—*Our Lady of Victory Missionary Sisters.*—O.L.V.M.
[3230]—*Poor Handmaids of Jesus Christ.*—P.H.J.C.
[0440]—*Sisters of Charity of Cincinnati, Ohio.*—S.C.
[0500]—*Sisters of Charity of Nazareth.*—S.C.N.
[0570]—*Sisters of Charity of Seton Hill, Greensburg, Pennsylvania.*—S.C.
[1000]—*The Sisters of Divine Providence of Kentucky.*—C.D.P.
[2360]—*Sisters of Loretto at the Foot of the Cross.*—S.L.
[2630]—*Sisters of Mercy of the Holy Cross.*—S.C.S.C.
[2580]—*Sisters of Mercy of the Union of the United States of America.*—R.S.M.
[2990]—*Sisters of Notre Dame.* (Covington Prov.).—S.N.D.
[3000]—*Sisters of Notre Dame de Namur.*—S.N.D.deN.
[3360]—*Sisters of Providence of Saint Mary-of-the-Woods, Indiana.*—S.P.
[1630]—*Sisters of St. Francis of Penance and Christian Charity, Stella Niagara, NY.*—O.S.F.
[3880]—*Sisters of St. Joseph of Medaille.* (Cincinnati Prov.).—C.S.J.
[3840]—*Sisters of St. Joseph of Medaille of Carondelet.* (Latham, NY).—C.S.J.
[1830]—*The Sisters of the Good Shepherd.*—R.G.S.
[2110]—*Sisters of the Humility of Mary.*—H.M.
[3260]—*Sisters of the Precious Blood (Dayton, Ohio).*—C.PP.S.
[1760]—*Sisters of the Third Order of St. Francis of Penance and Charity.*—O.S.F.
[2150]—*Sisters, Servants of the Immaculate Heart of Mary.*—I.H.M.
[4110]—*Ursuline Nuns (Roman Union).*—O.S.U.
[4120]—*Ursuline Nuns of the Congregation of Paris.* (Saint Martin).—O.S.U.
[4120-01]—*Ursuline Nuns of the Congregation of Paris (Cincinnati, OH).*—O.S.U.

CEMETERIES

CINCINNATI. *Calvary*, 1721 Duck Creek Rd., 45207. Tel: 513-961-2179.

Gate of Heaven, 11000 Montgomery Rd., 45242. Tel: 513-489-0300.

St. John, 701 Ross Ave., 45217. Tel: 513-242-4191.

St. Joseph, Eighth St. & Seton Ave., 45205. Tel: 513-921-3050.

St. Joseph New, 4500 Foley Ave., 45238. Tel: 513-251-3110.

St. Mary, 701 Ross Ave., 45217. Tel: 513-242-4191.

DAYTON. *Calvary*, Calvary & Dixie Ave., 45409. Tel: 513-293-1221.

SPRINGFIELD. *Calvary*, 3155 E. Possum Rd., 45502. Tel: 513-513-7474.

NECROLOGY

† Funk, Louis F., (Retired). —Died Jan. 24, 1997.
† Galvin, Paul G., Cincinnati, OH, St. John Fisher. —Died Nov. 13, 1997.
† Griese, Roger E., (Retired). —Died March 4, 1997.
† Krusling, Rev. Msgr. James L., (Retired). —Died April 27, 1997.
† Kylius, Ferdinand W., (Retired). —Died Jan. 19, 1997.
† McNicholas, Timothy J., (Retired). —Died March 29, 1997.
† Schaeper, Jerome A., Cincinnati, OH, Elder High School. —Died July 11, 1997.
† Tenoever, Donald A., (Retired). —Died July 21, 1997.
† Volker, Edward H., (Retired). —Died Oct. 3, 1997.

Diocese of Cleveland

(Dioecesis Clevelandensis)

Most Reverend

ANTHONY M. PILLA, D.D., M.A.

Bishop of Cleveland; ordained May 23, 1959; appointed Auxiliary and Titular Bishop of Scardona June 30, 1979; consecrated August 1, 1979; named Apostolic Administrator of Cleveland July 29, 1980; appointed Bishop of Cleveland November 18, 1980; installed January 6, 1981. *Office: 1027 Superior Ave., Cleveland, OH, 44114.* Tel.: 216-696-6525; 800-869-6525 (Ohio only); Fax: 216-696-6547.

Most Reverend

A. EDWARD PEVEC, Ph.D.

Auxiliary Bishop of Cleveland; ordained April 29, 1950; appointed Auxiliary and Titular Bishop of Mercia April 13, 1982; consecrated July 2, 1982. *Office: Center for Pastoral Leadership, 28700 Euclid Ave., Wickliffe, OH, 44092.* Tel.: 216-944-1400; Fax: 216-943-7577.

Most Reverend

A. JAMES QUINN, J.C.D., J.D.

Auxiliary Bishop of Cleveland; ordained May 24, 1958; appointed Auxiliary and Titular Bishop of Socia October 14, 1983; consecrated December 5, 1983. *Office: 2500 Elyria Ave., Lorain, OH, 44055.* Tel.: 216-244-2120; 579-0326 (Cleveland Line); Fax: 216-899-1122.

Established April 23, 1847.

Square Miles 3,414.

Comprises since July 22, 1943, eight Counties in the north-central part of the State of Ohio, namely Ashland, Cuyahoga, Geauga, Lake, Lorain, Medina, Summit and Wayne Counties.

For legal titles of parishes and diocesan institutions, consult the Chancery Office.

Chancery Building: 1027 Superior Ave., Cleveland, OH, 44114. Tel.: 216-696-6525; 800-869-6525 (Ohio only); Fax: 216-621-7332.

STATISTICAL OVERVIEW

Personnel	
Bishop	1
Auxiliary Bishops	2
Abbots	1
Priests: Diocesan Active in Diocese	366
Priests: Active Outside Diocese	18
Priests: Diocesan in Foreign Missions	5
Priests: Retired, Sick or Absent	112
Number of Diocesan Priests	501
Religious Priests in Diocese	141
Extern Priests in Diocese	30
Ordinations:	
Diocesan Priests	3
Religious Priests	1
Transitional Deacons	5
Permanent Deacons	7
Permanent Deacons in Diocese	164
Total Brothers	79
Total Sisters	1,617
Parishes	
Parishes	237
With Resident Pastor:	
Resident Diocesan Priests	212
Resident Religious Priests	16
Without Resident Pastor:	
Administered by Priests	6
Administered by Permanent Deacons	1
Administered by Professed Men Religious	1
Administered by Women Religious	1
Missions	1
Pastoral Centers	2
New Parishes Created	1
Professional Ministry Personnel:	
Brothers	3
Sisters	110
Lay Ministers	148
Welfare	
Catholic Hospitals	6
Total Assisted	635,704
Homes for the Aged	24
Total Assisted	3,198
Residential Care of Children	1
Total Assisted	236
Day Care and Extended Day Care Centers	7
Total Assisted	1,259
Specialized Homes	6
Total Assisted	1,334
Special Centers for Social Services	21
Total Assisted	457,521
Residential Care of Disabled	1
Total Assisted	138
Other Institutions	3
Total Assisted	33,431
Educational	
Seminaries, Diocesan	2
Students from This Diocese	52
Students from Other Diocese	1
Diocesan Students in Other Seminaries	1
Students Religious	6
Total Seminarians	59
Colleges and Universities	3
Total Students	6,309
High Schools, Diocesan and Parish	7
Total Students	4,436
High Schools, Private	16
Total Students	10,184
Elementary Schools, Diocesan and Parish	133
Total Students	49,540
Elementary Schools, Private	7
Total Students	2,469
Non-residential Schools for the Disabled	1
Total Students	72
Catechesis/Religious Education:	
High School Students	6,889
Elementary Students	45,214
Total Students Under Catholic Instruction	125,172
Teachers in the Diocese:	
Priests	15
Brothers	21
Sisters	233
Lay Teachers	3,196
Vital Statistics	
Receptions into the Church:	
Infant Baptism Totals	11,013
Adult Baptism Totals	1,057
Received into Full Communion	903
First Communions	12,336
Confirmations	9,620
Marriages:	
Catholic	2,815
Interfaith	1,701
Total Marriages	4,516
Deaths	8,876
Total Catholic Population	831,887
Total Population	2,821,580

Former Bishops—Rt. Rev. Amadeus Rappe, D.D., cons. Oct. 10, 1847; resigned Aug. 22, 1870; died Sept 8, 1877.—Rt. Rev. Richard Gilmour, D.D., cons. April 14, 1872; died April 13, 1891.—Rt. Rev. Ignatius F. Horstmann, D.D., cons. Feb. 25, 1892; died May 13, 1908.—Rt. Rev. John P. Farrelly, D.D., cons. May 1, 1909; died Feb. 12, 1921.—Most Rev. Joseph Schrembs, S.T.D., Archbishop-Bishop of Cleveland; cons. Feb. 22, 1911; transferred to the See of Cleveland, June 16, 1921; installed Sept. 8, 1921; appt. Archbishop, March 25, 1939; died November 2, 1945.—Most Rev. Edward F. Hoban, S.T.D., Ph.D., L.L.D., Archbishop-Bishop of Cleveland; cons. Dec. 21, 1921; transferred to Cleveland as Coadjutor Bishop "cum jure successionis" Nov. 14, 1942; succeeded to See of Cleveland, Nov. 2, 1945; appt. Archbishop, July 23, 1951; died Sept. 22, 1966.—Most Rev. Clarence G. Issenmann, S.T.D., cons. May 25, 1954; transferred to Cleveland as Coadjutor Bishop "cum jure successionis" and Titular Bishop of Filaca. Ap-Adm. Oct. 7, 1964; succeeded to See of Cleveland, Sept. 22, 1966; retired June 5, 1974; died July 27, 1982.—Most Rev. James A. Hickey, S.T.D., J.C.D., cons. April 14, 1967; appt. Bishop of Cleveland, June 5, 1974; installed July 16, 1974; appt. Archbishop of Washington, DC June 18, 1980; created Cardinal by Pope John Paul II in the consistory on June 28, 1988.

Vicars General—Most Rev. A. Edward Pevec, Ph.D., *Center For Pastoral Leadership, 28700 Euclid Ave., Wickliffe, 44092.* Tel: 216-944-1400. Most Rev. A. James Quinn, J.C.D., J.D., *2500 Elyria Ave., Lorain, 44055.* Tel: 216-244-2120; 579-0326 Cleveland Line. Rev. Ralph E. Wiatrowski, Chancellor, *1027 Superior Ave., Cleveland, 44114.* Tel: 216-696-6525.

College of Consultors—Rt. Rev. Roger Gries, O.S.B.;

Rev. Msgr. ROBERT BACHER; Revs. RAY BARTNIKOWSKI; JOHN CREGAN; MARK HOLLIS; JOSEPH H. KRAKER; THOMAS MCGOVERN; JOHN OLSAVSKY; PAUL ROSING; ROBERT SANSON; ANTHONY ZEPP; RALPH E. WIATROWSKI, Sec.

Presbyteral Council—Revs. MARK L. HOLLIS, Moderator; RICHARD C. ANTALL; ROBERT E. BACHER; LEONARD BACIK; RALPH L. COLETTA; EDWARD T. ESTOK; THOMAS A. MCGOVERN; STEPHEN RADECKY; LAWRENCE JURCAK; Rt. Rev. ROGER GRIES, O.S.B.; Revs. DANIEL F. SCHLEGEL; DAVID R. TRASK; ANTHONY W. ZEPP, Presbyteral Conveners: Revs. NELSON CALLAHAN; THOMAS A. HAREN; DENNIS J. KLEINWEBER; JOHN R. OLSAVSKY; WILLIAM B. PADAVICK; PAUL J. ROSING; JOHN J. CREGAN; MARK A. DINARDO; MARK L. HOLLIS; KEVIN LIEBHARDT; DANIEL L. BEGIN; DOUGLAS MAKOWSKI; ROBERT C. WOLFF.

Finance Council—Most Rev. ANTHONY M. PILLA, Pres.; Sr. MARY NATHAN, S.N.D.; ANTHONY LANG; JOHN P. MCGINTY; CASIMIR J. RUTT; KEVIN O'DONNELL; NORMAN T. PATTON; WILLIAM J. REIDY.

Diocesan Pastoral Council—Most Rev. ANTHONY M. PILLA; DONALD R. BECK, Pres.; MARY CHRISTINE JACKMAN, Vice Pres.; RICHARD KRIVANKA, Exec. Sec.

Conference of Religious Leadership—Sr. MARGARET TAYLOR, S.I.W., Chm., *6618 Pearl Rd., Parma Heights, 44130*. Tel: 440-886-1377. Sr. ROCHELLE GUERTAL, O.SS.T., Sec./Treas., *1355 W. 70th St., Cleveland, 44102*. Tel: 216-281-7146.

Diocese of Cleveland—

Chancery Building—1027 Superior Ave., Cleveland, 44114.

Catholic Center—1031 Superior Ave., Cleveland, 44114.

All Diocesan Offices in the Chancery Building or in the Catholic Center may be reached at Tel: 216-696-6525 or 800-869-6525 (Ohio only); Fax: 216-781-8243.

Address dispensations and all business communication to the Chancery Office.

Chancellor—Rev. RALPH E. WIATROWSKI, J.C.D., S.T.L., Office: *Chancery Building*. Fax: 216-621-7332.

Vice-Chancellor—Rev. DAVID J. WALKOWIAK, J.C.D., Office: *Chancery Building*.

Assistant Chancellors—Revs. THEODORE MARSZAL, Office: *Catholic Center*. JOSEPH E. LEHANE, Office: *40 University Ave., Akron, 44308*. Tel: 330-434-4114. Sr. LAURA BOUHALL, O.S.U., Office: *Chancery Building*.

Secretary to Bishop Pilla—Rev. THEODORE MARSZAL, Office: *Catholic Center*.

Judicial Offices—

Office of Mediation—Sr. DONNA MIKULA, O.S.U., *Chancery Building*. Tel: 216-696-6525; 800-869-6525.

Tribunal—Office: *1027 Superior Ave., Ste. 500, Cleveland, 44114*. Tel: 216-696-6525, Ext. 400; 800-869-6525 (Ohio only); 800-676-4431 (Outside Ohio); Fax: 216-696-3226.

Judicial Vicar—Rev. MARK Q. FEDOR, J.C.D.

Adjutant Judicial Vicars—Revs. DONALD P. BRICKMAN, J.C.L.; LAWRENCE JURCAK, J.C.L.; THOMAS A. MORAN, J.C.D.; GARY D. YANUS, J.C.D.; PETER D. WASLO, J.C.L.

Judges—Deacon LOUIS G. PECEK, Ph.D.; Sr. JEAN C. IFFARTH, O.S.U., J.C.L.

Defenders of the Bond—Revs. JOSEPH A. BACEVICE, M.Div.; WILLIAM M. JERSE, J.C.L.; Sr. CHRISTINE M. RODY, V.S.C., J.C.L.; Rev. MICHAEL J. TROHA, M.A., M.Div.

Associate Judicial Vicars—Revs. MIRKO HLADNI, J.C.L.; EDWARD J. LUCA, J.C.D.; JOHN R. OLSAVSKY, J.C.L.; WILLIAM P. O'NEILL, J.C.L.; ROBERT F. PFEIFFER, J.C.L.; ROBERT J. SANSON, J.C.D.; DAVID J. WALKOWIAK, J.C.D.; EDWARD F. WEIST, J.C.D.; RALPH E. WIATROWSKI, J.C.D.

Associate Judges—Deacon JAMES L. AGRIPPE; Rev. MARTIN J. AMOS; Sr. MARY ANN ANDREWS, C.S.A., J.C.L.; Revs. NELSON J. CALLAHAN, M.Div.; GARY D. CHMURA, M.Div.; CHARLES T. DIEDRICK, M.A.; JEROME J. DUKE; JOHN R. HENGLE; ALAN R. LAUBENTHAL, S.T.D.; JOHN E. MANNING, M.Div.; LAWRENCE N. MARTELLO, M.Div.; THOMAS W. MCCANN; JOHN J. MUELLER; CORNELIUS J. MURRAY, M.S.E.; PAUL J. ROSING, M.Div.; THOMAS R. SMITH, M.Div.; ARTHUR SNEDEKER, M.Div.; DONALD E. SNYDER, M.Div.; CHARLES J. STOLLENWERK, M.Div.; ALBERT J. TESEK; ROBERT M. WENDELKEN, M.Div.; ANTHONY W. ZEPP, M.Div.

Assessor—Mr. WILLIAM P. GILMORE, L.I.S.W.

Auditor/Assessor—Revs. ALLEN F. CORRIGAN, M.Div.; DONALD P. OLEKSIAK, M.Div.; DAVID R. TRASK, M.Div.

Procurators—Revs. JOSEPH HILINSKI, M.Div.; THEODORE MARSZAL, S.T.D.; DAVID J. WEBER, M.Div.

Promoter of Justice—Sr. CHRISTINE C. RODY, V.S.C., J.C.L.

Notaries—Ms. MARY M. BRYAN. Notary Public: Miss CYNTHIA M. QUINLAN; Miss DENISE C. RABATIN.

Translators—Mr. RIAD BAHUR; Revs. RICHARD R. BOBER, Ph.D.; EDWARD ESTOK, M.A., M.Div.; BEDE KOTLINSKI, O.S.B.; AUGUSTINE PHAM VAN LAN, Ph.D.; JOHN F. WESSEL.

Administrator of Buildings—MICHAEL E. SUHY, *Chancery Building*.

Archivist—Rev. RALPH E. WIATROWSKI; CHRISTINE L. KROSEL, Dir., *Chancery Building*.

Catholic Cemeteries Association—Rev. JAMES J. GRANDILLO, Dir.; THOMAS J. KELLEY, Admin., *10000 Miles Ave., Box 05310, Cleveland, 44105*. Tel: 216-641-7575.

Callistian Guild—P.O. Box 605044, Cleveland, 44105. Tel: 216-641-7575.

Central Purchasing—EDWARD J. ZAMISKA, Dir., *3020 Superior Ave., Cleveland, 44114*. Tel: 216-696-4811; 800-362-9016.

Communications Department—Rev. MICHAEL G. DIMENGO, Dir., *Chancery Building*. Tel: 216-696-6525, Ext. 454.

Office for Media Relations—ROBERT A. POLOMSKY, Assoc. Dir., *Chancery Building*.

Radio and Television Productions—MARY FLYNN, Assoc. Dir.

"Catholic Universe Bulletin"—Most Rev. ANTHONY M. PILLA, Publisher; Rev. MICHAEL G. DIMENGO, Assoc. Publisher; JOSEPH M. POLITO, Gen. Mgr., Office: *Chancery Building*. Tel: 216-696-6525, Ext. 587; 696-6525, Ext. 277 (after 5 p.m.).

Catholic Universe Bulletin Publishing Company, Inc.—Chancery Building.

Diocesan Pastoral Planning Office—RICHARD S. KRIVANKA, Dir.; MARIE HIRSCH, Coord., Special Projects; DAVID DE LAMBO, Consultant, Parish Pastoral Council Svcs.; JEAN S. CLEARY, Office Coord., Office: *Chancery Building*.

Mission Office, Society for the Propagation of the Faith—Rev. DENIS L. ST. MARIE, Dir., Office: *The Catholic Center*, Ext. 424.

Pontifical Programs—Society for the Propagation of the Faith; Society of St. Peter the Apostle; Missionary Union of the Clergy; Holy Childhood Assoc.

National Programs—Latin-American Program; Lay Mission Volunteers.

Diocesan Programs—Missionary Cooperation Plan; St. Francis Xavier Mission Assoc.; Cleveland Diocesan Mission, C.A.

National Shrine of Immaculate Conception—Washington, DC. Rev. RALPH E. WIATROWSKI, Chancellor, *Chancery Building*.

Financial & Legal

Financial—Rev. JOHN J. WRIGHT, J.D., C.E.O. & Financial/Legal Sec.; JOSEPH H. SMITH, Treasurer & C.F.O., *Ninth St. C.D.C.*

Legal—SANTIAGO FELICIANO, *Ninth St. C.D.C.*

Catholic Lawyers' Guild of Cleveland—Chancery Building.

Catholic Lawyers' Guild of Cleveland Endowment Trust—Chancery Building.

Diocesan Budget Committee—THOMAS GARVEY, Chm., *Chancery Building*.

Diocesan Building Commission—Rev. JOHN J. WRIGHT, J.D., Coord.

Department of Diocesan Fund Development—AUGUST A. NAPOLI, Jr., Coord.

Diocesan Insurance Service Committee—(DISC). Members: J. THOMAS HANNON; THOMAS MCGOWAN, III; DENNIS P. TOP.

Diocesan Financial Advisory Committee—JACK P. MCGINTY, Chm.

Health Benefits—PALMIRA JUREVICIUS, *Ninth St. C.D.C.*

Group Life and Pension Plans—LES KULIN, *Ninth St. C.D.C.*

Workers' Compensation Office—Vacant, *Ninth St. C.D.C.*

Informational Services Office—MICHAEL NOVICKY, Office: *Ninth St. C.D.C.*

Secretariat for Education

Secretary—Sr. CAROL ANNE SMITH, H.M., *The Catholic Center*. Tel: 216-696-6525, Ext. 328; Fax: 216-696-6217.

Departments—

School Food Services/Summer Food Service Program—RENE WEBER, Dir., *Catholic Center*.

Buildings and Grounds/Technology—DANIEL BRODNIK, Dir., *Catholic Center*.

Department of Fund Development—Mrs. KENDRA GEVRY, Dir., *Catholic Center*.

Catholic Education Endowment Trust—Catholic Center—

Inner-City School Fund—Catholic Center—

Newman Campus Ministry—WILLIAM FICHTER, Assoc. Dir., *Catholic Center*, Ext. 892.

Ministers—EMILY HOLTEL, *Akron University*. Tel: 330-376-3585. MARIE DE LABRUERE, *Case Western Reserve University, Hallinan Center*. Tel: 216-421-1522. MATTHEW MARUGGI, *Lakeland Community College*. Tel: 216-953-4803. Rev. EDWIN A. DOWLING, *Ashland University*. Tel: 419-994-4396. MAUREEN MASTERSON, *College of Wooster*. Tel: 216-263-2096. WILLIAM A. FICHTER, *Baldwin-Wallace College*. Tel: 216-243-4955. Rev. EDWARD KORDAS, *Oberlin College*. Tel: 216-775-8103. MAUREEN MASTERSON, *Cuyahoga Community College-West*. Tel: 216-886-1327. MATTHEW MARUGGI, *Case Western Reserve University, Hallinan Center*. Tel: 216-421-1522. WILLIAM FICHTER, *Cuyahoga Community College-Metro*. Tel: 216-987-4239. EMILY HOLTEL, *Lorain County Community College*. Tel: 440-365-5222, ext. 7661; 800-995-5222.

Religious Education Office—DENISE SMITHBERGER, Assoc. Dir., *Catholic Center*.

Area Religious Education Consultants—MARY ANN TYRER, *Western Area Office, 2500 Elyria Ave., Lorain, 44055*. Tel: 440-233-1612; 440-871-5246 (Cleveland line). DENISE SMITHBERGER; WILLIAM B. MILLER, *Southern Area, 1025 Clay St., Akron, 44301*. Tel: 330-773-7621. MARY LOU NECKEL, *Eastern Area Office, Hallinan Center, 11303 Euclid Ave., Cleveland, 44106*. Tel: 216-421-1522. MICHAEL YOUNGBLOOD, *Central Area Office, Catholic Center, 1031 Superior Ave., Cleveland, 44114*. Tel: 216-696-6525, Ext. 320.

Media Library—WILLIAM MILLER, *Catholic Center*. Tel: 216-696-6525, Ext. 433.

Office of Catholic Education—Sr. CAROL ANNE SMITH, H.M., Sec. for Education/Supt.; Sr. KATHLEEN SKUTA C.S.F.N., Sec. Asst., *Catholic Center*. Tel: 216-696-6525, Ext. 328.

Curriculum—Sr. MARY ELLEN RYAN, S.I.W., Dir. Catholic Ctr., Ext. 333.

Field Directors—Sr. BARBARA BROMEIER, H.M., *Eastern Area Office, Hallinan Center, 11303 Euclid Ave., Cleveland, 44106*. Tel: 216-421-1522. Sr. LUCIA BUCHOLTZ, S.S.J.-T.O.S.F., *Western Area Office, 2500 Elyria Ave., Lorain, 44055*. Tel: 440-244-1612; 871-5246 (Cleveland line). Sr. PATRICIA KIDDER, I.H.M., *Southern Area Office, 1025 Clay St., Akron, 44301*. Tel: 330-773-7621.

School Planning Process—Sr. ANNE GLASER, S.N.D., Dir., *Catholic Center*, Ext. 378.

Registrar/Special Projects—CASEY SCAFIDI, *Catholic Center*.

Catholic Parent Teacher League—ANITA WOZNIAK, Pres., *7120 Thorton Dr., Parma, 44129*. Tel: 216-845-9138. GAYLE JAKUBCZAK, Corresponding Sec. Tel: 216-901-0349.

Finance, Policy and Planning—LISA A.B. RACHUL, Business Mgr., *Catholic Center*, Ext. 630.

Secondary Education—MARGARET LYONS, Dir., *Catholic Center*, Ext. 245.

Government Programs—MICHAEL VOINOVICH, Dir., *Catholic Center*, Ext. 335.

Mandated Services—Consultants: CHERYL FASCIANO; RAY PUDELSKI; MICHELE WINTER-SHREFLER, *Catholic Center*.

Secretariat for Parish Life and Development

Secretary—Sr. RITA MARY HARWOOD, S.N.D., *Catholic Center*, Ext. 350.

Blue Army of Our Lady of Fatima—Marian Center, 6626 Pearl Rd., Parma Heights, 44130-3808. Tel: 440-888-8553.

Catholic Renewal Ministries—Rev. ROBERT FRANCO, *367 E. 260, Euclid, 44132-1495*. Tel: 216-731-1515. *Bishop's Delegate, Presentation House, 28706 Euclid Ave., #4, Wickliffe, 44092*. Tel: 440-944-9445.

Central City Ministry with Poor—Rev. JAMES P. O'DONNELL, *2186 E. 35th St., Cleveland, 44115*. Tel: 216-566-0531.

Cleveland Diocesan Council, NCCW—MARYALICE O'BRIEN, Pres., *Catholic Center*; Rev. RALPH HUDAK, Moderator, *4427 Rocky River Dr., Cleveland, 44135*. Tel: 216-251-8286.

Diocesan Interfaith Commission—Rev. JOSEPH J. HILINSKI, Delegate, *Catholic Center*, Ext. 511.

Enthronement of the Sacred Heart—Diocesan Center, St. John Cathedral Rectory, 1007 Superior Ave., Cleveland, 44114. Tel: 216-267-4713. MARGARET OLLE, Sec.

Ethnic Ministries—

Diocesan Hispanic Office—Sr. JOAQUINA CARRION, M.S.B.T., Dir., *Catholic Center*, Ext. 430.

Korean Catholic Apostolate—Rev. PETER YOUNG-KEU SIN, *St. Andrew Kim (Korean Pastoral Center), 2310 West 14th St., Cleveland, 44113*. Tel: 216-861-4630.

Native American Ministry—Sr. JOAN LANG, C.S.J., Dir., *Catholic Center*, Ext. 350.

Office of Ministry to African American Catholics—VANESSA GRIFFIN CAMPBELL, Dir., *Catholic Center*, Ext. 302.

Philippine-American Ministry—Rev. GREGORIO BANGA, Dir., *12021 Mayfield Rd., Cleveland, 44106*. Tel: 216-421-2995.

Vietnamese-American Apostolate—Rev. AUGUSTINE PHAM VAN LAN, Dir., *3545 W. 54th St., Cleveland, 44102*. Tel: 216-961-2713.

Office of Evangelization—Sr. VIRGINIA STASIUM, S.S.N.D., Dir., *Catholic Center,* Ext. 254.

Holy Name Societies, Cleveland Diocesan Union—Rev. THOMAS HAREN, Spiritual Dir., *15000 Lake Shore Blvd., Cleveland, 44110-1298.* Tel: 216-481-8200.

Pastoral Ministry Office—KATHLEEN HAASE-FALBO, Dir., *Center for Pastoral Leadership, 28700 Euclid Ave., Wickliffe, 44092.* Tel: 440-943-7670.

Legion of Mary—Rev. HERMAN B. PETERS, Spiritual Dir., Office: *1007 Superior Ave., Cleveland, 44114.*

Office for Pastoral Liturgy—Rev. J-GLENN MURRAY, S.J., Dir., *Catholic Center,* Ext. 412.

Office for Women in Church and Society—DEBRA MARSEY, Dir., *Catholic Center,* Ext. 303.

St. Joseph Christian Life Center—Rev. WALTER J. HYCLAK, Exec. Dir., *18485 Lake Shore Blvd., Cleveland, 44119.* Tel: 216-531-7370.

Secretariat for Clergy and Religious

Secretary—Rev. JOHN F. MURPHY, Ph.D., Vicar for Clergy and Religious, *The Catholic Center.*

Borromeo Seminary—See Seminaries.

Clergy Personnel Board—Rev. LAWRENCE JURCAK, J.C.L., M.Div., Dir., *The Catholic Center.*

Continuing Education and Formation of Ministers—Rev. EDWARD T. ESTOK, Dir., *The Center for Pastoral Leadership, 28700 Euclid Ave., Wickliffe, 44092.*

Office for Religious—Sr. CHRISTINE RODY, V.S.C., Delegate, *The Catholic Center.*

Permanent Diaconate—Deacon KENNETH PIECHOWSKI, Dir., *The Center for Pastoral Leadership, 28700 Euclid Ave., Wickliffe, 44092.*

Retirement Board—Revs. JAMES CONRY, Chm., *Sacred Heart Parish, 272 Broad St., Wadsworth, 44281.* Tel: 216-336-3049. Rev. THOMAS L. WEBER, Sec., *Holy Family, 7367 York Rd., Parma, 44130.* Tel: 216-842-5533.

St. Mary Seminary—See Seminaries.

Senior Priests—Rev. JOSEPH MCMAHON, Delegate, *St. Vincent Charity Hosp., 2351 E. 22nd St., Cleveland, 44115.* Tel: 216-861-6200.

Vocations Office—Co-Dirs.: Rev. ROBERT STEC; Sr. MARY ROSE KOCAB, S.I.W., *The Catholic Center.*

Avilas of the Diocese of Cleveland—RUTH MERRIMAN, Pres., *The Catholic Center.*

Parents of Priests—DONALD TRASK, Pres., *The Catholic Center.*

Secretariat for Health and Human Services

Secretary—J. THOMAS MULLEN, M.S.W., C.S.W., *1111 Superior Ave., Cleveland, 44114.* Tel: 216-696-6525, Ext. 416; Fax: 216-344-9962.

Catholic Charities Parish Services—TERRENCE FLANAGAN, Senior Dir., *1031 Superior Ave., Cleveland, 44114.* Tel: 216-696-6525, Ext. 503; Fax: 216-344-9962.

Office of Ministry for Persons with Disabilities—Rev. JOSEPH MCNULTY, M.Div., M.Th., Exec. Dir., *St. Augustine Church, 2486 W. 14th St., Cleveland, 44113.* Tel: 216-781-5530; Fax: 216-781-1124.

Marriage and Family Office—Rev. STEPHEN J. DOHNER, Dir., *1031 Superior Ave., Cleveland, 44114.* Tel: 216-696-6525, Ext. 357.

Catholic Information and Referral Service (CIRS)—JANE HORRIGAN, Dir., *1031 Superior Ave., Cleveland, 44114.* Tel: 216-696-HELP (4357); 800-869-6525, Ext. 243; 439; Fax: 216-344-9962.

Youth and Young Adult Ministry and CYO Office—GREG MOSER, Dir., *1031 Superior Ave., Cleveland, 44114.* Tel: 216-696-6525.

Migration and Refugee Services—DIANE SHERBAN, Dir., *1736 Superior Ave., Cleveland, 44114.* Tel: 216-566-9500; Fax: 216-566-9161.

Pro Life Office—COLLEEN GALLAGHER, Dir., *1031 Superior Ave., Cleveland, 44114.* Tel: 216-696-6525 (Ext. 360); 800-869-6525 (Central Office of Diocese); Fax: 216-781-8243. Satellite Office: *795 Russell, Akron, 44037.* Tel: 330-535-5767.

Catholic Charities Services Corporation—J. THOMAS MULLEN, Pres. & CEO; JOHN P. KLEE, Exec. Vice Pres. and COO, *1111 Superior Ave., Cleveland, 44114.* Tel: 216-696-6525, Ext. 416; Fax: 216-344-9962.

Children and Family Services—THOMAS WOLL, Senior Dir., Ext. 802.

Disabilities Services—DENNIS MCNULTY, Senior Dir., Ext. 249.

Emergency and Transitional Assistance Program—CHIP JOSEPH, Senior Dir., Ext. 352.

Other Adult Services—JEAN THERRIEN, Senior Dir., Ext. 393.

Catholic Charities Facilities Corp.—LAWRENCE E. MURTAGH, Pres. & CEO, *1111 Superior Ave., Cleveland, 44114.* Tel: 216-696-6525, Ext. 554; Fax: 216-344-9962.

Catholic Charities Corporation—AUGUST A. NAPOLI, JR., Pres. & CEO, *1111 Superior Ave., Cleveland, 44114.* Tel: 216-696-6525, Ext. 604; Fax: 216-348-0740.

The Catholic Charities Foundation—AUGUST A. NAPOLI, JR., Pres. & CEO, *1111 Superior Ave., Cleveland, 44114.* Tel: 216-696-6525, Ext. 604; Fax: 216-348-0740.

Diocesan Social Action Office—THOMAS J. ALLIO, Dir., *1031 Superior Ave., Cleveland, 44114.* Tel: 216-696-6525, Ext. 374; Fax: 216-781-8243.

Catholic Action Commission of Lorain County—SHARON KLEPPEL, Dir., *2500 Elyria Ave., Lorain, 44055.* Tel: 216-244-6037; Fax: 216-899-1122.

Catholic Commission of Lake and Geauga Counties—Sr. MADELINE SHEMO, H.M., Dir., *Schrembs Hall, 28706 Euclid Ave., Wickliffe, 44092.* Tel: 216-585-7745; Fax: 216-585-7747.

Catholic Commission (Summit County)—THOMAS J. ALLIO, Dir., *729 Russell Ave., Akron, 44307.* Tel: 330-535-2787; Fax: 330-535-9040.

Catholic Commission of Wayne, Ashland and Medina Counties—PATRICK O'BRIEN, Exec. Dir., *521 Beall Ave., P.O. Box 15, Wooster, 44691.* Tel: 330-263-6176; Fax: 330-262-4633. Satellite Office: *72 Public Square, Ste. 2, Medina, 44256.* Tel: 330-722-1851.

Campaign for Human Development—ROCKY ORTIZ, Coord., *1031 Superior Ave., Cleveland, 44114.* Tel: 216-696-6525, Ext. 228; Fax: 216-781-8243.

CLERGY, PARISHES, MISSIONS AND PAROCHIAL SCHOOLS

CITY OF CLEVELAND
(Cuyahoga County)

1—CATHEDRAL OF ST. JOHN THE EVANGELIST (1848), Rev. David C. Weber, Rector; Deacon Kenneth J. Piechowski. In res., Revs. Theodore Marszal; Lawrence Jurcak; John F. Murphy; Michael G. Dimengo; James J. Grandillo; Donald P. Brickman.
Res., 1007 Superior Ave., N.E., 44114-2582. Tel: 216-771-6666; Fax: 216-781-5646.
Church—E. 9th St. & Superior Ave. N.E., 44114.
Catechesis/Religious Programs—Students 150.

2—ST. ADALBERT (1883), Rev. Jerome Steinbrunner, C.PP.S.; Lemuel J. Walcott, Pastoral Assoc. In res., Bro. Richard Schaffner, C.PP.S.
Res., 2347 E. 83rd St., 44104. Tel: 216-881-7647.
School—2345 E. 83rd St., 44104. Tel: 216-881-6250; Fax: 216-881-9030. Ms. Elizabeth Dena Primer, Prin.
Lay Teachers 15; Students 378.

3—ST. AGNES - OUR LADY OF FATIMA (1980), Rev. Michael K. Barth, S.T. In res., Rev. John Ford, S.T.
Res., 6805 Quimby Ave., 44103. Tel: 216-391-3947; 391-1655 (Office); Fax: 216-391-7919.
Church—6800 Lexington Ave., 44103. Tel: 216-391-1655.

4—ST. ALOYSIUS - ST. AGATHA (1975), Revs. Michael Nartker, S.M.; Eldon Reichert, S.M.; Bro. Michael O'Grady, Admin.
Res., 10932 St. Clair Ave., 44108-1939. Tel: 216-451-3262; 3263; Fax: 216-268-3830.
Schools—640 Lakeview Rd., N.E., 44108. Tel: 216-451-2050; Fax: 216-541-1601. Sr. Sandra Lea Sabo, S.S.J.-T.O.S.F., Prin.
Sisters 2; Lay Teachers 8; Students 258; St. Joseph School, Tel: 216-451-2143; Fax: 216-451-8832.
Sisters 1; Lay Teachers 10; Students 241.
Convent—653 E. 109th St., 44108-1939. Tel: 216-791-9530.

5—ST. ANDREW (1906) (Slovak), Rev. Raphael Zbin, O.S.B.
Res., 5135 Superior Ave., 44103. Tel: 216-431-2057.

6—ST. ANDREW KIM (1988) (Korean), Rev. Peter Young Keu Sin; Sr. Benedicta Young Hee Ha, Admin. Pastoral Assocs.: Thomas Chan Jong; Dr. Cecilia Park.
Res., 2310 West 14th St., 44113. Tel: 216-861-4630; Fax: 216-241-6366.
Convent—2496 W. 14th St., 44113. Tel: 216-861-4408.

7—ANNUNCIATION (1924), Rev. Russell J. Banner. Pastoral Assocs.: Sr. Janet Bednar, C.S.J.; Sr. Marilyn Nickol, C.S.J.
Res., 4697 W. 130th St., 44135-3798. Tel: 216-671-2015; Fax: 216-941-1014.

8—ASCENSION (1946), Rev. Joseph J. Fortuna. Pastoral Assocs.: Ms. Laurel A. Jurecki; Ms. Lori Ashyk; Deacon John Koch.
Res., 14040 Puritas Ave., 44135. Tel: 216-671-5890; 5891; Fax: 216-671-2320.
School—4400 W. 140th St., 44135. Tel: 216-941-3715. Sr. Laura Bregar, O.S.U., Prin.
Sisters 2; Lay Teachers 20; Students 428.
Convent—4370 W. 140th St., 44135.

9—ST. AUGUSTINE (1860), Rev. Joseph D. McNulty. Pastoral Assocs.: Sr. Corita Ambro, C.S.J.; Mary Ellen Czelusniak; Sr. Audrey Koch, C.S.J.; Deacons John M. Rivera; Edmund J. Karecki; Louis Woyton.
Res., 2486 W. 14th St., 44113. Tel: 216-781-5530; Fax: 216-781-1124.
School—Metro Catholic Parish School. See Separate Listing under Elementary Schools, Parochial and Diocesan.
Catechesis/Religious Programs—Mrs. Sheila Gelzinis, D.R.E.
Students 413.
Convent—2432 W. 14th St., 44113. Tel: 216-579-1306.

10—ST. BARBARA (1905) (Polish), Revs. Michael S. Durcz, Admin.; Chester C. Cudnik, Pastor Emeritus.
Res., 1505 Denison Ave., 44109. Tel: 216-741-2067.
Convent—3855 W. 16th St., 44109. Tel: 216-661-0547.

11—ST. BENEDICT. Closed. For inquiries for parish records contact the Chancery.

12—BLESSED SACRAMENT (1903), Rev. Matthew A. Ischay; Deacon William E. Schill.
Res., 3381 Fulton Rd., 44109. Tel: 216-741-8338.
School—3389 Fulton Rd., 44109. Tel: 216-741-0172; Fax: 216-741-0172. Ms. Jane Bouman, Prin.
Lay Teachers 9; Students 150.

13—ST. BONIFACE (1903), Rev. Augustine Pham Van Lan; Sr. Dianne Skubby, C.PP.S., Pastoral Assoc. In res., Rev. Mark Q. Fedor.
Res., 3545 W. 54th St., 44102. Tel: 216-961-2713; 961-2714; Fax: 216-634-2844.
Convent—3588 W. 52nd St., 44102. Tel: 961-0669.

14—ST. CASIMIR (1891) (Polish), Rev. Msgr. Leo Telesz. In res., Rev. George Kusy, J.C.L.
Res., 8223 Sowinski Ave., 44103. Tel: 216-361-4322.
Convent—1116 East 82nd St., 44103. Tel: 216-361-5008.

15—ST. CATHERINE (1898), Revs. Walter H. Jenne, Admin.; Robert Wenz; William Dickinson. Pastoral Assocs.: Sr. Mary Jane Vovk, S.N.D.; Sr. Mary Janeta Stamper, S.N.D.
Res., 9412 Heath Ave., 44104-5512. Tel: 216-341-3353; 341-5542.
Church—E. 93rd & Catherine Ave., 44104.
School—See Archbishop Lyke School.

16—ST. CECILIA (1915), Revs. Daniel L. Begin; Herman B. Peters, Pastor Emeritus; Deacon William Ansley Love; Sr. Rosella Holloman, C.S.A., Pastoral Assoc.
Res., 3476 E. 152nd St., 44120. Tel: 216-921-3310; 921-3311.
Church—Kinsman Rd. & E. 152nd St., 44120.

17—ST. COLMAN (1880), Rev. Robert T. Begin; Deacon William H. Corrigan. Administrators: Sr. Carol English, C.S.J.; Sr. Lucy Dragonette, C.S.J.
Res., 2027 W. 65th St., 44102. Tel: 216-651-0550; Fax: 216-651-1663.
Convent—2007 W. 65th St., 44102. Tel: 216-961-1550.

18—CONVERSION OF ST. PAUL (1931), Revs. Senan Glass, O.F.M.Cap.; Andrew Hohman, O.F.M.Cap. In res., Revs. Eric Gauchet, O.F.M.Cap.; Gary Stakem, O.F.M.Cap.; Bro. James Allman.
Res., Connected with the monastery of the Poor Clares of Perpetual Adoration. 4120 Euclid Ave., 44103-3728. Tel: 216-431-8854; Fax: 216-361-1951.
Convent—4108 Euclid Ave., 44103-3728.

19—CORPUS CHRISTI (1935), Rev. Ronald J. Szudarek; Deacons David J. Lundeen; Charles Zawadzki.
Res., 5204 Northcliff Ave., 44144-4065. Tel: 216-351-8738; 8739; Fax: 216-741-5620.
School—5007 Archmere Ave., 44144. Tel: 216-351-2974; Fax: 216-661-9188. Sr. M. Maureen Ryba, S.S.J.-T.O.S.F., Prin.
Lay Teachers 10; Students 189.
Convent—Tel: 216-741-5001.

20—CRISTO REY, CAPILLA DE (1983) (Hispanic). Closed. For inquiries for parish records contact the Chancery.

21—ST. ELIZABETH (1892) (Magyar), Rev. Andras Antal (Hungary) Admin.
Mailing Address: P.O. Box 20175, 44120-0175.
Church—9016 Buckeye Rd., 44104. Tel: 216-231-0325; Fax: 216-231-0325.

22—ST. EMERIC (1904 & Territorial 1964) (Magyar), Rev. Sandor Siklodi (Hungary) Admin.; Deacon Geza J. Balassy.
Res., 1860 W. 22nd St., 44113. Tel: 216-861-1937.

23—EPIPHANY (1944), Rev. Daniel L. Begin; Deacon Troy F. Stokes; Sr. Sheila Marie Tobbe, O.S.U., Pastoral Assoc.
Res., 11901 Oakfield Ave., 44105. Tel: 216-561-3975.
School—See Mount Pleasant Catholic Elementary Education Center, 3845 E. 131st St., 44105. Tel: 216-991-1615.

24—ST. FRANCIS (1887), Rev. Thomas F. Martin; Deacon Frank Lozada.

Office: 7206 Myron Ave., 44103. Tel: 216-361-4133; Fax: 216-361-1673.
School—Tel: 216-361-4858. Sr. Karen Somerville, S.N.D., Prin.
Sisters of Notre Dame 6; Lay Teachers 5; Students 269.
Catechesis/Religious Programs—Students 266.
Convent—7119 Superior Ave., 44103. Tel: 216-361-5094.

25—ST. GEORGE (1901) (Lithuanian), Revs. Joseph A. Bacevice; Balys C. Ivanauskas, Pastor Emeritus.
Res., 6527 Superior Ave., 44103-2698. Tel: 216-431-5794; Fax: 216-391-8233.
Hunger Center—Tel: 216-391-9160.

26—ST. HENRY (1946), Rev. Robert J. Kropac. Pastoral Assocs.: Gerry Kynkor; Ms. Barbara Price. In res., Rev. J. Glenn Murray, S.J.; Deacon Shelby M. Friend.
Res., 18200 Harvard Ave., 44128. Tel: 216-921-0725; 921-0726; 921-7030; Fax: 216-991-9470.
School—Archbishop James P. Lyke Elementary School. See Elementary Schools, Parochial and Diocesan under Institutions Located in the Diocese.

27—HOLY FAMILY (1911). Closed. For inquiries for parish records contact the Chancery.

28—HOLY NAME (1854), Rev. Thomas V. O'Donnell; Deacon Martin J. Wendzicki. In res., Rev. John C. Dalton, Pastor Emeritus.
Res., 8328 Broadway Ave. S.E., 44105-3931. Tel: 216-271-4242; 4243; Fax: 216-271-0886.
School—Tel: 216-341-0084; Fax: 216-341-1122. Sr. Marie Patrice Joyce, S.C., Prin.
Sisters 2; Lay Teachers 8; Students 202.
Catechesis/Religious Programs—Students 78.

29—HOLY REDEEMER (1924) (Italian), Revs. Martin F. Polito; James J. Grandillo, Pastor Emeritus.
Res., 15712 Kipling Ave., 44110. Tel: 216-531-3313; Fax: 216-531-4717.
School—15720 Kipling Ave., 44110. Tel: 216-486-0935. Sr. Maureen Spillane, S.N.D., Prin.
Sisters of Notre Dame 1; Lay Teachers 7; Students 152.
Convent—924 Ruple Rd., 44110. Tel: 216-481-2740.

30—HOLY ROSARY (1892) (Italian), Rev. Philip G. Racco; Sr. Mary Johnica D'Amico, S.N.D., Pastoral Assoc. In res., Revs. Francis X. Klamet; Gregg Banaga, C.M.
Res., 12021 Mayfield Rd., 44106. Tel: 216-421-2995; 2996.

31—HOLY TRINITY - ST. EDWARD (1975), Revs. Senan Glass, O.F.M.Cap.; Peter J. Woll, Pastor Emeritus.
Res., 7211 Woodland Ave., 44104. Tel: 216-431-1134; 431-8854.

32—ST. HYACINTH (1906) (Polish), Rev. John S. Deka.
Res., 6114 Francis Ave., 44127. Tel: 216-641-3944.
Convent—2971 E. 61st St., 44127. Tel: 216-641-1508.

33—ST. IGNATIUS (1902), Rev. James R. McGonegal; Rev. Msgr. James P. McIntyre, Pastor Emeritus; Rev. Timothy M. Daw; Sr. Dianne Piunno, S.N.D., Pastoral Assoc.; Deacons Daniel J. Hancock; Billy Malcolm. In res., Rev. Gary D. Yanus.
Res., 10205 Lorain Ave., 44111-5470. Tel: 216-251-0300; 0301; 0302; Fax: 216-251-0302.
School—Tel: 216-671-0535. Sr. Theresine Cregan, C.S.J., Prin.
Religious 1; Lay Teachers 19; Students 418.
Convent—10212 Bernard Ave., 44111. Tel: 216-251-3446.

34—IMMACULATE CONCEPTION (1865), Revs. Michael J. Troha; Albert J. Mackert, Pastor Emeritus; Sr. Eileen Quinn, O.S.U., Pastoral Assoc. In res., Revs. John J. Hayes; David A. Novak.
Res., 4129 Superior Ave., 44103-1179. Tel: 216-431-5900; Fax: 216-881-4274.
School—Tel: 216-361-1883. Dr. Marlene M. Matis, Prin.
Lay Teachers 10; Students 202.
Convent—Tel: 216-541-3050.

35—IMMACULATE HEART OF MARY (1894) (Polish), Revs. Ralph Hudak; Marian Bendyk.
Res., 6700 Lansing Ave., 44105. Tel: 216-341-2734. [CEM]
School—Jesus and Mary Consolidated, (Grades 4-8). (See Sacred Heart of Jesus listing). 6804 Lansing Ave., 44105-3797. Tel: 216-441-0886; Fax: 216-441-1515. Mr. Frank W. Przybojewski, Prin.
Sisters 1; Lay Teachers 11; Students 291.
Convent—6804 Lansing Ave., 44105. Tel: 216-641-7121.

36—ST. JEROME (1919), Revs. Thomas A. Haren; Anthony Cassese; Deacon Peter Travalik.
Res., 15000 Lake Shore Blvd., 44110-1298. Tel: 216-481-8200; Fax: 216-481-8201.
School—15100 Lake Shore Blvd., 44110. Tel: 216-486-3587; Fax: 216-486-4288. Mr. Nicholas DiBartolemeo, Prin.
Ursuline Nuns of Cleveland 1; Lay Teachers 11; Students 262.
Convent—15025 Ridpath Ave., 44110. Tel: 216-531-6118.

37—ST. JOHN CANTIUS (1898) (Polish), Rev. Ralph A. Bodziony. In res., Rev. Msgr. Casimir S. Ciolek; Rev. Andrew Knapik.
Res., 906 College Ave., S.W., 44113. Tel: 216-781-9095; Fax: 216-696-6065.
School—2357 Tremont Ave., 44113. Tel: 216-861-0118. Miss Rosemary DiPetro, Prin.
Sisters 1; Lay Teachers 5; Students 69.
Convent—2265 W. 10th St., 44113. Tel: 216-861-1349.

38—ST. JOHN NEPOMUCENE (1902) (Bohemian), Revs. William F. Tezie; Joseph R. Spolny.
Res., 3785 Independence Rd., 44105-3357. Tel: 216-641-8444; 8445; Fax: 216-341-4466.
Church—Fleet Ave. & E. 50th St., 44105.
School—3777 Independence Rd., 44105. Tel: 216-341-1347; Fax: 216-341-4466. Mrs. Roswitha Wunker, Prin.
Lay Teachers 11; Students 239.
Convent—Tel: 216-341-6393.

39—ST. JOSAPHAT (1908), Rev. David A. Novak, Admin.; Rev. Msgr. Alexander I. Goldikovskis, Pastor Emeritus.
Res., 1411 E. 33rd St., 44114-4032. Tel: 216-579-0173.

40—ST. JOSEPH (Woodland). Closed. For inquiries for parish records contact the Chancery.

41—ST. JOSEPH (Collinwood) (1877). Closed. For inquiries for parish records contact St. Aloysius, Cleveland.

42—ST. LAWRENCE (1901) (Slovenian), Rev. Anthony Rebol. In res., Rev. Frank G. Godic.
Res., 3547 E. 80th St., 44105. Tel: 216-341-0496.
Church—3532 E. 81st St., 44105.
Convent—23531 E. 80th St., 44105. Tel: 216-341-1235.

43—ST. LEO THE GREAT (1948), Revs. Robert M. Bielek; William D. Eylar, Pastor Emeritus; John A. Ocilka; Kevin C. Shemuga; Sr. Joyce Joecken, C.S.J., Pastoral Assoc.; Deacon Thomas J. Waken.
Res., 4940 Broadview Rd., 44109. Tel: 216-661-1006; 1007; 1008; Fax: 216-661-7125.
School—4900 Broadview Rd., 44109. Tel: 216-661-2120. Michael Fasciano, Prin.
Lay Teachers 21; Students 638.
Catechesis/Religious Programs—Students 155.

44—COMMUNITY OF ST. MALACHI (1975). (Personal Parish). Revs. Anthony J. Schuerger; Paul J. Hritz, Pastor Emeritus.
Res., 2459 Washington Ave., 44113-2380. Tel: 216-781-3110; Fax: 216-861-5340.
Church—W. 25th & Detroit Ave., 44113.

45—ST. MALACHI (1865), Revs. Anthony J. Schuerger; Paul J. Hritz, Pastor Emeritus. Pastoral Assocs.: Donna K. Rego; Sr. M. Francis Borgia Allwine, O.S.U.
Res., 2459 Washington Ave., 44113-2380. Tel: 216-861-5343; 5344; Fax: 216-861-5340.
School—Urban Community School. (Intermediate Level) (See St. Wendelin listing for Primary Level) 2401 Washington Ave., 44113. Tel: 216-771-8014; Fax: 216-771-7888. Sr. Maureen Doyle, O.S.U., Prin.
Sisters 4; Lay Teachers 19; Students 391.
Convent—2456 Vermont Ave., 44113. Tel: 216-781-3481.

46—ST. MARK (1945), Revs. Douglas H. Koesel; Anthony J. Muzic, Pastor Emeritus; Joseph F. Wagner, Pastor Emeritus.
Res., 15800 Montrose Ave., 44111. Tel: 216-226-7577; 7578; Fax: 216-221-8664.
School—15724 Montrose Ave., 44111. Tel: 216-521-4115; Fax: 216-221-8664. Dr. Marilyn Kurnath, Prin.
Sisters of Immaculater Heart of Mary 1; Lay Teachers 19; Students 500.

47—ST. MARY (1905) (Slovenian), Revs. John M. Kumse; Victor N. Tomc, Pastor Emeritus; Sr. Nina Vitale, O.S.U., Pastoral Assoc. In res., Rev. Joze Cerne.
Res., 15519 Holmes Ave., 44110. Tel: 216-761-7740; 761-1837; 761-5524 (Ministry House); Fax: 216-451-7911.
School—716 E. 156th St., 44110. Tel: 216-451-1717. Sr. Mary Ellen Brinovec, O.S.U., Prin.
Religious 3; Lay Teachers 5; Students 129.
Convent—717 E. 155th St., 44110. Tel: 216-851-3234.
Catechesis/Religious Programs—Students 142.

48—ST. MARY OF CZESTOCHOWA (1913) (Polish). Closed. For inquiries for parish records contact the Chancery.

49—ST. MEL (1945), Revs. Edwin J. Schenkelberg; Ray J. Horley; Donna Winbiscus, Pastoral Assoc.
Res., 14436 Triskett Rd., 44111. Tel: 216-941-4313; 4314.
School—14440 Triskett Rd., 44111. Tel: 216-941-6879. Patricia Kelly, Prin.
Lay Teachers 18; Students 392.
Catechesis/Religious Programs—Students 367.
Convent—14538 Grapeland Ave., 44111. Tel: 216-941-6589.

50—ST. MICHAEL (1882), Revs. Dennis R. O'Grady; James H. McCreight; Sr. Mary Reean Coyne, S.N.D., Pastoral Assoc.; Deacon Miquel Figueroa. In res., Rev. Thomas V. O'Donnell.
Res., 3114 Scranton Rd., 44109. Tel: 216-861-6297; 6298; 621-3847 (Spanish); Fax: 216-696-9351.
Catechesis/Religious Programs—Students 152.
Convent—2202 Prame Ave., 44109. Tel: 216-351-0855.

51—NATIVITY OF THE BLESSED VIRGIN MARY. Closed. For inquiries for parish records contact the Chancery.

52—OUR LADY OF ANGELS (1922), Rev. John J. Cregan; Ann Steinbrunner, Pastoral Assoc. In res., Bro. Francis Fergus, O.S.B.
Res., 3644 Rocky River Dr., 44111. Tel: 216-252-2332; Fax: 216-252-2383.
School—Tel: 216-251-6841; Fax: 216-251-7831. Miss Kathleen A. Lynch, Prin.
Lay Teachers 24; Students 576.
Convent—3550 Rocky River Dr., 44111.

53—OUR LADY OF GOOD COUNSEL (1873), Revs. Leroy Moreeuw, C.PP.S.; John Zivjak, C.PP.S.; Deacon Patrick F. Berigan. In res., Rev. George J. Albers, C.PP.S.
Res., 4423 Pearl Rd., S.W., 44109. Tel: 216-749-2323; 2324; Fax: 216-741-7183.
School—4419 Pearl Rd., 44109. Tel: 216-741-3685. Sr. Margaret O'Brien, O.S.U., Prin.
Religious 2; Lay Teachers 16; Students 427.

54—OUR LADY OF LOURDES (1883) (Bohemian), Rev. James J. Masek. In res., Rev. Stephen F. Radecky.
Res., 3395 E. 53rd St., 44127-1692. Tel: 216-641-2829; 2830.
Church—E. 55th St. & Hamm Ave., 44127-1692.
Convent—3401 E. 53rd St., 44127.

55—OUR LADY OF MERCY (1922) (Slovak), Revs. Joseph T. Hilinski; Andrew P. Laheta, Pastor Emeritus.
Res., 2425 W. 11th St., 44113. Tel: 216-781-8277 (Parish House); 216-781-7928 (Parish Hall).

56—OUR LADY OF MOUNT CARMEL (East) (1936) (Italian). Officially closed as a parish on July 29, 1990, however, still in existence as an Oratory. Mrs. Rose Marie Criniti, Admin.
Res., 2615 Martin Luther King Blvd., 44104-2553. Tel: 216-421-0140.
Oratory—Cleveland, 11501 Mount Carmel Rd., 44104.

57—OUR LADY OF MOUNT CARMEL (West) (1926) (Italian), Revs. Richard Rasch, O.de.M.; James Mayer, O.de.M.; Deacon Clarence A. Chrosniak. In res., Rev. Vincent Caruso, O.de.M.; Bro. Martin Jarocinski, O.de.M.
Res., 6928 Detroit Ave., 44102-3093. Tel: 216-651-5043; 651-2547; 651-1611; Fax: 216-651-6641.
School—1355 W. 70th St., 44102. Tel: 216-281-7146; Fax: 216-281-6651. Sr. Rosario Vega, H.M.S.S., Prin.
Sisters of Most Holy Trinity 2; Lay Teachers 8; Students 236.
Convent—1355 W. 70th St., 44102.

58—OUR LADY OF PEACE (1919), Rev. Gary D. Chmura; Deacon William E. Dirk; Mrs. Nancy McIntosh, Pastoral Assoc. In res., Rev. Thomas A. Moran.
Res., 12503 Buckingham Ave., 44120-1498. Tel: 216-421-4211; 4212; Fax: 216-421-1612.
Church—Shaker Blvd. & E. 126th St., 44120.
School—12406 Buckingham Ave., 44120-1419. Tel: 216-795-7161; Fax: 216-795-7161. Mrs. Sheila Bolek, Prin.
Lay Teachers 10; Students 219.

59—OUR LADY OF PERPETUAL HELP (1929) (Lithuanian), Rev. Gediminas Kijauskas, S.J. Pastoral Assocs.: Nijole Kersnauskas; Stasys Ignatavicius.
Res., 18022 Neff Rd., 44119-2644. Tel: 216-531-4263; Fax: 216-531-8441.
Convent—18021 Marcella Rd., 44119.

60—ST. PATRICK (1853), Rev. Mark A. DiNardo; Deacon William Merriman; Mary Jane Treichel, Pastoral Assoc.
Res., 3602 Bridge Ave., 44113-3314. Tel: 216-631-6872; 6873; 6874; Fax: 216-281-8459.
School—Urban Community School. See St. Malachi listing. Tel: 216-771-8014.

61—ST. PATRICK (West Park) (1848), Revs. Thomas J. Hagedorn; Thomas D. Mahoney; Deacons Richard C. Beercheck; William Staab. In res., Rev. Joseph C. Pednekar, M.S.F.S.
Res., 4427 Rocky River Dr., 44135-2551. Tel: 216-251-8286; 8287; Fax: 216-251-8555. [CEM]
School—17720 Puritas Ave., 44135. Tel: 216-671-4314. Joyce Needham, Prin.
Ursuline Nuns of Cleveland 2; Lay Teachers 25; Students 629.

Convent—17712 Puritas Ave., 44135. Tel: 216-941-1088.

62—ST. PAUL (1902) (Croatian), Revs. Mirko Hladni; Stephen A. Mrakuzic, Pastor Emeritus.
Res., 1369 E. 40th St., 44103-1194. Tel: 216-431-1895; Fax: 216-431-1128.

63—ST. PETER (1853), Rev. Robert J. Marrone.
Res., 1533 E. 17th St., 44114. Tel: 216-861-1798; 861-1799.

64—SS. PHILIP AND JAMES (1950), Revs. J. Brendan McNulty; Robert F. Brennan, Pastor Emeritus, (Retired). In res., Rev. John F. McMahon.
Res., 10812 Adeline Rd., 44111-4806. Tel: 216-941-6808; 6809; Fax: 216-941-3808.
Church—3727 Bosworth Rd., 44111.
School—Tel: 216-941-7070. Miss Joan Woost, Prin.
Lay Teachers 8; Students 148.
Convent—10909 Oliver Rd., 44111. Tel: 216-941-7387.

65—ST. PHILIP NERI (1914), Rev. Gary Stakem, O.F.M.Cap.; Sr. Wilma Apack, C.S.J., Pastoral Assoc.
Res., 8215 St. Clair Ave., 44103. Tel: 216-431-2583.
School—St. Thomas Aquinas-St. Philip Neri, 9101 Superior Ave., 44106. Tel: 216-421-4668; Fax: 216-721-8444. Mrs. Berkely Dixon, Prin.
Lay Teachers 9; Students 320.
Convent—799 E. 82nd St., 44103. Tel: 216-431-0224.

66—ST. PROCOP (1872) (Bohemian), Rev. Mark J. Peyton.
Res., 3181 W. 41st St., 44109-1275. Tel: 216-631-0365; 631-0367.
School—Metro Catholic Parish School. See Separate Listing under Elementary Schools, Parochial and Diocesan.

67—ST. ROCCO (1922) (Italian), Revs. Michael Contardi, O.de.M.; Paschal Rosca, O.de.M.; Michael Perry, O.de.M.
Res., 3205 Fulton Rd., 44109-1495. Tel: 216-961-8331; 961-7384; Fax: 216-961-1845.
School—Tel: 216-961-8557; Fax: 216-961-1112. Sr. Judith Wulk, O.SS.T., Prin.
Sisters of Most Holy Trinity 3; Lay Teachers 8; Students 213.
Convent—Tel: 216-961-2378.

68—ST. ROSE (1899), Revs. James A. Viall; K. Francis Chinnappa, J.C.L.; Sr. Ruth Donnelly, O.S.U., Pastoral Assoc.
Res., 11411 Detroit Ave., 44102. Tel: 216-521-0133; Fax: 216-521-1306.
Church—Detroit Ave. & W. 114th St., 44102.
School—1441 W. 116th St., 44102. Tel: 216-226-4525; Fax: 216-226-0413. Sr. Maria Olga Palma, O.C.D., Prin.
Lay Teachers 10; Students 146.
Convent—1418 W. 114th St., 44102. Tel: 216-521-5605.

69—SACRED HEART OF JESUS (1888) (Polish), Rev. Francis M. Bednar.
Res., 6916 Krakow Ave., 44105. Tel: 216-341-2828; Fax: 216-271-1889.
Church—E. 71st & Kazimier Ave., 44105.
School—Jesus and Mary Consolidated, (Grades K-3). See Immaculate Heart of Mary listing. 6804 Lansing Ave., 44105.
Convent—Tel: 216-641-2797.

70—SAN JUAN BAUTISTA (1975) (Spanish-Non Territorial), Rev. David F. Fallon. Pastoral Assocs.: Sr. Florence Cremering, S.C.; Sr. Ann Dorenbusch, S.C.; Deacons Ceferino Medina; Epifanio Torres; Victor Colon; Ignacio Miranda.
Res., 1946 W. 32 St., 44113. Tel: 216-631-2888; Fax: 216-631-2999.
School—Metro Catholic Parish School. See Separate Listing under Elementary Schools, Parochial and Diocesan.
Catechesis/Religious Programs—Students 153.
Convent—3215 Carroll Ave., 44113. Tel: 216-281-7215.

71—ST. STANISLAUS (1873) (Polish), Revs. William E. Gulas, O.F.M.; Alcuin L. Mikulanis, O.F.M.
Res., 3649 E. 65th St., 44105-1293. Tel: 216-341-9091; 9092; Fax: 216-341-2688.
Church—Forman Ave. & E. 65th St., 44105.
School—6615 Forman Ave., 44105. Tel: 216-883-3307; Fax: 216-883-0514. Mrs. Alice Torrence, Prin.
Sisters 3; Lay Teachers 15; Students 402.
Convent—Tel: 216-341-0934.

72—ST. STEPHEN (1869) (German), Rev. S. Michael Franz; Sr. Carol Marie McHenry, S.N.D., Pastoral Assoc.
Res., 1930 W. 54th St., 44102. Tel: 216-631-5633; Fax: 216-631-5634.
School—Metro Catholic Parish School. See Separate Listing under Elementary Schools, Parochial and Diocesan.
Convent—1891 W. 57th St., 44102. Tel: 216-631-0754.

73—ST. THOMAS AQUINAS. Closed. For inquiries for parish records contact the Chancery.

74—TRANSFIGURATION (1943). Closed. For inquiries for parish records contact the Chancery.

75—ST. VINCENT DE PAUL (1922), Revs. John E. Manning; Urban A. Reichlin, Pastor Emeritus; Daniel P. Redmond; Deacons Kenneth J. Hill; Billy Malcolm.
Res., 13400 Lorain Ave., 44111. Tel: 216-252-2626; Fax: 216-251-0455.
Church—Lorain Ave. & Berea Rd., 44111.
School—13442 Lorain Ave., 44111. Tel: 216-251-3932. Sr. Caroline Kocur, O.S.U., Prin.
Sisters 1; Lay Teachers 18; Students 441.
Convent—3483 W. 135th St., 44111. Tel: 216-252-1080.

76—ST. VITUS (1893) (Slovenian), Rev. Joseph P. Boznar; Sr. Mary Avsec, S.N.D., Pastoral Assoc. In res., Rev. Vincent J. Moraghan.
Res., 6019 Glass Ave., 44103. Tel: 216-361-1444; 1445; Fax: 216-361-1445.
School—6111 Glass Ave., 44103. Tel: 216-881-1689. Mrs. Jeanette Polomsky, Prin.
Sisters of Notre Dame 1; Lay Teachers 11; Students 205.
Catechesis/Religious Programs—Students 212.
Convent—6104 Glass Ave., 44103. Tel: 216-361-7330.

77—ST. WENDELIN (1903) (Slovak), Rev. Jerome M. Lajack.
Res., 2281 Columbus Rd., 44113. Tel: 216-861-1141.
School—Urban Community School. (Primary and Junior High) (See St. Malachi listing for Intermediate Level) 2281 Columbus Rd., 44113. Tel: 216-861-4706; Fax: 216-781-0034.
Convent—2259 Columbus Rd., 44113. Tel: 216-241-1773.

OUTSIDE THE CITY OF CLEVELAND

Akron, Summit Co.,

1—ANNUNCIATION, (1907), Rev. Paul J. Rosing. Pastoral Ministers: Jean J. Jordan; Diana Herhold. In res., Revs. James J. Berardi; Augustine Ukwuoma.
Res., 87 Broad St., 44305. Tel: 330-535-4141; Fax: 330-762-8456.
Church—Broad St. & Kent St., 44305.
School—Annunciation-St. John the Baptist, 88 Kent St., 44305. Tel: 330-253-5311; Fax: 330-762-8456. Barbara Mesko, Prin.
Lay Teachers 13; Students 277.

2—ST. ANTHONY OF PADUA, (1933) (Italian), Revs. James V. Ragnoni; Robert Labella.
Res., 83 Mosser Pl., 44310. Tel: 330-762-7277.
School—80 E. York St., 44310. Tel: 330-253-6918. Sr. Elizabeth Szilvasi, M.P.F., Prin.
Religious Teachers Filippini 2; Lay Teachers 7; Students 220.
Convent—93 Mosser Pl., 44310. Tel: 216-376-1735.

3—ST. BERNARD, (1861), Rev. Paul E. Schindler; Deacon Daniel J. Matusicky. In res., Revs. Jude Onwana; Albert I. Reymann, M.M.
Res., 44 University Ave., 44308-1609. Tel: 330-253-5161; 5162; 253-5265; 253-5364; Fax: 330-253-6949. [CEM]

4—CHRIST THE KING, (1935), Revs. Francis J. Basa; Victor J. Cimperman, Pastor Emeritus.
Res., 1584 Creighton Ave., 44310-2699. Tel: 330-633-8418.
School—1558 Creighton Ave., 44310. Tel: 330-633-1383; Fax: 330-633-4512. Sr. Paula Krizancic, F.D.C., Prin.
Daughters of Divine Charity 3; Lay Teachers 6; Students 141.
Convent—Tel: 330-633-8217.

5—ST. FRANCIS DE SALES, (1948), Revs. James R. Schleicher; Sean Donnelly. In res., Rev. Charles L. Byrider.
Res., 4019 Manchester Rd., 44319. Tel: 330-644-2225.
School—4009 Manchester Rd., 44319. Tel: 330-644-0638. Carol Trifonoff, Prin.
Sisters Servants of Immaculate Heart of Mary 1; Lay Teachers 18; Students 463.
Catechesis/Religious Programs—Students 320.

6—ST. HEDWIG, (1912) (Polish), Rev. Thaddeus M. Swirski.
Res., 215 E. Glenwood Ave., 44310-3837. Tel: 330-376-6979.
Convent—211 E. Glenwood Ave., 44310.

7—ST. HILARY, (1958), Revs. Gordon A. Yahner; John P. Miceli; Deacon Lee F. Hindersheid. Pastoral Assocs.: Sr. Marlene LoGrasso; Mrs. Mary Lou Grossman; Ms. Christina Kitts; Mrs. Patricia Schnee.
Mailing Address: 2750 W. Market St., Fairlawn, 44333.
Res., 615 Moorfield Rd., Fairlawn, 44333. Tel: 330-867-1055; 1056; Fax: 330-869-2312.
Church—2750 W. Market St., Fairlawn, 44333.
School—645 Moorfield Rd., Fairlawn, 44333. Tel: 330-867-8720; Fax: 330-867-5081. Miss Patricia Nugent, Prin.
Lay Teachers 29; Students 606.
Catechesis/Religious Programs—Students 486.

8—IMMACULATE CONCEPTION, (1923), Rev. Arthur A. Snedeker; Melissa Keegan, Pastoral Assoc.; Deacon Dennis L. Smith. In res., Rev. Samuel R. Ciccolini.
Res., 2101 17th St. S.W., 44314-2315. Tel: 330-753-8429; Fax: 330-753-7440.
Church—2100 16th St. S.W., 44314. Tel: 800-311-8429.
School—2128 16th St. S.W., 44314. Tel: 330-745-3544; Fax: 330-745-2051. Mrs. Rosemary Capotosto, Prin.
Lay Teachers 10; Students 222.

9—ST. JOHN THE BAPTIST, (1907) (Slovak), Rev. Ralph V. Coletta.
Res., 1034 Brown St., 44301. Tel: 330-773-9114.
School—Annunciation-St. John the Baptist School, 88 Kent St., 44305. Tel: 330-253-5311. Barbara Mesko, Prin.
Lay Teachers 13; Students 277.

10—ST. MARTHA, (1919), Revs. Norman K. Douglas; Peter Colletti. Pastoral Assocs.: Sr. Eileen Keating, C.S.A.; Mrs. Kathleen Lux.
Res., 300 E. Tallmadge Ave., 44310-2399. Tel: 330-376-5144; 5145; 376-5858; Fax: 330-376-5311.
School—Tel: 330-535-8817. Mrs. Mary Dean, Prin.
Lay Teachers 12; Students 283.
Catechesis/Religious Programs—Students 220.

11—ST. MARY, (1887), Revs. John J. Hilkert; Raymond J. Smith.
Res., 750 S. Main St., 44311-1094. Tel: 330-762-9247; Fax: 330-253-1472.
School—Tel: 330-253-1233. Miss Joan Krill, Prin.
Lay Teachers 10; Students 224.
Convent—743 Dunbar Dr., 44311. Tel: 330-762-9496.

12—ST. MATTHEW, (1943), Rev. Thomas A. McGovern; Mrs. Patricia Flaherty, Pastoral Assoc. In res., Rev. William P. Lyons.
Res., 2603 Benton St., 44312-1694. Tel: 330-733-9944; Fax: 330-733-9424.
Church—Berne & Woolf St., 44312.
School—2580 Benton St., 44312. Tel: 330-784-1711. Mr. Thomas S. Maroon, Prin.
Dominican Sisters 1; Lay Teachers 20; Students 380.
Catechesis/Religious Programs—Students 150.
Convent—2578 Benton St., 44312. Tel: 330-733-1001.

13—NATIVITY OF THE LORD JESUS, (1977), Rev. David J. Halaiko; Sr. Susanne Gill, H.M., Pastoral Assoc.
Res., 2425 Myersville Rd., 44312. Tel: 330-699-5086.
Catechesis/Religious Programs—Students 252.

14—ST. PAUL, (1919), Revs. John M. Jenkins; Robert E. Stein; Therese Nesline, Pastoral Assoc.; Deacon Francis R. Lonteen.
Res., 433 Mission Dr., 44301-2798. Tel: 330-724-1263; Fax: 330-724-7680.
Church—1580 Brown St., 44301.
School—Tel: 330-724-1253. Mrs. Karen Sell-Virgin, Prin.
Lay Teachers 24; Students 454.

15—ST. PETER, (1917). Closed. For inquiries for parish records contact St. Mary Parish, Akron.

16—SACRED HEART OF JESUS, (1915) (Hungarian), Rev. Robert E. Clancy, Admin.; Deacon Geza Balassy.
Res., 212 E. Voris St., 44311. Tel: 330-434-4348.
Church—734 Grant St., 44311.

17—ST. SEBASTIAN, (1928), Revs. William D. Karg; John T. McDonough, Pastor Emeritus; Charles L. Byrider, Pastor Emeritus; Neil G. Walters; Chima Nwamadi; Deacon Terry W. Peacock.
Res., 476 Mull Ave., 44320-1299. Tel: 330-836-2233; 2234; 2235.
School—500 Mull Ave., 44320. Tel: 330-836-9107; Fax: 330-836-7690. Sr. Mary Patricia Leopold, H.M., Prin.
Sisters of the Humility of Mary 1; Lay Teachers 19; Students 464.
Catechesis/Religious Programs—Students 101.
Convent—352 Elmdale Ave., 44320. Tel: 330-864-2902.

18—ST. VINCENT, (1837), Revs. Joseph H. Kraker; Edward N. Schwet.
Res., 164 W. Market St., 44303-2395. Tel: 330-535-3135; Fax: 330-535-4160. [CEM]
Church—W. Market St. & Maple St., 44303.
School—17 S. Maple St., 44303. Tel: 330-762-5912; Fax: 330-535-2515. William D. Hackman, Prin.
Lay Teachers 14; Students 253.

Amherst, Lorain Co., St. Joseph (1864), Revs. Lawrence N. Martello; Anthony L. Kreps, Pastor Emeritus; James P. Schmitz; Sr. Mary Ann Burke, S.N.D., Pastoral Assoc. In res., Rev. Thomas V. Rath.
Res., 200 St. Joseph Dr., 44001-1663. Tel: 216-988-2848; 2849; 871-4415 (Cleveland); Fax: 216-984-2301. [CEM]

School—175 St. Joseph Dr., 44001. Tel: 216-988-4244. Sr. Mary Jo Ludwig, S.N.D., Prin.
Sisters of Notre Dame 1; Lay Teachers 14; Students 346.
Catechesis/Religious Programs—Students 500.
Convent—151 St. Joseph Dr., 44001. Tel: 216-988-2621.

Ashland, Ashland Co., St. Edward (1853), Rev. James M. Cassidy; Deacon James A. Kaniecki.
Res., 501 Cottage St., 44805-2167. Tel: 419-289-7224; Fax: 419-289-0515. [JC]
Administration Center—149 Pleasant St., 44805.
School—433 Cottage St., 44805. Tel: 419-289-7456. Douglas J. Mark, Prin.
Lay Teachers 8; Students 210.
Catechesis/Religious Programs—Students 149.
Convent—Tel: 419-289-8333.

Avon, Lorain Co., Holy Trinity (1833), Rev. John J. Gorski; Roger Camp, Pastoral Assoc.
Res., 33601 Detroit Rd., 44011-1999. Tel: 216-937-5363. [CEM]
School—2610 Nagel Rd., 44011. Tel: 216-937-6420. Sr. Patricia Vovk, S.N.D., Prin.
Notre Dame Sisters 2; Lay Teachers 9; Students 243.
Catechesis/Religious Programs—Students 247.
Convent—2620 Nagel Rd., 44011. Tel: 216-937-5005.

St. Mary of the Immaculate Conception (1841), Revs. Arthur B. Egan; John F. Wessel.
Res., 2640 Stoney Ridge Rd., 44011. Tel: 216-934-4212; Fax: 216-934-6246. [CEM]
School—2680 Stoney Ridge Rd., 44011. Tel: 216-934-6246. Miss Linda A. Kenzik, Prin.
Sisters of Notre Dame 2; Lay Teachers 8; Students 192.
Catechesis/Religious Programs—Students 180.
Convent—Tel: 216-934-5173.

Avon Lake, Lorain Co., Holy Spirit (1965), Revs. James H. Beatty; James J. Mosovsky, Pastor Emeritus; Deacon Harold R. Dietrich.
Res., 410 Lear Rd., 44012-2004. Tel: 440-933-3777; 871-8157; Fax: 440-871-8157.
Catechesis/Religious Programs—Students 363.

St. Joseph's (1949), Rev. Timothy J. O'Connor; Sr. Thomasine Antenucci, S.S.J.-T.O.S.F., Pastoral Assoc.; Deacon James R. Stewart.
Res., 32929 Lake Rd., 44012. Tel: 216-933-3152; 871-0616 (Cleveland); Fax: 216-933-8919.
School—Tel: 216-933-6233; Fax: 216-933-2463. Mrs. Patricia Vaccaro, Prin.
Religious 1; Lay Teachers 9; Students 274.
Catechesis/Religious Programs—Students 319.
Convent—32911 Lake Rd., 44012. Tel: 216-933-5769.

Barberton, Summit Co.,

1—St. Augustine, (1898), Revs. Richard Burchell; Robert W. Wisniewski; Paul J. Clines, Pastor Emeritus; Deacon Robin Adair.
Res., 204 Sixth St., N.W., 44203. Tel: 330-745-0011; 0012; Fax: 330-745-0012.
Church—Sixth St. & Lake St., 44203.
School—195 Seventh St., N.W., 44203. Tel: 330-753-6435. Lucille A. Liebman, Prin.
Lay Teachers 20; Students 437.
Catechesis/Religious Programs—Students 294.
Convent—633 W. Paige Ave., 44203. Tel: 330-745-5735.

2—SS. Cyril and Methodius, (1906), Revs. Edward F. Lajack; James A. Yavorsky, Pastor Emeritus.
Res., 189 15th St. N.W., 44203. Tel: 330-825-7089; Fax: 330-825-7181.
Church—183 15 St. N.W., 44203.

3—Holy Trinity, (1911) (Hungarian), Rev. Carl A. Ciprian.
Res., 398 Van St., 44203-2329. Tel: 330-745-4735.
Church—380 Wooster Rd. N., 44203-2329.

4—St. Mary's, (1912), Revs. Richard Arko, Admin.; Claude J. Gaebelein, Pastor Emeritus.
Res., 122 21st St. N.W., 44203. Tel: 330-825-6231.

5—Sacred Heart, (1916) (Slovenian), Rev. Albert A. Kunkel.
Res., 1263 Shannon Ave., N.W., 44203-6792. Tel: 330-825-9543.

Bay Village, Cuyahoga Co., St. Raphael (1946), Revs. Nelson J. Callahan; C. Thomas Cleaton; Sr. Ardath Blake, H.M., Pastoral Assoc.
Res., 525 Dover Center Rd., 44140-2366. Tel: 216-871-1100; Fax: 216-871-1358.
School—Tel: 216-871-6760. Beverly Nemec, Prin.
Lay Teachers 32; Students 778.
Catechesis/Religious Programs—Students 611.

Bedford, Cuyahoga Co., St. Mary (1910), Rev. Thomas J. Winkel; Rev. Msgr. Francis E. Gasbarre, Pastor Emeritus; Rev. Edward A. Burba.
Res., 300 Union St., 44146-4594. Tel: 216-232-9393; 9394; Fax: 216-232-2303.
Church—340 Union St., 44146.
School—270 Union St., 44146. Tel: 216-232-2303. Michelle Nowakowski, Prin.
Lay Teachers 11; Students 277.
Convent—36 Paul St., 44146. Tel: 216-439-1667.

St. Pius X (1952), Revs. Robert Wenz; James Mazanec; Deacon Willard C. Payne.
Res., 400 Center Rd., 44146-2296. Tel: 216-232-8166; 8167; Fax: 440-786-9929.
School—370 Center Rd., 44146-2297. Tel: 216-232-1531. Mrs. Mary Ann Murnyack, Prin.
Vincentian Sisters of Charity 1; Lay Teachers 9; Students 244.
Convent—Tel: 216-232-0571.

Bedford Heights, Cuyahoga Co., Holy Trinity (1965), Rev. Ernest C. Hepner; Rev. Msgr. Francis E. Gasbarre. Pastoral Assocs.: Josephine Jendrisak; Joan McGinty.
Res., 24821 Columbus Rd., 44146-2599. Tel: 440-232-2044; 2045; Fax: 440-232-3720.

Berea, Cuyahoga Co., St. Adalbert (1873) (Polish), Revs. Gerald J. Keller; Joseph Batkiewicz; Deacon Donald P. Butkovic; Sr. Thelma Gerhart, C.S.J., Pastoral Assoc.
Res., 66 Adelbert St., 44017-1799. Tel: 440-234-6830; Fax: 440-234-2588. [CEM]
School—56 Adelbert St., 44017. Tel: 440-234-5529. Mrs. Stephanie West, Prin.
Lay Teachers 10; Students 238.
Catechesis/Religious Programs—Students 137.
Convent—Tel: 216-234-1096.

St. Mary's (1852), Rev. John M. Garrity.
Res., 250 Kraft St., 44017-1449. Tel: 440-243-3877; 3878; Fax: 440-891-9417. [CEM]
School—265 Baker St., 44017-1515. Tel: 440-243-4555; Fax: 440-243-6214. Mrs. Nancy C. Kaesgen, Prin.
Lay Teachers 10; Students 336.
Catechesis/Religious Programs—Students 686.

Brecksville, Cuyahoga Co., St. Basil the Great (1960), Revs. Walter H. Jenne; Edward J. Camille, Pastor Emeritus; William R. Dickinson. Pastoral Assocs.: Sr. Maureen Grady, O.S.U.; Mrs. Carol Gaby. In res., Rev. Lloyd Boymer.
Res., 8700 Brecksville Rd., 44141. Tel: 216-526-1686; 1687; Fax: 216-526-2373.
Catechesis/Religious Programs—Tel: 216-526-3520; 526-3587.
Students 1007.
Convent—6901 Mill Rd., 44141. Tel: 216-526-2850; 2851.

Broadview Heights, Cuyahoga Co., Assumption (1857), Revs. Christopher Schwartz, O.S.B.; Clement Zeleznik, O.S.B.; Deacon Robert C. Bubnick, Sr.
Res., 9183 Broadview Rd., 44147. Tel: 216-526-1177; 1178.
School—Tel: 216-526-4877; Fax: 216-526-3752. Sr. Carol Tobler, S.I.W., Prin.
Sisters of Incarnate Word 2; Lay Teachers 9; Students 255.
Catechesis/Religious Programs—Students 380.
Convent—9139 Broadview Rd., 44147. Tel: 216-526-4069.

Brooklyn, Cuyahoga Co., St. Thomas More (1946), Revs. James J. Vesely; John S. Juhas; Gregory F. Schaut; Sr. Elaine Theresa Burrows, S.I.W., Pastoral Assoc.; Deacons Rudolph Jarosh, Jr.; Martin A. Thiel. In res., Rev. Andrew F. O'Boyle.
Res., 4170 N. Amber Dr., 44144-1399. Tel: 216-749-0414; Fax: 216-749-1001.
School—4180 N. Amber Dr., 44144. Tel: 216-749-1660; Fax: 216-398-4265. Nancy D. Brewer, Prin.
Sisters 1; Lay Teachers 19; Students 480.
Catechesis/Religious Programs—Students 270.

Brook Park, Cuyahoga Co., Assumption of Mary (1860), Revs. Thomas A. Boone; Dennis M. McNeil; Mrs. Joan Mahon, Pastoral Assoc.; Deacon Francis B. Wilson. In res., Rev. Anthony J. Dodd.
Res., 5445 Smith Rd., 44142-2077. Tel: 216-267-0630; Fax: 216-267-0632. [CEM]
Church—5555 Smith Rd., 44142. Tel: 216-267-1775.

St. Peter the Apostle (1968), Rev. George W. Balaun; Deacons Robert G. Sabol; James Vincent. In res., Rev. Dismas Boeff, O.S.B.
Res., 6455 Engle Rd., 44142-3503. Tel: 216-433-1440; 1441.
Catechesis/Religious Programs—Students 425.

Brunswick, Medina Co., St. Ambrose (1957), Revs. Robert C. Hilkert; Robert H. Jackson; Michael B. Smith; Deacons Clement J. Belter; John Miklosovic; Thomas J. Sheridan; Frank Weglicki.
Res., 929 Pearl Rd., 44212. Tel: 330-225-3116; Fax: 330-225-5425.
School—923 Pearl Rd., 44212. Tel: 330-225-2116. Sr. Mary Ann Senia, H.M., Prin.
Sisters of Humility of Mary 2; Lay Teachers 16; Students 454.
Catechesis/Religious Programs—Students 1,342.

St. Colette (1977), Rev. Thomas G. Montavon. In res., Rev. Joseph F. Wagner.
Res., 330 W. 130th St., 44212. Tel: 330-273-5500; Fax: 330-273-1355.
Catechesis/Religious Programs—Students 270.

Chagrin Falls, Holy Angels (1977), Rev. Joseph P. Labbe; Sr. Susan Javorek, S.N.D., Pastoral Assoc.
Res., 8390 Stoney Brook Dr., 44023-4851. Tel: 440-543-7227; 543-9540; Fax: 440-543-4876.
Church—18046 Chillicothe Rd., 44023-4851.
Catechesis/Religious Programs—Students 473.

St. Joan of Arc, Cuyahoga Co., (1948), Revs. John R. Olsavsky; John J. Kinkopf, Pastor Emeritus; John W. Wolf, Pastor Emeritus; David J. Majikas; Sr. Joanne Laurienzo, S.N.D., Pastoral Min.; Deacon Louis J. Capek.
Res., 496 E. Washington St., 44022-2999. Tel: 216-247-7183; 7184; Fax: 216-247-2327.
School—498 E. Washington St., 44022-2998. Tel: 216-247-6530; Fax: 216-247-2045. Mrs. Jean Takacs, Prin.
Sisters of Notre Dame 1; Lay Teachers 10; Students 232.
Catechesis/Religious Programs—Students 501.
Convent—456 E. Washington St., 44022. Tel: 216-247-4419.

Chardon, Geauga Co., St. Mary (1909), Revs. Thomas C. Gilles; David R. Durkee; Deacon Edward J. McCarthy, Jr.
Res., 400 North St., 44024. Tel: 440-285-7051; Fax: 440-285-2818.
School—401 North St., 44024. Tel: 440-286-3590. Sr. Mary Sandra Nativio, S.N.D., Prin.
Sisters of Notre Dame 2; Lay Teachers 18; Students 379.
Catechesis/Religious Programs—Students 483.
Convent—315 North St., 44024. Tel: 440-286-5641.

Chesterland, Geauga Co., St. Anselm (1961), Revs. Thomas M. Sweany; Eric B. Leissa; Deacons Dale A. Bacik; Donald E. Sill. In res., Rev. John F. Anderson, Pastor Emeritus.
Res., 12969 Chillicothe Rd., 44026-3199. Tel: 216-729-9575; Fax: 216-729-9103.
Church—13013 Chillicothe Rd., 44026.
School—Tel: 216-729-7806; Fax: 216-729-3524. Sr. Gretchen Rodenfels, O.S.U., Prin.
Sisters of Notre Dame 2; Lay Teachers 19; Students 414.
Catechesis/Religious Programs—Students 529.
Convent—13055 Chillicothe Rd., 44026. Tel: 216-729-0292.

Chippewa Lake, Medina Co., Jesus Divine Redeemer (1976). Attended by Our Lady Help of Christians, Litchfield.

Cleveland Heights, Cuyahoga Co., St. Ann (1915), Revs. James E. Singler; Robert J. Glepko; Sr. Donna Mikula, O.S.U., Pastoral Assoc.
Res., 2175 Coventry Rd., 44118-2898. Tel: 216-321-0024; 321-0025; 321-0048; 321-4599.
School—2160 Stillman Rd., 44118. Tel: 216-932-4177; Fax: 216-932-7439. Sr. Dorothy Ann Krolikowski, S.S.J.-T.O.S.F., Prin.
Sisters 3; Lay Teachers 18; Students 354.
Convent—12764 Cedar Rd., 44118-2899. Tel: 216-932-1438.

St. Louis (1947), Rev. Leonard J. Zamborsky; Deacon Richard E. Woods; Sr. Marie Manning, S.N.D., Pastoral Assoc. In res., Rev. Stephen J. Dohner.
Res., 2475 N. Taylor Rd., 44118-1397. Tel: 216-382-0440; Fax: 216-382-1605.
Church—2463 N. Taylor Rd., 44118.
School—Tel: 216-382-0033; Fax: 216-382-5933. Sr. Maurene Gilmore, S.N.D., Prin.
Sisters of Notre Dame 2; Lay Teachers 9; Students 197.
Convent—2425 N. Taylor Rd., 44118. Tel: 216-381-3034.

Clinton, Summit Co., St. George (1908), Rev. Msgr. Robert E. Bacher; Deacon Ronald J. Volek.
Res., 7615 Second Ave. N., 44216. Tel: 330-882-3353.
Church—7609 Second Ave. N., 44216.

Columbia Station, Lorain Co., St. Elizabeth Ann Seton (1976), Rev. Charles J. Ryba.
Mailing Address: P.O. Box 968, 44028-0968.
Res., 25777 Royalton Rd., 44028-0968. Tel: 440-236-8595.
Church—25801 Royalton Rd., 44028. Tel: 440-236-5095.
Catechesis/Religious Programs—Tel: 216-236-3711.
Students 176.

Concord Twp., Lake Co., St. Gabriel (1966), Revs. Frederick F. Pausche; Eric S. Orzech; Michael J. Guggenbiller; Deacon Norman H. Davis. In res., Rev. David G. Woost.
Res., 9925 Johnnycake Ridge Rd., 44060-6294. Tel: 216-352-8282; 953-3867 (Cleveland); Fax: 216-354-7558.
School—9935 Johnnycake Ridge Rd., 44060. Tel: 216-352-6169; Fax: 216-939-0143. Sr. Josephmarie Bunosky, S.N.D., Prin.

Sisters of Notre Dame 2; Lay Teachers 22; Students 573.
Catechesis/Religious Programs—Students 951.
Convent—9918 Johnnycake Ridge Rd., 44060. Tel: 216-354-7553.

Copley, Summit Co., Guardian Angels (1964), Rev. J. Norman Riley; Rev. Msgr. Robert C. Wolff, Pastor Emeritus.
Res., 1676 Cleveland-Massillon Rd., 44321-1976. Tel: 330-666-1373.
Church—1686 Cleveland-Massillon Rd., 44321-1976.
Catechesis/Religious Programs—Students 211.

Cuyahoga Falls, Summit Co., Immaculate Heart of Mary (1952), Revs. Thomas W. McCann; John R. Rathfon, Pastor Emeritus; Thomas G. Woost; Deacon J. David Seal.
Res., 1905 Portage Trail, 44223. Tel: 330-929-8361; Fax: 330-929-8496.
School—2859 Lillis Dr., 44223. Tel: 330-923-1220; Fax: 330-929-4373. Mr. John Mark, Prin.
Lay Teachers 22; Students 549.
Catechesis/Religious Programs—Students 218.

St. Eugene (1963), Rev. B. Thomas Zeisig.
Res., 1821 Munroe Falls Ave., 44221-3699. Tel: 330-923-5244; Fax: 330-923-8436.
Catechesis/Religious Programs—Students 209.

St. Joseph (1831), Revs. James J. Marsick; Raymond G. Hamlin; Deacon Robert Kochanski, Pastoral Assoc.
Res., 215 Falls Ave., 44221. Tel: 330-928-2173; Fax: 330-928-2173.
Church—1761 Second St., 44221.
School—1909 Third St., 44221-3894. Tel: 330-928-2151; Fax: 330-928-2151. Robert Kochanski, Prin.
Lay Teachers 15; Students 341.
Catechesis/Religious Programs—Students 153.

Doylestown, Wayne Co., SS. Peter and Paul (1827), Rev. David J. McCarthy.
Res., 161 W. Clinton St., 44230-1297. Tel: 330-658-2145; Fax: 330-658-2287. [CEM][JC]
School—169 W. Clinton St., 44230. Tel: 330-658-2804. Marian Gillen, Prin.
Lay Teachers 10; Students 192.
Catechesis/Religious Programs—Students 161.

East Cleveland, Cuyahoga Co., Christ the King (1928), Rev. Louis M. Papes; Deacon Raymond Daull. Pastoral Assocs.: Sr. Annette Amendolia, S.N.D.; Warrennette Reed.
Res., 1862 Noble Rd., 44112-1636. Tel: 216-851-4388; 4389; Fax: 216-851-4040.
School—Noble & Terrace Rd., 44112. Tel: 216-451-4756; Fax: 216-451-0831. Mr. Kevin James, Prin.
Lay Teachers 10; Students 195.
Convent—16005 Terrace Rd., 44112.

St. Philomena (1902), Rev. Dennis J. Kleinweber; Delores Breckenridge, Pastoral Assoc. In res., Rev. John R. McCarthy (STU).
Res., 13824 Euclid Ave., 44112. Tel: 216-541-3540; Fax: 216-541-3545.

Eastlake, Lake Co., St. Justin Martyr (1962), Rev. Kevin M. Liebhardt; Deacon Jerry J. Bals; Joanne E. Novak, Pastoral Assoc.
Mailing Address: 35781 Stevens Blvd., 44095.
Administration Center—Tel: 440-946-1177; Fax: 440-946-2074.
Res., 35701 Stevens Blvd., 44095.
School—35741 Stevens Blvd., 44095. Tel: 216-946-5414; Fax: 216-946-2074. Sr. Mary Quinlan, Prin.
Sisters of Notre Dame 4; Lay Teachers 8; Students 323.
Catechesis/Religious Programs—Students 399.
Convent—35711 Stevens Blvd., 44095. Tel: 440-946-1013.

Elyria, Lorain Co.,

1—St. Agnes, (1914), Rev. Michael D. Ausperk.
Res., 611 Lake Ave., 44035-3541. Tel: 440-322-5622; Fax: 440-322-0231.
Church—611 Lake Ave., 44035.

2—Holy Cross, (1922) (Polish), Rev. James D. Schorr, Admin.
Res., 417 West Ave., 44035. Tel: 440-323-1022; Fax: 440-323-8277.
Church—1417 West Ave., 44035.

3—St. Jude, (1943), Revs. Frank P. Kosem; Patrick J. O'Connor; Deacon Patrick J. Humphrey. Pastoral Assocs.: Sr. Marie Gillich, C.S.J.; Sr. Angela Nihill. In res., Rev. Robert W. Donohoe.
Res., 590 Poplar St., 44035. Tel: 440-366-5711; 366-6052; Fax: 440-366-1916.
School—594 Poplar St., 44035. Tel: 440-366-1681. Sr. Mary Berigan, S.N.D., Prin.
Sisters of Notre Dame 1; Lay Teachers 18; Students 540.
Catechesis/Religious Programs—Students 341.
Convent—628 Poplar St., 44035. Tel: 440-366-1551.

4—St. Mary, (1845), Revs. Joseph C. Weigand; Gary J. Malin; Deacon Frank A. Humphrey, III.
Res., 320 Middle Ave., 44035. Tel: 440-323-5530; 323-5539; 322-3054 (Cleveland); Fax: 440-322-2329. [CEM]
School—237 Fourth St., 44035. Tel: 440-322-2808; Fax: 440-323-0886. Sr. Geraldine M. Tengler, S.N.D., Prin.
Sisters of Notre Dame 1; Lay Teachers 13; Students 440.
Catechesis/Religious Programs—Tel: 216-322-3054.
Students 275.
Convent—Tel: 440-322-1423.

5—Sacred Heart of Jesus, (1922) (Magyar), Rev. George M. Guschwan; Deacon Edward R. Dillon.
Res., P.O. Box 417, 44036-0417. Tel: 216-323-3382.
Church—162 Irondale St., 44036.

Elyria Township, Lorain Co., St. Vincent de Paul (1949), Revs. James R. Ols; Liam J. Kitt, Pastor Emeritus.
Res., 41295 N. Ridge Rd., 44035. Tel: 440-324-4212; 277-5285; Fax: 440-324-2892.
School—41315 N. Ridge Rd., 44035. Tel: 440-277-6208; Fax: 440-324-9552. Mrs. Margaret Malenich, Prin.
Lay Teachers 10; Students 254.
Catechesis/Religious Programs—Students 186.

Euclid, Cuyahoga Co.,

1—St. Christine, (1925), Revs. Francis R. Sterk; Francis M. Paik, Pastor Emeritus; Keith M. Alberts.
Res., 840 E. 222nd St., 44123-3317. Tel: 216-261-1410; 261-6210; 261-6144; 261-6383; Fax: 216-261-9039.
School—860 E. 222nd St., 44123. Tel: 216-731-6244; Fax: 216-261-6003. Mrs. Mary Benns, Prin.
Lay Teachers 12; Students 249.

2—St. Felicitas, (1950), Pastoral Team: Revs. Richard J. Bober, Coord.; John J. Kraker; Deacon Thomas B. DeHaas, Jr.
Res., 140 Richmond Rd., 44143. Tel: 216-289-0770.
School—Tel: 216-261-1240; Fax: 216-261-5843.
Lay Teachers 25; Students 558.
Catechesis/Religious Programs—Students 271.

3—Holy Cross, (1924), Revs. John P. McNulty; Daniel F. Schlegel. Pastoral Assocs.: Sr. Kathleen Flannery, O.S.U.; Deacons Jerome B. Vrabel; Robert Payne; James Croniger.
Res., 19951 Lake Shore Blvd., 44119. Tel: 216-486-0850; Fax: 216-486-0851.
Church—Lake Shore Blvd. & E. 200th St., 44119.
School—Tel: 216-481-6824; Fax: 216-481-9841. Mrs. Sharon Stupica, Prin.
Ursuline Nuns of Cleveland 2; Lay Teachers 18; Students 465.
Catechesis/Religious Programs—Students 208.
Convent—19951 Lake Shore Blvd., 44119. Tel: 216-486-0088.

4—St. Paul, (1860), Rev. Francis C. Mulvanity; Deacon Louis G. Pecek. In res., Rev. William M. Jerse.
Res., 1231 Chardon Rd., 44117-1192. Tel: 216-531-0900; 0901; Fax: 216-481-0919. [CEM]
School—1200 E. 200th St., 44117. Tel: 216-481-6060. Sr. Donna Galetovich, S.N.D., Prin.
Ursuline Nuns of Cleveland 1; Lay Teachers 9; Students 218.
Convent—1050 E. 200th St., 44117. Tel: 216-531-9178.

5—St. Robert Bellarmine, (1950), Rev. John T. Burkley. In res., Rev. Peter J. Woll.
Res., 23802 Lake Shore Blvd., 44123-1200. Tel: 216-731-2606; 2607; Fax: 216-731-2109.
School—Tel: 216-731-2108; Fax: 216-731-2109. Mary A. Pittinger, Prin.
Lay Teachers 11; Students 258.
Convent—23805 Elmwood Dr., 44123. Tel: 216-731-3020.

6—St. William, (1946), Revs. David G. Baugh; Robert J. Franco. In res., Rev. John E. Lesniak, (Retired); Sr. Irene Charette, O.S.U., Pastoral Assoc.
Res., 367 E. 260th St., 44132-1495. Tel: 216-731-1515.
School—351 E. 260th St., 44132. Tel: 216-731-3060; Fax: 216-731-3061. Mary Heramb, Prin.
Lay Teachers 19; Students 417.
Catechesis/Religious Programs—Students 192.
Convent—584 Lloyd Rd., 44132. Tel: 216-261-1895.

Fairport Harbor, Lake Co., St. Anthony of Padua (1887), Revs. Peter M. Mihalec; William J. Englert, Pastor Emeritus; Deacon Clemens J. Urbanski.
Res., 316 Fifth St., 44077. Tel: 216-354-4525.

Fairview Park, Cuyahoga Co., St. Angela Merici (1923), Revs. Richard E. Hudak; Timothy W. Gareau; Douglas M. Proehl; Anthony Iezzi, Ph.D., Pastoral Assoc.; Deacon James L. Agrippe.
Res., 20970 Lorain Rd., 44126-2096. Tel: 216-333-2133; Fax: 216-333-8061.
School—20830 Lorain Rd., 44126. Tel: 216-333-2126; Fax: 216-333-8480. Mrs. Harriet Davis, Prin.
Lay Teachers 32; Students 650.
Catechesis/Religious Programs—Tel: 216-333-8061.
Students 400.
Convent—4317 W. 210th St., 44126. Tel: 216-331-1948.

Garfield Heights, Cuyahoga Co.,

1—St. Monica, (1952), Rev. John P. Seabold, Coord. of Pastoral Team. Pastoral Team: Rev. Donald P. Oleksiak; Deacon Ralph W. Netzband; Sr. Helen Weis, S.J.S.M.; Ms. Maureen Dowd.
Res., 13623 Rockside Rd., 44125-5197. Tel: 216-662-8685; 8686; 8687; 662-8625; Fax: 216-662-1245.
School—13633 Rockside Rd., 44125. Tel: 216-662-9380; Fax: 216-662-3137. Sr. Helen Weis, S.J.S.M., Prin.
Sisters of St. Joseph Third Order of St. Francis 3; Lay Teachers 18; Students 523.
Catechesis/Religious Programs—Students 284.

2—SS. Peter and Paul, (1927) (Polish), Rev. Anthony W. Zepp; Rev. Msgr. Casimir S. Ciolek, Pastor Emeritus; Rev. Lucjan Stokowski.
Res., 4750 Turney Rd., 44125. Tel: 216-429-1515; 1516; Fax: 216-429-1889.
School—4740 Turney Rd., 44125. Tel: 216-271-6564; Fax: 216-271-0504. Sr. M. Theresine Swigonski, S.S.J.-T.O.S.F., Prin.
Lay Teachers 19; Students 410.
Convent—Tel: 216-429-2666.

3—St. Therese, (1927), Revs. Norman A. Gajdzinski; Mark R. Blinn, Pastor Emeritus; Albert Veigas; Deacon Lawrence Cermak.
Res., 5276 E. 105th St., 44125. Tel: 216-581-2852; 2853.
School—10608 Penfield Ave., 44125. Tel: 216-581-3080; Fax: 216-581-3031. Sr. M. Anne Cecile Muldoon, O.S.U., Prin.
Ursuline Nuns of Cleveland 1; Lay Teachers 19; Students 410.
Catechesis/Religious Programs—Students 154.
Convent—10430 Granger Rd., 44125. Tel: 216-581-2864.

4—St. Timothy, (1923), Revs. Michael A. Matusz; John Wilson, Pastor Emeritus; Deacon Joseph H. Newman.
Res., 4341 E. 131st St., 44105. Tel: 216-581-0981; 0982; Fax: 216-581-8222.
School—Archbishop James P. Lyke Elementary School. See Elementary Schools, Parochial and Diocesan under Institutions Located in the Diocese. Tel: 216-991-9644.

Gates Mills, Cuyahoga Co., St. Francis of Assisi (1943), Revs. James L. Caddy; Sylvester W. Fridrich, Pastor Emeritus; Thomas J. Pajk; Ralph W. Thomas; Sr. Beverly Bodnar, C.PP.S., Pastoral Assoc.
Res., 6850 Mayfield Rd., P.O. Box 8003, 44040-8003. Tel: 216-461-0066; Fax: 216-461-9053.
School—Tel: 216-442-7450; Fax: 216-446-1132. Sr. Mary Patricia Griesmar, S.N.D., Prin.
Sisters of Notre Dame 2; Lay Teachers 10; Students 285.
Catechesis/Religious Programs—Students 313.
Convent—Tel: 216-449-1352.

Grafton, Lorain Co., Assumption (1894) (Polish), Rev. John M. Tezie.
Res., 1033 Elm St., 44044. Tel: 440-926-2364.

Immaculate Conception (1835), Rev. Robert R. Vieweg.
Res., 708 Erie St., 44044. Tel: 216-926-2268. [CEM]
Catechesis/Religious Programs—Students 244.

Green, Summit Co., Queen of Heaven (1964), Revs. Robert E. Pahler; Robert J. Teknipp, Pastor Emeritus; Deacons Francis R. Lonteen; James A. White.
Res., P.O. Box 296, 44232. Tel: 330-896-2345; Fax: 330-896-8882.
Church—1800 Steese Rd., 44232.
Catechesis/Religious Programs—Students 401.

Highland Heights, Cuyahoga Co., St. Paschal Baylon (1953), Revs. Mario Marzocchi, S.S.S.; Donald Jette, S.S.S.; William Young, S.S.S.; Bro. Scott Haig, S.S.S., Pastoral Assoc.; Deacon Robert J. Bowers.
Res., 5384 Wilson Mills Rd., 44143. Tel: 440-442-3410; 449-7532; 449-7758; Fax: 440-446-9037.
School—5360 Wilson Mills Rd., 44143. Tel: 440-442-6766. Mr. John V. Bednar, Prin.
Sisters of Notre Dame 1; Lay Teachers 27; Students 521.
Catechesis/Religious Programs—Students 428.
Convent—Tel: 440-442-2380.

Hinckley, Medina Co., Our Lady of Grace (1965), Rev. William P. O'Neill. In res., Rev. John T. McDonough.
Res., 1088 Ridge Rd., 44233-9602. Tel: 216-278-2834; 278-4121; Fax: 216-278-2834.
Catechesis/Religious Programs—Students 280.

Hudson, Summit Co., St. Mary (1860), Revs. Joseph J. Costello; Vincent P. O'Dea, Pastor Emeritus; Stephen K. Brunovsky; Kathee Sterbenz, Pastoral Assoc.
Res., P.O. Box 657, 44236. Tel: 216-653-8118; 656-2558 (Cleveland); 650-0722 (Akron); Fax: 216-463-5759. [CEM]

Church—340 N. Main St., 44236.
Catechesis/Religious Programs—Students 1,726.

Independence, Cuyahoga Co., St. Michael (1851), Revs. Carl L. D'Agostino; Denis L. St. Marie; Adelbert J. Gassert, Pastor Emeritus; Deacon Robert Weniger. In res., Rev. William F. Gibbons.
Res., 6912 Chestnut Rd., 44131-3399. Tel: 216-524-1394; 1395; Fax: 216-524-7538. [CEM]
Church—Brecksville Rd., 44131.
School—6906 Chestnut Rd., 44131. Tel: 216-524-6405. Sr. Carol Marek, S.N.D., Prin.
Sisters of Notre Dame 2; Lay Teachers 14; Students 403.
Parish Annex—6800 Chestnut Rd., 44131. Tel: 216-524-4212.
Catechesis/Religious Programs—Students 376.
Convent—Tel: 216-447-4406.

Kirtland, Lake Co., Divine Word (1977), Rev. Norman N. Smith; Deacons Carl M. Varga, Pastoral Assoc.; Lawrence Somrack. In res., Rev. John J. Kinkopf.
Res., 8100 Eagle Rd., 44094. Tel: 216-256-1412; 1413; Fax: 216-256-4929.
Catechesis/Religious Programs—Students 226.

Lakewood, Cuyahoga Co.,

1—St. Clement, (1922), Revs. Alfred H. Winters; Robert J. Jasany; Sr. Mary Jame Masterson, C.S.J., Pastoral Assoc.
Res., 2022 Lincoln Ave., 44107-6099. Tel: 216-226-5116; Fax: 216-226-9459.
Church—Madison & Lincoln Aves., 44107.
School—14505 Madison Ave., 44107. Tel: 216-226-1942. Mrs. Arlene Polen, Prin.
Lay Teachers 11; Students 239.
Catechesis/Religious Programs—Students 224.
Convent—14505 Madison Ave., 44107.

2—SS. Cyril and Methodius, (1902) (Slovak), Revs. Richard J. Ondreyka, M.S.; Jerome J. Duke.
Res., 12608 Madison Ave., 44107-4997. Tel: 216-521-7288; 521-9091; Fax: 216-221-8516.
Church—Madison Ave. & Lakewood Ave., 44107.
School—1639 Alameda Ave., 44107. Tel: 216-221-9409. Mrs. June Seman, Prin.
Lay Teachers 10; Students 195.
Convent—1635 Alameda Ave., 44107. Tel: 216-221-3164.

3—St. Hedwig, (1905) (Polish), Rev. John J. Bryk.
Res., 12903 Madison Ave., 44107. Tel: 216-521-5086; 521-4463.
Church—12905 Madison Ave., 44107.

4—St. James, (1908), Revs. John J. Weigand; Mark R. Riley; Miss Kathryn Haag, C.PP.S., Pastoral Assoc. In res., Rev. Thomas P. Kowatch.
Res., 17514 Detroit Ave., 44107. Tel: 216-221-0233; Fax: 216-529-7950.
Church—Detroit & Granger Ave., 44107.
School—17415 Northwood Ave., 44107. Tel: 216-221-1225; Fax: 216-529-7950. Miss Sheila Mannix, Prin.
Sisters of Humility of Mary 1; Lay Teachers 19; Students 351.
Catechesis/Religious Programs—Students 306.
Convent—17400 Northwood Ave., 44107. Tel: 216-521-4125.

5—St. Luke, (1922), Revs. Francis P. Walsh; Kenneth J. Jakubowski; Sr. Miriam Erb, C.S.A., Pastoral Assoc.; Deacon David A. Streeter. In res., Rev. Ralph E. Wiatrowski.
Res., 1212 Bunts Rd., 44107-2699. Tel: 216-521-0184; 0185; 0186.
School—13889 Clifton Blvd., 44107. Tel: 216-521-7033; Fax: 216-521-9124. Sr. Marilynn Kozak, O.S.U., Prin.
Ursuline Nuns of Cleveland 2; Lay Teachers 15; Students 306.
Catechesis/Religious Programs—Students 220.
Convent—1221 Chase Ave., 44107.

Litchfield, Medina Co., Our Lady Help of Christians Parish (1976), Rev. Robert A. Burge, Coord. Pastoral Team. Pastoral Team: Revs. Ronald J. Bryda; Michael A. Wittman; Edward F. Weist; Deacon John M. Buda; Sr. Margaret Duffy, O.S.U.; Sr. Mary Lou Misciasci, C.S.J.; Sandra J. Lynn.
Administration Center—9608 Norwalk Rd., 44253-9598. Tel: 330-722-1180; 273-1500 (Cleveland).
Catechesis/Religious Programs—Students 472.
Convent—9608 Norwalk Rd., 44253.
Missions—Litchfield, Jesus the Christ Child; Chippewa Lake, Jesus Divine Redeemer; Nova-Savannah, Jesus the Good Shepherd; Seville-Creston, Jesus Emmanuel; Spencer, Jesus Our Savior; Lodi, Jesus Our Teacher.

Lodi, Medina Co., Jesus Our Teacher (1976). Attended by Our Lady Help of Christians, Litchfield.

Lorain, Lorain Co.,

1—St. Anthony of Padua, (1923), Revs. Christian Moore, O.F.M.Conv.; Regis T. Schlagheck, O.F.M.Conv. In res., Bro. Campion Erdei, O.F.M.Cap.
Res., 1305 E. Erie Ave., 44052. Tel: 216-288-0106; Fax: 216-288-9550.
School—1339 E. Erie Ave., 44052. Tel: 216-288-2155; Fax: 216-288-2159. Mrs. Barbara Goebl, Prin.
Lay Teachers 11; Students 328.
Catechesis/Religious Programs—Students 133.

2—SS. Cyril and Methodius, (1905) (Slovenian), Rev. Paul Krajnik.
Res., 1709 E. 31st St., 44055. Tel: 216-277-8286.
Church—1705 E. 31st St., 44055.

3—Holy Trinity, (1906) (Slovak), Rev. Leonard M. Bacik.
Res., 2428 Elyria Ave., 44055-1392. Tel: 216-244-1253; 244-2418.

4—Sacred Heart Chapel, (1952) (Hispanic), Rev. Robert J. Reidy; Sr. Theresa Stegman, C.D.P., Pastoral Assoc.; Deacons Tomas Badillo; Jose A. Flores; Carlos Rivera; Prudo Vicens; Jose A. DeGracia; Juan Diaz, Sr.; Jose Luis Piniero.
Res., 3921 Seneca Ave., 44055. Tel: 216-277-7231; 7232; 277-7379 (Rectory); Fax: 216-277-7232.
Church—4301 Pearl Ave., 44055.
Catechesis/Religious Programs—Students 359.

5—St. John, (1900), Revs. Thomas V. Rath, Pastor Emeritus; Thomas R. Smith.
Res., 2143 Homewood Dr., 44055-2799. Tel: 440-277-7266.
School—2140 E. 36th St., 44055-2798. Tel: 440-277-6285. Mrs. Vera Darmafall, Prin.
Lay Teachers 10; Students 198.

6—St. Joseph, (1896) (German), Revs. Robert J. Reidy; Williams F. Gibbons, Pastor Emeritus; Deacon Luis Maldonado.
Res., 317 W. 15th St., 44052-3488. Tel: 216-244-2179.
Church—Reid Ave. & 15th St., 44052.

7—St. Ladislaus, (1890) (Hungarian), Revs. Patrick J. Shields, Admin. Pro Tem; Alex D. Demetzky, Pastor Emeritus.
Res., 1412 E. 29th St., 44055. Tel: 216-277-8187; 277-6607 (School).

8—St. Mary, (1873), Revs. Daniel O. Divis; John J. Kline, Pastor Emeritus; Mrs. Patricia Shullick, Pastoral Assoc.
Res., 310 Eighth St., 44052-1879. Tel: 216-245-5283; Fax: 216-246-0804.
School—307 Seventh St., 44052. Tel: 216-244-1697. Mr. Hobart Johnson, Prin.
Lay Teachers 11; Students 170.
Administration Center—309 Seventh St., 44052.

9—Nativity of the Blessed Virgin Mary, (1898) (Polish), Rev. Ronald J. Turek; Deacon Robert J. Dybo.
Res., 418 W. 15th St., 44052. Tel: 440-244-9090; 621-6445 (Cleveland); Fax: 440-244-0421.
Church—1454 Lexington Ave., 44052.

10—St. Peter, (1909), Revs. Kenneth J. Wolnowski; Patrick Henry; Deacon Ralph Krupp.
Res., 3501 Oberlin Ave., 44053-2759. Tel: 216-282-9103; 9104; 282-8104; 892-8641 (Cleveland); Fax: 216-892-1693.
School—3601 Oberlin Ave., 44053. Tel: 216-282-9909. Sr. Annamae Murphy, S.N.D., Prin.
Sisters of Notre Dame 2; Lay Teachers 32; Students 609.
Catechesis/Religious Programs—Students 354.
Convent—3651 Oberlin Ave., 44053. Tel: 216-282-2378.

11—St. Stanislaus, (1908) (Polish), Revs. Dennis J. Kristancic; Clyde K. Foster, Admin. Pro Tem.
Res., 2702 Elyria Ave., 44055. Tel: 216-244-4185.

12—St. Vitus, (1922) (Croatian), Rev. Simon J. Nekic.
Res., 1785 E. 32nd St., 44055. Tel: 216-277-8210.

Loudonville, Ashland Co., St. Peter (1870), Rev. Edwin A. Dowling.
Res., 132 N. Wood St., 44842. Tel: 419-994-4396. [CEM]
Catechesis/Religious Programs—Tel: 419-994-3329.
Students 167.

Lyndhurst, Cuyahoga Co., St. Clare (1944), Revs. Stanley J. Klasinski; Louis A. Pizmoht; Joseph Cappelletti; Deacons Ross C. DeJohn, Sr.; Bill Elwood; Leo F. McNulty; Robert J. Matoney, Jr.
Res., 5659 Mayfield Rd., 44124. Tel: 216-449-4242; 4243; 4244; Fax: 216-646-9648.
School—5655 Mayfield Rd., 44124. Tel: 216-449-1554; Fax: 216-449-1497. Miss Ruth Downey, Prin.
Ursuline Nuns of Cleveland 2; Lay Teachers 23; Students 492.
Catechesis/Religious Programs—Students 400.
Convent—5687 Mayfield Rd., 44124. Tel: 216-382-7409.

Macedonia, Summit Co., Our Lady of Guadalupe (1967), Revs. Joseph E. Lehane; Lloyd J. Boymer, Pastor Emeritus; Deacon Mario Vinciguerra; Mrs. Nancy Freibatt, Pastoral Assoc.
Res., 9080 Shepard Rd., 44056-1450. Tel: 216-468-2194; Fax: 216-468-2196.
Catechesis/Religious Programs—Students 314.

Madison, Lake Co., Immaculate Conception (1863), Rev. Luigi C. Miola; Deacons Thomas G. Hupertz; Richard F. Kuhlman.
Res., 2846 Hubbard Rd., 44057-2998. Tel: 440-428-5164; 5165; 975-0729 (Cleveland); Fax: 440-428-3075.
Catechesis/Religious Programs—Students 538.

Maple Heights, Cuyahoga Co., St. Martin of Tours (1960), Revs. John G. Vrana; John J. Gerrity, Pastor Emeritus; Allen F. Corrigan; Deacon John R. Bender.
Res., 14600 Turney Rd., 44137-4788. Tel: 216-475-4300; 4301; Fax: 216-475-8242. [CEM]
School—Tel: 216-475-3633; Fax: 216-475-2484. Rozann Swanson, Prin.
Lay Teachers 17; Students 250.
Catechesis/Religious Programs—Students 197.

St. Wenceslas (1923), Rev. Raymond B. Bartnikowski; Rev. Msgr. Joseph C. Heruday, Pastor Emeritus; Deacon Daniel C. Terrion; Derek Abrajano, Pastoral Assoc. In res., Rev. Stephen J. Walick.
Res., 17825 Libby Rd., 44137-1598. Tel: 216-475-2477; 2478; 475-3304; Fax: 216-662-8101.
Church—Libby Rd. & Cato St., 44137.
School—5254 Arch St., 44137. Tel: 216-662-0180. Sr. Mary Ellen Ryan, S.I.W., Prin.
Sisters 2; Lay Teachers 8; Students 261.

Medina, Medina Co., St. Francis Xavier (1860), Revs. Mark L. Hollis; Stephen Kaminski; Sue Kirkham, Pastoral Assoc.; Deacons Joseph E. Loutzenhiser; Leonard A. Sloan; James T. Schlund.
Res., 606 E. Washington St., 44256. Tel: 330-725-4968; 225-3940 (Cleveland); Fax: 330-725-5886. [CEM]
Church—600 E. Washington St., 44256.
School—612 E. Washington St., 44256. Tel: 330-725-3345. Sr. Sandra Bevec, C.S.S.F., Prin.
St. Felix of Cantalice 1; Lay Teachers 24; Students 554.
Catechesis/Religious Programs—Students 816.

Holy Martyrs (1980), Rev. Robert F. Pfeiffer. Pastoral Assocs.: Mary Frances Ehlinger; Suzanne Kozub.
Res., 3100 S. Weymouth Rd., 44256. Tel: 330-722-6633; 722-8951; 273-1188 (Cleveland).
Catechesis/Religious Programs—Students 599.

Mentor, Lake Co., St. Bede the Venerable (1964), Rev. John J. Sullivan. Pastoral Assocs.: Mrs. Judith A. Cox; Mrs. Lottie A. Sroczynski; Mrs. Karen J. Roman; Deacons Robert P. Ulman; John Burke, Jr.; Kenneth Knight.
Res., 9114 Lake Shore Blvd., 44060-1697. Tel: 216-257-5544; 5545; Fax: 216-257-2318.
Catechesis/Religious Programs—Tel: 216-257-6988.
Students 627.

St. John Vianney (1969), Revs. Robert W. Kline; Thomas W. Johns; Donald A. Rooney; Deacon Wayne W. Snyder.
Administration Office—7575 Bellflower Rd., 44060-3997. Tel: 216-943-3445 (Cleveland); 255-0600 (Cleveland Res.); Fax: 216-255-6482.
School—All Saints of St. John Vianney, Wickliffe. See separate listing under Institutions Located in the Diocese. Tel: 216-943-1395; Fax: 216-944-3341.
Catechesis/Religious Programs—Students 1,112.

St. Mary of the Assumption (1857), Revs. Wilfred T. Smith; Robert J. Lamby, S.S.C.; Deacons Raymond C. Beebe; James T. Martin.
Res., 8560 Mentor Ave., 44060-5853. Tel: 440-255-3404; 3405; 942-1774 (Cleveland); Fax: 440-974-8107.
School—8540 Mentor Ave., 44060. Tel: 440-225-9781. Mrs. Judy A. Tucci, Prin.
Ursuline Nuns of Cleveland 2; Lay Teachers 21; Students 473.
Catechesis/Religious Programs—Students 325.
Convent—Tel: 440-942-1656.

Middleburg Heights, Cuyahoga Co., St. Bartholomew (1956), Revs. John A. Leahy; Thomas G. Elsasser; Deacon Russell Glorioso; Bro. Thomas O'Malley, C.S.C., Pastoral Assoc.
Res., 14865 E. Bagley Rd., 44130. Tel: 216-842-5400; Fax: 216-842-2691.
School—Academy of St. Bartholomew, 14875 E. Bagley Rd., 44130. Tel: 216-845-6660; Fax: 216-845-6672. Mr. Frank E. Dobos, Prin.
Sisters 2; Lay Teachers 14; Students 457.
Catechesis/Religious Programs—Students 324.

Middlefield, Geauga Co., St. Lucy (1958), Rev. Harry S. Winca.
Mailing Address: P.O. Box 98, 44062-0178. Tel: 216-632-5824; 548-8091.
Church—16280 Kinsman Rd., 44062.

Newbury, Geauga Co., St. Helen (1949), Revs. James G. McPhillips; Andrew F. O'Boyle, Pastor Emeritus; Deacon Frederick F. Giel. In res., Rev. William J. Johnson.

Res., 12060 Kinsman Rd., 44065. Tel: 216-564-5805; 338-3358 (Cleveland); Fax: 216-338-1734.
School—Tel: 216-564-7125. Sr. Christin Alfieri, S.N.D., Prin.
Sisters of Notre Dame 2; Lay Teachers 8; Students 204.
Catechesis/Religious Programs—Students 288.

Northfield, Summit Co., St. Barnabas (1956), Revs. Charles T. Diedrick; Daniel McBride; Sr. Regina Kusnir, V.S.C., Pastoral Assoc.; Deacon Gerald Butler.
Res., 9451 Brandywine Rd., 44067. Tel: 440-467-7959; 467-7941; 467-6424; 650-0240 (Akron); Fax: 440-467-6424.
School—9200 Olde Eight Rd., 44067. Tel: 440-467-7921; Fax: 440-468-1926. Miss Beverly Tabacco, Prin.
Vincentian Sisters of Charity 1; Lay Teachers 24; Students 674.
Catechesis/Religious Programs—Students 736.

North Olmsted, Cuyahoga Co., St. Brendan (1964), Revs. Cornelius J. Murray; Stephen M. Spisak; Sr. Mary Ann Phillip, O.P., Pastoral Assoc. In res., Rev. Albert J. Myers.
Res., 3920 Brendan Ln., No. 615H, 44070-2999. Tel: 440-777-7222; 7223; Fax: 440-779-7997.
Church—4242 Brendan Ln., 44070.
School—Tel: 440-777-8433. Mary Mackin, Prin.
Lay Teachers 14; Students 305.
Catechesis/Religious Programs—Students 397.

St. Clarence (1978), Revs. Thomas A. Flynn; Allan R. Laubenthal, S.T.D.; Sr. Sonna M. Bradesca, O.S.U., D.Min., Pastoral Assoc.; Deacons Wayne A. Bosau; Homer L. Sherman.
Res., 30106 Lorain Rd., 44070-3986. Tel: 216-734-2414; Fax: 216-734-4255.
Catechesis/Religious Programs—Students 527.
Convent—30337 Lorain Rd., 44070. Tel: 216-777-5258.

St. Richard (1950), Revs. Charles J. Stollenwerk; George A. Vrabel; Deacon John Zdolshek; Sr. M. Jerome Fitzgerald, S.I.W., Pastoral Assoc.; Sr. Laurie Divoky, S.N.D. In res., Rev. Elmer E. Marquard.
Res., 26855 Lorain Rd., 44070. Tel: 216-777-5050; 5051; 5052; Fax: 216-777-3577.
School—Tel: 216-777-2922; Fax: 216-777-7374. Sr. Julie Demchak, H.M., Prin.
Sisters 3; Lay Teachers 21; Students 579.
Catechesis/Religious Programs—Students 295.
Convent—5053 Whitethorn Ave., 44070. Tel: 216-777-2168.

North Ridgeville, Lorain Co., St. Julie Billiart (1978), Rev. Richard A. Gonser; Deacon John M. Rivera.
Res., 5545 Opal Dr., 44039-2025. Tel: 440-327-1978; 1979; Fax: 440-327-1994. [JC]
Church—5500 Lear Nagle Rd., 44039.
Catechesis/Religious Programs—Students 130.

St. Peter (1875), Rev. Thomas J. Hyland.
Res., 35777 Center Ridge Rd., 44039. Tel: 216-327-2201; 327-2204 (Cleveland). [CEM]
School—35749 Center Ridge Rd., 44039. Tel: 216-327-3212; Fax: 216-327-6843. Sr. Marcia Wilkomm, S.N.D., Prin.
Sisters of Notre Dame 1; Lay Teachers 18; Students 435.
Catechesis/Religious Programs—Students 423.
Convent—Tel: 216-327-8713.

North Royalton, Cuyahoga Co., St. Albert the Great (1959), Revs. John L. Viall; Albert J. Tesek; Edward T. Holland; Russell P. Lowe.
Res., 6667 Wallings Rd., 44133. Tel: 216-237-6760; 6761; Fax: 216-237-5945.
School—Tel: 216-237-1032; Fax: 216-237-3308. Mr. John J. Krupinski, Prin.
Lay Teachers 26; Students 710.
Catechesis/Religious Programs—Students 1,006.

Norton, Summit Co., St. Andrew the Apostle (1951), Revs. James G. Maloney; John A. Wittreich, Pastor Emeritus.
Res., 4022 Johnson Rd., 44203. Tel: 330-825-2617; Fax: 330-825-5309.
Church—Johnson & Hametown Rd., 44203.
Catechesis/Religious Programs—Students 201.

Oberlin, Lorain Co., Sacred Heart (1880). Closed. Parish listings are included under Our Lady Help of Christians, Litchfield. Revs. William B. Padavick; Robert A. Bonnell, Pastor Emeritus.
Res., 410 W. Lorain St., 44074. Tel: 216-774-6791; Fax: 216-774-1337.

Olmsted Falls, Cuyahoga Co., St. Mary of the Falls (1854), Revs. Robert J. Cole; Daniel R. Fickes; Deacon Richard Mueller.
Res., 25615 Bagley Rd., 44138-1915. Tel: 440-235-2222; 2223; 235-2808; Fax: 440-235-2937. [CEM]
School—8262 Columbia Rd., 44138. Tel: 440-235-4580. Mrs. Priscilla Shields, Prin.
Lay Teachers 10; Students 250.
Catechesis/Religious Programs—Tel: 216-235-2808.
Students 626.

Orange Village, Cuyahoga Co., St. Margaret of Hungary (1921) (Hungarian), Rev. Ladislaus Rosko.
Res., 4680 Lander Rd., 44022. Tel: 440-248-2618; 248-8148.

Orrville, Wayne Co., St. Agnes (1879), Rev. Paul J. Wysocki.
Res., 541 Spring St., 44667. Tel: 216-682-3606; 682-2611.
Church—E. Oak St. & Lake St., 44667.
Catechesis/Religious Programs—Students 240.

Painesville, Lake Co., St. Mary (1848), Revs. R. Stephen Vellenga; Joseph S. Mecir; Robert G. Hanzo, Pastor Emeritus; Richard C. Antall.
Res., 242 N. State St., 44077-4095. Tel: 440-354-4381; 4382; Fax: 440-352-8712. [CEM]
School—268 N. State St., 44077. Tel: 216-352-9414; Fax: 216-352-8712. Sr. Mary Ann Raycher, V.S.C., Prin.
Vincentian Sisters of Charity 3; Lay Teachers 16; Students 293.
Catechesis/Religious Programs—Students 418.
Convent—339 Erie St., 44077-4095. Tel: 216-354-3762.

Parkman, Geauga Co., St. Edward (1928), Rev. Harry S. Winca.
Res., P.O. Box 709, 44080-0709. Tel: 440-548-8091.
Church—16150 Center St., 44080.

Parma, Cuyahoga Co.,

1—St. Anthony of Padua, (1959), Revs. Dale W. Staysniak; Robert A. Burge; William G. Bouhall; Deacons Thomas J. Senn; Robert J. Jasany. Pastoral Assocs.: Sr. Karen Kellereski, C.S.F.N.; Marie Mikovsky.
Res., 6750 State Rd., 44134-4518. Tel: 440-842-2666; 2667; 2668; Fax: 440-845-9549.
School—6800 State Rd., 44134. Tel: 440-845-3444; Fax: 440-884-4548. Mr. Frank M. Kuhar, Prin.
Lay Teachers 19; Students 527.
Catechesis/Religious Programs—Students 321.

2—St. Bridget, (1956), Revs. Lawrence J. Bayer; Jerome A. Lukachinsky. In res., Rev. William R. Krizner.
Res., 5620 Hauserman Rd., 44130. Tel: 216-886-4434; 4435; Fax: 216-886-5121.
School—Tel: 216-886-1468. Sr. Alice Rooney, C.S.J., Prin.
Sisters of St. Joseph 3; Lay Teachers 10; Students 322.
Convent—Tel: 216-886-2555.

3—St. Charles Borromeo, (1923), Revs. John T. Carlin; Dwayne Bednar; Richard A. Evans, M.Div.; Stephen P. Moran; Sr. Denise Marie Vlna, O.S.U., Pastoral Assoc.; Deacon John A. Talerico. In res., Rev. Dwayne A. Bednar.
Res., 5891 Ridge Rd., 44129-3642. Tel: 216-884-3030; 3031; 884-3232; Fax: 216-884-5326.
School—7107 Wilber Ave., 44129. Tel: 216-886-5546; Fax: 216-886-1163. Sr. Maryann Murphy, O.S.U., Prin.
Ursuline Nuns of Cleveland 3; Lay Teachers 27; Students 805.
Catechesis/Religious Programs—Students 444.
Convent—6902 Charles Ave., 44129. Tel: 216-886-0390.

4—St. Columbkille, (1956), Revs. Neil D. O'Connor; Stephen F. Radecky, Pastor Emeritus; John A. Misenko; James R. Stenger; Deacon Edward A. Telepak.
Res., 6740 Broadview Rd., 44134. Tel: 216-524-1987; 1988; 524-1516; Fax: 216-524-9146.
School—Tel: 216-524-4816. Miss Rita Klement, Prin.
Lay Teachers 22; Students 604.
Catechesis/Religious Programs—Students 394.
Convent—Tel: 216-524-1738.

5—St. Francis de Sales, (1931), Revs. Russell G. Rauscher; Donald J. Balogh, Pastor Emeritus; Robert L. Hoban; Neil P. Kookoothe; Deacon Robert J. Piskach.
Res., 3434 George Ave., 44134-2904. Tel: 440-884-2319; 2320; 2321; Fax: 440-884-1661.
Church—State & Snow Rd., 44134.
School—3421 Snow Rd., 44134-2596. Tel: 440-884-2340; Fax: 440-884-8211. Anne Sweeney, Prin.
Ursuline Nuns of Cleveland 1; Lay Teachers 19; Students 382.
Catechesis/Religious Programs—Students 313.
Convent—3425 Snow Rd., 44134. Tel: 440-884-7242.

6—Holy Family, (1872), Revs. James P. Costello; Thomas Sheehan; James McManamon, O.F.M.; Edwin M. Leonard; Thomas L. Weber; Sr. Mary Petronella, V.S.C., Pastoral Assoc.; Deacons Russell J. Glorioso; Joseph P. Litke.
Res., 7367 York Rd., 44130-5162. Tel: 216-842-5533; Fax: 216-842-6658. [CEM]
School—8, Tel: 216-842-7785; Fax: 216-842-3634. Kathleen Hrutkay, Prin.
Lay Teachers 32; Students 661.
Catechesis/Religious Programs—Students 523.
Convent—Tel: 216-843-9145.

7—St. Matthias, (1980), Rev. Raymond A. Sutter.
Res., 1200 W. Sprague Rd., 44134-6801. Tel: 216-888-8220; 8221; Fax: 216-888-8146.
Catechesis/Religious Programs—Students 269.

Parma Heights, Cuyahoga Co., St. John Bosco (1963), Revs. David D. Liberatore; Edward M. Tulley, Pastor Emeritus; Douglas T. Makowski; Stephen L. Shields; Deacon Roger Polefko.
Res., 6480 Pearl Rd., 44130. Tel: 440-886-3500; 3501; 3502; Fax: 440-886-0966.
School—6460 Pearl Rd., 44130. Tel: 440-886-0061; Fax: 440-884-4115. Mrs. Martha K. Jacobs, Prin.
Ursuline Nuns of Cleveland 2; Lay Teachers 20; Students 522.
Catechesis/Religious Programs—Students 387.
Convent—6485 Beverly Dr., 44130. Tel: 216-888-5229.

Peninsula, Summit Co., Mother of Sorrows (1882), Revs. John D. Terzano; Robert W. Donohoe, Pastor Emeritus; Rev. Msgr. Thomas J. Kelly, Pastor Emeritus; Sr. Mary Robert Clare, S.N.D., Pastoral Assoc.
Res., 6034 S. Locust St., 44264. Tel: 330-657-2631; 657-2075; 467-5549 (Cleveland Line); Fax: 330-657-2631.
Catechesis/Religious Programs—Students 95.

Perry, Lake Co., St. Cyprian (1968), Revs. James J. Patton; Anthony F. Alexander, Pastor Emeritus; Deacon Andrew Novak.
Res., 4223 Middle Ridge Rd., 44081. Tel: 216-259-2344; Fax: 216-259-2344.
Catechesis/Religious Programs—Students 372.

Richfield, Summit Co., St. Victor (1964), Rev. Arthur A. Bacher.
Res., P.O. Box 461, 44286-0461. Tel: 216-659-6591; 659-6321; Fax: 216-659-3618.
Church—3435 Everett Rd, 44286.
Catechesis/Religious Programs—Students 250.

Rittman, Wayne Co., St. Anne (1855), Revs. Phillip P. Pritt; Frank J. Kuta, Pastor Emeritus.
Res., 139 S. First St., 44270-1492. Tel: 216-927-2941. [CEM]
Church—E. Ohio & S. First St., 44270.

Rocky River, Cuyahoga Co., St. Christopher (1922), Revs. John C. Chlebo; Edward F. Prendergast, Pastor Emeritus; Thomas G. Fanta; Ms. Gayle Cilimburg, Pastoral Assoc. In res., Rev. Msgr. James P. McIntyre.
Res., 20141 Detroit Rd., 44116-2420. Tel: 440-331-4255; 4256; Fax: 440-331-0674.
School—1610 Lakeview Ave., 44116-2409. Tel: 440-331-3075. Sr. Patricia Twohig, Prin.
Sisters of Humility of Mary 1; Lay Teachers 22; Students 474.
Catechesis/Religious Programs—Tel: 216-331-6226.
Students 438.

Seville-Creston, Medina-Wooster Counties, Jesus Emmanuel (1976). Attended by Our Lady Help of Christians, Litchfield.

Shaker Heights, Cuyahoga Co., St. Dominic (1945), Rev. Martin J. Amos; Sr. Mary Ann Mehling, I.H.M., Pastoral Assoc. In res., Revs. Herman B. Peters; Edward T. Estok.
Res., 3450 Norwood Rd., 44122-4967. Tel: 216-991-1444; 991-1445; Fax: 216-561-9341.
Church—19000 Van Aken Blvd., 44122.
School—3455 Norwood Rd., 44122-4901. Tel: 216-561-4400; Fax: 216-561-1573. Sr. Mary Ann Mozser, C.PP.S., Prin.
Sisters of the Precious Blood 1; Lay Teachers 10; Students 246.
Catechesis/Religious Programs—Students 330.

Sheffield, Lorain Co., St. Teresa (1845), Revs. Edward J. Luca; Raymond J. Grismer, Pastor Emeritus; John H. Walker, Pastor Emeritus; Sr. Mary Floranne, S.N.D., Pastoral Assoc.
Church—1878 Abbe Rd., 44054-2322. Tel: 216-934-4227. [CEM]

Sheffield Lake, Lorain Co., St. Thomas the Apostle (1962), Revs. John J. McCaffrey; Stephen L. Shields, Admin. Pro Tem.
Res., 521 Harris Rd., 44054. Tel: 216-949-7744.
School—715 Harris Rd., 44054. Tel: 216-949-6275; Fax: 216-949-6275. Sr. Helene F. Minut, S.N.D., Prin.
Sisters of Notre Dame; Sisters 2; Lay Teachers 9; Students 185.
Catechesis/Religious Programs—Students 182.
Convent—4855 E. Lake Rd., 44054. Tel: 216-949-6232.

Solon, Cuyahoga Co., St. Rita (1929), Revs. Robert M. Wendelken; Robert A. Lorkowski; Clyde K. Foster; Deacons William Donlin; Gerard Ziemkiewicz; Robert Anderson; Mr. Albert E. Leko, Pastoral Assoc.
Res., 32820 Baldwin Rd., 44139-4098. Tel: 440-248-1350; Fax: 440-248-2094.

School—33200 Baldwin Rd., 44139. Fax: 440-248-9442. Mrs. Phyllis Nemetz, Prin.
Lay Teachers 23; Students 494.
Catechesis/Religious Programs—Students 758.
Resurrection of Our Lord (1971), Revs. J. Mark Hobson, Coord., Pastoral Team; Louis J. Trivison, Pastor Emeritus. Pastoral Team: Sr. Mary Jeanette Brown, S.N.D.; Ms. Elizabeth Frey.
Res., 31600 Farm Dr., 44139. Tel: 440-248-0980; 0981; Fax: 440-248-0992.
Church—32001 Cannon Rd., 44139.
Catechesis/Religious Programs—Students 381.
Convent—5710 Janet Blvd., 44139. Tel: 216-248-4364.

South Amherst, Lorain Co., Nativity of Blessed Virgin Mary (1933), Revs. Edward J. Kordas; Wallace F. Roth, Pastor Emeritus.
Res., 333 S. Lake St., 44001. Tel: 440-986-7011.
Catechesis/Religious Programs—Students 185.

South Euclid, Cuyahoga Co., St. Gregory the Great (1922), Rev. Msgr. William N. Novicky; Revs. Stephen A. Towell, Pastor Emeritus; Francis G. Van Bergen; John G. Crawford. Pastoral Assocs.: Sr. Monica Schmitt, S.N.D.; Sr. Mary Callista Antolik, S.N.D.; Sr. Lucille Myers, S.I.W.; Deacon John P. Sferry; Mrs. Mary Ann Trask.
Res., 1545 S. Green Rd., 44121-4085. Tel: 216-382-7601; Fax: 216-382-4992.
School—4478 Rushton Rd., 44121-4084. Tel: 216-381-0363; Fax: 216-691-0435. Miss Lucy Iemmolo, Prin.
Sisters of Notre Dame 1; Lay Teachers 35; Students 800.
Catechesis/Religious Programs—Students 320.
St. Margaret Mary (1948), Revs. Thomas J. Lusoski; Neal J. Buckon; Deacon John T. Wenzel. In res., Rev. Anselm Nzekwe.
Res., 4217 Bluestone Rd., 44121-3427. Tel: 216-382-4114; 4115.
School—4205 Bluestone Rd., 44121. Tel: 216-382-4272; Fax: 216-382-4559. Sr. Mary Barbara Morscher, S.N.D., Prin.
Sisters of Notre Dame 2; Lay Teachers 8; Students 200.
Catechesis/Religious Programs—Students 118.
Convent—4215 Bluestone Rd., 44121. Tel: 216-381-8787.

Spencer, Medina Co., Jesus Our Savior (1976). Attended by Our Lady Help of Christians, Litchfield.

Stow, Summit Co., Holy Family (1946), Revs. Edward J. Szabo; Joseph J. Lieberth; James F. Flood; Sr. Noel Marra, O.S.U., Pastoral Assoc.; Deacon Philip P. Kamlowsky.
Res., 3450 Sycamore Dr., 44224-3999. Tel: 330-688-6411; 6412; 6413; Fax: 330-688-3474.
Church—3179 Kent Rd., 44224.
School—3163 Kent Rd., 44224. Tel: 330-688-3816. Miss Susan Jelenic, Prin.
Lay Teachers 33; Students 717.
Catechesis/Religious Programs—Students 702.

Strongsville, Cuyahoga Co., St. John Neumann (1977), Revs. Robert J. Kraig; David R. Trask; Deacon Thomas Grasson. Pastoral Assocs.: Sr. Mary Popoczy S.N.D.; Sr. Patricia Sylvester, S.N.D.
Res., 16271 Pearl Rd., 44136. Tel: 440-238-1770; 1771; Fax: 440-238-2030.
School—SS. Joseph & John Interparochial. See St. Joseph, Strongsville. Tel: 440-238-4877; Fax: 440-238-8745.
Catechesis/Religious Programs—Students 925.
St. Joseph (1946), Revs. Robert J. Sanson; Charles F. Strebler; Sr. Betty Gulick, S.S.J.-T.O.S.F., Pastoral Assoc.; Deacons Alfred J. Koch; Howard Masony.
Res., 12700 Pearl Rd., 44136-3484. Tel: 440-238-5555; 5556; 238-1038; Fax: 440-238-1059.
School—SS. Joseph and John Interparochial, 12580 Pearl Rd., 44136. Tel: 440-238-4877; Fax: 440-238-8745. Mrs. Darlene Thomas, Prin.
Sisters of St. Joseph 1; Lay Teachers 30; Students 817.
Catechesis/Religious Programs—Tel: 216-238-5231.
Students 711.
Convent—12600 Pearl Rd., 44136. Tel: 440-238-6352.

Tallmadge, Summit Co., Our Lady of Victory (1944), Rev. John R. Hengle; Sr. Dolores Bourquin, H.M., Pastoral Assoc. & D.R.E.
Administration Center—73 North Ave., 44278-1996. Tel: 330-633-3637; 633-3672; Fax: 330-633-6978.
Church—105 North Ave., 44278.
Catechesis/Religious Programs—Students 558.

Thompson, Geauga Co., St. Patrick (1854), Rev. Paul F. Smith; Deacon Andrew J. Novak.
Res., 16550 Rock Creek Rd., Rte. 166, 44086-8753. Tel: 216-298-1327; Fax: 216-298-1846. [CEM]

Twinsburg, Summit Co., SS. Cosmas and Damian (1963), Rev. Robert E. Friedel; Deacon Vincent L. Belsito. In res., Rev. Joseph A. Goebel.
Res., 10419 Ravenna Rd., 44087-1726. Tel: 216-425-8141; 8142; Fax: 216-963-6597.
Church—10439 Ravenna Rd., 44087-1726. Tel: 216-425-8141.
School—Tel: 216-425-4279.
Lay Teachers 6; Students 89.
Catechesis/Religious Programs—Students 483.

University Heights, Cuyahoga Co., Gesu (1926), Revs. John V. White, S.J.; Edward M. Nemeth, S.J.; Joseph B. Kappes, S.J.; Deacon James K. O'Donnell. In res., Rev. Dennis T. Glasgow, S.J.
Res., 2470 Miramar Blvd., 44118. Tel: 216-932-0617; 0618; Fax: 216-932-0731.
Church—2490 Miramar Blvd., 44118.
School—2450 Miramar Blvd., 44118. Tel: 216-932-0620; Fax: 216-932-8326. Sr. Mary Reiling, S.N.D., Prin.
Sisters of Notre Dame 1; Lay Teachers 41; Students 797.
Catechesis/Religious Programs—Students 335.
Convent—2440 Miramar Blvd., 44118. Tel: 216-932-1660.

Valley City, Medina Co., St. Martin of Tours (1840), Rev. Thomas R. Dunphy; Deacon James E. Petrus.
Res., 1824 Station Rd., 44280. Tel: 330-483-3808; Fax: 330-483-3848. [CEM]
Catechesis/Religious Programs—Students 347.

Wadsworth, Medina Co., Sacred Heart (1866), Revs. Joseph L. Labak; James A. Conry; Neil A. Crosby; Deacon Roger N. Kiaas.
Res., 272 Broad St., 44281. Tel: 330-336-3049; Fax: 330-336-0143. [JC]
School—110 Humbolt Ave., 44281. Tel: 330-334-6272; Fax: 330-334-3236. Mrs. Joan Thompson, Prin.
Vincentian Sisters of Charity 1; Lay Teachers 14; Students 343.
Catechesis/Religious Programs—Students 396.
Convent—268 Broad St., 44281. Tel: 330-334-5063.

Warrensville Heights, Cuyahoga Co., St. Jude (1945), Rev. Thomas Carolan, O.F.M.; Susan Horvath, Pastoral Assoc. In res., Rev. Emmanuel Beunen, O.F.M.; Bro. Joseph DiSanto.
Res., 4760 Richmond Rd., 44128-5986. Tel: 216-292-6600; 6601; 6602.

Wellington, Lorain Co., St. Patrick (1851), Rev. James J. Reymann.
Res., 512 N. Main St., 44090-1198. Tel: 216-647-4375; Fax: 216-647-4675.
Catechesis/Religious Programs—Students 279.

Westlake, Cuyahoga, Co., St. Bernadette (1950), Revs. James F. Kramer; John W. Krasen; James T. Klein. Pastoral Assocs.: Sr. Theresa Sullivan, C.S.J.; Deacon Stanley J. Fulton; Mrs. Catherine Vaughan; Mrs. Diane Portorreal; Mrs. Mary Louis; Mrs. Marianne Betters; Mrs. Judy Head. In res., Rev. James A. O'Neill, Pastor Emeritus.
Res., 2256 Clague Rd., 44145-4328. Tel: 440-734-1300; Fax: 440-734-1584.
School—2300 Clague Rd., 44145. Tel: 440-734-7717; Fax: 440-734-9198. Mrs. Denise King, Prin.
Religious 1; Lay Teachers 18; Students 556.
Catechesis/Religious Programs—Students 541.
St. Ladislas (1973), Revs. Donald E. Snyder; Thomas F. Cullen, Pastor Emeritus. Pastoral Assocs.: Sr. Mary Joan Grisez, O.S.U.; Robert C. Hertl; Deacons David L. Kinzel; William Gorman. In res., Most Rev. A. James Quinn.
Res., 2335 Bassett Rd., 44145-2999. Tel: 216-835-2300; 2301; 2302; Fax: 216-835-2300.
Church—2345 Bassett Rd., 44145.
Catechesis/Religious Programs—Students 404.

West Salem, Wayne Co., St. Stephen (1952), Revs. Carl A. Uhler; Paul W. Hackman, Pastor Emeritus.
Res., 44 Britton St., 44287. Tel: 419-853-4946.
Catechesis/Religious Programs—Students 129.

Wickliffe, Lake Co., Our Lady of Mount Carmel (1921), Revs. David L. McCafferty; Dave R. Ireland; Nnamdi Nwankwo; Sr. Rosemary Diba, V.S.C., Pastoral Assoc.; Deacon John W. Strmac. In res., Rev. John M. Richards.
Res., 1730 Mount Carmel Dr., 44092-1835. Tel: 216-585-0700; Fax: 216-585-0870.
Church—29850 Euclid Ave., 44092.
School—29840 Euclid Ave., 44092. Tel: 216-585-0800. Mrs. Ellen Samuels, Prin.
Lay Teachers 16; Students 359.
Catechesis/Religious Programs—Students 245.

Willoughby, Lake Co., Immaculate Conception (1866), Revs. Francis D. Curran; Jeffrey M. Weaver.
Res., 37935 Wright St., 44094-5899. Tel: 216-942-4500.
School—37940 Euclid Ave., 44094. Tel: 216-942-2121; Fax: 216-942-6766. Mrs. Rosalie A. Lewis, Prin.
Ursuline Nuns of Cleveland 1; Lay Teachers 20; Students 423.
Catechesis/Religious Programs—Students 347.

Willoughby Hills, Lake Co., St. Noel (1980), Rev. George Smiga; Mr. Kevin Keil, Dir. Music. Pastoral Assocs.: Deacon Edward Feldkamp; Miss Alice Hinkel; Anthony Camino.
Res., 35200 Chardon Rd., Tel: 216-946-0887; Fax: 216-946-4331.
Catechesis/Religious Programs—Mrs. Marianne Slattery, D.R.E.
Students 356.

Willowick, Lake Co., St. Mary Magdalene (1949), Pastoral Team: Revs. John P. Singler, Coord. Pastoral Team; Ronald Wearsch; Theodore Lucas; Sr. Nancy Hendershot, C.S.A.; Sr. Joan Franklin, O.P.; Sr. Mercia Madigan, O.S.U.
Res., 460 East 321 St., 44095-3663. Tel: 440-943-2133; 943-7047; 943-2523; Fax: 440-943-3780.
Church—32114 Vine St., 44095.
School—Tel: 440-944-7222; Fax: 440-944-8416. Ms. Judy Novey, Prin.
Ursuline Nuns of Cleveland 1; Lay Teachers 15; Students 324.
Catechesis/Religious Programs—Tel: 216-944-2523.
Students 523.
Convent—32301 Willowick Dr., 44095. Tel: 440-944-1134.

Wooster, Wayne Co., St. Mary of the Immaculate Conception (1846), Revs. John J. Mueller; Kevin M. Conroy; Deacon Bernard E. Hosfeld. Pastoral Assocs.: Mrs. Jacquelynn Lee; Sr. Maria Kurrie, S.S.J.-T.O.S.F.
Res., P.O. Box 109, 44691. Tel: 330-264-8824; 264-8822; Fax: 330-262-4633. [CEM]
Church—527 Beall Ave., 44691.
School—535 E. Bowman St., P.O. Box 85, 44691. Tel: 330-262-8671. Cathleen Mark, Prin.
Lay Teachers 9; Students 250.
Catechesis/Religious Programs—Students 320.
Convent—546 E. Bowman St., 44691. Tel: 330-264-5569.

Cleveland Diocesan Mission

EL SALVADOR, C.A. *The Catholic Center*. Rev. Denis L. St. Marie, Dir. Society for the Propagation of the Faith.
Parroquial de Nuestra Senora de Guadalupe. Chirilagua Depto San Miguel, El Salvador. Revs. Joseph H. Callahan; John D. King; Sr. Lisa Marie Belz, O.S.U.
Parroquial Inmaculada Concepcion. Puerto de La Libertad, El Salvador. Revs. Albert Krupp; William A. Thaden; Sr. Roberta Goebel, O.S.U.
Senora del Pilar, Villa de Zaragoza. Rev. G. Michael Williamson.

Chaplains of Public Institutions

CLEVELAND. *Airport, Cleveland Hopkins International*. Rev. Msgr. Casimir Ciolek. Tel: 216-781-9095.
Cleveland Clinic Foundation. Revs. Vincent Moraghan Tel: 216-884-3030; Joseph P. Owens, S.J. Tel: 216-397-4689.
Cleveland House of Correction. Rev. Emmanuel Beunen, O.F.M. Tel: 216-292-6602.
Cleveland Psychiatric. (CPI). Rev. Thomas Gallagher. Tel: 216-361-1444.
Cuyahoga County Detention Home. Rev. James P. O'Donnell, on call. Tel: 216-566-9953.
Cuyahoga County Jail. Rev. Michael Perry, O.de.M. Tel: 216-961-8331.
Cuyahoga County Nursing Home Metro Health Pastoral Care. Vacant. Tel: 216-459-4663.
Cuyahoga Hills Boys School. Rev. Emmanuel Beunen, O.F.M. Tel: 216-292-6602.
Deaconess Hospital. Rev. Raymond Schultheis, C.PP.S. Tel: 216-749-2323.
Dept. of Youth Services. Rev. Emmanuel Beunen, O.F.M. Tel: 216-292-6602.
Fairview General Hospital. Bro. Francis Fergus, O.S.B. Tel: 216-252-2332.
Grace Hospital. Attended from St. Augustine. Tel: 216-781-5530.
Health Hill Hospital for Children. Attended from St. Andrew Abbey. Tel: 216-721-5300.
Kaiser Foundation Hospital. Attended from St. Ann, Fairhill. Tel: 216-321-0024.
Kaiser Foundation Hospital. Attended from St. Bridget. Snow Rd., 44129. Tel: 216-886-4434.
Lakewood Hospital. Tel: 216-226-5116. Rev. Thomas P. Kowatch. Tel: 216-221-0233.
Lutheran Medical Center. Rev. James Mayer, O. de M. Tel: 216-651-5043.
Meridia Euclid General Hospital. Deacon Jerome Vrabel. Tel: 216-486-0850.
Meridia Hillcrest Hospital. Attended from St. Francis of Assisi. Tel: 216-461-0066.
Meridia Huron Road Hospital. Attended from St. Philomena. Tel: 216-541-3540.
Meridia South Pointe Hospital. Rev. Stephen Walick. Tel: 216-475-1766.
Metro Health Center for Rehabilitation. Deacon Charles O. Johnson, Chap. Tel: 216-459-4663.
Metro Health Medical Center. (Hospital). Deacon

Charles O. Johnson, Chap. Tel: 216-671-9472.
Metzenbaum Children's Center. Attended from St. Augustine. Tel: 216-781-5330.
Mount Sinai Hospital. Tel: 216-486-8253. Deacon William Dirk, Chap.
Northeast Pre Release Center. Rev. James O'Donnell Tel: 216-566-9953.
Parma Community Hospital. Rev. James R. Semonin Tel: 216-843-8781.
Rainbow Hospital. (See University Hospitals).
Richmond Heights Mt. Sinai East. Attended from St. Felicitas. Tel: 216-289-0770.
St. Luke Hospital. Attended from Our Lady of Peace. Tel: 216-421-4211.
SouthWest General Hospital. Rev. Dismas Boeff. Tel: 216-433-0696.
Sunny Acres Skilled Nursing Facility. Rev. Emmanuel Beunen, O.F.M. Tel: 216-292-6602.
University Hospitals. Rev. John J. Hayes. Tel: 216-431-5900.
University Hospitals Bedford Medical Center. Rev. Stephen Walick. Tel: 215-475-1766.
Veterans Administration Hospitals, Brecksville V.A 1000 Brecksville Rd., 44141. Tel: 216-526-3030. Chaplains: Revs. Thomas Gallagher; John E. Bolan, C.PP.S., Cleveland V.A., 10701 East Blvd., 44106. Tel: 216-791-3800, Ext. 305.
AKRON. *Akron City Hospital*. Rev. James J. Berardi. Tel: 216-535-4141.
Akron General Hospital. Rev. Robert E. Clancy. Tel: 216-434-4348.
Edwin C. Shaw Hospital. Attended from Nativity of the Lord Jesus. Tel: 216-699-5086.
AMHERST. *Amherst Hospital*. Attended from St. Joseph. Tel: 216-988-2848.
APPLE CREEK. *Apple Creek State Institute*. Apostolate for Persons with Developmental Disabilities. Tel: 216-696-6525, Ext. 270.
ASHLAND. *Samaritan Hospital*. Attended from St. Edward. Tel: 419-289-0491.
AVON. *Our Lady of the Wayside*. Tel: 216-651-0550. Rev. Robert T. Begin.
BARBERTON. *Barberton Citizens Hospitals*. Attended from St. Augustine. Tel: 216-745-0011.
CHAGRIN FALLS. *Windsor Hospital*. Attended from St. Joan of Arc. Tel: 216-247-7183.
CHARDON. *Geauga Community Hospital*. Attended from St. Helen, Newbury. Tel: 216-564-5805; 338-3358 (Cleveland).
CUYAHOGA FALLS. *Fallsview Mental Health Center*. Attended from St. Eugene. Tel: 216-923-5244.
General Hospital. Attended from St. Joseph. Tel: 216-928-2173.
ELYRIA. *Elyria Memorial Hospital*. Sacred Heart, Elyria. Tel: 440-323-3221. Sr. Joan Tomchey, O.S.U., Chap., Pastoral Care. Tel: 216-933-5769.
GRAFTON. *Grafton Correctional Institution*. Deacon James Petrus, Chap. Tel: 330-723-6100.
HUDSON. *Youth Development Center*. Attended from St. Andrew Abbey. Tel: 216-721-5300.
LODI. *Lodi Hospital, Our Lady Help of Christians, Litchfield*. Vacant. Tel: 216-722-1180; 273-1500 (Cleveland).
LOUDONVILLE. *Kettering Hospital*. Attended from St. Peter. Tel: 419-994-4396.
MEDINA. *Medina Community Hospital*. Attended from St. Francis Xavier. Tel: 216-725-4968.
NORTHFIELD. *Western Reserve Psychiatric Habilitation Center* 44067. Tel: 216-467-7131. Rev. Adelbert Gassert.
OBERLIN. *Allen Memorial Hospital*. Attended from Sacred Heart. Tel: 216-774-6791.
ORRVILLE. *Dunlap Memorial Hospital*. Attended from St. Agnes. Tel: 216-682-3606.
PAINESVILLE. *Lake County Memorial Hospital-East*. Tel: 216-585-0700. Rev. John Richards.
SMITHVILLE. *Boys Village of Ohio*. Attended from St. Mary, Wooster. Tel: 216-264-8824.
WADSWORTH. *Wadsworth Health Care Center*. Attended from Sacred Heart of Jesus. Tel: 216-336-3049.
Wadsworth-Rittman Hospital. Attended from Sacred Heart of Jesus. Tel: 216-336-3049.
WILLOUGHBY. *Lake County Memorial Hospital-West*. Tel: 216-942-4500. Rev. John Richards Tel: 216-585-0700.
WOOSTER. *Wooster Community Hospital*. Attended from St. Mary. Tel: 216-264-8824.

Released from Diocesan Assignment:
Reverend Monsignors—
Broglio, Timothy, Secretariat of State, Vatican City State, 00120
Reverend Fathers—
Berthiaume, Gary D., Cenacle Retreat House, P.O. Box 340, Warrenville, IL 60555
Cooper, R. John, 4379 Plumwood Dr., North Olmsted, OH 44070
Klamet, Francis X., Holy Rosary, 12021 Mayfield Rd., Cleveland, OH 44106
Lang, Joseph J., Church of the Resurrection, 9504 100th Ave., Fort St. John, BC V1J 1X7 Canada
Lynch, James M., Casilla 53303, Santiago, Chile
Lyons, John F., 3175 W. 165th St., Cleveland, OH 44115
Myers, Kenneth C., Missionaries of Pastoral Charity Society, 1135 Mission Rd., San Antonio, TX 78210-4598
Obloy, Leonard G., Faculty & Vice Rector, St. Mary Seminary, Emmitsburgh, MD 21727
Patrick, William J., St. Jude Hospital & Rehabilitation Center, 101 E. Valencia Mesa Dr., Fullerton, CA 92634
Petcavage, Leonard, C.S.J., Order of Benedict, O.S.B., 10510 Buckeye Rd., Cleveland, OH 44104
Piskura, Joseph H., P.O. Box 33439, Fortsill, OK 73503-0439
Valley, John, 37825 Lake Shore Blvd., Eastlake, OH 44095
Zingales, Jonathan A., St. Andrew Abbey, 10510 Buckeye Rd., Cleveland, OH 44104

Military Chaplains:
Reverend Fathers—
Czech, Edward M.
McCausland, Joseph E.
Sheil, James

Graduate Studies:
Reverend Fathers—
Woost, Michael G.

Absent on Leave:
Reverend Fathers—
Baranek, Raymond
Brodnick, Joseph
Burg, Thomas R.
Chojnacki, David
Enzman, David
Esmurdoc, Christopher F.
Kristancic, Dennis
Lonteen, Daniel
Rupp, Edward F.

Retired:
Reverend Monsignors—
Ciolek, Casimir S., 906 College Ave., Cleveland, OH 44113
Gasbarre, Francis E., Holy Trinity, 24821 Columbus Rd., Bedford Heights, OH 44146
Goldikovskis, Alexander I., 21362 Milan Ave., Cleveland, OH 44119
Heruday, Joseph C., St. Wenceslas, 17825 Libby Rd., Maple Heights, OH 44137
Kelly, Thomas J., Issenmann Place, 4185 Brookway Ln., Brooklyn, OH 44144
McIntyre, James P., 20141 Detroit Rd., Rocky River, OH 44116
Moriarty, Joseph T., 6620 Pearl Rd., Parma Heights, OH 44130. Tel: 216-885-0320
Spitzig, Joseph, 1264 Tupelo Ln., West Salem, OH 44287
Wolff, Robert C., 4516 Rex Lake Dr., Akron, OH 44319
Reverend Fathers—
Alexander, Anthony F., 344 Sanford St., Painesville, OH 44077
Anderson, John F., 12969 Chillicothe Rd., Chesterland, OH 44026
Balogh, Donald J., 785 W. Perimeter Rd., Frewsburg, NY 14738
Becherer, James R., 4963 E. Lake Rd., Sheffield Lake, OH 44054
Blinn, Mark R., Harbor Side Manor, 27601 Westchester Pkwy., Westlake, OH 44145
Bonnell, Robert A., 143 E. College St., Apt. 313, Oberlin, OH 44074
Boymer, Lloyd J., St. Barnabas, 1105 Canyonview, #304, Sagamore, OH 44067
Brennan, Robert, 1076 Sylvan Ave., Lakewood, OH 44107
Bruening, Allen
Byrider, Charles L., St. Francis De Sales Parish, 4019 Manchester Rd., Akron, OH 44319
Camille, Edward J., St. Basil, 8700 Brecksville Rd., Brecksville, OH 44141
Cauley, Robert W., Eliza Jennings, 10603 Detroit Ave., Lakewood, OH 44107
Cimperman, Victor J., 1240 E. 61st St., Cleveland, OH 44103
Clines, Paul J., St. Augustine Parish, 965 Norton Ave., Barberton, OH 44203
Conroy, James A., 5891 Ridge Rd., Parma, OH 44129
Conway, Neil, 4045 Wetmore Rd., Cuyahoga Falls, OH 44223
Cook, William R., 15425 No. Tatum #126, Phoenix, AZ 85032
Cullen, Thomas F., 2284 Winward Dr., Westlake, OH 44145
Dalton, John, Holy Name, 8328 Broadway, Cleveland, OH 44105
Demetzky, Alex D., 7611 Eve Ave., Cleveland, OH 44102
Dodd, Anthony J., Assumption, 5445 Smith Rd., Brook Park, OH 44142
Donohue, Robert W., St. Jude, 590 Poplar St., Elyria, OH 44035
Englert, William J., 534 W. Bullard Ave., Fresno, CA 93704
Eylar, William D., 6163 E. Akron St., Mesa, AZ 85205
Gaebelein, Claude J., 4291 Richmond Rd., Warrenville Heights, OH 44122
Gassert, Adelbert, 925 Canyon View Dr., #205, Akron, OH 44067
Gerrity, John J., 4291 Richmond Rd., Warrensville Heights, OH 44122
Gibbons, William F., 6912 Chestnut Rd., Independence, OH 44131
Goebel, Joseph A., 10419 Ravenna Rd., Twinsburg, OH 44087-1726
Grandillo, James J., 1007 Superior Ave., Cleveland, OH 44144
Grismer, Raymond J., Issenmann Place, 4185 Brookway Ln., Brooklyn, OH 44144
Hackman, Paul W., 9901 Johnnycake Ridge Rd., Mentor, OH 44060
Hanzo, Robert, 5406 Pebble Creek Ln., Painesville, OH 44077
Hritz, Paul J., 28700 Euclid Ave., Wickliffe, OH 44092
Ivanauskas, Balys C., 200 S. Silvery Ln., Dearborn, MI 48124-1225
Jezeski, Henry, 7551 Pleasant Run Rd., Seven Hills, OH 44131-5906
Johnson, William J., 12060 Kinsman Rd., Newbury, OH 44065
Kilcoyne, John, Issenmann Place, 4185 Brookway Ln., Brooklyn, OH 44144
Kinkopf, John J., Divine Word, 8100 Eagle Rd., Kirtland, OH 44094
Kitt, William J., Castleblakeney, Ballinasloe, Co. Galway, Ireland
Kline, John J., 33803 Electric Blvd., #E-6, Avon Lake, OH 44012
Kreps, Anthony L., 2920 Hamlin Rd., Medina, OH 44256
Kuta, Frank J., 8795 N. Kane Rd., Warrensville, OH 44281
Laheta, Andrew P., 5232 Broadview Rd., Richfield, OH 44286
Lesniak, John E., 367 E. 260th St., Euclid, OH 44132
Lyons, William P., 2603 Benton St., Akron, OH 44312
Mackert, Albert J., 13719 Tartan Dr., Sun City West, AZ 85375
McDonough, John T., 1088 Ridge Rd., Hinckley, OH 44233
McMahon, John F., 10812 Adeline Rd., Cleveland, OH 44111
McShane, Patrick E., 180 Shawmut Ave, Apt. 707, Boston, MA 02118
Michalski, Thaddeus C., Issenmann Place, 4185 Brookway Ln., Brooklyn, OH 44144
Minnoggio, Ferrando, North American College, Vatican City State, 00120
Mosovsky, James J., 7801 Detroit Ave., Cleveland, OH 44102
Mrakuzic, Stephen A., Mailing Address: 4849 Grace Rd., North Olmsted, OH 44070
Mulica, James, 255 N. El Cielo Rd., No. 366, Palm Springs, CA 92262
Muzic, Anthony J., 1160 Broadway Ave., Bedford, OH 44146
Myers, Albert J., 3920 Brendan Ln., North Olmstead, OH 44070
O'Boyle, Andrew F., 4170 N. Amber Dr., Brooklyn, OH 44144
O'Dea, Vincent P., Issenmann Place, 4185 Brookway Ln., Brooklyn, OH 44144
O'Neill, James A., St. Bernadette Parish, 2225 Clague Rd., Westlake, OH 44145
Paik, Francis M., 12340 Bass Lake Rd., #B27, Chardon, OH 44024
Patragnoni, Ettore, Viale Principe di Piemonte No. 18, Stresa, (Novara) 28049 Italy
Peters, Herman B., St. Dominic Parish, 3450 Norwood Rd., Shaker Heights, OH 44122
Prendergast, Edward F., 33960 Daisy Ln., North Ridgeville, OH 44039
Radecky, Stephen F., 3395 E. 53rd St., Cleveland, OH 44127
Rath, Thomas V., 200 St. Joseph Dr., Amherst, OH 44001
Rathfon, John R., 263 Woodpecker Rd., Naples, FL 33961
Reichlin, Urban A., 76 Westshore Dr., Avon Lake, OH 44012
Roth, Wallace F., Issenmann Place, 4185 Brookway Lane, Brooklyn, OH 44144

Schneid, Michael, 10204 Grange Rd., Cleveland, OH 44125
Silva, David E., 2899 E. Ridgewood Dr., Seven Hills, OH 44131
Smith, James A., 5163 Broadway, Cleveland, OH 44127
Storey, John R., 5232 Broadview Rd., Richfield, OH 44286
Sullivan, Thomas F., 39 N. Portage Path, Akron, OH 44303
Teknipp, Robert J., 45 Lethbridge Ln., Akron, OH 44321-1369
Tomc, Victor N., 20654 Centuryway Rd., Maple Heights, OH 44137
Tomicky, Ronald, 6164 Westminster Dr., Parma, OH 44129-4924
Towell, Stephen A., 4483 Ardendale Rd., South Euclid, OH 44121
Trivison, Louis J., 283 Union St., Bedford, OH 44146
Tulley, Edward M., 4185 Brookway Ln., Brooklyn, OH 44144
Valentini, Francis M., 2749 Orchid Oaks Dr., #302-A, Sarasota, FL 34239
Wagner, Joseph F., St. Colette, 330 W. 130th St., Brunswick, OH 44212
Walker, John H., c/o 3200 Desiderata Ct., Plano, TX 75086
Wilson, John F., St. Edward Home, 3131 Smith Rd., Akron, OH 44313
Wittreich, John A., 18592 Edward Rd., 287 Tower, Doylestown, OH 44230
Wolf, John W., 5232 Broadview Rd., Richfield, OH 44286
Woll, Peter J., St. Robert Parish, 23802 Lake Shore Blvd., Euclid, OH 44123
Yavorsky, James A., 5232 Broadview Rd., Richfield, OH 44286

Permanent Deacons:
Adair, Robin, St.Augustine, Barberton
Agrippe, James L., St. Angela Merici, Fairview Park
Anderson, Robert C., St. Rita, Solon
Bacik, Dale A., St. Anselm, Chesterland
Badillo, Tomas, Sacred Heart Chapel, Lorain
Balassy, Geza J., St. Emeric, Cleveland; St. Albert the Great, North Royalton
Bals, Jerry J., Leave of Absence
Beebe, Raymond C., St. Mary, Mentor
Beercheck, Richard C., St. Patrick, (Rocky River), Cleveland
Belsito, Vincent L., Sts. Cosmas and Damian, Twinsburg; NADO Representative
Belter, Clement J., St. Ambrose, Brunswick
Bender, John R., St. Martin of Tours, Maple Heights
Berigan, Patrick F., Our Lady of Good Counsel, Cleveland
Boehnlein, Lawrence A., St. Mary, Chardon
Bosau, Wayne A., St. Clarence, North Olmsted
Bowers, Robert J., St. Paschal Baylon, Highland Heights
Broering, J. Harry, Jr., On Duty Outside the Diocese
Bubnick, Robert C., Sr., Apostolate for the Mentally Retarded, Assumption, Broadview Heights
Buda, John M., Our Lady Help of Christians, Litchfield
Burke, John Jr., St. Bede the Venerable, Mentor
Butkovic, Donald P., St. Adalbert, Berea; St. Thomas Hospital, Akron
Capek, Louis J., Rep. Diocesan Vocation Council, St. Joan of Arc, Chagrin Falls
Cermak, Lawrence, St. Therese, Garfield Heights
Chrosniak, Clarence A., Our Lady of Mount Carmel (West), Cleveland
Coleman, Gerald T., (Retired)
Colon, Victor R., San Juan Bautista, Cleveland
Corrigan, William H., St. Colman, Cleveland
Cowell, Bruce R., Leave of Absence
Croniger, James D., Holy Cross, Euclid
Damukaitis, Joseph B., Leave of Absence
Daull, Raymond L., Christ the King, Cleveland
Davis, Norman H., St. Gabriel, Mentor
Davison, John H., Leave of Absence
DeGracia, Jose A., Diaconate Staff, Sacred Heart Chapel, Lorain
DeHaas, Thomas B., Jr., St. Felicitas, Euclid
DeJohn, Ross C., Sr., St. Clare, Lyndhurst
Diaz, Juan A., Sacred Heart, Lorain
Dietrich, Harold R., Holy Spirit, Avon Lake
Dillon, Edward R., Sacred Heart of Jesus, Elyria
Dirk, William E., Our Lady of Peace, Cleveland; Mount Sinai Hospital; St. Luke Hospital
Donlin, William A., St. Rita, Solon
Duffy, James J., DPC Representative; St. John Vianney, Mentor
Dybo, Robert J., Nativity of the Blessed Virgin Mary, Lorain
Elwood, William T., St. Clare, Lyndhurst; Youth & Family Ministry, Eastern Region
Feldkamp, Edward J., St. Noel, Willoughby Hills
Figueroa, Miguel A., St. Michael, Cleveland
Flores, Jose A., Sacred Heart Chapel, Lorain
Friend, Shelby M., St. Henry, Cleveland
Fulton, Stanley J., St. Bernadette, Westlake
Giel, Frederick F., St. Helen, Newbury
Girard, Charles C., Tuscon, AZ
Glorioso, Russell J., Holy Family, Parma; St. Bartholomew, Middleburg Heights
Grasson, Thomas J., St. John Neumann, Strongsville
Hancock, Daniel J., Region VI Rep., St. Ignatius, Cleveland
Hill, Kenneth J., St. Vincent de Paul, Cleveland
Hinderscheid, Lee F., St. Hilary, Fairlawn
Hosfeld, Bernard E., St. Mary of the Immaculate Conception, Wooster
Humphrey, Frank A., III, St. Mary, Elyria
Humphrey, Patrick J., St. Jude, Elyria
Hupertz, Thomas G., Immaculate Conception, Madison
Jarosh, Rudolph, Jr., St. Thomas More, Brooklyn
Jasany, Robert J., St. Anthony of Padua, Parma
Johnson, Charles O., Metropolitan General Hospital; St. Aloysius-St. Agatha, Cleveland
Johnson, Joseph W., On Duty Outside the Diocese
Kamlowsky, Philip P., Holy Family, Stow
Kaniecki, James A., St. Edward, Ashland
Karecki, Edmund J., St. Augustine, Cleveland
Kinzel, David L., St. Ladislas, Westlake
Klaas, Roger N., Sacred Heart, Wadsworth
Knight, Kenneth, St. Bede the Venerable, Mentor
Koch, Alfred J., St. Joseph, Strongsville
Koch, John A., Ascension, Cleveland
Kochanski, Robert M., St. Joseph, Cuyahoga Falls
Krupp, Ralph J., St. Peter, Lorain
Kuhlman, Richard F., Immaculate Conception, Madison
Litke, Joseph P., Holy Family, Parma
Lobdell, Donald W., Nadeau, MI
LoCascio, Phillip A., Phoenix, AZ
Lonteen, Francis R., St. Paul, Akron; Queen of Heaven, Greensburg
Loutzenhiser, Joseph E., St. Francis Xavier, Medina
Love, Wm. Ansley, (Retired)
Lozada, Frank, St. Francis, Cleveland
Lundeen, David J., Corpus Christi, Cleveland
Malcolm, Billy J., St. Ignatius of Antioch & St. Vincent De Paul, Cleveland
Maldonado, Louis, St. Joseph Lorain
Martin, James T., St. Mary of the Assumption, Mentor
Masony, Howard J., Diaconate Staff, St. Jospeh the Worker, Strongsville
Matoney, Robert, Jr., St. Clare, Lyndhurst
Matusicky, Daniel J., St. Bernard, Akron
McCarthy, Edward J., Jr., Diaconate Staff, St. Mary, Chardon
McNulty, Leo F., St. Clare, Lyndhurst; St. Joseph Christian Life Center
Medina, Ceferino, San Juan Bautista, Cleveland
Merriman, William C., St. Patrick, Cleveland
Miklosovic, John, St. Ambrose, Brunswick
Miranda, Ignacio, San Juan Bautista, Cleveland
Mueller, Richard A., St. Mary of the Falls, Olmstead Falls
Netzband, Ralph W., St. Monica, Garfield Heights
Newman, Joseph H., Asst. Chap. Port of Cleveland, St. Timothy, Garfield Heights
Novak, Andrew J., St. Cyprian, Perry; St. Patrick, Thompson
O'Connell, Frank J., On Duty Outside the Diocese
O'Donnell, James K., Interfaith Commission, Diaconate Staff, Gesu, University Heights
Paroff, John A., Grand Rapids, MI
Payne, Robert H., Holy Cross, Euclid
Payne, Willard C., St. Pius X, Bedford
Peacock, Terry W., St. Sebastian, Akron
Pecek, Louis G., Diocesan Tribunal, St. Paul, Euclid
Petrus, James E., St. Martin of Tours, Valley City
Piechowski, Kenneth J., Dir. Diaconate & Cathedral of St. John
Pineiro, Jose L., Sacred Heart Chapel, Lorain
Piskach, Robert J., St. Francis de Sales, Parma
Polefko, Roger F., St. John Bosco, Parma Heights
Quiles, Rafael, St. Petersburg, FL
Rapp, Robert, Garrettsville, Ohio
Reiland, George J., Jr., (Retired)
Rivera, Carlos, Sacred Heart Chapel, Lorain
Rivera, John M., Diaconate Staff, St. Augustine, Cleveland; St. Julie Billiart, North Ridgeville
Rodriguez, Alfonso, Palm Bay, FL
Sabol, Robert G., St. Peter the Apostle, Brook Park
Savage, Joseph J., Plymouth, MI
Schad, Kenneth E., On Leave
Schill, William E., Blessed Sacrament, Cleveland
Seal, J. David, Immaculate Heart of Mary, Cuyahoga Falls
Senn, Thomas J., St. Anthony of Padua, Parma; Cuyahoga County Jail
Sferry, John P., St. Gregory, South Euclid
Sheridan, Thomas, St. Ambrose, Brunswick
Sherman, Homer L., St. Clarence, North Olmsted
Sill, Donald E., St. Anselm, Chesterland
Simon, Frederick F., Capilla de Cristo Rey, Cleveland
Skrha, Joseph W., M.D., Dir., Pastoral Care Dept., St. Michael Hospital, Cleveland
Sloan, Leonard A., St. Francis Xavier, Medina; University Hospitals
Smith, Dennis L., Immaculate Conception, Akron
Snyder, Wayne W., St. John Vianney, Mentor
Somrack, Lawrence A., St. Augustine Hunger Center, Cleveland; Divine Word, Kirtland
Staab, William M., St. Patrick, Cleveland
Stewart, James R., St. James, Lakewood
Stokes, Troy F., Epiphany, Cleveland
Streeter, David A., St. Luke, Lakewood
Strmac, John W., Diaconate Staff, Our Lady of Mount Carmel, Wickliffe
Talerico, John A., St. Charles Borromeo, Parma
Telepak, Edward A., Diaconate Staff, St. Columbkille, Parma
Terrion, Daniel C., St. Wenceslas, Maple Heights
Thiel, Martin A., St. Thomas More, Brooklyn
Torres, Epifanio, San Juan Bautista, Cleveland
Travalik, Peter M., St. Jerome, Cleveland
Ulman, Robert P., St. Bede the Venerable, Mentor
Urbanski, Clemens J., St. Anthony of Padua, Fairport Harbor
Varga, Carl M., Divine Word, Kirtland
Vicens, Prudo, Sacred Heart Chapel, Lorain
Vincent, James C., St. Peter the Apostle, Brook Park
Vinciguerra, Mario J., Our Lady of Guadelupe, Macedonia
Volek, Ronald J., St. George, Clinton
Vrabel, Jerome B., Holy Cross, Euclid
Waken, Thomas J., Pastoral Care Coord., St. Joseph Hospital; St. Leo, Cleveland
Walsh, John J. (Y), Pittsburgh, Pennsylvania
Weglicki, Frank L., Jr., St. Ambrose, Brunswick
Wendzicki, Martin J., Holy Name, Cleveland
Weniger, Robert L., St. Michael, Independence
Wenzel, John T., St. Margaret Mary, South Euclid
Wilson, Francis B., Assumption of Mary, Brook Park
Woods, Richard E., St. Louis, Cleveland Heights
Woyton, Louis M., St. Augustine, Cleveland
Zawadzki, Charles W., Corpus Christi, Cleveland
Zdolshek, John R., St. Richard, North Olmstead
Ziemkiewicz, Gerard J., St. Rita, Solon

INSTITUTIONS LOCATED IN THE DIOCESE

[A] SEMINARIES, DIOCESAN

WICKLIFFE. *Borromeo Seminary*, 28700 Euclid Ave., 44092-2585. Tel: 216-943-7600. Very Rev. Thomas M. Dragga, D.Min., Pres. & Rector; Rev. Robert Stec, M.A., M.Div.; Kathryn C. Simmons, Registrar; Revs. Donald Lippert, O.F.M.Cap., M.A.; John F. Loya, M.Div., Spiritual Dir.; Robert Marva, O.F.M.Cap., M.Div.; Mr. Brian F. Houlahan, Treas.; Rev. Timothy Plavac, M.Div.; Sr. Rosemarie Carfagna, O.S.U., Ph.D. Lay Teachers: Ed Kaczuk, M.M.; Ray Leopold; William Tighe, B.S. Priests 5; Sisters 1; Lay Teachers 3; Seminarians 32.

St. Mary Seminary and Graduate School of Theology. (Our Lady of the Lake), 28700 Euclid Ave., 44092-2585. Tel: 440-943-7600. Revs. Donald B. Cozzens, Ph.D., Pres. & Rector; Thomas W. Tifft, Ph.D., Vice Rector & Academic Dean; Peter M. Mihalic, S.T.D.; John F. Loya, M.A., M.Div., Spiritual Dir.; Ms. Kathryn C. Simmons, Registrar; Sr. Maribeth Howell, O.P., S.T.D.; Sr. Mary McCormick, O.S.U., Ph.D., Candidate; Revs. Gerald J. Bednar, Ph.D.; Donald Dunson, Ph.D.; Thomas Dragga, D.Min.; Mark Latcovich, Ph.D., Dean of Students; Thomas H. Weber, S.T.L., S.S.L.; Lorenzo Tosco, C.S.J., S.S.L.; Paul Hritz, Ph.D.; Mr. Edward J. Kaczuk, M.M.; Rev. David Walkowiak, J.C.D.; Mr. Alan K. Rome, M.L.S., Librarian; Mr. Brian F. Houlahan, Treas. Priests 12; Sisters 2; Adjunct Faculty 9; Students for Priesthood, Diocesan 27; Permanent Diaconate 25; Other 68.

[B] SEMINARIES, RELIGIOUS OR SCHOLASTICATES

CLEVELAND. *Blessed Sacrament Seminary, Congregation of the Blessed Sacrament*, 5384 Wilson Mills Rd., 44143-3092. Tel: 440-442-6311.
E-mail: aschueller@aol.com
Web site: blessedsacrament.com

Very Rev. Anthony L. Schueller, S.S.S., Provincial; Revs. Eugene LaVerdiere, S.S.S.; John Thomas Lane, S.S.S., Dir. of Vocations; Jack Dowling, Dir. of Scholasticates.

[C] COLLEGES AND UNIVERSITIES

CLEVELAND. *John Carroll Jesuit Community.*
E-mail: jesuits@jcvaxa.jcu.edu John Carroll University, University Heights, 44118. Tel: 216-397-1886; Fax: 216-397-4228.
For a complete listing, refer to the Colleges and Universities section.

John Carroll University, North Park & Miramar Blvd., 44118. Tel: 216-397-1886.
Web site: http://www.jcu.edu
For a complete listing, refer to the Colleges and Universities section.

Notre Dame College of Ohio.
E-mail: ndc.edu
Web site: www.ndc.edu
4545 College Rd. South Euclid, 44121. Tel: 216-381-1680; Fax: 216-381-3802.
For a complete listing, refer to the Colleges and Universities section.

Ursuline College 2550 Lander Rd. Pepper Pike, 44124. Tel: 440-449-4200; Fax: 440-646-8102.
For a complete listing, refer to the Colleges and Universities section.

[D] HIGH SCHOOLS, DIOCESAN

CLEVELAND. *Cleveland Central Catholic High School*, Administration: Forman Campus, 6550 Baxter Ave., 44105. Tel: 216-441-4700. Scranton Campus, 3146 Scranton Rd., 44109. Janice T. Roccosalva, Prin. Sisters 2; Lay Teachers 33; Students 550.

Villa Angela-St. Joseph High School, 18491 Lake Shore Blvd., 44119. Tel: 216-481-8414; Fax: 216-486-1035.
E-mail: vastjoe@connectinc.com
Sr. Maria Berlec, O.S.U., Prin. Marianists 2; Ursuline Nuns 2; Lay Teachers 32; Students 500.

BEDFORD. *St. Peter Chanel High School*, 480 Northfield Rd., 44146. Tel: 440-232-5900; Fax: 440-232-9283.
E-mail: chanelhs@aol.com
Web site: www.stpeterchanel.com
Mr. Roger R. Abood, Prin. Sisters of Notre Dame 2; Lay Teachers 29; Students 399.

ELYRIA. *Elyria Catholic High School.* (Coed), 725 Gulf Rd., 44035. Tel: 216-365-1821; Fax: 216-365-7536. Mr. Wayne Uehlein, M.A., Prin.
Serving Elyria, Avon, Sheffield, North Ridgeville, Grafton, Oberlin, and Amherst. Sisters of Notre Dame 1; Lay Teachers 35; Students 587.

LORAIN. *Lorain Catholic High School.* (Grades 7-12), 760 Tower Blvd., 44052. Tel: 440-282-8216. Rev. Leo Dechant, C.S.J., M.A., M.Div., Prin.; Mrs. Anna Marie Donley, B.A., Dean of Women; Mr. James W. Lawhead, B.A., M.S., Dean of Men; Revs. Giampietro Gasparin, C.S.J., M.Div., Chap.; Mark Withers, C.S.J., B.A., Religion Teacher. Priests 3; Sisters of Notre Dame 1; Lay Teachers 22; Students 352.

MENTOR. *Lake Catholic High*, 6733 Reynolds Rd., 44060. Tel: 440-951-0077; Fax: 440-974-9087. Sr. St. Ann Waldron, O.S.U., Prin.; Rev. David G. Woost, Chap. Priests 1; Ursuline Nuns of Cleveland (O.S.U.) 3; Lay Teachers 51; Students 912.

PARMA HEIGHTS. *Holy Name High School.* (Coed), 6000 Queens Hwy., 44130. Raymond R. Ramicone, Prin.; Rev. William R. Krinzner, Chap. Priests 1; Sisters 4; Lay Teachers 61; Students 1,191.

[E] HIGH SCHOOLS, PRIVATE

CLEVELAND. *Beaumont School.* 3301 N. Park Blvd., Cleveland Heights, 44118.
E-mail: beaumont@gwis.com
Web site: www.nw-ohio.net~beaumont
Beaumont Convent, 3240 Fairmount Blvd., 44118. Tel: 216-321-2157. Ursuline Sisters. Sr. Rita Mary Welsh, O.S.U., Pres.; Sr. Susan Mary Rathbun, O.S.U., Prin. Sisters 12; Lay Teachers 40; Students 440.

Benedictine High School, 2900 Martin Luther King Dr., 44104-4898. Tel: 216-421-2080; Fax: 216-421-1100. Rt. Rev. Roger W. Gries, O.S.B., Pres.; David A. Smith, Treas.; Mr. Timothy Evert, Chm., Board of Governors; Mr. Charles Reynolds, Prin.; Rev. Gerard Gonda, O.S.B., Vice Prin. Academic Affairs; Mr. Anthony Russ, Dean Student Affairs; Mr. Dereck Slesh, Business Mgr.; Revs. Albert Marflak, O.S.B.; Michael Brunovsky, O.S.B.; Timothy Buyansky, O.S.B.; Gary Hoover, O.S.B.; Bede Kotlinski, O.S.B.; Joachim Pastirik, O.S.B., School Chap.; Anselm Zupka, O.S.B.; Dominic Mondzelewski; Bros. Peter Ancel, O.S.B.; Theodore Girard, O.S.B.; Ignatius Isaac, O.S.B. Priests 9; Brothers 3; Lay Teachers 23; Students 371.

Magnificat High School. (Girls), 20770 Hilliard Rd., 44116. Tel: 440-331-1572; Fax: 440-331-7257. Sr. Mary Pat Cook, H.M., Prin. Sisters 4; Lay Teachers 63; Students 829.

Padua Franciscan High School, 6740 State Rd., 44134. Tel: 216-845-2444.
Web site: http://members.aol.com/paduahs
Rev. Walter Dolan, O.F.M., Pres.; Gerald R. Jindra, Vice Pres. for Development & Public Information; Timothy Giulivo, Prin.; Rev. Daniel Senger, O.F.M. Campus Ministry: Rev. Tony Posadas, O.F.M.; Bro. Tom Carroll, O.F.M., Academic Dean. Priests 3; Sisters 1; Brothers 1; Lay Teachers 63; Students 1,077.

Regina High School. (Girls), 1857 S. Green Rd., 44121. Tel: 216-382-2110; Fax: 216-382-3555.
E-mail: rhs@stratos.net
Sisters of Notre Dame. Sr. Maureen Burke, S.N.D., Prin. Sisters 12; Lay Teachers 24; Students 260.

St. Augustine Academy, 14808 Lake Ave., 44107. Tel: 216-221-4227. Sr. Patricia Lenard, C.S.F.N., Dir. Sisters of the Holy Family of Nazareth 4; Lay Teachers 25; Girls 311.

St. Edward High School. (Boys). 13500 Detroit Ave., Lakewood, 44107. Tel: 216-221-3776; Fax: 216-221-4609. Bro. James Spooner, C.S.C., Pres. Brothers 6; Lay Teachers 53; Students 888.

St. Ignatius High School, 1911 W. 30th St., 44113. Tel: 216-651-0222; Fax: 216-651-6313. Revs. Robert J. Welsh, S.J., Pres.; Bernard J. Streicher, S.J., Rector; Richard F. Clark, Prin.; Revs. Stephen J. Agostino, S.J.; Thomas J. Bain, S.J.; Henry F. Birkenhauer, S.J.; James Farrell, S.J.; John H. Kleinhenz, S.J.; James V. Lewis, S.J.; Lawrence M. Ober, S.J.; Glenn F. Williams, S.J.; Carl Bonk, S.J.; Dennis Dillon, S.J.; Michael Vincent, S.J. Priests 9; Lay Teachers 92; Students 1,357.

St. Joseph Academy, 3430 Rocky River Dr., 44111. Tel: 216-251-6788; Fax: 216-251-5809. Jacqualine Kasprowski, Prin. Sisters 14; Lay Teachers 49; Students 578.

Trinity High School, 12425 Granger, 44125. Tel: 216-581-1644.
E-mail: tmaher@ths.org
Web site: www.ths.org
Sisters of St. Joseph of the Third Order of St. Francis. Sr. Shawn Lee, S.S.J.-T.O.S.F., Pres.; Patrick J. Riley, D.Min., Vice Pres.; Thomas M. Maher, Ph.D., Prin.; Mr. Daniel J. Thomeier, Business Mgr.; Mr. Joseph A. Waler, M.A., M.Ed., Assoc. Prin. Sisters of St. Joseph 6; Lay Teachers 44; Students 675.

AKRON. *Archbishop Hoban High School.* (Coed), 400 Elbon Ave., 44306. Tel: 330-773-6658; Fax: 330-773-9100. Brothers of Holy Cross. Bro. Kenneth Haders, C.S.C., Pres.; Mrs. Mary Anne Beiting, Prin. Brothers 5; Lay Teachers 43; Students 674.

Our Lady of the Elms High School, 1375 W. Exchange St., 44313. Tel: 216-867-0880; Fax: 216-864-6488. Sisters of St. Dominic. Mrs. Connie Hardy, Prin. Sisters 3; Lay Teachers 31; Girls 336.

St. Vincent-St. Mary High School, 15 North Maple St., 44303. Tel: 330-253-9113; Fax: 330-996-0020. Margaret T. Lynch, Prin. Lay Teachers 36; Students 517.

CHARDON. *Notre Dame-Cathedral Latin School*, 13000 Auburn Rd., 44024. Tel: 440-286-6226; 888-214-8108 (toll free); Fax: 440-286-7199. Sisters of Notre Dame. Sr. Judith Lynne Mucheck, S.N.D., Prin. Sisters 8; Lay Teachers 51; Students 810.

CUYAHOGA FALLS. *Walsh Jesuit High School*, 4550 Wyoga Lake Rd., 44224. Tel: 216-929-4205; 800-686-4694 (Cleveland). Revs. Donald J. Petkash, S.J., Pres.; Emmett P. Holmes, S.J., Religious Supr.; Richard M. Rosenfelder, S.J.; Patrick F. Peppard, S.J.; Frederick J. Benda, S.J., Retreat Dir. Loyola of the Lakes Retreat House; James J. King, S.J.; Daniel D. Dunnigan, S.J.; Priests 7; Lay Teachers 60; Students 840.

GATES MILLS. *Gilmour Academy.* (Grades PreK-12). Private. 34001 Cedar Rd., 44040. Tel: 440-473-8000; Fax: 216-473-8010. Day and Resident College Preparatory School. Congregation of Holy Cross. Mr. Murlan J. Murphy, Jr., Chm., Board of Trustees; Bro. Robert Lavelle, C.S.C., Headmaster; Dr. Elizabeth Fesler, Ph.D., Dir. of Upper School; Ms. Monica Veto, Dir. of Lower School; Rev. John Blazek, C.S.C., Campus Minister. Priests 1; Brothers 8; Students 630; Residents 38; Lay Teachers 63.

[F] ELEMENTARY SCHOOLS

CLEVELAND. *Incarnate Word Academy*, 6618 Pearl Rd., 44130. Tel: 216-842-6818; Fax: 216-888-1377. Sr. Eileen Fitzgerald, S.I.W., Prin.; Rev. Msgr. Joseph T. Moriarty, Chap. Sisters 8; Lay Teachers 21; Students 621.

AKRON. *Our Lady of Elms Elementary School*, 1290 W. Market St., 44313. Tel: 330-864-7210. Dr. Hans Pesch, Prin. Sisters 3; Lay Teachers 19; Students 191.

CHARDON. *Notre Dame Elementary School*, 13000 Auburn Rd., 44024. Sr. Margaret Hartman, S.N.D., Prin. Sisters of Notre Dame 11; Lay Teachers 18; Students 443.

Notre Dame Montessori School, 13000 Auburn Rd., 44024. Tel: 216-286-7101, Ext. 592. Sr. Carol Urmetz, S.N.D., Prin. Sisters of Notre Dame 1; Lay Teachers 1; Students 48.

HUDSON. *Seton Catholic School of Hudson*, 6923 Stow Rd., 44236. Tel: 330-342-4200; Fax: 330-342-4276. Sr. Marie Damicone, Prin.; Rosemary Guerriero, Treas.

[G] ELEMENTARY SCHOOLS, PAROCHIAL AND DIOCESAN

CLEVELAND. *Archbishop James P. Lyke Elementary School.* St. Henry, St. Timothy and St. Catherine Schools consolidated to form Archbishop James P. Lyke Elementary School. 18230 Harvard Ave., 44128. Sr. Brigetta Waldron, O.S.U., Co-Prin.; Mrs. Margarete Smith, Co-Prin. Lay Teachers 32; Students 711.

St. Catherine Campus. (Grades K-1), 3443 E. 93rd St., 44104. Tel: 216-341-7212. Mr. Nash Thompson, Prin. Students 198.

St. Henry Campus. (Grades 2-4), 18230 Harvard Ave., 44128. Tel: 216-991-9644. Sr. Mary Pat Hable, S.J.S.M., Prin. Students 246.

St. Timothy Campus. (Grades 5-8), 4351 E. 131st St., Garfield Heights, 44105. Tel: 216-581-3517. Mrs. Margarete W. Smith, Prin. Students 267.

Urban Community School, 2401 Washington Ave., 44113. Tel: 216-771-8014; Fax: 216-771-7888. Sr. Maureen Doyle, O.S.U., Dir. Ursuline Nuns 4; Lay Teachers 21; Students 400.

WICKLIFFE. *All Saints of St. John Vianney School.* (Grades PreK-8), 28702 Euclid Ave., 44092. Tel: 216-943-1395. Mrs. Rosemary Wilson, Prin. Sisters 1; Lay Teachers 17; Students 385.

[H] SPECIAL SCHOOLS AND CENTERS

For Exceptional Children

CLEVELAND. *Julie Billiart.* 4982 Clubside Rd., Lyndhurst, 44124-2596. Tel: 216-381-1191. Non-graded school for children having learning problems. Sr. Agnesmarie, S.N.D., Prin. Sisters of Notre Dame of Chardon 10; Lay Staff 9; Students 115.

OLA-St. Joseph Center, 2346 W. 14th St., 44113. Tel: 216-621-3451; Fax: 216-621-6104. Non-graded school for developmentally handicapped children, ages 6-16. Mrs. Pamela Delly, Prin. Lay Teachers 10; Students 80.

[I] PRESCHOOL AND DAY CARE CENTERS

CLEVELAND. *Head Start Catholic Center*, 1031 Superior Ave., 44114. Tel: 216-696-6525, Ext. 287. Lois Reed, Dir. Lay Teachers 38; Children 1,294.

Villa Montessori Center, 5620 Broadway Ave., 44127. Tel: 216-641-4770; Fax: 216-641-4771. Sr. Marie Veres, H.M., Dir./Prin.

AKRON. *Our Lady of Elms Pre-School*, 1295 W. Exchange St., 44313. Tel: 330-864-6817. Miss Suzanne M. Scarpitti, Dir. Lay Teachers 12; Students 95.

GARFIELD HEIGHTS. *Marymount Child Care Center*, 12215 Granger Rd., 44125. Tel: 216-581-3540; Fax: 216-581-4264. Sr. Felicia Mann, S.S.J.-T.O.S.F., Dir. Total Assisted 200; Total Staff 19.

TWINSBURG. *Preschool Activity and Learning Sessions, Inc.*, 9550 Ravenna Rd., 44087. Florence Bonacci, Dir. Children 75; Total Staff 6.

[J] GENERAL HOSPITALS

(For information on other Catholic related hospitals please contact the Chancery Office.)

CLEVELAND. *Marymount Hospital, Inc.*, 12300 McCracken Rd., 44125. Tel: 216-581-0500
For a complete listing, refer to the Hospitals section.

St. Alexis Hospital Medical Center, 5163 Broadway Ave., 44127
For a complete listing, refer to the Hospitals section.

St. John Hospital, 2351 E. 22nd St., 44115. Tel: 216-696-5560
For a complete listing, refer to the Hospitals section.

LORAIN. *Community Health Partners of Ohio*, 3700 Kolbe Rd., 44053-1161. Tel: 440-960-3000
For a complete listing, refer to the Hospitals section.

Lorain Community/St. Joseph Regional Health Center, 205 W. 20th St., 44052
For a complete listing, refer to the Hospitals section.

[K] TRAINING SCHOOLS FOR NURSES

CLEVELAND. *Marymount School of Practical Nursing.* 12300 McCracken Rd., Garfield Heights, 44125. Tel: 216-587-8160.
E-mail: sleonard@marymount.org
Suzan Leonard, R.N., B.S.N., M.Ed., Dir. Students 33.

[L] SPECIAL HOSPITALS

CLEVELAND. *Holy Family Home*, 6707 State Rd., 44134. Tel: 216-885-3100; Fax: 216-885-0644
For a complete listing, refer to the Special Care Facilities section.

Rose Mary, The Johanna Grasselli Rehabilitation and Education Center, 19350 Euclid Ave., 44117. Tel: 216-481-4823
For a complete listing, refer to the Special Care Facilities section.

[M] PROTECTIVE INSTITUTIONS

CLEVELAND. *Christ Child - DePaul Day Care Center*, 2320 E. 24th St., 44115. Tel: 216-687-0006; Fax: 216-687-0403
For a complete listing, refer to the Special Care Facilities section.

INDEPENDENCE. *Marycrest*, 7800 Brookside Rd., 44131. Tel: 216-524-5280; Fax: 216-524-2127
For a complete listing, refer to the Special Care Facilities section.

PARMA. *Parmadale*, 6753 State Rd., 44134. Tel: 216-845-7700; Fax: 216-845-5910
For a complete listing, refer to the Special Care Facilities section.

[N] HOMES FOR AGED

CLEVELAND. *Jennings Hall Inc.*, 10204 Granger Rd., 44125. Tel: 216-581-2900; Fax: 216-581-1517.
E-mail: jenningshal@aol.com
For a complete listing, refer to the Special Care Facilities section.

Mount Alverna Home, Inc. & Mount Alverna Home Annex, Inc. 6765 State Rd. Parma, 44134. Tel: 216-843-7800; Fax: 216-843-7107.
For a complete listing, refer to the Special Care Facilities section.

Mount St. Joseph, 21800 Chardon Rd., 44117. Tel: 216-531-7426; Fax: 216-531-4033
For a complete listing, refer to the Special Care Facilities section.

St. Augustine Manor, 7801 Detroit Ave., 44102. Tel: 216-634-7400; Fax: 216-634-7483.
E-mail: p.gareau@worldnet.att.net
For a complete listing, refer to the Special Care Facilities section.

Sts. Mary and Joseph Home for the Aged, 4291 Richmond Rd., 44122-6199. Tel: 216-464-1222
For a complete listing, refer to the Special Care Facilities section.

AKRON. *Francesca Residence*, 39 N. Portage Path, 44303. Tel: 330-867-6334
For a complete listing, refer to the Special Care Facilities section.

BEACHWOOD. *Villa Sancta Anna Home for the Aged, Inc.*, 25000 Chagrin Blvd., 44122-5665. Tel: 216-464-9250
For a complete listing, refer to the Special Care Facilities section.

BEDFORD. *Light of Hearts Villa, Inc.*, 283 Union St., 44146. Tel: 216-232-1991
For a complete listing, refer to the Special Care Facilities section.

FAIRLAWN. *St. Edward Home dba The Village at Saint Edward Nursing Care and Assisted Living*, 3131 Smith Rd., 44333. Tel: 330-666-1183
For a complete listing, refer to the Special Care Facilities section.

RICHFIELD. *Regina Health Center*, 5232 Broadview Rd., 44286-9608. Tel: 216-659-4161; Fax: 216-659-5113
For a complete listing, refer to the Special Care Facilities section.

[O] RESIDENCE FOR RETIRED PRIESTS

BROOKLYN. *Issenmann Place*, 4185 Brookway Ln., 44144. Tel: 216-661-1470. William Brady, Asst. Admin. Total in Residence 7; Total Staff 3.

[P] MONASTERIES AND RESIDENCES OF PRIESTS AND BROTHERS

CLEVELAND. *Benedictine Order of Cleveland*, St. Andrew Abbey, 10510 Buckeye Rd., 44104. Tel: 216-721-5300. Rt. Rev. Roger W. Gries, O.S.B.; Very Rev. Joachim Pastirik, O.S.B., Prior; Revs. Clement Zeleznik, O.S.B.; Timothy Buyansky, O.S.B.; Dominic Mondzelewski, O.S.B.; Placid Pientek, O.S.B.; Dismas Boeff, O.S.B., Chap., Southwest General Hospital, St. Peter, 6455 Engle Rd., 44142. Revs. Gerard Gonda, O.S.B.; Armand E. Gress, O.S.B.; Gary Hoover, O.S.B.; Kenneth J. Katricak, O.S.B., Chap., Villa Santa Anna, 25000 Chagrin Blvd., 44122. Revs. Albert Marflak, O.S.B., Vocation Dir. & Abbey Procurator; Gregory Oravec, O.S.B.; Andrew Pier, O.S.B.; Benedict Sellers, O.S.B.; Lawrence Sevcik, O.S.B.; Bernard Slimak, O.S.B.; Robert Wilkes, O.S.B.; Anselm Zupka, O.S.B. Priests 25; Brothers 14.
Other Assignments: Revs. Bede Kotlinski, O.S.B.; William T. Matyas, O.S.B., Incarnate Word, 6618 Pearl Rd., Parma Heights, 44130. Revs. Ronald Mahnke, O.S.B.; Anthony Ozimek, O.S.B., St. Vincent Hospital, Billings, MT, 59107-5200. Rev. Christopher Schwartz, O.S.B., Assumption Church, 9183 Broadview Rd., 44147. Rev. Raphael Zbin, O.S.B., St. Andrew, 5135 Superior Ave., 44103. Rev. Michael Brunovsky, Novice Master.

Blessed Sacrament Community, 5384 Wilson Mills Rd., 44143-3092. Tel: 440-442-3411.
Web site: blessedsacrament.com
Revs. Anthony L. Schueller, S.S.S., Prov. Supr.; Patrick J. Fenton, S.S.S., Supr.; Donald J. Jette, S.S.S.; John Thomas Lane, Vocation Dir.; Mario T. Marzocchi; Raymond J. Dubois, S.S.S.; Edward J. Stapleton, S.S.S., Prov. Treas.; William F. Fickel, S.S.S.; William T. Young, S.S.S.; Frederick Roberge, S.S.S.; Bros. Eugene Blee, S.S.S.; Edmund Hardy, S.S.S.; Thomas F. Flanagan, S.S.S.; Gary L. Laverdiere, S.S.S.; Michael J. O'Leary, S.S.S.; Anthony Ornelas, S.S.S.; Ignatius J. Montgomery, S.S.S. Priests 10; Brothers 7. Regina Health Center, 5232 Broadview Rd., Richfield, 44286-9608. Revs. George Evans, S.S.S.; John Gartner, S.S.S.; Thomas E. Waldie, S.S.S.; Bros. Fernand Duquette, S.S.S.; Mark Proulx, S.S.S. Priests 3; Brothers 2.

Congregation of the Blessed Sacrament Provincial House. 5384 Wilson Mills Rd., Highland Heights, 44143-3092. Tel: 440-442-6311; Fax: 440-449-3862.
E-mail: aschueller@aol.com
Web site: blessedsacrament.com
Province of St. Ann. Very Rev. Anthony L. Schueller, S.S.S., Prov. Supr.; Rev. Edward J. Stapleton, S.S.S., Prov. Treas.
Priests Serving Outside Country: Very Rev. Norman Pelletier, S.S.S., General Supr.; Revs. Thomas Wiese, S.S.S., General Sec.; G. B. de Rossi (Rome, Italy); Ralph Roberts, S.S.S., Blessed Sacrament, P.O. Box 1000, Masaka, Uganda.
Priests attached to Provincialate: Revs. Frederick J. Ablog, S.S.S., Sabbatical; Andrew Beaudoin, S.S.S., 11487 Kerridale Ave., Spring Hill, FL, 34608-3111. Rev. Rene A. Belanger, S.S.S., 58 Dudley St., New Bedford, MA, 02744-1503. Rev. Peter Cops, S.S.S., Retreat House, Rte. 1, Box 110, Waverly, NE, 68462-9646. Rev. Edward Roberts, S.S.S., 36 Monument Sq., Apt. 4, Charlestown, MA, 02129-3429. Rev. John Keenan, S.S.S., Hampton House, 5300 S. Shore Dr., Apt. 95, Chicago, IL, 60615-5708. Rev. Robert S. Pittman, S.S.S., P.O. Box 410, Waldorf, MD, 20604. Rev. Joachim Viet-Chau, S.S.S., Vietnamese Apostolate, P.O. Box 1429, Gretna, LA, 70054-1419. Revs. John Gartner, S.S.S.; George Evans, S.S.S.; Thomas Waldie, S.S.S.; Bros. Fernand Duquette, S.S.S.; Mark Proulx, S.S.S., Regina Health Center, 5232 Broadview Rd., Richfield, 44286-9608.

Marianist Community, 18340 Marcella Rd., 44119-2622. Tel: 216-481-1007. Priests 2; Brothers 5.

Maryknoll Fathers, 10309 Edgewater Dr., 44102. Tel: 216-651-2121.
E-mail: mklcleve@igc.org
Web site: http://www.maryknoll.org
Rev. Robert L. Depinet, M.M., Dir., P.O. Box 80938, Davao City, Philippines, 8000. Revs. George H. Ratermann, M.M.; James H. Huvane, M.M.; Richard S. Kardian, M.M. Total in Residence 3; Total Staff 2.

Mercedarians, 6928 Detroit Ave., 44102. Tel: 216-651-5043. Order of Our Lady of Mercy. Rev. Richard Rasch, O.de.M., Supr. In res. Revs. Vincent Caruso, O.de.M., (Retired); James Mayer, O.de.M.; Bro. Martin Jarocinski, O.de.M. Priests 3; Brothers 1.

Missionary Servants of the Most Holy Trinity. St. Agnes-Our Lady of Fatima, 6800 Lexington Ave., 44103. Tel: 216-391-1655. Revs. Michael Barth, S.T.; John Ford, S.T.

Padua Franciscan Friary. 7022 State Rd., Parma, 44134. Tel: 216-888-7742. Revs. Eugene Katoski, O.F.M.; Walter Dolan, O.F.M.; Daniel Senger, O.F.M.; Jose Antonio Posadas, O.F.M.; Bro. Thomas Carroll, O.F.M., Guardian. Priests 6; Brothers 1.

St. Jude Friary, 4760 Richmond Rd., 44128. Tel: 216-292-6602. Revs. Emmanuel Beunen, O.F.M.; Thomas Carolan, O.F.M., Supr.; Bro. Joseph Di Santo, O.F.M. Priests 2; Brothers 1; Total Assisted 60.

St. Paul Friary, 4120 Euclid Ave., 44103. Tel: 216-431-8854. Revs. Senan Glass, O.F.M.Cap.; Gary Stakem, O.F.M.Cap.; Andrew Hohman, O.F.M.Cap.; Eric Gauchat, O.F.M.Cap.; Bro. James Allman, O.F.M.Cap. Priests 4; Brothers 1.

St. Stanislaus Friary, 3649 E. 65th St., 44105-1293. Tel: 216-341-9091; Fax: 216-341-2688.
E-mail: ststan@en.com
Revs. Alcuin L. Mikulanis, O.F.M.; William E. Gulas, O.F.M.; George Jaskulski, O.F.M. (Pulaski, WI), Chap., Marymount Convent, Garfield Heights. Rev. Lazarus Macior, O.F.M. (Pulaski, WI), Prof., University of Akron, Akron. The Franciscan Friars, Province of the Assumption of the Blessed Virgin. Priests 4.

AVON. *Congregation of St. Joseph*, 4076 Case Rd., 44011. Tel: 440-934-6270.
E-mail: lato@aol.com
Revs. Lawrence Tosco, C.S.J.; Leo Dechant, C.S.J.; Libero Ballestrazzi, C.S.J.; Gaetano Menegatto, C.S.J.; Giampietro Gasparin, C.S.J.; Mark Withers, C.S.J. Priests 6.

[Q] CONVENTS AND RESIDENCES FOR SISTERS

CLEVELAND. *Carmel of the Holy Family*, 3176 Fairmount Blvd., 44118-4199. Tel: 216-321-6568. Discalced Carmelite Nuns. Sr. Mary Lavin, O.C.D., Prioress. Professed Nuns 16; Vowed Religious Transfer Sisters in Formation 1.

Marymount Congregational Home. 12215 Granger Rd., Garfield Heights, 44125. Tel: 216-581-3535. Residence of the Sisters of St. Joseph, Third Order of St. Francis. Contact Persons: Sr. Esther Romalke; Sr. Dominica Fick; Rev. George Jaskulski, O.F.M., Chap. Sisters 80.

Monastery of the Poor Clares, 3501 Rocky River Dr., 44111-2998. Tel: 216-941-2820. Poor Clare Nuns (Colettine).
Observing the Primitive Rule of St. Clare (strictly cloistered solemn vows). Perpetual exposition of the Blessed Sacrament. Rev. Eugene Katoski, O.F.M., Chap. Cloistered Nuns 24; Extern Sisters 3.

Motherhouse and Novitiate of the Sisters of the Holy Spirit, 10102 Granger Rd., 44125. Tel: 216-581-2941. Sr. Assumpta Zabas, C.S.Sp., Supr. Gen.; Rev. John J. Wright, Chap. Professed Sisters 8.

Motherhouse and Novitiate of the Ursuline Sisters, 2600 Lander Rd., 44124. Tel: 440-449-1200. Sr. Virginia DeVinne, O.S.U., Gen. Supr. Legal Title: *The Ursuline Academy of Cleveland*. Professed Nuns 280; Noviates 1.

Motherhouse of the Sisters of St. Joseph, 3430 Rocky River Dr., 44111. Tel: 216-252-0440; Fax: 216-941-3430.
E-mail: ssj3430@aol.com
Exec. Team: Sr. Barbara Green; Sr. Donna Hawk; Sr. Marietta Starrie. Sisters 163.
St. Joseph Wellness Center. Total Staff 8.
Treasure Cove Resale Store. Total Staff 3.
Wellspring Bookstore. Total Staff 2.

Poor Clares of Perpetual Adoration, 4108 Euclid Ave., 44103. Tel: 216-361-0783. Mother Mary James, P.C.P.A., Supr. Cloistered Sisters 23; Novice 1. Monastery adjoins Conversion of St. Paul Church, where they maintain Perpetual Adoration.

Provincialhouse of Sisters of the Most Holy Trinity, 21281 Chardon Rd., 44117. Tel: 216-481-8232; Fax: 216-481-6577. Sr. M. Valentine, O.SS.T., Regl. Delegate.
Attended from Borromeo Seminary. Sisters 25; Total in Residence 15.

Sisters of St. Joseph of St. Mark. General Motherhouse and Novitiate of Sisters of St. Joseph of St. Mark-Generalate, Diocese of Cleveland. 21800 Chardon Rd., 44117. Tel: 216-531-7426; Fax: 216-531-4033. Mother M. Therese Trunk, Gen. Supr. Sisters 19.

Sisters of the Incarnate Word and Blessed Sacrament, 6618 Pearl Rd., 44130. Tel: 216-886-6440; Fax: 216-888-1377. Sr. Margaret Taylor, Congregational Leader. Legal Title: *Motherhouse and Novitiate of the Sisters of the Incarnate Word and and Blessed Sacrament*. Final Professed Sisters 41. In res. Rev. Msgr. Joseph T. Moriarty, 6620 Pearl Road, Parma Heights, 44130. Tel: 216-885-0320. Rev. William Matyas, O.S.B., 6634 Pearl Rd., Parma Heights, 44130. Tel: 216-886-6996.

AKRON. *Motherhouse of the Sisters of St. Dominic of the Immaculate Heart of Mary*, Our Lady of the Elms Convent, 1230 W. Market St., 44313-7185. Tel: 330-836-4908.
E-mail: srsstdomak@aol.com
Sisters 108.

Provincial Motherhouse and Novitiate of the Daughters of Divine Charity, 39 N. Portage Path, 44303-1183. Tel: 330-867-4960. Sr. Maria Bakich, F.D.C., Prov. Supr.; Rev. Thomas F. Sullivan, Chap. Tel: 330-864-6700. Sisters 22.

BEDFORD. *Motherhouse and Novitiate of the Vincentian Sisters of Charity*, Villa San Bernardo, 1160 Broadway, 44146-4523. Tel: 216-232-4755. Sr. Margaret Mach, Gen. Supr.; Sr. Dorothy Ann Blatnica, Formation Dir.; Sr. Ruthann Rody, Vocation-Contact Person. Sisters 75.

CHARDON. *Provincial House of the Sisters of Notre Dame, Juniorate, Novitiate*, Notre Dame Educational Center, 13000 Auburn Rd., 44024. Tel: 440-286-7101.
E-mail: fmurray@stratos.net
Web site: http://www.snd1.org
Rev. Paul J. Sciarrotta, Chap. Sisters 461.

INDEPENDENCE. *Contemplative Sisters of the Good Shepherd*. (Infirmary), 7800 Brookside Rd., 44131. Tel: 216-524-8692. Sr. Mary Josephine Fritz, C.G.S., Supr. Sisters 25.

Sisters of the Good Shepherd, Marycrest, 7800 Brookside Rd., 44131. Tel: 216-524-4578; Fax: 216-524-6669. Sr. Rose Catherine Wuensch, R.G.S., Supr., Marycrest Community Services, 1862 Noble Rd., East Cleveland, 44112. Tel: 216-687-0313. Sisters 4; Total in Residence 60; Total Staff 107.

RICHFIELD. *Mount Augustine, Motherhouse of the Sisters of Charity of St. Augustine*, 5232 Broadview Rd., 44286-9608. Tel: 216-659-5100; Fax: 216-659-3899.
E-mail: snh@srsofcharity.org
Sr. Nancy Hendershot, C.S.A., Major Supr.
Regina Health Center. Religious Congregations 22; Total Assisted Care 74; Skilled Nursing Beds 81.
Sisters of Charity of St. Augustine Health System.
Sisters of Charity of St. Augustine Foundation of Cleveland.
Saint Ann Foundation. Finally Professed Sisters 101.

[R] SECULAR INSTITUTES

CLEVELAND HEIGHTS. *Society of Our Lady of the Way*, c/o Mary Ann Tady, 1064 Oxford Rd., 44121. Tel: 216-381-5502.
E-mail: bryan@coffey.com
Web site: http://www.coffey.com/~bryan/main.html
Secular Institute for Single Women.

[S] HOMES FOR WOMEN

AKRON. *Leonora Hall*, 39 N. Portage Path, 44303. Tel: 330-867-1752
For a complete listing, refer to the Special Care Facilities section.

[T] LAY ASSOCIATIONS

CLEVELAND. *Community of Little Brothers and Sisters of the Eucharist, Inc.*, 2186 East 35th St., 44115-3039. Tel: 216-566-0531; Fax: 216-566-9370. Sr. Maggie Conrad, Dir.

[U] RETREAT HOUSES

CLEVELAND. *Jesuit Retreat House*, 5629 State Rd., 44134. Tel: 440-884-9300; Fax: 440-885-1055. Rev. James Riley, S.J., Dir. Spirituality Team: Revs. James Farrell, S.J.; Joseph Scharf, S.J.; Dennis Dillon, S.J.; Carl Bonk, S.J.; Henry F. Birkenhauer, S.J.
St. Joseph Christian Life Center, 18485 Lake Shore Blvd., 44119-1299. Tel: 216-531-7370; Fax: 216-531-0629. Rev. Walter J. Hyclak, Exec. Dir.; Jackie Cherep, Oper. Mgr. & Finance Coord.; Pat Kassay, Program Dir.; Andrea McGovern, Mktg. Dir.; Deacon Leo McNulty. Total Staff 34.

AKRON. *Loyola of the Lakes Jesuit Retreat House, Inc.* 700 Killinger Rd., Clinton, 44216-9628. Tel: 330-896-2315; 800-827-1416; Fax: 330-896-0858. Mrs. Elizabeth R. Flynt, Exec. Dir. In res. Rev. Vincent A. Hagarman, S.J.

BEDFORD. *Poustinia*, 1160 Broadway, 44146. Tel: 216-232-4755. Vincentian Sisters of Charity.
Tabor Center, 1160 Broadway, 44146. Tel: 216-232-4755. Vincentian Sisters of Charity. Sr. Irene Mraz, V.S.C., Contact Person. Maximum Capacity 5.

[V] SOCIAL SERVICE AGENCIES AND INSTITUTIONS

For information call Catholic Information and Referral Services (CIRS) Tel: 216-696-HELP (4357).

CLEVELAND. *Bishop William M. Cosgrove Center*, 1736 Superior Ave., 44114. Tel: 216-781-8262. Total Assisted 20,000; Total Staff 8.
Catholic Charities Corporation, 1111 Superior Ave., 44114. Tel: 216-696-6525. August Napoli, Jr., Pres.
Catholic Charities Facilities Corporation, 1111 Superior Ave., #420, 44114. Tel: 216-696-6525, Ext. 554. Lawrence E. Murtaugh, Pres.
The Catholic Charities Foundation, 1111 Superior Ave., 44114. Tel: 216-696-6525. August Napoli, Jr., Pres.
Catholic Charities Services Corporation, Eaton Center, 1111 Superior Ave., 44114. Tel: 216-696-6525; Fax: 216-344-9962. Provides management services and direction to Catholic Charities agencies and institutions to enhance the effectiveness and efficiency of human services within the Diocese. J. Thomas Mullen, M.S.W., Pres. & CEO; John Klee, Exec. Vice Pres. & COO; Patrick Ertle, Gen. Counsel; Jean Hutzler, M.S.W., Exec. Asst. to Pres.; Wayne Peel, CFO; Claire Gavin, Vice Pres. Human Resources; Paul Melian, Dir., MIS; Thomas Woll, Senior Dir., Children & Family Services; Jean Therrien, Senior Dir., Older Adult Services; Dennis McNulty, Senior Dir., Disability Services; Charles Joseph, III, Senior Dir., Emergency & Transitional Services; Patsy Holian, Vice Pres. System Devel.
Catholic Charities Services Corporation.
Bishop William M. Cosgrove Center, 1736 Superior Ave., 44114. Tel: 216-781-8262. Pat Wehner, Exec. Dir.
Catholic Social Services of Ashland, Medina, and Wayne Counties, 246 Northland Dr., Medina, 44256. Tel: 330-723-9615 (Medina); 419-289-1903 (Ashland); 330-262-7386 (Wooster). Timothy Putka, Dir.
Catholic Social Services of Cuyahoga County, 7800 Detroit Ave., 44102. Tel: 216-631-3499. Service Directors: Maureen Dee, Dir. Behavioral Health Services; David Mordarski, Dir. Community Services.
Catholic Services of Geauga County, 1077 Mayfield Rd., 44024. Tel: 800-242-9755. Anthony J. Marjenin, Dir.
Catholic Social Services of Lake County, 8 N. State St., Suite 455, Painesville, 44077. Tel: 216-946-7264; 352-6191. James R. Clements, Dir.
Catholic Social Services of Lorain County, 2136 N. Ridge Rd., Elyria, 44035. Tel: 216-324-2614; 277-7228. Bernadette Washington, Dir.
Fatima Community Center, 6707 Quimby Ave., 44103. Tel: 216-391-0505. LaJean Ray, Dir.
Hispanic Senior Center, 7800 Detroit Ave., 44102. Tel: 216-631-3599. Virginia Gomez, Acting Dir.
Matt Talbot Inn, 2270 Professor Ave., 44113. Tel: 216-781-0288. Ruby Black, Dir.
OLA/St. Joseph Center, 2346 W. 14th St., 44113-3697. Tel: 216-621-3451. Pamela Delly, Prin.
St. Martin de Porres Center, 1264 E. 123rd St., 44108. Tel: 216-268-3909. Marsha Banks, Dir.
Special Ministry to the Aged, 6804 Lansing Ave., 44105. Tel: 216-441-5402. Sr. Anna Kaszuba, Dir.
CATHOLIC CHARITIES PARISH SERVICES: Camps:
Camp Corde, 2901 Ridgewood Ave., Parma, 44134. Tel: 216-884-3950.
Camp Christopher, Ira & Hametown Rd., Bath, 44210. Tel: 800-CYO-CAMP.
AFFILIATED CORPORATIONS WITHIN THE SECRETARY FOR SOCIAL CONCERNS (Under membership structure of Bishop, Secretary for Social Concerns & Chairperson of Board of Trustees):
Catholic Social Services of Summit County.
CYO & Community Services of Summit County.
Jennings Hall, Inc.
The LeBlond Housing Corporation.
Parmadale.
Rose-Mary, The Johanna Grasselli Rehabilitation and Education Center.
St. Augustine Corporation.
The Village at St. Edward.
The Society of St. Vincent de Paul (not under membership structure). Total Staff 8; Total Assisted 20,000.
Catholic Social Services of Ashland, Medina, and Wayne Counties. 246 Northland Dr., Medina, 44256-1598. Medina. Tel: 330-723-9615. Ashland. Tel: 419-289-1903. Brunswick-Cleveland. Tel: 330-225-7100. Wadsworth-Akron. Tel: 330-336-6657. Wooster. Tel: 330-262-7836. Timothy J. Putka, M.S., Exec. Dir. Provides counseling, casework, and family life education in Ashland, Wayne, and Medina Counties.
Catholic Social Services of Cuyahoga County, St. Augustine Towers, 7800 Detroit Ave., 44102-2895. Tel: 216-631-3499. Maureen Dee, L.I.S.W., C.C.D.C. III, Dir. Behavioral Health Services; David J. Mordarski, A.C.S.W., L.I.S.W., Dir. Community Services; Sanford Waldman, M.D., Medical Dir. A multi-function social service agency which offers social service programs. Individual, family, and group counseling; marital counseling, psychiatric consultations; and outpatient psychiatric services for children, youth, and adults. Chemical dependency assessments and outpatient counseling for youth and families having alcohol and other drug-related problems. Bilingual services for Hispanic youth and families. Child day care; school for pregnant teens; pregnancy counseling and planning; adoption; big brothers/sisters; older adult programs, senior citizens counseling and respite care; employment services.
Satellite Offices: Midtown Center, 3135 Euclid Ave., Ste. 202, 44115-2507. 1414 S. Green Rd., Rm. 310, South Euclid, 44121. Parmadale, 6753 State Rd., Parma, 44134. Hispanic Services, 2012 W. 25th St., Rm. 517, 44113. St. Vincent School, 2320 E. 24th St., 44115. Total Assisted 3,500; Total Staff 94.
Catholic Social Services of Geauga County. 10771 Mayfield Rd., Chardon, 44024-9323. Tel: TDD: 440-285-3537; 800-242-9755 (Ohio); Fax: 440-285-4909. Anthony J. Marjenin, M.S.S.A., L.I.S.W., Exec. Dir. Outpatient counseling for families and individuals. Substance abuse counseling. Parenting programs. Services for the elderly. Services to strengthen and enrich the valued relationships of families and individuals for effective and healthy living.
Catholic Social Services of Lake County. 8 N. State St., No. 455, Painesville, 44077-3954. Tel: 440-352-6191; 946-7264. Anthony J. Marjenin, M.S.S.A., L.I.S.W., Exec. Dir.
Satellite Offices: 28706 Euclid Ave., Wickliffe, 44092. Tel: 440-943-5552; 800-394-4598.
Malachi House, Inc., 2810 Clinton Ave., 44113. Tel: 216-621-8831. Home for the Terminally Ill. Total assisted annually 60; Total Staff 15.
St. Malachi Center, Inc., 2459 Washington Ave., 44113. Tel: 216-771-3036. Total Assisted 65 per day (Neighborhood Center); 30 per Monday (Health Services); Total Staff 4.
Society of St. Vincent de Paul, Diocesan Central Council, Chancery Bldg., 1027 Superior Ave., 44114. Tel: 216-696-6525, Ext. 358. Rev. Msgr. Casimir S. Ciolek, A.C.S.W., Spiritual Dir.; Frank J. Fearon, Diocesan Pres.; Lawrence Lauter, A.C.S.W., L.I.S.W., M.Div, Exec. Dir.; Rev. James R. Schleicher, Spiritual Dir.; Frank Fearon, Pres.
Akron District Council, 200 Granger Rd., #6, Medina, 44256. Tel: 330-666-8039.
Cleveland District Council, Chancery Building, 1027 Superior Ave., 44114. Chancery Building, 1027 Superior Ave., 44114. Lawrence Lauter, Exec. Dir.
Lorain District Council, 221 Columbia, Elyria, 44035. Tel: 216-322-6250. Donald Smith, Pres.
St. Vincent de Paul Thrift Stores, 875 E. 70th, 44103. Tel: 216-391-9655. 16730 Lorain Ave., 44111. Tel: 216-252-8764. 5462 Broadway Ave., 44127. Tel: 216-341-3445. 4125 Lee Rd., 44128. Tel: 216-921-5550. 700 E. 185th St., 44119. Tel: 216-486-9122.

AKRON. *Catholic Social Services of Summit County, Inc.*, 640 N. Main St., 44310-3098. Tel: 216-762-7481. Susan E. Milne, M.S.W., Exec. Dir. Service sites throughout Summit County. Total Assisted 17,000; Total Staff 30.
CYO & Community Services, 812 Biruta St., 44307. Tel: 216-762-2961.
CYO Adult Day Care Services, 812 Biruta St., 44307. Tel: 216-762-2000. Donald P. Finn, Exec. Dir. Total Assisted 186; Total Staff 14.
Recreation (camping and athletics): Total Assisted 15,860; Total Staff 57.
Interval Brotherhood Home Alcohol-Drug Rehabilitation Center, 3445 S. Main St., 44319. Tel: 330-644-4095. Rev. Samuel R. Ciccolini, Dir. Total Assisted 385; Total Staff 72.
Leonora Hall. (Refer to Homes for Women).

ELYRIA. *Catholic Social Services of Lorain County*, 2136 N. Ridge Rd., 44035-1241. Tel: 216-324-2614; 277-7228 (Lorain); Fax: 216-324-2985. Barbara Alflen, Svc. Dir.
Senior Achievement Center, 3114 Pearl Ave., Lorain, 44055. Tel: 216-277-4860. Nancy Carrell, Prog. Dir.
Catholic Community Services, 203 Eighth St., Lorain, 44052. Tel: 216-244-9915. Peter Coffaro, Prog. Coord. Total Staff 8; Total Assisted 21,723.

GARFIELD HEIGHTS. *Brendan Manor, Inc.*, 13401 Cranwood Dr., 44105. Tel: 216-475-5230. Diane Kalchert, Admin. Licensed nonprofit, nondenominational shared living home for low to moderate income older adults. Total in Residence 16; Total Staff 7.

NORTHFIELD. *St. Barnabas Villa, Inc.*, 9234 Olde Eight Rd., 44067. Tel: 216-467-3758; 467-4044. A shared living facility for nine people over 60 years of age. Sr. M. Germaine Maximovich, V.S.C., Mgr.; Mrs. Jo Ann Smith, Asst. Mgr. Total in Residence 9; Total Staff 6.

[W] SHRINES

CLEVELAND. *Our Lady of Lourdes.* Euclid, (U.S. Rtes. 20 & 6). Administered by the Sisters of the Most Holy Trinity. 21281 Chardon Rd., 44117. Tel: 216-481-8232; Fax: 216-481-6577. Sr. M. Valentine, O.SS.T., Contact Person. Total in Residence 15.

BEDFORD. *Our Lady of Levocha.* (Ohio Rte. 14). Administered by the Vincentian Sisters of Charity (V.S.C.). 1160 Broadway, 44146. Tel: 216-232-4755. Sr. M. Gertrude, V.S.C., Contact Person.

GARFIELD HEIGHTS. *Our Lady of Czestochowa Shrine.* (Ohio Rte. 17). Administered by the Sisters of St. Joseph Third Order of St. Francis (S.S.J.), 12215 Granger Rd., 44125. Tel: 216-581-3535. Sr. Dominica, Shrine Contact.

PARMA. *Our Lady, Queen of the Holy Rosary.* (U.S. Rte. 42). Administered by the Sisters of the Incarnate Word and Blessed Sacrament (S.I.W.). 6618 Pearl Rd., 44130. Tel: 216-886-6440; Fax: 216-888-1377.

[X] MINISTRY TO THE SPANISH SPEAKING

CLEVELAND. *Diocesan Hispanic Office*, 1031 Superior Ave., 44114-2519. Tel: 216-696-6525, Ext. 253. Sr. Joaquina Carrion, M.S.B.T., Dir.
Hispanic Parishes: San Juan Bautista Parish, 1946 W. 32nd St., 44113. Tel: 216-631-2888. Rev. David F. Fallon.
Sacred Heart Chapel, 4301 Pear Ave., Lorain, 44055. Tel: 216-277-7231; 277-7379. Rev. Robert J. Reidy.
Parishes with Ministry to Spanish Speaking: St. Bernard, 47 University Ave., Akron, 44308. Tel: 216-253-5161. Rev. Paul E. Schindler.
St. Francis, 7119 Superior Ave., 44103. Tel: 216-361-4133. Rev. Thomas F. Martin; Deacon Frank Lozada.

St. Michael, 3114 Scranton Rd., 44109. Tel: 216-861-6297. Rev. Dennis R. O'Grady.
St. Mary's - Painesville, 242 N. State St., Painesville, 44077. Tel: 216-354-4381. Rev. Richard C. Antall.

[Y] NEWMAN CENTERS

BEREA. *Office of Newman Campus Ministry*, 170 E. Center St., 44017. Mr. William A. Fichter, Diocesan Dir.
Hallinan Center, 11303 Euclid Ave., Cleveland, 44106. Tel: 216-421-1522; Fax: 216-421-2925. Ms. Marie deLaBruere, Campus Min.
Case-Western Reserve Hallinan Chair of Catholic Studies, 2501 Kemper, Shaker Heights, 44106. Tel: 216-368-2210. Rev. James W. Flanagan (DUB).
Cleveland State University Newman Ministry, Hallinan Center, 11303 Euclid Ave., Cleveland, 44106. Tel: 216-421-1522; Fax: 216-696-2925. Mr. Matthew Maruggi, Campus Min.
Cuyahoga Community College, Metro Campus, 2900 Community College Dr., Cleveland, 44115. Tel: 440-243-4955. Mr. William A. Fichter, Assoc. Diocesan Dir.
Western Campus, 11000 Pleasant Valley, Parma, 44130. Tel: 216-886-1327. Maureen Masterson, Campus Min.
Lakeland Community College, Mentor, 44060. Tel: 216-953-4803. Mr. Matthew Maruggi, Campus Min.
University of Akron. (Akron), Newman Center, 44 University Ave., Akron, 44308. Tel: 330-376-3585. Ms. Emily Holtel, Campus Min.
Ashland College. (Ashland), c/o St. Peter Church, 132 N. Wood St., Loudonville, 44842. Rev. Edwin A. Dowling, Campus Min.
Baldwin-Wallace College Newman Center. (Berea), 170 E. Center St., 44017. Tel: 216-243-4955; Fax: 216-243-0354. Mr. William A. Fichter, Assoc. Diocesan Dir.
Oberlin College. (Oberlin), Office of Chaplains, 217 Wilder Hall, Oberlin, 44074. Tel: 440-775-8103. Rev. Edward J. Kordas, D.Min.
The College of Wooster. (Wooster), Box C-3135, Wooster, 44691. Tel: 330-263-2096. Ms. Maureen Masterson, Campus Min.
Lorain County Community College, 1005 N. Abbey Rd., Elyria, 44035. Tel: 440-365-5222, Ext. 7661; 800-995-5222. Emily Holtel, Campus Min. Total Staff for 12 Newman Centers 8.

[Z] ENDOWMENT TRUSTS

CLEVELAND. *Good Shepherd-Marycrest Endowment Fund*. 8010 Brookside Dr., Independence, 44131. Tel: 216-524-5280; Fax: 216-524-2127.
St. John Cathedral Endowment Trust, 1007 Superior Ave., 44114. Rev. David C. Weber.
Sisters of St. Joseph Community Support Charitable Trust, 3430 Rocky River Dr., 44111. Tel: 216-252-0440; Fax: 216-941-3430.
E-mail: ssj3430@aol.com
Sr. Marrieta Starrie, C.S.J., Contact Person.
St. Joseph Wellness Center. Total Staff 8.
Treasure Cove Resale Store. Total Staff 3.
Wellspring Bookstore. Total Staff 2.
Villa Angela - St. Joseph High School Education Endowment Foundation, 18491 Lake Shore Blvd., 44119.
E-mail: vastjoe@connectinc.com
AKRON. *The Daughters of Divine Charity, St. Mary Province, Charitable Trust*, 39 N. Portage Path, 44303-1183. Tel: 330-867-4960.
Our Lady of the Elms-Sisters of St. Dominic Foundation, 1230 W. Market St., 44313; Fax: 330-836-5913.
E-mail: srsstdomak@aol.com
St. Vincent-St. Mary High School Endowment Fund, 15 N. Maple St., 44303. Tel: 330-253-9113; Fax: 330-996-0020. Ann Garbor, Dir. Devel.
**St. Hilary Parish Foundation*, 657 Moorfield Rd., 44313. Tel: 330-666-2403. Mr. Edward F. Carter, Pres.
CHARDON. *The Sisters of Notre Dame Charitable Trust*, 13000 Auburn Rd., 44024. Tel: 440-942-6716.
E-mail: fmurray@stratos.net
Web site: http://www.snd1.org
Sr. Mary Frances Murray, S.N.D., Chm.
MENTOR. *St. Mary of the Assumption Parish Endowment Trust*, 8560 Mentor Ave., 44060-5853.
PARMA HEIGHTS. *Incarnate Word Endowment Trust*, 6618 Pearl Rd., 44130. Tel: 216-886-6440; Fax: 216-888-1377. Sr. Margaret Taylor, Chm. Total Staff 9; Total in Residence 28.
WELLINGTON. *St. Patrick Church Endowment Trust*, 512 N. Main St., 44090.
WOOSTER. *St. Mary of the Immaculate Conception Elementary Day School Endowment Trust*, 527 Beall Ave., P.O. Box 109, 44691.

[AA] MISCELLANEOUS

CLEVELAND. *Catholic Tours of Ohio, Inc.*, 17825 Libby Rd., 44137. Tel: 330-475-2478. Rev. Msgr. Joseph C. Heruday, Pres. & Sec.; Stanley Streiner, Treas. Nonprofit organization.
Christa Center, 18515 Underwood Ave., 44119. Tel: 216-481-1015.
E-mail: ik068@cleveland.freenet.edu
Sr. Elaine Wellinger, H.M., Dir.
Holistic Spirituality and Wellness Center. Total Assisted 1,220; Total Staff 2.
COAR Peace Mission, Inc., 4395 Rocky River Dr., 44135-2569. Tel: 216-252-5572. Sr. Ann Mary Brangan, C.C.V.I., Exec. Dir.; Margaret M. McBride, Office Mgr.; Mary Conroy, Sponsorship Coord.
COAR Children's Village. (Zaragoza, El Salvador, C.A.). Sr. Rose Ayala, C.C.V.I., Dir.; Rev. Kenneth C. Myers, Founder. COAR Children's Village is an orphanage in Zaragoza, El Salvador, serving 120 children whose parents have died in the violence or have been abandoned in refugee centers. 900 children attend the COAR school. This includes children from the surrounding area. The COAR Clinic serves the medical and dental needs of the resident orphaned children and assists 80 people on a weekly basis. COAR was begun in August 1980 by Rev. Kenneth C. Myers.
CSA St. John Ministries fka St. John West Shore Hospital, 2351 E. 22nd St., 44115. Tel: 888-223-1816; Fax: 216-696-2204. Sr. Mary Ann Andrews, CSA Pres. & CEO.
CSA St. Vincent Charity Ministries fka St. Vincent Charity Hospital, 2351 E. 22nd St., 44115. Tel: 888-223-1816; Fax: 216-696-2204. Sr. Mary Ann Andrews, CSA Pres. & CEO.
The Greater Cleveland/Akron Corporation United for Education, 1404 E. Ninth St., 8th Fl., 44114-1722. Tel: 216-696-6525, Ext. 436; Fax: 216-696-8084. Rev. John J. Wright, Exec. Dir.; Andrej N. Lah, Attorney; Joseph Smith, Treas.
H.M. Center for Women and Children, 2100 Broadway Ave., 44052. Tel: 216-356-5707. Sr. Cathleen Walsh, H.M., Chm., Board of Trustees; Kathryn Csank, Dir.
Heartbeats, 2259 Columbus Rd., 44113. Tel: 216-241-1504.
E-mail: heartbt@en.com
Web site: www.en.com/users/heartbt
Sr. Margaret Cessna, H.M., Dir.
L'Arche, Cleveland, 2634 E. 127 St., P.O. Box 20540, 44120. Tel: 216-721-2614. An ecumenical community providing homes for adults with mental retardation and developmental disabilities. Residents 9.
National Catholic Ministry to the Bereaved, Inc., 9412 Heath Ave., 44104. Tel: 216-441-2125. Total Staff 3; Total Assisted 1,200.
Ninth Street CDC, 1404 E. Ninth St., 8th Fl., 44114-1722. Tel: 216-696-6525. Rev. John J. Wright, Pres.
Sisters of Charity of St. Augustine Health Network, 2351 East 22nd St., 44115. Tel: 216-659-5560; Fax: 216-696-2204. Sr. Mary Ann Andrews, C.S.A., Pres. & CEO. Serves as the general partner to the joint venture ownership of Catholic healthcare providers.
Sisters of Charity of St. Augustine Health System, 2351 E. 22nd St., 44115. Tel: 216-696-5560; Fax: 216-696-2204. Sr. Mary Ann Andrews, C.S.A., Pres. & CEO.
Serves as the Member of foundations and human service corporations sponsored by the Sisters of Charity of St. Augustine, Richfield, OH.
**St. Augustine Development Corporation*, 7801 Detroit Ave., 44102-2895. Tel: 216-634-7400, Ext. 2345; Fax: 216-634-7483.
E-mail: p.gareau@worldnet.att.net
Mr. Patrick Gareau, CEO. Assisted Living Residents 99.
**St. Augustine Services Corporation*, 7801 Detroit Ave., 44102. Tel: 216-634-7400; Fax: 216-634-7483.
E-mail: p.gareau@worldnet.att.net
Provides administrative and support services to St. Augustine Manor and St. Augustine Development Corp. - both 509(a)(2) organizations. Mr. Patrick Gageau, Pres. Total Staff 55.
AKRON. *H.M. Housing Development Corporation*, 73 W. Market St., Ste. 106, 44303. Tel: 330-384-1555; Fax: 330-384-2144. Sr. Denise Maher, H.M., Pres. & CEO.
H.M. Life Opportunity Services, Box 8174, 44320. Central Office, 733 W. Market St., 44313. Tel: 330-376-5600; Fax: 330-869-8168. Sr. Loretta Rafter, H.M., Pres. & CEO.
Humility of Mary Housing, Inc., P.O. Box 22250, 44302-0250. Tel: 330-384-1555.
E-mail: dmhmhi@juno.com
Sr. Denise Maher, H.M., Pres. & CEO. Affordable housing and housing related services for low and moderate income individuals. Total Assisted 1,650; Total Staff 3.
BEDFORD. *Emmaus Conference Center*, Vincentian Sisters of Broadway, 1160 Broadway, 44146. Tel: 216-232-4755.
BROADVIEW HEIGHTS. *Alliance for Access dba Marymount South*, 2001 E. Royalton Rd., 44147. Tel: 440-526-3333; Fax: 440-526-1369. A corporation operating an urgent and ambulatory acute care facility sponsored by Marymount Hospital. Cynthia Boyton, Facility Dir.
CHARDON. *Christ Child Society-Geauga Chapter*, 12010 Burlington Glen, 44024. Linda L. Toth, Pres.
EUCLID. *Faith and Light U.S.A., Inc.*, 26351 Drakefield Ave., 44132. Pearl Cahoon; Posie O'Connor.
St. Robert's Holy Name Society Boosters, 23802 Lakeshore Blvd., 44123. Tel: 216-731-2606. Rev. John T. Burkley, Pastor. Total Staff 5; Total in Residence 100.
GARFIELD HEIGHTS. *Jennings Manor Housing Corporation*, 10204 Granger Rd., 44125. Tel: 216-581-2900; Fax: 216-581-1517. Marthe M. Kutik, Pres.
Marymount Health Care Systems. Provides comprehensive health and human services in response to the needs of the local community by owning, leasing, and operating health care facilities and services, including Marymount Place, a 104-unit Senior Living Community for the Well-elderly/Assisted Living, within the philosophy and objectives of the Sisters of St. Joseph of the Third Order of St. Francis and is the special Member of Marymount Hospital, Inc. 12200 McCracken Rd., 44125.
MHCS Real Estate Holding Company, 12300 McCracken Rd., 44125-2975. Tel: 216-587-8080; Fax: 216-587-8212. Mr. Thomas J. Trudell, Pres.
HUDSON.
**Laurel Lake Retirement Community, Inc.*, 200 Laurel Lake Dr., 44236. Tel: 330-656-3651. Paul Younger, Pres. & CEO. Independent Living Residents 363; Assisted Living Residents 18; Skilled Nursing Residents 75; Total Staff 270.
LORAIN. *Community Health Partners Foundation*, 3700 Kolbe Rd., 44053. Tel: 440-960-3980.
St. Joseph Health Care Foundation, Inc., 205 W. 20th St., 44052.
MIDDLEBURG HEIGHTS. *CHP - Humility of Mary Health Partners*, Plaza One South, 7251 Engle Rd., Ste. 410, 44130-3496. Tel: 800-884-9374; 440-234-0059. Sr. Frances Flanigan, H.M., Pres. & CEO.
St. Elizabeth Health Center, Youngstown. Medical Staff 547; Employees 2,700; Inpatient 20,298; Outpatient 260,908; Beds 550; Bassinets 60.
St. Joseph Health Center, Warren. Medical Staff 310; Employees 1,100; Inpatient 9,145; Outpatient 120,486; Bed Capacity 209; Bassinets 17.
Community Health Partners, Lorain. Medical Staff 295; Employers 2,201; Inpatient 13,745; Outpatient 183,030; Bed Capacity 303; Bassinets 23.
Laurel Lake Retirement Community, Hudson.
OBERLIN. *Common Ground Center for Community Renewal*, P.O. Box 613, 44074. Tel: 216-965-5551.
E-mail: rbator1625@aol.com
Sr. Rose Bator, H.M., Dir.
PARMA. *Society of St. Joseph the Worker*, 7033 State Rd., 44134-4952. Tel: 440-888-4872.
E-mail: bsjw@msn.com
Lawrence R. Verbiar, Dir.
PEPPER PIKE. *The O'Neill Brothers Foundation*, 3550 Lander Rd. #140, 44124. Tel: 216-464-2121; Fax: 216-464-1517. Mr. Robert K. Healey, Pres.
**Ursuline Sophia Center*, 2600 Lander Rd., 44124. Tel: 216-442-4160. Sr. Carolyn Clines, O.S.U., Dir. Total Staff 8; Total Assisted 2,000.
ROCKY RIVER. *The Center for Learning*, 21590 Center Ridge Rd., 44116. Tel: 440-331-1404; Fax: 440-331-5414.
E-mail: cfl@stratos.net
Web site: http://www.centerforlearning.org
Sr. Rose Schaffer, H.M., M.A., Pres. & CEO; Sr. Bernadette Vetter, H.M., M.A., Vice Pres.
Educational Development Center and Publisher of values-based instructional materials: Religion for Catholic schools and parishes; English/Language Arts, Social Studies, Novel/Drama, and Elementary Curriculum Units for all schools. Owned and operated by the Sisters of the Humility of Mary. Directed by an ecumenical lay board.
Administrative-Editorial Office in Rocky River. Shipping-Business Office, Evergreen Rd., P.O. Box 910, Villa Maria, PA, 16155. Tel: 800-767-9090; 412-964-8083; Fax: 888-767-8080.
SAN ANTONIO, TX, 1135 Mission Rd., 78210-4598. Rev. Kenneth C. Myers, Dir.
WICKLIFFE. *Center for Pastoral Leadership Services, Inc.*, 28700 Euclid Ave., 44092-2585. Tel: 216-943-7600. Rev. Donald B. Cozzens, Pres.; Mr. Brian F. Houlahan, Chief Operating Officer.

RELIGIOUS INSTITUTES OF MEN REPRESENTED IN THE DIOCESE

For further details refer to the corresponding bracketed number in the Religious Institutes of Men or Women section.
[0200]—*Benedictine Monks*. (St. Andrew Abbey).—O.S.B.
[0600]—*Brothers of the Congregation of Holy Cross*. (Midwest Prov.).—C.S.C.
[0470]—*The Capuchin Friars*.—O.F.M.Cap.

[1150]—*Congregation of St. Joseph.*—C.S.J.
[0220]—*Congregation of the Blessed Sacrament.*—S.S.S.
[0520]—*Franciscan Friars.* (Provs. of Sacred Heart & Assumption).—O.F.M.
[0480]—*Franciscan Friars (Conv.).*—O.F.M.Conv.
[0690]—*Jesuit Fathers and Brothers.* (Maryland Prov.).
[0690]—*Jesuit Fathers and Brothers.* (Detroit Prov.).
[0780]—*Marist Fathers.* (Washington Prov.).—S.M.
[0800]—*Maryknoll.*—M.M.
[0840]—*Missionary Servants of the Most Holy Trinity.*—S.T.
[0970]—*Order of Our Lady of Mercy.*—O.de.M.
[0610]—*Priests of the Congregation of the Holy Cross.* (Indiana Prov.).—C.S.C.
[0760]—*Society of Mary-Marianists.* (Dayton, OH).—S.M.
[1060]—*Society of the Precious Blood.* (Cincinnati Prov.).—C.PP.S.

RELIGIOUS INSTITUTES OF WOMEN REPRESENTED IN THE DIOCESE

[0230]—*Benedictine Sisters of Pontifical Jurisdiction.* (Erie, PA).—O.S.B.
[]—*Byzantine Nuns of St. Clare.*—B.N.S.C.
[0470]—*Congregation of the Sisters of Charity of the Incarnate Word.* (Houston).—C.C.V.I.
[1730]—*Congregation of the Sisters of the Third Order of St. Francis.* (Oldenburg).—O.S.F.
[1710]—*Congregation of the Third Order of St. Francis of Mary Immaculate, Joliet, IL.*—O.S.F.
[1830]—*Contemplative Sisters of the Good Shepherd.*—C.G.S.
[0420]—*Discalced Carmelite Nuns.*—O.C.D.
[1070-13]—*Dominican Sisters.*—O.P.
[1070-14]—*Dominican Sisters.*—O.P.
[1070-23]—*Dominican Sisters.*—O.P.
[1070-28]—*Dominican Sisters.*—O.P.
[1170]—*Felician Sisters.*—C.S.S.F.
[1210]—*Franciscan Sisters of Chicago.*—O.S.F.
[1840]—*Grey Nuns of Sacred Heart.*—G.N.S.H.
[2340]—*Little Sisters of the Poor.*—P.S.D.P.
[2790]—*Missionary Servants of the Most Blessed Trinity.*—M.S.B.T.
[3760]—*Order of St. Clare-Poor Clare Colettine Nuns.*—P.C.C.
[3130]—*Our Lady of Victory Missionary Sisters.*—O.L.V.M.
[0950]—*Pious Society Daughters of St. Paul.*—F.S.P.
[3210]—*Poor Clares of Perpetual Adoration.*—P.C.P.A.
[3420]—*Religious of the Eucharist.*—R.E.
[1830]—*Religious of the Good Shepherd.*—R.G.S.
[3430]—*Religious Teachers Filippini.*—M.P.F.
[2970]—*School Sisters of Notre Dame.*—S.S.N.D.
[0440]—*Sisters of Charity of Cincinnati, Ohio.*—S.C.
[0580]—*Sisters of Charity of St. Augustine.*—C.S.A.
[0990]—*Sisters of Divine Providence.*—C.D.P.
[2580]—*Sisters of Mercy of the Americas.* (Cincinnati & Detroit).—R.S.M.
[2990]—*Sisters of Notre Dame.*—S.N.D.
[1640]—*Sisters of St. Francis of Perpetual Adoration.*—O.S.F.
[3830-08]—*Sisters of St. Joseph.*—C.S.J.
[3910]—*Sisters of St. Joseph of St. Mark.*—S.J.S.M.
[3930]—*Sisters of St. Joseph of the Third Order of St. Francis.*—S.S.J.-T.O.S.F.
[1970]—*Sisters of the Holy Family of Nazareth.*—C.S.F.N.
[2030]—*Sisters of the Holy Spirit.*—C.S.Sp.
[2110]—*Sisters of the Humility of Mary.*—H.M.
[2210]—*Sisters of the Incarnate Word and Blessed Sacrament.*—S.I.W.
[2350]—*Sisters of the Living Word.*—S.L.W.
[2060]—*Sisters of the Most Holy Trinity.*—O.SS.T.
[3730]—*Sisters of the Order of St. Basil the Great.*—O.S.B.M.
[3260]—*Sisters of the Precious Blood.* (Dayton, Ohio).—C.PP.S.
[1490]—*Sisters of the Third Franciscan Order.*—O.S.F.
[3620]—*Sisters, Servants of Mary Immaculate.*—S.S.M.I.
[2150]—*Sisters, Servants of the Immaculate Heart of Mary.*—I.H.M.
[4120-04]—*Ursuline Nuns of the Congregation of Paris.*—O.S.U.
[4120-07]—*Ursuline Nuns of the Congregation of Paris.*—O.S.U.
[]—*Sisters of Divine Providence.* (Korea).
[4170]—*Vincentian Sisters of Charity.* (Bedford, OH).—V.S.C.

DIOCESAN CEMETERIES

CLEVELAND. *Assumption of Mary.*
Calvary.
St. John.
St. Joseph.
St. Mary.
St. Mary of the Falls.
AKRON. *Holy Cross.*
AVON. *Holy Trinity,* Detroit Rd.
Holy Trinity, Jaycox Rd.
BROOK PARK. *Holy Cross.*
CHARDON. *All Souls.*
CUYAHOGA HEIGHTS. *St. Mary.*
ELYRIA. *St. Mary.*
LORAIN. *Calvary.*
NORTHFIELD. *All Saints.*
VALLEY CITY. *Resurrection.*

NECROLOGY

† Andrews, William L., Lakewood, OH, St. James. —Died June 18, 1997.
† Fagan, Harry J., Madison, OH, Immaculate Conception. —Died Oct. 14, 1997.
† Ondik, Michael J., Avon, OH, Holy Trinity. —Died Jan. 16, 1997.
† Plafcan, Paul J., Lorain, OH, St. John. —Died May 26, 1997.

Diocese of Colorado Springs

Most Reverend

RICHARD C. HANIFEN, D.D., J.C.L.

Bishop of Colorado Springs; ordained June 6, 1959; appointed Titular Bishop of Abercorn and Auxiliary of Denver July 6, 1974; consecrated September 20, 1974; appointed First Bishop of Colorado Springs November 10, 1983; installed January 30, 1984. *Office: 29 West Kiowa, Colorado Springs, CO, 80903-1498.* Tel.: 719-636-2345; Fax: 719-636-1216.

Diocesan Offices: 29 West Kiowa, Colorado Springs, CO, 80903-1498. Tel.: 719-636-2345; Fax: 719-636-1216.

Legal Title: Diocese of Colorado Springs.

ESTABLISHED AND CREATED A DIOCESE JANUARY 30, 1984.

Square Miles Approximately 15,500.

Comprising the Counties of Chaffee, Cheyenne, Douglas, Elbert, El Paso, Kit Carson, Lake, Lincoln, Park and Teller.

For legal title of parishes and diocesan institutions, consult the Diocesan Offices.

STATISTICAL OVERVIEW

Personnel	
Bishop	1
Priests: Diocesan Active in Diocese	24
Priests: Active Outside Diocese	1
Priests: Retired, Sick or Absent	9
Number of Diocesan Priests	34
Religious Priests in Diocese	19
Extern Priests in Diocese	5
Ordinations:	
Diocesan Priests	4
Permanent Deacons in Diocese	20
Total Brothers	4
Total Sisters	145
Parishes	
Parishes	30
With Resident Pastor:	
Resident Diocesan Priests	13
Resident Religious Priests	8
Without Resident Pastor:	
Administered by Priests	3
Administered by Permanent Deacons	2
Administered by Professed Men Religious	4
Missions	9
Professional Ministry Personnel:	
Sisters	3
Lay Ministers	74
Welfare	
Catholic Hospitals	3
Total Assisted	292,014
Health Care Centers	2
Total Assisted	113
Homes for the Aged	2
Total Assisted	103
Educational	
Diocesan Students in Other Seminaries	3
Students Religious	3
Total Seminarians	6
Elementary Schools, Diocesan and Parish	4
Total Students	1,324
Catechesis/Religious Education:	
High School Students	2,409
Elementary Students	6,524
Total Students Under Catholic Instruction	10,263
Teachers in the Diocese:	
Sisters	1
Lay Teachers	78
Vital Statistics	
Receptions into the Church:	
Infant Baptism Totals	1,170
Adult Baptism Totals	218
Received into Full Communion	399
First Communions	1,311
Confirmations	645
Marriages:	
Catholic	204
Interfaith	154
Total Marriages	358
Deaths	254
Total Catholic Population	84,810
Total Population	669,303

Diocesan Offices—29 W. Kiowa St., Colorado Springs, 80903-1498. Tel: 719-636-2345; Fax: 719-636-1216. Office Hours: Mon.-Fri. 8:30-4:30.

Vicar General and Moderator of the Curia—Very Rev. DONALD F. DUNN.

Executive Assistant to the Bishop—Sr. PEG MALONEY, R.S.M.

Chancellor—Rev. GEORGE V. FAGAN, J.C.L., *29 W. Kiowa St., Colorado Springs, 80903.* Tel: 719-636-2345.

Diocesan Consultors—Most Rev. RICHARD C. HANIFEN; Very Rev. DONALD F. DUNN; Revs. JAMES A. BRACKE, C.S.C.; DONALD BROWNSTEIN; RICHARD BUHLER, S.J.; ROBERT JAEGER; KENNETH PRZYBYLA; AUGUST STEWART; Deacons DAVID KENNEY; GEORGE D. LINEHAN, JR.

Finance Officer—ROBERT G. DOERFLER, JR.

Archivist—Sr. JOSEPH MARIE JACOBSEN, O.S.B.

Judicial Vicar—Rev. GEORGE V. FAGAN, J.C.L.

Associate Judges—Revs. JAMES I. DONLON, J.C.D.; JOSEPH KOURY, S.J., J.C.D.

Defender of the Bond—Rev. MARK PLEWKA, J.C.L.

Procurator-Advocates—Revs. KARL USELDINGER; ERNEST W. BOND; Sr. JOSEPH MARIE JACOBSEN, O.S.B.; Deacon GEORGE D. LINEHAN, JR.

Auditors—Sr. JOSEPH MARIE JACOBSEN, O.S.B.

Ecclesiastical Notaries—Rev. GEORGE V. FAGAN, J.C.L.; Sr. JOSEPH MARIE JACOBSEN, O.S.B.; SHIRLEY WELLS.

Catholic Community Services, The Diocese of Colorado Springs, Inc.—GAIL DUSING, Exec. Dir.

Office of Pastoral Administration—ROBERT G. DOERFLER, JR., Dir.

Office of Stewardship and Development—HERMAN GUENTHER, Dir.

Office of Schools and Resource Center—Sr. JUDITH CAULEY, C.S.J., Supt. KAREN BAKER, Resource Ctr. Coord.

Propagation of the Faith—Very Rev. DONALD F. DUNN, Diocesan Dir.

Vocations Office—Rev. GEORGE V. FAGAN, JR., Dir.

Regionalization—Very Rev. DONALD F. DUNN, Vicar General; Northern Region: Rev. DENNIS DWYER, Vicar; Metro-Central Region (Colorado Springs): Rev. MICHAEL BUTER, Vicar; Metro-North Region (Colorado Springs): Rev. PAUL WICKER, Vicar; Metro-South Region (Colorado Springs): Very Rev. JOHN F. SLATTERY, Vicar; Western Region: Rt. Rev. WARREN HEIDGEN, O.S.B., Vicar; Eastern Region: Rev. R. WILLIAM RHINEHART, C.M., Vicar.

CLERGY, PARISHES, MISSIONS AND PAROCHIAL SCHOOLS

CITY OF COLORADO SPRINGS
(County of El Paso)

1—ST. MARY'S CATHEDRAL (1887), Very Revs. Donald F. Dunn, V.G., Rector; Theodore A. Haas, Rector Emeritus; Rev. Khanh Pham Nguyen. In res., Rev. Matthew T. Minh.
Res., 15 West View Pl., 80903.
Office: 22 W. Kiowa St., 80903. Tel: 719-473-4633.
Catechesis/Religious Programs—Kerry Susser, D.R.E.
Students 160.

2—CORPUS CHRISTI (1916), Rev. Lawrence W. Carmody; Deacon Benedict Cruise.
Res., 2318 N. Cascade Ave., 80907. Tel: 719-633-1457; Fax: 719-473-7567.
School—2410 N. Cascade Ave., 80907. Tel: 719-632-5092. Martha Frauenheim, Prin.
Lay Teachers 30; Students 430.
Catechesis/Religious Programs—Tel: 719-473-8363. Barb Maloney, D.R.E.
Students 120.

3—DIVINE REDEEMER (1950), Revs. Michael C. Butler; William Jarema; Deacon David Van Matre.
Res., 1520 E. Yampa St., 80909. Tel: 719-633-5559; Fax: 719-575-9180. [JC]
School—901 N. Logan, 80909. Tel: 719-471-7771; Fax: 719-575-9180. Patricia Beckert, Prin.
Lay Teachers 23; Students 461.
Catechesis/Religious Programs—Bernadette Tittle, D.R.E.
Students 186.

4—HOLY APOSTLES (1973), Rev. Paul F. Wicker.
Res., 4925 N. Carefree Cir., 80917. Tel: 719-597-4249; Fax: 719-591-1816.
Preschool—4925 N. Carefree, 80917. Tel: 719-591-1566; Fax: 719-591-1816. Mary Parsons, Dir.
Lay Teachers 13; Students 147.
Catechesis/Religious Programs—Mary Margaret Melanson, D.R.E.
Students 685.

5—HOLY TRINITY (1968), Ms. CoCo Soper, Parish Dir.
Office: 3122 Poinsetta Dr., 80907. Tel: 719-633-2132; Fax: 719-633-0975.
Res., 1522 Hollyhock, 80907.
School—3115 Larkspur Dr., 80907. Dr. Katherine Backe, Prin.
Lay Teachers 10; Students 217.
Catechesis/Religious Programs—Mary Ellen White, D.R.E.
Students 200.

6—KOREAN CATHOLIC COMMUNITY (1983). Closed. For inquiries for parish records contact the Chancery.

7—ST. ANDREW KIM QUASI PARISH (Korean), Rev. Berchmans Yong-Woo Lee, S.J. (Korea).

Office: 4514 E. Pikes Peak Ave., 80916. Tel: 719-638-0100; 638-0105 (Rectory); 638-0102 (Convent); Fax: 719-638-0101.

8—OUR LADY OF GUADALUPE (1948), Rev. Donald F. Dunn, V.G.; Deacon Dave Van Matre, Acting Parish Dir.
Res., 2715 E. Pikes Peak, 80909. Tel: 719-633-7204; Fax: 719-630-3184.
Catechesis/Religious Programs—Students 400.

9—OUR LADY OF THE PINES-BLACK FOREST (1965), Rev. Gerard J. Borer, S.J.; Deacons Gene Eastham; Lynn Sherman.
Res., 11020 Teachout Rd., 80908. Tel: 719-495-2351; Fax: 719-495-9062.
Catechesis/Religious Programs—D.R.E.: Mrs. Susan Ames; Mrs. Barbara Sherman.
Students 263.

10—SACRED HEART (1891), Revs. James A. Bracke, C.S.C.; Donald Dilg, C.S.C.
Office: 2021 W. Pikes Peak Ave., 80904. Tel: 719-633-8711; Fax: 719-633-1859.
Catechesis/Religious Programs—Kathleen Moriarty, D.R.E.
Students 280.
Missions—Manitou Springs, El Paso Co., Our Lady of Perpetual Help, 218 Ruxton Ave., Manitou Springs, 80829.; Cascade, El Paso Co., Holy Rosary, 4435 Holiday Trail, Cascade, 80809.

11—ST. FRANCIS OF ASSISI (1981), Dr. Maria Gatza, Parish Dir.; Rev. Owen J. McHugh; Deacon Michael Ciletti.
Office: 2650 Parish View, 80919. Tel: 719-599-5031; Fax: 719-559-3360.
Catechesis/Religious Programs—Terri Kowalczyk, D.R.E.
Students 650.

12—ST. JOSEPH'S (Southgate) (!968), Mr. David Kenney, Parish Dir.; Rev. Daniel Ayers; Deacon Albert E. Kimminau; Randall Brungardt, Pastoral Assoc.
Res., 1830 S. Corona Ave., 80906. Tel: 719-632-9903; Fax: 719-632-9170.
Catechesis/Religious Programs—Tel: 719-635-3166.
Students 258.

13—ST. PATRICK'S (1981), Revs. Donald Brownstein; Steve Parlet.
Office: 1925 Dominion Way, 80918. Tel: 719-598-3595; Fax: 719-599-5741.
Res., 6602 Snowbird Dr., 80918.
Catechesis/Religious Programs—Angelita M. Dykes, D.R.E.
Students 1,037.

14—SAINT PAUL (1925), Revs. John Auer; Khanh San Hoang; Deacon Patrick Bidon.
Office: 9 El Pomar Rd., 80906. Tel: 719-471-9700; Fax: 719-471-3009.
School—Pauline Memorial Catholic School, Tel: 719-632-1846; Fax: 719-632-0495.
Lay Teachers 15; Students 216.
Catechesis/Religious Programs—Deacon Dick Bowles, D.R.E.
Students 305.

15—THE VIETNAMESE HOLY MARTYRS QUASI-PARISH (1993), Rev. Matthew Minh Thanh Tran.
Res. & Mailing Address: 15 West View Pl., 80903. Tel: 719-634-6172.
Parish Center—29 W. Kiowa, 80903. Tel: 719-633-2274.

OUTSIDE THE CITY OF COLORADO SPRINGS

Bailey, Park Co., St. Mary's of the Rockies (1990), Rev. Ernest W. Bond.
Res., P.O. Box 319, 80421-8319. Tel: 303-838-2375; Fax: 303-838-2375.

Buena Vista, Chaffee Co., St. Rose of Lima (1880), Rt. Rev. Warren J. Heidgen, O.S.B.; Deacon Richard Willburn.
Res., 114 S. Gunnison, P.O. Box 458, 81211. Tel: 719-395-8424.
Catechesis/Religious Programs—Students 141.
Mission—Fairplay, Park Co., St. Joseph. (Send all correspondence to Buena Vista address.) 5th & Costello, Fairplay, 80440. Tel: 719-395-8424.

Burlington, Kit Carson Co., St. Catherine of Siena (1916), Rev. Jay L. Gibson, C.M.
Res., P.O. Box 57, Stratton, 80836. Tel: 719-348-5336; Fax: 719-348-5336.
Church—P.O. Box 38, 80836. Tel: 719-346-7156.
Catechesis/Religious Programs—Students 155.

Calhan, El Paso Co., St. Michael's (1920), Rev. James F. Halloran, Admin.
Res., Box 199, 80808. Tel: 719-347-2290; Fax: 719-347-2290.
Catechesis/Religious Programs—Students 57.

Castle Rock, Douglas Co., St. Francis of Assisi (1888), Revs. Dennis E. Dwyer; August Stewart; Deacon Robert Hunter.
Res., 2746 E Hwy. 86, 80104. Tel: 303-688-3025; 688-3057; Fax: 303-688-4016.
Catechesis/Religious Programs—Tel: 303-688-9522. Lynne K. Lane, D.R.E.
Students 435.

Cheyenne Wells, Cheyenne Co., Sacred Heart (1918), Rev. Thomas Kloppenborg, C.M.
Res., P.O. Box 819, 80810. Tel: 719-767-5272.
Mission—Kit Carson, Cheyenne Co., St. Augustine, P.O. Box 82, Kit Carson, 80825. Tel: 719-962-3552.
Catechesis/Religious Programs—D.R.E.: Dianne Smith; Sharon Baker; Eleanor Dechant.
Students 73.

Fountain, El Paso Co., St. Joseph (1970), Deacon Roger K. Eberwein, Parish Dir.
101 N. Main St., 80817. Tel: 719-382-7086.
Catechesis/Religious Programs—Students 125.

Highlands Ranch, Douglas Co., Pax Christi Catholic Church (1988), Mr. Jeff Kelling Parish Dir.
Office: 9777 S. Yosemite/Ste. 230, Littleton, 80124. Tel: 303-799-1036; Fax: 303-799-1072.
Catechesis/Religious Programs—Chris Holmes, D.R.E.
Students 572.

Leadville, Lake Co., Catholic Community of Leadville, Annunciation(1879) & St. Joseph(1899), Rev. Thomas M. Killeen, O.M.I., Admin.
Res., 609 Poplar St., 80461. Tel: 719-486-1382. [CEM]
Catechesis/Religious Programs—Students 179.

Limon, Lincoln Co., Our Lady of Victory(1925), Rev. R. William Rhinehart, C.M.
Res., 489 H Ave., P.O. Box 790, 80828. Tel: 719-775-2118.
Catechesis/Religious Programs—Limon & Missions.
Students 95.
Missions—Hugo, Lincoln Co., St. Anthony of Padua. (Send all correspondence to Limon address). 133 Fifth St., P.O. Box 275, Hugo, 80821. Tel: 719-743-2373. [CEM]
Flagler, Kit Carson Co., St. Mary. (Send all correspondence to Limon address.) Flagler, 80815.

Monument, El Paso Co., St. Peter (1911), Rev. Robert E. Jaeger.
Res., 55 N. Jefferson, Box 827, 80132. Tel: 719-481-2554; Fax: 719-481-9606.
Catechesis/Religious Programs—Tel: 719-481-3511. Kathy Campbell, D.R.E.
Students 478.

Parker, Douglas Co., Ave Maria (1983), Revs. Dennis E. Dwyer; Donald Sutton; James Williams; Jim Costello, S.J.; Kurt D. Bartley, Pastoral Admin.; Sr. Monica Marie Ehnie, S.C., Pastoral Assoc.; Deacons George D. Linehan, Jr.; Bob Hunter.
Res., 9056 E. Parker Rd., 80138-7209. Tel: 303-841-3750; Fax: 303-841-2412.
Catechesis/Religious Programs—Wavelyn Dreher, D.R.E.
Students 1,145.
Mission—Elizabeth, Our Lady of the Visitation, Elizabeth, 80107.

Salida, Chaffee Co., St. Joseph (1907), Rev. Kenneth Przybyla. In res., Rev. Anthony C. Uhl, Chap. Colorado Dept. of Corrections.
Res., P.O. Box 847, 81201. Tel: 719-539-6419; Fax: 719-539-7127.
Catechesis/Religious Programs—Students 145.

Security, El Paso Co., Holy Family (1957), Rev. Patrick W. Battiato.
Res., 331 Main St., 80911. Tel: 719-392-7653; Fax: 719-392-1651.
Catechesis/Religious Programs—Cathy Jane King, D.R.E.
Students 570.

Stratton, Kit Carson Co., St. Charles Borromeo (1910), Rev. Jay L. Gibson, C.M.
Res., P.O. Box 57, 80836. Tel: 719-348-5336; Fax: 719-348-5336.
Catechesis/Religious Programs—Students 128.

Woodland Park, Teller Co., Our Lady of the Woods (1954), Rev. Karl J. Useldinger; Deacon Allen Breaux.
Res., P.O. Box 416, 80866. Tel: 719-687-9345; Fax: 719-687-0893.
Catechesis/Religious Programs—Students 165.
Missions—Cripple Creek, Teller Co., St. Peter's. (Send all correspondence to Woodland Park address.); Victor, Teller Co., St. Victor's. (Send all correspondence to Woodland Park address.).

On Duty Outside Diocese:
Reverend Fathers—
Grabrian, Dennis, P.O. Box 347, Safford, AZ 85546

Retired:
Reverend Fathers—
Bruggeman, Gerald H., Chap., Penrose Hospital, 2215 N. Cascade Ave., Colorado Springs, CO 80907
Dresen, Arthur G., 4559 Sunnyhill Dr., Colorado Springs, CO 80916
Halloran, Joseph H., Fountain Terrace Apartments, 3211 E. Fountains Blvd., #103, Colorado Springs, CO 80910
Kekeisen, Robert E., 4895-B El Camino Dr., Colorado Springs, CO 80918
Leonard, Edward, 15 Hewlett Ave., New Castle, DE 19720
Myers, Rawley, St. Mary's Cathedral, 22 W. Kiowa, Colorado Springs, CO 80903

Permanent Deacons:
Bidon, Patrick, St. Paul's, Colorado Springs
Bowles, Richard, Unassigned
Breaux, Allen, Our Lady of the Woods, Woodland Park
Ciletti, Michael, Service to mentally and physically challenged communities, St. Francis of Assisi, Colorado Springs
Cruise, Ben, Corpus Christi & Fort Carson, Colorado Springs
Eastham, Eugene S., Our Lady of the Pines, Colorado Springs
Eberwein, Roger, Parish Dir., St. Joseph, Fountain
Huber, Robert A., Douglas/Elbert Counties Prison Ministry; Northern Region Ministry
Hunter, Robert, St. Francis of Assisi, Castle Rock
Kimminau, Albert E., St. Joseph's, Southgate, Colorado Springs
Leverington, Michael, Unassigned
Linehan, George D., Jr., Ave Maria, Parker
Martinez, Dan, Unassigned
Parrish, Thomas E., Jail Ministry
Reyes, Emilio, Unassigned
Sherman, Lynn, Our Lady of the Pines, Colorado Springs
Sherpa, Lee, (Retired)
Specht, Charles W., Dir., Office of Permanent Diaconate
Van Matre, Dave, Acting Parish Dir., Our Lady of Guadalupe, Colorado Springs
Willburn, Richard, St. Rose of Lima, Buena Vista

INSTITUTIONS LOCATED IN THE DIOCESE

[A] EDUCATIONAL INSTITUTIONS

COLORADO SPRINGS.
**The Center at Benet Hill Monastery*, 2577 N. Chelton Rd., 80909. Tel: 719-473-6184.
E-mail: benet@clsp.uswest.net
Web site: www.geocities.com/Wellesley/2815
Sr. Marilyn Carpenter, O.S.B., Contact Person. Sisters 6; Lay Staff 3.

[B] GENERAL HOSPITALS

COLORADO SPRINGS. *Centura Health-Penrose-St. Francis Health Services.*
For a complete listing, refer to the Hospitals section.
Penrose-St. Francis Healthcare Foundation, 7606 N. Union Blvd., Ste. D, 80920. Tel: 719-528-5883
For a complete listing, refer to the Hospitals section.
St. Francis Health Center, 825 E. Pikes Peak Ave., 80903. Tel: 719-776-8800; Fax: 719-636-8871
For a complete listing, refer to the Hospitals section.

[C] NURSING HOMES

*COLORADO SPRINGS. *St. Francis Nursing Center*, 7550 Assisi Heights, 80920. Tel: 719-598-1336
For a complete listing, refer to the Special Care Facilities section.

[D] SPECIAL CARE FACILITIES

COLORADO SPRINGS. *Centura Health-Namaste Alzheimer Center*, 2 Penrose Blvd., 80906. Tel: 719-560-2000
For a complete listing, refer to the Special Care Facilities section.
The Medalion (East), 1719 E. Bijou St., 80909. Tel: 719-471-4800; Fax: 719-471-4807
For a complete listing, refer to the Special Care Facilities section.
The Medalion (West), 417 E. Kiowa St., 80903. Tel: 719-471-2578; Fax: 719-471-4807
For a complete listing, refer to the Special Care Facilities section.

[E] RESIDENCES FOR MEN RELIGIOUS

CASCADE. *Holy Cross Novitiate*, Box 749, 80809. Tel: 719-684-9277. Congregation of Holy Cross (Indiana Prov., Marigreen Pines). Rev. Richard S. Wilkinson, C.S.C., Dir. Novices & Supr. Staff: Bros. Thomas Moser, C.S.C., Asst. Supr.; Thomas A. Dziekan, C.S.C., Steward. In res. Rev. Thomas A. Stella,

C.S.C. Priests 2; Brothers 2; Novices 11.

SEDALIA. *Sacred Heart Retreat House - Jesuit Community*, Box 185, 80135. Tel: 303-688-5196.
E-mail: shjesrh@aol.com
Revs. Richard O. Buhler, S.J., Supr.; Vincent E. Hovley, S.J.; Robert F. Houlihan, S.J.; James J. Costello, S.J.; William W. Williams, S.J.; Stephen E. Baird, S.J.; Bros. Richard P. May, S.J.; David L. Ward, S.J.

[F] RESIDENCES FOR WOMEN RELIGIOUS

COLORADO SPRINGS.

**Benet Hill Monastery*, 2555 N. Chelton Rd., 80909. Tel: 719-633-0655.
E-mail: benet@clsp.uswest.net
Web site: geocities.com/wellesley/2815
Motherhouse of the Sisters of St. Benedict (1963). Sr. Anne Stedman, O.S.B., Prioress; Sr. Diane Liston, O.S.B., Community Archivist. Professed Sisters 46; Novices 2.
Properties owned: The Center at Benet Hill Monastery and Benet Pines.

Mount St. Francis, 7665 Assisi Hts., 80919. Tel: 719-598-5486. Provincial and Formation House. Sisters of St. Francis of Perpetual Adoration, Province of St. Joseph (The Sisters of St. Francis of Colorado Springs). Sr. Clarice Gentrup, O.S.F., Prov.; Rev. George V. Fagan, Jr., Chap. Professed Sisters 118.

[G] RETREAT CENTERS

COLORADO SPRINGS.

**Benet Pines*, 15780 Hwy. 83, 80921. Tel: 719-495-2574. Sr. Jan Ginzkey, O.S.B.; Sr. Clare Carr, O.S.B.; Dick Pfalmer; Francie Pfalmer. Total in Residence 2; Total Staff 4; Total Assisted 20.

Franciscan Center, 7665 Assisi Hts., 80919-3836. Tel: 719-598-5486. Sr. Christine Hayes, O.S.F., Dir. Total Guests 13,000; Total Staff 7.

SEDALIA. *Sacred Heart Jesuit Retreat House*, Box 185, 80135. Tel: 303-688-4198.
E-mail: shjesrh@aol.com
Revs. Richard O. Buhler, S.J., Supr.; Vincent E. Hovley, S.J.; Robert F. Houlihan, S.J.; James J. Costello, S.J.; William W. Williams, S.J.; Stephen E. Baird, S.J.; Bros. David L. Ward, S.J.; Richard P. May, S.J. Total in Residence 8.

[H] MISCELLANEOUS LISTINGS

COLORADO SPRINGS. *Catholic Charismatic Renewal Services.* (CCRS), 926 Farragut Ave., 80909. Tel: 719-633-2302. Rev. William Jarema, Liaison to Bishop Hanifen for Charismatic Renewal.

The Catholic Foundation of the Diocese of Colorado Springs, Inc., 29 W. Kiowa, 80903-1498. Herman H. Guenther, Pres./Exec. Dir.

Colorado Springs Council of Black Catholics, 29 W. Kiowa St., 80909.

Colorado Springs Diocesan Council of Catholic Women, 720 Orion Dr., 80906. Tel: 719-635-7398. Phyllis E. Hinsey, Pres.

Franciscan Family Wellness Program, Inc., 7665 Assisi Hts., 80919. Sr. Judith Ann Schaeffer, Ph.D., Exec. Dir. Total Assisted 4,100; Total Staff 9.

The Franciscan Foundation of Colorado Springs, 7665 Assisi Hts., 80919-3836. Sr. Clarice Gentrup, O.S.F., Contact Person.

Jail Ministries, c/o Diocese of Colorado Springs, 29 W. Kiowa St., 80903. Tel: 719-636-2345. Deacon Thomas E. Parrish, Coord.

**Partners in Housing, Inc.*, 18 W. Bijou St., 80903.

S.E.T. of Colorado Springs, 2413 N. Cascade, 80907. Tel: 719-776-5476. Sr. Barbara Counts, Dir.

Theresians of the United States aka Theresians World Ministry, 2577 N. Chelton Rd., Ste. 207, 80909. Tel: 719-636-3643.
E-mail: tustwm@clsp.uswest.net
Sr. Rose Ann Barmann, Exec. Dir.

**Villa San Jose, Inc.*, 1810 S. Corona, 80906. Tel: 719-632-7444. Karla Ross, Admin. & Res. Svcs. Coord. Total in Residence 50; Total Staff 6.

NECROLOGY

(No Deaths)

Diocese of Columbus

(Dioecesis Columbensis)

Most Reverend

JAMES A. GRIFFIN, J.D., J.C.L.

Bishop of Columbus; ordained May 28, 1960; consecrated Titular Bishop of Holar and Auxiliary to the Bishop of Cleveland August 1, 1979; appointed Tenth Bishop of Columbus February 7, 1983; installed April 25, 1983. *Res., 198 E. Broad St., Columbus, OH, 43215.* Tel.: 614-224-2251.

Most Reverend

EDWARD J. HERRMANN, D.D.

Retired Bishop of Columbus; ordained June 12, 1947; appointed Auxiliary Bishop of Washington and Titular Bishop of Lamzella March 4, 1966; consecrated April 26, 1966; appointed Ninth Bishop of Columbus June 26, 1973; installed August 21, 1973; retired September 18, 1982; Apostolic Administrator September 1982 to April 1983. *Res., St. Raphael Home, 1550 Roxbury Rd., Columbus, OH, 43212.* Tel.: 614-224-2251.

ESTABLISHED 1868.

Square Miles 11,310.

Comprises the following 23 Counties in the State of Ohio: Hardin, Marion, Morrow, Knox, Holmes, Tuscarawas, Union, Delaware, Licking, Coshocton, Madison, Franklin, Muskingum, Fayette, Pickaway, Fairfield, Perry, Ross, Hocking, Pike, Jackson, Vinton and Scioto.

For legal titles of parishes and diocesan institutions, consult the Chancery Office.

Chancery Office: 198 E. Broad St., Columbus, OH, 43215. Tel.: 614-224-2251; 224-8718 (Sat.-Sun. and other times); Fax: 614-224-6306.

STATISTICAL OVERVIEW

Personnel	
Bishop	1
Retired Bishops	1
Priests: Diocesan Active in Diocese	139
Priests: Active Outside Diocese	8
Priests: Retired, Sick or Absent	52
Number of Diocesan Priests	199
Religious Priests in Diocese	41
Extern Priests in Diocese	8
Ordinations:	
Diocesan Priests	1
Transitional Deacons	2
Permanent Deacons	12
Permanent Deacons in Diocese	62
Total Brothers	8
Total Sisters	398
Parishes	
Parishes	108
With Resident Pastor:	
Resident Diocesan Priests	95
Resident Religious Priests	8
Without Resident Pastor:	
Administered by Priests	4
Administered by Women Religious	1
Missions	6
Professional Ministry Personnel:	
Brothers	1
Sisters	28
Lay Ministers	101
Welfare	
Catholic Hospitals	4
Total Assisted	907,461
Homes for the Aged	16
Total Assisted	1,011
Day Care and Extended Day Care Centers	2
Total Assisted	331
Specialized Homes	1
Total Assisted	499
Special Centers for Social Services	13
Total Assisted	323,348
Residential Care of Disabled	1
Total Assisted	135
Other Institutions	2
Total Assisted	3,197
Educational	
Seminaries, Diocesan	1
Students from This Diocese	9
Students from Other Diocese	94
Diocesan Students in Other Seminaries	3
Students Religious	8
Total Seminarians	20
Colleges and Universities	1
Total Students	1,949
High Schools, Diocesan and Parish	11
Total Students	4,771
Elementary Schools, Diocesan and Parish	45
Total Students	13,804
Elementary Schools, Private	1
Total Students	207
Catechesis/Religious Education:	
High School Students	1,619
Elementary Students	13,835
Total Students Under Catholic Instruction	36,205
Teachers in the Diocese:	
Priests	4
Sisters	39
Lay Teachers	994
Vital Statistics	
Receptions into the Church:	
Infant Baptism Totals	3,995
Adult Baptism Totals	556
Received into Full Communion	790
First Communions	4,164
Confirmations	3,516
Marriages:	
Catholic	566
Interfaith	734
Total Marriages	1,300
Deaths	1,732
Total Catholic Population	218,796
Total Population	2,297,396

Former Bishops—Rt. Rev. SYLVESTER HORTON ROSECRANS, D.D., cons. Titular Bishop of Pompeiopolis and Auxiliary to the Bishop of Cincinnati, March 25, 1862; transferred to Columbus, March 3, 1868; died Oct. 21, 1878.—Rt. Rev. JOHN AMBROSE WATTERSON, D.D., cons. Aug. 8, 1880; died April 17, 1899.—Most Rev. HENRY MOELLER, D.D., cons. Bishop of Columbus, Aug. 25, 1900; promoted to the Archiepiscopal See of Areopolis and made Coadjutor to the Archbishop of Cincinnati, with the right of succession, April 27, 1903; succeeded to the See of Cincinnati, Oct. 31, 1904; died Jan. 5, 1925.—Most Rev. JAMES JOSEPH HARTLEY, D.D., cons. Feb. 25, 1904; died Jan. 12, 1944.—Most Rev. MICHAEL JOSEPH READY, D.D., cons. Dec. 14, 1944; died May 2, 1957.—Most Rev. CLARENCE GEORGE ISSENMANN, S.T.D., cons. Titular Bishop of Phytea and Auxiliary Bishop of Cincinnati May 25, 1954; appt. Bishop of Columbus Dec. 5, 1957; transferred to Cleveland as Apostolic Administrator. "cum jure successionis," Oct. 7, 1964; died July 27, 1982.—His Eminence JOHN CARDINAL CARBERRY, D.D., appt. Titular Bishop of Elis and Coadjutor of Lafayette in Indiana "cum jure successionis," May 3, 1956; cons. July 25, 1956; succeeded to See Nov. 20, 1957; transferred to Columbus Jan. 20, 1965; transferred to the Archdiocese of St. Louis, March 24, 1968; created Cardinal April 28, 1969.—Most Rev. CLARENCE E. ELWELL, D.D., cons. Dec. 21, 1962; appt. to Columbus May 29, 1968; died Feb. 16, 1973.

Vicar General/Chancellor—Rev. Msgr. STEPHAN J. MOLONEY, M.A., M.Div., J.C.L.

Vicar General—Rev. Msgr. JOSEPH M. HENDRICKS, S.T.B., M.A.

Episcopal Vicar for Charities and Social Concerns—Rev. STANLEY BENECKI, Ph.D.

Episcopal Vicar for Education—Rev. PAUL A. NOBLE.

Episcopal Vicar for Church Ministry—Sr. JOAN M. HARPER, C.D.P.

Episcopal Vicar for Communications—Rev. THOMAS KESSLER, S.T.D.

Episcopal Vicar for Spiritual Life—Rev. Msgr. STEPHAN J. MOLONEY, M.A., M.Div., J.C.L.

Chancery Office—198 E. Broad St., Columbus, 43215. Office Hours: Mon.-Fri. 8-4:30. Tel: 614-224-2251 (Sat.-Sun.). Tel: 614-224-8718 (other times); Fax: 614-224-6306.

Chancellor—Rev. Msgr. STEPHAN J. MOLONEY, M.A., M.Div., J.C.L.

Assistant Chancellor—Rev. ROBERT E. WILLMANN, S.T.B., J.C.L., J.C.D.

Diocesan Consultors—Most Rev. JAMES A. GRIFFIN, J.D., J.C.L.; Rev. Msgr. JOSEPH M. HENDRICKS; Rev.Msgr. STEPHAN J. MOLONEY; Revs. RODNEY DAMICO; WILLIAM DUNN; JAMES GEIGER; MARK GHILONI; STEPHEN KRILE.

Parochial Examiners—Revs. CARL P. CLAGETT; CHARLES E. COTTON; Rev. Msgr. FRANK J. MEAGHER.

Vicars Forane—Vicariate 1: Center City: Rev. Msgr. LAWRENCE J. CORCORAN, *Holy Cross Church, 204 S.*

5th St., Columbus, 43215. Vicariate 2: Northwest: Rev. MARK J. HAMMOND, *St. Andrew Church, 1899 McCoy Rd., Columbus, 43220.* Vicariate 3: North High: Rev. Msgr. MARIO A. SERRAGLIO, *St. John the Baptist Church, 720 Hamlet St., Columbus, 43215.* Vicariate 4: Northland: Rev. RODRIC J. DIPIETRO, *St. Elizabeth Church, 1682 Lynnhurst Rd., Columbus, 43229.* Vicariate 5: West: Rev. JOHN L. BAKLE, S.M., *St. Agatha Church, 1860 Northam Rd., Columbus, 43221.* Vicariate 6: South: Rev. MICHAEL B. WATSON, *St. Mary Church, 684 S. 3rd St., Columbus, 43206.* Vicariate 7: East: Rev. DANIEL L. OCHS, *St. Pius X Church, 1051 Waggoner Rd., Reynoldsburg, 43068.* Vicariate 8: Marion: Rev. WILLIAM J. FAUSTNER, *Immaculate Conception Church, 215 E. North St., Kenton, 43326.* Vicariate 9: Zanesville: Rev. DWAYNE A. MCNEW, *St. Nicholas Church, 925 E. Main St., Zanesville, 43701.* Vicariate 10: Knox-Licking: Rev. G. MICHAEL GRIBBLE, *St. Edward Church, 785 Newark Rd., Granville, 43023.* Vicariate 11: Tusc.-Holmes: Rev. Msgr. GEORGE J. SCHLEGEL, *Sacred Heart Church, 139 3rd St., N.E., New Philadelphia, 44663.* Vicariate 12: Lancaster: Rev. MARTIN V. WEITHMAN, *132 S. High St., Lancaster, 43130.* Vicariate 13: Chillicothe: Rev. DONALD E. FRANKS, *St. Mary Church, 61 S. Paint St., Chillicothe, 45601.* Vicariate 14: Scioto County: Rev. MARK V. GHILONI, *Holy Redeemer Church, 1325 Gallia St., Portsmouth, 45662.* Vicariate 15: Perry County: Rev. Msgr. RICHARD F. DODD, *St. Patrick Church, 1170 State Rt. 668 South, Junction City, 43748.*

Priests' Senate—Rev. THOMAS SHONEBARGER, Chm.; Revs. WILLIAM D. HUBER, Vice Chm. & Treas.; JAMES A. WALTER, Sec.; THOMAS G. PETRY; THOMAS SHONEBARGER; CHARLES E. COTTON; DAVID E. GETREU; DANIEL J. MILLISOR; FRANK P. MILLER; DEAN MATHEWSON; MARTIN J. RALKO; RICHARD J. PENDOLPHI; JAMES L. COLOPY; PETER GIDEON. Ex Officio Members: Rev. Msgr. JOSEPH M. HENDRICKS; Rev. Msgr. STEPHAN J. MOLONEY.

Diocesan Pastoral Council—JOSEPH STEIGER, Chm.; Sr. PHYLLIS DUGAN, S.N.D.deN., Exec. Sec., *197 E. Gay St., Columbus, 43215.* Tel: 614-228-1646.

Tribunal—197 E. Gay St., Ste. 500, Columbus, 43215-3290. Tel: 614-241-2500. Commissions should be addressed to the Diocese of Columbus, Tribunal.

Judicial Vicar—Rev. MARK J. HAMMOND, S.T.L., J.C.L.

Adjutant Vicar Judicial—Rev. Msgr. JOHN G. JOHNSON, J.C.D.

Court of First Instance—

Diocesan Judges—Rev. Msgr. JOHN K. CODY, M.Div.; Rev. Msgr. F. THOMAS GALLEN, C.G.M.; Revs. LEO CONNOLLY, M.Div.; JOHN DITTOE, S.T.L.; WM. THOMAS KESSLER, S.T.D.; CHARLES F. KLINGER, M.Div., Ph.D.; WILLIAM A. METZGER, B.A.; CHARLES T. THOMAS, M.A., M.Div.; ROBERT E. WILLMANN, S.T.B., J.C.L.

Defenders of the Bond—Rev. DENNIS STEVENSON, M.Div., J.C.L.; Sr. WANDA SCHERER, O.S.F., M.A.

Auditors/Notaries—Sr. MARY LINDA LORENZ, O.P., M.A.; HELEN THOMAS; SAUNDRA BURNS.

Notaries—Sr. RAYMUNDA BROOKS, O.P., M.A.; ANGELA NESMITH.

Promoter of Justice—Rev. EDWARD F. TRENOR, J.C.L.

Court of Second Instance—

Presiding Judge—Rev. Msgr. JAMES L.T. RUEF, M.A., J.D., J.C.L.

Appellate Judges—Rev. Msgr. ANTHONY BORRELLI, J.C.L.; Rev. Msgr. JOHN J. DREESE, S.S.L.; Rev. Msgr. DAVID V. SOROHAN, M.A., S.T.L., Ph.D.; Rev. ROBERT E. WILLMANN, S.T.B., J.C.L.; Rev. Msgr. EDWARD F. TRENOR, J.C.L.; Rev. Msgr. JOHN V. WOLF, S.T.D.; Revs. THOMAS J. CADDEN, M.A.; JAMES A. GEIGER, A.B., Ph.D.

Defender of the Bond—Rev. LEO L. CONNOLLY, M.Div.

Apostleship of Prayer—Rev. Msgr. RICHARD DODD, Dir., *St. Patrick, Junction City, 43478.* Tel: 614-987-2691.

Building Commission—Rev. Msgr. EDWARD F. TRENOR, Chm. & Contact Person, *Christ the King, 2770 Dover Rd., Columbus, 43209.*

Catholic Center—Diocesan Office Building, 197 E. Gay St., Columbus, 43215. Tel: 614-228-2453.

Catholic Charities and Social Concerns—Rev. STANLEY BENECKI, Vicar, *197 E. Gay St., Columbus, 43215.* Tel: 614-241-2540; Fax: 614-268-8130.

Catholic Conference of Ohio—TIMOTHY V. LUCKHAUPT, Dir., *9 E. Long St., Ste. 201, Columbus, 43215.* Tel: 614-224-7147; Fax: 614-224-7150.

Catholic Record Society—DONALD SCHLEGEL, Sec., *197 E. Gay St., Columbus, 43215.* Tel: 614-241-2571.

Catholic Relief Services—MARK HUDDY, Diocesan Admin., *Dept. of Social Concerns, 197 E. Gay St., Columbus, 43215.* Tel: 614-241-2540.

Catholic Social Services—SARA K. MURPHY, Pres., *197 E. Gay St., Columbus, 43215.* Tel: 614-221-5891.

Cemeteries—RICHARD FINN, Dir., *6440 S. High St., Lockbourne, 43137.* Tel: 614-491-2751.

Censors of Books—Rev. Msgr. JOHN V. WOLF, S.T.D.; Rev. THOMAS KESSLER, S.T.D.

Central Purchasing Service, Inc.—STEPHEN DEEDRICK, Dir., *1567 Loretta Ave., Ste. 212, Columbus, 43211.* Tel: 1-800-842-8319; 614-262-0010.

Catholic Charismatic Renewal, Inc.—Rev. JUSTIN J. REIS, Bishop's Liaison, *St. Bernadette, 1343 Wheeling Rd., Lancaster, 43130-8701.* Tel: 614-654-1893. MAXINE POWERS, Dir., *Catholic Charismatic Center, 4207 E. Broad St., Ste. C, Columbus, 43213.* Tel: 614-224-7147; Fax: 614-237-6847.

Columbus Family and Child Guidance Centers—WILLIAM J. HAMBOR, Pres. & C.E.O., *1490 E. Main St., Columbus, 43205.* Tel: 614-252-0731.

St. Vincent Campus—1490 E. Main St., Columbus, 43205. Tel: 614-252-0731.

Franklinton Office—840 W. State St., Columbus, 43222. Tel: 614-221-7855.

Wayne Avenue Center—880 S. Wayne Ave., Columbus, 43204. Tel: 614-272-0018.

Communication Office—MARK MORETTI, Media Rels., *197 E. Gay St., Columbus, 43215.* Tel: 614-241-2555.

Council of Religious—Sr. WANDA SCHERER, O.S.F., Pres., *197 E. Gay St., Columbus, 43215.* Tel: 614-241-2500.

Deaf Apostolate—Rev. STANLEY BENECKI, *Sts. Augustine and Gabriel, 1567 Loretta Ave., Ste. 111, Columbus, 43211.* Tel: 614-261-0339 (TDD); 268-3123 (Voice); Fax: 614-268-8130.

Department of Education—Rev. PAUL A. NOBLE, Vicar-Supt., *197 E. Gay St., Columbus, 43215.* Tel: 614-221-5829.

Diocesan Council of Catholic Women—MARGUERITE KRAUSE, Pres., *197 E. Gay St., Columbus, 43215.* Tel: 614-228-8601.

Development Office—HELMUT J. NAUNHEIMER, Dir., *197 E. Gay St., Columbus, 43215.* Tel: 614-241-2550.

Diocesan Finance Committee—FRANK BETTENDORF, Chm.; Most Rev. JAMES A. GRIFFIN; Rev. Msgr. STEPHAN J. MOLONEY; Rev. Msgr. JOSEPH M. HENDRICKS; Rev. Msgr. EDWARD F. TRENOR; Revs. PAUL NOBLE; ROBERT E. WILLMANN; ANN O'ROURKE; DONALD BORROR; HUGH DORRIAN; WILLIAM HEROLD; THOMAS MCAULIFFE; JAMES J. NOLL; W. MATTHEW BROWN, *198 E. Broad St., Columbus, 43215.* Tel: 614-224-1221.

Diocesan Finance Council—Most Rev. JAMES A. GRIFFIN; Rev. Msgr. JOSEPH M. HENDRICKS; Rev. Msgr. STEPHAN J. MOLONEY; JAMES J. NOLL, *198 E. Broad St., Columbus, 43215.* Tel: 614-224-1221.

Priests Personnel Board—Rev. Msgr. DAVID R. FUNK, Chm., *1860 Northam Rd., Columbus, 43221.* Tel: 614-488-6149.

Diocesan Retirement Plans for Priests, Lay Employees and Lay Teachers—Rev. Msgr. EDWARD F. TRENOR, Chm. Admin. Board for Plans. Tel: 614-237-0401.

Family Life Office—STEPHANIE JENEMANN, Dir., *197 E. Gay St., Columbus, 43215.* Tel: 614-241-2560.

Finance Office—JAMES J. NOLL, Dir., *198 E. Broad St., Columbus, 43215.* Tel: 614-224-1221; 224-1235.

Foundation of the Catholic Diocese of Columbus—KATHLEEN SPENCER, Exec. Dir., *197 E. Gay St., Columbus, 43215.* Tel: 614-241-2566.

Health Affairs Department (Hospitals)—Rev. Msgr. ANTHONY BORRELLI, Coord., *197 E. Gay St., Columbus, 43215.* Tel: 614-279-1690.

Holy Childhood, Pontifical Association—Sr. M. PAULETTE BOLL, O.P., Dir., *197 E. Gay St., Columbus, 43215.* Tel: 614-228-8603.

House of Retreats—MARY E. MURPHY, Dir., *St. Therese Retreat Center, 5277 E. Broad St., Columbus, 43213.* Tel: 614-866-1611.

Insurance—Diocesan Finance Office, 198 E. Broad St., Columbus, 43215. Tel: 614-224-1221.

J.O.I.N. (Joint Organization for Inner-City Needs)—Mrs. RUTH BECKMAN, Dir., *197 E. Gay St., Columbus, 43215.* Tel: 614-241-2530.

Legion of Mary—Rev. Msgr. CHARLES J. FOELLER, Dir., *Sacred Hearts Church, 4680 U.S. Rt. 42, Cardington, 43315.* Tel: 419-946-3611.

Liturgical Commission—Rev. JAMES P. BLACK, Chm., *212 E. Broad St., Columbus, 43215.* Tel: 614-224-1295.

Liturgy Office—Rev. LARRY J. HEMMELGARN, C.PP.S., Dir., *197 E. Gay St., Columbus, 43215.* Tel: 614-221-4640.

Ministry Formation Office—LESLIE J. YOUNG, Ph.D., Dir. JAMES HATFIELD, Coord., *197 E. Gay St., Columbus, 43215.* Tel: 614-241-2544.

Newspaper—"The Catholic Times"; Rev. CHARLES T. THOMAS, Editor pro-tem, *P.O. Box 636, Columbus, 43216.* Tel: 614-224-5195.

Missions Office—Sr. M. PAULETTE BOLL, O.P., Dir., *197 E. Gay St., Columbus, 43215.* Tel: 614-228-8603.

Pastoral Services, Office of—Sr. PHYLLIS DUGAN, S.N.D-.deN., Dir., *197 E. Gay St., 4th Floor, Columbus, 43215.* Tel: 614-228-1646.

Permanent Diaconate Program—Deacons FRANK A. IANNARINO, Dir. THOMAS V. JOHNSTON, Assoc. Dir. Formation, Office: *197 E. Gay St., Columbus, 43215.* Tel: 614-241-2545., School: *Pontifical College Josephinum, 7625 N. High St., Columbus, 43085.* Tel: 614-885-5585.

Personnel Services—JOAN THORNTON PALKUTI, Sec., *197 E. Gay St., Columbus, 43215.* Tel: 614-241-2590.

Priests Continuing Education—Rev. G. MICHAEL GRIBBLE, *St. Edward Church, 785 Newark Rd., Granville, 43023.* Tel: 614-587-3254.

Propagation of the Faith and Opus Sancti Petri—Sr. M. PAULETTE BOLL, O.P., Dir., *197 E. Gay St., Columbus, 43215.* Tel: 614-228-8603.

Printing Services—NANCY EYERMAN, Mgr., *197 E. Gay St., Columbus, 43215.* Tel: 614-224-0261.

Real Estate—DONALD A. BORROR, Consultant, *5501 Frantz Rd., P.O. Box 7166, Dublin, 43017.* Tel: 614-761-6000.

Religious Education Office—BARBARA ROMANELLO-WICHTMAN, Dir., *197 E. Gay St., Columbus, 43215.* Tel: 614-221-4633.

Retreats—MARY E. MURPHY, Dir., *St. Therese Retreat Center, 5227 E. Broad St., Columbus, 43213.* Tel: 614-866-1611.

Rural Life Apostolate—Deacon RALPH L. PARSONS, Assoc. Dir., *P.O. Box 28, West Jefferson, 43162-0028.* Tel: 614-879-7601; Fax: 614-879-7605.

St. Stephen's Community House—JUDITH STATTMILLER, Dir., *1500 E. 17th Ave., Columbus, 43219.* Tel: 614-294-6347; Fax: 614-294-0258.

St. Vincent de Paul Society—BILL WISSE, Pres., *197 E. Gay St., Columbus, 43215.* Tel: 614-221-3554.

St. Vincent de Paul Shop—424 E. Locust St., Lancaster, 43130. Tel: 614-653-6037.

Scout Chaplain—Deacon PETER C. LABITA, Dir., *Christ the King Church, 2770 Dover Rd., Columbus, 43209.*

Department of Social Concerns—MARK H. HUDDY, Dir., *197 E. Gay St., Columbus, 43215.* Tel: 614-241-2540.

Spanish Speaking Apostolate—Rev. EUGENE CAHOUET, O.P., *St. Patrick Church, 376 E. Naghten St., Columbus, 43215.* Tel: 614-240-5914; Fax: 614-469-9178.

Vocations Office—Rev. THEODORE K. SILL, Dir., *197 E. Gay St., Columbus, 43215.* Tel: 614-221-5565.

Youth Ministry Office—PATRICIA M. CLANCY, Dir., *197 E. Gay St., Columbus.* Tel: 614-241-2565.

CLERGY, PARISHES, MISSIONS AND PAROCHIAL SCHOOLS

CITY OF COLUMBUS
(Franklin County)

1—ST. JOSEPH CATHEDRAL (1878), Rev. Msgr. Joseph N. Fete, Rector; Revs. James P. Black; David M. Gwinner; Deacon Thomas Johnston. In res., Rev. Paul A. Noble.
Res., 212 E. Broad St., 43215. Tel: 614-224-1295; Fax: 614-224-1176.
Church—E. Broad St. & N. Fifth St., 43215.

2—ST. AGATHA (Upper Arlington) (1940), Rev. Msgr. David R. Funk; Sr. Mary Catherine Kaeppner, Pastoral Min. In res., Revs. Robert J. Schuer; Robert E. Willmann; John L. Bakle, S.M.
Res., 1860 Northam Rd., 43221. Tel: 614-488-6149; Fax: 614-488-6596.
School—2767 Andover Rd., 43221. Tel: 614-488-9000; Fax: 614-488-5783. Mrs. Joan Mastell, Prin.
Lay Teachers 22; Students 408.
Catechesis/Religious Programs—Tel: 614-488-4975. Mrs. Jeanne Altiero, D.R.E.
Students 368.

3—ST. AGNES (1954), Rev. William A. Metzger.
Res., 2364 W. Mound St., 43204-2997. Tel: 614-276-5413; Fax: 614-276-5608.
Catechesis/Religious Programs—Students 12.

4—ST. ALOYSIUS (1906), Rev. Dennis E. Stevenson, J.C.L., Admin. In res., Rev. Msgr. Donald C. Schulz.
Res., 32 Clarendon Ave., 43223. Tel: 614-276-6587.
Catechesis/Religious Programs—2350 W. Mound St., 43204. Tel: 614-276-5413; Fax: 614-276-5608.
Students 27.

5—ST. ANDREW (1955), Rev. Msgr. J. Colby Grimes; Rev. Thomas Buffer. In res., Rev. Mark Hammond.
Res., 1899 McCoy Rd., 43220. Tel: 614-451-4290; Fax: 614-451-8300.
School—McCoy Rd. & Reed Rd., 43220. Tel: 614-451-1626. Raenita Kownacki, Prin.
Lay Teachers 27students525.
Catechesis/Religious Programs—Tel: 614-451-2855. Ann Brown, D.R.E.
Students 229.

6—SAINT ANTHONY (1963), Rev. John L. Swickard; Mrs.

Colleen Buzenski, Pastoral Asst.
Res., 4913 Atwater Dr., 43229. Tel: 614-885-4857.
School—(Grades K-8) 1300 Urban Dr., 43229. Tel: 614-888-4268; Fax: 614-888-4435. Richard Shisler, Prin.
Lay Teachers 9; Students 260.
Catechesis/Religious Programs—(Grades 1-8). Tel: 614-888-8190. Judy McElwee, D.R.E.
Students 86.

7—STS. AUGUSTINE AND GABRIEL (1984), Rev. Stanley Benecki; Deacon Roger Pry.
Office: 1567 Loretta Ave., Ste. 111, 43211-1507. Tel: 614-268-3123; Fax: 614-268-8130.
Church—1550 E. Hudson St., 43211. Tel: TDD 614-261-0339.
Catechesis/Religious Programs—Students 37.

8—ST. CATHARINE (1931), Rev. Msgr. David V. Sorohan; Rev. Joseph John Trapp, II; Sr. Christella Ritchey, O.S.F., Pastoral Assoc.; Donald Kegelmeyer, Chap., Pastoral Care, Tel: 614-235-7495.
Res., 500 S. Gould Rd., 43209. Tel: 614-231-4509; Fax: 614-231-8366.
School—2865 Fair Ave., 43209. Tel: 614-235-1396; Fax: 614-231-8366. Mrs. Margaret Crabtree, Prin.
Lay Teachers 14; Students 226.
Catechesis/Religious Programs—Tel: 614-231-4500. Sr. Christella Ritchey, O.S.F., D.R.E.
Students 217.

9—ST. CECILIA (1882), Rev. Craig R. Eilerman. In res., Rev. Jan C. Sullivan.
Res., 434 Norton Rd., 43228. Tel: 614-878-5353; Fax: 614-878-0459.
School—440 Norton Rd., 43228. Tel: 614-878-3555. Sr. Regina Snyder, O.S.F., Prin.
Lay Teachers 14; Students 296.
Catechesis/Religious Programs—Tel: 614-878-0133. Richard Keyes, D.R.E.
Students 27.

10—CHRIST THE KING (1946), Rev. Msgr. Edward F. Trenor; Rev. R. Michael Ellifritz; Deacon Peter C. Labita. In res., Rev. Msgr. Clement F. Faistl.
Res., 2770 Dover Rd., 43209. Tel: 614-237-0401; Fax: 614-237-4689.
School—2855 E. Livingston Ave., 43209. Tel: 614-231-3391. Ms. Chris Iaconis, Prin.
Sisters of St. Dominic 2; Lay Teachers 10; Students 295.
Catechesis/Religious Programs—Tel: 614-231-8374. Karen Laihr, D.R.E.
Students 90.

11—ST. CHRISTOPHER (1947), Revs. Michael J. Reis; Arthur W. Wiles. In res., Rev. Jerome D. Stluka.
Res., 1420 Grandview Ave., 43212. Tel: 614-486-0457; Fax: 614-486-0433.
School—Trinity, 1381 Ida Ave., 43212. Tel: 614-488-7650. Mrs. Diane Hayhurst, Prin.
Sisters 1; Lay Teachers 12; Students 248.
Catechesis/Religious Programs—Susan Bellotti, D.R.E.
Students 123.

12—CORPUS CHRISTI (1925), Rev. Samuel E. Ritchey; Deacon J. Jerry Butts.
Res., 1111 E. Stewart Ave., 43206. Tel: 614-444-9871.

13—SANTA CRUZ (1993) (Spanish), Rev. Eugene Cahouet, O.P.
Res., St. Patrick Church, 376 E. Naghten St., 43215. Tel: 614-224-9522; Fax: 614-240-5928.
Church—256 E. Rich St., 43215. Tel: 614-469-9178.

14—ST. DOMINIC (1889) (African American), Rev. Thomas G. Petry; Deacon Robert A. Neely.
Mailing Address: P.O. Box 83572, 43203-0572.
Res., 453 N. 20th St., 43203. Tel: 614-252-4913.

15—ST. FRANCIS OF ASSISI (1892), Rev. Msgr. John K. Cody.
Res., 386 Buttles Ave., 43215. Tel: 614-299-5781; Fax: 614-299-2933.

16—ST. ELIZABETH (1967), Rev. Rodric J. DiPietro; Deacons Frank X. Ball; John J. Rericha.
Res., 1682 Lynnhurst Rd., 43229. Tel: 614-882-1782; Fax: 614-882-1782.
Church—6077 Sharon Woods Blvd., 43229. Tel: 614-891-0150; Fax: 614-891-3243.
Catechesis/Religious Programs—Tel: 614-891-0151.
Students 131.

17—ST. GABRIEL. Merged with St. Augustine. See separate listing.

18—HOLY CROSS (1833) (German), Rev. Msgr. James M. Berendt. In res., Rev. Msgr. Lawrence J. Corcoran, P.A.
Res., 204 S. Fifth St., 43215. Tel: 614-224-3416.

19—HOLY FAMILY (1877), Rev. Kevin F. Lutz.
Res., 43 S. Skidmore St., 43215-2724. Tel: 614-221-4323; Fax: 614-221-1687.

20—HOLY NAME (1905), Rev. Msgr. James L.T. Ruef.
Res., 154 E. Patterson Ave., 43202. Tel: 614-262-0390.

21—HOLY SPIRIT (Whitehall) (1947), Rev. Raymond Larussa.
Res., 4383 E. Broad St., 43213. Tel: 614-861-1521; Fax: 614-861-3746.
School—4382 Duchene Ln., 43213. Tel: 614-861-0475. Sr. Shawn Fitzpatrick, O.P., Prin.
Lay Teachers 10; Students 294.
Catechesis/Religious Programs—Tel: 614-861-4559. D.R.E.: Michael T. Millisor; Mary G. Murtha.
Students 40.

22—IMMACULATE CONCEPTION (1957), Rev. Anthony N. Missimi; Rev. Msgr. Thomas Bennett.
Res., 414 E. North Broadway, 43214. Tel: 614-267-9241.
School—366 E. North Broadway, 43214. Tel: 614-267-6579. Suzanne Wettinger, Prin.
Lay Teachers 20; Students 480.
Catechesis/Religious Programs—440 E. North Broadway, 43214. Tel: 614-267-0279. Christopher Campbell, D.R.E.
Students 104.

23—ST. JAMES THE LESS (1947), Revs. James H. Dugal, C.PP.S.; Scott T. Kramer, C.PP.S.; Deacon Joseph P. Checca. In res., Rev. Richard Nieberding, C.PP.S.
Res., 1652 Oakland Park Ave., 43224. Tel: 614-262-1179; 1170; Fax: 614-262-6798.
School—1628 Oakland Park Ave., 43224. Tel: 614-268-3311; Fax: 614-262-6798. Kathleen O'Reilly, Prin.
Lay Teachers 20; Students 441.
Catechesis/Religious Programs—Mary Souder, D.R.E.
Students 80.

24—ST. JOHN THE BAPTIST (1896) (Italian), Rev. Mario Serraglio.
Res., 720 Hamlet St., 43215. Tel: 614-294-5319; Fax: 614-294-4303.

25—COMMUNITY OF HOLY ROSARY AND ST. JOHN (1979), Revs. Robert J. Scullin, S.J.; James W. Hasse, S.J.; John E. Beez, S.J.; Bro. James F. Gates; Deacon James R. Davis.
Res., 648 S. Ohio Ave., 43205. Tel: 614-252-5926; Fax: 614-252-5933.
Catechesis/Religious Programs—Sr. Diane Kozlowski, O.P., D.R.E.
Students 70.

26—ST. LADISLAS (1908) (Hungarian), Rev. William D. Huber; Sr. Andrew Marie, S.C.N., Pastoral Assoc.; Deacon Frank X. McDevitt.
Res., 260 Reeb Ave., 43207. Tel: 614-444-5009.

27—ST. LEO (1903) (German), Rev. Arvids Bernans.
Res., 221 Hanford St., 43206. Tel: 614-443-7685; Fax: 614-443-6791.

28—ST. MARGARET OF CORTONA (1921), Rev. Msgr. Anthony Borrelli; Sr. Julianna D'Amato, O.P., Pastoral Assoc.
Res., 1600 Hague Ave., 43204-1606. Tel: 614-279-1690; Fax: 614-279-2386.
Catechesis/Religious Programs—Sharon Curtin, D.R.E.
Students 144.

29—ST. MARY (1865) (German), Rev. Michael B. Watson; Mary Koors, Pastoral Assoc. In res., Rev. Arthur J. Dimond.
Res., 684 S. Third St., 43206. Tel: 614-445-9668; Fax: 614-445-9669.
School—700 S. Third St., 43206. Tel: 614-444-8994; Fax: 614-444-8145. Kathleen McClernon, Prin.
Lay Teachers 13; Students 308.

30—ST. MARY MAGDALENE (1928), Revs. Charles E. Cotton; Carmen J. Arcuri. In res., Rev. Theodore K. Sill.
Res., 473 S. Roys Ave., 43204. Tel: 614-274-1121; Fax: 614-274-1122.
School—2940 Parkside Rd., 43204. Tel: 614-279-9935. Mary Ann Piela, Prin.
Lay Teachers 26; Students 444.
Catechesis/Religious Programs—Tel: 614-875-0346.
Students 52.

31—ST. MATTHIAS (1956), Rev. James T. Smith; Sr. Marie Shields, S.N.D.deN., Pastoral Assoc.
Res., 1582 Ferris Rd., 43224. Tel: 614-267-3406.
School—1566 Ferris Rd., 43224. Tel: 614-268-3030; Fax: 614-268-4681. Mr. Daniel Kinley, Prin.
Sisters 1; Lay Teachers 10; Students 296.
Catechesis/Religious Programs—Nancy Mead, D.R.E.
Students 85.

32—ST. MICHAEL (1946), Revs. William A. Dunn; Willis E. Everett; Deacons John R. Crerand; John Vellani; Mrs. Lorie Zelina, C.S.J., Pastoral Min.
Res., 5750 N. High St., Worthington, 43085. Tel: 614-885-7814; Fax: 614-885-3446.
School—64 E. Selby Blvd., Worthington, 43085-3986. Tel: 614-885-3149; Fax: 614-885-1249. Miss Christine Armbrust, Prin.
Religious 2; Lay Teachers 22; Students 612.
Catechesis/Religious Programs—Tel: 614-888-5384. Mrs. Carol O'Connor, D.R.E.
Students 235.

33—OUR LADY OF THE MIRACULOUS MEDAL (1967), Rev. Carl P. Clagett; Deacon Joseph D. Poland. Pastoral Assocs.: Mrs. Anita Remy; Deacon Stephen A. Venturini.
Res., 5225 Refugee Rd., 43232. Tel: 614-861-1242.
Catechesis/Religious Programs—Tel: 614-868-1414. Mrs. Sandy Venturini, D.R.E.
Students 155.

34—OUR LADY OF PEACE (1946), Rev. Msgr. Kenneth F. Grimes; Rev. Francis M. Stanton; Deacon John D. Rankin; Sr. Mary Agnes Jones, O.P., Pastoral Min.
Res., 20 E. Dominion Blvd., 43214. Tel: 614-263-8824; Fax: 614-263-3383.
School—40 Dominion Blvd., 43214. Tel: 614-267-4535. Carol Folian, Prin.
Lay Teachers 12; Students 267.
Catechesis/Religious Programs—Andrea McAuliffe, D.R.E.
Students 32.

35—OUR LADY OF VICTORY (1922), Rev. Msgr. Paul P. Enke; Deacon Richard L. Baumann.
Res., 1559 Roxbury Rd., 43212. Tel: 614-488-2428; Fax: 614-488-0507.
School—Trinity. See St. Christopher, Columbus for details. Tel: 614-486-7650.
Catechesis/Religious Programs—Tel: 614-486-7678. Sr. Patricia Rooks, S.N.D.deN., D.R.E.
Students 160.

36—ST. PATRICK (1852) (Irish), Revs. Kenneth A. France-Kelly, O.P.; Stephen D. Hayes, O.P.; Eugene Cahouet, O.P.; William Luke Tancrell, O.P.; James Jordan Lenagham, O.P.
Res., 376 E. Naghten St., 43215. Tel: 614-224-9522; Fax: 614-240-5928.

37—ST. PETER (1970), Rev. Msgr. John G. Johnson; Rev. Matthew Hoover; Deacons Joseph E. Schermer; Philip M. Paulucci; James Rouse.
Res., 6899 Smoky Row Rd., 43235-1998. Tel: 614-889-2221; Fax: 614-889-6612.
Catechesis/Religious Programs—Tel: 614-889-1407; Fax: 614-889-0543.
Students 814.

38—ST. PHILIP THE APOSTLE (1956), Rev. Leo L. Connolly; Sr. Mary Caryl Perkinson, O.S.F., Pastoral Assoc.; Deacon Joseph W. Farry. In res., Rev. Patrick W. Rogers.
Res., 1573 Elaine Rd., 43227. Tel: 614-237-1671; Fax: 614-231-8416.
School—1555 Elaine Rd., 43227. Tel: 614-237-5278; Fax: 614-231-8416. Janet J. Nungesser, Prin.
Sisters of St. Francis 1; Lay Teachers 11; Students 235.
Catechesis/Religious Programs—Tel: 614-237-6500. Brad Walters, D.R.E.
Students 50.

39—SAINT STEPHEN THE MARTYR (1963), Sr. Anne McCarrick, S.N.D.deN., Pastoral Admin.; Rev. John L. Bakle, S.M.; Rev. Msgr. Stephan J. Moloney.
Res., 4031 Clime Rd., 43228. Tel: 614-272-5200.
Catechesis/Religious Programs—Students 84.

40—ST. TIMOTHY (1961), Rev. Thomas Shonebarger. In res., Rev. Msgr. Michael A. Nugent; Rev. Joseph F. Jerabek.
Res., 1088 Thomas Ln., 43220. Tel: 614-451-2671.
School—1070 Thomas Ln., 43220. Tel: 614-451-0739; Fax: 614-451-3108. Norma A. Horan, Prin.
Lay Teachers 10; Students 225.
Catechesis/Religious Programs—Tel: 614-451-3867. Margaret Gercke, D.R.E.
Students 85.

41—SACRED HEART (1875), Rev. William H. DeVille. In res., Rev. James W. Jones.
Res., 893 Hamlet St., 43201. Tel: 614-299-4191; 4192.

42—SHRINE OF BLESSED MARGARET OF CASTELLO (1957), Rev. Kenneth A. France-Kelly, O.P., Dir.
262 N. Grant Ave., 43215-2623. Tel: 614-240-5917; Fax: 614-240-5928.

43—ST. THOMAS THE APOSTLE (1900), Rev. Ronald J. Atwood.
Res., 2692 E. Fifth Ave., 43219. Tel: 614-252-0976; Fax: 614-252-0977.
School—767 N. Cassady Ave., 43219. Tel: 614-252-7136. Sr. Petra Flavin, Prin.
Lay Teachers 9; Students 250.

44—KOREAN CATHOLIC COMMUNITY. Unassigned.
Mailing Address: 5500 Broadview Rd., Gahanna, 43230. Tel: 614-476-9974.

OUTSIDE THE CITY OF COLUMBUS

Ada, Hardin Co., Our Lady of Lourdes (1874), Rev. Daniel J. Millisor; Deacon John P. Stahl.
Res., 222 E. Highland Ave., 45810. Tel: 419-634-2626.
Catechesis/Religious Programs—Students 114.

Bremen, Fairfield Co., St. Mary (1917), Rev. Msgr.

Thomas G. Bender.
Res., 602 Marietta St., 43107. Tel: 614-569-4272. [CEM]
Catechesis/Religious Programs—Tel: 614-569-7724. Patricia Davis, D.R.E.
Students 75.

Bolivar, Tuscarawas Co., Holy Trinity (1995), Rev. Michael F. Nimocks.
Res., 141 Water St. S.W., 44612. Tel: 330-874-4716; Fax: 330-874-4461. [CEM]

Buckeye Lake, Licking Co., Our Lady of Mt. Carmel (1929), Rev. Msgr. Frank J. Meagher. Pastoral Assocs.: Betty Friend; Deacon Joe Farmer.
Res., P.O. Box 45, 5133 Walnut Rd. S.E., 43008. Tel: 614-928-3266.
Catechesis/Religious Programs—Tel: 614-928-3264. Silvia Zaborowski, D.R.E.
Students 118.

Cardington, Morrow Co., Sacred Hearts (1868), Rev. Msgr. Charles J. Foeller.
Res., 4680 U.S. Rte. 42, 43315. Tel: 419-946-3611.
Catechesis/Religious Programs—D.R.E.: Gene McCurdy; Molly McCurdy.
Students 74.

Chillicothe, Ross Co., St. Mary (1837), Rev. Donald E. Franks; Deacon George L. Lovensheimer.
Res., 61 S. Paint St., 45601. Tel: 614-772-2061; Fax: 614-772-2061. [CEM][JC]
School—Tel: 614-774-2970; Fax: 614-774-2998. James Condron, Prin.
Sisters 1; Lay Teachers 22.
Catechesis/Religious Programs—570 Parsons Ave., 45601.
Students 121.

St. Peter (1845) (German), Rev. Msgr. A. Anthony Frecker; Deacon Richard T. Krick. In res., Rev. Charles R. Griffin.
Res., 122 Church St., 45601. Tel: 614-773-4391. [CEM][JC]
School—Bishop Flaget Consolidated, (Grades PreK-8) 570 Parsons Ave., 45601. Tel: 614-774-2970; Fax: 614-774-2889. Mr. James Condron, Prin.
Lay Teachers 20; Students 334.
Catechesis/Religious Programs—Tel: 614-773-3455.
Students 158.

Circleville, Pickaway Co., St. Joseph's (1840), Rev. Robert F. Reilly. Pastoral Assocs.: Mary Kay Wood; Nancy Plescia; Deacon Mark A. Scarpitti.
Res., 134 W. Mound St., P.O. Box 659, 43113. Tel: 614-477-2549. [CEM]
Catechesis/Religious Programs—Theresa Jenkins, D.R.E.
Students 205.

Corning, Perry Co., St. Bernard (1882), Rev. John L. Metzger; Sr. Diana Durling, S.C., Pastoral Min.; Sr. Assunta Ghiloni, O.S.F., D.R.E.
Res., 425 Adams St., 43730. Tel: 614-347-4700.

Coshocton, Coshocton Co., Sacred Heart (1897), Rev. Msgr. Robert E. Schneider; Sr. Mary Emma Muckensturm, Pastoral Assoc.; Deacon Frank A. Duda.
Res., 805 Main St., 43812. Tel: 614-622-8817.
School—39 Burt Ave., 43812. Tel: 614-622-3728; Fax: 614-622-9151. Mrs. Jo Ann Guida, Prin.
Sisters of St. Dominic 1; Lay Teachers 8; Students(K-6) 147; Students PreK 38.
Catechesis/Religious Programs—(Grades PreK-6) 128 Burt Ave., 43812. Tel: 614-623-0882. Veronica Guinther, D.R.E.
Students 95.
Mission—Wills Creek, Coshocton Co., Our Lady of Lourdes, 805 Main St., 43812.

Crooksville, Perry Co., Church of the Atonement (1896), Rev. John M. Fulcher.
Res., 320 Winter St., 43731. Tel: 614-982-3816. [CEM]
Catechesis/Religious Programs—Patricia Musick, D.R.E.
Students 119.

Danville, Knox Co., St. Luke (1820), Rev. F. Richard Snoke.
Res., 307 S. Market St., P.O. Box P, 43014. Tel: 614-599-6362. [CEM]
Catechesis/Religious Programs—St. Luke Community Center, 7 W. Rambo, P.O. Box P, 43014-0616. Tel: 614-599-7367. Thomas Harrmann, D.R.E.
Students 177.

Delaware, Delaware Co., St. Mary (1835), Rev. Kevin J. Kavanagh; Sr. Cecilia Taphorn, C.PP.S., Pastoral Assoc.; Deacon Felix Azzola. In res., Rev. Larry J. Hemmelgarn, C.PP.S Tel: 614-369-9778.
Res., 82 E. William St., 43015. Tel: 614-363-4641; 548-6050; Fax: 614-363-9915. [CEM]
School—66 E. William St., 43015. Tel: 614-362-8961; Fax: 614-363-9915. Eleanor Wagner, Prin. (Grades PreK-8).
Lay Teachers 16; Students 327.
Catechesis/Religious Programs—Tel: 614-369-8228. Sandra Murray, D.R.E. (Grades K-8).

Students 272.

Dennison, Tuscarawas Co., Immaculate Conception (1871), Rev. Martin J. Ralko. In res., Rev. Kenneth F. Wise.
Res., 206 N. First St., 44621. Tel: 614-922-3533; Fax: 614-922-2486. [CEM]
School—100 Sherman St., 44621. Tel: 614-922-3539; Fax: 614-922-2486. John Zucal, Prin.
Lay Teachers 9; Students 170.
Catechesis/Religious Programs—Brenda McCloud, D.R.E.
Students 30.

Dover, Tuscarawas Co., St. Joseph (1849), Rev. William L. Arnold; Sr. Barbara Sir, C.S.J., Pastoral Assoc.; Deacons Ronald H. Fondriest; Mark D. Allison.
Res., 613 N. Tuscarawas Ave., 44622. Tel: 330-364-6661. [CEM 2]
School—600 N. Tuscarawas Ave., 44622. Tel: 330-343-9134; Fax: 330-343-3704. Sr. Valerie Shaul, O.P., Prin.
Lay Teachers 14; Students 251.
Catechesis/Religious Programs—Tel: 330-364-8257. Mrs. Linda Allison, D.R.E.
Students 251.

Dresden, Muskingum Co., St. Ann's (1889), Rev. Frank P. Miller.
Res., 405 Chestnut St., Box 107, 43821. Tel: 614-754-2221.
Catechesis/Religious Programs—Tel: 614-754-3018.
Students 67.
Mission—Mattingly Settlement, Muskingum Co., St. Mary, 6280 St. Mary's Rd., Nashport, 43830. [CEM]

Dublin, Franklin Co., St. Brigid of Kildare (1987), Rev. Msgr. Joseph M. Hendricks; Rev. David W. Sizemore; Deacons Frank A. Iannarino; Thomas W. Gornick; Jean Bonk, Dir. Liturgy/Music. In res., Rev. Msgr. Frank P. Lane.
Res., 7179 Avery Rd., P.O. Box 3130, 43016-0062. Tel: 614-761-3734; Fax: 614-889-6638.
School—7175 Avery Rd., 43017. Tel: 614-718-5825; Fax: 614-718-5831. Mr. Kevan Hartman, Prin.
Lay Teachers 18; Students 458.
Catechesis/Religious Programs—Tel: 614-761-1176. Mary Fran Cassidy, D.R.E.
Students 1,107.

Gahanna, Franklin Co., St. Matthew (1959), Rev. Msgr. Edward J. McFarland; Rev. David E. Getreu. In res., Rev. Msgr. Stephan J. Moloney.
Res., 807 Havens Corners Rd., 43230. Tel: 614-471-0212; Fax: 614-471-0247.
School—795 Havens Corners Rd., 43230. Tel: 614-471-4930; Fax: 614-471-2067. Carole G. Marsh, Prin.
Lay Teachers 24; Students 597.
Catechesis/Religious Programs—Tel: 614-471-2067; Fax: 614-471-2067. Julie Zarichny, D.R.E.
Students 558.

Granville, Licking Co., St. Edward the Confessor (1946), Rev. G. Michael Gribble; Deacon Paul C. Belhorn.
Res., 785 Newark Rd., 43023. Tel: 614-587-3254; Fax: 614-587-0149.
Catechesis/Religious Programs—Linda Baus, D.R.E.
Students 292.

Grove City, Franklin Co., Our Lady of Perpetual Help (1954), Rev. Msgr. Romano Ciotola; Sr. Maxine Shonk, O.P., Pastoral Assoc.
Res., 3710 Broadway, 43123. Tel: 614-875-3322; Fax: 614-875-3329.
School—3752 N. Broadway, 43123. Tel: 614-875-6779. Mr. William R. Groce, Prin.
Sisters 1; Lay Teachers 15; Students 412.
Catechesis/Religious Programs—Tel: 614-875-9345. Mrs. Martha J. Hurd, D.R.E.
Students 392.

Groveport, Franklin Co., St. Mary's (1871), Rev. J. Lawrence Reichert; Deacon Frederick J. Schmitt.
Res., 5684 Groveport Rd., 43125. Tel: 614-497-1324; Fax: 614-497-2706.
Catechesis/Religious Programs—Tel: 614-497-1437. Alice Doran, D.R.E.
Students 257.

Heath, Licking Co., St. Leonard (1962), Rev. Harold E. Schneider; Deacon Albert E. Cain.
Res., 57 Dorsey Mill Rd., 43056. Tel: 614-522-5270.
Catechesis/Religious Programs—Betty Witalec, D.R.E.
Students 92.

Hilliard, St. Brendan (1957), Rev. Msgr. William J. Maroon; Rev. Thomas J. Brosmer; Deacons Patrick J. Wiggins; Gilbert L. Plummer.
Res., 4475 Dublin Rd., 43026. Tel: 614-876-1272; Fax: 614-876-1482.
School—(Grades 1-8). Tel: 614-876-6132; Fax: 614-529-8929. Mary Lang, Prin.
Lay Teachers 18; Students 368.
Catechesis/Religious Programs—Tel: 614-876-9533.

Students 1,230.

Jackson, Jackson Co., Holy Trinity (1875), Rev. Msgr. Robert E. Metzger.
Res., 215 Columbia St., 45640. Tel: 614-286-1428. [CEM]
Catechesis/Religious Programs—Karen Ochsenbein, D.R.E.
Students 62.

Johnstown, Licking Co., Church of the Ascension (1912), Rev. Richard L. Metzger.
Res., 276 S. Main St., 43031. Tel: 614-967-7871. [CEM]
Catechesis/Religious Programs—Tel: 614-967-1203. Kathy Wahlenmaier, D.R.E.
Students 100.

Junction City, Perry Co., St. Patrick (1820), Rev. Msgr. Richard F. Dodd; Mr. Al Kunkler, Pastoral Assoc.
Res., 1170 S.R.668, 43748. Tel: 614-987-2691.
Catechesis/Religious Programs—Tel: 614-342-4591. Mary Sawtelle, D.R.E.
Students 67.

Kenton, Hardin Co., Immaculate Conception (1836), Rev. William J. Faustner.
Res., 215 E. North St., 43326. Tel: 419-675-1162. [CEM]
Parish Center—220 E. North St., 44326. Tel: 419-675-9461.
Catechesis/Religious Programs—Tel: 419-675-1162. Jean M. Bruner, D.R.E.
Students 56.

Lancaster, Fairfield Co., St. Bernadette (1963), Rev. Justin J. Reis.
Res., 1343 Wheeling Rd., 43130-8701. Tel: 614-654-1893.
School—1325 Wheeling Rd., 43130. Tel: 614-654-3137. Pam Eltringham, Prin.
Lay Teachers 7; Students 173.
Catechesis/Religious Programs—Tel: 614-468-2268. Mary Good, D.R.E.
Students 100.

St. Mark (1960), Rev. Ronald L. Arter; Rev. Msgr. Robert Moon; Sr. Rita Walker, O.P., Pastoral Min. In res., Rev. Msgr. Robert L. Noon.
Res., 324 Gay St., 43130. Tel: 614-654-2874. [JC]
Catechesis/Religious Programs—331 Gay St., 43130. Tel: 614-653-1229. Cheryl Oelker, D.R.E.
Students 160.

St. Mary (1818), Revs. Martin V. Weithman; Jack G. Maynard, S.F.O.; Jeffrey J. Coning; Sr. Mary Cecil Grandpre, O.P., Pastoral Assoc.
Res., 132 S. High St., 43130. Tel: 614-653-0997; Fax: 614-653-0337. [CEM]
School—309 E. Chestnut St., 43130. Tel: 614-654-1632; Fax: 614-654-0877. Carlton B. Rider, Prin.
Sisters of St. Dominic 1; Lay Teachers 20; Students 438.
Catechesis/Religious Programs—Tel: 614-653-5054; Fax: 614-653-0337. Sr. Louis Mary Passeri, O.P., D.R.E.
Students 155.

La Rue, Marion Co., St. Joseph's (1864), Rev. Joseph F. Losh.
Res., 285 N. High St., P.O. Box 347, 43332-0347. Tel: 614-499-3614.

Logan, Hocking Co., St. John (1841) (German), Rev. Richard J. Pendolphi; Deacon Frank A. Paniccia.
Res., 351 N. Market St., 43138. Tel: 614-385-2549; Fax: 614-380-2837. [CEM]
School—321 N. Market St., 43138. Tel: 614-385-2767. Tonya C. Stump, Prin.
Lay Teachers 5; Students 79.
Catechesis/Religious Programs—Tel: 614-385-8852. Lisa Lanning, D.R.E.
Students 54.

London, Madison Co., St. Patrick (1865) (German-Irish), Rev. Donald M. Maroon.
Res., 61 S. Union St., 43140. Tel: 614-852-0942. [CEM]
School—(Grades K-8) 226 Elm St., 43140. Tel: 614-852-0161. James Moeller, Prin.
Lay Teachers 9; Students 170.
Catechesis/Religious Programs—Students 235.

Marion, Marion Co., St. Mary (1864), Revs. James A. Klima; Rodney M. Damico. In res., Rev. Frederick Furey, SS.CC.
Res., 251 N. Main St., 43302. Tel: 614-382-2118; Fax: 614-382-2110. [CEM]
School—274 North Prospect St., 44302. Tel: 614-382-1607. Robert Dendinger, Prin.
Lay Teachers 15; Students 205.
High School—(Grades 7-12). Tel: 614-389-2381.
Lay Teachers 15; Students 145.
Catechesis/Religious Programs—Tel: 614-382-2262; Fax: 614-389-2110.
Students 278.

Marysville, Union Co., Our Lady of Lourdes (1869), Rev. John B. Bentz; Deacon Gordon T. Kunkler.
Res., 1033 W. Fifth St., 43040. Tel: 513-644-6020; Fax: 513-644-6020.

Catechesis/Religious Programs—Tel: 513-644-6030. Maryanne Feeney, D.R.E.
Students 251.

Millersburg, Holmes Co., St. Peter (1877), Rev. Ronald J. Aubry.
Res., 379 S. Crawford St., 44654-1463. Tel: 330-674-1671. [CEM][JC]
Catechesis/Religious Programs—Tel: 330-674-0333. Patricia A. Huebner, D.R.E.
Students 133.
Mission—Glenmont, Holmes Co., SS. Peter and Paul, SR 520, Glenmont, 44628.

Mineral City, Tuscarawas Co., Saint Patrick. Closed. For sacramental records contact Holy Trinity, Bolivar.

Mt. Vernon, Knox Co., St. Vincent de Paul (1842), Rev. Charles Theodore Thomas; Sr. Jean Welling, S.C., Pastoral Assoc.
Res., 303 E. High St., P.O. Box 587, 43050. Tel: 614-392-4711. [CEM]
School—206 E. Chestnut St., 43050. Tel: 614-393-3611. Deborah Leibold, Prin.
Lay Teachers 11; Students 199.
Catechesis/Religious Programs—Tel: 614-393-0826. Shirley Lower, D.R.E.
Students 176.

Murray City, St. Philip Neri. Closed. For inquiries for parish records contact the Chancery.

New Albany, Franklin Co., Church of the Resurrection (1983), Rev. Jerome P. Rodenfels; Sr. Sarah Gass, S.C., Pastoral Assoc.
Res., 6300 E. Dublin-Granville Rd., 43054. Tel: 614-855-1400; Fax: 614-855-0779.
Catechesis/Religious Programs—(Grades K-6). Mrs. Diana Leister, D.R.E.
Students 236.

Newark, Licking Co., St. Francis de Sales (1842), Revs. Dean Mathewson; Richard C. Weyls; Sr. Barbara Catalano, O.P., Pastoral Assoc.
Res., 66 Granville St., 43055. Tel: 614-345-9874. [CEM 2]
School—38 Granville St., 43055. Tel: 614-345-4049. Gretchen O'Neil, Prin.
Sisters of St. Dominic 2; Lay Teachers 20; Students 511.
Catechesis/Religious Programs—Tel: 614-349-7978.
Students 280. D.R.E.: Michael Barone; Eddie Cotter, (Junior High School).

Church of the Blessed Sacrament (1904), Rev. Timothy M. Hayes; Deacons Charles F. Stevens, (Retired); Jack W. Elam; Robert W. Ghiloni.
Res., 378 E. Main St., 43055. Tel: 614-345-4290. [JC]
School—15 Penny Ave., 43055. Tel: 614-345-4125; Fax: 614-345-6168. Joseph A. Rogers, Prin.
Lay Teachers 10; Students 230.
Catechesis/Religious Programs—Tel: 614-763-4304. Debbie Wills, D.R.E.
Students 54.

New Boston, Scioto Co., St. Monica (1915), Rev. Peter M. Gideon; Sr. Theresa Kehres, O.S.F., Pastoral Assoc.
Res., 4252 Pine St., 45662. Tel: 614-456-5154. [CEM]

Newcomerstown, Tuscarawas Co., St. Francis de Sales (1918), Rev. Edward L. Keck.
Res., 440 River St., 43832. Tel: 614-498-7368. [JC]
Catechesis/Religious Programs—Tel: 614-498-5403. Cindy Branch, D.R.E.
Students 115.

New Lexington, Perry Co., St. Rose of Lima (1867), Rev. John J. Dreese; Sr. Diana Durling, S.C., Pastoral Min.
Res., 309 N. Main St., 43764. Tel: 614-342-1348. [JC]
School—119 W. Water St., 43764. Tel: 614-342-3043; Fax: 614-342-3206. J. Steven Holekamp, Prin.
Lay Teachers 9; Students 151.
Catechesis/Religious Programs—Tel: 614-342-4581; 342-3043. Sr. Assunta Ghiloni, O.S.F., D.R.E.
Students 87.

New Philadelphia, Tuscarawas Co., Sacred Heart (1895), Rev. Msgr. George J. Schlegel. In res., Rev. Robert T. Manning.
Res., 139 3rd St., N.E., 44663-3900. Tel: 330-343-6976. [CEM 2]
School—320 Fair Ave., N.E., 44663-3914. Tel: 330-343-1721; Fax: 330-364-4334. Scott Power, Prin.
Lay Teachers 12; Students 204.
Catechesis/Religious Programs—Tel: 330-364-2527.
Students 94.

Otway, Scioto Co., Our Lady of Lourdes (1917), Rev. David E. Young.
Res., 2215 Galena Pike, West Portsmouth, 45663. Tel: 614-858-4600. [CEM]
Otway Community Service Center—P.O. Box 8, 45657. Tel: 614-372-2202. Tom Loar, Mgr.

Pickerington, Fairfield Co., Seton Parish (1978), Revs. Stephen B. Hawkins; Dennis S. Kigozi.
Res., 600 Hill Rd., 43147. Tel: 614-833-0482; Fax: 614-833-4154.
Catechesis/Religious Programs—Tel: 614-833-0485. Mrs. Mary Houze, D.R.E.
Students 850.

Plain City, Madison Co., St. Joseph (1864), Rev. Patrick A. Toner.
Res., 6604 Perry Pk., 43064. Tel: 614-873-8850; Fax: 614-873-8850.
Catechesis/Religious Programs—Heidi Kellett, D.R.E.
Students 85.
Mission—Milford Center, Union Co., Sacred Heart, P.O. Box 166, 43064.

Portsmouth, Scioto Co., St. Mary (1841) (German), Rev. John J. Marquis; Sr. Gavin Hagan, Pastoral Assoc.; Deacon George E. Horsley.
Res., 524 Sixth St., 45662. Tel: 614-354-4551; Fax: 614-354-4552. [CEM]
Catechesis/Religious Programs—Students 176.

Holy Redeemer (1852), Rev. Mark Ghiloni; Sr. Rita Hawk, S.C., Pastoral Assoc., Tel: 614-353-4425.
Office: 805 Offnere St., 45662. Tel: 614-353-4425. [CEM][JC]
School—Notre Dame Elementary, (Grades PreK-6). Serving all 7 parishes in Scioto County. 1401 Gallia St., 45662. Tel: 614-353-8610; Fax: 614-353-6769. Kay Kern, Prin.
Lay Teachers 20; Students 448.

Powell, Delaware Co., St. Joan of Arc (1987), Revs. Jeffrey J. Rimelspach; Raymond E. Lavelle; Frederick A. Loyd; Deacons Thomas M. Berg; James A. Rouse.
Res., 10700 Liberty Rd. S., 43065-9303. Tel: 614-761-0905; Fax: 614-761-0850.
Catechesis/Religious Programs—Tel: 614-761-0903; Fax: 614-761-0850. Natalie Hutchison, D.R.E.
Students 642.

Reynoldsburg, Franklin Co., St. Pius X (1958), Revs. Daniel L. Ochs; Joseph A. Ehwald; Theodore F. Machnik. Pastoral Assocs.: Sr. Catherine Sullivan, O.P.; Ms. Regina Courey.
Res., 1051 Waggoner Rd., 43068. Tel: 614-866-2859; Fax: 614-866-1499.
School—1061 Waggoner Rd., 43068. Tel: 614-866-6050. Catherine Fields, Prin.
Lay Teachers 25; Students 638.
Catechesis/Religious Programs—Tel: 614-864-3505. Anne Grossman, D.R.E.
Students 450.

Roswell, Tuscarawas Co., St. Elizabeth. Closed. For sacramental records contact Sacred Heart Parish, New Philadelphia.

Shawnee, Perry Co., St. Mary & St. Augustine. Closed. For sacramental records contact St. Rose of Lima Parish, New Lexington.

Somerset, Perry Co., St. Joseph's (1818), Rev. Adrian L. Dionne, O.P.; Deacon Eugene O. Dawson.
Res., 5757 State Rte. 383 N.E., P.O. Box 190, 43783. Tel: 614-743-1317. [CEM]

Holy Trinity (1827), Rev. Adrian L. Dionne, O.P.; Deacon Eugene O. Dawson.
Res., 5757 State Rte. 383 N.E., P.O. Box 190, 43783. Tel: 614-743-1317. [CEM]
School—S. Columbus St., 43783. Tel: 614-743-1324. Mr. David Hartline, Prin.
Sisters of St. Dominic 1; Lay Teachers 7; Students 144.
Catechesis/Religious Programs—Tel: 614-246-5719.
Students 58.

Strasburg, Tuscarawas Co., St. Aloysius (1911). Closed. For sacramental records contact Holy Trinity, Bolivar.

Sugar Grove, Fairfield Co., St. Joseph (1892), Rev. James A. Geiger.
Res., 306 Elm St., 43155. Tel: 614-746-8302. [CEM][JC]
Catechesis/Religious Programs—Tel: 614-746-8302. Kathy Krile, D.R.E.
Students 63.

Sunbury, Delaware Co., St. John Neumann (1981), Rev. James A. Walter; Mrs. Linda K. Haas, Pastoral Assoc.
Res., 275 Carters Corner Rd., 43074-9536.
Church—9633 E. State Rte. 37, 43074-9593. Tel: 614-965-1358.
Catechesis/Religious Programs—Tel: 614-965-4877. Robert J. Steinbauer, D.R.E.
Students 258.

Utica, Licking Co., Church of the Nativity (1909), Rev. Stephen A. Metzger, Admin.
Res., 271 Jefferson St., P.O. Box 506, 43080. Tel: 614-892-2321.
Catechesis/Religious Programs—Rose Gorius, D.R.E.
Students 70.

Wainwright, Tuscarawas Co., Parish Community of St. Therese and St. Paul. Closed. For St. Therese's sacramental records contact Immaculate Conception, Dennison. For St. Paul's sacramental records contact Sacred Heart, New Philadelphia.

Washington Court House, Fayette Co., St. Colman (1885), Rev. Jerome K. Raiser; Deacon William T. Whalen.
Office: 219 S. North St., 43160. Tel: 614-335-5000.
Res., 223 E. East St., 43160. [CEM]
Catechesis/Religious Programs—Tel: 614-335-5005. D.R.E.: Kathy Henry, (Grades PreK-5); Rita Wheaton, (Grades 6-12); Willie Germann.
Students 173.

Waverly, Pike Co., St. Mary, Queen of the Missions (1878), Rev. William J. Metzger.
Res., 407 S. Market St., 45690. Tel: 614-947-2436. [JC]
Catechesis/Religious Programs—Students 18.

Wellston, Jackson Co., SS. Peter and Paul (1881), Rev. Stephen Krile.
Res., 227 S. New York Ave., 45692. Tel: 614-384-2359. [CEM]
School—229 S. New York Ave., 45692. Tel: 614-384-6354. Sr. Joellen Kohlmann, Prin.
Franciscan Sisters of Christian Charity 3; Lay Teachers 4; Students 135.
Catechesis/Religious Programs—Students 9.

Westerville, Delaware Co., St. Paul the Apostle (1913), Rev. Msgr. Edward J. Fairchild; Revs. Homer D. Blubaugh; David A. Poliafico; Deacons Thomas Barford; William J.F. Davis.
Res., 313 N. State St., 43082. Tel: 614-882-2109; Fax: 614-891-7476.
School—61 Moss Rd., 43082. Tel: 614-882-2710; Fax: 614-882-5998. Anne O'Flynn, Prin.
Lay Teachers 28; Students 792.
Catechesis/Religious Programs—Tel: 614-882-5045. Janet Brewer, D.R.E.
Students 637.

West Jefferson, Madison Co., SS. Simon and Jude (1866) (German-Irish), Rev. Michael J. Devaney, O.M.I.; Deacon Ralph L. Parsons.
Res., 95 W. Main St., 43162-1295. Tel: 614-879-8562. [CEM]
Catechesis/Religious Programs—Tel: 614-878-0611; Fax: 614-853-3553.
Students 120.

West Portsmouth, Scioto Co., Our Lady of Sorrows (1944), Rev. David E. Young.
Res., 2215 Galena Pike, 45663. Tel: 614-858-4600.
New To You Service Center—Mary Horn, Dir.
Catechesis/Religious Programs—P.O. Box 31, Otway, 45657. Tel: 614-372-7115.
Students 117.
Mission—Pond Creek, Scioto Co., Holy Trinity, 2215 Galena Pike, 45663.

Wheelersburg, Scioto Co., St. Peter (1855), Rev. Peter M. Gideon.
Res., 2167 Lick Run Lyra Rd., 45694. Tel: 614-574-5486. [CEM]
Catechesis/Religious Programs—Nancy Stegman, D.R.E.
Students 145.

Zaleski, Vinton Co., St. Sylvester (1862), Rev. James L. Colopy.
Res., 22 N. Second St., 45698. Tel: 614-596-5474. [CEM]

Zanesville, Muskingum Co., St. Nicholas (1842) (German), Revs. Charles F. Klinger; Dwayne A. McNew. Pastoral Assocs.: Sr. Anne Marie Selinsky, O.S.F.; Sr. Nadine Overbeck, O.S.F.; Deacons B. N. Peterson, Jr.; James P. Feerick.
Res., 925 E. Main St., 43701. Tel: 614-453-0597; Fax: 614-453-0590. [CEM]
School—1030 E. Main St., 43701. Tel: 614-453-2637. Sr. Leonette Kochan, O.S.F., Prin.
Franciscan Sisters of Christian Charity 4; Lay Teachers 12; Students 310.
Catechesis/Religious Programs—Tel: 614-453-3931. Judy Schiele, D.R.E.
Students 145.

St. Thomas Aquinas (1820), Revs. Thomas V. DiFede, O.P.; Joseph Ambrose Eckinger, O.P.; William P. Garrott, O.P. Pastoral Assocs.: Sr. Teresa Sommer, O.P.; Sr. Edwina Devlin, O.P.
Res., 130 N. Fifth St., 43701. Tel: 614-453-3301; Fax: 614-453-0333. [CEM 3]
School—139 N. Fifth St., 43701. Tel: 614-454-9731; Fax: 614-454-9732. Mr. Brad Changet, Prin.
Lay Teachers 9; Students 265.
Catechesis/Religious Programs—Melanie Von Gunten, D.R.E.
Students 150.
Mission—Philo, Muskingum Co., St. Ann, 79 Main St., Philo, 43771. Tel: 614-674-6448.

Chaplains of Public Institutions

COLUMBUS. *Children's Hospital*. Rev. Jan C.P. Sullivan.

Regency Manor. Rev. Samuel E. Ritchey.

CHILLICOTHE. *Chillicothe Correctional Institution*. Rev. Charles R. Griffin, Mailing Address: P.O. Box 5500, 45601. Tel: 614-773-2616, Ext. 248. Res., 122 Church St., 45601. Tel: 614-773-4391.

Ross Correctional Institution and Honor Camp. Rev. Charles R. Griffin, Mailing Address: P.O. Box 7010, 45601. Tel: 614-774-4182, Ext. 2519. Res., 122 Church St., 45601. Tel: 614-773-4391.

Veteran's Affairs Medical Center, 17273 S.R. 104, 45601. Tel: 614-773-1141. Rev. Jonathan D. Lao (Philippines).

LANCASTER. *Southeastern Correctional Institution*. Tel: 614-653-4324. Rev. Edward L. Kessler, Chap., Res., P.O. Box 264, Sugar Grove, 43155. Tel: 614-746-8007.

LONDON. *London Correctional Institution*. Rev. Patrick A. Toner Tel: 614-852-2454, Ext. 451.

LUCASVILLE. *Southern Ohio Correctional Facility*. Vacant. Tel: 614-259-5544.

MARION. *Marion Correctional Institution*. Rev. Frederick G. Furey, SS.CC. Tel: 614-382-5781, Ext. 346.

MARYSVILLE. *Ohio Reformatory for Women*. Rev. John B. Bentz. Tel: 513-642-1065; Deacon Gregory L. Eiden, 305 Acton Rd., Columbus, 43214. Tel: 614-267-7500.

MOUNT VERNON. *Mount Vernon State Institute*. St. Vincent de Paul Parish, 303 E. High St., 43050. Tel: 614-392-4711. Rev. P. Wayne Meyer Tel: 614-397-5094.

ORIENT. *Orient Correctional Institution*. Vacant.

Special Assignment:
Reverend Fathers—
Kessler, Thomas, Gethsemani Abbey, Trappist, KY
Sprenger, Alan M., Exec. Dir., Syntaxis, Inc., 5300 N. Hamilton Rd., Gahanna, OH 43230. Tel: 614-855-1224; 855-1333

On Duty Outside the Diocese:
Reverend Monsignors—
Spiers, Edward F., Chap., St. Joseph Hospital, 590 Central Dr., Southern Pines, NC 28387
Reverend Fathers—
Ascencio, Joseph A., Chap., Federal Prison System, CO
Byrne, Patrick J., Chap., V.A. Medical Center, 1202 N.W. 16th St., Miami, FL 33125. Tel: 305-324-4455, Ext. 3258
Martin, Thomas, St. Edward Church, Mendan, MI
Naughton, Patrick J., Holy Trinity, 520 S. Hanover St., Nanticoke, PA
Pickett, James, Good Sheperd Church, Pittsburg, CA
Schilder, David M., Chap., Elkton Federal Correctional Institution, Elkton

Military Chaplains:
Reverend Fathers—
Hummer, Lawrence L.

Graduate Studies:
Reverend Fathers—
Bay, Joseph N.
Klein, Terrance W.

Leave of Absence:
Reverend Fathers—
Hanrahan, Michael F.
Loyd, Frederick A.
Smith, Paul O.
Thomas, Raymond E.
Virginia, Stephen G.

Retired:
Reverend Monsignors—
Applegate, P.A Bennett, 793 W. State St., Columbus, OH 43222
Carroll, James, 12915 Galaxy Dr., Sun City W., AZ
Corcoran, Lawrence J., Holy Cross, 204 S. 5th St., Columbus, OH 43215
Dittoe, John T., 3547 Chowning Ct., Columbus, OH 43220
Faistl, Clement, Christ the King Church, 2770 Dover Rd., Columbus, OH 43209
Griffin, Patrick, 3881 Montorey Dr., Grove City, OH 43123
Hanley, James P., 2492 Timberside Dr., Columbus, OH 43235
Healey, Edward, 5415-B5 Yorkshire Terrace Dr., Columbus, OH 43232
Huntzinger, Ralph, 8797 State Rte. 273 W., Belle Center, OH 43310-9580
Noon, Robert L., St. Mark Church, 324 Gay St., Lancaster, OH 43130
Nugent, Michael A., St. Timothy Church, 1088 Thomas Ln., Columbus, OH 43220
Schmidt, Robert R., Seton Square East, 1235 Briarcliff Rd, #126, Reynoldsburg, OH 43068
Schulz, Donald C., St. Aloysius Church, 32 Clarendon Ave., Columbus, OH 43223
Schweitzer, Francis X.
Schwendeman, Francis J., 427 Strecker Ln., Marietta, OH 45750
Winel, Roland T., P.A., Nazareth Towers, 300 E. Rich St., Apt. 1306, Columbus, OH 43215
Wolf, John V., 104 N. Mulberry St., Fredericktown, OH 43019-1051. Tel: 614-694-2505
Reverend Fathers—
Buzek, Joseph L., 1858 Maywood Rd., Winter Park, FL 32792
Carter, Raymond J., 5325-301 Portland St., Columbus, OH 43235
Connor, William J., 10248 W. Snead Cir. N., Sun City, AZ 85351
Dermody, Ralph R., 2 Lake View Dr., Mt. Vernon, OH 43050
Dimond, Arthur, St. Mary, 684 S. 3rd St., Columbus, OH 43206
Durbin, Clement B., Sharon Brook Inn, 920 Sharon Vally Rd., #219, Newark, OH 43055
Engle, Richard F., 192 Grand Ave., Chillicothe, OH 45601
Essman, Charles P., Thurber Towers, 645 Neil Ave. #409, Columbus, OH 43215
Gamba, John J., P.O. Box 184, Doylestown, OH 44230
Gately, Robert E., P.O. Box 40232, St. Petersburg, FL 33743
Graf, John H., 155 Primrose Ln., McDermott, OH 45652
Haluska, Charles A., 37950 TR 344, Rte. 3, Warsaw, OH 43844
Jerabeck, Joseph F., St. Timothy Church, 1088 Thomas Ln., Columbus, OH 43220
Jones, Bernard P., c/o Desert Amethyst, 18170 N. 91st Ave., Apt. 1140, Peoria, AZ 18170
Kessler, Edward L., 107 W. 4th St., P.O. Box 264, Sugar Grove, OH 43155
Klee, Robert A., St. Charles Preparatory School, 2010 E. Broad St., Columbus, OH 43209
Laurinaitis, Saulius P., 4460 Dublin Rd., Columbus, OH 43221
Manning, Robert T., Sacred Heart, 139 3rd St. N.E., New Philadelphia, OH 44663
Marzluf, George J., 7807 Rockville Rd.S.W., Navarre, OH 44662
McClory, Bernard J.
McNulty, Edwin J., St. Rita Home, 880 Greenlawn Ave., Columbus, OH 43223
Meyer, Paul Wayne, 406 E. High St., Mount Vernon, OH 43050
Patterson, William C., St. Joseph Adoration Monastery, 2311 Stockham Ln., Portsmouth, OH 45662
Schaefer, Francis R., 11438 E. Huffman Rd. #4, Cleveland, OH 44130
Schuer, Robert J., St. Agatha, 1860 Northam Rd., Columbus, OH 43221
Stanton, Joseph, St. Leo Church, 221 Hanford St., Columbus, OH 43206
Tabit, Michael J., 617 Harrow St., Gahanna, OH 43230
Totten, Raymond F., 329 Carnegie Pl., Pittsburgh, PA 15208
Wise, Kenneth F., Immaculate Conception Church, 206 N. First St., Dennison, OH 44621

Permanent Deacons:
Allison, Mark D., St. Joseph, Dover
Azzola, Feliz F., St. Mary, Delaware
Ball, Frank X., St. Elizabeth, Columbus
Barford, Thomas M., St. Paul, Westerville
Baumann, Richard L., Our Lady of Victory, Columbus
Belhorn, Paul C., St. Edward, Granville
Berg, Thomas M., St. Joan of Arc, Powell
Bonacci, Anthony C., St. Joseph, Plain City
Butts, Jerome J., Corpus Christi, Columbus
Cain, Albert E., St. Leonard, Heath
Checca, Joseph P., St. James the Less, Columbus
Crerand, John R., St. Michael, Worthington
Davis, James R., Holy Rosary-St. John Community, Columbus
Davis, William J.F., St. Paul, Westerville
Dawson, Eugene O., St. Joseph, Somerset
Duda, Frank A., Sacred Heart, Coshocton
DuPrey, John L., Leave of Absence
Eiden, Gregory L., St. Francis of Assisi, Columbus
Elam, Jack W., Blessed Sacrament, Newark
Farmer, Joseph A., (Retired)
Farry, Joseph W., St. Philip, Columbus
Feerick, James P., (Retired)
Fondriest, Ronald H., St. Joseph, Dover
Franks, Michael J., Sr., St. Francis, Newark
Ghiloni, Robert W., Blessed Sacrament, Newark
Gorman, William J., Leave of Absence
Gornick, Thomas W., St. Brigid of Kildare, Dublin
Hann, Daniel W., Chap., Madison Correctional Institution
Horsley, George E., St. Mary, Portsmouth
Iannarino, Francis A., St. Brigid of Kildare, Dublin
Johnston, Thomas V., St. Joseph Cathedral, Columbus
Koebel, Lawrence F., Chap., Pickaway Correctional Institute
Krick, Richard T., St. Peter, Chillicothe
Kruse, David J., St. Elizabeth Ann Seton, Pickerington
Kunkler, Gordon T., Our Lady of Lourdes, Marysville
Labita, Peter C., Christ the King, Columbus
Lampe, Elmer L., Unassigned
Larcomb, Dwight T., Leave of Absence
Lovensheimer, George L., St. Mary, Chillicothe
McCurry, William E., County Sheriff's Office, Marion
McDevitt, Francis X., St. Ladislas, Columbus
Neely, Robert A., St. Dominic, Columbus
Paniccia, Frank A., St. John, Logan
Parsons, Ralph L., Sts. Simon & Jude, West Jefferson
Paulucci, Philip M., St. Peter, Columbus
Peterson, Burdette N., St. Nicholas, Zanesville
Plummer, Gilbert L., Sr., St. Brendan, Hilliard
Poland, Joseph D., Leave of Absence
Pry, Roger F., Sts. Augustine & Gabriel, Columbus
Rankin, John, Our Lady of Peace, Columbus
Rericha, John J., St. Elizabeth, Columbus
Rouse, James A., St. Peter, Columbus
Rzewnicki, Phil E., Unassigned
Scarpitti, Mark A., St. Joseph, Circleville
Schermer, Joseph E., St. Peter, Columbus
Schmitt, Frederick J., St. Mary, Groveport
Spina, Philip V., Jr., Leave of Absence
Stevens, Charles F., (Retired)
Vellani, Albert J., St. Michael, Worthington
Venturini, Stephen A., Our Lady of the Miraculous Medal, Columbus
Whalen, William T., St. Colman, Washington Court House
Wiggins, Patrick J., St. Brendan, Hilliard

INSTITUTIONS LOCATED IN THE DIOCESE

[A] SEMINARIES, DIOCESAN

COLUMBUS. *Pontifical College Josephinum*, 7625 N. High St., 43235-1498. Tel: 614-885-5585; Fax: 614-885-2307.

General Administrative Offices: Most Revs. Agostino Cacciavillan, Pro-Nuncio, Chancellor; James A. Griffin, J.D., J.C.L., Bishop of Columbus & Vice Chancellor; Rev. Msgr. Thomas J. Olmsted, J.C.D., Pres. & Rector; Mr. Patrick J. O'Reilly, Treas.; Dr. Byron W. Thorsen, Registrar; Mr. Peter Veracka, Dir. of the Library.

Theology Administrative Offices: Rev. Brian R. Moore, Ph.D. (DOD), Academic Dean; Mary Patricia Mulligan, M.A., Dir. Field Education School Theology & Dir. M.Div. Program; Revs. Richard J. Tomasek, S.J., S.T.L., Dir. Spiritual Formation; Roger P. Cooney, M.A. (COV), Vice Rector Theology & Dean of Men. Priests on Theology Teaching Staff: Revs. Robert J. Bauer, S.D.B., S.S.L.; John D. Corbett, O.P.; Jiri Kasny, S.D.B.; William D. Lynn, S.J., S.T.D.; William Dettling, O.P., S.T.D. Theology Teaching Staff: Sr. Carolyn Thomas, S.C.N., Ph.D.; Rev. James Keating, Ph.D.; Jose Pedrozo, Ph.D., Candidate; James A. Yeager, D.M.A.

College Administrative Offices: Steven Snyder, Ph.D., Academic Dean; Revs. Andrew J. Umberg, Dean of Students & Dir. of Pastoral Works; Robert A. Gonzales, Ph.D. (TUC); Thomas L. Gwozdz, S.D.B., Dir. Spiritual Formation; Charles A. Jackson, S.T.L., Coord. Personal Formation; John J. Moriarty, S.J. College Teaching Staff: Alma Amell, Ph.D.; David J. DeLeonardis, Ph.D. In res. Rev. Msgr. Anthony A. Kleinschmidt, B.L.S. (SCL). Total Staff 26; Total Enrollment 118.

[B] COLLEGES AND UNIVERSITIES

COLUMBUS. *Ohio Dominican College*, 1216 Sunbury Rd., 43219. Tel: 614-253-2741; Fax: 614-252-0776.
E-mail: admissions@odc.edu
Web site: http://www.odc.edu
For a complete listing, refer to the Colleges and Universities section.

[C] HIGH SCHOOLS, DIOCESAN OR INTERPAROCHIAL

COLUMBUS. *Bishop Hartley High School*, 1285 Zettler Rd., 43227. Tel: 614-237-5421.
E-mail: jsilcott@cd.pvt.k12.oh.us

Jim Silcott, Prin.; Don Burger, Dean of Students; Erskine Braggs, Athletic Dir. Religious 1; Lay Teachers 38; Students 540.

Bishop Ready High School, 707 Salisbury Rd., 43204. Tel: 614-276-5263; Fax: 614-276-5116. Celene A. Seamen, Prin. Lay Teachers 31; Students 475.

Bishop Watterson High School, 99 E. Cooke Rd., 43214. Tel: 614-268-8671.
Web site: http://www.cd.pvt.kiz.oh.us/schools/bw/
Mr. John J. Durant, Prin. Deacons 1; Sisters 1; Lay Teachers 63; Students 1,072. Convent, 100 Indian Springs Dr., 43214.

St. Charles Preparatory School, 2010 E. Broad St., 43209. Tel: 614-252-6714.
E-mail: dcavello@cd.pvt.k12.oh.us
Web site: www.cd.pvt.kiz.oh.us/schools/sc/index.html
Dominic J. Cavello, Prin.; Scott M. Pharion, Asst. Prin.; James Lower, Asst. Prin.; Rev. Msgr. Thomas M. Bennett; Rev. Msgr. F. Thomas Gallen; Sr. Margaret Hoffman. Lay Teachers 35; Students 487.

St. Francis de Sales High School, 4212 Karl Rd., 43224. Tel: 614-267-7808.
Web site: http://www.cd.pvt.kiz.oh.us
Mr. Patrick D. Rossetti, Prin.; Mr. Dan Garrick, Asst. Prin.; Ms. Molly Feesler, Asst. Prin. Convent, 4212 Karl Rd., 43224. Lay Teachers 48; Students 891.

LANCASTER. *William V. Fisher Catholic High School*, 1803 Granville Pike, 43130. Tel: 614-654-1231. Sr. Gail Morgan, O.P., Prin. Sisters 2; Lay Teachers 21; Students 309.

MARION. *Marion Catholic High School*, 1001 Mt. Vernon Ave., 43302; Fax: 614-389-5243.
E-mail: mchs@cd.pvt.k12.oh.us
Suzanne A. Emsweller, Prin. Lay Teachers 15; Students 145.

NEW PHILADELPHIA. *Central Catholic High School*, 777 Third St., N.E., 44663. Tel: 216-343-3302.
E-mail: NCCTJM@OMERESA.OHIO.GOV
Web site: http://webl.tusco.net/tcc/
Joe Martin, Prin. Lay Teachers 10; Students 178.

NEWARK. *Newark Catholic High School*, 1 Green Wave Dr., 43055. Tel: 614-344-3594.
E-mail: bhill@cd.pvt.K12.oh.us
Susie Gribble, Campus Min. Lay Teachers 24; Students 261.

PORTSMOUTH. *Notre Dame High School*. (Grades 7-12), 2220 Sunrise Ave., 45662. Tel: 614-353-0719. Kathleen Milligan, Prin. Sisters 1; Lay Teachers 18; Students 195.

ZANESVILLE. *Bishop Rosecrans High School*, 1040 E. Main St., 43701. Tel: 614-452-7504.
E-mail: jbrannon@cd.pvt.k12.oh.us
Joseph Brannon, Ph.D., Prin.; Rev. Dwayne A. McNew. Priests 1; Lay Teachers 16; Students 243.

[D] MONTESSORI SCHOOLS

COLUMBUS. *St. Joseph Montessori School*, 933 Hamlet St., 43201-3595. Tel: 614-291-8601.
E-mail: dbarton@cd.pvt.kiz.oh.us
Donna Barton, Admin. Lay Teachers 25; Students 267.

St. Mary of the Springs Montessori School, 2320 Airport Dr., 43219. Tel: 614-258-0024.
E-mail: pat.maloney@juno.com
Web site: http://www.odc.edu/sisters
Sr. Sheila Marie McIntyre, O.P., Sec.; Sr. Marietta Miller, O.P., Admin. Sisters 3; Lay Teachers 5; Students 75.

[E] GENERAL HOSPITALS

COLUMBUS. *Holy Cross Care Services, Inc. dba Northland Terrace Medical Center*, 5700 Karl Rd., 43229. Tel: 614-846-5420; Fax: 614-846-3247
For a complete listing, refer to the Hospitals section.

Mohun Health Care Center, 2320 Airport Dr., 43219. Tel: 614-253-8517.
E-mail: springscomm@juno.com
Web site: http://www.odc.edu/sisters
For a complete listing, refer to the Hospitals section.

Mount Carmel Health System, 793 W. State St., 43222. Tel: 614-234-5423; Fax: 614-234-5985
For a complete listing, refer to the Hospitals section.

ZANESVILLE. *Good Samaritan Medical Center*, 800 Forest Ave., 43701. Tel: 614-454-5000
For a complete listing, refer to the Hospitals section.

[F] PROTECTIVE INSTITUTIONS

COLUMBUS. *Rosemont Center*, 2440 Dawnlight Ave., 43211. Tel: 614-471-2626.
E-mail: rmarx@rosemont.org
Web site: http://www.rosemont.org
For a complete listing, refer to the Special Care Facilities section.

[G] HOMES FOR AGED AND HOUSING FOR ELDERLY

COLUMBUS. *Nazareth Towers*, 300 E. Rich St., 43215. Tel: 614-464-4780; Fax: 614-464-1733
For a complete listing, refer to the Special Care Facilities section.

St. Raphael Home for the Aged, Inc., 1550 Roxbury Rd., 43212. Tel: 614-486-0436; Fax: 614-486-1640
For a complete listing, refer to the Special Care Facilities section.

St. Rita Home, 880 Greenlawn Ave., 43223. Tel: 614-443-9433; Fax: 614-443-1196
For a complete listing, refer to the Special Care Facilities section.

Seton London, Inc. 350 Cambridge Dr. London, 43140. Tel: 614-852-4233.
For a complete listing, refer to the Special Care Facilities section.

Seton South Columbus, Inc., 155 Highview Blvd., 43207. Tel: 614-492-9944
For a complete listing, refer to the Special Care Facilities section.

Seton Square North, 1776 Drew Ave., 43235. Tel: 614-451-1995
For a complete listing, refer to the Special Care Facilities section.

Seton Washington Court House, Inc. 400 N. Glenn Ave. Washington Court House, 43160. Tel: 614-335-2292.
For a complete listing, refer to the Special Care Facilities section.

COSHOCTON. *Seton Coshocton, Inc.*, 377 Clow Ln., 43812. Tel: 614-451-1995
For a complete listing, refer to the Special Care Facilities section.

DOVER. *Seton Square Dover, I, Inc.*, 501 James St., 44622. Tel: 330-343-3611
For a complete listing, refer to the Special Care Facilities section.

Seton Square Dover, II, Inc., 139 Fillmore St., 44622. Tel: 330-343-3611
For a complete listing, refer to the Special Care Facilities section.

KENTON. *Seton Kenton, Inc.*, 699 Morningside Dr., 43326. Tel: 419-673-7202
For a complete listing, refer to the Special Care Facilities section.

LANCASTER. *Seton Lancaster, Inc.*, 232 Gay St., 43130. Tel: 614-681-1403
For a complete listing, refer to the Special Care Facilities section.

MARION. *Seton Square Marion, Inc.*, 255 Richland Rd., 43302. Tel: 614-389-4746
For a complete listing, refer to the Special Care Facilities section.

REYNOLDSBURG. *Seton Square East, Inc.*, 1235 Briarcliff Rd., 43068. Tel: 614-861-4860
For a complete listing, refer to the Special Care Facilities section.

WELLSTON. *Seton Square Wellston, Inc.*, 570 W. First St., 45692. Tel: 614-384-6174
For a complete listing, refer to the Special Care Facilities section.

ZANESVILLE. *Seton Housing, Inc.*, 516 Sheridan St., 43701. Tel: 614-453-4422
For a complete listing, refer to the Special Care Facilities section.

[H] MONASTERIES AND RESIDENCES OF PRIESTS AND BROTHERS

COLUMBUS. *Salesian Center*, 80 S. 6th St., 43215. Tel: 614-224-8000.
E-mail: sdbcol@aol.com
Web site: www.salesians.org
Revs. Steven Shafran, S.D.B., Dir.; Robert Bauer, S.D.B.; James Hurley, S.D.B., Exec. Dir. Boys & Girls Club; William Bucciferro, S.D.B., Youth Min. & Vice Dir.; Jiri Kasny, S.D.B.; Thomas L. Gwozdz, S.D.B. Students of Theology 6; Brothers 1; Total Staff 40; Total Assisted 15.

NEWARK. *P.I.M.E. Mission & Prayer Center*, 2734 Seminary Rd. S.E., 43056-9339. Tel: 614-928-4246; Fax: 614-928-1512. Revs. Dino S. Vanin, P.I.M.E., Rector; James Coleman, P.I.M.E.; Ronald Boccali, P.I.M.E.; Casto Marrapese, P.I.M.E.; Charles Sala, P.I.M.E. Total in Residence 5.

SOMERSET. *St. Joseph's Rectory*, 5757 State Rte. 383 N.E., P.O. Box 190, 43783. Tel: 614-743-1317. Rev. Adrian L. Dionne, O.P. Total Staff 2; Total in Residence 1.

WEST JEFFERSON. *SS. Simon and Jude*, 95 W. Main St., 43162-1225. Tel: 614-879-8562. Rev. Michael J. Devaney, O.M.I.; Deacon Ralph L. Parsons.

[I] CONVENTS AND RESIDENCES FOR SISTERS

COLUMBUS. *Our Lady of Bethlehem Convent*, 4567 Olentangy River Rd., 43214. Tel: 614-451-3900. American Region of the Sisters of the Poor Child Jesus. Sr. Frances Teresa Holzberger, P.C.J., Reg. Supr. Sisters 5.

Our Lady of Bethlehem Early Child Education Center. Sisters 1; Lay Teachers 17; Children 215.

St. Mary of the Springs, 2320 Airport Dr., 43219-2098. Tel: 614-252-2137.
E-mail: sheila.mcintyre@juno.com
Leadership Team: Sr. Mary Faith Geelan, O.P., Prioress; Sr. Anne Kilbride, O.P., Vicaress; Sr. Sheila Marie McIntyre, O.P., Councilor, Secretary-General; Sr. Ellen Dunn, O.P., Councilor; Sr. Arleen Kisiel, O.P., Councilor.
Sisters' Residence: Sr. Barbara Jinks, O.P., Supr.

Mohun Health Care Center. Sr. Jacqueline Baum, O.P., Admin.; Sr. Johanna Eberly, O.P., Dir. of Resident Life; Rev. Benedict Joseph, O.P., Chap. Sisters 120; Novices 1; Candidates 1; Total in Congregation 331.

Sisters of Notre Dame de Namur, 85 S. Roys Ave., 43204. Tel: 614-276-9521.

Sisters of the Good Shepherd, 2440 Dawnlight Ave., 43211. Tel: 614-471-2626. Sr. M. Denise Wigman, R.G.S., Supr. Sisters of Our Lady of Charity of the Good Shepherd 10; Total Staff 100.

Sisters of the Holy Cross, Our Lady of Mount Carmel Convent. 1750 Lane Rd., 43220. Tel: 614-459-0727. Sisters 4. 1381A Bluff Ave., 43221. Tel: 614-481-9390. Legal Title: *Sisters of the Holy Cross, Inc.*

PORTSMOUTH. Oratory. *St. Joseph Adoration Monastery, Poor Clares of Perpetual Adoration*, 2311 Stockham Ln., 45662-3049. Tel: 614-353-4713. Mother Mary Agnes, Abbess. Professed Cloistered Nuns 6; Extern Sisters 1.

[J] NEWMAN CENTERS

COLUMBUS. *Campus Ministry*. P.O. Box 587, Mt. Vernon, 43050. Tel: 614-291-4674. Ohio State University, 64 W. Lane Ave., 43201. Revs. David W. O'Brien, C.S.P., Dir.; Vincent W. McKiernan, C.S.P.; Donald A. Andrie, C.S.P.; Charles Theodore Thomas, Diocesan Dir. Campus Min., P.O. Box 587, Mt. Vernon, 43050.

[K] FOUNDATIONS

COLUMBUS.
**The Foundation of the Catholic Diocese of Columbus*, 197 E. Gay St., 43215. Tel: 614-241-2566. Kathy Spencer, Exec. Dir.

Legacy of Catholic Learning Endowment Program, 198 E. Broad St., 43215. Tel: 614-224-1221. Ann Ball, Coord.

LANCASTER.
**William V. Fisher Catholic High School Endowment Fund*, 1803 Granville Pike, 43130.

MARION. *Marion Catholic High School Endowment Fund*, 1001 Mount Vernon Ave., 43302.
E-mail: mchs@cd.pvt.k12.oh.us

NEW PHILADELPHIA. *Tuscarawas Central Catholic High School Endowment Fund*, 777 Third St. N.E., 44663.

NEWARK.
**Newark Catholic High School Endowment Fund*, One Green Wave Dr., 43055.

ZANESVILLE. *Bishop Rosecrans High School Foundation*, 1040 E. Main St., 43701. Tel: 614-452-7504.

[L] MISCELLANEOUS

COLUMBUS. *Blessed Margaret Guild, Inc.*, 262 N. Grant Ave., 43215. Tel: 614-240-5915; 240-5917; Fax: 614-240-5928. Rev. Kenneth A. France-Kelly, O.P., Exec. Dir. Total Staff 3.

Catholic Alumni Club, P.O. Box 695, 43216.
E-mail: rdardis@cas.org
Peggy Schano, Contact Person. Tel: 614-263-7686; Dan Doell, Contact Person. Tel: 614-846-7489; Rich Dardis. Tel: 614-851-0406.

The Christ Child Society of Columbus, Inc., P.O. Box 340091, 43234. Mrs. Susan L. Dilworth, Pres.

Diocesan Retirement Community Corp., 25 Noe-Bixby Rd., 43213. Mrs. Carol Oravec, Project Coord.

St. Stephen's Community House, 1500 E. 17th Ave., 43219. Tel: 614-294-6347; Fax: 614-294-0258.
E-mail: 75147.2073@cserve.org
Ms. Judith Stattmiller, Exec. Dir. Total Assisted 22,000; Total Staff 95.

The Villas at St. Therese Assisted Living, Inc., 25 Noe-Bixby Rd., 43213. Tel: 614-864-3576. Mrs. Carol Oravec, Project Coord.; Joseph M. Hendricks, Contact Person.

The Villas at St. Therese Independent Living, Inc., 25 Noe-Bixby Rd., 43213. Tel: 614-864-3576. Mrs. Carol Oravec, Project Coord.; Joseph M. Hendricks, Contact Person.

LANCASTER.
**St. Mary of the Assumption Foundation*, 132 S. High St., 43130. Tel: 614-653-0997; Fax: 614-653-0337. Martin V. Weithman, Contact Person.

ZANESVILLE. *St. Nicholas Foundation*, 925 E. Main St., 43701. Tel: 614-453-0597; Fax: 614-453-0590.
E-mail: charlie@nick@prodigy.net

RELIGIOUS INSTITUTES OF MEN REPRESENTED IN THE DIOCESE

For further details refer to the corresponding bracketed number in the Religious Institutes of Men or Women section.

[0350]—*Cistercians Order of the Strict Observance-Trappists.*—O.C.S.O.
[1140]—*Fathers of the Sacred Hearts.*—SS.CC.
[0690]—*Jesuit Fathers and Brothers.* (Detroit, Maryland, and Sri Lanka Provs.).—S.J.
[0910]—*Oblates of Mary Immaculate.*—O.M.I.
[0430]—*Order of Preachers-Dominicans.* (Prov. of St. Joseph).—O.P.
[1030]—*Paulist Fathers.*—C.S.P.
[1050]—*Pontifical Institute for Foreign Missions.*—P.I.M.E.
[1190]—*Salesians of St. John Bosco.*—S.D.B.
[0760]—*Society of Mary.*—S.M.
[1060]—*Society of the Precious Blood.* (Cincinnati Prov.).—C.PP.S.

RELIGIOUS INSTITUTES OF WOMEN REPRESENTED IN THE DIOCESE

[0330]—*Carmelite Sisters for the Aged and Infirm.*—O.Carm.
[1920]—*Congregation of the Sisters of the Holy Cross.*—C.S.C.
[1730]—*Congregation of the Sisters of the Third Order of St. Francis, Oldenburg, IN.*—O.S.F.
[1710]—*Congregation of the Third Order of St. Francis of Mary Immaculate, Joliet, IL.*—O.S.F.
[1070-02]—*Dominican Sisters.*—O.P.
[1070-13]—*Dominican Sisters.*—O.P.
[1070-25]—*Dominican Sisters.*—O.P.
[1230]—*Franciscan Sisters of Christian Charity.*—O.S.F.
[1440]—*Franciscan Sisters of the Poor.*—S.F.P.
[3790]—*Institute of the Sisters of St. Dorothy.*—S.S.D.
[3210]—*Poor Clares of Perpetual Adoration.*—P.C.P.A.
[1070-03]—*Sinsinawa Dominican Congregation of the Most Holy Rosary.*—O.P.
[0440]—*Sisters of Charity of Cincinnati, Ohio.*—S.C.
[0500]—*Sisters of Charity of Nazareth, Kentucky.*—S.C.N.
[0990]—*Sisters of Divine Providence.*—C.D.P.
[2575]—*Sisters of Mercy of the Americas.* (Detroit & St. Louis Provs.).—R.S.M.
[3000]—*Sisters of Notre Dame de Namur.*—S.N.D.deN.
[1630]—*Sisters of St. Francis of Penance and Christian Charity.* (Stella Niagara, NY).—O.S.F.
[1530]—*Sisters of St. Francis of the Congregation of Our Lady of Lourdes, Sylvania, OH.*—O.S.F.
[3830-05]—*Sisters of St. Joseph.*—C.S.J.
[3830-08]—*Sisters of St. Joseph.*—C.S.J.
[3830-13]—*Sisters of St. Joseph.*—C.S.J.
[1830]—*Sisters of the Good Sheperd.*—R.G.S.
[3220]—*Sisters of the Poor Child Jesus.*—P.C.J.
[3260]—*Sisters of the Precious Blood.* (Dayton, OH).—C.PP.S.
[3320]—*Sisters of the Presentation of the B.V.M.*—P.B.V.M.
[1760]—*Sisters of the Third Order of St. Francis of Penance and of Charity.*—O.S.F.
[1720]—*Sisters of the Third Order Regular of St. Francis of the Congregation of Our Lady of Lourdes.*—O.S.F.
[4120-04]—*The Ursuline Nuns of Cleveland.*—O.S.U.

DIOCESAN CEMETERIES

COLUMBUS. *Mount Calvary*, 581 Mt. Calvary Ave., 43223-2217. Tel: 614-491-2751. Rich Finn, Dir. & Gen. Mgr.

LEWIS CENTER. *Resurrection*, 9571 N. High St., 43035-9413. Tel: 614-888-1805. Rich Finn, Dir. & Gen. Mgr.

LOCKBOURNE. *St. Joseph*, 6440 S. High St., 43137-9208. Tel: 614-491-2751. Rich Finn, Dir. & Gen. Mgr.

PATASKALA. *Holy Cross*, 11539 National Rd. S.W., 43062-8304. Tel: 614-927-4442. Rich Finn, Dir. & Gen. Mgr.

NECROLOGY

† Emmert, Roger A., Columbus, OH, St. Joseph Cathedral. —Died Feb. 1, 1997.
† Miller, Wayne E., Columbus, OH, Our Lady of Victory. —Died May 28, 1997.

Diocese of Corpus Christi

(Dioecesis Corporis Christi)

Most Reverend

ROBERTO O. GONZALEZ, O.F.M.

Bishop of Corpus Christi; ordained May 1977; appointed Titular Bishop of Ursona and Auxiliary Bishop of Boston July 19, 1988; ordained Bishop October 3, 1988; appointed Coadjutor Bishop of Corpus Christi May 16, 1995; transferred to Corpus Christi June 26, 1995; succeeded to See April 1, 1997. *Res., 4109 Ocean Dr., Corpus Christi, TX, 78411. Office: 620 Lipan St., P.O. Box 2620, Corpus Christi, TX, 78403-2620.* Tel.: 512-882-6191.

Most Reverend

RENE H. GRACIDA, D.D.

Bishop Emeritus of Corpus Christi; ordained May 23, 1959; appointed Titular Bishop of Masuccaba and Auxiliary of Miami December 6, 1971; consecrated January 25, 1972; appointed Bishop of Pensacola-Tallahassee October 1, 1975; transferred to Corpus Christi May 19, 1983; installed July 11, 1983; retired April 1, 1997. *Res., 4126 Ocean Dr., Corpus Christi, TX, 78411-1224. Office: 620 Lipan St., P.O. Box 2620, Corpus Christi, TX, 78403-2620.* Tel.: 512-882-6191.

ERECTED A VICARIATE APOSTOLIC IN 1874; ELEVATED TO A DIOCESE MARCH 23, 1912.

Square Miles 17,294.

The territory embraced by the Diocese of Corpus Christi comprises the Counties of Aransas, Bee, Brooks, Duval, Jim Hogg, Jim Wells, Kleberg, Kenedy, Live Oak, Nueces, Refugio, San Patricio, Webb, Zapata, and parts of LaSalle and McMullen in the State of Texas.

For legal titles of parishes and diocesan institutions, consult the Chancery Office.

The Chancery Office: 620 Lipan St., P.O. Box 2620, Corpus Christi, TX, 78403-2620. Tel.: 512-882-6191; Fax: 512-882-1018; 883-8850.

Web site address: www.goccn.org

STATISTICAL OVERVIEW

Personnel	
Bishop	1
Retired Bishops	1
Abbots	1
Retired Abbots	1
Priests: Diocesan Active in Diocese	77
Priests: Active Outside Diocese	9
Priests: Diocesan in Foreign Missions	1
Priests: Retired, Sick or Absent	25
Number of Diocesan Priests	112
Religious Priests in Diocese	57
Extern Priests in Diocese	5
Ordinations:	
Diocesan Priests	3
Religious Priests	6
Transitional Deacons	1
Permanent Deacons	2
Permanent Deacons in Diocese	67
Total Brothers	18
Total Sisters	274
Parishes	
Parishes	86
With Resident Pastor:	
Resident Diocesan Priests	51
Resident Religious Priests	21
Without Resident Pastor:	
Administered by Priests	10
Administered by Permanent Deacons	4
Missions	59
Pastoral Centers	10
Professional Ministry Personnel:	
Brothers	7
Sisters	35
Lay Ministers	48
Welfare	
Catholic Hospitals	6
Total Assisted	405,685
Homes for the Aged	2
Total Assisted	151
Residential Care of Children	1
Total Assisted	59
Day Care and Extended Day Care Centers	3
Total Assisted	215
Specialized Homes	2
Total Assisted	1,120
Special Centers for Social Services	8
Total Assisted	27,141
Residential Care of Disabled	1
Total Assisted	4
Other Institutions	1
Total Assisted	2,120
Educational	
Seminaries, Diocesan	1
Students from This Diocese	1
Diocesan Students in Other Seminaries	27
Seminaries, Religious	1
Students Religious	4
Total Seminarians	32
High Schools, Diocesan and Parish	1
Total Students	550
High Schools, Private	1
Total Students	423
Elementary Schools, Diocesan and Parish	22
Total Students	3,456
Elementary Schools, Private	5
Total Students	1,120
Catechesis/Religious Education:	
High School Students	3,983
Elementary Students	15,256
Total Students Under Catholic Instruction	24,820
Teachers in the Diocese:	
Priests	3
Sisters	69
Lay Teachers	383
Vital Statistics	
Receptions into the Church:	
Infant Baptism Totals	5,497
Adult Baptism Totals	228
Received into Full Communion	1,025
First Communions	5,104
Confirmations	5,646
Marriages:	
Catholic	1,093
Interfaith	152
Total Marriages	1,245
Deaths	2,310
Total Catholic Population	362,500
Total Population	808,146

Former Bishops—Rt. Rev. DOMINIC MANUCY, cons. Dec. 8, 1874; transferred to Mobile March 9, 1884 reappointed to Vicariate Apostolic of Brownsville Feb. 1, 1885; died Dec. 4, 1885, before taking possession.—Rt. Rev. PETER VERDAGUER, cons. Nov. 9, 1890; died Oct. 26, 1911.—Rt. Rev. PAUL JOSEPH NUSSBAUM, C.P., D.D., cons. May 20, 1913; resigned March 26, 1920; Bishop of Marquette; appt. Nov. 14, 1922; died June 24, 1935.—Most Rev. EMMANUEL B. LEDVINA, D.D., LL.D., appt. April 30, 1921; cons. June 14, 1921; Assistant at Pontifical Throne May 30, 1931; resigned March 15, 1949; died Dec. 15, 1952.—Most Rev. MARIANO S. GARRIGA, D.D., LL.D., Coadjutor *cum jure successionis,* appt. June 20, 1936; cons. Sept. 21, 1936; succeeded to See March 15, 1949; assistant at Pontifical Throne April 14, 1951; died Feb. 21, 1965.—Most Rev. THOMAS J. DRURY, D.D., Fourth Bishop of Corpus Christi; Bishop of San Angelo; appt. Oct. 16, 1961; cons. Jan. 24, 1962; fourth Bishop of Corpus Christi; appt. July 19, 1965; installed Sept. 1, 1965; retired Bishop of Corpus Christi; appt. May 19, 1983; died July 22, 1992.—Most Rev. RENE H. GRACIDA, D.D., Bishop Emeritus; Fifth Bishop of Corpus Christi; appt. Titular Bishop of Masuccaba and Auxiliary of Miami Dec. 6, 1971; cons. Jan. 25, 1972; appt. Bishop of Pensacola-Tallahassee Oct. 1, 1975; transferred to Corpus Christi May 19, 1983; installed July 11, 1983; retired April 1, 1997.

Diocesan Curia—620 Lipan St., P.O. Box 2620, Corpus Christi, 78403-2620. Most Rev. ROBERTO O. GONZALEZ, O.F.M., Bishop of Corpus Christi; Rev. Msgr. RICHARD SHIRLEY, Vicar General; Rev. Msgr. THOMAS MEANY, Exec. Dir. to the Bishop's Office & Episcopal Vicar, Eastern Vicariate; Rev. THOMAS DAVIS, Episcopal Vicar, Western Vicariate; Rev. Msgr.

LEONARD D. PIVONKA, J.C.D., Judicial Vicar; Rev. ALEX SALAZAR, Chancellor; Mr. GREGOR SEAGRAVE, Fiscal Officer.

Bishop's Cabinet—620 Lipan St., P.O. Box 2620, Corpus Christi, 78403-2620. Tel: 512-882-6191. Mr. MARTY WIND, Sec. for Communications; Sr. KATHLEEN MCDONAGH, I.W.B.S., Sec. for Consecrated Life; Deacon STANLEY MILLSAP, Sec. for Deacons & Personnel Svcs.; Dr. FRANK LUCIDO, Sec. for Education; Rev. Msgr. LEONARD D. PIVONKA, J.C.D., Sec. for Health Care; Rev. Msgr. THOMAS MCGETTRICK, Sec. for Priests; Revs. ROBERT DUNN, Sec. for Pastoral Svcs. GLENN NULLAN, Sec. for Seminary Formation & Vocations; Rev. Msgr. ROBERT FREEMAN, P.A., Sec. for Social Svcs.

Consultative Bodies—620 Lipan St., P.O. Box 2620, Corpus Christi, 78403-2620.

Council Of Religious—Sr. KATHLEEN MCDONAGH, I.W.B.S.

Deans—Alice, Rev. EDUARDO GARCIA; *Beeville,* Rev. Msgr. JOHN KILEEN; *Corpus Christi Central,* Rev. Msgr. LAWRENCE WHITE; *Kingsville,* Rev. ROGER SMITH; *Laredo,* Rev. Msgr. JAMES HARRIS; *Refugio,* Rev. CELESTINE MURRAY.

Diaconal Screening Committee—Rev. BRADLEY BARBER, Clergy; Sr. KATHLEEN MCDONAGHUE; Ms. IRENE MEANY, Laity; Dr. MARSHALL VORIS; Dr. SHIRLEY GOOD; Mrs. SANDRA CARLISLE; Deacons JAMES CARLISLE; RICARDO COSTLEY; JERRY MORALES; STANLEY MILLSAP, Sec. for Deacons.

Finance Council—Most Rev. ROBERTO O. GONZALEZ, O.F.M.; Rev. Msgr. RICHARD SHIRLEY; Rev. Msgr. THOMAS MEANY; Rev. GREGORY DEAN; Sr. AGNES MARIE TENGLER, I.W.B.S.; Mrs. ROBIN PERRONE, C.P.A.; Mr. CECILE CARLISLE; Mr. THOMAS DURAN; Mr. J. PATRICK HEARN; Mr. CABAS B. ZAPATA, III; Mr. ARMENGOL GUERRA, III. Consultants: Mr. GREGOR SEAGRAVE; Mr. GARY A. RAMIREZ.

Personnel Board - Priests—Rev. Msgr. RICHARD SHIRLEY, V.G., Chm.; Rev. MATTHEW LYNG; Rev. Msgr. STANLEY SLIWIAK; Rev. MARK CHAMBERLIN; Rev. Msgr. JAMES HARRIS; Revs. RANDY CAIN; PAUL HESSE.

Presbyteral Council—Revs. ROGER SMITH, Chm. MARK CHAMBERLIN, Vice Chm. CELESTINE MURRAY, Sec.

Telecommunications Corporation—MARTY WIND, Exec. Vice Pres. & Gen. Mgr.

Tribunal—Rev. Msgr. LEONARD PIVONKA, J.C.D., V.J., Judicial Vicar; Sr. MARY WALDEN, O.S.U., Dir. Western Vicariate, *1901 Corpus Christi, Laredo, 78043.* Tel: 956-717-9968.

Judges—Revs. THOMAS P. FEENEY; JAMES HAMILTON; DONALD DOWNEY, J.C.L.; Deacon BRUCE AYCOCK.

Advocates—Rev. Msgr. JAMES HARRIS, V.E.; Rev. MORGAN ROWSOME; Sr. PATRICK BRUEN, O.L.C.; Sr. MARY WALDEN, O.S.U.; Sr. MARIE ELISE VAN DIJK, C.D.P.; Deacons ANTONIO CASTILLO; ANTONIO LARA; RAUL ROSALES; CRISPIN O. SOTO; JOHN SUTHERLAND; ANASTACIO BERNAL; LEONAL SAN MIGUEL; M. M. HORSEMAN; EMMA GONZALEZ; MARIO ALAMEIDA; MARY ALICE AMAYA; MARY C. CHRISTMAS; FRANCES COLLING; EVELYN MANSHEIM; BETTY PARKOS; BERNICE QUINTANILLA; CY RICHARDS; GRACIE SOSA; TED STRASSER, JR.; ELLEN STRASSER.

Defenders of the Bond—Rev. Msgr. MICHAEL HERAS; Rev. ROGER SMITH.

Notaries-Secretaries—SARA VARGAS; BELINDA HARRIS.

Villa Maria, Inc., Board—Rev. Msgr. ROBERT E. FREEMAN, P.A., Pres.; Sr. PATRICK BRUEN, O.L.C.; BRIAN CHAMBERLIN.

Administrative Offices

The Chancery Office—620 Lipan St., P.O. Box 2620, Corpus Christi, 78403-2620. Tel: 512-882-6191; Fax: 512-882-1018 (Admin.); 883-8850 (Fiscal Office). Office Hours: Mon.-Fri., 8:30-5. Closed holy days and holidays.

Office of the Bishop—Most Rev. ROBERTO O. GONZALEZ, O.F.M.

Office of the Bishop Emeritus—Most Rev. RENE H. GRACIDA, D.D.

Secretary for Canonical Affairs—Rev. Msgr. LEONARD D. PIVONKA, J.C.D.

Master Of Ceremonies to the Bishop—Rev. FRANCISCO LOPEZ.

Master of Ceremonies to the Bishop Emeritus—Rev. JOHN OUELLETTE.

Secretary to Bishops for Appointments—ANNA DE LEON.

Vicar General—Rev. Msgr. RICHARD SHIRLEY, V.G.

Judicial Vicar—Rev. Msgr. LEONARD D. PIVONKA, J.C.D.

Secretary for Pastoral Services—Rev. ROBERT DUNN.

Executive Director to the Bishop's Office—Rev. Msgr. THOMAS MEANY.

Secretary for Deacons—Deacon STANLEY MILLSAP.

Secretary for Priests—Rev. Msgr. THOMAS P. MCGETTRICK.

Chancellor—Rev. ALEX SALAZAR.

Family Life Office—Rev. ROBERT DUNN.

Fiscal Officer—GREGOR SEAGRAVE.

C.P.A.—PAUL A. DAMEROW.

Catholic Sharing Appeal—Mr. DALE BAIRD, Devel. Consultant.

Data Processing Office—PAUL DAMEROW, Supvr.

Human Life Office—Rev. ROBERT DUNN.

Office of Worship—NELDA CRUG MUNGUIA, Dir.

Personnel Office—Deacon STANLEY MILLSAP.

Propagation of the Faith Office—Rev. MICHAEL HOWELL.

Secretary for Seminary Formation & Vocations—Rev. GLENN MULLAN, *Corpus Christi Catholic Center, 3036 Saratoga, Corpus Christi, 78415.* Tel: 512-851-0908.

The Corpus Christi Pastoral Center—1200 Lantana St., Corpus Christi, 78407. Tel: 512-289-6501; Fax: 512-289-1867. Office Hours: Closed holy days and holidays.

Archives—Mr. CY RICHARDS, III, Archivist Mon.-Thurs. 9-2.

Catholic Schools Office—Dr. FRANK LUCIDO, Supt., *Corpus Christi Catholic Center, 3036 Saratoga, Corpus Christi, 78415.* Tel: 512-814-0444.

Catholic Cemeteries—Deacon LUIS TREVINO, Dir. Tel: 512-289-1528.

Diocesan Telecommunications Corporation—Tel: 512-289-6437. MARTY WIND, Sec. for Communications.

Education—Dr. FRANK LUCIDO, Supt., *Corpus Christi Catholic Center, 3036 Saratoga, Corpus Christi, 78415.* Tel: 512-814-0475.

Corpus Christi Catholic Center—3036 Saratoga, Corpus Christi, 78415. Tel: 512-814-0475. Office Hours: Mon.-Fri. 8:30-5. Closed holy days and holidays.

Natural Family Planning - Understanding Sexuality—4639 Corona, Ste. 13B, Corpus Christi, 78411. Tel: 512-852-0222; 852-2067. JANE TISDALE, Dir.

Maintenance & Construction Office—Mr. BILL TRBULA, Mgr.

Newspaper "The South Texas Catholic"—Most Rev. ROBERTO O. GONZALEZ, Publisher; PAULA ESPITIA, Editor. Tel: 512-289-1752.

Pastoral Institute For Ministry and Christian Service—Rev. BRADLEY A. BARBER, Dir., *Corpus Christi Catholic Center, 3036 Saratoga, Corpus Christi, 78415.* Tel: 512-814-5030.

Office for Persons with Disabilities—Rev. DAVID WALSH, C.Ss.R., Dir., *Corpus Christi Catholic Center, 3036 Saratoga, Corpus Christi, 78415.* Tel: 512-814-2181.

Real Property Office—WILLIAM TAGLIABUE, Mgr. Tel: 512-289-1528.

Religious Education—Dr. FRANK LUCIDO, Diocesan Coord., *Corpus Christi Catholic Center, 3036 Saratoga, Corpus Christi, 78415.* Tel: 512-814-5689.

Office of Youth And Young Adult Ministry—TONI CHAPA, Dir., *Corpus Christi Catholic Center, 3036 Saratoga, Corpus Christi, 78415.* Tel: 512-814-3806.

Episcopal Vicar for Western Vicariate for the Diocese of Corpus Christi—Rev. THOMAS DAVIS, *555 Del Mar Blvd., Laredo, 78041.* Tel: 956-722-6251.

Religious Education Office—Sr. MARIA GUADALUPE HERRERA, R.S.M., Laredo Area Coord., *1512 Logan St., Laredo, 78040.* Tel: 956-722-0950; Fax: 956-722-2238.

Other Offices and Organizations

Adoption Services—ROXANNA GUERRA, Admin., *1901 Corpus Christi St., Laredo, 78044.* Tel: 956-722-2443.

Alhambra—Mr. JAMES BRANNIGAN, Grand Commander, *429 Troy, Corpus Christi, 78412.* Tel: 512-991-8362. Dr. MARY MCCASKEY, Grand Sultana, *250 Cape Henry, Corpus Christi, 78412.* Tel: 512-991-6200.

Apostleship of The Sea—Rev. VINCENT PATRIZI, Dir., *Our Lady Star of the Sea, P.O. Box 1899, Corpus Christi, 78403.* Tel: 512-883-4507.

Birthright Counseling—ROXANNA GUERRA, Admin., *1901 Corpus Christi St., Laredo, 78044.* Tel: 956-722-2443. DONNA CISNEROS, Pres., *1422 Baldwin, Corpus Christi.* Tel: 512-884-2662.

Blue Army (World Apostolate of Fatima)—Mrs. AGNES BOCKHOLTZ, Pres., *Rte. 2, Box 885, Corpus Christi, 78410.* Tel: 512-265-9156.

Campus Ministries—Texas A&M University-Kingsville, St. Thomas Aquinas University Catholic Center; Rev. PIOTR KOZIEL, *1120 S. 8th St., Kingsville.* Tel: 512-592-5781. *Del Mar College, Collegiate Parish of St. Thomas More,* Rev. HANH VAN PHAM, *2045 18th St., Corpus Christi, 78404.* Tel: 512-883-9308. *The Cardinal John Henry Newman Catholic Student Center, at Texas A&M University-Corpus Christi,* Rev. BRUCE LINCON, *6300 Ocean Dr., Corpus Christi, 78412.* Tel: 512-993-5898. *Bee County College,* Rev. JAMES KELLEHER, *4000 N. St. Mary's St., Beeville, 78102.* Tel: 512-358-4968. *Laredo State University and Junior College,* Vacant, *P3, Fort McIntosh, Laredo, 78040.* Tel: 956-722-2324.

Catholic Daughters of the Americas—Ms. JUANITA AGUILAR, *District 15, 1201 Chihuahua, Laredo, 78040.* Tel: 956-723-3037. VICTORIA GONZALES, Dist. 16: *4442 Carlton, Corpus Christi, 78415.* Tel: 512-855-9646. ALICIA SALINAS, Dist. 23: *Rte. 3, Box 22, Alice, 78332.* Tel: 512-664-6932. DELPHA R. GONZALES, Dist. 36: *330 Cheyenne St., Corpus Christi, 78406.* Tel: 512-884-6970. TERRY SKORUPPA, Dist. 41: *4021 Pernitas Creek, Corpus Christi, 78410.* Tel: 512-242-2892.

Catholic Social Services of Corpus Christi, Inc.—Rev. Msgr. ROBERT E. FREEMAN, P.A.; Sr. PATRICK BRUEN, O.L.C., Admin., *1322 Comanche, Corpus Christi, 78401.* Tel: 512-884-0651; Fax: 512-884-3956.

Catholic Social Services of Laredo, Inc.—Rev. Msgr. ROBERT E. FREEMAN, P.A.; ROXANNA GUERRA, Admin., *1901 Corpus Christi St., Laredo, 78044.* Tel: 956-722-2443; Fax: 956-725-2238.

Cemeteries—(Laredo); Deacon LUIS TREVINO, Diocesan Dir. Tel: 956-723-6811.

Center For Spiritual Direction—Sr. JOAN MICHELE RAKE, C.D.P., Spiritual Dir., *4103 Ocean Dr., Corpus Christi, 78411.* Tel: 512-853-0171.

Charismatic Movement—Spiritual Directors: Deacons WALTER N. BRELAND; RAUL HINOJOSA; EDWARD NARTOWICZ; MARIO RIVERA, Area Coord. ANTONIO LARA, Diocesan Dir. Charismatic Renewal.

Diocesan Council Of Catholic Women—LORRAINE LUNCHEON, *P.O. Box 22, Beeville, 78102.*

Disaster Relief—Rev. Msgr. ROBERT E. FREEMAN, P.A., Dir., *1322 Comanche St., Corpus Christi, 78401.* Tel: 512-884-0651.

Emergency Aid—Sr. PATRICK BRUEN, O.L.C., Admin., *1322 Comanche, Corpus Christi, 78401.* Tel: 512-884-0651.

Family Counseling—Laredo Catholic Social Services: ROXANNA GUERRA, Admin., *1901 Corpus Christi, Laredo, 78044.* Tel: 956-722-2443. CSS-Corpus Christi Catholic Social Services: Sr. PATRICK BRUEN, O.L.C., Admin., *1322 Comanche St., Corpus Christi, 78401.* Tel: 512-884-0651.

Catholic Engaged Encounter—Rev. ROBERT DUNN, Dir., *P.O. Box 2620, Corpus Christi, 78403.* Tel: 512-882-6191, Ext. 356.

Immigration Services—Sr. PATRICK BRUEN, O.L.C., Admin., *1322 Comanche, Corpus Christi, 78401.* Tel: 512-884-0651. ROXANNA GUERRA, Admin., *Servicios Para Inmigrantes, 1901 Corpus Christi St., Laredo, 78044.* Tel: 956-722-2443.

Jail Ministries—Rev. MIGUEL ESQUIVEL, Chap., Three Rivers Federal Correctional Unit; Deacons ARMANDO CAVADA, Chap., McConnell Unit, Beeville; MADRIGAL SALVADOR, Assoc. Dir. Jail & Refugee Ministry, Laredo; JOSE RODRIGUEZ, JR., Dir. Ministry to Jails & Refugees, Laredo.

La Frontera Halfway House—ROXANNA GUERRA, Admin., *1616 Callaghan, Laredo, 78040.* Tel: 956-722-7271.

Lay Maryans—MANUEL GARCIA, Dir., *5310 Hitching Post Ln., Corpus Christi, 78415.* Tel: 512-855-9288.

Legion of Mary—BUNNIE HERMAN, Pres., *610 Wilshire, Corpus Christi, 78411.* Tel: 512-855-8321. JUAN VILLARREAL, Pres., *4415 Santa Maria, Laredo, 78041.* Tel: 956-723-9348.

Marriage Encounter—Rt. Rev. LUKE BUERGLER, O.S.B., Spiritual Dir., *Corpus Christi Abbey, HCR 2, Box 6300, Sandia, 78383.* Tel: 512-547-3257.

Pre-Release Prisoner Program—ROXANNA B. GUERRA, Admin., *1616 Callaghan, Laredo, 78040.* Tel: 956-722-7271.

Radio Stations - KLUX FM—RUSSEL WAYNE MARTIN, Dir. Broadcast Operations, *1200 Lantana St., Corpus Christi, 78407.* Tel: 512-289-2487.

KHOY FM—BENNETTE MCBRIDE, Mgr., *1901 Corpus Christi St., Laredo, 78040.* Tel: 956-722-4167.

Religious Education—Corpus Christi Area: Dr. FRANK LUCIDO, D.R.E., *Corpus Christi Catholic Center, 3036 Saratoga, Corpus Christi, 78415.* Tel: 512-289-5689. Laredo Area: Sr. M. GUADALUPE HERRERA, R.S.M., Coord., *1512 Logan St., Laredo, 78040.* Tel: 956-722-0959; Fax: 956-725-2238.

Serra International—Dr. GREG MCCASKEY, Pres., *250 Cape Henry, Corpus Christi, 78412.* Tel: 512-991-6200.

Theresians—ELLA NICHOLAS, Pres., *629 Moray, Corpus Christi, 78411.* Tel: 512-855-8656.

Villa Maria, Inc.—Deacon GARLAND FRAZIER, Dir., *Box 4, 3146 Saratoga Blvd., Corpus Christi, 78415.* Tel: 512-857-6171.

CLERGY, PARISHES, MISSIONS AND PAROCHIAL SCHOOLS

CITY OF CORPUS CHRISTI
(Nueces County)

1—CORPUS CHRISTI CATHEDRAL (1853), Revs. Michael Howell, Rector; Lowery A. Ross; Deacons Michael Mantz; Bruce Aycock.
Res., 505 N. Upper Broadway, 78401. Tel: 512-883-4213; Fax: 512-883-1918. [CEM]
Catechesis/Religious Programs—Tel: 512-883-4213; Fax: 512-883-1918.
Students 140.
Chapels—Emmanuel.; Blessed Sacrament.; Perpetual Eucharistic Adoration.

2—CHRIST THE KING (1946) (Mexican), Rev. Bernard Mlapah, O.SS.T.; Deacon Antonio Castillo.
Res., 3423 Rojo, 78415. Tel: 512-883-2821; Fax: 512-883-3448.
Catechesis/Religious Programs—Tel: 512-883-1404. Carol A. Enloe, D.R.E.
Students 250.
Convent—1625 Arlington, 78415. Tel: 512-883-0212.

3—HOLY CROSS (1914) (African American), Rev. Msgr. Patrick Higgins.
Res., 1109 N. Staples St., 78401. Tel: 512-888-4012; Fax: 512-888-5338.

4—HOLY FAMILY (1946), Revs. James E. Janecek, Pastor; Jesus Francisco Lopez.
Res., 2509 Nogales St., 78416. Tel: 512-882-3245; Fax: 512-882-4968.
Catechesis/Religious Programs—Tel: 512-882-3245.
Students 225.
Convent—1723 Frio St., 78417. Tel: 512-884-9142. Sisters of Mercy of the Blessed Sacrament 5.
Mission—Corpus Christi, Nueces Co., Mary, Mother of the Church, 1755 Frio St., Corpus Christi, 78417.

5—MOST PRECIOUS BLOOD (1966), Rev. Msgr. William Thompson; Rev. Bradley A. M. Barber.
Res., 3502 Saratoga Blvd., 78415. Tel: 512-854-3800; Fax: 512-854-9253.
Catechesis/Religious Programs—Tel: 512-854-9219. Sr. Margaret Hesse, D.R.E.
Students 450.

6—OUR LADY OF GUADALUPE (1969) (Hispanic), Deacons Alejandro Carrizales; Armando Botello.
Res., 540 Hiawatha, 78405. Tel: 512-882-1951; Fax: 521-888-5813.
Catechesis/Religious Programs—Tel: 512-882-8801. Estela Almeida, D.R.E.
Students 189.

7—OUR LADY OF THE ROSARY (1967) (Hispanic), Deacon Homer T. Martinez, Jr., Admin.
Res., 1123 Main Dr., 78409. Tel: 512-241-2004; Fax: 512-242-1099.
Catechesis/Religious Programs—Students 75.
Missions—Petronila, Nueces Co., St. Vivian, FM 665, Petronila, 78415.; Corpus Christi, Nueces Co., Our Lady of Mount Carmel, 1080 S. Clarkwood, Corpus Christi, 78406.

8—OUR LADY OF PERPETUAL HELP (1954), Rev. Msgr. Michael Heras, Pastor. In res., Rev. David Walsh, C.SS.R.
Res., 5830 Williams Dr., 78412-4415. Tel: 512-991-7891; Fax: 512-993-1211.
Catechesis/Religious Programs—Tel: 512-991-3261.
Students 120.

9—OUR LADY OF THE PILLAR (1964), Rev. Marcos Martinez; Deacon Armando Bolanos.
Res., 1101 Bloomington St., 78416. Tel: 512-852-6327; Fax: 512-852-2614.
Catechesis/Religious Programs—Tel: 512-852-6843.
Students 500.

10—OUR LADY STAR OF THE SEA (1950), Rev. Vincent M. Patrizi.
Res., 3110 E. Causeway Blvd., P.O. Box 1899, 78403. Tel: 512-883-4507; Fax: 512-888-6411.
Catechesis/Religious Programs—Students 60.

11—SACRED HEART (1936) (Hispanic), Rev. Jose M. Gutierrez.
Res., 422 N. Alameda, 78401. Tel: 512-883-6082; Fax: 512-883-6248. [CEM]
Catechesis/Religious Programs—Students 86.
Stations—Nueces County Jail.; Navarro Place.

12—SAINT ANDREW BY THE SEA PARISH (1986), Rev. Richard Filice.
Res., 14238 Encantada Ave., Padre Island, 78418-6432. Tel: 512-949-7193; Fax: 512-949-0717.

13—ST. ANSELM ANGLICAN USE COMMUNITY (1992), Rev. W.T. St. John Brown, Chap.
Res., 3036 Saratoga Blvd., 78415-5715. Tel: 512-854-3688; Fax: 512-852-8965.

14—SS. CYRIL AND METHODIUS (1947), Revs. Lawrence E. White; Robert DeCock, I.S.S.S.; Deacon Ron Dubuque.
Res., 3210 S. Padre Island Dr., 78415. Tel: 512-853-7371; Fax: 512-851-1438.
Catechesis/Religious Programs—Tel: 512-852-1651. Mona Lucido, D.R.E.
Students 450.

15—ST. JOSEPH (1952), Revs. David Tonary, M.S.F.; Joseph Lawless, M.S.F.; Deacon Pedro Ybarra; Bro. Rolland Kapsner, M.S.F.
Res., 710 S. 19th St., P.O. Box 5196, 78465-5196. Tel: 512-882-7912; Fax: 512-882-6853.
Catechesis/Religious Programs—Elizabeth Contreras, D.R.E.
Students 130.
Convent—2100 Morris St., 78405. Tel: 512-884-4027.
Sisters 2.

16—ST. MICHAEL THE ARCHANGEL LATIN MASS COMMUNITY (1995), Rev. Carlos S. Casavantes, F.S.S.P.
Res., 2233 Waldron Rd, 78418-4699. Tel: 512-937-2997; Fax: 512-939-7774.

17—ST. PATRICK (1944), Rev. Msgr. Robert E. Freeman; Rev. Manuel Hernandez, Jr.; Deacon W. Oliver.
Res., 3350 S. Alameda St., 78411. Tel: 512-855-7391; Fax: 512-855-7552.
Catechesis/Religious Programs—Tel: 512-855-7567.
Students 310.

18—ST. PAUL THE APOSTLE (1967), Rev. Bruno Mikolajczyk. In res., Rev. Carlos Casavantes, F.S.S.P.
Res., 2233 Waldron Rd., 78418. Tel: 512-937-3864; Fax: 512-939-7774.
Catechesis/Religious Programs—Tel: 512-937-6908. Sr. M. Purificion Palis, O.P., D.R.E.
Students 262.

19—ST. PETER PRINCE OF APOSTLES (1967), Rev. Morgan Rowsome.
Res. & Mailing Address—3901 Violet Rd., 78410. Tel: 512-241-3249; Fax: 512-241-0533.
Catechesis/Religious Programs—Tel: 512-241-3372; Fax: 512-241-0533. Marian Tajchman, D.R.E.
Students 568.
Mission—Corpus Christi, Nueces Co., St. Mary, 4849 Cynthia, 78410. Tel: 512-241-3432.

20—ST. PHILIP THE APOSTLE (1982), Rev. Msgr. Thomas P. McGettrick; Deacons Roy Grassedonio; Stacy Millsap.
Res., 6333 N. Washam St., 78414. Tel: 512-993-9474.
Church—3513 Cimarron Rd., 78414. Tel: 512-991-5146; Fax: 512-991-9135.
Catechesis/Religious Programs—Tel: 512-993-1710.
Students 395.

21—ST. PIUS X (1963), Rev. Msgr. Richard Shirley; Revs. J. Bruce Lincon, VG; John C. Ouellette, VG; Deacon Michael DeShetler.
Res., 5620 Gollihar Rd., 78412. Tel: 512-993-4053; Fax: 512-992-0352.
Catechesis/Religious Programs—Tel: 512-993-9024.
Students 260.

22—ST. THERESA (1947), Rev. Mark Chamberlin. In res., Rev. Msgr. Raymond F. Rau (BRK).
Res., 1302 Lantana St., 78407. Tel: 512-289-2759; Fax: 512-299-2018.
Catechesis/Religious Programs—Tel: 512-289-2238. Mrs. Josie Martinez, D.R.E.
Students 131.
Convent—1253 Lantana St., 78407. Tel: 512-289-5534.

23—COLLEGIATE PARISH OF ST. THOMAS MORE (1990), Rev. Hanh Van Pham.
Church—2045 18th St., 78404-3862. Tel: 512-888-9308; Fax: 512-888-6119.

OUTSIDE THE CITY OF CORPUS CHRISTI

Agua Dulce, Nueces Co., St. Frances of Rome (1934), Rev. James A. Hayes, M.S.C.
Mailing Address: P.O. Box 598, 78330. Tel: 512-998-2216.
Catechesis/Religious Programs—Mrs. Doretta McDonough, D.R.E.
Students 135.
Mission—Banquete, Nueces Co., St. Michael, Banquete, 78339. Tel: 512-998-2216.
Catechesis/Religious Programs—Otelia Pena, D.R.E.
Students 195.

Alice, Jim Wells Co., Our Lady of Guadalupe (1969), Rev. Thomas L. Goodwin.
Res., 1318 Guerra St., P.O. Box 411, 78332. Tel: 512-664-2953; Fax: 512-664-4001.
Catechesis/Religious Programs—Tel: 512-664-2957. D.R.E.: Rosaura Garcia; Delicia Rodriguez; Dora Rosales.
Students 327.
Convent—Tel: 512-664-0437. Carmelite Sisters.
Mission—Alice, Jim Wells Co., Santo Nino De Atocha, Rte. 3 Box 273, 78332. Tel: 512-664-2953.

St. Elizabeth (1918), Rev. James G. Stembler; Deacons James A. Carlisle; Alan K. Borse.
Res., 518 N. Almond St., P.O. Box 1009, 78333. Tel: 512-664-6481; Fax: 512-664-7243.
Catechesis/Religious Programs—Tel: 512-664-7719.
Students 281.
Convent—603 E. 5th St., 78332.
Mission—Ben Bolt, Jim Wells Co., St. Peter's Church, P.O. Box 1009, 78333.

St. Joseph (1911) (Hispanic), Revs. Eduardo H. Garcia; Raynaldo Yrlas, Jr.; Deacons Jose A. Vitela; Mario Rivera.
Res., 801 S. Reynolds St., P.O. Box 2026, 78333. Tel: 512-664-7551; Fax: 512-664-2388.
Catechesis/Religious Programs—Tel: 512-664-5625 (Elementary); 668-4567 (Junior High & High School).
Students 556.
Convent—311 Dewey St., P.O. Box 157, 78332. Tel: 512-664-6283.
Sisters 7.
Mission—Alice, Jim Wells Co., Sacred Heart, 110 S. Texas, 78332. Tel: 512-664-6225.
Chapel—Perpetual Eucharistic Adoration.

Aransas Pass, San Patricio Co., St. Mary, Star of the Sea (1948), Rev. Charles Doherty. In res., Rev. James Hamilton.
Res., 342 S. Rife St., 78336. Tel: 512-758-2662.
Catechesis/Religious Programs—Ginny Vega, D.R.E.
Students 278.

Beeville, Bee Co.,

1—OUR LADY OF VICTORY, (1908), Deacon Manuel G. Carranco. In res., Rev. John Fiala, S.O.L.T.
Res., 403 W. Carter St., 78102. Tel: 512-358-3761; Fax: 512-358-2028. [CEM 2][JC]
Catechesis/Religious Programs—Tel: 512-358-3761. Sr. Encarnacion D.R.E.
Students 80.
Mission—Pettus, Sacred Heart.

2—SACRED HEART MISSION, (1966) (Hispanic). (Independent). Rev. John Fiala, S.O.L.T.; Deacon Manuel G. Carranco.
403 W. Carter St., 78102. Tel: 512-375-2973; 375-2512 (Church); Fax: 512-358-2028.
Catechesis/Religious Programs—Guadalupe Aguirre, D.R.E.
Students 3.

3—ST. JAMES, (Alta Vista) (1966) (Hispanic), Rev. James Q. Dudley, M.S.C.; Deacon Juan Vasquez.
Res., 605 Alta Vista, 78102. Tel: 512-358-4825; Fax: 512-358-5150.
Catechesis/Religious Programs—Miss Mary Elizabeth Garcia, D.R.E.
Students 170.

4—ST. JOSEPH, (Alta Vista) (1891), Rev. Timothy J. Kinast; Deacons Luis Trevino; Rolando Salazar.
Res., 609 E. Gramman St., 78102. Tel: 512-358-3239; Fax: 512-358-4270. [CEM]
Catechesis/Religious Programs—Robin Pate, D.R.E.
Students 340.
Convent—610 E. Gramman St., 78102. Tel: 512-358-5089; 358-9405.
Sisters 4.

Benavides, Duval Co., St. Rose of Lima (1941) (Hispanic), Rev. Epifanio Rodriguez, O.P.
Res., Hackberry St., P.O. Drawer W, 78341. Tel: 512-256-3427.
Catechesis/Religious Programs—Tel: 512-256-3319. Gracie Garcia, D.R.E.
Students 165.
Mission—San Jose Ranch, Duval Co., St. Joseph, P.O. Box W, 78341.

Bishop, Nueces Co., St. James (1938), Rev. Patrick O'Connor, M.S.C.
Res., 601 W. 3rd St., P.O. Box 843, 78343. Tel: 512-584-3250. [CEM]
Catechesis/Religious Programs—Students 228.
Mission—Driscoll, Nueces Co., St. James, Driscoll, 78351.

Encinal, La Salle Co., Immaculate Heart of Mary, Rev. Pedro Nolasco Hinojosa, Jr.
Mailing Address: P.O. Box 5, 400 Santa Fe St., 78019-0005. Tel: 956-948-5328. [JC]
Catechesis/Religious Programs—Students 60.

Falfurrias, Brooks Co., Sacred Heart (1914), Rev. Matthew J. Stephan.
Res., 304 S. Caldwell St., 78355. Tel: 512-325-3455; Fax: 512-325-2486.
Catechesis/Religious Programs—Tel: 512-325-5067.
Students 512.
Mission—Encino, Brooks Co., St. Ann. c/o Sacred Heart Parish 78355.

Freer, Duval Co., St. Mary (1968), Rev. Gregory A. Boensch.

Res., 1500 Duval St., Box B, 78357. Tel: 512-394-6832.
Catechesis/Religious Programs—Tel: 512-394-7188. D.R.E.: Mrs. A. Bitoni; Mr. Teeka Mendiola. Students 260.

George West, Live Oak Co., St. George (1924), Rev. John P. Killeen.
Oratory—George West, Live Oak Co., Crockett St., P.O. Box 580, 78022. Tel: 512-449-1893; Fax: 512-449-1886. [CEM][JC]
Catechesis/Religious Programs—Tel: 512-449-2137. D.R.E.: Rev. John P. Killeen; Debbie Brown; Noreen Brown.
Students 250.
Mission—Gussetville, St. Joseph, Tel: 512-449-1893. [CEM][JC]

Gregory, San Patricio Co., Immaculate Conception (1926) (Hispanic), Rev. Robert Dunn.
Res., 107 Church St., P.O. Box 108, 78359-0108. Tel: 512-643-4505; Fax: 512-643-1509.
Catechesis/Religious Programs—Sr. Therese Cunnigham, S.H.Sp., D.R.E.
Students 372.

Hebbronville, Jim Hogg Co., Our Lady of Guadalupe (1926) (Hispanic), Revs. Adalberto Ramirez, O.F.M.; Eduardo Jayme, O.F.M.; Ricardo Rivera, O.F.M.; Bro. Jose Trinidad Gonzalez, O.F.M.
Res., 504 E. Santa Clara St., 78361. Tel: 512-527-3865; Fax: 512-527-5548. [CEM 2]
School—502 E. North St., 78361. Tel: 512-527-3611.
Little Flower Day Care Center—Tel: 512-527-3515. Mrs. Mary Garza, Prin.
Lay Teachers 5; Students 31.
Catechesis/Religious Programs—Beatriz (Bellita) Garza, D.R.E.
Students 230.
Missions—Hebbronville, Jim Hogg Co., Immaculate Conception; Mirando City, Webb Co., St. Agnes; Oilton, Webb Co., St. Bridget; Bruni, Webb Co., Sacred Heart; Realitos, Duval Co., Sacred Heart.

Ingleside, San Patricio Co., Our Lady of the Assumption (1970), Rev. Thomas Wellar.
Res., 2414 Main, 78362. Tel: 512-776-2644; 776-2446; Fax: 512-776-3963.
Catechesis/Religious Programs—Faith Repka, D.R.E.
Students 178.
Our Lady of the Assumption Early Learning Center—Tel: 512-776-3643.

Kingsville, Kleberg Co.,

1—Our Lady of Good Counsel, (1967) (Mexican), Rev. Michael Lenihan.
Res., 1102 E. Kleberg, 78363. Tel: 512-592-3489.
Catechesis/Religious Programs—Tel: 512-592-9546. Amparo Quintanilla, D.R.E.
Students 103.

2—St. Gertrude, (1908), Rev. Roger Smith.
Res., 1120 S. 8th St., 78363. Tel: 512-592-7351; Fax: 512-592-0028.
School—(Grades K4-6). Tel: 512-592-6522; Fax: 512-592-6591.
Students 196.
Catechesis/Religious Programs—Tel: 512-595-0974. Sr. Margaret Gerken, C.C.V.I., D.R.E.
Students 210.
Convent—400 E. Caesar Ave., 78363. Tel: 512-592-2443.

3—St. Joseph, (1973) (Hispanic), Rev. Richard Philion, O.M.I.
Res., 1400 Brookshire, P.O. Box 1602, 78364-1602. Tel: 512-592-5689.
Catechesis/Religious Programs—Tel: 512-592-5689. Rosalinda Vidal, D.R.E.
Students 200.

4—St. Martin, (1914) (Hispanic), Rev. James Foelker, O.M.I.; Deacons Tiburcio Garcia; Raul G. Rosales.
Res., 715 N. Eighth St., 78363. Tel: 512-592-4602; Fax: 512-592-4602.
Catechesis/Religious Programs—Tel: 512-592-0881. Gloria DeLeon, D.R.E.
Students 137.
Convent—919 N. Ninth St., 78363. Tel: 512-595-1087.
Sisters 8.

5—St. Thomas Aquinas, University Catholic Center, (1990), Rev. Piotr Koziel.
Res. & Mailing Address—1120 S. 8th, 78363. Tel: 512-592-5781; Fax: 512-592-8617.
Church—1119 W. Santa Gertrudis, 78363. Tel: 512-592-7351.

Laredo, Webb Co.,

1—Blessed Sacrament, (1950) (Hispanic), Rev. Msgr. Stanley A. Sliwak, Ph.D.; Rev. Pedro Nolasco Hinojosa, Jr., Pastoral Assoc.
Res., 2219 Galveston St., 78043. Tel: 956-722-1295; 722-1231; Fax: 956-722-2823.
Catechesis/Religious Programs—Tel: 956-725-7045. Eva Escamilla, D.R.E.
Students 216.

2—Christ the King, (1954), Rev. Daniel Ramirez-Portugal; Deacon Guillermo De La Garza.
Res., 1105 Tilden Ave., 78040. Tel: 956-723-4267; Fax: 956-791-8034. [JC]
School—Tel: 956-722-7821. Mrs. Mercedes Giddens, Prin.
Lay Teachers 4.
Catechesis/Religious Programs—Sr. Emilia Pastrano, M.C.D.P., D.R.E.
Students 312.

3—Holy Family, (1984) (Hispanic), Rev. Alejandro Salazar.
Res., 2705 McPherson, P.O. Box 1603, 78044. Tel: 956-724-6881; Fax: 956-724-5581.
Catechesis/Religious Programs—Students 161.

4—Holy Redeemer, (1940) (Hispanic), Revs. Jose Romero, O.S.A.; Ruben Zamudio, O.S.A.
Res., 1602 Garcia St., P.O. Box 1087, 78042. Tel: 956-723-7171; Fax: 956-723-7194. [CEM][JC]
Catechesis/Religious Programs—D.R.E.: Sonia Rendon; Josefina Garza.
Students 245.
Mission—Laredo, Webb Co., Santa Cruz, 2002 Lee Ave., 78040.

5—Our Lady of Guadalupe, (1910), Revs. Edward Ward, O.M.I.; Edward Vrazel.
Res., 1718 San Jorge Ave., P.O. Box 671, 78042. Tel: 956-723-6954; Fax: 956-723-6047.
Catechesis/Religious Programs—Olga Juarez, D.R.E.
Students 241.

6—San Augustin, (1879) (Mexican), Rev. Msgr. James E. Harris.
Res., 200 San Augustin Ave., 78040. Tel: 956-722-1382; Fax: 956-722-5599. [JC]
Catechesis/Religious Programs—Fax: 956-722-0441. Maria Elena Requejo, D.R.E.
Students 170.
Missions—Laredo, Webb Co., Santo Nino Mission, 2720 Ireland, 78043. Tel: 956-724-6638. Revs. Noel Davis; Vladimiro Manente, O.M.I.; Laredo, Webb Co., San Francisco Javier, 2502 Zargoza St., P.O. Box 1175, 78040. Tel: 956-723-3850.

7—San Luis Rey, (1958), Rev. Thomas Juarez, S.D.B.
Res., 3502 Sanders Ave., P.O. Box 2294, 78041. Tel: 956-723-6587; Fax: 956-723-6825.
Catechesis/Religious Programs—Tel: 956-722-3323. Mary Ann Gamez, D.R.E.
Students 503.

8—Santa Margarita De Escocia Independent Mission, (1991) (Mexican), Rev. Francis Stodola, Admin.; Deacon Leonel San Miguel.
Res., 320 Segovia Dr., 78046. Tel: 956-724-9669.
Catechesis/Religious Programs—Students 225.

9—San Martin De Porres, (1979), Rev. Domingo de Llano.
Res., 1704 Sandman, P.O. Box 2666, 78044-2666. Tel: 956-723-5215; Fax: 956-723-9443.
Catechesis/Religious Programs—Tel: 956-725-2440. Sr. Guadalupe Ramirez, M.C.D.P., D.R.E.
Students 425.

10—Santa Rita De Casia Independent Mission, Rev. Mariano Martinez.
Res., 1001 Espejo Molina, 78043. Tel: 956-725-7215.

11—St. Frances Cabrini, (1958), Rev. Alessandro DiTaddeo.
Res., 3018 Davis Ave., 78040. Tel: 956-722-2919; Fax: 956-791-5453.
Catechesis/Religious Programs—Tel: 956-722-8315. Agustina Bustos, D.R.E.
Students 259.

12—St. John Neumann, (1979), Rev. Randy Cain.
Mailing Address: 102 Hillside Rd., 78041.
Res., 5408 Gallagher, 78041. Tel: 956-726-9488; Fax: 956-726-0540.
Catechesis/Religious Programs—Cynthia Barreda, D.R.E.
Students 231.

13—St. Joseph, (1953), Rev. Jesus M. Madariaga, O.P., Admin.; Deacons Salvador Madrigal; Crispin O. Soto.
Res., 109 N. Meadow St., 78040. Tel: 956-723-4172; Fax: 956-728-8824.
Catechesis/Religious Programs—Mrs. Yolanda Molina, D.R.E.
Students 233.

14—St. Jude, Rev. Santiago Domingo.
Res., 2031 Lowry Rd., 78045. Tel: 956-722-2280; Fax: 956-726-8017.
Rectory—101 Biscayne Loop, 78045. Tel: 956-726-6318.
Catechesis/Religious Programs—Students 304.

15—St. Patrick, (1970) (Irish), Rev. Thomas A. Davis.
Res., 555 E. Del Mar Blvd., 78041. Tel: 956-722-6215; Fax: 956-722-6266. [CEM]
Catechesis/Religious Programs—Tel: 956-722-8451; Fax: 956-722-6266.
Students 495.

16—St. Peter the Apostle, (1897), Rev. Donald E. Critchlow.
Res., 1510 Matamoros St., P.O. Box 26, 78042. Tel: 956-723-6301; Fax: 956-723-6301.
Catechesis/Religious Programs—Students 210.

17—St. Vincent de Paul, (1969) (Hispanic), Revs. Roberto Vargas, O.S.A. (Mexico); Alberto Palmeno, O.S.A. (Mexico).
Res., 1119 S. Louisiana St., 78043. Tel: 956-722-3034; Fax: 956-722-4829.
Catechesis/Religious Programs—Tel: 956-726-4134. Graciela Ramirez, D.R.E.
Students 500.

Mathis, San Patricio Co., Sacred Heart (1942), Rev. Jose Angel Salazar.
Res., 114 S. Aransas, P.O. Box 608, 78368-0608. Tel: 512-547-9181; Fax: 512-547-6111. [JC]
Catechesis/Religious Programs—Rosie Aguilar, D.R.E.
Students 220.
Mission—San Patricio, San Patricio Co., St. Patrick, Tel: 512-547-5748.

Odem, San Patricio Co., Sacred Heart (1919), Rev. Paul A Hesse, Admin.
Res., 401 Willis St., P.O. Box 276, 78370. Tel: 512-368-9156; Fax: 512-368-2247.
Catechesis/Religious Programs—Tel: 512-368-2746. D.R.E.: Sr. Elsa Miranda, C.M.S.T.; Juan Orta, (Elementary); Manuela Cantu; Robert Mancias, (High School); Vicki Synovitz, (Junior High).
Students 367.
Convent—402 Borden, 78370. Tel: 512-368-2560.
Sisters 2.
Mission—Edroy, San Patricio Co., Our Lady of Guadalupe, P4D W. 5th, #N1, Edroy, 78352. Tel: 512-368-9156.

Orange Grove, Jim Wells Co., St. John of the Cross (1925), Rev. Brendan Ashe (Ireland).
Mailing Address: P.O. Box 329, 78372. Tel: 512-384-2795; Fax: 512-384-0056. [CEM]
Catechesis/Religious Programs—Tel: 512-384-2246.
Students 229.
Station—Sandia, St. Pius X.

Port Aransas, Nueces Co., St. Joseph (1860), Rev. Gregory S. Deane.
Mailing Address: 412 Lantana St., 78373. Tel: 512-749-5825; Fax: 512-749-5509. [JC]

Portland, San Patricio Co., Our Lady of Mount Carmel (1961), Rev. Mark Chamberlin; Deacon John W. Sutherland.
Res., 1008 Austin St., 78374. Tel: 512-643-7533; Fax: 512-643-5544.
Catechesis/Religious Programs—Tel: 512-643-3548. Mrs. Melanee Warner, D.R.E.
Students 263.

Premont, Jim Wells Co., St. Theresa of the Infant Jesus (1958), Rev. Jose A. Almazan, C.M. (Spain); Deacon Raul Hinojosa.
Res., 235 S.W. 4th St., P.O. Box 569, 78375. Tel: 512-348-2202; Fax: 512-348-2137.
Catechesis/Religious Programs—Tel: 512-348-3955. Fane Garza, D.R.E.
Students 247.
Missions—Concepcion, Duval Co., Immaculate Conception; Rios, Duval Co., St. Francis of Assisi; Ramirez, Duval Co., Our Lady of Guadalupe.

Refugio, Refugio Co., Our Lady of Refuge (1795), Rev. Thomas Feeney.
Res., 1008 S. Alamo St., 78377. Tel: 512-526-2083; Fax: 512-526-5653. [CEM][JC]
Catechesis/Religious Programs—106 W. Roca, 78377. Tel: 512-526-2053.
Students 233.
Mission—Blanconia, Bee Co., St. Catherine, 1008 S. Alamo, 78377.

St. James the Apostle (1886) (Hispanic), Rev. Thomas P. Feeney.
Res., 205 E. Santiago St., P.O. Box 326, 78377-0326. Tel: 512-526-2252; Fax: 512-526-5379. [CEM][JC]
Catechesis/Religious Programs—Tel: 512-526-2714.
Students 127.

Robstown, Nueces Co., St. Anthony (1914), Revs. Vincent Albano, S.O.L.T.; James Flanagan, S.O.L.T.; Robert Rank, S.O.L.T.; Isidore Usit Nyein, S.O.L.T.; Anthony Anderson, S.O.L.T.; Robert Copsey, S.O.L.T.; Paul Grala, S.O.L.T.; Alfredo Gaytan, S.O.L.T.
Res., 204 Dunne St., P.O. Box 792, 78380. Tel: 512-387-2774; Fax: 512-387-5114. [CEM]
Catechesis/Religious Programs—Tel: 512-387-9874. Eva Hernandez, D.R.E.
Students 395.
Convent—612 Indiana, 78380. Tel: 512-387-3810.

St. John Nepomucene, Rev. Joseph O'Connell, S.O.L.T.
Res., 603 N. First St., 78380. Tel: 512-387-3705; Fax: 512-387-3681.
Catechesis/Religious Programs—Joann Charba, D.R.E.
Students 127.

St. Thomas the Apostle (1980), Rev. Matthew Lyng.
Office: Rte. 5, Box 67-S, 78380. Tel: 512-387-1312; Fax: 512-387-9311.
Catechesis/Religious Programs—Shirley Syamken, D.R.E.
Students 230.

Rockport, Aransas Co., Sacred Heart (1838), Rev. Msgr. Louis F. Kihneman; Deacons Ciprian Martinez; Jerre Ledbetter; George Wiest.
Res., 704 Cornwall St., 78382. Tel: 512-729-2174; Fax: 512-729-1989.
Catechesis/Religious Programs—Tel: 512-729-8283.
Students 235.
Convent—114 N. Church St., 78382. Tel: 512-729-5311.
Sisters 2.

St. Peter Indo-Chinese Parish (1989) (Vietnamese), Rev. Peter Phan Van Nguyen, C.S.S.R. In res., Rev. Quang Dang Nguyen, (Retired).
Mailing Address: P.O. Box 1060, 78382. Tel: 512-729-3008.

San Diego, Duval Co., St. Francis de Paula (1866), Rev. Benito Retortillo, O.P.
Res., Victoria & St. Peter St., P.O. Box 279, 78384. Tel: 512-279-3596; Fax: 512-279-8288.
Catechesis/Religious Programs—411 S. Victoria St., 78384. Tel: 512-279-3586.
Students 518.
Mission—Palito Blanco, Jim Wells Co., St. Joseph.

Sarita, Kenedy Co., Our Lady of Guadalupe (1935), Rev. Angel Villalba, O.M.I.
Mailing Address: P.O. Box 6, 78385. Tel: 512-294-5350; Fax: 512-294-5350.
Mission—Norias Ranch, Santa Elena.

Sinton, San Patricio Co., Our Lady of Guadalupe (1954) (Hispanic), Rev. David Taurasi, Pastor.
Res., 725 Sodville Ave., 78387. Tel: 512-364-2210; Fax: 512-364-5818. [JC]
Catechesis/Religious Programs—Tel: 512-364-4542.
Students 378.

Sacred Heart (1918), Rev. Seamus J. McGowan.
Res., 906 E. Sinton St., P.O. Box 266, 78387. Tel: 512-364-1768; Fax: 512-364-5325. [JC 3]
Catechesis/Religious Programs—Tel: 512-364-1772. D.R.E.: Mary Connors; Marilyn Knox.
Students 163.
Mission—St. Paul, St. Paul.

Skidmore, Bee Co., Immaculate Conception (1915), Rev. James R. Kelleher, S.O.L.T.
Res., 600 First St., P.O. Box 189, 78389. Tel: 512-287-3256. [JC]
Catechesis/Religious Programs—Students 115.
Convent—Tel: 512-287-3146; 287-3570.
Sisters 8.
Mission—Tynan, Bee Co., St. Francis Xavier, 78384.

Taft, San Patricio Co., Holy Family (1957), Rev. Patrick K. Donohoe.
Mailing Address: P.O. Box 868, 78390-0868. Tel: 512-528-3132; Fax: 512-528-3907.
Res., 646 McIntyre, 78390-2904. Tel: 512-528-2584.
Catechesis/Religious Programs—Students 62.

Immaculate Conception (1928), Rev. Patrick K. Donohoe; Deacon Alonzo T. Rodriguez.
Mailing Address: 120 E. Escobedo, P.O. Box 868, 78390. Tel: 512-528-2626; Fax: 512-528-3907.
Res., 646 McIntyre, 78390. Tel: 512-528-2584.
Catechesis/Religious Programs—Tel: 512-528-5300.
Students 563.

Three Rivers, Live Oak Co., Sacred Heart (1948), Rev. Zenon Konowalek.
303 E. Alexandra, P.O. Box 729, 78071-0729. Tel: 512-786-3398; 786-1010.
Mission—Pawnee, Bee Co., Our Lady of Guadalupe, P.O. Box 729, 78071. Tel: 512-786-3398.

Tivoli, Refugio Co., Our Lady of Guadalupe (1936), Rev. John J. Feminelli.
Mailing Address: P.O. Box I, 77990. Tel: 512-286-3349; Fax: 512-286-3665.
Catechesis/Religious Programs—Joyce Lenhart, D.R.E.
Students 85.
Missions—Austwell, Refugio Co., St. Anthony of Padua, Drawer 1, 77990-0250; O'Connor Ranch, Refugio Co., St. Dennis.

Vattman, Kleberg Co., Our Lady of Consolation (1914), Rev. Wojciech Kosowicz.
Res., Rte. 1, Box 21, 78379. Tel: 512-297-5255; Fax: 512-297-5578. [CEM]
Catechesis/Religious Programs—Students 52.
Mission—Riviera, Kleberg Co., Our Lady of Guadalupe.

Violet, Nueces Co., St. Anthony (1910), Rev. Aidan J. Leddy.
Res., Rte. 3, P.O. Box 134, Robstown, 78380. Tel: 512-387-4434; Fax: 512-387-4434. [CEM]
Catechesis/Religious Programs—Students 36.

Woodsboro, Refugio Co., St. Therese, The Little Flower (1915), Rev. Celestine Murray.
Res., 315 Pugh St., Drawer 1076, 78393-1140. Tel: 512-543-4166; Fax: 512-543-5922. [CEM]
Catechesis/Religious Programs—Students 140.
Mission—Bayside, Refugio Co., St. Mary.

Zapata, Zapata Co., Our Lady of Lourdes (1940), Revs. Peter J. McNamara; Patrick Daniel Columba Mulligan, M.S.C.
Res., Hidalgo & 17th Ave., P.O. Box 3213, 78076. Tel: 956-765-4216; Fax: 956-765-6188. [JC 2]
Catechesis/Religious Programs—Tel: 956-765-6711.
Students 750.
Missions—San Ignacio, Zapata Co., St. Ignatius; Lopeno, Zapata Co., San Pedro; Falcon, Zapata Co., Santa Ana.

On Special Assignment:
Reverend Monsignors—
Flores, Daniel, North American College, Casa Santa Maria, Via dell'Umilta 30, 00187, Rome, Italy
Meany, Thomas, Chancery Office, 620 Lipan, P.O. Box 2620, Corpus Christi, TX 78403-2620
Reverend Fathers—
Downey, Donald, Spohn Shoreline Pastoral Care, 600 Elizabeth St., Corpus Christi, TX 78404
Esquivel, Miguel, Chap., Three Rivers Federal Correctional, P.O. Box 226, Sinton, TX 78387
Feminelli, John, Our Lady of Guadalupe Parish, P.O. Drawer 1, Tivoli, TX 77990
Gutierrez, Jose M., Chap., Spohn Hospital
Hamilton, James, St. Mary Star of the Sea, 342 S. Rife, Aransas Pass, TX 78336
Kenna, John Thomas, Mount Carmel Home, 4130 S. Alameda, Corpus Christi, TX 78411
Mullan, Glen, Sec., Seminary Formation & Vocations, 3036 Saratoga Blvd., Corpus Christi, TX 78415
Nguyen, Liep Van Joseph, Chap., Shoenstatt Retreat House, HCO, Box 101, Rockport, TX 78382
O'Donovan, Thomas P., Mercy Hospital, P.O. Drawer 2068, Laredo, TX 78041
Ramirez, Hernando, S.J., Mercy Regional Hospital, 1515 Logan, Laredo, TX 78041
Rodriguez, Antonio, I.Sch., 4343 Gains, Corpus Christi, TX 78412
Vega, Hector, I.Sch., 4343 Gaines, Corpus Christi, TX 78412
Walsh, David, C.SS.R., Dir., Office of Persons with Disabilities

On Duty Outside the Diocese:
Reverend Monsignors—
Flores, Daniel, North American College, Casa Santa Maria, Via Dell'Umilta 30, 08187, Rome, Italy
Reverend Fathers—
Bauta, Krzysztof T.
Bergin, Pascal
Martinez, Benjamin
Martinez, Francisco X., Divine Work College, 1025 Michigan Ave. N.E., Washington D.C., 20017-1895
Masin, Richard H., Russia
Masterson, Clyde
McGerity, Francis X., 26 Fairbanks St., Brighton, MA 02135
Mercer, Timmothy
Walsh, Arthur

Military Chaplains:
Reverend Fathers—
Chilen, Michael D., 17th ASG CM UNIT 45013, Box 2207, APO AP, 96338-5013
Shuley, Keith
Williams, Gary, Lt., Corpus Christi Naval Air Station, Bldg. 5, Corpus Christi, TX 78419

Retired:
Reverend Monsignors—
Adams, Michael, Mount Carmel Home, 4130 S. Alameda, Corpus Christi, TX 78411
Brasley, Lucian R., 9140 Timber Path, No. 2303, San Antonio, TX 78250
Clark, Robert, Villa Maria Apartments, 3146 Saratoga Blvd., Box 18, Corpus Christi, TX 78415
Clarke, Hugh, Coneyburro Rd., Lifford, Co. Donegal, Ireland
Kinlough, William C., St. Mary, P.O. Box 866, Lampasas, TX 76550
Tengler, Alvin, 1011 7th St., Corpus Christi, TX 78404
Reverend Fathers—
Arguelles, Antonio G., 3404 South Texas Ave., Laredo, TX 78043
Bradley, Robert, Villa Maria Apartments, 3146 Saratoga Blvd., Box 45, Corpus Christi, TX 78415. Tel: 512-855-3767
Brown, W.T. St. John, 1177 E. Mesquite Ave., Palm Springs, CA 92264-8416. Tel: 760-325-0354
Burke, Michael, St. Francis of Assisi, P.O. Box 878, Mount Kisco, NY 10549. Tel: 914-666-5986
DeAngelis, William, O.S.B., 6602 Everhard, #144, Corpus Christi, TX 78413
Fidalgo, Federico, 8326 N. Vandiver, #508, San Antonio, TX 78209
Iglesias, Luis Fernando, Villa Maria Apts., 3146 Saratoga Blvd., Box 39, Corpus Christi, TX 78415
Joseph, Louis, 4334 Ocean Dr., Corpus Christi, TX 78412. Tel: 512-814-3007
Kircher, Edward, 310 East Ward St., Refugio, TX 78377
McGowan, Seamus, Villa Maria Apts., 3146 Saratoga Blvd., Box 20, Corpus Christi, TX 78415
Nguyen, Quang Dang, P.O. Box 916, Fulton, TX 78358
Noone, Sean, Villa Maria Apartments, 3146 Saratoga Blvd., Box 12, Corpus Christi, TX 78415. Tel: 512-853-4814
Patrizi, Vincent, 15426 Fortuna Bay Dr., #102, Corpus Christi, TX 78418. Tel: 512-949-8862
Vidiella, Felix, 5702 Santa Clara, Santa Clara Estates, Robstown, TX 78380
Zagari, Joseph

Permanent Deacons:
Alvardo, Carlos, Our Lady of Perpetual Help, Corpus Christi
Aycock, J. Bruce, Corpus Christi Cathedral, Corpus Christi
Barbour, Tony R., St. Thomas Aquinas Collegiate Parish, Kingsville
Bernal, Anastacio, Our Lady of Guadalupe, Laredo
Bitoni, Eluterio, St. Mary Parish, Freer
Bolanos, Armando M., Our Lady of Pillar, Corpus Christi
Borse, Alan T., St. Elizabeth, Alice
Botello, Armando, Our Lady of Guadalupe, Corpus Christi
Breland, Walter N., Spiritual Dir., Cursillo Movement, St. John of the Cross, Orange Grove
Carlisle, James A., Dir., Diaconate Formation, St. Elizabeth, Alice
Carranco, Manuel G., Chap., Our Lady of Victory; Bee County Jail, Beeville.
Carrizales, Alejandro, Admin., Our Lady of Guadalupe, Corpus Christi
Castillo, Antonio M., Christ the King, Corpus Christi
Cavada, Armando, Chap., McConnell Unit, Beeville
Cavazos, Jesus Z., Our Lady of Lourdes, Zapata
Cleavelin, William, St. Thomas the Apostle, Robstown
Costley, Ricardo E., Assoc. Dir. of Formation, Sacred Heart, Falfurrias
de Anda, Candido, St. Francis of Rome, Agua Dulce
De la Garza, Guillermo, Mercy Regional Medical Center; Christ the King, Laredo
DeShelter, Michael, Liturgical Commission, St. Pius X, Corpus Christi
Dubuque, Roland, Deanery Representative, SS. Cyril & Methodius Parish, Corpus Christi
Flores, Arturo, Deanery Representative, St. Gertrude, Kingsville
Frazier, Garland, Exec. Dir. Villa Maria Apartments; St. Philip the Apostle, Corpus Christi
Garcia, Tiburcio, St. Martin, Kingsville
Garza, Jorge J., St. Francisco Javier Mission, Laredo
Gomez, Juan, Immaculate Conception, Taft
Grassedonio, Roy M., St. Philip the Apostle, Corpus Christi
Hinojosa, Raul, Spiritual Dir. Cursillo Movement, Mission of St. Theresa of the Infant Jesus, Premont
Horseman, M. M. (Pete), Our Lady Star of the Sea, Corpus Christi
Kaizen, Joseph, Our Lady of Guadalupe Chapel, N.A.S., Corpus Christi
Lara, Antonio S., Diocesan Dir. Charismatic Renewal, Immaculate Conception, Skidmore
Ledbetter, Jerre H., Sacred Heart, Rockport
Lickteig, Wayne, S.O.L.T., Dir., Lay Council of Society
Madrigal, Salvador, Assoc. Dir. Jail & Refugee Ministry, St. Joseph, Laredo
Mantz, Michael, Youth & Drug Abuse Prog. & Admin. Asst. to Vicar for Permanent Diaconate, Corpus Christi Cathedral, Corpus Christi
Martinez, Ciprian, Sacred Heart, Rockport
Martinez, Homer, Jr., Our Lady of the Rosary, Corpus Christi
Millsap, Stacy, St. Phillip the Apostle, Corpus Christi

Millsap, Stanley, Sec. to Personnel & Deacons
Morales, Gerardo, Assoc. Dir. of Formation of Western Vicariate, St. John Neumann, Laredo; St. Theresa, San Carlos, Sacred Heart, Catholic Community
Nartowicz, Edward, Catholic Social Services, Assoc. Spiritual Dir. Cursillo Movement, St. Paul the Apostle, Our Lady of Guadalupe Chapel, N.A.S., Corpus Christi
Nowicki, Edward, (Retired)
Oliver, Willard F., St. Patrick, Corpus Christi
Ouellette, Roland
Panas, George, Driscoll Childrens Hospital, Corpus Christi
Ponce, Cesar, Chap. for Catholic Scouting, St. Joseph, Beeville
Rivera, Gonzalo, Chap., Sacred Heart, Rockport; Brooks County Jail, Falfurrias
Rivera, Mario, Area Coord. Cursillo Movement, St. Joseph, Alice
Rodriguez, Alonzo, Immaculate Conception, Taft
Rodriguez, Fernando G., Most Precious Blood, Corpus Christi
Rodriguez, Jose, Jr., Outreach Coord. for La Frontera Halfway House & San Luis Rey, Laredo; Dir. Ministry to Jails & Refugees
Rodriguez, Reynaldo, Jr., Diocesan Chap., St. Therese, Woodsboro
Rosales, Raul G., Consultant for Mission 2000 Regional Dept. of Schools, St. Martin, Kingsville
Salazar, Rolando R., St. Joseph, Beeville
San Miguel, Leonel, Sr., Western Vicariate Deanery Representative, Santa Margarita De Escocia Independent Mission, Laredo
Sandlin, Larry, Blessed Sacrament, Laredo
Soto, Crispin O., St. Joseph, Laredo
Sutherland, John W., Deanery Representative, Our Lady of Mount Carmel, Portland
Trevino, Luis, Dir. Diocesan Cemeteries, Deanery Representative, St. Joseph, Beeville
Vallarata, David, San Augustin, Laredo; Asst. at Colonia San Carlos Mission
Vargas, David, Asst. at Colonia San Carlos Mission, Blessed Sacrament, Laredo
Vasquez, Juan, St. James, Beeville
Vasquez, Guadalupe C., Mary, Mother of the Church Mission, Corpus Christi
Vitela, Jose Angel, Deanery Representative, St. Joseph, Alice
Wiest, George Joe, Outreach Coord. for St. Vincent de Paul Society & Chap., Shoreline Treatment Facility, Taft, Sacred Heart, Rockport
Ybarra, Pedro M., St. Joseph, Corpus Christi

INSTITUTIONS LOCATED IN THE DIOCESE

[A] HIGH SCHOOLS

CORPUS CHRISTI. *Incarnate Word Academy High School.* (Private), 2910 S. Alameda, 78404. Tel: 512-883-0857; Fax: 512-883-2185.
E-mail: 1wa@mail.interconnect.net
Sr. Martha O'Gara, Prin. Sisters 9; Lay Teachers 32; Students 423.

LAREDO. *St. Augustine High School.* (Diocesan), 1300 Galveston St., 78040. Tel: 956-724-8131; Fax: 956-724-8131. Sr. Antoinette Billeaud, C.D.P., Prin. Lay Teachers 35; Students 550.

[B] JUNIOR HIGH AND ELEMENTARY SCHOOLS

CORPUS CHRISTI. *Bishop Garriga Middle School.* (Diocesan), 3114 Saratoga Blvd., 78415. Tel: 512-851-0853. Mrs. Margaret McGettrick, Prin.; Rev. Bradley Barber, Chap. Lay Teachers 13; Students 187.

Central Catholic School. (Parochial), 1218 Comanche St., 78401. Tel: 512-883-3873. Sr. Denise Cassidy, I.W.B.S., Prin. Sisters 2; Lay Teachers 7; Students 150.

Christ the King School. (Parochial), 1625 Arlington Dr., 78415. Tel: 512-883-5391. Sr. Colette Brehony, I.W.B.S., Prin. Sisters 1; Lay Teachers 8; Students 158.

Holy Family School. (Parochial), 2526 Soledad St., 78416. Tel: 512-884-9142. Sr. Bernadette Gomez, H.M.S.S., Prin. Sisters 4; Lay Teachers 17; Students 240.

Incarnate Word Elementary. (Private), 450 Chamberlain, 78404. Tel: 512-883-0857; Fax: 512-883-2185. Sr. Camelia Herlihy, Prin. Sisters 7; Lay Teachers 9; Students 231.

Incarnate Word Middle School. (Private), 2917 Austin St., 78404. Tel: 512-883-0857.
E-mail: sr.barbara@mail.interconnect.net
Sr. Barbara Netek, I.W.B.S., Prin. Sisters 2; Lay Teachers 20; Students 265.

Most Precious Blood School. (Parochial), 3502 Saratoga Blvd., 78415. Tel: 512-852-4800; Fax: 512-855-8707. Mrs. Anna Galvan, Prin. Religious Teachers 1; Lay Teachers 14; Students 270.

Our Lady of Perpetual Help School. (Parochial), 5814 Williams Dr., 78412. Tel: 512-991-3305. Ms. Linda Cantu, Prin. Lay Teachers 13; Students 201.

St. Patrick School. (Parochial), 3350 S. Alameda, 78411. Tel: 512-852-1211. Dr. Maria M. Barrera, Prin. Lay Teachers 19; Students 301.

St. Pius X School. (Parochial), 737 St. Pius Dr., 78412. Tel: 512-992-1343.
E-mail: dcccsspxscc@connectinc.com
Mrs. Patricia Stegall, Prin. Lay Teachers 13; Students 220.

SS. Cyril and Methodius School. (Parochial), 5002 Kostoryz Rd., 78415. Tel: 512-853-9392. Mrs. Nannette Hatch, Prin. Lay Teachers 13; Students 186.

ALICE. *St. Elizabeth School.* (Parochial), 615 E. Fifth, 78332. Tel: 512-664-6271. Ms. Julia Strubhart, Prin. Lay Teachers 12; Students 119.

St. Joseph School. (Parochial), P.O. Box 157, 78333. Tel: 512-664-4642. Mrs. Margarita Longoria, Prin. Sisters 4; Lay Teachers 7; Students 84.

BEEVILLE. *St. Mary's Academy School.* (Grades PreK-8). (Parochial), 410 N. Tyler, 78102. Tel: 512-358-5089; Fax: 512-358-7672. Mr. Bud Baker, Prin. Sisters 4; Lay Teachers 10; Students 128.

KINGSVILLE. *St. Gertrude School.* (Parochial), 400 E. Caesar St., 78363. Tel: 512-592-6522. Mrs. Jean Claire Turcotte, Prin. Lay Teachers 8; Students 146.

St. Martin Catholic School. (Parochial), 903 N. Ninth St., 78363. Tel: 512-592-5011. Sr. Marie Elise van Dijk, C.D.P., Prin. Sisters 1; Lay Teachers 4; Students 60.

LAREDO. *Blessed Sacrament School,* 1501 N. Bartlett St., 78043. Tel: 210-722-1222. Sr. Patrice Floyd, I.W.B.S., Prin. Lay Teachers 9; Students 100.

Mary Help of Christians School. (Private), 10 E. Del Mar Blvd., 78045. Tel: 210-722-3966. Sr. Barbara Campbell, F.M.A., Prin. Sisters 1; Lay Teachers 55; Students 724.

Our Lady of Guadalupe School. (Parochial), 400 Callaghan St., 78040-3834. Tel: 210-722-3915. Sr. Julia Hickey, O.S.U., Prin. Sisters 3; Lay Teachers 7; Students 125.

St. Augustine Elementary School. (Diocesan), 1300 Galveston, 78040. Tel: 210-724-1176; Fax: 210-725-9891. Sr. Marie Elise van Dijk, Prin. Sisters 1; Lay Teachers 11; Students 223.

St. Peter's Memorial School. (Diocesan), 1519 Houston St., P.O. Box 520, 78040. Tel: 210-723-6302. Ms. Alicia C. Valdez, Prin. Sisters 1; Lay Teachers 9; Students 116.

ROBSTOWN. *St. Anthony School.* (Parochial), 203 Dunne St., 78380. Tel: 512-387-3814. Rev. Robert Rank, Prin. Sisters 1; Lay Teachers 15; Students 140.

ROCKPORT. *Sacred Heart School.* (Parochial), 111 N. Church St., 78382. Tel: 512-729-2672; Fax: 512-729-1989. Mary E. Sierra-Lopez, Prin. Sisters 1; Lay Teachers 8; Students 170.

[C] DAY NURSERY, PRE-KINDER, KINDER

CORPUS CHRISTI. *Carmelite Learning Center of Corpus Christi.* (Private), 4015 MacArthur St., 78416-1907. Tel: 512-853-6970; Fax: 512-853-6670. Sr. M. Michelle, Carmel.D.C.J., Dir. Day Care and Kindergarten. Carmelite Sisters of the Divine Heart of Jesus 4; Lay Teachers 14; Students 75.

Our Lady of the Rosary Learning Center, 2237 Waldron Rd., 78418. Tel: 512-939-9847. Sr. Maria Paz Aribon, O.P., Dir. Sisters 7; Students 55.

LAREDO. *Christ the King Learning Center,* 1100 Hendricks, 78040. Tel: 210-722-7821. Mrs. Mary Martinez, Prin. Lay Teachers 3; Students 85.

[D] ORPHANAGES AND INFANT HOMES

LAREDO. *Sacred Heart Children's Home,* 3310 S. Zapata Hwy., 78046. Tel: 210-723-3343
For a complete listing, refer to the Special Care Facilities section.

[E] GENERAL HOSPITALS

CORPUS CHRISTI. *Spohn Hospital,* 600 Elizabeth St., 78404. Tel: 512-881-3000; Fax: 512-881-3149
For a complete listing, refer to the Hospitals section.

Spohn Hospital South, 5950 Saratoga Blvd., 78414. Tel: 512-985-5000; Fax: 512-985-5109
For a complete listing, refer to the Hospitals section.

Spohn Memorial Hospital Mailing Address: P.O. Box 5280, 78465-5280.
For a complete listing, refer to the Hospitals section.

BEEVILLE. *Spohn Bee County Hospital,* 1500 E. Houston Hwy., 78102. Tel: 512-354-2125
For a complete listing, refer to the Hospitals section.

KINGSVILLE. *Spohn-Kleberg Memorial Hospital,* 1300 General Cavazos Blvd., 78363. Tel: 512-595-1661; Fax: 512-595-9888
For a complete listing, refer to the Hospitals section.

LAREDO. *Mercy Regional Medical Center,* 1515 Logan, P.O. Box 2068, 78044. Tel: 210-718-6222; Fax: 210-718-6904
For a complete listing, refer to the Hospitals section.

[F] HOMES FOR THE AGED

CORPUS CHRISTI. *Casa San Lucas,* 222 Ocean View, 78412. Tel: 512-857-5758
For a complete listing, refer to the Special Care Facilities section.

Mount Carmel Home, 4130 S. Alameda St., 78411. Tel: 512-855-6243
For a complete listing, refer to the Special Care Facilities section.

Villa Maria, Inc., 3146 Saratoga Blvd., 78415. Tel: 512-857-6171; Fax: 512-857-6173
For a complete listing, refer to the Special Care Facilities section.

[G] RETREAT HOUSE

CORPUS CHRISTI. *Bishop Rene H. Gracida Retreat House,* 3036 Saratoga Blvd., 78415. Tel: 512-814-3806. Mr. William Tribula, Mgr.

Bishop Thomas J. Drury Retreat Center, 1200 Lantana St., 78407. Tel: 512-289-6501. Mr. William Tribula, Mgr.

LAREDO. *Holy Spirit Retreat and Conference Center,* 501 S. Century Dr., 78046. Tel: 956-726-4352; Fax: 956-726-4363.
E-mail: stjohn@border.net
Web site: http://www.stjean.com/laredo/hsrc/holy.htm
Rev. Dominic Peridans, F.J., Prior; Mr. Geoffrey Greenwell, Dir. Total Staff 4; Total in Residence 2.

SANDIA. *Benedictine Retreat Center,* HC 2, Box 6300, 78383-9989. Tel: 512-547-3257; Fax: 512-547-5184.
E-mail: ccabbey@aol.com
Very Rev. Michael De Leon, O.S.B., Prior. Total Staff 3.

SARITA. *Lebh Shomea House of Prayer,* La Parra Ranch, 78385-0009. Tel: 512-294-5369; Fax: 512-294-5791. Rev. Francis Kelly Nemeck, O.M.I. Total in Residence 4; Total Staff 7.

[H] MONASTERIES AND RESIDENCES OF PRIESTS AND BROTHERS

HEBBRONVILLE. *Catholic Solitudes,* Rancho Maria, P.O. Box 748, 78361. Tel: 512-527-4636; Fax: 512-527-4482.
E-mail: cath@aol.com
Rev. M. Brendan Meaney, F.J., Dir.; Jean-Baptiste LePichon, Dir. Special Apostolate: A fraternal community stressing eremitical contemplative prayer, welcoming eremitical vocations and spiritual formational retreats for young people under directives of Diocesan Bishop. Total Staff 1; Total in Residence 6.

Franciscan Friars - O.F.M., 504 E. Santa Clara St., 78361. Tel: 512-527-3865; Fax: 512-527-5548. Rev. Adalberto Ramirez, O.F.M., Pastor. Total Staff 7; Total Assisted 31.

LAREDO. *Marist Brothers,* 1511 E. Cherry Hill Dr., 78041. Tel: 210-724-2651; Fax: 210-724-1963. Bros. Philip R. Degagne, F.M.S., Dir.; Joseph E. Herrera, F.M.S.; Thomas W. Coyne, F.M.S.; John A. Allen, F.M.S.; Gregory Avina, F.M.S. Marist Brothers 5.

St. John's Priory, (F.J.), 505 Century Dr. S., 78046. Tel: 210-722-3399. Congregation of St. John. Revs. Dominique F. Peridans, F.J., Prior; Didier-Marie Dugas Viallis (France); Juan de Dios Saavedra (Spain); Deacon Emmanuel Durand (France); Bro. Louis-Mary Ketterhagen. Priests 3; Brothers in Formation (Postulants) 6; Total in Residence 11.

ROBSTOWN. *Society of Our Lady of the Most Holy Trinity,* P.O. Box 152, 78380-0792. Tel: 512-387-2774; Fax: 512-387-5114. Deacon Roy M. Grassedonio, Chancellor; Revs. Vincent Albano, S.O.L.T.; Anthony Anderson, S.O.L.T., Voc. Dir.; Peter J. Auer, S.O.L.T. (GF); James H.T. Brady, S.O.L.T. (WH); Alberto A. Brancaccio, S.O.L.T. (ALB); George Carlin, S.O.L.T.; Phillip Chavez, S.O.L.T.; Robert Copsey, S.O.L.T.; John Corapi, S.O.L.T. (SAC); Robert Cronin, S.O.L.T. (GLP); Jacques Dolbec, S.O.L.T. (FAR); James Flanagan, S.O.L.T.; Peter Fremont-Smith, S.O.L.T.; Alfredo Gaytan, S.O.L.T.; Thomas P. Gier, S.O.L.T.; Paul Grala, S.O.L.T.; Joseph Hadgkiss, S.O.L.T.; Gene Hart, S.O.L.T.; Edward Horan, S.O.L.T.; Jeffrey Johnson, S.O.L.T. (BO); Michael Jordan, S.O.L.T.; Eckley Macklin, S.O.L.T. (KC); John McHugh, S.O.L.T.; Glenn Meaux, S.O.L.T.; Christopher Myers, S.O.L.T.; Thien Chi Nguyen, S.O.L.T.; Vincent A. Nicosia, S.O.L.T. (SFE); Joseph O'Connell, S.O.L.T.; Frank Papa, S.O.L.T. (HRT); Tan Pham, S.O.L.T.; Santan Pinto, S.O.L.T. (SFE);

John Purtell, S.O.L.T. (BO); William Sharkey, S.O.L.T.; Gerald Sheehan, S.O.L.T.; Maurice Shepherd, S.O.L.T.; James Tamborino, S.O.L.T. (MIL); Deacon Wayne Lickteig, S.O.L.T. In res. Rev. Robert Rank, S.O.L.T.; Deacon Francis Hohenadel, S.O.L.T.

SAN DIEGO. *Vicariate of Holy Rosary*, St. Francis de Paul Church, P.O. Box 279, 78384. Tel: 512-279-3596. Order of Preachers, U.S. Foundation of the Province of Spain. Revs. Benito Retortillo, O.P., Local Supr.; Epifanio Rodriguez, O.P.

SANDIA. *Corpus Christi Abbey*. (Benedictine Monastery), HC2, Box 6300, 78383. Tel: 512-547-3257.
E-mail: ccabbey@aol.com
Order Saint Benedict-Swiss-American Congregation. Very Rev. Michael De Leon, O.S.B.; Rt. Revs. Louis Hacker, O.S.B., Abbot; Luke Buergler, O.S.B., (Retired); Revs. William DeAngelis, O.S.B.; Bartholomew Leon, O.S.B.; Augustine Linbeck, O.S.B.; John Harold McKenzie, O.S.B.; Sylvester Schad, O.S.B.; Gregory Yockey, O.S.B.; Maryon Jordan, O.S.B.; Deacon Dominic Mazoch, O.S.B. Brothers 13; Priests 10; Novices 1; Postulants 1.

[I] CONVENTS AND RESIDENCES FOR SISTERS

CORPUS CHRISTI. *Bethany Convent*, 2962 Austin St., 78404. Tel: 512-888-7537. Sisters of the Incarnate Word and Blessed Sacrament 2.

Blessed Sacrament Chapel, 4105 Ocean Dr., 78411-1223. Tel: 512-852-6212. Sr. Mary Margaret Friedl, S.Sp.S. de A.P., Supr. Sister-Servants of the Holy Spirit of Perpetual Adoration (Motherhouse, Steyl, Holland) 10.

Congregation of the Sisters of the Holy Cross, Holy Cross Convent, 1109 N. Staples, 78401-1836. Tel: 512-888-7753; 888-4012.

Corpus Christi Academy Convent, 3036 Saratoga Blvd., 78415. Tel: 512-853-5772. Sisters of St. Ann. Sr. Emiliana Mampallil, S.S.A., Supr.

Dominican Daughters of Santo Tomas de Aquino, 12201 Hearn Rd., 78410.

Incarnate Word Convent, 2930 S. Alameda, 78404. Tel: 512-882-5413. Sisters of the Incarnate Word and Blessed Sacrament. Legal Title: *Convent Academy of the Incarnate Word*. Sr. Michelle Marie Kuntscher, I.W.B.S., Supr. Tel: 512-882-5413; Rev. Robert McGrath, O.M.I. Sisters 33; Total Staff 17; Total in Residence 33.

Mount Carmel Home Convent, 4130 S. Alameda St., 78411. Tel: 512-855-6243. Carmelite Sisters of the Divine Heart of Jesus 9.

Mount Tabor Convent, 12940 Up-River Rd., 78410. Tel: 512-241-1955. Novitiate and Central Regional House of the Missionary Sisters of Jesus, Mary, and Joseph. Sr. Avelina Sosa, M.J.M.J., Delegation Supr.; Sr. Angeles Berrozpe, M.J.M.J., Supr. Sisters 5; Total Staff 5; Total Assisted 5.

Pax Christi Residence, 4601 Calallen Dr., 78410. Tel: 512-241-2833.
Pax Christi Institute. Mother Teresa Santoyo, P.C.I., Supr.; Rev. Msgr. Thomas Meany, Chap. Tel: 512-241-6329. Sisters 12; Total Staff 8; Total Assisted 3,640.

Religious Missionaries of St. Dominic, Inc. (Congregacion de Religiosas Misioneras de Santo Domingo), 2237 Waldron Rd., 78418. Tel: 512-939-8102; Fax: 512-939-8203.

Our Lady of the Rosary Learning Center. Sr. Mary Purificacion Palis, O.P., Contact Person, Delegate of the Supr. Gen.; Sr. Antonia Egar, Supr.

St. Joseph Home Convent, 4015 MacArthur St., 78416-1907. Tel: 512-853-6970; Fax: 512-853-6670. Carmelite Sisters of the Divine Heart of Jesus. Sr. M. Michelle Miranda Carmel, D.C.J., Supr. Total Staff 14; Sisters 5; Total Assisted 100.

Sisters of Our Lady of Charity Convent, 1201 Lantana St., 78407. Tel: 512-289-2611. Sisters of Our Lady of Charity. Sisters 2.

Spohn Hospital Convent, 1725 2nd St., 78404. Tel: 512-881-3000; 884-0702; Fax: 512-881-3634. Congregation of Sisters of Charity of the Incarnate Word - San Antonio. Sisters 3.

Stella Maris Convent, 1739 Second St., 78404. Tel: 512-887-7920; 887-0587. Congregation of Sisters of Charity of the Incarnate Word - San Antonio. Sr. Julia Delaney, C.C.V.I., Coord.

KINGSVILLE. *Missionary Daughters of the Most Pure Virgin Mary*, 919 N. Ninth St., 78363. Sr. Consuelo Ramirez, M.D.P.V.M., Supr. Sisters 11.

LAREDO. *Mary, Help of Christians Convent*, 10 E. Del Mar Blvd., 78041. Tel: 512-722-3966.
E-mail: fmasuolr@icsi.net
Daughters of Mary Help of Christians Salesian Sisters. Sr. Teresita Delgado, F.M.A., Supr.; Sr. Barbara Campbell, F.M.A., Prin.; Sr. Rosalba Garcia, F.M.A.; Sr. Ofelia Lozano, F.M.A.; Sr. Maria Guadalupe Medina, F.M.A.; Sr. Trinidad Reyes, F.M.A.; Sr. Assunta Sanchez, F.M.A.; Sr. Josephine Sanchez, F.M.A. Sisters 8; Total Staff 65.

Sacred Heart Children's Home Convent, 3310 S. Zapata Hwy., 78046. Tel: 210-723-3343. Servants of the Sacred Heart of Jesus and of the Poor. Sr. Maria Teresa Grajeda, S.S.H.J.P., Supr. Sisters 17.

St. Augustine's Convent, 1501 Cjuerrevo St., 78040. Tel: 956-722-3245. Sisters of Divine Providence. Sr. Maria Elise van Dijk, C.D.P.; Sr. Miriam Fidelis Mellein, C.D.P. Sisters 2.

Sisters of Mercy of the St. Louis Regional Community, Inc., 1414 Hendricks Ave., 78040. Tel: 210-723-1364. Religious Sisters of Mercy. Sr. Olivia M. Obregon, Local Coord. Sisters 16; Total Staff 11.

Mercy Hospital Convent, Sisters' Retirement Center.

Su Casa, 3906 Monterrey, 78043-6648. Tel: 210-718-8762.

Sisters of St. John, 504 Century Dr. S., 78046. Tel: 210-727-1028. Sr. Maria Immakulata Dziegielewska, Local Supr. Total in Residence 6.

Ursuline Convent, 2302 Corpus Christi St., 78043. Tel: 210-723-9185.
E-mail: mvitt2302@aol.com
1415 Jarvis St., 78043. Tel: 210-723-8968. Roman Union Central Province of the U.S. Sr. Margaret Mary Vitt, O.S.U., Prioress. Sisters 12.

ROCKPORT. *Schoenstatt Sisters of Mary*, 130 Front St., Lamar, HC 04, Box 100, 78382-9606. Tel: 512-729-1868; Fax: 512-729-1685. Secular Institute of the Schoenstatt Sisters of Mary. Sr. M. Antoinette Buffler, I.S.S.M., Prov. Supr. Sisters 27; Total in Residence 17.

SARITA. *Lebh Shomea, House of Prayer*, La Parra Ranch, 78385-0009. Tel: 512-294-5369; Fax: 512-294-5791. Total Staff 7; Total in Residence 4.

SKIDMORE. *Our Lady of the Most Holy Trinity Convent*, General Motherhouse, P.O. Box 189, 78389. Tel: 512-287-3570; 287-3830. Sr. Mary of the Redemption, S.O.L.T., Gen. Sister Servant; Sr. Mary Carmen Sandoval, S.O.L.T., Regional Sister Servant. Sisters 50.

[J] MISCELLANEOUS

CORPUS CHRISTI. *The Catholic Campaign of America, Inc.*, P.O. Box 2620, 78403-2620; Fax: 512-882-1018.

The Counseling Center, 1322 Commache, 78401. Tel: 512-894-0651. Ms. Gloria Garcia, Lead Counselor. Total Staff 2; Patients assisted annually 500.

Father Magsam Center for Spiritual Direction, 4103 Ocean Dr., 78411. Tel: 512-853-0170. Sr. Joan Michele Rake, C.D.P., Spiritual Dir. Total Assisted 2,120.

Hope, Faith & Love, Inc., 658 Robinson, 78404. Total Staff 2; Total Assisted 72.

Incarnate Word Academy Foundation, 2930 S. Alameda, 78404. Tel: 512-882-5413. Sr. Michelle Marie Kuntscher, I.W.B.S., Pres.

Pope John Paul, II Library, The Corpus Christi Catholic Center, 3036 Saratoga Blvd., 78415.

Secular Institute of the Schoenstatt Fathers aka Schoenstatt Fathers, 4343 Gains St., 78412-2541. Tel: 512-992-9841; Fax: 512-992-9842. Revs. Hector Vega, I.Sch., Supr. & Contact Person; Antonio Rodrigues, I.Sch.; Robert Decock, I.Sch.

LAREDO. *St. Augustine School Endowment Fund, Inc.*, 1300 Galveston, 78040. Tel: 210-724-5119. Sr. Antoinette Billeaud, Contact Person.

San Agustin Historical Preservation & Restoration Society, Inc., 200 San Agustin Ave., 78040. Tel: 956-722-1382. Rev. Msgr. James E. Harris, Contact Person.

RELIGIOUS INSTITUTES OF MEN REPRESENTED IN THE DIOCESE

For further details refer to the corresponding bracketed number in the Religious Institutes of Men or Women section.

[0140]—*The Augustinians*.—O.S.A.
[0200]—*Benedictine Monks*.—O.S.B.
[]—*Congregation of St. John*. (Priorato de San Juan).—F.J.
[0630]—*Congregation of the Missionaries of the Holy Family*.—M.S.F.
[0430]—*Dominican, Order of Preachers*. (Spain).—O.P.
[0520]—*Franciscan Friars*.—O.F.M.
[0770]—*The Marist Brothers*.—F.M.S.
[1110]—*Missionaries of the Sacred Heart*.—M.S.C.
[0910]—*Oblates of Mary Immaculate*. (Southwest Prov.).—O.M.I.
[1310]—*Order of the Holy Trinity*. (Province of Baltimore).—O.SS.T.
[]—*Priestly Fraternity of St. Peter, Society of Apostolic Life*.—F.S.S.P.
[1070]—*Redemptorists*.—C.Ss.R.
[1190]—*Salesians of St. John Bosco*.—S.D.B.
[]—*Schoenstatt Fathers*.—I.Sch.
[0690]—*Society of Jesus*.—S.J.
[0975]—*Society of Our Lady of the Most Holy Trinity, Society of Apostolic Life*.—S.O.L.T.

RELIGIOUS INSTITUTES OF WOMEN REPRESENTED IN THE DIOCESE

[0360]—*Carmelite Sisters of the Divine Heart of Jesus*.—Carmel.D.C.J.
[0406]—*Congregation of Sisters of Charity of Incarnate Word*. (Galveston/Houston, TX).—C.C.V.I.
[0406]—*Congregation of Sisters of Charity of the Incarnate Word*. (San Antonio, TX).—C.C.V.I.
[]—*Congregation of Sisters of St. John*.
[1920]—*Congregation of the Sisters of the Holy Cross*.—C.S.C.
[0850]—*Daughters of Mary Help of Christians*.—F.M.A.
[]—*Dominican Daughters of Santo Tomas de Aquino*.
[]—*Dominican Sisters of St. Thomas Aquinas*.—O.P.
[]—*Eucharistic Missionary Society*.—E.M.S.
[]—*Medical Missionaries Sisters of St. Joseph*. (Pittsburg, PA).—S.S.J.
[]—*Misioneras del Perpetua Socorro*.—M.P.S.
[0390]—*Missionary Carmelites of St. Teresa*.—C.M.S.T.
[]—*Missionary Daughters of the Most Pure Virgin Mary*. (U.S. Foundation-Mexico).—M.D.P.V.M.
[2770]—*Missionary Sisters of Jesus, Mary, and Joseph*.—M.J.M.J.
[]—*Pax Christi Institute*.—P.C.I.
[]—*Religious Missionaries of St. Dominic*. (Spanish Prov.).—O.P.
[2519]—*Religious Sisters of Mercy*.—R.S.M.
[]—*Schoenstatt Sisters of Mary Secular Institute*.—I.S.S.M.
[3660]—*Servants of the Sacred Heart of Jesus and of the Poor*.—S.S.H.J.P.
[1010]—*Sisters of Divine Providence of San Antonio, Texas*.—C.D.P.
[2590]—*Sisters of Mercy of the Blessed Sacrament*.—H.M.S.S.
[3070]—*Sisters of Our Lady of Charity*. (Dallas, TX).—O.L.C.
[]—*Sisters of Our Lady of the Rosary of Fatima, Zapata*.—H.M.R.F.
[3360]—*Sisters of Providence of Saint Mary-of-the-Woods, IN*.—S.P.
[3718]—*Sisters of St. Anne*.—S.S.A.
[1930]—*Sisters of the Holy Cross*.—C.S.C.
[2040]—*Sisters of the Holy Spirit*.—S.H.Sp.
[2205]—*Sisters of the Incarnate Word and Blessed Sacrament*.—I.W.B.S.
[]—*Sisters of the Society of Our Lady of the Most Holy Trinity, Society of Apostolic Life*.—S.O.L.T.
[3540]—*Sisters-Servants of the Holy Spirit of Perpetual Adoration*.—S.Sp.S.deA.P.
[4110]—*Ursuline Nuns (Roman Union)*.—O.S.U.

NECROLOGY

† Berger, Lawrence Joseph, (Retired). —Died July 24, 1997.

† Geisen, Bernard Sylvester, (Retired). —Died Jan. 12, 1997.

Diocese of Covington

(Dioecesis Covingtonensis)

Most Reverend

ROBERT W. MUENCH, D.D.

Bishop of Covington; ordained May 18, 1968; appointed Titular Bishop of Mactaris and Auxiliary of New Orleans May 8, 1990; consecrated June 29, 1990; appointed January 5, 1996; installed March 19, 1996. *Mailing Address: P.O. Box 18548, Erlanger, KY, 41018-0548.* Tel.: 606-283-6215.

Most Reverend

WILLIAM A. HUGHES, D.D.

Retired Bishop of Covington; ordained April 6, 1946; appointed Titular Bishop of Inis Cathaig and Auxiliary of Youngstown July 23, 1974; consecrated September 12, 1974; appointed Bishop of Covington April 13, 1979; transferred to Covington May 8, 1979; retired July 4, 1995. *Res., Cathedral Basilica of the Assumption, 1140 Madison Ave., Covington, KY, 41011-3116.*

ESTABLISHED JULY 29, 1853.

Square Miles 3,359.

Comprises 14 Counties of the Commonwealth of Kentucky in the north and east of the Commonwealth, including Bracken, Boone, Campbell, Carroll, Fleming, Gallatin, Grant, Harrison, Kenton, Lewis, Mason, Owen, Pendleton and Robertson Counties.

For legal titles of parishes and diocesan institutions, consult the Chancery Office.

The Catholic Center: P.O. Box 18548, Erlanger, KY, 41018-0548. Tel.: 606-283-6200; Fax: 606-283-6334.

STATISTICAL OVERVIEW

Personnel	
Bishop	1
Retired Bishops	1
Priests: Diocesan Active in Diocese	64
Priests: Active Outside Diocese	4
Priests: Retired, Sick or Absent	49
Number of Diocesan Priests	117
Religious Priests in Diocese	1
Ordinations:	
Diocesan Priests	1
Permanent Deacons in Diocese	18
Total Brothers	6
Total Sisters	440
Parishes	
Parishes	48
With Resident Pastor:	
Resident Diocesan Priests	41
Without Resident Pastor:	
Administered by Priests	4
Administered by Women Religious	3
Missions	9
Pastoral Centers	8
New Parishes Created	1
Closed Parishes	4
Professional Ministry Personnel:	
Brothers	2
Sisters	11
Lay Ministers	30
Welfare	
Catholic Hospitals	3
Total Assisted	323,402
Homes for the Aged	3
Total Assisted	576
Residential Care of Children	2
Total Assisted	78
Day Care and Extended Day Care Centers	1
Total Assisted	81
Special Centers for Social Services	4
Total Assisted	81,269
Other Institutions	1
Total Assisted	6,936
Educational	
Diocesan Students in Other Seminaries	5
Total Seminarians	5
Colleges and Universities	1
Total Students	1,505
High Schools, Diocesan and Parish	7
Total Students	2,450
High Schools, Private	2
Total Students	791
Elementary Schools, Diocesan and Parish	29
Total Students	8,049
Elementary Schools, Private	2
Total Students	498
Non-residential Schools for the Disabled	1
Total Students	20
Catechesis/Religious Education:	
High School Students	425
Elementary Students	4,267
Total Students Under Catholic Instruction	18,010
Teachers in the Diocese:	
Brothers	1
Sisters	63
Lay Teachers	647
Vital Statistics	
Receptions into the Church:	
Infant Baptism Totals	1,435
Adult Baptism Totals	216
Received into Full Communion	145
First Communions	1,545
Confirmations	1,620
Marriages:	
Catholic	373
Interfaith	220
Total Marriages	593
Deaths	844
Total Catholic Population	83,997
Total Population	401,127

Former Bishops—Rt. Rev. GEORGE ALOYSIUS CARRELL, S.J., D.D., cons. Nov. 1, 1853; died Sept. 25, 1868.—Rt. Rev. AUGUSTUS MARIA TOEBBE, D.D., cons. Jan. 9, 1870; died May 2, 1884.—Rt. Rev. CAMILLUS PAUL MAES, D.D., cons. Jan. 25, 1885; died May 11, 1915.—Rt. Rev. FERDINAND BROSSART, D.D., cons. Jan. 25, 1916; resigned March 14, 1923; died Aug. 6, 1930.—Most Rev. FRANCIS W. HOWARD, D.D., cons. July 15, 1923; died Jan. 18, 1944.—Most Rev. WILLIAM T. MULLOY, D.D., LL.D., cons. Jan. 10, 1945; died June 1, 1959.—Most Rev. RICHARD H. ACKERMAN, C.S.Sp., D.D., cons. May 26, 1956; transferred to Covington April 6, 1960; retired Nov. 28, 1978; died Nov. 18, 1992.—Most Rev. WILLIAM A. HUGHES, D.D., cons. Sept. 12, 1974; appt. April 13, 1979; retired July 4, 1995.

Vicar General and Chancellor—Very Rev. ROGER L. KRIEGE, S.T.B., V.G.

Assistant to Bishop and Assistant Chancellor—Rev. THOMAS B. SACKSTEDER.

Diocesan Tribunal—Very Rev. JOHN R. SCHULTE, J.C.L., Judicial Vicar; JOHN M. MEECE, Notary & Cast Promoter. Defenders of the Bond: Revs. GREGORY E. OSBURG, M.A., J.C.L.; GERALD E. TWADELL, Ph.D.; PAUL BERSCHIED; JOSEPH GALLENSTEIN.

Diocesan Consultors—Very Revs. ROGER L. KRIEGE, V.G.; EDWARD J. BRODNICK, V.F.; ROBERT J. HENDERSON, V.F.; JOHN H. KROGER, V.F.; Revs. JOSEPH N. BOSCHERT; ROBERT C. WEHAGE.

Deans—Rev. RAYMOND C. HOLTZ, Covington; Rev. Msgr. DONALD F. HELLMANN, Northern Kenton County; Rev. EDWARD J. BRODNICK, Southwest; Rev. JOHN H. KROGER, Newport, Bellevue, Dayton; Rev. ROBERT HENDERSON, Campbell County; Rev. WILLIAM HINDS, Southeast.

Diocesan Pastoral Council—Mrs. ELLEN CURTIN, Chm.; Sr. JO ANN MCMASTER, O.P., Exec. Sec.

Presbyteral Council—Rev. ROBERT C. WEHAGE, Chm.; Rev. Msgr. DONALD E. HELLMANN, Vice-Chm.; Rev. JOSEPH A. GALLENSTEIN, Sec.

Due Process Board of Administrative Review—Mr. MICHAEL HAMMONS, J.D., Chm.; Mr. STEPHEN KOPLYAY, Sec.

Diocesan Offices and Directors

The Catholic Center—*947 Donaldson Hwy., P.O. Box 18548, Erlanger, 41018-0548.* Tel: 606-283-6200; Fax: 606-283-6334. Office Hours: Mon.-Fri. 8:30-4:30.

Archives—DAVID E. SCHROEDER.

Board of Total Catholic Education—Mr. LAWRENCE W. BOWMAN, Ph.D.; SCOTT GROSSER, Chm.

Building Committee—Mr. JOSEPH SCHWAB, Chm.

Campus Ministry-Newman Centers—AL CUCCHETTI, Pastoral Admin., *Northern Kentucky Univ., 512 Johns Hill Rd., P.O. Box 76174, Highland Heights, 41076-1449.* Tel: 606-781-3775.

Cathedral Foundation, Inc.—CAROL SROCZYNSKI, Exec. Dir., *1140 Madison Ave., Covington, 41011-3116.* Tel: 606-431-2060; Fax: 606-431-8444.

Catholic Charities—Sr. JOAN MARIE BOBERG, C.D.P., Dir., *3629 Church St., Covington, 41015-1499.* Tel: 606-581-8974; Fax: 606-581-9595.

Catholic Scouting—Rev. JEROME BRITT, Chap.; Mrs. BETH WORLAND, Chm.

Cemeteries—JOHN NIENABER, Dir.

Censor Librorum—Rev. JAMES E. QUILL, S.T.D.
Charismatic Renewal—Contact Persons: HARRY HUMPERT; JOSEPH BESSLER.
Communication—Rev. THOMAS B. SACKSTEDER, Dir.
Continuing Education of Priests—Rev. RONALD KETTELER, Dir.
Corpus Central Purchasing—SANDRA NARE, Gen. Mgr. Buyers: MIKE FREUDENBERG; BRIAN NORTHCUTT, *845 Isabella St., Newport, 41071.* Tel: 606-491-8100; 800-955-2541; Fax: 606-491-6587.
Cursillo Movement—Rev. GERALD L. REINERSMAN, Spiritual Dir. DAVID ZERHUSEN, Lay Dir.
Development and Missions—SUE GRETHEL, Dir. Includes Pontifical Aid Societies, Campaign for Human Development, Catholic Relief Fund, Holy Childhood Assoc., Inner City Missions.
Disabilities Commission—J. DAVID MILLER, Chm.
Ecumenism—Rev. RONALD KETTELER, *Thomas More College, 333 Thomas More Pkwy., Crestview Hills, 41017-3428.* Tel: 606-344-3393.
Evangelization and Initiation Commission—MADONNA KLING, C.D.P., Chm.
Family Ministry—SUSAN VOGT, Dir.
Finance—ANTHONY G. DEPENBROCK, Dir.
Justice and Peace Office—Sr. RUTH KETTMAN, C.S.J., Dir.
Lay Retreat Movement—Deacon EDWARD STIERITZ, Dir., *945 Donaldson Hwy., Erlanger, 41018-1093.* Tel: 606-371-4224.
Legion of Mary—Rev. JOSEPH RUETER, Spiritual Dir.
Liaison for Retired Priests—Rev. ROBERT L. VATER.
Ministry Development Program—Sr. MONICA STUHLREYER, I.H.M., Dir.; Sr. MARY GALLAGHER, S.C., Assoc. Dir.
Mission Services, Pontifical Mission Aid Societies, Campaign for Human Development, Catholic Relief Fund, Holy Childhood Assoc., Inner City Missions—See Development and Missions.
Missions Among Black and Native Americans—Sr. JANET BUCHER, C.D.P.
Mustard Seed Community—Contact Persons: JOSEPH BESSLER; HARRY HUMPERT.
Newspaper "Messenger"—GERALD H. ENDERLE, Editor-in-Chief.
Pastoral Ministry Formation—Rev. GERALD L. REINERSMAN, Dir.
Pastoral Office for the Deaf—Sr. ROBIN CONNELL, C.S.J.
Pastoral Planning and Research—Sr. JO ANN MCMASTER, O.P., Dir., Consultant Parish Svcs.
Permanent Diaconate Formation—Rev. DONALD J. ENZWEILER, Dir.
Priest Personnel—Rev. GERALD L. REINERSMAN, Dir.
Priests' Eucharistic League—Rev. LOUIS B. BRINKER, Dir.
Priests' Retirement Board—Very Rev. ROGER L. KRIEGE, V.G., Chm.
Religious—Sr. M. JOAN DOHMEN, Dir.
Serra Club of Diocese of Covington—Rev. GERALD L. REINERSMAN, Chap.
St. Vincent de Paul Society—Rev. ROBERT J. REINKE, Spiritual Dir.
Total Catholic Education—LAWRENCE M. BOWMAN, Ph.D., Dir. Catholic Education & Supt. EUGENE A. KUEHNE, Dir. Business Svcs.; Sr. STELLA MARIE GOUGH, O.S.B., Dir. Catechetical Svcs.
Vocation Council—Rev. GERALD L. REINERSMAN, Dir.
Worship Commission—MADONNA MARIE KLING, C.D.P., Chm.
Office of Worship, Evangelization & Initiation—MADONNA MARIE KLING, C.D.P.
Office of Youth Ministry—Mrs. BETH WORLAND, Dir.

CLERGY, PARISHES, MISSIONS AND PAROCHIAL SCHOOLS

CITY OF COVINGTON
(Kenton County)

1—CATHEDRAL, BASILICA OF THE ASSUMPTION (1837), Very Rev. John W. Cahill; Deacon John Dunning.
Res., 1140 Madison Ave., 41011-3116. Tel: 606-431-2060; Fax: 606-431-8444.

2—ST. AGNES (1930), Rev. Msgr. Donald F. Hellmann; Revs. John J. Sterling; James E. Quill, (Retired); Deacons Joseph Cleves; David Flynn.
Res., 1680 Dixie Hwy., Fort Wright, 41011-2779. Tel: 606-431-1802; Fax: 606-291-7017.
School—Tel: 606-261-0543; Fax: 606-261-9778.
Lay Teachers 35; Students 515.
Catechesis / Religious Programs—Students 73.

3—ST. ANN (1860), Rev. Mark Steidle.
Res., 1274 Parkway, 41011-1060. Tel: 606-261-9548.

4—ST. AUGUSTINE (1870), Rev. Leo C. Schmidt. In res., Rev. Robert J. Reinke, (Retired).
Res., 1839 Euclid Ave., 41014-1162. Tel: 606-431-3943; Fax: 606-431-4036.
School—Tel: 606-261-5564; Fax: 606-261-5402.
Sisters of Notre Dame 3; Lay Teachers 7; Students 152.

5—ST. BENEDICT (1885), Rev. Mark A. Keene.
Res., 338 E. 17th St., 41014-1315. Tel: 606-431-5607; Fax: 606-431-5847.
Catechesis / Religious Programs—Students 160.

6—HOLY CROSS (1890), Rev. Thomas C. Barnes; Ms. Marg Wilburs, Pastoral Assoc. In res., Revs. Charles J. Garvey, (Retired); Charles Hoffer, (Retired); Deacon Ralph Colatrella.
Res., 3612 Church St., 41015-1431. Tel: 606-431-0636; Fax: 606-431-6917.
School—Tel: 606-581-6599.
Lay Teachers 12; Students 233.
Catechesis / Religious Programs—Students 70.

7—ST. JOHN (1854), Rev. David B. Gamm.
Res., 627 Pike St., 41011-1926. Tel: 606-431-5314; Fax: 606-431-8397.

8—MOTHER OF GOD (1841), Rev. Raymond C. Holtz; Deacon Thomas Runge.
Res., 119 W. 6th St., 41011-1409. Tel: 606-291-2288; Fax: 606-291-2065.

9—CHURCH OF OUR SAVIOR (1943), Sr. Janet Marie Bucher, C.D.P., Admin.; Rev. Robert C. Rosing.
Res., 246 E. 10th St., 41011-3026. Tel: 606-491-5872; Fax: 606-431-8444.
Catechesis / Religious Programs—Students 140.

OUTSIDE THE CITY OF COVINGTON

Alexandria, Campbell Co., St. Mary of the Assumption (1860), Revs. Joseph C. Brink; Ralph C. Hartman.
Res., 5 S. Jefferson St., 41001-1315. Tel: 606-635-4188; Fax: 606-635-4189. [CEM]
School—9 S. Jefferson St., 41001-1398. Tel: 606-635-9539; Fax: 606-635-4189.
Sisters of Notre Dame 2; Lay Teachers 27; Students 473.
Catechesis / Religious Programs—Students 248.

Augusta, Bracken Co., St. Augustine (1860), Very Rev. Daniel J. Saner; Deacon Frank Estill.
Res., 215 E. Fourth St., 41002-1117. Tel: 606-756-2377; Fax: 606-756-2377. [JC]
School—Tel: 606-756-3229; Fax: 606-756-2377.
Sisters of Notre Dame 3; Lay Teachers 5; Students 72.

Bellevue, Campbell Co., Sacred Heart (1874), Rev. Lawrence R. Robotnik. In res., Rev. Lawrence W. Keller, (Retired).
Res., 318 Division St., 41073-1104. Tel: 606-261-6172; Fax: 606-261-6172.

St. Anthony (1889), Rev. John H. Kroger.
Res., 320 Poplar St., 41073-1196. Tel: 606-431-7143; Fax: 606-491-4735.
Catechesis / Religious Programs—Students 20.

Brooksville, Bracken Co., St. James (1868), Rev. James L. McHugh.
Res., P.O. Box 27, 41004-0027. Tel: 606-735-2271. [CEM]
Catechesis / Religious Programs—Students 46.
Mission—Minerva, Mason Co., St. James, Kentucky Rd. 435-1235, Minerva, 41062.

California, Campbell Co., Sts. Peter and Paul (1854), Rev. Joseph N. Boschert.
Res., Rte. 2, Box 134, 41007-9713. Tel: 606-635-2924; Fax: 606-635-9184. [CEM 2]
School—Tel: 606-635-4382.
Lay Teachers 7; Students 117.
Mission—Stepstone, Pendleton Co., Immaculate Conception.

Camp Springs, Campbell Co., St. Joseph (1845), Rev. Paul F. Tenhundfeld, Admin.; Stephanie Zink, Pastoral Assoc.
Res., Box 225, 41059-9746. Tel: 606-635-2491; Fax: 606-635-7336. [CEM]
School—Tel: 606-635-5652.
Religious 1; Lay Teachers 3; Students 58.
Catechesis / Religious Programs—Students 58.

Carrollton, Carroll Co., St. John the Evangelist (1853), Rev. William B. Neuhaus.
Res., 507 Fifth St., 41008-1203. Tel: 502-732-5776; Fax: 502-732-5176. [CEM]
Catechesis / Religious Programs—Students 85.
Mission—Perry Park, Owen Co., Transfiguration.

Cold Spring, Campbell Co., St. Joseph (1870), Revs. Robert J. Henderson; James B. Egbers. In res., Rev. Joseph J. Rueter, (Retired).
Res., 4011 Alexandria Pk., 41076-1817. Tel: 606-441-1604; Fax: 606-441-7681. [CEM]
School—Tel: 606-441-2025; Fax: 606-441-7681.
Sisters of Notre Dame 4; Lay Teachers 37; Students 665.
Catechesis / Religious Programs—Students 80.

Crescent Springs, Kenton Co., St. Joseph (1916), Revs. Raymond S. Hartman; Douglas J. Lauer; Deacons Marvin Holstein; Joseph Baker. In res., Rev. Ronald M. Ketteler.
Res., 2470 Lorraine Ct., 41017-1406. Tel: 606-341-6609; Fax: 606-578-2741.
School—Tel: 606-578-2742; Fax: 606-578-2754.
Lay Teachers 30; Students 565.
Catechesis / Religious Programs—Students 175.

Cynthiana, Harrison Co., St. Edward (1872), Rev. Louis B. Brinker.
Res., 123 N. Walnut St., 41031-1225. Tel: 606-234-5444; Fax: 606-234-9823. [CEM]
School—Tel: 606-234-2731; Fax: 606-234-2731.
Sisters of Notre Dame 1; Lay Teachers 3; Students 77.

Dayton, Campbell Co., St. Bernard (1853), Revs. Michael E. Comer; Paul Brinker, (Retired); Deacon Charles Dietz.
Res., Fifth & Berry Sts., 41074-1139. Tel: 606-261-8506.
School—Tel: 606-581-6759; Fax: 606-581-7260.
Sisters of Divine Providence of Kentucky 2; Lay Teachers 3; Students 93.

Edgewood, Kenton Co., St. Pius X (1958), Revs. Douglas F. Fortner; Jeffrey D. Von Lehmen; Deacon Robert J. Hermann.
Res., 340 Dudley Rd., 41017-2609. Tel: 606-341-4888; Fax: 606-578-8597.
School—Tel: 606-341-3435.
Priests 2; Lay Teachers 33; Students 642.
Catechesis / Religious Programs—Students 232.

Erlanger, Kenton Co., St. Barbara (1967), Rev. G. Michael Greer; Deacon Bernard J. Kaiser.
Res., 4042 Turkeyfoot Rd., 41018-2921. Tel: 606-371-3100; Fax: 606-371-3101.
Catechesis / Religious Programs—Students 209.

St. Henry (1890), Revs. Robert C. Wehage; Michael D. Barth; Charlotte Berling, Pastoral Assoc.
Res., 3813 Dixie Hwy., 41018-1809. Tel: 606-342-2540; Fax: 606-342-2542.
School—Tel: 606-342-2551; Fax: 606-342-2554.
Religious 1; Lay Teachers 28; Students 523.
Catechesis / Religious Programs—Students 167.

Mary, Queen of Heaven, Boone Co., (1955), Rev. John J. McGuire. In res., Rev. James P. Gerrety, (Retired).
Res., 1150 Donaldson Hwy., 41018-1048. Tel: 606-525-6909; Fax: 606-525-7067.
School—Tel: 606-371-8100.
Sisters 1; Lay Teachers 8; Students 235.

Falmouth, Pendleton Co., St. Francis Xavier (1880), Rev. Louis H. Dickmann.
Res., 202 Second St., 41040-1118. Tel: 606-654-8241; Fax: 606-654-5203. [CEM]
Catechesis / Religious Programs—Students 81.

Flemingsburg, Fleming Co., St. Charles (1859), Rev. Verne F. Hogan.
Res., 211 Mt. Carmel Ave., 41041-1315. Tel: 606-845-4601.

Florence, Boone Co., St. Paul (1832), Revs. George E. Schneider; Joseph Gallenstein. In res., Rev. Robert L. Gruber, (Retired).
Res., 7301 Dixie Hwy., 41042-2126. Tel: 606-371-8051; Fax: 606-647-4073.
School—Tel: 606-647-4070.
Lay Teachers 26; Students 547.
Catechesis / Religious Programs—Students 437.

Fort Mitchell, Kenton Co., Blessed Sacrament (1920), Revs. Albert E. Ruschman; Mark G. Witte; Sr. Ann Middendorf, O.S.B., Pastoral Assoc.
Res., 2415 Dixie Hwy., 41017-2936. Tel: 606-331-4302; Fax: 606-578-4752.
School—Tel: 606-331-3062; Fax: 606-344-7323.
Lay Teachers 33; Students 565.
Catechesis / Religious Programs—Students 230.

Fort Thomas, Campbell Co., St. Catherine of Siena (1930), Rev. Daniel J. Vogelpohl; Deacon Edward Stieritz. In res., Rev. Robert L. Vater, (Retired).
Mailing Address: 1803 N. Ft. Thomas Ave., 41075-1170. Tel: 606-441-1352; Fax: 606-572-2685.
School—Tel: 606-572-2680; Fax: 606-572-2686.
Lay Teachers 17; Students 234.
Catechesis / Religious Programs—Students 234.

St. Thomas (1902), Revs. John J. Riesenberg; Richard W. Frazier; Deacon James Sweigart.
Res., 26 E. Villa Pl., 41075-2218. Tel: 606-441-1282; Fax: 606-572-4640.

School—Tel: 606-572-4641; Fax: 606-572-4644.
Sisters of Divine Providence of Kentucky 3; Lay Teachers 23; Students 271.
Catechesis/Religious Programs—Students 112.

Burlington, Boone Co., Immaculate Heart of Mary (1954), Rev. Jerome C. Britt.
Church—5876 Veterans Way, 41005-8824. Tel: 606-689-4488; Fax: 606-689-5636.
School—Tel: 606-689-4303.
Sisters of Divine Providence of Kentucky 2; Lay Teachers 20; Students 448.
Catechesis/Religious Programs—Students 345.

Independence, Kenton Co., St. Cecilia (1880), Rev. Paul L. Berschied.
Res., 5313 Madison Pk., P.O. Box 186, 41051-0186. Tel: 606-363-4311; Fax: 606-363-4312. [CEM]
School—Tel: 606-363-4314; Fax: 606-363-4315.
Lay Teachers 8; Students 194.
Catechesis/Religious Programs—Students 194.

Kenton, Kenton Co., St. Matthew (1909), Rev. Gregory E. Osburg.
Res., 13816 Decoursey Pk., P.O. Box 82, 41053-0082. Tel: 606-356-6530; Fax: 606-356-6530, Ext. 51. [CEM]
Catechesis/Religious Programs—Students 68.
Mission—Morning View, Kenton Co., Assumption of the Blessed Virgin, 3711 St. Mary Rd., Morning View, 41063.

Ludlow, Kenton Co., Sts. Boniface and James (1872), Rev. Allan W. Bradley.
Res., 304 Oak St., 41016-1417. Tel: 606-261-5340; Fax: 606-261-5340.

May's Lick, Mason Co., St. Rose of Lima (1864), Rev. Verne F. Hogan.
Church—P.O. Box 100, 41055-0100. Tel: 606-763-6304.

Maysville, Mason Co., St. Patrick (1847), Rev. William H. Hinds; Deacon Ernest B. Hillenmeyer.
Res., 110 E. Third St., P.O. Box 248, 41056-0248. Tel: 606-564-9015. [CEM]
School—Tel: 606-564-5949; Fax: 606-564-8795.
Lay Teachers 12; Students 242.
High School—Lay Teachers 13; Students 102.
Catechesis/Religious Programs—Students 45.

Melbourne, Campbell Co., St. Philip (1908), Rev. James M. Ryan.
Res., 1402 Mary Ingles Hwy., 41059-9701. Tel: 606-441-8949; Fax: 606-442-0290.
School—Tel: 606-441-3423; Fax: 606-441-2611.
Sisters of Divine Providence of Kentucky 3; Lay Teachers 4; Students 111.

Newport, Campbell Co.,

1—HOLY SPIRIT, (1997), Revs. Richard G. Bolte; Donald A. Enzweiler.
Res., 825 Washington Ave., 41071-1945. Tel: 606-431-2533; Fax: 606-431-3247.
School—840 Washington Ave., 41071-2485. Tel: 606-431-8745.
Religious Teachers 1; Lay Teachers 5; Students 107.
Junior High School—Grand & Chesapeake, 41071-2485. Tel: 606-292-0487; Fax: 606-292-0487.
Religious Teachers 2; Lay Teachers 4; Students 62.
Missions—Newport, Campbell Co., Corpus Christi, (1844) 841 Isabella St., 41071-1338; Newport, Campbell Co., St. Francis de Sales, (1911) Grand & Chesapeake, 41071-2418; Newport, Campbell Co., St. Stephen, (1854) 825 Washington Ave., 41071-2485; Newport, Campbell Co., St. Vincent de Paul, (1916) 115 Main St., 41071-2353.

2—CORPUS CHRISTI. Closed. For sacramental records contact Holy Spirit, Newport.

3—ST. FRANCIS DE SALES. Closed. For sacramental records contact Holy Spirit, Newport.

4—ST. STEPHEN. Closed. For sacramental records contact Holy Spirit, Newport.

5—ST. VINCENT DE PAUL. Closed. For sacramental records contact Holy Spirit, Newport.

Southgate, Campbell Co., St. Therese of the Infant Jesus (1927), Revs. Clarence J. Heitzman; Brian K. Wigger. In res., Rev. Msgr. Elmer J. Grosser, (Retired).
Res., 11 Temple Pl., 41071-3133. Tel: 606-441-1654; Fax: 606-441-2395.
School—Tel: 606-441-0449; Fax: 606-441-7988.
Sisters of Notre Dame 3; Lay Teachers 12; Students 296.
Catechesis/Religious Programs—Students 65.

Taylor Mill, Kenton Co., St. Anthony (1878), Rev. Thomas P. Robbins.
Res., Grand & Howard Ave., P.O. Box 15219, Covington, 41015-0219. Tel: 606-431-1773.
School—Tel: 606-431-5987.
Lay Teachers 10; Students 200.
Catechesis/Religious Programs—Students 60.

St. Patrick (1968), Rev. B. Gerald Witzemann.
Res., 3285 Mills Rd., Covington, 41015-2480. Tel: 606-356-2171.
Catechesis/Religious Programs—Students 185.

Union, Boone Co., St. Timothy (1989), Rev. Edward J. Brodnick; Deacon Thomas Nolan.
Res., 10272 Hwy. 42, P.O. Box 120, 41091-0120. Tel: 606-384-1100; Fax: 606-384-1709.
Catechesis/Religious Programs—Students 358.

Vanceburg, Lewis Co., Holy Redeemer (1965), Sr. Joseph Fillenwarth, S.P., Pastoral Admin.; Rev. Bruce Brylinski, Pastoral Supvr.
Res., P.O. Box 8, 41179-0008. Tel: 606-796-3052.

Walton, Boone Co., All Saints (1951), Rev. Edwin B. Heile.
Res., 46 Needmore St., 41094-1029. Tel: 606-485-4476; Fax: 606-485-4476. [CEM 2]
Catechesis/Religious Programs—Students 121.

Warsaw, Gallatin Co., St. Joseph (1864), Rev. George J. Schuhmacher.
Mailing Address: P.O. Box 495, 41095-0495.
Res., 602 Sparta Pike, 41095-0495. Tel: 606-567-2425. [CEM]
Mission—Owenton, Owen Co., St. Edward, (1958) 1335 Hwy. 22 E., R.R. 4, Box 35B, Owenton, 40359-9003. Tel: 606-567-2425.

Wilder, Campbell Co., St. John (1847), Rev. Richard H. McGrath; Ms. Margaret Quirk, Pastoral Assoc.
Res., 641 Licking Pike, 41076-9076. Tel: 606-781-2117; Fax: 606-781-2117. [CEM]

Williamstown, Grant Co., St. William (1912), Sr. Carol Leveque, S.C., Pastoral Admin.; Very Rev. Roger L. Kriege, V.G.
Res., 6 Church Dr., 41097. Tel: 606-824-5381; Fax: 606-824-0509. [CEM 2]
Catechesis/Religious Programs—Students 63.
Mission—Dividing Ridge, Pendleton Co., St. John's, (1956).

Chaplains of Public Institutions

COVINGTON. *Children's Psychiatric Hospital of Northern Kentucky*. Rev. Charles E. Weber.
St. John's Nursing Home. Attended by St. Augustine Church, Covington.

COLD SPRING. *Lakeside Place*. Attended by St. Joseph Parish, Cold Spring.

FLORENCE. *St. Luke West*. Rev. Charles E. Weber.

FORT THOMAS. *St. Luke Hospital East*. Rev. John A. Seiler.
Veterans Hospital. Attended by the Franciscan Fathers (O.F.M.), Cincinnati, Ohio.

On Duty Outside the Diocese:
Reverend Fathers—
Callahan, Leonard F., 3537 Townsend, Dallas, TX 75229
Cooney, Roger P., Pontifical College Josephinum, 7625 N. High St., Columbus, OH 43235-1499
Rutz, Gilbert J., 1224 E. Northern Ave., Phoenix, AZ 85020-4274

Leave of Absence:
Reverend Fathers—
Bierman, Earl C.
DeLange, Maurice
Goeke, John W.
Schott, Fred
Wilcoxson, Thomas J.

Military Chaplains:
Reverend Fathers—
Leslie, Larry B., MCMWTC, Chaplain's Office, Bridgeport, CA 93517-5001

Retired:
Most Rev.—
Hughes, William A., 1140 Madison Ave., Covington, KY 41011-3116
Reverend Monsignors—
Finn, Thomas B., Regina Cleri Home, 100 Carmel Manor Rd., Fort Thomas, KY 41075-2300
Fleming, W. Stanley, Regina Cleri Home, 100 Carmel Manor Rd., Fort Thomas, KY 41075-2300
Grosser, Elmer J., St. Therese Rectory, 11 Temple Pl., Southgate, KY 41071-3133
Hegenauer, John V., Carmel Manor, 100 Carmel Manor Rd., Fort Thomas, KY 41075-2300
Hickey, Edward T., Regina Cleri Home, 100 Carmel Manor Rd., Fort Thomas, KY 41075-2300
Meier, Allen J., Notre Dame Academy, 1699 Hilton Dr., Covington, KY 41011-2705
Murphy, John F., 2727 Leatherwood Ct., Crestview Hills, KY 41017-2274
Welp, Harry J., 726 Meadowood, Apt. 1, Villa Hills, KY 41017-4607
Reverend Fathers—
Bierman, Earl C., The Catholic Center, P.O. Box 18548, Erlanger, KY 41018-0548
Brinker, Paul J., P.O. Box 17321, Dayton, KY 41017-0321
Broering, Raymond L., 2 Cypress Run, Apt. 21B, Homosassa, FL 34446-4223
Deye, Anthony H., Regina Cleri Home, 100 Carmel Manor Rd., Fort Thomas, KY 41075-2300
Garvey, Charles J., Holy Cross Rectory, 3612 Church St., Covington, KY 41015-1431
Gerrety, James P., Mary, Queen of Heaven Rectory, 1150 Donaldson Hwy., Erlanger, KY 41018-1048
Gruber, Robert L., St. Paul's Rectory, 7301 Dixie Hwy., Florence, KY 41042-2126
Hoffer, Charles, Holy Cross Rectory, 3612 Church St., Covington, KY 41015-1431
Holtz, Louis J., 4594 State Rte. 276, Batavia, OH 45103
Jasper, Louis H., 1400 Sleepy Hollow, Apt. 4, Covington, KY 41011-2757
Kamlage, Herman, Hathaway Court, #416, 1200 Highway Ave., Covington, KY 41011-1095
Keller, Lawrence W., Sacred Heart Rectory, 318 Division St., Bellevue, KY 41073-1198
Klein, Robert P., 3516 Misty Creek Dr., Erlanger, KY 41018-2627
Krebs, Paul F., 14 Orchard St., Southgate, KY 41071-3126
McGrath, Richard H., 18 Woodland Hills, Apt. 5, Southgate, KY 41071-2969
Mertes, William H., 228 Covington Ave., Covington, KY 41011-1414
Mulhern, Raymond F., 6537 W. 173rd Pl., Apt. 1A, Tinley Park, IL 60477-3554
Nieman, Raymond L., 5419 Rattlesnake-Hammock Rd., F104, Naples, FL 33962-7401
Quill, James E., St. Agnes Rectory, 1680 Dixie Hwy., Covington, KY 41011-2779
Reifsnyder, John A., Sacred Heart Rectory, 310 Shady Ave., Pittsburgh, PA 15206-4306
Reinke, Robert J., St. Augustine Rectory, 1839 Euclid Ave., Covington, KY 41014-1162
Rooks, Charles W., 1601 Dixie Hwy., Covington, KY 41011-2798
Rosing, Robert C., Marydale Retreat Center, 945 Donaldson Rd., Erlanger, KY 41018-1093
Rueter, Joseph J., St. Joseph Rectory, 4011 Alexandria Pike, Cold Spring, KY 41076-1817
Shockey, David P., St. Joseph Convent, 13 Mulberry St., Walton, KY 41094-1026
Smith, R. Leroy, 5440 Moeller Ave., Norwood, OH 45212-1211
Steinhauser, Raymond W., 5419 Rattlesnake-Hammock Rd., F101, Naples, FL 33962-7401
Tenhundfeld, Paul F., Blessed Sacrament Rectory, 2415 Dixie Hwy., Fort Mitchell, KY 4107-2936
Toner, Edward R., 5614 Long Commons Cir., Sarasota, FL 34235-2401
Trimbur, Edwin H., P.O. Box 452, El Paso, TX 79943-0452
Urlage, Robert J., P.O. Box 75254, Fort Thomas, KY 41075-0254
Vater, Robert L., St. Catherine of Siena Rectory, 10 Wesley Hills Dr., Fort Thomas, KY 41075-1213
Werner, John P., 104 Highland Ave., Apt. 1, Fort Mitchell, KY 41017-2920
Witt, Robert G., P.O. Box 2844, Capistrano Beach, CA 92624-0844

Permanent Deacons:
Baker, Joseph, St. Joseph, Crescent Springs
Cleves, Joe, St. Agnes, Covington
Colatrella, Ralph, Holy Cross, Latonia
Dietz, Charles, St. Bernard, Dayton
Dunning, John, Cathedral, Covington
Estill, Andrew (Frank), St. Augustine, Augusta
Flynn, David, St. Agnes, Covington
Hermann, Robert J., St. Pius, Edgewood
Hillenmeyer, Ernest, St. Patrick, Maysville
Holstein, Marvin, St. Joseph, Crescent Springs
Kaiser, Bernard, St. Barbara, Erlanger
Kelly, Alfred John, Ph.D.
Lehmkuhl, Dennis, St. Mary, Alexandria
Nolan, Thomas, St. Timothy, Union
Norris, Eugene, (Retired)
O'Donnell, Richard, (Retired)
Runge, Thomas, Mother of God, Covington
Stieritz, Edward, St. Catherine, Fort Thomas
Sweigart, Jim, St. Thomas, Fort Thomas

PILGRIMAGE SHRINES

COVINGTON. *Shrine of St. Ann*. Attached to St. Ann Church.

SOUTHGATE. *Shrine of the Little Flower*. Attached to St. Therese Church.

INSTITUTIONS LOCATED IN THE DIOCESE

[A] COLLEGES AND UNIVERSITIES

COVINGTON. *THOMAS MORE COLLEGE*, Crestview Hills, 41017-3495. Tel: 606-341-5800; Fax: 606-344-3345. E-mail: clevesw@thomasmore.edu Web site: www.thomasmore.edu *For a complete listing, refer to the Colleges and Universities section.*

[B] HIGH SCHOOLS, DIOCESAN

COVINGTON. *Covington Catholic High School*, 1600 Dixie Hwy., 41011-2797. Tel: 606-431-5351; Fax: 606-655-4325. E-mail: TCKENVAN@ONE.NET Mr. Jack Kennevan, Prin.; Rev. John J. Sterling, Chap. Lay Teachers 33; Boys 532.

Covington Latin School, 21-23 E. 11th St., 41011-3196. Tel: 606-291-7044; Fax: 606-291-1939. E-mail: cls@fuse.net Web site: home.fuse.net/cls Mr. Richard Stewart, Dean; Mr. Robert R. Larcher, Headmaster; Rev. Mark Keene, Chap. Lay Teachers 16; Boys 116; Girls 80.

Holy Cross High School, 3617 Church St., 41015-1498. Tel: 606-431-1335; Fax: 606-655-2184. Mr. William Goller, Prin.; Rev. Thomas P. Robbins, Chap. Religious 2; Lay Teachers 30; Students 369.

ALEXANDRIA. *Bishop Brossart High School*, Jefferson St. & Grove St., 41001-1295. Tel: 606-635-2108; Fax: 606-635-2135. E-mail: DCBROSSART@connect.com Mr. Thomas H. Seither, Prin.; Rev. James Egbers, Chap. Sisters of Notre Dame 2; Lay Teachers 23; Students 413.

ERLANGER. *St. Henry District High School*, 3837 Dixie Hwy., 41018-1864. Tel: 606-342-2544; Fax: 606-342-2550. E-mail: sthenry@ix.netcom.com Mr. David M. Otte, Prin.; Rev. Michael D. Barth, Chap. Lay Teachers 33; Religious 1; Priests 1; Students 452.

MAYSVILLE. *St. Patrick High School*, 318 Limestone St., 41056-1248. Tel: 606-564-5949; Fax: 606-564-8795. Mrs. Sarah C. Kalb, Prin.; Rev. William H. Hinds, Chap. Lay Teachers 14; Students 100.

NEWPORT. *Newport Central Catholic High School*, 13 Carothers Rd., 41071-2497. Tel: 606-292-0001; Fax: 606-292-0656. E-mail:.NCCHS@ix.netcom.com Mr. Carl Foster, Prin.; Rev. Richard Bolte, Chap. Administrative Team: Mr. Greg Burwinkel; Mr. Robert Schneider. Lay Teachers 25; Students 420.

[C] HIGH SCHOOLS, PRIVATE

COVINGTON. *Academy of Notre Dame*, 1699 Hilton Dr., 41011-2705. Tel: 606-261-4300; Fax: 606-292-7722. E-mail: DCNDA@connectinc.com Web site: http://www.nda-cvg.org Sisters of Notre Dame. Sr. Mary Rita, S.N.D., Prin. Chaplains: Rev. Msgr. Allen J. Meier; Rev. Mark Witte. Sisters 12; Lay Teachers 35; Girls 647.

Villa Madonna High School. 2500 Amsterdam Rd., Villa Hills, 41017-3798. Tel: 606-331-6333; Fax: 606-331-8615. E-mail: vill@VMA.pvt.K12.US Web site: http://www.igloo.com/vma Sr. Victoria Eisenman, O.S.B., Dir.; Ms. Pamela McQueen, Prin.; Rev. Douglas J. Lauer, Chap. Sisters 5; Lay Teachers 13; Students 141.

[D] ELEMENTARY SCHOOLS, INTERPAROCHIAL

COVINGTON. *Holy Family Catholic School*, 338 E. 16th St., 41014-1304. Tel: 606-581-0290; Fax: 606-581-0624. E-mail: DCHOLYFAM@connectinc.com Lay Teachers 10; Students 162.

Prince of Peace School, 625 Pike St., 41011-2798. Tel: 606-431-5153; Fax: 606-431-0115. E-mail: DCPRINCE@connectinc.com Sr. Mary Sharron Goller, S.N.D., Prin. Sisters of Notre Dame 3; Lay Teachers 6; Students 134.

BELLEVUE. *St. Michael School*, 235 Division St., 41073-1101. Tel: 606-291-6937; Fax: 606-291-6970. E-mail: DCMICHAEL@connectinc.com Sr. M. Patrycia Sweeney, S.N.D., Prin. Sisters of Notre Dame 2; Lay Teachers 7; Students 124.

NEWPORT. *Holy Spirit Elementary School*, 840 Washington Ave., 41071-2485. Tel: 606-431-8745. E-mail: DCHOLYSPIR@connectinc.com Sr. Juanita Nadicksbernd, C.D.P., Prin. Sisters 2; Lay Teachers 5; Students 107.

Holy Spirit Junior High School, Chesapeake Ave. & Grand Ave., 41071-2485. Tel: 606-292-0487; Fax: 606-292-0487. Web site: http://www.igloo.com/vma Sr. Juanita Nadicksbernd, C.D.P., Prin. Sisters of Divine Providence 2; Lay Teachers 3; Students 65.

[E] ELEMENTARY SCHOOLS, DIOCESAN

FORT MITCHELL. *Guardian Angel*, P.O. Box 17007, Orphanage Rd., 41017-0007. Tel: 606-331-2040; Fax: 606-344-5022. Sr. Pamela Mae Geiger, S.N.D., Prin. School for the Emotional Behavioral Disabled. Sisters 2; Lay Teachers 5; Students 20.

[F] ELEMENTARY SCHOOLS, PRIVATE

COVINGTON. *Villa Madonna Elementary School*. 2500 Amsterdam Rd., Villa Hills, 41017-3798. Tel: 606-331-6333; Fax: 606-331-8615. E-mail: villa@wma.pvt.K12.ky.US Web site: http://www.igloo.com/vma Sr. Victoria Eisenman, O.S.B., Dir.; Mrs. Becky Moeller, Prin. Sisters 2; Lay Teachers 22; Students 273.

WALTON. *St. Joseph Academy*, 48 Needmore St., 41094-1028. Tel: 606-485-6444. Sisters of St. Joseph the Worker. Sr. Patricia Jean, S.J.W., Prin. Sisters 7; Lay Teachers 8; Students 243. Attended from All Saints, Walton; St. William, Williamstown; St. Joseph, Warsaw; and St. Timothy, Union.

[G] MONTESSORI SCHOOLS (PRESCHOOL)

VILLA HILLS. *Villa Madonna Montessori*, 2402 Amsterdam Rd., 41017-5316. Tel: 606-341-5145. Sr. Mary Peter, O.S.B., Prin. & Admin. Sisters of St. Benedict 2; Lay Teachers 5; Students 50.

[H] GENERAL HOSPITALS

COVINGTON. *St. Elizabeth Medical Center, North*, 401 E. 20th St., 41014-1585. Tel: 606-292-4000; Fax: 606-292-4487 *For a complete listing, refer to the Hospitals section.*

EDGEWOOD. *St. Elizabeth Medical Center, South*, One Medical Village Dr., 41017-3441. Tel: 606-344-2000; Fax: 606-344-3968 *For a complete listing, refer to the Hospitals section.*

WILLIAMSTOWN. *St. Elizabeth Medical Center, Grant County*, 238 Barnes Rd., 41097-9482. Tel: 606-824-2400; Fax: 606-823-0951 *For a complete listing, refer to the Hospitals section.*

[I] NURSING HOMES

COVINGTON. *Madonna Manor, Inc.* 2344 Amsterdam Rd. Villa Hills, 41017-3712. Tel: 606-341-3981. *For a complete listing, refer to the Special Care Facilities section.*

St. Charles Care Center, Inc., 500 Farrell Dr., 41011-3798. Tel: 606-331-3224; Fax: 606-578-2065 *For a complete listing, refer to the Special Care Facilities section.*

[J] PROTECTIVE INSTITUTIONS

COVINGTON. *Diocesan Catholic Children's Home*, Orphanage Rd., P.O. Box 17007, Fort Mitchell, 41017-2730. *For a complete listing, refer to the Special Care Facilities section.*

COLD SPRING. *Campbell Lodge Boys Home*, 150 Skyline Dr., 41076-2099. Tel: 606-781-1214; Fax: 606-781-1511 *For a complete listing, refer to the Special Care Facilities section.*

[K] HOMES FOR AGED

FORT THOMAS. *Carmel Manor*, 100 Carmel Manor Rd., 41075-2395. Tel: 606-781-5111; Fax: 606-781-2337 *For a complete listing, refer to the Special Care Facilities section.*

Regina Cleri Home for Retired Priests, 100 Carmel Manor Rd., 41075-2395. Tel: 606-781-5111; Fax: 606-781-2337 *For a complete listing, refer to the Special Care Facilities section.*

[L] MONASTERIES AND RESIDENCES OF PRIESTS AND BROTHERS

COVINGTON. *Brothers of the Poor of St. Francis*, 716 Bakewell St., 41011-1228. Tel: 606-431-3202; Fax: 606-431-7667. International Office. Bro. James Phelan, C.P.F., Res. Minister Gen. In res. Bros. James Phelan, C.P.F.; John Walsh, C.P.F.; Rock Larson, C.P.F.; Boniface Hracek, C.P.F.

[M] CONVENTS AND RESIDENCES FOR SISTERS

COVINGTON. *St. Joseph Heights Provincialate and Novitiate of the Sisters of Notre Dame*, 1601 Dixie Hwy., 41011-2798. Tel: 606-291-2040; Fax: 606-291-1774. E-mail: smshauna@juna.com Sr. Mary Shauna Bankemper, S.N.D., Prov. Supr.; Rev. Charles W. Rooks, Chap. Sisters in Community 182; Sisters in Prov. House 79.

St. Walburg Monastery, 2500 Amsterdam Rd., 41017-5316. Tel: 606-331-6324; Fax: 606-331-2136. E-mail: walburg@igloo.com Sisters of St. Benedict. Sr. Mary Catherine Wenstrup, O.S.B., Prioress; Rev. Gerald L. Reinersman, Chap. Professed Sisters 106.

ERLANGER. *Monastery of the Sacred Passion*, 1151 Donaldson Hwy., 41018-1000. Tel: 606-371-8568; Fax: 606-371-8568. Passionists Nuns. Sr. Margaret Mary, C.P., Supr.; Rev. John R. Schulte, Chap. Professed 9.

FORT THOMAS. *Sisters of the Good Shepherd*, Pelletier Hall, 930 Highland Ave., 41075-1776. Tel: 606-441-5531. Rev. Richard H. McGrath, Chap. Sisters of the Good Shepherd 22.

KENTON HILLS. *St. Vincent's Convent*, 630 Jerol Ave., 41011. Tel: 606-431-5388. Intercongregational Residence. Sisters 4.

MELBOURNE. *Holy Family Home*, Rte. 8, 2000 St. Anne Dr., 41059-9604. Tel: 606-781-0712. Rev. John Modica, Chap. Sisters in Residence 51.

St. Anne Convent, 1000 St. Anne Dr., 41059-9603. Tel: 606-441-0679. Provincial House and Novitiate of the Sisters of Divine Providence of Kentucky. Sr. Lynn Stenken, C.D.P., Prov. Supr. Sisters in Community 189; Sisters in Provincial House 34; Sisters in Residence 50.

WALTON. *St. William Convent*, One St. Joseph Ln., 41094-1036. Tel: 606-485-4914; 485-4256; Fax: 606-485-9302. Sisters of St. Joseph the Worker. Mother Ellen Curran, S.J.W., Supr.; Sr. Celeste Marie, Formation Dir.; Rev. David P. Shockey, Chap., 13 Mulberry St., 41094-1036. Tel: 606-485-7053. Sisters in Community 20; Sisters in Motherhouse 10.

[N] SECULAR INSTITUTES

COVINGTON. *Society of St. Vincent de Paul*, 2655 Crescent Springs Rd., 41017-1504. Tel: 606-341-3212. Vincent J. Bessler, Pres. District Council of Northern Kentucky. Executive Offices and Thrift Stores. 31 Parish Conferences in Northern Kentucky Thrift Stores, including Dayton, Newport, Crescent Springs, Latonia, Ludlow, Covington, and Walton. Total stores 7. A Catholic lay organization of over 875,000 members worldwide whose members meet in parish and district groups in order to help in a personal way those in need.

[O] SOCIAL SERVICES

COVINGTON. *Catholic Social Services*, 3629 Church St., 41015-1499. Tel: 606-581-8974; Fax: 606-581-9595. Sr. Joan Marie Boberg, C.D.P., Dir.; Anton Torres, Hispanic Min. Total Assisted 9,000; Staff 40.

Parish Kitchen, Pike St. & Russell St., P.O. Box 1234, 41011-1234. Tel: 606-581-7745. Ms. Molly Navin, Dir. Total Assisted 60,000.

Welcome House of Northern Kentucky, Inc., 141 Pike St., 41011-2521. Tel: 606-431-8717; Fax: 606-431-6297. 203-205 Pike St., 41011. Shelter for homeless women and their children, 24 hours a day. Emergency Assistance Center and Representative Payee Program, Family Case Management and Self-Suffiency Housing Programs. Total Assisted 12,269; Staff 40.

VANCEBURG. *Appalachian Apostolate, Inc.*, Rte. 3, Box 44, 41179-0008. Tel: 606-796-3289. Sr. Conall O'Connell, Dir. Persons assisted annually 1,200; Staff 5.

[P] DIOCESAN RETREAT HOUSES

ERLANGER. *Marydale Retreat Center*, 945 Donaldson Hwy., 41018-1093. Tel: 606-371-4224; Fax: 606-647-5682. Edward Stieritz, Dir.; Rev. Robert C. Rosing, Chap. Total Asssisted 6,936; Staff 21.

[Q] NEWMAN CENTERS

HIGHLAND HEIGHTS. *Catholic Newman Center - Northern Kentucky University*, 512 Johns Hill Rd., P.O. Box 76174, 41076-1449. Tel: 606-781-3775. Mr. Al Cucchetti, Pastoral Admin.

[R] INTERFAITH CENTERS

COVINGTON. *Interfaith Commission of Northern Kentucky*. P.O. Box 72296, Newport, 41072-0296. Tel: 606-581-2237. Rev. William C. Neuroth, Exec. Dir. Purpose: A religious organization committed to understanding the various faith traditions of our member bodies, while working together in response to the spiritual and human needs of all people of the Northern Kentucky area.

[S] MISCELLANEOUS

ERLANGER. *Women of Providence in Collaboration*, National Office, The Catholic Center, 947 Donaldson Rd., P.O. Box 18548, 41018-0548. Tel: 606-283-6303; Fax: 606-283-6334. Sr. Mary Catherine Hunt, C.D.P., Dir. Purpose: To investigate and develop intercongregationally a contemporary theology and spirituality of Providence and to undertake collaborative projects which communicate these understandings through our mission of witnessing Providence to the world.

FORT THOMAS. *Mission Share*, P.O. Box 242, 41075. Tel: 606-525-6909; Fax: 606-525-7067. Rev. John J. McGuire, Pres. Purpose: A mission society whose principal activity is to carry out and advance the function, practices, and liturgy of the Catholic Church in Cali, Colombia, and Latin America and for medical and dental programs, educational programs, the construction of parish and archdiocesan buildings, and the advancement of the Catholic faith and various other civic and social programs.

RELIGIOUS INSTITUTES OF MEN REPRESENTED IN THE DIOCESE

For further details refer to the corresponding bracketed number in the Religious Institutes of Men or Women section.

[0330]—*Brothers of the Christian Schools.*—F.S.C.

[0460]—*Brothers of the Poor of St. Francis.* (Aachen, Germany).—C.F.P.

[0570]—*Glenmary Home Missioners.*—Glmy.

[0690]—*Jesuit Fathers and Brothers.* (Chicago Prov.).—S.J.

RELIGIOUS INSTITUTES OF WOMEN REPRESENTED IN THE DIOCESE

[0230]—*Benedictine Sisters of Pontifical Jurisdiction.*—O.S.B.

[0330]—*Carmelite Sisters for the Aged and Infirm.* (Germantown, NY).—O.Carm.

[1070-01]—*Congregation of St. Catharine of Siena.* (Louisville, KY).—O.P.

[3180]—*Congregation of the Passion of Jesus Christ.*—C.P.

[1920]—*Congregation of the Sisters of the Holy Cross.* (Notre Dame, IN).—C.S.C.

[0440]—*Sisters of Charity of Cincinnati, Ohio.*—S.C.

[0500]—*Sisters of Charity of Nazareth.*—S.C.N.

[1000]—*Sisters of Divine Providence of Kentucky.*—C.D.P.

[2990]—*Sisters of Notre Dame.*—S.N.D.

[3360]—*Sisters of Providence of Saint Mary-of-the-Woods, IN.*—S.P.

[3880]—*Sisters of St. Joseph of Medaille.* (Cincinnati, OH).—C.S.J.

[3920]—*Sisters of St. Joseph the Worker.*—S.J.W.

[1830]—*Sisters of the Good Shepherd.*—R.G.S.

[3260]—*Sisters of the Precious Blood.* (Dayton, Ohio).—C.PP.S.

[1730]—*Sisters of the Third Order of St. Francis.* (Oldenburg, IN).—O.S.F.

[1720]—*Sisters of the Third Order Regular of St. Francis of the Congregation of Our Lady of Lourdes.* (Rochester, MN).—O.S.F.

[2150]—*Sisters, Servants of the Immaculate Heart of Mary.* (Monroe, MI).—I.H.M.

[4120]—*Ursuline Nuns, of the Congregation of Paris.* (Brown County, OH).—O.S.U.

DIOCESAN CEMETERIES

COLD SPRING. *St. Joseph.*

FORT MITCHELL. *St. John.*
St. Mary.

FORT THOMAS. *St. Stephen.*

WILDER. *St. Joseph.*

NECROLOGY

† Kelly, Francis Joseph, (Retired). —Died April 14, 1997.

† Schmidt, Vincent Francis, (Retired). —Died Jan. 27, 1997.

† Schutzman, John Stanley, (Retired). —Died Nov. 26, 1996.

Diocese of Crookston

(Dioecesis Crookstoniensis)

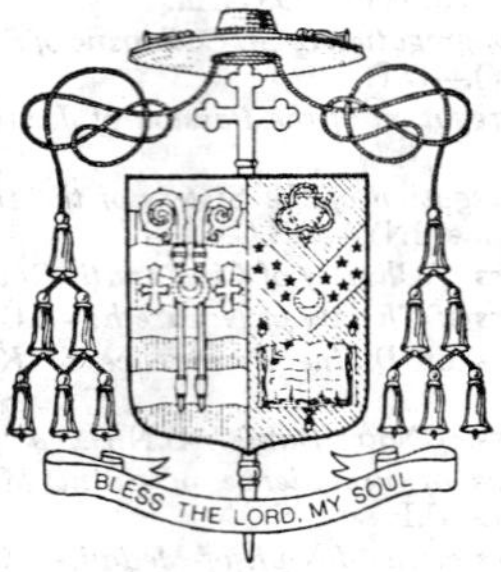

Most Reverend

VICTOR H. BALKE, D.D., PH.D.

Bishop of Crookston; ordained May 24, 1958; appointed July 7, 1976; Episcopal ordination September 2, 1976. *Res., 1200 Memorial Dr., Crookston, MN, 56716.* Tel.: 218-281-4533.

ESTABLISHED BY HIS HOLINESS PIUS X, DECEMBER 31, 1909.

Square Miles 17,210.

Comprises the Counties of Becker, Beltrami, Clay, Clearwater, Hubbard, Kittson, Lake of the Woods, Marshall, Mahnomen, Norman, Pennington, Polk, Red Lake and Roseau in the State of Minnesota.

PATRONESS OF THE DIOCESE: The Immaculate Conception.

Legal Title: Diocese of Crookston.

For legal titles of parishes and diocesan institutions, consult the Chancery Office.

Chancery Office: 1200 Memorial Dr., P.O. Box 610, Crookston, MN, 56716. Tel.: 218-281-4533; Fax: 218-281-3328.

STATISTICAL OVERVIEW

Personnel	
Bishop	1
Priests: Diocesan Active in Diocese	29
Priests: Active Outside Diocese	3
Priests: Diocesan in Foreign Missions	1
Priests: Retired, Sick or Absent	14
Number of Diocesan Priests	47
Religious Priests in Diocese	6
Extern Priests in Diocese	3
Ordinations:	
Transitional Deacons	2
Permanent Deacons in Diocese	8
Total Brothers	2
Total Sisters	182
Parishes	
Parishes	73
With Resident Pastor:	
Resident Diocesan Priests	22
Resident Religious Priests	5
Without Resident Pastor:	
Administered by Priests	37
Administered by Permanent Deacons	1
Administered by Women Religious	5
Administered by Lay People	3
Pastoral Centers	1
Professional Ministry Personnel:	
Brothers	2
Sisters	18
Lay Ministers	48
Welfare	
Catholic Hospitals	3
Total Assisted	53,505
Homes for the Aged	4
Total Assisted	317
Day Care and Extended Day Care Centers	1
Total Assisted	53
Educational	
Diocesan Students in Other Seminaries	6
Total Seminarians	6
High Schools, Diocesan and Parish	1
Total Students	148
Elementary Schools, Diocesan and Parish	8
Total Students	1,188
Elementary Schools, Private	1
Total Students	80
Catechesis/Religious Education:	
High School Students	2,458
Elementary Students	3,523
Total Students Under Catholic Instruction	7,403
Teachers in the Diocese:	
Sisters	6
Lay Teachers	87
Vital Statistics	
Receptions into the Church:	
Infant Baptism Totals	755
Adult Baptism Totals	20
Received into Full Communion	96
First Communions	651
Confirmations	750
Marriages:	
Catholic	122
Interfaith	140
Total Marriages	262
Deaths	606
Total Catholic Population	42,807
Total Population	236,100

Former Bishops—Most Rev. TIMOTHY CORBETT, D.D., ord. June 12, 1886; cons. May 19, 1910; resigned See Aug. 6, 1938; appt. Titular Bishop of Vita; died July 20, 1939.—Most Rev. JOHN H. PESCHGES, D.D., ord. April 15, 1905; cons. Nov. 9, 1938; died Oct. 30, 1944.—Most Rev. FRANCIS J. SCHENK, D.D., ord. June 13, 1926; cons. May 24, 1945; transferred to Duluth Jan. 27, 1960; died Oct. 28, 1969.—Most Rev. LAURENCE A. GLENN, D.D., ord. June 11, 1927; cons. Sept. 12, 1956; retired July 28, 1970; died Jan. 26, 1985.—Most Rev. KENNETH J. POVISH, D.D., ord. June 3, 1950; appt. Bishop of Crookston July 28, 1970; cons. Sept. 29, 1970; transferred to Lansing Oct. 21, 1975.

Vicar General—Rev. Msgr. ROGER L. GRUNDHAUS, J.C.L., *Cathedral of the Immaculate Conception, 702 Summit Ave., Crookston, 56716.*

Chancery Office—1200 Memorial Dr., P.O. Box 610, Crookston, 56716. Tel: 218-281-4533; Fax: 218-281-3328.

Chancellor—Rev. MICHAEL H. FOLTZ, J.C.L.

Moderator of the Curia—Rev. MICHAEL H. FOLTZ, J.C.L.

Episcopal Vicar for Canonical Affairs—Rev. MICHAEL H. FOLTZ, J.C.L.

Information Officer—Rev. MICHAEL H. FOLTZ, J.C.L.

Finance Manager—GEORGE NOEL.

Diocesan Tribunal—1200 Memorial Dr., P.O. Box 610, Crookston. Tel: 218-281-4533.

Judicial Vicar—Rev. MICHAEL SULLIVAN, J.C.L.

Defenders of the Bond—Revs. RICHARD BOYD; RICHARD LAMBERT.

Advocate—JOANNE TOLLEFSON.

Notary—KATHY MORVIG.

Psychological Consultant—ELIZABETH BARAGA SUPER, Ph.D.

Diocesan Offices And Directors

Diocesan Consultors—Rev. Msgr. ROGER L. GRUNDHAUS, J.C.L.; Revs. GARY LAMOINE; RAYMOND PALCISKO; JOHN KLEINWACHTER; TIMOTHY NOAH; AUGUST GOTHMAN.

Finance Council—Most Rev. VICTOR H. BALKE, D.D.; Rev. Msgr. ROGER L. GRUNDHAUS, V.G.; Rev. MICHAEL H. FOLTZ, J.C.L.; Rev. Msgr. MICHAEL PATNODE; Revs. DAVID SUPER; AL HENGER, O.M.I.; Sr. MARY DANIEL NEUMANN, O.S.B.; IRENE CAMPBELL; ELAINE WHITE; RICHARD TAYLOR; DEAN MITZEL.

Advocacy, Adoption Referral—BERNADETTE DUNN, *P.O. Box 610, Crookston, 56716.* Tel: 218-281-4533.

Beginning Experience—ROGER GANYO, Pres.; BERNADETTE DUNN, Bishop's Liaison, *P.O. Box 610, Crookston, 56716.* Tel: 218-281-4533.

Boy Scouts—DON VOTAVA, *Rte. 2, Box 172A, Warren, 56762.* Tel: 218-745-5423. Rev. MICHAEL SULLIVAN, Chap.

Campaign for Human Development—BERNADETTE DUNN, *P.O. Box 610, Crookston, 56716.* Tel: 218-281-4533.

Catholic Relief Services—Rev. MICHAEL H. FOLTZ, J.C.L., Dir., *P.O. Box 610, Crookston, 56716.* Tel: 218-281-4533.

Clergy Relief Society—Legal Title: *St. Joseph's Priest Fund Inc.* Rev. TIMOTHY MCGEE, Sec. & Treas.

Commission on Building and Planning—Rev. RICHARD LAMBERT; Sr. MARGUERITE STREIFEL, O.S.B.; RICHARD RUDE; JIM SHULIND; ROGER WINTER.

Commission on Catholic-Lutheran Rural Life—MILO MATHISON, Chm., *Rte. 1, Box 244, Mentor, 56736.* Tel: 218-637-6456.

Commission on Ecumenism—KEVIN ERPELDING, Chm.; JANICE SEMANKO; SUZANNE NELSON; ROY DUFAULT; MILDRED OVERGAARD; CHERYL YARNOTT; STEPHEN TAYLOR; AL OVERGAARD; RAY LAGASSE, Bishop's Liaison, *P.O. Box 610, Crookston, 56716.* Tel: 218-281-4533.

Commission on Liturgy, Sacred Music and Art—Sr. MARDELLE MOHS, O.S.B., Chm.; Sr. MARGUERITE STREIFEL, O.S.B., Dir.; Sr. PATRICE EBLEN, O.S.B.; JULIE MAREK; BONNIE LEE; JANEL KRESL; Rev. AUGIE GOTHMAN.

Commission on Respect Life—BERNADETTE DUNN, *P.O. Box 610, Crookston, 56716.* Tel: 218-281-4533.

Commission on Social Justice—Rev. DUANE PRIBULA, *P.O. Box 33, Warroad, 56763.* Tel: 218-386-1178.

Commission on Women—JOYCE STOLTMAN, *3807 Simonview Ct., Grand Forks, ND, 58201.* Tel: 701-746-0729.

Crookston Council of Women Religious—Sr. MAUREEN SUPRENANT, C.S.J., Pres.; Sr. MARY JEAN GUST, O.S.B., Sec.

Cursillo—OSCAR ELSHAUG, Chm. of the Secretariat, *602 S. Ash St., Crookston, 56716.*

Deans—Rev. MICHAEL SULLIVAN, Northwest; Rev. RAYMOND PALCISKO, Northeast; Rev. GERALD NOESEN, Western; Rev. ALCUIN HENGER, O.M.I., Eastern; Rev. DAVID SUPER, Southwest; Rev. JERRY ROGERS, Southeast.

Diaconate Office—Rev. ROBERT SCHREINER, Dir., *P.O. Box 507, Stephen, 56757.* Tel: 218-478-2231.

Diocesan Board of Conciliation and Arbitration—Rev. Msgr. WILLIAM MEHRKENS, *Red Lake, 56671.* Sr. DOREEN CHAREST, C.S.J., *Moorhead, 56560.* Judge MICHAEL KRAKER, *Mahnomen, 56557.*

School Board, Diocesan—MICHAEL STOLTMAN, Chm.; SUE WOYTASSEK, Vice Chm. Ex Officio Members:

Most Rev. VICTOR H. BALKE, D.D.; Sr. PAT MURPHY, C.S.J.,Members: Dr. JOHN HALCROW; JUDY SCHOENEBERGER; GREG KAISER; DAVID VIPOND; MICHELLE VOELLER; VICTORIA GRAVES; DAN OLSON; Rev. Msgr. MICHAEL PATNODE; Rev. DENNIS WIELAND.

Hispanic Ministry—Sr. TERESA ANN WOLF, O.S.B., Co-ord., *P.O. Box 610, Crookston, 56716*. Tel: 218-281-4533.

Holy Childhood Association—Rev. TIMOTHY BUSHY, Dir., *702 Summit Ave., Crookston, 56716*.

Native American Task Force—Rev. Msgr. WILLIAM MEHRKENS, Chm., *St. Mary's Mission Church, P.O. Box 189, Red Lake, 56671*. Tel: 218-679-3614.

Natural Family Planning—MARK WHELAN; JANE WHELAN, *RR 4, Box 78D, Detroit Lakes, 56501*. Tel: 218-847-6521.

Newspaper, "Our Northland Diocese"—CAROL EVENSON, Editor & Business Mgr., *Diocese of Crookston, 1200 Memorial Dr., P.O. Box 610, Crookston, 56716-0610*. Tel: 218-281-4533.

Pastoral Council—Most Rev. VICTOR H. BALKE, D.D.; Revs. JOE KIESELBACH; DENNIS WIELAND; Sr. MARY JEAN GUST, O.S.B.; Sr. DOREEN CHARIST, C.S.J.; GIL DIAZ; JUDY DUPREE; JOHN BRUGGEMAN; JAN DELAGE; ANDREW NISTLER; KERMIT ERICKSON; STEPHANIE WALTER; JOE NOEL; GINNY MCDOUGALL; JOANN KERSTING; WALLY LAMB, *P.O. Box 610, Crookston, 56716*. Tel: 218-281-4533.

Pastoral Office of Administration—GEORGE NOEL, Dir., *1200 Memorial Dr., P.O. Box 610, Crookston, 56716*. Tel: 218-281-4533.

Pastoral Office of Christian Service—BERNADETTE DUNN, Dir., *1200 Memorial Dr., P.O. Box 610, Crookston, 56716*. Tel: 218-281-4533.

Pastoral Office of the Word—Sr. PAT MURPHY, C.S.J., Dir., *1200 Memorial Dr., P.O. Box 610, Crookston, 56716*. Tel: 218-281-4533.

Pastoral Office of Worship—Sr. MARGUERITE STREIFEL, O.S.B., Dir., *1200 Memorial Dr., P.O. Box 610, Crookston, 56716*. Tel: 218-281-4533.

Priests' Council—Rev. AUGUST GOTHMAN, Chm., *St. Joseph's Church, 218 S. 10th St., Moorhead, 56560*. Tel: 218-236-5066. Rev. BERNARD FRIEDL, O.S.B., Sec.; Rev. Msgr. ROGER L. GRUNDHAUS; Revs. RAYMOND PALCISKO; JOHN KLEINWACHTER; GARY LAMOINE; TIMOTHY NOAH.

Priests' Personnel Board—Rev. Msgr. ROGER L. GRUNDHAUS, V.G. Ex Officio Members: Revs. JERRY ROGERS; GERALD NOESEN; DONALD BRAUKMANN; LARRY DELANEY.

Propagation of the Faith—Rev. MICHAEL H. FOLTZ, Dir., *P.O. Box 610, Crookston, 56716*.

Religious Education & Adult Faith Formation—RAY LAGASSE, Dir., *P.O. Box 610, Crookston, 56716*. Tel: 218-281-4533.

Schools—Sr. PAT MURPHY, C.S.J., Dir. Office of the Word, *1200 Memorial Dr., P.O. Box 610, Crookston, 56716*. Tel: 218-281-4533.

TEC (Teens Encounter Christ)—NANCY BOUCHER, Mgr., *P.O. Box 610, Crookston, 56716*. Tel: 218-281-4533.

Vocations—Rev. MICHAEL H. FOLTZ, J.C.L., Dir.; RAY HOLLCRAFT, Assoc. Dir., *P.O. Box 610, Crookston, 56716*. Tel: 218-281-4533.

Youth Ministry—RAY HOLLCRAFT, Dir., *P.O. Box 610, Crookston, 56716*. Tel: 218-281-4533.

CLERGY, PARISHES, MISSIONS AND PAROCHIAL SCHOOLS

CITY OF CROOKSTON
(Polk County)

1—CATHEDRAL OF THE IMMACULATE CONCEPTION, Rev. Msgr. Roger L. Grundhaus; Revs. Timothy F. Bushy; David Baumgartner; Sr. Mary Jean Gust, O.S.B., Pastoral Assoc.; Deacon Dennis Bivens.
Parish Office—702 Summit Ave., 56716. Tel: 218-281-1735; Fax: 218-281-1747.
Res., 319 S. Ash St., 56716. Tel: 218-281-2638. [JC]
School—The Cathedral School, (Grades K-6). Tel: 218-281-1835. Rev. Timothy F. Bushy, Prin.
Lay Teachers 8; Students 127.
Missions—Euclid, Polk Co., St. Mary; Gentilly, Polk Co., St. Peter; Ada, Norman Co., St. Joseph; Halstad, Norman Co., Holy Family; Twin Valley, Norman Co., St. William.

2—ST. ANNE'S. Closed. For inquiries for parish records contact the Cathedral of the Immaculate Conception, Crookston, for details.

OUTSIDE THE CITY OF CROOKSTON

Ada, Norman Co., St. Joseph's. Served by Cathedral of the Immaculate Conception, Crookston. Tel: 218-281-1735. Sr. Patrice Eblen, O.S.B., Pastoral Admin.
Res., 405 E. Thorpe Ave., 56510. Tel: 218-784-4131. [CEM]
Missions—Halstad, Norman Co., Holy Family; Twin Valley, Norman Co., St.William.

Akeley, Hubbard Co., St. John's, Rev. John Kleinwachter.
Res., P.O. Box 219, 56433. Tel: 218-652-2785.
Missions—Nevis, Hubbard Co., Immaculate Conception; Laporte, Hubbard Co., St. Theodore.

Alma, Marshall Co., St. John the Baptist. Served by St. Rose, Argyle. Tel: 218-437-6341.

Argyle, Marshall Co., St. Rose, Rev. Michael H. Foltz; Sr. Lorraine Kraft, O.S.B., Pastoral Assoc.
Res., P.O. Box 277, 56713. Tel: 218-437-6341. [CEM]
Mission—Alma.

Badger, Roseau Co., St. Mary's. Served by Sacred Heart, Roseau. Tel: 218-463-2441.

Bagley, Clearwater Co., St. Joseph. Served by St. Philip's, Bemidji. Sr. Joanne Johnson, C.S.J., Pastoral Admin.
Res., P.O. Box 67, 56621. Tel: 218-694-6416; Fax: 218-694-6416. [CEM]

Barnesville, Clay Co., Assumption, Rev. Msgr. Stanley C. Bourassa; Sr. Mardelle Mohs, O.S.B., Pastoral Min.
Res., 307 Front St. N., P.O. Box 339, 56514. Tel: 218-354-7320. [CEM]
Mission—Sabin, Clay Co., St. Cecilia.

Baudette, Lake of the Woods Co., Sacred Heart, Rev. Frank Ryan, O.M.I.; Deacon James Lukenbill.
Res., P.O. Box 738, 56623. Tel: 218-634-2689.
Mission—Williams, Lake of the Woods Co., St. Joseph. [CEM]

Beaulieu, Mahnomen Co., St. Joseph. Served by St. Michael, Mahnomen. Tel: 218-935-2503.

Bejou, Mahnomen Co., Immaculate Conception. Closed. For inquiries for parish records contact St. Michael's, Mahnomen.

Bemidji, Beltrami Co., St. Philip's, Rev. Msgr. Michael Patnode; Rev. James H.C. Lyons; Deacon John Schuiling. In res., Revs. William F. Lemen; Edward Nistler.
Res., 710 Beltrami Ave., 56601. Tel: 218-751-4262; Fax: 218-751-4262. [CEM]
School—Mrs. Carol Rettinger, Prin. Lay Teachers 17; Students 275.
Missions—Bagley, Clearwater Co., St. Joseph; Bemidji, Beltrami Co., Newman Center.

Benwood, Roseau Co., St. Joseph, The Worker. Served by Sacred Heart, Roseau. Tel: 218-463-2441.

Big Elbow Lake, Becker Co., St. Francis Cabrini. Served by St. Ann, Waubun. Tel: 218-473-2101.

Blackduck, Beltrami Co., St. Ann's, Rev. Alcuin J. Henger, O.M.I.
Res., P.O. Box G, 56630. Tel: 218-835-6673; Fax: 218-835-6675.
Missions—Kelliher, Beltrami Co., St. Patrick; Northome, Koochiching Co., St. Michael.

Brooks, Red Lake Co., St. Joseph. Served by St. Bernard, Thief River Falls. Tel: 218-681-3571.

Callaway, Becker Co., Assumption. Served by St. Mary of the Lakes, Lake Eunice Township. Tel: 218-532-2513. Deacon Randy Bauer, Pastoral Admin.
Res., P.O. Box 67, 56521. Tel: 218-375-3571; Fax: 218-847-6367.

Detroit Lakes, Becker Co., Holy Rosary, Rev. Jerry Rogers; Deacons Randall J. Bauer; James Thomas.
Res., 1016 Washington Ave., 56501. Tel: 218-847-1393; Fax: 218-847-6367. [CEM]
School—Tel: 218-847-5306; Fax: 218-847-6367. Kathleen Klindt, Prin.
Sisters of St. Benedict 1; Lay Teachers 9; Students 124.

Dilworth, Clay Co., St. Elizabeth, Rev. Joseph Kieselbach.
Res., P.O. Box 307, 56529. Tel: 218-287-2705.
Mission—Georgetown, Clay Co., St. John.

Dorothy, Red Lake Co., St. Dorothy. Served by St. Joseph's, Red Lake Falls. Tel: 218-253-2685.

East Grand Forks, Polk Co., Sacred Heart, Revs. Timothy H. McGee; Larry Delaney.
Res., 202 Third St. N.W., 56721. Tel: 218-773-0877; Fax: 218-773-8312. [CEM]
School—Tel: 218-773-1579. Mr. David Andrys, Prin. Lay Teachers 13; Students 154.
High School—Tel: 218-773-0230. Mr. Phillip E. Meyer, Prin.
Sisters 1; Lay Teachers 15; Students 148.
Convent—Sr. Marguerite Streifel, O.S.B., Coord.
Mission—Fisher, Polk Co., St. Francis.

Euclid, Polk Co., St. Mary. Served by the Cathedral of the Immaculate Conception, Crookston. Tel: 218-281-1735.

Falun, Roseau Co., St. Philip. Served by St. Mary's, Warroad. Tel: 218-386-1178.

Felton, Clay Co., St. Lawrence. Closed. For inquiries for parish records contact St. Joseph's, Ada.

Fertile, Polk Co., St. Joseph, Rev. Gerald L. Noesen.
Mailing Address: 201 S.E. Elm St., 56540. Tel: 218-945-6649.
Res., Rte. 1, Box 561, Mentor, 56736. Tel: 218-574-2424. [CEM]

Fisher, Polk Co., St. Francis. Served by Sacred Heart, East Grand Forks. Tel: 218-773-0877. Ms. Bernadette Dunn, Pastoral Admin.
Res., 304 Park Ave., 56723. Tel: 218-891-2406. [CEM]

Florian, Marshall Co., Assumption. Served by Blessed Sacrament, Greenbush. Tel: 218-782-2467. Rev. Donald Braukman.
Mailing Address: Rte. 2, Box 110, Strandquist, 56758. Tel: 218-478-3578.
Res., P.O. Box A, Greenbush, 56726. Tel: 218-782-2467.

Fosston, Polk Co., St. Mary's, Rev. Gerald L. Noesen.
Mailing Address: Rte. 3, Box 19A, 56542. Tel: 218-435-6484.
Res., Rte. 1, Box 561, Mentor, 56736. Tel: 218-574-2424. [CEM]

Frazee, Becker Co., Sacred Heart, Rev. Joseph DeCrans.
Res., P.O. Box 357, 56544. Tel: 218-334-4221. [CEM]

Gentilly, Polk Co., St. Peter's. Served by Cathedral of the Immaculate Conception, Crookston. Tel: 218-281-1735.
Mailing Address: Rte. 2, Box 80, Crookston, 56716. Tel: 218-281-1688. [CEM]

Georgetown, Clay Co., St. John. Served by St. Elizabeth's, Dilworth. Tel: 218-287-2705.

Goodridge, Pennington Co., St. Anne. Served by St. Bernard's, Thief River Falls. Tel: 218-681-3571.

Greenbush, Roseau Co., Blessed Sacrament, Rev. Donald Braukman.
Res., P.O. Box A, 56726. Tel: 218-782-2467; Fax: 218-782-5301. [CEM]
Missions—Leo, Roseau Co., St. Aloysius. [CEM] Middle River, Marshall Co., St. Joseph; Florian, Marshall Co., Assumption.

Grygla, Marshall Co., St. Clement. Served by St. Bernard's, Thief River Falls. Tel: 218-681-3571.

Hallock, Kittson Co., St. Patrick's, Rev. Timothy T. Noah.
Res., P.O. Box 519, 56728. Tel: 218-843-2323.
Mission—Lancaster, Kittson Co., Holy Rosary.

Halstad, Norman Co., Holy Family. Served by Cathedral of the Immaculate Conception, Crookston. Tel: 218-281-1735. Sr. Patrice Eblen, O.S.B., Pastoral Admin.
Res., 405 E. Thorpe Ave., Ada, 56510. Tel: 218-784-4131.

Hawley, Clay Co., St. Andrew. Served by St. Francis Xavier, Lake Park. Tel: 218-238-6639; Fax: 218-238-6028.
Mailing Address: 1419 Main St., P.O. Box 129, 56549. Tel: 218-483-4264.

Karlstad, Kittson Co., St. Edward the Confessor. Served by St. Stephen's, Stephen. Tel: 218-478-2231.

Kelliher, Beltrami Co., St. Patrick. Served by St. Ann's, Blackduck. Tel: 218-835-6673.

Lake Eunice Township, Becker Co., St. Mary of the Lakes, Rev. Eugene L. Wesely.
Mailing Address: R.R. 5, Box 364D, Detroit Lakes, 56501. Tel: 218-439-3938.
Mission—Callaway, Becker Co., Assumption.

Lake Itasca, Clearwater Co., St. Catherine. Closed. For inquiries for parish records contact St. Peter's, Park Rapids.

Lake Park, Becker Co., St. Francis Xavier's, Rev. Bernard Friedl, O.S.B.
Res., 2066 Second St., 56554-4402. Tel: 218-238-6639; Fax: 218-238-6028. [CEM]
Mission—Hawley, Clay Co., St. Andrew.

Lancaster, Kittson Co., Holy Rosary. Served by St. Patrick, Hallock. Tel: 218-843-2323.

Laporte, Hubbard Co., St. Theodore. Served by St. John's, Akeley. Tel: 218-652-2785.

Leo, Roseau Co., St. Aloysius. Served by Blessed Sacrament, Greenbush. Tel: 218-782-2467.

Mahnomen, Mahnomen Co., St. Michael's, Rev. Richard D. Lambert.
Res., Rte. 1, Box 22, 56557. Tel: 218-935-2503. [CEM]
School—Sisters of St. Benedict 2; Lay Teachers 6; Students 72.
Catechesis/Religious Programs—Sr. Yvonne Schafer, D.R.E.

Students 310.
Mission—Beaulieu, Mahnomen Co., St. Joseph. [CEM]

Mentor, Polk Co., St. Lawrence, Rev. Gerald L. Noesen; Deacon John A. Bruggeman.
Mailing Address: Box 51, 56736. Tel: 218-637-8178.
Res., Rte. 1, Box 561, 56736. Tel: 218-574-2424.

Middle River, Marshall Co., St. Joseph, Husband of Mary. Served by Blessed Sacrament, Greenbush. Mitch & Lee Walski, Pastoral Ministers.
Res., Rte. 2, Box 9, 56737. Tel: 218-222-3392.

Moorhead, Clay Co., St. Francis de Sales, Rev. David J. Super.
Res., 804 N. 13th St., 56560. Tel: 218-236-1505. [JC]
Church—601 15th Ave. N., 56560. Tel: 218-233-4780.

St. Joseph's, Rev. Msgr. Donald H. Krebs; Rev. August Gothman.
Office: 218 10th St. S., 56560. Tel: 218-236-5066; 236-9503 (Res.); Fax: 218-236-1624.
School—Tel: 218-233-0553. Sr. Mary Ann Welsch, Prin.
Sisters 2; Lay Teachers 13; Students 211.
Catechesis/Religious Programs—Tel: 218-236-1979. Barbara Schmidt, D.R.E.
Students 615.
Mission—Moorhead, Clay Co., St. Thomas Newman Center, 707-11th St. S., Tel: 218-236-9596.

Naytahwaush, Mahnomen Co., St. Anne. Served by St. Ann's, Waubun. Tel: 218-473-2101. Sr. Jean Schwartz, O.S.B., Pastoral Assoc.
Mailing Address: P.O. Box 157, 56566. Tel: 218-935-5676.

Nebish, Beltrami Co., St. John. Served by St. Mary's Mission, Red Lake. Tel: 218-679-3614.

Nevis, Hubbard Co., Immaculate Conception. Served by St. John's, Akeley. Tel: 218-652-2785.

Ogema, Becker Co., Most Holy Redeemer. Served by St. Benedict's, White Earth. Tel: 218-983-3519. Rev. Martin F. Machovec, O.M.I.
Mailing Address: P.O. Box 57, 56569. Tel: 218-983-3261. [CEM]

Oklee, Red Lake Co., St. Francis Xavier's. Served by St. Bernard's, Thief River Falls. Tel: 218-681-3571.
Mailing Address: P.O. Box 160, 56742. Tel: 218-796-5844; Fax: 218-796-5844. [CEM]

Oslo, Marshall Co., St. Joseph. Served by SS. Peter and Paul, Warren. Tel: 218-745-4511. Sr. Lucille Adelman, O.S.B., Pastoral Admin.
Res., P.O. Box 97, 56744. Tel: 218-695-2641. [CEM]

Park Rapids, Hubbard Co., St. Peter's, Rev. Richard Boyd.
Res., P.O. Box 353, 56470. Tel: 218-732-5142 (Office); 732-8852 (Res.). [CEM]
Mission—Two Inlets.

Pennington, Beltrami Co., St. Charles. (Under the jurisdiction of the Diocese of Crookston; administered by the Diocese of Duluth.). Rev. Michael T. Cotone, O.S.C.
P.O. Box 368, Cass Lake, 56633. Tel: 218-335-2359.

Plummer, Red Lake Co., St. Vincent de Paul. Served by St. Bernard, Thief River Falls. Tel: 218-681-3571.

Ponsford, Becker Co., St. Theodore. Served by St. Benedict's, White Earth. Tel: 218-983-3519.

Red Lake, Beltrami Co., St. Mary's Mission Church, Rev. Patrick A. Sullivan. In res., Rev. Msgr. William Mehrkens.
Res., P.O. Box 189, 56671. Tel: 218-679-3614. [CEM]
School—Tel: 218-679-3388. Sr. Philip Zimmer, Prin.
Sisters 1; Lay Teachers 6; Students 80.
Missions—Nebish, Beltrami Co., St. John; Wilton, Beltrami Co., Sacred Heart.

Red Lake Falls, Red Lake Co., St. Joseph's, Rev. Gary W. LaMoine; Sr. Lucille Schafer, O.S.B., Pastoral Assoc.
Res., P.O. Box 400, 56750. Tel: 218-253-2004. [CEM]
School—112 Edward Ave. N.W., Box 215, 56750. Tel: 218-253-2188; Fax: 218-253-2188. Val Gagnon, Prin.
Lay Teachers 7; Students 78.
Missions—Dorothy, Red Lake Co., St. Dorothy. [CEM]
Terrebonne, Red Lake Co., St. Anthony. [CEM]

Roseau, Roseau Co., Sacred Heart, Rev. Raymond Palcisko.
Res., P.O. Box 118, 403 Main Ave. N., 56751. Tel: 218-463-2441. [CEM]
Missions—Badger, Roseau Co., St. Mary's. [CEM]
Benwood, Roseau Co., St. Joseph, The Worker. [CEM]

Sabin, Clay Co., St. Cecilia. Served by Assumption, Barnesville. Tel: 218-354-7320.

Shevlin, Clearwater Co., Our Lady of Victory. Closed. For inquiries for parish records contact St. Joseph's, Bagley.

Stephen, Marshall Co., St. Stephen's, Rev. Robert C. Schreiner, S.T.L.
Res., 515 Fifth St., P.O. Box 507, 56757. Tel: 218-478-2231. [CEM]
Mission—Strandquist, Marshall Co., St. Edward the Confessor.

Tabor, Polk Co., Holy Trinity Catholic. Served by SS. Peter and Paul, Warren. Tel: 218-745-4511.

Terrebonne, Red Lake Co., St. Anthony. Served by St. Joseph's, Red Lake Falls. Tel: 218-253-2004.

Thief River Falls, Pennington Co., St. Bernards, Revs. Dennis J. Wieland; Robert J. LaPlante; Joseph Richards; Deacon John Eisbrenner; Ms. Sally Nelson, Pastoral Assoc.
Res., 105 Knight Ave. N., 56701. Tel: 218-681-3571. [CEM]
School—Tel: 218-681-1539. Sr. Kathy Kuchar, O.S.B., Prin.
Lay Teachers 8; Students 145.
Missions—Goodridge, Pennington Co., St. Ann; Grygla, Marshall Co., St. Clement.

Twin Valley, Norman Co., St. William. Served by Cathedral of the Immaculate Conception, Crookston. Tel: 218-281-1735. Sr. Patrice Eblen, O.S.B., Pastoral Admin.
Res., 405 E. Thorpe Ave., Ada, 56510. Tel: 218-784-4131.

Two Inlets, Becker Co., St. Mary's. Served by St. Peter's, Park Rapids. Tel: 218-732-5142. Rev. Rick Boyd, O.M.I.; Ms. Mary Ellen Kenney, Pastoral Admin.
Mailing Address: P.O. Box 287, Park Rapids, 56470. Tel: 218-732-4046.

Warren, Marshall Co., SS. Peter and Paul, Rev. Michael Sullivan.
Res., 208 N. Seventh St., 56762. Tel: 218-745-4511. [CEM]
Missions—Oslo, Marshall Co., St. Joseph, P.O. Box 97, 56744. Tel: 218-695-2641. Sr. Lucille Adelman, O.S.B., Admin.; Tabor, Polk Co., Holy Trinity Catholic.

Warroad, Roseau Co., St. Mary's, Rev. Duane Pribula; Deacon Robert Marvel.
Res., P.O. Box 33, 56763. Tel: 218-386-1178; Fax: 218-386-3054. [CEM]
Mission—Falun, Roseau Co., St. Philip.

Waubun, Mahnomen Co., St. Ann, Rev. Ronald J. Meyer, O.M.I.
Res., Rte. 2, Box 6, 56589. Tel: 218-473-2101; Fax: 218-473-2101. [CEM]
Missions—Naytahwaush, Mahnomen Co., St. Anne; Big Elbow Lake, Becker Co., St. Francis Cabrini.

White Earth, Becker Co., St. Benedict, Rev. Martin F. Machovec, O.M.I.; Bro. Craig Bonham, O.M.I., Pastoral Assoc.
Res., P.O. Box 417, 56591-0417. Tel: 218-983-3519. [CEM]
Missions—Ogema, Becker Co., Most Holy Redeemer; Ponsford, Becker Co., St. Theodore.

Williams, Lake of the Woods Co., St. Joseph. Served by Sacred Heart, Baudette. Tel: 218-634-2689.

Wilton, Beltrami Co., Sacred Heart. Served by St. Mary, Red Lake. Tel: 218-679-3614.

On Duty Outside the Diocese:
Reverend Fathers—
Bester, Robert
Foley, Gerald K.
Skoczylas, Walter
Wieseler, Lawrence A.

Leave of Absence:
Reverend Fathers—
Troska, Llewelyn J.

Retired:
Reverend Monsignors—
Mehrkens, William, P.O. Box 189, Red Lake, MN 56671. Tel: 218-679-3614
Stearns, John D., 5320 12th St. S., #227, Fargo, ND 58104
Reverend Fathers—
Archer, W. Donald, 1444 N. Recker Rd., #144, Mesa, AZ 85205
Bernauer, James, P.O. Box 7, Dent, MN 56528
Carriere, Henry G., 506 E. Esther St. #101, Badger, MN 56714
Felion, Jerome, 1514 Bamboo Cir., Harlingen, TX 78552
Keefe, William, Villa St. Vincent, 516 Walsh St. #212, Crookston, MN 56716. Tel: 218-281-5303
Kulhawik, Frank, St. William's, P.O. Box 306, Twin Valley, MN 56584. Tel: 218-584-5200
Lemen, William F., 710 Beltrami Ave., Bemidji, MN 56601. Tel: 218-751-4262
Nistler, Edward, 710 Beltrami Ave., Bemidji, MN 56601. Tel: 218-751-4262
Noah, Daniel, Rte. 2, Box 291, Crookston, MN 56716
Pryor, G. Robert, U.S.A.F, 286 Grantwood Dr., Henderson, NV 89014
Reid, Francis R., P.O. Box 474, Mahnomen, MN 56557

Permanent Deacons:
Bauer, Randall, Holy Rosary, Detroit Lakes
Bivens, Dennis, Cathedral of the Immaculate Conception, Crookston
Bruggeman, John, St. Lawrence, Mentor
Eisbrener, John, St. Bernard, Thief River Falls
Lukenbill, James, Sacred Heart, Baudette
Marvel, Robert, St. Mary's, Warroad
Schuiling, John, St. Philip, Bemidji
Thomas, James, Holy Rosary, Detroit Lakes

INSTITUTIONS LOCATED IN THE DIOCESE

[A] ELEMENTARY SCHOOLS, PRIVATE

RED LAKE. *St. Mary's Mission School*, 56671. Benedictine Sisters (St. Joseph, MN). Sr. Philip Zimmer, O.S.B., Prin.; Rev. Patrick A. Sullivan. Sisters 1; Lay Teachers 6; Students 85.

[B] CONFRATERNITY OF CHRISTIAN DOCTRINE

CROOKSTON. *Cathedral - Religious Education/Faith Formation*, 702 Summit Ave., 56716. Tel: 218-281-1735; Fax: 218-281-1747. Rev. Timothy F. Bushy, Dir.; Sr. Mary Jean Gust, Prog. Asst.; Michael Gerads, Junior High Coord.; Nancy Boucher, Senior High Coord. Students (Grades K-8) 275; High School Students (Grades 9-11) 138.

ADA. *St. Joseph Parish, R.E. Program*, 56510. Tel: 218-784-4131. Students 147.

ARGYLE. *St. Rose Parish, R.E. Program*, Box 277, 56713. Tel: 218-437-8336. Judy Adolphson, Dir. Students 136.

BEMIDJI. *St. Philips Parish, R. Formation Program*, 620 Beltrami Ave., 56601. Tel: 751-5849. D.R.E.: Kris Jensen, (Grades PreK-8); Mary Hoody, (Grades 9-12). Students (Grades PreK-5) 201; Students (Grades 6-12) 287.

DETROIT LAKES. *Holy Rosary Parish, R.E. Program*, 1032 Washington Ave., 56501. Tel: 218-847-8970. JoAnne Knuttila, Coord. Students 400.

EAST GRAND FORKS. *Sacred Heart Parish, R.E. Program*, 202 Third St., N.W., 56721. Tel: 218-773-0531. D.R.E.: Ginny Osowski, (Grades PreK-6); Sheryl Guzek, (Grades 7-12). Students 555.

GREENBUSH. *Religious Education Program*, P.O. Box A, 56726. Tel: 218-782-2263. Coordinators: Gerry Nubson. Students 127.

THIEF RIVER FALLS. *Religious Education Program*, 105 Knight Ave. N., 56701. Tel: 218-681-6268; 6269. Jan Halling, Coord. Students 224; High School Students 171.

[C] GENERAL HOSPITALS

BAUDETTE. *Lakewood Health Centers*, Rte. 1, Box 2120, 56623. Tel: 218-634-2120; Fax: 218-634-1307
For a complete listing, refer to the Hospitals section.

*DETROIT LAKES. *St. Mary's Regional Health Center*, 1027 Washington Ave., 56501. Tel: 218-847-5611; Fax: 218-847-7674
For a complete listing, refer to the Hospitals section.

PARK RAPIDS. *St. Joseph Area Health Services*, 600 Pleasant Ave., 56470. Tel: 218-732-3311
For a complete listing, refer to the Hospitals section.

[D] HOMES FOR THE AGED

CROOKSTON. *Villa St. Vincent*, 516 Walsh St., 56716
For a complete listing, refer to the Special Care Facilities section.

DETROIT LAKES. *St. Mary's Nursing Center*, 56501
For a complete listing, refer to the Special Care Facilities section.

[E] CONVENTS AND RESIDENCES FOR SISTERS

CROOKSTON. *Marywood Residential Community*. (Retirement Residence). Community, R.R. 2, Box 16, 56716-9603. Tel: 218-281-3093; Fax: 218-281-6123. Congregation of the Sisters of St. Joseph of Medaille (Pontifical Jurisdiction). Mr. William Larson, Admin.; Rev. Msgr. Roger L. Grundhaus, Chap. Marywood Residential Community 19; Crookston Regional Community 33.

Mount St. Benedict Monastery, 620 Summit Ave. E., 56716-2799. Tel: 218-281-3441; Fax: 218-281-3441, Ext. 26. Motherhouse of the Order of the Sisters of

St. Benedict of Pontifical Jurisdiction-The Federation of St. Gertrude. Sr. Michelle McGurran, O.S.B., Prioress; Sr. Lenore Paschke, Subprioress. Sisters in Community 149.

Sisters of St. Benedict Initial Formation. Sr. Lois Spors, O.S.B.

[F] NEWMAN CENTERS

CROOKSTON. *University of Minnesota Cooperative Campus Ministry*, 56716. Collette M. Conati, Dir. Coop. Campus Ministry.

BEMIDJI. *Holy Spirit Newman Center*, 1701 Birch Ln. N.E., 56601-2607. Tel: 218-751-3724. Rev. Msgr. Michael Patnode; Rev. James H.C. Lyons; Lois Jenkins, Pastoral Assoc.

MOORHEAD. *St. Thomas Aquinas Newman Center*, 707 11th St. S., 56560. Tel: 218-236-9596. Rev. August Gothman, Dir.; Shirley Wallace, Campus Minister.

[G] MISCELLANEOUS

CROOKSTON.

**Mount Saint Benedict Foundation*, 620 Summit Ave., 56716.

**The Diocese of Crookston Catholic Community Foundation*, 1200 Memorial Dr., 56716.

RELIGIOUS INSTITUTES OF MEN REPRESENTED IN THE DIOCESE

For further details refer to the corresponding bracketed number in the Religious Institutes of Men or Women section.

[0200]—*Benedictine Monks.*—O.S.B.

[0910]—*Oblates of Mary Immaculate.*—O.M.I.

RELIGIOUS INSTITUTES OF WOMEN REPRESENTED IN THE DIOCESE

[0230]—*Benedictine Sisters of Pontifical Jurisdiction.* (Congregation of St. Gertrude).—O.S.B.

[]—*Benedictine Sisters of Pontifical Jurisdiction (Federation of St. Benedict).*—O.S.B.

[3880]—*Sisters of St. Joseph of Medaille.*—C.S.J.

NECROLOGY

† Merth, John P., (Retired). —Died March 30, 1997.

Diocese of Dallas

(Dioecesis Dallasensis)

Most Reverend

CHARLES V. GRAHMANN, D.D.

Bishop of Dallas; ordained March 17, 1956; appointed Titular Bishop of Equilio and Auxiliary of San Antonio June 30, 1981; consecrated August 29, 1981; appointed First Bishop of Victoria April 14, 1982; installed May 29, 1982; appointed Coadjutor of Dallas December 18, 1989; Reception as Coadjutor of Dallas February 21, 1990; appointed Bishop of Dallas July 14, 1990.

Most Reverend

THOMAS TSCHOEPE

Retired Bishop of Dallas; ordained May 30, 1943; appointed Bishop of San Angelo January 12, 1966; consecrated March 9, 1966; transferred to Dallas August 27, 1969; resigned July 14, 1990. *Res., St. Joseph, P.O. Box 190, Waxahachie, TX, 75165.*

ESTABLISHED DIOCESE OF DALLAS ON JULY 15, 1890.

REDESIGNATED DIOCESE OF DALLAS-FORT WORTH ON OCTOBER 20, 1953.

REDESIGNATED DIOCESE OF DALLAS ON AUGUST 27, 1969.

Square Miles 7,523.

Comprises the following nine Counties in the State of Texas: Collin, Dallas, Ellis, Fannin, Grayson, Hunt, Kaufman, Navarro and Rockwall.

For legal titles of parishes and diocesan institutions, consult the Chancery Office.

Chancery Office: 3725 Blackburn, P.O. Box 190507, Dallas, TX, 75219. Tel.: 214-528-2240; Fax: 214-526-1743.

Web site address: http://www.diocese-of-dallas.org/

E-mail address: ccfc@cathdal.org

STATISTICAL OVERVIEW

Personnel	
Bishop	1
Retired Bishops	1
Abbots	1
Priests: Diocesan Active in Diocese	77
Priests: Active Outside Diocese	8
Priests: Retired, Sick or Absent	20
Number of Diocesan Priests	105
Religious Priests in Diocese	81
Extern Priests in Diocese	26
Ordinations:	
Diocesan Priests	5
Transitional Deacons	1
Permanent Deacons in Diocese	146
Total Brothers	5
Total Sisters	160
Parishes	
Parishes	65
With Resident Pastor:	
Resident Diocesan Priests	54
Resident Religious Priests	11
Without Resident Pastor:	
Missions	7
New Parishes Created	1
Professional Ministry Personnel:	
Brothers	2
Sisters	32
Lay Ministers	126
Welfare	
Catholic Hospitals	1
Total Assisted	43,303
Homes for the Aged	1
Total Assisted	58
Day Care and Extended Day Care Centers	5
Total Assisted	802
Special Centers for Social Services	16
Total Assisted	61,225
Educational	
Seminaries, Diocesan	1
Students from This Diocese	10
Diocesan Students in Other Seminaries	18
Total Seminarians	28
Colleges and Universities	1
Total Students	2,897
High Schools, Diocesan and Parish	3
Total Students	1,269
High Schools, Private	4
Total Students	1,844
Elementary Schools, Diocesan and Parish	30
Total Students	10,082
Elementary Schools, Private	3
Total Students	700
Non-residential Schools for the Disabled	1
Total Students	101
Catechesis/Religious Education:	
High School Students	4,273
Elementary Students	29,143
Total Students Under Catholic Instruction	50,337
Teachers in the Diocese:	
Priests	15
Scholastics	1
Brothers	2
Sisters	25
Lay Teachers	860
Vital Statistics	
Receptions into the Church:	
Infant Baptism Totals	10,644
Adult Baptism Totals	711
Received into Full Communion	656
First Communions	7,489
Confirmations	4,565
Marriages:	
Catholic	1,387
Interfaith	606
Total Marriages	1,993
Deaths	1,210
Total Catholic Population	544,441
Total Population	2,815,732

Former Bishops—Rt. Rev. THOMAS F. BRENNAN, D.D., cons. April 5, 1891; resigned Nov. 17, 1892; died March 21, 1916.—Rt. Rev. EDWARD JOSEPH DUNNE, D.D., cons. Nov. 30. 1893; died Aug. 5, 1910.—Most Rev. JOSEPH PATRICK LYNCH, D.D., LL.D., appt. June 8, 1911; cons. July 12, 1911; Assistant at Pontifical Throne, May 13, 1936; died Aug. 19, 1954.—Most Rev. THOMAS K. GORMAN, D.D., D.Sc.Hist., ord. June 23, 1917; Bishop of Reno; appt. April 24, 1931; cons. July 22, 1931; Assistant at the Pontifical Throne, May 4, 1942; appt. Titular Bishop of Rhasus and Coadjutor to the Bishop of Dallas, Feb. 8, 1952; succeeded to Aug. 19, 1954; resigned and appointed Titular Bishop of Pinhel, Aug. 27, 1969. (Title rescinded); died Aug. 16, 1980.

Vicar General—Rev. Msgr. GLENN D. GARDNER, J.C.D.

Chancery Office—3725 Blackburn, P.O. Box 190507, Dallas, 75219. Tel: 214-528-2240; Fax: 214-526-1743. Office Hours: 9-5.

Chancellor—Rev. Msgr. JOHN P. BELL, J.C.L.

Vice Chancellor—MARY EDLUND.

Diocesan Tribunal—P.O. Box 190507, Dallas, 75219. Tel: 214-528-9970.

Judicial Vicar—Rev. Msgr. JOHN P. BELL, J.C.L.

Assistant Judicial Vicar—Rev. JACK HOPKA, S.F.O., J.C.L.

Director of the Tribunal—WILLIAM C. HARE, III, J.C.L.

Secretary to the Tribunal—MARGARET GILLETT.

Defensores Vinculi—JOHN P. GARGAN, J.C.D.; Revs. JOSEPH MITCHELL, J.C.L.; MICHAEL DUCA, J.C.L.

Diocesan Judges—Rev. Msgr. GLENN D. GARDNER, J.C.D.; Rev. DAVID L. COLELLA, O.SS.T, J.C.D.

Notaries—MARGARET GILLETT; JANE HOFMEISTER.

Procurator-Advocates—SUSAN O'CONNOR BURKE; BEBE CANTU; ANN CARMODY; JUDY CLARK; VINCENT THIEN VAN DANG; Rev. JOHN F. DEEVES, S.J.; ANTHONY R. FLEO; Deacon DON FORBRICH; JEANNE MARIE GIRSCH; AGNES A. GLADBACH; Deacon WALLY GOVE; MARY CATHERINE HARE; VIRGINIA G. HEMMI; Rev. JOHN HOGAN, S.S.C.; Deacon JUAN IBARRA; MARY L. IZAK; MICHELLE JUNGWIRTH; Rev. GREG KELLY; Deacon JOHN PAUL KELLY; Deacon JOHN LEBLANC; LINDA MOSES; DENISE G. PHILLIPS; MARY A. RASINS; Deacon MICHAEL RASINS; PAUL W. REITTINGER; Deacon ROBERT RICARD; MARY KAY RITCHIE; LILY SALVATO; Deacons JOSEPH V. SALVO; ROBERT SANCHEZ; ED SCARBROUGH; WILLIAM J. SCHUSTER; Revs. MARK SEITZ; LUIS SERNA; CLIFFORD SMITH; ELAINE STIEBER; Deacon LEE J. STIEBER; Sr. DENISE THOMPSON, C.V.; MARY ELLEN

URIEGAS; FRANCIS XAVIER VUONG ANH THUONG; Deacon GARY M. VOGEL; MARGE WICK; DANNY WILCOX.

Consultors of Pastors—Rev. Msgr. RICHARD JOHNSON; Rev. Msgr. JOHN MEYERS; Revs. HENRY PETTER; TIM GOLLOB.

Diocesan Consultors—Rev. RAMON ALVAREZ; Rev. Msgr. JOHN BELL; Rev. TOM CLOHERTY; Rev. Msgr. DONALD FISCHER; Rev. Msgr. G. DUFFY GARDNER; Rev. HENRY PETTER; Rev. Msgr. DON ZIMMERMAN.

Presbyteral Council—Rev. Msgr. GLENN D. GARDNER, V.G., Ex-Offico; Revs. RAMON ALVAREZ; JAMES BALINT; Rev. Msgr. JOHN BELL; Revs. STEPHEN BIERSCHENK; IGNACIO CIZUR, O.F.M.Cap.; TOM CLOHERTY; MIKE DUCA; Rev. Msgr. DONALD FISCHER; Revs. TIM GOLLOB; ANDREW KOLZOW, O.P.; Rev. Msgr. JOHN MEYERS; Revs. HENRY PETTER; Rev. Msgr. DONALD ZIMMERMAN.

Censor Librorum—Rev. Msgr. GLENN D. GARDNER; Rev. ROBERT M. COERVER.

Diocesan Offices and Directors

Finance Council—Rev. DAVID FLORI, C.P.A.; EUGENE VILFORDI; LOUIS G. MUNIN; J. OLIVER MCGONIGLE; MICHAEL T. WEIS; TOM DORANS.

Building Commission—Rev. Msgr. JEROME P. DUESMAN; AL SALEM; DAVID FURLOW; MICHAEL T. WEIS. Tel: 214-528-2240.

Pastoral Concerns Board—Rev. Msgr. JOHN P. BELL; Rev. Msgr. JOHN F. MEYERS; Mrs. MARY EDLUND; Ms. Mr. BRONSON HAVARD; Mr. WILLIAM KEFFLER.

Personnel Board—Rev. Msgr. GLENN GARDNER; Rev. Msgr. DONALD ZIMMERMAN; Revs. RAMON ALVAREZ; HENRY PETTER; Deacon GEORGE ZACEK; Ms. BEVERLY J. BRADSHAW; Ms. BOZENA CLOUTIER; Mrs. MARY EDLUND; Mr. SHERBIE MATTHEWS.

Conduct Board—Rev. Msgr. GLENN GARDNER; Rev. Msgr. JOHN P. BELL; THERESA VO, Ph.D.

Ordination & Accreditation Board—Rev. THOMAS CLOHERTY; Sr. MARIA ELENA FERRER, S.S.N.D.; Deacon JOHN CATSORIS.

Teaching Division

I. Total Catholic Education—

Superintendent of Schools—Rev. LEONARD CALLAHAN, *P.O. Box 190507, Dallas, 75219.* Tel: 214-528-2360.

Associates—DOUGLAS J. HAMILTON; TONI UNDERWOOD; FRANK ROMERO.

Resource Center—Tel: 214-528-2360.

II. Media—

Media Division Head—Rev. Msgr. JOHN BELL, *P.O. Box 190507, Dallas, 75219.* Tel: 214-528-2240.

Newspaper—*"The Texas Catholic,"* Official Catholic Newspaper for the Diocese of Dallas; Most Rev. CHARLES V. GRAHMANN, D.D., Publisher; BRONSON HAVARD, Exec. Editor; ANTONIO RAMIREZ, JR., Business Mgr. Tel: 241-528-8792; Fax: 241-528-3411.

"El Catolico de Texas"—Spanish Language Paper.

Communications Office—MICHAEL MCGEE, Dir. Tel: 214-528-2240.

Santifying Division

Division Head—PATRICIA LENOIR, *P.O. Box 190507, Dallas, 75219.* Tel: 214-528-2360.

Worship Office—Rev. T. MICHAEL DUGAN, Dir. Tel: 214-528-2360.

Sacred Places—

Cemeteries—JAMES FOUCH, Exec. Dir., *3235 Lombardy Ln., 75220.* Tel: 214-357-5754.

Cathedral Santuario de Guadalupe—Rev. Msgr. LARRY PICHARD, Rector. Tel: 214-871-1362.

Catholic Conference and Formation Center—BARBARA LANDREGAN, Dir., *901 S. Madison Ave., Dallas, 75208. Mailing Address: P.O. Box 190507, Dallas, 75219.* Tel: 214-943-6585; Fax: 214-943-6587.

Sacramental Life Office—Rev. ROBERT COERVER, Dir. Tel: 214-582-2360.

Sacraments of Initiation & Healing—MARTY NOEL, *St. Patrick, 9643 Ferndale, Dallas, 75238.* Tel: 214-348-7380.

Seracments of Orders—

Seminary—Very Rev. MICHAEL DUCA, *Holy Trinity Seminary, P.O. Box 140309, Irving, 75014-0309.* Tel: 972-438-2212.

Seminarian Relations—Rev. JOHN LIBONE. Tel: 214-528-2240.

Vocations—Rev. GREG KELLY. Tel: 972-562-0638.

Diaconal Ministry—Deacon ARNOLD PICON, *901 S. Madison Ave., Dallas, 75208. Mailing Address: P.O. Box 190507, Dallas, 75219.* Tel: 214-943-6585.

Sacrament of Marriage—DIANE DANIELS. Tel: 214-528-2360.

Governing Division

Division Head—MICHAEL T. WEIS, *P.O. Box 190507, Dallas, 75219.* Tel: 214-528-2240.

Business Office—MICHAEL T. WEIS, Dir. Tel: 214-528-2240.

Catholic Community Appeal—R. MICHAEL GEORGE, Dir. Tel: 214-528-2240.

Pastoral Planning and Research—LYNN ROSSOL, Dir. Tel: 214-528-2240.

Tribunal—WILLIAM C. HARE, III, J.C.L., Dir. Tel: 214-528-2240.

Archives—ESTELLE METZGER, Archivist. Tel: 214-528-2240.

Mission Division

Division Head—Vacant, *P.O. Box 190507, Dallas, 75219.* Tel: 214-520-6590.

Catholic Charities—Sr. MARY ANN OWENS, S.S.N.D., Dir. Tel: 214-520-6590.

Mission Awareness / Justice and Peace—Sr. NANCY SULLIVAN, D.C., Dir. Tel: 214-528-2240.

CHD Coordinator—Sr. NANCY SULLIVAN, D.C. Tel: 214-528-2240.

Propagation of Faith and Holy Childhood—Sr. AGNES CHRISTINE MULLEN, C.PP.S., Dir. Tel: 214-528-2240.

Pastoral Care Ministries—

Addictions Ministry—PHIL PASCHKE. Tel: 972-960-2166.

Ministries to People with Disabilities—Rev. AUSTIN GREEN, O.P. Tel: 214-528-2240.

Hospital Ministry—SUE PARKER. Tel: 972-231-0869.

Prison Ministry—Rev. PAUL GRAY, *All Saints Parish, 5231 Meadowcreek, 75248.* Tel: 972-661-9282.

Networks

LYNN ROSSOL, Chm., *P.O. Box 190507, Dallas, 75219.* Tel: 214-528-2240

Family Life Network—SUE PARKER, Chm. Tel: 214-526-2772, Ext. 192.

Asian Network—VIVIEN RIVERA, Chm. Tel: 214-920-8384.

Black Network—Co-Chairs: LARI NEWMAN-WILLIAMS. Tel: 214-375-3715. PETER GRANGER. Tel: 972-227-4631.

Hispanic Network—MARGARET HERNANDEZ, Chm. Tel: 972-243-7104.

CLERGY, PARISHES, MISSIONS AND PAROCHIAL SCHOOLS

CITY OF DALLAS
(Dallas County)

1—CATHEDRAL-SANTUARIO DE GUADALUPE (1869), Rev. Msgr. Lawrence Pichard; Rev. Anibal Adorno; Deacons Juan Ibarra; Charles Stump.
Res., 2215 Ross Ave., 75201. Tel: 214-871-1362; Fax: 214-954-1557.
Catechesis / Religious Programs—Sr. Esther Guerrero, M.C.D.P., D.R.E.
Students 1,183.

2—ALL SAINTS (1976), Revs. Thomas Cloherty; Lonnie Honea; Paul Gray; Richard Weaver; Deacons Denis Simon; Vincent Bathea; William Friedman; John Costello.
Res., 5231 Meadowcreek, 75248. Tel: 972-661-9282; Fax: 972-233-5401.
Catechesis / Religious Programs—Students 451.

3—BLESSED SACRAMENT (1901), Rev. Paul L. Weinberger; Deacons Joe Vollmer-Konig; Jose R. Robles; Ismael A. Guerra. In res., Rev. Msgr. William A. Botik, (Retired).
Res., 231 N. Marsalis Ave., 75203. Tel: 214-948-6535; Fax: 214-948-1660.
Catechesis / Religious Programs—D.R.E.: Mr. Francisco Manzo.
Students 1,690.

4—CHRIST THE KING, Rev. Msgr. Donald F. Zimmerman; Deacon Sam Franklin; Mary Catherine Hare, Pastoral Assoc.
Res., 8017 Preston Rd., 75225. Tel: 214-365-1200; Fax: 214-365-1205.
School—4100 Colgate St., 75225. Tel: 214-365-1264; Fax: 214-365-1236.
Lay Teachers 32; Students 407.
Catechesis / Religious Programs—Students 255.

5—HOLY CROSS (1956), Rev. Timothy A. Gollob; Deacons Antonio Trevino; Henry Vault; Armando Murillo. In res., Rev. James George McKenna.
Res., 2926 E. Ledbetter Dr., 75216. Tel: 214-374-7952; Fax: 214-375-7457.
Catechesis / Religious Programs—Students 240.

6—HOLY TRINITY (1907), Revs. Paul W. Sauerbier, C.M.; George J. Weber, C.M.; Deacon Don Forbrich. In res., Rev. Warren F. Dicharry, C.M.
Mailing Address: 3826 Gilbert Ave., 75219.
Res., 3811 Oak Lawn Ave., 75219. Tel: 214-526-8555; Fax: 214-526-3477.
School—3815 Oak Lawn Ave., 75219.
Lay Teachers 21; Students 245.
Catechesis / Religious Programs—Students 475.

7—MARY IMMACULATE (1956), Rev. Msgr. Albert A. Cuschieri; Revs. Joseph Son Van Nguyen; Luis Gongora; Deacons Don Van-Scoy; Gerard L. Bauwens; Robert J. Dalton; Patrick Hayes.
Res., 14032 Dennis Ln., 75234. Tel: 972-243-7104; Fax: 972-406-1254.
School—Tel: 972-243-7105.
Lay Teachers 25; Students 571.
Catechesis / Religious Programs—Judy Grimmett, D.R.E.
Students 1,362.

8—OUR LADY OF LOURDES (1954), Revs. Jesse Torre, O.F.M.Cap. (Spain); Roberto Garcia, O.F.M.Cap. (Spain); Luis Gerardo Arraiza, O.F.M.Cap. (Spain). In res., Very Rev. Ignacio Cizur, O.F.M.Cap. (Spain).
Res., 5605 Bernal Dr., 75212. Tel: 214-637-6673.
Catechesis / Religious Programs—D.R.E.: Pete Rodriguez; Amy Rodriguez.
Students 925.

9—OUR LADY OF PERPETUAL HELP (1942), Revs. Juan Cruz Gaston, O.F.M.Cap.; Sabino Erro, O.F.M. (Spain); Deacons Albert Montes; Adolph Orozco, Jr.; Jesse J. Rojas. In res., Rev. Alfonso Casteig, O.F.M.Cap. (Spain).
Res., 7617 Cortland Ave., 75235. Tel: 214-352-6012; Fax: 214-351-3993.
School—7625 Cortland Ave., 75235. Tel: 214-351-3396; Fax: 214-351-9889.
School Sisters of Notre Dame 2; Lay Teachers 10; Students 174.
Catechesis / Religious Programs—Olivia Valenzuela, D.R.E.
Students 712.

10—OUR LADY OF SAN JUAN DE LOS LAGOS AND ST. THERESA (1928), Rev. Alfonso Casteig, O.F.M.Cap. (Spain).
Res., 2601 Singleton Blvd., 75212. Tel: 214-631-9627; Fax: 214-631-6267.
Catechesis / Religious Programs—Tel: 214-688-0942.
Students 220.

11—ST. ANDREW KIM (1977), Rev. John Hogan, S.S.C.
Res., 2712 Swiss Ave., 75204. Tel: 214-651-9150; Fax: 214-826-9099.
Catechesis / Religious Programs—Moses Chung, D.R.E.
Students 155.

12—ST. ANTHONY (1938), Rev. Anthony Nwaogu.
Res., 2711 Romine St., 75215. Tel: 214-428-6926.
School—3732 Myrtle St., 75215. Tel: 214-421-3645; Fax: 214-421-7416.
Lay Teachers 18; Students 215.

13—ST. AUGUSTINE (1937), Revs. Ernesto Torres; A. Oscar Diez; Deacon Robert Sanchez.
Res., 1047 N. St. Augustine Dr., 75217. Tel: 214-398-1583; Fax: 214-398-2580.
School—1064 N. St. Augustine Dr., 75217.
Sisters 2; Lay Teachers 10; Students 225.
Catechesis / Religious Programs—Sr. Catherine Killoran, D.R.E.
Students 1,119.

14—ST. BERNARD OF CLAIRVAUX (1947), Rev. August A. Melito; Deacons Robert Garcia; John Kelly.
Res., 1404 Old Gate Ln., 75218. Tel: 214-321-0454; Fax: 214-320-0119.
School—1420 Old Gate Ln., 75218. Tel: 214-321-2897; Fax: 214-321-4060.
Lay Teachers 22; Students 344.
Catechesis / Religious Programs—Juanita Mitchell, D.R.E.
Students 344.

15—ST. CECILIA (1933), Revs. Edmundo Paredes; H. Fred Caldwell; Deacons Gonzalo Gonzales; Onesimo Martinez.
Res., 1809 W. Davis St., 75208. Tel: 214-941-5821; Fax: 214-946-4466.
School—635 Marycliff Rd., 75208. Tel: 214-948-8628.
Sisters of St. Mary of Namur 1; Lay Teachers 10; Students 210.
Catechesis / Religious Programs—Students 1,175.

16—ST. EDWARD (1903), Revs. Eduardo Gonzalez, S.D.B.; Luis Serna; Deacons Juan G. Gonzalez; Guadalupe Carreon; Paul Johansen.
Res., 4014 Simpson St., 75246. Tel: 214-823-1291; Fax: 214-823-2911.
Catechesis / Religious Programs—Sylvia Orozco-Joseph, D.R.E.
Students 1,200.

17—ST. ELIZABETH (1956), Revs. T. Michael Dugan; Jonathan G. Austin; Deacons Joseph Vollmer-Konig; Denis Simon; Sr. Denise Thompson, Pastoral Assoc.
Res., 4015 S. Hampton Rd., 75224. Tel: 214-331-4328; Fax: 214-331-2464.

School—4019 S. Hampton Rd., 75224. Tel: 214-331-5139; Fax: 214-467-4346.
Lay Teachers 23; Students 411.
Catechesis/Religious Programs—Mr. Bebe Cantu, D.R.E.
Students 105.

18—ST. JAMES (1934), Rev. Efren Ortega; Deacon Vincent F. Jimenez.
Mailing Address: P.O. Box 763338, 75376.
Res., 1002 E. Saner Ave., 75216. Tel: 214-371-9209; Fax: 214-371-0226.
Catechesis/Religious Programs—Fax: 214-371-9672.
Students 510.

19—ST. JUDE CHAPEL AND INFORMATION CENTER (Downtown Dallas) (1968), Rev. Gilbert J. Graham, O.P., Admin.
Res., 1521 Main St., 75201. Tel: 214-742-2508; Fax: 214-748-5282.

20—ST. MARY OF CARMEL (1944), Rev. Jesus Sancho, O.C.D.
Res., 2900 Vilbig Rd., 75212. Tel: 214-747-1433; Fax: 214-748-7481.
School—1716 Singleton Blvd., 75212. Tel: 214-748-2934; Fax: 214-760-9052.
Sisters of the Holy Spirit 3; Lay Teachers 10; Students 206.
Catechesis/Religious Programs—Students 285.

21—ST. MONICA (1954), Revs. John F. Meyers; Brindley Mills; Joseph A. Mehan, Jr.; Deacons John M. Votruba; Larry Lucido; Bob Marrinan.
Res., 9933 Midway Rd., 75220. Tel: 214-358-1453; Fax: 214-351-1887.
School—4140 Walnut Hill Ln., 75229. Tel: 214-351-5688; Fax: 214-352-2608.
Lay Teachers 53; Students 810.
Catechesis/Religious Programs—Ms. Patricia Foley, D.R.E.
Students 366.

22—ST. PATRICK (1963), Rev. Msgr. Richard E. Johnson; Rev. Michael A. Guadagnoli; Deacons Clifford H. Kopinski; John C. Nordick.
Res., 9643 Ferndale Rd., 75238. Tel: 214-348-7380; Fax: 214-340-5956.
School—9635 Ferndale Rd., 75238. Tel: 214-348-8070; Fax: 214-503-7230.
Sisters of the Incarnate Word and Blessed Sacrament 2; Lay Teachers 31; Students 528.
Catechesis/Religious Programs—Mrs. Martha Noel, D.R.E.
Students 466.

23—ST. PETER (1905), Rev. Stanislaw Michalek, S.Ch.; Deacon Fred Delin.
Res., 2907 Woodall Rodgers Fwy., 75204. Tel: 214-855-1384; Fax: 214-855-1309.
Catechesis/Religious Programs—Mercy Hamilton, D.R.E.
Students 76.

24—ST. PHILIP (1954), Rev. Stephen J. Mocio.
Res., 8131 Military Pkwy., 75227. Tel: 214-388-5464; Fax: 214-388-2839.
School—8151 Military Pkwy., 75227. Tel: 214-381-4973.
Sisters of the Holy Spirit 3; Lay Teachers 13; Students 249.
Catechesis/Religious Programs—D.R.E.: Susan Laurence; Pat Kountz.
Students 208.

25—ST. PIUS X (1954), Revs. Ramon Alvarez; Michael D. Forge; Denis O'Brien, M.M.; Deacons David Leerssen; Michael Shaw; George Zacek; John Schell.
Res., 3030 Gus Thomasson Rd., 75228. Tel: 972-279-6155; Fax: 972-686-7510.
School—Tel: 972-279-2339; Fax: 972-613-2059.
Lay Teachers 30; Students 615.
Catechesis/Religious Programs—Tel: 972-279-2558. Virginia Hemmi, D.R.E.
Students 759.

26—ST. RITA (1961), Revs. Gerald Hughes, S.J.; W. Peter Bayhi, S.J.; Patrick H. Koch, S.J.; Deacons William Schuster; Charles Sylvester.
Office: 12521 Inwood Rd., 75244. Tel: 972-934-8388; Fax: 972-934-8965.
Res., 12626 Planters Glen, 75244. Tel: 972-239-5205.
School—12525 Inwood Rd., 75244. Tel: 972-239-3203; Fax: 972-934-3657.
Lay Teachers 38; Students 585.
Catechesis/Religious Programs—Deacon William Schuster, D.R.E.
Students 545.

27—ST. THOMAS AQUINAS (1952), Revs. Stephen W. Bierschenk; James R. Sharp. In res., Rev. Msgr. John T. Gulczynski.
Res., 6306 Kenwood Ave., 75214. Tel: 214-821-3360; Fax: 214-821-5395.
School—3741 Abrams Rd., 75214.
Lay Teachers 42; Students 555.
Catechesis/Religious Programs—Mrs. Mary Xuereb, D.R.E.
Students 169.

28—SANTA CLARA (1993), Revs. David L. Colella, O.SS.T.; Antonio Liberman Ormaza, S.C.S. (Ecuador); Deacon Alberto Villarreal.
Res., 321 Calumet St., 75211. Tel: 214-337-3936; Fax: 214-333-9148.
School—St. Clare of Assisi Catholic School, Tel: 214-333-9423. Amancio Cantu, Prin.
Catechesis/Religious Programs—Leo Landin, D.R.E.
Students 500.

OUTSIDE THE CITY OF DALLAS

Allen, Collin Co., St. Jude (1981), Revs. Bruce A. Bradley; Loyd Morris; Deacons Ronald Fejeran; Shawn French.
Mailing Address: P.O. Box 869, 75013.
Res., 1515 N. Greenville, 75002. Tel: 972-727-1177; Fax: 972-727-1401.
Catechesis/Religious Programs—Carole Anne Horstman, D.R.E.
Students 1,075.

Bonham, Fannin Co., St. Elizabeth, Rev. Jose Saldana; Deacon Joe Culling.
Res., 409 W. 10th St., 75418. Tel: 903-583-7359.

Commerce, Hunt Co., St. Joseph, Rev. D. Stanley Corcoran.
Res., 2904 Melmar Pk., 75428. Tel: 903-886-7135.
Catechesis/Religious Programs—Students 68.

Coppell, Dallas Co., St. Ann (1985), Rev. Msgr. Kilian J. Broderick; Rev. Tim Church, Assoc.; Deacons Ed Scarbrough; Joe Salvo.
Res., 129 Lansdowne Cir., 75019. Tel: 972-393-7951.
Church—180 Samuel Blvd., 75019. Tel: 972-393-5544; Fax: 972-462-1617.
Catechesis/Religious Programs—Sr. Ruth Ellen Dean, D.R.E.
Students 2,082.

Corsicana, Navarro Co., Immaculate Conception (1871), Rev. Robert Williams; Deacon Lewis Palos.
Res., 3000 Hwy. 22 W., P.O. Box 798, 75151. Tel: 903-874-4473; Fax: 903-874-2619.
School—James L. Collins Catholic School.
Sisters of St. Francis of Sylvania, OH 2; Lay Teachers 13; Students 191.
Catechesis/Religious Programs—Charles Bonin, D.R.E.
Students 130.

Denison, Grayson Co., St. Patrick (1872), Rev. George P. Monaghan; Deacon Gary Vogel.
Res., 314 N. Rusk Ave., 75020. Tel: 903-463-3275; Fax: 903-463-3447.
Catechesis/Religious Programs—Marge Orrick, D.R.E.
Students 181.

Duncanville, Dallas Co., Holy Spirit (1974), Rev. Timothy Heines, Admin.; Deacons Eugene Schlebach; Les Alt; Edward Armstead.
Res., 1111 W. Danieldale Rd., 75137-3719. Tel: 972-298-4971; Fax: 972-709-1443.
Catechesis/Religious Programs—Aggie Gladbach, D.R.E.
Students 869.

Ennis, Ellis Co., St. John Nepomucene (1902), Revs. Fred Sidler; John Dick; Deacons Dean Darnall; Don Griffith; Ralph Gordon.
Res., 401 E. Lampasas St., 75119. Tel: 972-878-2834; Fax: 972-875-2452. [CEM]
School—701 S. Paris St., 75119. Tel: 972-878-5411.
Sisters of Divine Providence 3; Lay Teachers 14; Students 142.
High School—Lay Teachers 15; Students 131.
Catechesis/Religious Programs—Students 400.

Ferris, Ellis Co., Corpus Christi, Rev. Raul Garza, C.M.
Res., 117 N. Wood, 75125. Tel: 972-842-2288.
Catechesis/Religious Programs—Students 152.

Forney, Kaufman Co., St. Martin (1891), Rev. Danilo G. Ramos, C.I.C.M. (Philippines); Deacons James Burkel; Hector Pena; Sergio Morales; Craig McAlister.
Res., 806 N. Washington St., P.O. Box 619, Kaufman, 75142. Tel: 972-962-3247; Fax: 972-962-3247.
Catechesis/Religious Programs—Students 67.

Frisco, Collin Co., St. Francis of Assisi (1966), Rev. Joseph Mitchell (Mexico); Deacon Stanley Storozuk.
Res., 8760 Third St., 75034. Tel: 972-335-6431.

Garland, Dallas Co.,

1—GOOD SHEPHERD, (1944), Revs. Robert R. Crisp; Ernesto Villarroya (Philippines); Deacons Leroy Berens; Walter R. Gove; Hugo Salinas. In res., Revs. Peter Kochery; Jose Moreno.
Res., 201 S. 13th St., 75040. Tel: 972-276-8587; Fax: 972-494-3653.
School—214 S. Garland Ave., 75040. Tel: 972-272-6533; Fax: 972-272-0512.
Brothers 1; Lay Teachers 27; Students 344.
Catechesis/Religious Programs—Students 650.

2—MOTHER OF PERPETUAL HELP, (Vietnamese), Revs. Augustine Nguyen; Hai Dinh, C.SS.R.; Thong Nguyen, C.SS.R.
Res., 2121 Apollo Rd., P.O. Box 451568, 75045. Tel: 972-614-7073.
Catechesis/Religious Programs—Bro. Hoa, D.R.E.
Students 420.

3—ST. MARY MALANKARA, (1996), Rev. Peter Kochery.
116 E. Ave. D, 75040. Tel: 972-494-5356.
Res., c/o Good Shepherd Church, 201 S. 13th St., 75040. Tel: 972-272-4641.

4—ST. MICHAEL THE ARCHANGEL, (1980), Rev. Msgr. Leon Duesman; Deacons Dave Beuerman; Joe Perez.
Res., 950 Trails Pkwy., 75043. Tel: 972-279-6581; 681-8026 (Rectory); Fax: 972-279-6647.
Catechesis/Religious Programs—Adela Miller, D.R.E.
Students 1,093.

5—ST. THOMAS THE APOSTLE, (1992), Rev. Jacob Angadiath.
Res., 4922 Rose Hill Rd., 75043. Tel: 972-270-4939.
Catechesis/Religious Programs—Students 106.

Grand Prairie, Dallas Co., Immaculate Conception (1916), Revs. Dennis O'Mara, S.S.C.; Bernard Toal, S.S.C.; Gerald Wilmsen, S.S.C.; Deacons Fernando L. Argumaniz; Manuel Veyna; Michael S. Rasins; Jesse Gonzales.
Res., 610 N.E. 17th St., 75050. Tel: 972-262-5137; Fax: 972-264-7657.
School—400 N.E. 17th St., 75050. Tel: 972-264-8777; Fax: 972-264-7742.
Sisters of the Holy Family of Nazareth 3; Lay Teachers 13; Students 227.
Catechesis/Religious Programs—Diane Gutierrez, D.R.E.
Students 725.

St. Joseph Vietnamese Catholic Community (1993), Rev. Peter Phong Nguyen.
Res., 1902 S.E. 8th St., 75051. Tel: 972-642-6747.

St. Michael the Archangel (1985), Rev. Joseph C. Lee; Deacons Robert Ricard; Dennis Bryant; Frank Eschbach.
2910 Corn Valley, 75052.
Res., 2925 Lake Park Dr., 75051. Tel: 972-262-0552; Fax: 972-642-5429.
Catechesis/Religious Programs—Tel: 972-262-6590.
Students 467.

Greenville, Hunt Co., St. William (1892), Rev. Robert M. Cox; Deacon Lee Davis.
Res., 4300 Stuart St., 75401. Tel: 903-450-1177; Fax: 903-455-7134.
Catechesis/Religious Programs—Tel: 903-455-8201. Carolyn Dorman, D.R.E.
Students 173.
Mission—Quinlan, Hunt Co., Our Lady of Fatima.

Irving, Dallas Co., Chapel of the Incarnation (1973), Ms. Christine G. Edmonds, Asst. Chap.
Res., University of Dallas, 75062. Tel: 972-721-5375; Fax: 972-721-5351.

Holy Family of Nazareth (1964), Rev. Msgr. Jerome P. Duesman; Rev. Aidan O'Donovan, M.S.C.; Deacons Lee Stieber; Kenneth Hale; Robert Miller.
Res., 2330 Cheyenne St., 75062. Tel: 972-252-5521; Fax: 972-252-5523.
School—2323 Cheyenne St., 75062. Tel: 972-255-0205; Fax: 972-252-4167.
Sisters of the Holy Family of Nazareth 3; Lay Teachers 27; Students 406.
Catechesis/Religious Programs—Monica Duyka, D.R.E.
Students 351.

St. Luke (1902), Revs. J. Douglas Deshotel; John W. Fowler, (Retired); Deacons Louis F. Adelmann; Marvin M. Barron; Jose Trevino; Daniel Segovia.
Res., 1015 Schulze Dr., 75060. Tel: 972-259-3222; Fax: 972-259-3339.
School—1023 Schulze Dr., 75060.
Sisters of the Holy Family of Nazareth 1; Lay Teachers 20; Students 350.
Catechesis/Religious Programs—Jo Ann Dreyer, D.R.E.
Students 887.

Kaufman, Kaufman Co., St. Ann (1935), Rev. Danilo G. Ramos, C.I.C.M. (Philippines); Deacons James Burkel; Hector Pena; Sergio Morales; Craig McAlister.
Res., 806 N. Washington St., P.O. Box 619, 75142. Tel: 972-962-3247.
Catechesis/Religious Programs—Nick Guigneaux, D.R.E.
Students 276.

Lancaster, Dallas Co., St. Francis of Assisi (1973), Rev. Arthur D. Mallinson; Deacon Jose F. Hernandez.
Res., 1001 Alicia, 75134. Tel: 972-227-4124; Fax: 972-227-2882.
Catechesis/Religious Programs—Tel: 972-227-0770. Jeannine McClellan, D.R.E.
Students 241.

McKinney, Collin Co., St. Gabriel the Archangel (1996), Rev. Gregory Kelly.

Mailing Address: 2214 Forest Creek, 75070. Tel: 972-562-0638; Fax: 972-540-1840.
Catechesis/Religious Programs—Students 423.
St. Michael (1892), Rev. J. Carl Vogel.
Res., 411 Paula Rd., 75069. Tel: 972-562-4444.
Catechesis/Religious Programs—Barbara Woodroof, D.R.E.
Students 373.
Mission—Van Alstyne, Grayson Co., Holy Family.

Plano, Collin Co., Prince of Peace (1991), Revs. R. James Balint; Lawrence A. Beyer; Deacons Robert Staib; Bernard Schroedle; Louis L. Munoz.
Res., 5100 W. Plano Pkwy., 75093. Tel: 972-380-2100; Fax: 972-380-5162.
School—Tel: 972-380-5505; Fax: 972-380-5162.
Lay Teachers 34; Students 340.
Catechesis/Religious Programs—Students 398.
St. Elizabeth Ann Seton (1976), Revs. Henry V. Petter; Paul Barrus; Robert Shortall (DAV); Deacons Ted Perez; Thomas Roche; Bill Flynn; Harry Pusateri.
Res., 2800 Piedra Ln., 75023. Tel: 972-596-5505; Fax: 972-985-7573.
Catechesis/Religious Programs—Tel: 972-596-1923. Mary Frazier, D.R.E.
Students 2,863.
St. Mark the Evangelist (1966), Revs. Thomas M. Speiser; Matthew A. Bagert; Deacons Bob Scoggins; Michael A. Carrell; Ed Putonti; Arnold Picon.
Res., 1201 Alma Dr., 75075. Tel: 972-423-5609; Fax: 972-423-5024.
School—Tel: 972-578-0610; Fax: 972-423-3299.
Lay Teachers 29; Students 575.
Catechesis/Religious Programs—Deacon Mike Carrell, D.R.E.
Students 1,476.

Richardson, Dallas Co., Mission of the Sacred Heart of Jesus (Chinese), Rev. John Chen.
Res., 14277 Preston Rd. #1027, Dallas, 75240. Tel: 972-716-0077; Fax: 972-980-8211.
St. Joseph (1976), Rev. Msgr. Don L. Fischer; Rev. Clifford G. Smith; Deacon Jim Daniels.
Res., 600 S. Jupiter Rd., 75081. Tel: 972-231-2951; Fax: 972-231-2875.
Catechesis/Religious Programs—Tel: 972-690-5588.
Students 734.
St. Paul the Apostle (1956), Revs. David J. Flori; Alejandro Buitrago; Deacon Carl Thelin.
Res., 709 James Dr., 75080. Tel: 972-235-6105; Fax: 972-480-8528.
School—720 S. Floyd Rd., 75080. Tel: 972-235-3263; Fax: 972-690-1542.
Lay Teachers 25; Students 448.
Catechesis/Religious Programs—Tel: 972-235-2598; Fax: 972-661-9993. Jeremy (Jerri) Brandenburg, D.R.E.
Students 638.

Rockwall, Rockwall Co., Our Lady of the Lake (1978), Rev. William Richard; Deacons John Catsoris; Jesus Cerrato.
Res., P.O. Box 191, 75087. Tel: 972-771-6671 (Office); Fax: 972-771-7283.
Catechesis/Religious Programs—Tel: 972-771-4253. Aline Kindle, D.R.E.
Students 455.

Rowlett, Dallas Co., Sacred Heart (1899), Rev. Daniel J. Clayton; Deacons Frank Dunlop, Sr.; James Welsh; Paul Husting.
Res., 3905 Hickox Rd., 75088. Tel: 972-475-4405; Fax: 972-475-6658.
Catechesis/Religious Programs—Sandy Guancial, D.R.E.
Students 432.

Sherman, Grayson Co., St. Mary (1872), Revs. Jeremy Myers; Juan R. Lira; Deacons John Le Blanc; Tomas Avila; Ron Fejeran.
Res., 727 S. Travis, 75090. Tel: 903-893-5148; Fax: 903-813-5489.
School—713 Travis St., 75090. Tel: 903-893-2127.
Lay Teachers 15; Students 165.
Catechesis/Religious Programs—Annie Kremer, D.R.E.
Students 335.
Mission—Whitesboro, Grayson Co., St. Francis of Assisi.

Terrell, Kaufman Co., St. John (1876), Rev. Raymond J. Scott.
Res., 701 N. Frances St., 75160. Tel: 972-563-3643.
Catechesis/Religious Programs—Susan Warner, D.R.E.
Students 170.

Waxahachie, Ellis Co., St. Joseph (1875), Rev. Mark Joseph Seitz; Most Rev. Thomas Tschoepe; Deacons Denver Crawley; Hugo Monsanto; Larry Hatch; Denis Corbin.
Res., 504 E. Marvin St., 75165. Tel: 972-938-1953; Fax: 972-938-1956.
School—St. Joseph Catholic School, 506 E. Marvin St., 75165. Tel: 972-938-2652. Edith Kosydar, Prin.
Lay Teachers 16; Students 132.
Catechesis/Religious Programs—Cheryl Bain, D.R.E.
Students 357.
Mission—Italy, Ellis Co., Epiphany, 434 S. Ward, Italy 76651.

Wylie, Collin Co., St. Anthony (1900), Deacons Peter Martinez; Warner Washington.
Res., 404 N. Ballard, 75098. Tel: 972-442-2765. [CEM]
Catechesis/Religious Programs—Students 400.

Chaplains of Public Institutions

DALLAS. *Veterans Administration Hospital* 2926 E. Ledbetter Dr., 75216. Tel: 214-374-7952. Rev. Timothy A. Gollob.

BONHAM. *Veterans Administration Hospital* 404 W. 10th St., 75418. Tel: 903-583-4942. Rev. Jose Saldana.

GRAND PRAIRIE. *Hensley Field Naval Base*. Vacant.

SEAGOVILLE. *Federal Correctional Institution*. Rev. Raymond Dowling.

TERRELL. *State Hospital* 702 N. Frances St., 75160. Tel: 972-563-3643. Rev. Raymond J. Scott.

Special Assignment:
Reverend Fathers—
Eades, B. G., 1503 Cedar Hills Ave., Dallas, TX 75205
Lucio, Justin, 5904 Ross Ave., Dallas, TX 75206
Pratt, Dean, Hospital Ministry, 218 Gwendola Dr., McKinney, TX 75070

On Duty Outside the Diocese:
Reverend Fathers—
Drozd, Henry J., P.O. Box 42063, Savannah, GA 31409-0001
Martin, Sean C., St. Mary's Seminary, Houston, TX
McKenna, James George, P.O. Box 190507, Dallas, TX 75219
Phan, Cho Dink Peter, Catholic University
Roberts, Kenneth J., 611 Rosetta, Florissant, MO 63031

Absent on Leave:
Reverend Fathers—
Brown, Richard
Tullius, Richard

Retired:
Reverend Monsignors—
Hughes, Gerald
Johnson, Edwin, 213 Goodford Rd., Philadelphia, PA 19154
McCallum, John V., 3406 Tipps Dr., Greenville, TX 75401
O'Rourke, John G.
Rehkemper, Robert
Reverend Fathers—
Fernandez, Edward P., 5392 Bramble Ln., Las Vegas, NV 89120
Fowler, John W., 6330 Shadybrook Ln., Apt. 2151, Dallas, TX 75206. Tel: 214-691-5407
Haberman, Lawrence R., 1518 E. Mulberry, Sherman, TX 75090
Slovacek, Emil C., 1815 Hamlet, Dallas, TX 75203
White, Gale, P.O. Box 699, Mineola, TX 75773

Permanent Deacons:
Adelman, Louis
Alt, Les
Argumaniz, Fernando L.
Armstead, Edward
Arredondo, Pastor G., (Retired)
Avila, Tomas
Barron, Marvin
Bathea, Val Vincent
Bauwens, Gerald
Berens, LeRoy J.
Beste, William B.
Bryant, Dennis Phillip
Burkel, James
Carrell, Michael A.
Carreon, Guadalupe A.
Catsoris, John A.
Cerrato, Jesus, Jr.
Chung, Hoan Moses
Coffey, Thomas, On Duty Outside the Diocese
Corbin, Denis D.
Costello, John R.
Crawley, Denver
Culling, Joseph
Dalton, Robert J.
Daniels, James
Darnall, Dean
Davis, Lee B.
Delin, Fred O.
Dorsey, Timothy, On Duty Outside the Diocese
Dunlop, Frank W., Sr.
Elsberg, Alick, On Duty Outside the Diocese
Eschbach, Frank
Fejeran, Ronald
Flynn, Bill
Forbrich, Donald
Franklin, Sam
Freeman, Mike
French, Shawn Patrick
Friedman, William L.
Garcia, Benito
Garcia, Robert
Gonzales, Gonzalo
Gonzales, Jesse
Gonzales, Juan G.
Gonzalez, Ronald, On Duty Outside the Diocese
Gordon, Ralph R.
Gove, Walter
Griffith, Don
Guerra, Ismael A.
Guerrero, Joseph D., Leave of Absence
Hale, Kenneth
Hancock, John, On Duty Outside the Diocese
Hatch, Larry G.
Hayes, Pat
Henvey, Thomas
Hernandez, Jose F.
Husting, Paul
Ibarra, Juan
Jimenez, Roberto, On Duty Outside the Diocese
Jimenez, Vincent
Johansen, Paul
Jones, Edward S.
Jorgensen, John, (Retired)
Kelly, John Paul
Kopinski, Clifford H.
LeBlanc, John D.
Leerssen, David
Leicht, Robert R., Jr., On Duty Outside the Diocese
Lincon, Jose
Lucido, Larry
Macero, Carl, On Duty Outside the Diocese
Marrinan, Robert, Sr.
Martinez, Onesimo
Martinez, Pete A., (Retired)
McAlister, Craig
McLean, Michael J.
Miller, Carl V., On Duty Outside the Diocese
Miller, J. Robert
Milliken, Frank M.
Monsanto, Hugo
Montes, Alberto
Morales, Sergio
Munoz, Louis L.
Murillo, Armando
Nordick, John C.
Noriega, Ramon, On Duty Outside the Diocese
Orozco, Adolph, Jr.
Palos, Lewis J.
Pena, Hector B.
Perez, Joe R.
Perez, Ted, Jr.
Picon, Arnold
Pilger, Rex, Jr., On Duty Outside the Diocese
Pusateri, Harry
Putonti, Edward
Rasins, Michael
Reisor, Kenneth
Rener, Bonnie Leo
Reyna, Frank
Ricard, Robert A.
Robles, Jose R.
Roche, Thomas
Rodriguez, Pedro P.
Rojas, Jessie
Ross, Donald, Leave of Absence
Salerno, John, On Duty Outside the Diocese
Salinas, Hugo A.
Salvo, Joseph
Sanchez, Robert
Scarbrough, Ed
Schell, John A.
Schlebach, Eugene M.
Schnurr, Don
Schroedle, Bernard E.
Schuster, William J.
Scoggins, Robert C., Jr.
Segovia, Daniel D.
Shaw, Michael, Jr.
Sifuentez, Stephen Q., Leave of Absence
Simon, Denis
Stabile, Benjamin, (Retired)
Staib, Bob
Stieber, Lee, (Retired)
Storozuk, Stanley
Stump, Charles, Jr.
Sykora, Richard
Sylvester, Charles T.
Thelin, Carl
Trevino, Antonio D.
Trevino, Jose
Valdes, Alfonso, (Retired)
Van Scoy, Donald G.
Vara, Rudolph R., (Retired)

Vault, Henry, Jr.
Veyna, Manuel
Villarreal, Albert
Vogel, Gary M.
Vollmer-Konig, Josef
Votruba, John M., (Retired)
Washington, Warner
Webb, Philip E., On Duty Outside the Diocese
Weithman, James C., (Retired)
Welsh, James L.
Wong, Peter
Wuenschel, Douglas
Zacek, George E.
Zoeller, William C., On Duty Outside the Diocese

INSTITUTIONS LOCATED IN THE DIOCESE

[A] SEMINARIES, DIOCESAN

IRVING. *Holy Trinity Seminary*, P.O. Box 140309, 75014-0309. Tel: 972-438-2212; Fax: 972-438-6530. Diocesan College and Pre-Theology Seminary. Very Rev. Michael Duca, Rector; Revs. James Orosco, Vice Rector; John Collet, Spiritual Dir. & Coord. Liturgy; Chris Eggleton, O.P., Assoc. Spiritual Dir.; Sr. St. John Begnaud, S.S.M.N., Academic Dean; Ms. Gail Tillman, M.Mus., Dir. Music. Priests 4; Seminarians 35.

[B] COLLEGES AND UNIVERSITIES

IRVING. *University of Dallas*, President's Office, 1845 E. Northgate, 75062. Tel: 972-721-5000; Fax: 972-721-5017
For a complete listing, refer to the Colleges and Universities section.

[C] HIGH SCHOOLS, DIOCESAN

DALLAS. *Bishop Dunne High School*. (Grades 8-12). (Coed), 3900 Rugged Dr., 75224. Tel: 214-339-6561; Fax: 214-339-1438. Kate C. Collins Dailey, Prin. Lay Teachers 42; Students 413.
Bishop Lynch High School, 9750 Ferguson Rd., 75228. Tel: 214-324-3607; Fax: 214-324-3600. Mr. Edward E. Leyden, Pres.; Dale Kennedy, Prin.; Rev. Victor Bartolotta. Lay Teachers 64; Students 927.

[D] HIGH SCHOOLS, PRIVATE

DALLAS. *Jesuit College Preparatory School*. (Boys), 12345 Inwood Rd., 75244. Tel: 214-387-8700; Fax: 214-661-9349.
Web site: http://www.jesuitcp.org
Society of Jesus. Revs. Eugene Sessa, S.J., Rector; Philip S. Postell, S.J., Pres.; John F. Deeves, S.J.; Michael D. Dooley, S.J.; Charles A. Leininger, S.J.; John G. Stack, S.J.; Mitchell Pacwa, S.J.; Bro. Gerald J. Landry, S.J. Priests 7; Lay Teachers 73; Students 864; Scholastics 1.
Ursuline Academy. (Girls), 4900 Walnut Hill Ln., 75229. Tel: 214-363-6551; Fax: 214-363-5524. Mrs. Shaun Underhill, Prin.; Sr. Margaret Ann Moser, O.S.U., Pres. Faculty 68; Students 787.
IRVING. *Cistercian Preparatory School*. (Boys), One Cistercian Rd., 75039-4599. Tel: 972-438-4956; Fax: 972-554-0736. Cistercian Fathers of Our Lady of Dallas Abbey. Rev. Peter Verhalen, O.Cist., Headmaster. Priests 8; Lay Teachers 22; Students 335.
Highland School, 1451 E. Northgate Dr., 75062. Tel: 972-554-1980; Fax: 972-721-1691. Rev. Steven Reilly, L.C., Pres.; Dr. Michael Dennell, Prin.; Rev. Eugene Gormley, L.C., Chap.

[E] SCHOOLS, PAROCHIAL

DALLAS. *Prince of Peace - Dallas*, 4500 W. Davis St., 75211. Tel: 214-337-0244. Mr. Christopher Cavnar, Prin.

[F] ELEMENTARY SCHOOLS, INTERPAROCHIAL

DALLAS. *John XXIII Regional School*, 4910 Bonnie View Rd., 75241. Tel: 214-371-8522. Dolores H. Costello, Prin. Lay Teachers 14; Students 191.

[G] ELEMENTARY SCHOOLS, PRIVATE

IRVING. *Cistercian Preparatory School*. (Boys), One Cistercian Rd., 75039. Tel: 214-438-4956; Fax: 214-554-0736. Cistercian Fathers of Our Lady of Dallas Abbey. Rev. Peter Verhalen, O.Cist., Headmaster. Priests 8; Lay Teachers 22; Students 335.
The Highland School, 1451 E. Northgate Drive, 75062. Tel: 972-554-1980; Fax: 972-721-1691. Rev. Steven Reilly, L.C., Pres.; Dr. Michael Pennell, Prin., (Upper School); Mark Salisbury, Prin., (Lower School); Rev. Eugene Gormley, L.C., Chap.

[H] SPECIAL SCHOOLS, PRIVATE

DALLAS. *Notre Dame of Dallas Schools, Inc.*, 2018 Allen St., 75204. Tel: 214-720-3911; Fax: 214-720-3913. Day School: Provides instructional education for mentally retarded children, ages 3-15. Ms. Theresa Francis, Prin. Students 118. Vocational Center: Provides vocational training for young adults, ages 15-21. Lay Staff 30.

[I] GENERAL HOSPITALS

DALLAS. *Parkland Hospital*, 5201 Harry Hines Blvd., 75235. Tel: 214-590-8512
For a complete listing, refer to the Hospitals section.
St. Paul Medical Center, 5909 Harry Hines Blvd., 75235. Tel: 214-879-1000
For a complete listing, refer to the Hospitals section.
St. Paul Medical Center, 5909 Harry Hines Blvd., 75235
For a complete listing, refer to the Hospitals section.
St. Paul Medical Center Foundation Inc., 2777 Stemmons Fwy., #957, 75207
For a complete listing, refer to the Hospitals section.

[J] CATHOLIC CHARITIES

DALLAS. *Catholic Charities*, 3725 Blackburn St., P.O. Box 190507, 75219. Tel: 214-520-6590; Fax: 214-520-6595. Sr. Mary Ann Owens, S.S.N.D.
Catholic Counseling Services, 3725 Blackburn St., P.O. Box 190507, 75219. Tel: 214-526-2772.
Immigration Counseling Services, 325 W. 12th St., 75208. Tel: 214-946-4889. Ms. Vanna Slaughter, M.S.W., Admin.
Marillac Social Center, 2827 Lapsley, 75212. Tel: 214-638-4997. Sr. Rose Ann Aguilar, D.C., Admin. Sisters 2; Lay Staff 58.
Migration Refugee Services; Refugee Resettlement; Refugee Job Placement, 325 W. 12th St., 75208. Tel: 214-946-2800. English as a second language. Mr. Art Granzeier, Admin.
Monsignor John P. Brady Center, 4009 Elm St., 75226. Tel: 214-826-8330. Mary N. Brown, Admin. Conducted by Catholic Charities. Lay Staff 23.
St. Joseph Adolescent & Family Counseling Center, 325 W. 12th St., 75208. Tel: 214-946-4896. Dr. Grant C. Hellyer, Admin. Treatment Center for adolescent boys and girls ages 13-17. Lay Staff 4; Capacity 20.
St. Joseph Residence, 330 W. Pembroke, 75208. Tel: 214-948-3597; Fax: 214-948-1209. Sr. Adelaide Bocanegra, Bethl., Admin. For elderly ladies, gentlemen, and couples. Conducted by Daughters of the Sacred Heart of Jesus (Bethlemitas). Sisters 6; Residents 45.
St. Jude, Inc., c/o Shamrock Mgmt., 16200 Dallas Pkwy., Ste. 270, 75248. Tel: 214-520-6590; Fax: 214-520-6595.
Purpose: To obtain housing for the elderly and needy in Dallas.
St. Martin Family Service Center, Inc., 325 W. 12th St., 75208. Tel: 214-520-6590; Fax: 214-520-6595.
Purpose: To provide social services to assist the poor and indigent families of Oak Cliff to become self-reliant.
Villa Santa Maria, Inc., c/o Shamrock Mgmt., 16200 Dallas Pkwy., Ste. 270, 75248. Tel: 214-520-6590; Fax: 214-520-6595.
Purpose: To obtain housing for the elderly and needy in Dallas.
COPPELL. *St. Martin de Porres, Inc.* c/o Shamrock Mgmt., 16200 Dallas Pkwy., Ste. 270, Dallas, 75248. Tel: 214-520-6590.
Purpose: To obtain housing for low-income families.

[K] EDUCATION CENTERS

DALLAS. *Mount Carmel Center*, 4600 W. Davis St., 75211-3498. Tel: 214-331-6224. Discalced Carmelite Fathers of the Southwestern Province. Revs. M. Philip Wurth, O.C.D., Dir.; Sam Anthony Morello, O.C.D.; John Michael Payne, O.C.D., Asst. Dir. In res. Rev. Joseph Neilson, O.C.D.
Mount St. Michael Spiritual Life Center, 4500 W. Davis St., 75211. Tel: 214-331-1754; Fax: 214-333-1659. Sr. Margaret McCaffrey, Major Supr. Sisters of Our Lady of Charity of Refuge 13.

[L] PERSONAL PRELATURES

DALLAS. *Marian Servants of the Holy Spirit*, 3930 Rugged Dr., 75224. Tel: 214-333-0410. Revs. Michael McDonagh, M.S.H.S., Supr. & Dir.; Matthew Riemer, M.S.H.S., Vocation Dir. Total in Residence 6.
IRVING. *Opus Dei*. (Prelature of the Holy Cross & Opus Dei), 3610 Wingren, 75062. Tel: 972-650-0064.
E-mail: info@opusdei.org
Web site: http://www.opusdei.org
Rev. Jack Solarski.

[M] MONASTERIES AND RESIDENCES OF PRIESTS

DALLAS. *Capuchin Franciscan Friars, Vice Province of Texas*, 2601 Singleton Blvd., 75212. Tel: 214-630-7933. Rev. Juan Cruz Gaston, O.F.M.Cap. Priests 16; Brothers 2.
Congregation of the Mission, Southern Province, 3826 Gilbert Ave., 75219. Tel: 214-526-2421; Fax: 214-526-3477.
E-mail: CongMissSP@aol.com
Rev. George J. Weber, C.M. Priests 33; Brothers 1.
IRVING. *Cistercian Abbey of Our Lady of Dallas*, One Cistercian Rd., 75039. Tel: 214-438-2044. Rt. Rev. Denis M. Farkasfalvy, O.Cist., S.S.L., M.S., S.T.D., Abbot, Vicar of the Abbot Pres. of Zirc; Revs. Peter Verhalen, O.Cist., M.A., Prior; Bernard Marton, O.Cist., Subprior; Christopher Rabay, O.Cist., S.T.L.; Damian Szodenyi, O.Cist., Ph.D.; Placid Csizmazia, O.Cist., Ph.D.; George Ferenczy, O.Cist., Ph.D.; Benedict Monostori, O.Cist., Ph.D.; Balthasar Szarka, O.Cist.; Bede Lackner, O.Cist., Ph.D.; Pascal Kis-Horvath, O.Cist.; Aloysius Kimecz, O.Cist.; David Balas, O.Cist., Ph.D., S.T.D.; Matthew Kovacs, O.Cist.; Melchior Chladek, O.Cist.; Rochus Kereszty, O.Cist., S.T.D.; Julius Leloczky, O.Cist., S.T.D.; Henry Marton, O.Cist., S.T.D.; James Lehrberger, O.Cist., Ph.D.; Robert Maguire, O.Cist., Ph.D.; Gregory Schweers, O.Cist., M.A.; Timothy Coble, O.Cist., M.A.; Mark Ripperger, O.Cist., M.A.; Paul McCormick, O.Cist., M.A. (STL); Bros. Patrick Griffin, O.Cist.; Gabriel Wagner, O.Cist.; Ambrose Young, O.Cist. Priests 25; Scholastics 3.
Priests of the Abbey Serving Abroad: Rev. Ralph March, O.Cist., Ph.D., Germany.
Dominican Priory of St. Albert the Great, Prior of Dominican Community, University of Dallas, 1845 E. Northgate Dr., 75062-4799. Tel: 972-438-1626; Fax: 972-554-7664. Very Rev. Andrew K. Kolzow, O.P., Prior; Revs. Paul G. Hinnebusch, O.P., Subprior; Thomas M. Cain, O.P.; Edward M. Robinson, O.P.; Daniel P. Brady, O.P.; Austin E. Green, O.P.; John B. Balsam, O.P.; Daniel A. Shanahan, O.P.; Thomas M. Cumiskey, O.P.; Joachim Culotta, O.P.; Christopher T. Eggleton, O.P.
Assigned to this Priory but residing elsewhere due to Ministry: Revs. Brian Pierce, O.P., (Tulsa, OK); Eduardo Gabriel, O.P., (Austin, TX).
Legionaries of Christ, 1451 E. Northgate Dr., 75062. Tel: 972-554-1980; Fax: 972-554-8729. Revs. Steven Reilly, L.C., Supr.; Eugene Gormley, L.C.; Andrew Mulchahey, L.C.; Bros. Jason Wallace, L.C.; Vu Pham, L.C.

[N] CONVENTS AND RESIDENCES FOR SISTERS

DALLAS. *Bethany House*, 3017 Mallory, 75216. Tel: 214-371-4867. Sisters of St. Mary of Namur. Sr. Patricia Ann Ridgley, S.S.M., Contact Person.
The Institute of Divine Mercy Convent, 8351 San Fernando Way, 75218. Tel: 214-969-7500. Sr. Maria Faustina; Sr. Mary Francis; Sr. Maria Barterte.
Marillac Daughters of Charity Residence, 2911 Lapsley St., 75212. Tel: 214-631-6757. Sr. Noreen Crean, D.C., Supr. Daughters of Charity of St. Vincent de Paul 7.
Missionaries of Charity, 2704 Harlandale, 75216. Tel: 214-374-3351. Sr. M. Bernice, M.C., Supr. Sisters 4.
Missionary Catechist of the Poor, 950 N. Montclair Ave., 75208. Tel: 214-942-6243. Sr. Ma. Guadalupe Martinez, M.C.P., Supr. Sisters 8.
Monastery of Discalced Carmelites, 600 Flowers Ave., 75211. Mother Celine, O.C.D., Prioress. Professed Sisters 9.
School Sisters of Notre Dame, P.O. Box 227275, 75222. Tel: 214-330-9152; Fax: 214-330-9197.
E-mail: daiglejuli@aol.com
Sr. Juliette Daigle, S.S.N.D.
Provincial House of the Dallas Province, 4500 W. Davis, 75211. Sr. Elizabeth Newman, S.S.N.D. Prov. Sisters 199.
Other Convents: 2930 Storey Ln., Apt. 101, 75220. 2810 Storey Ln., Apt. 101, 75220. 7625 Cortland, 75235. 4401 Highview, 75211. 1406 Glenwick, Irving, 75060. 2826 Storey Ln., Apts. 100 & 101, 75220. 2910 Storey Ln., Apt. 104, 75220. 7550 S. Westmoreland, #118, 75234. 2139 Estrada Pkwy., #311, Irving, 75061.
Ursuline Convent, 9905 Inwood Rd., 75220. Tel: 214-369-8159; Fax: 214-369-4004.
Ursuline Academy. (Grades 9-12), 4900 Walnut Hill Ln., 75229. Tel: 214-363-6551; Fax: 214-369-4034. Sr. Catherine Chandler, O.S.U., Prioress; Sr. Margaret Ann Moser, O.S.U., Pres. Nuns 20.
GRAND PRAIRIE. *Sisters of the Holy Family of Nazareth*. (Blessed Frances Siedliska Provincialate), 1814 Egyptian Way, P.O. Box 530959, 75053. Tel: 972-641-4496. Sr. M. Ancilla, C.S.F.N., Prov. Supr. Sisters 48.

[O] CAMPUS MINISTRY

IRVING. *Diocese of Dallas Campus Ministry*, University of Dallas, 75062. Tel: 972-721-5375. Rev. Thomas Cloherty, Diocesan Dir.; Christine Edmonds, Campus Min.

Southern Methodist University, P.O. Box 282, Dallas, 75275. Tel: 214-692-4504. Rev. Jeremiah J. Cullinane; Judy Henneberger, Campus Min.

East Texas State University, St. Joseph Church, 2904 Melmar Pk., Commerce, 75428. Tel: 903-886-7135. Rev. D. Stanley Corcoran.

[P] MISCELLANEOUS LISTINGS

DALLAS. *Cathedral Preservation Fund, Inc.*, 6517 Hillcrest Ave., Ste. 402, 75205. Tel: 214-361-8941. W. David Holliday, Contact.

Catholic Community Appeal, Inc., 3725 Blackburn St., P.O. Box 190507, 75219. Tel: 214-528-2240. Michael T. Weis, Treas.

Christian Community of God's Delight, 4500 W. Davis-Keating Hall, P.O. Box 225008, 75211. Tel: 214-333-2337; Fax: 214-333-2595.

Collin County Catholic High School Campaign, Inc., 3725 Blackburn St., P.O. Box 190507, 75219. Tel: 214-528-2240. Michael T. Weis, Treas.

Commission on Ecumenism, P.O. Box 190507, 75219. Tel: 214-528-2240. Rev. Robert Crisp, Chm.

Diocesan Charitable Trust, 3725 Blackburn, P.O. Box 190507, 75219. Tel: 214-528-2240. Sponsor of Rent Subsidizing Housing, Colonia Tepeyeac Apartments.

The Institute of Divine Mercy, Inc., 8351 San Fernando Way, 75218. Nonprofit corporation formed under the supervision of the diocese of Dallas for the purpose of starting a new order of cloistered nuns.

International Catholic Network, 419 Cockrell Hill Rd., 75211.

Ladies of Charity of Dallas, P.O. Box 595666, 75359-0666. Tel: 214-821-5713.

The National Cursillo Center and Office of the National Secretariat, 4500 W. Davis, 75211. Mailing Address: P.O. Box 210226, 75211. Tel: 214-339-6321. Thomas E. Sarg, Exec. Dir.; Joachim Thong Le, Vietnamese Coord., 9362 Asbery Cir., Westminster, CA, 92683. Tel: 714-891-6216. Juan Ruiz, Hispanic Coord., 15839 Hillgate Dr., Whittier, CA, 90604. Tel: 310-947-7824. Ken Sittenauer, English Coord., 3312 W. 50th Ter., Shawnee Mission, KS, 66205. Tel: 913-831-2936.

Patrons of the Arts in Vatican Museum, 5520 Park Ln., 75220.

School Sisters of Notre Dame of Dallas Charitable Trust, 4500 W. Davis, 75211. Tel: 214-330-9152; Fax: 214-330-9197. Mailing Address: P.O. Box 227275, 75222-7275.

Society of St. Vincent de Paul, 3826 Gilbert St., 75219. Tel: 214-528-7837. Central Office for all society activities in the Diocese of Dallas. Mr. Phillip Young, Pres.; Mr. Robert J. Little, Exec. Dir.

Southwestern Lieutenancy, Equestrian Order of the Holy Sepulchre of Jerusalem, 9716 Trailhill Dr., 75238. Tel: 214-341-4457; 349-6196; Fax: 214-341-6262. Albin J. Brezna, Lieutenant.

COMMERCE. *Apostleship of Prayer*, St. Joseph, 2904 Melmar Pk., 75428. Rev. Msgr. Robert Johnson, Dir.

GRAND PRAIRIE. *Sisters of the Holy Family of Nazareth - Blessed Frances Siedliska Province Charitable Trust*, 1814 Egyptian Way - P.O. Box 530959, 75053-0959. Tel: 214-641-4496. Sr. M. Ancilla Sojka, C.S.F.N., Prov. Supr.

RELIGIOUS INSTITUTES OF MEN REPRESENTED IN THE DIOCESE

For further details refer to the corresponding bracketed number in the Religious Institutes of Men or Women section.

[0470]—*The Capuchin Friars.*—O.F.M.Cap.

[0340]—*Cistercian Fathers.*—O.Cist.

[0260]—*Discalced Carmelite Friars.* (Oklahoma Prov.).—O.C.D.

[0690]—*Jesuit Fathers and Brothers.* (New Orleans Prov.).—S.J.

[0730]—*Legionaries of Christ.*—L.C.

[]—*Marian Servants of the Holy Spirit.*—M.S.H.S.

[1110]—*Missionaries of Sacred Heart.*—M.S.C.

[0430]—*Order of Preachers (Dominicans).* (Southern Dominican Prov.).—O.P.

[1260]—*Society of Christ.*—S.Ch.

[0370]—*Society of St. Columba.*—S.S.C.

[1330]—*Vincentian Fathers.* (Southern Prov.).—C.M.

RELIGIOUS INSTITUTES OF WOMEN REPRESENTED IN THE DIOCESE

[1810]—*Bernardine Sisters of the Third Order of St. Francis.*—O.S.F.

[1920]—*Congregation of the Sisters of the Holy Cross.*—C.S.C.

[0760]—*Daughters of Charity of St. Vincent de Paul.* (St. Louis Prov.).—D.C.

[]—*Daughters of the Sacred Heart of Jesus.*—S.C.I.F.

[0420]—*Discalced Carmelite Nuns.*—O.C.D.

[1070-03]—*Dominican Sisters.*—O.P.

[2710]—*Missionaries of Charity.*—M.C.

[]—*Missionary Catechists of the Poor.* (Mexico).

[3070]—*North American Union Sisters of Our Lady of Charity.*—N.A.U.-O.L.C.

[2970]—*School Sisters of Notre Dame.*—S.S.N.D.

[1010]—*Sisters of Divine Providence of San Antonio, Texas.*—C.D.P.

[3950]—*Sisters of Saint Mary of Namur.* (Western Prov.).—S.S.M.N.

[1970]—*Sisters of the Holy Family of Nazareth.* (Sacred Heart Vice Prov.).—C.S.F.N.

[2050]—*Sisters of the Holy Spirit and Mary Immaculate.*—S.H.Sp.

[4110]—*Ursuline Nuns (Roman Union).* (Central Prov.).—O.S.U.

DIOCESAN CEMETERIES

DALLAS. *Calvary Hill Cemetery & Mausoleum.*

DESOTO. *Holy Redeemer Cemetery & Mausoleum.*

ROWLETT. *Sacred Heart Cemetery & Mausoleum.*

WYLIE. *St. Paul.*

NECROLOGY

† Cusick, William F., Dallas, TX, Gate of Heaven. —Died May 1, 1997.

† Pondant, Anthony W., Wylie, TX, St. Anthony. —Died Aug. 24, 1997.

† Smyth, Rev. Msgr. Claude, Plano, TX, St. Mark the Evangelist. —Died Nov. 11, 1997.

Diocese of Davenport

(Dioecesis Davenportensis)

Most Reverend

WILLIAM E. FRANKLIN, D.D.

Bishop of Davenport; ordained February 4, 1956; appointed Titular Bishop of Surista and Auxiliary Bishop of Dubuque January 29, 1987; ordained Bishop April 1, 1987; transferred to Davenport November 12, 1993; installed January 20, 1994. *Res., 2761 Scott St., Davenport, IA, 52803.* Tel.: 319-324-4774. *Office: St. Vincent Center, 2706 N. Gaines St., Davenport, IA, 52804-1998.* Tel.: 319-324-1911.

Most Reverend

GERALD FRANCIS O'KEEFE, D.D.

Retired Bishop of Davenport; ordained January 29, 1944; appointed Auxiliary Bishop of St. Paul and Titular Bishop of Candyba May 5, 1961; consecrated July 2, 1961; transferred to Davenport October 20, 1966; installed January 4, 1967; retired November 12, 1993. *Res., 2706 N. Gaines St., Davenport, IA, 52804.*

ERECTED MAY 8, 1881.

Square Miles 11,438.

Comprises that part of the State of Iowa bounded on the east by the Mississippi River; on the west by the western boundaries of the counties of Jasper, Marion, Monroe and Appanoose; on the south by the State of Missouri; on the north by the northern boundaries of the Counties of Jasper, Poweshiek, Iowa, Johnson, Cedar and Clinton.

For legal titles of parishes and diocesan institutions, consult the Chancery.

Chancery: St. Vincent Center, 2706 N. Gaines St., Davenport, IA, 52804-1998. Tel.: 319-324-1911; Fax: 319-324-5842.

Web site address: davenportdiocese.org

STATISTICAL OVERVIEW

Personnel	
Bishop	1
Retired Bishops	1
Priests: Diocesan Active in Diocese	93
Priests: Active Outside Diocese	10
Priests: Diocesan in Foreign Missions	1
Priests: Retired, Sick or Absent	41
Number of Diocesan Priests	145
Religious Priests in Diocese	3
Extern Priests in Diocese	4
Ordinations:	
Diocesan Priests	3
Permanent Deacons in Diocese	48
Total Brothers	1
Total Sisters	250
Parishes	
Parishes	90
With Resident Pastor:	
Resident Diocesan Priests	59
Resident Religious Priests	1
Without Resident Pastor:	
Administered by Priests	28
Administered by Lay People	2
Pastoral Centers	1
Closed Parishes	3
Professional Ministry Personnel:	
Sisters	10
Lay Ministers	3
Welfare	
Catholic Hospitals	3
Total Assisted	276,000
Homes for the Aged	3
Total Assisted	597
Educational	
Seminaries, Diocesan	1
Students from This Diocese	3
Students from Other Diocese	1
Diocesan Students in Other Seminaries	5
Total Seminarians	8
Colleges and Universities	2
Total Students	3,358
High Schools, Diocesan and Parish	7
Total Students	1,683
Elementary Schools, Diocesan and Parish	45
Total Students	4,976
Catechesis/Religious Education:	
High School Students	3,200
Elementary Students	9,600
Total Students Under Catholic Instruction	22,825
Teachers in the Diocese:	
Priests	1
Sisters	12
Lay Teachers	355
Vital Statistics	
Receptions into the Church:	
Infant Baptism Totals	1,645
Adult Baptism Totals	217
Received into Full Communion	219
First Communions	2,122
Confirmations	1,957
Marriages:	
Catholic	372
Interfaith	411
Total Marriages	783
Deaths	1,105
Total Catholic Population	106,460
Total Population	726,646

Former Bishops—Rt. Rev. JOHN MCMULLEN, D.D., cons. July 25, 1881; died July 4, 1883.—Rt. Rev. HENRY COSGROVE, D.D., cons. Sept. 14, 1884; died Dec. 22, 1906.—Rt. Rev. JAMES DAVIS, D.D., cons. Nov. 30, 1904; died Dec. 2, 1926.—Most Rev. HENRY P. ROHLMAN, D.D., cons. July 25, 1927; appt. Coadjutor-Archbishop of Dubuque and Titular Archbishop of Macra in Rhodope, June 15, 1944; Archbishop of Dubuque, Nov. 18, 1946; appt. Titular Archbishop of Cotrada, Dec. 2, 1954; died Sept. 13, 1957.—Most Rev. RALPH LEO HAYES, D.D., ord. Sept. 19, 1909; appt. Bishop of Helena June 23, 1933; cons. Sept. 21, 1933; appt. Rector of North American College in Rome in Sept. 1935; transferred to Titular See of Hierapolis Oct. 26, 1935; transferred to Davenport Nov. 16, 1944; appt. Assistant at the Pontifical Throne April 30, 1958; transferred to Titular See of Naraggara; retired Oct. 20, 1966; died July 4, 1970.—Most Rev. GERALD FRANCIS O'KEEFE, D.D., ord. Jan. 29, 1944; appt. Auxiliary Bishop of St. Paul and Titular Bishop of Candyba May 5, 1961; cons. July 2, 1961; transferred to Davenport Oct. 20, 1966; installed Jan 4, 1967; retired Nov. 12, 1993.

Chancery—St. Vincent Center, 2706 N. Gaines St., Davenport, 52804-1998. Tel: 319-324-1911; Fax: 319-324-5842.

Vicar General—Rev. Msgr. MICHAEL J. MORRISSEY, J.C.L.

Chancellor—Rev. Msgr. LEO J. FEENEY.

Vice-Chancellor—Rev. Msgr. JAMES F. PARIZEK, J.C.L.

Diocesan Tribunal—St. Vincent Center, 2706 N. Gaines St., Davenport, 52804-1998. Tel: 319-324-1911.

Judicial Vicar—Rev. Msgr. JAMES F. PARIZEK, J.C.L.

Adjutant Judicial Vicar—Rev. Msgr. MICHAEL J. MORRISSEY, J.C.L.

Assistant to the Judicial Vicar—HELEN HART.

Promoter of Justice—Rev. FRANCIS C. HENRICKSEN.

Defenders of the Bond—Rev. Msgr. LEO J. FEENEY; Revs. JOHN P. GALLAGHER, J.C.L.; WILLIAM E. REYNOLDS, J.C.L.

Notaries—JOANN KAKERT; HELEN HART; BARBARA MORRISSEY; MARY FRICK.

Pro-Synodal Judges—Rev. Msgr. JAMES F. PARIZEK; Rev. Msgr. MICHAEL J. MORRISSEY; Rev. Msgr. LEO J. FEENEY; Revs. JOHN P. BOYLE; ROBERT J. BUSHER; JOSEPH B. DENNING; EDWARD J. FITZPATRICK; JOHN P. GALLAGHER; RUDOLPH T. JUAREZ; ROBERT T. MCALEER; GEORGE W. MCDANIEL; WILLIAM E. REYNOLDS.

Diocesan Consultors—Rev. Msgr. MICHAEL J. MORRISSEY, V.G.; Very Revs. JOHN M. HYLAND; MARVIN A. MOTTET; Revs. JOSEPH B. DENNING; FRANCIS C. HENRICKSEN; JOSEPH R. SPARKS.

Deans—Davenport: Very Rev. MARVIN A. MOTTET; Clinton: Very Rev. H. ROBERT HARNESS; Iowa City: Very Rev. EDWARD J. FITZPATRICK; Keokuk: Very Rev. JOHN M. HYLAND; Ottumwa: Very Rev. ANTHONY J. HEROLD; Grinnell: Very Rev. ERNEST E. BRAIDA.

Diocesan Administrative Council—Rev. Msgr. MICHAEL J. MORRISSEY; Rev. Msgr. LEO J. FEENEY; ROBERT VAN VOOREN; KATHY BUSH. Tel: 319-324-1911.

Finance Council—Most Rev. WILLIAM E. FRANKLIN; Rev. Msgr. MICHAEL J. MORRISSEY; JAMES MURPHY; MICHAEL BAUER; ROBERT VAN VOOREN; DON BLOUGH; KATHY BUSH.

Episcopal Vicar for Priests—Rev. Msgr. W. ROBERT SCHMIDT, E.V., *St. Vincent Center, 2706 N. Gaines St., Davenport, 52804-1998.* Tel: 319-324-1911.

Episcopal Vicar of Iowa City—Rev. KENNETH E. KUNTZ, *St. Mary Rectory, 220 E. Jefferson St., Iowa City, 52245-2137.*

Missionary Vicar—Rev. RUDOLPH T. JUAREZ, *516 Fillmore St., Davenport, 52802.*

Diocesan Offices and Directors

Operations—*St. Vincent Center, 2706 N. Gaines St., Davenport, 52804-1998.* Tel: 319-324-1911.

Director of Finance and Operations—STEPHEN J. SCHMALL.

Coordinating Director of Human Resource—Vacant.

Coordinating Director of Stewardship & Development—JENNIFER MAAS.

Director of Communication—DAVID MONTGOMERY.

Database / Publications Coordinator—CAROLINE BARTLING.

Technology Coordinator—ROBERT BUTTERWORTH.

Archivist—MICHELE TRAVER.

Departments—*St. Vincent Center, 2706 N. Gaines St., Davenport, 52804-1998.* Tel: 319-324-1911.

Parish Services Department—

Director of Pastoral Services & Ministry Formation—Deacon WILLIAM T. DITEWIG.

Coordinating Director of Social Action—DAN EBENER.

Ethnic Ministry Coordinator—MARTHA YERINGTON.

Immigration Program Coordinator—LAURA TORRES.

Coordinating Director of Education / Superintendent of Schools—MARY WIESER.

Director of Clergy Formation & Support—Rev. CHARLES A. ADAM.

Family Formation Coordinator—Vacant.

Youth Formation Coordinator—Vacant.

Adult Formation Coordinator—Sr. ANGELA IRELAND, S.S.S.F.

Religion Formation Coordinator—Vacant.

Curriculum / Media Coordinator—BOB PILCHER.

Coordinating Director of Worship—Rev. RICK POSTER.

Other Offices and Directors—

Boy Scouts—Deacon RICHARD J. RASMUSSEN, *3236 Somerset Dr., Bettendorf, 52722.* Tel: 319-332-7558.

Catholic Relief Services—Rev. Msgr. MICHAEL J. MORRISSEY, Dir., *St. Vincent Center, 2706 N. Gaines St., Davenport, 52804-1998.* Tel: 319-324-1911.

Catholic Woman's League—Rev. CHARLES E. GANNON, Chap., *St. Vincent Center, 2706 N. Gaines St., Davenport, 52804-1998.* Tel: 319-322-7837.

Cemetery Committee—JOHN MCCABE, Sec., *614 Main St., Davenport, 52801.* Tel: 319-322-4438.

Campaign for Human Development—DAN R. EBENER, *St. Vincent Center, 2706 N. Gaines St., Davenport, 52804-1998.* Tel: 319-324-1911.

Continuing Education of the Clergy—Rev. Msgr. MICHAEL J. MORRISSEY, *St. Vincent Center, 2706 N. Gaines St., Davenport, 52804-1998.* Tel: 319-324-1911.

Commission on Women in the Church—*St. Vincent Center, 2706 N. Gaines St., Davenport, 52804-1998.* Tel: 319-324-1911.

Commission on Worship and Prayer—Rev. RICK POSTER, *Sacred Heart Rectory, P.O. Box 127, Lost Nation, 52254-0127.* Tel: 319-678-2200.

Department of Communications—Rev. FRANCIS C. HENRICKSEN, Dir., *P.O. Box 460, 103 E. Second St., Davenport, 52805.* Tel: 319-323-9959.

D.C.C.W.—Rev. TIMOTHY J. REGAN, Dir., *109 N. Lincoln St., Keota, 52248-9757.* Tel: 515-636-3883.

Holy Childhood, Pontifical Association—Rev. Msgr. W. ROBERT SCHMIDT, Dir., *St. Vincent Center, 2706 N. Gaines St., Davenport, 52804-1998.* Tel: 319-324-1911.

Hospital Association—Rev. JAMES P. CONROY, Bishop's Rep., *St. Vincent Center, 2706 N. Gaines St., Davenport, 52804-1998.* Tel: 319-324-1911.

Legion of Mary—Chaplaincy Vacant. Contact Chancery.

Marriage Encounter—*St. Vincent Center, 2706 N. Gaines St., Davenport, 52804-1998.* Tel: 319-324-1911.

Newspaper—*"The Catholic Messenger"*; Rev. FRANCIS C. HENRICKSEN, Mng. Editor, *P.O. Box 460, Davenport, 52805.*

Pastoral Council—Most Rev. WILLIAM E. FRANKLIN, D.D., Chm., *St. Vincent Center, 2706 N. Gaines St., Davenport, 52804-1998.* Tel: 319-324-1911.

Permanent Diaconate—Deacon TERRY STARNS, *St. Vincent Center, 2706 N. Gaines St., Davenport, 52804-1998.* Tel: 319-324-1911.

Personnel Board—*St. Vincent Center, 2706 N. Gaines St., Davenport, 52804-1998.* Tel: 319-324-1911.

Presbyteral Council—Rev. ROBERT T. MCALEER, *St. Mary Rectory, 1013 Ave. E, Fort Madison, 52627-2816.* Tel: 319-372-3139.

Priests' Aid Society—Very Rev. ERNEST E. BRAIDA, *Sacred Heart Rectory, P.O. Box 1478, Newton, 50208-1478.* Tel: 319-792-2050.

Priests Eucharistic League—Rev. MICHAEL T. PHILLIPS, Dir., *Holy Family Rectory, 1923 N. Fillmore St., Davenport, 52804.* Tel: 319-322-0901.

Propagation of the Faith—Rev. Msgr. LEO J. FEENEY, Dir., *St. Vincent Center, 2706 N. Gaines St., Davenport, 52804-1998.* Tel: 319-324-1911.

Research and Development—Rev. Msgr. MICHAEL J. MORRISSEY, Dir., *St. Vincent Center, 2706 N. Gaines St., Davenport, 52804-1998.* Tel: 319-324-1911.

Respect Life—DAN R. EBENER, *St. Vincent Center, 2706 N. Gaines St., Davenport, 52804-1998.* Tel: 319-324-1911.

Rural Life—DAN R. EBENER, Dir., *St. Vincent Center, 2706 N. Gaines St., Davenport, 52804-1998.* Tel: 319-324-1911.

Serra Club—THOMAS E. MULLIN, *2604 West 38th Pl., Davenport, 52806.* Tel: 319-386-0911.

Sisters' Council—Sr. JANET KREBER, O.S.F., *Box 71, Richland, 52585.* Tel: 319-694-3209.

Substance Abuse Council—Rev. DANIEL C. MANNHARDT, Chm., *4105 N. Division, Davenport, 52806.* Tel: 319-391-4245.

Vicar for Indo-Chinese—Rev. JOSEPH KAHN V. NGUYEN, *St. Vincent Center, 2706 N. Gaines St., Davenport, 52804-1998.* Tel: 319-324-3134.

Vicar for Religious—Rev. FRANCIS C. HENRICKSEN, *4097 18th St., Bettendorf, 52722.* Tel: 319-332-7910; 323-9959.

Vocations—Rev. CHARLES ADAM, Dir., *St. Vincent Center, 2706 N. Gaines St., Davenport, 52804-1998.* Tel: 319-333-6151.

CLERGY, PARISHES, MISSIONS AND PAROCHIAL SCHOOLS

CITY OF DAVENPORT
(Scott County)

1—SACRED HEART CATHEDRAL (1856), Very Rev. Marvin A. Mottet; Sr. Charla Bulko, S.S.S.F., Pastoral Assoc. In res., Rev. Thomas F. Stratman.
Res., 422 E. 10th St., 52803-5499. Tel: 319-324-3257; Fax: 319-326-6014. [JC]
School—Tel: 319-326-6278. Dr. Joan Kuvaitis, Prin. Sisters 1; Lay Teachers 13; Students 203.
Catechesis / Religious Programs—Sr. Mary Schmidt, O.S.B., D.R.E.
Students 160.

2—OUR LADY OF VICTORY (1962), Revs. E. William Kaska; Christopher J. David; Deacons Paul Hittner; Marcel Mosse; William Ditewig. In res., Rev. Daniel C. Mannhardt.
Res., 4105 N. Division St., 52806. Tel: 319-391-4245; Fax: 319-445-1003 (Please call first). [JC]
School—John F. Kennedy Catholic, Tel: 319-391-3030. Judith C. Calcari, Prin.
Lay Teachers 22; Students 434.
Catechesis / Religious Programs—Tel: 319-391-8384. Kay Carruthers, D.R.E.
Students 306.

3—HOLY FAMILY (1897), Revs. Michael T. Phillips; Patrick Lumsden; Deacons Gerald Timmerman, Pastoral Assoc.; Joseph Rosenthal; Richard Rasmussen.
Res., 1923 Fillmore St., 52804. Tel: 319-322-0902 (Rectory); 322-0901; 326-3836 (Office); Fax: 319-322-1637.
School—1926 Marquette St., 52804. Tel: 319-324-3205; Fax: 319-324-9331. Mr. William R. Fox, Prin.
Lay Teachers 25; Students 474.
Catechesis / Religious Programs—Fax: 319-324-1637. Carol Kovach, D.R.E.
Students 190.

4—ST. ALPHONSUS, Revs. David G. Steinle; Joseph M. Wolf.
Res., 2618 Boies Ave., 52802. Tel: 319-322-0987; Fax: 319-323-1458.
School—Mrs. C. J. Albertson, Prin. Franciscan Sisters of Christ the Divine Teacher 2; Lay Teachers 9; Students 173.
Catechesis / Religious Programs—Mary Ann Hagemann, D.R.E.
Students 81.

5—ST. ANTHONY'S (1837) (Irish), Rev. James P. Conroy; Rev. Msgr. W. Robert Schmidt.
Res., 417 N. Main St., 52801. Tel: 319-322-3303; Fax: 319-326-5136.
Catechesis / Religious Programs—Students 307.

6—ST. JOSEPH'S (1855), Rev. E. James Wilson.
Res., 615 Marquette St., 52802. Tel: 319-322-3473; Fax: 319-323-7278.
School—Tel: 319-322-3723. William Meehan, Prin. Sisters 2; Lay Teachers 8; Students 128.
Catechesis / Religious Programs—516 Fillmore St., 52802. Tel: 319-322-3383.

7—ST. MARY'S (1867) (Irish), Very Rev. Rudolph T. Juarez; Deacons George D. Strader; Julian Gutierrez.
Res., 516 Fillmore St., 52802. Tel: 319-322-3383.
Catechesis / Religious Programs—Students 95.

8—ST. PAUL THE APOSTLE (1909), Revs. Joseph B. Denning; Patrick J. Hilgendorf; Deacons William Jones; Robert McCoy.
Res., 916 E. Rusholme St., 52803. Tel: 319-322-7994; Fax: 319-322-7995.
School—Tel: 319-322-2923; Fax: 319-322-9359. William Schneden, Prin.
Sisters of Charity of the Blessed Virgin Mary 1; Lay Teachers 21; Students 508.
Catechesis / Religious Programs—Tel: 319-322-3768. Terri Doran, D.R.E.
Students 514.

OUTSIDE THE CITY OF DAVENPORT

Albia, Monroe Co., St. Mary's (1874), Rev. Thomas R. Doyle.
Res., P.O. Box 365, 52531. Tel: 515-932-5130. [CEM]
Catechesis / Religious Programs—Tel: 515-932-5589. Jackie Maddy, D.R.E.
Students 272.

Ardon, Muscatine Co., St. Malachy. Closed. For sacramental records, inquiries should be addressed to St. Joseph Parish, 815 2nd St., Columbus Junction, IA, 52738.

Augusta, Des Moines Co., St. Mary's (1881). Closed. For inquiries for parish records contact the Chancery.

Bauer, Marion Co., St. Joseph. Closed. For inquiries for parish records contact the Chancery.

Bettendorf, Scott Co., Our Lady of Lourdes (1903), Revs. Thomas J. Spiegel; Gary L. Beckman; Sr. Rita Lenaghan, C.H.M., Pastoral Assoc.; Deacons Dennis Duff; Warren Jensen; Tom Nolan; Terry Starns.
Res., 1506 Brown St., 52722. Tel: 319-359-0345.
School—Tel: 319-359-3466. Mrs. Barbara Herter, Prin.
Sisters of the Humility of Mary 1; Lay Teachers 24; Students 430.
Catechesis / Religious Programs—Tel: 319-359-1869. Ms. Ada Davis, D.R.E.
Students 520.

St. John Vianney (1967), Rev. Francis C. Henricksen; Deacons William Donnelly; Thomas Sink.
Res., 4097 18th St., 52722. Tel: 319-332-7910; Fax: 319-332-8407. [JC]
Catechesis / Religious Programs—Tel: 319-332-7564. Sr. Phyllis Kernz, S.S.N.D., D.R.E. (Elementary).
Students 594.

Bloomfield, Davis Co., St. Mary Magdalen (1953). Attended by St.Patricks, Ottumwa.

Blue Grass, Scott Co., St. Andrew (1976), Revs. David Steinle; Joseph Wolf.
Mailing Address: 2618 Boies Ave., Davenport, 52802-2116. Tel: 319-322-0987; Fax: 319-322-1458.
Res., 333 W. Lotte St., 52726.
Catechesis / Religious Programs—Tel: 319-381-1363. D.R.E.: Dorothy Spiess; Deacons Allen Haut; Donald Frericks.
Students 144.

Brooklyn, Poweshiek Co., St. Patrick, Rev. Joseph Rogers.
Res., 215 Jackson St., 52211-0512. Tel: 515-522-7714. [CEM]

Bryant, Clinton Co., St. Mary. Consolidated with St. Joseph, Sugar Creek to form Sts. Mary and Joseph, Sugar Creek.

Buffalo, Scott Co., St. Peter's. Attended by St. Andrew, Blue Grass. Rev. Rudolph C. Berndt; Deacon Larry Dankert.
Mailing Address: 406 Fourth St., P.O. Box 488, 52728. Tel: 319-381-2265; 381-2865. [CEM]

Burlington, Des Moines Co., St. John's (1855), Very Rev. John M. Hyland, V.F.; Deacon Robert R. Gengenbacher.
Res., 700 Division St., 52601. Tel: 319-752-6733; Fax: 319-753-5211. [CEM]
Catechesis / Religious Programs—Tel: 319-753-0277.
Students 476.

St. Patrick's (1870), Revs. Gerald E. Stouvenel; John K. Sterling; Deacon Richard Hammer.
Res., 420 W. Mt. Pleasant St., P.O. Box 415, West Burlington, 52655. Tel: 319-752-4035. [JC]
Catechesis / Religious Programs—Tel: 319-753-0277. Sr. Mary Jean Assell, S.S.J., D.R.E.
Students 510.

St. Paul's (1840), Very Rev. John M. Hyland.
Res., 700 Division St., 52601-5415. Tel: 319-752-6733; Fax: 319-753-5211. [JC]

Catechesis/Religious Programs—Tel: 319-752-8771. Sr. Mary Assell, D.R.E.
Students 476.

Camanche, Clinton Co., Church of the Visitation (1966), Rev. John J. Stack; Deacon John H. Schmitt. 1032 Middle Rd., 52730-1032. Tel: 319-259-1188; Fax: 319-259-4462.
Catechesis/Religious Programs—Tel: 319-259-9401. Mrs. Diane Rink, D.R.E.
Students 170.

Centerville, Appanoose Co., St. Mary's, Rev. Joseph Miller, C.PP.S.
Res., 828 S. 18th St., 52544. Tel: 515-437-1984.
School—Tel: 515-437-1984. Robert Wells, Prin.
Sisters 1; Lay Teachers 6; Students 65.
Catechesis/Religious Programs—Students 150.

Charlotte, Clinton Co., Assumption of the Blessed Mary. Consolidated with St. Patrick's, Villa Nova to form Assumption and St. Patrick's, Charlotte.
Assumption and St. Patrick's, Rev. Charles J. Fladung.
Res., 147 Broadway St., 52731. Tel: 319-677-2758; Fax: 319-677-2739. [CEM]
Catechesis/Religious Programs—Students 121.

Clear Creek, Keokuk Co., SS. Peter & Paul. See Holy Trinity, Keota.

Clinton, Clinton Co., Jesus Christ, Prince of Peace, Revs. Ronald E. Young; Martin G. Goetz; Deacons Arthur Donart; Ramon Hilgendorf; Patrick Lennon; Aloysius Mueller.
Parish Office—(Maintained for all five churches in Clinton.) 505 Ninth Ave., S., 52732. Tel: 319-242-3311; Fax: 319-242-3323.
Churches—St. Mary's, 520 Ninth Ave., S., 52732.; Sacred Heart, 316 S. Fourth Ave., 52732.; St. Boniface, 2500 N. Pershing Blvd., 52732.; St. Irenaeus, 2811 N. Second St., 52732.; St. Patrick's, 240 Fourth Ave., N., 52732.
Catechesis/Religious Programs—Students 397.

Colfax, Jasper Co., Immaculate Conception (1898). Attended by Sacred Heart, Newton.
Mailing Address: P.O. Box 1478, Newton, 50208-1478. Tel: 515-792-2050.

Columbus Junction, Louisa Co., St. Joseph, Rev. Bernard E. Weir.
Res., 815 Second St., 52738. Tel: 319-728-8210.

Cosgrove, Johnson Co., St. Peter's. Attended by St. Mary, Oxford.
4022 Cosgrove Rd. S.W., Oxford, 52322. Tel: 319-628-4180.

Delmar, Clinton Co., St. Patrick's, Rev. Edward A. Botkin.
Res., 52037. Tel: 319-674-4240. [CEM]

DeWitt, Clinton Co., St. Joseph's (1880), Very Rev. H. Robert Harness, V.F.; Rev. David Brownfield; Sr. Theresa Ann Spitz, R.S.M., Pastoral Assoc.; Deacon Mike Sheil.
Res., 417 Sixth Ave., 52742. Tel: 319-659-3514; Fax: 319-659-2599. [CEM]
School—Tel: 319-659-3812. Patrick Meade, Prin.
Sisters of Mercy 1; Lay Teachers 12; Students 218.
Catechesis/Religious Programs—Kathy McGarry, D.R.E.
Students 218.

Dodgeville, Des Moines Co., St. Mary's (1850), Revs. Gerald E. Stouvenel; John K. Sterling; Deacon Clifford Beckman.
Res., 13204 Dodgeville Rd., Sperry, 52650-9875. Tel: 319-985-2122. [CEM]
Catechesis/Religious Programs—Tel: 319-865-7451. Frieda Vantiger, D.R.E.
Students 98.

East Pleasant Plain, Jefferson Co., St. Joseph's (1902). Attended by St. Francis Xavier Cabrini, Richland. Rev. Paul E. Connolly.
Mailing Address: P.O. Box 130, Richland, 52585. Tel: 319-456-3161; Fax: 319-456-6408. [CEM]
Catechesis/Religious Programs—Students 39.

Eddyville, Mahaska Co., St. Mary's. Closed. For inquiries for parish records contact the Chancery.

Eldon, Wapello Co., St. Aloysius. Closed. For inquiries for parish records contact the Chancery.

Fairfield, Jefferson Co., St. Mary's (1864), Rev. Stephen C. Page; Deacon Art Anderson.
Res., 402 N. Third, P.O. Box 903, 52556-0903. Tel: 515-472-3179.
Catechesis/Religious Programs—Tel: 515-472-5991. Therese Cummiskey, D.R.E.
Students 268.

Farmington, Van Buren Co., St. Boniface (1862), Rev. David F. Wilkening.
Res., 609 Washington St., 52626. Tel: 319-878-3736. [CEM]
Catechesis/Religious Programs—Students 129.

Fort Madison, Lee Co.,

1—St. Joseph's. Consolidated with St. Mary's to form SS.Mary & Joseph Parish.

2—St. Mary's. Consolidated with St. Joseph's to form SS. Mary & Joseph Parish.

3—SS. Mary & Joseph, Rev. Robert T. McAleer; Sr. Mary Helen Hotze, S.S.N.D., Pastoral Assoc.
Res., 1013 Ave. E, 52627. Tel: 319-372-3139.

4—Sacred Heart, (1893), Rev. Timothy J. Sheedy; Deacon Ronald Stein.
Res., 2204 Ave. I, 52627. Tel: 319-372-3179; Fax: 319-372-3321.
Catechesis/Religious Programs—Tel: 319-372-6428; 372-2486.
Students 377.

Georgetown, Monroe Co., St. Patrick's (1851) (Irish). Attended by St. Patrick, Melrose. Rev. Mark W. Swanson.
Mailing Address: P.O. Box 183, Albia, 52531. Tel: 515-726-3529. [CEM]

Grand Mound, Clinton Co., Church of St. Philip and James (1876), Rev. David L. Brownfield.
Res., 606 Fulton St., P.O. Box 287, 52751-0287. Tel: 319-847-2271. [CEM]
Catechesis/Religious Programs—Students 110.

Grinnell, Poweshiek Co., St. Mary's (1924), Rev. William E. Reynolds; Deacons Stephen J. Witt; William D. Olson.
Res., 1018 Broad St., P.O. Box 623, 50112. Tel: 515-236-5289. [CEM]
Catechesis/Religious Programs—Tel: 515-236-7486.
Students 200.

Harper, Keokuk Co., St. Elizabeth's. See Holy Trinity, Keota.

Hills, Johnson Co., St. Joseph's (1902), Rev. Louis J. Leonhardt.
Res., 52235. Tel: 319-679-2271.
Catechesis/Religious Programs—Students 76.

Holbrook, Iowa Co., St. Michael. Closed. For inquiries for parish records contact the Chancery.

Houghton, Lee Co., St. John's (1895), Rev. John D. Spiegel.
Res., Box 100, 52631. Tel: 319-469-2001. [CEM]
School—(Grades PreK-6). Tel: 319-469-3881. Sr. Pat Siepker, Prin.
Lay Teachers 12; Students 204.
High School—Tel: 319-837-6131. Mr. Dan Kieler, Prin.
Religious 2; Lay Teachers 16; Students 175.
Catechesis/Religious Programs—Tel: 319-469-2000.
Students 59.

Iowa City, Johnson Co.,

1—St. Mary of the Assumption, (1856) (German), Revs. Kenneth E. Kuntz; Brian J. Shepley; Sr. Mary Agnes Giblin, B.V.M., Pastoral Assoc.
Res., 220 E. Jefferson St., 52245. Tel: 319-337-4314. [CEM 2][JC]
Catechesis/Religious Programs—Tel: 319-351-7638.
Students 802.

2—St. Patrick's, (1872) (Irish), Rev. James J. Vrba.
Res., 228 E. Court St., 52240. Tel: 319-337-2856; Fax: 319-354-5590. [JC]

3—St. Thomas More, Rev. David F. Hitch; Sr. Margaret Kruse, O.S.F., Pastoral Assoc.
Res., 108 McLean St., 52246. Tel: 319-337-2173. [JC]
Catechesis/Religious Programs—Mary Lu Gallahan, D.R.E.
Students 533.

4—St. Wenceslaus, (1893) (Bohemian), Revs. Paul A. Deyo; Lawrence Smith.
Res., 623 Fairchild St., 52245. Tel: 319-337-4957. [JC]

Keokuk, Lee Co., All Saints (1982), Revs. Michael J. Spiekermeier; Dennis L. Hoffman; Deacon William Cosgrove.
Res., 310 S. Ninth St., 52632. Tel: 319-524-8334.
Catechesis/Religious Programs—Students 75.

Keota, Keokuk Co., Holy Trinity (1992), Rev. Timothy J. Regan.
Res., 109 N. Lincoln St., 52248-9757. Tel: 515-636-3883. [CEM 3]
Churches—St. Mary's, 109 N. Lincoln St., 52248-9757.; St. Elizabeth's, 20486 285th Ave., Harper, 52231. Tel: 515-635-2662; SS. Peter & Paul, 30832 242nd St., Harper, 52231. Tel: 515-635-2028.
Catechesis/Religious Programs—Tel: 515-636-3731.
Students 142.
St. Mary's. See Holy Trinity, Keota.

Keswick, Keokuk Co., Our Lady of Lourdes (N. European). Attended by St. Mary's, Sigourney. Rev. Philip R. Ryan.
Mailing Address: 415 E. Pleasant Valley St., Sigourney, 52591-1730. Tel: 515-622-3426.
Church—50136.
Catechesis/Religious Programs—Students 60 (Elementary).

Kinross, Keokuk Co., Sacred Heart. Closed. For inquiries for parish records contact the Chancery.

Knoxville, Marion Co., St. Anthony's (1870), Revs. Thomas L. Parlette; Robert D. Gruss.
Res., 1202 Woodland St., 50138. Tel: 515-828-7050; Fax: 515-828-7915. [CEM]
Catechesis/Religious Programs—Tel: 515-842-6249. Sr. Rachel Beeson, C.H.M., D.R.E.
Students 202.

Le Claire-Princeton, Scott Co., Our Lady of the River, Rev. John F. Hynes.
Res., 28225 226th St., LeClaire, 52753. Tel: 319-289-5736.
Catechesis/Religious Programs—Cheryl O'Klock, D.R.E.
Students 209.

Lone Tree, Johnson Co., St. Mary's. Unassigned.
Res., Box 187, Hills, 52235. Tel: 319-679-2271.

Long Grove, Scott Co., St. Ann's (1853), Rev. Stephen P. Ebel.
Res., 16550 290th St., 52756. Tel: 319-285-4596. [CEM]
Catechesis/Religious Programs—Tel: 319-285-4020. D.R.E.: Janice Uitenbroek; Fiona Wilson; Margaret Liske; Chris Behnke; Tammy Zimmer; Betty Zimmer.
Students 538.

Lost Nation, Clinton Co., Sacred Heart (1895), Rev. Richard J. Poster.
Res., P.O. Box 127, 52254. Tel: 319-678-2200. [CEM]

Lovilia, Monroe Co., St. Peter's, Rev. Thomas S. Doyle.
Mailing Address: P.O. Box 8, 50150. Tel: 515-946-8298. [CEM]

Marengo, Iowa Co., St. Patrick's (1878) (Irish), Rev. Joseph F. Roost.
Mailing Address: P.O. Box 183, 52301. Tel: 319-642-5438; Fax: 319-642-5648. [CEM]
Catechesis/Religious Programs—609 E. Randolph, 52301. Tel: 319-642-7680. Jayne Swift, D.R.E.
Students 121.

Mechanicsville, Cedar Co., St. Mary's (1872), Rev. William O. Meyer.
Res., 52306-0457. Tel: 319-432-6236.
Catechesis/Religious Programs—D.R.E.: Marilyn Fitzgerald; Dawn Weiland.
Students 75.

Melcher, Marion Co., Sacred Heart (1912), Revs. Thomas L. Parlette; Robert D. Gruss; Sr. Marian Joohum O.S.F., Pastoral Assoc.
315 S. Main, Box 277, 50163. Tel: 515-947-3261. [CEM]
Catechesis/Religious Programs—Tel: 515-947-2902. Jean Bishop, D.R.E.
Students 90.

Melrose, Monroe Co., St. Patrick's, Rev. Mark W. Swanson.
Res., P.O. Box 154, 52569. Tel: 515-726-3457.

Montrose, Lee Co., St. Joseph's, Rev. Gerald A. Hoenig.
Res., Box 206, 52639. Tel: 319-463-5443.

Mount Pleasant, Henry Co., St. Alphonsus (1862) (Irish), Rev. Nicholas Adam; Sr. Marilyn Schierbrock, C.H.M., Pastoral Min.; Deacon Joe Demeter.
Res., 607 S. Jackson St., 52641. Tel: 319-385-8410; Fax: 319-385-0545. [CEM]
Catechesis/Religious Programs—Tel: 319-385-4937. D.R.E.: Mary Hassenfritz, (Grades PreK-5); Cindy Riley, (Grades 6-8); Tammy Tyrrell, (Grades 9-10).
Students 294.

Muscatine, Muscatine Co., St. Mary's (1876), Rev. Mark P. Spring; Deacons Anton Tometich; James Becker.
Res., 417 Green St., 52761. Tel: 319-263-7788; Fax: 319-263-6287. [JC]
Catechesis/Religious Programs—Tel: 319-263-3848. Gayle Sayles, D.R.E.
Students 280.
St. Mathias (1842), Rev. George B. Hoenig.
Res., 215 W. Eighth St., 52761. Tel: 319-263-1878; Fax: 319-263-2321. [JC]
Our Lady of Guadalupe Catholic Mission, Rev. Alfonso Espino; Deacons Juan Leza; Juan Cadena.
Res., 501 E. Sixth St., P.O. Box 243, 52761. Tel: 319-263-0296.

Mystic, Appanoose Co., St. Francis. Closed. For inquiries for parish records contact the Chancery.

Newport, Johnson Co., St. Mary. Closed. For inquiries for parish records contact the Chancery.

Newton, Jasper Co., Sacred Heart (1867), Revs. Ernest E. Braida; Philip A. Cardenzana; Deacon William Schroeder. Pastoral Ministers: Tammy Norcross; Ila Mae Hanisch.
Mailing Address: P.O. Box 1478, 50208-1478. Tel: 515-792-4625; Fax: 515-792-5963. [CEM]
McCann Center—(Parish Office and Religious Education Center) 1115 S. Eighth Ave. E., P.O. Box 1478, 50208. Tel: 515-792-2050; Fax: 515-792-5963.
Catechesis/Religious Programs—D.R.E.: Cathi

Fouts, (Grades K-6); Marybeth Wagner, (Grades 7-12).
Students 360.

Nichols, Muscatine Co., St. Mary's. Unassigned.
Box 187, Hills, 52235. Tel: 319-679-2271. [CEM]

Nolan Settlement, Johnson Co., St. Bridget's. Closed. For inquiries for parish records contact the Chancery.

North English, Iowa Co., St. Joseph's (1963), Rev. John J. Whalen.
Res., 52316. Tel: 319-664-3325; Fax: 319-668-2582. [JC]
Catechesis/Religious Programs—Tel: 319-668-2241.
Students 110.

Oskaloosa, Mahaska Co., St. Mary's (1871), Rev. Robert J. Busher; Deacon William Wiegand.
Res., 311 First Ave. E., 52577. Tel: 515-673-6680; Fax: 515-672-2211. [CEM]
Catechesis/Religious Programs—Tel: 515-673-0659. Mrs. Madonna Bowie, D.R.E.
Students 200.

Ottumwa, Wapello Co., St. Mary of the Visitation (1851) (German), Rev. Robert M. Striegel.
Res., 216 N. Court St., 52501-2586. Tel: 515-682-4559; Fax: 515-682-4433.
Catechesis/Religious Programs—Tel: 515-682-4496.
Students 235.

St. Patrick's (1880), Rev. Anthony J. Herold, V.F.
Res., 222 N. Ward St., 52501. Tel: 515-682-4212.
Catechesis/Religious Programs—Tel: 515-682-0320. D.R.E.: Vickie Renfrew; Gail Bates.
Students 225.

Sacred Heart. Merged with St. Mary of the Visitation, Ottumwa.

Oxford, Johnson Co., St. Mary's (1860), Rev. Walter B. Helms.
Box 80, 52322. Tel: 319-628-4180; Fax: 319-628-4059. [CEM]

Parnell, Iowa Co., St. Joseph's. Attended by St. Joseph, North English. Rev. John J. Whalen.
52325. Tel: 319-668-2366. [CEM]

Pella, Marion Co., St. Mary's (1869), Revs. Thomas L. Parlette; Robert D. Gruss.
Res., 1104 Peace St., Box 144, 50219. Tel: 515-628-3078; Fax: 515-628-3165. [CEM]
Catechesis/Religious Programs—Students 199.

Petersville, Clinton Co., Immaculate Conception (1853), Rev. Edward A. Botkin.
Church—2885 145th St., Charlotte, 52731-9646. Tel: 319-674-4240. [CEM]

Rathbun, Appanoose Co., St. Anthony (1895). Closed. For inquiries for parish records contact the Chancery.

Richland, Keokuk Co., St. Frances Xavier Cabrini (1946), Rev. Paul E. Connolly.
Res., 308 W. Main St., P.O. Box 130, 52585-0130. Tel: 319-456-3161; Fax: 319-456-6408.

Richmond, Washington Co., Holy Trinity, Rev. Scott G. Lemaster.
Res., 580 Howard St., Kalona, 52247-9558. Tel: 319-656-2802. [CEM]
Catechesis/Religious Programs—Students 120.

Riverside, Washington Co., St. Mary of the Assumption, Rev. John P. Gallagher.
Res., 52327. Tel: 319-648-2331; Fax: 319-648-5024. [CEM]

St. Paul, Lee Co., St. James (1838). Attended by St. John, Houghton. Rev. John D. Spiegel. [CEM]
Catechesis/Religious Programs—1249 Hwy. 218, West Point, 52656. Tel: 319-469-2000. Rose Jennings, D.R.E.
Students 381.

Sigourney, Keokuk Co., St. Mary's (N. European), Rev. Philip V. Ryan; Deacon James Striegel.
Res., 415 E. Pleasant Valley St., 52591. Tel: 515-622-3426 (Rectory); 622-2316 (Business). [CEM][JC]
Catechesis/Religious Programs—Sr. Angela Keil, O.S.F., D.R.E.
Students 135.

Solon, Johnson Co., St. Mary's, Rev. Joseph R. Sparks.
Res., P.O. Box 69, 52333. Tel: 319-644-2228; Fax: 319-644-3564. [CEM]
Catechesis/Religious Programs—Students 364.

SS. Peter & Paul. Closed. For inquiries for parish records contact the Chancery.

String Prairie, Lee Co., St. Mary. Closed. For inquiries for parish records contact the Chancery.

Sugar Creek, Clinton Co., St. Joseph's. Consolidated with St. Mary, Bryant, to form Sts. Mary and Joseph, Sugar Creek.

Ss. Mary and Joseph (1993), Rev. Charles J. Fladung.
Res., 147 Broadway St., Charlotte, 52731-9686. Tel: 319-689-4355; Fax: 319-677-2739. [CEM 2]
Catechesis/Religious Programs—Tel: 319-689-6122. Barbara Skoff, D.R.E.
Students 121.

Tipton, Cedar Co., St. Mary's (1856), Rev. M. Eugene Benda; Deacons Adrian Panther; Robert Snavely.
Res., 52772. Tel: 319-886-2506. [CEM]
Catechesis/Religious Programs—Tel: 319-886-2506. Mary Wethington, D.R.E.
Students 245.

Toronto, Clinton Co., St. James (1855). Attended by Sacred Heart, Lost Nation. Rev. Richard J. Poster.
Mailing Address: P.O. Box 127, Lost Nation, 52254. Tel: 319-678-2200. [CEM]
Catechesis/Religious Programs—Mary Stevenson, D.R.E.
Students 62.

Valeria, Jasper Co., Sacred Heart (1892). Closed. For inquiries for parish records contact the Chancery.

Victor, Iowa Co., St. Bridget's (1886) (Belgian), Rev. Richard U.O. Okumu.
Res., 104 Third St., P.O. Box 266, 52347. Tel: 319-647-2220. [CEM][JC]

Villa Nova, Clinton Co., St. Patrick. Consolidated with Assumption of the Blessed Virgin Mary, Charlotte, to form Assumption and St. Patrick's, Charlotte.

Wapello, Louisa Co., St. Mary's (1867). Attended by St. Joseph, Columbus Junction. Rev. Bernard E. Weir.
Mailing Address: 815 Second St., Columbus Junction, 52738. Tel: 319-728-8210.

Washington, Washington Co., St. James (1860), Rev. Dennis C. Martin.
Res., 602 W. Second St., 52353-1994. Tel: 319-653-4504. [JC]
School—Tel: 319-653-3631; Fax: 319-653-3631. Ms. BethAnn McBride, Prin.
Lay Teachers 10; Students 148.
Catechesis/Religious Programs—Tel: 319-653-6213. Mary Langguth, D.R.E.
Students 197.

Wellman, Washington Co., St. Joseph, Rev. Scott G. Lemaster; Deacon David Reha.
Mailing Address: 580 Howard St., Kalona, 52247-9558. Tel: 319-656-2802.
Catechesis/Religious Programs—Tel: 319-646-2807. D.R.E.: Donna Johnson; Barry Johnson.
Students 64.

Weller, Monroe Co., St. Mary. Closed. For inquiries for parish records contact the Chancery.

Welton, Clinton Co., St. Anne (1910). Attended by St. Patrick, Delmar. Rev. Edward A. Botkin.
Mailing Address:Delmar, 52037. Tel: 319-674-4240.
Catechesis/Religious Programs—Students 56.

West Branch, Cedar Co., St. Bernadette (1960). Attended by St. Joseph, West Liberty. Rev. Edward A. O'Melia.
507 E. Orange, Box 103, 52358-0103.
Church & Mailing Address—307 E. Orange St., P.O. Box 103, 52358-0103. Tel: 319-643-2095; 627-2229 (Pastor Only).
Catechesis/Religious Programs—348 S. Maple St., Tel: 319-643-7296. Michael Hebl, D.R.E.
Students 115.

West Burlington, Des Moines Co., St. Mary's (1886), Revs. Gerald E. Stouvenel; John K. Sterling.
Res., 420 W. Mt. Pleasant St., P.O. Box 415, 52655. Tel: 319-752-4035. [CEM]
Catechesis/Religious Programs—520 W Mt. Pleasant St., 52655. Tel: 319-753-0277. Sr. Mary Jean Assell, S.S.J., D.R.E.
Students 510.

West Liberty, Muscatine Co., St. Joseph's (1892) (Hispanic), Rev. Edward A. O'Melia.
Res., 107 W. Sixth St., 52776-1246. Tel: 319-627-2229. [CEM]
Catechesis/Religious Programs—Students 210.

West Point, Lee Co., Assumption of the Blessed Virgin Mary, Rev. David F. Wilkening.
Res., 52656. Tel: 319-837-6808. [CEM]

What Cheer, Keokuk Co., St. Joseph's. Closed. For inquiries for parish records contact the Chancery.

Williamsburg, Iowa Co., St. Mary's (1891), Rev. Joseph F. Roost.
Res., 52361. Tel: 319-668-1397. [CEM]
Catechesis/Religious Programs—Tel: 319-668-2757.
Students 220.

Wilton, Muscatine Co., St. Mary's. Attended by St. Alphonsus, Davenport.
Res., 52778. Tel: 319-732-2271. [CEM]

Chaplains of Public Institutions

FORT MADISON. *Iowa State Penitentiary*. Rev. Gerald A. Hoenig.

IOWA CITY. *Oakdale Sanitorium*. Attended from St. Thomas More, Iowa City.
State University of Iowa Hospital. Revs. Vitolds Valainis; Jerry D. Lasley.
Veteran's Administration Hospital. Attended from Mercy Hospital, Iowa City. Revs. Andrew E. Kelly; Francis E. Bass; Louis J. Leonhardt.

KNOXVILLE. *Veteran's Administration Hospital*. Revs. Sylvester A. Conrad; Mark W. Swanson.

MOUNT PLEASANT. *Mental Health Institute, St. Dymphna Chapel*. Rev. Barnabas Barker, T.O.R.

Special Assignment:
Reverend Fathers—
Martinez, Frank R., 2706 N. Gaines St., Davenport, IA 52804
Mulligan, Louis J., 1140 E. 37th St., #114, Davenport, IA 52807

On Duty Outside the Diocese:
Reverend Fathers—
Bevenour, Richard F., 622 W. Escalon, Fresno, CA 93704
Beyer, Richard J., 1401 Chapelwood Dr., Waco, TX 76712
Cassidy, Dominic J., St. Joseph Hospital, 77 N. Airlite St., Elgin, IL 60120
Colonnese, Louis M., Apartado 109, Sonsonate, Depto. Sonsonate, El Salvador
Farrell, Anthony G., P.O. Box 301825, Veterans Dr. Anx., St. Thomas, USVI 00803
Otto, John A., 215 11th Ave., Apt. 5, Cold Springs, MN 56320
Shortall, Robert, 916 E. University, No. 147, Dallas, TX 75206
Steckel, Gregory A., 2351 McKinley Ave., Davenport, IA 52802-1769
Weibler, William F., 750 Burlington Ave., Apt. 3F, St. Petersburg Beach, FL 33701

Military Chaplains:
Reverend Monsignors—
Spiegel, Robert H., UNC/CFC/USFK/EUSA, PSC 303 Box 82, APO, 96204-0082
Reverend Fathers—
Burnett, James E., U.S. Air Force, PSC 50 Box 334, APO AE 09494, Croughton, AFB England

Absent on Leave:
Reverend Fathers—
Berndt, Rudolph C.
Leu, James E.

Retired:
Reverend Monsignors—
Burke, Ambrose J., B-6 Condo, 1014 Hickory Hill Ct., Clinton, IA 52732
Madsen, Cletus P., St. Vincent Center, 2706 N. Gaines St., Davenport, IA 52804
Menke, S. G., St. Vincent Center, 2706 N. Gaines St., Davenport, IA 52804
Walter, Robert J., 3406 Spring St., #3, Davenport, IA 52807-2117
Reverend Fathers—
Albers, Paul C., 611 Bel Aire Dr., West Point, IA 52656
Bass, Francis E., 109 N. Dodge St., Iowa City, IA 52245
Borger, Theodore R., 3265 Landis Ave., San Diego, CA 92104
Brothersen, Maynard J., St. Vincent Center, 2706 N. Gaines St., Davenport, IA 52804
Brownfield, Robert L., O'Keefe Hall, 104 E. Jefferson St., Iowa City, IA 52245
Collins, Edward F., Mercy McMahon Ter., 3856 J St., Sacramento, CA 95816
Conrad, Anthony J., St. Vincent Center, 2706 N. Gaines St., Davenport, IA 52804
Conrad, Sylvester A., 709 4th Ave., E., Albia, IA 52531-2455
Cross, Peter, 2220 10th St., Coralville, IA 52241
Dinh, Dominic, 602 B Gemini Ct., Arlington, TX 76011
Donahue, Paul H., St. Vincent Center, 2706 N. Gaines St., Davenport, IA 52804
Durkin, John R., 8927 Willmon Way, San Antonio, TX 78239
Egert, Clifford A., St. Vincent Center, 2706 N. Gaines St., Davenport, IA 52804
Ferrara, Pasquale L., Kahl Home, 1101 W. Ninth St., Davenport, IA 52804
Gannon, Charles E., St. Vincent Center, 2706 N. Gaines St., Davenport, IA 52804
Graham, John E., The Graham House, Belle Plaine, IA 52208
Grubb, James E., 514 Fahrney Blvd., Ottumwa, IA 52501-3254
Hratz, Joseph A., Kahl Home, 1101 W. Ninth St., Davenport, IA 52804
Janssen, James M., St. Vincent Center, 2706 N. Gaines St., Davenport, IA 52804
Kelleher, James P., A201, Canterbury Village, 1323 Derbyshire Ct., Naples, FL 33999

Kelly, Daniel J., 5645 Westwind Ln., Sarasota, FL 34231
Lawrence, James T., St. Vincent Center, 2706 N. Gaines St., Davenport, IA 52804
Lenoch, Francis J., 730 Market St, #11, Solon, IA 52333-8800
Leveling, Carlos F., St. Vincent Center, 2706 N. Gaines St., Davenport, IA 52804
Linnenbrink, Harry H., Cottage Gove Place, 2115 1st Ave., S.E., Apt. 304, Cedar Rapids, IA 52402
Manning, Martin B., St. Vincent Center, 2706 N. Gaines St., Davenport, IA 52804
Morrissey, John J., St. Vincent Center, 2706 N. Gaines St., Davenport, IA 52804
Ruppenkamp, Raymond, c/o 374 23rd Pl., Clinton, IA 52732-6901
Shepler, Charles C., 3004 Garfield St., Clinton, IA 52732-1637
Stratman, Thomas F., 422 E. 10th St., Davenport, IA 52803
Stratman, William J., 518 W. Locust St., Davenport, IA 52803
Strub, Herman A., Kahl Home, 1101 W. Ninth St., Davenport, IA 52804
Waldschmidt, Donald L., St. Vincent Center, 2706 N. Gaines St., Davenport, IA 52804
Weeg, Edmund J., 364 22nd Pl., Clinton, IA 52732-6104

Permanent Deacons:
Anderson, Arthur, Batavia
Barry, James T., Kansas City, MO
Becker, James L., Muscatine
Beckman, Clifford C., Sperry
Cadena, Juan J., Muscatine
Carl, Robert L., Muscatine
Clough, John R., West Point
Cord, Michael H., Des Moines
Cosgrove, William T., Keokuk
Dankert, Larry F., Davenport
Demeter, M. Joseph W., Mount Pleasant
Donart, Arthur C., Thomson, IL
Donnelly, William G., Bettendorf
Duff, Dennis L., Bettendorf
Frericks, Donald E., Blue Grass
Gengenbacher, Robert, Burlington
Gutierrez, Julian, Davenport
Hammer, Richard D., Burlington
Haut, Allen A., Bettendorf
Hilgendorf, Ramon, Clinton
Hittner, Paul F., Davenport
Jensen, Warren F., Davenport
Jones, William, Bettendorf
Larsen, Robert, Iowa City
Lennon, Patrick, Clinton
Leonard, Timothy, Lake Villa, IL
Lester, Jary, Sioux City
Leza, Juan B., Muscatine
McCoy, Robert C., Davenport
Mosse, Marcel G., Davenport
Mueller, Aloysius P., Clinton
Nolan, Thomas, Bettendorf
O'Connor, Arthur, Olatha, KS
Olson, William D., Grinnell
Pacha, Richard F., Washington
Panther, Adrian B., Tipton
Rasmussen, Richard J., Bettendorf
Reha, David, Wellman
Rosenthal, Joseph I., Davenport
Schmitt, John H., Low Moor
Schroeder, William E., Newton
Sheil, Michael D., DeWitt
Sink, Thomas, Bettendorf
Snavely, Robert E., Tipton
Starns, Terry L., Bettendorf
Stein, Ronald K., Donnellson
Strader, George D., Davenport
Striegel, James L., Delta
Timmerman, Gerald L., Davenport
Tometich, Anton I., Muscatine
Wiegand, William R., Oskaloosa
Witt, Stephen J., Grinnell

INSTITUTIONS LOCATED IN THE DIOCESE

[A] SEMINARIES, DIOCESAN

DAVENPORT. *St. Ambrose University Seminary*, 52803. Tel: 319-333-6151.
E-mail: cadam@saunix.sau.edu
Web site: www.davenportdiocese.org
Revs. Charles A. Adam, Rector; Edmond J. Dunn, Spiritual Dir. Students 5.

[B] COLLEGES AND UNIVERSITIES

DAVENPORT. *St. Ambrose University*, 52803-2898. Tel: 319-333-6300; Fax: 319-333-6243
For a complete listing, refer to the Colleges and Universities section.

CLINTON. *Mt. St. Clare College*, Bluff Blvd. & Springdale Dr., 52732. Tel: 319-242-4023.
E-mail: admissns@clare.edu
Web site: www.clare.edu
For a complete listing, refer to the Colleges and Universities section.

[C] SECULAR CAMPUSES

IOWA CITY. *Catholic Chair of Religion*, School of Religion, 314 Gilmore Hall, University of Iowa, 52242-1376. Tel: 319-335-2164. Rev. John P. Boyle, Ph.D, Res., 2413 Walden Ct., 52246-4118. Tel: 319-338-8634.

[D] ADULT RELIGIOUS EDUCATION

DAVENPORT. *New Horizons of Faith, Inc.*, 820 W. Central Park Ave., 52804. Tel: 319-336-8403. Sr. Joann K. Kuebrich, C.H.M. Total Enrollment 125.

[E] HIGH SCHOOLS, INTERPAROCHIAL

DAVENPORT. *Assumption High School*, 1020 W. Central Park Ave., 52804. Tel: 319-326-5313. Dr. Thomas Sunderbruch, Prin.; Ms. Colleen Blough, Campus Min. Sisters 1; Lay Teachers 43; Students 584.

BURLINGTON. *Notre Dame High School*, 702 S. Roosevelt Ave., 52601. Tel: 319-754-8431. William Bavery, Prin. Lay Teachers 20; Students 218.

CLINTON. *Mater Dei High School*, 525 Eighth Ave. S., 52732. Tel: 319-242-1663. Mr. David Burke, Prin. Sisters of Charity B.V.M. 2; Lay Teachers 6; Students 84.

FORT MADISON. *Aquinas Junior-Senior High School*, 2600 Ave. A, 52627. Tel: 319-372-2486. Mr. Thomas Walljasper, Prin. Lay Teachers 17; Students 192; Total Staff 21.

WEST POINT. *Marquette School, Inc.* (Marquette School System). See separate listing under Elementary Schools in the Institution section. Tel: 319-837-6131.

[F] EDUCATION CENTERS

CLINTON. *Trinity Early Learning Center*. (Grades PreK), 2520 Pershing Blvd., 52732. Tel: 319-242-9258. Mr. David Burke, Prin. Lay Teachers 1; Students 50.
Trinity Elementary. (Grades K-6), 312 S. Fourth St., 52732. Tel: 319-242-8929. Mr. David Burke, Prin. Teachers 9; Students 214.

IOWA CITY. *The Regina Catholic Education Center*, 2140 Rochester Ave., 52245. Tel: 319-337-2580. Mr. Raymond Pechous, Chief Admin. Tel: 319-358-2455; Ms. Sandra Feeney, Business Office.
Regina Junior Senior High School, 2150 Rochester Ave., 52245. Tel: 319-338-5436. Ms. Joy Kelly, Prin.; Rev. Paul A. Deyo. Sisters 2; Lay Teachers 25; Students 330.
Regina Elementary School, 2120 Rochester Ave., 52245. Tel: 319-337-5739. Ms. Celeste Cook, Prin. Lay Teachers 31; Students 500.
Regina Religious Education, 2140 Rochester Ave., 52245. Tel: 319-351-7638. Sr. Mary Frances Michalec.
Regina Fundraising Office, 2140 Rochester Ave., 52245. Tel: 319-358-2455. Ms. Ann Synan.
Regina Preschool-Daycare, 2140 Rochester Ave., 52245. Tel: 319-358-2455. Ms. Mary Pechous.
Regina Development Office. Tel: 319-354-5688.

KEOKUK. *Keokuk Catholic Schools, Inc.*, 2981 Plank Rd., 52632-2399. Tel: 319-524-2399. Jack Turner, Chief Admin.
St. Vincent's Elementary School. (Grades K-6). (Keokuk Catholic Schools, Inc.).
St. Vincent's Extended Day Care Program, 610 Timea St., 52632-5452. Tel: 319-524-6375. Paul Gaylord, Prin. Lay Teachers 9; Students 124.
Cardinal Stritch Junior Senior High School. (Grades 7-12). (Keokuk Catholic School, Inc.), 2981 Plank Rd., 52632-5452. Tel: 319-524-6375. Jack Turner, Prin. Lay Teachers 10; Students 118.

[G] ELEMENTARY SCHOOLS, INTERPAROCHIAL

DAVENPORT. *Holy Trinity Catholic Mission School*, 615 Marquette St., 52802. Tel: 319-322-3723. Sisters 2; Lay Teachers 7; Students 100.

BURLINGTON. *Burlington Area Catholic School System*. (Grades PreK-6), Notre Dame Elementary School, 700 S. Roosevelt Ave., 52601. Tel: 319-752-3776; 754-4417. Ms. Corinne Trautner, Prin. Lay Teachers 23; Students 342.

FORT MADISON. *Aquinas East and West*. (Grades PreK-3). (Primary), Aquinas East, 509 Avenue F, 52627. Tel: 319-372-5013. Mr. Robert Clifton, Prin. East and West. Lay Teachers 8; Students 161.
Aquinas West. (Grades 4-6). (Intermediate), 2213 Avenue J, 52627. Tel: 319-372-6428. Sisters 1; Lay Teachers 5; Students 86.

MUSCATINE. *Hayes Elementary School*, 2407 Cedar St., 52761. Tel: 319-263-3264. Mrs. Pauline Levine, Prin. Lay Teachers 6; Students 175.

OTTUMWA. *Seton Catholic School*, 117 E. Fourth St., 52501. Tel: 515-682-8826. Diane Reeves, Prin. Lay Teachers 7; Students 148.

WEST POINT. *Marquette School, Inc.* (Marquette School System), 52656.
Marquette School System: Marquette Primary. (K-3 at Houghton Center), P.O. Box 134, Houghton, 52631. Tel: 319-469-3581. Sr. Pat Siepker, Prin.
Marquette School System: Marquette Intermediate. (PreK, 4-6 at St. Paul Center), Box 71, St. Paul, 52657. Tel: 319-469-3881. Sr. Pat Siepker, Prin.
Marquette School System: Marquette Jr./Sr. High. (7-12, West Point), 413 Avenue C, 52656. Tel: 319-837-6131. Mr. Daniel J. Kieler, Prin. Religious 1; Lay Teachers 34; Students 379.

[H] CATHOLIC STUDENT CENTERS

IOWA CITY. *Newman Catholic Student Center*, 104 E. Jefferson St., 52245. Tel: 319-337-3106.
E-mail: newman-center@uiowa.edu
Revs. Edward J. Fitzpatrick, Dir.; John E. Stecher.

[I] RESIDENTIAL ADOLESCENT CARE CENTERS

*BURLINGTON. *Young House Family Services, Inc.*, Central Office, 724 N. 3rd St., P.O. Box 845, 52601. Tel: 319-752-4000; Fax: 319-752-6933
For a complete listing, refer to the Special Care Facilities section.

CLINTON. *Arch Office*, Box 278, 52733-0278. Tel: 319-243-9035.
E-mail: larchia@clinton.net
For a complete listing, refer to the Special Care Facilities section.

[J] GENERAL HOSPITALS

CENTERVILLE. *St. Joseph's Mercy Hospital*, One St. Joseph's Dr., 52544. Tel: 515-437-4111.
E-mail: stjocvil@se-iowa.net
For a complete listing, refer to the Hospitals section.

CLINTON. *Samaritan Health System, Inc.*, 1410 N. Fourth St., 52732. Tel: 319-244-5555
For a complete listing, refer to the Hospitals section.

IOWA CITY. *Mercy Hospital*, 52240. Tel: 319-339-0300; Fax: 319-339-3788
For a complete listing, refer to the Hospitals section.

[K] SOCIAL ACTION DEPARTMENTS

DAVENPORT. *John Lewis Coffee Shop/Miriam House*, 1202 W. 3rd St., P.O. Box 3245, 52808-3245. Tel: 319-322-0518.
E-mail: jlcsiowa@aol.com
Kate Ridge, Agent. Total Assisted 3,200; Total Staff 22.
Project Renewal of Davenport, Inc., Nazarath House, 906 W. Fifth St., 52802. Tel: 319-324-0800. Ann Schwickerath.
St. Vincent Center, 2706 N. Gaines St., 52804-1998. Tel: 319-324-1911. Mr. Dan R. Ebener.
Thomas Merton House, Inc., c/o 422 E. 10th St., 52803. Tel: 319-324-3257. Rev. Marvin A. Mottet.

[L] HOMES FOR AGED

DAVENPORT. *Kahl Home for the Aged and Infirm*, 1101 W. Ninth St., 52804. Tel: 319-324-1621
For a complete listing, refer to the Special Care Facilities section.

BURLINGTON. *St. Francis Continuation Care and Nursing Home*, 52601. Tel: 319-752-4564
For a complete listing, refer to the Special Care Facilities section.

CLINTON. *The Alverno Health Care Facility*, 52732. Tel: 319-242-1521; Fax: 319-243-3016.
E-mail: ruthcox@sanasys.com
For a complete listing, refer to the Special Care Facilities section.

[M] MONASTERIES AND RESIDENCES FOR PRIESTS AND BROTHERS

DAVENPORT. *St. Vincent Center*, 2706 N. Gaines St., 52804. Most Rev. Gerald O'Keefe; Rev. Msgr. Leo J. Feeney; Rev. Msgr. Cletus P. Madsen; Rev. Msgr. Sebastian J. Menke; Rev. Msgr. Michael J. Morrissey; Rev. Msgr. James F. Parizek; Rev. Msgr. W. Robert Schmidt; Revs. Maynard J. Brothersen; Anthony J. Conrad; Paul H. Donahue; Clifford A. Egert; Charles E. Gannon; James M. Janssen; James T. Lawrence; Carlos F. Leveling; Martin B. Manning; Frank R. Martinez; John J. Morrissey; Joseph Kahn V. Nguyen; Donald L. Waldschmidt.

IOWA CITY. *O'Keefe Hall*, #104 E. Jefferson St., 52245.
E-mail: newman-center@uiowa.edu

Rev. Edward J. Fitzpatrick. In res. Revs. John E. Stecher; Robert L. Brownfield; Mansuetus Setonga.

[N] CONVENTS AND RESIDENCES FOR SISTERS

DAVENPORT. *Franciscan Sisters of Christ the Divine Teacher*, 2605 Boies Ave., 52802. Tel: 319-323-1502. 4130 Nobis Dr., 52802. Tel: 319-323-7038. Sr. Bernadette Counihan, O.S.F., Superior. Sisters 5.

Humility Convent, 1310 W. Pleasant St., 52804. Tel: 319-326-3257.

Humility of Mary Center-Motherhouse of the Congregation of the Humility of Mary, 820 W. Central Park Ave., 52804. Tel: 319-323-9466; Fax: 319-323-5209. Sr. Jude Fitzpatrick, Pres. Total in Residence 31; Total Staff 9.

Humility of Mary Novitiate, 820 W. Central Park Ave., 52804. Tel: 319-323-8533; Fax: 319-323-5209.

CLINTON. *The Canticle*, 841 13th Ave., N., 52732-5162. Tel: 319-242-7903; Fax: 319-242-8024. Residence of the Sisters of St. Francis, Clinton. Sr. Marilyn Huegerich, O.S.F., Pres.; Rev. Thomas H. Mohr, Chap.; Anita Vaessen, Admin. Tel: 319-242-7903 Ext. 2343.

ELDRIDGE. *Carmel of the Queen of Heaven Discalced Carmelite Nuns*, 17937 250th St., 52748. Tel: 319-285-8387.
E-mail: solitude@netins.net
Web site: www.netins.net/showcase/solitude
Sr. Mary Joan Loebig, O.C.D., Prioress. Professed Sisters 12; Postulants 1; Novices 2.

IOWA CITY. *Dominican Sisters*, Provincial Office: 304 Oberlin St., 52245. Tel: 319-339-0993.
E-mail: jprovencher@regina.put.k12.ia.us
Web site: www.domcentral.org.roman
Sr. Marguerite Gregoire, O.P., Prioress; Sr. Jacqueline Provencher, O.P., Prov. Prioress. Sisters 18.

[O] RETREAT PROGRAMS-CENTERS

DAVENPORT. *Prayer and Spirituality Center*, 518 W. Locust St., 52803. Tel: 319-333-6189; Fax: 319-333-6234. Sr. Audrey Cleary, O.S.B., Dir.

BURLINGTON. *Beacon House, House of Prayer*, 915 N. Third, 52601. Tel: 319-752-2121. Sr. Mary Francis Houin, P.H.J.C.

IOWA CITY. *Emmanuel House of Prayer Country Retreat and Solitude Center*. Mailing Address: 4427 Kotts Ln. N.E., 52240. Tel: 319-351-5839. Betsy Coester, Dir.

WHEATLAND. *Our Lady of the Prairie Retreat*, 2774 145th Ave., 52777. Tel: 319-374-1092. Rev. Vincent J. Fabula, O.C.S.O., Dir.

[P] MISCELLANEOUS

DAVENPORT. *Assumption High School Foundation*, 1020 W. Central Park Ave., 52804. Tel: 319-326-5313. Dr. Thomas A. Sunderbruch.

Catholic Service Board, St. Vincent Center, 2706 N. Gaines St., 52804. Tel: 319-324-1911.

Commitment, St. Vincent Center, 2706 N. Gaines St., 52804. Tel: 319-324-1911. Rev. Louis M. Colonnese, Dir.; Sandy Carlson, Assoc. Dir.

Congregation of the Humility of Mary Charitable Trust, 820 W. Central Park Ave., 52804; Fax: 319-323-5209. Sr. Jude Fitzpatrick, C.H.M., Contact Person, Humility of Mary Shelter, Inc., 820 W. Central Park Ave., 52804. Tel: 319-323-9466; Fax: 319-323-5209. Sr. Jude Fitzpatrick, C.H.M., Contact Person. Total Assisted 160; Total Staff 9; Total in Residence 15.

Interfaith Housing, Ltd., 422 E. 10th St., 52803-5499. Tel: 319-324-3257. Rev. Marvin A. Mottet, Contact Person.

Kingdom Co., 2706 N. Gaines St., 52804-1998; Fax: 319-324-5842. Rev. Msgr. Michael J. Morrissey, Contact Person.

Quad Cities Catholic Deaf Ministry, 2706 N. Gaines St., 52804-1998. Rev. Msgr. James F. Parizek, Contact Person.

St. Vincent Home Corporation, 2706 N. Gaines St., 52804. Tel: 319-324-1911. Mr. Dan R. Ebener, Contact Person.

Spirit, Inc., 2219 E. Central Park, 52803. Tel: 319-324-9233. Mr. Harold Meier.

BROOKLYN. *St. Patrick Parish Foundation*, 215 Jackson St., 52211-0512. Tel: 515-522-7714. Rev. Joseph Rogers, Dir.

BURLINGTON. *Burlington Notre Dame Foundation*, 702 S. Roosevelt Ave., 52601. Tel: 319-752-8690. Debbie Trine.

St. Vincent De Paul Society, St. John the Baptist Church Conference, 712 Division St., 52601. Tel: 319-752-9332.

R.E.B.A. (Religious Education Burlington Area) Trust Fund, 700 Division St., 52601. Tel: 319-752-6733.

CENTERVILLE. *St. Mary School Foundation*, 838 S. 18th St., 52544.

CLINTON. *Amicare Home Health Services*, 562 Second Ave. S., 52732. Tel: 319-243-7261. Karen Roode, Dir.; Gary Baum, Chm.

Mount St. Clare Speech & Hearing Center, 562 N. Bluff Blvd., 52732. Tel: 319-242-4070; Fax: 319-242-2426. Sisters of St. Francis. Sr. Marcella Marie Narlock, Dir.

Sisters of St. Francis, Clinton, Iowa, Charitable Trust, 588 N. Bluff Blvd., 52732. Tel: 319-242-5631; 242-7609; Fax: 319-243-0007. Sr. Marilyn Huegerich, O.S.F., Pres.

IOWA CITY. *Mercy Hospital Foundation*, 500 E. Market St., 52245. Tel: 319-339-3540; Fax: 319-339-3788.
Mercy Hospital Guild of Iowa City, Iowa.
Mercy Outreach Iowa City, Inc.
Mercy Hospital, Iowa City, Iowa.
The Regina Foundation, 2140 Rochester Ave., 52245; Fax: 319-337-4109.

KEOKUK. *Ladies of Charity of Keokuk*, 1524 High St., 52632. Tel: 319-524-7517. Karen Taylor, Pres.; Lois Waldron, Welfare Chm.

WEST POINT. *Marquette Foundation*. Mailing Address: Box AA, 52656. Tel: 319-837-6749. Mr. Gene Winnike.

RELIGIOUS INSTITUTES OF MEN REPRESENTED IN THE DIOCESE

For further details refer to the corresponding bracketed number in the Religious Institutes of Men or Women section.

[0460]—*Brothers of the Poor of St. Francis*.—C.F.P.
[0350]—*Cistercian Order of the Strict Observance (Trappists)*.—O.C.S.O.
[1060]—*Society of the Precious Blood*.—C.PP.S.
[0560]—*Third Order Regular of Saint Francis*.—T.O.R.

RELIGIOUS INSTITUTES OF WOMEN REPRESENTED IN THE DIOCESE

[0230]—*Benedictine Sisters of Pontifical Jurisdiction*.—O.S.B.
[0330]—*Carmelite Sisters for the Aged and Infirm*.—O.Carm.
[2100]—*Congregation of the Humility of Mary*.—C.H.M.
[1780]—*Congregation of the Sisters of the Third Order of St. Francis of Perpetual Adoration*.—F.S.P.A.
[1710]—*Congregation of the Third Order of St. Francis of Mary Immaculate, Joliet, IL*.—O.S.F.
[0420]—*Discalced Carmelite Nuns*.—O.C.D.
[1070-03]—*Dominican Sisters*.—O.P.
[1120]—*Dominican Sisters of the Roman Congregation*.—O.P.
[]—*Franciscan Sisters of Christ the Divine Teacher*.—O.S.F.
[2575]—*Institute of the Sisters of Mercy of the Americas*. (Chicago).—R.S.M.
[2420]—*Marist Missionary Sisters*.—S.M.S.M.
[3230]—*Poor Handmaids of Jesus Christ*.—P.H.J.C.
[2970]—*School Sisters of Notre Dame*.—S.S.N.D.
[1680]—*School Sisters of St. Francis*.—O.S.F.
[0430]—*Sisters of Charity of the Blessed Virgin Mary*.—B.V.M.
[1540]—*Sisters of Saint Francis, Clinton, Iowa*.—O.S.F.
[1570]—*Sisters of St. Francis of the Holy Family*.—O.S.F.
[3830]—*Sisters of St. Joseph*.—C.S.J.
[3320]—*Sisters of the Presentation of the B.V.M.*.—P.B.V.M.
[1770]—*Sisters of the Third Order of St. Francis*. (Peoria, Illinois).—O.S.F.
[1705]—*Sisters of the Third Order of St. Francis of Assisi*.—O.S.F.
[1760]—*Sisters of the Third Order of St. Francis of Penance and of Charity*. (Tiffin, Ohio).—O.S.F.

NECROLOGY

† Bergthold, LeRoy, (Retired). —Died Jan. 29, 1997.
† McMahan, Frederick, Davenport, IA, St. Ambrose University. —Died Aug. 15, 1997.

Archdiocese of Denver

Archidioecesis Denveriensis

Most Reverend

CHARLES J. CHAPUT, O.F.M.Cap., D.D.

Archbishop of Denver; ordained August 29, 1970; Episcopal ordination July 26, 1988; appointed Bishop of Rapid City April 11, 1988; appointed Archbishop of Denver February 18, 1997.

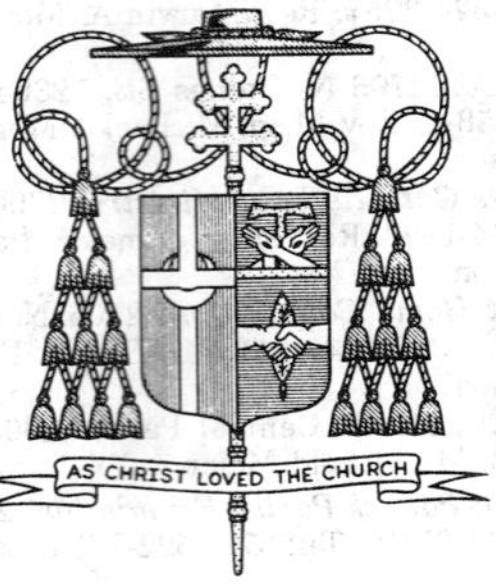

Pastoral Center: 1300 S. Steele St., Denver, CO, 80210.
Tel.: 303-715-2000; Fax: 303-715-2041.

Web site address: www.archden.org/archden

E-mail address: dcr@archden.org

ESTABLISHED A VICARIATE-APOSTOLIC IN 1868.

ERECTED A DIOCESE AUGUST 16, 1887; CREATED AN ARCHDIOCESE NOVEMBER 15, 1941.

Square Miles 40,154.

Comprises the northern part of the State of Colorado, including the 24 Counties of Adams, Arapahoe, Boulder, Clear Creek, Denver, Eagle, Garfield, Gilpin, Grand, Jackson, Jefferson, Larimer, Logan, Moffat, Morgan, Phillips, Pitkin, Rio Blanco, Routt, Sedgwick, Summit, Washington, Weld and Yuma.

For legal titles of parishes and archdiocesan institutions, consult the Chancery.

STATISTICAL OVERVIEW

Personnel	
Archbishop	1
Abbots	1
Priests: Diocesan Active in Diocese	119
Priests: Active Outside Diocese	5
Priests: Diocesan in Foreign Missions	1
Priests: Retired, Sick or Absent	36
Number of Diocesan Priests	161
Religious Priests in Diocese	133
Extern Priests in Diocese	12
Ordinations:	
Diocesan Priests	5
Permanent Deacons in Diocese	126
Total Brothers	22
Total Sisters	450
Parishes	
Parishes	112
With Resident Pastor:	
Resident Diocesan Priests	83
Resident Religious Priests	18
Without Resident Pastor:	
Administered by Priests	8
Administered by Permanent Deacons	1
Administered by Lay People	1
Administered by Pastoral Teams, etc.	1
Missions	38
Professional Ministry Personnel:	
Brothers	2
Sisters	20
Lay Ministers	202
Welfare	
Catholic Hospitals	3
Total Assisted	374,673
Health Care Centers	3
Total Assisted	490
Homes for the Aged	11
Total Assisted	1,410
Residential Care of Children	1
Total Assisted	70
Day Care and Extended Day Care Centers	24
Total Assisted	1,890
Specialized Homes	2
Total Assisted	75
Special Centers for Social Services	4
Total Assisted	7,550
Residential Care of Disabled	1
Total Assisted	60
Educational	
Diocesan Students in Other Seminaries	21
Seminaries, Religious	2
Students Religious	16
Total Seminarians	37
Colleges and Universities	1
Total Students	10,155
High Schools, Diocesan and Parish	2
Total Students	579
High Schools, Private	3
Total Students	1,950
Elementary Schools, Diocesan and Parish	36
Total Students	10,886
Elementary Schools, Private	1
Total Students	469
Catechesis/Religious Education:	
High School Students	3,222
Elementary Students	24,069
Total Students Under Catholic Instruction	51,367
Teachers in the Diocese:	
Priests	6
Brothers	8
Sisters	35
Lay Teachers	660
Vital Statistics	
Receptions into the Church:	
Infant Baptism Totals	9,778
Adult Baptism Totals	882
Received into Full Communion	969
First Communions	6,905
Confirmations	4,425
Marriages:	
Catholic	1,357
Interfaith	796
Total Marriages	2,153
Deaths	2,775
Total Catholic Population	330,662
Total Population	2,537,500

Former Bishops—Most Rev. JOSEPH PROJECTUS MACHEBEUF, D.D., cons. Titular Bishop of Epiphania and Vicar Apostolic of Colorado and Utah, Aug. 16, 1868; first Bishop of Denver in 1887; died July 10, 1889.—Most Rev. NICHOLAS CHRYSOSTOM MATZ, D.D., cons. Titular Bishop of Telmessa and Coadjutor of Denver *cum jure successionis,* Oct. 28, 1887; succeeded to the See of Denver, July 10, 1889; died Aug. 9, 1917.—Most Rev. J. HENRY TIHEN, D.D., ord. April 26, 1886; cons. Bishop of Lincoln, July 6, 1911; transferred to the See of Denver, Sept. 21, 1917; resigned Jan. 6, 1931; Apostolic Admin. until July 16, 1931; died Jan. 14, 1940.—Most Rev. URBAN J. VEHR, D.D., ord. May 29, 1915; Bishop of Denver; appt. April 17, 1931; cons. June 10, 1931; installed July 16, 1931; elevated to Archiepiscopal dignity, Nov. 15, 1941; installed as Archbishop of Denver; appt. Jan. 6, 1942; resigned Feb. 22, 1967; died Sept. 19, 1973.—Most Rev. JAMES V. CASEY, D.D., ord. Dec. 8, 1939; Titular Bishop of Citium and Auxiliary of Lincoln; appt. April 5, 1957; cons. April 24, 1957; promoted to Archbishop of Denver, Feb. 22, 1967; died March 14, 1986.—His Eminence J. FRANCIS CARDINAL STAFFORD, D.D., ord. Dec. 15, 1957; cons. Auxiliary Bishop of Baltimore, Feb. 29, 1976; installed Bishop of Memphis; appt. Nov. 16, 1982; installed Archbishop of Denver; appt. June 3, 1986; appt. President of the Pontifical Council for the Laity in Rome, Aug. 1996; elevated to cardinal Feb. 21, 1998.

The Pastoral Center—1300 S. Steele St., Denver, 80210. Tel: 303-715-2000; Fax: 303-715-2041.

Vicars General—Rev. Msgr. RAYMOND N. JONES; Rev. Msgr. R. WALKER NICKLESS.

Moderator of the Curia—Rev. Msgr. RAYMOND N. JONES.

Chancellor—FRANCIS X. MAIER.

Vice Chancellor—Rev. TIM J. MCCARTHY, J.C.L.

Executive Assistant to the Archbishop—PATRICIA J. MCDONALD.

Secretary for Permanent Deacons—Rev. MARCIAN T. O'MEARA.

Secretary Finance Administration and Planning—DENNIS D. RUSSELL.

Secretary for Priests and Seminarians—Rev. Msgr. R. WALKER NICKLESS.

Assistant Secretary for Priests—Rev. THOMAS S. FRYAR.

Secretary for Religious—Sr. SHARON FORD.

Secretary for Social Concerns—Vacant.

Secretary for Catholic Education—Rev. SAMUEL J. AQUILA.

Secretary for Hispanics—Vacant.

Archdiocesan Ecumenical Officer—Sr. MARIE REGIS, C.S.S.

Archdiocesan Master of Ceremonies—Rev. MICHAEL GLENN.

Presbyteral Council—Vacant.

Priest Personnel Board—Rev. Msgr. MICHAEL CHAMBERLAIN; Revs. THOMAS S. FRYAR; MICHAEL W. GASS; KENNETH KOEHLER; DONALD WILLETTE; Rev. Msgr. R. WALKER NICKLESS; Rev. REINHOLD WEISSBECK.

Priests' Continuing Education Committee—Rev. Msgr. R. WALKER NICKLESS; Revs. SAMUEL AQUILA; JAMES E. FOX; DORINO DELAZZER; ROGER LASCELLE; ANDREW KEMBERLING, O.S.B.; SEAN MCGRATH; GARY MUELLER, C.M.

Consultors—Rev. Msgr. EDWARD BUELT; Rev. Msgr. EDWARD M. HOFFMANN, V.F.; Rev. Msgr. RAYMOND N. JONES; Rev. Msgr. EDWARD T. MADDEN, V.F.; Rev. Msgr. R. WALKER NICKLESS; Rev. JOSEPH MONAHAN.

Archdiocesan Finance Council—RICHARD O. CAMPBELL; Dr. DORIS M. DRURY; DENNIS D. RUSSELL; JOHN P. BOX; Dr. LAWRENCE F. JOHNSON; GERALD J. LABER; JOHN YELENICK; Rev. Msgr. RAYMOND N. JONES; Rev. Msgr. R. WALKER NICKLESS.

Council for Religious—Rev. GEORGE FITZGERALD, C.S.P.; Sr. SHARON FORD, R.S.M., Sec.; Sr. CHRISTINE HOCK, R.G.S.; Sr. MACRINA SCOTT, O.S.F.; Bro. CHARLES MILLER, F.S.C.; Rev. LAWRENCE CHRISTENSEN C.M.; Sr. MARY DEL RAY EKLER, R.S.M.; Sr. LAVONNE

GUIDONI, S.C.L.; Rev. CHARLIE MARTINEZ, O.F.M.; Sr. ANN MARTIN KLEE, S.C.; Sr. MARGARET THOMAS, O.P.

Chairman of Deans—Rev. Msgr. R. WALKER NICKLESS, Sec. for Priests & Seminarians, *1300 S. Steele St., Denver, 80210.* Tel: 303-715-3197.

Deaneries—Very Rev. DARRELL SCHAFFER, V.F., East Denver; Very Rev. MARTIN LALLY, V.F., North Denver; Very Rev. MELVIN THOMPSON, V.F., West Denver; Rev. Msgr. EDWARD HOFFMANN S.T.D., J.C.L., Southeast Denver; Very Rev. THOMAS FRYAR, V.F., Southwest Denver; Very Rev. DAVID P. CROAK, V.F., Aurora; Rev. Msgr. EDWARD MADDEN, V.F., Boulder; Very Rev. ELBERT V. CHILSON, V.F., Fort Collins; Very Rev. ROBERT WHIPKEY, V.F., Eastern Plains; Very Rev. TIMOTHY GAINES, V.F., Greeley; Rev. Msgr. THOMAS F. DENTICI, V.F., Western Slope.

Metropolitan Tribunal

Judicial Vicar—Very Rev. JAMES S. MORENO, J.C.D.

Executive Director—TIMOTHY J. MCCARTHY, J.C.L.

Clerk of Due Process—TIMOTHY J. MCCARTHY, J.C.L., Pro Tem.

Promoters of Justice—Rev. Msgr. JOHN HARLEY SCHMITT, J.C.D.

Judges—Very Rev. JAMES S. MORENO, J.C.D.; Rev. RONALD F. WALTERS, O.F.M., J.C.L.; Rev. Msgr. MICHAEL J. CHAMBERLAIN, J.C.L.; Revs. GEORGE P. MILLER, J.C.L.; ROBERT P. HUNDT, J.C.L.; TIMOTHY J. MCCARTHY, J.C.L.

Defender of the Bond—Rev. THOMAS S. FRYAR.

Judicial Assessors—CATHERINE A. DAVISIO; JENNIFER A. RADCLIFFE.

Canonical Advisors—Revs. MARK PLEWKA, J.C.L.; J. ANTHONY MC DAID, J.C.D.

Advocates—Advocates appointed individually for particular cases.

Ecclesiastical Notary—RONDA WHITEHURST.

Coordinator of Second Instance—ELIZABETH O'MALLEY.

The Metropolitan Tribunal—Handles all marriage permissions and dispensations by delegation.

Archdiocesan Offices and Directors

The Archdiocese of Denver, a corporation sole—Rev. Msgr. RAYMOND N. JONES, Admin., *1300 S. Steele St., Denver, 80210.* Tel: 303-715-2000.

Archdiocesan Archives—Vacant, *1300 S. Steele St., Denver, 80210.* Tel: 303-715-3203.

Archdiocesan Campaign for Human Development—ANDREW PAGINI, Mission Coord., *1300 S. Steele St., Denver, 80210.* Tel: 303-715-3165.

Archdiocesan Liaison for Health Care—Vacant.

Chief Financial Officer—DENNIS D. RUSSELL, *1300 S. Steele St., Denver, 80210.* Tel: 303-715-3258.

Director of Construction and Engineering—WALTER E. WOSTENBERG, *1300 S. Steele St., Denver, 80210.* Tel: 303-715-3202.

Director of Property and Real Estate—DONNA BARR.

A.C.C.W.—VIC THORGREN, Spiritual Moderator, *3716 S. Forest Way, Denver, 80277.* Tel: 303-757-3722.

AIDS Task Force Members—Deacon JOSEPH BABISH, Chm.

Archdiocesan Housing Committee, Inc.—ANNA STROBEL, Exec. Dir., *1544 Pearl St., Denver, 80203.* Tel: 303-830-0215.

Boy and Girl Scouts—JAY ZOLITOR, *2071 S. Gray Dr., Denver, 80227.* Tel: 303-987-2306.

Building Committee—Rev. SAMUEL J. AQUILA; RAYMOND L. CRITES; RICHARD G. DUCEY; PETER J. FURSTENBERG; ALAN D. GILLAN; JAMES M. KLINK; JOHN F. MCGUIRE; GERHARD R. MUELLER; Rev. Msgr. JAMES W. RASBY; MICHAEL D. VANEK; WALTER E. WOSTENBERG.

Catholic Education Secretariat—Rev. SAMUEL J. AQUILA, Sec. Catholic Education; Dr. NORMAN RIDDER, Superintendent Office of Catholic Schools; WILLIAM BECKMAN, Dir., Office of Catechetics; Sr. MACRINA SCOTT, O.S.F., Coord., Catholic Biblical School, *1300 S. Steele St., Denver, 80210.* Tel: 303-715-3200. JEANETTE STACKHOUSE, Rites of Christian Initiation (RCIA); DAVID WARNER, Dir., Office of Catholic Adult Education; SYLVIA RAEL, Dir., Archbishop Vehr Theological Library; Rev. LAWRENCE M. FREEMAN, Dir. Special Religious Education & Pastoral Care, *3101 W. Hillside Pl., Denver, 80219.* Tel: 303-934-1999. Regional Catechetical Coords.: DON SCHNEIDER, North & Northeast Plains. Tel: 303-678-0900. Sr. MARY ANN FLAX, Western Slope. Tel: 970-824-4822. Archdiocesan Charismatic Ministries: Deacon RICHARD BAKER, Dir. Charismatic Renewal Services: Deacon RICHARD BAKER, *8213 Otis Ct., Arvada, 80003.* Tel: 303-940-8770. Christian Life Movement: Tel: 303-715-3252. Liturgy Office: Rev. CYPRIAN G. CONSTANTINE, O.S.B. Tel: 303-715-3156. Marriage and Family Life Office: CHRIS WEST. Tel: 303-715-3259. Youth/Young Adult and Campus Ministry: TOM MCCABE, Dir. Tel: 303-715-3178.

Mt. Olivet Cemetery Association—MICHAEL WRIGHT, Dir., *12801 W. 44th Ave., 80033.* Tel: 303-424-7785.

Catholic Charities and Community Services of the Archdiocese of Denver, Inc.—JAMES H. MAUCK, Pres., *2525 W. Alameda Ave., P.O. Box 19020, Denver, 80219.* Tel: 303-742-0828; Fax: 303-742-0774., *460 Linden Center Dr., Ft. Collins, 80524.* Tel: 303-484-5010. (For further details see Catholic Community Services-Northern, Inc. under Institutions located in the Archdiocese.).

Secretary for Social Concerns—DENISE MADDEN; DAN MONDRAGON, Assoc. Sec., *1300 S. Steele St., Denver, 80210.* Tel: 303-715-3171. Offices: Campaign for Human Development; Catholic Relief Services; Society for Propagation of the Faith; Holy Childhood; Justice and Peace. Liaison for: African American Liaisons; Archdiocesan AIDS Taskforce; The Hearing Challenged Community; Hmong Community; Kateri Catholic Indians; Korean Community; Rural Life Ministry; Vietnamese Community.

Colorado Catholic Conference 501(c)(4)—JIM TATTEN, *1300 S. Steele St., Denver, 80210.* Tel: 303-715-3206.

Secretary for Communications—GREGORY KAIL, *1300 S. Steele St., Denver, 80210.*

Office of Development—MOLLY MOORE, Dir. of Development, *1300 S. Steele St., Denver, 80210.* Tel: 303-715-3111; Fax: 303-715-2046.

Holy Childhood Assn.—DENISE MADDEN, Dir., *1300 S. Steele St., Denver, 80210.*

Archdiocesan Housing Committee, Inc.—(For further details see the listing under Institutions.).

John Paul II Center for the New Evangelization—MICHAEL MCKEE, *1300 S. Steele St., Denver, 80210.* Tel: 303-715-2007.

Legion of Mary—Vacant.

Migrant Ministry Archdiocesan Hispanic Center—*3600 Zuni, Denver, 80211.* Tel: 303-433-9013; 433-9028.

Archdiocesan Hispanic Center—Sr. IRENE MUNOZ, C.H.M., *3600 Zuni, Denver, 80211.* Tel: 303-433-9013; 433-9028.

Office of Liturgy—Revs. CYPRIAN CONSTANTINE, O.S.B., Dir. MICHAEL PAVLAKOVICH, Chm., Commission on the Sacred Liturgy, *1300 S. Steele St., Denver, 80210.* Tel: 303-715-3156.

Permanent Diaconate Program—Rev. MARCIAN T. O'MEARA, Sec. Associate Secretaries: Deacons JOHN PONTILLO; CLARENCE MCDAVID; GEORGE FORTUNATO; WARREN LYBARGER, *1300 S. Steele St., Denver, 80210.* Tel: 303-715-3198.

Priests' Eucharistic League—Rev. Msgr. JOHN V. ANDERSON, Dir., *1530 Logan St., Denver, 80202.* Tel: 303-831-7010.

Religious—Sr. SHARON FORD, R.S.M., Sec., *1300 S. Steele St., Denver, 80210.* Tel: 303-715-3239.

Rural Life Conference—RITA MAILANDER, *3990 S. Syracuse Way, Denver, 80237.* Tel: 303-741-2133.

Vocation Office—Rev. MICHAEL GLENN, Dir.; Sr. SHARON FORD, R.S.M., Assoc. Dir., *1300 S. Steele St., Denver, 80210.* Tel: 303-715-3239; Fax: 303-715-2048.

CLERGY, PARISHES, MISSIONS AND PAROCHIAL SCHOOLS

CITY OF DENVER
(County of Denver)

1—CATHEDRAL OF THE IMMACULATE CONCEPTION (1860), Rev. Msgr. John V. Anderson, Rector; Revs. James K. Goggins; Charles Martinez; Deacons Dominic Deprofio; Michael Dunn. In res., Rev. Msgr. Raymond N. Jones, V.G.; Rev. Samuel Aquila.
Res., 1530 Logan St., 80203. Tel: 303-831-7010; Fax: 303-831-9514.
Catechesis/Religious Programs—Students 91.

2—ALL SAINTS (1950), Rev. James R. Purfield; Deacon Arthur A. Vigil.
Res., 2559 S. Federal Blvd., 80219. Tel: 303-922-3758; Fax: 303-922-3750.
Parish Center—2560 S. Grove St., 80219.
Catechesis/Religious Programs—Students 353.

3—ANNUNCIATION (1883), Rev. Gene J. Emrisek, O.F.M.Cap. In res., Revs. Matthew Gross, O.F.M.Cap.; John P. Cousins, O.F.M.Cap.; Edward Judy, O.F.M.Cap.; Cyrus Gallagher, O.F.M.Cap.; Gregory Beyer, O.F.M.Cap.; David Songy, O.F.M.Cap.; John Toepfer, O.F.M.Cap.
Res., 3621 Humboldt St., 80205. Tel: 303-296-1024; Fax: 303-296-1026.
School—3536 Lafayette St., 80205. Tel: 303-296-2513. Sr. Jean Panisko, S.C.L., Prin.
Sisters of Charity of Leavenworth 5; Lay Teachers 9; Students 186.
Catechesis/Religious Programs—Students 88.
Mission—Denver, St. Patrick, 3401 Pecos St., 80211. Tel: 303-433-6328; Fax: 303-433-9627.

4—ASSUMPTION (1912), Revs. Hugh Guentner, O.S.M., Admin.; Gabriel M. Ramacciotti, O.S.M.; Mark M. Franceschini, O.S.M.
Res., 2361 E. 78th Ave., 80229. Tel: 303-288-2442; Fax: 303-289-2713.
School—2341 E. 78th Ave., 80229. Tel: 303-288-2159. Jane E. Schissel, Prin.
Lay Teachers 9; Students 143.
Catechesis/Religious Programs—Tel: 303-289-2713.
Students 91.

5—BLESSED SACRAMENT (1912), Revs. Roland Freeman; Lawrence Freeman; Deacon Nathan Coursey.
Res., 4930 Montview Blvd., 80207. Tel: 303-355-7361; Fax: 303-355-0894.
School—1973 Elm St., 80220. Tel: 303-377-8835.
Lay Teachers 18; Students 219.
Catechesis/Religious Programs—Students 192.

6—CHRIST THE KING (1947), Rev. J. Darrell Schaffer; Deacon Harold Del Real. In res., Revs. Donald Sutton; John Krenzke, (Retired).
Res., 845 Fairfax St., 80220. Tel: 303-388-1643; Fax: 303-355-0141.
School—860 Elm St., 80220. Tel: 303-321-2123. Elizabeth J. Begalla, Prin.
Lay Teachers 16; Students 252.
Catechesis/Religious Programs—Students 323.

7—CURE D'ARS (1952), Rev. John P. Cousins, O.F.M.Cap.; Deacon Clarence G. McDavid.
Office: 3050 Dahlia St., 80207. Tel: 303-322-1119; Fax: 303-322-9335.
Church—3201 Dahlia St., 80207. Tel: 303-322-7709.
Catechesis/Religious Programs—Students 75.

8—CHURCH OF THE GOOD SHEPHERD (1981). (Formerly St. John the Evangelist & St. Philomena). Revs. Marcian T. O'Meara; Michael Schlut; Deacon Stephen M. Blake.
Church and Res.—2626 E. Seventh Ave. Pkwy., 80206-3809. Tel: 303-322-7706; Fax: 303-399-1382.
Business and D.R.E. Offices—2626 E. Seventh Ave. Pkwy., 80206.
School—940 Fillmore St., 80206. Tel: 303-377-8018; Fax: 303-377-4034.
Middle School—620 Elizabeth St., 80206. Tel: 303-321-6231.
Lay Teachers 31; Students 351.

9—GUARDIAN ANGELS (1954), Rev. Robert J. Reycraft.
Res., 1843 W. 52nd Ave., 80221. Tel: 303-433-8361; Fax: 303-477-2066.
School—Tel: 303-480-9005. Mary Gold, Prin.
Lay Teachers 11; Students 233.
Catechesis/Religious Programs—Students 141.

10—HOLY CROSS (Thornton) (1957), Rev. Thomas Coyte; Deacons Tim Ritchey; Russell Halpine.
Res., 9371 Wigham St., 80229. Tel: 303-289-2258; 287-5204 (TDD); Fax: 303-289-2259.
Catechesis/Religious Programs—Students 412.

11—HOLY FAMILY (1889), Rev. Robert J. Greenslade; Deacon Leonard E. Polak. In res., Very Rev. James Moreno.
Res., 4377 Utica St., 80212. Tel: 303-455-1664; Fax: 303-455-7732.
Church—W. 44th Ave. & Utica St., 80212.
School—(Grades PreK-8) 4380 Utica St., 80212. Tel: 303-477-4023. Russell Plucinski, Prin.
Lay Teachers 16; Students 175.
Catechesis/Religious Programs—4377 Utica St., 80212. Tel: 303-433-9781.
Students 129.

12—HOLY GHOST (1905), Revs. Henry W. Grodecki, C.M.; Robert A. Schwane, C.M.; Gary A. Mueller, C.M.; Mark Pranaitis, C.M.; Deacon Vernon L. Rompot.
Res., 1900 California St., 80202. Tel: 303-292-1556; Fax: 303-292-5378.
Convent—2161 Tremont, 80202. Tel: 303-296-1740.
Missionary Sisters of Our Lady of Victory 2.
Catechesis/Religious Programs—Students 59.
Mission—Denver, Denver Co., St. Elizabeth of Hungary, 1060 St. Francis Way, Denver, 80204. Tel: 303-534-4014; Fax: 303-534-4140.

13—HOLY PROTECTION OF THE MOTHER OF GOD (Byzantine), Rev. Joseph Hutsko.
Mailing Address: 1074 S. Cook St., 80209. Tel: 303-778-8283.
Church—1201 S. Elizabeth St., 80209.

14—HOLY ROSARY (1918), Rev. Joseph A. Meznar.
Mailing Address: P.O. Box 8685, 80201-8685.
Res., 4695 Pearl St., 80216. Tel: 303-296-3283.
Catechesis/Religious Programs—Students 246.

15—MONTBELLO CATHOLIC PARISH-CHURCH OF THE ASCENSION (1972), Rev. John Gibbons, Admin.; Deacon Luis A. Usera. In res., Rev. Peter Urban.

Church—14050 Maxwell Pl., 80239. Tel: 303-371-0786; 303-373-4950 (Church); Fax: 303-373-4954. Rectory: 13190 E. 48th Ave., 80239.

16—MOST PRECIOUS BLOOD (1952), Rev. Kenneth Koehler; Deacons Joe Babish; Lewis Barbato, (Retired). Res., 2250 S. Harrison, 80210. Tel: 303-756-3083; Fax: 303-756-5628.
School—3959 E. Iliff, 80210. Tel: 303-757-1279. Martha Ellis, Prin.
Lay Teachers 20; Students 482.
Catechesis/Religious Programs—Students 158.

17—MOTHER OF GOD (1949), Rev. Msgr. Michael J. Chamberlain.
Res., 475 Logan St., 80203. Tel: 303-744-1715; Fax: 303-744-1716.

18—NOTRE DAME (1957), Revs. Leo R. Horrigan; Walter Huber, S.M.B.; Michael J. Flaska; Deacon Ken Hawkins.
Mailing Address: 5100 W. Evans Ave., 80219.
Church—2190 S. Sheridan Blvd., 80227.
Parish Center—Tel: 303-935-3900; Fax: 303-937-6699.
School—2165 S. Zenobia St., 80219. Tel: 303-935-3549; Fax: 303-937-4868. Stephen Furches, Prin.
Lay Teachers 24; Students 620.
Catechesis/Religious Programs—2160 S. Zenobia St., 80219. Tel: 303-922-9875; Fax: 303-937-6699. Students 319.

19—OUR LADY OF GRACE, Rev. Patrick Kennedy.
Res., 2645 E. 48th Ave., 80216. Tel: 303-297-3440; Fax: 303-297-3430.

20—OUR LADY OF GUADALUPE (1936) (Hispanic), Deacon Alfonso M. Sandoval, Pastoral Admin.
Res., 1209 W. 36th Ave., 80211. Tel: 303-477-1402; 477-8113; Fax: 303-477-4013.

21—OUR LADY OF LOURDES (1947), Rev. Robert D. Fisher, Admin.
Res., 2200 S. Logan St., 80210. Tel: 303-722-6861; Fax: 303-722-4810.
School—2256 S. Logan St., 80210. Tel: 303-722-7525. Joan Sheehan, Prin.
Sisters 1; Lay Teachers 12; Students 198.
Catechesis/Religious Programs—Students 102.

22—OUR LADY OF MT. CARMEL (1894) (Italian), Rev. Joseph M. Carbone, O.S.M., Admin. In res., Revs. Michael L. Doyle, O.S.M.; Larry E. Walling, O.S.M.; Gabriel M. Weber, O.S.M.
Res., 3549 Navajo St., 80211. Tel: 303-455-0447; Fax: 303-455-5487.

23—PRESENTATION OF OUR LADY, Rev. David A. Stahl. In res., Rev. James O. Abosike (Nigeria).
Res., 665 Irving St., 80204. Tel: 303-534-4882; Fax: 303-893-5056.
School—660 Julian St., 80204. Tel: 303-629-6562. Lay Teachers 12; Students 246.

24—CHURCH OF THE RISEN CHRIST (1967), Very Rev. Edward M. Hoffmann, S.T.D., V.F.; Rev. Sean J. McGrath.
Church—3060 S. Monaco Pkwy., 80222. Tel: 303-758-8826; Fax: 303-782-9667.
Catechesis/Religious Programs—Students 638.

25—SACRED HEART (1879) (Hispanic), Rev. Marcus Medrano; Deacons Henry Sandoval; Ron Ritter.
Res., 2760 Larimer St., 80205. Tel: 303-294-9830; Fax: 303-296-0171.

26—ST. ANTHONY OF PADUA (1947), Rev. Joseph C. Sullivan; Deacon A. Paul Garcia, (Retired).
Res., 3801 W. Ohio Ave., 80219. Tel: 303-935-2431; Fax: 303-935-8969.
Parish Center—775 S. Newton St., 80219.
Catechesis/Religious Programs—Tel: 303-936-5386; Fax: 303-935-8969.
Students 117.

27—ST. CAJETAN'S (Hispanic), Revs. James Prohens, C.R.; Tomas Fraile, C.R.; Deacon Filemon F. Gonzales, (Retired).
Res., 299 S. Stuart, 80219. Tel: 303-922-6306; Fax: 303-936-8285.
Church—299 S. Raleigh, 80219.
Catechesis/Religious Programs—4325 W. Alameda, 80219.
Students 334.

28—ST. CATHERINE OF SIENA (1912), Revs. Robert P. Meznar; Manuel Gabel; Deacon T. Patrick Bradley.
Res., 4200 Federal Blvd., 80211. Tel: 303-455-9090; Fax: 303-455-6651.
School—4280 Federal Blvd., 80211. Tel: 303-477-8035. Dilia Mapelli Taylor, Prin.
Lay Teachers 12; Students 203.
Catechesis/Religious Programs—Students 86.

29—ST. DOMINIC'S PARISH (1889), Revs. Jose M. Santiago, O.P.; John C. Risley, O.P. In res., Revs. Dennis Suzy, O.P.; John Keefer, O.P.; Michael G. Kyte, O.P., Novice Master; Ronald G. Kruel, O.P.; Bro. Henry A. Denier, O.P.
Res., 3005 W. 29th Ave., 80211. Tel: 303-455-3613; Fax: 303-455-3087.
Catechesis/Religious Programs—Students 104.

30—ST. FRANCIS DE SALES (1892), Rev. Msgr. Frank G. Morfeld.
Res., 301 S. Sherman St., 80209. Tel: 303-744-7211; Fax: 303-744-7211.
School—235 S. Sherman St., 80209. Tel: 303-744-7231. Sr. Eleanor O'Hearn, C.S.J., Prin.
Sisters of St. Joseph 4; Lay Teachers 10; Students 225.

31—ST. IGNATIUS LOYOLA (1924), Revs. Thomas Jost; John F. Brady, S.J.; Deacon Guffie Menogan. In res., Revs. J. Patrick Walsh, S.J.; Randel C. Hall, S.J.; Patrick Weis, S.J.
Res., 2305 Gaylord St., 80205. Tel: 303-322-8042; Fax: 303-322-2927.
School—2350 Gaylord, 80205.
Sisters of Charity of Cincinnati 4; Lay Teachers 7; Students 140.
Catechesis/Religious Programs—Students 137.

32—ST. JAMES (1909), Rev. Brian S. Morrow.
Res., 1314 Newport St., 80220. Tel: 303-322-7449; Fax: 303-399-2850.
School—Tel: 303-333-8275. Mary Win Aiton, Prin.
Lay Teachers 14; Students 227.
Catechesis/Religious Programs—Tel: 303-333-5189.
Students 184.

33—ST. JOSEPH'S (1882), Revs. Anthony Judge, C.SS.R.; Leopoldo Chavez, C.SS.R.; John P. Fahey, C.SS.R.; Deacon Alfredo Sanchez. In res., Revs. Michael McAndrew, C.SS.R.; John Morton, C.SS.R.
Res., 605 W. 6th Ave., 80204. Tel: 303-534-4408; Fax: 303-534-4412.
Catechesis/Religious Programs—Students 230.

34—ST. JOSEPH'S (1902) (Polish), Rev. Jan Mucha.
Res., 517 E. 46th Ave., 80216. Tel: 303-296-3217.

35—ST. MARY MAGDALENE'S (1907), Rev. Robert J. Greenslade; Deacon Richard Vieira. In res., Revs. William Brock; Albert Puhl; Robert Staes, O.P.; Thomas Noeson, O.P.
Res., 2771 Zenobia St., 80212. Tel: 303-477-4533; Fax: 303-477-2049.

36—ST. ROSE OF LIMA (1924), Rev. James Brennan; Deacon Sidney Atencio.
Res., 1320 W. Nevada Pl., 80223. Tel: 303-778-7673; Fax: 303-778-6601.
School—1345 W. Dakota Ave., 80223. Tel: 303-733-5806.
Lay Teachers 8; Students 142.
Catechesis/Religious Programs—Students 59.

37—ST. VINCENT DE PAUL, Revs. R. Christopher Hellstrom; Daniel W. Zimmerschied; Deacons Marvin A. Hegarty; Mark Salvato.
Res., 2375 E. Arizona Ave., 80210. Tel: 303-744-6119; Fax: 303-744-6124.
School—1164 S. Josephine St., 80210. Tel: 303-777-3812. Sr. Mary Angela Prin.
Sisters 4; Lay Teachers 35; Students 530.
Catechesis/Religious Programs—Students 283.

38—TRANSFIGURATION OF OUR LORD (Ukrainian), Rev. Basil Prakaiw.
Res., 4118 Shoshone St., 80211. Tel: 303-433-2347.

SUBURBAN PARISHES OF DENVER

Arvada, Jefferson Co., Shrine of St. Anne (1920), Rev. John D. McCormick; Deacons Michael Ritz, (Retired); Rodger Creel; Hugh Downey. In res., Rev. Kenneth J. Liuzzi.
Res., 7555 Grant Pl., 80002. Tel: 303-420-1280; Fax: 303-420-1341. [CEM]
School—Tel: 303-422-1800; Fax: 303-420-1341. Kathie Kuehl, Prin.
Lay Teachers 22; Students 502.
Catechesis/Religious Programs—Loretta Flom, D.R.E.
Students 439.

St. Joan of Arc (1967), Revs. James E. Kleiner; Walter Watson, S.J.; Deacons Gordon Hudec; John Smith.
Res., 12735 W. 58th Ave., 80002. Tel: 303-420-1232; Fax: 303-420-0126.
Catechesis/Religious Programs—Students 388.

Spirit of Christ Parish (1974), Revs. Robert J. Kinkel; Steve Padilla; James J. Cuneo; Deacons Michael Howard; Richard Baker.
Res., 7400 W. 80th Ave., 80003. Tel: 303-422-9173; Fax: 303-422-8251.
Catechesis/Religious Programs—Students 900.

Aurora, Arapahoe Co.,

1—QUEEN OF PEACE, (1968), Revs. William E. Breslin; Malachy R. McBride, O.F.M. Cap.; Rocco S. Porter; Deacons William Sorber; Martin A. Wilhelm.
Res., 13120 E. Kentucky Ave., 80012. Tel: 303-364-1056; Fax: 303-364-3944.
Catechesis/Religious Programs—Students 957.

2—ST. MICHAEL THE ARCHANGEL, (1978), Revs. Dorino De Lazzer; David W. Allen; Robert Syrianey, (Retired).
Res., 3320 S. Cathay St., 80013.
Parish Center and Office: 19099 E. Floyd Ave., 80013. Tel: 303-690-6797; Fax: 303-690-6932.
Catechesis/Religious Programs—Tel: 303-690-7697.
Students 1,030.

3—ST. PIUS X, (1956), Rev. Angelo Ossino; Deacons Gregory Martin; John Thunblom.
Res., 13670 E. 13th Pl., 80011. Tel: 303-364-7435; Fax: 303-340-0122.
School—13680 E. 14th Pl., 80011. Tel: 303-364-6515. Sr. Helen Weber, C.P.P.S., Prin.
Lay Teachers 24; Students 405.
Catechesis/Religious Programs—Students 207.

4—ST. THERESE, (1926), Revs. David P. Croak; Inde Geilenkirchen; Deacon Richard Brady.
Res., 1243 Kingston St., 80010. Tel: 303-344-0132; Fax: 303-344-0133.
School—Tel: 303-364-7494. Dr. Kelly Kelzenberg, Prin.
Sisters 2; Lay Teachers 21; Students 330.
Catechesis/Religious Programs—Students 118.

5—ST. LAWRENCE KOREAN CATHOLIC COMMUNITY, Rev. Andrew Myeong Rae Cho.
Res., 4310 S. Pitkin St., 80015-1974. Tel: 303-617-7555; Fax: 303-617-8265.

Broomfield, Boulder, Nativity of Our Lord (1958), Rev. Dennis K. Ryan; Deacon Richard Medenwaldt.
Church & School—900 W. Midway Blvd., 80020. Tel: 303-469-5171; Fax: 303-469-5172.
Parish Center Office—580 W. 3rd Ave. Dr., P.O. Box 302, 80020.
School—Tel: 303-466-4177. Mrs. Paula Beach, Prin.
Lay Teachers 16; Students 352.
Catechesis/Religious Programs—Students 402.

Commerce City, Adams Co., Our Lady Mother of the Church (1946), Rev. Terrence T. Kissell; Deacon Samuel R. Trujillo.
Res., 6690 E. 72nd Ave., 80022. Tel: 303-289-6489; Fax: 303-289-6480.
Catechesis/Religious Programs—Students 462.

Englewood, Arapahoe Co.,

1—ALL SOULS, (1955), Rev. Thomas S. Fryar. In res., Rev. Msgr. Thomas P. Barry; Deacon Gordon Milhone.
Res., 4950 S. Logan, 80110. Tel: 303-789-0007; Fax: 303-789-0491.
School—4951 S. Pennsylvania, 80110. Tel: 303-789-2155; Fax: 303-789-0491. William Moore, Prin.
Brothers 1; Lay Teachers 30; Students 461.
Catechesis/Religious Programs—Students 264.

2—HOLY NAME, (1894), Rev. William P. Murphy; Deacon Jack Sutton.
Res., 3290 W. Milan, 80110. Tel: 303-781-6093; Fax: 303-781-6398.
Catechesis/Religious Programs—Students 142.

3—ST. LOUIS, (1911), Rev. Roger W. Mollison; Deacons Dennis Kelly; Frank Bocovich; Marty Wager. In res., Rev. Simon Kalonga (Zaire).
Res., 3310 S. Sherman St., 80110. Tel: 303-761-3940; Fax: 303-781-7931.
School—3301 S. Sherman St., 80110. Tel: 303-762-8307.
Lay Teachers 11; Students 180.
Catechesis/Religious Programs—Students 88.

4—ST. THOMAS MORE, (1971), Revs. Michael Walsh; John J. McGinn; Patrick Dolan; Deacon Gary Rogge. In res., Rev. Martin Whealen, S.J.
Res., 8035 S. Quebec St., 80112. Tel: 303-770-1155; Fax: 303-220-3399.
School—7071 E. Otero Ave., 80112. Tel: 303-770-0441. Sue Roitman, Prin.
Lay Teachers 25; Students 516.
Catechesis/Religious Programs—Students 2,058.

Golden, Jefferson Co., St. Joseph (1867), Rev. Joseph E. Monahan, Admin.; Deacon William Ward.
Res., 969 Ulysses St., 80401. Tel: 303-279-4464; Fax: 303-273-9811.
Catechesis/Religious Programs—Students 382.

Lakewood, Jefferson Co.,

1—ST. BERNADETTE, (1947), Rev. Frank Deml; Deacons Gene Vitello; L. Kenneth Dreiling.
Res., 7240 W. 12th Ave., 80215. Tel: 303-233-1523; Fax: 303-233-7285.
Church—W. 12th Ave. & Teller St., 80215.
School—1100 Upham St., 80215. Tel: 303-237-0401. Henrietta Linenbrink, Prin.
Sisters 1; Lay Teachers 11; Students 184.
Catechesis/Religious Programs—Deacon Ken Dreiling, D.R.E.
Students 65.

2—CHRIST ON THE MOUNTAIN PARISH, (1975), Rev. John Gabrian, Admin.
Church—13922 W. Utah Ave., 80228-4110. Tel: 303-988-2222; Fax: 303-986-6956.
Catechesis/Religious Programs—Students 498.

3—OUR LADY OF FATIMA, Revs. Melvin F. Thompson; Tim I. Evans; Deacon Joseph W. Hawley. In res., Very Rev. R. Walker Nickless, V.G.

Res., 1985 Miller St., 80215. Tel: 303-233-6236; Fax: 303-237-6097.
School—Tel: 303-233-2500. Sr. Patricia Dunphy, C.S.J., Prin.
Lay Teachers 29; Students 445.
Catechesis/Religious Programs—Students 301.

4—ST. JUDE, (1967), Rev. Michael W. Gass; Deacons Joel J. Paulson; Tom Quinlan.
Office: 9405 W. Florida Ave., 80232. Tel: 303-988-6435; Fax: 303-988-6735.
Res., 1666 S. Jellison St., 80226.
Catechesis/Religious Programs—Students 556.

Littleton, Jefferson Co., St. Frances Cabrini Parish (1972), Rev. Kenneth Leone; Deacons Ronald Claussen; Craig Fucci; Paul Grimm.
Res., 6673 W. Chatfield Ave., 80128. Tel: 303-979-7688; Fax: 303-972-8566.
Catechesis/Religious Programs—Students 1,145.

Light of the World Parish (1979), Revs. Patrick Tierney; Jerome M. Rohr; Deacons Charles Lamar; Eugene Mooneyham; Chester Ubowski; Dick Kramb, (Retired).
Res., 5903 S. Kline St., 80127. Tel: 303-973-3969; Fax: 303-973-2122.
Catechesis/Religious Programs—Georgia Glover, D.R.E.
Students 909.

St. Mary, Arapahoe Co., (1901), Revs. David Blue Jacket, Admin.; Vincent Phung; John F. Wind; Deacons Edward Clements; William H. Ward.
Res., 6853 S. Prince, 80120. Tel: 303-798-8506; Fax: 303-347-2270. [JC]
School—(Grades K-8). Tel: 303-794-4757 (Grades K-3); 798-2375 (Grades 4-8). Donald McMaster, Prin.
Lay Teachers 40; Students 642.
Catechesis/Religious Programs—Students 784.

Northglenn, Adams Co., Immaculate Heart of Mary (1967), Very Rev. Martin Lally, V.F.; Rev. Gregory Beyer, O.F.M.Cap.; Deacons Leo Oehrle; Lynn Waring.
Offices & Mailing Address: 11385 Grant Dr., 80233. Tel: 303-452-2041; Fax: 303-452-7546.
Res., 335 E. 112th Dr., 80233. Tel: 303-452-9104.
Catechesis/Religious Programs—Students 650.

Westminster, Adams Co., Holy Trinity (1956), Revs. George M. Luznicky, O.S.M.; Mark Franceschini, O.S.M.; Hugh M. Guentner, O.S.M., Admin.; Deacon Lloyd Quintana. In res., Revs. Nicholas M. Norusis, O.S.M.; Roger M. Manning, O.S.M.
Res., 7595 N. Federal, 80030. Tel: 303-428-3594; Fax: 303-427-4125.
School—Tel: 303-427-5632. Sr. Anno La Mere, Prin.
Sisters 2; Lay Teachers 16; Students 292.
Friary—3100 W. 76th Ave., 80030. Tel: 303-428-1693.
Mission—Westminster, Adams Co., Our Lady of Visitation.
Catechesis/Religious Programs—Students 363.

St. Mark (1973), Rev. James R. Fox; Deacons John Pontillo; Darryl Dunn.
Res., 3141 W. 96th Ave., 80030. Tel: 303-466-8720; Fax: 303-466-0998.
Catechesis/Religious Programs—Students 311.

Wheat Ridge, Jefferson Co., Queen of Vietnamese Martyrs (1976) (Asian), Revs. Bartholomew Do Thai Hoa, C.M.C.; Louis M. Ha, C.M.C.; Deacon Joseph Van Le Tam.
Res., 4655 Harlan St., 80033. Tel: 303-431-0382; Fax: 303-431-1876.

SS. Peter and Paul (1949), Rev. John Hilton; Deacons Gary E. Miller; Jim Wall. In res., Rev. Michael Glenn.
Res., 3900 Pierce St., 80033. Tel: 303-424-3706; Fax: 303-424-0819.
School—Tel: 303-420-0402. Paula Wostenberg, Prin.
Lay Teachers 21; Students 380.
Catechesis/Religious Programs—Students 262.

OUTSIDE THE CITY OF DENVER

Akron, Washington Co., St. Joseph (1917), Rev. Thomas Clement.
Res., 551 W. 6th St., 80720. Tel: 970-345-6996; Fax: 970-345-6504. [CEM]
Catechesis/Religious Programs—Students 115.

Aspen, Pitkin Co., St. Mary (1892), Rev. Lawrence T. Solan.
Res., 104 S. Galena St., 81611. Tel: 970-925-7339; Fax: 970-925-1889.
Catechesis/Religious Programs—Students 71.
Mission—Aspen, Snowmass in Snowmass Village, Owl Creek Rd., 81615.

Ault, Weld Co., St. Mary. See Our Lady of Peace, Greeley.

Basalt, Eagle Co., St. Vincent (1970), Rev. Frank Maroney.
Res., P.O. 518, 81621. Tel: 970-927-3934; Fax: 970-927-3934.
Catechesis/Religious Programs—Students 45.
Mission—Carbondale, Garfield Co., St. Mary of the Crown, P.O. Box 64, 81623. Tel: 970-963-1270.

Boulder, Boulder Co.,

1—SACRED HEART OF JESUS, (1875), Very Rev. Edward T. Madden; Rev. Thomas L. McCormick; Deacon Robert J. Howard. In res., Rev. George L. Weibel.
Res., 2312 14th St., 80302. Tel: 303-442-6158; Fax: 303-442-7905. [JC]
School—(Grades PreK-8). Tel: 303-447-2362; Fax: 303-443-2466. Billie Middleton, Prin.
Lay Teachers 23; Students 428.
Catechesis/Religious Programs—Students 617.
Mission—Nederland, Boulder Co., St. Rita, P.O. Box 901, Nederland, 80466. Tel: 303-642-7348; Fax: 303-642-7348. Deacon Joseph Young, Admin.

2—SACRED HEART OF MARY, (1874), Revs. Andrew J. Kemberling, O.S.B.; Paul Montez, O.S.B.
Res., 6739 S. Boulder Rd., 80303. Tel: 303-494-7572; Fax: 303-494-7581. [CEM]
Rectory: Tel: 303-494-1266.
Catechesis/Religious Programs—Students 508.

3—ST. MARTIN DE PORRES, (1968), Rev. Hermanagild Jayachandra; Deacons Karl T. Matz; Francis A. Boselli.
Res., 3300 Table Mesa Dr., 80303. Tel: 303-499-7744; Fax: 303-494-8754.
Catechesis/Religious Programs—Students 119.

4—ST. THOMAS AQUINAS UNIVERSITY PARISH, (1950). (Campus Ministry), University of Colorado. Revs. George R. Fitzgerald, C.S.P.; Joseph A. Ciccone, C.S.P.; Thomas J. Holahan, C.S.P.
Pastoral Center: 904 14th St., 80302. Tel: 303-443-8383; Fax: 303-443-8399.
Catechesis/Religious Programs—Students 124.

Breckenridge, Summit Co., St. Mary (1875), Rev. Vincent Leo Smith.
Mailing Address: No. 2 W. Miner's Cr. Rd., P.O. Box 2670, Frisco, 80443. Tel: 970-668-3141; Fax: 970-668-3213.
Catechesis/Religious Programs—Students 180.
Mission—Dillon Valley, Summit Co., Our Lady of Peace.

Brighton, Adams Co., St. Augustine (1887), Rev. Reinhold B. Weissbeck; Deacon Gilbert Rael.
Res., 675 E. Egbert St., 80601. Tel: 303-659-1410; Fax: 303-659-6449.
Catechesis/Religious Programs—Tel: 303-659-1414.
Students 686.

Brush, Morgan Co., St. Mary (1911), Rev. James R. Baird.
Res., 340 Stanford St., 80723. Tel: 970-842-2216; Fax: 970-842-4461.
Catechesis/Religious Programs—Students 154.
Mission—Stoneham, Morgan Co., St. John, 340 Stanford, Brush 80723.

Byers, Arapahoe Co., Our Lady of the Plains (1978), Rev. Thomas M. Dona; Deacon William M. Sorber.
Res., 186 N. McDonnell, Box 519, 80103. Tel: 303-822-5880; Fax: 303-822-5780.
Catechesis/Religious Programs—Students 108.

Conifer, Jefferson Co., Our Lady of The Pines (1979), Rev. Reuben Payo; Deacon Frank W. Kullman.
Mailing Address: 9444 Eagle Cliff Rd., 80433. Tel: 303-838-0338; Fax: 303-697-5335.
Catechesis/Religious Programs—Students 295.
Mission—Buffalo Creek, Jefferson Co., St. Elizabeth, 9444 Eagle Cliff, 80433. Deacon Brian Kerby.

Craig, Moffat Co., St. Michael (1920), Rev. Cathal Longwill.
Res., 678 School St., 81625. Tel: 970-824-5330; Fax: 970-824-9724.
Catechesis/Religious Programs—Students 110.

Eagle, Eagle Co., St. Mary. See St. Clare of Assisi, Edwards.

Edwards, Eagle Co., St. Clare of Assisi (1993), Rev. Edward J. Poehlmann.
Mailing Address: P.O. Box 1390, 81632. Tel: 970-926-2821; Fax: 970-926-5350.
Res., 53 Old County Ln., 81631. Tel: 970-328-6396.
Catechesis/Religious Programs—Students 120.
Missions—Eagle, Eagle Co., St. Mary, 215 Capitol, Eagle, 81631.; Beaver Creek, Eagle Co., Beaver Creek Chapel. Not a mailing address. 33 Elktrack Rd., Tel: 970-845-9449.

Erie, Weld Co., St. Scholastica (1946). See St. Theresa, Frederick. Rev. G. Timothy Gaines.
Office: 436 Fifth St., Box 418, Frederick, 80530. Tel: 303-833-2966; 654-1106.
Church—615 Main St., 80516.
Catechesis/Religious Programs—Students 50.

Estes Park, Larimer Co., Our Lady of the Mountains (1947), Rev. James G. Simko; Deacon Jason Dorwart.
Res., P.O. Box 1706, 80517. Tel: 970-586-8111; Fax: 970-586-8112.
Catechesis/Religious Programs—Barry Emmett, D.R.E.
Students 49.

Evergreen, Jefferson Co., Christ the King (1932), Rev. John J. Murphy; Deacons George Fitterer (CHI); Norman Beabout (JOL).
Res., 4291 Evergreen Pkwy., 80439-7723. Tel: 303-674-3155; Fax: 303-674-3285.
Catechesis/Religious Programs—Tel: 303-674-5282.
Students 339.

Fort Collins, Larimer Co.,

1—ST. JOSEPH, (1879), Revs. Philip S. Meredith; Michael V. Delaney, S.J.; Deacon John Mckeown.
Res., 308 W. Mountain Ave., P.O. Box 502, 80522. Tel: 970-482-4148; Fax: 970-221-0635.
School—127 N. Howes St., 80522. Tel: 303-484-1171; Fax: 970-221-0635. Barbara Bullock, Prin.
Lay Teachers 18; Students 255.
Catechesis/Religious Programs—Students 571.
Mission—Red Feather Lakes, Larimer Co., Our Lady of the Lakes, P.O. Box 502, 80522.

2—HOLY FAMILY, (1924) (Hispanic), Rev. Joseph Romero, C.R.
Res., 326 N. Whitcomb St., 80521. Tel: 970-482-6599; Fax: 970-482-6599.
Catechesis/Religious Programs—Students 95.

3—JOHN XXIII UNIVERSITY PARISH, (1967), Rev. Robert L. Amundsen; Deacon Leonard Benzel.
Res., 1220 University Ave., 80521. Tel: 970-484-3356; Fax: 970-484-3434.
Catechesis/Religious Programs—Students 883.

4—ST. ELIZABETH ANN SETON, (1981), Very Rev. Elbert V. Chilson, V.F.; Deacon William Trewartha.
Res., 5450 S. Lemay Ave., 80525. Tel: 970-226-1303; Fax: 970-226-5780.
Catechesis/Religious Programs—Students 733.

Fort Lupton, Weld Co., St. William (1909), Rev. Gregario L. Mirto. In res., Rev. John Morton, C.SS.R.
Res., 1025 Fulton Ave., 80621. Tel: 303-857-6642; 659-3519; 785-6400; Fax: 303-857-6643.
Catechesis/Religious Programs—Students 282.
Mission—Platteville, Weld Co., St. Nicholas. See Wattenberg, Our Lady of Grace. 514 Marion, 80621. Tel: 970-785-2143; Fax: 970-857-6643.

Fort Morgan, Morgan Co., St. Helena (1910), Rev. Lawrence B. Kaiser.
Res., 917 W. 7th Ave., 80701. Tel: 970-867-2885.
Catechesis/Religious Programs—923 Pawnee, Ft. Morgan, 80701. Tel: 970-867-5768.
Students 354.
Mission—Weldona, Morgan Co., St. Francis of Assisi, 80701.

Frederick, Weld Co., St. Theresa (1923), Rev. G. Timothy Gaines.
Res., 436 Fifth St., P.O. Box 418, 80530. Tel: 970-833-2966; 303-654-1106 (Metro).
Catechesis/Religious Programs—Students 136.
Mission—Mead, Weld Co., Guardian Angels, 80530.

Glenwood Springs, Garfield Co., St. Stephen (1885), Rev. Cliff J. McMillan; Deacons Victor Kimminau; Charles Sprick.
Res., 1010 Grand Ave., 81601. Tel: 970-945-6673; Fax: 970-945-2089.
School—414 S. Hyland Park Dr., 81601. Tel: 970-945-7746. Cathye Woody, Prin.
Sisters 1; Lay Teachers 7; Students 102.
Catechesis/Religious Programs—Tel: 970-945-2580.
Students 145.

Grand Lake, Grand Co., St. Anne (1957), Rev. Francis J. Gerber, Jr.
Res., 219 Hancock St., P.O. Box 510, 80447. Tel: 970-627-3450; Fax: 970-627-3064.
Missions—Granby, Grand Co., Our Lady of the Snow, P.O. Box 510, 80447.; Winter Park, Grand Co., St. Bernard, P.O. Box 510, 80447.

Greeley, Weld Co., St. Mary (1965), Revs. Peter Quang Nguyen, Admin.; Warren Seedorf; Deacon Joseph H. Meilinger. In res., Rev. Robert Nevans, (Retired).
Res., 2222 23rd Ave., 80631. Tel: 970-352-1724; Fax: 970-352-1729.
Catechesis/Religious Programs—Students 592.

St. Peter (1903), Rev. Gregory K. Ames; Deacon Frederick Torrez. In res., Rev. Isaac Raney, M.Ss.A.
Office: 915 12th St., 80631. Tel: 970-352-1060; Fax: 970-352-1062.
Catechesis/Religious Programs—Tel: 970-346-9777.
Students 878.

Our Lady of Peace (1945), Rev. Kyle Fisher, C.SS.R. In res., Rev. Eugene Oates, C.SS.R.
Res., 1311 3rd St., 80631. Tel: 970-353-1747; Fax: 970-353-4830.
Catechesis/Religious Programs—1303 13th St., 80631. Tel: 970-351-6473; Fax: 970-353-4830.
Students 196.

Missions—Ault, Weld Co., St. Mary, 267 E. 4th St., 80610. Tel: 970-834-1609; Gilcrest, Weld Co., Sacred Heart, 4th St. & Starbird Rd., Gilcrest 80623; Eaton, Weld Co., St. Michael.

Holyoke, Phillips Co., St. Patrick (1893), Rev. Neal A. Pfister.
Res., 519 S. Interocean, 80734. Tel: 970-854-2762; 859-2866 (Hall); Fax: 970-854-2781; 854-2558 (R.E.). [CEM]
Catechesis/Religious Programs—Students 70.
Missions—Haxtun, Phillips Co., Christ the King, 306 N. Iris, Haxtun 80731. Tel: 974-774-7640; Fleming, Logan Co., St. Peter the Apostle, 40027 CR 18, Rte. 1, Fleming 80728. Tel: 970-265-2792. [CEM]

Idaho Springs, Clear Creek Co., St. Paul's (1881), Rev. Michael F. Kerrigan.
Res., P.O. Box 848, 1632 Colorado Blvd., 80452. Tel: 303-567-4662; Fax: 303-567-4662.
Catechesis/Religious Programs—Tel: 303-567-4138.
Students 51.
Missions—Central City, Gilpin Co., St. Mary of the Assumption, P.O. Box 848, 80452.; Georgetown, Clear Creek Co., Our Lady of Lourdes, P.O. Box 848, Idaho Springs 80452. [CEM]

Iliff, Logan Co., St. Catherine of Siena (1927), Very Rev. Robert G. Whipkey, Jr., V.F.; Rev. Adalberto DeGante (GLP).
Res., 111 S. Fifth St., P.O. Box 221, 80736. Tel: 970-522-8040; Fax: 970-334-2227.

Johnstown, Weld Co., St. John the Baptist (1937), Rev. Stephen E. Adams.
Res., 809 Charlotte St., 80534. Tel: 970-587-2879.
Catechesis/Religious Programs—Students 132.
Mission—Windsor, Weld Co., Our Lady of the Valley, P.O. Box 1018, 80534. Tel: 970-686-5084.

Julesburg, Sedgwick Co., St. Anthony (1907), Rev. Christopher A. Renner.
Res., 606 W. 3rd St., 80737. Tel: 970-474-2655; Fax: 970-474-2655.
Catechesis/Religious Programs—Students 54.
Mission—Crook, Logan Co., St. Peters, 612 E. 3rd, Crook, 80726.

Kremmling, Grand Co., St. Peter (1944), Rev. John Kauffman.
Church and Office: 106 S. 5th St., P.O. Box 428, 80459. Tel: 970-724-3428.
Mission—Walden, Grand Co., St. Ignatius, 80459.

Lafayette, Boulder Co., Immaculate Conception (1906), Rev. Joseph A. Hartmann; Deacon Merle Runck.
Res., 110 W. Simpson, 80026. Tel: 303-665-5103; Fax: 303-604-9077.
Catechesis/Religious Programs—Tel: 303-665-9334.
Students 127.

Longmont, Boulder Co., St. John the Baptist (1882), Revs. James E. Fox; Lawrence P. Christensen, C.M.; Deacons William Lee; Nehemias Ruiz.
Parish Center: 336 Emery St., 80501. Tel: 303-776-0737; 449-7745 (Metro); Fax: 303-772-5636. [JC]
School—350 Emory St., 80501. Tel: 303-449-7745. Dr. Paul Czaja, Prin.
Lay Teachers 19; Students 290.
Catechesis/Religious Programs—Tel: 303-772-5637.
Students 569.
Spirit of Peace Parish (1982), Revs. Donald Romero, Admin.; John J. Markey, O.P. Pastoral Team: Mary Franch; Sr. Dorothy Feehan, B.V.M.; Julie Lupien; Waldemar Perez; John Rejeske; Tom Shugrue.
Church and Office: 1500 Hover Rd., 80501. Tel: 303-772-6322; Fax: 303-772-9415. [JC]
Catechesis/Religious Programs—Students 392.

Louisville, Boulder Co., St. Louis (1884), Revs. Donald Willette; Thomas J. Burkett.
Res., 902 Grant Ave., 80027. Tel: 303-666-6401; Fax: 303-666-0826.
School—925 Grant Ave., 80027. Tel: 303-666-6220.
Lay Teachers 12; Students 210.
Preschool—901 Grant Ave., 80027. Tel: 303-665-0606.
Catechesis/Religious Programs—841 Grant Ave., 80027. Tel: 303-604-6055.
Students 526.

Loveland, Larimer Co., St. John the Evangelist (1902), Revs. Michael G. Palakovich, Admin.; Daniel J. Norick; Deacons Richard Johnson; Warren Lybarger; Robert Haigh.
Office: 1515 Hilltop Dr., 80537. Tel: 970-669-2720; Fax: 970-669-5743.
Res., 1523 Hilltop Dr., 80537. Tel: 970-663-3457.
School—1730 W. 12th St., Tel: 970-667-6846.
Sisters 1; Lay Teachers 10; Students 228.
Catechesis/Religious Programs—Students 445.

Meeker, Rio Blanco Co., Holy Family (1905), Rev. Roger L. Lasselle.
Res., 889 Park, Box 866, 81641. Tel: 970-878-3300; Fax: 970-878-3300.
Mission—Rangely, Rio Blanco Co., St. Ignatius, 109 S. Stanolind Ave., Rangely, 81648. Tel: 970-675-8935; Fax: 970-675-8935.

Minturn, Eagle Co., St. Patrick's (1913), Very Rev. Msgr. Thomas Dentici, V.F.
Res., 476 Pine St., P.O. Box 219, 81645. Tel: 970-827-5784; Fax: 970-827-9454.
Catechesis/Religious Programs—Students 140.
Missions—Red Cliff, Eagle Co., Our Lady of Mt. Carmel, P.O. Box 219, 81645.; Vail, Eagle Co., The Interfaith Chapel, P.O. Box 219, 81645.

Oak Creek, Routt Co., St. Martin of Tours. See Holy Name, Steamboat Springs.

Peetz, Logan Co., Sacred Heart, Very Rev. Robert G. Whipkey, Jr., V.F.; Rev. Adalberto DeGante (GLP).
Res., 621 Logan, P.O. Box D, 80747. Tel: 970-334-2227; Fax: 970-334-2227. [CEM]
Catechesis/Religious Programs—Students 52.

Platteville, Weld Co., St. Nicholas. See St. William, Fort Lupton.
Catechesis/Religious Programs—Students 120.

Rangely, Rio Blanco Co., St. Ignatius (1931), Rev. Roger L. Lascelle; Deacon George Fortunato.
Res., 109 S. Stanolind Ave., 81648. Tel: 970-675-8935; Fax: 970-675-8935.
Catechesis/Religious Programs—Students 46.

Red Feathers Lakes, Larimer Co., Our Lady of the Lakes. See St. Joseph, Fort Collins.

Rifle, Garfield Co., St. Mary's (1910), Rev. Robert E. Hehn.
Res., 323 1/2 E. Fifth St., P.O. Box 191, 81650. Tel: 970-625-2547. [JC]
Catechesis/Religious Programs—341 E. 5th St., 81650. Tel: 970-625-3914.
Students 235.
Missions—Silt, Garfield Co., Sacred Heart, P.O. Box 191, 81650.; Parachute, Garfield Co., St. Brendan, P.O. Box 191, 81650.

Roggen, Weld Co., Sacred Heart (1924), Rev. Joseph J. Blanco.
Res., 38044 Weld County Rd. 16, 80652. Tel: 303-849-5313; Fax: 303-849-5674.
Catechesis/Religious Programs—Students 41.
Missions—Keenesburg, Weld Co., Holy Family; Wiggins, Morgan Co., Our Lady of Lourdes .

Steamboat Springs, Routt Co., Holy Name (1907), Rev. George M. Schroeder.
Res., 504 Oak St., P.O. Box 774198, 80477-4198. Tel: 970-879-0671; Fax: 970-879-7406.
Catechesis/Religious Programs—Tel: 970-879-1225.
Students 259.
Mission—Oak Creek, Routt Co., St. Martin Church of Tours.

Sterling, Logan Co., St. Anthony (1888), Revs. Adalberto DeGante; Robert G. Whipkey, Jr., V.F.
Res., 327 S. 3rd St., 80751. Tel: 970-522-6422; Fax: 970-522-6442.
School—Tel: 970-522-7567.
Sisters of the Third Order of St. Francis of Assisi 1; Lay Teachers 9; Students 114.
Catechesis/Religious Programs—326 S. 3rd St., 80751. Tel: 970-522-7568.
Students 298.

Stoneham, Weld Co., St. John. See St. Mary, Brush.

Vail, Eagle Co., The Interfaith Chapel. See St. Patrick's, Minturn.

Walden, Jackson Co., St. Ignatius. See St. Peter, Kremmling.

Wattenberg, Fort Lupton Co., Our Lady of Grace. See St. William, Fort Lupton.

Weldona, Morgan Co., St. Francis of Assisi. See St. Helena, Fort Morgan.

Wiggins, Morgan Co., Our Lady of Lourdes. See Sacred Heart, Roggen.

Winter Park, Grand Co., St. Bernard of Montjoux. See St. Anne, Grand Lake.

Windsor, Weld Co., Our Lady of the Valley, Very Rev. Stephen E. Adams, V.F.; Deacon Harold Kimble.
Office: P.O. Box 1018, 80550. Tel: 970-686-5084; Fax: 970-587-2879.
Res., 809 Charlotte St., Johnstown, 80534. Tel: 303-587-2879.

Wray, Yuma Co., St. Andrew (1891), Rev. Gerald A. Young (LA).
Res., 412 Dexter St., 80758. Tel: 970-332-5858; Fax: 970-332-4604.
Catechesis/Religious Programs—Students 120.

Yuma, Yuma Co., St. John (1888), Rev. Gerald A. Young, Admin.
Res., 508 S. Ash St., 80759. Tel: 970-848-5973; Fax: 970-332-4604.
Catechesis/Religious Programs—Students 125.

Chaplains of Public Institutions

DENVER. *Veterans Hospital*. Rev. Thomas J. Woerth.
AURORA. *Fitzsimons Army Medical Center*. Rev. Edward Kucera, O.S.B.

On Duty Outside the Archdiocese:
Most Rev.—
Stafford, Francis J., Archbishop Emeritus of Denver, Pontifical Council for the Laity, Piazza San Calisto, 16, Vatican City State 00120 Italy
Reverend Monsignors—
Buelt, Edward L., Pontifical Council for Laity, Piazza San Calisto, 16, Vatican City State 00120 Italy
Reverend Fathers—
Denig, Philip, Chap. (Capt.), HHC 1 SB Unit, 31520, APO AE, 09832
Kelly, Thomas D., 15 ABW / HC, Hickam AFB, HI 96853-5112
McDaid, J. Anthony, Villa Stritch, Via Della Nocetta 63, Rome, 00164 Italy
Owlrich, Robert E., Casa Santa Maria, Via Dell' Umilta 30, Rome, 00187 Italy
Revello, James K.I., Chap. (Lt. Col.), USAF, 2703 San Juan Loop, Holloman, NM 88330
Schmitz, Bernard A., Monteria Mission, A.A. 1393, Monteria, Colombia

---

Absent on Leave:
Reverend Fathers—
Bradtke, Thomas A.
Dold, John F.
Fuller, Roger J.
McInerney, Maurice
Scezney, Leonard J.
St. Peter, Lawrence
White, Robert H.

Retired:
Reverend Monsignors—
Barry, Thomas P., 4950 S. Logan St., Englewood, CO 80110-6921
Foxhoven, Omer V., 3342 Marshall St., Wheat Ridge, CO 80033
Jones, William H., 7125 E. 11th Ave., Denver, CO 80220
Rasby, James W., 1011 S. Valencia, Villa 3, Denver, CO 80231
Schmitt, J. Harley, Chap., Mullen Home, 3629 W. 29th Ave., Denver, CO 80211
Reverend Fathers—
Banigan, Herbert, 5817 S. Mount Vernon, Spokane, WA 99223
Blach, Leo M., P.O. Box 371, Brighton, CO 80601
Breunig, Robert L., Villa Madeline, 2771 Zenobia St., Denver, CO 80212
Canjar, John A.
Durrie, Robert L., 1580 S. Dahlia, Denver, CO 80222
Flaherty, Daniel J., 902 Grant St., Louisville, CO 80027
Gibbons, John, 14050 Maxwell Pl., Denver, CO 80239
Herbert, Joseph, S.J., 1085 Zany St., Golden, CO 80401
Jones, Charles, 1129 Fillmore, Denver, CO 80206. Tel: 303-322-0624
Kane, James E., 2303 S. Vaughn Way, #208, Aurora, CO 80014
Kearney, George W., 3373 W. 36th Ave., Denver, CO 80211
McCallin, Frederick D., Mullen Home, 3629 W. 29th Ave., Denver, CO 80211
Mihelich, Leopold, 6305 W. 5th Pl., Lakewood, CO 80226
Nevans, Robert V., Villa Madeleine, 2771 Zenobia St., Denver, CO 80212
O'Malley, Joseph M., 1542 E. Nicholas Dr., Littleton, CO 80161
Puhl, Albert E., 800 Pennsylvania St., Denver, CO 80203
Salmon, Charles P., 2835 W. 32nd, Denver, CO 80211
Sanger, Charles P., 10450 Oakmont Dr., Sun City, AZ 85351
Scannell, John W., 6333 Rancho Mission Rd., San Diego, CA 92108
Sullivan, Patrick, Box 274, 8962 E. Hampden Ave., Denver, CO 80231-4996
Syrianey, Robert, 13902 E. Marina Ave., Apt. 207, Aurora, CO 80014
Weibel, George L., 2312 14th St., Boulder, CO 80304

Permanent Deacons:
Ansay, Ronald J., (Retired)
Atencio, Sidney, St. Rose of Lima, Denver
Babish, Joseph T., Most Precious Blood, Denver

Baca, Marcus, On Duty in the Archdiocese of Sante Fe
Baker, Richard L., Spirit of Christ, Arvada
Barbato, Lewis, M.D., (Retired)
Beabout, Norman, Christ the King, Evergreen
Becker, Henry Jr. (SAN), St. Thomas More, Englewood
Benzel, Leonard, John XXIII University, Fort Collins
Blake, Stephen M., Church of the Good Shepherd, Denver
Bocovich, Frank J., St. Louis, Englewood
Boselli, Francis A., St. Martin de Porres, Boulder
Bowles, Richard J., Jr., Diaconal Ministry Diocese of Colorado Springs
Bradley, Patrick (CAM), St. Catherine of Siena, Denver
Brady, Richard A., St. Therese, Aurora
Brown, James, St. Elizabeth of Hungary, Denver
Burgess, Lou A., Diaconal Ministry in Grenada
Clausson, Ronald L., St. Francis Cabrini, Littleton
Clements, Edward R., St. Mary, Littleton
Coker, Richard, Military Service
Combs, Richard E., On Duty in the Archdiocese of Seattle
Coursey, Nathan D., Contemplative Outreach Ministry, Blessed Sacrament Parish, Denver
Creel, Rodger L., Shrine of St. Anne, Arvada
Decker, Myles M., On Duty in the Diocese of Palm Beach
Del Real, Harold, Christ the King, Evergreen
DeProfio, Dominic, Immaculate Conception Cathedral, Denver
Dolan, L. Stephen, (Retired)
Dorwart, Jason, Our Lady of the Mountains, Estes Park
Downey, Hugh, Shrine of St. Anne, Arvada
Dreiling, L. Kenneth, St. Bernedette, Denver
Dunn, Darryl, St. Mark, Westminster
Dunn, Michael A., Immaculate Conception Cathedral, Denver
Fitterer, George (JOL), Christ the King, Evergreen
Fortunato, George R., St. Ignatius Parish, Rangely
Frisinger, Howard, (Retired)
Fucci, Craig (LA), St. Francis Cabrini, Littleton
Gamache, Robert K., On Duty in the Archdiocese of St. Louis
Garcia, A. Paul, (Retired)
Gonzales, Filemon F., (Retired)
Grimm, R. Paul, St. Francis Cabrini, Fort Logan Medical Center, Littleton
Haigh, Robert, St. John the Evangelist, Loveland
Halpine, Russell, Holy Cross, Thorton
Harrington, Philip, Notre Dame Parish, Denver
Hawkins, Kenneth I., Jr., Archdiocesan Family Center, Airport Ministry; Notre Dame, Denver
Hawley, Joseph W., Our Lady of Fatima, Lakewood
Hegarty, Marvin A., St. Vincent de Paul, Denver
Heissenbuttel, Thomas, St. Paul, Idaho Springs
Hillyer, Granby, On Duty in the Archdiocese of San Francisco
Howard, Michael J., Spirit of Christ, Arvada
Howard, Robert J., Sacred Heart of Jesus, Boulder
Hronek, Dennis R., Unassigned
Hudec, Gordon D., St. Joan of Arc, Arvada
Johnson, Richard, St. John the Evangelist, Loveland
Kelly, Dennis M., St. Louis, Englewood
Kerby, Brian J., Mt. Evans Hospice (Evergreen), St. Elizabeth, Buffalo Creek
Kimble, Harold, Our Lady of the Valley, Windsor
Kimminau, Victor H., St. Stephen, Glenwood Springs
Koch, Kenneth, (Retired)
Kramb, Richard F., (Retired)
Kulinski, Jerome N., (Retired)
Kullman, Frank W., Our Lady of the Pines Parish, Conifer
Lamar, Charles (CHI), Light of the World Parish, Littleton
Lee, William S., St. John the Baptist, Longmont
Linton, William J., (Retired)
Lujan, Edward, Sacred Heart, Denver
Lybarger, Warren G., St. John the Evangelist, Loveland
Martin, Gregory, St. Pius X, Aurora
Matz, Karl T., (Retired)
McDavid, Clarence G., Cure D'Ars, Denver
McKeown, John, St. Joseph, Fort Collins
Medenwaldt, Richard A., Nativity of Our Lord, Broomfield
Meilinger, Joseph H., St. Mary, Greeley
Menogan, Guffie E., St. Ignatius Loyola, Denver
Mich, Lawrence E., (Retired)
Milhone, Gordon G., All Souls, Denver
Miller, Gary E., Sts. Peter and Paul Parish, Wheat Ridge
Mooneyham, Eugene, Light of the World, Littleton
Oehrle, Leo A., Immaculate Heart of Mary, Northglenn
Padilla, Carlos L., (Retired)
Paulson, Joel J., St. Jude, Lakewood
Pelis, Richard F., St. Rita, Nederland
Pilger, Rex H., Jr., Unassigned
Polak, Leonard E., Holy Family, Denver
Pontillo, John E., St. Mark, Westminster
Power, Winfield S., (Retired)
Quinlan, Thomas, St. Jude, Lakewood
Quintana, Lloyd, Holy Trinity, Westminster
Rael, Gilbert E., Adams County Jail, St. Augustine, Brighton
Reynolds, Philip J., Diaconal Ministry in the Diocese of Pueblo
Ritchey, Ronald T., Denver County Jail, Holy Cross, Thornton
Ritter, Ron, Sacred Heart, Denver
Ritz, Michael P., Jr., (Retired)
Rogge, Gary, St. Thomas More, Englewood
Rompot, Vernon L., Holy Ghost Church, Denver
Ruiz, Nehemias (SEA), St. John the Baptist, Longmont
Runck, Merle, D.D.S., Immaculate Conception, Lafayette
Salvato, Mark, St. Vincent De Paul, Denver
Sanchez, Alfredo (SFE), St. Mark Parish, Westminister
Sanchez, Maclovio, (Retired)
Sanchez, Wilfred G., St. Elizabeth, Denver
Sandoval, Alfonso M., Our Lady of Guadalupe, Denver
Sandoval, Henry, (Retired)
Scholz, Franz, On Duty in the Diocese of San Diego
Smith, John L., St. Joan of Arc, Arvada
Sorber, William M., Queen of Peace Parish, Aurora
Sprick, Charles B., (Retired)
Stephenson, Billy C., (Retired)
Sutton, Jack, Holy Name, Sheridan
Thunblom, John, St. Pius X Parish, Aurora
Tirgrath, Howard L., On Duty in the Diocese of Las Vegas
Torrez, Frederick L., St. Peter, Greeley
Trewartha, William D.P.M., St. Elizabeth Ann Seton, Fort Collins
Trujillo, Samuel R., Our Lady Mother of the Church, Commerce City
Ubowski, Chester W., Light of the World Parish, Littleton
Usera, Luis A., Sr., Ascension, Denver
Van Tam Le, Joseph, (Retired)
Vieria, Richard, Jefferson County Jail, St. Mary Magdalene Parish, Denver
Vigil, Arthur A., All Saints Parish, Denver
Vitello, Eugene, St. Catherine of Siena, Denver
Wager, Martin A., St. Louis, Englewood, Handicapped Ministry
Wall, James R., Sts. Peter and Paul, Wheat Ridge
Ward, William (SLC), St. Mary, Littleton
Waring, Lynn E., Immaculate Heart of Mary, Northglenn
Webster, Earl, Denver International Airport Chapel
Wilhelm, Martin A., St. Michael the Archangel, Aurora
Young, John Joseph, St. Rita, Nederland

INSTITUTIONS LOCATED IN THE ARCHDIOCESE

[A] SEMINARIES, RELIGIOUS OR SCHOLASTICATES

DENVER. *Redemptoris Mater House of Formation*, 3434 E. Arizona Ave., 80210. Tel: 303-733-2220; Fax: 303-733-2223. Revs. Angel Molina, Vice Rector; Florian Martin-Calama; Patricio Puche, Spiritual Dir. Priests 3; Diocesan Seminarians 18.

St. Andrew's Theatine House, 1050 S. Birch St., 80246. Theatine Fathers. Very Rev. Patrick Valdez, C.R., Prov. Supr.; Rev. Bart Nadal, C.R., Rector. In res. Rev. Angelo Urdiain, C.R.

St. Dominic Priory, 3005 W. 29th Ave., 80211. Tel: 303-455-3613. Province of St. Albert the Great & St. Martin De Porres. Rev. Michael G. Kyte, O.P.

[B] COLLEGES AND UNIVERSITIES

DENVER. *Regis University*, 3333 Regis Blvd., 80221-1099. Tel: 303-458-4100

For a complete listing, refer to the Colleges and Universities section.

[C] INTER-PAROCHIAL HIGH SCHOOLS

DENVER. *Holy Family High School*, 4343 Utica St., 80212. Tel: 303-458-8822. Sr. Mary Rose Lieb, O.S.F., Prin. Priests 1; Sisters 3; Lay Teachers 25; Students 305.

Machebeuf Catholic High School, 1958 Elm St., 80220. Tel: 303-322-1810. Bill Giddings, Prin. Sisters 1; Lay Teachers 18; Students 274.

[D] HIGH SCHOOLS, PRIVATE

DENVER. *J.K. Mullen High School, Corp.*, 3601 S. Lowell Blvd., 80236. Tel: 303-761-1764. Legal Title: *The Christian Brothers of J.K. Mullen High School.* Coed Day School. Brothers of the Christian Schools. Vincent J. Greco, Jr., Prin. Brothers 4; Sisters 4; Lay Teachers 51; Students 918.

AURORA. *Regis Jesuit High School*, 16300 E. Weaver Pl., 80016. Tel: 303-699-1598. Day School for Boys. Revs. Walter T. Sidney, S.J., Pres.; Chris Pramuk, Head of Theology; James J. Burshek, S.J., Supr.; Patrick J. Weiss, S.J.; Mr. Rick Sullivan, Prin.; Bro. Joe Gockel, S.J. Priests 3; Jesuit Scholastics 2; Brothers 1; Lay Teachers 73; Students 831.

ENGLEWOOD. *St. Mary's Academy High School*, 4545 S. University Blvd., 80110. Tel: 303-762-8300; Fax: 303-783-6201. Sisters of Loretto at the Foot of the Cross. Judith Baenen, Pres.; Jenifer Fox, Prin. Lay Teachers 21; Girls 280.

[E] ELEMENTARY SCHOOLS, PRIVATE

DENVER. *St. Mary's Academy Lower School.* (Grades PreK-5), 4545 S. University Blvd., 80110. Tel: 303-762-8300; Fax: 303-761-4146. Sisters of Loretto at the Foot of the Cross. Sr. Susan Swain, S.L., Prin. Sisters 1; Lay Teachers 38; Students 300.

ENGLEWOOD. *St. Mary's Academy, Middle School.* (Grades 6-8), 4545 S. University Blvd., 80110. Tel: 303-762-8300. Mike Radigan, Prin. Lay Teachers 20; Students 167.

[F] SPECIAL EDUCATION

DENVER. *Mt. St. Vincent's Home*, 4159 Lowell Blvd., 80211. Tel: 303-458-7220.
E-mail: msvhome@concentrix.net
Web site: www.nahse.org/member/st.vincent
Sr. Vickie Perkins, Exec. Dir. Sisters of Charity of Leavenworth 7; Students 60.

[G] MINISTRY TO THE HANDICAPPED

DENVER. *The Carron Center*, 1050 S. Birch St., 80222. Tel: 303-759-5150. Mrs. Cary Carron, Supvr.

Religious Education-Pastoral Care of Developmentally Disabled Persons, 3101 W. Hillside Pl., 80219. Tel: 303-934-1999. Rev. Lawrence M. Freeman, Dir.; Sr. Mary Catherine Widger, S.L., Assoc. Dir.; Sr. Sue Rogers, S.L., Asst. Dir.; Risna Dimas, Dir. Bridge Community Group Home. Religious education of approximately 400 mentally retarded children and adults; One 8 bed group home.

[H] GENERAL HOSPITALS

*DENVER. *Centura Health*, 1601 Lowell Blvd., 80204
For a complete listing, refer to the Hospitals section.

Mercy Medical Center, 1650 Fillmore St., 80206
For a complete listing, refer to the Hospitals section.

Provenant Acute Long Stay Hospital, 1601 Lowell Blvd., 80204
For a complete listing, refer to the Hospitals section.

Provenant Home Health and Eldercare Services, 1560 Meade St., 80204
For a complete listing, refer to the Hospitals section.

St. Anthony Hospital Central, 4231 W. 16th Ave., 80204
For a complete listing, refer to the Hospitals section.

St. Anthony Hospital North, 2551 W. 84th Ave., 80030
For a complete listing, refer to the Hospitals section.

St. Joseph Hospital, 1835 Franklin St., 80218. Tel: 303-837-7111
For a complete listing, refer to the Hospitals section.

The Villas at Sunny Acres, 2501 E. 104th Ave., 80233
For a complete listing, refer to the Hospitals section.

[I] HOMES FOR AGED

DENVER. *Francis Heights, Inc.*, 2626 Osceola St., 80212. Tel: 303-433-6268
For a complete listing, refer to the Special Care Facilities section.

**Gardens at St. Elizabeth*, 2835 W. 32nd Ave., 80211. Tel: 303-477-4442.
Web site: www.centura.org
For a complete listing, refer to the Special Care Facilities section.

Mullen Home, 3629 W. 29th Ave., 80211. Tel: 303-433-7221; Fax: 303-455-9184
For a complete listing, refer to the Special Care Facilities section.

[J] HOMES AND SERVICES FOR AGED AND INFIRM

DENVER. *Hospice of Peace*, 1601A Lowell Blvd., 80204-1545. Tel: 303-575-8393; 575-8350
For a complete listing, refer to the Special Care Facilities section.

[K] HOUSING FOR THE ELDERLY AND FOR FAMILIES (LOW INCOME)

DENVER. *Archdiocesan Housing Committee*, 1544 Pearl St., 80203. Tel: 303-830-0215; Fax: 303-830-2885
For a complete listing, refer to the Special Care Facilities section.

Clare Gardens, Inc., 2626 Osceola St., 80212. Tel: 303-433-6268
For a complete listing, refer to the Special Care Facilities section.
Damen House, P.O. Box 11580, 80211. Tel: 303-433-4280
For a complete listing, refer to the Special Care Facilities section.
Dayspring Villa, Inc., 3777 W. 16th Ave., 80211. Tel: 630-455-5066
For a complete listing, refer to the Special Care Facilities section.

WESTMINSTER. *Clare of Assisi Homes - Westminster, Inc.*, 2451 W. 82 Pl., 80003. Tel: 303-427-4406; 462-9271 (Corporate)
For a complete listing, refer to the Special Care Facilities section.
Villa Maria, Inc., 2461 W. 82nd Pl., 80030-4065. Tel: 303-426-1518; Fax: 303-426-4301
For a complete listing, refer to the Special Care Facilities section.

[L] CATHOLIC CHARITIES & COMMUNITY SERVICES

DENVER. *Catholic Charities and Community Services of the Archdiocese of Denver, Inc.*, 2525 W. Alameda Ave., 80219. Tel: 303-742-0828; Fax: 303-742-0774.
E-mail: ccaofd@aol.com
James H. Mauck, Pres., Admin. Day Care Centers 4; Total Assisted 500. Special Centers for Social Services 12; Total Assisted 50,000.
Samaritan House, 2301 Lawrence St., 80205. Tel: 303-294-0241. Employment Resource Center, 2525 W. Alameda Ave., 80219. Tel: 303-742-0828.
Shelter for Homeless.
Transitional Housing, Courtyard Commons, 1122 Pearl St., 80203. Tel: 303-860-9098.
The Carron Center, 1050 S. Birch St., 80246. Tel: 303-759-5150.
Catholic Charities Child Development Center, 1155 Decatur St., 80204. Tel: 303-629-5466.
The Family Center, 2525 W. Alameda Ave., 80219. Tel: 303-742-0828. Counseling, Adoption, Foster Care & Senior Services.
Camp Santa Maria, Grant. Tel: 303-238-0521. 2525 W. Alameda Ave., 80219. Tel: 303-642-0828. Camping for Children, Youth & Seniors.
Immigration Services, 2525 W. Alameda Ave., 80219. Tel: 303-458-0222.
Community Organizing Center, 2525 W. Alameda Ave., 80219. Tel: 303-742-0828.
Mulroy Neighborhood Center, 3550 W. 13th Ave., 80204. Tel: 303-892-1540.
Employment Resource Center, 2525 W. Alameda Ave., 80219. Tel: 303-742-0828.
SHARE Colorado, 9360 Federal Blvd., Federal Heights, 80221. Tel: 303-428-0400.
Homeless Prevention Services, 9360 Federal Blvd., 80219. Tel: 303-412-9809.
Catholic Charities Northern, 460 Linden Center Dr., Fort Collins, 80524. Tel: 970-484-5010. Shelter for Homeless, Job Bank, Emergency Assistance, Senior Services, Farm Labor Housing Corp.
Catholic Charities - Western Slope, P.O. Box 966, Minturn, 81645. Tel: 970-479-1741.
Catholic Charities Northern - Greely, 1311 11th St., Greely, 80631. Tel: 970-353-6433. Shelter for the Homeless & Senior Services.
Aurora Family Assistance Center, 1468 Iola St., Aurora, 80010. Tel: 303-363-9543. Services for Developmentally Disabled Adults.
North Area Cares Emergency Assistance, 7280-A Irving, #106-A, Westminster, 80030. Tel: 303-427-6256. Services for Developmentally Disabled Adults.
Northeast E.A. Center, 6621 E.72nd Ave., Commerce City, 80022. Tel: 303-287-1127. Services for Developmentally Disabled Adults.
Central Emergency Assistance Center, 1440 Poplar St., 80220. Tel: 303-399-1558. Services for Developmentally Disabled Adults.
Southwest Emergency Assistance Center, 902 S. Sheridan Blvd., 80601. Tel: 303-922-5205. Services for Developmentally Disabled Adults.
Brighton Emergency Assistance Center, 178 S. Sixth St., Brighton, 80601. Tel: 303-654-1040. Services for Developmentally Disabled Adults.
Archdiocesan Housing Committee, Inc.: Archdiocesan Family Housing, Inc., 1544 Pearl St., 80203. Mr. Donald A. Smith, Contact Person.
Archdiocesan Housing Committee, Inc.: Cathedral Plaza, Inc., 1544 Pearl St., 80203. Mr. Donald A. Smith, Contact Person.
Archdiocesan Housing Committee, Inc.: Marian Plaza, Inc., 1544 Pearl St., 80203. Mr. Donald A. Smith, Contact Person.
Archdiocesan Housing Committee, Inc.: Holy Family Plaza, Inc., 1544 Pearl St., 80203. Mr. Donald A. Smith, Contact Person.

[M] MONASTERIES AND RESIDENCES OF PRIESTS AND BROTHERS

DENVER. *Annunciation Friary*, 3621 Humboldt St., 80205. Tel: 303-296-1024. Capuchin Friars. In res. Revs. Gene J. Emrisek, O.F.M.Cap., Guardian; Edward Judy, O.F.M.Cap., Vicar; Matthew Gross, O.F.M.Cap.; David Songy, O.F.M.Cap.; Gregory Beyer, O.F.M.Cap.; Cyrus Gallagher, O.F.M.Cap.; John Toepfer, O.F.M.Cap.
Christian Brothers (F.S.C.)- St. Joseph Community, 3601 S. Lowell Blvd., 80236. Tel: 303-295-2515; 761-1764. Bro. Mariano Lopez, Contact.
Congregation of the Mission Midwest Province: De Paul House, 2340 S. University Blvd., 80210. Tel: 303-698-1618; Fax: 303-777-0468. Revs. John H. Karssen, C.M., Supr.; Richard R. Ryan, C.M.; E. Hartrick Sullivan, C.M.; Thomas J. Nelson, C.M.; John Q. O'Connell, C.M.
Holy Trinity Friary, 2924 W. 43rd Ave., 80211. Tel: 303-561-1474.
E-mail: Charlieofm@aol.com
Rev. Chas. Martinez, O.F.M., Guardian. Priests 3; Brothers 2; Students 2.
Loyola Parish - Jesuit Community, 2305 Gaylord St., 80205-5627. Tel: 303-322-8042; Fax: 303-322-2927. Revs. C. Thomas Jost, S.J.; John F. Brady, S.J.; Randall C. Hall, S.J.
Maryknoll Fathers, Catholic Foreign Mission Society of America (Legal Title), 4460 Federal Blvd., 80211. Tel: 303-455-5669; Fax: 303-455-5753.
E-mail: mkldenver@igc.org
Rev. Joseph J. McGahren, M.M.; Bro. Francis Dolphin, M.M.
The Redemptorists/Denver Province, Provincial Residence, Box 300399, 80203-0399. Tel: 303-370-0035; Fax: 303-370-0036. Res., 2130 E. Fourteenth Ave., 80206. Very Rev. Richard Thibodeau, C.Ss.R., Prov. Supr.; Revs. J. Robert Fenili, C.Ss.R., Prov. Vicar; Stephen Meyer, C.Ss.R., Prov. Consultor; John Steingraeber, C.Ss.R., Co-Dir., Financial Svcs.; Bro. Thomas Wright, C.Ss.R., Co-Dir., Financial Svcs. Priests 21; Brothers 2.
Serving abroad: Most Rev. Clarence Duhart, C.Ss.R., 123/19 Ruam Rudi Ln., Bangkok, Thailand, 10330. Rev. Alfred Novak, C.Ss.R., Rua Consulheiro Sinimbu, 83200 Paranagua, Parana, Brazil. Revs. Anthony Smith, C.Ss.R.; Joseph W. Tobin, C.Ss.R., Casa Sant'Alfonso, C.P. 2458, 00100 Rome, Italy. Revs. William Cleary, C.Ss.R.; William Peterson, C.Ss.R.; Robert Wirth, C.Ss.R.; John Willett, C.Ss.R.; Bro. Daniel Hall, C.Ss.R., P.O. Box 29585 Secretariat, Bodija, Ibadan, Oyo State, Nigeria. Rev. William Fitzgerald, C.Ss.R., C.P. 400, 48900 Juazeiro, Bahia, Brazil. Rev. Harold Thiel, C.Ss.R., 88 Chotana Rd., T. Chang Phuek A. Muang, Chaing Mai 50300, Thailand.
Serving elsewhere, not listed: Rev. John McPhee, C.Ss.R., 61847 Glenwood Ter., Washington, MI, 49084. Rev. Thomas Fransiscus, C.Ss.R., The Tribunal, 515 Court St., Reno, NV, 89501. Rev. Pascal Dreici, C.Ss.R., 1035 E. Walthen, Fresno, CA, 93710. Rev. Ricardo Elford, C.Ss.R., P.O. Box 574, Cortaro, AZ, 85652. Rev. Joseph Nuttmann, C.Ss.R., P.O. Box 235, Carlin, NV, 89822. Revs. Richard Strass, C.Ss.R.; Roderick Garvey, C.Ss.R., P.O. Box 207, Seward, AK, 99664.
Regis Jesuit Community (The Jesuits at Regis University), Jesuit House M12, 3333 Regis Blvd., 80221-1099. Tel: 303-458-4100; Fax: 303-964-5525. Revs. Richard W. Dunphy, S.J., Rector; John J. Callahan, S.J.; David M. Clarke, S.J.; Thomas W. Cummings, S.J.; James B. Guyer, S.J.; Edward L. Maginnis, S.J.; Edward T. Oakes, S.J.; Patrick H. O'Liddy, S.J.; James S. Richard, S.J.; John K. Ridgway, S.J.; James G. Sampson, S.J.; Michael J. Sheeran, S.J.; Charles M. Shelton, S.J.; John J. Vowells, S.J.
St. Francis of Assisi Friary, 3553 Wyandot St., 80211-2948. Tel: 303-477-5542; Fax: 303-477-6925. In res. Rev. Harvey P. Dinkel, O.F.M.Cap., Vicar, Exec. Sec./Treas.; Very Rev. David Gottschalk, O.F.M.Cap., Prov. Min., Guardian; Revs. Thomas More Janeck, O.F.M.Cap., Chap. Poor Clares; John Lager, O.F.M.Cap., Dir. Devel.; Eric Lindbloom, O.F.M.; Malachy R. McBride, O.F.M. Cap.; Regis Scanlon, O.F.M.Cap., Preaching Ministry; William Kraus, O.F.M.Cap., Vocations. Total In Res. 8; Total Staff 1.
Xavier Jesuit Center, 3450 W. 53rd, 80221-6568. Tel: 303-480-3900; Fax: 303-433-6235. Revs. Thomas W. Cummings, S.J., Supr.; Richard F. Bocklage, S.J.; Joseph F. Bona, S.J.; John J. Campbell, S.J.; Robert R. DeRouen, S.J.; Edward F. Flaherty, S.J.; John C. Futrell, S.J.; Harry E. Hoewischer, S.J.; Carl G. Kloster, S.J.; Timothy J. Lawless, S.J.; William T. Miller, S.J.; Anthony J. Short, S.J.; James C. Sunderland, S.J.; John P. Teeling, S.J.; Edward A. Thro, S.J.; William S. Udick, S.J.; James P. Walsh, S.J.; Stephen T. Yavorsky, S.J.; Bros. Herbert A. Bussen, S.J.; John C. Fava, S.J.; A. Albert Knoll, S.J.

AURORA. *Regis Jesuit High School - Jesuit Community*, 16810 E. Caley Ave., 80016. Tel: 303-699-1598; 690-4782. Revs. Philip G. Steele, S.J., Supvr.; Walter T. Sidney, S.J.; David A. Wayne, S.J.; Bro. Joseph L. Gockel, S.J.

SNOWMASS. *St. Benedict's Monastery*, 1012 Monastery Rd., 81654. Tel: 970-927-3311; Fax: 970-927-3399.
E-mail: retreat@rof.net
Web site: www.snowmass.org
The Order of Cistercians of the Strict Observance (Trappists). Rt. Rev. Joseph Boyle, O.C.S.O.; Revs. Thomas Keating, O.C.S.O.; Theophane Boyd, O.C.S.O.; Daniel Kelliher, O.C.S.O.; William Meninger, O.C.S.O. Professed Monks 12; Novices 1.

[N] CONVENTS AND RESIDENCES FOR SISTERS

DENVER. *Dominican Sisters of Hope*, 2501 Gaylord St., 80205. Tel: 303-322-1413; Fax: 303-322-1608. Sr. Anne Frances Goedert, O.P., Contact. Dominican Sisters Home Health Agency of Denver, Inc. served 105 patients. Sisters 3.
Marycrest Convent Franciscan Sisters, 2851 W. 52nd Ave., 80221. Tel: 303-433-2276; 458-6270; Fax: 303-433-5865. Sr. Gloria Shuffer, O.S.F., Provincial Min. Provincial Motherhouse of Sisters of St. Francis of Penance and Christian Charity, Province of the Sacred Heart #1630. Sr. Helen Cassino, Min. Special Center for Social Assistance. Total Assisted 5,000; Total Staff 2. Retreat Center. Total In Res. 100. Sisters 30.
Missionaries of Charity, 1840 Grant St., 80203. Tel: 303-860-8040. Sr. M. Shanti Prabha, M.C., Supr. & Contact. Total Assisted 50.
Monastery of Our Lady of Light (Capuchin Poor Clares). (Strict Enclosure), 3325 Pecos, 80211. Tel: 303-458-6339. Legal Title: *Capuchin Poor Clares of Denver, Inc.* Mother Maria de Cristo Palafox, O.S.C.Cap., Abbess; Rev. Thomas More Janeck, O.F.M.Cap., Chap. Sisters 9.
Queen of Peace Convent, 5360 Columbine Rd., 80221. Tel: 303-477-9139. Sisters of St. Francis of Penance and Christian Charity. Sr. Lucy King, O.S.F. Sisters 4.
Sisters of the New Covenant, 10620 Livingston Dr., 80234. Tel: 303-451-8677; Fax: 303-438-9556. Pious Union. Sr. Angeline Bukowiecki, S.N.C. Sisters 3.

GOLDEN. *Mother Cabrini Shrine*, 20189 Cabrini Blvd., 80401. Tel: 303-526-0758; Fax: 303-526-9795.
E-mail: mcshrine@den-cabrini-shrine.org
Web site: www.den-cabrini-shrine.org
Sr. Bernadette Casciano, M.S.C., Contact; Thomas M. James, Registered Agent. Missionary Sisters of the Sacred Heart of Jesus (M.S.C.) 4.

LAKEWOOD. *Benedictine Sisters of Denver, Inc.*, Spirit of Life Monastery, 10760 W. Glennon Dr., 80226. Tel: 303-986-9234. Sr. Charlotte Redpath, O.S.B., Prioress. Sisters 2; Total Staff 2; Total Assisted in Counselling 60.

LITTLETON. *Carmel of Holy Spirit*, 6138 S. Gallup St., 80120-2702. Tel: 303-798-4176. Discalced Carmelites (O.C.D.). Mother Judith of the Immaculate Heart, D.C., Prioress; Rev. Gaston Muyombo (Zaire), Chap. Sisters 9.
Loretto Center, 4000 S. Wadsworth, 80123-1309. Tel: 303-986-1541; Fax: 303-986-8453. Sr. Ann Lucille Ryan, S.L., Coord. Sisters 34.
Sisters of Benedict of Colorado, Inc., 4264 W. Ponds View Dr., 80123. Tel: 303-795-2378. Sr. Judith Elms, O.S.B., Supr.

VIRGINIA DALE. *Abbey of St. Walburga*, 32109 N. U.S. Hwy. 287, 80536-8942. Tel: 970-472-0612. Mother Maria-Thomas Beil, O.S.B., Abbess. Benedictine Nuns 20; Novices 2; Postulants 1.

[O] RETREAT CENTERS

ALLENSPARK. *St. Malo Conference, Retreat Center*, 10758 Hwy. 7, 80510. Tel: 303-747-2892; 970-586-6061 (Estes Park); 303-444-5177 (Denver); Fax: 303-747-2892. Blake Fischer, Dir.

[P] CAMPUS MINISTRY

DENVER. *Auraria Campus.*
Community College of Denver.
Metropolitan State College.
University of Colorado at Denver. Rev. Gary A. Mueller, C.M.
Vincentian Fathers.
St. Elizabeth Parish.
St. Francis Center, 1030 St. Francis Center, 80204. Tel: 303-534-4014; 556-3864.
Director of Campus Ministry, 1300 S. Steele St., 80210. Tel: 303-715-3178; Fax: 303-715-2042.
Web site: www.archden.org/archden
Mr. Thomas McCabe, Dir. Youth, Adult & Campus Ministry.
Regis University (Denver), 3333 Regis Blvd., Ste. 200, 80221. Tel: 303-458-4153; Fax: 303-964-5530.
E-mail: kschaefer@regis.edu
Rev. John Vowells, S.J.; Mrs. Kathleen Schaefer, Dir.; Mr. Ken Phillips, Asst. Dir.

University of Denver, Catholic Campus Ministry House, 1795 S. Williams St., 80210. Tel: 303-778-7657. Sr. Maria Regis, S.C.J.

BOULDER. *University of Colorado (Boulder)*, St. Thomas Aquinas Parish, 904 Fourteenth St., 80302. Tel: 303-443-8383; Fax: 303-443-8399. Revs. Thomas J. Holahan, C.S.P.; George R. Fitzgerald, C.S.P.; Joseph A. Ciccone, C.S.P.; Ms. Sandy Swegel; Ms. Kathleen Ahl.

FORT COLLINS. *Colorado State University (Fort Collins)*, John XXIII University Center, 1220 University Ave., 80521. Tel: 303-484-3356; Fax: 303-484-3434. Rev. Robert L. Amundsen; Ms. Kathy Kautzky.

GOLDEN. *Colorado School of Mines (Golden)*, 15755 W. 3rd Ave., 80401. Tel: 303-273-3460. Mr. Edward Mantz.

GREELEY. *University of Northern Colorado (Greeley)*, St. Peter's Parish, 915 12th St., 80631. Tel: 970-352-1060; Fax: 970-352-1062. Rev. Gregory K. Ames.

LITTLETON. *Arapahoe Community College*, c/o Al Rodriguez, 2500 W. College Ave., P.O. Box 9002, 80160-9002. Tel: 303-797-5910; Fax: 303-797-5935.

RANGELY. *Colorado Northwestern Community College (Rangely)*, 109 S. Stanolind Ave., P.O. Box 370, 81648. Tel: 303-675-8935; Fax: 303-878-5736 (Meeker). Rev. Roger L. Lascelle; Deacon George G. Fortunato.

STEAMBOAT SPRINGS. *Colorado Mountain College*, c/o Holy Name Catholic Church, P.O. Box 774198, 80477-4198. Tel: 970-879-0671; Fax: 970-879-7406. Rev. George M. Schroeder.

STERLING. *Northeastern Junior College (Sterling)*, St. Anthony Church, 327 S. Third St., 80751. Tel: 303-525-6422. Very Rev. Robert G. Whipkey, Jr., V.F.; Michael Wolsbauer.

WESTMINSTER. *Front Range Community College*, c/o Mr. Frank Sullivan, 3645 W. 112 Ave., 80030. Tel: 303-404-5282; Fax: 303-404-2178.
E-mail: fsulliva@mosquito.frcc.cccoes.edu
Web site: http://frcc.cc.co.us

[Q] MISCELLANEOUS LISTINGS

DENVER. *Blessed Sacrament Catholic Educational Foundation*, 4930 Montview Blvd., 80207. Tel: 303-355-7361. Rev. Roland Freeman, Exec. Officer & Contact Person.

Catholic Alumni Club of Denver, Inc. P.O. Box 6111, Cherry Creek Station, 80206. Tel: 303-756-7659.

Catholic Health Initiatives, 1999 Broadway, Ste. 2605, 80202. Tel: 303-298-9100; Fax: 303-298-9690. Patricia A. Cahill, J.D., Pres. & CEO.

**Colorado Vincentian Volunteers*, 1732 Pearl St., 80203. Tel: 303-863-8141. Bill Jaster, Exec. Dir.

Denver Catholic Register, Archdiocesan Religious Newspaper, 1300 S. Steele St., 80210. Tel: 303-715-3123. Greg Kail, General Mgr.

Francis of Assisi Foundation of Colorado, Inc., 2626 Osceola St., 80211. Tel: 303-433-6268. Franciscan Sisters, Daughters of the Sacred Hearts of Jesus and Mary, (Wheaton, IL). Linda Hilton, Admin.

Hmong Catholic Community, All Saints Parish, 2559 S. Federal Blvd., 80219. Tel: 303-922-3758; 429-6427.

Kateri Catholic Indian Community of Colorado, 2340 S. University Blvd #32, 80210. Tel: 303-778-5966.
E-mail: quentin@priest.com
Rev. John Q. O'Connell, C.M.

Marycrest Health System, 2861 W. 52nd Ave., 80221. Tel: 303-458-8611; Fax: 303-477-4105. Dale Budde, Pres.

Mercy Housing, Inc., 601 E. 18th Ave., Ste. 150, 80203. Tel: 303-830-3300; Fax: 303-830-3301.
E-mail: mail@mercyhousing.org
Affordable Housing Properties. Sr. Lillian Murphy, Pres. Units 677; Total Served 1,700. Day Care Centers 3; Total Served 200.

Mercy Services Corp., 601 E. 18th Ave., Ste. 150, 80203. Tel: 303-830-3300. Sr. Lillian Murphy, R.S.M., Pres.

Decatur Place, 601 E. 18th Ave., Ste. 150, 80203. Tel: 303-830-3300. Gloria Munoz, R.S.M., Pres.

Homes Again Program, 601 E. 18th Ave., Ste. 150, 80203. Tel: 303-830-3300. Gloria Munoz, Pres.

Mercy Housing Colorado, 601 E. 18th Ave., Ste. 150, 80203. Tel: 303-830-3300. Gloria Munoz, Pres.

Mercy Properties, Inc., 601 E. 18th Ave., Ste. 150, 80203. Tel: 303-830-3397. Lillian Murphy, R.S.M., Pres.

Willow Street Apartments, 601 E. 18th Ave., Ste. 150, 80203. Tel: 303-830-3397. Eddie Muniz, Contact.

Mercy Holly Park East, 601 E. 18th Ave., Ste. 150, 80203. Tel: 303-830-3397. Eddie Muniz, Contact.

Mercy Holly Park West, 601 E. 18th Ave., Ste. 150, 80203. Tel: 303-830-3397. Eddie Muniz, Contact.

Mercy Green Mountain Manor, 601 E. 18th Ave., Ste. 150, 80203. Tel: 303-830-3397. Eddie Muniz, Contact.

S.E.T. of Colorado, Inc., dba Health S.E.T., Raleigh Bldg., 4200 N. Conejos #436, 80204. Tel: 303-534-8002. Jim Elfline, Exec. Dir. Total Staff 6; Total Volunteers 130; Total Assisted 4,400.

Sacred Heart House of Denver, 2844 Lawrence, 80205. Tel: 303-296-6686. Sr. Maureen Kottenstette, C.S.J., Exec. Dir.

Saint Joseph Hospital Foundation, 1835 Franklin St., 80218. Tel: 303-837-7043; Fax: 303-837-7115. Roger A. Goodwin, Exec. Dir.

St. Vincent de Paul Stores, Inc., 2525 W. Alameda Ave., 80219. Tel: 303-742-0828; Fax: 303-742-0774. Mr. James Mauck, C.E.O.

St. Vincent DePaul Society Denver-Metro Council, 1300 S. Steele St., 80210. Tel: 303-777-8367. Leonard J. Langenderfer, Pres.; Robert S. Huff, Exec. Sec.

Seeds of Hope Charitable Trust Fund, 1300 S. Steele St., 80210. Tel: 303-715-3199; Fax: 303-715-2041.
E-mail: seeds@archden.org
Mr. Haven C. Moses, Exec. Dir.

**Sisters of St. Francis Foundation*, 2851 W. 52nd Ave., 80221. Tel: 303-458-6270; Fax: 303-433-5865. Sisters of St. Francis. Sr. Kathryn Zochol, Contact.

ARVADA.
**Buena Vista, Inc.*, P.O. Box 745475, 80006-5475. Tel: 303-426-6622; 941-947-8545; Fax: 303-657-9428.
E-mail: 74541.165@compuserve
Web site: www.buenavista.org
Peg Bisgrove, Pres.

ENGLEWOOD. *Queen of the Apostles Mission Association, Inc.*, 8035 S. Quebec St., 80112-3118. Tel: 303-770-3240; Fax: 303-770-0415.
E-mail: qama@aol.com
Matt Werner, Pres.

Sisters of Charity Health Services Colorado - SCHSC, 5570 DTC Pkwy., 80111. Tel: 303-290-6500. Mr. Gary Susnara, Pres. & CEO. Affiliate of Catholic Health Initiatives.

ESTES PARK.
**Our Lady of Tenderness, Poustinia*, Box 4311, 80517. Tel: 970-227-5513. Lucille Dupuis, Dir.

GLENDALE.
**Havican Insurance Co.*, 4100 E. Mississippi Ave., Ste. 1500, 80222. Sisters of the Holy Cross.

LITTLETON. *Auxiliary of Mother Cabrini Shrine*, 7295 S. Steele Cir., 80122. Tel: 303-771-4386. Zoraide Scordo, Founder.

RELIGIOUS INSTITUTES OF MEN REPRESENTED IN THE ARCHDIOCESE

For further details refer to the corresponding bracketed number in the Religious Institutes of Men or Women section.

[0200]—*Benedictine Monks.* (Canon City, CO).—O.S.B.
[]—*Bethlehem Fathers.*—S.M.B.
[0330]—*Brothers of the Christian Schools.*—F.S.C.
[0460]—*Brothers of the Poor of St. Francis.*—C.F.P.
[0470]—*The Capuchin Friars.* (Denver, CO).—O.F.M.Cap.
[0350]—*Cistercians of the Strict Observance-Trappists.* (St. Benedict Abbey).—O.C.S.O.
[]—*Congregation of Mother Coredemptrix.* (Carthage, MO).—C.M.C.
[1330]—*Congregation of the Mission.* (Western Prov.).—C.M.
[0520]—*Franciscan Friars.* (Provs. of the Most Holy Name of Jesus & Our Lady of Guadalupe).—O.F.M.
[0690]—*Jesuit Fathers and Brothers.* (Missouri, Milwaukee, Oregon, Maryland Provs.).—S.J.
[0800]—*Maryknoll.* (Denver).—M.M.
[0430]—*Order of Preachers-Dominicans.* (Prov. of St. Albert the Great).—O.P.
[1030]—*Paulist Fathers.*—C.S.P.
[1070]—*Redemptorist Fathers.* (St. Louis Prov.).—C.SS.R.
[1240]—*Servites.* (Western Prov.).—O.S.M.
[1300]—*Theatine Fathers.* (Rome, Italy).—C.R.

RELIGIOUS INSTITUTES OF WOMEN REPRESENTED IN THE ARCHDIOCESE

[0190]—*Benedictine Nuns.*—O.S.B.
[0230]—*Benedictine Sisters of Pontifical Jurisdiction.* (Colorado Springs, CO; Boulder, CO; Denver, CO; Oklahoma City, OK).—O.S.B.
[]—*Capuchin Poor Clares.*—O.S.C.Cap.
[3110]—*Congregation of Our Lady of the Retreat in the Cenacle.*—R.C.
[2100]—*Congregation of the Humility of Mary.* (Davenport, IA).—C.H.M.
[1780]—*Congregation of the Sisters of the Third Order of St. Francis of Perpetual Adoration.* (La Crosse, WI).—F.S.P.A.
[0760]—*Daughters of Charity of St. Vincent de Paul.*—D.C.
[0960]—*Daughters of Wisdom.*—D.W.
[0420]—*Discalced Carmelite Nuns.*—O.C.D.
[1070-14]—*Dominican Sisters.*—O.P.
[1070-16]—*Dominican Sisters.*—O.P.
[1070-18]—*Dominican Sisters.*—O.P.
[1070-24]—*Dominican Sisters.*—O.P.
[1070-28]—*Dominican Sisters.*—O.P.
[1070-03]—*Dominican Sisters.* (Sinsinawa).—O.P.
[]—*Dominican Sisters of the Congregation of St. Cecilia.* (Nashville).
[1240]—*Franciscan Sisters, Daughters of the Sacred Hearts of Jesus and Mary.* (Wheaton, IL).—O.S.F.
[2575]—*Institute of the Sisters of Mercy of the Americas.*—R.S.M.
[2340]—*Little Sisters of the Poor.*—L.S.P.
[2710]—*Missionaries of Charity.*—M.C.
[]—*Missionaries of Charity of Mary Immaculate.*—M.C.M.I.
[2860]—*Missionary Sisters of the Sacred Heart.*—M.S.C.
[3130]—*Our Lady of Victory Missionary Sisters.*—O.L.V.M.
[1680]—*School Sisters of St. Francis.* (Milwaukee, WI).—O.S.F.
[0440]—*Sisters of Charity of Cincinnati, Ohio.*—S.C.
[0480]—*Sisters of Charity of Leavenworth, Kansas.*—S.C.L.
[0430]—*Sisters of Charity of the Blessed Virgin Mary.*—B.V.M.
[2360]—*Sisters of Loretto at the Foot of the Cross.* (Nerinx, KY).—S.L.
[2990]—*Sisters of Notre Dame.*—S.N.D.
[1705]—*Sisters of St. Francis of Assisi.* (Milwaukee, WI).—O.S.F.
[1630]—*Sisters of St. Francis of Penance and Christian Charity.*—O.S.F.
[1640]—*Sisters of St. Francis of Perpetual Adoration.* (Colorado Springs, CO).—O.S.F.
[3830-05]—*Sisters of St. Joseph.*—C.S.J.
[3830-15]—*Sisters of St. Joseph.*—C.S.J.
[3840]—*Sisters of St. Joseph of Carondelet.*—C.S.J.
[3930]—*Sisters of St. Joseph of the Third Order of St. Francis.* (Immaculate Conception Prov.).—S.S.J.-T.O.S.F.
[1830]—*Sisters of the Good Shepherd.*—R.G.S.
[]—*Sisters of the New Covenant.*—S.N.C.
[3260]—*Sisters of the Precious Blood.* (Dayton, OH).—C.PP.S.
[1720]—*Sisters of the Third Order Regular of St. Francis of the Congregation of Our Lady of Lourdes.* (Rochester, MN).—O.S.F.

ARCHDIOCESAN CEMETERIES

WHEAT RIDGE. *Archdiocese of Denver Mortuary at Mt. Olivet, Inc.*, 12801 W. 44th Ave., 80033. Tel: 303-425-9511.

Mount Olivet Cemetery, 12801 W. 44th Ave., 80033. Tel: 303-424-7785.

NECROLOGY

† Hoffman, Rev. Msgr. Robert F., (Retired). —Died May 12, 1997.

Diocese of Des Moines

(Dioecesis Desmoinensis)

Most Reverend

JOSEPH L. CHARRON, C.PP.S., S.T.D.

Bishop of Des Moines; ordained June 3, 1967; appointed Titular Bishop of Bencenna and Auxiliary Bishop of Saint Paul and Minneapolis November 6, 1989; consecrated January 25, 1990; appointed Bishop of Des Moines November 12, 1993.

Chancery: 601 Grand Ave., P.O. Box 1816, Des Moines, IA, 50306. Tel.: 515-243-7653; Fax: 515-237-5070.

Web site address: http://members.aol.com/cathdiodm

E-mail address: cathdiodm@aol.com

ERECTED BY POPE S. PIUS X, AUGUST 12, 1911.

Square Miles 12,446.

Legal Title: "The Roman Catholic Diocese of Des Moines."

Comprises that part of the State of Iowa which is bounded on the east by the eastern boundaries of the Counties of Polk, Warren, Lucas and Wayne; on the south by the State of Missouri; on the west by the Missouri River; and on the north by the northern boundaries of the Counties of Harrison, Shelby, Audubon, Guthrie, Dallas and Polk.

PATRONS OF THE DIOCESE: I. BLESSED VIRGIN MARY QUEEN; II. POPE SAINT PIUS X. Diocese solemnly consecrated to the Immaculate Heart of Mary on May 16, 1948.

For legal titles of parishes and diocesan institutions, consult the Chancery Office.

STATISTICAL OVERVIEW

Personnel	
Bishop	1
Priests: Diocesan Active in Diocese	87
Priests: Active Outside Diocese	4
Priests: Diocesan in Foreign Missions	1
Priests: Retired, Sick or Absent	24
Number of Diocesan Priests	116
Religious Priests in Diocese	10
Extern Priests in Diocese	3
Ordinations:	
Diocesan Priests	3
Permanent Deacons	6
Permanent Deacons in Diocese	61
Total Brothers	8
Total Sisters	119
Parishes	
Parishes	87
With Resident Pastor:	
Resident Diocesan Priests	58
Resident Religious Priests	3
Without Resident Pastor:	
Administered by Priests	25
Administered by Permanent Deacons	1
Missions	1
Professional Ministry Personnel:	
Brothers	5
Sisters	12
Lay Ministers	5
Welfare	
Catholic Hospitals	3
Total Assisted	302,963
Health Care Centers	1
Total Assisted	522,056
Homes for the Aged	1
Total Assisted	201
Specialized Homes	1
Total Assisted	200
Special Centers for Social Services	4
Total Assisted	37,082
Educational	
Diocesan Students in Other Seminaries	4
Total Seminarians	4
Colleges and Universities	1
Total Students	440
High Schools, Diocesan and Parish	2
Total Students	1,468
Elementary Schools, Diocesan and Parish	15
Total Students	4,644
Catechesis/Religious Education:	
High School Students	2,099
Elementary Students	9,822
Total Students Under Catholic Instruction	18,477
Teachers in the Diocese:	
Priests	5
Brothers	1
Sisters	11
Lay Teachers	302
Vital Statistics	
Receptions into the Church:	
Infant Baptism Totals	1,977
Adult Baptism Totals	238
Received into Full Communion	485
First Communions	2,054
Confirmations	1,985
Marriages:	
Catholic	336
Interfaith	333
Total Marriages	669
Deaths	738
Total Catholic Population	95,596
Total Population	671,091

Former Bishops—Most Rev. AUSTIN DOWLING, D.D., first Bishop of Des Moines; ord. June 24, 1891; appt. Bishop Jan. 31, 1912; cons. April 25, 1912; promoted to the See of St. Paul, Jan., 1919.—Most Rev. THOMAS W. DRUMM, D.D., Bishop of Des Moines; ord. Dec. 21, 1901; cons. May 21, 1919; died Oct. 24, 1933.—Most Rev. GERALD T. BERGAN, D.D., ord. Oct. 28, 1915; appt. Mar. 24, 1934; cons. June 13, 1934; enthroned June 21, 1934; elevated to Archiepiscopal dignity and promoted to Omaha Feb. 9, 1948.—Most Rev. EDWARD C. DALY, O.P., S.T.M., Bishop of Des Moines; ord. June 12, 1921; appt. March 13, 1948; cons. May 13, 1948; named Asst. at Papal Throne, May 23, 1958; died Nov. 23, 1964.—Most Rev. GEORGE J. BISKUP, D.D., ord. March 19, 1937; appt. Auxiliary Bishop of Dubuque, March 9, 1957; cons. April 24, 1957; appt. Bishop of Des Moines, Feb. 3, 1965; appt. Coadjutor Archbishop of Indianapolis, July 26, 1967; succeeded to See Jan. 14, 1970.—Most Rev. MAURICE J. DINGMAN, D.D., Retired Bishop of Des Moines; ord. Dec. 8, 1939; appt. Bishop of Des Moines April 2, 1968; cons. June 19, 1968; installed July 7, 1968; retired Oct. 14, 1986; died Feb. 1, 1992.—Most Rev. WILLIAM H. BULLOCK, ord. June 7, 1952; appt. Auxiliary Bishop of St. Paul and Minneapolis and Titular Bishop of Natchez June 3, 1980; cons. Aug. 12, 1980; appt. Bishop of Des Moines Feb. 10, 1987; installed April 2, 1987; appt. to Diocese of Madison April 13, 1993.

Vicar General and Moderator of the Curia—Rev. Msgr. STEPHEN ORR, *P.O. Box 1816, Des Moines, 50306.* Tel: 515-237-5044; 222-9577(Residence).

Chancery—601 Grand Ave., P.O. Box 1816, Des Moines, 50306. Tel: 515-243-7653; Fax: 515-237-5070. Office Hours: Mon.-Fri. 8:30-4:30.

Chancellor—LAWRENCE BREHENY,All Matrimonial Correspondence to Tribunal.

Secretary to the Bishop—PATRICIA ROSS, *P.O. Box 1816, Des Moines, 50306.* Tel: 515-237-5039; Fax: 515-237-5071.

Finance Officer—MARY LOU HERRING, *P.O. Box 1816, Des Moines, 50306.* Tel: 515-237-5012.

Vicar for Finance—Rev. Msgr. EDWARD HURLEY.

Diocesan Tribunal—601 Grand Ave., P.O. Box 1816, Des Moines, 50306. Tel: 515-237-5030.

Judicial Vicar—Rev. Msgr. LAWRENCE BEESON, J.C.D.

Director of Tribunal—Sr. CAMILLA HUBER, O.S.M.

Defenders of the Bond—Revs. MICHAEL AMADEO, J.C.L.; LAWRENCE R. HOFFMANN; DANIEL F. KRETTEK, J.C.L.; SAMUEL PALMER, J.C.L.; DAVID J. POLICH; Deacon ROBERT L. HOWE.

Judges—Rev. Msgr. LAWRENCE A. BEESON, J.C.D.; Revs. DANIEL L. CLARKE; GARRY A. CULVER, J.C.L.; DANIEL KRETTEK; Rev. Msgr. STEPHEN L. ORR; Rev. SAMUEL I. PALMER, J.C.L.; Rev. Msgr. EDWARD B. PFEFFER, J.C.L.; Rev. THOMAS J. PFEFFER, J.C.L.

Notary—DORIS KLANG.

Advocates—Revs. EUGENE R. KOCH; JOHN P. LUDWIG; VINCE G. ROSONKE; JOHN DORTON; Sr. CAMILLA HUBER, O.S.M.; Deacons ROBERT BRAY; GREGG ERICKSON; JOAN BERNER; PATRICIA CORNWELL; SARAH LUFT.

Diocesan Consultors—Rev. Msgr. LAWRENCE BEESON; Rev. Msgr. FRANK BOGNANNO; Rev. Msgr. GERALD STESSMAN; Rev. Msgr. JOHN MCILHON; Revs. JOHN ACREA; PAUL BIANCHI; GORDON GITTINS.

Diocesan Corporation Board—Most Rev. JOSEPH L. CHARRON; Rev. Msgr. STEPHEN ORR; CYNTHIA EISENHAUER; MICHAEL RILEY; MARY LOU HERRING; LAWRENCE BREHENY.

Diocesan Offices and Directors

Catholic Charities—LAWRENCE BREHENY, Exec. Dir.; Rev. DUANE WEILAND, Assoc. Dir., *601 Grand Ave., P.O. Box 723, Des Moines, 50303.* Tel: 515-237-5058.

Social Service Division—Des Moines Office, 601 Grand Ave., P.O. Box 723, Des Moines, 50303. Tel: 515-237-5055.

Council Bluffs Office—411 E. Broadway, Council Bluffs, 51503. Tel: 712-328-3086; Fax: 712-322-1388.

Charismatic Renewal Liaison—Rev. Msgr. FRANK E. BOGNANNO, *St. Augustin, 545 42nd, Des Moines, 50312.* Tel: 515-255-1175.

Communications, Office of—THOMAS CHAPMAN, Dir., *P.O. Box 1816, Des Moines, 50306.* Tel: 515-237-5041; Fax: 515-237-5071.

Continuing Education for Clergy—Rev. JAMES KIERNAN, Dir., *St. Ambrose Cathedral, 607 High St., Des Moines, 50309.* Tel: 515-288-7411.

Deaf-Handicapped, Office of—Sr. HELEN SEIVERT, O.S.F.,

Dir., *315 W. Pierce St., Council Bluffs, 51501.* Tel: 712-328-3086.

Advancement Office—JACK JONES, Exec. Dir., *P.O. Box 1816, Des Moines, 50306.* Tel: 515-237-5007.

Diocesan Council of Catholic Women—ELIZABETH SCHMID, Pres., *1503 Birchwood, Red Oak, 51566.* Tel: 712-623-3209. Rev. GORDON GITTINS, *St. Michael's Church, 1912 18th St., Harlan, 51537.* Tel: 712-755-5244.

Diaconate (Permanent)—Deacon GENE JAGER, Dir.

Evangelization, Office of—JIM BOND, Dir., *P.O. Box 1816, Des Moines, 50306.* Tel: 515-237-5046.

Hispanic Ministry, Office of—Rev. KEVIN CAMERON, *Visitation, 1271 E. 9th St., Des Moines, 50316.* Tel: 515-266-6695.

Holy Childhood, Pontifical Association—Dr. LUVERN GUBBELS, *P.O. Box 1816, Des Moines, 50306.* Tel: 515-237-5013.

Legislative Activities, Office of—PATRICK FINAN, *601 Grand Ave., P.O. Box 723, Des Moines, 50303.* Tel: 515-237-5047.

Newspaper—"The Catholic Mirror", TOM CHAPMAN, Editor, *601 Grand Ave., P.O. Box 10372, Des Moines, 50306.* Tel: 515-237-5060.

Priests' Pension Fund Society—Most Rev. JOSEPH L. CHARRON; Rev. ED KELLY; Rev. Msgr. EDWARD HURLEY; Rev. ROBERT SCHOEMANN; Rev. Msgr. RAYMOND CONLEY.

Propagation of the Faith—Rev. PAUL BIANCHI, Dir., *Box 1816, Des Moines, 50306-1816.* Tel: 515-237-5058.

Religious Education Office—JOANNE DALHOFF, Dir., *P.O. Box 1816, Des Moines, 50306.* Tel: 515-237-5052.

St. Vincent de Paul Society—Rev. JOHN LUDWIG, Chap., *St. Catherine of Siena Catholic Student Center, 1150 28th St., Des Moines, 50311-4142.* Tel: 515-271-4747.

Schools—Dr. LUVERN GUBBELS, Supt./Dir. Educ. Elementary School Coords.: Sr. JUDITH SHEAHAN, B.V.M.; MARJ CANAN, *P.O. Box 1816, Des Moines, 50306.* Tel: 515-237-5013.

Office of Social Justice—PATRICK FINAN, *P.O. Box 723, Des Moines, 50303.* Tel: 515-237-5047.

Vocations—Rev. DAVID FLEMING, Dir.; Sr. EILEEN MALLOY, C.S.C., Assoc. Dir., *P.O. Box 1816, Des Moines, 50306.* Tel: 515-237-5014.

Office of Worship (Liturgy, Music, Art and Architecture)—JIM BOND, Dir., *601 Grand Ave., P.O. Box 1816, Des Moines, 50306.* Tel: 515-237-5046.

Youth Ministry, Office of—Rev. JAMES WILWERDING, *St. Thomas More Center, 6177 Panorama Rd., Panora, 50216.* Tel: 515-755-3164.

CLERGY, PARISHES, MISSIONS AND PAROCHIAL SCHOOLS

CITY OF DES MOINES
(Polk County)

1—ST. AMBROSE CATHEDRAL (1856), Revs. James W. Kiernan, Rector; Felix Onuora, C.S.Sp.; Sr. Patricia Scherer, Pastoral Min.; Sr. Virginia Jennings, O.S.F., D.R.E.; Deacons Lee Pao Yang; Robert Bray; Dave Garza; Joseph Huynh; Michael McCarthy.
Res., 607 High St., 50309. Tel: 515-288-7411. [JC]

2—ALL SAINTS (1914), Rev. Anthony Aiello.
650 N.E. 52nd Ave., 50313. Tel: 515-265-5001; Fax: 515-265-5636. [JC]

3—CHRIST THE KING (1939), Rev. Albert G. Sherbo. Pastoral Ministers: Sr. Barbara L. Marshall, S.F.C.C.; Deacon Daniel McGuire.
Res., 5711 S.W. 9th St., 50315. Tel: 515-285-2888.
School—701 Wall St., 50315. Tel: 515-285-3349; Fax: 515-285-0381.
Lay Teachers 18; Students 223.
Catechesis/Religious Programs—Students 266.

4—HOLY TRINITY (1920), Rev. Msgr. Gerald J. Stessman; Rev. Mike McLaughlin; Deacons Robert Howe; Jeff Boehlert.
Res., 2926 Beaver Ave., 50310. Tel: 515-255-3162; Fax: 515-255-1381.
School—Lay Teachers 30; Students 552.
Catechesis/Religious Programs—Students 145.

5—ST. ANTHONY'S (1905), Revs. Lawrence R. Hoffmann; Robert Harris.
Res., 15 Indianola Rd., 50315. Tel: 515-244-4709.
School—16 Columbus Ave., 50315. Tel: 515-243-1874.
Sisters 2; Lay Teachers 23; Students 377.
Catechesis/Religious Programs—Tel: 515-244-1119.
Students 225.

6—ST. AUGUSTIN'S (1923), Rev. Msgr. Frank E. Bognanno; Rev. John F. Lorenz; Deacon Dennis Luft.
Res., 545 42nd St., 50312. Tel: 515-255-1175; Fax: 515-255-7969.
School—4320 Grand Ave., 50312. Tel: 515-279-5947; Fax: 515-279-8049.
Lay Teachers 16; Students 290.

7—ST. CATHERINE OF SIENNA CATHOLIC STUDENT CENTER (1969). (Non-Territorial University Parish). Rev. John Ludwig.
Church—1150-28th St., 50311-4142. Tel: 515-274-4747; Fax: 515-271-1918.

8—BASILICA OF SAINT JOHN (1905), Rev. Msgr. Frank E. Chiodo; Rev. Richard Wagner; Deacons John Jarvis; Patrick Kirkman; Charles Putbrese.
Res., 1915 University Ave., 50314. Tel: 515-244-3101; Fax: 515-244-3165.
School—Holy Family School, (Grades PreK-3). (Consolidated) 1913 University Ave., 50314. Tel: 515-288-6455.
Lay Teachers 18; Students 213.

9—ST. JOSEPH'S (1924), Rev. Msgr. Robert J. Chamberlain; Rev. Remigius Okere; Deacons Marvin Brewer; William Smith.
Res., 3300 Easton Blvd., 50317. Tel: 515-266-2226.
School—Tel: 515-266-3433; Fax: 515-266-8348.
Lay Teachers 14; Students 192.
Catechesis/Religious Programs—Students 121.

10—ST. MARY OF NAZARETH (1964), Revs. Gerald E. Ryan; David Santoro, O.P.
Res., 4605 N.W. 47th Ct., P.O. Box 13170, 50310. Tel: 515-276-4042; Fax: 515-252-1995.
Catechesis/Religious Programs—Tel: 515-276-7589.
Students 403.

11—ST. PETER'S (1915), Rev. John Dorton; Deacon Eugene Jager.
Res., 607 E. 18th St., 50316. Tel: 515-266-4265.

12—ST. THERESA OF THE CHILD JESUS (1951), Revs. Robert A. Hoefler; Tan Van Tran; James Kirby.
Res., 1230 Merle Hay Rd., 50311. Tel: 515-279-4654; Fax: 515-277-0838. [JC]
School—5810 Carpenter, 50311. Tel: 515-277-0178; Fax: 515-277-0838.
Lay Teachers 20; Students 386.
Catechesis/Religious Programs—Students 150.

13—VISITATION (1882), Revs. Thomas Pfeffer; Kevin Cameron, Hispanic Ministry.
Res., 1271 E. 9th St., 50316. Tel: 515-266-6695.
School—Holy Family, (Grades 4-8). (Consolidated). Tel: 515-262-8025.
Lay Teachers 15; Students 213.
Catechesis/Religious Programs—Tel: 515-266-1027.
Students 256.
Mission—Des Moines, Polk Co., Our Lady of Guadalupe, 601 S.E. 8th St., 50316. Tel: 515-243-9585.

OUTSIDE THE CITY OF DES MOINES

Adair, Adair Co., St. John (1879). Attended by St. Mary, Anita. Rev. Christopher Hartshorn.
Res., P.O. Box 277, Anita, 50020. Tel: 712-762-3484; 762-3773 (Office).

Adel, Dallas Co., St. John (1917), Rev. Martin G. Chevalier.
Mailing Address: P.O. Box 151, 50003-0151. Tel: 515-993-4482.
Catechesis/Religious Programs—Students 124.

Afton, Union Co., St. Edward (1878). Attended by Paul VI Pastoral Ministry from Creston.
Mailing Address: 406 W. Clark, Creston, 50801. Tel: 515-782-5278; Fax: 515-782-5924.
Church—104 W. Union, 50830. Tel: 515-347-8452.

Altoona, Polk Co., SS. John and Paul (1983), Rev. Vince G. Rosonke.
Res., 114 13th St., S.E., 50009. Tel: 515-967-3796; Fax: 515-967-7197.
Catechesis/Religious Programs—Students 360.

Anita, Cass Co., St. Mary (1924), Rev. Christopher Hartshorn.
Church—P.O. Box 277, 50020. Tel: 712-762-3484; 762-3773 (Office).

Ankeny, Polk Co., Our Lady's Immaculate Heart (1961), Revs. Gregory Leach; Randy Richman; Deacon Richard Ziller.
Res., 510 E. First St., 50021. Tel: 515-964-3038; Fax: 515-964-5997.
Catechesis/Religious Programs—Tel: 515-964-3545.
Students 1,079.

Atlantic, Cass Co., SS. Peter and Paul (1871), Rev. Msgr. Lawrence A. Beeson; Deacon Fred Cornwell, Pastoral Assoc.
Res., 106 W. 6th St., 50022. Tel: 712-243-4721.
Catechesis/Religious Programs—Tel: 712-243-2144.
Students 280.

Audubon, Audubon Co., St. Patrick (1918), Rev. John C. Maier.
Res., 116 E. Division St., 50025. Tel: 712-563-2283; Fax: 712-563-3238. [CEM]
Catechesis/Religious Programs—Students 180.

Avoca, Pottawattamie Co., St. Mary, Mediatrix of All Graces (1882), Rev. Fred P. Reischl; Deacon Clarence Christensen.
Res., 326 N. Maple St., P.O. Box 38, 51521. Tel: 712-343-6948.
Catechesis/Religious Programs—Students 95.

Bayard, Guthrie Co., St. Patrick (1882), Rev. Tan Van Tran.
Res., 214 Prairie St., P.O. Box 274, 50029. Tel: 712-651-2676.

Bedford, Taylor Co., Sacred Heart. Attended by St. Clare, Clarinda. Rev. Thomas Coenen.
Mailing Address: 300 E. Lincoln Blvd., Clarinda, 51632.

Carlisle, Warren Co., St. Elizabeth Seton (1979), Rev. Nelo A. Leto.
Mailing Address: 256 Scotch Ridge Rd., P.O. Box 35, 50047. Tel: 515-989-0659.
Catechesis/Religious Programs—Students 105.

Carter Lake, Pottawattamie Co., Our Lady of Carter Lake (1970). Attended by Our Lady, Queen of Apostles, Council Bluffs. Rev. Dennis Trausch.
Church—3501 N. 9th St., 51510. Tel: 712-347-6631; Fax: 712-325-2411.

Casey, Guthrie Co., St. Joseph (1898). Attended by St. Mary, Anita. Rev. Christopher Hartshorn.
Mailing Address: P.O. Box 277, Anita, 50020. Tel: 712-762-3484.

Chariton, Lucas Co., Sacred Heart (1869), Rev. Allan Stetz. Pastoral Ministers: Sr. Mary Lenz, O.S.F.; Sr. Mary Ellen Schulte, B.V.M. Tel: 515-774-5486.
Res., 407 N. Main, 50049. Tel: 515-774-5486 or 515-766-6786.

Churchville, Warren Co., Assumption of the Blessed Virgin Mary (1855), Rev. John O. Bertogli.
Res., P.O. Box 88, St. Mary's, 50241. Tel: 515-297-2267.

Clarinda, Page Co., St. Clare (1942), Rev. Tom Coenen.
Res., 300 E. Lincoln Blvd., 51632. Tel: 712-542-2030.
Catechesis/Religious Programs—Students 61.

Corning, Adams Co., St. Patrick's, Rev. Daniel E. Siepker.
Res., 504 Grove Ave., 50841. Tel: 515-322-3363. [CEM]

Corydon, Wayne Co., St. Francis (1969). Attended by Chariton of the South Central Catholic Ministry Team.
Mailing Address: 213 W. Jackson, 50060. Tel: 515-774-4978.

Council Bluffs, Pottawattamie Co.,

1—HOLY FAMILY, (1908), Rev. Kenneth A. Gross; Deacon Joseph Scurlock.
Res., 2217 Ave. B, 51501. Tel: 712-328-3869.

2—OUR LADY, QUEEN OF APOSTLES, (1957), Revs. Thomas Crowley; William Dolan; Deacon Monty Montagne.
Res., 3304 4th Ave., 51501. Tel: 712-323-2916; Fax: 712-328-0228.
Catechesis/Religious Programs—Students 230.

3—ST. PATRICK, (1924), Rev. Msgr. Edward Kelly; Rev. Raphael Masabakhwa; Deacon Charles Hannan.
Res., 223 Harmony St., 51503. Tel: 712-323-1484.
Catechesis/Religious Programs—Students 274.

4—ST. PETER, (1887) (German), Rev. Charles Kottas; Deacon Stephen Rallis, Pastoral Min.
Res., One Bluff St., 51503. Tel: 712-322-8889; Fax: 712-323-1442.
St. Francis Worship Center—238 6th St., 51501. Tel: 712-328-7272.

Creston, Union Co., Holy Spirit (1975), Revs. Leonard A. Kenkel; John W. Acrea.
Res., 406 W. Clark, 50801. Tel: 515-782-5278.
Church—Also serving the parish of St. Edward, Afton. 107 W. Howard St., Afton, 50801. Tel: 515-782-2716.
School—St. Malachy, Tel: 515-782-7125; Fax: 515-782-5924.
Lay Teachers 11; Students 113.

Cumberland, Cass Co., St. Timothy (Reno) (1883), Rev. Paul Mahowald, S.J.
Mailing Address: P.O. Box 605, Griswold, 51535-0605. Tel: 712-778-4540.

Cumming, Warren Co., St. John (1892), Rev. Robert J. Aubrey; Deacon David O'Brien.
Res., P.O. Box 5, 50061. Tel: 515-981-4855.
Catechesis/Religious Programs—Students 240.

Defiance, Shelby Co., St. Peter (1882), Rev. Joseph L. Brown, C.PP.S.
Res., P.O. Box 127, 51527. Tel: 712-748-3501.

Dunlap, Harrison Co., St. Patrick, Rev. Howard Fitzgerald.

Res., 509 S. 3rd St., 51529. Tel: 712-643-5808.
Catechesis/Religious Programs—Students 164.

Earling, Shelby Co., St. Joseph (1882) (German), Rev. Michael Berner.
Res., P.O. Box 225, 51530. Tel: 712-747-2091.
School—See Shelby County Board of Catholic Education under Education Centers in the Institution section. Tel: 712-747-3081.

Elkhart, Polk Co., St. Mary/Holy Cross (1914), Rev. Daniel J. Kirby.
Res., 214 Washington, P.O. Box 110, 50073. Tel: 515-367-2685.

Exira, Audubon Co., Holy Trinity. Attended by St. Patrick.
116 E. Division St., Audubon, 50025. Tel: 712-563-2283; Fax: 712-268-3238.

Glenwood, Mills Co., Our Lady of the Holy Rosary (1955), Rev. Paul Monahan; Deacons Joseph Blankenship; Ronald Kohn; Richard Maiers; James Parr.
Res., 24116 Marian Ave., 51534-5291. Tel: 712-527-5211.
Catechesis/Religious Programs—Students 236.

Grand River, Decatur Co., St. Patrick, Rev. John M. Frost.
Res., 222 E. Pearl, Osceola, 50213. Tel: 515-342-2850.

Granger, Dallas Co., Assumption of the Blessed Virgin Mary (1871), Rev. Eugene R. Koch.
Res., 1906 Sycamore, P.O. Box 177, 50109. Tel: 515-999-2239; Fax: 515-999-2208.
School—Tel: 515-999-2211.
Lay Teachers 7; Students 85.
Mission—Woodward, Dallas Co., St. Ann.

Greenfield, Adair Co., St. John (1907), Rev. Dean Nimerichter.
Res., 303 N.E. Elm St., 50849. Tel: 515-743-2641.
Catechesis/Religious Programs—Students 129.

Griswold, Cass Co., Our Lady Of Grace (1911), Rev. Paul Mahowald, S.J.
Mailing Address: P.O. Box 605, 51535-0605. Tel: 712-778-4540.

Guthrie Center, Guthrie Co., St. Mary (1906), Rev. Benedict J. Kenkel.
Res., 603 Main St., 50115. Tel: 515-747-2569.

Hamburg, Fremont Co., St. Mary (1874). Attended by St. Mary, Shenandoah. Rev. Donald Bruck.
Res., 1306 Washington St., 51640. Tel: 712-382-2871.

Harlan, Shelby Co., St. Michael (1888), Rev. Gordon Gittins; Deacons Patrick Davitt; Donald Jacobi; John Stessman.
Res., 1912-18th St., 51537. Tel: 712-755-5244; Fax: 712-755-3332.
School—See Shelby County Board of Catholic Education under Education Centers in the Institution section.
Catechesis/Religious Programs—Tel: 712-755-5366; Fax: 712-755-3332.
Students 325.

Imogene, Fremont Co., St. Patrick (1880), Rev. John W. Clarke.
Res., P.O. Box 205, 51645. Tel: 712-386-2123.
Catechesis/Religious Programs—Students 105.

Indianola, Warren Co., St. Thomas Aquinas (1958), Rev. Frank S. Palmer.
Res., 1202 W. Iowa Ave., 50125. Tel: 515-961-3026; Fax: 515-961-3458.
Catechesis/Religious Programs—Tel: 515-961-0447.
Students 287.

Irish Settlement, Madison Co., St. Patrick (1852), Rev. John O. Bertogli.
Res., P.O. Box 88, St. Marys, 50241. Tel: 515-297-2267.

Jamaica, Guthrie Co., St. Joseph (1903). Attended by St. Patrick, Bayard.
214 Prairie, P.O. Box 274, Bayard, 50029. Tel: 712-651-2676.

Lacona, Warren Co., Holy Trinity Church of Southeast Warren County (1978), Rev. Frank Cordaro.
Res., P.O. Box 145, 50139. Tel: 515-534-4691.
Worship Centers—St. Mary of the Assumption Church, Lacona; St. Augustine Church, Milo; St. Mary of Perpetual Help Church, Rosemont.

Lenox, Taylor Co., St. Patrick (1875). Attended by St. Patrick, Corning.
Church—600 W. Michigan, 50851. Tel: 515-336-2893.

Leon, Decatur Co., St. Brendan (1865) (Irish), Rev. Thomas V. Dooley.
Res., 1001 N.W. Church St., 50144. Tel: 515-446-4789.

Logan, Harrison Co., St. Anne, Rev. John Harmon.
Res., 112 W. 3rd St., 51546. Tel: 712-644-2535.

Maloy, Ringgold Co., Immaculate Conception (1874), Rev. Thomas V. Dooley.
Res., 103 Shay St., 50836. Tel: 515-446-4789. [CEM]

Massena, Cass Co., St. Patrick (1888), Deacon Fred Cornwell.
Res., P.O. Box 180, 50853. Tel: 712-779-3397.

Missouri Valley, Harrison Co., St. Patrick (1877), Rev. James F. Kleffman.
Res., 215 N. Seventh St., 51555. Tel: 712-642-3124; Fax: 712-642-2518.
School—219 N. Seventh St., 51555. Tel: 712-642-3155.
Lay Teachers 5; Students 86.

Mondamin, Harrison Co., Holy Family. Attended by St. Anne.
112 W. 3rd St., Logan, 51546.

Mt. Ayr, Ringgold Co., St. Joseph (1913). Attended by St. Brendan.
Church—100 N. Polk, 50854. Tel: 515-446-4789.

Neola, Pottawattamie Co., St. Patrick (1882), Rev. Wayne Gubbels; Deacon Mark Stageman.
Res., P.O. Box 127, 51559. Tel: 712-485-2124.

Orient, Adair Co., St. Mark. Attended by St. John, Greenfield. Rev. Dean Nimerichter.
Res., 303 N.E. Elm, Greenfield, 50849. Tel: 515-743-2641.

Osceola, Clarke Co., St. Bernard (1885), Rev. John M. Frost.
Res., 222 E. Pearl, 50213. Tel: 342-2850.

Panama, Shelby Co., St. Mary of the Assumption (1899) (German), Rev. Michael G. Peters.
Res., Box 130, 51562. Tel: 712-489-2030.
School—See Shelby County Board of Catholic Education under Education Centers in the Institution section.

Panora, Guthrie Co., St. Cecilia (1907). Attended by St. Mary, Guthrie Center.
Church—220 N. First St., 50216. Tel: 515-755-2658.

Perry, Dallas Co., St. Patrick (1881), Rev. Raymond Higgins.
Res., 1312 3rd St., 50220. Tel: 515-465-4387; Fax: 515-465-4387.
School—1324 5th St., 50220. Tel: 515-465-4186; Fax: 515-465-7771.
Lay Teachers 11; Students 138.

Portsmouth, Shelby Co., St. Mary (1885), Rev. Paul Bianchi.
Res., P.O. Box 98, 51565. Tel: 712-743-2625; Fax: 712-743-2010.
Catechesis/Religious Programs—Students 114.

Red Oak, Montgomery Co., St. Mary (1902), Rev. Jon Kautzky.
Res., 1510 Highland Ave., 51566. Tel: 712-623-2744.
Catechesis/Religious Programs—Students 158.

St. Marys, Warren Co., Immaculate Conception (1871), Rev. John O. Bertogli.
Res., P.O. Box 88, 50241. Tel: 515-297-2267.

Shenandoah, Page Co., St. Mary, Rev. Donald Bruck; Deacon Ed Miller.
Res., 512 W. Thomas Ave., 51601. Tel: 712-246-1718.
Catechesis/Religious Programs—Students 165.

Stuart, Guthrie Co., All Saints (1876), Rev. Daniel Clark.
Res., P.O. Box 605, 50250. Tel: 515-523-1497.
Catechesis/Religious Programs—Students 75.

Urbandale, Polk Co., St. Pius X (1955), Rev. Msgr. Joseph McDonnell; Rev. Samuel Palmer. Pastoral Ministers: Mary Sue Lone; Barbara Mease; June Wilwert.
Res., 3663 66th St., Des Moines, 50322. Tel: 515-276-2059; Fax: 515-276-8351.
School—3601 66th St., Des Moines, 50322. Tel: 515-276-1061. Roberta Harvey, Prin.
Sisters 1; Lay Teachers 26; Students 399.
Catechesis/Religious Programs—Tel: 515-278-5684. D.R.E.: Mary Heinrich; Mary Green.
Students 600.

Villisca, Montgomery Co., St. Joseph (1947). Attended by St. Clare, Clarinda. Rev. Thomas Coenen.
304 E. Lincoln St., Clarinda, 51632. Tel: 712-826-8841.

Walnut, Pottawattamie Co., St. Patrick (1882). Attended by St. Mary, Mediatrix of All Graces, Avoca. Rev. Fred P. Reischl.
Mailing Address: 326 N. Maple St., P.O. Box 38, Avoca, 51521. Tel: 712-343-6948.
Catechesis/Religious Programs—Students 74.

Waukee, Dallas Co., St. Boniface (1880), Rev. Robert L. Schoemann; Sr. Theresa Engel, S.S.S.F., Pastoral Min.
Res., 250 4th St., 50263-9623. Tel: 515-987-4597; Fax: 515-987-5272.
Catechesis/Religious Programs—Students 245.

West Des Moines, Polk Co., Sacred Heart (1892), Revs. Phillip Kruse; Emeka Akabueze; Garry Culver; Deacon Chris Rohwer; Sr. Mary Margaret O'Toole, Pastoral Assoc.
Res., 1627 Grand Ave., 50265. Tel: 515-225-6414; Fax: 515-225-0286.
School—1601 Grand Ave., 50265. Tel: 515-223-1284; Fax: 515-223-9413.
Sisters 2; Lay Teachers 26; Students 533.
Catechesis/Religious Programs—Tel: 515-225-7030; Fax: 515-225-0286.
Students 394.

St. Francis of Assisi, Dallas Co., (1991), Rev. Msgr. Stephen Orr; Rev. Christopher Fontanini.
7075 Ashworth Rd., 50266. Tel: 515-223-4577; Fax: 515-223-4768.
Catechesis/Religious Programs—Students 505.

Weston, Pottawattamie Co., St. Columbanus (1883). Attended by St. Patrick. Rev. Wayne Gubbels.
Res., St. Patrick's Church, P.O. Box 127, Neola, 51559. Tel: 712-485-2124.

Westphalia, Shelby Co., St. Boniface (1873), Rev. Joseph Brown, C.PP.S.
Church—207 Duren Strasse, P.O. Box 86, 51578. Tel: 712-627-4255.

Winterset, Madison Co., St. Joseph (1893), Rev. Msgr. Edward B. Pfeffer.
Res., 607 W. Green St., 50273. Tel: 515-462-1083; Fax: 515-462-2378.
Catechesis/Religious Programs—Students 144.

Woodbine, Harrison Co., Sacred Heart. Attended by St. Patrick's, Dunlap. Rev. Howard Fitzgerald.
33 Seventh St., 51579.

Woodward, Dallas Co., St. Ann (1934). Attended by Assumption of the Blessed Virgin Mary.
1906 Sycamore St., P.O. Box 177, Granger, 50109. Tel: 515-999-2239; Fax: 515-999-2208.

Chaplains of Public Institutions

DES MOINES. *City Chaplaincy Program,* 1610 60th St., 50322. Rev. Arthur McCann.
United States Veterans Hospital, 3019 Pleasant, 50310. Rev. Paul Holt.

CLARINDA. *State Hospital.* Served from St. Clare Church, Clarinda.

COUNCIL BLUFFS. *Iowa School for the Deaf,* 411 E. Broadway, 51503. Tel: 712-322-2449. Sr. Helen Seivert, Chap. & D.R.E.

GLENWOOD. *Glenwood State School.* Vacant.

MITCHELLVILLE. *Iowa Correctional Institution for Women.* Deacon Jim Doyle, Chap. & Coord., Svcs. to Catholic Residents.

On Special Assignment:
Reverend Fathers—
Amadeo, Michael, Diocesan Tribunal Office
Fleming, David, Diocesan Dir. Vocations
Weiland, Duane J., Clinical Therapist, Catholic Charities

On Duty Outside the Diocese:
Reverend Fathers—
Fitzgerald, P. Timothy, Notre Dame Center for Pastoral Liturgy, P.O. Box 81, Notre Dame, IN 46556
Freeman, James, Holy Trinity Church, 1300 N. Greasewood, Tucson, AZ 85745
Grant, Robert, St. Ambrose University, Davenport, IA 52803
Koch, Paul M., Casilla 919, Santa Cruz, Bolivia
Polich, James, Conception Seminary College, Conception, MO 64433

Retired:
Reverend Monsignors—
Conley, Raymond J., 1390 Buffalo Rd., West Des Moines, IA 50265
Connelly, Paul J., 615 Park St., #1501, Des Moines, IA 50309
Deere, Gerald, 128 Baughn St., Council Bluffs, IA 51503
Devine, W. J., Sagamore Towers No. 2, 95 Squantum St., Apt. 609, Quincy, MA 02169
Gorman, John, 1390 Buffalo Rd., West Des Moines, IA 50265
Kovacs, John F., 1390 Buffalo Rd., West Des Moines, IA 50265
McIlhon, John J., 1390 Buffalo Rd., West Des Moines, IA 50265
Ring, Arthur R., 4317 Ovid Ave., Des Moines, IA 50310
Ryan, Joseph P., 1390 Buffalo Rd., West Des Moines, IA 50265
Schulte, Joseph M., 1390 Buffalo Rd., West Des Moines, IA 50265
Schwarte, Michael W., P.O. Box 43, Portsmouth, IA 51565
Wadsworth, James, 600 Locust, Atlantic, IA 50022
Reverend Fathers—
Cunningham, John E., 1390 Buffalo Rd., West Des Moines, IA 50265

Daleke, Don, 9125 Meadow Run Way, San Diego, CA 92100
Elias, Woodrow, 100 W. Moore Rd., No. 414, Pharr, TX 78577
Fenelon, David, 934 Lincoln St., Waterloo, IA 50703
Gaul, Cornelius, P.O. Box 59, R.R., Earling, IA 51530
Klein, Eugene J., R.R. 1, Box 83, Earling, IA 51530
Peterson, Cyril P., Longview Home, Inc., Rm. 20, 1010 Longview Dr., Missouri Valley, IA 51555
Reece, Frederick W., 2929-35th St., Des Moines, IA 50310
Reisz, Adam, R.R. 2, Dunlap, IA 51529
Ryan, John R., 1173 20th Pl., West Des Moines, IA 50265

Permanent Deacons:
Blankenship, Joseph
Boehlert, Jeffrey
Bray, Robert
Brewer, Marvin
Catanzano, George
Christensen, Clarence
Coan, Joseph
Cord, Michael
Cornwell, Fred
Cortese, Joseph
Critelli, Anthony
Davitt, Patrick
Doyle, James
Erickson, Gregg
Garza, David
Gaul, Leo
Hannan, Charles
Heitkotter, Jerome
Herman, James
Howe, Robert
Huynh, Joseph
Jacobi, Donald
Jager, Gene
Jarvis, John
Kirkman, Patrick
Kirlin, Dennis
Klein, Marvin
Knotek, Lawrence
Kohn, Ronald
Leininger, Jerry
Lovell, David
Lovell, Dennis
Luft, Dennis
Maiers, Richard
Maly, Tom
McCarthy, Michael
McGuire, Dan
Miller, Edward
Montagne, Monty
O'Brien, David
Parr, James
Pins, Fred
Putbrese, Charles
Rallis, El
Richardson, Alan
Rohwer, Chris
Scurlock, Joseph
Smith, William
Stageman, Mark
Starbuck, Tom
Stessman, Gail
Stessman, John
Sullivan, Robert
Von Behren, Lyle
Webering, James
Wolford, Charles
Yang, LyPao
Ziller, Richard

INSTITUTIONS LOCATED IN THE DIOCESE

[A] EDUCATION CENTERS

COUNCIL BLUFFS. *Council Bluffs Area Catholic Education Systems, Inc.*, 400 Gleason Ave., 51503. Tel: 712-329-9000. John F. Cronin, Ph.D., Pres.
St. Albert Junior High School. (Grades 7-8), 400 Gleason Ave., 51503. Tel: 712-328-2316. Rev. Phillip Hobt. Lay Teachers 8; Students 138.
St. Albert Intermediate School. (Grades 4-6), 3330 Fourth Ave., 51501. Tel: 713-322-7004. Lay Teachers 8; Students 193.
St. Albert Primary School. (Grades PreK-3), 2912 9th Ave., 51501. Tel: 712-323-3703. Lay Teachers 15; Students 370.
Religious Education Center, 424 Gleason Ave., 51503. Tel: 712-322-4339. Mary B. Fisher, Dir.

PANAMA. *Shelby County Board of Catholic Education*, 208 St. Mary's Ave., 51562-0183.
Elementary Schools: Shelby County Catholic Schools. Attendance Centers:
St. Mary's Center. (Grades PreK-3), 208 St. Mary's Ave., 51562-0183. Tel: 712-489-2727. Lay Teachers 5; Students 126.
St. Joseph's Center. (Grades 4-8), 208 Main St., Earling, 51530-0227. Tel: 712-747-3081. Lay Teachers 5; Students 102.
St. Michael's Center. (Grades PreK-6), 205 College Blvd., Harlan, 51537. Tel: 712-755-5634. Lay Teachers 8; Students 140.

WEST DES MOINES. *St. Joseph Educational Center*, 1400 Buffalo Rd., 50265. Tel: 515-225-3000. Rev. Msgr. Michael N. Hess, Pres.; Rev. James M. Laurenzo.
Religious Education. Rev. James M. Laurenzo, Dir. Adult and Youth Ministries.

[B] COLLEGES AND UNIVERSITIES

DES MOINES. *Mercy College of Health Sciences*, 928-6th Ave., 50309-1239. Tel: 515-247-3180; Fax: 515-362-6698.
E-mail: mercy@mchs.edu
Web site: http://www.mchs.edu
For a complete listing, refer to the Colleges and Universities section.

[C] HIGH SCHOOLS, INTERPAROCHIAL

COUNCIL BLUFFS. *Saint Albert Catholic Schools*, 400 Gleason Ave., 51503. Tel: 712-328-2316. John F. Cronin, Ph.D., Pres., Saint Albert High School (Grades 9-12).
Serving all parishes in Council Bluffs; St. Patrick, Missouri Valley; St. Patrick, Neola; Holy Rosary, Glenwood; St. Columbanus, Weston. Priests 1; Lay Instructors 33; Students 315.

WEST DES MOINES. *Dowling High School*, 1400 Buffalo Rd., 50265. Tel: 515-225-3000; Fax: 515-222-1056. Rev. Msgr. Michael N. Hess, Pres.; James Dowdle, Prin.; Mary Bustin, Registrar; Rev. Lyle Peters.
Serving all parishes in Des Moines; Sacred Heart, West Des Moines; St. Francis of Assisi, West Des Moines; St. Boniface, Waukee; Assumption, Granger; St. John, Cumming; St. Mary, Elkhart; Holy Cross, Elkhart; SS. John and Paul, Atoona; Immaculate Heart, Ankeny. Priests 3; Sisters 3; Lay Teachers 61; Students 1,070.

[D] GENERAL HOSPITALS

DES MOINES. *Mercy Hospital Medical Center*, 400 University Ave., 50314. Tel: 515-247-3121
For a complete listing, refer to the Hospitals section.

CORNING. *Mercy Midlands: Mercy Hospital*, Rosary Dr., P.O. Box 368, 50841. Tel: 515-322-3121; Fax: 515-322-4872
For a complete listing, refer to the Hospitals section.

COUNCIL BLUFFS. *Bergan Mercy-Alegant Health System: Mercy Hospital*, 800 Mercy Dr., 51502. Tel: 712-328-5000; Fax: 712-328-5202
For a complete listing, refer to the Hospitals section.

[E] HOMES FOR AGED

JOHNSTON. *Bishop Drumm Retirement Center - Affiliate of Catholic Health Initiatives*, 5837 Winwood Dr., 50131. Tel: 515-270-1100; Fax: 515-276-1714
For a complete listing, refer to the Special Care Facilities section.

[F] SPECIAL CARE FACILITIES

DES MOINES. *House of Mercy*, 1409 Clark St., 50314-1964. Tel: 515-362-6500; Fax: 515-243-0318
For a complete listing, refer to the Special Care Facilities section.

[G] SECULAR INSTITUTES

DES MOINES. *Institute of the Heart of Jesus*, P.O. Box 4634, 50306. Secular Priests and Lay People. Rev. John F. Lorenz.

[H] SPIRITUAL MINISTRY TO THE DIOCESE

DES MOINES. *Emmaus House*, 1521 Center St., 50314. Tel: 515-282-4839. Sr. Mary Dingman, S.S.S.F., Dir.

[I] NEWMAN CENTERS

DES MOINES. *St. Catherine of Siena Catholic Student Center.* (Drake Newman Community), 1150-28th St., 50311-4142. Tel: 515-271-4747.
E-mail: newman@acad.drake.edn
Rev. John Ludwig. Students 750; Non-Students 250.

[J] MISCELLANEOUS LISTINGS

DES MOINES. *Bishop's Endowment Fund Foundation*, 601 Grand Ave., 50309.
City Hospital Chaplaincy Service, 1610 60th St., 50322-6106. Tel: 515-255-1846. Rev. Arthur McCann.
Serving all non-Catholic hospitals in Des Moines.
Dowling-St. Joseph Alumni Foundation, 1400 Buffalo Rd., 50265. Tel: 515-225-3000. Larry Reelitz, Pres.; Rev. Msgr. Michael N. Hess, Sec.; Bob Ligouri, Vice Pres. Devel.
Life in the Spirit Community, Inc., 4601 Ovid Ave., 50310. Tel: 515-255-7534. Michael Freilinger, Co-ord.
Mercy Child Development Center, 6th & University, 50314. Tel: 515-247-4200. Diane Kraemer, Mgr.
Mercy Foundation of Des Moines - Affiliate of Catholic Health Initiatives, 921 Sixth Ave., Ste. A, 50314-1200. Tel: 515-247-3248. Sheila Smith, Ed.D., Pres.
National Catholic Rural Life Conference, 4625 Beaver Ave., 50310. Tel: 515-270-2634; Fax: 515-270-9447.
E-mail: ncrlc@aol.com
Web site: www.ncrle.com
Most Rev. Raymond L. Burke, D.D., J.C.D., (Bishop of LaCrosse); Bro. David G. Andrews, C.S.C., Exec. Dir.
Roman Catholic Pastoral Center Foundation, 601 Grand Ave., 50309. Rev. Msgr. Stephen Orr, Vicar Gen.
Roman Catholic Priests' Medical Fund Foundation, 601 Grand Ave., 50309.
Roman Catholic Seminary Fund Foundation, 601 Grand Ave., 50309.
St. Joseph Emergency Shelter, 1535 - 11th St., 50314.
St. Mary Family Center, 1248 E. 12th, 50316.
Society of Saint Vincent de Paul, 1426 6th Ave., 50314. Tel: 515-282-8327. Virginia Klemm, District Pres.; Larry Schmitz, Vice Pres.
Society of St. John (Brothers of Saint Benedict), 1915 University Ave., 50314. Tel: 515-244-3101. Rev. Msgr. Frank E. Chiodo, Supr. Brothers 6; Oblates 1.

COUNCIL BLUFFS. *Mercy Hospital Foundation, Council Bluffs*, 800 Mercy Dr., P.O. Box 1C, 51502. Tel: 712-328-5585. Richard A. Hachten, II, Pres.
St. Albert Educational Foundation, 400 Gleason Ave., 51503. Tel: 712-329-9000. John F. Cronin, Ph.D., Pres.
St. Joseph Catholic Cemetery Association, 17510 Sunnydale Rd., 51501. Tel: 712-322-7963. John E. O'Connor, Mgr.

GRISWOLD. *Wakonda Prayer House*, Box 370, 51535. Tel: 712-778-4325. Rev. La Vern Wingert.

HARLAN. *Shelby County Catholic Education Foundation*, 711 Court St., 51537.

JOHNSTON. *Bishop Drumm Foundation - Affiliate of Catholic Health Initiatives*, 5837 Winwood Dr., 50131. Tel: 515-270-1100.

PANORA. *St. Thomas More Center*, 6177 Panorama Rd., 50216. Tel: 515-755-3164.
E-mail: stmg@netins.net
Rev. James Wilwerding.

RELIGIOUS INSTITUTES OF MEN REPRESENTED IN THE DIOCESE

For further details refer to the corresponding bracketed number in the Religious Institutes of Men or Women section.

[0600]—*Brothers of the Congregation of the Holy Cross.*—C.S.C.

[0690]—*Jesuit Fathers and Brothers.* (Wisconsin Prov.).—S.J.

[0430]—*Order of Preachers-Dominicans.*—O.P.

[0200]—*Order of St. Benedict.* (Conception, MO).—O.S.B.

RELIGIOUS INSTITUTES OF WOMEN REPRESENTED IN THE DIOCESE

[0230]—*Benedictine Sisters of Pontifical Jurisdiction.*—O.S.B.

[2100]—*Congregation of the Holy Humility of Mary.*—C.H.M.

[1920]—*Congregation of the Sisters of the Holy Cross.*—C.S.C.

[1070-14]—*Dominican Sisters.*—O.P.

[1070-03]—*Dominican Sisters.*—O.P.

[1070-13]—*Dominican Sisters.*—O.P.

[1120]—*Dominican Sisters of the Roman Congregation.*—O.P.

[2575]—*Institute of the Sisters of Mercy of the Americas.* (Cedar Rapids, IA; Omaha, NE; Chicago, IL).—R.S.M.

[1680]—*School Sisters of St. Francis.*—O.S.F.

[3580]—*Servants of Mary.*—O.S.M.

[0480]—*Sisters of Charity of Leavenworth, Kansas.*—S.C.L.

[0430]—*Sisters of Charity of the Blessed Virgin Mary.*—B.V.M.
[2630]—*Sisters of Mercy of the Holy Cross.*—S.C.S.C.
[3000]—*Sisters of Notre Dame de Namur.*—S.N.D.de.N.
[3320]—*Sisters of Presentation of the Blessed Virgin Mary.*—P.B.V.M.
[1540]—*Sisters of Saint Francis, Clinton, Iowa.*—O.S.F.
[1705]—*The Sisters of St. Francis of Assisi.*—O.S.F.
[2960]—*Notre Dame Sisters.* (Omaha, NE).—N.D.
[1570]—*Sisters of St. Francis of the Holy Family.*—O.S.F.

NECROLOGY

† Kane, Rev. Msgr. Bartholomew, P.A., (Retired). —Died April 23, 1997.

Archdiocese of Detroit

(Archidioecesis Detroitensis)

Most Reverend

ARTHUR H. KRAWCZAK, D.D.

Retired Auxiliary Bishop of Detroit and Titular Bishop of Subbar; ordained May 18, 1940; appointed February 8, 1973; consecrated April 3, 1973; resigned August 17, 1982. *Res., Marywood Nursing Care, 36975 Five Mile Rd., Livonia, MI, 48154.*

Most Reverend

THOMAS J. GUMBLETON, D.D.

Auxiliary Bishop of Detroit, Titular Bishop of Ululi; ordained June 2, 1956; appointed March 8, 1968; consecrated May 1, 1968. *Office: 1234 Washington Blvd., Detroit, MI, 48226.*

Most Reverend

WALTER J. SCHOENHERR, D.D.

Retired Auxiliary Bishop of Detroit, Titular Bishop of Timidana; ordained October 27, 1945; appointed March 8, 1968; consecrated May 1, 1968; retired March 7, 1995. *Office: 1234 Washington Blvd., Detroit, MI, 48226.*

Most Reverend

MOSES B. ANDERSON, S.S.E., D.D.

Auxiliary Bishop of Detroit, Titular Bishop of Vatarba; ordained May 30, 1958; appointed December 3, 1982; consecrated January 27, 1983. *Office: 1234 Washington Blvd., Detroit, MI, 48226.*

Most Reverend

KEVIN M. BRITT, D.D.

Auxiliary Bishop of Detroit, Titular Bishop of Esco; ordained June 28, 1970; appointed November 23, 1993; consecrated January 6, 1994. *Office: 1234 Washington Blvd., Detroit, MI, 48226.*

His Eminence

ADAM CARDINAL MAIDA, J.C.L., J.D., S.T.L.

Archbishop of Detroit; ordained May 26, 1956; appointed to Green Bay November 8, 1983; consecrated January 25, 1984; installed as Archbishop of Detroit June 12, 1990; created Cardinal on November 26, 1994.

Cardinal's Office: 1234 Washington Blvd., Detroit, MI, 48226; Fax: 313-237-4642.

Web site address: www.archdioceseofdetroit.org

Most Reverend

BERNARD J. HARRINGTON, D.D.

Auxiliary Bishop of Detroit, Titular Bishop of Uzali; ordained June 6, 1959; appointed November 23, 1993; consecrated January 6, 1994. *Office: 1234 Washington Blvd., Detroit, MI, 48226.*

Most Reverend

ALLEN J. VIGNERON, D.D.

Auxiliary Bishop of Detroit, Titular Bishop of Sault Ste. Marie; ordained July 27, 1975; appointed June 12, 1996; consecrated July 9, 1996. *Office: 1234 Washington Blvd., Detroit, MI, 48226.*

Most Reverend

JOHN C. NIENSTEDT

Auxiliary Bishop of Detroit, Titular Bishop of Alton; ordained July 27, 1974; appointed June 12, 1996; consecrated July 9, 1996. *Office: 1234 Washington Blvd., Detroit, MI, 48226.*

ESTABLISHED MARCH 8, 1833; CREATED AN ARCHBISHOPRIC AUGUST 3, 1937.

Square Miles 3,901.

Comprises the Counties of Lapeer, Macomb, Monroe, Oakland, St. Clair and Wayne.

For legal titles of parishes and archdiocesan institutions, consult the Cardinal's Office.

STATISTICAL OVERVIEW

Personnel	
Cardinal	1
Auxiliary Bishops	6
Retired Bishops	2
Priests: Diocesan Active in Diocese	335
Priests: Active Outside Diocese	13
Priests: Diocesan in Foreign Missions	1
Priests: Retired, Sick or Absent	138
Number of Diocesan Priests	487
Religious Priests in Diocese	236
Extern Priests in Diocese	42
Ordinations:	
Diocesan Priests	7
Religious Priests	1
Transitional Deacons	7
Permanent Deacons in Diocese	143
Total Brothers	97
Total Sisters	2,091
Parishes	
Parishes	307
With Resident Pastor:	
Resident Diocesan Priests	261
Resident Religious Priests	30
Without Resident Pastor:	
Administered by Priests	16
Missions	5
Pastoral Centers	6
New Parishes Created	1
Professional Ministry Personnel:	
Brothers	6
Sisters	140
Lay Ministers	443
Welfare	
Catholic Hospitals	11
Total Assisted	1,523,477
Health Care Centers	8
Total Assisted	9,927
Homes for the Aged	13
Total Assisted	2,017
Residential Care of Children	8
Total Assisted	1,456
Day Care and Extended Day Care Centers	2
Total Assisted	529
Specialized Homes	8
Total Assisted	1,998
Special Centers for Social Services	11
Total Assisted	17,223
Residential Care of Disabled	1
Total Assisted	118
Educational	
Seminaries, Diocesan	2
Students from This Diocese	41
Students from Other Diocese	80
Diocesan Students in Other Seminaries	2
Seminaries, Religious	2
Students Religious	12
Total Seminarians	55
Colleges and Universities	4
Total Students	19,526
High Schools, Diocesan and Parish	18
Total Students	6,268
High Schools, Private	14
Total Students	7,778
Elementary Schools, Diocesan and Parish	132
Total Students	40,030
Elementary Schools, Private	6
Total Students	1,124
Catechesis/Religious Education:	
High School Students	7,347
Elementary Students	72,206
Total Students Under Catholic Instruction	154,334
Teachers in the Diocese:	
Priests	35
Brothers	21
Sisters	154
Lay Teachers	2,484
Vital Statistics	
Receptions into the Church:	
Infant Baptism Totals	16,907
Adult Baptism Totals	1,327
Received into Full Communion	1,846
First Communions	16,084
Confirmations	12,508
Marriages:	
Catholic	4,229
Interfaith	1,778
Total Marriages	6,007
Deaths	10,324
Total Catholic Population	1,452,100
Total Population	4,266,650

Former Bishops—Rt. Rev. FREDERIC RESE, D.D., cons. Oct. 6, 1833; resigned Aug. 19, 1840; died Dec. 30, 1871.—Rt. Rev. PETER PAUL LEFEVERE, D.D., cons. Nov. 22, 1841; Bishop of Zela, coadjutor and admin. of Detroit; died March 4, 1869.—Rt. Rev. CASPAR HENRY BORGESS, D.D., cons. April 24, 1870; Bishop of Calydon, coadjutor and admin. of Detroit; became Bishop of Detroit Dec. 30, 1871; resigned April 16, 1887; died May 3, 1890.—Rt. Rev. JOHN SAMUEL FOLEY, D.D., cons. Nov. 4, 1888; died Jan. 5, 1918.—Most Rev. MICHAEL JAMES GALLAGHER, D.D., cons. Sept. 8, 1915; Bishop of Tipasa, coadjutor of Grand

Rapids; became Bishop of Grand Rapids Dec. 26, 1916; transferred to Detroit July 18, 1918; died Jan. 20, 1937.—His Eminence EDWARD CARDINAL MOONEY, D.D., appt. Apostolic Delegate in India Jan. 8, 1926; appt. Titular Archbishop of Irenopolis Jan. 18, 1926; cons. Jan. 31, 1926; appt. Apostolic Delegate in Japan Feb. 25, 1931; transferred to the Diocese of Rochester, Aug. 28, 1933; transferred to the Archdiocese of Detroit, Aug. 3, 1937; created Cardinal Priest of the title of S. Susanna, Feb. 18, 1946; died Oct. 25, 1958.—His Eminence JOHN CARDINAL DEARDEN, D.D., ord. Dec. 8, 1932; cons. Titular Bishop of Sarepta and coadjutor Bishop of Pittsburgh Dec. 22, 1950; installed Archbishop of Detroit Jan. 29, 1959; created Cardinal April 28, 1969; resigned as Archbishop July 15, 1980; died Aug. 1, 1988.—His Eminence EDMUND CARDINAL SZOKA, J.C.L., D.D., Archbishop Emeritus of Detroit; ord. June 5, 1954; appt. Bishop of Gaylord June 15, 1971; cons. July 20, 1971; installed July 20, 1971; promoted to See of Detroit March 28, 1981; installed May 17, 1981; created Cardinal June 28, 1988; appt. Pres., Prefacture for Economic Affairs of the Holy See June 25, 1990.

Archdiocesan Departments and Divisions

Information and Reference—Tel: 313-237-5800.

Cardinal's Office—1234 Washington Blvd., Detroit, 48226; Fax: 313-237-4642. All official mail should be directed to this office. Rev. G. MICHAEL BUGARIN, Cardinal's Appointments Sec. Tel: 313-237-5816. Rev. Msgr. JOHN P. ZENZ, Moderator of the Curia. Tel: 313-237-5783. Sr. BARBARA CELESKEY, S.J., Chancellor. Tel: 313-237-5847; Fax: 313-237-4643.

Auxiliary Bishops—Most Rev. BERNARD J. HARRINGTON, D.D., Region 2. Tel: 313-237-5859. Most Rev. KEVIN M. BRITT, D.D., Region 3. Tel: 313-237-5848. Most Rev. MOSES B. ANDERSON, D.D., Region 1. Tel: 313-342-5292. Most Rev. JOHN C. NIENSTEDT, D.D., Region 4. Tel: 313-237-5788. Most Rev. ALLEN J. VIGNERON, D.D., Region 2. Tel: 313-883-8501.

College of Consultors—Revs. JEROME A. BRZEZINSKI; FRANCIS BURNS; DONALD HANCHON; Rev. Msgr. JAMES MOLONEY; Rev. KEVIN O'BRIEN; Rev. FREDERICK SCHWEIHOFER; Rev. Msgr. ANTHONY TOCCO; Rev. Msgr. JOHN P. ZENZ.

Presbyteral Council—Revs. LOUIS E. GRANDPRE; DAVID BUERSMEYER; Rev. Msgr. JOHN P. ZENZ; Sr. BARBARA CELESKEY, S.J.; Revs. RAYMOND SAYERS; THOMAS SUTHERLAND; Revs. DONALD ARCHAMBAULT; FRANCIS BURNS; PATRICK HALFPENNY; MICHAEL HRYDZIUSZKO; Rev. Msgr. F. GERALD MARTIN; Revs. MICHAEL MOLNAR; JOHN LEO PHALEN; DAVID PRUESS, O.F.M.Cap.; JAMES SCHEICK; TIMOTHY SZOTT; Rev. Msgr. ANTHONY TOCCO; Revs. STANLEY ULMAN; RONALD WILLIAMS; JEROME A. BRZEZINSKI; Rev. Msgr. WILLIAM EASTON; Revs. DONALD HANCHON; DENNIS LAESCH; KEVIN O'BRIEN; FREDERICK SCHWEIHOFER; Rev. Msgr. WILLIAM SHERZER; Revs. DANIEL TRAPP; MICHAEL VERSHAEVE; JAMES WRIGHT; LAWRENCE ZUREK.

Archdiocesan Vicars—Revs. TIMOTHY F. BABCOCK, Pontiac Area (3); RICHARD BARTOSZEK, Downriver (4); GERARD BECHARD, Western Wayne (4); JAMES L. BJORUM, Serf (2); MARK BRAUER, West Detroit (1); JAMES E. COMMYN, Belle River (2); RONALD DEHONDT, Northwest Detroit (1); RENE L. DESMARAIS, Port Huron (2); SIDNEY J. ECKERT, Gratiot (1); NEIL EMON, O.S.C., Southland (4); WILLIAM FISHER, O.S.F.S., Monroe (4); VALENTINE GATTARI, East Side (1); Rev. Msgr. ROBERT S. HUMITZ, Vicariate of the Lakes (3); Revs. LAWRENCE KAISER, Dearborn (4); TIMOTHY KANE, North Central (1); KENNETH KAUCHECK, Birmingham-Bloomfield-Troy (3); GERALD A. MCENHILL, Farmington-Southfield (3); RICHARD MEVISSEN, C.Ss.R., The Hub (1); RONALD MILLIGAN, North Macomb (2); TIMOTHY MURRAY, Warren-Centerline (2); DUANE NOVELLY, Detroit-Grosse Pointe (1); Rev. Msgr. JAMES ROBINSON, S.S.E., West Side Inner City (1); Revs. THOMAS F. SLOWINSKI, Northwest Wayne (4); GARY T. SMETANKA, East Macomb (2); DOUGLAS J. TERRIEN, Thumb (3); EDWARD F. ZAORSKI, Southwest (1); LAWRENCE ZURAWSKI, Southeast Oakland (3).

Archdiocesan Pastoral Council—Rev. RICHARD G. THOMPSON, O.S.C.; Ms. CATHERINE WAGNER.

The Metropolitan Tribunal—305 Michigan Ave., Detroit, 48226. Tel: 313-237-5865; Fax: 313-237-5872. Office Hours: Mon.-Fri. 8:30-4:30.

Judicial Vicar—Very Rev. NORMAN D. NAWROCKI, J.C.L.

Adjutant Judicial Vicars—Revs. GEORGE P. MILLER, J.C.L.; RONALD J. JOZWIAK, J.C.L.

Diocesan Judges—Revs. WILLIAM CARNAGO, J.C.L.; JEROME SLOWINSKI, J.C.L.; Rev. Msgr. JOHN WEIER, J.C.L.; Revs. TIMOTHY BABCOCK; JAMES BJORUM, J.C.L.; ROBERT BURKE, J.C.L.; JOHN GAGALA, J.C.L.; KENNETH KAUCHECK, J.C.D.; MICHAEL A. MOLNAR, J.C.L.; GARY TIERNEY, J.C.L.; ROBERT H. WILLIAMS, J.C.L.

Office Manager—SALLY BAIRD.

Notaries—GLORIA ANFIELD; SALLY BAIRD; ALICE LILEY; ANDREA PINTO; MARJORIE SEERY; DARNELL MCQUEEN.

Defenders of Bond—Revs. RICHARD CAVELLIER, J.C.L.; FRANCIS REISS, J.C.L.; Rev. Msgr. RICARDO BASS, J.C.L.; FRANCIS SYLVESTER; Rev. Msgr. WALTER A. HURLEY, J.C.L.; Rev. RONALD T. BROWNE, J.C.L.; Sr. DIANE MASSON, C.S.S.F., J.C.L.

Auditors—Rev. MAREK STOCHMAL; ROBERT CADOTTE.

Court Expert—Sr. JUDITH MCMANUS, O.P., A.C.S.W., C.S.W.

Department of Christian Service—DANIEL PIEPSZOWSKI, Dir., *305 Michigan Ave., Detroit, 48226.* Tel: 313-237-5900; Fax: 313-237-5866.

Office of Human Services and Pastoral Care—KRISTA BAJOKA. Tel: 313-237-5962.

Office of Institutions and Agencies—PHIL WELLS. Tel: 313-237-5903.

Office of Social Ministries—Sr. JUDE VAN BAALEN. Tel: 313-237-5958.

Department of Communications—NED MCGRATH, Dir., *305 Michigan Ave., Detroit, 48226.* Tel: 313-237-5943; Fax: 313-237-4644.

Office of Information Technology—CLIFF TRUDEAU. Tel: 313-237-5797; Fax: 313-237-5979.

Office of Public Relations—NED MCGRATH. Tel: 313-237-5943; Fax: 313-237-4644.

Office of Printing and Mailing—DENNIS MILLIGAN. Tel: 313-237-5967; Fax: 313-965-8471.

Office of Television—KEN KOLB. Tel: 313-237-5943; Fax: 313-237-5928.

Department of Education—Rev. Msgr. JOHN M. QUINN, Dir., *305 Michigan Ave., Detroit, 48226.* Tel: 313-237-4675; Fax: 313-237-5867.

Catholic Schools—Sr. FRANCES NADOLNY, O.P., Ph.D., Supt. Tel: 313-237-5775.

Office of Catechetics / Religious Education—Sr. ELIZABETH FLAHERTY, O.P. Tel: 313-237-4670.

Office of Family Life / Youth Ministry—FRANCIS OZAR. Tel: 313-237-5892.

St. John Center for Family and Youth—Rev. JOHN WEST, Rector. Tel: 734-237-4668; Fax: 734-414-1154.

Department of Development—MICHAEL E. MURPHY, Dir., *1234 Washington Blvd., Detroit, 48226.* Tel: 313-883-8657; Fax: 313-883-8681.

Catholic Services Appeal—THERESA J. KACH. Tel: 313-883-8656.

Stewardship Education—KAREN D. WILLIAMS. Tel: 313-883-8657.

Planned Giving—THOMAS P. SCHOLLER. Tel: 313-883-8657.

Donor Relations—DAVID P. CASNOVSKY. Tel: 313-883-8657.

Sacred Heart Major Seminary— Institutional Advancement; MICHAEL G. MCGLINNEN, Dir., *2701 Chicago Blvd., Detroit, 48206.* Tel: 313-883-8532.

Department of Finance and Administrative Services—Sr. MARY V. KORB, R.S.M., Dir., *1234 Washington Blvd., Detroit, 48226.* Tel: 313-237-5834; Fax: 313-237-5868.

Archdiocesan Buildings—DONALD J. SCHEIBLE. Tel: 313-237-5845. JEMAR HARVILLE, Asst. Dir. Bldgs. Tel: 313-237-5806.

Archdiocesan Properties—GERALD T. CHUHRAN. Tel: 313-237-5820.

Financial Services—ABELARDO B. BUSQUE. Tel: 313-237-5828.

Human Resources—CAROL MEYERS. Tel: 313-237-5947.

Sacred Heart Building Administration—JOHN DUNCAN. Tel: 313-883-8599.

Archdiocese of Detroit Endowment Foundation—1234 Washington Blvd., Detroit, 48226.

Administration—Sr. MARY V. KORB, R.S.M., Dir. Tel: 313-237-5834; Fax: 313-237-5868.

Development—MICHAEL E. MURPHY, Dir. Tel: 313-883-8657; Fax: 313-883-8681.

Department of Parish Life—CATHERINE WAGNER, Dir. LORY MCGLINNEN, Assoc. Dir., *305 Michigan Ave., Detroit, 48226.* Tel: 313-237-5934; Fax: 313-237-5869.

Evangelization—Rev. DANIEL HAVRON, O.F.M. Tel: 313-237-4686.

Office of Christian Worship—DANIEL MCAFEE. Tel: 313-237-5932.

Council of Catholic Women—PATRICIA KENDRO, Pres. Tel: 313-237-5896.

Hispanic Catholic Ministries—RAUL FELICIANO. Tel: 313-237-5761.

Black Catholic Ministries—Rev. CLARENCE WILLIAMS, C.PP.S. Tel: 313-237-5934.

Office of Leadership Formation—Rev. RICHARD THOMSON, O.S.C. Tel: 313-237-5887.

Office of Pastoral Ministers and Permanent Diaconate—Deacon JOHN BALL. Tel: 313-237-5778.

Delegate for Religious—Sr. MARGARET STECHSHULTE, O.P. Tel: 313-237-4682.

Pastoral Resources—Dr. MICHAEL MCCALLION. Tel: 313-237-5760.

"The Michigan Catholic" Newspaper—KAREN M. PITTON, Editor, *305 Michigan Ave., Detroit, 48226.* Tel: 313-224-8000.

Archivist—ROMAN P. GODZAK, *1234 Washington Blvd., Detroit, 48226.* Tel: 313-237-5846; Fax: 313-237-4643.

Propagation of the Faith (Missions)—Rev. Msgr. JAMES A. MOLONEY, *17650 W. Outer Dr., Dearborn Heights, 48127.*

Holy Childhood Association—1230 Washington Blvd., Detroit, 48226. Tel: 313-237-5807.

Catholic Youth Organization—Detroit: *Gabriel Richard Bldg., 305 Michigan Ave., Detroit, 48226.* Tel: 313-963-7172. Branch office, RAYMOND HILLEN, Dir., *22235 Fenkell, Detroit.* Tel: 313-534-4620. Neighborhood Development, Brightmoor Community.

Archdiocesan Theological Commission—Rev. Msgr. JOHN P. ZENZ. Tel: 313-237-5783.

Vocation Office—Rev. ROBERT J. FISHER, Dir. Tel: 313-237-5875. Sr. ANGELA CERNA-PLATA, I.H.M., Asst. Dir., . Fax: 313-237-6070.

Office of Pastoral Services for Clergy—Most Rev. KEVIN M. BRITT, Dir.; Deacon EUGENE KRZEMINSKI, Exec. Asst., *1234 Washington Blvd., Detroit, 48226.* Tel: 313-237-5848; Fax: 313-237-5844.

Office of Parish Support Services—GERALD STEBBINS. Tel: 313-237-6059; Fax: 313-237-4643.

CLERGY, PARISHES, MISSIONS AND PAROCHIAL SCHOOLS

CITY OF DETROIT
(Wayne County)

1—CATHEDRAL, CHURCH OF THE MOST BLESSED SACRAMENT, Rev. Msgr. James P. Robinson, S.S.E., Rector.
Res., 9844 Woodward Ave., 48202. Tel: 313-865-6300; Fax: 313-867-4613.

2—ALL SAINTS, Rev. Edward F. Zaorski.
Res., 7824 W. Fort St., 48209. Tel: 313-841-1428; Fax: 313-841-3009.

3—ST. ALOYSIUS, Revs. Mark Soehner, O.F.M.; Mel P. Brady, O.F.M. In res., Rev. Charles Smiech, O.F.M.; Bro. James Ebaugh, O.F.M.
Res., Chancery Bldg., 1234 Washington Blvd., 48226. Tel: 313-237-5810; Fax: 313-963-9076.

4—ST. ANDREW (Polish), Rev. Julian Chmura.
Res., 7060 McGraw Ave., 48210. Tel: 313-361-1717; Fax: 313-361-9816.

5—SS. ANDREW AND BENEDICT (Slovak), Rev. Edward F. Zaorski.
Res., 2430 S. Beatrice St., 48217. Tel: 313-381-1184; Fax: 313-831-0416.

6—STE. ANNE, Revs. Robert J. Duggan, C.S.B.; Maurice Restivo, C.S.B.
Res., 1000 Ste. Anne St., 48216. Tel: 313-496-1701; Fax: 313-496-0429.

7—ANNUNCIATION, Rev. Valentine A. Gattari.
Res., 1265 Parkview Ave., 48214. Tel: 313-822-1262; Fax: 313-824-1908.
Stapleton Center—9341 Agnes, 48214. Tel: 313-822-0397.

8—ST. ANTHONY, Rev. Michael Nkackukwu; Deacon Elgia L. McCoy, Exec. Admin.
Office: 5247 Sheridan Ave., 48213. Tel: 313-921-0263; Fax: 313-924-4040.

9—ST. ANTHONY (Lithuanian), Rev. Alphonse Babonas.
Res., 1750 25th St., 48216. Tel: 313-554-1284.

10—ASSUMPTION GROTTO, Rev. Eduard Perrone. In res., Rev. Boleslaus Lipczewski; Bro. Matthew Hincks, O.R.C.
Res., 13770 Gratiot Ave., 48205. Tel: 313-372-0762; Fax: 313-372-2064. [CEM]

11—ST. AUGUSTINE AND ST. MONICA, Rev. Daniel J. Trapp, Admin.
Res., 4151 Seminole St., 48214. Tel: 313-921-4107; Fax: 313-921-1115.

12—ST. BARTHOLOMEW, Rev. Boleslaus Krol. In res., Rev. Edward Kaszak.
Res., 2291 E. Outer Dr., 48234. Tel: 313-892-1446; Fax: 313-892-1149.
School—Tel: 313-366-3640. Sr. Albina, Prin.
Lay Teachers 8; Students 158.
Convent—2251 E. Outer Dr., 48234. Tel: 313-366-0525.
Sisters 4.

13—St. Brendan, Rev. Sidney Eckert, Admin. In res., Rev. Luis Resma.
Res., 11433 Beaconsfield, 48224. Tel: 313-372-1644; Fax: 313-372-7195.

14—St. Cecilia, Rev. Msgr. Thomas J. Finnigan.
Res., Box 04209, 10400 Stoepel Ave., 48204. Tel: 313-933-6788; Fax: 313-933-1439.
Church—Livernois at Stearns, 48204.
School—Tel: 313-933-2400; Fax: 313-933-9332. Sr. Margaret Sweeney, I.H.M., Prin.
Sisters-Servants of the Immaculate Heart of Mary 2; Lay Teachers 16; Students 400.
High School—Tel: 313-864-3330; Fax: 313-864-3648. Sunbeam Hughes, Prin.
Priests 1; Sisters 3; Lay Teachers 24.
Convent—6336 Burlingame Ave., 48204.

15—St. Charles Borromeo, Revs. David Preuss, O.F.M.Cap.; Augustine Cops, O.F.M.Cap.; Sr. Francis W. Schnell, O.P., Pastoral Assoc.
Res., 1491 Baldwin Ave., 48214. Tel: 313-331-0253; Fax: 313-331-4834.

16—St. Christine, Rev. Mark S. Brauer.
Office: 22303 Fenkell St., 48223. Tel: 313-535-7272; Fax: 313-535-3439.
Res., 23450 W. Davison, 48223.
School—13550 Virgil, 48223. Tel: 313-535-9342; Fax: 313-455-7355. Sr. M. Josephine Lechowicz, C.S.S.F., Prin.
Felician Sisters 2; Lay Teachers 11; Students 246.

17—Christ the King, Rev. Victor Clore. Pastoral Assocs.: Sr. Fiorentina D'Amore; Mrs. Katherine Paul.
Res., 16805 Pierson, 48219. Tel: 313-532-1211; Fax: 313-532-1216.
Church—20800 Grand River & Burt Rd., 48219. Tel: 313-532-1213.
School—Tel: 313-532-1213. Mrs. Margaret Pic-Kell, D.R.E.
Lay Teachers 18; Students 267.

18—St. Christopher, Rev. Richard A. Hartmann; Deacons John Marku; Norbert Motowski; Sr. Celeste Hupert.
Res., 7800 Woodmont Ave., 48228. Tel: 313-584-7460; Fax: 313-584-6361.
School—Tel: 313-846-1430. Ronald Mysliwiec, Prin. Sisters of the Holy Family of Nazareth 1; Lay Teachers 7; Students 217.
Convent—7800 Woodmont Ave., 48228.

19—St. Cunegunda, Rev. Mitchell Szarek.
Res., 5900 St. Lawrence Ave., 48210. Tel: 313-841-4000.
School—Tel: 313-843-0004. Sr. Mary Alexander, C.S.S.F., Prin.
Lay Teachers 8; Religious 3; Students 159.

20—St. Dominic, Revs. Malcolm S. Willoughby, O.P.; James Murray, O.P.; Charles D. Farrell, O.P. In res., Revs. Daniel Casey, O.P.; Francis Maguire, O.P.; Jesse Cox, O.P.
Res., 4844 Trumbull Ave., 48208. Tel: 313-831-8790; Fax: 313-831-2965.
Shrine—Rosary Shrine of St. Jude, Tel: 313-831-7566; Fax: 313-831-2965.
Convent—4835 Lincoln Ave., 48208. Tel: 313-831-1028. Missionaries of Charity
Sisters 4.

21—St. Elizabeth, Rev. John W. Markham.
Res., 3138 E. Canfield Ave., 48207. Tel: 313-921-9225; Fax: 313-921-9475.

22—St. Francis D'Assisi, Rev. Robert J. Wojciechowski.
Res., 4500 Wesson St., 48210. Tel: 313-897-7229; Fax: 313-897-7485.
School—Tel: 313-897-8720. Mrs. Marlene Garrett, Prin.
Lay Teachers 8; Lay Librarian 1; Students 187.

23—St. Francis de Sales, Rev. James E. O'Reilly, S.J.
Res., 10600 Fenkell Ave., 48238. Tel: 313-861-4020; Fax: 313-861-4718.

24—St. Gabriel, Rev. Donald F. Hanchon. In res., Rev. Anthony F. Bologna.
Res., 8118 W. Vernor Hwy., 48209-1524. Tel: 313-841-0753; Fax: 313-841-0916.
Catechesis/Religious Programs—Students 395.

25—St. Gemma Galgani, Rev. Mark S. Brauer.
Res., 23450 W. Davison, 48223. Tel: 313-255-3666; Fax: 313-537-0598.
School—13550 Virgil, 48223. Tel: 313-535-9342.
Lay Teachers 10; Students (Grades K-8) 189.

26—St. Gerard, Rev. Donald Archambault; Deacon Alfons Hogrebe.
Res., 19800 Pembroke, 48219. Tel: 313-537-5770; Fax: 313-537-5773.
School—19900 Evergreen Rd., 48219. Tel: 313-533-4353; Fax: 313-533-2190.
Sisters 2; Lay Teachers 11; Students 204.
Catechesis/Religious Programs—Tel: 313-533-0197. Sr. Laura Kendrick, H.V.M., D.R.E.
Students 252.
Convent—19900 Evergreen Rd., 48219.

27—Gesu, Rev. Norman Dickson, S.J.; Deacon Ronald McIntyre. In res., Revs. John A. Hardon, S.J.; Kenneth J. Noetzel, S.J.; John C. Kehres, S.J.; Bro. Richard C. Conroy, S.J.
Res., 17204 Oak Dr., 48221. Tel: 313-862-4400; Fax: 313-862-1083.
School—Sr. Stella Rabaut, I.H.M., Prin., Tel: 313-863-4677. Sisters-Servants of the Immaculate Heart of Mary 2; Lay Teachers 28; Students 546.
Convent—17180 Oak Dr., 48221. Tel: 313-861-8877.

28—St. Gregory, Rev. Ronald J. DeHondt; Deacon Benjamin Prince.
Res., 15031 Dexter, 48238. Tel: 313-861-0363; Fax: 313-862-6805.

29—Guardian Angels, Rev. Sidney J. Eckert.
Res., 12545 Kelly Rd., 48224. Tel: 313-526-0735; Fax: 313-526-7382.

30—St. Hedwig, Rev. Kenneth M. Chase.
Res., 3245 Junction Ave., 48210. Tel: 313-894-5409; Fax: 313-894-4730.

31—Holy Cross (Hungarian), Revs. Barnabas G. Kiss, O.F.M.; Angelus Ligeti, O.F.M.
Res., 8423 South St., 48209. Tel: 313-842-1133; Fax: 313-842-2773.

32—Holy Family (Italian), Rev. John Stopponi, Admin.
Res., 641 Walter P. Chrysler Expwy., 48226. Tel: 313-963-2046; Fax: 313-961-0065.

33—Holy Redeemer, Revs. Robert Halter, C.SS.R.; Lawrence Sanders, C.SS.R.; Richard Mevissen, C.SS.R.; Gregory May, C.SS.R. In res., Revs. Robert Hirsch, C.SS.R.; John E. Bellon, C.SS.R.; Bros. Gerard Patin, C.SS.R.; Robert Ruffing, C.SS.R.
Res., 1721 Junction Ave., 48209. Tel: 313-842-3450; Fax: 313-849-0539.
School—Tel: 313-841-5230. Sr. Elizabeth Fleckenstein, I.H.M., Prin.
Sisters Servants of the Immaculate Heart of Mary 8; Lay Teachers 13; Students 360.
High School—Tel: 313-841-4433. John Conley, Prin. Sisters 5; Lay Teachers 9; Students 185.
Convent—5678 Eldred Ave., 48209. Tel: 313-841-8420.

34—St. Hyacinth (Polish), Rev. Francis S. Skalski.
Res., 3151 Farnsworth Ave., 48211. Tel: 313-922-1507; Fax: 313-922-2459.

35—Immaculate Heart of Mary, Rev. William J. Carnago; Mary Caroline Jonah, Pastoral Assoc.
Res., 16000 Pembroke Ave., 48235. Tel: 313-272-0990; Fax: 313-272-9772.
School—19940 Mansfield, 48235. Tel: 313-835-0258. Sr. Stephanie Holub, R.S.M., Prin.
Sisters of Mercy of the Union 3; Lay Teachers 15; Students 144.
Convent—19960 Mansfield Ave., 48235. Tel: 313-272-6810; Fax: 313-272-6811.

36—St. Jerome. Closed. For inquiries for parish records contact the Chancery.

37—St. John Berchmans-St. Juliana, Rev. Luke Stano, O.S.M.
Res., 9801 Chalmers, 48213. Tel: 313-526-7254; Fax: 313-526-7553.
School—St. Juliana, 9755 Chalmers, 48213. Tel: 313-526-0062.
Servite Sisters 1; Lay Teachers 10; Students 260.

38—St. John Cantius (Polish), Rev. Edwin A. Szczygiel.
Res., 844 Harbaugh Ave., 48209. Tel: 313-842-2276; Fax: 313-842-2268.

39—St. Josaphat (Polish), Rev. Ronald J. Jozwiak.
Res., 691 E. Canfield Ave., 48201. Tel: 313-831-1072; Fax: 313-831-1072.

40—St. Joseph, Rev. Msgr. John F. Schweder.
Res., 1828 Jay St., 48207. Tel: 313-393-8212; Fax: 313-393-8294.

41—St. Jude, Revs. Raymond J. Sayers; Christopher Maus; Sr. Judy Lieder, O.P., Pastoral Assoc.
Res., 15889 E. Seven Mile Rd., 48205. Tel: 313-527-0380; Fax: 313-527-3511.
School—15865 E. Seven Mile, 48205. Tel: 313-839-6792.
Sisters 2; Lay Teachers 22; Students 421.
Catechesis/Religious Programs—Students 210.

42—St. Leo, Most Rev. Thomas J. Gumbleton. Pastoral Assocs.: William Morrow; Daniel Maxwell.
Church & Res.: 4860 15th St., 48208. Tel: 313-894-0357; Fax: 313-896-2804.
School—4851 14th St., 48208. Mary Lou Van Antwerp, Prin., Tel: 313-896-6078.
Sisters 2; Lay Teachers 7; Students 200.

43—St. Louis the King, Revs. Boleslaus Krol; Ron Borg, C.S.B.
Res., 18891 St. Louis Ave., 48234. Tel: 313-891-1766; Fax: 313-891-7959.

44—St. Luke, Rev. Robert Kotlarz; Sr. Judith Mouch, R.S.M., Parish Nurse Ministry; Sr. Marie Roy, S.S.J., Pastoral Assoc.
Res., 8017 Ohio Ave., 48204. Tel: 313-935-6161; Fax: 313-935-0788.
School—St. Luke & St. Brigid Elementary School, St. Brigid Montessori Preschool, 8091 Ohio, 48204. Tel: 313-933-9611; Fax: 313-983-9522. Clima Fields, Prin.
Lay Teachers 10; Students 171.

45—Madonna, Rev. Charles G. Kosanke, Admin.; Sr. Ellen Ann Gardner, S.C.
Res., 1125 Oakman Blvd., 48238. Tel: 313-868-4308; Fax: 313-868-9771.

46—Martyrs of Uganda, Rev. Tyrone Robinson; Deacons Douglas Jackson; Allen McNeeley.
Res., 7601 Rosa Parks Blvd., 48206. Tel: 313-896-2335; Fax: 313-896-0925.
School—Martyrs of Uganda Catholic Academy, 4317 Blaine, 48204. Tel: 313-361-1065.
Lay Teachers 14; Students 180.
Catechesis/Religious Programs—Mrs. Mary Brown, D.R.E.
Students 17.

47—St. Mary, Revs. Norman G. Hannahs, C.S.Sp.; Martin J. Conroy, C.S.Sp.
Res., 646 Monroe Ave., 48226. Tel: 313-961-8711; Fax: 313-961-4994.

48—St. Mary's of Redford, Rev. Ronald R. Williams.
Mailing Address: 14750 St. Mary's, 48227. Tel: 313-273-1100; Fax: 313-273-2002.
School—St. Mary of Redford Grade School, 14751 Mansfield, 48227. Tel: 313-835-6834; Fax: 313-836-4184. Sr. Joan McGrath, I.H.M., Prin.
Religious 4; Lay Teachers 21; Students 416.
Convent—14601 Mansfield, 48227. Tel: 313-272-2727.
Sisters 4.

49—St. Matthew, Rev. Duane R. Novelly; Sr. Karen Eklund, I.H.M., Pastoral Min.; Deacon William H. Johr.
Res., 6021 Whittier Ave., 48224. Tel: 313-884-4470; Fax: 313-884-4276.
School—Ann O'Grady, Prin. Lay Teachers 10; Students 154.

50—Most Holy Trinity, Revs. Russell E. Kohler; Grace Agius.
Res., 1050 Porter St., 48226. Tel: 313-965-4450; Fax: 313-965-4453.
Schools—Tel: 313-961-8855. Sr. Irene Therese Gumbleton, Prin.
Sisters 3; Lay Teachers 5; Students 152; St. Vincent Middle School, (Grades 5-8) 2020 14th St., 48216. Tel: 313-961-6773. Ms. Kathleen McBride, Prin.
Lay Teachers 4; Students 90.
Convent—1234 Porter St., 48226. Tel: 313-961-6683.

51—Nativity of Our Lord, Rev. Jerome C. Singer.
Res., 5900 McClellan Ave., 48213. Tel: 313-922-0033; Fax: 313-922-0033.

52—Our Lady Gate of Heaven, Rev. Dennis D. Duggan, Admin.; Sr. Rosemarie Kieffer, O.P., Pastoral Assoc.; Sr. Nancy Jureck, O.P., Pastoral Assoc.; Deacons William Krauskoff; Wyatt Jones.
Church—9555 St. Mary's, 48227. Tel: 313-270-5350; Fax: 313-838-3207.

53—Our Lady of Good Counsel, Revs. David E. Weisner; Emiliano Ahurwendeire; Deacon Donald Sandstrom, Pastoral Assoc.
Res., 17142 Rowe Ave., 48205. Tel: 313-372-1698; Fax: 313-372-1211.

54—Our Lady Help of Christians (Polish), Rev. George A. Rutkowski.
Res., 12635 McDougall Ave., 48212. Tel: 313-892-6116.
Convent—12541 McDougall Ave., 48212. Tel: 313-891-5280.

55—Our Lady of Mt. Carmel, Rev. Bartolomeo Santino Ferrero. Pastoral Associates: Ms. Mary Jane Jarczak; Tom Di Giacomo; Rosalie DeLoye; Cyndy Guerra.
Res., 555 Oakwood Blvd., 48217. Tel: 313-841-8478.

56—Our Lady of the Rosary, Rev. Robert Morand.
Res., 5930 Woodward Ave., 48202. Tel: 313-875-6011; Fax: 313-872-0758.

57—Our Lady of Sorrows, Revs. David Preuss, O.F.M.Cap.; Augustine Cops, O.F.M.Cap.
Mailing Address: 2965 Meldrum, 48207. Tel: 313-571-4643 (parish).
Res., 1491 Baldwin, 48214. Tel: 313-331-0253; Fax: 313-331-4834.

58—Our Lady Queen of Angels, Rev. James Henning, O.F.M.Conv.
Res., 4200 Martin Ave., 48210. Tel: 313-897-8160; Fax: 313-897-8126.
School—Tel: 313-894-6266. Mr. Carl E. Weiss, Prin.
Franciscan Sisters of St. Joseph 2; Lay Teachers 7; Students 219.
Convent—4108 Martin Ave., 48210. Tel: 313-894-3462.

59—OUR LADY QUEEN OF HEAVEN, Rev. Donald A. Sopiak.
Res., 8200 Rolyat Ave., 48234. Tel: 313-891-4553; Fax: 313-891-5782.

60—ST. PATRICK, Rev. Thomas J. Duffey; Floria Ellison, Pastoral Assoc.
Church—58 Parsons, 48201. Tel: 313-833-0857; Fax: 313-833-0128.
St. Patrick Senior Center, Inc.—Tel: 313-833-7080. Sr. Mary Watson, O.P., Pres.

61—SS. PETER AND PAUL JESUIT, Rev. Robert R. Hartigan, S.J. In res., Revs. Arthur E. Loveley, S.J.; Francis X. Budovic, S.J.; George R. Follen, S.J.
Res., 438 St. Antoine St., 48226. Tel: 313-961-8077; Fax: 313-961-5134.

62—SS. PETER AND PAUL (West Side), Revs. Francis R. Reiss; John M. Kubik.
Res., 7685 Grandville Ave., 48228. Tel: 313-846-2222; Fax: 313-584-1484.
School—Tel: 313-336-3600. Patricia Gajewski, Prin. Sisters 2; Lay Teachers 7; Students 133.

63—ST. PHILOMENA, Rev. Peter S. Lentine.
Res., 4281 Marseilles Ave., 48224. Tel: 313-882-4300; Fax: 313-882-1661.
Catechesis/Religious Programs—Kathleen McKenzie, D.R.E., Tel: 313-884-2422.
Students 189.

64—PRECIOUS BLOOD, Most Rev. Moses B. Anderson, S.S.E.
Res., 13305 Grove Ave., 48235. Tel: 313-342-5292; Fax: 313-342-3513.

65—PRESENTATION-OUR LADY OF VICTORY, Rev. Kenneth C. Stewart, O.F.M.Cap.
Res., 19760 Meyers Rd., 48235. Tel: 313-342-1333; Fax: 313-342-4182.
School—Tel: 313-864-0595; Fax: 313-864-2271.
Lay Teachers 10; Students 169.

66—ST. RAYMOND, Rev. David E. Weisner.
Res., 20103 Joann Ave., 48205. Tel: 313-527-0525; Fax: 313-527-9776.
Community House—20055 Joann Ave., 48205. Tel: 313-521-4615.

67—ST. RITA, Rev. Timothy Kane.
Res., 1000 E. State Fair, 48203. Tel: 313-366-2340; Fax: 313-891-0677.

68—SACRED HEART-CHALDEAN PARISH, Rev. Jacob O. Yasso.
Res., 310 W. Seven Mile Rd., 48203. Tel: 313-368-6214; Fax: 313-891-0132.

69—SACRED HEART OF JESUS, Rev. Norman P. Thomas.
Res., 1000 Eliot St., 48207. Tel: 313-831-1356; Fax: 313-831-8603.
Catechesis/Religious Programs—Barbara Hunt, D.R.E.
Students 111.

70—ST. SCHOLASTICA, Rev. Livius Paoli, O.S.B.
Res., 17320 Rosemont Rd., 48219. Tel: 313-531-0140; Fax: 313-531-0739.
Church—Southfield Rd. & West Outer Dr., 48219.
School—Tel: 313-532-1916. Eric Westley, Elementary Prin.
Sisters of St. Dominic (Adrian) 1; Lay Teachers 25; Students 425.
High School—Benedictine High School, Tel: 313-532-1274; Fax: 313-532-5767. Sam Walker, High School Prin.
Sisters 1; Lay Teachers 18; Students 330.
Catechesis/Religious Programs—Students 755.
Convent—17305 Ashton, 48219. Tel: 313-531-3694.

71—ST. STEPHEN-MARY MOTHER OF THE CHURCH, Revs. Mark Gawronski; Rafael Jimenez.
Res., 4311 Central Ave., 48210. Tel: 313-841-0783; Fax: 313-841-4868.
School—Tel: 313-841-2739. Sr. Mary Laurene Smolinski, C.S.S.F., Prin.
Religious 3; Lay Teachers 8; Students 190.
Convent—4329 Central Ave., 48210. Tel: 313-843-9080.

72—ST. SUZANNE, Rev. Dennis D. Duggan; Sr. Lucy Abbey, I.H.M., Pastoral Assoc.
Res., 9357 Westwood Ave., 48228. Tel: 313-838-6780; Fax: 313-838-1063.
School—Sr. Jordan Schaefer, O.S.F., Prin., Tel: 313-836-7030. Lay Teachers 9; Students 180.

73—SWEETEST HEART OF MARY (Polish), Rev. Msgr. John Schweder, Admin.
Res., 4440 Russell St., 48207. Tel: 313-831-6659; Fax: 313-831-8522. [CEM]

74—ST. THOMAS AQUINAS, Rev. William J. Promesso. Pastoral Assocs.: Bro. Michael Graf, O.F.M.; Micheleen Troutman.
Parish Center—5780 Evergreen Rd., 48228. Tel: 313-271-3266; Fax: 313-271-8773.
Rectory—5890 Evergreen Rd., 48228. Tel: 313-336-4559.
School—Tel: 313-271-4170. Sr. Jan Stocking, R.S.M., Prin.
Sisters of Mercy 2; Lay Teachers 12; Students 239.
Catechesis/Religious Programs—Tel: 313-271-0813. Clare Cooper, D.R.E.
Students 159.

75—TRANSFIGURATION, Rev. Andrew Wesley; Deacon Don Sobolewski.
Res., 5830 Simon K. St., 48212. Tel: 313-892-1310; Fax: 313-893-2478.
School—Sr. Angelica Zajkowski, Prin. Sisters of the Holy Family of Nazareth 2; Lay Teachers 10; Students 300.
Convent—5821 Rupert, 48212. Tel: 313-891-9273.

OUTSIDE THE CITY OF DETROIT

Algonac, St. Clair Co., St. Catherine, Rev. Leo P. Broderick.
Res., 1103 Washington, 48001. Tel: 810-794-3301; Fax: 810-794-1849. [CEM]
School—1106 St. Clair Blvd., 48001. Joseph LaLonde, Prin., Tel: 810-794-4966.
Sisters 2; Lay Teachers 7; Students 130.
Catechesis/Religious Programs—Tel: 810-794-3843. Anna Mae Lines, D.R.E.
Students 220.

Allen Park, Wayne Co., St. Frances Cabrini, Revs. Gary Bueche; Gerard J. LeBoeuf; P. Larry Siroskey. In res., Rev. Michael Gormley, S.A.C.
Res., 9000 Laurence Ave., 48101. Tel: 313-381-5601; Fax: 313-381-7837.
School—Tel: 313-928-6610. Bernadette Sugrue, Prin.
Lay Teachers 24; Students 479.
High School—Tel: 313-388-0110. R. Edward Smith, Prin.
Lay Teachers 21; Students 360.
Catechesis/Religious Programs—Jerome Green, D.R.E.
Students 501.

Allenton, St. Clair Co., St. John the Evangelist, Rev. Salvino Briffa.
Res., 872 Capac Rd., 48002. Tel: 810-395-7074; Fax: 810-395-7718.
Catechesis/Religious Programs—Tel: 810-395-2301.
Students 237.

Anchorville, St. Clair Co., Immaculate Conception, Rev. Sigismund Kowalczyk.
Mailing Address: P.O. Box 106, 48004. Tel: 810-725-3051; 725-1121; Fax: 810-725-2474. [CEM]
School—7403 Church Rd., 48004. Tel: 810-725-0078; Fax: 810-725-2474. Irene Heidtke, Prin.
Lay Teachers 12; Students 298.
Catechesis/Religious Programs—Jane Petitpren, D.R.E., Tel: 810-725-1762.
Students 263.

Armada, Macomb Co., St. Mary Mystical Rose, Rev. Bradley Forintos.
Res., 24040 Armada Ridge, 48005. Tel: 810-784-5966; Fax: 810-784-9330.
Catechesis/Religious Programs—Students 252.

Auburn Hills, Oakland Co., Sacred Heart, Rev. James A. Mayworm; Sr. Sharon Simon, O.P., Pastoral Assoc.
Res., 3400 Adams Rd., 48326. Tel: 248-852-4170; Fax: 248-852-5745.
Catechesis/Religious Programs—Tel: 248-852-3620.
Students 334.

St. John Fisher Chapel University Parish, Rev. Jerome A. Brzezinski. Pastoral Assocs.: Sr. Mary Bodde; Sr. Mary Van Gilder; Sr. Mary Ann Dixon; Ms. Linda Coleman; Mr. Eugene Mahon; Mrs. Susan Burrato.
Res., 3665 Walton Blvd., 48326. Tel: 248-373-6457; Fax: 248-373-5479.
Catechesis/Religious Programs—Tel: 248-373-3130. Sr. Mary Ann Dixon, O.P., D.R.E.
Students 809.

Belleville, Wayne Co., St. Anthony, Rev. Thomas H. Cusick; Terrence D. Taylor, Pastoral Assoc.; Deacon Peter Cornell.
Res., 409 W. Columbia Ave., 48111. Tel: 313-697-1211; Fax: 313-697-6217.
School—Tel: 313-699-4313; Fax: 313-699-0824. Sr. Denise Seymour, Prin.
Sisters of St. Joseph of the Third Order of St. Francis 2; Lay Teachers 10; Students 259.
Convent—371 W. Columbia Ave., 48111. Tel: 313-697-6661.

Berkley, Oakland Co., Our Lady of La Salette, Rev. Lawrence Zurawski; Deacon Daniel Darga.
Res., 2600 Harvard Rd., 48072. Tel: 248-541-3762; Fax: 248-541-4250.
School—Tel: 248-542-3757. Mrs. Sue Perna, Prin.
Sisters 2; Lay Teachers 9; Students 268.
Catechesis/Religious Programs—Tel: 248-547-1150.
Students 162.

Beverly Hills, Franklin Co., Our Lady of Albanians, Rev. Primus P. Ndrevashay.
Res., 20855 W. Thirteen Mile Rd., 48025. Tel: 248-642-0816; Fax: 248-642-0251.

Birmingham, Oakland Co., St. Columban, Very Rev. Msgr. John A. Trese; Patricia Costigan, Pastoral Assoc.; Deacon Robert Ovies.
Res., 2200 Dunstable, 48009. Tel: 248-642-1148; Fax: 248-642-4636.
Church—1775 Melton, 48009. Tel: 248-646-5224.
Catechesis/Religious Programs—Tel: 248-646-5225. Nancy Sullivan, D.R.E.
Students 222.

Holy Name, Rev. Robert E. Burke. Pastoral Assocs.: Sr. Shirlee Hoski, S.S.J.-T.O.S.F.; Deacon Michael J. McKale; Donna M. Hansen; Mary A. Pineau.
Parish Office—630 Harmon St., 48009.
Res., 645 Woodland Ave., 48009. Tel: 248-646-2244; Fax: 248-646-2286.
School—Tel: 248-644-2722. Sr. Annice Mordenski, O.P., Prin.
Sisters 2; Lay Teachers 20; Students 417.
Catechesis/Religious Programs—Mary Morian, D.R.E.
Students 490.

Our Lady Queen of Martyrs, Revs. Robert F. Wyzgoski; Michael J. Heppen, C.S.C.
Res., 32340 Pierce Ave., Beverly Hills, 48025. Tel: 248-644-8620; Fax: 248-644-8623.
School—32460 Pierce Ave., Beverly Hills, 48025. Tel: 248-642-2616; Fax: 248-642-3671. Peter J. Ferguson, Prin.
Lay Teachers 15; Students 330.
Catechesis/Religious Programs—Tel: 248-647-6068. Marie Therese Walbridge, D.R.E.
Students 246.

Bloomfield Hills, Oakland Co., St. Hugo of the Hills, Rev. Msgr. Anthony M. Tocco; Rev. James Bilot; Sr. Barbara Rund, O.P., Pastoral Assoc.; Deacon Michael T. Smith.
Res., 2215 Opdyke Rd., 48304. Tel: 248-644-5460; Fax: 248-644-1758.
School—380 E. Hickory Grove, 48304. Tel: 248-642-6131; Fax: 248-642-4457. Sr. Margaret Van Velzen, I.H.M., Prin.
Sisters, Servants of the Immaculate Heart of Mary 5; Lay Teachers 34; Students 877.
Catechesis/Religious Programs—Tel: 248-642-6062.
Students 430.

St. Owen, Rev. Msgr. Edward J. Baldwin. Pastoral Ministers: Sr. Carolyn Nelson; Sr. Anne McGinn. In res., Rev. Msgr. William J. Sherzer, (Retired).
Res., 6869 Franklin Rd., 48301. Tel: 248-626-0840; Fax: 248-626-0345.
Catechesis/Religious Programs—Tel: 248-626-2300. D.R.E.: Sue Fredenberg; Karen Heuer.
Students 412.

St. Regis, Revs. Daniel J. Murphy; Patrick J. Connell; Deacon Brian Carroll. In res., Rev. Duane Doherty, O.F.M.Conv.
Res., 3695 Lincoln, 48301. Tel: 248-646-2686; Fax: 248-646-4643.
School—Tel: 248-644-4466. Barbara S. Stork, Prin.
Lay Teachers 18; Students 342.
Catechesis/Religious Programs—Robert Metz, D.R.E.
Students 158.

Canton, Wayne Co., Saint John Neumann, Rev. George Charnley; Eugene Kijek, Pastoral Min. In res., Rev. Jack J. Quinlan.
Res., 44800 Warren Rd., 48187. Tel: 313-455-5910; Fax: 313-455-6779.
Catechesis/Religious Programs—Ms. Fran Dawson, D.R.E.
Students 1,356.

Resurrection, Rev. Richard A. Perfetto.
48755 Warren Rd., 48187-1216. Tel: 313-451-0444; Fax: 313-451-0454.
Catechesis/Religious Programs—Students 130.

St. Thomas a Becket, Rev. C. Richard Kelly.
Res., 555 S. Lilley Rd., 48188. Tel: 313-981-1333; Fax: 313-981-1481.
Catechesis/Religious Programs—Tel: 313-981-6680.
Students 962.

Capac, St. Clair Co., St. Nicholas, Rev. Bogdan Milosz.
Res., 4331 Capac Rd., 48014.
Church—4331 Capac Rd., Tel: 810-395-7572; Fax: 810-395-7572.

Carleton, Monroe Co., St. Patrick, Rev. Robert A. Bauer.
Res., 2996 Labo Rd., 48117. Tel: 313-654-2500; Fax: 313-654-6594. [CEM]
School—Tel: 313-654-2522. Sr. Jeanne Twomey, S.S.J., Prin.
Sisters 1; Lay Teachers 11; Students 205.
Catechesis/Religious Programs—Tel: 313-654-6444. Diane Janssens, D.R.E.
Students 250.
Convent—2970 Labo Rd., 48117. Tel: 313-654-2904.

Centerline, Macomb Co., St. Clement, Revs. Jeffrey Anifer; David J. Blazek; Carl J. Yagley; Sr. Emeline Bash, O.P., Pastoral Assoc.
Res., 8075 Ritter Ave., 48015-1499. Tel: 810-757-3306; Fax: 810-757-5390. [CEM]
School—Tel: 810-757-7500; Fax: 810-757-4724. Patricia A. Downey, Prin.
Lay Teachers 22; Students 469.
High School—Tel: 810-757-1739; Fax: 810-757-1797. Deborah A. Michon, Prin.
Lay Teachers 20; Students 273.
Catechesis/Religious Programs—Tel: 810-757-3306; Fax: 810-757-5390. Linda Braman, D.R.E.
Students 200.

Clarkston, Oakland Co., St. Daniel, Rev. Msgr. Robert S. Humitz; Deacon Alexander Jablonowski.
Res., 7010 Valley Park Dr., 48346. Tel: 248-625-4580; Fax: 248-620-9839.
Catechesis/Religious Programs—Tel: 248-625-1750. Frieda Arpoika, D.R.E.
Students 850.

Clawson, Oakland Co., Guardian Angels, Revs. Gary M. Tierney; Robert R. Spezia; Deacon Eugene Tombler. In res., Revs. Vincent Nguyen An Ninh (Vietnamese); Bernard A. Schroll; John A. Blaska.
Res., 581 E. 14 Mile Rd., 48017. Tel: 248-588-1222; Fax: 248-588-8767.
School—Tel: 248-588-5545. Mr. Frank Spencer, Prin.
Dominican Sisters (Adrian) 1; Lay Teachers 19; Students 345.
Catechesis/Religious Programs—Eilleen Burke, D.R.E.
Students 292.

Clinton Twp., Macomb Co.,

1—St. Claude, Rev. Edward J. Wilk.
Res., 33826 Beaconsfield, 48035. Tel: 810-791-6630; Fax: 810-791-0017.
Catechesis/Religious Programs—Donna Hartner, D.R.E.
Students 98.

2—St. Louis, Rev. Pasquale LoGrasso; Sr. Rose Arnold, S.C., Pastoral Assoc.; Deacon Donald C. Junak. In res., Rev. Thomas R. Physician.
Res., 24415 Crocker Blvd., 48036. Tel: 810-468-8734; Fax: 810-468-9647.
Catechesis/Religious Programs—Tel: 810-468-4332. Joyce Appelt, D.R.E.
Students 365.
Convent—39173 Ormsby St., 48036. Tel: 810-468-4574.

3—St. Paul of Tarsus, Rev. Louis E. Grandpre; Rev. Msgr. Eugene Edyk; Rev. Clifford Ruskowski; Deacon Edward Wilson.
Res., 41300 Romeo Plank Rd., 48038. Tel: 810-228-1210; Fax: 810-228-8935.
Catechesis/Religious Programs—Tel: 810-228-0047. Audrey Wentz, D.R.E.
Students 1,099.

4—St. Ronald, Rev. Ralph L. Quane.
Res., 17701 15 Mile Rd., 48035-2401. Tel: 810-792-1190; Fax: 810-792-0765.
Catechesis/Religious Programs—Tel: 810-792-1276.
Students 130.

5—St. Thecla, Revs. Gary T. Smetanka; Michael Hrydziuszko; Sr. M. Francesca, C.S.S.F., Pastoral Assoc.
Res., 20740 Nunneley Rd., 48035-1628. Tel: 810-791-3930; Fax: 810-791-3890.
School—Tel: 810-791-2170.
Felician Sisters 3; Lay Teachers 22; Students 527.
Catechesis/Religious Programs—Tel: 810-792-0550.
Students 480.

6—St. Valerie of Ravenna, Rev. Richard Cavellier.
Res., 23300 King Dr., 48035. Tel: 810-791-5450; Fax: 810-791-6876.

7—San Francesco Community, Rev. Giulio Schiavi, P.I.M.E.
Res., 22870 S. Nunneley Rd., 48035. Tel: 810-792-5346; Fax: 810-792-5119.
Catechesis/Religious Programs—Students 150.

Columbus, St. Clair Co., St. Philip Neri, Rev. Francis A. Zielinski.
Res., 9735 Dolan Rd., 48063. Tel: 810-727-7263. [CEM]
Mission—Smiths Creek, St. Clair Co., Holy Rosary.

Dearborn, Wayne Co.,

1—St. Alphonsus, Rev. Michael W. Quaine.
Res., 7455 Calhoun Ave., 48126. Tel: 313-581-5218; Fax: 313-584-9560.
School—Tel: 313-581-1886. Sr. Carol Hane, O.P., Grade School Prin.
Lay Teachers 12; Students 271.
High School—Tel: 313-582-4266; Fax: 313-584-9589. Terrence George, High School Prin.
Adrian Dominican Sisters 1; Lay Teachers 19; Students 296.
Catechesis/Religious Programs—Tel: 313-581-5218. Kevin Tishier, D.R.E.
Students 100.
Convent—13541 Gould Ave., 48126. Tel: 313-584-4350.

2—St. Barbara, Rev. Zbigniew W. Grankowski; Deacon Richard B. Hulan, Pastoral Assoc. In res., Revs. Celedonio G. Melicor; Wojciech J. Zolnowski.
Res., 13534 Colson Ave., 48126. Tel: 313-582-8383; Fax: 313-582-1581.

3—St. Bernadette, Rev. Robert Cini, M.S.S.P. (Malta).
Res., 2600 Saulino Court, 48120. Tel: 313-841-0400; Fax: 313-841-2140.

4—St. Clement, Rev. Arnold V. Dachille; Sr. Ann Dineen, S.M., Pastoral Assoc.
Res., 5275 Kenilworth Ave., 48126. Tel: 313-581-7495; Fax: 313-581-4233.
Catechesis/Religious Programs—Tel: 313-846-2443. Tim Pilon, D.R.E.
Students 120.

5—Divine Child, Rev. Msgr. Herman W. Kucyk; Rev. John C. Riccardo.
Res., 25001 Hollander, 48128. Tel: 313-277-3110; Fax: 313-277-3211.
School—Tel: 313-562-1090; Fax: 313-562-2045. Sr. Cecilia Bondy, Elementary Prin.
Bernardine Sisters 9; Lay Teachers 25; Students 835.
High School—Tel: 313-562-1990. Sr. Elena Sabalausky, High School Prin.
Bernardine Sisters 8; Lay Teachers 57; Students 920.
Catechesis/Religious Programs—Sr. Helen Therese Bodziak, D.R.E.
Students 272.
Convent—1045 N. Silvery Ln., 48128. Tel: 313-561-5455.

6—St. Joseph, Rev. Adolph Redwick.
Res., 16101 Rotunda Dr., 48120. Tel: 313-336-3227; Fax: 313-441-6769.

7—St. Martha, Rev. John F. Child.
Res., 18200 Oakwood Blvd., 48124. Tel: 313-336-4090; Fax: 313-336-3318.

8—Sacred Heart, Revs. James P. Kenneally; Robert J. McCabe; Fran Helner, Pastoral Assoc.
Res., 22430 W. Michigan Ave., 48124. Tel: 313-278-5555; Fax: 313-278-8582. [CEM]
School—22513 Garrison, 48124. Tel: 313-561-9192; Fax: 313-561-1598. Keiren Stoller, Prin.
Sisters 2; Lay Teachers 19; Students 407.
Catechesis/Religious Programs—Denise Daniel, D.R.E.
Students 407.

Dearborn Heights, Wayne Co.,

1—St. Albert the Great, Rev. Lawrence Kaiser; Sr. Mary Downey, I.H.M., Pastoral Assoc.; Deacon Ray Gabel.
Res., 4855 Parker, 48125. Tel: 313-292-0430; Fax: 313-292-8565.
School—Tel: 313-292-1144.
Sisters, Servants of the Immaculate Heart of Mary 1; Lay Teachers 9; Students 237.
Catechesis/Religious Programs—Tel: 313-292-9370. Mrs. Barbara Brown, D.R.E.
Students 215.
Convent—4864 Parker, 48127. Tel: 313-292-0493.

2—St. Anselm, Rev. Msgr. James A. Moloney, Pastor and Dir., Society for The Propagation of The Faith; Sr. Mary Ann Thue, R.S.M., Pastoral Assoc. & Prin.
Res., 17650 W. Outer Dr., 48127. Tel: 313-565-4808; Fax: 313-565-7514.
School—Tel: 313-563-3430.
Sisters 4; Lay Teachers 6; Students 250.
Catechesis/Religious Programs—Tel: 313-561-0512. Sr. Mary Ann Thue, R.S.M., D.R.E.
Students 175.
Convent—20495 Brooklawn, 48127. Tel: 313-271-2287.

3—St. John the Baptist, Rev. Edwin W. Balazy.
Res., 26123 McDonald Ave., 48125. Tel: 313-292-9693; Fax: 313-292-1755.

4—St. Linus, Rev. Randall R. Phillips; Deacon George Cochrane. In res., Rev. George Miller.
Parish Office: 6466 Evangeline, 48127-2086. Tel: 313-274-4500; Fax: 313-562-2821.
School—Tel: 313-274-5320. Thomas Judd, Prin.
Lay Teachers 11; Students 303.
Catechesis/Religious Programs—Tel: 313-274-5778.
Students 230.
Convent—25450 Hass, 48127.

5—St. Mel, Rev. James G. Livingston; Sr. Carmen Dominguez, O.P., Pastoral Assoc.
Church—7506 Inkster Rd., 48127. Tel: 313-274-0684; Fax: 313-274-9080.
School—Tel: 313-274-6270. Mrs. Georgene Wojciechowski, Prin.
Lay Teachers 9; Students 147.
Catechesis/Religious Programs—Tel: 313-274-3977. Nancy Liebau, D.R.E.
Students 220.

6—Our Lady of Grace, Rev. Ronald Cyprys; Deacon Robert DeWitt. In res., Rev. Charles O'Neill.
Res., 8679 Riverview, 48127. Tel: 313-561-6373; Fax: 313-359-2727.
Church—23700 Joy Rd., 48127.
School—Tel: 313-562-6524.
Lay Teachers 10; Students 150.

7—St. Sabina, Rev. Joseph L. Romano.
Res., 25605 Ann Arbor Tr., 48127. Tel: 313-561-1977; Fax: 313-561-7898.
School—Tel: 313-274-5628.
Sisters 2; Lay Teachers 8; Students 217.
Catechesis/Religious Programs—Tel: 313-274-5635.
Students 80.

8—St. Sebastian, Revs. William B. Brennan; John Cusmano; Rita Oleksiak, Pastoral Min.
Res., 3850 Merrick Ave., Dearborn, 48124. Tel: 313-562-5356; Fax: 313-562-0058.
School—Tel: 313-563-6640.
Franciscan Sisters of St. Joseph 4; Lay Teachers 16; Students 443.
Catechesis/Religious Programs—Tel: 313-563-0960. Judy Valiguette, D.R.E.
Students 445.
Convent—20700 Colgate Ave., 48125. Tel: 313-562-7733.

Dryden, Lapeer Co., St. Cornelius, Rev. Wayne G. Ureel.
Res., 3834 Mill St., P.O. Box 208, 48428. Tel: 810-796-2926; Fax: 810-796-9713.

Dundee, Monroe Co., St. Irene, Rev. Ronald J. Alder.
Res., 576 Main St., 48131. Tel: 313-529-2160.

Eastpointe, Macomb Co., St. Barnabas, Rev. William J. Keveney; Deacon Thomas M. Thomas.
Res., 24800 Phlox Ave., 48021. Tel: 810-775-2284; Fax: 810-775-6933.
Catechesis/Religious Programs—Geraldine Combetta, D.R.E.
Students 180.

St. Basil, Rev. James H. Profota.
Parish Center—22851 Lexington Ave., 48021. Tel: 810-777-5610; Fax: 810-779-3341.
Catechesis/Religious Programs—Tel: 810-772-5434.
Students 222.

St. Veronica, Revs. Stanley L. Pachla, Jr.; Keith Priestly; Januscz Iwan; Kulan-Daisamy Arokiasamy.
Res., 21440 Universal Dr., 48021. Tel: 810-777-0331; Fax: 810-777-0615.
School—Tel: 810-775-8333. Sr. Gloria Jean Zieske, Prin.
Sisters of St. Joseph 4; Adrian Dominican 1; Sisters of Charity 1; Lay Teachers 14; Students 399.
Catechesis/Religious Programs—D.R.E.: Sr. Mary Ann Ankoviak, S.S.J.; Sr. Geraldine Arnold, S.S.J.
Students 267.
Convent—21357 Redmond, 48021. Tel: 810-777-0321.

Ecorse, Wayne Co., St. Francis Xavier, Rev. Victor Roman.
Res., 4250 W. Jefferson Ave., 48229. Tel: 313-383-8514; Fax: 313-383-7508. [CEM]
Catechesis/Religious Programs—Cathy Borsch, D.R.E.
Students 174.

Emmett, St. Clair Co., Our Lady of Mount Carmel, Rev. Jasper F. Sirianni.
Res., 10828 Brandon Rd., 48022. Tel: 810-384-1338; Fax: 810-384-1338.
Catechesis/Religious Programs—Tel: 810-384-6925.
Students 199.
Convent—10832 Brandon Rd., 48022. Tel: 313-384-6925.

Erie, Monroe Co., St. Joseph, Rev. Joseph Plawecki.
Res., 2214 Manhattan Ave., 48133. Tel: 313-848-6125; Fax: 313-848-2784. [CEM]
School—Tel: 313-848-6985.
Sisters 2; Lay Teachers 12; Students 216.
Convent—2238 Manhattan Ave., 48133. Tel: 313-848-8754.

Farmington, Oakland Co., St. Colman, Rev. Norbert V. Kendzierski; Mrs. Kathleen O. Daray, Pastoral Assoc.
Res., 32500 Middlebelt Rd., Farmington Hills, 48334. Tel: 248-626-0285; Fax: 248-626-5420.
Catechesis/Religious Programs—Tel: 248-626-0287.
Students 61.

St. Gerald, Rev. Gerald A. McEnhill.
Res., 21300 Farmington Rd., 48336. Tel: 248-477-7470; Fax: 248-477-3878.
Catechesis/Religious Programs—Tel: 248-476-7677. Mary Taylor, D.R.E.
Students 394.

Our Lady of Sorrows, Rev. Msgr. Walter A. Hurley; Revs. David F. West; Douglas J. Bignall; Loren F. O'Dea; Sr. Christine Mihelcic, S.J., Dir. In res., Rev. Arthur W. Fauser.
Res., 23815 Power Rd., 48336. Tel: 248-474-5720; Fax: 248-474-1340.
School—(Grades K-8). Tel: 248-476-0977 (Elem.); 248-615-5574 (Middle). Roberta Clemak, Prin. (Grades K-8).
Lay Teachers 40; Students 785.
Catechesis/Religious Programs—Tel: 248-474-6480. Bette Jannott, D.R.E.
Students 491.

Farmington Hills, Oakland Co., St. Alexander, Rev. James B. Wright.
Res., 27835 Shiawassee, 48336. Tel: 248-474-5748; Fax: 248-474-5776.
Catechesis/Religious Programs—Tel: 248-474-8126; Fax: 248-474-8231.
Students 155.

St. Clare of Assisi, Rev. Frederick J. Klettner.
Res., 29200 W. Ten Mile, 48336. Tel: 248-477-9870; Fax: 248-477-4785.

St. Fabian, Rev. Brian J. Chabala.
Church—32200 W. 12 Mile Rd., 48334. Tel: 248-553-4610; Fax: 248-553-6296.
Res., 32265 Red Clover Rd., 48334.
School—Tel: 248-553-2750. Sr. M. Loretelle, O.S.F., Prin.
Bernardine Sisters 3; Lay Teachers 13; Students 330.
Catechesis/Religious Programs—Gina Karl, D.R.E.
Students 612.
Convent—32170 Twelve Mile Rd., 48334. Tel: 248-553-4186.

Ferndale, Oakland Co., St. James, Rev. Robert L. Wurm; Sr. Eveleen Forkin, Pastoral Min.; W. Michael O'Neill, Pastoral Assoc.
Res., 241 W. Pearson Ave., 48220. Tel: 248-542-8835; Fax: 248-542-0267.
Catechesis/Religious Programs—W. Michael O'Neill, D.R.E.
Students 241.

Flat Rock, Wayne Co., St. Roch, Rev. Frederick Misiolek; Deacon Harold Goodhue.
Res., 25022 Gibraltar Rd., 48134. Tel: 313-782-4471; Fax: 313-782-5450.

Fraser, Macomb Co., Our Lady Queen of All Saints, Rev. Ronald J. Babich; Sr. Nancy Zajac, O.P., Pastoral Assoc.
Res., 31740 Cyril Dr., 48026. Tel: 810-293-4050; Fax: 810-293-1041.
Catechesis/Religious Programs—Tel: 810-294-6180; Fax: 810-293-1041.
Students 421.

Garden City, Wayne Co., St. Dunstan, Rev. Donald Demmer; Deacon Michael Markulike.
Res., 1646 Belton Ave., 48135. Tel: 313-425-6720; Fax: 313-425-8411.
School—1615 Belton Ave., 48135. Tel: 313-425-4380. Sr. Mariella Chrusciel, Prin.
Sisters 3; Lay Teachers 10; Students 231.
Catechesis/Religious Programs—Tel: 313-425-4396. Sr. Mary Martin, D.R.E.
Students 160.

St. Raphael the Archangel, Rev. Edward Prus; Sr. Ritamary Pyzick, Pastoral Min.
Parish Center—31530 Beechwood, 48135. Tel: 313-427-1533; Fax: 313-427-8594.
Parish Hall—5875 Merriman, 48135. Tel: 313-422-9617.
School—Tel: 313-425-9771. Judith McBride, Prin.
Lay Teachers 20; Students 440.
Catechesis/Religious Programs—Tel: 313-425-5550. Sr. Patricia Donnelly, D.R.E.
Students 375.

Gibraltar, Wayne Co., St. Victor, Rev. Roger A. Knapp.
Res., 14100 Navarre, 48173. Tel: 313-675-0100; Fax: 313-675-6952.

Grosse Ile, Wayne Co., Sacred Heart, Rev. Thomas P. Flynn; Sr. Mary Ann Kasper, S.J., Pastoral Assoc.; Deacon Robert Tremmel.
Res., 21526 E. River Rd., 48138. Tel: 313-671-3043; Fax: 313-676-3623. [CEM]
Parish Center—21599 Parke Ln., 48138. Tel: 313-676-1378; Fax: 313-676-3623.
Catechesis/Religious Programs—Students 663.
Convent—21537 Parke Ln., 48138. Tel: 313-671-3056.

Grosse Pointe, Wayne Co., Our Lady Star of the Sea, Rev. Msgr. Dennis Harrity; Rev. John J. Mech.
Church—467 Fairford, 48236. Tel: 313-884-5554; Fax: 313-885-5591.
School—Tel: 313-884-1070. Dr. Lois Masouris, Prin.
Lay Teachers 27; Students 427.
Catechesis/Religious Programs—Tel: 313-884-7407. Helen L. Goettl, D.R.E.
Students 490.
Convent—19950 Morningside Dr., 48236. Tel: 313-884-4074.

Grosse Pointe Farms, Wayne Co., St. Paul Catholic Church, Rev. Msgr. Leonard P. Blair; Rev. George W. Williams. Pastoral Assocs.: Deacon Richard Shubick; Sr. Ruthanne Reed, O.P. In res., Rev. Michael G. O'Leary.
Res., 157 Lake Shore Rd., 48236. Tel: 313-885-8855; Fax: 313-886-6467. [CEM]
School—170 Grosse Pointe Blvd., 48236. Tel: 313-885-3430; Fax: 313-885-9357. Elizabeth A. Burns, Prin.
Sisters 3; Lay Teachers 27; Students 504.
Catechesis/Religious Programs—Carol Jadach, D.R.E.
Students 596.

Grosse Pointe Park, Wayne Co., St. Ambrose, Rev. Timothy R. Pelc. Pastoral Assocs.: Sr. Irene Kerich, O.P.; Deacons John Schaible, Emeritus; William Jamieson.
Res., 15020 Hampton, 48230. Tel: 313-822-2814; Fax: 313-822-9838.
School—Tel: 313-823-0177. Sr. Marie Cyril DeLisi, I.H.M., Prin.
Religious 6; Lay Teachers 7; Students 200.
Catechesis/Religious Programs—Julie Telang, D.R.E.
Students 225.

St. Clare of Montefalco, Rev. Joseph E. McCormick, O.S.A. In res., Revs. John J. Burkhart, O.S.A.; Joseph F. Hartman, O.S.A.; Francis R. McDonnell, O.S.A.; Robert Gardella, O.S.A.
Res., 1401 Whittier Rd., 48230. Tel: 313-885-4960; Fax: 313-885-8533.
School—16231 Charlevoix, 48230. Tel: 313-886-1440; Fax: 313-886-1437.
Catechesis/Religious Programs—Tel: 313-884-2110. Paula Miller, D.R.E.
Students 385.

Hamtramck, Wayne Co., St. Florian, Revs. Wojciech Baryski, S.Ch.; Julian Kaczowka.
Res., 2626 Poland Ave., 48212. Tel: 313-871-2778; Fax: 313-871-5947.
Church—Florian and Latham Aves., 48212.
School—Tel: 313-875-3040.
Felician Sisters 2; Lay Teachers 10; Students 261.
High School—Tel: 313-875-6347. Sr. Mary Estelle, C.S.S.F., Prin.
Felician Sisters 2; Lay Teachers 12; Students 148.
Convent—2622 Florian Ave., 48212. Tel: 313-872-5775.

St. Ladislaus (Polish), Rev. Stanley A. Ulman. In res., Rev. Stanislaus Czapiewski, S.J.
Res., 2730 Caniff Ave., 48212. Tel: 313-872-0709; Fax: 313-872-5906.
Convent—2697 Caniff Ave., 48212. Tel: 313-365-6610. Sisters of St. Francis (Sylvania, OH)

Our Lady Queen of Apostles (Polish), Revs. Gary M. Michalik; Wojciech Wojcicki.
Res., 3851 Prescott Ave., 48212-3115. Tel: 313-891-1520; 1521; Fax: 313-891-3552.
School—11420 Conant, 48212. Tel: 313-892-8130. Sr. M. Gloria Ertman, C.S.S.F., Prin.
Sisters 4; Lay Teachers 8; Students 236.
Convent—3891 Prescott Ave., 48212-3115. Tel: 313-891-7121.

Harper Woods, Wayne Co., Our Lady Queen of Peace, Rev. Daniel C. Complo. In res., Revs. John M. Fee, SS.CC.; Eugene F. Fedewa; John T. Gordon.
Res., 20955 Bournemouth Ave., 48225. Tel: 313-881-5212; Fax: 313-881-7813.
School—Tel: 313-881-3629. Richard Flaherty, Prin. & D.R.E.
Lay Teachers 11; Students 187.
Catechesis/Religious Programs—Tel: 313-884-8744.
Students 205.

St. Peter the Apostle, Rev. Robert J. Keller.
Res., 19851 Anita St., 48225. Tel: 313-886-1771; Fax: 313-886-1489.
School—Tel: 313-885-8062. Sr. Kathleen DeSmedt, I.H.M., Prin.
Lay Teachers 18; Students 252.

Harrison Twp., Macomb Co., St. Hubert, Rev. James J. O'Leary; Sr. Susan Ouwerkerk, O.P., Pastoral Assoc.
Res., 38775 Prentiss, 48045. Tel: 810-463-5877; 463-7796; Fax: 810-463-1734.
Catechesis/Religious Programs—Tel: 810-463-5875. Mr. Allan Ranusch, D.R.E.
Students 608.

Harsens Island, St. Clair Co., St. Mark, Rev. Erwin J. Bauer, Admin.
Res., Church and Rectory, 4190 Green Dr., Harsen's Island, 48028. Tel: 810-748-3828; Fax: 810-748-9148.

Hazel Park, Oakland Co., St. Justin, Rev. Robert Hayes Williams.
Res., 1631 E. Elza St., 48030. Tel: 248-542-2129; Fax: 248-542-2715.

St. Mary Magdalen, Revs. Michael Bertram, O.F.M.Cap.; Raymond Stadmeyer, O.F.M.Cap.
Res., 50 E. Annabelle, 48030. Tel: 248-542-8060; Fax: 248-542-4563.
School—Tel: 248-547-3363. Suzanne Kisseberth, Prin.
Sisters 1; Lay Teachers 8; Students 200.
Catechesis/Religious Programs—Tel: 248-547-0323. Elaine Duellette, D.R.E.
Students 210.

Highland, Oakland Co., Church of the Holy Spirit, Rev. Leo T. Lulko.
Church—3700 Harvey Lake Rd., 48356.
Res., 1673 Apollo Dr., 48356. Tel: 248-887-9029; Fax: 248-889-1374.
Catechesis/Religious Programs—Joann Dalton, D.R.E.
Students 666.

Highland Park, Wayne Co., St. Benedict, Rev. Robert B. McGrath; Deacon Richard Conlin.
Res., 60 Church Ave., 48203. Tel: 313-868-3876; Fax: 313-868-0110.
School—53 Candler, 48203. Tel: 313-868-7502. Kathleen Freeman, Prin.
Sisters 1; Lay Teachers 13; Students 280.

Holly, Oakland Co., St. Rita, Rev. Joseph P. Killeen.
Res., 309 E. Maple, 48442. Tel: 248-634-4841; Fax: 248-634-4858.
Catechesis/Religious Programs—Tel: 248-634-1658. Dawn M. Sliwa, D.R.E.
Students 219.

Ida, Monroe Co., St. Joseph, Rev. John P. LaCasse, Admin.
Res., 8295 Van Akin St., 48140. Tel: 313-269-3895. [CEM]
Catechesis/Religious Programs—Tel: 313-269-3414. Linda Wilson, D.R.E.
Students 275.

Imlay City, Lapeer Co., Sacred Heart, Rev. Ezequiel Mondragon.
Res., 700 Maple Vista, 48444. Tel: 810-724-1135; Fax: 810-724-0870. [CEM]
Catechesis/Religious Programs—Tel: 810-724-1145.
Students 278.

Inkster, Wayne Co., Holy Family Parish, Revs. John Lehner, O.S.F.S.; Festus Ejimadu.
Res., 27800 Annapolis Rd., 48141. Tel: 313-563-8242.

St. Kevin and St. Norbert, Revs. John Lehner, O.S.F.S.; Festus Ejimadu.
Office: 27355 Woodsfield, 48141.
Res., 604 Sherbourne Dr., 48141. Tel: 313-563-0993; Fax: 313-563-3148.
Catechesis/Religious Programs—Tel: 313-278-4924; Fax: 313-563-3148.
Students 95.

Lake Orion, Oakland Co., St. Joseph, Revs. John L. Phalen; Bernard J. Mullen. Pastoral Assocs.: Sr. Barbara Jean Pelak, O.P.; William Chamberlin; Deacon Thomas Yezak.
Res., 715 N. Lapeer Rd., 48362. Tel: 248-693-0440; Fax: 248-693-3724.
School—Tel: 248-693-6215; Fax: 248-693-0958. Sr. Theresa Darga, O.S.F., Prin.
Lay Teachers 12; Students 286.
Catechesis/Religious Programs—Regina Moskal, D.R.E.
Students 826.

Lakeport, St. Clair Co., St. Edward's on the Lake, Rev. Leonard P. Wallace.
Res., 6945 Lakeshore Rd., 48059. Tel: 810-385-4340; Fax: 810-364-3472.
School—(Grades K-5). For grades 6-8 please refer to McCormick Consolidated Academy, Port Huron, under Elementary Schools, Inter-Parochial in the Institutions Located in the Archdiocese section. Tel: 810-385-4461; Fax: 810-385-6972.
Students 103.
Convent—6975 Lakeshore Rd., 48059. Tel: 810-385-9531.

Lapeer, Lapeer Co., Immaculate Conception of the Blessed Virgin Mary, Revs. Douglas J. Terrien; Josef Mitek; Deacon Gerald Deshaw.
Res., 814 Nepessing, 48446. Tel: 810-664-8594; Fax: 810-664-4564. [CEM]
School—Bishop Kelley School, Tel: 810-664-5011. Miss Barbara Davis, Prin.
Lay Teachers 9; Students 198.
Catechesis/Religious Programs—Tel: 810-664-0868.
Students 540.

Lincoln Park, Wayne Co., Christ the Good Shepherd, Revs. David A. Buersmeyer; Marek P. Stochmal; Sr. Marge Zacharias, Pastoral Assoc.

Res., 1540 Riverbank Ave., 48146. Tel: 313-928-1324; Fax: 313-928-1326.
School—Tel: 313-386-0633. Thomas Caruso, Prin.
Lay Teachers 24; Students 466.
Catechesis/Religious Programs—Tel: 313-382-1818. Sr. Rebecca Vonderhaas, D.R.E.
Students 310.

St. Henry, Rev. Gerard J. Cupple.
Res., 1358 Council Ave., 48146. Tel: 313-381-0711; 0712; Fax: 313-381-6746.
Catechesis/Religious Programs—Anne Martus, D.R.E.
Students 95.

Livonia, Wayne Co.,

1—St. Aidan, Rev. Gerald K. Flannery; Dr. Jerard E. Delaney, II, Pastoral Assoc. & D.R.E.; Deacon Robert Rowland.
Res., 17500 Farmington Rd., 48152. Tel: 313-425-5950; Fax: 313-425-3687.
Catechesis/Religious Programs—Tel: 313-425-9333. Mary Ellen Skene, Assoc. D.R.E.
Students 657.

2—St. Colette, Revs. Henry W. Roodbeen; Arthur H. Jacobi; Deacons Al Morad; Leo D'Argis.
Res., 17600 Newburgh, 48152-2699. Tel: 313-464-4433; Fax: 313-464-1694.
Catechesis/Religious Programs—Tel: 313-464-4435; Fax: 313-464-7817. Joanne Plant, D.R.E.
Students 894.

3—St. Edith, Revs. James C. Scheick; John Castelot; Deacons John Kenny; Ric Misiak.
Res., 15089 Newburgh, 48154. Tel: 313-464-1222; Fax: 313-464-7582.
School—Tel: 313-464-1250. Sr. Margaret Kijek, C.S.S.F., Prin.
Felician Sisters 1; Lay Teachers 8; Students 300.
Catechesis/Religious Programs—Tel: 313-464-2020. Elizabeth Nowak, D.R.E.
Students 505.

4—St. Genevieve, Rev. Kean D. Cronin; Deacon R. P. Piro, Pastoral Assoc.
Res., 29015 Jamison, 48154. Tel: 313-427-5220; Fax: 313-422-1763.
School—Tel: 313-425-4420. Sr. M. Juanita Szymanski, C.S.S.F., Prin.
Sisters 2; Lay Teachers 8; Students 200.
Catechesis/Religious Programs—Tel: 313-261-5920. D.R.E.: Diana Tarnacki; Paula Brach.
Students 315.

5—St. Maurice, Rev. John P. Maierle; Darlene Bellmore, Pastoral Assoc.
Res., 32765 Lyndon Ave., 48154. Tel: 313-522-1616; Fax: 313-522-5092.
Catechesis/Religious Programs—Tel: 313-421-5240. Lezlie Allison, D.R.E.
Students 135.

6—St. Michael, Rev. Alberto P. Bondy; Deacon Robert C. Fitzgerald.
Res., 11441 Hubbard Ave., 48150. Tel: 313-261-1455; Fax: 313-522-1123.
School—Tel: 313-421-7360. Sr. M. Carolyn Ratkowski, C.S.S.F., Prin.
Felician Sisters 6; Lay Teachers 26; Students 786.
Religious Education—Tel: 313-261-1790.
Students 277.
Catechesis/Religious Programs—Students 246.
Convent—11400 Fairfield, Tel: 313-421-7522.

7—St. Priscilla, Rev. Kevin P. O'Brien; Deacon Ray Kunik.
Res., 19120 Purling Brook Rd., 48152. Tel: 248-442-9419; Fax: 248-476-7831.
Catechesis/Religious Programs—Tel: 248-476-4702.
Students 490.

Macomb, Macomb Co., St. Isidore, Revs. Frank J. Berge; Kevin Thomas, M.M.; Karl DeLisle, Pastoral Assoc.
Res., 18201 Twenty-three Mile Rd., 48042. Tel: 810-286-1700; Fax: 810-286-8753.
Catechesis/Religious Programs—Tel: 810-286-4433. Betty Frei, D.R.E.
Students 1,217.

Madison Heights, Oakland Co., St. Vincent Ferrer, Rev. Steven C. Koehler; Deacon Ralph Hardwick; Sr. Mary Jo Sieg, O.P., Pastoral Assoc.
Res., 1087 E. Gardenia Ave., 48071. Tel: 248-542-8720; Fax: 248-542-8721.
School—1075 E. Gardenia, 48071. Tel: 248-398-4191; Fax: 248-398-4190. Mrs. Suzanne Pientak, Prin.
Lay Teachers 15; Students 157.
Catechesis/Religious Programs—Michael Novak, D.R.E.
Students 221.

Marine City, St. Clair Co., Holy Cross, Rev. James R. Wysocki; Deacon Gary Krueger.
Res., 610 S. Water St., 48039. Tel: 810-765-3568; Fax: 810-765-2974. [CEM]
School—Holy Cross Elementary, Tel: 810-765-3591. Mrs. Dianne Lovette, Prin.
Dominican Sisters 1; Lay Teachers 12; Students 186.
High School—Cardinal Mooney Catholic. Fax: 810-765-8825. Dr. Elsie L. Ogden, Prin.
Priests 1; Sisters 5; Lay Teachers 13; Students 193.
Catechesis/Religious Programs—Tel: 810-765-8300. Sr. Kathleen Mulso, O.S.F., D.R.E.
Students 280.

Marysville, St. Clair Co., St. Christopher, Rev. Arthur R. Baranowski; Sr. Doris Wood, S.S.J., Pastoral Min.
Res., 1000 Michigan Ave., 48040. Tel: 810-364-4100; Fax: 810-364-5947.
Catechesis/Religious Programs—Tel: 810-364-7080. Amy Miles, D.R.E.
Students 458.

Maybee, Monroe Co., St. Joseph, Rev. Michael D. Malawy.
Res., 9207 Joseph St., Box 118, 48159. Tel: 313-587-8835; Fax: 313-587-3490. [CEM]
Convent—9147 Joseph St., Box 126, 48159. Tel: 313-587-8785.

Melvindale, Wayne Co., St. Conrad, Rev. Joseph A. Gagnon.
Res., 3320 Melwood, 48122. Tel: 313-383-0303; Fax: 313-383-5704.

St. Mary Magdalen, Revs. James E. Curtin; John Melepuram (India).
Res., 19624 Wood St., 48122. Tel: 313-381-8566; Fax: 313-381-1319.
School—Tel: 313-382-6060. James A. Bouvy, Prin.
Lay Teachers 11; Students 326.
Catechesis/Religious Programs—Tel: 313-382-1099. Mrs. Patricia Dincau, D.R.E.
Students 103.
Mission—Melvindale, St. Thomas Indian Catholic Mission, Tel: 313-381-1773.

Memphis, Macomb Co., All Saints, Rev. Dennis Nowinski.
Church—79780 Main St., 48041. Tel: 810-392-2056; 392-3232; Fax: 810-392-3043.
Catechesis/Religious Programs—Toni Zweng, D.R.E.
Students 210.

Milford, Oakland Co., St. Mary, Our Lady of the Snows, Rev. Ronald Anderson; Sr. Lucille Janowiak, O.P., Pastoral Assoc.; Deacon Archie Noon.
Res., 1851 E. Commerce, 48381. Tel: 248-685-1482; Fax: 248-684-5642. [CEM]
Catechesis/Religious Programs—Tel: 248-685-2702. Michael Maras, D.R.E.
Students 996.

Monroe, Monroe Co.,

1—St. Anne, Revs. William F. Fisher, O.S.F.S.; Robert C. Mossett, O.S.F.S.
Res., 2420 N. Dixie Hwy., 48161. Tel: 313-289-2910; Fax: 313-289-1098.
Catechesis/Religious Programs—Students 122.

2—St. John The Baptist, Rev. Terrence D. Kerner.
Res., 511 S. Monroe St., S., 48161. Tel: 313-241-8910; Fax: 313-241-1943.
School—Tel: 313-241-1670. Rita Linnenkugel, Prin.
Lay Teachers 10; Students 224.
Catechesis/Religious Programs—D.R.E.: Sharon DuVall; Karon Kinsey.
Students 251.

3—St. Joseph's, Rev. William F. Fisher, O.S.F.S.; Sr. Harriet Fitzmaurice, I.H.M., Pastoral Assoc.
Res., 924 E. Second St., 48161. Tel: 313-241-9590; Fax: 313-241-5296. [JC]
Catechesis/Religious Programs—Mrs. Judy Collins, D.R.E.
Students 150.

4—St. Mary's, Rev. Anthony P. Sulkowski; Sr. Jean M. O'Connor, I.H.M., Pastoral Assoc.
Res., 127 N. Monroe St., 48162. Tel: 313-241-1644; Fax: 313-241-3077. [JC]
School—Mary Ann Lapinski, Prin. Lay Teachers 14; Students 297.
Catechesis/Religious Programs—Ellen Licavoli, D.R.E.
Students 352.

5—St. Michael, Rev. Stephen Rooney; Deacon Michael M. Ingels; Sr. Dorothy Jayne. Krupp, O.S.F., Pastoral Assoc.
Res., 502 W. Front St., 48161. Tel: 313-241-8645; Fax: 313-241-6132. [JC]
School—Tel: 313-241-3923; Fax: 313-241-3924. Karen Pilon, Prin.
Lay Teachers 12; Students 252.
Catechesis/Religious Programs—Susan Pacitti, D.R.E.
Students 128.

Mount Clemens, Macomb Co., St. Peter, Rev. Michael N. Cooney; Sheila Roy, Pastoral Min.; Doris Kallek, Admin.
Admin. Bldg.—98 New St., 48043. Tel: 810-468-4578; Fax: 810-468-3199.
Res., 100 New St., 48043. [CEM]
School—St. Mary, Tel: 810-468-4570. Elizabeth McMillan, Prin.
Lay Teachers 20; Students 513.
Catechesis/Religious Programs—Judy Coll, D.R.E.
Students 420.

New Baltimore, Macomb Co., St. Mary Queen of Creation, Revs. Nicholas Zukowski; Patrick P. Casey; Mary Frances Van Hollenbeck, Parish Nurse Coord.; Deacon Anthony Lewandoski.
Res., 51041 Maria St., 48047. Tel: 810-725-2441; Fax: 810-725-3647. [CEM]
Catechesis/Religious Programs—Carolyn Bissett, D.R.E.
Students 850.

New Boston, Wayne Co., St. Stephen, Revs. Alexander J. Wytrwal; Joseph Szewczyk.
Res., 18800 Huron River Dr., 48164-9599. Tel: 313-753-4305; Fax: 313-753-5828. [CEM]
School—Tel: 313-753-4175. Sr. M. Virginia Gola, C.S.S.F., Prin.
Felician Sisters 2; Lay Teachers 9; Students 209.
Catechesis/Religious Programs—Tel: 313-753-4722. D.R.E.: Sr. Mary Patricia Pyszynski, C.S.S.F.; Sr. Mary Rosanne Krzesicki, C.S.S.F.
Students 138.
Convent—Tel: 313-753-9937.

New Haven, Macomb Co., St. Francis of Assisi, Rev. Daniel O'Sullivan.
Res., 57775 Main St., P.O. Box 308, 48048. Tel: 810-749-9584; Fax: 810-749-6021.

Newport, Monroe Co., St. Charles Borromeo, Rev. William H. Tindall.
Res., 8109 Swan Creek Rd., 48166. Tel: 313-586-2531; Fax: 313-586-3900. [CEM]
School—Tel: 313-586-2171. Krista Seibert, Prin.
Lay Teachers 10; Students 202.
Catechesis/Religious Programs—Tel: 313-586-3304. Mrs. Marshia Valleau, D.R.E.
Students 217.

North Branch, Lapeer Co., St. Mary's Burnside, Rev. Richard M. Schmidberger.
Res., 5622 Summers Rd., 48461. Tel: 810-688-3648; Fax: 810-688-3654. [CEM]
Mission—Brown City, Sanilac Co., Sacred Heart. [CEM]

SS. Peter and Paul, Rev. Jude T. Ellinghausen.
Res., Box 208, 6645 Washington, 48461. Tel: 810-688-3797. [CEM]
Catechesis/Religious Programs—Tel: 810-688-9019. Charlotte Kalbfleisch, D.R.E.
Students 244.
Mission—Clifford, St. Patrick's. [CEM]

Northville, Wayne Co., Our Lady of Victory, Revs. Ernest M. Porcari; James F. Kean; Patricia Ernst, Pastoral Assoc.
Res., 770 Thayer, 48167. Tel: 248-349-2621; Fax: 248-349-7329.
School—Tel: 248-349-6610.
Lay Teachers 20; Students 272.
Catechesis/Religious Programs—Ms. Eileen Moss, D.R.E.
Students 590.
Convent—103 Orchard Dr., 48167. Tel: 248-349-8587.

St. Andrew Kim Korean Catholic Church, Rev. Blase Lee.
Res., 21177 Halsted Rd., 48167. Tel: 248-442-9026; Fax: 248-442-9020.

Novi, Oakland Co., Holy Family, Revs. John G. Budde; Denis B. Theroux; Deacon William Waldmann.
Res., 24505 Meadowbrook, 48375. Tel: 248-349-8847; Fax: 248-349-3711.
Catechesis/Religious Programs—Tel: 248-349-8837. Dorothy Morse, D.R.E.
Students 1,312.

St. James, Rev. James F. Cronk.
46325 Ten Mile Road, 48374-3007.
Res., 24491 Riverview Ln., 48374-3052. Tel: 248-347-7778; Fax: 248-347-9625.
Catechesis/Religious Programs—Wendy Duvall-Angelocci, D.R.E.
Students 851.

Oak Park, Oakland Co., Our Lady of Fatima, Rev. Paul F. Chateau; Sr. Jane Zoltek, S.S.J., Pastoral Assoc.
In res., Rev. Nicholas H. Amico (Ecuador).
Res., 13500 Oak Park Blvd., 48237. Tel: 810-545-2310; Fax: 810-545-2312.

Orchard Lake, Oakland Co., Our Lady of Refuge, Rev. William J. Murphy.
Res., 3663 Erie Dr., P.O. Box 240485, 48324. Tel: 248-682-0920; Fax: 248-682-3794.
School—Tel: 248-682-3422; Fax: 248-682-0479. Sr. Mary Ruth Koralewski, C.S.S.F., Prin.
Sisters 3; Lay Teachers 22; Students 502.
Catechesis/Religious Programs—Gloria Boesch, D.R.E.
Students 345.
Convent—3725 Erie Dr., 48324. Tel: 248-682-1876.

Orion Township, Oakland Co., Christ the Redeemer, Rev. Joseph E. Dailey.
Res., 4005 Baldwin, Orion, 48359. Tel: 248-391-1621; Fax: 248-391-3412.
Catechesis/Religious Programs—Tel: 248-391-4074. Henry Mucha, D.R.E.
Students 528.

Ortonville, Oakland Co., St. Anne, Rev. A. Frank Pollie; Deacon Bernard Braun.
Res., 825 Ortonville Rd., 48462. Tel: 248-627-3965; Fax: 248-627-3965.
Catechesis/Religious Programs—Tel: 248-627-3753. Elaine Young, D.R.E.
Students 385.

Plymouth, Wayne Co., Our Lady of Good Counsel, Revs. John J. Sullivan; Stanislaw Tokarski; Deacon Don Leach.
Res., 1062 Church St., 48170. Tel: 313-453-0326; Fax: 313-416-9257.
School—Tel: 313-453-3053. Theodore Behn, Prin.
Lay Teachers 22; Students 562.
Catechesis/Religious Programs—Tel: 313-455-0242.
Students 625.

St. Kenneth, Rev. Joseph S. Mallia; Deacon Eugene Krzeminski.
Res., 14951 Haggerty Rd., 48170. Tel: 313-420-0288; Fax: 313-420-2921.
Catechesis/Religious Programs—Tel: 313-420-3031. Mrs. Laurel McGrane, D.R.E.
Students 410.

Pontiac, Oakland Co., St. Joseph, Revs. John P. Wynnycky; Charles P. Farrar; Fabian B. Slominski, Liturgical Presider; Deacon John M. Fleming; Sr. M. Patricia Malone, R.S.M., Pastoral Assoc.
400 S. Blvd. W., 48341-2465. Tel: 248-332-9872.
Res., 150 E. Wide Track Dr., 48342. Tel: 248-332-0283; Fax: 248-334-0528.

St. Michael, Rev. John P. Wynnycky; Deacons Edward Strye; Richard Vestuto, Pastoral Assoc.
Res., 120 Lewis, 48342. Tel: 248-332-9167; Fax: 248-332-3901.

St. Vincent de Paul, Revs. John P. Wynnycky; Charles P. Farrar. Pastoral Assocs.: Sr. Carmen Coccimiglio, S.L.W.; Maria Jimenez; Willie McCray, Minister of Service; Deacons Fernando Valdez; Jesus Vasquez; Brigido Rodriguez; Norman LaLone.
Res., 150 E. Wide Track Dr., 48342. Tel: 248-332-0283; Fax: 248-332-7041.

Port Huron, St. Clair Co., St. Joseph, Rev. Rene Desmarais; Mary Fran Canza, Pastoral Assoc.
Res., 1317 7th St., 48060. Tel: 810-985-9616; Fax: 810-985-9807. [JC]
School—Tel: 810-982-3701.
Sisters 1; Lay Teachers 7; Students 77.
Catechesis/Religious Programs—Tel: 810-982-2343. Mrs. Fran Warsalla, D.R.E.
Students 99.

St. Mary, Rev. Stanley Wyczawski.
Res., 1505 Ballentine St., 48060. Tel: 810-982-7906; Fax: 810-987-8255.
School—Tel: 810-982-1091. Mrs. Karen Pawlak.
Lay Teachers 8; Students 168.

St. Stephen, Rev. David Lesniak.
Res., 325 32nd St., 48060. Tel: 810-984-2689; 984-3220; Fax: 810-984-8559.
Parish Center—2865 Henry, 48060. Tel: 810-984-2689.
Catechesis/Religious Programs—Rose Marie Miller, D.R.E.
Students 294.

Redford, Wayne Co.,

1—St. Agatha, Rev. Thomas F. Slowinski.
Parish Office—19750 Beech Daly Rd., 48240.
Res., 19650 Beech Daly Rd., 48240. Tel: 313-531-0371; Fax: 313-531-1805.
School—Tel: 313-532-6940. Lorelei Darga, Prin.
Sisters 1; Lay Teachers 10; Students 290.
High School—Robert Snowden, High School Prin.
Sisters 2; Lay Teachers 7; Students 158.
Catechesis/Religious Programs—Students 145.

2—St. John Bosco, Rev. Richard A. Osebold.
Res., 12100 Beech-Daly Rd., 48239. Tel: 313-937-9690; Fax: 313-937-2927.
School—Tel: 313-937-3856. Sr. Rita Sieg, O.P., Prin.
Lay Teachers 7; Students 109.

3—Our Lady of Loretto, Rev. Joseph M. Esper; Sr. Margretta Wojcik, O.S.F., Pastoral Assoc.; Deacon Gary Pardo.
Res., 17116 Olympia Ave., 48240. Tel: 313-534-9000; Fax: 313-534-6744.
School—Tel: 313-532-4764; Fax: 313-794-1506.
Lay Teachers 14; Students 287.
Catechesis/Religious Programs—Tel: 313-532-3707. Carol Wojciak, D.R.E.
Students 160.

4—St. Valentine, Rev. Thomas A. Belczak. In res., Rev. Norman Nawrocki.
Res., 25881 Dow, 48239. Tel: 313-532-4394; Fax: 313-532-2237.
School—25800 Dow St., 48239. Tel: 313-533-7149. Carol Budchuk, Prin.
Lay Teachers 21; Students 320.
Catechesis/Religious Programs—Tel: 313-538-9161. Sharon Larkin, D.R.E.
Students 312.
Convent—25900 Dow St., 48239. Tel: 313-533-7828.

Redford Township, Wayne Co., St. Robert Bellarmine, Revs. John B. Zwers; Donald L. Walker.
Res., 27101 W. Chicago, 48239. Tel: 313-937-1500; Fax: 313-937-1185.
School—Tel: 313-937-1655. Michael Reece, Prin.
Lay Teachers 19; Students 330.
Catechesis/Religious Programs—Tel: 313-937-1531. Jan Lopata, D.R.E.
Students 256.

St. Hilary, Rev. John T. Nowlan; Sr. Marie Miller, I.H.M.
Res., 23901 Elmira, 48239. Tel: 313-533-1560; Fax: 313-533-1735.

Richmond, Macomb Co., St. Augustine, Rev. James E. Commyn.
Res., 68035 Main St., 48062. Tel: 810-727-5215; Fax: 810-727-3760. [CEM]
School—Tel: 810-727-9365.
Sisters 1; Lay Teachers 13; Students 252.
Catechesis/Religious Programs—Tel: 810-727-9290.
Students 274.
Convent—67900 Howard St., 48062. Tel: 810-727-1517.

River Rouge, Wayne Co., Our Lady of Lourdes, Rev. James F. Wieging; Dr. Paul D. Bodrie, Pastoral Assoc.
Res., 1440 Coolidge Highway, 48218. Tel: 313-842-3320; 3321; Fax: 313-842-4507.

Riverview, Wayne Co., St. Cyprian, Rev. Jude Verley, O.S.C. In res., Revs. Neil J. Emon, O.S.C.; Dale H. Redwanski, O.S.C.; Richard M. Leliaert, O.S.C.
Res., 13249 Pennsylvania, 48192. Tel: 313-283-1366; Fax: 313-283-2809.
School—Tel: 313-283-9442. Ann Roush, Prin.
Lay Teachers 14; Students 186.
Catechesis/Religious Programs—Mrs. Kathleen Duford, D.R.E.
Students 392.

Rochester, Oakland Co., St. Andrew, Revs. Timothy F. Babcock; Dennis C. Laesch; Sr. Carmela Whitton, O.S.F., Pastoral Assoc.; Deacon Charles G. Skubick.
Res., 1400 Inglewood, 48307. Tel: 248-651-7486; Fax: 248-651-3950.
Catechesis/Religious Programs—Tel: 248-651-6401. Nancy Clancy, D.R.E.
Students 1,262.

St. Irenaeus, Rev. Edward J. Mitchell; Patricia Egan-Myers, Pastoral Assoc. & D.R.E.
Res., 771 Old Perch Rd., Rochester Hills, 48309. Tel: 248-651-9595; Fax: 248-651-1504.
Catechesis/Religious Programs—Tel: 248-651-2443.
Students 671.

Rochester Hills, St. Mary's of the Hills, Rev. Eugene Strain.
Res., 2675 John R, 48307-4652. Tel: 248-853-5390; Fax: 248-853-7989.
Catechesis/Religious Programs—Tel: 248-853-5390. Nancy A. Mason, D.R.E.
Students 615.

Rockwood, Wayne Co., St. Mary, Rev. Thomas M. Sauter; Deacon Thomas C. Murphy.
Res., P.O. Box 249, 48173. Tel: 313-379-9248; Fax: 313-379-6548. [CEM]
School—Tel: 313-379-9285. Michelle E. Seward, Prin.
Lay Teachers 11; Students 189.
Catechesis/Religious Programs—Tel: 313-379-9406. Ms. Theresa Borawski, D.R.E.
Students 200.
Convent—32477 Church St., 48173.

Romeo, Macomb Co., St. Clement of Rome, Rev. Stephen C. Reckker.
Res., 343 S. Main St., 48065. Tel: 810-752-9611; Fax: 810-752-7795.
Catechesis/Religious Programs—Tel: 810-752-6951; Fax: 810-752-7485. Deborah Knoblock, D.R.E.
Students 690.

Romulus, Wayne Co., St. Aloysius, Rev. Michael D. Malawy.
Res., 11280 Ozga Rd., 48174. Tel: 734-941-5056; Fax: 734-941-6018.
School—Tel: 734-941-3340. Dorian Mantei, Prin.
Lay Teachers 6; Students 96.

Roseville, Macomb Co.,

1—St. Angela, Revs. George T. Browne; Zdzislaw Gnat.
Res., 25001 Chippendale, 48066. Tel: 810-445-6360; Fax: 810-445-6366.
Church—Ten Mile Rd. and Chippendale, 48066.
School—Tel: 810-445-6375; Fax: 810-445-6382. Sr. M. LaVerne, C.S.B., Prin.
Sisters 8; Lay Teachers 14; Students 359.
Catechesis/Religious Programs—Tel: 810-445-6377. Diane McDonald, D.R.E.
Students 307.
Convent—25165 Chippendale, 48066. Tel: 810-445-6370.

2—St. Athanasius, Rev. William P. Siebert; Deacon Ron Channell.
Res., 18720 Thirteen Mile Rd., 48066. Tel: 810-772-1170; Fax: 810-776-2945.
Catechesis/Religious Programs—Sr. Theresa Bray, O.P., D.R.E.
Students 333.

3—St. Donald, Rev. Michael A. Donovan.
Res., 16330 Twelve Mile Rd., 48066. Tel: 313-773-3440; Fax: 810-773-1235.

4—Holy Innocents, Rev. Richard C. Welsh. Pastoral Assocs.: Deacon James Pallarito; Lena Kocis.
Res., 26100 Ridgemont Rd., 48066. Tel: 810-777-7543; Fax: 810-777-1536.
School—Tel: 810-777-5266.
Lay Teachers 10; Students 233.
Catechesis/Religious Programs—Robert Dugas, D.R.E.
Students 194.

5—Sacred Heart, Rev. William Bonnici; Sr. Anne Momienski, Pastoral Assoc.
Res., 18430 Utica Rd., 48066. Tel: 810-777-9116; Fax: 810-777-7958.
Catechesis/Religious Programs—Tel: 810-777-8150; Fax: 810-777-3288. Patricia DeBruce, D.R.E.
Students 102.

Royal Oak, Oakland Co., St. Dennis, Revs. John P. Christ, O.S.C.; Gerald Thaar, O.S.C.; Sr. Connie Parran, I.H.M., Pastoral Assoc.
Res., 2200 E. 12 Mile Rd., 48067-1504. Tel: 248-544-2181; Fax: 248-544-9443.
School—1415 N. Stephenson, 48067-1504. Tel: 248-398-6555; Fax: 248-398-2878. Cheryl Hermann, Prin.
Sisters 2; Lay Teachers 18; Students 443.
Catechesis/Religious Programs—Tel: 248-545-1926. Mrs. B. Gutowski, D.R.E.
Students 225.

St. Mary, Rev. Michael A. Woroniewicz; Rev. Msgr. Thomas H. Villerot; Deacon James A. Cron; Sr. Therese Allgeyer, O.P.
Res., 730 Lafayette Ave., S., 48067. Tel: 248-547-1818; Fax: 248-547-4577. [CEM]
School—628 Lafayette Ave., S., 48067. Tel: 248-545-2140. William R. Farrand, Prin.
Lay Teachers 12; Students 147.
Catechesis/Religious Programs—Tel: 248-547-1810. Ms. Bridget Gasior, D.R.E.
Students 105.

Shrine of the Little Flower, Rev. Msgr. William M. Easton; Revs. Reginald Brady; Joseph R. Horn. In res., Rev. Lambert H. Smits.
Res., 2123 Roseland Ave., 48073. Tel: 248-541-4122 (Office); Fax: 248-541-2838.
Church—2123 Roseland, 48067.
School—Tel: 248-541-4622. Patricia Crowe, Prin.
Lay Teachers 26; Students 609.
Academy—Tel: 248-549-2928. Timothy Kelly, Dir.
Lay Teachers 7; Students 159.
High School—3500 W. Thirteen Mile Rd., 48073. Tel: 248-549-2925; Fax: 248-549-2953. Thomas Kirkwood, Prin.
Lay Teachers 21; Students 327.
Catechesis/Religious Programs—Judy Dantzer, D.R.E.
Students 433.

St. Clair, St. Clair Co., St. Mary, Rev. Edward W. Ritter; Sr. Eileen Meyers, O.P., Pastoral Assoc.
Res., 415 N. 6th St., 48079. Tel: 810-329-2255; Fax: 810-329-5997. [CEM]
School—Tel: 810-329-4150. Mrs. Marilynn Pavlov, Prin.
Lay Teachers 14; Students 345.
Catechesis/Religious Programs—Tel: 810-329-7801. Sr. Janice Marie Peer, O.S.F., D.R.E.
Students 547.
Convent—811 Orchard St., 48079. Tel: 810-329-2400.

St. Clair Shores, Macomb Co.,

1—St. Germaine, Rev. James L. Bjorum; Deacon Terrance Downey, Pastoral Assoc.
Office: 28301 Little Mack, 48081. Tel: 810-771-1750; Fax: 810-771-7634.
School—Tel: 810-771-0890. Mrs. Kay O'Leary, Prin.
Sisters 2; Lay Teachers 18; Students 450.

Catechesis/Religious Programs—Sr. Helen Williams, I.H.M., D.R.E.
Students 167.

2—ST. GERTRUDE, Revs. Thomas J. Johnston, O.P.; Gerald B. Morahan, O.P.; Michael Monshau, O.P.
Res., 28839 Jefferson Ave., 48081. Tel: 810-777-9120; Fax: 810-777-8390. [CEM]
Catechesis/Religious Programs—Tel: 810-775-5820. Paul Lippard, D.R.E.
Students 244.

3—ST. ISAAC JOGUES, Revs. Ronald J. Victor; Francisco Restrepo Diaz (Mexico); Ms. Alice Murphy, Pastoral Assoc.
Parish Center—21120 Benjamin Dr., 48081. Tel: 810-778-5100; Fax: 810-778-4458.
School—Tel: 810-771-3525; Fax: 810-778-8183.
Lay Teachers 25; Students 389.
Catechesis/Religious Programs—Mrs. Claudia Givinsky, D.R.E.
Students 415.

4—ST. JOAN OF ARC, Rev. Msgr. Ricardo E. Bass; Revs. Roman Pasieczny (Poland); Michael J. Byrnes; Deacons Eugene E. DiCresce; Robert F. Busch.
Parish Center—22412 Overlake, 48080. Tel: 810-777-3670; Fax: 810-774-5528.
School—22415 Overlake, 48080. Tel: 810-777-8370; Fax: 810-447-3574. Mr. Don Ancypa, Prin.
Sisters of St. Joseph (Nazareth) 1; Lay Teachers 31; Students 773.
Catechesis/Religious Programs—Tel: 810-772-1282. Sr. Marie Houle, O.P., D.R.E.
Students 677.

5—ST. LUCY, Rev. John C. Esper; Deacon Robert Herta. In res., Rev. Robert Fisher.
Res., 23401 Jefferson, 48080. Tel: 810-771-8300; Fax: 810-447-4220.
Catechesis/Religious Programs—Sr. Kathy Payne, O.S.M., D.R.E.
Students 514.

6—ST. MARGARET OF SCOTLAND, Rev. Ronald W. Kurzawa. In res., Rev. Mark A. Borkowski.
Res., 21201 Thirteen Mile Rd., 48082. Tel: 810-293-2240; Fax: 810-293-0116.
Catechesis/Religious Programs—Tel: 810-293-3280. Mary Paonessa, D.R.E.
Students 601.

Shelby Twp., St. John Vianney Church, Rev. Jerome J. Machlik.
Res., 54045 Schoenherr Rd., 48315. Tel: 810-781-6525; Fax: 810-781-6527.
Catechesis/Religious Programs—Tel: 810-781-2627. D.R.E.: Fritzi Bohlman; Mary Lundgaard; Ida Johns.
Students 1,032.

St. Kieran, Rev. H. Thomas Johnson; Deacon Ronald W. Cook, Pastoral Assoc.
Res., 53600 Mound Rd., 48316. Tel: 810-781-4901; Fax: 810-781-6516.
Catechesis/Religious Programs—Patricia Radacsy, D.R.E.
Students 931.

St. Therese of Lisieux, Rev. Thomas J. Sutherland.
Res., 49230 Arlington Ct., 48315-3903. Tel: 810-247-5428.
Church—48115 Schoenherr Rd., 48315-4225. Tel: 810-254-4433; Fax: 810-254-5463.
Catechesis/Religious Programs—Students 582.

Southfield, Oakland Co.,

1—ST. BEATRICE, Rev. John Gagala.
Res., 17235 Mt. Vernon, 48075. Tel: 248-557-3342; Fax: 248-557-3427.

2—ST. BEDE, Rev. Lawrence A. Pettke. In res., Rev. Toma A. Behman.
Res., 18290 Twelve Mile Rd. W., 48076. Tel: 248-559-0577; Fax: 248-559-0752.
Church—Twelve Mile and Southfield Rds., 48076.
School—Tel: 248-559-0572. Beth Fischer, Prin.
Lay Teachers 9; Students 181.
Catechesis/Religious Programs—Tel: 248-559-0578. Pat Metz, D.R.E.
Students 70.

3—DIVINE PROVIDENCE, Rev. Aloyzas Volskis.
Res., 25335 W. 9 Mile Rd., 48034. Tel: 248-354-3429; Fax: 248-354-1773.

4—ST. IVES, Rev. William D. Sinatra; Deacon Brian J. Black; Linda Simonelli, Pastoral Assoc.
Res., 29350 Lahser, 48034. Tel: 248-353-3410; Fax: 248-353-5412.
Catechesis/Religious Programs—Students 125.

5—ST. MICHAEL, Revs. Lawrence W. Zurek, O.F.M.; John C. Market, O.F.M., (Retired); Theophane Dattilo, O.F.M., (Retired); Roch Farland, O.F.M., (Retired); Bro. Michael Schebeci, O.F.M., Pastoral Assoc.
Res., 25225 Code Rd., 48034. Tel: 248-356-8787; Fax: 248-356-1240.
School—Tel: 248-356-6113. Sr. M. Presentine, Prin.
Sisters 1; Lay Teachers 11; Students 273.
Convent—22750 10 Mile Rd., 48034. Tel: 248-356-8785.

Southgate, Wayne Co., St. Pius X, Rev. Peter Petroske.
Office: 14101 Superior Ave., 48195. Tel: 313-285-1100; Fax: 313-285-5310.
Res., 14160 Longtin Ave., 48195.
School—Tel: 313-285-1100. Clara Seeley, Elementary Prin.
Lay Teachers 20; Students 400.
High School—Sue Kodyk, Interim Prin. Religious 1; Lay Teachers 16; Students 202.
Catechesis/Religious Programs—Carol Buboi, D.R.E.
Students 299.

St. Hugh, Eugene E. Wojtewicz.
Res., 11300 Reeck Rd., 48195. Tel: 313-287-6990; Fax: 313-287-8109.

South Lyon, Oakland Co., St. Joseph, Rev. Howard L. Vogan. Pastoral Assocs.: Sr. Eleanor Furman, O.S.F.; Deacon William Otto.
Res., 810 S. Lafayette, 48178. Tel: 248-437-1121; Fax: 248-437-3784.
Catechesis/Religious Programs—Mary Ann Sikorski, D.R.E.
Students 849.

Sterling Heights, Macomb Co.,

1—ST. BLASE, Rev. Msgr. Michael C. LeFevre; Rev. Thomas P. Kirwan; Sr. Megan McElroy, O.P., Pastoral Assoc.
Res., 12151 E. 15 Mile Rd., 48312-5120. Tel: 810-268-2244; Fax: 810-268-1174.
Catechesis/Religious Programs—Students 868.

2—SS. CYRIL AND METHODIUS, Rev. Elemir Joseph Mikus.
Res., 41233 Ryan Rd., 48314. Tel: 810-726-6911; Fax: 810-726-5913.

3—ST. EPHREM, Rev. Ronald Milligan.
Res., 38900 Dodge Rd., 48312. Tel: 810-264-1230; Fax: 810-264-2757.
Catechesis/Religious Programs—Tel: 810-264-2777.
Students 371.

4—ST. JANE FRANCES DE CHANTAL, Revs. Leon J. Page; John Vargas.
Res., 38750 Ryan Rd., 48310. Tel: 810-977-8080; Fax: 810-977-9305.

5—ST. MALACHY, Rev. Joseph J. Gembala. Pastoral Assocs.: Sr. Alys Currier, I.H.M.; Sr. Pat McCarthy, S.F.C.C.
Res., 14115 14 Mile Rd., 48312-6506. Tel: 810-264-1220; Fax: 810-264-1656.
Catechesis/Religious Programs—Tel: 810-268-4430. Ms. Patricia Whelan, D.R.E.
Students 331.

6—ST. MATTHIAS, Revs. Richard E. Cyr; Thomas J. Moloney, S.A.C.
Res., 12509 Nineteen Mile Rd., 48313. Tel: 810-731-1300; Fax: 810-731-2576.
Catechesis/Religious Programs—Tel: 810-731-0650. Mary A. Lang, D.R.E.
Students 789.

7—ST. MICHAEL, Revs. Lawrence J. Jackson; Thomas Kuehnemund; Deacon Lawrence Healy; Carrie Orlando, Pastoral Assoc.
Church—40501 Hayes Rd., 48313. Tel: 810-247-0020; Fax: 810-247-4081.
Res., 39443 Heatherheath, Clinton Twp., 48038. Tel: 810-286-3322.
Catechesis/Religious Programs—Tel: 810-247-0098. D.R.E.: Emily Gordon; Catherine McInerney.
Students 1,127.

8—OUR LADY OF CZESTOCHOWA, Revs. Jan Rudzewicz, S.Ch.; Jacek Nowak, S.Ch.; Konrad Urbanowski, S.Ch.
Res., 3100 18 Mile Rd., 48314-3810. Tel: 810-977-7267; Fax: 810-977-2074.
Catechesis/Religious Programs—Sr. Bernadetta Gosciniak, D.R.E.
Students 400.

9—ST. RENE GOUPIL, Revs. Frederick J. Schweihofer; Steven A. Wertanen; Sr. Mary Schmidlin, O.S.F., Pastoral Assoc.; Deacon John Santeramo.
Res., 35955 Ryan Rd., 48310. Tel: 810-939-7500; Fax: 810-939-7839.
Catechesis/Religious Programs—Tel: 810-939-7688. Mary Gagnon, D.R.E.
Students 583.

Taylor, Wayne Co.,

1—ST. ALFRED, Revs. C. Michael Verschaeve; Neil Emon, O.S.C.
Res., 9500 Banner, 48180. Tel: 313-291-6464; Fax: 313-291-2733.
School—Tel: 313-291-0247; 291-4600. A. Francis Bontumasi, Prin.
Sisters 1; Lay Teachers 21; Students 409.
Catechesis/Religious Programs—Tel: 313-291-3210. Beth A. Oley, D.R.E.
Students 223.

2—ST. CONSTANCE, Rev. Leo F. Sabourin; Deacon Joseph Mouro.
Res., 21555 Kinyon Rd., 48180. Tel: 313-291-4050; Fax: 313-291-5655.

3—ST. CYRIL OF JERUSALEM, Rev. Gary Morelli; Deacons Daniel J. Hurley; William A. Thome. Pastoral Assocs.: Sr. Marion Therese Mackey, O.P.; Joan Forrest.
Parish Center—20170 Pinecrest, 48180.
Res., 6442 Pelham Rd., 48180. Tel: 313-381-3000; Fax: 313-381-5528.
School—Tel: 313-383-8585. John Champion, Prin.
Lay Teachers 10; Students 190.
Catechesis/Religious Programs—Tel: 313-383-5663. Stacie Battaglia, D.R.E.
Students 216.

4—ST. PASCHAL, Rev. Robert Cislo.
Res., 22210 Champaign St., 48180. Tel: 313-291-4880; Fax: 313-291-7514.
School—Tel: 313-291-6650. Marcia Guerra, Prin.
Lay Teachers 10; Students 150.

Temperance, Monroe Co., St. Anthony, Rev. Gregory J. Deters; Deacon Robert J. Snyder.
Res., 4605 St. Anthony Rd., 48182. Tel: 313-854-1143; Fax: 313-854-4622. [CEM]
School—Tel: 313-854-1160. Sr. M. Joan Furlong, S.N.D., Prin.
Sisters of Notre Dame 5; Dominican Sisters 1; Lay Teachers 10; Students 152.
Catechesis/Religious Programs—Students 104.
Convent—4607 St. Anthony Rd., 48182. Tel: 313-854-2779.

Our Lady of Mt. Carmel, Rev. Alfred J. Miller; Sr. Pam Nosbusch; Hazel Destatte, Pastoral Assoc.
Res., 810 Donna Dr., 48182. Tel: 313-847-2805; Fax: 313-847-8970.
Catechesis/Religious Programs—Tel: 313-847-1725.
Students 542.

Trenton, Wayne Co., St. Joseph, Rev. James A. Vedro, O.S.C.; Sr. Ellen Baker, I.H.M., Pastoral Assoc.
Parish Center—250 Elm St., 48183. Tel: 313-676-3082.
Res., 2623 3rd St., 48183. Tel: 313-676-9082; Fax: 313-676-6255. [JC]
School—Tel: 313-676-2565; Fax: 313-676-9744. Wanda Rovenskie, Prin.
Lay Teachers 8; Students 227.
Catechesis/Religious Programs—Tel: 313-676-7115. Jacqueline Pangborn, D.R.E.
Students 322.

St. Timothy, Rev. Charles S. Fontana.
Parish Office: 2901 Manning Dr., 48183. Tel: 313-676-5115; Fax: 313-676-6863.
Catechesis/Religious Programs—D.R.E.: Fritzi Bohlmann; Geraldine Mooney.
Students 213.

Troy, Oakland Co.,

1—ST. THOMAS MORE, Rev. Edward A. Belczak; Deacon John Ball.
Res., 4580 Adams Rd., 48098. Tel: 248-647-2222; Fax: 248-647-8192.
Catechesis/Religious Programs—Tel: 248-647-4680.
Students 1,413.

2—ST. ALAN, Revs. Thaddeus J. Blaszczyk; Edward F. Konopka, Pastor Emeritus; Sr. Mary Choiniere, S.S.J., Pastoral Assoc.
Church—3077 Glouchester, 48084. Tel: 248-649-5511; Fax: 248-649-6729.
Res., 2345 Coolidge Rd., 48084.

3—ST. ANASTASIA, Rev. Kenneth R. Kaucheck. Pastoral Assocs.: Sr. Kay Allberry, O.P.; Deacon Mark Springer. In res., Rev. William B. Davidson.
Res., 4571 John R. Rd., 48098. Tel: 248-689-8380; Fax: 248-689-7489.
Catechesis/Religious Programs—Tel: 248-689-1431. Elizabeth Murray, D.R.E.
Students 1,070.

4—ST. ELIZABETH ANN SETON, Rev. Ronald J. Essman; Deacon Kenneth Braman.
Res., 280 E. Square Lake Rd., 48098. Tel: 248-879-1310; Fax: 248-879-2886.
Catechesis/Religious Programs—Tel: 248-879-1314.
Students 302.

5—ST. LUCY, Rev. Slaven Mijatovic, O.F.M.
Res., 200 E. Wattles, 48098. Tel: 248-619-9910; Fax: 248-619-9912.

Utica, Macomb Co., St. Lawrence, Revs. Timothy J. Szott; Robert C. Schuster; Sr. Janet Sullivan, I.H.M., Pastoral Assoc.
Res., 44633 Utica Rd., 48317. Tel: 810-731-5347; Fax: 810-731-5393.
School—Tel: 810-731-0135. Paul Gielow, Prin.
Lay Teachers 22; Students 587.
Catechesis/Religious Programs—Tel: 810-731-5072. Linda Sheets, D.R.E.
Students 662.

Walled Lake, Oakland Co., St. William, Rev. Michael G. Savickas; Deacons Richard T. Smith; Timothy J. Pilon. In res., Rev. Christopher N. Chukwu.
Res., 531 Common St., 48390. Tel: 248-624-1421; Fax: 248-624-5273.
School—135 O'Flaherty, 48390. Tel: 248-669-4440; Fax: 248-669-2245. Alexandra Leidlein, Prin.
Lay Teachers 15; Students 269.
Catechesis/Religious Programs—Tel: 248-624-1371. Joni Benson, D.R.E.
Students 575.

Warren, Macomb Co.,

1—St. Anne's, Revs. Michael Kazer; Jerome Slowinski; Sr. Alice Miller, I.H.M., Pastoral Assoc.; Deacon Marvin Strzyzewski.
Res., 32000 Mound Rd., 48092. Tel: 810-268-3434; Fax: 810-268-4142.
School—Tel: 810-264-2911. Dr. Thomas Engel, Prin.
Intercommunity Sisters 1; Lay Teachers 30; Students 881.
Catechesis/Religious Programs—Patricia Berry, D.R.E.
Students 436.

2—Ascension, Rev. Norbert Maciejewski.
Res., 21050 Ascension St., 48089. Tel: 810-754-4000; Fax: 810-757-2342.
Catechesis/Religious Programs—Tel: 810-754-6741.
Students 69.

3—St. Cletus, Rev. Philip Briffa.
Office: 26256 Ryan Rd., 48091. Tel: 810-755-1313; Fax: 810-756-0724.
Res., 26262 Ryan Rd., 48091.
Catechesis/Religious Programs—Tel: 810-755-1350. Virginia Filar, D.R.E.
Students 230.

4—St. Dorothy, Revs. Francis A. Weingartz; Thomas Puzio; Sr. Carlotta Lammers, Pastoral Assoc.
Res., 12255 Frazho, 48089. Tel: 810-754-3232; Fax: 810-754-3152.
Catechesis/Religious Programs—Tel: 810-759-1040.
Students 265.

5—St. Edmund, Revs. Robert J. Witkowski; Eugene T. Katcher; Deacon Val Buyle.
Res., 14025 Twelve Mile Rd., 48093. Tel: 810-772-2720; Fax: 810-772-5576.
Catechesis/Religious Programs—Tel: 810-773-9220.
Students 611.

6—St. Leonard of Port Maurice, Rev. Andrew J. Tomasko; Sr. Patricia Eeckhout, Pastoral Assoc.; Deacon Edward Swartz.
Res., 14057 E. Nine Mile, 48089. Tel: 810-777-1350; Fax: 810-777-1247.

7—St. Louise, Rev. Thomas G. Rice; Deacons Wilhelm Kessler; Anthony Morici.
Res., 2500 Twelve Mile Rd., 48092. Tel: 810-751-3340; Fax: 810-751-0603.
Catechesis/Religious Programs—Tel: 810-751-3486. Mrs. Irmgard Kovacs, D.R.E.
Students 180.

8—St. Mark, Rev. Robert A. Ruedisueli; Deacon George R. Posavetz.
Res., 4257 Bart, 48091. Tel: 810-759-3020; Fax: 810-759-3024.
Catechesis/Religious Programs—Tel: 810-759-3022. Suzanne Cornelius, D.R.E.
Students 400.

9—St. Martin de Porres, Revs. Timothy J. Murray; Timothy Mazur. Pastoral Assocs.: Mrs. Cynthia Branch; Sr. Joan Popovits, O.P.; Deacon Larry Sullivan.
Res., 31555 Hoover Rd., 48093. Tel: 810-264-7515; Fax: 810-264-4013.
Catechesis/Religious Programs—Tel: 810-264-7970. Mrs. Diane Bucko, D.R.E.
Students 420.
Convent—31014 Shaw, 48093. Tel: 810-264-4894.
Sisters 2.

10—St. Paul Albanian Catholic Community, Rev. Anton Kcira, Admin.
Office: 3411 Twelve Mile Rd., 48092. Tel: 810-573-8110; Fax: 810-573-4107.
Res., 3239 E. Twelve Mile Rd., 48092. Tel: 810-573-8799.

11—St. Sylvester, Revs. Gary Schulte; Stanislaw J. Obloj; Deacon John L. Skladanowski, Pastoral Min.
Res., 11200 Twelve Mile Rd., 48093. Tel: 810-751-3636; Fax: 810-751-1766.
Catechesis/Religious Programs—Tel: 810-751-3510.
Students 442.

Washington, Macomb Co., SS. John and Paul, Rev. Terence F. Treppa.
Res., 7777 W. 28 Mile Rd., 48094. Tel: 810-781-9010; Fax: 810-781-7061.
Catechesis/Religious Programs—Tel: 810-781-9488. Bernadine Biske, D.R.E.
Students 341.

Waterford, Oakland Co., Our Lady of the Lakes, Revs. Lawrence Delonnay; Jacek Brewczynski; Deacon Charles F. Johnson.
Res., 5481 Dixie Hwy., 48329. Tel: 248-623-0274; Fax: 248-623-2723.
School—Tel: 248-623-0250. Carol Hanrahan, Elementary Prin.
Lay Teachers 15; Students 466.
High School—Tel: 248-623-0340. Carl Uberti, Prin.
Sisters 1; Lay Teachers 23; Students 327.
Catechesis/Religious Programs—Tamzien Tallenger, D.R.E.
Students 433.

St. Benedict, Rev. James P. O'Hagan; Maria Geryk, Pastoral Assoc.
Parish Office—80 S. Lynn, 48328. Tel: 248-681-1534; Fax: 248-681-4501.
Res., 1160 Myrtle St., 48328.
School—Tel: 248-682-5580. Dr. Eugene Mignacca, Prin.
Lay Teachers 10; Students 184.
Catechesis/Religious Programs—Tel: 248-681-1536. Patricia Tola, D.R.E.
Students 198.

St. Perpetua, Rev. Richard S. Rakoczy.
Res., 134 Airport Rd., 48327. Tel: 248-682-6431; Fax: 248-682-7088.
Catechesis/Religious Programs—Joseph Leddy, D.R.E.
Students 370.

Wayne, Wayne Co., St. Mary, Rev. Jack H. Baker. Pastoral Assocs.: Sr. Eleanor Sekol, I.H.M.; Sr. Patricia Hergenroether, S.S.J.; Deacon William Meahan.
34530 Michigan Ave., 48184. Tel: 313-721-8745; Fax: 313-721-0260.
School—34516 Michigan Ave., 48184. Tel: 313-721-1240; Fax: 313-467-7381. Ms. Catherine Myszka, Prin.
Lay Teachers 10; Students 297.
Catechesis/Religious Programs—Tel: 313-326-8180.
Students 335.

West Bloomfield, Oakland Co., Prince of Peace, Rev. Arnold J. Kosco.
Res., 4300 Walnut Lake Rd., 48323. Tel: 248-681-9424; Fax: 248-681-5543.
Catechesis/Religious Programs—Tel: 248-681-5070. Irma Macy, D.R.E.
Students 575.

Westland, Wayne Co.,

1—St. Bernardine, Rev. Ronald Sayes.
Res., 31463 Ann Arbor Trail, 48185. Tel: 313-427-5150; Fax: 313-427-3319.
Catechesis/Religious Programs—Tel: 313-261-3050. Mary Jane Ayotte, D.R.E.
Students 275.

2—St. Damian, Rev. William J. Pettit, Admin.
Res., 29825 Joy Rd., 48185. Tel: 313-421-6130; Fax: 313-513-4916.
School—Tel: 313-427-1680. Sr. M. Pauline, C.S.S.F., Prin.
Felician Sisters 2; Lay Teachers 11; Students 248.
Catechesis/Religious Programs—Elaine O'Neill, D.R.E.
Students 205.
Convent—30055 Joy Rd., 48185. Tel: 313-427-0031.

3—Church of the Divine Savior, Rev. Alexander A. Kuras; Deacon Paul F. Pelchat.
Church—39375 Joy Rd., 48185. Tel: 313-455-3620; Fax: 313-455-7998.
Res., 9249 Caprice, Plymouth, 48170. Tel: 313-455-6964.
Catechesis/Religious Programs—Mary Ann Newton, D.R.E.
Students 255.

4—St. Richard, Rev. John F. Hall.
Res., 35637 Cherry Hill, 48185. Tel: 313-729-2240.
Church & C.C.D. Office—35851 Cherry Hill Rd., 48185. Tel: 313-729-4412; Fax: 313-729-3132.
Catechesis/Religious Programs—Tel: 313-729-4411. Jeanne Martin, D.R.E.
Students 286.

5—SS. Simon and Jude, Rev. Gerard V. Bechard.
Office: 32500 Palmer Rd., 48186. Tel: 313-722-1343; Fax: 313-326-5466.
Res., 1700 Hubbard Ave., 48186.
Catechesis/Religious Programs—D.R.E.: Mary Ann Kocsis; Margaret Reyez.
Students 150.

6—St. Theodore of Canterbury, Revs. Michael A. Molnar; Daniel Zaleski; Deacon Anthony Kendzierski.
Res., 8200 Wayne Rd., 48185. Tel: 313-425-4421; Fax: 313-425-0650.
Catechesis/Religious Programs—Tel: 313-425-7310.
Students 394.

White Lake, Oakland Co., St. Patrick, Rev. Thomas L. Meagher.
Res., 9086 Hutchins Rd., 48386. Tel: 248-698-3100; Fax: 248-698-2350.
School—9040 Hutchins Rd., 48386. Tel: 248-698-2340. Mrs. Linda Meese, Prin.
Lay Teachers 10; Students 295.
Catechesis/Religious Programs—Students 942.

Woodhaven, Wayne Co., Our Lady of the Woods, Rev. Richard J. Bartoszek.
Res., 21892 Gudith Rd., 48183. Tel: 313-671-5102; Fax: 313-671-2901.
Catechesis/Religious Programs—Tel: 313-671-0525. Patricia Butler, D.R.E.
Students 1694.

Wyandotte, Wayne Co.,

1—St. Elizabeth, Rev. Charles M. Morris.
Res., 138 Goodell St., 48192. Tel: 313-284-7727; Fax: 313-284-7891.

2—St. Helena, Rev. George Kowalski.
Res., 753 Forest St., 48192. Tel: 313-284-4988.

3—St. Joseph, Rev. Gerard Frawley, S.A.C.
Res., 353 Elm St., 48192. Tel: 313-285-9840; Fax: 313-285-9745.
School—Tel: 313-285-2030; Fax: 313-285-0327. Mary Swinkey, Prin.
Lay Teachers 10; Students 169.
Catechesis/Religious Programs—Doreen Calvin, D.R.E.
Students 225.

4—Our Lady of Mt. Carmel, (Polish), Rev. Walter J. Ptak.
Res., 976 Superior Blvd., 48192. Tel: 313-284-9135; Fax: 313-284-1367. [CEM]
School—2609 Tenth St., 48192. Tel: 313-285-5520; Fax: 313-285-9245. Sr. Mary Anita Niemiec, C.S.S.F., Elementary Prin.
Felician Sisters 3; Lay Teachers 15; Students 240.
High School—Tel: 313-284-7311; Fax: 313-284-6235. Sr. Mary Cordelia, C.S.S.F., High School Prin.
Felician Sisters 2; Lay Teachers 12; Students 130.
Catechesis/Religious Programs—Tel: 313-284-6145. Sr. Mary Adonia, C.S.S.F., D.R.E.
Lay Teachers 13; Students 150.
Convent—2609 Tenth St., 48192. Tel: 313-284-7253.

5—St. Patrick, Rev. Raymond H. Lewandowski.
Office: 135 Superior Blvd., 48192.
Res., 105 Superior Blvd., 48192. Tel: 313-285-9472; Fax: 313-285-1623. [JC]
School—Wyandotte Catholic Consolidated School, Tel: 313-285-2030. Mary Swinkey, Elementary Prin.
Lay Teachers 9; Students 176.
High School—Gabriel Richard H.S., Tel: 313-284-1875. John Bres, High School Prin.
Students 520.

6—St. Stanislaus Kostka, (Polish), Rev. John P. Hedges.
Res., 266 Antoine St., 48192. Tel: 313-285-9509.
School—240 Antoine St., 48192. Tel: 313-282-3105.
Sisters 1; Lay Teachers 8; Students 153.

Yale, St. Clair Co., Sacred Heart, Rev. Lawrence E. Dunn.
Res., 310 N. Main St., 48097. Tel: 810-387-2998. [CEM]
Catechesis/Religious Programs—Tel: 810-387-3361. Marian Boike, D.R.E.
Students 156.

Chaplains of Public Institutions

Detroit. *Alexander Blaine Memorial*. Attended from St. Peter and Paul. Tel: 313-961-8077.
Annapolis. Rev. Bernard Pilarski.
Art Centre Hospital. Attended from Lady of the Rosary. Tel: 313-875-6011.
Beaumont Hospital. Revs. Christopher Welch; Lloyd Thiel, O.F.M. Cap.
Bi-County Osteopathic. Revs. Theo Meyer; Luke Krotkiewicz.
Bon Secours. Rev. Donald J. Kresmer; Sr. Therese Tighe, O.P., Chap.; Rita McEachen Neal, Chap.
Children's Hospital. Tel: 313-745-5917. Sr. Janet Ryan, I.H.M., Dir.; Sr. Beverly Hindson, I.H.M., Chap.
Clinton Valley Center. Tel: 810-338-7241, Ext. 425. Rev. Daniel Thottakara, C.M.I.
Cottage Hospital. Attended from St. Paul's. Tel: 810-785-8855.
Crittendon Hospital. Rev. Walter Lezochowski.
Detroit General Hospital, 48226. Tel: 313-224-0541. Sr. Adelaide Eiden, Chap.
Detroit Osteopathic Hospital. Attended from Cathedral of the Most Blessed Sacrament. 48226. Tel: 313-865-6300.

Detroit Psychiatric Institute, 48226. Tel: 313-427-1533. Rev. Daniel O'Sullivan.
Detroit Receiving Hospital, 48226. Rev. Bernard Backiel, M.I.C.; Sr. Janet Hudspeth, Chap.
Detroit Riverview Hospital. Attended from St. Charles.
Doctor's Hospital. Vacant. St. Peter and Paul, 48226. Tel: 313-961-8077.
Garden City Osteopathic Hospital. Rev. Bernard Pilarski.
Glen Eden Hospital. Attended from the Capuchin Community.
Grace Hospital-Northwest University. Deacon Dan Sweeney, Chap.; Mary Bartnik, Chap.
Harper Hospital and Rehabilitation Center. Revs. Gabriel Cohelo, O.F.M.Cap.; Anthony Abgali.
Henry Ford Hospital. Rev. Charles Hart, O.F.M.; Sr. Fran Pokreifka, I.H.M., Chap.; Mrs. Marie Handley, Chap.
Heritage Hospital. Tel: 810-295-6700. Sherri Christ.
Hutzel Hospital. Tel: 313-831-3139. Rev. James L. Meyer.
Kirkwood Hospital. Attended from St. Gregory. Tel: 313-861-0363.
Lapeer Regional. Attended from Immaculate Conception. Tel: 810-664-8594.
Lincoln Hospital. Attended from Holy Redeemer. Tel: 313-842-3450.
Macomb Hospital Center. Mrs. Katherine Breslin, Chap.
Martin Place East Hospital. Attended from St. Vincent Ferrer. Tel: 810-542-8720.
McNamara Hospital. Attended from the Capuchin Community. Tel: 810-751-0410.
Mercy Hospital Detroit, 48226. Sr. Rose Petrozzo, O.P., Chap.
Michigan Health Care Corporation. Rev. Bernard Backiel, M.I.C.
North Woodward Hospital. Attended from Blessed Sacrament Cathedral. Tel: 313-865-6300.
Northville State Hospital. Tel: 810-349-1800. Rev. Stanislaus C. Kukulski.
Oakland General Osteopathic. Sr. Stephanie Thompson, Chap.
Oakwood Hospital. Revs. Michael Gormley, S.A.C.; Richard Lileart; Sr. Ann Foley, Chap.
Palmer Osteopathic Hospital. Attended from St. Benedict. Tel: 313-868-3876.
Palmer Osteopathic Hospital-East. Attended from St. Matthew. Tel: 313-881-4049.
Pontiac Correction Camp. Attended from St. Patrick, Union Lake. Tel: 810-363-2441.
Pontiac General Hospital. Diane Guappone, Chap.
Pontiac Osteopathic Hospital. Diane Guappone, Chap.
Redford Community Hospital. Attended from St. Agatha. Tel: 313-531-0371.
Rehabilitation Institute. Sr. Therese LeBlanc, Dir.; Sr. Leslie Hartway, Chap.
Riverside Osteopathic Hospital. Attended from St. Joseph. Vacant. Tel: 313-676-9082.
Saratoga General Hospital. Rev. Louis Resma.
Sinai Hospital. Rev. Kenneth Noetzel, S.J.
Southwest Detroit Hospital, 48226. Tel: 313-963-4539. Rev. Thomas Lumpkin.
Veterans Administration Hospital. Vacant.
Warren Memorial Hospital. Vacant.
Wayne and Monroe County-Adults, 305 Michigan Ave., 48226. Tel: 313-237-4684. John Humphrey, Chap.
Wayne Co., 305 Michigan Ave., 48226. Tel: 313-237-4684. Abdulami Osman, Outreach Coord.
Wayne County Juvenile Justice, c/o Team for Justice, 1035 St. Antoine, 48226. Tel: 313-965-3242. Bill Kresse, Chap.
Wayne County Youth Home. Tel: 313-831-1356. Rufus Knighton, Chap.
Wyandotte General Hospital. Attended from St. Helena. Tel: 313-284-4988. Rev. George Kowalski.
Yale Community Hospital. Attended from Sacred Heart. Tel: 810-387-2998.
Zieger Osteopathic Hospital. Attended from Our Lady Queen of Angels. Tel: 313-825-4696.

CLINTON TOWNSHIP. *State Prisons,* 24415 Crocker Blvd., 48036. Tel: 810-755-9359. Rev. Thomas R. Physician.

FARMINGTON. *Botsford General Hospital.* St. Alexander's. Tel: 810-474-5748. Rev. Louis Resma.

MOUNT CLEMENS. *Macomb County Adults,* c/o Macomb County Jail, 43565 Elizabeth Rd., 48043. Tel: 810-307-9326. Jo Kudela, Chap.
Macomb County Jail and Macomb County Youth Home. Attended from St. Peter's, Mount Clemens. Tel: 313-237-5962.
Mount Clemens General Hospital. Ms. Connie Walker, Dir.

PONTIAC. *Oakland and Lapeer County-Adults,* 14 Judson St., 3rd Floor, P.O. Box 431366, 48343-1366. Tel: 810-338-9310. Peggy Devaney, Chap.
Oakland, Lapeer, and St. Clair County, 14 Judson St., 3rd Floor, P.O. Box 431366, 48343-1366. Tel: 810-338-9310. Chaplains: Betty Clark; Miguel Rivera.
Oakland, Lapeer, Macomb, and St. Clair Counties-Juveniles, 14 Judson St., 3rd Floor, P.O. Box 431366, 48343-1366. Tel: 810-338-9310. Carleen Ward, Chap.

PORT HURON. *Mercy Hospital Port Huron,* 48060. Sr. Margaret Weber, R.S.M., Chap.; Sr. M. Frances Villerot, R.S.M., Chap.
Port Huron Hospital. Attended from St. Joseph. 48060. Tel: 810-985-7750.

Special Assignment:
Reverend Monsignors—
Quinn, John M., Dept. of Education
Sable, Robert M., Prelate Auditor of the Roman Rota, Vatican
Zenz, John P., Moderator of the Curia
Reverend Fathers—
Browne, Ronald, Tribunal & Faculty, Sacred Heart Major Seminary
Bugarin, Michael, Sec. Cardinal
Carnago, William J., Tribunal & Pastor, Immaculate Heart of Mary, Detroit
DePorres-Cox, Jesse, O.P., Dept. of Parish Life
Fisher, Robert J., Vocations Office
Havron, Daniel, O.F.M., Office of Evangelization
Jozwiak, Ronald J., Tribunal & Admin., St. Josaphat, Detroit
Kosnik, Anthony, Marygrove College
Miller, George, Tribunal
Nawrocki, Norman, Tribunal
Slowinski, Jerome, Tribunal
Taube, Sylvester, Family Life Office
Thomson, Richard G., O.S.C., Dept. of Parish Life
West, John H., Rector, St. John's Center for Youth & Families
Williams, Clarence E., C.PP.S., African American Catholic Ministries Office
Williams, Robert Hayes, Tribunal & Pastor, St. Justin, Hazel Park

---

On Duty Outside the Archdiocese:
Reverend Fathers—
Cassidy, Richard, East Aurora, NY
Singelyn, Robert K., Recife, Brazil
Trent, James F., Chaplaincy Admin., Federal Bureau of Prisons-Western Region, 7950 Dublin Blvd., Dublin, CA 94568. Tel: 510-803-4776
Walsh, Jerome, Jackson Heights, NY

Military Chaplains:
Reverend Fathers—
Bjorklund, Brian, U.S. Navy
Borycz, Edmund S., U.S. Army
Hogan, Timothy D., U.S. Navy
Jagielski, James, U.S. Army
Kaul, John, U.S. Naval Reserves

Awaiting Assignment:
Reverend Fathers—
Jones, Daniel J., 1234 Washington Blvd., Detroit, MI 48226-1825

Graduate Studies:
Reverend Fathers—
Kasza, John, Pontifical Intl. Inst. of San Anselmo
Monforton, Jeffrey, Pontifical Gregorian Univ.

Absent on Leave:
Reverend Fathers—
Crepeau, John J.
Ellis, Matthew
Hogan, Richard
Kramer, Thomas
Loyson, Michael
McLaughlin, Andrew
Shirilla, Gerald

Absent on Sick Leave:
Reverend Fathers—
Lipczewski, Boleslaus
MacLennan, Donald
Morgan, Colum

Retired:
Reverend Monsignors—
Canfield, Francis X., 821 Neff Rd., Grosse Pointe, MI 48230
DeCneudt, Ferdinand, Father Tallieu Senior Citizen Residence, Apt. B104, 18740 Thirteen Mile Rd., Roseville, MI 48066
Flanigan, Gerald A., 14469-B Levan Rd., Livonia, MI 48154
Horkan, Vincent J., 36800 Schoolcraft, Livonia, MI 48150
Lorenz, Victor O., Lourdes Nursing Home, 2300 Watkins Lake Rd., Waterford, MI 48328
Sawher, Clifford F., 716 Clinton Ave., St. Clair, MI 48079
Sherzer, William J., St. Owen Parish, 6869 Franklin Rd., Bloomfied Hills, MI 48301
Villerot, Thomas H., 14453-A Levan Rd., Livonia, MI 48154-5022
Weier, John A., Maryhaven, 11350 Reeck Rd., Rm. 73, Southgate, MI 48195
Reverend Fathers—
Bartone, Donald E., 1715 N. River Rd., Apt. 21, St. Clair, MI 48079
Bauer, Erwin J., 75 S. Channel, Harsens Island, MI 48028
Berg, Paul, Sacred Heart Major Seminary, 2701 Chicago Blvd., Detroit, MI 48206
Blaska, John A., 541 E. 14 Mile Rd., Clawson, MI 48017
Bodde, Frederick A., 6116 N. River Rd., East China, MI 48054-4731
Bologna, Anthony F., St. Gabriel Parish, 8118 W. Vernor, Detroit, MI 48209
Borowski, Ladislaus, DeSerrano Res., C-226, 17255 Common Rd., Roseville, MI 48066
Bresnahan, Thomas J., 14453-B Levan Rd., Livonia, MI 48154-5022
Britz, Gerald F., 8781 Lakeshore, Lexington, MI 48450
Brock, David F., 41464 Whitetail Ln., Canton, MI 48188-2073
Burke, Walter E., 17582 N. Whitefish Point Rd., Paradise, MI 49768
Burkholder, Robert, 84 - 770 Kili Dr., Apt. 632, Waianae, HI 96792
Burns, Francis H., 810 North Shore, St. Clair Shores, MI 48080
Butkus, Casimir, 6467 Warwick, Detroit, MI 48228
Byrne, Thomas, P.O. Box 375, Flat Rock, MI 48134
Canavan, John D., 11395 Oakwood Dr., Jerome, MI 49249-9516
Castelot, John, 42555 Plymouth Hollow, Plymouth, MI 48170
Ciesniewski, Richard P., St. Elizabeth Seton Parish, 9728 Palmeras Ln., Sun City, AZ 85373
Dacey, Donald, Fairlane Meadows, 5148 Heather Dr., #116, Dearborn, MI 48126
Davidson, William, St. Anastasia Parish, 4571 John Rd., Troy, MI 48098
Decker, Maurice C., Rapalo North Condominiums, 306, 1701 S. Flagler, West Palm Beach, FL 33401
Dietz, Francis, 14453-C Levan Rd., Livonia, MI 48154-5022
Dorr, Richard J., 38110 John P. Rd., Clinton Twp., MI 48036-1218
Dowell, William J., 14467-A Levan Rd., Livonia, MI 48154-5022
Drogowski, Joseph, P.O. Box 372, Cohoctah, MI 48816-0372
Dunn, John, Casa Maria, 670 Maple Vista, Imlay City, MI 48444
Edwards, Lawrence A., 8181 Wayne Rd., Apt. K-1093, Westland, MI 48185
Erpelding, Martin L., 4309 Pratt, Grand Blanc, MI 48439
Esper, Thomas, 164 Shoreline Rd., East Port Sanilac, MI 48469-9769
Fares, Lawrence, 36773 Kelly Rd., Clinton Township, MI 48035-1325
Fauser, Arthur W., Our Lady of Sorrows Parish, 23815 Powers, Farmington, MI 48336
Fedewa, Eugene F., Our Lady Queen of Peace Parish, 20955 Bournemouth, Harper Wds., MI 48225
Femminineo, Joseph P.
Ferens, Joseph F., 1870 Lakesview Blvd., Oxford, MI 48371
Forish, Andrew, 19450 Mayfield, Apt. 104, Livonia, MI 48152
Fortuna, George B., 14467-C Levan Rd., Livonia, MI 48154-5022
Gierut, Joseph A., 9106 Del Prado Dr., Palos Hills, IL 60525-0807
Goentges, Charles J., 14468-A Levan Rd., Livonia, MI 48154-5022
Goodrow, Robert A., Chap., USNR, 1809 Marquis Loop, Lady Lake, FL 32159
Hadad, Gerard A., 20941 Persimmons Pl., Estero, FL 33928
Haener, Robert W., 14467-B Levan Rd., Livonia, MI 48154-5022
Haney, Richard M., Loudres Nursing Home, 2300 Watkins Lake Rd., Waterford, MI 48328
Hardy, John J., P.O. Box 488, Ortonville, MI 48462
Hayes, James L., Villa Maria, Apt. 1, 15131 Newburg Rd., Livonia, MI 48154
Heidelberger, Ronald, 1431 Washington Blvd., Apt. 1402, Detroit, MI 48226-1723
Hennes, Paul R., 5325 Pointe Dr., East China, MI 48504-4161
Herman, Jerome A., 1604 E. 9th St., Stuart, FL 34996
Higdon, C. Paul, 3900 Aspen Dr., #345, Port Huron, MI 48060
Hillebrand, Albert J., 1116 Shore Club Dr., St. Clair Shores, MI 48080

Hoffmaster, Harry, 2500 River Rd. #41, Marysville, MI 48040
Hubble, Karl D., 1593 N. River Rd., Apt. 1-D, St. Clair, MI 48079
Immel, William A., 7300 Orchard St., P.O. Box 236, Port Sanilac, MI 48469
Janiga, Joseph, 7039 Sarena, Detroit, MI 48210
Jones, Raymond, 207 Golf Villas Ct., N.W., Lake Placid, FL 33852
Kaznowski, Valentine J., 7758 Colony Dr., Algonac, MI 48001
Kenna, John A., Maryhaven, 11350 Reeck Rd., Apt. 74, Southgate, MI 48195
Koenig, Robert B., Chalet Apts., 33373 Utica Rd., Apt. 2, Fraser, MI 48026
Koltuniak, Michael P., 14454-C Levan Rd., Livonia, MI 48154-5022
Konopka, Edward F., 7950 N. McNab, Bldg.10, Apt. 210, Tamarac, FL 33321
Kosicki, Bohdan, 5630 Klettner, St. Clair Twp., MI 48079
Kowalski, Ralph E., 14467-D Levan Rd., Livonia, MI 48154-5022
Kreft, Henry S., 3621 Port Austin Rd., Port Austin, MI 48467
Kresmer, Donald J., Maryhaven #26, 11350 Reeck Rd., Southgate, MI 48195-2285
Krieg, Jerome L., 2300 Watkins Lake Rd., Waterford, MI 48328
Krisciunevicius, Victor, 12942 Brixham, Warren, MI 48093
Kubik, John M., St. Peter & Paul Parish, 7685 Grandville, Detroit, MI 48228
Kundrat, Michael J., 81393 Belle River Rd. #15, Memphis, MI 48041
Kuntz, Donald B., 9245 North River Rd., Algonac, MI 48001
Lederman, Paul, 14455-C Levan Rd., Livonia, MI 48154
Lombardi, Albert U., 14465-B Levan Rd., Livonia, MI 48154-5022
Malaric, Stephen L., 5325 Pointe Dr., E. China, MI 48054-4161
Maliszewski, Francis S., 986 Wexford Way, Rochester Hills, MI 48309
Maloney, Richard E., 390 Mt. Vernon, Grosse Pointe Farms, MI 48236
Marshall, Raymond, 19650 Eastland Village Dr., Apt.#1, Harper Woods, MI 48225
Matlenga, Joseph, Sacred Heart Home for the Aged, 4900 Navarre, Oregon, OH 43616
McGoldrick, William J., 467 Fairford Rd., Grosse Pointe, MI 48236
Muir, Edmund D., 443 Cerromar Ln., Apt. 300, Venice, FL 34293
Neffy, Arthur, 17825 15 Mile Rd. #25, Clinton Twp., MI 48035
O'Callaghan, John F., 14469-D Levan Rd., Livonia, MI 48154-5022
O'Hara, Michael J., 22612 St. Joan, St. Clair Shores, MI 48080-3866
O'Leary, Michael G., St. Paul Parish, 157 Lake Shore Dr., Grosse Pointe Farms, MI 48236
O'Neill, Charles F., Our Lady of Grace Parish, 8679 Riverview, Dearborn Heights, MI 48127
Partensky, Leonard J., 6747 N. Wayne Rd., 440A-3, Westland, MI 48185
Perkowski, Joseph, 16113 Inla Ln., Ocqueoc, MI 49759
Pettit, William J., 19120 Purling Brook Rd., Livonia, MI 48152
Reckinger, Robert A., 3300 Jeffries Fwy., Detroit, MI 48208
Redwick, Stanislaus J., Marywood Nursing Center, 36975 W. Five Mile Rd., Livonia, MI 48154
Rybinski, Marvin, Marybrook, 36975 Five Mile Rd., Livonia, MI 48154
Ryder, Joseph F., 3015 Moonlake Dr., W. Bloomfield, MI 48323
Sadler, Alfred H., 5571 Pointe Dr., E. China, MI 48054
Samonie, Jacob, 34644 Spring Valley, Westland, MI 48185
Scheuerman, Edward L., 14453-D Levan Rd., Livonia, MI 48154
Schmitt, Thomas G., 53880 Sunderlund Dr., Shelby Township, MI 48316
Schroll, Bernard A., Guardian Angels Parish, 581 E. 14 Mile, Clawson, MI 48017
Schweihofer, Walter J., 49310 Bay Shore Dr., New Baltimore, MI 48047
Sierocki, Paul E., 1723 N. Lafayette, Dearborn, MI 48128
Sirianni, Jasper F., Our Lady of Mt. Carmel Parish, 10828 Brandon Rd., Emmett, MI 48022
Sito, Joseph, 14455-B Levan Rd., Livonia, MI 48154-5022
Slominski, Fabian B., 5405 Christi Dr., Warren, MI 48091
Stanievich, J. Walter, 22295 Green Hill, Apts. 29, Farmington Hills, MI 48335
Stine, Jerome E., 20198 Omira, Detroit, MI 48203
Tucci, Italo, Fr. Taillieu Sr. Citizens #107, 18700 13 Mile Rd., Roseville, MI 48066
Ugolik, Richard, 57088 Copper Creek Dr., Washington Township, MI 48094-2822
Van Der Linden, Peter J., 1370 Aspen Dr., Apt. 4, Marysville, MI 48040
Villerot, Henry E., De Serrano Residence, 17255 Common Rd. B-200, Roseville, MI 48066
Welch, William F., 14455-A Levan Rd., Livonia, MI 48154-5022
Wittstock, John J., 3603 Villa Knolls Dr., Las Vegas, NV 89120
Wolber, Ferdinand A., Woodlore Condominiums, 33399 Fargo, Livonia, MI 48152
Xuereb, Paul, 16900 Paul Revere, Clinton Twp., MI 48035
Zdrodowski, Francis, 976 Superior, Wyandotte, MI 48192-4926
Zeeb, Charles, 18569 Manorwood West, Clinton Township, MI 48039
Ziemba, Walter J., SS. Cyril & Methodius Seminary, 3535 Indian Trail, Orchard Lake, MI 48324

Permanent Deacons:
Abler, Donald, VA Medical Center, Allen Park
Ball, John H., St. Thomas More, Troy
Barbera, John, St. Valerie/St. Claude, Clinton Twp.
Black, Brian J., St. Ives, Southfield
Braman, Kenneth, St. Elizabeth Ann Seton, Troy
Braun, Bernard, St. Anne, Ortonville
Bruen, Patrick T., St. Stanislaus Kostka, Wyandotte
Busch, Robert F., St. Joan of Arc, St. Clair Shores
Buyle, Valere, St. Edmund, Warren
Carroll, Brian, St. Regis, Birmingham
Channell, Ronald, St. Athanasius, Roseville
Cochrane, George, St. Linus, Dearborn Heights
Cominotto, Anthony, St. Augustine, Richmond
Conlin, Richard R., St. Benedict, Highland Park
Connors, John J., St. Stephen, Port Huron
Cook, Ronald W., St. Kieran, Utica
Cornell, Peter, St. Anthony, Belleville
Cousino, Wesley, St. Joseph, Erie
Cox, Donald J., St. Blase, Sterling Heights
Cron, James A., St. Mary, Royal Oak
D'Argis, Leo, St. Colette, Livonia
Daratony, Joseph J., Resurrection, Canton
Darga, Daniel J., Our Lady of La Salette, Berkley
Delbeke, Robert G., St. Rita, Detroit
Deshaw, Gerald, Immaculate Conception, Lapeer
Desjarlais, Eugene B., Madonna University, Livonia
Desmedt, Frank, St. Lawrence, Utica
DeWitt, Robert N., Our Lady of Grace, Dearborn Heights
DiCresce, Eugene, St. Joan of Arc, St. Clair Shores
Downey, Terrance E., St. Germaine, St. Clair Shores
Dullinger, Aloysius, Senior Status
Fitzgerald, Robert C., St. Michael, Livonia
Fleming, John Michael, St. Joseph, Pontiac
Fraser, Daniel, St. Mary, Monroe
Gabel, Raymond, St. Albert the Great, Dearborn Heights
Girard, Lawrence, St. Sebastian, Dearborn Heights
Gonzalez, Norman, Senior Status
Goodhue, Harold, St. Roch, Flat Rock
Hardwick, Ralph, St. Vincent Ferrer, Madison Heights
Healy, Lawrence, St. Michael, Sterling Heights
Hensel, James L., Senior Status
Herta, Robert, St. Lucy, St. Clair Shores
Hulan, Richard, St. Barbara, Dearborn
Hurley, Daniel, St. Cyril, Taylor
Igoe, James, St. Richard, Westland
Ingels, Michael M., St. Michael, Monroe
Iskra, Joseph, St. Raymond, Detroit
Jablonowski, Alexander, St. Daniel, Clarkston
Jackson, Douglas, Jr., Martyrs of Uganda, Detroit
Jamieson, William E., St. Ambrose, Grosse Point Park
Jimenez, Rafael, St. Stephen, Mary Mother of the Church
Johnson, Charles, Our Lake of the Lakes, Waterford
Johr, William H., St. Matthew, Detroit
Jones, Wyatt, Our Lady Gate of Heaven, Detroit
Junak, Donald C., St. Louis, Mount Clemens
Kendzierski, Anthony, St. Theodore, Westland
Kenny, John, St. Edith, Livonia
Kessler, Wilhelm, St. Louise, Warren
Krauskoff, William, Our Lady Gate of Heaven, Detroit
Krueger, Gary R., Holy Cross, Marine City
Krzeminski, Eugene, St. Kenneth, Plymouth
Kunik, Raymond L., St. Priscilla, Livonia
LaLone, Norman C., Senior Status
Leach, Donald, Our Lady of Good Counsel, Plymouth
Lennon, Joseph, St. Stanislaus Kostka, Wyandotte
Lewandoski, Anthony, St. Mary Church, New Baltimore
Lubien, Raymond J., St. Bartholomew, Detroit
Machus, Paul H., St. William, Walled Lake
Maiuri, Rocco, St. Isaac Joques, St. Clair Shores
Marku, John, St. Christopher, Detroit
Markulike, Michael J., St. Dunstan, Garden City
Marquis, Joseph, St. Paul of the Cross Retreat Center, Detroit
Martin, John, Senior Status
McCoy, Elgia, St. Anthony, Detroit
McIntyre, Ronald L., Gesu, Detroit
McKale, Michael, Holy Name, Birmingham
McLeod, Robert E., St. Mary, St. Clair
Meahan, William, St. Mary, Wayne
Misiak, Richard, St. Edith, Livonia
Modes, Robert, St. Mel, Dearborn Heights
Morad, Alfred J., Senior Status
Morello, Steven, St. Agatha, Redford
Morici, Anthony, St. Louise, Warren
Motowski, Norbert, St. Christopher, Detroit
Mouro, Joseph, St. Constance Parish, Taylor
Murphy, Thomas, St. Mary, Rockwood
Noon, Archie J., St. Mary, Milford
Nowicki, Kenneth, St. Catherine, Algonac
Otto, William, St. Joseph, South Lyon
Ovies, Robert, St. Columban, Birmingham
Pallarito, James R., Holy Innocents, Roseville
Pardo, Gary, Our Lady of Loretto, Redford
Pelchat, Paul, Divine Savior, Westland
Pickett, Brock, St. Irene, Dundee
Piro, Rudolph P., St. Genevieve, Livonia
Posavetz, George, St. Mark, Warren
Prince, Benjamin, St. Gregory the Great, Detroit
Riopelle, Ernest, St. Conrad, Melvindale
Rivier, Robert, St. Elizabeth, Wyandotte
Rodriguez, Brigido, St. Vincent de Paul, Pontiac
Rohlman, Ronald, St. Ives, Southfield
Rowland, Robert, St. Alban, Livonia
Sandstrom, Donald, Our Lady of Good Counsel, Detroit
Santeramo, John, St. Rene Goupil, Sterling Heights
Schaible, John, Senior Status
Schlesser, Peter, Annunciation, Detroit
Shubik, Richard, St. Paul, Grosse Pointe Farms
Skladanowski, John L., St. Sylvester, Warren
Skubick, Charles G., St. Andrew, Rochester
Smith, Michael T., St. Hugo of the Hills, Bloomfield Hills
Smith, Richard, St. William, Walled Lake
Snyder, Robert J., St. Anthony, Temperance
Sobolewski, Don F., Transfiguration, Detroit
Solomon, James, Redemption, Melkite, Warren
Springer, Mark, St. Anastasia, Troy
Stankiewicz, Clement, St. Christine/St. Gemma, Detroit
Stimpson, Bill, Jr., Precious Blood, Detroit
Strye, Edward, St. Michael, Pontiac
Strzyzewski, Marvin, St. Anne, Warren
Sullivan, Lawrence, St. Martin de Porres, Warren
Swartz, Edward, St. Leonard, Warren
Thomas, Thomas M., St. Barnabas, Eastpointe
Thome, William A., St. Cyril of Jerusalem, Taylor
Tombler, Eugene, Guardian Angels, Clawson
Tremmel, Robert, Sacred Heart, Grosse Ile
Valdez, Ferando, St. Vincent de Paul, Pontiac
Van Brook, Arthur, Holy Spirit, Highland
Vanneste, Johnny M., St. Jane Frances DeChantal, Sterling Heights
Vasquez, Jesus, St. Vincent de Paul, Pontiac
Vestuto, Richard, St. Benedict, Waterford
Waldmann, William L., Holy Family, Novi
Wilson, Edward C., Jr., St. Paul of Tarsus, Clinton Township
Yezak, Thomas, St. Joseph, Lake Orion

INSTITUTIONS LOCATED IN THE ARCHDIOCESE

[A] SEMINARIES, ARCHDIOCESAN

DETROIT. *Sacred Heart Major Seminary, Inc.*, 2701 Chicago Blvd., 48206. Tel: 313-883-8500. Most Rev. Allen H. Vigneron, Rector & Pres.; Revs. Patrick F. Halfpenny, Vice Rector & Dean of Seminarians; Earl Boyea, Dean of Studies; Sr. Mary Ward, O.P., Registrar.

The College of Liberal Arts. Revs. Charles Kosanke, Dir. Undergraduate Seminarians; Richard Mocry, Spiritual Dir.; Stephen Vileo; Zbigniew Liana; Sr. Mary Finn, H.V.M., Dir. The Apostolic Experience Program; Mrs. Karen Mehaffey, Dir. of Libraries; Dr. Deborah Friauff; Ms. Jane Schaub; Mr. John Goyette.

The School of Theology. Revs. Paul Kreimes, Dir.

Graduate Seminarians; Daniel J. Trapp, Spiritual Dir.; Clifford Ruskowski; Ronald Browne; Sr. Kathleen Ronan; Revs. Ronald De Hondt; James Jorgenson, (Orthodox Church in America); Dr. Patricia Cooney-Hathaway; Mr. Mark Latkovic; Sr. Mary Lou Putrow, O.P.; Dr. William Riordan.

The Institute for Pastoral Ministry. Mrs. Patricia A. Rennie, Dean of The Institute for Ministry; Ms. Suzanne Schreiber, Asst. Dean of The Institute for Recruitment & Retention.

Seminary Total: Priests 10; Sisters 4; Lay Faculty 7; Students 293.

ORCHARD LAKE. *SS. Cyril and Methodius Seminary*, 3535 Indian Trail, 48324. Tel: 248-683-0311; 313-963-8075. Rev. Msgr. Stanley E. Milewski, D.H.L., Chancellor; Rev. Msgr. Francis B. Koper, D.Min. (WIL), Rector, Vice Chancellor; Rev. Adam Dalack, Dir. Formation; Gary Lovid, Comptroller; Rev. Albin J. Grous, S.T.D. (PH), Academic Dean; Mrs. Mary Jo Wagener, Registrar; Rev. Msgr. Jan Jagodzinski, M.A. (Poland); Revs. Stanislaw Flis, S.T.D. (Poland), Dir. Admissions and Recruitment; James K. Mazurek, M.Div. (PIT), Devel. Exec. Sec., Natl. Alumni Assoc.; Roman Nir (Poland), Archivist; Kathleen Castillo, M.A., Dir. Field Ed.; David Troiano, Dir. Liturgical Music; Nancy Ward, M.S.L.S., Librarian. Full Time Resident Faculty: Rev. Msgr. Zdzislaw Peszkowski, Ph.D. (Poland), Emeritus; Revs. Gregory Banazak, S.T.D.; Czeslaw M. Krysa, S.T.L. (BUF); Janusz Kukulka, M.A. (Poland); Michael Monshau, O.P., Ph.D.; Walter J. Ziemba, Ph.D., Emeritus. Students 95.

[B] SEMINARIES, RELIGIOUS OR SCHOLASTICATES

DETROIT. *Duns Scotus*. (Corporate Title: Duns Scotus), St. Aloysius Friary, 1234 Washington Blvd., 48226. Tel: 313-237-5811. Order of Friars Minor, St. John Baptist Province (Cincinnati). Revs. Maynard Tetreault, O.F.M., Pres.; Daniel Havron, O.F.M., Sec.; Bro. James Baugh, O.F.M., Resident Agent. Priests 2; Brothers 1.

BERKLEY. *Loyola House*. (Novitiate of the Chicago-Detroit Provinces of the Society of Jesus), 2599 Harvard Rd., 48072. Tel: 248-399-8132. Revs. Joseph H. Boel, S.J., Supr.; Timothy J. Shepard, S.J., Dir. Formation & Novices; Mark J. Andrews, S.J., Asst. Dir. Novices; Norman J. Dickson, S.J., Dir. Vocations; Jerome K. Odbert, S.J., Minister; Sr. Melaine Svoboda, S.N.D., Spirituality & Min. Priests 6; Sisters 1; Scholastics 13.

OXFORD. *St. Benedict Monastery*, 2711 E. Drahner Rd., 48370. Tel: 248-628-2249. Headquarters Novitiate House of Sylvestrine Benedictine Monks in the United States. Revs. Daniel J. Homan, O.S.B., Conventual Prior & Retreat Dir.; Michael R. Green, O.S.B., Subprior. Priests 3; Brothers 8; Chapels 2.

[C] COLLEGES AND UNIVERSITIES

DETROIT. *Marygrove College*, 8425 W. McNichols Rd., 48221. Tel: 313-862-8000.

For a complete listing, refer to the Colleges and Universities section.

University of Detroit Mercy, McNichols Campus, 4001 W. McNichols Rd. at Livernois, 48219-0900. Tel: 313-993-1000.

For a complete listing, refer to the Colleges and Universities section.

LIVONIA. *Madonna University*, 36600 Schoolcraft Rd., 48150. Tel: 734-432-5300; Fax: 734-432-5393.

For a complete listing, refer to the Colleges and Universities section.

ORCHARD LAKE. *Saint Mary's College*, 3535 Indian Trail, 48324. Tel: 248-682-1885.

For a complete listing, refer to the Colleges and Universities section.

[D] HIGH SCHOOLS, INTER-PAROCHIAL

DETROIT. *Bishop Borgess High School*, 11685 Appleton, 48239. Tel: 313-255-1100; Fax: 313-255-1102. Sr. Joan Charnley, I.H.M., Prin.; Ms. Patrice Evans, Youth Minister. Priests 1; Sisters 2; Lay Teachers 18; Lay Admin. & Personnel 4; Students 297.

East Catholic High School, 7320 St. Anthony Pl., 48213. Tel: 313-921-9650. R. Munson-Griffin, S.L.W., Prin. Sisters 1; Lay Teachers 11; Students 169.

St. Martin de Porres High, 13436 Grove, 48235. Tel: 313-864-3330; Fax: 313-864-3648. Ms. Sunbeam Hughes, Prin. Priests 1; Sisters 2; Lay Teachers 23; Students 350.

St. Vincent Middle School, 2020 14th St., 48216. Tel: 313-961-6773. Ms. Kathleen McBride, Prin. Lay Teachers 4; Students 100.

HARPER WOODS. *Bishop Gallagher High School*, 19360 Harper, 48225. Tel: 313-886-0855; Fax: 313-886-9650. Francis Turk, Prin. Sisters 2; Lay Teachers 13; Students 221.

MADISON HEIGHTS. *Bishop Foley High School*, 32000 Campbell Rd., 48071. Tel: 248-585-1210; Fax: 248-585-3667. Alex M. Gajewski, Prin. Priests 1; Sisters 12; Lay Teachers 48; Students 622.

Bishop Foley Venture Fund, 32000 Campbell Rd., 48071. Tel: 248-585-1210. Paul Marzec, Pres.

MARINE CITY. *Cardinal Mooney Catholic College Preparatory School*, 660 S. Water St., 48039. Tel: 810-765-8825; Fax: 810-765-7164. Dr. Elsie L. Ogden, Prin. Priests 1; Sisters 4; Lay Teachers 16; Students 197.

MONROE. *St. Mary Catholic Central High School*. (Coed), 108 W. Elm Ave., 48161. Tel: 313-241-0663; Fax: 313-241-0342. Bro. Robert Livernois, C.S.C., Prin. Brothers 1; Sisters 4; Lay Teachers 28; Students 468.

PONTIAC. *Notre Dame Preparatory High School and Marist Academy*, 1300 Giddings Rd., 48340-2108. Tel: 248-373-5300; Fax: 248-373-8024. Revs. Leon M. Olszamowski, S.M., Prin.; Juan J. Gonzales, S.M. Priests 2; Brothers 1; Lay Teachers 48; Students 802.

RIVERVIEW. *Gabriel Richard High School*, 15325 Pennsylvania Rd., 48192. Tel: 313-284-1875; Fax: 313-284-9304. John A. Bres., Prin. Brothers 2; Sisters 4; Lay Teachers 33; Students 494.

ROYAL OAK. *Shrine High School*, 3500 W. 13 Mile Rd., 48073. Tel: 248-549-2925; Fax: 248-549-2953. Mr. Thomas P. Kirkwood, Prin. Lay Teachers 25; Students 327.

SOUTHGATE. *Aquinas High School*, 15601 Northline Rd., 48195. Tel: 313-283-3190; Fax: 313-283-1752. Susan M. Kotyk, Prin. Lay Teachers 17; Students 204.

[E] HIGH SCHOOLS, PRIVATE

DETROIT. *Dominican High School and Academy*, 9740 McKinney Ave., 48224. Tel: 313-882-8500 (High School & Academy). Adrian Dominican Sisters. Admin. Team: Ms. Rose Horowitz, Prin. Sisters 12; Lay Teachers 12; Students 290.

Loyola High School, 15325 Pinehurst, 48238-1633. Tel: 313-861-2407; Fax: 313-861-4718. Revs. Michael A. Evans, S.J., Pres.; David F. Mostrangelo, S.J., Prin. Priests 4; Brothers 2; Sisters 1; Lay Teachers 14; Students 145.

University of Detroit Jesuit High School and Academy, 8400 S. Cambridge, 48221. Tel: 313-862-5400; Fax: 313-862-3299. Revs. Timothy T. Shannon, S.J., Pres.; Kenneth A. Styles, S.J., Rector; R. James Kurtz, S.J.; John F. Libens, S.J.; Patrick J. Rice, S.J.; Keith Esenther, S.J.; Martin T. Connell, S.J.; Edward A. Flint, S.J.; Thomas M. Ryan, S.J.; Ronald F. Torina, S.J.; Bro. James J. Boynton, S.J. Priests 10; Scholastics 1; Lay Teachers 38; Students 656; Chapels 2.

BLOOMFIELD HILLS. *Academy of the Sacred Heart*, 1250 Kensington Rd., 48304. Tel: 248-646-8900; Fax: 248-646-4143. Religious of the Sacred Heart. Sr. Margaret Mary Canty, R.S.C.J., Headmistress. Sisters 5; Lay Teachers 54; Students 418.

Brother Rice Endowment Fund. (The "Foundation"), 7101 Lahser Rd., 48301-4045. Tel: 248-647-2526. Bro. William A. Dogan, C.F.C.; Mr. Thomas Sklut, Contact Person.

Brother Rice High School, 7101 Lahser Rd., 48301-4045. Tel: 248-647-2526. Congregation of Christian Brothers. Bro. William A. Dogan, C.F.C., Prin. Brothers 8; Sisters 2; Lay Teachers 42; Students 725.

Marian High School for Young Women, 7225 Lahser Rd., 48301. Tel: 248-644-1750; Fax: 248-644-6107. Sr. Lenore Pochelski, I.H.M., Prin. Sisters 2; Lay Teachers 32; Students 460.

FARMINGTON HILLS. *Mercy High School for Girls*, 29300 Eleven Mile Rd., 48336. Tel: 248-476-8020; Fax: 248-476-3691. Sisters of Mercy. Sr. Regina Marie Doelker, R.S.M., Prin. Faculty 63; Students 875.

HARPER WOODS. *Notre Dame High School*, 20254 Kelly Rd., 48225-1287. Tel: 313-371-8965. Marist Fathers. Revs. John Sajdak, S.M., Prin.; John Bryson, S.M.; Raymond Ouellette, S.M.; John Kiselica, S.M.; Normand Martin, S.M.; Frank Reitter, S.M. Priests 6; Sisters 3; Lay Teachers 27; Students 430.

Regina High School for Girls, 20200 Kelly Rd., 48225-1284. Tel: 313-526-0220; Fax: 313-526-5850. Sr. Mary Leanne, Prin. Sisters of St. Joseph of the Third Order of St. Francis 10; Lay Teachers 44; Students 780.

LIVONIA. *Ladywood High School*, 14680 Newburgh Rd., 48154. Tel: 313-591-1544. (Private School for Girls). Sr. Mary Ann Smith, C.S.S.F., Prin. Students 528.

ORCHARD LAKE. *St. Mary's Preparatory*, 3535 Indian Trail, 48324. Tel: 248-683-0530. Rev. Msgr. Stanley E. Milewski, Chancellor; Larry Reeside, Prin.; Mr. Richard Rychcik, Dean of Residence. Priests 1; Lay Teachers 39; Students 400.

REDFORD. *The Catholic Central Endowment Trust* 48239-2999, 14200 Breakfast Dr. Tel: 313-534-0660. Gregory Grabowski, Dir.

Catholic Central High School, 14200 Breakfast Dr., 48239. Tel: 313-534-0660; 261-3387 (Res); Fax: 313-534-2683. Basilian Fathers. Revs. Harold B. Gardner, C.S.B., Prin.; Richard J. Elmer, C.S.B., Supr.; John J. Ward, C.S.B.; Frank H. Bredeweg, C.S.B.; Edward Donoher, C.S.B.; Kenneth B. McKernan, C.S.B.; John H. Menner, C.S.B.; Raymond Paramo, C.S.B.; Charles C. Smith, C.S.B. Priests 9; Lay Teachers 60; Students 991.

WARREN. *De La Salle Collegiate for Boys*, 14600 Common Rd., 48093-3397. Tel: 810-778-2207. High School Brothers of the Christian Schools. Bros. Joseph Jozwiak, F.S.C., Prin.; Kevin Gilhooly, F.S.C., Supr. Brothers 6; Sisters 1; Lay Teachers 40; Students 800.

La Salle Warren, Inc., 14600 Common Rd., 48093. Tel: 908-842-7420. Bro. Kevin Gilhooly, F.S.C., Contact Person.

[F] ELEMENTARY SCHOOLS, INTER-PAROCHIAL

DETROIT. *Genesis Catholic Elementary School*, 20045 Joann, 48205. Tel: 313-839-2330. (Combined Parish Schools from Our Lady of Good Counsel and St. Raymond). Mr. Joseph Iskra, Prin. Lay Teachers 10; Total Enrollment 249.

Our Help of Christians Elementary School, 12634 McDougall Ave., 48212.

CANTON. *All Saints Regional School*, 48735 Warren Rd., 48187-1233. Tel: 313-459-2490; Fax: 313-459-0981. Mrs. Mary Rita Allen, Prin.

PORT HURON. *McCormick Catholic Academy*. (Grades 6-8), 2865 Henry, 48060. Tel: 810-985-9599. Mrs. Deborah A. Krueger, Prin. Lay Teachers 11; Students 90. A consolidation of the following three parish schools in Port Huron: St. Edward (Lakeport), St. Joseph and St. Mary.

ROCHESTER. *Holy Family Regional School*, 1240 Inglewood, 48307. Tel: 248-656-1234; Fax: 248-656-3494. (Regional). Sr. Karen Hawver, S.C., Prin. Students 553.

[G] ELEMENTARY, PRIVATE

BLOOMFIELD HILLS. *Academy of the Sacred Heart*, 1250 Kensington Rd., 48304. Tel: 248-646-8900; Fax: 248-646-4143. Religious of the Sacred Heart. Sr. Margaret Mary Canty, R.S.C.J., Headmistress. Sisters 4; Lay Teachers 54; Students 418.

[H] GENERAL HOSPITALS

DETROIT. *Holy Cross Hospital*, 4777 E. Outer Dr., 48234. Tel: 313-369-9100

For a complete listing, refer to the Hospitals section.

Mercy Family Care Program Unit, 5555 Conner Ave., 48213. Tel: 313-579-4300

For a complete listing, refer to the Hospitals section.

Mercy Hospital, 5555 Conner Ave., 48213. Tel: 313-579-4000

For a complete listing, refer to the Hospitals section.

St. John Hospital and Medical Center, 22101 Moross Rd., 48236. Tel: 313-343-4000

For a complete listing, refer to the Hospitals section.

CLINTON TOWNSHIP. *Mercy Mount Clemens Corporation*, 15855 Nineteen Mile Rd., 48038. Tel: 810-263-2707

For a complete listing, refer to the Hospitals section.

GROSSE POINTE. *Bon Secours Hospital*, 468 Cadieux Rd., 48230. Tel: 313-343-1000

For a complete listing, refer to the Hospitals section.

LIVONIA. *Marian Village Corporation*, 36475 Five Mile Rd., 48154. Tel: 313-464-4800, Ext. 2300

For a complete listing, refer to the Hospitals section.

St. Mary Hospital, 36475 W. Five Mile Rd., 48154. Tel: 313-655-4800

For a complete listing, refer to the Hospitals section.

PONTIAC. *St. Joseph Mercy - Oakland*, 900 Woodward Ave., 48341-2985. Tel: 248-858-3000

For a complete listing, refer to the Hospitals section.

PORT HURON. *Mercy Hospital of Port Huron*, 2601 Electric, 48060-6518. Tel: 810-985-1500

For a complete listing, refer to the Hospitals section.

SOUTHFIELD. *Providence Hospital*, 16001 W. Nine Mile Rd., P.O. Box 2043, 48037. Tel: 810-424-3000

For a complete listing, refer to the Hospitals section.

[I] SPECIAL HOSPITALS AND SANATORIA FOR INVALIDS

LAKE ORION. *Guest House for Women Religious*, 1840 W. Scripps Rd., Box 68, 48360. Tel: 248-391-3100; Fax: 248-391-1553.

..For a complete listing, refer to the Special Care Facilities section.

LIVONIA. *Marycrest Manor*, 15475 Middlebelt Rd., 48154. Tel: 313-427-9175.

..For a complete listing, refer to the Special Care Facilities section.

Marywood Nursing Care Center, 36975 W. Five Mile Rd., 48154. Tel: 313-464-0600.

..For a complete listing, refer to the Special Care Facilities section.

MOUNT CLEMENS. *St. Joseph Mercy Living Care Center,* 37700 Harper, 48043. Tel: 810-468-0827.
For a complete listing, refer to the Special Care Facilities section.

ST. CLAIR SHORES. *Sisters of Bon Secours Nursing Care Center,* 26001 E. Jefferson, 48081. Tel: 810-779-7000.
For a complete listing, refer to the Special Care Facilities section.

WATERFORD. *Lourdes Nursing Home,* 2300 Watkins Lake Rd., 48328. Tel: 810-674-2241.
For a complete listing, refer to the Special Care Facilities section.

[J] HOUSING AND/OR COMMUNITY FACILITIES FOR THE AGING

DETROIT. *St. Catherine's House,* 1641 Webb Ave., 48206. Tel: 313-868-4505.
For a complete listing, refer to the Special Care Facilities section.

St. Joseph's Home, 4800 Cadieux Rd., 48224. Tel: 313-882-3800; Fax: 313-882-6944.
For a complete listing, refer to the Special Care Facilities section.

ALLEN PARK. *Little Sisters of the Poor,* P.O. Box 610, 48101.
For a complete listing, refer to the Special Care Facilities section.

BLOOMFIELD HILLS. *St. Elizabeth's Briarbank,* 1315 N. Woodward Ave., 48304. Tel: 248-644-1011.
For a complete listing, refer to the Special Care Facilities section.

Villa Francesca, 565 W. Long Lake Rd., 48302. Tel: 248-644-5390.
For a complete listing, refer to the Special Care Facilities section.

CLINTON TWP. *A Friends House Adult Day Care Center,* 16931 19 Mile Rd., Ste. 140, 48038. Tel: 810-412-8494.
For a complete listing, refer to the Special Care Facilities section.

FARMINGTON HILLS. *Mercy Services for Aging,* 34605 Twelve Mile Rd., 48331-3221. Tel: 248-305-7920.
For a complete listing, refer to the Special Care Facilities section.

LIVONIA. *Marybrook Manor,* 36975 W. Five Mile Rd., 48154. Tel: 313-464-9667.
For a complete listing, refer to the Special Care Facilities section.

Ryan Senior Residences of the Archdiocese of Detroit. Inc., Central Office, 36800 Schdolcraft, 48150. Tel: 313-953-5873.
For a complete listing, refer to the Special Care Facilities section.

ST. CLAIR SHORES. *Sisters of Bon Secours Nursing Care Center,* 26001 E. Jefferson, 48081. Tel: 810-779-7000.
For a complete listing, refer to the Special Care Facilities section.

SOUTHFIELD. *Sheltering Arms,* 18310 W. 12 Mile, 48076. Tel: 248-557-7373.
For a complete listing, refer to the Special Care Facilities section.

WATERFORD. *Fox Manor, Inc.,* 2350 Watkins Lake Rd., 48238. Tel: 810-674-9590.
For a complete listing, refer to the Special Care Facilities section.

St. Jude Home, Inc., 2270 Marwood, 48328. Tel: 248-673-5179.
For a complete listing, refer to the Special Care Facilities section.

[K] MONASTERIES AND RESIDENCES OF PRIESTS AND BROTHERS

DETROIT. *Jesuit Community at the University of Detroit,* Lansing-Reilly Hall, 4001 W. McNichols Rd., 48221. Tel: 313-993-1000.
(Corporate Title: The Jesuit Community Corporation at the University of Detroit Mercy). Mailing Address: P.O. Box 19900, 48219. Revs. Mark G. Henninger, S.J.; Arthur F. McGovern, S.J.; Gary R. Wright, S.J.; Gregory Chisholm, S.J.; Malcolm Carron, S.J.; Gerald F. Cavanagh, S.J.; Terrence M. Curry, S.J.; Paulinus F. Forsthoefel, S.J.; George F. Lundy, S.J.; Brian P. O'Donnell, S.J.; Oswald A. Mascarenhas, S.J. (India); Norman G. McKendrick, S.J.; Herman J. Muller, S.J.; John D. O'Neill, S.J.; Sushil Sah India; John A. Saliba, S.J. (Malta); D. Clayton Schario, S.J.; Raphael Shen, S.J. (China); John M. Staudenmaier, S.J.; R. Gerard Albright, S.J.; Joseph P. Daoust, S.J.; John E. Dister, S.J.; Eugene L. Donahue, S.J.; Bro. Henry C. Kuhn, S.J.

Jesuit Provincial Office-Detroit Province of the Society of Jesus, 7303 W. Seven Mile, 48221-2198. Tel: 313-861-7500. Very Rev. John F. Libens, S.J., Prov.; Revs. Keith J. Esenther, S.J., Exec. Asst. & Asst. for Higher Education; Norman J. Dickson, S.J., Asst. Intl. Missions & Vocations; John E. Dister, S.J., Asst. for Pastoral & Social Ministries; Walter L. Farrell, S.J., Treas.; Timothy J. Shepard, S.J., Asst. for Formation; James E. Von Tobel, S.J., Asst. for Health Care. Priests 162; Brothers 19; Scholastics 21. Priests assigned outside the U.S.: Rev. Richard M. Mackowski, S.J., Piazza S. Maria Maggiore 7, Rome, Italy, 00185. Tel: 39-6-6701-7140; Fax: 3964465576. Rev. Thomas H. Radloff, S.J., Spiritual Dir. at North American College, 000120 Vatican City State. Tel: 3966869441; Fax: 3966867561. Rev. W. Jared Wicks, S.J., Piazza della Pilotta 4, Rome, Italy, 00187. Tel: 39667015454; Fax: 39667015413. Rev. Kenneth M. Kunert, S.J., Xavier House, P.O. Box 7300, Kampala, Uganda, 25641267614. Rev. Michael J. Vjecha, S.J., American Refugee Committee, P.O. Box 39694, Nairobi, Kenya. Rev. Theodore W. Walters, S.J., Nyegezi Social Training Institute, P.O. Box 307, Mwanza, Tanzania. Tel: 2556850560. Rev. Martin L. Chase, S.J., Niels Steensens Gymnasium, Niels Steensens Kollegium Sankt Kjeldsgade 3, DK210D Kobenhavn O, Denmark. Tel: 45-3120-9337; Fax: 45-3927-3501. Rev. Kevin L. Flannery, S.J., Pontificia Universita Gregoriana, Piazza Della Pilotta 4, 00187 Rome, Italy. Tel: 39-6-6701-5213; Fax: 39-6-6701-5413. Rev. Joseph E. Mulligan, S.J., Colegio Centroamericano, Apdo. 2419, Managua, Nicaragua. Tel: 5052786965; Fax: 5052783359. Rev. Joseph G. Mueller, S.J., 9, Rue Raynouard, Paris, France, 75016. Tel: 33144146620; 33144146626 (private); Fax: 33144146622. Members in the U.S. residing outside the Province: Revs. Thomas S. Acker, S.J.; David C. Bayne, S.J.; Peter J. Bernardi, S.J.; Martin J. Calkins, S.J.; Joseph F. Downey, S.J.; Thomas W. Gedeon, S.J., Exec. Dir., Retreats International; Thomas W. Gensler, S.J.; Francis T. Gignac, S.J.; Howard J. Gray, S.J.; Fred M. Henley, S.J.; Francis J. Houdek, S.J.; John L. Kieffer, S.J.; William F. King, S.J.; Karl J. Kiser, S.J.; John P. Langan, S.J.; Brian J. Lehane, S.J.; Daniel P. Liderbach, S.J.; John A. Lucal, S.J.; Mark S. Massa, S.J.; Edward J. Mattimoe, S.J.; George C. Maynard, S.J.; J. Thomas McClain, S.J.; Richard A. McCormick, S.J.; John M. McManamon, S.J.; Timothy J. Meier, S.J.; George B. Murray, S.J.; John W. O'Malley, S.J.; Philip C. Rule, S.J.; Donald M. Serva, S.J.; Edward J. Siebert, S.J.; Michael F. Steltenkamp, S.J.; Earl A. Weis, S.J.; Eric A. Zimmer, S.J.; Bros. Jerome J. Pryor, S.J.; Joseph Shubitowski.

Maryknoll Fathers and Brothers, 12709 Pembroke, 48235. Tel: 313-342-0330. Rev. Paul Brien, M.M., Dir.

P.I.M.E. College Community, 17330 Quincy Ave., 48221. Tel: 313-861-2866; Fax: 313-342-6816. Rev. Giorgio Paleari, P.I.M.E., Formation. Seminarians 5. P.I.M.E. Missionaries. (Pontifical Institute for Foreign Missions). P.I.M.E. Mission Center, 17330 Quincy Ave., 48221. Tel: 313-342-4066; Fax: 313-342-6816. Revs. Bruno Piccolo, P.I.M.E., Mission Office Dir.; Claudio Corti, P.I.M.E., Vocation Dir. Vocations Office; Foster Parents Mission Club; Leprosy Relief Society; Printing Press; P.I.M.E. World Magazine; Public Relations Office.

P.I.M.E. Missionaries of SS. Peter and Paul. (Pontifical Institute for Foreign Missions). P.I.M.E. Motherhouse in Detroit, 17330 Quincy, 48221. Tel: 313-342-4066; Fax: 313-342-6816. Revs. Bruno Piccolo, P.I.M.E., Prov. Supr.; Steven Baumbusch, P.I.M.E., Procurator; Angelo Villa, P.I.M.E., Asst. Rector; John B. Boracco, P.I.M.E., House Rector; Luigi Acerbi, P.I.M.E.; Raffaele Magni, P.I.M.E.; Dominic Rossi, P.I.M.E.; Giorgio Paleari, P.I.M.E.; Luigi Maggioni, P.I.M.E.; Edward Miley, P.I.M.E. Brothers 1; Franciscan Sisters of St. Joseph (Mexico City) 4.

St. Bonaventure Friary, 1740 Mt. Elliott Ave., 48207-3496. Tel: 313-579-2100; Fax: 313-579-2275. Legal Title: *Province of St. Joseph of the Capuchin Order, Inc.* Provincialate: Revs. Daniel Fox, O.F.M.Cap., Prov. Min.; Perry McDonald, O.F.M.Cap., Prov. Vicar; Bros. Mark McDonough, Sec. & Treas.; David Swab, O.F.M.Cap., Sec. Religious Affairs; Larry LaCross, O.F.M.Cap., Public Rels. & Devel.; Revs. Loran Miller, O.F.M.Cap., Mission Secretariat; James Wolf, O.F.M.Cap., Archivist.
Priests of the Province Assigned Outside the U.S.: Rev. Charles Bantle, O.F.M.Cap., Diocese of Naha - Chancery, 3 chome 7-2 Asato (Naha), Okinawa, Japan, 902; Fax: 011-098-863-8474. Rev. Carmel Flora, O.F.M.Cap., St. Lawrence Community, 545 Tingal Rd., Wynnum North, Qld. 4178, Australia; Fax: 011-61-7-893-2905. Rev. Patrick McSherry, O.F.M.Cap., Capuchin General Curia, Via Piemonte, 70, Rome, Italy, 00187; Fax: 011-39-6-482-8267. Rev. John Myers, O.F.M.Cap., St. Lawrence Community, 392 Albert St., Balcatta, Perth, West Australia, 6021. In Residence in the Archdiocese of Detroit (excluding parishes): Rev. Blase Gitzen, O.F.M.Cap., 4030 W. 13 Mile Rd., Apt. J-3, Royal Oak, 48073-6638. Bro. Sam Ciraulo, O.F.M.Cap, Canterbury Woods, 700 Tobin Dr., Apt. 15, Inkster, 48141. Bro. Michael Graf, O.F.M.Cap., Canterbury Woods, 700 Tobin Dr., Apt. 15, Inkster, 48141. Assigned to St. Bonaventure Friary: Rev. James Hast, O.F.M.Cap., Local Min.; Bro. Richard Merling, O.F.M.Cap., Vicar; Revs. Gabriel Prashant Coelho, O.F.M.Cap.; Daniel Fox, O.F.M.Cap.; Charles Hart, O.F.M.; James Leary, O.F.M.Cap.; Joseph Maloney, O.F.M.Cap.; Perry McDonald, O.F.M.Cap.; Philip Naessens, O.F.M.Cap.; Albert Sandor, O.F.M.Cap.; Lloyd Thiel, O.F.M.Cap.; Donald Wiest, O.F.M.Cap.; James Wolf, O.F.M.Cap.; Bros. Gabriel Badalamenti, O.F.M.Cap.; Michael Drobnicki, O.F.M.Cap.; Paul Hanisko, O.F.M.Cap.; Joseph Howe, O.F.M.Cap.; Thomas Kroll, O.F.M.Cap.; Ignatius Milne, O.F.M.Cap.; Joseph Monachino, O.F.M.Cap.; John Raniszewski, O.F.M.Cap.; Daniel Vena, O.F.M.Cap.; Leo Wollenweber, O.F.M.Cap.

St. Mary's Friary, 5275 Kensington, 48224. Tel: 313-653-4700. Revs. Michael Gaffney, O.F.M.Cap., Local Min.; James Zelinski, O.F.M.Cap., Prov. Asst.; Lawrence Abler, O.F.M.Cap.; Patrick McSherry, O.F.M.Cap.

St. Paul of the Cross Community, Congregation of the Passion, 23300 W. Davison Ave., 48223. Tel: 313-531-0562; Fax: 313-531-6911. A center for the Passionist Fathers & Brothers in mid-western & north central United States. Members of this community conduct parish missions, renewals & retreats for laity, clergy & religious, Forty Hours, Devotion & other ministries. Revs. Sebastian MacDonald, C.P., Supr.; Rene Champagne, C.P.; Ronald Corl, C.P.; John Devany, C.P.; Michael Higgins, C.P., Dir., Retreat Center; Randal Joyce, C.P.; John Anthony Parenza, C.P., St. Mary's Hospital, Livonia; Philip Schaefer, C.P.; Robert Weiss, C.P.; Emil Womack, C.P.; William Baalman, C.P.; Bros. John Gebauer, C.P.; Patrick Keeney, C.P.; Jerome Milazzo, C.P. Priests 10; Brothers 4.

St. Sylvester Monastery, 17320 Rosemont Rd., 48219. Tel: 313-532-6064. Revs. Livius Paoli, O.S.B., Prior; Bartholomew Kraemer, O.S.B.; John Stopponi, O.S.B.; Leo Cornelli, O.S.B.; John Colautti, O.S.B.; Dom Bernard Schinn, O.S.B., Holy Family Church, 641 Chrysler Express Way.

BLOOMFIELD HILLS. *Congregation of Christian Brothers, Brother Rice Community,* Carroll Hall, 3575 Lincoln Dr., 48301. Tel: 248-647-1547. Bros. Arthur M. Arndt, C.F.C., Supr.; William A. Dogan, C.F.C., Prin. In res. Bros. Robert E. Beckstrom, C.F.C.; Norbert B. Hueller, C.F.C.; E. Vincent Kelly, C.F.C.; David A. MacIntyre, C.F.C.; Robert L. Stanick, C.F.C.; W. Rudolph Younghans, C.F.C. Brothers 8.

DEARBORN. *Society of St. Paul,* 7050 Pinehurst, 48126. Tel: 313-582-2033. Revs. Joseph Chircop, S.S.P., Supr.; Joseph A. Triano, S.S.P.; Ernesto Tigreros, S.S.P.; Bros. Gerard T. Roche, S.S.P.; Emmanuel Canas. Priests 3; Brothers 2.

DEARBORN HEIGHTS. *Our Lady of Grace Monastery,* Mariannhill Mission Society, 23715 Ann Arbor Trail, 48127. Tel: 313-561-7140; 561-8888; Fax: 313-561-9486. Vocation Office: Tel: 313-274-2893. Revs. Francis Claerr, C.M.M.; Egbert Heinlein, C.M.M., (Retired); Anthony Kirschner, C.M.M.; Anthony Gathen, C.M.M., Supr.; Raymond Lucasinsky, C.M.M., Mission Procurator; Timothy Mock, C.M.M., Prov. Treas.; Thomas Szura, C.M.M., Asst. Prov. Treas.; Aloysius Blonigen, C.M.M., Prov., Retreat Dir.; Reinhold Schmitt, C.M.M.; Thomas Heier, C.M.M., Editor of LEAVES; Vergil Heier, C.M.M. In res. Bros. Otto Waldmueller, C.M.M.; Jamie Miller, C.M.M.; Francis Berridge, C.M.M.; Kenneth Lansing, C.M.M.; William Simon, C.M.M. Priests 11; Brothers 3; Seminarians 2.

LIVONIA. *Marist Fathers & Brothers Community,* 32509 Scone, 48154-4165.

RIVERVIEW. *Crosier Community of Riverview,* 13249 Pennsylvania Rd., 48192. Tel: 313-283-0112; Fax: 313-283-2809. Revs. Jude Verley, O.S.C.; John P. Christ, O.S.C.; Bruce C. Maxwell, O.S.C., U.S. Navy; Neil J. Emon, O.S.C.; Gordon Van Hoof, O.S.C.; Richard M. Leliaert, O.S.C.; Dale H. Redwanski, O.S.C.; Very Rev. James A. Vedro, O.S.C., Supr.; Revs. Steven Henrich, O.S.C.; Gerald Thaar, O.S.C.; Richard Thompson, O.S.C. Priests 11.

STERLING HEIGHTS. *Society of Christ Provincial Home,* Provincial Home, 3000 18 Mile Rd., 48314. Tel: 810-939-5022. Revs. Andrzej Maslejak, S.Ch., Prov.; Stanislaw Kuczaik, S.Ch., Asst. Prov.; Gerald Grupczynski, S.Ch., Treas.

WYANDOTTE. *Pallottine Fathers,* 3352 Fourth St., 48192. Tel: 313-285-2966. Rev. Stephen Keogh, S.A.C., Rector & Mission Promotions Dir.; Bro. Faustino Paez, S.A.C.

[L] CONVENTS AND RESIDENCES FOR SISTERS

DETROIT. *Adrian Dominican Sisters - Great Lakes Mission Chapter,* 9400 Courville, 48224-2517. Tel: 313-882-8484; Fax: 313-882-0436. Sr. Rosemary Asaro, O.P., Chapter Prioress.

Franciscan Sisters of St. Joseph (Mexico City), 17330 Quincy Ave., 48221. Tel: 313-342-0825; Fax: 313-342-6816. Sr. Magdalena Santiago Chenete, F.S.S.J., Supr. Sisters 4.

Missionaries of Charity, 4835 Lincoln St., 48208. Tel: 313-831-1028. Sr. M. Christophine, M.C., Supr.

Sisters, Home Visitors of Mary Convent, 121 E. Boston, 48202. Tel: 313-875-1123. Sr. Barbara Dakoske, H.V.M., Admin.

BLOOMFIELD HILLS. *Daughters of Divine Charity - Holy Trinity Province* (1972), Holy Trinity Provincialate, 1315 N. Woodward Ave., 48304. Tel: 248-644-1011; Fax: 248-644-1596. Sr. M. Paschal Grand, F.D.C., Prov. Supr. Sisters in Community 30.

CLARKSTON. *Servants of Jesus,* 9075 Big Lake Rd., Box 128, 48347. Tel: 810-625-8483. Leadership Team: Sr. Virginia Skurski, S.J., Pres.; Sr. Corinne Weiss, S.J.; Sr. Karen Shirilla, S.J.

S.J. Charitable Trust (Retired & Infirm Sisters), Servants of Jesus Community Support Trust, 9075 Big Lake Rd., Box 128, 48347.

CLINTON TWP. *Monastery of St. Therese of the Child Jesus,* 35750 Moravian Dr., 48035-2138. Tel: 810-790-7255. Discalced Carmelite Nuns. Mother Therese Marie, O.C.D., Prioress. Professed Nuns 8; Extern Sisters 2; Extern Novice 1.

DEARBORN HEIGHTS. *Adrian Dominican Sisters, Nokomis Mission Chapter,* 7506 N. Inkster Rd., 48127-1668. Tel: 313-274-3543; Fax: 313-791-0319. Sr. Nancyann Turner, O.P., Chapter Prioress.

FARMINGTON HILLS. *Adrian Dominican Sisters, Southeast Adrian Mission Chapter,* 28650 Eleven Mile Rd., 48336-1502. Tel: 248-426-9185; Fax: 248-426-9186. Sr. Lorraine Mordenski, O.P., Chapter Prioress.

Bernardine Franciscan Sisters, 27405 W. 10 Mile Rd., 48336. Tel: 810-476-4111. Our Lady of the Rosary Convent Sisters of the Third Order of St. Francis. Sr. Maria Christine Keller, O.S.F., Province Min. Sisters in Area 55.

Mercy Center, 28650 Eleven Mile Rd., 48336.

Monastery of the Blessed Sacrament, 29575 Middlebelt Rd., 48334-2311. Tel: 810-626-8253; Fax: 810-626-8724. Dominican Nuns of Perpetual Adoration (Strictly Cloistered). Sr. Mary Thomas, O.P., Prioress; Rev. Martin F. McCormick, O.P., Chap. Cloistered Sisters 37; Extern Sister 3.

Sisters of Mercy-Regional Community of Detroit, Inc., 29000 Eleven Mile Rd., 48336. Tel: 248-476-8000; Fax: 248-476-4222. Sr. Gretchen Elliott, R.S.M., Pres. Sisters 294; U.S.Professed 264; In Argentine-Professed 30; Candidates 1.

Sisters of Mercy of the Americas. Regional Community of Detroit, Charitable Trusts 1 & 2.

IDA. *St. Joseph's Convent,* 2882 Southwick, Box 187, 48140. Tel: 313-269-2505. Missionary Sisters of Our Lady of Victory 2.

LIVONIA. *Provincial House and Novitiate of the Sisters of St. Felix,* 36800 Schoolcraft Rd., 48150. Tel: 734-591-1730. Sr. Mary Dennis Glonek, C.S.S.F., Prov. Min.; Rev. Michael Daly, Res. Chap.; Rev. Msgr. Vincent J. Horkan, Infirmary Chap. Legal Title: *Provincial House and Novitiate of the Congregation of the Sisters of St. Felix, C.S.S.F., Felician Sisters.* Professed Sisters 258; Novices 3.

MONROE. *Sisters, Servants of the Immaculate Heart of Mary, Leadership Council,* 610 W. Elm Ave., 48162-9909. Tel: 313-241-0092; Fax: 313-241-9114. Sr. Mary M. McCann, I.H.M., Pres.; Sr. Nancy Sylvester, I.H.M., Vice Pres.; Sr. Frances Mlocek, I.H.M., CFO; Sr. Paula Cathcart, I.H.M., Leadership Council; Sr. Anne Crimmins, I.H.M., Leadership Council; Sr. Mary Ann Markel, I.H.M., Leadership Council; Sr. Kathleen O'Brien, I.H.M., Leadership Council; Sr. Mary Agnes Ryan, I.H.M., Leadership Council.

ORTONVILLE. *Our Lady of Mt. Thabor Monastery,* 1295 Bald Eagle Lake Rd., 48462. Tel: 248-627-4355. Dominican Sisters of Mt. Thabor. Sr. Mary Martin, Prioress.

OXFORD. *Dominican Sisters, Congregation of St. Rose of Lima, St. Joseph Convent,* 775 W. Drahner Rd., Box 167, 48371. Tel: 248-628-2872; Fax: 248-628-1725. Sr. Frances Mary Kernasovich, O.P., Pres.; Sr. Teresita Lipar, O.P., First Vice Pres.; Sr. Sue McMahon, O.P., Second Vice Pres. Professed Sisters 46. General Mother House and Novitiate of the Dominican Sisters; St. Mary Retreat House; Dominican Center; St. Raphael's.

RIVERVIEW. *Sisters of Mary Reparatrix,* 17320 Grange Rd., 48192. Tel: 810-364-3326; Fax: 810-364-0970. Sisters 2.

Full Circle House of Prayer.

[M] HOMES FOR MEN AND WOMEN

DETROIT. *St. Mary's Residence,* 2120 Orleans St., 48207. Tel: 313-259-6874; 259-0459
For a complete listing, refer to the Special Care Facilities section.

[N] CATHOLIC SOCIAL SERVICE AGENCIES

DETROIT. *Catholic Social Services of Wayne County,* 9851 Hamilton Ave., 48202. Tel: 313-883-2339; Fax: 313-883-3957. Patrick J. Heron, Pres. & CEO. Family service, marriage counseling, adoption services, services to unwed mothers, planned respite care, substance abuse counseling, foster family care & services to youth & older persons including Foster Grandparent, Senior Companion & Retired Senior Volunteer Programs.
Branches: 24331 Van Born Rd., Taylor, 48180. Tel: 313-292-5690. 17332 Farmington Rd., Livonia, 48152. Tel: 313-421-3730. 15200 E Jefferson, Ste. 105, Grosse Point Park, 48230. Tel: 313-821-2590.

LAPEER. *Christian Family Services of Lapeer County, Inc.,* 441 Clay St., 48446. Tel: 810-664-4557.

MONROE. *Catholic Social Services of Monroe County,* 16 E. Fifth St., 48161. Tel: 313-242-3800; Fax: 313-242-6203. Mark T. Robinson, M.S.W., A.C.S.W., Pres. & CEO. South County Office: 8330 Lewis Ave., P.O. Box 10, Temperance, 48182. Tel: 313-847-1523.

Head Start Office, 502 W. Elm St., 48162.

MOUNT CLEMENS. *Catholic Services of Macomb,* 235 S. Gratiot, 48043. Tel: 810-468-2616. Mr. Thomas Reed, Pres. & CEO.
Branch Offices: 12434 Twelve Mile Rd., Ste. 202, Warren, 48093. Tel: 810-558-7551. 18720 Thirteen Mile Rd., Roseville, 48066. Tel: 810-558-7551. 45100 Sterrit, Ste. 104, Utica, 48087. Tel: 810-254-2900.

Friend's House Adult Day Care for the Elderly, 16931 Nineteen Mile Rd., Ste. 140, Clinton Township, 48038. Tel: 810-412-8494.

PONTIAC. *Catholic Social Services of Oakland County,* 50 Wayne St., 3rd Floor, 48342. Tel: 248-333-3700. Margaret A. Huggard, M.S.W., Pres.
Branches: 53 Franklin Blvd., 48341. Tel: 248-334-3595. 6637 Highland Rd., Waterford, 48327. Tel: 248-666-8870. 26105 Orchard Lake Rd., Ste. 303, Farmington, 48334. Tel: 248-471-4140. 1424 E. Eleven Mile Rd., Royal Oak, 48067. Tel: 248-548-4044.

Sheltering Arms Adult Day Care, 18310 W. 12 Mile Rd., Southfield, 48076. Tel: 248-557-7373.

PORT HURON. *Catholic Social Services of St. Clair County, Inc.,* 2601 Thirteenth St., 48060. Tel: 810-987-9100. Patrick L. Cogley, M.A., Pres.

[O] SPECIALIZED CHILD CARE FACILITIES AND SCHOOLS

DETROIT. *Christ Child House,* 15751 Joy Rd., 48228. Tel: 313-584-6077; Fax: 313-584-1148.
For a complete listing, refer to the Special Care Facilities section.

Don Bosco Hall, Inc., 10001 Petosky, 48204. Tel: 313-834-8677.
For a complete listing, refer to the Special Care Facilities section.

DEARBORN HEIGHTS. *Vista Maria,* 20651 W. Warren Ave., 48127. Tel: 313-271-3050.
For a complete listing, refer to the Special Care Facilities section.

FARMINGTON HILLS. *Marillac Programs,* 22255 Greenfield, Ste. 330 Southfield, 48334. Tel: 810-559-2272; Fax: 810-559-2226.
For a complete listing, refer to the Special Care Facilities section.

St. Vincent and Sarah Fisher Center, 27400 W. Twelve Mile Rd., 48334. Tel: 313-538-6000; 810-626-7527.
For a complete listing, refer to the Special Care Facilities section.

Seton Nursery School and Infant-Toddler Child Care Center, 29475 Inkster Rd., 48018. Tel: 810-626-6990.
For a complete listing, refer to the Special Care Facilities section.

NORTHVILLE. *Our Lady of Providence Center,* 16115 Beck Rd., 48167. Tel: 313-453-1300.
For a complete listing, refer to the Special Care Facilities section.

SOUTHFIELD. *Boysville of Michigan, Inc.,* Community Resource Office, 17117 W. Nine Mile Rd., Ste. 1111, 48075. Tel: 248-569-6630; Fax: 248-569-8171.
For a complete listing, refer to the Special Care Facilities section.

St. Francis Family Services, 17500 W. Eight Mile Rd., 48075. Tel: 810-552-0750.
For a complete listing, refer to the Special Care Facilities section.

[P] RETREAT HOUSES

DETROIT. *St. Paul of the Cross Retreat Center.* Conducted by the Passionist Community. 23333 Schoolcraft, 48223-2499. Tel: 313-535-9563; Fax: 313-535-9207. Rev. Michael Higgins, C.P., Retreat Dir. Team Members: Revs. Rene Champagne, C.P.; Ronald Corl, C.P., Asst. Retreat Dir.; Bro. William Bahlman, C.P.

BLOOMFIELD HILLS. *Manresa Jesuit Retreat House,* 1390 Quarton Rd., 48304-3554. Tel: 313-564-6455; 810-644-4933; Fax: 810-644-8291. Revs. James K. Serrick, S.J., Dir. Supr.; John A. McGrail, S.J., Retreat Dir.; Bernard J. Owens, S.J., Retreat Dir.; John T. Schuett, S.J., Retreat Dir.; Benno G. Kornely, S.J., Retreat Dir.; Eugene P. Simon, S.J. Priests 6.

CLARKSTON. *Colombiere Center,* 9075 Big Lake Rd., Box 139, 48347. Tel: 810-625-5611; Fax: 810-625-3526. Spirituality Conference Center and Jesuit Health Care Community for the Detroit Province and Chicago Province. Revs. James E. Von Tobel, S.J., Supr. & Dir.; Paul L. Allen, S.J.; Thomas F. Ankenbrandt, S.J.; Joseph M. Becker, S.J.; Leo J. Belanger, S.J.; Thomas C. Biecker, S.J.; John L. Blanchard, S.J.; Robert C. Broome, S.J.; Edward W. Burke, S.J.; Joseph M. Casey, S.J., Asst. Supr.; Edward E. Cincoski, S.J.; Jerome A. Clifford, S.J.; Paul F. Conan, S.J.; Thomas P. Conry, S.J.; George A. Curran, S.J.; Stanislaus Czapiewski, S.J., St. Ladislaus, 2730 Caniff, Hamtramck, 48212. Tel: 313-872-0709. Revs. J. Richard Dempsey, S.J.; Edward L. Fergus, S.J.; Henry C. Gelin, S.J.; Francis X. Grollig, S.J.; Cletus F. Hartmann, S.J.; Fred M. Henley, S.J.; Lawrence E. Isenecker, S.J.; Joseph V. Loftus, S.J.; Edward M. Loveley, S.J.; John E. Mahoney, S.J.; Oswald J. Marshall, S.J.; David F. McCarthy, S.J.; Stephen A. Meder, S.J.; David E. Meier, S.J.; Harold R. Meirose, S.J., Pastoral Care, Asst. Dir.; Edmund J. Montville, S.J.; Francis M. Moore, S.J.; Edwin A. Mousbrugger, S.J.; Joseph J. Peters, S.J.; Robert A. Pollauf, S.J.; Francis D. Rabaut, S.J.; LeRoy F. Ryan, S.J., St. James, P.O. Box 145, Beaver Island, 49782. Tel: 616-448-2230. Revs. William F. Schmoldt, S.J.; George T. Tolbert, S.J.; Jules J. Toner, S.J.; William G. Topmoeller, S.J.; Jerome F. Treacy, S.J.; Bros. Philip J. Anton, S.J.; William J. Balconi, S.J.; Rev. Donald J. Butler, S.J.; Bros. Tomasz Dziemba, S.J.; Herman F. Elsaesser, S.J.; John E. Foy, S.J.; Frederick A. Frowerk, S.J.; Charles W. Hocter, S.J.; Bruno W. Karpinski, S.J.; Daniel J. McCullough, S.J.; Clayton P. Morell, S.J.; John J. Petrus, S.J.; Bernard L. Polinak, S.J.; Frederick F. Readence, S.J.; Albert J. Savoie, S.J. Priests 43; Brothers 13.

MONROE. *Visitation,* 529 Stewart Rd., 48162. Tel: 313-242-5520; Fax: 313-242-5530. Sponsorship of I.H.M. Congregation. Sisters 4.

WASHINGTON. *Capuchin Retreat,* 62460 Mt. Vernon Rd., P.O. Box 188, 48094. Tel: 248-651-4826. Revs. Jogues Constance, O.F.M.Cap.; James R. Andres, O.F.M.Cap.; Gerald Kessel, O.F.M.Cap.; Gerald Pehler, O.F.M.Cap.

[Q] SPECIAL SERVICES

DETROIT. *Capuchin Soup Kitchen,* 1760 Mt. Elliott, 48207. Tel: 313-579-2100. Rev. James Leary, O.F.M.Cap., Dir.; Mr. Lewis Hickson, Exec. Dir.

Jefferson House, 8311 E. Jefferson, 48214. Tel: 313-331-8900. Transitional alcohol-drug residence. Mr. James Fleming, Site Dir.

Catholic Community Services of the Archdiocese of Detroit, Inc., 1234 Washington Blvd., 48226. Tel: 313-237-5885; Fax: 313-237-4642. His Eminence Adam J. Maida, Pres.; Rev. Msgr. John P. Zenz, Sec.; Sr. Mary V. Korb, R.S.M., Treas.

Community Food Depots, Society of St. Vincent de Paul, 2929 E. Grand Blvd., 48202. Tel: 313-972-3100. Ellen Kennedy, Dir.

Manna Community Meal. (Soup Kitchen), 1950 Trumbull, 48226. Tel: 313-963-8708.

Pope John XXIII Hospitality House, 3977 2nd Ave., 48201. Tel: 313-832-HELP. Cancer outpatient-residents, Transportation for Area Pediatric Cancer Patients. Rev. Russell E. Kohler.

St. Mary's Residence, 2120 Orleans, 48207. Tel: 313-259-6874; 259-0459. Sr. M. Fidelis, F.D.C., Admin. Conducted by the Daughters of Divine Charity. A licensed adult foster care home for mentally or physically handicapped women, ages 30-65. Staff 6; Residents 60.

St. Patrick's Senior Center, Inc., 58 Parsons, 48201. Tel: 313-833-7080. Sr. Mary Watson, O.P., Pres.; Rev. Thomas J. Duffey, Vice Pres. Lay Staff 10; Patients assisted annually 1,400.

St. Vincent de Paul Society, Archdiocesan Council, 2929 E. Grand Blvd., 48202. Tel: 313-972-3100; Fax: 313-972-3147. James Dumont, Pres.; Rev. Msgr. F. Gerald Martin, Spiritual Dir.; Patrick Adamcik, Exec. Sec.

MEMPHIS. *Sacred Heart Rehabilitation Center, Inc.,* 400 Stoddard Rd., Box 41038, 48041-1038. Tel: 810-392-2167. John Sass, Jr., Pres. Beds 98. Treatment for alcoholism and drug dependency to adult men and women. Detox and residential services.

ONSTED. *St. Patrick's Retreat,* 11528 Killarney Hwy., 49265. Tel: 517-467-7492. Rev. Russell E. Kohler, Dir. Tel: 313-832-4357. Retreats for Family with cancer outpatient; small groups of handicapped-developmentally disabled; small parish team meetings; hospice & chaplain's meetings.

TROY. *Gabriel Richard Institute*, 2820 W. Maple #101, 48084. Tel: 810-643-4039; 800-382-8609; Fax: 810-643-4045. Adult and youth Christopher Leadership training for Catholic laymen, women, clergy & religious. Rev. Thomas J. Bresnahan, Dir.; Dolores Ammar, Natl. Mgr.

WARREN. *St. John's Deaf Center*, 8245 Fisher, 48089. Tel: 810-758-0710 (TDD); 758-0714 (Voice). Revs. Richard J. Yost, O.S.F.S., Dir.; Kenneth N. McKenna, O.S.F.S., Assoc.

WATERFORD. *Lourdes Alzheimers Special Care Center*, 2300 Watkins Lake Rd., 48328. Tel: 810-674-2241. Sr. Sue McMahon, O.P., Contact.

[R] CAMPS AND COMMUNITY CENTERS

DETROIT. *C.Y.O. Boys Camp*, CYO Camps, Catholic Youth Organization, 305 Michigan Ave., 48226. Tel: 313-963-7172. Brian Cokonougher, Camp Dept. Dir.

C.Y.O. Girls Camp, CYO Camps, Catholic Youth Organization, 305 Michigan Ave., 48226. Tel: 313-963-7172. Brian Cokonougher, Camp Svcs. Dir.

Camp Ozanam, Central Office-St. Vincent de Paul Society, 2929 E. Grand Blvd., 48202-0518. Tel: 313-972-3100. A free week long christian camping experience for boys 8-12. Recruitment through Parish Conferences of the Society of St. Vincent de Paul.

Camp Stapleton-St. Vincent de Paul Society, Central Office, 2929 E. Grand Blvd., 48202. Tel: 313-972-3100. A free week long christian camping experience for girls 8-12. Recruitment through Parish Conferences of the Society of St. Vincent de Paul.

[S] CAMPUS MINISTRIES

DETROIT. *Marygrove College Campus Ministry*, 8425 West McNichols Rd., 48221. Tel: 313-862-8000, Ext. 275. Sr. Marie Sweeney, I.H.M., Campus Ministry.

University of Detroit Mercy Campus Ministry. Mailing Address: P.O. Box 19900, 48219-0900.

McNickols Campus. Tel: 313-993-1560. Rev. Gary R. Wright, S.J., Dir.

Outer Drive Campus. Tel: 313-993-6216. C. Sylvia Shorter, Campus Min.

Wayne State University, Newman Center, 761 Student Center, 48202. Tel: 313-577-3462. Sr. Martha M. Curry, R.S.C.J., Dir.

AUBURN HILLS. *St. John Fisher Chapel University Parish*, 3665 Walton Blvd., 48326. Tel: 248-373-6457. Campus Ministry for Oakland University. Rev. Jerome A. Brzezinski; Sr. Mary Bodde, S.C.; Mrs. Susan Burrato; Sr. Mary Dixon, O.P.; Sr. Mary Van Gilder, I.H.M.; Mr. Eugene Mahon.

DEARBORN. *Univ. of Michigan, Dearborn, Henry Ford Community College Newman Center*. Gabriel Richard Campus Ministry Center, 5001 Evergreen Rd., 48128. Tel: 313-271-6000. Shannon Dyer, B.A., Campus Min.

LIVONIA. *Madonna University Newman Center*, 36600 Schoolcraft, 48150. Tel: 313-591-5000. Deacon Eugene Desjarlais, Dir. Campus Min.

Schoolcraft College, Newman House. (Campus Ministry), 17300 Haggerty Rd., 48152. Tel: 313-464-2160. Rev. J. Robert Schaden; Ms. Bert Kelly.

PORT HURON. *John Courtney Murray Newman Center*, 505 Huron Ave., 48060. Tel: 810-948-5195. Rev. Rene L. Desmarais.

WARREN. *Macomb Community College Campus Ministry*, 14500 Twelve Mile Rd., 48093. Tel: 810-445-7378. Sr. Joyce Campbell, I.H.M.; Julie Telang; Michael Lauchlan.

[T] MISCELLANEOUS LISTINGS

DETROIT. *American Friends of the Vatican Library*, 2701 W. Chicago Blvd., 48206. Tel: 313-883-8586. Rev. Charles Kosanke, Contact.

The Black Catholic Televangelization Network, 11430 Morang, 48224. Tel: 313-521-7777. Rev. Clarence E. Williams, C.PP.S., Pres. Search, Black and Catholic (TV) and the Catholic African World Network.

Cardinal Club, 1234 Washington, 48226. An organization of Catholic laymen in business and professional fields.

Christ Child Society, 15751 Joy Rd., 48228; Fax: 313-584-1148. Rev. Msgr. John P. Zenz, Spiritual Dir.; Darcy Connolly, Pres.

Clergy Health Plan, Chancery Building, 1234 Washington Blvd., 48226. Rev. Jack Fabian, Dir.

Council of Catholic Women, 305 Michigan Ave., 48226. Tel: 313-237-5896. Patricia A. Kendro, Pres.

Detroit Federation of Christian Life Communities, 1234 Washington Blvd., 48226. Mrs. Shirley Boots, Pres.

Dominican Literacy Center, 9400 Courville, 48224. Tel: 313-882-4853. Sr. Marie Schdenlein, O.P., Dir.

Foster Parents Mission Club, 17330 Quincy Ave., 48221. Tel: 313-342-4066; Fax: 313-342-6816. Rev. Bruno Piccolo, P.I.M.E., Dir.; Alice Marino, Exec. Sec. An agency of the P.I.M.E. Missionaries.

The Franciscan Project, Inc., 4603 Vinewood, 48208-1879. Tel: 313-896-7103. Sr. Patricia Mary Hackett, S.A., Pres.

Jesuit Seminary Association, 7303 W. Seven Mile Rd., 48221. Tel: 313-861-4438. Rachel M. Brennan, Dir. of Development & of Jesuit Seminary Assoc.

Jesuit International Missions. Rev. Norman J. Dickson.

Jesuit Volunteer Corps. Midwest, Inc., 438 St. Antoine, 48226-4318. Tel: 313-963-4112; Fax: 313-963-9620. Timothy McCabe, Exec. Dir. Mailing Address: P.O. Box 32692, 48232.

Latino Catholic Pastoral Center, 5680 Konkel, 48210. Tel: 313-897-5277; Fax: 313-897-8279. Raul Feliciano, Dir.

Leprosy Relief Society, 17330 Quincy Ave., 48221. Tel: 313-342-4066; Fax: 313-342-6816. Barbara J. Rubaie, Dir. An agency of the P.I.M.E. Missionaries.

**Mercy Education Project*, 2020 14th St., 48216. Tel: 313-963-5881; Fax: 313-963-0209. Sr. Candice Johnson, R.S.M., Exec. Dir.

Pope John Paul II Cultural Foundation, Inc., 2701 Chicago Blvd., 48206. Tel: 313-883-8518. His Eminence Adam J. Maida, Episcopal Moderator; Rev. Msgr. Michael R. Dylag, Admin. Asst.

St. John Health System. Holding Company Sponsored by Sisters of St. Joseph which operates: St. John Hospital & Medical Center; St. John Ambulatory Corp.; The Oxford Institute; The St. John Dialysis Center Corporation; St. John Hospital-Macomb Center; Affiliated Health Services; St. John-Bon Secours Senior Community; Eastwood Community Clinics; Holy Cross Hospital; Oakland General Hospital; Saratoga Community Hospital. 22101 Moross Rd., 48236. Tel: 313-343-4000. Rev. James Krasman, O.F.M., Chap.; Dr. Anthony R. Tersigni, Ed.D., Pres. & CEO.

St. John Newco, 22101 Moross, 48236. Tel: 313-343-7880. Arthur F. deVaux, Contact Person.

St. Mary Magdalen Catholic Community, Ryan Correctional Facility, 305 Michigan Ave., 48226. Tel: 313-237-4688. Rev. Thomas R. Physician, Chaplaincy Coord.

SS. Peter & Paul Jesuit Church Historical Fund, 438 St. Antoine, 48226. Tel: 313-961-8077. Rev. Robert R. Hartigan, S.J., Contact Person.

BLOOMFIELD HILLS. *Amicare Home Health Care - Metro Detroit*, 281 Enterprise Dr., Ste. 200, 48302. Tel: 248-858-7735. Gary Baum, Pres.

Ladies of Charity of St. Vincent de Paul Oakland County Associaton, 1466 Glengarry, 48301. Patricia Hurlbert, Contact Person.

The Legion of Christ, Inc., 2460 Opdyke Rd., 48304. Tel: 248-644-2954. Rev. Lorenzo Gomez, Contact.

Logos, Inc. (Michigan), 2460 Opdyke Rd., 48304. Tel: 203-281-4798. Rev. Lorenzo Gomez, L.C., Contact.

Opdyke, Inc., 2460 Opdyke Rd., 48103. Tel: 248-644-2954. Rev. Lorenzo Gomez, Contact.

DEARBORN. *Archdiocesan Catholic Campus Ministry Association, Gabriel Richards Campus Ministry*, University of Michigan-Dearborn, 5001 Evergreen, 48128. Tel: 313-271-6000. Leadership Team: Shannon Dyer; Michael Laughlin; Silvia Shorter; Kathy Eubanks.

Leo XIII Society, 1734 N. Waverly, 48128. Tel: 313-561-2155. Ernie Scarano, Contact Person.

DEARBORN HEIGHTS. *Dominican Center for Religious Development*, 7430 N. Inkster Rd., 48127. Tel: 313-730-8759. Sr. Charlotte Hoefer, O.P.

EASTPOINTE. *Detroit Catholic Charismatic Renewal*, Coordinating Center, 22851 Lexington, 810-777-7780. Rev. John Esper, Assoc. Liason. Diocesan Service Committee: Arlene Apone; Al Schindler; John Sherry.

FARMINGTON HILLS.

**Amicare Home Health Services, Inc.*, P.O. Box 9185, 48333-9185; Fax: 248-305-7632. Gary Baum, Pres.

**Amicare Hospice Services, Inc.*, 34605 Twelve Mile Rd., 48331; Fax: 248-489-6204. Gary Baum, Pres.

Mercy Health Foundation, 34605 Twelve Mile Rd., 48331-3292. Tel: 810-489-6084. Nancy Van Zant, M.S.Ed., V.P. Devel. Svcs.

Mercy Health Services (Formerly Sisters of Mercy Health Corporation), 34605 Twelve Mile Rd., 48331. Tel: 810-489-6000. Judith Pelham, Pres. Organization owns & operates 13 hospital divisions in Michigan & Iowa. Owns & operates 13 nursing home facilities, manages senior housing facilities, alternative health financing activities, home care services, hospice services, rehabilitation services and foundation activities.

Mercy Information Systems, 34605 Twelve Mile Rd., 48331. Tel: 248-489-6500.

Mercy International Health Services, 34605 Twelve Mile Rd., 48331. Tel: 248-489-6100. David Vellinga, Pres.

Mercy Services for Aging. Wholly-owned subsidiary of Mercy Health Services, 34605 Twelve Mile Rd., 48331. Tel: 248-305-7920. Gerald Bruen, Pres.

Mercy Services for Aging, Non-profit Housing Corporation. Wholly owned subsidiary of Mercy Services for Aging, 34605 Twelve Mile Rd., 48331. Tel: 248-305-7920. Gerald Bruen, Pres.

GROSSE POINTE. *John Paul II Foundation of Michigan, Inc.*, 35 Warner Rd., 48236. Tel: 313-882-2140. Mrs. Frank A. Germack, Jr., Pres. Conducts religious, cultural, educational, humanitarian and fund raising activities in Michigan in liaison with the John Paul Foundation in Rome. Regular, supporting and life memberships.

LAKE ORION. *Guest House Alumni Association*, 1601 Joslyn Rd., Box 420, 48361. Tel: 248-391-4445. Daniel Webster, Dir. Communications; William C. Morgan, Dir. Rochester Treatment Facility; Sr. Mae Kierans, C.S.J., Clinical Svcs. Coord.; Rev. Andrew J. Tomasko, Pres. Alumni Assoc.

LIVONIA.

**Angela Hospice Home Care, Inc.*, 14100 Newburgh Rd., 48154-1871. Tel: 313-464-7810.

MARYSVILLE. *National Alliance of Parishes Restructuring into Communities*, 1000 Michigan Ave., 48040-1466. Tel: 810-364-3500; Fax: 810-364-3555. Rev. Art Baranowski, Pres.; Margaret Steinhaus, Mgr.; Larry & Judy Berch, Editors. The N.A.P.R.C. networks and supports American & intl. parishes developing small church communities as the primary restructuring of the parish.

MONROE. *SSIHM Charitable Trust (Retired and Infirm Sisters)*, 610 Elm Ave., 48162-7907. Tel: 313-241-0092. Sr. Suzanne Sattler, I.H.M., Trustee.

NEWPORT. *Companions of Christ the Lamb*, P.O. Box 115, 48166. Tel: 248-486-5051. Rev. Jack Fabian, Dir.

NOVI.

**Mission Health Corporation*, 47601 Grand River Ave., 48374. Tel: 248-380-4850; Fax: 248-380-4859. Brian Connolly, Pres.

REDFORD. *Siena Literacy Center*, 11685 Appleton, 48239. Tel: 313-532-8404. Sr. Mary Hemmen, O.P., Dir.

ROSEVILLE. *Cursillos in Christianity Movement of the Archdiocese of Detroit*, 18430 Utica Rd., 48066. Tel: 810-776-4533. Rev. Charles M. Morris, Spiritual Advisor; Mr. William Pfannes, Lay Dir. Tel: 810-524-1951.

ST. CLAIR SHORES. *Catholic Kolping Society of America, Detroit Branch, Inc.*, 24409 Jefferson, 48080. Tel: 810-775-9159. Mary Margaret Hubert, Pres. Tel: 248-689-7975; Thekla Abels, Contact Person. Tel: 313-885-1189; Revs. James Leary, O.F.M.Cap., Praeses; Bohdan W. Kosicki.

**Celebrate Life Ministries*, 28111 Jefferson, A6, 48081. Tel: 810-778-4446. Mrs. Patricia Haas, Coord.

Dominican Consultation Center, 22811 Greater Mack, Ste. L-11, 48080. Tel: 810-775-5620. 24225 W.Nine Mile Rd., Ste. 114A, Southfield, 48034-3990. Tel: 248-353-9080. Sr. Diane Burgermeister, O.P.

SOUTHFIELD. *Seton Health Corporation of Southeast Michigan*, 16001 W. Nine Mile Rd., 48037. Tel: 248-424-3011. Brian Connolly, Pres.

WATERFORD. *Voluntas Dei Institute*, 4557 Fairway Ct., 48328. Tel: 248-682-0097; Fax: 248-682-5201. Rev. George F. Hazler, Contact Person.

[U] CLOSED INSTITUTIONS

DETROIT. *Archdiocesan Archives*. The following institutional sacramental records can be found at the following address unless otherwise indicated. 1234 Washington Blvd., 48226. Tel: 313-237-5846; Fax: 313-237-4643.

St. Agnes.
St. Albertus.
Anawim Community.
Assumption of the Blessed Virgin Mary.
St. Augustine.
St. Benedict the Moor.
St. Bernadette Chapel.
St. Bernard.
St. Boniface.
St. Brigid.
St. Camillus.
Cardinal Leger Community.
St. Catherine.
St. Casimir.
Corpus Christi.
St. David.
St. Edward.
Emmaus Community.
Epiphany.
St. Eugene.
St. Francis Hospital.
Holy Ghost.
Holy Name of Jesus.
St. Ignatius of Antioch.
Immaculate Conception.
St. Joachim.
St. John the Evangelist.
St. John Nepomucene.
St. John Vianney.
St. Lawrence.
St. Margaret Mary.
St. Martin.
St. Mary Hospital - Detroit Memorial Hospital.
St. Monica.
Mother of Consolation.

Mother of Our Savior.
Mount Carmel Mercy Hospital.
Our Lady of Guadalupe.
Our Lady of Help.
Our Lady of the Hills.
Our Lady Queen of Hope.
St. Paul Maltese.
Patronage of St. Joseph.
St. Peter (Lithuanian).
St. Philip Neri.
Resurrection.
St. Rose of Lima.
St. Stanislaus Bishop and Martyr.
St. Theresa.
St. Thomas the Apostle.
St. Vincent de Paul.
Santa Maria.
Vida Nueva Community.
Visitation.
St. Wenceslaus.

RELIGIOUS INSTITUTES OF MEN REPRESENTED IN THE ARCHDIOCESE

For further details refer to the corresponding bracketed number in the Religious Institutes of Men or Women section.

[0140]—*The Augustinians.* (Chicago).—O.S.A.
[0170]—*Basilian Fathers.* (Toronto, Ont.).—C.S.B.
[0200]—*Benedictine Monks.* (Detroit Prov.).—O.S.B.
[0330]—*Brothers of the Christian Schools.* (New York Prov., Chicago, IL).—F.S.C.
[0600]—*Brothers of the Congregation of Holy Cross.* (Midwest Prov.).—C.S.C.
[0460]—*Brothers of the Poor of St. Francis.*—C.F.P.
[0400]—*Canons Regular of the Order of the Holy Cross.* (Prov. of St. Odilia).—O.S.C.
[0470]—*The Capuchin Friars.* (St. Joseph Prov.).—O.F.M.Cap.
[0275]—*Carmelites of Mary Immaculate.*—C.M.I.
[0310]—*Congregation of Christian Brothers.* (American Prov.).—C.F.C.
[0750]—*Congregation of Marianhill Missionaries.*—C.M.M.
[0740]—*Congregation of Marians of the Immaculate Conception.* (St. Stanislaus Kostka Prov.).—M.I.C.
[1000]—*Congregation of the Passion.* (Western Prov.).—C.P.
[1140]—*Congregation of the Sacred Hearts of Jesus and Mary.*—SS.CC.
[0480]—*Conventual Franciscans.*—O.F.M.Conv.
[0520]—*Franciscan Friars (Custody of St. John Capristran; Prov. of St. Stephen, King; Custody of the Holy Family / Croatian).*—O.F.M.
[0650]—*Holy Ghost Fathers.* (Eastern Prov.).—C.S.Sp.
[0690]—*Jesuit Fathers and Brothers.* (Detroit Prov.).—S.J.
[0730]—*Legionaries of Christ.*—L.C.
[]—*Little Brothers of Jesus.*
[0780]—*Marist Fathers.* (Northeastern Prov.).—S.M.
[0800]—*Maryknoll.*—M.M.
[0720]—*The Missionaries of Our Lady of La Salette.*—M.S.
[0860]—*Missionhurst Congregation of the Immaculate Heart of Mary.*—C.I.C.M.
[0920]—*Oblates of St. Francis De Sales.*—O.S.F.S.
[0430]—*Order of Preachers-Dominicans.* (Provs. of St. Joseph & St. Albert the Great).—O.P.
[1020]—*Pauline Fathers and Brothers.*—S.S.P.
[1050]—*Pontifical Institute for Foreign Missions.*—P.I.M.E.
[1070]—*Redemptorist Fathers.* (St. Louis Prov.).—C.SS.R.
[1260]—*Society of Christ.* (American-Canadian Prov.).—S.Ch.
[0440]—*Society of Saint Edmund.*—S.S.E.
[0990]—*Society of the Catholic Apostolate.*—S.A.C.
[1060]—*Society of the Precious Blood.* (Cincinnati Prov.).—C.PP.S.

RELIGIOUS INSTITUTES OF WOMEN REPRESENTED IN THE ARCHDIOCESE

[1810]—*Bernardine Sisters of the Third Order of St. Francis.*—O.S.F.
[0360]—*Carmelite Sisters of the Divine Heart of Jesus Carmel.*—D.C.J.
[3810]—*Catholic Mission Sisters of St. Francis Xavier.*—X.S.
[0270]—*Congregation of Bon Secours.*—C.B.S.
[2410]—*Congregation of the Marianites of Holy Cross.*—M.S.C.
[1730]—*Congregation of the Sisters of the Third Order of St. Francis Oldenburg, IN.*—O.S.F.
[1710]—*Congregation of the Third Order of St. Francis of Mary Immaculate, Joliet, IL.*—O.S.F.
[1830]—*Contemplative Sisters of the Good Shepherd.*—C.G.S.
[0760]—*Daughters of Charity of St. Vincent de Paul.*—D.C.
[0790]—*Daughters of Divine Charity.*—F.D.C.
[]—*Daughters of Mary Immaculate (Chaldean).*—D.M.I.
[0940]—*Daughters of St. Mary of Providence.*—D.S.M.P.
[0810]—*Daughters of the Heart of Mary.*—D.H.M.
[0420]—*Discalced Carmelite Nuns.*—O.C.D.
[1050]—*Dominican Contemplative Nuns.*—O.P.
[1070-13]—*Dominican Sisters (Adrian, MI).*—O.P.
[1070-02]—*Dominican Sisters (Columbus,OH).*—O.P.
[1070-17]—*Dominican Sisters (Elkin Park).*—O.P.
[1070-14]—*Dominican Sisters (Grand Rapids, MI).*—O.P.
[1070-16]—*Dominican Sisters (Hope).*—O.P.
[1070-26]—*Dominican Sisters (Oxford, MI).*—O.P.
[1070-09]—*Dominican Sisters (Racine, WI).*—O.P.
[]—*Dominican Sisters of Mt. Thabor.*—O.P.
[1170]—*Felician Sisters.*—C.S.S.F.
[1470]—*Franciscan Sisters of St. Joseph.*—F.S.S.J.
[1480]—*Franciscan Sisters of St. Joseph.* (Mexico).—.F.S.S.J.
[1440]—*Franciscan Sisters of the Poor.*—S.F.P.
[2430]—*Marist Sisters Congregation of Mary.*—S.M.
[2720]—*Mission Helpers of the Sacred Heart.*—M.H.S.H.
[2710]—*Missionaries of Charity.*—M.C.
[]—*Missionaries of the Kingship of Christ.*—S.I.M.
[]—*Missionary Sisters of Christ the King for Polonia.*—M.S.K.C.P.
[3130]—*Our Lady of Victory Missionary Sisters.*—O.L.V.M.
[2970]—*School Sisters of Notre Dame.*—S.S.N.D.
[3560]—*Servants of Jesus.*—S.J.
[3590]—*Servants of Mary (Servite Sisters).*—O.S.M.
[0440]—*Sisters of Charity of Cincinnati, Ohio.*—S.C.
[0520]—*Sisters of Charity of Our Lady, Mother of Mercy.*—S.C.M.M.
[0990]—*Sisters of Divine Providence.*—C.D.P.
[2575]—*Sisters of Mercy of the Americas.*—R.S.M.
[2990]—*Sisters of Notre Dame.*—S.N.D.
[1530]—*Sisters of St. Francis of the Congregation of Our Lady of Lourdes, Sylvania, Ohio.*—O.S.F.
[1570]—*Sisters of St. Francis of the Holy Family.*—O.S.F.
[1600]—*Sisters of St. Francis of the Martyr St. George.*—O.S.F.
[3830-11]—*Sisters of St. Joseph.*—S.S.J.
[3930]—*Sisters of St. Joseph of the Third Order of St. Francis.*—S.S.J.-T.O.S.F.
[1830]—*Sisters of the Good Shepherd.*—R.G.S.
[1970]—*Sisters of the Holy Family of Nazareth.*—C.S.F.N.
[1990]—*Sisters of the Holy Names of Jesus and Mary.*—S.N.J.M.
[2350]—*Sisters of the Living Word.*—S.L.W.
[3730]—*Sisters of the Order of St. Basil the Great.*—O.S.B.M.
[3260]—*Sisters of the Precious Blood (Dayton, Ohio).*—C.PP.S.
[2090]—*Sisters, Home Visitors of Mary.*—H.V.M.
[3610]—*Sisters, Servants of Mary Immaculate.*—S.S.M.I.
[2150]—*Sisters, Servants of the Immaculate Heart of Mary.*—I.H.M.
[2460]—*Society of Mary Reparatrix.*—S.M.R.
[4070]—*Society of the Sacred Heart.*—R.S.C.J.
[4120-06]—*Ursuline Nuns of the Congregation of Paris.*—O.S.U.
[]—*Vestiarski Sisters of Jesus.*—V.S.

ARCHDIOCESAN CEMETERIES

DETROIT. *Owned and Operated by the Archdiocese of Detroit.*
Holy Cross.
Holy Sepulchre, Southfield.
Our Lady of Hope, Southgate.
Owned and Operated by the Mt. Elliott Cemetery Association.
Mt. Elliott.
Mt. Olivet.
Resurrection, Clinton Township.
All Saints, Waterford.
Owned and Operated by the Conventual Franciscan Friars.
St. Hedwig, Dearborn Heights.

NECROLOGY

† Bell, Arthur, (Retired). —Died Aug. 12, 1997.
† Cunningham, William, Detroit, MI, Church of the Madonna. —Died May 26, 1997.
† David, Basilio, (Retired). —Died Jan. 23, 1997.
† Foley, John, (Retired). —Died March 29, 1997.
† Fraser, Thomas, (Retired). —Died May 31, 1997.
† Gordon, Rev. Msgr. John T., Dir., Southfield, MI, Archdiocesan Cemeteries. —Died Oct. 27, 1997.
† Kress, Joseph, (Retired). —Died May 27, 1997.
† Matheson, Paul, (Retired). —Died April 25, 1997.
† Rebain, Daniel, Auburn Hills, MI, Sacred Heart. —Died Jan. 18, 1997.
† Wiercioch, Casimir, Maybee, MI, St. Joseph. —Died July 10, 1997.

Diocese of Dodge City

(Dioecesis Dodgepolis)

Most Reverend

STANLEY G. SCHLARMAN, D.D.

Bishop of Dodge City; ordained July 13, 1958; appointed to the Titular See of Capri and Auxiliary Bishop of Belleville, March 13, 1979; consecrated May 14, 1979; appointed Bishop of Dodge City March 1, 1983; installed May 4, 1983. *Office: 910 Central Ave., Box 137, Dodge City, KS, 67801.*

Most Reverend

MARION F. FORST, D.D.

Retired Bishop of Dodge City; ordained June 10, 1934; consecrated Bishop of Dodge City March 24, 1960; installed April 5, 1960; resigned from Dodge City; appointed Auxiliary Bishop of Kansas City in Kansas October 16, 1976; retired as Auxiliary Bishop December 23, 1986. *Res., St. Joseph Care Center, 759 Vermont Ave., Kansas City, KS, 66601.*

Catholic Church Offices: 910 Central Ave., P.O. Box 137, Dodge City, KS, 67801-0137. Tel.: 316-227-1500; Fax: 316-227-1570.

ESTABLISHED MAY 19, 1951.

Square Miles 23,000.

Comprises the following Counties in the State of Kansas: Barton, Stafford, Pratt, Barber, Rush, Ness, Lane, Scott, Wichita, Greeley, Hamilton, Kearny, Finney, Hodgeman, Pawnee, Edwards, Ford, Gray, Haskell, Grant, Stanton, Morton, Stevens, Seward, Meade, Clark, Kiowa and Comanche.

Principal Patron: Our Lady of Guadalupe.

Secondary Patron: St. John the Baptist.

For legal titles of parishes and diocesan institutions, consult the Chancery Office.

STATISTICAL OVERVIEW

Personnel	
Bishop	1
Retired Bishops	1
Priests: Diocesan Active in Diocese	26
Priests: Active Outside Diocese	3
Priests: Retired, Sick or Absent	20
Number of Diocesan Priests	49
Religious Priests in Diocese	2
Extern Priests in Diocese	5
Permanent Deacons in Diocese	4
Total Sisters	116
Parishes	
Parishes	51
With Resident Pastor:	
Resident Diocesan Priests	26
Resident Religious Priests	2
Without Resident Pastor:	
Administered by Priests	19
Administered by Permanent Deacons	2
Administered by Professed Men Religious	2
Closed Parishes	6
Professional Ministry Personnel:	
Sisters	5
Lay Ministers	5
Welfare	
Catholic Hospitals	3
Total Assisted	120,480
Special Centers for Social Services	4
Total Assisted	77,895
Educational	
Diocesan Students in Other Seminaries	2
Total Seminarians	2
Elementary Schools, Diocesan and Parish	10
Total Students	1,251
Catechesis/Religious Education:	
High School Students	1,609
Elementary Students	4,122
Total Students Under Catholic Instruction	6,984
Teachers in the Diocese:	
Sisters	2
Lay Teachers	87
Vital Statistics	
Receptions into the Church:	
Infant Baptism Totals	842
Adult Baptism Totals	236
Received into Full Communion	97
First Communions	887
Confirmations	604
Marriages:	
Catholic	132
Interfaith	88
Total Marriages	220
Deaths	324
Total Catholic Population	44,504
Total Population	215,920

Former Bishops—Most Rev. JOHN BAPTIST FRANZ, D.D., cons. Aug. 29, 1951; transferred to the See of Peoria Aug. 8, 1959.—Most Rev. MARION F. FORST, D.D., cons. March 24, 1960; transferred to See of Kansas City, KS as Auxiliary Oct. 16, 1976; retired as Auxiliary Bishop Dec. 23, 1986.—Most Rev. EUGENE J. GERBER, D.D., cons. Dec. 14, 1976; transferred See of Wichita, KS Nov. 23, 1982.

Vicar General—Rev. JOHN J. MAES.

Chancellor & Director of the Catholic Chancery—Sr. PATRICIA MCGREEVY, O.S.B., J.C.L.

Vice Chancellor—Sr. LORETTA GEGEN, A.S.C., Ph.D.

Catholic Church Offices—910 Central Ave., P.O. Box 137, Dodge City, 67801-0137. Tel: 316-227-1500; Fax: 316-227-1570. Office Hours: Mon.-Fri. 9-4:30 All rogatonial commissions should be sent to the Catholic Church Offices.

Finance Director—Mr. DANIEL M. STREMEL, C.P.A., *Catholic Church Offices, 910 Central Ave., P.O. Box 137, Dodge City, 67801-0137.* Tel: 316-227-1500.

Presbyteral Council & Diocesan Board of Consultors—Most Rev. STANLEY G. SCHLARMAN; Revs. DENNIS REED, Chm.; TED SKALSKY, Vice Chm.; JAMES E. BAKER, J.C.L., Sec. & Treas.; BRIAN D. HIPP; MICHAEL L. HELMS; GILBERT HERRMAN; HENRY HILDEBRANDT; PASCAL L. KLEIN; GREGORY LEBLANC; JOHN J. MAES, V.G.; FRANCIS KHOI NGUYEN; WARREN L. STECKLEIN.

Deans—Rev. JAMES E. BAKER, V.F., Garden City; Rev. JOSEPH E. BAHR, V.F., Great Bend; Sr. PATRICIA MCGREEVY, Dodge City.

Council of Administration—Sr. LORETTA GEGEN, A.S.C., Ph.D.; Rev. JOHN J. MAES, V.G.; Mr. DANIEL M. STREMEL, C.P.A.; Sr. PATRICIA MCGREEVY, O.S.B., J.C.L.

Matrimonial Tribunal—910 Central Ave., P.O. Box 137, Dodge City, 67801-0137.

Judicial Vicar—Rev. JAMES E. BAKER, J.C.L.

Synodal Judge—Rev. JAMES E. BAKER, J.C.L.

Promotor of Justice—Rev. GERALD A. HAMMEKE, *1015 Harding, Great Bend, 67530.* Tel: 316-793-7497.

Defender of the Bond—Rev. DAVID H. KRAUS, J.C.L., *723 S. Baca Ave., P.O. Box 570, Elkhart, 67950-0570.* Tel: 316-697-4622.

Advocates—All priests in active ministry in the diocese.

Notary—LYNETTE KESSEN; PAMELA POLLEY.

Diocesan Offices and Directors

Catholic Education Office and Superintendent of Schools - Elementary School Religious Education—Sr. ROSEMARY HENRICHS, A.S.C., *P.O. Box 137, Dodge City, 67801-0137.* Tel: 316-227-1500.

Catholic Social Service Offices—Rev. TED A. SKALSKY, Exec. Dir., *805 Ave. J, Dodge City.* Tel: 316-227-3442. DEBBIE SNAPP, Program Dir., *P.O. Box 137, Dodge City, 67801-0137.* Tel: 316-227-1500.

Commission for Continuing Education for Priests—Revs. JAMES E. BAKER, J.C.L.; JOHN P. KOWAL; GREGORY LEBLANC.

Commission for Ministry to Priests—Revs. JOHN J. MAES, V.G.; CHARLES MAZOUCH; TED SKALSKY.

Council of Catholic Women—Sr. LORETTA GEGEN, A.S.C., Moderator.

Development Office—JACK SCHRAMM, *P.O. Box 137, Dodge City, 67801-0137.* Tel: 316-227-1500.

Diocesan Attorney—Frigon Chartd., *208 W. Wyatt Earp Blvd., P.O. Box 1695, Dodge City, 67801.* Tel: 316-225-0600.

Diocesan Commission for the Promotion of Christian Unity—Vacant.

Diocesan Finance Council—Most Rev. STANLEY G. SCHLARMAN, Ex-Officio; ED MICHEL, C.P.A., Chm.; Rev. GERALD A. HAMMEKE, Vice Chm.; Mr. DANIEL M. STREMEL, C.P.A., Ex-Officio, Sec. & Treas. JOHN ACKERMAN, Ex-Officio; EUGENE BERNING; CLARINE HEIMAN; EUGENE HEIMAN; CARL HELFRICH, C.P.A.; JACK SCHRAMM; SID SHRIWISE; Rev. WARREN STECKLEIN; ANN STEGMAN; RON VRATIL, C.P.A.

Due Process—Vacant.

Diocesan Fitness Review Board—DAVID H. SNAPP, Admin. Tel: 316-225-5051 (Office); 316-225-2412 (Home).

Diocesan Pastoral Council—Most Rev. STANLEY G. SCHLARMAN, Ex-Officio; Sr. LORETTA GEGEN, A.S.C., Coord.; Rev. JOSEPH E. BAHR, V.F.; Sr. JOEL CHRISTOPH, O.P., Ex-Officio; DEBBIE HELFRICH; RITA HITT, Ex-Officio, DCCW/NCCW; JEANETTE SIEMENS; LEROY THILLI; Rev. JAMES E. BAKER, V.F.; BECKY HESSMAN; Mrs. PAT KRIER; KEITH WIERMAN; VICTOR GRAFF; GENE JUNO; JOHN BROWER.

Diocesan Priests' Trust Fund—Revs. ROBERT A. SCHREMMER, Chm.; JOHN R. STRASSER, Vice Chm.; JAMES P. DIEKER, Sec.; Rev. Msgr. A. F. PREISNER, Treas.; Revs. EUGENE P. KENNY; GEORGE E. MUELLER; MARVIN W. REIF.

Diocesan School Council—Most Rev. STANLEY G. SCHLARMAN, Ex-Officio; Sr. ROSEMARY HENRICHS, A.S.C., Supt. of Schools; Revs. ROBERT A. SCHREMMER; CHRIS HIMMELWRIGHT; JAMES E. BAKER; BECKY HORNUNG; DENNIS REED; MARVIN W. REIF; CRAIG ROBL; JANICE SCOTT; WARREN L. STECKLEIN; JOHN STROBEL.

Health Affairs Office—Sr. BETTY WERNER, O.P., Dir., *3600 Broadway, Great Bend, 67530.*

Lay Employees' Retirement Plan—Mr. DANIEL M. STREMEL, C.P.A.

League of the Apostleship of Prayer—Vacant.

Newspaper Office—"The Southwest Kansas Register," Diocesan Weekly, TIM WENZL, Editor, *P.O. Box 137, Dodge City, 67801-0137.* Tel: 316-227-1500.

Office of Family Ministries—Co-Directors: Sr. ROSE MARY STEIN, O.P.; STEVEN POLLEY, *P.O. Box 137, Dodge City, 67801-0137.* Tel: 316-227-1500.

Office of Leadership Formation and Planning—Sr. LORETTA GEGEN, A.S.C., Dir., *P.O. Box 137, Dodge City, 67801-0137.* Tel: 316-227-1500.

Office of Liturgy and Worship (R.C.I.A.)—Rev. DAVID A. FLAGOR, Dir., *St. Mary Parish, P.O. Box 7, Marienthal, 67863-0007.* Tel: 316-379-4431. JANE STEIN, Coord., *523 W. 6th, Ashland, 67831.* Tel: 316-635-4060.

Ministry to Parents and the Aging—Sr. ROSE MARY STEIN, O.P., *910 Central, P.O. Box 137, Dodge City, 67801-0137.* Tel: 316-227-1500.

Catholic Agency - Migration and Refugee Services—LEVITA ROHLMAN, Exec. Dir., *1510 Taylor Plaza E., Garden City, 67846.* Tel: 316-276-7610; Fax: 316-276-9228.

Permanent Diaconate Office—Rev. BRIAN D. HIPP, Dir., *P.O. Box 137, Dodge City, 67801-0137.* Tel: 316-227-1500.

Propagation of the Faith and Pontifical Association of the Holy Childhood—Sr. KAREN ACKERMAN, A.S.C., *St. Lawrence Parish, P.O. Box 278, Jetmore, 67854-0278.* Tel: 316-357-8791.

High School Religious Education, Youth Ministry, Confirmation Retreats—STEVEN D. POLLEY, Dir., *P.O. Box 137, Dodge City, 67801-0137.* Tel: 316-227-1500.

Scouting—Rev. JAMES E. BAKER, *P.O. Box 278, Jetmore, 67854-0278.* Tel: 316-357-8791.

Vigilance for the Faith—The Rev. Deans.

Vocation Director—Rev. BRIAN HIPP, *P.O. Box 137, Dodge City, 67801-0137.* Tel: 316-227-1500.

CLERGY, PARISHES, MISSIONS AND PAROCHIAL SCHOOLS

CITY OF DODGE CITY
(Ford County)

1—CATHEDRAL OF THE SACRED HEART (1882), Revs. John R. Strasser; Louis Trung Hoang; Sr. Rose Hacker, S.S.S.F., Pastoral Min.
Office: 903 Central Ave., 67801. Tel: 316-225-4802.
Res., 903 Central, 67801. Tel: 316-227-3772.
School—905 Central Ave., 67801. Tel: 316-227-6532. Mrs. Kathryne Germscheid, Prin.
Religious 1; Lay Teachers 20; Students 404.
Catechesis/Religious Programs—Selene Shumacher, D.R.E.
Students 225.

2—OUR LADY OF GUADALUPE (1915), Rev. Ted A. Skalsky; Sr. Patricia Schlarman, A.S.C., Pastoral Assoc.
Res., 805 Ave. J, 67801. Tel: 316-227-3442 (Office).
Catechesis/Religious Programs—Elaine Campbell, D.R.E.
Students 403.

OUTSIDE THE CITY OF DODGE CITY

Ashland, Comanche Co., Holy Spirit Station (1984). Attended by St. Joseph, Ashland. Rev. Zeno Ye Swe, Admin.
Mailing Address: c/o St. Joseph Church, 514 Main St., Box 577, 67831. Tel: 316-635-2338; Fax: 316-635-4066. [JC]

St. Joseph, Clark Co., (1886), Rev. Xeno Ye Swe, Admin.
Res., 514 Main St., P.O. Box 577, 67831-0577. Tel: 316-635-2338; Fax: 316-635-4066.
Catechesis/Religious Programs—Tel: 316-635-2565. Della Marie Moore, D.R.E.
Students 36.

Beaver, Barton Co., St. Joseph. Closed. Sacramental records can be found at St. John, Hoisington.

Belpre, Edwards Co., St. Bernard (1921), Rev. Robert A. Schremmer; Deacon Richard Rondeau.
Res., 203 Hudson St., P.O. Box 188, 67519-0188. Tel: 316-995-4305.
Catechesis/Religious Programs—Tel: 316-348-3578. Eileen Loomis, D.R.E.
Students 82.

Bucklin, Ford Co., St. George. Closed. Sacramental records can be found at Our Lady of Guadalupe, Dodge City.

Burdett, Pawnee Co., Holy Rosary. Closed. Sacramental records can be found at Sacred Heart, Larned.

Claflin, Barton Co., Immaculate Conception (1904), Rev. Joseph E. Bahr; Sr. Catherine Therese Paulie, C.S.J., Pastoral Min.
Mailing Address: P.O. Box 197, 67525. Tel: 316-587-3628.
Catechesis/Religious Programs—Students 145.

Coldwater, Holy Spirit. Closed. Sacramental records can be found at St. Joseph, Ashland.

Deerfield, Kearney Co., Christ the King (1937), Rev. James E. Baker, J.C.L.
Mailing Address: P.O. Box 455, 67838. Tel: 316-275-4204.
Catechesis/Religious Programs—Tel: 316-426-6397. Marilyn Danler, D.R.E.
Students 70.

Dighton, Lane Co., St. Theresa (1927). Attended by St. Joseph, Scott City. Rev. Francis Khoi Nguyen.
Res., 322 S. First St., P.O. Box 787, 67839. Tel: 316-397-5357. [JC]
Catechesis/Religious Programs—Tel: 316-397-5711. Annette Wilson, D.R.E.
Students 57.

Dubuque, Barton Co., St. Catherine. Closed. Sacramental records can be found at St. John the Evangelist, Hoisington.

Elkhart, Morton Co., St. Joan of Arc (1921), Rev. David H. Kraus, J.C.L.
Res., 723 S. Baca Ave., P.O. Box 570, 67950-0570. Tel: 316-697-4622.
Catechesis/Religious Programs—Tel: 316-697-4587. Cristina Quijano, D.R.E.
Students 52.

Ellinwood, Barton Co., St. Joseph (1876), Rev. Joseph E. Bahr.
Res., 214 N. Main St., 67526. Tel: 316-564-2534.
School—111 W. Third, 67526. Tel: 316-564-2721. Sr. Noella Blick, A.S.C., Prin.
Adorers of the Blood of Christ 2; Lay Teachers 6; Students 80.
Catechesis/Religious Programs—Tel: 316-564-3632. Mary Tudor, D.R.E.
Students 73.

North Ellinwood, Barton Co., Sts. Peter & Paul. Closed. Sacramental records can be found at St. Joseph, Ellinwood.

Fowler, Meade Co., St. Anthony (1910). Attended by St. John the Baptist, Meade. Rev. George E. Mueller; Deacon Dwaine Lampe.
Res., 310 Fourth St., P.O. Box 80, 67844. Tel: 316-646-5297; Fax: 316-646-5207. [JC]
Catechesis/Religious Programs—Pat Dierking, D.R.E.
Students 99.

Garden City, Finney Co., St. Dominic (1965), Revs. Dennis L. Reed; Gregory S. LeBlanc.
Office: 615 J. C. St., 67846. Tel: 316-276-2024; Fax: 316-276-2086.
School—617 J. C. St., 67846. Tel: 316-276-8981.
Lay Teachers 9; Students 153.
Catechesis/Religious Programs—Tel: 316-276-3500. Michael Dorsey, D.R.E.
Students 352.

St. Mary (1898), Revs. James E. Baker, J.C.L.; Orestes Huerta.
Res., 509 St. John St., 67846. Tel: 316-275-4204; Fax: 316-272-9971. [CEM]
School—503 W. St. John St., 67846. Tel: 316-276-2241; Fax: 316-276-7067. Trina Delgado, Prin.
Lay Teachers 7; Students 87.
Catechesis/Religious Programs—Tel: 316-276-2716. Patricia Nieman, D.R.E.
Students 424.
Mission—Deerfield, Kearny Co., Christ the King, 812 Main St., Deerfield, 67838. Tel: 316-426-6996.

Great Bend, Barton Co., St. Patrick (1960), Rev. Warren L. Stecklein. In res., Rev. Dermot F. Tighe.
Res., 4100 Broadway, 67530. Tel: 316-792-1396; Fax: 316-792-1397. [JC]
School—4200 Broadway, 67530. Tel: 316-793-3265. Mr. Fred Meyers, Prin.
Lay Teachers 10; Students 156.
Catechesis/Religious Programs—Debra Hecht, D.R.E.
Students 167.

St. Rose of Lima (1878), Revs. Charles J. Mazouch; Pius Mahn Tacaw.
Res., 1423 Holland St., P.O. Box 1007, 67530. Tel: 316-792-3641. [JC]
School—1400 Baker Ave., 67530. Tel: 316-793-5662. Mr. Fred Meyers, Prin.
Lay Teachers 7; Students 101.
Catechesis/Religious Programs—Joyce Haberman, D.R.E.
Students 130.

Greensburg, Kiowa Co., St. Joseph (1952). Attended by St. Joseph, Ashland. Rev. David A. Flagor.
Res., 514 Main St., P.O. Box 577, Ashland, 67831-0577. Tel: 316-635-2338; Fax: 316-635-4066.

Hanston, Hodgeman Co., St. Anthony (1908). Attended by St. Lawrence, Jetmore. Rev. Michael Helms.
Mailing Address: c/o St. Lawrence Church, P.O. Box 278, Jetmore, 67854. Tel: 316-357-8791. [CEM]

Hoisington, Barton Co., St. John the Evangelist (1892), Rev. John J. Maes, V.G. Pastoral Ministers: Sr. Alvina Miller, O.P.; Sr. Marie Zoglman, A.S.C.
Office: 122 E. 5th St., 67544. Tel: 316-653-2963; Fax: 316-653-2934.; Rectory: 108 E. 5th St., 67544. Tel: 316-653-2695. [CEM]
Catechesis/Religious Programs—Ms. Judy Linsner, D.R.E.
Students 203.

Hugoton, Stevens Co., St. Helen (1948), Rev. Emil Dinkel, C.PP.S.
Parish Office: 1011 S. Jefferson St., 67951-2823. Tel: 316-544-2551.
Catechesis/Religious Programs—Tel: 316-544-4644. Phyllis Ackerman, D.R.E.
Students 84.

Ingalls, Gray Co., St. Stanislaus (1909), Revs. Dennis L. Reed; Gregory LeBlanc.
Mailing Address: P.O. Box 175, 67853. Tel: 316-335-5202. [JC]
Catechesis/Religious Programs—Kathy Hornung, D.R.E.
Students 163.

Jetmore, Hodgeman Co., St. Lawrence (1923), Rev. Michael Helms.
Mailing Address: P.O. Box 278, 67854. Tel: 316-357-8791. [JC]
Catechesis/Religious Programs—P.O. Box 655, 67854. Tel: 316-357-6109. Amy Rudzik, D.R.E.
Students 78.

Johnson, Stanton Co., St. Bernadette (1949) (Hispanic). Attended by Mary Queen of Peace, Ulysses. Rev. John P. Kowal.
Mailing Address: c/o Mary, Queen of Peace Church, 804 Colorado, Ulysses, 67880. Tel: 316-356-1532; Fax: 316-424-1065.
Catechesis/Religious Programs—Tel: 316-495-2471. Jana Brady, D.R.E.
Students 65.

Kinsley, Edwards Co., St. Nicholas (1883), Rev. William Vogel.
Res., 706 E. Sixth St., 67547. Tel: 316-659-2692. [CEM]
School—720 E. Sixth St., 67547. Tel: 316-659-2521. Mrs. Rebecca Burcher, Prin.
Lay Teachers 5; Students 63.

Kiowa, Barber Co., St. John the Apostle (1885). Attended by Holy Rosary, Medicine Lodge and St. Boniface, Sharon. Rev. Anthony J. Suellentrop.
Res., 920 E. Main St., 67070. Tel: 316-825-4361; Fax: 316-886-5517.
Catechesis/Religious Programs—Tel: 316-825-4836. Linda Forester, D.R.E.
Students 60.

LaCrosse, Rush Co., St. Michael (1911), Rev. Benjamin Martin, Admin.
Res., 918 Lincoln St., P.O. Box 309, 67548. Tel: 913-222-2561. [JC]
Catechesis/Religious Programs—Tel: 913-222-3202. Twila Herman, D.R.E.
Students 113.

Lakin, Kearny Co., St. Anthony (1909), Rev. Gilbert P. Herrman.
Res., 600 Soderberg St., P.O. Box 983, 67860. Tel: 316-355-6405. [JC]
Catechesis/Religious Programs—Tel: 316-355-7119. Delia Stahlecker, D.R.E.
Students 135.

Larned, Pawnee Co., Sacred Heart (1912), Rev. Robert A. Schremmer.
Res., 1111 State St., 67550. Tel: 316-285-2035. [JC]
School—527 W. 12th St., 67550. Tel: 316-285-3025. Diane Dodez, Prin.
Lay Teachers 6; Students 72.
Catechesis/Religious Programs—Students 120.

Leoti, Wichita Co., St. Anthony of Padua (1887), Rev. David A. Flagor.
Res., P.O. Box D, 67861. Tel: 316-779-4431. [CEM]
Catechesis/Religious Programs—Tel: 316-375-2791. Connie Tankersley, D.R.E.
Students 90.

Liberal, Seward Co., St. Anthony (1916), Rev. Henry F. Hildebrandt; Deacon Erasmo Rodriguez.
Res., 419 W. First St., 67901. Tel: 316-624-4135; Fax: 316-624-3553.
Catechesis/Religious Programs—Bob Berry, D.R.E.
Students 256.

Liebenthal, Rush Co., St. Joseph (1905). Attended by St. Michael, LaCrosse. Rev. Benjamin Martin, Admin.
Mailing Address: P.O. Box 98, 67553. Tel: 785-222-3160. [CEM]

Loretto, St. Mary, Help of Christians. Closed. Sacramental records can be found at St. Joseph, Liebenthal.

Marienthal, Wichita Co., St. Mary (1886), Rev. David A. Flagor.
Mailing Address: P.O. Box 7, 67863. Tel: 316-379-4431; Fax: 316-379-4479. [CEM]
Catechesis/Religious Programs—Tel: 316-379-4446. Jolene Berning, D.R.E.
Students 76.

McCracken, Rush Co., St. Mary (1905), Rev. Eugene P. Kenny.
Mailing Address: P.O. Box 157, 67556. Tel: 913-394-2251. [CEM][JC]

Meade, Meade Co., St. John the Baptist (1889), Rev. George E. Mueller; Deacon Dwaine Lampe.
Res., 412 W. Carthage St., P.O. Box 706, 67864. Tel: 316-873-2003. [JC]

Medicine Lodge, Barber Co., Holy Rosary (1952). Attended by St. John the Apostle, Kiowa and St. Boniface, Sharon. Rev. Anthony J. Suellentrop.
Mailing Address: 808 N. Cedar, 67104. Tel: 316-886-3596; Fax: 316-886-5517.
Catechesis/Religious Programs—Tel: 316-886-3171. Jo Boor, D.R.E.
Students 61.

Ness City, Ness Co., Sacred Heart (1912), Rev. Marvin W. Reif.
Res., 606 S. School St., P.O. Box 310, 67560. Tel: 913-798-3195. [CEM]
School—510 S. School St., 67560. Tel: 913-798-3530. Ann Depperschmidt, Prin.
Adorers of the Blood of Christ 2; Lay Teachers 6; Students 65.
Catechesis/Religious Programs—Joby Henning, D.R.E.
Students 79.

North Kinsley, Edwards Co., SS. Peter and Paul. Closed. Sacramental records can be found at St. Nicholas, Kinsley.

Odin, Barton Co., Holy Family (1879), Rev. John J. Maes, V.G.
Mailing Address: c/o St. John the Evangelist Parish, 122 E. 5th St., Hoisington, 67544. [CEM]
Catechesis/Religious Programs—Teresa Hickel, D.R.E.
Students 72.

Offerle, Edwards Co., St. Joseph (1876), Rev. William Vogel.
Mailing Address: P.O. Box 7, 67563. Tel: 316-659-2692. [CEM 2]

Olmitz, Barton Co., St. Ann (1889), Rev. Ultan P. Murphy.
Res., 115 Cleveland St., P.O. Box 8, 67564. Tel: 316-586-3306. [CEM]
Catechesis/Religious Programs—Tel: 316-586-3282. Terese Frieb, D.R.E.
Students 118.

Plains, Meade Co., St. Patrick (1916). Attended by St. John the Baptist, Meade. Rev. George E. Mueller; Deacon Dwaine Lampe.
Res., St. John the Baptist, 412 W. Carthage, P.O. Box 706, Meade, 67864. Tel: 316-873-2003.
Church—601 Superior, P.O. Box 247, 67869. Tel: 316-563-7663. [CEM]
Catechesis/Religious Programs—P.O. Box 102, 67869. Tel: 316-563-9473. Ann Amerin, D.R.E.
Students 80.

Pratt, Pratt Co., Sacred Heart (1887), Rev. James P. Dieker.
Res., 332 N. Oak St., 67124. Tel: 316-672-6352.
School—(Grades PreK-5) 330 N. Oak St., 67124. Tel: 316-672-3687. Mr. Dallas Woolf, Prin.
Lay Teachers 6; Students 60.
Catechesis/Religious Programs—Tel: 316-672-6352. Rita Hitt, D.R.E.
Students 180.

Ransom, Ness Co., St. Aloysius (1903). Attended by Sacred Heart, Ness City. Rev. Marvin W. Reif.
Mailing Address: P.O. Box 96, 67572. Tel: 913-731-2497. [CEM]
Catechesis/Religious Programs—Loretta Flax, D.R.E.
Students 59.

St. John, Stafford Co., St. John the Apostle (1947). Attended by St. Francis Xavier, Steward. Rev. Rene Guesnier, O.S.B.
Res., 609 E. Fourth St., Rte. 2, Box 100, 67576. Tel: 316-549-3538.
Catechesis/Religious Programs—Johnna Stanford, D.R.E.
Students 63.

St. Mary, Hodgeman Co., St. Mary. Closed. Sacramental records can be found at St. John the Baptist, Spearville.

Satanta, Haskell Co., St. Alphonsus (1946), Rev. Emil Dinkel, C.PP.S.
Res., 603 Tecumseh, Box 65, 67870. Tel: 316-649-2692.
Church—601 Tecumseh, 67870.
Catechesis/Religious Programs—Students 88.

Scott City, Scott Co., St. Joseph (1911), Rev. Francis X. Khoi Nguyen.
Res., 1004 Main St., P.O. Box 228, 67871. Tel: 316-872-3644. [JC]
Catechesis/Religious Programs—Tel: 316-872-5405. Marilee Cramer, D.R.E.
Students 193.

Seward, Stafford Co., St. Francis Xavier (1886), Rev. Rene Guesnier, O.S.B.
Mailing Address: 504 Main St., 67576. Tel: 316-458-5691.

Sharon, Barber Co., St. Boniface (1904). Attended by Holy Rosary, Medicine Lodge and St. John the Apostle, Kiowa. Rev. Anthony J. Suellentrop.
Res., 410 N. Main St., P.O. Box 118, 67138. Tel: 316-294-5526; Fax: 316-886-5317. [CEM]
Catechesis/Religious Programs—Tel: 316-294-5566; Fax: 316-886-5517. Marge Rankin, D.R.E.
Students 77.

Spearville, Ford Co., St. John the Baptist (1904), Rev. Michael Helms.
Res., 100 Main St., P.O. Box 187, 67876. Tel: 316-385-2212. [CEM][JC 2]
Catechesis/Religious Programs—Tel: 316-385-2674. Carol Durler, D.R.E.
Students 176.

Syracuse, Hamilton Co., St. Raphael (1906), Rev. Gilbert P. Herrman.
Mailing Address: P.O. Box 731, 67878. Tel: 316-384-7357. [CEM][JC]
Catechesis/Religious Programs—Mary Ann Fair, D.R.E.
Students 70.

Timken, Rush Co., Holy Trinity (1904) (Czech). Attended by St. Ann, Olmitz. Rev. Ultan P. Murphy.
Mailing Address: c/o St. Ann Church, P.O. Box 8, Olmitz, 67564. Tel: 316-586-3306. [CEM]
Catechesis/Religious Programs—Tel: 913-387-2552. Marie Stremel, D.R.E.
Students 49.

Tribune, Greeley Co., St. Joseph (1950). Attended by St. Mary's, Marienthal. Rev. David A. Flagor.
Mailing Address: c/o St. Mary's, P.O. Box 7, Marienthal, 67863. Tel: 316-376-2292.
Catechesis/Religious Programs—Helen Govert, D.R.E.
Students 60.

Ulysses, Grant Co., Mary Queen of Peace (1948) (Hispanic), Rev. John P. Kowal.
Res., 804 N. Colorado, 67880. Tel: 316-356-1532; Fax: 316-424-1065.
Catechesis/Religious Programs—Tel: 316-356-4911. Toney Hernandez, D.R.E.
Students 328.

Windthorst, Ford Co., Immaculate Heart of Mary. Closed. Sacramental records can be found at St. John the Baptist, Spearville.

Wright, Ford Co., St. Andrew (1909), Rev. Brian D. Hipp.
Mailing Address: 10893 St. Andrew Rd., P.O. Box 125, 67882. Tel: 316-227-3363. [CEM]
Parish Center—11792 Jewel Rd., 67882. Tel: 316-225-7345.
Catechesis/Religious Programs—Diane Lix, D.R.E.
Students 69.

On Duty Outside the Diocese:
Reverend Fathers—
Fiedler, Donald J.
Joyce, Thomas J.
Moore, Brian R.

Retired:
Reverend Monsignors—
Leahy, Patrick J., 6900 E. 45th St. N., Wichita, KS 67226
Preisner, A. F., 105 Kent, Dodge City, KS 67801
Stewart, George N., 6900 E. 45th St. N., Wichita, KS 67226. Tel: 316-744-0289
Weller, Arnold J., Manor of the Plains, 200 Campus Dr., HCC 42, Dodge City, KS 67801. Tel: 316-225-1928
Reverend Fathers—
Birzer, W. L., 308 E. Third St., P.O. Box 37, Ellinwood, KS 67526
Dreher, Jacob J., 3706 Meadowlark, Great Bend, KS 67530
Haberthier, John A., 3440 Cottonwood C-9, San Jacinto, CA 92582
Kelly, James, 6900 E. 45th St. N., Apt. D-4, Wichita, KS 67226
Klenke, Elmer A., 205 N. Lakin St., P.O. Box 1213, Lakin, KS 67860-1213
Lavrih, John, 6900 E. 45th St. N., Apt. D-2, Wichita, KS 67226
O'Neill, Rory, 6900 E. 45th St. N., Wichita, KS 67226
Pottorff, Lisle J., Rte. 2, Box 247, Douglass, KS 67039
Tuzicka, Fred M., 2611 27th St., Apt. 3-38, Great Bend, KS 67530
van Sloun, Eugene G., Rijksweg C.10, 6161EE, Geleen, Netherlands
Wylie, Stephen, 6900 E. 45th St. N., Apt. D-3, Wichita, KS 67226

Permanent Deacons:
Crowley, Norman, (Retired)
Lampe, Dwaine, St. Anthony, Fowler
Rodriguez, Erasmo, St. Anthony, Liberal
Rondeau, Richard, St. Bernard, Belpre
Stickney, Harold, (Retired)

INSTITUTIONS LOCATED IN THE DIOCESE

[A] GENERAL HOSPITALS

GARDEN CITY. *St. Catherine Hospital*, 410 E. Walnut, 67846-5672. Tel: 316-272-2222; Fax: 316-272-2566
For a complete listing, refer to the Hospitals section.

GREAT BEND. *Central Kansas Medical Center*, 3515 Broadway, 67530. Tel: 316-792-2511
For a complete listing, refer to the Hospitals section.

LARNED. *Central Kansas Medical Center, St. Joseph Campus*, 923 Carroll St., 67550. Tel: 316-285-3161
For a complete listing, refer to the Hospitals section.

[B] RETREAT CENTERS

GREAT BEND. *Heartland Center for Spirituality*, 3600 Broadway, 67530-3692. Tel: 316-792-1232; Fax: 316-792-1746.
E-mail: ksdom@midusa.net
Retreat Center. Sr. Louise Hageman, O.P., Dir.; Sr. Geraldine Eakes. Total Staff 6.

[C] EDUCATIONAL ENDOWMENT FUNDS

DODGE CITY. *The Sacred Heart School Endowment*, 903 Central, 67801.

ELLINWOOD. *St. Joseph School Education Endowment Fund*, 214 N. Main St., 67526.

GARDEN CITY. *St. Dominic Grade School Endowment Fund*, 615 J.C. St., 67846.
The St. Mary Catholic Education Endowment Fund, 509 St. John St., 67846.

GREAT BEND. *Catholic Social Services Endowment Fund*, 2546 20th St., 67530.
The St. Patrick Grade School Education Endowment Fund, 4100 Broadway, 67530.

The St. Rose of Lima Grade School Education Endowment Fund, 1423 Holland St., Box 1007, 67530.

LARNED. *The Sacred Heart Grade School of Larned Education Endowment Fund*, 527 W. 12th St., 67550.

PRATT. *The Sacred Heart School Education Endowment, Inc.*, 332 N. Oak St., 67124.

[D] CONVENTS AND RESIDENCES FOR SISTERS

GREAT BEND. *Immaculate Conception Convent*, 3600 Broadway, 67530-3692. Tel: 316-792-1232; Fax: 316-792-1746.
E-mail: ksdom@midusa.net
Dominican Sisters of Great Bend. Legal Title: *Immaculate Conception Convent, Motherhouse and Novitiate of the Nuns of the Third Order of St. Dominic*. Sr. Betty Werner, O.P., Prioress; Sr. Peggy Ann Martin, Asst. Prioress. Council Members: Sr. LeAnn Probst, O.P.; Sr. Rita Brizer, O.P.; Sr. Terence Wasinger, O.P. Final Professed Sisters 130; Novices 1; Lay Associates 54.

Great Bend Dominican Sisters Office of Mission and Ministry, 3600 Broadway, 67530-3692. Tel: 316-792-8661. Total in Residence 50. Retreat Center.

[E] SERVICES FOR THE ELDERLY

GREAT BEND. *Cedar Park Place, Inc.*, 3910 Cedar Park Pl., 67530-3692. Tel: 316-793-8115; Fax: 316-792-1746. Low and Middle Income Housing for Elderly and Handicapped.

[F] MISCELLANEOUS

DODGE CITY. *Manna House*, 1012 First, 67801. Tel: 316-227-6707. Margaret Witsken, Exec. Dir. Short-term housing and food distribution for those in need. Total Staff 3; Total Assisted 2,964.

GARDEN CITY. *Catholic Agency-Migration & Refugee Service*, 1510 Taylor Plaza E., 67846. Tel: 316-276-7610; Fax: 316-276-9228. Ms. Levita Rohlman, Exec. Dir. Total Staff 1; Assisted 2,000.

Emmaus House, 802 N. Fifth St., 67846-5638. Tel: 316-275-2008. Special Center for Social Services & Assistance. Mrs. Marjorie R. Williams, Dir. Total Staff 3; Total Assisted 72,291.

GREAT BEND. *Family Crisis Center*, 1300 Kansas, 67530. Tel: 316-793-1965; 1966; 792-1885 (Crisis Line). Patty Linsner, Contact Person. Total Staff 7; Total Assisted 640.

Sommerset Place, 5803 16th Terrace, 67530. 60 Unit Apartment Complex.

RELIGIOUS INSTITUTES OF MEN REPRESENTED IN THE DIOCESE

For further details refer to the corresponding bracketed number in the Religious Institutes of Men or Women section.

[0200]—*Benedictine Monks.*—O.S.B.

[0430]—*Dominican Fathers.*—O.P.

[1060]—*Society of the Precious Blood.* (Kansas City Prov.).—C.PP.S.

RELIGIOUS INSTITUTIONS OF WOMEN REPRESENTED IN THE DIOCESE

[0100]—*Adorers of the Blood of Christ.*—A.S.C.

[]—*Benedictine Sisters of Erie.* (Mt. St. Benedict Monastery).—O.S.B.

[2100]—*Congregation of the Humility of Mary.*—C.H.M.

[1070-24]—*Nuns of the Third Order of St. Dominic.*—O.P.

[1680]—*School Sisters of St. Francis.*—S.S.S.F.

[3830-18]—*Sisters of St. Joseph.*—C.S.J.

NECROLOGY

† Downey, Patrick Michael, Dubuque, KS, St. Catherine. —Died Jan. 1, 1997.

Archdiocese of Dubuque

(Archidioecesis Dubuquensis)

Most Reverend

JEROME HANUS, O.S.B., D.D.

Archbishop of Dubuque; ordained July 30, 1966; appointed Bishop of St. Cloud July 6, 1987; ordained and installed August 24, 1987; appointed Coadjutor Archbishop of Dubuque August 23, 1994; welcomed October 27, 1994; succeeded to the See October 16, 1995. *Office: Box 479, Dubuque, IA, 52004-0479.*

Most Reverend

DANIEL W. KUCERA, O.S.B., PH.D., D.D.

Retired Archbishop of Dubuque; ordained May 26, 1949; appointed Titular Bishop of Natchez and Auxiliary Bishop of Joliet June 6, 1977; ordained Bishop July 21, 1977; appointed Bishop of Salina March 11, 1980; installed May 7, 1980; appointed Archbishop of Dubuque December 20, 1983; installed February 23, 1984; retired October 16, 1995. *13952 E. Marina Dr., #612, Aurora, CO, 80014.*

ESTABLISHED JULY 28, 1837.; CREATED AN ARCHDIOCESE JUNE 15, 1893.

Square Miles 17,403.

PATRONS OF THE ARCHDIOCESE: Primary: St. Raphael, the Archangel; Secondary: St. John Mary Vianney, Cure of Ars.

Corporate Title: "The Archdiocese of Dubuque."

Comprises 30 Counties, that part of the State of Iowa north of the Counties of Polk, Jasper, Poweshiek, Iowa, Johnson, Cedar and Clinton and east of the Counties of Kossuth, Humboldt, Webster and Boone.

For legal titles of parishes and archdiocesan institutions, consult the Chancery.

Chancery-Archdiocesan Center: P.O. Box 479, Dubuque, IA, 52004-0479. Tel.: 319-556-2580; Fax: 319-556-5464.

E-mail address: dbqcco@connectinc.com

STATISTICAL OVERVIEW

Personnel	
Archbishop	1
Retired Archbishops	1
Abbots	1
Retired Abbots	4
Priests: Diocesan Active in Diocese	163
Priests: Active Outside Diocese	6
Priests: Diocesan in Foreign Missions	1
Priests: Retired, Sick or Absent	93
Number of Diocesan Priests	263
Religious Priests in Diocese	36
Extern Priests in Diocese	1
Ordinations:	
Diocesan Priests	4
Transitional Deacons	3
Permanent Deacons	6
Permanent Deacons in Diocese	66
Total Brothers	30
Total Sisters	1,040
Parishes	
Parishes	212
With Resident Pastor:	
Resident Diocesan Priests	128
Resident Religious Priests	1
Without Resident Pastor:	
Administered by Priests	74
Administered by Permanent Deacons	3
Administered by Women Religious	6
Missions	2
Pastoral Centers	1
Closed Parishes	2
Professional Ministry Personnel:	
Brothers	2
Sisters	66
Lay Ministers	491
Welfare	
Catholic Hospitals	6
Total Assisted	880,423
Health Care Centers	3
Total Assisted	374
Homes for the Aged	5
Total Assisted	382
Day Care and Extended Day Care Centers	1
Total Assisted	61
Educational	
Seminaries, Diocesan	1
Students from This Diocese	3
Students from Other Diocese	3
Diocesan Students in Other Seminaries	19
Seminaries, Religious	1
Students Religious	112
Total Seminarians	134
Colleges and Universities	3
Total Students	4,074
High Schools, Diocesan and Parish	8
Total Students	3,181
Elementary Schools, Diocesan and Parish	54
Total Students	12,446
Catechesis/Religious Education:	
High School Students	5,515
Elementary Students	14,932
Total Students Under Catholic Instruction	40,282
Teachers in the Diocese:	
Priests	2
Brothers	1
Sisters	45
Lay Teachers	976
Vital Statistics	
Receptions into the Church:	
Infant Baptism Totals	3,378
Adult Baptism Totals	164
Received into Full Communion	434
First Communions	3,677
Confirmations	2,806
Marriages:	
Catholic	931
Interfaith	658
Total Marriages	1,589
Deaths	2,167
Total Catholic Population	217,856
Total Population	923,000

Former Bishops—Most Rev. MATHIAS LORAS, D.D., cons. Dec. 10, 1837; died Feb. 19, 1858.—Most Rev. CLEMENT SMYTH, O.C.S.O., D.D., cons. May 3, 1857; died Sept. 22, 1865.—Most Rev. JOHN HENNESSY, D.D., First Archbishop, cons. Sept. 30, 1866; raised to the Archiepiscopal Dignity, June 16, 1893; died March 4, 1900.—Most Rev. JOHN J. KEANE, D.D., cons. Bishop of Richmond, Aug. 25, 1878; transferred to the Titular See of Jasso, Aug. 12, 1888; elevated to the Archiepiscopal Dignity with the title of Archbishop of Damascus, Jan. 9, 1897; transferred to the See of Dubuque, July 24, 1900; resigned April 3, 1911; appt. Titular Archbishop of Cios, April 28, 1911; died June 22, 1918.—Most Rev. JAMES JOHN KEANE, D.D., ord. Dec. 23, 1882; cons. Bishop of Cheyenne, Oct. 28, 1902; elevated to the Archiepiscopal Dignity and transferred to Dubuque, Aug. 11, 1911; died Aug. 2, 1929.—Most Rev. FRANCIS J. L. BECKMAN, S.T.D., Titular Archbishop of Phulli; ord. June 20, 1902; appt. Bishop of Lincoln, Dec. 23, 1923; cons. Bishop of Lincoln, May 1, 1924; Apostolic Administrator of Omaha, June 1, 1926 to July 4, 1928; elevated to Archiepiscopal Dignity and transferred to Dubuque, Jan. 17, 1930; appt. Assistant at the Pontifical Throne, April 21, 1928; resigned Nov. 11, 1946; died Oct. 17, 1948.—Most Rev. HENRY P. ROHLMAN, D.D., appt. Bishop of Davenport, May 20, 1927; cons. July 25, 1927; appt. Coadjutor Archbishop of Dubuque "cum jure successionis" and Apostolic Administrator, July 15, 1944; installed Sept. 12, 1944; succeeded to Nov. 11, 1946; named Assistant at Pontifical Throne, Sept. 2, 1950; resigned and named Titular Archbishop of Cotrada, Dec. 2, 1954; died Sept. 13, 1957.—Most Rev. LEO BINZ, D.D., ord. March 15, 1924; appt. Titular Bishop of Pinara, Coadjutor Bishop and Apostolic Administrator of Winona, Nov. 21, 1942; cons. Dec. 21, 1942; named Titular Archbishop of Silyum and Coadjutor to the Archbishop of Dubuque "cum jure successionis," Oct. 15, 1949; named Assistant at the Pontifical Throne, June 11, 1954; Archbishop of Dubuque, Dec. 2, 1954; Pallium conferred, June 12, 1958; appt. Archbishop of St. Paul, Dec. 16, 1961; retired July, 1975; died Oct. 9, 1979.—Most Rev. JAMES J. BYRNE, S.T.D., appt. Titular Bishop of Etenna and Auxiliary Bishop of St. Paul, May 10, 1947; ord. Bishop, July 2, 1947; transferred Boise, ID, June 16, 1956; appt. Archbishop of Dubuque, March 19, 1962; retired Aug. 23, 1983; named Apostolic Administrator; died Aug. 2, 1996.—Most Rev. DANIEL KUCERA, O.S.B., Ph.D., D.D., ord. May 26, 1949; appt. Titular Bishop of Natchez and Auxiliary Bishop of Joliet, June 6, 1977; ord. Bishop, July 21, 1977; appt. Bishop of Salina, KS, March 11, 1980; installed May 7, 1980; named Archbishop of Dubuque, Dec. 20, 1983; installed Feb. 23, 1984; retired Oct. 16, 1995.

Archbishop—Most Rev. JEROME HANUS, O.S.B., *Archdiocesan Center, 1229 Mt. Loretta Ave., P.O. Box 479, Dubuque, 52004-0479.* Tel: 319-556-2580.

Vicar General and Episcopal Vicar for Dubuque Region—Rev. Msgr. DAVID A. WHEELER, J.C.D., *Archdiocesan Center, 1229 Mt. Loretta Ave., P.O. Box 479, Dubuque, 52004-0479.* Tel: 319-556-2580.

Episcopal Vicar for Cedar Rapids Region—Rev. Msgr. JAMES O. BARTA, Ph.D., *P.O. Box 8293, Cedar Rapids, 52408-8293.* Tel: 319-366-1647; Fax: 319-366-0426.

Episcopal Vicar for Waterloo Region—Rev. Msgr. W. DEAN WALZ, J.C.L., *320 Mulberry St., Waterloo, 50703.* Tel: 319-235-5566; Fax: 319-235-5567.

Judicial Vicar—Rev. JOSEPH L. HAUER, J.C.L., *Archdiocesan Center, 1229 Mt. Loretta Ave., P.O. Box 479, Dubuque, 52004-0479.* Tel: 319-556-2580.

Chancellor—Rev. JOSEPH L. HAUER, J.C.L., *Archdiocesan Center, 1229 Mt. Loretta Ave., P.O. Box 479, Dubuque, 52004-0479.* Tel: 319-556-2580.

Finance Officer—RICHARD L. RUNDE, *Archdiocesan Center, 1229 Mt. Loretta Ave., P.O. Box 479, Dubuque, 52004-0479.* Tel: 319-556-2580.

College of Consultors—Most Rev. JEROME HANUS, O.S.B.; Rev. Msgr. W. DEAN WALZ; Rev. Msgr. DAVID A. WHEELER; Rev. Msgr. JAMES O. BARTA; Rev. Msgr. JOSEPH J. SLEPICKA; Rev. DONALD L. KLEIN; Rev. Msgr. WALTER L. BRUNKAN.

Deans—Very Rev. DENNIS R. CAIN, Bellevue; Very Rev. CHARLES E. LANG, Cedar Rapids; Very Rev. GARY F. KRAPFL, Decorah; Very Rev. JOSEPH V. O'BRIEN, Dubuque; Rev. Msgr. NEIL W. TOBIN, Dyersville; Very Rev. FREDERICK C. FANGMANN, Elkader; Very Rev. RALPH P. SIMINGTON, Independence; Very Rev. EVERETT HEMANN, Marshalltown; Rev. Msgr. JOSEPH J. SLEPICKA, Mason City; Very Rev. ROGER R. RETHAMEL, New Hampton; Very Rev. PATRICK G. GEARY, Waterloo; Very Rev. GERALD A. CONDON, Webster City; Rev. Msgr. ROBERT R. VOGL, Loras College.

Archdiocesan Central Offices

Archdiocesan Pastoral Center—Mailing Address: P.O. Box 479, Dubuque, 52004-0479. 1229 Mt. Loretta Ave., Dubuque, 52003-7800. Tel: 319-556-2580; Fax: 319-556-5464. Office Hours: Mon.-Fri. 8:30-4:30; Most Rev. JEROME HANUS, O.S.B.; BETTY SCHUELLER, Sec.; Rev. Msgr. DAVID A. WHEELER, Vicar Gen.; JUDY KLEINSCHMIDT, Sec.; Rev. JOSEPH L. HAUER, Chancellor; BEV RECH, Sec.; Rev. THOMAS E. TOALE, Moderator of the Curia; PHYLLIS BERTHEL, Sec.

Adult Catechesis/Special Needs—Archdiocesan Center, 1229 Mt. Loretta Ave, P.O. Box 479, Dubuque, 52004-0479. Tel: 319-556-2580. Sr. MARCI BLUM, O.S.F., Dir.; NANCY TRUMM, Sec.

Archives—Rev. LORAS OTTING, Dir.; Rev. Msgr. EDGAR J. KURT, Archivist Emeritus; LINDA MATHEWSON, Sec.

Archdiocesan Educational System—

Office of Catholic Schools and Catechetical Services—Rev. THOMAS E. TOALE, Ph.D., Dir., Educational Svcs. & Supt. of Schools; JAMES OSTERBERGER, Dir., Educational Planning and Technology; Sr. NONA MEYERHOFER, O.S.F., M.Ed., Administrative Asst., Boards of Educ.; JOAN MANTERNACH, Curriculum Coord. Secretaries: PHYLLIS BERTHEL; PATSY BURKEN.

Catholic Schools (in addition to the above)—CHERIE CASEY, M.A., Secondary Coord., Dubuque Regl. Dir. of Educational Svcs.; ANNE MCCLAIN, Sec.; Sr. JEAN MARIE BRADY, B.V.M., Cedar Rapids Regl. Dir. of Educational Svcs.; MARY DUSTERHOFT, Sec.; LORETTA RYAN, M.A., Waterloo Regl. Dir. of Educational Svcs. MARY WERNER, Sec.

Catechetical Services (in addition to above)—ROBERT HOFFMAN, D.Min., Dir., Catechetical Svcs.; Assoc. Directors of Catechetical Services: Sr. MILDRED STREIF, R.S.M., Dubuque; JULIE JOHNSON, Cedar Rapids; BETH DERR, Dyersville; Sr. MARGARET ANNE KRAMER P.B.V.M., Waukon; HELEN ENGELKEN, Sec.

Boy Scouts—Rev. LYLE L. WILGENBUSCH, Archdiocesan Chap. & Spiritual Dir., *St. Joseph the Worker, 60 S. Algona St., Dubuque, 52001-5605.* Tel: 319-588-1433.

Campaign for Human Development—JAMES L. YEAST, Dir., *1229 Mt. Loretta Ave., P.O. Box 1309, Dubuque, 52004-1309.* Tel: 319-556-2580; 588-0558. KEN RAHE, Admin. Asst.

Campus Ministry—Rev. JOHN S. HAUGEN, Dir., *St. Stephen the Witness Catholic Student Center, 1019 W. 23rd St., Cedar Falls, 50613-3550.* Tel: 319-266-9863; Fax: 319-266-3706.

Catholic Cemeteries of the Archdiocese of Dubuque—RICHARD L. RUNDE, Dir., Finance Office: *1229 Mt. Loretta Ave., Dubuque, 52003-7800.* Tel: 319-556-2580.

Catholic Charities—

Administrative Offices—JAMES L. YEAST, A.C.S.W., Dir. JUDE PANSINI, Housing Admin. JOE FEATHERSTON, M.A., Dir., Professional Svcs. KEN RAHE, Admin. Asst. Office Secs.: MARTHA DEVEAUX; SUE HIRD, Business Mgr.; CAROL CALLAHAN, Business Office: *1229 Mt. Loretta Ave., P.O. Box 1309, Dubuque, 52004-1309.* Tel: 319-556-2580.

Branch Offices—

Dubuque—JOSEPH FEATHERSTON, Supvr.; JOYCE CONNORS; TOM SHEA; ANGELLA LINK, *P.O. Box 1309, Dubuque, 52004-1309.* Tel: 319-556-2580.

Decorah—DONALD KLAUKE, *P.O. Box 1309, Dubuque, 52004-1309.* Tel: 800-772-2758.

Cedar Rapids—GARY STEJSKAL, Supvr.; CHRISTY JOHNSON; LYN PIOTROWSKI, Sec., *1430 Second Ave. S.E., Cedar Rapids, 52403.* Tel: 319-364-7121.

Ames—JULIA PETERS, *208 Fifth St., Ames, 50010.* Tel: 515-232-7421.

Waterloo—THOMAS FLAHERTY, Supvr.; ORLYN WATHIER; Rev. KENNETH STECHER; MICHELLE SPRIO, Sec., *Kimball Ridge Center, 2101 Kimball Ave., Ste. LL-11, Waterloo, 50702.* Tel: 319-272-2080.

Mason City—THOMAS FLAHERTY, *Will F. Muse Center, 600 First St. N.W., Mason City, 50401.* Tel: 515-424-9683.

Special Programs—

Adoption—NANCY KINLEY, Dubuque Office.

Family Ministry—CHARLOTTE MCCOY, Coord. Tel: 319-556-2580.

Refugee Resettlement—JOE FEATHERSTON, Dubuque Office.

Social Concerns/Parish-Based Social Service—JAMES L. YEAST, Dubuque Office. *Catholic Charities may be telephoned toll-free from anyplace in Iowa: 800-772-2758.*

Communications—Sr. CAROL HOVERMAN, O.S.F., Coord., *Archdiocesan Center, 1229 Mt. Loretta Ave., Dubuque, 52003-7800.* Tel: 319-556-2580. LARRY GAUL, Media Technician.

Continuing Formation of Clergy and Young Priests Program—Rev. DAVID H. O'CONNOR, Dir., *Archdiocesan Center, 1229 Mt. Loretta Ave., Dubuque, 52003-7800.* Tel: 319-556-2580. BEV RECH, Sec.

Council of Catholic Women—Rev. Msgr. W. DEAN WALZ, Moderator; ELSIE DIESEL, Exec. Pres., *1425 US Hwy. 52, Ossian, 52161.* Tel: 319-532-9409. Office: *Archdiocesan Center, 1229 Mt. Loretta Ave., Dubuque, 52003-7800.* Tel: 319-556-2580. Bellevue Deanery: HELEN ZEIMET, Springbrook. Tel: 319-689-4466. Cedar Rapids Deanery: HELEN HANSON, Cedar Rapids. Tel: 319-393-8105. Decorah Deanery: DENISE HAGER, Waukon. Tel: 319-568-4765. Dubuque Deanery: CALLISTA HOPPMAN, Dubuque. Tel: 319-582-8701. Dyersville Deanery: JANAAN KRAUS, Monticello. Tel: 319-465-4699. Elkader Deanery: NEVA FISCHER, Strawberry Point. Tel: 319-933-4957. Independence Deanery: MARY ANN JAEGER, Manchester. Tel: 319-927-4049. Marshalltown Deanery: MARY ANN HUSAK, Toledo. Tel: 515-484-2159. Mason City Deanery: BARBARA WHARAM, Plymouth. Tel: 515-592-5182. New Hampton Deanery: ELEANOR GANSEN, Elma. Tel: 515-393-2137. Waterloo Deanery: JACKIE REITER, LaPorte City. Tel: 319-342-2367. Webster City Deanery: MARY ANN SPITLER, Belmond. Tel: 515-444-4003.

Development Office—PAUL FROMMELT, Dir., *P.O. Box 479, Dubuque, 52004-0479.* Tel: 319-556-2580. LOIS THILMANY, Office Mgr.; LUANN LECONTE, Sec.

Education Resource Center—MARY MESCHER, Dir., *1229 Mt. Loretta Ave., Dubuque, 52003-7800.* Tel: 319-556-2580; 800-876-3546. Media Clerks: KIM FELDMANN; CONNIE MCDERMOTT.

Family Life Office—Rev. MELVIN D. HEMANN, Dir.; GINNY NEUWOHNER, Office Sec., *Archdiocesan Center, 1229 Mt. Loretta Ave., Dubuque, 52003-7800.* Tel: 319-556-2580.

Engaged Encounter—Coords.: JUDY BECK; PAUL BECK, *2485 Maryville Dr., Dubuque, 52001.* Tel: 319-556-1438. BARB LUDESCHER; JACK LUDESCHER, *2780 Andrew Ct., Dubuque, 52001.* Tel: 319-583-7039. Rev. PHIL SCHMITT, Spiritual Advisor, *St. Mark, 415 Main St., Iowa Falls.* Tel: 515-648-9547.

For Registration—Family Life Office, 1229 Mt. Loretta Ave., Dubuque, 52003-7800. Tel: 319-556-2580.

Marriage Encounter—Family Life Office, 1229 Mt. Loretta Ave., Dubuque, 52003-7800. Tel: 319-556-2580.

Marriage Retorno—Dirs.: Deacon MICHAEL OATES; MAUREEN OATES, *127 Kaspend Pl., Cedar Falls, 50613.* Tel: 319-268-0202. For Registration contact—*Family Life Office, 1229 Mt. Loretta Ave., Dubuque, 52003-7800.* Tel: 319-556-2580.

Natural Family Planning—COREY WESTHOFF; MICHELLE WESTHOFF, *1691 300th Ave., Dyersville, 52040.* Tel: 319-875-8363.

NEET Experience—GINNY WEBER, *3477 Kingswood Pl., Waterloo, 50701.* Tel: 319-235-1247. For registration contact—*Family Life Office, 1229 Mt. Loretta Ave., Dubuque, 52003-7800.* Tel: 319-556-2580.

Pre-Cana—Family Life Office, 1229 Mt. Loretta Ave., Dubuque, 52003-7800. Tel: 319-556-2580. AREA I: Dubuque Deanery, SANDY ERNSDORFF, *2085 Hale St., Dubuque, 52001.* Tel: 319-556-2859. AREA II: Dyersville Deanery, Dirs.: JERRY BECKER; CATHY BECKER, *2275 310th Ave., Earlville, 52041.* Tel: 319-875-8656. AREA III: Elkader, New Hampton, Decorah Deaneries, For registration contact—*Family Life Office, 1229 Mt. Loretta Ave., Dubuque, 52003-7800.* Tel: 319-556-2580. AREA IV: Independence & Waterloo Deaneries, For registration contact—*Family Life Office, 1229 Mt. Loretta Ave., Dubuque, 52003-7800.* Tel: 319-556-2580. AREA V: Cedar Rapids Deanery, Dirs.: PAT MURPHY; SANDY MURPHY, *1130 33rd St. S.E., Cedar Rapids, 52403.* Tel: 319-365-9839. AREA VI: Marshalltown & Webster City Deaneries, For registration contact—*Family Life Office, 1229 Mt. Loretta Ave., Dubuque, 52003-7800.* Tel: 319-556-2580. AREA VII: Mason City Deanery, Dirs.: CHUCK COOPER; JENNY COOPER, *710 N. Adams, Mason City, 50401.* Tel: 515-424-6251.

Retrouvaille—Contacts: STEVE LAWSON; MARY LAWSON, *424 Ardmore, Waterloo, 50701.* Tel: 319-232-8475. DICK SMITH; JOYCE SMITH, *420 10th Ave., S.E., Dyersville, 52040.* Tel: 319-875-8791.

Sponsor Couple—Family Life Office, 1229 Mt. Loretta Ave., Dubuque, 52003-7800. Tel: 319-556-2580.

To Trust Again—Family Life Office, 1229 Mt. Loretta Ave., Dubuque, 52003-7800. Tel: 319-556-2580.

Finance Office—RICHARD L. RUNDE, Finance Officer; JULIE KNIPPER, Controller; EDWARD HABERKORN, Financial Svcs. Clerk; JANICE TUEGEL, Accounting Clerk; MARY FLECKENSTEIN, Bookkeeper/Sec., *P.O. Box 479, Dubuque, 52004-0479.* Tel: 319-556-2580.

Health Care—JANINE MARIE IDZIAK, Ph.D., Consultant, *P.O. Box 479, Dubuque, 52004-0479.* Tel: 319-556-2580. NANCY TRUMM, Sec.

Hispanic Ministry—Cedar Rapids: ROSA MARIA SMITH, *866 4th Ave. S.E., Cedar Rapids, 52403.* Tel: 319-362-8689. Dubuque: ROBERTO GUTIERREZ, *1425 Iowa St., Dubuque, 52001-4890.* Tel: 319-584-0640. Marshalltown: Rev. LLOYD PAUL OUDERKIRK; Sr. ANNE MARIE MANTERNACH, O.S.F., *12 W. Linn, Marshalltown, 50158-0642.* Tel: 515-753-7815; Fax: 515-753-7815. Waterloo: Sr. KATHLEEN GRACE, O.S.F., *329 Mulberry St., Waterloo, 50703.* Tel: 319-234-6744. Webster City Deanery: Sr. CAROL BESCH, O.S.F., *13 Second Ave., N.W., Hampton, 50441.* Tel: 515-456-2797.

Holy Childhood, Pontifical Association—Rev. Msgr. ROBERT L. FERRING, Dir., *Archdiocesan Center, 1229 Mt. Loretta Ave., Dubuque, 52003-7800.* Tel: 319-556-2580. NANCY EISBACH, Sec.

Insurance: Property and Liability (Dubuque Archdiocesan Protection Program)—DAVID ROTH, Field Rep., *Archdiocesan Center, 1229 Mt. Loretta Ave., Dubuque, 52003-7800.* Tel: 319-556-2580. PATSY BURKEN, Sec.

Lay Ministry Formation—Sr. CARLA POPES, P.B.V.M., Dir. CAROL RAUSCH, Sec., *Archdiocesan Center, 1229 Mt. Loretta Ave., P.O. Box 479, Dubuque, 52004-0479.* Tel: 319-556-2580.

Legion of Mary—Rev. JOHN R. HUSSMANN, *P.O. Box 479, Dubuque, 52004-0479.* Tel: 319-556-2580.

Metropolitan Tribunal—P.O. Box 479, Dubuque, 52004-0479. Tel: 319-556-2580. (Please send all dispensation requests to the Tribunal.).

Judicial Vicar—Rev. JOSEPH L. HAUER, J.C.L.

Director of the Metropolitan Tribunal—Sr. FRANCINE QUILLIN, P.B.V.M., J.C.L.; CHARLOTTE NEISES, Asst. to the Dir. and Notary.

Defenders of the Bond—Rev. Msgr. RICHARD P. FUNKE, J.C.L.; Rev. DONALD J. PLAMONDON, J.C.L.; Rev. Msgr. DAVID A. WHEELER, J.C.D.

Auditor—Deacon GERALD JORGENSEN, Ph.D.

Judges—Revs. SCOTT E. BULLOCK, J.C.L.; JOSEPH HAUER, J.C.L.; MARK R. NEMMERS; Rev. Msgr. ROBERT L. SPAIGHT, J.C.D.; Rev. Msgr. W. DEAN WALZ, J.C.L.; Rev. THOMAS R. ZINKULA, J.D.; Sr. FRANCINE QUILLEN, P.B.V.M., J.C.L.

Ecclesiastical Attorneys—Rev. Msgr. W. DEAN WALZ, J.C.L.; Rev. Msgr. RICHARD P. FUNKE, J.C.L.; Rev. MARK R. NEMMERS.

Promoter of Justice—Rev. Msgr. DAVID A. WHEELER, J.C.D.

Notary and Office Secretary—THERESA HOUSELOG.

Management Information Services—JEFF WEINBERG, Dir.; PEG HENNAGIR, Sec.

Newspaper "The Witness"—Rev. Msgr. THOMAS J. RALPH, Editor, *Archdiocesan Center, 1229 Mt. Loretta Ave., P.O. Box 917, Dubuque, 52004-0917.* Tel: 319-588-0556. Staff: JUDY BANDY; BRET FEAR; STEVE MCMAHON; BETTY BERRIE, Circulation.

Pastoral Planning Office—Sr. MARY MONTGOMERY, O.P., Dir.; JUDY KLEINSCHMIDT, Sec., *P.O. Box 479, Dubuque, 52004-0479.* Tel: 319-556-2580.

Permanent Diaconate Program—Deacon LEN FROYEN, Dir.; ANETTE MYERS, Sec., *St. Stephen the Witness Student Center, 1019 W. 23rd St., Cedar Falls, 50613.* Tel: 319-266-9863. Asst. Directors: Deacons GERALD JORGENSEN; MICHAEL OATES.

Print Shop—ROBERT GOLDTHORPE, Mgr., *P.O. Box 479, Dubuque, 52004-0479.* Tel: 319-556-2580.

Propagation of the Faith—Rev. Msgr. ROBERT L. FERRING; NANCY EISBACH, Sec., *Archdiocesan Center, 1229 Mt. Loretta Ave., Dubuque, 52003-7800.* Tel: 319-556-2580.

Respect Life Office—JAMES L. YEAST, Dir., Catholic Charities; KEN RAHE, Admin. Asst., *P.O. Box 1309, Dubuque, 52004-1309.* Tel: 319-556-2580; 800-772-2758.

Rural Life Office—DONALD KLAUKE, Archdiocesan Dir.; MARY KLAUKE, Sec., *1229 Mt. Loretta Ave., P.O. Box 479, Dubuque, 52004-0479.* Tel: 319-556-2580.

St. Mary's Home, Inc.—JAMES L. YEAST, A.C.S.W., Dir.; JUDE PANSINI, Admin., *1229 Mt. Loretta Ave., P.O. Box 1309, Dubuque, 52003-7800.* Tel: 319-556-2580.

Saint Raphael Priest Fund Society—Most Rev. JEROME HANUS, O.S.B., Pres.; Rev. Msgr. DAVID A. WHEELER, Vice Pres.; Rev. Msgr. JAMES O. BARTA, Sec. & Treas., *P.O. Box 8293, Cedar Rapids, 52408-8293.* Dirs.: Rev. Msgr. RICHARD P. FUNKE; Rev. Msgr. STANLEY J. HAYEK; Rev. Msgr. JOSEPH P. HERARD; Rev. Msgr. NEIL W. TOBIN; Rev. Msgr. ROBERT G. HOGAN; Very Rev. GARY F. KRAPFL; Very Rev. RALPH P. SIMINGTON; Revs. GERALD A. CONDON; JERRY KOPACEK; KARL L. GLOVIK; CHARLES W. WHALEN.

Seminarians—Revs. JOSEPH L. HAUER, Dir.; SCOTT E. BULLOCK, Assoc. Dir.; BEV RECH, Sec., *1229 Mt. Loretta Ave., Dubuque, 52003-7800.* Tel: 319-556-2580.

Stewardship Program—Rev. Msgr. ROBERT G. HOGAN, Dir., *2310 First Ave. N.E., Cedar Rapids, 52402.* Tel: 319-363-8269.

Vocations—Revs. JOSEPH L. HAUER, Dir., Seminarians; SCOTT E. BULLOCK, Assoc. Dir., Seminarians; Deacon JOHN MCCULLY, Dir.; Revs. DOUGLAS J. LOECKE, Assoc. Dir., Waterloo Region; JON M. SEDA, Assoc. Dir., Cedar Rapids Region; JAMES E. HAYES, Assoc. Dir., Dubuque Region; BEV RECH, Sec., *Archdiocesan Center, 1229 Mt. Loretta Ave., Dubuque, 52003-7800.* Tel: 319-556-2580.

Worship Office—Rev. NEIL J. MANTERNACH, Dir.; THERESA HARVEY, Assoc. Dir., *1229 Mt. Loretta Ave., P.O. Box 479, Dubuque, 52004-0479.* Tel: 319-556-2580. GINNY NEUWOHNER, Sec.

Youth Formation/Young Adult Ministry—BENEDICT WEISSE, Dir.; JUDY ARLEN, Sec., *Archdiocesan Center, 1229 Mt. Loretta Ave., Dubuque, 52003.* Tel: 319-556-2580.

Archdiocesan Boards

Archdiocesan Administrative Board—Most Rev. JEROME HANUS, O.S.B.; Rev. Msgr. DAVID A. WHEELER; Rev. JOSEPH L. HAUER; Sr. MARY MONTGOMERY, O.P.; RICHARD L. RUNDE.

Archdiocesan Advisory Committee of Persons with Disablities—MITZI BAKER; Sr. MARCI BLUM, O.S.F.; BOB BRUNKAN; FRANCES BRUNKAN; Sr. MARGE BURKLE, O.S.F.; MARSHA FISCHER; MICHAEL FISCHER; D. J. JAEGER; KELLY KANE; Rev. JERRY KOPACEK; NANCY KNIPPER; Deacon STEVE MACDONALD; KIM MAJERUS; RUTH PALMER; ANNE SCHMIEDER; KAREL THOME; KEVIN WILLE; LINDA WOODCOCK; JERRY WOODCOCK.

Archdiocesan Board of Education—BRIAN KANE, Pres., Dubuque Deanery; Sr. HELEN NELSON, O.S.F., Vice-Chair; GLENDA NICKOL, Sec., Dyersville Deanery; RANDY BENDER, Bellevue Deanery; CAROL VOLK, Cedar Rapids Deanery; MARY HOLTHAUS, Decorah Deanery; LARRY MURPHY, Elkader Deanery; PATRICIA KAYSER, Independence Deanery; MARGARET BOWMAN, Marshalltown Deanery; MARY KOPACEK, Mason City Deanery. New Hampton Deanery: STEVEN LAURES; PAM POPELKA; DEB BARSCHOW, Waterloo Deanery; CLEONE MENAGE, Webster City Deanery. Appointed by the Archbishop: MATT BRANDES; ROSA MARIA DE FINDLEY; FRANCIS "CHIP" MURRAY; MARTHA NASH. Priest Council Representative: Rev. DONALD P. SCHMITT. Sister Representatives: Sr. THERESE BECK, B.V.M.; Sr. FRANCESCA OLDHAM, R.S.M. Ex-Officio Members: Most Rev. JEROME HANUS, O.S.B.; Rev. Msgr. DAVID A. WHEELER; Rev. Msgr. JAMES O. BARTA; Rev. Msgr. W. DEAN WALZ; Revs. THOMAS E. TOALE; Sr. NONA MEYERHOFER, O.S.F.; ROBERT HOFFMAN.

Archdiocesan Building Commission—Rev. Msgr. JAMES O. BARTA, Chair; RICHARD L. RUNDE, Exec. Sec.; Rev. Msgr. STANLEY HAYEK; Rev. Msgr. ROBERT G. HOGAN; Rev. Msgr. NEIL TOBIN; Rev. JOHN R. GALLAGHER; JAMES HYNES; JOHN D. KILBY; Rev. NEIL J. MANTERNACH; WAYNE SNYDER; LEO THEISEN; JAMES YOUNGBLUT.

Archdiocesan Campaign for Human Development Board of Directors—JAMES YEAST, Chm.; JOANN MILLER; Rev. WILLIAM JOENSEN; HELEN SORENSEN; TOM HOMAN; RANDALL KREIG; ANN MICHALSKI; STEVE HINDMAN; Rev. Msgr. RICHARD FUNKE; COLLEEN MACFARLAND.

Archdiocesan Chemical Dependency Board—Rev. Msgr. ROBERT L. SPAIGHT, Chm.; Revs. DENNIS J. COLTER; PAUL C. MCMANUS; STEVEN J. ROSONKE; CARL L. SCHMITT.

Archdiocesan Church Design/Renovation Commission—Rev. NEIL J. MANTERNACH, Exec. Sec.; PAM JOHNSTON; Rev. DENNIS D. JUHL; Rev. LYLE L. WILGENBUSCH.

Archdiocesan Continuing Formation of Clergy—Rev. DAVID H. O'CONNOR, Chm.; Rev. Msgr. RUSSELL M. BLEICH; Rev. Msgr. JOSEPH P. HERARD; Revs. WALTER J. KLEINFEHN; GARY KRAPFL; MICHAEL J. MESCHER; JAMES SECORA; THOMAS E. TOALE, Ex-Officio; DAVID J. AMBROSY, Liaison to Priests' Council.

Archdiocesan Diaconal Council—Most Rev. JEROME HANUS, O.S.B., Pres.; Deacons MATT BERRY, Chm.; LEN FROYEN, Ph.D., Exec. Sec.

Ames Region—Deacons KEN SIMMONS; IRV VASKE.

Cedar Rapids Region—Deacons BOB HURYCH; ED PANTALONI.

Dubuque Region—Deacons STEVE MACDONALD; BILL BIVER.

Elkader Region—Deacon RICHARD GEHRKE.

Mason City Region—Deacons MATT BERRY; JIM SINNWELL.

Waterloo Region—Deacons JOHN BAKER; JOHN HERMAN.

Appointed—Deacons DARYL FORTIN; MICHAEL OATES; MICHAEL BLOUIN, APC Liaison.

Archdiocesan Due Process Board—REX REYNOLDS, Chair; MIKE BLOUIN; Rev. JOHN FRIEDERICK; Sr. KATHLEEN GRACE, O.S.F.; Rev. JERRY KOPACEK; Bro. BRIAN MCLAUGHLIN, S.V.D.; JOYCE MERRITT; Sr. ELIZABETH PRESSLER, P.B.V.M.; LEO ROLING; JOHN WHALEN.

Archdiocesan Finance Commission—Most Rev. JEROME HANUS, O.S.B., Chm.; RICHARD L. RUNDE, Exec. Sec.; Rev. THOMAS E. TOALE, Recording Sec.; PAUL J. FROMMELT; Rev. Msgr. RICHARD P. FUNKE; Rev. Msgr. ROBERT G. HOGAN; ARTHUR NIXA; ANN OSTERHAUS; ROBERT VERHILLE; DAN WELU.

Archdiocesan Lay Ministry Advisory Board—Deacon DARYL FORTIN; Rev. DENNIS JUHL; JANET O'MEARA; Sr. CARLA POPES, P.B.V.M.; DENNIS RYAN; CATHY SCHMITZ; Deacon KEN SIMMONS; MARTHA SIMMONS; Rev. Msgr. W. DEAN WALZ.

American Martyrs Retreat House Advisory Board—Sr. M. JEANINE KUHN, P.B.V.M, Dir.; ROGER KEUTER, Chm.; JOAN GLAZ, Sec.; BETTIE FERGUSON; EDWARD J. GALLAGHER, JR.; RON LEIBOLD; JANINE WHIPPS; Rev. Msgr. W. DEAN WALZ, Ex-Officio.

Archdiocesan Medical-Moral Commission—JANINE MARIE IDZIAK, Ph.D., Chm.; KEVIN HEALY, M.D.; STEPHEN HOY, M.D.; Rev. WILLIAM JOENSEN; Very Rev. DANIEL A. KRAPFL; Rev. STEPHEN A. LUNDGREN; RICHARD V. MCKAY, M.D.; GERALD ODEFEY, Ph.D.; Sr. DOLORES ULLRICH, O.S.F.; BETTY WEBER, R.N.; RICHARD WHITTY, J.D.

Archdiocesan Pastoral Council—Most Rev. JEROME HANUS, O.S.B., Pres.; CARLOS LEDESMA, Chm.; SANDRA SCOTT, Vice-Chm.; TOM BOCK, Sec.; Sr. MARY MONTGOMERY O.P., Exec. Sec.; Rev. Msgr. DAVID A. WHEELER; Rev. Msgr. JAMES O. BARTA; Rev. Msgr. W. DEAN WALZ; Deacon MICHAEL BLOUIN; PATRICK BYRNE; RAY COLEMAN; Sr. LOUANN DOERING, P.B.V.M.; Sr. MARY LIANA GLYNN, O.P.; Sr. NORMA JEAN HOLTHAUS, O.S.F.; DONNA JORDAN; LUCILLE KRUSE; Sr. KATHRYN LAWLOR, B.V.M.; Rev. DOUGLAS J. LOECKE; THOMAS MCGREAL; NORMA MCDONELL; CHARLES MAZUR; JOYCE MERRITT; Revs. MICHAEL J. MESCHER; TERRENCE RASSMUSSEN, O.F.M.Conv.; RICHARD REDING; JUDY SZUMLAS; PEGGY SWIFT; Dr. LOREN WILL.

Archdiocesan Permanent Diaconate Formation Board—Deacon LEN FROYEN, Chm.; Deacons IRV FROST; GERALD JORGENSEN; MAUREEN OATES; MARY JENNEY; Rev. JOHN S. HAUGEN.

Archdiocesan Personnel Advisory Board—Revs. JOSEPH V. O'BRIEN, Chm.; JAMES L. MILLER, Sec.; Rev. Msgr. RUSSELL M. BLEICH; Revs. MARK OSTERHAUS; WAYNE A. RESSLER.

Archdiocesan Priests' Council—Most Rev. JEROME HANUS, O.S.B., Pres.; Rev. JAMES DUSTER, Chm. Episcopal Vicars: Rev. Msgr. DAVID A. WHEELER; Rev. Msgr. W. DEAN WALZ; Rev. Msgr. JAMES O. BARTA.

Appointed—Rev. Msgr. JOSEPH SLEPICKA; Revs. DONALD BRUGGEMAN; DONALD L. KLEIN.

Age Group Representatives—Age Group 1- Rev. Msgr. ROBERT R. VOGL; Age Group 2- Rev. HERBERT L. TEGELER; Age Group 3- Rev. Msgr. WALTER L. BRUNKAN; Age Group 4- Rev. RICHARD J. AMENT; Age Group 5- Rev. MARK OSTERHAUS.

Religious Priests Representative—Rev. XAVIER DIETER, O.C.S.O.

Deanery Representatives—Bellevue Deanery: Rev. DANIEL J. KNEPPER; Cedar Rapids Deanery: Rev. JAMES J. DUSTER; Decorah Deanery: Rev. LEO P. RILEY; Dubuque Deanery: Rev. LYLE L. WILGENBUSCH, Dyersville Deanery: Rev. LOUIS M. JAEGER; Elkader Deanery: Rev. RICHARD G. GAUL; Independence Deanery: Rev. GABRIEL C. ANDERSON; Loras College Deanery: Rev. DOUGLAS O. WATHIER; Marshalltown Deanery: Rev. RONALD G. FRIEDELL; Mason City Deanery: Rev. STEPHEN L. MEYER; New Hampton Deanery: Rev. JOHN A. MOSER; Waterloo Deanery: Rev. JOHN R. FLAHERTY; Webster City Deanery: Rev. RAY A. BURKLE. Consultors Ex-Officio: Rev. Msgr. WALTER BRUNKAN; Rev. DONALD KLEIN; Rev. Msgr. JOSEPH SLEPICKA.

Archdiocesan Seminary Board—Rev. JOSEPH L. HAUER, Chm.; Revs. SCOTT E. BULLOCK; JOHN GOSSMAN; JAMES E. HAYES; DOUGLAS J. LOECKE; JON M. SEDA; LYLE WILGENBUSCH; Deacon JOHN MCCULLY; Rev. DENNIS J. COLTER, Ex-Officio.

Archdiocesan Worship Commission—Rev. NEIL MANTERNACH, Exec. Sec.; Sr. KATE HENDEL, B.V.M., Chm.; BOB BURKE, Vice Chm.; Revs. ROBERT R. BECK; DAVID M. BECKMAN; EVERETT HEMANN; DANIEL J. KNEPPER; Deacon MICHAEL MOETSCH; CRYSTAL CARUANA-SULLIVAN; LORRAINE LOECHER, O.S.F.; MARY BETH SIEMANN; TERRY SLADE; Sr. BETTY TRANEL, S.Sp.S.

Archdiocesan Young Adult Advisory Board—Rev. JOHN HAUGEN; DAVE HEUPEL; KRISTEN HEUPEL; STEVE HILL; Rev. LOUIS M. JAEGER; AMY KIES; COLLEEN MCENEANY; CHRIS MILLER; JULIE MODDE; JOHN MOSHER; MARCIA REILLY; SUE SCHLADER; BEN WEISSE.

Archdiocesan Youth Commission—BEN WEISSE, Exec. Dir.; DIANE FLAHERTY, Chm.; MATT FELDMANN, Vice Chm. Adult Members: RODNEY BLUML; JOYCE CONNORS; BETH DERR; Rev. CLAYTON LANDHERR; GENE MEALHOW; LYNN MEALHOW; BRENDA MOSHER; JOHN MOSHER; KIM VOGEL. Youth Members: JANA BODENSTEINER; BILL DAVIS; LAURA FARMER; AMY HUINKER; BOBBI ANN RUBA; GINA SCHMIDT; AMBER THIBODEAUX; LAURA PEDERSEN; DENAE WHITE; PETER YURKO; HEATHER ZIMMERMAN.

Catholic Charities and St. Mary's Home Boards of Directors—Most Rev. JEROME HANUS, O.S.B., Pres.; Rev. Msgr. DAVID A. WHEELER, Vice Pres.; JAMES YEAST, Treas.; ALFRED HUGHES, Sec.; JUDY BOWLING; ROBERT BRUNKAN; JEFFREY FITZPATRICK; FRITZ GANSHIRT; ELDON HERRIG; MICHAEL HOUSER; CONNIE MAHONEY; LAWRENCE MCGRATH; LARRY MURPHY; ANNETTE SIMONSON.

CLERGY, PARISHES, MISSIONS AND PAROCHIAL SCHOOLS

CITY OF DUBUQUE
(Dubuque County)

1—ST. RAPHAEL'S CATHEDRAL (1833), Very Rev. Joseph V. O'Brien, Rector; Barbara Gatch, Pastoral Assoc.; Sr. Ruth Jackson, S.V.M., Music Dir. & Liturgist. In res., Rev. James E. Hayes.
Res., 231 Bluff St., 52001-6918. Tel: 319-582-7646. [JC]
Catechesis/Religious Programs—Barbara Gatch, D.R.E.
Students 86.

2—ST. ANTHONY'S (1867), Rev. Eugene C. Kutsch. Pastoral Assocs.: Sr. Anne Sedgwick, O.S.F.; Sr. Barbara Rastatter, P.B.V.M.; Deacon William Mauss.
Res., 1870 St. Ambrose St., 52001-4196. Tel: 319-588-0571. [JC]
Church—1880 St. Ambrose St., 52001.
School—2175 Rosedale, 52001-4147. Tel: 319-556-2820. Lori Apel, Prin.
Lay Teachers 22; Students 395.
Catechesis/Religious Programs—Carol A. Witry, D.R.E.
Students 176.

3—ST. COLUMBKILLE'S (1887), Rev. Msgr. Richard P. Funke; Deacon William Biver; Diane Kramer, Pastoral Assoc. In res., Rev. Ardel H. Barta.
Res., 1240 Rush St., 52003-7598. Tel: 319-583-9117. [JC]
School—1198 Rush St., 52003-7598. Tel: 319-583-3532. Randy Althoff, Prin.
Lay Teachers 21; Students 331.
Catechesis/Religious Programs—Linda Frommelt, D.R.E.
Students 106.

4—ST. MARY'S (1850), Rev. Florian J. Schmidt. In res., Rev. Wilfred W. Schmidt.
Res., 1584 White St., 52001-4905. Tel: 319-582-5469. [JC]
School—St. Mary-St. Patrick Consolidated. See

separate listing under Institutions Located in the Archdiocese for details.
Catechesis/Religious Programs—Patti Steuer, D.R.E.
Students 102.

5—ST. PATRICK'S (1862), Very Rev. Joseph V. O'Brien; Rev. Ardel H. Barta; Deacon Tim LoBianco, Pastoral Admin.
Res., 1425 Iowa St., 52001-4890. Tel: 319-583-9749. [JC]
School—St. Mary-St. Patrick Consolidated. See separate listing under Institutions Located in the Archdiocese for details.
Catechesis/Religious Programs—Patti Steuer, D.R.E.
Students 20.

6—CHURCH OF THE RESURRECTION (1857), Rev. Msgr. Joseph P. Herard; Rev. Clayton R. Landherr; Sr. Eileen Brynda, O.P., Pastoral Assoc.; Deacon Gerald Jorgensen.
Res., 4300 Asbury Rd., 52002-0414. Tel: 319-556-7511. [CEM]
School—Steven P. Cornelius, Prin. Sisters of the Presentation 1; Lay Teachers 21; Students 533.
Catechesis/Religious Programs—Sue Van De Casteele, D.R.E.
Students 374.

7—SACRED HEART (1879), Revs. James T. Chappell; Alexander Wild. In res., Rev. Harold J. Drexler.
Res., 2215 Windsor Ave., 52001-1698. Tel: 319-583-1709. [JC]
School—Holy Trinity-Sacred Heart Consolidated. See separate listing under Institutions Located in the Archdiocese for details.
Catechesis/Religious Programs—Sr. Mary Kivlahan, O.S.F., D.R.E.
Students 67.

8—HOLY GHOST (1896), Revs. Paul J. Otting; Paul C. Baldwin; Sr. Susan Ivis, O.S.F., Pastoral Min.
Res., 2917 Central Ave., 52001-1999. Tel: 319-582-5443. [JC]
School—Carol Streif, Prin. Priests 1; Sisters of St. Francis of the Holy Family 1; Lay Teachers 21; Students 399.
Catechesis/Religious Programs—Joseph N. White, D.R.E.
Students 119.

9—HOLY TRINITY (1910), Rev. Paul L. Weis.
Res., 1700 Lincoln Ave., 52001-2104. Tel: 319-556-0733. [JC]
School—Holy Trinity-Sacred Heart Consolidated. See separate listing under Institutions Located in the Archdiocese for details.
Catechesis/Religious Programs—Sr. Mary Kivlahan, O.S.F., D.R.E.
Students 51.

10—NATIVITY (1923), Revs. Wayne A. Ressler; Francis Bashyam; Deacon David McGhee, Pastoral Assoc.
Office: 1225 Alta Vista St., 52001-4398. Tel: 319-582-1839. [JC]
Res., 1075 University, 52001. Tel: 319-582-1714.
School—Tel: 319-582-7236. Lynn Devaney, Prin. Sisters 1; Lay Teachers 22; Students 415.
Catechesis/Religious Programs—Sr. Beth Kress, P.B.V.M., D.R.E.
Students 118.

11—ST. JOSEPH THE WORKER (1949), Revs. Lyle L. Wilgenbusch; David J. Ambrosy; Deacon Stephen MacDonald.
Res., 90 S. Algona St., 52001-5605. Tel: 319-588-2934. [JC]
Office: 60 S. Algona, 52001-5605. Tel: 319-588-1433.
Church—2001 St. Joseph St., 52001.
School—Tel: 319-588-4194. David J. Clark, Prin. Lay Teachers 25; Students 472.
Catechesis/Religious Programs—Sr. Kathleen Long, O.P., D.R.E.
Students 214.

OUTSIDE THE CITY OF DUBUQUE

Ackley, Franklin Co., St. Mary's (1891), Rev. Rick D. Dagit; Deacon David Jones.
Res., 614 N. Washington St., Eldora, 50627-1257. Tel: 515-847-2406. [CEM]
Church—611 Sherman Ave.
Catechesis/Religious Programs—Kathy Jones, D.R.E.
Students 73.

Allison, Butler Co., Immaculate Conception. Closed. For inquiries for parish records contact St. Mary's, Greene.

Alta Vista, Chickasaw Co., St. Bernard (1897), Very Rev. Roger R. Rethamel.
Res., 203 Seventh St., P.O. Box 38, Elma, 50628-0038. Tel: 515-393-2520. [CEM]
Church—114 E. Washington.
Catechesis/Religious Programs—Irene Huegel, D.R.E.
Students 73.

Ames, Story Co., St. Cecilia (1899), Revs. Terrence Rassmussen, O.F.M.Conv.; Howard Hansen, O.F.M.Conv.; Bro. Randy Kin, O.F.M.Conv., Pastoral Assoc.; Deacons Gary Aitchison; Tom Lang; John McCully; Kenneth Simmons; Richard Tondra.
Res., 2900 Hoover Ave., 50010-4498. Tel: 515-233-3092; Fax: 515-233-6423.
School—Tel: 515-232-5290. Loretta Tracy, Prin. Lay Teachers 14; Students 182.
Catechesis/Religious Programs—Tel: 515-232-5290. Jacek Soroka, D.R.E.
Students 514.

St. Thomas Aquinas Church (and Catholic Student Center) (1947), Revs. Everett Hemann; Jon M. Seda; Deacon Steve VanKerckvoorde. In res., Rev. Msgr. James Supple, (Retired). Campus Ministry: Mr. John Donaghy; Crystal Caruana-Sullivan.
Church—2210 Lincoln Ave., 50014-7184. Tel: 515-292-3810.
Res., 129 Ash, 50014-7125. Tel: 515-292-1192.
Catechesis/Religious Programs—Mary Ricke, D.R.E.
Students 221.

Anamosa, Jones Co., St. Patrick's (1861), Very Rev. Charles E. Lang; Rev. James J. Duster; Sr. Patricia McNamara, B.V.M., Pastoral Admin.; Regina Bonifazi, Pastoral Assoc.
Res., 215 N. Garnavillo St., 52205-1122. Tel: 319-462-2141. [CEM]
School—Tel: 319-462-2688. Linda Vaughn, Prin. & D.R.E.
Brothers 1; Lay Teachers 9; Students 103.
Catechesis/Religious Programs—Students 139.
Oratory—Stone City, St. Joseph. Sacramental Records are located at St Patrick's, Anamosa.

Andrew, Jackson Co., St. John (1914), Rev. Dwayne J. Thoman.
Res. and Mailing Address—St. John Rectory, 507 Elm St., P.O. Box 26, Lamonte, 52054-0026. Tel: 319-773-2323.
Church—204 Main St. [CEM]
Catechesis/Religious Programs—Phyllis Gerlach, D.R.E.
Students 65.

Balltown, Dubuque Co., St. Francis of Assisi (1891), Rev. Melvin D. Hemann; Sr. Mildred Leuenberger, O.S.F., Pastoral Admin.
Res. and Mailing Address—5131 Sherrill Rd., Sherrill, 52073-9612. Tel: 319-552-2611.
Church—468 Balltown Rd. [CEM]
School—Balltown-Sherrill Consolidated School. See separate listing under Institutions Located in the Archdiocese for details.
Catechesis/Religious Programs—Mary Anne Manternach, D.R.E.
Students 20.

Bankston, Dubuque Co., St. Clement's (1859), Rev. Linus E. Rasing.
Res., 24287 New Vienna Rd., P.O. Box 283, Epworth, 52045-0283. Tel: 319-744-3314. [CEM]
School—Seton Catholic Elementary School, Epworth. See separate listing under Institutions Located in the Archdiocese for details.
Catechesis/Religious Programs—Betty Pins, D.R.E.
Students 72.

Barclay, Blackhawk Co., St. Francis (1862), Rev. Donald P. Schmitt.
Res., 7837 E. Airline Hwy., Dunkerton, 50626-9715. Tel: 319-822-4614. [CEM]
Catechesis/Religious Programs—D.R.E.: Margaret Miller; Debra Thurman.
Students 88.

Belle Plaine, Benton Co., St. Michael (1885), Very Rev. Charles E. Lang; Rev. Steven G. O'Brien; Deacon J.C. Otto, Pastoral Admin.
Mailing Address: 1304 Ninth Ave., 52208-1614. Tel: 319-444-3106; Fax: 319-444-3734.
Catechesis/Religious Programs—Sandy Wedmore, D.R.E.
Students 147.

Bellevue, Jackson Co., St. Joseph's (1841), Rev. Daniel J. Knepper. In res., Rev. Msgr. Ernest P. Ament.
Res., 405 Franklin St., 52031-1596. Tel: 319-872-3234. [CEM]
School—Bellevue Area Catholic Elementary School. See separate listing under Institutions Located in the Archdiocese for details.
Catechesis/Religious Programs—Bro. Stephen Markham, F.S.M., D.R.E.
Students 157.

Belmond, Wright Co., St. Francis Xavier (1870), Rev. John C. Paisley; Deacon Nick Schmit.
Res., 1207 Third St. N.E., 50421-1608. Tel: 515-444-3249. [CEM]
Catechesis/Religious Programs—Julie M. Jonas, D.R.E.
Students 106.

Blairstown, Benton Co., St. John (1948), Rev. Louis C. Zee; Sr. Nora Rochford, O.S.F., Pastoral Assoc.; Deacon James Naso.
Mailing Address: 105 West St. N.W., 52209-0340. Tel: 319-454-6431.
Res., 405 4th Ave., Van Horne, 52346-0250.
Catechesis/Religious Programs—Patricia Angerman, D.R.E.
Students 62.

Blessing, Blackhawk Co., Immaculate Conception (1875), Revs. Lloyd Reuter; Paul C. McManus.
Res. and Mailing Address—1435 E. Eagle Rd., R.R. 4, Waterloo, 50701-9447. Tel: 319-342-2481.
Church—14004 S. Hudson Rd. [CEM]
Catechesis/Religious Programs—Rita Schmidt, D.R.E.
Students 65.

Bluffton, Winneshiek Co., St. Bridget (1858), Rev. Michael L. Tauke; Sr. Mary Hargrafen, O.S.F., Pastoral Assoc.
Res. and Mailing Address—116 Third St. E., Cresco, 52136. Tel: 319-547-3243.
Church—3094 253 Ave., Ridgeway. [CEM]
Catechesis/Religious Programs—Marie O'Shea, D.R.E.
Students 38.

Britt, Hancock Co., St. Patrick's (1880), Rev. Marvin J. Bries.
Res., 139 Third St. S.E., 50423-1726. Tel: 515-843-3215. [CEM]
Church—335 First Ave. S.E.
Catechesis/Religious Programs—Kathryn Smith, D.R.E.
Students 122.

Buffalo Center, Winnebago Co., St. Patrick's (1899), Rev. Craig E. Steimel; Sr. M. Dolores Moes, P.B.V.M., Pastoral Assoc.
Res. and Mailing Address—St. James Rectory, Bancroft Rd., P.O. Box 310, Forest City, 50436-0310. Tel: 515-582-4856.
Church—115 5th Ave. N.W.
Catechesis/Religious Programs—Jody Smith, D.R.E.
Students 47.

Calmar, Winneshiek Co., St. Aloysius (1875), Rev. Donald J. Hawes.
Res., 304 S. Maryville, P.O. Box 819, 52132-0819. Tel: 319-562-3603. [CEM]
School—Calmar-Festina-Spillville (CFS) Catholic Elementary School. See separate listing under Institutions Located in the Archdiocese for details.
Catechesis/Religious Programs—Jenn Shimek, D.R.E.
Students 103.

Cascade, Dubuque Co., St. Matthias, Rev. Daniel J. Krapfl; Deacon Joseph D. Hayes; Sr. Marlene McDonnell, S.F.C.C., Pastoral Assoc.
Res., 206 Grant St. S.W., P.O. Box 699, 52033-0699. Tel: 319-852-3524. [CEM]
School—Aquin Educational System. See separate listing under Institutions Located in the Archdiocese for details.
Catechesis/Religious Programs—D.R.E.: Joann Harry; Lindan Laban.
Students 177.

Castle Grove, Jones Co., Immaculate Conception (1877), Rev. Msgr. Neil W. Tobin; Sr. M. Damian O'Brien, P.B.V.M., Pastoral Assoc.
Mailing Address: 22178 County Rd. D-62, Monticello, 52310-7827. Tel: 319-465-5570.
Res., Sacred Heart, 328 N. Sycamore St., Monticello, 52310. Tel: 319-465-5944. [CEM]
Catechesis/Religious Programs—Sr. M. Damian O'Brien, P.B.V.M., D.R.E.
Students 22.

Cedar Falls, Blackhawk Co., St. Patrick (1855), Rev. James L. Secora; Deacons Michael Oates; Daryl Fortin; Michael Moetsch.
Res., 122 W. Seventh St., 50613-2902. Tel: 319-266-3523. [CEM]
School—Tel: 319-277-6781. Sr. Mary Louise Scieszinski, P.B.V.M., Prin.
Sisters 2; Lay Teachers 21; Students 384.
Catechesis/Religious Programs—D.R.E.: Marie Lemka; Jean Ripplinger.
Students 399.

Cedar Rapids, Linn Co.,

1—IMMACULATE CONCEPTION, (1858), Rev. Karl L. Glovik. Pastoral Assoc.: Deacon Gerald D. Pettit; Mary Ann McEniry. In res., Revs. Steven G. O'Brien; Valerian Gonsalves, O.S.B.
Res., 857 Third Ave. S.E., Box 1247, 52406-1247. Tel: 319-362-7181. [JC]
Catechesis/Religious Programs—Mary Ann McEniry, D.R.E.
Students 36.

2—ALL SAINTS, (1947), Very Rev. Charles E. Lang; Rev. James L. Blocklinger; Deacon Mike Blouin.
Res., 720 29th St. S.E., 52403-3099. Tel: 319-363-6130; Fax: 319-363-9547. [JC]

School—Tel: 319-363-4110. Cindy Machado, Prin. Sisters 1; Lay Teachers 24; Students 394.
Catechesis/Religious Programs—Elaine Collins, D.R.E.
Students 223.

3—St. Jude, (1962), Revs. Donald R. Bruggeman; Dennis J. Quint; Mark McDermott, Pastoral Assoc.
Res., 3601 First Ave. S.W., 52405. Tel: 319-396-8827. [JC]
Church and Office—50 Edgewood Rd. N.W., 52405-4539. Tel: 319-396-3520.
School—Holy Family Consolidated Catholic School. See separate listing under Institutions Located in the Archdiocese.
Catechesis/Religious Programs—D.R.E.: Mary Beth Siemann; Diane Morse.
Students 348.

4—St. Ludmila's, (1922), Rev. Harry A. Koelker; Deacons Richard Manning; James Berger.
Res., 2107 J St. S.W., 52404-3615. Tel: 319-362-7282. [JC]
Church—211 21st Ave. S.W.
School—Holy Family Consolidated Catholic School.
Catechesis/Religious Programs—Sue Berger, D.R.E.
Students 176.

5—St. Matthew's, (1922), Rev. Msgr. Robert G. Hogan; Roseann Wiley, Pastoral Assoc.; Deacon Phil Saunders.
Res., 2310 First Ave. N.E., 52402-4999. Tel: 319-363-8269; Fax: 319-362-8260. [JC]
School—Tel: 319-362-3021. Joe Wolf, Prin.
Lay Teachers 21; Students 302.
Catechesis/Religious Programs—Betsy Schmuck, D.R.E.
Students 201.

6—St. Patrick's, (1886), Rev. Steven J. Rosonke; Sr. Lucy Kurt, O.S.F., Pastoral Assoc.; Deacon Daniel Hoeger.
Parish Office: 516 A Ave. N.W., 52405-3935. Tel: 319-362-7966; 366-5369. [JC]
Catechesis/Religious Programs—Unita Schliemann, D.R.E.
Students 95.

7—St. Pius X, (1959), Revs. Donald L. Klein; Philip G. Gibbs; Deacons Albert Scharosch; Paul Zimmerman. Pastoral Assocs.: Sr. Karen Lueck, F.S.P.A.; Sr. Eileen Schoehnerr, O.S.F.
Office: 4949 Council St. N.E., 52402-2492. Tel: 319-393-4445; Fax: 319-393-9424. [JC]
School—Tel: 319-393-4507. Candace Kent, Prin.
Lay Teachers 25; Students 444.
Catechesis/Religious Programs—D.R.E.: Julie Johnson; Liz Pollard.
Students 425.

8—St. Wenceslaus, (1874), Rev. Karl L. Glovik; Sr. Rosemary Riesberg, F.S.P.A., Pastoral Assoc.; Deacon William Cisler.
Mailing Address: 510 16th Ave. S.E., 52401-2697. Tel: 319-362-8061. [JC]
Catechesis/Religious Programs—Sr. Rosemary Riesberg, F.S.P.A., D.R.E.
Students 39.

Central City, Linn Co., St. Stephen's (1932), Rev. Richard J. Ament; Sr. Anne Kisting, O.S.F., Pastoral Assoc.
Res. and Mailing Address—410 Terrace Dr., P.O. Box S, 52214-0420. Tel: 319-438-6625.
Catechesis/Religious Programs—Monica Carpenter, D.R.E.
Students 126.

Charles City, Floyd Co., Immaculate Conception (1857), Rev. Msgr. Stanley J. Hayek; Sr. M. Jennifer Rausch, P.B.V.M., Pastoral Assoc.; Deacon James Sinnwell.
Res., 106 Chapel Ln., 50616-2898. Tel: 515-228-1071. [CEM]
School—Tel: 515-228-1225. Sr. M. Dianne Michels, P.B.V.M., Prin.
Sisters of the Presentation 2; Lay Teachers 16; Students 235.
Catechesis/Religious Programs—Patricia Rottinghaus, D.R.E.
Students 260.

Chelsea, Tama Co., St. Joseph's (1867), Very Rev. Charles E. Lang; Rev. Steven G. O'Brien; Deacon J.C. Otto, Pastoral Admin.
Mailing Address: 1304 9th Ave., Belle Plaine, 52208-1614. Tel: 319-444-3106.
Church—307 Station St., 52215-0098. [CEM]
Catechesis/Religious Programs—Skip Ledvina, D.R.E.
Students 52.

Cherry Mound, Allamakee Co., St. Pius (1863), Rev. Robert J. Levenhagen.
Res. and Mailing Address—St. Mary's Rectory, 311 7th St., McGregor, 52157-9999. Tel: 319-873-2287. [CEM]
Religious Education Office: 699 State Forest Rd., Harper's Ferry, 52146.
Catechesis/Religious Programs—Mary Ann Kelly, D.R.E.
Students 64.

Chester, Howard Co., St. Stephen's (1916), Rev. John A. Moser.
Res. and Mailing Address—Our Lady of Lourdes Rectory, P.O. Box 146, Riceville, 50466-0146. Tel: 515-985-2028.
Church—408 Main St.
Catechesis/Religious Programs—Debra Meyer, D.R.E.
Students 35.

Clarion, Wright Co., St. John's (1883), Rev. Wayne J. Droessler; Deacon Michael Whitters; Sr. Mary K. Doughan, R.S.M., Pastoral Assoc.
Mailing Address: P.O. Box 26, 50525-0026. Tel: 515-532-3586. [CEM]
Res., Sacred Heart, 204 S. Jackson, Eagle Grove, 50533. Tel: 515-448-4765.
Catechesis/Religious Programs—Sue Moss, D.R.E.
Students 115.

Clear Lake, Cerro Gordo Co., St. Patrick's (1901), Rev. Msgr. Joseph J. Slepicka; Deacon Leo W. Stattelman.
Res., 1001 Ninth Ave. S., 50428-2615. Tel: 515-357-3214.
Catechesis/Religious Programs—D.R.E.: Christine Carrier; Virginia Copas; Delores Orozco.
Students 160.

Clermont, Fayette Co., St. Peter's (1855), Rev. Leo P. Riley.
Mailing Address: 608 Larrabee, 52135-0025. Tel: 319-423-7293.
Res., St. Bridget, 135 W. Williams, P.O. Box 369, Postville, 52162. Tel: 319-864-3138. [CEM]
Catechesis/Religious Programs—Mary Olson, D.R.E.
Students 105.

Clutier, Tama Co., Immaculate Conception (1900), Rev. John R. Tilp.
Res. and Mailing Address—1102 Walnut St., Traer, 50675. Tel: 319-478-2222.
Church—501 5th St. [CEM]
Catechesis/Religious Programs—Jane Svoboda, D.R.E.
Students 62.
Oratory—Carroll Township, St. Wenceslaus. Sacramental Records are located at Immaculate Conception, Clutier.

Coggon, Linn Co., St. John the Evangelist (1912), Rev. Richard J. Ament; Sr. Anne Kisting, O.S.F., Pastoral Assoc.
Mailing Address: P.O. Box 47, 52218-0047. Tel: 319-435-2236. [CEM]
Res., 410 Terrace Dr., Central City, 52214. Tel: 319-438-6625.
Church—211 Third St. N., 52218.
Catechesis/Religious Programs—Pamela Klima, D.R.E.
Students 37.

Colesburg, Delaware Co., St. Patrick's (1862), Rev. John J. Friederick.
Res., St. Mark Rectory, 205 S. Locust, P.O. Box 345, Edgewood, 52042-0345. Tel: 319-928-7200. [CEM]
Church—Delaware St.
Catechesis/Religious Programs—D.R.E.: Gene Kruse; Ramona Engelken.
Students 101.

Colo, Story Co., St. Mary's, Rev. John M. Herzog; Sr. Jeanne Marie Roche, R.S.M., Pastoral Assoc.
Res., 410 Bailey, P.O. Box 236, 50056-0236. Tel: 515-377-2710. [CEM]
Church—422 Fourth St.

Corwith, Hancock Co., St. Mary's (1912), Rev. Marvin J. Bries.
Mailing Address: 139 Third St. S.E., Britt, 50423. Tel: 515-843-3215. [CEM]
Church—404 Wayne St.
Catechesis/Religious Programs—Judy Weber, D.R.E.
Students 15.

Cresco, Howard Co., Assumption of the Blessed Virgin Mary (1858), Rev. Michael L. Tauke; Sr. Mary Hargrafen, O.S.F., Pastoral Assoc.
Office: 116 Third St. E., Box 198, Crecso, 52136-1699. Tel: 319-547-3243.
Res., 221 Third Ave. W., 52136. Tel: 319-547-5826. [JC]
Church—229 Third Ave. W.
School—Notre Dame System of Education. See separate listing under Institutions Located in the Archdiocese for details.
Catechesis/Religious Programs—Bruce Kingsley, D.R.E.
Students 314.

St. Joseph's (1870), Rev. Michael L. Tauke; Sr. Mary Hargrafen, O.S.F., Pastoral Assoc.
Office: 116 Third St. E., Box 198, 52136-1699. Tel: 319-547-5826.
Res., 221 Third St. W., 52136. Tel: 319-547-5826. [JC]
Church—223 Second Ave. E.
School—Notre Dame System of Education. See separate listing under Institutions Located in the Archdiocese for details.
Catechesis/Religious Programs—Bruce Kingsley, D.R.E.
Students 314.
Oratory—Plymouth Rock, St. Agnes. Sacramental Records at Assumption Parish, Cresco.

Decorah, Winneshiek Co., St. Benedict's (1864), Very Rev. Gary Krapfl. In res., Rev. John F. McTarsney.
Res., 307 W. Main St., 52101-1778. Tel: 319-382-9631. [CEM]
School—Tel: 319-382-4668. Sr. Francesca Oldham, R.S.M., Prin.
Sisters of Mercy 2; Lay Teachers 14; Students 178.
Catechesis/Religious Programs—Colleen Wetli, D.R.E.
Students 371.

Delhi, Delaware Co., St. John's (1872), Rev. John R. Kremer.
Res., 307 South St., 52223-0187. Tel: 319-922-2251. [CEM]
Catechesis/Religious Programs—D.R.E.: Marilyn Wilson; Lynn Lechtenberg.
Students 159.

Dike, Grundy Co., St. Mary (1880), Rev. Kenneth C. Stecher.
Res. and Mailing Address—702 Grant St., P.O. Box E, Parkersburg, 50665. Tel: 319-346-1411.
Church—680 Main St. [CEM]
Catechesis/Religious Programs—Elaine Folkerts, D.R.E.
Students 38.

Dorchester, Allamakee Co., St. Mary's (1865), Rev. Henry W. Charipar; Sr. Erma Rottinghaus, O.S.F., Pastoral Assoc.
Mailing Address: P.O. Box 21, 52140-0021. Tel: 319-497-3332. [CEM]
Church—590 Waterloo Creek Rd., Dorcester.
Catechesis/Religious Programs—Sr. Erma Rottinghaus, D.R.E.
Students 58.

Dougherty, Cerro Gordo Co., St. Patrick's (1870), Rev. Stephen L. Meyer; Deacon Victor Groh.
Mailing Address: P.O. Box 208, 50433-0208.
Church—410 Patrick St., Dougherty, 50433.
Res., Sacred Heart Rectory, P.O. Box 30, 305 Elm St. E., Rockwell, 50469-0030. Tel: 515-822-4957. [CEM]
Catechesis/Religious Programs—Dolores Marzen, D.R.E.
Students 67.

Dumont, Butler Co., St. Francis (1890), Very Rev. Gerald A. Condon.
Res. and Mailing Address—St. Patrick, 1405 N. Federal St., Hampton, 50441-1005. Tel: 515-456-4857; 456-3406.
Church—720 Pine St., 50625.
Catechesis/Religious Programs—Judy Nelson, D.R.E.
Students 21.

Duncan, Hancock Co., St. Wenceslaus (1900), Rev. John W. Hemann.
Res. and Mailing Address—St. Bonafice Rectory, 660 Bush Ave., Garner, 50438-1513. Tel: 515-923-2329.
Church—2343 Navy Ave. [CEM]
Catechesis/Religious Programs—Esther Hadacek, D.R.E.
Students 50.

Dyersville, Dubuque Co., Basilica of St. Francis Xavier (1859), Revs. Edward C. Petty; Ray E. Atwood. Pastoral Assocs.: Sr. Mary Clare Miller, O.S.F.; Sr. Marian Einck, O.S.F.
Res., 104 Third St. S.W., 52040-1696. Tel: 319-875-7325. [CEM]
School—Tel: 319-875-7376. Ralph Pauly, Prin.
Sisters of St. Francis of the Holy Family 3; Lay Teachers 20; Students 324.
Catechesis/Religious Programs—D.R.E.: John F.E. Steger; Jennifer Rahe.
Students 165.

Dysart, Tama Co., St. Joseph (1878), Rev. Joseph E. McGuire.
Mailing Address: 2200 S. Second Ave., Vinton, 52349. Tel: 319-472-4448. [CEM]
Church—101 Clark St.
Catechesis/Religious Programs—Lynn McGivern, D.R.E.
Students 61.

Eagle Center, Blackhawk Co., St. Mary of Mt. Carmel (1859), Rev. Lloyd E. Reuter.
Mailing Address: 1435 E. Eagle Rd., Waterloo, 50701-9447. Tel: 319-342-2481. [CEM]
Catechesis/Religious Programs—Sr. Betty Tranel, S.Sp.S., D.R.E.
Students 119.

Eagle Grove, Wright Co., Sacred Heart (1882), Rev. Wayne J. Droessler; Louise Russell, Pastoral Assoc.
Res., 204 S. Jackson St., 50533. Tel: 515-448-4765. [CEM]
Catechesis/Religious Programs—Jacquelyn Zigrang, D.R.E.
Students 129.

Earlville, Delaware Co., St. Joseph's (1887), Rev. Frank M. Benda; Sr. Lenore Gardner, R.S.M., Pastoral Assoc.; Deacon James Steger.
Res. and Mailing Address—P.O. Box 187, 52041-0187. Tel: 319-923-3135. [CEM]
School—Sandra Klaus, Prin. Lay Teachers 9; Students 78.
Catechesis/Religious Programs—Joan Steger, D.R.E.
Students 102.

Edgewood, Delaware Co., St. Mark's (1916), Rev. John J. Friederick.
Res., 205 S. Locust St., P.O. Box 365, 52042-0365. Tel: 319-928-6938; 928-7200. [CEM]
Catechesis/Religious Programs—Judith Kintzle, D.R.E.
Students 163.

Eldora, Hardin Co., St. Mary's (1868), Rev. Rick D. Dagit; Deacon Wayne Cashatt.
Res., 614 Washington St., 50627-1257. Tel: 515-858-5666. [CEM]
Catechesis/Religious Programs—Mary Reece, D.R.E.
Students 90.

Elkader, Clayton Co., St. Joseph's (1844), Rev. Paul R. Peters; Sr. Rosanna Gleason, O.P., Pastoral Assoc.
Res., 330 First St., 52043. Tel: 319-245-2548. [CEM]
Catechesis/Religious Programs—D.R.E.: Patty Engelhardt; Kathy Schutte.
Students 158.
Oratory—Wadena, St. Joseph. Sacramental Records at St. Joseph, Elkader.

Elma, Howard Co., Immaculate Conception (1887), Very Rev. Roger R. Rethamel; Betty Boehmer, Pastoral Assoc.
Res., 203 Seventh St., P.O. Box 38, 50628-0038. Tel: 515-393-2520. [CEM]
Catechesis/Religious Programs—Eleanor Burke, D.R.E.
Students 110.

Epworth, Dubuque Co., St. Patrick's (1879), Rev. Louis M. Jaeger; Deacon James Kean.
Res., 104 First St. S.E., P.O. Box 286, 52045-0286. Tel: 319-876-5540. [CEM]
School—Seton Catholic Elementary School, Epworth. See separate listing under Institutions Located in the Archdiocese for details.
Catechesis/Religious Programs—D.R.E.: Lori Kramer; Diane McDermott.
Students 68.

Evansdale, Blackhawk Co., St. Nicholas (1951), Rev. Msgr. Cletus J. Hawes; Deacon William Jenney.
Res., 443 S. Roosevelt Rd., 50707-1259. Tel: 319-232-9737. [JC]
School—St. John-St. Nicholas Consolidated. See St. John, Waterloo for details.
Catechesis/Religious Programs—Dave Cushing, D.R.E.
Students 58.

Fairbank, Buchanan Co., Immaculate Conception (1858), Rev. Mark J. McGovern.
Res., 302 W. Main St., P.O. Box 505, 50629-0505. Tel: 319-635-2211. [CEM]
Catechesis/Religious Programs—Kim Weepie, D.R.E.
Students 217.

Fairfax, Linn Co., St. Patrick's (1875), Rev. Thomas J. Schwinn; Sr. Sheila Fitzgerald, O.P., Pastoral Assoc.; Deacon John Malone.
Parish Office: 620 Church St., P.O. Box 219, 52228-0219. Tel: 319-846-2025.
Church—324 Church St., 52228. [CEM]
Catechesis/Religious Programs—Betty Regan, D.R.E.
Students 137.

Farley, Dubuque Co., St. Joseph's (1914), Rev. John P. Ptacek.
Res., 204 Second Ave. S.E., P.O. Box 67, 52046-0067. Tel: 319-744-3715. [CEM]
School—Seton Catholic Elementary School, Epworth. See separate listing under Institutions Located in the Archdiocese for details.
Catechesis/Religious Programs—D.R.E.: Joanne Dardis; Deb Jasper; Monica Lynch.
Students 265.

Fayette, Fayette Co., St. Francis of Assisi (1879), Rev. Dale J. Rausch.
Mailing Address: P.O. Box 276, 52142-3184. Tel: 319-425-3228.
Res., 128 N. Walnut St., West Union, 52175-1347. Tel: 319-422-3184. [CEM]
Church—205 Lovers Ln.
Catechesis/Religious Programs—Holly Streeter, D.R.E.
Students 105.

Festina, Winneshiek Co., Our Lady of Seven Dolors (1843), Rev. Richard W. Kuhn.
Mailing Address: 2348 Co. Rd. B 3, 52144-7701. Tel: 319-532-9366. [CEM]
School—Calmar-Festina-Spillville (CFS) Elementary. See separate listing under Institutions Located in the Archdiocese for details.

Fillmore, Dubuque Co., Sacred Heart (1890), Rev. Neil J. Manternach.
Res., 19661 Sacred Heart Ln., Bernard, 52032-9722. Tel: 319-879-3103. [CEM]
School—Aquin Elementary School. See separate listing under Institutions Located in the Archdiocese for details.

Forest City, Winnebago Co., St. James (1870), Rev. Craig E. Steimel; Sr. Mary Dolores Moes, P.B.V.M., Pastoral Assoc.
Res., 906 W. O St., P.O. Box 310, 50436-0310. Tel: 515-582-4856. [CEM]
Catechesis/Religious Programs—Rita Kleemeier, D.R.E.
Students 147.

Fort Atkinson, Winneshiek Co., St. John Nepomucene's (1875), Rev. Allen M. Schmitt.
Res., 202 Second St. S.E., 52144-0157. Tel: 319-534-7298. [CEM]
School—Trinity Catholic School, Protivin. See separate listing under Institutions Located in the Archdiocese for details.

Garber, Clayton Co., St. Michael's (1917), Rev. Richard G. Gaul.
Res. and Mailing Address—402 S. Washington, P.O. Box 7, Garnavillo, 52049-0007. Tel: 319-964-2168.
Church—800 Main. [CEM]
Catechesis/Religious Programs—Ann Armstrong, D.R.E.
Students 30.

Garnavillo, Clayton Co., St. Joseph's (1846), Rev. Richard G. Gaul.
Res., 402 S. Washington St., P.O. Box 7, 52049-0007. Tel: 319-964-2168. [CEM]
Church—204 W. Oak St.
Catechesis/Religious Programs—Darlene Wille, D.R.E.
Students 88.

Garner, Hancock Co., St. Boniface (1883), Rev. John W. Hemann.
Res., 660 Bush Ave., 50438-1513. Tel: 515-923-2329. [CEM]
Catechesis/Religious Programs—Rebecca Rolling, D.R.E.
Students 227.

Garryowen, Jackson Co., St. Patrick's (1840), Rev. Thomas R. Bisenius.
Res., 28914 46th Ave., Bernard, 52032-9289. Tel: 319-879-3303. [CEM]
School—Aquin Elementary School. See separate listing under Institutions Located in the Archdiocese for details.
Catechesis/Religious Programs—Joanne Harry, D.R.E.
Students 44.

Garwin, Tama Co., St. Boniface (1884), Rev. Lloyd Paul Ouderkirk.
Office and Mailing Address—306 Rider St., 50632. Tel: 515-499-2180.
Res., St. Mary Church, 9 W. Linn St., Marshalltown, 50158. Tel: 515-753-6278. [JC]
Catechesis/Religious Programs—Diane Jones, D.R.E.
Students 42.

Geneva, Franklin Co., St. Paul. Closed. Sacramental records are located at St. Mary, Ackley.

Gilbert, Story Co., SS. Peter and Paul (1882). Conventual Franciscan Friars. Revs. Terrence Rassmussen, O.F.M.Conv.; Howard Hanson, O.F.M.Conv.
Res., St. Cecilia Rectory, 2900 Hoover, Ames, 50010-4498. Tel: 515-233-3092. [CEM]
Church—14238 500th Ave., Rte. 38.
Catechesis/Religious Programs—D.R.E.: Jean Johnson; Peg Stowell.
Students 74.

Gilbertville, Blackhawk Co., Immaculate Conception (1875), Rev. Philip E. Thompson.
Res., 311 15th Ave., 50634-0136. Tel: 319-296-1092. [CEM]
School—Immaculate Conception-St. Joseph. (Gilbertville-Raymond Consolidated). See separate listing under Institutions Located in the Archdiocese for details.
Catechesis/Religious Programs—Dessie Rottinghaus, D.R.E.
Students 36.

Greeley, Delaware Co., St. Joseph's (1870), Rev. Frank M. Benda; Deacon Jim Steger; Sr. Charmaine Plotz, O.S.F., Pastoral Assoc.
Mailing Address: P.O. Box 187, Earlville, 52041-0187. Tel: 319-923-3135. [CEM]
Church—208 E. 2nd Ave.
Catechesis/Religious Programs—Sr. Charmaine Plotz, O.S.F., D.R.E.
Students 71.

Greene, Butler Co., St. Mary's (1872), Rev. Msgr. Walter L. Brunkan.
Res., 105 N. Main, P.O. Box 480, 50636-0480. Tel: 515-823-4146. [CEM]
Catechesis/Religious Programs—Sherilyn Backer, D.R.E.
Students 127.

Grundy Center, Grundy Co., Sacred Heart (1885), Rev. Douglas J. Loecke.
Res., 204 G Ave., 50638-1939. Tel: 319-824-3571. [CEM]
Catechesis/Religious Programs—D.R.E.: Sharon Davidson; Cheryl Osterhaus.
Students 51.

Guttenberg, Clayton Co., St. Mary's (1851), Rev. Msgr. John R. McClean; Deacon James Pfaffly.
Res., 520 S. Second, P.O. Box 847, 52052-0847. Tel: 319-252-1247. [CEM]
School—Guttenberg-North Buena Vista Consolidated. See separate listing under Institutions Located in the Archdiocese for details.
Catechesis/Religious Programs—Julie Rastetter, D.R.E.
Students 185.

Hampton, Franklin Co., St. Patrick's (1870), Very Rev. Gerald A. Condon.
Res., 1405 N. Federal, 50441-1005. Tel: 515-456-3406; 456-4857.
Catechesis/Religious Programs—Judy Nelson, D.R.E.
Students 143.

Hanover, Allamakee Co., St. Mary's (1875), Rev. Henry W. Charipar; Sr. Erma Rottinghaus, O.S.F., Pastoral Assoc.
Mailing Address: P.O. Box 21, Dorchester, 52140-0021. Tel: 319-497-3332.
Res., 114 3rd N.E., Box D, New Albin, 52160-0404. Tel: 319-544-4855. [CEM]
Church—2096 Hwy. 76.
Catechesis/Religious Programs—Mary Teresa Klauke, D.R.E.
Students 20.

Harpers Ferry, Allamakee Co., St. Ann-St. Joseph (1855), Rev. Louis J. Trzil.
Res. and Mailing Address—Immaculate Conception (Wexford) 1416 Great River Rd., Lansing, 52151-7519. Tel: 319-586-2150.
Church—307 W. Orange, Harper's Ferry. [CEM]
Catechesis/Religious Programs—Bernadine Heffern, D.R.E.
Students 32.

Haverhill, Marshall Co., Immaculate Conception (1877), Rev. William D. O'Brien.
Res., 101 Second Ave., 50120-5009. Tel: 515-475-3341. [CEM]
School—Marshalltown Area Consolidated Catholic. See separate listing under Institutions Located in the Archdiocese for details.
Catechesis/Religious Programs—Rev. William O'Brien, D.R.E.
Students 23.

Hawkeye, Fayette Co., St. Francis Xavier (1891), Rev. John J. Purtell.
Res. and Mailing Address—Immaculate Conception, 413 W. First St., Sumner, 50674-1313. Tel: 319-578-5366.
Church—304 E. Main.
Catechesis/Religious Programs—Donna Scholbrock, D.R.E.
Students 13.

Hazleton, Buchanan Co., St. Mary's (1881), Rev. Dennis Juhl; Deacon Richard Gehrke.
Mailing Address: 207 Benton, 50641-0146. Tel: 319-636-2131. [CEM]
Parish Office: 305 Worth St., Lamont, 50650-0180. Tel: 319-924-2691.
Church—209 Benton.

Hiawatha, Linn Co., St. Elizabeth Ann Seton Parish (1989), Rev. John A. Gossman; Marlene Myers, Pastoral Assoc.
Res., 1045 Eisenhower Rd., 52233-1927. Tel: 319-393-3778. [JC]
Church—1350 Lyndhurst Dr.

Holy Cross, Dubuque Co., Holy Cross (1845), Rev. Donald J. Plamondon.
Res., 875 Church St., P.O. Box 398, 52053-0398. Tel: 319-870-2155. [CEM]
School—Rickardsville-Holy Cross-Luxemburg (RHCL) Catholic. See separate listing under Institutions Located in the Archdiocese for details.

Hopkinton, Delaware Co., St. Luke's (1922), Rev. John R. Kremer; Patricia Hucker, Pastoral Assoc.
Mailing Address: P.O. Box 159, 52237-0159.
Res. and Parish Office—202 First St. S.E., 52237. Tel: 319-926-2613.
Church—206 First St. S.E.
Catechesis/Religious Programs—Patricia Hucker, D.R.E.
Students 158.
Oratory—Sand Springs, Immaculate Conception. Sacramental Records at St John's, Delhi.

Independence, Buchanan Co., St. John Evangelist (1856), Rev. Aloysius J. Vorwald; Sharon Bainbridge, Pastoral Assoc.
Res., 209 Fifth Ave. N.E., 50644-1998. Tel: 319-334-7191. [CEM]
School—Christine Beumer, Prin. Sisters 1; Lay Teachers 10; Students 125.
Catechesis/Religious Programs—Christine Beumer, D.R.E.
Students 225.

Ionia, Chickashaw Co., St. Boniface's (1899), Rev. Francis J. Perry.
Mailing Address: 200 E. Prairie, P.O. Box 160, 50645-0160. Tel: 515-394-2078.
Res., 114 N. Wapsie, North Washington, 50661. Tel: 515-394-2078. [CEM]
Catechesis/Religious Programs—Bonnie Boggess, D.R.E.
Students 35.

Iowa Falls, Hardin Co., St. Mark's (1855), Rev. Phillip E. Schmitt.
Res., 415 Main St., P.O. Box 368, 50126-0368. Tel: 515-648-9547. [CEM]
Catechesis/Religious Programs—Judith Connell, D.R.E.
Students 129.

Jesup, Buchanan Co., St. Athanasius (1880), Rev. Donald P. Schmitt; Sr. Donna Burke, O.S.F., Pastoral Assoc.
Res., 634 Stevens St., P.O. Box 316, 50648-0316. Tel: 319-827-6682. [CEM]
School—Gladys Oppold, Prin. Sisters 1; Lay Teachers 10; Students 133.
Catechesis/Religious Programs—Lynda Westemeier, D.R.E.
Students 149.

Jewell, Hamilton Co., Good Shepherd (1915), Rev. Raymond A. Burkle.
Res., St. Mary, 404 Fourth St., P.O. Box 157, Williams, 50271-0157. Tel: 515-827-5612.
Church—503 Edwards St.
Catechesis/Religious Programs—Students 35.

Key West, Dubuque Co., St. Joseph's (1872), Rev. James J. Goedken.
Res., 10234 Key West Dr., Dubuque, 52003-8936. Tel: 319-582-7392.
Church—10334 Key West Dr., Dubuque, 52003.
School—10244 Key West Dr., Dubuque, 52003. Tel: 319-582-2866. Connie Kessler, Prin.
Sisters 1; Lay Teachers 12; Students 215.
Catechesis/Religious Programs—Students 138.

Lake Mills, Winnebago Co., St. Patrick (1870), Rev. Craig E. Steimel; Sr. Mary Dolores Moes, P.V.B.M., Pastoral Assoc.
Res. and Mailing Address: 906 West St., P.O. Box 310, Forest City, 50436-0310. Tel: 515-582-4856. [CEM]
Church—406 S. Grant St.
Catechesis/Religious Programs—Regina Adams, D.R.E.
Students 68.

Lamont, Buchanan Co., St. Mary's (1894), Rev. Dennis Juhl; Robin Ballard, Pastoral Assoc.
Res. and Mailing Address—305 Worth St., P.O. Box 180, 50650-0180. Tel: 319-924-2691.
Church—845 Pearl St. [CEM]
Catechesis/Religious Programs—Julia Gamm, D.R.E.
Students 111.

La Motte, Jackson Co., Holy Rosary (1893), Rev. Dwayne J. Thoman.
Res., 507 Elm St., P.O. Box 26, 52054-0026. Tel: 319-773-2323. [CEM]
School—Bellevue Area Catholic Elementary. See separate listing under Institutions Located in the Archdiocese for details.
Catechesis/Religious Programs—Marla Kilburg, D.R.E.
Students 35.

Lansing, Allamakee Co., Immaculate Conception (1855), Rev. Herbert L. Tegeler; Sr. Catherine Schmitz, F.S.P.A., Pastoral Assoc.
Res., 648 Main St., 52151-9685. Tel: 319-538-4171. [CEM]
Catechesis/Religious Programs—Karen Weber, D.R.E.
Students 136.

La Porte City, Blackhawk Co., Sacred Heart (1887), Rev. Lloyd E. Reuter.
Res., 1021 Poplar St., 50651-1732. Tel: 319-342-2991.
Catechesis/Religious Programs—Barb Oberhauser, D.R.E.
Students 125.

Lawler, Chickasaw Co., Our Lady of Mt. Carmel (1869), Rev. Marvin C. Salz; Sr. Lois Erpelding, O.S.F., Pastoral Assoc.
Res., 2940 Iowa Hwy. 24, Box 119, 52154-0119. Tel: 319-238-3444. [CEM]
Catechesis/Religious Programs—Leslie Cuvelier, D.R.E.
Students 153.

Little Turkey, Chickasaw Co., Assumption of the B. V. M. (1902), Rev. Allen M. Schmitt.
Res. and Mailing Address: 110 Commercial Ave., P.O. Box 205, Protivin, 52163-0205. Tel: 319-569-8259. [CEM]
Church—3303 160th St., Lawler.
Catechesis/Religious Programs—Kathy Ball, D.R.E.
Students 50.
Oratory—Reilly Settlement, Sacred Heart. Sacramental Records at Holy Trinity, Protivin.

Lourdes, Howard Co., Our Lady of Lourdes (1875), Very Rev. Roger R. Rethamel; Betty Boehmer, Pastoral Assoc.
Res. and Mailing Address—P.O. Box 38, Elma, 50628. Tel: 515-393-2520. [CEM]
Church—14068 175th St., Elma, 50628.
Catechesis/Religious Programs—Sam Kramer, D.R.E.
Students 57.

Luxemburg, Dubuque Co., Holy Trinity (1865), Rev. Donald J. Plamondon.
Res. and Mailing Address—875 Church St., P.O. Box 398, Holy Cross, 52053-0398. Tel: 319-870-2155. [CEM]
Church—103 S. Andres St.
School—Rickardsville-Holy Cross-Luxemburg (RHCL) Catholic. See separate listing under Institutions Located in the Archdiocese for details.
Catechesis/Religious Programs—Students 22.

Lycurgus, Allamakee Co., St. Mary's (1859), Rev. Msgr. Edward W. Lechtenberg; Sr. Margaret Anne Kramer, P.B.V.M., Pastoral Assoc.
Res. and Mailing Address—109 Second St. S.W., P.O. Box 158, Waukon, 52172-0158. Tel: 319-568-3671. [CEM]
Church—1831 Lycurgus Rd., Waukon, 52172-0146.
Catechesis/Religious Programs—Rita Whalen, D.R.E.
Students 40.

Manchester, Delaware Co., St. Mary's (1872), Very Rev. Ralph P. Simington; Sr. Mary Klisart, O.S.F., Pastoral Assoc.
Res., 119 W. Fayette St., 52057-1596. Tel: 319-927-4710. [CEM]
School—Sr. Marilou Irons, P.B.V.M., Prin. Sisters 1; Lay Teachers 17; Students 234.
Catechesis/Religious Programs—Dianne Larsen, D.R.E.
Students 445.

Manly, Worth Co., Sacred Heart (1883), Rev. Thomas F. McAndrew; Deacon Robert Mega.
Res., 120 E. North, 50456-0160. Tel: 515-454-2586. [CEM]
Catechesis/Religious Programs—Tammy Nettleton, D.R.E.
Students 56.

Maquoketa, Jackson Co., Sacred Heart (1873), Very Rev. Dennis R. Cain; Sr. Nancy Anderson, O.S.B., Pastoral Assoc.; Deacon Robert Head.
Res., 200 S. Vermont St., 52060-2709. Tel: 319-652-6931. [CEM]
School—Sr. Rita Green, O.S.F., Prin. Brothers 1; Sisters 2; Lay Teachers 8; Students 141.
Catechesis/Religious Programs—Karen Steffen, D.R.E.
Students 164.
Oratory—Baldwin, Holy Trinity. Closed. Sacramental Records are located at Sacred Heart, Maquoketa.

Marion, Linn Co., St. Joseph's (1890), Revs. Michael C. Fitzgerald; James P. Brokman; Deacons Leo Schmall; Ed Pantaloni; Barbara McGrane, Pastoral Assoc.
Res., 1790 14th St., 52302-2267. Tel: 319-377-4869; Fax: 319-377-9043. [JC]
School—Sr. Margaret Weigel, R.S.M., Prin. Sisters of Mercy 1; Lay Teachers 23; Students 377.
Catechesis/Religious Programs—D.R.E.: Ruth Ard; Mary Hauschildt.
Students 584.

Marshalltown, Marshall Co., St. Henry's (1959), Rev. Thomas E. Braak; Deacon Irvin Vaske. Pastoral Assoc: Toni Waters; Karen Mrozand.
Parish Center: 221 W. Olive St., 50158-4248. Tel: 515-753-7374; Fax: 515-753-1499. [JC]
Res., 212 Huisman Cir., 50158. Tel: 515-752-2043.
School—Marshalltown Area Consolidated Catholic. See separate listing under Institutions Located in the Archdiocese for details.
Catechesis/Religious Programs—Karen Koorsen, D.R.E.
Students 281.

St. Mary's (1869), Rev. Jerry F. Kopacek; Deacon Edward J. Mead. In res., Rev. Lloyd Paul Ouderkirk.
Res., 9 W. Linn St., P.O. Box 642, 50158-0642. Tel: 515-753-6278. [JC]
School—Marshalltown Area Consolidated Catholic. See separate listing under Institutions Located in the Archdiocese for details.
Catechesis/Religious Programs—Sr. Sheila Geraghty, R.S.M., D.R.E.
Students 213.

Mason City, Cerro Gordo Co., St. Joseph's (1873), Revs. Carl A. Ries; Michael G. Schueller; Sr. LaVerne Dolphin, B.V.M., Pastoral Assoc.; Deacon Jack Barlow.
Res., 302 Fifth St. S.E., 50401-4005. Tel: 515-423-5001.
School—Newman Catholic. See separate listing under Institutions Located in the Archdiocese for details.
Catechesis/Religious Programs—Ginny Verstegen, D.R.E.
Students 158.

Holy Family (1908), Revs. Dennis H. Cahill; David M. Beckman; Deacons Charles Cooper; Matthew Berry.
Res., 714 N. Adams St., 50401-2199. Tel: 515-423-7301. [JC]
School—Newman Catholic. See separate listing under Institutions Located in the Archdiocese for details.
Catechesis/Religious Programs—Ginny Verstegen, D.R.E.
Students 266.

Masonville, Delaware Co., Immaculate Conception (1883), Rev. Ivan R. Nienhaus; Sr. Mary Valentine Smith, O.S.F., Pastoral Assoc.
Res. and Mailing Address—555 First St., P.O. Box 236, Winthrop, 50682-0236. Tel: 319-935-3523.
Church—Bernhardt St., 50654. [CEM]
Catechesis/Religious Programs—Julie Francois, D.R.E.
Students 71.

McGregor, Clayton Co., St. Mary's (1873), Rev. Robert J. Levenhagen.
Res., 311 Seventh St., 52157-9999. Tel: 319-873-2287. [CEM]
Catechesis/Religious Programs—Mary Young, D.R.E.
Students 71.

Meyer, Mitchell Co., Sacred Heart (1900), Rev. Joseph M. Schneider.
Mailing Address: 2697 480th St. W., McIntire, 50455-8024.
Res., 604 N. Broad St., Stacyville, 50476-5019. Tel: 515-737-2262. [CEM]
School—Visitation (Stacyville-Meyer) Consolidated. See separate listing under Institutions Located in the Archdiocese for details.
Catechesis/Religious Programs—Barbara Brumm, D.R.E.
Students 58.

Monona, Clayton Co., St. Patrick's (1856), Rev. Daniel J. Keppler.
Res., 403 East St. S., P.O. Box U, 52159-0557. Tel: 319-539-4442. [CEM]
Catechesis/Religious Programs—D.R.E.: Marilyn Ryan; Don Montgomery.
Students 203.

Monti, Buchanan Co., St. Patrick's (1855), Rev. John W. Carpender.
Res. and Mailing Address—615 Howard St., P.O. Box 219, Ryan, 52330-0219. Tel: 319-932-2151.
Church—2856 Washington Ave., Masonville, 50654. [CEM]
Catechesis/Religious Programs—Linda Dolan, D.R.E.
Students 61.

Monticello, Jones Co., Sacred Heart (1868), Rev. Msgr. Neil W. Tobin.
Office and Res.—328 N. Sycamore, 52310-1213. Tel: 319-465-5944. [CEM]
Church—302 N. Sycamore.
School—(Grades PreK-6). David E. Bertling, Prin. Brothers 1; Lay Teachers 11; Students 176.
Catechesis/Religious Programs—Guy E. Woodward, D.R.E.
Students 176.

Mount Vernon, Linn Co., St. John's the Baptist (1843), Rev. James J. Duster. In res., Rev. Ernest Engler.
Res., 212 7th St. S.E., P.O. Box 169, 52314-0169. Tel: 319-895-6246. [CEM]
Catechesis/Religious Programs—Sue Schettler, D.R.E.
Students 209.

Nashua, Chickasaw Co., St. Michael's (1870), Rev. Msgr. Robert L. Spaight.
Res., 612 Cedar St., P.O. Box 308, 50658-0308. Tel: 515-435-2070. [CEM]
Catechesis/Religious Programs—Kendra Gilbert, D.R.E.
Students 139.

Nevada, Story Co., St. Patrick's (1870), Rev. John M. Herzog; Sr. Carole Freking, O.S.F., Pastoral Assoc.
Mailing Address: 1127 10th St., 50201-1708. Tel: 515-382-2974. [CEM]
Res., St. Mary, 410 Bailey St., Colo, 50056. Tel: 515-377-2710.
Catechesis/Religious Programs—Belinda Hansen, D.R.E.
Students 138.

New Albin, Allamakee Co., St. Joseph's (1910), Rev. Henry W. Charipar; Sr. Erma Rottinghaus, O.S.F., Pastoral Assoc.
Res., 114 3rd N.E., Box D, 52160-0404. Tel: 319-544-4855. [CEM]
Catechesis/Religious Programs—Rita Krzbietke, D.R.E.
Students 65.

Newhall, Benton Co., St. Paul's (1914), Rev. Louis C. Zee; Sr. Nora Rochford, O.S.F., Pastoral Assoc.; Deacons Robert F. Hurych; James Naso.
Mailing Address: P.O. Box 447, 52315-0447. Tel: 319-223-5576.
Res., Immaculate Conception, 405 Fourth Ave., P.O. Box 250, Van Horne, 52346. Tel: 319-228-8131.
Church—303 Third St. E.
Catechesis/Religious Programs—D.R.E.: Joan Stien; Mary Wilhelmi.
Students 126.

New Hampton, Chickasaw Co., St. Joseph's (1870), Rev. Carl L. Schmitt. Pastoral Assocs.: Sr. Lorraine Loecher, O.S.F.; Sr. Phyllis Ann Hackman, F.S.P.A.; Deacon Robert Baltes.
Res., 202 N. Broadway, 50659-1111. Tel: 515-394-2105. [CEM]
School—Alice Conlon, Prin. Sisters 1; Lay Teachers 16; Students 233.
Catechesis/Religious Programs—Sr. Lois Erpelding, O.S.F., D.R.E.
Students 158.

St. Mary's (1894), Rev. Marvin C. Salz.
Res., 239 S. Walnut Ave., P.O. Box 66, 50659-0066. Tel: 515-394-2195. [CEM]
Catechesis/Religious Programs—Sr. Lois Erpelding, O.S.F., D.R.E.
Students 176.

New Haven, Mitchell Co., St. Peter's (1876), Rev. John A. Moser.
Mailing Address: 2985 360th St., Osage, 50461-8517.
Office: 209 E. Main St., Riceville, 50466-0146. Tel: 515-985-2028. [CEM]
Church—2985 360th St., Osage.
Catechesis/Religious Programs—Pat Wickham, D.R.E.
Students 32.

New Melleray, Dubuque Co., Holy Family (1850), Rev. Carl J. Manternach.
Res., St. John the Baptist, 10761 Sundown Rd., Peosta, 52068-9507. Tel: 319-582-4217.
Church—16500 Holy Family Ln., Peosta. [CEM]
Catechesis/Religious Programs—Kay Goedken, D.R.E.
Students 62.

New Vienna, Dubuque Co, St. Boniface's (1845), Rev. John J. O'Connor.
Mailing Address: P.O. Box 200, 52065-0114. Tel: 319-921-2465.
Res., SS. Peter and Paul, 1625-300th Ave., Petersburg, 52040-8736. Tel: 319-875-7992. [CEM]
Church—7401 Columbus St.
School—Archbishop Hennessy Catholic. See separate listing under Institutions Located in the Archdiocese for details.

North Buena Vista, Clayton Co., Immaculate Conception (1898), Rev. Msgr. John R. McClean.
Mailing Address: P.O. Box 847, Guttenberg, 52052. Tel: 319-252-1247. [CEM]
Church—218 Main St. N., Buena Vista.

North Washington, Chickasaw Co., Immaculate Conception (1868), Rev. Francis J. Perry.
Res., 114 N. Wapsi, 50661. Tel: 515-394-2078. [CEM]
Catechesis/Religious Programs—Mary Roethler, D.R.E.
Students 66.

Norway, Benton Co., St. Michael's (1867), Rev. Walter J. Kleinfehn.
Res., 512 Evergreen, P.O. Box 09, 52318-0009. Tel: 319-227-7169. [CEM]
Catechesis/Religious Programs—Cathy Maile, D.R.E.
Students 118.

Oelwein, Fayette Co., Sacred Heart (1876), Rev. Frederick C. Fangmann; Carol Hamilton, Pastoral Assoc.
Res., 628 S. Frederick Ave., 50662. Tel: 319-283-3743.
School—(Grades K-6). Sr. Benjamin Duschner, P.B.V.M., Prin.
Sisters of Mercy 2; Lay Teachers 4; Students 192.
Catechesis/Religious Programs—Students 253.

Osage, Mitchell Co., Sacred Heart (1878), Rev. Philip F. Recker; Sr. Rosanne Rottinghaus, P.B.V.M., Pastoral Assoc.
Res., 1209 State St., 50461-1844. Tel: 515-732-4342. [CEM]
School—(Grades PreK-6). Sr. Lenore Ostdiek, O.S.F., Prin.
Sisters 1; Lay Teachers 9; Students 134.
Catechesis/Religious Programs—D.R.E.: Eve Kenny; Jane Krabbe.
Students 185.

Ossian, Winneshiek Co., St. Francis de Sales (1876), Rev. Richard W. Kuhn.
Res., 418 E. Main St., 52161-9998. Tel: 319-532-9366. [CEM]
School—Mae Becker, Prin. Lay Teachers 8; Students 144.
Catechesis/Religious Programs—Jennifer Shimek, D.R.E.
Students 67.

Otter Creek, Jackson Co., St. Lawrence (1854), Rev. Msgr. Thomas J. Ralph.
Res., 17486 Bellevue-Cascade Rd., Zwingle, 52079-9688. Tel: 319-686-4228. [CEM]
Catechesis/Religious Programs—Mary Gansen, D.R.E.
Students 67.

Oxford Junction, Jones Co., Sacred Heart (1890), Rev. Richard J. Poster.
Res. and Mailing Address—301 Hwy. 136, P.O. Box 127, Lost Nation, 52254-0127. Tel: 319-678-2200.
Church—309 Church St.
Catechesis/Religious Programs—Patti Manuel, D.R.E.
Students 65.

Parkersburg, Butler Co., St. Patrick's (1889), Rev. Kenneth C. Stecher.
Res., 702 Grant St., P.O. Box E, 50665. Tel: 319-346-1411. [CEM]
Church—304 Second St.
Catechesis/Religious Programs—Darcy Bertram, D.R.E.
Students 60.

Peosta, Dubuque Co., St. John the Baptist (1874), Rev. Carl J. Manternach.
Res., 10761 Sundown Rd., 52068-9507. Tel: 319-582-4217. [CEM]
School—Seton Catholic Elementary School, Epworth. See separate listing under Institutions Located in the Archdiocese for details.
Catechesis/Religious Programs—Sr. Mary Kent Pearson, O.P., D.R.E.
Students 103.
Oratories—Lattnerville, Annunciation. Sacramental Records are located at St. John, Peosta.; Prairie, St. Joseph. Closed. Sacramental Records are located at St. John, Peosta.

Petersburg, Delaware Co., SS. Peter and Paul (1867), Rev. John J. O'Connor.
Res. and Mailing Address—1625 300th Ave., 52040-8736. Tel: 319-875-7992. [CEM]
School—Archbishop Hennessy Catholic, New Vienna. See separate listing under Institutions Located in the Archdiocese for details.

Placid, Dubuque Co., St. John's (1874), Rev. Joseph L. Hauer; Deacon Gerald Koopmann.
Res., 22453 E. Pleasant Grove Rd., Epworth, 52045-9603. Tel: 319-876-5501. [CEM]
School—Seton Catholic Elementary School, Epworth. See separate listing under Institutions Located in the Archdiocese for details.
Catechesis/Religious Programs—Lori Kramer, D.R.E.
Students 48.

Plymouth, Cerro Gordo Co., St. Michael (1872), Rev. Thomas F. McAndrew; Deacon Robert Mega.
Res., Sacred Heart, 120 E. North, Manly, 50456-0160. Tel: 515-454-2586.

Plymouth Rock, Winneshiek Co., St. Agnes (1857). Closed. Sacramental records are located at Assumption, Cresco.

Postville, Allamakee Co., St. Bridget's (1872), Rev. Leo P. Riley.
Res., 135 W. Williams, P.O. Box 369, 52162-0369. Tel: 319-864-3138.
Catechesis/Religious Programs—Mary Koopmann, D.R.E.
Students 105.

Prairieburg, Linn Co., St. Joseph's (1874), Rev. Richard J. Ament; Sr. Anne Kisting, O.S.F., Pastoral Assoc.
Mailing Address: P.O. Box 4248, 52219-4248.
Parish Office: 410 Terrace Dr., Central City, 52214-0420. Tel: 319-438-6625. [CEM]
Church—300 West Ave.

Preston, Jackson Co., St. Joseph's (1881), Rev. Donald V. Bakewell.
Res. and Mailing Address: 250 S. Faith St., P.O. Box 309, 52069-0309. Tel: 319-689-5161. [CEM]
Catechesis/Religious Programs—D.R.E.: Irene Entsminger; Rosemary Sievers.
Students 194.

Protivin, Howard Co., Holy Trinity (1878), Rev. Allen M. Schmitt.
Res. and Mailing Address—110 Commercial Ave., P.O. Box 205, 52163-0205. Tel: 319-569-8259. [CEM]
School—Julie Franzen, Prin. Lay Teachers 9; Students 167.
Catechesis/Religious Programs—Christopher Weber, D.R.E.
Students 69.
Oratory—Schley, Holy Cross. Sacramental Records at Holy Trinity, Protivin.

Raymond, Blackhawk Co., St. Joseph's (1905), Rev. John R. Flaherty.
Res. and Mailing Address—313 E. Central St., P.O. Box 158, 50667-0158. Tel: 319-233-5395. [CEM]
School—Immaculate Conception-St. Joseph (Gilbertville-Raymond Consolidated Elementary). See separate listing under Institutions Located in the Archdiocese for details.

Reinbeck, Grundy Co., Queen of Heaven (1958), Rev. Douglas J. Loecke.
Res., Sacred Heart, 204 G Ave., Grundy Center, 50638-1939. Tel: 319-824-3571. [CEM]
Church—1006 Blackhawk St., 50669.
Catechesis/Religious Programs—Gloria Rickert, D.R.E.
Students 53.

Riceville, Howard Co., Immaculate Conception (1879), Rev. John A. Moser.
Res. and Mailing Address: 209 E. Main St., Box 146, 50466-0146. Tel: 515-985-2028. [CEM]
Catechesis/Religious Programs—Deborah Oulman, D.R.E.
Students 169.

Rickardsville, Dubuque Co., St. Joseph's (1840), Rev. Melvin D. Hemann.
Res., 20245 St. Joseph Dr., 52039-9757. Tel: 319-552-2233. [CEM]
School—Rickardsville-Holy Cross-Luxemburg (RHCL) Catholic. See separate listing under Institutions Located in the Archdiocese for details.
Catechesis/Religious Programs—Mary Anne Manternach, D.R.E.
Students 74.

Rockford, Floyd Co., Holy Name (1910), Rev. Roger L. Katz.
Res., 507 First Ave. N.W., 50468-1132. Tel: 515-756-3569.
Catechesis/Religious Programs—Brenda Schmitt, D.R.E.
Students 134.

Rockwell, Cerro Gordo Co., Sacred Heart (1878), Rev. Stephen L. Meyer; Deacon Victor Groh.
Res. and Mailing Address: 305 Elm St. E., P.O. Box 30, 50469-0030. Tel: 515-822-4957. [CEM]
Catechesis/Religious Programs—Eleanor Nelson, D.R.E.
Students 82.
Oratory—Cartersville, St. John. Sacramental Records at Sacred Heart, Rockwell.

Roseville, Floyd Co., St. Mary (1867), Rev. Msgr. Walter L. Brunkan.
Res., 105 N. Main, Greene, 50636. Tel: 515-823-4146. [CEM]
Church—2397 Hwy. 14, Marble Rock.
Catechesis/Religious Programs—Betty Jo Staudt, D.R.E.
Students 57.

Rowley, Buchanan Co., All Saints (1896), Rev. Aloysius J. Vorwald.
Mailing Address: 3103 Michael, 52329-0206.
Res., 209 Fifth Ave. E., Independence, 50644. Tel: 319-334-7191. [CEM]
Church—219 Park Ave.
Catechesis/Religious Programs—Brenda Corkery, D.R.E.
Students 46.

Ryan, Delaware Co., St. Patrick's (1882), Rev. John W. Carpender.
Res. and Mailing Address: 615 Howard St., P.O. Box 219, 52330-0219. Tel: 319-932-2151. [CEM]
Church—606 Franklin St.
Catechesis/Religious Programs—Kathy Zimmerman, D.R.E.
Students 132.

Sabula, Jackson Co., St. Peter (1840), Rev. Donald V. Bakewell; Sr. Susan Dunnwald, R.S.M., Pastoral Admin.
Res., 504 Elk St., P.O. Box 429, 52070-0429. Tel: 319-687-2525. [CEM]
Catechesis/Religious Programs—Sr. Susan Dunnwald, R.S.M., D.R.E.
Students 23.

St. Ansgar, Mitchell Co., St. Ansgar (1951), Rev. Joseph M. Schneider; Sr. Burnita Kaschmitter, O.S.F.
Mailing Address: P.O. Box 396, 50472-0396.
Parish Office: 604 N. Broad St., Stacyville, 50476-5019. Tel: 515-737-2262.
Church—704 E. Fourth St.
Catechesis/Religious Programs—Mary Wilder, D.R.E.
Students 72.

St. Anthony, Marshall Co., Sacred Heart (1878), Rev. Richard J. Hess.
Res., 418 Main St., P.O. Box 300, 50239-0300. Tel: 515-477-8227. [CEM]
Catechesis/Religious Programs—Rev. Richard J. Hess, D.R.E.
Students 21.

St. Catherine, Dubuque Co., St. Catherine's (1887), Very Rev. Dennis R. Cain; Rev. Sean Bullock; Sr. Romaine Pickart, O.S.F., Pastoral Assoc.
Res., 5177 St. Catherine Rd., Dubuque, 52003-9566. Tel: 319-583-0092. [CEM]
School—Bellevue Area Catholic Elementary. See separate listing under Institutions Located in the Archdiocese for details.
Catechesis/Religious Programs—Sr. Dolores McAllister, O.S.F., D.R.E.
Students 50.

St. Cecilia, Howard Co., St. Patrick's. Closed. Sacramental records are located at Immaculate Conception, Elma.

St. Donatus, Jackson Co., St. Donatus (1853), Very Rev. Dennis R. Cain; Rev. Scott E. Bullock; Sr. Dolores McAllister, O.S.F., Pastoral Admin.
Res. and Mailing Address—5177 St. Catherine Rd., Dubuque, 52003-9566. Tel: 319-583-0092.
Church—E. First St.
School—Bellevue Area Catholic Elementary. See separate listing under Institutions Located in the Archdiocese for details.

St. Lucas, Fayette Co., St. Luke's (1855), Rev. Raphael A. Ludwig.
Res., 207 E. Main St., P.O. Box 187, 52166-0187. Tel: 319-778-2370. [CEM]
School—Trinity Catholic School, Protovin. See separate listing under Institutions Located in the Archdiocese for details.
Catechesis/Religious Programs—D.R.E.: Trudy Smith; Deb Dietzenbach.
Students 79.

St. Theresa, Jackson Co., St. Theresa's (1853), Rev. Mark R. Nemmers.
Res., 34257 230th Ave., LaMotte, 52054-9794. Tel: 319-773-2341. [CEM]
Catechesis/Religious Programs—Patricia Puetz, D.R.E.
Students 39.

Sand Springs, Delaware Co., Immaculate Conception (1884). Closed. Sacramental records are located at St. John's, Delhi.

Schley, Howard Co., Holy Cross (1928). Closed. Sacramental records are located at Holy Trinity, Protivin.

Shell Rock, Butler Co., Holy Name. Closed. Sacramental records are located at St. Mary's, Waverly.

Sherrill, Dubuque Co., SS. Peter and Paul (1852), Rev. Melvin D. Hemann; Sr. Mildred Leuenberger, O.S.F., Pastoral Admin.
Res., 5131 Sherrill Rd., 52073-9612. Tel: 319-552-2611. [CEM]
School—Balltown-Sherrill Catholic. See separate listing under Institutions Located in the Archdiocese for details.
Catechesis/Religious Programs—Mary Anne Manternach, D.R.E.
Students 64.

Spillville, Winneshiek Co., St. Wenceslaus (1860), Rev. Donald J. Hawes.
Res., 207 Church St., Box 128, 52168-0128. Tel: 319-562-3637. [CEM]
School—Calmar-Festina-Spillville (CFS) Catholic Elementary. See separate listing under Institutions Located in the Archdiocese for details.
Catechesis/Religious Programs—Helen Pinter, D.R.E.
Students 80.

Springbrook, Jackson Co., SS. Peter and Paul (1864), Rev. Donald V. Bakewell; Sr. Susan Dunnwald, R.S.M., Pastoral Assoc.
Mailing Address: 105 E. Main St., 52075. Tel: 319-872-3875.
Res., 205 Faith St., Preston, 52069-0309. Tel: 319-689-5161. [CEM]
School—Bellevue Area Catholic Elementary. See separate listing under Institutions Located in the Archdiocese for details.

Springville, Linn Co., St. Isidore's (1961), Revs. Michael C. Fitzgerald; James P. Brockman.
Res. and Mailing Address—St. Joseph Rectory, 1790 14th St., Marion, 52302-2267. Tel: 319-377-4860.
Church—603 6th St. S.
Catechesis/Religious Programs—Marilyn Andersen, D.R.E.
Students 67.

Stacyville, Mitchell Co., Church of the Visitation (1894), Rev. Joseph M. Schneider; Sr. Burnita Kaschmitter, O.S.F., Pastoral Assoc.
Res., 604 N. Broad St., 50476-5019. Tel: 515-737-2262. [CEM]
School—Visitation (Stacyville-Meyer) Consolidated. See separate listing under Institutions Located in the Archdiocese for details.
Catechesis/Religious Programs—Julie Brumm, D.R.E.
Students 48.

State Center, Marshall Co., St. Joseph's (1870), Rev. Ronald G. Friedell.
Res., 607 Third St. S.W., P.O. Box 694, 50247-0694. Tel: 515-483-2464. [CEM]
Catechesis/Religious Programs—Judy Eggers, D.R.E.
Students 45.

Strawberry Point, Clayton Co., St. Mary's (1876), Rev. Dennis Juhl; Robin Ballard, Pastoral Assoc.
Mailing Address: 314 W. Mission St., 52076-9432. Tel: 319-933-6166. [CEM]
Catechesis/Religious Programs—Bonnie Hayes, D.R.E.
Students 198.

Sumner, Bremer Co., Immaculate Conception (1894), Rev. John J. Purtell; Eloyce Munk, Pastoral Assoc.
Res., 413 W. First St., 50674-1313. Tel: 319-578-5366. [CEM]
Catechesis/Religious Programs—Barbara Hennessey, D.R.E.
Students 155.
Oratory—Pinhook, St. Bridget. Sacramental Records at Immaculate Conception, Sumner.

Sylvia, Dubuque Co., Assumption (1896), Rev. Mark R. Nemmers.
Res., 34257 230th Ave., La Motte, 52054-9794. Tel: 319-773-2341. [CEM]
Catechesis/Religious Programs—Patricia Puetz, D.R.E.
Students 34.

Tama-Toledo, Tama Co., St. Patrick's (1864), Rev. Keith L. Birch; Patti Hoffman, Pastoral Assoc.
Res., 900 Park St., Tama, 52339-1238. Tel: 515-484-3039; 484-4242. [CEM]
Catechesis/Religious Programs—Patricia Green, D.R.E.
Students 202.

Temple Hill, Jones Co., St. Peter's (1852), Rev. Thomas E. Toale.
Res., 20189 Temple Hill Rd., 52033-9802. Tel: 319-852-3448. [CEM]
School—Aquin Elementary School. See separate listing under Institutions Located in the Archdiocese for details.
Catechesis/Religious Programs—Julie Orris, D.R.E.
Students 61.

Traer, Tama Co., St. Paul's (1912), Rev. John R. Tilp.
Res., 1102 Walnut St., 50675-1440. Tel: 319-478-2222. [CEM]
Catechesis/Religious Programs—Cecilia Podhajsky, D.R.E.
Students 128.

Urbana, Benton Co., St. Mary (1872), Rev. Garbiel C. Anderson.
Res. and Mailing Address—Sacred Heart, 516 Rowley St., P.O. Box 116, Walker, 52352-0116. Tel: 319-448-4316.
Church—401 Ash Ave. [CEM]
Catechesis/Religious Programs—Linda Van Etten, D.R.E.
Students 106.

Van Horne, Benton Co., Immaculate Conception (1869), Rev. Louis C. Zee; Deacon James Naso.
Res., 405 Fourth Ave., P.O. Box 250, 52346-0250. Tel: 319-228-8131. [CEM]
Catechesis/Religious Programs—Sr. Nora Rochford, O.S.F., D.R.E.
Students 99.

Vining, Tama Co., St. Mary's (1874), Rev. John R. Tilp.
Res. and Mailing Address—1102 Walnut St., Traer, 50675-1440. Tel: 319-478-2222.
Church—405 2nd Ave. [CEM]
Catechesis/Religious Programs—Barbara Cibula, D.R.E.
Students 27.

Vinton, Benton Co., St. Mary's (1878), Rev. Joseph E. McGuire.
Res., 2200 S. Second Ave, 52349. Tel: 319-472-4448. [CEM]
Catechesis/Religious Programs—Lynn Mealhow, D.R.E.
Students 166.

Volga, Clayton Co., Sacred Heart (1889), Rev. Paul R. Peters; Sr. Rosanna Gleason, O.P., Pastoral Assoc.
Mailing Address: 330 First St. P.O. Box 135, Elkader, 52043-0626. Tel: 319-245-2548. [CEM]
Church—304 White St.
Catechesis/Religious Programs—Sr. Rosanna Gleason, O.P., D.R.E.
Students 17.

Walford, Linn Co., Holy Trinity (1890), Rev. Thomas J. Schwinn; Sr. Sheila Fitzgerald, O.P., Pastoral Assoc.; Deacon John Malone.
Mailing Address: 110 First St. S., 52351-0126. Tel: 319-846-2270.

Walker, Linn Co., Sacred Heart (1885), Rev. Gabriel C. Anderson.
Res., 516 Rowley St., P.O. Box 116, 52352-0116. Tel: 319-448-4316. [CEM]
Catechesis/Religious Programs—Linda Van Etten, D.R.E.
Students 95.

Waterloo, Blackhawk Co.,

1—St. Joseph's, (1868), Revs. Leon Connolly; Robert E. Hilmer; Deacon Clarence Gram. In res., Rev. Msgr. W. Dean Walz.
Res., 320 Mulberry St., 50703-3598. Tel: 319-234-4439. [JC]

2—St. Mary's, (1898), Revs. Daniel J. Knipper; Robert E. Hilmer.
Res., 2127 E. Fourth St., 50703-2699. Tel: 319-232-1326. [JC]
School—Tel: 319-232-2418. Patricia Powell, Prin.
Lay Teachers 11; Students 153.
Catechesis/Religious Programs—Bev Byford, D.R.E.
Students 56.

3—Sacred Heart, (1909), Rev. Michael Mescher; Sr. Louann Doerning, P.B.V.M., Pastoral Assoc. In res., Rev. Arthur W. Kleve.
Res., 627 W. Fourth St., 50702-1501. Tel: 319-234-4996. [JC]
School—Julie Niemeyer, Prin. Sisters 1; Lay Teachers 17; Students 339.
Catechesis/Religious Programs—Pamela Johnston, D.R.E.
Students 117.

4—St. Edward's, (1945), Rev. Msgr. Russell M. Bleich; Rev. Thomas J. McDermott; Karol Rae Hoth, Pastoral Assoc.; Deacon John Baker. In res., Rev. Justin T. Kane.
Res., 1423 Kimball Ave., 50702-3837. Tel: 319-233-8060. [JC]
School—Chris Mitchell, Prin. (Elementary). Sisters 1; Lay Teachers 25; Students 455.
Catechesis/Religious Programs—Mary Ann Helie, D.R.E.
Students 120.

5—St. John's, (1923), Rev. George W. Karnik; Sr. JoAnn O'Connell, B.V.M., Pastoral Assoc.; Deacon Edward Weber.
Res., 1701 Mulberry St., 50703-4991. Tel: 319-233-5241. [JC]
School—St. John-St. Nicholas Consolidated. Barbara Emerson, Prin.
Lay Teachers 20; Students 358.
Catechesis/Religious Programs—Dave Cushing, D.R.E.
Students 24.

6—Blessed Sacrament, (1947), Revs. Patrick G. Geary; Paul E. Lippstock; Sr. Madonna M. Friedman, O.S.F., Pastoral Assoc.; Deacons John Herman; James Freet.
Res., 650 Stephan Ave., 50701-2099. Tel: 319-233-6179. [JC]
School—Tel: 319-233-7863. Georgine Hurt, Prin.
Sisters 1; Lay Teachers 13; Students 261.
Catechesis/Religious Programs—Anne Phillips, D.R.E.
Students 89.

Watkins, Benton Co., St. Patrick's (1880), Rev. Walter J. Kleinfehn.
Res. and Mailing Address—St. Michael, 512 Evergreen St., P.O. Box 9, Norway, 52318-0009. Tel: 319-227-7169.
Church—2nd St., 52354. [CEM]
Catechesis/Religious Programs—Yvonne Brecht, D.R.E.
Students 30.

Waucoma, Fayette Co., St. Mary's (1898), Rev. Raphael A. Ludwig.
Res. and Mailing Address—207 E. Main, P.O. Box 187, St. Lucas, 52166-0187. Tel: 319-778-2370.
Church—218 3rd St. N.W. [CEM]
Catechesis/Religious Programs—Christin Bouska, D.R.E.
Students 76.

Waukon, Allamakee Co., St. Patrick's (1851), Rev. Msgr. Edward W. Lechtenberg; Sr. Margaret Anne Kramer, P.B.V.M., Pastoral Min. & D.R.E.
Res., 109 Second St. S.W., Box 146, 52172-0146. Tel: 319-568-3671. [CEM]
School—Tel: 319-568-2415. Michael Ward, Prin. Lay Teachers 14; Students 172.
Catechesis/Religious Programs—Students 260.
Oratory—West Ridge, St. John the Baptist. Sacramental Records at St. Patricks, Waukon.

Waverly, Bremer Co., St. Mary's (1856), Rev. James L. Miller; Sr. Bernadette Engelhaupt, Pastoral Assoc.
Res., 112 Second Ave. S.E., 50677-3404. Tel: 319-352-2493. [CEM]
Catechesis/Religious Programs—Deacon Guy Beck, D.R.E.
Students 446.

Webster City, Hamilton Co., St. Thomas Aquinas (1870), Rev. John J. Walsh.
Res., 1010 Des Moines St., 50595-2147. Tel: 515-832-1190. [CEM]
School—Tel: 515-832-1346. Duane Siepker, Prin. Lay Teachers 11; Students 124.
Catechesis/Religious Programs—D.R.E.: Cathy Olson; Mary Becker.
Students 167.

West Union, Fayette Co., Holy Name (1870), Rev. Dale J. Rausch.
Res., 128 N. Walnut St., 52175-1347. Tel: 319-422-3184. [CEM]
Catechesis/Religious Programs—Mike Woodson, D.R.E.
Students 218.

Wexford, Allamakee Co., Immaculate Conception (1851), Rev. Louis J. Trzil.
Res. and Mailing Address—1416 Great River Rd., Lansing, 52151-7519. Tel: 319-586-2150. [CEM]
Catechesis/Religious Programs—Patty Manning, D.R.E.
Students 40.

Williams, Hamilton Co., St. Mary's (1875), Rev. Raymond A. Burkle.
Res., 404 Fourth St., P.O. Box 157, 50271-0157. Tel: 515-854-2241. [CEM]
Catechesis/Religious Programs—Marty Doerning, D.R.E.
Students 22.

Winthrop, Buchanan Co., St. Patrick's (1894), Rev. Ivan R. Nienhaus; Sr. Mary Valentine Smith, O.S.F., Pastoral Assoc.
Res., 555 First St., P.O. Box 236, 50682-0236. Tel: 319-935-3523. [CEM]
Catechesis/Religious Programs—D.R.E.: Phil and Deb Steffen.
Students 165.

Woden, Hancock Co., Sacred Heart (1900), Rev. Marvin J. Bries.
Res. and Mailing Address—139 Third St. S.E., Britt, 50423-1726. Tel: 515-843-3215.
Church—147 Howard Ave., 50484.
Catechesis/Religious Programs—Kathryn Smith, D.R.E.
Students 27.

Worthington, Dubuque Co., St. Paul's (1875), Rev. Mark Osterhaus.
Res., 314 Third Ave. S.W., P.O. Box 38, 52078-0038. Tel: 319-855-2405. [CEM]
School—Sandra Klaus, Prin. Lay Teachers 10; Students 82.
Catechesis/Religious Programs—Julie Bries, D.R.E.
Students 89.

Zearing, Story Co., St. Gabriel (1904), Rev. Richard J. Hess.
Res. and Mailing Address—Sacred Heart, 418 Main St., P.O. Box 300, St. Anthony, 50239-0300. Tel: 515-477-8227.
Church—302 N. Center.
Catechesis/Religious Programs—D.R.E.: Rev. Richard J. Hess; Rex Gogerty.
Students 42.

Chaplains of Public Institutions

ANAMOSA. *Iowa State Men's Reformatory.* Vacant.
INDEPENDENCE. *Mental Health Institute.* P.O. Box 505, 302 W. Main St., Fairbanks, 50629. Tel: 319-635-2211. Rev. Mark J. McGovern, Part-Time Chap.
MARSHALLTOWN. *Veterans' Home.* Rev. Ronald G. Friedell, Chap., 607 Third St. S.W., State Center, 50247. Tel: 515-483-2464.

On Special or Other Archdiocesan Assignment:
Reverend Monsignors—
Barta, James O., Episcopal Vicar, Cedar Rapids Region
Walz, W. Dean, Episcopal Vicar, Waterloo Region

On Duty Outside the Archdiocese:
Reverend Fathers—
Burke, Clement, 2321 Aldrich Ave. S., #315, Minneapolis, MN 55405
Flanagan, James W., Dept. of Religion, Mather House, Case Western Reserve Univ., Cleveland, OH 44106
Grady, Bernard C., Padres San Columbano, Apartado 1041, Lima, 100, Peru, S.A.

Military Chaplains:
Reverend Fathers—
Remy, David P., U.S.N., C.H.C., L.C.D.R., Naval Station Washington, Anacostia, Office of the Chaplain, Bldg. 72, Washington D.C., 20374
Schueller, La Verne L., Ch. Col., 96 ABW/HC, 202 N. Eighth St., Ste. 1, Eglin AFB, FL 32542-5651

Graduate Studies:
Reverend Fathers—
Joensen, William, Casa Santa Maria, Via dell'Umilta 30, 00187, Rome, Italy
Zinkula, Thomas R., Edifice Deschatelets, 175, Rue Main, Ottawa, ONT. K1S1C3 Canada

Unassigned:
Reverend Fathers—
DeVenney, Timothy
Goltz, William

On Leave of Absence:
Reverend Fathers—
Lynch, Maurice J.

On Medical Leave:
Reverend Fathers—
McTarsney, John F.

Retired:
Reverend Monsignors—
Ament, Ernest P., 405 Franklin St., Bellevue, IA 52031
Blessington, William H., Villa Raphael, 1235 Mt. Loretta, Dubuque, IA 52003-8785
Chihak, John P., 420 W. Lyon St., Garner, IA 50438
Collins, Bernard G., 3160 E. Main St., Village Grove #8, Mesa, AZ 85213
Dalton, John W., 1301 Rhodes, Naperville, IL 60540
Ferring, Robert L., 3400 Dana Dr., #4, Dubuque, IA 52002
Friedl, Francis P., 3400 Dana Dr., #3, Dubuque, IA 52002
Halbach, A. A., Stonehill Care Center, 3485 Windsor Ave., Dubuque, IA 52001-1312
Heineman, Donald P., 108 3rd St., S.E., P.O. Box 187, Fort Atkinson, IA 52144-0187
Heles, Frederic G., 107 Martin Dr., Apollo, PA 15613-8516
Heuring, Alvan P., 3458 Edison St., San Mateo, CA 94403-3401
Kress, Justin A., Villa Raphael, 1235 Mt. Loretta Ave., Dubuque, IA 52003-8785
Kurt, Edgar J., Villa Raphael, 1235 Mt. Loretta, Dubuque, IA 52003-8785
Leonard, William P., 971 Mt. Loretta Ave., Dubuque, IA 52003
Manternach, Albert V., 617 1st Ave., W., Cascade, IA 52033
McAvoy, Ambrose A., Stonehill Care Center, 3485 Windsor Ave., Dubuque, IA 52001-1312
O'Brien, Roger E., Villa Raphael, 1235 Mt. Loretta, Dubuque, IA 52003-8785
Raker, Clarence J., Stonehill Care Center, 3485 Windsor Ave., Dubuque, IA 52001-1312
Reicks, Leander H., 105 E. Rural St., P.O. Box 223, St. Lucas, IA 52166
Steimel, Paul T., 3709 W. 9th St., Apt. 8, Waterloo, IA 50702
Sullivan, Joseph A., 2245 Chaney Rd., #1, Dubuque, IA 52001
Supple, James A., 129 Ash St., #2, Ames, IA 50010
Sweeney, Donald F., Villa Raphael, 1235 Mt. Loretta Ave., Dubuque, IA 52003-8785
Vogl, Robert R., Loras College, 1450 Alta Vista, Dubuque, IA 52004-0178
Zachar, Albert L., 3031 Sixth St., S.W., Apt. 12, Cedar Rapids, IA 52404

Reverend Fathers—
Ament, Robert J., 1375 273rd Ave., Fort Atkinson, IA 52144-7405
Arquitt, William A., 1715 Edgewood Dr., NW, Apt. 3, Cedar Rapids, IA 52405
Auer, Robert F., 1027 N. Third St., Guttenberg, IA 52052
Axen, Ronald J., St. Francis Village, 105 Trinity Cir., Crowley, TX 76036
Bahning, Frederick C., Windsor Park, # 408, 801 Davis St., Dubuque, IA 52001
Barnes, John G., 114 Sheakley, New Hampton, IA 50659
Bierie, Elwyn L., P.O. Box 198, Bullshoals, AR 72619
Bodensteiner, Peter C., 108 W. Spring St., Apt. A-1, Lawler, IA 52154
Brickley, John J., Villa Raphael, 1235 Mt. Loretta Ave., Dubuque, IA 52003-8785
Brosius, Alfred G., Villa Raphael, 1235 Mt. Loretta Ave., Dubuque, IA 52003-8785
Carpender, Thomas J., Brookwood, Apt. 413, 1320 E. 48th Pl., Tulsa, OK 74105
Cross, Vern F., Stonehill Care Center, 3485 Windsor Ave., Dubuque, IA 52001-1312
Currier, Thomas F., 925 N. Harrison Ave., Mason City, IA 50401
Devine, William P., 22623 V Ave., Eldora, IA 50627-8012
Drexler, Harold J., Sacred Heart, 2215 Windsor Ave., Dubuque, IA 52001-1698
Dunkel, Henry N., Lourdes R.F.D. 1, Elma, IA 50628
Einck, Gregory J., Windsor Park Apartments, No. 109, 801 Davis Ave., Dubuque, IA 52001
Engler, Ernest J., St. John Rectory, 212 Seventh St. S.E., Mt. Vernon, IA 52314-0169
Evans, Paul J., 400 Blunt St., Charles City, IA 50616
Frana, Clarence L., 3031 Sixth St., S.W., Apt. 9, Cedar Rapids, IA 52404
Goedken, Nestor B., Windsor Park, 801 Davis, Dubuque, IA 52001
Griffin, Joseph F., Villa Rafael, 1235 Mount Loretta Ave., Dubuque, IA 52003-8785
Guter, Lawrence, Stonehill Care Center, 3485 Windsor Ave., Dubuque, IA 52001-1312
Hamilton, Philip A., 12 Padgett Ct., Bluffton, SC 29910
Heimerman, Francis D., 151 Main St., P.O. Box 623, Nashua, IA 50658
Hirsch, Robert M., 411 N. Jefferson St., P.O. Box 609, Calmar, IA 52132-0609
Holzer, Wm., 292 Northpointe Dr., N.E. 118, Cedar Rapids, IA 52405-6215
Hussmann, John R., Villa Raphael, 1235 Mt. Loretta Ave., Dubuque, IA 52003-8785
Kalb, Bertram J., Stonehill Care Center, 3485 Windsor Ave., Dubuque, IA 52001-1312
Kane, Justin J., 1423 Kimball Ave., Waterloo, IA 50702-3837
Karal, John W., Maple View, 613 W. Main St., Apt. 1, Marshalltown, IA 50158
Kissling, John M., P.O. Box 356, Chetek, WI 54728-0356
Klein, Karl J., Cedar River Tower, Apt. 905, 100 First Ave., N.E., Cedar Rapids, IA 52401
Kleve, Arthur W., Sacred Heart, 627 W. Fourth St., Waterloo, IA 50702
Kruse, Clarence, Villa Raphael, 1235 Mt. Loretta Ave., Dubuque, IA 52003-8785
Kurt, Allan J., P.O. Box 479, Dubuque, IA 52004-0479
LaBarge, Charles F., 1538 Kehl Ct., Dubuque, IA 52003
Laughlin, Martin T.,
Laughlin, Daniel, 4614 E. Hamblin Dr., Phoenix, AZ 85024
Maichen, Richard F., 1112 E. Main, Troy, OH 45373
McDonald, J. Robert, 718 Crystal Dr., N.E., Cedar Rapids, IA 52402
McDonald, Paul F., U.S.A.F., 8915 Willmon Way, San Antonio, TX 78239
Menster, William J., 703 Bluff St., Dubuque, IA 52001
Merfeld, Vincent C., 4536 Wilshire Blvd., #4, Los Angeles, CA 90010
Moran, John W., 507 Cherry Dr., P.O. Box 970, Monona, IA 52159
Most, William G., 9210 Park Ave., Manassas, VA 22110
Norton, Claude B., Villa Raphael, 1235 Mt. Loretta Ave., Dubuque, IA 52003-8785
Otting, Loras C., Villa Raphael, 1235 Mt. Loretta Ave., Dubuque, IA 52003-8785
Palen, Robert L., 19 W. 230 Governors Trail, Oak Brook, IL 60521

Pepper, David J., 102 W. Spring, Box 120, Lawler, IA 52154

Pitzen, John J., 215 Vanderbilt St., Fairfax, IA 52228

Purtell, Thomas W., Villa Raphael, 1235 Mt. Loretta Ave., Dubuque, IA 52003-8785

Raftis, J. Duane, Stonehill Care Center, 3485 Windsor Ave., Dubuque, IA 52001-1312

Rhomberg, Thomas W., 1510 Kell Ct., Apt. 6, Dubuque, IA 52003

Rogers, Daniel J., 3839 St. Catherine Rd., Bellevue, IA 52031

Roth, Jacob P., 3285 S. Liberty St., Apt. B, Canton, MS 39046

Ruhland, Carl J., 3955 Creston St., Dubuque, IA 52002

Saunders, Robert J., 710 Anderson St., Manchester, IA 52057

Schmidt, Wilfred W., 1584 White St., Dubuque, IA 52001

Schroeder, Karl G., Loras College, 1450 Alta Vista St., P.O. Box 178, Dubuque, IA 52001-0178

Schwartz, William T., 6421 S. Oakmont Dr., Chandler, AZ 85249

Sigwarth, Reynold J., Villa Raphael, 1235 Mt. Loretta Ave., Dubuque, IA 52003

Simon, Vincent J., 100 South St., P.O. Box 304, Ossian, IA 52161

Smith, John P., 203 First St. E., Cresco, IA 52136

Stark, John W., 3312 Carlton Dr., Cedar Falls, IA 50613

Weydert, Donald D., 2249 Del Monaco Dr., Dubuque, IA 52002

Whalen, Charles W., 2245 Chaney Rd., #4, Dubuque, IA 52001-2939

Permanent Deacons:

Aitchison, Gary, St. Cecilia, Ames
Ayers, John, Clear Lake
Baker, John, St. Edward, Waterloo
Baltes, Robert, St. Joseph, New Hampton
Barlow, Jack, St. Joseph, Mason City
Bassler, Eugene, (Retired), Maquoketa
Berger, James, St. Ludmila, Cedar Rapids
Berry, Matthew, Holy Family, Mason City
Biver, William, St. Columbkille, Dubuque
Blouin, Mike, All Saints, Cedar Rapids
Brustkern, Leo J., (Retired), La Porte City
Cashatt, Wayne, St. Mary, Eldora
Cisler, William, St. Wenceslaus, Cedar Rapids
Cooper, Charles, Holy Family, Mason City
DiPietre, Dennis, Columbia, MO
Dutcher, Frank, (Retired), St. Louis, MO
Fessler, Ray, (Retired), Dubuque
Fortin, Daryl, St. Patrick, Cedar Falls
Freet, James, Blessed Sacrament, Waterloo
Frost, Irwin, (Retired), Waterloo
Froyen, Leonard, St. Stephen The Witness Student Center, Cedar Falls
Gehrke, Richard, St. Mary, Hazleton
Gram, Clarence, St. Joseph, Waterloo
Groh, Victor, Sacred Heart, Rockwell; St. Patrick, Dougherty
Hayes, Joseph, St. Matthias, Cascade
Head, Robert, Sacred Heart, Maquoketa
Herman, John, Blessed Sacrament, Waterloo
Hoeger, Daniel, St. Patrick, Cedar Rapids
Hurych, Robert F., St. Paul, Newhall
Jenney, William, St. Nicholas, Evansdale
Jones, David, St. Mary, Ackley
Jorgensen, Gerald, Resurrection, Dubuque
Karsten, Thomas M., (Retired), Independence
Knepper, Walter, (Retired), Cascade
Koopmann, Gerald, St. John, Placid
LoBianco, Timothy, St. Patrick, Dubuque
MacDonald, Stephen, St. Joseph the Worker, Dubuque
Malone, John, St. Patrick, Fairfax; Holy Trinity, Walford
Manning, Richard, St. Ludmila, Cedar Rapids
Mauss, William, St. Anthony, Dubuque
McCully, John, St. Cecilia, Ames
McGhee, David, Nativity, Dubuque
Mead, Edward, St. Mary, Marshalltown
Mega, Robert, Sacred Heart, Manly
Moetsch, Michael, St. Patrick, Cedar Falls
Naso, James, Immaculate Conception, Van Horne; St. Paul, Newhall; St. John, Blairstown
Oates, Michael, St. Patrick, Cedar Falls
Otto, J. C., St. Michael, Belle Plaine; St. Joseph, Chelsea
Pantaloni, Ed, St. Joseph, Marion
Pettit, Gerald, Immaculate Conception, Cedar Rapids
Pfaffly, James, St. Mary, Guttenberg
Saunders, Phil, St. Matthew, Cedar Rapids
Scharosch, Albert, St. Pius X, Cedar Rapids
Schmall, Leo, St. Joseph, Marion
Schmit, Nick, St. Francis Xavier, Belmond
Simmons, Kenneth, St. Cecilia, Ames
Sinnwell, James E., Immaculate Conception, Charles City
Stattelman, Leo W., St. Patrick, Clear Lake
Steger, James, St. Joseph, Earlville; St. Joseph, Greeley
Tondra, Richard, St. Cecilia, Ames
Vaske, Irvin, St. Henry, Marshalltown
Weber, Edward, St. John, Waterloo
Whitters, Michael, St. John, Clarion
Wilson, James, (Retired), Waterloo
Zimmerman, Paul, St. Pius X, Cedar Rapids

INSTITUTIONS LOCATED IN THE ARCHDIOCESE

[A] SEMINARIES, ARCHDIOCESAN

DUBUQUE. *Seminary of St. Pius X,* Loras College, 1450 Alta Vista St., P.O. Box 179, 52001-0178. Tel: 319-588-7782. Revs. Dennis J. Colter, Rector; Mark A. Ressler, Vice Rector; David H. O'Connor, Spiritual Dir.; Scott E. Bullock, Dir. Pre-theology Formation. Students for Archdiocese of Dubuque 9; Seminarians 12.

[B] SEMINARIES, RELIGIOUS OR SCHOLASTICATES

EPWORTH. *Divine Word College,* 102 Jacoby Dr. S.W., P.O. Box 380, 52045-0380. Tel: 319-876-3353.
E-mail: hutch@mwci.net
Web site: www.svd.org
Society of the Divine Word (S.V.D.). Very Rev. William Shea, S.V.D., Rector; Revs. Michael Hutchins, S.V.D., Pres.; Kenneth Anich, S.V.D., Vice Pres. & Vice Pres. for Academic Affairs; Bros. Dennis Newton, S.V.D., Vice Pres. of Recruitment & Admissions; Leonard Bauer, S.V.D.; Rev. James Heiar, S.V.D., Vice Pres. for Devel.; Bro. Daniel Holman, S.V.D.; Rev. Joseph McDermott, S.V.D.; Bros. Henry Oeser, S.V.D.; James Zabransky, S.V.D.; Rev. John Tra, S.V.D.; Bros. Rodney Bowers, S.V.D.; Tony Kreinus, S.V.D.; Rogers Hannan, S.V.D.; Revs. Quang Duc Dinh, S.V.D., Vice Pres. for Formation & Dean of Students; John-Hue Tran, S.V.D., Assoc. Development Dir.; Joseph Dang, S.V.D.; Walter Bunofsky, S.V.D.; Francis Kuttikattukunnel, S.V.D.; Gus Wall, S.V.D.; Thanh Van Nguyen, S.V.D. Priests 13; Brothers 7; Sisters 2; Lay Teachers 24; Students 112.

[C] COLLEGES AND UNIVERSITIES

DUBUQUE. *Clarke College,* 1550 Clarke Dr., 52001. Tel: 319-588-6300; Fax: 319-588-6789.
Web site: www.clarke.edu
For a complete listing, refer to the Colleges and Universities section.

Loras College, 1450 Alta Vista St., P.O. Box 178, 52004-0178. Tel: 319-588-7100; Fax: 319-588-7964
For a complete listing, refer to the Colleges and Universities section.

CEDAR RAPIDS. *Mount Mercy College,* 1330 Elmhurst Dr., N.E., 52402. Tel: 319-363-8213; Fax: 319-368-6492.
E-mail: admission@mmc.mtmercy.edu
Web site: http://www.mtmercy.edu
For a complete listing, refer to the Colleges and Universities section.

[D] HIGH SCHOOLS, INTERPAROCHIAL

DUBUQUE. *Wahlert High School,* 2005 Kane St., 52001. Tel: 319-583-9771. Mr. Donald Miller, Prin.; Rev. James E. Hayes, Spiritual Dir. Priests 1; Sisters 3; Lay Teachers 60; Students 931.
Serving all Parishes in Dubuque; Holy Family, New Melleray; St. Joseph's, Key West; SS. Peter and Paul, Sherrill.

BELLEVUE. *Marquette High School,* 502 Franklin St., 52031. Tel: 319-872-3356. Rev. Donald V. Bakewell, Exec. Coord. Priests 1; Sisters 1; Lay Teachers 8; Students 118.
Serving St. John's, Andrew; St. Joseph's, Bellevue; St. Catherine's, St. Catherine; St. Donatus, St. Donatus; Holy Rosary, LaMotte; St. Peter's, Sabula; SS. Peter and Paul, Springbrook.

CEDAR RAPIDS. *Metropolitan Office of Catholic Education,* Cedar Rapids Metro Office, 516 A Ave. N.W., 52405. Tel: 319-366-2517. Sr. Jean Brady, B.V.M., Assoc. Dir.

Regis LaSalle Foundation, 516 A Ave. N.W., P.O. Box 1394, 52406. Tel: 319-366-0491; Fax: 319-366-4068. Anne Cunningham, Exec. Dir.; Rev. Msgr. Robert G. Hogan, Exec. Coord.

Xavier High School dba Regis High School and LaSalle High School Center, 735 Prairie Dr., N.E., 52402. Tel: 319-365-6991. Rev. Donald R. Bruggeman, Exec. Coord.; Jeff Henderson, Chief Admin. & Contact Person; Rev. Steven G. O'Brien, Campus Minister.

LaSalle High School Center. (Coed), 3700 First Ave., N.W., 52405. Tel: 319-396-7791. Joe Steepleton, Prin. Priests 1; Lay Teachers 16; Students 220.
Serving Holy Trinity, Walford; St. Patrick's, Fairfax; St. Jude's, St. Ludmila's and St. Patrick's, Cedar Rapids.

Regis High School Center, 735 Prairie Dr., N.E. Mr. Richard Breitbach, Prin.; Mr. David Glynn, Asst. Prin.; Mr. Justin Kramer, Guidance Dir. Priests 1; Lay Teachers 35; Students 477.
Serving the following parishes in Cedar Rapids: Immaculate Conception, St. Wenceslaus, St. Matthew, All Saints, St. Pius X, St. Joseph, Marion; St. Elizabeth Ann Seton, Hiawatha.

DYERSVILLE. *Beckman High School.* (Grades 7-12). (Coed), 1325 Ninth St. SE, 52040. Tel: 319-875-7188. Steve Schute, Prin.; Mr. Wayne Wilgenbusch, Asst. Prin. Priests 1; Sisters 1; Lay Teachers 34; Students 494.
Serving the following Parishes: St. Francis Xavier, Dyersville; St. Joseph, Earlville; St. Boniface, New Vienna; Ss. Peter and Paul, Petersburg; St. Paul, Worthington.

GILBERTVILLE. *Don Bosco High School,* 405 16th Ave., 50634. Tel: 319-296-1692.
E-mail: dons@forbin.com
Web site: http://homeforbin.com/ndons
Rev. Philip Thompson, Exec. Coord.; James Hrabe, Prin.; Rev. John Flaherty, Spiritual Dir.; Stacey Staton, Guidance Counselor. Priests 1; Lay Teachers 19; Students 236.
Serving St. Francis, Barclay, Dunkerton; Immaculate Conception, Gilbertville; St. Athanasius, Jesup; Sacred Heart, LaPorte City; St. Joseph's, Raymond; St. Mary of Mt. Carmel, Eagle Center.

WATERLOO. *Columbus High School,* 3231 W. Ninth St., 50702. Tel: 319-233-3358. Rev. Msgr. Russell M. Bleich, Exec. Coord.; Mr. D. Michael Palmer, Prin.; David Sharp, Assoc. Prin.; Rev. Paul E. Lippstock. Sisters 1; Lay Teachers 45; Students 576.
Serving all parishes in Waterloo; St. Nicholas, Evansdale; St. Patrick's, Cedar Falls.

[E] SCHOOLS OF RELIGION

CALMAR. *Christian Family School,* 52312. Tel: 319-562-3045. Rev. Richard W. Kuhn, Exec. Coord.; Susan Wiley, Youth Min. Priests 1; Lay Teachers 1; Students 208.

CASCADE. *Aquin Religious Education Center,* 608 Third Ave. NW, 52033-0460. Tel: 319-852-3005. Rev. Daniel A. Krapfl, Exec. Coord.; Jo Ann Harry, D.R.E. Lay Teachers 3; Students 135.

LANSING. *Lansing School of Religion,* 52151. Tel: 319-538-4668; 538-4360. Rev. Herbert L. Tegeler; Karen Weber, Dir. Priests 1; Sisters 1; Lay Teachers 11; Students 122.

MANCHESTER. *St. Paul's School of Religion,* 408 Clara Ave., 52057. Tel: 319-927-2900. Rev. Ralph P. Simington, Exec. Coord.; Wilma Billhorn, Dir. Priests 1; Lay Teachers 2; Students 474.

NEW HAMPTON. *St. John's School,* 823 W. Main St., Box 108, 50659. Tel: 515-394-3171. Rev. Marvin C. Salz, Dir.; Marjorie Zipsie, Coord. Lay Teachers 3; Students 185.

[F] CONSOLIDATED PARISH SCHOOLS

DUBUQUE. Consolidation of the following parishes: St. John Nepomucene, Fort Atkinson; St. Luke, St. Lucas.

Holy Trinity-Sacred Heart Consolidation. (Grades PreK-8), 2222 Queen St., 52001. Tel: 319-588-4657. Jean Burgmeier, Prin. Sisters 2; Lay Teachers 12; Students 290.

St. Mary-St. Patrick Catholic School. Martha Wightman, Prin., St. Patrick Attendance Center, 180 W. 15th St., 52001. Tel: 319-582-2127. St. Mary's Attendance Center, 1600 White St., 52001. Tel: 319-582-1053. Sisters 1; Lay Teachers 11; Students 168.

BALLTOWN. *Balltown-Sherrill Catholic School.* (Grades PreK-6). 5135 Sherrill Rd., Box 49, Sherrill, 52073. Tel: 319-552-2166. Sr. Paula Maloy, S.V.M., Prin.; Sr. Mildred Leuenberger, O.S.F., Exec. Coord.
Consolidation of the following parishes: St. Francis, Balltown; SS. Peter & Paul, Sherrill. Sisters 2; Lay Teachers 5; Students 68.

BELLEVUE. *Bellevue Area Catholic Elementary School.* (Grades K-8), 403 Park St., 52031. Tel: 319-872-3284. Jim Squires, Prin.; Rev. Donald V. Bakewell, Exec. Sec.
Consolidation of the following parishes: St. Donatus, St. Donatus; St. Peter, Springbrook; St. Joseph, Bellevue (School location); Holy Rosary, LaMotte. Lay Teachers 22; Students 275.

CALMAR. *Calmar-Festina-Spillville (CFS) Catholic Elementary School,* Box 815, 52132. Tel: 319-562-3291; Fax: 319-562-3292. Katie Schmitt, Prin.; Rev. Donald J. Hawes, Exec. Sec.
Consolidation of the following parishes: Our Lady of Seven Dolors (St. Mary's), Festina; St. Wenceslaus, Spillville; St. Aloysius, Calmar; St. Wenceslaus (Grades 1-4); St. Aloysius (Grades 5-8). Lay Teachers 10; Students 137.

CASCADE. *Aquin Elementary School,* 608 Third Ave., N.W., 52033-0460. Tel: 319-852-3331. Rev. Daniel A. Krafl, Exec. Coord.; Peter Smith, Prin.
Consolidation of the following parishes: St. Matthias, Cascade; Sacred Heart, Fillmore; St. Patrick, North Garryowen; St. Peter, Temple Hill. Sisters of St. Francis of the Holy Family 2; Lay Teachers 19; Students 256.

CEDAR RAPIDS. *Holy Family Catholic Consolidated School.* Rev. Harry A. Koelker, Exec. Sec. Lay Teachers 50; Students 731.
St. Ludmila Center. (Grades PreK-5), 215 21st Ave., S.W., 52404. Tel: 319-362-1943. Mike Welch, Prin.
St. Jude Center. (Grades PreK-5), 50 Edgewood Rd., N.W., 52405. Tel: 319-396-7818. Jack Luensman, Prin.
St. Patrick Center. (Grades PreK & 6-8), 509 A Ave., N.W., 52405. Tel: 319-363-1027. John Krumbholz, Prin.

CRESCO. *Notre Dame System of Education.* (Grades PreK-6), 221 Second Ave., E., 52136. Tel: 319-547-4513. Rev. Michael L. Tauke, Exec. Coord.; Alice M. Bartow, Prin. Lay Teachers 13; Students 237.

EPWORTH. *Seton Catholic Elementary School,* 52045.
E-mail: seton@hwcl.net
Deb Fleckenstein, Prin.; Rev. Louis Joeger, Exec. Sec.
Consolidation of the following parishes: St. Patrick, Epworth; St. John, Peosta; St. John, Placid; St. Joseph, Farley; St. Clement, Bankston. Sisters of the Presentation 1; Lay Teachers 24; Students 345.

GILBERTVILLE. *Immaculate Conception-St. Joseph School.* (Gilbertville-Raymond Consolidated Elementary School), 311 16th Ave., 50634-0256. Tel: 319-296-1089. Ruth Palmer, Prin.
Consolidation of the following parishes: St. Joseph, Raymond; Immaculate Conception, Gilbertville; St. Joseph (Grades K-2); Immaculate Conception (Grades 3-8). Sisters 1; Lay Teachers 19; Students 350.

GUTTENBERG. *Guttenberg-North Buena Vista Consolidated School.* (Grades K-8), 502 S. Second St., 52052. Tel: 319-252-1577. Sr. Suzanne Gallagher, P.B.V.M., Prin.; Rev. Msgr. John R. McClean, Exec. Sec.
Consolidation of the following parishes: St. Mary's, Guttenberg; Immaculate Conception, North Buena Vista. Lay Teachers 11; Students 158.

HOLY CROSS. *Rickardsville-Holy Cross-Luxemburg (RHCL) Catholic School,* 835 Church St., P.O. Box 368, 52053. Tel: 319-870-2405. Rev. Donald J. Plamondon, Exec. Coord.; Mary Smock, Prin.
Consolidation of the following parishes: St. Joseph, Rickardsville; Holy Cross, Holy Cross; Holy Trinity, Luxemburg (Grades K-3); Holy Cross (Grades 4-8). Sisters 1; Lay Teachers 8; Students 190.

MARSHALLTOWN. *Marshalltown Area Consolidated Catholic School,* 10 W. Linn St., P.O. Box 512, 50158. Tel: 515-753-7977. Mrs. Patricia Fox, Prin.; Rev. Thomas E. Braak, Exec. Sec.
Consolidation of the following parishes: St. Mary, Marshalltown; St. Henry, Marshalltown; Immaculate Conception, Haverhill; St. Henry, 310 Columbus (Grades K-2); St. Marys, 10 W. Linn St. (Grades 3-6). Lay Teachers 20; Students 277.

NEW VIENNA. *Archbishop Hennessy Catholic School,* Box 210, 52065. David Gross, Prin.; Rev. John J. O'Connor, Exec. Sec.
Consolidation of the following parishes: St. Boniface Center (Grades K-3), New Vienna; SS. Peter & Paul (Grades 4-6), Petersburg. Sisters 1; Lay Teachers 6; Students 121.

PROTOVIN. *Trinity Catholic School,* 116 Main St., 52163-0246. Tel: 319-569-8556. Julie Franzen, Prin.

STACYVILLE. *Visitation School.* (Grades 1-8), 603 N. Broad St., 50476. Tel: 515-737-2380. Sr. Lenore Ostdiek, O.S.F., Prin.
Consolidation of the following parishes: Church of the Visitation, Stacyville; Sacred Heart, Meyer. Sisters 2; Lay Teachers 8; Students 65.

[G] CONSOLIDATED K-12 SYSTEMS

MASON CITY. *Newman Catholic.* Newman High and Middle School. (Grades 5-12), 2245 19th St., S.W., 50401. Tel: 515-423-6939. St. Joseph Center. (Grades K-4), 320 Fifth St., S.E., 50401-4005. Tel: 515-423-3101. Newman Catholic Child Care, 713 N. Adams, 50401. Tel: 515-423-0168. Revs. Dennis H. Cahill, Exec. Coord.; David M. Beckman; Vicki Steil, Secondary Prin.; Kathy Lloyd, Early Childhood Dir. Parishes served: Holy Family, St. Joseph, Mason City: St. Patrick, Clear Lake; Sacred Heart, Manly; St. Michael, Plymouth; Sacred Heart, Rockwell; St. Patrick, Dougherty. Priests 1; Sisters 3; Lay Teachers 45; Elementary 468; High School 215.

[H] GENERAL HOSPITALS

DUBUQUE. *Mercy Health Center-St. Joseph's Unit,* 250 Mercy Dr., 52001. Tel: 319-589-8000; Fax: 319-589-8073
For a complete listing, refer to the Hospitals section.

CEDAR RAPIDS. *Mercy Medical Center, Cedar Rapids, Iowa,* 701 Tenth St., S.E., 52403. Tel: 319-398-6011.
E-mail: mercylib@crpl.cedar-rapids.lib.ia.us
Web site: http.//www.mercycare.org
For a complete listing, refer to the Hospitals section.
Mercy Medical Center, Cedar Rapids, Iowa, Endowment Foundation, Inc., 701 Tenth St., S.E., 52403. Tel: 319-398-6278
For a complete listing, refer to the Hospitals section.
Mercycare Service Corporation, 701 10th St., S.E., 52403. Tel: 319-398-6011
For a complete listing, refer to the Hospitals section.

DYERSVILLE. *Mercy Health Center-St. Mary's Unit,* 1111 Third St., S.W., 52040. Tel: 319-875-7101; Fax: 319-875-2957
For a complete listing, refer to the Hospitals section.

MASON CITY. *North Iowa Mercy Health Center,* 1000 4th St. S.W., 50401. Tel: 515-422-7000; Fax: 515-422-7827
For a complete listing, refer to the Hospitals section.

NEW HAMPTON. *St. Joseph Community Hospital,* 308 N. Maple Ave., 50659. Tel: 515-394-4121; Fax: 515-394-5628
For a complete listing, refer to the Hospitals section.

OELWEIN. *Mercy Hospital of Franciscan Sisters,* 50662. Tel: 319-283-6000; Fax: 319-283-6004
For a complete listing, refer to the Hospitals section.

WATERLOO. *Covenant Medical Center,* 3421 W. Ninth St., 50702. Tel: 319-272-8000
For a complete listing, refer to the Hospitals section.

[I] SPECIAL HEALTH CENTERS

DUBUQUE. *Holy Family Hall Infirmary,* 3340 Windsor Ave., 52001-1300. Tel: 319-583-9786; Fax: 319-583-3250.
E-mail: mtstfran@mwci.net
Web site: www.osfdbg.org
For a complete listing, refer to the Special Care Facilities section.
Marian Hall Infirmary, 1050 Carmel Dr., 52003. Tel: 319-556-5474
For a complete listing, refer to the Special Care Facilities section.
St. Dominic Villa, Cardiff St. and Mazzuchelli Heights, 52001-7399
For a complete listing, refer to the Special Care Facilities section.

[J] HOMES FOR AGED

DUBUQUE. *Padre Pio Health Care Center, Inc. dba Stonehill Care Center,* 3485 Windsor Ave., 52001-1312. Tel: 319-557-7180; Fax: 319-557-8934
For a complete listing, refer to the Special Care Facilities section.
Villa Raphael, 1235 Mt. Loretta Ave., 52003. Tel: 319-583-4904
For a complete listing, refer to the Special Care Facilities section.

CEDAR RAPIDS. *Hallmar-Mercy Medical Center,* 701 Tenth St., S.E., 52403
For a complete listing, refer to the Special Care Facilities section.

CRESCO. *Elder Hospitality of Iowa, Inc.,* Village Apartments, 301 First Ave., 52136. Tel: 319-547-3325
For a complete listing, refer to the Special Care Facilities section.

DYERSVILLE. *Mercy Health Center St. Mary's Unit-Oakcrest Manor,* 1111 Third St., S.W., 52040. Tel: 319-875-7101; Fax: 319-875-2957
For a complete listing, refer to the Special Care Facilities section.

[K] MONASTERIES AND RESIDENCES OF PRIESTS AND BROTHERS

PEOSTA. *New Melleray Abbey, Order of Cistercians of the Strict Observance,* 6500 Melleray Cir., 52068. Tel: 319-588-2319.
E-mail: melleray@mwci.net
Web site: www.osb.org/osb/cist/melleray
Legal Title: *Corporation of New Melleray.* Rt. Revs. Brendan J. Freeman, O.C.S.O., Abbot; David R. Bock, O.C.S.O., Retired Abbot; James J. Kerndt, O.C.S.O., Retired Abbot; David L. Wechter, O.C.S.O., Retired Abbot; Philip J. O'Connor, O.C.S.O., Retired Abbot; Revs. Timothy L. Welsh, O.C.S.O.; Bernard J. Cullen, O.C.S.O.; Daniel F. Lenihan, O.C.S.O.; Kenneth F. Tietjen, O.C.S.O.; Thomas J. McCarty, O.C.S.O.; James E. O'Connor, O.C.S.O.; Thaddeus J. Kennedy, O.C.S.O.; Xavier L. Dieter, O.C.S.O.; Joseph P. Bauwens, O.C.S.O.; Thomas A. MacMaster, O.C.S.O., Prior; Joseph G. Knapp, O.C.S.O.; James B. Henderson, O.C.S.O.; Neil Paquette, O.C.S.O. Total Residents 37; Priests 18; Brothers 19; Scholastics 1.

[L] CONVENTS AND RESIDENCES FOR SISTERS

DUBUQUE. *Mt. Loretto Convent.* Motherhouse and Novitiate of the Sisters of the Presentation of the B.V.M. 2360 Carter Rd., 52001-2997. Tel: 319-588-2008. Sr. Mary Jacqueline Quillin, P.B.V.M., Major Supr.; Sr. Mary Sharon Kelchen, P.B.V.M., Dir.; Rev. Douglas O. Wathier, Chap. Professed Sisters 80.
International Presentation Association.
Mt. St. Francis, 3390 Windsor Ave., 52001-1311. Tel: 319-583-9786; Fax: 319-583-3250. Motherhouse and Novitiate of the Sisters of St. Francis of the Holy Family. Sr. Margaret Jungers, O.S.F., Pres.; Sr. Marge Staudt, O.S.F., Dir. Sister Support Svcs.; Rev. Dennis J. Colter, Chap. Professed Sisters 128.
Sisters of St. Francis of the Holy Family Charitable Trust.
Our Lady of the Mississippi Abbey, 8400 Abbey Hill, 52003. Tel: 319-582-2595; Fax: 319-582-5511.
E-mail: misisip@mwci.com
The Cistercian Nuns of the Strict Observance. (Monastery of Trappistine Nuns). Rev. Mother Gail Marie Fitzpatrick, O.C.S.O., Abbess; Rt. Rev. James Kerndt, O.C.S.O., Chap. Professed Nuns 27; Novices 2.
St. Joseph's Convent, Mount Carmel, 1150 Carmel Dr., 52003. Tel: 319-556-3240; Fax: 319-557-1349.
E-mail: bvmcenter@bvmcong.org
Web site: http://www.bvm.cong.org
Motherhouse of the Sisters of Charity of the Blessed Virgin Mary. Sr. Floria Shannon, B.V.M., Admin.; Sr. Donard Collins, B.V.M., Admin.; Sr. Eileen Healy, B.V.M., Pastoral Care; Rev. Msgr. David A. Wheeler, Chap. Professed Sisters 125.
Sisters of Charity of the Blessed Virgin Mary, BVM Center, Mount Carmel, 1100 Carmel Dr., 52003. Tel: 319-588-2351; Fax: 319-588-4832.
E-mail: bvmcenter@bvmcong.org
Web site: http://www.bvmcong.org
Sr. Dolores Marie McHugh, B.V.M., Pres. Congregation; Sr. Mary McCauley, B.V.M., 1st Vice Pres.; Sr. Mary Joellen McCarthy, B.V.M., 2nd Vice Pres.; Sr. Margaret Zimmerman, B.V.M., Admin., B.V.M. Center.
Sisters of Charity of the Blessed Virgin Mary: Retirement Trust Plan and Charitable Trust. Total Staff 20.
Visitation Convent, 2950 Kaufmann Ave., 52001-1655. Tel: 319-556-2440. Sisters of the Visitation of the Congregation of the Immaculate Heart of Mary. Sr. Ruth Jackson, S.V.M., Pres.; Rev. Robert Beck, Chap. Professed Sisters 9.

CEDAR RAPIDS. *Sacred Heart Convent,* 1125 Prairie Dr., N.E., 52402-4737. Tel: 319-364-5196; Fax: 319-364-7383. Motherhouse of the Sisters of Mercy (Cedar Rapids Regional Community). Sr. Susan O'Connor, R.S.M., Pres.; Sr. Delores Marie Hannon, R.S.M., Vice Pres.; Marianne Arndorfer, Admin. Sacred Heart Convent. Professed Sisters 109; Total Staff 4.
Sisters of Mercy, Cedar Rapids.
Sisters of Mercy Charitable Trust.
Catherine McAuley Center for Women, Cedar Rapids.
Mount Mercy College, Cedar Rapids.

HIAWATHA. *Central Region of Franciscan Sisters of Perpetual Adoration,* Box 190, 52233-0190. Tel: 319-393-6092.
E-mail: KarenF@aol.com
Web site: www.fspa.org
Sr. Karen Flottmeier, F.S.P.A., Reg. Supr. Tel: 319-393-5982. Professed Sisters 167.

[M] RETREAT HOUSES

DUBUQUE. *New Melleray Guest House,* 6500 Melleray Cir., 52068. Tel: 319-588-2319.
E-mail: melleray@mwci.net
Web site: www.osb.org/osb/cist/melleray

Shalom Retreat Center, 1001 Davis St., 52001-1398. Tel: 319-582-3592. Sr. Marie Therese Kalb, O.S.F., Dir. Total Staff 10; Retreatants 6,532.

CEDAR FALLS. *American Martyrs Retreat House*, 2209 North Union Rd., P.O. Box 605, 50613-0605. Tel: 319-266-3543. Sr. Jeanine Kuhn, P.B.V.M., Dir. Total Staff 13.

HIAWATHA. *Prairiewoods Franciscan Spirituality Center*, 120 E. Boyson Rd., 52233. Tel: 319-395-6700; Fax: 319-393-7602. Sr. Joanne Moeller, F.S.P.A., Contact Person.

[N] NEWMAN CENTERS

AMES. *St. Thomas Aquinas Church and Catholic Student Center (Iowa State University)*, 2210 Lincoln Way, 50014-7184. Tel: 515-292-3810. Revs. Everett Hemann; Jon M. Seda; Rev. Msgr. James A. Supple, (Retired); Deacon Steve Vankerckvoorde; Sr. Mary Lou Specha, Parish Family Life & Youth Min.; John Donaghy, Dir. Campus Ministry & Charity, Justice and Peace Coord.; Robert LeBlanc, Church Business Admin.; Dawn Martin, Marriage Preparation; Jack Alexander, Coord. of Order of Christian Initiation of Adults & Liturgist; Crystal Caruana Sullivan, Campus Min.; Mary Ricke, D.R.E.; Nicole Cortazzo, Development Coord.

CEDAR FALLS. *St. Stephen the Witness Catholic Student Center, University of Northern Iowa*, 1019 W. 23rd St., 50613-3550. Tel: 319-266-9863; Fax: 319-266-3706. Rev. John S. Haugen, Dir. & Campus Pastor; Deacon Leonard Froyen, Dir. Permanent Diaconate; Joan E. Farstad, Dir. Education; David Marchesani, Dir. Alumni & Development.

WEST UNION. *Upper Iowa University*, c/o St. Francis of Assisi Church of Fayette, 128 N. Walnut, 52175. Tel: 319-422-3184. Rev. Dale J. Rausch, Chap., Holy Name Parish, 52175.

[O] MISCELLANEOUS

DUBUQUE. *Archdiocese of Dubuque Deposit and Loan Fund*, 1229 Mt. Loretta, 52003-7800. Richard L. Runde, Finance Officer.

Archdiocese of Dubuque Education Fund, 1229 Mt. Loretta, 52003-7800. Richard L. Runde, Finance Officer.

Archdiocese of Dubuque Perpetual Care Fund, 1229 Mt. Loretta, 52003-7800. Richard L. Runde, Finance Officer.

Archdiocese of Dubuque Seminarian Education Fund, 1229 Mt. Loretta, 52003-7800. Richard L. Runde, Finance Officer.

Heartland Housing Initiative, 696 Central Ave., 52001. Tel: 319-583-9653; Fax: 319-583-6490. (A member of the Mercy Housing System, Heartland Housing Initiative.). Sr. Mary Martensen, R.S.M., Regional Pres. Total Staff 2; Total Assisted 172.

Hennessy Charitable Trust, 2360 Carter Rd., 52001-2297. Tel: 319-588-2008. Sr. Mary Jacqueline Quillin. Sponsored by the Sisters of the Presentation.

National Communicators Network for Women Religious, 17027 Mountain Ridge, 52002. Tel: 319-557-8033. Sandy Wilgenbusch, Contact Person. Sponsor: Communication personnel of congregations of Women Religious who are members. Purpose: NCNWR is organized to promote and assist in the understanding of women religious and specifically, to enhance their image and advance their mission. The organization is also organized to provide a network of professional support and education for its members.

St. Vincent de Paul Society of the Archdiocese of Dubuque.

Dubuque Council, 1351 Iowa St., 52001. Tel: 319-583-8701. Paul Hoppman, Natl. Trustee & Pres.

Waterloo Council, 4114 Heritage Rd., Cedar Falls, 50613. Tel: 319-232-8662. Richard McGrane, Pres.

Cedar Rapids Council, 339 22nd Ave. S.W., Cedar Rapids, 52404. Tel: 319-364-0748. Robert Crawford, Pres.

WATERLOO. *Ridgeway Place, Inc.*, 155 E. Ridgeway Ave., 50702. Mr. Rod Acardi, Pres.
Sponsored by the Wheaton Franciscan Sisters, Wheaton, IL and a corporation of Wheaton Franciscan System. Purpose: To provide assisted living and economical housing, and related services, for elderly people and individuals.

RELIGIOUS INSTITUTES OF MEN REPRESENTED IN THE ARCHDIOCESE

For further details refer to the corresponding bracketed number in the Religious Institutes of Men or Women section.

[1180]—*Brothers of Saint Pius X.*—C.S.P.X.

[0350]—*Cistercians Order of the Strict Observance-Trappists.* (Our Lady of New Melleray).—O.C.S.O.

[0480]—*Conventual Franciscans.* (Prov. of Our Lady of Consolation).—O.F.M.Conv.

[0430]—*Dominican Fathers.* (Prov. of St. Albert the Great).—O.P.

[0420]—*Society of the Divine Word.* (Northern Prov.).—S.V.D.

RELIGIOUS INSTITUTES OF WOMEN REPRESENTED IN THE ARCHDIOCESE

[0230]—*Benedictine Sisters of Pontifical Jurisdiction.* (Yankton, SD).—O.S.B.

[0670]—*Cistercian Nuns of the Strict Observance.*—O.C.S.O.

[2100]—*Congregation of the Humility of Mary.* (Davenport, IA).—C.H.M.

[1780]—*Congregation of the Sisters of the Third Order of St. Francis of Perpetual Adoration.*—F.S.P.A.

[1070-03]—*Dominican Sisters Congregation of the Most Holy Rosary.* (Sinsinawa).—O.P.

[1820]—*Hospital Sisters of the Third Order of St. Francis.*—O.S.F.

[3530]—*Missionary Sisters Servants of the Holy Spirit.*—S.Sp.S.

[2960]—*Notre Dame Sisters.* (Omaha).—N.D.

[3130]—*Our Lady of Victory Missionary Sisters.*—O.L.V.M.

[2970]—*School Sisters of Notre Dame.* (Mankato, MN).—S.S.N.D.

[1680]—*School Sisters of St. Francis.* (Milwaukee, WI).—O.S.F.

[]—*Sisters for Christian Communities.* (Cincinnati).

[0430]—*Sisters of Charity of the Blessed Virgin Mary.*—B.V.M.

[2575]—*Sisters of Mercy of the Americas.* (Cedar Rapids).—R.S.M.

[2575.2]—*Sisters of Mercy of the Americas.*—R.S.M.

[1540]—*Sisters of St. Francis.* (Clinton).—O.S.F.

[1570]—*The Sisters of St. Francis of Assisi.*—O.S.F.

[3320]—*Sisters of the Presentation of the B.V.M.* (Dubuque; Aberdeen, SD).—P.B.V.M.

[1720]—*Sisters of the Third Order Regular of St. Francis of the Congregation of Our Lady of Lourdes.*—O.S.F.

[4200]—*Sisters of the Visitation of the Congregation of the Immaculate Heart of Mary.* (Dubuque, IA).—S.V.M.

CEMETERIES

DUBUQUE. *Mount Calvary.*
Mount Olivet.

CEDAR RAPIDS. *Calvary.*
St. John.
St. Joseph.

CRESCO. *Calvary.*

MARSHALLTOWN. *St. Mary.*

MCINTIRE. *St. Mel.*
St. Patrick.

WATERLOO. *Catholic Cemeteries, Inc.*

NECROLOGY

† Kissling, Joseph L., (Retired). —Died June 16, 1997.
† Kunsch, William C., (Retired). —Died April 29, 1997.
† Peters, John M., (Retired). —Died May 31, 1997.
† White, Alphonse P., (Retired). —Died July 10, 1997.

Diocese of Duluth

(Dioecesis Duluthensis)

Most Reverend

ROGER L. SCHWIETZ, O.M.I., D.D.

Bishop of Duluth; ordained December 20, 1967; appointed Bishop of Duluth December 12, 1989; consecrated and installed February 2, 1990. *Res., 2830 E. Fourth St., Duluth, MN, 55812.* Tel.: 218-724-9111; Fax: 218-724-1056.

Corporate title: *Diocese of Duluth.*

ESTABLISHED OCTOBER 3, 1889.

Square Miles 22,354.

Comprises the counties of Aitkin, Carlton, Cass, Cook, Crow Wing, Itasca, Koochiching, Lake, Pine and St. Louis in the State of Minnesota.

For legal titles of parishes and diocesan institutions, consult the Chancery Office.

Pastoral Center: 2830 E. Fourth St., Duluth, MN, 55812. Tel.: 218-724-9111; Fax: 218-724-1056.

E-mail address: bpschwietz@aol.com

STATISTICAL OVERVIEW

Personnel	
Bishop	1
Priests: Diocesan Active in Diocese	55
Priests: Active Outside Diocese	4
Priests: Retired, Sick or Absent	22
Number of Diocesan Priests	81
Religious Priests in Diocese	16
Extern Priests in Diocese	2
Ordinations:	
Diocesan Priests	1
Transitional Deacons	1
Permanent Deacons	3
Permanent Deacons in Diocese	22
Total Brothers	1
Total Sisters	179
Parishes	
Parishes	94
With Resident Pastor:	
Resident Diocesan Priests	49
Resident Religious Priests	11
Without Resident Pastor:	
Administered by Priests	34
Missions	3
Closed Parishes	1
Professional Ministry Personnel:	
Sisters	2
Lay Ministers	11
Welfare	
Catholic Hospitals	2
Total Assisted	158,000
Health Care Centers	2
Total Assisted	1,500
Homes for the Aged	2
Total Assisted	305
Educational	
Diocesan Students in Other Seminaries	7
Total Seminarians	7
Colleges and Universities	1
Total Students	1,749
Elementary Schools, Diocesan and Parish	13
Total Students	1,938
Catechesis/Religious Education:	
High School Students	4,605
Elementary Students	5,385
Total Students Under Catholic Instruction	13,684
Teachers in the Diocese:	
Priests	1
Sisters	2
Lay Teachers	161
Vital Statistics	
Receptions into the Church:	
Infant Baptism Totals	1,190
Adult Baptism Totals	52
Received into Full Communion	228
First Communions	1,269
Confirmations	1,241
Marriages:	
Catholic	298
Interfaith	265
Total Marriages	563
Deaths	1,468
Total Catholic Population	81,878
Total Population	416,781

Former Bishops—Rt. Rev. JAMES MCGOLRICK, D.D., cons. Dec. 27, 1889; died Jan. 23, 1918.—Rt. Rev. JOHN T. MCNICHOLAS, O.P., S.T.D., cons. Sept. 8, 1918; appt. Archbishop of Cincinnati July 8, 1925.—Most Rev. THOMAS A. WELCH, D.D., cons. Feb. 3, 1926; died Sept. 9, 1959.—Most Rev. FRANCIS J. SCHENK, D.D., cons. May 24, 1945; appt. to Duluth Jan. 19, 1960; resigned April 30, 1969; died Oct. 28, 1969.—Most Rev. PAUL F. ANDERSON, D.D., appt. Titular Bishop of Polignando and Co-adjutor Bishop with right of succession July 19, 1968; cons. Oct. 17, 1968; succeeded to See April 10, 1969; resigned Aug. 7, 1982; appt. Apostolic Administrator Aug. 7, 1982; appt. Auxiliary Bishop of Sioux Falls, SD March 25, 1983; died Jan. 4, 1987.—Most Rev. ROBERT H. BROM, D.D., cons. May 23, 1983; appt. Coadjutor Bishop of San Diego, CA, May 9, 1989.

Vicar General—Rev. DAVID TUSHAR.

Chancellor—Rev. DALE NAU, J.C.L.

Pastoral Center—2830 E. Fourth St., Duluth, 55812. Tel: 218-724-9111; Fax: 218-724-1056. Office Hours: Mon.-Fri. 8:30-12 & 1-4:30.

Deans—Rev. PAUL FRUTH, Brainerd; Rev. CORNELIUS KELLEHER, Cloquet; Rev. JEROME WEISS, Duluth; Rev. RONALD GAGNE, Hibbing; Rev. JAMES SCHEUER, Virginia.

Diocesan Tribunal—2830 E. Fourth St., Duluth, 55812. Tel: 218-724-9111.

Judicial Vicar—Rev. JAMES BISSONETTE, J.C.L.

Associate Judge and Vicar for Canonical Affairs—Rev. DALE NAU, J.C.L.

Defenders Of Bond—Rev. PATRICK MORAN, J.C.L.

Advocate—BETTE DAMBERG.

Notary—ROSE MARIE EICHMUELLER.

College of Consultors—Most Rev. ROGER SCHWIETZ, O.M.I.; Revs. DAVID TUSHAR; RONALD GAGNE; MICHAEL HAYES; ANDREW KNOP, O.M.I; FREDRICK METHOD; KENTON SAILSTAD; JEROME WEISS.

Priests' Pension Board—Most Rev. ROGER L. SCHWIETZ, O.M.I.; Revs. WILLIAM FIDER; FREDRICK METHOD; DALE NAU; DAVID TUSHAR, V.G.; JERRY WEISS; Mr. ROBERT MILLER.

Presbyteral Council—Rev. FREDRICK METHOD, Chm.

Corporate Board—Most Rev. ROGER L. SCHWIETZ, O.M.I.; Revs. DALE NAU; DAVID TUSHAR; Mrs. MARILYN GRATTO; Mr. ROBERT MILLER.

Finance Council—Most Rev. ROGER L. SCHWIETZ, O.M.I.; Revs. DALE NAU; LAWRENCE O'SHEA; SANDY SONDGEROTH, O.M.I.; DAVID TUSHAR, V.G.; JAMES BARTKOWSKI; GARY BUBALO; MARILYN GRATTO; DOUG HILDENBRAND; RONALD KARLEN; MICHAEL MARRIN; Mr. ROBERT MILLER; JOHN R. RYAN.

Finance Officer—Rev. LAWRENCE O'SHEA.

Diocesan Offices and Directors

Archivist—Rev. PATRICK J. MORAN, J.C.L., *2830 E. Fourth St., Duluth, 55812.* Tel: 218-724-9111.

Boy Scouts—Deacon GREGORY HUTAR, *604 E. Boundary St., Ely, 55731.* Tel: 218-365-5906.

Campus Ministry—Rev. DALE NAU, Dir., *421 W. Ste. Marie, Duluth, 55811.* Tel: 218-728-3757.

Cemeteries—Rev. DALE NAU, Dir., *2830 E. Fourth St., Duluth, 55812.* Tel: 218-724-9111.

Censor of Books—Rev. J. W. EVANS, Ph.D., *2830 E. Fourth St., Duluth, 55812.* Tel: 218-724-9111.

Continuing Formation of Priests—Rev. DAVE TUSHAR, *2830 E. Fourth St., Duluth, 55812.* Tel: 218-724-9111.

Coordinator of Catechesis—DENISE MACIEJ, *2830 E. Fourth St., Duluth, 55812.* Tel: 218-724-9111.

Coordinator of Youth Ministry—JANICE KILGORE, *2830 E. Fourth St., Duluth, 55812.* Tel: 218-724-9111.

Council of Catholic Women—Rev. PAUL FRUTH, Moderator, *1108 Willow St., S.E., Brainerd, 56401.* Tel: 218-829-8932.

Cursillo Movement—Rev. ROMAN SPORS, Spiritual Advisor, *Box 266, Emily, 56477.* Tel: 218-763-2101. BRYON HARKER, Lay Dir., *Rte. 1, Box 245, Longville, 56655.* Tel: 218-363-2567.

Diocesan Pastoral Council—Most Rev. ROGER L. SCHWIETZ, O.M.I., Pres.; ROSE EICHMUELLER, Sec.

Ecumenical and Inter-faith Affairs—Sr. CLAUDIA RIEHL, O.S.B., *2830 E. Fourth St., Duluth, 55812.* Tel: 218-724-9111.

Finance Officer—Rev. LAWRENCE O'SHEA, *2830 E. Fourth St., Duluth, 55812.* Tel: 218-724-9111.

Health Affairs—Rev. JOHN WHITNEY EVANS, *1200 Kenwood Ave., Duluth, 55811.* Tel: 218-723-6000.

Liturgy and Spirituality—Rev. KENT SAILSTAD, S.T.L., Dir., *2830 E. Fourth St., Duluth, 55812.* Tel: 218-724-9111.

Mission Outreach and Propagation of the Faith—Rev. LAWRENCE O'SHEA, Dir., *2830 E. Fourth St., Duluth, 55812.* Tel: 218-724-9111.

Newspaper "Catholic Outlook"—Rev. PETER MUHICH, Editor, *2830 E. Fourth St., Duluth, 55812.* Tel: 218-724-9111.

Office of Indian Ministry—Sr. MARIE ROSE MESSINGSCHLAGER, C.D.P., Dir., *2830 E. Fourth St., Duluth, 55812.* Tel: 218-724-9111.

Office for Clergy Vocations—Deacon MIKE KNUTH, *2830 E. Fourth St., Duluth, 55812.* Tel: 218-724-9111.

Office for Communications—Rev. DALE NAU, Dir., *2830 E. Fourth St., Duluth, 55812.* Tel: 218-724-9111.

Office for Education—Deacon MIKE KNUTH, Coord.; Mr. TERRY CHURCHILL, (Schools), *2830 E. Fourth St., Duluth, 55812.* Tel: 218-724-9111.

Office for Marriage and Family Life—Mr. DICK FROST, *2830 E. Fourth St., Duluth, 55812.* Tel: 218-724-9111.

Office for Development—MICHAEL MARRIN, Dir., *2830 E. Fourth St., Duluth, 55812.* Tel: 218-724-9111.

Office for the Permanent Diaconate—Deacon DAVID CRAIG, Dir., *2830 E. Fourth St., Duluth, 55812.* Tel: 218-724-9111.

Office for the Social Apostolate of the Church—Mr. DICK FROST, *2830 E. Fourth St., Duluth, 55812.* Tel: 218-724-9111.

Rural Life—Rev. MICHAEL HAYES, Dir., *112 Cedar, Moose Lake, 55767.* Tel: 218-485-5909.

CLERGY, PARISHES, MISSIONS AND PAROCHIAL SCHOOLS

CITY OF DULUTH
(St. Louis County)

1—CATHEDRAL OF OUR LADY OF THE ROSARY, Revs. David Tushar, Rector; Thomas Foster. In res., Rev. James Crossman.
Res., 2801 E. Fourth St., 55812. Tel: 218-728-3646.
School—Sisters 3; Lay Teachers 17; Students 307.
Catechesis/Religious Programs—D.R.E.: Mr. Patrick Bliss; Ms. Amy Kane.
Students 177.
Convent—443 Lakeview Ave., 55812. Tel: 218-724-4370. Sisters of the Third Order of St. Dominic (Springfield, IL)

2—GOOD SHEPHERD. Closed. For inquiries for parish records contact the Chancery.

3—HOLY FAMILY,. Consolidated with Ss. Peter and Paul, and St. Clement. Revs. Andrew Knop, O.M.I.; Anthony Wroblewski, O.M.I.
Parish Office: 518 N. 24th Ave., 55806. Tel: 218-722-4445.
Res., 2423 W. Third St., 55806. Tel: 218-722-0730.
Church—2401 W. Fifth St., 55806.
Catechesis/Religious Programs—Desiree Taylor, D.R.E.
Students 134.

4—OUR LADY OF MERCY, Rev. Patrick McDowell. In res., Rev. John C. Petrich.
Res., 325 E. Third St., 55805. Tel: 218-722-3078.
Church—2002 Minnesota Ave., 55805.

5—ST. ANTHONY. Closed. Sacramental records are located at St. Benedict.

6—ST. BENEDICT'S, Rev. Jon Wild; Deacon Dennis Anderson.
Office: 1419 St. Benedict St., 55811. Tel: 218-728-4325; 724-4828.
Res., 1419 Arrowhead Rd., 55811. Tel: 218-724-8926.
Catechesis/Religious Programs—Bob Huot, D.R.E.
Students 360.
Station—Duluth, Aftenro Home.

7—ST. ELIZABETH'S, Rev. Patrick J. Moran.
Res., 610 99th Ave. W., Duluth, 55808. Tel: 218-626-2283.
Catechesis/Religious Programs—Mrs. Ann Menart, D.R.E.
Students 51.

8—ST. JAMES, Rev. Charles Flynn.
Res., 721 N. 57th Ave. W., Duluth, 55807. Tel: 218-624-0125.
School—Catherine Clark, Prin. Lay Teachers 8; Students 102.
Catechesis/Religious Programs—Cheryl Foldesi, D.R.E.
Students 144.

9—ST. JOHN'S (Woodland), Rev. Jerome P. Weiss. In res., Rev. Joseph A. Hughes.
Res., 4230 St. John's Ave., 55803. Tel: 218-724-6332.
School—Tel: 218-724-9392. Mrs. Marie McCarthy, Prin.
Lay Teachers 6; Students 182.
Catechesis/Religious Programs—Students 308.
Mission—Gnesen, St. Joseph. [CEM]

10—ST. JOSEPH'S (Duluth Heights), Rev. Noel Stretton.
Res., 151 W. Linden St., 55811. Tel: 218-722-1021.
Catechesis/Religious Programs—Denise Maciej, D.R.E.
Students 120.

11—ST. LAWRENCE'S, Rev. William Fournier.
Res., 2404 Morris Thomas Rd., 55811. Tel: 218-722-1900; 722-2259.
Catechesis/Religious Programs—D.R.E.: Shawna Hansen; Sybil Zimmerman, (Grades K-6).
Students 270.

12—ST. MARGARET MARY (Morgan Park), Rev. Richard Partika.
Res., 1467 88th Ave. W., 55808. Tel: 218-626-2379.
Catechesis/Religious Programs—Janet Stanley, D.R.E.
Students 65.

13—ST. MARY STAR OF THE SEA, Rev. Patrick McDowell.
Res., 325 E. Third St., 55805. Tel: 218-722-3078.
Catechesis/Religious Programs—Shirley Baker, D.R.E.
Students 70.

14—ST. MICHAEL'S, Revs. William P. Fider; Frank Melovasich.
Office: 4901 E. Superior St., 55804. Tel: 218-525-1902.
Res., 4931 E. Superior, 55804. Tel: 218-525-7513.
School—4924 Pitt St., 55804. Tel: 218-525-1931.
Catechesis/Religious Programs—Joan Homstad, D.R.E.
Students 350.

15—ST. PETER'S, Rev. Patrick McDowell.
Res., 325 E. Third St., 55805. Tel: 218-722-3078.
Church—Third St. & Eighth Ave. W., 55805.

16—SS. PETER AND PAUL. See separate listing. Holy Family, Duluth.

17—ST. RAPHAEL'S, Rev. Lawrence O'Shea.
Parish Center: 5779 Seville Rd., 55811. Tel: 218-729-7537.
Res., 4458 Midway Rd., 55811. Tel: 218-729-5546.
Catechesis/Religious Programs—Rachelle Benoit, D.R.E.
Students 285.

18—WEST END CATHOLIC PARISH OF SS. CLEMENT AND JEAN. See separate listing for Holy Family, Duluth.

OUTSIDE THE CITY OF DULUTH

Aitkin, Aitkin Co., St. James, Rev. Patrick Coyle.
Res., 309 Second St., N.W., 56431. Tel: 218-927-6581. [CEM]
Catechesis/Religious Programs—Mary Ellen Moriarty, D.R.E.
Students 129.

Aurora, St. Louis Co., Holy Rosary, Rev. Joseph Sirba.
Res., 16 W. Fifth Ave. N., 55705. Tel: 218-229-3210.
Catechesis/Religious Programs—Students 62.

Babbitt, St. Louis Co., St. Pius X, Rev. James Scheuer. In res., Rev. John Sustarsic.
Res., 15 Ash Blvd., 55706. Tel: 218-827-2291.
Catechesis/Religious Programs—Mary Zupancich, D.R.E.
Students 59.

Ball Club, Itasca Co., St. Joseph's, Rev. Athanase Fuchs, O.S.B.
Res., HC4 Box 104, Deer River, 56636. Tel: 218-246-1805. [CEM]
Missions—Federal Dam, Sacred Heart; Bena, St. Anne's.

Beroun, Pine Co., St. Joseph's, Rev. Cornelius Kelleher.
Res. and Mailing Address—203 Lawler Ave. S., P.O. Box 490, Hinckley, 55037. Tel: 320-384-6313.
Church—250 Praha Ave., 55063. [CEM]

Bigfork, Itasca Co., Our Lady of the Snows, Rev. Stephen Solors; Deacon Jerome Sura.
Res., P.O. Box 11, 56628. Tel: 218-743-3255.
Chapel—Squaw Lake, St. Catherine's.

Biwabik, St. Louis Co., St. John's, Rev. Frank Perkovich; Deacon Herb Riley.
Res., Box 569, 55708. Tel: 218-865-6774.

Brainerd, Crow Wing Co., St. Andrew's, Rev. Paul Fruth.
Res., 1122 11th St., S.E., 56401. Tel: 218-829-0723; 829-8932 (Office).
Catechesis/Religious Programs—D.R.E.: Veronica Besmehn; Cheryl Hawkinson.
Students 400.

St. Francis, Revs. Roland J. Antus; Mark Coen.
Office: 412 N. Eighth St., 56401. Tel: 218-829-8753.
Res., 1-913 Juniper St., 56401. Tel: 218-829-3833.
Res., 2-921 Juniper St., 56401. Tel: 218-829-0184.
School—817 Juniper St., 56401. Tel: 218-829-2344. Faye Buffepta, Prin.
Lay Teachers 12; Students 157.
Catechesis/Religious Programs—Kim Koning, D.R.E.
Students 548.
Convent—625 N. Third St., 56401. Tel: 218-829-2437. Sisters of St. Benedict
Chapel—Pine Beach, St. Thomas of the Pines. [CEM]

Carlton, Carlton Co., St. Francis, Rev. James Bissonette.
Res., 509 Sunrise Dr., 55718. Tel: 218-384-4563. [CEM]
Catechesis/Religious Programs—Students 194.
Mission—Cromwell-Wright, Immaculate Conception. [CEM]

Cass Lake, Cass Co., St. Charles, Rev. Michael Cotone, O.S.C.
Res., 308 Central Ave. N., Box 368, 56633. Tel: 218-335-2359.
Catechesis/Religious Programs—Students 40.
Mission—Pennington, St. Charles.

Chisholm, St. Louis Co., St. Joseph's, Rev. Steven Daigle. In res., Rev. Clement Gustin, O.S.C.
Res., 113 S.W. Fourth St., 55719. Tel: 218-254-5703. [CEM]
Catechesis/Religious Programs—D.R.E.: Deanne Hildenbrand; Kathy Gregorich.
Students 425.
Mission—Buhl, Our Lady of the Sacred Heart, Tel: 218-258-3279.

Cloquet, Carlton Co., Holy Family, Rev. Eugene Francis Lyttle.
Res., 280 Reservation Rd., 55720. Tel: 218-879-9047. [CEM]
Mission—Sawyer, SS. Mary & Joseph.

Queen of Peace. Consolidated from the following two parishes: St. Casimir and Our Lady of the Sacred Heart. Rev. Kenton Sailstad.
102 4th St., 55720. Tel: 218-879-6958. [CEM]
Office: Tel: 218-879-6793.
School—Tel: 218-879-8516. Mother Colleen Kimbro, F.S.E., Prin.
Sisters 2; Lay Teachers 6; Students 125.
Catechesis/Religious Programs—Irene McKay, D.R.E.
Students 340.
Convent—5613 Lilac Hill Rd., Duluth, 55810. Tel: 218-624-9038. Franciscan Sisters of the Eucharist

Coleraine, Itasca Co., Mary Immaculate, Rev. Paul J. Larson.
Res., Box 290, 55722. Tel: 218-245-1684.

Cook, St. Louis Co., St. Mary's, Rev. Lawrence T. Antus, O.M.I.
Res., Box 609, 55723. Tel: 218-666-5334. [CEM]

Crosby, Crow Wing Co., St. Joseph's, Rev. Howard P. Eisel, S.S.C.
Res., 619 Poplar St., 56441. Tel: 218-546-6559.
Mission—Deerwood, St. Joseph.

Crosslake, Crow Wing Co., Immaculate Heart, Rev. Dennis Hoffman.
Res., Box 155, 56442. Tel: 218-692-3731.
Catechesis/Religious Programs—Students 95.

Deer River, Itasca Co., St. Mary's, Rev. Anselm Thevarkunnel.
Res., Box 98, 56636. Tel: 218-246-8582.
Catechesis/Religious Programs—Students 115.

Ely, St. Louis Co., St. Anthony's, Rev. James Scheuer; Deacon Gregory Hutar.
Res., 231 E. Camp St., 55731. Tel: 218-365-4017.
Catechesis/Religious Programs—Barbara Condor, D.R.E.
Students 226.

Emily, Crow Wing Co., St. Emily's, Rev. Roman Spors.
Res., Box 25, 56447. Tel: 218-763-2101.

Eveleth, St. Louis Co., Resurrection, Rev. Eamonn Boland.
Res., Box 586, 55734. Tel: 218-744-3277.
Catechesis/Religious Programs—D.R.E.: Pam Rapacz, (Grades K-6); Mary Dosan, (Grades 7-12).
Students 250.

Floodwood, St. Louis Co., St. Louis, Rev. John Doyle.
Res., Box 378, 55736. Tel: 218-476-2367.
Mission—Meadowlands, St. Mary's.
Chapel—Elmer, St. Joseph's.

Garrison, Crow Wing Co., Our Lady of Fatima, Rev. Vincent Ott, O.M.I.; Deacon Roger Marks.
Res., St. Therese Church, Onamia, 56359. Tel: 612-532-3614; 692-4466.

Gilbert, St. Louis Co., St. Joseph's, Rev. Frank Perkovich.
Res., Box 788, 55741. Tel: 218-741-9551.
Catechesis/Religious Programs—Students 141.

Grand Marais, Cook Co., St. John's, Rev. Walter O'Connell, O.P.
Res., Box 549, 55604-0549. Tel: 218-387-1409. [CEM]
Catechesis/Religious Programs—Students 70.
Mission—Grand Portage, Holy Rosary. [CEM]

Grand Rapids, Itasca Co., St. Joseph's, Revs. Thomas Radaich; James H. Hauver.
Parish Center: 613 First Ave., N.W., 55744. Tel: 218-326-2843.
Res., 726 Second Ave. N.W., 55744.
School—Sr. Mary Rochefort, O.S.B., Prin. Lay Teachers 10; Students 169.
Catechesis/Religious Programs—D.R.E.: Mary Gunderson; Mary Prudhomme; Lori Dowling; Edna Trunt.
Students 504.
Mission—Cohasset, St. Augustine's.

Hibbing, St. Louis Co., Blessed Sacrament, Rev. John O'Donnell.

Res., 2328 Seventh Ave. E., 55746. Tel: 218-263-3681.
School—Assumption.
Lay Teachers 7; Students 137.
Catechesis/Religious Programs—Dan Turnbloom, D.R.E.
Students 330.
Convent—718 E. 23rd St., 55746.
Station—Side Lake, Blessed Sacrament Chapel.

Immaculate Conception, Rev. John O'Donnell, Admin.
Res., 1928 Fifth Ave. E., 55746. Tel: 218-263-4319.

St. Leo's, Rev. Fredrick Method.
Res., 218 E. 39th St., 55746. Tel: 218-262-5541.
School—Rita Perry, Prin. Lay Teachers 10; Students 122.
Catechesis/Religious Programs—Students 438.
Convent—(Duluth) 2503 W. Third Ave., 55746. Sisters of St. Benedict

Hill City, Aitkin Co., St. John, Rev. Edward Buczynski.
Res., Box 156, 55748. Tel: 218-697-2465.
Catechesis/Religious Programs—Students 52.
Mission—Warba, St. Paul's.

Hillman, Crow Wing Co., Holy Family, Rev. Vincent Ott, O.M.I.
Res., Rte. 1, Box 188, 56338. Tel: 612-277-3386.

Hinckley, Pine Co., St. Patrick's, Rev. James W. Scheuer.
Res., Box 490, 55037-0490. Tel: 320-384-6313.
Catechesis/Religious Programs—Students 100.

Hoyt Lakes, St. Louis Co., Queen of Peace, Rev. Joseph Sirba.
Res., 513 Hampshire Dr., P.O. Box 211, 55750. Tel: 218-225-2867.
Catechesis/Religious Programs—Students 115.

International Falls, Koochiching Co., St. Thomas Aquinas, Revs. Louis Sondgeroth, O.M.I.; Wilfrid Upson, O.M.I.
Res., 810 Fifth St., 56649. Tel: 218-283-3293.
School—Rev. Thomas Belanger, O.M.I., Admin. Lay Teachers 10; Students 110.
Catechesis/Religious Programs—D.R.E.: Dawn Fausz; Jo McLaughlin.
Students 316.

Keewatin, Itasca Co., St. Mary's, Rev. Ronald Gagne.
Res., Box 219, 55753. Tel: 218-778-6379.

Littlefork, Koochiching Co., St. Columban, Rev. Louis Sondgeroth, O.M.I.
Res., Box C, 56653. Tel: 218-278-6638.

Longville, Cass Co., St. Edward's, Rev. Thomas J. Kisting.
Res., Box 38, 56655-0038. Tel: 218-363-2799.
Mission—Remer, St. Paul.

McGregor, Aitkin Co., Holy Family, Rev. John J. Fleischhacker, O.S.C.
Res., 55760. Tel: 218-768-2702.
Catechesis/Religious Programs—Students 55.
Chapel—McGrath, Our Lady of Fatima.

Marble, Itasca Co., St. Mary's, Rev. Paul J. Larson, Admin.
Res., Box 411, 55764. Tel: 218-247-7368.
Mission—Taconite, St. Joseph's.

Moose Lake, Carlton Co., Holy Angels, Rev. Michael T. Hayes.
Res., P.O. Box 487, 55767. Tel: 218-485-4909.
Catechesis/Religious Programs—D.R.E.: Peggy Rosera; Mary Rose Rosc.
Students 180.

Nashwauk, Itasca Co., St. Cecilia's, Rev. Ronald Gagne.
Res., 326 Second St., 55769. Tel: 218-885-1126.
Catechesis/Religious Programs—Students 134.
Mission—Pengilly, St. Kevin.

Northome, Koochiching Co., St. Michael's. (Under the jurisdiction of the Duluth Diocese; administered by the Crookston Diocese.). Rev. Alcuin J. Henger, O.M.I.
Res., St. Ann, P.O. Box G, Blackduck, 56630. Tel: 218-835-6673.

Orr, St. Louis Co., Holy Cross, Rev. Lawrence T. Antus, O.M.I.
Res., Box 218, 55771. Tel: 218-757-3273.
Chapel—Buyck, St. Joseph's.

Pequot Lakes, Crow Wing Co., St. Alice's, Rev. James Walsh; Deacon David Craig.
Res., Box 159, 56472. Tel: 218-568-4760.
Catechesis/Religious Programs—Amber Sechser, D.R.E.
Students 445.
Mission—Nisswa, St. Christopher's.

Pine City, Pine Co., Immaculate Conception, Rev. Michael J. Lyons; Deacon Eugene Biever.
Res., 535 Eighth St., 55063. Tel: 612-629-2935. [CEM]
School—St. Mary's, 815 W. Sixth Ave., 55063. Tel: 612-629-3953. Mary Beth Badowich, Prin.
Lay Teachers 4; Students 73.
Catechesis/Religious Programs—Students 140.

Pine River, Cass Co., Our Lady of Lourdes, Rev. Edward M. Foster.
Res., Box 44, 56474. Tel: 218-587-4163; 587-4203.

Proctor, St. Louis Co., St. Rose Catholic Church, Rev. Peter Muhich.
Res., 3 Sixth Ave., 55810. Tel: 218-624-0007.
School—Tel: 218-624-0818. Peggy Frederickson, Prin.
Lay Teachers 7; Students 78.
Catechesis/Religious Programs—Janice Rohweder, D.R.E.
Students 183.
Mission—Saginaw, St. Philip Neri.

St. Mathias, Crow Wing Co., St. Mathias, Rev. Henry A. Miller, O.S.C.
Res., 9988 Co. Rd. 121 S.W., Fort Ripley, 56449. Tel: 218-829-4061.
Station—St. Mathias, Crow Wing State Park.

Sandstone, Pine Co., St. Luke's, Rev. Jerome Datko, O.M.I.
Res., P.O. Box 644, 55072. Tel: 320-245-5175.
Catechesis/Religious Programs—Students 105.
Missions—Finlayson, St. Joseph's. [CEM]
Bruno, Sacred Heart. [CEM]

Silver Bay, Lake Co., St. Mary's, Rev. Francis Paquette; Deacon Fred Wright.
Res., 57 Horn Blvd., 55614. Tel: 218-226-3100.
Catechesis/Religious Programs—Students 68.

Tower, St. Louis Co., St. Martin's, Rev. Rudolph Pakiz.
Res., Box 757, 55790. Tel: 218-753-4310.
Catechesis/Religious Programs—Students 74.

Two Harbors, Lake Co., Holy Spirit, Rev. George Zeck.
Res., 227 Third St., 55616. Tel: 218-834-4313.
Catechesis/Religious Programs—Students 270.

Virginia, St. Louis Co., Holy Spirit, Revs. Lloyd Mudrak; Timothy Deutsch.
Res., 306 S. Second St., 55792. Tel: 218-741-6344.
School—Marquette, 311 3rd St. S., 55792. Tel: 218-741-6811.
Catechesis/Religious Programs—Linda Strukel, D.R.E.
Students 250.

Sacred Heart, Revs. Lloyd Mudrak; Timothy Deutsch.
Res., 603 12th St. N., 55792. Tel: 218-741-2322.
Catechesis/Religious Programs—Sally Strle, D.R.E.
Students 185.
Mission—Mountain Iron, Sacred Heart.

Walker, Cass Co., St. Agnes, Rev. Bruce Engen.
Res., Box 874, 56484. Tel: 218-547-1054.
Mission—Hackensack, Sacred Heart.
Station—Walker, Ah-Gwah Ching State Nursing Home.

Willow River, Pine Co., St. Mary's, Rev. Norman Pahl, O.M.I.
Res., Box 97, 55795. Tel: 218-372-3446. [CEM]
Mission—Sturgeon Lake, St. Isidore's.
Station—Willow River, Youth Conservation Camp.

INDIAN MISSIONS

Duluth, St. Louis Co., Indian Missions,
c/o Chancery Office: 2830 E. Fourth St., 55812. Sr. Marie Rose Messingschlager, C.D.P.
Missions—Cloquet, Carlton Co., Holy Family Church, Reservation Rd., P.O. Box 280, Cloquet, 55720. Tel: 218-879-9047. [CEM]
Rev. Eugene Lyttle.
Sawyer, Carlton Co., SS. Mary and Joseph, 280 Reservation Rd., Cloquet, 55720. Rev. Eugene Lyttle.; Ball Club, Itasca Co., St. Joseph's. [CEM]
Rev. Athanase Fuchs, O.S.B.
Federal Dam, Sacred Heart, HC4 Box 104, Deer River, 56636. Rev. Athanase Fuchs, O.S.B.; Grand Portage, Cook Co., Holy Rosary, P.O. Box 549, Grand Marais, 56604. [CEM]
Rev. Walter O'Connel, O.P.
Walker, Ah-Gwah-Ching State Nursing Home, Box 874, Walker, 56484. Rev. Bruce Engen; Nett Lake, St. Louis Co., Immaculate Conception. (Indian Apostolate) Holy Cross, Box 218, Orr, 55771. Rev. Lawrence Antus, O.M.I.

Chaplains of Public Institutions

Hospitals

DULUTH. *Miller Dwan Hospital*. Rev. John C. Petrich, Chap. Tel: 218-727-1089.
St. Luke's Hospital, 2002 Minnesota Ave., 55802. Tel: 218-727-1089. Rev. John C. Petrich, Chap.

BRAINERD. *Brainerd Regional Human Services Center*. Vacant.

MOOSE LAKE. *Moose Lake State Hospital*, 112 Cedar, 55767. Tel: 218-485-4909. Rev. Michael T. Hayes, Chap. Tel: 218-485-4411.

Correctional Institutions

DULUTH. *Duluth Federal Prison*. Rev. Noel Stretton. Tel: 218-722-1021.

SAGINAW. *Northeast Regional Correctional Institution*. Rev. John C. Petrich, Chap. Tel: 218-727-1089.

WILLOW RIVER. *Youth Conservation Camp*. Rev. Norman Pahl, O.M.I., Chap. Tel: 218-372-3446.

Special Assignment:
Reverend Fathers—
Evans, John Whitney, College of St. Scholastica, 1200 Kenwood Ave., Duluth, MN 55811. Tel: 218-723-6000

On Duty Outside the Diocese:
Reverend Fathers—
Graham, William C., 47 E. 129th St., New York City, NY 10035
Johnson, Lawrence P., 7752 Clarmont Dr., No. 1634, San Diego, CA 92122
Kaster, Alfred D., St. Patrick, 235 Chapel St., Grass Valley, CA 95945
Kottiry, Alphonsus, Ramapuran Bazaar, P.O. Box Kattayam Dist., Kerala State S., India

Military Chaplains:
Reverend Fathers—
Lambert, Peter, Chap., U.S.A.F., PSC 41 Box 1938, APO, AE 09464

On Leave Without Assignment:
Reverend Fathers—
Klein, Robert W., Albuquerque Villa, Albuquerque, NM 87150
Makowski, Mark, 389 Dayton Ave., St. Paul, MN 55102

Retired:
Reverend Monsignors—
Popesh, Bernard, 609 E. Chapman St., Ely, MN 55731. Tel: 218-365-6085
Reverend Fathers—
Bouchard, Thomas, Box 38, Remer, MN 56672. Tel: 218-566-2954
Cossette, Raymond, 1599 County Rd. 8 SE., Brainerd, MN 56401. Tel: 218-764-2941
Dolsina, Stanley, 2423 Morris Thomas Rd., Duluth, MN 55811
Faith, Rudolph, 330 E. 3rd St., Duluth, MN 55805. Tel: 218-733-0988
Fox, Fredrick, 330 E. 3rd St., Duluth, MN 55805. Tel: 218-724-9228
Gaber, Francis, 250 Praha, Beroun, MN 55004. Tel: 612-629-3342
Golden, James, 204-4th Ave., Keewatin, MN 55753. Tel: 218-778-6949
Golobich, John, 524 N. Oak Bend Drive, #102, Duluth, MN 55811. Tel: 218-723-1566
Hughes, Joseph A., 4230 St. John's Ave., Duluth, MN 55803. Tel: 218-728-3068
Kuras, Felix, 330 E. 3rd St., Duluth, MN 55805. Tel: 218-723-7125
Marincel, Frank, 8521 Park Villa Drive, #105 W, Mt. Iron, MN 55768. Tel: 218-749-6750
McEnery, Dennis, Abbeyfeale, Co. Limerick, Ireland
Vovk, Joseph, 16 W. Fifth Ave. N., Aurora, MN 55705. Tel: 218-229-3210
Zorichak, William, 330 E. Third St., Duluth, MN 55805

Permanent Deacons:
Anderson, Dennis, St. Benedict, Duluth
Anderson, H. L., St. John, Duluth
Beier, Walter, St. John's, Duluth
Biever, Eugene, Immaculate Conception Church, Pine City
Birkland, Roger, St. Joseph, Gnesen
Christensen, Robert, (Retired)
Craig, David, St. Alice, Pequot Lakes
Ferris, Jack, St. Mary's, Silver Bay
Griffiths, James, St. Leo's, Hibbing
Hume, Michael, Central City Parishes, Duluth
Hutar, Gregory, St. Anthony, Ely
Knuth, Michael, St. Alice, Pequot Lakes
Laumeyer, Richard, St. Michael's, Duluth
Marks, Roger, Holy Family, Hillman
Mayer, Philip, St. Joseph's, Crosby
Olson, Barry, Immaculate Heart, Cross Lake
Paine, Richard, St. Alice, Pequot Lakes
Riley, Herbert, St. John, Biwabik
Sura, Jerome, Our Lady of the Snows, Bigfork
Szyman, Robert, Queen of Peace, Cloquet
Windus, Theodore, Sr., St. James, Duluth
Woznick, Gregory, St. Paul, Remer
Wright, Fred, St. Mary's, Silver Bay

INSTITUTIONS LOCATED IN THE DIOCESE

[A] COLLEGES AND UNIVERSITIES

DULUTH. *College of St. Scholastica*, 1200 Kenwood Ave., 55811. Tel: 218-723-6000; Fax: 218-723-6290.
For a complete listing, refer to the Colleges and Universities section.

[B] ELEMENTARY SCHOOLS, INTERPAROCHIAL

VIRGINIA. *Marquette Catholic School*, 311 Third St. S., 55792. Tel: 218-741-6811. Serving the parishes of Holy Spirit & Sacred Heart. Marianne Runkle, Prin. Lay Teachers 10; Students 126.

[C] GENERAL HOSPITALS

DULUTH. *St. Mary's Medical Center*, 407 E. Third St., 55805. Tel: 218-726-4000; Fax: 218-726-4383.
For a complete listing, refer to the Hospitals section.

BRAINERD. *St. Joseph's Medical Center*, 523 N. Third St., 56401. Tel: 218-829-2861; Fax: 218-828-3103.
For a complete listing, refer to the Hospitals section.

[D] HOMES FOR AGED

DULUTH. *Benedictine Health Center*, 935 Kenwood Ave., 55811. Tel: 218-723-6408; Fax: 218-723-6449.
For a complete listing, refer to the Special Care Facilities section.

St. Ann's Senior Residence, 330 E. Third St., 55805. Tel: 218-727-8831; Fax: 218-727-8833.
For a complete listing, refer to the Special Care Facilities section.

[E] CONVENTS AND RESIDENCES FOR SISTERS

DULUTH. *Benedictine Sisters Benevolent Association.* (Minnesota Corporation), 1001 Kenwood Ave., 55811-2300. Tel: 218-728-1817; Fax: 218-723-5902. Sr. Danile Lynch, O.S.B., Pres.

Motherhouse and Novitiate of the Sisters of Saint Benedict, St. Scholastica Monastery, 1001 Kenwood Ave., 55811. Tel: 218-723-6555. Sr. Aelred Roehl, O.S.B., Archivist.
In community: Professed Sisters 164.

[F] NEWMAN CENTERS

DULUTH. *University of MN-Duluth*, 421 W. Ste. Marie St., 55811. Tel: 218-728-3757. Rev. Dale Nau, Dir.; Deacon Chico Anderson, Assoc. Dir.

College of St. Scholastica, 1200 Kenwood Ave., 55811. Tel: 218-723-6000. Campus Ministry Directors: John O'Connor; Mary O'Connor.

Brainerd Community College, 921 Juniper St., Brainerd, 56401. Tel: 218-829-8753.

Itasca Community College, St. Joseph's, Box 110, Grand Rapids, 55744.

Hibbing Community College, 2328 Seventh Ave. E., Hibbing, 55746. Tel: 218-263-3681. Rev. John O'Donnell.

Mesabi Community College, 603 12th St. N., Virginia, 55792. Tel: 218-741-2322. Rev. Timothy Deutsch.

Vermilion Community College, St. Anthony's Catholic Church, 231 E. Camp St., Vermilion, 55731. Rev. James Scheuer.

[G] MISCELLANEOUS LISTINGS

DULUTH. *Benedictine Sisters Benevolent Association.* (Parent Co.), 1001 Kenwood Ave., 55811-2300. Tel: 218-728-1817; Fax: 218-723-5902. Sr. Danile Lynch, O.S.B., Pres.

Benedictine Health System. (Sub. of Benedictine Sisters Benevolent Association), 503 E. Third St., Ste. 400, 55805. Tel: 218-720-2370; Fax: 218-720-2373. Barry J. Halm, Pres. & CEO.

St. Mary's Medical Center. (Sub. of Benedictine Health System), 407 E. Third St., 55805. Tel: 218-726-4000; Fax: 218-726-4383. Sr. Kathleen Hofer, O.S.B., Pres. & CEO.

St. Joseph's Medical Center, Brainerd. (Sub. of Benedictine Health System), 323 N. Third St., Brainerd, 56401. Tel: 218-829-2861; Fax: 218-828-3103. Thomas Prusak, Pres. & CEO.

Benedictine Foundation, Inc. (Sub. of Benedictine Health System), 407 E. Third St., 55805. Tel: 218-720-2396; Fax: 218-726-4018. Steve Yorde, Pres. & CEO.

Benedictine Health Center. (Sub. of Benedictine Health System), 935 Kenwood Ave., 55811. Tel: 218-723-6408; Fax: 218-723-6449. Joseph Devore, Exec. Dir.

St. Francis Regional Medical Center. (Sub. of Benedictine Health System), 1455 St. Francis Ave., Shakopee, 55379. Tel: 612-403-3000; Fax: 612-403-3820. Venetia Kudrle, Pres. & CEO.

St. Mary's Regional Health Center. (Sub. of Benedictine Health System), 1027 Washington, Detroit Lakes, 56501. Tel: 218-847-5611; Fax: 218-847-7674. John Solheim, Pres. & CEO.

Polinsky Medical Rehabilitation Center, (Sub. of St. Mary's Medical Center), 530 E. Second St., 55805. Tel: 218-727-5083; Fax: 218-727-1167. Ann Bussey, Dir.

St. Mary's/Polinsky Center for Personal Fitness. (Sub. of St. Mary's Medical Center), 5th Ave. E. & 2nd St., Duluth, 55805. Tel: 218-725-5400.

BHS Long Term Care, Inc. (Sub. of Benedictine Health System), 503 E. Third St., Ste. 400, 55805. Tel: 218-720-2370; Fax: 218-720-2373. Dennis Acrea, Pres. & CEO.

St. Mary's Hospital. (Sub. of Benedictine Health System), P.O. Box 137, Cottonwood, ID, 83522. Tel: 208-962-3251; Fax: 208-962-3722. Mrs. Casey Uhling, Admin.

Madonna Towers of Rochester, Inc. (Sub. of Benedictine Health System), 4001 19th Ave. N.W., Rochester, 55901. Tel: 507-288-3911; Fax: 507-288-0393. Mark Cairns, Admin.

Tekawitha Nursing Center, Inc. (Sub. of Benedictine Health System), 6 E. Chestnut, Sisseton, SD, 57262. Tel: 605-698-7693; Fax: 605-698-3091. Patrick Rafferty, Admin.

The Blessed Nuno Society, P.O. Box 3484, 55803. Tim Heinan, Dir.

Holy Rosary Parish Endowment Fund, 2801 E. Fourth St., 55812.

The Human Life and Development Fund of the Diocese of Duluth, 2830 E. Fourth St., 55812. Tel: 218-724-9111; Fax: 218-724-1056. Most Rev. Roger Schwietz, O.M.I., Pres.; Revs. David Tushar, V.G., Vice Pres.; Dale Nau, Chancellor, Sec. & Treas.

John S. Duss Memorial Music Conservatory, 2211 Greysolon Rd., 55812. Tel: 218-724-2052. Franciscan Sisters of the Eucharist. Part of Franciscan Life Center Network, Inc.

McCabe Renewal Center, 2125 Abbotsford Ave., 55803. Tel: 218-724-5266. Sr. Mary Stephen Eckes, O.S.B., Dir.

Port Area Catholic Education (PACE), 2830 E. Fourth St., 55812. PACE is a consortium of Catholic parish elementary schools (St. Rose, Proctor; Holy Rosary, St. Michael, St. John, & St. James, Duluth; Queen of Peace, Cloquet).

St. Vincent de Paul Society, 109 W. Fourth St., 55806. Tel: 218-727-9145. Joseph Jodouin, Pres.

WALKER. *S.W. Deanery Chapter of Magnificat of the Diocese of Duluth*, P.O. Box 1030, 56484. Incorporators: Rosemary Ellis; Betty Garoutte.

RELIGIOUS INSTITUTES OF MEN REPRESENTED IN THE DIOCESE

For further details refer to the corresponding bracketed number in the Religious Institutes of Men or Women section.

[0200]—*Benedictine Monks.*—O.S.B.

[0400]—*Canons Regular of the Order of Holy Cross.*—O.S.C.

[0430]—*Dominican Fathers.* (Northern Prov.).—O.P.

[0910]—*Oblates of Mary Immaculate.* (Central Prov.).—O.M.I.

[0370]—*Society of St. Columban.*—S.S.C.

RELIGIOUS INSTITUTES OF WOMEN REPRESENTED IN THE DIOCESE

[0230]—*Benedictine Sisters of Pontifical Jurisdiction.* (St. Joseph, MN; Watertown, SD; St. Paul, MN; Duluth, MN).—O.S.B.

[1070-10]—*Dominican Sisters.*—O.P.

[1070-13]—*Dominican Sisters.*—O.P.

[1250]—*The Institute of the Franciscan Sisters of the Eucharist.* (Meriden, CT).—F.S.E.

[2970]—*School Sisters of Notre Dame.* (Mankato Prov.).—S.S.N.D.

[0430]—*Sisters of Charity of the Blessed Virgin Mary.*—B.V.M.

[]—*Sisters of Divine Providence of KY.*—C.D.P.

[1990]—*Sisters of the Holy Names of Jesus and Mary.*—S.N.J.M.

[1720]—*Sisters of the Third Order Regular of St. Francis of the Congregation of Our Lady of the Lourdes.*—O.S.F.

[2150]—*Sisters Servants of the Immaculate Heart of Mary.*—I.H.M.

DIOCESAN CEMETERIES

DULUTH. *Calvary Cemetery*, 1312 Howard Gnesen Rd., 55803. Tel: 218-724-3376. Rev. Dale Nau, Dir.; Mr. Tim Stresow, Supt.

NECROLOGY

† Hogan, Michael Jerome, (Retired). —Died May 8, 1997.

† O'Doherty, Dermot Augustine, (Retired). —Died June 25, 1997.

Diocese of El Paso

(Dioecesis Elpasensis)

Most Reverend

ARMANDO X. OCHOA, D.D.

Bishop of El Paso; ordained May 23, 1970; appointed Titular Bishop of Sitifi and Auxiliary of the Archdiocese of Los Angeles December 29, 1986; ordained Bishop February 23, 1987; appointed Bishop of El Paso April 1, 1996; installed June 26, 1996.

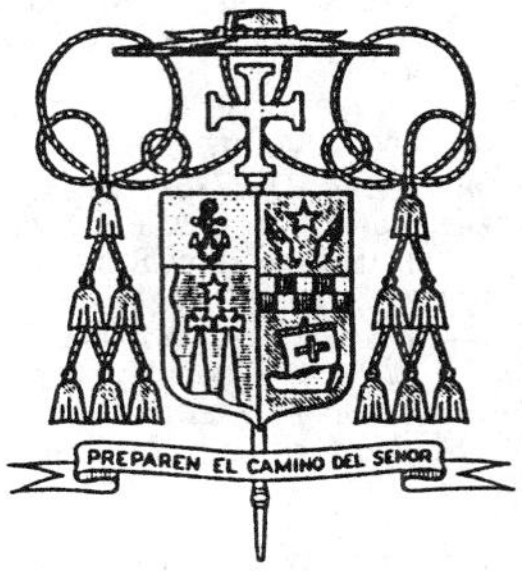

ERECTED MARCH 3, 1914.

Square Miles 26,686.

Comprises in Texas, the Counties of El Paso, Brewster, Culberson, Hudspeth, Jeff Davis, Loving, Presidio, Reeves, Ward and Winkler.

For legal titles of parishes and diocesan institutions, consult the Chancery Office.

Chancery Office: 499 St. Matthews St., El Paso, TX, 79907. Tel.: 915-595-5000; Fax: 915-595-5095.

STATISTICAL OVERVIEW

Personnel	
Bishop	1
Priests: Diocesan Active in Diocese	65
Priests: Active Outside Diocese	2
Priests: Retired, Sick or Absent	25
Number of Diocesan Priests	92
Religious Priests in Diocese	40
Ordinations:	
Diocesan Priests	3
Transitional Deacons	2
Permanent Deacons in Diocese	15
Total Brothers	17
Total Sisters	243
Parishes	
Parishes	58
With Resident Pastor:	
Resident Diocesan Priests	40
Resident Religious Priests	15
Without Resident Pastor:	
Administered by Priests	2
Administered by Women Religious	1
Missions	22
Professional Ministry Personnel:	
Sisters	12
Lay Ministers	23
Welfare	
Health Care Centers	1
Total Assisted	18,870
Homes for the Aged	2
Total Assisted	97
Day Care and Extended Day Care Centers	1
Total Assisted	73
Specialized Homes	1
Total Assisted	67
Special Centers for Social Services	5
Total Assisted	75,600
Educational	
Seminaries, Diocesan	1
Students from This Diocese	1
Diocesan Students in Other Seminaries	3
Seminaries, Religious	2
Students Religious	18
Total Seminarians	22
High Schools, Diocesan and Parish	1
Total Students	657
High Schools, Private	2
Total Students	340
Elementary Schools, Diocesan and Parish	9
Total Students	3,410
Elementary Schools, Private	3
Total Students	850
Catechesis/Religious Education:	
High School Students	5,062
Elementary Students	12,686
Total Students Under Catholic Instruction	23,027
Teachers in the Diocese:	
Priests	9
Brothers	9
Sisters	33
Lay Teachers	283
Vital Statistics	
Receptions into the Church:	
Infant Baptism Totals	8,473
Adult Baptism Totals	127
Received into Full Communion	256
First Communions	5,433
Confirmations	3,642
Marriages:	
Catholic	1,163
Interfaith	101
Total Marriages	1,264
Deaths	1,816
Total Catholic Population	591,361
Total Population	780,608

Former Bishops—Most Rev. JOHN J. BROWN, S.J., preconized Bishop of El Paso, Jan. 22, 1915; resigned June 16, 1915.—Most Rev. ANTHONY J. SCHULER, S.J., D.D., cons. Oct. 28, 1915; died June 3, 1944.—Most Rev. SIDNEY M. METZGER, S.T.D., J.C.D., cons. April 10, 1940; succeeded to See, Nov. 29, 1942; retired May 29, 1978; died April 12, 1986.—Most Rev. PATRICK F. FLORES, D.D., cons. May 5, 1970; installed Bishop of El Paso, May 29, 1978; appt. Archbishop of San Antonio, Aug. 28, 1979.—Most Rev. RAYMUNDO J. PENA, D.D., cons. Dec. 13, 1976; appt. Bishop of El Paso, April 29, 1980; appt. Bishop of Brownsville, May 23, 1995.

Vicars General—Rev. Msgr. FRANCIS J. SMITH; Rev. RICHARD A. MATTY.

Moderator of the Curia—Rev. RICHARD A. MATTY.

Chancellor—Rev. RICHARD A. MATTY.

Vice Chancellor—Sr. HELEN SANTAMARIA, S.L.

Canonical Consultant—Rev. RICHARD ZAMORANO.

Diocesan Pastoral Staff—Rev. RICHARD A. MATTY, Chancellor; Sr. HELEN SANTAMARIA, S.L., Assoc. Chancellor.

Diocesan Pastoral Center—499 St. Matthews St., El Paso, 79907. Tel: 915-595-5000; Fax: 915-595-5095. Refer all official business to this address.

Diocesan Tribunal—499 St. Matthews St., El Paso, 79907. Tel: 915-595-5038. Rev. JOSE C. GUERRERO, J.C.L., Judicial Vicar. Adjutant Vicars: Revs. STEPHEN PETERS; ROBERT S. KOBE.

Presbyteral Council—Rev. Msgr. DAVID G. FIERRO; Rev. Msgr. JOHN PETERS; Revs. THOMAS DEVINE, O.A.R.; RAFAEL FARRERA, S.M.; FRANK LOPEZ; JOE MOLINA; JOHN RINI; LEONIDES RIVERO; RICARDO RUIZ; RICHARD ZAMORANO. Ex-Officio Members:: Rev. Msgr. FRANCIS J. SMITH; Rev. RICHARD A. MATTY.

Judges—Revs. JOSE C. GUERRERO, J.C.L.; STEPHEN PETERS; ROBERT S. KOBE; JAMES W. HALL; GILES CARIE, O.F.M.Conv.

Defenders of the Bond—Rev. Msgr. DAVID G. FIERRO; Revs. TRINI FUENTEZ; DEMETRIO PONCE; RICK ZAMORANO; Deacon GEORGE LEVY.

Advocates—Rev. Msgr. FRANCIS J. SMITH; Revs. JUVENTINO CELINO; MICHAEL DONNELLY, S.S.C.; FRANCISCO LOPEZ; JOHN LUCIDO.

Lay Advocates—ROBERT ARMENDARIZ; OUISA DAVIS; CARMEN RODRIGUEZ; PATRICIA ROYBAL.

Tribunal Ecclesiastical Notary—YOLANDA RUIZ.

Peritus—RICHARD B. PATTERSON, Ph.D.; Dr. CHESTER L. REYNOLDS, M.D.

Vicar for Clergy and Religious—Vacant.

Vicars-Vicariates—St. Peter: Rev. TRINDAD FUENTEZ, *Queen of Peace Parish, 1551 Belvidere, El Paso, 79912.* Tel: 915-584-5817. St. Paul: Rev. HECTOR CRUZ, S.M., *Santa Lucia Parish, 519 Gallagher, El Paso.* Tel: 915-592-5245. St. John: Rev. SANTOS PEREZ, O.F.M., *Our Lady of Guadalupe Parish, 2709 Alabama, El Paso, 79930.* Tel: 915-562-4304. St. Mark: Vacant, *St. Thomas - St. Joseph Parish, 838 Bellaire, Kermit, 79745.* Tel: 915-586-4694. St. Luke: Rev. RAUL TRIGUEROS, *Cristo Rey Parish, 8011 Williamette, El Paso, 79907.* Tel: 915-591-0688. St. Mark: Rev. RALPH SOLIS, JR., *Our Lady of Fatima, P.O. Box 398, Van Horn, 79855.* Tel: 915-283-2042. Our Lady of Guadalupe: Rev. Msgr. FRANCIS J. SMITH, *St. Raphael Parish, 2301 Zanzibar, El Paso, 79925.* Tel: 915-598-3431.

Diocesan Master of Ceremonies—Rev. MARCUS MCFADIN.

Finance Council—Most Rev. ARMANDO X. OCHOA; Rev. Msgr. FRANCIS J. SMITH; Rev. JOSEPH HERMOSO; E. H. BAEZA; FRANK GORMAN; TED HOUGHTON, JR.; PHILLIP MULLIN.

Diocesan Building Committee—Most Rev. ARMANDO X. OCHOA; Rev. JUVENTINO CELINO; FRANK ALDERETE; ERNESTO ARMENDARIZ; RICARDO BACA; PEDRO HERRERA; ROSIE TORRES.

Priests' Personnel Advisory Committee—Rev. Msgr. FRANCIS J. SMITH; Revs. RICHARD A. MATTY; TRINI FUENTEZ; HECTOR CRUZ, S.M.; SANTOS PEREZ, O.F.M.; RALPH SOLIS, JR.; RAUL TRIGUEROS.

Catholic Ministry in Hospitals & Nursing Homes—Revs. ANTHONIO CONCHA, S.J., Dir.; RODOLFO LACERNA; RICHARD WAIWOOD. Tel: 915-532-5447.

Laity, Office of the—Rev. Msgr. ARTURO BANUELAS, *Youth Services, 499 St. Matthew St., El Paso, 79907.* Tel: 915-595-5020; Youth: 915-595-5000. The following associations are under the direction of the Office of the Laity:

Adoracion Nocturna (Nocturnal Adoration)—Rev. SANTOS PEREZ, O.F.M.

Apostolado de la Cruz (Apostolate of the Cross)—Vacant.

Blue Army—Rev. RICHARD WAIWOOD.

Catholic Daughters of America—Rev. BENJAMIN FLORES-RUIZ.

Catholic Knights of America—Rev. BENJAMIN FLORES-RUIZ.

Cursillos de Cristianidad—Rev. Msgr. RAFAEL MIRANDA, *San Judas Tadeo Parish, 4006 Hidden Way, El Paso, 79922.*
Franciscans, Secular Order of Franciscans—Rev. SANTOS PEREZ, O.F.M.
Knights of Columbus—Rev. Msgr. FRANCIS J. SMITH.
Knights of the Holy Sepulchre—Rev. Msgr. FRANCIS J. SMITH.
Knights of St. Gregory—Vacant.
Ladies of Charity; Daughters of Charity; Ladies of the Holy Sepulchre—Rev. Msgr. FRANCIS J. SMITH.
Legion of Mary—Rev. VINCENT ASCHERL.
Serra Club—Rev. BENJAMIN FLORES-RUIZ.
St. Vincent de Paul Society—Mr. TOM WALTERS.
Young Adults-Singles—Vacant.

Catholic Communications Ministry—Rev. RAUL TRIGUEROS, *499 St. Matthews St., El Paso, 79907.* Tel: 915-595-5056.

Diocesan Newspaper—*"Rio Grande Catholic", 499 St. Matthews St., El Paso, 79907.* Tel: 915-595-5056.

Persons with Disabilities—Vacant.

Evangelization & Renewal Center—Sr. ASUNTA LABRADO, C.D.P., *499 St. Matthews St., El Paso, 79907.* Tel: 915-595-5063.

Villa Maria - Home for Aged Women & Men—Sr. MARY ANN HAMOR, C.S.J., Dir., *920 S. Oregon, El Paso, 79901.* Tel: 915-533-5152.

Catholic Charities—Sr. MARIAN KLUESNER, F.S.P.A., *1013 E. San Antonio, El Paso, 79901.* Tel: 915-532-9532.

Campaign for Human Development—Rev. RICHARD A. MATTY, *499 St. Matthews St., El Paso, 79907.* Tel: 915-595-5007.

Office of Marriage and Family Life—Rev. JAMES W. HALL, *499 St. Matthews St., El Paso, 79907.* Tel: 915-595-5032.

Historical Archives & Diocesan Museum—Rev. RICHARD A. MATTY, *499 St. Matthews St., El Paso, 79907.* Tel: 915-595-5007; 915-595-5000.

Campus Ministry—Sr. ANN FRANCIS MONADERO, O.S.F., *400 E. Robinson, El Paso, 79902.* Tel: 915-544-3888.

Permanent Diaconate Office—Vacant, *499 St. Matthews St., El Paso, 79907.* Tel: 915-595-5000.

Priests' Retirement and Disability Plan—Rev. Msgr. JOHN PETERS; Rev. Msgr. FRANCIS J. SMITH, Pres.; Rev. Msgr. WILLIAM RYAN; Rev. RICHARD ZAMORANO; Mr. YAZBIK DAW; ROBERT ORTEGA.

Missions Office—Sr. HELEN SANTAMARIA, S.L., *499 St. Matthews St., El Paso, 79907.* Tel: 915-595-5007.

Office of Education—Sr. ELIZABETH SWARTZ, S.S.N.D., Supt., *499 St. Matthews St., El Paso, 79907.* Tel: 915-595-5026.

Tepeyac Institute—Rev. Msgr. ARTURO BANUELAS, S.T.D., Dir.; Sr. ROSEANNE KOSKIE, Assoc. Dir.; Sr. ESTHER ORTEGA, O.P., Assoc. Dir.; Sr. DONNA KUSTUSCH, O.P., Teacher, *499 St. Matthews St., El Paso, 79907.* Tel: 915-595-5020.

Retreat House—*499 St. Matthews St., El Paso, 79907.* Tel: 915-595-5006.

Reverence for Life Ministry—Rev. RAFAEL GARCIA, S.J., *499 St. Matthews St., El Paso, 79907.* Tel: 915-595-5046.

Vocations & Seminarians—Rev. BENJAMIN FLORES, *499 St. Matthews St., El Paso, 79907.* Tel: 915-595-5003.

Jail Ministry—Vacant.

West Texas Ministry—Team Ministry: Sr. MARGIE SILGUERO, M.J.M.J.; Sr. LUZ DONEZ, M.J.M.J., *Box 1118, Marfa, 79843.* Tel: 915-729-3385. Sr. JOSEPHA DWYER, *P.O. Box 1747, Pecos, 79772.* Tel: 915-445-3208.

Cursillo—Rev. Msgr. JOSE GOMEZ, *5649 Dailey, El Paso, 79905.* Tel: 915-779-1583.

Movimiento Familiar Cristiano—Rev. Msgr. JOSE GOMEZ, Dir., *St. Patrick Cathedral, 1118 N. Mesa, El Paso, 79902.* Tel: 915-533-4451.

CLERGY, PARISHES, MISSIONS AND PAROCHIAL SCHOOLS

CITY OF EL PASO
(El Paso County)

1—ST. PATRICK'S CATHEDRAL, Revs. Richard A. Matty, Rector; Anthony Celino; Alfred Villanueva; Deacon Ken Flynn.
Res., 1118 N. Mesa St., 79902. Tel: 915-533-4451; Fax: 915-532-8761.
School—(Grades K-8) 1111 N. Stanton St., 79902. Mr. Ben Brooks, Prin.
Sisters 1; Lay Teachers 22; Students 404.
Catechesis / Religious Programs—Students 544.

2—ALL SAINTS, Rev. Kennon Y. Ducre, S.T.L.
Res., 1415 Dakota St., 79930. Tel: 915-566-9711.

3—BLESSED JUAN DIEGO PARISH, Rev. Edward G. Roden-Lucero.
Res., 14520 E. Montana, 79938. Tel: 915-855-2217.

4—BLESSED SACRAMENT, Revs. Stephen Peters; Jose F. Molina.
Res., 9025 Diana Dr., 79924. Tel: 915-755-7658; Fax: 915-755-0434.
School—(Grades PreK-8). Tel: 915-755-2711. Ms. Guadalupe Varela.
Franciscan Sisters of Our Lady of Perpetual Help 1; Lay Teachers 14; Students 252.
Catechesis / Religious Programs—Teri Valdez, D.R.E. Students 600.

5—CHRIST THE SAVIOR, Rev. Robert S. Kobe; Deacon Paul Andrade.
Res., 5301 Wadsworth Ave., 79924. Tel: 915-821-3766.

6—CORPUS CHRISTI, Rev. Wilson Cuevas.
Res., 9205 N. Loop Dr., 79907. Tel: 915-858-0488.
Catechesis / Religious Programs—Students 783.

7—CRISTO REY CHURCH, Revs. Raul Trigueros; Jose Martinez-Mata (Mexico).
Res., 8011 Williamette, 79907. Tel: 915-591-0688; Fax: 915-593-0470.

8—GUARDIAN ANGEL, Revs. Thomas Devine; Jesus Maria P. Arrilucea, O.A.R.
Res., 3021 Frutas Ave., 79905. Tel: 915-533-2077; Fax: 915-533-3649.

9—HOLY FAMILY, Administrators: Revs. Trini Fuentez; Alejandro Reyes. In res., Rev. Richard Waiwood.
Res., 104 Fewel St., 79902. Tel: 915-532-8462.

10—IMMACULATE CONCEPTION, Rev. Msgr. William H. Ryan.
Res., 118 N. Campbell St., 79901-2404. Tel: 915-533-3427.

11—LA PURISIMA, Rev. Rafael Farrera, S.M.
Res., 328 S. Nevarez St., 79927. Tel: 915-859-7718.

12—SAINT THERESE OF THE LITTLE FLOWER PARISH, Rev. Francisco Siguenza, O.A.R.
Church—171 Polo Inn, 79915.
Res., 3021 Frutas, 79901. Tel: 915-772-1285.

13—MOST HOLY TRINITY, Rev. Msgr. Robert S. Calles; Rev. Fidel Cervantes.
Res., 10000 Pheasant Rd., 79924. Tel: 915-751-6416; Fax: 915-751-3242.
School—(Grades K-8). Tel: 915-751-2566.
Lay Teachers 13; Students 183.

14—OUR LADY OF ASSUMPTION, Revs. John Telles; Jose Guerrero.
Res., 4800 Byron St., 79930. Tel: 915-566-4040; Fax: 915-566-4049.
School—(Grades K-8). Tel: 915-565-3411.
Sisters 1; Lay Teachers 10; Students 123.

15—OUR LADY OF GUADALUPE, Revs. Santos Perez, O.F.M.; Ricardo Rodriguez, O.F.M.; Jorge Frausto, O.F.M.; Bro. Bernardo Alvarado, O.F.M.
Res., 2709 Alabama St., 79930. Tel: 915-562-4304; Fax: 915-562-3509.
Catechesis / Religious Programs—Mrs. Zenaida Servin, D.R.E.
Students 457.

16—OUR LADY OF THE LIGHT, Rev. Msgr. David G. Fierro.
Res., 4700 Delta Dr., 79905. Tel: 915-532-1757.

17—OUR LADY OF MT. CARMEL, Revs. John Stowe, O.F.M.Conv., Admin.; Giles Carie, O.F.M.Conv.; Marcos Reyna, O.F.M.Conv.
Res., 131 S. Zaragoza, 79907. Tel: 915-859-9848; Fax: 915-860-9340. [CEM]
School—(Grades K-8) 9101 Socorro Rd., 79907. Tel: 915-859-9812.
Sisters 1; Lay Teachers 12; Students 177.

18—OUR LADY OF SORROWS, Revs. Ruben M. Torres, O.S.M.; Jorge Palacio, O.S.M.; Andres Ponso, O.S.M.
Res., 7712 Rosedale St., 79915. Tel: 915-772-4834; Fax: 915-772-9078.

19—OUR LADY OF THE VALLEY, Revs. John Rini; Michael Rodriguez.
Res., 8600 Winchester, 79907. Tel: 915-859-7939.
School—Tel: 915-859-6448; Fax: 915-859-3908. Sr. Caroline Vasquez, O.S.F., Prin.
Lay Teachers 11; Students 203.

20—QUEEN OF PEACE, Rev. Trinidad Fuentez.
Res., 1551 Belvidere, 79912. Tel: 915-584-5817; Fax: 915-584-7761.
Catechesis / Religious Programs—Pat Fowler, D.R.E.
Students 586.

21—SACRED HEART, Revs. Rafael Garcia, S.J.; John Paul, S.J.; Louis J. Lambert, S.J.; Bro. Manuel Cabral, S.J. In res., Revs. Edward Schott, S.J.; Michael Gallagher, S.J.; Antonio Concha, S.J.
Res., 602 S. Oregon St., 79901. Tel: 915-532-5447; Fax: 915-533-0013.

22—ST. FRANCES XAVIER CABRINI PARISH, Rev. Frank Lopez; Sr. Julia Donez, Pastoral Assoc.
Res., 12037 Picasso, 79936. Tel: 915-857-1263.

23—ST. FRANCIS XAVIER, Rev. Esteban Sescon; Deacon Luis Montes.
Res., 519 S. Latta St., 79905. Tel: 915-532-2761; Fax: 915-544-5103.

24—ST. IGNATIUS OF LOYOLA, Revs. Jeronimo Melendez, O.S.M.; Franco Tentori, O.S.M.; Francisco DiTomasi, O.S.M.
Res., 408 Park St., 79901. Tel: 915-532-9534; Fax: 915-577-0433.

25—ST. JOSEPH'S, Revs. Joseph Hermoso; Francisco Herrera. In res., Rev. Vincent Ascherl.
Res., 1315 Travis St., 79903. Tel: 915-566-9396; Fax: 915-566-5606.
School—(Grades K-8) 1300 Lamar, 79903. Tel: 915-566-1661; Fax: 915-566-1664. Bro. Edwin Gallagher, Prin.
Brothers 3; Lay Teachers 26; Students 489.

26—ST. LUKE, Rev. Msgr. John Peters.
Res., 930 E. Redd Rd., 79912. Tel: 915-585-0255.

27—ST. MARK, Rev. Leonides Rivero.
Res., 11609 John Weir, 79936. Tel: 915-857-2955; Fax: 915-857-2955.
Church—11700 Pebble Hills, 79936.

28—ST. MATTHEW, Rev. Msgr. A. Dixon Hartford; Rev. Miguel Luna.
Res., 400 W. Sunset Rd., 79922. Tel: 915-584-3461; Fax: 915-584-2107.
Catechesis / Religious Programs—D.R.E.: Mrs. Alice Teran; Mrs. Allyn Echaniz.
Students 466.

29—ST. PAUL THE APOSTLE, Rev. Emanuel Alcazar; Deacon Vicente Aguirre.
Res., 7424 Mimosa, 79915. Tel: 915-778-5304.

30—ST. PIUS X, Rev. Msgr. Arturo Banuelas; Rev. Marcus McFadin; Deacon Jim Szostek.
Res., 1050 N. Clark Rd., 79905. Tel: 915-772-3226; Fax: 915-771-6665.
School—(Grades PreK-8). Tel: 915-772-6598.
Sisters 4; Lay Teachers 31; Students 511.
Catechesis / Religious Programs—Students 332.

31—ST. RAPHAEL, Rev. Msgr. Francis J. Smith, P.A.; Revs. Vicente Calderon, Jr.; Paul Garcia; Deacons George Levy; Frank Mares; John Paddenburg; Bernard Rulong. In res., Rev. Rodolfo Lacerna.
Res., 2301 Zanzibar Rd., 79925. Tel: 915-598-3431; 3432; Fax: 915-598-0944.
School—(Grades PreK-8) 2310 Woodside, 79925. Tel: 915-598-2241; Fax: 915-598-3002. Elizabeth Wiehe, Prin.
Lay Teachers 53; Students 578.
Catechesis / Religious Programs—Students 1,023.

32—ST. STEPHEN, DEACON AND MARTYR, Revs. Juventino C. Celino; Edward C. Carpenter; Deacon Gus Rodriguez, Sr.
Res., 1651 Janet Coles Ln., 79936.
Church—1700 George Dieter, 79936. Tel: 915-855-1661; Fax: 915-857-5800.

33—ST. THOMAS AQUINAS, Revs. James W. Hall; Richard Zamorano.
Church—10970 Bywood, 79936. Tel: 915-592-1313.
Catechesis / Religious Programs—Sr. Carmen Moreno, A.S.C., D.R.E.
Students 585.

34—STS. PETER AND PAUL, Rev. Saul de Jesus Uribe. In res., Rev. Celimo Osorio.
Res., 673 Old Hueco Tanks Rd., 79927. Tel: 915-859-3758.

35—SAN ANTONIO, Revs. Luis Martin; Santiago Alonso.
Res., 503 Hunter, 79915. Tel: 915-598-1457; Fax: 915-590-1312.

36—SAN JOSE, Rev. Jose Alcocer.
Res., 8100 San Jose Rd., 79907. Tel: 915-598-6285.

37—SAN JUAN BAUTISTA, Rev. Msgr. Jose A. Gomez. In res., Rev. Ignacio Echave.
Res., 5649 Dailey Ave., 79905. Tel: 915-779-1583.

38—SAN JUDAS TADEO, Rev. Msgr. Rafael Miranda; Rev. Richard Weiss.
Res., 4006 Hidden Way, 79922. Tel: 915-584-1095.
Mission—El Paso, El Paso Co., Santa Teresita, 3400 Lomont Dr., 79912. Rev. Richard Weiss.

39—SANTA LUCIA, Rev. Hector J. Cruz, S.M. (Mexico). In res., Rev. Richard Zamorano.
Res., 518 Gallagher St., 79915. Tel: 915-592-5245.

40—SANTO NINO DE ATOCHA, Rev. J. Alfredo Olivas.
Res., 210 S. Clark, 79905. Tel: 915-779-3164; Fax: 915-779-1811.

OUTSIDE THE CITY OF EL PASO

Alpine, Brewster Co., Our Lady of Peace, Revs. Ricardo Ruiz; Edilberto Lopez.
Res., Box 89, 79831. Tel: 915-837-3304; Fax: 915-837-1752. [CEM]
Mission—Terlingua, Brewster Co., St. Mary, P.O. Box 268, Marathon, 79842.

Balmorhea, Reeves Co., Christ the King. Unassigned.
Res., Rte. 1, Box 3, 79718. Tel: 915-375-2347.
Mission—Saragosa, Our Lady of Guadalupe. Tel: 915-375-2636.

Canutillo, El Paso Co., St. Patrick, Rev. Jose Velasquez.
Res., 7065 Second St., P.O. Box 10, 79835. Tel: 915-877-3997.
Mission—Westway, El Paso Co., Immaculate Heart of Mary, 8701 Joplin Rd., 79835. Tel: 915-886-3539.

Clint, El Paso Co., San Lorenzo, Rev. Joseph Nam Kim, Admin.
Res., P.O. Box 215, 79836. Tel: 915-851-2255.

Fabens, El Paso Co., Our Lady of Guadalupe, Rev. Michael Donnely, S.S.C. In res., Rev. John Wanaurny, S.S.C.
Res., P.O. Box 356, 127 W. Main St., 79838. Tel: 915-764-3942. [CEM]
Missions—Cuadrilla, San Jose; Tornillo, Santa Rita; La Isla, San Luis.

Fort Davis, Jeff Davis Co., St. Joseph, Rev. Demetrio Ponce, Admin.
Res., P.O. Box 787, 79734. Tel: 915-426-3284. [CEM]

Fort Hancock, Hudspeth Co., Santa Teresa, Sr. Maureen Jerkowski, O.S.F., Pastoral Coord., Tel: 915-769-3711.
Res., P.O. Box 215, 79839.

Horizon City, El Paso Co., Holy Spirit. (Independent Mission). Revs. Pablo Matta; Miguel Meneses.
Res., 1608 McMahon St., El Paso, 79927. Tel: 915-852-3582.

Kermit, Winkler Co., St. Thomas & St. Joseph, Revs. John Lucido, Admin.; Ralph Barranger.
Res., 838 Bellaire Rd., 79745. Tel: 915-586-3922.
St. Joseph the Worker. Consolidated with St. Thomas in 1990.

Marfa, Presidio Co., St. Mary's, Rev. Demetrio Ponce.
Res., Box 356, 79843. Tel: 915-729-4694. [CEM]

Monahans, Ward Co., St. John the Apostle and Evangelist, Revs. John Lucido; Ralph Barranger.
Res., 5th & S. Ike St., 79756. Tel: 915-943-5114. [JC]
Mission—Grandfalls, Ward Co., St. Gertrude, P.O. Box 181, Grandfalls, 79742. Tel: 915-547-2484.

Pecos, Reeves Co., St. Catherine, Deacon George Vasquez.
Res., P.O. Box 670, 79772. Tel: 915-447-9231.
Mission—Toyah, St. Emily.
Santa Rosa Church, Revs. Antonio Mena; Juan Narez; Roberto Alvarado.
Res., 620 E. 4th St., Box 686, 79772. Tel: 915-445-2309. [CEM]
Mission—Barstow, Our Lady of Refuge.

Presidio, Presidio Co., Santa Teresa de Jesus, Revs. Arturo Bustamante, O.F.M.; Rafael Rincon, O.F.M.
Res., P.O. Box 2049, 79845. Tel: 915-229-3235. [CEM]
Missions—Shafter, Sgdo. Corazon de Jesus; Redford, San Jose; Candelaria, Our Lady of Peace; Lajitas, Lajitas Mission.

San Elizario, El Paso Co., San Elceario, Rev. Lorenzo Lucero.
Res., P.O. Drawer 910, 79849. Tel: 915-851-2333. [JC]
San Felipe de Jesus, Rev. Celimo Osorio.
Res., P.O. Box 1070, 79849. Tel: 915-851-3039.

Van Horn, Culberson Co., Our Lady of Fatima, Revs. Ralph Solis, Jr.; Alejandro Reyes.
Res., 308 Almond St., P.O. Box 398, 79855. Tel: 915-283-2042.
Missions—Sierra Blanca, Our Lady of Miracles, P.O. Box 1, Sierra Blanca, 79851.; Dell City, San Isidro; Valentine, Sacred Heart, General Delivery, Valentine, 79854.

Chaplains of Public Institutions

El Paso. *El Paso County Jail*. Vacant.
El Paso Juvenile Detention Center. Vacant.

Anthony. *La Tuna Federal*. Vacant. 7045 Second St., P.O. Box 10, Canutillo, 79835.

On Duty Outside of Diocese:
Reverend Fathers—
Aguilera, Salvador, U.S. Navy, U.S. Naval Academy, Annapolis, MD 21402
Lopez, Jairo, St. William's, 1000 McNeil Rd., Round Rock, TX 78681
Rowland, Thomas, Madonna House, Ontario, Combermere K0J 1L0 Canada

---

Absent on Leave:
Reverend Fathers—
Bengert, Anthony L.
Kleinworth, Robert
Knopp, John
Madrid, Jaime
Maraya, Felipe
Marin, Miguel
Ramirez, Jose Nieves

Retired:
Reverend Fathers—
Acevedo, Luis H.
Ascherl, Vincent
Bertasius, Anthony
Burkus, John
Camacho, Gilbert
Finochietto, Arnold
Lafrenz, James
Perera, Paul
Saez, Jose
Stegman, Leonard F.

Permanent Deacons:
Aguirre, Vicente G., St. Paul, El Paso
Andrade, Paul, Christ the Savior, El Paso
Flynn, Ken, St. Patrick's Cathedral, El Paso
Guerrero, Teofilo, Prison Ministry
Holbritter, Milton A., (Retired)
Levy, George, St. Raphael, El Paso
Mares, Frank J., St. Raphael, El Paso
Montes, Louis A., St. Francis Xavier, El Paso
Paddenburg, John A., St. Raphael, El Paso
Rodriguez, Gus J., St. Stephen, El Paso
Rulong, Bernard, St. Raphael, El Paso
Schuffer, George M., Jr., William Beaumont Army Medical Center, El Paso
Solis, Ralph, St. Joseph, El Paso
Szostek, James T., St. Pius X, El Paso
Vasquez, George, St. Catherine, Pecos
Wauson, Thomas J., Christ the Savior, El Paso

INSTITUTIONS LOCATED IN THE DIOCESE

[A] SEMINARIES, DIOCESAN

El Paso. *St. Charles Seminary College Program*, P.O. Box 17548, 79917. Tel: 915-591-9821. Very Rev. Juan Garcia, Rector. Priests 1; Students 1.

[B] SEMINARIES, RELIGIOUS OR SCHOLASTICATES

El Paso. *Roger Bacon College* (1940), 2400 Marr St., 79903. Tel: 915-565-2921. Minor Seminary of the Franciscan Fathers, Province of the Holy Gospel. Revs. Alberto Hernandez, O.F.M.; Guillermo Ordenes, O.F.M.; Aaron Martinez, O.F.M. Priests 3; Brothers 1.
St. Anthony's School of Theology, Hastings St. and Crescent Dr., 79903. Tel: 915-566-2261. Franciscan Fathers of St. Peter and St. Paul Province, Michoacan, Mexico. Revs. Alejandro Juarez, O.F.M.; Martin Arriage, O.F.M., Guardian; Jaime Yanez, O.F.M.; Hugo Cordova, O.F.M.; Jorge Rivas, O.F.M.; Fernando Mendoza, O.F.M.; Joaquin Acevedo, O.F.M. Priests 7; Scholastics 20; Brothers 3.

[C] HIGH SCHOOLS, DIOCESAN

El Paso. *Cathedral High School*. (Boys), 1309 N. Stanton St., 79902. Tel: 915-532-3238. Mr. Leo Cancellare, Prin. Sisters 2; Brothers 6; Lay Teachers 35; Students 660.

[D] HIGH SCHOOLS, PRIVATE

El Paso. *Father Yermo High School*, 250 Washington St., 79905. Tel: 915-533-3185. Servants of the Sacred Heart of Jesus and of the Poor. Sisters 3; Lay Teachers 13; Students 163.
Loretto Academy, 1300 Hardaway, 79903. Tel: 915-564-0211. Sisters of Loretto at the Foot of the Cross. Sisters 8; Lay Teachers 60; Students 851; Priests 1.

[E] ELEMENTARY SCHOOLS, PRIVATE

El Paso. *Father Yermo Elementary School*. (Grades K-8), 237 Tobin Pl., 79905. Tel: 915-533-4693. Servants of the Sacred Heart and of the Poor. Sisters 4; Lay Teachers 10; Students 169.
Loretto Academy Middle School, 1300 Hardaway, 79903. Tel: 915-566-5453. Sisters of Loretto at the Foot of the Cross. Sr. Patricia Williams, S.L., Prin. Sisters 2; Lay Teachers 9; Students 105.
Loretto Elementary School-Loretto Academy. (Grades PreK-5), 4625 Clifton, 79903. Tel: 915-565-2765. Sisters of Loretto at the Foot of the Cross. Mrs. Karla Onick, Prin. Lay Teachers 16; Students 208.
St. Michael School, 616 S. Virginia, 79901. Tel: 915-542-1253; Fax: 915-532-1121. Servants of the Sacred Heart of Jesus and of the Poor: Father Yermo delegation. Sr. Maria Angelica Omana, S.S.H.J.P. Sisters 4; Lay Teachers 5; Students 80.

[F] CLINICS

El Paso. *Centro San Vicente*, 8061 Alameda, 79915. Tel: 915-859-7545.
For a complete listing, refer to the Hospitals section.
La Clinica Guadalupana, Inc., 901 Ascencion, 79927. Tel: 915-852-3328.
For a complete listing, refer to the Hospitals section.

[G] AGENCIES AND INSTITUTIONS OF THE CHARITIES OF THE DIOCESE

El Paso. *Catholic Charities*, 1013 E. San Antonio St., 79901. Tel: 915-532-9532. Sr. Marian Kluesner, F.S.P.A., Dir.

[H] DAY CARE CENTERS

El Paso. *St. Joseph of the Valley*, 7681 Barton, 79915. Tel: 915-778-3407. Sisters 3; Lay Teachers 7; Students 65.

[I] HOMES FOR AGED

El Paso. *Nazareth Hall*, 4614 Trowbridge, 79903. Tel: 915-565-4677; Fax: 915-566-7530.
For a complete listing, refer to the Special Care Facilities section.
Villa Maria, 920 S. Oregon St., 79901. Tel: 915-533-5152.
For a complete listing, refer to the Special Care Facilities section.

[J] MONASTERIES & RESIDENCES FOR PRIESTS & BROTHERS

El Paso. *Christian Brothers*, 1204 N. Mesa, 79902-4012. Tel: 915-532-9314.
E-mail: brothernick@juno.com

[K] CONVENTS AND RESIDENCES FOR WOMEN

El Paso. *Adorers of the Blood of Christ (A.S.C.)*, 2209 Pittsburg, 79930. Tel: 915-566-5855. Sr. Darlene Stoecklein, A.S.C., Contact Person. Sisters 2.
Adrian Dominican Sisters (O.P.), 1011 E. Nevada, 79902. Tel: 915-533-4744. Sr. Donna Kustusch, O.P., Contact Person; Sr. Eleanor Stech, O.P., Contact Person. Sisters 3.
Association of Mary Immaculate (A.I.M.), 3900 La Luz St., 79903. Tel: 915-566-0447. Sr. Sue Castaneda, A.I.M., Contact Person.
Daughters of Charity of St. Vincent De Paul (D.C.), 1020 N. Campbell St., 79902. Tel: 915-533-9013; Fax: 915-859-9862. Sisters 4.
Franciscan Sisters of Our Lady of Perpetual Help (O.S.F.), Blessed Sacrament Convent, 9005 Diana Dr., 79904. Tel: 915-755-4871. Sr. M. Jeanette Danielewicz, O.S.F. Sisters 3.
Hermanas Contemplativas del Buen Pastor (H.B.P.). (Cloistered), Good Shepherd Convent, 8824 Old County Rd., P.O. Box 17254, 79917. Tel: 915-859-3683. Sr. Ernestina Estrada, Supr. Sisters 11.
Hermanas del Servicio Social, 6372 Saint Lo Dr., 79925-1807. Tel: 915-771-0780. Sr. Carmen Aurora Gomez.
Hermanas Dominicas de la Doctrinia Cristiana (O.P.), San Alberto Magno Convent, P.O. Box 17391, 79917. Sr. Celia Gonzalez, Provincial Supr.; Sr. Guadalupe Garcia, O.P., Local Supr. Sisters 19.
Missionary Sisters of Jesus, Mary & Joseph (M.J.M.J.), 7681 Barton Dr., 79915. Tel: 915-778-3407. Sr. Gloria Rodriquez, Supr. Sisters 6.
North American Union Sisters of Our Lady of Charity, 415 N. Glenwood Dr., 79905. Tel: 915-772-0737. Sr. Yolanda Martinez, Supr. Sisters 12.
San Juan Day Care Center, 5636 Frutas St., 79905. Tel: 915-772-1681. Sr. Cruz Celia Gomez, Admin.
School Sisters of St. Francis (O.S.F.), 124 Bauxite, 79932. Tel: 915-581-2776. Sr. Imelda Kaufman, Contact Person; Sr. Bernadette Halbur, Contact Person; Sr. Maureen Jerkowski. Sisters 3.
Servants of the Sacred Heart of Jesus and of the Poor (S.S.H.J.P.), Father Yermo Convent, 237 Tobin Pl., 79905. Tel: 915-533-3338. Sr. Marie de la Luz Fernandez, Supr. Sisters 14.
Queen of Peace Convent, 3119 Pera Ave., 79905. Tel: 915-533-0590. Sr. Gloria Margarita Rodriguez, Supr. Sisters 17.
Sisters of Loretto at the Foot of the Cross (S.L.),

Loretto Convent, 1400 Hardaway St., 79903. Tel: 915-566-1628. M. Judith Flood, Facilities Mgr. Sisters 13.

Sisters of Our Lady of Charity of the Good Shepherd (R.G.S.), Good Shepherd Convent, 8824 Old County Rd., P.O. Box 17635, 79917. Tel: 915-859-6004. Sr. Ma. Emanuel Galvan, Supr. Sisters 10.

Sisters of Perpetual Adoration (A.P.). (Cloistered), Corpus Christi Monastery, 451 Mockingbird Ln., 79907. Tel: 915-591-5662. Mother Maria Sagrario Perez, A.P., Supr. Sisters 15; Novices 3.

Cristo Rey Monastery of Perpetual Adoration, 145 Cotton St., 79901. Tel: 915-533-5323. Mother Maria de Jesus Armendariz, A.P., Supr. Sisters 15; Novices 2; Postulants 2.

Sisters of St. Joseph of Carondelet (C.S.J.), 4704 Caples, 79903. Tel: 915-566-7635. Sr. Jacqueline Lawson, C.S.J.; Sr. J. Sue Smith, C.S.J.; Sr. Kate Forbes, 4904 Gary Owen, 79903. Tel: 915-565-1258. Sisters 4.

MARFA. *Missionary Sisters of Jesus, Mary & Joseph*, P.O. Box 1118, 79843. Tel: 915-729-3385. Sisters 2.

PRESIDIO. *Sisters of the Most Precious Blood of O'Fallon, Missouri*, P.O. Box 893, 79845. Tel: 915-229-3409; 915-229-4246.

SIERRA BLANCA. *School Sisters of St. Francis, (S.S.S.F.)*, P.O. Box 303, 79851. Tel: 915-369-2062; 369-2651.

[L] RESIDENCES FOR WOMEN

EL PASO. *Queen of Angels Residence for College Girls and Business Women*, 119 W. Nevada Ave., 79902. Tel: 915-533-3173; Fax: 915-541-1123. Sr. Grace I. Vargas, R.J.M., Supr. Residence for Ladies conducted by the Religious of Jesus and Mary. Sisters 12; Residents 15.

[M] NEWMAN CENTERS

EL PASO. *University of Texas at El Paso Catholic Campus Ministry*, Archbishop Oscar Romero Center, 400 E. Robinson, 79902-2619. Tel: 915-544-3883. Sr. Ann Francis Monedero, O.S.F., Dir.

ALPINE. *Sul Ross State University Newman Center*, P.O. Box C 78, 79832. Tel: 915-837-2905.
E-mail: plister@sul-ross.edu
Dr. Paul Lister.

[N] MISCELLANEOUS LISTINGS

EL PASO. *Annunciation House*, 1003 E. San Antonio, 79901. Tel: 915-545-4509. Mr. Ruben Garcia, Dir.

Casa Vides. (Shelter for Refugees), 325 Leon St., 79901. Mr. Ruben Garcia, Dir.

Catholic Counseling Services, Inc., 499 St. Matthews St., 79907. Tel: 915-595-5096; Fax: 915-595-5098. Mr. Jose Castrellon, Exec. Dir.

The Catholic Diocese of El Paso Foundation, 499 St. Matthews, 79907. Tel: 915-595-5054; Fax: 915-595-5095. Mr. Gilber Morales.

Catholic Legal Immigration Network, Inc. (CLINIC). Subsidiary of the NCCB/USCC Southwest Regional Office. 1205 N. Oregon, 79902. Tel: 915-533-3971; Fax: 915-533-3974.
E-mail: clinictx@aol.com
Lily Gutierrez, S.W. Reg. Clinic Coord. Services: National immigration support network to the Catholic Dioceses throughout the U.S. Southwest regional CLINIC office provides technical assistance, basic organizational program services, management assessments, and immigration law training for its diocesan affiliates. CLINIC assists dioceses in applying for agency recognition and staff accreditation before the Immigration Board of Appeals. CLINIC assists dioceses and religious congregations in obtaining legal status for foreign clergy as non-immigrant and legal permanent residents.

Catholic Properties of El Paso, Inc., 499 St. Matthews St., 79907. Tel: 915-595-5006; Fax: 915-595-5095. Mr. Jorge Virgen, Exec. Dir.

Christ Child Society, 8317 Hopewell, 79925.

Historic Missions Restoration, Inc., 499 St. Matthews St., 79907.

La Posada Home, 248 Francis St., 79905-4416. Tel: 915-544-4595. Shelter for Displaced Women. Sisters 3.

The Office of Migrant and Refugee Services, 1117 N. Stanton, 79902. Tel: 915-532-3975; 3976; Fax: 915-532-4071.

Our Lady's Youth Center, 501 E. Paisano, P.O. Box 1422, 79948. Tel: 915-533-5260; 533-9122.
E-mail: kjes@aol.com
Rev. Richard M. Thomas, S.J., Dir. The Lord's Ranch & The Lord's Food Bank.

Progress for the Diocese of El Paso, 499 St. Matthews St., 79907. Tel: 915-585-5054; Fax: 915-595-5095.
E-mail: gmorales@whc.net
Mr. Gilberto Morales, Exec. Dir.

RELIGIOUS INSTITUTES OF MEN REPRESENTED IN THE DIOCESE

For further details refer to the bracketed number in the Religious Institutes of Men or Women section.

[0330]—*Brothers of the Christian Schools.* (New Orleans and Santa Fe Provs.).—F.S.C.
[0460]—*Brothers of the Poor of St. Francis.*—C.F.P.
[0480]—*Conventual Franciscan Friars.* (Custody of Our Lady of Guadalupe).—O.F.M.Conv.
[]—*Diocesan Laborer Priests.*—D.L.P.
[0520]—*Franciscan Friars.* (Holy Gospel Prov. and St. Peter & Paul Prov.).—O.F.M.
[0690]—*Jesuit Fathers and Brothers.* (Prov. of New Orleans).—S.J.
[0780]—*Marist Fathers.*—S.M.
[0150]—*Order of the Augustinian Recollects.* (Prov. of San Nicolas of Tolentino, Italy).—O.A.R.
[1070]—*Redemptorist Fathers.*—C.SS.R.
[1240]—*Servites.* (Province of Mexico).—O.S.M.

RELIGIOUS INSTITUTES OF WOMEN REPRESENTED IN THE DIOCESE

[0100]—*Adorers of the Blood of Christ.*—A.S.C.
[]—*Association of Mary Immaculate.*—A.I.M.
[1010]—*Congregation of Divine Providence of San Antonio, Texas.*—C.D.P.
[1780]—*Congregation of the Sisters of the Third Order of St. Francis of Perpetual Adoration.* (Central Region).—F.S.P.A.
[0760]—*Daughters of Charity of St. Vincent de Paul.*—D.C.
[1070-13]—*Dominican Sisters.*—O.P.
[1070-14]—*Dominican Sisters.*—O.P.
[1430]—*Franciscan Sisters of Our Lady of Perpetual Help.*—O.S.F.
[]—*Franciscan Sisters of the Sorrowful Mother.*—F.S.S.M.
[]—*Hermanas Contemplativas del Buen Pastor.*—H.B.S.
[]—*Hermanas del Buen Pastor.*—S.G.S.
[]—*Hermanas del Servico Social.*—H.S.S.
[]—*Hermanas Dominicanas de la Doctrina Cristiana.*—O.P.
[2770]—*Missionaries of Jesus, Mary and Joseph.*—M.J.M.J.
[3070]—*North American Union of the Sisters of Our Lady of Charity.*—N.A.U.-O.L.C.
[3190]—*Nuns of the Perpetual Adoration of the Blessed Sacrament.*—A.P.
[3450]—*Religious of Jesus and Mary.*—R.J.M.
[1680]—*School Sisters of St. Francis.*—S.S.S.F.
[3660]—*Servants of the Sacred Heart of Jesus and of the Poor.*—S.S.H.J.P.
[2360]—*Sisters of Loretto at the Foot of the Cross.*—S.L.
[4090]—*Sisters of Social Services.*—S.S.S.
[3830-15]—*Sisters of St. Joseph.*—C.S.J.
[3840]—*Sisters of St. Joseph of Carondelet.* (Prov. of St. Paul).—C.S.J.
[1830]—*The Sisters of the Good Shepherd.* (St. Louis Province).—R.G.S.
[3270]—*Sisters of the Most Precious Blood (O'Fallon, MO).*—C.PP.S.
[4100]—*Sisters of the Sorrowful Mother (Third Order of St. Francis).*—S.S.M.

DIOCESAN CEMETERY

EL PASO. *Mount Carmel*, Box 17655, 79917. Tel: 915-859-7734.

NECROLOGY

(No Deaths)

Diocese of Erie

(Dioecesis Eriensis)

Most Reverend

DONALD W. TRAUTMAN, S.T.D., S.S.L.

Bishop of Erie; ordained April 7, 1962; appointed Titular Bishop of Sassura and Auxiliary Bishop of Buffalo February 27, 1985; consecrated April 16, 1985; appointed to Erie June 12, 1990; installed July 16, 1990. *Res., 205 West 9th St., Erie, PA, 16501.* Tel.: 814-824-1120; Fax: 814-824-1124.

Most Reverend

MICHAEL J. MURPHY, D.D., S.T.L.

Retired Bishop of Erie; ordained February 28, 1942; appointed Titular Bishop of Arindela and Auxiliary Bishop of Cleveland April 20, 1976; consecrated June 11, 1976; appointed Coadjutor Bishop of Erie November 28, 1978; succeeded to See July 16, 1982; retired July 16, 1990. *Mailing Address: St. Patrick/St. Hedwig Parish Cluster, 130 East 4th St., Erie, PA, 16507.* Tel.: 814-454-8085.

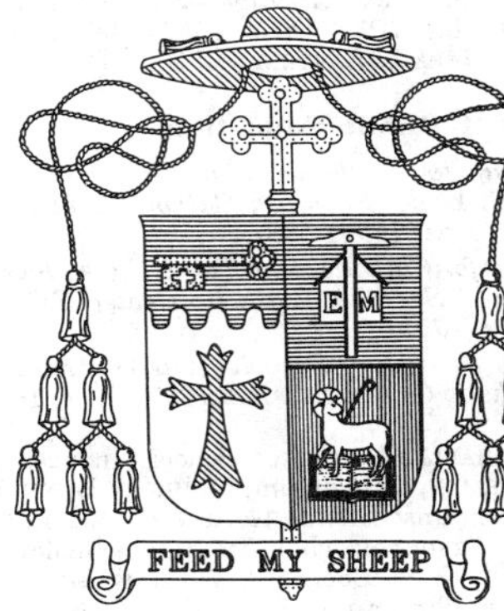

ESTABLISHED 1853.

Square Miles 9,936.

Comprises the following Counties in Northwestern Pennsylvania: Erie, Crawford, Mercer, Venango, Forest, Clarion, Jefferson, Clearfield, Cameron, Elk, McKean, Potter and Warren.

For legal titles of parishes and diocesan institutions, consult the Chancery.

Chancery: St. Mark Catholic Center, P.O. Box 10397, Erie, PA, 16514. Tel.: 814-824-1111; Fax: 814-824-1128.

Web site address: http://www.eriercd.org

E-mail address: cprehoda@eriercd.org

STATISTICAL OVERVIEW

Personnel	
Bishop	1
Retired Bishops	1
Priests: Diocesan Active in Diocese	180
Priests: Active Outside Diocese	10
Priests: Diocesan in Foreign Missions	1
Priests: Retired, Sick or Absent	58
Number of Diocesan Priests	249
Religious Priests in Diocese	14
Extern Priests in Diocese	3
Ordinations:	
Diocesan Priests	3
Transitional Deacons	1
Permanent Deacons	3
Permanent Deacons in Diocese	4
Total Brothers	2
Total Sisters	550
Parishes	
Parishes	127
With Resident Pastor:	
Resident Diocesan Priests	106
Resident Religious Priests	7
Without Resident Pastor:	
Administered by Priests	14
Missions	24
Pastoral Centers	1
Professional Ministry Personnel:	
Sisters	23
Lay Ministers	29
Welfare	
Catholic Hospitals	1
Total Assisted	223,178
Homes for the Aged	4
Total Assisted	610
Day Care and Extended Day Care Centers	1
Total Assisted	173
Specialized Homes	2
Total Assisted	200
Special Centers for Social Services	9
Total Assisted	110,067
Other Institutions	1
Total Assisted	623
Educational	
Seminaries, Diocesan	1
Students from This Diocese	15
Diocesan Students in Other Seminaries	8
Total Seminarians	23
Colleges and Universities	2
Total Students	6,177
High Schools, Diocesan and Parish	6
Total Students	1,773
High Schools, Private	2
Total Students	1,400
Elementary Schools, Diocesan and Parish	42
Total Students	10,521
Elementary Schools, Private	1
Total Students	411
Catechesis/Religious Education:	
High School Students	7,092
Elementary Students	12,658
Total Students Under Catholic Instruction	40,055
Teachers in the Diocese:	
Priests	31
Sisters	27
Lay Teachers	793
Vital Statistics	
Receptions into the Church:	
Infant Baptism Totals	2,497
Adult Baptism Totals	326
Received into Full Communion	264
First Communions	2,949
Confirmations	2,574
Marriages:	
Catholic	730
Interfaith	548
Total Marriages	1,278
Deaths	2,643
Total Catholic Population	230,848
Total Population	878,400

Former Bishops—Rt. Rev. MICHAEL O'CONNOR, cons. Bishop of Pittsburgh, Aug. 15, 1843; transferred from Pittsburgh as first Bishop of Erie in 1853; transferred back to Pittsburgh in 1854; died Oct. 18, 1872.—Rt. Rev. JOSUE M. YOUNG, cons. April 23, 1854; died Sept. 18, 1866.—Rt. Rev. TOBIAS MULLEN, D.D., cons. Aug. 2, 1868, Bishop of Erie; resigned Aug. 10, 1899, and appt. to Titular See of Germanicopolis; died April 22, 1900.—Rt. Rev. JOHN E. FITZMAURICE, D.D., cons. Feb. 24, 1898; died June 18, 1920.—Most Rev. EDWARD P. MCMANAMAN, S.T.D., Titular Bishop of Floriana and Auxiliary Bishop of Erie; cons. Oct. 28, 1948; died July 18, 1964.—Most Rev. JOHN MARK GANNON, D.D., Archbishop-Bishop of Erie; ord. Dec. 21, 1901; appt. Titular Bishop of Nilopolis, Nov. 13, 1917; cons. Feb. 6, 1918; transferred to Erie, Aug. 26, 1920; installed Dec. 16, 1920; appt. Assistant at the Pontifical Throne Nov. 4, 1944; appt. Archbishop "ad personam" Nov. 25, 1953; resigned Sept. 21, 1966 and transferred to Titular See of Tacarata, Dec. 14, 1966; died Sept. 5, 1968.—Most Rev. JOHN F. WHEALON, D.D., appt. Titular Bishop of Andrapa and Auxiliary Bishop of Cleveland, June 2, 1961; cons. July 6, 1961; transferred to the See of Erie, Dec. 14, 1966; transferred to the Archdiocese of Hartford; died Aug. 2, 1991.—Most Rev. ALFRED M. WATSON, D.D., Bishop of Erie; ord. May 10, 1934; Titular Bishop of Nationa and Auxiliary Bishop of Erie; appt. May 17, 1965; cons. June 29, 1965; succeeded to See, March 19, 1969; retired July 16, 1982; died Jan. 4, 1990.—Most Rev. MICHAEL J. MURPHY, D.D., S.T.L., Titular Bishop of Arindela and Auxiliary Bishop of Cleveland; appt. April 20, 1976; cons. June 11, 1976; Coadjutor Bishop of Erie; appt. Nov. 28, 1978; succeeded to See, July 16, 1982; retired July 16, 1990.

Vicar General—Rev. Msgr. ROBERT J. SMITH, J.C.L., *St. Mark Catholic Center, P.O. Box 10397, Erie, 16514.* Tel: 814-824-1130.

Office of the Bishop—NANCY HAMILTON, Sec. to the Bishop, *St. Mark Catholic Center, P.O. Box 10397, Erie, 16514.* Tel: 814-824-1120.

Chancery—St. Mark Catholic Center, P.O. Box 10397, Erie, 16514. Tel: 814-824-1135; Fax: 814-824-1124.

Chancellor—Rev. Msgr. LAWRENCE E. BRANDT, J.C.D., Ph.D.

Vice Chancellor—Rev. GREGORY KIRSCH.

Diocesan Archivist and Historian—Rev. ROBERT G. BARCIO, Ph.D. All Diocesan Offices and Personnel listed in Directory can be reached at: *St. Mark*

Catholic Center, 429 E. Grandview Blvd., P.O. Box 10397, Erie, 16514-0397. Tel: 814-824-1111, unless otherwise indicated.

Episcopal Vicars—

Northern Vicariate—Rev. Msgr. ROBERT J. SMITH, J.C.L., *St. Mark Catholic Center, P.O. Box 10397, Erie, 16514.* Tel: 814-824-1130.

Eastern Vicariate—Rev. Msgr. CHARLES A. KAZA, *1100 Hewett St., Brockway, 15824.* Tel: 814-265-1374.

Western Vicariate—Rev. Msgr. ROBERT L. BRUGGER, *967 Chancery Ln., Meadville, 16335.* Tel: 814-333-6382.

Administrative Coordinator—Mr. FRANK E. HAKEL, *St. Mark Catholic Center, P.O. Box 10397, Erie, 16514.* Tel: 814-824-1245.

Vicar for Religious—Sr. MARY RITA KUHN, S.S.J., *St. Mark Catholic Center, P.O. Box 10397, Erie, 16514-0397.* Tel: 814-824-1125.

Director of Planning—WALTER SPILLER, *St. Mark Catholic Center, P.O. Box 10397, Erie, 16514-0397.* Tel: 814-824-1116.

Mission Office and Society for the Propagation of the Faith—Sr. THERESA ZOKY, O.S.B., *St. Mark Catholic Center, P.O. Box 10397, Erie, 16514-0397.* Tel: 814-824-1230.

Advisory To Bishop

Administrative Cabinet—Rev. Msgr. ROBERT J. SMITH, J.C.L., V.G.; Rev. Msgr. CHARLES A. KAZA; Sr. MARY RITA KUHN, S.S.J.; Rev. Msgr. ANDREW H. KARG; Rev. Msgr. LAWRENCE E. BRANDT, J.C.D., Ph.D.; Mr. FRANK HAKEL; Rev. Msgr. MICHAEL D. MCGRAW, L.S.W., M.Ss.A.; Rev. CONRAD KRAUS; DAVID MURPHY; Rev. Msgr. ROBERT A. BRUGGER. Special Consultants: WALTER SPILLER; GARY LONCKI.

Consultors—Rev. Msgr. WILLIAM C. KARG; Rev. Msgr. ROBERT L. BRUGGER; Rev. Msgr. HENRY A. KRIEGEL; Rev. Msgr. ROBERT W. COHAN, V.F.; Rev. Msgr. LOUIS J. HEBERLEIN; Rev. Msgr. ROBERT J. SMITH, J.C.L.

Finance Council—Most Rev. DONALD W. TRAUTMAN; Rev. Msgr. A. JOSEPH BOOK; Rev. Msgr. RICHARD E. BUTRYN; Rev. Msgr. JOHN R. SNYDER; WILLIAM P. BOLASH; THOMAS GUELCHER; HAROLD LANZEL; PATRICIA LIEBEL; Sr. LEONELLA GINGENBACH, S.S.J.; JAMES F. TOOHEY, Esq. Ex-Officios: Rev. Msgr. ROBERT J. SMITH, J.C.L.; FRANK HAKEL; DAVID MURPHY.

Deans—Rev. Msgr. ROBERT W. COHAN, V.F., Erie East; Rev. Msgr. WILLIAM E. BIEBEL, V.F., Erie West; Very Rev. CHARLES H. DREXLER, S.T.D., V.F., Gannon University; Rev. Msgr. EDWARD J. ZEITLER, V.F., Sharon; Very Rev. THOMAS L. TYLER, V.F., Oil City; Very Rev. THOMAS M. ALEKSA, V.F., Bradford; Rev. Msgr. JOSEPH K. BOBAL, V.F., Clearfield; Rev. Msgr. JOHN J. LUCAS, V.F., Meadville; Rev. Msgr. HENRY L. KREBS, Dubois; Rev. Msgr. JOSEPH K. BOBAL, V.F., St. Marys; Rev. Msgr. EDWARD J. KOSIK, V.F., Warren.

Presbyteral Council—Most Rev. DONALD W. TRAUTMAN, Pres.; Rev. Msgr. DANIEL ARNOLD, Chm.; Rev. WILLIAM LASKA, Sec.

Priest Personnel Board—Rev. Msgr. ROBERT BRUGGER, Chm.; Rev. Msgr. RICHARD MAYER, Vice Chm.; Rev. JEFF NOBLE, Sec.

Priest Retirement Board—Most Rev. DONALD W. TRAUTMAN, Chm. Members: WILLIAM BOLASH; Sr. JEAN BAPTISTE DILUZIO, S.S.J.; JAMES HOLLAND; Rev. Msgr. JOHN J. SLATER; JAMES TOOHEY, Attorney. Ex-Officio: Rev. Msgr. LAWRENCE E. BRANDT; Rev. DANIEL K. ARNOLD. Staff: DAVID J. MURPHY; Rev. Msgr. ROBERT L. BRUGGER.

Pennsylvania Catholic Conference—Rev. Msgr. LAWRENCE E. BRANDT, J.C.D., Ph.D., Personal Rep. of the Bishop, *St. Mark Catholic Center, P.O. Box 10397, Erie, 16514.*

The Bishop's Theologial Advisory Committee—Rev. Msgr. GERALD L. ORBANEK, M.A., Chm.; Revs. JOHN P. SCHANZ, Ph.D.; CHARLES H. DREXLER, S.T.D.; EDWARD KRAUSE, Ph.D.; CASIMIR J. WOZNIAK, Ph.D.; RICHARD J. SULLIVAN, M.A.; SCOTT P. DETISCH, Ph.D.; Mr. PATRICK O'CONNELL, Ph.D.; Sr. MICHELLE HEALY, S.S.J., M.A.

Lake Shore Visitor Advisory Board—Most Rev. DONALD W. TRAUTMAN; GINA ADAMS; GARY LONCKI, Editor; Rev. Msgr. WILLIAM E. BIEBEL; JOSEPH MASSA, District Attorney; PATRICK C. BOYLE; DAVID SLOMSKI; JILL T. SLOMSKI; Rev. Msgr. LAWRENCE BRANDT, Chancellor; Sr. MARY LOUIS EICHENLAUB, O.S.B.; TOM BRENNAN.

Matrimonial Concerns

All requests for marriage dispensations, permissions, and rogatory commissions should be sent to this office

Diocesan Tribunal—*St. Mark Catholic Center, P.O. Box 10397, Erie, 16514.* Tel: 814-824-1140; Fax: 814-824-1140.

Bishop's Delegate for Dispensations—Rev. GEORGE L. GROUCUTT.

Judicial Vicar—Rev. MARK L. BARTCHAK, J.C.D.

Adjutant Judicial Vicar—Rev. SCOTT T. STROUPE, J.C.L.

Promoter of Justice—Rev. Msgr. LAWRENCE E. BRANDT, J.C.D., Ph.D.

Defenders of the Bond—Rev. Msgr. LAWRENCE E. BRANDT, J.C.D., Ph.D.; Revs. CHARLES MURCKO; JOSEPH RICCARDO.

Matrimonial Judges—Rev. Msgr. ROBERT J. SMITH, J.C.L.; Rev. Msgr. RICHARD J. STACK, J.C.L.; Revs. MARK L. BARTCHAK, J.C.D.; JOHN P. BEAL, J.C.D.; CHARLES SCHMITT, M.A.; L. THOMAS SNYDERWINE, Ph.D.; Rev. SCOTT T. STROUPE, J.C.L.; Deacon RICHARD D. SHEWMAN, J.C.L.

Auditors—Rev. JAMES P. RUHLING; Sr. REBECCA ANN COSTA, S.S.J.; Sr. JEAN BAPTISTE DILUZIO, S.S.J.

Secretary / Notary—CAROL GRYGIER; CINDY MANGIARACINA.

Office of Conciliation & Arbitration—*St. Mark Catholic Center, P.O. Box 10397, Erie, 16514.* Tel: 814-824-1140. Rev. MARK L. BARTCHAK, J.C.D., Dir.

Catholic Education

Episcopal Vicar for Catholic Education—Rev. Msgr. ANDREW H. KARG, *St. Mark Catholic Center, P.O. Box 10397, Erie, 16514-0397.*

Superintendent for Catholic Schools—Sr. MARY ARNOLD TANN, S.S.J., *St. Mark Catholic Center, P.O. Box 10397, Erie, 16514-0397.*

Coordinator of Secondary Schools—FRANK HAKEL, *St. Mark Catholic Center, P.O. Box 10397, Erie, 16514-0397.*

Directors—CHARLES BANDUCCI, School Finance; JANICE WHITEMAN, Curriculum; MAUREEN DUNN, Dir. Govt. Programs; Sr. MARY ANN BADER, R.S.M., Teacher Personnel; NED SMITH, Technology & Community Rels. Coord.; J. WILLIAM JONES, Coord. Athletic Programs, *St. Mark Catholic Center, P.O. Box 10397, Erie, 16514-0397.*

Youth Athletic Director—J. WILLIAM JONES, *St. Mark's Catholic Center, P.O. Box 10397, Erie, 16514-0397.* Tel: 814-824-1213.

Religious Education—Mr. JOSEPH STREETT, Dir., Religious Education, Curriculum & Catechist Formation; Sr. NANCY FISCHER, S.S.J., Dir., Community Formation & Ministry Training; GREGORY SCHLUETER, Dir., Youth Ministry Heart & Soul Program; Vacant, Dir., Youth Ministry, *St. Mark Catholic Center, P.O. Box 10397, Erie, 16514-0397.* KAREN LESLIE, Media Resource Coord. Mktg., *St. Mark Catholic Center, P.O. Box 10397, Erie, 16514-0397.*

Campus Ministry—Diocesan Co-Dirs.: RENEE J. LABAKI, *Gannon University, University Sq., Erie, 16541.* Tel: 814-871-7435. Rev. MICHAEL ALLISON, *Penn State Erie, The Behrend College, Sta. Rd., Erie, 16563.* Tel: 814-898-6245. See separate listing in the institution section for details on Campus Ministry and Newman Centers.

Catholic Charities
Affiliated Offices, Agencies and Institutions
Central Administration

Office of Catholic Charities—Rev. Msgr. MICHAEL D. MCGRAW, M.Ss.A., L.S.W., Exec. Dir., *St. Mark Catholic Center, P.O. Box 10397, Erie, 16514-0397.*

Catholic Charities of the Diocese of Erie, Inc.—Rev. Msgr. MICHAEL D. MCGRAW, M.Ss.A., L.S.W., Exec. Dir., *St. Mark Catholic Center, P.O. Box 10397, Erie, 16514-0397.* Charities program and fiscal development corporation.

Development and Grantwriting; STEVEN C. DEHART, Dir., *St. Mark Catholic Center, P.O. Box 10397, Erie, 16514-0397.* Rev. MICHAEL G. BARLETTA, Devel. & Pub. Rels. Assoc., *St. Mark Catholic Center, P.O. Box 10397, Erie, 16514-0397*

Parish Social Services

Family Ministries—MARY MAXWELL, M.A., Dir., *St. Mark Catholic Center, P.O. Box 10397, Erie, 16514-0397.* Office includes Marriage Preparation and Enrichment Programs, Divorced Ministry, Retrouvaille, Parenting and Rainbows.

Respect Life / Justice and Peace—RITA M. SCRIMENTI, M.S.W., Dir., *St. Mark Catholic Center, P.O. Box 10397, Erie, 16514-0397.* Office includes advocacy, parish-based social justice education programs and respect life efforts.

Parish Social Ministry—Sr. ANN AMEN, S.S.J., Ph.D., Dir., *St. Mark Catholic Center, P.O. Box 10397, Erie, 16514-0397.* Consultant for Parish Care and Concern model and training program for volunteers.

Natural Family Planning—Diocesan Coords.: EDWARD BURKETT; BARBARA BURKETT, *St. Mark Catholic Center, P.O. Box 10397, Erie, 16514-0397.* Natural Family Planning training and education, Teen Chastity educational programs.

Rainbows-Services to Children of Separation / Divorce—ROSE JONES, M.A., Dir., *St. Mark Catholic Center, P.O. Box 10397, Erie, 16514-0397.*

Campaign for Human Development—RITA M. SCRIMENTI, M.S.W., Dir., *St. Mark Catholic Center, P.O. Box 10397, Erie, 16514-0397.*

Persons with Disabilites Ministries—JACKLYN JOHNSON, R.N., Coord.

Clinical Services

Catholic Charities Counseling and Adoption Services—NANCY MONICATTI, A.C.S.W., L.S.W., Agency Dir. ROSEMARIE RADOMSKI, M.A., M.S., Clinical Dir.

Northern Vicariate - Erie Office—*329 W. Tenth St., Erie, 16502.* Tel: 814-456-2091., Satellite Office - Warren: *213 W. Third Ave., Office 105, Warren.* Tel: 814-726-9799.

Western Vicariate - Sharon Office—MARTHA CONSLA, M.Ed., Reg. Supvr., *786 E. State St., Sharon, 16146.* Tel: 412-346-4142., Satellite Office - Meadville: *967 Chancery Ln., Meadville, 16335.* Tel: 814-337-5551.

Eastern Vicariate - DuBois Office—JOHN S. PETKAC, M.A., *90 Beaver Dr., DuBois, 15801.*

Institutional Care of Elderly

John XXIII Home—ROBERTA T. LAMONT, Admin., *2250 Shenango Fwy., Hermitage, 16148.* Tel: 814-981-3200.

Christ the King Manor—Rev. Msgr. JOHN W. MIGNOT, Admin., *1100 W. Long Ave., Du Bois, 15801.* Tel: 814-371-3180.

Community Services

**St. Martin Center*—CHERYL WEBER, M.A., Dir., *1701 Parade St., Erie, 16503.* Tel: 814-452-6113.

Harborcreek Youth Services—JAMES E. HENRY, A.C.S.W., L.S.W., Dir., *5712 Iroquois Ave., Harborcreek, 16421.* Tel: 814-899-7664.

Prince of Peace Center—Sr. CLARE MARIE BEICHNER, S.S.J., Dir., *502 Darr Ave., Box 89, Farrell, 16121.* Tel: 412-346-5777.

Better Housing for Erie, c/o H.A.N.D.S.—CHARLES SCALISE, SR., Dir., *139 E. 12th St., Erie, 16501.* Tel: 814-459-1047.

Good Samaritan Center—Rev. JAMES C. MCKEE, S.J., Dir., *Clearfield.* Tel: 814-236-1896; 768-7229.

Other Charitable/Social Agencies and Institutions

Gannondale Residential Center for Girls—LOUIS J. GRANDE, A.C.S.W., Exec. Dir., *4635 E. Lake Rd., Erie, 16511.* Tel: 814-899-7659.

St. Mary's Home—Sr. ANASTASIA VALIMONT, S.S.J., Admin., *607 E. 26th St., Erie, 16504.* Tel: 814-459-0621.

Mercy Center For Women—PATRICIA DONZE, Dir., *1039 E. 27th St., Erie, 16507.* Tel: 814-455-4577.

Young People Who Care—Sr. THERESE DUSH, C.A., Dir., *Frenchville, 16836.* Tel: 814-263-4177.

Maria House Projects—Rev. Msgr. JAMES PETERSON, Dir., *P.O. Box 10682, Erie, 16514.* Tel: 814-454-0891.

Emmaus Ministries—Sr. MARY MILLER, O.S.B., Dir., *218 E. 11th St., Erie, 16501.* Tel: 814-459-8754.

St. Patrick Haven—Sr. MARY EILEEN MOYER, S.S.J., Dir., *147 E. 12th St., Erie, 16501.* Tel: 814-454-7219.

Parish Services

Liturgy & Worship—Rev. CONRAD KRAUS, Dir., *St. Mark Catholic Center, P.O. Box 10397, Erie, 16514-0397.*

Community Formation—Sr. NANCY FISCHER, S.S.J., Dir., *St. Mark Catholic Center, P.O. Box 10397, Erie, 16514-0397.*

Lay Ministry Training—Sr. NANCY FISCHER, S.S.J., Dir. JOSEPH STREETT, *St. Mark Catholic Center, P.O. Box 10397, Erie, 16514-0397.*

Rite of Christian Initiation for Adults—Rev. GERARD H. KREBS, *St. Mark Catholic Center, P.O. Box 10397, Erie, 16514-0397.* Tel: 814-824-1272.

Finance and Development

Director—DAVID J. MURPHY, *St. Mark Catholic Center, P.O. Box 10397, Erie, 16514-0397.*

Finance Office—DAVID J. MURPHY, Dir.; JAMES L. BOGNIAK, Mgr., Accounting & Budgeting; THOMAS E. BURIK, Parish Accountant & Auditor, *St. Mark Catholic Center, P.O. Box 10397, Erie, 16514-0397.* Tel: 814-824-1180.

Development Office—WILLIAM F. GRANT, II, Dir., *St. Mark Catholic Center, P.O. Box 10397, Erie, 16514-0397.* Consultants: JACK DWYER; Rev. Msgr. ERNEST J. DALEY. Tel: 814-824-1193.

Diocesan Attorney—FRANK L. KROTO, JR., ESQ., *Quinn, Buseck, Leemhuis, Toohey & Kroto, Inc., 2222 W. Grandview Blvd., Erie, 16506.* Tel: 814-833-2222.

Erie Diocesan Cemeteries—Board of Members: Most Rev. DONALD W. TRAUTMAN; Rev. Msgr. ROBERT J. SMITH, J.C.L.; Rev. Msgr. LAWRENCE E. BRANDT, J.C.D., Ph.D.; DAVID J. MURPHY; THOMAS L. COPECK, Dir.; JOHN HROMYAK, Operations Mgr., *3325 West Lake Rd., Erie, 16505.* Tel: 814-838-7724.

Clergy Formation

Clergy Personnel—Rev. Msgr. ROBERT L. BRUGGER, Dir.

Clergy Continuing Education and Formation—Rev. THOMAS J. WHITMAN, Dir., *St. Mark Catholic Center, P.O. Box 10397, Erie, 16514-0397.*

Seminary Program

Vocation Office—Rev. EDWARD M. LOHSE, Dir., *St. Mark Catholic Center, P.O. Box 10397, Erie, 16514-0397.*

St. Mark's College Formation Program—Rev. Msgr. LAWRENCE T. SPEICE, Rector, *St. Mark Catholic Center, P.O. Box 10397, Erie, 16514-0397.*

Continuum Program & Spiritual Formation—Rev. MICHAEL T. KESICKI, Dir., *St. Mark Catholic Center, P.O. Box 10397, Erie, 16514-0397.* Sr. MARY ANDREW HIMES, R.S.M., Dir., Liturgical Music.

Special Apostolates

Spiritual Apostolates—Rev. JOHN T. CARTER, Dir., *5145 Peach St., Erie, 16509.* Tel: 814-864-0622.

Black Apostolate—Rev. EDWARD C. KRAUSE, C.S.C., *233 E. 16th St., Erie, 16503.* Tel: 814-454-1615.

Hispanic Apostolate—Rev. JORGE VILLEGAS, Dir., *1237 W. 21st St., Erie, 16502.* Tel: 814-459-0543.

Apostleship of the Sea and Chaplain to the Port of Erie—Rev. L. THOMAS SNYDERWINE, Dir., *c/o St. Paul Church, 1617 Walnut St., Erie, 16502.* Tel: 814-459-3173.

Blue Army of Our Lady of Fatima—Rev. OTTO B. PISONI, Dir., *502 Peach St., Erie, 16501-1104.* Tel: 814-454-6494.

Cursillo Movement—Rev. JOHN J. HILBERT, Dir., *695 Smithson Ave., Erie, 16511.* Tel: 814-899-3000.

Legion of Mary—Rev. JOHN T. CARTER, Dir., *5145 Peach St., Erie, 16509.* Tel: 814-864-0622.

Charismatic Movement—MICHAEL VEHEC, Diocesan Liaison, *St. Mark Catholic Center, P.O. Box 10397, Erie, 16514-0397.*

Special Ministries—Rev. Msgr. JAMES W. PETERSON, Dir., *P.O. Box 10682, Erie, 16514.* Tel: 814-454-0891.

Bread of Life Community—Rev. LAWRENCE RICHARDS, Moderator, *830 W. 9th St., Erie, 16502.* Tel: 814-456-5698. GENE KOBAL, Pres.

Word of Life Charismatic Renewal—*St. Mark Catholic Center, 429 E. Grandview Blvd., P.O. Box 10397, Erie, 16514-0397.* Tel: 814-824-1286.

Ecumenism

Pennsylvania Conference on Inter-Church Cooperation—Rev. Msgr. LAWRENCE E. BRANDT, J.C.D., Ph.D., Diocesan Rep.

Ecumenical Officers—

Eastern Vicariate—Rev. DENNIS C. HADBERG.

Western Vicariate—Rev. Msgr. WILLIAM C. KARG, *St. Joseph, 79 Case Ave., Sharon, 16146.* Tel: 412-981-3232.

Northern Vicariate—Rev. Msgr. WILLIAM E. BIEBEL, *St. Peter Cathedral, 230 W. 10th St., Erie, 16501.* Tel: 814-453-6677.

Communication

Office of Communications—GARY C. LONCKI, Dir., *P.O. Box 10668, Erie, 16514-0668.* Tel: 814-824-1160; Fax: 814-824-1128.

"Lake Shore Visitor" - Diocesan Newspaper—GARY C. LONCKI, Editor; ANDREA BARAN, Asst. Editor, *P.O. Box 10668, Erie, 16514-0668.* Tel: 814-824-1160; Fax: 814-824-1128.

CLERGY, PARISHES, MISSIONS AND PAROCHIAL SCHOOLS

CITY OF ERIE
(Erie County)

1—ST. PETER CATHEDRAL (1893), Rev. Msgr. William E. Biebel, V.F., Rector; Rev. Joseph P. Reigel; Sr. Mary McCarthy, R.S., D.R.E.; Sr. Martha Howick, S.S.J., Pastoral Assoc. In res., Rev. Msgr. Edward H. Latimer, (Retired); Revs. Gregory A. Kirsch, Vice Chancellor; Robert Barcio, Archivist.
Res., 230 W. 10th St., 16501. Tel: 814-453-6677; Fax: 814-456-1351.
Church—10th St. & Sassafras St., 16501.
School—Tel: 814-452-4276; Fax: 814-452-0479.
Sisters 1; Lay Teachers 28; Students 347.

2—BLESSED SACRAMENT (1938), Rev. Msgr. Daniel K. Arnold; Rev. John J. Detisch; Sr. Mary Rose Romeo, S.S.J., Music Dir.
Res., 1626 W. 26th St., 16508. Tel: 814-454-0171; Fax: 814-459-6832.
School—Tel: 814-455-1387; Fax: 814-455-1388.
Sisters of St. Joseph 2; Lay Teachers 20; Students 471.

3—HOLY FAMILY/ST. ANN/ST. CASIMIR (1902) (Slovak), Rev. James T. O'Hara.
Office: 913 Fulton St., 16503. Tel: 814-452-4832.
School—Tel: 814-452-4720.
Lay Teachers 10; Students 175.

4—HOLY ROSARY (1927), Very Rev. Richard D. Lynch; Rev. William M. Laska.
Res., 2701 East Ave., 16504. Tel: 814-456-4254; Fax: 814-456-4255.
School—Tel: 814-456-7212; Fax: 814-454-5467.
Lay Teachers 17; Students 209.

5—HOLY TRINITY (1903) (Polish), Rev. David J. Maciukiewicz; Sr. Teresita Langowski, C.S.S.F., Pastoral Min.
Res., 2220 Reed St., 16503. Tel: 814-456-0671.

6—IMMACULATE CONCEPTION (1946) (African American), Rev. Edward Krause, C.S.C., Admin.
Res., 109 University Square, 16541. Tel: 814-871-7545.
Church—233 E. 16th St., 16503. Tel: 814-454-1615.

7—MOUNT CALVARY (1951), Rev. Msgr. Daniel E. Magraw.
Res., 2004 East Lake Rd., 16511. Tel: 814-454-0061; Fax: 814-454-7177.
School—Tel: 814-455-1268.
Lay Teachers 13; Students 178.

8—OUR LADY OF MERCY (1946), Rev. Gerald T. Ritchie; Sr. Rosemary O'Brien, S.S.J., Pastoral Min.; Sr. Irene Lucas, O.S.B., D.R.E.; Sr. Mary Daniel Meahl, O.S.B., Dir. Music.
Res., 837 Bartlett Rd., Harborcreek, 16421. Tel: 814-899-5342; Fax: 814-898-3306.

9—OUR LADY OF MT. CARMEL (1960), Rev. Thomas M. Fialkowski; Rev. Msgr. Joseph V. Reszkowski; Sr. Carol Wilcox, S.S.J.
Res., 1553 E. Grandview Blvd., 16510. Tel: 814-825-7313; Fax: 814-825-4190.
School—Tel: 814-825-2822.
Lay Teachers 22; Students 332.

10—OUR LADY OF PEACE (1955), Rev. Msgr. Ernest J. Daley; Rev. Michael G. DeMartinis; Sr. Elizabeth Bauer, O.S.F., Pastoral Assoc. In res., Rev. Msgr. Andrew H. Karg; Rev. James Ruhling.
Res., 2401 W. 38th St., 16506. Tel: 814-833-7701; Fax: 814-833-7702.
School—Tel: 814-838-3548.
Lay Teachers 25; Students 454.

11—SACRED HEART (1894), Revs. David Findlay; Thomas M. Brooks; Sr. Ricarda Vincent, S.S.J., Pastoral Assoc. In res., Revs. Jerome S. Simmons; Daniel Dymski.
Res., 816 W. 26th St., 16508. Tel: 814-456-6256.
School—Tel: 814-459-7247; Fax: 814-459-8838.
Sisters 2; Lay Teachers 24; Students 420.

12—ST. ANDREW (1871), Rev. Richard J. Sullivan. In res., Revs. Scott T. Stroupe; John E. Santor.
Res., 1116 W. Seventh St., 16502. Tel: 814-454-2486; Fax: 814-456-4443.
School—Tel: 814-454-2454; Fax: 814-456-3737.
Sisters 1; Lay Teachers 10; Students 187.

13—ST. ANN (1887). (See Holy Family for Ministry Team.). Rev. James T. O'Hara. In res., Revs. Chester J. Gawronski; Gerald J. Koos; Edward Feeney, (Retired).
Church—921 East Ave., 16503. Tel: 814-453-4681.

14—ST. BONIFACE (1857), Rev. Leo J. Gallina. In res., Rev. Raymond W. Hahn.
Res., 7615 Wattsburg Rd., 16509. Tel: 814-825-4439; Fax: 814-825-4430. [CEM]
School—Tel: 814-825-4238; Fax: 814-825-8101.
Lay Teachers 19; Students 263.

15—ST. CASIMIR (1914) (Polish), Rev. James T. O'Hara.
Church—629 Hess Ave., 16503. Tel: 814-459-7361.

16—ST. GEORGE (1922), Rev. Msgr. Jan C. Olowin; Revs. John P. Malthaner; John T. Carter; Sr. Maria O'Connor, R.M.S., Pastoral Min.; Sr. Regina Przestrzelski, R.M.S., D.R.E.
Res., 5145 Peach St., 16509. Tel: 814-864-0622; Fax: 814-866-7532.
School—Tel: 814-864-4821; Fax: 814-866-7532.
Sisters 2; Lay Teachers 33; Students 604.

17—ST. HEDWIG/ST. PATRICK (1910), Rev. Msgr. John M. Dollinger.
Res., 521 E. 3rd St., 16507. Tel: 814-454-8096.

18—ST. JAMES (1921), Rev. Msgr. Robert W. Cohan, V.F.; Sr. Colette Hilow, C.D.S., D.R.E. In res., Rev. James McCormick.
Res., 2635 Buffalo Rd., 16510. Tel: 814-899-6178; Fax: 814-899-7681.
School—Tel: 814-899-3429.
Sisters of the Congregation of the Divine Spirit 7; Lay Teachers 16; Students 286.

19—ST. JOHN THE BAPTIST (1870), Rev. Philip M. Oriole.
Res., 509 E. 26th St., 16504. Tel: 814-454-2873; Fax: 814-456-7073.
School—Tel: 814-452-6874; Fax: 814-456-7033.
Sisters 1; Lay Teachers 12; Students 228.

20—ST. JOSEPH (1867) (German), Rev. Jeffery J. Lucas. In res., Rev. Msgr. John M. Gannon, (Retired); Rev. Gerard H. Krebs.
Res., 147 W. 24th St., 16502. Tel: 814-452-2982; Fax: 814-452-4400.
School—Tel: 814-452-3119.
Sisters 1; Lay Teachers 11; Students 121.

21—ST. JUDE THE APOSTLE (1955), Rev. Msgr. Henry A. Kriegel. In res., Rev. Thomas J. Whitman.
Res., 2801 W. 6th St., P.O. Box 8408, 16505. Tel: 814-833-0927; Fax: 814-833-9692.
School—Our Lady's Christian, 814-838-7676.
Sisters 1; Lay Teachers 25; Students 480.

22—ST. JULIA (1938), Rev. Msgr. Richard J. McGuire.
Res., 638 Roslyn Ave., 16505. Tel: 814-833-4347; Fax: 814-833-4347.
School—Our Lady's Christian. (See St. Jude the Apostle for details.).

23—ST. LUKE (1954), Revs. L. Thomas Snyderwine; Lawrence Richards; Sr. Margaret Mary Wagner, C.D.P., Pastoral Min. & D.R.E. In res., Rev. Msgr. Robert D. Goodill; Rev. David E. Prenatt.
Res., 421 East 38th St., 16504. Tel: 814-825-6920; Fax: 814-825-6920.
School—Tel: 814-825-7105.
Lay Teachers 26; Students 435.

24—ST. MARK THE EVANGELIST (Lawrence Park) (1938), Rev. John J. Hilbert.
Res., 695 Smithson Ave., 16511. Tel: 814-899-3000; Fax: 814-899-5212.

25—ST. MARY (1840) (German), Rev. Msgr. Robert J. Reilly; Sr. Mary Louis Eichenlaub, O.S.B., Pastoral Min.; Sr. Lucia B. Serrano, R.M.S.
Res., 315 E. 9th St., 16503. Tel: 814-452-2410.

26—ST. MATTHEW IN THE WOODS (1966), Rev. Richard E. Powers, S.J.
Res., 1290 Townhall Rd. West, 16509. Tel: 814-866-6248.

27—ST. PATRICK/ST. HEDWIG (1834), Rev. William E. Sutherland, Admin.; Sr. Mary Pascal Gray, S.S.J., Pastoral Assoc.; Sr. Marie Stephen Kebort, S.S.J., D.R.E. In res., Most Rev. Michael J. Murphy; Rev. Msgr. Joseph V. Wardanski; Revs. Michael G. Barletta; Thomas E. Smith.
Res., 130 E. 4th St., 16507. Tel: 814-454-8085; Fax: 814-459-8685.

28—ST. PAUL (1891) (Italian), Rev. Msgr. Richard J. Stack; Sr. Martha Howick, S.S.J., Pastoral Min. In res., Rev. Michael P. Allison.
Res., 1617 Walnut St., 16502. Tel: 814-459-3173.

29—ST. STANISLAUS (1885) (Polish), Rev. Msgr. Bernard J. Urbaniak; Sr. Elizabeth Oettel, O.S.B., D.R.E.; Sr. Rosemary Modzelewski, C.S.F.N., Parish Min. In res., Rev. Mark L. Bartchak.
Res., 516 E. 13th St., 16503. Tel: 814-452-6606; Fax: 814-452-6606. [CEM]
School—Tel: 814-452-4825.
Lay Teachers 11; Students 178.

30—ST. STEPHEN (1917), Rev. Jorge C. Villegas; Sr. Laura Villarreal, O.L.C., Patoral Assoc.
Res., 1237 W. 21 St., 16502. Tel: 814-459-0543.

OUTSIDE THE CITY OF ERIE

Albion, Erie Co., St. Lawrence (1914), Rev. John M. Fischer.
Res., 180 E. State St., 16401. Tel: 814-756-3623.
St. Lawrence Catechetical Center—129 E. Pearl St., 16401. Tel: 814-756-4840.

Anita, Jefferson Co., St. Joseph (1898), Rev. Paul Schill.
Res., Box 24, Walston, 15781. Tel: 814-938-9687. [CEM]

Bradford, McKean Co., St. Bernard (1880), Very Rev. Thomas M. Aleksa, V.F. In res., Revs. Christopher C. Merry; William J. O'Brien.
Res., 98 E. Corydon St., 16701. Tel: 814-362-6825; Fax: 814-362-1479. [CEM]
School—Tel: 814-368-5891; Fax: 814-368-1464.
Lay Teachers 17; Students 366.

St. Francis of Assisi (1846), In res., Rev. Howard J. King; Bro. Michael W. Hicks, D.R.E.
Res., 574 E. Main St., 16701. Tel: 814-368-6959; Fax: 814-368-6959. [JC]

Brandy Camp, Elk Co., Holy Cross (1908) (Italian), Rev. Msgr. Louis Heberlein, Admin.; Rev. John R. Neff. Mailing Address: P.O. Box 65, 15822. Tel: 814-265-4331.
Res., 287 Treasure Lake, Du Bois, 15821. Tel: 814-371-2899. [CEM]

Brockway, Jefferson Co., St. Tobias (1898), Rev. Msgr. Louis J. Heberlein; Deacon Thomas Jackson. In res., Rev. Msgr. Charles A. Kaza.
Res., 1100 Hewett St., 15824. Tel: 814-268-3655; Fax: 814-268-1147. [CEM]

Brookville, Jefferson Co., Immaculate Conception (1852), Rev. Joseph P. Staszewski.
Res., 129 Graham Ave., 15825. Tel: 814-849-8697. [CEM]
Missions—Corsica, Jefferson Co., St. Ann. [CEM]
Sigel, Jefferson Co., St. Dominic. [CEM]

Cambridge Springs, Crawford Co., St. Anthony (1899), Rev. Robert F. Bower, Admin. In res., Revs. Mark A. Nowak; Robert G. Craig.
Res., 165 Beach Ave., 16403. Tel: 814-398-4234.

Clarion, Clarion Co., Immaculate Conception (1855), Revs. Frank J. Przepierski; Brian E. Vossler; Sr. Virginia Cummings, O.S.F.; Sr. Bernadine Gehinger, S.S.J., Pastoral Assoc.
Res., 720 Liberty St., 16214. Tel: 814-226-8433; Fax: 814-226-1090. [CEM]
School—Tel: 814-226-9690.
Lay Teachers 22; Students 125.
Catechesis/Religious Programs—Students 395.

Clearfield, Clearfield Co., St. Francis (1830), Rev. David L. Poulson.
Res., 212 S. Front St., 16830. Tel: 814-765-9671; Fax: 814-765-9489. [CEM]
School—Tel: 814-765-2618.
Lay Teachers 16; Students 190.

Coalport, Clearfield Co., St. Basil the Great (1887), Rev. Alexander D. Amico.
Res., Box 395, 16627. Tel: 814-672-5561; Fax: 814-672-5954. [CEM]

Conneaut Lake, Crawford Co., Our Lady Queen of the Americas (1958), Rev. Msgr. John J. Lucas, V.F.
Res., 9th & Water Sts., Box 110, 16316. Tel: 814-382-7252; Fax: 814-382-9575. [CEM]

Conneautville, Crawford Co., St. Peter (1853) (Irish), In res., Rev. Robert P. Fedor.
Res., 626 Washington St., P.O. Box F, 16406. Tel: 814-587-3435. [CEM]
Convent—High St., P.O. Box 305, 16406. Tel: 814-587-2011. Sacred Heart

Corry, Erie Co., St. Thomas The Apostle (1856), Revs. William M. Kuba; Richard J. Allen.
Res., 203 W. Washington St., 16407. Tel: 814-663-3041; Fax: 814-663-0505. [CEM]
School—Tel: 814-665-7375.
Lay Teachers 13; Students 143.
St. Elizabeth (1876), Rev. Joseph F. Finucane.
Res., 26 W. Pleasant St., 16407. Tel: 814-664-7105. [CEM]
Mission—Spartansburg, Crawford Co., Our Lady of Victory, Spartansburg, 16434. Tel: 814-664-7105.

Coudersport, Potter Co., St. Eulalia (1891), Rev. John F. Weibel.
Res., 16915. Tel: 814-274-8646. [CEM]
Mission—Austin, Potter Co., St. Augustine. [CEM]

Crossingsville, Crawford Co., St. Philip (1840), Rev. Thaddeus T. Kondzielski.
Res., Crossingville, R.D. 2, Edinboro, 16412. Tel: 814-734-7395. [CEM]

Crown, Clarion Co., St. Mary (1848), Rev. Thomas S. Hoderny.
Res., 16220. Tel: 814-744-9919; Fax: 814-744-8624. [CEM 2]
Mission—Marienville, Forest Co., St. Anne.

Curwensville, Clearfield Co., St. Timothy (1915), Rev. Gregory P. Passaure. In res., Rev. James C. McKee, S.J.
Res., 306 Walnut St., 16833. Tel: 814-236-1845; Fax: 814-236-1845. [CEM]

Daguscahonda, Elk Co., St. Benedict. Closed. Effective April 30, 1995, St. Benedict in Daguscahonda became a Public Oratory (Cannon 1223).

Delancey, Jefferson Co., St. Adrian, Rev. Paul A. Schill, Jr., Admin.
Res., Box 24, Walston, 15781. Tel: 814-938-9687.

Du Bois, Clearfield Co., St. Catherine (1877), Rev. Richard R. Siefer. In res., Revs. Edward J. Walk; Patrick J. Healy.
Res., 116 S. State St., 15801. Tel: 814-371-8556; Fax: 814-371-0592. [CEM]
School—Tel: 814-371-2570. Joseph Ryan, Prin.
Lay Teachers 20; Students 253.
St. Joseph (1893) (Lithuanian), Rev. James J. Kennelley.
Res., 15 South Ave., 15801. Tel: 814-371-7956; 371-7604. [CEM]
St. Michael (1912), Rev. Msgr. Henry L. Krebs, V.F. In res., Revs. Mark S. Swoger; Michael G. DeMartinis.
Res., 15 Robinson St., 15801. Tel: 814-371-5773; Fax: 814-371-5794. [CEM]

East Brady, Clarion Co., St. Eusebius (1877), Rev. Joseph J. Kalinowski.
Res., R.D. 1, Box 747, 16028. Tel: 412-526-3366. [CEM]
Mission—Rimersburg, Clarion Co., St. Richard.

Edinboro, Erie Co., Our Lady of the Lake (1950), Rev. John B. Jacquel; Sr. Mary Ann White, S.S.J., D.R.E.
Res., Box 838, 128 Sunset Dr., 16412. Tel: 814-734-3113; Fax: 814-734-3085.

Eldred, McKean Co., St. Raphael (1847), Rev. Samuel B. Slocum.
Res., 22 First St., Box No. 252, 16731. Tel: 814-225-4231; Fax: 814-225-4298. [CEM 2]
Mission—Sartwell, McKean Co., St. Mary. [CEM]

Emlenton, Venango Co., St. Michael (1867), Rev. Mark E. Rusnak, Admin.
Res., Chestnut St., P.O. Box 177, 16373. Tel: 412-867-2422. [CEM]

Emporium, Cameron Co., St. Mark (1888), Rev. Paul S. Siebert; Sr. Mercedes Muskovish, O.S.B., Parish Min.
Res., 235 E. 4th St., 15834. Tel: 814-486-0569; Fax: 814-486-3298. [CEM]
Mission—Driftwood, Cameron Co., St. James.

Fairview, Erie Co., Holy Cross (1963), Rev. J. Thomas Dugan.
Res., 3627 Shauna Ave., P.O. Box 10, 16415. Tel: 814-474-2605; Fax: 814-474-1256.

Falls Creek, Jefferson Co., St. Bernard (1952), Rev. Stanley J. Swacha.
Res., 205 Taylor Ave., 15840. Tel: 814-371-7419.

Farrell, Mercer Co.,

1—HOLY TRINITY, (1915) (Hungarian), Rev. John R. Boeckman.
Res., 1132 Fruit Ave., 16121. Tel: 412-342-0794; Fax: 412-342-0831. [CEM]

2—OUR LADY OF FATIMA, (1952), Rev. Donald E. Berdis. In res., Rev. Joseph A. Ciaiola.
Res., 601 Roemer Blvd., 16121. Tel: 412-346-3359. [CEM 2]
School—Monsignor Geno Monti School, Tel: 412-347-1440.
Lay Teachers 9; Students 102.
Mission—Farrell, Mercer Co., St. Paul.

3—ST. ADALBERT, (1913), Rev. John R. Boeckman.
Res., 1035 Fruit Ave., 16121. Tel: 412-346-5379; Fax: 412-342-0831. [CEM]

4—ST. ANN, (1904) (Slovak), Rev. Richard C. Tomasone.
Res., 1035 Fruit Ave., 16121. Tel: 412-346-5979. [CEM]

Force, Elk Co., St. Joseph (1906), Rev. Donald J. Cooper.
Res., 15841. Tel: 814-787-4151. [CEM]

Franklin, Venango Co., St. Patrick (1867), Revs. John J. Herbein; Mark A. Hoffman.
Res., 949 Liberty St., 16323. Tel: 814-437-5763; Fax: 814-437-6326. [CEM]
School—Tel: 814-432-8689.
Lay Teachers 13; Students 187.

Frenchtown, Crawford Co., St. Hippolyte (1838), Rev. Monty Sayers.
Res., R.D. 2, Guys Mills, 16327. Tel: 814-789-2022; Fax: 814-789-2025.
Mission—Cochranton, Crawford Co., Our Lady of Lourdes.

Frenchville, Clearfield Co., St. Mary of the Assumption (1840), Rev. Samuel Bungo; Sr. Therese Dush, C.A.
Res., P.O. Box 159, 16836. Tel: 814-263-4354; Fax: 814-263-4219. [CEM]
Missions—Karthaus, Clearfield Co., SS. John & Paul; Grass Flats, Clearfield Co., SS. Peter & Paul. [CEM]
Drifting, Clearfield Co., St. Severin. [CEM]

Fryburg, Clarion Co., St. Michael (1846), Rev. John A. Walsh.
Res., P.O. Box 46, Main St., Rte. 208, 16326. Tel: 814-354-2467. [CEM]
School—Tel: 814-354-2523.
Lay Teachers 6; Students 72.

Galeton, Potter Co., St. Bibiana (1888) (Italian), Rev. Thomas E. Brown.
Res., 111 Germania, 16922. Tel: 814-435-2303. [CEM]
Mission—Genesee, Potter Co., Sacred Heart.

Girard, Erie Co., St. John the Evangelist (1853), Rev. Glenn R. Whitman; Sr. Geraldine Kasper, O.S.F., D.R.E. In res., Rev. Conrad L. Kraus.
Res., 142 E. Main St., Box 336, 16417. Tel: 814-774-4108. [CEM]
School—Tel: 814-774-8865; Fax: 814-774-0604.
Sisters 1; Lay Teachers 13; Students 208.

Grampian, Clearfield Co., St. Bonaventure (1833), Rev. Gregory P. Passauer.
Res., P.O. Box 127, 16838. Tel: 814-236-0364. [CEM]

Greenville, Mercer Co., St. Michael (1850), Rev. Msgr. A. Joseph Book; Rev. Dennis J. Veltri; Sr. Mary Gertrude McElhinny, S.C., Pastoral Min.; Deacon Dillworth Davis.
Res., 85 N. High St., 16125. Tel: 412-588-9800; Fax: 412-588-7053. [CEM]
School—Tel: 412-588-7050.
Lay Teachers 20; Students 256.
Mission—Jamestown, Mercer Co., St. Margaret.

Grove City, Mercer Co., Beloved Disciple (1925), Rev. Msgr. Edward J. Zeitler, V.F.; Rev. James A. Wiley.
Res., 321 N. Broad St., 16127. Tel: 412-458-7145. [CEM]

Hermitage, Mercer Co., Church of Notre Dame (1960), Rev. Msgr. John B. Hagerty; Rev. James F. Bird.
Res., 2325 Highland Rd., 16148. Tel: 412-981-5566; Fax: 412-981-3215.
School—Tel: 412-342-2205.
Lay Teachers 15; Students 278.

Houtzdale, Clearfield Co., Christ the King (1970), Rev. John G. Chaplin, C.S.C. In res., Rev. William A. Rice.
Res., 123 Good St., 16651. Tel: 814-378-7653. [CEM]
Mission—Madera, Clearfield Co., Immaculate Conception.

Johnsonburg, Elk Co., Holy Rosary (1896), Rev. David J. Wilson. In res., Sr. Angela Marie Serviden, S.S.J.
Res., 606 Penn St., 15845. Tel: 814-965-2819; Fax: 814-965-5528. [CEM]
School—Tel: 814-965-2812.
Lay Teachers 9; Students 113.

Kane, McKean Co., St. Callistus (1878), Rev. Phillip A. Pinczewski; Sr. Francis Therese Matia, S.S.J., D.R.E.
Res., 342 Chase St., 16735. Tel: 814-837-6694. [CEM]
Convent—116 Haines St., 16735.

Kersey, Elk Co., St. Boniface (1832), Rev. John A. Kuzilla.
Res., 355 Main St., 15846. Tel: 814-885-8941. [CEM]
School—Tel: 814-885-8093.
Sisters of St. Benedict 1; Lay Teachers 11; Students 79.

Lewis Run, McKean Co., Our Mother of Perpetual Help (1946), Rev. Howard J. King.
Res., 31 Lafayette, 16738. Tel: 814-368-6355.

Linesville, Crawford Co., St. Philip (1957), Rev. William J. Driscoll.
Res., R.D. 1, Box 1C, 16424. Tel: 814-683-5313. [CEM]

Lucinda, Clarion Co., St. Joseph (1840), Rev. Joseph R. Czarkowski.
Res., 16235. Tel: 814-226-7288. [CEM]
School—Tel: 814-226-8018. Sr. Monica Steiner, O.S.B., Prin., D.R.E.
Sisters 1; Lay Teachers 6; Students 87.

McKean, Erie Co., St. Francis Xavier (1838), Rev. Msgr. John A. Kirk; Sr. Jane Matheis, S.S.J., Pastoral Min.
Res., 16426. Tel: 814-476-7657. [CEM]

Meadville, Crawford Co., St. Agatha (1849), Rev. Msgr. Henry J. Schauerman; Rev. Richard J. Allen.
Res., 353 Pine St., 16335. Tel: 814-336-1112. [CEM]
School—Seton School. Consolidation of St. Agatha Elementary and St. Brigid Elementary. Tel: 814-336-2320; Fax: 814-336-2328.
Sisters 1; Lay Teachers 19; Students 251.
Mission—Saegertown, Crawford Co., St. Bernadette, 222 Renner Ln., Saegertown, 16433. Tel: 814-763-2831. Rev. Mark A. Nowak.
St. Brigid (1865), Rev. Msgr. Richard E. Butryn; Rev. James E. Piszker. In res., Rev. Msgr. Robert L. Brugger.
Res., 967 Chancery Ln., 16335. Tel: 814-336-4459; Fax: 814-724-2996. [CEM]
St. Mary (1909), Rev. Msgr. Casimir A. Bogniak.
Res., 1085 Water St., 16335. Tel: 814-333-6161.

Mercer, Mercer Co., Immaculate Heart (1838), Rev. Charles S. Murcho.
Res., 16137. Tel: 412-662-2999. [CEM]

Morrisdale, Clearfield Co., St. Agnes (1891), Rev. Mark R. Anderson.
Res., 16858. Tel: 814-342-2583; Fax: 814-342-6377. [CEM]
Mission—Hawk Run, Clearfield Co., SS. Peter & Paul. [CEM]

Mount Jewett, McKean Co., St. Joseph (1898), Rev. John G. Barwin.
Res., P.O. Box 520, 17 Division St., 16740. Tel: 814-778-5520.

New Bethlehem, Clarion Co., St. Charles (1872), Very Rev. Thomas L. Tyler, V.F.
Res., 201 Washington St., 16242. Tel: 814-275-3446. [CEM]
Mission—Crates, Clarion Co., St. Nicholas. [CEM]

North East, Erie Co., St. Gregory Thaumaturgus (1875), Revs. Michael T. Gaines; Regis J. Meenihan.
Res., 136 W. Main St., 16428. Tel: 814-725-9691; Fax: 814-725-1225. [CEM]
School—140 W. Main St., 16428. Tel: 814-725-4571.
Sisters of St. Benedict 1; Lay Teachers 13; Students 173.

Oil City, Venango Co.,

1—Assumption of the Blessed Virgin Mary, (1899) (Polish), Rev. F. Thomas Suppa.
Res., 210 Emerald St., 16301. Tel: 814-677-2032.
Mission—Rouseville, Venango Co., St. Venantius.

2—Our Lady Help of Christians, (1914), Rev. John M. Schultz.
Res., 69 Willow St., 16301. Tel: 814-677-3078.

3—St. Joseph, (1865), Revs. William C. Miller; Mark J. Mastrian.
Res., 35 Pearl Ave., 16301. Tel: 814-677-4004; Fax: 814-677-5977. [CEM 2]

4—St. Stephen, (1898), Revs. Jeffrey J. Noble; Scott E. Katren.
Res., 210 Reed St., 16301. Tel: 814-677-3020; Fax: 814-678-8841.
School—Tel: 814-677-2053.
Lay Teachers 16; Students 249.

Port Allegany, McKean Co., St. Gabriel the Archangel (1876), Rev. Charles R. Schmitt.
Res., 203 Arnold Ave., 16743. Tel: 814-642-2847. [CEM]
Mission—Roulette, Potter Co., St. Mary.

Punxsutawney, Jefferson Co., SS. Cosmas and Damian (1885), Rev. Joseph J. Riccardo.
Res., 616 W. Mahoning St., 15767. Tel: 814-938-6540; Fax: 814-938-7439. [CEM]
School—Tel: 814-938-4224; Fax: 814-939-3759.
Lay Teachers 12; Students 138.

Ramey, Clearfield Co., Holy Trinity (1937), Rev. Killian E. Shuman, T.O.R.
Res., Box 196, 16671. Tel: 814-378-7193. [CEM]

Reynoldsville, Jefferson Co., St. Mary (1872), Rev. Msgr. John W. Mignot.
Res., 607 Main St., 15851. Tel: 814-653-8586. [CEM]

Ridgway, Elk Co., St. Leo the Great (1874), Rev. Msgr. Joseph K. Bobal; Revs. Robert Horgas; James G. Faluszak; Sr. Mary Joan Beauseigneur, S.S.J., Prin.
Res., 111 Depot St., 15853. Tel: 814-772-3135; Fax: 814-772-3225. [CEM]
School—Tel: 814-772-9775.
Sisters 1; Lay Teachers 13; Students 167.
Convent—117 Depot St., 15853.

Rouseville, Venango Co., St. Venantius (1870), Rev. F. Thomas Suppa, Admin.
Res., 210 Emerald St., Oil City, 16301. Tel: 814-677-2032.
Church—403 Main St., 16344.

St. Marys, Elk Co., St. Mary (1842) (German), Revs. Jude W. Brady, O.S.B.; Alfred Patterson, O.S.B.; Bro. Edward Alton; Sr. Josephine DePetro, S.S.J., Coord. Inter Parish Svcs.
Res., 144 Church St., St. Mary, 15857. Tel: 814-781-1019; Fax: 814-834-6795. [CEM]
School—Tel: 814-834-2665.
Lay Teachers 18; Students 272.

Queen of the World (1954), Revs. Leon Hont, O.S.B.; Jeremy Bolha, O.S.B.; Sr. Josephine DiPetro, S.S.J., Coord. Inter Parish Svcs.
Res., 134 Queens Rd., 15857. Tel: 814-834-4701; Fax: 814-834-3422.
School—Tel: 814-834-4169.
Lay Teachers 29; Students 376.

Sacred Heart of Jesus (1876), Revs. Chad R. Ficorilli, O.S.B.; Ananius G. Buccicone, O.S.B.; Scott W. Jabo; Sr. Josephine DePetro, S.S.J., Coord. Inter Parish Svcs.
Res., 323 Center St., 15857. Tel: 814-834-7861; Fax: 814-834-1376.
School—Tel: 814-834-4017.
Lay Teachers 23; Students 291.

Sharon, Mercer Co.,

1—Sacred Heart, (1864), Rev. Daniel J. Kresinski; Rev. Msgr. Donald J. Scully.
Res., 40 S. Irvine Ave., 16146. Tel: 412-346-3567. [CEM]

2—St. Anthony, (1924) (Croatian), Rev. Matthew Ruyechan, O.F.M.
Res., 804 Idaho St., 16146. Tel: 412-342-7391; Fax: 412-342-7981. [CEM]

3—St. Joseph, (1892), Rev. Msgr. William C. Karg; Revs. Jerry S. Priscaro; Patrick J. Damond. In res., Rev. Msgr. Raymond O. Meier, (Retired).
Res., 79 Case Ave., 16146. Tel: 412-981-3232; Fax: 412-981-4174. [CEM][JC]
School—Tel: 412-938-8382.
Lay Teachers 22; Students 307.

4—St. Stanislaus Kostka, (1931) (Polish), Rev. Victor Maksimovich, O.F.M.
Res., 370 Spruce Ave., 16146. Tel: 412-347-7526; Fax: 412-347-1760. [CEM]
Catechesis/Religious Programs—Rose DeSantis, D.R.E.
Students 180.

Sharpsville, Mercer Co., St. Bartholomew (1874), Rev. John S. Lynch.
Res., 311 W. Ridge Ave., 16150. Tel: 412-962-7130; Fax: 412-962-1771.

Sheffield, Warren Co., St. Anthony (1878), Rev. John F. Bauer; Sr. Kathleen Warner, O.S.B., D.R.E.
Res., P.O. Box 518, Four Mile Rd., 16347. Tel: 814-968-5915.

Shinglehouse, Potter Co., St. Theresa (1901), Rev. Samuel B. Slocum.
Res., P.O. Box 277, 16748. Tel: 814-697-6900.

Smethport, McKean Co., St. Elizabeth (1875), Rev. Theodore B. Marconi, Admin.
Res., 307 Franklin St., 16749. Tel: 814-887-9254; Fax: 814-887-1930. [CEM]

Stoneboro, Mercer Co., St. Columbkille (1874), Rev. Henry C. Andrae, Admin.
Res., Franklin St., P.O. Box 206, 16153. Tel: 412-376-3393. [CEM]

Sykesville, Jefferson Co., Assumption of Blessed Virgin Mary (1923), Rev. William F. Presley.
Res., 20 Shaffer St., 15865. Tel: 814-894-2772; Fax: 814-894-7981. [CEM]

Tidioute, Warren Co., St. John (1866), Rev. V. David Foriadori.
Res., 25 First St., 16351. Tel: 814-484-7747; Fax: 814-484-7231. [CEM]
Mission—Tionesta, Forest Co., St. Anthony.

Titusville, Crawford Co., St. Titus (1962), Rev. James G. Gutting; Sr. Edith Hirsch, R.M.S., Pastoral Min.
Res., 513 W. Main St., 16354. Tel: 814-827-4636; Fax: 814-827-4637. [CEM][JC]
School—Tel: 814-827-3312.
Lay Teachers 11; Students 131.
Christian Activities Center—505 W. Walnut St., 16354. Tel: 814-827-7223.
Mission—Mageetown, Crawford Co., Immaculate Conception, Tel: 814-827-2075.

St. Walburga (1872) (German), Rev. Rocco A. Tito.
Res., 120 Brook St., 16354. Tel: 814-827-3958. [CEM]

Union City, Erie Co., St. Teresa of Avila (1906), Rev. Daniel J. Prez.
Res., 9 Third Ave., 16438. Tel: 814-438-2924. [CEM]
Mission—Canadohta Lake, Crawford Co., Our Lady of Fatima.

Walston, Jefferson Co., St. Anthony (1898), Rev. Paul A. Schill, Admin.
Res., Box 24, 15781. Tel: 814-938-9687.

Warren, Warren Co., Holy Redeemer (1912), Rev. Msgr. Edward J. Kosik, V.F.
Res., 11 Russell St., 16365. Tel: 814-726-3360; Fax: 814-726-3361.

St. Joseph (1858), Rev. Walter E. Packard; Rev. Msgr. H. Desmond McGee; Sr. Mary Winkelbauer, C.D.P., D.R.E.
Res., 600 Penna. Ave. W., 16365. Tel: 814-723-2090; Fax: 814-723-6042. [CEM][JC]
School—Tel: 814-723-2030.
Lay Teachers 13; Students 191.

Waterford, Erie Co., St. Cyprian (1878), Rev. Richard E. Powers, S.J.
Church—12775 Donation Rd., Box 535, 16641. Tel: 814-796-4329.

West Middlesex, Mercer Co., Good Shepherd (1955), Rev. Msgr. Richard G. Mayer.
Res., P.O. Box 226, 16159. Tel: 412-528-3539. [JC]

Wilcox, Elk Co., St. Anne (1890), Rev. Norbert K. Wolf.
Res., P.O. Box 65, Clarion St., 15870. Tel: 814-929-5577. [JC]
Mission—Rasselas, Elk Co., Holy Cross. [CEM]

Winburne, Clearfield Co., SS. Cyril and Methodius (1904) (Slovak-Hungarian), Rev. Msgr. Michael E. Tutokie, Admin.
Res., 16879. Tel: 814-345-5674. [CEM][JC]

Youngsville, Warren Co., St. Luke (1958), Rev. John W. Swoger, Admin.
Res., 420 N. Main St., 16371. Tel: 814-563-4432.

Chaplains of Public Institutions

Erie. *Erie County Geriatric Center Annex*, St. Paul, 1617 Walnut St. Rev. L. Thomas Snyderwine.
Erie County Geriatrics Center. Vacant.
Erie County Prison. Rev. Msgr. John M. Dollinger.
Hamot Medical Center, 201 State St., 16550. Rev. Gerald J. Koos.
St. Vincent's Health Center, 232 W. 25th St., 16544. Revs. Dennis A. Martin, Chap.; Raymond Gramata, Chap.
Shriners Hospital for Crippled Children. Vacant. 1116 W. 7th St., 16550.
Soldiers and Sailors Home. Rev. James Ruhling.
Veterans Administration Hospital. Rev. Thomas M. Fialkowski, Chap.

Albion. *Albion State Correctional Facility*. Vacant.

Bradford. *Federal Correction Institution*, P.O. Box 5000, 16701-0950. Rev. John G. Barwin.

Cambridge Springs. *Cambridge Springs Correction Institution*. Rev. Robert G. Craig.

Du Bois. *Du Bois Regional Hospital*, 100 Hospital Ave., 15801. Rev. John R. Neff, Chap.

Lewis Run. *Federal Correction Institution*. Vacant. P.O. Box 5000, 16738.

Meadville. *Crawford Country Home*, 967 Chancery Ln., 16335. Rev. Richard E. Butryn, Chap.

Mercer. *State Correctional Facility*, Box 530, 16137. Rev. Patrick J. Healy, Chap.

Polk. *Polk Center*, Box 94, 16342. Rev. Mark J. Mastrian.

Warren. *Warren State Hospital*. Rev. John F. Bauer.

Special or Diocesan Assignment:
Reverend Fathers—
Fischer, G. William, O.S.F.S., 10018 Seeley St., Lake City, PA 16423-1546

On Duty Outside Diocese:
Reverend Monsignors—
Sanner, James E., Army
Reverend Fathers—
Beal, John P., Washington, DC
Burke, John R., Mexico
Humenay, Robert, WY
Jeselnick, Stephen, AFB
Kelley, Thomas, TX
Malene, Robert, AZ
Milewski, Robert, Navy

On Leave of Absence:
Reverend Fathers—
Collins, Stephen L., III
Roseto, James
Weiss, James F.

Retired:
Reverend Monsignors—
Daniszewski, John D.
Enright, Vincent L.
Gannon, James J.
Gannon, John M.
Goodill, Robert D.
Latimer, Edward H.
Martin, Daniel J.
Meier, Raymond O.
Mitchell, Salvatore P.
Ritchie, G. Carlton
Schriefer, Robert F.
Slater, John J.
Snyder, John R.
Sperry, James E.
Tutokie, Michael E.
Reverend Fathers—
Anderson, Emil
Barcio, Robert G.
Capozzelli, Anthony M.
Cici, William
Cray, Kevin, S.D.S.
Dobosiewicz, Stephen J.
Donovan, Edmund J.
Feeney, J. Edward
Fin, Robert G.
Groucutt, George L.
Jerge, Joseph W.
Kacprowicz, Joseph A.
Kotyuk, Stephen
Kozlowski, Louis
Levis, Robert J.
Lohse, Walter H.
Maloney, William J.
Maryland, Joseph A.
Murray, John L.
Obenrader, Paul F.

Pisoni, Otto B.
Sharpe, Patrick F.
Skinner, Charles D.
Somers, Eldon K.
Stutz, Edward J.
Varga, George
Weber, James H.
Wiley, Joseph
Wilson, Edward M.

INSTITUTIONS LOCATED IN THE DIOCESE

[A] SEMINARIES, DIOCESAN

ERIE. *St. Mark's Seminary*. Mailing Address: 429 E. Grandview Blvd., P.O. Box 10397, 16514. Tel: 814-824-1200. Rev. Msgr. Lawrence T. Speice, Rector & Dir. Seminarians; Revs. Michael T. Kesicki, Dir. Spiritual Formation & Continuum Office; Edward M. Lohse, Vocation Dir.

[B] COLLEGES AND UNIVERSITIES

ERIE. *Gannon University*, University Square, 16541. Tel: 814-871-7000.
For a complete listing, refer to the Colleges and Universities section.
Mercyhurst College, 501 E. 38th St. Blvd., 16546. Tel: 814-824-2000.
E-mail: jgower@paradise.mercy.edu
Web site: www.mercy.edu
For a complete listing, refer to the Colleges and Universities section.

[C] HIGH SCHOOLS, DIOCESAN

ERIE. *Cathedral Preparatory School*, 225 W. Ninth St., 16501. Tel: 814-453-7737. Rev. Msgr. Bruce Allison, Headmaster; Mrs. Joann Mullen, Prin.
Faculty: Revs. Raymond W. Hahn; Lawrence Richards; James McCormick; Regis J. Meenihan; William Fischer; Sr. James Francis Mulligan. Priests 7; Sisters 2; Laymen 26; Laywomen 9; Students 637.

BRADFORD. *Bradford Central Christian High School*, 450 W. Washington St., 16701. Tel: 814-362-3815. Rev. H. Desmond McGee, Jr., Prin. Priests 1; Lay Teachers 16; Students 73.

DU BOIS. *Du Bois Area Catholic Schools*, 204 Hospital Ave., 15801. Tel: 814-371-3060. Mrs. Lorraine Mack, Prin.; Revs. Edward J. Walk, Asst. Prin.; Mark S. Swoger.
Central Christian High School.
Central Christian Middle School. Priests 2; Sisters 1; Lay Teachers 42; Students 674.

HERMITAGE. *Kennedy Christian High School*, 2120 Fwy., 16148. Tel: 412-346-5531. Mr. Peter Iacino, Pres.; Rev. Richard C. Tomasone, Asst. Headmaster; Mrs. Christine Perry, Prin. Priests 3; Lay Teachers 23; Students 394.

OIL CITY. *Venango Christian High School*, 1505 W. 1st St., 16301. Tel: 814-677-3098.
E-mail: vchs1@mail.usachoice.net
Rev. John M. Schultz, Headmaster. Priests 1; Lay Teachers 12; Students 87.

SAINT MARYS. *Elk County Christian High School*, 600 Maurus St., 15857. Tel: 814-834-7800; Fax: 814-781-3441. Mr. John W. Kowach, Headmaster. Campus Ministers: Revs. Scott W. Jabo; James G. Faluszczak. Priests 2; Lay Teachers 27; Students 386.

[D] HIGH SCHOOLS, PRIVATE

ERIE. *Mercyhurst Preparatory School*, 538 E. Grandview Blvd., 16504. Tel: 814-824-2210; Fax: 814-824-2116. Georgia C. Johnson, Pres.; Edward Zenewicz, Prin. Sisters 4; Lay Teachers 55; Students 830.
Villa Maria Academy, 2403 W. 8th St., 16505. Tel: 814-838-2061. Sr. Ann Marie Joint, S.S.J., Prin.; Mrs. Kathleen DiNicola, Asst. Admin.; Mr. John Gardner, Asst. Admin. Sisters 4; Lay Teachers 39; Students 570.

[E] ELEMENTARY SCHOOLS, PRIVATE

ERIE. *Villa Maria Elementary School*, 2551 W. 8th St., 16505. Tel: 814-838-5451. Sr. Margaret Frank, S.S.J., Prin. Sisters of St. Joseph 4; Lay Teachers 27; Students 411.

[F] SPECIAL MINISTRY

ERIE. *Erie East Coast Migrant Programs*, 345 E. 9th St., 16503. Tel: 814-454-4514. Benedictine Sisters of Erie. Sr. Diane Rabe, O.S.B., Dir. Students 30.
L'Arche Community, 523 W. 8th, 16502. Tel: 814-452-2064.
E-mail: larche@velocity.net
Rev. George E. Strohmeyer, Pastoral Min., Eastern U.S. Communities.
Mercy Center of the Arts, 444 E. Grandview Blvd., 16504. Tel: 814-824-2519.
St. Benedict Child Development Center, 345 E. 9th St., 16503. Tel: 814-454-4515. Sr. Diane Rabe, O.S.B., Admin.
St. Benedict Education Center, 330 E. 10th St., 16503. Tel: 814-452-4072; Fax: 814-454-2686. Sr. Miriam Mashank, O.S.B., Dir. Students 90.
Villa Maria Center, 2551 W. 8th St., 16505. Tel: 814-838-5514. Sr. Leonie Shanley, S.S.J., Admin.

[G] GENERAL HOSPITALS

*ERIE. *Saint Vincent Health Center*, 232 W. 25th St., 16544. Tel: 814-452-5000.
For a complete listing, refer to the Hospitals section.

[H] PROTECTIVE INSTITUTIONS

ERIE. *Gannondale Residential Center for Girls*, 4635 E. Lake Rd., 16511. Tel: 814-899-7659.
For a complete listing, refer to the Special Care Facilities section.

HARBORCREEK. *Harborcreek Youth Services*, 5712 Iroquois Ave., 16421. Tel: 814-899-7664; Fax: 814-899-3075.
For a complete listing, refer to the Special Care Facilities section.

[I] APARTMENTS FOR SENIOR CITIZENS

ERIE. *Mercy Terrace Apartments*, 430 E. Grandview Blvd., 16504. Tel: 814-825-6791.
For a complete listing, refer to the Special Care Facilities section.

*HARBORCREEK. *Benetwood Apartments for Persons Elderly and Handicapped*, 641 Troupe Rd., 16421-1048. Tel: 814-899-0088.
For a complete listing, refer to the Special Care Facilities section.

[J] RESIDENCES FOR RETIRED PRIESTS

ERIE. *Bishop Michael J. Murphy Residence for Retired Priests*, 400 E. Gore Rd., 16509. Tel: 814-825-0680.
For a complete listing, refer to the Special Care Facilities section.

[K] NURSING HOMES

ERIE. *St. Mary's Home of Erie*, 607 E. 26th St., 16504. Tel: 814-459-0621; Fax: 814-454-0909.
For a complete listing, refer to the Special Care Facilities section.

DU BOIS. *Christ the King Manor, Inc.*, 1100 W. Long Ave., 15801. Tel: 814-371-3180.
For a complete listing, refer to the Special Care Facilities section.

HERMITAGE. *John XXIII Home*, 2250 Shenango Fwy., 16148. Tel: 412-981-3200.
For a complete listing, refer to the Special Care Facilities section.

[L] SHELTERS FOR MEN AND WOMEN

ERIE. *Community House Inc.*, 521 W. 7th St., 16502. Tel: 814-459-5853; Fax: 814-452-3416.
For a complete listing, refer to the Special Care Facilities section.
Mercy Center for Women, 1039 E. 27th St., 16504. Tel: 814-453-3668.
For a complete listing, refer to the Special Care Facilities section.
St. Patrick Haven, Inc., 147 E. 12th St., 16501. Tel: 814-454-7219; 838-5430.
For a complete listing, refer to the Special Care Facilities section.

[M] CONVENTS AND RESIDENCES FOR SISTERS

ERIE. *Congregation of the Divine Spirit*, 409 W. 6th St., 16507. Tel: 814-455-3590; Fax: 814-454-8899. Mother Patricia O'Connor, C.D.S., Supr. Gen.; Rev. John E. Santor. Members 47.
Erie Dawn, 330 E. 10th St., 16503. Tel: 814-453-5921. Sr. Phyllis Hilbert, S.S.J., Admin.
Gannondale Residential Center for Girls, 4635 E. Lake Rd., 16511.
Holy Family Monastery, 510 E. Gore Rd., 16509-3799. Mother Emmanuel of the Mother of God, O.C.D., Prioress; Rev. Michael Barletta, Chap. Discalced Carmelites 9.
Kraus House Priory, 436 E. 9th St., 16503. Sisters of St. Benedict. Sisters 4.
Mount Saint Benedict Monastery, 6101 E. Lake Rd., 16511. Tel: 814-899-0614; Fax: 814-898-4004.
E-mail: msbsecretary@compuserve.com
Web site: www.bison.com/benedic/msb
Sr. Phyllis Schleicher, O.S.B., Prioress. Sisters of St. Benedict of Erie. Professed Sisters in Community 138; Sisters in Formation 9.
North American Union Sisters of Our Lady of Charity, 4635 E. Lake Rd., 16511. Tel: 814-899-1052. Sr. Mother Teresa Gomez, Local Supr.
Om Shanti, 1239 W. 7th St., 16502. Tel: 814-459-3215. Sr. Diane Cook, O.S.B. Sisters of St. Benedict 2.
Sophia House, 1245 W. 10th St., 16502. Tel: 814-454-1212.
Bethany House, 218 E. 11th St., 16503. Tel: 814-455-4574.
Peace House, 103 E. 35th St., 16504. Tel: 814-455-6066.
Benedicta Riepp Priory, 2108 Poplar St., 16502. Tel: 814-455-5699.
St. Scholastica Priory, 355 E. 9th St., 16503. Tel: 814-454-4052.
Sisters of Mercy Motherhouse, 444 E. Grandview Blvd., 16504. Tel: 814-824-2516; Fax: 814-824-2127. Sr. Joanne Courneen, R.S.M. Professed Sisters 83.
Villa Maria, 5031 W. Ridge Rd., 16506-1249. Tel: 814-838-4100; Fax: 814-838-5167.
E-mail: ssjmaryf@erie.net
Sr. Mary Fromknecht, S.S.J., Congregational Admin.; Rev. Msgr. Gerald L. Orbanek, Chap. The Sisters of St. Joseph of Northwestern PA. Professed Sisters in Community 180.
World of Life Catholic Charismatic Renewal, St. Mark Catholic Center, 429 E. Grandview Blvd., P.O. Box 10397, 16514-0397. Tel: 814-824-1286.

ST. MARYS. *Benedictine Sisters of Elk County O.S.B. St. Joseph Monastery*, 303 Church St., 15857. Tel: 814-834-2267. Sr. M. Raphael Baker, Prioress.
Pax Priory, 345 E. 9th St., Erie, 16503. Tel: 814-452-6318.
E-mail: benedictine@igc.apc.org
Benedictine Sisters of Erie 7. Professed Sisters 44.

[N] SOCIOLOGICAL

ERIE. *Emmaus Ministries*, 345 E. 9th St., 16503. Tel: 814-459-8349. Sr. Mary Miller, O.S.B., Dir.
Mercy Center for Women, 1039 E. 27th St., 16504. Tel: 814-453-3668. Tish Donze, Exec. Dir.
Mercy Center on Aging, 444 E. Grandview Blvd., 16504-2604. Tel: 814-824-2214; Fax: 814-824-2127. Sr. Mary Dolores, R.S.M., Exec. Dir.

[O] RETREAT & RENEWAL CENTERS

ERIE. *Ecclesia Center/Renewal Center*, 9101 Ridge Rd., 16417-9625. Tel: 814-774-9691. Rev. Jerome S. Simmons.
Glinodo Center, 6270 E. Lake Rd., 16511. Tel: 814-899-4584; Fax: 814-898-4004. Sr. Carolyn Gorny-Kopkowski, O.S.B., Admin. Benedictine Sisters of Erie.
Special Ministries, P.O. Box 10682, 16514. Tel: 814-456-0891. Rev. Msgr. James W. Peterson, Dir.
Theophilus, Theophilus House, 4115 Royal Ave., 16509-1428. Tel: 814-866-6891. Rev. Anthony M. Capozzelli, Dir.

DU BOIS. *Nazareth In The Woods, Inc.*, R.D. #8, Box 23, 15801. Tel: 814-375-0268. Rev. F. Thomas Suppa, 814-677-2032. A center of renewal and the Spirituality of the Hidden Life of Nazareth.

FRENCHVILLE. *Young People Who Care Center, Caritas Mission*, 16836. Tel: 814-263-4177.
E-mail: caritasm@phoenix.vicon.net
Web site: http://vicon-net-caritasm
Sr. Theresa Dush, Dir.

UNION CITY. *Avila House Retreat Center*, 61 E. High St., 16438. Tel: 814-438-7020. Mr. & Mrs. Larry Pline, Dir.

[P] CAMPUS MINISTRY

ERIE. *Newman Centers and Campus Ministry*. Office of Education, P.O. Box 10397, 429 E. Grandview Blvd., 16514-0397.
Allegheny College, 147 Crimson Dr., R.D. 1, Meadville, 16335. Tel: 814-332-2800. Mr. David Roncolato, Dir.
Bradford Extension. (University of Pittsburgh), St. Bernard Parish, 98 E. Corydon St., Bradford, 16701. Tel: 814-362-6825.
Clarion University of Pennsylvania, 720 Liberty St., Clarion, 16214. Tel: 814-226-6869. Rev. Brian E. Vossler, Dir.
Clearfield Extension. (Lockhaven University), St. Francis Parish, 212 S. Front St., 16830. Tel: 814-765-9671.
Du Bois Extension. (Penn State University), St. Catherine Parish, 116 State St., DuBois, 15801. Tel: 814-371-8556.
Edinboro University of PA, P.O. Box 820, Edinboro, 16412. Tel: 814-734-1651. Rev. Mark A. Nowak, Dir.
Gannon University, University Sq., 16541. Tel: 814-871-7547. Ms. Renee Boltri, Diocesan Co-Dir.; Heidi Chen, Graduate Asst.; Sandy Honick, Graduate Asst.
Grove City College, Beloved Disciple Parish, 321 N. Broad St., Grove City, 16127. Tel: 412-458-7145. Sr. Marilyn Uline, Assoc.
Mercyhurst College, 501 E. 38th St., 16546. Tel: 814-824-2301. Sr. Elisabeth Lintsen, M.S.O.L.A., Dir.; Rev. Stephen A. Anderson, Chap. & Dir. Tel: 814-824-2467; Michelle Garvey, Asst.

Oil City Extension. (Clarion State University of PA), St. Stephen Parish, 210 Reed St., Oil City, 16301. Tel: 814-677-3020.
Penn State University, The Behrend College, Station Rd., 16563-0901. Tel: 814-898-6245. 1113 Brewster St., 16503-1522. Tel: 814-455-9985. Rev. Michael P. Allison, Chap. Tel: 814-825-4850.
Punxsutawney Extension. (Indiana University of PA), S.S. Cosmos & Damian Parish, 616 W. Mahoning St., Punxsutawney, 15767. Tel: 814-938-6540.
Sharon Extension. (Penn State University), St. Joseph Parish, 74 Case Ave., Sharon, 16146. Tel: 412-981-3232.
Thiel College. Joanne Schell.
Titusville Extension. (University of Pittsburgh), St. Titus Parish, 513 W. Main St., Titusville, 16354. Tel: 814-827-4636.

[Q] MISCELLANEOUS

ERIE. *Alliance for International Monasticism (AIM)*, 345 E. 9th St., 16503. Tel: 814-453-4724.
E-mail: aimusa1@juno.com
Web site: www.csbsju.edu/osb/intl/aimusa.html
AIM is an organization founded to assist Benedictine and Cistercian monasteries in the Third World. Sr. Mary Lou Kownacki, O.S.B., Exec. Dir.
St. Thomas More Society, 429 E. Grandview Blvd., 16514. Judge Ernest Desantis, Pres.

FRENCHVILLE. *Anawim Community of Frenchville*, P.O. Box 129, 16836.

ST. MARYS. *Opportunity for Parochial Education Network (OPEN)*, 575 Charles St., 15857. Tel: 814-834-6181. Richard J. Reuscher, Trustee.

RELIGIOUS INSTITUTES OF MEN REPRESENTED IN THE DIOCESE

For further details refer to the corresponding bracketed number in the Religious Institutes of Men or Women section.

[0200]—*Benedictine Monks.* (St. Vincent's Archabbey).—O.S.B.
[1330]—*Congregation of the Mission.*—C.M.
[0480]—*Conventual Franciscans.* (Anthony of Padua Prov.).—O.F.M.Conv.
[0520]—*Franciscan Friars.*—O.F.M.
[0690]—*Jesuit Fathers and Brothers.*—S.J.
[0610]—*Priests of the Congregation of Holy Cross.*—C.S.C.
[1070]—*Redemptorist Fathers.* (Baltimore Prov.).—C.SS.R.
[1200]—*Society of Divine Savior.*—S.D.S.
[0560]—*Third Order Regular of Saint Francis.* (Most Sacred Heart Prov.).—T.O.R.

RELIGIOUS INSTITUTES OF WOMEN REPRESENTED IN THE DIOCESE

[0230]—*Benedictine Sisters of Elk Co.*—O.S.B.
[0160]—*Benedictine Sisters of Erie.*—O.S.B.
[]—*Congregation of Divine Providence.* (Pittsburgh).—C.D.P.
[]—*Congregation of the Divine Providence.*—C.D.P.
[]—*Congregation of the Divine Spirit.*—C.D.S.
[0420]—*Discalced Carmelite Nuns.*—O.C.D.
[1170]—*Felician Sisters.*—C.S.S.F.
[1840]—*Gray Nuns of the Sacred Heart.*—G.N.S.H.
[2720]—*Mission Helpers of the Sacred Heart.*—M.H.S.H.
[2820]—*Missionary Sisters of Our Lady of Africa.*—M.S.O.L.A.
[3070]—*North American Union of Sisters of Our Lady of Charity.*—N.A.U.-O.L.C.
[1690]—*School Sisters of the Third Order of St. Francis.*—O.S.F.
[0507]—*Sisters of Charity of Seton Hill, Greenburg, PA.*—S.C.
[2570]—*Sisters of Mercy.*—R.S.M.
[1620]—*Sisters of St. Francis of Millvale, PA.*—O.S.F.
[3830]—*Sisters of St. Joseph.*—S.S.J.
[1970]—*Sisters of the Holy Family of Nazareth.*—C.S.F.N.

DIOCESAN CEMETERIES

ERIE. *Queen of Peace.*
Trinity, Calvary & Gate of Heaven.

NECROLOGY

† Toven, Ronald D., (Retired). —Died Oct. 8, 1997.

Diocese of Evansville

(Dioecesis Evansvicensis)

Most Reverend

GERALD ANDREW GETTELFINGER

Bishop of Evansville; born October 20, 1935; ordained May 7, 1961; appointed Fourth Bishop of Evansville March 11, 1989; ordained and installed April 11, 1989. *Res., 3980 Woodcastle, Evansville, IN, 47711. Mailing Address: Catholic Center, 4200 N. Kentucky Ave., P.O. Box 4169, Evansville, IN, 47724-0169.*

Catholic Center: 4200 N. Kentucky Ave., P.O. Box 4169, Evansville, IN, 47724-0169. Tel.: 812-424-5536; Fax: 812-421-1334.

Web site address: www.evansville-diocese.org

E-mail address: dioevv@aol.com

ESTABLISHED NOVEMBER 11, 1944.

Square Miles 5,010.

Comprises twelve Counties in the Southwestern part of Indiana: Daviess, Dubois, Gibson, Greene, Knox, Martin, Pike, Posey, Spencer (except township of Harrison), Sullivan, Vanderburgh, Warrick.

The Diocese of Evansville was established by decree of Pope Pius XII, November 11, 1944, and the See was fixed at Evansville.

For legal titles of parishes and diocesan institutions, consult the Chancery.

STATISTICAL OVERVIEW

Personnel	
Bishop	1
Priests: Diocesan Active in Diocese	69
Priests: Active Outside Diocese	4
Priests: Retired, Sick or Absent	31
Number of Diocesan Priests	104
Religious Priests in Diocese	10
Permanent Deacons in Diocese	22
Total Brothers	2
Total Sisters	321
Parishes	
Parishes	70
With Resident Pastor:	
Resident Diocesan Priests	57
Resident Religious Priests	3
Without Resident Pastor:	
Administered by Priests	6
Administered by Permanent Deacons	1
Administered by Women Religious	3
Pastoral Centers	6
Closed Parishes	3
Professional Ministry Personnel:	
Sisters	25
Lay Ministers	40
Welfare	
Catholic Hospitals	2
Total Assisted	320,428
Health Care Centers	1
Total Assisted	60
Homes for the Aged	3
Total Assisted	249
Day Care and Extended Day Care Centers	1
Total Assisted	432
Special Centers for Social Services	15
Total Assisted	24,000
Educational	
Diocesan Students in Other Seminaries	11
Total Seminarians	11
High Schools, Diocesan and Parish	4
Total Students	1,702
High Schools, Private	1
Total Students	133
Elementary Schools, Diocesan and Parish	24
Total Students	5,947
Non-residential Schools for the Disabled	1
Total Students	22
Catechesis/Religious Education:	
High School Students	2,017
Elementary Students	7,881
Total Students Under Catholic Instruction	17,713
Teachers in the Diocese:	
Priests	2
Brothers	2
Sisters	24
Lay Teachers	410
Vital Statistics	
Receptions into the Church:	
Infant Baptism Totals	1,524
Adult Baptism Totals	147
Received into Full Communion	173
First Communions	1,523
Confirmations	1,506
Marriages:	
Catholic	343
Interfaith	252
Total Marriages	595
Deaths	907
Total Catholic Population	88,903
Total Population	475,953

Former Bishops—Most Rev. HENRY JOSEPH GRIMMELSMAN, D.D., appt. Nov. 11, 1944; cons. Dec. 21, 1944; retired and named Titular Bishop of Tabla Oct. 20, 1965; died June 26, 1972.—Most Rev. PAUL F. LEIBOLD, D.D., appt. Titular Bishop of Trebenna and Auxiliary of Cincinnati April 10, 1958; cons. June 17, 1958; appt. to Evansville April 6, 1966; translated to Archbishop of Cincinnati July 23, 1969; died June 1, 1972.—Most Rev. FRANCIS R. SHEA, appt. Dec. 10, 1969; retired; died Aug. 18, 1994.

Catholic Center—4200 N. Kentucky Ave., P.O. Box 4169, Evansville, 47724-0169. Tel: 812-424-5536; Fax: 812-421-1334. Office Hours: Mon.-Fri. 8-5.

Vicar General—Rev. Msgr. KENNETH R. KNAPP, A.C.S.W., M.S.

Chancellor—JUDITH A. NEFF.

Executive Director of Diocesan Services—KENNETH W. KRASAVAGE.

Secretary to the Bishop—DEANNA RUSTON.

Treasurer—ROBERT J. COX.

Associate Treasurer—SCOTT BRITT.

Senior Consultant to the Treasurer—Rev. Msgr. OMER MEYER.

Assistant Treasurer—RITA REXING.

Diocesan Tribunal—P.O. Box 4169, Evansville, 47724-0169.

Director of Operations—Rev. JAMES R. ENDRESS.

Judicial Vicar—Rev. Msgr. CHARLES J. KOCH, S.T.L., J.C.L.

Adjutant Judicial Vicar—Rev. J. KENNETH WALKER, B.A., M.Div., M.C.L., J.C.L.

Promoter Justitiae—Rev. Msgr. CHARLES SCHOETTELKOTTE, M.S., M.S.W.

Defender of the Bond—Rev Msgr. CLINTON F. HIRSCH, J.C.L.; Rev. JAMES ENDRESS, S.T.L., M.S., M.A.

Judges—Revs. RAYMOND L. KUPER; STEPHEN P. LINTZENICH; WILLIAM M. SCHWENK; MARY GEN BLITTSCHAU, M.A., M.C.L., J.C.L.

Advocates—Revs. JOHN H. SCHIPP; MICHAEL MADDEN.

Secretary and Notary—CHARLEEN HEBERT.

Archivist—JUDITH A. NEFF.

Diocesan Consultors—Rev. Msgr. KENNETH R. KNAPP; Rev. Msgr. CHARLES KOCH; Revs. DAVID NUNNING; JOSEPH ZILIAK; JAMES ENDRESS; DAVID FLECK; FRANCIS SCHROERING.

Diocesan Council of Priests—Rev. Msgr. KENNETH R. KNAPP; Rev. Msgr. CHARLES J. KOCH; Revs. DAVID H. NUNNING; JOSEPH ZILIAK; GREGORY CHAMBERLIN, O.S.B.; DAVID FLECK; JACK DURCHHOLZ; JAMES ENDRESS; STEPHEN P. LINTZENICH; LOWELL WILL; JOHN SCHIPP; BERNARD LUTZ.

Personnel Board—Revs. DONALD ACKERMAN; KENNETH KNAPP; JAMES KORESSEL; HENRY KUYKENDALL; PATRICK FOSTER; JAMES BLESSINGER; TIMOTHY TENBARGE.

Deans—Rev. KENNETH R. KNAPP, Evansville, East; Rev. DAVID NUNNING, Evansville, West; Rev. PATRICK FOSTER, Jasper; Rev. JOSEPH ZILIAK, Newburgh; Rev. FRANCIS SCHROERING, Princeton; Rev. DONALD K. ACKERMAN, Vincennes; Rev. LEO KIESEL, Washington.

Censors Of Books—Rev. Msgr. CHARLES J. KOCH, J.C.L., S.T.L.; Rev. JOSEPH ZILIAK, S.T.L.

Diocesan Offices And Directors

Boy Scouts—JACK THOMPSON, Chap.

Campus Ministry—MICHAEL H. EPPLER, Coord.

Catholic Charities—JAMES F. COLLINS, Exec. Dir., *Court Building, Suite 603, 123 N.W. Fourth St., Evansville, 47708.* Tel: 812-423-5456.

Catholic Diocese of Evansville, Inc.—Most Rev. GERALD A. GETTELFINGER.

Catholic Education Endowment, Inc. (Washington)—ROBERT GRAHAM, JR.

Catholic Education Foundation, Inc. (Evansville)—THOMAS CORCORAN, Pres.

The Catholic Foundation of Southwestern Indiana, Inc.—DONNA LEADER, Exec. Dir., *P.O. Box 4169, Evansville, 47724-0169.*

Holy Family Catholic School Foundation, Inc.—WILFRED WEINZAPFEL, Pres., *950 Church Ave., Jasper, 47546.*

Catholic Education, Office of—PHYLLIS BESHEARS, Dir. Schools; MARIE BRANDLE, Asst. Dir.; ANN WOLBER, Sec.; MARYLOU ULRICH, Coord. Media Svcs.; MARY GARRETT, Media Clerk.

Catholic Communication Office—PAUL LEINGANG, Dir., *P.O. Box 4169, Evansville, 47724-0169.*

Catholic Hospitals, Diocesan Representative for—Rev.

RALPH SCHIPP, *St. Mary's Medical Center, 3700 Washington Ave., Evansville, 47750.* Tel: 812-479-4342.

Catholic Relief Services—JAMES F. COLLINS, *Court Building, Suite 603, 123 N.W. Fourth St., Evansville, 47708.* Tel: 812-423-5456.

Cemeteries—Rev. EUGENE SCHROEDER, Dir., *600 Herndon Dr., Evansville, 47711.* Tel: 812-422-8211.

Christian Educational Foundation of Vincennes, Inc.—Dr. DAVID GRUNDMAN, Pres.

Continuing Education of Clergy—Revs. JAMES SAUER; JAMES KORESSEL, *P.O. Box 4169, Evansville, 47724-0169.*

Cursillos in Christianity—JOANN SCHLACHTER, Lay Dir., *1337 Thompson, Evansville, 47715.* Tel: 812-476-1980.

Deaf Ministry—Rev. HENRY KUYKENDALL, *3635 Pollack, Evansville, 47714.* Tel: 812-476-4646.

Diocesan Finance Council—Ex-Officio: Most Rev. GERALD A. GETTELFINGER; Rev. Msgr. KENNETH R. KNAPP; KEN KRASAVAGE; ROBERT COX; GARY BECKMAN; ALAN HOFFMAN; MARGARET CONWAY; CHRIS MELTON; KEN ELLSPERMANN; STEVE WITTING.

Diocese of Evansville Retirement Trust Agreement and Plan for Priests—Office of the Vicar General, 4200 N. Kentucky Ave., P.O. Box 4169, Evansville, 47724-0169. Tel: 812-424-5536.

Ecumenism—4200 N. Kentucky Ave., P.O. Box 4169, Evansville, 47724-0169. Tel: 812-424-5536.

Evangelization, Office of—4200 N. Kentucky Ave., P.O. Box 4169, Evansville, 47724-0169. Tel: 812-424-5536.

Girl Scouts—JACK THOMPSON, Chap.

Spanish Speaking Apostolate—Rev. EUGENE HEERDINK.

Propagation of the Faith and Holy Childhood Association—Rev. Msgr. CLARENCE A. SCHLACHTER, Dir., *4200 N. Kentucky Ave., P.O. Box 4169, Evansville, 47724-0169.* Tel: 812-424-5536.

Justice and Peace—(Please refer to Catholic Charities for further information).

Legion of Mary—Vacant.

Message, The—Catholic Press of Evansville; Publisher, Most Rev. GERALD A. GETTELFINGER; PAUL LEINGANG, Editor.

National Shrine of the Immaculate Conception Washington, D.C.—Vacant.

Permanent Diaconate Program—Deacon THOMAS HOLSWORTH, *1066 W. Tenth, Jasper, 47546.*

Adult Formation—Sr. GERALDINE HEDINGER, O.S.B., Dir. DONNA GISH, Asst. Dir.

Rural Life Conference—Rev. JOHN BOEGLIN, Dir., *Holy Family Church, 950 E. Church Ave., Jasper, 47546-3797.*

St. Vincent De Paul Society—Rev. RAYMOND BRENNER, Diocesan Chap.; Deacon CHARLES SEIFERT, Spiritual Dir., Jasper District Council; Rev. DONALD ACKERMAN, Spiritual Dir., Vincennes District Council.

Sarto Retreat House—GEORGE ANNE RYDER, Dir.; CAROLYN SINGER, Sec.

Secretariat for Charismatic Renewal—CAROL VOLLMAN, *771 Tulip Ave., Evansville, 47711.*

Stewardship/Development, Office of—JUSTIN CLEMENTS, Dir., *P.O. Box 4169, Evansville, 47724-0169.* Tel: 812-424-5536.

Vocation Office—Rev. BERNARD ETIENNE, Vocation Dir., *P.O. Box 4169, Evansville, 47724-0169.* Tel: 812-424-5536.

Worship/RCIA—Rev. WILLIAM DEERING, Dir., *4200 N. Kentucky, P.O. Box 4169, Evansville, 47724-0169.* Tel: 812-424-5536.

Youth and Young Adult Ministry—MICHAEL H. EPPLER, Dir., *4200 N. Kentucky, P.O. Box 4169, Evansville, 47724-0169.* Tel: 812-424-5536.

CLERGY, PARISHES, MISSIONS AND PAROCHIAL SCHOOLS

CITY OF EVANSVILLE
(Vanderburgh County)

1—PRO-CATHEDRAL OF THE MOST HOLY TRINITY, Rev. Msgr. Michael O.J. Wolf, Rector.
Res., 305 Court St., 47708-1233. Tel: 812-422-5150.

2—ASSUMPTION CATHEDRAL. Closed. For inquiries for parish records contact Holy Trinity Pro-Cathedral.

3—CHRIST THE KING, Rev. Msgr. Kenneth R. Knapp.
Res., 3109 Bayard Park Dr., 47714-2602. Tel: 812-476-3061; Fax: 812-476-3062.
School—Lay Teachers 22; Students 305.

4—CORPUS CHRISTI, Rev. John Breidenbach; Deacon David A. Franklin.
Res., 5528 Hogue Rd., 47712-3298. Tel: 812-422-2027; Fax: 812-421-8316.
School—Lay Teachers 13; Students 177.

5—GOOD SHEPHERD, Rev. Theodore G. Tempel; Deacons Edward Wilkerson; Cyril Will.
Res., 2301 N. Stockwell, 47715. Tel: 812-477-5405; Fax: 812-476-2907.
School—Lay Teachers 19; Students 318.

6—HOLY REDEEMER, Rev. William Wargel.
Res., 918-A W. Mill Rd., 47710. Tel: 812-424-8344.
School—Lay Teachers 20; Students 264.

7—HOLY ROSARY, Revs. James Sauer; Brian Holtz; Rev. Msgr. Maurilius Bilskie, Pastor Emeritus; Deacons Richard Preske; Robert Thurgood.
Res., 1301 S. Green River Rd., 47715. Tel: 812-477-8923; Fax: 812-471-7226.
School—Lay Teachers 26; Students 418.

8—HOLY SPIRIT, Rev. Michael Madden; Sr. Joan Scheller, O.S.B., Pastoral Assoc.
Res., 1800 S. Lodge Ave., 47714. Tel: 812-477-1738; Fax: 812-477-2085.
School—Lay Teachers 16; Students 200.
Convent—Sisters of St. Benedict 4.

9—NATIVITY, Rev. Henry Kuykendall; Sr. Jane McConnell, O.S.F., Pastoral Assoc.
Res., 3635 Pollack, 47714. Tel: 812-476-7186; Fax: 812-476-7956.
Catholic Ministry of the Deaf Office—Tel: 812-476-4646.

10—RESURRECTION, Rev. Raymond A. Brenner; Deacon Joseph Schapker.
Res., 5301 New Harmony Rd., 47720-1774. Tel: 812-963-3121; Fax: 812-963-1141.
School—Sisters of St. Benedict 1; Lay Teachers 16; Students 321.

11—SACRED HEART, Rev. Eugene Dewig; Rev. Msgr. Omer F. Meyer.
Res., 2701 W. Franklin St., 47712. Tel: 812-425-5505.
School—Westside Catholic Consolidated, (Grades PreK-K).
Lay Teachers 10; Students 143.

12—ST. AGNES, Rev. Raymond L. Kuper; Deacon Richard Grannan.
Res., 1600 Glendale Ave., 47712. Tel: 812-425-9140; Fax: 812-423-4240.
School—Westside Catholic Consolidated, (Grades 1-4).
Lay Teachers 10; Students 120.

13—ST. ANTHONY, Rev. John Davidson; Sr. Joan Miller, O.S.F., Pastoral Assoc. In res., Revs. James Lex; Earl Rohleder.
Res., 704 First Ave., 47710. Tel: 812-423-5209; Fax: 812-424-5498.

14—ST. BENEDICT, Rev. Gregory D. Chamberlin, O.S.B.; Sr. Mary Agnes Semersheim, Pastoral Assoc.
Parish Center—1328 Lincoln Ave., 47714-1598. Tel: 812-425-3369; Fax: 812-425-3378.
Res., 1312 Lincoln Ave., 47714.
School—530 S. Harlan Ave., 47714-1598. Tel: 812-425-4596.
Lay Teachers 23; Students 295.

15—ST. BONIFACE, Rev. William M. Schwenk. In res., Rev. Robert Wannemuehler.
Res., 418 N. Wabash Ave., 47712. Tel: 812-425-8375.
School—Westside Catholic Consolidated, (Grades 5-8). Serves St Agnes, St. Boniface and Sacred Heart Parishes. 2031 W. Michigan St., 47712.
Lay Teachers 11; Students 131.

16—ST. JOHN, Rev. Kenneth Herr; Sr. Jane Nesmith, S.B.S., Pastoral Life Coord.
Church—617 Bellemeade Ave., 47713-1707. Tel: 812-424-9261; Fax: 812-424-5933.

17—ST. JOHN THE EVANGELIST, Rev. Robert A. Deig; Robert Vollmer, Pastoral Assoc.
Church—5301 Daylight Dr., 47711. Tel: 812-867-3718.
Res., 4020 E. Boonville-New Harmony Rd., 47711. Tel: 812-867-3987.

18—ST. JOSEPH, Rev. Wilfred Englert. Pastoral Staff: Jeffrey T. Ward; Sr. Agnes Marie Dauby, O.S.B.
Res., 600 E. Virginia St., 47711. Tel: 812-422-5668; Fax: 812-425-2730.

19—ST. MARY, Rev. Stephen P. Lintzenich. Pastoral Assocs.: Sr. Darlene Boyd, S.F.C.C.; Sr. Mary Mundy, S.P.; Deacon James Cavera.
Res., 609 Cherry St., 47713. Tel: 812-425-1577; Fax: 812-426-1416.

20—ST. THERESA, Rev. Eugene Schroeder; Sr. Annette Langenderfer, O.S.F., Pastoral Assoc.
Mailing Address: 600 Herndon Dr., 47711-3897.
Res., Tel: 812-422-8211; Fax: 812-422-5345.
School—Lay Teachers 16; Students 263.
Convent—Sisters of St. Benedict 4.

OUTSIDE CITY OF EVANSVILLE

Bicknell, Knox Co., St. Philip Neri, Rev. Frank G. Renner.
Res., 605 W. Fourth St., 47512. Tel: 812-735-4069.

Bloomfield, Greene Co., Holy Name, Sr. Diane Fischer, O.S.B., Pastoral Life Coord.; Rev. Hilary F. Vieck, Pastoral Moderator.
Res., 700 Lincoln Dr., 47424-0124. Tel: 812-384-8415.

Boonville, Warrick Co., St. Clement, Rev. James Koressel; Deacon Tom Lambert; Sr. Rachel Neveu, O.S.B., Pastoral Assoc.
Res., 216 N. Seventh St., 47601. Tel: 812-897-4653; Fax: 812-897-4653.
Religious Education Center—Tel: 812-897-1843.
Convent—Sisters 3.

Cannelburg, Daviess Co., All Saints. Attended by St. Peter, Montgomery. Rev. Lowell Will, Temp. Admin. Tel: 812-486-3149.

Celestine, Dubois Co., St. Celestine, Rev. Robert S. Bultman.
Res., 6864 E. State Rd. 164, P.O. Box 1, 47521-0001. Tel: 812-634-1875; Fax: 812-634-1875. [CEM]

Chrisney, Spencer Co., St. Martin, Rev. Gordon Mann.
Res., P.O. Box 147, 47611-0147. Tel: 812-362-7313. [CEM]

Dale, Spencer Co., St. Joseph, Rev. Eugene Heerdink.
Res., 8 E. Maple St., R.R. 1, Box 308, 47523. Tel: 812-937-2200; Fax: 812-937-4349.

Dubois, Dubois Co., St. Raphael, Rev. Donald E. Spaulding.
Res., 5564 E. St. Raphael St., 47527. Tel: 812-678-2011. [CEM]

Ferdinand, Dubois Co., St. Ferdinand, Revs. Philip J. Kreilein; Jack J. Durchholz; Sr. Ruth Ellen Doane, S.P., Pastoral Assoc.
Res., 840 Maryland, P.O. Box 156, 47532. Tel: 812-367-1212; Fax: 812-367-1066.
Spiritual Life Center—Tel: 812-367-1092.

Fort Branch, Gibson Co., Holy Cross, Rev. Bernard A. Lutz; Rev. Msgr. Charles Kaiser, Pastor Emeritus; Deacon Stephen Hall.
Res., 305 E. Walnut St., 47648. Tel: 812-753-3548. [CEM]
School—Sisters 1; Lay Teachers 11; Students 112.

Haubstadt, Gibson Co., SS. Peter and Paul, Rev. Francis A. Schroering.
Res., 201 Vine St., 47639. Tel: 812-768-6457; Fax: 812-768-6521.
School—(Grades PreK-5).
Lay Teachers 9; Students 175.

Huntingburg, Dubois Co., Visitation of the Blessed Virgin Mary, Rev. Pius Klein, O.S.B.
Res., 313 Washington St., 47542. Tel: 812-683-2372.
Convent—Daughters of Charity 4.

Ireland, Dubois Co., Annunciation of the Blessed Virgin Mary. (St. Mary's). Rev. Kenneth Betz.
Res., P.O. Box 67, 47545. Tel: 812-482-7041. [CEM]

Jasonville, Greene Co., St. Joan of Arc. Attended by St. Mary, Sullivan. Tel: 812-268-4088.

Jasper, Dubois Co., Holy Family, Rev. John Boeglin; Deacon Charles Seifert.
Res., 950 E. Church Ave., 47546-3797. Tel: 812-482-3076; Fax: 812-634-6998.
School—Sisters of St. Benedict 3; Lay Teachers 21; Students 328.
Convent—Sisters of St. Benedict 7.

Precious Blood, Rev. Joseph E. Kane; Sr. Betty Koressel, S.P., Pastoral Assoc.
Res., 1458 Gregory Ln., 47546.
Church—1385 W. Sixth St., 47546. Tel: 812-482-3589; Fax: 812-482-3589.
School—(Grades PreK-5).
Sisters 3; Lay Teachers 10; Students 201.
Convent—Sisters of Providence 5.

St. Joseph, Revs. Patrick Foster; Michael Allen; Kenneth Steckler. Pastoral Staff: Sr. Mary Jane Kiesel, O.S.B.; Sr. Therese Mary Rebstock, S.S.N.D.
Res., 1020 Kundek St., 47546. Tel: 812-482-1805; Fax: 812-482-1814. [CEM]

Linton, Greene Co., St. Peter, Rev. Hilary F. Vieck.
Res., 489 E St. N.E., 47441. Tel: 812-847-7821; Fax: 812-847-8892.

Loogootee, Martin Co., St. John, Rev. Leo C. Kiesel.
Res., 408 Church St., 47553. Tel: 812-295-2225; Fax: 812-295-2031. [CEM]
Chapel—St. Mary, St. Mary.

Mariah Hill, Spencer Co., Mary, Help of Christians, Rev. Paul Roos.
Church—Spaeth Rd., 47556. Tel: 812-937-4326.

Montgomery, Daviess Co., St. Peter, Rev. Lowell C. Will.
Res., P.O. Box 38, 47558. Tel: 812-486-3149. [CEM]
Convent—Sisters of St. Benedict 3.
Chapels—St. Michael, St. Michael's; St. Patrick, St. Patrick's.

Mount Vernon, Posey Co., St. Matthew, Rev. Joseph Swartz.
Res., 421 Mulberry St., 47620. Tel: 812-838-2535. [CEM]
School—Sr. Christine Kempf, O.S.B., Prin. Sisters 1; Lay Teachers 11; Students 112.
Convent—.Sisters 3.

New Boston, Spencer Co., St. John Chrysostom, Rev. Micheas Langston, O.S.B.
Mailing Address: R.R. 1, Box 156, Evanston, 47531. Tel: 812-357-6531.

Newburgh, Warrick Co., St. John the Baptist, Rev. Joseph L. Ziliak. Pastoral Assocs.: Sr. Jeanne Voges, O.S.B.; Lynda Provence. In res., Rev. J. Kenneth Walker; Deacon Joseph Siebert.
Res., 625 Frame Rd., 47630. Tel: 812-853-6181; Fax: 812-853-6182.
School—Lay Teachers 20; Students 333.

New Harmony, Posey Co., Holy Angels, Rev. Earl Rohleder.
Mailing Address: 423 South St., P.O. Box 548, 47631. Tel: 812-682-4224.

Oakland City, Gibson Co., Blessed Sacrament. Attended by St. Bernard, St. Bernard.
Res., Rte. 1, Box 72-A, 47660. Tel: 812-749-4474.

Petersburg, Pike Co., SS. Peter and Paul, Rev. Edward Schneider; Deacon Donald Haag.
Res., 711 Walnut St., 47567. Tel: 812-354-6942.

Poseyville, Posey Co., St. Francis Xavier, Rev. William Dietsch; Sr. Leta Zeller, O.S.B., Pastoral Assoc.
Res., 10 N. St. Francis Ave., 47633. Tel: 812-874-2258. [CEM]

Princeton, Gibson Co., St. Joseph, Rev. Bernard Etienne.
Res., 410 S. Race St., P.O. Box 47, 47670. Tel: 812-385-2617; Fax: 812-385-2603. [CEM]
School—Lay Teachers 9; Students 121.

Red Brush, Warrick Co., St. Rupert, Rev. Sylvester Loehrlein.
Church—1244 Red Brush Rd., Newburgh, 47630. Tel: 812-853-3040.

Rockport, Spencer Co., St. Bernard, Rev. Edward C. Schnur; Charles Marks, Pastoral Assoc.
Res., 547 Elm St., 47635. Tel: 812-649-4811. [CEM]
School—Sisters of St. Benedict 1; Lay Teachers 8; Students 125.

St. Anthony, Dubois Co., St. Anthony, Rev. Timothy Tenbarge.
Res., P.O. Box 98, 4444 S. Ohio St., 47575-0098. Tel: 812-326-2777. [CEM]

St. Bernard, Gibson Co., St. Bernard, Rev. William Deering; Deacon Stephen Hall, Jr.
Res., R.R. 2, Box 115, Fort Branch, 47648. Tel: 812-753-4568. [CEM]

St. Henry, Dubois Co., St. Henry, Rev. Camillus Ellspermann, O.S.B.; Sr. Edith Hohl, O.S.B., Pastoral Assoc.
Res., 1311 W. 1100 S., Ferdinand, 47532-9710. Tel: 812-367-2731. [CEM]

St. James, Gibson Co., St. James, Rev. Joseph F. Erbacher.
Res., R.R. 1, Box 280, Haubstadt, 47639. Tel: 812-867-5175. [CEM]
School—Lay Teachers 11; Students 134.

St. Joseph, Martin Co., St. Joseph's, Rev. Thomas Kessler.
Mailing Address: 408 Church St., Loogootee, 47553. Tel: 812-295-2225.

St. Joseph's, Vanderburgh Co., Rev. Richard J. Wildeman; Deacons Gilbert Fehrenbacher; Francis Hillenbrand.
Res., 6202 W. St Joseph Rd., Evansville, 47720. Tel: 812-963-3273; Fax: 812-963-6254. [CEM]
School—Sisters 2; Lay Teachers 10; Students 160.
Convent— Sisters of St. Benedict
Sisters 3.

St. Martin, Martin Co., St. Martin's, Rev. Thomas Kessler.
Mailing Address: 408 Church St., Loogootee, 47553. Tel: 812-295-2225. [CEM]

St. Philip, Posey Co., St. Philip's, Rev. David Fleck; Gary O'Neill, Pastoral Assoc.
Res., 3500 S. St. Philip Rd., Mt. Vernon, 47620. Tel: 812-985-2275; Fax: 812-985-2590. [CEM]
School—Lay Teachers 18; Students 292.

St. Wendel, Posey Co., St. Wendel, Rev. David H. Nunning; Deacon Joseph Blankenberger.
Res., 10542 W. Boonville-New Harmony Rd., Evansville, 47720-7901. Tel: 812-963-3733; Fax: 812-963-3835. [CEM]
School—Sisters of the Third Order of St. Francis 1; Lay Teachers 12; Students 163.
Convent—Sisters of St. Francis 2.

Santa Claus, Spencer Co., St. Nicholas, Rev. Gordon Mann, Pastoral Moderator; Sr. Mary Terence Knapp, Pastoral Life Coord.
Res., P.O. Box 351, 181 Balthazar, 47579. Tel: 812-937-2380; Fax: 812-937-2385.

Schnellville, Dubois Co., Sacred Heart, Rev. Firmus Dick.
Res., 2504 Walnut St., 47580. Tel: 812-389-2535. [CEM]

Shoals, Martin Co., St. Mary's. Attended by St. John, Loogootee, Tel: 812-295-2225.

Sullivan, Sullivan Co., St. Mary, Rev. Kenneth Graehler.
Res., 105 E. Jackson St., P.O. Box 506, 47882. Tel: 812-268-4088.

Vincennes, Knox Co.,

1—Sacred Heart, Rev. James C. Blessinger. In res., Rev. Robert Nemergut.
Res., 2004 N. Second St., 47591. Tel: 812-882-8382; Fax: 812-886-4676.
School—Vincennes Schools Consolidated. See St. John the Baptist for details.

2—Basilica of St. Francis Xavier, Rev. John H. Schipp.
Res., 205 Church St., 47591. Tel: 812-882-5638; Fax: 812-882-4042. [JC]
School—Vincennes Schools Consolidated. See St. John the Baptist for details.

3—St. John the Baptist, Rev. Donald K. Ackerman.
Res., 803 Main St., 47591. Tel: 812-882-1762; Fax: 812-886-9151. [JC]
Parish Center—828 Vigo St., 47591.
School—Vincennes Schools Consolidated.
Lay Teachers 15; Students 286.

4—St. Thomas, Revs. Donald K. Ackerman, Pastoral Moderator; Mark A. Kurzendoerfer, Sacramental Min.; Deacon Joseph Sturgis, Pastoral Life Coord.
Res., R.R. 5, Box 102, 47591. Tel: 812-882-2478. [CEM]

5—St. Vincent de Paul, Rev. Albert J. Scheller.
Res., R.R. 3, Box 267, 47591. Tel: 812-882-8968. [CEM]

Washington, Daviess Co., Immaculate Conception, Rev. Ronald S. Zgunda; Yvonne Evans, Pastoral Assoc.
Res., 114 W. Van Trees St., 47501. Tel: 812-254-3187; Fax: 812-257-1133.
School—Elementary & Middle - Washington Catholic Interparochial Schools. See St. Simon Parish for details.
High School—Washington Catholic Interparochial Schools. See High Schools, Diocesan under Institutions Located in the Diocese for details.

St. Simon, Rev. David A. Martin; Sr. Rose Anne Muller, O.S.U., Pastoral Assoc.; Deacon Michael Morris.
Res., 315 N.E. Third St., 47501. Tel: 812-254-2883; Fax: 812-254-2884.
Schools—Schools Operated jointly by St. Mary & St. Simon Parishes. Washington Catholic Interparochial Schools Elementary. 310 N.E. Second St., 47501.
Lay Teachers 18; Students 274; Washington Catholic Interparochial Schools Middle, (Grades 6-8) 200 W. Main St., 47501.
Sisters 1; Lay Teachers 11; Students 93.
High School—See High Schools, Diocesan under Institutions Located in the Diocese for details.

Special Assignment:
Reverend Monsignors—
Knapp, Kenneth R., Vicar General, 3109 Bayard Pk. Dr., Evansville, IN 47714
Koch, Charles J., Judicial Vicar, P.O. Box 4169, Evansville, IN 47724-0169
Meyer, Omer F., 2701 W. Franklin, Evansville, IN 47712
Schlachter, Clarence A., Dir., Propagation of the Faith & Holy Childhood Association, 1508 Greenfield Rd., Evansville, IN 47715
Reverend Fathers—
Deering, William, R.R. 2, Box 115, Fort Branch, IN 47648
Endress, James R., 600 Cullen Ave., Apt. 510, Evansville, IN 47715
Herr, Kenneth, Faculty Residence, 1500 Lincoln Ave., Evansville, IN 47714
Kurzendoerfer, Mark A., 1500 Lincoln Ave., Evansville, IN 47714
Schipp, Ralph, 856 S. Lombard, Evansville, IN 47714
Walker, J. Kenneth, 625 Frame Rd., Newburgh, IN 47630

On Duty Outside the Diocese:
Reverend Monsignors—
Neufelder, Jerome M., St. Meinrad School of Theology, St. Meinrad, IN 47577
Reverend Fathers—
Kissel, Anthony, Fishermen's Cove, 36112 Angler Ln., Dade City, FL 33525
Kress, Robert, 2845 Hikes Ln., Apt. 102, Louisville, KY 40218
O'Brien, Christopher, 5850 Cameron Run Ter., Apt. 1415, Alexandria, VA 22303

Sabbatical:
Reverend Fathers—
Traylor, William A.

On Leave of Absence:
Reverend Fathers—
Verkamp, Bernard J.
Vogler, Jean

Retired:
Reverend Monsignors—
Bilskie, Maurilius, 1301 S. Green River Rd., Evansville, IN 47715
Clarke, Thomas J., Little Sisters of the Poor, 1236 Lincoln Ave., Evansville, IN 47714
Conti, Leo J., P.O. Box 2485, Evansville, IN 47728
Hirsch, Clinton F., Villa Maria, 1640 Lincoln Ave., Apt. 102, Evansville, IN 47714
Kaiser, Charles, 305 E. Walnut St., Fort Branch, IN 47648
Kilfoil, Patrick, 6161 Sunset Ln., North Crow's Nest, Indianapolis, IN 46208
Lindauer, Clarence, 1236 Lincoln Ave., Evansville, IN 47714
Schoettelkotte, Charles T., Little Sisters of the Poor, 1236 Lincoln Ave., Evansville, IN 47714
Shetler, Carl A., 104 E. 35th St., Jasper, IN 47546
Vollmer, Roman, Regina Continuing Care, 3900 Washington, Evansville, IN 47714
Reverend Fathers—
Bauer, Francis, Regina Continuing Care, 3900 Washington, Evansville, IN 47714
Brune, James, Villa Maria, 1640 Lincoln Ave., Apt. 101, Evansville, IN 47714
Busch, August, 5221 New Harmony Rd., Evansville, IN 47720
Clauss, Joseph, Guadalupe Retreat Center, 39100 Orchard Ave., Cherry Valley, CA 92223
Dilger, Donald, 6621 Smith Diamond Rd., Evansville, IN 47712
Egloff, Adolph, 2017 N. Second St., Vincennes, IN 47591
Emge, John P., Villa Maria, 1640 Lincoln Ave., Apt. 205, Evansville, IN 47714
Finis, John, R.R. 2, Box T 42, Taswell, IN 47175
Hoffman, Richard L., 3943 Aspen Dr., Evansville, IN 47711
Hut, Clemens, 1711 E. Grandview, Mesa, AZ 85203
Lefler, John, 7788 Taylorville Rd., Tennyson, IN 47637
Lex, James, St. Anthony Church, 704 First Ave., Evansville, IN 47710
Reising, Raymond, 901-C Erie Ave., Evansville, IN 47715
Rogers, James, 801 N. Shortridge Rd., Apt. F4, Indianapolis, IN 46219
Schroering, Raymond A., Villa Maria, 1640 Lincoln Ave., Apt. 201, Evansville, IN 47714
Wannemuehler, Robert, 418 N. Wabash, Evansville, IN 47712

Permanent Deacons:
Blankenberger, Joseph V., St. Wendel Parish, Evansville
Cavera, James, St. Mary Parish, Evansville
Dow, Lancaster, Jr., Unassigned
Fehrenbacher, Gilbert, St. Joseph Parish, Vanderburgh County
Franklin, David, Corpus Christi Parish, Evansville
Grannan, Richard, St. Agnes Parish, Evansville
Haag, Donald, SS. Peter & Paul Parish, Petersburg
Hall, Stephen, St. Bernard Parish & Holy Cross, Fort Branch
Hayden, Robert, Unassigned
Hillenbrand, Francis, St. Joseph Parish, Vanderburgh County
Holsworth, Thomas, Permanent Deacon Coord.
Lambert, Thomas, St. Clement, Boonville
McFall, Gerald D., Unassigned
Morris, Michael, St. Simon, Washington
Preske, Richard, Holy Rosary, Evansville
Schapker, Joseph, Resurrection Parish, Evansville

Seibert, Joseph S., St. John, Newburgh
Seifert, Charles, Holy Family Parish, Jasper
Sturgis, Joseph V., St. Thomas Parish, Vincennes
Thurgood, Robert, Holy Rosary Parish, Evansville
Wilkerson, Edward, Good Shepherd, Evansville
Will, Cyril, Good Shepherd, Evansville

INSTITUTIONS LOCATED IN THE DIOCESE

[A] HIGH SCHOOLS, DIOCESAN

EVANSVILLE. *Mater Dei High School*, 1300 Harmony Way, 47712. Tel: 812-426-2258; Fax: 812-421-5717. Web site: www.MaterDei.pvt.K12.IN.W
Mr. Herb Neighbors, M.A., Prin.; Rev. Mark A. Kurzendoerfer, Chap. Priests 1; Sisters 2; Lay Teachers 41; Students 613.

Reitz Memorial High School, 1500 Lincoln Ave., 47714. Tel: 812-476-4973; Fax: 812-474-2942. Mr. Gerry Adams, M.A., Ed.S., Prin.; Del Schiavone, Asst. Prin.; Rev. Kenneth Herr, Chap.; Mrs. Lisa Popham, Admin. Assist. Brothers 2; Lay Teachers 54; Students 850.

VINCENNES. *Jean Francois Rivet High School*. (Vincennes Area), 210 Barnett St., 47591. Tel: 812-882-6215.
Web site: www.cntwk.net/vcs
Richard Kapiszka, Prin. Sisters 1; Lay Teachers 17; Students 222.

WASHINGTON. *Washington Catholic Interparochial Schools*, 201 N.E. Second St., 47501. Tel: 812-254-2050.
Web site: www.dmrtc.net/~wchsb
Lay Teachers 19; Students 123.

[B] HIGH SCHOOLS, PRIVATE

FERDINAND. *Marian Heights Academy*, 812 E. Tenth St., 47532. Tel: 812-367-1431.
Web site: www.thedome.org
High School for Girls. Sisters of St. Benedict. Sr. Jane Ann Breen, Prin. Sisters 7; Lay Teachers 8; Students 133.

[C] SCHOOLS OF SPECIAL EDUCATION

EVANSVILLE. *Marian Day School*, 700 Herndon Dr., 47711. Tel: 812-422-5346. Bev Williamson, Dir. Lay Teachers 2; Students 22.

[D] DAY CARE CENTERS

EVANSVILLE. *St. Vincent Day Care Center*, 611 First Ave., 47710. Tel: 812-424-4780. Sr. Patricia Dunne, D.C., Admin.; Sr. Evelyn Boyd, Supr. Daughters of Charity of St. Vincent de Paul 5; Children 432.

[E] GENERAL HOSPITALS

EVANSVILLE. *St. Mary's Medical Center of Evansville, Inc.*, 3700 Washington Ave., 47750. Tel: 812-485-4000.
For a complete listing, refer to the Hospitals section.

JASPER. *Memorial Hospital and Health Care Center, Little Company of Mary of Indiana, Inc.*, 800 W. Ninth St., 47546. Tel: 812-482-2345.
For a complete listing, refer to the Hospitals section.

Memorial Hospital Foundation, Inc., 47546.
For a complete listing, refer to the Hospitals section.

[F] HOMES FOR AGED

EVANSVILLE. *The Regina Continuing Care Center*, 3900 Washington Ave., 47714. Tel: 812-485-4226.
For a complete listing, refer to the Special Care Facilities section.

St. John's Home for the Aged, 1236 Lincoln Ave., 47714. Tel: 812-464-3607.
For a complete listing, refer to the Special Care Facilities section.

Seton Residence, 9200 New Harmony Rd., 47720-8918. Tel: 812-963-7600.
For a complete listing, refer to the Special Care Facilities section.

JASPER. *Providence Home, Nursing Home for the Needy*, 520 W. Ninth St., 47546. Tel: 812-482-6603.
For a complete listing, refer to the Special Care Facilities section.

[G] RETREAT HOUSES

EVANSVILLE. *Sarto Retreat House*, 4200 N. Kentucky Ave., P.O. Box 4169, 47724-0169. Tel: 812-424-5536. Mrs. George-Anne Ryder, Dir.; Mrs. Carolyn Singer, Sec.

FERDINAND. *Kordes Enrichment Center*, 841 E. 14th St., 47532-9216. Tel: 812-367-2777. Sr. Barbara C. Schmitz, O.S.B., Dir.

[H] CONVENTS AND RESIDENCES FOR SISTERS

EVANSVILLE. *Daughters of Charity of St. Vincent de Paul of Indiana, Inc.*, 9400 New Harmony Rd., 47720. Tel: 812-963-3341. Sr. Catherine Madigan, D.C., Visitatrix; Rev. Patrick Harrity, C.M., Prov. Dir. Legal Title: *Daughters of Charity of St. Vincent de Paul of Indiana, Inc., Mater Dei Provincialate, Inc.*

Monastery of St. Clare, 6825 Nurrenbern Rd., 47712. Tel: 812-425-4396. Franciscan Poor Clare Nuns. Sr. Jeanne Maffet, O.S.C., Supr. Solemnly Professed Cloistered Nuns 17.

FERDINAND. *Sisters of St. Benedict of Ferdinand, IN, Inc., Monastery Immaculate Conception*, 802 E. Tenth St., 47532. Tel: 812-367-1411.
Web site: www.thedome.org
Sisters of St. Benedict. Sr. Kathryn M. Huber, O.S.B., Prioress; Rev. Matthias Neuman, O.S.B., Chap., St. Meinrad Chaplain Team. Professed Sisters in Community 211; Temporary Commitment 10; Novices 3; Postulants 4.

[I] NEWMAN CENTERS & CAMPUS MINISTRY

EVANSVILLE. *Newman Center for the University of Evansville*, 1901 Lincoln Ave., 47714. Tel: 812-477-6446. Joe Cook, Dir.

University of Southern Indiana Newman Center, 8113-A O'Daniel Ln., 47712. Tel: 812-464-1871.

Vincennes University-Newman Center, c/o P.O. Box 4169, 47724-0169. Tel: 812-424-5536.

OAKLAND CITY. *Oakland City College Newman Center*, Blessed Sacrament Church, R.R. 1, Box 72-A, 47660. Tel: 812-749-4474.

[J] MISCELLANEOUS

EVANSVILLE. *Catholic Education Foundation, Inc.*, P.O. Box 4169, 47724-0169. Linda Montejano, Dir.

Daughters of Charity National Health System-East Central, Inc., 9400 New Harmony Rd., 47720. Sr. Catherine Madigan, D.C., Board Chm.

Seton Health Corporation of Southern Indiana, 3700 Washington Ave., 47750. Sr. Veronica Ann Brown, D.C., Chm.

LOOGOOTEE. *American-Innsbruck Alumni Association*, St. John Parish Church, 408 Church St., 47553. Tel: 812-295-2225. Rev. Leo C. Kiesel, Contact Person.

SANTA CLAUS. *The Outpost*, P.O. Box 64, 47579. Tel: 812-937-2723. Michael H. Eppler; John "Jack" Thompson, Camp Dir.

VINCENNES. *Old Cathedral Library & Museum, Inc.*, 205 Church St., 47591. Tel: 812-882-7016.
Web site: http://birch.palni.edu/~oldcath/oldcath.htm
Rev. John H. Schipp, Registered Agent; Steve Cochran, Librarian & Conservator.

RELIGIOUS INSTITUTES OF MEN REPRESENTED IN THE DIOCESE

For further details refer to the corresponding bracketed number in the Religious Institutes of Men or Women section.

[0200]—*Benedictine Monks*.—O.S.B.
[0600]—*Brothers of the Congregation of Holy Cross*. (Midwest Prov.).—C.S.C.
[1330]—*Congregation of the Mission*.—C.M.
[0410]—*Sons of Divine Providence*.—F.D.P.

RELIGIOUS INSTITUTES OF WOMEN REPRESENTED IN THE DIOCESE

[0230]—*Benedictine Sisters of Pontifical Jurisdiction*.—O.S.B.
[1730]—*Congregation of the Third Order of St. Francis*.—O.S.F.
[0760]—*Daughters of Charity of St. Vincent de Paul*.—D.C.
[2340]—*Little Sisters of the Poor*.—L.S.P.
[3760]—*Order of St. Clare*.—O.S.C.
[2970]—*School Sisters of Notre Dame*.—S.S.N.D.
[]—*Sisters for Christian Community*.—S.F.C.C.
[3360]—*Sisters of Providence of Saint Mary-of-the-Woods, Indiana*.—S.P.
[0260]—*Sisters of the Blessed Sacrament*.—S.B.S.
[2270]—*Sisters of the Little Company of Mary*.—L.C.M.
[1760]—*Sisters of the Third Order of St. Francis, of Penance and Charity*.—O.S.F.
[4120]—*Ursuline Nuns of the Congregation of Paris*. (Louisville, KY).—O.S.U.

JOINT CEMETERIES

EVANSVILLE. *St. Joseph*, 2500 Mesker Park Dr., 47712.
JASPER. *Fairview*, 1215 Newton St., 47546.
VINCENNES. *Calvary*, P.O. Box 4, 47591.
WASHINGTON. *St. John*, 101 N. Meridian St., 47501-2931.

NECROLOGY

† Lautner, Rev. Msgr. William A., (Retired). —Died May 15, 1997.

Diocese of Fairbanks

Most Reverend

MICHAEL J. KANIECKI, S.J., D.D.

Bishop of Fairbanks; ordained June 5, 1965; appointed March 8, 1984; consecrated May 1, 1984; installed July 28, 1985. *Office: 1316 Peger Rd., Fairbanks, AK, 99709.* Tel.: 907-474-0753.

Most Reverend

ROBERT LOUIS WHELAN, S.J., D.D.

Retired Bishop of Fairbanks; ordained June 17, 1944; appointed Titular Bishop of Sicilibba and Coadjutor Bishop of Fairbanks, *"cum jure successionis"* December 6, 1967; consecrated February 22, 1968; succeeded to November 30, 1968; retired July 28, 1985. *Mailing Address: Regis Community, 1107 N. Astor, Spokane, WA, 99202.*

Corporate Title: "Catholic Bishop of Northern Alaska."

ESTABLISHED AS THE PREFECTURE APOSTOLIC OF ALASKA, JULY 27, 1894.

ERECTED INTO THE VICARIATE OF ALASKA, DEC. 22, 1916; ELEVATED TO A DIOCESE, AUG. 8, 1962

Square Miles 409,849.

Comprises all of the State of Alaska, north of the old Territorial Third Judicial Division whose boundary extended in a northwesterly direction from the Canadian Border along the crest of the Alaska range to Mount McKinley, thence southwesterly to Cape Newenham and west along the 58 parallel north of the Pribilof Islands.

For legal titles of parishes and diocesan institutions, consult the Chancery Office.

Chancery Office: 1316 Peger Rd., Fairbanks, AK, 99709. Tel.: 907-474-0753; Fax: 907-474-8009.

Web site address: http://www2.polarnet.com/~cbna

E-mail address: chancelr@cbna.org

STATISTICAL OVERVIEW

Personnel	
Bishop	1
Retired Bishops	1
Priests: Diocesan Active in Diocese	4
Priests: Active Outside Diocese	1
Number of Diocesan Priests	5
Religious Priests in Diocese	23
Extern Priests in Diocese	5
Permanent Deacons in Diocese	41
Total Brothers	4
Total Sisters	15
Parishes	
Parishes	48
With Resident Pastor:	
Resident Diocesan Priests	9
Resident Religious Priests	4
Without Resident Pastor:	
Administered by Priests	13
Administered by Permanent Deacons	2
Administered by Professed Men Religious	1
Administered by Women Religious	5
Administered by Lay People	14
Missions	7
Pastoral Centers	1
Professional Ministry Personnel:	
Brothers	2
Sisters	15
Lay Ministers	14
Welfare	
Special Centers for Social Services	1
Total Assisted	5,900
Educational	
Diocesan Students in Other Seminaries	2
Total Seminarians	2
High Schools, Diocesan and Parish	1
Total Students	225
Elementary Schools, Diocesan and Parish	1
Total Students	270
Catechesis/Religious Education:	
High School Students	657
Elementary Students	1,956
Total Students Under Catholic Instruction	3,110
Teachers in the Diocese:	
Sisters	2
Lay Teachers	37
Vital Statistics	
Receptions into the Church:	
Infant Baptism Totals	427
Adult Baptism Totals	31
Received into Full Communion	50
First Communions	343
Confirmations	141
Marriages:	
Catholic	45
Interfaith	25
Total Marriages	70
Deaths	126
Total Catholic Population	17,095
Total Population	141,759

Former Bishops—Most Rev. JOSEPH RAPHAEL CRIMONT, S.J., D.D., Vicar-Apostolic of Alaska; ord. Aug. 26, 1888; appt. Prefect-Apostolic March 28, 1904; appt. Vicar-Apostolic of Alaska Feb. 15, 1917; preconized Titular Bishop of Ammaedera, March 22, 1917; cons. July 25, 1917; died May 20, 1945.—Most Rev. WALTER J. FITZGERALD, S.J., D.D., Vicar-Apostolic of Alaska; ord. May 16, 1918; appt. Coadjutor Vicar-Apostolic of Alaska *cum jure successionis,* Dec. 14, 1938; cons. Titular Bishop of Tymbrias, Feb. 24, 1939; succeeded to as Vicar-Apostolic of Alaska, May 20, 1945; died July 19, 1947.—Most Rev. GEORGE T. BOILEAU, S.J., D.D., appt. Coadjutor Bishop *cum jure successionis,* April 21, 1964; cons. Titular Bishop of Ausuccura, July 31, 1964; died Feb. 25, 1965.—Most Rev. FRANCIS D. GLEESON, S.J., D.D., ord. July 29, 1926; appt. Titular Bishop of Cotenna and Vicar-Apostolic of Alaska Jan. 8, 1948; cons. April 5, 1948; appt. First Bishop of Fairbanks Aug. 8, 1962; retired Nov. 30, 1968; transferred to Titular See of Cuicul in Numidia and Assistant at the Pontifical Throne by Pope Paul VI, Feb. 3, 1969; died April 30, 1983.—Most Rev. ROBERT LOUIS WHELAN, S.J., D.D., retired Bishop of Fairbanks; ord. June 17, 1944; appt. Titular Bishop of Sicilibba and Coadjutor Bishop of Fairbanks, *cum jure successionis* Dec. 6, 1967; cons. Feb. 22, 1968; succeeded to Nov. 30, 1968; retired July 28, 1985.

Vicar General—Vacant, *1316 Peger Rd., Fairbanks, 99709.*

Superior Regular—Rev. THEODORE E. KESTLER, S.J., *Bro. Joe Prince Jesuit Community, St. Mary's Mission Center, St. Marys, 99658.*

Chancery Office—1316 Peger Rd., Fairbanks, 99709. Tel: 907-474-0753; Fax: 907-474-8009.

Chancellor—Sr. MARILYN MARX, S.N.J.M.

Secretary to Bishop—THERESE BURIK.

Treasurer—GEORGE W. BOWDER.

Matrimonial Tribunal—Sr. CAROLYN ROEBER, O.P., Tribunal Dir.

Judicial Vicar—Rev. FRANCIS E. MUELLER, S.J., J.C.D.

Defender of the Bond—Rev. JOSEPH E. LAUDWEIN, S.J.

Promotor of Justice—Rev. RICHARD L. MCCAFFREY, S.J.

Notaries—BARBARA THIEME TOLLIVER; Sr. CAROLYN ROEBER, O.P.; Sr. MARILYN MARX, S.N.J.M.

Bishop's Council; Diocesan Consultors—Bro. KIRBY BOONE, C.F.X.; Revs. PATRICK BERGQUIST; RICHARD D. CASE, S.J.; JAMES M. KOLB, C.S.P.; JACK DE VERTEUIL; Sr. MARILYN MARX, S.N.J.M.; Bro. ROBERT RUZICKA, O.F.M.

Diocesan Archivist—Sr. MARILYN MARX, S.N.J.M.; BECKY MESSINA, Sec.

Diocesan Offices and Directors

Apostleship of Prayer—Rev. J. ALBERT LEVITRE, JR., Dir.

"Alaskan Shepherd" Office—Rev. LOUIS L. RENNER, S.J., Editor, *1312 Peger Rd., Fairbanks, 99709.* Tel: 907-474-9649.

Campaign for Human Development—Sr. MARILYN MARX, S.N.J.M.

Campus Ministry—Rev. GERALD ORNOWSKI, M.I.C., *P.O. Box 750166, Fairbanks, 99775.* Tel: 907-474-6776.

Catholic Community Resources—Vacant, *1316 Peger Rd., Fairbanks, 99709.* Tel: 907-474-0656.

Fairbanks Counseling and Adoption—MARLENE THIBODEAU, Dir., *912 Barnette, P.O. Box 1544, Fairbanks, 99707.* Tel: 907-456-4729.

Beginning Experience—Rev. TIMOTHY SANDER, O.S.B., Dir., *Box 74401, Fairbanks, 99707.* Tel: 907-452-1215.

Ecumenical Commission—Rev. JAMES M. KOLB.

Communications, Radio and TV—THOMAS BUSCH, Dir., KNOM Radio Station, *P.O. Box 988, Nome, 99762.* Tel: 907-443-5221.

Cursillo Movement—PEGGY MANTEI, Lay Dir.; Rev. J. ALBERT LEVITRE, Spiritual Dir.

The Children and Family Life Center—MADELINE NANCE.

Construction Committee—GEORGE W. BOWDER; Deacon PAUL PERREAULT, Chm. GEORGE SUNDBORG, JR.

Engaged Encounter—KELLY HUGHES; CRAIG HUGHES, *Fairbanks*. Tel: 907-479-6402.

Finance Advisory Board—Most Rev. MICHAEL J. KANIECKI, S.J., Chm. DONALD HOOVER; JAMES LYNCH; JOAN OSTERKAMP; Sr. MARILYN MARX, S.N.J.M.; MICHAEL KELLIHER; JOSEPH PASKVAN.

Hispanic Ministry—Rev. NORMAND PEPIN, S.J.

Native Alaskan Ministries Coordinators—Bro. KIRBY BOONE, C.F.X., *St. Aloysius, Tanana, 99777*. Sr. KATHLEEN RADICH, O.S.F., *St. Mary's Conf. Ctr., P.O. Box 172, St. Marys, 99658*.

Marriage Encounter—Vacant.

Ministry of Sick, Aged and Imprisoned—Rev. JOSEPH LAUDWEIN, S.J.; Sr. MARITA SOUCY, C.S.J.

Office of Religious Education—GERALD FINKLER, Dir., *1316 Peger Rd., Fairbanks, 99709*. Tel: 907-474-0753.

Office of Native Permanent Diaconate—Rev. RICHARD D. CASE, S.J., Dir., *Jesuit Community, P.O. Box 173, St. Marys, 99658*. Tel: 907-438-2536.

Office of Urban Permanent Diaconate—Sr. ALITA LISBETH, O.P., Dir., *1316 Peger Rd., Fairbanks, 99709*. Tel: 907-474-0753; Fax: 907-474-8009.

Office of Worship—Sr. ALITA LISBETH, O.P.

Personnel—Sr. MARILYN MARX, S.N.J.M.

Pontifical Association of the Holy Childhood—Chancery Office.

Pontifical Society for Propagation of the Faith—Sr. MARILYN MARX, S.N.J.M., Chancery Office.

Schools—NANCY COOK, Supt., *615 Monroe St., Fairbanks, 99701*. Tel: 907-456-8571.

Vocations—Ordained Ministries Formation Board: Most Rev. MICHAEL J. KANIECKI, S.J.; Rev. AL LEVITRE; Sr. MARILYN MARX, S.N.J.M.

Vocation Director—Rev. JOHN HINSVARK.

CLERGY, PARISHES, MISSIONS AND PAROCHIAL SCHOOLS

CITY OF FAIRBANKS NORTH STAR BOROUGH

1—SACRED HEART CATHEDRAL (1966), Rev. Edward J. Hartmann; Deacon Paul Perreault.
Res., 1316 Peger Rd., 99709. Tel: 907-474-0836; Fax: 907-479-3327.
Church—2501 Airport Way, 99709. Tel: 907-474-9032.
Catechesis/Religious Programs—Tel: 907-474-9033. Gigi Martinez, D.R.E.
Students 224.

2—IMMACULATE CONCEPTION (1904), Rev. Andrew L. Maddock, S.J.; Deacon Robert Mantei.
Res., 115 N. Cushman St., 99701. Tel: 907-452-3533; Fax: 907-456-3336. [JC]
Catechesis/Religious Programs—Kathleen Kohler-Balko, D.R.E.
Students 154.

3—ST. MARK UNIVERSITY PARISH (1977), Rev. Gerald Ornowski, M.I.C.
Res., Box 750166, 99775. Tel: 907-474-6776.
Catechesis/Religious Programs—Dorothy Hebard, D.R.E.
Students 30.

4—ST. RAPHAEL'S (1991), Rev. James M. Kolb; Mrs. Betty Johnson, Admin.
Res., P.O. Box 10508, 99710. Tel: 907-457-6603.
Catechesis/Religious Programs—D.R.E.: Richelle Schruf, (Grades K-6); Mary Schwetz, (Jr. High School); Greg Gibson, (High School).
Students 100.

OUTSIDE CITY OF FAIRBANKS

Alakanuk, St. Ignatius (1954) (Yup'ik), Rev. Thomas G. Provinsal, S.J.; Deacons Joseph Phillip, (Retired); Emmanuel Stanislaus; Denis Sheldon; Charles Clyde Smith.
Res., P.O. Box 53, 99554. Tel: 907-238-3914. [CEM][JC]
Mission—Sheldon Point, St. Peter's, P.O. Box 45, Sheldon Point, 99666. Tel: 907-498-4246.

Aniak, St. Theresa (1935) (Yup'ik), Rev. William E. Cardy, O.F.M.
Res., P.O. Box 308, 99557. Tel: 907-675-4448. [CEM]
Mission—Kalskag, Box 11, Kalskag, 99607. Tel: 907-471-2298. Sr. Anne Hogan, S.S.J., Pastoral Min.

Barrow, North Slope Borough, St. Patrick (1954), Rev. Francis E. Mueller, S.J.
Mailing Address: P.O. Box 389, 99723. Tel: 907-852-3515. [JC]

Bethel, Immaculate Conception (1942), Rev. Richard L. McCaffrey, S.J.; Deacons Bob Aloysius; Peter Aluska.
Res., 790 River St., P.O. Box 428, 99559. Tel: 907-543-2464.
Catechesis/Religious Programs—Susan Murphy, D.R.E.
Students 120.

Chefornak, St. Catherine (Yup'ik), Rev. Mark Hoelsken, S.J.; Agnes Kairaiuak, Admin.; Deacons David Panruk; Cyril Alexie, (Retired); David Erik, (Retired).
Res., P.O. Box 90, 99561. Tel: 907-867-8702. [CEM]
Catechesis/Religious Programs—Students 165.

Chevak, Sacred Heart (1952) (Cup'ik), Rev. Gregg D. Wood, S.J.; Doris A. Atchak, Acting Parish Admin.; Deacons Frank Smart; David Boyscout.
Res., 99563. Tel: 907-858-7826; 858-7265. [CEM]
Catechesis/Religious Programs—Tel: 907-858-7265.
Students 269.

Delta Junction, Our Lady of Sorrows (1959), Rev. Don M. Balquin.
Res., 2565 Deborah St., Box 446, 99737. Tel: 907-895-5232.
Catechesis/Religious Programs—Students 40.
Mission—Tok, Holy Rosary, P.O. Box 369, Tok, 99780. Tel: 907-883-4111. Sr. Linda Hogan, C.S.J., Pastoral Admin.
Stations—Northway, St. Ann.; Eagle, St. Francis Xavier.

Emmonak, Sacred Heart (1953) (Yup'ik), Rev. Thomas G. Provinsal, S.J.; Mr. Patrick C.W. Tam, Dir. Youth Ministry; Deacons Bart Agathluk, Sr.; Raymond Waska.
Res., P.O. Box 190, 99581. Tel: 907-949-1012. [JC]
Catechesis/Religious Programs—D.R.E.: Virginia Kassock; Nora Westlock.
Students 179.

Galena, St. John Berchman (1923) (Athabascan), Rev. Patrick D. Bergquist (BAL); Bro. Robert Ruzicka, O.F.M.
Res., P.O. Box 131, 99741. Tel: 907-656-1240; Fax: 907-656-1240.
Catechesis/Religious Programs—Students 40.
Station—Huslia, St. Francis Regis, Tel: 907-829-2234.

Healy, Holy Mary of Guadalupe (1984), Rev. Jack de Verteuil; Barbara Walters, Pastoral Min.
Mailing Address: P.O. Box 32, 99743.
Church—P.O. Box 32, 99743. Tel: 907-683-2535; 683-1018 (Rectory).
Mission—Cantwell, Denali National Park, General Delivery, 99743. [JC]

Holy Cross, Holy Cross (1888), Rev. William E. Cardy, O.F.M., (Visiting); Sr. Frances McCarron, I.B.V.M., Pastoral Admin.; Sr. Anne Hogan, S.S.J., Pastoral Min.
Res., P.O. Box 101, 99602. Tel: 907-476-7144.
Catechesis/Religious Programs—Students 31.

Hooper Bay, Little Flower of Jesus (1928) (Yup'ik), Rev. Gregg D. Wood, S.J.; Deacon James Gump; Jerry Moses, Parish Admin.
Res., 99604. Tel: 907-758-4620; Fax: 907-758-4620. [JC]
Catechesis/Religious Programs—Students 14.

Kaltag, St. Teresas (Athabaskan), Rev. Joseph Hemmer, O.F.M.
Res., 99748. Tel: 907-534-2218. [JC]
Catechesis/Religious Programs—Students 36.

Kotlik, St. Joseph (1949) (Yup'ik), Rev. Eugene Delmore, S.J.; Deacons Henry Teeluk, (Retired); David Mike; Raymond Teeluk; Aloysius Wasuli; Mary Ann Mike, Acting Parish Admin.
Church—99620. Tel: 907-899-4715.
Catechesis/Religious Programs—Bibiana Prince, D.R.E.
Students 144.

Kotzebue, Northwest Arctic Borough, St. Francis Xavier (1929), Rev. John B. Martinek (CHI).
Res., Box 358, 99752. Tel: 907-442-3239; Fax: 907-442-3239. [CEM][JC]

Koyukuk, St. Patrick (Athabascan), Rev. James E. Falsey.
Res., P.O. Box 10, 99754. Tel: 907-927-2240.

Marshall, Immaculate Heart of Mary (Yup'ik), Rev. Paul Cochran, S.J.; Deacon Alvin Owleyuk; Ms. Clara Shorty, Acting Parish Admin.
Mailing Address:99585. Tel: 907-679-6639.
Mission—Our Lady of Guadalupe Russian Mission.

McGrath, St. Michael (1960), Rev. Thomas Gallagher, S.J.; Sr. Frances McCarron, I.B.V.M., Pastoral Min.
Res., P.O. Box 141, 99627. Tel: 907-524-3928.
Station—Takotna, Tel: 907-298-2328.

Mountain Village, Northwest Arctic Borough, St. Lawrence (1918) (Yup'ik), Rev. Eugene Delmore, S.J.; Deacon Elmer Beans; Susie Luke, Parish Admin.
Res. & Mailing Address—P.O. Box 32205, 99632. Tel: 907-591-2348; 549-3231 (Pilot Station).

Nenana, St. Theresa (1922). Served out of Healy, AK. Sr. Agnes Anne Wilcox, S.M.S.M., Pastoral Admin.; Rev. Jack deVerteuil, Visiting Priest.
P.O. Box 312, 99760. Tel: 907-832-5617. [JC]
Catechesis/Religious Programs—P.O. Box 32, Healy, 99743. Tel: 907-683-2535.
Students 21.

Newtok, Holy Family (1950) (Yup'ik), Rev. Mark Hoelsken, S.J.; Deacons Larry Charles; Mark Tom; Katherine Charles, Admin.
Res., 99559. Tel: 907-237-2427. [CEM]
Catechesis/Religious Programs—Sophie John, D.R.E.
Students 110.

Nightmute, Our Lady of Perpetual Help (1950), Rev. Henry Hargreaves, S.J.; Cecilia Anthony, Acting Parish Admin.; Deacons Thomas Jumbo; Camillus Tulik.
Res., 99690. Tel: 907-647-6428. [CEM]
Catechesis/Religious Programs—Students 56.

Nome, St. Joseph (1901), Revs. John Hinsvark; Andrzej Maslanka; Bro. Philip Drouin, (Retired).
Res., P.O. Box 1010, 99762. Tel: 907-443-5527; Fax: 907-443-5757. [CEM]
Catechesis/Religious Programs—Students 55.
Mission—Diomede, St. Jude, General Delivery, 99762-7999.

North Pole, North Star Borough, St. Nicholas (1975), Rev. J. Albert Levitre, Jr.; Deacon Walt Gelinas.
Res., 707 St. Nicholas Dr., 99705. Tel: 907-488-2595; Fax: 907-488-9625.
Catechesis/Religious Programs—Students 130.
Station—Manley Hot Springs.

Nulato, Our Lady of the Snows (1877) (Athabascan), Rev. James E. Falsey (SAG).
Res., P.O. Box 89, 99765. Tel: 907-898-2242.
Catechesis/Religious Programs—Students 50.

Pilot Station, St. Charles Spinola (1914) (Yup'ik), Rev. Richard D. Case, S.J.
Mailing Address: P.O. Box 5120, 99650. Tel: 907-549-3231; Fax: 907-549-3231. [JC]

Ruby, St. Peter-in-Chains (1912) (Athabascan), Rev. Joseph Hemmer, O.F.M.
Res., P.O. Box 45, 99768. Tel: 907-468-4482; 468-4413. [JC]

St. Marys, Church of the Nativity, Rev. Theodore E. Kestler, S.J.; Deacon Patrick L. Beans, Sr., (Retired).
Res., P.O. Box 105, 99658. Tel: 907-438-2133; Fax: 907-438-2536. [CEM]
Catechesis/Religious Programs—Students 65.

St. Michael, St. Michael (1900) (Yup'ik), Rev. Thomas F. Carlin, S.J.
Res., P.O. Box 29, 99659. Tel: 907-923-3151. [JC]
Catechesis/Religious Programs—Students 46.

Scammon Bay, Blessed Sacrament (1930) (Yup'ik), Sr. Darlene Cholok, Admin.; Rev. Gregg D. Wood, S.J., Itinerant Min.; Deacon Francis Charlie.
Res., P.O. Box 133, 99662. Tel: 907-558-5229. [JC]

Stebbins, St. Bernard (1908) (Yup'ik), Rev. Thomas F. Carlin, S.J.; Margaret Marlin, Acting Admin.
Res., 99671. Tel: 907-934-3151. [JC]
Catechesis/Religious Programs—Students 57.

Tanana, St. Aloysius (1887) (Athabascan), Bro. Kirby Boone, C.F.X., Pastoral Min.; Rev. Joseph Laudwein, S.J.
Res., P.O. Box 6, 99777. Tel: 907-366-7238. [JC]

Teller, St. Ann (1909), Revs. John Hinsvark; Andrzej Maslanka.
Res., P.O. Box 529, 99778.

Toksook Bay, St. Peter the Fisherman (1964) (Central Yup'ik), Deacon James Charlie, Admin.; Rev. Mark Hoelsken, S.J.; Deacons Joseph Asuluk, Sr.; Nick Therchik, Sr.; Gregory Charlie; Maggie John, Acting Parish Admin.
P.O. Box 37046, 99637. Tel: 907-427-7813. [CEM]
Catechesis/Religious Programs—Tel: 907-427-7826; Fax: 907-427-7820. Marie Hopstad, D.R.E.
Students 164.
Station—Umkumute.

Tununak, Northwest Arctic Borough, St. Joseph, Rev. Henry Hargreaves, S.J.; Sophie Oscar, Admin.; Deacons Dick Lincoln; Mike Angaiak, (Retired).
Res., P.O. Box 113, 99681. Tel: 907-652-6214. [CEM]
Catechesis/Religious Programs—Tel: 907-652-6237.
Students 75.

Unalakleet, Northwest, Church of the Holy Angels (1952), Rev. Thomas F. Carlin, S.J.
Res., 99684.

Leave of Absence:
Reverend Fathers—
Wallner, Gerhard

Permanent Deacons:
Agathluk, Bart, Sacred Heart, Emmonak
Alexie, Cyril, St. Catherine's, Chefornak
Aloysius, Bob, Immaculate Conception, Bethel
Altsik, Maxie, Our Lady of Perpetual Help, Nightmute
Aluska, Peter, Sr., Immaculate Conception, Bethel
Angaiak, Michael, St. Joseph Church, Tununak
Asuluk, Joe, St. Peter Fisherman, Toksook Bay
Beans, Elmer, St. Lawrence Church, Mountain Village
Beans, Patrick L., Church of the Nativity, St. Mary
Boyscout, David, Sacred Heart Church, Chevak
Charles, Larry, Holy Family Church, Newtok
Charlie, Francis, Blessed Sacrament, Scammon Bay
Charlie, Gregory, St. Peter the Fisherman, Toksook Bay
Charlie, James, St. Peter the Fisherman, Toksook Bay
Edwards, Patrick, St. Charles Spinola, Pilot Station
Eric, David, St. Catherine's, Chefornak
Gelinas, Walt, St. Nicholas, North Pole
Gump, James, Little Flower Mission, Hooper Bay
Jumbo, Thomas, Our Lady of Perpetual Help, Nightmute
Kelly, Norman, St. Charles Spinola Church, Pilot Station
Lincoln, Dick, St. Joseph's, Tununak
Mantei, Robert, Immaculate Conception, Fairbanks
Mike, David, St. Joseph, Kotlik
Owletuk, Alvin, Immaculate Heart of Mary Church, Marshall
Panruk, David, St. Catherine, Chefornak
Perreault, Paul, Sacred Heart Cathedral, Fairbanks
Phillip, Joseph, St. Ignatius, Alakanuk
Sheldon, Denis, St. Ignatius, Alakanuk
Smart, Frank, Sacred Heart Church, Chevak
Smith, Clyde, St. Ignatius, Alakanuk
Stanislaus, Emmanuel, Alakanuk
Steve, Charlie, St. Bernard Church, Stebbins
Teeluk, Henry, St. Joseph Church, Kotlik
Teeluk, Raymond, St. Joseph, Kotlik
Therchik, Nick, St. Peter the Fisherman, Toksook Bay
Tom, Mark, Holy Family, Newtok
Tommy, Nicholas, Holy Family, Newtok
Tulik, Camillus, Our Lady of Perpetual Help, Nightmute
Waska, Ray, Sacred Heart, Emmonak
Wasuli, Aloysius, St. Joseph, Kotlik

INSTITUTIONS LOCATED IN THE DIOCESE

[A] HIGH SCHOOLS, DIOCESAN

FAIRBANKS. *Monroe Catholic Junior-Senior High School*, 615 Monroe St., 99701. Tel: 907-452-2044.
E-mail: monroehs@polarnet.com
Mr. John Hoffman, Prin.; Rev. Normand A. Pepin, S.J. Priests 1; Lay Teachers 21; Religious 1; Students 225.

[B] GRADE SCHOOLS, DIOCESAN

FAIRBANKS. *Immaculate Conception Grade School*, 715 Monroe St., 99701. Tel: 907-456-4574; Fax: 907-456-7481.
E-mail: monroehs@polarnet.com
Ms. Nancy Cook, Prin. Sisters 1; Lay Teachers 16; Students 270.

[C] RESIDENCES FOR PRIESTS AND BROTHERS

FAIRBANKS. *Jesuit Residence*, 2890 N. Kobuk Ave., 99709. Tel: 907-474-9320; 438-2146; Fax: 907-479-6848. Very Rev. Theodore E. Kestler, S.J., Alaska Jesuit Supr.; Revs. William C. Dibb, S.J., Local Supr.; Francis E. Mueller, S.J.; Joseph Laudwein, S.J.; Normand A. Pepin, S.J.; Louis L. Renner, S.J.; Andrew L. Maddock, S.J.; Francis W. McGuigan, S.J.; Bro. Ignatius Jakes, S.J. Regional Offices of the Society of Jesus, Alaska.

[D] CONVENTS AND RESIDENCES OF SISTERS

FAIRBANKS. *Diocesan Convent*, 1316 Peger Rd., 99709. Tel: 907-474-9538. Sr. Alita Lisbeth, O.P.; Sr. Marilyn Marx, S.N.J.M.; Sr. Carolyn Roeber, O.P. Sisters 3.
Immaculate Conception Convent, 615 Betty St., 99701. Tel: 907-452-2750. Sisters 4.
Xavier Hall, 417 Monroe St., 99701. Tel: 907-452-1322.

NOME. *Little Sisters of Jesus*, Box 845, 99762. Sr. Odette, L.S.J.; Sr. Damiene, L.S.J.; Sr. Yoshie, L.S.J. Sisters 3.

[E] MISCELLANEOUS LISTINGS

FAIRBANKS. *Bishop's Attic, III*, 4523 Old Airport Way, 99709. Tel: 907-474-0209.
E-mail: treasure@cbna.org
Web site: www2.polarnet.com/~cbna/
Doris Lundin, Dir. Oper.
House of Prayer, 1316 Peger Rd., 99709. Tel: 907-474-9379. Rev. Normand A. Pepin, S.J., Dir.; Sr. Marie Teresa Boulet, O.P.
**Monroe Foundation, Inc.*, P.O. Box 71620, 99707. Tel: 907-456-7970; Fax: 907-456-7481. Rev. Francis W. McGuigan, S.J., Exec. Dir., 718 Betty St., 99701.
Voice in the Wilderness Prayer Community, 2501 Airport Rd., 99709.

NOME. *Alaska Radio Mission, Station KNOM*, Box 988, 99762. Tel: 907-443-5221.
E-mail: busch@knom.org
Web site: www.knom.org
Thomas Busch, Gen. Mgr. Total Staff 8; Total in Residence 2.

ST. MARYS. *Brother Joe Prince Jesuit Community*, P.O. Box 173, 99658. Tel: 907-438-2536.
E-mail: kestlersj@aol.com
Very Rev. Theodore E. Kestler, S.J., Alaska Jesuit Supr., Asst. in Native Ministry Training Prog., Pastoral Ministry, St. Mary's, AK; Revs. Rene Astruc, S.J., Pastoral Ministry, Mountain Village & Kotlik, AK; Thomas F. Carlin, S.J., Pastoral Ministry, St. Michael's, Stebbins, & Unalakleet, AK; Richard D. Case, S.J., Dir. of Native Deacon Prog. & Pastoral Ministry, Pilot Station, AK; Paul M. Cochran, S.J., Asst. in Native Ministry Training Prog., Pastoral Ministry, Marshall & Russian Mission, AK; Eugene P. Delmore, S.J., Pastor, Immaculate Conception, Bethel, AK; Thomas N. Gallagher, S.J., Pastoral Ministry, McGrath, AK & Outreach to Urban Native, Anchorage, AK; Henry G. Hargreaves, S.J., Pastoral Ministry, Tununak & Nightmute, AK; Mark A. Hoelsken, S.J., Pastoral Ministry, Chefornak, Newtok, & Toksook Bay, AK; Richard L. McCaffrey, S.J., Sabbatical; Thomas G. Provinsal, S.J., Pastoral Ministry, Alakunuk, Emmonak, & Sheldon Point, AK; Gregg D. Wood, S.J., Pastoral Ministry, Hooper Bay, Scammon Bay, & Chevak, AK.
Native Ministry Training Program, P.O. Box 172, 99658. Tel: 907-438-2832; Fax: 907-438-2536.
E-mail: nmtp@juno.com
Very Rev. Theodore E. Kestler, S.J.; Rev. Paul Cochran, S.J.; Mrs. Lilly Afcan. Total Staff 5; Total in Residence 4.
St. Marys Conference Center, P.O. Box 172, 99658. Tel: 907-438-2712. Erik Weingarth, Admin. Total in Residence 8; Total Staff 15.

RELIGIOUS INSTITUTES OF MEN REPRESENTED IN THE DIOCESE

For further details refer to the corresponding bracketed number in the Religious Institutes of Men or Women section.

[0200]—*Benedictine Monks.*—O.S.B.
[0320]—*Brothers of Christian Instruction.*—F.I.C.
[0520]—*Franciscan Friars.*—O.F.M.
[0690]—*Jesuit Fathers and Brothers.*—S.J.
[0740]—*Marian Fathers.*—M.I.C.
[1350]—*Xaverian Brothers.*—C.F.X.

RELIGIOUS INSTITUTES OF WOMEN REPRESENTED IN THE DIOCESE

[1070-03]—*Dominican Sisters.*—O.P.
[1070-21]—Dominican Sisters.—O.P.
[2370]—*Institute of the Blessed Virgin Mary.*—I.B.V.M.
[2330]—*Little Sisters of Jesus.*—L.S.J.
[2420]—*Missionary Sisters Society of Mary.*—S.M.S.M.
[0590]—*Sisters of Charity of Saint Elizabeth, Convent Station.* (Northern Prov.).—S.C.
[1650]—*The Sisters of St. Francis of Philadelphia.*—O.S.F.
[3830-12]—*Sisters of St. Joseph.* Ogdensburg.—S.S.J.
[3840, 3850]—*Sisters of St. Joseph of Carondelet.*—C.S.J.
[1990]—*Sisters of the Holy Names of Jesus and Mary.*—S.N.J.M.

NECROLOGY

(No Deaths)

Diocese of Fall River

(Dioecesis Riverormensis)

Most Reverend

SEAN O'MALLEY, O.F.M.CAP., PH.D.

Bishop of Fall River; ordained August 29, 1970; named Coadjutor May 30, 1984; appointed Bishop of St. Thomas, Virgin Islands; ordained August 2, 1984; installed October 16, 1985; appointed Bishop of Fall River June 16, 1992; installed August 11, 1992.

ESTABLISHED MARCH 12, 1904.

Square Miles 1,194.

Comprises Bristol, Barnstable, Dukes and Nantucket Counties, and the Towns of Marion, Mattapoisett and Wareham in Plymouth County, Massachusetts.

For legal titles of parishes and diocesan institutions, consult the Chancery Office.

Chancery Office: Box 2577, Fall River, MA, 02722. Tel.: 508-675-1311; Fax: 508-679-9220.

E-mail address: Chancery@dioc-fr.org

STATISTICAL OVERVIEW

Personnel	
Bishop	1
Priests: Diocesan Active in Diocese	134
Priests: Active Outside Diocese	3
Priests: Diocesan in Foreign Missions	1
Priests: Retired, Sick or Absent	43
Number of Diocesan Priests	181
Religious Priests in Diocese	103
Ordinations:	
Diocesan Priests	5
Transitional Deacons	3
Permanent Deacons	21
Permanent Deacons in Diocese	56
Total Brothers	31
Total Sisters	385
Parishes	
Parishes	111
With Resident Pastor:	
Resident Diocesan Priests	98
Resident Religious Priests	10
Without Resident Pastor:	
Administered by Priests	3
Missions	13
Closed Parishes	1
Professional Ministry Personnel:	
Sisters	14
Lay Ministers	52
Welfare	
Catholic Hospitals	1
Total Assisted	169,825
Health Care Centers	1
Total Assisted	120
Homes for the Aged	5
Total Assisted	988
Residential Care of Children	1
Total Assisted	150
Day Care and Extended Day Care Centers	2
Total Assisted	60
Special Centers for Social Services	4
Total Assisted	2,400
Educational	
Diocesan Students in Other Seminaries	20
Total Seminarians	20
Colleges and Universities	1
Total Students	2,715
High Schools, Diocesan and Parish	4
Total Students	2,550
Elementary Schools, Diocesan and Parish	24
Total Students	5,791
Elementary Schools, Private	1
Total Students	158
Catechesis/Religious Education:	
High School Students	5,642
Elementary Students	33,809
Total Students Under Catholic Instruction	50,685
Teachers in the Diocese:	
Priests	11
Brothers	4
Sisters	23
Lay Teachers	566
Vital Statistics	
Receptions into the Church:	
Infant Baptism Totals	5,391
Adult Baptism Totals	114
Received into Full Communion	132
First Communions	5,264
Confirmations	4,300
Marriages:	
Catholic	1,723
Interfaith	356
Total Marriages	2,079
Deaths	3,950
Total Catholic Population	356,972
Total Population	718,000

Former Bishops—Rt. Rev. WILLIAM STANG, D.D., cons. May 1, 1904; died Feb. 2, 1907.—Most Rev. DANIEL F. FEEHAN, D.D., cons. Sept. 19, 1907; died July 19, 1934.—Most Rev. JAMES E. CASSIDY, D.D., appt. Titular Bishop of Ibora and Auxiliary, March 21, 1930; cons. May 27, 1930; succeeded to the See, July 28, 1934; died May 17, 1951.—Most Rev. JAMES L. CONNOLLY, D.D., D.Sc.H., ord. Dec. 21, 1923; appt. Titular Bishop of Mylasa and Coadjutor "cum jure successionis," April 18, 1945; cons. May 24, 1945; succeeded to See, May 17, 1951; retired Oct. 30, 1970; died Sept. 12, 1986.—Most Rev. DANIEL A. CRONIN, D.D., S.T.D., ord. Dec. 20, 1952; appt. Titular Bishop of Egnatia and Auxiliary Bishop of Boston, June 10, 1968; cons. Sept. 12, 1968; transferred Fall River, Oct. 30, 1970; installed Dec. 16, 1970; transferred Hartford, Dec. 9, 1991.

Vicar-General—Rev. Msgr. GEORGE W. COLEMAN, V.G., *P.O. Box 2577, Fall River, 02722.*

Cabinet Secretaries—

Secretary for Community Service—Rev. JOSEPH M. COSTA, *327 Second St., Fall River, 02721.* Tel: 508-673-2833.

Secretary for Health Care—Very Rev. EDMUND J. FITZGERALD, V.F., *368 N. Main St., Fall River, 02720.* Tel: 508-679-8154; Fax: 508-679-1422.

Secretary for Spiritual Development/Apostolates—Rev. Msgr. THOMAS J. HARRINGTON, J.C.L., *121 Mt. Pleasant St., New Bedford.* Tel: 508-992-3184.

Secretary for Youth—Rev. GEORGE E. HARRISON, *984 Taunton Ave., Seekonk, 02771.* Tel: 508-336-9022; Fax: 508-336-9010.

Secretary for Temporalities—Rev. MICHAEL K. MCMANUS, *P.O. Box 2577, Fall River, 02722.* Tel: 508-675-1311; Fax: 508-679-9220.

Secretary for Communications—Rev. JOHN F. MOORE, *P.O. Box 7, Fall River, 02720.* Tel: 508-675-0211; Fax: 508-675-7048.

Secretary for Education/Evangelization—Rev. Msgr. JOHN J. OLIVEIRA, P.A., *106 Illinois St., New Bedford, 02745.* Tel: 508-995-3593; Fax: 508-995-2453.

Secretary for Ministerial Personnel—Rev. JOHN A. PERRY, *P.O. Box 718, E. Freetown, 02717.* Tel: 508-763-2240; Fax: 508-763-3040.

Vicar for Clergy—Very Rev. FRANCIS L. MAHONEY, *709 Hanover St., Fall River, 02720.*

Chancery Office—Mailing Address: P.O. Box 2577, Fall River, 02722-2577. Tel: 508-675-1311; Fax: 508-679-9220.

Chancellor—Rev. MICHAEL K. MCMANUS.

Secretary to the Bishop—Rev. STEPHEN J. AVILA, *394 Highland Ave., Fall River, 02720.*

Diocesan Tribunal—887 Highland Ave., Fall River, 02720. Tel: 508-675-7150; Fax: 508-675-7295.

Judicial Vicar—Rev. JAY T. MADDOCK, J.C.L.

Adjutant Judicial Vicar—Rev. PAUL F. ROBINSON, O.Carm., J.C.D.

Promotor Justitiae—Rev. Msgr. DANIEL F. HOYE, J.C.L.

Judges—Revs. RICHARD W. BEAULIEU; THOMAS L. RITA; GERARD A. HEBERT, J.C.L.; MARK R. HESSION, J.C.L.; THOMAS E. MCGLYNN, J.C.L.; Rev. Msgr. HENRY T. MUNROE, P.A.; Rev. JOSE M. SOUSA, J.C.L.

Defenders of the Bond—Rev. ROLAND BOUSQUET, S.T.L.; Rev. Msgr. THOMAS J. HARRINGTON, J.C.L.; Rev. Msgr. DANIEL F. HOYE, J.C.L.

Advocates—Revs. MARC H. BERGERON; BRUCE M. NEYLON; Rev. Msgr. JOHN J. OLIVEIRA, P.A.; Revs. LUCIO B. PHILLIPINO; HORACE J. TRAVASSOS.

Advocate/Auditor—Rev. DAVID M. ANDRADE.

Auditors—Revs. DANIEL W. LACROIX; JOHN J. PERRY; HENRY J. DAHL; Deacons PAUL FOURNIER; ROBERT LEMAY; ROBERT PELLAND; THOMAS J. SOUZA; THOMAS SURPRENANT.

Notaries—DENISE BERUBE; HELEN BEAUDOIN.

Diocesan Consultors—Rev. Msgr. GEORGE W. COLEMAN, V.G.; Rev. PETER N. GRAZIANO; Rev. Msgr. THOMAS J. HARRINGTON, J.C.L.; Rev. Msgr. DANIEL F. HOYE, J.C.L.; Rev. Msgr. HENRY T. MUNROE, P.A.; Rev. Msgr. JOHN J. OLIVEIRA, P.A.; Rev. Msgr. JOHN J. SMITH.

Presbyteral Council—Revs. JOHN J. STEAKEM, Chm. MARC H. BERGERON, Vice Chm. EDWARD J. HEALEY, Sec., *P.O. Box 2577, Fall River, 02722.* Members: Very Rev. HENRY S. ARRUDA, V.F.; Rev. JOSEPH M. COSTA; Very Rev. EDMUND J. FITZGERALD, V.F.; Very Rev. BENTO R. FRAGA, V.F.; Revs. JON-PAUL GALLANT; MICHAEL K. MCMANUS; BRUCE M. NEYLON; JOHN J. OLIVEIRA, P.A.; Very Rev. ROBERT A. OLIVEIRA, V.F.; Revs. JOHN A. PERRY; CRAIG A. PREGANA;

DAVID REID, SS.CC.; RICHARD M. ROY; STEPHEN B. SALVADOR; Very Rev. GERALD T. SHOVELTON, V.F.; Rev. RONALD A. TOSTI.

Deans—Fall River Deanery: Very Rev. EDMUND J. FITZGERALD, V.F., *945 Main Rd., P.O. Box 3328, Wstport, 02790.* Taunton Deanery: Very Rev. BENTO R. FRAGA, V.F., *261 Tremont St., Taunton, 02780.* Attleboro Deanery: Very Rev. ROBERT A. OLIVEIRA, V.F., *P.O. Box 1027, North Attleboro, 02761.* Cape Cod Deanery: Very Rev. GERALD T. SHOVELTON, V.F., *246 Main St., West Harwich, 02671.* New Bedford Deanery: Very Rev. HENRY S. ARRUDA, V.F., *230 Bonney St., New Bedford, 02744.*

Diocesan Offices and Directors

Apostolate for Persons with Disabilities—Rev. JOSEPH VIVEIROS, Dir., *243 Forest St., Fall River, 02721.* Tel: 508-679-8373; 674-5741, Ext. 2270.

Campus Ministry—Rev. RICHARD W. BEAULIEU, Dir., *529 Eastern Ave., Fall River, 02723.* Tel: 508-679-1991; Fax: 508-676-5276.

Bristol Community College—Sr. ANNETTE BIBEAU, S.S.A., *777 Elsbree St., Fall River, 02720.* Tel: 508-678-2811, Ext. 301.

University of Massachusetts Dartmouth—Rev. MICHAEL CARVILL; Sr. MADELEINE TACY, O.P. Tel: 508-999-8872.

Wheaton College—Rev. THOMAS M. FEELEY, C.S.C.

Massachusetts Maritime Academy—Rev. Msgr. NORMAN J. FERRIS, *300 North Eastern Ave., Fall River, 02723.*

Cape Cod Community College—Vacant.

Catholic Youth Organization—Rev. JAY T. MADDOCK, Dir., *403 Anawan St., Fall River, 02720.*

Catholic Charities Appeal—Rev. Msgr. THOMAS J. HARRINGTON, Dir., Office: *344 Highland Ave., Fall River, 02720.*

Diocesan Apostolate to Hispanics—Rev. PAUL E. CANUEL, Diocesan Dir., *P.O. Box 40605, New Bedford, 02744.* Area Offices, Fall River: Rev. GUSTAVO DOMINGUEZ, I.V.E., Dir., *327 2nd St., Fall River, 02721.* Tel: 508-672-9303. Attleboro: Rev. KEVIN J. HARRINGTON, Dir., *208 S. Main St., Attleboro, 02703.* Tel: 508-266-1115. Taunton: Rev. WILLIAM M. COSTELLO, Dir., *14 St. Mary's Square, Taunton, 02780.* Tel: 508-822-7116. New Bedford: Rev. PAUL E. CANUEL, Dir., *P.O. Box 40605, New Bedford, 02744.* Tel: 508-996-5862; Fax: 508-992-2208. Rev. JOSE IGNACIO DEL VAL, Asst. Dir., *306 Ashley Blvd., New Bedford, 02746.* Cape Cod: Rev. EDWARD HEALEY, Dir., *P.O. Box 1800, Mashpee, 02649.* Tel: 508-477-7710; Fax: 508-477-8158.

Director of Ministry to Sick, Retired, and Senior Priests—Rev. JOHN P. CRONIN, *818 Middle St., Fall River, 02721.*

Director of Portuguese Ministry—Rev. JOHN J. OLIVEIRA, P.A., *344 Country St., New Bedford, 02740.*

Diocesan Archives—Rev. MICHAEL K. MCMANUS, *Chancery, P.O. Box 2577, Fall River, 02722.*

Diocesan Office of Communications—Rev. JOHN F. MOORE, Dir. JOHN E. KEARNS, JR., Asst. to the Dir., *887 Highland Ave., Fall River, 02720.* Tel: 508-675-7151., *Mailing Address: P.O. Box 7, Fall River, 02722.*

Diocesan Director of Cemeteries—Rev. JOHN P. CRONIN, *818 Middle St., Fall River, 02721.* Tel: 508-673-0377.

Diocesan Education Center—Rev. WILLIAM T. GARLAND, O.S.A., Dir., Schools; JAMES A. MCNAMEE, Supt., Schools; Sr. ANNE M. LANDRY, C.N.D., Supt., Elementary Schools; Deacon BRUCE J. BONNEAU, Dir., Religious Education; LISA M. GULINO, Dir., Adult Education, *Office, 423 Highland Ave., Fall River, 02720.* Tel: 508-678-2828; Fax: 508-674-4218.

Diocesan Department of Pastoral Care for the Sick—Rev. GEORGE C. BELLENOIT, Dir.; Sr. SHIRLEY AGNEW, R.S.M., Asst. Dir., Office: *330 Pratt St., Mansfield, 02048.* Tel: 508-339-2981.

Diocesan Department of Catholic Social Services and Special Apostolates—ARLENE A. MCNAMEE, Exec. Dir., Office: *783 Slade St., Box M, S. Station, Fall River, 02724.* Tel: 508-674-4681; Fax: 508-675-2224.

Diocesan Finance Council—Most Rev. SEAN O'MALLEY, O.F.M.Cap., Chm.; Rev. Msgr. HENRY T. MUNROE, P.A.; Rev. Msgr. JOHN J. OLIVEIRA, P.A.; FREDERIC J. TORPHY, ESQ.; LAURENCE T. FLYNN, C.P.A., Consultant, *P.O. Box 2577, Fall River, 02722.* Tel: 508-675-1311.

Diocesan Guild for the Blind—Rev. BRUCE M. NEYLON, *385 Central Ave., Seekonk, 02771.* Tel: 508-399-8440.

Diocesan Health Facilities—Very Rev. EDMUND J. FITZGERALD, V.F., Dir., Office: *368 N. Main St., Fall River, 02720.* Tel: 508-679-8154; Fax: 508-679-1422.

Diocesan Insurance Department—Rev. MICHAEL K. MCMANUS; JOSEPH A. FIGLOCK, *P.O. Box 2577, Fall River, 02722.* Tel: 508-675-3850; Fax: 508-672-3802.

Diocesan Newspaper, "The Anchor"—Rev. JOHN F. MOORE, Editor, Office: *887 Highland Ave., Fall River, 02722.* Tel: 508-675-7151. *Mailing Address: P.O. Box 7, Fall River, 02722.*

Episcopal Representative for Religious—Sr. MARY NOEL BLUTE, R.S.M., *500 Slocum Rd., N. Dartmouth, 02747.* Tel: 508-992-9921.

Family Ministry—Rev. HORACE J. TRAVASSOS, Dir., *Family Life Center, 500 Slocum Rd., N. Dartmouth, 02747.* Tel: 508-999-6420.

Holy Childhood Association, The—Rev. Msgr. JOHN J. OLIVEIRA, P.A., Dir., *106 Illinois St., New Bedford, 02745.* Tel: 508-995-3593.

Missionary Cooperative Plan—Rev. Msgr. JOHN J. OLIVEIRA, P.A., Dir., *106 Illinois St., New Bedford, 02745.* Tel: 508-995-3593.

Office for Divine Worship—Rev. JON-PAUL GALLANT, S.L.L., Dir., *311 Somerset Ave., Taunton, 02780.* Tel: 508-823-2521.

Office of AIDS Ministry, Inc.—243 Forest St., Clemence Hall, Rm. 225, Fall River, 02721.

Office of Pastoral Planning & Urban Ministry—Rev. JOSEPH M. COSTA, *327 Second St., Fall River, 02721.* Tel: 508-673-2833.

Permanent Diaconate Program—Rev. JOHN F. MOORE, Dir.; Rev. CRAIG A. PREGANA, Assoc. Dir.; Deacon LAWRENCE A. ST. ONGE, Asst. Dir., *500 Slocum Rd., N. Dartmouth, 02747.* Tel: 508-993-9935; 993-9938.

Propagation of the Faith—Rev. Msgr. JOHN J. OLIVEIRA, P.A., Dir., Office: *106 Illinois St., New Bedford, 02745.* Tel: 508-995-3593; Fax: 508-995-2453.

St. Vincent De Paul Society—Rev. JOSEPH M. COSTA, *327 Second St., Fall River, 02721.* Tel: 508-673-2833.

Vocations—Rev. CRAIG A. PREGANA, Dir., *160 Seabury St., Fall River, 02720.* Tel: 508-673-0852.

Commissions and Councils

Campaign for Human Development—ARLENE A. MCNAMEE, *P.O. Box M, S. Station, Fall River, 02724.* Tel: 508-674-4681; Fax: 508-675-2224.

Catholic Scouting Program—Rev. STEPHEN B. SALVADOR, Dir., *71 Linden St., Attleboro, 02703.* Tel: 508-222-3266.

Continuing Education of the Clergy—Rev. MARK R. HESSION, Dir., *19 Kilmer Ave., Taunton, 02780.* Tel: 508-824-5435.

Diocesan Council of Catholic Nurses—Rev. MARK R. HESSION, Moderator, *19 Kilmer Ave., Taunton, 02780.* Tel: 508-824-5435.

Diocesan Council of Catholic Women—Rev. BRIAN J. HARRINGTON, Moderator, *494 Slocum Rd., North Dartmouth, 02747.* Tel: 508-993-2351.

Diocesan Ecumenical Commission—Rev. MARC H. BERGERON, Chm., *818 Middle St., Fall River, 02721.* Tel: 508-674-5651.

Diocesan Liaison to the Committee on Evangelization—Rev. Msgr. JOHN J. OLIVEIRA, P.A., *106 Illinois St., New Bedford, 02745.* Tel: 508-995-3593.

Diocesan Liaison with Marriage Encounter—Vacant.

Diocesan Liaison with Charismatic Groups—Rev. ROBERT S. KASZYNSKI, Dir., *36 Rockland St., Fall River, 02724.* Tel: 508-672-0423.

Diocesan Liaison with Cursillo—Very Rev. EDMUND J. FITZGERALD, V.F., *945 Main Rd., P.O. Box 3328, Westport, 02790.* Tel: 508-636-2251.

Diocesan Pastoral Council—Rev. Msgr. GEORGE W. COLEMAN, V.G., *P.O. Box 2577, Fall River, 02722.*

Legion of Mary—Rev. BARRY W. WALL, *22 Barstow St., Mattapoisett, 02739.* Tel: 508-758-3719.

Pastoral Ministry to the Sick—Rev. GEORGE C. BELLENOIT, Dir., *330 Pratt St., Mansfield, 02048.* Sr. SHIRLEY AGNEW, R.S.M., Asst. Dir.; Revs. ROBERT A. ROCHON; JOSEPH MAURITZEN; Sr. CAROLE V. M. MELLO, O.P.; Sr. LORNA RIORDAN, O.P.; Sr. PATRICIA ANNE CONLAN, R.S.M., *St. Anne's Hospital, 795 Middle St., Fall River, 02721.* Revs. STEVEN R. FURTADO; HERBERT T. NICHOLS; Sr. JACQUELINE DUBOIS, S.S.A.; Sr. LUCILLE SOCCIARELLI, R.S.M., *Charlton Memorial Hospital, Fall River.* Rev. JOHN M. SULLIVAN; Sr. ANNETTE LANGLOIS, S.A.S.V., Sturdy Memorial Hospital, Attleboro. Rev. EDWARD J. HEALEY; Sr. DYMPNA SMITH, R.S.M., *Cape Cod Hospital, Hyannis.* Revs. FRANCIS J. MCMANUS, S.J.; JOHN F. DIAS, C.S.C.; Sr. ROBERTA O'CONNELL, F.C.J.; Sr. KATHLEEN SCHMITH, R.S.M.; Sr. M. HOPE HUGHES, R.S.M., *St. Luke's Hospital, New Bedford.* Rev. DAVID J. LANDRY; Bro. RONALD CHRISTENSON, C.S.C., *Morton Hospital, Taunton.* Sr. SHIRLEY AGNEW, R.S.M., *Tobey Hospital, Wareham and Rehabilitation Hospital of Cape & Islands, Sandwich;* Rev. TIMOTHY P. REIS, *Falmouth Hospital, Falmouth.*

Divine Worship Commission—Rev. JON-PAUL GALLANT, S.L.L., Chm., *311 Somerset Ave., Taunton, 02780-4822.* Tel: 508-823-2521.

Pro-Life-Respect Life Program—Rev. STEPHEN A. FERNANDES, Dir., *SS. Peter and Paul, 500 Slocum Rd., N. Dartmouth, 02747.* Tel: 508-997-2290.

Television Apostolate—Rev. STEPHEN J. AVILA, Coord., *394 Highland Ave., Fall River, 02720.*

Diocesan Office of Youth Ministry—LOUIS MILLER, Dir., *P.O. Box 1167, Fall River, 02722.* Tel: 508-678-2828.

CLERGY, PARISHES, MISSIONS AND PAROCHIAL SCHOOLS

CITY OF FALL RIVER
(Bristol County)

1—CATHEDRAL OF ST. MARY OF THE ASSUMPTION (1838), Rev. Joseph M. Costa, Rector. In res., Rev. Jose M. Sousa.
Res., 327 Second St., 02721. Tel: 508-673-2833.
Catechesis/Religious Programs—467 Spring St., 02721. Tel: 508-672-5531.
Students 135.

2—BLESSED SACRAMENT (1902) (French), Rev. Gerald P. Barnwell.
Res., 2492 S. Main St., 02724. Tel: 508-672-5473.
Catechesis/Religious Programs—Students 70.

3—ESPIRITO SANTO (1904) (Portuguese), Rev. James Ferry; Deacon John de Amaral Moniz. In res., Rev. Steven R. Furtado, Chap.
Res., 311 Alden St., 02723. Tel: 508-672-3352.
School—143 Everett St., 02723. Tel: 508-672-3362; Fax: 508-672-7724. Mrs. Patricia Benoit, Prin.
Lay Teachers 17; Students 232.
Catechesis/Religious Programs—Beverly Tavares, D.R.E.
Students 460.

4—HOLY CROSS (1916) (Polish). Merged with SS. Peter & Paul, Fall River.

5—HOLY NAME (1923), Rev. Francis L. Mahoney; Deacon Edward A. Murphy.
Res., 709 Hanover St., 02720. Tel: 508-679-6732; Fax: 508-675-4755.
School—850 Pearce St., 02720. Tel: 508-674-9131; Fax: 508-679-0571.
Religious Sisters of Mercy 1; Lay Teachers 11; Students 221.
Catechesis/Religious Programs—Tel: 508-679-6732.
Students 570.

6—NOTRE DAME DE LOURDES (1874) (French), Rev. Richard W. Beaulieu.
Res., 529 Eastern Ave., 02723. Tel: 508-679-1991; Fax: 508-676-5276.
School—34 St. Joseph St., 02723. Tel: 508-672-5461.
Lay Teachers 12; Students 210.
Catechesis/Religious Programs—Students 237.

7—OUR LADY OF THE ANGELS (1915) (Portuguese), Rev. Evaristo Tavares; Deacon John F. Branco.
Res., 221 Kilburn St., 02724. Tel: 508-676-8883; Fax: 508-677-9078.
Catechesis/Religious Programs—Tel: 508-679-8292. Marion Carrier, D.R.E.
Students 352.

8—OUR LADY OF HEALTH (1924) (Portuguese), Rev. Jose A.F. dos Santos.
Res., 642 Cambridge St., 02721. Tel: 508-672-2793.
Catechesis/Religious Programs—49 Somerset St., 02721. Tel: 508-673-8987.
Students 375.

9—OUR LADY OF THE HOLY ROSARY (1904) (Italian), Rev. Vincent F. Diaferio.
Res., 120 Beattie St., 02723. Tel: 508-672-7232; Fax: 508-672-1506.
Catechesis/Religious Programs—84 Beattie St., 02723. Tel: 508-672-7267. Ernest DiGiammo, D.R.E.
Students 167.

10—OUR LADY OF THE IMMACULATE CONCEPTION (1882), Rev. Kenneth J. Delano.
Res., 15 Thomas St., P.O. Box 4127, 02723. Tel: 508-673-2122; Fax: 508-730-1694.
Catechesis/Religious Programs—Tel: 508-672-3254. Mrs. Colleen Laliberte, D.R.E.
Students 175.

11—SACRED HEART (1872), Rev. David A. Costa; Sr. Eugenia Margaret Ready, S.U.S.C., Pastoral Asst. In res., Rev. Craig A. Pregana.
Res., 160 Seabury St., 02720. Tel: 508-673-0852; Fax: 508-678-0873.
Catechesis/Religious Programs—Mrs. Maureen Costa, D.R.E.
Students 140.

12—ST. ANNE'S (1869) (French), Revs. Marc H. Bergeron; Pierre E. Lachance, O.P.; Jean Dominique Pare, O.P.; Herbert T. Nichols.
Res., 818 Middle St., 02721. Tel: 508-674-5651; 678-5322; Fax: 508-672-0939.
School—Tel: 508-678-2152; Fax: 508-674-5190. Mrs. Denise Gagne, Prin.

Sisters 1; Lay Teachers 24; Students 458.
Catechesis/Religious Programs—Tel: 508-678-1510. Susan Chapdelaine, D.R.E.
Students 280.

13—ST. ANTHONY OF PADUA (1911) (Portuguese), Rev. John C. Martins.
Res., 48 Sixteenth St., 02723. Tel: 508-673-2402.
Catechesis/Religious Programs—Tel: 508-764-1986. D.R.E.: Jorgelina B. Krupa; Deborah Polselli.
Students 417.

14—ST. ELIZABETH'S (1915) (Portuguese), Rev. Raymond Cambra.
Res., 515 Tucker St., 02721. Tel: 508-679-6903; Fax: 508-675-8983.
Catechesis/Religious Programs—Tel: 508-672-6602.
Students 73.

15—ST. JEAN BAPTISTE (1901) (French), Rev. David M. Andrate, Admin.
Res., 951 Stafford Rd., 02721. Tel: 508-672-6552; Fax: 508-673-5518.
School—Lamphor St., 02721. Tel: 508-673-6772; Fax: 508-730-1864. Kathleen Barboza, Prin.
Lay Teachers 11; Students 230.
Catechesis/Religious Programs—Tel: 508-672-4822.
Students 91.

16—ST. JOSEPH'S (1873), Rev. John J. Perry. In res., Rev. Msgr. George W. Coleman, V.G.
Res., 1335 N. Main St., 02720. Tel: 508-673-1123; Fax: 508-646-1060.
Catechesis/Religious Programs—Students 198.

17—ST. LOUIS (1885), Revs. Michael Carvill; Vincent Nagle; Antonio Lopez.
Res., 420 Bradford Ave., 02721. Tel: 508-676-8603; Fax: 508-324-1702.
Catechesis/Religious Programs—Students 107.

18—ST. MICHAEL'S (1902) (Portuguese), Revs. Luis A. Cardoso; Dermut Rodgers. In res., Rev. Manuel T. Faria.
Res., 189 Essex St., 02720. Tel: 508-672-6713; Fax: 508-679-1841. [CEM]
School—Tel: 508-678-0266.
Religious of the Holy Union of the Sacred Hearts 1; Lay Teachers 10; Students 187.
Catechesis/Religious Programs—Tel: 508-678-0266.
Students 355.

19—ST. PATRICK'S (1873), Rev. James M. Fitzpatrick, Admin.
Res., 1598 S. Main St., 02724-2596. Tel: 508-672-2302; Fax: 508-673-1280.
Catechesis/Religious Programs—John J. Fortin, D.R.E.
Students 203.

20—SS. PETER AND PAUL (1882), Revs. Stephen A. Fernandes; Charles Porada, O.F.M. Conv.; Deacon David M. Sharland.
Res., 250 Snell St., 02721. Tel: 508-676-8463; Fax: 508-678-8070.
School—240 Dover St., 02721. Tel: 508-672-7258; Fax: 508-674-6042.
Sisters of Mercy 1; Lay Teachers 12; Students 200.
Catechesis/Religious Programs—Tel: 508-672-3720.
Students 191.

21—ST. STANISLAUS (1898) (Polish), Rev. Robert S. Kaszynski; Deacon Franciszek W. Mis.
Res., 36 Rockland St., P.O. Box 111, 02724. Tel: 508-672-0423; Fax: 508-677-1378.
School—37 Rockland St., 02724. Tel: 508-674-6771; Fax: 508-677-1622. Mrs. Denita Tremblay, Prin.
Lay Teachers 11; Students 200.
Catechesis/Religious Programs—Students 110.

22—ST. WILLIAM'S (1905), Rev. Horace J. Travasses.
Res., 42 Chicago St., 02721. Tel: 508-675-7503; Fax: 508-675-9209.
Catechesis/Religious Programs—Tel: 508-675-0695.
Students 142.

23—SANTO CHRISTO (1891) (Portuguese), Rev. Gastao A. Oliveira.
Res., 185 Canal St., 02721. Tel: 508-676-1184; Fax: 508-676-9701.
Catechesis/Religious Programs—Tel: 508-675-3007. Mr. Osvaldo Pacheco, D.R.E.
Students 681.

OUTSIDE THE CITY OF FALL RIVER

Acushnet, Bristol Co., St. Francis Xavier's (1915), Rev. Paul A. Caron; Deacon Michael P. Guy.
Res., 125 Main St., 02743. Tel: 508-995-7600; Fax: 508-995-1794.
School—223 Main St., 02743. Tel: 508-995-4313. Mrs. Susan Boulay, Prin.
Religious 2; Lay Teachers 10; Students 217.
Catechesis/Religious Programs—Tel: 508-998-7445.
Students 400.

Assonet, Bristol Co., St. Bernard's (1938), Rev. Timothy J. Goldrick; Deacon Lawrence A. St. Onge.
Res., 32 S. Main St., P.O. Box 370, 02702. Tel: 508-644-5585; Fax: 508-644-2136.
Catechesis/Religious Programs—Tel: 508-644-2032. John G. Lanctot, D.R.E.
Students 480.

Attleboro, Bristol Co.,

1—ST. JOHN THE EVANGELIST, (1883), Rev. Msgr. Daniel F. Hoye, V.E.; Rev. David A. Pregana; Deacon A. Anthony Cipriano.
Res., 155 N. Main St., 02703-2251. Tel: 508-222-1206; Fax: 508-226-6461. [CEM]
School—13 Hodges St., 02703. Tel: 508-222-5062; Fax: 508-223-1737. Sr. Ann Therese Connolly, C.D.P., Prin.
Congregation of Divine Providence 1; Lay Teachers 10; Students 251.
Catechesis/Religious Programs—Tel: 508-222-0707.
Students 658.

2—ST. JOSEPH'S, (1905), Rev. Kevin J. Harrington.
Res., 208 S. Main St., 02703. Tel: 508-226-1115; Fax: 508-226-0234.
Catechesis/Religious Programs—10 Maple St., Tel: 508-222-1730.
Students 212.

3—ST. STEPHEN'S, (1875), Rev. William L. Boffa; Deacon Robert W. Pelland.
Res., 683 S. Main St., 02703-6397. Tel: 508-222-0641; Fax: 508-222-1815. [CEM]
Catechesis/Religious Programs—Mrs. Irene Pelland, D.R.E.
Students 275.

4—HOLY GHOST, (1921), Rev. Stephen B. Salvador; Deacon Paul M. Fournier.
Res., 71 Linden St., 02703. Tel: 508-222-3266; Fax: 508-222-3292.
Catechesis/Religious Programs—Tel: 508-222-6756. Jacqueline DaSilva, D.R.E. & Coord.
Students 168.

5—ST. THERESA OF THE CHILD JESUS, (1925), Rev. James W. Fahey.
Res., 18 Baltic St., S. Attleboro, 02703. Tel: 508-761-8111; Fax: 508-761-5475.
Catechesis/Religious Programs—Tel: 508-761-5367. Deacon Robert E. Nicholson, D.R.E.
Students 435.

Attleboro Falls, Bristol Co., St. Mark's (1967), Revs. Peter N. Graziano; Thomas A. Frechette.
Res., 105 Stanley St., Box 1240, 02763. Tel: 508-699-7566; Fax: 508-643-0103.
Catechesis/Religious Programs—Tel: 508-695-7773. Mrs. Elaine Corvese, D.R.E.
Students 860.

Brewster, Barnstable Co., Our Lady of the Cape (1961), Revs. Bernard Baris, M.S.; Raymond Vaillancourt, M.S.; Roger Leroux, M.S.; Deacons Loren King, Jr.; R. Donald Biron.
Res., Stony Brook Rd., P.O. Box 1799, 02631. Tel: 508-385-3252; Fax: 508-385-6864.
Catechesis/Religious Programs—Tel: 508-385-2115. Elizabeth M. McCullough, D.R.E.
Students 596.
Mission—East Brewster, Barnstable Co., Immaculate Conception, Rte. 6A, 02631.

Buzzards Bay, Barnstable Co., St. Margaret (1915), Rev. James C. Tuxbury, O.F.M.
Res., 141 Main St., 02532. Tel: 508-759-7777; Fax: 508-759-3920. [JC]
Catechesis/Religious Programs—Tel: 508-759-2065. Roberta Smolinsky, D.R.E.
Students 470.
Mission—Onset, St. Mary Star of the Sea.

Centerville, Barnstable Co., Our Lady of Victory (1957), Rev. Msgr. Henry T. Munroe, P.A.; Revs. William W. Norton; Marek Chmurski; Deacons Joseph P. Stanley; James M. Barrett.
Res., 230 S. Main St., 02632. Tel: 508-775-5744; Fax: 508-771-0170.
Catechesis/Religious Programs—Tel: 508-771-1614. D.R.E.: Jessie duMont; Claudia Anderson.
Students 1,226.
Mission—West Barnstable, Barnstable Co., Our Lady of Hope, Rte. 6A, West Barnstable, 02668. Tel: 508-362-8112.

Chatham, Barnstable Co., Holy Redeemer (1955), Rev. James F. Buckley; Deacon Joseph F. Mador.
Res., 57 Highland Ave., Box 687, 02633. Tel: 508-945-0677; Fax: 508-945-3186. [JC]
Catechesis/Religious Programs—Students 110.
Mission—South Chatham, Barnstable Co., Our Lady of Grace, P.O. Box 687, 02633.

Dighton, Bristol Co., St. Peter's (1904), Rev. Bernard Vanasse.
Res., 2039 County St., 02715. Tel: 508-669-6463; Fax: 508-669-6463.
Catechesis/Religious Programs—Tel: 508-669-6925.
Students 187.

East Falmouth, Barnstable Co., St. Anthony's (1923), Rev. Leonard Mullaney.
Res., 167 E. Falmouth Hwy., 02536. Tel: 508-548-0108; Fax: 508-548-7734. [CEM]
Catechesis/Religious Programs—Tel: 508-548-3515.
Students 518.

East Freetown, Bristol Co., St. John Neumann (1984), Rev. John A. Perry; Deacon Robert L. Surprenant.
Res., Middleboro Rd., Box 718, 02717. Tel: 508-763-2240; Fax: 508-763-3040.
Catechesis/Religious Programs—Tel: 508-763-8122. D.R.E.: Dr. Doris Thibault; Mrs. Madeleine Oliver.
Students 510.

East Taunton, Bristol Co., Holy Family (1908), Rev. Jay Maddock; Deacon John J. Fitzpatrick.
Res., 370 Middleboro, P.O. Box 619, 02718. Tel: 508-824-5707; Fax: 508-824-5665.
Catechesis/Religious Programs—Tel: 508-824-4207. Sr. Anita Marie, M.S.B.T., D.R.E.
Students 554.

Edgartown, Dukes Co., St. Elizabeth (1925), Revs. Michael R. Nagle, D.Min.; Michael O'Hearn.
Res., 86 Main St., P.O. Box 156, 02539. Tel: 508-627-5017; Fax: 508-627-6021.
Catechesis/Religious Programs—Pease Point Way, 02539. Tel: 508-627-5871.
Students 103.

Fairhaven, Bristol Co., St. Joseph's (1905), Revs. William Heffron, SS.CC.; Frederick Meyers, SS.CC. In res., Rev. Leo King, SS.CC.; Bro. Chris Santangelo, SS.CC., Pastoral Assoc.
Res., 41 Walnut St., 02719. Tel: 508-994-9714; Fax: 508-979-4659.
School—Spring St. and Homestead Ave., 02719. Tel: 508-996-1983. Sr. Muriel Ann Lebeau, SS.CC., Prin.
Sisters 1; Lay Teachers 10; Students 249.
Catechesis/Religious Programs—Tel: 508-994-8679. Ms. Jane Ayer, D.R.E.
Students 420.

St. Mary's (1933), Rev. Robert Charlton, SS.CC. In res., Rev. Alphonsus McHugh, SS.CC.
Res., 41 Harding Rd., 02719. Tel: 508-992-7300; Fax: 508-992-8721.
Catechesis/Religious Programs—Tel: 508-992-7300. Sr. Eleanor Cyr, SS.CC., D.R.E.
Students 362.

Falmouth, Barnstable Co., St. Patrick's (1899), Rev. Msgr. John J. Regan; Revs. George B. Scales; Timothy P. Reis; Deacon Patrick J. Mahoney.
Res., 511 E. Main St., P.O. Box 569, 02541. Tel: 508-548-1065; Fax: 508-495-0875. [CEM]
Catechesis/Religious Programs—Tel: 508-548-2306. Cynthia O'Connor, D.R.E.
Students 387.
Chapel—Falmouth Heights, St. Thomas, Tel: 508-548-8539.

Hyannis, Barnstable Co., St. Francis Xavier's (1904), Revs. Edward J. Byington; Paul T. Lamb.
Res., 347 South St., 02601. Tel: 508-775-0818.
Catechesis/Religious Programs—Tel: 508-775-6200. Mrs. Mary Offiler, D.R.E.
Students 274.
Mission—Yarmouth Port, Barnstable Co., Sacred Heart Chapel, Summer St., Yarmouth Port, 02675.

Mansfield, Bristol Co., St. Mary's (1894), Revs. George C. Bellenoit; Daniel W. Lacroix; Sr. Ann William Publicover, M.S.B.T., Pastoral Min.; Deacons Thomas P. Palanza; Walter D. Thomas.
Res., 330 Pratt St., 02048-1581. Tel: 508-339-2981; Fax: 508-339-0612. [CEM]
Catechesis/Religious Programs—Tel: 508-339-4621. Mrs. Ellen Westlund, D.R.E.
Students 1,800.

Marion, Plymouth Co., St. Rita's (1972), Rev. William G. Campbell.
Res., 113 Front St., Box 902, 02738. Tel: 508-748-1497; Fax: 508-748-0604.
Catechesis/Religious Programs—Tel: 508-748-2196.
Students 210.

Mashpee, Barnstable Co., Christ The King (1984), Rev. Ronald A. Tosti; Deacon Robert D. Lemay. In res., Rev. Edward J. Healey.
Res., The Commons, P.O. Box 1800, 02649. Tel: 508-477-7710; Fax: 508-477-8158.
Catechesis/Religious Programs—Tel: 508-477-6565. D.R.E.: Sr. Annette Roach, O.P.; Sr. Claire Sinotte, O.P.
Students 809.

Mattapoisett, Plymouth Co., St. Anthony's (1908), Rev. Barry W. Wall; Deacon Louis A. Bousquet.
Mailing Address: P.O. Box 501, 02739-0501. Fax: 508-758-3019.

Res., 22 Barstow St., 02739. Tel: 508-758-3719. [CEM]
Catechesis/Religious Programs—Tel: 508-758-3735. Mrs. Natalie Taber, D.R.E.
Students 277.

Nantucket, Nantucket Co., St. Mary's, Our Lady of the Isle (1903), Rev. Thomas C. Lopes.
Res., 6 Orange St., P.O. Box 1168, 02554. Tel: 508-228-0100; Fax: 508-325-7991. [CEM]
Catechesis/Religious Programs—Tel: 508-228-4852.
Students 256.
Station—Siasconset.

New Bedford, Bristol Co.,

1—Holy Name, (1909), Rev. Msgr. Thomas J. Harrington.
Res., 121 Mt. Pleasant St., 02740. Tel: 508-992-3184; Fax: 508-984-3406.
Catechesis/Religious Programs—Tel: 508-996-8654. D.R.E.: Mrs. Nancy Davis; Mrs. Heidi Kuliga.
Students 200.

2—Nuestra Senora de Guadalupe, (1993) (Hispanic), Rev. Paul E. Canuel.
Mailing Address: P.O. Box 40605, 02744-0006. Tel: 508-996-5862; Fax: 508-992-2208.
Res., 344 County St., 02740. Tel: 508-994-2521; Fax: 508-992-2208.
Catechesis/Religious Programs—Tel: 508-997-8729. Sr. Candelaria Hernandez, M.G.Sp.S., D.R.E.
Students 60.

3—Our Lady of the Assumption, (1905) (Cape Verdean), Revs. David P. Reid, SS.CC.; Richard Lifrak, SS.CC.; Deacons Eduardo M. Pacheto; Antonio M. Da Cruz.
Res., 54 S. 6th St., 02740.
Parish Center—47 S. 6th St., 02740. Tel: 508-994-7602; Fax: 508-994-9461.
Catechesis/Religious Programs—Students 237.

4—Our Lady of Fatima, (1966), Rev. James F. Greene.
Res., 4254 Acushnet Ave., 02745. Tel: 508-995-7351; Fax: 508-995-4401.
Catechesis/Religious Programs—Tel: 508-995-6685. Mrs. Pearl Enos, D.R.E.
Students 198.
Parish Center—980 Tobey St., New Bedord, 02745.

5—Our Lady of the Immaculate Conception, (1914) (Portuguese), Revs. Daniel O. Reis; Brian E. Albino, S.J.
Res., 136 Earle St., 02746. Tel: 508-992-9892; Fax: 508-992-9907.
Catechesis/Religious Programs—156 Davis St., 02746. Tel: 508-990-0249.
Students 962.

6—Our Lady of Mt. Carmel, (1902) (Portuguese), Very Rev. Henry S. Arruda; Revs. Michael Camara, O.F.M.; Marek S. Tuptynski; Antonino C. Tavares, (Retired); Deacons Paul Macedo; Abilio Pires.
Parish Center: 238 Bonney St., 02744. Tel: 508-993-0529.
Res., 230 Bonney St., 02744. Tel: 508-993-4704; Fax: 508-991-5536.
School—103 Crapo St., 02744. Tel: 508-997-9612. Mrs. Rosemary da Silva, Prin.
Lay Teachers 11; Students 160.
Catechesis/Religious Programs—Tel: 508-984-7097.
Students 900.

7—Our Lady of Perpetual Help, (1905) (Polish), Revs. Roman Chwaliszewski, O.F.M.Conv.; Sebastian Slesinski, O.F.M.Conv. In res., Rev. Isidore Kowalski, O.F.M.Conv.
Res., 235 N. Front St., 02746. Tel: 508-992-9378; Fax: 508-993-4881.
Catechesis/Religious Programs—Students 62.

8—Sacred Heart, (1874) (French), Rev. Clement E. Dufour; Deacon Eugene H. Sasseville.
Res., 341 Summer St., 02740. Tel: 508-993-1204; Fax: 508-999-4140.
Catechesis/Religious Programs—Tel: 508-999-4140.
Students 64.

9—St. Anne, (1908) (French), Rev. Martin L. Buote; Deacon Marcel Morency.
Res., 890 Brock Ave., 02744. Tel: 508-997-9271.

10—St. Anthony of Padua's, (1895) (French), Rev. Edmond R. Levesque.
Res., 1359 Acushnet Ave., 02746. Tel: 508-993-1691; Fax: 508-999-4775.
School—109 Ashley Blvd., 02746. Tel: 508-994-5121; Fax: 508-979-5923. Sr. Elizabeth Lavigne, Prin.
Lay Teachers 15; Students 325.
Catechesis/Religious Programs—Students 125.
Convent—106 Bullard St., 02746. Mother of God Sisters of Capuchin Recollect 8.

11—St. Casimir, (1927) (Polish), Rev. Henry K. Kropiwnicki.
Res., 2048 Acushnet Ave., 02745-6139. Tel: 508-995-0345.

12—St. Francis of Assisi Church, (1928) (Italian), Rev. Albert J. Ryan.
Res., 247 North St., 02740. Tel: 508-997-7732; Fax: 508-991-6630.
Catechesis/Religious Programs—Mrs. Natalie Arsenault, D.R.E.
Students 30.

13—St. Hedwig, (1908) (Polish), Rev. Paul E. Canuel.
Mailing Address: P.O. Box 40605, New Bedord, 02744-0006. Tel: 508-996-8703; Fax: 508-992-2208.
Res., 344 County St., 02740. Tel: 508-994-2521.

14—St. James, (1888), Rev. Edward E. Correia. In res., Rev. Francis J. McManus, S.J., Chap.
Res., 233 County St., 02740. Tel: 508-992-9408.
School—St. James-St. John, 180 Orchard St., 02740. Tel: 508-996-0534.
Sisters of Mercy 1; Lay Teachers 10; Students 250.
Catechesis/Religious Programs—Tel: 508-992-7122.
Students 208.

15—St. John the Baptist, (1871) (Portuguese), Revs. John J. Oliveira; James S. Medeiros. In res., Rev. Paul E. Canuel.
Res., 344 County St., 02740. Tel: 508-992-7727; Fax: 508-997-1462. [CEM]
School—See listing for St. James, New Bedford.
Catechesis/Religious Programs—Tel: 508-996-3087. Ms. Marge Ferreira, D.R.E.
Students 272.

16—St. Joseph's, (1910) (French), Rev. Roger J. Levesque; Deacon Maurice Lavallee.
Res., 51 Duncan St., 02745-6108. Tel: 508-995-5235.
School—35 Kearsarge St., 02745-6117. Tel: 508-995-2264. Paulette S. Dansereau, Prin.
Lay Teachers 11; Students 240.
Catechesis/Religious Programs—Students 125.

17—St. Kilian, (1896), Revs. Benito M. Lagos, I.V.E.; Jose Del Val; Gustavo Dominguez.
Res., 306 Ashley Blvd., 02746. Tel: 508-992-7587; Fax: 508-994-8201.
Catechesis/Religious Programs—Students 87.

18—St. Lawrence Martyr, (1821), Revs. John P. Driscoll; Thomas E. O'Dea.
Res., 110 Summer St., 02740. Tel: 508-992-4251; Fax: 508-993-8277.
School—Holy Family-Holy Name, 91 Summer St., 02740. Tel: 508-993-3547. Ms. Cecilia Felix, Prin. & D.R.E.
Sisters 2; Lay Teachers 15; Students 272.
Catechesis/Religious Programs—Tel: 508-993-3577.
Students 242.

19—St. Mary's, Rev. Msgr. John J. Oliveira, P.A.; Rev. John C. Ozug; Deacon Claude A. Leblanc.
Res., 106 Illinois St., 02745. Tel: 508-995-3593; Fax: 508-995-2453.
School—115 Illinois St., 02745. Tel: 508-995-3696.
Sisters 1; Lay Teachers 10; Students 201.
Catechesis/Religious Programs—Students 460.

20—St. Theresa, (1926) (French), Rev. Roland Bousquet, S.T.L.; Deacon Leo T. Racine.
Res., 2693 Acushnet Ave., 02745. Tel: 508-995-0403; Fax: 508-998-2957.
Catechesis/Religious Programs—Tel: 508-995-3790.
Students 150.

North Attleboro, Bristol Co., St. Mary's (1890), Rev. Robert A. Oliveira; Deacon James J. Meloni. In res., Revs. John M. Sullivan; William T. Babbitt.
Mailing Address: P.O. Box 1027, 02761-1027. Tel: 508-695-6161; Fax: 508-695-5248.
Res., 14 Park St., P.O. Box 1027, 02760. Tel: 508-695-6161. [CEM]
School—See St. Mary-Sacred Heart. Tel: 508-695-3072.
Catechesis/Religious Programs—14 Park St., P.O. Box 1027, 02761-1027. Tel: 508-695-3823.
Students 470.
Convent—125 Broad St., 02760. Tel: 508-695-7989. Sisters of the Holy Union 14.

Sacred Heart (1904) (French), Rev. Richard E. Degagne.
Res., 58 Church St., P.O. Box 470, 02761-0470. Tel: 508-699-8383; Fax: 508-699-7016.
School—St. Mary's-Sacred Heart Consolidated School, 57 Richards Ave., 02760. Tel: 508-695-3072. Mrs. Denise M. Peixoto, Prin.
Lay Teachers 16; Students 236.
Catechesis/Religious Programs—Tel: 508-643-9009.
Students 194.

North Dartmouth, Bristol Co., St. Julie Billiart (1969), Revs. Brian J. Harrington; Christopher Stanibula; Deacon Bruce J. Bonneau.
Res., 494 Slocum Rd., 02747. Tel: 508-993-2351; Fax: 508-993-2437.
Catechesis/Religious Programs—Tel: 508-990-0287. Ms. Jane Ayer, D.R.E.
Students 900.

North Dighton, Bristol Co., St. Joseph's (1913), Rev. James McLellan.
Res., 499 Spring St., P.O. Box 564, 02764-0564. Tel: 508-822-1425; Fax: 508-822-3886.
Catechesis/Religious Programs—Tel: 508-824-6581. Sr. Judith Costa, S.S.D., D.R.E.
Students 295.

North Easton, Bristol Co., Immaculate Conception (1871), Rev. Lucio B. Phillipino.
Res., 193 Main St., 02356. Tel: 508-238-3232; Fax: 508-238-7849. [CEM]
Catechesis/Religious Programs—Tel: 508-238-3230; Fax: 508-238-7849. Maryann Dziekiewicz, D.R.E.
Students 289.

North Falmouth, Barnstable Co., St. Elizabeth Seton (1977), Rev. John F. Moore; Deacons Paul K. Roma; Frank D. Fantasia.
Res., 481 Quaker Rd., Box 861, 02556. Tel: 508-563-7770; Fax: 508-563-7794.
Catechesis/Religious Programs—Tel: 508-563-7774.
Students 275.

Norton, Bristol Co., St. Mary's (1925), Revs. Arnold R. Medeiros; Gregory A. Mathias.
Res., 133 S. Worcester St., Box 430, 02766-0430. Tel: 508-285-4462; Fax: 508-285-5589.
Catechesis/Religious Programs—Tel: 508-285-3237. Mrs. Rose E. Collette, D.R.E.
Students 944.

Oak Bluffs, Dukes Co., Sacred Heart (1880), Revs. Michael R. Nagle; Michael O'Hearn.
Res., 259 Circuit Ave., P.O. Box 1565, 02557. Tel: 508-693-0342. [CEM]
Catechesis/Religious Programs—Tel: 508-693-3995.
Students 116.

Orleans, Barnstable Co., St. Joan of Arc (1947), Rev. Richard M. Roy; Deacon Norman McEnaney.
Res., 61 Canal Rd., P.O. Box 336, 02653. Tel: 508-255-0170; Fax: 508-240-6741.
Catechesis/Religious Programs—Tel: 508-255-7442.
Students 280.
Mission—North Eastham, Barnstable Co., Church of the Visitation, Masasoit Rd., North Eastham, 02651. Tel: 508-255-6588.

Osterville, Barnstable Co., Our Lady of the Assumption (1906), Rev. Thomas L. Rita.
Res., 76 Wianno Ave., P.O. Box E., 02655. Tel: 508-428-2011.
Catechesis/Religious Programs—Students 156.

Pocasset, Barnstable Co., St. John the Evangelist (1969), Rev. Robert C. Donovan; Deacons James Marzelli, Jr.; Leonard C. Dexter, Jr.
Res., 15 Virginia Rd., P.O. Box 1558, 02559. Tel: 508-563-3121; 563-5887; Fax: 508-563-3102.
Catechesis/Religious Programs—841 Shore Rd., P.O. Box 1558, 02559. Tel: 508-563-5536. Bette Songer, D.R.E.
Students 300.

Provincetown, Barnstable Co., St. Peter the Apostle (1874), Rev. John A. Raposo; Deacon Chester O. Cook.
Res., 11 Prince St., 02657. Tel: 508-487-0095; Fax: 508-487-2564. [CEM]
Catechesis/Religious Programs—Students 100.

Raynham, Bristol Co., St. Ann (1961), Revs. Philip A. Davignon; Pawel A. Swiercz; Deacon John Welch.
Res., 660 N. Main St., P.O. Box 247, 02768. Tel: 508-823-9833; 823-9834; Fax: 508-823-8935.
Catechesis/Religious Programs—725 N. Main St. Box 247, Raynham Center, 02768. Tel: 508-824-9021. Donna Martyniak, D.R.E.
Students 741.

Sandwich, Barnstable Co., Corpus Christi (1830), Revs. Marcel H. Bouchard; Henry J. Dahl; Felician Plichta, O.F.M.Conv.; Deacons Richard J. Murphy, Sr.; John J. Emmert; Robert Alence.
Res., 251 Service Rd., P.O. Box 1170, East Sandwich, 02537-2170. Tel: 508-888-0209; Fax: 508-888-8961. [CEM]
Parish Center—324 Quaker Meetinghouse Rd., East Sandwich, 02537.
Catechesis/Religious Programs—Tel: 508-888-8267. Sr. Doreen Donegan, D.R.E.
Students 1,200.
Mission—Sagamore, Barnstable Co., St. Theresa.

Seekonk, Bristol Co., Our Lady of Mt. Carmel (1922), Revs. George E. Harrison; Thomas M. Kocik.
Res., 984 Taunton Ave., 02771. Tel: 508-336-9022; Fax: 508-336-9010.
Catechesis/Religious Programs—1040 Taunton Ave., 02771. Tel: 508-336-8608. Sr. Irene Rivard, F.C.S.C.J., D.R.E.
Students 786.

St. Mary's (1906), Revs. Bruce M. Neylon; Michael F. Kuhn.
Res., 385 Central Ave., 02771. Tel: 508-399-8440; Fax: 508-399-7398.
Catechesis/Religious Programs—Tel: 508-399-7534.
Students 807.

Somerset, Bristol Co., St. John of God (1928) (Portuguese), Rev. Raul M. Lagoa. In res., Rev. Luciano J. de M. Pereira, (Retired).
Res., 996 Brayton Ave., Box 113, 02726. Tel: 508-678-5513; Fax: 508-678-6458.
Catechesis/Religious Programs—1036 Brayton Ave., 02726. Tel: 508-678-5139. Edward Medeiros, D.R.E.
Students 362.

St. Thomas More (1949), Rev. John J. Steakem; Deacon Victor Haddad. In res., Revs. John J. Murphy; Michael K. McManus.
Res., 386 Luther Ave., 02726. Tel: 508-673-7831; Fax: 508-730-1396.
Catechesis/Religious Programs—Tel: 508-679-1236. Mrs. Patricia Pasternak, M.A., D.R.E.
Students 320.

St. Patrick's (1883), Rev. Marc P. Tremblay; Deacon Edward Hussey.
Res., 306 South St., 02726-5617. Tel: 508-672-1523; Fax: 508-675-5787. [CEM]
Catechesis/Religious Programs—Tel: 508-675-1073.
Students 287.

South Dartmouth, Bristol Co., St. Mary's (1930), Rev. Terence Keenan; Deacon Jeremiah J. Reardon.
Res., 783 Dartmouth St., 02748. Tel: 508-992-7163; Fax: 508-992-5209.
Catechesis/Religious Programs—Tel: 508-992-7505. Sr. Joan Blazevich, C.J.C., D.R.E.
Students 550.

South Easton, Bristol Co., Holy Cross (1967), Revs. Richard C. Hockman, C.S.C.; Daniel Kayajan, C.S.C.; Deacon George H. Zarella.
Res., 225 Purchase St., 02375. Tel: 508-238-2235; Fax: 508-238-0500.
Catechesis/Religious Programs—Tel: 508-238-2131. D.R.E.: Lorraine Gryniuk; Kathy Hohl; Janet Merriam.
Students 945.

South Yarmouth, Barnstable Co., St. Pius Tenth (1954), Rev. Msgr. John J. Smith; Rev. Hugh J. McCullough, S.J.B.; Deacons David Akin; Richard J. Hasey; Thomas Bailey.
Res., 5 Barbara St., 02664. Tel: 508-398-2248; Fax: 508-398-7233.
Catechesis/Religious Programs—Station Ave., 02664. Tel: 508-394-0709; 0708. D.R.E.: Mrs. Joan Robinson; Mrs. Jean Kelly.
Students 672.
Chapel—Bass River, Our Lady of the Highway, Tel: 508-760-3332.

Swansea, Bristol Co.,

1—St. Dominic's, (1911), Rev. Joseph F. Viveiros.
Res., 1277 Grand Army Hwy., P.O. Box 205, 02777. Tel: 508-675-7206.
Catechesis/Religious Programs—Tel: 508-675-7002.
Students 263.

2—St. Louis de France, (1928) (French), Rev. Roger D. LeDuc; Deacon Robert G.L. Normandin.
Res., 56 Buffington St., 02777. Tel: 508-674-1103; Fax: 508-674-1103.
Catechesis/Religious Programs—66 Buffington St., 02777. Tel: 508-672-0615. Mrs. Lucia C. Marcille, D.R.E.
Students 523.

3—St. Michael's, (1922), Rev. Richard R. Gendreau; Deacon Thomas F. Prevost.
Res., 270 Ocean Grove Ave., 02777. Tel: 508-673-2808; Fax: 508-672-1642.
Catechesis/Religious Programs—Tel: 508-674-0024.
Students 250.

4—Our Lady of Fatima, (1958), Rev. George F. Almeida; Deacon Mark G. Shea.
Res., 530 Gardner Neck Rd., 02777. Tel: 508-676-1541; Fax: 508-676-0289.
Catechesis/Religious Programs—Tel: 508-678-7011. Sr. Mary Denisita Sullivan, R.S.M., D.R.E.
Students 275.

Taunton, Bristol Co.,

1—Our Lady of the Holy Rosary, (1909) (Polish), Revs. David M. Stopyra, O.F.M.Conv.; Joseph Grzybowski, O.F.M.Conv.
Res., 80 Bay St., 02780. Tel: 508-823-3046; Fax: 508-823-0585.
Catechesis/Religious Programs—Tel: 508-824-3910.
Students 94.

2—Our Lady of the Immaculate Conception, (1883), Rev. William P. Blottman; Deacon Michael Murray. In res., Rev. David J. Landry.
Res., 387 Bay St., 02780-1718. Tel: 508-824-8794; Fax: 508-821-7616.
Catechesis/Religious Programs—Tel: 508-824-4545. Mrs. Kathleen A. Peterson, D.R.E.
Students 300.

3—Our Lady of Lourdes, (1905) (Portuguese), Rev. John A. Gomes.
Res., 49 First St., 02780. Tel: 508-822-0357; Fax: 508-823-4999.
School—52 First St., 02780. Tel: 508-822-3746. Mrs. Arleen Booker, Prin.
Sisters 3; Lay Teachers 5; Students 203.
Catechesis/Religious Programs—Students 220.
Convent—55 First St., 02780. Tel: 508-822-9206.

4—Sacred Heart, (1873), Rev. Jon-Paul Gallant.
Res., 311 Somerset Ave., 02780. Tel: 508-823-2521; Fax: 508-823-2522.
Catechesis/Religious Programs—29 First St., 02780. Tel: 508-824-6791.
Students 300.

5—St. Anthony's, (1910) (Portuguese), Revs. Manuel P. Ferreira; Maurice O. Gauvin; Deacon Thomas J. Souza.
Res., 126 School St., 02780. Tel: 508-822-0714; Fax: 508-828-5844.
Catechesis/Religious Programs—Students 375.

6—St. James, (1904) (French), Rev. Thomas E. Morrissey.
Res., 249 Whittenton St., 02780. Tel: 508-824-7794; Fax: 508-822-8014.
Catechesis/Religious Programs—Tel: 508-824-7808.
Students 62.
Convent—279 Whittenton St., 02780. Tel: 508-824-8946.

7—St. Joseph's, (1896), Rev. Mark R. Hession; Deacon Robert J. Hill.
Res., 19 Kilmer Ave., 02780. Tel: 508-824-5435; Fax: 508-880-1903.
Catechesis/Religious Programs—Tel: 508-823-6819. Margaret Travers, D.R.E.
Students 400.

8—St. Mary's, (1828), Rev. William M. Costello.
Res., 14 St. Mary's Square, 02780. Tel: 508-822-7116; Fax: 508-822-7117.
School—Tel: 508-822-9480; Fax: 508-822-7164. Mr. Brian Cote, Prin.
Lay Teachers 26; Students 487.
Catechesis/Religious Programs—Tel: 508-880-5062.
Students 214.
Dolan Parish Center—Tel: 508-880-5062.

9—St. Paul's, (1904), Very Rev. Bento R. Fraga, V.F.; Deacon John H. Schondek.
Res., 261 Tremont St., 02780. Tel: 508-824-7166; Fax: 508-822-9618.
Catechesis/Religious Programs—Tel: 508-822-9672.
Students 316.

Vineyard Haven, Dukes Co., St. Augustine (1962), Revs. Michael R. Nagle, D.Min.; Michael O'Hearn.
Res., 56 Franklin St., P.O. Box 1058, 02568. Tel: 508-693-0103; Fax: 508-693-8517.
Catechesis/Religious Programs—Students 157.

Wareham, Plymouth Co., St. Patrick's (1911), Rev. Freddie Babiczuk, Jr., Admin.; Deacon William A. Martin.
Res., 82 High St., P.O. Box 271, 02571-0271. Tel: 508-295-2411; Fax: 508-295-2417. [CEM]
Catechesis/Religious Programs—Tel: 508-295-0780; Fax: 508-295-2417. Mrs. Ann MacDonald, D.R.E.
Students 790.
Mission—West Wareham, Plymouth Co., St. Anthony, P.O. Box 271, 02571-0271.

Wellfleet, Barnstable Co., Our Lady of Lourdes (1910), Rev. John F. Andrews.
Res., 335 Main St., P.O. Box 1414, 02667-1414. Tel: 508-349-2222. [CEM 2]
Catechesis/Religious Programs—Students 21.
Missions—North Truro, Barnstable Co., Our Lady of Perpetual Help, Pond Rd., North Truro, 02652.; Truro, Barnstable Co., Sacred Heart, 40 Truro Center Rd., Truro, 02666.

Westport, Bristol Co., Our Lady of Grace (1954), Rev. Richard L. Chretien.
Res., 569 Sanford Rd., 02790. Tel: 508-674-6271.
Catechesis/Religious Programs—Tel: 508-675-5857. Teresa Alexander, D.R.E.
Students 438.

St. George's (1914), Rev. Gerard A. Hebert.
Res., 12 Highland Ave., P.O. Box 1530, 02790. Tel: 508-636-4965; Fax: 508-636-4188.
Catechesis/Religious Programs—Tel: 508-636-4909.
Students 250.

St. John the Baptist (1930), Rev. Edmund J. Fitzgerald.
Res., 945 Main Rd., Box 3328, 02790. Tel: 508-636-2251; Fax: 508-636-8306.
Catechesis/Religious Programs—924 Main Rd., P.O. Box 3328, 02790. Tel: 508-636-5506.
Students 220.

West Harwich, Barnstable Co., Holy Trinity (1918), Very Rev. Gerald T. Shovelton, V.F.; Rev. Joseph J. Blyskosz. In res., Rev. Oscar Clemente (Brazil); Deacons Ralph F. Cox; Dana G. McCarthy.
Res., S. Main St., 02671. Tel: 508-432-4000; Fax: 508-432-3494.
School—Sisters 3; Lay Teachers 4; Students 139.
Catechesis/Religious Programs—Tel: 508-432-2898. Marie Mann, D.R.E.
Students 330.
Mission—Dennis Port, Barnstable Co., Our Lady of the Annunciation, P.O. Box 428, Dennis Port, 02639. [CEM]

Woods Hole, Barnstable Co., St. Joseph's (1882), Rev. Bernard R. Kelly.
Res., 33 Millfield St., P.O. Box 3, 02543. Tel: 508-548-0990.
Catechesis/Religious Programs—Tel: 508-540-3723.
Students 59.

Chaplains of Public Institutions

Barnstable. *Barnstable County House of Correction.* Deacon Richard J. Murphy, Coord., 347 South St., Hyannis, 02601.

New Bedford. *Bristol Co. House of Correction & Eastern Massachusetts Correctional Alcohol Center.* Rev. Matthew Sullivan, SS.CC., 3 Adams St., P.O. Box 111, Fairhaven, 02719. Tel: 508-993-2442.

Awaiting Assignment:
Reverend Fathers—
Racine, Michael S.

Special Assignment:
Reverend Fathers—
Bowen, Donald J., St. James Society, Latin America
Cwiekowski, Bruce W., Catholic Charities, 213 S.E. 12th St., Portland, OR 97214
Morse, James H.
Morse, Richard D., Rome
Wilson, Richard D., Pontifical North American College, Via Del Gianicolo, 14, 00120 Vatican City State, Rome, Italy

---

Absent on Leave:
Reverend Fathers—
Andrade, Richard G.
Baker, William F.
Boulet, Norman J., 2402 Highland Ave., Fall River, MA 02720
Faria, Andre H., Jr.
Hamel, Philip N.
Robillard, Raymond A., 2402 Highland Ave., Fall River, MA 02720
Simoes, Gilbert, Box 706, Falmouth, MA 02541
Sousa, Douglas H.
Tripp, Kevin F.

Absent on Sick Leave:
Reverend Fathers—
de Mello, Arthur T., P.O. Box 40905, New Bedford, MA 02744-0005
McGlynn, Thomas E.

Retired:
Reverend Fathers—
Babbitt, William T., P.O. Box 1027, North Attleboro, MA 02761
Boivin, Louis R., 375 Elsbree St., Fall River, MA 02720
Boule, Roland B., 375 Elsbree St., Fall River, MA 02720
Burns, Edward J., 418-21 Quinaquisset Ave., Mashpee, MA 02649
Chabot, Bertrand R., 57 Wilfin Rd., South Yarmouth, MA 02135
Clark, James W., P.O. Box 139, Monument Beach, MA 02635-0169
Connors, Francis B., 9 Bayside Ln., Pocasset, MA 02559
d'Entremont, Clarence J., Middle West Pubnico, Yarmouth County, Nova Scotia B0W 1M0 Canada
Dalzell, James P., 161 Clark Ave., Hyde Park, MA 02136
Denehy, John F., 460 Grant Ave., Satellite Beach, FL 32937
Freitas, Daniel L., P.O. Box 411154, Melbourne, FL 32941-1154
Gamache, Daniel, 375 Elsbree St., Fall River, MA 02720
Joseph, Louis, 2022 San Angelo St., Fairfield, CA 94533

Jussaume, Andre P., 32 Churchill Rd., Lakeville, MA 02347
Jussaume, Lucien, 2400 S. Main St., Fall River, MA 02724
Kirby, Robert F., 375 Elsbree St., Fall River, MA 02720
Levesque, Rene R., P.O. Box 169, Cotuit, MA 02635-0169
Lyons, James F., 287 Cory St., Fall River, MA 02720
Maguire, Joseph D., P.O. Box 750, North Falmouth, MA 02556-0750
McCarthy, James, P.O. Box 3176, Pocasset, MA 02559
McIsaac, Edward F., 2446 Highland Ave., Fall River, MA 02720
Murphy, Clarence, 900 VFW Pkwy., West Roxbury, MA 02132
Murphy, John J., 386 Luther Ave., Somerset, MA 02726
O'Neill, Cornelius J., 2446 Highland Ave., Fall River, MA 02720
Oliveira, Joseph, 2446 Highland Ave., Fall River, MA 02720
Pereira, Luciano J., 996 Brayton Ave., Somerset, MA 02721
Powers, Joseph L., 15 Widgeon Rd., Falmouth, MA 02540
Robida, Raymond A., 375 Elsbree St., Fall River, MA 02720
Shovelton, William J., P.O. Box 1284, Harwich, MA 02645
Tavares, Antonino C., 230 Bonney St., New Bedford, MA 02744
Tetrault, Ralph D., 2402 Highland Ave., Fall River, MA 02720
Wallace, Francis X., P.O. Box 3737, Pocasset, MA 02559

Permanent Deacons:
Akin, David P., St. Pius X, South Yarmouth
Barrett, James M., Jr., Our Lady of Victory, Centerville
Bonneau, Bruce J., St. Julie Billiart, North Dartmouth
Bousquet, Louis A., St. Anthony, Mattapoisett
Branco, John F., Our Lady of the Angels, Fall River
Cipriano, A. Anthony, St. John the Evangelist, Attleboro
Cook, Chester O., St. Peter the Apostle, Provincetown
Cox, Ralph
Cwiekowski, John W., (Retired)
daCruz, Antonio, Our Lady of the Assumption, New Bedford
Dexter, Leonard C., Jr., St. John the Evangelist, Pocasset
Dresser, Richard M., St. Francis Xavier, Hyannis
Drinkwater, Oscar T., Unassigned
Emmert, John J., Corpus Christi, East Sandwich
Fantasia, Frank D., St. Elizabeth Seton, North Falmouth
Faria, Robert A., Our Lady of Health, Fall River
Fitzpatrick, John J., Holy Family, East Taunton
Fournier, Paul M., Holy Ghost, Attleboro
Guy, Michael P., St. Francis Xavier, Acushnet
Haddad, Victor, St. Thomas More, Somerset
Hill, Robert J., St. Joseph, Taunton
Hussey, Edward J., St. Patrick, Somerset
Lavallee, Maurice, St. Joseph, New Bedford
LeBlanc, Claude A., St. Mary, New Bedford
Lemay, Robert D., Christ the King, Mashpee
Macedo, Paul J., Our Lady of Mt. Carmel, New Bedford
Mador, Joseph F., Holy Redeemer, Chatham
Martin, William A., St. Patrick, Wareham
Marzelli, James, Jr., St. John the Evangelist, Pocasset
McCarthy, Dana G., Holy Trinity, West Harwich
McEnaney, Norman F., St. Joan of Arc, Orleans
Medeiros, Joseph P., Our Lady of Lourdes, Taunton
Meloni, James J., Jr., St. Mary's, North Attleboro
Mis, Franciszek W., St. Stanislaus Church, Fall River
Moniz, John de A., Espirito Santo, Fall River
Morency, Marcel G., St. Anne, New Bedford
Murphy, Richard J., Corpus Christi, East Sandwich
Murray, Michael E., Immaculate Conception, Taunton
Normandin, Robert G.L., St. Louis de France, Swansea
Pacheco, Eduardo M., Our Lady of the Assumption, New Bedford
Palanza, Thomas P., St. Mary, Mansfield
Pelland, Robert W., St. Stephen, Attleboro
Pires, Abilio dos A., Our Lady of Mt. Carmel, New Bedford
Prevost, Thomas F., St. Michael, Swansea
Racine, Leo W., St. Theresa, New Bedford
Reardon, Jeremiah J., St. Mary, South Dartmouth
Roma, Paul K., St. Elizabeth Seton, North Falmouth
Sasseville, Eugene H., Sacred Heart, New Bedford
Schondek, John H., St. Paul, Taunton
Shea, Mark G., Our Lady of Fatima, Swansea
Souza, Thomas J., St. Anthony, Taunton
St. Onge, Lawrence A., St. Bernard, Assonet
Stanley, Joseph P., Our Lady of Victory, Centerville
Surprenant, Robert L., St. John Neumann, East Freetown
Thomas, Walter D., St. Mary, Mansfield
Welch, John, St. Ann, Raynham
Zarella, George H., Holy Cross, South Easton

INSTITUTIONS LOCATED IN THE DIOCESE

[A] COLLEGES AND UNIVERSITIES

NORTH EASTON. *Holy Cross Fathers Religious*, 480 Washington St., 02356. Tel: 508-238-5942; Fax: 508-238-1297
For a complete listing, refer to the Colleges and Universities section.
Stonehill College, 02357. Tel: 508-238-1081; Fax: 508-230-3732
For a complete listing, refer to the Colleges and Universities section.

[B] HIGH SCHOOLS, DIOCESAN

FALL RIVER. *Bishop Connolly High School*, 373 Elsbree St., 02720. Tel: 508-676-1071; Fax: 508-676-8594. Mr. Anthony S. Nunes, Prin.; Bro. Richard J. Lunny, C.F.X., Academic Vice Prin. Priests 1; Brothers 4; Lay Teachers 30; Students 430.

ATTLEBORO. *Bishop Feehan High School*, 70 Holcott Dr., 02703. Tel: 508-226-6223; Fax: 508-226-7696. Mr. George Milot, Prin.; Rev. Michael F. Kuhn, Chap. Priests 1; Sisters 9; Lay Teachers 54; Students 828.
Our Lady of Mercy Convent, 70 Holcott Dr., 02703. Tel: 508-226-4608. Sr. Rose Angela McLellan, R.S.M., Supr. Sisters 28.

NORTH DARTMOUTH. *Bishop Stang High School*, 500 Slocum Rd., 02747-2999. Tel: 508-996-5602; Fax: 508-994-6756.
E-mail: admits@bishopstang.com
Web site: http://www.bishopstang.com
Theresa E. Dougall, Pres.; Mary Ann Miskel, Academic Prin.; Robert Zukowski, Prin. of Students; Rev. James S. Medeiros, Chap. Priests 1; Sisters 1; Lay Teachers 50; Support Staff 16; Students 570.

TAUNTON. *Coyle and Cassidy High School*, 2 Hamilton St., 02780. Tel: 508-823-6164.
E-mail: coyle@aol.com
Web site: http://www.coylecassidy.com
Mr. Dennis R. Poyant, Headmaster; Rev. John Denning, C.S.C. Priests 1; Sisters 2; Lay Teachers 53; Students 722.

[C] ELEMENTARY SCHOOLS, DIOCESAN

TAUNTON. *Taunton Catholic Middle School*, 61 Summer St., 02780. Tel: 508-822-0491; Fax: 508-824-0469.
E-mail: tcms@ici.net
Kathleen A. Simpson, Prin.; Rev. Pawel A. Swiercz, Chap. Lay Teachers 17; Students 300.

[D] ELEMENTARY SCHOOLS, PRIVATE

FALL RIVER. *Dominican Academy*, 37 Park St., 02721. Tel: 508-674-6100. Sr. Louise Synan, O.P., Prin. Sisters 1; Lay Teachers 9; Girls 158.

[E] RESIDENTIAL CHILD CARE FACILITIES

FALL RIVER. *St. Vincent's Home Corp.*, Main Campus: 2425 Highland Ave., 02720. Tel: 508-679-8511; Fax: 508-672-2558. Mr. John T. Weldon, Exec. Dir. Sisters 8; Total Staff 360; Children Residents 150.

[F] NURSERIES

NEW BEDFORD. *St. Saviour's Day Nursery*, 405 County St., 02740-4935. Tel: 508-997-0233. Sr. Marcella Rostkowski, C.R., Supr. Congregation of the Resurrection 5; Students 30.

[G] GENERAL HOSPITALS

FALL RIVER. *Saint Anne's Health Care Management Services, Inc.*, 795 Middle St., 02721-1798.
For a complete listing, refer to the Hospitals section.
Saint Anne's Health Care System, Inc., 795 Middle St., 02721-1798.
For a complete listing, refer to the Hospitals section.
Saint Anne's Hospital, 795 Middle St., 02721-1798. Tel: 508-674-5741.
For a complete listing, refer to the Hospitals section.

[H] SPECIAL HOSPITALS AND SANATORIA FOR INVALIDS

FALL RIVER. *Rose Hawthorne Lathrop Home*, 1600 Bay St., 02724. Tel: 508-673-2322; Fax: 508-679-5830.
For a complete listing, refer to the Special Care Facilities section.

[I] HOMES FOR AGED

FALL RIVER. *Catholic Memorial Home Inc.*, 2446-2474 Highland Ave., 02720-4599. Tel: 508-679-0011; Fax: 508-672-5858.
For a complete listing, refer to the Special Care Facilities section.

FAIRHAVEN. *Our Lady's Haven of Fairhaven Inc.*, 71 Center St., 02719. Tel: 508-999-4561.
For a complete listing, refer to the Special Care Facilities section.

NEW BEDFORD. *Sacred Heart Home*, 359 Summer St., 02740. Tel: 508-996-6751.
For a complete listing, refer to the Special Care Facilities section.

NORTH ATTLEBORO. *Madonna Manor Inc.*, 85 N. Washington St., 02760. Tel: 508-699-2740; Fax: 508-699-0481.
For a complete listing, refer to the Special Care Facilities section.

TAUNTON. *Bethany House Adult Day Care*, 72 Church Green, 02780. Tel: 508-822-9200.
For a complete listing, refer to the Special Care Facilities section.
Marian Manor Inc., 33 Summer St., 02780. Tel: 508-822-4885.
For a complete listing, refer to the Special Care Facilities section.

[J] MONASTERIES AND RESIDENCES OF PRIESTS AND BROTHERS

FALL RIVER. *Brothers of Christian Instruction*, 555 Eastern Ave., 02723. Tel: 508-672-5763. Bros. Daniel Caron, Supr.; Raymond Berube, Asst. Supr.; Walter Zwierchowski; Roger Millette; Norman Simoneau. Brothers 5; Faculty of Bishop Connolly High 3.
Cardinal Medeiros Residence-Retirement Facility for Priests, 375 Elsbree St., 02720. Tel: 508-675-1050; Fax: 508-675-2181.
Dominican House, 818 Middle St., 02721. Tel: 508-678-5322. Rev. Pierre E. Lachance, O.P., Supr.
Priests' Hostel, 2402 Highland Ave., 02720. Tel: 508-672-1632; Fax: 508-679-1422. In res. Revs. Raymond A. Robillard; Norman J. Boulet; Herbert T. Nichols.
St. John Vianney House, 818 Middle St., 02721-1734. Tel: 508-673-0377. Revs. John P. Cronin; Richard G. Andrade. Priests 5; Total Staff 3.
Vincentian Fathers Mission House, 601 June St., 02720. Tel: 508-672-1122.

ATTLEBORO. *La Salette Missionary Association*, 947 Park St., 02703. Tel: 508-222-0027. Very Rev. Dennis J. Loomis, M.S., Dir.
La Salette Provincial House, 947 Park St., P.O. Box 2965, 02703-0965. Tel: 508-222-6682. Immaculate Heart of Mary Province. Very Rev. Dennis J. Loomis, M.S., Prov. Supr.; Revs. Andre Patenaude, M.S.; William Slight, M.S. Priests 3; Brothers 2.
Priests of the Province serving outside the U.S.: Rev. Gerald Baril, M.S., John Paul II Residence, 1243 Kilborn Pl., #307, Ottawa, Canada, K1H 6K9. Rev. Gerard Comeau, M.S., Sanctuario de Nuestra Senora de LaSalette Siador-Silleda, Ponte Vedra, Espana. Rev. Camille Doucet, M.S., 3535 Park Ave., Montreal, Canada, PQ H2X 2H8. Rev. George Dube, M.S., Our Lady of LaSalette, 3535 Park Ave., Quebec H2Z-2H8, Canada. Rev. Andre Lussier, M.S., La Salette Fathers, P.O. Box AC 59, Quezon City 1100, Philippines. Rev. Joseph Gosselin, M.S., 229 Cadillac St., Ontario N8Y-2S8, Canada. Rev. Fernand Langevin, M.S., 270 Deragon St., Granby, Canada, PQ J2G 5J5. Rev. Paul M. Roy, M.S., 490 Charles St., Buckingham, PQ J8L-2K5, Canada. Rev. Robert Vachon, M.S., 4917 St. Urbain, Montreal, PQ H2T-2W1, Canada. Rev. Theodule Richard, M.S., 200 Baul. Roberts, Granby, Canada, PQ J2G 9I6. Rev. Roland Vandal, M.S., 3535 Park Ave., Montreal, Quebec H2X-2H8, Canada.
La Salette Shrine, 947 Park St., 02703. Tel: 508-222-5410; Fax: 508-222-6770. Revs. Rene Gelinas, M.S., Supr. & Gen. Counselor; Ernest J. Corriveau, M.S., Dir. In res. Revs. George Brennan, M.S.; Paul Dalbec, M.S.; Richard Delisle, M.S.; Gerald Forest, M.S.; Albert Fredette, M.S.; Joseph Fredette, M.S.; Armand Giroux, M.S.; Armand Gonthier, M.S.; Richard Landry, M.S.; Raymond Moquin, M.S.; Thomas Paris, M.S.; Manuel Pereira, M.S.; Joseph Ross, M.S.; Normand Theroux, M.S.; Bros. Armand Binette, M.S.; Lucien Brodeur, M.S.; Charles Caillouette, M.S.; Roger Moreau, M.S.; Leonard Melanson, M.S.; Robert Nichols, M.S.; Ronald Taylor, M.S.; Raymond Tetreault, M.S. Priests 16; Brothers 8.

FAIRHAVEN. *National Center of the Enthronement*, P.O. Box 111, 02719-01111. Tel: 508-999-2680.
E-mail: keane@sscc.org

Web site: http://www.sscc.org or www.ici.net.mantle
Bro. William F. Keane, SS.CC., Treas. Total Staff 2.
Sacred Hearts Provincial House, 77 Adams St., P.O. Box 111, 02719-0111. Tel: 508-993-2442; Fax: 508-996-5499.
Web site: http://www.sscc.org
Congregation of the Sacred Hearts of Jesus and Mary. Very Rev. Patrick F. Fanning, SS.CC., Prov.; Revs. David P. Reid, SS.CC., Treas.; William T. Penderghest, SS.CC.; Gabriel Healy, SS.CC., Mission Procurator & Dir. Devel.; David Lupo, SS.CC., Vocation Dir.; Matthew Sullivan, SS.CC.; Columban Crotty, SS.CC. Fathers 5. Damien Residence, 73 Adams St., P.O. Box 111, 02719-0111. Tel: 508-999-0500. Congregation of the Sacred Hearts of Jesus and Mary. Revs. William Davis, SS.CC., Dir.; Albert Dagnoli, SS.CC.; Albert Evans, SS.CC.; William Mitchell, SS.CC.; Roy Yurco, SS.CC.; Rene Gaudin, SS.CC.; Owen Goodwin, SS.CC.; Henry Creighton, SS.CC.; Bros. Damien O'Hare, SS.CC.; William Keane, SS.CC. Fathers 8; Brothers 2.
Priests of the Province Serving Abroad - In Japanese Missions: Very Rev. Michael Narita, SS.CC., Vice Prov.; Revs. Michael Coleman, SS.CC.; Cornelius Biffar, SS.CC.; John Yamada, SS.CC.; Lawrence Craig, SS.CC.; William Donegan, SS.CC.; William Ducey, SS.CC.; Louis Kawamata, SS.CC.; Edward Keeney, SS.CC.; Augustine Kobayashi, SS.CC.; Peter Kusunoki, SS.CC.; James E. McDonough, SS.CC.; Philip Murphy, SS.CC.; Daniel Perry, SS.CC.; Kenji Honma, SS.CC.; Bro. Francis Nakazawa, SS.CC.
In the Philippines: Rev. Andrew Healey, SS.CC.
In Nassau, Bahamas: Revs. Martin Gomes, SS.CC.; Michael Kelly, SS.CC.; Brian Marggraf, SS.CC.
In Abaco, Bahamas: Rev. Stanley Kolasa, SS.CC.
In Eleuthera, Bahamas: Revs. Patrick Killilea, SS.CC.; Patrick Fanning, SS.CC.
In India: Revs. William Petrie, SS.CC.; Michael Shanahan, SS.CC.; Bro. James Rukavina, SS.CC.
In Rome, Italy: Rev. Richard McNally, SS.CC., General Councillor.
Chaplains in Military Facilities: Rev. James Keefe, SS.CC., William Beaumont Army Medical Center, Chaplains Office, P.O. Box 70005, El Paso, TX, 79920-0005. Rev. Jude Morgan, SS.CC., V.A. Medical Center, First Ave., at 24th St., New York, NY, 10010-5050. Rev. Austin Nagle, SS.CC., V.A. Hospital, Belmont St., Brockton, 02401-5599.

NEW BEDFORD. *Marian Friary of Our Lady, Queen of the Seraphic Order*, 600 Pleasant St., 02740-6299. Tel: 508-996-8274. Mailing Address: P.O. Box 3003, 02741-3003. Revs. Peter Damian M. Fehlner, F.F.I., Guardian; Maximilian M. Warnisher, F.F.I., Vicar; Francis M. Pimental, F.F.I.; Alphonsus M. Sutton, F.F.I.; Martin M. Fonte, F.F.I. Priests 5; Brothers 16; Novices 2.

NORTH DARTMOUTH. *Holy Cross Mission House*, 824 Tucker Rd., 02747. Tel: 508-993-2238. Residence for Religious Priests and Brothers. Revs. Charles L. Wallen, C.S.C., Dir.; Thomas L. Campbell, C.S.C.; Mortimer A. Ferrick, C.S.C.; J. Marc Herbert; Thomas J. Tobin; John F. Dias, C.S.C.; Francis E. Grogan, C.S.C.; Bro. Joseph L. Morris, C.S.C.
St. Joseph's Hall, 800 Tucker Rd., 02747-3599. Tel: 508-996-2413. Revs. J. Robert Rioux, C.S.C., Dir. of Province Dev. & St. Joseph's Hall; William Condon, C.S.C. Tel: 508-993-1302; Bro. Thomas Mahon, C.S.C. Priests 2; Brothers 1.

ONSET. *St. Joseph Novitiate-Franciscan Friars*, Robinwood Rd., P.O. Box 63, 02558. Tel: 508-759-7280. Rev. Regis Gallo, O.F.M., Supr., Dir. of Novices; Bro. Juniper O'Connor, O.F.M., Cook. Novices: Bros. Rudolfo Borja, O.F.M.; Michael Corcione, O.F.M.; Roger Hall, O.F.M. Total Staff 1; Total in Residence 5.

[K] CONVENTS AND RESIDENCES FOR SISTERS

FALL RIVER. *Bishop's Residence Convent*, 394 Highland Ave., 02720. Tel: 508-675-1311. Sisters of St. Jeanne d'Arc. Sisters 3.
Convent of Dominican Sisters of Hope, 37 Park St., 02721. Tel: 508-676-3096. Sr. Catherine Walsh, O.P., Prioress Gen.
Convent of the Sacred Hearts, 47 Prospect Pl., 02720. Tel: 508-679-1044; 1045. Sisters of the Holy Union of the Sacred Hearts 20.
Holy Union Provincialate, 550 Rock St., 02720-3436. Tel: 508-678-3616; Fax: 508-324-0686.
E-mail: tmb@ici.net
Sr. Theresa M. Horvath, S.U.S.C., Prov. Holy Union Sisters.
Other Convents: Our Lady of Mercy Convent, 70 Holcott Dr., Attleboro, 02703. 18 Pear St., 02720. 161 Shawmut St., 02720. Sisters 3. Sacred Hearts Convent, 47 Prospect Pl., 02720-5403. Sisters 20. Catholic Memorial Home, 2446 Highland Ave., 02720. Sisters 7. 527 Rock St., 02720. Sisters 4. 570 Rock St., 02720. Sisters 7. St. Patrick's Convent, 55 Tuttle St., 02720. 601 King Philip St., Apt. #37, Raynham, 02767. 12 Woodridge Rd., Sandwich, 02563. 7 Bradford St., Taunton, 02780. Sisters 2. 34 Mitchell Dr., Apt. 71H, 02724. St. Anthony Convent, Taunton. Sisters 7. 82 Eldridge St., Taunton, 02780. 898 Robeson St., 02720.
St. Patrick's Convent, 55 Tuttle St., 02724. Tel: 508-673-0796. Sr. M. Romana Murphy, R.S.M., Coord. Sisters 8.
Sisters of Mercy, 2425 Highland Ave., 02720. Tel: 508-679-8511, Ext. 319. Sr. M. Lourdette Harrold, Contact. Sisters of Mercy of the Americas 5; Total Assisted 103; Total Staff 250.

ATTLEBORO. *Our Lady of Mercy Convent*, 70 Holcott Dr., 02703. Tel: 508-226-4608. Sr. Rose Angela McLellan, R.S.M., Local Coord. Sisters 21.

DIGHTON. *Dominican Sisters of Charity of the Presentation of the Blessed Virgin*, 3012 Elm St., 02715. Tel: 508-669-5425; 669-5023 (Novitiate); Fax: 508-669-6521. Sr. Joanna Fernandes, O.P., Prov. Supr. Provincial House-Residence, Residence for Aged Sisters, Novitiate. Sisters 23.

FAIRHAVEN. *Franciscan Sisters of the Immaculate*, 382 Main St., 02719. Tel: 508-992-0482.
E-mail: fsi@ici.net
Web site: http://www.connix.com/'/.FIsisters/
Sisters of the Sacred Hearts. Regional Headquarters, 35 Huttleston Ave., 02719-3154. Tel: 508-994-9341; Fax: 508-990-1967. Legal Title: *Sisters of the Sacred Hearts of Jesus and Mary and of Perpetual Adoration, SS.CC.* Sr. Dolores Pavao, SS.CC., Regional Supr., 44 Adams St., 02719. Tel: 508-994-5917. Sr. Lillian Cookson, SS.CC., Local Supr., 491 Hood St., Fall River, 02720. Tel: 508-675-7716. Sr. Margaret Woods, SS.CC., Local Supr. Sisters in Region 14.

HARWICHPORT. *Contemplative Sisters of the Good Shepherd*, 88 Bank St., 02646. Tel: 508-432-5582.

NEW BEDFORD. *Misioneras Guadalupanas del Espiritu Santo*, 2 Acushnet Ave., 02744. Tel: 508-997-8729. Sr. Aida Sansor A., M.G.Sp.S., Supr.; Sr. M. Candelaria Hernandez; Sr. Soledad Mendoza; Sr. Ladivel Diaz; Sr. Obdulia Olivar. Sisters 5.
Our Lady of Mercy Convent, 14 Summer St., 02740. Tel: 508-992-3694. Sr. Jeannette Thomas, R.S.M., Coord. Sisters 4.
Sisters of Mercy, 15 Lemos St., 02740. Tel: 508-992-4947. Sr. M. Nathan Doherty, R.S.M., Contact Person. Sisters 3.

NORTH DARTMOUTH. *Diocesan Family Life Center*, 500 Slocum Rd., 02747. Tel: 508-999-4620; Fax: 508-999-6430. Total Staff 3.
Dominican Sisters of Hope, 856 Tucker Rd., 02747. Tel: 508-996-1305. Sisters 7.

TAUNTON. *Our Lady of Lourdes Convent*, 55 First St., 02780. Tel: 508-822-9206. Sr. M. Margretta Sol, Contact Person. Sisters of Mercy of the Union 3.
Villa Fatima, 90 County St., 02780. Tel: 508-822-6282. Sisters of St. Dorothy. Sr. Rosalie Patrello, S.S.D., Local Coord. Professed Sisters 10.

WAREHAM. *St. Patrick's Missionary Cenacle*, 86 High St., 02571. Tel: 508-295-0780. Outreach to the homebound handicapped. Missionary Servants of the Most Blessed Trinity 1.

[L] RETREAT HOUSES

ATTLEBORO. *La Salette Center for Christian Living*, 947 Park St., 02703-0965. Tel: 508-222-8530; Fax: 508-222-8558.
E-mail: lasalett@ma.ultranet.com
Web site: http://www.ultranet.com/~lasalett
Revs. Richard Landry, M.S., Dir.; Fern Cassista, M.S.; Mrs. Karen Laroche; Mr. Mark Morisseau; Bros. David Dumaine, M.S.; Roger A. Moreau, M.S. In res. Rev. Normand Theroux, M.S. Priests 2; Total Staff 12; Total Assisted 4,200.

EAST FREETOWN. *Cathedral Camp Retreat Center*, 167 Middleboro Rd., P.O. Box 428, 02717-0428. Tel: 508-763-3994.
E-mail: joseph_marie2@juno.com
Sr. Joseph Marie Levesque, O.P., Dir. Total Staff 6; Total in Residence 1.

NORTH EASTON. *Holy Cross Fathers Retreat House*, 490 Washington St., Rte. 138, 02356-1294. Tel: 508-238-2051. Revs. Thomas E. Lawton, C.S.C., Dir.; Richard H. Sullivan, C.S.C., Asst. Dir. Priests 2.

WAREHAM. *Sacred Hearts Retreat Center*, 226 Great Neck Rd., 02571. Tel: 508-295-0100; 295-1450.
E-mail: retreats@sscc.org
Web site: http://www.sscc.org/wareham
Congregation of the Sacred Hearts of Jesus and Mary and of the Perpetual Adoration of the Most Blessed Sacrament. Revs. Thomas McElroy, SS.CC., Dir.; Gabriel Healy, SS.CC.; David Lupo, SS.CC.; Bro. Joseph Fandel, SS.CC. Priests 3; Brothers 1; Sisters 1.

[M] DEPARTMENT OF CATHOLIC SOCIAL SERVICES AND SPECIAL APOSTOLATES

FALL RIVER. *Catholic Social Services of Fall River*, 783 Slade St., P.O. Box M-S, Station, 02724. Tel: 508-674-4681; Fax: 508-675-2224.
E-mail: arlmac@aol.com
Arlene A. McNamee, Exec. Dir. Program Directors: Mary Lou Mancini, M.Ed., L.C.S.W., Pregnancy & Adoption Services; Maria C. Pereira, M.S.W., L.I.C.S.W., Counseling Services; Susan E. Desrosiers, M.S.W., L.S.W., Sexual Abuse Prevention.
Catholic Social Services of Attleboro, 10 Maple St., Attleboro, 02703. Tel: 508-226-4780.
Catholic Social Services of New Bedford, 59 Rockland St., New Bedford, 02740. Tel: 508-997-7337.
Catholic Social Services of Cape Cod, 261 South St., Hyannis, 02601. Tel: 508-771-6771.
Catholic Social Services of Taunton, 78 Broadway, Taunton, 02780. Tel: 508-824-3264.
Reaching Out, 311 Hooper St., Tiverton, RI, 02878. Tel: 401-624-9270.
St. Mathieu's Residence for Women, 189 Wellington St., 02720. Tel: 508-675-1868.
Special Apostolates, Department of, 783 Slade St., P.O. Box M-S, Station, 02724. Tel: 508-674-4681. Arlene A. McNamee, Executive Dir.
Campaign For Human Development Apostolate. Craig Gaspard, Community Organizer.
Apostolate for Persons with Developmental Disabilities, 243 Forest St., 02721. Tel: 508-679-8373 (Voice); 679-4277 (TTY). Rev. Joseph F. Viveiros, Dir.
Spanish Apostolate, 2 Acushnet Ave., New Bedford, 02744. Tel: 508-997-8729. Gloria Rodriquez; Rev. Paul E. Canuel, Dir., P.O. Box 40605, New Bedford, 02744-0006. Tel: 508-997-8729.

[N] CAMPS AND COMMUNITY CENTERS

FALL RIVER. *Diocesean Catholic Youth Organization*, 42 Chicago St., 02721. Tel: 508-675-7503. Rev. Jay T. Maddock, Diocesan & Area Dir.
Fall River Area Catholic Youth Organization, 403 Anawan St., 02720. Tel: 508-672-9644.
New Bedford Area Catholic Youth Organization, Kennedy Youth Center, 377 County St., New Bedford, 02740. Tel: 508-996-0536.
Taunton Area Catholic Youth Organization, 61 Summer St., Taunton, 02780. Tel: 508-822-5218. Deacon Thomas J. Souza, Area Dir.

[O] NEWMAN CENTERS AND CAMPUS MINISTRY

FALL RIVER. *Bristol Community College Newman Center*, 777 Elsbree St., 02720-7395.
E-mail: srannett@bristol.mass.edu
Sr. Annette Bibeau, S.S.A., (Full Time). Total Staff 1.
Diocesan Education Center, 423 Highland Ave., 02720. Tel: 508-678-2828; Fax: 508-674-4218.
E-mail: diocese@ultranet.com
Rev. William T. Garland, O.S.A., Dir. of Education; Mr. James A. McNamee, Supt. of Schools; Deacon Bruce Bonneau, Dir. Religious Education; Rev. Mark R. Hession, Dir. Continuing Formation of Clergy; Sr. Anne M. Landry, C.N.D., Asst. Supt. of Schools; Lisa M. Gulino, Dir. of Adult Education.

BUZZARDS BAY. *Massachusetts Maritime Academy Newman Center*, 141 Main St., 02532.

NORTH DARTMOUTH. *University of Massachusetts Dartmouth Catholic Campus Ministry*, 285 Old Westport Rd., 02747-2300. Tel: 508-999-8872.
E-mail: mcarvill@umassd.edu
Web site: http://www.umassd.edu/2Student/CampusCenter/CatholicCampus/
Campus Ministers: Rev. Michael Carvill; Sr. Madeleine Tacy, O.P. Total Staff 2.

NORTON. *Wheaton College Newman Center.*
E-mail: whanawalt@stonehill.edu
Web site: http://www.stonehill.edu
Rev. Thomas M. Feeley, C.S.C., Chap., Holy Cross Residence, 480 Washington St., N. Easton, 02356.

TAUNTON. *Paul A. Dever State School (For Retarded) Newman Center*, Box 631, 02780. Tel: 508-824-5881. Rev. William J. Beston, C.S.C., Chap.

WEST BARNSTABLE. *Cape Cod Community College Newman Center.*

[P] MISCELLANEOUS LISTINGS

FALL RIVER. *Carmelite Convent of Dartmouth, Inc.*, c/o P.O. Box 2577, 02722.
Community Action for Better Housing, Inc., 783 Slade St., P.O. Box M, S. Station, 02724.
Diocesan Facilities Self-Insurance Group, Inc., P.O. Box 1110, 02722.
Priestly Fraternity of the Missionaries of St. Charles Borromeo, Inc., 420 Bradford Ave., 02721. Tel: 508-676-8603.
E-mail: mcarvill@umassd.edu
Revs. Michael Carvill; Vincent Nagle; Antonio Lopez.
St. Francis' Residence. A program of Catholic Social Services. 166, 182 and 196 Whipple St., 02721. Tel: 508-676-9332. Arlene A. McNamee, Executive Dir.; Susan E. Desrosiers, Coord.; Mrs. Zilda Fagundes, House Mgr. Residence for Women. Boarders 34.

Saint Mary's Education Fund, Inc., P.O. Box 2577, 02722. Tel: 508-675-1311.

Youth Apostles, c/o Deacon David Sharland, 327 2nd St., 02721-2007. Tel: 508-672-2755.
E-mail: dmsharland@juno.com
Web site: http://www.catholic.org/youth/youthapostles
Deacon David Sharland, Dir. Total in Residence 4.

NEW BEDFORD. *The Institute of the Incarnate Word, Inc.*, 306 Ashley Blvd, 02746. Tel: 508-672-9303.
E-mail: benoive@aol.com
Web site: http://www.ive.org
Revs. Benito M. Lagos, I.V.E.; Jose Del Val, I.V.E.; Gustavo Dominguez, I.V.E.

Missionaries of Charity, 556 County St., 02740. Shelter for homeless women. Total in Residence 4; Total Assisted 54.

St. Mary's Home of New Bedford, Inc. c/o P.O. Box 2577, Fall River, 02722. Tel: 508-675-1311.

RELIGIOUS INSTITUTES OF MEN REPRESENTED IN THE DIOCESE

For further details refer to the corresponding bracketed number in the Religious Institutes of Men or Women section.

[0320]—*Brothers of Christian Instruction.*—F.I.C.
[0330]—*Brothers of the Christian Schools.*
[0600]—*Brothers of the Congregation of Holy Cross.*
[]—*Capuchin Recollects Friars.*
[1330]—*Congregation of the Mission.*—C.M.
[1140]—*Congregation of the Sacred Hearts of Jesus and Mary.*—SS.CC.
[0480]—*Conventual Franciscans.* (Buffalo, NY).—O.F.M.Conv.
[0470]—Franciscan (Order of Friars Minor Capuchin). (St. Augustine Prov.).—O.F.M.Cap.
[0520]—*Franciscan Friars.* (Immaculate Conception Prov.).—O.F.M.
[0533]—*Franciscan Friars of the Immaculate.*—F.F.I.
[]—*The Institute of the Incarnate Word.*—I.V.E.
[0690]—*Jesuit Fathers and Brothers.*—S.J.
[0720]—*The Missionaries of Our Lady of La Salette.*—M.S.
[0870]—*Montfort Missionaries.*—S.M.M.
[0430]—*Order of Preachers (Dominicans).*—O.P.
[]—*Priestly Fraternity of the Missionaries of St. Charles Borromeo Order.*—C.S.
[0610]—*Priests of the Congregation of the Holy Cross.* (Eastern Prov.).—C.S.C.

RELIGIOUS INSTITUTES OF WOMEN REPRESENTED IN THE DIOCESE

[]—*Capuchin Recollects Sisters.*
[0330]—*Carmelite Sisters of the Aged and Infirm.*—O.Carm.
[3815]—*Congregation of the Sisters of St. Joan of Arc.*—S.J.A.
[1830]—*Contemplative Sisters of the Good Shepherd.*—C.G.S.
[0750]—*Daughters of the Charity of the Sacred Heart of Jesus.* (Sacred Heart Prov.).—F.C.S.C.J.
[1070-23]—*Dominican Sisters.*—O.P.
[1100]—*Dominican Sisters of Charity of the Presentation of the Blessed Virgin.*—O.P.
[]—*Dominican Sisters of Hope.*—O.P.
[2580]—*Institute of the Sisters of Mercy of the Americas.* (Hartford, CT; Manchester, NH).—R.S.M.
[3790]—*Institute of the Sisters of St. Dorothy.*—S.S.D.
[2790]—*Missionary Servants of the Most Blessed Trinity.*—M.S.B.T.
[]—*Missioneras Guadalupanas del Espirito Santo.*
[3240]—*Poor Sisters of Jesus Crucified and the Sorrowful Mother.*
[3410]—*Religious of Christian Education.*—R.C.E.
[3450]—*Religious of Jesus and Mary.*—R.J.M.
[2070]—*Religious of the Holy Union of the Sacred Hearts.* (Immaculate Heart and Sacred Heart Provs.).—S.U.S.C.
[3650]—*Servants of Our Lady, Queen of the Clergy.*—S.R.C.
[0560]—*Sisters of Charity of Quebec (Grey Nuns).*—S.C.Q.
[0590]—*Sisters of Charity of Saint Elizabeth (Convent Station).*—S.C.
[0640]—*Sisters of Charity of St. Vincent de Paul (Halifax).*—S.C.
[3000]—*Sisters of Notre Dame De Namur.*—S.N.D.deN.
[3720]—*Sisters of Saint Anne.*—S.S.A.
[1705]—*The Sisters of St. Francis of Assisi.*—O.S.F.
[3830-16]—*Sisters of St. Joseph.*—S.S.J.
[3860]—*Sisters of St. Joseph of Cluny.*—S.J.C.
[2980]—*Sisters of the Congregation of Notre Dame.*—C.N.D.
[3180]—*Sisters of the Cross and Passion.*—C.P.
[1830]—*Sisters of the Good Shepherd.*—R.G.S.
[]—*Sisters of the Holy Cross.*
[]—*Sisters of the Holy Cross and of the Seven Dolors.*—C.S.C.
[3480]—*Sisters of the Resurrection.*—C.R.
[3690]—*Sisters of the Sacred Hearts of Perpetual Adoration.*—SS.CC.
[4048]—*Society of the Sisters, Faithful Companions of Jesus.*—F.C.J.

DIOCESAN CEMETERIES

FALL RIVER. *Notre Dame.*
St. John.
St. Mary.
St. Patrick.
ATTLEBORO. *St. John.*
St. Stephen.
EAST FALMOUTH. *St. Anthony.*
HYANNIS. *St. Francis.*
MANSFIELD. *St. Mary.*
MATTAPOISETT. *St. Anthony.*
NANTUCKET. *St. Mary.*
NEW BEDFORD. *St. John Sacred Heart.*
St. Mary.
NORTH ATTLEBORO. *St. Mary.*
NORTH EASTON. *Immaculate Conception.*
OAK BLUFFS. *Sacred Heart.*
PROVINCETOWN. *St. Peter.*
SANDWICH. *St. Peter.*
SOMERSET. *St. Patrick.*
TAUNTON. *St. Francis.*
St. James.
St. Joseph.
St. Mary.
TRURO. *Sacred Heart.*
WAREHAM. *St. Patrick.*
WELLFLEET. *Our Lady of Lourdes.*
WEST HARWICH. *Holy Trinity.*

NECROLOGY

† Bessette, Ernest N., (Retired). —Died July 17, 1997.
† Gauthier, Rene G., Fall River, MA, St. Jean Baptiste. —Died Jan. 6, 1997.
† Mendonca, Rev. Msgr. Luiz G., (Retired). —Died Feb. 21, 1997.
† Sullivan, Walter A., South Dartmouth, MA, St. Mary. —Died May 1, 1997.

Diocese of Fargo

(Dioecesis Fargensis)

Most Reverend

JAMES S. SULLIVAN, D.D.

Bishop of Fargo; ordained June 4, 1955; consecrated Auxiliary Bishop of Lansing September 21, 1972; appointed Bishop of Fargo April 2, 1985; installed May 30, 1985. *Res., Bishop's House, 608 Broadway, P.O. Box 1750, Fargo, ND, 58107.*

Chancery Office: 1310 Broadway, Box 1750, Fargo, ND, 58107. Tel.: 701-235-6429; Fax: 701-235-0296.

Web site address: www.fargodiocese.org

E-mail address: web@fargodiocese.org

Corporate title: *The Diocese of Fargo.*

FORMERLY DIOCESE OF JAMESTOWN.

ESTABLISHED NOVEMBER 12, 1889; TRANSFERRED TO FARGO, APRIL 6, 1897

Square Miles 35,786.

Comprises the Counties of Barnes, Benson, Bottineau, Cass, Cavalier, Dickey, Eddy, Foster, Grand Forks, Griggs, Kidder, LaMoure, Logan, McHenry, McIntosh, Nelson, Pembina, Pierce, Ramsey, Ransom, Richland, Rolette, Sargent, Sheridan, Steele, Stutsman, Towner, Traill, Walsh and Wells in the State of North Dakota.

For legal titles of parishes and diocesan institutions, consult the Chancery Office.

STATISTICAL OVERVIEW

Personnel	
Bishop	1
Priests: Diocesan Active in Diocese	107
Priests: Active Outside Diocese	8
Priests: Diocesan in Foreign Missions	1
Priests: Retired, Sick or Absent	40
Number of Diocesan Priests	156
Religious Priests in Diocese	7
Ordinations:	
Diocesan Priests	9
Religious Priests	3
Transitional Deacons	2
Permanent Deacons in Diocese	35
Total Brothers	8
Total Sisters	153
Parishes	
Parishes	159
With Resident Pastor:	
Resident Diocesan Priests	82
Resident Religious Priests	14
Without Resident Pastor:	
Administered by Priests	63
Closed Parishes	1
Professional Ministry Personnel:	
Brothers	1
Sisters	12
Lay Ministers	44
Welfare	
Catholic Hospitals	8
Total Assisted	77,712
Health Care Centers	51
Total Assisted	904
Homes for the Aged	5
Total Assisted	485
Day Care and Extended Day Care Centers	35
Total Assisted	280
Special Centers for Social Services	2
Total Assisted	16,071
Other Institutions	9
Total Assisted	270
Educational	
Seminaries, Diocesan	1
Students from This Diocese	13
Students from Other Diocese	7
Diocesan Students in Other Seminaries	29
Students Religious	4
Total Seminarians	46
High Schools, Diocesan and Parish	1
Total Students	318
Elementary Schools, Diocesan and Parish	13
Total Students	2,022
Catechesis/Religious Education:	
High School Students	4,073
Elementary Students	7,652
Total Students Under Catholic Instruction	14,093
Teachers in the Diocese:	
Brothers	4
Sisters	9
Lay Teachers	174
Vital Statistics	
Receptions into the Church:	
Infant Baptism Totals	1,052
Adult Baptism Totals	48
Received into Full Communion	224
First Communions	1,409
Confirmations	1,748
Marriages:	
Catholic	275
Interfaith	281
Total Marriages	556
Deaths	857
Total Catholic Population	79,141
Total Population	391,000

Former Bishops—Rt. Rev. JOHN SHANLEY, D.D., ord. 1874; cons. Dec. 27, 1889; died July 16, 1909.—Most Rev. JAMES O'REILLY, D.D., ord. June 24, 1880; cons. May 19, 1910; installed June 1, 1910; died Dec. 19, 1934.—His Eminence ALOISIUS CARDINAL MUENCH, ord. June 8, 1913; appt. Bishop of Fargo, Aug. 10, 1935; cons. Oct. 15, 1935; installed Nov. 6, 1935; appt. Apostolic Visitator for Germany, July 8, 1946 granted personal title of Archbishop, Nov. 1, 1950; appt. Papal Nuncio to Germany, March 10, 1951; created Cardinal Priest and elevated to the Roman Curia, Dec. 14, 1959; died Feb. 15, 1962.—Most Rev. LEO F. DWORSCHAK, ord. May 29, 1926; appt. Coadjutor Bishop of Rapid City, June 23, 1946; cons. August 22, 1946; appt. Auxiliary Bishop of Fargo, April 10, 1947; succeeded to See, May 10, 1960; resigned and retired Sept. 8, 1970; died Nov. 5, 1976.—Most Rev. JUSTIN A. DRISCOLL, ord. July 28, 1945; appt. Bishop of Fargo, Sept. 8, 1970; ord. Bishop of Fargo and installed Oct. 28, 1970; died Nov. 19, 1984.

Chancery Office—1310 Broadway, Box 1750, Fargo, 58107. Tel: 701-235-6429; Fax: 701-235-0296.

Vicar General—Rev. Msgr. WENDELYN VETTER, V.G.

Moderator of the Curia—Rev. Msgr. WENDELYN VETTER.

Chancellor—Very Rev. ROBERT IRWIN.

Vice-Chancellor—Rev. DANIEL PILON, J.C.L.

Vice-Chancellor/Priest Secretary to the Bishop—Rev. STEVEN REISKE.

Vice-Chancellor for Supra Diocesan Affairs—J. RITTER HARSY.

Archivist—Very Rev. ROBERT IRWIN; Sr. MARY JAMES MERRICK, O.S.F.

Fiscal Manager—SCOTT HOSELTON, C.P.A.

Diocesan Tribunal—2537 S. University Dr., Fargo, 58103. Tel: 701-235-7279.

Officialis—Rev. Msgr. WENDELYN VETTER, V.G.

Vice-Officialis—Rev. DANIEL PILON, J.C.L., Adjutant Judicial Vicar.

Promotor Justitiae—Very Rev. VALERIAN PACZEK, J.C.D.

Defensor Vinculi—Very Rev. VALERIAN PACZEK, J.C.D.

Judges—Rev. ALBERT H. BINDER; Very Rev. JOHN D. ANDERSON; Rev. Msgr. WENDELYN VETTER, V.G.; Very Rev. VAL GROSS; Revs. AL M. BITZ; LEONARD BURCKHARD; DANIEL PILON.

Advocates—MARILYN BITTNER; Sr. CELINE FOY, P.B.V.M.; ELLEN O'CONNOR; Deacon DONALD TINGUELY; IONE NIELAND.

Notaries—Very Rev. ROBERT IRWIN; SCOTT HOSELTON, C.P.A.

Diocesan College of Consultors—Rev. Msgr. WENDELYN VETTER, V.G.; Very Rev. VAL GROSS; Revs. DONALD LEIPHON; BRIAN DONAHUE; FRANKLIN MILLER; Revs. DALE KINZLER; GERALD MCCARTHY; PETER HUGHES, C.S.Sp.

Deans—Southeast: Very Rev. JOHN D. ANDERSON, Hankinson; East Central South: Very Rev. VAL GROSS, West Fargo; East Central North: Very Rev. ROMAN E. LUDWIG, Larimore; North East: Very Rev. GERALD MYERS, Walhalla; North Central: Very Rev. ROBERT SKAROHLID, Lakota; North West: Very Rev. GEORGE SCHNEIDER, Rolla; West Central: Very Rev. JOSEPH P. SENGER, Velva; South Central: Very Rev. BERNARD PFAU, Jamestown; South West: Very Rev. ADAM HASEY, Oakes.

Diocesan Pastoral Council—Most Rev. JAMES S. SULLIVAN, Pres. Priest Representatives: Area 1, Rev. DONALD A. LEIPHON, Area 2, Very Rev. ROMAN LUDWIG, Area 3, Rev. LEO KINNEY, Area 4, Rev. CHAD WILHELM. Deacon Representatives: Deacon GEORGE ETHIER. Sister Representatives: Sr. PAULA RINGUETTE, P.B.V.M.; Sr. MARLYSS DIONNE, S.M.P. Lay Representatives: Deanery 1, KATHLEEN SKROCH, Deanery 2, STUART LONGTIN, Deanery 3, SUSAN SPICER, Deanery 4, JEFFREY BATES, Deanery 5, LINDA CULLMER, Deanery 6, JAMIE BRADLEY, Deanery 7, BETTY REGSTAD, Deanery 8, DARLENE WESHNEVSKI, Deanery 9, GARY HORSAGER; FRANCIS MLARNIK, Lay Member at Large; Deacon DAVID EBLEN, Chm. Ex-Officio Members: Rev. Msgr. WENDELYN VETTER, V.G.; Very Rev. ROBERT IRWIN, Chancellor; Rev. TIMOTHY SCHROEDER; JO RITTER HARSY, Vice Chancellor & DPC Sec.; SCOTT HOSELTON, Fiscal Mgr.; Rev. GREGORY SCHLESSELMANN; Dr. SHERRYL HOUDEK; TERRY KNOEPFLE. Emeritus Members: ROBERT ARTZ; Revs. PETER HUGHES, C.S.Sp.; JAMES MEYER; Sr. MARY JAMES MERRICK, O.S.F.; BERNIE WAGNER; RALPH ERICKSON.

Diocesan Offices and Directors

Corporate Board—Most Rev. JAMES S. SULLIVAN; Rev. Msgr. WENDELYN VETTER, V.G.; Very Rev. ROBERT IRWIN; Rev. Msgr. ALLAN F. NILLES; Very Rev. JOHN D. ANDERSON; TERRY W. KNOEPFLE; SCOTT HOSELTON, C.P.A.

Administration Board of Minor Seminary—Rev. Msgr. ANTHONY R. PESCHEL; Rev. Msgr. WENDELYN VETTER, V.G.,Consilium pro Re Temporali; Very Rev. VAL GROSS, Oeconomus.

Apostleship of Prayer—Very Rev. ROMAN LUDWIG, Dir.

Diocesan Finance Council—Most Rev. JAMES S. SULLIVAN, Pres.; Rev. Msgr. WENDELYN VETTER, V.G.; Very Rev. ROBERT IRWIN; GERALD F. HAMERLIK; GARY DIETZ; MICHAEL FIX; RAY SIMON; SCOTT A. HOSELTON, C.P.A.; Very Rev. VAL GROSS; TERRY W. KNOEPFLE; Rev. FRANKLIN MILLER.

The Catholic Church Expansion Fund of the Diocese of Fargo—Most Rev. JAMES S. SULLIVAN; Rev. Msgr. WENDELYN VETTER, V.G.; Very Rev. ROBERT IRWIN; Rev. Msgr. ALLAN F. NILLES; Very Rev. JOHN D. ANDERSON; SCOTT A. HOSELTON, C.P.A.; TERRY W. KNOEPFLE.

Censor Librorum—Rev. ROBERT LALIBERTE.

Catholic Family Service—ROGER E. SCHWINGHAMMER, Dir., *2537 S. University Dr., Fargo, 58103.* Tel: 701-235-4457; Fax: 701-239-8266., Grand Forks Office: *505 University Ave., Ste. 1, Grand Forks, 58203.* Tel: 701-775-4196; Fax: 701-775-0129.

Office of Liturgy and Worship—Bro. VINCENT LOMONACO, O.S.F., Dir. Tel: 701-235-6429.

Continuing Education of Priests—Rev. PAUL DUCHSCHERE, Chm.

Due Process Board Members (Conciliators)—Rev. Msgr. ALLAN F. NILLES, Chm.; Revs. EDWARD SHERMAN; GERALD MCCARTHY; JOSEPH AXTMANN; PETER GRADY; Sr. MARY JANE REIBER, O.S.F.; Sr. LEONIDA SCHMIDT, O.S.F.; Sr. ELIZABETH ROSE MUSCHA, S.M.P.; JOHN D. KELLY; PAUL CRARY; JOSEPH BLACK.

Ecumenical Commission—Rev. PAUL SCHUSTER.

Vicar for Diocesan Development—Very Rev. VAL GROSS. *Director of Development*—DOUG TOLLEFSON. Tel: 701-235-6429.

Director of God's Gift Appeal—DOUG TOLLEFSON.

Catholic School Network Office—DOUG JACOBSON, Prin.; Dr. SHERRYL HOUDEK, Supt., *705 13th Ave. N., P.O. Box 7100, Fargo, 58109.* Tel: 701-293-3780.

Villa Nazareth—Sr. PAULA RINGUETTE, P.B.V.M., Pres., *3004 11th St. S., Fargo, 58103.* Tel: 701-235-8217.

Holy Childhood Association—Rev. JOSEPH J. SENGER, Dir., *St. Cecilia's Church, 201 Second Ave. W., Velva, 58790.* Tel: 701-338-2663.

Migrant Workers Apostolate—Rev. C. JAMES JEFFREY, Dir., All mail to go to: *Church of St. Bridget, 201 1st St. S., Box 280, Cavalier, 58220.*

Media Office—GREG SMITH.

The "New Earth"-Diocesan Newspaper—CHARLES ELDREDGE.

North Dakota Catholic Conference—CHRISTOPHER DODSON, *227 W. Broadway, Ste. 2, Bismarck, 58501.*

Parish Liaisons—GREG SMITH.

Permanent Diaconate—Deacons DAVE EBLEN; MATT PROM.

Priests Mutual Aid Fund—Most Rev. JAMES S. SULLIVAN, Chm.; Very Rev. VAL GROSS, Sec. & Treas.

Priests Eucharistic League—Rev. JOSEPH R. HUEBSCH, Dir.

Priests Personnel Board—Very Rev. JOHN D. ANDERSON, Chm.; Revs. PHILLIP ACKERMAN; Rev. THOMAS KRUPICH; MATT LANZ; GERALD MYERS.

Presbyteral Council—Rev. TIMOTHY SCHROEDER, Chm., All mail to go to: *Church of the Nativity, 1825 S. 11th St., Fargo, 58103.*

Propagation of the Faith—Rev. JOSEPH SENGER, Dir., *St. Cecilia's Church, 201 Second Ave. W., Velva, 58790.*

Retreats—GEORGE LACHER, Bldg. Dir., *Queen of Peace Retreat Center, 1310 Broadway, Fargo, 58102.* Tel: 701-293-9286.

Rural Life Conference—Deacon JAMES WEST, Coord., *Reynolds, Rte. 1, Box 104C, Thompson, 58278.* Tel: 701-599-2501.

St. Vincent de Paul Society—ORVILLE KELLY, Pres., *1425 First Ave. S., Fargo, 58102.* Tel: 701-235-5944. DELORES HACKENBERG, *3627 9th Ave. N., Grand Forks, 58203.* Tel: 701-775-9911.

Technology/Computer Coordinator—WILLIAM LAGE.

Office for Evangelization—*P.O. Box 1750, Fargo, 58107.* Tel: 701-235-6429.

Department for Catholic Education and Formation—Rev. GREGORY SCHLESSELMANN.

Catechesis—Rev. MICHAEL HICKIN, S.T.B.

Youth/Young Adults—KURT GUNWALL, B.A.

Evangelization/Adult Ed.—Deacon DAVID EBLEN.

Resource Center-Department Admin. Asst.—JACINTA GOERING, B.S.

Catechesis/Youth Secretary—JENNY KORZMO.

School Dept. Secretary—ANDRE HORST.

Department for Catholic Schools—Dr. SHERRYL HOUDEK, Supt. THOMAS FREI, Asst. Supt.

Vicar for Religious—Rev. DONALD A. LEIPHON, All mail to: *Carmel of Mary, 17775 78th St., S.E., Wahpeton, 58075.*

Vocation Coordinator—Rev. FRANKLIN MILLER, *Cardinal Muench Seminary, 100-35th Ave. N.E., Fargo, 58102.*

Office of Priestly Formation—Rev. BRIAN DONAHUE.

Office of Permanent Deacon Formation—Rev. BRIAN DONAHUE.

Diocesan Pension Plan for Lay Employees—SCOTT A. HOSELTON, C.P.A.

Pro-Life—RACHELLE SAUVAGEAU, Coord. Tel: 701-235-6429.

Catholic Cemeteries—Very Rev. ROBERT IRWIN.

Diocesan Planning and Survey Board—Very Revs. JOHN D. ANDERSON; VAL GROSS; JOSEPH T. SENGER; DALE LAGODINSKI; ROBERT SKAROHLID; GEORGE SCHNEIDER; ROMAN LUDWIG; BERNARD PFAU; ADAM HASEY.

Diocesan Choir—Bro. VINCENT LOMONACO, O.S.F.

Diocesan Building Committee—Rev. LEONARD LOEGERING, Chm.

World Apostolate of Fatima (Blue Army)—Rev. DAMIAN HILS.

Cursillo Movement—Very Rev. JOHN D. ANDERSON.

Engaged Encounter—Rev. GERALD A. MCCARTHY.

Marriage Encounter—Rev. DALE KINZLER.

Catholic Scouting—GREG SMITH.

Apostolate for Spanish Speaking—Rev. C. JAMES JEFFREY, *St. Bridget Church, Box 280, Cavalier, 58220.*

Apostolate for Migrant Workers—Rev. C. JAMES JEFFREY.

Beginning Experience Apostolate—Rev. Msgr. WENDELYN VETTER, V.G.

Clergy Credit Union (Carmel of Mary, Wahpeton)—Rev. DONALD LEIPHON.

Prison Apostolate—Very Rev. JOSEPH SENGER.

Liaison with Charismatic Movement—Very Rev. ADAM J. HASEY.

CLERGY, PARISHES, MISSIONS AND PAROCHIAL SCHOOLS

CITY OF FARGO
(Cass County)

1—ST. MARY'S CATHEDRAL (1880). Also serving Argusville and Merit Care Hospital. Revs. Peter Hughes, C.S.Sp.; Armand L. Brooks; Michael W. Hickin, S.T.B.; Deacon Julian Mrozla.
Office: 619 7th St. N., 58102. Tel: 701-235-4289; 235-4280; Fax: 701-235-2986.
Res., 679 6th Ave. N., 58102. [JC]
Mission—Argusville, St. William.

2—HOLY SPIRIT (1951). Also serving Vets' Hospital. Revs. Phillip Ackerman; Damien Schill; Deacon James Perius.
Res., 1420 N. 7th St., 58102. Tel: 701-232-5900; Fax: 701-232-5902. [JC]
School—1441 8th St. N., 58102. Mr. Tim Jacobson, Prin.
Lay Teachers 10; Students 135.

3—NATIVITY (1960). Also serving Manor Care & Villa Maria Nursing Homes, Dakota Heartland Hospital. Revs. Dale Kinzler; Timothy C. Schroeder; Sr. Ruth Gerates, P.B.V.M., Pastoral Assoc.
Res., 1825 11th St. S., 58103. Tel: 701-232-2414; Fax: 701-232-4491. [JC]
School—Tel: 701-232-7461. Cindy Hutchins, Prin.
Lay Teachers 20; Students 320.

4—SS. ANNE & JOACHIM (1995). Also serving Kindred. Very Rev. Val Gross; Rev. Brian M. Bachmeier.
3329 S. University Dr., 58103. Tel: 701-235-5757; Fax: 701-235-0651.
Res., 2501 58th Ave. S.W., 58104. Tel: 701-235-1514.

5—ST. ANTHONY OF PADUA (1917). Also serving Heartland Medical Center (formerly St. John Hospital), and Cass County Jail. Revs. James R. Ermer; Jared C. Kadlec; Deacon Math Prom.
Res., 710 S. 10th St., 58103. Tel: 701-237-6063; Fax: 701-237-6064. [JC]
School—St. Anthony's Junior High, 719 9th St., 58103. Tel: 701-232-3296. Mr. Doug Jacobson, Prin.
Lay Teachers 12; Students 231.
Mission—Kindred, St. Maurice.

6—ST. PAUL NEWMAN CENTER, N.D.S.U. (1928), Rev. Paul Duchschere.
Res., 1141 N. University Dr., 58102. Tel: 701-298-9775.
Church—1141 N. University Dr., 58102. Tel: 701-235-0142. [JC]

OUTSIDE THE CITY OF FARGO

Alice, Cass Co., St. Henry (1902). Served from Enderlin.
c/o 302 Bluff St., Enderlin, 58027.
Church—58003. [CEM]

Anamoose, McHenry Co., St. Francis Xavier (1899). Also serving Drake and Esmond. Rev. Leo Kinney. In res., Rev. Eugene Fish.
Res., 605 1st St., Box 49, 58710-0049. Tel: 701-465-3780; Fax: 701-465-0217. [CEM]
Missions—Drake, McHenry Co., St. Margaret Mary. [CEM]
Esmond, Benson Co., St. Boniface, P.O. 37, Esmond, 58332-0037. Tel: 701-249-3459.

Aneta, Nelson Co., Sacred Heart. Served from Cooperstown.
c/o P.O. Box 548, Cooperstown, 58425. Tel: 701-797-2624.

Ardoch, Walsh Co., St. John the Baptist (1883). Served from Minto.
c/o 629 3rd St., Box 316, Minto, 58261.

Argusville, Cass Co., St. William (1942). Served from St. Mary's Cathedral, Fargo. Revs. Armand L. Brooks; Michael W. Hickin, S.T.B.
c/o 619 7th St. N., Fargo, 58102. Tel: 701-235-4289.
Church—107 Drake Ave., 58005. Tel: 701-484-5211. [JC]

Ashley, McIntosh Co., St. David (1960). Served from Zeeland.
c/o P.O. Box 1, Zeeland, 58581. Tel: 701-423-5494.

Balfour, McHenry Co., St. Joseph's (1906). Closed. For inquiries for parish records contact the Chancery.

Balta, Pierce Co., Our Lady of Mount Carmel (1902). Also serving Fulda and Orrin. Rev. Vincent J. Tuchscherer.
Res., Box 428, 58313. Tel: 701-542-3326. [CEM]
Missions—Fulda, McHenry Co., St. Anselm. [CEM]
Orrin, Pierce Co., Sacred Heart. [CEM]

Bathgate, Pembina Co., St. Anthony (1883). Served from Walhalla.
c/o 801 Central Ave., Box 228, Walhalla, 58282. Tel: 701-549-2729. [CEM]

Bechyne, SS. Peter & Paul. Served from Michigan, ND.
c/o P.O. Box 332, Michigan, 58259. Tel: 701-259-2248.

Belcourt, Rolette Co., St. Ann (1885), Revs. Fred Underwood, S.O.L.T.; Dale Kraig, S.O.L.T.; Robert J. Cronin, S.O.L.T.; Bro. John DeMay, S.O.L.T.
Res., Box 2000, 58316. Tel: 701-477-5601; Fax: 701-477-5602. [CEM]
Mission—Belcourt, Rolette Co., St. Anthony Indian Mission. [CEM]
St. Anthony (1895). Attended by St. Ann, Belcourt.
c/o P.O. Box 2000, 58316. Tel: 701-477-5601. [CEM]

Bisbee, Towner Co., Holy Rosary (1889). Served from Rolette.

Bottineau, Bottineau Co., St. Mark's (1905). Also serving Westhope. Rev. Kevin J. Boucher.
Res., 322 Sinclair St., 58318. Tel: 701-228-3164. [CEM]
Mission—Westhope, Bottineau Co., St. Andrew.

Bremen, Wells Co., St. Joseph (1896). Served from Fessenden.
c/o P.O. Box 325, Fessenden, 58438. Tel: 701-547-3430.

Brocket, Ramsey Co., St. Joseph's (1910). Served from Lakota.
c/o 109 East Ave. E., P.O. Box 509, Lakota, 58344. Tel: 701-247-2594. [CEM]

Buchanan, Stutsman Co., St. Margaret. Served from Jamestown.
c/o 622 1st Ave. S., Box 347, Jamestown, 58402. Tel: 701-252-0119.

Buffalo, Cass Co., St. Thomas (1900). Served from Casselton.
c/o 712 2nd St. N., Box 340, Casselton, 58012.

Burnstad, Logan Co., St. Clara (1915). Served from Napoleon.
c/o 401 Broadway, Napoleon, 58561-7013. Tel: 701-754-2860.

Cando, Towner Co., Sacred Heart (1893), Rev. John Sutton.
Res., 310 3rd Ave., P.O. Box 399, 58324. Tel: 701-968-3462. [CEM]

Carrington, Foster Co., Sacred Heart (1887). Also serving Kensal, St. John's. Rev. Lawrence Haas.
Res., 663 1st St. S., P.O. Box 420, 58421. Tel: 701-652-2519. [CEM]
Mission—Kensal, Stutsman Co.

Casselton, Cass Co., St. Leo (1880). Also serving Buffalo. Rev. Al Bitz; Deacons Donald Tinguely; George Loegering.
Res., 712 2nd St. N., P.O. Box 340, 58012. Tel:

701-347-4609. [CEM]
Mission—Buffalo, St. Thomas. St. Leo's Religious Education Center, 152 8th Ave., N., 58012. Tel: 701-347-4611.

Cavalier, Pembina Co., St. Bridget's (1881). Also serving Neche. Rev. C. James Jeffrey.
Res., 201 First St., S., P.O. Box 280, 58220. Tel: 701-265-8877. [CEM]
Mission—Neche, Pembina Co., SS. Nereus and Achilleus. [CEM]

Cayuga, Sargent Co., SS. Peter and Paul (1916). Served from Forman.
c/o Box 175, Forman, 58032-0175. Tel: 701-724-3319.

Cogswell, Sargent Co., Our Lady of Mercy (1903). Served from Forman.
c/o Box 175, Forman, 58032-0175. Tel: 701-724-3319.

Conway, Walsh Co., St. Mark. Served from Pisek.
c/o Box 27, Pisek, 58273. Tel: 701-284-6060; Fax: 701-284-6331.

Cooperstown, Griggs Co., St. George's (1939). Also serving Aneta, Jessie. Rev. James Cheney.
Res., P.O. Box 548, 58425. Tel: 701-797-2624. [CEM]
Missions—Jessie, Griggs Co., St. Lawrence. [CEM]
Aneta, Nelson Co., Sacred Heart. [CEM]

Courtenay, Stutsman Co., St. Mary's. Served from Sanborn.
c/o 1324 95 Ave. S.E., Sanborn, 58426. [CEM]

Crow Hill, St. Jerome. Served from Fort Totten.

Crystal, Pembina Co., St. Patrick (1892). Served from Park River.
c/o Hwy. 17 E., P.O. Box 110, Park River, 58270. Tel: 701-284-6165.

Dazey, Barnes Co., St. Mary (1899). Served from Sanborn.
Church—c/o P.O. Box 35, Sanborn, 58480.

Devils Lake, Ramsey Co., St. Joseph's (1884). Also serving Rutten (sometimes called Crary). Revs. Jeffrey Wald; Robert F. Smith, Jr.; Emmanuel M. Okonmah; Deacon Lawrence Lange.
Res., 515 Fourth St., Box 898, 58301. Tel: 701-662-7558. [CEM]
School—Tom Burckhard, Prin. Lay Teachers 9; Students 176.
Missions—Rutten, Ramsey Co., St. Benedict. [CEM]
Starkweather, Ramsey Co., Assumption of the Blessed Virgin Mary. [CEM]

Dickey, LaMoure Co., Assumption (1909). Served from LaMoure.
c/o 209 First St., S.E., Box 217, La Moure, 58458. Tel: 701-883-5987.

Drake, McHenry Co., St. Margaret Mary's (1910). Attended by St. Francis Xavier, Anamoose.
Res., 605 Main St., P.O. Box 197, 58736. Tel: 701-465-3281. [CEM]
Catechesis/Religious Programs—Students 63.

Drayton, Pembina Co., St. Edward's (1889). Also serving St. Thomas, St. Thomas and Pembina, Assumption. Rev. Charles Fisher.
Res., 211 N. Main St., P.O. Box 215, 58225. Tel: 701-454-6171. [CEM]
Mission—St. Thomas, Pembina Co., St. Thomas. [CEM]

Dunseith, Rolette Co., St. Louis (1882). Also serving Immaculate Heart of Mary (Rolette Co.). Rev. Joseph H. Zimmer, S.A.C.
Res., 112 First St., N.W., Box 160, 58329. Tel: 701-244-5738. [CEM]
St. Mary's Mission Center—P.O. Box 130, 58329.

Edgeley, LaMoure Co., Transfiguration (1915). Also serving Nortonville, Manor St. Joseph. Rev. Duaine M. Cote; Deacon Thurston Ham.
Res., 205 Second St., P.O. Box 347, 58433. Tel: 701-493-2387. [CEM]
Mission—Nortonville, LaMoure Co., Holy Spirit.

Ellendale, Dickey Co., St. Helena's (1888). Also serving Fullerton. Rev. Gary Luiten.
Res., 421 Second St. N., P.O. Box 796, 58436. Tel: 701-349-3297. [CEM]
Mission—Fullerton, Dickey Co., St. Patrick. [CEM]

Enderlin, Ransom Co., St. Patrick's (1908). Also serving Alice, Sheldon. Rev. James F. McKinney.
Res., 302 Bluff St., 58027. Tel: 701-437-2791. [CEM]
Missions—Alice, St. Henry. [CEM]
Sheldon, St. Mary & Our Lady of the Scapular. [CEM]

Esmond, Benson Co., St. Boniface (1909), In res., Rev. Eugene J. Fish.
c/o Box 37, 58332-0033.

Fairmount, Richland Co., St. Anthony's (1909). Also serving Carmel Convent. Rev. Donald A. Leiphon.
Res., 204 Second St. N., Box 292, 58030. Tel: 701-474-5518. [CEM]

Fessenden, Wells Co., St. Augustine's (1896). Also serving Bremen and Maddock. Rev. George B. Billman.
Res., P.O. Box 325, 58438. Tel: 701-547-3430.
Missions—Bremen, Wells Co., St. Joseph. [CEM]
Maddock, Benson Co., St. William.

Fingal, Barnes Co., Holy Trinity (1889). Attended by St. Bernard, Oriska.
c/o 606 Fifth St., Oriska, 58063. Tel: 701-845-3713.

Finley, Steele Co., St. Olaf. Served from Hope.
c/o P.O. Box 99, Hope, 58046. Tel: 701-945-2652.

Forman, Sargent Co., St. Mary's (1913). Also serving Cayuga, Cogswell, and Milnor. Revs. Kazimierz Kopacz; Joy Chakian; Deacons Richard Biss; David Gates.
Res., Box 175, 58032-0175. Tel: 701-724-3319. [CEM]
Missions—Cayuga, Sts. Peter & Paul. [CEM]
Cogswell, Our Lady of Mercy. [CEM]
Milnor, Sargent Co., St. Arnold. [CEM]

Fort Totten, Benson Co., Seven Dolors (1875). Also serving Crow Hill, Tokio. Rev. Charles J. Leute, O.P.; Deacon Anthony McDonald.
Res., P.O. Box 299, 58335. Tel: 701-766-4314.
Mission—Tokio, Benson Co., Christ the King.
Memorial Station, Crow Hill, St. Jerome—.

Fried, Stutsman Co., Sacred Heart (1888). Served from Jamestown.
c/o 622 First Ave. S., Box 347, Jamestown, 58402. Tel: 701-252-0119.

Fulda, McHenry Co., St. Anselm (1901). Served from Balta.
c/o Box 428, Balta, 58313.

Fullerton, Dickey Co., St. Patrick (1921). Served from Ellendale.
c/o 421 Second St. N., P.O. Box 796, Ellendale, 58436. Tel: 701-349-3297.

Gackle, Logan Co., St. Anne. Served from Windsor.
Mailing Address: c/o 207 Washington Ave., Cleveland, 58424. Tel: 701-763-6192.

Geneseo, Sargent Co., St. Martin's (1907). Served from Lidgerwood.
c/o 118 Second Ave. N.W., Box 449, Lidgerwood, 58053. Tel: 701-538-4608.
Church—58037. [CEM]

Grafton, Walsh Co., St. John the Evangelist's (1881). Also serving State School. Rev. Bert Miller; Margaret Bruce, Pastoral Assoc.
Res., 344 15th St. W., P.O. Box 636, 58237. Tel: 701-352-1648. [CEM]
St. John's Catechetical Center—58237. D.R.E.: Cindy Jononsek; John Halvorson.
Lay Associates and Workers 11.

Grand Forks, Grand Forks Co.,

1—Holy Family, (1960), Revs. Leonard Loegering; Anthony C. Odozi, Jr.; Deacon Samuel Pupino.
Res., 1018 18th Ave. S., 58201. Tel: 701-746-1454. [JC]
School—Mr. Charles Scherr, Prin. Sisters 1; Lay Teachers 10; Students 123.

2—St. Mary's, (1915), Rev. Jerald L.C. Finnestad; Deacon Don Litzinger.
216 Belmont Rd., 58201. Tel: 701-775-9318; Fax: 701-775-7568. [JC]
School—Dixie Klein, Prin. Lay Teachers 6; Students 85.

3—St. Michael's, (1872), Revs. William C. Sherman; Mathew Pamplaniyil; Anthony J. Dudzinski; Deacon Albert Schmisek.
Res., 520 N. Sixth St., 58203. Tel: 701-772-2624; Fax: 701-772-0211. [JC]
School—Tel: 701-772-1822. Sharon Litchy, Prin.
Lay Teachers 14; Students 121.
St. James Religious Center—211 S. Fourth St., Rm. 105, 58203. Tel: 701-775-4261. Sr. M. Beata Seil, O.S.F., Admin.; Lois Stoltman, Dir.

4—St. Thomas Aquinas Parish, UND, (1951), Rev. Raymond P. Courtright.
Res., 410 Cambridge St., 58201. Tel: 701-777-6850; Fax: 701-777-8905. [JC]

Granville, McHenry Co., Our Lady of Perpetual Help. Served from Towner.
c/o 503 First St., SW., Box 267, Towner, 58788. Tel: 701-537-5133.

Gwinner, Sargent Co., St. Vincent (1984). Served from Lisbon.
707 Oak St., P.O. Box 226, Lisbon, 58054-0226. Tel: 701-683-4620.

Hankinson, Richland Co., St. Philip's (1889), Very Rev. John D. Anderson.
Res., 612 S. Main, P.O. Box 419, 58041. Tel: 701-242-7327. [CEM]
St. Philip's Religious Education Center—(Grades K-12) St. Francis Convent, Hankison, 58041. Tel: 701-242-7800. Mr. William Hrdlicka, Prin.; Sr. Edwardine O.S.F., D.R.E.
Lay Teachers 34; Students 143.

Hansboro, Towner Co., Sacred Heart. Closed. For inquiries for parish records contact the Chancery.

Harvey, Wells Co., St. Cecilia's (1895). Also serving St. Aloisius Hospital and Selz, St. Anthony's. Rev. Vernon Smith; Deacon Jeffrey M. Faul.
Res., 413 E. Brewster St., 58341. Tel: 701-324-2144; Fax: 701-324-4640. [CEM]
St. Cecilia Religious Education Center—413 E. Brewster St., 58341. Tel: 701-324-2637.
Teachers 21; Students (Grades 1-8) 137; Students (Grades 9-12) 71.
Mission—Selz, Pierce Co.

Hillsboro, Traill Co., St. Rose of Lima (1892), Rev. Msgr. Wendelyn Vetter.
Res., 503 Third St. S.E., Box 459, 58045. Tel: 701-436-4541. [CEM]

Hope, Steele Co., St. Agatha's (1907). Also serving Finley and Page. Rev. Steven Meyer.
Res., P.O. Box 99, 58046. Tel: 701-945-2652. [CEM]
Missions—Finley, Steele Co., St. Olaf; Page, Cass Co., St. James. [CEM]

Hunter, Cass Co., St. Agnes (1898). Attended by Our Lady of Peace, Mayville.
c/o 435 E. Main St., Mayville, 58257. Tel: 701-874-2226. [CEM]

Hurdsfield, Wells Co., St. Patrick (1969). Served from Sykeston.
c/o P.O. Box 397, Sykeston, 58486. Tel: 701-984-2266.

Jamestown, Stutsman Co., The Basilica of St. James (1881). Also serving Buchanan, Fried, and Pingree. Very Rev. Bernard A. Pfau; Revs. Ignatius Sebastian; James S. Goodwin; Sr. Michaeleen Jantzer, O.S.B., Pastoral Min.; Deacon Tim Marcy.
Res., 622 First Ave. S., Box 347, 58402. Tel: 701-252-0119; Fax: 701-252-4453. [CEM]
School—St. John's Grade School. Sr. Dorothy Zeller, S.S.N.D., Prin.
Lay Teachers 13; Students (Grades PreK-6) 201.
St. James Religious Education—622 First Ave. S., P.O. Box 2093, 58042. Rita Kenna, D.R.E., Tel: 701-252-0478.
Lay Teachers 35.
Missions—Fried, Sacred Heart; Buchanan, St. Margaret; Pingree, St. Michael. [CEM]
Deacon Timothy Marcy.

Jessie, Griggs Co., St. Lawrence (1888). Served from Cooperstown.
c/o P.O. Box 548, Cooperstown, 58425. Tel: 701-797-2624.

Karlsruhe, McHenry Co., SS. Peter and Paul's (1903). Served from Velva.
c/o 201 Second Ave., W., Box K, Velva, 58790. [CEM]

Kensal, Stutsman Co., St. John's (1917). Served by Carrington.
c/o P.O. Box 420, Carrington, 58421.
Church—58455. Tel: 701-435-2876.

Kindred, Cass Co., St. Maurice (1965). Served from SS. Anne & Joachim, Fargo. Rev. Brian M. Bachmeier.
5313 165 Ave. N.E., 58081. Tel: 701-428-3094.

Kintyre, Logan Co., St. Boniface's (1906), Rev. John A. Bacevicius.
Res., 7013 26th Ave. S.E., 58549. Tel: 701-332-6636. [CEM]

Knox, Benson Co., St. Mary's (1936). Served from Leeds.
Mailing Address: Box 97, 58343. Tel: 701-583-2808.

Lake Williams, Kidder Co., Our Lady of the Lake (1946). Served from Tappen.
c/o P.O. Box 98, Tappen, 58487. Tel: 701-327-8344.

Lakota, Nelson Co., St. Mary's (1902). Also serving Brocket and Tolna. Rev. Robert F. Skarohlid.
Res., 109 East Ave., E., P.O. Box 509, 58344. Tel: 701-247-2594. [CEM]
Missions—Brocket, Ramsey Co., St. Joseph. [CEM]
Tolna, Nelson Co., St. Joseph.

La Moure, La Moure Co., Holy Rosary (1890). Also serving Dickey and Marion. Revs. Kevin Willis; Joseph Allen.
Res., 209 First St., S.E., Box 217, 58458. Tel: 701-883-5987. [CEM]
Missions—Marion, LaMoure Co., St. Francis, (1910); Dickey, LaMoure Co., Assumption. [CEM]

Langdon, Cavalier Co., St. Alphonsus (1888). Also serving Nekoma. Rev. Michael Schommer.
Res., 1010 Third St., 58249. Tel: 701-256-5966; Fax: 701-256-2358. [CEM]
School—Tel: 701-256-2354. Sr. Anne Frawley, P.B.V.M., Prin.
Sisters 1; Lay Teachers 11; Students 96.
Mission—Nekoma, Cavalier Co., St. Edwards, (1907).

Lankin, Walsh Co., St. Joseph's (1906). Attended by St. John Nepomucene, Pisek.
Church—Box 216, 58250. Tel: 701-593-6212. [CEM]
Box 27, Pisek, 58273.

Larimore, Grand Forks Co., St. Stephen's (1885), Very Rev. Roman E. Ludwig; Rev. Arulando Thainese.
Res., 311 W. Front St., P.O. Box 778, 58251. Tel: 701-343-2377. [CEM]

Leeds, Benson Co., St. Vincent de Paul (1897). Also serving Knox and Minnewaukan. Rev. Mathias F. Lanz.
Res., 315 Central Ave., P.O. Box 307, 58346. Tel: 701-466-2777. [CEM]
Missions—Minnewauken, Benson Co., St. James. [CEM]
Knox, Benson Co., St. Mary. [CEM]

Leroy, Pembina Co., St. Joseph's (1848). Served from Walhalla.
c/o 801 Central Ave., Box 228, Walhalla, 58282. Tel: 701-549-3750.
Church—58252. [CEM]

Lidgerwood, Richland Co., St. Boniface's (1887). Also serving Geneseo. Rev. Eugene Gilles, S.A.C.
Res., 118 Second Ave., N.W., P.O. Box 449, 58053. Tel: 701-538-4608. [CEM]
Mission—Geneseo, Sargent Co., St. Martin. [CEM]

Lisbon, Ransom Co., St. Aloysius (1884). Also serving Gwinner. Rev. John L. Evans, II.
Res., 707 Oak, P.O. Box 226, 58054-0226. Tel: 701-683-4620. [CEM]
Mission—Gwinner, Sargent Co., St. Vincent. [CEM]

Lomice, Walsh Co., St. Catherine (1936). Served from Michigan, ND.
c/o P.O. Box 332, Michigan, 58259. Tel: 701-259-2248. [CEM]

Maddock, Benson Co., St. William (1954). Served from Fessenden.
c/o P.O. Box 325, Fessenden, 58438. Tel: 701-547-3430.

Mantador, Richland Co., SS. Peter and Paul's (1906). Served from Mooreton.
c/o 204 Mooreton Ave., N., Mooreton, 58061. Tel: 701-274-8259.
Church—58058. [CEM]

Manvel, Grand Forks Co., St. Timothy's (1882). Served from St. Timothy's. Rev. Paul Schuster.
Church—511 Eighth St. W., P.O. Box 28, 58256. Tel: 701-696-2219. [CEM]

Marion, La Moure Co., St. Francis (1910). Served from LaMoure.
c/o 209 First St., S.E., Box 217, LaMoure, 58458.
Church—58466. [CEM]

Mayville, Traill Co., Our Lady of Peace (1945). Also serving Hunter. Rev. Bernard R. Schneider.
Res., 435 E. Main St., 58257. Tel: 701-786-3234. [CEM]
Missions—Hunter, Cass Co., St. Agnes. [CEM]
Mayville, State University Newman Club.

McClusky, Sheridan Co., Holy Family (1932). Served from Sykeston.
c/o P.O. Box 397, Sykeston, 58486. Tel: 701-984-2266. [CEM]

McHenry, Foster Co., SS. Peter & Paul (1912). Served from New Rockford.
c/o 116 First Ave., N., P.O. Box 389, New Rockford, 58356. Tel: 701-947-5325. [CEM]

Medina, Stutsman Co., St. Mary. Served from Windsor.
c/o 207 Washington Ave., Cleveland, 58424. Tel: 701-763-6192. [CEM]

Michigan, Nelson Co., St. Lawrence O'Toole (1883). Also serving Bechyne and Lomice. Rev. Alfred Allmaras.
Res., P.O. Box 332, 58259. Tel: 701-259-2248. [CEM]
Missions—Bechyne, Walsh Co., SS. Peter & Paul. [CEM]
Lomice, Walsh Co., St. Catherine. [CEM]

Milnor, Sargent Co., St. Arnold's (1905). Attended by St. Mary, Forman.
c/o Box 175, Forman, 58032-0175.
Church—Box 295, 58060. Tel: 701-427-9288. [CEM]

Milton, Cavalier Co., St. Clotilde. Served from Wales.
Mailing Address: c/o P.O. Box 127, Wales, 58281. Tel: 701-283-5352. [CEM]

Minnewaukan, Benson Co., St. James (1899). Served from Leeds.
c/o 315 Central Ave., P.O. Box 307, Leeds, 58346. Tel: 701-466-2777. [CEM]

Minto, Walsh Co., Sacred Heart (1905). Also serving Ardoch. Rev. Feliks Lubas.
Res., 629 Third St., P.O. Box 316, 58261. Tel: 701-248-3589. [CEM]
Mission—Ardoch, Walsh Co., St. John the Baptist. [CEM]

Mooreton, Richland Co., St. Anthony's (1885). Also serving Mantador. Rev. Jan Klimek.
Res., 204 Mooreton Ave., N., 58061. Tel: 701-274-8259. [CEM]
Mission—Mantador, Richland Co., Sts. Peter & Paul. [CEM]

Mount Carmel, Cavalier Co., Our Lady of Mount Carmel (1888). Served from Wales.
c/o P.O. Box 127, Wales, 58281. Tel: 701-283-5352. [CEM]

Munich, Cavalier Co., St. Mary's (1916), Rev. Joseph S. Axtmann.
Res., P.O. Box 159, 58352. Tel: 701-682-5178. [CEM]

Napoleon, Logan Co., St. Philip Neri (1906), Rev. James P. Lauerman, M.R.E.; Deacon Howard Hunkler.
Res., 401 Broadway, 58561-7013. Tel: 701-754-2860. [CEM]
Mission—Burnstad, Logan Co., St. Clara. [CEM]

Neche, Pembina Co., SS. Nereus and Achilleus (1884). Attended by St. Bridget, Cavalier.
c/o 201 First St. S., Box 280, Cavalier, 58220. Tel: 701-886-7471. [CEM]

Nekoma, Cavalier Co., St. Edward (1907). Served from Langdon.
c/o 1010 Third St., Langdon, 58249. Tel: 701-256-5966. [CEM]

New Rockford, Eddy Co., St. John's (1896). Also serving McHenry. Rev. Jerome Hunkler.
Res., 116 First Ave. N., P.O. Box 389, 58356. Tel: 701-947-5325. [CEM]
Mission—McHenry, Foster Co., SS. Peter & Paul. [CEM]

Nortonville, LaMoure Co., Holy Ghost (Spirit) (1912). Served from Edgeley.
c/o 205 Second St., P.O. Box 347, Edgeley, 58433. Tel: 701-493-2387.

Oakes, Dickey Co., St. Charles Borromeo (1905). Also serving Oakes Community Hospital, Oakes. Very Rev. Adam J. Hasey.
Res., 410 N. Seventh St., 58474. Tel: 701-742-2418. [CEM]
Mission—Verona, LaMoure Co., St. Raphael. [CEM]

Oakwood, Walsh Co., Sacred Heart (1881). Unassigned.
Res., 7010 County Rd. 4, Grafton, 58237-8860. Tel: 701-352-1392. [CEM]

Olga, Cavalier Co., Our Lady of the Sacred Heart (1882). Served from Walhalla.
Res., H.C. 2, Box 102, Langdon, 58249. Tel: 701-549-3465. [CEM]

Oriska, Barnes Co., St. Bernard's (1908). Also serving Fingal. Rev. Kevin Willis.
Res., 606 Fifth St., 58063. Tel: 701-845-3713. [CEM]
Mission—Fingal, Barnes Co., Holy Trinity.

Orrin, Pierce Co., Sacred Heart (1903). Served from Balta.
c/o Box 428, Balta, 58313.
Church—58368. [CEM]

Osnabrock, Cavalier Co., St. Joseph (1909). Served from Wales.
c/o P.O. Box 127, Wales, 58281. Tel: 701-282-5352. [CEM]

Page, Cass Co., St. James (1909). Served from Hope.
c/o Box 99, Hope, 58046. Tel: 701-945-2652.
Church—58064. [CEM]

Park River, Walsh Co., St. Mary's (1888). Also serving St. Ansgar Hospital, Crystal. Rev. Msgr. Allan F. Nilles; Deacon Gerald F. Sobolik.
Res., Hwy. 17 E., P.O. Box 110, 58270. Tel: 701-284-6165. [CEM]
Mission—Crystal, Pembina Co., St. Patrick. [CEM]

Pembina, Pembina Co., Assumption of the Blessed Virgin Mary (1818). Served from Drayton.
Church—143 Hayden St., Box 151, 58271. Tel: 701-825-6266. [CEM]

Penn, Ramsey Co., Immaculate Conception. Closed. For inquiries for parish records contact St. Vincent de Paul, Leeds.

Pingree, Stutsman Co., St. Michael's (1905). Served from Jamestown.
c/o 622 First Ave. S., Box 347, Jamestown, 58402. Tel: 701-252-0119.
Church—58476. [CEM]

Pisek, Walsh Co., St. John Nepomucene (1886). Also serving Conway and Lankin. Rev. John Fallon.
Res., Box 27, 58273. Tel: 701-284-6060; Fax: 701-284-6331. [CEM]
Missions—Conway, Walsh Co., St. Marks. [CEM]
Lankin, Walsh Co., St. Joseph. [CEM]

Reynolds, Grand Forks Co., Our Lady of Perpetual Help (1895). Also serving Thompson. Rev. Kenneth F. Knoke.
Res., 424 Fifth St., Box 96, 58275. Tel: 701-847-2371. [CEM]
Mission—Thompson, Grand Forks Co., St. Jude. [CEM]

Rock Lake, Towner Co., Immaculate Heart of Mary. Served from Rolla.
c/o P.O. Box 788, Rolla, 58367. Tel: 701-477-5277.

Rolette, Rolette Co., Sacred Heart (1918). Also serving Willow City and Bisbee. Rev. Thomas Graner; Deacon Conrad Schuster.
Res., Box 127, 58366. Tel: 701-246-3449; Fax: 701-246-3449. [CEM]
Missions—Willow City, Bottineau Co., Notre Dame. [CEM]
Bisbee, Towner Co., Holy Rosary.
Immaculate Heart of Mary (1948). Attended by St. Louis, Dunseith.
c/o 112 First St., N.W., Box 160, Dunseith, 58329. Tel: 701-244-5738.

Rolla, Rolette Co., St. Joachim's (1894). Also serving Rock Lake and Rolla Community Hospital. Very Rev. George D. Schneider.
Res., 207 Second Ave. N.E., P.O. Box 788, 58367. Tel: 701-477-5277. [CEM]
St. Joachim Religious Education Center—P.O. Box 788, 58367. Tel: 701-477-3568.
Mission—Rock Lake, Towner Co.

Rugby, Pierce Co., St. Therese, Little Flower (1910), Revs. Daniel Miho Mrnarevic; Clement Perianayagam; Deacon Edward Eberle.
Res., 218 Third St., S.E., 58368. Tel: 701-776-5327. [CEM]
School—306 Third Ave., S.E., 58368. Tel: 701-776-6740. Sr. Donna Welder, Admin.
Sisters of St. Francis of the Immaculate Heart of Mary (Hankinson, ND) 2; Lay Teachers 8; Students 114.
Little Flower Parish School of Religious Education—306 Third Ave., S.E., 58368. Tel: 701-776-6258.
Lay Teachers 25.

Rutten, Ramsey Co., St. Benedict. Served from Devils Lake. Revs. Emmanuel M. Okonmah; Robert F. Smith, Jr.
c/o 515 Fourth St., Box 898, Devils Lake, 58301. Tel: 701-662-7558. [CEM]

St. John, Rolette Co., St. John the Baptist (1882). Also serving St. Benedict Indian Mission (Rolette Co.). Rev. Gerald McCarthy.
Church—Box 170, 58369. Tel: 701-477-3081. [CEM]
Mission—Belcourt, Rolette Co., St. Benedict. [CEM]

St. Michael, Benson Co., St. Michael's (1874), Revs. Edward Sherman; Theodore Brune, O.S.B.
Res., P.O. Box 84, 58370. Tel: 701-766-4151. [CEM]

St. Thomas, Pembina Co., St. Thomas (1886). Served from Drayton.
c/o 211 N. Main St., P.O. Box 215, Drayton, 58225. Tel: 701-454-6171.
Church—58276. Tel: 701-257-6492. [CEM]

Sanborn, Barnes Co., Sacred Heart (1904). Also serves Dazey, Courtenay and Wimbledon. Rev. Chad Wilhelm.
Res., P.O. Box 35, 58480. Tel: 701-646-6306. [CEM]
Missions—Dazey, Barnes Co., St. Mary. [CEM]
Courtenay, Stutsman Co., St. Mary; Wimbledon, Barnes Co., St. Boniface.

Selz, Pierce Co., St. Anthony's (1917). Served from Harvey.
c/o 29 Girard St., Harvey, 58341-7316.

Sheldon, Ransom Co., St. Mary, Our Lady of the Scapular (1884). Served from Enderlin.
c/o 302 Bluff St., Enderlin, 58027. Tel: 701-437-2791.
Church—58068.

Starkweather, Ramsey Co., Assumption of the Blessed Virgin Mary (1905). Served from Devils Lake. Revs. Emmanuel M. Okonmah; Robert F. Smith, Jr.
c/o 515 Fourth St., Box 898, Devils Lake, 58301. Tel: 701-662-7558.
Church—58377. Tel: 701-292-4301. [CEM]

Steele, Kidder Co., St. Francis de Sales (1958). Served from Tappen.
c/o P.O. Box 98, Tappen, 58487. Tel: 701-327-8344. [CEM]

Stirum, Sargent Co., St. Vincent. Closed. 1986. For inquiries for parish records contact St. Aloysius, Lisbon.

Sykeston, Wells Co., St. Elizabeth's (1905). Also serving Hurdsfield and McCluskey. Rev. Julian F. Kupisz.
Res., P.O. Box 397, 58486. Tel: 701-984-2266. [CEM]
Missions—Hurdsfield, Wells Co., St. Patrick; McClusky, Sheridan Co., Holy Family.

Tappen, Kidder Co., St. Paul's (1908). Also serving Lake Williams and Steele. Rev. Thomas J. Krupich.
Res., P.O. Box 98, 58487. Tel: 701-327-8344.

Missions—Lake Williams, Kidder Co., Our Lady of the Lake. [CEM]
Steele, Kidder Co., St. Francis de Sales. [CEM]

Thompson, Grand Forks Co., St. Jude's (1895). Served from Reynolds.
c/o 424 Fifth St., Box 96, Reynolds, 58275.
Church—58278. [CEM]

Tokio, Benson Co., Christ the King (Indian Mission). Served from Fort Totten.
c/o P.O. Box 299, Fort Totten, 58335. Tel: 701-766-4314.

Tolna, Nelson Co., St. Joseph's (1911). Served from Lakota.
c/o 109 E. E Ave., Box 509, Lakota, 58344.
Church—58380. [CEM]

Towner, McHenry Co., St. Cecilia's (1906). Also serving Granville. Rev. Ronald Yee Mon.
Res., 503 First St., S.W., Box 267, 58788. Tel: 701-537-5133. [CEM]
Mission—Granville, McHenry Co., Our Lady of Perpetual Help.

Valley City, Barnes Co., St. Catherine's (1882). Also serving Newman Center. Rev. H. Gerard Braun; Deacons Arlie Braunberger; Raphael Grim; Eugene Klein.
524 Third Ave., N.E., 58072. Tel: 701-845-0354. [CEM]
School—(Grades K-6). Tel: 701-845-1453. Mr. Ralph Dyrness, Prin.
Lay Teachers 6; Students 59.
St. Catherine's Parish Education Center—540 Third Ave. N.E., 58072. Ralph Dyrness, Parish Education Dir.
Lay Teachers 22.

Velva, McHenry Co., St. Cecilia's (1906). Also serving Karlsruhe. Very Rev. Joseph P. Senger.
Res., 201 Second Ave. W., P.O. Box K, 58790. Tel: 701-338-2663. [CEM]
Mission—Karlsruhe, McHenry Co., Sts. Peter & Paul. [CEM]

Verona, LaMoure Co., St. Raphael (1898). Served from Oakes.
c/o 410 N. Seventh St., Oakes, 58474. Tel: 701-742-2418. [CEM]

Veseleyville, Walsh Co., St. Luke (1880). Served from Warsaw. Rev. Damian J. Hils.
Mailing Address: 14207 63rd St., N.E., Grafton, 58237. Tel: 701-248-3981. [CEM]

Wahpeton, Richland Co., St. John's (1876), Rev. Dale Lagodinski; Deacons Gene Hoefs; George Ethier; Ignatz Zach.
Office: 115 Second St. N., 58075. Tel: 701-642-6982. [CEM]
Res., 222 Dakota Ave., 58075. Tel: 701-642-4985.
School—122 Second St., N., 58075. Tel: 701-642-6116. Wilfred Sauer, Prin.
Lay Teachers 11; Students 156.
St. John Day Care Center—Tel: 701-642-4922. Bobbi Jo Neiber, Dir.
Staff 24; Students 111.

Newman Student Parish (1968), Rev. Dale Lagodinski, Campus Min. North Dakota State College of Science.
Office: 701 N. Seventh St., 58075. Tel: 701-642-3410.

Wales, Cavalier Co., St. Michael's (1905). Also serving Mount Carmel, Milton, and Osnabrock. Rev. Vincent J. Fitzpatrick.
Res., P.O. Box 127, 58281. Tel: 701-283-5352. [CEM]
Missions—Mount Carmel, Cavalier Co., Our Lady of Mount Carmel. [CEM]
Milton, Cavalier Co., St. Clothilde. [CEM]
Osnabrock, Cavalier Co., St. Joseph. [CEM]

Walhalla, Pembina Co., St. Boniface's (1850), Rev. Gerald Myers; Deacons Jim Carpenter; Alan Storey.
Res., 801 Central Ave., Box 228, 58282. Tel: 701-549-2729. [CEM]
Missions—Bathgate, Pembina Co., St. Anthony. [CEM]
Leroy, Pembina Co., St. Joseph. [CEM]
Olga, Cavalier Co., Our Lady of the Sacred Heart. [CEM]

Warsaw, Walsh Co., St. Stanislaus (1882). Also serves Veselyville. Rev. Damian J. Hils.
6098 County Rd. 4, Minto, 58261. Tel: 701-248-3981. [CEM]

West Fargo, Cass Co., Blessed Sacrament (1945), Revs. John Cavanaugh; Fernando Sayasaya.
Res., 210 Fifth Ave. W., 58078. Tel: 701-282-4554; Fax: 701-282-6503. [JC]

Holy Cross (1981), Rev. James A. Leith, J.C.D.; Sr. Ruth Wirtzfield, Pastoral Assoc.; Deacon James Uline.
Res., 1420 Cross Way, 58078. Tel: 701-282-7217; Fax: 701-277-9337. [JC]

Westhope, Bottineau Co., St. Andrew's (1904). Served from Bottineau.
Mailing Address: Box 365, 58793. Tel: 701-245-6171.

Wild Rice, Cass Co., St. Benedict's (1870), Rev. Daniel J. Pilon; Sr. Ann O'Brien, Pastoral Assoc.
Res., 11705 38th St., S., Horace, 58047. Tel: 701-588-4288. [CEM]

Willow City, Bottineau Co., Notre Dame des Victoires (1895). Attended by Sacred Heart, Rolette.
c/o Box 127, Rolette, 58366.
Church—R.R. 1, Box 167, 58384. Tel: 701-366-4771. [CEM]

Wimbledon, Barnes Co., St. Boniface's (1886). Unassigned. Served from Sanborn.
P.O. Box 9, 58492. Tel: 701-435-2310. [CEM]

Windsor, Stutsman Co., St. Mathias (1910). Also serving Gackle and Medina. Rev. Andrew Roehrich.
Res., 207 Washington Ave., Cleveland, 58424. Tel: 701-763-6192. [CEM]
Missions—Medina, Stutsman Co., St. Mary. [CEM]
Gackle, Logan Co., St. Anne.

Wishek, McIntosh Co., St. Patrick (1952). Served from Zeeland.
c/o Box 1, Zeeland, 58581. Tel: 701-423-5494. [CEM]

Wyndmere, Richland Co., St. John the Baptist (1912), Rev. James A. Meyer.
Res., 630 Sixth St., Box 68, 58081. Tel: 701-439-2200. [CEM]

Zeeland, McIntosh Co., St. Andrew's (1906). Also serving Ashley and Wishek. Rev. John Lewandowski.
Res., P.O. Box 1, 58581. Tel: 701-423-5494. [CEM]
Missions—Ashley, McIntosh Co., St. David; Wishek, McIntosh Co., St. Patrick. [CEM]

INDIAN MISSIONS

Turtle Mountain Reservation, (Chippewa Indians), *Missions*—Belcourt, St. Ann. Revs. Fred Underwood, S.O.L.T.; Dale Kraig, S.O.L.T.; Robert J. Cronin, S.O.L.T.; Bro. John DeMay, S.O.L.T.; St. Anthony, Rolette Co., St. Anthony. Served from Belcourt.

Fort Totten Reservation, (Sioux Indians), *Missions*—Tokio, Christ the King. Rev. Charles J. Leute, O.P.; Fort Totten Reservation, Benson Co., Seven Dolors Indian Mission. Also serving Crow Hill, Tokio. Seven Sorrows Dr., Box 299, 58335-0299. Tel: 701-766-4314. Rev. Charles J. Leute, O.P.

St. Michael, St. Michael's Indian Mission, Revs. Edward Sherman; Theodore Brune, O.S.B.; Bro. Roman Sleger, O.S.B.

Chaplains of Public Institutions

FARGO. *Meritcare Hospital in Fargo*. Served from St. Mary Cathedral, Fargo. 619 N. Seventh St., 58102.
Veterans Administration Facility. Rev. Phillip Ackerman, Res., Holy Spirit Church, 1420 N. Seventh St., 58102.

DEVILS LAKE. *School for the Deaf*. Rev. Jeffrey Wald, Res., St. Joseph's Rectory, 515 Fourth St., Box 898, 58301.

GRAFTON. *Grafton State School*. Rev. Burt Miller, Res., St. John the Evangelist Church, 344 15th St. W., P.O. Box 636, 58237.

GRAND FORKS. *Grand Forks Air Force Base*. Rev. Gary R. Breig, Res., 1699 J. St., GFAFB, 58205.
School for the Blind. Rev. William C. Sherman, Res., St. Michael Church, 520 N. 6th St., 58203.

JAMESTOWN. *State Hospital*. Rev. Ignatius Sebastian.

LISBON. *Soldier's Home*. Rev. John L. Evans, II, Res., St. Aloysius Church, 707 Oak St., Box 226, 58054.

Special Assignment:
Reverend Fathers—
Donahue, Brian G., Cardinal Muench Seminary, 100 35th Ave. N.E., Fargo, ND 58102
Gross, Richard J., Chap., United Hospital, 1220 S. Columbia Rd., Grand Forks, ND 58201
Irwin, Robert, Chancellor, 608 Broadway, P.O. box 1750, Fargo, ND 58102
Laliberte, Robert L., Cardinal Muench Seminary, 100 35th Ave. N.E., Fargo, ND 58102
Miller, Franklin, Cardinal Muench Seminary, 100 35th Ave. N.E., Fargo, ND 58102
Potter, Gerald L., U.N.D., Box 7128 University Station, Grand Forks, ND 58202
Reiske, Steven, Vice-Chancellor, 1129 N. University Dr., Fargo, ND 58102
Schlesselmann, Gregory, Dir. Catholic Education & Formation, 1129 N. University Dr., Fargo, ND 58102
Skonseng, Dennis A., Cardinal Muench Seminary, 100 35th Ave. NE, Fargo, ND 58102

On Duty Outside the Diocese:
Reverend Fathers—
Bachmeier, Bernard A., Mercy Hospital & Medical Center, 4077 Fifth Ave., San Diego, CA 92103
Bushy, Timothy F., Immaculate Conception Church, 702 Summit Ave., Crookston, MN 56716-2736
Cosentino, Jack A., St. Ambrose, P.O. Box 999, Deerfield Beach, FL 33441
Davis, John E., Apartado 134, Chimbote, Peru
Graven, John P., St. Polycarp Church, 8100 Chapman Ave., Stanton, CA 90680
LaCorte, Richard P., St. John the Cross Rectory, 950 82nd Ave., Vero Beach, FL 32966
McCauley, David, 475 University Ave., St. Paul, MN 55103

Military Chaplains:
Reverend Fathers—
Herron, Jack B. (CPT), Chap., USACHCS, CHOAC, 95-001, Fort Monmouth, NJ 07703-5612
Kawczynski, Ronald (LT), Chap., Asst. Regt. Chaplains, 3942 Roebling Ln., Virginia Beach, VA 23452

Absent on Leave:
Reverend Fathers—
Feltis, Jerome
Haenke, Roger, 5501 Queens Ave. S., Minneapolis, MN 55410
Pietrus, Henryk

Retired:
Reverend Monsignors—
McNamee, William J., 715 Washington, Larimore, ND 58251
Peschel, Anthony R., 150 County Rd. 34 #210B, Arthur, ND 58006
Reverend Fathers—
Aleksonis, Vladas, Riverview Pl., 5300 12th St. S. # 303A, Fargo, ND 58104
Binder, Albert, Riverview Place, 5320 12th St. S., #121, Fargo, ND 58104
Bolte, George, Holy Trinity, 417 First Ave., Fingal, ND 58031
Campbell, Joseph, 4 Lakeview Ave., Bella Vista, AR 72714
Conway, John, 3500 Dupont Ave. S., #203, Minneapolis, MN 55408
Cote, Donald J., RR #1, Hatton, ND 58240
Cullen, Martin T., R.R. 2, Box 271, Lake Park, MN 56554
Dickinson, Stephen, P.O. Box 667, Valley City, ND 58072-0667
Duffy, Patrick, Box 63, Neche, ND 58265
Engelhardt, Adam J., Good Samaritan Center, 1414 20 St., N.W., E. Grand Forks, MN 56721
Filteau, Jerome E., Riverview Pl., 5320-12th St. S., Box 318E, Fargo, ND 58104
Grady, Peter W., Riverview Pl., 5220-12th St. S #206C, Fargo, ND 58104
Gregory, Joseph F., S.J., Rt. 1, Box 99, Minto, ND 58261
Huebsch, Joseph R., 514 First Ave. S.W., P.O. Box 98, Hankinson, ND 58041
King, Stephen D., Good Samaritan Nursing Home, Hwy. 18, Arthur, ND 58006
Koehler, Paul L., St. Gerard Nursing Home, P.O. Box 279, Hankinson, ND 58041
Krile, George F., Brentwood West, 3104 E. Broadway #211, Mesa, AZ 85204
Lang, Julius, P.O. Box 126, Naples, FL 33939
Lommel, George D., 509 Almeron Ave., Drayton, ND 57225
Mehok, William J., S.J., Riverview Place, 5320 12th St. S., #218, Fargo, ND 58104
Mentel, Joseph C., 912 27th St. N., Bismarck, ND 58501
Moore, John E., Riverview Pl., 5320 12th St. S. #322, Fargo, ND 58104
Mueller, Maurice M., Riverview Pl., 5320 12th St. S., #217E, Fargo, ND 58104
Mullins, Robert J., 1451 Third St., S.E., Apt. 306B, St. Cloud, MN 56301
Neva, Roman G., 417 Second St., N., Wahpeton, ND 58078
Paczek, Valerian, 24 Third Ave. S.W., Lidgerwood, ND 58053
Potter, Gerald, 615 39th St. N., #206C, Grandforks, ND 58202
Proeller, Ullric, Padua Place, 100 Peter Baque Rd., San Antonio, TX 78209
Richard, Antonio J., Riverview Place, 5300 12 St. S., #328E, Fargo, ND 58104
Rudd, Richard, 2802 15th St. S., Unit B, Fargo, ND 58103
Scheller, Raymund B., 101 28th Ave., #15, San Mateo, CA 94403
Schill, Victor J., P.O. Box 12, Walhalla, ND 58282
Schue, Dennis L., Mercy Hospital, 1031 Seventh St., Devils Lake, ND 58301
Sendell, John, 2115 32nd Ave. S., Fargo, ND 58103
Sinner, Richard W., 625 21st St., #1, Fargo, ND 58103

Snell, Roger K., 404 Fourth Ave., Edgeley, ND 58433
Stelten, Leo F., Rt. 2, Box 651, Frazee, MN 54544
Studzinski, Lambert V., Riverview Place, 5320 12th St. S., #127E, Fargo, ND 58104
Walz, Julius J., 29259 Elias Ct., Chicago, IL 60608
Wild, David D.

Permanent Deacons:
Biss, Richard, St. Arnold, Milnor
Braumberger, Arlie, St. Catherine, Valley City
Buresh, Leonard, St. John the Evangelist, Grafton
Carpenter, Stanley, St. Boniface, Walhalla
Davis, Francis R., St. Ann, Belcourt
Didier, Harry, Jr., Sacred Heart, Sanborn
Eberle, Edward, St. Therese Little Flower, Rugby
Eblen, David, St. Rose of Lima, Hillsboro
Ethier, George, St. John, Wahpeton
Faul, Jeffrey, St. Cecilia, Harvey
Gates, David, St. Arnold, Milnor
Grim, Raphael, St. Catherine, Valley City
Ham, Thurston, Transfiguration, Edgeley
Hoefs, Gene, St. John, Wahpeton
Hunkler, Howard, St. Philip Neri, Napolean
Klein, Eugene, St. Catherine, Valley City
La Rocque, Dorian, St. Boniface, Walhalla
Lange, Lawrence, St. Joseph's, Devils Lake
Litzinger, Donald, St. Mary, Grand Forks
Loegering, George, St. Leo, Casselton
Marcy, Timothy, Sacred Heart, Fried
McDonald, Anthony, Seven Dolors, Fort Totten
Mrozla, Julian, St. Mary Cathedral, Fargo
Perius, James, Holy Spirit, Fargo
Prom, Mathias, St. Anthony, Fargo
Pupino, Samuel, Holy Family, Grand Forks
Schmisek, Albert, St. Michael, Grand Forks
Schuster, Conrad, Notre Dame, Willow City
Sobolick, Gerald, St. Mary, Park River
Storey, Alan, St. Boniface, Walhalla
Tinguely, Donald, St. Leo, Casselton
Uline, James, Holy Cross, West Fargo
West, James, St. Jude, Thompson
Zach, Ignatz, St. John, Wahpeton

INSTITUTIONS LOCATED IN THE DIOCESE

[A] SEMINARIES, DIOCESAN

FARGO. *Cardinal Muench Seminary*, 100 35th Ave., N.E., 58102. Tel: 701-232-8969.
Corporate Title: The Cardinal Muench Seminary. Revs. Brian G. Donahue, Rector & Pres.; Dennis A. Skonseng; Robert L. Laliberte. Sisters 1; Priests 3; Lay Teachers 4; 4-year College Students 21.

[B] HIGH SCHOOLS, DIOCESAN

FARGO. *Fargo Catholic Schools Network*, 705 13th Ave. N., P.O. Box 2085, 58107. Dr. Sherry Houdek, Supt.; Elaine Borud, Bus. Mgr.; Don Fischer, Transportation Supr.; Trent Baalke, Athletic Dir.
Shanley High School, 705 13th Ave. N., 58102. Tel: 701-235-5581; Fax: 701-293-3613. Douglas Jacobson, Prin. Priests 1; Brothers 1; Lay Teachers 23; Students 326.

[C] PROTECTIVE INSTITUTIONS

FARGO. *Villa Nazareth dba Friendship, Inc.*, 3004 S. 11th St., 58103. Tel: 701-235-8217.
For a complete listing, refer to the Special Care Facilities section.

[D] GENERAL HOSPITALS

BOTTINEAU. *St. Andrew's Health Center*, 316 Ohmer St., 58318. Tel: 701-228-2255.
For a complete listing, refer to the Hospitals section.
CARRINGTON. *Carrington Health Center*, 800 N. Fourth St., 58421. Tel: 701-652-3141.
For a complete listing, refer to the Hospitals section.
DEVILS LAKE. *Mercy Hospital*, 1031 Seventh St., 58301. Tel: 701-662-2131; Fax: 701-662-4862.
For a complete listing, refer to the Hospitals section.
HARVEY. *St. Aloisius Medical Center*, 325 E. Brewster St., 58341. Tel: 701-324-4651.
For a complete listing, refer to the Hospitals section.
OAKES. *Oakes Community Hospital*, 314 S. Eighth St., 58474. Tel: 701-742-3291.
For a complete listing, refer to the Hospitals section.
PARK RIVER. *St. Ansgar's Health Center*, 115 Vivian St., 58270. Tel: 701-284-7500.
For a complete listing, refer to the Hospitals section.
ROLLA. *Presentation Medical Center*, 213 N.E. Third St., 58367. Tel: 701-477-3161.
For a complete listing, refer to the Hospitals section.
VALLEY CITY. *Mercy Hospital*, 570 Chautauqua Blvd., 58072. Tel: 701-845-0440.
For a complete listing, refer to the Hospitals section.

[E] HOMES FOR AGED

FARGO. *Riverview Place, Inc.*, 5300 12th St., S., 58103. Tel: 701-237-4700.
For a complete listing, refer to the Special Care Facilities section.
EDGELEY. *Manor St. Joseph*, 404 Fourth Ave., 58433. Tel: 701-493-2477.
For a complete listing, refer to the Special Care Facilities section.
ELLENDALE. *Ellendale Nursing Center*, 201 8th St. N., 58436. Tel: 701-349-3312; Fax: 701-349-3944.
For a complete listing, refer to the Special Care Facilities section.
GRAND FORKS. *St. Anne's Guest Home*, 524 N. 17th St., 58203. Tel: 701-746-9401.
For a complete listing, refer to the Special Care Facilities section.
HANKINSON. *St. Gerard Community Nursing Home*, 613 First Ave. S.W., 58041. Tel: 701-242-7891.
For a complete listing, refer to the Special Care Facilities section.
LA MOURE. *La Moure Healthcare Manor*, Hwy. 13, P.O. Box 627, 58458. Tel: 701-883-5363; Fax: 701-883-5711.
For a complete listing, refer to the Special Care Facilities section.
ROLETTE. *Presentation Care Center*, 304 John St., 58366. Tel: 701-246-3786.
For a complete listing, refer to the Special Care Facilities section.
WAHPETON. *Wahpeton Health Care Center*, 1307 N. Seventh St., 58075. Tel: 701-642-6667.
For a complete listing, refer to the Special Care Facilities section.

[F] MONASTERIES AND RESIDENCES FOR PRIESTS AND BROTHERS

PISEK, ND. *Franciscan Friars of Mary Immaculate*, St. Francis Friary, 119 Clement Avenue, 58273-7301.

[G] CONVENTS AND RESIDENCES FOR SISTERS

FARGO. *Prairieland Home Health Agency, Inc.*, 1102 Page Dr., P.O. Box 10007, 58106-0006. Tel: 701-237-9290. Margaret A. Kaltefleiter, Pres.
Presentation Center-Sacred Heart Convent, 1101 32nd Ave. S., 58103. Tel: 701-237-4857; Fax: 701-237-9822. Sr. Paula Ringuette, Pres.; Rev. Maurice M. Mueller. Sisters 63. Sisters of Mary of the Presentation Health Corporation, 1102 Page Dr., P.O. Box 10007, 58106-0006. Tel: 701-237-9290. Aaron Alton, Pres.
Sisters Minor of Mary Immaculate, 1131 N. University Dr., 58102. Tel: 701-239-4669. Sr. Donna Marie, S.M.M.I., Supr. Sisters 1; Novices 2.
BELCOURT. *Queen of Peace Monastery*. Sisters of St. Benedict, P.O. Box 370, 58316. Tel: 701-477-6167. Sr. Judith Emge, O.S.B., Prioress. Sisters 6.
HANKINSON. *Sisters of St. Francis of the Immaculate Heart of Mary*, P.O. Box 447, 58041-0447. Sr. Ann Marie Friederichs, O.S.F., Prov. Sisters 76.
VALLEY CITY. *Sisters of Mary of the Presentation*, 11550 River R. Rd., 58072. Sr. Marlyss Dionne, S.M.P., Prov. Supr.; Rev. John Odermann, O.S.B., Chap. Sisters 60.
WAHPETON. *Carmel of Mary*, 17765 78th St. S.E., 58075. Tel: 701-642-2360. Carmelite Nuns of the Ancient Observance. Mother Rose of the Sacred Heart, O.Carm., Prioress; Rev. Donald A. Leiphon, Chap. Solemn Professed Nuns 13; Junior Professed Nuns 1; Postulants 1.

[H] RETREAT HOUSES

FARGO. *Presentation Prayer Center*, 1101 32nd Ave. S., 58103. Tel: 701-237-4857. Sr. Andrea Arendt, P.B.V.M., Dir. Sisters 2.
Queen of Peace Retreat Center, 1310 Broadway, 58102. Tel: 701-293-9286. Diocesan sponsored retreat house operated by the Diocese of Fargo. George Lacher, Bldg. Dir.

[I] NEWMAN FOUNDATIONS

FARGO. *St. Paul's Catholic Chapel*, 1141 N. University Dr., 58102. Rev. Paul Duchschere, Dir. Campus Ministry. Staff 3.
GRAND FORKS. *Univ. of North Dakota Newman Center*, St. Thomas Aquinas Parish, UND. St. Thomas Aquinas Newman Center, UND, 410 Cambridge St., 58201. Rev. Raymond P. Courtright. Staff 6; Catholic Students 2,500.
MAYVILLE. *Mayville State University Newman Center*. c/o Our Lady of Peace, 435 E. Main St., 58257. Rev. Bernard R. Schneider. Catholic Students 180.
WAHPETON. *State College of Science Newman Student Parish*, 701 N. Seventh St., 58075. Rev. Dale Lagodinski.

[J] MISCELLANEOUS LISTINGS

FARGO. A self-assessment evangelizing vocational tool designed to aid vocation recruitment in discerning individuals for service to the church as priest or religious.
Catholic Development Foundation. c/o Chancery, 1310 Broadway, Box 1750, 58107. A non-profit foundation for religious charitable and educational purposes.
Catholic Family Service, 2537 S. University Dr., 58103. Tel: 701-235-4457.
Catholic School Network Foundation, Office, 705-13th Ave. N., P.O. Box 2085, 58107-2085. A non-profit foundation for religious charitable and educational purposes.
The Presentation Foundation, Sacred Heart Convent, 1101 32nd Ave. S., 58103. Sr. Paula Ringuette, Supr. & Pres.
BOTTINEAU. *Minot State University-Bottineau*, c/o St. Mark, 322 Sinclair St., 58318. Rev. Kevin J. Boucher. Catholic Students 70.
DEVILS LAKE. *UND-Lake Region*, c/o St. Joseph's, 515 Fourth St., P.O. Box 898, 58301. Rev. Jeffrey Wald. Catholic Students 90.
GRAND FORKS. *Air Force Base, Our Lady of the Snows Catholic Community*, 319 ARW/HC, 1699 J ST. (Sunflower Chapel), 58205-6335. Tel: 701-747-3074. Rev. Gary R. Breis, Catholic Chap.
Grand Forks Catholic Schools Association, 216 Belmont Rd., 58201. Pamela Neppel, Sec. A non-profit organization developing, curriculum study, scholarship, transportation, personnel and fund raising.
JAMESTOWN. *Jamestown College*, 6052 College Ln., 58405. Rev. Bernard A. Pfau; Sr. Michaeleen Jantzer, O.S.B., Pastoral Min. & Campus Min. Catholic Students 235.
VALLEY CITY. *Valley City State University*, St. Catherine's, 58072. Ralph Dyrness. Catholic Students 314.

RELIGIOUS INSTITUTES OF MEN REPRESENTED IN THE DIOCESE

For further details refer to the corresponding bracketed number in the Religious Institutes of Men or Women section.
[0200]—*Benedictine Monks*. (Marvin, SD; Collegeville, MN).—O.S.B.
[]—*Bethlehem Community*. (Minto, ND).—.
[]—*Franciscan Brothers of the Sacred Heart*.—O.S.F.
[]—*Franciscan Friars of Mary Immaculate*.—O.F.M.I.
[]—*Franciscan Monks of the Conventional*.—O.F.M.Conv.
[0650]—*Holy Ghost Fathers*.—C.S.Sp.
[0430]—*Order of Preachers-Dominicans*.—O.P.
[]—*Society of Our Lady of the Most Holy Trinity*.—S.O.L.T.
[0990]—*Society of the Catholic Apostolate*. (Mater Dei Prov.).—S.A.C.

RELIGIOUS INSTITUTES OF WOMEN REPRESENTED IN THE DIOCESE

[0230]—*Benedictine Sisters of the Pontifical Jurisdiction*. (Belcourt, ND).—O.S.B.
[0300]—*Calced Carmelites*.—O.Carm.
[2575]—*Institute of the Sisters of Mercy of the Americas*. (Omaha, NE).—R.S.M.
[]—*Sisters Minor of Mary Immaculate*. (Fargo, ND).—S.M.M.I.
[2450]—*Sisters of Mary of the Presentation*. (Maryvale)—S.M.P.
[1590]—*Sisters of St. Francis of the Immaculate Heart of Mary*. (Hankinson, ND).—O.S.F.
[3320]—*Sisters of the Presentation of the B.V.M.* (Fargo, ND).—P.B.V.M.

NECROLOGY

† Duda, Stanislaus J., (Retired). —Died March 3, 1997.
† Strandenses, Lawrence, (Retired). —Died April 20, 1997.

Diocese of Fort Wayne - South Bend

(Dioecesis Wayne Castrensis-South Bendensis)

Most Reverend

JOHN M. D'ARCY, D.D., M.A., S.T.D.

Bishop of Fort Wayne-South Bend; ordained February 2, 1957; appointed Auxiliary Bishop of Boston and Titular Bishop of Mediana December 31, 1974; consecrated February 11, 1975; appointed Bishop of Fort Wayne-South Bend February 26, 1985; installed May 1, 1985. *Mailing Address: P.O. Box 390, Fort Wayne, IN, 46801.*

Chancery Office: 1103 S. Calhoun St., P.O. Box 390, Fort Wayne, IN, 46801. Tel.: 219-422-4611; Fax: 219-423-3382.

Most Reverend

DANIEL R. JENKY, C.S.C.

Auxiliary Bishop of Fort Wayne-South Bend; ordained April 6, 1974; appointed Auxiliary Bishop of Fort Wayne-South Bend and Titular Bishop of Amantia October 21, 1997; consecrated December 16, 1997. *Res., St. Matthew's Cathedral, 1701 Miami St., South Bend, IN, 46613.*

Most Reverend

JOSEPH R. CROWLEY, D.D.

Retired Auxiliary Bishop of Fort Wayne-South Bend; ordained May 1, 1953; appointed Titular Bishop of Maraguia June 16, 1971; consecrated August 24, 1971; retired July 15, 1990. *Mailing Address: 1240 Honan Dr., South Bend, IN, 46614.* Tel.: 219-299-9155.

Most Reverend

LEO ALOYSIUS PURSLEY, D.D.

Retired Bishop of Fort Wayne-South Bend; appointed Titular Bishop of Hadrianopolis and Auxiliary July 22, 1950; consecrated September 19, 1950; appointed Bishop February 26, 1957; retired October 19, 1976. *Res., 2 Northway Dr., Huntington, IN, 46750.*

Most Reverend

JOHN R. SHEETS, S.J.

Retired Auxiliary Bishop of Fort Wayne-South Bend; completed theological studies at St. Mary Jesuit School in Kansas and was ordained in 1953; received his Doctorate in Theology in 1957 in Innsbruck, Austria; ordained to the Episcopacy for the Diocese of Fort Wayne-South Bend on June 25, 1991; and Titular Bishop of Murkona, Province of Maurtitania Cesariense. *Res., St. Matthew Cathedral, 1701 Miami St., South Bend, IN, 46613.* Tel.: 219-289-5539.

ESTABLISHED SEPT. 22, 1857.

Square Miles 5,792.

REDESIGNATED DIOCESE OF FORT WAYNE-SOUTH BEND ON JULY 22, 1960.

Comprises the Counties of Adams, Allen, Dekalb, Elkhart, Huntington, Kosciusko, La Grange, Marshall, Noble, St. Joseph, Steuben, Wabash, Wells, Whitley in the State of Indiana.

For legal titles of parishes and diocesan institutions, consult the Chancery Office.

STATISTICAL OVERVIEW

Personnel	
Bishop	1
Auxiliary Bishops	1
Retired Bishops	2
Priests: Diocesan Active in Diocese	72
Priests: Active Outside Diocese	1
Priests: Retired, Sick or Absent	28
Number of Diocesan Priests	101
Religious Priests in Diocese	178
Ordinations:	
Diocesan Priests	1
Religious Priests	4
Transitional Deacons	3
Permanent Deacons in Diocese	32
Total Brothers	225
Total Sisters	658
Parishes	
Parishes	89
With Resident Pastor:	
Resident Diocesan Priests	65
Resident Religious Priests	24
Without Resident Pastor:	
Pastoral Centers	2
Closed Parishes	1
Professional Ministry Personnel:	
Sisters	21
Lay Ministers	97
Welfare	
Catholic Hospitals	5
Total Assisted	396,192
Health Care Centers	1
Total Assisted	20,000
Homes for the Aged	4
Total Assisted	515
Day Care and Extended Day Care Centers	2
Total Assisted	428
Specialized Homes	1
Total Assisted	19
Special Centers for Social Services	3
Total Assisted	12,919
Educational	
Diocesan Students in Other Seminaries	8
Seminaries, Religious	1
Students Religious	25
Total Seminarians	33
Colleges and Universities	5
Total Students	13,805
High Schools, Diocesan and Parish	4
Total Students	3,405
Elementary Schools, Diocesan and Parish	40
Total Students	10,875
Catechesis/Religious Education:	
High School Students	2,483
Elementary Students	10,114
Total Students Under Catholic Instruction	40,715
Teachers in the Diocese:	
Priests	2
Brothers	1
Sisters	25
Lay Teachers	718
Vital Statistics	
Receptions into the Church:	
Infant Baptism Totals	2,679
Adult Baptism Totals	390
Received into Full Communion	456
First Communions	3,115
Confirmations	2,952
Marriages:	
Catholic	603
Interfaith	501
Total Marriages	1,104
Deaths	1,565
Total Catholic Population	162,756
Total Population	1,156,129

Former Bishops—Rt. Rev. JOHN HENRY LUERS, D.D., cons. Jan. 10, 1858; died June 29, 1871.—Rt. Rev. JOSEPH DWENGER, C.PP.S., D.D., cons. April 14, 1872; died Jan. 27, 1893.—Rt. Rev. JOSEPH RADEMACHER, D.D., cons. Bishop of Nashville, June 24, 1883; transferred to Fort Wayne, July 14, 1893; died Jan. 12, 1900.—Rt. Rev. HERMAN JOSEPH ALERDING, D.D., cons. Nov. 30, 1900; died Dec. 6, 1924.—Most Rev. JOHN FRANCIS NOLL, D.D., cons. June 30, 1925; promoted to rank of Archbishop "ad personam," Sept. 2, 1953; died July 31, 1956.—Most Rev. LEO A. PURSLEY, D.D., cons. Sept. 19, 1950; retired Oct. 19, 1976.—Most Rev. WILLIAM E. MCMANUS, D.D., ord. April 15, 1939; appt. Auxiliary Bishop of Chicago, June 21, 1967; appt. Bishop of Fort Wayne, Aug. 31, 1976; installed as 7th Bishop of Fort Wayne, Oct. 19, 1976; retired Feb. 25, 1985; died March 3, 1997.

Diocese of Fort Wayne-South Bend, Inc.—(Incorporated Aug. 29, 1955). *Board of Directors:* Most Rev. JOHN M. D'ARCY, Pres.; Rev. Msgr. J. WILLIAM LESTER P.A., Vice Pres.; Rev. Msgr. JAMES J. WOLF, Sec. *Finance Council:* Mr. JOSEPH RYAN; ARTHUR DECIO; LOUIS PACH; Sr. M. THERESA SOLBACK, O.S.F.; Mr. JERRY HAMMES; JOSEPH DAHM; MICHAEL HAMMES; THOMAS BLEE; RICHARD DOERMER; VINCENT TIPPMANN; Mr. JERRY KEARNS.

Chancery Office—1103 S. Calhoun St., P.O. Box 390, Fort Wayne, 46801. Tel: 219-422-4611; Fax: 219-423-3382. Office Hours: Mon.-Fri. 8:30-4:30. Other times by appointment.

Vicar General-Chancellor—Rev. Msgr. JAMES J. WOLF; Rev. Msgr. J. WILLIAM LESTER, P.A.

Episcopal Vicar for Education—Rev. Msgr. J. WILLIAM LESTER, P.A., *1103 S. Clinton St., Box 390, Fort Wayne, 46801.* Tel: 219-422-4611; Fax: 219-423-3382.

South Bend Chancery—114 W. Wayne St., S. Bend, 46624. Tel: 219-234-0687; Fax: 219-232-8483.

Diocesan Tribunal—1103 S. Calhoun St., P.O. Box 390, Fort Wayne, 46801. Tel: 219-422-4611., South Bend Office: *114 W. Wayne St, P.O. Box 1432, S. Bend, 46624.* Tel: 219-287-6531; Fax: 219-423-3382.

Judicial Vicar—Rev. BRUCE PIECHOCKI.

Defenders of the Bond—Deacon LOUIS B. MCDOUGALL; Rev. VIGNY J. BELLERIVE.

Pro-Synodal Judges—Revs. PHILIP DEVOLDER; LAWRENCE KRAMER; BRUCE PIECHOCKI; ROBERT SCHULTE.

Court Consultants—JOHN NEWBAUER, Ph.D.; PHIL SUTTON, Ph.D.

Fort Wayne Office Secretary—JANICE BRELL. Office Auditors: VICKI FERRIER; MONICA KLUESNER; WILLIAM PLATTER; JAMES SHERRON.

Notary—JANICE BRELL.

South Bend Office Secretary—DIANA HEIDT. Office Auditors: SANDRA LAVIOLETTE; JANET LATTREZ.

Consultors—Rev. Msgr. J. WILLIAM LESTER, P.A.; Rev. Msgr. JAMES J. WOLF; Rev. Msgr. JOHN N. SUELZER; Revs. BRUCE PIECHOCKI; WILLIAM HODDES; RAYMOND BALZER; BERNARD GALIC.

Diocesan Offices and Directors

Business Administration Office—JOSEPH RYAN, Chief Fin. Officer; Vacant, Controller, *P.O. Box 390, Ft. Wayne, 46801.* Tel: 219-422-4611.

Buildings and Improvements—Advisory Board: Rev. Msgr. JAMES WOLF; Rev. Msgr. J. WILLIAM LESTER, P.A.; Rev. Msgr. ROBERT CONTANT; Revs. ANTHONY LETKO; LAURENCE TIPPMANN; DAVID CARKENORD; ROBERT YAST; ELDEN J. MILLER; Mr. JOSEPH RYAN; JAMES SCHENKEL.

Budget Committee—Rev. Msgr. J. WILLIAM LESTER, P.A.; Rev. Msgr. JAMES J. WOLF; Rev. JOHN PFISTER; Rev. Msgr. JOHN SUELZER; Rev. BERNARD GALIC; Mr. JOSEPH RYAN.

Diocesan Services Agency—JOHN KLEIN; MARY LOU O'KEEFFE, Purchasing, *P.O. Box 390, Fort Wayne, 46801.* Tel: 219-422-4611; 800-856-4611.

Diocesan Office of Development—JOHN BARRETT, *1103 S. Calhoun St., P.O. Box 390, Fort Wayne, 46801.* Tel: 219-422-4611. *219-420-6306.*

Campus Ministry—LINDA FURGE, Dir., *1330 E. Washington Center Rd., Fort Wayne, 46825.* Tel: 219-483-3661.

Campaign for Human Development—Rev. THOMAS O'CONNOR, *P.O. Box 11383, Fort Wayne, 46857-1383.* Tel: 219-424-8231; Fax: 219-426-2406.

Catholic Charities—KATHLEEN DONNELLAN, Dir., *315 E. Washington, Fort Wayne, 46802.* Tel: 219-439-0242; 800-686-7459; Fax: 219-439-0250.

Censor Librorum—Rev. JOHN KUZMICH, *8669 Auburn Rd., Ft. Wayne, 46825.* Tel: 219-489-3537.

Cemeteries—Rev. DAVID CARKENORD, Dir., *1098 Co. Rd. 39, Waterloo, 46793.* Tel: 219-837-7115; 800-570-8080; Fax: 219-837-7727.

Catholic Cemetery Association of Fort Wayne, Inc.—*3500 Lake Ave., Fort Wayne, 46805.* Tel: 219-426-2044.

Charismatic Movement—Rev. GEORGE KAMINSKI, *St. Vincent de Paul, 8669 Auburn Rd., Fort Wayne, 46825.* Tel: 219-489-3537. Deacon KEVIN RANAGHAN, *1003 St. Vincent, South Bend, 46617.* Tel: 219-234-2465.

Clergy Relief Association—Revs. ROBERT YAST, Pres.; DANIEL LEEUW, Sec.; JAMES KOONS, Treas. Directors: Revs. ROBERT VAN KEMPEN; EDWARD J. KRASON; PHILLIP WIDMANN; JOHN PFISTER.

Communications—CHRISTINE BONAHOOM, *150 Doan Dr., Fort Wayne, 46816.* Tel: 219-744-0012; Fax: 219-744-1473.

Continuing Education of the Clergy—Rev. Msgr. J. WILLIAM LESTER, P.A., *P.O. Box 390, Fort Wayne, 46801.* Tel: 219-422-4611; Fax: 219-423-3382.

Council of Priests—Most Rev. JOHN D'ARCY; Most Rev. JOHN SHEETS, S.J.; Rev. Msgr. J. WILLIAM LESTER, P.A.; Rev. Msgr. JAMES J. WOLF; Revs. PHILIP DEVOLDER; BARRY C. ENGLAND; MICHAEL HEINTZ; THOMAS JONES, C.S.C.; WILLIAM KUMMER; JOHN KUZMICH; THOMAS LEMOS, C.S.C.; RONALD RIEDER, O.F.M.Cap.; ROBERT SCHULTE; DERRICK SNEYD; WILLIAM SULLIVAN, C.S.C.; LAURENCE TIPPMANN.

Cursillo—Rev. PAUL BUETER, *114 W. Monroe, Goshen, 46526.* Tel: 219-533-3385.

Hispanic Ministry Services—Rev. PAUL BUETER, Diocesan Coord., *114 W. Monroe, Goshen, 46526.* Tel: 219-533-3385.

Fort Wayne—Rev. GLENN KOHRMAN; Sr. ELIZABETH GARCIA, S.N.D., *St. Paul, 416 W. Washington Blvd., Fort Wayne, 46858.* Tel: 219-744-1450.

Milford—Rev. PAUL R. BUETER; Sr. M. VICTOR KERCHER, O.S.B., *Our Lady of Guadalupe, 4th & Main St., Milford, 46542.* Tel: 219-658-9384; 658-9594.

South Bend—Rev. THOMAS LEMOS, C.S.C., *St. Stephen, 1102 W. Thomas St., South Bend, 46625.* Tel: 219-287-7681.

La Casa de Amistad, Inc.—CHRIS NANNI, Dir., *746 S. Meade St., S. Bend, 46619.* Tel: 219-233-2120.

Diocesan Council of Catholic Women—Rev. EDWARD NARCOWICH, *5790 E. 1100 S., Geneva, 46740.* Tel: 219-997-6558. BETTY LOMONT, Pres., *15412 Dawkins Rd., New Haven, 46774.* Tel: 219-749-9396.

Diocesan Family Life—FRED EVERETT; LISA EVERETT, *114 W. Wayne St., S. Bend, 46601.* Tel: 219-234-0687; Fax: 219-232-8483.

Ecumenical Affairs—Rev. ROBERT C. SCHULTE, Dir., *10700 Aboite Center Rd., Fort Wayne, 46804.* Tel: 219-432-0268.

Human Development Commission—Rev. THOMAS O'CONNOR, *P.O. Box 11383, Fort Wayne, 46857-1383.* Tel: 219-424-8231; Fax: 219-426-2406.

Liturgical Commission—Rev. WILLIAM SCHOOLER, Chm.

Environment and Art—Dr. ROBERT AMICO; Dr. JAIME BELLATA; Revs. JOSE MARTELLI, C.S.C.; JAMES FLANIGAN, C.S.C.; RICHARD BULLENE, C.S.C.

Liturgy—Revs. WILLIAM SCHOOLER; WILLIAM KUMMER.

Music—JUDY THROM; Dr. EDWARD KLINE; STEVE WARNER.

R.C.I.A.—Ms. GERVAISE BASTIAN; Sr. BETTY KORESSEL, S.P.

Office of Worship—Vacant; Dir., *1103 S. Calhoun St., Box 390, Fort Wayne, 46801.* Tel: 219-422-4611.

Official Publication "Today's Catholic"—JOHN ANKENBRUCK, Editor; MURRAY HUBLEY, JR., News Editor, *150 Doan Dr., Fort Wayne, 46816., Mailing Address: P.O. Box 11169, Fort Wayne, 46856.* Tel: 219-456-2824; Fax: 219-744-1473.

Permanent Diaconate—Rev. WILLIAM KUMMER, *St. John, 4525 Arlington Ave., Fort Wayne, 46807.* Tel: 219-744-4393.

Priests' Eucharistic League—Vacant, *P.O. Box 390, Fort Wayne, 46801.* Tel: 219-422-4611.

Pro-Life—FRED EVERETT; LISA EVERETT, *114 W. Wayne St., S. Bend, 46601.* Tel: 219-234-0687., Birthline phones: Tel: 219-422-1818 (Fort Wayne); 356-3322 (Huntington); 289-1034 (South Bend).

Propagation of the Faith and Holy Childhood Association—Rev. PHILLIP WIDMANN, *641 N. Main, P.O. Box 250, Roanoke, 46783-0250.* Tel: 219-672-2838; Fax: 219-672-3069.

Religious Education, Office of—Sr. M. JANE CAREW, O.V., Diocesan Dir., Religious Education Fort Wayne: DONNA MACINO, Assoc. Dir., *P.O. Box 390, Fort Wayne, 46801.* Tel: 219-422-4611.

South Bend-Mishawaka Area Office of Religious Education—Vacant, *1328 W. Dragoon Trail, Mishawaka, 46554.* Tel: 219-259-9994; Fax: 219-256-2709.

Refugee Resettlement Program—KATHLEEN DONNELLAN, Dir., *315 E. Washington, Fort Wayne, 46802.* Tel: 219-422-7511; 800-686-7459; Fax: 219-439-0250.

Retired Clergy Committee—Revs. WILLIAM GIERANOWSKI, Pres. BARRY ENGLAND; JAMES WOLF; JOHN SUELZER; Rev. Msgr. J. WILLIAM LESTER, P.A.

Retired Senior Volunteer Program (RSVP)—Auburn: PATTI SHEPPARD, Coord., *500 E. 7th St., Auburn, 46706.* Tel: 219-925-0917.

Serra International—Rev. GLENN KOHRMAN, *Sacred Heart Parish, 1020 Capitol Ave., Fort Wayne, 46806.* Tel: 219-744-2519. Rev. ROBERT YAST, *225 S. Mill St., Mishawaka, 46544.* Tel: 219-255-6134.

Single Catholic Adult Club—Rev. GEORGE KAMINSKI, *1103 S. Calhoun St., P.O. Box 390, Fort Wayne, 46801.* Tel: 219-422-4611.

Schools—Dr. JEANETTE KAM, Supt. CANDACE SCHEIDT, Assoc. JOHN GAUGHAN, Asst. Dir. High Schools, *1102 S. Clinton St., Box 390, Ft. Wayne, 46801.* Tel: 219-422-4611; Fax: 219-420-6306. South Bend Office: LARRY BARTEK, Assoc. Supt., *1328 W. Dragoon Trail, Mishawaka, 46544.* Tel: 219-255-1387; Fax: 219-256-2709.

School Board, Diocesan—

Vicariate A, B, C—Rev. DARYL RYBICKI; MARY JANE STANLEY.

Vicariate D, E, F—Rev. KENNETH ALT, C.P.P.S.; DANIEL ARNOLD; LIZ BROWN; DENNIS ZENT.

At-Large Representatives—STEPHEN SMITH; Sr. ELAINE BROTHERS, O.S.F.; JANE BAKER.

Catholic Schools Office—LARRY BARTEK; Dr. JEANETTE KAM; CANDACE SCHEIDT; JOHN GAUGHAN.

Ex Officio Members—Most Rev. JOHN M. D'ARCY; Rev. Msgr. J. WILLIAM LESTER, P.A.

Scouting—Fort Wayne: Rev. TIMOTHY WROZEK, *207 North Cass St., Wabash, 46992-2441.* Tel: 219-563-4750; Fax: 219-563-0313. South Bend: Rev. ELDEN J. MILLER, *Queen of Peace, 4508 Vistula Rd., Mishawaka, 46555.* Tel: 219-255-9674; Fax: 219-255-1029.

St. Vincent de Paul Society—Rev. THOMAS O'CONNOR, *P.O. Box 11383, Fort Wayne, 46857-1383.* Tel: 219-424-8231; Fax: 219-426-2406.

Spiritual Development—Fort Wayne: Sr. ANN KIHSLINGER S.S.N.D., Co-Dir.; South Bend: Sr. MARY BROOKS, Co-Dir., *114 W. Wayne St., S. Bend, 46601.* Tel: 219-234-0687.

Office of Youth Ministry and Spiritual Development—STEVEN J. WEIGAND, Assoc., *P.O. Box 390, Fort Wayne, 46801.* Tel: 219-422-4611; Fax: 219-420-6306.

Vocations—Rev. BERNARD GALIC, Dir., *114 W. Wayne St., South Bend, 46601.* Tel: 219-234-0687; Fax: 219-232-8483.

Youth Organizations—Rev. GEORGE KAMINSKI, Moderator, *8669 Auburn Rd., Fort Wayne, 46825.* Tel: 219-489-3537. Rev. PETER A. JARRET, C.S.C., *St. Pius X Parish, 52553 Fir Rd., Granger, 46530.* Tel: 219-272-8462; Fax: 219-272-8493.

CLERGY, PARISHES, MISSIONS AND PAROCHIAL SCHOOLS

CITY OF FORT WAYNE
(Allen County)

1—CATHEDRAL OF THE IMMACULATE CONCEPTION (1836). (Calhoun, between Lewis and Jefferson Sts.). Rev. Msgr. James J. Wolf, Co-Rector; Rev. Msgr. J. William Lester, Co-Rector; Sr. Sally Soules, S.F.C.C., Pastoral Min.; Deacon Joseph R. Zickgraf. In res., Rev. Peter Kaija (Uganda).
Res., 1122 Clinton St., P.O. Box 10898, 46854. Tel: 219-424-1485; Fax: 219-423-3382.
Catechesis/Religious Programs—Students 127.
Chapel—MacDougall Memorial Chapel.

2—ST. ANDREW (1910), Rev. John H. Delaney, Admin. 518 E. DeWald, 46803. Tel: 219-744-2765; Fax: 219-744-1972.
Res., 2610 New Haven Ave., 46803. Tel: 219-422-0380. Sr. Rose Clare Ehrlich, C.S.A., Pastoral Assoc.

3—ST. CHARLES BORROMEO (1957), Rev. Msgr. John N. Suelzer; Revs. Polycarp Fernando (Sri Lanka); Michael Heintz; Rev. Msgr. Edward I. Hession, Pastor Emeritus, (Retired); Sr. Kathleen Morrissey, O.P., Pastoral Assoc.; Deacon Louis B. McDougall.
Res., 4916 Trier Rd., 46815. Tel: 219-482-2186; Fax: 219-471-2144.
School—3700 Reed Rd., 46815. Tel: 219-484-3392; Fax: 219-482-2006. Mrs. Michelle Hittie, Prin.
Franciscan Sisters of the Sacred Heart 2; Lay Teachers 33; Students 719.
Catechesis/Religious Programs—Tel: 219-484-7322. Kathy Monagle, D.R.E.
Students 550.

4—ST. ELIZABETH ANN SETON (1988), Revs. Robert Schulte; John Overmyer.
Office: 10700 Aboite Center Rd., 46804. Tel: 219-432-0268; Fax: 219-436-5851.
Res., 10517 Unita Dr., 46804. Tel: 219-436-9819.
Catechesis/Religious Programs—Tel: 219-432-0268. Michelle Kriss, D.R.E.
Students 849.

5—ST. HENRY (1956), Rev. Kenneth Sarrazine.
Res., 2929 E. Paulding Rd., 46816. Tel: 219-447-4100.

6—ST. HYACINTH (1910). Closed. For inquiries for parish records contact the Chancery.

7—ST. JOHN BAPTIST (1929), Revs. William Kummer; Charles A. Herman; Mary L. Glowaski, Pastoral Assoc.
Res., 4525 Arlington Ave., 46807. Tel: 219-744-4393; Fax: 219-456-3072.
School—4500 Fairfield Ave., 46807. Tel: 219-456-3321. Mr. J. Mark Mugg, Prin.
Sisters 1; Lay Teachers 22; Students 389.
Catechesis/Religious Programs—4501 Arlington Ave., 46807. Tel: 219-744-3578. Kelley Renz, D.R.E.
Students 61.

8—ST. JOSEPH (1914) (Italian), Revs. Laurence Tippmann; Adam Schmitt.
Res., 1910 Hale Ave., 46802. Tel: 219-432-5113; Fax: 219-432-4711.
School—2213 Brooklyn Ave., 46802. Tel: 219-432-4000; Fax: 219-432-8642. Ms. Mary Schreiber, Prin.
Sisters of St. Agnes 2; Lay Teachers 16; Students 350.

9—ST. JUDE (1929), Revs. William C. Schooler; Eric Van Meter; Mary Pohlman, Pastoral Assoc.; Deacon Fred J. Larson. In res., Revs. Robert L. Traub; Robert D'Souza (India).
Res., 2101 Pemberton Dr., 46805. Tel: 219-484-6609.
School—2110 Pemberton Dr., 46805. Tel: 219-484-4611. Sr. Alice Marie Willman, S.N.D., Prin.
Sisters of Notre Dame 4; Lay Teachers 35; Students 620.
Catechesis/Religious Programs—Tel: 219-484-6609. Mary Barnes, D.R.E.
Students 261.

10—ST. MARY (1848), Rev. Thomas P. O'Connor.
Mailing Address: P.O. Box 11383, 46857-1383.
Res., 422 E. Jefferson St., 46802. Tel: 219-424-8231; Fax: 219-426-2406.

11—MOST PRECIOUS BLOOD (1897), Revs. Kenneth G. Alt, C.PP.S.; Werner F. Verhoff, C.PP.S.
Res., 1515 Barthold St., 46808. Tel: 219-424-5535.
School—1529 Barthold St., 46808. Tel: 219-424-4832. Corinne Tessman, Prin.
Lay Teachers 12; Students 200.
Catechesis/Religious Programs—Students 60.

12—OUR LADY OF GOOD HOPE (1969), Rev. David Voors.
Res., 7215 St. Joe Rd., 46835. Tel: 219-485-9615; Fax: 219-485-4463.
Catechesis/Religious Programs—Tel: 219-485-3732. D.R.E.: Mary Kay Matasky; Donna Maroney.
Students 280.

13—ST. PATRICK (1889) (Vietnamese), Rev. James W. Koons. In res., Rev. Matthew S. Kafka.

Res., 2120 S. Harrison St., 46802. Tel: 219-744-1450; Fax: 219-744-6231.

14—ST. PAUL (1865) (Hispanic), Rev. Glenn Kohrman, Admin.; Sr. Elizabeth Garcia, S.N.D., Pastoral Assoc.; Deacon Justo Donias.
Office: 416 W. Washington Blvd., 46802.
Res., 1020 Capitol Ave., 46802. Fax: 219-744-2519.
Catechesis/Religious Programs—Tel: 219-422-0118; Fax: 219-422-0118.
Students 95.

15—ST. PETER (1872), Rev. John Delaney; Sr. Melanie Raul, P.H.J.C., Pastoral Assoc.
Res., 518 E. De Wald St., 46803. Tel: 219-744-2765; Fax: 219-744-1972.

16—QUEEN OF ANGELS (1947), Rev. John F. Pfister; Sr. Joan Bakle, S.S.N.D., Pastoral Min. In res., Rev. Bruce Piechocki.
Res., 1500 W. State St., 46808. Tel: 219-482-9411; Fax: 219-471-0005.
School—1600 W. State Blvd., 46808. Tel: 219-483-8214. Mrs. Sandra Koziol, Prin.
Lay Teachers 14; Students 340.
Catechesis/Religious Programs—Students 82.

17—SACRED HEART (1947), Rev. Glenn Kohrman.
Res., 1020 Capitol, 46806. Tel: 219-744-2519; Fax: 219-744-2519.
School—Julian Benoit Academy, 3029 E. Paulding Rd., 46816. Tel: 219-447-5121.

18—ST. THERESE (1947), Rev. Michael J. Rosswurm.
Res., 2304 Lower Huntington Rd., 46819. Tel: 219-747-9139; Fax: 219-747-1494.
School—2222 Lower Huntington Rd., 46819. Tel: 219-747-2343; Fax: 219-747-4767. Charles A. Grimm, Prin.
Lay Teachers 12; Students 248.
Catechesis/Religious Programs—Tel: 219-747-9139.
Students 93.

19—ST. VINCENT DE PAUL (1846), Revs. John M. Kuzmich; George Kaminski; Mark Allen Gurtner. Pastoral Assocs.: Sr. Mary Catherine Jarema, S.S.N.D.; Mrs. Judy Mockenhaupt.
Res., 8669 Auburn Rd., 46825. Tel: 219-489-3537; Fax: 219-489-9405. [CEM]
School—8905 Auburn Rd., 46825. Tel: 219-489-4591; Fax: 219-489-5318. Mrs. Barbara McClure, Prin.
Sisters 1; Lay Teachers 30; Students 700.
Catechesis/Religious Programs—Tel: 219-489-1684. Elizabeth Balbo-Ryan, D.R.E.
Students 580.

CITY OF SOUTH BEND
(St. Joseph County)

1—ST. MATTHEW CATHEDRAL (1921), Most Rev. John R. Sheets, S.J., D.D.; Rev. Thomas R. Shoemaker.
Res., 1701 Miami St., 46613. Tel: 219-289-5539; Fax: 219-289-0227.
School—1015 E. Dayton, 46613. Tel: 219-289-4535. Ms. Mary Ann Retseck, Prin.
Lay Teachers 23; Students 470.

2—ST. ADALBERT (1910) (Polish), Revs. Daryl Rybicki; John Klimczyk; Sr. M. Anthony Kubat, C.S.S.F., Pastoral Min. In res., Rev. James Fahey, C.S.C.
Res., 2420 W. Huron St., 46619. Tel: 219-288-5708.
School—519 S. Olive St., 46619. Tel: 219-288-6645. Sr. Dian Majsterek, S.S.J.-T.O.S.F., Prin.
Felician Sisters 1; Sisters of St. Joseph 1; Lay Teachers 8; Students 110.

3—ST. ANTHONY DE PADUA (1949), Revs. Barry England; Joseph Gaughan; Deacon Brian Miller.
Res., 2120 E. Jefferson Blvd., 46617. Tel: 219-282-2308; Fax: 219-288-8877.
School—2310 E. Jefferson Blvd., 46615. Tel: 219-233-7169; Fax: 219-288-8877. Ms. Martha Lewallen, Prin.
Lay Teachers 22; Students 454.
Catechesis/Religious Programs—Tel: 219-282-2308.
Students 100.

4—ST. AUGUSTINE (1928) (African American), Rev. Daryl Rybicki; Deacon Paul Baumgartner.
Mailing Address: P.O. Box 3198, 46619-0198. Tel: 219-234-6334.
Res., 1130 W. Thomas St., 46601. Tel: 219-234-0295.

5—ST. CASIMIR (1899) (Polish), Revs. Thomas F. Lemos, C.S.C.; John Arthur Steele, C.S.C. In res., Rev. Robert C. Steigmeyer, C.S.C.
Res., 1308 W. Dunham St., 46619. Tel: 219-287-9551.

6—CHRIST THE KING (1933), Revs. Thomas J. Jones, C.S.C.; Gary Chamberland, C.S.C.; John P. Riley, C.S.C.; Sr. Diane C. Jamison, O.S.F., (Dir. of Christian Formation).
Res., 52473 U.S. 33 N., 46637. Tel: 219-272-3113; Fax: 219-273-6702.
School—Tel: 219-272-3922. Jacqueline M. Klaybor, Prin.
Lay Teachers 25; Students 517.
Catechesis/Religious Programs—Students 174.

7—CORPUS CHRISTI (1961), Rev. Camillo Tirabassi. In res., Rev. Walter J. Bly.
Res., 2822 Corpus Christi Dr., 46628. Tel: 219-272-9982.
School—2817 Corpus Christi Dr., 46628. Tel: 219-272-9868; Fax: 219-272-9894. Mrs. Marilyn Gibbs, Prin.
Daughters of Divine Charity 1; Lay Teachers 27; Students 526.
Catechesis/Religious Programs—Students 60.

8—ST. HEDWIG (1877) (Polish), Rev. Leonard F. Chrobot.
Res., 331 S. Scott St., 46601. Tel: 219-287-8932; Fax: 219-232-9787.

9—HOLY CROSS (1929), Revs. Michael Belinski, C.S.C.; Richard Conyers, C.S.C.
Res., 1520 Vassar Ave., 46628. Tel: 219-233-2179; Fax: 219-237-6736.
School—(Grades PreK-8) 1020 Wilber St., 46628. Tel: 219-234-3422. Mrs. Karen Van Meter, Prin.
Lay Teachers 20; Students 465.
Catechesis/Religious Programs—920 Wilber St., 46628. Tel: 219-233-2954.
Students 100.

10—HOLY FAMILY (1945), Revs. Bernard J. Galic; Paul Butler (Ireland); Deacon Eugene Szynski, Pastoral Assoc. In res., Rev. Paul Miller.
Res., 56405 Mayflower Rd., 46619. Tel: 219-282-2317; Fax: 219-282-2318. [JC]
School—Tel: 219-289-7375. Sr. Joan Marie Shillinger, C.S.S.F., Prin.
Felician Sisters of Livonia, MI 2; Lay Teachers 18; Students 416.
Catechesis/Religious Programs—Tel: 219-289-7375. Ann Schramm, D.R.E.
Students 195.

11—ST. JOHN THE BAPTIST (1956), Rev. Terry E. Place.
Res., 3526 St. John Way, 46628. Tel: 219-233-5414.
School—3616 St. John Way, 46628. Tel: 219-232-9849. Sr. Connie Bach, Prin.
Lay Teachers 10; Students 100.

12—ST. JOSEPH (1853), Revs. Anthony V. Szakaly, C.S.C.; Timothy L. O'Connor, C.S.C.; Regina Wilson, M.Div., Pastoral Assoc. In res., Rev. Richard P. Zang, C.S.C.; Bro. Steve Nani, C.S.C.
Res., 226 N. Hill St., 46617. Tel: 219-234-3135.
Parish Office: 211 N. St. Louis Blvd., 46617. Tel: 219-234-3134; Fax: 219-234-2822.
School—216 N. Hill St., 46617. Tel: 219-234-0451. Mrs. Suzanne Wiwi, Prin.
Lay Teachers 20; Students 348.

13—ST. JUDE (1948), Revs. James Stoyle; Robert Muhiirwa, C.S.C. (Uganda).
Res., 19704 Johnson Rd., 46614. Tel: 219-291-0570; Fax: 219-299-3051.
School—19657 Hildebrand St., 46614. Tel: 219-291-3820. Ms. Judi Cole, Prin.
Lay Teachers 10; Students 246.
Catechesis/Religious Programs—Tel: 219-291-2797.
Students 98.

14—ST. MARY OF THE ASSUMPTION (1882) (German), Rev. Paul McCarthy.
Res., 3501 S. Locust Rd., 46614. Tel: 219-287-0225.
School—3402 S. Locust Rd., 46614. Tel: 219-287-1472.
Lay Teachers 10; Students 190.

15—OUR LADY OF HUNGARY (1921), Rev. Thaddeus Kwak; Deacon Ervin Kuspa. In res., Rev. Anthony Molnar.
Res., 829 W. Calvert St., 46613. Tel: 219-287-1700. [CEM]
School—735 W. Calvert St., 46613. Tel: 219-289-3272. Mr. Clem Wroblewski, Prin.
Lay Teachers 10; Students 180.

16—ST. PATRICK (1858), Rev. Charles J. Lavely, C.S.C. In res., Revs. Richard A. Laurick, C.S.C.; Donald J. Bielby, C.S.C. (Canada).
Res., 309 S. Taylor St., 46625. Tel: 219-232-5839; Fax: 219-232-5830.
Catechesis/Religious Programs—Tel: 219-289-3700.
Students 73.

17—FAITH & HOPE & CHARITY CHAPEL (1975), Revs. James F. Blaes, C.S.C.; Raymond Cour, C.S.C.; William A. Botzum, C.S.C.
Res., 114 W. Wayne St., P.O. Box 143, 46624. Tel: 219-289-4263.

18—ST. STANISLAUS (1899) (Polish), Revs. David J. Porterfield, C.S.C.; Ronald R. Tripi, C.S.C.; Daniel C. Coughlin, C.S.C.; Sr. Linda Bellemore, C.S.C., Pastoral Assoc.
Res., 415 N. Brookfield St., 46628. Tel: 219-233-1217; 233-5490; Fax: 219-233-5490.

19—ST. STEPHEN (1909) (Hispanic), Revs. Thomas F. Lemos, C.S.C.; John Steele, C.S.C. In res., Rev. Bob Steigmeyer, C.S.C.
Res., 1102 W. Thomas St., 46601. Tel: 219-287-7681.
Catechesis/Religious Programs—Tel: 219-287-7681. Sr. Clare Alfred, C.S.C., D.R.E., Pastoral Min.
Students 260.

20—ST. THERESE, LITTLE FLOWER (1937), Revs. Paul LeBrun, C.S.C.; Donald Guertin, C.S.C.
Res., 54191 N. Ironwood Dr., 46635. Tel: 219-272-7070; Fax: 219-243-3434.
Catechesis/Religious Programs—Tel: 219-272-7070.
Students 325.

OUTSIDE THE CITIES OF FORT WAYNE AND SOUTH BEND

Albion, Noble Co., Blessed Sacrament (1875), Rev. Dale Bauman; Deacon Ramiro Reyes.
Res., 300 Ravine Park Dr., Ligonier, 46767-1301. Tel: 219-894-4946. [JC]
Church—State Rd. 9 S., Box 102, 46701-0102. Tel: 219-636-2072.
Catechesis/Religious Programs—Students 77.

Angola, Steuben Co., St. Anthony (1926), Rev. Fred Pasche, O.F.M.Conv. In res., Revs. Conrad L. Schweibold, O.F.M.Conv.; Philip Schneider, O.F.M.Conv.
Res., 700 W. Maumee St., 46703. Tel: 219-665-2259; Fax: 219-665-2268.
Catechesis/Religious Programs—Tel: 219-665-6129. Kathy Dowe, D.R.E.
Students 175.
Mission—Clear Lake, Steuben Co., St. Paul Chapel, 46703.

Arcola, Allen Co., St. Patrick (1846), Rev. Eugene A. Koers.
Res., 12305 Arcola Rd., Fort Wayne, 46818. Tel: 219-625-4151. [CEM]
Catechesis/Religious Programs—Students 102.

Auburn, De Kalb Co., Immaculate Conception (1872), Rev. Raymond J. Balzer.
Res., 500 E. 7th St., 46706. Tel: 219-925-3930. [CEM]
Catechesis/Religious Programs—Tel: 219-925-1621. D.R.E.: Phyllis Gurtner; Karen Wrona.
Students 283.

Avilla, Noble Co., St. Mary of the Assumption (1853), Rev. Daniel Durkin. In res., Rev. Herman J. Schnurr.
Res., 228 N. Main St., Box 700, 46710-0700. Tel: 219-897-3261; Fax: 219-897-3261. [CEM]
School—232 N. Main St., 46710. Tel: 219-897-3481; Fax: 219-897-3481. Sr. Theresa Renninger, O.S.F., Prin.
Franciscan Sisters of the Sacred Heart 2; Lay Teachers 7; Students 173.
Catechesis/Religious Programs—Students 97.

Besancon, Allen Co., St. Louis (1846), Rev. Stephen E. Colchin.
Res., 15535 Lincoln Hwy. E., New Haven, 46744. Tel: 219-749-4525. [CEM 2]
School—15529 Lincoln Hwy. E., New Haven, 46744. Tel: 219-749-5815. Ms. Agnes Hart, Prin.
Lay Teachers 4; Students 68.
Catechesis/Religious Programs—15412 Dawkins Rd., New Haven, 46774. Tel: 219-749-9396.
Students 157.

Big Long Lake, LaGrange Co., St. Mary of the Angels (1937), Rev. Conrad L. Schweibold, O.F.M.Conv.
Res., St. Anthony Rectory, 700 W. Maumee, Angola, 46703. Tel: 219-665-2259. [JC]
Church—Hudson, 46747. Tel: 219-351-2404.
Catechesis/Religious Programs—Students 52.

Bluffton, Wells Co., St. Joseph (1875), Rev. Lawrence A. Kramer.
Res., 1700 N. Main St., 46714. Tel: 219-824-1380. [JC]
Catechesis/Religious Programs—Students 162.

Bremen, Marshall Co., St. Dominic (1947), Rev. Robert J. Dombrowski.
Church—212 N. Maryland St., 46506. Tel: 219-546-3601; Fax: 219-546-3659.
Catechesis/Religious Programs—903 W. Bike St., 46506.
Students 195.

Bristol, Elkhart Co., St. Mary of the Annunciation (1942), Rev. James F. Seculoff.
Res., 411 W. Vistula St., Box 245, 46507. Tel: 219-848-4305; Fax: 219-848-4305.
Catechesis/Religious Programs—Students 401.

Churubusco, Whitley Co., St. John Bosco (1971), Rev. Danny Pinto (Sri Lanka).
Res., 216 N. Main St., 46723. Tel: 219-693-9578; Fax: 219-693-1608.
Catechesis/Religious Programs—Students 175.

Clear Lake, Steuben Co., St. Paul Chapel (1941), Rev. Philip Schneider, O.F.M.Conv., Admin.
Res., St. Anthony Rectory, 700 W. Maumee, Angola,

46703. Tel: 219-665-2259; Fax: 219-848-4305.
Church—8780 E. 700 N., 46703. Tel: 219-495-9913.
Catechesis/Religious Programs—Students 56.

Columbia City, Whitley Co., St. Paul of the Cross (1860), Rev. Sextus Don, Admin.
Res., 307 S. Line St., 46725. Tel: 219-244-5723. [CEM]
Catechesis/Religious Programs—Students 282.

Culver, Marshall Co., St. Mary of the Lake, Rev. Jeffery Largent.
Res., 124 College Ave., 46511. Tel: 219-842-2522.
Catechesis/Religious Programs—Students 108.

Decatur, Adams Co., St. Mary (1840), Revs. Philip DeVolder; Joseph Lawrence (India); Sr. Margaret Rose Donnelly, S.S.N.D., Pastoral Assoc.
Res., 414 W. Madison St., P.O. Box 207, 46733. Tel: 219-724-9159; Fax: 219-724-8948. [CEM]
School—St. Joseph, 127 N. Fourth St., 46733. Tel: 219-724-2765; Fax: 219-724-4953. Mr. Daniel Swygart, Prin.
Lay Teachers 17; Students 381.
Catechesis/Religious Programs—Tel: 219-724-9159; Fax: 219-724-9380. Teresa Schurger, D.R.E.
Students 179.

Ege, Noble Co., Immaculate Conception (1876). Attended by St. John Bosco, Churubusco. Rev. Danny Pinto (Sri Lanka).
216 N. Main St., Churubusco, 46723. Tel: 219-693-9578; Fax: 219-693-1608. [CEM]
Catechesis/Religious Programs—Students 105.

Elkhart, Elkhart Co., St. Thomas the Apostle (1949), Revs. Richard P. Hire; Thomas Ryan (Ireland); Sr. Marcianne Targonski, C.S.S.F., Pastoral Assoc.
Res., 1405 N. Main St., 46514. Tel: 219-262-1505. [JC]
School—1331 N. Main St., 46514. Tel: 219-264-4855; Fax: 219-262-8477. Robert J. Sikorski, Prin.
Felician Sisters 2; Lay Teachers 24; Students 368.
Catechesis/Religious Programs—Tel: 219-264-0491.
Students 325.

St. Vincent de Paul (1868), Revs. Joseph A. Rulli; James R. Myers (Ghana).
Res., 1108 S. Main St., 46516. Tel: 219-293-8231; Fax: 219-293-1105. [CEM]
School—(Grades PreK-6) 1114 S. Main St., 46516. Tel: 219-293-8451; Fax: 219-293-1105. Mrs. Diane S. Gorman, Prin.
Lay Teachers 9; Students 197.
Catechesis/Religious Programs—Tel: 219-293-8071. D.R.E.: Miss Lisa Kloska; Mrs. Nancy DeMarco; Mrs. Kristi Ward.
Students 430.

Garrett, De Kalb Co., St. Joseph (1876), Rev. Thomas Lombardi; Deacon Harris Hoeffel.
Office: 300 W. Houston, 46738-1424. Tel: 219-357-3122.
Res., 307 S. Ijams St., 46738. Tel: 219-357-3122. [CEM]
School—(Grades K-6) 301 W. Houston, 46738. Tel: 219-357-5137. Ms. Linda Speer, Prin.
Lay Teachers 7; Students 130.

Geneva, Adams Co., St. Mary of the Presentation (1883), Rev. Edward Narcowich.
Res., 5790 E. 1100 S., 46740-9132. Tel: 219-997-6558; Fax: 219-997-6558. [CEM]
Catechesis/Religious Programs—Students 93.

Goshen, Elkhart Co., St. John the Evangelist (1840), Rev. Edward J. Krason; Deacons N. Arthur Bleau; Ricardo Medina, III. In res., Revs. Paul Bueter; Martin A. Horvath.
Res., 114 W. Monroe St., 46526. Tel: 219-533-3385; Fax: 219-533-1814.
School—117 W. Monroe, 46526. Tel: 219-533-9480. Mrs. Diane Gorman, Prin.
Sisters 1; Lay Teachers 6; Students 113.
Catechesis/Religious Programs—Tel: 219-533-0020. Mr. James Finnigan, D.R.E.
Students 230.

Granger, St. Joseph Co., St. Pius X (1955), Revs. Peter A. Jarret, C.S.C.; William J. Neidhart, C.S.C.; Deacon William G. Gray. In res., Rev. James G. Karaffa, C.S.C.
Res., 52553 Fir Rd., 46530. Tel: 219-272-8462; Fax: 219-272-8493.
Catechesis/Religious Programs—Tel: 219-277-5760; Fax: 219-272-8493.
Students 1,300.

Hessen Cassel, Allen Co., St. Joseph (1851), Rev. Robert A. Van Kempen.
Res., 11337 Old U.S. 27 S., Fort Wayne, 46816. Tel: 219-639-3748. [CEM]
School—11521 Old U.S. 27 S., Fort Wayne, 46816. Tel: 219-639-3580. Miss Lois Widner, Prin.
Lay Teachers 9; Students 196.
Catechesis/Religious Programs—Students 43.

Huntington, Huntington Co., St. Mary (1896), Rev. Gary L. Sigler.
Res., 903 N. Jefferson St., 46750. Tel: 219-356-4398; Fax: 219-356-3529. [JC]
School—Huntington Catholic School. (Consolidated with SS. Peter and Paul) Primary Building, 820 Cherry St., 46750. Tel: 219-356-2320.
Sisters 4; Lay Teachers 10; Students 192.
Middle Building: 960 Warren St., 46750. Tel: 219-356-1926. Sr. Moira McGinley, O.S.F., Prin.
Catechesis/Religious Programs—Students 137.

SS. Peter and Paul (1843), Revs. Ronald Rieder, O.F.M.Cap.; Thomas Zelinski, O.F.M.Cap.
Res., 860 Cherry St., 46750. Tel: 219-356-4798; Fax: 219-356-7154. [CEM]
School—Huntington Catholic School. (See St. Mary for details). Tel: 219-356-2320.
Catechesis/Religious Programs—Sr. Miriam Gill, S.S.N.D., D.R.E.
Students 388.

Kendallville, Noble Co., Immaculate Conception (1867), Rev. Jacob M. Gall.
Res., 319 E. Diamond St., 46755. Tel: 219-347-2522.
Catechesis/Religious Programs—Students 99.

LaGrange, LaGrange Co., St. Joseph (1934), Rev. Paul Faroh, O.F.M.Conv.
Res., 100 E. 50 N., P.O. Box 69, 46761. Tel: 219-463-3472. [JC]
Catechesis/Religious Programs—Students 78.

Lagro, Wabash Co., St. Patrick (1838). Closed. For inquiries for parish records contact the Chancery.

Lakeville, St. Joseph Co., Sacred Heart (1932), Rev. James Stoyle, Admin.
Res., 63568 U.S. 31 S., South Bend, 46614. Tel: 219-291-2826. [CEM]
Catechesis/Religious Programs—Tel: 219-784-2579.
Students 68.

Ligonier, Noble Co., St. Patrick (1860), Rev. Dale Bauman.
Res., 300 Ravine Park Dr., 46767-1301. Tel: 219-894-4946. [JC]
Catechesis/Religious Programs—Students 80.

Milford, Kosciusko Co., Our Lady of Guadalupe (1972) (Hispanic), Rev. Paul Bueter.
Res. & Church: P.O. Box 605, 46542. Tel: 219-658-9594.

Mishawaka, St. Joseph Co.,

1—St. Bavo, (1903), Rev. James A. Shafer; Gus Zuehlke, Pastoral Assoc.; Deacon Kevin M. Ranaghan.
Res., 511 W. 7th St., 46544. Tel: 219-255-1437.
School—513 W. 7th St., 46544. Tel: 219-259-4214. Dr. Susan Bryant, Prin.
Lay Teachers 13; Students 230.
Catechesis/Religious Programs—Students 105.

2—St. Joseph, (1848), Rev. Robert A. Yast; Deacon Ronald Moser.
Res., 225 S. Mill St., 46544. Tel: 219-255-6134. [CEM]
School—220 W. 4th St., 46544. Tel: 219-255-5554. Mrs. Mary Geist, Prin.
Lay Teachers 13; Students 245.
Catechesis/Religious Programs—Students 100.

3—St. Monica, (1915), Rev. William Sullivan; Sr. Eileen Daudlin, S.S.N.D., Pastoral Assoc.; Deacon Carl Lenzo.
Res., 222 W. Mishawaka Ave., 46545. Tel: 219-255-2247; Fax: 219-255-8375.
Parish Center: 214 W. Mishawaka Ave., 46545. Tel: 219-255-1957.
School—223 W. Grove St., 46545. Tel: 219-255-0709. Sr. Pat Gavin, S.S.N.D., Prin.
Sisters 1; Lay Teachers 13; Students 251.
Catechesis/Religious Programs—Jane Cors Smith, D.R.E.
Students 121.

4—Queen of Peace, (1957), Rev. Elden J. Miller; Deacon Eugene Egendoerfer; Carol Cone, Pastoral Assoc.
Res., 4508 Vistula Rd., 46544. Tel: 219-255-9674; Fax: 219-255-9675.
Catechesis/Religious Programs—Tel: 219-255-0392; Fax: 219-255-1029. Betty S. Whitson, D.R.E.
Students 310.

5—St. Michael Ukrainian Catholic Church, (1916) (Ukrainian), Rev. Richard L. Kirovac.
Res., 712 E. Lawrence St., 46545-6835. Tel: 219-259-7173.

Monroeville, Allen Co., St. Rose of Lima (1888), Rev. Babasino Fernandes (India) Admin.
Res., P.O. Box 406, 46773. Tel: 219-623-6437; Fax: 219-623-2370. [CEM]
School—St. Joseph, 209 Mulberry St., 46773. Tel: 219-623-3447. Ms. Carolyn Kirkendall, Prin.
Lay Teachers 4; Students 82.
Catechesis/Religious Programs—Students 48.

Napanee, Elkhart Co., St. Isidore. Closed. For inquiries for parish records contact the Chancery.

New Carlisle, St. Joseph Co., St. Stanislaus Kostka (1884) (Polish), Rev. Eugene J. Kazmierczak.
Res., 55756 Tulip Rd., 46552. Tel: 219-654-3781; Fax: 219-654-3781.
Catechesis/Religious Programs—Tel: 219-654-8738. Barbara Mireles, D.R.E.
Students 120.

New Haven, Allen Co., St. John the Baptist (1859), Rev. Derrick Sneyd.
Res., 943 Powers St., 46774. Tel: 219-493-4553; Fax: 219-749-6164. [CEM]
School—206 Rufus St., 46774. Tel: 219-749-9903; Fax: 219-749-6047. Robert Sordelet, Prin.
Lay Teachers 14; Students 346.
Catechesis/Religious Programs—Students 205.

Nix Settlement, Whitley Co., St. Catharine (1850), Rev. Phillip A. Widmann.
Res., St. Joseph Rectory, 641 N. Main St., P.O. Box 250, Roanoke, 46783-0250. Tel: 219-672-2838; Fax: 219-672-3069.
Church—Ind. Hwy. 9 & Whitley Co. Rd., 1,000 S., 46783. Tel: 219-672-2838. [CEM]

North Manchester, Wabash Co., St. Robert Bellarmine (1963), Rev. Ronald Ramenaden.
Res., 1203 State Rd., 114 E., 46962. Tel: 219-982-4404.

Notre Dame, St. Joseph Co., Sacred Heart (1842), Revs. Jose M. Martelli, C.S.C.; James W. Thorton, C.S.C.; Christoper Miller, Pastoral Assoc.
Res., Presbytery, 46556. Tel: 219-631-7511; 7512; Fax: 219-631-9687. [CEM][JC]
Catechesis/Religious Programs—Tel: 219-631-9436.
Students 125.

Pierceton, Kosciusko Co., St. Francis Xavier (1841), Rev. Bruce Piechocki; Deacon H. Dean Tucker.
Mailing Address: P.O. Box 376, 46562. Tel: 219-594-5750.
Church—408 W. Catholic St., 46562. [CEM]
Catechesis/Religious Programs—Students 87.

Plymouth, Marshall Co., St. Michael (1862), Revs. Anthony Gillespie, Admin.; Emile Perera; Deacons Ed Lyczak; Victor Carrillo.
Res., 612 N. Walnut St., 46563. Tel: 219-936-4935; Fax: 219-936-9293. [CEM]
School—(PreK-5) 612 N. Center St., 46563. Tel: 219-936-4329. Miss Gertrude Nawara, Prin.
Lay Teachers 8; Students 161.
Catechesis/Religious Programs—Sr. Rose Andre Miller, D.R.E.
Students 191.

Roanoke, Huntington Co., St. Joseph (1867), Rev. Phillip A. Widmann.
Res., 641 N. Main St., P.O. Box 250, 46783-0250. Tel: 219-672-2838; Fax: 219-672-3069. [CEM]
Catechesis/Religious Programs—Dr. Kathleen Schneider, D.R.E.
Students 99.

Rome City, Noble Co., St. Gaspar del Bufalo (1957), Rev. Charles F. Mullen, C.PP.S.
Res., 10871 N. State Rd. 9, 46784. Tel: 219-854-3100. [CEM]
Catechesis/Religious Programs—Students 70.

Syracuse, Kosciusko Co., St. Martin de Porres (1966), Rev. Edward Erpelding.
Res., 6941 E. Waco Dr., 46567-9496. Tel: 219-457-3528.
Catechesis/Religious Programs—Students 105.

Wabash, Wabash Co., St. Bernard (1864), Rev. Timothy A. Wrozek; Deacon Ted Krizman.
Res., 207 N. Cass St., 46992. Tel: 219-563-4750; Fax: 219-563-0313.
School—191 N. Cass St., 46992. Tel: 219-563-5746. Mr. Kenneth Bond, Prin.
Lay Teachers 8; Students 119.
Catechesis/Religious Programs—Tel: 219-563-4495.
Students 118.

Walkerton, St. Joseph Co., St. Patrick (1856), Rev. Michael J. Winkowski, C.PP.S.
Res., 801 Tyler St., 46574. Tel: 219-586-7404.
School—811 Tyler St., 46574. Tel: 219-586-7405. Mrs. Judith Miller, Prin.
Sisters of St. Joseph of the Third Order of St. Francis 1; Lay Teachers 4; Students 65.
School Annex—807 Tyler St., 46574.
Catechesis/Religious Programs—Students 90.

Warsaw, Kosciusko Co., Sacred Heart (1852), Rev. Terry A. Fisher; Mary Jo Gremling, Pastoral Min.
Res., 125 N. Harrison St., 46580. Tel: 219-267-5842; Fax: 219-267-2589. [JC]
School—135 N. Harrison, 46590. Tel: 219-267-5874. Mrs. Cheryl Zale, Prin.
Lay Teachers 13; Students 215.
Catechesis/Religious Programs—Students 251.

Waterloo, DeKalb Co., St. Michael the Archangel (1880), Rev. David Carkenord.
Res., 1098 County Road 39, 46793-9779. Tel: 219-837-7115. [CEM]
Catechesis/Religious Programs—Students 206.

Yoder, Allen Co., St. Aloysius (1859), Rev. William G. Hodde.
Res., 14623 Bluffton Rd., 46798-9741. Tel: 219-622-4491. [CEM]
School—14607 Bluffton Rd., 46798-9741. Tel: 219-622-7151. Mr. Robert Kelty, Prin.
Lay Teachers 5; Students 92.
Catechesis/Religious Programs—Students 84.

Chaplains of Public Institutions

FORT WAYNE. *Lutheran Hospital*, 3024 Fairfield Ave., 46807. Tel: 219-458-2117; 458-2001. Sr. Adele Mann, S.P.; Deacon Thomas Doell.
Parkview Memorial Hospital. Tel: 219-484-6636, Ext. 26311. Rev. Robert D'Souza (India); Roseann Bloomfield, Chap.
Veterans Administration Hospital. Rev. Daniel Leeuw.

On Duty Outside the Diocese:
Reverend Fathers—
Kruger, Brent Allan, C.S.C., Andre House, Phoeniz, AZ
Wilbright, Stephen Sullivan, C.S.C., St. John Vianney, Goodyear, AZ

On Special Assignment:
Reverend Fathers—
Doriot, Thomas E., 2637 Fulton Ave., #232, Sacramento, CA 95821
McNulty, Patrick J., Madonna House, Combermere, Ontario K0J 1L0
Piechocki, Bruce, Officialis of Diocese, Chancery

Retired:
Reverend Monsignors—
Faber, William, Summer, 728 S. Main, Kendallville, IN 46755. Tel: 219-347-5041
Hession, Edward I., 4827 Woodmark Ct., Fort Wayne, IN 46815. Tel: 219-483-2567
Voors, William J., 4837 Greenfield, Fort Wayne, IN 46815. Tel: 219-485-5587
Reverend Fathers—
Bell, Milford C., Vindobona Nursing Home, P.O. Box 318, Braddock Heights, MD 21714-0318
Cardinali, Fred, 4520 S. Hanna St., Fort Wayne, IN 46806. Tel: 219-456-6889
Cis, James, 6930 Whiteoak Ave., Apt. 216, Hammond, IN 46324. Tel: 219-845-5091
Gieranowski, William, Parliament House, 405 N. Ocean Blvd., Apt. 1004, Pompano Beach, FL 33062-5116. Tel: 954-784-1455
Gillig, John, 612 N. Second St., Decatur, IN 46733. Tel: 219-724-3545
Hinckley, Christopher, 4924 S. Wayne, Fort Wayne, IN 46807. Tel: 219-456-7785
Hoevel, Robert J., 1104 New England Dr., Fort Wayne, IN 46815. Tel: 219-749-8245
Horvath, Joseph P., R.R. No. 4, Box 136 B, Walkerton, IN 46574. Tel: 219-586-3678
Horvath, Martin A., 114 W. Monroe, Goshen, IN 46526. Tel: 219-533-3385
Jacobs, Joseph A., 2722 Rock Maple Ct., South Bend, IN 46628. Tel: 219-271-1288
Lange, Matthew, 1149 Co. Rd. 39, Waterloo, IN 46793. Tel: 219-837-7766
Letko, Anthony, 8545 N. Tippecanoe St., Walkerton, IN 46574
Molnar, Anthony, 829 W. Calvert, South Bend, IN 46613. Tel: 219-289-6704
O'Connor, James J., 6006 Chapel Pines Run, Fort Wayne, IN 46804. Tel: 219-436-1703
Peil, William, 1841 N. Anthony, Fort Wayne, IN 46805. Tel: 219-422-1950
Rose, James, 2781 Huycks, Coldwater, MI 49036
Ruetz, Edward J., 621 Portage, South Bend, IN 46616. Tel: 219-234-5652
Schnurr, Herman J., St. Mary Parish, 228 N. Main St., P.O. Box 700, Avilla, IN 46710-0700
Urbine, Richard, 533 S. Main St., Bourbon, IN 46504. Tel: 219-342-8012

Permanent Deacons:
Baumgartner, Paul E., 417 Howard St., South Bend, IN 46617
Bleau, N. Arthur, 64429 Pleasant Pl., Goshen, IN 46526
Crowder, Richard E., 2005 Camelot Dr., Las Cruces, NM 88005
Dits, Paul, 17433 Battles Rd., Mishawaka, IN 46544
Doehrman, Michael J., 902 Lake, Ft. Wayne, IN 46805
Egendoerfer, Eugene, 1302 Cantondale Ln., Mishawaka, IN 46544
Folds, Milton, 3286 West, #50, Columbia City, IN 46725
Gizzi, Emilio, 238 Eckman, South Bend, IN 46614
Hilger, Edward, 5321 Yorkshire Dr., Fort Wayne, IN 46816
Hoeffel, Harris H., 401 S. Harrison, Garrett, IN 46738
Krizman, Ted, Box 134 W. Sinclair, Wabash, IN 46992
Kuspa, Ervin, 434 S. Liberty, South Bend, IN 46619
Larson, Fred J., 1001 Bell, New Haven, IN 46774
Loving, Peter, 3730 Stillwater Pl., Ft. Wayne, IN 46808
Lyczak, Edward, 4460 Pleasant Point Ln., Bremen, IN 46506
Madey, Robert T., 5217 Country Trail, Raleigh, NC 27609
McDougall, Louis, 3419 Sanibel Dr., Fort Wayne, IN 46815
Medina, Ricardo, III, 323 Stocker, Elkhart, IN 46516
Miller, Brian L., 1115 N. St. Peter St., South Bend, IN 46617
Moser, Ronald J., 51793 Whitestable, South Bend, IN 46637
Ranaghan, Kevin, 1003 St. Vincent, South Bend, IN 46617
Salinas, Rogelio, 30492 Co. Rd. 38, Wakarusa, IN 46573
Sanborn, Phillip J., R.R. 2, 814 Apple Hill, Angola, IN 46703
Tucker, H. Dean, 8378 E. 350 North, Pierceton, IN 46562
Walsh, Francis, 2515 Cliffton Hills Dr., Fort Wayne, IN 46808. Tel: 219-471-2446
Walsh, James M., 2222 Broadmoor Dr., Elkhart, IN 46514
Zickgraf, Joseph R., 289 N. Columbia Pkwy, Columbus City, IN 46725

INSTITUTIONS LOCATED IN THE DIOCESE

[A] SEMINARIES, RELIGIOUS, OR SCHOLASTICATES

NOTRE DAME. *Moreau Seminary*, P.O. Box 668, 46556. Tel: 219-631-7735; Fax: 219-631-9233. This is a college level and Theological Seminary run by the Indiana Province of the Congregation of Holy Cross for Religious Priesthood and Brotherhood candidates.
Formation Staff: Revs. John F. Lahey, C.S.C., Supr.; David L. Guffey, C.S.C., Asst. Supr.; Robert H. Moss, C.S.C.; Peter D. Rocca, C.S.C.; Patrick Neary, C.S.C.; James A. Rigert, C.S.C.; William D. Seetch, C.S.C. In res. Bros. James E. Gormley, C.S.C.; James Lakofka, C.S.C.; John Platte, C.S.C.; Chester Ziemba, C.S.C.; Robert Ewald, C.S.C.; Richard Kyle, C.S.C.; Joseph Dougherty, F.S.C.; Revs. John J. Croston, C.S.C.; Robert A. Kreig, C.S.C.; Anthony J. Lauck, C.S.C.; James Trepanier, C.S.C.; Jerome Wilson, C.S.C.; James T. Rahilly, C.S.C.; Charles B. Gordon, C.S.C.; Robert Sullivan (BO); Mark B. Thesing, C.S.C.
Vocations Office: Revs. James B. King, C.S.C., Dir.; William A. Wack, C.S.C., Asst. Dir., Mailing Address: Moreau Seminary, Box 541, 46556. Priests 8; Sisters 3; Seminarians 36.
Old College. Mailing Address: Box 638, 46556. Tel: 219-631-8403. College candidates study here for up to three years before entering Moreau Seminary. Rev. Robert H. Moss, C.S.C., Dir. & Contact Person. Priests 2; Sisters 1; Candidates for the Priesthood in the First Three Years of Undergraduate Formation 9.

[B] COLLEGES AND UNIVERSITIES

FORT WAYNE. *University of St. Francis*, 2701 Spring St., 46808-3994. Tel: 219-434-3100; Fax: 219-434-3183; 434-3194.
E-mail: ekriss@sfc.edu
Web site: http://www.sfc.edu
For a complete listing, refer to the Colleges and Universities section.

DONALDSON. *Ancilla Domini College* Mailing Address: P.O. Box 1, 46513.
For a complete listing, refer to the Colleges and Universities section.

NOTRE DAME. *Holy Cross College, Holy Cross College, Inc.*, 1801 N. Michigan, P.O. Box 308, 46556-0308. Tel: 219-239-8400; Fax: 219-233-7427.
E-mail: richard.b.gilman.1@nd.edu
Web site: http://www.hcc-nd.edu
For a complete listing, refer to the Colleges and Universities section.
Saint Mary's College, 46556. Tel: 219-284-4000; Fax: 219-284-4716.
E-mail: 1hitch@saintmarys.edu
For a complete listing, refer to the Colleges and Universities section.
**University of Notre Dame Du Lac*, (1842) Corby Hall, 46556. Tel: 219-631-5000.
Web site: http://www.nd.edu/ndhomepage/ndhomepage.html
For a complete listing, refer to the Colleges and Universities section.

[C] HIGH SCHOOLS, DIOCESAN

FORT WAYNE. *Bishop Dwenger High School*, 1300 E. Washington Center Rd., 46825. Tel: 219-483-1108. Mr. J. Fred Tone, Prin.; Mr. Eva Merkel, Asst. Prin. Lay Teachers 54; Students 942.
Bishop Luers High School, 333 E. Paulding Rd., 46816. Tel: 219-456-1261; Fax: 219-456-1262. Mary Keefer, Prin.; Jo Ann Roscoe, Asst. Prin. Chaplains: Revs. Lawrence Tippmann; Glenn Kohrman; Deacon Charles Herman. Lay Teachers 42; Students 584.

SOUTH BEND. *Saint Joseph's High School*, 1441 N. Michigan St., 46617. Tel: 219-233-6137; Fax: 219-232-3482.
E-mail: sbdstjoehs@connectinc.com
Mrs. Barbara Jemielity, Prin.; Mrs. Kathleen Ratliff, Vice Prin.; Rev. Walter J. Bly. Priests 1; Brothers of Holy Cross 3; Sisters of the Holy Cross 2; Lay Teachers 60; Students 861.

MISHAWAKA. *Marian High School*, 1311 S. Logan St., 46544. Tel: 219-259-5257.
E-mail: marianhs.1@nd.edu
Mr. Joseph Brettnacher, Prin.; Karen LeMire, Pastoral Min. Priests 2; Sisters 5; Lay Teachers 46; Students 699.

[D] DIOCESAN ELEMENTARY SCHOOLS

FORT WAYNE. *Monsignor Julian Benoit Academy*, 3029 E. Paulding Rd., 46816. Tel: 219-447-5121. Ms. Jeanette Donovan, Prin. Consolidation of Sacred Heart, St. Patrick's & St. Henry's Schools. Lay Teachers 14; Students 260.

[E] CONSOLIDATED SCHOOL DAY CARE CENTER RESIDENTIAL TREATMENT CENTER

FORT WAYNE. *Catholic Charities Children's Services*, 2820 Reed St., 46806. Tel: 219-745-4929. Theresa Harvey, Dir. Lay Teachers 5; Aides 6; Enrollment 82.
The Children's Cottage, 2820 Reed St., 46806. Tel: 219-745-4929. Licensed day care facility with a capacity for 82 children, ages 2 to 7. Serves families of all faiths. Lay Teachers 5; Aides 6.

[F] GENERAL HOSPITALS

FORT WAYNE. *St. Joseph Medical Center*, 700 Broadway, 46802. Tel: 219-425-3000; Fax: 219-425-3222
For a complete listing, refer to the Hospitals section.

SOUTH BEND. *Saint Joseph's Medical Center, Inc.*, 801 E. LaSalle St., 46617. Tel: 219-237-7111.
E-mail: breedenm@sjcg.org
For a complete listing, refer to the Hospitals section.
St. Mary Community Hospital, 2515 E. Jefferson Blvd., 46615. Tel: 219-288-8311.
E-mail: khobgood@skynet.net
Web site: http://www.specialtymile.com/ancillahealthcare/index.html
For a complete listing, refer to the Hospitals section.

*MISHAWAKA. *St. Joseph Community Hospital*, 215 W. 4th St., 46544. Tel: 219-259-2431.
E-mail: khabgood@skynet.net
Web site: http://www.specialtymile.com/ancillahealthcare/index.html
For a complete listing, refer to the Hospitals section.

PLYMOUTH. *Saint Joseph's Hospital of Marshall County, Inc.*, 1915 Lake Ave., P.O. Box 670, 46563. Tel: 219-936-3181.
For a complete listing, refer to the Hospitals section.

[G] SPECIAL HOSPITALS

NOTRE DAME. *University Health Services*, 46556. Tel: 219-239-8013.
For a complete listing, refer to the Special Care Facilities section.

[H] HOMES FOR THE AGED

FORT WAYNE. *Saint Anne Home & Retirement Community*, 1900 Randallia Dr., 46805. Tel: 219-484-5555.
For a complete listing, refer to the Special Care Facilities section.
St. Anne Home of the Diocese of Fort Wayne - South Bend, 1900 Randalia Dr., 46805. Tel: 219-422-4611.
For a complete listing, refer to the Special Care Facilities section.

AVILLA. *LaVerna Terrace Apartments*, 517 N. Main St., 46710. Tel: 219-897-2093.
For a complete listing, refer to the Special Care Facilities section.
Sacred Heart Home, 515 N. Main St., 46710-9602. Tel: 219-897-2841.
For a complete listing, refer to the Special Care Facilities section.

[I] PERSONAL PRELATURES

SOUTH BEND. *Prelature of the Holy Cross and Opus Dei*, Windmoor Center, 1121 N. Notre Dame Ave., 46617. Tel: 219-232-0550.
Web site: opusdei.com
Legal Title: *The Work of God, Inc.* Rev. Gerry Kolf. Staff 7.

[J] MONASTERIES AND RESIDENCES OF PRIESTS AND BROTHERS

FORT WAYNE. This is the residence of the Brothers employed in various appointments at the University of Notre Dame & is also a house of retirement for Holy Cross Brothers, Midwest Prov.

SOUTH BEND. *Congregation of Holy Cross Indiana Province Provincial House*, 1304 E. Jefferson Blvd., 46617. Tel: 219-289-6850. Legal Title: *Priests of Holy Cross, Indiana Province, Inc.* Revs. William D. Dorwart, C.S.C., Prov.; Robert L. Epping, C.S.C., First Asst. Prov.; James F. Flanigan, C.S.C., Second Asst. Prov. Councilors: Revs. David L. Guffey, C.S.C.; Peter A. Jarret, C.S.C.; Wilson D. Miscamble, C.S.C.; Robert S. Pelton, C.S.C.; David T. Tyson, C.S.C.; Bro. John J. Platte, C.S.C.
Holy Cross Priests Serving in Foreign Countries: Chile:
Congregacion de Santa Cruz, Casilla 1271, Santiago 1, Chile. Revs. Jorge A. Canepa, C.S.C., District Supr.; Jose E. Ahumanda, C.S.C.; Thomas V. Bednar, C.S.C.; Sergio E. Concha, C.S.C.; Charles A. Delaney, C.S.C.; Joseph M. Doherty, C.S.C.; Fermin J. Donoso, C.S.C.; Joseph A. Dorsey, C.S.C.; Erwin A. Fonseca, C.S.C.; Roberto M. Gilbo, C.S.C.; Malcolm D. Johnson, C.S.C.; Gerald T. Papen, C.S.C.; Bro. Joaquin R. Parada, C.S.C.; Revs. Robert L. Plasker, C.S.C.; Robert G. Simon, C.S.C.; Romulo E. Vera, C.S.C.; Gerald J. Whelan, C.S.C.
Peru: Rev. Diego J. Yrarrazaval, C.S.C.
Instituto de Estudios Aymaras, Apartado 295, Puno, Peru. Rev. Philip T. Devlin, C.S.C., Apartado 3872, Lima 100, Peru. Rev. Gerald R. Barmasse, C.S.C., Apartado 317, Chimbote, Peru.
On Leave for Higher Studies: Rev. Robert A. Dowd, C.S.C.
St. Monica's Parish, 725 California Ave., Santa Monica, CA, 90403. Rev. Jeffrey A. Cooper, C.S.C., Miami Manor Apartments, 330 E. Chesnut, #205B, Oxford, OH, 45056. Rev. Charles B. Gordon, C.S.C., Catholic Rectory, Hills Rd., Cambridge, CB2 1JR, England. Rev. Daniel G. Groody, C.S.C., Holy Cross Center, 2597 Virginia St., Berkeley, CA, 94709. Rev. Paul V. Kollman, C.S.C, Andre House, P.O. Box 1037, Jinja, Uganda. Rev. William M. Lies, C.S.C., 4720 Fifth Ave., Pittsburgh, PA, 15213. Rev. Russell K. McDougall, C.S.C., Via Framura 85, 00168 Rome, Italy. Rev. Francis J. Murphy, C.S.C. *Loyola House*, Box 245, Guelph, Ontario, Canada, N1H6J9. Rev. Mark B. Thesing, C.S.C., 211 McCauley St., Chapel Hill, NC, 27516.
Military Chaplains: Rev. S. Douglas Smith, C.S.C., NAS Whidbey Island (N9), Bldg. 960, Oak Harbor, WA, 98278-1600. Rev. Robert E. Roetzel, C.S.C., HHT, 3-4 Calvary Squadron, 25th Infantry Division (L), Wheeler AAF, Hawaii, 96854.
Priests of the Province in Residences Not Listed Elsewhere: Rev. Maurice E. Amen, C.S.C., College of Comparative Culture, Sophia University, 4 Yonbancho Chiyoda-Ku, Tokyo 102, Japan. Rev. Robert C. Antonelli, C.S.C., Congregazione di Santa Croce, Via Framura, 85, 00168 Rome, Italy. Rev. James T. Burtchaell, C.S.C., Our Lady of Princeton, Great Rd. at Drakes Corner, Princeton, NJ, 08540. Rev. Joseph H. Carey, C.S.C., Washington Theological Union, 6896 Laurel St., N.W., Washington, DC, 20012. Rev. LeRoy E. Clementich, C.S.C., 225 Cordova St., Anchorage, AK, 99501. Rev. Charles W. Corso, C.S.C., Box 3908, Fremont, CA, 94539. Rev. Ralph F. Dunn, C.S.C., 655 W. Irving Park Rd., Apt. 3916, Chicago, IL, 60613. Rev. Thomas Elliott, C.S.C., St. Vincent's Medical Center, P.O. Box 6016, Bridgeport, CT, 06606. Rev. John T. Ford, C.S.C., Mailing Address: Catholic University, Cardinal Station, Box 236, Washington, DC, 20064. Rev. William W. Faiella, C.S.C., 73-955 Santa Rosa Way, Palm Desert, CA, 92260. Rev. Thomas E. Hewitt, C.S.C., 5714 Prentiss St., San Antonio, TX, 78240. Rev. James W. Irwin, C.S.C., c/o Calle Puebla 844 Norte, Ciudad Obregon, Mexico. Rev. George G. Kahle, C.S.C., St. Paul's Retirement Community, 3602 S. Ironwood Dr., 46614. Rev. John P. Keefe, C.S.C., Hispanic Ministry, 384 S. Reese St., P.O. Box 428, Battle Mountain, NV, 89820-0428. Rev. Edward C. Krause, C.S.C., Gannon University, Erie, PA, 16541. Rev. Robert J. Lochner, C.S.C., 325 Arthur Ave., Cocoa Beach, FL, 32931. Rev. John W. Lubbers, C.S.C., St. Joseph Hall Community, St. Edward's University, Austin, TX, 78704. Rev. Walter L. McInerney, C.S.C., 51 Joan Rd., Centerville, MA, 02632. Rev. John M. Mulcahy, C.S.C., Morris Camp, Box 550, Ontario, Canada. Rev. Edward J. Reidy, C.S.C., 73441 Fred Waring Dr., Palm Desert, CA, 92260. Rev. David E. Schlauer, C.S.C., St. Michael's Community, 13270 Maple Dr., 63127. Most Rev. Charles A. Schleck, C.S.C., Piazza di Spagna 48, Rome, Italy. Rev. Norbert J. Sinski, C.S.C., 319 Ave. C, Apt. 2B, New York, NY, 10009. Rev. John A. Struzzo, C.S.C., Mission Hospital Regional Medical Center, 27700 Medical Center Rd., Mission Viejo, CA, 92691. Rev. James N. Watzke, C.S.C., 400 E. Randolph St., Apt. 3230, Chicago, IL, 60601. Rev. Herbert C. Yost, C.S.C., Solitude of the Savior, 9033 N. County Rd., 600E, Rolling Prairie, 46371.
Holy Cross House, Notre Dame, 46556. Revs. Andre E. Leville, C.S.C., Supr.; William P. Melody, C.S.C., Asst. Supr.; Lawrence T. Bauer, C.S.C.; William J. Beston, C.S.C.; Paul E. Beichner, C.S.C.; James F. Blaes, C.S.C.; Claude L. Boehm, C.S.C.; Ferdinand L. Brown, C.S.C.; Edward A. Buenger, C.S.C.; John C. Burke, C.S.C.; Jeremiah R. Buttomer, C.S.C.; Allen L. Cormier, C.S.C.; David H. Fosselman, C.S.C.; Paul E. Fryberger, C.S.C.; Arthur S. Harvey, C.S.C.; William F. Hickens, C.S.C.; Albin L. Hosinski, C.S.C.; Joseph A. Kehoe, C.S.C.; Roman S. Ladewski, C.S.C.; Gregory J. Lombardo, C.S.C.; Charles J. Mahoney, C.S.C.; Walter G. Michalik, C.S.C.; Michael G. O'Brien, C.S.C.; Paul B. Rankin, C.S.C.; Bernard E. Ransing, C.S.C.; Joseph A. Rogusz, C.S.C.; George E. Schidel, C.S.C.; Chester A. Soleta, C.S.C.; Edgar S. Szymanski, C.S.C.; John V. VandenBossche, C.S.C.; Andrew B. Wohman, C.S.C.; Bros. Remy Aydt, C.S.C.; Clarence J. Breitenbach, C.S.C.; Thomas J. Combs, C.S.C.; Andrew Corsini Fowler, C.S.C.; Orlando Gozdowski, C.S.C.; Paul H. Loos, C.S.C.

NOTRE DAME. *Congregation of Holy Cross, Midwest Province*, Provincial House, 1801 N. Michigan St., Box 460, 46556. Tel: 219-239-8312; Fax: 219-289-0487.
E-mail: wgeenen@hcc-nd.edu
Legal Title: *Brothers of Holy Cross, Inc.* Bros. William Geenen, C.S.C., Prov. Supr.; Donald Gibbs, C.S.C., Asst. Prov. & Vicar; Donald Bailer, C.S.C., Prov. Steward; Joseph Fox, C.S.C., Prov. Sec.; Kenneth Haders, C.S.C., Prov. Councilor.
Holy Cross Brothers Center, P.O. Box 716, 46556. Tel: 219-239-8330; Fax: 219-239-8372. Bros. Joseph Fox, C.S.C., Supr.; Rex Hennel, C.S.C., Asst. Supr.; Rev. Kenneth Grabner, C.S.C., Chap. Total in Residence 25.
Dujarie House, Infirmary, P.O. Box 706, 46556. Tel: 219-287-1838; Fax: 219-289-7277. Bro. Thomas Shaughnessy, C.S.C., Admin. Total in Residence 26.
Schubert Villa, Assisted Living, P.O. Box 1020, 46556. Tel: 219-287-1986; Fax: 219-289-7277. Bro. Thomas Shaughnessy, C.S.C., Admin. Total in Residence 16.
Columba Hall, University of Notre Dame, 46556. Tel: 219-631-6284. Bros. Donald Allen, C.S.C., Supr.; Raymond Trottman, C.S.C., Asst. Supr.; Rev. Roman Ladewski, C.S.C., Chap. Total in Residence 40. Total in Residence 9.
Holy Cross Community, Corby Hall, University of Notre Dame, 46556. Tel: 219-631-7325. Revs. Robert J. Austgen, C.S.C.; Nicholas Ayo, C.S.C.; Leonard N. Banas, C.S.C.; Ernest J. Bartell, C.S.C.; Michael J. Baxter, C.S.C.; E. William Beauchamp, C.S.C.; Thomas E. Blantz, C.S.C.; William A. Botzum, C.S.C.; Richard Bullene, C.S.C.; David B. Burrell, C.S.C.; Charles M. Carey, C.S.C.; Austin I. Collins, C.S.C.; John E. Conley, C.S.C.; Raymond F. Cour, C.S.C.; Alfred F. D'Alonzo, C.S.C.; Paul F. Doyle, C.S.C.; Deacon Thomas P. Doyle, C.S.C.; Revs. John S. Dunne, C.S.C.; Clarence R. Durbin, C.S.C.; Joseph Fey, C.S.C.; Mark J. Fitzgerald, C.S.C.; James K. Foster, C.S.C.; Patrick Gaffney, C.S.C.; David A. Garrick, C.S.C.; Thomas E. Gaughan, C.S.C.; Mark R. Ghyselinck, C.S.C.; Bro. Francis J. Gorch, C.S.C.; Rev. Gregory A. Green, C.S.C.; Bro. Valery Greenwell, C.S.C.; Revs. Robert Griffin, C.S.C.; Carl G. Hager, C.S.C.; Bro. Edward Hagus, C.S.C.; Rev. Theodore M. Hesburgh, C.S.C.; Bro. Louis F. Hurcik, C.S.C.; Revs. John I. Jenkins, C.S.C., Religious Supr.; Daniel R. Jenky, C.S.C.; Edmund P. Joyce, C.S.C.; Thomas P. King, C.S.C.; Jerome E. Knoll, C.S.C.; Jim M. Lies, C.S.C.; Bro. Edward C. Luther, C.S.C.; Revs. James E. McDonald, C.S.C., Steward; James J. McGrath, C.S.C.; Most Rev. Mark G. McGrath, C.S.C.; Revs. Donald P. McNeill, C.S.C.; Edward A. Malloy, C.S.C.; Patrick H. Maloney, C.S.C.; Jose M. Martelli, C.S.C.; Leon J. Mertensotto, C.S.C.; Bro. Dennis Meyers, C.S.C.; Revs. Matthew M. Miceli, C.S.C.; Wilson D. Miscamble, C.S.C.; Robert H. Moss, C.S.C.; Michael J. Murphy, C.S.C.; Stephen Newton, C.S.C.; Martin Lam Nguyen, C.S.C.; Edward D. O'Connor, C.S.C.; John H. Pearson, C.S.C.; Robert S. Pelton, C.S.C.; Mark L. Poorman, C.S.C.; Louis J. Putz, C.S.C.; Herman R. Reith, C.S.C.; James L. Riehle, C.S.C.; James A. Rigert, C.S.C.; George A. Rozum, C.S.C.; David J. Scheidler, C.S.C.; Bro. Beatus Schlenker, C.S.C.; Revs. Timothy R. Scully, C.S.C., William D. Seetch, C.S.C.; Thomas G. Streit, C.S.C.; Michael B. Sullivan, C.S.C.; Thomas Tallarida, C.S.C.; Merwyn J. Thomas, C.S.C.; James W. Thornton, C.S.C.; Bro. Thomas P. Tucker, C.S.C.; Revs. William A. Wack, C.S.C.; Joseph L. Walter, C.S.C.; Richard V. Warner, C.S.C.; Charles F. Weiher, C.S.C.; Oliver F. Williams, C.S.C.; George C. Wiskirchen, C.S.C.

[K] CONVENTS AND RESIDENCES OF SISTERS

FORT WAYNE. *Marian Convent.* (St. Joseph Medical Center Convent, P.H.J.C.), 4138 S. Harrison, 46807. Tel: 219-745-4041.
E-mail: MarianConvent@juno.com
Sr. Marybeth Martin; Sr. Mary Conrad Kirchhoff; Sr. Julienne Smith; Sr. Laura Banet. Poor Handmaids of Jesus Christ 4.
Sisters of Providence Residences, 813 1-2 Kinnaird St., 46807-1250. Tel: 219-744-0780. Other Location: 2440 Fairfield, 46807-1250. Tel: 219-744-5586.
Sisters of St. Benedict. Mailing Address: 802 E. Tenth St., Ferdinand, 47532-9239.
Sisters of St. Joseph of the Third Order of St. Francis Residences S.S.J.-T.O.S.F., 2425 Chestnut St., 46803. Tel: 219-422-6675. Sisters 3. Other Location: 2419 Chestnut St., 46803. Tel: 219-424-5084. Sisters 2.

SOUTH BEND. *Handmaids of the Most Holy Trinity Monastery-Hermitage*, 23089 Adams Rd., 46628-9674. Tel: 219-272-9425. Sr. Mary Emmanuel Baggoo, H.T., Rep.; Sr. Mary Magdalene Sladicka, H.T. Contemplative Community; Prayer Ministry; Prayer Witness which includes Retreats and Spiritual Direction.
St. Joseph High School Convent, 1445 N. Michigan, 46617. Tel: 219-234-0149. Legal Title: *Sisters of the Holy Cross, Inc.*
Sisters of the Holy Cross Convents, 821 N. Blaine Ave., 46617. Tel: 219-287-6703. Sisters 4. 1104 N. Notre Dame Ave., 46617. Tel: 219-288-2665. Sisters 7. Legal Title: *Sisters of the Holy Cross, Inc.*, 919 St. Vincent St., 46617. Tel: 219-232-6084. Sisters 2. 52700 Shellbark Ave., 46628. Tel: 219-277-1877; 277-1646. Sisters 3. 2558 Flint Ct., #5. Tel: 219-273-5289. Sisters 2. 831 W. Colfax St., 46601. Tel: 219-246-0673. Sisters 4. La Casa de Amistad, 746 S. Meade St., 46619. Tel: 219-287-0531. Sisters 2. 303 Waterfall Dr., Elkhart, 46514. Tel: 219-262-0336. 190 Village Dr., 46545. Tel: 219-258-5974. St. Joseph's Towers, 316 S. St. Joseph's St., #116, 46601-2342. Tel: 219-232-8170. Sisters 5.
The Sisters of St. Joseph of the Third Order of St. Francis Central Offices, S.S.J.-T.O.S.F.
Sisters of St. Joseph of the Third Order of St. Francis Residences, 2419 Chestnut St., Fort Wayne, 46806. Tel: 219-744-5773. Sisters 2. 2425 Chestnut St., Fort Wayne, 46803. Tel: 219-422-6675. Sisters 3. 1208 Thomas St., 46601. Tel: 219-287-7341. 1042 Patty Ln., 46615. Tel: 219-289-2735. 617 W. Wayne St., 46601-9998. Tel: 219-232-6573. Sisters 3. 1445 N. Michigan St., 46617. Tel: 219-234-0149. Sisters 2. 1043 Thomas St., 46601. Tel: 219-288-5071. Sisters 2.
Chiara Home, Inc., 1105 W. Jefferson St., 46601-2618. Tel: 219-287-3184. Sisters 2.

AVILLA. *St. Mary Convent*, 226 N. Main St., P.O. Box 109, 46710. Tel: 219-897-3484. Franciscan Sisters of the Sacred Heart. Sr. M. Debrah, Funfsinn, Supr.; Sr. Theresa Renninger, Prin. Sisters 2.

DONALDSON. *Convent Ancilla Domini*, 46513. Tel: 219-936-9936; Fax: 219-935-1785.
E-mail: phjc@skynet.net
Web site: http://poorhandmaids.com
Provincialate, Poor Handmaids of Jesus Christ (The Ancilla Domini Sisters). Sr. Jolise May, P.H.J.C., Prov. Professed Sisters 42.
Catherine Kasper Home. Retired Sisters 66.
Ancilla Domini Hospitals Insurance Trust.
Maria Center. Senior Apartments (Efficiency and Singles), 46513. Apartments 15.
Poor Handmaids of Jesus Christ Community Support Trust.
Ancilla College.
Lindenwood, Retreat & Conference Center.

ELKHART. *Sisters of the Holy Cross*, 303 Waterfall Dr., 46514. Tel: 219-262-0336. 303 Waterfall Dr., 46516.

HUNTINGTON. *Victory Noll—Motherhouse of Our Lady of Victory Missionary Sisters*, 1900 W. Park Dr., Box 109, 46750. Tel: 219-356-0628; Fax: 219-356-0628, Ext. 157. Rev. Thomas C. Fahey, Chap.; Sr. Lucy Regalado, O.L.V.M., Pres.
Legal Holding: Victory Noll Sisters Community Support Trust. Sr. Mary Elise Allmaras, O.L.V.M.; Sr. Margarita Aragon, O.L.V.M.; Sr. Joan Arnold, O.L.V.M.; Sr. Helen Marie Beall, O.L.V.M.; Sr. Jean Brosnan, O.L.V.M.; Sr. Marie Jean Chettle, O.L.V.M.; Sr. Helen Collis, O.L.V.M.; Sr. Camilla Cray, O.L.V.M.; Sr. Kathleen Cummings, O.L.V.M.; Sr. Marjorie Curran, O.L.V.M.; Sr. Adriana Daskoski, O.L.V.M.; Sr. Evelyn Marie Davis, O.L.V.M.; Sr.

Denise Dean, O.L.V.M.; Sr. Madeline DeGroot, O.L.V.M.; Sr. Mary Barbara Desch, O.L.V.M.; Sr. Mary Ellen Descourouez, O.L.V.M.; Sr. Theresa Egidy, O.L.V.M.; Sr. Marie Celine Ernst, O.L.V.M.; Sr. Sharon Rose Eshleman, O.L.V.M.; Sr. Celestine Feik, O.L.V.M.; Sr. Mary Paula Fortier, O.L.V.M.; Sr. Catherine Marie Ganse, O.L.V.M.; Sr. Agatha Gerlits, O.L.V.M.; Sr. Mary Joan Ginsterblum, O.L.V.M.; Sr. Antoinette Golabowski, O.L.V.M.; Sr. Grace Golenberke, O.L.V.M.; Sr. Victoria Grabler, O.L.V.M.; Sr. Beatrice Haines, O.L.V.M.; Sr. Elizabeth Hann, O.L.V.M.; Sr. Mary Magdelan Heim, O.L.V.M.; Sr. Veronica Hirjak, O.L.V.M.; Sr. Rose Elizabeth Hohner, O.L.V.M.; Sr. Mary Lucille Huegel, O.L.V.M.; Sr. Carolyn Issenmann, O.L.V.M.; Sr. Mary Karl, O.L.V.M.; Sr. Isabelle Kestler, O.L.V.M.; Sr. Justine Kiefer, O.L.V.M.; Sr. Josephine Konrad, O.L.V.M.; Sr. Mary Dolores Kotas, O.L.V.M.; Sr. Frances Kowalewski, O.L.V.M.; Sr. Rosario Lara, O.L.V.M.; Sr. Vivian Lembeck, O.L.V.M.; Sr. Dorothy Anne Lengerich, O.L.V.M.; Sr. Mary Rosella Lengerich, O.L.V.M.; Sr. Callista Ley, O.L.V.M.; Sr. Florentine Lohr, O.L.V.M.; Sr. Madelon LoRang, O.L.V.M.; Sr. Florence Luechtefeld, O.L.V.M.; Sr. Trinidad Luna, O.L.V.M.; Sr. William Ann Maloney, O.L.V.M.; Sr. Clarice May, O.L.V.M.; Sr. Barbara McCord, O.L.V.M.; Sr. Lurlien McCoy, O.L.V.M.; Sr. Deborah McGinley, O.L.V.M.; Sr. Frances Meyer, O.L.V.M.; Sr. Anna Rita Montoya, O.L.V.M.; Sr. Carmen Montoya, O.L.V.M.; Sr. Carolyn Louise Neff, O.L.V.M.; Sr. Mary Cecelia Niehaus, O.L.V.M.; Sr. Lorraine Noon, O.L.V.M.; Sr. Marcella Poydock, O.L.V.M.; Sr. Mary Isabel Quinn, O.L.V.M.; Sr. John Francis Radler, O.L.V.M.; Sr. Lucy Regaldo, O.L.V.M.; Sr. Cecilia Marie Renk, O.L.V.M.; Sr. Anna Marie Richter, O.L.V.M.; Sr. Mary Lawrence Rochel, O.L.V.M.; Sr. Mary Helen Rogers, O.L.V.M.; Sr. Mary Esther Rosenbeck, O.L.V.M.; Sr. Gertrude Salitrik, O.L.V.M.; Sr. Grace Marie Samblanet, O.L.V.M.; Sr. Eva Maria Sanchez, O.L.V.M.; Sr. Marie Schene, O.L.V.M.; Sr. Clare Marie Schnedecker, O.L.V.M.; Sr. Marguerite Sheilds, O.L.V.M.; Sr. Martha Sijota, O.L.V.M.; Sr. Gertrude Spetter, O.L.V.M.; Sr. Mary Matilda Spetter, O.L.V.M.; Sr. Germaine Stadler, O.L.V.M.; Sr. Joachim Stetar, O.L.V.M.; Sr. Mary John Sullivan, O.L.V.M.; Sr. Janet Thill, O.L.V.M.; Sr. Regina Torzewski, O.L.V.M.; Sr. Monica Ulibarri, O.L.V.M.; Sr. Margaret Urhausen, O.L.V.M.; Sr. Lucy Marie Vega, O.L.V.M.; Sr. Amelia Villanueva, O.L.V.M.; Sr. Henrietta Wilke, O.L.V.M.; Sr. Barbara Marie Witt, O.L.V.M.; Sr. Dorothy Louise Wortmann, O.L.V.M.

FORT WAYNE: Sr. Rita Musante, O.L.V.M.; Sr. Judith Ann Turnock, O.L.V.M.; Sr. Angeline Walczyk, O.L.V.M.; Sr. Martha Wordeman, O.L.V.M.

SYRACUSE: Sr. Dolores Carlos, O.L.V.M. Professed Sisters 90.

MISHAWAKA. *Our Lady of the Angels Convent*, 1515 Dragoon Ter., P.O. Box 766, 46546-0766. Tel: 219-259-5427. Convent for retired and infirm sisters. Sr. M. Julitta, O.S.F., Supr.; Rev. Maynard Kolodziej, O.F.M., Chap. Sisters 57.

St. Francis Provincialate, Box 766, 46546-0766. Tel: 219-259-5427.
Web site: www.ssfpa.org
Sisters of St. Francis of Perpetual Adoration, Inc. St. Francis Convent and Novitiate of Immaculate Heart of Mary Province. Sr. M. Rose Agnes Pfautsch, O.S.F., Prov.; Revs. George Dubowski, O.F.M., In Res. Tel: 219-255-4068; Francis Affelt, O.F.M., Chap. Sisters 40.

NOTRE DAME. *Saint Mary's of the Immaculate Conception*, Bertrand Hall, 46556. Tel: 219-284-5550; Fax: 219-284-5779. Sr. Catherine O'Brien, C.S.C., Pres.; Sr. Aline Marie, C.S.C., Councilor; Sr. M. Genevra, C.S.C., General Sec.; Sr. Joan Marie Steadman, C.S.C., Councilor; Sr. Kathleen Moroney, C.S.C., Councilor Fin.; Sr. M. Veronique, C.S.C., Councilor. Professed Sisters in Congregation 642; Temporarily Incorporated 36; Novices 8. Generalate, Candidate Program, Associate Program. Legal Title: *Sisters of the Holy Cross, Inc.; Sisters of the Holy Cross, Inc. dba CSC Consultation Services; Holy Cross Health System Corporation; The Corporation of Saint Mary's College, Notre Dame; Holy Cross Services Corporation.*

Sisters of the Holy Cross Other Residences and Programs:

Andre House-East. Tel: 219-284-5644. Sisters 4.

Andre House-West. Tel: 219-284-5645. Sisters 3.

Holy Cross Hall. Tel: 219-284-4520.

Immaculata Hall Convent. Tel: 219-284-5676. Sisters 9.

Lourdes Convent. Tel: 219-284-5589. Sisters 21.

Marian Convent. Tel: 219-284-5614. Sisters 5.

Mary's Solitude. Tel: 219-284-5599.

Moreau Convent. Tel: 219-284-5663. Sisters 6.

Queen of Peace Convent. Tel: 219-284-5579. Sisters 10.

Rosary Convent. Tel: 219-284-5845. Sr. John Margaret, Supr. Sisters 34.

Shalem House. Tel: 219-284-5358. Sisters 3.

St. Bridget's Convent. Tel: 219-232-2683. Sisters 2.

St. John's Convent. Tel: 219-284-5695. Sisters 4.

St. Joseph's Convent. Tel: 219-284-5719. Sisters 5.

Bethany House. Tel: 219-284-3674. Sisters 6.

Saint Mary's Convent. Tel: 219-284-5688; 5689; 284-5736. Sr. Patricia Mulvaney, C.S.C., Supr. Sisters 86.

Loretto Convent. Tel: 219-284-5677. Sisters 6.

Welsh Family Hall, Notre Dame. Tel: 219-631-5158.

University Health Services, Notre Dame. Tel: 219-631-6358. Sisters 3.

University of Notre Dame, 46556. Sisters 2.

WALKERTON. *St. Patrick School Annex*, 807 Tyler St., 46574.

[L] MISSION HOUSES

NOTRE DAME. *Holy Cross Mission House*, 46556. Tel: 219-232-6005. Revs. William B. Simmons, C.S.C., Supr.; William G. Blum, C.S.C., Asst. Supr.; Michael Connors, C.S.C.; Stephen C. Gibson, C.S.C.; Andrew Guljas, C.S.C.; Casimir Grabarz, C.S.C.; Robert Hoffman, C.S.C.; Charles W. Kohlerman, C.S.C.; William M. Schreiner, C.S.C.; Paul G. Wendel, C.S.C., Asst. Supr.; John H. Wilson, C.S.C.

[M] RETREAT HOUSES & EDUCATIONAL CENTERS

DONALDSON. *Lindenwood Retreat*, PHJC Ministry Center.
E-mail: lindenwo@skynet.net
Web site: www.poorhandmaids.com
Mailing Address: P.O. Box 1, 46513. Tel: 219-935-1780; Fax: 219-935-1728. Carole Wielosinski, Dir. Overnight facilities for 100, Conference rooms for 250, Handicapped accessibility. Total Staff 9.

NOTRE DAME. *Mary's Solitude-Prayer Center*, 46556. Tel: 219-284-5599. Sr. Arlene Kniola, Dir. Center for spiritual direction, days and evenings of recollection, weekend retreats, individually-directed retreats, private & group retreats, scripture & special interest programs, 30-day retreat. Rooms 15. Total Staff 8.

Our Lady of Fatima Retreat Center, P.O. Box 929, 46556-0929. Tel: 219-631-8288.
E-mail: nd.fatima.1@nd.edu
Web site: www.nd.edu/~Fatima
Directors: Revs. Michael E. Connors, C.S.C.; Stephen C. Gibson, C.S.C.; Charles W. Kohlerman, C.S.C.; Paul G. Wendel, C.S.C., Spiritual Dir. in Res.; Sr. Rose Edward Goodrow, C.S.C. Retreats for men, women, husbands and wives, special interest groups, professional groups, youth groups and religious. Total Staff 6; Total in Residence 11.

[N] MISCELLANEOUS

FORT WAYNE. *Catholic Charities.*

Fort Wayne Community Service Center, 315 E. Washington Blvd., 46802. Tel: 219-439-0242. Kathleen Donnellan, M.S.W., Exec. Dir. Total Staff 98; Total Assisted 18,358.

South Bend Community Service Center, 425 N. Michigan, Ste. 222, South Bend, 46601. Tel: 219-234-3111; Fax: 219-289-1034. Carl Lenzo, Admin. Total Staff 23; Total Assisted 3,400.

Elkhart Community Service Center, 201 S. Second St., Elkhart, 46516. Tel: 219-295-5284. Cheryl Murphy, M.S.W., Contact Person.

Villa of the Woods-Catholic Charities Residential Living, 5610 Noll Ave., 46806. Tel: 219-745-7039. Cheryl Smith, Admin. Total Staff 10; Residents 27. Residential facilities for the elderly including housing, meals, laundry services and planned activities.

Crosier Fathers of Fort Wayne, 1721 Magnavox Way, 46802. William G. Niezer, Registered Agent. Total Staff 1.

The Diocese of Fort Wayne-South Bend, Endowment Trust, Inc., 1103 S. Calhoun Street, P.O. Box 390, 46801. Tel: 219-422-4611. Most Rev. John M. D'Arcy, Contact Person.

Foundation For Catholic Secondary Schools of Fort Wayne, Inc., Mailing Address: P.O. Box 11632, 46859-1632. Tel: 219-424-8112. Donald J. Mauch, Pres.; Michael E. Millikan, Contact Person-Dir.

St. Joseph Medical Center of Fort Wayne, Inc., 700 Broadway, 46802. Tel: 219-425-3000. John T. Farrell, Sr., Contact Person-Pres. & CEO.

St. Joseph's Health Foundation, Inc., 700 Broadway, 46802.
E-mail: cmarsh@ancilla.org
Cindi Marsh, Exec. Dir.

St. Vincent de Paul Society Store, 1600 S. Calhoun St., 46802. Tel: 219-456-3561. Steve R. App, Mgr. Total Assisted 500.

**The Christ Child Society of Fort Wayne, Inc.*, 1103 S. Calhoun St., 46802. Shirley Vorndran, Contact Person.

SOUTH BEND. *Chiara Home, Inc.*, 1105 W. Jefferson Blvd., 46601-2618. Tel: 219-287-5435. Contact Persons: Sr. Sharon E. Dillon, S.S.J.-T.O.S.F.; Sr. Gretchen Clark, S.S.J.-T.O.S.F. Respite Care for people with special needs. Total Staff 7; Total Assisted 1,500.

Christ Child Society of South Bend. Tel: 219-288-6028. Mailing Address: P.O. Box 1286, 46624. Mrs. Thomas Cahir, Res. Agent.

The Foundation of Ancilla Health Care. 215 W. Fourth St., Mishawaka, 46544; Fax: 219-239-4908. Edward Newman, Pres. Housing for the elderly 202; Residents 84.

Holy Cross Care Services, Inc., 105 Jefferson Ctr., Ste. 700, 46601-1916. Tel: 219-232-3512. Edward B. Newman, Pres. & CEO.

Holy Cross Community Services, Inc., 610 N. Michigan, Ste. 310, 46601. Tel: 219-232-9534. Bro. Christopher J. Dreyer, C.S.C., Pres. & Contact Person. Total Staff 13; Total Assisted 525.

Holy Cross Health System Corporation, 3606 E. Jefferson Blvd., 46615. Tel: 219-233-8558; Fax: 219-233-8891.
E-mail: dgh222@hchsc.org
Sr. Patricia Vandenberg, C.S.C., Pres. & CEO. Sponsored by Congregation of the Sisters of the Holy Cross, St. Mary's, Notre Dame.

Saint Joseph's Care Foundation, Inc., 801 E. LaSalle, P.O. Box 1935, 46634-1935.

Saint Joseph's Care Group, Inc., 801 E. LaSalle, 46617. Robert L. Beyer, Pres. & CEO. Total Staff 22; Total Assisted 135.

St. Vincent de Paul Referral Services, 230 E. Sample St., 46601. Tel: 219-234-6211. Mrs. Joan M. Eash, Exec. Dir. Total Staff 7; Volunteers 186.

St. Vincent de Paul Society of St. Joseph County, Inc., 230 E. Sample St., 46601. Tel: 219-234-6211. Total Staff 7; Volunteers 180; Total assisted 24,000.

St. Vincent de Paul Thrift Shop, 230 E. Sample St., 46601. Tel: 219-234-6009. Alicia McMurtrie, Mgr.

GRANGER. *Jesuit Community*, 16203 Candlewycke Ct., 46530. Tel: 219-243-0601. Rev. Jerome H. Neyrey, S.J., Contact Person.

St. Joseph's Farm, 52682 Current Rd., 46530. Tel: 219-272-0962. Brothers of the Congregation of Holy Cross, South-West Province. Bro. Donald Dunleavy, C.S.C., Dir. This farm is operated in the interests of the Congregation of Holy Cross, South-West Province. Brothers 1; Total Staff 2.

HUNTINGTON. *Our Sunday Visitor, Inc.*, 200 Noll Plaza, 46750. Tel: 219-356-8400. Publishers of Catholic Periodicals, Books and Religious Education Materials. Robert P. Lockwood, Pres. & CEO; Most Rev. John M. D'Arcy, Chm. Bd.

MISHAWAKA. *Alverno Administrative Services, Inc.*, 1515 Dragoon Tr., P.O. Box 1290, 46546-1290.

Alverno Health Corporation, 1515 Dragoon Tr., P.O. Box 1290, 46546-1290.

Alverno-Louisville Corporation, 1515 Dragoon Tr., P.O. Box 1290, 46546-1290. Tel: 219-256-3935.

Alverno Memphis Corporation, 1515 Dragoon Tr., P.O. Box 1290, 46546-1290.

Sisters of St. Francis Health Services, Inc. Mailing Address: P.O. Box 1290, 46546-1290.

St. Anthony Medical Center Foundation, 1515 Dragoon Tr., P.O. Box 1290, 46546-1290. Tel: 219-256-3935.

Ancilla Health Care, Inc.
dba St. Joseph Community Hospital of Mishawaka.
dba St. Mary Community Hospital, South Bend.
215 W. Fourth St., 46544. Tel: 219-259-2431.

St. Joseph Hospital of Mishawaka Foundation, Inc., 215 W. Fourth St., 46544. William B. Killilea, Foundation Dir.

St. Joseph's Visiting Nurse Association, Inc., 810 E. Park Pl., P.O. Box 5006, 46546-5006. Mr. Steve Kastner, Exec. Vice Pres.

Sisters of St. Francis of Perpetual Adoration, Inc., Mailing Address: P.O. Box 766, 46546-0766.

Sisters of St. Francis of Perpetual Adoration, Inc., Medical Benefits Trust.

Sisters of St. Francis of Perpetual Adoration, Inc. Capital Improvements Trust, 1515 Dragoon Ter., Box 766, 46546-0766. Tel: 219-256-3935.
Web site: www.ssfpa.org

Sisters of St. Francis Charitable Mission Trust.

Sisters of St. Francis Retirement Fund.

SSFPA Ministry Corporation, 1515 Dragoon Trail, P.O. Box 766, 46546. Tel: 219-258-5048; 258-5427. Sr. M. Rose Agnes Pfautsch, O.S.F., Prov. Supr.

**St. Margaret Mercy Health Care Center, Inc.*, 1515 Dragoon Tr., 46544. Tel: 219-256-3935.

Yves R. Simon Institute, 508 Travers Cir., 46545. Tel: 219-259-1864. Mr. Anthony O. Simon, Dir. & Contact Person. Catholic academic institute.

NOTRE DAME. *Association of St. Joseph*, Mailing Address: P.O. Box 985, 46556-0985. Tel: 219-631-7830. Bro. Flavius Ellison, C.S.C., Contact Person.

Ave Maria Press, Inc., P.O. Box 428, 46556. Tel: 219-287-2831; Fax: 219-239-2904. Frank J. Cunningham, Pres. & Publisher. Owned and operated by the Congregation of Holy Cross, Indiana Province, Inc.

Brothers of Holy Cross Life Development Trust, Mailing Address: P.O. Box 460, 46556. Tel: 219-239-8300; Fax: 219-289-0487. Trustees: Bros. Donald Bailer; William Dygert; Paul Kelly; Stanley Olszowka; Lawrence Skitzki.

Holy Cross Associates, Mailing Address: Moreau Seminary, P.O. Box 668, 46556. Tel: 219-631-5521.
E-mail: nd.hcassoc.1.@nd.edu
Web site: www.nd.edu:80/~hcassoc/
John Pinter, Contact Person-Dir. Total Staff 2; Total in Residence 55.

Holy Cross Services Corp., Bertrand Hall, St. Mary's, 46556. Tel: 219-284-5550. Sisters of the Holy Cross.

Midwest Hispanic Catholic Commission, N.C.C.B. Regions VI and VII, 18965 Douglas Rd., P.O. Box 703, 46556. Tel: 219-271-7459; 271-7593; Fax: 219-631-6947.

PLYMOUTH. *Earthworks, Inc.*, 9815 Union Rd., 46563. Tel: 219-936-9936. Sr. Janis Yaekel, A.S.C., Dir. An environmental education center; a sponsored entity of the Poor Handmaids of Jesus Christ (P.H.J.C.) affiliated with Convent Ancilla Domini, Donaldson, IN.

RELIGIOUS INSTITUTES OF MEN REPRESENTED IN THE DIOCESE

For further details refer to the corresponding bracketed number in the Religious Institutes of Men or Women section.

[0600]—*Brothers of the Congregation of Holy Cross.* (Midwest Province).—C.S.C.

[0470]—*The Capuchin Friars.* (Prov. of St. Joseph).—O.F.M.Cap.

[0480]—*Conventual Franciscans.* (Prov. of Our Lady of Consolation).—O.F.M.Conv.

[0520]—*Franciscan Friars.* (Prov. of St. John the Baptist).—O.F.M.

[0690]—*Jesuit Fathers and Brothers.*—S.J.

[0610]—*Priests of the Congregation of Holy Cross.* (Indiana Province).—C.S.C.

[1060]—*Society of the Precious Blood.* (Cincinnati Province).—C.PP.S.

RELIGIOUS INSTITUTES OF WOMEN REPRESENTED IN THE DIOCESE

[0230]—*Benedictine Sisters of Pontifical Jurisdiction.* (Ferdinand, IN).—O.S.B.

[3710]—*Congregation of the Sisters of Saint Agnes.*—C.S.A.

[1920]—*Congregation of the Sisters of the Holy Cross.*—C.S.C.

[1710]—*Congregation of the Third Order of St. Francis of Mary Immaculate.* (Joliet, IL).—O.S.F.

[0760]—*Daughters of Charity of St. Vincent de Paul.* (East Central Province).—D.C.

[0790]—*Daughters of Divine Charity.* (Holy Trinity Province).—F.D.C.

[1070-03]—*Dominican Sisters.*—O.P.

[1070-13]—*Dominican Sisters.*—O.P.

[1170]—*Felician Sisters.* (Presentation of the B.V.M. Province).—C.S.S.F.

[1450]—*Franciscan Sisters of the Sacred Heart.*—O.S.F.

[]—*Handmaids of the Most Holy Trinity.*—H.T.

[3130]—*Our Lady of Victory Missionary Sisters.*—O.L.V.M.

[3230]—*Poor Handmaids of Jesus Christ.*—P.H.J.C.

[2970]—*School Sisters of Notre Dame.*—S.S.N.D.

[2990]—*Sisters of Notre Dame.* (Province of Toledo).—S.N.D.

[3000]—*Sisters of Notre Dame de Namur.* (Chesapeake Province).—S.N.D.deN.

[3360]—*Sisters of Providence of Saint Mary-of-the-Woods, Indiana.*—S.P.

[1640]—*Sisters of St. Francis of Perpetual Adoration.* (Province of the Immaculate Heart of Mary).—O.S.F.

[3830]—*Sisters of St. Joseph.*—C.S.J.

[3880]—*Sisters of St. Joseph of Medaille.* (New Orleans).—C.S.J.

[3930]—*Sisters of St. Joseph of the Third Order of St. Francis.*—S.S.J.-T.O.S.F.

[2110]—*Sisters of the Humility of Mary.*—H.M.

[3260]—*Sisters of the Precious Blood.* (Dayton, Ohio).—C.PP.S.

DIOCESAN CEMETERY

FORT WAYNE. *Catholic*, 3500 Lake Ave., 46805. Tel: 219-426-2044.

NECROLOGY

✠ McManus, Most Rev. William E., (Retired). —Died March 3, 1997.

† Hayes, James E., (Retired). —Died Jan. 30, 1997.

† Zenz, Louis J., (Retired). —Died Nov. 12, 1996.

Diocese of Fort Worth

(Dioecesis Arcis-Vorthensis)

Most Reverend

JOSEPH P. DELANEY, D.D.

Bishop of Fort Worth; ordained December 18, 1960; appointed Bishop of Fort Worth July 10, 1981; ordained Bishop September 13, 1981. *Mailing Address: 800 West Loop 820 S., Fort Worth, TX, 76108.* Tel.: 817-560-3300.

ESTABLISHED AUGUST 22, 1969.

Square Miles 23,950.

Comprises the following twenty-eight Counties in the State of Texas: Archer, Baylor, Bosque, Clay, Comanche, Cooke, Denton, Eastland, Erath, Foard, Hardeman, Hill, Hood, Jack, Johnson, Knox, Montague, Palo Pinto, Parker, Shackleford, Stephens, Somervell, Tarrant, Throckmorton, Wichita, Wilbarger, Wise and Young.

For legal titles of parishes and diocesan institutions, consult the Chancery Office.

The Catholic Center: 800 West Loop 820 S., Fort Worth, TX, 76108. Tel.: 817-560-3300; Fax: 817-244-8839.

STATISTICAL OVERVIEW

Personnel	
Bishop	1
Priests: Diocesan Active in Diocese	45
Priests: Active Outside Diocese	3
Priests: Diocesan in Foreign Missions	1
Priests: Retired, Sick or Absent	9
Number of Diocesan Priests	58
Religious Priests in Diocese	50
Extern Priests in Diocese	9
Ordinations:	
Diocesan Priests	1
Permanent Deacons in Diocese	64
Total Brothers	11
Total Sisters	113
Parishes	
Parishes	87
With Resident Pastor:	
Resident Diocesan Priests	38
Resident Religious Priests	22
Without Resident Pastor:	
Administered by Priests	22
Administered by Permanent Deacons	3
Administered by Professed Men Religious	1
Administered by Women Religious	1
Missions	2
Professional Ministry Personnel:	
Brothers	3
Sisters	18
Lay Ministers	80
Welfare	
Catholic Hospitals	1
Total Assisted	65,000
Health Care Centers	1
Total Assisted	1,200
Homes for the Aged	5
Total Assisted	506
Day Care and Extended Day Care Centers	1
Total Assisted	63
Special Centers for Social Services	16
Total Assisted	30,621
Educational	
Diocesan Students in Other Seminaries	13
Total Seminarians	13
High Schools, Diocesan and Parish	4
Total Students	1,572
Elementary Schools, Diocesan and Parish	15
Total Students	4,758
Elementary Schools, Private	1
Total Students	232
Catechesis/Religious Education:	
High School Students	5,491
Elementary Students	17,983
Total Students Under Catholic Instruction	30,049
Teachers in the Diocese:	
Priests	2
Brothers	8
Sisters	20
Lay Teachers	636
Vital Statistics	
Receptions into the Church:	
Infant Baptism Totals	4,891
Adult Baptism Totals	461
Received into Full Communion	649
First Communions	4,080
Confirmations	2,290
Marriages:	
Catholic	732
Interfaith	405
Total Marriages	1,137
Deaths	982
Total Catholic Population	200,461
Total Population	2,264,487

Former Bishops—Most Rev. JOHN J. CASSATA, D.D., ord. Dec. 8, 1932; Titular Bishop of Bida and Auxiliary of Dallas-Fort Worth; appt. March 20, 1968; cons. June 5, 1968; first Bishop, Fort Worth; appt. Aug. 22, 1969; retired Sept. 16, 1980; died Sept. 8, 1989.

Vicar General—Rev. Msgr. JOSEPH A. SCHUMACHER.

Chancellor and Moderator of the Curia—Rev. ROBERT WILSON.

Deans—Rev. THOMAS CRAIG, North; Rev. RAY MULLAN, Southwest; Rev. WILLIAM WINASKI, Northwest; Rev. PHILIP JOHNSON, East; Rev. TIMOTHY THOMPSON, Central.

Diocesan Pastoral Advisory Council—(Includes Presbyteral Council listed below). Lay Persons: Ms. JAMES GAGLIARDO; Mr. ROBERT GARRISON; Mr. PETE GUERRERO; Ms. JO ANN HARRIS; Ms. JOSIE HERNANDEZ; Ms. KAY KEGLOVITS; Ms. MARGARITA LUNA; Ms. LINDA RAINOSEK. Career Ministers: Ms. SHARON CASTLEBERRY; Mr. PAUL COMBEST; Ms. MARY HELEN FRANKO; Ms. KAY FUHRMAN; Sr. BERNICE KNAPEK, S.S.M.N.; Mr. RALPH MCCLOUD; Deacon JAMES POOLE; Ms. LEONA SCHWARTZ; Ms. CHARMAINE WILLIAMS, Facilitator.

Presbyteral Council and Consultors—Revs. ESTEBAN JASSO, T.O.R.; RAYMUND MULLAN; WARREN MURPHY, T.O.R.; KEN ROBINSON; JONATHAN SCALONE; JOSEPH SCANTLIN; KARL SCHILKEN; JOSEPH A. SCHUMACHER; ROBERT WILSON; WILLIAM WINASKI.

Diocesan Finance Council—Mr. CHUCK BARTUSH, JR.; Mr. JOHN HERNANDEZ; Rev. Msgr. CHARLES KING; Ms. BARBARA MAY; Mr. DAVID MORITZ; Ms. ELAINE PETRUS; Mr. ROBERT SCHUMACHER; Mr. EARLE SHIELDS, JR.; Mr. PETER FLYNN, Staff; Rev. ROBERT WILSON, Ex-Officio; Rev. Msgr. JOSEPH A. SCHUMACHER, Chm. Ex-Officio.

Catholic Foundation of North Texas—Mr. PETER FLYNN, Exec. Dir.; Mr. JERRY KRAMER, Planned Giving; Mr. CHUCK BARTUSH, JR.; Mr. JOHN HERNANDEZ; Rev. Msgr. CHARLES KING; Ms. BARBARA MAY; Mr. DAVID MORITZ; Ms. ELAINE PETRUS; Mr. ROBERT SCHUMACHER; Mr. EARLE SHIELDS, JR.; Rev. ROBERT WILSON; Rev. Msgr. JOSEPH A. SCHUMACHER.

Catholic Schools Trust—Mr. EARLE SHIELDS, JR., Chm.; Mr. MARSHALL WHITEHEAD; Mr. NOEL ARAGON; Mr. JOSEPH MONTELEONE; Mr. RICK BONDURANT; Dr. CAROL CARLSON DEAN; Ms. JANELLE KAVANAUGH; Mr. JOHN CRUMLEY, Attorney; Mr. PAUL GREENWELL, Investment Mgr.; Sr. MARGUERITE CONNORS, S.H.Sp., Supt. of Schools; Mr. PETER FLYNN, Finance Officer.

Catholic Cemeteries Trust—Mr. HENRY PENNARTZ; Mr. BILL METZLER; Mr. DAN SHINE; Mr. JOHN PRIBYLA; Ms. JOLEEN RAMPY; Mr. RAY LINDEMANN; Ms. CAROLYN JONES, Staff.

St. Joseph's Health Care Trust—Rev. ROBERT W. WILSON.

North Texas San Benito, Inc.—Mr. PETER FLYNN.

Division Directors, Diocesan Offices

Christian Formation—Dr. DAN LUBY.

Clergy and Religious Personnel Services—Rev. Msgr. JOSEPH A. SCHUMACHER.

Executive Services—Rev. ROBERT WILSON.

Financial Services—Mr. PETER FLYNN.

Pastoral and Community Services—Mr. RALPH MCCLOUD.

Pastoral Planning and Human Resources—Mrs. CHARMAINE WILLIAMS.

Schools—Sr. MARGUERITE CONNORS, S.H.Sp.

The Catholic Center—800 West Loop 820 S., Fort Worth, 76108. Tel: 817-560-3300; Fax: 817-244-8839. Departments and programs below, which are part of one of the divisions above, are listed alphabetically. Unless specifically noted the address and phone numbers are as above.

Boards and Associations

Board of Arbitration and Conciliation—Mr. PHIL RECORD, Chm.; Ms. SANDRA LEIGHTON; Mr. STEVE WILCOX; Mr. CLE ROYAL; Ms. Taylor.

Building Commission—Rev. Msgr. HUBERT NEU, Chm.; Rev. Msgr. JOSEPH A. SCHUMACHER; Mr. JACK DREWETT; Ms. DEBORAH GAGLIARDI; Mr. CREIGHTON PICKETT; Mr. BRAD RUPAY; Mr. PETER FLYNN; Mr. GARY FRAGOSSO, Staff.

Diocesan Pastoral Finance Council (Budgets)—Rev. ROBERT WILSON, Chm.

Diocesan School Board—Mr. HOWARD NEEB, Pres.

Priests' Personnel Board—Rev. JOSEPH SCANTLIN, Chm., *2100 N. Davis Dr., Arlington, 76012-1803.* Tel: 817-460-2751.

Priests' Retirement Board—Rev. Msgr. JOSEPH A. SCHUMACHER, Chm.; Rev. JAMES O'TOOLE; Mr. EARLE

SHIELDS; Rev. Msgr. HUBERT NEU; Mr. FRANKLIN MOORE.

Diocesan Programs

Christian Formation—Dr. DAN LUBY, Div. Dir.
Adult Formation—Dr. DAN LUBY, Dir.
Campus Ministry—Mr. PAUL COMBEST, Contact Person.
Children's Catechesis—Sr. DOROTHY POWERS, S.S.M.N., Dir.; Ms. NANCY RISTUCCIA, Dir.
Cursillo—Rev. ERIC AZCONA, O.F.M.Cap., *Cursillo Center, 2221 N.W. 26th St., Fort Worth, 76106*. Tel: 817-624-9411.
Hispanic Pastoral Services—Sr. GABRIELA MARTINEZ, S.S.M.N., Dir.
Rural Hispanic Ministry—Mr. ANDRES ARANDA, Dir.
Light of Christ Institute for Lay Ministry Development—Dr. ANN HEALEY, Dir.
Media Library—Ms. DANETTE SARTORI.
Scouting—Rev. JOHN GREMMELS, *2016 Willis Ln., Keller, 76248*. Tel: 817-431-3857.
Worship—Ms. MARY MCLARRY, Dir.
Young Adult Ministry—Mr. PAUL COMBEST, Dir.
Youth Ministry and Adolescent Catechesis—Mr. KEVIN PREVOU, Dir.
Clergy and Religious Personnel Services—Rev. Msgr. JOSEPH A. SCHUMACHER, Div. Dir.
Clergy Relief Association—Rev. Msgr. JOSEPH A. SCHUMACHER.
Continuing Pastoral Formation—Rev. WILLIAM HOPKINS.
Permanent Diaconate, Office of—Deacon JOSEPH MILLIGAN, Dir.
Seminarians—Sr. DONNA FERGUSON, S.S.M.N., Dir.
Vicar for Religious—Sr. THERESA KHIRALLAH, S.S.N.D.
Vocations—Rev. WILLIAM HOPKINS, Dir.
Executive Services—Rev. ROBERT WILSON, Div. Dir.
Development Office—Mr. JERRY KRAMER, Dir.
Foundation Relations—Ms. BARBARA M. SHELTON, Dir.
Parish Stewardship—Ms. DIANA FRANCO, Dir.
Newspaper "North Texas Catholic"—Mr. JEFF HENSLEY, Editor; Ms. MARY MARTIN, Assoc. Editor.
Propagation of the Faith—Rev. ROBERT WILSON, Acting Dir.
Tribunal—Rev. TIMOTHY THOMPSON, Judicial Vicar; Mrs. SANDRA LEIGHTON, Dir.
Financial Services—Mr. PETER FLYNN, Div. Dir.
Accounting/Budgeting—Ms. CAROLYN JONES.
Construction and Property Management—Mr. GARY FRAGOSSO, Dir.
Cemeteries—Ms. CAROLYN JONES, Dir.
Planning and Human Resources—Ms. CHARMAINE WILLIAMS, Div. Dir.
Pastoral Planning Office—Ms. CHARMAINE WILLIAMS, Dir.
Benefits Coordinator—Ms. SHARON FIELDER.
Parish Pastoral Planning—Ms. MARY RALEY, Dir.
Personnel Officer—Ms. MARY MILLS.
Pastoral and Community Services—Mr. RALPH MCCLOUD, Div. Dir.
African American Ministries—Mr. RALPH MCCLOUD, Dir.
Catholic Women, Council of—Rev. IVOR KOCH, *Sacred Heart Parish, 1504 10th St., Wichita Falls, 76301*. Tel: 817-723-5288.
Campaign for Human Development—Mr. RALPH MCCLOUD.
Ecumenism, Office of—Rev. Msgr. CHARLES KING, *St. John the Apostle, 7341 Glenview Dr., Fort Worth, 76180*. Tel: 817-284-4811.
Family Life and Pre-Cana—Vacant.
Hospital Chaplaincy—Rev. RAPHAEL EAGLE, T.O.R., *St. Mary of the Assumption, 509 W. Magnolia Ave., Fort Worth, 76104*. Tel: 817-923-1911. Sr. TERESA NASCHE, S.H.Sp., *3416 Brady, Fort Worth, 76109*. Tel: 817-926-7180.
Jail Ministry—Mr. RALPH MCCLOUD, Dir.
Laotian Pastoral Center—*3508 Maurice Ave., Fort Worth, 76111*. Tel: 817-831-4404.
Peace and Justice Office—Mr. RALPH MCCLOUD, Coord.
Prolife—Vacant.
Rural Life—Mr. RALPH MCCLOUD, Contact Person.
St. Vincent de Paul—Deacon JOE RAETZ, *5013 Emerald Dr., Fort Worth, 76103*. Tel: 817-457-6948.
Wichita Falls-Bethania Regional Health Care Center-Chaplain—Rev. AIDAN DONLON, S.A.C., *1600 11th St., Wichita Falls, 76301*. Tel: 817-723-4111.
Schools—Sr. MARGUERITE CONNORS, S.H.Sp., Div. Dir. & Supt. of Catholic Schools.
Associate Superintendent—Sr. BERNICE KNAPEK, S.S.M.N.
Holy Childhood Association—Sr. MARGUERITE CONNORS, S.H.Sp., Dir.
New Schools Coordinator—Vacant.

CLERGY, PARISHES, MISSIONS AND PAROCHIAL SCHOOLS

CITY OF FORT WORTH
(Tarrant County)

1—ST. PATRICK CATHEDRAL (1870), Rev. Msgr. Hubert Neu; Revs. Dennis Smith; Albert Tyl; Robert Strittmatter.
Res., 1206 Throckmorton St., 76102. Tel: 817-332-4915; Fax: 817-338-1988.
Catechesis/Religious Programs—Tel: 817-338-4441.
Students 399.

2—ALL SAINTS (1902) (Hispanic), Revs. Stephen Jasso, T.O.R.; Bernardo Nicolau, T.O.R. (Spain); Amando Trujillo, T.O.R. (Mexico).
Res., 214 N.W. 20th St., 76106. Tel: 817-626-3055; Fax: 817-626-3056.
School—2006 N. Houston St., 76106-8195. Tel: 817-624-2670; 624-3471; Fax: 817-624-1221.
Sisters 1; Lay Teachers 11; Students 174.
Catechesis/Religious Programs—2022 Houston St., 76106. Tel: 817-626-1711.
Students 725.

3—HOLY FAMILY (1942), Rev. Joseph Pemberton; Deacon Joseph L. Milligan, Jr.
Res., 6150 Pershing Ave., 76107. Tel: 817-737-6768; Fax: 817-737-6876.
School—Tel: 817-737-4201.
Lay Teachers 13; Students 225.
Catechesis/Religious Programs—Students 285.

4—HOLY NAME OF JESUS (1952), Rev. Lawrence Breedlove.
Res., 2637 Avenue L., 76105. Tel: 817-536-9604.
Catechesis/Religious Programs—Tel: 817-535-8495.
Students 390.

5—IMMACULATE HEART OF MARY (1961), Revs. Francisco X. Fernandez, O.F.M.Cap. (Spain); Greg Goicoechea, O.F.M.; Jose Maria Oroquieta, O.F.M. (Spain).
Res., 100 E. Pafford St., 76110. Tel: 817-923-6323.
Catechesis/Religious Programs—Tel: 817-923-8582.
Students 1,312.

6—OUR LADY OF GUADALUPE (1977) (Hispanic), Revs. Claudio Zudaire, O.F.M.Cap.; Francis Garces, O.F.M.Cap. In res., Rev. Eric Azcona, O.F.M.Cap.
Res., 3301 Clinton, 76106. Tel: 817-626-7421; Fax: 817-625-8032.
Catechesis/Religious Programs—Tel: 817-624-3240.
Students 1,270.

7—OUR MOTHER OF MERCY (1929) (African American), Rev. Michael J. Farrell, S.S.J.
Res., 1007 E. Terrell Ave., 76104-3788. Tel: 817-335-1695.
School—1003 E. Terrell Ave., 76104-3799. Tel: 817-336-2880.
Sisters of the Holy Spirit 3; Lay Teachers 8; Students 212.

8—ST. ANDREW (1953), Revs. Warren Murphy, T.O.R.; Joseph Janiszeski, T.O.R. In res., Revs. Benjamin Medeiros, T.O.R.; Theodore J. Bradower, T.O.R.
Res., 3717 Stadium Dr., 76109. Tel: 817-927-5383; Fax: 817-927-8507.
School—St. Andrew Catholic School, 3304 Dryden Rd., 76109. Tel: 817-924-8917; Fax: 817-927-8507.
Lay Teachers 37; Students 704.
Catechesis/Religious Programs—Students 628.

9—ST. BARTHOLOMEW (1969), Revs. Richard Beaumont; Gary Geurtz; Deacon Gerald M. Barry.
Res., 3601 Altamesa Blvd., 76133. Tel: 817-292-7703; Fax: 817-292-2568.
Catechesis/Religious Programs—Students 370.

10—ST. GEORGE (1941), Bro. Paul McMullen, T.O.R., Pastoral Admin.; Deacon Ruben Curiel.
Res., 825 Karnes, 76111. Tel: 817-831-4404; Fax: 817-834-0121.
School—824 Hudgins St., 76111. Tel: 817-838-5685; Fax: 817-834-0121.
Lay Teachers 9; Students 123.
Catechesis/Religious Programs—Tel: 817-831-4404.
Students 260.

11—ST. JOHN THE APOSTLE (North Richland Hills) (1964), Rev. Msgr. Charles B. King; Revs. Phillip Magaldi; Danny Kelley; Deacon Tom Giovannetti.
Res., 7341 Glenview Dr., 76180. Tel: 817-284-4811; Fax: 817-284-1729.
School—7421 Glenview Dr., 76180. Tel: 817-284-2228.
Lay Teachers 41; Students 629.
Catechesis/Religious Programs—Tel: 817-590-0915.
Students 1,060.

12—ST. MARY OF THE ASSUMPTION (1909), Rev. Gerald Haby, S.M.; Bro. Robert Minges, S.M. In res., Raphael Eagle, T.O.R.
Res., 509 W. Magnolia Ave., 76104. Tel: 817-923-1911; Fax: 817-923-0769.
Catechesis/Religious Programs—Students 315.

13—ST. PAUL (1952), Rev. Ellsworth T. Wigginton; Deacon Ron Aziere.
Res., 925 Yale St., 76114. Tel: 817-738-9925; Fax: 817-735-8579.
Church—5508 Black Oak Ln., 76114.
Catechesis/Religious Programs—Students 170.

14—ST. PETER THE APOSTLE (1952), Rev. D. Timothy Thompson; Mrs. Fran Bresler, Pastoral Assoc.; Deacons Louis Poth; Pat Bresler.
Office: 1201 S. Cherry Ln., 76108. Tel: 817-246-3622; Fax: 817-246-4900.
Res., 7828 Abbott, 76108. Tel: 817-246-3442.
School—Tel: 817-246-2032. Mrs. Deborah Herrera, Prin.
Lay Teachers 14; Students 157.
Catechesis/Religious Programs—Students 216.

15—ST. RITA (1910), Revs. Richard Flores; Mark Bau, C.M.C.
Res., 5550 E. Lancaster, 76112. Tel: 817-451-9395; Fax: 817-451-9421.
School—712 Weiler Blvd., 76112. Tel: 817-451-9383.
Lay Teachers 20; Students 248.
Catechesis/Religious Programs—Students 170.

16—ST. THOMAS (1937), Rev. Salvator Stefula, T.O.R.
Res., 2920 Azle Ave., 76106. Tel: 817-624-2184; Fax: 817-624-9688.
Catechesis/Religious Programs—Students 550.
Mission—Azle, Tarrant Co., Holy Trinity, 800 Highcrest, Azle, 76020.
Mailing Address: P.O. Box 136038, Forth Worth, 76136.

17—ST. THOMAS MORE, Rev. Edward James Hart.
Res., 2728 Merida Ave., 76109. Tel: 817-927-2414.

18—SAN MATEO (1939) (Hispanic), Sr. Felipa Guadalupe Lara, M.C.
Rectory—2909 Photo Ave., 76107. Tel: 817-737-5470.
Res., 2640 Avenue L., 76105. Tel: 817-535-8495.
Catechesis/Religious Programs—Students 138.

19—CHRIST THE KING. (Quasi-Parish). Rev. Matthias Tinh An Tran Man.
Res., 1112 Eagle Dr., 76111. Tel: 817-831-7200.

OUTSIDE THE CITY OF FORT WORTH

Abbott, Hill Co., Immaculate Heart of Mary (1946), Rev. James G. Ryan, O.S.A.
Res., Rte. 2, Box 82A, 76621. Tel: 817-582-3092. [CEM]
Catechesis/Religious Programs—Students 80.

Albany, Shackelford Co., Jesus of Nazareth (1970), Deacon Ruben L. Castaneda.
Res., P.O. Box 1584, 76430. Tel: 915-762-2632. [JC]
Catechesis/Religious Programs—Students 63.

Arlington, Tarrant Co.,

1—CHURCH OF ST. MARY THE VIRGIN, (1994), Rev. Allan R.G. Hawkins.
Res., 1408 N. Davis Dr., 76012. Tel: 817-460-2278; Fax: 817-277-9927.

2—MOST BLESSED SACRAMENT, (1978), Rev. Joseph S. Scantlin.
Res., 2100 N. Davis Dr., 76012. Tel: 817-460-2751; Fax: 817-460-2761.
Catechesis/Religious Programs—Students 580.

3—ST. JOSEPH'S, (1988), Rev. James Miller.
Office: 1927 S.W. Green Oaks Blvd., 76017-2734. Tel: 817-472-5181; Fax: 817-467-9319.
Res., 5108 Winterberry, 76018. Tel: 817-468-7521.

4—ST. MARIA GORETTI, (1941), Rev. James Gigliotti, T.O.R.
Res., 1200 S. Davis Dr., 76013. Tel: 817-274-0643; Fax: 817-277-4193.
School—Tel: 817-275-5081.
Lay Teachers 26; Students 460.
Catechesis/Religious Programs—Tel: 817-460-0048.
Students 280.

5—ST. MATTHEW, (1964), Rev. Msgr. Joseph A. Schumacher; Revs. Hilary M. Tran-cong-Ly, C.M.C.; D. Leo Bonsall, O.S.B.; Deacons Eduardo Garcia; Benito Serenil.
Res., 2021 New York Ave., 76010-6097. Tel: 817-860-0130; Fax: 817-277-7159.
Catechesis/Religious Programs—Students 1,538.

6—ST. VINCENT DE PAUL, (1976), Rev. Philip L. Johnson; Deacons George R. Nicklas, Jr.; Charles Castleberry.
Res., 5819 W. Pleasant Ridge Rd., 76016. Tel: 817-478-8206; Fax: 817-478-8513.

Catechesis/Religious Programs—Tel: 817-478-8208.
Students 1,538.

Bedford, Tarrant Co., St. Michael (1977), Revs. James O'Toole; Mel Bessellieu; E. James Hart; Deacons Harry Heinz; Lonnie Weaver.
Res., 3713 Harwood, 76021-4097. Tel: 817-283-8666; Fax: 817-283-9306.
Catechesis/Religious Programs—Students 1,255.

Bowie, Montague Co., St. Jerome (1986). Attended by St. Mary, Henrietta. Rev. John S. Stasiowski.
Mailing Address: 105 S. Barrett, Henrietta, 76365. Tel: 817-538-4214.
Catechesis/Religious Programs—Students 62.

Breckenridge, Stephens Co., Sacred Heart (1920), Rev. Anh Q. Tran.
Res., 208 S. Miller St., 76424. Tel: 254-559-2860; Fax: 254-559-5289.
Catechesis/Religious Programs—Students 76.

Bridgeport, Wise Co., St. John the Baptizer (1889), Rev. Gonzalo Morales.
Res., 1801 Irvin, 76426. Tel: 940-683-2743; Fax: 940-683-2743.
Catechesis/Religious Programs—Tel: 817-627-2743.
Students 135.

Burkburnett, Wichita Co., St. Jude Thaddeus (1965), Rev. Severius Blank.
Res., 600 Davey Dr., 76354. Tel: 817-569-1222.
Catechesis/Religious Programs—Students 58.

Burleson, Tarrant Co., St. Ann (1971), Rev. John Hennessy.
Res., 100 S.W. Alsbury Blvd., 76028. Tel: 817-295-5621.
Catechesis/Religious Programs—Students 308.

Carrollton, Denton Co., St. Catherine of Siena (1981), Revs. George Thennattil, T.O.R.; Thomas Panickaurparampil, T.O.R.; Deacons Philip Webb; Robert Stuart.
Mailing Address: 1705 Peters Colony, 75007-3704. Tel: 972-492-3237; Fax: 972-394-0676.
Catechesis/Religious Programs—Students 845.

Cisco, Eastland Co., Holy Rosary (1920). Attended by St. Rita, Ranger. Rev. Vincent Inametti.
1109 Blackwell St., Ranger, 76470. Tel: 817-647-3167.

Cleburne, Johnson Co., St. Joseph (1888), Rev. Sergio Rizo.
Mailing Address: 807 N. Anglin St., 76031. Tel: 817-645-4478.
Catechesis/Religious Programs—Students 240.

Clifton, Bosque Co., Holy Angels (1954), Rev. Salvador Perez, O.S.A.
Church—Box 431, 76634. Tel: 254-675-8877.
Catechesis/Religious Programs—Students 70.

Colleyville, Good Shepherd (1992), Rev. Robert Wilson. Administrators: Sr. Dorothy Eggering, S.S.N.D.; Sr. Theresa Khirallah, S.S.N.D.
1000 Tinker Rd., 76034. Tel: 817-421-1387; Fax: 817-421-4709.
Catechesis/Religious Programs—Students 890.

The Colony, Denton Co., Holy Cross (1981), Rev. Publius Xuereb.
Church—7000 Morning Star, P.O. Box 560156, 75056. Tel: 972-625-5252; Fax: 972-370-5524.
Catechesis/Religious Programs—Students 390.

Comanche, Comanche Co., Sacred Heart (1964). Attended by St. Brendan, Stephenville. Deacon William Bolf.
Church—1444 W. Washington Ave., Stephenville, 76401. Tel: 817-965-5693.
Catechesis/Religious Programs—Students 127.

Crowell, Foard Co., St. Joseph (1910). Attended by Holy Family, Vernon. Rev. Oren W. Key, S.J.
Church—2200 Roberts, P.O. Box 1377, Vernon, 76384. Tel: 817-552-2895; Fax: 817-552-6084.

Decatur, Wise Co., Assumption of the Blessed Virgin Mary (1938), Rev. Gonzalo Morales.
Res., 1305 Deer Park Rd., 76234-9701. Tel: 940-627-3307; Fax: 940-683-2743.
Church Rectory: 1801 Irvin, Bridgeport, 76426. Tel: 817-627-2561.
Catechesis/Religious Programs—Students 175.

De Leon, Comanche Co., Our Lady of Guadalupe (1975). Attended by St. Brendan, Stephenville.
Mailing Address: c/o St. Brendan, 1444 W. Washington, Stephenville, 76401. Tel: 817-965-5693.
Church—Hwy. 16, 2 miles S. of Hwy. 6, 76444. Tel: 817-893-5511.
Catechesis/Religious Programs—Students 58.

Denton, Denton Co., Immaculate Conception (1894), Rev. Juan Rivero; Deacon Popo Gonzalez. In res., Rev. Robert M. Lewandowski, S.M.
Res., 1215 N. Elm St., 76201. Tel: 940-565-1770; Fax: 940-382-7939.
Catechesis/Religious Programs—Sr. Helen Stejskal, S.S.N.D., D.R.E.
Students 375.

St. Mark (1995), Rev. Eugene Sweeney, S.M.
2800 Pennsylvania, 76205. Tel: 940-387-6223; Fax: 940-382-1641.

Dodson Prairie, Palo Pinto Co., St. Boniface (1913). Attended by Sacred Heart, Breckenridge. Rev. Anh Q. Tran.
Mailing Address: 208 S. Miller, Breckenridge, 76424. Tel: 254-559-2860.

Dublin, Erath Co., St. Mary (1916). Attended by St. Brendan, Stephenville.
1444 W. Washington Ave., Stephenville, 76401. Tel: 817-965-5693.
Catechesis/Religious Programs—Students 112.

Eastland, Eastland Co., St. Francis Xavier (1920). Attended by St. Rita, Ranger. Rev. Vincent Inametti.
1109 Blackwell St., Ranger, 76470. Tel: 817-647-3167; Fax: 817-647-3167.

Electra, Wichita Co., St. Paul (1966), Deacon Patrick Burke, Admin.
Mailing Address: P.O. Box 991.
Res., 709 W. Rebecca St., Iowa Park, 76367. Tel: 940-592-2930. [JC]
Church—500 N. Bailey, 76360. Tel: 940-495-3464; 592-2802.

Gainesville, Cooke Co., St. Mary (1879), Rev. Richard Sternemann, O.S.B. In res., Rev. David Petraitis, O.S.A., Hispanic Min.
Res., 805 N. Weaver St., 76240. Tel: 940-665-2413; Fax: 940-665-0957.
School—931 N. Weaver St., 76240. Tel: 817-668-7898; Fax: 817-668-1881.
Sisters of St. Mary of Namur 1; School Sisters of Notre Dame 2; Lay Teachers 13; Students 186.
Catechesis/Religious Programs—Tel: 817-665-5395.
Students 199.
Convent—825 N. Weaver St., 76240.

Glen Rose, Somervell Co., St. Rose of Lima (1969). Attended by St. Frances Cabrini. Rev. Lawrence Gould, S.A.C.
P.O. Box 757, Granbury, 76048. Tel: 817-326-2131. [JC]

Graford, Palo Pinto Co., St. Francis of Assisi (1949). Attended by Sacred Heart, Breckenridge. Rev. Anh Q. Tran.
Res., P.O. Box 404, 76449. Tel: 940-779-2023.

Graham, Young Co., St. Mary (1922), Rev. Raymund A. Mullan.
Res., 1218 S. Rodgers Dr., Box 547, 76450. Tel: 940-549-4314. [JC]
Catechesis/Religious Programs—Students 152.

Granbury, Hood Co., St. Frances Cabrini (1976), Rev. Lawrence Gould, S.A.C.; Deacon Ed Bevers.
Res., 812 Shadygrove Dr., P.O. Box 757, 76048. Tel: 817-326-2131. [JC]
Catechesis/Religious Programs—76048. Tel: 817-326-2131.
Students 220.

Grapevine, Tarrant Co., St. Francis of Assisi (1949), Rev. Ken Robinson.
Res., P.O. Box 56, 76099-0056. Tel: 817-481-2685; Fax: 817-488-3169.
Catechesis/Religious Programs—Students 1,039.

Henrietta, Clay Co., St. Mary (1879), Rev. John S. Stasiowski.
Res., 105 S. Barrett St., 76365. Tel: 817-538-4214. [CEM]

Hillsboro, Hill Co., Our Lady of Mercy (1887), Rev. Alfred LaFleur, O.S.A.
Res., Interstate 35, P.O. Box 567, 76645. Tel: 254-582-5640.
Catechesis/Religious Programs—Students 65.

Iowa Park, Wichita Co., Christ the King (1980), Deacon Patrick Burke, Admin.
Mailing Address: P.O. Box 239, 76367.
Office: 1008 First St., 76367. Tel: 940-592-2802.
Res., 709 W. Rebecca St., 76367. Tel: 940-592-2930; Fax: 940-592-2802.
Catechesis/Religious Programs—Students 51.

Jacksboro, Jack Co., St. Mary (1911), Rev. Gonzalo Morales.
Mailing Address: c/o St. John the Baptizer, 1801 Irvin St., Bridgeport, 76426. Tel: 940-683-2743; Fax: 940-683-2743.
Church—Hwy. 148 N., 76458.

Keller, Tarrant Co., St. Elizabeth Ann Seton (1985), Rev. John Gremmels.
Office: 2016 Willis Ln., 76248. Tel: 817-431-3857; Fax: 817-431-9568.
Catechesis/Religious Programs—Tel: 817-431-6023.
Students 1,060.

Knox City, Knox Co., Santa Rosa (1948). Attended by St. Joseph, Rhineland. Rev. Kevin Fagan; Deacon Julian Estrada.
Mailing Address: Rte. 1, Box 79, 79529. Tel: 940-658-5062.
Church—N. 3rd and Ave. G, 79521. Tel: 817-658-5062. [JC]
Catechesis/Religious Programs—Students 100.

Lewisville, Denton Co., St. Philip the Apostle (1976), Rev. Jonathan Scalone; Deacon Raymond G. Lamarre.
Office: 1773 Canterbury Ln., 75067. Tel: 972-436-9581; Fax: 972-436-5302.
Catechesis/Religious Programs—1897 W. Main, 75067.
Students 986.

Lindsay, Cooke Co., St. Peter (1902), Rev. Eugene Luke, O.S.B.
Res., 424 Main St., P.O. Box 148, 76250. Tel: 940-668-7609; Fax: 940-668-7723. [CEM]
Catechesis/Religious Programs—P.O. Box 95, 76250.
Students 328.

Mansfield, Tarrant Co., St. Jude (1898), Rev. Karl Schilken.
Res., 500 E. Dallas St., 76063. Tel: 817-473-6709; Fax: 817-477-2088. [CEM]
Catechesis/Religious Programs—Tel: 817-473-0768.
Students 376.
Parish Hall: Tel: 817-473-9463.

Megargel, Archer Co., St. Mary (1909). Attended by Sacred Heart. Rev. Bart J. Landwermeyer.
205 N. Cedar, Seymour, 76380. Tel: 817-888-5252; Fax: 817-888-2136. [CEM]

Mineral Wells, Palo Pinto Co., Our Lady of Lourdes (1960), Rev. John Nagle, S.A.C.
Res., 108 N.W. 4th Ave., P.O. Box 1327, 76068. Tel: 940-325-4789.
Catechesis/Religious Programs—Students 200.

Montague, Montague Co., St. William (1899). Attended by St. Mary, Henrietta. Rev. John S. Stasiowski.
Mailing Address: 105 S. Barrett, Henrietta, 76365. Tel: 817-538-4214. [CEM]
Catechesis/Religious Programs—Students 66.

Morgan, Bosque Co., Our Lady of Guadalupe (1987), Rev. Salvador Perez.
Mailing Address: P.O. Box 431, Clifton, 76634. Tel: 817-675-8877.
Church—Jessup St.

Muenster, Cooke Co., Sacred Heart (1889), Rev. Tom Craig.
Res., 714 N. Main St., 76252. Tel: 940-759-2511. [CEM]
Preschool—.
Lay Teachers 2; Students 25.
School—Tel: 940-759-4121.
Benedictine Sisters 1; Lay Teachers 14; Students 190.
High School—Benedictine Sisters 1; Priests 1; Lay Teachers 11; Students 93.
Catechesis/Religious Programs—Tel: 940-759-2511, Ext. 37.
Students 229.

Nocona, Montague Co., St. Joseph (1948). Attended by St. Mary, Henrietta. Rev. John S. Stasiowski.
105 S. Barrett, Henrietta, 76365. Tel: 817-538-4214.

Olney, Young Co., St. Theresa of the Infant Jesus (1935). Attended by St. Mary, Graham. Rev. Raymund A. Mullan.
Mailing Address: P.O. Box 547, Graham, 76450. Tel: 940-549-4314. [JC]
Church—Oak & Avenue E, 76374. Tel: 940-564-5426.

Penelope, Hill Co., Nativity of the Blessed Virgin Mary (1909), Rev. James G. Ryan, O.S.A.
Mailing Address: P.O. Box 98, 76676. Tel: 817-533-2325. [CEM 2]
Catechesis/Religious Programs—Students 71.

Pilot Point, Denton Co., St. Thomas Aquinas (1891), Rev. Donald Brennan, O.S.A.
Res., 925 N. Charcut, 76258. Tel: 817-686-2088. [CEM]
Catechesis/Religious Programs—400 E. Gibbons, 76258. Tel: 817-686-2360.
Students 257.

Quanah, Hardeman Co., St. Mary (1914). Attended by Holy Family, Vernon. Rev. Oren W. Key, S.J.
2200 Roberts, P.O. Box 1377, Vernon, 76384. Tel: 817-552-2895; Fax: 817-552-6084. [JC]

Ranger, Eastland Co., St. Rita (1919), Rev. Vincent B. Inametti.
Res., 1109 Blackwell St., 76470. Tel: 817-647-3167.

Rhineland, Knox Co., St. Joseph (1895), Rev. Kevin Fagan; Deacon Julian Estrada.
Res., Rte. 2, P.O. Box 15, Rhineland, Munday, 76371. Tel: 940-422-4270. [CEM]
Catechesis/Religious Programs—Students 134.

Scotland, Archer Co., St. Boniface (1911). Attended by St. Mary, Windthorst. Rev. David Kraeger, T.O.R.
Church—76379. Tel: 817-423-6687; Fax: 817-423-6657. [CEM]

Seymour, Baylor Co., Sacred Heart (1910), Rev. Bart J. Landwermeyer.
Res., 205 N. Cedar St., 76380. Tel: 817-888-3902. [CEM]
Sacred Heart Pastoral Center—207 W. Pecan, 76380. Tel: 817-888-5252; Fax: 817-888-2136.
Catechesis / Religious Programs—Students 129.

Stephenville, Erath Co., St. Brendan (1958), Rev. Philip McNamara, S.A.C.
Res., 1444 W. Washington Ave., 76401. Tel: 817-965-5693.
Catechesis / Religious Programs—Students 202.

Strawn, Palo Pinto Co., St. John (1912). Attended by St. Rita. Rev. Vincent Inametti.
Res., 1109 Blackwell Rd., Ranger, 76470. Tel: 817-647-3167.

Throckmorton, Throckmorton Co., San Patricio (1964). Attended by Sacred Heart, Breckenridge. Rev. Anh Q. Tran.
Mailing Address: 208 S. Miller, Breckenridge, 76024. Tel: 254-559-2860; Fax: 254-559-5289.

Valley View, Cooke Co., St. John (1946), Rev. Harry W. Fisher.
Res., 709 Lee St., 76272. Tel: 940-726-3524. [JC]

Vernon, Wilbarger Co., Holy Family (1891), Rev. Oren W. Key, S.J.
Res., 2200 Roberts, P.O. Box 1377, 76384. Tel: 817-552-2895; Fax: 817-552-6084.
Catechesis / Religious Programs—Students 180.

Weatherford, Parker Co., St. Stephen (1882), Rev. Philip McNamara, S.A.C.
Mailing Address: P.O. Box 1743, 76086.
Office: 1802 Bethel Rd., 76086. Tel: 817-596-9585.
Res., 105 E. Columbia St., 76086. Tel: 817-596-9586.
Catechesis / Religious Programs—Students 520.

Wichita Falls, Wichita Co., Our Lady of Guadalupe (1927) (Hispanic), Rev. Hector Medina.
Res., 421 Marconi, 76301. Tel: 817-766-2735. [JC]
Parish Hall: Tel: 817-322-0143.
Catechesis / Religious Programs—Students 307.

Our Lady Queen of Peace (1956), Rev. William Winaski; Deacons Richard A. Arndt; Larry W. Bills.
Res., 4040 York Ave., 76309. Tel: 940-696-1253; Fax: 940-696-1216. [JC]
Catechesis / Religious Programs—Students 265.

Sacred Heart (1891), Revs. Ivor Koch; John Vu Quang Huy, C.M.C.; Deacon Russell W. Detwiler.
Mailing Address: 1504 Tenth St., 76301. Tel: 940-723-5288; Fax: 940-767-0160.
Res., 1505 Ninth St., 76301. Tel: 940-723-5288; Fax: 940-767-0160.
Catechesis / Religious Programs—Students 378.
Mission—Wichita Falls, Wichita Co., The Assumption of Mary, 909 Lincoln St., 76304. Tel: 940-322-2500. [CEM][JC]

Windthorst, Archer Co., St. Mary (1892), Rev. David Kraeger, T.O.R.
Res., P.O. Drawer 230, 76389. Tel: 817-423-6687; Fax: 817-423-6657. [CEM]
Catechesis / Religious Programs—Students 305.

Chaplains of Public Institutions

DENTON. *State School*, 1215 E. Elm St., 76201. Tel: 817-387-1755. Rev. Juan Rivero.

GAINESVILLE. *Texas Youth Council Youth Facility*. Vacant. 805 N. Weaver, 76240. Tel: 817-665-2413.

WICHITA FALLS. *State Hospital*. Tel: 817-723-4111. Rev. Aidan Donlon, S.A.C.

On Duty Outside the Diocese:
Reverend Fathers—
Renteria, Rudy, 4050 Glenridge Rd., Dallas, TX 75220
Spong, William, Ogdensburg, NY
Thames, Robert, Residencia Episcopal, C.P. 34, Trinidad, Bolivia

---

Absent on Leave:
Reverend Fathers—
Miranda, Luke
Owen, David

Retired:
Reverend Monsignors—
Hartnett, Donald, Retirement Inn, 8000 Calmont Apt. 113, Fort Worth, TX 76116
Reilly, James J., 321 W. Butler Ave., Chalfont, PA 18914
Reverend Fathers—
Boyle, James A., Wildwood Springs, 305 Springdale Village, Bradenton, FL 34207
Cooney, Gerald, c/o 1824 Clark Rd., Crowley, TX 76036-9714
Curtsinger, George, 3015 Lubbock #5, Fort Worth, TX 76109
Stephens, Gerald, 208 Martin St., Wylie, TX 75098

Permanent Deacons:
Amos, Clarence
Armknecht, William
Arndt, Richard
Aziere, Ronald
Barry, Gerald
Bell, James
Bevers, Eddy
Bills, Larry
Bolf, William
Bowden, Edgar
Bressler, Patrick
Burke, Patrick
Casias, Arturo
Castaneda, Ruben
Castellon, Damaso
Castleberry, Charles
Christian, Phil
Curiel, Ruben
Detwiler, Russell
Firth, John
Friedman, William
Garcia, Eduardo
Garcia, Raul
Giovannitti, Thomas
Gonzalez, Emilio
Greene, Clifford
Griego, Richard
Gutbier, Klaus
Guzman, John
Hatch, Larry
Heinz, Harry
Junginger, George
Konar, Albert
Kunath, Wolfgang
Lamarre, Raymond
Luna, Andres
Marquez, Mario
McDermott, John
Milligan, Joseph
Nicklas, George
Novak, Jim
Perez, Anastasio
Poole, James
Poth, Louis J.
Raetz, Joseph
Salva, Hector
Serenil, Benito
Stojak, Richard
Stuart, Robert
Tassin, Terry
Torrez, Simon
Vicroy, Clarence
Warner, Don
Weaver, Lonnie, Jr.
Webb, Philip
Wolf, George
Wuenschel, Douglas

INSTITUTIONS LOCATED IN THE DIOCESE

[A] HIGH SCHOOLS, DIOCESAN

FORT WORTH. *Cassata Learning Center*. (Coed Secondary). 1400 Hemphill St., 76104-4796. Tel: 817-926-1745; Fax: 817-926-3132. Ms. Cynthia Morton, Exec. Dir. Teachers 8; Students 455.

Nolan Catholic High School. (Grades 7-12). (Coed), 4501 Bridge St., 76103. Tel: 817-457-2920; Fax: 817-496-9775. Society of Mary. Bros. Eugene Meyerpeter, S.M., Pres.; Oscar Vasquez, S.M., Prin.; Revs. Paul Newman, S.M.; James Young, S.M. Priests 1; Brothers 8; Sisters 4; Lay Teachers 72; Students 1,100.

Nolan School Trust.

WICHITA FALLS. *Notre Dame Middle-High School*, 2821 Lansing Blvd., 76309. Tel: 817-692-6041; Fax: 817-692-2811. Mr. Joe Cluley, Prin. Lay Teachers 20; Students 254.

[B] HIGH SCHOOLS, PAROCHIAL

MUENSTER. *Sacred Heart School*. (Grades Prek-12), 141 E. Sixth, Box 588. Mr. Jack Murdock, Prin. Priests 1; Olivetan Benedictine Sisters 3; Lay Teachers 20; Students 297.

**Sacred Heart Teachers Trust Fund*.

[C] ELEMENTARY AND SECONDARY SCHOOLS, PAROCHIAL

ARLINGTON. *South Arlington Catholic School*, 2015 S.W. Green Oaks Blvd., 76017. Tel: 817-419-6800; Fax: 817-459-3690. Total Staff 24; Students 220.

DENTON. *Immaculate Conception Catholic School*, 1212 Bolivar, 76201. Tel: 940-381-1155; Fax: 940-381-1837. Lay Teachers 9; Students 110.

GRAPEVINE. *Holy Trinity Catholic School*,. Mailing Address: P.O. Box 3338, 76099-3338. 3450 William D. Tate Blvd., 76051. Tel: 817-421-8000; Fax: 817-421-4468. Lay Teachers 19; Students 300.

WICHITA FALLS. *Notre Dame Elementary School*, 4060 York Ave., 76309. Sisters 2; Lay Teachers 17; Students 298.

[D] ELEMENTARY SCHOOLS, PRIVATE

FORT WORTH. *Our Lady of Victory Elementary*, 3320 S. Hemphill St., 76110. Tel: 817-924-5123; Fax: 817-922-6598. Lay Teachers 15; Students 232.

[E] CHILDREN'S GROUP CARE

FORT WORTH. *Catholic Charities, Inc*. An Independent Corporation Founded by the Diocese of Fort Worth, 2701 Burchill Rd. N., 76105-3012. Tel: 817-534-0814; Fax: 817-535-8779. Karen Spicer, LMSW-ACP, Exec. Dir.
Emergency Financial Assistance, 1404 Hemphill, 76104. Tel: 817-921-5381. Carolyn Henry, Dept. Dir. Provides direct financial and material assistance to families in financial crisis.
Office Sites: 401 W. Sanford, Arlington, 76011. Tel: 817-274-2560. 349 N.W. Renfro, Burleson, 76028. Tel: 817-295-6252. 6201 Camp Bowie Blvd., 76116. Tel: 817-737-9338. 208 Miller, 76105. Tel: 817-534-5610.
Special Services Department: 2701 Burchill Rd., N., 76105-3012. Tel: 817-534-0814; Fax: 817-535-8779. Ann Tucker, Ph.D., Dept. Dir. Administers residential programs for the elderly, disabled, and additional programs for special populations.
Program Sites: Nuestro Hogar, Inc., 709 Magnolia St., Arlington, 76012. Tel: 817-216-0608; Fax: 817-861-6178. CASA, Inc., 3201 Sondra Dr., 76107. Tel: 817-332-7276; Fax: 817-877-0487. CASA Brendan and CASA II, Inc., 1300 Hyman St., Stephenville, 76401. Tel: 817-965-6964; Fax: 817-968-3072.
Department of Health & Family Services, 2701 Burchill Rd., N., 76105. Tel: 817-534-0814; Fax: 817-535-8779. Mary Smith, LMSW-ACP. Provides a wide range of clinical and supportive services.
Program Sites: St. Teresa's Group Home, 2701 Burchill Rd., N., 76105-3012. Tel: 817-534-0814. Assessment Center of Tarrant County (children's shelter), 2000 McKenzie, 76105. Extended Day Treatment & Family Support Services, 2701 Burchhill Rd., 76105. Tel: 817-534-0814. Therapeutic Foster and Respite Care, 2701 Burchill Rd., N., 76105. Tel: 817-534-0814. Family Preservation Unit, 1208 W. Magnolia, 76104. Anne Simon Reeves Children's Center, 2641 Ave. L, 76105. Tel: 817-534-0814.
Clinical Counseling Department, 1216 W. Magnolia, 76104. Tel: 817-536-6857; Fax: 817-923-8211.
Immigration and Refugee Services Department, 1216 W. Magnolia, 76104. Tel: 817-338-0774; Fax: 817-335-9749. Katy Burns, LMSW-ACP, Dept. Dir. Immigration Counseling, Refugee Resource Center and Refugee Resettlement. Assistance in migration matters: family reunification, adjustment of status, naturalization, ESL, and employment services.
Community Support Services Department, 1404 Hemphill, 76104. Carolyn Henry, LMSW-AP, Dept. Dir. Coordinates the Emergency Assistance Association of Tarrant County, Social Concerns, Holiday Network, Disaster Relief, Public Relations.

[F] GENERAL HOSPITALS

WICHITA FALLS. *Bethania Regional Health Care Center*, 1600 Eleventh St., 76301. Tel: 817-723-4111.
For a complete listing, refer to the Hospitals section.

[G] RETIREMENT & DISABILITY HOUSING

FORT WORTH. *Casa del Cor, Inc.*, 2701 Burchill Rd., N., 76105. Tel: 817-534-0814; Fax: 817-535-8779.
For a complete listing, refer to the Special Care Facilities section.

Casa, Inc. Housing for the Elderly and Handicapped, 3201 Sondra Dr., 76107. Tel: 817-332-7276.
For a complete listing, refer to the Special Care Facilities section.

ARLINGTON. *Nuestro Hogar, Inc. Catholic Charities*, 709 Magnolia St., 76012. Tel: 817-261-0608.
For a complete listing, refer to the Special Care Facilities section.

CROWLEY. *St. Francis Village, Inc.*, 1 Chapel Plaza, 76036. Tel: 817-292-5786.
For a complete listing, refer to the Special Care Facilities section.

STEPHENVILLE. *CASA Brendan and CASA II, Inc. Catholic Charities*, 1300 Hyman, 76401. Tel: 817-965-6964.
For a complete listing, refer to the Special Care Facilities section.

[H] MONASTERIES AND RESIDENCES OF PRIESTS AND BROTHERS

CROWLEY. *St. Maximilian Kolbe Friary* (Fort Worth), 1 Marquard Cir. & 2 Marquard Cir., St. Francis Village, 76036. Tel: 817-370-9747; Fax: 817-370-1914. Revs. Peter Fritz, O.F.M., Guardian; Raymar Bobber, O.F.M.; Vincent Elsen, O.F.M; Jovian Lang, O.F.M; Armand Lubanski, O.F.M; Donald Werr, O.F.M.; Mathias Kiemen, O.F.M; Bros. Earl Benz, O.F.M.; Allan Haiar, O.F.M.

[I] CONVENTS AND RESIDENCES FOR SISTERS

FORT WORTH. *Hermanas Catequistas Guadalupanas*, 3203 Clinton, 76106. Tel: 817-740-0038. Sr. Maria Martinez, H.C.G., Supr. Sisters 3.
Missionary Catechists of the Sacred Hearts of Jesus and Mary, 2640 Avenue L., 76105. Tel: 817-535-8495. Sr. Felipa Guadalupe Lara, Supr. Sisters 4.
Provincialate, Our Lady of Victory Center, 909 W. Shaw St., 76110. Tel: 817-923-8393; Fax: 817-921-5064. Provincial House of the Western Province, Sisters of St. Mary of Namur. Sr. Joan Markey, S.S.M.N., Prov. Supr.; Rev. James Young, S.M., Chap.
Sisters of St. Mary Namur, 3233 College Ave., 76110. Tel: 817-921-0305; 923-8393. Sisters of St. Mary of Namur.

ARLINGTON. *Monastery of the Most Holy Trinity, Discalced Carmelites*, 5801 Mt. Carmel Dr., 76017. Tel: 817-468-1781. Mother Anne Teresa Kulinski, O.C.D., Prioress. Solemn Professed Nuns 9; Novices 1.

WICHITA FALLS. *Mercy Convent*, 3000 Lansing Blvd., 76309. Sisters 2; Associates 1.
Notre Dame Convent, 2820 Lansing Blvd., 76309. Sisters 3.

[J] RETREAT HOUSES

LAKE DALLAS. *Montserrat Jesuit Retreat House*, P.O. Box 398, 75065. Tel: 817-321-6020; 321-6030; Fax: 817-321-6040. Rev. George Wiltz, S.J. Associate Directors: Revs. Walter C. McCauley, S.J.; Niel J. Jarreau, S.J.; Charles G. Coyle, S.J. In res. Rev. John P. Koeplin, S.J.

[K] RENEWAL CENTERS

FORT WORTH. *The Catholic Renewal Center of North Texas, Inc.*, 4503 Bridge St., 76103. Tel: 817-429-2920 (Metro).
Beginning Experience.
Retorno.
Special Days for Special People.
National Marriage Encounter of North Texas.
Engaged Encounter of North Texas.
Stepping Stones.

[L] SOCIETY OF ST. VINCENT DE PAUL

FORT WORTH. *St. Vincent de Paul Diocesan Council of Fort Worth*, 6336 Genoa, 76116. Tel: 817-737-9167. Mr. Robert Churchill, Contact Person.

WICHITA FALLS. *Particular Council of Wichita Falls, St. Vincent de Paul Society*, 4516 Lake Park Dr., 76302. Tel: 817-322-2920. Mr. Walter Brady.

[M] NEWMAN CENTERS

FORT WORTH. *Texas Christian University Catholic Community*, TCU Station, P.O. Box 297310, 76129-0001. Tel: 817-921-7830, Ext. 5100; Fax: 817-921-7333. Rev. Charles L. Calabrese (STU). E-mail:c.calabrese@tcu.edu.

ARLINGTON. *University of Texas at Arlington*, 303 Lampe, 76010. Tel: 817-460-1155. Rev. Robert M. Lewandowski, S.M., Chap.; Mr. Tuyen Nguyen, Campus Min. Legal Title: *University of Texas at Arlington University Catholic Community.*

DENTON. *University of North Texas and Texas Woman's University*, 1303 Eagle Dr., 76201. Tel: 817-566-0004. Rev. Robert M. Lewandowski, S.M., Chap.; Mr. Tuyen Nguyen, Campus Min. Legal Title: *University of North Texas and Texas Woman's University.*

HILLSBORO. *Hill College Newman Center.* Attended from Our Lady of Mercy as United Christian Fellowship. P.O. Box 567, 76645. Tel: 817-582-5640. Deacon Jim Poole, Campus Min.

WICHITA FALLS. *Catholic Campus Ministry*, Midwestern State University, 3410 W. Campus Dr., 76308. Tel: 817-692-9778. Rev. Christopher Davis, O.S.B.

[N] MISCELLANEOUS

FORT WORTH. *Community Hospice of Texas*, 1000 Summit Ave., 76102. Tel: 817-870-2795; Fax: 817-878-3713. Ms. Andrea Green.
Loaves and Fishes, The Metroplex Food Bank, 3200 Yuma St., 76119. Tel: 817-924-FEED; Fax: 817-924-3210.
Soup Kitchen, 1709 E. Hattie, 76104. Tel: 817-536-9100.
North Texas San Benito, Inc., The Catholic Center, 800 W. Loop, 820 S., 76108.
Sister of St. Mary of Namur Marion House, 3353 College Ave., 76110.

RELIGIOUS INSTITUTES OF MEN REPRESENTED IN THE DIOCESE

For further details refer to the corresponding bracketed number in the Religious Institutes of Men or Women section.

[0140]—*The Augustinians.*—O.S.A.
[0200]—*Benedictine Monks.*—O.S.B.
[0470]—*The Capuchin Friars.*—O.F.M.Cap.
[0520]—*Franciscan Friars.*—O.F.M.
[0690]—*Jesuit Fathers and Brothers.*—S.J.
[]—*Missionaries of St. Paul.*—M.S.P.
[0897]—*Paris Foreign Mission Society.*—M.E.P.
[]—*Priests and Brothers of the Mother Coredemptrix.*—C.M.C.
[0760]—*Society of Mary (Marianists).*—S.M.
[0990]—*Society of the Catholic Apostolate.*—S.A.C.
[0560]—*Third Order Regular of Saint Francis.*—T.O.R.

RELIGIOUS INSTITUTES OF WOMEN REPRESENTED IN THE DIOCESE

[0100]—*Adorers of the Blood of Christ.*—A.S.C.
[0230]—*Benedictine Sisters of Pontifical Jurisdiction.*—O.S.B.
[]—*Congregation of Missionary Catechists of the Sacred Heart of Jesus and Mary.*—M.C.
[0420]—*Discalced Carmelite Nuns.*—O.C.D.
[1170]—*Felician Sisters.*—C.S.S.F.
[1900]—*Hermanas Catequistas Guadalupanas.*—H.C.G.
[2970]—*School Sisters of Notre Dame.*—S.S.N.D.
[1010]—*Sisters of Divine Providence of San Antonio, Texas.*—C.D.P.
[3950]—*Sisters of Saint Mary of Namur.*—S.S.M.N.
[1970]—*Sisters of the Holy Family of Nazareth.*—C.S.F.N.
[2050]—*Sisters of the Holy Spirit and Mary Immaculate.*—S.H.Sp.
[1110]—*Cabra Dominican Sisters.*—O.P.
[0460]—*Congregation of Sisters of Charity of the Incarnate Word.*—C.C.V.I.
[2150]—*Servants of the Immaculate Heart of Mary.*—I.H.M.

NECROLOGY

† Wolf, Rev. Msgr. Vincent Joseph, Fort Worth, TX, Holy Family. —Died July 8, 1997.

Diocese of Fresno

(Dioecesis Fresnensis)

Most Reverend

JOHN T. STEINBOCK, D.D.

Bishop of Fresno; ordained May 1, 1963; appointed Titular Bishop of Midila and Auxiliary Bishop of Orange May 29, 1984; consecrated July 14, 1984; installed as Bishop of Santa Rosa March 31, 1987; installed as Bishop of Fresno November 24, 1991. *Office: 1550 N. Fresno St., Fresno, CA, 93703-3788.* Tel.: 209-488-7400; Fax: 209-488-7464.

Chancery Office: 1550 N. Fresno St., Fresno, CA, 93703-3788. Tel.: 209-488-7400; Fax: 209-488-7464.

ESTABLISHED DECEMBER 15, 1967.

FORMERLY DIOCESE OF MONTEREY-FRESNO.

Square Miles 35,239.

Comprises the Counties of Fresno, Inyo, Kern, Kings, Madera, Mariposa, Merced and Tulare in the State of California.

Diocesan Patroness: St. Therese of the Child Jesus.

Legal titles of parishes and institutions, the Roman Catholic Bishop of Fresno, a Corporation Sole, Diocese of Fresno Education Corporation (for schools).

STATISTICAL OVERVIEW

Personnel	
Bishop	1
Priests: Diocesan Active in Diocese	83
Priests: Active Outside Diocese	1
Priests: Retired, Sick or Absent	24
Number of Diocesan Priests	108
Religious Priests in Diocese	44
Extern Priests in Diocese	16
Ordinations:	
Diocesan Priests	3
Transitional Deacons	2
Permanent Deacons	1
Permanent Deacons in Diocese	7
Total Brothers	10
Total Sisters	109
Parishes	
Parishes	84
With Resident Pastor:	
Resident Diocesan Priests	69
Resident Religious Priests	8
Without Resident Pastor:	
Administered by Priests	6
Administered by Permanent Deacons	1
Missions	40
Professional Ministry Personnel:	
Brothers	10
Sisters	109
Lay Ministers	175
Welfare	
Catholic Hospitals	3
Total Assisted	576,663
Health Care Centers	2
Homes for the Aged	1
Total Assisted	124
Specialized Homes	1
Total Assisted	100
Special Centers for Social Services	5
Total Assisted	277,103
Educational	
Diocesan Students in Other Seminaries	17
Total Seminarians	17
High Schools, Diocesan and Parish	1
Total Students	775
High Schools, Private	1
Total Students	719
Elementary Schools, Diocesan and Parish	23
Total Students	5,720
Catechesis/Religious Education:	
High School Students	7,070
Elementary Students	23,268
Total Students Under Catholic Instruction	37,569
Teachers in the Diocese:	
Priests	1
Brothers	4
Sisters	28
Lay Teachers	245
Vital Statistics	
Receptions into the Church:	
Infant Baptism Totals	17,707
Adult Baptism Totals	466
Received into Full Communion	593
First Communions	8,481
Confirmations	3,195
Marriages:	
Catholic	1,909
Interfaith	410
Total Marriages	2,319
Deaths	2,881
Total Catholic Population	323,743
Total Population	2,225,050

Former Prelates of Diocese of Monterey-Fresno—Most Rev. JOHN B. MACGINLEY, ord. June 8, 1895; cons. May 10, 1910; First Bishop of Monterey-Fresno, July 31, 1924; resigned Sept. 30, 1932; died Oct. 19, 1969.—Most Rev. PHILIP G. SCHER, ord. June 6, 1903; appt. April 28, 1933; cons. June 29, 1933; died Jan. 3, 1953.—Most Rev. ALOYSIUS J. WILLINGER, C.Ss.R., ord. July 2, 1911; cons. Bishop of Ponce, Puerto Rico, Oct. 28, 1929; Coadjutor Bishop of Monterey/Fresno *"cum jure successionis,"* Dec. 17, 1946; succeeded to the See, Jan. 3, 1953; resigned Oct. 25, 1967; died July 25, 1973.—Most Rev. HARRY ANSELM CLINCH, D.D., ord. June 6, 1936; appt. Auxiliary to the Bishop of Monterey-Fresno, Dec. 5, 1956; transferred to the See of Monterey, Dec. 14, 1967.

Former Bishops of Fresno—His Eminence TIMOTHY CARDINAL MANNING, D.D., appt. Titular Bishop of Lesvi and Auxiliary of Los Angeles, Aug. 3, 1946; cons. Oct. 15, 1946; installed as First Bishop of Fresno, Dec. 15, 1967; elevated to Coadjutor Archbishop of Los Angeles *"cum jure successionis,"* June 11, 1969; succeeded to the See, Jan. 21, 1970; created Cardinal, March 5, 1973; died June 23, 1989.—Most Rev. HUGH A. DONOHOE, D.D., ord. June 14, 1930; appt. Auxiliary in San Francisco, Aug. 2, 1947; cons. Oct. 7, 1947; appt. Bishop of Stockton, Feb. 21, 1962; appt. Second Bishop of Fresno, Aug. 28, 1969; resigned July 1, 1980; died Oct. 26, 1987.—His Eminence ROGER CARDINAL MAHONY, D.D., ord. May 1, 1962; appt. Auxiliary, Jan. 7, 1975; ord. Bishop, March 19, 1975; transferred to Diocese of Stockton, CA April 17, 1980; appt. Archbishop of Los Angeles, July 16, 1985; created Cardinal, June 28, 1991.—Most Rev. JOSEPH J. MADERA, D.D., cons. March 4, 1980 and; succeeded to the See on July 1, 1980; transferred to Archdiocese for the Military Services, Washington, DC May 28, 1991.

Vicar General and Moderator of the Curia—Rev. SERGIO P. NEGRO, V.G.

Vicar for Insurance and Retirement Matters—Rev. Msgr. J. WAYNE HAYES, P.A.

Chancellor—Sr. SANDRA ANN SILVA, S.H.F.

Chancery Office—*1550 N. Fresno St., Fresno, 93703-3788.* Tel: 209-488-7400; Fax: 209-488-7464.

Diocesan Tribunal—NANCY STEVENS, J.C.L., Dir. Tribunal, *1550 N. Fresno St., Fresno, 93703-3788.* Tel: 209-488-7490; Fax: 209-488-7498.

Judicial Vicar—Rev. Msgr. HERBERT ELMLINGER.

Adjutant Judicial Vicar—Rev. Msgr. STEPHEN A. FROST, J.C.L.

Promoter of Justice—Rev. Msgr. SEAMUS MCMULLAN.

Defensores Vinculi—Rev. Msgr. PATRICK G. DOHERTY; Rev. Msgr. HERBERT ELMLINGER; Rev. Msgr. JOHN O'FRIEL; Rev. Msgr. MICHAEL R. BRAUN; Rev. Msgr. STEPHEN A. FROST, J.C.L.; Rev. Msgr. THOMAS G. KLEINHANS; Rev. PATRICK MCCORMICK.

Judges—Rev. Msgr. RICHARD RYAN, J.C.D.; Rev. Msgr. HERBERT ELMLINGER; Revs. STEPHEN A. FROST, J.C.L.; THOMAS FRANSISCUS, C.SS.R., J.C.L.

Notaries—Revs. PERRY KAVOOKJIAN; THOMAS M. TIMMINGS; Mrs. NANCY CLEMONS; GLORIA MARSCHALL.

Approved Advocates—Rev. Msgr. JOHN ESQUIVEL; Rev. Msgr. WALTER MINHOTO; Rev. Msgr. STEPHEN A. FROST, J.C.L.; Rev. Msgr. THOMAS G. KLEINHANS; Revs. JOHN GRIESBACH; PATRICK MCCORMICK; CHARLES F. SMITH; RICHARD URIZALQUI.

Diocesan Consultors—Rev. Msgr. ED POSCHEN; Rev. Msgr. JOHN MORETON, V.U.; Revs. JEAN-MICHAEL LASTIRI, V.F.; SERGIO P. NEGRO, V.G.; ROBERT WENZINGER, V.F.; JOHN GRIESBACH, V.F.; RICHARD URIZALQUI, V.F.

Vicars Forane—Rev. Msgr. JOHN MORETON, V.U.; Revs. JOHN GRIESBACH, V.F.; RICHARD URIZALQUI, V.F.; ROBERT WENZINGER, V.F.; JEAN-MICHAEL LASTIRI, V.F.

Diocesan Offices and Directors

Catholic Charities—Mr. ROLLIE SMITH, Dir., *149 N. Fulton, Fresno, 93701.* Tel: 209-237-0851; Fax: 209-237-7144.

Channel 49 (KNXT)—MARV HARRISON, Gen. Mgr., *1550 N. Fresno St., Fresno, 93703-3788.* Tel: 209-488-7440; Fax: 209-488-7444.

Continuing Formation of Priests—Rev. SERGIO P. NEGRO, *1550 N. Fresno St., Fresno, 93703.* Tel: 209-488-7400. Rev. JEAN-MICHAEL LASTIRI, *P.O. Box 2087, Merced, 95344.* Tel: 209-383-3924.

Cursillo Movement—Rev. RONALD ALVES, C.M.F., *P.O. Box 97, Laton, 93242.* Tel: 209-923-4935.

Diocese of Fresno Education Corporation—*1550 N. Fresno St., Fresno, 93703-3788.*

Diocesan Newspaper—BILL LUCIDO, Editor, *"Central California Catholic Life", 1550 N. Fresno St., Fresno, 93703-3788.*

Ecumenical Affairs—Rev. DAVID J. NORRIS, *1572 E. Barstow Ave., Fresno, 93710.* Tel: 209-436-3434.

Finance Committee—Rev. SERGIO P. NEGRO, V.G.; Rev. Msgr. J. WAYNE HAYES, P.A.; Rev. Msgr. MICHAEL BRAUN; Mr. JOSEPH ZIEMANN; LEROY GILSDORF; GARY BETHKE; LARRY STEFANI; GARY RENNER, *1550 N. Fresno St., Fresno, 93703-3788.* Tel: 209-488-7400.

Deposit and Loan Fund—Rev. SERGIO NEGRO, V.G.; Rev. Msgr. MICHAEL BRAUN; Rev. Msgr. J. WAYNE HAYES, P.A.; Mr. JAMES F. SWEENEY; Mrs. ROSEMARY MCCAVE; Mr. JOSEPH ZIEMANN; Mr. GARY BETHKE.

Health and Hospitals—Rev. SERGIO P. NEGRO, V.G.

Hispanic Apostolate—Mr. ZEFERINO GONZALES, Coord. Migrant Prog., *1530 N. Fresno St., Fresno, 93703-3788.* Tel: 209-488-7455.

Holy Childhood, Pontifical Association—Rev. SERGIO NEGRO, V.G.; Dir., *1550 N. Fresno St., Fresno, 93703-3788.* Tel: 209-488-7400; Fax: 209-488-7464.

Italian Catholic Federation—Rev. Msgr. J. WAYNE HAYES, P.A., Diocesan Chap.

Legion of Mary—Rev. Msgr. LASERIAN BYRNE, Diocesan Dir., *5770 N. Maroa, Fresno, 93704.* Tel: 209-439-0124.

Marian Federation of Guadalupe—Rev. Msgr. DANIEL LOPEZ, Diocesan Chap., *213 Orange Ave., Chowchilla, 93610.*

Ministry to Priests—Rev. SERGIO P. NEGRO, V.G.

Newman Apostolate—Rev. PERRY KAVOOKJIAN, *1572 E. Barstow Ave., Fresno, 93710.*

Office of Development—BILL LUCIDO, *1550 N. Fresno St., Fresno, 93703-3788.* Tel: 209-488-7414.

Office of Diocesan Properties—TIM TILLMAN, *1550 N. Fresno St., Fresno, 93703-3788.* Tel: 209-488-7470.

Office of Finances—GARY BETHKE, Fiscal Mgr., *1550 N. Fresno St., Fresno, 93703-3788.* Tel: 209-488-7476; Fax: 209-488-7461.

Office of Human Resources—PAT GORDON, S.P.H.R., Dir., *1550 N. Fresno St., Fresno, 93703-3788.* Tel: 209-488-7488.

Office of Insurance—GARY BETHKE, *1550 N. Fresno St., Fresno, 93703-3788.* Tel: 209-488-7476; Fax: 209-488-7461.

Office of Ministries—JAMES GRANT, Dir. PAUL MENTLEWSKI, Admin. Asst. Tel: 209-488-7474.

Campesino and Youth Ministry (Spanish)—Mr. ZEFERINO GONZALEZ.

Youth Ministry (English)—CHARISE HANSEN.

Family Life and Social Justice (Bi-lingual)—PATRICIA RODRIGUEZ, Dir.

Ministry Formation Coord.—Deacon MAURY MCCAFFREY. Tel: 209-488-7474.

Office of Worship—Rev. GERALD AMERANDO, Dir., *4870 E. Belmont, Fresno, 93727.* Tel: 209-255-3871.

Pastoral Center—TIM TILLMAN, *1530 N. Fresno St., Fresno, 93703.* Tel: 209-488-7470.

Personnel Committee—Rev. Msgr. JOHN MORETON, V.U.; Rev. Msgr. LASERIAN BYRNE; Rev. Msgr. JOSEPH BARNES; Revs. SERGIO P. NEGRO, V.G.; JEAN-MICHAEL LASTIRI; JOHN GRIESBACH; MYRON COTTA; PATRICK MCCORMICK; ROBERT WENZINGER; RICHARD URIZALQUI.

Priests' Council—Rev. Msgr. JOHN MORETON, V.U.; Revs. JOHN GRIESBACH, V.F.; ROBERT WENZINGER, V.F.; RICHARD URIZALQUI, V.F.; Rev. Msgr. JEAN-MICHAEL LASTIRI, V.F.; Rev. Msgr. MICHAEL BRAUN; Rev. Msgr. JOHN ESQUIVEL, Chm.; Rev. Msgr. JOHN STEPHEN FROST, J.C.D.; Rev. Msgr. ED POSCHEN; Revs. SERGIO P. NEGRO, V.G.; JERRY AMERANDO; JEFF HARVEY, C.M.; Sr. SANDRA ANN SILVA, S.H.F.

Propagation of the Faith and St. Peter Society—Rev. SERGIO NEGRO, V.G., *1550 N. Fresno St., Fresno, 93703-3788.*

Retreats—Rev. IGNATIUS DEGROOT, O.F.M., Dir. Retreat Masters: Revs. JUAN LEON, O.F.M.; DAVID JOHNSON, O.F.M.; Bros. JOE BRAND, O.F.M.; NICHOLAS HEINRICH, O.F.M., *P.O. Box 249, Three Rivers, 93271.* Tel: 209-561-4595.

Schools—RICHARD SEXTON, Supt.; Miss ADRIENNE LOPES, Asst. Supt.

Diocesan Advisory Board of Education—Mrs. JAYNE TACKE, Pres., *1510 N. Fresno St., Fresno, 93703.* Tel: 209-488-7420; Fax: 209-488-7422.

Vicar for Insurance and Retirement Affairs—Rev. Msgr. J. WAYNE HAYES, P.A., *1109 5th. St., Los Banos, 93635.* Tel: 209-826-4246; Fax: 209-826-5335.

Vicar for Religious—Sr. SANDRA SILVA, S.H.F., *1550 N. Fresno St., Fresno, 93703.* Tel: 209-488-7400; Fax: 209-488-7464.

Vocations—Rev. ROD CRAIG, Dir., *1550 N. Fresno St., Fresno, 93703-3788.* Tel: 209-488-7400; Fax: 209-488-7475.

CLERGY, PARISHES, MISSIONS AND PAROCHIAL SCHOOLS

CITY OF FRESNO
(Fresno County)

1—ST. JOHN CATHEDRAL, Rev. Msgr. John Harguindeguy, Rector; Rev. Edgar Jimenez. In res., Rev. Umberto Nespolo, O.M.I., (Hmong Ministry); Rev. Msgr. Walter Minhoto, (Retired).
Res., 2814 Mariposa St., 93721. Tel: 209-485-6210; Fax: 209-485-8409.
Catechesis/Religious Programs—Students 566.
Mission—Fresno, St. Francis, Ninth & Lowe, 93702. Tel: 209-485-9467. Rev. Joseph Cong Hoan, (Vietnamese Ministry).

2—HOLY SPIRIT (1981), Rev. Msgr. James T. Logan; Stephanie Hacnik, Business Mgr.
Mailing Address: 355 E. Champlain Dr., 93720-1273.
Res., 8781 N. Millbrook, 93720-1718. Tel: 209-434-7701 (Office); 435-2278 (Rectory); Fax: 209-434-7734.
Catechesis/Religious Programs—Judy Bedrosian, D.R.E.
Students 464.
Mission—Pinedale, Fresno Co., St. Agnes, 111 W. Birch St., Pinedale, 93650. Tel: 209-439-2100.
Stations—Tollhouse, Shaver Lake, Tel: 209-841-3524; Tollhouse, Auberry, Tel: 209-855-5011.

3—THE CATHOLIC COMMUNITY OF MT. CARMEL & ST. ALPHONSUS (1996) (Spanish). Merged Our Lady of Mt. Carmel with St. Alphonsus. Revs. Phil Van Linden, C.M.; Jeff Harvey, C.M.
Office: 816 Pottle Ave., 93706. Tel: 209-264-2587; Fax: 209-264-2539.
Catechesis/Religious Programs—1207 E. Trinity, 93706. Tel: 209-486-1049.
Students 210.

4—OUR LADY OF VICTORY (1950), Rev. Msgr. John Moreton; Deacon Ignacio Villafan.
Res., 1215 W. Michigan Ave., 93705. Tel: 209-226-1163.
Parish Center—2850 N. Crystal, 93705. Fax: 209-229-2093.
School—1626 W. Princeton Ave., 93705. Tel: 209-229-0205. Ms. Patricia Baldwin, Prin.
Lay Teachers 11; Students 245.
Catechesis/Religious Programs—Tel: 209-229-0024.
Students 371.

5—SACRED HEART (1947), Revs. Charles F. Smith; Raja Perera.
Res., 2240 N. Cedar Ave., 93703-2668. Tel: 209-237-4121; Fax: 209-237-0122.
School—4460 E. Yale, 93703. Tel: 209-251-3171. Connie McGhee, Prin.
Sisters of the Love of God 3; Lay Teachers 6; Students 153.
Catechesis/Religious Programs—Tel: 209-237-4365.
Students 500.
Convent—4305 E. Union, 93703. Tel: 209-454-1864.

6—ST. ALPHONSUS. Merged with Our Lady of Mt. Carmel to form Catholic Community of Mt. Carmel/ St. Alphonsus.

7—ST. ANTHONY OF PADUA (1953), Rev. Msgr. Laserian Byrne; Revs. Loren Blessing, O.F.M.; Patrick Joel Davadilla, S.V.D.
Res., 5770 N. Maroa St., 93704. Tel: 209-439-0124; Fax: 209-439-3050.
School—Tel: 209-437-0700; Fax: 209-435-6749. Mr. Shawn Carey, Prin.
Lay Teachers 23; Students 600.
Catechesis/Religious Programs—5680 N. Maroa St., 93704. Tel: 209-431-8512.
Students 775.

8—ST. ANTHONY CLARET (Calwa Area) (1952), Revs. Arturo S. Gomez, C.M.F.; Ronald Alves, C.M.F. In res., Revs. Fernando Vega, C.M.F.; Cecil Barron, C.M.F.
Res., 2494 S. Chestnut Ave., 93725. Tel: 209-255-4260; Fax: 209-255-4274.
Catechesis/Religious Programs—Students 416.
Mission—Malaga, Fresno Co., Christ the King, 3565 Calvin St., 93725.

9—ST. GENEVIEVE, Rev. Vincent Lau (Hong Kong).
Res., 1127 Tulare St., 93706. Tel: 209-486-2988. [CEM]

10—ST. HELEN (1955), Rev. Eric Swearingen. In res., Revs. Joseph Nguyen (Vietnam); Jerry Amerando.
Office: 4875 E. Grant Ave., 93727.
Res., 4870 E. Belmont, 93727. Tel: 209-255-3871; Fax: 209-255-7625.
School—4888 E. Belmont, 93727. Tel: 209-251-5855; Fax: 209-251-5948. Toni Amodio, Prin.
Franciscan Hospitalers of the Immaculate Conception 1; Lay Teachers 10; Students 243.
Junior Kindergarten:—Tel: 209-251-2422. Mrs. Linda Stuart, Dir.
Catechesis/Religious Programs—Tel: 209-251-4978.
Students 215.

11—ST. MARY (1967), Rev. Patrick Joseph McCormick.
Res., 4636 W. Dakota, 93722. Tel: 209-275-2022; Fax: 209-275-2040. [CEM]

12—ST. PAUL (1964), Revs. Perry Kavookjian; Jerry Amerando.
Church—California State University, St. Paul Newman Center, 1572 E. Barstow St., 93710. Tel: 209-436-3434; Fax: 209-436-3430.

13—ST. THERESE (1927), Rev. Msgr. Edward Poschen.
Mailing Address: 1444 N. Wishon, 93728. Tel: 209-268-6388; Fax: 209-268-6389.
Res., 855 E. Floradora Ave., 93728. Tel: 209-485-2199.
Catechesis/Religious Programs—Students 144.

OUTSIDE THE CITY OF FRESNO

Arvin, Kern Co., St. Thomas (1939) (Mexican), Rev. Lucas Azpericueta, Admin.
Res., 350 E. Bear Mountain, 93203. Tel: 805-854-6150; Fax: 805-854-2564.
Catechesis/Religious Programs—Students 317.

Atwater, Merced Co., St. Anthony (1909), Rev. Thomas Timmings.
Office: 1799 Winton Way, 95301. Tel: 209-358-5743.
Res., 1999 Juniper Ave., 95301.
School—Tel: 209-358-3341. Miss Dianne Silva, Prin.
Lay Teachers 6; Students 115.
Preschool:—Tel: 209-358-3341. Mrs. Debbie Flores, Dir.
Catechesis/Religious Programs—Tel: 209-358-3382.
Students 660.
Mission—Buhach, Merced Co., Immaculate Conception, 1799 Winton Way, 95301.

Avenal, Kings Co., St. Joseph (1941) (Spanish), Rev. Gregory Kareta, O.F.M. Con.
Res., P.O. Box 219, 93204. Tel: 209-386-9523.
Mission—Kettleman City, St. Cecilia. Milham & 8th St.

Bakersfield, Kern Co.,

1—OUR LADY OF GUADALUPE, (1925), Revs. James Catalano, O.S.J.; Chummar Chirayath, O.S.J. (India).
Res., 601 E. California Ave., 93307. Tel: 805-323-3148; Fax: 805-323-6016.
School—609 E. California Ave., 93307. Tel: 805-323-6059. Sr. Teresa Juarez, S.J.S., Prin.
Sisters 3; Lay Teachers 6; Students 177.
Catechesis/Religious Programs—Tel: 805-637-0601. Sofia Mendez, D.R.E.
Students 670.
Missions—Bakersfield, Kern Co., Holy Spirit, 720 E. Belle Terrace, 93307. Tel: 805-834-7095; Bakersfield, Kern Co., St. Jude, 825 Chapman, 93307. Tel: 805-323-2347.

2—OUR LADY OF PERPETUAL HELP, (1948), Rev. Msgr. Michael R. Braun.
Res., 124 Columbus St., 93305. Tel: 805-323-3108; Fax: 805-325-7067.
School—Tel: 805-327-7741. Mrs. Elenor Etcheverry, Prin.
Lay Teachers 12; Students 290.
Catechesis/Religious Programs—Students 331.
Mission—Bakersfield, Kern Co., San Clemente, 1305 Water St., 93305. Tel: 805-871-9190. Rev. Msgr. Ralph Belluomini.

3—SACRED HEART, (1952), Rev. Dan Coyle.
Res., 9915 Ramos St., 93307. Tel: 805-831-8905; Fax: 805-837-8075.
Catechesis/Religious Programs—Tel: 805-831-6223.
Students 235.

4—ST. FRANCIS, (1881), Revs. A. Joseph Heffernan; Leonard J. Trindade.
Res., 900 H St., 93304. Tel: 805-327-4734; Fax: 805-327-4930.
School—2516 Palm St., 93304. Tel: 805-326-7955; Fax: 805-327-0395. Mrs. Fabienne Esparza, Prin.
Sisters 2; Lay Teachers 20; Students 439.
Daycare/Preschool—Tel: 805-326-7958. Mrs. Mary Johnson, Dir.
Students 68.
Catechesis/Religious Programs—Tel: 805-323-8800. Mrs. Alice Fry, D.R.E.
Students 515.

5—ST. JOSEPH, (1907) (English-Spanish), Revs. Robert D. Wenzinger; Patrick Persinger.
Res., 1515 Baker St., 93305. Tel: 805-327-2744; Fax: 805-327-0133.

6—ST. PHILIP THE APOSTLE, (1968), Rev. Msgr. Ronald J. Swett; Rev. Robert Davis.
Mailing Address: 7100 Stockdale Hwy., 93309-1399. Tel: 805-834-7483; Fax: 805-834-2214.
Preschool:—Tel: 805-835-6930. Mrs. Debbie Anderson, Dir.
Catechesis/Religious Programs—D.R.E.: Leila Hunzman, (Elementary); Joan Lund.
Students 1,050.

Bass Lake, Madera Co., St. Dominic Savio (1961), Rev. Herman O. Bezunartea.
Res., P.O. Box 410, 93604. Tel: 209-642-3452.

Mission—North Fork, Madera Co., St. Joseph the Worker, 56522 Rd. 200, North Fork, 93643.

Bishop, Inyo Co., Our Lady of Perpetual Help (1947), Rev. Gerald F. Chavez.
Res., 849 N. Home St., 93514. Tel: 760-872-7231; Fax: 760-872-9222.
Catechesis/Religious Programs—Tel: 760-873-8862.
Students 210.
Mission—Big Pine, Inyo Co., St. Stephen, 461 S. Main St., Bishop 93513. Tel: 760-938-2724.

Boron, Kern Co., St. Joseph (1969), Rev. Robert E. Gamel.
Mailing Address: Drawer D, 93596. Tel: 760-762-5453.
Catechesis/Religious Programs—David Romero, D.R.E. (California City).
Students 116.
Station—California City, Our Lady of Lourdes, Tel: 760-373-2256; Fax: 760-373-1365.

Buttonwillow, Kern Co., St. Mary (1941), Rev. Msgr. Loydell J. Marth, Admin.
Res., 420 N. Main St., Box 875, 93206. Tel: 805-764-5486.

Chowchilla, Madera Co., St. Columba (1921) (Anglo-Saxon-Spanish-Portuguese), Rev. Msgr. Daniel M. Lopez.
Res., 213 Orange Ave., 93610. Tel: 209-665-3376. [JC]
Catechesis/Religious Programs—Tel: 209-665-5104.
Students 285.

Clovis, Fresno Co., Our Lady of Perpetual Help (1929), Rev. Msgr. Raymond C. Dreiling; Rev. George Berendt, P.I.M.E.
Res., 929 Harvard, 93612. Tel: 209-299-4270; Fax: 209-299-7126.
Church—Ninth & DeWitt.
School—836 DeWitt, 93612. Tel: 209-299-7504.
Immaculate Conception Sisters 5; Lay Teachers 6; Students 278.
Catechesis/Religious Programs—Tel: 209-297-8506.
Students 578.

Coalinga, Fresno Co., St. Paul The Apostle (1907) (English), Rev. Nobert Rockensperger, O.F.M.Conv.
Res., 637 Sunset St., P.O. Box 812, 93210. Tel: 209-935-1872; Fax: 209-935-3763. [JC]

Corcoran, Kings Co., Our Lady of Lourdes (1939) (Hispanic), Rev. Richard D. Magdaleno.
Res., 1404 Hanna, 93212. Tel: 209-992-4414; Fax: 209-992-2512.
Catechesis/Religious Programs—Tel: 209-992-4698.
Students 581.

Cutler, Tulare Co., St. Mary (1953), Rev. Jose Luis Vega.
Res., 12588 Avenue 407, P.O. Box 6, 93615. Tel: 209-528-3566.
Catechesis/Religious Programs—Tel: 209-528-3077.
Students 225.

Delano, Kern Co., St. Mary's of the Miraculous Medal (1920), Rev. Rick Fierros, M.Div.
Res., 916 Lexington St., 93215. Tel: 805-725-8456; Fax: 805-725-8485.
School—Tel: 805-725-9055; Fax: 805-725-3224. Ken Thomas, Prin.
Sisters 1; Lay Teachers 9; Students 150.
Catechesis/Religious Programs—Tel: 805-725-9041. Mrs. Alex Guerrero, D.R.E.
Students 750.
Mission—Richgrove, Tulare Co., St. Vincent.

Our Lady of Guadalupe (1954) (Mexican-American-Filipino), Rev. Emerito Gomez, O.F.M.
Res., 1015 Clinton St., 93215. Tel: 805-725-9087; 725-9115.
Catechesis/Religious Programs—Students 437.

Del Rey, Fresno Co., St. Katherine. (Quasi-parish included with St. Mary, Sanger). Rev. John Bruno, R.C.J.
Res., 828 "O" St., P.O. Box 335, Sanger, 93657. Tel: 209-888-2889; 875-2025.

Dinuba, Tulare Co., St. Catherine (1948), Rev. Msgr. Anthony Janelli.
Res., 356 N. Villa Ave., 93618. Tel: 209-591-0931; Fax: 209-591-2965.
Catechesis/Religious Programs—Tel: 209-591-2988. D.R.E.: Tomi Castilleja; Laura Rico; Mary Todd; Cindy Todd; Ray Montanez; Salvador Vargez.
Students 700.

Dos Palos, Merced Co., Sacred Heart (1924), Rev. Robert R. Vanoncini.
Res., 1650 Lucerne, 93620. Tel: 209-392-2724; Fax: 209-392-1037.

Earlimart, Tulare Co., St. Jude (1968), Rev. Raul Sanchez.
Res., P.O. Box 12187, 93219. Tel: 805-849-3170.

Easton, Fresno Co., St. Jude Mission. See St. Alphonsus, Fresno for details. Rev. Roderick L. Craig.
208 W. Jefferson, 93706. Tel: 209-485-3870.

Exeter, Tulare Co., Sacred Heart (Hispanic) (1950), Rev. Msgr. Nicolas Herrero.
Res., 417 North E St., 93221. Tel: 209-592-2465; Fax: 209-592-2465.
Catechesis/Religious Programs—Tel: 209-592-1020.
Students 502.
Mission—Farmersville, Tulare Co., St. Anthony of Egypt, 821 W. Visalia Rd., Farmersville, 93223. Tel: 209-747-0234.

Firebaugh, Fresno Co., St. Joseph (1950) (Hispanic), Rev. Craig F. Harrison.
Res., 1558 12th St., 93622. Tel: 209-659-2225; Fax: 209-659-0408.
School—1900 Saipan, 93622. Tel: 209-659-2841.
Sisters 4; Lay Teachers 5; Students 195.
Catechesis/Religious Programs—Students 578.

Fowler, Fresno Co., St. Lucy (1965), Rev. Msgr. John Esquivel; Rev. John Gracey; Deacon Ed Harmon, III. In res., Deacon Maury McCaffrey.
Res., P.O. Box 295, 93625. Tel: 209-834-2624.
Catechesis/Religious Programs—Tel: 209-834-9124; Fax: 209-896-3975.
Students 123.

Frazier Park, Kern Co., Our Lady of the Snows. (Quasi-parish). Rev. Charles Casale, Admin.
7115 Lakewood Dr. Lake of the Woods, P.O. Box 995, 93225. Tel: 805-245-3741.

Goshen, Tulare Co., St. Thomas the Apostle (1963), Revs. Raphael G. Farrow; Fernando Meza; Deacon Julian Ponce.
Res., 1908 N. Court, Visalia, 93291. Tel: 209-732-8089; Fax: 209-732-0969. [CEM]

Gustine, Merced Co., Our Lady of Miracles (1919) (Portuguese), Rev. Myron Cotta.
Res., 370 Linden Ave., 95322. Tel: 209-854-6692; Fax: 209-854-1344.
School—Tel: 209-854-3180. Sarah Howard, Prin.
Lay Teachers 10; Students 200.
Preschool:—Tel: 209-854-3180. Mrs. Connie Rayan, Dir.
Catechesis/Religious Programs—Students 220.

Hanford, Kings Co., St. Brigid (1886), Rev. Daniel C. Avila.
Office & Mailing Address: 200 E. Florinda, 93230. Fax: 209-582-9193.
Res., 1005 N. Douty St., 93230. Tel: 209-582-2533. [CEM]
School—St. Rose-McCarthy Catholic School, 1000 N. Harris St., 93230. Tel: 209-584-5218; Fax: 209-584-5273. Ms. Debra Cabral, Prin.
Sisters of Our Lady of Nazareth 2; Lay Teachers 9; Students 190.
Catechesis/Religious Programs—Students 502.

Immaculate Heart (1948) (Mexican-Portuguese), Rev. Victor V. Piansay.
Res., 10355 Hanford Armona Rd., 93230. Tel: 209-584-8576; Fax: 209-584-0436.
Catechesis/Religious Programs—Students 342.

Hilmar, Merced Co., Holy Rosary (1948) (Portuguese), Rev. David J. Norris.
Res., P.O. Box 429, 95324. Tel: 209-667-8961; Fax: 209-667-5239.
Catechesis/Religious Programs—Tel: 209-632-7163; Fax: 209-632-7163.
Students 250.
Mission—Stevinson, Merced Co., St. Mary.

Huron, Fresno Co., St. Frances Cabrini (1961) (Hispanic), Rev. Stephen M. Devine.
Res., 36986 Los Angeles St., P.O. Box 939, 93234. Tel: 209-945-2507.
Catechesis/Religious Programs—Students 210.

Kerman, Fresno Co., St. Patrick (1943), Revs. John Griesbach; Gregory Bede DeSilva.
Mailing Address: P.O. Box 375, 93630. Tel: 209-846-8190; Fax: 209-846-7705.
Res., 567 S. Sixth St., 93630.
Catechesis/Religious Programs—Students 320.

Kingsburg, Fresno Co., Holy Family (1950), Rev. Kenneth J. Bozzo.
Res., 1301 Smith St., P.O. Box 798, 93631-0798. Tel: 209-897-5953; Fax: 209-897-8599. [JC]
Catechesis/Religious Programs—Tel: 209-897-7620.
Students 150.
Missions—London, Tulare Co., Santa Cruz, 5625 Ave. 378, 93631; Traver, Tulare Co., St. John the Baptist Educational Center, 4204 Merritt Dr., Traver, 93673. Tel: 209-897-2716.

Lamont, Kern Co., St. Augustine (1962) (Mexican), Rev. John Schmoll.
Res., 10601 Myrtle Ave., 93241-2198. Tel: 805-845-0003; Fax: 805-845-0259.
Catechesis/Religious Programs—Tel: 805-845-3622.
Students 588.

Laton, Fresno Co., Shrine of Our Lady of Fatima (1953), Rev. Timothy A. Gallemore.
Res., P.O. Box 97, 93242. Tel: 209-923-4935.
Catechesis/Religious Programs—Students 300.

Lemoore, Kings Co., St. Peter (1912), Rev. Msgr. John O'Friel.
Res., P.O. Box 100, 93245. Tel: 209-924-2562; Fax: 209-924-5727.
School—884 N. Lemoore Ave., 93245. Tel: 209-924-3424; Fax: 209-924-7848. Sr. Marion Abraham, C.S.S.T., Prin.
Carmelite Sisters of St. Teresa 4; Lay Teachers 6; Students 250.
Catechesis/Religious Programs—Tel: 209-924-2826. Cathy Hammond, D.R.E.
Students 800.
Missions—Stratford, Kings Co., St. Joseph; Tache Indian Reservation, Kings Co., St. Rosa. [CEM]
Chapel—St. Rose of Lima.

Lindsay, Tulare Co., Sacred Heart (1925), Rev. Alex C. Ignacio.
Res., 217 Lindero Ave., 93247-2623. Tel: 209-562-4008; Fax: 209-562-5511.
Catechesis/Religious Programs—Tel: 209-562-2082.
Students 250.
Mission—Tonyville, St. Anthony. 21631 Brooks Ave.
Stations—Plainview; Strathmore.

Livingston, Merced Co., St. Jude Thaddeus (1937) (Portuguese-Hispanic), Rev. Harvey Fonseca.
Res., 330 Franci St., 95334. Tel: 209-394-7512; Fax: 209-394-3089.
Catechesis/Religious Programs—Rosa Maria Mercado, D.R.E.
Students 638.

Lone Pine, Inyo Co., Santa Rosa (1919), Deacon John Burns, Admin.
Res., P.O. Box 246, 93545. Tel: 619-876-4350; Fax: 760-876-4350.
Missions—Shoshone-Tecopa, Inyo Co., St. John the Baptist, P.O. Box 12, Shoshone, 92384; Independence, Inyo Co., St. Vivian, P.O. Box 192, Lone Pine, 93526.
Station—Lone Pine, Death Valley.

Los Banos, Merced Co., St. Joseph (1905), Rev. Msgr. J. Wayne Hayes, P.A.; Rev. Joaquin Arriaga.
Res., 1109 Fifth St., 93635. Tel: 209-826-4246; Fax: 209-826-5335.
School—Tel: 209-826-2709; Fax: 209-826-7320. Ms. Kathy Nerell, Prin.
Franciscan Sisters 1; Lay Teachers 9; Students 267.
Catechesis/Religious Programs—1625 Center Ave., 93635. Tel: 209-826-1512.
Students 469.

Madera, Madera Co., St. Joachim (1881), Revs. Arnold Ortiz, O.S.J.; Guadalupe Sanchez, O.S.J.
Res., 401 W. Fifth St., 93637. Tel: 209-673-3290; Fax: 209-673-6471.
School—Tel: 209-674-7628. Sr. Carmen Santuiste, R.C.M., Prin.
Immaculate Conception Sisters 2; Lay Teachers 7; Students 271.
Catechesis/Religious Programs—Tel: 209-674-5871.
Students 1,925.
Missions—Madera, Madera Co., St. Agnes, 7308 Hwy 145, 93637; Raymond, Madera Co., St. Anne, Raymond-Knowles, Raymond, 93653.

Mariposa, Mariposa Co., St. Joseph (1857), Rev. Stephen C. Bulfer.
Mailing Address: P.O. Box 215, 95338-0215. Tel: 209-966-2522.
Res., 4985 Bullion St. [CEM 3]
Mission—Hornitos, Mariposa Co., St. Catherine of Sienna.

McFarland, Kern Co., St. Elizabeth (1966), Rev. Jose Luis Varo, O.F.M., (Spain) Admin.
Res., 835 E. Perkins, 93250. Tel: 805-792-3225.
Catechesis/Religious Programs—Tel: 805-792-3429. Rosa Carmona, D.R.E.
Students 520.

Mendota, Fresno Co., Our Lady of Guadalupe (1953) (Hispanic), Rev. Msgr. Ricardo Barajas.
Res., P.O. Box 248, 93640. Tel: 209-655-3631.
Mission—Three Rocks, Fresno Co., Our Lady of Lourdes, 161015 S. Derrick, Three Rocks, 93608. Tel: 209-829-3358.

Merced, Merced Co., Our Lady of Mercy/St. Patricks, Revs. Jean-Michael Lastiri; Michael Burchfield.
Mailing Address: P.O. Box 2087, 95344.
Churches—Our Lady of Mercy, (1867), 435 W. 21st St., 95340. Tel: 209-383-3930 (Mass Recording). [JC]
St. Patrick, (1968), 671 E. Yosemite, 95340. Tel: 209-726-3216.
Res., 610 Rambler Rd., 95348. Tel: 209-383-3924; Fax: 209-723-6510.
School—Our Lady of Mercy Elementary, 1400 E. 27th St., 95340. Tel: 209-722-7496; Fax: 209-722-7532. Mrs. Brenda Feehan, Prin.

Lay Teachers 22; Students 481.
Preschool:—Tel: 209-722-6657. Mrs. Jill Serpa, Dir.
Catechesis/Religious Programs—Tel: 209-723-8888. Sr. Mary Kinsinger, D.R.E.
Students 609.
Mission—Hopeton, St. John the Baptist.

Sacred Heart (1945) (English-Hispanic), Rev. Jose M. Montiel.
Res., 1220 M St., 95340. Tel: 209-383-6604; Fax: 209-383-6147.
Catechesis/Religious Programs—Tel: 209-383-1528. Sr. Gabriel Ann Tamayo, D.R.E.
Students 612.
Missions—Merced, Merced Co., El Nido, 95340.; Merced, Merced Co., St. George.

Mojave, Kern Co., St. Mary's, Rev. Leslie F. Shenoy.
Res. & Mailing Address—3100 15th St., Rosamond, 93560. Tel: 805-256-4505; Fax: 805-256-7127.
Catechesis/Religious Programs—Students 173.
Mission—Mojave, St. Francis, Tel: 805-824-2073.

Oildale, Kern Co., Christ the King (1952), Rev. Stephen A. Frost, J.C.L., Admin.
Res., 1800 Bedford Way, 93308. Tel: 805-391-4640; Fax: 805-391-4649.

Orange Cove, Fresno Co., St. Isidore the Farmer (1978), Rev. Angel L. Sotelo, Admin.
Mailing Address: P.O. Box 309, 93646. Tel: 209-626-4943; Fax: 209-626-4648.
Res., 480 Adams Ave., 93646.
Catechesis/Religious Programs—Students 366.
Mission—Squaw Valley, Fresno Co., St. Rita, 30673 George Smith Rd., Squaw Valley, 93675.

Parlier, Fresno Co., Our Lady of Sorrows (1963), Rev. Rodolfo Orozco.
Res., 830 Tulare St., 93648. Tel: 209-646-2161.

Planada, Merced Co., Sacred Heart (1939) (Hispanic-Italian), Rev. John Fluetsch.
Res., 9317 Amistad, P.O. Box 278, 95365. Tel: 209-382-0459. [JC]
Catechesis/Religious Programs—Students 400.
Mission—Le Grand, Merced Co., Our Lady of Lourdes.

Porterville, Tulare Co., St. Anne (1896), Revs. Scott Daugherty; Martin A. McGagh; Raul Diaz.
Res., 378 North F St., 93257. Tel: 209-784-2800; Fax: 209-784-4338.
School—369 North F St., 93257. Tel: 209-784-4096. Sr. Rosario Mediavilla, R.A.D., Prin.
Sisters of the Love of God 4; Lay Teachers 8; Students 192.
Preschool:—Tel: 209-781-8614. Mrs. Rhonda Dotters, Dir.
Catechesis/Religious Programs—Students 650.
Missions—Porterville, Our Lady of Guadalupe, 217 S. Wallace, 93257; Tule Indian Reservation, Tulare Co., Mater Dolorosa; Terra Bella, Blessed Miguel Agustin Pro, 9120 Rd. 236, Terra Bella, 93270.
Station—At Methodist Church, 35725 Hwy 190, Springville, 93265.

Reedley, Fresno Co., St. Anthony (1906), Rev. Msgr. Francis G. Tasy, V.S.; Rev. Angel Gonzalez, S.P.
Res., P.O. Box 188, 93654. Tel: 209-638-2012.
School—St. La Salle Grammar School, 404 E. Manning Ave., 93654. Tel: 209-638-2621; Fax: 209-638-5542.
Sisters 2; Lay Teachers 12; Students 221.
Catechesis/Religious Programs—Tel: 209-638-5608. D.R.E.: Sr. Sandra Ann Silva, S.H.F.; Laura Rivera; Margaret Silva.
Students 480.

Ridgecrest, Kern Co., St. Ann (1946), Rev. Msgr. Kevin Cleary.
Res., 446 W. Church St., P.O. Box 127, 93556. Tel: 760-375-2110; Fax: 760-375-6345. [JC]
School—(Grades K-6). Tel: 760-375-4713.
Lay Teachers 7; Students 183.
Catechesis/Religious Programs—Students 305.
Mission—Randsburg, Kern Co., Santa Barbara, 72 Lexington Ave., Randsburg, 93554.

Riverdale, Fresno Co., St. Ann (1928), Revs. Raymond J. Duffy; Pedro M. Mancilla.
Res., P.O. Box 335, 93656. Tel: 209-867-3035. [JC]
Catechesis/Religious Programs—Tel: 209-867-4996.
Students 372.
Missions—Diener Ranch At Five Points, Fresno Co., Holy Family Chapel; Caruthers, Fresno Co., Our Lady of the Assumption, West & Herndon, P.O. Box 26, Caruthers, 93609.

Sanger, Fresno Co., St. Mary (1922), Revs. Salvatore Ciranni, R.C.J.; John Bruno, R.C.J.; Loji Pilones, R.C.J.
Res., 828 O St., P.O. Box 335, 93657. Tel: 209-875-2025; Fax: 209-875-1281. [JC]
Catechesis/Religious Programs—2590 North Ave., 93657. Tel: 209-875-6340.
Students 780.
Mission—Del Rey, St. Katherine's.

Selma, Fresno Co., St. Joseph (1913), Rev. Msgr. John Esquivel; Rev. John Gracey; Deacons Maury McCaffrey; Ed Harmon, III.
Res., 2441 Dockery Ave., P.O. Box 179, 93662. Tel: 209-896-1052; Fax: 209-896-3975.
Catechesis/Religious Programs—Tel: 209-896-2620.
Students 296.

Shafter, Kern Co., St. Therese (1952), Rev. Thomas O'Neill.
Res., 300 W. Lerdo, P.O. Box 1355, 93263. Tel: 805-746-4471.
Catechesis/Religious Programs—Students 328.

Taft, Kern Co., St. Mary (1918), Rev. Msgr. Loydell J. Marth.
Res., 110 E. Woodrow St., 93268. Tel: 805-765-4292.

Tehachapi, Kern Co., St. Malachy (1887), Rev. Msgr. Joseph C. Barnes; Rev. Msgr. Seamus O. McMullan, Pastor Emeritus; Rev. Msgr. Francis J. Pointek, Pastor Emeritus; Revs. Neil Adolfo (Philippines) Prison Chap.; Godfrey Raffel, (Retired).
Res., 407 W. "E" St., 93561-1642. Tel: 805-822-3060; Fax: 805-822-3159.
Catechesis/Religious Programs—Tel: 805-822-6327.
Students 400.

Tipton, Tulare Co., St. John (1945) (Portuguese-Hispanic), Rev. Warren Hengel, Jr.
Res., 232 S. Adams Rd., Box 159, 93272. Tel: 209-752-4544; Fax: 209-752-1409.
Catechesis/Religious Programs—Students 375.
Mission—Woodville, Tulare Co., St. Francis of Assisi, 16410 Ave. 168, Woodville, 93258.
Station—Tipton, Pixley.

Tranquillity, Fresno Co., St. Paul (1924), Revs. John Griesbach; Gregory Bede DeSilva.
Res., P.O. Box 575, 93668. Tel: 209-698-7429.
Catechesis/Religious Programs—Students 155.
Mission—San Joaquin, Fresno Co., St. Vincent de Paul.

Tulare, Tulare Co., St. Aloysius (1905), Revs. Richard Urizalqui; Raul Marta.
Res., 125 E. Pleasant Ave., 93274. Tel: 209-688-1796; 1797; Fax: 209-688-0948.
School—Tel: 209-686-6250; Fax: 209-686-0479. Sr. Kay O'Brien, O.P., Prin.
Dominican Sisters of Tacoma, WA 1; Lay Teachers 9; Students 274.
Catechesis/Religious Programs—Students 500.

St. Rita (1967), Rev. Timothy N. Cardoza.
Res., 954 S. O St., 93274. Tel: 209-686-3847; Fax: 209-686-9672.

Visalia, Tulare Co., Holy Family (1950), Revs. Raphael G. Farrow; Fernando Meza; Deacon Julian Ponce.
Res., 1908 N. Court St., 93291. Tel: 209-732-8089; Fax: 209-732-0969. [JC]
Catechesis/Religious Programs—Tel: 209-732-9651.
Students 620.

St. Mary (1861), Rev. Msgr. Thomas G. Kleinhans; Rev. Gregory Beaumont.
Res., 608 N. Church St., P.O. Box 287, 93279. Tel: 209-734-9522; Fax: 209-734-3435.
School—George McCann Memorial School, 200 E. Race St., 93291. Tel: 209-732-5831; Fax: 209-741-1562. Mr. Victor Suarez, Prin.
Lay Teachers 9; Students 242.
Catechesis/Religious Programs—Tel: 209-733-3929. Mrs. Joan Bell, D.R.E.
Students 871.

Wasco, Kern Co., St. John the Evangelist (1919) (Hispanic), Rev. Msgr. Dino F. Riccomini.
Res., 1300 Ninth Pl., 93280. Tel: 805-758-6688.
School—Tel: 805-758-6467. Mrs. Joanne Todd, Prin.
Lay Teachers 4; Students 63.
Preschool:—Tel: 805-758-6829. Mrs. Donna Ward, Dir.
Catechesis/Religious Programs—Students 430.
Mission—Blackwell's Corner, Kern Co., Nuestra Senora de la Paz, 14846 Hwy. 33, Lost Hills, 93249.

Wofford Heights, Kern Co., St. Jude (1969), Rev. James Kudilil.
Res., 86 Nellie Dent Dr., 93285. Tel: 760-376-2416; Fax: 760-376-1369.

Woodlake, Tulare Co., St. Frances Cabrini (1963) (Spanish), Rev. Jesse C. Venzor.
Res., 599 N. Valencia Blvd., P.O. Box 459, 93286. Tel: 209-564-2647.
Catechesis/Religious Programs—Students 319.
Mission—Three Rivers, Tulare Co., St. Clair, Alta Acres Dr., Three Rivers, 93271.

Yosemite National Park, Mariposa Co., Our Lady of the Snows (1963), Rev. Dennis M. Alvernaz; Deacon Christian DeVos.
Res., P.O. Box 457, 95389. Tel: 209-372-4729.
Station—Yosemite National Park, Wawona.

Chaplains of Public Institutions

FRESNO. *Community Hospital, Veterans' Hospital.* Attended by Capuchin Fathers. Revs. David LaPierre, O.F.M.Cap., Supr.; Alejandro Magallanes, O.F.M.Cap.; Donal Burke, O.F.M.Cap.; Perry Burke, O.F.M.Cap.

AVENAL. *California State Prison, Kings Co.* Rev. Romuald Perera, O.S.B., Chap.

BAKERSFIELD. *Kern Medical Center, Bakersfield Memorial Hospital & San Joaquin Community Hospital.* Rev. Patrick Persinger.

CHOWCHILLA. *Department of Corrections, Central California Women's Facility.* Rev. Dominic T. Pontolillo, O.F.M.Cap.

COALINGA. *Pleasant Valley State Prison*, 601 C Washington, 93210. Rev. James Cadera.

CORCORAN. *Calif. State Prison.* Tel: 209-992-8800. Rev. John J. Moore.
Prison Medical Facility. Rev. Paul McCarthy; Sr. Christine McNamara, S.S.L.

DELANO. *North Kern State Prison.* Tel: 805-721-2345, Ext. 6862. Bro. "Ponchie" Vasquez, O.F.M.

PORTERVILLE. *State Hospital.* Vacant. P.O. Box 2000, 93258.

TEHACHAPI. *California Correctional Institution*, P.O. Box 426, 93581. Tel: 209-822-4402, Ext. 4387. Rev. Hermengildo Adolfo, Chap.

WASCO. *Prison Facility*, P.O. Box 8800, 93280-8800. Tel: 805-758-8400. Rev. Paul L. Manzano.

On Special Assignment:
Reverend Fathers—
Craig, Rod, Vocations Dir., 1550 N. Fresno St., Fresno, CA 93703-3788
Frost, Stephen A., J.C.L., Adjutant Judicial Vicar & Dir. of Tribunal, 1550 N. Fresno St., Fresno, CA 93703-3788
Negro, Sergio P., Vicar Gen., 1550 N. Fresno St., Fresno, CA 93703-3788
Nespolo, Umberto, Asian Ministry in Fresno, 2814 Mariposa, Fresno, CA 93721
Peterson, E. James, Dir., Renew 2000; Rector, San Joaquin Memorial H.S.; Vice Pres. TV Station KNXT

Faculties Only:
Reverend Fathers—
Da Costa, Joseph Dinis, O.F.M.
Drieci, Pat, C.SS.R.
Harris, Edward, S.J.
Peters, Noel, O.M.I.
Schindler, Robert
Vespa, Bauttista
Vogt, William

On Duty Outside the Diocese:
Reverend Fathers—
Flickinger, Don D., 15333 Woodard Rd., San Jose, CA 95124

Absent on Sick Leave:
Reverend Fathers—
Bray, Kevin

Retired:
Reverend Monsignors—
Balker, Joseph W., 2401 N. Kaweah, Exeter, CA 93221
Doherty, Patrick G., P.O. Box 348, Visalia, CA 93279
Elmlinger, Herbert, 188A W. Barstow, Fresno, CA 93704
Flood, Patrick, 2550 W. Clinton, Fresno, CA 93705
Herdegen, Anthony, 5660 N. River Forrest Dr., Milwaukee, WI 53209
Lahey, Maurice, 2121 N. 1st St., Fresno, CA 93703
Lee, Howard T.
McHugh, Martin, Knock Inverin, County Galway, Ireland
McMullan, Seamus O., St. Malachy, 542 Jacobson Ct., Tehachapi, CA 93581
Meyer, Gilbert, P.O. Box 117, Olancha, CA 93548
Minhoto, Walter F., 2814 Mariposa, Fresno, CA 93721
O'Connor, Michael, P.O. Box 6751 PMC, Frazier Park, CA 93274
Pointek, Francis J., P.O. Box 1240, Tehachapi, CA 93581
Ryan, John F.C., 2121 N. First St., Fresno, CA 93703

Reverend Fathers—
Alabart, Francis X., 722 Dover Pl., Delano, CA 93215

Costabile, George, 2307 Colston Dr., Silver Spring, MD 20910
Cummins, Timothy, 2121 N. First St., Fresno, CA 93703
Gonzales, Antonio, 715 E. Elm St., Tulare, CA 93274
Grupa, Henry, 2121 First St., Fresno, CA 93703
Leitheiser, Douglas, P.O. Box 639, Lindsay, CA 93247
McGagh, Martin, P.O. Box 52, Porterville, CA 93258
McKee, John, c/o Hugent Summerhill, Athlone, Ireland
Pascual, Manuel, 4701 S. Mooney Blvd., Sp.R7, Visalia, CA 93277
Raffel, Godfrey, P.O. Box 387, Tehachapi, CA 93581
Schindler, Robert

INSTITUTIONS LOCATED IN THE DIOCESE

[A] HIGH SCHOOLS, PRIVATE

FRESNO. *The San Joaquin Memorial High School of Fresno, Inc.*, 1406 N. Fresno St., 93703. Tel: 209-268-9251; Fax: 209-268-1351. Bros. Gary Hough, F.S.C., Dir.; Ricardo Palacio, F.S.C., Campus Min. Dir.; Cecil-Charles Duncan, F.S.C., Instructor; Austin Gili, F.S.C., Instructor; DeSales Benning, F.S.C., Instructor; Andrew Steele, F.S.C., Faculty Devel. In res. Bro. Lawrence Haley, F.S.C. Brothers of the Christian Schools 7; Sisters 3; Lay Teachers 40; Students 719.

[B] HIGH SCHOOLS, INTERPAROCHIAL

BAKERSFIELD. *Garces Memorial High School*, 2800 Loma Linda Dr., 93305. Tel: 805-327-2578. John Kvasnicka, Prin.; David West, Campus Ministry Coord. Lay Teachers 43; Students 775.

[C] GENERAL HOSPITALS

FRESNO. *Saint Agnes' Medical Center*, 1303 E. Herndon, 93720. Tel: 209-449-3000.
For a complete listing, refer to the Hospitals section.

BAKERSFIELD. *Mercy Healthcare Bakersfield*, 2215 Truxtun Ave., 93301. Tel: 805-632-5000; Fax: 805-327-2592.
Web site: www.chw.edu
For a complete listing, refer to the Hospitals section.

MERCED. *Mercy Hospital & Health Services*, 2740 M St., 95340. Tel: 209-384-6444; Fax: 209-722-2902.
For a complete listing, refer to the Hospitals section.

[D] HOMES FOR INVALID AND AGED

FRESNO. *Nazareth House*, 2121 N. First St., 93703. Tel: 209-237-2257.
For a complete listing, refer to the Special Care Facilities section.

[E] CATHOLIC CHARITIES

FRESNO. *Catholic Charities of the Diocese of Fresno.* Vacant. 149 N. Fulton St., 93701. Tel: 209-237-0851.
Catholic Social Services, 149 N. Fulton St., 93701. Tel: 209-264-6414. Anita Tomlinson, Dir. Total Staff 1; Total Assisted 2,548.
Francis X. Singleton Emergency Food Assistance Program, 149 N. Fulton St., 93701. Tel: 209-233-3663. Peter P. Hagel, Dir. Total Staff 2; Total Assisted 65,000.
Immigration & Refugee Services, 149 N. Fulton St., 93701. Tel: 209-264-6400.
E-mail: FRESM@lightspeed.net
Tam Nguyen, Dir. Total Staff 6; Total Assisted 1,200.
Senior Companion Program. Tel: 209-498-6377. Patricia A. Strahl, Dir. Total Staff 2; Total Assisted 112.

BAKERSFIELD. *Bakersfield Big Brothers*, 415 E. 19th St., 93305. Tel: 805-323-3025. George San Miguel, Dir. Staff 2; Total Assisted 130.
Catholic Social Services, 310 Baker St., 93305. Tel: 805-323-2941. Joan Garabaldi, Prog. Chm. Total Staff 3; Total Assisted 73,000.
Homemaker Program, Cabrini League. Vacant. 310 Baker St., 93305. Tel: 805-323-2941. Staff 20; Total Assisted 250.
Immigration & Refugee Services, 415 E. 19th St., 93305. Tel: 805-325-7751. Delfina Granados, Dir. Total Staff 1; Total Assisted 1,200.
Junipero Serra Inn-Half Way House, 700 19th St., 93301. Tel: 805-324-6125; 323-4646. Hassan Kowwasar, Dir. Halfway/Work Furlough Community Correctional Re-entry Center (CCRC). Total Staff 17; Total Assisted 100.

DELANO. *Kaleidoscope.* (Drug Counseling Program), 1206 High St., 93215. Tel: 805-725-0969. Hector Vela, Prog. Dir. Total Staff 4; Total Assisted 135.

FARMERSVILLE. *St. Vincent de Paul Center*, 468 E. Visalia Rd., P.O. Box 106, 93223. Tel: 209-594-4932. Mary G. Flores. Total Staff 3; Total Assisted 1,150.

MERCED. *Catholic Charities*, 1810 Canal St., 95340. Tel: 209-383-2494; 383-5220. Ramiro Coronado, Dir. Total Staff 5; Total Assisted 2,500.
Direct Services, 1810 Canal St., 95340. Tel: 209-383-2494. Ramiro Coronado, Dir.
Migrant and Refugee Services, 1810 Canal St., 95340. Tel: 209-383-0283. Ramiro Coronado, Dir. Tel: 209383-5220.

PORTERVILLE. *Catholic Social Services*, 1309 S. Main, Bldg. B, 93257. Tel: 209-781-5778. Mary Meisel, Dir. Total Staff 2; Total assisted annually 35,778.

VISALIA. *Catholic Social Services*, 1638 N. Dinuba Blvd., 93291. Tel: 209-734-1572; Fax: 209-234-4921. Sr. Kenneth Quinn, D.C., M.S.W., Dir. Total Staff 18; Total Assisted 94,000.
Good News Medical Clinic, 1638 N. Dinuba Blvd., 93291. Tel: 209-734-1572.
Good News Center (Sr. Ursula's Kitchen & Thrift Store), 1724 N. Dinuba Blvd., 93291. Tel: 209-738-8922.
Good News Inn (Shelter), 1718 & 1722 N. Dinuba Blvd., 93291. Tel: 209-734-6470.

[F] CONVENTS AND RESIDENCES FOR SISTERS

FRESNO. *Franciscan Hospitallers*, 6020 N. Flora Ave., 93722. Tel: 209-261-1782. Sisters 2.
Poor Sisters of Nazareth, 2121 N. First St., 93703. Tel: 209-237-2257. Sr. Rose Hoye, P.S.N., Supr. Sisters 5.
St. Agnes Hospital Convent, 1261 E. Los Altos Ave., 93710. Tel: 209-431-3376. Sisters of the Holy Cross, Inc. 9.
Sister Disciples of the Divine Master, 3700 N. Cornelia Ave., 93722. Tel: 209-275-1656. Sr. M. Peter Mendes, P.D.D.M., Supr. Sisters 13.
Sisters of the Love of God (RAD), 4305 E. Union Ave., 93703. Tel: 209-454-1864.

ATWATER. *Our Lady of the Atonement Convent*, 1694 Grove Ave., 95301. Tel: 209-358-2109. Sr. Helena Horwood, S.A. Franciscan Sisters of the Atonement 4.

BAKERSFIELD. *Sister Servants of the Blessed Sacrament (SJS)*, 1100 S. Kern St., 93307. Tel: 805-323-6059.

CLOVIS. *Sisters of the Immaculate Conception (RCM)*, 859 Harvard Ave., 93612. Tel: 209-299-8407.

FIREBAUGH. *Carmelite Sisters of St. Teresa (CSST)*, 1900 Saipan Ave., 93622. Tel: 209-924-2440.

LEMOORE. *Carmelite Sisters of St. Teresa (CSST)*, 884 N. Lemoore Ave., 93245. Tel: 209-924-2347.

LOS BANOS. *Franciscan Hospitallers (FHIC)*, 1625 Center Ave., 93635. Tel: 209-826-5298.

MADERA. *Sisters of the Immaculate Conception (RCM)*, 224 N. J St., 93637. Tel: 209-674-4085.

MERCED. *Daughters of the Holy Spirit (DHS)*, 2987 Tahoe Dr., 95340. Tel: 209-384-2705.
Sisters of the Third Order of St. Dominic, 2635 Piedmont Dr., 95340. Tel: 209-723-6564. Sisters 3.
Sisters of the Third Order of St. Dominic, 2231 Lecco Way, 95340. Sisters 3.

PORTERVILLE. *Sisters of the Love of God (RAD)*, 385 N. F St., 93257. Tel: 209-784-6889.

REEDLEY. *Daughters of Divine Zeal (FDZ)*, 379 E. Manning Ave., 93654. Tel: 209-638-1916.

THREE RIVERS. *Daughters of Charity of St. Vincent de Paul (DC)*, 40534 Cherokee Oaks Dr., 93271-9743. Tel: 209-561-1204.

[G] RETREAT HOUSES

THREE RIVERS. *St. Anthony's Retreat House*, P.O. Box 249, 93271. Tel: 209-561-4595. Revs. Ignatius DeGroot, O.F.M., Dir. & Supr.; David Johnson, O.F.M.; Juan Leon, O.F.M.; Bros. Joseph Brand, O.F.M.; Nicholas Heinrich, O.F.M. Priests 3; Brothers 2.

[H] NEWMAN CENTERS

FRESNO. *St. Paul Newman Center*, 1572 E. Barstow Ave., 93710. Tel: 209-436-3434; Fax: 209-436-3430.
E-mail: Padre@fresno.edu
Web site: http://www.csufresno.edu/CSA
Rev. Perry Kavookjian. Campus Ministers: Rev. Jerry Amerando; Tina Fridley.
California State University at Fresno.
Fresno City College.

BAKERSFIELD. *Bakersfield College Newman Center*, 124 Columbus, 93305. Tel: 805-323-3108. Rev. Msgr. Michael R. Braun, Chap.

[I] SOCIETY OF ST. VINCENT DE PAUL

FRESNO. *St. Vincent's Lemonaid Shoppe of Valley Catholic Charities*, 149 N. Fulton St., 93701-1607. Tel: 209-237-0851.
Society of St. Vincent de Paul, 149 N. Fulton St., 93701. Tel: 209-237-0851. Parish Conferences are located in parishes throughout the Diocese.
Fresno District Council, 149 N. Fulton St., 93701. Alice M. Thoms, Trustee.
Kern District Council, 300 Baker St., 93305. Tel: 805-323-7340.
Merced-Mariposa District Council, 131 W. Main St., Merced, 95340. Tel: 209-723-6077. Legal Title: *Merced-Mariposa District Council of St. Vincent de Paul Society.* Dolores Schwerdferger, Pres.

BAKERSFIELD. *Bakersfield St. Vincent de Paul Thrift Store*, 300 Baker St., 93305. Tel: 805-323-7340. Don Border, Pres.

[J] MISCELLANEOUS & AGENCIES

FRESNO. *Apostolate of Christian Action*, P.O. Box 24, 93707. Tel: 209-291-0400; Fax: 209-291-1650. Roger Oraze, Pres.; Rev. Msgr. James T. Logan, Spiritual Dir.
Catholic Truth International, 5654 E. Westover, Suite 103, 93727. Tel: 209-291-0400; Fax: 209-291-1650. Christopher Knuffke, Pres.; Rev. Stephen A. Frost, Spiritual Dir.
St. Anthony's Bread Basket, Inc., P.O. Box 6045, 93703. Tel: 209-252-4929. James R. Johnson, Pres.

CLOVIS. *Catholic Professional & Business Breakfast Club of the Fresno Diocese*, c/o Our Lady of Perpetual Help, Ninth and DeWitt Ave. Mailing Address: 929 Harvard Ave., 93612. Tel: 209-299-4270. Rev. Msgr. Raymond C. Dreiling, Contact Person.

SANGER. *Fr. Hannibal House Social Service Center*, 1501 14th St., P.O. Box 37, 93657. Tel: 209-875-0564; Fax: 209-875-1281.

RELIGIOUS INSTITUTES OF MEN REPRESENTED IN THE DIOCESE

For further details refer to the corresponding bracketed number in the Religious Institutes of Men or Women section.

[0200]—*Benedictine Monks.*—O.S.B.
[0330]—*Brothers of the Christian Schools.* (San Francisco Prov.).—F.S.C.
[0470]—*The Capuchin Friars.*—O.F.M.Cap.
[0360]—*Claretian Missionaries.* (Western Prov.).—C.M.F.
[0480]—*Conventual Franciscans.* (St. Joseph Cupertino Prov.).—O.F.M.Conv.
[0260]—*Discalced Carmelite Friars.*—O.C.D.
[0520]—*Franciscan Friars.* (St. Barbara Prov.).—O.F.M.
[0650]—*Holy Ghost Fathers.* (Western Prov.).—C.S.Sp.
[0690]—*Jesuit Fathers and Brothers.*—S.J.
[0910]—*Oblates of Mary Immaculate.*—O.M.I.
[0930]—*Oblates of St. Joseph.* (Asti, Italy).—O.S.J.
[0430]—*Order of Preachers.*—O.P.
[1050]—*Pontifical Institute for Foreign Missions.*—P.I.M.E.
[1070]—*Redemptorists.*—C.SS.R.
[1090]—*Rogationist Fathers.*—R.C.J.
[1200]—*Society of the Divine Savior.*—S.D.S.
[0420]—*Society of the Divine Word.*—S.V.D.
[1330]—*Vincentians (Congregation of the Mission).*—C.M.

RELIGIOUS INSTITUTES OF WOMEN REPRESENTED IN THE DIOCESE

[0230]—*Benedictine Sisters of Pontifical Jurisdiction.* (Mt. Angel, OR).—O.S.B.
[]—*Carmelite Sisters of St. Teresa.* (Gidellahalli, Bangalore-India).—C.S.S.T.
[1920]—*Congregation of the Sisters of the Holy Cross.* (Notre Dame, IN).—C.S.C.
[0760]—*Daughters of Charity of St. Vincent de Paul.* (Los Altos Hills, CA) (Western Prov.).—D.C.
[0795]—*Daughters of Divine Zeal.* (Rome, Italy).—F.D.Z.
[0820]—*Daughters of the Holy Spirit.* (France) (Putnam, CT Prov. House).—D.H.S.
[1070-20]—*Dominican Sisters.* (Congregation of St. Thomas Aquinas, Marymount, Tacoma, WA).—O.P.
[1070-25]—*Dominican Sisters.* (Congregation of the Dominican Sisters of St. Catherine of Siena of Kenosha).—O.P.
[1270]—*Franciscan Hospitaller Sisters of the Immaculate Conception.* (San Jose, CA).—F.H.I.C.
[1190]—*Franciscan Sisters of the Atonement.* (Graymoor, NY).—S.A.
[2180]—*Immaculate Heart Community.* (Los Angeles, CA).—I.H.M.
[2570]—*Institute of the Sisters of Mercy of the Americas.* (Burlingame, CA).—R.S.M.
[2690]—*Missionary Catechists of Divine Providence.* (San Antonio, TX).—M.C.D.P.
[0980]—*Pious Disciples of the Divine Master.* (Staten Island, NY).—P.D.D.M.
[3242]—*Poor Sisters of Nazareth.* (Los Angeles, CA).—P.S.N.
[2970]—*School Sisters of Notre Dame.* (St. Louis, MO).—S.S.N.D.

[3499]—*Servants of the Blessed Sacrament.* (El Secondo, CA).—S.J.S.

[0430]—*Sisters of Charity of Blessed Virgin Mary.* (Dubuque, IA).—B.V.M.

[1010]—*Sisters of Divine Providence of San Antonio, Texas.*—C.D.P.

[2560]—*Sisters of Mercy.*—S.M.

[]—*Sisters of Our Lady of Nazareth.* (Fiji, South Pacific).—S.O.L.N.

[3840]—*Sisters of St. Joseph of Carondelet.* (Los Angeles, CA & Baden, PA).—C.S.J.

[1960]—*Sisters of the Holy Family.* (Mission San Jose, CA).—S.H.F.

[2130]—*Sisters of the Immaculate Conception.* (San Francisco, CA).—R.C.M.

[]—*Sisters of the Love of God.* (La Puente, CA).—R.A.D.

[4120-06]—*Ursuline Nuns of the Congregation of Paris.* (Toledo, OH).—O.S.U.

DIOCESAN CEMETERIES

FRESNO. *Fresno Catholic Cemeteries,* 264 N. Blythe, 93706. Tel: 209-488-7449; Fax: 209-488-7466. Michael Orlando, Dir.

NECROLOGY

† McMullan, Rev. Msgr. Seamus, (Retired). —Died Nov. 27, 1997.

† Sancho-Boyles, Anthony, (Retired). —Died Aug. 2, 1997.

Diocese of Gallup

(Diocesis Gallupiensis)

Most Reverend

DONALD E. PELOTTE, S.S.S., D.D., PH.D.

Bishop of Gallup; ordained September 2, 1972; appointed Coadjutor Bishop of Gallup February 24, 1986; consecrated May 6, 1986; succeeded to See, March 20, 1990. *Office: P.O. Box 1338, Gallup, NM, 87305. Res., 433 Camino Del Sol, P.O. Box 1317, Gallup, NM, 87305.* Tel.: 505-722-3047.

ESTABLISHED DECEMBER 16, 1939.

Square Miles 55,468.

Comprises Apache, Navajo and those parts of the Navajo and Hopi Reservations in Coconino Counties in the State of Arizona; San Juan, McKinley, Catron, Cibola and those parts of Rio Arriba, Sandoval, Bernalillo and Valencia Counties lying west of 106, 52', 41" meridian in the State of New Mexico.

Legal Title: New Mexico: Roman Catholic Church of the Diocese of Gallup. Arizona: Bishop of the Roman Catholic Church of the Diocese of Gallup.

For legal titles of parishes and diocesan institutions, consult the Chancery Office.

Chancery: 711 S. Puerco Dr., P.O. Box 1338, Gallup, NM, 87305. Tel.: 505-863-4406; Fax: 505-722-9131.

STATISTICAL OVERVIEW

Personnel	
Bishop	1
Priests: Diocesan Active in Diocese	30
Priests: Active Outside Diocese	19
Priests: Retired, Sick or Absent	9
Number of Diocesan Priests	58
Religious Priests in Diocese	31
Extern Priests in Diocese	8
Ordinations:	
Permanent Deacons	1
Permanent Deacons in Diocese	32
Total Brothers	12
Total Sisters	155
Parishes	
Parishes	59
With Resident Pastor:	
Resident Diocesan Priests	28
Resident Religious Priests	19
Without Resident Pastor:	
Administered by Priests	9
Completely Vacant	3
Missions	41
Pastoral Centers	38
Professional Ministry Personnel:	
Brothers	2
Sisters	30
Lay Ministers	13
Welfare	
Homes for the Aged	1
Total Assisted	42
Specialized Homes	2
Total Assisted	200
Special Centers for Social Services	4
Total Assisted	22,348
Educational	
Diocesan Students in Other Seminaries	2
Total Seminarians	2
High Schools, Private	3
Total Students	303
Elementary Schools, Diocesan and Parish	2
Total Students	302
Elementary Schools, Private	8
Total Students	1,320
Catechesis/Religious Education:	
High School Students	1,030
Elementary Students	3,400
Total Students Under Catholic Instruction	6,357
Teachers in the Diocese:	
Sisters	22
Lay Teachers	102
Vital Statistics	
Receptions into the Church:	
Infant Baptism Totals	936
Adult Baptism Totals	298
Received into Full Communion	107
First Communions	914
Confirmations	667
Marriages:	
Catholic	140
Interfaith	71
Total Marriages	211
Deaths	512
Total Catholic Population	43,824
Total Population	355,640

Former Bishop—Most Rev. BERNARD T. ESPELAGE, O.F.M., D.D., ord. May 16, 1918; appt. Bishop of Gallup, July 20, 1940; cons. Oct. 9, 1940; resigned Sept. 3, 1969; died Feb. 19, 1971.—Most Rev. JEROME J. HASTRICH, D.D., ord. Feb. 9, 1941; cons. Auxiliary Bishop of Madison and Titular Bishop of Gurza, July 31, 1963; transferred to the See of Gallup, Sept. 3, 1969; installed Dec. 3, 1969; retired March 20, 1990; died May 12, 1995.

Vicar General—Rev. Msgr. LEO GOMEZ, V.G.

Vicar for Indian Affairs—Rev. CARON VOLLMER, O.F.M.

Office of the Bishop—711 S. Puerco Dr., P.O. Box 1338, Gallup, 87305. Tel: 505-863-4406.

Chancery—711 S. Puerco Dr., P.O. Box 1338, Gallup, 87305. Tel: 505-863-4406; Fax: 505-722-9131. Office Hours: Mon.-Thurs. 8:30-12 & 1-4:30; Fri. 8:30-12.

Chancellor—Bro. DUANE A. TORISKY, O.F.M.

Financial Secretary—Mrs. ANNA J. DIGREGORIO.

Diocesan Tribunal (First Instance)—711 S. Puerco Dr., P.O. Box 1338, Gallup, 87305. Tel: 505-863-4406; Fax: 505-722-9324.

Judicial Vicar—Rev. LAWRENCE J. O'KEEFE, J.C.D.

Adjutant Judicial Vicar—Rev. ALFRED A. TACHIAS, J.C.L.

Judges—Revs. ALFRED A. TACHIAS, J.C.L.; Deacon PAUL DOOLEY; Rev. Msgr. LEO GOMEZ; Rev. Msgr. JAMES LINDENMEYER.

Defenders of the Bond—Revs. MELDON HICKEY, O.F.M.; MICHAEL VIGIL; THOMAS MAIKOWSKI, Ph.D.; EMERIC NORDMEYER, O.F.M.

Notary—MARY ALICE SALAZ.

Episcopal Vicars—Very Rev. DIEGO MAZON, O.F.M., V.F., McKinley Vicariate; Very Rev. MARTAN RADEMAKER, O.F.M., V.F., Apache Vicariate; Very Rev. MICHAEL VIGIL, V.F., Navajo Vicariate; Very Rev. JOSE RODRIQUEZ, V.F., Lower Arizona Vicariate; Very Rev. TIMOTHY FARRELL, San Juan Vicariate; Very Rev. EMERIC NORDMEYER, O.F.M., Cibola Vicariate.

Vicaress for Religious—Sr. MARY LOUISE HOELSCHER, C.PP.S., *P.O. Box 120, Manuelito, 87318-0120.* Tel: 505-863-1918.

Presbyteral Council—Most Rev. DONALD E. PELOTTE, S.S.S., D.D., Ph.D.; Rev. Msgr. LEO GOMEZ, V.G.; Very Revs. LAWRENCE O'KEEFE, Moderator; DIEGO MAZON, O.F.M.; EMERIC NORDMEYER, O.F.M.; Rev. EDWARD FRONSKE, O.F.M.; Very Revs. LOUIS FRANZ, C.M.; TIMOTHY FARRELL; Revs. THOMAS MAIKOWSKI; MICHAEL VIGIL; JOSE RODRIQUEZ; Very Rev. MARTAN RADEMAKER, O.F.M.; Bro. DUANE TORISKY O.F.M., Sec., *P.O. Box 1338, Gallup, 87305.*

Diocesan Consultors—Rev. Msgr. LEO GOMEZ, V.G.; Revs. LAWRENCE O'KEEFE; JOSE RODRIGUEZ; EDWARD FRONSKE, O.F.M.; THOMAS MAIKOWSKI; Very Revs. DIEGO MAZON, O.F.M.; LOUIS FRANZ, C.M.

Diocesan Navajo Mission Board—Most Rev. DONALD E. PELOTTE, S.S.S.; Very Rev. MARTAN RADEMAKER, O.F.M.; Revs. CARON VOLLMER, O.F.M.; DAVIN VON HAGEL, O.F.M.

Diocesan Offices and Directors

Archivist—Bro. DUANE TORISKY, O.F.M.

Boy Scouts—Rev. THOMAS MAIKOWSKI, Ph.D., Dir. & Chap., *P.O. Box 1028, Gallup, 87305.* Tel: 505-863-3563.

Budget and Finance—Deacon JAMES P. HOY, Dir.

Cemeteries—Rev. Msgr. JAMES LINDENMEYER, *Box 2840, Farmington, 87401.*

Catholic Charities—Sr. BETTY MARIE DUNKEL, D.C., Dir., *Main Office, Gallup, P.O. Box 1589, Gallup, 87305.* Tel: 505-722-5272. Chinle: *P.O. Box 417, Chinle, AZ, 86053.* Tel: 520-674-3238. Grants-Milan: *2595 W. Hwy. 66, P.O. Box 124, Grants, 87020.* Tel: 505-285-5451. Farmington: *119 W. Broadway, Farmington, 87401.* Tel: 505-325-3724. Holbrook: *P.O. Box 41, Holbrook, AZ, 86025.* Tel: 520-524-9720. White Mountain: *P.O. Box 600, McNary, AZ, 85930.* Tel: 520-334-2219.

Cursillos—Rev. MELDON HICKEY, O.F.M., *P.O. Drawer 60, Fort Defiance, AZ, 86504.* Tel: 520-729-5068.

Diocesan Pastoral Council—Most Rev. DONALD E. PELOTTE, S.S.S., D.D., Ph.D.; Bro. DUANE TORISKY, O.F.M.; KATHLEEN BEATON, Chm.; MARY ANN MONTOYA, Vice Chm.; Sr. FRANCELLA MARY GRIGGS, Sec.; ROGER RIDGEWAY, Consultant; Revs. THOMAS MAIKOWSKI; WALTER OPALEWSKI; MICHAEL VIGIL; Deacon JORGE CAMPOS; Bro. DUANE TORISKY, O.F.M.; Sr. SARAH PAGE, O.S.F.; PAULINE BACA; JUDY DAVIS; JULIA GORMAN; BARBARA KOZELISKI; JERRY LINDSAY; FRANCIS J. PAWLOWSKI; SAM ROTOLO.

Director of Education, (Catholic Schools and Religious Education)—Rev. THOMAS MAIKOWSKI, Ph.D., Director of Education, *P.O. Box 1028, Gallup, 87305.* Tel: 505-863-3563.

Ecumenical Affairs in Arizona, Arizona Ecumenical Council—Rev. ALBERTO AVELLA, *P.O. Box 1449, Showlow, 85901.* Tel: 520-537-2543.

Ecumenical Affairs in New Mexico, New Mexico Council of Churches—Rev. DANIEL DALEY, *307 N. Church St., Bloomfield, 87413.* Tel: 505-632-2014.

Newspaper—"Voice of the Southwest"; Rev. TIMOTHY FARRELL, *P.O. Box 1338, Gallup, 87305.* Tel: 505-863-4406.

Permanent Deacon Program—Most Rev. DONALD E. PELOTTE, S.S.S., D.D., Ph.D.; Deacons TIMOTED P. LUJAN, Deacon Dir. PAUL DOOLEY, Asst. Dir.

Priests' Retirement Fund—WILLIAM DAY, Chm.; Revs. JOSE RODRIQUEZ; PATRICK WEDEKING; OLIVER CURRAN; FRANK CHACON.

Propagation of the Faith—Rev. MICHAEL MACK, *P.O. Box 1338, Gallup, 87305.*

Radio and Television—Rev. CORMAC ANTRAM, O.F.M., *P.O. Box 517, Kayenta, AZ, 86033.*

Search—TED GOMEZ, Dir., *2103 Lynwood Dr., Farmington, 87401.*

Serra Club—Vacant.

Social Justice and Outreach—FRANCIS J. PAWLOWSKI, *P.O. Box 1338, Gallup, 87305.*

Vocations—For Priesthood: Rev. JOACHIM BLONSKI, *414 N. Allen Ave., Farmington, 87401.* Deacon Vocations: Deacon TIMOTED LUJAN, *P.O. Box 2612, Milan, 87021-2612.* MAGDA GARCIA, H.N.S.G., *217 E. Wilson, Gallup, 87301.*

Youth Ministry—DOUGLAS CLAPPER; LENA CLAPPER, *P.O. Box 1615, Aztec, 87410.*

CLERGY, PARISHES, MISSIONS AND PAROCHIAL SCHOOLS

CITY OF GALLUP (McKinley County)

1—CATHEDRAL OF THE SACRED HEART. (Dedicated June 19, 1955). Rev. Msgr. Leo Gomez, V.G., Rector; Deacon Joseph Krikawa.
Mailing Address: P.O. Box 1029, 87305.
Res., 415 E. Green Ave., 87301. Tel: 505-722-6644; Fax: 505-722-6645.
Catechesis/Religious Programs—Barbara Kozeliski, D.R.E.
Students 327.

2—ST. FRANCIS OF ASSISI, Revs. Diego Mazon, O.F.M.; Ulric Pax, O.F.M.; Bro. George Ward, O.F.M. In res., Bro. Duane Torisky, O.F.M.
Res., 411 N. Second, 87301. Tel: 505-863-3033.
School—215 W. Wilson, 87301. Tel: 505-863-3145. Rev. Thomas Maikowski, Prin.
Sisters 2; Lay Teachers 6; Students 87.
Catechesis/Religious Programs—Sr. Annette O'Donnell, D.R.E.
Students 400.
Mission—Gamerco, St. Joseph the Worker.

3—ST. JEROME. Closed. For inquiries for parish records contact the Chancery.

4—ST. JOHN VIANNEY (1973), Rev. Walter Opalewski; Deacon Timothy Kelley.
Res., 3408 Zia Dr., 87301. Tel: 505-722-3361.
Catechesis/Religious Programs—Tel: 505-722-5085.
Students 149.
Mission—Bluewater, McKinley Co., Risen Savior, HC 62, Box 7129, Thoreav, 87323.

OUTSIDE THE CITY OF GALLUP, NEW MEXICO

Acoma, Cibola Co., San Esteban, Acoma Catholic Indian Mission (1629) (Native American), Revs. Antonio Trujillo, O.F.M.; Gary German, O.F.M. Pastoral Team: Ernest Vallo; Miriam Pritchard; Regina Shatira.
Res., P.O. Box 448, Pueblo of Acoma, 87034-0448. Tel: 505-552-6403. [CEM]
Catechesis/Religious Programs—Students 66.
Missions—Acomita, Cibola Co., St. Anne, P.O. Box 448, 87034.; McCartys, Cibola Co., Santa Maria de Acoma, 87034.

Aragon, Catron Co., Santo Nino, Rev. Patrick C. Wedeking; Deacon Juan Aragon.
Res., P.O. Box 493, 87830. Tel: 505-533-6240.
Missions—Lower San Francisco, San Isidro; Reserve, St. Francis; Horse Springs, St. Anne.
Station—Apache Creek.

Aztec, San Juan Co., St. Joseph (1946) (Hispanic), Rev. Luis J. Garcia, J.C.L.; Deacon Charles Peterson.
Res., 500 N. Mesa Verde St., 87410. Tel: 505-334-6535.
Catechesis/Religious Programs—Tel: 505-334-3542. Deacon Frank Chavez, D.R.E.
Students 267.

Blanco, San Juan Co., St. Rose, Rev. Daniel P. Daley.
Res., P.O. Box 417, 87412. Tel: 505-632-2064.
Catechesis/Religious Programs—Ms. Monique Bryant, D.R.E.
Students 87.
Mission—Los Martinez, Our Lady of Guadalupe.

Bloomfield, San Juan Co., St. Mary, Rev. Daniel P. Daley.
Res., 307 N. Church St., 87413. Tel: 505-632-2014.
Catechesis/Religious Programs—Sr. Edith Stichler, D.R.E.
Students 290.

Chichiltah, McKinley Co., St. Patrick Navajo Mission, Rev. Jeffrey King.
Res., P.O. Box 267, Vanderwagon, 87326. Tel: 505-778-5410.

Church Rock, McKinley Co., St. Philip Benizi, Rev. Francis C. Buck, S.J.
Res., P.O. Box 310, 87311. Tel: 505-488-5515.
Station—Pinedale.

Crownpoint, McKinley Co., St. Paul, Rev. Patrick J. Universal.
Res., P.O. Box 268, 87313. Tel: 505-786-7110; Fax: 505-786-5376.
Catechesis/Religious Programs—Peg Perez, M.R.E., D.R.E.
Students 35.
Mission—Star Lake, San Ignacio.
Station—Lake Valley.

Cuba, Sandoval Co., Immaculate Conception (Nacimiento), Rev. Eugene Bowski.
Res., P.O. Box 40, 87013. Tel: 505-289-3803.
Missions—La Jara, Santo Nino; San Luis, Saint Aloysius Gonzaga; Cabezon, San Jose; Guadalupe, Sacred Heart of Mary.
Station—Torrcon, Counselors.

Farmington, San Juan Co., Sacred Heart, Rev. Timothy Farrell.
Res., 414 N. Allen Ave., 87401. Tel: 505-325-9743; Fax: 505-325-8860.
Catechesis/Religious Programs—Sr. Rene Backe, C.S.A., D.R.E.
Students 433.

St. Mary's, Rev. Msgr. James Lindenmeyer; Deacon Paul Berhost. In res., Rev. Raymond Mahlmann.
Res., P.O. Box 2840, 87499-2840. Tel: 505-325-0287.
Catechesis/Religious Programs—James Hornecker, D.R.E.
Students 200.

Flora Vista, San Juan Co., Holy Trinity (1986) (Hispanic), Rev. Luis J. Garcia, J.C.L.; Deacons Frank Chavez; Charles Peterson.
Res., 500 N. Mesa Verde Ave., Aztec, 87410. Tel: 505-334-6535.

Fort Wingate, McKinley Co., St. Eleanor. Closed. For inquiries for parish records contact the Chancery.
Station—Iyanbito.

Grants, Cibola Co., St. Teresa, Rev. Emeric Nordmeyer, O.F.M. In res., Rev. Maurus Pax, O.F.M.; Bro. Arthur Puthoff, O.F.M.; Deacons Larry Chavez; Paul Sanchez.
Res., 213 Smith St., P.O. Box 668, 87020. Tel: 505-285-6645; Fax: 505-285-6646.
Catechesis/Religious Programs—Dina Calonge, D.R.E.
Students 450.

Laguna, Cibola Co., St. Joseph (Indian Pueblo), Revs. Antonio Trujillo, O.F.M.; Gary German, O.F.M.
Res., P.O. Box 1000, 87026. Tel: 505-552-9330.
Catechesis/Religious Programs—D.R.E.: Sr. Marcia Huber, S.M.I.C., (Youth); Sr. Virginia Adler, C.S.A, (Adult).
Students 120.
Missions—Encinal, Nativity of the Blessed Virgin Mary; Mesita, Sacred Heart; Paguate, St. Elizabeth; Paraje, St. Mary Margaret; Seama, St. Anne.

Lumberton, Rio Arriba Co., St. Francis of Assisi, Rev. Stephan B. Perzan (PH).
Res., P.O. Box 68, 87547. Tel: 505-759-3498.
Catechesis/Religious Programs—Sr. Carmelita Erdman, D.R.E.
Students 55.
Mission—Dulce, St. Anthony.

Milan, Cibola Co., St. Vivian, Rev. William Day; Deacon Timoteo P. Lujan.
Res., P.O. Box 2938, 87021. Tel: 505-287-9327.
Catechesis/Religious Programs—Sr. Angelita Rivera, H.N.S.G., D.R.E.
Students 165.

Navajo, McKinley Co., St. Berard, Rev. Niles E. Kraft, O.F.M.; Deacon Wilson Gorman. In res., Rev. Davin W. Von Hagel, O.F.M.
Res., P.O. Box 1284, 87328. Tel: 505-777-2251.
Catechesis/Religious Programs—Sr. Dorothy Dowd, S.B.S., D.R.E.
Students 60.
Mission—Sawmill, Apache Co., St. Francis Mission, P.O. Box 41, Sawmill, AZ 86549. Tel: 602-729-5224.
Station—Crystal.

Pinehaven, McKinley Co., Good Shepherd Catholic Mission, Rev. Jeffrey King.
Res., P.O. Box 2170, Gallup, 87305. Tel: 505-778-5658.
Convent—Box 267, Vanderwagen, 87326. Tel: 505-778-5740. Missionaries of Charity
Sisters 4.

Quemado, Catron Co., Sacred Heart, Rev. Thomas Coleman.
Res., P.O. Box 338, 87829. Tel: 505-773-4631.
Mission—Datil, Nativity of the Blessed Virgin Mary.

San Fidel, Cibola Co., St. Joseph. Unassigned.
Res., P.O. Box 370, 87049. Tel: 505-552-6236.
Mission—Cubero, Our Lady of Light.

San Mateo, Cibola and McKinley Cos., San Mateo, Rev. William Day.
Mailing Address: P.O. Box 14, 87050.
Res., P.O. Box 2938, Milan, 87021.

San Rafael, Cibola Co., San Rafael, Rev. William Day.
Res., P.O. Box 145, 87051. Tel: 505-287-8164.
Catechesis/Religious Programs—Sr. Ana Lilia Zuniga, H.N.S.G., D.R.E.
Students 88.

Seboyeta, Cibola Co., Our Lady of Sorrows, Rev. John Boland.
Res., P.O. Box 13, 87055. Tel: 505-552-6301.
Missions—Bibo, Our Lady of Loretto; Moquino, Santa Rosalia.
Station—Marquez.

Shiprock, San Juan Co., Christ the King, Rev. John Sauter.
Res., P.O. Box 610, 87420. Tel: 505-368-4532.

Thoreau, McKinley Co., St. Bonaventure. Unassigned.
Res., P.O. Box 1389, 87323. Tel: 505-862-7449.
Station—Smith Lake, Holy Spirit.

Tinaja, Cibola Co., San Lorenzo, Rev. Steve Pispeky.
Res., State Rte. 2, Box 47, Ramah, 87321. Tel: 505-783-4301.
Mission—Fence Lake, El Morro.

Tohatchi, McKinley Co., St. Mary Church, Revs. John Mittelstadt, O.F.M.; Pacian Meyer, O.F.M.; Bro. Michael Haag, O.F.M.; Deacon Sherman Manuelito.
Res., Box 39, 87325. Tel: 505-733-2243. [CEM]
Catechesis/Religious Programs—Sr. Patricia Bietsch, O.S.F., D.R.E.
Students 92.
Mission—Naschitti, St. Anthony.
Stations—Coyote Canyon; Mexican Springs; Twin Lakes; Sheep Springs; Chuska.

Waterflow, San Juan Co., Sacred Heart, Rev. Joachim Blonski.
Res., Rte. 1, Box 10, 87421. Tel: 505-598-5454.
Catechesis/Religious Programs—Gretchen Hohenberg, D.R.E.
Students 70.
Mission—Kirtland, San Juan Catholic Center Ojo Amarillo Mission.

Zuni, McKinley Co., St. Anthony Indian Mission, Our Lady of Guadalupe (Indian Pueblo), Revs. Dale Jamison, O.F.M.; Terence Rhodes, O.F.M.; Richard Maguire, Pastoral Min.
Res., P.O. Box 486, 87327. Tel: 505-782-2888.
School—St. Anthony Indian School, Tel: 505-782-4596. Sr. Patricia Glynn, F.S.P., Prin.
Sisters 4; Lay Teachers 10; Students 215.

ARIZONA

Alpine, Apache Co., St. Helena, Rev. Msgr. Arthur F. MacDonald.
Res., P.O. Box 229, 85920. Tel: 520-339-4363.
Missions—Glenwood, Catron Co., Santo Nino, P.O. Box 284, Glenwood, NM 88039.; Mogollon, Our Lady.

Chinle, Apache Co., Our Lady of Fatima, Indian Mission, Revs. Blane Grein, O.F.M.; Pio O'Connor, O.F.M.
Res., P.O. Box 2119, 86503. Tel: 520-674-5413.
Missions—Many Farms, St. Anthony, Tel: 520-781-6350; Pinon, Navajo Co., St. Mary of the Rosary, P.O. Box 432, Pinon, AZ 86510. Tel: 520-725-3365.
Stations—Salina Springs; Rough Rock; Black Mountain; Canyon Del Muerto; Cotton Wood; Nazlini.

Cibecue, Navajo Co., St. Catherine, Rev. Bernard Green, S.D.S.
Res., P.O. Box 156, 85911. Tel: 520-332-2311.
Mission—Cedar Creek, St. Anthony. (TUC).

Concho, Apache Co., San Rafael, Rev. Frank Chacon.
Church—P.O. Drawer C, 85924. Tel: 520-337-2515.

Fort Defiance, Apache Co., Our Lady of Blessed Sacrament, Revs. Martan Rademaker, O.F.M.; Meidon Hickey, O.F.M.; Deacon Dan Martin.
Res., P.O. Box 60, 86504-0060. Tel: 520-729-5068.
Catechesis/Religious Programs—Sr. Theresa Chato, S.B.S., D.R.E.
Students 98.

Ganado, Apache Co., All Saints, Rev. Flann O'Neil, O.F.M.
Res., P.O. Box 119, 86505. Tel: 520-755-3401.
Catechesis/Religious Programs—Sr. Maria Sarto Moreau, O.P., D.R.E.
Students 135.
Missions—Klagetoh, St. Anne. Bro. John Hotstream, S.C. Tel: 520-654-3236.; Greasewood, Our Lady of the Rosary. Bro. Paul O'Brien, O.F.M.
Stations—Cornfields; Wide Ruins.

Holbrook, Navajo Co., Our Lady of Guadalupe, Rev. Lawrence O'Keefe.
Res., 212 E. Arizona St., P.O. Box 250, 86025. Tel: 520-524-3261; Fax: 520-524-1507.
Catechesis/Religious Programs—Students 230.

Houck, Apache Co., St. John (Tekakwitha Mission), Rev. Valentine Young, O.F.M. In res., Rev. Conall P. Lynch, O.F.M.
Res., P.O. Box 48, 86506. Tel: 520-688-2921.
Catechesis/Religious Programs—Students 50.
Mission—Pine Springs, St. Rose.

Kayenta, Navajo Co., Our Lady of Guadalupe, Rev. Jerome Herff, C.M.
Res., P.O. Box 517, 86033. Tel: 520-697-3429.
Catechesis/Religious Programs—Students 74.
Stations—Chilchinbito; Shonto.

Keams Canyon, Navajo Co., St. Joseph's Indian Mission, Rev. Clayton F. Kilburn, C.M.
Res., P.O. Box 128, 86034. Tel: 520-738-2325.
Station—Toyei.

Lukachukai, Apache Co., St. Isabel Mission for Navajo Indians, Rev. Caron Vollmer, O.F.M.
Res., P.O. Box 128, 86507. Tel: 520-787-2322.
Missions—Round Rock, Our Lady of Guadalupe; Tsaile, St. Ann; Wheatfields, Our Lady of the Lake.

McNary, Apache Co., St. Anthony, Rev. Cyril Levy.
Res., P.O. Box 628, 85930. Tel: 520-334-2394.
Stations—Hawley Lake; The Ranch (Summer); Sunrise Ski Lodge (Winter).

Overgaard, Navajo Co., Our Lady of Assumption, Rev. Jose Rodriguez.
Res., P.O. Box 628, 85933. Tel: 520-535-5329.

Page, Coconino Co., Immaculate Heart of Mary, Revs. Mark Ford, C.M.; Louis Franz, C.M.; Deacon Roy Stringfellow.
Res., P.O. Box 1387, 86040. Tel: 520-645-2301.
Catechesis/Religious Programs—Students 110.

Pinetop, Apache Co., St. Mary of the Angels, Rev. Oliver Curran.
Res., Box 819, 85935. Tel: 520-367-2080; Fax: 520-367-2085.
Catechesis/Religious Programs—Mindy Savoia, D.R.E.
Students 161.

Pinon, Navajo Co., St. Mary of the Rosary. Attended by Chinle, AZ.
Res., P.O. Box 432, 86510. Tel: 520-725-3365.
Stations—Tachee; Blue Gap; Forest Lake; Whippoorwill Spring; Hardrock; Kits'iiLi.

Show Low, Navajo Co., St. Rita, Rev. Alberto Avella; Deacon John Heal.
Res., P.O. Box 1449, 85901. Tel: 520-537-2543.
Catechesis/Religious Programs—D.R.E.: Mary Sexton; Lucy Coen.
Students 79.

Snowflake, Navajo Co., Our Lady of the Snows, Rev. Jose Rodriguez; Deacons William J. Rogers; Anthony Scarabino.
Res., P.O. Box 1060, 85937. Tel: 520-536-4559.
Catechesis/Religious Programs—Mrs. John M. Heal, D.R.E.
Students 65.

Springerville, Apache Co., St. Peter, Rev. Robert Mathieu; Deacon George Campos.
Res., P.O. Box 1566, 85938. Tel: 520-333-4423.

St. Johns, Apache Co., St. John the Baptist, Rev. Frank Chacon.
Res., P.O. Box 309, 85936. Tel: 520-337-4390.
Catechesis/Religious Programs—Students 230.

St. Michaels, Apache Co., St. Michael, Rev. Simon Conrad, O.F.M. In res., Revs. Cormac Antram, O.F.M.; Lorenzo Ruiz, O.F.M.; Bros. John Friebel, O.F.M.; Francis Evans, O.F.M.; Gerald Grantner, O.F.M.; Maynard Shurley, O.F.M.
Res., P.O. Box 680, 86511-0680. Tel: 520-871-4171.
Catechesis/Religious Programs—D.R.E.: Sr. Josephine Goebel, C.S.A; Sr. Frances Rose Dinkel, C.S.A.
Students 90.
Mission—St. Michaels, St. Michael's Mission for Navajo Indians.

Tuba City, Coconino Co., St. Jude, Revs. Mark Ford, C.M.; J. Godden Menard, C.M.
Res., P.O. Box 248, 86045. Tel: 520-283-5391.

Whiteriver, Navajo Co., St. Francis Apache Indian, Rev. Edward Fronske, O.F.M.
Res., P.O. Box 778, 85941. Tel: 520-338-4432.
Catechesis/Religious Programs—Sr. Mary Hottenroth, S.B.S., D.R.E.
Students 87.

Winslow, Navajo Co., St. Joseph's, Rev. Michael A. Vigil.
Res., 300 W. Hillview St., 86047. Tel: 520-289-2350.
Catechesis/Religious Programs—Students 257.
Stations—Leupp; Dilcon; Seba Dalkai.
Madre de Dios, Rev. William Welch.
Res., 1015 Central St., 86047. Tel: 520-289-2010.
Catechesis/Religious Programs—J. Lopez, D.R.E.
Students 68.

Chaplains of Public Institutions

GALLUP. *Gallup Area Hospitals & Nursing Homes*, 506 W. 66 Ave., 87301. Tel: 505-722-0999. Rev. Hugh O'Neill.

Special Assignment:
Reverend Fathers—
Maikowski, Thomas, Dir. of Education

On Duty Outside of Diocese:
Reverend Fathers—
Bezzina, Benjamin, St. Mary's Catholic Church, 56 Burton St., Concord, New South Wales 2137 Australia
Casimano, Santino, Chap., Navsubase Nlon, Groton, CT 06349-5013
Coutu, Joseph, Most Holy Trinity Monastery, Dugway Rd., Petersham, MA 01366
DeGante, Adalberto, St. Anthony Parish, 327 South St., Sterling, CO 80751. Tel: 303-522-6422
Hussey, Daniel, CHC, USNR, 779-229 East Shore Terrace, Chula Vista, CA 91913
Llano, Isidoro
Mangampo, Gil, 2901 E. Yorba Linda Blvd., Fullterton, CA 92631. Tel: 714-985-1463
Morello, Peter, VA Medical, 650 E. Indian School Rd., Phoenix, AZ 85012
Perez, Rafael, St. Joseph Parish, 416 E. Second St., Lordsburg, NM 88045
Sanchez, Raul, Ch. Capt., USAF, 6933 Borderbrook Dr., Apt. 1313, San Antonio, TX. Tel: 210-670-7373
Turner, Robert, Blessed Sacrament Parish, 3100 S. 41st St., Milwaukee, WI 53215

Absent on Leave:
Reverend Fathers—
Buckley, James, P.O. Box 71037, Sanger, TX 76266
Finnegan, Kevin, St. Paul University Seminary, 249 Main St., Ottawa, Ontario, K1S 1C5 Canada
Kassis, Daniel, P.O. Box 4742, Laguna Beach, CA 92652-4742
Kugler, Michael, 304 N. 74th St., Milwaukee, WI 53213
Lopez, Adolfo
McConvey, Michael, 3 Argyll Ave., Bustin Brae Larne, Co. Antrim, Ireland
McNeill, Douglas, 488 7th Ave., Brooklyn, NY 11215
Mesley, Jerry
Obersteiner, Ernest, 67-918 Arden Dr., Cathedral City, CA 92234
Wollersheim, David, 1222 A Washington St., Apt. 1, Manitowoc, WI 54220

Retired:
Reverend Fathers—
Brackett, Joseph, Good Shepherd Manor, P.O. Box 10248, Albuquerque, NM 87184-0284
Budai, Frank A., 149530 Seneca Tr., P.O. Box 2709, Big River, CA 92242
Burns, James, P.O. Box 2155, Wickenburg, AZ 85378
Doyle, Gerald, P.O. Box 2131, Swansboro, NC 28584
Hart, William, P.O. Box 413, Castine, ME 04421
Manero, Ismael, Eladio Perlado 26-8C, Burgos, 09007
McLaughlin, Joseph
Smith, Norman, Mullen Home, 3629 W. 29th Ave., Denver, CO 80211
Stanfield, Francis E., 309 E. Logan Ave., Gallup, NM 87301

Permanent Deacons:
Aragon, Juan, Gen. Del., Aragon, NM
Aragon, Vidal, 324 Jane N.E., Albuquerque, NM 87123
Berhost, Paul, 2104 E. 17th St., Farmington, NM 87020
Bloomfield, John, P.O. Box 5024, Gallup, NM 87305
Calonge, Elie, 206 Smith St., Grants, NM 87020
Campos, George, P.O. Box 1254, Eagar, AZ 85925
Chavez, Frank, 341 Arnold Dr., Aztec, NM 87410
Chavez, Larry, P.O. Box 1883, Grants, NM 87020
Dooley, Paul, P.O. Box 2954, Gallup, NM 87301
Gorman, Wilson C., P.O. Box 218, Fort Defiance, AZ 86504-0218
Guoladdle, Bobby, HC61, Box 240, Winslow, NM 86047
Heal, John, P.O. Box 1429, Snowflake, AZ 85937
Hernandez, Arnold, St. Edwards Church, 610 W. Stevens, Carlsbad, NM 88220
Hoy, James, P.O Box 1084, Gallup, NM 87305
Kelley, Timothy, 416 Valentina Dr., Gallup, NM 87301
Krikawa, Joseph, P.O. Box 651, Gallup, NM 87305
Lane, John F., P.O. Box 1750, Fargo, ND 58107-1750
Lucero, Levy, 414 San Andreas, Alamogordo, NM 88310
Lujan, Timoteo, P.O. Box 2612, Milan, NM 87021-2612
Majesky, Russel, P.O. Box 139, Greer, AZ 85927
Manuelito, Sherman, P.O. Box 296, Tohatchi, NM 87325-0296
Martin, Daniel Nez, P.O. Box 724, Window Rock, AZ 86515
Moffett, Stephen, P.O. Box 4383, North Las Vegas, NV 89036
Peterson, Charles, 28 Rd. 3009, Aztec, NM 87410
Resendes, Daniel, 4514 N. Carlin Springs Rd., Arlington, VA 22203
Rogers, Earl, P.O. Box 283, La Plata, NM 87418
Rogers, William, P.O. Box 217, Taylor, AZ 85939-0217
Sanchez, Paul, 203 N. Nimitz, Grants, NM 89020
Scarabino, Anthony, P.O. Box 1278, Taylor, AZ 85939
Stando, Matthew, 2446 Harlem Rd., Cheektowaga, NY 14225
Starrs, William, 4580 N. Aqua Fria Dr., #A, Prescott Valley, AZ 86314
Stringfellow, Roy, P.O. Box 2559, Page, AZ 86040
Valencia, Ernest, P.O. Box 461, Blanco, NM 87412

INSTITUTIONS LOCATED IN THE DIOCESE

[A] SEMINARIES, DIOCESAN

GALLUP. *Diocesan Diaconate Formation Program*, P.O. Box 1338, 87305. Tel: 505-863-4406. Most Rev. Donald E. Pelotte; Deacons Timoteo Lujan, Dir.; Paul Dooley, Asst. Dir. Faculty: Revs. Alfred A. Tachias; Lawrence O'Keefe; Berard Doerger, O.F.M.; Meldon Hickey, O.F.M.; Dr. Emerine Glowienka, Ph.D.; Sr. Dolores Wright, O.S.F.; Sr. Ruth Battaglia, C.S.A.; Sr. Rene Bache, C.S.A.; Sr. Sarah Page, O.S.F., Ed.D. Diaconate Students 7.

CHINLE, AZ. *Native American Lay Ministry and Diaconate Program*, P.O. Box 2119, 86503. Rev. Blane Grein, O.F.M., Dir. Faculty: Rev. Pio O'Connor, O.F.M.; Bro. John Horstream, S.C.; Sr. Maureen Farrar, A.S.C.; Sr. Barbara Smith, A.S.C.; Sr. Dolores Wright, O.S.F.; Sr. Gloria Davis, S.B.S.; Sr. Marcia Huber, S.M.I.C. Students 57.

[B] HIGH SCHOOLS, PRIVATE

ST. MICHAELS, AZ. *St. Michael High School*, P.O. Box 650, 86511. Tel: 520-871-4443. John K. Reilly, Prin. Sisters 8; Lay Teachers 11; Students 149.

THOREAU. *St. Bonaventure High School*, 25 Navarre Blvd., Box 909, 87323. Tel: 505-862-7466. Steve Ward, Prin. Lay Teachers 11; Students 80.

[C] ELEMENTARY SCHOOLS, PRIVATE

GALLUP. *Gallup Catholic School*. (Grades PreK-11), 515 Park Ave., 87301. Tel: 505-863-6652. Donald Sparks, Prin. Lay Teachers 17; Students 254.

CUBA. *Immaculate Conception School*. (Grades K-8), P.O. Box 218, 87013. Tel: 505-289-3749. Robert Gutierrez, Prin. Sisters 1; Lay Teachers 6; Students 97.

FARMINGTON. *Sacred Heart School*. (Grades K-6), 404 N. Allen Ave., 87401. Tel: 505-325-7152. William Francis, Prin. Lay Teachers 9; Students 159.

GRANTS. *St. Teresa of Avila School*. (Grades K-8), P.O. Box 729, 87020. Tel: 505-287-2261. Marcia Lackey, Prin. Lay Teachers 13; Students 130.

LUMBERTON. *St. Francis School*. (Grades K-8), P.O. Box 26, 87528. Tel: 505-759-3252; Fax: 505-759-3844. Sr. Rose Marie Deibel, S.N.D.deN., Prin. Sisters 3; Lay Teachers 8; Students 85.

ST. MICHAELS, AZ. *St. Michael Indian School*, P.O. Box 650, 86511. Tel: 520-871-4636. Sr. Kathleen Kajer, Prin. (Elementary). Sisters 8; Lay Teachers 7; Students 265.

SAN FIDEL. *St. Joseph School*. (Grades K-6), P.O. Box 370, 87049. Tel: 505-552-6362. Sr. Michelle Geerken, Prin. Sisters 1; Lay Teachers 8; Students 103.

THOREAU. *St. Bonaventure School*. (Grades K-8), 25 Navarre Blvd., W., P.O. Box 909, 87323. Tel: 505-862-7465. Sr. Natalie Bussiere, S.N.D.deN., Prin. Sisters 2; Faculty 18; Students 190.

[D] CONVENTS AND RESIDENCES FOR SISTERS

GALLUP. *Carmelite Monastery*, P.O. Box 690, 191 Twin Buttes Rd., 87305-0690. Tel: 505-722-4516.

E-mail: mt.carmel@concentric.net
Discalced Carmelite Nuns. Mother Mary of the Angels, O.C.D., Prioress; Rev. Louis D. Konechne, Chap. Sisters 6.
Casa Reina, 217 E. Wilson, 87301. Tel: 505-722-5511. Sisters of Guadalupe and St. Joseph. Mother Magda, H.N.S.G., Supr.
Perpetual Adoration Chapel. Immigration and Naturalization Services, Hispanic Ministry. Sisters 16.
Our Lady of Mt. Carmel, 208 Cedar Ave., 87301. Tel: 505-722-9411; Fax: 505-863-5017. Sr. Rose Marie Holden, O.S.F., Dir. Residence for Indian girls.
St. Valerians Catholic Indian Center, 506 W. 66th Ave., 87301. Deacon James Hoy, Dir. Tel: 505-722-0999.

[E] HOMES FOR THE AGED

GALLUP. *Villa Guadalupe Home for the Aged*, 1900 Mark Ave., 87301. Tel: 505-863-6894. Sr. Celine Therese, L.S.P.; Rev. Alfred A. Tachias, Chap. Little Sisters of the Poor 8.

[F] MISCELLANEOUS LISTINGS

GALLUP. *Blue Army*. (Fatima Apostolate), 217 E. Wilson Ave., 87301. Tel: 505-722-5511. Mrs. Lillie Yepez, Pres.; Sr. Magda Leticia Garcia, Spiritual Dir.
Casa San Martin, 411 W. Wilson St., 87301. Tel: 505-722-5156. Soup Kitchen & Shelter for Native American Clients. Missionaries of Charity. Sr. M. Crispina, M.C., Supr. Convent, 207 E. Wilson Ave., 87301. Tel: 505-722-5261.
Gallup Catholic School Foundation, Inc., 515 Park Ave., 87301.
Sacred Heart Retreat, Zuni Hwy. S., P.O. Box 1989, 87305. Tel: 505-722-6755. Sr. Sarah Page, O.S.F.
Southwest Indian Foundation, 100 W. Coal Ave., P.O. Box 307, 87305. Tel: 505-863-9568.
E-mail: swif@cia-g.com
Mr. William McCarthy, Exec. Dir. Board of Directors: Mr. John Dowling, Pres.; Mr. James Mason, Vice Pres.; Mrs. Fred Melton, Sec.; Rev. Conall P. Lynch, O.F.M.; Hon. Judge Homer Bluehouse; Hon. Judge Marie Nezwood; Mrs. Mary Constant; Rev. Francis E. Stanfield; Mr. Daniel Deschiney; Sr. Beata Maria Stones, S.B.S.; Rev. Caron Vollmer, O.F.M.
CHINLE, AZ. *Talbot House-Catholic Charities*, P.O. Box 417, 86503. Tel: 520-674-3238. Sr. Adelaide Link, S.F.P., C.I.S.W., Dir. (Affiliated with Catholic Charities).
GRANTS-MILAN. *Casa San Jose*, 2595 W. Hwy. 66, P.O. Box 124, 87020. Tel: 505-285-5451. Sr. Francine Schuster, A.S.C., Admin. Residence of Pregnant teenagers. Operated by Catholic Charities. Sisters Adorers of the Blood of Christ 4.
PINETOP, AZ. *St. Vincent DePaul Society*. Thrift Shop & Emergency Aid Office. St. Mary of the Angels, P.O. Box 819, 85935. Tel: 520-367-2029; 3057. Ann C. Schultz, Pres.; Bill Schultz, Shop Mgr.; Barbara Parris, Emergency Aid Contact Person.
THOREAU. *St. Bonaventure Indian Mission & School*, 25 Navarre Blvd. W., P.O. Box 610, 87323. Tel: 505-862-7847; Fax: 505-862-7029. Hubert O'Reilly, Pres.; Barbara Morales; Dr. Franklin Freeland, Sec.; George Hanosh, Treas.
WINSLOW, AZ. *La Casa de Nuestra Senora*. Mission of Madonna House Apostolate Combermere, Ontario, Canada. 213 Jefferson St., 86047. Tel: 520-289-3007. Mariann Dunsmore, Dir.
Prayer and Social Service Center.

RELIGIOUS INSTITUTES OF MEN REPRESENTED IN THE DIOCESE

For further details refer to the corresponding bracketed number in the Religious Institutes of Men or Women section.
[1100]—*Brothers of the Sacred Heart*.—S.C.
[1330]—*Congregation of the Mission*.—C.M.
[0520]—*Franciscan Friars*. (Provs. of Our Lady of Guadalupe & St. Barbara).—O.F.M.
[1200]—*Society of the Divine Savior*.—S.D.S.

RELIGIOUS INSTITUTES OF WOMEN REPRESENTED IN THE DIOCESE

[0100]—*Adorers of the Blood of Christ*.—A.S.C.
[1810]—*Bernardine Sisters of the Third Order of St. Francis*.—O.S.F.
[3710]—*Congregation of the Sisters of Saint Agnes*.—C.S.A.
[0420]—*Discalced Carmelite Nuns*.—O.C.D.
[1070-03]—*Dominican Sisters*.—O.P.
[1070-06]—*Dominican Sisters*.—O.P.
[1070-13]—*Dominican Sisters*.—O.P.
[1070-09]—*Dominican Sisters*.—O.P.
[1070-14]—*Dominican Sisters*.—O.P.
[1120]—*Dominican Sisters of the Roman Congregation*.—O.P.
[1390]—*Franciscan Missionary Sisters of Our Lady of Sorrow*.—O.S.F.
[1350]—*Franciscan Missionary Sisters of the Immaculate Conception*.—O.S.F.
[1425]—*Franciscan Sisters of Peace*.—F.S.P.
[2340]—*Little Sisters of the Poor*.—L.S.P.
[2470]—*Maryknoll Sisters of St. Dominic*.—M.M.
[2710]—*Missionaries of Charity*.—M.C.
[2760]—*Missionary Sisters of the Immaculate Conception of the Mother of God*.—S.M.I.C.
[2850]—*Missionary Sisters of the Precious Blood*.—C.P.S.
[1640]—*Poor Sisters of St. Francis Seraph of the Perpetual Adoration*.—O.S.F.
[2970]—*School Sisters of Notre Dame*.—S.S.N.D.
[]—*Sisters for Christian Community*.—S.F.C.C.
[2360]—*Sisters of Loretto at the Foot of the Cross*.—S.L.
[2570]—*Sisters of Mercy*. (Erie, PA).—R.S.M.
[3000]—*Sisters of Notre Dame de Namur*.—S.N.D.deN.
[]—*Sisters of Our Lady of Guadalupe and St. Joseph, Inc.*
[1510]—*Sisters of St. Francis*.—O.S.F.
[1705]—*Sisters of St. Francis of Assisi*.
[1730]—*Sisters of St. Francis of Oldenburg*.—O.S.F.
[1650]—*The Sisters of St. Francis of Philadelphia*.—O.S.F.
[1550]—*Sisters of St. Francis of the Holy Cross*.—O.S.F.
[1660]—*Sisters of St. Francis of the Providence of God*.—O.S.F.
[0260]—*Sisters of the Blessed Sacrament for Indians and Colored People*.—S.B.S.
[1100]—*Sisters of the Divine Providence of Kentucky*.—C.D.P.
[1030]—*Sisters of the Divine Savior*.—S.D.S.
[1830]—*The Sisters of the Good Shepherd*.—R.G.S.
[1990]—*Sisters of the Holy Names of Jesus and Mary*.—S.N.J.M.
[2940]—*Sisters of the Most Holy Sacrament*.—M.H.S.
[1440]—*Sisters of the Poor of St. Francis*.—S.F.P.
[3260]—*Sisters of the Precious Blood (Dayton, OH)*.—C.PP.S.
[1800]—*Sisters of the Third Order Regular*.—O.S.F.
[4120-05]—*Ursuline Nuns of the Congregation of Paris*.—O.S.U.

NECROLOGY

† Quintana, Edward, (Retired). —Died Oct. 6, 1997.

Diocese of Galveston—Houston

(Dioecesis Galvestoniensis Houstoniensis)

Most Reverend

JOSEPH A. FIORENZA, D.D.

Bishop of Galveston-Houston; ordained May 29, 1954; appointed Bishop of San Angelo September 4, 1979; consecrated and installed October 25, 1979; appointed Bishop of Galveston-Houston December 18, 1984; installed February 18, 1985. *Office: 1700 San Jacinto, Houston, TX, 77002-8291. Mailing Address: P.O. Box 907, Houston, TX, 77001-0907.* Tel.: 713-659-5461.

Most Reverend

CURTIS JOHN GUILLORY, S.V.D., D.D.

Auxiliary Bishop of Galveston-Houston; ordained December 16, 1972; appointed Titular Bishop of Stagno and Auxiliary Bishop of Galveston-Houston December 29, 1987; consecrated February 19, 1988. *Mailing Address: P.O. Box 907, Houston, TX, 77001-0907. Office: 1700 San Jacinto, Houston, TX, 77002-8291.* Tel.: 713-659-5461.

Most Reverend

JAMES A. TAMAYO, D.D.

Auxiliary Bishop of Galveston-Houston; ordained June 11, 1976; appointed Titular Bishop of Ita and Auxiliary Bishop of Galveston-Houston January 26, 1993; consecrated March 10, 1993. *Mailing Address: P.O. Box 907, Houston, TX, 77001-0907. Office: 1700 San Jacinto, Houston, TX, 77002-8291.* Tel.: 713-659-5461.

Chancery Office: P.O. Box 907, Houston, TX, 77001-0907. Tel.: 713-659-5461; Fax: 713-759-9151.

ESTABLISHED IN 1847.

Square Miles 9,354.

REDESIGNATED DIOCESE OF GALVESTON-HOUSTON ON JULY 25, 1959.

Comprises the Counties of Madison, Walker, San Jacinto, Galveston, Grimes, Montgomery, Waller, Harris, Fort Bend, Brazoria and Austin in the State of Texas.

For legal titles of parishes and diocesan institutions, consult the Chancery Office.

STATISTICAL OVERVIEW

Personnel	
Bishop	1
Auxiliary Bishops	2
Priests: Diocesan Active in Diocese	144
Priests: Active Outside Diocese	9
Priests: Diocesan in Foreign Missions	1
Priests: Retired, Sick or Absent	37
Number of Diocesan Priests	191
Religious Priests in Diocese	225
Extern Priests in Diocese	38
Ordinations:	
Diocesan Priests	2
Religious Priests	1
Transitional Deacons	4
Permanent Deacons in Diocese	256
Total Brothers	19
Total Sisters	517
Parishes	
Parishes	151
With Resident Pastor:	
Resident Diocesan Priests	95
Resident Religious Priests	55
Without Resident Pastor:	
Administered by Priests	1
Missions	9
Pastoral Centers	18
New Parishes Created	1
Welfare	
Catholic Hospitals	4
Total Assisted	307,364
Health Care Centers	6
Total Assisted	68,946
Homes for the Aged	3
Total Assisted	275
Residential Care of Children	3
Total Assisted	166
Day Care and Extended Day Care Centers	34
Total Assisted	3,184
Specialized Homes	4
Total Assisted	1,428
Special Centers for Social Services	10
Total Assisted	446,647
Educational	
Seminaries, Diocesan	1
Students from This Diocese	15
Students from Other Diocese	32
Diocesan Students in Other Seminaries	20
Seminaries, Religious	5
Students Religious	20
Total Seminarians	55
Colleges and Universities	1
Total Students	2,506
High Schools, Diocesan and Parish	2
Total Students	410
High Schools, Private	6
Total Students	3,142
Elementary Schools, Diocesan and Parish	47
Total Students	12,372
Elementary Schools, Private	3
Total Students	748
Catechesis/Religious Education:	
High School Students	14,603
Elementary Students	62,835
Total Students Under Catholic Instruction	96,671
Teachers in the Diocese:	
Priests	15
Brothers	3
Sisters	58
Lay Teachers	1,263
Vital Statistics	
Receptions into the Church:	
Infant Baptism Totals	17,053
Adult Baptism Totals	1,285
Received into Full Communion	955
First Communions	14,793
Confirmations	7,078
Marriages:	
Catholic	2,716
Interfaith	1,075
Total Marriages	3,791
Deaths	3,405
Total Catholic Population	862,369
Total Population	4,298,663

Former Bishops—Rt. Rev. J. M. ODIN, C.M., D.D., cons. Bishop of Claudiopolis and Vicar-Apostolic of Texas, March 6, 1842; transferred to Galveston 1847; promoted to New Orleans in 1861; died in Ambierle, France, May 25, 1870; Rt. Rev. C. M. DUBUIS, D.D., cons. Nov. 23, 1862; resigned 1881 remained Titular Bishop of Galveston till 1892, when he was promoted to an Archbishopric *i.p.i.; died May 21, 1895* at Vernaison, France; Rt. Rev. P. DUFAL, C.S.C., D.D., cons. Nov. 25, 1860; Bishop of Delcon, and Vicar-Apostolic of Eastern Bengal; transferred to Galveston as Coadjutor of Rt. Rev. C. M. DUBUIS, *cum jure successionis,* May 14, 1878; resigned 1880; died in Paris 1898; Rt. Rev. NICHOLAS A. GALLAGHER, D.D., cons. Titular Bishop of Canopus, April 30, 1882; succeeded to Galveston, Dec. 16, 1892; died Jan. 21, 1918; Most Rev. CHRISTOPHER E. BYRNE, D.D., appt. July 18, 1918; cons. Nov. 10, 1918 made Assistant at the Pontifical Throne, May 8, 1941; died April 1, 1950.—Most Rev. WENDELIN J. NOLD, S.T.D., appt. Nov. 29, 1947; cons. Feb. 25, 1948; died Oct. 1, 1981; Most Rev. JOHN L. MORKOVSKY, S.T.D., ord. Dec. 5, 1933; Titular Bishop of Hieron and Auxiliary Bishop of Amarillo; appt. Dec. 22, 1955; cons. Feb. 22, 1956; succeeded to See Aug. 18, 1958; transferred to Galveston-Houston as Titular Bishop of Tigava and Coadjutor and Apostolic Administrator *"cum jure successionis"*April 1963; installed June 11, 1963; succeeded to the See of Galveston-Houston, April 22, 1975; retired Aug. 16, 1984; died March 24, 1990.

Chancery Office—1700 San Jacinto St., Houston, 77002-8291., P.O. Box 907, Houston, 77001-0907. Office Hours: Mon.-Fri. 8:30-4:30. Tel: 713-659-5461; Fax: 713-759-9151.

Chancellor and Moderator of the Curia—Rev. FRANK H. ROSSI, S.T.L., *1700 San Jacinto St., Houston, 77002-8291., P.O. Box 907, Houston, 77001-0907.* Tel: 713-659-5461.

Vice Chancellor—Rev. R. TROY GATELY, *1700 San Jacinto St., Houston, 77002-8291., P.O. Box 907, Houston, 77001-0907.* Tel: 713-659-5461., *Christ the King Rectory, 4419 N. Main, Houston, 77009-5199.* Tel: 713-869-1440; 863-3140.

Vicars General—Most Rev. CURTIS JOHN GUILLORY, S.V.D., *1700 San Jacinto St., Houston, 77002-8291., P.O. Box 907, Houston, 77001-0907.* Tel: 713-659-5461. Most Rev. JAMES A. TAMAYO, D.D., *1700 San Jacinto St., Houston, 77002-8291., P.O. Box 907, Houston, 77001-0907.* Tel: 713-659-5461. Rev. Msgr. VINCENT M. RIZZOTTO, *11720 Joan of Arc, Houston, 77024-2602.* Tel: 713-465-3414.

Ethnic Vicars—Most Rev. CURTIS JOHN GUILLORY, S.V.D., Vicar of African American Catholics; Most Rev. JAMES A. TAMAYO, D.D., Vicar of Hispanic Catholics; Rev. ANTHONY CHINH QUANG DAO, O.P., Vicar of Vietnamese Catholics; Rev. Msgr. SETH HERMOSO, Vicar of Filipino Catholics.

Vicar for Religious—Sr. M. ADELINE O'DONOGHUE, C.C.V.I., *6510 Lawndale, Houston, 77023.* Tel: 713-928-6053.

Spiritual Director for Priests—Vacant.

Parish Priest Consultor—Rev. Msgr. JOSEPH H. CROSTHWAIT, *P.O. Box 1302, New Ulm, 78950.* Tel: 409-992-3821.

Finance Officer and Business Manager—Mr. THOMAS B. O'TOOLE, *1700 San Jacinto St., Houston, 77002-8291., P.O. Box 907, Houston, 77001-0907.* Tel: 713-659-5461.

Diocesan Tribunal—1700 San Jacinto St., Houston, 77002-8291., P.O. Box 907, Houston, 77001-0907. Tel: 713-659-5461.

Judicial Vicar—Rev. LAWRENCE JOZWIAK, J.C.L., *Chancery Bldg., P.O. Box 907, Houston, 77001-0907.* Tel: 713-659-5461.

Adjutant Judicial Vicar—Rev. FRED CHALUPA, J.C.L., *P.O. Box 907, Houston, 77001-0907.* Tel: 713-659-5461.

Diocesan Judges—Rev. Msgr. T. JOSEPH CULVER; Rev. Msgr. PHILIPPE LE-XUAN THUONG, J.C.D.; Revs. ROBERT BARRAS; ERIC PITRE; ANTON SHELTZ; STEPHEN P. ZIGRANG, J.C.L.

Promotor of Justice—Rev. Msgr. VINCENT M. RIZZOTTO, J.C.L.

Defender of the Bond—Rev. FRED CHALUPA, J.C.L.

Censor Librorum—Rev. TERENCE BRINKMAN, S.T.D., *2302 Oak Shores Dr., Kingwood, 77339-1801.* Tel: 281-358-6637.

Deans and Vicariates—

Central Vicariate—Most Rev. CURTIS J. GUILLORY, S.V.D., V.G., Episcopal Vicar. Tel: 713-659-5461. Rev. ISIDORE GARCIA, O.M.I., V.F., Central Dean. Tel: 713-224-5291. Rev. GARY F. WANZONG, V.F., Northeast Dean. Tel: 713-631-3681. Rev. PAUL CHOVANEC, V.F., Southeast Dean. Tel: 713-645-6614.

Northern Vicariate—Rev. GEORGE A. SHELTZ, Episcopal Vicar. Tel: 281-469-2686. Rev. Msgr. DAVID W. KENNEDY, V.F., Northern Dean. Tel: 409-756-8186. Rev. JOHN A. ZABELSKAS, V.F., Eastern Dean. Tel: 281-843-2422. Rev. PAUL PROCELLA, V.F., San Jacinto Dean. Tel: 281-446-8211.

Southern Vicariate—Rev. Msgr. T. JOSEPH CULVER, E.V., Episcopal Vicar. Tel: 409-938-7000. Rev. Msgr. MILAM E. KLEAS, V.F., Galveston-Mainland Dean. Tel: 281-337-4112. Rev. TOM RAFFERTY, V.F., Bay Area Dean. Tel: 281-471-2000. Rev. Msgr. LEO WLECZYK, V.F., Southern Dean. Tel: 409-297-3041.

Western Vicariate—Rev. Msgr. WILLIAM M. PICKARD, E.V., Episcopal Vicar. Tel: 713-774-7475. Rev. DANIEL WARDEN, V.F., Western Dean. Tel: 281-342-3089. Rev. Msgr. EDWARD RANDALL, V.F., Southwest Dean. Tel: 713-789-1250. Rev. ADAM S. MCCLOSKEY, V.F., Northwest Dean. Tel: 281-955-7324. Rev. EDWARD KUCERA, V.F., Bluebonnet Dean. Tel: 409-826-2275.

Secretariat Directors—

Secretariat For Christian Formation—Sr. MARY GRACE O'BRIEN, C.V.I., Dir., *2403 Holcombe Blvd., Houston, 77021-2099.* Tel: 713-741-8786.

Secretariat for Family and Social Concerns—Mrs. SUSAN STROMATT, Dir., *2403 Holcombe Blvd., Houston, 77021-2099.* Tel: 713-741-8769.

Secretariat For Administration—Mr. THOMAS B. O'TOOLE, Dir., *1700 San Jacinto St., Houston, 77002-8291., P.O. Box 907, Houston, 77001-0907.* Tel: 713-659-5461.

Secretariat For Communication—Mr. RON REGAN, Dir., *1700 San Jacinto St., Houston, 77002-8291., P.O. Box 907, Houston, 77001-0907.* Tel: 713-659-5461.

Secretariat For Special Services—Rev. FRANK H. ROSSI, Dir., *1700 San Jacinto St., Houston, 77002-8291., P.O. Box 907, Houston, 77001-0907.* Tel: 713-659-5461.

Diocesan Councils, Commissions and Committees—

Diocesan Presbyteral Council—Rev. HUGH KEALY, Chm., *1700 San Jacinto St., Houston, 77002-8291., P.O. Box 907, Houston, 77001-0907.* Tel: 281-498-4653.

Presbyteral Council—Most Rev. CURTIS J. GUILLORY, S.V.D.; Most Rev. JAMES A. TAMAYO, D.D.; Revs. DREW WOOD; MARIO ARROYO; DOUGLAS J. HYPOLITE, S.J.; GEORGE A. SHELTZ; Rev. Msgr. WILLIAM M. PICKARD; Revs. ANTHONY DAO, O.P.; HUBERT KEALY; Rev. Msgr. T. JOSEPH CULVER; Revs. DAVID CARDENAS; DON KUDER, C.S.B.; PAUL PROCELLA; Rev. Msgr. VINCENT M. RIZZOTTO; Rev. FRANK H. ROSSI; Rev. Msgr. DANIEL SCHEEL; Rev. DAN WARDEN.

College of Consultors—Most Rev. CURTIS J. GUILLORY, S.V.D.; Most Rev. JAMES A. TAMAYO, D.D.; Rev. Msgr. JOSEPH H. CROSTHWAIT; Rev. Msgr. DANIEL SCHEEL; Rev. Msgr. CHESTER L. BORSKI; Rev. Msgr. T. JOSEPH CULVER; Rev. Msgr. VINCENT M. RIZZOTTO, J.C.L.; Rev. FRANK H. ROSSI, S.T.L.

Priests Personnel Committee—Rev. Msgr. VINCENT M. RIZZOTTO, J.C.L., Chm., *11720 Joan of Arc, Houston, 77024-2602.* Tel: 713-465-3414. Rev. Msgr. GENE FRANCIS; Revs. DENNIS PETERSON; STEVE TIEMANN; FRANK H. ROSSI; GEORGE A. SHELTZ, V.F.; PHILIP WILHITE.

Building Commission—Rev. Msgr. CHARLES C. DOMEC, Chm., *26777 Glen Loch Rd., The Woodlands, 77381-2921.* Tel: 281-367-9885. Rev. Msgr. T. JOSEPH CULVER; Rev. Msgr. EDWARD RANDALL; Mr. TONY ROURKE; Mr. BILL MAREK; Rev. ANTON SHELTZ.

Board of Education—Mr. JAMES MCLAIN, Pres., *Chancery Bldg., at St. Dominic Center.* Tel: 713-741-8786.

Ecumenism and Interreligious Affairs Commission—Mrs. GARLAND POHL, Chm., *8003 Mobud, Houston, 77036-6403.* Tel: 713-774-0097.

Liturgical Commission—Rev. WILLIAM OLIVER, Coord.

Diocesan Departments and Offices

Archives—Ms. LISA MAY, Dir., *1700 San Jacinto St., Houston, 77002-8291., P.O. Box 907, Houston, 77001-0907.* Tel: 713-659-5461.

Accounting Department—Mrs. NANCY HEISLER, Dir., *1700 San Jacinto St., Houston, 77002-8291., P.O. Box 907, Houston, 77001-0907.* Tel: 713-659-5461.

African American Ministry—Ms. CHARLOLETTE DAVIS, Dir., *2403 Holcombe Blvd., Houston, 77021-2098.* Tel: 713-741-8733.

Aging Ministry—Sr. DOROTHY SACHNIK, C.V.I., Dir., *2403 Holcombe Blvd., Houston, 77021-2098.* Tel: 713-741-8712.

Apostleship of Prayer—Vacant.

Apostleship of the Sea (Port Ministry)—Rev. RIVERS PATOUT, Houston Dir., *9217 E. Ave. L., Houston, 77012-2727.* Tel: 713-923-5843; 926-7669 (Rectory)., *Houston International Seaman's Center, P.O. Box 9506, Houston, 77261.* Tel: 713-672-0511. Galveston: Mrs. KAREN LAI, *2002 Mechanic, Galveston, 77550.* Tel: 409-762-0021.

Boy and Girl Scouts—Rev. Msgr. T. A. WENDLAND, Dir., *3600 Brinkman Rd., Houston, 77018-6329.* Tel: 713-692-9123.

Campus Ministry—Sr. MARY GRACE O'BRIEN, Sec.-Dir., *2403 Holcombe Blvd., Houston, 77021-2098.* Tel: 713-741-8786.

Catholic Cemeteries—Mr. TERRANCE D. MULCARE, Dir., *P.O. Box 965 (Gulf Fwy. at Hughes Rd.), Dickinson, 77539.* Tel: 281-337-1641; 409-948-1455.

Catholic Chaplain Corps (Hospital Chaplains)—Rev. ALCUIN E. GREENBURG, Dir., *4206 MacGregor Way S., Houston, 77021-1598.* Tel: 713-526-6438.

Associated Catholic Charities—Mrs. ANNA BABIN, Dir., *3520 Montrose Blvd., Houston, 77006-4387.* Tel: 713-526-4611; Fax: 713-526-1546.

Associate Executive Director Program Services—YOLANDA SANTOS, P.H.

Associate Executive Director Finance and Support Services—MICHAEL J. PIERI, C.P.A.

Director, Fund Development/Marketing—JULIE PLATEK, M.S.W.

Children Services—VALERIE PERALES, L.M.S.W.-A.C.P., Admin.

Children Placement Services Adoption and Foster Care—SHARON JORGESON, L.M.S.W., Supvr., *St. Joseph Inn, P.O. Box 8275, Galveston, 77553.* ELLEN HANLEY, Prog. Coord. Tel: 409-765-5343.

Services to Pregnant Adolescents and Their Families—SYLVIA ALANIS, L.M.S.W.-A.C.P., A.C.S.W., Supvr.

Post Adoption Services—MARY LOU KELLY, L.M.S.W., Supvr.

Community Outreach Services—KATHERINE BINGHAM, M.P.H.

Diocesan AIDS Ministry—THERESA GOMEZ, Prog. Coord.-Interim Dir., *3400 Montrose #400, Houston, 77006.* Tel: 713-524-0182.

Guadalupe Area Social Services—YOLANDA GUTIERREZ, L.M.S.W., Supvr., *326 S. Jensen, Houston, 77003-1599.* Family Assistance Program, La Casita, Villa Guadalupe-Transitional Housing for Women.

Parish Social Ministry—ESMERALDA CERVANTES, Coord.

Serenity House—Temporary housing for medical center patient's families. KATHERINE BINGHAM, M.P.H.

Services to the Alone and Frail Elderly—KATHERINE BINGHAM, M.P.H., In Formation: Tel: 713-520-7835.

Family Counseling—CAROL KELLEHER, Ph.D., Admin. CAROL KELLEHER, Ph.D., Supvr., Prevention Services; DAVID QUIROZ, L.M.S.W.-A.C.P., L.P.C., Supervising Family Counseling. Tel: 713-668-5763; 526-4611, Ext. 3500 (Appointments); Fax: 713-527-9198 (Family Counseling).

Immigration Services—JANET WAITES, Admin.

Texas Center for Immigrant Legal Assistance—SUSIE MAXWELL, Supvr. Tel: 713-529-9382.

Parish Social Ministry—

St. Joseph's Inn—

Project Learn—JANET WAITES, Supvr. Tel: 713-229-0220.

Refugee Resettlement Services—JANET WAITES, Supvr. Tel: 713-526-5812.

Undocumented and Unaccompanied Juvenile Foster Care—CONNIE HIDALGO, Supvr. Tel: 713-526-4611.

Outreach Services—KATHY BINGHAM. Tel: 713-520-7835.

Needy Family Services—YOLANDA GUITIERREZ, Supvr. Tel: 713-520-9561.

Services to the Elderly—KATHY BINGHAM, Supvr. Tel: 713-520-9561.

Serenity House—KATHY BINGHAM. Tel: 713-526-4611, Ext. 3268.

Direct Services: Counseling, Adoption, Foster Care, Services to Young Parents—SHARON JORGESON, Admin.

Catholic Charities Galveston—Mrs. JANE AYALA, Dir., *4418 Ave. M, Galveston, 77550-3726.* Tel: 409-762-2062.

Catholic Relief Services—Mrs. HILDA HERNANDEZ, Dir., *Chancery Bldg., 1700 San Jacinto St., Houston, 77002-8921. P.O. Box 907, Houston, 77001-0907.* Tel: 713-659-5461.

Computer Network Manager—Mr. ED HERRERA, *Chancery Bldg., 1700 San Jacinto St., Houston, 77002-8921. P.O. Box 907, Houston, 77001-0907.* Tel: 713-659-5461.

Community Relations—Mrs. SUSAN STROMATT, *2403 Holcombe Blvd., Houston, 77021-2099.* Tel: 713-741-8731.

Continuing Christian Education—Mrs. JOANNE SANDERS, Dir., *2403 Holcombe Blvd., Houston, 77021-2099.* Tel: 713-741-8730.

Construction/Preventative Maintenance—Mr. TONY ROURKE, Dir., *Chancery Bldg., 1700 San Jacinto St., Houston, 77002-8291. P.O. Box 907, Houston, 77001-0907.* Tel: 713-659-5461. Mr. RANDY ALLEN, Preventive Maintenance.

Correctional Ministries (Jail Chaplains)—Rev. RONALD F. CLOUTIER, Dir. (Chaplain Office at Harris County Jail), Office and Mailing Address: *2403 E. Holcombe Blvd., Houston, 77021-2098.* Tel: 713-869-1449., *215 E. 10th St., Houston, 77008-7025.* Tel: 713-864-2653.

Council of Catholic Women—Rev. Msgr. THOMAS A. WENDLAND, Dir., *3600 Brinkman Rd., Houston, 77018-6329.* Tel: 713-692-9123. Rev. Msgr. LEO WLECZYK, Assoc. Moderator, *100 Oak Dr., S., Lake Jackson, 77566-5630.* Tel: 409-297-3041.

Cursillos in Christianity—Rev. JOSE MARIA FERNANDEZ, Dir., *4419 N. Main, Houston, 77009-5199.* Tel: 713-869-1449. *St. Paul Cursillo Center, 4000 Belk St., Houston, 77087.* Tel: 713-643-7682.

Deaf Apostolate—Rev. ROBERT BEK, C.SS.R., Dir., *St. Dominic Center, 2401 Holcombe Blvd., Houston, 77021-2099.* Tel: 713-741-8721.

Development Office—Vacant, *1700 San Jacinto St., Houston, 77002-8291. P.O. Box 907, Houston, 77001-0907.* Tel: 713-659-5461.

Diaconal Formation/Diaconal Ministry—Rev. Msgr. JACK M. DINKINS, Dir., *1530 Norwalk Dr., Katy, 77450-4999.* Tel: 281-578-0707.

Permanent Deacons—Mr. FRED SHETZ, Dir., *1700 San Jacinto St., Houston, 77002-8291. P.O. Box 907, Houston, 77001-0907.* Tel: 713-659-5461.

Diocesan Services Fund—Mrs. BARBARA SCIONEAUX, Dir., *Lock Box 200562, Houston, 77216. 1700 San Jacinto St., Houston, 77002-8291.* Tel: 713-659-5461.

Disaster Relief—Rev. REGINALD PETRASH, Dir., *St. Mary Star of the Sea Church, 1019 W. 6th St., Freeport, 77541-5423.* Tel: 409-233-5271.

Family Life Ministry—Mrs. WINIFRED HONEYWELL, Dir., *St. Dominic Center, 2403 Holcombe Blvd., Houston, 77021-2099.* Tel: 713-741-8710.

Hispanic Ministry—Mr. PEDRO MORENO, Dir., *2403 E. Holcombe Blvd., Houston, 77021-2099.* Tel: 713-741-8727.

Risk Manager/Legal Services—Mr. ROBERT SCAMARDO, Dir., *Chancery Bldg., 1700 San Jacinto St., Houston, 77002-8291. P.O. Box 907, Houston, 77001-0907.* Tel: 713-659-5461.

Internal Auditor—Mr. CHARLES ROBINSON, Dir., *1700 San Jacinto St., Houston, 77002-8291. P.O. Box 907, Houston, 77001-0907.* Tel: 713-659-5461.

Land Specialist—Mr. KEN SYKES, *1700 San Jacinto St., Houston, 77002-8291. P.O. Box 907, Houston, 77001-0907.* Tel: 713-659-5461.

Marian Activities—Mrs. LEE BOWERS, *St. Dominic Center, 2403 Halcombe Blvd., Houston, 77021-2099.* Tel: 281-741-8721.

Media Center—Mrs. GALE HANKS, Dir., *2403 E. Holcombe Blvd., Houston, 77021-2099.* Tel: 713-741-8781.

Mission Office—Mrs. HILDA HERNANDEZ, Dir., *Chancery Bldg., 1700 San Jacinto St., Houston, 77002-8291., P.O. Box 907, Houston, 77001-0907.* Tel: 713-659-5461. Holy Childhood, Propagation of the Faith.

Oremus Pro Invicem—Rev. Msgr. FRANCIS G. WEARDEN, Dir., *1100 Parthenon Pl., New Caney, 77357-3039.* Tel: 281-399-0270.

Parish Accounting Services (PAS)—Mrs. PAT MITCHELL, Dir., *1700 San Jacinto St., Houston, 77002-8291. P.O. Box 907, Houston, 77001-0907.* Tel: 713-659-5461.

Parish Social Ministry / (CHD)—*Chancery at St. Dominic's Diocesan Center, 2403 E. Holcombe Blvd., Houston, 77021-2099.* Tel: 713-741-8730.

Personnel—Mr. FRED SHETZ, Dir.

Benefits—Mrs. DAWN GIBLIN, Dir.

Parish Development—Mr. THOM JONES, Dir., *1700 San Jacinto St., Houston, 77002-8291. P.O. Box 907, Houston, 77001-0907.* Tel: 713-659-5461.

Radio—Mrs. MADELINE JOHNSON, Dir., *1700 San Jacinto St., Houston, 77002-8291. P.O. Box 907, Houston, 77001-0907.* Tel: 713-659-5461.

Records—Miss MARY ANN ACOSTA, Dir., *1700 San Jacinto St., Houston, 77002-8291. P.O. Box 907, Houston, 77001-0907.* Tel: 713-659-5461.

Respect Life Office—Mrs. MARCELLA COLBERT, Dir., *2403 Holcombe Blvd., Houston, 77021-2098.* Tel: 713-225-5826; 741-8730 (Main Tel.).

Claims Risk Manager—Mr. JAMES QUATTRINI, Dir., *2403 Holcombe Blvd., Houston, 77021-2099.* Tel: 713-741-8758; 800-856-4040; Fax: 713-748-3205.

Rural Life Bureau—Rev. FRANK H. ROSSI, *1700 San Jacinto St., Houston, 77002-8291. P.O. Box 907, Houston, 77001-0907.* Tel: 713-659-5461.

Seminarian Support—Rev. STEPHEN E. TIEMANN, Dir., *1700 San Jacinto St., Houston, 77002-8291. P.O. Box 907, Houston, 77001-0907.* Tel: 713-659-5461.

Catholic School Office—Sr. COLLEEN HENNESSEY, S.S.N.D., Supt., *2403 Holcombe Blvd., Houston, 77021-2099.* Tel: 713-741-8704.

School of Environmental Education - Camp Kappe—Sr. THOMAS ANN LACOUR, O.P., Dir., *Rte. 2, Box 3197, Navasota, 77868.* Tel: 409-894-2141.

St. Dominic Diocesan Center—Mr. JIM HORSTMAN, Mgr., *2401 E. Holcombe Blvd., Houston, 77021-2024.* Tel: 713-741-8741.

St. Vincent de Paul Society—Sr. YVONNE WUENSCHE, Dir., *2403 Holcombe Blvd., Houston, 77021-2099.* Tel: 713-741-8783.

Stewardship—Mr. ADAM MARTINEZ, Dir., *1700 San Jacinto St., Houston, 77002-8291.* Tel: 713-659-5461., *P.O. Box 907, Houston, 77001-0907.*

Texas Catholic Herald—Ms. JACQUELINE SROUJI, Editor, *1700 San Jacinto St., Houston, 77002-8291. P.O. Box 907, Houston, 77001-0907.* Tel: 713-659-5461. Saturdays & Holidays. Tel: 713-659-3702; Fax: 713-659-3444.

Vocations Office—Rev. STEPHEN E. TIEMANN, Dir., *1700 San Jacinto St., Houston, 77002-8291. P.O. Box 907, Houston, 77001-0907.* Tel: 713-659-5461.

Worship—Mrs. PAT KERWIN, Dir., *2403 Holcombe Blvd., Houston, 77021-2099.* Tel: 713-741-8760.

Youth Ministry—Bro. JIM BARRETTE, S.M., Dir., *2403 E. Holcombe Blvd., Houston, 77021-2099.* Tel: 713-741-8723.

Special Youth Services (Juvenile Detention Ministry)—MARILU BALLOW, Dir., *2403 Holcombe Blvd., Houston, 77021-2099.* Tel: 713-527-1894; 762-7192 (Pager).

CLERGY, PARISHES, MISSIONS AND PAROCHIAL SCHOOLS

CITY OF GALVESTON
(Galveston County)

1—ST. MARY'S CATHEDRAL BASILICA (1847), Rev. Charles J. Coffey, C.S.Sp. In res., Revs. Edward Baur, S.V.D.; Gerald Lewis, S.V.D.; Deacon John S. Pistone.
Res., 2011 Church St., 77550-2091. Tel: 409-762-9611; Fax: 409-765-8585.

2—HOLY ROSARY (1888), Rev. Paul H. Banet, S.S.J. In res., Revs. Robert DeGrandis, S.S.J.; Charles H. Banet, C.PP.S.
Res., 1420 31st St., 77550-4399. Tel: 409-762-2478; Fax: 409-762-8383.

3—OUR LADY OF GUADALUPE. Closed. August 1992. Contact Chancery for further information.

4—ST. PATRICK (1870), Revs. Page E. Polk, O.F.M.; Matthew Holahan, O.F.M.; Deacon Tom Hunter.
Church—1010 35th St., 77550. Fax: 409-765-7636.
Res., 3420 Avenue K, 77550-4091. Tel: 409-762-9646.
Catechesis / Religious Programs—Jo Anita Jefferies, D.R.E.
Students 264.
Mission—Galveston, Galveston Co., Queen of Peace Mission, 706 51st St., 77551. Tel: 409-762-2833; Fax: 409-765-9747. Rev. Serafin Cejudo.

5—ST. PETER THE APOSTLE (1967), Rev. William D. Bartniski; Deacon William J. Bobb.
Res., 1805 Driftwood Ln., 77551-1399. Tel: 409-744-3561; Fax: 409-744-4286.
Catechesis / Religious Programs—Tel: 409-744-7250. Randy Adams, D.R.E.
Students 142.
Mission—Jamaica Beach, Galveston Co., Mary, Star of the Sea.

6—SACRED HEART (1884), Rev. Frank T. Fabj.
Res., 1302 Broadway, 77550-6198. Tel: 409-762-6374; Fax: 409-762-0919.
Catechesis / Religious Programs—Students 212.

CITY OF HOUSTON
(Harris County)

1—SACRED HEART CO-CATHEDRAL (1896), Rev. Msgr. Philippe La-Xuan-Thuong, J.C.D., S.T.L.; Rev. Stephen E. Tiemann; Deacon Marvin R. Fikac. In res., Rev. R. Troy Gately.
Res., 1111 Pierce St., 77002-8195. Tel: 713-659-1561; 1562; Fax: 713-739-1306.
Catechesis / Religious Programs—Paul Parker, D.R.E.
Students 140.

2—ALL SAINTS (1908), Rev. Carl Tenhundfeld; Deacon Frank Matula. In res., Rev. Ronald F. Cloutier.
Res., 215 E. 10th St., 77008-7025. Tel: 713-864-2653; Fax: 713-864-0761.
Catechesis / Religious Programs—Natalia Pena, D.R.E.
Students 315.

3—ST. ALBERT OF TRAPANI (1970), Revs. Mark J. Schaffner, O.Carm.; Sylvan Boyle, O.Carm.
Res., 11027 S. Gessner Dr., 77071-3599. Tel: 713-771-3596; Fax: 713-270-0441.
Catechesis / Religious Programs—Peggy Popkey, D.R.E.
Students 395.

4—ST. ALPHONSUS (1968), Rev. Rivers A. Patout, Coord. Port Min.; Sr. Lucinda Gonzalez, Admin. & Pastoral Assoc.
Res., 9217 E. Ave. L, 77012-2299. Tel: 713-923-5843; Fax: 713-923-5843.
Catechesis / Religious Programs—Tel: 713-644-7008. Ophelia Martinez, D.R.E.
Students 203.

5—ST. AMBROSE (1958), Revs. Joseph A. Gietl; Philip A. Wilhite, S.T.L. In res., Rev. Franklin Simmons, Chap. Corps.
Res., 4213 Mangum Rd., 77092-5599. Tel: 713-686-3497; Fax: 713-686-6604.
School—Tel: 713-686-6990; Fax: 713-686-6902. Mrs. Mary Kay Volker, Prin.
Sisters 2; Lay Teachers 29; Students 498.
Catechesis / Religious Programs—Tel: 713-686-3857. Alicia I. Perez, D.R.E.
Students 590.

6—ST. ANDREW KIM (1981) (Korean), Rev. Paul Chun-Ho Kim.
Res., 1706 Bingle Rd., 77055-2336. Tel: 713-465-5974.

7—ST. ANNE (1925), Revs. Charles A. Christopher, C.S.B.; Thomas B. Mailloux, C.S.B.; Thomas J. McReavy, C.S.B.; David J. Zapalac, C.S.B.
Res., 2140 Westheimer, 77098-1496. Tel: 713-526-3276; Fax: 713-526-3079.
School—Tel: 713-526-3279.
Sisters 1; Lay Teachers 26; Students 350.
Catechesis / Religious Programs—Tel: 281-286-2369. Arlene Holm, D.R.E.
Students 484.

8—ST. ANNE DE BEAUPRE (1948), Revs. Kenneth Howard, S.S.J.; Paul E. Kluthe, S.S.J.
Res., 2810 Link Rd., 77009-1196. Tel: 713-869-1319; Fax: 713-869-1319.

9—ANNUNCIATION (1869), Rev. Msgr. James L. Golasinski; Deacons Joseph Jachimcyk; David Adame.
Mailing Address: P.O. Box 214, 77001-0214. Tel: 713-222-2289; Fax: 713-222-2280.
Res., 1618 Texas Ave., 77003.

10—ASCENSION CHINESE MISSION (1988) (Chinese), Rev. Francis X. Chang, S.J.
Res., 4605 Jetty Ln., 77072-1222. Tel: 281-575-8855; Fax: 281-575-8866.

11—ASSUMPTION (1948), Revs. Italo Dell'Oro, C.R.S. (Italy); Narciso Bordignon, C.R.S.; John Peter Borsari; Deacon Albert Bottijer.
Res., 901 Rose Ln., 77037. Tel: 281-447-6381; Fax: 281-447-6382. [CEM]
Catechesis / Religious Programs—Tel: 281-445-1268. Betty Blazek, D.R.E.
Students 665.

12—ST. AUGUSTINE (1955), Rev. Msgr. Seth Hermoso, (Vicar for Filipinos); Rev. Joseph T.P. Bui; Deacon Joe Zamora.
Res., 5560 Laurel Creek Way, 77017-6729. Tel: 713-946-8968; Fax: 713-946-0080.
School—Terry Smith, Prin. Sisters 1; Lay Teachers 25; Students 308.
Catechesis / Religious Programs—Tel: 713-946-7636. Mrs. Bea Zamora, D.R.E.
Students 330.

13—ST. BENEDICT THE ABBOT (1963), Rev. Nicolas Pasadilla.
Office: 4025 Grapevine, 77045-6320. Tel: 713-433-9836; Fax: 713-433-3949.
Catechesis / Religious Programs—Tel: 713-433-2436. Brenda Wade, D.R.E.
Students 475.

14—ST. BERNADETTE SOUBIROUS (1977), Revs. Joseph J. McCarthy, O.Carm.; Joseph Joyce, O.Carm.; Roger Bonneau.
Mailing Address: 15500 El Camino Real, 77062. Tel: 281-486-0337; Fax: 281-486-7664.
Catechesis / Religious Programs—Tel: 281-486-0337. Sally Johnson, D.R.E.
Students 1,224.

15—CHRIST, THE INCARNATE WORD MISSION, Rev. John Hoang Minh Toan, Admin.; Deacon Bach Si Nguyen.
Res., c/o 7720 Boone Rd., 77072-3595. Tel: 281-498-4653; Fax: 281-879-1527.

16—CHURCH OF THE BLESSED SACRAMENT (1910), Rev. Jose Isidore Garcia, O.M.I., V.F.; Deacon Pedro Lerma. In res., Bro. Patrick Vilim, O.M.I.
Res., 4015 Sherman Ave., 77003-2695. Tel: 713-224-5291; Fax: 713-224-5292.
Catechesis / Religious Programs—Tel: 713-947-2515. Mary T. Martinez, D.R.E.
Students 334.

17—ST. CATHERINE OF SIENA (1975), Rev. Robert S. Barras; Deacon John Coussirat.
Mailing Address: 10688 Shadow Wood, 77043-2826. Tel: 713-467-8170; Fax: 713-467-7149.
Catechesis / Religious Programs—Tel: 713-467-8170. Dorris Desroche, D.R.E.
Students 165.

18—ST. CECILIA (1956), Rev. Msgr. Vincent M. Rizzotto, J.C.L., Vicar Gen.; Revs. Octavio Muguerza; Guido Anthony Fregeau; Deacons Don Bradley; Cade Nelms.
Res., 11720 Joan of Arc, 77024-2602. Tel: 713-465-3414; Fax: 713-465-1305.
School—Tel: 713-468-9515; Fax: 713-468-4695. Ms. Bridget Collins, Prin.
Lay Teachers 31; Students 502.
Catechesis / Religious Programs—Lee Renaud, D.R.E.
Students 880.

19—ST. CHARLES BORROMEO (1962), Revs. John E. Cahoon; Edwin Coreas; Deacon Rodrigo Lozano.
Res., 501 Tidwell, 77022. Tel: 713-692-6303; Fax: 713-692-6314.
School—Tel: 713-692-4898. Mrs. Angelina Karpinski, Prin.
Sisters 3; Lay Teachers 20; Students 270.
Catechesis / Religious Programs—Tel: 281-442-1334. Linda Schulle, D.R.E.
Students 750.

20—CHRIST THE KING (1928), Rev. Stephen B. Reynolds. In res., Rev. Jose Maria Fernandez.
Res., 4419 N. Main St., 77009-5199. Tel: 713-869-1449; Fax: 713-869-1491.
School—Ms. Nikki Spedale, Prin. Lay Teachers 3; Students 32.
Catechesis / Religious Programs—Tel: 713-869-3140. Daniel Schwieterman, D.R.E.
Students 910.

21—CHRIST THE REDEEMER (1980), Revs. Dominic A. Peluse, S.C.J.; Howard Melzer, S.C.J.; Deacons Richard L. Leach; Jim Osterhaus.
Res., 12402 Bexhill, 77065.
Church—11507 Huffmeister, 77065-1051. Tel: 281-469-5533; Fax: 281-469-8441.
Catechesis / Religious Programs—Tel: 281-469-5533. Mary Lou Lietzau, D.R.E.
Students 1,001.

22—ST. CHRISTOPHER (1924), Revs. Paul R. Chovanec, B.S., M.Th.; Michael Berlowski. In res., Rev. Denis A. Osuagwu, C.M.F.; Deacons Peter J. Kelleher; Jose Aranda; Merce C. Leal, Jr.; Henry T. Gramann; Terrance D. Mulcare.
Res., 8150 Park Place Blvd., 77017-3033. Tel: 713-645-6614; Fax: 713-640-1640.
School—8134 Park Place Blvd., 77017. Tel: 713-649-0009. Therese Cutrer, Prin.
Sisters 2; Lay Teachers 21; Students 352.
Catechesis / Religious Programs—D.R.E.: Gloria Leal; Tammy Juarez.
Students 606.

23—ST. CLARE OF ASSISI (1990), Rev. John H. Kappe; Deacons Wilfred J. Hargraves; Daniel Q. Guerra.
Res., 15922 Hillside Falls Tr., 77062.
Mailing Address: 3131 El Dorado Blvd., 77059-5100. Tel: 281-286-7729; Fax: 281-286-1256.
School—Tel: 281-286-3395. Ann Jackson, Prin.
Lay Teachers 7; Students 95.

Catechesis/Religious Programs—Tel: 281-486-0874. Celia Guadiano, D.R.E.
Students 545.

24—ST. CYRIL OF ALEXANDRIA (1963), Rev. Msgr. Edward Randall, V.F.; Revs. Jesus Bahena; Isaac O. Francis. In res., Rev. Jacques Weber., S.J., S.T.L., M.S.; Deacon Woods Martin.
Res., 10503 Westheimer, 77042-3502. Tel: 713-789-1250; Fax: 713-780-0967.
Catechesis/Religious Programs—Tel: 713-789-1250. Margaret McDermott, D.R.E.
Students 606.

25—CORPUS CHRISTI (1956), Revs. Roger C. Prefontaine, S.S.S.; Dominic Phu Nguyen, S.S.S.; Deacon Joseph Bourgeois. In res., Revs. Robert P. Rousseau, S.S.S.; Donald J. Jette, S.S.S.
Res., 9900 Stella Link Rd., 77025-4798. Tel: 713-667-0497; Fax: 713-668-4742.
School—4005 Cheena St., 77025. Tel: 713-664-3351; Fax: 713-664-6095. Theresa Rourke, Prin.
Lay Teachers 20; Students 245.
Catechesis/Religious Programs—Tel: 713-667-1911. Peggy Marroquin, D.R.E.
Students 310.

26—ST. DOMINIC (1965), Rev. Anton R. Sheltz, M.Th.; Deacon Philip Arlen Wiles.
Res., 8215 Reservoir St., 77049-1728. Tel: 281-458-2910; Fax: 281-458-7114.
Catechesis/Religious Programs—George T. McDonald, D.R.E.
Students 156.

27—ST. ELIZABETH ANN SETON (1977), Revs. Frank Wittouck, S.C.J.; Richard DiLeo, S.C.J.; Leonard Elder, S.C.J.; Deacons Francis Adams; Charles G. Pennell.
Res., 6646 Addicks-Satsuma Rd., 77084-1599. Tel: 281-463-7878; Fax: 281-463-4822.
School—Tel: 281-463-1444. Mary Crenshaw, Prin.
Lay Teachers 9; Students 133.
Catechesis/Religious Programs—Tel: 281-463-7356. Mrs. Bernadette Bacak, D.R.E.
Students 2,470.

28—ST. FRANCES CABRINI (1962), Revs. Norbert Maduzia, D. Min.; Joseph Thanh Vu; Deacons John Rooney; Frank Moreno; Robert Gregory Stevens; Fernando Ramirez; Charles Roessler.
Mailing Address: 10727 Hartsook St., 77034-3523. Tel: 713-946-5768; Fax: 713-946-3282.
Res., 10726 Bessemer, 77034.
Catechesis/Religious Programs—Patricia Weimer, D.R.E.
Students 823.

29—ST. FRANCIS DE SALES (1962), Rev. Msgr. William M. Pickard, J.C.D., E.V.; Revs. Jhon Jairo Arroyave; Pavel Mikes; Deacons Albert G. Bothe; Frank Comer; Hugo Klein.
Res., 8018 Roos Rd., 77036. Tel: 713-774-7475; Fax: 713-774-6591. [JC]
School—8100 Roos Rd., 77036. Tel: 713-774-4447; Fax: 713-271-6744.
Lay Teachers 31; Students 539.
Catechesis/Religious Programs—Tel: 713-774-9631. Janet Pitcaithly, D.R.E.
Students 686.

30—ST. FRANCIS OF ASSISI (1950), Rev. Patrick R. Wells; Deacon Ignatius Joseph.
Res., 5102 Dabney St., 77026-3015. Tel: 713-672-7773; Fax: 713-673-1913.
School—5100 Dabney St., 77026. Tel: 713-631-3681; Fax: 713-631-6114.
Sisters 1; Lay Teachers 16; Students 205.
Catechesis/Religious Programs—Tel: 713-674-5314. Shirley M. Rene, D.R.E.
Students 130.

31—ST. FRANCIS XAVIER (1952), Revs. Brian Fox, S.S.J.; Emmanuel Agbor, M.S.P.; Deacons Daniel W. Gilbert; Albert Henry; Michael V. Jenkins.
Res., 9202 Cullen Blvd., 77051-3399. Tel: 713-738-2311; Fax: 713-738-2312.
Catechesis/Religious Programs—Tel: 281-495-7458. Grenda Williams, D.R.E.
Students 212.

32—ST. GREGORY THE GREAT (1962), Rev. Gary F. Wanzong, V.F.; Deacon Julio Ramirez.
Res., 10500 Nold Dr., 77016-2921. Tel: 713-631-3681; Fax: 713-631-6114.
Catechesis/Religious Programs—Tel: 713-631-0058. D.R.E.: Raquel Castillo; Jessica Dargin.
Students 225.

33—HOLY CROSS CHAPEL (Downtown), Rev. Msgr. Albert J. Beck, Dir.; Rev. Msgr. George A. Beck.
Chapel—905 Main St., 77002. Tel: 713-650-1323; Fax: 713-650-8836.

34—HOLY GHOST (1946), Revs. Alton T. Carr, C.Ss.R.; John M. Farnik, C.Ss.R.; Peter H. Voelker, C.Ss.R.; Edward Glebe, C.Ss.R. In res., Revs. A. J. Chandonnet, C.Ss.R.; Robert Bek, C.Ss.R.; Deacon Robert Brueggerhoff.
Res., 6921 Chetwood Dr., 77081-5697. Tel: 713-668-0463; Fax: 713-661-4645.
School—6920 Chimney Rock, 77081. Tel: 713-668-5327. Susan Sanchez, Prin.
Lay Teachers 16; Students 244.
Catechesis/Religious Programs—Tel: 713-668-8001. Anne W. Brown, D.R.E.
Students 253.

35—HOLY NAME (1920), Revs. Charles Kelly, S.C.J.; Vincent McDonald, S.C.J. In res., Rev. Philip Elmer, S.C.J.
Res., 1917 Cochran St., 77009-8497. Tel: 713-222-1255; Fax: 713-222-1260.
School—1912 Marion St., 77009-8649. Tel: 713-227-9529. Sr. Angelica Garza, S.S.C.J., Prin.
Sisters 3; Lay Teachers 12; Students 173.
Catechesis/Religious Programs—Tel: 713-223-4059. Mrs. Alicia Bernal, D.R.E.
Students 593.

36—HOLY ROSARY (1913), Revs. Joseph D. Konkel, O.P.; William H. Brenda, O.P.; Joseph Nguyen Ngoc Tu, O.P.
Res., 3600 Travis St., 77002-9591. Tel: 713-529-4854; Fax: 713-522-3967.

37—IMMACULATE CONCEPTION (1911), Revs. Charles Borski, O.M.I.; James Miller, O.M.I.; Deacons Joseph G. Morin; Leslie Bart Hock.
Res., 7250 Harrisburg Blvd., 77011-4791. Tel: 713-921-1261; Fax: 713-921-2304.
Catechesis/Religious Programs—Tel: 713-645-5932. Ms. Teresa Martinez, D.R.E.
Students 739.

38—IMMACULATE HEART OF MARY (1926), Revs. Adolph Kaler, O.M.I.; William Davis, O.M.I.; Deacon Raul G. Navarro.
Res., 7539 Ave. K, 77012-1033. Tel: 713-923-2394; Fax: 713-923-2395.
School—7535 Ave. L, 77012-1098. Tel: 713-921-5431; Fax: 713-923-2395. Dora Tillman, Prin.
Sisters 1; Lay Teachers 6; Students 72.
Catechesis/Religious Programs—Tel: 713-928-5238. Theresa Godoy, D.R.E.
Students 549.

39—ST. JEROME (1960), Rev. Msgr. Daniel Scheel, S.T.L., M.Ch.A.; Revs. Douglas Smith; Lee Flores; Deacons Alden Knobloch; Jim Rutledge; Juan Pareja.
Res., 8825 Kempwood, 77080-4199. Tel: 713-468-9555; Fax: 713-464-0325.
School—Tel: 713-468-7946. Sharon Makulski, Prin.
Sisters 2; Lay Teachers 19; Students 357.
Catechesis/Religious Programs—Tel: 713-464-5029. Sr. Araceli Diaz, O.P., D.R.E.
Students 1,180.

40—ST. JOHN NEUMANN (1977), Rev. Msgr. Eugene G. Francis, M.R.E.; Rev. Francis Huan Ton Ngo; Deacon Klaus W. Petereit.
2730 Nelwood Drive, 77038-1025.
Res., 2715 Nelwood Dr., 77038-1025. Tel: 281-931-0684; Fax: 281-931-5363.
Catechesis/Religious Programs—Tel: 281-931-0684. Mrs. Kathy Kimich, D.R.E.
Students 355.

41—ST. JOHN VIANNEY (1966), Revs. John N. Morfin; John C. Upton; Doakim Nguyen; Deacons Dale Steffes; Albert Vacek, Jr.
Res., 625 Nottingham Oaks Tr., 77079-6299. Tel: 281-497-1500; Fax: 281-584-2024.
Catechesis/Religious Programs—Tel: 281-497-6665. Frances Contello, D.R.E.
Students 1,861.

42—ST. JOSEPH (1880), Revs. Ferdinand Derrera, S.J.; Donald G. Bahlinger, S.J.; Bro. Walter A. Eckler, S.J.; Deacons Geronimo Flores; Martin Sanchez.
Res., 1505 Kane St., 77007-7711. Tel: 713-222-6193; Fax: 713-222-6195.
Catechesis/Religious Programs—Marina Ramirez, D.R.E.
Students 280.

43—ST. JUSTIN MARTYR (1982), Revs. John T. Keller, M.Th., M.R.E.; Francis Pham, C.Ss.R.; Deacons Robert C. Keller; Gene Festa; Cornelius C. Llorens; J. M. Baker, C.S.
Res., 13350 Ashford Point Dr., 77082-5100. Tel: 281-556-5116; Fax: 281-556-6932.
Rectory: 12809 Sunset Dunes, 77082.
Catechesis/Religious Programs—Carole Polzer, D.R.E.
Students 910.

44—ST. LEO THE GREAT (1973), Revs. Louis Piran, C.S.; Rafael Becera, C.S.
Res., 2131 Lauder Rd., 77039-3199. Tel: 281-449-2344; Fax: 281-449-3664.
Catechesis/Religious Programs—Alicia Perez, D.R.E.
Students 420.

45—ST. LUKE THE EVANGELIST (1975), Revs. Stephen R. Horn, M.Div.; Thu Ngoc Nguyen; Deacons John E. Devine, Jr.; James Sharpless; Paul J. Robison, Jr.
11011 Hall Rd., 77089-2999.
Res., 10914 Sagemeadow, 77089. Tel: 281-481-6816; Fax: 281-481-8969.
Catechesis/Religious Programs—Tel: 281-481-4735.
Students 840.

46—ST. MARK THE EVANGELIST (1974), Rev. Roosevelt Martin.
Res., 5302 Castlecreek Ln., Houston, 77053. Tel: 281-437-9114; 437-4828; Fax: 281-835-6303.
Church—5430 W. Ridgecreek Dr., Houston, 77053-3211.
Catechesis/Religious Programs—Tel: 281-438-0350. Zulema Perez, D.R.E.
Students 219.

47—ST. MARY OF THE PURIFICATION (1929), Revs. Michael J. Fritzen, S.V.D.; John Duah Prempeh, S.V.D. In res., Rev. Stanley J. Gootee, S.V.D.
Res., 3006 Rosedale Ave., 77004-6199. Tel: 713-528-0571; Fax: 713-528-0572.
School—3002 Rosedale, 77004. Tel: 713-522-9276; Fax: 713-522-1879. Mae Smith, Ed.D., Prin.
Lay Teachers 18; Students 232.
Catechesis/Religious Programs—Tel: 281-437-4110. Mrs. Evelyn Hunter, D.R.E.
Students 117.

48—ST. MATTHEW THE EVANGELIST (1974), Revs. Richard Johnston, S.C.J.; Robert Tucker, S.C.J.; Deacons John Adams; Adolph Zuk.
Res., 9915 Hollister Dr., 77040-1702. Tel: 713-466-4030; Fax: 713-896-7235.
Catechesis/Religious Programs—Tel: 713-466-4030. Virginia Diehl, D.R.E.
Students 620.

49—ST. MAXIMILIAN KOLBE (1983), Rev. Adam S. McClosky; Deacon Ronald J. Frazier.
Res., 10218 Great Plains, 77064.
Church—10135 West Rd., 77064-5361. Tel: 281-955-7324; Fax: 281-850-7328.
Catechesis/Religious Programs—Ginger Tamborello, D.R.E.
Students 990.

50—ST. MICHAEL (1925), Revs. Laurence Connelly; Fred P. Valone; Stephen V. Cooley, O.Carm.
Res., 1801 Sage Rd., 77056-3598. Tel: 713-621-4370; Fax: 713-850-8341.
School—1833 Sage Rd., 77056-3599. Tel: 713-621-6847; Fax: 713-877-8812. Dean Karns, Prin.
Lay Teachers 39; Students 517.
Catechesis/Religious Programs—Tel: 713-840-8213. Patricia Jantz, D.R.E.
Students 521.

51—ST. RAPHAEL THE ARCHANGEL (1961), Rev. James C. Arrambide, C.Ss.R.
Mailing Address: P.O. Box 630787, 77263. Tel: 713-781-9511.
Res., 3915 Ocee, 77063-5417.
Catechesis/Religious Programs—Ana Oliva, D.R.E.
Students 430.

52—ST. MONICA (1960), Rev. Alphonsus Bakyil, S.O.L.T.
Res., 8421 W. Montgomery Rd., 77088-7116. Tel: 281-447-5837; Fax: 281-447-8410.
Catechesis/Religious Programs—Students 170.

53—ST. NICHOLAS, Rev. Donatus Anosike, M.S.P.
Res., 2508 Clay Ave., 77003-4498. Tel: 713-223-5210; Fax: 713-223-5210.

54—NOTRE DAME (1969), Revs. Hubert J. Kealy; Charles J. Samperi; Deacon Arturo M. Gomez. In res., Rev. John Hoang Toan.
Res., 11226 Pompano Ln., 77072-3595.
Church—7720 Boone Rd., 77072-3595. Tel: 281-498-4653; Fax: 281-879-1527.
Catechesis/Religious Programs—Robby Lantz, D.R.E.
Students 440.

55—OUR LADY OF CZESTOCHOWA (1982) (Polish), Rev. Jerzy Frydrych, S.Ch.
Res., 1712 Oak Tree, 77080-7240. Tel: 713-973-1081; Fax: 713-973-1081.

56—OUR LADY OF GUADALUPE (1912), Revs. James D. Steffes, S.C.J.; Francis Strafalace, S.C.J.
Res., 2405 Navigation Blvd., 77003-1599. Tel: 713-222-0203; Fax: 713-225-2235. [JC]
School—Tel: 713-224-6904. Chris Skowronek, Prin.
Sisters 4; Lay Teachers 12; Students 204.
Catechesis/Religious Programs—Sr. Lelia Martinez, M.C.D.P., D.R.E.
Students 725.

57—OUR LADY OF LAVANG CHURCH (1985) (Vietnamese), Revs. Anthony Chinh Quang Dao, O.P., Vicar for Vietnamese; Anthony Hung Ngoc Tran, O.P.; Bro. Peter Mai Van To, O.P.; Deacon Michael Nguyen K. Khanh.
Res., 12320 Old Foltin Rd., 77086-3513. Tel: 281-999-1672; Fax: 281-999-1670.
Catechesis/Religious Programs—Nam Hoang Luong, D.R.E.
Students 550.

58—OUR LADY OF MT. CARMEL (1953), Revs. Roy Ontiveros, O.Carm.; Bill Harry, O.Carm.; Gregory

Battafarano, O.Carm.
Res., 6723 Whitefriars Dr., 77087-6598. Tel: 713-645-6673; Fax: 713-645-6674.
School—6703 Whitefriars Dr., 77087. Tel: 713-643-0676. Cecilia King, Prin.
Lay Teachers 13; Students 239.
Catechesis/Religious Programs—Tel: 713-645-6010. Rebecca Gotting, D.R.E.
Students 192.

59—Our Lady of St. John (1947), Rev. Armando J. Rodriguez; Deacon Julio Suriano.
Res., 7500 Hirsch Rd., 77016-6215. Tel: 713-631-0810; Fax: 713-631-0781.
Catechesis/Religious Programs—Students 264.

60—Our Lady of Sorrows (1936), Rev. Norberto Conde.
Res., 3006 Kashmere St., 77026-5999. Tel: 713-673-5622; Fax: 713-673-5667.
Catechesis/Religious Programs—Diana Ruiz, D.R.E.
Students 215.

61—Our Lady of Walsingham (1984), Rev. James T. Moore; Deacon James M. Barnett.
Res. & Mailing Address: 7809 Shady Villa Ln., 77055-5011. Tel: 281-821-0423; Fax: 713-683-9407.

62—Our Mother of Mercy (1930), Revs. Kenneth J. Howard, S.S.J.; Eugene R. Moynihan, S.S.J. In res., Revs. John E. Hardman, S.S.J.; Francis McCarthy, S.S.J.; Deacon Charles J. Allen, Sr.
Res., 4000 Sumpter St., 77020-2497. Tel: 713-672-0026; Fax: 713-672-2031.
School—Sr. Dorothy Marie Stuart, S.S.F., Prin.
Sisters 5; Lay Teachers 11; Students 197.
Catechesis/Religious Programs—D.R.E.: Sr. Theresa Healy; Tom Davis.
Students 314.

63—Our Lady Star of the Sea (1958), Rev. Louis R. Saporito, S.S.J.
Res., 1401 Fidelity St., 77029. Tel: 713-674-9206; Fax: 713-675-7842.

64—St. Patrick (1880), Revs. Henry Walker, O.M.I.; Salvatore F. DeGeorge.
Res., 4918 Cochran St., 77009-2117. Tel: 713-695-0631; Fax: 713-695-6255.
Catechesis/Religious Programs—Students 831.

65—St. Paul (1964), Revs. Dominic J. Pistone, Jr.; Walter N. Sheffield; Deacons Ray Sanders; Richard Labrecque; Robert G. Alexander.
Church—18223 Point Lookout Dr., 77058. Tel: 281-333-3891; Fax: 281-333-3815.
Rectory: 18326 Point Lookout Dr., 77058.
Catechesis/Religious Programs—Students 544.

66—St. Peter the Apostle (1941), Revs. Paul N. Ofoa, M.S.P.; Patrick Oter, M.S.P.; Deacon Clarence Johnson. In res., Rev. Msgr. Goodwin Akpan, M.S.P.
Res., 6220 La Salette Dr., 77021-1323. Tel: 713-747-7800; Fax: 713-747-9671.
School—Tel: 713-747-9484; Fax: 713-747-8754. Mr. Lucius M. Guillory, Prin.
Lay Teachers 10; Students 161.

67—St. Peter Claver (1964), Rev. Larry A. Gutierrez, S.S.J.
Mailing Address: 6005 N. Wayside Dr., 77028-4494. Tel: 713-674-3338; Fax: 713-674-6524.
Catechesis/Religious Programs—Students 145.

68—St. Philip Neri (1961), Rev. Tom Byrne, C.S.Sp., D.Min.; Deacon Ronald Simon.
Res., 10950 Martin Luther King Blvd., 77048-1815.
Mailing Address: P.O. Box 330190, 77233-0190. Tel: 713-733-0320; Fax: 713-734-0331.
School—Tel: 713-733-2343. Melina G. Harris, Prin.
Lay Teachers 12; Students 94.
Catechesis/Religious Programs—Mrs. Mary Freeman, D.R.E.
Students 125.

69—St. Philip of Jesus (1958), Rev. Timothy Gray, S.C.J., (Hispanic Ministry Hechos Program); Deacon Roy Breaux.
Res., 3526 La Retama Dr., 77013-3818. Tel: 713-672-6141; Fax: 713-672-8675.
Catechesis/Religious Programs—Tel: 713-674-1664. Leticia Davila, D.R.E.
Students 318.

70—Prince of Peace (1971), Revs. George A. Sheltz, V.F.; Thomas V. Ponzini.
Res., 8300 Dorrcrest Ln., 77070-3510. Tel: 281-469-2686; Fax: 281-469-8418.
Church—19222 Tomball Pkwy., 77070-3510.
Catechesis/Religious Programs—Students 1,298.

71—Queen of Peace (1942), Rev. Michael J. Carmody; Deacon Jose Liendo.
Res., 3011 Telephone Rd., 77023-5395. Tel: 713-921-6127; Fax: 713-921-6128.
School—Tel: 713-921-1558. Sr. M. Alberta Novosad, Prin.
Sisters 3; Lay Teachers 8; Students 87.
Catechesis/Religious Programs—Tel: 713-921-1917. Sr. Gisela Rivera, C.M.S.T., D.R.E.
Students 672.

72—Resurrection (1920), Revs. David J. Cardenas; Blas P. Herrador; Deacons Gregory Garcia; Jose J. Ramirez.
Res., 915 Zoe St., 77020-6898. Tel: 713-675-5333; Fax: 713-673-3605.
School—916 Majestic St., 77020. Tel: 713-674-5545. Maria Elena Cuchapin, Prin.
Sisters 2; Lay Teachers 12; Students 178.
Catechesis/Religious Programs—Tel: 713-674-2151. Gloria Hewitt, D.R.E.
Students 250.
Station—Port Houston, La Divina Providencia.

73—St. Rose of Lima (1947), Rev. Msgr. Thomas A. Wendland; Rev. Patrick John Cummings.
Res., 3600 Brinkman, 77018-6329. Tel: 713-692-9123; Fax: 713-692-5638.
School—Mrs. Judy McCullough, Prin. Lay Teachers 21; Students 385.
Catechesis/Religious Programs—Mary Jo Wilt, D.R.E.
Students 300.

74—Our Lady of Lourdes (1994) (Vietnamese), Rev. Dominic Trinh The Huy, O.P.; Deacon Joseph Chuong Nguyen Do.
Mailing Address: 6550 Fairbanks N. Houston Rd., 77040-4307. Tel: 713-939-1906; Fax: 713-939-0771.
Catechesis/Religious Programs—Students 350.

75—St. Stephen (1941), Revs. Ignatio Garzon, M.J.; Angel Montano, M.J.
Mailing Address: 2019 Center St., 77007-6106.
Res., 1910 Center St., 77007. Tel: 713-864-4075; Fax: 713-880-8611.
Catechesis/Religious Programs—Tel: 281-445-8830. Sr. Soledad Arellano, C.M.S.T., D.R.E.
Students 294.

76—St. Theresa (1947), Revs. Benjamin Smaistrla; James M. Burkart; Deacons Larry A. Vaclavik; John M. Baker; Jay Vocelka. In res., Rev. Dennis L. Peterson.
Res., 6622 Haskell St., 77007-2097. Tel: 713-869-3783; Fax: 713-869-3784.
School—Tel: 713-864-4536. Mrs. Judy Fritsch, Prin.
Lay Teachers 18; Students 228.
Catechesis/Religious Programs—Tel: 713-869-9725. Deacon Jay Vocelka, D.R.E.
Students 259.

77—St. Thomas More (1963), Revs. William L. Young, III; Kenneth Heberlein; Stanislaus Bieniek. In res., Revs. Joseph T. O'Malley; Joseph Meledom; Deacons Anthony Alessi; Edwin Gosline; Thomas Newhouse; Edward Stoessel.
Res., 10330 Hillcroft, 77096-4795. Tel: 713-729-0221; Fax: 713-729-3294.
School—5927 Wigton, 77096. Tel: 713-729-3434. Mrs. Nadine Mouser, Prin.
Lay Teachers 32; Students 638.
Catechesis/Religious Programs—Tel: 713-729-3435. Mrs. Chris Twardowski, D.R.E.
Students 767.

78—St. Vincent de Paul (1941), Rev. Msgr. James A. Jamail; Revs. Howard Drabek; Richard Barker. In res., Most Rev. James A. Tamayo; Deacons Dr. Joseph Lorino; George Sheltz.
Res., 6800 Buffalo Speedway, 77025-1499. Tel: 713-667-9111; Fax: 713-667-3453.
School—6802 Buffalo Speedway, 77025. Tel: 713-666-2345. Virginia Malloy, Prin.
Sisters 3; Lay Teachers 32; Students 527.
Catechesis/Religious Programs—Sr. Jean Marie Goukas, C.V.I., D.R.E.
Students 500.

79—Vietnamese Martyrs (1986) (Vietnamese), Rev. J. B. Huynh Ngoc Tran; Deacon Joseph Nguyen Pham.
Res., 10610 Kingspoint Rd., 77075-4114. Tel: 713-941-0521; Fax: 713-941-0521.
Catechesis/Religious Programs—Students 350.

OUTSIDE THE CITIES OF GALVESTON AND HOUSTON

Alvin, Brazoria Co., St. John the Baptist (1952), Revs. Daniel McKenna, O.M.I.; Stanley Guzik, O.M.I.; Deacons Robert Kacz; Diego Gutierrez, Sr.
Res., 110 E. South St., 77511-3500. Tel: 281-331-3751; Fax: 281-331-5430.
Catechesis/Religious Programs—Tel: 281-331-0181. Sr. Charles Marie Flores, S.S.C.J., D.R.E.
Students 844.

Anderson, Grimes Co., St. Stanislaus (1866), Rev. Louis S. Sikorski, D.R.E.; Deacons Anton Sicinski; Peter Sechelski.
Res., P.O. Box 210, 77830-0210. Tel: 409-873-2291; Fax: 409-873-2291. [CEM]
Catechesis/Religious Programs—Students 142.

Angleton, Brazoria Co., St. Basil (1960), Revs. Vincent Dulock, C.S.B.; Frederick L. Clay, C.S.B.; Gerald F. Dillon, C.S.B.; Deacon Andrew J. Shefts.
Res., 1713 N. Tinsley, 77515-3598. Tel: 409-849-2421; Fax: 409-849-2425.
Catechesis/Religious Programs—Tel: 409-849-1764. D.R.E.: Bernetta Cook; Norma Mata.
Students 435.

Barrett Station, Harris Co., St. Martin de Porres (1944), Rev. Anthony Ekanem, M.S.P.; Deacon Steve Arceneaux, Jr.
Mailing Address: P.O. Box 3459, 77532-2459. Tel: 281-328-4451; Fax: 281-328-7306.
Res., 12606 Crosby-Lynchburg Rd., 77532.
Catechesis/Religious Programs—Mrs. Jude Arceneaux, Jr., D.R.E.
Students 232.

Beasley, Ft. Bend Co., St. Wenceslaus Mission (1923). (Independent Mission). Rev. Henry C. Rachunek.
Res., P.O. Box 121, Hungerford, 77448-0121. Tel: 409-532-4767; Fax: 409-532-8713. [CEM]

Baytown, Harris Co., St. John the Evangelist (1974), Rev. William A. Oliver; Deacons Justin Wewer; John William Singer.
Res., 800 W. Baker Rd., 77521-2311. Tel: 281-837-8180; Fax: 281-837-8181.
Catechesis/Religious Programs—Jan Allison, D.R.E.
Students 320.

St. Joseph (1924), Rev. Stephen A. Mandry, S.T.D.; Deacons John William Singer, Jr.; Rudy Venegas.
Res., 1907 Carolina St., 77520-6098. Tel: 281-420-3588; Fax: 281-420-3044.
School—1811 Carolina St., 77520. Tel: 281-422-9749. Joe W. Connealy, Prin.
Lay Teachers 8; Students 145.
Catechesis/Religious Programs—Fax: 281-427-5720. Judy Arceneaux, D.R.E.
Students 188.

Our Lady of Guadalupe (1958), Rev. Ramon Martinez, O.S.A.; Deacon Fernando Gonzalez.
Res., 1124 Beech St., 77520-4198. Tel: 281-428-1507; Fax: 281-422-4554.
Catechesis/Religious Programs—Tel: 281-427-5836. Dahlia & Hector Meza, D.R.E.
Students 681.

Bellville, Austin Co., SS. Peter & Paul (1860), Rev. Timothy P. Bucek.
Res., P.O. Box 176, 77418-0176. Tel: 409-865-2368; Fax: 409-865-9929. [CEM]
Catechesis/Religious Programs—Tel: 409-865-8601. Cristina Pier, D.R.E.
Students 187.
Mission—Industry, Austin Co., Immaculate Conception, (1875).

Brazoria, Brazoria Co., St. Joseph (1840), Rev. William P. Sommerville; Deacons Raul A. Castillo; Jimmy Smith.
Res., Rte. 4, Box 4100, 77422-8699. Tel: 409-798-2288; Fax: 409-798-4702. [CEM]
Catechesis/Religious Programs—Betty Castillo, D.R.E.
Students 173.

Channelview, Harris Co., St. Andrew (1970), Rev. Stephen P. Ziqrang, J.C.L.; Deacons Jack Rook; John Santos; Steve Miller; Javier Gomez.
Res., 827 Sheldon Rd., 77530-3511. Tel: 281-452-9865; Fax: 281-452-2157. [JC]
Catechesis/Religious Programs—Tel: 281-452-0618. Sr. Helen Spanos, D.R.E.
Students 898.

Clute, Brazoria Co., St. Jerome (1969), Rev. James F. Lynes.
Mailing Address: 107 N. Lazy Ln., 77531. Tel: 409-265-5179; Fax: 409-265-4601. [JC]
Catechesis/Religious Programs—Tel: 409-233-0520. Dina Tonche, D.R.E.
Students 359.

Conroe, Montgomery Co., Sacred Heart (1916), Rev. Msgr. David W. Kennedy, V.F.; Rev. Manuel La Rosa-Lopez.
Res., 109 N. Frazier St., 77301-2889. Tel: 409-756-8186; Fax: 409-756-8105.
School—615 McDade, 77301. Tel: 409-756-3848. Margaret Looper, Prin.
Sisters 2; Lay Teachers 12; Students 311.
Spanish Ministry—Tel: 409-756-8288.
Catechesis/Religious Programs—Becki Lipari, D.R.E.
Students 464.

Crosby, Harris Co., Sacred Heart (1935), Rev. Msgr. Fred P. O'Connor.
Res., 915 Runneburg Rd., 77532-5826. Tel: 281-328-4871; Fax: 281-328-1075. [CEM]
School—907 Runneberg Rd., 77532. Tel: 281-328-6561. Margaret Burke Cotrone, Prin.
Sisters 2; Lay Teachers 7; Students 146.
Catechesis/Religious Programs—Tel: 409-756-8186. Margaret Benham, D.R.E.
Students 236.

Damon, Brazoria Co., SS. Cyril and Methodius (1925), Rev. James Ramsey.
Mailing Address & Res.—P.O. Box 309, 77430-0309. Tel: 409-742-3383; Fax: 409-742-3383.
Church—603 Parrott Ave., 77430.

Danbury, Brazoria Co., St. Anthony de Padua (1911), Rev. Msgr. Boleslaus Zientek; Deacon Gerald Peltier.
Res., P.O. Box 288, 77534-0288. Tel: 409-922-1240; Fax: 409-922-8643. [CEM]
Catechesis/Religious Programs—Tel: 409-922-1241. Catine Peltier, D.R.E.
Students 153.

Deer Park, Harris Co., St. Hyacinth (1965), Rev. Msgr. Elmer T. Quinters; Rev. Anthony A. Castro; Deacons Dennis M. Hickey; Richard F. Camunez.
Res., 2921 Center St., 77536-4997. Tel: 281-479-4298; Fax: 281-479-4132.
Catechesis/Religious Programs—Tel: 713-479-8832. Mary Wilson, D.R.E.
Students 929.

Dickinson, Galveston Co., Shrine of the True Cross (1909), Rev. Msgr. Milam E. Kleas; Rev. Robert C. Ramon; Deacon Sam Ausmus, III.
Mailing Address: P.O. Box 687, 77539.
Res., 3720 Spruce, 77539. Tel: 281-337-4112; Fax: 281-337-5779.
Church—300 Pine Dr., 77539-0687.
School—400 Pine Dr., 77539. Tel: 281-337-5212. Susan Callaway, Prin.
Lay Teachers 13; Students 302.
Catechesis/Religious Programs—Tel: 713-337-3130. Jane Hebert, D.R.E.
Students 776.

Freeport, Brazoria Co., St. Mary: Star of the Sea (1925), Rev. Reginald F. Petrash; Deacon Wallace Shaw.
Mailing Address: 1019 West 6th St., 77541.
Res., 914 W. 7th St., 77541. Tel: 409-233-5271; Fax: 409-233-5272.
Catechesis/Religious Programs—Tel: 409-233-5271. Barbara Flores, D.R.E.
Students 317.

St. Henry (1932), Rev. Jose M. Sanchez.
Mailing Address: P.O. Box 857, 77542.
Res., 318 E. 5th St., 77541-0857. Tel: 409-233-2887; Fax: 409-233-2887.

Friendswood, Galveston Co., Mary, Queen (1964), Revs. Paul Mandziuk, M.S.; Phil M. Negley, M.S.; Bro. Robert Belliveau, M.S.; Deacon Darrell Moulton.
Res., P.O. Box 207, 77549. Tel: 281-482-1391; Fax: 281-482-4886.
Catechesis/Religious Programs—Tel: 713-482-5875. Donna Patlach, D.R.E.
Students 973.

Frydek, Austin Co., St. Mary's (1908), Rev. Bernard C. Snock.
Res., 124 Zaruba Rd., Sealy, 77474-0337. Tel: 409-885-3131; Fax: 409-885-4555. [CEM]

Galena Park, Harris Co., Our Lady of Fatima (1946), Revs. Robert D. Carlson; Faustino Maramot.
Res., 1705 Eighth St., P.O. Box 644, 77547-0644. Tel: 713-675-0981; Fax: 713-675-0982.
School—1702 Ninth St., 77547. Tel: 713-674-5832. Sr. Martini Hoare, S.H.Sp., Prin.
Lay Teachers 11; Students 169.
Catechesis/Religious Programs—Rachel Gonzalez, D.R.E.
Students 460.

Hempstead, Waller Co., Mary, Mother of God (1879), Rev. Edward C. Kucera, Jr., M.Th., B.A.
Mailing Address: P.O. Box 576, 77445. Tel: 409-826-2275; Fax: 409-826-2275.
Res., 604 14th St., 77445.
Catechesis/Religious Programs—D.R.E.: Carmen Karisch; Rosemary Thompson.
Students 225.

Highlands, Harris Co., St. Jude Thaddeus (1946), Rev. John A. Zabelskas. In res., Rev. Luis Chia.
Res., 800 S. Main St., 77562-4236. Tel: 281-843-2422; Fax: 281-426-3671.
Catechesis/Religious Programs—Tel: 713-426-6800. Theresa A. Cashion, D.R.E.
Students 196.

Hitchcock, Galveston Co., Our Lady of Lourdes (1954), Revs. John C. DeForke; Peter A. Ferguson, Admin.
Res., 10114 Hwy. 6, 77563-4515. Tel: 409-925-3579; Fax: 409-925-5094.
School—Theresa "Terry" Bogar, Prin. Sisters 2; Lay Teachers 8; Students 147.
Catechesis/Religious Programs—Sr. Mary Anne C.V.I., D.R.E.
Students 279.

Huffman, Harris Co., St. Philip the Apostle (1977), Rev. George J. Olsovsky, M.Th.
Mailing Address: P.O. Box 292, 77336-0292. Tel: 281-324-1478; Fax: 281324-2775.
Res., 2308 Third St., 77336.
Catechesis/Religious Programs—Tel: 281-334-4401. Maureen Schuster, D.R.E.
Students 156.

Humble, Harris Co., St. Mary Magdalene (1911), Revs. Paul Procella; Tom McKinney; Deacons James N. Caruso; Jader de Jesus Cardenas.
Mailing Address: 527 S. Houston Ave., 77338-4763.
Res., 525 S. Houston Ave., 77338-4763. Tel: 281-446-8211; Fax: 281-446-8213.
Catechesis/Religious Programs—Tel: 281-446-2933. Jean Johnson, D.R.E.
Students 1,072.

Huntsville, Walker Co., St. Thomas the Apostle (1963), Rev. Stephen J. Payne. In res., Rev. Robert P. Zawacki, S.S.J.
Res., 1323 16th St., 77340-4431. Tel: 409-295-8159; Fax: 409-295-3543.
Catechesis/Religious Programs—Tel: 409-295-2298. Janet Johnson, D.R.E.
Students 205.

Katy, Harris Co., St. Bartholomew The Apostle (1965), Rev. Alberto A. Maullon, Jr.; Deacons William C. Wagner; L. William Hamilton.
Res., 5356 11th St., 77493-1797. Tel: 281-391-4758; Fax: 281-391-3978.
Catechesis/Religious Programs—Tel: 281-391-0839. Bill Wagner, D.R.E.
Students 861.

Epiphany of the Lord (1981), Rev. Msgr. Jack M. Dinkins; Deacons Don Kish; Leonard Broussard.
Res., 1530 Norwalk Dr., 77450-4999. Tel: 281-578-0707; Fax: 281-578-9161.
Catechesis/Religious Programs—Tel: 281-578-8271. Bonnie Caruso, D.R.E.
Students 1,748.

Kingwood, Harris Co., St. Martha (1979), Revs. Terence Brinkman, S.T.D.; Jimmy B. Hababag. In res., Rev. Romanus O. Muoneke.
Res., 2302 Oak Shores Dr., 77339-1801. Tel: 281-358-6637; Fax: 281-358-7973.
School—P.O. Box 6354, 77325-6354. Tel: 281-358-5523. Fred Schumacher, Prin.
Sisters 1; Lay Teachers 19; Students 197.
Catechesis/Religious Programs—Tel: 713-358-1959. Francine Puglia, D.R.E.
Students 2,184.

Lake Jackson, Brazoria Co., St. Michael (1966), Rev. Msgr. Leo Wleczyk, V.F.; Deacon Vincent A. Rowan.
Res., 100 Oak Dr., S., 77566-5630. Tel: 409-297-3041; Fax: 409-297-7895.
Catechesis/Religious Programs—Tel: 409-297-3043. Marsha Jacklitsch, D.R.E.
Students 929.

La Marque, Galveston Co., Our Lady Queen of Peace (1951), Rev. Msgr. T. Joseph Culver, E.V.; Deacons James Bonura; Earl Llewellyn. In res., Rev. Joseph Howard.
Mailing Address: 1224 Cedar Dr., 77568.
Res., 626 Laurel, 77568. Tel: 409-938-7000; Fax: 409-935-9791.
Church—1200 Cedar Dr., 77568.
Catechesis/Religious Programs—Tel: 409-935-3535. Maira Compean, D.R.E.
Students 194.

La Porte, Harris Co., St. Mary of the Immaculate Conception (1954), Rev. Thomas F. Rafferty; Deacons Hector Cantu; Thomas Lewis.
Res., 816 Park Ave., 77571-5811. Tel: 281-471-2000; Fax: 281-471-9365. [JC]
Catechesis/Religious Programs—Joan Westbeld, D.R.E.
Students 419.

League City, Galveston Co., St. Mary (1910), Rev. Msgr. Eugene Cargill; Deacons Robert Garza; Jerome McAllister.
Res., 1612 E. Walker St., 77573-4137. Tel: 281-332-3031; Fax: 281-332-8328.
School—Lay Teachers 20; Students 208.
Catechesis/Religious Programs—Tel: 281-332-4014. Rosa Guerrero, D.R.E.
Students 661.

McNair, Harris Co., Holy Family (1945), Rev. Lawrence A. Ebuk, M.S.P. (Nigeria).
Mailing Address: P.O. Box 307, Highlands, 77562-0307. Tel: 281-426-8448; Fax: 281-426-8449.
Res., 7122 Whiting Rock Dr., Baytown, 77521. [JC]

Madisonville, Madison Co., St. Elizabeth Ann Seton (1980), Rev. Joseph Phiet The Nguyen; Deacon Burke J. Landry.
Res., 209 S. Tammye Ln., 77864-3011. Tel: 409-348-5570.

Magnolia, Montgomery Co., St. Matthias the Apostle (1978), Rev. Frank W. Jones; Deacon Theodore Otis Baker.
Res., 302 S. Magnolia Blvd., 77355-8535. Tel: 281-356-2000; Fax: 281-356-7818.
Catechesis/Religious Programs—Students 241.

Manvel, Brazoria Co., Sacred Heart of Jesus (1945), Revs. James J. Gaunt, C.S.B.; John S. Broussard, C.S.B.
Res., 6502 Co. Rd. 48, 77578-2902. Tel: 281-489-8720; Fax: 281-489-8727.
Catechesis/Religious Programs—Tel: 281-489-7603. Theresa Garza, D.R.E.
Students 424.

Missouri City, Ft. Bend Co., Holy Family (1915), Revs. William E. Coughlin, C.S.B.; Jesse Santiago, C.S.B.; Hugh J. Curran, C.S.B.; Thaddeus T. Valencia, C.S.B.; Deacons Leonard Ramirez; William Seifert.
Res., 1510 Fifth St., 77489-1298. Tel: 281-499-9688; Fax: 281-499-9680.
Catechesis/Religious Programs—Tel: 281-499-4612.
Students 970.

Navasota, Grimes Co., Christ Our Light (1869), Rev. Paul G. Felix; Deacons Grant E. Holt; Gregory N. Jelinek, M.D.; William Leonard Sheffield.
Mailing Address: 510 Manley St., 77868-3926.
Res., 615 Church St., 77868-3905. Tel: 409-825-3920; Fax: 409-825-7612.
Church—1705 S. Loop 6, 77868.
Catechesis/Religious Programs—Mrs. Lucille Pavlock, D.R.E.
Students 308.

Needville, Fort Bend Co., St. Michael (1926), Rev. James Ramsey.
Res., P.O. Box 95, 77461-0095. Tel: 409-793-4477; Fax: 409-793-7456. [CEM]
Church—9202 Main St., 77461.
Catechesis/Religious Programs—Lynn Sury, D.R.E., Tel: 281-232-4006 (Res.).
Students 509.

New Caney, Montgomery Co., St. John of the Cross (1989), Rev. Frank Guenter.
Mailing Address: 20000 Loop 494, 77357. Tel: 281-399-9008; Fax: 281-399-9008.
Catechesis/Religious Programs—Linda Jochec, D.R.E.
Students 207.

New Waverly, Walker Co., St. Joseph (1869), Rev. Joseph K. Kalladan.
Res., P.O. Box 188, 77358-0188. Tel: 409-344-6104; Fax: 409-344-2818. [CEM 2]
Church—101 Elmore, 77358.
Catechesis/Religious Programs—Kathy Craig, D.R.E.
Students 157.
Mission—Point Blank, St. Stephen the Martyr.

Pasadena, Harris Co., St. Pius the Fifth (1941), Revs. Mario J. Arroyo; Miguel Solarzano.
Res., 824 Main St., 77506-3532. Tel: 713-473-9484; Fax: 713-473-2731.
School—Tel: 713-472-5172. Ms. Anne Bryant, Prin.
Lay Teachers 25; Students 182.
Catechesis/Religious Programs—D.R.E.: Sr. Felice Mojica, M.C.D.P.; Sr. Frances Jean Terrazas, M.C.D.P.
Students 1,140.

Blessed Juan Diego (1954). (Formerly Guardian Angel). Revs. J. Francisco Leon, O.S.A.; Leonel Martinez, O.S.A. (Mexico); Deacon Valeriano Leija.
Res., 3301 Pasadena Blvd., 77503-3201. Tel: 713-477-6693; Fax: 713-477-0523.
Catechesis/Religious Programs—Tel: 713-472-0356. Beatrice Canas, D.R.E.
Students 466.

Pattison/Brookshire, Waller Co., Sacred Heart (1914), Rev. Kenneth E. Mikulik, Admin., Pro-Tem.
Mailing Address: P.O. Box 300, Pattison, 77466-0300.
Res., 4445 F.M. 359 N., Pattison, 77466. Tel: 281-934-2888; Fax: 281-375-5799.
Catechesis/Religious Programs—Tel: 281-375-6638. Mrs. Marie Pattison, D.R.E.
Students 157.

Pearland, Brazoria Co., St. Helen (1966), Rev. Msgr. Leroy H. Braden; Rev. Gary A. Rickles; Deacons Gilbert Villarreal; Darvin Bordelon.
Res., 2209 Old Alvin Rd., 77581. Tel: 281-485-2421; Fax: 281-485-6789.
School—Tel: 281-485-2845. Merri Shaaf-Morales, Prin.
Lay Teachers 4; Students 60.
Catechesis/Religious Programs—Patsy Morales, D.R.E.
Students 1,458.

Plantersville, Grimes Co., St. Mary (1894), Rev. James F. Burke, C.S.Sp.
Res., Rte. 2, Box 3160, Navasota, 77868-9604. Tel: 409-894-2223; Fax: 409-894-2223. [CEM]
Mission—Stonehan, Grimes Co., St. Joseph.

Port Bolivar, Galveston Co., Our Mother of Mercy, Rev. John J. Connolly.
Mailing Address: P.O. Drawer C, 77650-0703.
Church—18th St. at Madison, Port Boliver, 77650.
Res., 1313 18th St., 77650-0703. Tel: 409-684-8962; Fax: 409-684-8962.
Mission—Crystal Beach, Galveston Co., St. Therese of Lisieux, 2400 Hwy. 87, 77650-0703.

Prairie View, Waller Co., St. Martin de Porres (1962), Rev. Robert B. Fisher, S.V.D.
Church—708 Thompson Dr., 77446.
Res., P.O. Box 3027, 77446-3027. Tel: 409-857-3351; Fax: 409-857-3351. [CEM]

Richmond, Fort Bend Co., Sacred Heart (1935), Rev. Eric J. Pitre; Deacons Don Ries; Joe Kelly.
Res., 507 S. Fourth St., 77469-3599. Tel: 281-342-3609; Fax: 281-342-9833.
Catechesis/Religious Programs—Tel: 281-342-8371. Virginia Ewald, D.R.E.
Students 936.

St. John Fisher (1952), Rev. Wencil C. Pavlovsky, C.S.B.
Mailing Address: 410 Clay St., 77469-1708.
Res., 610 North Fourth St., 77469. Tel: 281-342-5092; Fax: 281-232-2607.
Catechesis/Religious Programs—Tel: 281-232-0348. Janie Taylor, D.R.E.
Students 417.

Rosenberg, Fort Bend Co., Holy Rosary (1911), Rev. Daniel L. Warden, V.F.; Deacon David D. Mitchell.
Res., 1416 George St., 77471-3198. Tel: 281-342-3089; Fax: 281-342-7688.
School—1408 James St., 77471. Tel: 281-342-5813. Mrs. Elizabeth Anthony, Prin.
Lay Teachers 13; Students 241.
Catechesis/Religious Programs—Ms. Kelly Horner, D.R.E., Tel: 281-342-3089 Ext. 106.
Students 264.

Our Lady of Guadalupe (1936), Revs. Jamie M. Abercrombie, C.S.B.; Charles E. Lynch, C.S.B.
Mailing Address: 514 Carlisle St., 77471. Tel: 281-342-4008; Fax: 281-342-4008.
Catechesis/Religious Programs—Tel: 281-232-4322. Dolores Yanz, D.R.E.
Students 565.

Sealy, Austin Co., Immaculate Conception (1889), Rev. Joseph Limanni; Deacon Frank Laredo.
Mailing Address: P.O. Box 337, 77474.
Church—525 5th St., 77474.
Res., 517 Fifth St., 77474. Tel: 409-885-3868; Fax: 409-885-2246. [CEM]
Catechesis/Religious Programs—Donna Brown, D.R.E.
Students 369.

South Houston, Harris Co., Our Lady of Grace (1971), Rev. Jose Maria Asenjo.
Mailing Address: P.O. Box 164, 77587.
Church—1211 Michigan Ave., 77587.
Res., 1206 Michigan St., 77587. Tel: 713-946-6461; Fax: 713-946-0647.
Catechesis/Religious Programs—Tel: 281-333-4174. Amailia D. Parra, D.R.E.
Students 293.

Spring, Harris Co.,

1—Christ the Good Shepherd, (1978), Rev. Msgr. William P. Robertson; Rev. Francisco Quezada; Deacons Steve La Bonte; Pat Camerino.
Res., 18511 Klein Church Rd., 77379-4998. Tel: 281-376-7319; Fax: 281-376-8945.
Catechesis/Religious Programs—Lorelei Guerin, D.R.E.
Students 975.

2—St. Edward, (1969), Rev. Msgr. Al R. Doga; Rev. Dwight Canizares; Deacons Kenneth Martin; Joe Mignogna.
Res., 2601 Spring Stuebner Rd., 77389-4824. Tel: 281-353-9774; Fax: 281-353-9786.
School—Tel: 281-353-4570; Fax: 281-353-8255. Ann Henthorn, Prin.
Lay Teachers 22; Students 385.
Catechesis/Religious Programs—Tel: 281-353-4930. Joe Wappelhorst, D.R.E.
Students 663.

3—St. Ignatius of Loyola, (1985), Revs. Francis X. Pistorius, S.J.; Daniel Croagan, S.J.; Joseph M. Nasser, S.J.; Deacons Glen Cupier; Jim Hite.
Church—7810 Cypresswood Dr., 77379-7101. Tel: 281-370-3401 (Office); Fax: 281-370-9306.
Catechesis/Religious Programs—Deacon James L. Hite, D.R.E.
Students 1,725.

4—St. James the Apostle, (1976), Revs. John Francis Ulm; Tin Cosmas Pham; Deacons Steven Griesmyer; Michael Schmidt.
Res., 22800 Aldine Westfield Rd., 77373-6500. Tel: 281-353-5053; Fax: 281-355-8847.
Catechesis/Religious Programs—Tel: 281-353-3497. Jan Skrehot, D.R.E.
Students 742.

Sugar Land, Fort Bend Co., St. Laurence (1985), Revs. John T. Weyer, B.A., M.Th.; Stuart Emmert; Chacko Puthumayil; Deacons Lee Tollett; Bob Dunham; Steve Harper.
Res., 3100 Sweetwater Blvd., 77479-2630. Tel: 281-980-9812; Fax: 281-980-0686.
School—2630 Austin Pkwy., Sugar Land, 77479. Tel: 281-980-0550; Fax: 281-980-0026.
Lay Teachers 28; Students 537.
Catechesis/Religious Programs—Tel: 281-265-5774. Eleanor Notz, D.R.E.
Students 1,640.

St. Theresa (1924), Revs. Robert J. Matzinger, C.S.B.; Robert G. Ritz, C.S.B.; George E. Silvester, C.S.B.; Robert W. Moslousky, C.S.B.; Deacons Gerald DuPont; Don Burns.
Res., 115 Seventh St., P.O. Box 968, 77487-0968. Tel: 281-494-1156; Fax: 281-242-1393.
Catechesis/Religious Programs—Tel: 281-494-2717. Kathleen Barnosky, D.R.E.
Students 1,647.

St. Thomas Aquinas (1978), Rev. Kevin C. Thissen, O.P.
Church & Mailing Address:—12627 W. Bellfort, 77478.
Res., 10415 Huntington Wood Dr., Houston, 77099-3721. Tel: 281-240-6721; Fax: 281-240-6733.
Catechesis/Religious Programs—Christy Wright, D.R.E.
Students 702.

Sweeny, Brazoria Co., Our Lady of Perpetual Help (1954), Rev. Peter Mastrobuono, S.C.J.
Res., 310 N. McKinney St., 77480-2899. Tel: 409-548-2020; Fax: 409-548-2020.
Catechesis/Religious Programs—Tel: 409-548-4470. Mary Wooderson, D.R.E.
Students 115.
Mission—West Columbia, Brazoria Co., St. John the Apostle, 807 Loggins, West Columbia, 77486-3843. Tel: 409-345-3600.

Texas City, Galveston Co., St. Mary (1911), Rev. Ralph G. Schmidt, Jr. In res., Rev. Msgr. Thomas J. Cullen (Mobile); Rev. John C. DeForke; Deacons Michael Satterwhite; Jose Duplan, Jr.
Mailing Address: 1604 Ninth Ave., N., 77590-5468.
Res., 722 Third Ave. N., 77590. Tel: 409-948-8448; Fax: 409-945-8662.
School—Our Lady of Fatima, 1600 Ninth Ave., N., 77590. Tel: 409-945-3326. Mary Ann Cullen, Prin.
Lay Teachers 20; Students 163.
Catechesis/Religious Programs—Joe Hensley, D.R.E.
Students 525.

The Woodlands, Montgomery Co., Sts. Simon and Jude (1979), Rev. Msgr. Charles C. Domec; Rev. Niall Nolan; Deacons Ken Carlson; Robert Flynn; Fred Shetz; Sid Sandiford; John Charnisky.
Res., 26777 Glen Loch Dr., 77381-2921. Tel: 281-367-9885; Fax: 281-367-9888.
Catechesis/Religious Programs—Tel: 281-292-9801. Robin Walker, D.R.E.
Students 2,264.

St. Anthony of Padua, Rev. John-Vincent Rouse.
Res., 75 W. Sandalbranch Cir., 77382. Tel: 409-273-6979; Fax: 409-321-0314.

Tomball, Harris Co., St. Anne (1964), Rev. David J. DuBois; Deacon J. R. (Bob) Crawford.
Res., 1111 S. Cherry St., 77375-6675. Tel: 281-351-8106; Fax: 281-351-8142.
School—Tel: 281-351-0093. Richard Moran, Prin.
Lay Teachers 23; Students 274.
Catechesis/Religious Programs—Selma De Marco, D.R.E.
Students 570.

Wallis, Austin Co., Guardian Angel (1892), Rev. Albert Walsh.
Res., 5610 Demel St., P.O. Box 487, 77485-0487. Tel: 409-478-6532; Fax: 409-478-7275. [CEM]
Catechesis/Religious Programs—Tel: 409-478-6843. Angelica Flores, D.R.E.
Students 223.

Chaplains of Public Institutions

Prison Chaplains

Galveston. *Galveston County Jail.* Vacant. 715 19th St., 77550. Tel: 409-766-2315.

Angleton. *Retrieve Unit.* Deacon Earl Llewellyn, Rte. 4, Box 1500, 77515. Tel: 713-595-3465.

Brazoria. *Clemens Unit.* Vacant. Rte. 1, Box 1077, 77422. Tel: 409-798-2188.

Huntsville. *Diagnostic Unit.* Deacon Frank Ortego, Box 77340, 76054. Tel: 409-295-8159.
Ellis I Unit. Deacon Richard Lopez, Rte. 6, 77343. Tel: 409-295-5756, Ext. 155.
Ellis II Unit. Rev. Robert Zawacki, S.S.J., Tel: 409-295-8159.
Goree Unit. Deacon Frank Ortego, Box 38, 77340. Tel: 409-295-8159.
Walls Unit. Rev. Robert Zawacki, S.S.J., Box 32, 77340. Tel: 409-295-8159.
Wynne Unit. Rev. Robert Zawacki, S.S.J., Rte. 1, Box 1, 77340. Tel: 409-295-8159.

Midway. *Ferguson Unit.* Deacon Gerardo Garcia, Rte. 2, Box 20, 75852. Tel: 409-348-3751; 295-8159.

Navasota. *Pack I Unit.* Deacon Peter Sechelski, Rte. 3, Box 300, 77686. Tel: 409-825-3728.
Pack II Unit. Deacon Peter L. Sechelski, Rte. 1, Box 1000, 77686. Tel: 409-825-7548.

Richmond. *Jester I Unit.* Rev. Donald McNally, O.M.I., Rte. 2, 77469.
Jester II Unit. Rev. Donald McNally, O.M.I., Rte. 2, 77469.
Jester III Unit. Rev. Donald McNally, O.M.I., Rte. 2, 77469.
Jester IV Unit. Rev. Donald McNally, O.M.I., Rte. 2, 77469. Tel: 713-277-3700.

Rosharon. *Darrington Unit.* Deacon Earl Llewellyn, Rte. 3, Box 59, 77583. Tel: 713-595-2465.
Ramsey I Unit. Deacon Robert Leicht, Rte. 4, Box 1100, 77583.
Ramsey II Unit. Deacon Robert Leicht, Rte. 4, Box 1200, 77583.
Ramsey III Unit. Deacon Robert Kacz, Rte. 4, Box 1300, 77583.

Sugar Land. *Central Unit.* Deacon Emilio Gonzales, One Circle Dr., 77478. Tel: 713-491-2146.

Jail Chaplains

Houston. *Harris County Jail.* Bro. John Cosgrove, O.P. Tel: 713-755-8562; Rev. Ronald F. Cloutier. Tel: 713-755-5326, Res., 215 E. 10th St., 77008.
Juvenile Detention Center. Ms. Marilu Ballow. Tel: 713-762-7192.

On Special Assignment:
Reverend Fathers—
Beck, Albert J., Downtown Chapel, 906 Main St., Houston, TX 77002
Gately, R. Troy, Vice Chancellor
Jozwiak, Lawrence, Tribunal
Rossi, Frank H., Chancellor

On Duty Outside the Diocese:
Reverend Monsignors—
Broussard, William L., Texas Catholic Conference
Fruge, Donald J., P.O. Box 13327, Capitol Station, Austin, TX 78711
Reverend Fathers—
Cahill, Brendan J., Casa Santa Maria, Via dell'Umilta, 30 00187, Rome, Italy. Tel: (06) 68-69-441
Cantu, Oscar, Casa Santa Maria, Via dell'Umilta, 30 00187, Rome, Italy. Tel: (06) 68-69-441
Corrigan, Michael T., St. Anne, 300 Ashton Ave., Kingstree, SC 29556. Tel: 803-354-7798
Hughes, Royce, 745 E. U.S. Hwy. 90, Schulenburg, TX 78956-5233. Tel: 409-743-3722
McGinnis, Jack P., Chap., The Meadows, P.O. Box 637, Wickenburg, AZ 85358. Tel: 602-684-3926
Nguyen, Trung, Divine Word College, Catholic University of America, Washington, D.C.
Perez, Joseph, The Chancery, P.O. Box 907, Houston, TX 77001
Ressler, Clint C., Casa Santa Maria, Via dell'Umilta 30 00187, Rome, Italy. Tel: (06) 68-69-441

Military Chaplains:
Reverend Fathers—
Schwarting, J. Donald, Pastoral Care Services, National Naval Medical Center, Bethesda, MD 20889

Retired:
Reverend Monsignors—
Alleman, C. J., 501 13th St., Galveston, TX 77550-5034. Tel: 409-763-2588
Barzyk, Robert R., 212 Oakdale, Shoreacres, TX 77571-7347
Beck, George A., 8045 Holiday, Houston, TX 77075
Crosthwait, Joseph H., P.O. Box 1302, New Ulm, TX 78950. Tel: 409-992-3821
Donovan, Thomas A., Pope John XXIII Residence, 2407 E. Holcombe Blvd., Houston, TX 77021-2023. Tel: 409-748-4608
Fuchs, Sylvester, Lost Prairie Villa, 9901 FM 2086, Temple, TX 76501-3528. Tel: 817-984-2312
Jones, John B., Pope John XXIII Residence, 2407 E. Holcombe Blvd., Houston, TX 77021-2023. Tel: 713-747-1746
Lagana, Frank A., Pope John XXIII Residence, 2407 E. Holcombe Blvd., Houston, TX 77021-2023. Tel: 713-748-4608
Madden, James J., Pope John XXIII Residence, 2407 E. Holcombe Blvd., Houston, TX 77021-2023. Tel: 713-748-3115
Peguero, Lawrence, Pope John XXIII Residence, 2407 E. Holcombe Blvd., Houston, TX 77021-2023. Tel: 713-748-4608
Rhein, George V., 2407 E. Holcombe Blvd., Houston, TX 77021-2023. Tel: 713-747-7308
Schoppe, Charles K. Tel: 713-748-4596
Wearden, Francis G., 1100 Parthenen Pl., New Caney, TX 77357-3039. Tel: 713-399-0270
Reverend Fathers—
Antle, Nicholas C., Pope John XXIII Residence, 2407 E. Holcombe Blvd., Houston, TX 77021-2023. Tel: 713-748-1553
Banet, Charles, C.PP.S., Holy Rosary Church, 1420 31st St., Galveston, TX 77550-4399. Tel: 409-762-2478
Burns, Charles E., 343 Bobolink, New Braunfels, TX 78130-3868
Burns, David E.

Carreon, Albert S., P.O. Box 15836, Santa Ana, CA 92705
Chandonnet, A. J., C.SS.R., Holy Ghost, 6921 Chetwood, Houston, TX 77081-5697. Tel: 713-668-0463
Clemens, Norbert H., C.S.B., Dillon House, 1302 Kipling St., Houston, TX 77006-4297. Tel: 713-529-3994; 529-3970
Daigle, Robert E., 6505 O'Bannon Dr., Las Vegas, NV 89102-0854
del Val, Feliciano, Pope John XXIII Residence, 2407 East Holcombe Blvd., Houston, TX 77021-2023. Tel: 713-748-4608
Dougherty, George Patrick, 7228 Comanche Trail, Austin, TX 78732-1011. Tel: 512-266-2186
Ferguson, Carlos, c/o Chancery
Freret, Warren Joseph, P.O. Box 850, Hawthorne, NV 89415. Tel: 702-945-2020
Gillece, Alfred F., 630 N. Via Lucia, Tucson, AZ 85745. Tel: 602-792-0122
Gillgannon, Patrick, P.O. Box 300923, Houston, TX 77230-0923. Tel: 713-799-8350
Greenwald, Alfred F., 630 N. Via Lucia, Tucson, AZ 85745. Tel: 602-792-0122
Guillermo, Rodrigo J., M.S.Ch.E., M.B.A., c/o Chancery
Hebert, Marvin A., c/o Mr. Jude C. Hebert, 415 Jeannette Dr., Bridge City, TX 77611-3742
Horacek, Mark, Notre Dame, 7720 Boone Rd., Houston, TX 77072-3595. Tel: 713-498-4653
Hosko, George H., C.S.B., Supr., Dillon House, 1302 Kipling St., Houston, TX 77006-4297. Tel: 713-529-3994; 529-3970
Joubert, Gerard, O.P., 9946 Village Bell, Houston, TX 77038-2612. Tel: 713-820-3871
Kellick, John W., 6517 Burdock Dr., Santa Fe, TX 77510-9340. Tel: 409-925-6817
Lee, Lawrence, Pope John XXIII Residence, 2407 E. Holcombe Blvd., Houston, TX 77021-2023. Tel: 713-748-3115
Leonard, Lawrence J., C.M., Pope John Paul XXIII Residence, 2407 E. Holcombe Blvd., Houston, TX 77021-2023. Tel: 713-747-4844
Lynch, Denis
Madden, John F., C.S.B., Campus Ministry, Dillon House, 1302 Kipling St., Houston, TX 77006-4297. Tel: 713-529-3994; 529-3970
Murphy, Joseph R., S.S.J., 100 Ferol Ln., Highlands, TX 77562-3934 7. Tel: 713-426-3433
Natho, Clifton J., 8326 Autumn Wind Dr., Houston, TX 77040-1474
O'Loughlin, S. Raphael, C.S.B., Dillon House, 1302 Kipling St., Houston, TX 77006-4297. Tel: 713-529-3994; 529-3970
Roussel, Joseph P., C.S.B., 1302 Kipling St., Houston, TX 77006-4297. Tel: 713-529-3994; 529-3970
Stredny, Anthony G., B.A.
Tran, John Chinh Chan, 8138 Lynn St., Houston, TX 77017-3050. Tel: 713-645-2834
Van Der Peet, Michael, S.C.J., Aids Ministry Support Group, St. Matthew Church, Scotland Yard Apts., 8450 Cambridge, #1174, Houston, TX 77054-3919. Tel: 713-797-1830
Volpe, Rocco C., C.S.B., Dillon House, 1302 Kipling St., Houston, TX 77006-4297. Tel: 713-529-3994; 529-3970
Walker, Anselm, 1817 Parker, Houston, TX 77093. Tel: 713-697-7109
Weihrer, John A., Pope John XXIII Residence, 2407 East Holcombe Blvd., Houston, TX 77021-2023. Tel: 713-748-3130

Permanent Deacons:
Abram, Alfred, Sr., Unassigned
Acosta, Angel R., St. Mary, Texas City
Adame, David, Annunciation/St. Joseph Hospital, Houston
Adams, Francis E., St. Elizabeth Anne Seton, Houston
Adams, John W., St. Matthew the Evangelist, Houston
Aiuvalasit, Anthony George, St. John Vianney, Houston
Alessi, Anthony V., St. Thomas More, Houston
Alexander, Robert George, Mary Queen, Friendswood
Allen, Charles J., Sr., Our Mother of Mercy, Houston
Aranda, Jose Francisco, St. Christopher, Houston
Arceneaux, Leon M., Jr., St. Pius V, Pasadena
Arceneaux, Steve, Jr., St. Martin de Porres, Barrett Station
Arellano, Jose, Immaculate Heart of Mary, Houston
Ausmus, Sam, III, Shrine of the True Cross, Dickinson
Baker, J. M., St. Theresa/St. Justin Martyr, Houston
Baker, Theodore Otis, St, Matthias the Apostle, Magnolia
Barnett, James, Our Lady of Walsingham, Houston
Bart, James, St. Augustine, Houston
Betancourt, Manuel, Unassigned
Bobb, William J., St. Peter the Apostle, Galveston
Bonura, James L., Sr., TDC/Queen of Peace, La Marque
Bordelon, Darvin A., St. Helen, Pearland
Bothe, Albert G., St. Francis de Sales, Houston
Bottjer, Albert, Assumption, Houston/Ben Taub Hospital
Bradley, Donald E., St. Cecilia, Houston
Breaux, Roy, St. Phillip of Jesus, Houston
Brinkman, Fred H., TDC-Ramsey Units I, II, III/Drug Trustee Camp
Broussard, Leonard J., Epiphany of the Lord, Katy; Holy Name Retreat Center, Houston
Brueggerhoff, Robert T., Holy Ghost, Houston
Burns, Don, St. Theresa, Sugar Land
Cabler, Paul Stephen, Unassigned
Calonge, Elie, Texas Dept. of Corrections, Palestine, TX
Calvo, Clement S., Hispanic Ministry Office, Houston
Camerino, Pat W., Christ the Good Shepherd, Spring
Camunez, Richard F., St. Hyacinth, Deer Park
Cantu, Hector, St. Mary, La Porte
Carlson, Kenneth D., Sts. Simon & Jude, The Woodlands
Carranza, Joe M., Archdiocese of St. Paul and Minneapolis
Caruso, James, St. Mary, Humble
Castaneda, Guillermo F., Jr., St. John Fisher, Richmond
Castillo, Raul A., St. Joseph, Brazoria
Charnisky, John E., Jr., Sts. Simon & Jude, The Woodlands
Cooper, Leslie F., Christ the Good Shepherd, Spring
Coussirat, John F., St. John Vianney, Houston
Crawford, J. R., St. Anne, Tomball
Cromer, Frank P., St. Francis de Sales, Houston
Cuiper, Glen H., St. Ignatius of Loyola, Spring
Dalecki, Robert, Prince of Peace, Houston
Despania, Raymond L., Sr., St. Peter Claver, Houston
Devine, John E., Jr., St. Luke the Evangelist, Houston
Do, Joseph Chuong Nguyen, Our Lady of Lourdes, Houston
Duck, Charles, Prince of Peace, Houston
Dunham, Robert K., St. Laurence, Sugarland
Duplan, Jose, Jr., St. Mary's, Texas City
Dupont, Gerald W., St. Theresa, Sugar Land
Duron, Jose, St. Alphonsus, Houston
Ehrman, John W., Jr., Sacred Heart, Conroe
Evon, William J., Sr., St. Ignatius of Loyola, Spring
Festa, Gene, St. Justin Martyr, Houston
Fikac, Marvin R., Sacred Heart Co-Cathedral, Houston
Flores, Geronimo, St. Joseph, Houston
Floyd, Ivy C., St. Thomas the Apostle, Huntsville
Flynn, Robert E., Sr., Sts. Simon & Jude, The Woodlands
Fraser, Ronald J., St. Maximilian Kolbe, Houston
Garcia, Gerardo J., Christ the King, Houston
Garcia, Gregory C., Resurrection, Houston
Garza, Robert, St. Mary, League City
Gilbert, Daniel W., St. Francis Xavier, Houston
Glor, Richard J.L., Unassigned
Gomez, Arturo M., Notre Dame, Houston
Gomez, Javier, St. Andrew, Channelview
Gonzales, Emiliano, TDC Prison Chaplain, Houston
Gonzalez, Enrique, St. Charles Borromeo, Houston
Gonzalez Bangs, Fernando, Our Lady of Guadalupe, Baytown
Gosline, Edwin F., St. Thomas More, Houston
Graham, Michael G., St. John the Evangelist, Baytown
Gramann, Henry T., St. Christopher, Houston
Granado, Alfred E., Jr., Leave of Absence
Griesmyer, Steven, Sr., St. James the Apostle, Spring
Guajardo, Fredrico, Our Lady of Mt. Carmel, Houston
Guerra, Daniel, Sr., St. Clare of Assisi, Houston
Gutierrez, Diego, Sr., St. John the Baptist, Alvin
Hall, Raymond J., St. James the Apostle, Spring
Hamilton, L. William, Unassigned
Hargraves, Wilfred J., Jr., St. Clare of Assisi, Houston
Harper, Stephen Edwin, St. Laurence, Sugarland
Hart, Donald J., St. Pius V, Pasadena; Catholic Charismatic Center, Houston
Hennessy, Robert, St. John the Evangelist, Baytown
Henry, Albert, St. Francis Xavier, Houston
Herrera, Rolando, Unassigned
Hickey, Dennis, St. Hyacinth, Deer Park
Hite, James, St. Ignatius Loyola, Spring
Hock, Leslie Bart, Immaculate Conception, Houston
Hodapp, Cyril J., St. Bernadette, Houston
Holt, Grant E., Christ Our Light, Navasota
Horbowy, Thaddeus J., Chaplain-Fed. Bureau of Prisons, Richmond, VA
Horr, Louis Eugene, St. Jerome, Houston
Housholder, John, St. Helen, Pearland
Hubisz, John Lawrence, NC State University Catholic Center
Hunsucker, Paul David, St. Thomas the Apostle, Canyon Lake, TX
Hunter, Thomas Alexander, Hospital/Port/St.Patrick, Galveston
Husch, John M., Leave of Absence
Jachimczyk, Joseph A., Annunciation, Houston
Jackson, Clifford X., Our Lady of Sorrows, Houston
Jelinek, Gregory N., M.D., Christ Our Light-Navasota; O.C. LutherTDC
Jenkins, Michael V., St. Francis Xavier, Houston
Johnson, Clarence B., St. Peter the Apostle, Houston
Joseph, Ignatius, St. Francis of Assisi, Houston
Kacz, Robert, St. John the Baptist, Alvin
Kelleher, Peter J., St. Christopher, Houston
Keller, Robert C., St. Justin Martyr, Houston
Kelly, Joseph R., Sr., Sacred Heart, Richmond
Kish, Don, Epiphany of the Lord, Katy
Klein, Hugo L., St. Francis de Sales, Houston
Knobloch, Alden J., St. Jerome, Houston
Koch, William E., Sr., Leave of Absence
Kulhanek, Jerry Peter, Sr., Our Lady of Fatima, Galena Park
Kutach, Emil W., Leave of Absence
LaBonte, Stephen L., Christ the Good Shepherd, Spring
Labrecque, Richard, St. Paul, Houston
Landry, Burke J., St. Elizabeth Ann Seton, Madisonville
Lansch, John, St. Justin Martyr, Houston
Laredo, Frank, Immaculate Conception, Sealy
Laugermann, Frank J., Jr., St. Benedict the Abbot, County Jail, Houston
Leach, Richard L., Christ the Redeemer; St. John Neumann, Houston
Leal, Merce C., Jr., St. Christopher, Houston
Leblanc, Irvin, St. Mary of the Purification, Houston
Leicht, Robert, Ramsey III Unit - TDC
Leija, Valeriano, Blessed Juan Diego, Pasadena
Lerma, Pedro, Sr., Blessed Sacrament, Houston
Lewis, Edward Thomas, St. Mary, La Porte
Liendo, Jose L., Queen of Peace, Houston
Llewellyn, Earl, Jr., TDCJ Hospital Chaplain, Galveston; Queen of Peace, LaMarque
Llorens, Cornelius C., St. Justin Martyr, Houston
Lopez, Richard, St. Thomas the Apostle, Huntsville
Lorino, Joseph E., St. Vincent de Paul, Houston
Lozano, Rodrigo, St. Charles Borromeo, Houston
Lugo, Loni G., Holy Family, Missouri City
Lynch, Philip F., Unassigned
Marquez, Antonio, St. Raphael, Houston
Martin, Henry Woods, St. Cyril of Alexandria, Houston
Martin, Kenneth, St. Edward, Spring
Matula, Francis L., All Saints, Houston
McAllister, Jerome, St. Mary, League City
McKinney, Thomas K., Ellis Unit TDC; St. Mary Magdalene, Humble
Mignogna, Joe, St. Edward, Spring
Miller, Arthur, Harris Co. Psychiatric Center, Houston
Miller, Stephen, St. Andrew, Channelview
Mitchell, David D., Holy Rosary, Rosenberg
Morales, Hector Hernando, Our Lady of Fatima, Galena Park
Moreno, Aurelio Frank, Jr., St. Frances Cabrini, Houston
Moreno, Leopold R., Catholic Charismatic Center, Houston
Morin, Joseph G., Immaculate Conception, Houston
Motley, John M., Unassigned
Moulton, Darrell, Mary Queen, Friendswood; Covenant House, Houston
Mulcare, Terrance D., St. Christopher, Houston
Navarro, Raul G., Immaculate Heart of Mary, Houston
Nelms, D. Cade, St. Cecilia, Houston
Newhouse, Thomas C., St. Thomas More, Houston
Nguyen Kim Khanh, Michael, Our Lady of Lavang, Houston
Nguyen Pham, Joseph, Vietnamese Martyrs, Houston
Nguyen Si Bach, Joseph, Notre Dame, Houston
O'Brien, Alfred J., Prison Chaplain Stiles Unit-Beaumont
Ortego, Frank P., St. Thomas the Apostle, Huntsville
Osterhaus, James H., Christ the Redeemer, Houston
Ostrand, Gerard, St. Martha, Kingwood
Pareja, Juan Francisco, St. Jerome, Houston

Parr, Kenneth, Catholic Charismatic Center, Houston
Payne, George, Leave of Absence
Peltier, Gerald, St. Anthony, Danbury
Pennell, Charles G., St. Elizabeth Ann Seton, Houston
Petereit, Klaus, St. John Newmann, Houston
Pistone, John Salvadore, St. Mary's Cathedral Basilica, Galveston
Ramirez, Fernando, St. Frances Cabrini, Houston
Ramirez, Jose J., Resurrection, Houston
Ramirez, Julio M., St. Gregory the Great, Houston
Ramirez, Leonard, Holy Family, Missouri City
Ries, Donald G., Sacred Heart, Richmond
Rincon, George, Our Lady of Guadalupe, Baytown
Robison, Paul L., Jr., St. Luke the Evangelist, Houston
Roessler, Charles F., Jr., St. Frances Cabrini, Houston
Romeu, Hector J., St. John Vianney, Houston
Rook, R. Jack, St. Andrew, Channelview
Rooney, John, St. Frances Cabrini, Houston
Rowan, Vincent A., St. Michael, Lake Jackson
Rutledge, James E., St. Jerome, Houston
Salazar, Mariano, St. Joseph, Houston
Saltzmann, Peter, Catholic Charismatic Center, Houston
Sanchez, Martin G., St. Joseph, Houston
Sanders, Raymond L., Jr., St. Paul, Houston
Sandiford, Sid, Sts. Simon & Jude, The Woodlands
Santos, John, St. Andrew, Channelview
Satterwhite, Michael, St. Mary, Texas City
Schmidt, Glendon Michael, St. James, Spring
Sechelski, Peter, TDC/St. Stanislaus, Anderson
Seifert, William E., Jr., Holy Family, Missouri City
Sharpless, James, St. Luke the Evangelist, Houston
Shaw, Wallace, St. Mary Star of the Sea, Freeport
Sheffield, William Leonard, Christ Our Light, Navasota
Shefts, Andrew, St. Basil, Angleton
Sheltz, George A., Sr., St. Joseph Hospital/St. Vincent de Paul, Houston
Shetz, Fred T., Dir. Perm. Deacons, Sts. Simon & Jude, The Woodlands
Sicinski, Anton, St. Stanislaus, Anderson
Simon, Ronald, St. Philip Neri, Houston
Singer, John William, Jr., St. Joseph, Baytown
Smaistrla, Denis J., St. Mary's Seminary, Houston
Smith, Jimmy, St. Joseph, Brazoria
St. Aubin, Leo F., Sacred Heart, Conroe
Stanley, John, Terrell Unit, Livingston; St. Joseph's Livingston
Steffes, Dale W., St. John Vianney, Houston
Stevens, Robert Gregory, St. Francis Cabrini, Houston
Stoessel, Edward T., St. Thomas More, Houston
Stubbs, Peter, Holy Ghost Hall, Houston
Suriano, Julio S., Our Lady of St. John, Houston
Tollett, Lee Joseph, St. Laurence, Sugar Land
Trosclair, George, Prince of Peace, Houston
Vacek, Albert E., Jr., St. John Vianney, Houston
Vaclavik, Larry A., St. Theresa, Houston
Vanderslice, Ron, Leave of Absence
Venegas, Rudy, St. Joseph, Baytown
Vicknair, Tom Jude, Catholic Charismatic Center, Houston
Villarreal, Gilbert R., St. Helen, Pearland
Villarreal, Marcelino, St. Benedict the Abbot, Houston
Vocelka, Frank Jay, Jr., St. Theresa, Houston
Wagner, William C., St. Bartholomew, Katy
Watkins, Rollo J., Christ the King, Houston
Weaver, William A., St. Elizabeth Ann Seton, Houston
Wewer, Justin J., St. John the Evangelist, Baytown
Wiles, Philip Arlen, St. Dominic, Houston
Wright, Jim, St. Thomas Aquinas, Sugar Land
Zamora, Joe, St. Augustine, Houston
Zuk, Adolph J., St. Matthew the Evangelist, Houston

INSTITUTIONS LOCATED IN THE DIOCESE

[A] SEMINARIES, DIOCESAN

HOUSTON. *St. Mary's Seminary*, 9845 Memorial Dr., 77024-3498. Tel: 713-686-4345. Rev. Msgr. Chester L. Borski, Rector; Rev. Msgr. Reginald Nesvadba, Vice Rector; Revs. Leon Strieder (AUS), Formation Dir.; John Kha Tran, Formation Dir.; Drew Wood, Spiritual Dir.; Edward Abell, Spiritual Dir.; Sr. Barbara Tovar, M.C.D.P., Dir., Cultural Formation; Deacon Denis J. Smaistrla, Treas.-Plant Mgr.; Revs. Louis T. Brusatti, C.M., Dean, School of Theology; James B. Anderson, Asst. Prof., Systematic Theology; Dr. Frances Panchok, Prof., Church History; Dr. Michael Prokurat, Asst. Prof., Sacred Scripture; Dr. Sandra Magie, Asst. Prof., Moral Theology; Dr. Richard Gaillardetz, Asst. Prof. Systematic Theology; Revs. Jack Gallagher, C.S.B.; Sean C. Martin, Asst. Prof. Sacred Scripture. Lay Teachers 4; Diocesan Seminarians 45; Religious Seminarians 7; Total Enrollment 52.

[B] SEMINARIES, RELIGIOUS OR SCHOLASTICATES

HOUSTON. *Casa San Basilio*, 1910 W. Alabama, 77098. Tel: 713-522-1736.
E-mail: sinasac@earthlink-net
Rev. Alvin A. Sinasac, C.S.B., Dir.
Purpose: House of formation for Hispanic men in Religious life discernment. Apostolate of the Basilian Fathers. Total Enrollment 5.

Holy Ghost Fathers, Holy Ghost Seminary, 4410 Yoakum Blvd., 77006-5820. Tel: 713-529-0405. Rev. John J. Walsh, C.S.Sp.; Deacon Peter Stubbs, C.S.Sp., Dir. of House Formator; Mrs. Judy Stubbs, Bursar Formator; Revs. Frankie L. G. Santos, C.S.Sp., Formation Dir.; Anton Morgenroth, C.S.Sp., (Retired); Ron Groschen, M.S.; Vincent O'Grady, C.S.Sp.; Bro. Robert W. Hassel, C.S.Sp. Priests 1; Deacons 1; Lay Teachers 1.

St. Basil Novitiate, 106 Fifth St., 77478-2631. Tel: 713-491-8700.

[C] COLLEGES AND UNIVERSITIES

HOUSTON. *University of St. Thomas*, 3800 Montrose Blvd., 77006-4696. Tel: 713-522-7911.
Web site: stthom.edu
For a complete listing, refer to the Colleges and Universities section.

[D] HIGH SCHOOLS, DIOCESAN

GALVESTON. *O'Connell Catholic High School*, 1320 Tremont St., 77550-4513. Tel: 409-765-5534; Fax: 409-765-5536. Rev. Joseph Howard; Mr. Thomas E. Ducote, Prin. Priests 1; Sisters 1; Lay Teachers 16; Students 185.

HOUSTON. *Mt. Carmel High School*, 6700 Mt. Carmel Dr., 77087. Tel: 713-649-2745; Fax: 713-649-6851. Mr. William Knapick, Prin. Priests 1; Lay Teachers 20; Students 227.

[E] JUNIOR HIGH SCHOOLS, DIOCESAN

HOUSTON. *Seton Catholic Jr. High School*, 801 Rose Ln., 77037-4696. Tel: 281-447-2132; Fax: 281-447-1825. Miss Mary Jo Smith, Prin. Sisters 2; Principals 1; Assistant Principals; 1; Counselors 1; Development Directors 1; Lay Teachers 16; Total Staff 21; Students 267.

[F] HIGH SCHOOLS, PRIVATE

HOUSTON. *Academy of the Incarnate Word*, 609 Crawford St., 77002-3668. Tel: 713-227-3637; Fax: 713-227-1014. Sisters of the Incarnate Word and Blessed Sacrament. Ms. Mary Welch, Prin. Sisters 2; Lay Teachers 19; Girls 250.

Duchesne Academy of the Sacred Heart, 10202 Memorial Dr., 77024-3299. Tel: 713-468-8211. Religious of the Sacred Heart. Sr. Jan Dunn, R.S.C.J., Headmistress. Sisters 2; Lay Teachers 32; Girls 206.

St. Agnes Academy, 9000 Bellaire Blvd., 77036-4683. Sr. Jane Meyer, O.P., Prin. Tel: 713-219-5450. Dominican Sisters 1; Lay Teachers 57; Girls 732.

St. Pius X High School, Inc., 811 W. Donovan, 77091-5699. Tel: 713-692-3581. Sr. Donna M. Pollard, O.P., Prin. Dominican Sisters 2; Lay Teachers 55; Total Staff 70; Students 636.

St. Thomas High School, 4500 Memorial Dr., 77007-7332. Tel: 713-864-6348 (School); 868-9209 (Residence); Fax: 713-864-5750. Basilian Residence, Basilian Fathers. Revs. Jack H. Hanna, C.S.B., Supr.; Carl L. Belisch, C.S.B.; Edward A. Doser, C.S.B.; William Vela, C.S.B.; Norbert C. Reuss, C.S.B.; Total Enrollment 650.

Strake, Jesuit College Preparatory Inc., 8900 Bellaire Blvd., 77036-4699. Tel: 713-774-7651; Fax: 713-774-6427. Rev. Brian F. Zinnamon, S.J., Pres.; Mr. Richard Nevle, Prin.; Revs. Christopher A. Billac, S.J.; Edward T. Coles, S.J.; John N. Folzenlogen, S.J.; Douglas J. Hypolite, S.J., Rector; Joseph B. Leininger, S.J.; Vincent A. Orlando, S.J.; D. Richard Toye, S.J.; Bros. Castenzio A. Ferlita, S.J.; Jeff Pouzar, S.J. Scholastics: Harlan W. Fails, S.J. Teachers: Priests 7; Brothers 1; Lay Teachers 49; Boys 700.

[G] ELEMENTARY SCHOOLS, PRIVATE

HOUSTON. *Duchesne Academy of the Sacred Heart*, 10202 Memorial Dr., 77024-3299. Tel: 713-468-8211. Sr. Jan Dunn, R.S.C.J., Headmistress. Lay Teachers 29; Total Staff 52; Girls 403.

John Paul II Catholic School, 1400 Parkway Plaza Dr., 77077. Tel: 713-496-1500; Fax: 713-496-2943. Clarice Franke, Prin. Lay Teachers 32; Students 530.

The Regis School, 7330 Westview Dr., 77055-5122. Tel: 713-682-8383; Fax: 713-682-8388. Catholic School for Boys. Anne Storey Carty, Headmistress. Lay Teachers 19; Students 140.

St. Catherine's Montessori, 2510 Westridge, 77054. Tel: 713-665-2195. Mailing Address: P.O. Box 20728, 77225-0728. Sisters 2; Lay Teachers 8; Students 206.

[H] ELEMENTARY SCHOOLS, CONSOLIDATED

GALVESTON. *Galveston Catholic School*, 2601 Ursuline Ave., 77550-4398. Tel: 409-765-6607. Mrs. Mary Frances Bernardoni, Prin. Lay Teachers 27; Students 383.
Serving the parishes of Holy Rosary, Sacred Heart, St. Mary Cathedral Basilica, St. Patrick, Queen of Peace Mission, St. Peter the Apostle, Our Lady of Lourdes, Reina de la Paz, Queen of Peace, La Marque, Shrine of True Cross, St. Mary's/League City, St. Mary's/Texas City, Our Mother of Mercy/Bolivar.

NAVASOTA. *School of Environmental Education - Camp Kappe.* (Grade 5), Rte. 2, Box 3197, 77868-9604. Tel: 409-894-2141. Sr. Thomas Ann LaCour, O.P., Prin. Lay Teachers 2.

RICHWOOD. *Our Lady Queen of Peace*, 1600 Hwy. 2004, 77531. Tel: 409-265-3909. Mr. Jack Hawthorne, Prin. Lay Teachers 21; Students 330.
Serving the parishes of St. Basil; St. Jerome, Clute; St. Anthony, Danbury; St. Henry; St. Mary, Star of the Sea, Freeport; St. Michael, Lake Jackson; Our Lady of Perpetual Help, Sweeney; St. John the Apostle Mission, West Columbia.

[I] SOCIAL AGENCIES CATHOLIC CHARITIES

HOUSTON. *Associated Catholic Charities of the Diocese of Galveston-Houston*, 3520 Montrose Blvd., P.O. Box 66508, 77266. Tel: 713-526-4611; Fax: 713-526-1546. Anna M. Babin, Exec. Dir.
Diocesan AIDS Ministry.
Catholic Charities, Galveston.
St. Joseph's Inn, Galveston.
Guadalupe Area Social Services.
Children's Placement Services.
Services to Pregnant Adolescents and Their Families.
Post Adoption Services.
Family Counseling.
Prevention Services.
Texas Center for Immigrant Legal Assistance.
Refugee Resettlement Program.
Unaccompanied Juvenile Foster Care Program.
Services to the Alone and Frail Elderly.
Serenity House.
Parish Social Ministry. Total Assisted 44,000.

[J] HEALTH AND HOSPITALS

HOUSTON. *St. Joseph Hospital*, 1919 LaBranch, 77002. Tel: 713-757-1000
For a complete listing, refer to the Hospitals section.
Sisters of Charity of the Incarnate Word, Houston, Texas, 2600 N. Loop W., 77092. Tel: 713-681-8877
For a complete listing, refer to the Hospitals section.

MADISONVILLE. *Madison Acquisition Company dba St. Francis Health Center*, P.O. Box 698 - 100 W. Cross St., 77864-0698
For a complete listing, refer to the Hospitals section.

NASSAU BAY. *St. John Hospital*, 2050 Space Park Dr., 77058. Tel: 281-333-5503; Fax: 281-333-8891
For a complete listing, refer to the Hospitals section.

[K] CATHOLIC CHAPLAIN CORPS

HOUSTON. *The Catholic Chaplain Corps*, 4206 S. MacGregor Way, 77021-1598. Tel: 713-526-6438; Fax: 713-747-3642. Rev. Alcuin E. Greenburg, Dir. Houston Hospitals: St. Luke's Episcopal, Texas Heart Institute, Texas Children's Hospital, Methodist, M. D. Anderson Cancer Center - Hospital of University of Texas, Diagnostic, Shriners Hospital for Crippled Children, The Institute of Rehabilitation and Research, Ben Taub Hospital, Hermann Hospital, Diagnostic Center Hospital, Vencor Hospital.

Catholic Chaplain Corps, Texas Medical Center. Revs. Alcuin E. Greenburg; Joseph Dean; Elias E. Doroin; Joseph Haley; Bruce H. Noble; David H. Noble; Don A. Neumann; Donald E. Kuder, C.S.B.; Teodoro Tim Y. Prado; Jose A. Joseph, C.M.I.; Sr. Beatrice Cruz, I.W.B.S.; Sr. Josephine Nolan, C.V.I.

Chaplain Corps, Southwest Memorial Center Complex, 10330 Hillcroft, 77096-4795. Rev. Joseph T. O'Malley.

Chaplain Corps, Lyndon B. Johnson Hospital. Tel: 713-526-6438 (24-hour paging). Rev. A. Ed Doser, C.S.B.; Sr. Martha Christina Mejia, C.V.I.

Chaplain Corps. Tel: 713-526-6438 (24 hour paging). Rev. Franklin Simmons.
Memorial City/Spring Branch Medical Complexes: Memorial City Medical Center Hospital.

Chaplain Corps: John Sealy Medical Center, U.T.M.B. Hospital, 2011 Ave. F (Church St.), Galveston, 77550-2091; Fax: 409-762-9612. Revs. Gerald Lewis, S.V.D.; Edward Baur, S.V.D.

[L] CLINICS

HOUSTON. *San Jose Clinic*, 301 Hamilton St., 77002. Tel: 713-228-9411; Fax: 713-228-6371. Sr. Margaret Bulmer, C.C.V.I., Exec. Dir. Sisters of Charity of the Incarnate Word 1; Patients assisted annually 29,453; Lay Staff 35.

[M] PROTECTIVE INSTITUTIONS

HOUSTON. *Casa de Esperanza, De Los Ninos, Inc.*, Mailing Address: P.O. Box 66581, 77006. Tel: 713-529-0639.
For a complete listing, refer to the Special Care Facilities section.
Casa Juan Diego, 4818 Rose, 77007. Tel: 713-869-7376.
For a complete listing, refer to the Special Care Facilities section.
Casa Maria de Guadalupe Medical Clinic and Social Service Center, 6101 Edgemoor, 77081. Tel: 713-995-9414.
For a complete listing, refer to the Special Care Facilities section.
Covenant House Texas, 1111 Lovett Blvd., 77006. Tel: 713-523-2231.
For a complete listing, refer to the Special Care Facilities section.
Santa Maria Hostel, 807 Paschall St., 77009. Tel: 713-228-0125.
For a complete listing, refer to the Special Care Facilities section.

[N] HOMES FOR THE AGED

HOUSTON. *Pope John XXIII Priest Residence*, 2407 Holcombe Blvd., 77021-2023. Tel: 713-748-4608
For a complete listing, refer to the Special Care Facilities section.
St. Dominic Nursing Home, St. Dominic Center, 2409 E. Holcombe Blvd., 77021-2023. Tel: 713-741-8701
For a complete listing, refer to the Special Care Facilities section.
St. Dominic Residence Hall, St. Dominic Diocesan Center, 2401 E. Holcombe Blvd., 77021-2023. Tel: 713-741-8700
For a complete listing, refer to the Special Care Facilities section.

[O] RESIDENTIAL TREATMENT AND RENEWAL CENTERS

SPLENDORA. *Shalom Center, Inc.*, 13516 Morgan Dr., 77372-3121. Tel: 713-399-0520; Fax: 713-399-0520. A residential treatment center for clergy and religious. Sr. Gina Marie Iadanza, M.S.C., Exec. Dir.

[P] PERSONAL PRELATURES

HOUSTON. *Opus Dei.* (Prelature of the Holy Cross and Opus Dei), 5505 Chaucer Dr., 77005. Tel: 713-528-4081. Very Rev. Michael J. Barrett, Delegate Vicar; Revs. Jose Gomez; George W. Crafts.

[Q] MONASTERIES AND RESIDENCES OF PRIESTS AND BROTHERS

HOUSTON. *Carmelite Priory*, Casa Santa Teresita, 6725 Reed Rd., 77087-6830. Tel: 713-644-5561. Revs. Gregory Battafarano, O.Carm., Dir. & Prior; William Harry, O.Carm.; Bro. Stephen DieKemper, O.Carm. College level pre-novitiate house and program of formation for Hispanic candidates seeking admission to the Most Pure Heart of Mary Province of the Carmelite Order (O.Carm.). Students 4; Total in Residence 3; Total Staff 1.
Dillon House, 1302 Kipling, 77006-4297. Tel: 713-529-3994; 529-3970 (Ans. machine); Fax: 713-942-7623. Basilian Fathers. Revs. George H. Hosko, C.S.B., Supr.; Norbert H. Clemens, C.S.B., (Retired); John F. Madden, C.S.B., (Retired); S. Raphael O'Loughlin, C.S.B., (Retired); Wilfred S. Canning, C.S.B., (Retired); Joseph B. Courtney, C.S.B., (Retired); Rocco C. Volpe, C.S.B., (Retired).
Dominican Fathers and Brothers, St. Mark Priory, Inc., 1702 Bolsover Rd., 77005-1726. Tel: 713-526-6411. Revs. Richard Martin Patrick, O.P., Prior; Joseph Ngoc Tu Nguyen, O.P.; Thomas D. Sheehan, O.P.; Isidore V. Vicente, O.P.; Daniel Ulloa, O.P.; Wilfred S. Canning, C.S.B., (Retired); Joseph B. Courtney, C.S.B., (Retired); Rocco C. Volpe, C.S.B., (Retired).
Assigned to St. Mark Priory, Residing Elsewhere: Rev. Terence A. Holachek, O.P., Corpus Christi, TX; Bro. John M. Cosgrove, O.P.; Rev. Stephen T. Smithers, O.P., Houston, TX. Total Assisted 100; Total Staff 10.
Franciscan Friars, 2508 Wilshire St., 77023-5246. Tel: 713-921-0259; Fax: 713-526-6010. Rev. Jeffrey Scheeler, O.F.M.
Franciscan Friars, 4643 Wild Indigo, #409, 77027-7058. Tel: 713-355-1319. Mailing Address: P.O. Box 66669, 77266-6669. Bros. Robert Hozie, O.F.M., Supr.; David Crank, O.F.M.
Marianist Community, 6409 Brookside Dr., 77023-3323. Tel: 713-926-5925. Society of Mary. Revs. Robert E. Hackel, S.M.; Agustin Guzman, S.M.; Bros. James E. Barrette, S.M.; Michael H. Gillespie, S.M.
Maryknoll Fathers and Brothers, 2360 Rice Blvd., 77005-2652. Tel: 713-529-1912; Fax: 713-529-0372. Revs. Rafael R. Davila, M.M., Dir.; Kyungsu Son, M.M.; Paul R. Masson, M.M.; Bro. Mark Gruenke, M.M. Total in Residence 4; Total Staff 5. Catholic Charismatic Center, 2500 Bell St., 77003. Tel: 713-236-9977. Rev. Richard E. Paulissen, M.M.
Residence of the Basilian Fathers of the University of St. Thomas, 4019 Yoakum Blvd., 77006-4696. Tel: 713-525-3515; Fax: 713-529-0844. Revs. John C. Gallagher, C.S.B., Supr.; Dennis M. Andrews, C.S.B.; Edward A. Bader, C.S.B.; Edward J. Baenziger, C.S.B.; Patrick O. Braden, C.S.B.; Victor B. Brezik, C.S.B.; Daniel D. Callam, C.S.B.; Robert W. Crooker, C.S.B.; Mark R. Gazin, C.S.B.; George H.Hosko, C.S.B.; James J. Keon, C.S.B.; John E. McManus, C.S.B.; Joseph L. Meyers, C.S.B.; J. Michael Miller, C.S.B.; Harold V. O'Leary, C.S.B.; Joseph E. Pilsner, C.S.B.; Joseph P. Roussel, C.S.B.; Richard J. Schiefen, C.S.B.; T. Patrick Warden, C.S.B.; Walter M. Werbylo, C.S.B.; William J. Young, C.S.B.; Janusz Ihnatowicz (Poland).
Western Province of the Congregation of the Holy Ghost, 1700 West Alabama St., 77098-2808. Tel: 713-522-2882; Fax: 713-522-8063.
E-mail: spiritars@aol.com
Very Rev. Donald S. Nesti, C.S.Sp., Supr. Total in Residence 20.

BARRETT STATION. *Missionary Society of St. Paul, Inc. - U.S. Region.* Rev. Paul N. Ofoha, M.S.P., Local Supr.

MANVEL. *The Basilian Fathers' Monastery of Citeaux*, Mailing Address: 6502 County Rd. 48, 77578-2908. Rev. James J. Gaunt, C.S.B., Dir.

NEW CANEY. *Congregation of the Mother Coredemptrix*, Holy Family House, Rte. 4, Box 265 B (Oak Shadow), 77357. Tel: 281-354-4764. Rev. Anselm Dinh Vuong Can, C.M.C. Total in Residence 2.

SUGAR LAND. *Basilian Mission Center*, 414 Main St., P.O. Box 708, 77487-0708. Tel: 713-242-3148. Revs. John R. Whitley, C.S.B., Supr., Mission Procurator, Treas.; Robert J. Klem, C.S.B.; W. Maximus Murphy, C.S.B.; Joseph P. Shannon, C.S.B.; Roy J Oggero, C.S.B.; Edward X. Ronan, C.S.B.
Priests Serving in Foreign Missions: Revs. Francis A. Amico, C.S.B.; John L. Boscoe, C.S.B.; M. Marciano Dominguez, C.S.B.; Thomas P. Dugan, C.S.B.; Rene J. Espejel, C.S.B.; William J. Frankenberger, C.S.B.; Marco A. Hernandez, C.S.B.; Leonard A. Kennedy, C.S.B.; Kevin J. Kirley, C.S.B.; Francis J. Launtrie, C.S.B.; Rafael I. Lopera, C.S.B.; Francisco S. Mauricio, C.S.B.; W. Lawrence Moran, C.S.B.; Francois J. Morfin, C.S.B.; Jesse Owens, C.S.B.; W. Wallace Platt, C.S.B.; Roberto P. Rojas, C.S.B.; A. John Ruth, C.S.B.; Robert J. Seguin, C.S.B.; Thomas W. Sepulveda, C.S.B.; J. Vincent Thompson, C.S.B.; Clarence E. Watrin, C.S.B. Associates 20; Scholastics 15; Novices 6.

[R] CONVENTS AND RESIDENCES FOR SISTERS

HOUSTON. *Carmelite Sisters of the Sacred Heart (O.C.D.)*, 22 Farrell, 77022. Tel: 713-697-6020. Sr. Antonia Albarran; Sr. Mary Esther Alonso; Sr. Aurora Gonzalez; Sr. Rosa Maria Neri; Sr. Gloria Diaz. Total Staff 5.
Congregation of Divine Providence (C.D.P.), 2008 Southgate, 77030-2126. Tel: 713-659-5461.
Other Addresses: 2800 West T.C. Jester, No. 15, 77018. Tel: 713-683-9762. 6427 Pinehurst, 77023-3329. Tel: 713-926-2829. 2425 Sage, #174, 77056. Tel: 713-621-5269.
Congregation of the Incarnate Word & Blessed Sacrament (C.V.I.) (Houston), Incarnate Word Convent, 3400 Bradford Pl., 77025-1398. Tel: 713-668-0423. Casa Pacis Convent, 3428 Bradford Pl., 77025. Tel: 713-661-3785. Sisters 2. Incarnate Word Academy, 609 Crawford St., 77002. Tel: 713-223-4143. Sisters 6. St. Christopher Convent, 8711 Glen Loch, 77061. Tel: 713-649-4700. Sisters 2. Visitation Convent, 3418A Bradford Pl., 77025-1398. Tel: 713-664-8370. Sisters 4. Our Lady of Lourdes Convent, 10114 Hwy 6, Hitchcock, 77563. Tel: 409-925-7237. Sisters 3. Sacred Heart Convent, 1015 N. Frazier, Conroe, 77301. Tel: 409-756-3051. Sisters 3. St. Joseph Convent, 1811 Carolina, Baytown, 77520. Tel: 713-422-7700. St. Michael Convent, 5515 W. 43rd, 77092. Tel: 713-682-2242. Sisters 40.
Congregation of the Lovers of the Cross of Thaibinh Diocese, N. Vietnam, 1919 Runnels, No. 268, 77003. Tel: 713-224-7233. Sisters 4.
Congregation of the Sisters of Charity of the Incarnate Word (C.C.V.I.), 6510 Lawndale, P.O. Box 230969, 77223-0969. Tel: 713-928-6053; Fax: 713-928-8148. Total Sisters in Congregation 248. St. Jeanne Convent. Sisters 2. Caritas Convent. Sisters 5. Marian Convent. Sisters 21. St. Anne Convent. Sisters 21. Ruah Community. Sisters 4. Villa de Matel. Sisters 9. St. Placidus Convent, 1500 S. Wayside Dr., P.O. Box 230969, 77223-0969. Tel: 713-928-6053. Sisters 29. Shalom Hermitage, 6510 Lawndale, P.O. Box 230969, 77223-0969. Tel: 713-921-5305. Sisters 2. Edith Stein Convent, 6405 Pinehurst, 77023. Tel: 713-926-6024. Sisters 2. Dubuis Convent, 6510 Lawndale Ave., P.O. Box 230696, 77223-0969. Tel: 713-748-8814. Sisters 3. St. Joseph Convent, 1919 La Branch St., 77002. Tel: 713-757-7485. Sisters 20. St. John Convent, 1623 Antigua Ln., 77058. Tel: 713-333-9363. Sisters 3. St. Mary's Convent, 4400 Ave. N., Galveston, 77550. Tel: 409-763-1971. Sisters 2.
Evelyn Malloy Education Fund for The Sisters of Charity of the Incarnate Word, 6510 Lawndale Ave., P.O. Box 230969, 77223-0969. Tel: 713-928-6053. Sr. John Marie Crowley, C.C.V.I.
Incarnate Word Charitable Trust, 6510 Lawndale, P.O. Box 230969, 77223-0969. Sr. John Marie Crowley, Chairperson.
Congregation of the Sisters of Charity of the Incarnate Word (C.C.V.I.), Mailing Address: P.O. Box 230969, 77223-0969. Villa de Matel, 6510 Lawndale Ave., 77023. Tel: 713-928-6053.
Incarnate Word Charitable Trust.
Evelyn Malloy Education Fund for the Sisters of Charity of the Incarnate Word, 6510 Lawndale Ave., P.O. Box 230969, 77023-0969. Tel: 713-928-6053. Sr. John Marie Crowley, C.C.V.I.
Dominican Sisters of Houston, Motherhouse Complex & Administrative Offices: 6501 Almeda Rd., 77021-2095. Tel: 713-747-3310; Fax: 713-747-4707. Legal Title: *Dominican Sisters of Houston, Texas Inc. (O.P.) Dominican Convent.* The Sacred Heart Convent Retirement Trust.
Other Addresses: Aquinas House, 7400 Bellerive, No. 1306, 77036. Tel: 713-266-5106. Sisters 2. Gannon House Community, 2604 White Oak Dr., 77009. Tel: 713-868-5124. Sisters 3. Genesis House (Formation), 6505 Almeda Rd., 77021. Tel: 713-741-8298; 665-2195. Sisters 5. Magevney Convent, 6509-B Almeda Rd., 77021. Tel: 713-741-8342. Sisters 4. Queen of Peace Convent, 2330 Oakcliff, 77023. Tel: 713-923-8255. Sisters 4. Rose Lynch Convent, 6509-A Almeda Rd., 77021. Tel: 713-741-8369. Sisters 5. St. Benedict Convent, 3927 Grapevine, 77045. Tel: 713-433-8368. St. Catherine Convent, 6503 Almeda Rd., 77021. Tel: 713-748-8649. Sisters 5. St. Dominic Villa, 6504 Almeda Rd., 77021. Tel: 713-747-9425. Sisters 36. Dominican Sisters, 6506 Tam O'Shanter, 77036. Tel: 713-774-3674. Sisters 3. St. Joseph Convent, 6507 Almeda Rd., 77021. Tel: 713-741-8310; 747-3310. Sisters 5. Seton Convent, 801 Rose Ln., 77037. Tel: 713-447-2617. Sisters 3. Siena House, 2415 Willowby Dr., 77008. Tel: 713-522-8416. Sisters 3. Sojourner House, 1039 LeGreen, 77009. Tel: 713-861-3870. Sisters 4. Dominican Convent, 2210 Avenue M, Galveston, 77550. Tel: 409-762-4878. Sisters 2. Camp Kappe, Rte. 2, Box 3197, 77868. Tel: 409-894-2141. Sisters 1. Wellsprings, P.O. Box 66463, 77266. Tel: 713-529-6559. Sisters 2. 3809 N. Braeswood, #11, 77025. Tel: 713-661-1534. 2800 W. T.C. Jester, #18, 77018. Tel: 713-957-0239. 3809 N. Braeswood #8, 77025. Tel: 713-665-6457. 4102 Cherry Oak Cir., 77088. Tel: 713-847-9263. 109 N. Frazier, Conroe, 77301. Tel: 409-756-3051; 756-8186. 1660 W. T.C. Jester #623, 77008. Tel: 713-864-1905; 686-4345, Ext. 269. Dominican Sisters Convent, 2217 Hollister #215, 77080. Tel: 713-973-7817; 686-6990. Sisters 2. 7992 Locke Ln. #8, 77063. Tel: 713-784-5447; 771-8392. 1607 Avenue M, Rosenburg, 77471-3316. Tel: 281-232-4863. Benincasa, 1802 Rosedale, 77004-5631. Tel: 713-521-9623. Sisters 2. Circle Lake Retreat, P.O. Box 1408, Pinehurst, 77362-1408. Tel: 713-356-6764. 9988 Windmill Lakes #1607, 77075. Tel: 713-910-5227.
St. Agnes Academy; St. Agnes Academy Foundation; St. Pius X High School; St. Pius X High School Foundation, Inc.; The Sacred Heart Convent Retirement Trust.
Dominican Sisters-Vietnamese (O.P.), Inc., St. Catherine Convent, 5250 Gasmer Dr., 77035. Tel: 713-723-8250. Sisters 57. Vietnamese Dominican Sisters Novitiate & House of Study, 5250 Gasmer Dr., 77035. Tel: 713-723-8250. Mary Immaculate Convent, 5900 Chippewa Blvd., 77086. Tel: 713-445-9574. Sisters 7.
Eucharistic Missionaries of St. Theresa-Mexico (M.E.S.T.), St. John of the Cross Convent, 430 Bunker Hill, 77024. Tel: 713-461-8337. Sr. Olegaria Romero, M.E.S.T., Supr. Sisters 4.
Handmaids of the Sacred Heart of Pohang (H.S.H.), St. Andrew Kim Convent, 1706 Bingle Rd., 77055. Tel: 713-465-1196. Rev. Paul Chun Ho Kim. Sisters 2.

Incarnate Word Convent, 3400 Bradford Pl., 77025-1398. Tel: 713-668-0423.
Maryknoll Sisters of St. Dominic (M.M.), 7490 Brompton, No. 265, 77025. Tel: 713-793-2480 (Office); 666-5245 (Home). 14515 Wunderlick Rd., No. 1603, 77069. Tel: 713-376-6831 (Office); 440-9994 (Home). Total in Residence 2.
Missionary Carmelites of St. Teresa (C.M.S.T.), Holy Family Provincial House, 9548 Deer Trail Dr., 77038. Tel: 281-445-5520; Fax: 281-445-5748. Divine Providence Convent, 9600 Deer Trail Dr., 77038. Tel: 713-847-3328. Mt. Carmel House of Prayer, 9600 Deer Trail Dr., 77038. Tel: 281-445-8830. Sisters 8. Postulancy St. Teresa, 9600 Deer Trail Dr., 77038. Tel: 713-820-3732.
Missionary Catechists of the Sacred Hearts of Jesus and Mary (M.C.S.H.S.M.). Our Lady of Guadalupe Convent, 502 Carlisle St., Rosenberg, 77471. Tel: 713-232-5500. Sisters 3.
Missionary Sisters of the Immaculate Conception (S.M.I.C.), 6414 Ludington Dr., 77035-3919. Tel: 713-729-6971. Total Assisted 151; Total Staff 1.
Our Lady of Sorrows Convent, 4703 Lelia St., 77026. Tel: 713-676-2630. 3907 Rotman, 77003. Tel: 713-227-2555. 5102 Irvington Blvd., 77009. Tel: 713-692-8266. St. Pius V Convent, 812 S. Main, 77506. St. Mary's Convent, 1400 Wilkins St., 77445. Tel: 409-826-2275. 1719 Knightwick, 77008. Tel: 713-862-2376.
Our Lady of the Cenacle (R.C.), Cenacle Retreat House, 420 N. Kirkwood, 77079. Tel: 713-497-3131. Sr. Lois Dideon, Supr.; Sr. Mary Dennison; Sr. Thressa Heard; Sr. Emily Katz; Sr. Margaret Byrne; Sr. Elizabeth Mozina; Sr. Catherine Quinn. Sisters 30.
Religious of the Sacred Heart (R.S.C.J.), Duchesne Community, 10204 Memorial Dr., 77024. Tel: 713-467-5312; Fax: 713-465-9809. 1830 Arlington, 77008. Tel: 713-880-5230. Sisters 5. 2020 Harvard, 77008. Tel: 713-868-9607. Sisters 3. Sisters 4.
School Sisters of Notre Dame (S.S.N.D.) Community, 4010 Linkwood Dr., #902, 77025. Tel: 713-660-9317. Sisters 1.
Sisters for Christian Community (S.F.C.C.). SFCC Community, 109 N. Frazier, Conroe, 77301. Tel: 409-756-3051. Sacred Heart Convent, 105 N. Frazier St., 77301. Tel: 409-756-3051. St. Gregory the Great Convent, 5123 Calgary, 77016. Sr. Natalia Adame, S.F.C.C., 2200 Fountainview, #60, 77057. Sr. Ginny Braniff, S.F.C.C., 510 Manley St., Navasola, 77868-3905. Sr. Josefina Gutierrez, M.C-.S.C.J.M., Sacred Heart Convent, 105 N. Frazier, Conroe, 77301. Sr. Isidra Hernandez, S.F.C.C., 3709 Lila, 77026. Sr. Juanita Martinez, S.F.C.C., 502 29th Ave. N., Texas City, 77590. Sr. Laurine Murragh, S.F.C.C.
Sisters of Providence of St. Mary of the Woods (Indiana) (S.P.), 4727 Oakshire, No. 2, 77027. Tel: 713-850-1687.
Sisters of St. Francis of the Providence of God (O.S.F., Whitehall, PA), P.O. Box 66581, 77266. Tel: 713-529-0639 (Work); 713-528-2940 (Res.).
Sisters of St. Mary of Namur (S.S.M.N.), Casa de Esperanza, 1807 Wichita, 77004. Tel: 713-529-0639. Sisters of St. Mary, 4119 Graustark, #3, 77006. Tel: 713-526-8175. Sisters of St. Mary, 3822 Braeswood, #135, 77025. Tel: 713-349-8901. Sisters 3.
Sisters of the Holy Family (S.S.F.), Our Mother of Mercy Convent, 2000 Benson St., 77020. Tel: 713-674-6560. Sisters 8.
Sisters of the Holy Spirit and Mary Immaculate (S.H.Sp.), St. Charles Borromeo Convent, 9601 McGallon, 77076. Tel: 713-694-4264. Sr. Anne Finnerty, S.H.Sp., Gen. Supr. Tel: 210-533-5149; 533-5522; Fax 210-533-3434; Sr. Muriel Clarke; Sr. Pauline Hynes; Sr. Hilda Mangan, Our Lady of Fatima Convent, 1701 Ninth St., 77547. Tel: 713-674-1811. Sr. Martina Hoase, S.H.Sp.; Sr. Teresa Healy, S.H.Sp. Tel: 713-672-2037. Sisters 3.
Sisters of the Sacred Heart (S.S.C.J.), Holy Name Convent, 1217 Hogan, 77009. Tel: 713-228-4500. Sisters 3. Immaculate Heart of Mary Convent, 7535 Ave. L, 77012. Tel: 713-921-5431. Sisters 4; Total Staff Both Addresses 5.

MISSOURI CITY. *Schoenstatt Sisters of Mary (I.S.S.M.)*, Holy Family Church, 1510 Fifth St., 77489. Tel: 713-499-6246.

NEW CANEY. *Discalced Carmelite Nuns (O.C.D.) Carmel of the Holy Trinity*, 1100 Parthenon Pl., 77357-3039. Tel: 281-399-0270; Fax: 281-689-3615. Sisters 12.

[S] RETREAT HOUSES

HOUSTON. *Cenacle Retreat House*, 420 N. Kirkwood, 77079. Tel: 713-497-3131. Congregation of Our Lady of the Retreat in the Cenacle. Sr. Lois Dideon, R.C., Supr.; Sr. Thressa Heard, R.C., Coord. of Ministry. Sisters 7.
Holy Name Retreat Center, 430 Bunker Hill Rd., 77024-6399. Tel: 713-464-0211; Fax: 713-464-0671. Revs. John Schork, C.P., Retreat Dir.; John P. Conley, C.P.; David Colhour, C.P., Assoc. Dir., Congregation of the Passion, Holy Name Retreat, 430 Bunker Hill Road, 77024-6399. Tel: 713-464-4932; Fax: 713-932-7303. Very Rev. Blaise Czaja, C.P., Local Supr.; Revs. Leo Patrick Brady, C.P.; Simon Herbers, C.P.; Alfonso San Juan, C.P.; John Conley, C.P.; John Schork, C.P.; Bernard Weber, C.P.; David Colhour, C.P.; Deacon James Griffith, C.P.; Bro. Joachim Saunders, C.P. Total in Residence 1; Total Staff 5.
Shalom House of Prayer, 6510 Lawndale Ave., P.O. Box 230969, 77223. Tel: 921-5305. Sr. Genevieve Marheineke, Hermit. Total in Residence 2.

DICKINSON. *Christian Renewal Center*, 1515 Hughes Rd., P.O. Box 635, 77539-0635. Tel: 281-337-1312 (Center); Fax: 281-337-2615. Rev. Edward W. Couch, O.M.I., Dir. Associate Directors: Revs. Maurice Lange, O.M.I.; Bernard Doyon, O.M.I. In res. Rev. John Ward, O.M.I. Total in Residence 4; Total Staff 17.

[T] NEWMAN CENTERS

GALVESTON. *Newman Apostolate Center*, 1402 Broadway, 77550. Tel: 409-762-4202.
Texas A & M, University of Galveston, University of Texas, Medical Branch of Galveston College, College of the Mainland. Mr. James Bonura.

HOUSTON. *Rice University / Texas Medical Center Schools; Catholic Student Center*, 1703 Bolsover Rd., 77005. Tel: 713-526-3809; Fax: 713-526-6010. Sr. Antoinette "Kitty" Carter, O.P., Co-Dir. Total Staff 1.
San Jacinto Community College North Campus Newman Center, 5800 Uvalde, 77049. Tel: 713-458-2398. Ms. Delores Fischer.
San Jacinto Community College South Campus, Catholic Newman Association, 13735 Beamer Rd., 77089. Tel: 713-484-1900, Ext. 3509.
E-mail: kwood@south.sjcd.cc.tx.us
Ms. Kathleen Wood. Total Staff 1.
Texas Southern University Catholic Newman Hall, 3535 Wheeler, 77004. Tel: 713-747-9595. Rev. John J. Walsh, C.S.Sp. Total in Residence 1; Total Staff 4.
University of Houston Central Campus Catholic Newman Association, 203 A.D. Bruce Religion Center, 77204-3621.
Web site: http://www.uh.edu/catholic
Catholic Center. Tel: 713-748-2529; 748-2342. Rev. Paul Gallagher, O.F.M. Campus Ministers: Rev. Isidore V. Vicente; Pamela Krinock.
University of Houston Downtown Catholic Campus Ministry, 1 Main St., Room 280 S., 77002. Tel: 713-221-8592. Total Staff 1.
University of Houston, Clear Lake City Newman Center. 1515 Hughes Rd., P.O. Box 635, Dickinson, 77539. Student Activities, 18519 Egret Bay, No. 1609, 77058. Tel: 713-488-9466. Rev. John Ward, O.M.I.
University of St. Thomas Campus Ministry, 3800 Montrose Blvd., 77006. Tel: 713-525-3589.
E-mail: gazing@stthom.edu
Web site: www.stthom.edu
Rev. Mark R. Gazin, C.S.B., Dir., Campus Ministry.

ALVIN. *Alvin Community College Newman Center*, 3110 Mustang Rd., 77511. Tel: 713-388-4646. Gillian Callen.

HUNTSVILLE. *Catholic Student Center, S.H.S.U.*, 1310 17th St., 77340-4415. Tel: 409-291-2620. Total Assisted 500.

LAKE JACKSON. *Brazosport College Newman Club*, 500 College Dr., 77566. Tel: 409-297-1821; 265-6131, Ext. 33F. Ms. Nelda Thrash.

PRAIRIE VIEW. *Prairie View A & M University Catholic Center*, P.O. Box 3027, 77446-3027. Tel: 409-857-3351. Rev. Robert B. Fisher, S.V.D. Total Staff 3.

SPRING. *North Harris College Newman Center*, 2700 W. Thorne Dr., 77073. Tel: 713-443-5546. Mrs. Bertha Parle.

[U] MISCELLANEOUS

HOUSTON. *A.I.I.L.S.* (Adult Institute of Independent Living Skills), 2403 E. Holcome Blvd., 77021-2024. Tel: 713-741-8725.
Asociacion Nacional de Sacerdotes Hispanos, 2472 Bolsover, Ste. #442, 77005. Tel: 713-528-6517. Rev. Jose H. Gomez, Pres.
Berakah Alternative Investment Fund, 2476 Bolsover #272, 77005. Tel: 713-522-8028; Fax: 713-529-8411. Paul Degler, Exec. Dir. The Berekah Fund makes loans to spur economic development in low-income neighborhoods.
Catholic Charismatic Center, 1949 Cullen P.O. Box 230287, 77223-0287. Tel: 713-236-9977; 921-2736 (Res.). Rev. Richard E. Paulissen, M.M., Dir.
Catholic Clerical Student Fund, 9845 Memorial, 77024. Most Rev. Joseph A. Fiorenza, Chm.; Margaret Sustala, Pres. Higher learning for the priesthood.
Charity Guild of Catholic Women, 1203 Lovett Blvd., 77006. Tel: 713-529-0995.
Charity Guild of St. Joseph, 7607 Meadowglen, 77063. Tel: 713-626-9788. Mrs. Catherine Cash, Pres., 4234 Whitman, 77027. Tel: 713-623-2935.
Education Foundation of the Diocese of Galveston-Houston, 1700 San Jacinto, 77002-8291. Tel: 713-659-5461. Thomas B. O'Toole, Treas.
Equestrian Order of the Holy Sepulchre of Jerusalem, 309 Knipp Rd., 77024. Tel: 713-468-5602.
E-mail: AnneKendall@compuserve.com
Mr. F. Russell Kendall, Knight of the Collar, Vice Gov. Gen., Member of the Grand Magisterium.
Southwestern Lieutenancy, Equestrian Order of the Holy Sepulchre of Jerusalem, 9716 Trailhill Dr., Dallas, 75238-1444. Tel: 214-341-4457 (office); 349-6196 (res). Mr. Albin Brezna, Jr.
Jesuit Volunteer Corps: South, P.O. Box 3126, 77253-3126. Tel: 713-756-5095; Fax: 713-756-8928.
E-mail: jvcsouth@aol.com
Web site: http://guweb.georgetown.edu/jvc
Mr. Kevin O'Brien, Dir. Volunteer service organizations.
Kolbe Project, Inc., 1030 Heights Blvd., 77008-6669. P.O. Box 6669, 77266-6669. Tel: 713-851-7212; Fax: 713-861-1800. Bro. David Crank, O.F.M.
Martha's Kitchen Food Services, 322 S. Jensen Dr., 77003. Tel: 713-224-2522. Rev. Terence P. Brinkman, S.T.D. Sisters 4.
Sacred Military Constantinian Order of Saint George, American Delegation, 3731 Olympia, 77019-3029. Tel: 713-888-0242; Fax: 713-888-0345. Mr. David L. Garrison, Delegate.
St. Dominic Center, Inc., 2401 E. Holcombe, 77021. Tel: 713-741-8741. Jim Horstman, Admin.
St. Francis de Sales School Foundation, 8100 Roos, 77036. Tel: 713-774-7474.
St. Mary's Orphanage Board, Chancery Bldg., 1700 San Jacinto, P.O. Box 907, 77001. Tel: 713-659-5461. Most Rev. Joseph A. Fiorenza, Pres.; Rev. Msgr. Frank A. Lagana, Vice Pres.
St. Pius X High School Foundation, Inc., 811 W. Donovan, 77091-5699. Tel: 713-692-3581.
Web site: www.stpiusx.org
Jim Clepper, Pres.
Sociedad San Martin de Porres, P.O. Box 7788, 77270-7788. Tel: 713-880-0091; Fax: 713-880-0091.
Southern Dominican Volunteer Program.
Corporate Office: 6501 Almeda Rd., 77021-2095. Tel: 713-747-3310.
Placement Office: 5401 St. Bernard Ave., New Orleans, LA, 70122. Tel: 504-283-5768. Sr. Robin Richard, O.P., Pres.; Sr. Kathleen McNally, O.P., Prog. Admin.
Spiritan House, 6707 Salta Dr., 77083-1400.

CONROE. *Dogwood Foundation, Inc.*, P.O. Box 2774, 77305-2774. Tel: 409-588-2078. Ben J. Petru, Pres.

RELIGIOUS INSTITUTES OF MEN REPRESENTED IN THE DIOCESE

For further details refer to the corresponding bracketed number in the religious Institutes of Men or Women section.

[0140]—*The Augustinians*.—O.S.A.
[0170]—*Basilian Fathers*. (Toronto, Canada).—C.S.B.
[0470]—*The Capuchin Friars*.—O.F.M.Cap.
[0270]—*Carmelite Fathers & Brothers*. (Prov. of Most Pure Heart of Mary).—O.Carm.
[0350]—*Cistercians of the Strict Observance-Trappists*.—O.C.S.O.
[0220]—*Congregation of the Blessed Sacrament*.—S.S.S.
[1330]—*Congregation of the Mission*. (Southern Prov.).—C.M.
[]—*Congregation of the Mother Coredemptrix*.—C.M.C.
[1000]—*Congregation of the Passion*. (Chicago).—C.P.
[1130]—*Congregation of the Priests of the Sacred Heart*.—S.C.J.
[0520]—*Franciscan Friars*.—O.F.M.
[0650]—*Holy Ghost Fathers*. (Western Prov.).—C.S.Sp.
[0690]—*Jesuit Fathers and Brothers*. (New Orleans Prov.).—S.J.
[0800]—*Maryknoll*.—M.M.
[0720]—*The Missionaries of Our Lady of La Salette*. (Prov. of Mary Queen).—M.S.
[]—*Missionaries of St. Joseph*. (Mexico).—M.J.
[]—*Missionaries of St. Paul*.—M.S.P.
[0910]—*Oblates of Mary Immaculate*.—O.M.I.
[0430]—*Order of Preachers-Dominicans*. (Prov. of St. Albert the Great).—O.P.
[1310]—*Order of the Holy Trinity*.—O.SS.T.
[1030]—*Paulist Fathers*.—C.S.P.
[0610]—*Priests of the Congregation of Holy Cross*. (Houston).—C.S.C.
[1070]—*Redemptorist Fathers*. (New Orleans Vice Prov.).—C.SS.R.
[0700]—*St. Joseph's Society of the Sacred Heart*. (Baltimore, MD).—S.S.J.
[]—*Scalabrinians*.—C.S.

[1260]—*Society of Christ.*—S.Ch.
[0420]—*Society of the Divine Word.*—S.V.D.
[1250]—*Somascan Fathers.*—C.R.S.

RELIGIOUS INSTITUTES OF WOMEN REPRESENTED IN THE DIOCESE

[1070]—*Dominican Sisters.* (Adrian, MI).—O.P.
[]—*Benedictine Sisters of the Sacred Heart.*—O.S.B.
[0390]—*Carmelite Missionaries of St. Teresa.*—C.M.S.T.
[]—*Carmelite Sisters of the Sacred Heart.*—C.S.C.
[]—*Congregation of Divine Providence.*—C.D.P.
[3110]—*Congregation of Our Lady of the Retreat in the Cenacle.*—R.C.
[3830-08]—*Congregation of St. Joseph.* (Cleveland, OH).—C.S.J.
[]—*Congregation of the Lovers of the Cross.* (N. Vietnam).—H.C.L.
[3830-01]—*Congregation of the Sisters of St. Joseph of Boston.*—C.S.J.
[]—*Cordi-Marian Missionary Sisters.*—M.C.M.
[]—*Daughters of Divine Love.*—D.D.L.
[0420]—*Discalced Carmelite Nuns.*—O.C.D.
[]—*Dominican Sisters.* (Congregation of the Sacred Heart).—O.P.
[]—*Eucharistic Missionaries of St. Theresa.* (Mexico).—M.E.S.T.
[]—*Handmaids of the Sacred Heart.* (N. Korea).—H.S.H.
[2470]—*Maryknoll Sisters of St. Dominic.*—M.M.
[2690]—*Missionary Catechists of Divine Providence.*—M.C.D.P.
[2700]—*Missionary Catechists of the Sacred Hearts of Jesus and Mary.*—M.C.
[2760]—*Missionary Sisters of the Immaculate Conception.*—S.M.I.C.
[2860]—*Missionary Sisters of the Sacred Heart.*—M.S.C.
[4070]—*Religious of the Sacred Heart.*—R.S.C.J.
[4110]—*Roman Union of the Order of St. Ursula.*—O.S.U.
[]—*Schoenstatt Sisters.* (Rockport, TX).—I.S.S.M.
[2970]—*School Sisters of Notre Dame.* (South Central Prov.).—S.S.N.D.
[]—*Sisters for the Christian Community.*—S.F.C.C.
[0440]—*Sisters of Charity.* (Cincinnati, OH).—S.C.
[0590]—*Sisters of Charity of St. Elizabeth.*—S.C.
[]—*Sisters of Charity of the Incarnate Word.*—C.C.V.I.
[]—*Sisters of Charity of the Incarnate Word.* (San Antonio).—C.C.V.I.
[]—*Sisters of Our Lady of Mt. Carmel.* (Vietnamese).—O.C.A.
[3360]—*Sisters of Providence.* (St. Mary of the Woods, IN).—S.P.
[1530]—*Sisters of St. Francis.* (Sylvania, OH).—O.S.F.
[3840]—*Sisters of St. Joseph of Carondelet.*—C.S.J.
[3950]—*Sisters of St. Mary of Namur.*—S.S.M.N.
[1950]—*Sisters of the Holy Family.*—S.S.F.
[2050]—*Sisters of the Holy Spirit and Mary Immaculate.*—S.H.Sp.
[]—*Sisters of the Immaculate Heart of Mary.*—I.H.M.
[2190]—*Sisters of the Incarnate Word and Blessed Sacrament.*—C.V.I.
[2200]—*Sisters of the Incarnate Word and Blessed Sacrament.* (Corpus Christi).—I.W.B.S.
[3310]—*Sisters of the Presentation of Mary.*—P.M.
[3670]—*Sisters of the Sacred Heart of Jesus.*—S.S.C.J.
[]—*Vietnamese Dominican Sisters.*—O.P.
[]—*Whitehall Franciscan Sisters.*—O.S.F.

DIOCESAN CEMETERIES

GALVESTON. *Old Catholic, Calvary.*
HOUSTON. *Holy Cross.*
St. Vincent.
DICKINSON. *Mount Olivet.*

NECROLOGY

† Brumleu, Ernest J., (Retired). —Died Nov. 10, 1997.
† Gillgannon, Patrick, (Retired). —Died Sept. 11, 1997.
† Pekar, Rev. Msgr. Gilbert F., (Retired). —Died July 31, 1997.
† Posluszny, Sylvester, (Retired). —Died Jan. 7, 1997.
† Prill, John, Houston, TX, St. John Neumann.—Died Feb. 10, 1997.
† Tran, Mark That, (Retired). —Died Jan. 19, 1997.

Diocese of Gary

(Dioecesis Gariensis)

Most Reverend

DALE J. MELCZEK, D.D.

Bishop of Gary; ordained June 6, 1964; appointed Auxiliary Bishop of Detroit and Titular Bishop of Trau December 3, 1982; consecrated January 27, 1983; appointed Apostolic Administrator of Gary August 19, 1992; appointed Coadjutor Bishop of Gary October 20, 1995; succeeded to the See of Gary June 1, 1996. *Office: 9292 Broadway, Merrillville, IN, 46410.* Tel.: 219-769-9292; Fax: 219-769-2066.

Most Reverend

NORBERT F. GAUGHAN, D.D., PH.D.

Retired Bishop of Gary; ordained November 4, 1945; appointed Auxiliary Bishop of Greensburg and Titular Bishop of Taraqua April 2, 1975; consecrated June 26, 1975; appointed Bishop of Gary July 9, 1984; retired June 1, 1996. *The Chancery: 9292 Broadway, Merrillville, IN, 46410.*

ESTABLISHED DECEMBER 17, 1956.

Square Miles 1,807.

Comprises the Counties of Lake, LaPorte, Porter and Starke in the State of Indiana.

For legal titles of parishes and diocesan institutions, consult the Chancery.

Chancery: 9292 Broadway, Merrillville, IN, 46410. Tel.: 219-769-9292; Fax: 219-738-9034.

STATISTICAL OVERVIEW

Personnel	
Bishop	1
Retired Bishops	1
Priests: Diocesan Active in Diocese	96
Priests: Active Outside Diocese	5
Priests: Diocesan in Foreign Missions	1
Priests: Retired, Sick or Absent	26
Number of Diocesan Priests	128
Religious Priests in Diocese	52
Extern Priests in Diocese	7
Ordinations:	
Diocesan Priests	2
Permanent Deacons in Diocese	25
Total Brothers	20
Total Sisters	126
Parishes	
Parishes	78
With Resident Pastor:	
Resident Diocesan Priests	72
Resident Religious Priests	3
Without Resident Pastor:	
Administered by Priests	3
Missions	3
Pastoral Centers	7
Closed Parishes	1
Professional Ministry Personnel:	
Brothers	4
Sisters	17
Lay Ministers	49
Welfare	
Catholic Hospitals	6
Total Assisted	513,939
Homes for the Aged	3
Total Assisted	478
Residential Care of Children	3
Total Assisted	128
Day Care and Extended Day Care Centers	1
Total Assisted	200
Specialized Homes	1
Total Assisted	700
Special Centers for Social Services	7
Total Assisted	10,000
Educational	
Diocesan Students in Other Seminaries	7
Seminaries, Religious	1
Students Religious	7
Total Seminarians	14
Colleges and Universities	1
Total Students	1,035
High Schools, Diocesan and Parish	3
Total Students	2,007
Elementary Schools, Diocesan and Parish	30
Total Students	8,039
Elementary Schools, Private	1
Total Students	110
Catechesis/Religious Education:	
High School Students	693
Elementary Students	10,125
Total Students Under Catholic Instruction	22,023
Teachers in the Diocese:	
Priests	6
Brothers	4
Sisters	16
Lay Teachers	550
Vital Statistics	
Receptions into the Church:	
Infant Baptism Totals	2,345
Adult Baptism Totals	210
Received into Full Communion	262
First Communions	2,393
Confirmations	2,048
Marriages:	
Catholic	570
Interfaith	318
Total Marriages	888
Deaths	1,641
Total Catholic Population	184,106
Total Population	759,673

Former Bishops—Most Rev. ANDREW GREGORY GRUTKA, D.D., ord. Dec. 5, 1933; appt. Bishop of Gary Dec. 29, 1956; cons. February 25, 1957; retired July 9, 1984; died Nov. 11, 1993.—Most Rev. NORBERT F. GAUGHAN, D.D., Ph.D., ord. Nov. 4, 1945; appt. Auxiliary Bishop of Greensburg April 2, 1975; cons. June 26, 1975; appt. Bishop of Gary July 9, 1984; retired June 1, 1996.

Vicar General—Rev. SAMMIE L. MALETTA, J.D., J.C.L.

Deans—Rev. ROBERT P. GEHRING, Gary-Hobart Deanery; Rev. STANLEY J. DOMINIK, North Lake County Deanery; Rev. RICHARD A. EMERSON, South Lake County Deanery; Rev. Msgr. RICHARD F. ZOLLINGER, Porter-Starke County Deanery; Rev. RICHARD H. AMELING, LaPorte County Deanery.

Chancery—9292 Broadway, Merrillville, 46410. Tel: 219-769-9292; Fax: 219-738-9034.

Chancellor/Moderator of the Curia—Rev. SAMMIE L. MALETTA, J.D., J.C.L.

Bishop's Delegate for Sexual Abuse Matters—Rev. Msgr. JOHN J. SIEKIERSKI, J.C.L.

Director of Finance and Administration—KARL P. DYTRYCH.

Secretary to the Bishop—VALERIE D. MCMANUS. Tel: 219-769-9181; Fax: 219-769-2066.

Diocesan Tribunal—9292 Broadway, Merrillville, 46410. Tel: 219-769-9292.

Judicial Vicar—Rev. JOSEPH F. GAZARKIEWICZ, J.C.L.

Judges—Revs. MATTHEW C. IWUJI, J.U.D.; JAMES W. MEADE, J.D., S.T.L., J.C.L.; Sr. THERESE GUERIN SULLIVAN, S.P., D.Min., J.C.L.

Defenders of the Bond—Revs. JAMES P. MCGROGAN; SAMMIE L. MALETTA, J.D., J.C.L.

Advocates—DONNA V. CALLAWAY; LINDA PLANER.

Promoter of Justice—Rev. JAMES P. MCGROGAN.

Notaries—VALERIE MCMANUS; MARY LESKO; DONNA CALLAWAY; MARY ANN O'CONNELL; JENNIFER POTCHEN.

Bishop's Council of Priests—Rev. Msgr. RICHARD F. ZOLLINGER; Rev. Msgr. F. J. MELEVAGE; Rev. Msgr. DON C. GRASS; Revs. JOHN T. AMBRE; RICHARD H. AMELING; DOMINIC V. BERTINO; ALFRED J. DETTMER; STANLEY J. DOMINIK; RICHARD A. EMERSON; ROBERT P. GEHRING; DAVID H. GOSNELL; EDWARD J. KENNEDY; SAMMIE L. MALETTA, V.G.; DOUGLAS J. MAYER; JAMES W. MEADE; JOSEPH V. MURPHY; MICHAEL VENEKLASE, O.C.D.; MICHAEL J. YADRON.

Consultors—Rev. Msgr. RICHARD F. ZOLLINGER; Revs. ROBERT P. GEHRING; STANLEY J. DOMINIK; RICHARD A. EMERSON; SAMMIE L. MALETTA, V.G.; RICHARD H. AMELING.

Priests' Personnel Board—Rev. Msgr. JOSEPH F. SEMANCIK, M.S.W., Ph.D.; Rev. Msgr. RICHARD F. ZOLLINGER; Rev. Msgr. DON C. GRASS; Revs. RICHARD A. EMERSON; RICHARD H. AMELING; STANLEY J. DOMINIK; ROBERT P. GEHRING; SAMMIE L. MALETTA, V.G.; DOUGLAS J. MAYER; PATRICK J. CONNOLLY.

Diocesan Offices and Directors

African American Catholic Ministry—Rev. CHARLES A. MOSLEY, Dir., *525 N. Broad St., Griffith, 46319*. Tel: 219-924-4163.

Benefits—KAREN WALSH, Coord., *9292 Broadway, Merrillville, 46410*. Tel: 219-769-9292; Fax: 219-738-9034.

Blue Army—Rev. MARK G. MAZZA, Chap., *303 Keller Ave., North Judson, 46366*. Tel: 219-896-2195.

Boy Scouts Liaison—Deacon WILLIAM E. JONES, *1977 David Dr., Chesterton, 46307*. Tel: 219-921-1780.

Campaign for Human Development—Rev. DERRICK F. DUDASH, Dir., *302 N. Madison, Hebron, 46341*. Tel: 219-996-4611.

Campus Ministry—St. Teresa of Avila Catholic Student Center (Valparaiso University); Rev. KEVIN P. MCCARTHY, Dir., *1511 LaPorte St., Valparaiso, 46383*. Tel: 219-464-4042. Indiana University Northwest; Rev. JOHN T. AMBRE, Dir., *501 W. Ridge Rd., Gary, 46408*. Tel: 219-887-0514.

Catholic Marriage Preparation—Coordinators: RITA MAYER; BARBARA PAWLAK, *Catholic Family Service, 973 W. 6th Ave., Gary, 46402*. Tel: 219-882-2759.

Catholic Youth Organization (CYO) Office—FRANK R. KONTOR, Dir., *7725 Broadway, Ste. G, Merrillville, 46410*. Tel: 219-736-8931; Fax: 219-736-9457.

Cemeteries—Rev. STANLEY J. DOMINIK, Dir., *7113 Columbia Ave., Hammond, 46324*. Tel: 219-844-9027.

Charismatic Apostolate—Rev. JOHN V. SCOTT, Dir., *2949 Willowcreek Rd., Portage, 46368*. Tel: 219-762-4858.

Charities—Rev. Msgr. JOSEPH F. SEMANCIK, M.S.W., Ph.D., Dir., *973 W. Sixth Ave., Gary, 46402*. Tel: 219-882-2720.

Communications Office—BRIAN T. OLSZEWSKI, Dir., *9292 Broadway, Merrillville, 46410*. Tel: 219-769-9292.

Council of Catholic Women—Rev. ROY T. BEECHING, Diocesan Moderator, *5304 Hohman Ave., Hammond, 46320*. Tel: 219-932-0702.

Cursillos in Christianity—Revs. JUAN GONZALEZ, C.PP.S., Dir. (Spanish); EDWARD J. KENNEDY, (English), *1445 Hoffman St., Hammond, 46327*. Tel: 219-931-5229.

Development—JUDY WILLIAMSON, Dir., *9292 Broadway, Merrillville, 46410*. Tel: 219-769-9292; Fax: 219-738-9034.

Diaconate—Rev. J. PATRICK GAZA, Dir., *9292 Broadway, Merrillville, 46410*. Tel: 219-769-9292.

Ecumenical Officer—Rev. DOUGLAS J. MAYER, *356 W. Seven Mile Rd., Valparaiso, 46383*. Tel: 219-759-2400.

Engaged Encounter—GREG CASIMER; LISA CASIMER, *6365 Venus Ave., Portage, 46368*. Tel: 219-762-2039.

Family Life Ministry—RITA MAYER, Coord., *973 W. Sixth Ave., Gary, 46402*. Tel: 219-882-2720.

Finance Council—Rev. SAMMIE L. MALETTA, V.G.; DENNIS BIELFELDT; CALVIN E. BELLAMY; T. CLIFFORD FLEMING; JOSEPH F. GLOTZBACH, C.P.A.; KARL DYTRYCH; FELICIA FLOWERS SMITH; Rev. JOSEPH M. PAWLOWSKI.

Girl Scout Liaison—Rev. THEODORE A. NORDQUIST, *109 C St., LaPorte, 46350*. Tel: 219-362-9595.

Health Care, Bishop's Representative—Rev. SAMMIE L. MALETTA, *9292 Broadway, Merrillville, 46410*. Tel: 219-769-9292; Fax: 219-769-2066.

Heartland Center—Revs. THOMAS GANNON, S.J.; JAMES SCHULZ, S.J., *7128 Arizona Ave., Hammond, 46323*. Tel: 219-844-7515; Fax: 219-844-7566.

Holy Childhood Association—cf. Mission Office.

Hispanic Diocesan Ministries—ANGEL TORRES, Dir. ADELINE TORRES, Asst., *P.O. Box 3027, East Chicago, 46312*. Tel: 219-397-2125; Fax: 219-397-2168.

Indiana Catholic Conference—Rev. JAMES W. SCHULZ, S.J., Diocesan Coord., *7128 Arizona Ave., Hammond, 46323*. Tel: 219-844-7515; Fax: 219-844-7566.

Lay Ministry Formation Office—ANNE VERBEKE, Dir., *9292 Broadway, Merrillville, 46410*. Tel: 219-769-9292.

Legal Counsel—Rev. SAMMIE L. MALETTA, J.D., J.C.L., *9292 Broadway, Merrillville, 46410*. Tel: 219-769-9292; Fax: 219-769-2066.

Liturgy Office—Rev. MARTIN J. DOBRZYNSKI, Dir.; JULIE VOLKMANN, Admin. Asst., *9292 Broadway, Merrillville, 46410*. Tel: 219-769-9292.

Marriage Dispensations—Rev. GERALD H. SCHWEITZER, *P.O. Box 386, Wanatah, 46390*. Tel: 219-733-2955.

Marriage Encounter—MARK GORE; SUSAN GORE, *270 E. Stoneridge Ct., Chesterton, 46304*. Tel: 219-395-9955.

Ministry with the Physically and Mentally Challenged—Rev. JOHN J. ZEMELKO, Dir., *638 N. Calumet Rd., Chesterton, 46304*. Tel: 219-926-1282.

Mission Office—Rev. JOSEPH E. VAMOS, Dir., *8303 Taft St., Merrillville, 46410*. Tel: 219-769-2785.

Newspaper—*"Northwest Indiana Catholic"*, BRIAN T. OLSZEWSKI, Editor; CAROL MACINGA, Circulation Mgr., *9292 Broadway, Merrillville, 46410*. Tel: 219-769-9292.

Parish Pastoral Councils—ANNE VERBEKE, Dir., *9292 Broadway, Merrillville, 46410*. Tel: 219-769-9292; Fax: 219-738-9034.

Peace and Social Justice, Office of—Rev. THOMAS GANNON, S.J., Dir., *7128 Arizona Ave., Hammond, 46323*. Tel: 219-844-7515; Fax: 219-844-7566.

Priestly Life Coordinator—Rev. Msgr. WILLIAM L. MARTIN, *11000 W. 133rd Ave., Cedar Lake, 46303*. Tel: 219-374-7160.

Prison Ministries—Rev. WALTER M. CIESLA, Coord., *1001 W. 8th St., Michigan City, 46360*. Tel: 219-874-3491.

Pro-Life Activities—Rev. THEODORE J. MENS, Diocesan Dir., *525 N. Broad St., Griffith, 46319*. Tel: 219-924-4163.

Propagation of the Faith and Holy Childhood Association—cf. Mission Office.

Religious Education Office—Sr. CAROLINE CERVENY, S.S.J.-T.O.S.F., Dir., *9292 Broadway, Merrillville, 46410*. Tel: 219-769-9292.

Religious, Liaison for Women and Men—Sr. THERESE G. SULLIVAN, S.P., J.C.L., *9292 Broadway, Merrillville, 46410*. Tel: 219-769-9292.

Retirement Plan of the Diocese of Gary, Indiana—JOSEPH F. GLOTZBACH, C.P.A., *9292 Broadway, Merrillville, 46410*. Tel: 219-769-9292.

Rural Life Conference—Rev. ANTHONY L. SPANLEY, *P.O. Box 230, Hamlet, 46532*. Tel: 219-867-2461.

St. Vincent de Paul Society—DIANE MCKERN, Pres., *7132 Arizona Ave., Hammond, 46324*. Tel: 219-845-7531.

Schools Office—Dr. JOHN M. SHIELDS, Supt. of Schools; KIM PRYZYBYLSKI, Assoc. Supt. Schools, *9292 Broadway, Merrillville, 46410*. Tel: 219-769-9292.

Spiritual Life Center—Rev. MICHAEL W. COOPER, S.J., Dir., *1441 Hoffman St., Hammond, 46327*. Tel: 219-932-8321.

Stewardship—Rev. JOSEPH V. MURPHY, *10996 Four Seasons Place, Crown Point, 46307*. Tel: 219-661-0644; Fax: 219-661-0645.

Vocations—Rev. STEPHEN G. GIBSON, Dir., *812 W. 144th St., East Chicago, 46312*. Tel: 219-398-2409; Fax: 219-391-8999.

Youth Ministry—FRANK J. ZOLVINSKI, Dir., *9292 Broadway, Merrillville, 46410*. Tel: 219-769-9292.

CLERGY, PARISHES, MISSIONS AND PAROCHIAL SCHOOLS

CITY OF GARY
(Lake County)

1—CATHEDRAL OF HOLY ANGELS (1907), Rev. Robert P. Gehring.
Res., 640 Tyler St., 46402-2299. Tel: 219-882-6079; Fax: 219-882-0133.

2—BLESSED SACRAMENT (1947), Rev. Robert J. Tokarz.
Res., 1775 W. 41st Ave., 46408. Tel: 219-980-3081; Fax: 219-980-5646.
School—Tel: 219-980-5635.
Poor Handmaids of Jesus Christ 2; Lay Teachers 13; Students 222.
Catechesis/Religious Programs—Mrs. Lucille Highsmith, D.R.E.
Students 40.
Convent—6001 W. 25th Ave., 46406. Tel: 219-844-3212.

3—HOLY FAMILY (1926) (Polish), Rev. Stanley J. Milewski.
Res., 416 E. Ridge Rd., 46409. Tel: 219-884-1733.

4—HOLY ROSARY (1931), Rev. Frank D. Torres; Deacons Martin Gomez; Frederick Romanski.
Res., 719 Clark Rd., 46406. Tel: 219-944-1084.
Catechesis/Religious Programs—Sr. Rose Ann Kaiser, O.L.V.M., D.R.E.
Students 80.

5—HOLY TRINITY (1911) (African American). Closed. For inquiries for parish records contact Cathedral of Holy Angels, Gary.

6—SACRED HEART (1918) (Polish). Closed. For inquiries for parish records contact Cathedral of Holy Angels, Gary.

7—ST. ANN (1942), Rev. Stephen D. Kosinski.
Res., 6025 W. 25th Ave., 46406. Tel: 219-844-2448; Fax: 219-844-2897.

8—ST. ANTHONY (1918). Closed. For inquiries for parish records contact Cathedral of Holy Angels, Gary.

9—ST. CASIMIR (1916) (Lithuanian), Rev. Msgr. Ignatius L. Urbonas.
Res., 1390 W. 15th Ave., 46407. Tel: 219-882-1171.

10—ST. EMERIC (1911). Closed. For inquiries for parish records contact Holy Trinity (Hungarian), East Chicago.

11—ST. HEDWIG (1908) (Polish),
Serviced by Salvatorian Fathers. 1746 Pennsylvania St., 46407. Tel: 219-882-2584.; 5755 Pennsylvania St., Merrillville, 46410. Tel: 219-884-0714; Fax: 219-981-9224. [JC]

12—ST. JOSEPH THE WORKER (1912) (Croatian), Revs. Benedict Benakovic, O.F.M.Conv.; Stephen Loncar, O.F.M.Conv.
Res., 330 E. 45th Ave., 46409. Tel: 219-980-1846.

13—ST. LUKE (1917). See St. Monica, Gary.

14—ST. MARK (1921), Revs. John T. Ambre; Joseph J. Montoro; Sr. Rose Ann O.L.V.M., Pastoral Assoc.
Res., 501 W. Ridge Rd., 46408. Tel: 219-887-0514.
School—3880 Jackson St., 46408. Maria E. Vazquez, Prin.
Lay Teachers 8; Students 150.

15—ST. MARY OF THE LAKE (1929), Rev. Joseph M. Pawlowski.
Res., 6060 Miller Ave., 46403. Tel: 219-938-1373.
Catechesis/Religious Programs—Tel: 219-938-9115. Mary K. Mauer, D.R.E.
Students 63.

16—SS. MONICA-ST. LUKE (1927; 1917), Rev. J. Patrick Gaza; Deacons Melvin Clark; Michael Richardson.
Res., 645 Rhode Island, 46402. Tel: 219-883-1861.
Catechesis/Religious Programs—Students 42.

OUTSIDE THE CITY OF GARY

Beverly Shores, Porter Co., St. Ann (1956), Rev. Charles E. Doyle.
Res., P.O. Box 727, 46301. Tel: 219-879-7565; Fax: 219-874-4349.

Cedar Lake, Lake Co., Holy Name (1859), Rev. Msgr. William L. Martin.
Res., 11000 W. 133rd Ave., 46303. Tel: 219-374-7160; Fax: 219-374-7165. [CEM]
Parish Center—13209 Schneider St., 46303. Tel: 219-374-8798.
Catechesis/Religious Programs—Tel: 219-374-8798.
Students 260.

Chesterton, Porter Co., St. Patrick (1858), Revs. Lawrence S. Heeg; John J. Zemelko; Deacons Nicholas Juracevich; William Jones.
Res., 638 N. Calumet Rd., 46304. Tel: 219-926-1282. [CEM]
School—640 N. Calumet Rd., 46304. Tel: 219-926-1707. Ruth McCullough, Prin.
Lay Teachers 14; Students 213.
Catechesis/Religious Programs—Tel: 219-926-1265. Norma Dvorscak, D.R.E.
Students 640.

Crown Point, Lake Co., St. Mary (1865) (German), Rev. Msgr. Don C. Grass; Rev. Robert T. Naglich, S.C.J.
Res., 321 E. Joliet St., 46307. Tel: 219-663-0044; Fax: 219-663-0676. [CEM]
School—405 E. Joliet St., 46307. Tel: 219-663-0676. Sr. Kathleen Burke, S.P., Prin.
Lay Teachers 23; Students 612.
Catechesis/Religious Programs—Mrs. Jan Mucha, D.R.E.
Students 282.
Convent—222 E. Walnut St., 46307. Tel: 219-661-0735.

St. Matthias (1967), Rev. Terrence J. Steffens; Deacon Gregory Fabian.
Mailing Address: 2449 W. 125th Ave., 46307.
Res., 12505 Marshall St., 46307. Tel: 219-663-2201; Fax: 219-663-2567.
Catechesis/Religious Programs—Christine Nienhaus, D.R.E.
Students 340.

Dyer, Lake Co., St. Joseph (1867), Rev. Mark S. Pavlina.
Res., 440 Joliet St., 46311. Tel: 219-865-2271; Fax: 219-865-2350. [CEM]
School—Tel: 219-865-2750; Fax: 219-865-2750. Mr. Daniel McCabe, Prin.
Lay Teachers 12; Students 186.
Catechesis/Religious Programs—430 Joliet St., 46311. Tel: 219-865-2355.
Students 315.

St. Maria Goretti (1977), Rev. Alfred J. Dettmer.
Res., 500 Northgate Dr., 46311. Tel: 219-865-8956; Fax: 219-322-1670.
Catechesis/Religious Programs—Tel: 219-322-6124. Joyce Peterson, D.R.E.
Students 340.

East Chicago, Lake Co.,

1—ASSUMPTION, (1915) (Slovak), Rev. Larry J. Kew.
Res., P.O. Box I, 46312. Tel: 219-398-0420.

2—HOLY TRINITY, (1916) (Croatian), Rev. Msgr. Paul P. Bogovich.
Res., 4754 Carey St., 46312. Tel: 219-398-3061.

3—HOLY TRINITY, (1906) (Hungarian), Rev. Alphonse Skerl.
Res., 4759 McCook Ave., 46312. Tel: 219-397-1907.

4—IMMACULATE CONCEPTION, (1933) (Italian). Closed. For inquiries for parish records contact St. Stanislaus, East Chicago.

5—OUR LADY OF GUADALUPE, (1927) (Hispanic), Revs. Juan Gonzalez, C.PP.S.; Diego J. Getting, C.PP.S.; Bro. Jerry Schwieterman, C.PP.S., Pastoral Assoc.
Office: 3510 Deodar St., P.O. Box 3400, 46312. Tel: 219-398-0253; Fax: 219-398-0266.
Res., 4001 Fir St., 46312. Tel: 219-398-5640.
School—Interparochial Consolidated, Tel: 219-397-1122.
Catechesis/Religious Programs—Tel: 219-397-3293. Sr. Josephine Espinos, D.R.E.
Students 285.

6—SACRED HEART, (1926) (Slovak), Rev. Msgr. Joseph F. Semancik.
Res., 4423 Olcott Ave., 46312. Tel: 219-397-5857.

7—ST. FRANCIS, (1913) (Lithuanian). Closed. For inquiries for parish records contact St. John Cantius, East Chicago.

8—ST. JOHN CANTIUS, (1906) (Polish), Rev. Joseph R. Niezgoda. In res., Rev. Matthew J. Kish.
Res., 3903 Main St., 46312. Tel: 219-398-1370.
School—Indiana Catholic Elementary School, Tel: 219-397-1122.

9—ST. JOSEPH, (1916) (Polish). Closed. For inquiries for parish records contact St. John Cantius, East Chicago.

10—ST. JUDE, (1933). Closed. For inquiries for parish records contact Our Lady of Guadalupe, East Chicago.

11—ST. MARY, (1890), Revs. Stephen G. Gibson; Dave W. Kime.
822 W. 144th St., 46312. Tel: 219-398-2409.
School—Tel: 219-397-4404. Mr. Donald Domsich, Prin.
Lay Teachers 10; Students 225.
Catechesis/Religious Programs—Students 215.

12—ST. PATRICK, (1902) (Hispanic), Rev. Fernando de Cristobal; Sr. Irene DeMeulenaere, Pastoral Assoc.
Res., 3810 Grand Blvd., 46312. Tel: 219-398-1036; Fax: 219-398-1036.
School—Interparochial, Tel: 219-397-1122.
Catechesis/Religious Programs—3916 Pulaski St., 46312. Tel: 219-397-3293.
Students 81.

13—ST. STANISLAUS, (1896) (Polish), Rev. Msgr. John J. Siekierski; Rev. Stanley Witek.
Res., 808 W. 150th St., 46312. Tel: 219-398-2341.
School—4930 Indianapolis Blvd., 46312. Tel: 219-398-1316. Patricia Panozzo, Prin.
Sisters of St. Joseph of the Third Order of St. Francis 3; Lay Teachers 14; Students 240.
Convent—4940 Indianapolis Blvd., 46312. Tel: 219-397-7059.

East Gary, Lake Co., . (Name change - refer to Lake Station, Lake Co., IN, for all information.).

Fish Lake, La Porte Co., St. Anthony (1948), Rev. Michael G. Heimer.
Res., (Fish Lake) 7732 E. State Rd. 4, Walkerton, 46574. Tel: 219-369-1210.

Griffith, Lake Co., St. Mary (1928), Rev. Theodore J. Mens. In res., Rev. Charles A. Mosley.
Res., 525 N. Broad St., 46319. Tel: 219-924-4163; Fax: 219-922-2291.
School—Tel: 219-924-8633. Sr. Helen Minich, Prin.
Sisters of St. Francis of Perpetual Adoration 3; Lay Teachers 18; Students 361.
Catechesis/Religious Programs—Tel: 219-922-2277. Mrs. Barbara Letts, D.R.E.
Students 402.
Convent—508 N. Lafayette St., 46319. Tel: 219-922-2278.

Hamlet, Starke Co., Holy Cross (1888), Rev. Anthony L. Spanley.
Res., P.O. Box 230, 46532. Tel: 219-867-2461. [CEM]
Mission—Koontz Lake, Starke Co., St. Dominic, (1981) P.O. Box 230, 46532.

Hammond, Lake Co.,

1—ALL SAINTS, (1896), Rev. J. Antonio Valtierra.
Res., 570 Sibley St., P.O. Box 836, 46325-0836. Tel: 219-932-0204; Fax: 219-932-4507.
Catechesis/Religious Programs—Josephine Perez, D.R.E.
Students 132.

2—OUR LADY OF PERPETUAL HELP, (1937), Revs. John R. Winterlin; Andrew Corona. In res., Deacon Thomas Kreidler.
Res., 7132 Arizona St., 46323. Tel: 219-844-3438; Fax: 219-844-3580.
Catechesis/Religious Programs—7128 Arizona St., 46323. Ruth Rossi, D.R.E.
Students 140.

3—ST. CASIMIR, (1890) (Polish), Revs. Vladimir Janeczek; Richard M. Penczynski.
Res., 4340 Johnson St., 46327. Tel: 219-931-2589.
School—4329 Cameron St., 46327. Tel: 219-932-2686. Mrs. Stasia Krempa, Prin.
Lay Teachers 8; Students 204.
Catechesis/Religious Programs—Students 50.

4—ST. CATHERINE OF SIENA, (1956), Rev. Richard A. Orlinski.
Res., 6605 Kentucky Ave., 46323. Tel: 219-845-1939; Fax: 219-845-4772.
School—6525 Kentucky Ave., 46323. Tel: 219-845-1217; Fax: 219-845-1591. Christine Nielsen, Prin.
Poor Handmaids of Jesus Christ 1; Lay Teachers 8; Students 198.
Catechesis/Religious Programs—Tel: 219-845-2207. Susan Bates, D.R.E.
Students 120.
Convent—Tel: 219-845-5341.

5—ST. JOHN BOSCO, (1934), Revs. Stanley J. Dominik; Peter J. Muha; Deacon Robert DeVore.
Res., 7113 Columbia Ave., 46324. Tel: 219-844-9027; Fax: 219-844-6986.
Pastoral Center: 1247-171st Pl., 46324.
School—(Grades K-8) 1231-171st Pl., 46324. Tel: 219-845-6226. James O'Donnell, Prin.
Lay Teachers 14; Students 200.
Catechesis/Religious Programs—Tel: 219-844-7874. Mrs. Kathy Hocker, D.R.E.
Students 140.

6—ST. JOSEPH, (1879), Rev. Roy T. Beeching; Deacon James F. Etter.
Res., 5304 Hohman Ave., 46320. Tel: 219-932-0702; Fax: 219-932-0059.
Catechesis/Religious Programs—Tel: 219-932-7294. Sr. Barbara Koza, S.S.J.-T.O.S.F., D.R.E.
Students 100.

7—ST. MARGARET MARY, (1947), Rev. Matthew C. Iwuji.
Res., 1445 Hoffman St., 46327. Tel: 219-931-5229; Fax: 219-937-4357.
Catechesis/Religious Programs—Students 120.

8—ST. MARY, (1912) (Polish). Unassigned.
Res., 931 Merrill St., 46320. Tel: 219-932-2511.
Church—Morris & Tapper Aves., 46320.

Hebron, Porter Co., St. Helen (1946), Rev. Derrick F. Dudash.
Res., 302 N. Madison St., 46341. Tel: 219-996-4611.
Catechesis/Religious Programs—Tel: 219-996-4612. Susan Witt, D.R.E.
Students 142.

Highland, Lake Co., Our Lady of Grace (1949), Revs. Edward J. Moszur; Edward J. Kennedy.
Office: 3005 Condit St., 46322. Tel: 219-838-0395; Fax: 219-972-6372.
School—3025 Highway Ave., 46322. Tel: 219-838-2901. Marilyn Tomko, Prin.
Sisters 1; Lay Teachers 18; Students 293.
Catechesis/Religious Programs—Tel: 219-838-6790. Mrs. Diane Foster, D.R.E.
Students 224.

St. James the Less (1967), Revs. Francis M. Lazar; Joseph A. Angotti; Deacons Martin Denkhoff; Raymond Dec.
Mailing Address: 9640 Kennedy Ave., 46322.
Res., 2703 45th St., 46322. Tel: 219-924-4220; Fax: 219-924-4295.
Catechesis/Religious Programs—Theresa A. Zarndt, D.R.E.
Students 405.

Hobart, Lake Co., St. Bridget (1873), Revs. Dominic V. Bertino; Andrew Malarz.
Res., 568 E. Second St., 46342. Tel: 219-942-6441; Fax: 219-942-4573.
School—107 Main St., 46342. Tel: 219-942-1894. Sr. Rita Marie Malachinski, S.S.J., Prin.
Lay Teachers 16; Students 286.
Catechesis/Religious Programs—Students 300.

Kingsford Heights, La Porte Co., Immaculate Heart of Mary (1953), Rev. Michael G. Heimer, Admin.
c/o 7732 E. State Road 4, Walkerton, 46574. Tel: 219-393-5061; 369-1210.
Catechesis/Religious Programs—Students 47.

Knox, Starke Co., St. Thomas Aquinas (1923), Rev. Msgr. Richard F. Zollinger.
Res., 406 E. Washington St., 46534. Tel: 219-772-4134.
Catechesis/Religious Programs—Students 64.

Kouts, Porter Co., St. Mary (1884), Rev. Thomas T. Tibbs.
Res., P.O. Box 663, 46347. Tel: 219-766-3680. [CEM]
Catechesis/Religious Programs—Mary Martin, D.R.E.
Students 110.

Lake Station, Lake Co., St. Francis Xavier (1930), Rev. Robert B. Evers; Deacon Leonard Holland.
Res., 2447 Putnam St., 46405. Tel: 219-962-8626. [CEM]
School—2453 Putnam St., 46405. Tel: 219-962-4507. Carol Brendza, Prin.
Lay Teachers 5; Students 107.
Catechesis/Religious Programs—Kenneth Mayner, D.R.E.
Students 164.

La Porte, La Porte Co., St. Joseph (1858), Rev. Theodore A. Nordquist; Deacon Robert Bucheit.
Res., 109 C St., 46350. Tel: 219-362-9595. [CEM]
School—101 C St., 46350. Tel: 219-362-6472. Sr. M. James Kuzell, Prin.
Sisters of St. Francis of Perpetual Adoration 2; Lay Teachers 11; Students 188.
Catechesis/Religious Programs—Sr. M. Robertann, D.R.E.
Students 120.
Convent—102 B St., 46350. Tel: 219-362-2587.

St. Peter (1853), Rev. George M. Vrabely.
Res., 1104 Monroe St., 46350. Tel: 219-362-6186.
Catechesis/Religious Programs—1110 Monroe St., 46350. Tel: 219-362-2509. Patricia Poleski, D.R.E.
Students 357.

Sacred Heart (1912) (Polish), Rev. Gerald A. Sroka.
Res., 128 Bach St., 46350. Tel: 219-362-2815; Fax: 219-362-4822. [JC]
Catechesis/Religious Programs—Joan Kowalczyk, D.R.E.
Students 135.

Lowell, Lake Co., St. Edward (1870), Rev. Thomas E. Mischler.
Res., 216 S. Nichols St., 46356. Tel: 219-696-7307; Fax: 219-696-3525. [CEM]
School—210 S. Nichols St., 46356. Tel: 219-696-9876; Fax: 219-696-2524.
Lay Teachers 11; Students 121.
Catechesis/Religious Programs—Tel: 219-696-4282; Fax: 219-696-3525. Veronica Grubb, D.R.E.
Students 266.
Mission—Shelby, Lake Co., St. Theresa, 23315 Shelby Rd., Shelby, 46377.

Merrillville, Lake Co.,

1—OUR LADY OF CONSOLATION, (1947), Rev. Joseph E. Vamos; Deacon Robert E. Gill.
Res., 8303 Taft St., 46410. Tel: 219-769-2785; Fax: 219-769-2607.
Catechesis/Religious Programs—Tel: 219-769-1755. Bridget Bowman, D.R.E.
Students 423.

2—ST. ANDREW, (1965), Rev. Terrence R. Chase.
Res., 801 W. 73rd Ave., 46410. Tel: 219-769-8534; Fax: 219-769-8543.
School—Tel: 219-769-2049. June Kachur, Prin.
Lay Teachers 8; Students 140.
Catechesis/Religious Programs—Tel: 219-769-2049.
Students 233.

3—ST. JOAN OF ARC, (1968), Rev. Sammie L. Maletta.
Res., 200 E. 78th Ave., 46410. Tel: 219-769-1973; Fax: 219-769-9056.
Catechesis/Religious Programs—Tel: 219-769-2037. Joyce Martinez, D.R.E.
Students 68.
St. Joan of Arc Center—.

4—SS. PETER AND PAUL, (1850), Rev. Dennis J. Teles.
Res., 5885 Harrison St., 46410. Tel: 219-980-2693; Fax: 219-980-2851. [CEM]
Catechesis/Religious Programs—Tel: 219-887-2940. Paula Burrell, D.R.E.
Students 102.

5—ST. STEPHEN, MARTYR, (1968), Rev. David G. Nowak; Deacon Joseph Codespoti.
Res., 5920 Waite St., 46410. Tel: 219-980-9348.
Catechesis/Religious Programs—5885 Harrison, 46410. Tel: 219-887-2940.
Students 53.

Michigan City, La Porte Co.,

1—ST. MARY OF THE IMMACULATE CONCEPTION, (1849), Rev. James P. McGrogan. In res., Rev. John B. Barasinski.
Res., 411 W. 11th St., 46360. Tel: 219-874-7231.
School—321 W. 11th St., 46360. Tel: 219-873-1321; Fax: 219-873-1329. James L. Faroh, Sr., Prin.
Lay Teachers 10; Students 192.

2—NOTRE DAME, (1953), Rev. Richard H. Ameling.
Res., 1010 Moore Rd., 46360. Tel: 219-872-4844.
School—Tel: 219-872-6216. William Davis, Prin.
Lay Teachers 13; Students 268.
Catechesis/Religious Programs—Students 28.

3—QUEEN OF ALL SAINTS, (1950), Revs. Michael J. Yadron; William F. O'Toole.
Res., 526 S. Woodland Ave., 46360. Tel: 219-872-9196; Fax: 219-872-9176.
School—1715 E. Barker Ave., 46360. Tel: 219-872-4420. Theresa J. Glowacki, Prin.
Sisters of Holy Cross 1; Lay Teachers 20; Students 470.
Catechesis/Religious Programs—Tel: 219-878-9348. Bro. James Drangsholt, O.S.F., D.R.E.

Students 200.
Convent—606 S. Woodland Ave., 46360. Tel: 219-872-5401.

4—ST. STANISLAUS KOSTKA, (1891) (Polish), Rev. Msgr. Michael J. Tomaszewski; Deacon Daniel Bowmar.
Res., 109 Ann St., 46360. Tel: 219-879-9281.
School—1506 Washington St., 46360. Tel: 219-872-2258. Margaret Clifford, Prin.
Lay Teachers 9; Students 174.
Catechesis/Religious Programs—Tel: 219-879-6561. Antoinette Sajewski, D.R.E.
Students 100.

5—SACRED HEART, (1915) (Lebanese), Rev. Walter Ciesla.
Res., 1001 W. Eighth St., 46360. Tel: 219-874-3491.
Catechesis/Religious Programs—Students 50.

Munster, Lake Co., St. Thomas More (1945), Revs. Richard A. Emerson; Keith M. Virus; Ian J. Williams; Jon J. Plavcan; Deacon Joseph Sobek.
Res., 8501 Calumet Ave., 46321. Tel: 219-836-8610; Fax: 219-836-0945.
School—Tel: 219-836-9151; Fax: 219-836-0982. Kevin T. Zajdel, Ed.D., Prin.
Lay Teachers 30; Students 561.
Catechesis/Religious Programs—Tel: 219-836-9152. Sr. Marilyn Hettinger, D.R.E.
Students 625.

New Chicago, Lake Co., Assumption of the Blessed Virgin Mary (P.O. Hobart) (1917) (Polish), Rev. Martin J. Dobrzynski.
Res., 3530 Illinois St., Hobart, 46342. Tel: 219-962-1073.
Catechesis/Religious Programs—Tel: 219-962-6678.
Students 68.

North Judson, Starke Co., Ss. Cyril and Methodius (1881), Rev. Mark G. Mazza.
Res., 303 Keller Ave., 46366. Tel: 219-896-2195. [CEM]
Catechesis/Religious Programs—Students 60.

Otis, La Porte Co., St. Mary (1873), Rev. Joseph E. Pusateri.
Res., 101 N. Church St., 46391. Tel: 219-785-2212; Fax: 219-785-4743. [CEM]

Portage, Porter Co., Nativity of Our Savior (1964), Revs. John V. Scott; Patrick J. Kalich; Deacons Robert J. Bonta; Alexander A. Saims; Sr. Kay Kelly, S.P., Pastoral Assoc.
Res., 2949 Willowcreek Rd., 46368. Tel: 219-762-4858.
School—2929 Willowcreek Rd., 46368. Tel: 219-763-2400. Jo Ann Abbott, Prin.
Lay Teachers 10; Students 213.
Catechesis/Religious Programs—Students 581.

Rolling Prairie, Laporte Co., St. John Kanty (1888) (Polish), Rev. James W. Meade, Admin.
Res., P.O. Box 236, 46371. Tel: 219-778-2935. [CEM]

Saint John, Lake Co., St. John Evangelist (1839), Revs. Stephen J. Titko; Kevin R. Huber.
Mailing Address: P.O. Box 360, 46373.
Res., 11211 W. 93rd St., 46373. Tel: 219-365-5678; Fax: 219-365-2703. [CEM]
Parish Office: 11350 School St., P.O. Box 360, St. John, 46373.
School—9400 Wicker Ave., St. John, 46373. Tel: 219-365-5451; Fax: 219-365-6173. Sr. Angela Mellady, Prin.
Sisters of St. Francis of Perpetual Adoration 3; Lay Teachers 18; Students 358.
Catechesis/Religious Programs—Tel: 219-365-3709. Arlene Crilley, D.R.E.
Students 332.
Convent—11340 School St., 46373. Tel: 219-365-3882.

San Pierre, Starke Co., All Saints (1858), Rev. William J. Spranger.
Res., P.O. Box 56, 46374. Tel: 219-828-4281. [CEM]

Schererville, Lake Co., St. Michael (1874), Revs. Patrick J. Connolly; James E. Wozniak. In res., Rev. Joseph F. Gazarkiewicz.
Res., One Wilhelm St., 46375. Tel: 219-322-4505; Fax: 219-322-4508. [CEM]
Preschool—(Good Shepherd Program).
Students 20.
School—16 W. Wilhelm St., 46375. Tel: 219-322-4531.
Franciscan Sisters of the Sacred Heart 1; Lay Teachers 14; Students 322.
Catechesis/Religious Programs—Tel: 219-322-3077.
Students 626.

Shelby, Lake Co., St. Theresa (1939), Revs. Thomas E. Mischler; Bede Hepnar, O.F.M.
Res., 216 S. Nichols St., Lowell, 46356. Tel: 219-696-7307; Fax: 219-696-3525.

Valparaiso, Porter Co., Our Lady of Sorrows (South Haven) (1967), Rev. Douglas J. Mayer; Deacon Sherman Brown.
Res., 356 W. Seven Mile Rd., 46383. Tel: 219-759-2400.
Catechesis/Religious Programs—Tel: 219-759-2286.
Students 150.

St. Paul (1858), Rev. Msgr. John J. Charlebois; Deacon John McGuckin.
Mailing Address: P.O. Box 1475, 46384-1475. Tel: 219-464-4831; Fax: 219-464-4833.
Res., 452 W. Chicago St., 46383. Tel: 219-465-3723. [CEM]
Church—1855 Harrison Blvd., 46383. Tel: 219-464-4831; Fax: 219-464-4833.
School—352 W. Chicago St., 46383. Tel: 219-462-3374; Fax: 219-477-1763. Nancy Dennis, Prin.
Lay Teachers 12; Students 210.
Catechesis/Religious Programs—Tel: 219-464-8502.
Students 858.
Child Development Center—Tel: 219-465-0882. Janet McCorkle, Dir.
St. Agnus Day Service Center—1859 Harrison Blvd., 46383. Barbara Kubiszak, Dir.

St. Elizabeth Seton (1978), Revs. Gerald A. Sroka; David H. Gosnell; Deacon James J. Keough.
Res., 509 W. Division Rd., 46383. Tel: 219-464-1624; Fax: 219-465-7673.
Catechesis/Religious Programs—Tel: 219-462-2202. MaryAnn Kelley, D.R.E.
Students 782.

Wanatah, La Porte Co., Sacred Heart (1887), Rev. Gerald H. Schweitzer.
Res., 202 N. Ohio St, P.O. Box 386, 46390. Tel: 219-733-2955. [CEM]
Catechesis/Religious Programs—Tel: 219-733-2315.
Students 160.
Mission—LaCrosse, LaPorte Co., St. Martin, (1860) Lowell & Dominic Sts., LaCrosse, 46348.

Whiting, Lake Co.,

1—IMMACULATE CONCEPTION, (1922) (Slovak), Rev. Anthony D. Ficko.
Res., 2006 Schrage Ave., 46394. Tel: 219-659-0724.

2—SACRED HEART, (1889), Rev. Msgr. F. Raymond Fowerbaugh.
Res., 1731 Laporte Ave., 46394. Tel: 219-659-0733.
School—1723 Laporte Ave., 46394. Tel: 219-659-0705. Phillip Kokandy, Prin.
Lay Teachers 8; Students 110.
Convent—1717 Laporte Ave., 46394. Tel: 219-659-1648.

3—ST. ADALBERT, (1902) (Polish), Rev. Walter J. Rakoczy.
Res., 1340 121st St., 46394. Tel: 219-659-3848.

4—ST. JOHN THE BAPTIST, (1897) (Slovak), Revs. John E. Kalicky, C.PP.S.; Edward C. Homco, C.PP.S.; Matthew W. Jozefiak, C.PP.S.; Deacons David Hajduch; Joseph Manchak. In res., Rev. Leon Flaherty, C.PP.S.
Res., P.O. Box 70, 46394. Tel: 219-659-0023; Fax: 219-473-7551.
School—1844 Lincoln Ave., 46394. Tel: 219-659-3042. Thomas J. Puplava, Prin.
Lay Teachers 22; Students 469.
Catechesis/Religious Programs—Tel: 219-659-1889; Fax: 219-473-7553. Miss Lenore R. Lazur, D.R.E.
Students 125.

5—STS. PETER AND PAUL, (1910), Rev. Charles W. Niblick.
Res., 1709 Center St., 46394. Tel: 219-659-1291.
Catechesis/Religious Programs—Students 70.

Chaplains of Public Institutions

MICHIGAN CITY. *Indiana State Prison.* Revs. Joseph M. Lanzalaco, C.S.B.; Joseph Ross, C.S.C., 5959 Broadway, Merrillville, 46410. Tel: 219-887-5281; 887-5284.

ROLLING PRAIRIE. *Sharing Meadows.* Dennis J. Blaney, P.O. Box 400, 46371. Tel: 219-778-9130.

WESTVILLE. *Westville Correctional Center.* Rev. Walter M. Ciesla, Coord., 1001 W. 8th St., Michigan City, 46360. Tel: 219-874-3491.

On Duty Outside the Diocese:
Reverend Monsignors—
Charlebois, Robert L., 161 E. Chicago Ave., Chicago, IL 60611
Reverend Fathers—
Coriden, James A., 6896 Laurel St., N.W., Washington, DC 20012
Hand, Dennis M., Parroquia de los Santos Inocentes, Apartado Postal #102, La Libertad, El Salvador
Hendricks, Clare, P.O. Box 8066, Columbia, TN 38401

Military Chaplains:
Reverend Fathers—
Nondorf, Aloysius J., 1962 Bay City Pl., El Paso, TX 79936

Graduate Studies:
Reverend Fathers—
Danforth, Clarence E., Convitto San Tommaso, Via degli Ibernesi, 20, Rome, 00184 Italy

---

Absent on Leave:
Reverend Fathers—
Murzyn, John A., Sick Leave, P.O. Box 817, Flagler Beach, FL 32136

Retired:
Reverend Monsignors—
Doody, Timothy F., 1501 Hoffman St., Hammond, IN 46327
Hoffmann, Ralph G., 2103 Hawthorne Ln., Chesterton, IN 46304
Lengerich, Vincent L., 301 S. Main St., Knox, IN 46534
Litot, Edward F., 317 Waverly Rd., La Porte, IN 46350
Melevage, F. J., 3214 Milestone Creek Ct., Valparaiso, IN 46383
Morales, John F., 333 N. Palm Dr., #305, Beverly Hills, CA 90210
Van Nevel, Albert H., 11652 Patterson St., Cedar Lake, IN 46303
Witte, John C., 3713 S. State Rd. 104, La Porte, IN 46350
Reverend Fathers—
Bargielski, John C., Albertine Home, 1501 Hoffman St., Hammond, IN 46327
Daniels, John W., 425 Birch St., N.W., DeMotte, IN 46310
Fusco, Philip N., 3132 100th Pl., Highland, IN 46322
Kashmer, George B., 2501 Chelwood, N.E., Albuquerque, NM 87112
Kish, Matthew J., 3903 Main St., East Chicago, IN 46312
Kronkowski, Leonard J., 1 Cambridge Ct., Apt. 8, Michigan City, IN 46360
Lukaszewski, Leonard, 21-163rd St., Calumet City, IL 60409
Madejczyk, Louis S., 3599 Kingsway Dr., Crown Point, IN 46307
McGinnity, Ambrose T., 6450 S. State Rd. 10, Knox, IN 46534
Meneghello, Serafino, Via Oliosi, 13 San Massimo, Verona, Italy
Minnich, John F., P.O. Box 537, Georgetown, IN 47122
Peil, William L., 1841 N. Anthony Blvd., Fort Wayne, IN 46805
Pogorzelski, Eugeniusz, 1501 Hoffman St., Hammond, IN 46327
Strebig, John J., 135 Kingsbury Ave., LaPorte, IN 46350
Till, Joseph E., 317 W. 10th St., Michigan City, IN 46360
Vogt, William E., 965 E. Sutton Dr., Fresno, Ca 93720
Zimmerman, Albert J., Albertine Home, 1501 Hoffman St., Hammond, IN 46327

Permanent Deacons:
Bonta, Robert J.
Bowmar, Daniel L.
Brown, Sherman W.
Bucheit, Robert J.
Clark, Melvin
Codespoti, Joseph
Dec, Raymond
Delgado, Juan, On Duty Outside the Diocese
Denkhoff, Martin J.
DeVore, Robert S.
Etter, James, On Leave
Fabian, Gregory G.
Gill, Robert E.
Godinez, Rafael, On Duty Outside the Diocese
Gomez, Martin
Hajduch, David A.
Hawkins, Dennis, On Leave
Holland, Leonard D.
Jones, William E., Jr.
Jurasevich, Nicholas J.
Keough, James J.
Kreidler, Thomas
Maldonado, Felipe
Manchak, Joseph C.
McGuckin, John D.
Modrak, George V.
Neely, Vincent, On Duty Outside the Diocese

O'Donnell, Robert, On Leave
Paulson, Joel, On Duty Outside the Diocese
Perez, Gilberto, On Duty Outside the Diocese
Richardson, Michael E.
Romanski, Frederick, On Leave
Roscoe, John, On Duty Outside the Diocese
Saims, Alexander A.
Sobek, Joseph J., Sr.
Vendl, Leslie, On Duty Outside the Diocese

INSTITUTIONS LOCATED IN THE DIOCESE

[A] COLLEGES AND UNIVERSITIES

WHITING. *Calumet College of St. Joseph*, 2400 New York Ave., 46394. Tel: 219-473-7770.
Web site: www.ccsj.edu
For a complete listing, refer to the Colleges and Universities section.

[B] HIGH SCHOOLS, DIOCESAN

HAMMOND. *Bishop Noll Institute*, 1519 Hoffman St., 46327. Tel: 219-932-9058; Fax: 219-853-1736.
E-mail: sowen.bni@ash.palni.edu
Web site: www.bishopnoll.com
Suzan LaPeer, Prin.; Rev. Andrew Corona. Priests 3; Lay Teachers 61; Students 916.

MERRILLVILLE. *Andrean High School*, 5959 Broadway, 46410. Tel: 219-887-5281. Rev. Paul E. Quanz, C.S.B., Prin.; Sr. Fabian Philothea, S.S.C.M., Asst. Prin.; Revs. John J. Fiore, C.S.B.; Ralph C. Koehler, C.S.B.; Joseph M. Lanzalaco, C.S.B. Basilian Fathers 4; Sisters of Sts. Cyril and Methodius 3; Lay Teachers 59;; Students 827.

MICHIGAN CITY. *Marquette Catholic High School*, 306 W. Tenth St., 46360. Tel: 219-873-1325.
E-mail: mhsoff@adsnet.com
Patrick Cannon, Prin. Priests 2; Lay Teachers 17; Students 245.

[C] ELEMENTARY SCHOOLS, DIOCESAN

GARY. *Sr. Thea Bowman Elementary School*, 975 W. Sixth Ave., 46402-1799. Tel: 219-883-1331. Mrs. Hazel Holmes, Prin. Lay Teachers 14; Total Staff 32; Students 386.

[D] ELEMENTARY SCHOOLS, PRIVATE

ROLLING PRAIRIE. *Le Mans Academy*. (Grades 5-9), 46371. Tel: 219-778-2521.
E-mail: LMASpartan@aol.com
Web site: www.asgusa.com/lemans
Private boarding school for boys. Bro. William Dygent, C.S.C., Pres.; Mr. Steve Cash, Headmaster. Priests 1; Brothers 4; Lay Teachers 20; Total Staff 50; Enrollment 107.

[E] ELEMENTARY SCHOOLS, INTERPAROCHIAL

EAST CHICAGO. *Indiana Harbor Catholic Elementary School*, 3916 Pulaski St., 46312. Tel: 219-397-1122. Mrs. Francisca C. Phelps, Prin. Lay Teachers 8; Students 180. Serving the parishes of Assumption, Our Lady of Guadalupe, St John Cantius, and St. Patrick in East Chicago.

[F] GENERAL HOSPITALS

CROWN POINT. *St. Anthony Medical Center, Inc.*, 1201 S. Main St., 46307-8483. Tel: 219-738-2100
For a complete listing, refer to the Hospitals section.

DYER. *St. Margaret Mercy Healthcare Centers, South Campus*, 24 Joliet, 46311. Tel: 219-932-2300
For a complete listing, refer to the Hospitals section.

EAST CHICAGO. *St. Catherine Hospital*, 4321 Fir St., 46312. Tel: 219-392-1700; Fax: 219-392-7002
For a complete listing, refer to the Hospitals section.

HAMMOND. *St. Margaret Mercy Healthcare Centers - North Campus*, 5454 Hohman Ave., 46320. Tel: 219-932-2300
For a complete listing, refer to the Hospitals section.

HOBART. *St. Mary Medical Center*, 1500 S. Lake Park Ave., 46342. Tel: 219-942-0551; Fax: 219-947-6037
For a complete listing, refer to the Hospitals section.

MICHIGAN CITY. *St. Anthony Hospital and Health Centers*, 301 W. Homer St., 46360. Tel: 219-879-8511.
Web site: www.sahhc.org
For a complete listing, refer to the Hospitals section.

[G] PROTECTIVE INSTITUTIONS

EAST CHICAGO. *Carmelite Home for Girls*, 4840 Grasselli Ave., 46312. Tel: 219-397-1085; Fax: 219-392-3574
For a complete listing, refer to the Special Care Facilities section.

HAMMOND. *Carmelite Home for Boys*, 4007 Sheffield Ave., 46327. Tel: 219-931-6451
For a complete listing, refer to the Special Care Facilities section.

SCHERERVILLE. *Hoosier Boys' Town*, 7403 Cline Ave., 46375. Tel: 219-838-7723
For a complete listing, refer to the Special Care Facilities section.

[H] HOMES FOR THE AGED

CROWN POINT. *St. Anthony Home, Inc.*, 203 Franciscan Dr., 46307-4824. Tel: 219-757-6281
For a complete listing, refer to the Special Care Facilities section.

HAMMOND. *Albertine Home*, 1501 Hoffman St., 46327. Tel: 219-937-0575
For a complete listing, refer to the Special Care Facilities section.

SAN PIERRE. *Holy Cross Care Services dba Little Company of Mary Health Facility, Inc.*, 7520 S. U.S. Hwy. 421, 46374-4275. Tel: 219-828-4111; Fax: 219-828-4172
For a complete listing, refer to the Special Care Facilities section.

[I] PERSONAL PRELATURES

VALPARAISO. *Opus Dei*, 359 West 200 North, 46383. Tel: 219-462-6594; 462-0931. Prelature of the Holy Cross and Opus Dei, Shellbourne Conference Center. Legal Title: *The Work of God, Inc.*

[J] MONASTERIES AND RESIDENCES OF PRIESTS AND BROTHERS

CEDAR LAKE. *Our Lady of Lourdes Friary*, 12915 Parrish St., P.O. Box 156, 46303. Tel: 219-374-5931. Franciscan Friars of the Assumption of the B.V.M. Province (Order of Friars Minor). Revs. Anthony F. Janik, O.F.M., Guardian; Francis Appelt; George Dubowski, O.F.M.; Bede Hepnar, O.F.M.; Bronislaus Jaskulski, O.F.M.; Maynard Kolodziej, O.F.M.; Myron Lowisz, O.F.M.; Andrew Meronek; Bert Pepowski; Clarence Mazur, O.F.M.; Patrick Szemla, O.F.M.; Carmen Scuderi, O.F.M. Priests 12; Brothers 3.

San Damiano Friary, 12921 Parrish St., P.O. Box 500, 46303. Tel: 219-374-5741; Fax: 219-374-9650. Cedar Lake Franciscan Friars (Order of Friars Minor). Interprovinicial Novitiate. Revs. Donald P. Blaeser, O.F.M., Guardian; Thomas W. Luczak, O.F.M., Dir. Novices; Ronald F. Walters, O.F.M., J.C.L., Treas.; Bro. Edward Demyanovich, Vicar. Priests 3; Brothers 1; Novices 7.

EAST CHICAGO. *Roque Gonzalez Residence-Jesuit Fathers*, 3905 Fir St., 46312. Tel: 219-397-1885; 397-3906; Fax: 219-932-8321.
E-mail: xctb29c@prodigy.com
Revs. Michael W. Cooper, S.J., Supr.; Thomas M. Gannon, S.J.; James W. Schulz, S.J.

MERRILLVILLE. *Basilian Fathers Residence*, 5959 Broadway, 46410. Tel: 219-887-5284; Fax: 219-981-5072. Revs. John J. Fiore, C.S.B., Rector; Michael A. Buentello, C.S.B., First Councillor; Ralph C. Koehler, C.S.B., Treas.; Joseph M. Lanzalaco, C.S.B.; Paul E. Quanz, C.S.B. Priests 5.

Salvatorian Fathers (Society of the Divine Savior), 5755 Pennsylvania St., 46410. Tel: 219-884-0714; Fax: 219-981-9224. Mission House for Polish Priests and Brothers. Revs. Emil Jarco, S.D.S., Supr.; Joseph R. Zuziak, S.D.S., Vice Supr. & Treas.; Norbert Stawowy, S.D.S.; Edward Kawa, S.D.S.; Zenon Boczek, S.D.S.; Marek Wiorkiewicz, S.D.S.; Bros. Marek Miazga, S.D.S.; Piotr Bogawski, S.D.S. Priests 6; Brothers 2.

MUNSTER. *Discalced Carmelite Fathers Monastery*, 1628 Ridge Rd., 46321. Tel: 219-838-7111; Fax: 219-838-7214. Revs. Thomas I. Balys, O.C.D., Prior; Bronislaw F. Socha, O.C.D., Subprior; Casimir Adalbert Borcz, O.C.D., Second Consultor; Michael G. Veneklase, O.C.D., Master of Novices; Waclaw L. Lech, O.C.D., Treas.; John Baptista Kolaczek, O.C.D.; Edward C. Spyrka, O.C.D.; Joseph Ivans, O.C.D.; Mark Nojek, O.C.D.; Jacek Palica, O.C.D. Priests 10; Postulants 2.

[K] CONVENTS AND RESIDENCES OF SISTERS

EAST CHICAGO. *St. Catherine Convent*, 4325 Elm St., 46312. Tel: 219-398-0403. Poor Handmaids of Jesus Christ 5; Dominican Sister 1; Sisters of St. Joseph 1.

Saint Patrick Convent, 3814 Grand Blvd., 46312. Tel: 219-398-1983. Teaching and Parish Ministry, Our Lady of Victory Missionary Sisters; Health Ministry and Home Nursing, Poor Handmaids of Jesus Christ; Religious Educ., Sisters of St. Joseph, TOSF. Sisters 4.

HAMMOND. *Albertine Sisters (Prov. of Krakow, Poland)*, 1501 Hoffman St., 46327. Tel: 219-937-0575. Sr. Sigmunda Wojtusiak, Supr. Sisters 11.

MERRILLVILLE. *Convent of Sts. Cyril and Methodius*, 5959 Broadway, 46410. Tel: 219-887-5287. Teaching at Andrean High School. Sisters 6.

[L] RETREAT HOUSES

EAST CHICAGO. *Bethany Retreat House*, 2202 Lituanica Ave., 46312. Tel: 219-398-5047.
E-mail: bethanyrh@sprynet.com
Sr. Joyce Diltz, P.H.J.C. Total Staff 4; Guests 126.

MICHIGAN CITY. *Angela House*, 412 W. 10th St., 46360. Tel: 219-873-1324. Sr. Anna Clare O'Connor, C.S.C., Dir.; Sr. Cyril Dubala, C.S.C. Total Staff 2; Total in Residence 2.

[M] DIOCESAN CHARITIES

GARY. *Catholic Charities*, 973 W. Sixth Ave., 46402. Tel: 219-882-2720; Fax: 219-886-2428. Rev. Msgr. Joseph F. Semancik, M.S.W., Ph.D., Dir. Coordination and supervision of social welfare program; Francis M. Moynihan, M.A., Admin.

Catholic Family Service, 973 W. Sixth Ave., 46402. Tel: 219-882-2723. Marcella Walters, M.S.W., Exec. Dir.

St. Mark's Center, 509 W. Ridge Rd., 46408. Tel: 219-980-1318. 3901 Fir St., East Chicago, 46312. Tel: 219-397-5803. 6919 Indianapolis Blvd., Hammond, 46324. Tel: 219-844-4883. 2967 Willowcreek Rd., Portage, 46368. Tel: 219-762-1177. 1501 Franklin St., Michigan City, 46360. Tel: 219-879-9312. 166 S. West St., Crown Point, 46307. Tel: 219-662-7677.

Family Life Ministry. Legal Title: *Family Life Ministry, Immigrant Documentation Program, Refugee Assistance Program, Rainbows For All God's Children, Caretaker Program, and Pastor's Emergency Fund.* 973 W. Sixth Ave., 46402. Tel: 219-882-2720.

Services to the Aging, Retired Senior Volunteer Program. LaPorte & Starke Co., 1501 Franklin St., Michigan City, 46360. Tel: 219-874-8195. Lake Co., 973 W. Sixth Ave., 46402. Tel: 219-882-2737.

Senior Companion Program. Lake Co., 973 W. Sixth Ave., 46402. Tel: 219-882-7331.

Society of St. Vincent DePaul.

Particular Council of Gary, 973 W. Sixth Ave., 46402. Tel: 219-882-2720. Rev. Theodore A. Nordquist, Moderator.

[N] NEWMAN APOSTOLATES

GARY. *Indiana University Northwest*, 501 W. Ridge Rd., 46408. Tel: 219-887-0514.
E-mail: nsuman@juno.com
Rev. John T. Ambre. For Catholic students attending Indiana University, Northwest. Students 5,000.

VALPARAISO. *Newman Apostolate-Valparaiso University*, 1511 La Porte Ave., 46383-5818. Tel: 219-464-4042. St. Teresa, Catholic Student Center of Avila. Chapel and Center for Catholic Students attending Valparaiso University. Rev. Kevin P. McCarthy, Chap. Students 738.

[O] MISCELLANEOUS

DYER. *Amicare Home Health Services, Inc.*, 24 Joliet St., 46311. Tel: 219-322-1323. Mr. Gary Baum, Pres.

EAST CHICAGO. *Lakeshore Health System Incorporated (the "Corporation")*. dba St. Catherine Hospital of East Chicago; dba St. Mary Medical Center (Hobart), 4321 Fir St., 46312. Tel: 219-392-7004; Fax: 219-392-7037. Affiliate of Ancilla Systems, Inc. Sponsored by the Poor Handmaids of Jesus Christ.

Office of Hispanic Ministry, 1709 E. 138th St., P.O. Box 3027, 46312. Tel: 219-397-2125; Fax: 219-397-2168. Angel Torres, Dir.; Adeline Torres, Asst.

HAMMOND. *Alverno-Hammond Corporation*. 1515 Dragoon Tr., P.O. Box 1290, Mishawaka, 46546-1290.

Heartland Center, 7128 Arizona Ave., 46323. Tel: 219-844-7515; Fax: 219-844-7566.
E-mail: heartlandc@aol.com
Web site: www.heartlandc@aol.com
Office of Peace and Social Justice of the Diocese of Gary. Revs. Thomas M. Gannon, S.J.; James W. Schulz, S.J. Total Staff 5.

Seimetz Center, 1441 Hoffman, 46327. Tel: 219-933-0226. Rev. Michael W. Cooper, S.J.

Spiritual Life Center, 1441 Hoffman St., 46327. Tel: 219-932-8321; 932-0191.
E-mail: xctb29c@prodigy.com
Rev. Michael W. Cooper, S.J., Dir.; Karen McMahon, Asst. Dir. Total Staff 6.

HOBART. *Ancilla Systems, Inc.*, 1000 S. Lake Park Ave., 46342.

Ancilla Systems Foundation, Inc.

MICHIGAN CITY. *Alverno-Michigan City Corp.* 1515 Dragoon Tr., P.O. Box 1290, Mishawaka, 46546-1290.

VALPARAISO. *Camp Lawrence*. Diocesan Spiritual Center and Youth Camp. 68 E. 700 N., 46383. Tel: 219-462-8243; 462-5261. Catholic Youth Organization, 5284 Broadway, Merrillville, 46410. Tel: 219-887-9581.

RELIGIOUS INSTITUTES OF MEN REPRESENTED IN THE DIOCESE

For further details refer to the corresponding bracketed number in the Religious Institutes of Men or Women section.

[0170]—*Basilian Fathers.* (Toronto).—C.S.B.
[0600]—*Brothers of the Congregation of Holy Cross.*—C.S.C.
[0275]—*Carmelites of Mary Immaculate.* (India).—C.M.I.
[1130]—*Congregation of the Priests of the Sacred Heart.*—S.C.J.
[0480]—*Conventual Franciscans.* (Croatia).—O.F.M.Conv.
[0260]—*Discalced Carmelite Friars.* (Holy Ghost Prov., Poland).—O.C.D.
[0520]—*Franciscan Friars.* (Prov. of Assumption of B.V.M.; Prov. of St. John the Baptist; Prov. of the Sacred Heart).—O.F.M.
[0690]—*Jesuit Fathers and Brothers.*—S.J.
[0610]—*Priests of the Congregation of Holy Cross.*—C.S.C.
[1200]—*Society of the Divine Savior.*—S.D.S.
[1060]—*Society of the Precious Blood.*—C.PP.S.

RELIGIOUS INSTITUTES OF WOMEN REPRESENTED IN THE DIOCESE

[]—*Albertine Sisters.* (Prov. of Krakow, Poland).—C.S.A.
[0230]—*Benedictine Sisters of the Pontifical Jurisdiction.*—O.S.B.
[0360]—*Carmelite Sisters of the Divine Heart of Jesus.*—Carmel D.C.J.
[3710]—*Congregation of the Sisters of Saint Agnes.*—C.S.A.
[1920]—*Congregation of the Sisters of the Holy Cross.*—C.S.C.
[1070-03]—*Dominican Sisters.*—O.P.
[1070-13]—*Dominican Sisters.*—O.P.
[1210]—*Franciscan Sisters of Chicago.*—O.S.F.
[1450]—*Franciscan Sisters of the Sacred Heart.*—O.S.F.
[3130]—*Our Lady of Victory Missionary Sisters.*—O.L.V.M.
[3230]—*Poor Handmaids of Jesus Christ.*—P.H.J.C.
[2970]—*School Sisters of Notre Dame.*—S.S.N.D.
[3340]—*Sisters of Providence.*—S.P.
[3780]—*Sisters of Saints Cyril and Methodius.*—SS.C.M.
[]—*Sisters of St. Anne of Bangalore.*—S.A.B.
[1640]—*Sisters of St. Francis of Perpetual Adoration.*—O.S.F.
[3930]—*Sisters of St. Joseph of the Third Order of St. Francis.* (Immaculate Conception Prov.).—S.S.J.-T.O.S.F.

DIOCESAN CEMETERIES

HAMMOND. *Saint John-Saint Joseph,* 1547 167th St., 46324. Tel: 219-844-9475.

MICHIGAN CITY. *Saint Stanislaus,* 1015 Greenwood, 46360. Tel: 219-874-4310.

NECROLOGY

† Mastey, Walter S., (Retired). —Died April 14, 1997.
† Senderak, Rev. Msgr. Casimir E., (Retired). —Died Dec. 14, 1996.
† Shank, Bernard F., (Retired). —Died Sept. 13, 1997.
† Wozniak, Louis B., (Retired). —Died May 11, 1997.

Diocese of Gaylord

(Dioecesis Gaylordensis)

Most Reverend

PATRICK R. COONEY, S.T.D., S.T.L.

Bishop of Gaylord; ordained December 20, 1959; appointed Titular Bishop of Hodelm and Auxiliary Bishop of Detroit December 3, 1982; consecrated January 27, 1983; appointed Bishop of Gaylord November 21, 1989; installed January 28, 1990. *Res., 1665 W. M-32, Seton Building, Gaylord, MI, 49735.*

ESTABLISHED JULY 20, 1971.

Square Miles 11,171.

Comprises the following 21 Counties in the State of Michigan: Alcona, Alpena, Antrim, Benzie, Charlevoix, Cheboygan, Crawford, Emmet, Grand Traverse, Iosco, Kalkaska, Leelanau, Manistee, Missaukee, Montmorency, Ogemaw, Oscoda, Otsego, Presque Isle, Roscommon and Wexford.

For legal titles of parishes and diocesan institutions, consult the Chancery Office.

Diocesan Pastoral Center: 1665 W. M-32, Gaylord, MI, 49735. Tel.: 517-732-5147; Fax: 517-732-1706.

E-mail address: msteffel@dioceseofgaylord.org

STATISTICAL OVERVIEW

Personnel	
Bishop	1
Priests: Diocesan Active in Diocese	47
Priests: Active Outside Diocese	2
Priests: Retired, Sick or Absent	24
Number of Diocesan Priests	73
Religious Priests in Diocese	16
Extern Priests in Diocese	8
Ordinations:	
Diocesan Priests	3
Transitional Deacons	1
Permanent Deacons in Diocese	12
Total Brothers	2
Total Sisters	66
Parishes	
Parishes	81
With Resident Pastor:	
Resident Diocesan Priests	45
Resident Religious Priests	12
Without Resident Pastor:	
Administered by Priests	19
Administered by Women Religious	5
Closed Parishes	1
Professional Ministry Personnel:	
Brothers	1
Sisters	16
Lay Ministers	40
Welfare	
Catholic Hospitals	3
Total Assisted	222,179
Specialized Homes	2
Total Assisted	417
Special Centers for Social Services	19
Total Assisted	9,008
Educational	
Diocesan Students in Other Seminaries	8
Total Seminarians	8
High Schools, Diocesan and Parish	4
Total Students	657
Elementary Schools, Diocesan and Parish	18
Total Students	2,921
Catechesis/Religious Education:	
High School Students	1,342
Elementary Students	5,227
Total Students Under Catholic Instruction	10,155
Teachers in the Diocese:	
Sisters	8
Lay Teachers	207
Vital Statistics	
Receptions into the Church:	
Infant Baptism Totals	1,021
Adult Baptism Totals	174
Received into Full Communion	267
First Communions	1,357
Confirmations	1,421
Marriages:	
Catholic	377
Interfaith	237
Total Marriages	614
Deaths	964
Total Catholic Population	85,533
Total Population	458,130

Former Bishops—Most Rev. EDMUND C. SZOKA, J.C.L., D.D., First Bishop of Gaylord; ord. June 5, 1954; cons. July 20, 1971; installed July 20, 1971; appt. Archbishop of Detroit March 28, 1981; installed May 17, 1981; named Cardinal Priest May 29, 1988; elevated June 28, 1988 Assigned to the Vatican, 1990—Most Rev. ROBERT J. ROSE, S.T.L., D.D., ord. Dec. 21, 1955; appt. Bishop of Gaylord Oct. 13, 1981; installed Dec. 6, 1981; transferred to Diocese of Grand Rapids July 11, 1989; installed Aug. 30, 1989.

Vicar General—Vacant.

Diocesan Offices and Departments

Diocesan Pastoral Center—1665 W. M-32, Gaylord, 49735. Tel: 517-732-5147; Fax: 517-732-1706. Office Hours: 8-4:30 Mon.-Fri. All business should be directed to this office.

Consultors, Diocesan Board of—Revs. JAMES L. BRUCKSCH; ANDREW G. BUVALA, O.F.M.; FRANCIS J. MURPHY; RAYMOND C. MULKA; THOMAS A. NEIS; DENNIS R. STILWELL.

Members of the Presbyteral Council—

Elected Members—Revs. ALEXANDER BORUTA, O.F.M.; ANDREW G. BUVALA, O.F.M.; CHARLES DONAJKOWSKI; GERALD F. MICKETTI; ISADORE J. MIKULSKI; FRANCIS J. MURPHY; THOMAS A. NEIS; FRANCIS C. PARTRIDGE; DENNIS R. STILWELL; CASIMIR J. ZAWACKI.

Appointed Members:—Revs. JAMES L. BRUCKSCH; WALTER W. DERYLO; RAYMOND C. MULKA.

Vicars (by region)—Alpena: Rev. JOSEPH P. GRAFF; Gaylord: Rev. ROBERT W. NALLEY; Manistee: Rev. MICHAEL P. CONNER; Petosky: Rev. DONALD PAULUS, O.F.M.; Traverse City: Rev. EDWIN A. THOME; West Branch: Rev. JOHN O. LADD.

Administrative Services, Secretariat for—MICHAEL E. STEFFEL, Dir., *1665 W. M-32, Gaylord, 49735.* Tel: 517-732-5147.

Audio-Visual Resource Center—Ms. TERI HALL, *1665 W. M-32, Gaylord, 49735.* Tel: 517-732-5147.

Archivist—Rev. GERALD F. MICKETTI, *1665 W. M-32, Gaylord, 49735.* Tel: 517-732-5147.

Catechesis—(See Education-Formation.).

Communications, Secretariat for—SAM BARBARO, Dir., *1665 W. M-32, Gaylord, 49735.* Tel: 517-732-5147.

Council of Catholic Women, Diocesan—GENEVIEVE SIETING, Pres., *5739 Sieting Rd. S.W., South Boardman, 49680.* Tel: 616-369-4123.

Cursillo—Rev. ANTHONY CITRO, *P.O. Box 248, Roscommon, 48653.* Tel: 517-275-5212.

Ecumenical Apostolate—Vacant.

Education-Formation, Secretariat for—Miss MARLENE PEPLINSKI, Dir.; Rev. JOHN E. MCCRACKEN, Assoc. Dir. (Includes Catechesis, Ministries and Schools). *1665 W. M-32, Gaylord, 49735.* Tel: 517-732-5147.

Finance Council, Diocesan—Most Rev. PATRICK R. COONEY; BARBARA BENSON; SHARON R. STACK; JANICE SMOLINSKI; MARY LOU NADON; BERNARD BAK; RENE HOENSCHEID; WILLIAM CORBETT.

Financial Development and C.S.A., Secretariat for—RALPH SORENSEN, Dir., *1665 W. M-32, Gaylord, 49735.* Tel: 517-732-5147.

Holy Childhood Pontifical Association—Rev. Msgr. GERARD F. GUZIKOWSKI, *371 Fifth St., Manistee, 49660.* Tel: 616-723-2165.

Native American Apostolate—Rev. ANDREW G. BUVALA, O.F.M., Coord., *Blessed Kateri Tekakwitha Parish, P.O. Box 369, Suttons Bay, 49682.* Tel: 616-271-6651.

Knights of Columbus—ROBERT S. SLUSARSKI, Eastern Diocesan Prog. Dir., *1901 Deeter Rd., Luzerne, 48636.* Tel: 517-826-5088. E. JAMES WEBB, Western Diocesan Prog. Dir., *207 Hersey St., Cadillac, 49601-2321.* Tel: 616-775-6244.

Liturgy and Evangelization, Secretariat for—Sr. ARLENE BENNETT R.S.M., Dir., *1665 W. M-32, Gaylord, 49735.* Tel: 517-732-5147.

Migrant Apostolate—Rev. CHAD W. ZIELINSKI; GLADYS MUNOZ, *Immaculate Conception Parish, 720 W. Second, Traverse City, 49684.* Tel: 616-946-1205.

Parish Social Ministries and Youth Ministry—Sr. T. J. SEMMERLING, S.C.S.C., Dir., *1665 W. M-32, Gaylord, 49735.* Tel: 517-732-5147.

Pastoral Support Services for Priests and Pastoral Administrators—Rev. ROBERT W. NALLEY, Dir., *1665 W. M-32, Gaylord, 49735.* Tel: 517-732-5147.

Priests' Retirement Fund—Most Rev. PATRICK R. COONEY, Chm. Board of Directors. Elected Members: Revs. THOMAS M. DOMINIAK; RAYMOND C. MULKA; EDWIN J. FREDERICK; JAMES P. HAYDEN; MARGE WAGNER, Appointed Member.

Priestly Vocations—Rev. JAMES P. HAYDEN, Dir., *Diocese of Gaylord, 1665 W. M-32, Gaylord, 49735.* Tel: 517-732-5147.

Propagation of the Faith—Rev. Msgr. GERARD F. GUZIKOWSKI, Dir., *Guardian Angels Parish, 317 Fifth St., Manistee, 49660.* Tel: 616-723-2165.

St. Vincent De Paul, Society of—Particular Council of Tawas, *115 First St., Tawas City, 49763.* Roscommon County, *Box 644, Prudenville, 48651.* Tel: 517-366-7613., *1028 Hannah, Traverse City, 49684.* Also particular councils in Cheboygan, Hillman, Hale, Prescott, Mikado and Alpena.

Tribunal Diocesan—Rev. ROBERT W. NALLEY, Judicial Vicar. Judges: Revs. DENNIS R. STILWELL; R. DALE MAGOON; WILLIAM L. ZWIEFKA; Revs. JAMES A.

HOLTZ, Defender of the Bond. Procurators-Advocates: JAMES P. HAYDEN; CHARLES G.DONAJKOWSKI; RHONDA KLEE, Auditor; MARY DICKERSON, Notary Inquiries may be made through the local pastors or directed to this office., *1665 W. M-32, Gaylord, 49735.* Tel: 517-732-5147.

CLERGY, PARISHES, MISSIONS AND PAROCHIAL SCHOOLS

CITY OF GAYLORD
(Otsego County)

1—ST. MARY CATHEDRAL, Rev. John E. McCracken, Rector; Sr. Cecilia Faber, O.P., Pastoral Min.
Res., 606 N. Ohio Ave., 49735. Tel: 517-732-5448. [CEM]
Catechesis/Religious Programs—Diana Peffers, D.R.E.
Students 149.
Convent—211 N. Otsego, 49735. Tel: 517-732-4989.

OUTSIDE THE CITY OF GAYLORD

Acme, Grand Traverse Co., Christ the King, Rev. Edwin A. Thome.
Res., P.O. Box 95, 49610. Tel: 616-938-9214; Fax: 616-938-3266.
Church—3801 Shore Rd., 49610.
School—Grand Traverse Area Schools. See separate listing under Institutions Located in the Diocese.
Catechesis/Religious Programs—Patricia Cesere, D.R.E.
Students 390.

Afton, Cheboygan Co., St. Monica, Rev. Thomas M. Dominiak.
Res., P.O. Box 130, Onaway, 49765. Tel: 517-733-4043. [CEM]
Church—M-68, 49705.

Alpena, Alpena Co.,

1—ST. ANNE, Revs. Joseph P. Graff; Gregory Paul McCallum.
Res., 203 S. Ninth Ave., 49707. Tel: 517-356-0622; Fax: 517-354-3918. [JC]
Church—201 S. Ninth Ave., 49707.
Catechesis/Religious Programs—Jeri Standen, D.R.E.
Students 266.

2—ST. BERNARD, Rev. Joseph P. Graff; Sylvia Owens, Pastoral Min.
Res., 322 Chisholm St., 49707. Tel: 517-354-2676; Fax: 517-354-6087. [JC]
Catechesis/Religious Programs—Tel: 517-354-8018. Geraldine LaCross, D.R.E.
Students 94.

3—ST. JOHN THE BAPTIST, Rev. Kenneth R. Stachnik; Patricia Przeslawski, Pastoral Assoc.
Res., 2425 Frederick St., 49707. Tel: 517-354-3019; Fax: 517-358-9079.
Catechesis/Religious Programs—2550 S. First, 49707. Tel: 517-354-3292. Judith H. Burns, D.R.E.
Students 240.

4—ST. MARY, Rev. Walter W. Derylo.
Res., 516 N. Second Ave., 49707. Tel: 517-354-2322; Fax: 517-356-9637. [JC]
Catechesis/Religious Programs—Tel: 517-354-8655. Mrs. Cherie Smigelski, D.R.E.
Students 278.
Convent—120 E. Miller St., 49707.

Alverno, Cheboygan Co., St. Francis of Assisi. Closed. For sacramental records contact St. Mary-St. Charles Parish, Cheboygan.

Atlanta, Montmorency Co., Jesus the Good Shepherd, Rev. Raymond J. Pilarski.
Res., P.O. Box 216, Hillman, 49746. Tel: 517-742-4542.
Church—4521 County Rd. 491, 49746.

Bay Shore, Emmet Co., St. Francis Solanus, Rev. Andre Schludecker, O.F.M.
Res., 415 State St., Petoskey, 49770. Tel: 616-347-4133; Fax: 616-347-4134.
Church—Townline Rd., 49770.

Beaver Island, Charlevoix Co., Holy Cross. Unassigned.
Res., P.O. Box 145, St. James, 49782. [CEM]
Church—St. James, Kings Highway, 49782. Tel: 616-448-2230.

Bellaire, Antrim Co., St. Luke, Sr. Celine Goessl, S.C.S.C., Admin.
Res., 3078 M-88, P.O. Box 799, 49615-0799. Tel: 616-533-8121; Fax: 616-533-8759.

Black River, Alcona Co., St. Gabriel, Rev. Lawrence A. Kelleher.
Res., 2188 W. Nicholson Hill Rd., Ossineke, 49766-9736. Tel: 517-471-2556. [CEM]
Church—5570 N. Lake Shore Dr., 48721.

Boyne City, Charlevoix Co., St. Matthew, Rev. Francis C. Partridge.
Res., 1303 Boyne Ave., 49712. Tel: 616-582-7718; Fax: 616-582-7490. [JC]
Catechesis/Religious Programs—Tel: 616-582-6589. Suzanne Dzwik, D.R.E.
Students 134.

Boyne Falls, Charlevoix Co., St. Augustine, Rev. Francis C. Partridge.
Res., 1303 Boyne Ave., Boyne City, 49712. Tel: 616-582-7718; Fax: 616-582-7490. [CEM]
Church—Grove St., 49713. Tel: 616-549-2350.
Catechesis/Religious Programs—Frank Wasylewski, D.R.E.
Students 49.

Burt Lake, Cheboygan Co., Assumption of St. Mary, Rev. Sylvester Micek, O.F.M.
Res., P.O. Box 122, Pellston, 49769. Tel: 616-539-8805.

Cadillac, Wexford Co., St. Ann, Rev. Francis J. Murphy; Sr. Hilda Sucher, R.S.M., Pastoral Min.
Res., 800 W. 13th St., 49601-9281. Tel: 616-775-2471; Fax: 616-775-2452. [CEM]

Cedar, Leelanau Co., Holy Rosary. Unassigned.
Res., 3919 E. Gatzke Rd., 49621. Tel: 616-228-5429; Fax: 616-228-5429. [CEM]

Charlevoix, Charlevoix Co., St. Mary, Rev. Thomas A. Neis.
Res., 102 W. Garfield, 49720. Tel: 616-547-6652.
Catechesis/Religious Programs—Students 150.

Cheboygan, Cheboygan Co., St. Mary-St. Charles, Revs. Dennis R. Stilwell; Donald R. Geyman. Pastoral Assocs.: Mrs. Patricia Watson; Mr. Joseph T. Fortin; Deacon Stan Szczepanski.
Mailing Address: P.O. Box 40, 49721. Tel: 616-627-2105; Fax: 616-627-5362. [JC]
Catechesis/Religious Programs—Mrs. Deby Frato, D.R.E.
Students 187.

Copemish, Manistee Co., St. Raphael, Rev. Richard A. Kosterman.
Res., P.O. Box 204, 49625. Tel: 616-378-2984. [CEM]
Church—M-115, 49765.

Cross Village, Emmet Co., Holy Cross, Rev. Albert Langheim, O.F.M.
Res., 6624 N. Lake Shore, 49740-9745. Tel: 616-526-2030. [CEM]

East Jordan, Charlevoix Co., St. Joseph, Rev. William McKeon.
Res., P.O. Box 379, 49727. Tel: 616-536-2934. [CEM]

East Tawas, Iosco Co., St. Joseph. Merged with Immaculate Heart of Mary, Tawas City to form Holy Family, Tawas City.

Elk Rapids, Antrim Co., Sacred Heart, Rev. Robert J. Zuchowski.
Res., 143 Charles St., 49629. Tel: 616-264-8087. [CEM]
Catechesis/Religious Programs—Sandea S. Boals, D.R.E.
Students 157.

Elmira, Antrim Co., St. Thomas Aquinas, Rev. Richard T. Hannon, Admin.
Res., P.O. Box 128, 49730. Tel: 616-546-3326. [CEM]
Church—M-32, 49730.

Empire, Leelanau Co., St. Philip Neri, Rev. John B. Tupper.
Res., P.O. Box 257, 49630. Tel: 616-326-5255. [CEM]
Church—11411 La Core Ave., 49630.
Catechesis/Religious Programs—Mary Boissoneau, D.R.E.
Students 43.

Fife Lake, Grand Traverse Co., St. Aloysius, Rev. James A. Holtz.
Res., 438 County Rd. 612, Kalkaska, 49646. Tel: 616-258-5021; Fax: 616-258-2842. [CEM]
Church—Merritt St., 49633. Tel: 616-258-2752.

Frankfort, Benzie Co., St. Ann, Rev. Msgr. David W. Gemuend.
Res., P.O. Box 1168, 508 Crystal Ave., 49635. Tel: 616-352-4421; Fax: 616-352-9940.
Catechesis/Religious Programs—Tel: 616-352-4541.
Students 52.

Gills Pier, Leelanau Co., St. Wenceslaus, Rev. Gerard A. Hunko.
Mailing Address: P.O. Box 340, Lake Leelanau, 49653. Tel: 616-256-9676; Fax: 616-256-7812.
Res., 8500 E. Kolarik, Suttons Bay, 49682. Tel: 616-271-3574. [CEM]
Church—County Rds. 637 & 626, 49682.

Glennie, Alcona Co., St. Francis of Assisi. Closed. For inquiries for parish records contact the Chancery.

Good Hart, Emmet Co., St. Ignatius, Rev. Albert Langheim, O.F.M.
Res., 6624 N. Lake Shore Dr., Cross Village, 49740. Tel: 616-526-2030. [CEM]

Grayling, Crawford Co., St. Mary, Rev. Robert W. Nalley.
Res., 708 Peninsular St., 49738. Tel: 517-348-7291; 348-7657 (Office).
Catechesis/Religious Programs—Tel: 517-348-8669.
Students 117.

Hale, Iosco Co., St. Pius X, Rev. J. August Franczek.
Res., P.O. Box 428, 48739. Tel: 517-728-3106.
Church—3900 M-65, 48739.
Catechesis/Religious Programs—Tel: 517-728-2278. Karol Shellenbarger, D.R.E.
Students 42.

Hannah, Grand Traverse Co., St. Mary, Rev. Albin J. Gietzen.
Res., 2962 M-113 West Rd., Kingsley, 49649. Tel: 616-263-5640. [CEM]
Catechesis/Religious Programs—Sr. Geneva Marie Schaub, O.P., D.R.E.
Students 67.
Convent—2912 M-113 West Rd., Kingsley, 49649. Tel: 616-263-5287.

Harbor Springs, Emmet Co., Holy Childhood of Jesus, Rev. Frank Kordek, O.F.M.; Bro. Patrick Kendrick, O.F.M.
Res., 150 W. Main St., 49740. Tel: 616-526-2017. [CEM]
Catechesis/Religious Programs—Tel: 616-526-7181. Ginny Day, D.R.E.
Students 152.

Harietta, Wexford Co., St. Edward, Rev. Francis J. Murphy.
Res., 800 W. 13th St., Cadillac, 49601-9281. Tel: 616-775-2471; Fax: 616-775-2452.
Church—207 W. Gaston, 49638.

Harrisville, Alcona Co., St. Anne, Rev. Lawrence E. Boks.
Res., P.O. Box 345, 48740. Tel: 517-724-6713. [CEM]
Church—110 State St., 48740.

Herron, Alpena Co., St. Rose of Lima, Sr. Carmelita Switzer, O.P., Pastoral Admin.
Church—3439 Herron Rd., 49744. Tel: 517-379-4316.

Higgins Lake, Roscommon Co., St. Hubert, Sr. Ann Christopher Herald, O.P., Pastoral Admin.
Res., P.O. Box 75, 48627. Tel: 517-821-5591; Fax: 517-821-5895.
Church—7612 W. Higgins Lake Dr., 48627.

Hillman, Montmorency Co., St. Augustine, Rev. Raymond J. Pilarski.
Res., P.O. Box 216, 49746. Tel: 517-742-4542. [CEM]
Church—24140 Veterans Memorial Hwy., 49746.
Catechesis/Religious Programs—Jean Davis, D.R.E.
Students 116.

Houghton Lake, Roscommon Co., St. James, Sr. Ann Christopher Herald, O.P., Pastoral Admin.
Res., P.O. Box 75, Higgins Lake, 48627. Tel: 517-821-5591; Fax: 517-821-5895.
Church—7878 E. Houghton Lake Dr., 48629. Tel: 517-422-3925.

Indian River, Cheboygan Co., Cross in the Woods Catholic Shrine, Revs. Donard Paulus, O.F.M.; Flavius Czuba, O.F.M.; Elstan Coghill, O.F.M.; Deacon John B. Wallace.
Res., 7078 M-68, 49749. Tel: 616-238-8973; Fax: 616-238-7012. [CEM]
Catechesis/Religious Programs—49749. Tel: 616-238-8542. Mrs. Kenya Swiss, D.R.E.
Students 80.

Kalkaska, Kalkaska Co., St. Mary of the Woods, Rev. James A. Holtz.
Res., 438 County Rd. 612, 49646. Tel: 616-258-5021; Fax: 616-258-2842. [CEM]
Catechesis/Religious Programs—Donalda Barrett, D.R.E.
Students 109.

Klacking Creek, Ogemaw Co., Holy Family, Rev. Miro Wiese, O.F.M.
Res., 402 W. Peters Rd., West Branch, 48661. Tel: 517-345-3422. [CEM]
Catechesis/Religious Programs—Rose Quackenbush, D.R.E.
Students 70.

Lake City, Missaukee Co., St. Stephen, Rev. Roy Zebrowski, O.F.M.
Res., P.O. Box 379, 49651. Tel: 616-839-2121.
Church—506 Union St., 49651.
Catechesis/Religious Programs—Joan Boomgaard, D.R.E.
Students 66.

Lake Leelanau, Leelanau Co., St. Mary, Rev. Gerard A. Hunko.
Mailing Address: P.O. Box 340, 49653. Tel: 616-256-9676; Fax: 616-256-7812.
Res., 8500 E. Kolarik, Suttons Bay, 49682. Tel: 616-271-3574. [CEM]
Church—403 S. St. Mary St., 49653.

Larks Lake, Emmet Co., St. Nicholas, Rev. Albert Langheim, O.F.M.
Res., 6624 N. Lake Shore Dr., Cross Village, 49740. Tel: 616-526-2030. [CEM]

Lewiston, Montmorency Co., St. Francis of Assisi, Rev. Gregory Kurutz, O.F.M.
Res., P.O. Box 182, 49756. Tel: 517-786-2235. [CEM]
Church—4086 Salling Ave., 49756. Tel: 517-786-3081.
Catechesis/Religious Programs—Eva Claeys, D.R.E. Students 62.

Mackinaw City, Emmet Co., St. Anthony of Padua, Rev. Leonard Jocys. In res., Rev. John J. Adomaitis.
Res., P.O. Box 460, 49701. Tel: 616-436-5561; 436-5601. [CEM]
Church—600 W. Central Ave., 49701.
Catechesis/Religious Programs—Eileen Raymond, D.R.E.
Students 51.

Mancelona, Antrim Co., St. Anthony, Rev. R. Dale Magoon.
Mailing Address: P.O. Box 677, 49659-0677.
Church—209 Jefferson St., 49659. Tel: 616-587-8401. [CEM]

Manistee, Manistee Co., Guardian Angels, Rev. Msgr. Gerard Guzikowski.
Res., 371 Fifth St., 49660. Tel: 616-723-2165. [JC]
Convent—501 Michael St., 49660. Tel: 616-723-6332.
St. Joseph, Revs. William L. Zwiefka; James M. Bearss.
Res., 254 Sixth St., 49660. Tel: 616-723-2619. [JC]
Catechesis/Religious Programs—Tel: 616-723-3732. Shirley Skiera, D.R.E.
Students 131.
St. Mary of Mt. Carmel Shrine, Rev. Gabriel Fox.
Res., 260 St. Mary Pkwy., 49660. Tel: 616-723-3345; Fax: 616-723-2157. [JC]
Catechesis/Religious Programs—Sr. Ann Porter, O.P., D.R.E.
Students 60.

Manton, Wexford Co., St. Theresa, Rev. Roy Zebrowski, O.F.M.
Res., P.O. Box 379, Lake City, 49651. Tel: 616-839-2121.
Church—9475 14th & 1/4 Rd., 49663.

Maple City, Leelanau Co., St. Rita-St. Joseph. Unassigned.
Res., 3919 Gatzke Rd., Cedar, 49621. Tel: 616-228-5429. [CEM]
Church—8707 Hill St., 49664. Tel: 616-228-5823.
Catechesis/Religious Programs—Rita Wilson, D.R.E.
Students 125.

Mapleton, Grand Traverse Co., St. Joseph, Rev. Patrick J. Barrett.
Mailing Address: 13400 Center Rd., Traverse City, 49686. Tel: 616-223-4303. [CEM]
Catechesis/Religious Programs—Peggy Stinnet, D.R.E.
Students 75.

McBain, Missaukee Co., St. Rita. Closed. For inquiries for parish records contact the Chancery.

Metz, Presque Isle Co., St. Dominic, Sr. Rita Epple, R.S.M., Pastoral Admin.
Res., 9269 County Rd. 441, Posen, 49776. Tel: 517-766-2694; Fax: 517-766-2694. [CEM]
Catechesis/Religious Programs—Carolyn Haske, D.R.E.
Students 48.

Mikado, Alocona Co., St. Raphael, Rev. Lawrence E. Boks.
Res., P.O. Box 345, Harrisville, 48740. Tel: 517-724-6713. [CEM]
Church—2531 E. Mikado Rd., 48745. Tel: 517-736-6071.

Mio, Oscoda Co., St. Mary, Rev. Regis Burzynski, O.F.M.
Res., P.O. Box 189, 48647. Tel: 517-826-5509.
Ministry Office—Tel: 517-826-6057.

North Port, Leelanau Co., St. Gertrude, Rev. Wayne H. Dziekan.
Res., P.O. Box 9, Suttons Bay, 49682. Tel: 616-271-3744.
Church—701 Warren, Northport, 49670.

Onaway, Presque Isle Co., St. Paul, Rev. Thomas M. Dominiak.
Res., 3856 Oak St., P.O. Box 130, 49765. Tel: 517-733-4043. [CEM]

Onekama, Manistee Co., St. Joseph, Rev. Michael P. Conner.
Res., P.O. Box 150, 49675. Tel: 616-889-4254. [CEM]
Church—8380 Fifth St., 49675.

Oscoda, Iosco Co., Sacred Heart, Rev. James L. Brucksch.
Res., 5300 N. U.S.-23, 48750. Tel: 517-739-9511; Fax: 517-739-3010. [CEM]
Catechesis/Religious Programs—Tel: 517-739-5523. Mrs. Jackie Welles, D.R.E.
Students 36.

Ossineke, Alpena Co., St. Catherine, Rev. Lawrence A. Kelleher.
Res., 2188 W. Nicholson Hill Rd., 49766-9736. Tel: 517-471-2556. [CEM]
Catechesis/Religious Programs—Tel: 517-471-5121. D.R.E.: Mary Kay Lee; Cynthia Prevo.
Students 202.

Pellston, Emmet Co., St. Clement, Rev. Sylvester Micek, O.F.M.
Res., P.O. Box 122, 49769. Tel: 616-539-8805. [CEM]
Church—202 Maple, 49769.

Peshabestown, Leelanau Co., Blessed Kateri Tekakwitha, Rev. Andrew Buvala, O.F.M.
Res., P.O. Box 369, Suttons Bay, 49682. Tel: 616-271-6651.

Petoskey, Emmet Co., St. Francis Xavier, Revs. Andre Schludecker, O.F.M.; Wilbert Hegener, O.F.M.; Robert Dentzman, O.F.M.; Bro. Daniel Badsing, O.F.M.
Res., 513 Howard St., 49770. Tel: 616-347-4133; Fax: 616-347-4134. [CEM]
School—414 Michigan St., 49770. Tel: 616-347-3651. Pamela Dickerson, Prin.
Students 260.
Catechesis/Religious Programs—Tel: 616-347-2681. Julie Wyrembelski, D.R.E.
Students 260.

Posen, Presque Isle Co., St. Casimir, Rev. Stanislaw J. Bereda.
Res., P.O. Box 217, 49776. Tel: 517-766-2660. [CEM]
Church—10075 M-65 North, 49776-0217.
Catechesis/Religious Programs—Joan Chappa, D.R.E.
Students 135.

Praga, Antrim Co., St. John Nepomucene, Rev. William McKeon.
Res., P.O. Box 379, East Jordan, 49727. Tel: 616-536-2934. [CEM]

Prudenville, Roscommon Co., Our Lady of the Lake, Rev. John O. Ladd.
Res., 1037 W. Houghton Lake Dr., P.O. Box 800, 48651. Tel: 517-366-5533.
Catechesis/Religious Programs—D.R.E.: Vernon Anderson; Fern Anderson.
Students 109.
Convent—1039 W. Houghton Lake Dr., 48651. Tel: 517-366-5592.

Riggsville, Cheboygan Co., Sacred Heart, Rev. Leonard Jocys.
Mailing Address: P.O. Box 460, Mackinaw City, 49701-0460.
Res., St. Anthony of Padua, P.O. Box 460, Mackinaw City, 49701. Tel: 616-436-5561.
Church—Polish Line Rd., Cheboygan, 49721.

Rogers City, Presque Isle Co., St. Ignatius, Rev. Charles G. Donajkowski.
Res., 175 W. Ira Ave., 49779. Tel: 517-734-3388. [CEM]
Catechesis/Religious Programs—Tel: 517-734-7768. Robert Chapdelaine, D.R.E.
Students 74.
Convent—585 S. Third St., 49779. Tel: 517-734-3605.

Roscommon, Roscommon Co., St. Michael, Rev. Anthony M. Citro.
Res., 104 N. 6th St., P.O. Box 248, 48653. Tel: 517-275-5212.
Catechesis/Religious Programs—Tel: 517-275-5212. Kathleen Butler, D.R.E.
Students 160.

St. Helen, Roscommon Co., St. Helen, Rev. Albert Couturier.
Res., 737 N. M-76, 48646. Tel: 517-389-3495; 389-4959 (Office); 389-3441 (Church); Fax: 517-389-3495.

Skidway Lake, Ogemaw Co., St. Stephen of Hungary, Rev. Alexander Boruta, O.F.M.
Res., 2811 E. Greenwood Rd., Prescott, 48756. Tel: 517-873-3340; Fax: 517-873-5209.

Suttons Bay, Leelanau Co., St. Michael the Archangel, Rev. Wayne H. Dziekan.
Res., P.O. Box 9, 49682. Tel: 616-271-3744. [CEM]
Church—315 Broadway, 49682.
Catechesis/Religious Programs—Tel: 616-271-3733. Nita Send, D.R.E.
Students 250.

Tawas City, Iosco Co., Holy Family. Consolidation of St. Joseph, East Tawas and Immaculate Heart of Mary, Tawas City. Rev. Ronald V. Gronowski.
Mailing Address: P.O. Box 472, East Tawas, 48730.
Church—501 Lake St., 48763. Tel: 517-362-3162; Fax: 517-362-9077.
Immaculate Heart of Mary. Merged with St. Joseph, East Tawas to form Holy Family, Tawas City.

Traverse City, Grand Traverse Co., Immaculate Conception, Revs. James P. Hayden; Chad W. Zielinski.
Res., 720 W. Second, 49684. Tel: 616-946-4211; Fax: 616-946-0567.
Catechesis/Religious Programs—Tel: 616-946-2782. Dannie Brzezinski, D.R.E.
Students 240.
St. Francis of Assisi, Rev. James K. Gardiner; Sr. Katherine Murphy, R.S.M., Pastoral Assoc. In res., Rev. William W. Lipscomb.
Res., 1025 S. Union St., 49684. Tel: 616-947-4620; Fax: 616-947-4693.
St. Patrick, Rev. Gerald F. Micketti.
Res., 630 W. Silver Lake Rd. S., 49684-8526. Tel: 616-943-4633; Fax: 616-943-8886.
Catechesis/Religious Programs—Students 275.

Vanderbilt, Otsego Co., Holy Redeemer, Rev. Richard T. Hannon; Mrs. Carolyn Zecchin, Admin. & D.R.E.
Res., 606 N. Ohio St., Gaylord, 49735. Tel: 517-732-5448.

West Branch, Ogemaw Co., St. Joseph, Rev. Robert H. Bissot.
Res., 907 Houghton Ave., 48661. Tel: 517-345-0064. [CEM]
School—Tel: 517-345-0220.
Catechesis/Religious Programs—Tel: 517-345-0670.
Students 115.
Convent—961 W. Houghton, 48661. Tel: 517-345-0221.

Whittemore, Iosco Co., St. James, Rev. Patrick Bascio, C.S.Sp.
Res., P.O. Box 206, 48770. Tel: 517-756-2591; Fax: 517-756-3255. [CEM]
Church—202 E. Sherman, 48770.

Special Assignment:
Reverend Fathers—
Hayden, James P., Dir. Priestly Vocations, 1665 W. M-32, Gaylord, MI 49735
Holtz, James A., Defender of the Bond, 1665 W. M-32, Gaylord, MI 49735
McCracken, John E., Assoc. Dir. of Education & Formation, 1665 W. M-32, Gaylord, MI 49735
Nalley, Robert W., Judicial Vicar & Dir. Pastoral Support Svcs. for Priests & Pastoral Admin., 1665 W. M-32, Gaylord, MI 49735
Suchocki, James A.
Zwiefka, William L., Tribunal Judge, 1665 W. M-32, Gaylord, MI 49735

Absent on Leave:
Reverend Fathers—
Cotter, Raymond C.
Greene, John C.
McLaughlin, James C., II
Pelky, Theron E.

Retired:
Reverend Fathers—
Adomaitis, John J., St. Anthony Parish, P.O. Box 460, Mackinaw City, MI 49701-0460
Dieninis, Lionginas, 3016 Risdale, Lansing, MI 48911
Frederick, Edwin J., P.O. Box 733, Traverse City, MI 49685-0733
Gaj, Zygmut, 2733 Bullock Rd., Bay City, MI 48708
Harnish, Lionel, 4039 26th St., Dorr, MI 49323
Kluonius, Joseph V., 2013 Hess, Holiday, FL 34691
Machcinski, Anthony J., 7826 Homer Ave., Hudson, FL 34667
Marciulonis, Benedict J., 1407 Chilean Ln., Winter Park, FL 32792
Marek, Walter, P.O. Box 203, Whitehall, MI 49461
Mausolf, James H., 703 W. Seventh St., Traverse City, MI 49684
Mikulski, Isadore J., 7718 Westwood Dr., Oscoda, MI 48750
Mulka, Arthur C., 2388 Emmett, Alpena, MI 49707
Mulka, Raymond C., 300 Washington, Alpena, MI 49707
Reitz, Joseph A., 52 Marble Rd., Lowell, MI 49331
Rushman, John, P.O. Box 646, East Tawas, MI 48730
Sarosiek, John H., 4468 Lincoln, Dearborn Heights, MI 48125
Seifferly, Richard R., P.O. Box 422, West Branch, MI 48661-0422

Sitar, Richard T., 1484 Spring Lake Rd., Fruitland, FL 34731
Smolinski, Clarence D., 14692 Lakeside Dr., Presque Isle, MI 49777
Tamulis, John J., 1189 S. 35 Mile Rd., Cadillac, MI 49601
Wiekierak, Joseph F., 1470 West Norton, Apt. H-5, Muskegon, MI 49441-4362
Zawacki, Casimir J., 305 Fifth Ave., #8, Manistee, MI 49660

Permanent Deacons:
Barbaro, Sam, St. Mary Cathedral, Gaylord
Bousmara, Thomas, Immaculate Conception, Traverse City
Friend, Harry, St. Philip, Empire
Goetz, Robert, Unassigned
LePain, Andrew, Unassigned
LoVetere, Arthur, Jesus the Good Shepherd, Atlanta
Nelson, Joseph B., Holy Cross, Cross Village
Szczepanski, Stanley T., St. Mary-St. Charles, Cheboygan
Trapp, Richard, Unassigned
Vondra, Edward, Unassigned
Wallace, John, Catholic Shrine, Indian River
Wendell, Max, Unassigned

INSTITUTIONS LOCATED IN THE DIOCESE

[A] INTERPAROCHIAL SCHOOLS

CHEBOYGAN. *Bishop Baraga Elementary.* (Grades K-6), 421 State St., 49721. James Leinbach, Prin. Lay Teachers 7; Students 173.
Bishop Baraga Preschool, 120 C St., 49721. Lay Teachers 3; Students 58.

MANISTEE. *Manistee Catholic Central Schools.* (Grades PreK-12), 1200 U.S. 31 South (at 12th St.), 49660. Tel: 616-723-2529. Michael Buell, Admin. Sisters 1; Lay Teachers 20; Students 242; Preschool 19.

TRAVERSE CITY. *Grand Traverse Area Catholic Schools*, 123 E. 11th St., 49684. Tel: 616-946-8100. Mary Oosterhouse, Admin. Sisters 2; Lay Teachers 56; Students 1040.
Immaculate Conception Middle School. (Grades 5-8), 218 Vine, 49684. Tel: 616-947-1252. Kenneth J. Knudsen, Prin. Lay Teachers 19; Students 317.
St. Francis Elementary. (Grades K-4), 130 E. 10th, 49684. Tel: 616-946-5961. Mr. William J. Gorney, Prin. Sisters 1; Lay Teachers 20; Students 427.
St. Francis High School, 123 E. 11th St., 49684. Tel: 616-946-8038; Fax: 616-946-1878. Mark Esper, Prin. Sisters 1; Lay Teachers 17; Students 296.

[B] PAROCHIAL SCHOOLS

GAYLORD. *St. Mary Cathedral Elementary School.* (Grades K-6), 321 N. Otsego Ave., 49735. Sr. Jean Karen Woloszyk, O.P., Prin. Lay Teachers 13; Students 286.
St. Mary Cathedral High School. (Grades 7-12), 310 W. Mitchell, 49735. Mr. James Kerfoot, Prin. Sisters 1; Lay Teachers 11; Students 203.

ALPENA. *Alpena Catholic Middle School.* (Grades 6-8), 319 Lockwood St., 49707. Tel: 517-354-6861. Mr. William Morford, Jr., Prin. Lay Teachers 3; Students 58.
St. Anne Elementary. (Grades K-5), 205 S. 9th, 49707. Mr. William Morford, Jr., Prin. Lay Teachers 6; Students 142.
St. Mary Elementary. (Grades PreK-6), 500 N. Second, 49707. Sr. Mary Edwardine Stoppa, C.S.S.F., Prin. Sisters 1; Lay Teachers 7; Students 104.

CADILLAC. *St. Ann Elementary.* (Grades K-5), 800 W. 13th, 49601. Mary Ann Palacios, Prin. Lay Teachers 6; Students 158.

CEDAR. *Holy Rosary Elementary.* (Grades K-6), 6982 Schomberg, 49621. Heidi Sleder, Prin. Lay Teachers 4; Students 51.

CHARLEVOIX. *St. Mary Elementary.* (Grades PreK-5), 1005 Bridge St., 49720. Sr. Margaret Schneider, O.P., Prin. Sisters 2; Lay Teachers 8; Students 98.

EAST TAWAS. *Holy Family Elementary School.* (Grades K-6), 411 N. Wilkinson, 48730. Sr. Monica Meyer, O.P., Prin. Lay Teachers 5; Students 95.

HANNAH. *St. Mary's Hannah School.* (Grades K-6), 2912 M-113, 49649. Deanna Couture, Prin. Lay Teachers 6; Students 73.

LAKE LEELANAU. *St. Mary's Schools.* (Grades PreK-12), 303 S. St. Mary St., 49653. Mailing Address: P.O. Box 340, 49653. Therese Lichty, Prin. Lay Teachers 12; Students 208.

PETOSKEY. *St. Francis Xavier Elementary.* (Grades K-8), 414 Michigan, 49770. Pamela Dickerson, Prin. Sisters 1; Lay Teachers 15; Students 219.

PRUDENVILLE. *Our Lady of the Lake Elementary.* (Grades K-8), 1039 W. Houghton Lake, 48651. Sr. Mary Lourdes Campbell, R.S.M., Prin. Lay Teachers 6; Students 84.

ROGERS CITY. *St. Ignatius Elementary.* (Grades 1-8), 545 S. Third, 49779. David Giles, Prin. Lay Teachers 10; Students 136.

WEST BRANCH. *St. Joseph Elementary.* (Grades K-8), 935 W. Houghton Ave., 48661. Lorrene Spaulding, Prin. Lay Teachers 9; Students 208.

[C] GENERAL HOSPITALS

CADILLAC. *Mercy Hospital*, 400 Hobart St., 49601. Tel: 616-779-7200.
For a complete listing, refer to the Hospitals section.

GRAYLING. *Mercy Hospital*, 1100 Michigan Ave., 49738. Tel: 517-348-5461; Fax: 517-348-4839.
For a complete listing, refer to the Hospitals section.

*TAWAS CITY. *Saint Joseph Huron Home Health and Hospice*, 716 German St., Ste. B, P.O. Box 208, 48764. Tel: 517-362-4611.
For a complete listing, refer to the Hospitals section.
Tawas St. Joseph Hospital, 200 Hemlock, M-55, 48764-0659. Tel: 517-362-3411; Fax: 517-362-7277.
For a complete listing, refer to the Hospitals section.

[D] CONVENTS AND RESIDENCES FOR SISTERS

CONWAY. *Sacramentine Monastery of Perpetual Adoration*, 49722. Tel: 616-347-0447. Sr. Mary Rosalie, O.S.S., Prioress. Sacamentine Sisters 4.

TRAVERSE CITY. *Infant Jesus of Prague Monastery*, 3501 Silver Lake Rd., 49684-8949. Tel: 616-946-4960. Rev. Valerian J. Rykowski, Chap. Tel: 616-947-6935. Carmelite Nuns. Solemn Vows 6.

[E] CHILD CARE FACILITIES

ALPENA. *Huron House / Boysville of Michigan, Inc.*, 4761 U.S. 23 N., 49707. Tel: 517-356-3573; Fax: 517-356-4910. Residential and community-based treatment programs for troubled youth and families, with facilities located throughout the state of Michigan and one in the state of Ohio under the auspices of the Brothers of the Holy Cross at Notre Dame. Parent company, Boysville of Michigan, Inc. Bro. Francis Boylan, C.S.C., Exec. Dir.; Joseph Martinus, Pastoral Min.; Rick Boone, Regional Dir. Boys 14.
Boysville's Family & Community Support Program. Includes specialized foster care, supervised independent living, in-home family treatment, Families First and Nokomis Challenge.

TRAVERSE CITY. *Non-Secure Detention / Boysville of Michigan, Inc.*, 207 W. Grandview Pkwy., Ste. 200, 49684. Tel: 616-922-9664; 800-235-9664. Bro. Francis Boylan, C.S.C., Exec. Dir.; Rick Boone, Regional Dir. Youth 403.

[F] RETREAT HOUSES

CONWAY. *Augustine Center*, P.O. Box 84, 49722-0084. Tel: 616-347-3657. Sr. Barbara Hubeny, O.P., Dir.

ST. JAMES. *Brother Damian Lodge* (Beaver Island), 49782. Tel: 616-448-2204. Open June, July and August. Bro. Kevin Mackey, F.S.C., Dir.

[G] CATHOLIC SOCIAL SERVICE AGENCIES

GAYLORD. *Catholic Human Services*, 111 S. Michigan Ave., Ste. A, 49735. Tel: 517-731-2877. Mr. Clement C. Veeser, Pres. & CEO; Mrs. Anita Lawnichak, Dir. Accounting & Financial Svcs.
Area Offices: 154 S. Ripley Blvd., Alpena, 49707. Tel: 517-356-6385. Dr. Russ Wood, Admin., 140 W. River St., #7, Cadillac, 49601. Tel: 616-775-6581. Mr. David Martin, Admin., 111 S. Michigan, 49735. Tel: 517-732-6761. Dr. Russ Wood, Admin., 1000 Hastings St., Traverse City, 49686. Tel: 616-947-8110. Mr. David Martin, Admin.

[H] MISCELLANEOUS

GAYLORD. *Camp Sancta Maria.* (Sponsored by the Archdiocese of Detroit), P.O. Box 338, 49735. Mike Hickey, Mgr., 3002 N. Connecticut, Royal Oak, 48073. Tel: 810-589-2306.

ALPENA. *Madonna House Apostolate*, 309 Lockwood, 49707. Tel: 517-354-4073. Rosemary Horan, Dir.

FARMINGTON HILLS. *Mercy Housing Michigan*, 29000 Eleven Mile Rd., 48336. Tel: 810-476-8000. Sr. Theresa Blaquiere, R.S.M., Contact Person.

HARBOR SPRINGS. *Christ Child Society of Northern Michigan, Inc.*, P.O. Box 132, 49740-0132. Tel: 616-526-7271. Allison Hooton, Pres.

JOHANNESBURG. *Stella Maris Hermitage*, 19920 Black River Rd., 49751-9645. Tel: 517-732-9580. Rev. Richard Kropf.

PRESCOTT. *House of the Holy Shroud*, 1629 Beach Rd., 48756. Tel: 517-873-4000. Bro. Michael W. Whitman, Dir.

RELIGIOUS INSTITUTES OF MEN REPRESENTED IN THE DIOCESE

For further details refer to the corresponding bracketed number in the Religious Institutes of Men or Women section.

[0520]—*Franciscan Friars.* (Assumption, Sacred Heart Provs.).—O.F.M.
[0650]—*Holy Ghost Fathers.*—C.S.Sp.

RELIGIOUS INSTITUTES OF WOMEN REPRESENTED IN THE DIOCESE

[0420]—*Discalced Carmelite Nuns.*—O.C.D.
[1070]—*Dominican Sisters.*—O.P.
[1170]—*Felician Sisters.*—C.S.S.F.
[1230]—*Franciscan Sisters of Christian Charity.* (Manitowac, WI).—O.S.F.
[2580]—*Institute of the Sisters of Mercy of the Americas.*—R.S.M.
[3490]—*Sacramentine Nuns.*—O.S.S.
[3560]—*Servants of Jesus.*—S.J.
[3580]—*Servants of Mary (Servite Sisters).*—O.S.M.
[2630]—*Sisters of Mercy of the Holy Cross.* (Merill, WI).—S.C.S.C.
[3830]—*Sisters of St. Joseph.*—S.S.J.

NECROLOGY

† Thomas, Frederick Joseph, (Retired). —Died Feb. 23, 1997.

Diocese of Grand Island

(Dioecesis Insulae Grandis)

Most Reverend

LAWRENCE J. MCNAMARA, D.D., S.T.L.

Bishop of Grand Island; ordained May 30, 1953; appointed January 10, 1978; consecrated and installed March 28, 1978. *Mailing Address: Box 1531, Grand Island, NE, 68802.*

Most Reverend

JOHN L. PASCHANG, D.D., PH.D., J.C.D.

Retired Bishop of Grand Island; ordained June 12, 1921; appointed July 28, 1951; consecrated October 9, 1951. *Res., 320 E. Decatur St., West Point, NE, 68788.*

Chancery Office: 311 W. 17th St., P.O. Box 996, Grand Island, NE, 68802. Tel.: 308-382-6565; Fax: 308-382-6569.

ERECTED AT KEARNEY, MARCH 8, 1912; SEE TRANSFERRED TO GRAND ISLAND, APRIL 11, 1917.

Square Miles 40,000.

Comprises the Counties of Arthur, Banner, Blaine, Box Butte, Brown, Buffalo, Cherry, Cheyenne, Custer, Dawes, Deuel, Garden, Garfield, Grant, Greeley, Hooker, Howard Keyapaha, Kimball, Logan, Loup, McPherson, Morrill, Rock, Scotts Bluff, Sheridan, Sherman, Wheeler, Sioux, Thomas, Valley, and those portions of Dawson, Hall, Lincoln and Keith lying north of the South Platte River in the State of Nebraska.

For legal titles of parishes and diocesan institutions, consult the Chancery Office.

STATISTICAL OVERVIEW

Personnel	
Bishop	1
Retired Bishops	1
Priests: Diocesan Active in Diocese	48
Priests: Active Outside Diocese	3
Priests: Retired, Sick or Absent	29
Number of Diocesan Priests	80
Religious Priests in Diocese	1
Total Sisters	98
Parishes	
Parishes	43
With Resident Pastor:	
Resident Diocesan Priests	43
Without Resident Pastor:	
Missions	40
Welfare	
Health Care Centers	2
Total Assisted	136,368
Homes for the Aged	1
Total Assisted	69
Educational	
Diocesan Students in Other Seminaries	3
Total Seminarians	3
High Schools, Diocesan and Parish	4
Total Students	1,086
Elementary Schools, Diocesan and Parish	7
Total Students	716
Catechesis/Religious Education:	
High School Students	2,421
Elementary Students	5,481
Total Students Under Catholic Instruction	9,707
Teachers in the Diocese:	
Sisters	2
Lay Teachers	73
Vital Statistics	
Receptions into the Church:	
Infant Baptism Totals	1,152
Adult Baptism Totals	111
Received into Full Communion	143
First Communions	1,235
Confirmations	833
Marriages:	
Catholic	201
Interfaith	177
Total Marriages	378
Deaths	520
Total Catholic Population	56,523
Total Population	290,429

Former Bishops—Most Rev. JAMES ALBERT DUFFY, D.D., cons. April 16, 1913; resigned See, May 7, 1931; appt. Titular Bishop of Silando; died Feb. 12, 1968.—Most Rev. STANISLAUS V. BONA, D.D., appt. Bishop of Grand Island, Dec. 18, 1931; cons. Feb. 25, 1932; appt. Coadjutor Bishop of Green Bay and Titular Bishop of Mela, Dec. 2, 1944; succeeded to See, March 3, 1945; died Dec. 1, 1967.—Most Rev. EDWARD J. HUNKELER, D.D., ord. June 14, 1919; appt. March 10, 1945; cons. May 1, 1945; transferred to Kansas City in Kansas, March 31, 1951; died Oct. 1, 1970.—Most Rev. JOHN L. PASCHANG, D.D., Ph.D., J.C.D., ord. June 12, 1921; appt. July 28, 1951; cons. October 9, 1951; resigned July 25, 1972.—Most Rev. JOHN J. SULLIVAN, D.D., ord. Sept. 23, 1944; appt. July 25, 1972; cons. Sept. 19, 1972; transferred to Kansas City-St. Joseph in Missouri, Aug. 17, 1977.

Vicar General—Rev. JAMES D. O'KANE, *St. Agnes, Scottsbluff, 69363.* Tel: 308-632-3541.

Chancery Office—311 W. 17th St., P.O. Box 996, Grand Island, 68802. Tel: 308-382-6565; Fax: 308-382-6569. Office Hours: 9-5.

Moderator of the Curia—Rev. RICHARD L. PIONTKOWSKI, JR., S.T.L., J.C.L.

Diocesan Tribunal—P.O. Box 996, Grand Island, 68802. Tel: 308-382-6364.

Vicar-Judicial—Rev. MICHAEL F. MCDERMOTT, J.C.L.

Adjutant Vicars-Judicial—Revs. RICHARD L. PIONTKOWSKI, JR., S.T.L., J.C.L.; CHARLES L. TORPEY, S.T.L., J.C.L.

Defenders of the Bond—Revs. THOMAS RYAN; DONALD E. LARMORE, J.C.D.

Promoter Justitiae—Rev. DONALD E. LARMORE, J.C.D.

Judges—Revs. CHARLES L. TORPEY, S.T.L., J.C.L.; RICHARD PIONTKOWSKI, JR., S.T.L., J.C.L.; MICHAEL F. MCDERMOTT, J.C.L.

Procurator—Rev. JAMES M. HUNT.

Advocates—Rev. JAMES M. HUNT; RUTH NOZICKA; CONNIE RUHLMAN.

Associate Director-Notary—JOYCE M. PROUTY.

Diocesan Consultors—Revs. JOHN E. SCHLAF; DON BUHRMAN; CHARLES L. TORPEY, S.T.L., J.C.L.; JOSEPH HANNAPPEL; MICHAEL F. MCDERMOTT, S.T.L., J.C.L.; ROBERT B. ROONEY; JAMES D. O'KANE.

Vicar for Religious Communities of Women—Rev. FRANK L. HOELCK, Spalding.

Diocesan Offices and Directors

Building Committee—Revs. ANDREW GONDA; STANLEY GORAK; JOHN SCHLAF; JAMES D. O'KANE.

Charismatic Renewal—Rev. HAROLD KURTENBACH, Dir., *Box 936, Grand Island, 68802.* Tel: 308-382-2523.

Charities—Rev. JOSEPH M. WALSH, Dir., Catholic Soc. Svc. Bureau; JAMES R. BLUE, Asst. Dir., Catholic Soc. Svcs., *335 N. 27th St., Lincoln, 68503.* Tel: 402-474-1600.

Communications—Rev. DONALD E. LARMORE, Dir., *1724 N. Walnut, Grand Island, 68801.* Tel: 308-384-0532.

Continuing Education for the Clergy—Revs. ARTHUR FAESSER, *821 W. 27 St., Kearney, 68848.* ROBERT ROONEY, *Box 405, Broken Bow, 68822.*

Council of Catholic Women, Diocesan—Rev. STEPHEN F. DEAVER, Diocesan Moderator.

Family Life—EUGENE GILSDORF, Dir., *214 W. 5th, P.O. Box 1064, North Platte, 69103.* Tel: 308-532-2707.

Hispanic Ministry—Mr. ADOLFO BARROS, Dir., *Box 651, North Platte, 69103.* Tel: 308-532-2707. Rev. PAUL J. COLLING, Asst. Dir., *1103 12th Ave., Scottsbluff, 69361.* Tel: 308-632-2845.

Holy Childhood Association—Rev. REGINALD URBAN, Dir.

Liturgical Commission—Revs. CHARLES L. TORPEY, S.T.L., J.C.L., Chm. JAMES D. O'KANE, Vice Chm.

Marriage Encounter—Rev. WALTER W. PHILLIPS, *701 Student Dr., Ogallala, 69153.* Tel: 308-284-2458.

Newspaper—*"The West Nebraska Register"*. Co-Editors: MARY PARLIN; MARILYN ZASTROW,address all correspondence to, *P.O. Box 608, Grand Island, 68802.* Tel: 308-382-4660; Fax: 308-382-4746.

Personnel Board—Revs. BRYAN D. ERNEST; JOHN R. RADEMACHER; JAMES C. SCHMITT; CHARLES L. TORPEY; JOHN E. SCHLAF; BERNARD M. BERGER; HAROLD KURTENBACH; ROBERT KARNISH.

Priests' Advisory Board (Presbyteral Council)—Revs. DON BUHRMAN; MICHAEL F. MCDERMOTT; JOSEPH HANNAPPEL; RAYMOND M. KOSMICKI; RODNEY L. PRUSS; PAUL J. COLLING; BERNARD M. BERGER; JOHN E. SCHLAF; CHARLES L. TORPEY; LOUIS NOLLETTE; EDWARD CORTNEY; JAMES O'KANE.

Catholic Relief Services—Rev. FRANCIS T. CURRAN, Dir.

Priests' Pension and Welfare Board—Address all mail to: Rev. JAN SMUTNY, *P.O. Box 194, Pleasanton, 68866.*

Propagation of the Faith—Rev. MICHAEL D. MCDONALD, Dir., *1210 E. 11th, Kearney, 68847.* Tel: 308-236-9171.

Remex-Media Center—214 W. 5th St., P.O. Box 1617, North Platte, 69103. Tel: 308-532-2707.

Religious Education—DONALD KURRE, Dir.; Sr. MARIETTA SPENNER, O.S.F., Assoc. Dir., *214 W. 5th St., P.O. Box 1617, North Platte, 69103.* Tel: 308-532-2707.

Rural Life Conference—Rev. NEAL P. NOLLETTE, Dir., *Box 530, Elm Creek, 68836.*

Schools—Rev. THOMAS A. RYAN, Diocesan Supt. of Schools, *311 W. 17th, P.O. Box 996, Grand Island, 68802.* Tel: 308-682-6565; Fax: 308-382-6569.

Sisters Council, Administrative Team—Sr. PAULETTE KUTA; Sr. ROBERTA ANN SEMPER; Sr. MARY CHAMBERLAIN.

Vocations—Rev. BRYAN D. ERNEST, Dir., *1104 Cheyenne Ave., Alliance, 69301.* Tel: 308-762-1418.

Youth—JENNIFER HOSTLER, Dir., *P.O. Box 1721, Grand Island, 68802.* Tel: 308-382-4660; Fax: 308-382-4746.

CLERGY, PARISHES, MISSIONS AND PAROCHIAL SCHOOLS

CITY OF GRAND ISLAND
(Hall County)

1—CATHEDRAL OF THE NATIVITY OF THE BLESSED VIRGIN MARY (1864), Revs. Thomas A. Ryan; Harold Kurtenbach.
Res., 207 S. Elm St., 68801. Tel: 308-384-2523.
Catechesis/Religious Programs—502 West Division, 68801. Tel: 308-382-1198. Sr. Barbara Bader, C.S.J., D.R.E.
Students 505.

2—BLESSED SACRAMENT (1949), Revs. Donald E. Larmore; Martin L. Egging.
Res., 1724 N. Walnut, 68801. Tel: 308-384-0532; Fax: 308-384-0424.
Catechesis/Religious Programs—518 W. State St., 68801. Tel: 308-384-2086. Ms. Mary Jane Spirk, D.R.E.
Students 414.
Chapel—Geer-Sterne, 801 Stoeger Dr., 68803.

3—RESURRECTION (1973), Rev. James C. Schmitt.
Res., 4110 Cannon Rd., 68803. Tel: 308-382-8644.
Catechesis/Religious Programs—Tel: 308-382-0976. Therese Stump, D.R.E.
Students 288.

4—ST. LEO (1972), Rev. John R. Rademacher; Sr. Leona Augustyn, Pastoral Min.
Res., 2410 S. Blaine, 68801. Tel: 308-382-4753. [CEM]
Catechesis/Religious Programs—D.R.E.: Beata Nabity, (Grades PreK-5); Kevin M. Fuller, (Grades 6-12).
Students 447.

OUTSIDE THE CITY OF GRAND ISLAND

Ainsworth, Brown Co., St. Pius X, Rev. James M. Hunt.
Res., P.O. Box 7, 69210. Tel: 402-387-1275.
Catechesis/Religious Programs—Tel: 402-387-2260. D.R.E.: Linda Schumacher, (St. Pius X); Sue Jilg, (Holy Cross).
Students 150.
Mission—Bassett, Rock Co., Holy Cross, P.O. Box 7, 69210.

Alliance, Box Butte Co., Holy Rosary (1894), Revs. Bryan D. Ernest; Timothy L. Stoner.
Parish Offices: 1104 Cheyenne Ave., 69301. Tel: 308-762-2009; Fax: 308-762-7474.
Res., 916 Cheyenne Ave., 69301. Tel: 308-762-1418. [CEM]
School—St. Agnes Academy, Tel: 308-762-2315.
Sisters 3; Lay Teachers 14; Students 178.
Catechesis/Religious Programs—Tel: 308-762-2830. Shari Harris, D.R.E.
Students 400.

Anselmo, Custer Co., St. Anselm's, Rev. Mark A. Maresh.
Res., P.O. Box 157, 68813. Tel: 308-749-2254. [CEM]
Catechesis/Religious Programs—D.R.E.: Connie Chandler, (High School); Cindy Hempstead, (Elementary).
Students 118.
Mission—Merna, Custer Co., St. Paul, P.O. Box 157, 68813. [CEM]

Ashton, Sherman Co., St. Francis, Rev. Frederick N. Snyder.
Res., 245 Howells Ave., P.O. Box 147, 68817. Tel: 308-738-2198.
Catechesis/Religious Programs—Mrs. Eddy Krzycki, D.R.E.
Students 55.
Mission—Paplin, Howard Co., Our Lady of Mt. Carmel.

Bridgeport, Morrill Co., All Souls (1919), Rev. Christopher R. Keith.
Res., P.O. Box 250, 69336-0250. Tel: 308-262-0709. [CEM]
Catechesis/Religious Programs—D.R.E.: Sheri Hopkins; Michelle Lempke; Janet Dailey; Meline Jackson.
Students 140.
Missions—Dalton, Cheyenne Co., St. Mary, P.O. Box 346, 69131-0346. Tel: 308-377-2440; Bayard, Morrill Co., Sacred Heart, P.O. Box 190, 69334-0190. Tel: 308-586-1160.

Broadwater, Cheyenne Co., St. Dominic. Closed. For inquiries for parish records contact the Chancery.

Broken Bow, Custer Co., St. Joseph's (1888), Rev. Robert Rooney.
Mailing Address: P.O. Box 405, 68822.
Res., 1407 S. E St., 68822. Tel: 308-872-5716; Fax: 308-872-5809. [CEM]
Catechesis/Religious Programs—Students 215.
Missions—Ansley, Custer Co., Sacred Heart, 68822.; Mason City, Custer Co., St. Thomas, 68822.

Burwell, Garfield Co., Sacred Heart (1910), Rev. Bernard M. Berger.
Res., 747 I St., P.O. Box 667, 68823. Tel: 308-346-4190.
Catechesis/Religious Programs—Betty Kovorik, D.R.E.
Students 89.
Missions—Ericson, Wheeler Co., St. Theresa of the Child Jesus, 68823.; Sargent, Custer Co., Assumption of the Blessed Virgin Mary, P.O. Box 397, Sargent, 68874. [CEM]

Chadron, Dawes Co., St. Patrick's (1886), Rev. Edward P. Cortney.
Office: 340 Cedar St., P.O. Box 231, 69337. Tel: 308-432-2626. [CEM]
Catechesis/Religious Programs—Tel: 308-432-2161. Linda Yeradi, D.R.E.
Students 153.

Chappell, Deuel Co., St. Joseph's (1909), Rev. Joseph A. Hannappel.
Office: Tel: 308-874-3407.
Res., 1049 2nd St., P.O. Box 586, 69129. Tel: 308-874-3221. [CEM]
Catechesis/Religious Programs—Students 43.
Missions—Lodgepole, Cheyenne Co., Sacred Heart; Oshkosh, Garden Co., St. Elizabeth, 300 W. 4th, P.O. Box 17, 69154.; Lisco, Garden Co., St. Gall, 307 1st St., 69148.

Cozad, Dawson Co., Christ the King (1951), Rev. Donald J. O'Brien; Sr. Juana O'Brien, O.P., Pastoral Assoc., Tel: 308-537-3364.
Res., 1220 Ave. M, 69130. Tel: 308-784-3959.
Catechesis/Religious Programs—512 E. 19th, Tel: 308-784-2696. Donna Kolbo, D.R.E.
Students 211.
Mission—Gothenburg, Dawson Co., Our Lady of Good Counsel, Gothenburg, 69138.

Crawford, Dawes Co., St. John the Baptist (1896), Rev. Todd K. Philipsen.
Res., 808 4th St., 69339. Tel: 308-665-1584. [CEM]
Catechesis/Religious Programs—Linda Moloney, D.R.E.
Students 42.
Mission—Harrison, Sioux Co., Church of the Nativity of the Blessed Virgin Mary, 69339.

Elm Creek, Buffalo Co., Immaculate Conception (1879), Rev. Neal P. Nollette.
Res., P.O. Box 530, 68836. Tel: 308-856-4375. [CEM]
Catechesis/Religious Programs—Vickie Sullwold, D.R.E.
Students 120.
Missions—Overton, Dawson Co., Holy Rosary, Overton, 68863.; Amherst, Buffalo Co., St. John Capistran, Jefferson & Ash, Amherst, 68812.; Eddyville, Custer Co., St. Patrick. [CEM]

Elyria, Valley Co., St. Mary's. Closed. For inquiries for parish records contact the Chancery.

Farwell, Howard Co., St. Anthony of Padua (1877), Rev. Lawrence W. Coulter.
Res., 103 Kearns Ave., Box 156, 68838. Tel: 308-336-3323. [CEM 4]
Catechesis/Religious Programs—D.R.E.: Kathy Gorecki Tel: 308-336-3351; Tami Morrow Tel: 308-863-2320; Sharon Krzycki Tel: 308-738-2167.
Students 187.
Missions—Elba, Howard Co., St. Joseph, 68838.; Ashton, Sherman Co., St. Francis, 68838. [CEM] Paplin, Howard Co., Our Lady of Mount Carmel, 68838.; Geranium, Valley Co., St. Wenceslaus.

Gering, Scotts Bluff Co., Christ the King (1958), Rev. Gerald J. Harr.
Res., 1730 N St., P.O. Box 33, 69341. Tel: 308-436-4000; Fax: 308-436-2923. [CEM]
Catechesis/Religious Programs—18th & N St., P.O. Box 33, 69341. Tel: 308-436-2290. Pat Schumacher, D.R.E. & Dir. Youth Ministry.
Students 302.

Gordon, Sheridan Co., St. Leo's (1887), Rev. Robert A. Karnish.
Res., 228 N. Maverick, 69343. Tel: 308-282-0427. [JC]
Catechesis/Religious Programs—Students 147.
Missions—Rushville, Sheridan Co., Immaculate Conception, 606 Church St., Tel: 308-327-2430; Hay Springs, Sheridan Co., St. Columbkille. 545 N. Main.

Greeley, Greeley Co., Sacred Heart (1893) (Irish), Rev. Gerald J. Carlson.
Res., 302 W. Wicklow, P.O. Box 99, 68842. Tel: 308-428-2855. [JC]
Catechesis/Religious Programs—Tel: 308-428-3015.
Students 33.
Missions—Scotia, Greeley Co., St. Patrick, 68842.; O'Connor, Greeley Co., Our Lady of the Visitation, 68842.

Hemingford, Box Butte Co., St. Bridget (1888), Rev. Hubert J. Spanel.
Res., 801 Niobrara Ave., P.O. Box 67, 69348. Tel: 308-487-3617. [CEM]
Catechesis/Religious Programs—Judy Gonzalez, D.R.E.
Students 100.
Mission—Hay Springs, Sacred Heart.

Kearney, Buffalo Co., St. James (1881), Revs. Charles L. Torpey; James R. Golka.
Res., 7 Sioux Ln., P.O. Box 128, 68848. Tel: 308-234-5536; 234-5354. [JC]
High School—Kearney Catholic, (Grades 7-12). Tel: 308-234-2610; Fax: 308-234-4986. Mr. Terrence Torson, Admin.
Sisters 1; Lay Teachers 21; Students 322.
Catechesis/Religious Programs—Tel: 308-234-9695. Deb Kratochvil, D.R.E.
Students 517.

Prince of Peace (1986), Rev. Michael D. McDonald; Sr. Roberta Ann Semper, O.P., Pastoral Min.
Res., 1210 E. 11th St., 68847. Tel: 308-236-9171.
Catechesis/Religious Programs—Ms. Carolynn Smallcomb, D.R.E.
Students 144.

Kimball, Kimball Co., St. Joseph's (1921), Rev. Francis T. Curran.
Res., 507 S. Howard, 69145. Tel: 308-235-2162.
Catechesis/Religious Programs—Students 85.

Lexington, Dawson Co., St. Ann's (1883), Rev. Donald A. Buhrman.
Res., 303 E. 6th St., P.O. Box 578, 68850. Tel: 308-324-4648. [CEM]
Catechesis/Religious Programs—St. Ann's Parish Center, 10th & Taft St., 68850. Tel: 308-324-2616; Fax: 308-324-5320. Joan Karre, D.R.E. (Grades K-12).
Students 399.

Loup City, Sherman Co., St. Josaphat's (1882) (Polish), Rev. Reginald A. Urban.
Res., Rte. 2, P.O. Box 38A, 68853. Tel: 308-745-0315.
Catechesis/Religious Programs—Tel: 308-745-1235.
Students 410.

Merriman, Cherry Co., St. Elizabeth. Closed. For inquiries for parish records contact the Chancery.

Mitchell, Scotts Bluff Co., St. Theresa's, Rev. Stephen F. Deaver.
Res., 1715 17th St., 69357. Tel: 308-623-1745.
Catechesis/Religious Programs—Students 67.
Missions—Morrill, Scotts Bluff Co., St. Ann, Hwy. 26 & Walsh, Morrill, 69358.; Lyman, Scotts Bluff Co., Sacred Heart.

Mullen, Hooker Co., St. Mary's, Rev. Louis A. Nollette.
Res., 302 S. Blaine, P.O. Box 191, 69152. Tel: 308-546-2250; Fax: 308-546-2327.
Catechesis/Religious Programs—Students 121.
Missions—Brownlee, Cherry Co., St. Joan of Arc, 69152.; Hyannis, Grant Co., All Saint's, 69152.; Thedford, Thomas Co., St. Thomas of Canterbury, 69152.

North Platte, Lincoln Co., Holy Spirit (1973), Rev. James H. Heithoff.
Res., P.O. Box 427, 69103. Tel: 308-534-4334; 534-7906; Fax: 308-534-6525.
Catechesis/Religious Programs—Kathy Schroeder, D.R.E.
Students 235.

St. Patrick (1875), Rev. Richard L. Piontkowski, Jr.
Res., 415 N. Chestnut, P.O. Box 399, 69103. Tel: 308-532-0942; Fax: 308-532-0944. [CEM]
School—(Grades K-6). Tel: 308-532-0622. Mr. Tom Rhodes, Prin.
Lay Teachers 19; Students 210.
High School—(Grades 7-12). Tel: 308-532-1874;

Fax: 308-532-1875. Mr. William McGahan, Jr., Supt.
Lay Teachers 18; Students 215.
Catechesis/Religious Programs—Tel: 308-532-6388. Rebecca Wing, D.R.E.
Students 149.

Ogallala, Keith Co., St. Luke's (1887), Rev. John E. Schlaf.
Res., 417 E. Third, 69153. Tel: 308-284-3196. [JC]
School—Tel: 308-284-4841.
Ursuline Sisters 1; Lay Teachers 3; Students 71.
Catechesis/Religious Programs—Lay Teachers 22; Students 165.

Ord, Valley Co., Our Lady of Perpetual Help, Rev. James L. Warner.
Res., P.O. Box 123, 68862. Tel: 308-728-3351. [CEM]
School—Tel: 308-728-5389.
Sisters 1; Lay Teachers 5; Students 74.
Catechesis/Religious Programs—Students 132.

Pleasanton, Buffalo Co., St. Mary's (1909) (German), Rev. Loren G. Pohlmeier.
Res., 504 N. Sycamore St., Box 134, 68866. Tel: 308-388-2181. [CEM][JC]
Catechesis/Religious Programs—Tel: 308-388-3062. D.R.E.: Delores Paitz; Claudette Sekutera; Darlene Schulte.
Students 132.
Missions—Hazard, Sherman Co., St. Gabriel, Market St. & DeWitt St., 68844.; Prairie Center, Buffalo Co., St. Mary, 3125 190 Rd., Kearney 68847. Tel: 308-237-0857. [CEM]

Ravenna, Buffalo Co., Our Lady of Lourdes (1887) (German), Rev. Rodney Lee A. Pruss.
Res., 515 Sicily Ave., Box 90, 68869. Tel: 308-452-3314.
Catechesis/Religious Programs—Tel: 308-452-3109.
Students 105.
Mission—Rockville, Sherman Co., St. Mary's, 406 Fair St., Rockville, 68871. [CEM]

St. Libory, Howard Co., St. Libory's (1884), Rev. David L. Rykwalder.
Res., P.O. Box 7, 68872. Tel: 308-687-6276. [CEM]
Catechesis/Religious Programs—Students 125.
Mission—Wolbach, St. Joseph's.

St. Paul, Howard Co., SS. Peter and Paul (1878), Rev. Michael F. McDermott.
Res., 405 7th St., 68873. Tel: 308-754-4649. [JC]
Catechesis/Religious Programs—713 Elm St., 68873. Tel: 308-754-4002. Sr. Maria del Rey Mangan, O.P., D.R.E.
Students 175.

Scottsbluff, Scotts Bluff Co., St. Agnes (1912), Rev. James D. O'Kane.
Res., 2314 3rd Ave., P.O. Box 349, 69363. Tel: 308-632-2541.
School—Tel: 308-632-6918.
Lay Teachers 9; Students 95.
Catechesis/Religious Programs—Kathleen Roehl, D.R.E.
Students 212.

Our Lady of Guadalupe (1955) (Hispanic), Rev. Paul J. Colling.
Res., 1103 12th Ave., 69361. Tel: 308-632-2845. [CEM]
Catechesis/Religious Programs—Elizabeth Salazar, D.R.E.
Students 151.

Sidney, Cheyenne Co., St. Patrick's (1978), Rev. Ted A. Nekoliczak; Sr. Esther Fehringer, Pastoral Assoc.
Res., 1039 14th Ave., P.O. Box 99, 69162. Tel: 308-254-2828; Fax: 308-254-5318. [JC]
Catechesis/Religious Programs—D.R.E.: Sheila Hrnchir, (Grades K-6); Pat Mertz, (Grades 7-12).
Students 315.

Spalding, Greeley Co., St. Michael's (1887), Rev. Frank Hoelck.
Res., 68665. Tel: 308-497-2662. [CEM 2]
Schools—Spalding Academy, Tel: 308-497-2103; Fax: 308-497-2105.
Sisters of St. Dominic 2; Lay Teachers 16; Students 87; (Grades K-6).
Lay Teachers 5; Students 50.
High School—Lay Teachers 9; Students 37.
Catechesis/Religious Programs—Students 112.

Stapleton, Logan Co., St. John the Evangelist (1913), Rev. James E. Novakowski.
Res., P.O. Box 309, 69163. Tel: 308-636-2421. [CEM]
Catechesis/Religious Programs—Students 90.
Missions—Arnold, St. Agnes, 69163.; Callaway, St. Boniface; Oconto, St. Mary, 69163.

Sutherland, Lincoln Co., Sacred Heart, Rev. Thomas J. Dillon.
Res., 69165. Tel: 308-386-4300.
Catechesis/Religious Programs—Tel: 308-386-2401.
Students 90.
Missions—Paxton, Keith Co., St. Patrick, 69165.; Hershey, Lincoln Co., Our Lady of Guadalupe, 69165.

Valentine, Cherry Co., St. Nicholas (1893), Rev. James J. Janovec.
Res., 69201. Tel: 402-376-1672. [JC]
Catechesis/Religious Programs—Tel: 402-376-1938. Mary Lou Stauffer, D.R.E.
Students 218.
Mission—Nenzel, Cherry Co., St. Mary, P.O. Box 510, 69201. [CEM]

Wood River, Hall Co., St. Mary's (1884), Rev. Raymond M. Kosmicki.
Res., P.O. Box 37, 68883. Tel: 308-583-2464. [CEM]
Catechesis/Religious Programs—Students 128.
Mission—Shelton, Sacred Heart, 68883.
Catechesis/Religious Programs—Students 101.

Chaplains of Public Institutions

GRAND ISLAND. *Nebraska Veterans Home*. Rev. James C. Schmitt.
U.S. Veterans' Hospital. Rev. Walter M. Phelan.
KEARNEY. *Youth Development Center*, W. Hwy. 30, 68847. Tel: 308-237-3181. Rev. Arthur A. Faesser, Chap.

On Duty Outside the Diocese:
Reverend Fathers—
Fenton, Lawrence E., Holy Name of Jesus Church, 345 S. Military Trail, West Palm Beach, FL 33415
Whalen, Joseph E., 512 Gibson Ave., Lexington, KY 40517

Military Chaplains:
Reverend Fathers—
Borzych, Alexander J.

Retired:
Reverend Monsignors—
Hayden, Carl T., 111 Emerson #1225, Denver, CO 80218
Portrey, Lawrence A., 816 W. First, North Platte, NE 69101
Reverend Fathers—
Abele, Joseph P., Box 168, Oshkosh, NE 69154
Augustyn, Andrew M., 2517 W. Phoenix, Grand Island, NE 68803
Bauer, Jacob F., 2106 W. Cottage, Grand Island, NE 68803
Chamberlain, Robert F., Box 803, Sutherland, NE 69165
Cook, John N., Box 242, Greeley, NE 68842
Cortney, Kevin J., 510 Centennial Circle, Rm 110, North Platte, NE 69101
Dennett, John A., Box 1323, Lusk, WY 82225
Dowd, Thomas M., 2516 Commerce Ave., Grand Island, NE 68801
Ferris, Carl A., Valentine, NE 69201
Foster, Robert L., P.O. Box 241, Greeley, NE 68842
Gonda, Andrew, 1111 E. Nebraska Ave., Grand Island, NE 68801
Gorak, Stanley C., 318 E. 22nd St., Kearney, NE 68847
Guevara, Miguel H., Box 399, North Platte, NE 69103
Hargarten, Joseph F., No. 12 Pinewood Grove, Gering, NE 69341
Koprowski, Mitchell J., Mullen, NE 69152
Kremeier, James, 200 Swink Ave., Rocky Ford, CO 81067
Krystosek, Robert H., Box 425, Clara City, MN 56222
McSweeney, James, P.O. Box 100A, Rte. 1, Stapleton, NE 69163
Mullowney, Thomas E., 110 E. 39th St., E7, Kearney, NE 68847
Murphy, James E., Rte. 1, Box 131, Spalding, NE 68665
Phelan, Walter M., 1111 E. Nebraska Ave., Grand Island, NE 68801
Phillips, Walter W., 701 Student Dr., Ogallala, NE 69153
Smutny, Jan, Box 194, Pleasanton, NE 68866
Snyder, Frederick, St. Mary's Convent, 2649-US20, Swanton, OH 43558
Szczesny, Michael S., 1405 W. Koenig, No. 307, Grand Island, NE 68801
Valdez, Max E., 3010 Ave. D, Scottsbluff, NE 69361
Whalen, James R., 314 East E, Ogallala, NE 69153

INSTITUTIONS LOCATED IN THE DIOCESE

[A] HIGH SCHOOLS, DIOCESAN

GRAND ISLAND. *Central Catholic Middle School-High School*. (Grades 6-12), 1200 Ruby Ave., 68803. Tel: 308-384-2440. Dr. R. L. Ripp, Supt.; John Golka, Prin.; Howard Schumann, Asst. Prin.; Rev. Martin L. Egging. Lay Teachers 34; Students 517.

[B] GENERAL HOSPITALS

GRAND ISLAND. *Saint Francis Medical Center*, 2620 W. Faidley Ave., P.O. Box 9804, 68802. Tel: 308-384-4600; Fax: 308-389-5589.
E-mail: dsanders@sfmc-gi.org
Web site: www.sfmc-gi.org
For a complete listing, refer to the Hospitals section.

KEARNEY. *Good Samaritan Health Systems dba Good Samaritan Hospital*, 10 E. 31st St., P.O. Box 1990, 68848-1990. Tel: 308-865-7100
For a complete listing, refer to the Hospitals section.

[C] HOMES FOR THE AGED

KEARNEY. *Mount Carmel Home-Keens' Memorial*, 412 W. 18th St., 68847. Tel: 308-237-2287
For a complete listing, refer to the Special Care Facilities section.

[D] NEWMAN CENTERS

CHADRON. *Chadron State College-Newman Club*, 907 Main St., 69337. Tel: 308-432-4286; 432-3846.
E-mail: gggolka@bbc.net
Mr. Gregory Golka. Total in Residence 1; Total Staff 1.

KEARNEY. *University of Nebraska at Kearney Newman Apostolate*, 821 W. 27th St., 68847. Tel: 308-234-1539. Rev. Arthur A. Faesser. Total in Residence 9; Total Staff 3.

RELIGIOUS INSTITUTES OF WOMEN REPRESENTED IN THE DIOCESE

For further details refer to the corresponding bracketed number in the Religious Institutes of Men or Women section.

[0350]—*Carmelite Sisters (Corpus Christi)*.—O.Carm.
[1070-01]—*Dominican Sisters*.—O.P.
[1070-13]—*Dominican Sisters*.—O.P.
[3580]—*Servants of Mary*. (Omaha, NE).—O.S.M.
[0480]—*Sisters of Charity of Leavenworth, Kansas*.—S.C.L.
[3710]—*Sisters of St. Agnes*.—C.S.A.
[1630]—*Sisters of St. Francis of Penance and Christian Charity*.—O.S.F.
[1640]—*Sisters of St. Francis of Perpetual Adoration*.—O.S.F.
[3830]—*Sisters of St. Joseph*.—C.S.J.
[2110]—*Sisters of the Humility of Mary*.—H.M.
[4120-03]—*Ursuline Nuns of the Congregation of Paris*. (Louisville, KY).—O.S.U.

NECROLOGY

† Wiest, Robert E., (Retired). —Died Jan. 3, 1997.

Diocese of Grand Rapids

(Dioecesis Grandormensis)

Most Reverend

ROBERT J. ROSE, S.T.L., D.D.

Bishop of Grand Rapids; ordained December 21, 1955; appointed Bishop of Gaylord October 13, 1981; consecrated December 6, 1981; appointed Bishop of Grand Rapids July 11, 1989; installed August 30, 1989. *Office: 660 Burton St., S.E., Grand Rapids, MI, 49507.* Tel.: 616-243-0491.

Most Reverend

JOSEPH M. BREITENBECK, D.D.

Retired Bishop of Grand Rapids; ordained May 30, 1942; appointed Titular Bishop of Tepelta and Auxiliary of Detroit October 18, 1965; consecrated December 20, 1965; appointed Bishop of Grand Rapids October 15, 1969; installed December 2, 1969; retired August 3, 1989. *Mailing Address: 660 Burton St., S.E., Grand Rapids, MI, 49507.*

Most Reverend

JOSEPH C. MCKINNEY, D.D.

Titular Bishop of Lentini and Auxiliary of Grand Rapids; ordained December 20, 1953; appointed Auxiliary July 24, 1968; consecrated September 26, 1968. *Res., 4865 Eleven Mile Rd., Rockford, MI, 49341.* Tel.: 616-866-0931.

ESTABLISHED MAY 19, 1882.

Square Miles 6,795.

Comprises the following Counties of the Lower Peninsula of the State of Michigan: Ionia, Kent, Lake, Mason, Mecosta, Montcalm, Muskegon, Newaygo, Oceana, Osceola, Ottawa.

For legal titles of parishes and diocesan institutions, consult the Chancery Office.

Administrative Office of Diocese of Grand Rapids: 660 Burton St., S.E., Grand Rapids, MI, 49507. Tel.: 616-243-0491; Fax: 616-243-4910.

STATISTICAL OVERVIEW

Personnel	
Bishop	1
Auxiliary Bishops	1
Retired Bishops	1
Priests: Diocesan Active in Diocese	92
Priests: Active Outside Diocese	5
Priests: Retired, Sick or Absent	32
Number of Diocesan Priests	129
Religious Priests in Diocese	21
Extern Priests in Diocese	12
Ordinations:	
Diocesan Priests	2
Permanent Deacons in Diocese	21
Total Brothers	2
Total Sisters	300
Parishes	
Parishes	90
With Resident Pastor:	
Resident Diocesan Priests	86
Resident Religious Priests	3
Without Resident Pastor:	
Administered by Priests	1
Missions	12
Pastoral Centers	2
Professional Ministry Personnel:	
Brothers	1
Sisters	26
Lay Ministers	78
Welfare	
Catholic Hospitals	2
Total Assisted	773,842
Homes for the Aged	1
Total Assisted	150
Specialized Homes	9
Total Assisted	652
Special Centers for Social Services	22
Total Assisted	25,500
Residential Care of Disabled	1
Total Assisted	75
Other Institutions	2
Total Assisted	1,400
Educational	
Seminaries, Diocesan	1
Students from This Diocese	3
Diocesan Students in Other Seminaries	7
Total Seminarians	10
Colleges and Universities	1
Total Students	2,458
High Schools, Diocesan and Parish	4
Total Students	1,912
Elementary Schools, Diocesan and Parish	41
Total Students	8,974
Catechesis/Religious Education:	
High School Students	2,346
Elementary Students	12,649
Total Students Under Catholic Instruction	28,349
Teachers in the Diocese:	
Brothers	1
Sisters	27
Lay Teachers	654
Vital Statistics	
Receptions into the Church:	
Infant Baptism Totals	3,188
Adult Baptism Totals	350
First Communions	3,138
Confirmations	2,406
Marriages:	
Catholic	629
Interfaith	504
Total Marriages	1,133
Deaths	1,443
Total Catholic Population	145,021
Total Population	1,167,900

Former Bishops—Most Rev. HENRY JOSEPH RICHTER, D.D., cons. April 22, 1883; died Dec. 26, 1916.—Most Rev. MICHAEL JAMES GALLAGHER, D.D., ord. March 19, 1893; appt. titular Bishop of Tipasa and Coadjutor Bishop of Grand Rapids July 5, 1915; cons. Sept. 8, 1915; succeeded to the Diocese of Grand Rapids, Dec. 26, 1916; transferred to the See of Detroit, July 18, 1918; died Jan. 20, 1937.—Most Rev. EDWARD D. KELLY, ord. June 16, 1886; cons. auxiliary Bishop of Detroit, Jan. 26, 1911; transferred to the See of Grand Rapids, Jan. 16, 1919; died March 26, 1926.—Most Rev. JOSEPH G. PINTEN, D.D., ord. Nov. 1, 1890; cons. Bishop of Superior May 3, 1922; transferred to See of Grand Rapids June 25, 1926; resigned and appt. Titular Bishop of Sela Nov. 1, 1940; died Nov. 6, 1945.—Most Rev. JOSEPH CASIMIR PLAGENS, ord. July 5, 1903; cons. Sept. 30, 1924, Auxiliary Bishop of Detroit and Titular Bishop of Rhodiopolis; transferred to See of Marquette Nov. 16, 1935; transferred to See of Grand Rapids Dec. 16, 1940; installed as Bishop of Grand Rapids Feb. 18, 1941; died March 31, 1943.—Most Rev. FRANCIS J. HAAS, D.D., ord. June 11, 1913; appt. Sept. 26, 1943; cons. and installed as Bishop of Grand Rapids, Nov. 18, 1943; died Aug. 29, 1953.—Most Rev. ALLEN J. BABCOCK, D.D., ord. March 7, 1925; appt. Titular Bishop of Irenopolis and Auxiliary of Detroit Feb. 15, 1947; cons. March 25, 1947; appt. to Grand Rapids March 23, 1954; died June 27, 1969.

Administrative Office of Diocese of Grand Rapids—660 Burton St., S.E., Grand Rapids, 49507. Tel: 616-243-0491; Fax: 616-243-4910. Office Hours: Mon.-Fri. 8-4:30 All official communications to be directed to this office.

Moderator of the Curia—Rev. Msgr. TERRENCE L. STEWART.

Chancellor—Sr. PATRICE KONWINSKI, O.P.

Director of Finance—JOHN S. CZACHORSKI.

Vicars General—Most Rev. JOSEPH C. MCKINNEY, *4865 Eleven Mile Rd., Rockford, 49341.* Tel: 616-866-0931. Rev. Msgr. TERRENCE L. STEWART, *660 Burton St., S.E., Grand Rapids, 49507.* Tel: 616-243-0491.

Clergy Fund—Rev. DONN TUFTS, *10224 Maple Island Rd., Fremont, 49412-9116.* Tel: 616-924-3389.

Deans—Rev. ROCK BADGEROW, Big Rapids; Rev. JOHN F. PORTER, Grand Haven, *12285 Heights Ravenna Rd., Ravenna, 49451-0216.* Tel: 616-853-6222. Rev. JOSEPH W. KENSHOL, Grand Rapids North, *1 Maple St., P.O. Box 140, Sand Lake, 49343.* Tel: 616-636-5671. Rev. ROBERT L. PINKSTON, C.S.P., Grand Rapids South, *246 Ionia N.W., Grand Rapids, 49583.* Tel: 616-459-7267. Rev. Msgr. ERNEST SCHNEIDER, Grand Rapids East, *6477 Ada Dr. P.O. Box 369, Ada, 49301.* Tel: 616-676-9111. STEVEN D. CRON, Grand Rapids West; Rev., *733 Bridge N.W., Grand Rapids, 49504.* Tel: 616-458-3213. Rev. THOMAS F. BOUFFORD, Ionia, *531 Jordan Lake St., Lake Odessa, 48849.* Tel: 616-374-7253. Rev. THOMAS C. NIEDZWIECKI, Ludington, *1 Oak St., P.O. Box 155, Irons, 49644.* Tel: 616-266-5155. Rev. RICHARD J. VAN LENTE, Montague, *510 Iroquois, Fremont, 49412.* Tel: 616-924-0160. Rev. JAMES WYSE, Muskegon, *1292 Jefferson St., Muskegon, 49441-2027.* Tel: 616-722-2793.

Presbyteral Council—Rev. ROBERT L. PINKSTON, C.S.P., *246 Ionia N.W., Grand Rapids, 49503.* Tel: 616-459-7267.

Finance Council—Most Rev. ROBERT J. ROSE, *660 Burton St., S.E., Grand Rapids, 49507.* Tel: 616-243-0491.

Vicar For Religious—Vacant.

Catholic Services Appeal—660 Burton St., S.E., Grand Rapids, 49507. Tel: 616-243-0491.

Tribunal Office—Rev. DENNIS A. WAGNER, Officialis, *265 Sheldon Ave., S.E., Grand Rapids, 49503.* Tel: 616-459-4509.

Vicar For Priests—Rev. DONALD E. WEBER, *1630 Godfrey S.W., Wyoming, 49509.* Tel: 616-241-6489.

Moderator of the Curia—Rev. Msgr. TERRENCE L. STEWART, *660 Burton St., S.E., Grand Rapids, 49507.* Tel: 616-243-0491.

Secretariat for Christian Life and Ministry Formation

Secretary—Rev. RICHARD J. LAWIE, *600 Burton St., S.E., Grand Rapids, 49507.* Tel: 616-243-0491.

Bishop Baraga Bookstore and Religious Education Resource Center—MARGARET A. DEVITO, Coord. Tel: 616-245-2251.

Youth, Young Adult and Family—Vacant.

Worship and Spirituality—Vacant.

Theology, Curriculum, Methods—Vacant.

Permanent Diaconate—Rev. RICHARD J. LAWIE.

Christopher House—Rev. MICHAEL DANNER, *723 Rosewood Ave., S.E., East Grand Rapids, 49506.* Tel: 616-243-6538.

Continuing Formation of Priests and Vocation Director—Rev. MICHAEL DANNER, Dir., *600 Burton St., S.E., Grand Rapids, 49507.* Tel: 616-243-0491.

Pastoral Council Formation—Rev. DENNIS A. WAGNER, Dir.

Secretariat of Diocesan Schools

Secretary—JAMES O'DONNELL.

Supt. of Schools—JAMES O'DONNELL, *600 Burton St., S.E., Grand Rapids, 49507.* Tel: 616-243-0491.

Associate Supt.—CHRISTINE BURNS.

Secretariat for Social Justice

Secretary—JAMES RADEMAKER, Dir., *650 Burton St., S.E., Grand Rapids, 49507.* Tel: 616-243-0491.

Catholic Social Services, Grand Rapids—RICHARD V. LIBERATORE, Exec. Dir., *1152 Scribner N.W., Grand Rapids, 49504.* Tel: 616-456-1443.

Catholic Social Services, Muskegon—ROBERT H. MILLS, Exec. Dir., *Suite 125, 1095 Third St., Muskegon, 49441.* Tel: 616-726-4735.

Catholic Human Development Outreach—JOHN OTT, Exec. Dir., *650 Burton St., S.E., Grand Rapids, 49507.* Tel: 616-248-3030.

Christian Community Center—540 E. Hackley, Muskegon, 49444. Tel: 616-725-7579.

Rose Haven Ministry—650 Burton S.E., Grand Rapids, 49507. Tel: 616-246-6445.

Office of Social Justice—650 Burton St., S.E., Grand Rapids, 49507. Tel: 616-243-0491.

Bishops Overseas Appeal—

Catholic Relief Services—

Project Rachel—650 Burton St., S.E., Grand Rapids, 49507.

Office of Black Catholic Ministry—WILLIAM L. RAWLINGS, Ph.D., Dir., *650 Burton St., S.E., Grand Rapids, 49507.* Tel: 616-248-3030.

Native American Ministry—SHARON DETZ, Staff Coord., *650 Burton St., S.E., Grand Rapids, 49507.* Tel: 616-248-3030.

Hispanic Ministry—LUIS BETETA, *650 Burton S.W., Grand Rapids, 49507.* Tel: 616-243-0491.

Vietnamese Ministry—Rev. PETER NGHIEM, *1653 Leestma, S.W., Wyoming, 49509.* Tel: 616-241-9148.

Prison/Jail Ministry—GERTRUDE STAWICK, Dir., *650 Burton St., S.E., Grand Rapids, 49507.* Tel: 616-243-0491.

Secretariat for Administration

Secretary—Sr. PATRICE KONWINSKI, O.P., *660 Burton St., S.E., Grand Rapids, 49507.* Tel: 616-243-0491.

Archivist—Rev. DENNIS W. MORROW, *660 Burton St., S.E., Grand Rapids, 49507.* Tel: 616-243-0491.

Building and Planning Committee—Sr. PATRICE KONWINSKI, O.P., *660 Burton St., S.E., Grand Rapids, 49507.* Tel: 616-243-0491.

Cemeteries—Rev. JAMES C. CUSACK, *660 Burton St., S.E., Grand Rapids, 49507.* Tel: 616-243-0491. Resurrection Cemetery: ROBERT R. MENZEL, Mgr., *Res., 4100 Clyde Park, S.W., Grand Rapids, 49509.* Tel: 616-531-9320.

Director of Finance—JOHN S. CZACHORSKI, *660 Burton St., S.E., Grand Rapids, 49507.* Tel: 616-243-0491.

Self-Insurance Program—Sr. PATRICE KONWINSKI, O.P., *660 Burton St., S.E., Grand Rapids, 49507.* Tel: 616-243-0491.

Tribunal—Rev. DENNIS A. WAGNER, Officialis, *265 Sheldon, S.E., Grand Rapids, 49503.* Tel: 616-459-4509.

Council of Catholic Women—ARLENE THOMAS, *650 Burton St., S.E., Grand Rapids, 49507.* Tel: 616-243-0491.

Ecumenical Commission—Rev. CHARLES R. DAUTREMONT, *150 E. Summit St., Muskegon Hts., 49444.* Tel: 616-733-2440.

Hospital Apostolate—Rev. EUGENE S. GOLAS, Chap., *Res., 2110 Leonard, N.E., Grand Rapids, 49505.* Tel: 616-242-4832. Rev. MARK E. MITCHELL, Assoc. Chap., *Res., 628 Diamond N.E., Grand Rapids, 49503.* Tel: 616-242-4832.

Director of Communications and Stewardship/Development—KATHERINE KEATING.

CLERGY, PARISHES, MISSIONS AND PAROCHIAL SCHOOLS

CITY OF GRAND RAPIDS
(Kent County)

1—CATHEDRAL OF ST. ANDREW, Rev. M. Thomas Bolster.
Res., 267 Sheldon Ave., S.E., 49503. Tel: 616-456-1454. [CEM]
School—305 Sheldon Ave., S.E., 49503.
Sisters 3; Lay Teachers 13; Students 214.
Catechesis/Religious Programs—Karen Noguera, D.R.E.
Students 182.

2—BASILICA OF ST. ADALBERT (Polish), Rev. Thomas J. DeYoung.
Res., Box 1, Basilica Center, 671 Davis, N.W., 49504-5137. Tel: 616-458-3065; Fax: 616-458-3065. [JC]
School—640 Fifth St., N.W., 49504. Tel: 616-459-7988; Fax: 616-459-9619.
Sisters 1; Lay Teachers 10; Students 120.

3—ST. ALPHONSUS, Revs. Daniel L. Lowery, C.SS.R.; Bernard Rooney, C.SS.R.; Bernie Carlin, C.SS.R.; Rudy Papes, C.SS.R.; Thomas O'Connor, C.SS.R.; Robert Balser, C.SS.R.; Patrick Grile, C.SS.R.
Res., 224 Carrier St., N.E., 49505. Tel: 616-451-3043. [JC]
School—228 Carrier St., N.E., 49505. Tel: 616-454-4904.
Sisters 1; Lay Teachers 20; Students 375.
Catechesis/Religious Programs—Lucio Caruso, D.R.E.
Students 240.

4—ST. ANTHONY OF PADUA, Revs. Edmund Goldbach, O.F.M.Conv.; John Raphael Hadnagy, O.F.M. Conv.; Sr. Eileen Golos, O.S.F., Pastoral Min. In res., Rev. Raymond Oosdyke, O.F.M.Conv.
Res., 2510 Richmond St., N.W., 49504. Tel: 616-453-8229; Fax: 616-453-8053.
School—Tel: 616-453-4062.
Lay Teachers 15; Students 334.
Catechesis/Religious Programs—Tel: 616-453-6647. Cecilia Rinkevich, D.R.E.
Students 300.

5—BLESSED SACRAMENT, Rev. John J. Wisneski; Deacon George LeMire.
Res., 2275 Diamond Ave. N.E., 49505-4313. Tel: 616-361-7339; Fax: 616-361-1327. [JC]
School—2233 Diamond N.E., 49505-4313. Tel: 616-364-9453.
Lay Teachers 25; Students 410.

6—ST. FRANCIS XAVIER, Rev. Charles R. Antekeier.
Res., 250 Brown St. S.E., 49507. Tel: 616-241-2485; Fax: 616-241-2079. [JC]
School—240 Brown St. S.E., 49507. Tel: 616-241-5474. Sr. Winifred Wheeler, S.J., Prin.
Lay Teachers 14; Students 186.
Convent—(Detroit Prov.) 245 Griggs S.E., 49507. Tel: 616-245-9279. Sisters of Mercy

7—HOLY NAME OF JESUS, Rev. Donald E. Weber.
Res., 1630 Godfrey Ave. S.W., 49509. Tel: 616-241-6489; Fax: 616-241-6480. [JC]
School—1650 Godfrey Ave. S.W., 49509. Tel: 616-243-1126. Sr. Adele Labiotka, Prin.
Sisters 1; Lay Teachers 12; Students 170.

8—HOLY SPIRIT, Revs. Leonard Sudlik; Ronald Hutchinson; Daryl E. Nowicki, Business Mgr.
Res., 2230 Lake Michigan Dr. N.W., 49504. Tel: 616-453-6369; Fax: 616-453-0244.
School—Lay Teachers 27; Students 564.
Catechesis/Religious Programs—Tel: 616-453-1591. Patricia Frisk, D.R.E.
Students 260.

9—IMMACULATE HEART OF MARY, Revs. Julian Reginato; Peter Vu; Deacon Virgil Glocheski.
Res., 1935 Plymouth Rd. S.E., 49506. Tel: 616-241-4477; Fax: 616-241-2832.
School—Lay Teachers 20; Students 489.
Catechesis/Religious Programs—Tel: 616-241-0863. Teri D'Orazio, D.R.E.
Students 150.

10—ST. ISIDORE'S (Polish), Rev. Donald E. Lomasiewicz.
Res., 628 Diamond Ave. N.E., 49503. Tel: 616-459-4731; Fax: 616-454-5832. [JC]
School—625 Spring Ave. N.E., 49503. Tel: 616-454-1236.
Lay Teachers 12; Students 155.

11—ST. JAMES, Rev. Steven D. Cron; Norm Szubinski, Pastoral Assoc.
Res., 733 Bridge St. N.W., 49504. Tel: 616-458-3213; Fax: 616-458-9002.
School—751 First St. N.W., 49504. Tel: 616-454-2567.
Lay Teachers 13; Students 195.

12—ST. JOHN VIANNEY, Revs. Larry King; Chris Rouech.
Res., 4135 Clyde Park S.W., 49509. Tel: 616-534-5449; Fax: 616-530-8224. [JC]
School—Harry Hudson, Prin. Lay Teachers 20; Students 449.
Catechesis/Religious Programs—Tel: 616-530-8224; 532-2397. Mark Kranenberg, D.R.E.
Students 300.

13—ST. JOSEPH THE WORKER, Rev. Pedro V. Garcia.
Res., 333 Rumsey St., S.W., 49503-4935. Tel: 616-456-7982; Fax: 616-456-1445.

14—ST. DOMINIC, Rev. Charles R. Dautremont.
Office: 50 Bellevue, S.W., 49548-3144. Tel: 616-531-1480; Fax: 616-531-0759.
Res., 59 Thurston, S.W., 49548-3163.
Catechesis/Religious Programs—Students 100.

15—ST. JUDE, Rev. Thomas S. Vesbit.
Office: 1120 Four Mile N.E., 49505. Tel: 616-363-6885.
School—Lay Teachers 18; Students 255.
Catechesis/Religious Programs—1110 Four Mile N.E., 49505. Tel: 616-363-6897.
Students 372.

16—ST. MARY'S, Rev. Dick Host.
Res., 423 First St., N.W., 49504. Tel: 616-459-7390; Fax: 616-459-9630.
Catechesis/Religious Programs—Tel: 616-451-4215. Dick Bulkowski, D.R.E.
Students 46.

17—ST. MARY MAGDALEN, Revs. Louis L. Anderson; Loc Trinh; Sr. Beverly Pety, O.P., Pastoral Assoc.; Deacon Michael L. Wood.
Res., 1213 52nd St., S.E., 49508. Tel: 616-455-9310; Fax: 616-455-4139.
Catechesis/Religious Programs—Students 535.

18—OUR LADY OF SORROWS (Italian), Rev. Theodore Kozlowski.
Res., 101 Hall St., S.E., 49507. Tel: 616-243-0222.
Catechesis/Religious Programs—Joseph Amante, D.R.E.
Students 75.

19—ST. PAUL THE APOSTLE, Rev. R. Louis Stasker.
Res., 2750 Burton St., S.E., 49546. Tel: 616-949-4170; Fax: 616-949-5295.
School—Tel: 616-949-1690.
Lay Teachers 17; Students 260.
Catechesis/Religious Programs—Beth Kolenda, D.R.E.
Students 165.

20—SS. PETER AND PAUL'S (Lithuanian), Rev. Dennis Morrow. In res., Rev. Joseph J. Pettit, (Retired).
Res., 520 Myrtle St., N.W., 49504. Tel: 616-454-6000. [CEM]
School—1433 Hamilton Ave., N.W., 49504. Mrs. Nancy Kryger, Prin.
Sisters of St. Francis of the Providence of God 2; Lay Teachers 10; Students 183.
Catechesis/Religious Programs—Students 55.

21—SACRED HEART, Rev. Edward A. Hankiewicz; Sr. Marie Bernarde Salazar, O.P., Pastoral Assoc. In res., Rev. Msgr. James P. Moran, P.A.
Res., 156 Valley Ave., S.W., 49504. Tel: 616-459-8362. [JC]
School—Tel: 616-459-0948; Fax: 616-459-0899. Richard E. Kosla, Prin.
Lay Teachers 14; Students 192.
Catechesis/Religious Programs—Mrs. Mary Ann Cichewicz, D.R.E.
Students 64.

22—ST. STEPHEN'S, Rev. Mark C. Przybysz.
Res., 750 Gladstone Ave., S.E., 49506. Tel: 616-243-8998; Fax: 616-243-8998. [JC]

School—740 Rosewood Ave., S.E., 49506. Tel: 616-243-9013; Fax: 616-243-0451. Nannette Swanson, Prin.
Lay Teachers 12; Students 270.
Catechesis/Religious Programs—Tel: 616-243-9012. Mrs. Rhonda Lomonaco, D.R.E.
Students 284.

23—St. Thomas the Apostle, Rev. James A. Chelick.
Res., 1449 Wilcox Park Dr., S.E., 49506. Tel: 616-459-4662; Fax: 616-458-4047. [JC]
School—Tel: 616-458-4228; Fax: 616-458-4583. David A. Faber, Prin.
Sisters of the Third Order of St. Dominic 3; Lay Teachers 10; Students 311.

OUTSIDE THE CITY OF GRAND RAPIDS

Ada, Kent Co., St. Robert, Rev. Msgr. Ernest P. Schneider; Rev. James C. Kowalski. Pastoral Assocs.: Sr. Joan Brown, O.P.; Sr. Ann Michael Farnsworth, O.P.; Dorothy Powell.
Res., 49301. Tel: 616-676-9111; Fax: 616-676-9112.
Catechesis/Religious Programs—Tel: 616-676-1488. Mary Ann Snyder, D.R.E.
Students 1,062.

Alpine, Kent Co., Holy Trinity, Rev. Daniel R. DePew.
Res., 1200 Alpine Church Rd., N.W., 49321. Tel: 616-784-0677.
School—Comstock Park, 49321. Tel: 616-784-0696. Julie Whelan, Prin.
Lay Teachers 8; Students 200.
Catechesis/Religious Programs—Eric Egeler, D.R.E.
Students 235.

Baldwin, Lake Co., St. Ann's, Rev. Joseph J. Fix.
Res., 740 E. Ninth St., 49304. Tel: 616-745-7997.
Mission—Luther, St. Ignatius.

Belding, Ionia Co., St. Joseph's, Rev. George E. Darling.
Office: 409 S. Bridge St., 48809. Tel: 616-794-2145; Fax: 616-794-0930. [CEM]
School—St. Joseph-St. Mary, Tel: 616-794-1910. Kathy Rand, Prin.
Lay Teachers 4; Students 75.

Belmont, Kent Co., Assumption of the Blessed Virgin Mary, Rev. James M. Bozung, Admin.
Res., 6369 Belmont Ave., 49306. Tel: 616-361-5126; Fax: 616-361-5503. [CEM]
School—6393 Belmont Ave., 49306. Tel: 616-361-5483; Fax: 616-361-2553. Sr. Rosemary Smith, R.S.M., Prin.
Lay Teachers 9; Students 220.

Big Rapids, Mecosta Co., St. Mary's, Rev. Michael G. McKenna.
1009 Marion Ave., 49307. Tel: 616-796-5202; Fax: 616-796-9231. [CEM 2]
School—Robert C. King, Prin. Sisters 2; Lay Teachers 9; Students 145.
Catechesis/Religious Programs—Students 49.
St. Paul's Campus Parish, Rev. Thomas P. Page.
Res., One Damascus Rd., 49307. Tel: 616-796-7393; Fax: 616-796-3990.
Catechesis/Religious Programs—Students 156.

Brunswick, Newaygo Co., St. Michael's, Rev. Donn P. Tufts.
Res., 10224 Maple Island Rd., R.R. #5, Fremont, 49412. Tel: 616-924-3389; 924-9803. [CEM]
School—Tel: 616-924-0268. Sr. M. Theresa Pelky, R.S.M.
Sisters 4; Lay Teachers 1; Students 82.
Catechesis/Religious Programs—Students 102.
Mission—Hesperia, Christ the King.

Byron Center, Kent Co., St. Sebastian's, Rev. Msgr. Gaspar F. Ancona.
Res., 9408 Wilson, 49315. Tel: 616-878-1893; Fax: 616-878-4019. [CEM]
Catechesis/Religious Programs—Theresa Dekker, D.R.E.
Students 132.

Caledonia, Kent Co., Holy Family, Rev. David E. LeBlanc.
Res., 9669 Kraft Ave., S.E., 49316. Tel: 616-891-1160; 891-9259 (Office); Fax: 616-891-1346. [CEM]
Catechesis/Religious Programs—Tel: 616-891-8867. Judy France, D.R.E.
Students 495.

Carson City, Montcalm Co., St. Mary's, Rev. William J. Reitz.
Res., 404 N. Division St., 48811. Tel: 517-584-3553. [CEM]
Catechesis/Religious Programs—Tel: 517-981-6668. Kathleen Copp, D.R.E.
Students 70.

Conklin, Ottawa Co., St. Francis Xavier, Rev. John F. Porter.
Res., 2044 Gooding Rd., 49403. Tel: 616-899-2471; Fax: 616-853-2191.

Coopersville, Ottawa Co., St. Michael's, Rev. Mark F. Bauer.
Res., 17151 88th Ave., 49404. Tel: 616-837-8792; 837-8158 (Parish Office); Fax: 616-837-7893.
School—Tel: 616-837-6346. Wendy Sipka, Prin.
Lay Teachers 6; Students 106.

Custer, Mason Co., St. Mary's, Rev. William F. McKnight.
Res., 85 S. Madison, P.O. Box 68, 49405. Tel: 616-757-4709. [CEM]
Catechesis/Religious Programs—Tel: 616-757-3078. Roberta Edel, D.R.E.
Students 86.
Mission—Round Lake, St. Joseph.

Edmore, Montcalm Co., St. Margaret Mary, Rev. Vincent Bryce, O.P.
Res., 1051 E. Howard City Rd., 48829. Tel: 517-427-5645; Fax: 517-427-3268.

Evart, Osceola Co., Sacred Heart, Rev. Rock J. Badgerow.
Res., 9878 E. US 10, P.O. Box 778, 49631. Tel: 616-734-3171; Fax: 616-734-6880.

Free Soil, Mason Co., St. John Cantius, Rev. Isidro T. Gargantiel (Philippines).
Res., 2845 E. Michigan, 49411-9602. Tel: 616-464-5672. [CEM]
Catechesis/Religious Programs—Tel: 616-464-5567. Mary Kovalcik, D.R.E.
Students 65.

Fremont, Newaygo Co., All Saints, Rev. Richard J. Van Lente.
Res., 510 Iroquois Dr., P.O. Box 248, 49412. Tel: 616-924-0160; Fax: 616-924-0996.
Catechesis/Religious Programs—Students 135.

Grand Haven, Ottawa Co., St. Patrick's, Rev. William A. Langlois; Deacons Dale Hollern; Richard Fett.
Res., 920 Fulton St., 49417. Tel: 616-842-0001.
Catechesis/Religious Programs—Tel: 616-842-8230. William Dunn, D.R.E.
Students 303.
Mission—Robinson Township, St. Anthony, 13421 Green St., 49417.

Grandville, Kent Co., St. Pius X, Rev. Msgr. John A. Najdowski.
Res., 3937 Wilson Ave., S.W., 49418. Tel: 616-532-9344; Fax: 616-538-6340.
Catechesis/Religious Programs—Linda Vanden Berg, D.R.E.
Students 659.

Greenville, Montcalm Co., St. Charles, Rev. Thomas A. McKinney.
Res., 102 W. Oak, 48838. Tel: 616-754-4194; Fax: 616-754-2857. [CEM]
School—501 S. Franklin St., 48838. Tel: 616-754-3196; Fax: 616-754-9262. Sr. David Therese Korson, O.P., Prin.
Sisters of St. Dominic, Grand Rapids, MI 1; Lay Teachers 8; Students 140.
Catechesis/Religious Programs—Diane Hamel, D.R.E.
Students 147.
Mission—Harvard, Kent Co., St. Margaret, 10195 16 Mile Rd., Cedar Springs, 49319. Tel: 616-696-3904. [CEM]

Hart, Oceana Co., St. Gregory's, Rev. Ronald F. Schneider.
Res., 316 Peach St., 49420. Tel: 616-873-2660.
Catechesis/Religious Programs—Linda Foster, D.R.E.
Students 113.
Mission—Elbridge, St. Joseph Church.

Holland, Ottawa Co., St. Francis de Sales, Revs. Stephen S. Dudek; Jose Luis Quintana; Sr. M. Therese Harum, I.H.M., Pastoral Assoc.; Deacon Juan Garcia.
Office: 195 W. 13th St., 49423. Tel: 616-396-7641; Fax: 616-392-2474.
Res., 284 Maple Ave., 49423. Tel: 616-392-3985.
School—183 W. Thirteenth St., 49423. Tel: 616-396-4725. Mitre Zainea, Prin.
Lay Teachers 13; Students 233.
Catechesis/Religious Programs—195 1/2 W. 13th St., 49423. Tel: 616-392-6700. Marilyn Torborg, D.R.E.
Students 671.
Our Lady of the Lake, Rev. William H. Duncan.
Res., 480 152nd Ave., 49424. Tel: 616-399-1062; Fax: 616-399-5766.
Catechesis/Religious Programs—Mark E. Peacock, D.R.E.
Students 629.

Howard City, Montcalm Co., Christ the King, Rev. Phong Q. Pham.
Res., 9596 Reed Rd., 49329. Tel: 616-937-5757; Fax: 616-937-9268.
Catechesis/Religious Programs—Katherine P. Miller, D.R.E.
Students 100.

Hubbardston, Ionia Co., St. John the Baptist, Rev. William J. Reitz.
Res., 404 N. Division, Carson City, 48811. Tel: 517-584-3553. [CEM]
Catechesis/Religious Programs—Kathleen Copp, D.R.E.
Students 70.

Ionia, Ionia Co., SS. Peter and Paul, Rev. Melvin E. Fox; Deacon Zenon Cardenas, Sr.
Parish Office: 434 High St., 48846. Tel: 616-527-3610; Fax: 616-527-3611. [CEM]
School—317 Baldie, 48846. Tel: 616-527-3561; Fax: 616-527-3562.
Lay Teachers 11; Students 248.

Irons, Lake Co., St. Bernard's, Rev. Thomas C. Niedzwicki.
Res., One Oak St., P.O. Box 155, 49644. Tel: 616-266-5155; Fax: 616-266-8948.
Catechesis/Religious Programs—Students 16.

Jenison, Ottawa Co., Holy Redeemer, Rev. Denis P. Nash.
Res., 2700 Baldwin Dr., 49428. Tel: 616-669-9220; Fax: 616-669-9360.
Catechesis/Religious Programs—Tel: 616-669-0820. Therese Carroll, D.R.E.
Students 612.

Lake Odessa, Ionia Co., St. Edward's, Rev. Thomas F. Boufford.
Res., 531 Jordan Lake St., 48849-6200. Tel: 616-374-7253; Fax: 616-374-1559.
Catechesis/Religious Programs—Dee Manshum, D.R.E.
Students 110.

Lakeview, Montcalm Co., St. Francis de Sales, Rev. Phong Q. Pham.
Res., 9596 N. Reed Rd., Howard City, 49329.
Church—829 E. Richardson, 48850. Tel: 517-352-7293.
Catechesis/Religious Programs—Katherine Miller, D.R.E., Tel: 616-937-5757.
Students 80.

Lakewood Club, Muskegon Co., St. Mary of the Woods, Rev. Henry J. Dondzila.
Res., 150 Church St., Twin Lake, 49457. Tel: 616-894-5887.

Lowell, Kent Co., St. Mary's, Rev. George J. Fekete; Deacon John Paroff.
Res., 402 Amity St., 49331-1308. Tel: 616-897-9820. [CEM]
Catechesis/Religious Programs—Maggie Walsh, D.R.E.
Students 132.

Ludington, Mason Co., St. Simon's, Rev. Kenneth H. Schichtel.
Res., 702 E. Bryant Rd., 49431. Tel: 616-843-8606; Fax: 616-843-2052. [CEM]
School—Cindy Bollman, Prin. Lay Teachers 10; Students 173.
St. Stanislaus, Rev. Dennis O'Donnell.
Res., 503 Third St., 49431. Tel: 616-845-7666. [JC]

Marion, Osceola Co., St. Agnes, Rev. Rock J. Badgerow.
Res., P.O. Box 778, Evart, 49631. Tel: 616-734-3171.
Church—Tel: 616-743-6401; Fax: 616-734-6880.

Marne, Ottawa Co., St. Mary's, Rev. Msgr. Terrence L. Stewart; Sr. Bernadine Gazda, S.S.J., Pastoral Assoc.
Res., 15164 Juniper Dr., 49435. Tel: 616-677-3934; Fax: 616-677-5866. [CEM]
Catechesis/Religious Programs—Students 174.

Miriam, Ionia Co., St. Mary's, Rev. George E. Darling.
Office: 409 S. Bridge St., Belding, 48809. Tel: 616-794-2145. [CEM]
School—St. Joseph-St. Mary. See St. Joseph, Belding. 616-794-1910.

Montague, Muskegon Co., St. James, Rev. Thomas A. Schiller.
Res., 5179 Dowling St., 49437. Tel: 616-893-3085; Fax: 616-894-9929. [CEM]
School—Tel: 616-893-2972. Mitzi Luttrull, Prin.
Lay Teachers 6; Students 87.
Catechesis/Religious Programs—Tel: 616-894-8771. Joyce Richards, D.R.E.
Students 200.
Mission—Claybanks, St. John.

Muskegon, Muskegon Co.,

1—Our Lady of Grace, Rev. Michael P. Olson; Michael A. Pehar, Jr., Pastoral Assoc.
Res., 451 S. Getty St., 49442. Tel: 616-722-2803; Fax: 616-722-3622. [JC]
Catechesis/Religious Programs—Students 80.

2—St. Francis de Sales, Revs. Thomas G. Simons; Phillip A. Sliwinski; Deacon William McCabe.
Res., 2929 McCracken St., 49441. Tel: 616-755-1953; Fax: 616-759-7074.
Catechesis/Religious Programs—Tel: 616-755-1307. Suzanne Southworth, D.R.E.
Students 375.

3—St. Jean Baptiste, Rev. James B. Wyse; Michael Stacy, Pastoral Assoc.
Res., 1292 Jefferson St., 49441. Tel: 616-722-2793; Fax: 616-726-5976. [JC]

Catechesis/Religious Programs—Barbara Miles, D.R.E.
Students 130.

4—St. Joseph's, Rev. John A. Johnson; Theresa Secord, D.R.E.
Res., 1224 Fifth St., 49441. Tel: 616-722-2556. [CEM]
Catechesis/Religious Programs—Students 80.

5—St. Mary's, Rev. John A. Johnson.
Res., 239 W. Clay Ave., 49440-1213. Tel: 616-722-2844; Fax: 616-722-0733. [JC]

6—St. Michael's, Rev. Thomas J. Hack.
Res., 1716 Sixth St., 49441. Tel: 616-722-3071. [JC]
Catechesis/Religious Programs—Sr. Agnes Mary Wojtkowiak, O.P., D.R.E.
Students 480.

7—St. Thomas the Apostle, Rev. Phillip J. Witkowski; Deacon David Kasprzyk.
Office: 3252 Apple Ave., 49442. Tel: 616-773-3160; Fax: 616-777-7866.
Catechesis/Religious Programs—Students 151.

Muskegon Heights, Muskegon Co., Sacred Heart, Rev. Norman P. Droski.
Res., 150 E. Summit Ave., 49444. Tel: 616-733-2440.
School—Lay Teachers 5; Students 105.
Convent—2900 Leahy St., 49444.

Newaygo, Newaygo Co., St. Bartholomew's, Rev. Paul A. Milanowski; Sr. Jean Marie Wojtas, S.J., Pastoral Min.
Res., 599 Brooks St., 49337. Tel: 616-652-1286; Fax: 616-652-6669. [CEM]
Catechesis/Religious Programs—Janet Vile, D.R.E.
Students 223.
Mission—Grant, Our Lady of Guadalupe Church.

North Muskegon, Muskegon Co., Prince of Peace, Rev. Robert A. Hart. Pastoral Assocs.: Sr. Judie Schuett, S.J.; Deacons Wesley Hewitt; Simon Rodriguez.
Res., 1110 Dykstra, 49445. Tel: 616-744-3321; Fax: 616-744-4859.
Catechesis/Religious Programs—Sandra Finkelstein, D.R.E.
Students 422.

Parnell, Kent Co., St. Patrick's, Rev. Wayne B. Wheeler, Jr.; Sr. Bonita Janiszewski, Pastoral Assoc.
Res., 4351 Parnell Ada, 49301. Tel: 616-691-8541; Fax: 616-691-6309. [CEM]
School—Mr. Thomas O'Brien, Prin. Students 190.

Pewamo, Ionia Co., St. Joseph's, Rev. Charlon O. Mason, Admin.
Res., 106 East St., 48873. Tel: 517-593-3440. [CEM]
School—Tel: 517-593-3400. Sr. Mary Catherine Quick, Prin.
Lay Teachers 5; Students 85.

Portland, Ionia Co., St. Patrick's, Revs. Charles D. Hall; Troy Nevins.
Res., 140 Church St., 48875. Tel: 517-647-6505; Fax: 517-647-7807.
School—122 West St., 48875. Tel: 517-647-7551.
Lay Teachers 16; Students 190.
High School—Lay Teachers 14; Students 202.
Catechesis/Religious Programs—Nancy Gleason, D.R.E.
Students 223.

Ravenna, Muskegon Co., St. Catherine, Rev. John F. Porter.
Res., 49451. Tel: 616-853-6222; Fax: 616-853-2191. [CEM]
School—Sr. Peter Mary Korson, O.P., Prin. Sisters 1; Lay Teachers 3; Students 58.
Catechesis/Religious Programs—Students 70.

Reed City, Osceola Co., St. Philip Neri, Rev. Daniel C. Aerts.
Res., 831 S. Chestnut, 49677. Tel: 616-832-5544; Fax: 616-832-5545. [CEM]
Catechesis/Religious Programs—Elizabeth Marek, D.R.E.
Students 136.
Mission—Paris, Mecosta Co., St. Anne.

Remus, Mecosta Co., St. Michael's, Rev. William F. Zink.
Res., 5045 Nine Mile Rd., 49340. Tel: 517-967-3520; Fax: 517-967-8246. [CEM]
School—(Grades PreK-6). Mr. Robert Cathcart, Prin.
Sisters 3; Lay Teachers 8; Students 180.
Catechesis/Religious Programs—Tel: 517-967-3681.
Students 120.

Rockford, Kent Co., Our Lady of Consolation, Most Rev. Joseph C. McKinney; Mary Ellen Koziol, Pastoral Assoc.
Office: 5001 Eleven Mile Rd., 49341. Tel: 616-866-0931; Fax: 616-866-3668.
School—(Grades PreK-6). Tel: 616-866-2427. Carolyn Hardy, Prin.
Lay Teachers 8; Students 166.
Catechesis/Religious Programs—Tammy Graves, D.R.E.
Students 582.

Rothbury, Oceana Co., Our Lady of the Assumption, Rev. John F. Vallier.
Res., 1372 S. Oceana Dr., Shelby, 49455. Tel: 616-861-2620.
Church—3000 Winston Rd., 49452. Tel: 616-893-0905.

Sand Lake, Kent Co., Mary Queen of Apostles, Rev. Joseph W. Kenshol.
Res., P.O. Box 140, 49343. Tel: 616-636-5671; Fax: 616-636-4570. [CEM]
Catechesis/Religious Programs—Pat Patin, D.R.E.
Students 224.
Mission—Coral, St. Clara.

Saranac, Ionia Co., St. Anthony, Rev. Norbert L. Leyrita (Phillipines).
Res., 3927 Jackson Rd., 48881. Tel: 616-642-6119.
Catechesis/Religious Programs—Tel: 616-642-6402. D.R.E.: Janice Diaz; Monty Simpson; Sharon Basset.
Students 107.

Scottville, Mason Co., St. Jerome, Rev. Isidro T. Gargantiel.
Res., 203 W. State St., 49454. Tel: 616-757-2855.
Catechesis/Religious Programs—Kathy Papes, D.R.E.
Students 84.

Shelby, Oceana Co., Our Lady of Fatima, Rev. John F. Vallier.
Res., 1372 S. Oceana Dr., 49455. Tel: 616-861-2620.
Catechesis/Religious Programs—Paula Michalko, D.R.E.
Students 62.

Sparta, Kent Co., Holy Family, Rev. Philip A. Shangraw.
Res., 425 S. State St., 49345. Tel: 616-887-8222.
Catechesis/Religious Programs—Students 242.

Spring Lake, Ottawa Co., St. Mary's, Rev. Anthony C. Vainavicz.
Res., 406 E. Savidge, 49456. Tel: 616-842-1702; Fax: 616-842-3392.
School—Sr. Mary Lou Houghton, O.P., Prin. Dominican Sisters 3; Lay Teachers 11; Students 215.
Catechesis/Religious Programs—Tel: 616-842-2840. Peggy Secory, D.R.E.
Students 370.
Convent—421 E. Exchange St., 49456.

Stanton, Montcalm Co., St. Bernadette of Lourdes, Rev. Vincent Bryce, O.P.
Res., 1051 E. Howard City, Edmore, 48829. Tel: 517-427-5645; Fax: 517-427-3268.

Weare Twp., Oceana Co., St. Joseph's, Rev. Charles D. Brown.
Res., 2380 W. Jackson Rd., Hart, 49420. Tel: 616-873-2683. [CEM]
Mission—Pentwater, St. Vincent, Tel: 616-869-2601.

White Cloud, Newaygo Co., St. Joseph's, Rev. Richard J. VanLente.
Res., 965 Newell St., 49349. Tel: 616-689-6061. [CEM]

Wright Township, Ottawa Co., St. Joseph's, Rev. Leo S. Rosloniec.
Res., 18876 Eighth Ave., Conklin, 49403. Tel: 616-899-2286; Fax: 616-899-2212.
School—Tel: 616-899-5300; Fax: 616-899-5491. Mrs. Ann Rutowski, Prin.
Dominican Sisters 2; Lay Teachers 4; Students 89.

CHAPELS

Grand Rapids. *Chapel of Our Lady of Aglona, Latvian Apostolate*, 507 Broadway Ave., N.W., 49504. Tel: 616-454-5921.

Chapel of St. Paul-Catholic Information Center, 246 Ionia, N.W., 49503. Tel: 616-459-7267. Revs. Robert L. Pinkston, C.S.P.; Robert Sirico, C.S.P.; Joseph W. Gallagher, C.S.P.; Michael Martin, C.S.P.; Deacon Elmer Zinn; Sr. Carmen Rostar, O.P.

Michigan Veterans' Facility Catholic Chapel, 3000 Monroe Ave., N.E., 49505. Tel: 616-363-2691.

On Special Assignment:
Reverend Monsignors—
Stewart, Terrence L., Moderator of the Curia & Vicar Gen., 660 Burton, S.E., Grand Rapids, MI 49507. Tel: 616-243-0491
Reverend Fathers—
Bolster, M. Thomas, In charge of Hispanic Community, Our Lady of Guadalupe, 267 Sheldon S.E., Grand Rapids, MI 49503. Tel: 616-456-1454
Danner, Michael A., Dir. Continuing Formation of Priests, Dir. Vocations & Dir. Christopher House, Christopher House, 723 Rosewood, S.E., Grand Rapids, MI 45906. Tel: 616-243-6538
Darling, George E., Rural Life Dir., 409 S. Bridge St., Belding, MI 48809. Tel: 616-794-2145
Dudek, Stephen S., Assoc. Dir. Hispanic Apostolate, Res., 3252 Apple Ave., Muskegon, MI 49442. Tel: 616-777-1621
Duncan, William H., Asst. Chancellor, 660 Burton S.E., Grand Rapids, MI 49507. Tel: 616-243-0491
Fekete, George J., Dir. Missions, 402 Amity, Lowell, MI 49331. Tel: 616-897-9820
Golas, Eugene S., Chap., Blodgett & Butterworth Hospitals, 2110 Leonard, N.E., Rm. 416, Grand Rapids, MI 49505. Tel: 616-242-4732
Hankiewicz, Edward, Tribunal Office. Tel: 616-459-4509
Heydens, Donald J., Tribunal Office. Tel: 616-459-4509
Lawie, Richard J., Dir. Secretariat for Christian Life and Ministry Formation, 660 Burton, S.E., Grand Rapids, MI 49507. Tel: 616-243-0491
Leyrita, Norbert L., Dir. Hispanic Ministry
Mitchell, Mark E., Assoc. Chap., Blodgett & Butterworth Hospitals, 628 Diamond N.E., Grand Rapids, MI 49503. Tel: 616-242-4832
Morrow, Dennis, Adjutant Judicial Vicar for the Tribunal; Diocesan Archivist; Chap. Grand Rapids Fire Dept. & Grand Rapids Police Dept.
Nghiem, Peter Hoan-Xuan, Dir. Vietnamese Apostolate, 1653 Leetsma S.W., Grand Rapids, MI 49509. Tel: 616-241-9148
Nguyen, Phillip D., Chap. U.S. Air Force
Page, Thomas P., Diocesan Coord. Campus Ministry, One Damascus Rd., Big Rapids, MI 49307
Porter, John, Officialis Diocesan Tribunal
Shangraw, Philip A., Coord. Planning & Direction Diocesan Third Millenium Prog.
Wagner, Dennis A., Officialis, Diocesan Tribunal Office, 265 Sheldon, S.E., Grand Rapids, MI 49503. Tel: 616-459-4509
Weber, Donald E., Vicar Priests

On Duty Outside the Diocese:
Reverend Fathers—
Cook, Daniel
Hartwig, Lawrence N.
Kurylowicz, Martin
Nguyen, Phillip D.
Turner, Robert

Retired:
Reverend Monsignors—
Brophy, Charles D., 1247 Rennslaer, N.W., Grand Rapids, MI 49504
Giammona, John J., 5916 Bayberry Farms Dr. #8, Grandville, MI 49418
Jude, Walter F., R.R. #2, Box 76-1, Irons, MI 49644
Moran, James P., 156 Valley S.W., Grand Rapids, MI 49504
Powers, William E., 3033 N.W. 33rd Ave., Fort Lauderdale, FL 33311
Sniegowski, Thaddeus R., 17885 Apple Ave., Casnovia, MI 49318
Zerfas, Herman H., 3888 44th St., S.W., Grandville, MI 49418
Reverend Fathers—
Allen, Joseph A., 1631 Ferdinand, Detroit, MI 48209
Alvesteffer, Eugene
Baudone, Louis
Bernott, Albert R., 1409 Quarry, N.W., Grand Rapids, MI 49504
Bernott, Ernest J.
Bielskas, Edward J., 4101 Clyde Park, S.W., Wyoming, MI 49509
Branigan, Francis H., 2110 E. Leonard, Apt. 214, Grand Rapids, MI 49505
Cawley, Patrick
Cusack, James C.
Farrell, Edmund J., 307 57th St. Ct., West Bradenton, FL 34209
Feltman, Harold R., 504 S.E. 14 Ter., Cape Coral, FL 33990
Flynn, Francis J., 1060 Becker Rd., North Muskegon, MI 49445
Gillespie, Robert B., 1305 Walker, N.W., Apt. 5315, Grand Rapids, MI 49504
Hall, Bernard
Hoogterp, M. James, 3278 Roosevelt Rd., Muskegon, MI 49442
Johnson, Paul T., 823 W. River Rd., North Muskegon, MI 49445
Kubiak, Edward J., 437 First St., N.W., Grand Rapids, MI 49504
Malewitz, Joseph M., 17444 A Dunewood Ct., Spring Lake, MI 49456
Ostrowski, Max J., 2044 Gooding Rd., Conklin, MI 49403
Pettit, Joseph J.
Plewka, Edwin J., 2161 Leonard, N.W., Grand Rapids, MI 49504
Statkus, Edward, 541 Broadway, Grand Rapids, MI 49504

Toolis, Martin, 3028 Piney Ridge Rd., Ludington, MI 49431

Wing, Kenneth A., 625 Lake Forest Ln., Apt. A5, Muskegon, MI 49441

Yager, James P., 3062 W. Leonard St., Grand Rapids, MI 49504

Permanent Deacons:

Cardenas, Zenon, SS. Peter and Paul, Ionia

Fett, Richard, Jail Ministry, Ottawa Co.

Garcia, Juan, St. Francis de Sales, Holland

Glocheski, Virgil, Immaculate Heart of Mary, Grand Rapids

Herrera, Manuel E., SS. Peter and Paul, Grand Rapids

Hewitt, Wesley, Prince of Peace, North Muskegon

Hollern, Dale, St. Patrick, Grand Haven

Jankowski, Leon, (Retired)

Jurek, Thomas, Basilica of St. Adalbert, Grand Rapids

Kasprzyk, David, St. Thomas the Apostle, Muskegon

LeMire, George, Blessed Sacrament, Grand Rapids

Mauer, Michael J., St. James, Grand Rapids

McCabe, William, St. Francis de Sales, Muskegon

McGinnity, Michael, All Saints, Fremont

Paroff, John, St. Mary, Lowell

Radecki, Richard, St. Paul the Apostle, Grand Rapids

Riksen, Norman, St. Pius X, Grandville

Rodriguez, Simon, Prince of Peace, North Muskegon

Scheid, Howard, St. Joseph, Belding

Wood, Michael, St. Mary Magdalen, Grand Rapids

Zinn, Elmer, Catholic Information Center, Grand Rapids

INSTITUTIONS LOCATED IN THE DIOCESE

[A] SEMINARY, DIOCESAN

GRAND RAPIDS. *Christopher House-College Department of St. Joseph's Seminary*, 723 Rosewood Ave., S.E., 49506. Tel: 616-243-6538. Rev. Michael A. Danner, Dir. Students 3.
Students attend area colleges.

[B] COLLEGES AND UNIVERSITIES

GRAND RAPIDS. *Aquinas College*, 1607 Robinson Rd., S.E., 49506. Tel: 616-459-8281
For a complete listing, refer to the Colleges and Universities section.

[C] HIGH SCHOOLS, DIOCESAN

GRAND RAPIDS. *Catholic Central High School*, 319 Sheldon Ave., S.E., 49503. Tel: 616-459-4559. Paul Guild, Prin.; Mr. Steve Passinault, Asst. Prin. Sisters of St. Dominic 2; Lay Teachers 46; Students 915.

West Catholic High School, 1801 Bristol, N.W., 49504. Tel: 616-453-4467. Mr. Bernard T. Stanko, Prin.; Mr. John Kolassa, Asst. Prin. Lay Teachers 32; Students 560.

MUSKEGON. *Muskegon Catholic Central Junior High and High School*. Greater Muskegon Catholic Schools. 1145 W. Laketon, 49441. Tel: 616-755-2201. Thomas Powers, Chief School Officer & Exec. Dir.; Patricia O'Toole, Prin. Lay Teachers 27; High School Students 279; Junior High Students 244.

[D] GRADE SCHOOL INTERPAROCHIAL

MUSKEGON. *St. Francis de Sales Elementary School*. (Grades PreK-6). Greater Muskegon Consolidated School. 2947 McCracken Ave., 49441. Tel: 616-755-1045. Mrs. Marcy Henehan, Prin. Lay Teachers 12; Students 251.

St. Michael Elementary School. (Grades PreK-5). Greater Muskegon Consolidated School. 215 W. Dale Ave., 49441. Tel: 616-722-4666. Elaine Bertram, Prin. Lay Teachers 7; Students 190.

[E] GENERAL HOSPITALS

GRAND RAPIDS. *St. Mary's Health Services*, 200 Jefferson, S.E., 49503. Tel: 616-752-6090
For a complete listing, refer to the Hospitals section.

MUSKEGON. *Mercy Hospital*, 1500 E. Sherman Blvd., P.O. Box 358, 49443. Tel: 616-739-9341; Fax: 616-733-0957
For a complete listing, refer to the Hospitals section.

[F] PROTECTIVE INSTITUTIONS

GRAND RAPIDS. *Contemplative Sisters of the Good Shepherd*, 1355 Walker Ave., N.W., 49504. Tel: 616-454-6268
For a complete listing, refer to the Special Care Facilities section.

[G] HOMES FOR THE AGED

GRAND RAPIDS. *St. Ann's Home*, 2161 Leonard St., N.W., 49504. Tel: 616-453-7715; Fax: 616-453-7359
For a complete listing, refer to the Special Care Facilities section.

[H] MONASTERIES AND RESIDENCES OF PRIESTS AND BROTHERS

MUSKEGAN. *Dominican Friars*, 1145 West Laketon, 49441. Tel: 616-755-5238. Dominicans Province of St. Albert the Great, U.S.A. Bros. Benedict Baer, O.P.; Joachim M. Thiel, O.P.

[I] CONVENTS AND RESIDENCES FOR SISTERS

GRAND RAPIDS. *Aquinata Hall*, 153 Lakeside, N.E., 49503-3894. Tel: 616-456-5038. Ms. Jacqueline Ghysels, Admin. Sisters 42; Beds 54.

Contemplative Sisters of the Good Shepherd, 1400 Morgan St., N.W., 49504. Tel: 616-453-4315. Sr. Genevieve Heart of Mary, C.G.S., Supr. Sisters 6.

Dominican Center, 2025 E. Fulton St., 49503-3895. Tel: 616-454-1241; Fax: 616-454-2861. Mark Clarke, Dir.

Motherhouse of the Dominican Sisters, Marywood, 2025 E. Fulton St., 49503-3895. Tel: 616-459-2910. Motherhouse and Novitiate for the Sisters of the Order of St. Dominic of the Congregation of Our Lady of the Sacred Heart. Legal Titles: *Sisters of St. Dominic of the Congregation of Our Lady of the Sacred Heart (The Religious Institute).*; *Sisters of the Order of St. Dominic of Grand Rapids, Michigan (The Corporation)*. Sr. Barbara Hansen, O.P., Prioress; Rev. Paul Colloton, O.P., Coord. Pastoral Life; Sr. Diane Zerfas, O.P., Coord. Pastoral Life. Sisters 348.

ADA. *Discalced Carmelite Nuns, Monastery of Our Lady of Guadalupe*, 4300 Mount Carmel Dr., N.E., 49301-9784. (Parnell). Mother Elizabeth Ann, O.C.D., Prioress. Professed Carmelite Nuns 20; Extern Sisters 3.

BELMONT. *Motherhouse of the Consolata Missionary Sisters*, 6801 Belmont Rd., P.O. Box 371, 49306. Tel: 616-361-2072; Fax: 616-361-2049. Sr. Felicia Bertaina, M.C., Supr. Consolata Sisters 22.

[J] RETREAT HOUSES

SPRING LAKE. *St. Lazare Retreat House*, 18600 W. Spring Lake Rd., 49456-0462. Tel: 616-842-3370. Revs. Michael J. Shea, C.M.; Alfred Pehrsson, C.M.

[K] NEWMAN CENTERS

COOPERSVILLE. *Grand Valley State University Catholic Campus Ministry*, Allendale Campus, 17151-88th Ave., 49404. Tel: 616-837-8158. Rev. Mark F. Bauer, Campus Priest; Deacon Dale Holleran, Campus Min.

EDMORE. *Montcalm Community College Newman Center*, 1051 E. Howard City Rd., 48829. Rev. Isidro T. Gargantiel.

[L] MISCELLANEOUS LISTINGS

GRAND RAPIDS. *Bishops' Housing Corporation*, 660 Burton St., S.E., 49507.

The Catholic Foundation of West Michigan, 660 Burton, S.E., 49507. Tel: 616-243-0491; Fax: 616-243-4910. Sr. Patrice Konwinski, O.P.

**Dominican Land Company*, 2025 E. Fulton St., 49503-3895. Tel: 616-459-2910; Fax: 616-454-6105. Sr. Ann Walters, O.P.

Educational Foundation of St. Francis Xavier School, Inc., 240 Brown St., S.E., 49507.

The Foundation for Catholic Education of Greater Grand Rapids, Inc., 410 Bridge St., N.W., 49504.

Fund for Faith, 660 Burton St., S.E., 49507. Foundation established in 1976 for various apostolic works.

Marywood Academy, 2025 E. Fulton St., 49503-3895. Tel: 616-454-2910; Fax: 616-454-6105. Sr. Ann Walters, O.P.

SS. Peter and Paul Parish Education Endowment Fund, 520 Myrtle St., N.W., 49504. Tel: 616-454-6000.

Sisters of St. Dominic Charitable Trust, 2025 E. Fulton Rd., 49503-3895. Tel: 616-459-2910; Fax: 616-454-6105. Sr. Barbara Hansen, O.P. Legal Title: *Sisters of St. Dominic of the Congregation of Our Lady of the Sacred Heart Charitable Trust (The Trust).*

Steepletown Neighborhood Services, Inc., 423 First St., N.W., 49504.

West Michigan Catholic Education Foundation Funds, Inc., 660 Burton St., S.E., 49507. Tel: 616-243-0491.

LOWELL. *Franciscan Life Process Center*, 11650 Downes St., 49331-9489. Tel: 616-897-7842; Fax: 616-897-7054. Sr. Colleen Ann Nagle, F.S.E., Dir.

MUSKEGON HEIGHTS. *Christian Community Center*, 540 E. Hackley, 49444. Tel: 616-725-7579.

Madonna House Apostolate, 3201 Peck St., 49444. Tel: 616-733-1129. Theresa Marsey, Dir.

PORTLAND. *The Father Flohe Foundation*, 140 Church St., 48875.

RELIGIOUS INSTITUTES OF MEN REPRESENTED IN THE DIOCESE

For further details refer to the corresponding bracketed number in the Religious Institutes of Men or Women section.

[1330]—*Congregation of the Mission*. (Eastern Prov.).—C.M.

[0480]—*Conventual Franciscans*. (Louisville).—O.F.M.Conv.

[0430]—*Order of Preachers-Dominicans*. (Central Prov.).—O.P.

[1030]—*Paulist Fathers*.—C.S.P.

[]—*Priests of the Holy Cross*. (Indiana Prov.).—C.S.C.

[1070]—*Redemptorist Fathers*. (Prov. of St. Louis).—C.SS.R.

RELIGIOUS INSTITUTES OF WOMEN REPRESENTED IN THE DIOCESE

[0360]—*Carmelite Sisters of the Divine Heart of Jesus*.—Carmel.D.C.J.

[0720]—*Consolata Missionary Sisters*.—M.C.

[1830]—*Contemplative Sisters of the Good Shepherd*.—C.G.S.

[0420]—*Discalced Carmelite Nuns*.—O.C.D.

[1070-14]—*Dominican Sisters*.—O.P.

[1250]—*Institute of the Franciscan Sisters of the Eucharist*.—F.S.E.

[2575]—*Institute of the Sisters of Mercy of the Americas*.—R.S.M.

[3130]—*Our Lady of Victory Missionary Sisters*.—O.L.V.M.

[2970]—*School Sisters of Notre Dame*.—S.S.N.D.

[3560]—*Servants of Jesus*.—S.J.

[1530]—*Sisters of St. Francis*.—O.S.F.

[3830-11]—*Sisters of St. Joseph of Nazareth*.—S.S.J.

[1830]—*Sisters of the Good Shepherd*.—R.G.S.

[2150]—*Sisters of the Immaculate Heart of Mary*.—I.H.M.

[3260]—*Sisters of the Precious Blood*.—C.PP.S.

NECROLOGY

† Pattok, Raymond J., (Retired). —Died Oct. 14, 1997.

† Sikorski, Andrew, (Retired). —Died June 8, 1997.

† Zvirblis, John, (Retired). —Died March 4, 1997.

Diocese of Great Falls—Billings

(Dioecesis Magnocataractensis-Billingensis)

Most Reverend

ANTHONY M. MILONE, D.D.

Bishop of Great Falls-Billings; ordained December 15, 1957; appointed Titular Bishop Plestia and Auxiliary of Omaha November 10, 1981; Episcopal ordination January 6, 1982; appointed Bishop of Great Falls-Billings December 14, 1987; installed February 23, 1988. *Office: 121-23rd St. S., Great Falls, MT, 59401.* Tel.: 406-727-6683.; (Corporation title: "Roman Catholic Bishop of Great Falls, Montana a corporation sole.")

Most Reverend

ELDON BERNARD SCHUSTER, D.D.

Former Bishop of Great Falls; ordained May 27, 1937; appointed Titular Bishop of Amblada October 30, 1961; consecrated December 21, 1961; appointed Bishop of Great Falls December 2, 1967; resigned December 27, 1977. *Res., 1325 Smelter Ave., Black Eagle, MT, 59414.* Tel.: 406-453-8425.

ERECTED MAY 18, 1904.

Square Miles 94,158.

Comprises the eastern part of the State of Montana and is made up of the following Counties: Big Horn, Blaine, Carbon, Carter, Cascade, Chouteau, Custer, Daniels, Dawson, Fallon, Fergus, Garfield, Golden Valley, Hill, Judith Basin, Liberty, McCone, Musselshell, Park, Petroleum, Phillips, Powder River, Prairie, Richland, Roosevelt, Rosebud, Sheridan, Stillwater, Sweet Grass, Treasure, Valley, Wibaux, Yellowstone and parts of Teton and Toole.

For legal titles of parishes and diocesan institutions, consult the Pastoral Office .

Pastoral Office: 121 23rd St. S., Great Falls, MT, 59401-3997. Mailing Address: P.O. Box 1399, Great Falls, MT, 59403-1399. Tel.: 406-727-6683; 800-332-9998 (Toll Free Montana Only); Fax: 406-454-3480.

Web site address: http://www.mcn.net/~dioceseofgfb

E-mail address: dioceseofgfb@mcn.net

STATISTICAL OVERVIEW

Personnel	
Bishop	1
Retired Bishops	1
Retired Abbots	1
Priests: Diocesan Active in Diocese	36
Priests: Active Outside Diocese	7
Priests: Retired, Sick or Absent	34
Number of Diocesan Priests	77
Religious Priests in Diocese	14
Extern Priests in Diocese	3
Ordinations:	
Diocesan Priests	1
Permanent Deacons in Diocese	3
Total Sisters	79
Parishes	
Parishes	54
With Resident Pastor:	
Resident Diocesan Priests	32
Resident Religious Priests	12
Without Resident Pastor:	
Administered by Priests	5
Administered by Women Religious	4
Administered by Lay People	1
Missions	72
Professional Ministry Personnel:	
Sisters	25
Lay Ministers	40
Welfare	
Catholic Hospitals	2
Total Assisted	24,906
Health Care Centers	1
Total Assisted	18,400
Day Care and Extended Day Care Centers	8
Total Assisted	476
Special Centers for Social Services	3
Total Assisted	81,200
Educational	
Diocesan Students in Other Seminaries	4
Total Seminarians	4
Colleges and Universities	1
Total Students	1,253
High Schools, Diocesan and Parish	1
Total Students	391
High Schools, Private	1
Total Students	154
Elementary Schools, Diocesan and Parish	8
Total Students	1,646
Elementary Schools, Private	3
Total Students	476
Catechesis/Religious Education:	
High School Students	2,575
Elementary Students	4,906
Total Students Under Catholic Instruction	11,405
Teachers in the Diocese:	
Priests	2
Sisters	6
Lay Teachers	254
Vital Statistics	
Receptions into the Church:	
Infant Baptism Totals	872
Adult Baptism Totals	116
Received into Full Communion	187
First Communions	946
Confirmations	879
Marriages:	
Catholic	172
Interfaith	179
Total Marriages	351
Deaths	973
Total Catholic Population	57,165
Total Population	392,900

Former Bishops—Most Rev. MATHIAS C. LENIHAN, D.D., ord. Dec. 20, 1879; cons. First Bishop of Great Falls, Sept. 21, 1904; resigned Jan. 18, 1930; created Titular Archbishop of Preslavo, Feb. 14, 1930; died Aug. 19, 1943.—Most Rev. EDWIN V. O'HARA, D.D., ord. June 10, 1905; appt. Aug. 1, 1930; cons. Oct. 28, 1930; appt. Bishop of Kansas City April 15, 1939 made asst. at the Pontifical Throne Jan. 5, 1949; appt. Archbishop "Ad Personam" June 29, 1954; died Sept. 11, 1956, Milan, Italy.—Most Rev. WILLIAM J. CONDON, D.D., ord. Oct. 14, 1917; appt. Aug. 5, 1939; cons. Oct. 18, 1939 asst. at the Pontifical Throne Dec. 9, 1964; died Aug. 17, 1967.—Most Rev. ELDON BERNARD SCHUSTER, D.D., ord. May 27, 1937; appt. Titular Bishop of Amblada; cons. Dec. 21, 1961; appt. Bishop of Great Falls Dec. 2, 1967; resigned Dec. 27, 1977.—Most Rev. THOMAS JOSEPH MURPHY, S.T.D., D.D., appt. Bishop of Great Falls July 5, 1978 Episcopal ordination and installation Aug. 21, 1978; appt. co-adjutor Archbishop of Seattle May 26, 1987; died June 26, 1997.

Vicars General—Very Rev. DAVID F. DWYER; Very Rev. GILBERT HEMAUER, O.F.M.Cap.; Very Rev. EUGENE P. HRUSKA.

Pastoral Office—121 23rd St. S., P.O. Box 1399, Great Falls, 59403. Tel: 406-727-6683; 800-332-9998 (Montana Toll Free Number Only); Fax: 406-454-3480. All applications for dispensations and official communications should be addressed to this office.

Chancellor—Sr. PAT CORMACK, S.C.S.C.

Moderator of the Curia—Rev. EUGENE P. HRUSKA, V.G.

Business Manager—JOSEPH LONCKI.

Diocesan Tribunal—121 23rd St. S., P.O. Box 1399, Great Falls, 59403. Tel: 406-727-6683; 800-332-9998 (Montana Toll Free Number Only).

Judicial Vicar—Rev. ROBERT D. GROSCH, J.C.L.

Promoter of Justice—Rev. JOHN W. ROBERTSON, J.C.L.

Defenders of the Bond—Revs. DAVID DWYER, V.G.; ROBERT FOX; MARGARET ROMANO-HOGAN.

Tribunal Director—TERRYAL ANN REAVLEY.

Notary—TERRYAL ANN REAVLEY.

Diocesan Consultors—Most Rev. ELDON B. SCHUSTER; Revs. ROBERT GROSCH; THOMAS HARNEY; JAMES O'NEIL; DALE YURKOVIC; PATRICK ZABROCKI; STEPHEN ZABROCKI.

Personnel Board—Most Rev. ANTHONY M. MILONE; Revs. DICK SCHLOSSER, Chm. KIRK C. MORGAN; JAMES

O'NEIL; GREGORY R. STAUDINGER, Sec. RICHARD OSTERMAN; ROGER VEIK, O.F.M.Cap., Vicar of Clergy Personnel (Ex Officio).

Regional Deans & Vicar Delegates—Rev. STEPHEN L. TOKARSKI, Billings; Rev. JAY PETERSON, Great Falls; Rev. PATRICK ZABROCKI, Havre; Rev. KIRK MORGAN, Miles City; Rev. STEPHEN ZABROCKI, Wolf Point.

Cemetery Board—Revs. EUGENE HRUSKA, V.G., Great Falls: JOSEPH LONCKI.

Vicar of Clergy Personnel—Rev. ROGER VEIK, O.F.M.Cap., *1122 N. 30th St., Billings, 59101.* Tel: 406-259-9902.

Cum Christo—Rev. WAYNE PITTARD, Diocesan Spiritual Dir., *503 Main St., Roundup, 59072.* Tel: 406-323-1019. Rev. JAY PETERSON, Assoc. Diocesan Spiritual Dir., *P.O. Box 421, Lewistown, 59457.* Tel: 406-538-9306.

Vicar for Ministry to Native Americans—Rev. PETER E. GUTHNECK, *Rocky Boy CPU-Box 3009, Box Elder, 59521-3009.* Tel: 406-395-4380.

Diocesan Offices and Directors

Apostleship of Prayer—Vacant.

Boy Scouts—Rev. LEO MCDOWELL, Chap., *215 N. 31st St., Billings, 59101.* Tel: 406-259-3389; Fax: 406-248-1185.

Campaign for Human Development—BRUCE DAY, Diocesan Dir.; Rev. EUGENE P. HRUSKA, Consultant, *121 23rd St. S., Great Falls, 59401., P.O. Box 1399, Great Falls, 59403.* Tel: 406-727-6683; Fax: 406-454-3480.

Care & Share Committee—STELLA ZIEGLER, Chm.

Catechesis—PAUL F. KAISER, Dir., *Pastoral Center, P.O. Box 1399, Great Falls, 59403.* Tel: 406-727-3386. Sr. BARBARA BROWN, O.P., Assoc. Dir., *1109 Orr St., Miles City, 59301.* Tel: 406-232-2116.

Catholic Relief Services—JOSEPH LONCKI, Dir., Pastoral Center.

Catholic University, Friends of—Rev. ROBERT J. FOX, S.T.L., Ph.D., *P.O. Box 53, Poplar, 59255.*

Clerical Benefit Association—Most Rev. ANTHONY M. MILONE, Ex Officio; Revs. ANTHONY SCHUSTER, Chm. STEPHEN ZABROCKI; THOMAS HARNEY; JAMES SIKORA; LOTHAR KRAUTH, Sec. TERRANCE REGAN; JOSEPH LONCKI, Consultant; Rev. MICHAEL GUINAN, Retired Priests' Rep.

Continuing Education for Clergy—Rev. JOHN J. HOULIHAN, *St. Patrick's Co-Cathedral, 215 N. 31st St., Billings, 59101-9920.*

Diocesan Pastoral Council—Sr. PAT CORMACK, S.C.S.C., Exec. Dir. KIMBERT LARSEN, Chm., *121-23rd St. S., P.O. Box 1399, Great Falls, 59403-1399.* Tel: 406-727-6683; Fax: 406-454-3480.

D.C.C.W.—ADRIANA "ANN" O'BRIEN, Pres.; Most Rev. ANTHONY M. MILONE, Episcopal Moderator; Rev. JOHN J. HOULIHAN, Priest Moderator.

Ecumenical Officer—PAUL F. KAISER.

Education—Sr. JEAN DAWSON, S.C.L., Diocesan School Supt., *P.O. Box 31158, Billings, 59107.* Tel: 406-252-9595; 800-682-2218 (Montana Toll Free Number Only); Fax: 406-252-9875.

Finance Council—Most Rev. ANTHONY M. MILONE; JOSEPH LONCKI, Consultant; WILLIAM ARTZ; Rev. DAVID F. DWYER, V.G.; MARILYN HARMON; Rev. EUGENE P. HRUSKA, V.G.; THOMAS LANE; JOHN NELSON; Most Rev. ELDON B. SCHUSTER; ALBERT MARTENS; THOMAS PELATT; MARILYN ROSE; ELLEN SOLEM; Rev. STEPHEN ZABROCKI.

Holy Childhood Association—Vacant.

Lay Ministry Program—Sr. PAULINE SCHWANDT, O.S.F., Pastoral Center.

Liturgy Commission—REGINA GABRIEL; Sr. MARGARET MARY O'DOHERTY, O.P.; DIANA O'HARA; Rev. TERRANCE REGAN; JOE SULLIVAN; MICHAEL PRENDERGAST, Chm. JAN WOOD, Vice-Chm. ANN O'BRIEN; Most Rev. ANTHONY MILONE; Rev. KEVIN CHRISTOFFERSON.

Liturgy Office—MICHAEL PRENDERGAST.

Missions—Vacant.

Newspaper—*"Harvest"*; Rev. EUGENE HRUSKA, V.G.

Social Justice and Peace Office—BRUCE DAY, Dir., *121-23rd St. S., P.O. Box 1399, Great Falls, 59403-1399.* Tel: 406-727-6683; Fax: 406-454-3480.

RCIA—MICHAEL PRENDERGAST, Consultant, Pastoral Center.

Pastoral Outreach—PAUL F. KAISER, Coord.; Sr. BARBARA BROWN, O.P.; Sr. PAT CORMACK, S.C.S.C.; BRUCE DAY; Rev. EUGENE HRUSKA; SUZANNE JOHNSON; MICHAEL PRENDERGAST; Sr. PAULINE SCHWANDT, O.S.F.

Priests' Council—Most Rev. ANTHONY M. MILONE; Revs. STEPHEN ZABROCKI, Chm. ANTHONY GREGORI, Vice-Chm. PASCHAL SILER, O.F.M.Cap.; ROBERT GROSCH; JAMES O'NEIL; DALE YURKOVIC; PATRICK ZABROCKI; THOMAS HARNEY; EUGENE P. HRUSKA, V.G.; GILBERT HEMAUER, O.F.M.Cap., V.G.; MICHAEL SCHNEIDER.

Sister's Council—Sr. ELIZABETH FARRER, S.S.J., Pres.; Sr. CLAVER EHREN, O.S.F., Vice Pres.; Sr. LORETTA SEDLMAYER, R.S.M., Sec.; Sr. VALERIE MCGEOUGH, R.S.M., Treas.

Director of Vocations—Rev. DALE E. YURKOVIC, *St. Mary's Church, P.O. Box 646, Livingston, 59047.* Tel: 406-222-1393.

Inter-Diocesan Organizations

Montana Catholic Conference—SHARON HOFF, Dir., *P.O. Box 1708, Helena, 59624.* Tel: 406-442-5761; Fax: 406-442-9047.

Montana Catholic Social Services—MARILYN MCKIBBEN, Dir., *P.O. Box 907, Helena, 59624.* Tel: 406-442-4130. Provides adoption and counseling services for families, children and infants.

Billings Office—BECKY HUBBERT, *2703 11th Ave. N., Ste. 2, Billings, 59101.* Tel: 406-252-3399.

Great Falls Office—KYLA KALANICK, *P.O. Box 7410, Great Falls, 59403.* Tel: 406-771-7805.

Helena Office—Sr. NOEL BRUCH; SHIRLEY COLE, *P.O. Box 907, Helena, 59601.* Tel: 406-442-4130.

Missoula Office—BETSY ROBEL-GOMEZ, *St. Patrick's Hospital, 554 W. Broadway, Missoula, 59802.* Tel: 406-329-5629.

Montana Association of Churches—Rev. KENNETH W. MOORE, Pres. MARGARET E. MACDONALD, Exec. Dir., *Andrew Square, Ste. G, 100 24th St. W., Billings, 59102.* Tel: 406-656-9779.

CLERGY, PARISHES, MISSIONS AND PAROCHIAL SCHOOLS

CITY OF GREAT FALLS
(Cascade County)

1—ST. ANN'S CATHEDRAL, Most Rev. Anthony M. Milone, D.D.; Rev. William A. Hogan, Rector; Sr. M. Genevieve Garvin, S.M., Pastoral Min.
Res., 715 Third Ave. N., P.O. Box 1708, 59403. Tel: 406-761-5456; Fax: 406-761-5457.

2—EASTSIDE CATHOLIC COMMUNITIES, Rev. Richard Schlosser; Rev. Msgr. Joseph Gluszek, (Retired).
Office: 2816 Central Ave., 59401-3498. Tel: 406-452-6491; Fax: 406-452-6495.
Churches—St. Gerard Majella, 2211-5th Ave. N., 59401.; Holy Family, 2800 Central Ave., 59401.; Sts. Peter & Paul, 200-44th St. S., 59405.
Catechesis/Religious Programs—Kathy Malby, D.R.E.
Students 210.

3—ST. JOSEPH'S, Rev. Anthony J. Shuster.
Res., 420-22nd Ave. N.E., 59404. Tel: 406-453-6546.
Church—420-2nd Ave. S.W., 59404. Tel: 406-453-9331.
Catechesis/Religious Programs—Tel: 406-453-9331. Jean Sobolik, D.R.E.
Students 150.

4—OUR LADY OF LOURDES, Rev. Lothar Krauth; Sr. Marian Lorang, O.S.U., Pastoral Assoc.
Res., 409 13th St. S., 59405. Tel: 406-452-6464; Fax: 406-761-7180.
School—(Grades PreK-8) 1305 Fifth Ave. S., 59405. Tel: 406-452-0551. Mrs. Adele Meister, Prin.
Ursuline Nuns 1; Lay Teachers 18; Students 266.
Catechesis/Religious Programs—Sena Bozlee, D.R.E.
Students 120.

5—ST. LUKE THE EVANGELIST, Rev. Anthony J. Schuster.
Pastoral Assocs.: Mary Anne Sladich-Lantz; Donna Wilson.
Res., 420 22nd Ave. N.E., 59404. Tel: 406-453-6546; Fax: 406-453-0323.
Catechesis/Religious Programs—Aubrey Rearden, D.R.E.
Students 400.

CITY OF BILLINGS
(Yellowstone County)

1—ST. PATRICK'S CO-CATHEDRAL, Revs. John J. Houlihan; Leo George McDowell; Richard J. Hopkins; Sr. Lillian Maguire, S.C.L., Pastoral Assoc.
Res., 215 N. 31st St., 59101. Tel: 406-259-3389; Fax: 406-248-1185.
Catechesis/Religious Programs—Jean Ott, D.R.E.
Students 95.

2—HOLY ROSARY, Sr. Eileen Hurley, S.C.L., Pastoral Admin.; Virginia Jeanotte, Pastoral Assoc.; Deacon Melvin A. Melius. Sacramental Ministers: Revs. John J. Houlihan; Leo George McDowell.
Office: 521 Custer Ave., 59101. Tel: 406-259-7611.
Catechesis/Religious Programs—Jean Ott, D.R.E.
Students 57.

3—LITTLE FLOWER, Rev. Paul Reichling, O.F.M.Cap.
Res., 209 S. 35th St., 59101. Tel: 406-245-4717.
Catechesis/Religious Programs—Tel: 406-259-7611. Jean Ott, D.R.E.
Students 80.

4—ST. BERNARD'S, Rev. David Reichling, O.F.M.Cap.; Deacon Tim Birkle.
Office: 226 Wicks Ln., 59105. Tel: 406-259-4350; Fax: 406-259-0443.
Catechesis/Religious Programs—D.R.E.: Sandra Stokoe; Mary Newpower.
Students 630.
Mission—Ballantine, Sts. Cyril & Methodius.

5—OUR LADY OF GUADALUPE, Rev. Paul Reichling, O.F.M.Cap.
Res., 209 S. 35th St., 59101. Tel: 406-245-4717.
Catechesis/Religious Programs—Tel: 406-259-7611.
Students 95.

6—ST. PIUS X, Rev. Stephen L. Tokarski; Deacon Robert W. Daem; Don Foster, Pastoral Assoc.
Parish Center: 717 18th St. W., 59102. Tel: 406-656-2522; Fax: 406-656-2584.
Catechesis/Religious Programs—Cheryl Daem, D.R.E.
Students 470.

7—ST. THOMAS THE APOSTLE, Rev. Nathaniel J. Bourke; Jim Downs, Pastoral Assoc.
Res., 2055 Woody Dr., 59102. Tel: 406-656-5578.
Church—2055 Woody Dr., 59102. Tel: 406-656-5800.
Catechesis/Religious Programs—Joyce Hollowell, D.R.E.
Students 420.

OUTSIDE THE CITIES OF GREAT FALLS AND BILLINGS

Ashland, Rosebud Co., St. Labre's, Rev. Paschal Siler, O.F.M.Cap.
Res., Tongue River Rd., 59003. Tel: 406-784-2755.
Station—Ashland, Birney Post.

Baker, Fallon Co., St. John the Evangelist, Rev. Thomas Tobin.
Res., P.O. Box 1519, 59313. Tel: 406-778-2297.
Catechesis/Religious Programs—Norma Losing, D.R.E.
Students 193.
Missions—Ekalaka, St. Joan of Arc; Plevna, St. Anthony. [CEM]

Belt, Cascade Co., St. Mark the Evangelist, Rev. Ted F. Szudera.
Res., P.O. Box 213, 59412. Tel: 406-277-3537.
Catechesis/Religious Programs—Patty Kolar, D.R.E.
Students 100.
Missions—Highwood, St. Jane Frances; Monarch, St. Clement; Raynesford, St. Mary.

Big Sandy, Chouteau Co., St. Margaret Mary, Rev. Peter E. Guthneck; Sr. Margaret Mary O'Doherty, O.P., Pastoral Assoc. & D.R.E.
Res., St. Mary's Rocky Boy Indian Reservation, Rocky Boy CPU-Box 3009, Box Elder, 59521. Tel: 406-395-4380.
Catechesis/Religious Programs—Students 115.
Missions—Box Elder, St. Anthony; Rocky Boy Indian Reservation, St. Mary.

Big Timber, Sweet Grass Co., St. Joseph, Sr. Catherine Kinsella, O.P., Pastoral Admin.
Res., P.O. Box 871, 59011. Tel: 406-932-4728.

Black Eagle, Cascade Co., Most Blessed Sacrament, Rev. Raymond J. Nyquist. In res., Most Rev. Eldon B. Schuster, D.D., (Retired).
Res., 1325 Smelter Ave., Great Falls, 59414. Tel: 406-453-8425; Fax: 406-453-8425.

Bridger, Carbon Co., Sacred Heart, Sr. Mary Lou Mendel, S.C.L., Pastoral Admin.
Res., P.O. Box 309, 59014-0309. Tel: 406-662-3550.
Catechesis/Religious Programs—Students 140.
Missions—Fromberg, St. Joseph; Joliet, St. John.

Broadus, Powder River Co., St. David's, Rev. Chester Poppa, O.F.M.Cap.
Mailing Address: P.O.Box 52, 59317. Tel: 406-436-2348. [CEM]
Mission—Alzada.

Centerville, Cascade Co., Holy Trinity, Rev. Ted Szudera.
Mailing Address: P.O. Box 125, Stockett, 59480-0125. Tel: 406-736-5491.
Res., P.O. Box 213, Belt, 59412.
Catechesis/Religious Programs—Tel: 406-736-5114. D.R.E.: Bev Pepos; Cynthia Ingman.
Students 71.

Chester, Liberty Co., St. Mary's, Rev. Joseph Marmion.
Res., P.O. Box 647, 504 Main, 59522. Tel: 406-759-5377.
Catechesis/Religious Programs—D.R.E.: Natalie Ghekiere; Dianne Folk.
Students 154.
Missions—Hingham, Our Lady of Ransom; Inverness, Sacred Heart; Rudyard, Holy Family Center.

Chinook, Blaine Co., St. Gabriel's, Rev. Marcel J. Vogel.
Res., 152 Eighth St., P.O. Box 1089, 59523. Tel: 406-357-2073; Fax: 406-357-2173.

Catechesis/Religious Programs—D.R.E.: Mrs. Ellen Pyette, (Elementary); Mrs. Norma Fritz, (High School).
Students 110.
Education Center—Tel: 406-353-2407.
Missions—Harlem, St. Thomas the Apostle, P.O. Box 819, Harlem, 59526.; Hogeland, St. Thomas Aquinas.

Circle, McCone Co., St. Francis Xavier, Rt. Rev. Robert West, O.S.B.
Res., P.O. Box 160, 59215-0160. Tel: 406-485-3520.
Missions—Jordan, St. John the Baptist, Tel: 406-557-6135; Richey, St. Francis de Sales.

Colstrip, Rosebud Co., St. Margaret Mary, William Medved, Pastoral Admin.
Res., P.O. Box 305, 59323. Tel: 406-748-2234; Fax: 406-748-2234.
Catechesis/Religious Programs—Students 65.

Columbus, Stillwater Co., St. Mary's, Sr. Mary Francis Kirkpatrick, S.C.L., Pastoral Admin.
Mailing Address: P.O. Box 956, 59019. Tel: 406-322-5541.
Catechesis/Religious Programs—D.R.E.: Jeanne Harsha; Jeanne Babcock; Geri Turk.
Students 80.
Mission—Absarokee, St. Michael.

Crow Agency, Big Horn Co., St. Dennis, Rev. Charles Robinson, O.F.M.Cap.; Sr. Loretta Sedlmayer, R.S.M., Pastoral Assoc.
Res., P.O. Box 57, 59022. Tel: 406-638-2641.
Catechesis/Religious Programs—Students 60.
Mission—St. Xavier, St. Francis Xavier, P.O. Box 138, St. Xavier, 59075. Tel: 406-666-2380. Sr. Claver Ehren, O.S.F., Pastoral Assoc.

Culbertson, Roosevelt Co., St. Anthony's, Rev. Benjamin Lobo.
Res., P.O. Box 30, 59218. Tel: 406-787-6666; Fax: 406-787-6183.
Catechesis/Religious Programs—Lynn Finnicum, D.R.E.
Students 52.
Missions—Bainville, Sacred Heart; Froid, Immaculate Conception; Medicine Lake, St. Patrick.

Forsyth, Rosebud Co., Immaculate Conception, Rev. Gilbert Hemauer, O.F.M.Cap., V.G.
Res., 591 N. 12th Ave. N., P.O. Box 166, 59327. Tel: 406-356-2101 (Church); 356-9239 (Parish Center).
Catechesis/Religious Programs—Renee Steinberger, D.R.E.
Students 97.
Mission—Hysham, St. Joseph.

Fort Benton, Chouteau Co., Immaculate Conception, Rev. Denis J. Keane; Trish Eklund, Pastoral Assoc.
Res., P.O. Box 868, 59442. Tel: 406-622-3726.
Catechesis/Religious Programs—Tel: 406-622-5288. D.R.E.: Vicky O'Hara; Michelle Schneider.
Students 120.
Mission—Geraldine, St. Margaret.

Fort Shaw, Cascade Co., St. Ann, Rev. Eugene P. Hruska, V.G.
Res., P.O. Box 99, 59443. Tel: 406-264-5554.
Catechesis/Religious Programs—D.R.E.: JoAnn Holmes, (St. Ann), Tel: 406-264-5495; David Konecny, (Sacred Heart), Tel: 406-468-2368.
Students 105.
Mission—Cascade, Sacred Heart.

Glasgow, Valley Co., St. Raphael's, Rev. Thad Kozikowski.
Office: 412 Third Ave. N., P.O. Box 1047, 59230. Tel: 406-228-4651.
Catechesis/Religious Programs—Tel: 406-228-4651. Bernardine Sullivan, D.R.E.
Students 198.
Missions—Fort Peck, Our Lady of the Lake; Hinsdale, St. Albert; Nashua, Queen of the Angels.

Glendive, Dawson Co., Sacred Heart, Rev. Joseph Ponessa; Gene Fitzpatrick, Pastoral Assoc.
Res., 316 W. Benham St., P.O. Box 36, 59330. Tel: 406-365-2585; Fax: 406-365-4033.
Catechesis/Religious Programs—Tel: 406-365-4569. Monica Christianson, D.R.E.
Students 300.
Missions—Wibaux, St. Peter, P.O. Box 217, Wibaux, 59353. Tel: 406-795-2215; Wibaux, St. Philip, P.O. Box 217, Wibaux, 59353. Tel: 406-795-8188.

Hardin, Big Horn Co., St. Joseph's, Rev. Fabian Fehring, O.F.M.Cap.
Res., 710 N. Custer, P.O. Box 510, 59034. Tel: 406-665-1432.
Catechesis/Religious Programs—Students 100.
Mission—Custer, St. Mary.

Havre, Hill Co., St. Jude Thaddeus, Revs. Robert D. Grosch; Patrick Zabrocki.
Res., 624 Fourth St., P.O. Box 407, 59501. Tel: 406-265-4261; Fax: 406-265-4408.
School—(Grades PreK-8). Tel: 406-265-4613. Mrs. Therese Cowdery, Prin.
Lay Teachers 12; Students 225.
Catechesis/Religious Programs—Timothy Maroney, D.R.E.
Students 160.
Mission—Cottonwood, St. John.

Hays, Blaine Co., St. Paul's Indian Mission, Rev. Joseph R. Retzel, S.J.
Res., P.O. Box 40, 59527. Tel: 406-673-3300.
School—Tel: 406-673-3123. Sr. Helen Durso, O.P., Prin.
Sisters 5; Lay Teachers 5; Students 135.
Catechesis/Religious Programs—Sr. Nora McCarthy, O.P., D.R.E.
Students 138.
Missions—Zortman, St. Joseph; Dodson, St. Thomas, Lodgepole Rte., Dodson, 59524. Tel: 406-673-3454. Sr. Laura Fucito, O.P., Pastoral Assoc.; Fort Belknap Agency, Sacred Heart, Tel: 406-353-2927. Pastoral Assocs.: Sr. Nancy Maclean, S.P.; Sr. Mary Eileen Boyle, O.S.U.

Lame Deer, Rosebud Co., Blessed Sacrament, Rev. Daniel Crosby, O.F.M.Cap. Pastoral Assocs. & D.R.E.: Sr. Mary Ann Stoffregen, O.S.F.; Mary K. Manger.
Res., P.O. Box 100, 59043. Tel: 406-477-6384.
Catechesis/Religious Programs—Students 23.
Mission—Busby, Christ the King.

Laurel, Yellowstone Co., St. Anthony's, Rev. Thomas C. Harney.
Res., P.O. Box 955, 59044. Tel: 406-628-7182. [CEM]
Catechesis/Religious Programs—Tel: 406-628-7484. Barb Hoppel, D.R.E.
Students 255.

Lewistown, Fergus Co., St. Leo's, Rev. Jay H. Peterson; Sr. Anne Walch, O.S.F.
Res., P.O. Box 421, 59457. Tel: 406-538-9306; Fax: 406-538-7624. [CEM]
Catechesis/Religious Programs—D.R.E.: Judy Marxer, (Grades K-6); Denise Goodwyn, (Grades 7-12).
Students 460.
Mission—Winifred, Holy Family.
Chapels—Danvers, St. Wenceslaus.; Hilger, St. Victor.; Roy, Sacred Heart.

Livingston, Park Co., St. Mary's, Rev. Dale E. Yurkovic; Joannie Lee, Pastoral Assoc. & D.R.E.
Res., S F St., P.O. Box 646, 59047-0646. Tel: 406-222-1393; Fax: 406-222-1405. [CEM]
School—(Grades PreK-8). Tel: 406-222-3303. Michelle Moore, Prin.
Lay Teachers 10; Students 144.
Catechesis/Religious Programs—Students 62.
Missions—Clyde Park, St. Margaret; Gardiner, St. William.

Lodge Grass, Big Horn Co., Our Lady of Loretto, Rev. James Antoine, O.F.M.Cap.
Res., P.O. Box N, 59050. Tel: 406-639-2254; Fax: 406-639-2254.
Catechesis/Religious Programs—Rosaline Old Bear, D.R.E.
Students 35.
Mission—Wyola, Blessed Kateri Tekakwitha.

Malta, Phillips Co., St. Mary's, Rev. Jim O'Neil.
Res., 27 S. Seventh St. W., P.O. Box 70, 59538. Tel: 406-654-1446; Fax: 406-654-1446.
Catechesis/Religious Programs—Dianne Salsbery, D.R.E.
Students 130.
Missions—Dodson, Sacred Heart; Saco, St. Francis of Assisi; Whitewater, St. John.

Miles City, Custer Co., Sacred Heart, Revs. Kirk Morgan; Kevin Lane Christofferson. Pastoral Assocs.: Sr. Janice Steiger, S.C.L.; Mrs. Carol Green.
Res., P.O. Box 1016, 59301. Tel: 406-232-1691; Fax: 406-232-5687.
School—(Grades K-8). Tel: 406-232-3850. Mrs. Kay Plummer, Prin.
Lay Teachers 7; Students 50.
Catechesis/Religious Programs—Mrs. Janice Wood, D.R.E.
Students 200.
Mission—Terry, Sacred Heart, P.O. Box 526, Terry, 59349. Tel: 406-637-5569.
Stations—Pine Hills School, Tel: 406-232-1377; Fax: 406-232-7432; Holy Rosary Extended Care, Tel: 406-233-2600; Fax: 406-233-2621; Holy Rosary Hospital.; Veterans' Administration Hospital, Tel: 406-232-3060; Miles City, Friendship Villa Rest Home, Tel: 406-232-2687.

Plentywood, Sheridan Co., St. Joseph's, Rev. Jerry P. Connolly; Kordelia French, Admin. Asst.
Res., P.O. Box 6, 59254. Tel: 406-765-2250.
Catechesis/Religious Programs—Kathleen Jensen, D.R.E.
Students 164.
Missions—Outlook, St. Boniface; Wesby, St. Elizabeth. [CEM]

Poplar, Roosevelt Co., Our Lady of Lourdes, Rev. Michael Schneider; Sr. Mary Hourigan, O.P., Pastoral Assoc.
Res., P.O. Box 187, 59255. Tel: 406-768-3244 (Rectory); 768-3305 (Office).
Catechesis/Religious Programs—Yvonne Shields, D.R.E.
Students 95.
Missions—Brockton, St. Thomas; Brockton, Roosevelt Co., St. Anthony, P.O. Box 86, Fort Kipp, 59213. Tel: 406-786-3265.

Pryor, Big Horn Co., St. Charles Borromeo Mission, Rev. Randolph Graczyk, O.F.M.Cap.
Res., P.O. Box 29, 59066. Tel: 406-259-9747; Fax: 406-259-7092.
School—(Grades K-8). Tel: 406-259-9976; Fax: 406-259-7092. Larry Cunningham, Prin.
Sisters 1; Lay Teachers 12; Students 138.

Red Lodge, Carbon Co., St. Agnes, Rev. Richard D. Osterman.
Res., P.O. Box 1067, 59068. Tel: 406-446-1237; Fax: 406-446-1237.
Catechesis/Religious Programs—Students 59.
Mission—Roberts, St. Thomas Aquinas.

Roundup, Musselshell Co., St. Benedict's, Rev. Wayne Pittard.
Res., 503 Main St., 59072. Tel: 406-323-1019.
Catechesis/Religious Programs—Ann Newell, D.R.E.
Students 79.
Missions—Melstone, Our Lady of Mercy; Musselshell, St. Honorata; Winnett, St. Aloysius; Broadview, Little Flower; Ryegate, St Mathias.

Scobey, Daniels Co., St. Philip Bonitus, Rev. Daniel J. O'Rourke.
Res., P.O. Box 827, 59263. Tel: 406-487-5525; Fax: 406-487-5566.
Catechesis/Religious Programs—D.R.E.: Diana Carney; Terry Risa; Ronnalee Harrold.
Students 106.
Missions—Flaxville, St. Louis; Glentana, Holy Family; Peerless, St. Ann. [CEM]

Sidney, Richland Co., St. Matthew, Rev. Greg Staudinger.
Res., 219 Seventh St. S.E., 59270. Tel: 406-482-1068; Fax: 406-482-4373. [CEM]
Catechesis/Religious Programs—Tel: 406-482-2510. D.R.E.: Barbara Olson; Valerie Wentz; Yvonne Volkman; Leslie Bieber.
Students 424.
Missions—Fairview, St. Catherine; Lambert, St. Theresa; Charley Creek, St. Bernard's; Savage, St. Michael.

Stanford, Judith Basin Co., St. Rose of Lima, Rev. Terrence P. Regan.
P.O. Box 250, 59479. Tel: 406-566-2531.
Catechesis/Religious Programs—Students 170.
Missions—Denton, St. Anthony, P.O. Box 386, Denton, 59430. Tel: 406-567-2438; Geyser, St. Cyril, P.O. Box 35, Geyser, 59447. Tel: 406-735-4388; Moore, St. Mathias, P.O. Box 104, Moore, 59464. Tel: 406-374-2468; Hobson, Sacred Heart, P.O. Box 286, Hobson, 59452. Tel: 406-423-5431.

Wolf Point, Roosevelt Co., Immaculate Conception, Rev. Stephen J. Zabrocki.
Res., 500 Fifth Ave. S., P.O. Box 789, 59201. Tel: 406-653-2610. [CEM]
Catechesis/Religious Programs—Linda Johnson, D.R.E.
Students 170.
Missions—Frazer, St. Joseph; Vida, St. Ann; Riverside, Sacred Heart.

Special Assignment:
Reverend Fathers—
Bailey, Larry, 315 72nd St. N., Malmastrom AFB, MT 59402-7514
Taylor, Jon, University of Great Falls, 1302 20th St. S., Great Falls, MT 59405
Vogel, Marcel, St. Gabriel's Church, P.O. Box 1089, Chinook, MT 59523-1089

On Duty Outside of the Diocese:
Reverend Fathers—
Cawley, William, St. Patrick Rectory, 231 S. Beaver St., York, PA 17403
Dobbin, Jay D., P.O. Box 27084 GMF, Barrigada, Guam 96921
Kirkness, Michael D., 136 N G St., Lompoc, CA 93436
Krier, John P., Immaculate Conception Church, P.O. Box 910, Davenport, WA 99122-0910
Moore, John J., 1520 Wigdal Ave., Corcoran, CA 93212-2378
Papes, Joseph T., 5201 Raubinger Rd., Swartz Creek, MI 48473

Military Chaplains:
Reverend Fathers—
Munsell, Richard F., 114 Patrick Drive, Biloxi, MS 39531

Absent on Leave:
Reverend Fathers—
Rutan, Albert E., P.O. Box 50, Liberty Center, IA 50145-0050

Retired:
Reverend Monsignors—
Gluszek, Joseph, Mailing Address: P.O. Box 7204, Great Falls, MT 59403
Werner, Martin E., Mailing Address: 820 32nd St. S., Great Falls, MT 59405
Reverend Fathers—
Arbanas, Harold P., 3475 16th St., #1, San Francisco, CA 94114-0011
Beggin, Thomas M., Regina Cleri, 2003 Woody Dr., No. 2, Billings, MT 59102
Bezdicek, Valerian V., Regina Cleri, 2003 Woody Dr., No. 3, Billings, MT 59102
Bofto, Robert C., 3001 S. 288th St., #230, Federal Way, WA 98003
Clausen, Kenneth J., 3729 Second Ave. N., Billings, MT 59101
Coady, John, 5734 E.19th St., Tucson, AZ 85711
Dwyer, David F., 1701 26th St. S., #3, Great Falls, MT 59405
Fisher, Martin, 507 Parkhill Dr., Billings, MT 59102
Fox, Robert J., P.O. Box 53, Poplar, MT 59255
Galour, Joseph L., 4630 S. Lakeshore, #116, Tempe, AZ 85282
Gedvila, Izidorius, 426 Randolph, Sunny Hills, FL 32428
Gorman, Charles L., Moate, Ballinakill, Portlaois, Laois, Ireland
Gregori, Anthony F., 1711 1/2 Smelter Ave., Great Falls, MT 59414
Guinan, Michael, 1701 26th St. S., #4, Great Falls, MT 59405
Hanrahan, John A., 1701 26th St. S., #2, Great Falls, MT 59405
Heretick, Joseph S., c/o Diocese of Great Falls-Billings, P.O. Box 1399, Great Falls, MT 59403
Hoffman, Emmett G., Golden Sun Estates, 40-985 Sun Estates, Palm Desert, CA 92211
Hopkins, Richard J., St. Patrick's Co-Cathedral, 215 N. 31st St., Billings, MT 59101
Janson, Leo F., Regina Cleri, 2003 Woody Dr., No. 1, Billings, MT 59102
Kaminski, Joseph M., 649 21st St., Black Eagle, MT 59414
Kelly, Frank F., 1701 26th St. S., #1, Great Falls, MT 59405
Marmion, Joseph B., P.O. Box 647, Chester, MT 59522
McInnis, Francis L., 4126 3rd Ave. S., Great Falls, MT 59405
McTague, Thomas, P.O. Box 225, Hysham, MT 59038
Mears, Charles T., 1430 E. El Parque, Tempe, AZ 85282
Moran, Patrick A., 1464 Green Trails Dr., No. 1, Naperville, IL 60540
O'Hanlon, Michael A., Danesfort, Dromahane Mallow, County Cork, Ireland
O'Reilly, Patrick J., 823 Leisure World, Mesa, AZ 85206
Powers, Thomas F., Aspen Village Retirement Residence, 3075 Ave. C, #230, Billings, MT 59102
Sampson, Patrick, 596 Acorn Pl., Billings, MT 59102
Shinnick, Edward P., RR 2 - Box 156A, Savage, MT 59262
Tarrant, Patrick J., P.O. Box 275, Yarmouth Port, MA 02675

Permanent Deacons:
Birkle, Timothy J., 1216 Claim Jumper, Billings, MT 59101
Daem, Robert W., 220 34th St. W., Billings, MT 59102
Melius, Melvin A., 1437 Avenue D, Billings, MT 59102

INSTITUTIONS LOCATED IN THE DIOCESE

[A] COLLEGES AND UNIVERSITIES

GREAT FALLS. *University of Great Falls,* (1932) 1301 20th St. S., 59405. Tel: 406-761-8210.
E-mail: adminrec@ugf.edu
Web site: www.ugf.edu
For a complete listing, refer to the Colleges and Universities section.

[B] HIGH SCHOOLS, DIOCESAN

BILLINGS. *Central Catholic High School,* 3 Broadwater Ave., 59101. Tel: 406-245-6651; Fax: 406-259-3124. Jo Ellen Estenson, Prin.; Mr. Donald Dundas, Asst. Prin. Sisters 1; Lay Teachers 33; Students 391.

[C] HIGH SCHOOLS, PRIVATE

ASHLAND. *St. Labre Indian Catholic High School,* Mission Rd., 59003. Tel: 406-784-2347; Fax: 406-784-2199. Dr. Russell Alexander, Dir. of Schools; Mr. Sean Flynn, Prin. Lay Teachers 15; Students 154.

[D] ELEMENTARY SCHOOLS, DIOCESAN

GREAT FALLS. *Blessed Trinity School,* 2820 Central Ave., 59401. Tel: 406-761-5775; Fax: 406-761-7180. Mrs. Patricia Scotson, Prin. Lay Teachers 21; Students 302.

BILLINGS. *St. Francis Intermediate School.* (Grades 3-5), 1734 Yellowstone Ave., 59101. Tel: 406-656-2300; Fax: 406-656-2301. Ed Rachac, Prin. Lay Teachers 11; Students 195.
St. Francis Primary School. (Grades PreK-2), 511 Custer Ave., 59101. Tel: 406-259-6421. Sr. Elizabeth Young, S.C.L., Head Prin.; Karen Petermann, Assoc. Prin. Lay Teachers 13; Students 275.
St. Francis Upper School. (Grades 6-8), 205 N. 32nd St., 59101. Tel: 406-259-5037; Fax: 406-259-7981. Martha Zauher, Prin. Lay Teachers 13; Students 229.

[E] ELEMENTARY SCHOOLS, PRIVATE

ASHLAND. *St. Labre Indian Catholic Elementary School,* Mission Rd., 59003. Tel: 406-784-2746; Fax: 406-784-2199. Dr. Russell Alexander, Dir. of Schools; Scott Gion, Prin. Lay Teachers 20; Students 315.

PRYOR. *St. Charles Mission School,* P.O. Box 29, 59066. Tel: 406-259-9976; Fax: 406-259-7092. Larry Cunningham, Prin. Sisters 1; Lay Teachers 16; Students 136.

ST. XAVIER. *Pretty Eagle Catholic School,* 59075. Tel: 406-666-2215; Fax: 406-666-2245. Veronica Small, Prin. Sisters 1; Lay Teachers 18; Students 148.

[F] CHILD CARE & YOUTH SERVICES

GREAT FALLS. *St. Thomas Child and Family Center,* 416 23rd St. N., 59401. Tel: 406-761-6538.
E-mail: stcfc@mcn.net
Sisters of Providence. Ms. Crystalle Ebbinga, Admin.
Child Care Center; Family Life Education; Prevention and Treatment of Child Abuse; Education, Information, and Referral Service; Summer Food Program for Low-Income Children; Before- and After-School Care Programs. Lay Staff 62; Child Care & Nursery Children 550.

BILLINGS. *Little Flower Day Care,* 120 S. 34th St., P.O. Box 31158, 59107. Tel: 406-252-5697. Sr. Elizabeth Young, S.C.L., Dir.
St. Francis Day Care, 511 Custer Ave., 59101. Tel: 406-259-6421. Sr. Anita Sullivan, S.C.L., Dir.
Saint Francis Day Care West, 2821 Augusta Ln., 59102. Tel: 406-256-3562. Sr. Anita Sullivan, S.C.L., Dir.

[G] GENERAL HOSPITALS

GREAT FALLS. *Benefis Health Care,* 500-15th Ave. S., P.O. Box 5013, 59403. Tel: 406-727-3333
For a complete listing, refer to the Hospitals section.

BILLINGS. *Saint Vincent Hospital and Health Center,* 1233 N. 30th St., P.O. Box 35200, 59107-5200. Tel: 406-657-7000
For a complete listing, refer to the Hospitals section.

MILES CITY. *Holy Rosary Health Center,* 2600 Wilson St., 59301. Tel: 406-233-2600; Fax: 406-233-2601
For a complete listing, refer to the Hospitals section.

[H] CONVENTS AND RESIDENCES FOR SISTERS

GREAT FALLS. *Our Lady of Lourdes Convent,* 319 14th St. S., 59405. Tel: 406-761-6443. Ursuline Nuns 2.
Ursuline Convent, 2300 Central Ave., 59401. Tel: 406-452-8585. Sr. Daniel Ryan, O.S.U., Supr. Ursuline Sisters 8.

BILLINGS. *Mercy Convent,* 2420 Elm St., 59101. Tel: 406-259-2550. Sisters of Mercy 2.
Sisters of Charity of Leavenworth, 1134 N. 31st St., 59101. Tel: 406-252-0395. Sisters 3.

[I] RENEWAL CENTERS

BILLINGS. *Sacred Heart Renewal Center,* 26 Wyoming Ave., P.O. Box 153, 59103-0153. Tel: 406-252-0322. Val King, Admin.; Polly Eaton, Spiritual Dir.

[J] RETREAT HOUSES

GREAT FALLS. *Ursuline Retreat Centre,* 2300 Central Ave., 59401. Tel: 406-452-8585. Harry J. Tholen, Dir.

[K] MISCELLANEOUS LISTINGS

GREAT FALLS. *Big Sky Cum Christo,* P.O. Box 1248, 59403. Tel: 406-452-1964. Mike Ferradas, Contact Person.
Cascade County Council of the St. Vincent de Paul Society, P.O. Box 1562, 500 Central Ave. W., 59403. Tel: 406-761-0870; 761-0966. Reggie Lantz, Operations Mgr.
Eastside Catholic Community of Great Falls, 2820 Central Ave., 59401. Tel: 406-761-5775. Education Trust for Blessed Trinity Catholic School. Peggy Tremper, Pres.
Frank & Isabell Stites Memorial Center. (Retired Priests & Lay People Living). Mailing Address: Pastoral Center, P.O. Box 1399, 59403. Tel: 406-727-6683. 1701 26th St. S., 59403. Joseph Loncki, Contact Person.
Great Falls City-Wide Ministry to Native Americans, 121 23rd St. S., P.O. Box 1399, 59403. Tel: 406-727-6683. Linda Kovar, Dir.
Heisey Memorial Trust Fund, 313 Seventh St. N., 59401. Tel: 406-453-1211. Mr. Kirby Crosley, Dir.
Heisey Memorial Youth Center, 313 Seventh St. N., 59401. Tel: 406-453-1211. Mr. Kirby Crosley, Dir. Recreation center serving the adults and youth of the community.
St. Joseph's Education Trust, 500 2nd Ave. S.W., 59404. Tel: 406-453-5558. Rev. Anthony J. Schuster, Chm.
Tekakwitha Conference, P.O. Box 6768, 59406. Tel: 406-727-0147; Fax: 406-452-9845.

BILLINGS. *Billings Area Catholic Education Trust.* (BACET), P.O. Box 31158, 59107-1158. Tel: 406-252-0252. Ms. Marilyn Miller, Exec. Dir.; Ms. Patte Paquette, Chair; Mr. Clay Skurdal, Vice Chair; Mr. Jim Winchell, Treas.
Kateri Indian Ministry, 1015 Broadwater, #12, 59102. Tel: 406-256-5142. Sr. Catherine A. Dorsey, O.P., Dir.
Mayfair Auction, Billings Catholic Schools. Mailing Address: P.O. Box 31158, 59107. Tel: 406-245-5463. Joni Harman, Exec. Dir.
Newman Center, 1500 N. 30th St., Box 55 MSU-Billings, 59101. Tel: 406-657-2276.
Regina Cleri. Pastoral Center, P.O. Box 1399, Great Falls, 59403. Tel: 406-727-6683. 2003 Woody Dr., 59102. (Retired Priests Living). Joseph Loncki, Contact Person.
St. Vincent de Paul Society of Yellowstone County, 2610 Montana Ave., 59101. Tel: 406-252-1855. Harold W. Merchant, Exec. Dir.; Sr. Monica McCormilla, R.S.M., Spiritual Advisor.
Saint Vincent Foundation, P. O. Box 35200, 59107-5200. Tel: 406-657-7997. Carolyn K. Ennis, Exec. Dir.; Mike Gustafson, Chm., Board of Trustees.

ASHLAND. *St. Labre Home for Indian Children and Youth,* P.O. Box 458, 59003. Tel: 406-784-2746; Fax: 406-784-2217. Mr. Anthony J. Vegh, Acting Prog. Dir. Children 23.
St. Labre Indian School Educational Association, P.O. Box 216, 59003. Tel: 406-784-2746; Fax: 406-784-6161. A nonprofit Corporation. Mr. Curtis Yarlott, Pres & Exec. Dir.; Rev. Emmett G. Hoffmann, (Retired). Four Catholic schools for Native Americans: St. Labre Indian School at Ashland (Grade School Students 315); (High School Students 150); Pretty Eagle School, St. Xavier (Students 148); St. Charles Mission School, Pryor (Students 138).

GLENDIVE. *Sacred Heart Educational Endowment Trust,* P.O. Box 36, 59330. Tel: 406-365-2585. Rev. Joseph Ponessa.

HAVRE. *St. Jude's Education Trust,* 811-6th St., 59501. Tel: 406-265-9445. M. F. Clancey, Chm.

LEWISTOWN. *St. Leo's Catholic Education Trust,* P.O. Box 421, 59457. Tel: 406-538-9306.
E-mail: stleos@tein.net
Rev. Jay H. Peterson, Chm.

MALTA. *St. Mary's Catholic Education Trust,* P.O. Box 70, 59538. Rev. James O'Neil.

MILES CITY. *Custer County Conference of the Society of Saint Vincent de Paul and Thrift Store,* 407 Main St., 59301. Tel: 406-232-3011. Dorothy Buck, Pres. Store Managers: Mathel Jager; Marcia Rudolph; Mrs. Marjorie Shipp.

MONARCH. *Thieltges-St. Thomas Camp,* P.O. Box 46, 59463. Tel: 406-236-5385.

RELIGIOUS INSTITUTES OF MEN REPRESENTED IN THE DIOCESE

For further details refer to the corresponding bracketed number in the Religious Institutes of Men or Women section.
[0200]—*Benedictine Monks.* (Assumption Abbey, Richardton, ND).—O.S.B.
[0470]—*The Capuchin Friars.* (Prov. of St. Joseph, Detroit).—O.F.M.Cap.
[0690]—*Jesuit Fathers and Brothers.* (Oregon Prov.).—S.J.

RELIGIOUS INSTITUTES OF WOMEN REPRESENTED IN THE DIOCESE

[0230]—*Benedictine Sisters of Pontifical Jurisdiction*. (Rapid City, SD and St. Paul, MN).—O.S.B.

[2100]—*Congregation of the Humility of Mary*. (Davenport, IA).—C.H.M.

[1730]—*Congregation of the Sisters of the Third Order of St. Francis*. (Oldenburg, IN).—O.S.F.

[1070-11]—*Dominican Sisters, Congregation of Our Lady of the Rosary*. (Sparkill, NY).—O.P.

[1070-03]—*Dominican Sisters, Sinsinawa Dominican Congregation of the Most Holy Rosary*. (Sinsinawa, WI).—O.P.

[1430]—*Franciscan Sisters of Our Lady of Perpetual Help*. (St. Louis, MO).—O.S.F.

[1680]—*School Sisters of St. Francis*. (Milwaukee, WI).—S.S.S.F.

[0480]—*Sisters of Charity of Leavenworth, Kansas*.—S.C.L.

[]—*Sisters of Mercy of Ballyshannon*. (Ballyshannon, Ireland).—R.S.M.

[2575]—*Sisters of Mercy of the Americas*. (Omaha, NE).—R.S.M.

[2630]—*Sisters of Mercy of the Holy Cross*. (Merrill, WI).—S.C.S.C.

[3350]—*Sisters of Providence*. (Spokane, WA).—S.P.

[3830-11]—*Sisters of St. Joseph of Nazareth*. (Nazareth, MI).—S.S.J.

[3320]—*Sisters of the Presentation of the B.V.M.*. (Aberdeen, SD).—P.B.V.M.

[1720]—*Sisters of the Third Order Regular of St. Francis of the Congregation of Our Lady of Lourdes*. (Rochester, MN).—O.S.F.

[4110]—*Ursuline Nuns*. (Santa Rosa, CA).—O.S.U.

[4120-04]—*Ursuline Nuns*. (Cleveland, OH).—O.S.U.

DIOCESAN CEMETERIES

GREAT FALLS. *Calvary*.
Mount Olivet.

BILLINGS. *Calvary*.
Holy Cross.

NECROLOGY

† McFarlane, Dale Floyd, (Retired). —Died April 25, 1997.

Diocese of Green Bay

(Dioecesis Sinus Viridis)

Most Reverend

ROBERT J. BANKS, D.D.

Bishop of Green Bay; ordained December 20, 1952; consecrated September 19, 1985; appointed Auxiliary Bishop to the Archbishop of Boston and Titular Bishop of Taraqua on June 26, 1985; appointed to Green Bay October 16, 1990. *Office: 1910 S. Webster Ave., P.O. Box 23825, Green Bay, WI, 54305-3825.* Tel.: 920-437-7531.

Most Reverend

ALOYSIUS J. WYCISLO, D.D.

Retired Bishop of Green Bay; ordained April 7, 1934; appointed Titular Bishop of Stadia and Auxiliary of Chicago October 17, 1960; consecrated December 21, 1960; appointed to Green Bay March 8, 1968; retired May 10, 1983; appointed Apostolic Administrator of Green Bay Diocese June 16, 1983. *Res., 1825 Riverside Dr., Green Bay, WI, 54301.* Tel.: 920-435-3685.

Most Reverend

ROBERT F. MORNEAU, D.D.

Auxiliary Bishop of Green Bay and Titular Bishop of Massa Lubrense; ordained May 28, 1966; appointed December 19, 1978; consecrated February 22, 1979. *Res., 1825 Riverside Dr., P.O. Box 23825, Green Bay, WI, 54305-3825. Office: 1910 S. Webster, P.O. Box 23825, Green Bay, WI, 54305-3825.* Tel.: 920-437-7531.

Chancery: 1910 S. Webster Ave., P.O. Box 23825, Green Bay, WI, 54305-3825. Tel.: 920-437-7531; Fax: 920-435-1330.

Web site address: www.gbdioc.org

E-mail address: jdewane@gbdioc.org

ESTABLISHED MARCH 3, 1868.

Square Miles 10,728.

Incorporated January 16, 1907.

Legal Title: Catholic Diocese of Green Bay.

Comprises these 16 Counties: Brown, Calumet, Door, Florence, Forest, Kewaunee, Langlade, Manitowoc, Marinette, Menominee, Oconto, Outagamie, Shawano, Waupaca, Waushara and Winnebago in the State of Wisconsin.

For legal titles of parishes and diocesan institutions, consult the Chancery Office.

STATISTICAL OVERVIEW

Personnel	
Bishop	1
Auxiliary Bishops	1
Retired Bishops	1
Abbots	1
Retired Abbots	3
Priests: Diocesan Active in Diocese	160
Priests: Active Outside Diocese	9
Priests: Diocesan in Foreign Missions	5
Priests: Retired, Sick or Absent	61
Number of Diocesan Priests	235
Religious Priests in Diocese	147
Extern Priests in Diocese	4
Ordinations:	
Diocesan Priests	3
Religious Priests	2
Transitional Deacons	2
Permanent Deacons	1
Permanent Deacons in Diocese	79
Total Brothers	46
Total Sisters	690
Parishes	
Parishes	201
With Resident Pastor:	
Resident Diocesan Priests	119
Resident Religious Priests	30
Without Resident Pastor:	
Administered by Priests	45
Administered by Permanent Deacons	1
Administered by Women Religious	6
Missions	4
Pastoral Centers	18
Professional Ministry Personnel:	
Sisters	71
Lay Ministers	92
Welfare	
Catholic Hospitals	7
Total Assisted	493,106
Homes for the Aged	10
Total Assisted	1,173
Day Care and Extended Day Care Centers	2
Total Assisted	100
Specialized Homes	4
Total Assisted	658
Special Centers for Social Services	8
Total Assisted	218,575
Residential Care of Disabled	1
Total Assisted	7
Educational	
Diocesan Students in Other Seminaries	10
Seminaries, Religious	1
Students Religious	4
Total Seminarians	14
Colleges and Universities	2
Total Students	5,066
High Schools, Diocesan and Parish	5
Total Students	1,483
High Schools, Private	1
Total Students	826
Elementary Schools, Diocesan and Parish	79
Total Students	13,333
Catechesis/Religious Education:	
High School Students	8,961
Elementary Students	18,584
Total Students Under Catholic Instruction	48,267
Teachers in the Diocese:	
Priests	1
Brothers	3
Sisters	39
Lay Teachers	926
Vital Statistics	
Receptions into the Church:	
Infant Baptism Totals	4,792
Adult Baptism Totals	187
Received into Full Communion	474
First Communions	5,304
Confirmations	3,914
Marriages:	
Catholic	1,533
Interfaith	535
Total Marriages	2,068
Deaths	3,296
Total Catholic Population	387,868
Total Population	898,050

Former Bishops—Rt. Rev. JOSEPH MELCHER, D.D., cons. July 12, 1868; died Dec. 20, 1873.—Rt. Rev. FRANCIS XAVIER KRAUTBAUER, D.D., cons. June 29, 1875; died Dec. 17, 1885.—Rt. Rev. FREDERICK XAVIER KATZER, D.D., appt. July 13, 1886; cons. Sept. 21, 1886; appt. Archbishop of Milwaukee, Jan. 30, 1891; died July 20, 1903.—Rt. Rev. SEBASTIAN GEBHARD MESSMER, D.D., cons. Bishop of Green Bay, March 27, 1892; appt. Archbishop of Milwaukee, Nov. 28, 1903; died Aug. 4, 1930.—Rt. Rev. JOSEPH J. FOX, D.D., cons. Bishop of Green Bay, July 25, 1904; resigned Dec. 4, 1914; appt. Titular Bishop of Ionopolis; died March 14, 1915.—Most Rev. PAUL P. RHODE, D.D., ord. June 17, 1894; cons. Titular Bishop of Barca and Auxiliary to the Archbishop of Chicago, July 29, 1908; transferred to the See of Green Bay, July 5, 1915; died March 3, 1945.—Most Rev. STANISLAUS V. BONA, D.D., ord. Nov. 1, 1912; appt. Bishop of Grand Island, NE Dec. 18, 1931; cons. Feb. 25, 1932; appt. Coadjutor Bishop of Green Bay, Dec. 2, 1944; succeeded to See, March 3, 1945; died Dec. 1, 1967.—Most Rev. ALOYSIUS J. WYCISLO, D.D., ord. April 7, 1934; appt. Titular Bishop of Stadia and Auxiliary Bishop of Chicago Oct. 17, 1960; cons. Dec. 21, 1960; appt. to Green Bay, March 8, 1968; retired May 10, 1983.—Most Rev. ADAM J. MAIDA, J.C.L., J.D., S.T.L., Bishop of Green Bay; ord. May 26, 1956; appt. to Green Bay, Nov. 8, 1983; cons. Jan. 25, 1984.

Vicars General—Most Rev. ROBERT F. MORNEAU, D.D.; Rev. Msgr. JOHN B. DEWANE, M.A., S.T.L., D.Min.

Chancery—1910 S. Webster Ave., P.O. Box 23825, Green Bay, 54305-3825. Tel: 920-437-7531; Fax: 920-435-1330. Office Hours: Mon.-Fri. 9-5; other times by appointment only.

Vicar for Administration—Rev. Msgr. JOHN B. DEWANE, M.A., S.T.L., D.Min.

Chancellor—Sr. LISA LUCHT, O.P., M.M., D.Min.

Vice-Chancellor—Rev. Msgr. JOHN H. SCHUH.

Archivist—Sr. ELLA KASTER, C.S.J., M.A., , Ext. 8186.

Secretary to Bishop—TERRI WICKMAN, , Ext. 8194.

Chancery Secretary—MARY JO KRUEGER, , Ext. 8188.

Diocesan Tribunal—Mailing Address: *1910 S. Webster Ave., P.O. Box 23825, Green Bay, 54305-3825.* Tel: 920-437-7531.

Presiding Judge and Officialis—Rev. Msgr. BRIAN P. COLEMAN, J.C.L.
Associate Judicial Vicar—Rev. ROBERT J. KABAT, J.C.L.
Vice-Officialis and Assoc. Presiding Judge—Rev. RICHARD GETCHEL, J.C.L.
Defenders of the Bond—Revs. LEE J. KAHRS; PHILIP HOFFMANN.
Prosynodal Judges—Rev. Msgr. DENNIS M. LALLY; Revs. DENNIS M. BURKE, O.Praem, S.T.D., J.C.D.; ARTHUR J. DANKS; ROBERT KABAT, J.C.L.; RICHARD C. SHAFER, M.A.; WILLIAM L. VAN DE KREEKE, J.C.L.
Notaries—MARGIE GANTZ; RITA VANDEN AVOND; KATHLEEN SCHUMACHER.
Diocesan Consultors—Most Rev. ROBERT F. MORNEAU, V.G.; Rev. JOHN B. DEWANE, M.A., S.T.L., D.Min.; Revs. C. TERRENCE LACOMBE; MICHAEL BETLEY; PAUL DEMUTH; DENNIS DRURY; DAVID BAETEN; EARL BROUCHOUD; Rev. Msgr. ROY KLISTER.
Secretary to Consultors—Sr. LISA LUCHT, O.P.
Pastor Consultors—Rev. Msgr. PETER N. KLAUCK; Rev. Msgr. CARL E. STEINER; Revs. JOHN P. BERGSTADT; JAMES A. HABLEWITZ; JOSEPH A. MATTERN; PAUL A. SCHUMACHER; WILLARD J. VAN DE LOO.
Regional Vicars—Revs. RALPH GILLIS, Vicariate I; LEONARD M. EVERS, Vicariate II; PAUL J. RADETSKI, Vicariate III; PHILIP DINH-VAN-THIEP, Vicariate IV; DENNIS M. RYAN, Vicariate V; JAMES A. HABLEWITZ, Vicariate VI; DEAN DOMBROSKI, Vicariate VII; DAVID SCHMIDT, Vicariate VIII; JOHN T. MULLARKEY, Vicariate IX; MICHAEL KOCH, Vicariate X; RALLEN STENCIL, Vicariate XI; RALPH C. MERKATORIS, Vicariate XII.
Diocesan Pastoral Council—Sr. BARBARA BELINSKI.
Presbyteral Council—Rev. Msgr. JAMES DILLENBURG, Chm.
Appointed Representatives—Rev. Msgr. ROY M. KLISTER; Rev. Msgr. BRIAN COLEMAN; Revs. DAVID HOFFMAN; LOREN NYS, S.D.S.; JOHN ZICKERT, O.F.M.Cap.; MICHAEL INGOLD; EARL SCHUH; JOHN HARPER.
Elected Representatives—Rev. GERALD SCHMIDT, O.F.M.Cap, Vicariate I; Rev. MICHAEL CARROLL, Vicariate II; Rev. JOHN GALLAGHER, Vicariate III; Rev. MICHAEL BETLEY, Vicariate IV; Rev. GARY DANTINNE, Vicariate V; Rev. Msgr. JAMES DILLENBURG, Vicariate VI; Rev. DENNIS DRURY, Vicariate VII; Rev. JAMES GILSOUL, Vicariate VIII; Rev. TOM POMEROY, Vicariate IX; Rev. MARTIN CARR, Vicariate X; Rev. GARY NEW, S.D.S., Vicariate XI; Rev. JOHN PUODZIUNAS, O.F.M., Vicariate XII. Ex-Officios: Most Rev. ROBERT F. MORNEAU; Rev. Msgr. JOHN B. DEWANE.
Bishop's Finance Council—Rev. ROBERT K. FINNEGAN, O.Praem.; MARY STAUDENMAIER; MICHAEL ARIENS; JAMES LIETHEN; JOHN F. BERGSTROM; ROBERT C. GALLAGHER; WILLIAM FRIEDER.
Resource—Most Rev. ROBERT F. MORNEAU; THOMAS KURKOWSKI.

Ministry Personnel

Vicar for Religious—Rev. Msgr. JOHN H. SCHUH, *P.O. Box 23825, Green Bay, 54305-3825.* Tel: 920-437-7531, Ext. 8179.
Representative for Religious—Sr. MARY JO KIRT, *P.O. Box 23825, Green Bay, 54305-3825.* Tel: 920-437-7531, Ext. 8292.
Vicar for Priests—Rev. WILLARD J. VAN DE LOO, *P.O. Box 23825, Green Bay, 54305-3825.* Tel: 920-437-7531, Ext. 8322.
Vicar for Senior Priests—Rev. PHILIP HOFFMANN, *P.O. Box 23825, Green Bay, 54305-3825.* Tel: 920-437-7531, Ext. 8183.
Ministry to Priests Program—Rev. WILLARD J. VAN DE LOO, Dir., *P.O. Box 23825, Green Bay, 54305-3825.* Tel: 920-437-7531, Ext. 8322.
Department of the Permanent Diaconate—Deacon MAURICE REED, Dir., Prog. Coord. & Vicar for Deacons, *P.O. Box 23825, Green Bay, 54305-3825.* Tel: 920-437-7531, Ext. 8290.
Vocations—*P.O. Box 23825, Green Bay, 54305-3825.* Tel: 920-437-7531. Rev. DOUGLAS LECAPTAIN, Dir.; Sr. MARY JO KIRT, Assoc. Dir.
Department for Parish Ministers—Sr. FLORENCE YOUNGWIRTH, A.N.G., Dir., *P.O. Box 23825, Green Bay, 54305-3825.* Tel: 920-437-7531, Ext. 8268.

Education

Education—*1825 Riverside Dr., P.O. Box 23825, Green Bay, 54305-3825.* Tel: 920-437-7531; Fax: 920-437-0694.
Total Catholic Education Department—Mr. LELAND NAGEL, Dir., , Ext. 8269.
Consultants—
Youth Ministry—TONY PICHLER, , Ext. 8218.
Staff Development Services—Sr. PAT MCCORMICK, , Ext. 8271.
Personnel Services—ANN FOX, , Ext. 8273.
Instructional Leadership—Sr. PAT BECKMAN, , Ext. 8284.
Educational Programs—CHRIS BROSLAVICK, , Ext. 8283.
Young Adult/Adult Catechesis—Sr. PEG GABIK, , Ext. 8270.
Religious Education (K-6)—JEANNINE GOGGIN, , Ext. 8274.
Catechist Formation—Sr. STEPHANIE SPENCE, , Ext. 8277.
Liaisons-Office of Education—
Priests Eucharistic League—Rev. DONALD FELLER, *2496 Mary Jo Dr., Green Bay, 54311.* Tel: 920-465-3460.
The Diocesan Charismatic Renewal Center—Rev. Msgr. JAMES VANDEN HOGEN, *Res., St. John Nepomucene Parish, 323 S. Pine St., Little Chute, 54140-1896.* Tel: 920-788-9061.
Serra Clubs—Rev. DOUGLAS LECAPTAIN, *P.O. Box 23825, Green Bay, 54305-3825.* Tel: 920-437-7531.
Blue Army - World Apostolate of Fatima—Rev. ARTHUR DANKS, *2616 He-Nis-Ra Ln., Green Bay, 54304.* Tel: 920-499-9309.
Cursillo—Rev. DAVID PLEIER, *2040 Hillside Ln., Green Bay, 54302-4098.* Tel: 920-468-4811.
Xavier Guild—Rev. DENNIS M. RYAN, Chap., *St. Nicholas Parish, N4088 Cty. Tr. E., P.O. Box 1006, Freedom, 54131-1006.* Tel: 920-788-1492.
Diocesan Council of Catholic Women—SUE WINTER, Pres., *N4135 Hwy. 32, Krakow, 54137.* Tel: 920-899-3680.

Pastoral Services

Pastoral Services—*1825 Riverside Dr., P.O. Box 23825, Green Bay, 54305-3825.* Tel: 920-437-7531; Fax: 920-437-0694. MARK MOGILKA, Dir., , Ext. 8297.
Family Life Department (Voice & TDD)—TOM RINKOSKI, Dir., , Ext. 8304.
Marriage Preparation, Parenting—MARY STUBLER, , Ext. 8315.
Consultants—
Ecumenism—Rev. PHILIP HOFFMANN, Ecumenical Officer, , Ext. 8183.
Evangelization/Renew 2000—JACKIE STALEY, , Ext. 8316.
Ministry with Persons with Disabilities—SUE PERRAULT, , Ext. 8306.
Pastoral Care—MARK MITCHELL, , Ext. 8300.
Respect Life—HELEN URBAN, , Ext. 8308.
Rural Life—PATRICIA POSBRIG, Consultant, *N256 State Hwy. 55, Seymour, 54165.* Tel: 920-833-7557.
Social Concerns—PAUL GRIMM, Consultant, , Ext. 8299.
Worship Department—DIANN WIMMER, Dir., , Ext. 8311.
RCIA—CINDE BECKER, Consultant, , Ext. 8301.
Sacred Music—PAUL GRIMM, Consultant, , Ext. 8299.
Campus Ministry—Rev. JEFFREY VANDEN HEUVEL, Dir., *717 W. Irving, Oshkosh, 54901.* Tel: 920-233-5555.
Department of World Mission Services—CLAIRE THOMAS, Dir., *P.O. Box 23825, Green Bay, 54305-3825.* Tel: 920-437-7531, Ext. 8192; Fax: 920-435-1330.
Agencies—Propagation of the Faith, St. Peter the Apostle, Holy Childhood Association, Catholic Relief Services.
Holy Name Retreat House—MICHAEL CHERF, Co-Admin. MARY CHERF, Co-Admin.
Evangelization Commission—CINDE BECKER.
Liturgical Commission—DIANN WIMMER.
Ecumenical Commission—Rev. PHILIP HOFFMAN.
Justice & Peace Commission—PAUL GRIMM.

Community Services

Community Services—KAREN JOHNSTON, Dir., *1825 Riverside Dr., P.O. Box 23825, Green Bay, 54305-3825.* Tel: 920-437-7531, Ext. 8226; Fax: 920-437-0694.
Department of Catholic Social Services—KAREN JOHNSTON, Dir. JANE KOEFERL, Clinical Svcs. Coord., , Ext. 8242.
Department of Refugee, Migration and Hispanic Services—BARBARA B. BIEBEL, Dir., , Ext. 8252.
Apostleship of the Sea—Deacon GLENN TESKE, Dir., *2839 S. Broadway, Green Bay, 54304-5309.* Tel: 920-499-0035.
Diocesan Health Services—Rev. DAVID BEAUDRY, Coord., *8109 Northeim Rd., Newton, 53063-9630.* Tel: 920-726-4228.
McCormick Memorial Home for the Aged—*212 Iroquois St., Green Bay, 54301.* Tel: 920-437-0883. JAMES GENRICH, Admin.; Rev. THADDEUS J. KOSZAREK, Chap.
Liaisons - Community Services—
Sign of God Deaf Ministry—Rev. ANTHONY WIECZOREK, O.Praem., Chap. MARY E. ZUPANSIC, Pastoral Assoc., *1016 N. Broadway, De Pere, 54115.* Tel: 920-337-9454.
Society of St. Vincent de Paul—ROGER HEROLD, Pres. & Trustee; Rev. ARTHUR J. DANKS, Spiritual Dir. (Council of the Green Bay Diocesan, Society of St. Vincent de Paul, Inc.); EVERETT JOHNSON, Exec. Sec., *834 Gross Ave., Green Bay, 54304.* Tel: 920-490-9360.
Knights of Columbus—DON BETTINE, District Deputy, Council 5382, *1243 Valley View Rd., Green Bay, 54304.* Tel: 920-499-2811. Rev. STANLEY BROWNE, Chap.
Our Lady of Charity Center, Inc.—Sr. BARBARA JEAN ARNSMEYER, O.L.C., Dir., *2560 Shawano Ave., P.O. Box 10357, Green Bay, 54313.* Tel: 920-434-8208.
Daughters of Isabella—MADELINE CENTEN, Local Regent, *820 Marvin Ln., Green Bay, 54311-5944.* Tel: 920-468-0269.
Catholic Veterans of War—RAYMOND WOZNICK, Commander, *418 Forrest Ave., Fond du Lac, 54935.* JOSEPH RICKERT, District 3 Commander, *936 W. Marquette St., Appleton, 54911.* Tel: 920-734-9684.
Menominee Pastoral Program—Rev. DAVID S. BARRETT, *St. Michael Church, P.O. Box 610, Keshena, 54135-0160.* Tel: 715-799-3811.

Support Services

Support Services—*1910 S. Webster Ave., P.O. Box 23825, Green Bay, 54305-3825.* Tel: 920-437-7531; Fax: 920-435-1330. Rev. Msgr. JOHN B. DEWANE, M.A., S.T.L., D.Min., Vicar for Admin., , Ext. 8171.
Annual Bishop's Appeal—CINDI BRAWNER, , Ext. 8173.
Medical Insurance and Benefits—MARY VANKAUWENBERG, *Box 23825, Green Bay, 54305-3825.* Tel: 920-437-7531, Ext. 8260.
Bishop's Charities Game—JAMES HOGAN, *P.O. Box 23825, Green Bay, 54305-3825.* Tel: 920-437-7531, Ext. 8219.
Camp Tekawitha—ROBERTA LARSON, *P.O. Box 23825, Green Bay, 54305-3825.* Tel: 920-437-7531, Ext. 8511.
Cemeteries—JOHN C. NELSON, *1825 Riverside Dr., P.O. Box 23825, Green Bay, 54305-3825.* Tel: 920-437-7531, Ext. 8229.
Communications—*P.O. Box 23825, Green Bay, 54305-3825.* Tel: 920-437-7531. TONY KUICK, Dir., , Ext. 8214. RENAE WUERGER, Pub. Rels. Coord., , Ext. 8213.
Diocesan Newspaper—*"The Compass", P.O. Box 23825, Green Bay, 54305-3825.* Tel: 920-437-7531. Appleton Area: Tel: 920-233-5555. TONY KUICK, Gen. Mgr., , Ext. 8214. ANTON STALEY, Editor, , Ext. 8210.
Computer Services—TONY KUICK, Dir. BEA SEIDL, Database Admin., , Ext. 8255. DAN LEE, P.C. Specialist, *Box 23825, Green Bay, 54305-3825.* Tel: 920-437-7531.
Financial Services—THOMAS KURKOWSKI, Dir., , Ext. 8267. MIKE SPEEL, Sr. Acct., , Ext. 8259., *P.O. Box 23825, Green Bay, 54305-3825.* Tel: 920-437-7531.
Personnel—JAMES HOGAN, Dir., *P.O. Box 23825, Green Bay, 54305-3825.* Tel: 920-437-7531, Ext. 8219.
Property Management and Real Estate—JOHN C. NELSON, Dir. Temporalities, *P.O. Box 23825, Green Bay, 54305-3825.* Tel: 920-437-7531, Ext. 8229.
Sacred Heart Seminary, Inc.—*P.O. Box 23825, Green Bay, 54305-3825.* Tel: 920-437-7531.
Sacrificial Giving Program—CINDI BRAWNER, Dir., *P.O. Box 23825, Green Bay, 54305-3825.* Tel: 920-437-7531, Ext. 8173.
St. Joseph Corporation and Central Services—VINCE PELLETIER, *P.O. Box 23825, Green Bay, 54305-3825.* Tel: 920-437-7531, Ext. 8246.
Stewardship and Development—CINDI BRAWNER, *P.O. Box 23825, Green Bay, 54305-3825.* Tel: 920-437-7531, Ext. 8173.
Priests' Personnel Board—Revs. JOHN H. VAN DEUREN, Chm. RONALD COLOMBO; RALPH MERKATORIS; MICHAEL BETLEY; WILLIAM SPALDING; JOHN MULLARKEY; Rev. Msgr. JOHN H. SCHUH; Rev. WILLARD J. VAN DE LOO, Resource Person.
Conciliation and Arbitration Board—Rev. JOHN T. MULLARKEY, Pres. ROBERT J. KABAT, Clerk, *P.O. Box 23825, Green Bay, 54305-3825.* Tel: 920-437-7531.
Liaisons—Personnel—
Association of Pastoral Associates—Sr. FLORENCE YOUNGWIRTH, *P.O. Box 23825, Green Bay, 54305-3825.* Tel: 920-437-7531, Ext. 8268.
Leo Benevolent Association—Rev. WILLIAM J. SPALDING, Chm., *310 Alpine Dr., Apt. 9, Shawano, 54166.* Tel: 715-524-5904.
Clergy Credit Union—Rev. CHARLES W. MOCCO, Treas., *Res., UWGB Ecumenical Center, 2420 Nicolet Dr., Green Bay, 54311-7001.* Tel: 920-465-5133.
Community of Our Lady—Rev. REGIS N. BARWIG, Prior, *2804 Oakwood Ln., Oshkosh, 54904.* Tel: 920-233-5633.
A New Genesis—Sr. STEPHANIE SPENCE, Moderator, *1701 N. McDonald St., Appleton, 54911.* Tel: 920-731-3523. Most Rev. ALOYSIUS J. WYCISLO, Chap.

CLERGY, PARISHES, MISSIONS AND PAROCHIAL SCHOOLS

CITY OF GREEN BAY
(Brown County)

1—ST. FRANCIS XAVIER CATHEDRAL, Rev. Msgr. Peter N. Klauck; Rev. John Doerfler; Deacon Paul Plantico.
Res., 139 S. Madison St., 54301-4588. Tel: 920-324-4348; Fax: 920-435-5068.
School—St. Thomas More. Consolidated with St. Mary and Ss. Peter & Paul 650 S. Irwin Ave., 54301. Tel: 920-432-8242. Barbara Schneider, Prin.
Catechesis/Religious Programs—Students 77.

2—NATIVITY OF OUR LORD, Revs. James A. Hablewitz; Donald Everts; Sr. Louise Kwaterski, Pastoral Assoc.
Res., 2270 S. Oneida St., 54304-4712. Tel: 920-995-5156; Fax: 920-490-1352.
Catechesis/Religious Programs—Lorraine Cann, D.R.E.
Students 1,433.

3—ST. AGNES, Rev. Richard Getchel; Deacon Robert Arnold.
Res., 1484 9th St., 54304-3098. Tel: 920-942-2534.
School—Holy Family. Serving the parishes of St. Elizabeth Seton & St. Agnes. 1204 S. Fisk St., 54304. Tel: 920-494-1931. Sr. Kathryn Klackner, O.S.F., Prin.
Franciscan Sisters of Christian Charity 4; Lay Teachers 26; Students 477.
Catechesis/Religious Programs—Students 377.
Convent—1208 S. Fisk St., 54304.

4—ANNUNCIATION OF THE BLESSED VIRGIN MARY, Rev. Joseph R. Coopmans, O.Praem.
Res., 401 Gray St., 54303-3099. Tel: 920-992-2333.
School—1087 Kellogg St., 54303. Tel: 920-499-1919. Alice Jacques, Prin.
Lay Teachers 12; Students 221.
Catechesis/Religious Programs—Students 111.

5—ST. BERNARD, Revs. David Pleier; John Schuetze; Sr. Pauline Feiner, S.D.S., Pastoral Assoc.; Deacons Lawrence Mastalish; John Laurant.
Res., 2040 Hillside Ln., 54302-4098. Tel: 920-684-4811; Fax: 920-468-1396.
School—2020 Hillside Ln., 54302. Tel: 920-468-5026. Mrs. Pat Ford, Prin.
Sisters 1; Lay Teachers 20; Students 488.
Catechesis/Religious Programs—Sr. Mary Ramone Blahnik, D.R.E.
Students 752.

6—ST. JOHN, Rev. Msgr. James B. Feely.
Res., 413 St. John St., 54301-4195. Tel: 920-366-6380.

7—ST. JOSEPH, In res., Rev. Douglas LeCaptain.
Res., 936 9th St., 54304-3499. Tel: 920-977-7042.
School—1224 12th Ave., 54304. Tel: 920-497-7085. Mrs. Patricia Brault, Prin.
Lay Teachers 13; Students 174.
Catechesis/Religious Programs—Eugene Mailhiot, D.R.E.
Students 128.

8—ST. JUDE, Rev. Ronald C. Belitz; Ann Froelich, Pastoral Min.
Res., 1423 Kellogg St., 54303-3197. Tel: 920-962-2160.
School—1420 Division St., 54303-3113. Tel: 920-296-2162. Jane Schueller, Prin.
Religious 1; Lay Teachers 14; Students 259.
Catechesis/Religious Programs—Carolyn Whitcomb, D.R.E.
Students 246.

9—HOLY MARTYRS OF GORCUM, Rev. Robert E. Rhyner; Deacon William Burkel.
Res., 3562 Finger Rd., 54311-7733. Tel: 920-685-5718; Fax: 920-468-5713. [CEM]
School—3542 Finger Rd., 54311-7733. Tel: 920-468-7262. Sr. Therese Kulas, Prin.
Lay Teachers 9; Students 141.
Catechesis/Religious Programs—Tim Younk, D.R.E.
Students 138.

10—ST. MARY OF THE ANGELS, Revs. Finian Zaucha, O.F.M.; Brendan Wroblewski, O.F.M.; Deacon Earl Charlier.
Res., 645 S. Irwin Ave., 54301-3397. Tel: 920-371-1979.
School—St. Thomas More, (Grades PreK-8). Consolidated with Cathedral and Ss. Peter & Paul. 650 S. Irwin, 54301. Tel: 920-432-8242. Barbara Schneider, Prin.
Religious 1; Lay Teachers 22; Students 255.
Catechesis/Religious Programs—Students 105.

11—ST. MATTHEW, Rev. David Baeten.
Res., 130 Saint Matthews St., 54301-2999. Tel: 920-356-6811.
School—2575 S. Webster Ave., 54301. Tel: 920-432-5223. Sr. Carmelyn Gentrup, Prin.
Religious 1; Lay Teachers 15; Students 198.
Catechesis/Religious Programs—Mike Westenberg, D.R.E.
Students 275.

12—ST. PATRICK, Rev. John F. O'Brien; Sr. Jeanne Vander Boomen, O.S.F., Pastoral Assoc.
Res., 211 N. Maple Ave., 54303-2783. Tel: 920-373-3911; Fax: 920-437-3356.
Catechesis/Religious Programs—Marge Vander Steeg, D.R.E.
Students 165.

13—SS. PETER AND PAUL, Rev. Msgr. Roy M. Klister, J.C.L.; Revs. Joseph E. Dorner; John G. Van Der Horst; Earl J. Schuh, Pastor Emeritus; Sr. Lucy Andre, O.S.F., Pastoral Assoc.; Deacon Kenneth D. Kopydlowski.
Res., 710 N. Baird St., 54302-1997. Tel: 920-357-7548; Fax: 920-432-1321.
Schools—St. Thomas More Elementary. Consolidation of SS. Peter & Paul,St. Mary,& Cathedral. Tel: 920-432-8242. Mrs. Barbara Schneider, Prin.
Sisters 1; Lay Teachers 24; SSPP Students 81; St. Thomas More School System, (Grades PreK-8) 650 S. Irwin Ave., 54301.
Lay Teachers 7; SSPP Students 42.
Catechesis/Religious Programs—Associated with Holy Martyrs (for Confirmation). Mike & Doris Vincent, D.R.E.
Students 234.

14—ST. PHILIP THE APOSTLE, Revs. Lawrence J. Canavera; Paul E. Du Charme; Sr. Dorothy Wagner, Pastoral Assoc.; Deacon Terry Dineen.
Res., 312 Victoria St., 54302-2818. Tel: 920-687-7848; Fax: 920-468-1025.
School—Tel: 920-468-7755. Sr. Mary Ann Tupy, Prin.
Sisters 2; Lay Teachers 14; Students 279.
Catechesis/Religious Programs—D.R.E.: Mary Terrien; Sandy Mangin.
Students 354.
Convent—312 Victoria St., 54302. Franciscan Sisters of Christian Charity

15—RESURRECTION, Rev. Paul E. Demuth; Sr. Helen Plum, S.S.N.D., Pastoral Assoc. & Liturgist; Deacon Timothy Reilly.
Res., 333 Hilltop Dr., 54301-2799. Tel: 920-367-7768; Fax: 920-336-1949.
School—Tel: 920-336-3230. Brian Jones, Educ. Dir.
Lay Teachers 18; Students 229.
Catechesis/Religious Programs—Brian Jones, D.R.E.
Students 374.

16—ST. ELIZABETH ANN SETON, Rev. Msgr. James Dillenburg; Rev. John Van Deuren; Sr. Madonna Schmelzle, O.S.F., Pastoral Assoc.; Deacon James Gauthier.
Res., 2771 Oakwood Dr., 54304-1699. Tel: 920-991-1546; Fax: 920-499-2207.
School—Holy Family. Consolidated with St. Agnes. 1204 Fisk St., 54304. Tel: 920-494-1931. Sr. Kathryn Klackner, Prin.
Religious 5; Lay Teachers 26; Students 259.
Catechesis/Religious Programs—Carol Vanden Bush, D.R.E.
Students 675.

17—ST. WILLEBRORD, Revs. Kenneth J. DeGroot, O.Praem.; Harvey H. Toonen, O.Praem.; Albin V. Veszelovszky, O.Praem. In res., Rev. Willard Van De Loo. Pastoral Assocs.: Sr. Melanie Maczka, S.S.C.; Sr. Sharon Stecker, S.S.N.D.; Sr. Elizabeth Koszarek, S.S.J., T.O.S.F.; Mary Funk.
Res., 209 S. Adams St., 54301-4584. Tel: 920-352-2016; Fax: 920-435-2039.

OUTSIDE THE CITY OF GREEN BAY

Abrams, Oconto Co., St. Louis. Attended by St. John Cantius, Sobieski. Rev. Gerald Prusakowski, O.F.M.
Mailing Address: 6051 Noble St., Sobieski, 54171-9724. Tel: 920-267-7425. [JC]
Catechesis/Religious Programs—Associated with St. John Cantius, Sobieski.
Students 65.

Algoma, Kewaunee Co., St. Mary, Rev. Michael Flanary.
Res., 118 Church St., 54201-1033. Tel: 920-875-5005; Fax: 920-487-5002. [CEM]
School—214 Church St., 54201. Tel: 920-487-5004. Mrs. Mary Mayheu, Prin.
Lay Teachers 9; Students 115.
Catechesis/Religious Programs—Students 130.

Alverno, Manitowoc Co., St. Joseph. (Also serves St. Casimir, Northeim). Rev. David Beaudry.
Mailing Address: 8109 Northeim Rd., Newton, 53063-9630. Tel: 920-824-4217; Fax: 920-682-6264. [CEM]
Church—2413 S. Alverno Rd., Manitowoc, 54220-9340. [CEM]
School—Tel: 920-682-4217. Mr. John Pavek, Prin.
Lay Teachers 6; Students 52.
Catechesis/Religious Programs—Students 131.

Amberg, Marinette Co., St. Agnes. Attended by St. Augustine, Wausaukee. Rev. John F. McLaughlin.
Mailing Address: P.O. Box 375, Wausaukee, 54177-0375. Tel: 715-565-5276.

Aniwa, Shawano Co., St. Boniface. Attended by St. Philomena, Birnamwood. Rev. Everard S. Scesney, O.F.M.
Res., P.O. Box K, Birnamwood, 54414-0911. Tel: 715-492-2104. [CEM]
Catechesis/Religious Programs—Students 84.

Antigo, Langlade Co., St. John, Rev. Charles G. Hoffmann.
Res., 426 Hudson St., 54409-2197. Tel: 715-232-2024. [JC]
School—420 Fulton St., 54409. Tel: 715-623-4835; Fax: 715-627-2969. John Cerny, Prin.
Lay Teachers 12; Students 261.
Catechesis/Religious Programs—Gerald Bahar, D.R.E.
Students 249.

St. Hyacinth, Rev. Msgr. Paul P. Koszarek.
Res., 819 3rd Ave., 54409-1930. Tel: 715-232-2425. [JC]
Catechesis/Religious Programs—Students 74.

St. Mary. (Also serves St. Wencaslaus, Neva). Rev. Jeremiah F. Worman; Deacon Thomas J. Hanley.
Res., 735 Deleglise St., 54409-1497. Tel: 715-232-2522.
School—723 Deleglise St., 54409. Tel: 715-623-5629. Vicki Koeppel, Prin.
Sisters of Mercy of the Holy Cross 1; Lay Teachers 5; Students 71.
Catechesis/Religious Programs—Students 94.

Appleton, Outagamie Co.,

1—ST. BERNADETTE, Rev. Harold Berryman.
Church—2331 E. Lourdes Dr., 54915-3698. Tel: 920-394-4157.
School—1810 W. Prospect Ave., 54914. Tel: 920-735-9380. Jennifer Rohlf, Prin.
Lay Teachers 26; Students 218.
Catechesis/Religious Programs—D.R.E.: Lorna Davel; Donna Cherry.
Students 510.

2—ST. BERNARD, Revs. John Bergstadt; Peter Mastalir; Deacon Maurice Reed. In res., Rev. Michael Simonini.
Parish Center: 1617 W. Pine St., 54914-5118. Tel: 920-390-0331; Fax: 920-749-9771.
Catechesis/Religious Programs—Students 697.

3—ST. JOSEPH, Revs. John Holly, O.F.M.Cap.; David Belongea, O.F.M.Cap.; Sr. Lynne Marie Simonich, O.S.F., Pastoral Assoc.; Deacon Roy Baumruk. In res., Rev. Kurt Gessner, O.F.M.Cap.
Res., 404 W. Lawrence St., 54911-5855. Tel: 920-347-7195; Fax: 920-734-0227. [CEM]
School—Appleton Catholic Education System, 300 N. Woods Edge Dr., 54914. Tel: 920-735-9380. William O'Brien, Exec. Dir.
Catechesis/Religious Programs—(Associated with St. Mary's, Appleton.). D.R.E.: Sr. Maxine Bauer, S.S.N.D., (Grades K-5); Peter Reinl, Dir.; Doug Lynott, (Grades 6-10).
Students 167.

4—ST. MARY, Rev. Michael K. O'Rourke. Pastoral Assocs.: Sr. Joanne Goessl; Ms. Barbara Kratz; Deacon William Burke.
Church—312 S. State St., 54911-5926. Tel: 920-395-5119; Fax: 920-739-5111. [CEM]
School—Catholic Central. Member of Appleton Catholic Education System. 313 S. State St., 54911. Tel: 920-733-3709; Fax: 920-733-8142. Rosemary Perrino, Prin.
Religious 1; Lay Teachers 23; Students 226.
Catechesis/Religious Programs—Associated with St. Joseph-St. Mary Interparish. Peter Reinl, D.R.E.
Students 307.

5—ST. PIUS X, Revs. Donald M. Zuleger; David Funk, O.F.M.Cap.; John Blaha.
Office: 500 W. Marquette St., 54911-1997. Tel: 920-330-0575.
School—Tel: 920-733-4918. Sr. Mary Shawn Fagan, A.N.G., Prin.
Lay Teachers 16; Students 332.
Catechesis/Religious Programs—Students 726.

6—SACRED HEART, Rev. William M. Kuhr; Deacon Donald Gigure.
Res., 222 E. Fremont St., 54915-1890. Tel: 920-393-3196.
Catechesis/Religious Programs—Students 304.

7—ST. THERESE, Rev. Daniel C. Gilsdorf; Deacon Patrick Whitcomb.
Res., 216 E. Summer St., 54911-4864. Tel: 920-338-8568; Fax: 920-954-5727.
Rectory: 213 E. Wisconsin Ave., 54911. Tel: 920-738-0376.
School—Member of Appleton Catholic Education System. 1810 W. Prospect Ave., 54914. Tel: 920-735-9380.

Catechesis/Religious Programs—Tel: 414-739-0794. Marie Loberger, D.R.E.
Students 156.

8—ST. THOMAS MORE, Rev. Gerald R. Falk; Sr. Betty Reinders, Pastoral Assoc.; Deacons Paul Klein; Reinhart Wessing; Donald Wetzel.
Res., 1810B N. McDonald St., 54911-3499. Tel: 920-397-7758.
School—1810 N. McDonald St., 54911. Tel: 920-739-7826; Fax: 920-739-2376. Sr. Mary Barbara Loch, Prin.
Sisters 2; Lay Teachers 19; Students 229.
Catechesis/Religious Programs—Peggy LeClair, D.R.E.
Students 415.
Convent—1226 E. Pauline St., 54911.

Argonne, Forest Co., St. Mary. Attended by St. Joseph, Crandon. Rev. Ralph J. Gillis.
Res., 208 N. Park Ave., Crandon, 54520-1351. Tel: 715-783-3396. [CEM]

Armstrong Creek, Forest Co., St. Stanislaus Kostka. (Also serves St. Joan of Arc, Goodman). Rev. Edward S. Nowakowski.
Mailing Address: P.O. Box 39, 54103-0039. Tel: 715-362-2334.
Catechesis/Religious Programs—Associated with St. Joan of Arc, Goodman.
Students 67.

Askeaton, Brown Co., St. Patrick, Rev. Allen Geiser.
Res., 7815 Saint Patrick Church Rd., Greenleaf, 54126-9611. Tel: 920-326-6665. [CEM]

Aurora, Florence Co., Sacred Heart. Attended by Immaculate Conception, Florence. Rev. Leo R. Lessard.
Mailing Address: P.O. Box 85, Florence, 54121-0085.
Res., 308 Florence Ave., Florence, 54121-0085. Tel: 715-283-3310.
Catechesis/Religious Programs—Students 63.

Baileys Harbor, Door Co., St. Mary of the Lake, Rev. Chester Cappucci, O.M.I.
Mailing Address: P.O. Box 405, 54202-0405. Tel: 920-392-2041. [CEM]
Station—Washington Island, Door Co., St. Michael. (Also serves St. Rosalia, Sister Bay.).

Bay Settlement, Brown Co., Holy Cross, Rev. Timothy D. Shillcox, O.Praem.
Res., 3009 Bay Settlement Rd., Green Bay, 54311-7301. Tel: 920-680-0595. [CEM]
School—3002 Bay Settlement Rd., Green Bay, 54311. Tel: 920-468-0625; Fax: 920-468-0625. Mrs. Jane Wicker, Prin.
Lay Teachers 10; Students 193.
Catechesis/Religious Programs—Students 195.

Bear Creek, Outagamie Co., St. Mary. Attended by St. Rose, Clintonville. Rev. Msgr. Mark J. Schommer.
Mailing Address: P.O. Box 27, 54922-0027. Tel: 715-752-4177. [CEM]
School—P.O. Box 216, 54922-0027. Tel: 715-752-4168. Sr. Jane Resop, Prin.
Sisters 1; Lay Teachers 2; Students 35.
Convent—Tel: 715-752-3585.
Catechesis/Religious Programs—Associated with St. Rose, Clintonville.
Students 68.

Birnamwood, Shawano Co., St. Philomena. (Also serves St. Boniface, Aniwa). Rev. Everard S. Scesney, O.F.M.
Res., P.O. Box K, 54414-0911. Tel: 715-492-2104. [CEM]
Catechesis/Religious Programs—Students 170.

Black Creek, Outagamie Co., St. Mary, Rev. Paul Paider.
Res., P.O. Box 217, 54106-0217. Tel: 920-843-3319. [CEM]
Catechesis/Religious Programs—Rita Theobald, D.R.E.
Students 202.

Brillion, Calumet Co., St. Mary, Rev. Thomas Long.
Res., 215 Center St., 54110-1222. Tel: 920-562-2535. [CEM 2]
School—209 N. Custer St., 54110. Tel: 920-756-2502. Mrs. Kathy Van Vonderen, Prin.
Lay Teachers 11; Students 115.
Catechesis/Religious Programs—Mrs. Roberta Whittaker, D.R.E.
Students 228.

Brussels, Door Co., St. Francis and St. Mary Parish. (Worship sites in Brussels and Namur.). Rev. Pius Cotter, O.F.M.Cap., Admin.
Res., 9716 Cemetery Rd., 54204-9749. Tel: 920-257-7555. [CEM 3]
Catechesis/Religious Programs—Sue Johnson, D.R.E.
Students 247.

Casco, Kewaunee Co., Holy Trinity, Rev. Thomas Farrell.
Res., 506 Church Ave., 54205-9709. Tel: 920-377-7234. [CEM]
School—510 Church Ave., 54205-9700. Tel: 920-837-7531. Mrs. Kaye Jacobs, Prin.
Lay Teachers 7; Students 111.
Catechesis/Religious Programs—Students 152.

Cecil, Shawano Co., St. Martin. Attended by Sacred Heart, Shawano. Rev. Leonard M. Evers; Deacon Charles Daily.
Mailing Address: 321 S. Sawyer St., Shawano, 54166-2437. Tel: 715-262-2023.
Church—107 S. Warrington, P.O. Box 157, 54111. [CEM]

Champion, Brown Co., St. Joseph. Attended by St. Killian, New Franken. Rev. Roger Zach, O.F.M.Cap., Admin.
Mailing Address: 5996 County Rd. K, New Franken, 54229-9456. Tel: 920-669-9961. [CEM]
Catechesis/Religious Programs—Mrs. Bonnie Agahaite, D.R.E.
Students 125.

Charlesburg, Calumet Co., St. Charles Borromeo. (Linked with all 6 Chilton area parishes). Revs. Gary New, S.D.S.; Fred Peters, S.D.S.
Mailing Address: 62 E. Main St., Chilton, 53014-1499. Tel: 920-499-9363. [CEM]
School—Chilton Catholic. Consolidated with all 6 Chilton area parishes. See St. Mary, Chilton. Tel: 920-849-4141. Sr. Betty Ann Heegman, O.P.

Charlestown, Calumet Co., St. Martin. (Linked with all 6 Chilton area parishes). Revs. Gary New, S.D.S.; Fred Peters, S.D.S.
Mailing Address: 62 E. Main St., Chilton, 53014-1499. Tel: 920-499-9363. [CEM]
School—Chilton Catholic. Consolidated with all 6 Chilton area parishes. See St. Mary, Chilton. Tel: 920-849-4141. Sr. Betty Ann Heegman, O.P.

Chase, Oconto Co., St. Joseph. Attended by St. John Cantius, Sobieski. Rev. Gerald Prusakowski, O.F.M.
Res., 6051 Noble St., Sobieski, 54171-9724. Tel: 920-225-5255. [CEM]

Chilton, Calumet Co., St. Augustine. (Linked with all 6 Chilton area parishes). Revs. Gary New, S.D.S.; Fred Peters, S.D.S.
Mailing Address: 62 E. Main St., 53014-1499. Tel: 920-499-9363. [CEM]
School—Chilton Catholic. Consolidated with all 6 Chilton parishes. See St. Mary, Chilton. 60 E. Washington St., 53014. Tel: 920-849-4141. Sr. Betty Ann Heegman, O.P.

St. Mary. (Linked with all 6 Chilton area parishes). Revs. Gary New, S.D.S.; Fred Peters, S.D.S.
Res., 62 E. Main St., 53014-1499. Tel: 920-499-9363. [CEM]
School—Chilton Catholic School. Consolidated with all 6 Chilton parishes. 60 E. Washington St., 53014. Tel: 920-849-4141. Sr. Betty Ann Heegman, O.P., Prin.
Sisters 1; Lay Teachers 10; Students 155.
Catechesis/Religious Programs—Consolidated with all area parishes.
Students 574.
Convent—(Catholic Inter-Parish Ministry of Chilton includes the following parishes: St. Charles, Charlesburg; St. Martin, Charlestown; St. Elizabeth, Kloten; Holy Trinity, Jericho; and St. Augustine and St. Mary, Chilton.) 38 E. Washington St., 53014. School Sisters of St. Francis

Clarks Mills, Manitowoc Co., Immaculate Conception, Rev. John F. Conrad.
Res., 15 S. County Rd. J, Cato, 54206-9612. Tel: 920-754-4365. [CEM]
School—19 S. CTH J, Cato, 54206. Tel: 414-775-4366. Sr. Marie Bernadette Dorn, Prin.
Franciscan Sisters of Christian Charity 4; Lay Teachers 5; Students 88.
Catechesis/Religious Programs—Students 116.

Cleveland, Manitowoc Co., St. Wendel, Rev. Gilbert H. Jacobs, O.Praem., Admin.
Res., P.O. Box 236, 53015-0236. Tel: 920-938-8552. [JC 2]
Catechesis/Religious Programs—Associated with grades 1-12 w/Osman; grades 9-12 w/Alverno & Northeim. Janice Batchelder, D.R.E.
Students 128.

Clintonville, Waupaca Co., St. Rose. Also serves St. Mary, Bear Creek. Rev. Msgr. Mark J. Schommer; Deacon Thomas Jozwiak.
Res., 24 7th St., 54929-1733. Tel: 715-233-3416. [CEM]
School—140 Auto St., 54929. Tel: 715-823-3416; Fax: 715-823-7160. Robert J. Bootz, Prin.
Lay Teachers 9; Students 77.
Catechesis/Religious Programs—D.R.E.: Dawn Kratzke; Gemma Niemuth.
Students 149.

Coleman, Marinette Co., Ss. Francis/Wenceslaus, Rev. John Hephner; Sr. Carleen Peters, S.S.N.D., Pastoral Assoc.
Res., 228 E. Main St., 54112-9407. Tel: 920-973-3226. [CEM 2]
Catechesis/Religious Programs—Students 221.

Combined Locks, Outagamie Co., St. Paul, Rev. Robert H. Vandenberg; Deacon George Schraufnagel, D.R.E.
Res., 410 Wallace St., 54113-1128. Tel: 920-884-4553; Fax: 920-788-6822. [CEM]
Catechesis/Religious Programs—Ms. Mary Ann Jasiak, D.R.E.
Students 254.

Cooperstown, Manitowoc Co., St. James, Rev. Ronald A. Colombo, Admin.
Res., 18228 County Rd. R, Denmark, 54208-9519. Tel: 920-632-2585; Fax: 920-863-5445. [CEM]
Catechesis/Religious Programs—Jean Schleis, D.R.E.
Students 224.

Crandon, Forest Co., St. Joseph. (Also serves St. Mary, Argonne and St. Michael at Hiles.). Rev. Ralph J. Gillis.
Res., 208 N. Park Ave., 54520-1351. Tel: 715-783-3396.
Catechesis/Religious Programs—Students 155.

Crivitz, Marinette Co., St. Mary, Rev. Donald R. Burkart.
Mailing Address: P.O. Box 159, 54114-0159. Tel: 715-542-2501. [CEM]
Catechesis/Religious Programs—Students 265.
Station—Caldron Falls.

Darboy, Outagamie Co. (Appleton P.O.), Holy Angels, Rev. Donald F. Fuller.
Res., W. 5831 County Road KK, Appleton, 54915-9345. Tel: 920-336-6214. [CEM]
School—W2796 KK, Appleton, 54915-9407. Tel: 920-733-2651. Doris Vincent, Prin.
Religious 1; Lay Teachers 16; Students 280.
Catechesis/Religious Programs—Sr. Elise Cholewinski, D.R.E.
Students 311.

Denmark, Brown Co., All Saints, Rev. Msgr. Robert F. Gulig, Admin.; Mary Burns, Pastoral Assoc. & D.R.E.
Res., P.O. Box 787, 54208-0787. Tel: 920-632-2357. [CEM]
Office: Tel: 414-863-5256.
School—Tel: 920-863-2449. Jeffrey Staddler, Prin.
Lay Teachers 8; Students 112.
Catechesis/Religious Programs—Associated with Holy Trinity, New Denmark. Tel: 414-863-5256.
Students 191.
Mission—New Denmark, Holy Trinity.

De Pere, Brown Co.,

1—ST. FRANCIS XAVIER, Rev. V. Anthony Dolski; Kenneth Trinkner, Admin. Asst. In res., Rev. Msgr. Brian P. Coleman.
Res., 220 S. Michigan St., 54115-2794. Tel: 920-361-1813. [JC]
School—Notre Dame of De Pere Middle School. Consolidated with St. Mary, De Pere. 221 S. Wisconsin St., 54115. Tel: 920-337-1100. William Matchefts, Prin.
Religious 1; Lay Teachers 26; Students 243.
Catechesis/Religious Programs—Students 274.

2—ST. MARY, Rev. John H. Harper; Deacon Frank W. Kremer.
Mailing Address: P.O. Box 70, 54115-0070. Tel: 920-372-2330; Fax: 920-337-2332. [JC]
School—Notre Dame. Consolidated with St. Francis Xavier, De Pere. 100 S. Huron St., 54115. Tel: 920-337-1100. William Matchefts, Prin.
Sisters of St. Francis of the Holy Cross 1; Lay Teachers 26; Students 484.
Catechesis/Religious Programs—Marge Frase, D.R.E.
Students 266.

3—ST. JOSEPH. Merged with St. Boniface, De Pere to form Our Lady of Lourdes, De Pere.

4—ST. BONIFACE. Merged with St. Joseph, De Pere to form Our Lady of Lourdes, De Pere.

5—OUR LADY OF LOURDES, (1996), Revs. Conrad J. Kratz, O. Praem.; James T. Baraniak, O. Praem.; Robin Cribb, Pastoral Assoc.; Deacons Glenn Teske; Harvey Quinette.
Res., 1307 Lourdes Ave., 54115-1018. Tel: 920-364-4033; Fax: 920-336-3910.
School—1305 Lourdes Ave., 54115-1099. Tel: 920-336-3091. Mrs. Susan Sands, Prin.
Lay Teachers 25; Students 311.
Catechesis/Religious Programs—Students 407.

6—ST. NORBERT COLLEGE PARISH, Revs. Gery G. Meehan, O.Praem.; Mark Payne, O.Praem.; Tami Schmitz, Pastoral Assoc.
Mailing Address: Campus Ministry, St. Norbert College, 100 Grant St., 54115-2099.
Res., 402 3rd St., 54115-2142. Tel: 920-337-3010.
Catechesis/Religious Programs—Students 78.

Dyckesville, Kewaunee Co., St. Louis, Rev. Richard Mauthe.
Res., N8726 County Line Rd., Luxemburg, 54217-8629. Tel: 920-662-2410. [CEM 2]

School—N8710 Cty. Line Rd., Luxemburg, 54217. Tel: 920-866-2611. Mrs. Mary Rechek, Prin.
Lay Teachers 6; Students 60.
Catechesis/Religious Programs—Students 125.

Eaton, Brown Co., SS. Cyril and Methodius. (Also serves Our Lady Queen of Peace, Humboldt). Rev. Dean W. Dombroski.
Res., 3041 S. County Rd. T, Green Bay, 54311-9429. Tel: 920-632-2593; Fax: 920-863-2593. [CEM]
Catechesis/Religious Programs—Students 169.

Egg Harbor, Door Co., St. John the Baptist. (Also serves St. Paul, Fish Creek, and St. Michael, Jacksonport). Rev. George Kuryvial, O.M.I.
Mailing Address: P.O. Box 49, 54209-0049. Tel: 920-683-3241. [CEM]
Catechesis/Religious Programs—Students 60.

Eland, Shawano Co., St. William. Attended by Holy Family, Wittenberg. Rev. Claude A. Zabinski, O.F.M.
Res., 106 N. Ellms St., Wittenberg, 54499-9099. Tel: 715-532-2050.

Elcho, Langlade Co., Holy Family, Rev. Joseph C. Bauschka.
Mailing Address: P.O. Box 128, 54428-0128. Tel: 715-275-3750. [CEM][JC]
Mission—Pickerel, St. Mary.

Fish Creek, Door Co., St. Paul. Attended by St. John the Baptist, Egg Harbor. Rev. George Kuryvial, O.M.I.
Mailing Address: P.O. Box 49, Egg Harbor, 54209-0049. Tel: 920-683-3241.

Flintville, Brown Co., SS. Edward and Isidore, Rev. David D. Kasperek; June Ingold, Pastoral Assoc.; Deacon Earl Kunzer.
Res., 3667 Flintville Rd., Green Bay, 54313-8330. Tel: 920-657-7677; Fax: 920-865-4375. [CEM]
Rectory: 3752 Elm Tree Rd., Green Bay, 54313. Tel: 920-865-7019.
Catechesis/Religious Programs—D.R.E.: Nancy Nelson; Mary Neckuty; June Ingold.
Students 656.

Florence, Florence Co., Immaculate Conception. (Also serves Sacred Heart, Aurora). Rev. Leo R. Lessard.
Res., P.O. Box 166, 54121-0166. Tel: 715-283-3310; Fax: 715-528-3310. [CEM]
Catechesis/Religious Programs—Students 139.

Francis Creek, Manitowoc Co., St. Anne. (Also serves St. Augustine, Kossuth.). Rev. Theodore J. Hendricks.
Res., P.O. Box 217, 54214-0217. Tel: 920-826-6640. [CEM]
School—202 Packer Dr., 54214. Tel: 920-682-1454. Mr. Charles Vaughan, Prin.
Franciscan Sisters of Christian Charity 4; Lay Teachers 4; Students 95.
Catechesis/Religious Programs—Students 109.

Freedom, Outagamie Co., St. Nicholas, Rev. Dennis M. Ryan; Deacon Donald Newhouse.
Res., P.O. Box 1006, 54131-1006. Tel: 920-881-1492. [CEM]
School—P.O. Box 1022, 54131-1022. Tel: 920-788-9371. Phyllis Techlin, Prin.
Lay Teachers 12; Students 189.
Catechesis/Religious Programs—Sr. Charlene Hockers, D.R.E.
Students 355.

Gillett, Oconto Co., St. John, Rev. John M. Gallagher.
Res., P.O. Box 377, 54124-0377. Tel: 920-552-2542. [CEM]
Catechesis/Religious Programs—Students 122.

Glenmore, Brown Co., Immaculate Conception. (Also serves St. Mary, Stark). Rev. Lee J. Kahrs.
Res., 5840 Big Apple Rd., De Pere, 54115-9766. Tel: 920-647-7641. [CEM]
Catechesis/Religious Programs—Judy Hoida, D.R.E.
Students 172.

Goodman, Marinette Co., St. Joan of Arc. Attended by St. Stanislaus Kostka, Armstrong Creek. Rev. Edward S. Nowakowski.
Mailing Address: P.O. Box 39, Armstrong Creek, 54103-0039. Tel: 715-362-2334.
Catechesis/Religious Programs—Associated with St. Stanislaus Kosta, Armstrong Creek.
Students 50.

Greenleaf, Brown Co., St. Mary, Rev. Robert J. Kabat.
Res., 2212 Day St., 54126-9200. Tel: 920-642-2550; Fax: 920-864-2979. [CEM 2]
School—2218 Day St., 54126-9200. Tel: 920-864-2586. Sr. Margaret Mary Halbach, Prin.
Religious 1; Lay Teachers 6; Students 64.
Catechesis/Religious Programs—Lois Trad, D.R.E.
Students 159.

Greenville, Outagamie Co., St. Mary, Rev. John Zickert, O.F.M.Cap.
Mailing Address: P.O. Box 195, 54942-0195. Tel: 920-576-6555. [CEM]
Res., N2343 Municipal Dr., 54942. Tel: 920-757-6333.
School—(Grades PreK-8) N2387 Municipal Dr., 54942. Tel: 920-757-5516. Mary Lou Kalaus, Prin.
Lay Teachers 5; Students 146.
Catechesis/Religious Programs—Jane Angha, D.R.E.
Students 305.

Gresham, Shawano Co., St. Francis Solanus. Attended by St. Mary, Leopolis. Rev. Harry G. Hafeman; Deacon Paul Boucher.
Mailing Address: P.O. Box 177, 54128-0177. Tel: 715-873-3250. [CEM]
Catechesis/Religious Programs—Students 63.

Hilbert, Calumet Co., St. Mary, Rev. Rallen H. Stencil.
Res., P.O. Box 386, 54129-0386. Tel: 920-533-3252. [CEM]
School—154 S. 6th St., P.O. Box 249, 54129-0249. Tel: 920-853-3216. Sr. Elise Zettel, Prin.
Religious 1; Lay Teachers 4; Students 51.
Catechesis/Religious Programs—Students 155.

Hofa Park, Shawano Co., St. Stanislaus. Attended by Assumption BVM, Pulaski. Rev. Albert Lis, O.F.M.
Res., N1302 Maple Rd., Seymour, 54165-9506. Tel: 920-225-5512. [CEM]
Catechesis/Religious Programs—Students 69.

Hollandtown, Brown Co., St. Francis, Rev. Stanley Browne, Admin.
Res., 439 County Rd. CE, Kaukauna, 54130-8964. Tel: 920-661-1222. [CEM]
School—Rte. 4, Kaukauna, 54130. Tel: 920-766-3469. Mrs. Jennie Eggleston, Prin.
Franciscan Sisters of Christian Charity 2; Lay Teachers 5; Students 54.
Catechesis/Religious Programs—Associated with St. Aloysius, Kaukauna.
Students 58.

Hortonville, Outagamie Co., SS. Peter and Paul, Rev. Thomas Pomeroy.
Res., P.O. Box 238, 54944-0238. Tel: 920-796-6133; Fax: 920-779-4425. [CEM]
School—107 N. Olk St., 54944. Tel: 920-779-4425; Fax: 920-799-4425. Donna Koeller, Prin.
Sisters of St. Agnes 1; Lay Teachers 8; Students 110.
Catechesis/Religious Programs—Ms. Catherine Benoy, D.R.E.
Students 214.

Howard, Brown Co., St. John the Baptist, Revs. William Swichtenberg, Co-Pastor; Gregory J. Smith, Co-Pastor; Deacons Nicholas Williams; David LeMere.
Res., 2597 Glendale Ave., Green Bay, 54313-6899. Tel: 920-342-2145; Fax: 920-434-5015. [CEM]
School—2561 Glendale Ave., Green Bay, 54313. Tel: 920-434-2145; Fax: 920-434-5016. Sherilyn M. Moon, Prin.
Lay Teachers 21; Students 342.
Catechesis/Religious Programs—D.R.E.: Patricia A. Vanden Boogaard, (Grades 1-6); Mary A. Vanden Busch, (Grades 7-12).
Students 652.

Humboldt, Brown Co., Our Lady Queen of Peace. Attended by Ss. Cyril & Methodius, Eaton. Rev. Dean H. Dombroski; Sr. Marlene Dimmerling, O.P., Pastoral Assoc.
Res., 5930 Humboldt Rd., Luxemburg, 54217-9325. Tel: 920-636-6113. [CEM 3]
Catechesis/Religious Programs—Associated with Ss. Cyril & Methodius, Eaton.
Students 229.

Institute, Door Co., SS. Peter and Paul, Rev. Patrick Gawrylewski, O.F.M.Cap.; Deacon Roger Madsen.
Res., 4767 Dunn Rd., Sturgeon Bay, 54235-8822. Tel: 920-434-4842; Fax: 920-743-3885. [CEM]
School—4761 Dunn Rd., Sturgeon Bay, 54235. Tel: 920-743-6335; Fax: 920-743-3885. Kathryn LaChapell, Prin.
Sisters of St. Francis of the Holy Cross 1; Lay Teachers 6; Students 119.

Isaar, Outagamie Co., St. Sebastian, Rev. David Ashbeck.
Res., N9269 Isaar Rd., Seymour, 54165-9428. Tel: 920-332-2558. [CEM]
Catechesis/Religious Programs—Students 161.

Jacksonport, Door Co., St. Michael. Attended by St. John the Baptist, Egg Harbor. Rev. George Kuryvial, O.M.I.
Mailing Address: P.O. Box 49, Egg Harbor, 54209-0049. Tel: 920-683-3241. [CEM]

Jericho, Calumet Co., Holy Trinity. (Linked with all 6 Chilton area parishes). Revs. Gary New, S.D.S.; Fred Peters, S.D.S.
Mailing Address: 62 E. Main St., Chilton, 53014-1499. Tel: 920-499-9363. [CEM]
School—Chilton Catholic. Consolidated with all 6 Chilton area parishes. See St. Mary, Chilton. Tel: 920-849-4141. Sr. Betty Ann Heeggan, O.P., Prin.

Kaukauna, Outagamie Co., Holy Cross, Revs. John T. Mullarkey; David Hoffman.
Res., 309 Desnoyer St., 54130-2187. Tel: 920-663-3773; Fax: 920-766-3774. [CEM]
School—Kaukauna Catholic Schools System, Tel: 920-766-0186. Sr. Camilla Wolfgram, Prin. (Grades PreK-5).
Sisters 5; Lay Teachers 14; Students 237.
Catechesis/Religious Programs—Elaine Huss, D.R.E.
Students 502.

St. Aloysius, Rev. David Schmidt, Admin.
Res., 2401 Main Ave., 54130-3599. Tel: 920-665-5111.
School—Kaukauna Catholic Schools System, Tel: 920-766-5199. Sr. Camilla Wolfgram, Prin.
Franciscan Sisters of Christian Charity 3; Lay Teachers 12; Students 125.
Catechesis/Religious Programs—Maxine Geiger, D.R.E.
Students 309.

St. Mary of the Annunciation, Rev. Robert Udulutsch, O.F.M.Cap.; Sr. Mary Rose O'Connell, Pastoral Assoc.; Deacon Steven Vande Hey. In res., Revs. Irvin Udulutach, O.F.M.Cap.; Kieran Hickey, O.F.M.Cap.
Res., 119 W. 7th St., 54130-2356. Tel: 920-661-1445; Fax: 920-766-1476. [JC]
School—Kaukauna Catholic Schools System, 112 W. 8th St., 54130. Tel: 920-766-1545; Fax: 920-766-1476. Mrs. Susan Knier, Prin.
Sisters 1; Lay Teachers 13; Students 153.
Catechesis/Religious Programs—Students 369.
Convent—Tel: 414-766-2952. Franciscan Sisters of Christian Charity

Kellnersville, Manitowoc Co., St. Joseph, Rev. Ronald A. Colombo; Deacon Richard Meidl; Sr. Marlene Greatens, Dir.
Res., P.O. Box 27, 54215-0027. Tel: 920-323-3770. [CEM 2]
Catechesis/Religious Programs—Students 68.

Keshena, Menominee Co., St. Michael (Indian), Rev. David S. Barrett; Sr. Kathleen Walli, O.P., Pastoral Assoc.
Mailing Address: P.O. Box 610, 54135-0610. Tel: 715-993-3811. [CEM]
Catechesis/Religious Programs—Students 113.
Mission—Keshena, Menominee Co., St. Joseph of the Lake, South Branch, P.O. Box 610, 54135-0610.

Kewaunee, Kewaunee Co., Holy Rosary, Rev. Daniel Dewane; Deacon Dana Gallenberger.
Res., 521 Juneau St., 54216-1397. Tel: 920-882-2285; Fax: 920-388-3822. [CEM]
School—519 Kilbourn St., 54216. Tel: 920-388-2285. Mrs. Nancy Leifer, Prin.
Lay Teachers 11; Students 175.
Catechesis/Religious Programs—D.R.E.: Phylis Gencius; Evy Walecka; Barbara Puzdera.
Students 178.

Kiel, Manitowoc Co., SS. Peter and Paul, Revs. Loren G. Nys, S.D.S.; Cletus LaMer.
Res., 413 Fremont St., 53042-1398. Tel: 920-943-3553; Fax: 920-894-4462. [CEM]
School—423 Fremont St., 53042. Tel: 920-894-3533; Fax: 920-894-4462. Sr. Rosalyn Geenen, Prin.
Sisters 2; Lay Teachers 9; Students 135.
Catechesis/Religious Programs—D.R.E.: Barb Graf; Kathy Pritzl.
Students 254.

Kimberly, Outagamie Co., Holy Name of Jesus, Revs. Dennis Bergsbaken; Robert Stegmann.
Res., 602 E. Kimberly Ave., 54136-1599. Tel: 920-887-7640. [CEM]
School—614 E. Kimberly Ave., 54136. Tel: 920-788-7650. Sr. Mary Barbieur, Prin.
Lay Teachers 24; Students 276.
Catechesis/Religious Programs—Students 436.

King, Waupaca Co., St. George, Rev. Paul A. Vanden Hogen.
Res., P.O. Box 152, 54946-0152. Tel: 715-585-5586.

Klondike, Oconto Co., St. Wenceslaus. Merged with St. Francis of Assisi, Coleman, to form Ss. Francis of Assisi and Wenceslaus.

Kloten, Calumet Co., St. Elizabeth. (Linked with all 6 Chilton area parishes). Revs. Gary New, S.D.S.; Fred Peters, S.D.S.
Mailing Address: 62 E. Main St., Chilton, 53014-1499. Tel: 920-499-9363. [CEM]
School—Chilton Catholic. Consolidated with all 6 Chilton area parishes. See St. Mary, Chilton. Tel: 920-849-4141. Sr. Betty Ann Heegman, O.P.

Kossuth, Manitowoc Co., St. Augustine. Attended by St. Anne, Francis Creek. Rev. Theodore J. Hendricks.
Mailing Address: P.O. Box 217, Francis Creek, 54214-0217. Tel: 920-826-6640. [CEM]

Krakow, Shawano Co., St. Casimir, Rev. James J. Esser, O.F.M.
Mailing Address: P.O. Box 66, 54137-0066. Tel: 920-993-3621. [CEM]
Catechesis/Religious Programs—Students 106.

Krok, St. John. Merged with St. Joseph, Monteplier to form St. Joseph-St. John, Montpelier.

Lakewood, Oconto Co., St. Mary of the Lake. Attended by St. Ambrose, Wabeno. Rev. Gerald Schmidt, O.F.M.Cap.; Deacon Harold Orlowski.
Res., P.O. Box 219, 54138-0219. Tel: 715-767-7364. [CEM]
Stations—Crooked Lake.; Silver Cliff.
Catechesis/Religious Programs—Students 75.

Langlade, Langlade Co., St. Stanislaus Kostka. Merged with St. James, White Lake.

Laona, Forest Co., St. Leonard, Rev. John W. Cerkas.
Res., Rte. 1, Box 344, 54541-9641. Tel: 715-743-3241. [JC]
Catechesis/Religious Programs—Students 137.
Mission—Newald, Argonne Co., St. Hubert. (Also serves St. Norbert, Long Lake).

Lebanon Township, Waupaca Co., St. Patrick, Rev. Msgr. Dennis Lally, Admin.
Res., N5705 County Rd. T, New London, 54961-8464. Tel: 920-825-5475. [CEM]
Catechesis/Religious Programs—Students 99.

Lena, Oconto Co., Holy Cross, Rev. Harold A. Beerntsen; Deacon James Kostichka.
Res., P.O. Box 30, 54139-0030. Tel: 920-295-5222. [JC 2]
School—221 E. Main St., 54139. Tel: 920-829-6027. Mary Jane Klister, Prin.
Lay Teachers 4; Students 68.
Catechesis/Religious Programs—Students 211.

Leopolis, Shawano Co., St. Mary. (Also serves St. Francis Solanus, Gresham.). Rev. Harry G. Hafeman; Deacon Paul Boucher.
Res., P.O. Box 39, 54948-0039. Tel: 715-873-3377. [CEM]
Catechesis/Religious Programs—Students 64.

Lincoln, Kewaunee Co., St. Peter. Merged with St. Hubert, Rosiere.

Little Chute, Outagamie Co., St. John, Rev. Msgr. James Vanden Hogen; Rev. David C. Ruby; Deacon Vincent M. DeGroot.
Res., 323 Pine St., 54140-1896. Tel: 920-889-9061; Fax: 920-687-0851. [CEM]
School—328 Grand Ave., 54140. Tel: 920-788-9082. Peter Spaeth, Prin.
Sisters 4; Lay Teachers 25; Students 584.
Catechesis/Religious Programs—Colleen Mitchell, D.R.E.
Students 533.

Little Suamico, Oconto Co., St. Pius. Attended by St. Benedict, Suamico. Rev. Gary J. Dantinne.
Mailing Address: P.O. Box 66, Suamico, 54173-0066. Tel: 920-342-2024.
Catechesis/Religious Programs—Students 80.

Long Lake, Florence Co., St. Norbert. Attended by St. Leonard, Laona. Rev. John W. Cerkas.
Res., R.R.1, Box 344, Laona, 54541-9641. Tel: 715-743-3241.

Montpelier, Kewaunee Co., St. Joseph-St. John. Unassigned.
Res., E. 860 State Hwy. 29, Luxemburg, 54217-7462. Tel: 414-845-2565. [CEM]

Luxemburg, Kewaunee Co., Immaculate Conception, Rev. Milton M. Suess.
Res., 1412 Main St., 54217-1308. Tel: 920-452-2056. [CEM]
School—St. Mary, 1406 Main St., 54217-1308. Tel: 920-845-2224. Linda Gerlach, Prin.
Lay Teachers 8; Students 161.
Catechesis/Religious Programs—Students 232.

Mackville, Outagamie Co., St. Edward, Rev. Charles Brooks.
Res., N2921 State Rd. 47, Appleton, 54915-9564. Tel: 920-339-9266. [CEM]
School—N2944 State Rd. 47, Appleton, 54915. Tel: 920-733-6276. Jaclyn Behnke, Prin.
Lay Teachers 6; Students 45.
Catechesis/Religious Programs—Students 232.

Manawa, Waupaca Co., Sacred Heart, Rev. Bert Samsa, O.F.M.Cap.
Res., P.O. Box 10, 54949-0010. Tel: 920-963-3323. [JC]
Catechesis/Religious Programs—Students 118.

Manitowoc, Manitowoc Co.,

1—St. Boniface, Rev. Carl Meulemans, M.M., Admin.; Sr. Mary Kevin, Pastoral Assoc. In res., Rev. Richard H. Klingeisen.
Res., 1110 S. 10th St., 54220-5288. Tel: 920-843-3718.
School—See Consolidated Schools under Institutions Located in the Diocese. 1418 Grand Ave., 54220. Tel: 920-683-6888.
Religious 2; Lay Teachers 9; Students 40.
Catechesis/Religious Programs—Associated with St. Paul,St. Mary, & St. Andrew.
Students 60.
Convent— Franciscan Sisters of Christian Charity *Holy Family Conservatory*—1015 S. 11th St., 54220.

2—Holy Innocents, Revs. Gerald J. Foley; Matthew Simonar; Sr. Connie Wavrunek, O.S.F., Pastoral Assoc.; Deacons Rahlf Proulx; Paul Kieffer; Ken Nelesen.
Res., 1121 N. 14th St., 54220-3298. Tel: 920-820-0031. [CEM]
School—St. Francis de Sales. See Consolidated Schools under Institutions Located in the Diocese. 1408 Waldo Blvd., 54220. Tel: 920-683-6892. Sr. Paulyn Vanden Hogen.
Religious 1; Lay Teachers 22; Students 381.
Catechesis/Religious Programs—Claudia Maly, D.R.E.
Students 354.

3—St. Mary, Revs. Roman Zbieranski, O.F.M.; John Puodziunas, O.F.M.; Deacon Robert Drobka.
Res., 1114 S. 21st St., 54220-4994. Tel: 920-843-3558.
School—St. Frances Cabrini. See Consolidated Schools under Institutions Located in the Diocese. 2109 Marshall St., 54220. Tel: 920-683-6884. James Clark, Prin.
Lay Teachers 20; Students 229.
Catechesis/Religious Programs—Associated with St. Boniface, Manitowoc.
Students 210.

4—Sacred Heart, Rev. William H. Zimmer.
Res., 520 N. 7th St., 54220-4099. Tel: 920-848-8692. [JC]
Catechesis/Religious Programs—Sr. Rose Marie Buscemi, D.R.E.
Students 220.

5—St. Andrew, Rev. Camillus Janas, O.F.M., Admin.
Res., 1416 Grand Ave., 54220-6199. Tel: 920-820-0023; Fax: 920-682-1452.
School—St. Francis Xavier. See Consolidated Schools under Institutions Located in the Diocese. 1418 Grand Ave., 54220. Tel: 920-683-6888. Mrs. Linda Bender, Prin.
Religious 2; Lay Teachers 11; Students 216.
Catechesis/Religious Programs—Associated with St. Boniface, St. Paul, St. Mary, and St. Andrew.
Students 60.

6—St. Paul, Rev. Ronald P. Reimer; Deacons Alan Boeldt; William D. Klein.
Res., 712 S. 24th St., 54220-4498. Tel: 920-846-6714. [JC]
Catechesis/Religious Programs—Associated with St. Boniface.
Students 72.

Maple Grove, Manitowoc Co., St. Patrick. Merged with St. Mary, Reedsville. Rev. Nicholas A. Johannes; Deacon Donald Schneider.
Mailing Address: P.O. Box 248, Reedsville, 54230-0248. Tel: 414-754-4665. [CEM]

Maplewood, Door Co., St. Mary, Rev. Wilbert L. Buhl.
Mailing Address: P.O. Box 308, 54226-0308. Tel: 920-566-6440. [CEM 2]
Catechesis/Religious Programs—D.R.E.: Sharon McNulty; Joan Schley.
Students 209.

Marchand, Door Co., St. Francis de Paul (Duvall). Closed. For inquiries for parish records contact St. Louis, Dyckesville.

Marinette, Marinette Co.,

1—Holy Family. (Includes the combined parishes of Our Lady of Lourdes, St. Anthony, Sacred Heart, and St. Joseph). Revs. Lawrence T. Marto; David Zimmerman; Sr. Donna Marie Botz, S.S.N.D., Pastoral Assoc.; Deacons Jerry Thetreau; Byron Otradovec.
Office: 1223 Carney Blvd., 54143-2512. Tel: 715-359-9100; Fax: 715-735-9650. [CEM 2]
School—1232 Garfield Ave., 54143. Tel: 715-735-7174. Mrs. Judith Urbanski, Prin.
Students 210.
Catechesis/Religious Programs—D.R.E.: Kathryn Lieburn; Sabrina Schmidt; Charlotte Duran.
Students 470.

2—Our Lady of Lourdes. Merged with Holy Family Parish.

3—St. Joseph. Merged with Holy Family Parish.

4—Sacred Heart Congregation. Merged with Holy Family Parish.

5—St. Anthony. Merged with Holy Family Parish.

Marion, Waupaca Co., St. Mary. Served from St. Anthony, Tigerton. Rev. Michael R. Carroll, Admin.
Mailing Address: P.O. Box 206, 54950. Tel: 715-542-2116. [CEM]
Catechesis/Religious Programs—Students 87.

Mattoon, Shawano Co., Holy Family. Attended by St. Anthony, Neopit. Rev. R. David Kiefer; Deacon Tom Hartman.
Mailing Address: P.O. Box 21, 54450-0021. Tel: 715-893-3579; Fax: 715-754-2116. [CEM]

Menasha, Winnebago Co., St. Patrick, Rev. Roy J. Geenen; Mary Doverspike, Pastoral Assoc.; Deacon Howard Bricco.
Res., 320 Nicolet Blvd., 54952-3394. Tel: 920-258-8381; Fax: 920-727-5544. [JC]
School—Seton Catholic Middle School, 312 Nicolet Blvd., 54952. Tel: 920-727-0279; Fax: 920-727-1215. Ms. Monica Bausom, Prin.
Lay Teachers 16; Students 160.
Catechesis/Religious Programs—Barb Mauthe, D.R.E.
Students 205.

St. Mary, Revs. Robert Lussier, S.S.S.; Michael Noreika, S.S.S. In res., Bros. Allen Broeckman, S.S.S.; Michael Galligan, S.S.S.
Res., 212 Appleton St., 54952-3189. Tel: 920-257-7714; Fax: 920-725-7612. [CEM]
School—(Grades PreK-5) 540 Second St., 54952. Tel: 920-725-5351; Fax: 920-722-5940. Michael Buss, Prin.
Lay Teachers 17; Students 187.
Catechesis/Religious Programs—Mary Gyrion, D.R.E.
Students 175.

St. John, Rev. R. Thomas Golden.
Res., 516 Depere St., 54952-2899. Tel: 920-228-8922. [CEM]
School—628 Fifth St., 54952. Tel: 920-722-9370. Mr. Jon M. Streu, Prin.
Lay Teachers 15; Students 168.
Catechesis/Religious Programs—Patricia Jakubek, D.R.E.
Students 163.

Mishicot, Manitowoc Co., Holy Cross, Rev. John Neuser.
Res., 423 S. Main St., 54228-9777. Tel: 920-552-2550. [CEM]
School—423 Church St., 54228. Tel: 920-755-2487. Joseph Linsmeier, Prin.
Lay Teachers 6; Students 102.
Catechesis/Religious Programs—Corrine Duffek, D.R.E.
Students 180.

Montpelier, Kewaunee Co., St. Joseph/St. John. (Also serves St. Lawrence, Stangelville & St. Hedwig, West Kewaunee). Rev. Michael Ingold, Admin.
Res., E860 State Hwy. 29, Luxemburg, 54217-7462. Tel: 920-452-2565. [CEM]

Namur, Door Co., St. Mary. Closed. See St. Frances and St. Mary, Brussels, for details.

Navarino, Shawano Co., St. Lawrence, Rev. Paul Paider; Sr. Charlotte Rebbe, O.P., Dir.
Res., W5125 State Hwy. 156, Bonduel, 54107-8614. Tel: 715-588-8161. [CEM]
Catechesis/Religious Programs—Students 90.

Neenah, Winnebago Co., St. Margaret Mary, Rev. David J. Koch; Joan Bartman, Pastoral Assoc.; Deacon Norman Spielbauer.
Res., 439 Washington Ave., 54956-3398. Tel: 920-294-4560; Fax: 920-729-4572. [JC]
Church—666 Division St., 54956-3398.
School—610 Division St., 54956. Tel: 920-729-4565. Gretchen Schaeffer, Prin.
Lay Teachers 18; Students 169.
Catechesis/Religious Programs—D.R.E.: Cathy Poirier; Peggy Lemberg; Kathy Kellerman.
Students 230.

St. Gabriel I, Rev. Richard L. Allen.
Res., 151 Andrew Ave., 54956-2289. Tel: 920-224-4914; Fax: 920-722-2566. [JC]
School—900 Geiger St., 54956. Tel: 920-725-4161. Selene Finch, Prin.
Lay Teachers 18; Students 224.
Catechesis/Religious Programs—Kurt Grube, D.R.E.
Students 688.

Neopit, Menominee Co., St. Anthony. (Also serves St. Joseph, Phlox, and Holy Family, Mattoon). Rev. R. David Kiefer; Sr. Michael Ann O'Donnel, Pastoral Assoc.; Deacon Thomas Hartman.
Mailing Address: P.O. Box 241, 54150-0241. Tel: 715-562-2361. [CEM]
Catechesis/Religious Programs—Students 104.

Neva, Langlade Co., St. Wenceslaus. Attended by St. Mary, Antigo. Rev. Jeremiah F. Worman; Deacon Thomas Hanley.
Mailing Address: 735 Deleglise St., Antigo, 54409-1497. Tel: 715-232-2522. [CEM]
Res., N5340 Church Rd., Deerbrook, 54424-9413. Tel: 715-623-7019. [CEM]
Catechesis/Religious Programs—Tina Bures, Coord.
Students 160.

Newald, Argonne Co., St. Hubert, Rev. John W. Cerkas.
Res., R.R. 1, Box 344, Laona, 54541-9641. Tel: 715-743-3241.
Mission—Laona, St. Leonard.

New Denmark, Brown Co., Holy Trinity, Rev. Msgr. Robert Gulig, Admin.
Res., P.O. Box 787, Denmark, 54208-0787. Tel: 920-632-2357. [CEM]
Mission—Denmark, All Saints.

New Franken, Brown Co., St. Kilian. (Also serves St. Joseph, Champion). Rev. Roger Zach, O.F.M.Cap., Admin.

Res., P.O. Box 83, 54229-0083. Tel: 920-663-3541. [CEM]
Catechesis/Religious Programs—Mrs. Nancy Meltzer, D.R.E.
Students 122.

New Holstein, Calumet Co., Holy Rosary. (Also serves St. Ann, St. Anna). Rev. Frank Weber.
Res., 1724 Madison St., 53061-1326. Tel: 920-984-4884. [CEM]
School—1814 Madison St., 53061-1347. Tel: 920-898-4210. Sr. Anna Tisler, Prin.
Sisters 4; Lay Teachers 10; Students 150.
Catechesis/Religious Programs—Mrs. Gail Welter, D.R.E.
Students 158.

New London, Waupaca Co., Most Precious Blood, Rev. Tito Sammut; Deacon David De Young.
Res., 808 S. Pearl St., 54961-1863. Tel: 920-822-2346. [CEM]
School—102 E. Washington St., 54961. Tel: 414-982-2134.
Lay Teachers 12; Students 156.
Catechesis/Religious Programs—Mary Kleist, D.R.E.
Students 332.

Niagara, Marinette Co., St. Anthony. (Also serves St. Margaret, Pembine). Rev. Patrick A. Bernardy.
Res., 1432 River St., 54151-1599. Tel: 715-513-3879.
Catechesis/Religious Programs—D.R.E.: Mary Ann Brasure, (Grades K-8); Joetta Bartolac, (Grades 9-12).
Students 251.

Norman, Kewaunee Co., St. Joseph. Attended by Nativity BVM, Tisch Mills. Rev. Gerald Kempen, O.Praem.
Res., E3295 County Rd. G, Kewaunee, 54216-9538. Tel: 920-761-1600. [CEM]

Northeim, Manitowoc Co., St. Casimir. Attended by St. Joseph, Alverno. Rev. David Beaudry.
Res., 8109 Northeim Rd., Newton, 53063-9630. Tel: 920-264-4228. [CEM]
Catechesis/Religious Programs—Students 50.

Oconto, Oconto Co., Holy Trinity (1996), Rev. C. Terrence LaCombe; Deacon Walter Kaszynski.
Res., 716 Madison St., 54153-1668. Tel: 920-345-5900; Fax: 920-834-5907.
School—310 Arbitus Ave., 54153. Tel: 920-834-5910. Mrs. Sallie Barta, Prin.
St. Joseph. Merged with St. Peter, Oconto to form Holy Trinity Parish, Oconto.
St. Peter. Merged with St. Joseph, Oconto to form Holy Trinity Parish, Oconto.

Oconto Falls, Oconto Co., St. Anthony. Attended by St. Patrick, Stiles. Rev. Msgr. Carl E. Steiner.
Church—239 N. Franklin St., 54154-1042. Tel: 920-462-2152. [CEM]
School—253 N. Franklin St., 54154. Tel: 414-846-2276. Ms. Rosemary Marifke, Prin.
Lay Teachers 5; Students 48.
Catechesis/Religious Programs—Mary Holtzberger, D.R.E.
Students 191.

Omro, Winnebago Co., St. Mary, Rev. Joseph A. Mattern.
Res., 233 E. Scott, 54963-1705. Tel: 920-852-2258; Fax: 920-685-7343.
Catechesis/Religious Programs—Beth Winkel, D.R.E.
Students 218.

Oneida, Brown Co., St. Joseph, Rev. George G. Lenzner.
Res., 145 St. Joseph Dr., 54115-8914. Tel: 920-692-2244. [CEM]
Catechesis/Religious Programs—Andrea Sabor, D.R.E.
Students 258.

Oneida Township, Outagamie Co., Immaculate Conception, Rev. Richard L. Thomas, Admin.
Res., N5589 County Rd. E., De Pere, 54115-8529. Tel: 920-692-2626. [CEM]
Catechesis/Religious Programs—Students 83.

Oshkosh, Winnebago Co.,

1—St. Peter, Rev. John J. Becker; Sr. Diane Faust, Pastoral Assoc.; Deacon Gerald Kuborn.
Res., 435 High Ave., 54901-4796. Tel: 920-319-9782; Fax: 920-231-9808. [JC]
Catechesis/Religious Programs—Students 274.

2—St. Mary, Rev. John Becker; Deacon Robert Penzenstadler; Sr. Judith Miller, Dir.
Res., 442 Monroe St., 54901-5198. Tel: 920-315-5317.
School—St. Francis Cabrini Elementary. Part of the Oshkosh Area Catholic Educational System. Includes St. Vincent, St. Peter & St. Raphael. 619 Merritt Ave., 54901-5100. Tel: 920-235-0637. Dr. Roger Herold, Prin.
Lay Teachers 12; Students 227.
Catechesis/Religious Programs—Students 150.
Convent—441 Boyd St., 54901-5135. Tel: 414-231-3388.

3—St. Josaphat, Rev. Stanley F. Kolbusz.
Res., 1333 Walnut St., 54901-3699. Tel: 920-353-3363; Fax: 920-235-3363.
Catechesis/Religious Programs—Mrs. M. Wichmann, D.R.E.
Students 173.

4—St. Vincent de Paul, Rev. William Van De Kreeke; Deacon Raymond Brandenstein.
Res., 216 W. South Park Ave., 54901-6598. Tel: 920-318-8855. [JC]
School—St. Elizabeth Seton Elementary. (Part of the Oshkosh Area Catholic Educational System. Includes St. Vincent, St. Peter, St. Raphael, and St. Mary) 1207 Oregon St., 54901. Tel: 920-235-4060. Dr. Roger Herold, Prin.
Religious 1; Lay Teachers 10; Students 233.
Catechesis/Religious Programs—Students 109.

5—St. John. (Also serves St. Vincent de Paul, Oshkosh). Rev. William L. Van De Kreeke.
Res., 434 W. South Park Ave., 54901-6569. Tel: 920-318-8596. [JC]
Catechesis/Religious Programs—Students 232.

6—Sacred Heart, Rev. Martin Fox.
Res., 1020 W. 6th Ave., 54901-5794. Tel: 920-352-2073. [CEM]
Catechesis/Religious Programs—Students 112.

7—St. Raphael, Rev. Daniel J. Felton; Deacon Lee Vanden Heuvel. In res., Rev. Jeffrey M. Vanden Heuvel.
Mailing Address: 2355 W. Ninth Ave., 54904. Tel: 920-235-7158. [JC]
Church—830 Westhavan Dr., 54904-7977. Tel: 920-338-8044; Fax: 920-233-2360.
School—Unified Catholic Schools of Oshkosh, P.O. Box 1513, 54902-1513. Tel: 920-426-3626.
Catechesis/Religious Programs—Students 785.

Osman, Manitowoc Co., St. Isidore, Rev. Gilbert Jacobs, O.Praem.
Mailing Address: 701 Westview St., P.O. Box 236, Cleveland, 53063-0236. Tel: 920-938-8552. [CEM 2]

Pembine, Marinette Co., St. Margaret. Attended by St. Anthony, Niagara. Rev. Patrick A. Bernardy.
Res., 1432 River St., Niagara, 54151-1599. Tel: 715-324-5849.

Peshtigo, Marinette Co., St. Mary, Rev. Paul J. Radetski.
Res., 600 Thompson St., 54157-1430. Tel: 715-823-3876.
School—141 S. Wood, 54157. Tel: 715-582-4041. Mr. Frank C. Kotecki, Prin.
Sisters 1; Lay Teachers 7; Students 89.
Catechesis/Religious Programs—Mrs. Janice Vande Hei, D.R.E.
Students 251.

Phlox, Langlade Co., St. Joseph. Attended by St. Anthony, Neopit. Rev. R. David Kiefer; Deacon Tom Hartman.
Mailing Address: P.O. Box 73, 54464-0073. Tel: 715-893-3330. [CEM]
Catechesis/Religious Programs—Students 83.

Pine Grove, Brown Co., Holy Trinity, Rev. Ralph C. Merkatoris.
Res., 4767 Stagecoach Rd., Denmark, 54208-9181. Tel: 920-632-2545. [CEM]
Catechesis/Religious Programs—D.R.E.: Jane Lyon; Tammy Vanderloop.
Students 340.

Plainfield, Waushara Co., St. Paul, Rev. Michael E. Betley.
Res., 622 S. Beach St., 54966-9637. Tel: 715-354-4314. [CEM]
Catechesis/Religious Programs—Students 200.

Poy Sippi, Waushara Co., Sacred Heart of Jesus. Attended by St. Mark, Redgranite. Rev. Francis P. Reinke, Admin.
Mailing Address: P.O. Box 273, Redgranite, 54970-0273. Tel: 920-664-4442. [CEM]

Pulaski, Brown Co., Assumption of the Blessed Virgin Mary, Revs. Albert Lis, O.F.M.; Edward Tlucek, O.F.M.; Mr. Michael Vincent, Pastoral Min.; Deacon William Doran.
Res., P.O. Box 379, 54162-0379. Tel: 920-223-3279; Fax: 920-822-8030. [CEM]
School—109 E. Pulaski St., P.O. Box 57, 54162. Tel: 920-822-5650. Mrs. Mary Terrien, Prin.
Sisters 2; Lay Teachers 10; Students 125.
Catechesis/Religious Programs—Robert Berchmans, D.R.E.
Students 290.

Redgranite, Waushara Co., St. Mark. (Also serves Sacred Heart of Jesus, Poy Sippi). Rev. Francis P. Reinke, Admin.
Mailing Address: P.O. Box 273, 54970-0273. Tel: 920-664-4442.
Catechesis/Religious Programs—Students 72.

Reedsville/Maple Grove, Manitowoc Co., St. Mary-St. Patrick. St. Mary, Reedsville, and St. Patrick, Maple Grove, merged to become St. Mary-St. Patrick. Rev. James Massart, Admin.; Deacon Donald Schneider.
Res., P.O. Box 248, Reedsville, 54230-0248. Tel: 920-544-4665. [CEM 3]
School—628 Menasha St., Reedville, 54230. Tel: 920-754-4124. Daniel O'Rourke, Prin.
Lay Teachers 8; Students 118.
Catechesis/Religious Programs—Students 152.

Rosiere, Kewaunee Co., St. Peter and St. Hubert. Merged with St. Peter, Lincoln. Rev. Dennis G. Drury.
Res., E3085 County Rd. X, Casco, 54205-9757. Tel: 920-372-2852. [CEM 4]
Catechesis/Religious Programs—Students 279.

St. Anna, Calumet Co., St. Ann. Attended by Holy Rosary, New Holstein. Rev. Frank Weber.
Res., N188 School St., New Holstein, 53061-9776. Tel: 920-943-3147; Fax: 920-894-3147. [CEM]
Catechesis/Religious Programs—Students 54.

St. John, Calumet Co., St. John the Baptist Parish. Merged with Sacred Heart, Sherwood, to form St. John-Sacred Heart, Sherwood/St. John.

St. Nazianz, Manitowoc Co., St. Gregory, Rev. Gerald Sirois, S.D.S.; Deacon James Steffen.
Mailing Address: 208 Church St., 54232-0199. Tel: 920-732-2511. [CEM]
School—212 School St., 54232. Tel: 920-773-2530. Mrs. Judy Phillip, Prin.
Lay Teachers 10; Students 90.
Catechesis/Religious Programs—Fran Durkee, D.R.E.
Students 154.

School Hill, Manitowoc Co., Holy Trinity, Rev. Gerald Sirois, S.D.S.; Deacon James Steffen.
Res., 11928 Marken Rd., Kiel, 53042-9750. Tel: 920-732-2380. [CEM]
Catechesis/Religious Programs—Mrs. Barbara Graf, D.R.E.
Students 168.

Seymour, Outagamie Co., St. John, Rev. Francis R. Kerscher; Deacon Orvell DeBruin.
Mailing Address: 915 Ivory St., 54165-1629.
Res., 904 S. Main St., 54165. Tel: 920-366-6140. [CEM]
School—928 S. Main St., 54165. Tel: 920-833-2122. Mary Jo Brown, Prin.
Lay Teachers 8; Students 109.
Catechesis/Religious Programs—Theresa Hebert, D.R.E.
Students 222.

Shawano, Shawano Co., Sacred Heart. (Also serves St. Martin, Cecil). Revs. Leonard M. Evers; Robert Kollath; Sr. Evelyn Antoine, O.P., Pastoral Assoc.; Deacon Charles Daily.
Mailing Address: Office, 321 S. Sawyer St., 54166-2437. Tel: 715-262-2023.
Res., 325 S. Main St., 54166. Tel: 715-526-4106. [CEM 2]
School—124 E. Center St., 54166. Tel: 715-526-5328. Mary Jo Ambrosius, Prin.
Lay Teachers 13; Students 220.
Catechesis/Religious Programs—Mrs. Mary Ellen Waldvogel, D.R.E.
Students 350.

Sherwood/St. John, Calumet Co., St. John-Sacred Heart, Rev. Kenneth R. Frozena.
Res., P.O. Box 58, Sherwood, 54169-0058. Tel: 920-891-1515. [CEM]
School—N361 Military Rd., P.O. Box 78, Sherwood, 54169. Tel: 920-989-1373. Kerry Sievert, Prin.
Lay Teachers 9; Students 125.
Catechesis/Religious Programs—Students 113.

Shiocton, Outagamie Co., St. Denis, Revs. Thomas Pomeroy; Frank Schrage; Sr. Mary Bride Grubbs, A.N.G., Dir.
Mailing Address: N5591 2nd St., 54170. Tel: 920-863-3369; Fax: 920-986-3364. [JC]
Catechesis/Religious Programs—Jennifer Nooker, D.R.E.
Students 166.

Sister Bay, Door Co., St. Rosalia. Attended by St. Mary of the Lake, Baileys Harbor. Rev. Chester Cappucci, O.M.I.
Mailing Address: P.O. Box 405, Baileys Harbor, 54202-0405. Tel: 920-545-5264. [CEM]
Catechesis/Religious Programs—Students 95.

Slovan, Kewaunee Co., St. Adalbert. Merged with Holy Trinity, Casco.

Sobieski, Oconto Co., St. John Cantius. (Also serves St. Joseph, Chase, and St. Louis, Abrams). Rev. Gerald Prusakowski, O.F.M.
Res., 6051 Noble St., 54171-9724. Tel: 920-225-5255. [CEM]
Catechesis/Religious Programs—Students 101.

South Branch, Menominee Reservation, St. Joseph of the Lake. (Mission of St. Michael, Keshena.). Rev. David S. Barrett; Sr. Kathleen Walli, O.P., Pastoral Assoc.

Mailing Address: P.O. Box 610, Keshena, 54135-0610. Tel: 715-993-3811. [CEM]

Spruce, Oconto Co., Sacred Heart of Jesus. Merged with St. Charles Borromeo, Lena.

Stangelville, Kewaunee Co., St. Lawrence. Served from St. Joseph-St. John, Montpelier. Rev. Michael Ingold, Admin.
Mailing Address: N2085 State Hwy. 163, Denmark, 54208-7705. Tel: 920-638-8747. [CEM]
Catechesis/Religious Programs—Associated with St. Joseph-St. John, Montpelier/Krok.
Students 50.

Stark, Brown Co., St. Mary. Attended by Immaculate Conception, Glenmore. Rev. Lee J. Kahrs.
Res., 5840 Big Apple Rd., De Pere, 54115-9746. Tel: 920-647-7641. [CEM]

Stephensville, Outagamie Co., St. Patrick, Revs. Thomas Pomeroy; John Kastenholz, O.Praem.; Sr. Mary Bride Grubbs, A.N.G., Dir.
Res., N3686 State Rd. 76, Hortonville, 54944-9707. Tel: 920-575-5090. [CEM]
Catechesis/Religious Programs—Students 120.

Stiles, Oconto Co., St. Patrick. (Also serves St. Anthony, Oconto Falls). Rev. Msgr. Carl E. Steiner.
Res., 5246 St. Patrick Rd., Lena, 54139-9105. Tel: 920-342-2575. [JC]
Catechesis/Religious Programs—Associated with St. Anthony, Oconto Falls.
Students 51.

Stockbridge, Calumet Co., St. Mary, Rev. Leander F. Nickel.
Res., P.O. Box 8, 53088-0008. Tel: 920-391-1515. [CEM]
Catechesis/Religious Programs—Students 125.

Sturgeon Bay, Door Co., St. Joseph, Rev. Robert J. Karuhn; Sr. Sandra Peterson, S.S.N.D., Pastoral Assoc.; Deacon Kenneth Hunsader.
Res., 526 Louisiana St., 54235-1796. Tel: 920-432-2062; Fax: 920-743-6786.
School—130 N. 5th Ave., 54235. Tel: 920-743-9219; Fax: 920-743-9297. Michael Taylor, Prin.
Lay Teachers 11; Students 112.
Catechesis/Religious Programs—Students 263.

Corpus Christi, Rev. Anthony J. Birdsall; Deacon Paul Zenefski.
Oratory—Sturgeon Bay, 25 N. Elgin Ave., 54235-2963. Tel: 920-434-4716; Fax: 920-743-3711.
Res., 722 W. Maple St., 54235. [JC]
School—731 W. Juniper, 54235. Tel: 920-743-4144. Sr. Mary Kabat, Prin.
Lay Teachers 9; Students 171.
Catechesis/Religious Programs—Karen Stookinger, D.R.E.
Students 169.

Suamico, Brown Co., St. Benedict. (Also serves St. Pius, Little Suamico). Rev. Gary J. Dantinne; Deacon John Maloney.
Mailing Address: P.O. Box 66, 54173-0066. Tel: 920-342-2024. [CEM]
Catechesis/Religious Programs—Students 143.

Suring, Oconto Co., St. Michael, Revs. John Gallagher; Mike Clifford; Sr. Karen Vollmer, O.P., Dir.
Mailing Address: P.O. Box 248, 54174-0248. Tel: 920-422-2580. [CEM]
Catechesis/Religious Programs—Students 128.
Station—Chute Lake.

Thiry Daems, Kewaunee Co., St. Odile. Closed. For inquiries for parish records contact the Chancery.

Tigerton, Shawano Co., St. Anthony. (Also serves St. Mary, Marion). Rev. Michael R. Carroll, Admin.; Deacons Ken Sambs; Hilary Hayek.
Mailing Address: P.O. Box 106, 54486-0106. Tel: 715-352-2571; Fax: 715-535-2571.
Catechesis/Religious Programs—Students 70.

Tisch Mills, Manitowoc Co., Nativity of the Blessed Virgin Mary, Rev. Gerald B. Kempen, O.Praem.
Mailing Address: 18424 Tisch Mills Rd., Denmark, 54208-9508. Tel: 920-761-1555. [CEM]
Catechesis/Religious Programs—Students 145.

Tonet, Kewaunee Co., St. Martin. Closed. For inquiries for parish records contact the Chancery.

Two Rivers, Manitowoc Co.,

1—St. Luke. (Also serves St. Mark, Two Rivers). Rev. Larry J. Seidl; Deacon Kenneth Coenen.
Res., 1814 Jefferson St., 54241-2699. Tel: 920-932-2236.
School—Two Rivers Catholic Central. Consolidated with St. Mark, Two Rivers. 1800 Jefferson St., 54241. Tel: 920-794-7266. Mrs. Kay Franz, Prin.
Lay Teachers 16; Students 255.
Catechesis/Religious Programs—Associated with Holy Redeemer, Two Rivers.
Students 93.

2—Sacred Heart, Rev. William O'Brien.
Res., 2208 Washington St., 54241-2241. Tel: 920-947-7869.

3—St. Mark. Attended by St. Luke, Two Rivers. Rev. Larry J. Seidl.
2214 11th St., 54241-3718. Tel: 920-941-1717.
School—Two Rivers Catholic Central. Consolidated with St. Luke, Two Rivers. 2203 12th St., 54241. Tel: 920-794-7622. Kay Franz, Prin.
Students 95.
Catechesis/Religious Programs—Associated with Most Holy Redeemer, Two Rivers.
Students 128.

4—Most Holy Redeemer, Rev. William O'Brien; Donna Treml, Pastoral Assoc.; Deacon James E. Sustman.
Church—3210 Tannery Rd., 54241-1648. Tel: 920-931-1755. [CEM]
Catechesis/Religious Programs—Associated with St. Luke, St. Mark & Sacred Heart, Two Rivers. Sr. Maria Casetta, O.S.F., D.R.E.
Students 684.

Wabeno, Forest Co., St. Ambrose. (Also serves St. Mary of the Lake, Lakewood). Rev. Gerald Schmidt, O.F.M.Cap.
Mailing Address: P.O. Box 219, Lakewood, 54138-0219. Tel: 715-732-2511. [CEM]
Catechesis/Religious Programs—Students 67.

Wagner, Marinette Co., St. Edward. Attended by St. Joseph, Walsh. Rev. Roger Strebel, Admin.
Res., W3308 County Rd. G, Porterfield, 54159-9736. Tel: 715-892-2254. [CEM]
Catechesis/Religious Programs—Students 37.

Walhain, Kewaunee Co., St. Amand. Closed. For inquiries for parish records contact the Chancery.

Walsh, Marinette Co., St. Joseph. (Also serves St. Edward, Wagner). Rev. Roger Strebel, Admin.
Res., W3308 County Rd. G, Porterfield, 54159-9736. Tel: 715-892-2254. [CEM]
Catechesis/Religious Programs—Students 106.

Waupaca, Waupaca Co., St. Mary Magdalene, Rev. James F. Vennix.
Office and Mailing Address: 223 S. Division St., 54981-1594. Tel: 715-583-3000; Fax: 715-258-5708. [CEM]
Res., E. 1277 Cleghorn Rd., 54981. Tel: 715-258-4928.
Catechesis/Religious Programs—Students 440.

Wausaukee, Marinette Co., St. Augustine. (Also serves St. Agnes, Amberg). Rev. John F. McLaughlin.
Mailing Address: P.O. Box 375, 54177-0375. Tel: 715-565-5276.
Catechesis/Religious Programs—Mrs. Joy Duhey, D.R.E.
Students 170.

Wautoma, Waushara Co., St. Joseph, Rev. Philip Dinh-Van-Thiep. Pastoral Assocs. & D.R.E.: Sr. Mary Ellen Doherty; Sr. Veronica Horvat, S.S.N.D.
Res., R.R. 1, Box 426, 54982-9581. Tel: 920-873-3848. [CEM]
Catechesis/Religious Programs—Students 236.

West Kewaunee, Kewaunee Co., St. Hedwig. Attended by St. Joseph-St.John, Montpelier. Rev. Michael Ingold, Admin.
Res., E3306 Krok Rd., Kewaunee, 54216-9687. Tel: 920-761-1555. [CEM]

Weyauwega, Waupaca Co., SS. Peter and Paul, Rev. Bertin L. Samsa, O.F.M.Cap.
Res., P.O. Box 548, 54983-0548. Tel: 920-672-2179; Fax: 920-867-2179. [CEM]
Catechesis/Religious Programs—Shirley Sexton, D.R.E.
Students 175.

White Lake, Langlade Co., Ss. James & Stanislaus, Deacon Thomas Craig, Dir.; Rev. Omer Kelley.
Mailing Address: P.O. Box 36, 54491-0036. Tel: 715-822-2551. [CEM 2]
Res., 252 Bissell St., 54491.

Whitelaw, Manitowoc Co., St. Michael, Rev. Richard H. Heymen.
Mailing Address: P.O. Box 206, 54247-0206. Tel: 920-323-3901. [CEM]
School—132 W. Menasha Ave., 54247. Tel: 920-732-4442. Mrs. Arlene Rhein, Prin.
Lay Teachers 5; Students 53.
Catechesis/Religious Programs—Students 124.

Winneconne, Winnebago Co., St. Mary, Rev. Leroy R. Smet.
Res., 205 Pleasant Dr., 54986-0640. Tel: 920-824-4246; Fax: 920-582-7712.
Church—P.O. Box 640, 54986-0640. [JC]
Catechesis/Religious Programs—Students 291.

Wittenberg, Shawano Co., Holy Family. (Also serves St. William, Eland). Rev. Claude A. Zabinski, O.F.M.
Res., 106 N. Ellms St., 54499-9099. Tel: 715-532-2050. [CEM]
Catechesis/Religious Programs—D.R.E.: Sr. Therese Lukas; Joyce Zaverorsky.
Students 116.

Wrightstown, Brown Co., St. Paul, Rev. Elroy Reimer.
Res., P.O. Box 187, 54180-0187. Tel: 920-324-4374. [JC 2]
School—425 Main St., 54180. Tel: 920-532-4833. Mrs. Carol Hoard, Prin.
Lay Teachers 8; Students 105.
Catechesis/Religious Programs—Students 131.

Chaplains of Public Institutions

Green Bay. *Green Bay Correctional Institution.* Rev. Jerome Taddy, 2615 Washington St., Two Rivers, 54241-2140. Tel: 920-794-7273.

King. *Wisconsin Veterans Home* P.O. Box 152, 54946-0152. Tel: 715-258-5586, Ext. 381. Rev. Paul A. Vanden Hogen.

Special Assignment:
Reverend Monsignors—
Coleman, Brian P., P.O. Box 23825, Green Bay, WI 54305-3825
Dewane, John B., P.O. Box 23825, Green Bay, WI 54305-3825
Maufort, Richard A., Charlestown Pointe I, 1975 Ridgeway Dr., Apt. 30, De Pere, WI 54115-4109
Schuh, John H., P.O. Box 23825, Green Bay, WI 54305-3825
Reverend Fathers—
Carr, Martin P., 1965 Oshkosh Ave., Oshkosh, WI 54901-2659
Clifford, Michael J., 10653 Green Meadow Ln., Coleman, WI 54112-9623
Gilsdorf, Gordon J., Notre Dame de la Baie Academy, 610 Maryhill Dr., Green Bay, WI 54303-2092
Gilsdorf, Richard W., N9599 Bay Shore Ln., Luxemburg, WI 54217
Groher, Robert C., 6202 Dogwood Ln., Oconto, WI 54153-9590
Hoffmann, Philip A., P.O. Box 23825, Green Bay, WI 54305-3825
Koch, Michael R., Chap. for Sisters of the Sorrowful Mother, Oshkosh, 890 Graceland Dr., Apt. 8, Oshkosh, WI 54904
Krutzik, Norman, 622 E. Pershing St., Appleton, WI 54911-8270
Mocco, Charles W., UW-Green Bay Ecumenical Center, 2420 Nicolet Dr., Green Bay, WI 54311-7001
Samter, James, P.O. Box 23825, Green Bay, WI 54305-3825. Tel: 920-437-7531
Smith, Ivan E., 3416 County Rd. V, Sturgeon Bay, WI 54235-8832
Van De Loo, Willard, P.O. Box 23825, Green Bay, WI 54305-3825
Vanden Heuvel, Jeffrey M., Newman Center, 717 W. Irving, Oshkosh, WI 54901-4319
Ver Bust, Richard M., Faculty St. Norbert College, 824 Voelker St., De Pere, WI 54115-3618
Werner, Justin N., N1682 Ridgeway Dr., Greenville, WI 54942

On Duty Outside the Diocese:
Reverend Monsignors—
Dewane, Frank J., Pontificio Consiglio Cor Unum, 00120 Vatican City, Rome, Italy. Tel: 011-396-6988-7331
Polc, Jaroslav, Tha Kurova 3, 16000 Prague 6, Czech Republic
Reverend Fathers—
Blaha, John F., P.O. Box 23825, Green Bay, WI 54305-3825
Conard, Raymond J., Apartado Postal 13, San Juan de la Maguana, Dominican Republic
Dowling, Raymond G., 9707 Kingsley Rd., Apt. 514, Dallas, TX 75238
Hoffmann, William A., Casa Curiel, Parroquia Santa Teresa, Elias Pina, Dominican Republic
Mayefske, Thomas, 6041 Sequoia Rd. N.W., Apt. A18, Albuquerqe, NM 87120-3406
Rank, Robert F., 203 Dunne Ave., Robstown, TX 78380-3501
Reuter, John F., Apartado 46, Tlaxiaco, Oaxaca Mexico
Schiavone, Robert W., 10430 W. Plum Tree Cir., #203, Hales Corners, WI 53130-2670
Seis, Michael, Casa Curiel, Pannoquia Santa Teresa, Elias Pina, Dominican Republic
Taylor, Peter, Box 768, Bagdad, AZ 86321
Vander Heyden, William F., Chap., V.A. Medical Center, 3001 Green Bay Rd., North Chicago, IL 60064-3049

Military Chaplains:
Reverend Fathers—
Dory, Michael, Lt. Cmdr., Bldg. #3, Naval Training Center #5, 2701 Sheridan Rd., Great Lakes, IL 60088-5135

Absent on Leave:
Reverend Monsignors—
Witczak, Edward
Reverend Fathers—
Eberhardy, William
Pawelski, John
Resheske, Florian

Scherer, Steven J.
Schneider, Ronald
Shebuski, Charles
Somers, Michael
Stocker, Thomas
Thompson, Robert

Retired:
Most Rev.—
Wycislo, Aloysius, P.O. Box 23825, Green Bay, WI 54305-3825
Reverend Monsignors—
Hotchkiss, Eugene, 1400 S. Park Ave., Neenah, WI 54956-4651
Rose, Donald, 865 Mill Rd., Sturgeon Bay, WI 54235-9267
Schneider, Alfred, 224 Iroquois Ave., #11, Green Bay, WI 54301-1918
Reverend Fathers—
Bablitch, Michael, 3100 Ellis St., Apt. 8, Stevens Point, WI 54481
Barcome, Earl, 1326 S. Fisk St., Green Bay, WI 54304-3055
Bedessem, Henry W., 1851 Eldorado Dr., Apt. 6, Green Bay, WI 54302-5554
Bestler, Joseph, 224 Iroquois Ave., #14, Green Bay, WI 54301-1918
Brouchoud, Earl, 1136 S. Lake St., Manitowoc, WI 54220-5328
Danks, Arthur J., 2616 He Nis Ra Ln., Green Bay, WI 54304-1308
Feeney, John P., 3333 W. 2nd St., 56/123, Los Angeles, CA 90004-6149
Feller, Donald J., 2496 Mary Jo Dr., Green Bay, WI 54311-5208
Flatley, Eugene T., 2153 Calle Buena Ventura, Oceanside, CA 92056-3216
Gartska, Joseph A., N8778 Forest Rd., Deerbrook, WI 54424-9613
Geigel, Francis, Rte. 1, Box 396, Wabeno, WI 54566-9742
Gerend, Lawrence, 216 Catherine St., Kaukauna, WI 54130-3126
Gitter, Aloysius A., P.O. Box 98, Harper, TX 78631-0098
Gomulka, Henry J., Alvernia Manor, 1598 Main St., Lemont, IL 60439-3701
Hietpas, Raymond, 224 Iroquois Ave., #7, Green Bay, WI 54301-1918
Hogan, LeRoy, 220 W. 4th St., Kaukauna, WI 54130
Jacobs, James T., P.O. Box 86, Crandon, WI 54520-0086
Janssen, Orville, 1500 Oakcrest Ct., Appleton, WI 54914
Johanek, John, 1137 Edgewood Dr., Green Bay, WI 54311-5524
Kelley, Omer C., 1215 Spanish Fort Ave., Antigo, WI 54409-1566
Kerch, Rudolph S., 1331 Bellevue St., Lot 225 Huguet, Green Bay, WI 54302-2145
Kilsdonk, Edward, 2249 W. Cortland Dr., Appleton, WI 54914-1932
Kleiber, Richard, 3920 Libal St., Green Bay, WI 54301-1048
Knier, Aloysius M., 1910 W. Ohio Ave., Room 251, Milwaukee, WI 53215-4933
Koehne, David, 1051 Main St., Wrightstown, WI 54180-1007
Koszarek, Thaddeus J., 224 Iroquois Ave., #1, Green Bay, WI 54301-1918
Kutiuk, Casimir, 259 Westhaven Dr., Apt. 101, Oshkosh, WI 54904-7858
Laux, Donald, P.O. Box 219, Birnamwood, WI 54414-0219
Lexa, Robert, 2320 Woodrow Ct., #7, Appleton, WI 54915
Marquardt, Donald, 224 Iroquois Ave., #3, Green Bay, WI 54301-1918
Melchior, Frank, E2783 Rockledge Rd., Casco, WI 54205
Peeters, R. Thomas, 224 Iroquois Ave., #6, Green Bay, WI 54301-1918
Rickert, William, 224 Iroquois Ave., #5, Green Bay, WI 54301-1918
Rodgers, Kenneth, 441 St. Mary Blvd., Green Bay, WI 54301-2607
Scanlan, Lambert, 1499 Capitol Dr., #105, Green Bay, 54303-2244
Schmidt, Eugene, 2650 Vinland Rd., Oshkosh, WI 54901-1524
Schmitt, John P., 2819 35th St., Two Rivers, WI 54241-1521
Schneider, Donald, 509 Laurel Dr., P.O. Box 163, Francis Creek, WI 54214-0163
Schreiter, Daniel A., 4616 Basswood St., Land O'Lakes, FL 34639-5603
Schuh, Earl, 2470 Mary Jo Dr., Green Bay, WI 54311-5208
Schumacher, Paul, 2427 County Rd. J, Abrams, WI 54101
Shafer, Richard, 1515 Capitol Dr., #105, Green Bay, WI 54303-2246
Sladek, Robert, 520 S. Kensington Dr., Appleton, WI 54915
Spalding, William, 310 Alpine Dr., #9, Shawano, WI 54166-2011
Staudenmaier, Wilbert, 214 E. Summer St., Appleton, WI 54911-4814
Steckbauer, Linus J., 1411 N. Superior St., Antigo, WI 54409-2359
Stingle, Lawrence A., 2777 He Nis Ra Ln., Green Bay, WI 54304-1357
Worzalla, Dennis, St. Peter Parish, 800 4th Ave., Stevens Point, WI 54481-1627

Permanent Deacons:
Andrastek, Phil, 1607 Hamilton St., Manitowoc, WI 54220-5029
Arnold, Robert, St. Agnes Church, Green Bay
Asmuth, James, (Retired), 1615 Nicolet Blvd., Neenah, WI 54956-2984
Baumruk, Roy, St. Joseph Church, Appleton
Beaudry, Glenn, (Retired), 221 E. Fairview, Green Bay, WI 54301-1269
Boeldt, Alan, St. Paul Church, Manitowoc
Boucher, Paul, St. Francis Solanus Church, Gresham and St. Mary Church, Leopolis
Brandenstein, Raymond, St. Vincent de Paul Church, Oshkosh
Bricco, Howard, St. Patrick Church, Menasha
Burke, William, St. Mary Church, Appleton
Burkel, William, Holy Martyrs of Gorcum Church, Green Bay
Charlier, Earl, 733 S. Clay St., Green Bay, WI 54301-3415
Coenen, Kenneth, St. Luke Church, Two Rivers
Craig, Thomas, Dir., Ss. James & Stanislaus Church, White Lake
Daily, Charles, Sacred Heart Church, Shawano and St. Martin Church, Cecil
De Bruin, Orvell, St. John Church, Seymour
De Groot, Vincent M., St. John Church, Little Chute
DeYoung, David, Most Precious Blood Church, New London
Dineen, Terry, St. Philip the Apostle Church, Green Bay
Doran, William, Assumption BVM Church, Pulaski
Drobka, Robert, St. Mary Church, Manitowoc
Ellis, Robert, 1372 Nienhaus Dr., DePere, WI 54115-9802
Garcia, Benjamin, 612 E. Smith St., Iron Mountain, MI 49801-1954
Gauthier, James, St. Elizabeth Ann Seton Church, Green Bay
Gigure, Donald, Sacred Heart Church, Appleton
Goetz, Claude, (Retired), 538 N. 8th St., Manitowoc, WI 54220-1906
Hanley, Thomas, St. Mary Church, Antigo and St. Wenceslaus Church, Neva
Hartman, Thomas, St. Joseph Church, Phlox; Holy Family Church, Mattoon; St. Anthony Church, Neopit
Hayek, Hilary, St. Anthony Church, Tigerton
Hunsader, Kenneth, St. Joseph Church, Sturgeon Bay
Jacqmin, Robert, (Retired), 2212 Nicolet Dr., #3, Green Bay, WI 54311-5585
Jozwiak, Thomas, St. Rose Church, Clintonville
Kaszynski, Walter, Holy Trinity Church, Oconto
Kieffer, Paul, Holy Innocents Church, Manitowoc
Klein, Paul, St. Thomas More Church, Appleton
Klein, William, St. Paul Church, Manitowoc
Koehler, Daniel, 1302 W. Ajo Way, #14, Tucson, AZ 85713-5704
Kopydlowski, Kenneth, SS. Peter & Paul Church, Green Bay
Kostichka, James, Holy Cross Church, Lena
Kremer, Frank, Jr., St. Mary Church, De Pere
Kuborn, Gerald, St. Peter Church, Oshkosh
Kunzer, Earl, Ss. Edward/Isidore Church, Flintville
Laurant, John, St. Bernard Church, Green Bay
Le Mere, David, St. John Baptist Church, Howard
Lowe, Russ, (Retired), N2280 Country Ln., Waupaca, WI 54981-9526
Ludke, David, 3518 Glasscock Ave., Bossier City, LA 71112
Madsen, Roger, Ss. Peter/Paul Church, Institute
Maloney, John, St. Benedict Church, Suamico
Mastalish, Larry, St. Bernard Church, Green Bay
Meidl, Richard, St. Joseph Church, Kellnersville
Nass, Donald, (Retired), 946 Debbie Ln., Redgranite, WI 54970-0273
Nelesen, Ken, Holy Innocents Church, Manitowoc
Newhouse, Don, St. Nicholas Church, Freedom
Orlowski, Harold, St. Mary/Lake Church, Lakewood
Otradovec, Byron, Holy Family Church, Marinette
Paulick, Don, 915 N. Locust St., Green Bay, WI 54303-4427
Penzenstadler, Robert, St. Mary Church, Oshkosh
Peronteau, B., (Retired), 1787 Cecil Ave., Wabeno, WI 54566
Plantico, Paul, St. Francis Xavier Cathedral, Green Bay
Proulx, Rahlf, Holy Innocents Church, Manitowoc
Quinette, Harvey, Our Lady of Lourdes Church, De Pere
Reed, Maurice, Dir. Office of Permanent Diaconate, St. Bernard Church, Appleton
Reilly, Timothy, Resurrection Church, Green Bay
Rocchi, Steven, (Retired), N4297 Cty. WW, Wild Rose, WI 54984-9418
Sambs, Kenneth, St. Anthony Church, Tigerton
Sauve, Willard, (Retired), 107 Park Rd., Two Rivers, WI 54241-3811
Schneider, Donald, Sr., St. Mary-St. Patrick Church, Reedsville/Maple Grove
Schraufnagel, George, St. Paul Church, Combined Locks
Spielbauer, Norman, St. Margaret Mary Church, Neenah
Steffen, James, Holy Trinity Church, School Hill and St. Gregory Church, St. Nazianz
Sustman, James, Most Holy Redeemer Church, Two Rivers
Swinford, Norval, (Retired), N1764 County Rd. D, Hortonville, WI 54944-9802
Teske, Glenn, Our Lady of Lourdes, De Pere
Thetreau, Jerome, Holy Family Church, Marinette
Vande Hey, Steven, St. Mary Church, Kaukauna
Vanden Heuvel, Lee P., St. Raphael the Archangel Church, Oshkosh
Wessing, Reinhart, St. Thomas More Church, Appleton
Wetzel, Donald, St. Thomas More Church, Appleton
Whitcomb, Patrick, St. Theresa Church, Appleton
Wildenberg, Clay, 115 Professional Plaza, Apt. 138, Neenah, WI 54956-4064
Williams, Nick, St. John the Baptist Church, Howard
Zenefski, Paul, Corpus Christi Church, Sturgeon Bay

INSTITUTIONS LOCATED IN THE DIOCESE

[A] SEMINARIES, RELIGIOUS OR SCHOLASTICATES

GREEN BAY. *St. Mary of the Angels Friary*, 645 S. Irwin Ave., 54301-3303. Tel: 920-437-7411. Bro. James Buda, O.F.M., Guardian. Priests 3; Brothers 4.

DE PERE. *St. Norbert Abbey*, 1016 N. Broadway, 54115-2697. Tel: 920-337-4300; Fax: 920-337-4328. Rt. Revs. E. Thomas De Wane, O.Praem., Abbot; Benjamin T. Mackin, O.Praem., Abbot Emeritus; Sylvester M. Killeen, O.Praem., Abbot Emeritus; Jerome G. Tremel, O.Praem., Abbot Emeritus; Very Rev. David F. Strenski, O.Praem., Prior; Revs. Robert K. Finnegan, O.Praem., Provisor, Sec. & Treas.; James T. Baraniak, O.Praem., Vocation Coord.; Donald C. Noel, O.Praem., Subprior & House Supr.; Lawrence A. Mayer, O.Praem., Dir. Formation & Novice Master; Thomas O. Meulemans, O.Praem., Mission Procurator.

[B] COLLEGES AND UNIVERSITIES

DE PERE. *St. Norbert College*, 54115-2099. Tel: 920-403-3181.
E-mail: opatpjcsncad.snc.edu
Web site: http://www.snc.edu
For a complete listing, refer to the Colleges and Universities section.

MANITOWOC. *Silver Lake College of the Holy Family*, 2406 S. Alverno Rd., 54220-9319. Tel: 920-684-6691; Fax: 920-684-7082.
E-mail: adm@sl.edu
Web site: http://sl.edu/slc
For a complete listing, refer to the Colleges and Universities section.

[C] HIGH SCHOOLS, DIOCESAN

APPLETON. *Xavier High School*. Coed, 1600 W. Prospect Ave., 54914. Tel: 920-733-6632.
E-mail: mreynebeau@xavier.k12.wi.us
Web site: http://www.xavier.k12.wi.us
Mr. Matt Reynebeau, Prin.; Mrs. Donna Fahrenkrug, Assoc. Prin.; Andrew Mahoney, Dir. Guidance Dept.; Ms. Sarah Simon, Campus Min. Lay Teachers 45; Students 548.

MANITOWOC. *Roncalli High School*, 2000 Mirro Dr., 54220-6799. Tel: 920-682-8801. Christian Brothers and Franciscan Sisters of Christian Charity. Bro. Patrick Conway, Pres.; Mr. Tim Olson, Prin.; Mr. Ron Klestinski, Dean of Students.
Campus Ministers: Bro. Larry Zeman; Mrs. Jennifer Nooker. Brothers 4; Sisters 7; Lay Teachers 28;

Students 399.

MARINETTE. *Marinette Catholic Central High School*, 1200 Main St., 54143-2594. Tel: 715-735-7481. Sr. Rose Adler, Prin. Lay Teachers 15; Students 109.

NEENAH/MENASHA. *St. Mary Central High School*. 1050 Zephyr Dr., Neenah, 54956-1389. Tel: 920-722-7796; Fax: 920-722-5940. Mrs. Sue Simonsen, Prin. Sisters 1; Lay Teachers 18; Students 240.

OSHKOSH. *Lourdes High School*. (Coed.), 110 N. Sawyer St., 54901-5696. Tel: 920-235-5670.
E-mail: Lourdes@vbe.com
Web site: www.vbe.com/~Lourdes
(Part of Unified Catholic Schools of Oshkosh). Bro. Roger Betzold, F.S.C., Prin.; Mr. Tom Baum, Vice Prin.; Carol Staszkiewicz, Dev. Dir. Lay Teachers 21; Students 184.

[D] HIGH SCHOOLS, PRIVATE

GREEN BAY. *Notre Dame de la Baie Academy*, 610 Maryhill Dr., 54303-2092. Tel: 920-498-6464; Fax: 920-498-6456.
E-mail: mschmidt@mail.wiscnet.net
Web site: http://www.geocities.com/athens/6330/
Sr. Patricia Clement, C.S.J., Prin. Priests 2; Lay Teachers 49; Students 826.

[E] CONSOLIDATED SCHOOLS

APPLETON. *Appleton Catholic Educational System (ACES)*, 300 N. Woods Edge Dr., #3, 54914. Tel: 920-735-9380. William O'Brien, Exec. Dir.

MANITOWOC. *Manitowoc Area Catholic System (MACS)*, 1418 Grand Ave., 54220-6197. Tel: 920-683-6888. Linda Bender, Contact Person & Prin.

St. Francis de Sales School. (Grades K-5), 1408 Waldo Blvd., 54220-2610.

St. Francis Xavier School. (Grades PreK-5), 1418 Grand Ave., 54220-6197.

St. Frances Cabrini Middle School. (Grades 6-8), 2109 Marshall St., 54220-4959. Consolidation of Holy Innocents, Sacred Heart, St. Andrew, St. Paul, St. Mary and St. Boniface grade schools in Manitowoc.

NEENAH/MENASHA. *Twin Cities Catholic Educational System (TCCES)*. 528 Second St., Menasha, 54952-3112. Tel: 920-722-7922; Fax: 920-722-1838. Michelle Uitenbroek, Contact Person. Consolidation of St. Gabriel, St. Margaret Mary, St. Mary Elementary, Seton Catholic Middle School and St. Mary Central High School.

OSHKOSH. *Unified Catholic Schools of Oshkosh*, 110 N. Sawyer St., 54901. Tel: 920-426-3626.

[F] GENERAL HOSPITALS

GREEN BAY. *Libertas Treatment Center for Chemically Dependent*, 1701 Dousman St., 54303-3282. Tel: 920-498-8600
For a complete listing, refer to the Hospitals section.

St. Mary's Hospital-Medical Center, 1726 Shawano Ave., 54303-3282. Tel: 920-498-4200; Fax: 920-498-1861
For a complete listing, refer to the Hospitals section.

St. Vincent Hospital, P.O. Box 13508, 54307-3508. Tel: 920-433-0111; 433-8162; Fax: 920-431-3215
For a complete listing, refer to the Hospitals section.

ANTIGO. *Langlade Memorial Hospital*, 112 E. 5th Ave., 55409. Tel: 715-623-2331; Fax: 715-623-9359
For a complete listing, refer to the Hospitals section.

APPLETON. *St. Elizabeth Hospital*, 1506 S. Oneida St., 54915-1305. Tel: 920-738-2665; Fax: 920-738-0949
For a complete listing, refer to the Hospitals section.

KEWAUNEE. *St. Mary Kewaunee Area Memorial Hospital*, 810 Lincoln St., P.O. Box 117, 54216-0117. Tel: 920-388-2210; Fax: 920-388-2302
For a complete listing, refer to the Hospitals section.

MANITOWOC. *Holy Family Memorial, Inc.*, 2300 Western Ave., P.O. Box 1450, 54221-1450. Tel: 920-684-2011; Fax: 920-684-2522
For a complete listing, refer to the Hospitals section.

OSHKOSH. *Mercy Medical Center*, 631 Hazel St., P.O. Box 1100, 54902-1100. Tel: 920-236-2000; Fax: 920-231-5677
For a complete listing, refer to the Hospitals section.

[G] PROTECTIVE INSTITUTIONS

GREEN BAY. *McClosky Program, Inc.*, 2560 Shawano Ave., P.O. Box 10357, 54313. Tel: 920-434-8208
For a complete listing, refer to the Special Care Facilities section.

Our Lady of Charity Center, Inc., 2560 Shawano Ave., P.O. Box 10357, 54313. Tel: 920-434-8208
For a complete listing, refer to the Special Care Facilities section.

OSHKOSH. *The Convent Project, Inc.*, 435 High Ave., 54901. Tel: 920-235-6002
For a complete listing, refer to the Special Care Facilities section.

TWO RIVERS. *Sisters Treatment Group Home*, 3904 Martin Ln., 54241. Tel: 920-794-1524
For a complete listing, refer to the Special Care Facilities section.

[H] HOMES FOR AGED

GREEN BAY. *The McCormick Memorial Home for the Aged*, 212 Iroquois Ave., 54301-1918. Tel: 920-437-0883; Fax: 920-437-2696
For a complete listing, refer to the Special Care Facilities section.

APPLETON. *Franciscan Care and Rehabilitation Center, Inc.*, 2915 N. Meade St., 54911-1598. Tel: 920-831-8700; Fax: 920-731-3206.
E-mail: osh.screech@affinity.com
For a complete listing, refer to the Special Care Facilities section.

KAUKAUNA. *St. Paul Home, Inc.*, 1211 Oakridge Ave., 54130-9961. Tel: 920-766-6020; Fax: 920-766-9161
For a complete listing, refer to the Special Care Facilities section.

MANITOWOC. *Felician Village Inc.*, 1700 S. 18th St., 54220. Tel: 920-684-7171
For a complete listing, refer to the Special Care Facilities section.

St. Mary's Home for the Aged, 2005 Division St., 54220-5699. Tel: 920-684-7171; Fax: 920-684-0240
For a complete listing, refer to the Special Care Facilities section.

NEENAH. *Assisi Homes of Neenah, Inc.*, 210 Byrd Ave., 54946. Tel: 920-821-0336
For a complete listing, refer to the Special Care Facilities section.

Villa Saint Clare, Inc., 130 Byrd Ave., 54952
For a complete listing, refer to the Special Care Facilities section.

NEW LONDON. *St. Joseph Residence, Inc., New London*, 107 E. Beckert Rd., 54961. Tel: 920-982-5354.
E-mail: sjradm@athenet.net
For a complete listing, refer to the Special Care Facilities section.

NIAGARA. *Maryhill Manor (SNF)*, 501 Madison Ave., 54151. Tel: 715-251-3178; Fax: 715-251-1200
For a complete listing, refer to the Special Care Facilities section.

[I] MONASTERIES AND RESIDENCES OF PRIESTS AND BROTHERS

GREEN BAY. *St. Mary of the Angels Friary*, 645 S. Irwin Ave., 54301-3303. Tel: 920-437-7411. Franciscan Friars, Assumption of the Blessed Virgin Mary Province (Order of Friars Minor). Revs. Finian Zaucha, O.F.M., Vicar & Pastor; Brendan Wroblewski, O.F.M., Asst. Pastor; Campion Kluczynski, Chap. St. Vincent's Hospital; Lawrence Karcz, O.F.M., Preaching Ministry; Bros. James Buda, O.F.M., Vicar & Guardian; Columban Sokolowski, O.F.M.; Joseph Krymkowski, O.F.M.; Theodore Tokarz, O.F.M. Priests 3; Brothers 4.

APPLETON. *St. Fidelis Friary*, 1100 N. Ballard Rd., 54911-5100. Tel: 920-954-8954. Revs. Simeon Keogh, Guardian; Donald Brody; Ambrose De Groot; Joseph Doerfler; Silas Baumann; William Lulloff; Pius Pulvermacher; Ambrose Simon; Giles Soyka; Jerome Tuller; Joel Tuller; Vianney Thibedeau; Anthony Thoma; Grigion Wenning; Bros. Thomas Heegeman; Carmel Labadie; Cyrus Toschik; Richard McDaniel; Conrad Heinen. Priests 14; Brothers 5; Staff 3.

St. Joseph Friary, 404 W. Lawrence St., 54911-5855. Tel: 920-734-7195. Order of Friars Minor Capuchin. Revs. John Holly, O.F.M.Cap.; Kurt Gessner, O.F.M.Cap.; David Belongia, O.F.M.Cap.

DE PERE. *St. Joseph Priory*, 103 Grant St., 54115-2001. Tel: 920-403-3258. Residence for Norbertine Community. Revs. James T. Baraniak; John Bostwick, O.Praem., House Supr.; Dennis M. Burke, O.Praem.; Robert J. Cornell, O.Praem.; Rowland C. De Peaux, O.Praem.; George J. Feldman, O.Praem.; David M. Komatz, O.Praem.; Conrad J. Kratz, O.Praem.; Brendan J. McKeough; Gery G. Meehan, O.Praem.; Thomas O. Meulemans; Gilbert Mihayli, O.Praem.; Mark Payne, O.Praem.; Dane Radecki, O.Praem.; Joseph Rekasi; Alan Scheible, O.Praem.; Timothy Shillcox, O.Praem.; Harvey H. Toonen, O.Praem.; Louis J. Vande Castle, O.Praem.; Robert Vande Hey, O.Praem.; Bro. Robert Craanen. Priests 20; Brothers 1.

St. Norbert Abbey, 1016 N. Broadway, 54115-2697. Tel: 920-337-4300; Fax: 920-337-4328. Canons Regular of Premontre. Legal Titles: *The Premonstratensian Fathers.; NORBERT & CO., a nominee of The Premonstratensian Fathers, Norbertine Fathers.; St. Norbert Abbey, Inc.; Augustine Stewardship Fund Trust.; Norbertine Retirement Fund Trust.; St. Norbert Abbey Seminarian and Education Fund Trust.; The Walnut Markets, Inc.; Los Amigos del Peru, Inc.* Rt. Revs. E. Thomas De Wane, O.Praem., Abbot; Benjamin T. Mackin, O.Praem., Abbot Emeritus; Sylvester M. Killeen, O.Praem., Abbot Emeritus; Jerome G. Tremel, O.Praem., Abbot Emeritus; Very Rev. David F. Strenski, O.Praem., Prior; Revs. Robert K. Finnegan, O.Praem., Provisor & Sec.-Treas.; Donald C. Noel, O.Praem., Subprior & House Supr.; Laurence A. Mayer, O.Praem., Dir. Formation & Novice Master; Thomas O. Meulemans, O.Praem., Mission Procurator; Bartholomew A. Agar, O.Praem.; Jordan R. Blecha, O.Praem.; Robert E. Carson, O.Praem.; Angelo J. Feldkamp, O.Praem.; Jay J. Fostner, O.Praem.; Michael F. Frisch, O.Praem.; Isadore M. Gosz, O.Praem.; Eugene E. Gries, O.Praem.; Guy E. Guyon, O.Praem; Gabriel A. Hinkes, O.Praem.; Robert L. Hyde, O.Praem.; Fabian A. Jolicoeur, O.Praem.; Stanislaus N. Joppe, O.Praem; John P. Kastenholz, O.Praem.; Alfred A. McBride, Weston, MA; Francis B. McHugh, O.Praem.; Gilbert E. Mihalyi, O.Praem., (Kecskemet, Hungary); Emmanuel F. Mulhall, O.Praem.; Conan P. Mulrooney, O.Praem.; Richard D. Mulroy, O.Praem.; James P. Nielson, O.Praem.; Gary J. Neville, O.Praem.; Ambrose J. Peeters, O.Praem.; Peter J. Renard, O.Praem.; Robert B. Reppen, O.Praem.; Julian C. Resch, O.Praem.; Joseph A. Rohlinger, O.Praem; Stephen J. Rossey, O.Praem.; Glen F. Siebers, O.Praem; Milton C. Strebel, O.Praem.; Roman R. Vanasse, O.Praem.; Achilles E. Van Hoof, O.Praem., (Tongerlo, Belgium); Albin V. Veszelovszky, O.Praem., (Godollo, Hungary); Michael J. Weber, O.Praem., (Chap., United States Air Force, Montgomery, AL); Anthony J. Wieczorek, O.Praem.; Bros. Steven J. Herro, O.Praem.; Gerlac J. Riess, O.Praem.; Clement G. Tourangeau, O.Praem. Brothers 6; Priests 86; Priests at St. Norbert Abbey 40; Seminarians 4.

Retreats, Missions and Renewals: Rev. Robert E. Carson, O.Praem.; Rt. Rev. Jerome G. Tremel, O.Praem.

Priests serving in foreign Countries: Archdiocese of Lima, Peru, South America, Padres Norbertinos, Correo Las Flores, Lima 36. Tel: 011-511-992-4323 (Cellular); 011-511-458-0715 (Regular); Fax: 011-511-459-5905. Revs. Roderick R. Fenzl, O.Praem.; William J. Fischer, O.Praem.; Sebastian R. Schalk, O.Praem., Archidiocese of Iquitos, Peru, South America, Santa Clotilde, Rio Napo, Apartado 216. Tel: 011-51-94-25-1932; Fax: 011-51-94-25-1932. Revs. Lambert C. Baeten, O.Praem.; John P. MacCarthy, O.Praem.

NEW HOLSTEIN. *Salvatorian Center Residence*, 53061-0001. Tel: 920-898-5635. Brothers 6.

Salvatorian Public Relations, Salvatorian Center, 53062. Tel: 920-898-4201. Rev. Gregory Coulthardt, S.D.S.

Salvatorian Mission Warehouse, 53061. Tel: 920-898-5898. Bro. Regis Fust, S.D.S., Dir. Mission Supply Prog.

OSHKOSH. *Community of Our Lady*. (Diocesan Pious Union), 2804 Oakwood Ln., 54904-8406. Tel: 920-233-5633; Fax: 920-233-5604. Very Rev. Regis N. Barwig, Prior; Revs. Eugene E. Kalinski; Augustine Serafini.

PULASKI. *Assumption of B.V.M. Friary*, 143 E. Pulaski St., P.O. Box 100, 54162-0100. Tel: 920-822-5422; Fax: 920-822-5423.
E-mail: 70640.3237@compuserve.com
Web site: www.pulaskiofm.org
Headquarters of the Assumption of the Blessed Virgin Mary Province, Franciscan Friars (Order of Friars Minor). Revs. Paul Reczek, O.F.M., Minister Prov.; Thomas W. Luczak, O.F.M., Vicar Prov.; John Puodziunas, O.F.M., Treasurer; Richard Tulko, O.F.M., Prov. Sec.

Friary, 54162. Tel: 414-822-8125. Revs. Edward Tlucek, O.F.M., Guardian; Melvin Wierzbicki, O.F.M.; Adalbert Kalenty, O.F.M.; De Paul Sobotka, O.F.M.; Bros. Herman-Joseph Peplinski, O.F.M.; Anthony Gancarz, O.F.M.; Peter Rydza, O.F.M.; Gregory Stasinski, O.F.M.; David Typek, O.F.M.; Henry Kolbok, O.F.M.; Austin Mysliwiec, O.F.M.; Andrew Brophy, O.F.M.; Michael Janiak, O.F.M.

Retired-Infirm - Elsewhere: St. Mary's Home, Manitowoc: Revs. Thomas Wojciechowski, O.F.M., Chap.; Herman J. Ziemba, O.F.M.; Josaphat Ledwon, O.F.M.; Gerard Kotula, O.F.M.; Damien Rybka, O.F.M.; Sylvester E. Makarewicz, O.F.M.; Bros. Eugene Lacny, O.F.M.; Miles Brainer, O.F.M.; Lambert Gorczycki, O.F.M.

Outside of Diocese: Revs. Ladislaus Szepe, S.F.O., Sarasota, FL; Lazarus Macior, O.F.M., Univ. of Akron, Biology Dept., 44325. Rev. Adam Szufel, O.F.M., Warner Robins, GA, 31088.

Priests of the Province Serving Abroad: Revs. Lyle Chrobak, O.F.M., Guaymas, Mexico; Arcadius Smolinski, O.F.M., Europe; Henry Howaniec, O.F.M., Kazakstan; Liguori Mierzwiak, O.F.M., Holy Land; James Heinsch, O.F.M., Holy Land.

Military Chaplains: Revs. Conrad Targonski, O.F.M.; Adam E. Szufel, O.F.M., (Retired); Randall Roberts, O.F.M.

Franciscan Publishers. Tel: 920-822-5833.

ST. NAZIANZ. *Religious House of the Society of the Divine Savior S.D.S.* Salvatorian Community. 206 Church, 54232. Tel: 920-773-2794. Bros. Thaddeus

Huebner, S.D.S.; Florian Schueth, S.D.S. Brothers 2.

[J] CONVENTS AND RESIDENCES FOR SISTERS

GREEN BAY. *Hospital Sisters of the Third Order of St. Francis,* 304 David Dr., 54303. Tel: 920-497-1882. Sisters 3. 1015 S. Webster St., 54305. Tel: 920-432-1337. Sisters 2.

St. Francis Convent of Sisters of St. Francis of the Holy Cross, 3025 Bay Settlement Rd., 54311-7301. Tel: 920-468-1828; Fax: 920-468-1207.
E-mail: sisters@gbonline.com
Sr. Sally Ann Brickner, Pres. Sisters 95; In Diocese 88.

Sisters of Our Lady of Charity of the North American Union, Inc., 2560 Shawano Ave., P.O. Box 10357, 54313. Tel: 920-434-8208. Sr. Barbara Jean Arnsmeyer, Supr.; Sr. Ellen Patrick Stapleton, Business Mgr. Sisters 30.

MANITOWOC. *Holy Family Convent of Franciscan Sisters of Christian Charity.* Motherhouse and Novitiate dedicated to the Holy Family, 2409 S. Alverno Rd., 54220-9320. Tel: 920-682-7728; Fax: 920-682-4195. Revs. Louis Fronczek, O.F.M., Chap.; Samuel D. Jadin, O.Praem.; Sr. Paula Vanden Hogen, Community Dir. Sisters 538; In Diocese 373; Novices 2; Postulants 1; Total in Residence 192.

St. Clare Convent, 3 Riverview Dr., 54220. Tel: 920-682-5145. Sr. Mary Noel Brown, Dir. Franciscan Sisters of Christian Charity. Sisters 8.

St. Francis Convent, 6835 Hwy. 151, 54220. Tel: 920-684-7884. Sr. Debra Shepeck, Sec. Franciscan Sisters of Christian Charity. Sisters 45.

NEW FRANKEN. *Monastery of the Holy Name of Jesus, Ltd.,* Carmelite Monastery, 4047 Chapel Dr., 54229-9768. Tel: 920-866-2571. Mother Marie Bernard, Prioress; Sr. Mary Elizabeth, Contact Person. Total 10.

OSHKOSH. *SSM Franciscan Courts,* 815 Westhaven Dr., 54904-7978. Tel: 920-426-2440; Fax: 920-426-3196.
E-mail: franct@athenet.net
Sisters of the Sorrowful Mother. Brenda Retzlaff, Human Resources Mgr.; Rev. Michael R. Koch, Chap. Sisters 50.

ST. NAZIANZ. *St. Mary's Convent-Sisters of the Divine Savior.* (Home for retired sisters), 300 S. 2nd Ave., 54232. Tel: 920-773-2515. Sr. Jane Barman, S.D.S., Coord. Sisters 13.

[K] CAMPS AND COMMUNITY CENTERS

SHAWANO. *Camp Tekawitha.* (Located on Loon Lake, Shawano). Mailing Address: P.O. Box 23825, Green Bay, 54305-3825. Tel: 920-437-7531, Ext. 8511. Mrs. Roberta Larson, Dir. Capacity 160. (Boys & Girls ages 7 to 14).

[L] SHRINES

ROBINSONVILLE. *The Chapel of Our Lady of Good Help (Diocesan Shrine)-Robinsonville,* 4047 Chapel Dr., 54229-9768. Tel: 920-866-2571. Mother Marie Bernard, Prioress; Sr. Mary Elizabeth, Contact Person.

[M] RETREAT HOUSES

APPLETON. *Monte Alverno Retreat Center,* 1000 N. Ballard Rd., 54911-5148. Tel: 920-733-8526; Fax: 920-733-7562.
E-mail: montealverno@juno.com
The Province of St. Joseph of the Capuchin Order, Inc. Revs. Gabriel Diefenbach, O.F.M.Cap.; Werner Wolf, O.F.M.Cap., Dir.; Lester Bach, O.F.M.Cap.; Timon Costello, O.F.M.Cap.; Ellis Zimmer, O.F.M.Cap.; Mel Hermanns, O.F.M.Cap; Bro. John Kocian, O.F.M.Cap. Priests 6; Brothers 1; Retreatants Annually 2,500; Total in residence 7; Total Staff 13.

BAILEYS HARBOR. *St. Joseph Retreat Center,* 3035 O'Brien Rd., 54202-9132. Tel: 920-839-2391.
E-mail: malbert.mail@wiscnet.net
Sr. Mary Anne Albert, S.S.S.F., Dir.; Rev. Byron Haaland, S.C.J., Admin. Retreats & Coord. Community; Sr. Lorraine Aspenleiter, S.S.S.F.; Bros. John Monek, S.C.J.; Andrew Lewandowski, S.C.J. Lay Missioners: Priests of the Sacred Heart. Ms. Maria Galang; Ms. Karen Powers. In res. Rev. Joseph Dean, S.C.J. Priests 2; Brothers 2; Sisters 2; Total in residence 8; Total staff 11.

CHAMBERS ISLAND. *Holy Name Retreat House.* Mailing Address: 1825 Riverside Dr., P.O. Box 23825, Green Bay, 54305-3825. Tel: 920-437-7531; Fax: 920-437-0694. Conducted by Diocese of Green Bay. Michael & Mary Cherf, Admin.

DE PERE. *Norbertine Center for Spirituality.* (An Apostolate of the Norbertine Fathers), St. Norbert Abbey, 1016 N. Broadway, 54115-2697. Tel: 920-337-4315; Fax: 920-337-4328.
E-mail: ncs@sneac.snc.edu
Web site: http://www.snc.edu/norbertines/
Rev. Alan D. Scheible, O.Praem., Dir. Total in residence 1; Total staff 5.

MENASHA. *LaSalle Center,* 522 2nd St., 54952. Tel: 920-722-8918. Bro. Richard D. Roller, F.S.C., Dir. of Dev.; Mrs. Jenifer A. Plath, Admin. Total in Residence 3; Total Staff 10.

OSHKOSH. *Jesuit Retreat House,* 4800 Fahrnwald Rd., Hwy. 45, 54901-7598. Tel: 920-231-9060. Society of Jesus. Revs. Richard F. McCaslin, S.J., Dir.; Cornelius Carr, S.J.; Robert Dufford, S.J.; Orville J. Catuso, S.J.; Sr. Marie Schwan, C.S.J. In res. Bro. Anthony Simon, S.J.

[N] NEWMAN CENTERS

GREEN BAY. *University of Wisconsin G.B. Ecumenical Center,* 2420 Nicolet Dr., 54311-7001. Tel: 920-465-5133. Rev. Charles W. Mocco, Catholic Campus Min.

Lawrence University Newman Center. (Appleton).

University of Wisconsin Manitowoc Campus Newman Center. (Manitowoc).

University of Wisconsin Marinette Campus Newman Center. (Marinette).

University of Wisconsin Fox Valley Campus Newman Center. (Menasha).

University of Wisconsin Newman Center, 717 W. Irving Ave., Oshkosh, WI, 54901. Tel: 920-233-5555. Rev. Jeffrey Vanden Heuvel, Dir. & Chap.

[O] MISCELLANEOUS LISTINGS

GREEN BAY. *The Diocesan Charismatic Renewal Center,* 1227 13th Ave., 54304. Tel: 920-405-1960. Rev. Msgr. James Vanden Hogen, Liaison; Mrs. Karen Wautlet, Pres.; Judy Goolsbey, Office Mgr.

Green Bay Area Catholic High School Foundation, L.T.D., P.O. Box 23825, 54305-3825. Tel: 920-437-7531. Mr. Dick White, Pres.; Rev. Edward J. Smith, O.Praem., Exec. Dir.

A New Genesis (ANG). An Association of the Faithful, 1825 S. Riverside Dr., P.O. Box 23825, 54305-3825. Tel: 920-437-7531.
E-mail: sspence@gbdioc.org
Sr. Stephanie Spence, Pres., St. Joseph Chapel; Most Rev. Aloysius J. Wycislo. Total Members 24.

Sacred Heart Seminary, Inc., P.O. Box 23825, 54305-3825. Tel: 920-437-7531; Fax: 920-435-1330. Rev. Msgr. John B. Dewane, Admin.; Sr. Lisa Lucht, Chancellor.

St. Joseph Corporation, Diocesan Central Offices, P.O. Box 23825, 54305-3825. Tel: 920-437-7531; Fax: 920-437-0694. Mr. Vincent Pelletier, Admin.

Teens Encounter Christ (TEC), Green Bay Chapter, P.O. Box 23825, 54305-3825. Tel: 920-437-7531; Fax: 920-437-0694.
E-mail: tpichler@gbdioc.org
Mr. Tony Pichler, Diocesan Liaison.

APPLETON.

**First Care North, Inc.,* 1506 S. Oneida St., 54915. Tel: 920-738-2094. Judy Westphal, Pres.; Rosemary Dorachek, Dir.

St. Elizabeth Hospital Community Foundation, Inc., 1506 S. Oneida, 54915-1305. Tel: 920-738-2365; Fax: 920-738-0949. Franciscan Sisters, Daughters of the Sacred Heart of Jesus and Mary (Wheaton, IL). Mr. Otto Cox, Pres.; Lisa Weiner, Dir. of Devel.

DE PERE. *Augustine Stewardship Fund Trust,* 1016 N. Broadway, 54115-2697. Tel: 920-337-4300; Fax: 920-337-4328.

Canons Regular of Magnovarad, Ltd., 1016 N. Broadway, 54115-2697. Tel: 920-337-4300; Fax: 920-337-4328. Rev. Albin V. Veszelovszky, O.Praem., Pres.; Rt. Rev. Jerome G. Tremel, O.Praem., Vice Pres.; Revs. Joseph S. Rekasi, O.Praem.; Robert K. Finnegan, O.Praem., Sec. & Treas.

Los Amigos del Peru, Inc., 1016 N. Broadway St., 54115-2697. Tel: 920-337-4300; Fax: 920-337-4328.

NORBERT & CO. A nominee of The Premonstratensian Fathers, 1016 N. Broadway, 54115-2697. Tel: 920-337-4300; Fax: 920-337-4328. Rt. Rev. E. Thomas DeWane, O.Praem.; Very Rev. David F. Strenski, O.Praem.; Rev. Robert K. Finnegan, O.Praem.

Norbertine Generalate, Inc., 1016 N. Broadway, 54115-2697. Tel: 920-337-4300; Fax: 920-337-4328. Most Rev. Hermenegild J. Noyens, O.Praem., Pres., Rome, Italy; Rt. Rev. Benjamin T. Mackin, O.Praem., Vice Pres.; Rev. Robert K. Finnegan, O.Praem., Sec. & Treas.

Norbertine Retirement Fund Trust, 1016 N. Broadway, 54115-2697. Tel: 920-337-4300; Fax: 920-337-4328.

St. Norbert Abbey Seminary and Education Fund Trust, 1016 N. Broadway, 54115-2697. Tel: 920-337-4300; Fax: 920-337-4328.

DEERBROOK.

**Living Waters International, Inc.,* N7544 County Rd. S., 54424. Tel: 715-627-4782. Dr. Stephen L. Zimmerman, Ph.D., Pres.

MANITOWOC. *Franciscan Sisters of Christian Charity Healthcare Ministry, Inc.,* 1415 S. Rapids Rd., 54220-9302. Tel: 920-684-7071; Fax: 920-684-6417.
E-mail: fhcm@dataplusnet.com
Sr. Laura J. Wolf, O.S.F., Pres.

NEENAH. *Global Outreach, Inc.,* 433 Hawthorne St., 54956. Tel: 920-727-1207. James Catlin, Pres.; Gary Elmer, Vice Pres. & Treas.; Barbara Bartz, Sec.; Mary Piette, Dir.

St. Mary High School Foundation, Inc., 1050 Zephyr Dr., 54956-1389.

OSHKOSH. *Affinity Health System,* P.O. Box 1100, 54902. Tel: 920-236-2010; Fax: 920-231-5677. Mr. Otto Cox, Pres. & CEO. Sponsored by Franciscan Sisters, Daughters of the Sacred Hearts of Jesus and Mary, Wheaton, IL and Sisters of the Sorrowful Mother, Milwaukee, WI.

RELIGIOUS INSTITUTES OF MEN REPRESENTED IN THE DIOCESE

For further details refer to the corresponding bracketed number in the Religious Institutes of Men or Women section.

[0140]—*The Augustinians.*—O.S.A.

[0330]—*Brothers of the Christian Schools.*—F.S.C.

[0900]—*Canons Regular of Premontre.*—O.Praem.

[0470]—*The Capuchin Friars.* (Province of St. Joseph).—O.F.M.Cap.

[0220]—*Congregation of the Blessed Sacrament.*—S.S.S.

[1130]—*Congregation of the Priests of the Sacred Heart.*—S.C.J.

[0690]—*Franciscan Friars.*—O.F.M.

[0690]—*Jesuit Fathers and Brothers.* (Wisconsin Province).—S.J.

[0800]—*Maryknoll Fathers and Brothers.*—M.M.

[0910]—*Oblates of Mary Immaculate.*—O.M.I.

[1200]—*Society of the Divine Savior.*—S.D.S.

RELIGIOUS INSTITUTES OF WOMEN REPRESENTED IN THE DIOCESE

[3710]—*Congregation of the Sisters of St. Agnes.*—C.S.A.

[0420]—*Discalced Carmelite Nuns.*—O.C.D.

[1070-03]—*Dominican Sisters.*—O.P.

[1070-09]—*Dominican Sisters.*—O.P.

[1070-13]—*Dominican Sisters.*—O.P.

[1070-14]—*Dominican Sisters.*—O.P.

[1170]—*Felician Sisters.*—C.S.S.F.

[1230]—*Franciscan Sisters of Christian Charity.*—O.S.F.

[1240]—*Franciscan Sisters, Daughters of the Sacred Hearts of Jesus and Mary.*—O.S.F.

[1820]—*Hospital Sisters of the Third Order of St. Francis.*—O.S.F.

[3070]—*North American Union Sisters of Our Lady of Charity.*—N.A.U.-O.L.C.

[3440]—*Religious Hospitallers of Saint Joseph.*—R.H.S.J.

[2970]—*School Sisters of Notre Dame.*—S.S.N.D.

[1680]—*School Sisters of St. Francis.*—O.S.F.

[0500]—*Sisters of Charity of Nazareth.*—S.C.N.

[0430]—*Sisters of Charity of the Blessed Virgin Mary.*—B.V.M.

[2630]—*Sisters of Mercy of the Holy Cross.*—S.C.S.C.

[3800]—*Sisters of St. Elizabeth.*—S.S.E.

[1705]—*The Sisters of St. Francis of Assisi.*—O.S.F. - S.S.S.F.

[1550]—*Sisters of St. Francis of the Holy Cross.*—O.S.F.

[3840]—*Sisters of St. Joseph of Carondelet.* (Prov. of St. Louis).—C.S.J.

[3880]—*Sisters of St. Joseph of Medaille.*—C.S.J.

[3930]—*Sisters of St. Joseph of the Third Order of St. Francis.*—S.S.J.-T.O.S.F.

[1030]—*Sisters of the Divine Savior.*—S.D.S.

[4100]—*Sisters of the Sorrowful Mother (Third Order of St. Francis).*—S.S.M.

DIOCESAN CEMETERIES

GREEN BAY. *Diocesan Cemeteries,* P.O. Box 23825, 54305-3825. Tel: 920-437-7531, Ext. 8229. Mr. John C. Nelson, Diocesan Dir.

Allouez Catholic Cemetery, 2121 Riverside Dr., 54301.

Allouez Chapel Mausoleum, 2121 Riverside Dr., 54301.

Queen of Peace Cemetery & Mausoleum, Box 535, Antigo, 54409.

St. Joseph Cemetery, P.O. Box 2676, Appleton, 54913-2676.

Mount Calvary Cemetery, 1307 Lourdes Ave., De Pere, 54115.

Mount Olivet Cemetery, S. Erie St., De Pere, 54115.
Calvary Cemetery & Calvary Chapel Mausoleum, 2601 S. 14th St., Manitowoc, 54220-6467.
Oconto Catholic Cemetery, c/o 716 Madison St., Oconto, 54153. Tel: 414-834-5750.
Oshkosh Catholic Cemetery, 1905 Roosevelt Ave., Oshkosh, 54901.
St. Joseph Cemetery & Mausoleum, 25 N. Elgin, Sturgeon Bay, 54235.

NECROLOGY

† Guillette, Ronald P., Reedsville, WI, St. Mary-St. Patrick. —Died Jan. 7, 1997.

† Hemauer, William G., (Retired). —Died Sept. 21, 1997.

† Loehr, Alfred M., (Retired). —Died July 30, 1997.

† Schmitt, Leo J., (Retired). —Died Feb. 5, 1997.

† Watry, Jerome R., (Retired). —Died Nov. 9, 1997.

Diocese of Greensburg

(Dioecesis Greensburgensis)

Most Reverend

ANTHONY G. BOSCO, D.D., J.C.L.

Bishop of Greensburg; ordained June 7, 1952; appointed Auxiliary Bishop of Pittsburgh and Titular Bishop of Labico May 14, 1970; consecrated June 30, 1970; appointed Bishop of Greensburg April 14, 1987; installed June 30, 1987. *Office: 723 E. Pittsburgh St., Greensburg, PA, 15601.*

ESTABLISHED MARCH 10, 1951.

Square Miles 3,334.

Comprises the Counties of Armstrong, Fayette, Indiana and Westmoreland in the State of Pennsylvania.

For legal titles of parishes and diocesan institutions, consult the Chancery Office.

Chancery Office: 723 E. Pittsburgh St., Greensburg, PA, 15601. Tel.: 724-837-0901; Fax: 724-837-0857.

Web site address: www.catholicgbg.org

STATISTICAL OVERVIEW

Personnel	
Bishop	1
Abbots	1
Retired Abbots	1
Priests: Diocesan Active in Diocese	111
Priests: Active Outside Diocese	11
Priests: Retired, Sick or Absent	34
Number of Diocesan Priests	156
Religious Priests in Diocese	89
Ordinations:	
Diocesan Priests	3
Religious Priests	2
Transitional Deacons	1
Total Brothers	43
Total Sisters	291
Parishes	
Parishes	107
With Resident Pastor:	
Resident Diocesan Priests	82
Resident Religious Priests	10
Without Resident Pastor:	
Administered by Priests	15
Professional Ministry Personnel:	
Brothers	1
Sisters	13
Lay Ministers	48
Welfare	
Catholic Hospitals	1
Total Assisted	53,926
Homes for the Aged	2
Total Assisted	58
Residential Care of Disabled	1
Total Assisted	95
Other Institutions	3
Total Assisted	4
Educational	
Diocesan Students in Other Seminaries	13
Seminaries, Religious	1
Students Religious	15
Total Seminarians	28
Colleges and Universities	2
Total Students	2,302
High Schools, Diocesan and Parish	2
Total Students	795
Elementary Schools, Diocesan and Parish	27
Total Students	5,708
Elementary Schools, Private	4
Total Students	302
Catechesis/Religious Education:	
High School Students	1,314
Elementary Students	10,824
Total Students Under Catholic Instruction	21,273
Teachers in the Diocese:	
Priests	22
Brothers	6
Sisters	34
Lay Teachers	311
Vital Statistics	
Receptions into the Church:	
Infant Baptism Totals	2,348
Adult Baptism Totals	144
Received into Full Communion	373
First Communions	2,592
Confirmations	2,828
Marriages:	
Catholic	583
Interfaith	467
Total Marriages	1,050
Deaths	2,827
Total Catholic Population	193,098
Total Population	679,144

Former Bishops—Most Rev. HUGH L. LAMB, S.T.D., First Bishop of Greensburg; ord. May 29, 1915; appt. Titular Bishop of Helos and Auxiliary of Philadelphia Dec. 19, 1935; cons. March 19, 1936; promoted to Greensburg May 28, 1951; installed Jan. 16, 1952; died Dec. 8, 1959.—Most Reverend WILLIAM G. CONNARE, D.D., ord. June 14, 1936; appt. Feb. 23, 1960; cons. May 4, 1960; retired Jan. 20, 1987; died June 12, 1995.

Chancery Office—723 E. Pittsburgh St., Greensburg, 15601. Tel: 724-837-0901; Fax: 724-837-0857. Office Hours: Mon.-Fri. 8:45-5.

Vicar General / General Executive Director, Moderator of the Curia—Rev. ROGER A. STATNICK, V.G., S.T.L., Ph.D. Tel: 724-837-9521.

Chancellor / Associate General Executive Director—Rev. LAWRENCE T. PERSICO, J.C.L. Tel: 724-837-9522.

Executive Director of Finance—MICHAEL J. MCGEE.

Deaneries—Rev. JOHN T. SWEENEY, V.F., Pro-Tem, Deanery 1-Alle Kiski; Rev. Msgr. WILLIAM G. CHARNOKI, V.F., Deanery 2-Indiana; Rev. Msgr. JOHN L. CONWAY, V.F., Deanery 3-Westmoreland West; Rev. LAWRENCE R. KINIRY, V.F., Deanery 4-Westmoreland East; Rev. JOHN R. CINDRIC, V.F., Deanery 5-Mon Yough; Rev. JOHN A. REGOLI, V.F., Deanery 6-Fayette.

Director for Religious—Vacant, Office: *723 E. Pittsburgh St., Greensburg, 15601.*

Tribunal—Address all correspondence to, *723 E. Pittsburgh St., Greensburg, 15601.* Tel: 724-837-9523.

Judicial Vicar—Rev. WILLIAM R. RATHGEB, J.C.L.

Defender of Bond—Rev. LAWRENCE T. PERSICO, J.C.L.

Judges—Revs. LAWRENCE T. PERSICO, J.C.L.; WILLIAM R. RATHGEB, J.C.L.; RICHARD J. KOSISKO, J.C.L.; Rev. Msgr. WILLIAM G. CHARNOKI, V.F.; Bro. DAVID KELLY, O.S.B.

Advocates—Rev. DANIEL C. MAHONEY; Sr. MARY HALLORAN, S.C.

Notaries—CINDY J. OZZELLO; KATHLEEN POLOSKY.

Assesor—Rev. ANTHONY J. CARBONE.

Advisory Bodies

Board of Consultors—Most Rev. ANTHONY G. BOSCO, Presider; Revs. ROGER A. STATNICK, V.G.; THADDEUS J. KACZMAREK, V.F.; Rev. Msgr. JOHN L. CONWAY, V.F.; Revs. LAWRENCE R. KINIRY, V.F.; RICHARD G. CURCI; MICHAEL J. BEGOLLY; JAMES D. TRINGHESE; GEORGE W. SWAST.

Diocesan Pastoral Council—In process of restructuring.

Bishop's Priests Council—Rev. ROGER A. STATNICK, V.G.; Rev. Msgr. JOHN L. CONWAY, V.F.; Revs. LAWRENCE R. KINIRY, V.F.; JOHN T. SWEENEY, V.F., Pro-Tem; Rev. Msgr. WILLIAM G. CHARNOKI, V.F.; Revs. JOHN A. REGOLI, V.F.; GEORGE W. SWAST; Rev. Msgr. DAVID L. FISHER; Revs. RICHARD G. CURCI; FRANCIS A. LESNIOWSKI; JOHN R. CINDRIC, V.F.; ALEXANDER L. PLEBAN; RICHARD E. MACKIEWICZ; RONALD L. SIMBOLI; LARRY J. KULICK.

Finance Council—Most Rev. ANTHONY G. BOSCO; Rev. ROGER A. STATNICK, V.G.; JOSEPH G. KLOCEK; JOHN A. ROBERTSHAW, JR.; Mrs. BERNARD F. SCHERER; MICHAEL J. MCGEE; Rev. Msgr. JOHN L. CONWAY; ADOLPH BARTOLOMUCCI; CHARLES A. FAGAN, III; JACK L. HADLEY; Sr. GERTRUDE FOLEY, S.C.

Diocesan Offices, Commissions and Special Programs

The Catholic Foundation Trust for the Diocese of Greensburg—Under Declaration of Trust dated 1st day of November, 1988, as amended 2nd day of November 1992 having as its purpose the support of any Roman Catholic benevolent, charitable, educational or missionary undertaking. Most Rev. ANTHONY G. BOSCO, D.D., J.C.L., Chm. Board of Trustees; Revs. ROGER A. STATNICK, V.G., S.T.L., Ph.D., Vice Chm. LAWRENCE T. PERSICO, J.C.L., Assoc. Vice Chm. JOHN A. ROBERTSHAW, JR., Pres. CHARLES A. FAGAN, III, Sec. MICHAEL J. MCGEE, Treas., *723 E. Pittsburgh St., Greensburg, 15601.*

The Catholic Institute of Greensburg—A Corporation, not-for-profit, incorporated under the law of the Commonwealth of Pennsylvania on the 4th day of June, 1954 having as its purpose the support of any Roman Catholic benevolent, charitable, educational or missionary undertaking. Most Rev. ANTHONY G. BOSCO, D.D., J.C.L., Pres.; Revs. ROGER A. STATNICK, V.G., Vice Pres. LAWRENCE T. PERSICO, Sec. MICHAEL J. MCGEE, Treas., *723 E. Pittsburgh St., Greensburg, 15601.*

Greensburg Catholic Accent and Communications, Inc.—A corporation, not-for-profit, under the laws of the Commonwealth of Pennsylvania having as its purpose the support of any Roman Catholic benevolent, charitable, educational or missionary undertaking. Most Rev. ANTHONY G. BOSCO, D.C., J.C.L., CEO; Rev. ROGER A. STATNICK, V.G., Vice Pres. MICHAEL J. MCGEE, Treas., *723 E.*

Pittsburgh St., Greensburg, 15601. Tel: 724-837-0901.

Catholic Charities of the Diocese of Greensburg, PA, Inc.—A corporation not-for-profit incorporated under the law of the Commonwealth of Pennsylvania on the 27th day of August, 1954, having as its purpose, the support of any Roman Catholic benevolent, charitable, educational or missionary undertaking. Most Rev. ANTHONY G. BOSCO, D.D., J.C.L., Chm. of the Members of the Corp. CHARLES DELUZIO, Pres. Bd. of Trustees; Rev. RAYMOND E. RIFFLE, Exec. Dir., *115 Vannear Ave., Greensburg, 15601.* Tel: 724-837-1840.

Archives—ALBINA GUERRIERI, Sec.

Catholic Charities—Rev. RAYMOND E. RIFFLE, M.S.W., M.P.A., Exec. Dir. ROBERT MCHENRY, Dir. Operations & Finance, *115 Vannear Ave., Greensburg, 15601.* Tel: 724-837-1840; Fax: 724-837-4077.

Catholic Relief Services Representative—Rev. Msgr. DAVID L. FISHER, *723 E. Pittsburgh St., Greensburg, 15601.* Tel: 724-837-0901.

Communications—Ms. ANGELA J. BURROWS, Exec. Dir. DAVID MALONEY, Mgr. Television & Radio, *723 E. Pittsburgh St., P.O. Box 850, Greensburg, 15601.* Tel: 724-834-4010; Fax: 724-836-5650.

Services and Facilities—EDWARD J. BLASZKOWSKI, Assoc. Exec. Dir., *723 E. Pittsburgh St., Greensburg, 15601.*

Department of Education and Spiritual Formation—Rev. JAMES T. GASTON, Exec. Dir., *723 E. Pittsburgh St., Greensburg, 15601.* Tel: 724-837-9543.

Office of Catholic Schools—Dr. PHILIP BOGGIO, Supt.; Sr. MARGUERITE COYNE, C.S.J., Acting Supt. THERESE TELEPAK, Coord. Drug & Alcohol Prevention, *723 E. Pittsburgh St., Greensburg, 15601.* Tel: 724-836-1281.

Office of Initiation and Spiritual Formation—MICHAEL J. GRAMMER, Dir. THERESE TELEPAK, Assoc. Dir. for Youth Formation; SALLY LOUGHRAN, Coord. Marriage Formation; ANGELO DIPPOLITO, Coord. Athletics; Rev. LAWRENCE L. MANCHAS, Coord. Scouts, *723 E. Pittsburgh St., Greensburg, 15601.* Tel: 724-837-9543.

Office of Parish Life and Ministry—MARY ANN GUBISH, Dir.; Sr. SUSAN JENNY, S.C., Assoc. Dir., *723 E. Pittsburgh St., Greensburg, 15601.* Tel: 724-837-9543.

Office of Worship—Rev. MICHAEL J. BEGOLLY, Dir. MARIE KONOPKA, Diocesan Liturgy Coord.; Rev. ANTHONY J. CARBONE, *723 E. Pittsburgh St., Greensburg, 15601.* Tel: 724-837-0901.

Office of Vocations—JAMES S. HAGEDER, Dir. Vocations, *723 E. Pittsburgh St., Greensburg, 15601.* Tel: 724-837-0901.

Office of Clergy Formation—Rev. JOSEPH P. MADDALENA, Dir., *723 E. Pittsburgh St., Greensburg, 15601.* Tel: 724-837-0901.

Missions—Society for the Propagation of the Faith and Holy Childhood, Rev. Msgr. DAVID L. FISHER, *723 E. Pittsburgh St., Greensburg, 15601.* Tel: 724-837-0901.

Newspaper—*"The Catholic Accent", 723 E. Pittsburgh St., P.O. Box 850, Greensburg, 15601.* Tel: 724-834-4010; Fax: 724-836-5650. VINCENT A. CAPOZZI, Editor.

Parish Facilities Management Office—EDGAR R. TURNER, Dir. Engrg. & Parish Facilities Mgmt.; Mr. PETER L. PEZZIN, Asst. Dir., *2900 Seminary Dr., Greensburg, 15601.* Tel: 724-836-2900.

Stewardship—ROBERT P. MUELLER, Dir. Stewardship & Devel. JAMES A. SCHUCOLSKY, Assoc. Dir. Stewardship & Devel. JOSEPH W. HOAG, Dir. Devel. for Catholic Schools, *723 E. Pittsburgh St., Greensburg, 15601.*

SPECIAL PROGRAMS:

Apostleship of Prayer—Rev. J. EDWARD MCCULLOUGH, Dir., *R.D.#1, Ranch Road, Dunbar, 15431.*

Apostolate for the Deaf—Rev. JOSEPH P. TRAYNOR, Dir., *47 Morris St., Clymer, 15728.*

Catholic Business and Professional Women's Association—Rev. JOSEPH P. MADDALENA, Chap., *723 E. Pittsburgh St., Greensburg, 15601.*

Catholic Daughters of America—Rev. Msgr. DAVID L. FISHER, Dir., *P.O. Box 398, 201 Church St., Penn, 15675.* Tel: 724-523-3450.

Cemeteries—*723 E. Pittsburgh St., Greensburg, 15601.*

Charismatic—Sr. ANN INFANGER, S.C., Moderator, *Seton Hill College, Greensburg, 15601.*

Cursillo—Vacant.

Diocesan Council of Catholic Women—Rev. DONALD J. MONDELLO, Dir., *1204 Ligonier St., Latrobe, 15650.*

Holy Childhood Association—Rev. Msgr. DAVID L. FISHER, Dir., *723 E. Pittsburgh St., Greensburg, 15601.*

Holy Name Society—Rev. GEORGE K. ALDERSON, Dir., *50 Jefferson St., Uniontown, 15401.*

Legion of Mary—Rev. HENRY P. DINICCO, Dir., *135 Carriage Dr., North Huntington, 15642.*

Pilgrimages—Rev. J. EDWARD MCCULLOUGH, Dir., *R.D.#1, Ranch Road, Dunbar, 15431.*

Priests' Eucharistic League—Rev. J. EDWARD MCCULLOUGH, *R.D. 1, Ranch Rd., Dunbar, 15431.*

St. Thomas More Guild for Lawyers—*723 E. Pittsburgh St., Greensburg, 15601.*

St. Vincent de Paul Society—Rev. JOHN A. SEDLAK, Spiritual Dir., *St. Hedwig Church, P.O. Box 251, Smock, 15480.*

CLERGY, PARISHES, MISSIONS AND PAROCHIAL SCHOOLS

CITY OF GREENSBURG
(Westmoreland County)

1—BLESSED SACRAMENT CATHEDRAL, Rev. Msgr. Robert J. Shuda; Rev. Michael P. Sikon. In res., Rev. James S. Hageder.
Res., 300 N. Main St., 15601. Tel: 724-834-3710; Fax: 724-834-1518. [CEM]
Convent—350 N. Main St., 15601. Tel: 724-834-0894. Sisters of Charity
School—Aquinas Academy. See separate listing under Elementary Schools in the Institution section.

2—ST. BRUNO, Rev. Blane L. Resko, O.S.B.
Res., 1707 Poplar St., 15601. Tel: 724-836-0690.
School—Aquinas Academy. See separate listing under Elementary Schools in the Institution section.

3—OUR LADY OF GRACE, Revs. Lawrence R. Kiniry; Salvatore Lamendola. In res., Rev. James T. Gaston.
Res., 1001 Mount Pleasant Rd., 15601. Tel: 724-838-9480; Fax: 724-838-1842.
School—Aquinas Academy. See separate listing under Elementary Schools in the Institution section.

4—ST. PAUL, Rev. Leonard W. Stoviak. In res., Revs. Daniel L. Blout; Raymond E. Riffle.
Res., 820 Carbon Rd., 15601. Tel: 724-834-6880; Fax: 724-834-1492.
School—Aquinas Academy. See separate listing under Elementary Schools in the Institution section.

OUTSIDE THE CITY OF GREENSBURG

Apollo, Armstrong Co., St. James the Greater, Rev. Ronald L. Simboli.
Res., 109 Owens View, 15613. Tel: 724-478-4958; Fax: 724-478-1802.
School—109 Owens View, 15613. Tel: 724-478-4851; Fax: 724-478-1802. Mr. Thomas J. Shearon, Prin.
Sisters 1; Lay Teachers 5; Students 83.
Convent—715 Rte. 56 E., 15613. Tel: 724-478-3287. Sisters of Charity

Arnold, Westmoreland Co., All Saints (Slovak), Rev. George W. Swast, Admin.
Res., 1700 Leishman Ave., 15068. Tel: 724-335-8232.

Avonmore, Westmoreland Co., St. Ambrose, Rev. William J. Homolak.
Res., P.O. Box 617, 505 Cambria Ave., 15618. Tel: 724-697-4129.

Belle Vernon, Westmoreland Co., St. Sebastian, Revs. John R. Cindric, V.F.; E. George Saletrik.
Res., 801 Broad Ave., 15012. Tel: 724-929-9300; Fax: 724-930-7611.
School—815 Broad Ave., 15012. Tel: 724-929-5143; Fax: 724-929-3038. Sr. Madonna Helbling, O.S.F., Prin.
Sisters of St. Francis Millvale 1; Lay Teachers 10; Students 221.
Chapel—Belle Vernon, Our Lady of Perpetual Help.

Blairsville, Indiana Co., SS. Simon and Jude, Rev. Chester J. Raimer.
Res., 155 N. Brady St., 15717. Tel: 724-459-7103; Fax: 724-459-5314.

Bovard, Westmoreland Co., St. Bede, Rev. Brinstan G. Takach, O.S.B.
Res., c/o St. Vincent Archabbey, 300 Fraser Purchase Rd., Latrobe, 15650. Tel: 724-532-6629; 837-3690.

Brady's Bend, Armstrong Co., St. Patrick, Rev. Thomas A. Federline.
Res., R.D. 1, Box 78, 16028. Tel: 724-526-5079. [CEM]
Chapel—Sugar Creek, Chapel of St. Patrick, Brady's Bend. [CEM]

Brownsville, Fayette Co., St. Peter, Rev. Vincent J. Gigliotti.
Res., 304 Shaffner Ave., 15417. Tel: 724-785-7781; Fax: 724-785-8161. [CEM 2]
School—Brownsville Catholic School. See separate listing under Elementary Schools in the Institution section.
Convent—302 Shaffner Ave., 15417. Tel: 724-785-7172.

St. Mary, Rev. John S. Szczesny.
Res., 118 Church St., 15417. Tel: 724-785-5932. [CEM]
School—Brownsville Catholic School. See separate listing under Elementary Schools in the Institution section.

Cadogan, Armstrong Co., St. Lawrence, Rev. Edward Volz, O.S.P.P.E.
Res., Box 114, 16212. Tel: 724-763-1089. [CEM]
Chapel—Nicholson Run, Chapel of the Holy Guardian Angel.

Calumet, Westmoreland Co., St. Stanislaus (Polish), Rev. John M. Foriska, Admin.
Res., P.O. Box 56, 15621. Tel: 724-423-4052. [CEM]

Cardale, Fayette Co., Madonna of Czestochowa, Rev. Ronald J. Rutkowski.
Res., P.O. Box 8, 15420. Tel: 724-246-9657. [CEM]

Clymer, Indiana Co., Church of the Resurrection, Revs. Micah E. Kozoil; Joseph P. Traynor; Stephen R. Bugay.
Administration Center: 47 Morris St., 15728. Tel: 724-254-3041; Fax: 724-254-3045. [CEM]
Chapel—Camerons Bottom,Chapel of Church of the Resurrection,Clymer.

Connellsville, Fayette Co.,

1—IMMACULATE CONCEPTION, Rev. Michael J. Sciberras.
Res., 148 E. Crawford Ave., 15425. Tel: 724-628-8550; Fax: 724-628-3410. [CEM]
School—Conn-Area Catholic School. See separate listing under Elementary Schools in the Institution section.
Chapel—Dawson, Chapel of Immaculate Conception, Connellsville.

2—HOLY TRINITY, (Polish), Rev. Benjamin S. Babula, Admin.
Res., 109 N. Seventh St., 15425. Tel: 724-628-7061. [CEM]
School—Conn-Area Catholic School. See seperate listing under Elementary Schools in the Institution section.

3—ST. JOHN THE EVANGELIST, (Slovak), Rev. John M. Butler.
Res., 908 W. Crawford Ave., 15425. Tel: 724-628-2112. [CEM]
School—Conn-Area Catholic School. See separate listing under Elementary Schools in the Institution section.

4—ST. RITA, (Italian), Rev. Francis A. Lesniowski.
Res., 116 S. Second St., 15425. Tel: 724-628-4015. [CEM]
School—Conn-Area Catholic School. See separate listing under Elementary Schools in the Institution section.

Coral, Indiana Co., St. Francis, Rev. Elmer A. Kacinko.
Res., Box G, 15731. Tel: 724-479-9161; Fax: 724-479-0449. [CEM]
Chapel—Blacklick, Chapel of St. Francis, Coral.

Crabtree, Westmoreland Co., St. Bartholomew, Rev. Augustine Flood O.S.B.
Res., P.O. Box A, 15624. Tel: 724-834-0709. [CEM]

Delmont, Westmoreland Co., St. John Baptist de La Salle, Rev. William C. McGuirk.
Res., St. John Square, 497 Athena Dr., 15626. Tel: 724-468-4221; Fax: 724-468-4221.

Derry, Westmoreland Co., St. Joseph, Rev. Kenneth G. Zaccagnini. In res., Roger A. Statnick, V.G., S.T.L., Ph.D.
Rectory: 117 S. Ligonier St., 15627. Tel: 724-694-5359. [CEM]
St. Joseph Residence: 209 Broad St., 15627. Tel: 724-694-0320; Fax: 724-694-0320.

Donegal, Westmoreland Co., St. Raymond, Rev. Edward C. Tojc.
Res., P.O. Box 194, 15628. Tel: 724-593-7479. [CEM]

Dunbar, Fayette Co., St. Aloysius, Rev. J. Edward McCullough.
Res., R.D. 1, Ranch Rd., 15431. Tel: 724-277-4236; Fax: 724-277-0192. [CEM]

East Vandergrift, Westmoreland Co., Our Lady, Queen of Peace, Rev. Joseph Minsterman.
Res., 400 Kennedy Ave., 15629. Tel: 724-567-7603.

Ernest, Indiana Co., Church of the Assumption. Closed. For inquiries for parish records contact Church of the Resurrection, Clymer.

Everson, Fayette Co., St. Joseph, Rev. Joseph L. Sredzinski, M.Div.
Res., 201 Painter St., 15631. Tel: 724-887-6714. [CEM]

Export, Westmoreland Co., St. Mary, Rev. Dismas Young, O.F.M.Cap. In res., Revs. John Carey, O.F.M.Cap.; Gabriel Giles, O.F.M.Cap.; Bro. John Donatelli, O.F.M.Cap.
Res., 5900 Kennedy Ave., 15632. Tel: 724-327-0647; Fax: 724-325-3784.

Fairchance, Fayette Co., SS. Cyril and Methodius, Rev. Anthony A. Wozniak.
Res., 50 Morgantown St., 15436. Tel: 724-564-7436. [CEM]
Chapel—Shoaf, Chapel of SS. Cyril & Methodius, Fairchance.

Farmington, Fayette Co., St. Joan of Arc, Rev. Paul A. Whalen.
Res., P.O. Box 92, 15437. Tel: 724-329-4522. [CEM]

Fayette City, Fayette Co., Holy Spirit, Rev. Leonard McAlpin.
Res., P.O. Box 639, 139 S. High St., 15438. Tel: 724-326-4352.

Footedale, Fayette Co., St. Thomas (Polish), Rev. James L. Popochock, Admin.
Res., P.O. Box 547, New Salem, 15468. Tel: 724-245-9244; Fax: 724-245-9289. [CEM]

Forbes Road, Westmoreland Co., St. Mary, Rev. Anthony J. Burlas, O.S.B.
Res., c/o St. Vincent Archabbey, 300 Fraser Purchase Rd., Latrobe, 15650. Tel: 724-539-9761; 532-6648.

Ford City, Armstrong Co., St. Mary, Rev. Terry A. Hercik.
Res., 718 Fourth Ave., 16226. Tel: 724-763-1631. [CEM]
School—Divine Redeemer School. See separate listing under Elementary Schools in the Institution section.

St. Francis of Paola (Polish), Rev. Lawrence L. Hoppe, Admin.
Res., P.O. Box 327, 736 Fifth Ave., 16226. Tel: 724-763-1196. [CEM]
School—Divine Redeemer School. See separate listing under Elementary Schools in the Institution section.

Holy Trinity (Slovak), Rev. Robert E. Feeney.
Res., 1008 Sixth Ave., 16226. Tel: 724-763-9141. [CEM]
School—Divine Redeemer School. See separate listing under Elementary Schools in the Institution section.
Convent—1016 Sixth Ave., 16226. Tel: 724-763-1109. Vincentian Sisters of Charity

Freeport, Armstrong Co., St. Mary, Rev. Denis R. Sweeney, M.Div., M.S.W.
Res., 608 High St., 16229. Tel: 724-295-2281; Fax: 724-295-2281. [CEM]
School—610 High St., 16229. Tel: 724-295-3003; Fax: 724-295-3003. Mrs. Adrienne Ofcharsky, Prin.
Lay Teachers 7; Students 101.

Glen Campbell, Indiana Co., St. Michael. Closed. For inquiries for parish records contact Church of the Resurrection, Clymer.

Grindstone, Fayette Co., St. Cecilia (Slovak), Rev. John A. Sedlak, Admin.
c/o P.O. Box 251, Smock, 15480. Tel: 724-677-2110; Fax: 724-677-0146.

Harrison City, Westmoreland Co., St. Barbara, Revs. V. Paul Fitzmaurice; Anthony W. Ditto.
Res., 34 Raymaley Rd., 15636. Tel: 724-744-7474; Fax: 724-744-3056. [CEM]

Heilwood, Indiana Co., St. John the Baptist. Closed. For inquiries for parish records contact Church of the Resurrection, Clymer.

Herminie, Westmoreland Co., St. Edward, Revs. Lawrence L. Manchas; Edward J. Lewis.
Res., 87 Sixth St. Ext., 15637. Tel: 724-446-5197; Fax: 724-446-1433.
School—89 Sixth St., 15637. Tel: 724-446-5381. Sr. MaryLou Witkowski, S.H.S., Prin.
Sisters of the Holy Spirit 2; Lay Teachers 9; Students 173.
Convent—87 Sixth St., 15637. Tel: 724-446-5359. Sisters of the Holy Spirit

Indiana, Indiana Co., St. Bernard, Rev. Msgr. William G. Charnoki, J.C.L., V.F.; Rev. Paul R. Stivason.
Res., 200 Clairvaux Dr., 15701. Tel: 724-465-2210; Fax: 724-465-0422. [CEM]
School—300 Clairvaux Dr., 15701. Tel: 724-465-7139; Fax: 724-465-0803. Mrs. Lucinda Copeland, Prin.
Lay Teachers 15; Students 180.

St. Thomas More University Parish. (Newman Center). Rev. Michael J. Begolly.
Res., Indiana University of PA, 1200 Oakland Ave., 15701. Tel: 724-463-2277; Fax: 724-463-7116.

Irwin, Westmoreland Co., Immaculate Conception, Rev. Msgr. John L. Conway, V.F.; Rev. William J. Lechnar.
Res., 305 Second St., 15642. Tel: 724-863-9550; Fax: 724-863-9552. [CEM]
School—Queen of Angels Regional Catholic School. See separate listing under Elementary Schools in the Institution section.

Iselin, Indiana Co., Holy Cross. Closed. For inquiries for parish records contact Church of the Good Shepherd, Kent.

Jeannette, Westmoreland Co., Sacred Heart, Revs. William A. Beaver, O.S.B.; James H. Loew, O.S.B.; Bro. James Cartwright, O.S.B., Parish Min. In res., Rev. Dominic J. Petroy, O.S.B.
Res., 504 Cowan Ave., 15644. Tel: 724-523-2560; Fax: 724-523-9400. [CEM]

Ascension (Italian), Rev. Msgr. Nicholas A. Mitolo.
Res., 615 Division Ave., 15644. Tel: 724-523-6567; 6568.

Kent, Indiana Co., Church of the Good Shepherd, Rev. Larry J. Kulick.
Res., P.O. Box 99, 15752. Tel: 724-479-3881; Fax: 724-479-3882.

Kittanning, Armstrong Co., St. Mary, Our Lady of Guadalupe, Rev. William J. Kiel.
Res., 101 W. High St., 16201. Tel: 724-548-7640; 548-7649; Fax: 724-545-3262. [CEM]
Convent—348 N. Water St., 16201. Tel: 724-543-4518. Sisters of St. Joseph

Maxwell, Fayette Co., St. James, Rev. James F. Petrovsky.
Res., Box 247, LaBelle, 15450. Tel: 724-785-3617.
Chapel—Isabella, Chapel of St. James, Maxwell.

Latrobe, Westmoreland Co.,

1—HOLY FAMILY, Revs. Donald J. Mondello; Alan W. Grote; Paul E. Rubadue, O.S.B.
Res., 1204 Ligonier St., 15650. Tel: 724-539-9751; Fax: 724-539-8044. [CEM]
School—Christ the Divine Teacher School. See separate listing under Elementary Schools in the Institution section.

2—ST. VINCENT BASILICA, Revs. Mario A. Fulgenzi, O.S.B.; John-Mary Tompkins, O.S.B.; Stanley T. Markiewicz, O.S.B.
Res., 300 Fraser Purchase Rd., 15650. Tel: 724-539-8629; Fax: 724-539-3810. [CEM]
School—Christ the Divine Teacher School. See separate listing under Elementary Schools in the Institution section.

3—ST. JOHN THE EVANGELIST, Rev. Thomas M. Lukac. In res., Rev. Stephen C. West.
Res., 306 St. John Dr., 15650. Tel: 724-537-8909.
School—Christ the Divine Teacher School. See separate listing under Elementary Schools in the Institution section.
Convent—310 St. John Dr., 15650. Tel: 724-537-7580.

4—ST. ROSE, Rev. William P. Donahue.
Res., 1112 Hillview Ave., 15650. Tel: 724-537-3709. [CEM]
School—Christ the Divine Teacher School. See separate listing under Elementary Schools in the Institution section.

5—ST. BONIFACE. (Chestnut Ridge). Rev. Simon J. Toth, O.S.B. Tel: 724-593-7869.
Res., c/o St. Vincent Archabbey, 300 Fraser Purchase Rd., 15650. Tel: 724-532-6600.
School—Christ the Divine Teacher School. See separate listing under Elementary Schools in the Institution section.

Leckrone, Fayette Co., Our Lady of Perpetual Help (St. Mary), Rev. Andrew M. Kawecki.
Res., P.O. Box 248, 15454. Tel: 724-737-5736; Fax: 724-737-1042. [CEM]

Leechburg, Armstrong Co., St. Catherine of Alexandria, Rev. Dominic G. Pozzuoli.
Res., 612 Second St., 15656. Tel: 724-845-8191. [CEM]
Chapel—Hyde Park, Chapel of St. Catherine, Leechburg.

Church of the Assumption, Rev. Robert R. Byrnes.
Res., R.D. 5, Box 1235, 15656. Tel: 724-842-3521; 845-6593 (Church Hall).

St. Martha (Slovak), Rev. Richard E. Mackiewicz.
Res., 368 Third St., 15656. Tel: 724-842-1791. [CEM]

Leisenring, Fayette Co., St. Vincent de Paul, Rev. Peter L. Peretti.
Res., Box 24, 15455. Tel: 724-628-7361. [CEM]
Chapel—West Leisenring, Chapel of St. Vincent de Paul, Leisenring.

Ligonier, Westmoreland Co., Holy Trinity, Rev. Joseph P. Maddalena, S.T.L.
Res., 342 W. Main St., 15658. Tel: 724-238-6434; Fax: 724-238-6688. [CEM]
School—327 W. Vincent St., 15658. Tel: 724-238-6430; Fax: 724-238-6341. Mr. Steven Smith, Prin.
Lay Teachers 9; Students 118.
Chapel—Wilpen, Chapel of Holy Trinity, Ligonier.

Lower Burrell, Westmoreland Co., St. Margaret Mary, Rev. John T. Sweeney.
Res., 201 Park Dr., 15068. Tel: 724-335-2336; Fax: 724-337-9908.
School—3055 Leechburg Rd., 15068. Tel: 724-335-6700. Mrs. Darlene Scopel, Prin.
Lay Teachers 9; Students 188.

Lucernemines, Indiana Co., St. Louis, Rev. James M. Goldberg.
Res., P.O. Box 197, 15754. Tel: 724-479-9542; Fax: 724-479-0983. [CEM]

Marguerite, Westmoreland Co., St. Benedict, Rev. Stephen R. Honeygosky, O.S.B.
Res., R.D. 8, Box 560, Greensburg, 15601. Tel: 724-834-9045; Fax: 724-834-1880.

Masontown, Fayette Co., All Saints, Revs. Edward C. Tajc; James F. Bump.
Res., 101 W. Church Ave., 15461. Tel: 724-583-7866; Fax: 724-583-0373. [CEM]
School—100 S. Washington St., 15461. Tel: 724-583-2141; Fax: 724-583-2141. Sr. Maria Estelle Chopnak, V.S.C., Prin.
Vincentian Sisters 1; Lay Teachers 9; Students 140.
Convent—100 S. Washington St., 15461. Tel: 724-583-9891.
Chapel—McClellandtown, Chapel of All Saints, Masontown.

Monessen, Westmoreland Co., The Epiphany of Our Lord, Revs. Paul A. Lisik; David J. Nazimek.
Res., 618 Knox Ave., 15062. Tel: 724-684-7661; Fax: 724-684-8981. [CEM 2]
School—701 Schoonmaker Ave., 15062. Tel: 724-684-5610; Fax: 724-684-5464. Mrs. Kathleen Warfield, Prin.
Lay Teachers 10; Students 162.

Mount Pleasant, Westmoreland Co., St. Pius X, Rev. Michael W. Matusak.
Res., 216 Spruce St., 15666. Tel: 724-547-3533. [CEM]
School—Holy Trinity Catholic School. See separate listing under Elementary Schools in the Institution section.

Transfiguration (Polish), Rev. Robert M. Washko.
Res., 35 N. Hitchman St., 15666. Tel: 724-547-2556. [CEM]
School—Holy Trinity Catholic School. See separate listing under Elementary Schools in the Institution section.
Convent—409 Smithfield St., 15666. Tel: 724-547-8112. Felician Sisters

Visitation of the Blessed Virgin Mary (Slovak), Rev. Gregory F. Premoshis. In res., Rev. Nicholas Trongo.
Res., 740 Walnut St., 15666. Tel: 724-547-5735. [CEM]
School—Holy Trinity Catholic School. See seperate listing under Elementary Schools in the Institution section.

Murrysville, Westmoreland Co., Mother of Sorrows, Revs. Daniel C. Mahoney; Joseph V. Trupkovich.
Res., 4200 Old William Penn Hwy., 15668. Tel: 724-733-8870; Fax: 724-733-8108.
School—3264 Evergreen Dr., 15668. Tel: 724-733-8840; Fax: 724-733-8807. Patricia A. Sheahan, Ed.D., Prin.
Lay Teachers 23; Students 322.

New Alexandria, Westmoreland Co., St. James, Rev. Lawrence T. Persico, J.C.L., Admin.
Res., R.D. 3, Box 400, 15670. Tel: 724-668-2829; Fax: 724-668-7327.

New Derry, Westmoreland Co., St. Martin, Rev. Arthur Holtz, O.S.B.
Res., R.D. 1, Box 100, 15671. Tel: 724-694-5716. [CEM]

New Kensington, Westmoreland Co., St. Mary of Czestochowa (Polish), Rev. Richard P. Karenbauer.
Res., 857 Kenneth Ave., 15068. Tel: 724-335-8212; 335-2626; Fax: 724-335-1314. [CEM]
Convent—837 Kenneth Ave., 15068. Tel: 724-339-9868. Felician Sisters

St. Joseph, Revs. George W. Swast; James W. Clark.
Res., 1125 Leishman Ave., 15068. Tel: 724-337-6412; Fax: 724-337-4022.
School—1129 Leishman Ave., 15068. Tel: 724-339-4411; Fax: 724-337-6457. Sr. Marie Corde Denny, C.S.J., Prin.
Sisters 5; Lay Teachers 10; Students 215.
Convent—1129 Leishman Ave., 15068. Tel: 724-335-7433. Sisters of St. Joseph

Mt. St. Peter (Italian), Revs. Richard G. Curci; Robert T. Lubic.
Res., 100 Freeport Rd., 15068. Tel: 724-335-9877; Fax: 724-335-9138.
School—Tel: 724-335-5911. Sr. Mariella Bradley, R.S.M., Prin.
Sisters of Mercy 2; Lay Teachers 15; Students 333.

New Salem, Fayette Co., St. Procopius, Rev. James L. Popochock.
Res., 20 Church St., P.O. Box 547, 15468. Tel: 724-245-9244; Fax: 724-245-9289. [CEM]

North Huntingdon, Westmoreland Co., St. Agnes, Revs. Thaddeus J. Kaczmarck; Thomas S. Trupkovich.
Res., 11400 St. Agnes Ln., 15642. Tel: 724-863-2626; 863-2630; Fax: 724-863-1057.
School—Queen of Angels Catholic School. See separate listing under Elementary Schools in the Institution section.
Convent—501 Crestwood Dr., 15642. Tel: 724-863-1670. Sisters of St. Joseph
St. Elizabeth Ann Seton, Rev. Michael J. Crookston.
Res., 200 Leger Rd., 15642. Tel: 724-864-6364; Fax: 724-864-4580.

Palmer, Fayette Co., St. Albert, Rev. Ronald J. Rutkowski.
Res., Box 295, Adah, 15410. Tel: 724-737-6720.

Parker, Armstrong Co., St. Mary, Our Lady of the Snows, Rev. Thomas A. Federline, Admin.
Res., c/o R.D. 1, Box 78, Brady's Bend, 16028. Tel: 724-526-5079.

Penn, Westmoreland Co., St. Boniface, Rev. Msgr. David L. Fisher.
Res., 201 Church St., Box 398, 15675. Tel: 724-523-3450. [CEM]

Perryopolis, Fayette Co., St. John the Baptist, Rev. John T. Euker.
Res., P.O. Box 606, 15473. Tel: 724-736-4442. [CEM]

Point Marion, Fayette Co., St. Hubert, Rev. Dennis A. Bogusz.
Res., 9 Sadler St., 15474. Tel: 724-725-3655.

Republic, Fayette Co., Holy Rosary, Rev. Mark E. Purnell.
Res., Main St., P.O. Box 400, 15475. Tel: 724-246-9639; Fax: 412-246-8081. [CEM]
School—Abigail St., P.O. Box 797, 15475. Tel: 724-246-9083; Fax: 412-246-2500. Sr. Corrine Giel, V.S.C., Prin.
Sisters 2; Lay Teachers 8; Students 180.
Convent—P.O. Box 797, 15475. Tel: 724-246-2500. Vincentian Sisters of Charity

Rossiter, Indiana Co., St. Francis of Assisi. Closed. For inquiries for parish records contact the Church of the Resurrection, Clymer.

Rostraver, Westmoreland Co., St. Anne, Rev. Thomas W. Rogers.
Res., 1870 Rostraver Rd., Belle Vernon, 15012. Tel: 724-929-9599.
Chapel—Webster, Chapel of St. Anne, Rostraver.

Sagamore, Armstrong Co., Sacred Heart, Rev. Robert E. Moslener, Admin.
Res., Box 327, Yatesboro, 16263. Tel: 724-783-7191. [CEM]

Saltsburg, Indiana Co., St. Matthew, Rev. Gregory J. Flohr.
Res., 703 Indiana Ave., 15681. Tel: 724-639-3690. [CEM]

Scottdale, Westmoreland Co., St. John the Baptist, Rev. Emil S. Payer.
Res., 416 S. Broadway, 15683. Tel: 724-887-6321; Fax: 724-887-6324. [CEM]
School—504 S. Broadway, 15683. Tel: 724-887-9550; Fax: 724-887-9553. Joseph Dreliszak, Prin.
Benedictine Sisters 3; Lay Teachers 14; Students 156.
Convent—408 S. Broadway, 15683. Tel: 724-887-6612. Benedictine Sisters

Seward, Westmoreland Co., Holy Family, Rev. John E. Wilt.
Res., Box 336, 15954. Tel: 814-446-5759; Fax: 814-446-4481. [CEM]
Chapels—New Florence, Chapel of Holy Family, Seward.; Bolivar, Chapel of Holy Family, Seward.

Slickville, Westmoreland Co., St. Sylvester, Rev. Richard J. Kosisko, J.C.L.
Res., Box 307, 15684. Tel: 724-468-5794; Fax: 724-468-5765.

Smithton, Westmoreland Co., St. Timothy, Rev. James D. Vasil.
Res., Peer & Third St., Box 776, 15479. Tel: 724-872-8070. [CEM]

Smock, Fayette Co., St. Hedwig, Rev. John A. Sedlak.
Res., Box 251, 15480. Tel: 724-677-2110; Fax: 724-677-0146. [CEM]
Chapel—Keisterville, Chapel of St. Hedwig, Smock.

Starford, Indiana Co., St. Elizabeth. Closed. For inquiries for parish records contact Church of the Resurrection, Clymer.

Sutersville, Westmoreland Co., St. Charles Borromeo, Rev. John A. Moineau.
Res., Fifth Ave., P.O. Box 413, 15083. Tel: 724-872-5286.

Trafford, Westmoreland Co., St. Regis, Rev. James D. Tringhese.
Res., 517 Homewood Ave., 15085. Tel: 412-372-4577; Fax: 412-373-5979.
Convent—424 Edgewood Ave., 15085. Tel: 412-372-3198. Sisters of Charity

Trauger, Westmoreland Co., Forty Martyrs, Rev. Joel R. Lieb, O.S.B.
Res., c/o St. Vincent Archabbey, 300 Fraser Purchase Rd., Latrobe, 15650. Tel: 724-423-3282; 532-6725; Fax: 724-537-4554. [CEM]

Uniontown, Fayette Co.,

1—St. John The Evangelist, Revs. George K. Alderson; John J. Harrold.
Res., 50 Jefferson St., 15401. Tel: 724-437-7569; Fax: 724-437-6277.
School—88 Pennsylvania Ave., 15401. Tel: 724-438-8598; Fax: 724-438-8585. Sr. M. Kevin Berdis, O.S.F., Prin.
Sisters 3; Lay Teachers 14; Students 281.
Convent—88 Pennsylvania Ave., 15401. Tel: 724-438-5271. School Sisters of St. Francis

2—St. Joseph, (Polish), Rev. Alexander L. Pleban, S.T.L.
Res., R.D. 4, Walnut Hill Rd., 15401. Tel: 724-437-3927; Fax: 724-437-5354. [CEM]

3—Nativity of the Blessed Virgin Mary, (Slovak), Rev. Msgr. Andrew A. Chupela.
Res., 61 N. Mount Vernon Ave., 15401. Tel: 724-437-1512; Fax: 724-437-7482. [CEM]
School—17 Gilmore St., 15401. Tel: 724-438-8471; Fax: 724-438-8338. Sr. Mary Jean Kubilus, V.S.C., Prin.
Sisters 2; Lay Teachers 11; Students 239.
Convent—7 Gilmore St., 15401. Tel: 724-437-5478; Fax: 724-439-9328. Vincentian Sisters of Charity
Chapel—Lemont Furnace, Chapel of St. Mary, Uniontown.

4—St. Therese, the Little Flower of Jesus, (Italian), Revs. John A. Regoli; Joseph E. Bonafed.
Res., 61 Mill St., 15401. Tel: 724-438-2341; Fax: 724-438-2361.

United, Westmoreland Co., St. Florian, Rev. John M. Foriska.
Res., P.O. Box 187, 15689. Tel: 724-423-4431; Fax: 724-423-4438. [CEM]
School—P.O. Box 188, 15689. Tel: 724-423-4437; Fax: 724-423-2207. Mrs. Lucy Hastings, Prin.
Lay Teachers 7; Students 132.
Convent—P.O. Box 188, 15689. Tel: 724-423-5087. Vincentian Sisters of Charity

Vandergrift, Westmoreland Co., St. Gertrude, Rev. Thaddeus E. Rettger, O.S.B.
Res., 303 Franklin Ave., 15690. Tel: 724-568-2331. [CEM]
School—315 Franklin Ave., 15690. Tel: 724-568-3304. Mr. Thomas J. Kazmeraski, Prin.
Lay Teachers 9; Students 103.

West Newton, Westmoreland Co., Holy Family, Rev. Robert F. Brannon.
Res., 225 N. Second St., P.O. Box 216, 15089. Tel: 724-872-6123; Fax: 724-872-6133.

Whitney, Westmoreland Co., St. Cecilia, Rev. Mark M. Peters, O.S.B.
Res., P.O. Box 80, 15693. Tel: 724-423-3777; 423-2289; Fax: 724-423-3778.

Yatesboro, Armstrong Co., St. Mary, Rev. Robert E. Moslener.
Res., P.O. Box 327, 16263. Tel: 724-783-7191. [CEM]

Youngstown, Westmoreland Co., Sacred Heart, Rev. Aelred J. Beck, O.S.B.
Res., P.O. Box 328, 15696. Tel: 724-537-7358; Fax: 724-537-7358.
School—P.O. Box 328, 15696. Tel: 724-539-5561; Fax: 724-539-5561. Sr. Grace Marie Spera, C.S.S.F., Prin.
Felician Sisters 3; Lay Teachers 5; Students 148.
Convent—Main St., P.O. Box 328, 15696. Tel: 724-537-8958. Felician Sisters

Youngwood, Westmoreland Co., Holy Cross, Rev. Angelo G. Ciuffoletti.
Res., 701 Depot St., 15697. Tel: 724-925-7811.
School—S. Eighth St., 15697. Tel: 724-925-7253. Mrs. Audrey Quinlan, Prin.
Lay Teachers 8; Students 154.
Chapel—Hunker, Chapel of Holy Cross, Youngwood.

Yukon, Westmoreland Co., Seven Dolors, Rev. Dennis E. Sheehy.
Res., Center & Hill St., P.O. Box 308, 15698. Tel: 724-722-3141; 722-3140 (Hall). [CEM]

Chaplains of Public Institutions

Greensburg. *Westmoreland Hospital* Tel: 724-832-4000. Rev. Jacques de Paul Daley, O.S.B., Chap., Assoc. Chaplains: Rev. Justin Withrow, O.S.B.; Sr. Mary Ann Thimons, C.S.J.

Brownsville. *Brownsville General Hospital.* Attended by St. Peter, Brownsville, Tel: 724-785-7200; 785-7781 (Res.).

Connellsville. *Highlands Hospital & Health Center* Tel: 724-628-1500. Rev. Nicholas Trongo, Chap., Tel: 724-547-5735 (Res.).

Indiana. *Indiana Hospital.* Attended by St. Bernard, Indiana, Tel: 724-357-7000; 724-465-2210 (Res.). Tel: 724-357-7000.

Jeannette. *Jeannette District Memorial Hospital* Tel: 724-527-3551. Revs. Dominic J. Petroy, O.S.B., Chap., Tel: 724-523-2560 (Res.); Justin Withrow, O.S.B., Assoc. Chap., Tel: 724-539-9761 (Res.).
Monsour Medical Center Tel: 724-527-1511. Revs. Dominic J. Petroy, O.S.B., Chap., Tel: 724-523-2560 (Res.); Justin Withrow, O.S.B., Assoc. Chap., Tel: 724-539-9761 (Res.).

Kittanning. *Armstrong County Hospital* Tel: 724-543-8500. Rev. Raphael Glinkowski, O.S.P.P.E., Chap., Tel: 724-763-1375 (Res.).

Latrobe. *Latrobe Area Hospital* Tel: 724-537-1000. Rev. Ermin R. Smith, O.S.B., Chap., Assoc. Chaplains: Revs. Justin Withrow, O.S.B.; Michael A. McIlwain, O.S.B. Tel: 724-539-9761 (Res.).

Mount Pleasant. *Frick Community Health Center* Tel: 724-547-1500. Rev. Nicholas Trongo, Chap., Tel: 724-547-5735 (Res.).

New Kensington. *Citizens General Hospital.* Attended by St. Mary, New Kensington, Tel: 724-335-8212 (Res.); St. Joseph, New Kensington, Tel: 724-337-6412 (Res.); Mount St. Peter, New Kensington, Tel: 724-335-9877 (Res.). Tel: 724-337-3541.

Torrance. *Torrance State Hospital* Tel: 724-459-8000. Rev. Chester J. Raimer, Chap., Tel: 724-459-7103 (Res.).

Uniontown. *Uniontown Hospital* Tel: 724-430-5000. Rev. Marion L. Herrick, O.F.M., Chap., Tel: 724-438-0500 (Res.).

On Duty Outside the Diocese:
Reverend Monsignors—
DeAndrea, Joseph A., Villa Stritch, Via della Nocetta 63, 00164 Rome, Italy. Tel: 011-39-6-66162662
Dylag, Michael R., One Kenberton Dr., Pleasant Ridge, MI 48069. Tel: 810-547-2006
Reverend Fathers—
Boley, Edward J., Marian Hall, 529 Martin Luther King Ave., Flint, MI 48532. Tel: 313-235-8574
Conroy, Donald B., Dir., Nat'l. Institute for Family, 3019 4th St., N.E., Washington, DC 20017. Tel: 202-269-3461
Marzilli, Raphael, Chap. to the Franciscan Missionaries of Mary, 399 Fruit Hill Ave., North Providence, RI 02911-2842. Tel: 401-354-4254
Preneta, Henry S., St. Paul Church, 128 N. McKean St., Butler, PA 16001
Survil, Bernard, Convento Santo Domingo, Primer Ave. 1-31, Zona 3, 16001 Coban Ave., Guatemala C.A.
Waczula, Michael F., HC 33 Box 4, Tilly, AR 72679

Military Chaplains:
Reverend Fathers—
Koser, Rudolph J., Jr., Maj. CH., A 25 ABS/HC, Unit 6870 Box 55, APO, AE 09821-6870. Tel: 011-90-232-445-6310, Ext. 3201/3633
Mandock, Patrick H., CH. (LTC), HQ, 19th TAACOM, Unit 15015, Box 2023, APO, AP 96218-0171
Sinclair, Roger A., 150 S. Huntington Ave., Boston, MA 02130

Retired:
Reverend Monsignors—
Garred, John L., Neumann House, 2900 Seminary Dr., Greensburg, PA 15601
Hanicak, Robert A., Neumann House, 2900 Seminary Dr., Greensburg, PA 15601
McCarren, Stephen A., Rte. 2, Box 390, Kearneysville, WV 25430
Ramellini, P. Lino, 19 Rex Blvd., Monessen, PA 15062
Reverend Fathers—
Bahleda, Aloysius J., Neumann House, 2900 Seminary Dr., Greensburg, PA 15601
Bienia, Michael A., Neumann House, 2900 Seminary Dr., Greensburg, PA 15601
Borkowski, Aloysius J., R.D. 3, Box 138D, Derry, PA 15627
Bratus, Walter N., 723 East Pittsburgh St., Greensburg, PA 15601
Bucci, Michael J., 1319 Walnut St., South Connellsville, PA 15425
Casaliggi, John R., Casa Del Clero Cerati, Via Torta 28, 29100 Piacenza, Italy
Charnoki, Andrew J., St. Anne Home, 685 Angela Dr., Greensburg, PA 15601
Cheatham, Louis W., Neumann House, 2900 Seminary Dr., Greensburg, PA 15601
Curry, Edward V., P.O. Box 14697, Jacksonville, FL 32238-4097
Dinnico, Henry P., 135 Carriage Ln., North Huntington, PA 15642
Drab, Stephen J., R.D. 1, Box 228-N, Connellsville, PA 15425

Gearing, Edward P., 1088 Greentree Rd., Apt. #101, Pittsburgh, PA 15220

Higgins, Edward F., P.O. Box 4388, 1934 Southridge Way, Hidden Valley, PA 15502

Hirt, Edwin H., St. Anne Home, 685 Angela Dr., Greensburg, PA 15601

Horvath, Andrew B., 735 Mace St., Greensburg, PA 15601

Murawski, Apolinary, Neumann House, 2900 Seminary Dr., Greensburg, PA 15601

Murphy, Harry J., Nazareth House-St. Michael's, Rancho Mission Rd., San Diego, CA 92108-2099

Oris, Fabian G., RD 2, Box 476E, Uniontown, PA 15401

Ott, Francis M., Neumann House, 2900 Seminary Dr., Greensburg, PA 15061

Pirulli, Francis D., Neumann House, 2900 Seminary Dr., Greensburg, PA 15601

Rivi, Geno G., Sailwind Condo #416, 1200 Shoreline Dr., Gulf Breeze, FL 32561

Stofcik, John A., 304 Stacey Dr., Mount Pleasant, PA 15666

Vallor, Robert, 9 Third St., Rossiter, PA 15772

Weiksner, Jerome M., P.O. Box 875, Greensburg, PA 15601

INSTITUTIONS LOCATED IN THE DIOCESE

[A] SEMINARIES, RELIGIOUS OR SCHOLASTICATES

LATROBE. *St. Vincent Seminary*, 300 Fraser Purchase Rd., 15650. Tel: 724-537-4592; Fax: 724-532-5052. Very Rev. Thomas Acklin, O.S.B., Rector; Revs. Justin M. Matro, O.S.B., Dir. Spiritual Life; William J. Fay, Vice Rector & Dean of Students; Sr. Cecilia Murphy, R.S.M., Academic Dean; Rev. Richard Michel, O.S.B., Dir. of Field Education. Professors 30; Theology Students 19; Seminarians 69; Benedictines 15.

[B] COLLEGES AND UNIVERSITIES

GREENSBURG. *Seton Hill College*, 15601. Tel: 724-834-2200; Fax: 724-830-4611
For a complete listing, refer to the Colleges and Universities section.

LATROBE. *St. Vincent College*, 300 Fraser Purchase Rd., 15650-2690. Tel: 724-539-9761
For a complete listing, refer to the Colleges and Universities section.

[C] HIGH SCHOOLS, DIOCESAN

GREENSBURG. *Greensburg Central Catholic High School*, 901 Armory Dr., 15601. Tel: 724-834-0310; Fax: 724-834-2472. Sr. Brigid Marie Grandey, S.C., Prin.; Rev. Daniel L. Blout, Asst. Prin., Chap. Priests 1; Sisters 2; Lay Teachers 28; Students 425.

CONNELLSVILLE. *Geibel Catholic High School*, 611 E. Crawford Ave., 15425. Tel: 724-628-5600; Fax: 724-626-5700. Mr. Stephen Fusco, Prin.; Rev. Gregory F. Premoshis, Chap. Priests 1; Sisters 1; Lay Teachers 30; Students 417.

[D] ELEMENTARY SCHOOLS, INTER-PAROCHIAL

GREENSBURG. *Aquinas Academy*, 330 N. Main St., 15601. Tel: 724-834-7940; Fax: 724-836-0497. Sr. Brycelyn Eyler, S.C., Prin.; Mr. Daniel Mahoney, Vice-Prin. Sisters 1; Lay Teachers 38; Students 603.

CONNELLSVILLE. *Conn-Area Catholic School*, 110 N. Prospect St., 15425. Tel: 724-628-5090. Sr. Catherine Meinert, S.C., Prin. Lay Teachers 11; Students 191.

FORD CITY. *Divine Redeemer School*, 726 Fourth Ave., 16226. Tel: 724-763-3761. Paul J. Caruso, Prin. Lay Teachers 9; Students 105.

LATROBE. *Christ the Divine Teacher School*. (Grades PreK-8), 323 Chestnut St., 15650. Tel: 724-539-1561. Sr. Donna Marie Palya, V.S.C., Prin. Sisters 4; Lay Teachers 20; Students 370.

MOUNT PLEASANT. *Holy Trinity Catholic*, 222 Summit St., 15666. Tel: 724-547-9871; 547-9474. Sr. Kathleen McCauley, S.C., Prin. Sisters 1; Lay Teachers 9; Students 103.

NORTH HUNTINGDON. *Queen of Angels Regional Catholic School*, 11410 St. Agnes Ln., 15642. Tel: 724-863-2628; 863-9581; Fax: 724-861-8858. Sr. Grace Hartzog, S.C., Prin. Sisters 1; Lay Teachers 23; Students 526.

[E] SPECIAL EDUCATION

GREENSBURG. *Clelian Heights School for Exceptional Children*, R.D. 9, Box 607, 15601. Tel: 724-837-8120. Apostles of the Sacred Heart of Jesus. Sr. M. Adrianne DiLonardo, A.S.C.J., Dir.; Sr. Linda Pettinella, A.S.C.J., Prin.; Rev. William R. Rathgeb, J.C.L., Chap. Sisters 13; Lay Teachers 6; Students 83.

Elizabeth Seton Montessori School of Westmoreland County, Inc., R.D. 7, P.O. Box 268, 15601. Tel: 724-837-8500. Sisters of Charity. Sr. Anita Schulte, S.C., Dir. Sisters 1; Lay Teachers 3; Students 52.

MOUNT PLEASANT. *Verna Montessori School*, R.D. 2, Box 348, 15666. Tel: 724-887-8810; Fax: 724-887-0220. Ivrea Sisters of Charity of the Immaculate Conception. Sr. M. Letizia Tribuzio, S.C.I.C., Prin.; Sr. Virginia Tortora, Admin. Sisters 5; Lay Teachers 3; Students 135.

[F] GENERAL HOSPITALS

JEANNETTE. *Jeannette District Memorial Hospital*, Jefferson Ave., 15644. Tel: 724-527-3551
For a complete listing, refer to the Hospitals section.

[G] HOMES FOR AGED

GREENSBURG. *Neumann House*, 2900 Seminary Dr., 15601 Fax: 724-834-7351
For a complete listing, refer to the Special Care Facilities section.

St. Anne Home, 685 Angela Dr., 15601. Tel: 724-837-6070; Fax: 724-837-6099
For a complete listing, refer to the Special Care Facilities section.

[H] MONASTERIES AND RESIDENCES OF PRIESTS AND BROTHERS

KITTANNING. *Pauline Fathers Monastery*, Bunker Hill Rd., P.O. Box 66, 16201. Tel: 724-763-1375. Revs. Edward Volz, O.S.P.P.E., Prior; Raphael K. Glinkowski, O.S.P.P.E., Admin. Priests 2.

LATROBE. *Saint Vincent Archabbey*, 300 Fraser Purchase Rd., 15650-2686. Tel: 724-539-9761; 532-6600; Fax: 724-539-2110. Legal Titles: *The Benedictine Society of Westmoreland County.*; *Saint Vincent College Corporation.*; *The Wimmer Corporation.*; *The Saint Vincent Cemetery Corporation.* Rt. Revs. Douglas R. Nowicki, O.S.B., Archabbot; Paul R. Maher, O.S.B., Archabbot (Retired); Egbert H. Donovan, O.S.B., Archabbot (Retired); Very Rev. Earl J. Henry, O.S.B., Prior; Bro. David A. Kelly, O.S.B., Subprior; Revs. Sebastian A. Samay, Master of Novices; Reginald G. Bender, O.S.B., Procurator; Thomas Acklin, O.S.B., Rector of the Seminary; Martin R. Bartel, O.S.B., Pres. of the College; Aelred J. Beck, O.S.B.; Kurt J. Belsole, O.S.B.; Joseph P. Bronder, O.S.B.; Gilbert J. Burke, O.S.B.; Godfrey F. Burkhardt, O.S.B.; Anthony J. Burlas, O.S.B.; Julian F. Burt, O.S.B.; Aaron N. Buzzelli, O.S.B.; Andrew S. Campbell, O.S.B.; Athanasius C. Cherry, O.S.B., Sec. to the Archabbot; Wulfstan F. Clough, O.S.B.; Millard S. Cook, O.S.B.; Vincent de Paul Crosby, O.S.B.; Jacques de Paul Daley, O.S.B.; Thomas W. Devereux, O.S.B.; Alvin T. Downey, O.S.B.; Demetrius R. Dumm, O.S.B.; Bertin L. Emling, O.S.B.; Marion J. Emling, O.S.B.; John R. Erickson, O.S.B.; Mario A. Fulgenzi, O.S.B.; Clair F. Gannon, O.S.B.; Campion P. Gavaler, O.S.B.; David R. Griffin, O.S.B., Dir. of College Campus Ministry; Alfred L. Grotzinger, O.S.B.; Mark F.X. Gruber, O.S.B.; Thomas M. Hart, O.S.B.; Bede J. Hasso, O.S.B.; Clement J. Heid, O.S.B.; Roland L. Heid, O.S.B.; Lawrence H. Hill, O.S.B.; Vernon A. Holtz, O.S.B.; Cuthbert A. Jack, O.S.B.; Myron M. Kirsch, O.S.B.; Omer U. Kline, O.S.B., Admin. Asst. to the Archabbot; Rene M. Kollar, O.S.B.; Germain L. Lieb, O.S.B.; Joel R. Lieb, O.S.B.; Stanley T. Markiewicz, O.S.B.; Justin M. Matro, O.S.B., Spiritual Dir. (Seminary); Michael A. McIlwain, O.S.B.; Alphonse H. Meier, O.S.B.; Richard B. Michel, O.S.B.; Jonathan J. Murrman, O.S.B.; Warren D. Murrman, O.S.B.; Justin Nolan, O.S.B.; Daniel Paul O'Keefe, O.S.B.; Emeric J. Pfiester, O.S.B.; James Podlesny, O.S.B.; Donald Raila, O.S.B.; Emmeran A. Rettger, O.S.B.; Roland R. Ripoli, O.S.B.; Noel H. Rothrauff, O.S.B., Dir. of Foreign Missions; Chrysostom V. Schlimm, O.S.B.; Louis S. Sedlacko, O.S.B.; Paulinus J. Selle, O.S.B.; Thomas More Sikora, O.S.B., Dir. of Vocations; Brendan L. Smetana, O.S.B.; Ermin R. Smith, O.S.B.; Ralph Tajak, O.S.B.; Brinstan G. Takach, O.S.B.; Paul R. Taylor, O.S.B.; John-Mary Tompkins, O.S.B.; Simon J. Toth, O.S.B.; Herman F. Ubinger, O.S.B.; Remigius B. Verostko, O.S.B.; Damian J. Warnock, O.S.B.; Charles A. Weber, O.S.B.; Canice T. Welsh, O.S.B.; Justin Withrow, O.S.B.; William Wurm, O.S.B.; Flavian G. Yelinko, O.S.B.; Frank E. Ziemkiewicz, O.S.B., Dean of Students at the College.
On Leave for Study and Teaching: Revs. Millard S. Cook, O.S.B., Fordham Univ.; Patrick T. Cronauer, O.S.B., Ecole Biblique, Jerusalem, Israel; Michael McKay, O.S.B., Johns Hopkins Univ.; Nathan Munsch, O.S.B.; Mark Edward Wenzinger, O.S.B., Catholic Univ. of America.
Priests of the Archabbey Serving Abroad: Very Rev. Cristiano Brito, O.S.B., Prior; Revs. Mauro de Souza Fernandes, O.S.B.; Leo P. Rothrauff, O.S.B.; Claudio Moraes, O.S.B.; Luiz Antonio Carqueijo Se, O.S.B.
Priests on Leave: Revs. Ambrose G. Eberz, O.S.B.; Becket G. Senchur, O.S.B.
Priests on Loan: Revs. Cornelius P. Chang, O.S.B., Archdiocese of New York; Cyprian G. Constantine, O.S.B., Archdiocese of Denver; Christian G. Le Frois, O.S.B., Diocese of Savannah; Job-John Forte, O.S.B., Honduras, C.A. Priests in Archabbey 81; Community: Priests 138; Deacons 3; Solemn Professed Choir-Monks 24; Junior Professed Monks 12; Choir Novices 4; Brothers 7.

NEW FLORENCE. *Mount Carmel Hermitage*, Pineland, R.D. No. 3, Box 36, 15944. Tel: 724-235-2157. Revs. Bede J.K. Mulligan, O.Carm.; Simeon D. Marro, O.Carm. Priests 2.

UNIONTOWN. *St. Anthony Friary*, 115 Oakland Ave., 15401-2818. Tel: 724-438-0500; Fax: 724-438-4251. Friars Richard A. Portasik, O.F.M., Local Min.; Joseph L. Portasik, O.F.M., Vicar; Matthew Brozovic, O.F.M.; Marion J. Herrick, O.F.M., Hospital Chap.; Paul Wild, O.F.M.; Bros. Damien Murkley, O.F.M., Assistance; Juniper Crouch, O.F.M.

[I] CONVENTS AND RESIDENCES FOR SISTERS

GREENSBURG. *Apostles of the Sacred Heart of Jesus*, Clelian Heights Convent, R.D. 9, Box 607, 15601. Tel: 724-837-8120. Sr. M. Adrianne DiLonardo, A.S.C.J., Local Supr.; Rev. William R. Rathgeb, J.C.L., Chap. Sisters 13.

Benedictine Sisters (Eichstatt, Bavaria), St. Emma Monastery, 1001 Harvey Ave., 15601-1494. Tel: 724-834-3060; Fax: 724-834-5772. Mother Mary Anne Noll, O.S.B., Prioress; Rev. Lawrence T. Persico, J.C.L., Chap. Sisters 18; Novices 2.

Doran Hall, Mount Thor Rd., 15601. Tel: 724-837-8645; Fax: 724-836-0766. Sisters of Charity. Sr. Mary Jude McColligan, S.C., Sr. Servant.

Ennis Hall, 447 Mount Thor Rd., 15601. Tel: 724-836-7940. Sisters of Charity 12.

Regina House (Sisters of Charity Generalate), DePaul Center, Administrative Offices, Mount Thor Rd., 15601. Tel: 724-836-0406. Sr. Gertrude Foley, S.C., Pres. Sisters 500; Novices 27; Postulants 18.

Sisters of Charity, Sisters of Charity Center, Mount Thor Rd., 15601. Tel: 724-837-8645. Sr. Annette Frey, S.C., Sister Servant; Sr. Vincent Marie Sidick, S.C., Admin.; Rev. Stephen C. West, Chap. Sisters 77.

Sisters of Charity Formation House, Marian Hall, 451 Mount Thor Rd., 15601. Tel: 724-837-5863. Sisters of Charity 1.

Sisters of Mary Immaculate (Krishnagar, India), St. Joseph Center Convent, 2900 Seminary Dr., 15601. Tel: 724-836-0449. Sr. Tracy Vattakuzhiyil, S.M.I., Local Supr. Sisters 3.

LATROBE. *Discalced Carmelite Nuns*, Carmel of the Assumption, R.D. 6, Box 28, Center Dr., 15650. Tel: 724-539-1056. Sr. Barbara Sitter, O.C.D., Prioress; Rev. Michael A. McIlwain, O.S.B., Chap. Professed Nuns of Solemn Vows 14; Extern 1.

LEECHBURG. *Sisters of Mary Immaculate (West Bengal, India)*, R.D. 5, Box 1231, 15656. Tel: 724-845-2828. Sr. Tracy Vattakuzhiyil, S.M.I., Local Supr. Sisters 3.

MOUNT PLEASANT. *Ivrea Sisters of Charity of the Immaculate Conception*, Immaculate Virgin of Miracles Convent, R.D. 2, Box 348, 15666. Tel: 724-887-6753; Fax: 724-887-0220. Sr. Letizia Garruba, S.C.I.C., Local Supr. Sisters 8.

[J] RETREAT HOUSES

GREENSBURG. *St. Emma Retreat House*, 1001 Harvey Ave., 15601. Tel: 724-834-3060; Fax: 724-834-5772. Benedictine Sisters (Eichstatt, Bavaria). Mother Mary Anne Noll, O.S.B., Prioress.

[K] MISCELLANEOUS LISTINGS

GREENSBURG. *Gilbert Straub Plaza*, 620 Reamer Ave., 15601. Tel: 724-832-2280; Fax: 724-836-8280. Sisters of Charity. Co-Managers: Sr. Andrew Mary, S.C.; Sr. Isabelle, S.C.; Sr. Miriam David, S.C. Sisters 3.

St. Joseph Center, 2900 Seminary Dr., 15601. Tel: 724-834-7350; Fax: 724-834-7351. Mr. Gerald R. Bertig, Dir. Facilities Mgmt.

INDIANA. *Clairvaux Commons*, 100 Clairvaux Dr., 15701. Tel: 724-349-2920; Fax: 724-349-2921. Sisters of St. Joseph 2.

LEECHBURG. *Bishop Morrow Personal Care Home*, R.D. #5, Box 1231, 15656. Sisters of Mary Immaculate. Sr. Tracy Vattakuzhiyil, S.M.I., Dir.

SMOCK. *Ladies of Charity*, Box 251, 15480. Tel: 724-677-2110. Rev. John A. Sedlak, Spiritual Dir.

RELIGIOUS INSTITUTES OF MEN REPRESENTED IN THE DIOCESE

For further details refer to the corresponding bracketed number in the Religious Institutes of Men or Women section.

[0200]—*Benedictine Monks.* (St. Vincent Archabbey).—O.S.B.

[0270]—*Carmelite Fathers and Brothers.*—O.Carm.

[0520]—*Franciscan Friars.*—O.F.M.

[1010]—*Pauline Fathers.*—O.S.P.P.E.

RELIGIOUS INSTITUTES OF WOMEN REPRESENTED IN THE DIOCESE

[0130]—*Apostles of the Sacred Heart of Jesus.*—A.S.C.J.

[0190]—*Benedictine Sisters.*—O.S.B.

[0230]—*Benedictine Sisters of Pontifical Jurisdiction.*—O.S.B.

[0420]—*Discalced Carmelite Nuns.*—O.C.D.

[1070]—*Dominican Sisters, St. Mary of the Springs.* (Columbus, OH).—O.P.

[1170]—*Felician Sisters.*—C.S.S.F.

[2575]—*Institute of the Sisters of Mercy of the Americas.* (Pittsburgh, PA).—R.S.M.

[1690]—*School Sisters of the Third Order of St. Francis.*—O.S.F.

[0570]—*Sisters of Charity of Seton Hill, Greensburg, Pennsylvania.*—S.C.

[0450]—*Sisters of Charity of the Immaculate Conception of Ivrea.*—S.C.I.C.

[0990]—*Sisters of Divine Providence.* (St. Peter Prov.).—C.D.P.

[2440]—*Sisters of Mary Immaculate.*—S.M.I.

[1660]—*Sisters of Saint Francis of the Providence of God.*—O.S.F.

[1620]—*Sisters of Saint Francis, Millvale, Pennsylvania.*—O.S.F.

[3830-13]—*Sisters of St. Joseph.*—C.S.J.

[2040]—*Sisters of the Holy Spirit.*—S.H.S.

[3730]—*Sisters of the Order of St. Basil the Great.*—O.S.B.M.

[4160]—*Vincentian Sisters of Charity.*—V.S.C.

NECROLOGY

† Bertolina, Thomas J., North Huntingdon, PA, St. Agnes. —Died Dec. 2, 1996.

Diocese of Harrisburg

(Dioecesis Harrisburgensis)

Most Reverend

NICHOLAS C. DATTILO, D.D.

Bishop of Harrisburg; ordained May 31, 1958; appointed Eighth Bishop of Harrisburg November 21, 1989; consecrated January 26, 1990. *Res., 4800 Union Deposit Rd., P.O. Box 2153, Harrisburg, PA, 17105.* Tel.: 717-657-4804.

LOVE LIFE AND DO GOOD

ESTABLISHED MARCH 3, 1868.

Square Miles 7,660.

Comprises the Counties of Dauphin, Lebanon, Lancaster, York, Adams, Franklin, Cumberland, Perry, Juniata, Mifflin, Snyder, Northumberland, Union, Montour and Columbia in the State of Pennsylvania.

PATRON OF DIOCESE: St. Patrick, Bishop and Confessor.

For legal titles of parishes and diocesan institutions, consult the General Secretariat.

Diocesan Center: P.O. Box 2153, Harrisburg, PA, 17105-2153. Tel.: 717-657-4804; Fax: 717-657-7673.

STATISTICAL OVERVIEW

Personnel	
Bishop	1
Priests: Diocesan Active in Diocese	129
Priests: Active Outside Diocese	10
Priests: Retired, Sick or Absent	23
Number of Diocesan Priests	162
Religious Priests in Diocese	34
Extern Priests in Diocese	11
Ordinations:	
Diocesan Priests	2
Transitional Deacons	2
Permanent Deacons in Diocese	63
Total Brothers	1
Total Sisters	564
Parishes	
Parishes	89
With Resident Pastor:	
Resident Diocesan Priests	74
Resident Religious Priests	12
Without Resident Pastor:	
Administered by Priests	3
Missions	7
Welfare	
Catholic Hospitals	2
Total Assisted	335,772
Homes for the Aged	6
Total Assisted	828
Residential Care of Children	1
Total Assisted	86
Day Care and Extended Day Care Centers	1
Total Assisted	9
Specialized Homes	4
Total Assisted	182
Special Centers for Social Services	6
Total Assisted	2,801
Other Institutions	1
Total Assisted	41
Educational	
Diocesan Students in Other Seminaries	11
Total Seminarians	11
High Schools, Diocesan and Parish	7
Total Students	3,708
High Schools, Private	1
Total Students	30
Elementary Schools, Diocesan and Parish	40
Total Students	10,864
Elementary Schools, Private	2
Total Students	47
Catechesis/Religious Education:	
High School Students	2,104
Elementary Students	20,899
Total Students Under Catholic Instruction	37,663
Teachers in the Diocese:	
Priests	2
Sisters	99
Lay Teachers	743
Vital Statistics	
Receptions into the Church:	
Infant Baptism Totals	3,565
Adult Baptism Totals	297
Received into Full Communion	551
First Communions	3,816
Confirmations	3,432
Marriages:	
Catholic	620
Interfaith	648
Total Marriages	1,268
Deaths	2,221
Total Catholic Population	230,871
Total Population	1,940,954

Former Bishops—Rt. Rev. JEREMIAH F. SHANAHAN, D.D., cons. July 12, 1868; died Sept. 24, 1886.—Rt. Rev. THOMAS MCGOVERN, D.D., cons. March 11, 1888; died July 25, 1898.—Rt. Rev. JOHN W. SHANAHAN, D.D., cons. May 1, 1899; died Feb. 19, 1916.—Most Rev. PHILIP R. MCDEVITT, D.D., cons. Sept. 21, 1916; died Nov. 11, 1935.—Most Rev. GEORGE L. LEECH, D.D., J.C.D., appt. Auxiliary of Harrisburg July 6, 1935; cons. Oct. 17, 1935; succeeded to See Dec. 19, 1935; retired Oct. 19, 1971; died March 12, 1985.—Most Rev. JOSEPH T. DALEY, D.D., cons. Jan. 7, 1964; appt. Coadjutor Bishop July 31, 1967; succeeded to See Oct. 19, 1971; died Sept. 2, 1983.—Most Rev. WILLIAM H. KEELER, ord. July 17, 1955; cons. Sept. 21, 1979; appt. Bishop of Harrisburg, Nov. 10, 1983; succeeded to See Jan. 4, 1984; transferred Baltimore May 23, 1989.

Diocese of Harrisburg Officials

Bishop—Most Rev. NICHOLAS C. DATTILO, D.D., *P.O. Box 2153, Harrisburg, 17105-2153.* Tel: 717-657-4804.

Vicar General—Very Rev. JAMES M. LYONS, M.Div., M.Ed., *4800 Union Deposit Rd., Box 2153, Harrisburg, 17105-2153.* Tel: 717-657-4804.

General Secretary—Very Rev. JAMES M. LYONS, M.Div., M.Ed., *P.O. Box 2153, Harrisburg, 17105-2153.*

Secretary for Canonical Services—Very Rev. WILLIAM J. KING, J.C.L., *P.O. Box 2557, Harrisburg, 17105-2557.* Tel: 717-657-4804.

Secretary for Catholic Charities—Rev. Msgr. FRANCIS M. KUMONTIS, M.S.W., M.B.A., Ph.D., *P.O. Box 3551, Harrisburg, 17105-3551.* Tel: 717-657-4804.

Secretary for Clergy and Religious Life—Very Rev. PAUL C. HELWIG, M.Div., *P.O. Box 2161, Harrisburg, 17105-2161.*

Secretary for Communications—Very Rev. T. RONALD HANEY, M.A., *4800 Union Deposit Rd., P.O. Box 2555, Harrisburg, 17105-2555.* Tel: 717-657-4804.

Secretary for Education—Very Rev. EDWARD J. QUINLAN, III, M.Div., *4800 Union Deposit Road, Box 3553, Harrisburg, 17105-3553.* Tel: 717-657-4804; 944-3133 (Res.).

Secretary for Parish and Special Ministries—Very Rev. JOSEPH F. GOTWALT, M.Ed., S.T.B., *4800 Union Deposit Road, Box 3557, Harrisburg, 17105-3557.* Tel: 717-657-4804.

Judicial Vicar—Very Rev. WILLIAM J. KING, J.C.L., *P.O. Box 2557, Harrisburg, 17105-2557.* Tel: 717-657-4804.

Chancellor—CAROL HOUGHTON, S.T.D., J.C.D., *P.O. Box 2557, Harrisburg, 17105-2557.* Tel: 717-657-4804.

Diocesan Offices, Commissions, Boards and Programs

Adult Religious Formation, Department for—Dr. MARY ANN BOYARSKI, Dir., *P.O. Box 2161, Harrisburg, 17105-2161.*

Archives—KATHLEEN SIGNOR, Archivist, *4800 Union Deposit Rd., P.O. Box 2153, Harrisburg, 17105-2153.* Tel: 717-657-4804.

Black Catholic Ministry—GWEN SUMMERS, Coord., *4800 Union Deposit Rd., P.O. Box 3557, Harrisburg, 17105.* Tel: 717-657-4804.

Buildings and Properties—LES ZIMMERMAN, Dir., *4800 Union Deposit Rd., P.O. Box 3651, Harrisburg, 17105.* Tel: 717-657-4804.

Campus Ministry—Very Rev. JOSEPH F. GOTWALT, Coord., *P.O. Box 3557, Harrisburg, 17105.* Tel: 717-657-4804.

Catholic Charities Administration, Department for—THOMAS J. D'ANNUNZIO, Dir., *P.O. Box 3551, Harrisburg, 17105.*

Catholic Charities Counseling/Field Services, Department for—Reg. Directors: PETER BIASUCCI, L.S.W.; FRANK KOEBER, M.S., M.F.; THOMAS THORPE, *P.O. Box 3551, Harrisburg, 17105.*

Catholic Schools, Department for—Sr. MARILOU MCDONALD, I.H.M., Supt., *P.O. Box 3553, Harrisburg, 17105.*

The "Catholic Witness"—Very Rev. T. RONALD HANEY, Exec. Editor, *4800 Union Deposit Road, Box 2555, Harrisburg, 17105.* Tel: 717-657-4804.

Catholic Women, Diocesan Council of—LOUISE CONDON, *1205 Livingston Rd., York, 17404.* Tel: 717-848-6444.

Cemeteries—EDWARD G. FARADAY, Dir., *4800 Union Deposit Road, Box 3651, Harrisburg, 17105.* Tel: 717-652-0539.

Charismatic Movement—Rev. Msgr. ROBERT E. LAWRENCE, Liaison, *P.O. Box 3553, Harrisburg, 17105.*

Consultors, College—Rev. Msgr. THOMAS R. BRENNER, V.F.; Very Rev. PHILIP G. BURGER, V.F.; Very Rev. PATRICK A. DEVINE, V.F.; Very Rev. PAUL C. HELWIG; Rev. LAWRENCE J. HEMLER; Very Rev. KENNETH F. LAWRENCE, V.F.; Very Rev. JAMES M. LYONS, V.G.; Rev. J. MICHAEL MCFADDEN; Rev. Msgr. HUGH A. OVERBAUGH; Revs. CHESTER A. SNYDER; ALLAN F. WOLFE; Rev. Msgr. RICHARD A. YOUTZ, V.F.

Cursillo Movement—Rev. Msgr. THOMAS H. SMITH, Moderator.

Deans—Very Rev. JOSEPH C. HILBERT, V.F., Adams Deanery; Very Rev. RICHARD P. WALDRON, V.F., Cumberland/Perry Deanery; Rev. Msgr. WILLIAM

M. RICHARDSON, V.F., Dauphin Deanery; Rev. Msgr. THOMAS R. BRENNER, V.F., Franklin Deanery; Very Rev. KENNETH F. LAWRENCE, V.F., North Lancaster Deanery; Very Rev. WILLIAM J. SULLIVAN, V.F., South Lancaster Deanery; Very Rev. DAVID T. MCANDREW, V.F., Lebanon Deanery; Very Rev. PATRICK A. DEVINE, V.F., Northern Deanery; Very Rev. THOMAS R. HOKE, V.F., York Deanery.

Diocesan Center—LES ZIMMERMAN, Coord., *4800 Union Deposit Rd., P.O. Box 3651, Harrisburg, 17105.* Tel: 717-657-4804.

Ecumenical and Interreligious Affairs—Deacon CHARLES CLARK, Dir., *P.O. Box 3557, Harrisburg, 17105.*

Family Ministries, Department for—VICTORIA LASKOWSKI, J.D., Dir., *P.O. Box 3557, Harrisburg, 17105.* Tel: 717-657-4804.

Finance Council—

Financial Administration, Department for—EDWARD G. FARADAY, Dir., *4800 Union Deposit Rd., P.O. Box 3651, Harrisburg, 17105.* Tel: 717-657-4804.

Health Care Ministry—*P.O. Box 3557, Harrisburg, 17105.*

Holy Name Societies—NORMAND RABOIN, Liaison, *334 Frederick St., Hanover, 17331.* Tel: 717-637-6491.

Knights of Columbus—PATRICK MONAGHAN, Pres., *1304 Foerster Dr., New Cumberland, 17070.* Tel: 717-774-3489.

Ministry Development, Department for—MARY ANN O'DONNELL, Dir., *4800 Union Deposit Rd., P.O. Box 3557, Harrisburg, 17105.* Tel: 717-657-4804.

Lay Personnel, Department for—Very Rev. JAMES M. LYONS, M.Div., M.Ed., *Box 2153, Harrisburg, 17105.* Tel: 717-657-4804.

Legion of Mary—Rev. WALTER SEMPKO, Moderator, *1051 Avila Rd., Harrisburg, 17109.* Tel: 717-652-5900.

Missions, Office of (Home and Foreign)—Rev. ROBERT F. SHARMAN, S.T.L., Dir., *P.O. Box 3657, Harrisburg, 17105.* Tel: 717-657-4804.

Pastoral Council, Diocesan—ANNA BIANCO; DANIEL P. ERNST; VERONICA FABIAN; LAWRENCE P. GEMMELL; Rev. ARTHUR P. GILDEA, C.SS.R.; Very Rev. JOSEPH F. GOTWALT; Deacon MICHAEL A. GRELLA; Dr. CAROL L. HOUGHTON; SARAH C. KANASKIE; ERNEST P. KLINE; JOSEPH C. LAMONT; NINH V. LE; BLANDINA LECCE; Very Rev. JAMES M. LYONS; Dr. HUGH F. MCKEEGAN; LORRAINE MITRICK; ALBERTA COSTA NORTON; MARY ANN O'DONNELL; Rev. EDWARD J. QUINLAN, III; THOMAS ROBEL; Dr. WALTER SEVERS; Rev. ROBERT F. SHARMAN; Sr. MARY AGNES SHURER, S.C.C.

Permanent Diaconate, Office for—Very Rev. PAUL C. HELWIG, Dir., *P.O. Box 2161, Harrisburg, 17105.* Tel: 717-657-4804.

Presbyteral Council—Rev. Msgr. FRANCIS J. HUDAK; Rev. CHESTER P. SNYDER; Rev. Msgr. HUGH A. OVERBAUGH; Rev. Msgr. THOMAS R. BRENNER, V.F.; Rev. J. MICHAEL MCFADDEN; Very Rev. KENNETH F. LAWRENCE, V.F.; Very Rev. BERNARDO PISTONE; Rev. JOSEPH A. CELIA; Very Rev. PHILIP J. BURGER, V.F.; Rev. LAWRENCE J. HEMLER; Very Rev. PATRICK A. DEVINE, V.F.; Revs. SAMUEL E. HOUSER; EDWARD R. LAVELLE; EDWARD C. MALESIC; WILLIAM J. NESSEL, O.S.F.S.; Rev. Msgr. VINCENT J. TOPPER; Rev. ALLAN F. WOLFE; Rev. Msgr. RICHARD A. YOUTZ.

Prison Ministry—*P.O. Box 3557, Harrisburg, 17105.*

Project: Head, Elder Council—VICTORIA LASKOWSKI, Coord., *P.O. Box 3557, Harrisburg, 17105.*

Respect Life/Human Growth and Development, Office for—MARY SHRIVER, M.A., Dir., *P.O. Box 3553, Harrisburg, 17105.*

Public Relations, Department for—Very Rev. T. RONALD HANEY, M.A., Dir., *P.O. Box 2555, Harrisburg, 17105.*

Religious Education (CCD), Department for—TERRY KLUGH, Dir., *P.O. Box 3553, Harrisburg, 17105.*

Religious Life, Department for—Sr. MARION DOLORES, Dir., *P.O. Box 2161, Harrisburg, 17105.*

Saint Thomas More Society—JOHN NANORTA Esq., *17 Spring Creek Manor, Hershey, 17033.* Tel: 717-787-8491.

Saint Vincent de Paul Society—JOSEPH MERLINA, Pres., *40 Hickorytown Rd., Carlisle, 17013.* Tel: 717-243-1090.

Spanish Speaking Ministry—Very Rev. BERNARDO PISTONE, Vicar, *Assumption B.V.M., 119 S. Prince St., Lancaster, 17603.* Tel: 717-392-2578.

Special Ministries, Department for—Very Rev. JOSEPH F. GOTWALT, Dir., *P.O. Box 3557, Harrisburg, 17105.*

Telecommunications—JOSEPH APONICK, Dir., *4800 Union Deposit Rd., Box 2555, Harrisburg, 17105.* Tel: 717-657-4804.

Tribunal—

Judicial Vicar—Very Rev. WILLIAM J. KING, J.C.L., *4800 Union Deposit Rd., P.O. Box 2557, Harrisburg, 17105.* Tel: 717-657-4804.

Diocesan Judges—Rev. Msgr. DAMIEN E. MCGOVERN, J.C.L.; Revs. MICHAEL F. BARRETT; DAVID M. O'CONNELL, C.M., J.C.L.; CAROL HOUGHTON, S.T.D., J.C.D.; Rev. Msgr. RICHARD A. YOUTZ, J.C.L.

Defender of the Bond—Rev. EDWARD R. LAVELLE, S.T.L.

Notaries—BARBARA ROTH; KATHRYN GOULDY; RITA PATACKIS.

Vietnamese Ministry—Rev. JOSEPH HOA VAN NGUYEN, Coord., *Our Lady of the Blessed Sacrament, 2121 N. Third St., Harrisburg, 17110.* Tel: 717-233-1014.

Vocations, Office for—Rev. THOMAS J. ROZMAN, S.T.B., Dir., *P.O. Box 2161, Harrisburg, 17105.* Tel: 717-657-4804.

World Apostolate of Fatima—Rev. JOHN A. SZADA, JR., Spiritual Moderator, *St. Francis of Assisi, 1439 Market St., Harrisburg, 17103.* Tel: 717-232-1003.

Worship, Office of—Rev. THOMAS J. ROZMAN, S.T.B., Dir., *P.O. Box 2161, Harrisburg, 17105.* Tel: 717-657-4804.

Youth and Young Adult Ministry, Department for—LUCILLE SMITH, Dir., *4800 Union Deposit Rd., Box 3551, Harrisburg, 17105.* Tel: 717-657-4804.

CLERGY, PARISHES, MISSIONS AND PAROCHIAL SCHOOLS

CITY OF HARRISBURG
(Dauphin County)

1—CATHEDRAL PARISH OF ST. PATRICK (1995), Rev. Msgr. William M. Richardson, V.F.; Rev. John Schmalhofer; Margaret Danner, Pastoral Assoc.; Deacons J. Leo Dunn; James E. Bogdan; Charles W. Clark. In res., Very Rev. Joseph F. Gotwalt; Rev. Thomas J. Rozman.
Res., 212 State St., 17101. Tel: 717-232-2169; Fax: 717-232-2799.

2—ST. CATHERINE LABOURE (1948). (Shrine of the Miraculous Medal). Rev. Msgr. Hugh A. Overbaugh; Rev. Philip DeChico; Deacons Thomas H. Flannery; William E. Whale; Thomas A. Fedor. In res., Very Rev. James M. Lyons, V.G.
Res., 4000 Derry St., 17111. Tel: 717-564-1321.
School—4020 Derry St., 17111. Tel: 717-564-1760; Fax: 717-564-3010. Sr. Suzanne Duzen, SS.C.M., Prin.
Sisters of SS. Cyril and Methodius 3; Lay Teachers 27; Students 531.
Catechesis/Religious Programs—D.R.E.: Sr. Carol Marie, SS.C.M.; Sr. Deborah Marie, SS.C.M. Students 477.
Convent—4010 Derry St., 17111. Tel: 717-564-0721.

3—ST. FRANCIS OF ASSISI (1901), Revs. Daniel C. Mitzel; John Bateman; Hilda Gomez, Pastoral Assoc.; Deacon Miguel Marroquin.
Res., 1439 Market St., 17103. Tel: 717-232-1003; Fax: 717-232-1003.
Catechesis/Religious Programs—Tel: 717-233-7912.
Students 118.

4—HOLY FAMILY (1958), Rev. Bernard P. McGinley, M.A.
Church—555 S. 25th St., 17104. Tel: 717-232-4237.
Rectory: 2501 Barkley Ln., 17104. Tel: 717-561-8250.
School—Tel: 717-232-2551. Sr. Joseph Marie Carter, I.H.M., Prin.
Sisters Servants of the Immaculate Heart of Mary 2; Lay Teachers 9; Students 234.
Catechesis/Religious Programs—Students 286.
Convent—2473 Adrian St., 17104. Tel: 717-564-7236.

5—HOLY NAME OF JESUS (Lower Paxton Twp.) (1960), Revs. Daniel J. Mahoney; Dennis G. Dalessandro; Francis M. Lahout; Deacons Jerome Foerster; Joseph J. Wrabel.
Res., 6150 Allentown Blvd., 17112. Tel: 717-652-4211; Fax: 717-652-6941.
School—(Lower Paxton Twp.) 6190 Allentown Blvd., 17112. Tel: 717-657-1704; Fax: 717-697-8834. Tom Nissley, Prin.
Sisters of St. Joseph 1; Lay Teachers 54; Students 852.
Catechesis/Religious Programs—Evelyn Alviani, D.R.E.
Students 1,042.
Convent—Tel: 717-545-4357.
Pastoral Associates 3; Teachers 1; Diocesan Administrators 2.

6—ST. LAWRENCE (1859) (German). Closed. See St. Patrick Cathedral, Harrisburg.

7—ST. MARGARET MARY ALACOQUE (Penbrook) (1948), Revs. John G. Allen; Michael M. Laicha; Mrs. Karen Hurley, Pastoral Assoc. In res., Rev. Edward C. Malesic.
Res., 2848 Herr St., 17103-1817. Tel: 717-233-3062; Fax: 717-238-5633.
School—Tel: 717-232-3771; Fax: 717-232-0776. Mrs. Kathleen McKenna, Ph.D., Prin.
Sisters of Mercy 2; Lay Teachers 19; Students 370.
Catechesis/Religious Programs—Tel: 717-232-3800. Mrs. Suzanne Fonner, D.R.E.
Students 164.

8—OUR LADY OF THE BLESSED SACRAMENT (1906), Rev. Paul R. Shuda; Deacon John Mowery. In res., Revs. Edward R. Lavelle; Joseph Hoa Nguyen.
Res., 2121 N. Third St., 17110-1812. Tel: 717-233-1014; Fax: 717-233-0420.
Catechesis/Religious Programs—Students 166.
Convent—2900 N. Green St., 17110. Tel: 717-236-3354. Sisters of Mercy
Sisters 2.

9—SACRED HEART OF JESUS (1901). Closed. See St. Patrick Cathedral, Harrisburg.

OUTSIDE THE CITY OF HARRISBURG

Abbottstown, York Co., Immaculate Heart of Mary (1809), Rev. Thomas F. Langan; Deacon Raymond J. Smith; Karen Kreller, Pastoral Assoc. & D.R.E.
Res., R.D. 1, Box 343, Canal Rd., 17301-9051. Tel: 717-259-0611; Fax: 717-259-6371. [CEM]
Catechesis/Religious Programs—Tel: 717-259-9426.
Students 275.

Annville, Lebanon Co., St. Paul the Apostle (1928), Rev. John D. Hoke; Deacon Richard A. Ryan. In res., Rev. Dennis M. Young (STA).
Res., 125 S. Spruce St., 17003. Tel: 717-867-1525.
Catechesis/Religious Programs—Tel: 717-867-7471.
Students 229.
Stations—Fort Indiantown Gap, Our Lady of Victory, Tel: 717-861-2241; Lebanon Valley College, Miller Chapel, Tel: 717-867-6135.

Berwick, Columbia Co., Immaculate Conception of the Blessed Virgin Mary (1906), Rev. Joseph H. Fennessy.
Res., 1730 Fowler Ave., 18603-1462. Tel: 717-759-8113; Fax: 717-759-6637. [CEM]
School—Holy Family Consolidated School, Tel: 717-752-2021; Fax: 717-752-2914.
Catechesis/Religious Programs—Tel: 717-759-9225.
Students 230.

St. Joseph's (1928), Rev. Dominick A. Mammarella; Sr. M. Carmelina, D.M., Pastoral Assoc.
Res., 721 Monroe St., 18603. Tel: 717-752-5684.
School—Holy Family Consolidated School, Tel: 717-752-2021. Sr. M. Ambrogina, D.M., Prin.
Catechesis/Religious Programs—Students 163.
Convent—728 Washington St., 18603. Tel: 717-752-2112. Daughters of Mercy
Sisters 3.

Bloomsburg, Columbia Co., St. Columba (1882) (Irish), Revs. Patrick A. Devine; Ronald J. Moratelli.
Mailing Address: P.O. Box 829, 17815.
Res., 42 E. Third St., 17815. Tel: 717-784-0801; Fax: 717-387-2604. [CEM]
School—40 E. Third St., 17815. Tel: 717-784-5932. Sr. Rita Polchin, S.S.C.M., Prin.
Sisters 3; Lay Teachers 5; Students 161.
Catechesis/Religious Programs—Tel: 717-387-4068.
Students 345.
Convent—342 Iron St., 17815. Tel: 717-784-1385.
Mission—Benton, Columbia Co., Christ the King, Mendenhall Ln., Benton, 17814. Tel: 717-925-6969.

Blue Ridge Summit, Franklin Co., St. Rita (1919), Revs. Michael A. Messaro, M.SS.CC.; Antony Attumaly, M.SS.CC.
Immaculate Conception:Fairfield, 17320. Tel: 717-642-8815. [JC]

Bonneauville, Adam Co., St. Joseph (1859), Revs. Brian P. Conrad; Paul N. Miller; Deacon Richard J. Weaver.
Res., 12 E. Hanover St., Gettysburg, 17325-7750. Tel: 717-334-2510. [CEM]
Catechesis/Religious Programs—Students 108.

Buchanan Valley, Adams Co., St. Ignatius Loyola (Orrtanna) (1817), Rev. Carl J. Steffen.
Res., 1095 Church Rd., Orrtanna, 17353. Tel: 717-677-8012. [CEM]
Catechesis/Religious Programs—Tel: 717-677-8012.
Students 83.

Camp Hill, Cumberland Co., Good Shepherd (1951), Rev. Msgr. Vincent J. Smith; Rev. Alfred P. Sceski; Deacon Francis Gorman. In res., Very Rev. William J. King, J.C.L., J.V.
Res., 3435 Trindle Rd., 17011. Tel: 717-761-1167; Fax: 717-761-5313.
School—Tel: 717-737-7261; Fax: 717-761-4673. Mrs. Maretta K. Schmidt, Prin.
Lay Teachers 15; Students 267.

Catechesis/Religious Programs—3400 Market St., 17011. Tel: 717-737-8216.
Students 267.

Carlisle, Cumberland Co., St. Patrick (1779), Revs. Andrew J. Fontanella; Joseph T. Scanlin; Curtis R. Delarm; Deacon Gerard J. Kole. In res., Rev. Daniel J. Menniti.
Res., 140 E. Pomfret St., 17013. Tel: 717-243-4411; Fax: 717-245-0522. [CEM 2]
School—87 Marsh Dr., 17013. Tel: 717-249-4826. Sr. Karen Washabaugh, S.S.J., Prin.; Sr. Dorothy Kelm, S.S.J., Asst. to the Prin.
Lay Teachers 2; Students 430.
Catechesis/Religious Programs—Tel: 717-243-4891. Mrs. Helen Richards, D.R.E.
Students 405.
Chapel—Pine Grove Furnace, St. Eleanor Regina.

Centralia, Columbia Co., St. Ignatius (1869). Closed. See Our Lady of Mount Carmel, Mount Carmel.

Chambersburg, Franklin Co., Corpus Christi (1792), Rev. Msgr. Thomas R. Brenner, V.F.; Revs. Daniel F. Lawler, S.J.; Jude Dawson-Amoah, O.P.
Res., 320 Philadelphia Ave., 17201. Tel: 717-264-6317; Fax: 717-264-1787. [CEM]
School—305 N. Second St., 17201. Tel: 717-263-5036; Fax: 717-263-6079. Mr. Thomas F. Yurkovic, Prin.
Lay Teachers 18; Students 278.
Catechesis/Religious Programs—Tel: 717-263-9541. Mrs. Jean M. Brigham, D.R.E.
Students 352.
Mission—Doylesburg, Franklin Co., Our Lady of Refuge, 21169 Cross Rd., Doylesburg, 17219. Tel: 717-349-7953. Rev. John R. Campion, Admin.
Station—Scotland School for Veterans' Children, Tel: 717-264-7187; Fax: 717-264-0322.

Coal Township, Northumberland Co., Our Lady of Hope, Very Rev. Philip G. Burger, V.F.; Rev. Edward J. Keating.
Res., 863 W. Chestnut St., 17866-1995. Tel: 717-648-4432.

St. Stephen Protomartyr, Northumberland Co., (1898) (Polish). Closed. See Our Lady of Hope, Coal Township.

Columbia, Lancaster Co., St. Peter (1828), Rev. John F. Smith; Sr. George Ann Biscan, A.S.C., Pastoral Assoc.; Deacon Michael J. Lydon.
Res., 217 Maple St., Wrightsville, 17368. Tel: 717-252-3806; Fax: 717-684-3102. [CEM 2]
School—121 S. Second St., 17512. Tel: 717-684-2433; Fax: 717-684-5039. Mrs. Theresa M. Burg, Prin.
Lay Teachers 9; Students 176.
Catechesis/Religious Programs—Mr. John J. Campbell, III, D.R.E.
Students 92.
Convent—Tel: 717-684-2707.
Mission—Wrightsville, York Co., Mother of Holy Purity, 217 Maple St., 17368.

Holy Trinity (1860), Very Rev. Kenneth F. Lawrence; Sr. Anna Cosgrave, O.S.F., Pastoral Assoc.
Res., 409 Cherry St., 17512. Tel: 717-684-2711; Fax: 717-684-9612. [CEM]
School—404 Cherry St., 17512. Tel: 717-684-2664. Shirley A. Meley, Prin.
Lay Teachers 10; Students 179.
Catechesis/Religious Programs—Students 122.
Convent—548 Cherry St., 17512. Tel: 717-684-2232. Sisters of St. Francis of Philadelphia

Conewago Township, Adams Co., Basilica of the Sacred Heart of Jesus (1730), Rev. Msgr. George W. Rost.
Res., 30 Basilica Dr., Hanover, 17331-8924. Tel: 717-637-2721. [CEM]
School—Tel: 717-632-8715. Sr. Eileen Kean, Prin.
Sisters of St. Joseph 3; Lay Teachers 8; Students 244.
Convent—55 Basilica Dr., Hanover, 17331. Tel: 717-637-3370. Sisters of St. Joseph
Sisters 4.

Cornwall, Lebanon Co., Sacred Heart of Jesus (1886), Rev. Andrew P. Marinak.
Res., 2596 Cornwall Rd., P.O. Box 136, 17016-0136. Tel: 717-273-1574. [CEM]
Parish Center—Tel: 717-274-3239.
Catechesis/Religious Programs—Tel: 717-273-2160. Sr. Helen Ann Gaidos, D.R.E.
Students 95.

Dallastown, York Co., St. Joseph (1850), Revs. Robert S. Panza; Daniel P. O'Brien; Deacon John Weaver.
Res., 251 E. Main St., 17313. Tel: 717-246-3007; Fax: 717-244-5278. [CEM][JC]
School—271 E. Main St., 17313. Tel: 717-244-9386. Donna Phillips, Prin.
Lay Teachers 12; Students 211.
Catechesis/Religious Programs—Tel: 717-244-6279.
Students 450.

Danville, Montour Co., St. Joseph (1848), Revs. William M. Weary; Lawrence C. Gross.
Res., 18 E. Center St., 17821. Tel: 717-275-2512; Fax: 717-275-6840. [CEM 3]
School—511 Ferry St., 17821. Tel: 717-275-2435. Sisters 1; Lay Teachers 8; Students 164.
Catechesis/Religious Programs—Students 380.
Convent—9 Bloom St., 17821. Tel: 717-275-0562.

Dauphin, Dauphin Co., St. Matthew, Apostle and Evangelist (1976), Rev. David T. Lawlor, O.Praem.; Deacon Richard Aull.
Res., 420 Stony Creek Rd., P.O. Box 459, 17018. Tel: 717-921-2363; Fax: 717-921-2364.

Doylesburg, Franklin Co., Our Lady of Refuge Mission (1802), Rev. John R. Campion, Admin.
Res., 21169 Cross Rd., 17219. Tel: 717-349-7953. [CEM]

Elizabethtown, Lancaster Co., St. Peter (1752), Rev. Joseph D. Blascovich. In res., Rev. Thomas J. Kujovsky.
Res., One Saint Peter's Pl., 17022-1956. Tel: 717-367-1255; Fax: 717-367-1270. [CEM]
School—61 E. Washington St., 17022. Tel: 717-367-1678. Mrs. Paula Fish, Prin.
Lay Teachers 7; Students 112.
Catechesis/Religious Programs—Tel: 717-367-5538.
Students 301.

Elysburg, Northumberland Co., Queen of the Most Holy Rosary (1950), Rev. Charles R. Slough; Deacon Robert Mack.
Res., 103 W. Center St., 17824. Tel: 717-672-2302; Fax: 717-672-3310. [JC]
Catechesis/Religious Programs—Tel: 717-672-9930.
Students 210.

Enhaut, Dauphin Co., St. John the Evangelist (1902). Closed. See Prince of Peace, Steelton.

Enola, Cumberland Co., Our Lady of Lourdes (1926), Rev. John A. Acri; Ms. Celeste Hamilton, Pastoral Assoc.; Deacon Edwin L. Fitzpatrick.
Res., 225 Salt Rd., 17025. Tel: 717-732-9642; Fax: 717-732-8184.
Catechesis/Religious Programs—Students 420.

Ephrata, Lancaster Co., Mother of Perpetual Help (1914), Very Rev. Arthur P. Gildea, C.SS.R.; Revs. Edward W. Jackson, C.SS.R.; William F. Rosner, C.SS.R.; John J. Dorff, C.SS.R.
Res., 300 Pine St., P.O. Box 209, 17522-0209. Tel: 717-733-6596; Fax: 717-733-0502. [JC]
School—Tel: 717-738-2414; Fax: 717-738-3280. Sr. Ann Damien, O.S.F., Prin.
Bernardine Sisters of the Third Order of St. Francis 5; Lay Teachers 10; Students 340.
Catechesis/Religious Programs—Tel: 717-738-4517; Fax: 717-733-2119.
Students 450.
Convent—310 Church Ave., 17522. Tel: 717-733-1291.

Fairfield, Adams Co., Immaculate Conception of the Blessed Virgin Mary (1823), Revs. Michael A. Messaro, M.SS.CC.; Antony Attumaly, M.SS.CC.
Res., 17320. Tel: 717-642-8815. [CEM][JC]
Catechesis/Religious Programs—Students 110.

Gettysburg, Adams Co., St. Francis Xavier's (1831), Very Rev. Joseph C. Hilbert, V.F.; Rev. Caesar A. Belchez; Deacon James Sneeringer.
Res., 22 W. High St., 17325. Tel: 717-334-3919; 334-7711; Fax: 717-338-0831. [CEM]
School—45 W. High St., 17325. Tel: 717-334-4221; Fax: 717-334-8883. Sr. Phyllis R.S.M., Prin.
Sisters of Mercy 3; Lay Teachers 16; Students 240.
Catechesis/Religious Programs—Tel: 717-334-1221.
Students 214.
Convent—Tel: 717-334-4310.

Greencastle, Franklin Co., St. Mark the Evangelist (1965), Rev. Joseph L. Stahura.
Res., 395 S. Ridge Ave., P.O. Box 218, 17225. Tel: 717-597-2705. [JC]
Catechesis/Religious Programs—Students 185.
Mission—Mercersburg, Franklin Co., St. Luke the Evangelist.

Hanover, York Co., St. Joseph (1864), Rev. Msgr. Robert C. Gribbin; Revs. Robert M. Gillelan, Jr.; Norman C. Hohenwarter, Jr.
Res., 244 Baltimore St., 17331. Tel: 717-637-5236; Fax: 717-637-6615. [CEM]
School—236 Baltimore St., 17331. Tel: 717-632-1335. Mrs. Susan M. Mummert, Prin.
Sisters of St Joseph 3; Lay Teachers 10; Students 270.
Catechesis/Religious Programs—Students 490.
Convent—252 Baltimore St., 17331. Tel: 717-637-4233.

St. Vincent (1904), Rev. Bernard Quinn.
Res., 220 Third St., 17331. Tel: 717-637-4625. [CEM]
School—224 Third St., 17331. Tel: 717-637-5190.
Lay Teachers 8; Students 214.
Catechesis/Religious Programs—Students 85.

Hershey, Dauphin Co., St. Joan of Arc (1920), Rev. Msgr. Leo N. Bierster; Rev. John Trigilio, Jr.; Deacon Thomas S. Oliver. In res., Rev. Stephen D. Weitzel; Rev. Msgr. Francis M. Kumontis.
Res., 359 W. Areba Ave., 17033. Tel: 717-533-7168; Fax: 717-520-0526.
School—305 W. Areba Ave., 17033. Tel: 717-533-2854. Sr. Eileen M. McGowan, Prin.
Daughters of Our Lady of Mercy 4; Lay Teachers 24; Students 325.
Catechesis/Religious Programs—Tel: 717-533-8578.
Students 460.
Convent—Tel: 717-533-2864.
Sisters 4.

Kulpmont, Northumberland Co., Assumption of the Blessed Virgin Mary (1909). Closed. See Holy Angels, Kulpmont.

St. Casimir (1915). Closed. See Holy Angels, Kulpmont.

Holy Angels (1995), Rev. Raymond J. Orloski.
Res., 855 Scott St., 17834. Tel: 717-373-1221; Fax: 717-373-1226. [CEM 3]
Catechesis/Religious Programs—863 Scott St., 17834. Tel: 717-373-1512.
Students 197.

Lancaster, Lancaster Co.,

1—St. Anne, (1923), Rev. Msgr. Leo A. Beierschmitt; Rev. Gerald A. Lytle; Deacons Frank Eckman; Joseph L. Anders.
Res., 929 N. Duke St., 17602. Tel: 717-392-2225.
School—Cherry & Liberty St., 17602. Tel: 717-394-6711; Fax: 717-394-8628.
Lay Teachers 11; Students 263. Principals: Donna Power, (Elementary); Dermot Garrett, (High School).
Catechesis/Religious Programs—Tel: 717-397-8755. Mrs. Suzanne Ganse, D.R.E.
Students 110.

2—St. Anthony of Padua, (1870), Revs. Charles McDonald, C.SS.R.; James Small, C.SS.R.; William Geiger, C.SS.R.
Res., 501 E. Orange St., 17602. Tel: 717-394-0669; Fax: 717-394-4507. [CEM]
School—Resurrection. See Assumption of the Blessed Virgin Mary, Lancaster, and report of Resurrection School for details. Tel: 717-392-3083.
Catechesis/Religious Programs—Tel: 717-392-2930. Patricia Meyer, D.R.E.
Students 286.
Convent—533 E. Orange St., 17602. Tel: 717-397-1043. Sisters of the Holy Cross
Stations—Lancaster, Lancaster County Prison, Tel: 717-299-7800; Conestoga View Nursing Home, Tel: 717-299-7850.

3—Assumption of the Blessed Virgin Mary, (1741), Very Rev. Bernardo Pistone; Revs. Thomas J. Gralinski; Allan F. Wolfe; Ignacio Palomino (Peru); Mrs. Frances Sescilla, Pastoral Assoc.; Deacon Manuel Velazquez.
Res., 119 S. Prince St., 17603. Tel: 717-392-2578; Fax: 717-394-6549.
School—Resurrection. Consolidation of St. Anthony, St. Joseph and St. Mary. 32 W. Vine St., 17603. Tel: 717-397-3136. Mary Jo Moczulski, Prin.
Religious 2; Lay Teachers 20; Students 417.
Catechesis/Religious Programs—Ann Bleistine, D.R.E.
Students 325.

4—St. John Neumann, (1978), Rev. Msgr. Richard A. Youtz, J.C.L.; Rev. Neil S. Sullivan; Sr. Helen E. McCormac, Pastoral Assoc.; Deacon Matthew P. Culley.
Res., 601 E. Delp Rd., 17601. Tel: 717-569-8531; Fax: 717-569-2135.
Catechesis/Religious Programs—Tel: 717-569-8533; Fax: 717-569-9156.
Students 933.

5—St. Joseph, (1849), Rev. Msgr. Thomas H. Smith; Rev. Msgr. Cletus H. Wagman, Senior Priest; Mrs. Patricia Weaver, Pastoral Assoc. In res., Revs. James Muthuplakel; Michael F. Barrett.
Res., 440 St. Joseph St., 17603-5298. Tel: 717-397-6921. [CEM]
School—Resurrection. See Assumption of the Blessed Virgin Mary, Lancaster, for details.
Catechesis/Religious Programs—Students 118.

6—Sacred Heart of Jesus, (1900), Rev. Michael J. Grab; Sr. Anne Hodgson, S.N.D., Pastoral Assoc.
Res., 558 W. Walnut St., 17603. Tel: 717-394-0757; Fax: 717-394-3589.
School—235 Nevin St., 17603. Tel: 717-393-8433. Sr. Ellen Thomas, I.H.M., Prin.
Servants of the Immaculate Heart of Mary 3; Lay Teachers 11; Students 230.
Catechesis/Religious Programs—Sr. Mary Canavan, I.H.M., D.R.E.
Students 82.
Convent—565 W. Walnut St., 17603. Tel: 717-392-4522.

Lebanon, Lebanon Co.,

1—ASSUMPTION OF THE BLESSED VIRGIN MARY, (1810), Very Rev. David T. McAndrew, V.F.; Rev. Robert F. Sharman; Deacon Richard Wentzel. In res., Rev. Walter A. Halaburda.
Office: 12 N. Eighth St., 17046. Tel: 717-272-5674.
Res., 2 N. Eighth St., 17046. [CEM][JC]
Catechesis/Religious Programs—Mrs. Julie Shuyler, D.R.E.
Students 525.
Mission—Jonestown, Lebanon Co., Our Lady of Fatima.

2—ST. BENEDICT THE ABBOT, (1995), Rev. Msgr. Mercurio A. Fregapane.
Res., 1300 Lehman St., 17046-3331. Tel: 717-272-0623; Fax: 717-270-6926.
Catechesis/Religious Programs—Tel: 717-272-1242.
Students 169.

3—ST. CECILIA, (1995), Rev. J. Michael McFadden.
Res., 202 E. Lehman St., 17046. Tel: 717-272-4412; Fax: 717-272-3206. [CEM]
Catechesis/Religious Programs—Students 336.

4—ST. GERTRUDE, (1906). Closed. See St. Cecilia, Lebanon.

5—ST. GREGORY THE GREAT, (1965). Closed. See St. Cecilia, Lebanon.

6—SS. CYRIL AND METHODIUS, (1905) (Slavonic). Closed. See St. Benedict the Abbot, Lebanon.

Lewisburg, Union Co., Sacred Heart of Jesus (1935), Revs. William J. Nessel, O.S.F.S.; Patrick J. Shannon.
Res., 814 St. Louis St., 17837. Tel: 717-523-3104; Fax: 717-524-5156.
Catechesis/Religious Programs—Sr. Karen Wilson, SS.C.M., D.R.E.
Students 371.
Station—Laurelton, Laurelton Center, Tel: 717-922-5100.

Lewistown, Mifflin Co., Sacred Heart of Jesus (1830), Revs. Thomas C. Marickovic; Thaddeus B. Strzelec.
Res., 106 N. Dorcas St., 17044. Tel: 717-242-2781; Fax: 717-248-0260. [CEM]
School—110 N. Dorcas St., 17044. Tel: 717-248-5351; 248-0260.
Lay Teachers 12; Students 155.
Mission—Burnham, Mifflin Co., Mary Queen of All Saints. Closed.

Lititz, Lancaster Co., St. James (1977), Revs. Gerard J. Szymkowiak, C.SS.R.; John Creaven, C.SS.R.; Deacon Donald Hackman.
Res., 505 Woodcrest Ave., 17543. Tel: 717-626-5580; Fax: 717-626-2146.
Catechesis/Religious Programs—Tel: 717-626-0244. Catherine M. Trusz, D.R.E.
Students 370.

Littlestown, Adams Co., St. Aloysius (1884), Rev. James M. Sterner.
Res., 29 S. Queen St., 17340. Tel: 717-359-4513. [CEM]
Catechesis/Religious Programs—Faith Redding, D.R.E.
Students 180.

Locustdale, Columbia Co., St. Joseph (1913). Closed. See Our Lady of Mount Carmel, Mount Carmel.

Locust Gap, Northumberland Co., St. Joseph (1870). Closed. See Our Lady of Mount Carmel, Mount Carmel.

Lykens, Dauphin Co., Our Lady Help of Christians (1853), Rev. Francis J. Karwacki, M.Ed., M.Div.
Res., 732 E. Main St., 17048. Tel: 717-453-7895. [CEM 2][JC 3]
Catechesis/Religious Programs—Tel: 717-453-9931.
Students 224.
Mission—Williamstown, Dauphin Co., Sacred Heart of Jesus, 140 E. Market St., Williamstown, 17098. Tel: 717-647-2645.

McSherrystown, Adams Co., Annunciation of the Blessed Virgin Mary (1899), Rev. Andre J. Meluskey; Deacon Joseph F. Lawrence.
Res., 26 N. Third St., 17344. Tel: 717-637-1191. [CEM]
School—316 North St., 17344. Tel: 717-637-3135; Fax: 717-637-1715. Sr. Ann Marie Wierman, S.S.J., Prin.
Lay Teachers 18; Students 300.
Catechesis/Religious Programs—Students 105.

Manheim, Lancaster Co., St. Richard (1978), Rev. Raymond J. Christ, O.S.F.S. In res., Rev. John F. Kenny, O.S.F.S.
Res., 201 Adele Ave., 17545. Tel: 717-665-2465.
Catechesis/Religious Programs—D.R.E.: Margaret D. Haines, (Grades K-12); Theresa M. Griffith, (Grades K-12).
Students 101.

Marietta, Lancaster Co., Presentation of the Blessed Virgin Mary (1869). Closed. See Mary, Mother of the Church, Mount Joy.

Marion Heights, Northumberland Co., Our Lady of Perpetual Help (1905). Closed. See Holy Angels, Kulpmont.

Marysville, Perry Co., Our Lady of Good Counsel (1956), Rev. John F. Greaney.
Res., 121 William St., 17053. Tel: 717-957-2662.
Catechesis/Religious Programs—Tel: 717-834-4519. Sally Robert, D.R.E.
Students 168.
Mission—Duncannon, Perry Co., St. Bernadette, 901 High St., Duncannon, 17020. Tel: 717-834-4519.

Mechanicsburg, Cumberland Co., Blessed Katharine Drexel (1988), Rev. James R. O'Brien; Deacons Melvin Dowdy; Joseph Gorini.
Res., One Clover Ln., 17055. Tel: 717-697-8716.
Mailing Address: One Peter Dr., 17055. Fax: 717-697-3702.
Catechesis/Religious Programs—Tel: 717-795-8572. Carolyn Keffer, D.R.E.
Students 431.

St. Elizabeth Ann Seton (1977), Very Rev. Richard P. Waldron, V.F.; Rev. Leo M. Goodman, III.
Res., 310 Hertzler Rd., 17055. Tel: 717-697-2614; Fax: 717-795-0800.
Catechesis/Religious Programs—Tel: 717-697-3545. D.R.E.: Carol Holder; Judy Olinger.
Students 438.

St. Joseph (1952), Revs. Chester P. Snyder; Daniel F. X. Powell; Darius G.C. Moss; Rose Baker, Pastoral Assoc.; Deacons Andrew Fine; Jack Paruso.
Res., 200 S. Filbert St., P.O. Box 2012, 17055. Tel: 717-766-9433; Fax: 717-795-9123.
Church—400 E. Simpson St., 17055.
School—410 E. Simpson St., 17055. Tel: 717-766-2564; Fax: 717-766-1226.
Sisters of SS. Cyril and Methodius 3; Lay Teachers 19; Students 504.
Catechesis/Religious Programs—Tel: 717-766-2472.
Students 533.
Convent—302 S. Chestnut St., 17055. Tel: 717-766-6221.

Middletown, Dauphin Co., Seven Sorrows of the Blessed Virgin Mary (1855), Very Rev. Edward J. Quilan, III; Rev. Louis P. Ogden.
Res., 280 N. Race St., 17057. Tel: 717-944-3133; Fax: 717-944-1170. [CEM]
School—(Grades PreK-8) Race & Conewago St., 17057. Tel: 717-944-5371; Fax: 717-944-5419. Mr. Thomas Frey, Prin.
Lay Teachers 12; Students 220.
Catechesis/Religious Programs—Students 275.

Mifflintown, Juniata Co., St. Jude (1959), Rev. Thomas C. Marickovic; Deacon John A. Rocco.
Res., Box 187, 17059. Tel: 717-436-6722.

Millersburg, Dauphin Co., Queen of Peace (1952), Rev. Joseph A. Kelly, O.Praem.
Res., 202 Zimmerman, 17061. Tel: 717-692-3504.
Catechesis/Religious Programs—Tel: 717-692-3504. Mrs. Cynthia Miskinis, D.R.E.
Students 157.

Millersville, Lancaster Co., St. Philip the Apostle (1965), Revs. Michael E. Homola; Stephen A. Sheetz; Deacons Martin C. Light, Sr.; Ross Beighley.
Res., 2111 Millersville Pike, Lancaster, 17603. Tel: 717-872-2166.
Catechesis/Religious Programs—Tel: 717-872-9892. Sr. Charlotte O.S.F., D.R.E.
Students 421.

Milton, Northumberland Co., St. Joseph (1805), Rev. Thomas A. Scala.
Res., 109 Broadway, 17847. Tel: 717-742-4356; Fax: 717-742-9171. [CEM]
Catechesis/Religious Programs—Tel: 717-742-4481. Belinda Stefl, D.R.E.
Students 182.

Mount Carmel, Northumberland Co.,

1—DIVINE REDEEMER, (1995), Revs. Joseph M. Pease; Robert A. Yohe.
Res., 438 West Ave., 17851. Tel: 717-339-3450. [CEM]
Catechesis/Religious Programs—250 West Ave., 17851. Tel: 717-339-3823.
Students 256.

2—HOLY CROSS, (1892) (Lithuanian). Closed. See Divine Redeemer, Mount Carmel.

3—ST. JOHN THE BAPTIST, (1892) (Slovak). Closed. See Divine Redeemer, Mount Carmel.

4—ST. JOSEPH, (1875) (Polish). Closed. See Our Lady of Mount Carmel, Mount Carmel.

5—OUR LADY OF MOUNT CARMEL, (1886), Rev. Msgr. Lawrence R. Overbaugh.
Res., 47 S. Market St., 17851. Tel: 717-339-1031. [JC 4]
Catechesis/Religious Programs—Tel: 717-339-2325. Sr. Mary Carol Kerdell, D.R.E.
Students 150.

6—OUR MOTHER OF CONSOLATION, (1895) (Polish). Closed. See Divine Redeemer, Mount Carmel.

7—ST. PETER, (1905) (Italian). Closed. See Divine Redeemer, Mount Carmel.

Mount Joy, Lancaster Co., Assumption of B.V.M. (1979). Closed. See Mary, Mother of the Church, Mount Joy.

Mary, Mother of the Church (1995), Rev. Paul T. Rindos.
Res., 625 Union School Rd., 17552-9712. Tel: 717-653-4903.

Myerstown, Lebanon County, Mary, Gate of Heaven (1926), Rev. Robert F. Berger.
Res., 188 W. McKinley Ave., P.O. Box 227, 17067. Tel: 717-866-5640.
Catechesis/Religious Programs—Students 153.

New Bloomfield, Perry Co., St. Bernard (1942), Rev. Anthony J. Larry, O.S.F.S.
Res., W. McClure St., P.O. Box 25, 17068. Tel: 717-582-4113; Fax: 717-582-3797.
Catechesis/Religious Programs—Alice Vilk, D.R.E.
Students 230.

New Cumberland, Cumberland Co., St. Theresa of the Infant Jesus (1928), Rev. Msgr. Robert E. Lawrence; Revs. Lawrence R. Coakley; Luis R. Rodriguez; Deacon Joseph J. Kramer. In res., Very Rev. Thomas R. Haney.
Res., 1300 Bridge St., 17070. Tel: 717-774-5918; Fax: 717-774-5915.
School—1210 Bridge St., 17070. Tel: 717-774-7464; Fax: 717-774-3154.
Sisters of Mercy 4; Lay Teachers 21; Students 524.
Principals: Sr. Bernadette Bergen, R.S.M., (Elementary); Sr. Francine Gagne, I.H.M., (High School).
Catechesis/Religious Programs—Tel: 717-774-7296.
Students 395.
Convent—1200 Bridge St., 17070. Tel: 717-774-6583. Sisters of Mercy
Sisters 4.

New Freedom, York Co., St. John the Baptist (1841), Revs. Sylvan P. Capitani; Robert J. Kobularik; Deacon Michael Bahn.
Res., 315 N. Constitution Ave., 17349. Tel: 717-235-2156; Fax: 717-235-2223. [CEM]
Catechesis/Religious Programs—Tel: 717-235-2439.
Students 650.

New Holland, Lancaster Co., Our Lady of Lourdes (1972), Rev. Patrick J. McGarrity, C.SS.R.
Res., 737 Walnut St., 17557. Tel: 717-354-2540; Fax: 717-354-4170.
Catechesis/Religious Programs—Tel: 717-354-4686.
Students 241.

New Oxford, Adams Co., Immaculate Conception of the Blessed Virgin Mary (1852), Rev. Msgr. Francis J. Hudak.
Res., 106 Carlisle St., 17350. Tel: 717-624-4121; Fax: 717-624-9711. [CEM]
School—101 N. Peter St., 17350. Tel: 717-624-2061. Sr. Ann Leonard, Prin.
Lay Teachers 9; Students 174.
Catechesis/Religious Programs—Sr. Paula Mary D.R.E.
Students 141.
Convent—5 Carlisle St., 17350. Tel: 717-624-7531.

Northumberland, Northumberland Co., St. Thomas More (1955). Closed. See St. Monica, Sunbury.

Palmyra, Lebanon Co., Holy Spirit (1955), Rev. David L. Danneker, Ph.D.
Res., 245 W. Pine St., 17078. Tel: 717-838-3369; Fax: 717-838-3065.
Catechesis/Religious Programs—Mrs. Helen Remington, D.R.E.
Students 154.

Quarryville, Lancaster Co., St. Catherine of Siena (1843), Rev. Joseph C. Coyne; Deacon Ed Leszczynski.
Res., 15 E. Third St., 17566-1255. Tel: 717-786-2695. [CEM]
Catechesis/Religious Programs—Mrs. Diane Dalgaard, D.R.E.
Students 231.

Ranshaw, Northumberland Co., St. Anthony of Padua (1919). Closed. See Mother Cabrini, Shamokin.

Roaring Creek, Columbia Co., Our Lady of Mercy (1923), Rev. Thomas Ignatius Mannion.
Res., R.R. #1, Box 56, Catawissa, 17820. Tel: 717-799-5642. [CEM]

Catechesis/Religious Programs—Mrs. Margaret Jessick, D.R.E.
Students 66.

Rohrerstown, Lancaster Co., St. Leo the Great (1964), Very Rev. William J. Sullivan, V.F.; Rev. Kenneth G. Smith; Deacon Eugene Vannucci.
Res., 2427 Marietta Ave., Lancaster, 17601. Tel: 717-394-1742; Fax: 717-394-1779.
School—Tel: 717-392-2441. Mrs. Joyce Redington, Prin.
Lay Teachers 18; Students 286.
Catechesis/Religious Programs—Tel: 717-394-7354.
Students 631.

Selinsgrove, Snyder Co., St. Pius X (1964), Rev. Joseph A. Celia.
Res., 610 University Ave., 17870. Tel: 717-374-4113; Fax: 717-374-4113.
Catechesis/Religious Programs—Students 240.
Missions—Susquehanna, Snyder Co., Susquehanna University, 17870. Tel: 717-372-4113; Selinsgrove, Snyder Co., Selinsgrove Center, 17870.

Shamokin, Northumberland Co.,

1—ASSUMPTION OF THE BLESSED VIRGIN MARY, (1892) (Slovak). Closed. See Mother Cabrini, Shamokin.

2—ST. EDWARD, (1866). Closed. See Mother Cabrini, Shamokin.

3—ST. JOSEPH, (1913). Closed. See Our Lady of Hope, Coal Township.

4—ST. MICHAEL ARCHANGEL, (1894) (Lithuanian). Closed. See Mother Cabrini, Shamokin.

5—MOTHER CABRINI, (1995), Rev. David Grumsey, O.F.M.Conv.
Res., 214 N. Shamokin St., 17872. Tel: 717-648-4512; Fax: 717-648-1209. [JC 4]

6—ST. STANISLAUS KOSTKA, (1874) (Polish). Closed. See Mother Cabrini, Shamokin.

Shippensburg, Cumberland Co., Our Lady of the Visitation (1950), Rev. Lawrence W. Sherdel; John Boyle, Pastoral Assoc.
Res., 305 N. Prince St., 17257. Tel: 717-532-2912; Fax: 717-532-3905.
Catechesis/Religious Programs—Students 108.

South Mountain, Franklin Co., Most Holy Rosary. Closed. See St. Ignatius, Buchannon Valley.

Spring Grove, York Co., Sacred Heart (1976), Rev. Hugh J. McLaughlin.
Res., 152 N. Main St., Box 42, 17362. Tel: 717-225-1704.
Catechesis/Religious Programs—Tel: 717-225-6404. Peggy Rizzuto, D.R.E.
Students 146.

Steelton, Dauphin Co.,

1—ST. ANN, (1901) (Italian). Closed. See Prince of Peace, Steelton.

2—ASSUMPTION OF THE BLESSED VIRGIN MARY, (1898) (Croatian). Closed. See Prince of Peace, Steelton.

3—ST. JAMES, (1878). Closed. See Prince of Peace, Steelton.

4—ST. PETER, (1909) (Slovenian). Closed. See Prince of Peace, Steelton.

5—PRINCE OF PEACE, (1995), Revs. Samuel E. Houser; William Waltersheid; Deacon Michael Grella. In res., Very Rev. Paul C. Helwig.
Res., 815 S. Second St., 17113. Tel: 717-985-1330; Fax: 717-985-1333.
School—245 Reynders St., 17113. Tel: 717-939-6357; Fax: 717-939-3660. Mr. Ultan Ohman, Prin.

Sunbury, Northumberland Co., St. Michael Archangel (1863). Closed. See St. Monica, Sunbury.
St. Monica (1995), Rev. William T. Haviland.
Res., 20 N. Front St., 17801. Tel: 717-286-0761; Fax: 717-286-8588.
School—109 Market St., 17801. Tel: 717-286-5983; Fax: 717-286-7351. Theodore J Andrewlevich, Prin.
Lay Teachers 13; Students 239.
Catechesis/Religious Programs—Mrs. Peggy Walker, D.R.E.
Students 183.

Trevorton, Northumberland Co., St. Patrick (1850), Revs. Philip G. Burger; Edward J. Keating.
Res., 331 W. Shamokin St., 17881-1523. Tel: 717-797-8251. [CEM]
Catechesis/Religious Programs—Tel: 717-797-1882. Mrs. Bernadette Dry, D.R.E.
Students 72.

Waynesboro, Franklin Co., St. Andrew (1893), Rev. Thomas J. Hemler.
Res., 12 N. Broad St., P.O. Box 167, 17268. Tel: 717-762-1914; Fax: 717-762-3319. [CEM]
School—213 E. Main St., 17268. Tel: 717-762-3221. Mrs. Eileen M. Sullivan, Prin.
Sisters of SS. Cyril & Methodius 2; Lay Teachers 9; Students 144.
Catechesis/Religious Programs—Tel: 717-762-5958.
Students 185.
Convent—Tel: 717-762-4935.

Williamstown, Dauphin Co., Sacred Heart of Jesus (1875), Rev. Francis J. Karwacki.
Res., 140 E. Market St., 17098. Tel: 717-647-2645. [CEM][JC]
Catechesis/Religious Programs—Tel: 717-647-2447. Sr. Carlotta, R.S.M., D.R.E.
Students 87.

York, York Co.,

1—IMMACULATE CONCEPTION OF THE BLESSED VIRGIN MARY, (1852), Revs. Lawrence J. Hemler; Michael C. Letteer. Pastoral Assocs.: Deacon Catalino Gonzalez; Mrs. Marilynn Trauger.
Res., 309 S. George St., 17403. Tel: 717-845-7629; Fax: 717-845-2433. [CEM][JC]
Catechesis/Religious Programs—Tel: 717-846-6001. Marilynn Trauger, D.R.E.
Students 140.
Convent—26 E. College Ave., 17403. Tel: 717-848-1232.

2—ST. JOSEPH, (1913), Revs. John Daya, O.F.M.Cap.; Victor Kriley, O.F.M.Cap.; Reginald Russo, O.F.M.Cap. In res., Bro. Thomas Wells, O.F.M.Cap.
Res., 2935 Kingston Rd., 17402-4003. Tel: 717-755-7503; Fax: 717-757-1900.
School—2945 Kingston Rd., 17403. Tel: 717-755-1797; Fax: 717-751-0136. Sr. Dorita Slaughter, O.S.F., Prin.
Sisters 3; Lay Teachers 21; Students 365.
Catechesis/Religious Programs—Tel: 717-757-1707. Sr. Jean Holtz, S.S.J., D.R.E.
Students 594.
Convent—405 Quaker Dr., 17402. Tel: 717-757-3667. Sisters of St. Francis
Sisters 3. Missionary Sisters of the Sacred Heart.

3—ST. PATRICK, (1776), Revs. C. Anthony Miller; JohnBosco Ikemeh, O.P.; Sr. Monica Imgrund, R.S.M., Pastoral Assoc.; Deacon Sam Moschella. In res., Rev. William M. Cawley (GF).
Res., 231 S. Beaver St., 17403. Tel: 717-848-2007; Fax: 717-854-8263. [CEM]
School—219 S. Beaver St., 17403. Tel: 717-854-8263. Sr. Ann Harrison, I.H.M., Prin.
Sisters, Servants of the Immaculate Heart of Mary 2; Lay Teachers 10; Students 194.
Catechesis/Religious Programs—Tel: 717-854-6653. Mrs. Connie Egan, D.R.E.
Students 195.
Convent—Tel: 717-848-1911. Sisters, Servants of the Immaculate Heart of Mary
Sisters 7.

4—ST. ROSE OF LIMA, (1907), Revs. Thomas J. Hoke; Martin O. Moran, III; Thomas Macauley; Deacon Joseph Sferrella. In res., Rev. Carl T. Tancredi.
Res., 950 W. Market St., 17404. Tel: 717-846-4935; Fax: 717-843-4391. [JC]
School—944 W. Market St., 17404. Tel: 717-854-7979. Sr. Joan Mickey, Prin.
Sisters of St. Joseph 4; Lay Teachers 18; Students 291.
Catechesis/Religious Programs—Tel: 717-843-3043. D.R.E.: Patricia Drawbaugh; Sr. Jane Keller.
Students 442.
Convent—Tel: 717-854-0378. Sisters of St. Joseph
Sisters 14.

York Haven, York Co., Holy Infant (1972), Rev. Clarence A. Olszewski.
Res., 34 Third St., 17370. Tel: 717-266-5286.
Catechesis/Religious Programs—Tel: 717-266-1643.
Students 195.

Chaplains of Public Institutions

HARRISBURG. *Community General Osteopathic Hospital*. Vacant.
Harrisburg Hospital Tel: 717-782-3333. Rev. John A. Szada, Jr. Tel: 717-233-1014.
Polyclinic Medical Clinic Tel: 717-782-4141. Rev. John A. Szada, Jr. Tel: 717-233-1014.
State Hospital Pouch A, 17105. Tel: 717-787-9232. Deacon Frank Parr.

CAMP HILL. *State Correctional Institution* P.O. Box 200, 17011. Tel: 717-737-4531, Ext. 307. Deacon Manuel Velazquez.

DANVILLE. *Geisinger Medical Center* Tel: 717-275-2512. Rev. Francis Tamburro.
State Hospital P.O. Box 219, 17821. Tel: 717-275-7011. Rev. Thomas Ignatius Mannion Tel: 717-799-5642.

HERSHEY. *Milton J. Hershey Medical Center* 500 University Blvd., 17033. Tel: 717-534-8177. Rev. Stephen D. Weitzel Tel: 717-533-7168.

LANCASTER. *Lancaster County Prison* 625 E. King St., 17602. Tel: 717-534-8177. Deacon William J. Jordan.
Lancaster General Hospital and Lancaster Community Hospital. Rev. James Muthuplakel.

LEBANON. *Veterans Administration Hospital* R.D. No. 1, 17042. Tel: 717-272-6621. Rev. Dennis M. Young.

LEWISBURG. *U.S. Penitentiary* Tel: 717-523-1251. Robert Bierowski, Liason.

SELINSGROVE. *Selinsgrove Center* Box 500, 17870. Tel: 717-374-2911, Ext. 425. Rev. Joseph A. Celia; Deacon Samuel Sica.

SOUTH MOUNTAIN. *Restoration Center* Tel: 717-749-5773. Rev. Joeseph C. Carolin.

YORK. *York Hospital* 1001 S. George St., 17405. Tel: 717-771-2345. Rev. Lawrence Hemler.

On Duty Outside the Diocese:
Reverend Fathers—
Barrett, Edward J., Wadsworth VA Hospital, Los Angeles, CA 90073
Blackwell, Edward, 520 N.E. 20th St., #408, Fort Lauderdale, FL 33305-2195
Kemper, John C., S.S., Sts. Cyril & Methodius Seminary, 3535 Indian Tr., Orchard Lake, MI 48324
McLernon, Thomas M., Sacred Heart University, 5151 Park Ave., Fairfield, CT 06432-1000
Sperber, Timothy (MIA), St. Gregory Church, 200 N. University Dr., Plantation, FL 33324-2085
Topper, Charles J., 467 Bloomfield Ave., Bloomfield, CT 06002

Absent on Leave:
Reverend Fathers—
Bennett, Michael X.

Retired:
Reverend Monsignors—
Kujovsky, Thomas
McGough, Thomas J., Misericordia Convalescent Home, 998 S. Russell St., York, PA 17402. Tel: 717-757-3455
Topper, Vincent J., 915 S. Lincoln Ave., Lebanon, PA 17042. Tel: 717-273-1295
Reverend Fathers—
Beeman, James W.
Burakowski, Anthony E., 13 Pratt St., Fairfield, CT 06430
Farace, Frederick A., P.O. Box 276, Mount Carmel, PA 17851
McGinley, Anthony J.
Sawdy, Wallace E., 222 Herr St., Harrisburg, PA 17102
Zangari, Salvatore V.

Permanent Deacons:
Anders, Joseph L., St. Anne, Lancaster
Aull, Richard H., St. Matthew's, Dauphin
Bahn, Michael P., St. Joseph, York
Bankos, Stephen, St. Mary, York
Beighley, Ross W., St. Catherine of Siena, Quarryville
Bertollo, Edward L., Jr., Immaculate Conception BVM, Berwick
Clark, Charles W., St. Patrick, Harrisburg
Colonell, Arthur W., Our Mother of Perpetual Help, Ephrata
Culley, Matthew P., St. John Neumann, Lancaster
Dunn, J. Leo, St. Patrick, Harrisburg
Eckman, Frank M., St. Anne, Lancaster
Fedor, Thomas A., Holy Family, Harrisburg
Fine, Andrew V., St. Joseph, Mechanicsburg
Fitzpatrick, Edwin L., Our Lady of Lourdes, Enola
Flannery, Thomas H., St. Catherine, Harrisburg
Foerster, Jerome T., Holy Name of Jesus, Harrisburg
Gonzales, Catalino, Spanish-Speaking Apostolate, Harrisburg; Cristo Salvador, York
Gorman, Francis, Good Shepherd, Camp Hill
Grella, Michael A., St. Peter, Steelton
Hackman, Donald D., St. James, Lititz
Hayes, Arthur Hull, Jr.
Jordan, William J., Lancaster County Prison & St. Anthony of Padua, Lancaster
Kenski, Francis G., Holy Spirit Hospital, Camp Hill; Our Lady of Good Counsel, Marysville
Kole, Gerard J., Chap., County Nursing Home, Cumberford; County Prison, Carlisle
Kramer, Joseph J., St. Theresa, New Cumberland
Lawrence, Joseph F., Annunciation BVM, McSherrystown
Leszczynski, Edward A., St. Catherine of Siena, Quarryville
Light, Martin C., St. Philip, Millersville
Lydon, Michael, St. Peter, Columbia
MacAdam, Morris D., Sacred Heart of Jesus, Harrisburg
Mack, Robert P., St. Edward, Shamokin
Marroquin, Miguel, Spanish-Speaking Apostolate, Harrisburg
Miller, Gene R., Immaculate Conception BVM, New Oxford

Mordecai, Philip B.
Moschella, Sabino E., St. Patrick, York
Mowery, John, Our Lady of the Blessed Sacrament, Harrisburg
Oliver, Thomas S., St. Joan of Arc, Hershey
Parr, Frank J., Harrisburg State Hospital, Harrisburg
Paruso, John L., St. Joseph, Mechanicsburg
Ramos, Felix, San Juan Bautista, Lancaster
Rocco, John, St. Jude Thaddeus, Mifflintown; Sacred Heart, Lewistown
Runkle, Ralph H., St. Patrick, York
Ryan, Richard A., St. Paul the Apostle, Annville
Sahd, Joseph A., St. Joseph Hospital, Lancaster
Santiago, Expidito, San Juan Bautista, Lancaster
Sferrella, Joseph, St. Rose of Lima, York
Sica, Samuel A., St. Pius X & Selinsgrove Center, Selinsgrove
Smith, Raymond, Immaculate Heart, Abbottstown
Sneeringer, James, St. Francis Xavier, Gettysburg
Vannucci, Eugene D., St. Leo the Great, Rohrerstown
Velazquez, Manuel, Camp Hill State Correctional Institution, Camp Hill
Weaver, John A., St. Joseph, Dallastown
Weaver, Richard J., St. Joseph, Bonneauville
Weaver, Robert E., St. Joseph Hospital, Lancaster
Wentzel, Richard W., Assumption BVM & Lebanon Catholic High School, Lebanon
Whale, William E., St. Catherine Laboure, Harrisburg
Wrabel, Joseph J., Holy Name, Harrisburg

INSTITUTIONS LOCATED IN THE DIOCESE

[A] HIGH SCHOOLS

HARRISBURG. *Bishop McDevitt High School*, 2200 Market St., 17103-2499. Tel: 717-236-7973.
E-mail: mcdevitthbg@juno.com
Mr. John D. Brixius, Prin. Sisters 8; Lay Teachers 44; Students 709.

CAMP HILL. *Trinity High School*, 3601 Simpson Ferry Rd., 17011. Tel: 717-761-1116; Fax: 717-761-7309.
E-mail: fgagne@trinityhs.k12.pa.us
Web site: www.paonline.com/trinity
Sr. Francine Gagne, I.H.M., Prin. Sisters 5; Lay Teachers 32; Students 555.

COAL TOWNSHIP. *Our Lady of Lourdes Regional High School*, 2001 Clinton Ave., 17866-1699. Tel: 717-644-0375; Fax: 717-644-7655.
E-mail: lourdes@postoffice.ptd.net
Web site: http://home.ptd.net/ lourdes/
Sr. Rita O'Leary, I.H.M., Prin. Sisters 5; Lay Teachers 25; Students 292.

DANVILLE. *St. Cyril Academy*, Railroad St., 17821. Tel: 717-275-1505. Sr. Mary Anne Nemic, SS.C.M., Prin. Sisters of SS. Cyril & Methodius 8; Lay Teachers 7; Girls 30.

LANCASTER. *Lancaster Catholic High School*, 650 Juliette Ave., 17601. Tel: 717-393-0454. Mr. Dermot Garrett, Prin. Sisters 3; Lay Teachers 37; Students 646.

LEBANON. *Catholic Junior-Senior High School*, 1400 Chestnut St., 17042. Tel: 717-273-3731. Mr. Mark J. Freund, Prin. Sisters of St. Joseph 2; Lay Teachers 24; Students 341; Total Staff 7.

MCSHERRYSTOWN. *Delone Catholic High School*, 140 S. Oxford Ave., 17344. Tel: 717-637-5969; Fax: 717-637-0442. Mrs. Maureen C. Thiec, Ed.D., Prin. Sisters 3; Lay Teachers 32; Students 530.

YORK. *York Catholic High School*, 601 E. Springettsbury Ave., 17403. Tel: 717-846-8871. Rev. William M. Cawley (GF), Teacher. Priests 2; Sisters 7; Lay Teachers 37; Total Staff 50; Students 664.

[B] CONSOLIDATED ELEMENTARY SCHOOLS

HARRISBURG. *Cathedral School*, 212 State St., 17101. Tel: 717-234-3797. Sr. Mary Agnes Shurer, S.C.C., Prin.
Upper School. (Includes Kindergarten). Sisters 1; Lay Teachers 5.
Lower School. Sisters 1; Lay Teachers 3.

LEBANON. *Our Lady of the Valley School*, 740 Willow St., 17042. Tel: 717-272-8961. Mrs. Karen Smoker, Prin. Sisters 1; Lay Teachers 21; Total Staff 32; Students 418.

MOUNT CARMEL. *Holy Spirit Consolidated School*, 250 West Ave., 17851. Tel: 717-339-3823; Fax: 717-339-0606.
E-mail: dove@sunlink.net
Web site: www.sunlink.net/~dove
Sr. Mary Rene Procopio, Prin. Sisters 2; Lay Teachers 10; Students 222.

SHAMOKIN. *Queen of Peace Consolidated School*. (Grades PreK-8), 201 N. Shamokin St., 17872. Tel: 717-648-6672; 648-0182 (Convent). Sr. Jeanne Patrick, I.H.M., Prin. Serves the parishes of Our Lady of Hope, Coal Township; Queen of the Most Holy Rosary, Elysburg; Mother Cabrini, Shamokin; and St. Patrick, Treverton. Sisters 5; Lay Teachers 18; Students 335.

[C] PRESCHOOLS AND DAY NURSERIES

MCSHERRYSTOWN. *St. Joseph Academy*. (Preschool), Main St., 17344. Tel: 717-637-2227. Sisters of St. Joseph. Sr. Alma Bernadette Hurley, S.S.J., Dir. Sisters 1; Students 30.

YORK. *Holy Child Nursery*, 1141 E. Market St., 17403. Tel: 717-848-1691. Daughters of Our Lady of Mercy. Sr. M. Clare, D.M., Admin. Sisters 5; Lay Aides 5; Students 65.

[D] RELIGIOUS RESOURCE CENTERS

CAMP HILL. *Trinity High School*, 17011. Tel: 717-761-1116; Fax: 717-761-7309.
Web site: www.paonline.com/trinity

COLUMBIA. *Religious Education Resource Center*, St. Joseph Convent, 3950 Columbia Ave., 17512-9714. Tel: 717-285-3217. Sr. Hilda Marie, A.S.C.

DANVILLE. *Villa Sacred Heart*, 17821-1698. Tel: 717-275-7513; Fax: 717-275-5997. Sr. Virginia Zapotocky, SS.C.M.

MCSHERRYSTOWN. *Delone Catholic High School*, 140 S. Oxford Ave., 17344. Tel: 717-632-7510. Religious Education Resource Center. Sr. Ann Vincentia Snyder, S.S.J.

[E] CATHOLIC CHARITIES COUNSELING & FIELD SERVICES

HARRISBURG. *Department for Catholic Charities Counseling/Field Services*, P.O. Box 3551, 17105.
Adoption Services, 4800 Union Deposit Rd., P.O. Box 3551, 17105. Tel: 717-657-4804. Kay Eisenhour, M.S.W., L.S.W., Prog. Dir.
Capital Region Office, 223 North St., 17101. Tel: 717-233-7978. Frank Koerber, M.S., District Dir.
Cenacle Youth Shelter, 1611 Boas St., 17103. Tel: 717-236-8211. Tim Wolfe, B.A., Prog. Dir.
Evergreen House and Day Care Program, 100 Evergreen St., 17104. Tel: 717-238-6343. Program Directors: Willamae Williams; Sr. Marie Aimee Finnegan, R.S.M.
Specialized Foster Care, 806-C South 29th St., 17111. Tel: 717-654-7115. Nancy Jamison, M.S.W., Prog. Dir.
Immigration and Refugee Services, 900 N. 17th St., 17103. Tel: 717-232-0568. Norman Lederer, Prog. Dir.
Interfaith Shelter for Homeless Families, Harrisburg St. Hospital, Hemlock Bldg. #26, 17105. Tel: 717-236-6783. Michele O'Neill, Prog. Dir.
Lourdeshouse Maternity Services, 100 B. Livingston St., Enhaut, 17113. Tel: 717-986-9510. Marilyn Bellesfield, Prog. Dir.
Paradise School, R.D. 1, Box 341, Abbottstown, 17301. Tel: 717-259-9537. Michael Langley, M.S., Prog. Dir.
Chambersburg Office, 336 Philadelphia Ave., Chambersburg, 17201. Tel: 717-263-3765. Carolyn George, M.Div., District Dir.
Chambersburg Family Outreach, 336 Philadelphia Ave., Chambersburg, 17201. Tel: 717-264-2332. Wendy Mellott, M.S., Prog. Dir.
Lancaster Office, 925 N. Duke St., Lancaster, 17602. Tel: 717-299-3659. Kirk Reider, A.C.S.W., L.S.W., District Dir.
Intensive Day Treatment, 47 S. Mulberry St., Lancaster, 17603. Tel: 717-295-9630. Joe Paskovich, M.S., Prog. Dir.
Lancaster In-Home Intensive Services, 417 Poplar St., Lancaster, 17603. Tel: 717-392-3619. Chris Vandenberg, M.H.S., Prog. Dir.
Lebanon Office, 1431 Walnut St., Lebanon, 17042. Tel: 717-273-8514. Kirk Reider, A.C.S.W., L.S.W., District Dir.
Lebanon Family FOCUS, 1431 Walnut St., Lebanon, 17042. Tel: 717-273-3011. D.J. Dunlap, M.S.W., Prog. Dir.
Northern Office, 900 N. Shamokin St., Shamokin, 17872. Tel: 717-648-6431. Loretta Stefanovage, M.S.W., L.S.W., District Dir.
York Office, 253 E. Market St., York, 17403. Tel: 717-845-2696. Donna Dillon, M.S.W., District Dir.
York Intensive Family Services, 253 E. Market St., York, 17403. Tel: 717-845-2696. Connie Krout, M.H.S., Prog. Dir.
HOPE House, 1509 Cresent Ave., Lancaster, 17601. Tel: 717-293-9089. Judy Wendler, L.P.N.A.P., Co-ord. Total Assisted 600; Total Staff 6.

[F] GENERAL HOSPITALS

CAMP HILL. *Holy Spirit Hospital and Community Mental Health Center*, 503 N. 21st St., 17011-2288. Tel: 717-763-2100; Fax: 717-763-2183.
E-mail: mcicco@hsh.org
For a complete listing, refer to the Hospitals section.

LANCASTER. *St. Joseph Hospital and Health Care Center*, 250 College Ave., P.O. Box 3509, 17604. Tel: 717-291-8211; Fax: 717-291-8516
For a complete listing, refer to the Hospitals section.

[G] CONVALESCENT & RETIREMENT HOMES

HARRISBURG. *Villa Teresa Nursing Home*, 1051 Avila Rd., 17109. Tel: 717-652-5900; Fax: 717-652-5941
For a complete listing, refer to the Special Care Facilities section.

COLUMBIA. *St. Anne's Home*, 3952 Columbia Ave., 17512-9715. Tel: 717-285-5443
For a complete listing, refer to the Special Care Facilities section.

DANVILLE. *Holy Family Convent and Infirmary*, One Montour St., 17821. Tel: 717-275-3141
For a complete listing, refer to the Special Care Facilities section.
Maria Hall, Maria Hall Dr., 17821. Tel: 717-275-1120
For a complete listing, refer to the Special Care Facilities section.
Maria Joseph Manor, 875 Montour Blvd., 17821. Tel: 717-275-4221; Fax: 717-275-4711
For a complete listing, refer to the Special Care Facilities section.

LEBANON. *Villa Vianney*, 915 S. Lincoln Ave., 17042. Tel: 717-273-1295
For a complete listing, refer to the Special Care Facilities section.

YORK. *Misericordia Convalescent Home*, 998 S. Russell St., 17402. Tel: 717-755-1964
For a complete listing, refer to the Special Care Facilities section.

[H] MONASTERIES AND RESIDENCES OF PRIESTS AND BROTHERS

EPHRATA. *St. Clement's Mission House*, P.O. Box 209, 17522-0209. Tel: 717-733-6596; Fax: 717-733-0502.
E-mail: omph@ptd.net
Redemptorist Fathers and Brothers. Very Rev. Arthur P. Gildea, C.SS.R.; Revs. Edward W. Jackson, C.SS.R.; John J. Creaven, C.SS.R.; William F. Rosner, C.SS.R.; Patrick J. McGarrity, C.SS.R.; Gerard J. Szymkowiak, C.SS.R.; John J. Dorff, C.SS.R.; John H. Wright.
Mission Preaching Band: Revs. Arthur J. Mahoney, C.SS.R.; John W. Kelly, C.SS.R.

[I] CONVENTS AND RESIDENCES FOR SISTERS

HARRISBURG. *Bishops' Residence*, 4800-A Union Deposit Rd., 17105. Tel: 717-671-9323. Sr. M. Patricia Bonner, A.S.C., Supr. Adorers of the Blood of Christ 2.
Immaculate Heart of Mary Convent, 603 N. Second St., 17101. Tel: 717-236-4821. Sr. Rose Patrice Kuhn, I.H.M. Sisters, Servants of the Immaculate Heart of Mary 12.
St. Joseph Convent, 605 N. Second St., 17101. Tel: 717-232-0204. Sisters of Christian Charity. Sr. Mary Agnes Shurer, S.C.C., Supr. Sisters of St. Francis (Aston, PA) 1; Total in Residence 7; Total Staff 7.
Saint Margaret Mary Convent, 2836 Herr St., 17103. Tel: 717-232-0204. Adorers of the Blood of Christ. Total in Residence 5; Total Staff 4.

COLUMBIA. *Adorers of the Blood of Christ*, 3950 Columbia Ave., 17512-9714. Tel: 717-285-4536; Fax: 717-285-9789.
E-mail: agathagrft@redrose.net
Province Center of the Adorers of the Blood of Christ. Sr. Agatha Marie Groft, A.S.C., Prov. Supr.
The Precious Blood Spiritual Center, 3950 Columbia Ave., 17512-9714. Tel: 717-285-2215; Fax: 717-285-9789. S. Constance Sophy, R.S.M., Dir. Columbia Province 83.

DANVILLE. *Villa Sacred Heart*, 17821-1698. Tel: 717-275-3581; 275-4929; Fax: 717-275-5997. Motherhouse of the Sisters of SS. Cyril and Methodius. Sr. M. Paracleta Amrich, SS.C.M., Gen. Supr.; Rev. Frederick A. Farace, Chap. Sisters 42.
Villa Sacred Heart Formation Center. Tel: 717-275-3702. Sr. Virginia DeWan, SS.C.M., Vocation Dir.
Villa Sacred Heart Music Conservatory, 17821-1698. Tel: 717-275-5185. Sr. M. Michaelette, SS.C.M., Dir.
Villa Preschool and Kindergarten, 17821-1698. Tel: 717-275-1667. Sr. Judy Therese, SS.C.M., Prin. This building houses the Diocesan Religious Education Resource Center.
Religious Education Resource Center. Tel: 717-275-7513. Sr. Virginia Zapotocky, SS.C.M., Dir.

ELYSBURG. *Carmelite Monastery*, 70 Monastery Rd., 17824-9697. Tel: 717-672-2935. Discalced Carmelite Nuns. Sr. Christine O'Brien, O.C.D., Prioress. Nuns in Solemn Vows 18.

LANCASTER. *Monastery of the Dominican Nuns of the Perpetual Rosary*, 1834 Lititz Pike, 17601-6585. Tel: 717-569-2104. Mother Mary Veronica, O.P.,

Prioress; Rev. Francis R. Mullin, O.P., Chap. Solemnly Professed Nuns 13; Novices 2; Postulants 1.
St. Francis Convent, 903 W. Walnut St., 17603. Tel: 717-392-1740. Sisters of St. Francis of Philadelphia 5.

LEBANON. *Assumption-Hill Convent*, 1430 Chestnut St., 17042. Tel: 717-272-8262. Sr. S. Loretta Marchetti, S.S.J., Supr. Sisters of St. Joseph 4.

[J] QUASI-PARISHES

LANCASTER. *Iglesia de San Juan Bautista*, 425 S. Duke St., 17602. Tel: 717-392-4118. Very Rev. Bernardo Pistone, Diocesan Vicar for the Hispanics; Revs. Ignacio Palomino; Allan F. Wolfe; Deacons Expedito Santos; Manuel Velazquez; Felix Ramos.

[K] NEWMAN CENTERS

HARRISBURG. *Catholic Campus Ministry*, P.O. Box 3557, 17105-3557. Tel: 717-657-4804. Very Rev. Joseph F. Gotwalt, Coord.
Lebanon Valley College, 125 S. Spruce St., Annville, 17003. Tel: 717-867-1525. Rev. John D. Hoke.
Bloomsburg University of Pennsylvania, 353 College Hill, Bloomsburg, 17815. Tel: 717-784-3123. Rev. Lawrence J. McNeil; Anita McGowan.
Dickinson School of Law, 140 E. Pomfret St., Carlisle, 17013. Tel: 717-243-4411. Rev. Joseph T. Scanlin.
Wilson College Chambersburg, 320 Philadelphia Ave., Chambersburg, 17201. Rev. Msgr. Thomas R. Brenner. Tel: 717-264-6317.
Elizabethtown College, Park St. & Cherry Ave., Elizabethtown, 17022. Tel: 717-367-1255. Rev. Joseph D. Blascovich; Thomas Fertal.
Gettysburg College, 12 E. Hanover St., Gettysburg, 17325-0136. Tel: 717-334-2510. Rev. Brian Conrad; Susan Collinge.
Hershey Medical Center, 359 W. Areba Ave., 17033. Tel: 717-533-7168. Rev. Stephen D. Weitzel.
Franklin and Marshall College, Lancaster, 227 N. George St., Millersville, 17551. Tel: 717-291-3880. Rev. William C. Forrey.
Bucknell University, Newman Center, 610 St. George St., Lewisburg, 17837. Tel: 717-524-7951. Rev. John J. Kelly, O.S.F.S.
Penn State University, Harrisburg Campus, 401 Conewago St., Middletown, 17057. Tel: 717-944-3133.
Millersville University, Newman Center, 227 N. George St., Millersville, 17551. Tel: 717-872-3350. Rev. William C. Forrey.
Susquehanna University Catholic Campus Ministry, 610 University Ave., Selinsgrove, 17870. Tel: 717-374-4113. Rev. Joseph A. Celia.
Shippensburg University, 305 N. Prince St., Shippensburg, 17257. Tel: 717-532-1244. Rev. Lawrence Sherdel; Roxanne Dennis.
Penn State University, Mont Alto Campus, South Mountain, Campus Ministry Office, Mont Alto, 17237. Tel: 717-749-6135. Roxanne Dennis.
Penn State University, York Campus, 850 E. Princess St., York, 17403. Tel: 717-848-1797. Rev. Carl T. Tancredi, D.Min.
York College, 950 W. Market St., York, 17404. Tel: 717-846-4935. Rev. Carl T. Tancredi, D.Min.

[L] MISCELLANEOUS LISTINGS

HARRISBURG. *Pennsylvania Catholic Conference*, 223 North St., P.O. Box 2835, 17105. Tel: 717-238-9613; Fax: 717-238-1473.
Pennsylvania Catholic Health Association, 223 North St., P.O. Box 2835, 17105. Tel: 717-238-9613; Fax: 717-238-1473.
E-mail: PennCHA@aol.com
Sr. Clare Christi Schiefer, O.S.F., Pres.

LANCASTER. *Neumann Services, Inc.*, 830 Marietta Ave., 17603. Tel: 717-291-8395. Miss Karen M. Leque, Dir.

PHILADELPHIA. *St. Joseph Village Corporation*, Mount Saint Joseph Convent, 9701 Germantown Ave., 19118-2694. Village location, 90 Main St., McSherrystown, 17344. Sr. Eugenie Madeleine Gaddi, Gen. Sec.

SHIREMANSTOWN. *Trinity Spiritual Center*, 3609 Simpson Ferry Rd., 17011. Tel: 717-761-7355. Mrs. Mary Ann O'Donnell, Admin.; Mrs. Esther Fitzgerald, Facility Mgr. Total Staff 3.

RELIGIOUS INSTITUTES OF MEN REPRESENTED IN THE DIOCESE

For further details refer to the corresponding bracketed number in the Religious Institutes of Men or Women section.

[0200]—*Benedictine Monks.*—O.S.B.
[0470]—*The Capuchin Friars.*—O.F.M.Cap.
[0480]—*Conventual Franciscans.* (Buffalo, NY).—O.F.M.Conv.
[0650]—*Holy Ghost Fathers.* (Eastern Prov.).—C.S.Sp.
[0690]—*Jesuit Fathers and Brothers.*—S.J.
[1120]—*Missionaries of the Sacred Hearts of Jesus and Mary.*—M.SS.CC.
[0920]—*Oblates of St. Francis De Sales.* (American Prov.).—O.S.F.S.
[0430]—*Order of Preachers (Dominicans).*—O.P.
[1070]—*Redemptorist Fathers.* (Baltimore Prov.).—C.SS.R.
[0700]—*St. Joseph's Society of the Sacred Heart.*—S.S.J.
[1060]—*Society of the Precious Blood.* (Cincinnati Prov.).—C.PP.S.
[0560]—*Third Order Regular of Saint Francis.* (Prov. of the Most Sacred Heart).—T.O.R.

RELIGIOUS INSTITUTES OF WOMEN REPRESENTED IN THE DIOCESE

[0100]—*Adorers of the Blood of Christ.*—A.S.C.
[1810]—*Bernardine Sisters of the Third Order of St. Francis.*—O.S.F.
[1920]—*Congregation of the Sisters of Holy Cross.*—C.S.C.
[0890]—*Daughters of Our Lady of Mercy.*—D.M.
[0420]—*Discalced Carmelite Nuns.*—O.C.D.
[1050]—*Dominican Contemplative Nuns.*—O.P.
[1170]—*Felician Sisters.*—C.S.S.F.
[1470]—*Franciscan Sisters of St. Joseph.*—F.S.S.J.
[2575]—*Institute of the Sisters of Mercy of the Americas.*—R.S.M.
[2970]—*School Sisters of Notre Dame.*—S.S.N.D.
[0660]—*Sisters of Christian Charity.*—S.C.C.
[3780]—*Sisters of Saints Cyril and Methodius.*—SS.C.M.
[1650]—*The Sisters of St. Francis of Philadelphia.*—O.S.F.
[3830-13]—*Sisters of St. Joseph.*—C.S.J.
[2110]—*Sisters of the Humility of Mary.*—H.M.
[2170]—*Sisters, Servants of the Immaculate Heart of Mary.*—I.H.M.

NECROLOGY

† Ceponis, Joseph A., Lebanon, PA, St. Benedict the Abbot. —Died June 11, 1997.
† Kealy, Rev. Msgr. Joseph P., (Retired). —Died July 19, 1997.
† Lentocha, Rev. Msgr. George V., Middletown, PA, Seven Sorrows of the B.V.M. —Died May 26, 1997.
† McGough, Rev. Msgr. Thomas J., (Retired). —Died Aug. 29, 1997.
† Procopio, Charles A., Mount Carmel, PA, Our Lady of Mt. Carmel. —Died July 18, 1997.
† Taylor, Rev. Msgr. Francis J., New Cumberland, PA, St. Theresa of the Infant Jesus. —Died June 7, 1997.

Archdiocese of Hartford

(Archidioecesis Hartfortiensis)

Most Reverend

DANIEL A. CRONIN, S.T.D.

Archbishop of Hartford; ordained December 20, 1952; appointed Titular Bishop of Egnatia and Auxiliary Bishop of Boston June 10, 1968; ordained Bishop September 12, 1968; transferred to Fall River October 30, 1970; installed December 16, 1970; transferred to Hartford December 10, 1991; installed January 28, 1992. *Office: 134 Farmington Ave., Hartford, CT, 06105-3784.* Tel.: 860-541-6491; Fax: 860-541-6293.

Most Reverend

PETER A. ROSAZZA, D.D., V.G.

Auxiliary Bishop of Hartford and Titular Bishop of Oppido Nuovo; ordained June 29, 1961; appointed February 28, 1978; ordained Bishop June 24, 1978. *Office & Res.: 1450 Chapel St., New Haven, CT, 06511.* Tel.: 203-789-5970.

Most Reverend

CHRISTIE A. MACALUSO, D.D., V.G.

Auxiliary Bishop of Hartford and Titular Bishop of Grassy Valley; ordained May 22, 1971; appointed March 18, 1997; ordained Bishop June 10, 1997. *Office: 134 Farmington Ave., Hartford, CT, 06105-3784.* Tel.: 860-541-6491; Fax: 860-541-6293.

Chancery Office: 134 Farmington Ave., Hartford, CT, 06105-3784. Tel.: 860-541-6491; Fax: 860-541-6309.

Web site address: http://www.archdiocese-hartford.org

E-mail address: chancllr@connix.com

ESTABLISHED NOVEMBER 28, 1843; CREATED ARCHDIOCESE AUGUST 6, 1953.

Square Miles 2,288.

Corporate Title: *"The Hartford Roman Catholic Diocesan Corporation."*

Comprises the Counties of Hartford, Litchfield and New Haven in the State of Connecticut.

For legal titles of parishes and archdiocesan institutions, consult the Chancery Office.

STATISTICAL OVERVIEW

Personnel	
Archbishop	1
Auxiliary Bishops	2
Priests: Diocesan Active in Diocese	301
Priests: Active Outside Diocese	16
Priests: Diocesan in Foreign Missions	1
Priests: Retired, Sick or Absent	98
Number of Diocesan Priests	416
Religious Priests in Diocese	113
Extern Priests in Diocese	15
Ordinations:	
Diocesan Priests	2
Religious Priests	1
Transitional Deacons	6
Permanent Deacons in Diocese	333
Total Brothers	46
Total Sisters	995
Parishes	
Parishes	220
With Resident Pastor:	
Resident Diocesan Priests	192
Resident Religious Priests	20
Without Resident Pastor:	
Administered by Priests	8
Missions	4
Closed Parishes	2
Professional Ministry Personnel:	
Brothers	2
Sisters	36
Lay Ministers	94
Welfare	
Catholic Hospitals	3
Total Assisted	715,286
Homes for the Aged	6
Total Assisted	855
Residential Care of Children	1
Total Assisted	500
Day Care and Extended Day Care Centers	1
Total Assisted	80
Specialized Homes	1
Total Assisted	8
Special Centers for Social Services	20
Total Assisted	24,000
Residential Care of Disabled	8
Total Assisted	34
Educational	
Seminaries, Diocesan	1
Students from This Diocese	6
Diocesan Students in Other Seminaries	10
Seminaries, Religious	1
Students Religious	145
Total Seminarians	161
Colleges and Universities	3
Total Students	3,920
High Schools, Diocesan and Parish	4
Total Students	1,851
High Schools, Private	7
Total Students	3,062
Elementary Schools, Diocesan and Parish	70
Total Students	18,831
Elementary Schools, Private	2
Total Students	330
Non-residential Schools for the Disabled	1
Total Students	47
Catechesis/Religious Education:	
High School Students	8,619
Elementary Students	43,752
Total Students Under Catholic Instruction	80,573
Teachers in the Diocese:	
Priests	17
Brothers	4
Sisters	111
Lay Teachers	1,207
Vital Statistics	
Receptions into the Church:	
Infant Baptism Totals	10,956
Adult Baptism Totals	256
Received into Full Communion	370
First Communions	10,354
Confirmations	7,402
Marriages:	
Catholic	2,770
Interfaith	563
Total Marriages	3,333
Deaths	8,840
Total Catholic Population	756,663
Total Population	1,806,705

Former Bishops—Rt. Rev. WILLIAM TYLER, D.D., first Bishop; cons. March 17, 1844; died June 18, 1849.—Rt. Rev. BERNARD O'REILLY, D.D., second Bishop; cons. Nov. 10, 1850 perished at sea, Jan., 1856.—Rt. Rev. FRANCIS P. MCFARLAND, D.D., third Bishop; cons. March 14, 1858; died Oct. 12, 1874.—Rt. Rev. THOMAS GALBERRY, D.D., fourth Bishop; cons. March 19, 1876; died Oct. 10, 1878.—Rt. Rev. LAWRENCE S. MCMAHON, D.D., fifth Bishop; cons. Aug. 10, 1879; died Aug. 21, 1893.—Rt. Rev. MICHAEL TIERNEY, D.D., sixth Bishop; cons. Feb. 22, 1894; died Oct. 5, 1908.—Most Rev. JOHN J. NILAN, D.D., seventh Bishop; cons. April 28, 1910; died April 13, 1934.—Most Rev. MAURICE F. MCAULIFFE, D.D., eighth Bishop; ord. July 29, 1900; appt. Auxiliary to the Bishop of Hartford, Dec. 17, 1925; cons. April 28, 1926; appt. Bishop of Hartford, April 25, 1934; installed May 29, 1934; died Dec. 15, 1944.—Most Rev. HENRY J. O'BRIEN, D.D., ninth Bishop, first Archbishop; ord. July 8, 1923; appt. Titular Bishop of Sita and Auxiliary to Bishop of Hartford, March 19, 1940; cons. May 14, 1940; appt. Bishop of Hartford, April 7, 1945; appt. Archbishop of Hartford, Aug. 6, 1953; appt. at Pontifical Throne, April 29, 1955; resigned and appt. Titular Archbishop of Utina, Nov. 20, 1968 Given title "Former Archbishop of Hartford", Nov. 14, 1970; died July 23, 1976.—Most Rev. JOHN F. WHEALON, D.D., S.T.L., S.S.L., tenth Bishop, second Archbishop; ord. May 26, 1945; appt. Titular Bishop of Andrapa and Auxiliary of Cleveland, June 2, 1961; cons. July 6, 1961; appt. Bishop of Erie, Nov. 30, 1966; installed March 7, 1967; appt. Archbishop of Hartford, Dec. 28, 1968; installed March 19, 1969; died Aug. 2, 1991.

Vicars General—Most Rev. PETER A. ROSAZZA, D.D.; Most Rev. CHRISTIE A. MACALUSO, D.D.

Episcopal Vicars—Rev. Msgr. DANIEL J. PLOCHARCZYK, Hartford Vicariate; Rev. Msgr. JAMES G. COLEMAN,

New Haven Vicariate; Rev. Msgr. JOSEPH A. DEVINE, Waterbury Vicariate.

Chancery Office—134 Farmington Ave., Hartford, 06105-3784. Tel: 860-541-6491; Fax: 860-541-6293 (Bishop's Office); Fax: 860-541-6309 (Chancery). All applications for dispensations and correspondence on diocesan business should be sent to this address. Office Hours: Mon.-Fri. 8:30-4:30.

Moderator of the Curia—Most Rev. CHRISTIE A. MACALUSO.

Chancellor—Rev. Msgr. THOMAS M. GINTY.

Vice-Chancellor—Rev. ROBERT B. VARGO, J.C.L.

Archbishop's Delegate for Special Needs—Sr. HELEN MARGARET FEENEY, C.S.J.

Chief Financial Officer—MICHAEL R. ST. DENIS C.P.A.

Accounts Manager—THERESA MROCZKOWSKI.

Accounts Payable—ROBERT D. NEWBERY.

Accounts Receivable—MARIE C. LUTHER.

Group Benefits—KATHLEEN A. ANDERSON.

Archivist—Sr. MARJORIE FALLON, R.S.M.

Secretary to the Archbishop—Rev. Msgr. THOMAS M. GINTY.

Metropolitan Tribunal—134 Farmington Ave., Hartford, 06105-3784. Tel: 860-541-6491.

Judicial Vicar (Officialis)—Rev. JOHN J. MCCARTHY, J.C.L., J.D.

Adjutant Judicial Vicar (Vice Officialis)—Rev. ALVIN J. LEBLANC, J.C.L.

Defenders of the Bond—Revs. CHRISTOPHER M. FORD, J.C.L.; MICHAEL H. GOSSELIN, S.T.M., J.C.L.

Promoter of Justice—Rev. ROBERT B. VARGO, J.C.L.

Judges—Rev. Msgr. WILLIAM J. MULLEN, J.C.D.; Revs. LAWRENCE G. WRENN, J.C.D.; JAMES F. KINNANE, J.C.L.; THOMAS J. BARRY, J.C.L.

Case Instructors (part-time)—Revs. LAWRENCE R. BOCK; BRADFORD COLTON; WILLIAM E. DUDACK; JOHN F. EDWARDS; RONALD A. FERRARO; GENE E. GIANELLI; VITTORIO GUERRERA; BERNARD KILLEEN; LEONARD KVEDAS; DANIEL MCLEAREN; TIMOTHY A. O'BRIEN; THOMAS E. PTASZYNSKI; THOMAS J. SAS; BRIAN A. SHAW; RONALD T. SMITH; ADAM C. SUBOCZ; ROBERT F. TUCKER; WILLIAM C. WHALEN; PETER J. ZIZKA; Deacon PAUL B. LAUER; Sr. IRENE FORTIER, D.H.S.; Mr. ANTHONY SYLVESTER; Ms. DIAN GRANT.

Secretary—CAROLE BERTRAND.

College of Consultors—Most Rev. PETER A. ROSAZZA, D.D., V.G.; Most Rev. CHRISTIE A. MACALUSO; Rev. Msgr. DANIEL J. PLOCHARCZYK; Rev. Msgr. JOSEPH A. DEVINE; Rev. Msgr. JAMES G. COLEMAN; Revs. CHRISTOPHER M. TIANO; HOWARD M. NASH.

Deans—Hartford Vicariate: Rev. RICHARD R. RUSSELL, Farmington Valley; Rev. FRANCIS T. CARTER, New Britain; Rev. NICHOLAS J. CESARO, Hartford; Rev. HENRY P. CODY, Suburban Hartford; Rev. JOHN S. GOLAS, Manchester; Rev. ROBERT T. RUSSO, Enfield New Haven Vicariate: Rev. DAVID J. BARANOWSKI, Hamden-North Haven; Rev. VINCENT A. BROWN, East Shore Line; Rev. ARTHUR J. DUPONT, Meriden; Rev. THOMAS A. SIEVEL, West Shore Line; Rev. HOWARD J. NASH, New Haven Waterbury Vicariate: Rev. JOHN M. COONEY, Suburban Waterbury; Rev. LEONARD J. KVEDAS, Ansonia-Derby; Rev. JOSEPH E. LOONEY, Waterbury; Rev. JAMES F. PILON, Litchfield; Rev. ROBERT J. ROUSSEAU, Bristol; Rev. PHILIP A. SHERIDAN, Naugatuck-Cheshire.

Ecumenical Affairs Commission for—Rev. KENNETH H. SHINER, Ecumenical Officer, *St. Elizabeth Rectory, 65 Burban Dr., Branford, 06405.* Tel: 203-488-1661.

Evangelization Office—Rev. MICHAEL J. MOTTA, Dir., *650 Willard Ave., Newington, 06111.* Tel: 860-667-0891; Fax: 860-667-2595.

Holy Childhood Association—Rev. BRIAN W. MONNERAT, Dir., *467 Bloomfield Ave., Bloomfield, 06002.* Tel: 860-243-9184; Fax: 860-243-9460.

Office for Divine Worship—Rev. Msgr. THOMAS M. GINTY, Dir. LUCY ZOCCO, Asst. to the Dir., *467 Bloomfield Ave., Bloomfield, 06002.* Tel: 203-242-4020; Fax: 860-286-0513.

Newspaper—"The Catholic Transcript"; Rev. CHRISTOPHER M. TIANO, Exec. Editor, *467 Bloomfield Ave., Bloomfield, 06002.* Tel: 860-286-2828; 800-726-2391; Fax: 860-726-0000. Most Rev. DANIEL A. CRONIN, D.D., Pres. & Publisher; CAROLE CRONSELL, Business Mgr. DEBRA DURBIN, Asst. Editor; ROY J. ROWLAND, Advertising Mgr.

Office for AIDS Ministries—Sr. DOROTHY STRELCHUN, S.N.D.deN., *Catholic Charities, 467 Bloomfield Ave., Bloomfield, 06002-2999.* Tel: 860-242-9816.

Office for Black Catholics—Vacant Contact office of the Moderator of the Curia, *134 Farmington Ave., Hartford, 06105-3784.* Tel: 860-541-6491; Fax: 860-541-6309.

Office of Continuing Formation of Priests—Rev. GERARD G. SCHMITZ, Dir., *134 Farmington Ave., Hartford.* Tel: 860-541-6491.

Office of Radio and Television—Rev. JOHN P. GATZAK, Exec. Dir., *785 Asylum Ave., Hartford, 06105.* Tel: 860-246-7295; Fax: 860-246-9455.

Office of Family Life, Marriage and Family Apostolate—Co-Dirs.: DONALD PAGLIA; CHRISTINE PAGLIA, *412 Ridge Rd., Hamden, 06517.* Tel: 203-230-2460; Fax: 203-230-2472.

Archbishop's Annual Appeal—Rev. DOUGLAS P. CLANCY, Exec. Dir. BERNADETTE EGAN, Sec., *134 Farmington Ave., Hartford.* Tel: 860-541-6268; Fax: 860-541-6289.

Office of Religious Education (CCD)—Rev. MICHAEL J. MOTTA, Dir., *650 Willard Ave., Newington, 06111.* Tel: 860-667-0891; Fax: 860-667-2595.

Priests Eucharistic League—Rev. THOMAS E. MCCARTHY, Dir., *St. Ann, 289 Arch Rd., Avon, 06001.* Tel: 860-673-9858.

Commission for Priests' Retreats—Revs. FREDERICK M. ANIELLO, Chm. TERENCE KRISTOFAK, C.P.; GERARD G. SCHMITZ; DANIEL JEREMIAH SULLIVAN.

Office of Ministry for Priests—Rev. JOHN P. CONTE, Minister for Priests, *St. Thomas Seminary, 467 Bloomfield Ave., Bloomfield, 06002.* Tel: 860-286-8644.

Mission Cooperative Planning Office—Sr. HELEN MARGARET FEENEY, C.S.J., *Chancery, 134 Farmington Ave., Hartford, 06105-3784.* Tel: 860-541-6491.

Pro-Life Activities—Rev. JAMES J. CRONIN, Dir., *70 Gulf St., P.O. Box 230, Milford, 06460-0230.* Tel: 203-878-3571.

Propagation of the Faith, Society for—(The Catholic Mission Aid Society of Hartford)—Rev. BRIAN W. MONNERAT, Dir., *467 Bloomfield Ave., Bloomfield, 06002.* Tel: 860-243-9184; Fax: 860-243-9460.

Radio Apostolate—Radio Station WJMJ—JOHN L. ELLINGER, Station Mgr., *467 Bloomfield Ave., Bloomfield, 06002.* Tel: 860-242-8800. Licensed by St. Thomas Seminary, Bloomfield. (Hartford).

Office of Catholic Schools—Rev. ZIGFORD J. KRISS, Supt.; Dr. JOSEPH A. BOUND, Asst. Supt., Spec. Svcs. and Secondary Schools; Sr. LORETTA FRANCIS MANN, O.S.F., Asst. Supt., Elementary Education; JEANNINE V. DASH, Dir., Devel., *467 Bloomfield Ave., Bloomfield, 06002.* Tel: 860-242-4362; Fax: 860-242-8683.

Diocesan Labor Institute—Rev. DANIEL E. JOHNSON, Dir., *115 Pond Hill Rd., Wallingford, 06492.* Tel: 203-265-1694.

Social Service—PATRICK J. JOHNSON, Dir., *467 Bloomfield Ave., Bloomfield, 06002.* Tel: 860-242-9577.

Office for Catholic Relief Services—PATRICK J. JOHNSON, Coord., *467 Bloomfield Ave., Bloomfield, 06002.* Tel: 860-242-9577.

Vocations—Rev. JOHN J. DIETRICH, Dir., *Pope Paul VI House of Formation, 469 Bloomfield Ave., Bloomfield, 06002.* Tel: 860-286-7670; Fax: 860-242-9701.

Office of the Permanent Diaconate—Deacon RICHARD L. SANTELLO, Dir., *467 Bloomfield Ave., Bloomfield, 06002.* Tel: 860-243-8005; Fax: 860-243-5287.

Office for Religious—Rev. JAMES F. KINNANE, Vicar; Sr. HELEN MARGARET FEENEY, C.S.J., Dir., *134 Farmington Ave., Hartford, 06105-3784.* Tel: 860-541-6491.

Office of Vicar For Priests—Rev. Msgr. CHARLES B. JOHNSON, *467 Bloomfield Ave., Bloomfield, 06002.* Tel: 860-242-2510; Fax: 860-242-3785.

Censor Librorum—Rev. DAVID Q. LIPTAK.

Archdiocesan Offices and Directors

Archdiocesan Dispute Resolution Office—Most Rev. CHRISTIE A. MACALUSO, Moderator of the Curia, *134 Farmington Ave., Hartford, 06105-3784.* Tel: 860-541-6491.

Archdiocesan Office of Urban Affairs—P. JOSEPH SMYTH, Exec. Dir., *81 Saltonstall Ave., New Haven, 06513.* Tel: 203-777-7279; Fax: 203-776-3233.

Office for Hispanic Evangelization—Most Rev. PETER A. ROSAZZA, Vicar; Deacon RAFAEL LOPEZ, Dir. EMY J. RODRIGUEZ, Office Mgr., *467 Bloomfield Ave., Bloomfield, 06002.* Tel: 860-243-0940; Fax: 860-286-2797.

Cana Conferences—DONALD PAGLIA; CHRISTINE PAGLIA, *412 Ridge Rd., Hamden, 06517.* Tel: 203-230-2460; Fax: 203-230-2472.

Catholic Cemeteries Association—Rev. DAVID M. WALKER, Dir. ROBERT S. MAREK, Exec. Dir., *700 Middletown Ave., P.O. Box 517, North Haven, 06473-0517.* Tel: 203-239-2557; Fax: 203-239-5035.

Catholic Deaf Apostolate—Rev. ROBERT D. BERGIN, Dir.; Sr. MAURA JOSEPH, R.S.M., Coord., *243 Steele Rd., W. Hartford, 06117.* Tel: 860-523-7530 (TDD or Voice); 236-3503.

Catholic Library and Information Center—Rev. EDWARD J. MCLEAN, Dir., *125 Market St., Hartford, 06103.* Tel: 860-522-0602; 246-5628; 800-308-3300; Fax: 860-247-3490.

Connecticut Catholic Conference—Dr. MARIE HILLIARD, Exec. Dir., *134 Farmington Ave., Hartford, 06105-3784.* Tel: 860-524-7882; Fax: 860-525-0750.

Office for People with Disabilities—GEORGE DUCHARME, Ph.D., Co-Dir. MARY ANN LANGTON, Co-Dir., *467 Bloomfield Ave., Bloomfield, 06002.* Tel: 860-242-3304; Fax: 860-521-3688.

Small Christian Communities—Bro. ROBERT K. MORIARTY, S.M., Coord., *467 Bloomfield Ave., Bloomfield, 06002.* Tel: 860-243-9642; Fax: 860-286-0289.

Cursillo Movement, Archdiocesan Director of—Rev. JOHN M. COONEY, Dir., *St. John the Evangelist, 21 Academy Hill, Watertown, 06795-2101.* Tel: 860-274-8836.

Computer Services, Ministry of—Rev. EUGENE J. CHARMAN, Archdiocesan Consultant, *Computer Learning Center, 50 Knowles Ave., P.O. Box 455, Plantsville, 06479.* Tel: 860-628-7385; Fax: 860-276-0722.

CLERGY, PARISHES, MISSIONS AND PAROCHIAL SCHOOLS

CITY OF HARTFORD (Hartford County)

1—CATHEDRAL OF ST. JOSEPH (1872), Rev. Msgr. Daniel J. Plocharczyk; Rev. Dennis J. Vincenzo. In res., Revs. John J. McCarthy; John P. Gatzak.

Res., 140 Farmington Ave., 06105-3783. Tel: 860-249-8431; Fax: 860-249-5910.

School—Cathedral Regional, 809 Asylum Ave., 06105. Tel: 860-522-2678. Mr. Thomas Gersz, Prin. Sisters of Mercy 1; Daughters of Widsom 1; Lay Teachers 13; Students 203.

2—HOLY TRINITY (1900) (Lithuanian), Rev. Christopher M. Tiano, Admin.

Res., 53 Capitol Ave., 06106-1798. Tel: 860-246-4162.

3—IMMACULATE CONCEPTION (1899), Revs. Joseph J. Baxer, M.S., Co-Pastor; James Aherne, M.S., Co-Pastor; Bro. Benedict Roy, S.C.; Deacons Carmelo Hernandez; Adolfo G. Carrero.

Res., 574 Park St., Box 260610, 06126. Tel: 860-525-1522; Fax: 860-728-6995.

Catechesis/Religious Programs—Tel: 860-525-1522; Fax: 860-728-6995.

Students 202.

4—OUR LADY OF FATIMA (1957) (Portuguese), Revs. Jose D. Silva; Rui M. Carrico.

Res., Fatima Sq., 06106-2042. Tel: 860-236-1443; Fax: 860-236-1443.

5—OUR LADY OF SORROWS (1895), Revs. Joseph M. O'Neil, M.S., Co-Pastor & Admin.; Francis C. Cooney, M.S., Co-Pastor; Deacons Domingo Delgado; Rafael Lopez; Peter J. Klimanowski. In res., Rev. Stephen G. Dressell, M.S.

Res., 16 Greenwood St., 06106-2109. Tel: 860-233-4424; Fax: 860-236-0149.

Church—79 New Park Ave., 06106-2109. Tel: 860-233-4424.

Catechesis/Religious Programs—Students 104.

6—SACRED HEART (1872) (Spanish), Revs. Albert Zanatta, C.R.S., Admin.; Franco Cecchini, C.R.S.; Deacons Isidro DeJesus; Edwin Ortiz.

Res., 49 Winthrop St., 06103-1030. Tel: 860-527-6459; Fax: 860-527-6450.

Catechesis/Religious Programs—Tel: 860-527-6459; Fax: 860-527-6450.

Students 240.

7—ST. ANNE (1889) (French), Revs. Joseph J. Baxer, M.S., Co-Pastor & Admin.; James Aherne, M.S., Co-Pastor.

Res., 820 Park St., 06106-2388. Tel: 860-728-7445.

8—ST. AUGUSTINE (1902), Revs. Nicholas J. Cesaro; Charles E. Jacobs; Deacons Jose A. Morales; John F. Dempsey.

Res., 10 Campfield Ave., 06114-1832. Tel: 860-522-7128; Fax: 860-246-1753.

School—20 Clifford St., 06114-1798. Tel: 860-249-5661; Fax: 860-293-2981. Sr. Joan Crowley, C.S.J., Prin.

Priests 1; Brothers 1; Sisters 4; Lay Teachers 14; Students 367.

Catechesis/Religious Programs—Tel: 860-249-3430.

Students 100.

9—SS. CYRIL AND METHODIUS (1902) (Polish), Revs. William P. Przybylo; Kazimierz Heisig (Poland); Ronald P. Zepecki.

Res., 55 Charter Oak Ave., 06106-1902. Tel: 860-522-9157.

School—35 Groton St., 06106. Tel: 860-522-8490; Fax: 860-493-7409.

Sisters 5; Lay Teachers 8; Students 200.

Catechesis/Religious Programs—Tel: 860-522-8490.

Students 220.

Convent—45 Groton St., 06106. Tel: 860-527-3775. Felician Sisters

10—St. Justin (1924) (African American), Rev. Christopher M. Ford.
Res., 230 Blue Hills Ave., 06112-1836. Tel: 860-246-6897; Fax: 860-246-6898.

11—St. Lawrence O'Toole (1885), Revs. John P. Tracy; Paul F. Kenefick; Deacons Robert H. Godlewsky; Pedro S. Rivera.
Res., 494 New Britain Ave., 06106-3797. Tel: 860-522-1129; Fax: 860-549-4261.
Catechesis/Religious Programs—Tel: 860-522-1120; Fax: 860-549-4261.
Students 256.

12—St. Luke (1930), Rev. John J. Peruti; Deacon James E. Hickey, Jr. In res., Rev. Msgr. Charles W. Daly.
Res., 66 Bolton St., 06114. Tel: 860-296-8681.
Catechesis/Religious Programs—Students 143.

13—St. Michael (1900) (African American-Hispanic), Rev. Alfred J. Jaenicke; Deacon Valentine Perez, (Spanish Apostolate).
Res., 98 Capen St., 06120-2075. Tel: 860-522-6184; Fax: 860-278-8410.
Catechesis/Religious Programs—Tel: 860-522-6184; Fax: 860-278-8410.
Students 232.

14—St. Patrick-St. Anthony (1829), Revs. Jerome Massimino, O.F.M.; John Murphy, O.F.M.; Andrew Giardino, O.F.M.; Cornelius Conti, O.F.M.; Bro. Kevin McGoff, O.F.M.; Sr. Regina Whalen, S.N.D., Pastoral Assoc.
Franciscan Center for Urban Ministry: 285 Church St., 06103. Tel: 860-246-6874; Fax: 860-249-6487.

15—St. Peter (1859) (Irish), Rev. Michael S. Galasso; Deacon Bruce Thompson.
Res., 160 Main St., 06106-1894. Tel: 860-525-2683.
Catechesis/Religious Programs—Students 350.
Convent—11 Charter Oak Pl., 06106. Tel: 860-522-8428. Sisters of Mercy Mercedarian Missionary Sisters (Spanish).

OUTSIDE THE CITY OF HARTFORD

Ansonia, New Haven Co.,

1—Assumption, (1870), Team Ministry: Revs. George P. Burnett; Robert F. Condron; Deacons John F. Brady, Jr.; Joseph L. DiPiro; Robert C. Johnson. In res., Rev. Albert J. Zanavich.
Res., 61 N. Cliff St., 06401-1698. Tel: 203-735-7857; Fax: 203-734-5521.
School—Tel: 203-734-0855; Fax: 203-734-5521. Mrs. Kathleen Molner, Prin.
Lay Teachers 11; Students 279.
Catechesis/Religious Programs—51 N. Cliff St., 06401. Tel: 203-735-2701.
Students 252.

2—Holy Rosary, (1908) (Italian), Revs. Ronald L. Genua; Raymond F. Paul; Carlos Garces-Henao; Deacons Ralph A. Aconfora; Michael Impellitteri; Victor M. Lembo.
Res., Fr. Salemi Dr., 06401-2396. Tel: 203-735-7875; Fax: 203-732-2212.
Catechesis/Religious Programs—Tel: 203-736-0242. Verna Ingrassia, D.R.E.
Students 443.

3—St. Anthony's, (1915) (Lithuanian), Revs. Lee W. Hellwig, Admin.; Patrick J. Berkery.
Res., 199 N. Main St., 06401-1696. Tel: 203-734-4759.

4—St. Joseph's, (1925) (Polish), Revs. Marek W. Sobczak; Joseph Szpilski, C.M.
Res., 32 Jewett St., 06401-2499. Tel: 203-734-0402.
School—36 Jewett St., 06401. Tel: 203-734-3821. Sr. M. Adrianne, C.S.F.N., Prin.
Lay Teachers 10; Students 164.
Catechesis/Religious Programs—Students 85.
Convent—Tel: 203-736-9573. Sisters of the Holy Family of Nazareth

Avon, Hartford Co., St. Ann's (1917), Revs. Thomas E. McCarthy; Kevin G. Donovan; Deacons William A. Farrell; John E. Thayer; Alan D. Campbell.
Res., 289 Arch Rd., 06001-4209. Tel: 860-673-9858; Fax: 860-675-4350. [CEM]
Catechesis/Religious Programs—Tel: 860-673-2137; Fax: 860-675-4350. Patricia Piano, D.R.E.
Students 820.

Bantam, Litchfield Co., Our Lady of Grace (1949), Rev. John H. McCann, S.M.M., Admin.
Res., P.O. Box 427, Rte. 202, 06750. Tel: 203-567-9522. [CEM]
Catechesis/Religious Programs—Students 96.
Mission—Morris, Litchfield Co., Our Lady of Hope, Rte. 109, 06750. Tel: 860-567-5717.

Beacon Falls, New Haven Co., St. Michael's (1899), Rev. Leonard J. Kvedas; Deacon Frank J. Krasnicki. In res., Rev. James F. O'Dea.
Res., 25 Maple Ave., 06403-1145. Tel: 203-729-2504.
Catechesis/Religious Programs—Tel: 203-729-2504.
Students 306.

Bethlehem, Litchfield Co., Church of the Nativity (1921), Rev. Richard L. Shellman; Deacon William McGrath.
Res., 48 East St., Box 192, 06751-0192. Tel: 203-266-5211.
Catechesis/Religious Programs—Tel: 203-266-5212.
Students 237.

Bloomfield, Hartford Co., Christ the King (1936). Closed. For inquiries for sacramental records contact Sacred Heart, Bloomfield.

Sacred Heart (1878), Revs. Joseph C. Gengras; Joseph V. DiSciacca; Bro. Paul Gauvin, S.C., Pastoral Assoc.; Sr. Rosemary Ryan, Pastoral Assoc.; Deacon Joseph Whittel.
Res., 25 Foothills Way, 06002-2488. Tel: 860-242-1942.
Church—26 Wintonbury Ave., 06002. Tel: 860-242-4142; Fax: 860-286-0044.
Catechesis/Religious Programs—Students 141.

Branford, New Haven Co., St. Elizabeth (1966), Rev. Kenneth H. Shiner; Deacon Joseph F. Coyne.
Res., 65 Burban Dr., 06405. Tel: 203-488-1661; Fax: 203-483-9248.
Catechesis/Religious Programs—Tel: 203-488-1661; Fax: 203-483-9248.
Students 261.

St. Mary (1868), Revs. Vincent A. Brown; Shawn T. Daly; Deacons Paul V. Prete; Robert P. Tartaris.
Res., 731 Main St., 06405-3693. Tel: 203-488-1607; Fax: 203-488-1608. [CEM 2]
School—(Grades PreK-8). Tel: 203-488-8386.
Lay Teachers 16; Students 265.
Catechesis/Religious Programs—Tel: 203-488-7412.
Students 729.

St. Therese (1947), Rev. Raymond J. Barry; Deacons Paul C. Eschrich, (Retired); Gerald S. Walton.
Office: 105 Leetes Island Rd., 06405.
Res., 82 Thimble Island Rd., 06405. Tel: 203-488-2998; Fax: 203-488-8542.
Catechesis/Religious Programs—Students 290.

Bristol, Hartford Co.,

1—St. Ann, (1908) (French), Revs. Robert J. Rousseau; Dennis C. Gingras; Deacons Joseph E. Levesque; Albert Lozier.
Res., 215 West St., 06010-5754. Tel: 860-582-8169; Fax: 860-585-7139.
Catechesis/Religious Programs—Tel: 860-582-3524. Carol Gignac, D.R.E.
Students 182.

2—St. Anthony's, (1920) (Italian), Revs. Nicholas P. Melo; Louis S. Paturzo; Deacon Laurent J. Cote.
Res., 111 School St., 06010-6078. Tel: 860-583-1349; Fax: 860-582-3861.
School—30 Pleasant St., 06010. Tel: 860-582-7874; Fax: 860-582-7124.
Lay Teachers 13; Students 297.
Catechesis/Religious Programs—20 Pleasant St., 06010. Tel: 860-583-4495.
Students 218.

3—St. Gregory's, (1957), Revs. Charles R. Mullins; Joseph H. Keating; Daniel H. Connaghan; Deacons Roy Dungan; Roger Albert.
Res. & Mailing Address: St. Gregory Rectory, Maltby St., 06010-3892. Tel: 860-589-2295; Fax: 860-589-6692.
Catechesis/Religious Programs—1043 Stafford Ave., 06010. Tel: 860-589-4232; Fax: 860-584-4786. Barbara Sergio, D.R.E.
Students 1,149.

4—St. Joseph, (1864), Revs. James F. Leary; Louis S. Paturzo; Deacon Robert M. Pallotti.
Res., 149 Goodwin St., 06010-5115. Tel: 860-583-1369; Fax: 860-583-1360. [CEM]
School—335 Center St., 06010. Tel: 860-582-8696. Mark J. Monnerat, Prin.
Lay Teachers 19; Students 431.
Catechesis/Religious Programs—Tel: 860-582-2888.
Students 355.

5—St. Stanislaus, (1919) (Polish), Rev. Brian A. Shaw, D.Min.; Rev. Msgr. John P. Wodarski, S.T.D., (Retired); Rev. Lech Kuna (Poland).
Res., 510 West St., P.O. Box 1860, 06011-1860. Tel: 860-583-4242; Fax: 860-583-9464.
Catechesis/Religious Programs—Students 218.

Broad Brook, Hartford Co., St. Catherine's (1886), Rev. David Q. Liptak; Deacons Vincent Motto; John Abdalla.
Res., 6 Windsorville Rd., 06016-0359. Tel: 860-623-4636; Fax: 860-623-4636. [CEM]
Catechesis/Religious Programs—7 Rye St., 06016. Tel: 860-623-1974.
Students 280.

Canaan, Litchfield Co., St. Joseph's (1920), Revs. Edmund Ansaloni, O.F.M.; Marion Cascino, O.F.M. In res., Rev. Michael A. Malley.
Res., 4 Main St., P.O. Box 845, 06018-2459. Tel: 860-824-7078; Fax: 860-824-7078. [CEM][JC]
Mission—Falls Village, Litchfield Co., St. Patrick, (1851) Beebe Hill Rd. [CEM][JC]
Catechesis/Religious Programs—Students 160.

Cheshire, New Haven Co., Church of the Epiphany (1967), Rev. Norman L. Brockett; Deacon Edward J. Pantalena.
Res., 1777 Old Waterbury Rd., 06410-1399. Tel: 203-272-5211.
Church & Parish Center—1750 Huckins Rd., 06410. Tel: 203-272-4355; Fax: 203-272-4878.
Catechesis/Religious Programs—Tel: 203-272-4355, Ext. 2.
Students 213.

St. Bridget's (1871), Revs. James B. Gunnoud; John K. Lynch; Deacons Wesley Baxter; Burdon Lowe; Richard Wilber.
Res., 175 Main St., 06410-2446. Tel: 203-272-3531; Fax: 203-271-3356. [CEM]
Parish Center—Tel: 203-271-9994.
Catechesis/Religious Programs—Tel: 203-272-6504.
Students 955.

St. Thomas Becket (1971), Rev. Kenneth J. Frisbie.
Res., 511 Sharon Dr., 06410-4244. Tel: 203-272-3324.
Catechesis/Religious Programs—Tel: 203-272-5777.
Students 440.

Collinsville, Hartford Co., St. Patrick's (1856), Rev. Ronald P. May; Deacon Robert N. Blair.
Res., 7 Burlington Ave., P.O. Box 287, 06022-0287. Tel: 860-693-8727; Fax: 860-693-4538. [CEM] [JC 2]
Catechesis/Religious Programs—Tel: 860-693-1068.
Students 382.

Cornwall Bridge, Litchfield Co., St. Bridget (1883), Rev. James F. Pilon.
Res., 7 River Rd., P.O. Box 52, 06754-1903. Tel: 203-672-6515. [CEM]

Derby, New Haven Co., St. Jude (1961), Rev. William J. Killeen; Deacon Robert Fitzgerald.
Res., 71 Pleasant View Rd., 06418-2455. Tel: 203-735-8725; Fax: 203-735-4402.
Catechesis/Religious Programs—Students 123.

St. Mary's (1851), Revs. James H. Smith; Peter G. Mitchell, Pastor Emeritus; Deacon Frederick M. Grant.
Res., 212 Elizabeth St., 06418-1834. Tel: 203-735-3341; Fax: 203-736-6492.
School—St. Mary-St. Michael, (Grades K-8) St. Mary Campus, 14 Seymour Ave., P.O. Box 397, 06418. Tel: 203-735-6471.
Lay Teachers 14; Students 316.
Catechesis/Religious Programs—Tel: 203-736-0794.
Students 221.

St. Michael (1905) (Polish), Revs. Ronald A. Wiktor, C.M.; Walenty Pieczka, C.M.; John Kuczynski, C.M.
Res., 75 Derby Ave., 06418-2098. Tel: 203-734-0005. [CEM]
School—St. Mary-St. Michael, (Grades 4-8) St. Michael Campus, 73 Derby Ave., P.O. Box 397, 06418. Tel: 203-734-2017.
Lay Teachers 5; Students 127.
Catechesis/Religious Programs—Students 184.

East Berlin, Hartford Co., Sacred Heart (1896), Rev. Thomas C. Culotta.
Res., 48 Cottage St., 06023. Tel: 860-828-0159.
Church—66 Cottage St., 06023.
Catechesis/Religious Programs—Fax: 860-828-5305.
Students 243.

East Hartford, Hartford Co.,

1—Blessed Sacrament, (1948), Rev. Jeffrey T. Walsh.
Res., 36 Cambridge Dr., 06118-2699. Tel: 860-568-2747.

2—Our Lady of Peace, (1971), Rev. James J. Nock.
Res., 370 May Rd., 06118-3496. Tel: 860-568-4414.
Catechesis/Religious Programs—Students 183.

3—St. Christopher, (1965), Revs. James G. Fanelli; William E. McGrath, Pastor Emeritus; Sr. Joan Bernier, S.N.D., Pastoral Assoc.; Deacon William Gilles.
Res., 538 Brewer St., 06118-2399. Tel: 860-568-5240.
School—570 Brewer St., 06118. Tel: 860-568-4100. Sr. Valerie Noone, O.P., Prin.
Lay Teachers 14; Students 277.
Catechesis/Religious Programs—Tel: 860-568-0546; 895-8692 (Youth Ministry).
Students 316.

4—St. Isaac Jogues, (1964), Rev. Emilio P. Padelli.
Res., 1 Community St., 06108-2808. Tel: 860-528-6749.

Catechesis/Religious Programs—Tel: 860-528-7976.
Students 116.

5—ST. MARY'S, (1873), Revs. Martin J. Scholsky; Frank E. Papa, S.O.L.T.; Deacon Ronald R. Daigle.
Res., 15 Maplewood Ave., 06108-4021. Tel: 860-289-7916.
Parish Center—30 Maplewood Ave., 06108. Tel: 860-289-7510.
Catechesis/Religious Programs—Students 142.

6—ST. ROSE'S, (1920), Revs. Ronald J. Osborne; Robert P. Ricciardi; Deacon William J. Brown.
Res., 33 Church St., 06108-3794. Tel: 860-289-8616; Fax: 860-289-3966.
School—Tel: 860-528-4169; Fax: 860-528-4160.
Lay Teachers 10; Students 166.
Catechesis/Religious Programs—Tel: 860-528-3967.
Students 192.

East Haven, New Haven Co., Our Lady of Pompeii (1947), Revs. Dennis R. Hussey; Matthew R. Shanley; Deacons Nicholas DelCorte; Joseph LaPierre; Henry Lotto.
Res., Foxon Rd., 06513. Tel: 203-469-0764.
Catechesis/Religious Programs—Students 650.

St. Clare (1947), Rev. William A. Bray; Deacon Wayne E. Sandford.
Res., 234 Coe Ave., 06512-4112. Tel: 203-467-5136.
Catechesis/Religious Programs—Tel: 203-467-0600.
Students 335.

St. Vincent de Paul's (1915), Revs. Gary F. Simeone; Robert J. Burbank, Pastor Emeritus; Alphonso R. Fontana; Deacons Norman H. Singer; William Eyles.
Res., 80 Taylor Ave., 06512. Tel: 203-467-6394; Fax: 203-467-6716.
School—35 Bishop St., 06512. Tel: 203-467-1606; 467-1607; Fax: 203-467-8851.
Lay Teachers 11; Students 247.
Catechesis/Religious Programs—Students 589.

East Windsor, Hartford Co., St. Philip's (1959), Rev. Robert T. Russo.
Res., 150 S. Main St., 06088-9760. Tel: 860-623-0408; Fax: 860-623-8937.
Catechesis/Religious Programs—Students 125.

Enfield, Hartford Co.,

1—HOLY FAMILY, (1965), Rev. Francis T. Kerwan; Deacons Robert Linehan; Raymond J. McGivney; Donald H. Pond, Jr.; Arthur J. Dickman.
Res., 23 Simon Rd., 06082-5903. Tel: 860-741-2101.
Catechesis/Religious Programs—Tel: 860-745-1018. Elizabeth McGivney, D.R.E.
Students 1,139.

2—ST. ADALBERT'S, (1915) (Polish), Rev. Adam Subocz.
In res., Rev. Anthony J. Bruno Tel: 860-745-9966.
Res., 90 Alden Ave., 06082-2865. Tel: 860-745-4837; Fax: 860-745-1787. [CEM]
School—Tel: 860-745-6135.
Sisters 3; Lay Teachers 7; Students 150.
Catechesis/Religious Programs—Students 72.
Convent—82 Alden Ave., 06082. Tel: 860-745-4169. Felician Sisters

3—ST. BERNARD'S, (1870), Revs. Brian W. Monnerat; William F. O'Keefe; Deacons J. Gerard Mon; Hobart T. Stadtlander; Suzanne O. Cannon, Pastoral Assoc.
Res., 426 Hazard Ave., 06082-4719. Tel: 860-749-8353; Fax: 860-749-6456. [CEM]
School—Tel: 860-749-8182 (East Campus); 745-5275 (West Campus).
Sisters 3; Lay Teachers 20; Students 395.
Catechesis/Religious Programs—Tel: 860-749-2993.
Students 300.
Convent—376 Hazard Ave., 06082. Tel: 860-749-4214. Felician Sisters

4—ST. MARTHA'S, (1961), Revs. John B. O'Connell; Stanley Smolenski; Deacons Rene Kieda; Robert Lambert; Robert Bernd.
Res., 214 Brainard Rd., 06082-2609. Tel: 860-745-5616.
School—Tel: 860-745-3833.
Felician Sisters 1; Lay Teachers 9; Students 260.
Catechesis/Religious Programs—Tel: 860-745-5616.
Students 325.

5—ST. PATRICK'S, (1866), Revs. Francis J. Browne, C.Ss.R.; Thomas G. Sullivan, C.Ss.R.; Sr. Mary O'Neill, R.S.M., Pastoral Assoc.
Res., 64 Pearl St., 06082-3594. Tel: 860-745-2411; Fax: 860-253-9483. [CEM]
Catechesis/Religious Programs—Tel: 860-741-0572.
Students 300.

Farmington, Hartford Co., St. Patrick's (1871), Revs. Thomas P. Quinn; James V. Hickey; Deacon Joseph E. Kane.
Res., 110 Main St., P.O. Box 523, 06034-0523. Tel: 860-677-2639.
Catechesis/Religious Programs—Fax: 860-677-2672.
Students 568.

Forestville, Hartford Co., St. Matthew (1891), Revs. Robert J. Lysz; Arthur J. Audet; Deacons John E. Pahl; Richard J. O'Day; Sr. Judith Mulhall, C.S.J., Pastoral Assoc.
Res., 120 Church Ave., Box 9216, 06011-9216. Tel: 860-583-1833; Fax: 860-582-6152.
School—Welch Dr., 06010. Tel: 860-583-5214.
Sisters 5; Lay Teachers 9; Students 295.
Parish Resource Center—101 Church Ave., 06010. Tel: 860-583-1241.
Catechesis/Religious Programs—Tel: 860-583-7806.
Students 630.
Convent—119 Church Ave., 06010. Tel: 860-583-2004. Sisters, Servants of the Immaculate Heart of Mary

Glastonbury, Hartford Co., St. Dunstan (1971), Rev. William L. Traxl.
Res., 1345 Manchester Rd., 06033-2604. Tel: 860-633-3317; Fax: 860-659-8611.
Catechesis/Religious Programs—Tel: 860-633-6876; Fax: 860-659-8611.
Students 659.

St. Paul's (1954), Revs. L. Randall Blackall; John P. Gwozdz; Deacon John W. McKaig.
Res., 2577 Main St., 06033-2023. Tel: 860-633-9419; Fax: 860-633-0040.
Catechesis/Religious Programs—Tel: 860-659-3029; Fax: 860-633-0040. Joan Flannery, D.R.E.
Students 718.

Goshen, Litchfield Co., St. Thomas of Villanova (1880), Rev. Raymond G. Proulx; Deacon Nick Diorio.
Res., 71 North St., P.O. Box 177, 06756-0177. Tel: 860-491-2756. [CEM]
Catechesis/Religious Programs—Tel: 860-491-9276.
Students 138.

Granby, Hartford Co., St. Therese's (1958), Rev. Ronald R. Yelle; Deacon Robert D. Newbery.
Res., 120 W. Granby Rd., 06035-2907. Tel: 860-653-3371.
Catechesis/Religious Programs—Tel: 860-653-5780.
Students 407.

Guilford, New Haven Co., St. George (1870), Rev. Msgr. James G. Coleman; Rev. John W. McHugh; Deacons Jose A. Rivera; Adam J. Michaele; James F. O'Neill.
Res., 33 Whitfield St., 06437-2698. Tel: 203-453-2788; Fax: 203-453-4985. [CEM]
Catechesis/Religious Programs—Tel: 203-453-3496.
Students 1,040.

Hamden, New Haven Co.,

1—ASCENSION, (1964), Rev. Thomas J. O'Rourke; Deacon Kenneth McCusker.
Res., 1040 Dunbar Hill Rd., 06514-1410. Tel: 203-288-7516.
Catechesis/Religious Programs—Tel: 203-288-5761.
Students 166.

2—BLESSED SACRAMENT, (1939), Revs. David M. McDonald; Stuart H. Pinette; Deacon James A. Tripp, Sr.
Res., 321 Circular Ave., 06514-3428. Tel: 203-288-1652; Fax: 203-248-0873.
Catechesis/Religious Programs—306 Circular Ave., 06514. Tel: 203-288-5228.
Students 412.

3—OUR LADY OF MT. CARMEL, (1869), Revs. Neil F. Fitzgerald; Daniel James Sullivan; Deacon John O'Donovan.
Res., 2819 Whitney Ave., 06518-2598. Tel: 203-248-0141. [CEM]
Parish Center—2809 Whitney Ave., 06518. Tel: 203-287-9017.
Catechesis/Religious Programs—Tel: 203-287-9017. Sr. Ann O'Neill, R.S.M., D.R.E.
Students 915.

4—ST. ANN'S, (1919) (Italian), Rev. Kenneth P. Bonadies.
Res., 930 Dixwell Ave., 06514-4990. Tel: 203-865-0886.

5—ST. JOAN OF ARC, (1971), Rev. Robert G. Heffernan; Deacon John P. Twerago.
Res., 450 W. Todd St., 06518. Tel: 203-288-4543.
Catechesis/Religious Programs—Tel: 203-230-1926.
Students 264.

6—ST. RITA'S, (1928), Revs. David M. Walker; Robert M. Kwiatkowski; Deacon Joseph E. Rolando.
Res., 1620 Whitney Ave., 06517. Tel: 203-248-5513; Fax: 203-248-2684.
School—1601 Whitney Ave., 06517. Tel: 203-248-3114; Fax: 203-248-1016.
Priests 1; Dominican Sisters of St. Mary of the Springs 2; Apostles of the Sacred Heart 3; Lay Teachers 16; Students 513.
Catechesis/Religious Programs—Tel: 203-281-7522; Fax: 203-248-2684. Dianne Breen, D.R.E.
Students 424.

7—ST. STEPHEN'S, (1953), Rev. David J. Baranowski; Deacon Richard Santello.
Res., 400 Ridge Rd., 06517-2941. Tel: 203-288-6439; Fax: 203-288-4152.
School—Tel: 203-288-6792.
Sisters of Mercy 2; Lay Teachers 10; Students 213.

Harwinton, Litchfield Co., Immaculate Heart of Mary (1956), Rev. Allan J. Hill; Deacons Jose L. Dlugokinski; John L. Dembishack.
Res., 78 Litchfield Rd., 06791-2230. Tel: 860-485-1588; Fax: 860-485-1004.
Catechesis/Religious Programs—Tel: 860-485-9264. Christine Rousseau, D.R.E.
Students 411.

Kensington, Hartford Co., St. Paul's (1878), Team Ministry: Revs. Herman Czaster, O.F.M.Conv.; Herbert Obijiski, O.F.M.Conv.; Thomas Lavin, O.F.M.Conv.; Deacons Oral Talbot; Carmen Guzzardi.
Res., 479 Alling St., 06037-2100. Tel: 860-828-0331; Fax: 860-828-7620.
School—(Grades PreK-8). Tel: 860-828-4343; Fax: 860-828-1226. Mrs. Patricia O'Neill-Tiezzi, Prin.
Daughters of Mary of the Immaculate Conception 3; Lay Teachers 16; Students 298.
Catechesis/Religious Programs—Tel: 860-828-1934. Louann Warren, D.R.E.
Students 1,177.

Kent, Litchfield Co., Sacred Heart (1970), Rev. William R. Metzler; Deacon Roland Miller.
Res., 90 Cobble Rd., P.O. Box 186, 06757-0186. Tel: 860-927-3003; Fax: 860-927-3985. [CEM]
Church—17 Bridge St., 06757.
Catechesis/Religious Programs—Students 78.

Lakeville, Litchfield Co., St. Mary's (1874), Rev. Edmund M. O'Brien; Deacon Wayne F. Griffin.
Res., 76 Sharon Rd., 06039-0466. Tel: 860-435-2659. [CEM]
Catechesis/Religious Programs—Students 132.

Litchfield, Litchfield Co., St. Anthony's (1882), Rev. Robert F. Tucker; Deacon Kenneth DosSantos.
Res., 49 South St., P.O. Box 97, 06759-0097. Tel: 860-567-5209. [CEM]
Catechesis/Religious Programs—Students 306.

Madison, New Haven Co., St. Margaret (1937), Revs. Gerard G. Schmitz; Francis R. Fador; Deacons Joseph M. Regan; William A. Elder.
Res., 24 Academy St., P.O. Box 814, 06443-2647. Tel: 203-245-7301; Fax: 203-245-8568.
Catechesis/Religious Programs—Tel: 203-245-7971.
Students 781.

Manchester, Hartford Co.,

1—ASSUMPTION, (1955), Rev. John S. Golas; Deacons J. Fernand Chamberland; Leo R. LaRocque.
Res., 285 W. Center St., 06040-4898. Tel: 860-643-2195; Fax: 860-646-4360.
School—Tel: 860-649-0889. Sr. Martin Prin.
Sisters 3; Lay Teachers 6; Students 167.
Catechesis/Religious Programs—Students 245.
Convent—21 S. Adams St., 06040. Tel: 860-643-0452. Sisters of Charity of Our Lady, Mother of the Church

2—ST. BARTHOLOMEW'S, (1958), Rev. Peter J. Zizka.
Res., 45 Ludlow Rd., 06040-4542. Tel: 860-646-1613; Fax: 860-646-7121.
Catechesis/Religious Programs—Tel: 860-643-9178.
Students 333.

3—ST. BRIDGET'S, (1870), Rev. Joseph T. Donnelly.
Res., 80 Main St., 06040-3180. Tel: 860-643-2403; Fax: 860-646-6936.
School—74 Main St., 06040. Tel: 860-649-7731; Fax: 860-646-6936.
Sisters 1; Lay Teachers 10; Students 288.
Catechesis/Religious Programs—Tel: 860-643-5454; Fax: 860-646-6936.
Students 467.

4—ST. JAMES, (1874), Revs. Douglas P. Clancy; William F. Lynch; Louis D. Cremonie; Deacon Edward Giard.
Res., 896 Main St., 06040-6079. Tel: 860-643-4129; Fax: 860-643-4120.
School—Tel: 860-643-5088. Sr. Louise Kelly, R.S.M., Prin.
Sisters 4; Lay Teachers 20; Students 508.
Catechesis/Religious Programs—73 Park St., 06040. Tel: 860-643-9605.
Students 400.

Marlborough, Hartford Co., St. John Fisher (1972), Rev. Mario P. Pepe; Deacons Peter Klein; Ray Parenteau.
Res., 24 Cheney Rd., 06447-1327. Tel: 860-295-0067.

Catechesis/Religious Programs—Tel: 860-295-0067.
Students 360.

Meriden, New Haven Co.,

1—OUR LADY OF MOUNT CARMEL, (1894) (Italian), Rev. David J. Borino; Deacon Robert Gale.
Res., 109 Goodwill Ave., 06451-3000. Tel: 203-235-6381; Fax: 203-238-3629.
School—Tel: 203-235-2759.
Sisters 1; Lay Teachers 10; Students 170.
Catechesis/Religious Programs—Tel: 203-235-6381; Fax: 203-237-6225.
Students 185.
Convent—109 Goodwill Ave., Apt. 2, 06451-3000. Tel: 203-235-3622. Apostles of the Sacred Heart of Jesus
Sisters 3.

2—ST. JOSEPH, (1900), Revs. Mark R. Jette; Robert P. Roy; Deacon John J. Suzio. In res., Rev. Daniel G. Keefe.
Res., 22 Goodwill Ave., 06451. Tel: 203-237-5593.
School—Tel: 203-237-6800. Sr. Georgeann Vumbaco, Prin.
Sisters of Mercy 5; Lay Teachers 8; Students 240.
Catechesis/Religious Programs—Tel: 203-237-5593.
Students 325.

3—ST. LAURENT, (1880) (French), Rev. Maurice P. Soucy.
Res., 121 Camp St., 06450-3279. Tel: 203-634-1583.
School—Tel: 203-235-3192. Mrs. Rita Barry, Prin.
Sisters 1; Lay Teachers 9; Students 132.
Catechesis/Religious Programs—Students 123.

4—ST. MARY, (1890) (German), Revs. Mark R. Jette; Robert P. Roy.
Res., 5 Sherman Pl., 06451. Tel: 203-235-0519. [CEM]
School—Tel: 203-237-2931.
Lay Teachers 7; Students 75.

5—ST. ROSE OF LIMA, (1848), Rev. Joseph E. Vujs; Deacons Raul Cardona; Charles E. Cunniff, Jr.; Jacinto Ortiz.
Res., 35 Center St., 06450-1504. Tel: 203-235-1644; Fax: 203-235-1360.
Catechesis/Religious Programs—Tel: 203-235-6887.
Students 427.

6—ST. STANISLAUS, (1891) (Polish), Revs. Edmund S. Nadolny; Joseph K. Parzymies. In res., Revs. Joseph C. Paciorek, C.M.; Walter Kaminski.
Res., 82 Akron St., 06450-5796. Tel: 203-235-6341; Fax: 203-235-6342. [CEM]
School—Tel: 203-235-1005; Fax: 203-235-6341.
Sisters of St. Joseph of the Third Of St. Francis (Garfield Heights, OH) 4; Lay Teachers 25; Students 456.
Catechesis/Religious Programs—Tel: 203-235-6341; Fax: 203-235-6342.
Students 180.

Middlebury, New Haven Co., St. John of the Cross (1904), Revs. John D. Regan; Robert F. Birmingham; Deacon Neil Culhane.
Res., 1089 Whittemore Rd., P.O. Box 361, 06762-0361. Tel: 203-758-2659; Fax: 203-758-1121.
Catechesis/Religious Programs—Tel: 203-758-1326.
Students 425.

Milford, New Haven Co.,

1—CHRIST THE REDEEMER, (1966), Rev. John T. Moskus; Deacon Edmund J. Ramos.
Res., 325 Oronoque Rd., 06460-1798. Tel: 203-878-7431; Fax: 203-878-0677.
Catechesis/Religious Programs—Students 170.

2—ST. ANN'S, (1924), Rev. Thomas J. Baylis.
Res., 501 Naugatuck Ave., Devon, 06460-5095. Tel: 203-874-0634; Fax: 203-874-1919.
School—Tel: 203-878-2738.
Lay Teachers 10; Students 190.
Catechesis/Religious Programs—Students 349.

3—ST. GABRIEL, (Wildemere Beach) (1946), Rev. Maurice J. Maroney; Deacons Calvin Croll; Henry Doyle.
Res., 26 Shorefront, 06460-5968. Tel: 203-877-6096; Fax: 203-878-9700.
School—(Grades PreK-8) 1 Tudor Rd., 06460. Tel: 203-874-3811; Fax: 203-874-0416.
Religious 1; Lay Teachers 16; Students 261.
Catechesis/Religious Programs—Tel: 203-876-9355; Fax: 203-876-9355.
Students 237.

4—ST. MARY'S, (Wildemere Beach) (1874), Revs. James J. Cronin; Vito C. DeCarolis; Frederick M. Langlois; Deacons George A. Puskas; Paul E. Sabo; Richard M. Sennett; Paul Lauer.
Res., 70 Gulf St., Box 230, 06460-0230. Tel: 203-878-3571; Fax: 203-877-8741. [CEM]
School—Tel: 203-878-6539.
Sisters of Mercy 2; Lay Teachers 22; Students 473.
Catechesis/Religious Programs—Tel: 203-877-5874. Sue Marra, D.R.E.
Students 755.

Naugatuck, New Haven Co., St. Francis of Assisi (1866), Revs. William L. Burns; William O. Seery; Faron Calumba. In res., Rev. Joseph P. Donahue; Deacon William F. Mingrone.
Res., 318 Church St., 06770. Tel: 203-729-4543.
School—Tel: 203-729-2247. Mrs. Lorraine Hurley, Prin.
Lay Teachers 12; Students 317.
Catechesis/Religious Programs—D.R.E.: Mr. Joseph Guarino; Mr. John Paret.
Students 610.

St. Vincent Ferrer (1975), Rev. Jeremiah N. Murasso; Deacon Nicholas J. Iassogna, Jr.; Sr. Susan Carlin, R.S.M., Pastoral Min.
Res., 1006 New Haven Rd., 06770-4731. Tel: 203-723-7497; Fax: 203-729-4475.
Catechesis/Religious Programs—Sr. Susan Carlin, R.S.M., D.R.E.
Students 554.

New Britain, Hartford Co.,

1—ALL SAINTS, (1918) (Slovak), Rev. Augustine H. Giusani.
Res., 15 Wilcox St., 06051. Tel: 860-229-0135.

2—HOLY CROSS, (1927) (Polish), Revs. Peter S. Sobiecki; Darius Goscinak; Edward Ziemnicki. In res., Rev. Henry P. Fiedorczyk.
Res., 31 Biruta St., 06053-2899. Tel: 860-229-2011; Fax: 860-826-5887.
School—221 Farmington Ave., 06053. Tel: 860-225-4275; Fax: 860-225-5073.
Sisters of St. Joseph of the Third Order of St. Francis 6; Lay Teachers 16; Students 416.
Catechesis/Religious Programs—Students 197.

3—SACRED HEART OF JESUS, (1894) (Polish), Rev. Paul P. Wysocki.
Res., 158 Broad St., 06053-4195. Tel: 860-229-0081; 826-4721; Fax: 860-826-6201. [CEM]
School—Tel: 860-229-7663. Sr. M. Alma Sakowicz, Prin.
Daughters of Mary of the Immaculate Conception 3; Lay Teachers 21; Students 447.
Catechesis/Religious Programs—Students 190.

4—ST. ANDREW'S, (1895) (Lithuanian), Rev. John E. Rikteraitis. In res., Rev. Ronald T. Smith.
Res., 396 Church St., Box 515, 06050-0515. Tel: 860-224-0341; Fax: 860-826-6201.

5—ST. ANN, (1938) (Italian), Revs. Augustine H. Giusani; J. Thomas Walsh; Nathaniel C. Labarda; Deacon Carl Lickwar.
Res., 47 Clark St., 06051-1903. Tel: 860-225-7625.
Catechesis/Religious Programs—Tel: 860-229-1929.
Students 174.

6—ST. FRANCIS OF ASSISI, (1941), Revs. Bruce C. Czapla, O.F.M.; Richard Donovan, O.F.M.
Res., 1755 Stanley St., 06053-2099. Tel: 860-225-6449; Fax: 860-225-2315.
Middle School—Tel: 860-225-8729.
School Sisters of Notre Dame 3; Lay Teachers 9; Students 179.
Catechesis/Religious Programs—Students 100.

7—ST. JEROME'S, (1958), Revs. Edward M. LaRose; Joseph Varickamackal; Deacon Reginald Roy.
Res., 1010 Slater Rd., 06053-1698. Tel: 860-224-2411; Fax: 860-224-6838.
Catechesis/Religious Programs—Students 106.

8—ST. JOHN THE EVANGELIST, (1916), Rev. Harold D. Heinrich; Deacon Albert Kristopik.
Res., 655 East St., 06051-2108. Tel: 860-223-3667; 3668.
Catechesis/Religious Programs—Students 128.

9—ST. JOSEPH'S, (1896), Rev. Thomas F. Gaffney.
Res., 195 S. Main St., 06051-3199. Tel: 860-229-4851; Fax: 860-225-1403.
School—Tel: 860-223-5959; Fax: 860-225-1403.
Lay Teachers 10; Students 230.
Catechesis/Religious Programs—Tel: 860-229-4851; Fax: 860-225-1403.
Students 156.

10—ST. MARY'S, (1848), Revs. Salvatore J. Rosa; Francis T. Carter; Deacons Chester Roman; Ronald Camden.
Res., 544 Main St., 06051-1814. Tel: 860-229-4894.
Catechesis/Religious Programs—Students 200.

11—ST. MAURICE, (1946), Rev. Joseph V. Napolitano.
Res., 100 Wightman Rd., 06052-1597. Tel: 860-225-8419; Fax: 860-224-1947.
Catechesis/Religious Programs—Tel: 860-225-4477. Linda E. Tower, D.R.E.
Students 175.

12—ST. PETER'S, (1873) (German-French), Rev. Michael H. Gosselin, S.T.M., J.C.L.
Res., 98 Franklin Sq., 06051-2607. Tel: 860-224-1446; Fax: 860-223-8717.

New Hartford, Litchfield Co., Immaculate Conception (1869), Rev. James R. Emerling.
Res., Town Hill Rd., 06057. Tel: 860-379-5215. [CEM]
Catechesis/Religious Programs—Tel: 860-379-0144.
Students 375.

New Haven, New Haven Co.,

1—SACRED HEART, (1876), Revs. Robert V. Newman, S.C.; James Richardson, S.C.
Res., 74 Liberty St., 06519-2299. Tel: 203-562-7592; Fax: 203-562-1737.
School—208 Columbus Ave., 06519. Tel: 203-777-8137; Fax: 203-776-5018.
Lay Teachers 10; Students 206.

2—ST. AEDAN'S, (1900), Revs. Joseph H. McCann; Cyriac Maliekal; Deacons Edward Taddei; Joseph R. Ryzewski.
Res., 112 Fountain St., 06515-0156. Tel: 203-389-2619; Fax: 203-389-1235.
School—Tel: 203-387-5693; Fax: 203-387-1609. Miss Nancy Bourgoin, Prin.
Lay Teachers 17; Students 247.
Catechesis/Religious Programs—Students 120.

3—ST. ANTHONY'S, (1904) (Italian), Revs. Joseph G. Moffo, C.S.; Antonio LiCastro.
Res., 25 Gold St., 06519. Tel: 203-624-1418.

4—ST. BERNADETTE'S, (1938), Revs. Howard J. Nash; Stephen A. Krugel; Deacon Gabriel Azzaro.
Res., 385 Townsend Ave., 06512-3998. Tel: 203-467-1007; Fax: 203-467-3719.
School—Tel: 203-469-2271.
Lay Teachers 20; Students 274.
Catechesis/Religious Programs—Tel: 203-467-8763.
Students 250.

5—ST. BONIFACE'S, (1868) (German), Rev. John D. Casey. In res., Rev. Johannes B. Hari Kustanto, S.J. (Indonesia).
Res., 630 State St., 06511-6599. Tel: 203-865-3365.

6—ST. BRENDAN'S, (1913), Rev. Donald J. French; Deacon Robert Brunell.
Res., 455 Whalley Ave., 06511-3080. Tel: 203-865-0561.
School—342 Ellsworth Ave., 06511. Tel: 203-562-6128.
Sisters 6; Lay Teachers 5; Students 257.
Convent—455 1/2 Whalley Ave., 06511. Tel: 203-787-4631. Sisters of Our Lady of the Garden

7—ST. CASIMIR'S, (1912) (Lithuanian), Rev. John D. Casey. In res., Revs. Ralph M. Colicchio; Geoffrey Smith.
Res., 339 Greene St., 06511-6599. Tel: 203-624-8085.

8—ST. DONATO'S, (1915) (Italian), Rev. Louis Anthony Evangelisto.
Res., 505 Lombard St., 06513-2910. Tel: 203-789-1576.

9—ST. FRANCIS, (1868), Rev. William J. Brenza.
Res., 397 Ferry St., 06513-3698. Tel: 203-777-5356; Fax: 203-777-5357.
School—Tel: 203-777-5352. Dr. Robert Schreck, Prin.
Religious 3; Lay Teachers 8; Students 277.
Catechesis/Religious Programs—Tel: 203-865-5179.
Students 75.

10—ST. JOHN THE BAPTIST, (1893), Rev. John J. Keane; Deacon Ronald Gurr. In res., Rev. Daniel J. Scott, M.S.
Res., 782 Dixwell Ave., 06511-1098. Tel: 203-624-3097; Fax: 203-562-0433.
Parish Center—20 Elizabeth St., 06511. Tel: 203-562-3908. Sr. Rosalie Shields, O.P., Pastoral Min.
Catechesis/Religious Programs—Students 72.

11—ST. JOHN THE EVANGELIST. Merged with St. Peter, New Haven.

12—ST. JOSEPH'S, (1900), Rev. John P. Sullivan, Temp. Admin.
Res., 129 Edwards St., 06511-2299. Tel: 203-777-2548.

13—SAINT MARTIN DE PORRES, (1942) (African American), Rev. Joseph M. Elko.
Res., 136 Dixwell Ave., 06511-3400. Tel: 203-624-9944.

14—ST. MARY'S PRIORY, (1832), Very Rev. Carleton Parker Jones, Prior; Revs. Paul J. Keller, O.P.; Thomas Q. Shanley, O.P.; Paul A. Bernardin, O.P.; Charles T. Shannon, O.P.; Gabriel O'Donnell, O.P.; Peter M. Girard, O.P.; Bernard T. Confer, O.P.; William B. Ryan, O.P.; Bro. Gerard Thayer, O.P.; Deacon Martin J. O'Connor.
Mailing Address: P.O. Box 1202, 06505-1202.

Res., 5 Hillhouse Ave., 06511. Tel: 203-562-6193; Fax: 203-562-1273.
Shrine—The Shrine of the Infant Prague (Inc.), Tel: 203-562-9326; Fax: 203-562-1273.

15—ST. MICHAEL'S, (1889) (Italian), Rev. Michael Tarro, C.S.
Res., 29 Wooster Pl., 06511-6998. Tel: 203-562-7178; Fax: 203-752-0157.
Parish Center—Tel: 203-789-9453.

16—ST. PETER, (1902). Closed. For inquiries for sacramental records contact Sacred Heart, New Haven.

17—ST. ROSE OF LIMA, (1907), Rev. William Burbank; Deacons Julio Vazquez; Julius Marcarelli.
Res., 115 Blatchley Ave., 06513-4298. Tel: 203-865-6149; Fax: 203-865-6140.
School—12 Richard St., 06513. Tel: 203-624-5075; Fax: 203-624-1686. Mary Joy Walsh, Prin.
Lay Teachers 10; Students 199.
Catechesis/Religious Programs—Students 180.

18—ST. STANISLAUS, (1901) (Polish), Revs. Waclaw Hlond, C.M.; Henry Sawicki, C.M.; Roman Kmiec, C.M.
Res., 9 Eld St., 06511-3899. Tel: 203-562-2828; Fax: 203-752-0217.
Catechesis/Religious Programs—Students 72.

Newington, Hartford Co., Holy Spirit (1964), Revs. John T. O'Connor; James F. Kinnane; Faron P. Calumba (Philippines); Deacon James A. Fortier. In res., Rev. Raymond S. Smialowski.
Res., 183 Church St., 06111-4898. Tel: 860-666-5671; Fax: 860-666-9784.
Catechesis/Religious Programs—Tel: 860-666-3562. Mary Marsan, D.R.E.
Students 720.

St. Mary (1924), Revs. Thomas J. Barry; Michael J. Dolan; James M. Moran; Deacons Michael J. O'Toole; Peter A. Cenci; Barry T. Skipp.
Res., 626 Willard Ave., 06111. Tel: 860-666-1591; Fax: 860-666-5720.
School—Tel: 860-666-3844; Fax: 860-666-5570.
Religious 3; Lay Teachers 13; Students 282.
Maryhouse—(Sisters of Mercy) 21 Hartford Ave., #9, 06111. Tel: 860-666-1085.
Convent—168 Cedar St., 06111. Tel: 860-667-1790. Sisters of Charity
Catechesis/Religious Programs—Tel: 860-666-6347. Susan Skipp, D.R.E.
Students 620.

New Milford, Litchfield Co., St. Francis Xavier's (1871), Rev. Mario F. Julian, O.F.M.
Res., 26 Chestnut Land Rd., P.O. Drawer 390, 06776-0390. Tel: 860-354-2202; 350-1611.
Catechesis/Religious Programs—Tel: 860-354-5372.
Students 725.

Our Lady of the Lakes (1990), Rev. Thomas E. Ptaszynski; Deacon Robert E. Muro.
Res., 3 Old Town Park Rd., 06776-4212. Tel: 860-354-5239; Fax: 860-354-2968.
Catechesis/Religious Programs—Tel: 860-355-5365.
Students 438.

Norfolk, Litchfield Co., Immaculate Conception (1889), Rev. John S. Ahern; Deacon Michael T. Sponzo.
Res., 4 North St., P.O. Box 583, 06058-1009. Tel: 860-542-5442. [CEM]
Catechesis/Religious Programs—Students 95.

North Branford, New Haven Co., St. Augustine (1941), Rev. Daniel F. McSheffery.
Res., 30 Caputo Rd., 06471-1027. Tel: 203-484-0403; Fax: 203-484-0132.
Catechesis/Religious Programs—Students 548.

Northford, New Haven Co., St. Monica's (1964), Rev. Joseph Parel; Sr. Judith Mulhall, C.S.J., Pastoral Assoc.; Deacons Louis P. Fusco; William B. Bergers.
Res., 1331 Middletown Ave., Box 160, 06472-0160. Tel: 203-484-9226.
Catechesis/Religious Programs—Tel: 203-484-2434.
Students 410.

North Haven, New Haven Co., St. Barnabas (1922), Revs. Hugh J. MacDonald; John J. Daly, Pastor Emeritus; Deacons James Stanley; James Taylor; William Bartlett; Paul T. Koch.
Res., 44 Washington Ave., 06473-1799. Tel: 203-239-5378; Fax: 203-239-3510.
Catechesis/Religious Programs—Tel: 203-239-3804. Karin Tierney, D.R.E.
Students 409.

St. Frances Cabrini (1967), Rev. John J. Georgia; Deacons Eugene Labagnara; George Stephens.
Res., 6 Welch Rd., 06473-2896. Tel: 203-239-5700; Fax: 203-239-6463.
Church & Parish Center—Pond Hill Rd., 06473. Tel: 203-239-5644.
Catechesis/Religious Programs—94 Chapel Hill Rd., 06473. Tel: 203-239-8012.
Students 368.
Nursery School—90 Chapel Hill Rd., 06473.
Convent— Sisters of the Sacred Heart of Jesus

St. Therese's (1925), Revs. Timothy A. Meehan; Alexander J. Cherukarakunnel; Deacons Carmine A. Angeloni; Louis J. Florio; Frank X. Paturzo.
Res., 555 Middletown Ave., 06473-4000. Tel: 203-239-1671; Fax: 203-234-2220.

Oakville, Litchfield Co., St. Mary Magdalen (1900), Revs. Joseph T. Kaminsky; William O. Seery.
Res., 145 Buckingham St., 06779-1797. Tel: 860-274-9273; Fax: 860-274-2013.
School—Tel: 860-945-0621; Fax: 860-945-6162.
Lay Teachers 11; Students 297.
Catechesis/Religious Programs—Students 444.

Orange, New Haven Co., Holy Infant (1952), Revs. Peter S. Dargan; Bernard D. Killeen, Pastor Emeritus; Deacons Americo Bichi; William Shaffer; Bernard J. Hayden; Harold J. Hoffman; Joseph D. Sullivan.
Res., 450 Race Brook Rd., 06477. Tel: 203-799-2379; Fax: 203-799-9720.
Catechesis/Religious Programs—Tel: 203-777-2417.
Students 883.

Oxford, New Haven Co., St. Thomas the Apostle (1966), Rev. Dominic J. Valla.
Res., 733 Oxford Rd., 06478. Tel: 203-888-2382; Fax: 203-881-5518.
Catechesis/Religious Programs—Students 585.

Plainville, Hartford Co., Our Lady of Mercy (1881), Revs. Richard P. McGann; Edmund K Karwowski; Deacon Gerald Geraci. In res., Rev. Francis E. Martens, C.I.C.M.
Res., 15 S. Canal St., 06062-2799. Tel: 860-793-1399; Fax: 860-747-5407. [CEM]
Parish Center: 19 S. Canal St., 06062. Tel: 860-747-6825; Fax: 860-747-5407.
Catechesis/Religious Programs—Tel: 860-747-6010. Jeanne Gionfriddo, D.R.E.
Students 202.

Plantsville, Hartford Co., Mary Our Queen (1961), Rev. Arthur J. DuPont; Deacons Frank Casey; Joseph DiMauro; Paul J. Kulas.
Res., 248 Savage St., P.O. Box 46, 06479-0046. Tel: 860-628-4901; Fax: 860-621-0610.
Catechesis/Religious Programs—Tel: 860-628-0437.
Students 515.

St. Aloysius (1961), Rev. John P. Blanchfield. In res., Rev. Donald J. O'Leary.
Res., 254 Burritt St., 06479-1426. Tel: 860-276-9208. [JC]
Catechesis/Religious Programs—Students 395.

Poquonock, Hartford Co., St. Joseph's (1874), Rev. William J. Hilliard; Deacon Joseph S. Sloan. In res., Rev. Robert B. Vargo.
Res., 1747 Poquonock Ave., P.O. Box 253, 06064-0253. Tel: 860-688-9566; Fax: 860-683-2225. [CEM]
Catechesis/Religious Programs—Tel: 860-683-0366.
Students 457.

Prospect, New Haven Co., St. Anthony's (1939), Revs. Philip J. Cascia; Joseph R. DeCarolis; Deacons Paul Iadarola; George Dinkle.
Res., 4 Union City Rd., P.O. Box 7117, 06712-0117. Tel: 203-758-4056; Fax: 203-758-4594.
Catechesis/Religious Programs—Tel: 203-758-4848; Fax: 203-758-4594.
Students 895.

Rocky Hill, Hartford Co., St. James (1880), Revs. Thomas B. Shepard; Anthony R. DeFronzo; Deacon Michael Shelto.
Res., 767 Elm St., 06067-1902. Tel: 860-529-8655; Fax: 860-257-1754.
Catechesis/Religious Programs—(Grades K-10). Tel: 860-529-1274. Thomas Sacerdote, D.R.E.
Students 686.

St. Elizabeth Seton (1985), Rev. James A. Shanley; Deacon Stephen L. Weaver.
Res., 280 Brook St., 06067-0485. Tel: 860-529-3222; Fax: 860-529-6421.
Catechesis/Religious Programs—Students 199.

Seymour, New Haven Co., Good Shepherd (1967), Rev. Edward S. Jaksina; Deacons John R. Maffeo; Alan C. Baldwin.
Res., 135 Mountain Rd., 06483-2038. Tel: 203-888-9243.
Catechesis/Religious Programs—D.R.E.: Glenn Durette; Debra Durette.
Students 423.

St. Augustine's (1866), Rev. Brian E. Jeffries; Deacon John R. Saffo, Sr.
Res., 35 Washington Ave., 06483-3198. Tel: 203-888-2081; Fax: 203-888-9681. [CEM]
Catechesis/Religious Programs—Tel: 203-888-7003.
Students 221.

Sharon, Litchfield Co., St. Bernard's (1885), Rev. James F. Pilon.
Res., 52 New St., Box 218, 06069-0218. Tel: 860-364-5244; Fax: 860-364-9893. [CEM]

Simsbury, Hartford Co., St. Mary's (1921), Team Ministry: Revs. Lawrence R. Bock; William E. Dudack; Deacons Joseph Gabriele; John Sweeney.
Res., 940 Hopmeadow St., P.O. Box 575, 06070-1819. Tel: 860-658-7627; Fax: 860-658-7626.
School—St. Mary School, 946 Hopmeadow St., 06070. Tel: 860-658-9412. Mrs. Maria Maynard, Prin.
Lay Teachers 15; Students 286.
Catechesis/Religious Programs—Tel: 860-658-5919.
Students 1,031.

Southbury, New Haven Co., Sacred Heart (1884), Rev. Mark F. Flynn; Deacons Joseph Lavoie, (Retired); Vincent Cassidy; Charles Dietsch; Michael Kulas.
Res., 68 Georges Hill Rd., 06488-0686. Tel: 203-264-5071; Fax: 203-264-5005. [CEM]
Catechesis/Religious Programs—Tel: 203-264-5065; Fax: 203-264-5005. Eileen Dignazio, D.R.E.
Students 860.
Station—Southbury, Southbury Training School, Tel: 203-264-8231.

South Glastonbury, Hartford Co., St. Augustine (1877), Rev. John F. McDonald.
Res., 55 Hopewell Rd., P.O. Box 175, 06073-0175. Tel: 860-633-9505. [CEM]
Catechesis/Religious Programs—Hopewell School, (Grades K-8). Tel: 860-633-9505.
Students 275.

Southington, Hartford Co., Immaculate Conception (1915) (Polish), Rev. David J. Lewandowski; Deacon Andrew Galiette. In res., Rev. Eugene J. Charman Tel: 203-628-7385.
Res., 130 Summer St., 06489. Tel: 203-628-2181. [CEM]
Catechesis/Religious Programs—Judy Telesmanic, D.R.E.
Students 227.
Father Kolbe Catechetical Center—152 Summer St., Plantsville, 06479. Tel: 860-628-6973.

St. Dominic (1971), Rev. Henry C. Frascadore; Deacons John L. Crowley; Eugene P. Nebiolo.
Res., 1050 Flanders Rd., 06489-1344. Tel: 860-628-0349; Fax: 860-276-8390.
Catechesis/Religious Programs—Tel: 860-628-6555. Jacqueline Marenholz, D.R.E.
Students 665.

St. Thomas (1860), Revs. George F. Lauretti; Joseph F. Keough; Deacons James P. Quinn; Angelo J. Coppola.
Res., 99 Bristol St., 06489-4599. Tel: 860-628-4713; Fax: 860-628-7341. [CEM]
School—Tel: 860-628-2485. Mrs. Joan Murphy, Prin.
Lay Teachers 7; Students 155.
Catechesis/Religious Programs—Tel: 860-628-9679.
Students 635.

South Meriden, New Haven Co., Holy Angels (1887), Rev. Roland M. LaPlante; Deacons Donald H. Smith; George Kraussman.
Res., 915 Main St., 06451-4999. Tel: 203-235-5311 (Rectory); 235-3822 (Office); Fax: 203-630-3041.
Catechesis/Religious Programs—585 Main St., 06451. Tel: 203-237-8697. Stephen N. Filippo, D.R.E.
Students 195.

South Windsor, Hartford Co., St. Francis of Assisi (1941), Rev. John P. Rohan; Deacon David F. Dwyer.
Res., 673 Ellington Rd., 06074-4166. Tel: 860-528-8288; Fax: 860-528-1685.
Catechesis/Religious Programs—Tel: 860-289-3671. Mark F. Cerrato, D.R.E.
Students 465.

St. Margaret Mary (1961), Revs. Daniel Jeremiah Sullivan; Francis V. Krukowski; Deacons Robert R. LaRochelle; Thomas J. Conklin.
Res., 80 Hayes Rd., 06074-1499. Tel: 860-644-2411; Fax: 860-644-5765.
Catechesis/Religious Programs—Tel: 860-644-2549.
Students 1,038.

Suffield, Hartford Co., Sacred Heart (1884), Revs. Theodore T. Raczynski; Timothy A. O'Brien; Deacons Benedict Winiarski; Valentino Bertolini.
Res., 446 Mountain Rd., 06078-0626. Tel: 860-668-4246; Fax: 860-668-1337. [JC]
Catechesis/Religious Programs—Tel: 860-668-7766.
Students 662.

St. Joseph's (1916) (Polish), Rev. William L. Baldyga; Deacon Edward Szewczyk.
Res., 140 S. Main St., 06078-2218. Tel: 860-668-2880. [CEM]
Convent—156 S. Main St., 06078. Tel: 860-668-2503. Felician Sisters

Tariffville, Hartford Co., St. Bernard's (1878), Rev. Thomas A. Flower; Deacons Andrew J. Anthony; Thomas P. Scanlon.
Res., 7 Maple St., P.O. Box 85, 06081-0085. Tel: 860-658-5142; Fax: 860-658-2804. [CEM]
Catechesis/Religious Programs—Students 237.

Terryville, Litchfield Co., Immaculate Conception (1882), Rev. Gerald H. Dziedzic.
Res., 21 Maple St., 06786-1197. Tel: 860-583-4697. [CEM 2]
Catechesis/Religious Programs—Students 120.

St. Casimir (1906), Rev. Daniel J. Karpiey.
Res., 19 Allen St., 06786-1503. Tel: 860-583-4660.

Thomaston, Litchfield Co., St. Thomas (1869), Revs. Harold M. Kearns; John E. Cockayne; Deacons Gerald Wooton; Robert Gordon.
Parish Center—(CEM) 19 Electric Ave., 06787-1651. Tel: 860-283-5817; Fax: 860-283-1009.
School—30 N. Main St., 06787. Tel: 860-283-5955.
Lay Teachers 10; Students 149.
Catechesis/Religious Programs—Tel: 860-283-4296.
Students 433.

Torrington, Litchfield Co.,

1—St. Francis of Assisi, (1877), Revs. Robert W. Ladish; John G. Weaver; Deacon Edward Dickson; Sr. Helen Marie Clark, R.S.M., Pastoral Assoc.
Res., 160 Main St., 06790-5299. Tel: 860-482-5571.
School—Tel: 860-489-4177. Mrs. Margaret Carabelli, Prin.
Lay Teachers 8; Students 205.
Catechesis/Religious Programs—360 Prospect St., 06790. Tel: 203-482-3121.
Students 430.

2—Sacred Heart, (1910) (Slovak), Revs. Gerard G. Masters; Stephen M. Sledesky.
Res., 116 Grove St., 06790-5047. Tel: 860-482-8246.
Parish Center—119 Grove St., 06790. Tel: 860-489-4070.
Catechesis/Religious Programs—Students 69.

3—St. Mary's, (1919) (Polish), Revs. Robert W. Ladish; John G. Weaver.
Res., 61 Forest Ct., 06790-4698. Tel: 860-482-3583.
Catechesis/Religious Programs—Students 50.

4—St. Peter's, (1910) (Italian), Revs. Gerard G. Masters; Stephen M. Sledesky.
Res., 107 E. Main St., 06790-5493. Tel: 860-482-4433; Fax: 860-482-1891.
School—Tel: 860-489-8735; Fax: 860-482-9406.
Maestre Pie Filippini 2; Lay Teachers 8; Students 175.
Catechesis/Religious Programs—Students 189.

Union City, New Haven Co., St. Hedwig (Naugatuck) (1906) (Polish), Rev. George F. Ziezulewicz; Deacon Michael Szumigala.
Res., 32 Golden Hill St., 06770-3099. Tel: 203-729-2490; Fax: 203-720-2161.
School—Tel: 203-729-2403; Fax: 203-720-2161. Ms. Patricia Dayner, Prin.
Lay Teachers 6; Students 128.
Catechesis/Religious Programs—Students 106.

St. Mary's (Naugatuck) (1907), Rev. Philip A. Sheridan; Deacon Thomas J. Clifford.
Res., 338 N. Main St., 06770-3235. Tel: 203-729-2279.
Catechesis/Religious Programs—Students 150.

Unionville, Hartford Co., St. Mary's (1874), Rev. Robert J. St. Martin.
Res., 16 Bidwell Sq., 06085-1116. Tel: 860-673-2422; Fax: 860-673-2001. [CEM]
Catechesis/Religious Programs—Students 650.

Wallingford, New Haven Co., Holy Trinity (1869), Revs. Charles J. MacDonald; John J. Williams; Luis M. Jaramillo; Deacons Joseph Cretella; Efrain DeJesus; Eugene Riotte.
Res., 68 N. Colony St., 06492-3696. Tel: 203-269-8791; Fax: 203-269-0880.
School—11 N. Whittlesey Ave., 06492. Tel: 203-269-4476; Fax: 203-294-4983. Sr. Kathleen Kelly, R.S.M., Prin.
Sisters of Mercy 1; Lay Teachers 9; Students 270.
Catechesis/Religious Programs—Tel: 203-265-6300. Frances Selmecki, D.R.E.
Students 985.

Resurrection (1963), Revs. Dawson D. Trenchard; Daniel E. Johnson, Pastor Emeritus. In res., Rev. Mark J. Bonsignore (Peru).
Res., 115 Pond Hill Rd., 06492-4836. Tel: 203-265-1694; Fax: 203-284-9766.
Catechesis/Religious Programs—Tel: 203-481-8029. Mary Ann Marchitto, D.R.E.
Students 591.

SS. Peter and Paul (1924) (Polish), Rev. Stephen Bzdyra; Deacon Louis P. Sill, Jr.
Res., 139 N. Orchard St., 06492-3617. Tel: 203-269-4617; Fax: 203-265-6751. [CEM]
Catechesis/Religious Programs—Students 98.

Washington Depot, Litchfield Co., Our Lady of Perpetual Help (1893), Rev. Thomas F. Bennett; Deacon George H. Streib.
Res., 34 Green Hill Rd., P.O. Box 303, 06794. Tel: 860-868-2600. [CEM]
Catechesis/Religious Programs—Students 163.
Mission—Roxbury, Litchfield Co., St. Patrick's, Church St., Roxbury 06783.

Waterbury, New Haven Co.,

1—Blessed Sacrament, (1911), Rev. Walter A. Vichas; Deacon George Wilcox.
Res., 192 Robbins St., 06708. Tel: 203-753-3149.
School—Tel: 203-756-5313.
Sisters 3; Lay Teachers 9; Students 265.
Catechesis/Religious Programs—Tel: 203-757-1656.
Students 91.
Convent—407 Robinwood Rd., 06708. Tel: 203-753-1472. Sisters of the Third Order Regular of St. Francis

2—Immaculate Conception, (1848), Revs. John J. Bevins; Raymond Pitruzzello, Pastor Emeritus; George M. White, O.M.I.; John Curry Gay; Maximo Asencios-Pablo, M.Ss.A.; Thomas Simon, M.Ss.A.
Res., 74 W. Main St., 06721-1670. Tel: 203-574-0017.
School—St. Mary's, Tel: 203-753-2574.
Sisters 2; Lay Teachers 18; Students 512.
Catechesis/Religious Programs—Students 169.
Convent—55 Cole St., 06702. Tel: 203-754-2913. Maryknoll Sisters

3—Our Lady of Fatima, (1971) (Portuguese), Rev. Nelson Ribeiro, C.M.
Res., 2071 Baldwin St., 06706. Tel: 203-753-1424; Fax: 203-753-1424.
Catechesis/Religious Programs—Students 410.

4—Our Lady of Loreto, (1971), Rev. Msgr. Joseph A. Devine.
Res., 12 Ardsley Rd., 06708-1825. Tel: 203-757-6112; Fax: 203-756-9656.
Catechesis/Religious Programs—Students 206.

5—Our Lady of Lourdes, (1899) (Italian), Rev. Ronald A. Ferraro; Deacon George M. Pettinico.
Res., 309 S. Main St., 06706-1090. Tel: 203-754-4134.

6—Our Lady of Mt. Carmel, (1923) (Italian), Revs. Carmine B. Raneri; Daniel J. McLearen; Deacon Daniel A. Sloan.
Res., 785 Highland Ave., 06708-4199. Tel: 203-756-8981; Fax: 203-756-2074.
School—645 Congress Ave., 06708. Tel: 203-755-6809. Sr. Daniella Marie O'Sullivan, S.S.N.D., Prin.
Lay Teachers 10; Students 267.
Catechesis/Religious Programs—Tel: 203-753-1713.
Students 220.
Convent—656 Congress Ave., 06708. Tel: 203-754-1947.

7—Sacred Heart, (1855), Rev. Joseph E. Looney; Deacon Earle Kimball. In res., Rev. Richard C. Bollea.
Res., 13 Wolcott St., 06702-1790. Tel: 203-757-8737; Fax: 203-754-5862.

8—St. Anne, (1886) (French), Rev. Alvin J. LeBlanc; Deacons Francis X. Bandeira; Gaspard D. LeBlanc.
Res., 515 S. Main St., 06706-1089. Tel: 203-756-4439; Fax: 203-754-3244.

9—St. Cecilia's, (1893) (German), Rev. John C. Blackall, (Spanish Apostolate); Deacon Alejandro Lopez.
Res., 83 Cherry St., 06702-1699. Tel: 203-574-5156.
Catechesis/Religious Programs—Tel: 203-754-1124.
Students 367.

10—St. Francis Xavier's, (1896), Rev. Paul J. Pace; Deacon Donald E. Cruess.
Res., 625 Baldwin St., 06706-1597. Tel: 203-756-7804.
School—605 Baldwin St., 06706. Tel: 203-753-3197. Mr. J. Brian Lally, Prin.
Religious 1; Lay Teachers 9; Students 240.
Catechesis/Religious Programs—Tel: 203-754-6996.
Students 165.

11—St. Joseph, (1894) (Lithuanian), Rev. Francis V. Karvelis. In res., Rev. Paul P. Sabulis, (Retired).
Res., 46 Congress Ave., 06708. Tel: 203-754-1557.
School—Lay Teachers 10; Students 219.

12—St. Leo the Great, (1974), Rev. Joseph F. Gorman; Deacons Modesto Rosello; Charles Colella.
Res., 14 Bentwood Dr., 06705-3612. Tel: 203-573-0511.
Catechesis/Religious Programs—Tel: 203-573-0511.
Students 220.

13—St. Lucy's, (1926) (Italian), Rev. Paul Mangiafico.
Res., 24 Branch St., 06704-3626. Tel: 203-574-5903.
School—58 Griggs St., 06704. Tel: 203-756-3831. Mr. John J. Petto, Prin.
Lay Teachers 10; Students 240.
Parish Center: 64 Division St., 06704. Tel: 203-755-8420.
Catechesis/Religious Programs—Students 90.

14—St. Margaret's, (1910), Rev. Kevin J. Gray; Sr. Rosemary McKenna, D.W., Pastoral Min.; Deacon George Hajjar.
Res., 289 Willow St., 06710. Tel: 203-754-6101.
School—Tel: 203-753-3708. Ms. Margaret Sheehy, Prin.
Lay Teachers 11; Students 236.
Catechesis/Religious Programs—Students 150.

15—St. Michael, (1897), Rev. Ronald Gliatta, O.F.M.; Friar Larry Parent, O.F.M.; Deacon Domenic Stolfi.
Res., 62 St. Michael Dr., 06704-1295. Tel: 203-753-0689; Fax: 203-573-9101.
Catechesis/Religious Programs—Students 180.

16—St. Patrick, (1880), Rev. Richard M. Taberski; Deacon Thomas F. Johnson.
Mailing Address: P.O. Box 271, 06720-0271. Tel: 203-756-8837; Fax: 203-756-4690.
Res., 50 Charles St., 06708. Tel: 203-756-8837.
Catechesis/Religious Programs—Students 50.

17—SS. Peter and Paul, (1920), Revs. Edward F. Hyland; Kevin V. Walsh; John Meaney, M.M. In res., Rev. Robert J. Grant.
Res., 67 Southmayd Rd., 06705. Tel: 203-756-7919; Fax: 203-755-3535.
School—Tel: 203-755-0881. Janet Curry, Prin.
Lay Teachers 14; Students 345.
Catechesis/Religious Programs—114 Beecher Ave., 06705. Tel: 203-753-4242.
Students 255.

18—St. Stanislaus Kostka, (1913) (Polish), Rev. George F. Ziezulewicz, Admin.
Res., 86 East Farm St., 06704. Tel: 203-574-0871; Fax: 203-575-0107.

19—St. Thomas, (1898). Closed. For inquiries for sacramental records contact St. Michael, Waterbury.

Watertown, Litchfield Co., St. John the Evangelist (1878), Revs. John M. Cooney; Kevin J. Forsyth; Deacons George Simonin; Daniel Camerota; John Chartes.
Res., 21 Academy Hill, 06795-2101. Tel: 860-274-8836. [CEM]
School—Tel: 860-274-9208; Fax: 860-945-1082. Sr. Eileen Eden, S.S.N.D., Prin.
School Sisters of Notre Dame 5; Lay Teachers 7; Students 197.
Catechesis/Religious Programs—Tel: 860-274-4123. Theresa N. Morgado, D.R.E.
Students 795.

West Hartford, Hartford Co.,

1—St. Brigid's, (1919), Revs. Edward J. McLean; Richard B. Sherer, Pastor Emeritus; Deacon Robert J. Hilliard. In res., Rev. Msgr. Charles B. Johnson.
Res., 1088 New Britain Ave., 06110-2489. Tel: 860-236-5965.
School—100 Mayflower St., 06110. Tel: 860-561-2130.
Sisters 1; Lay Teachers 16; Students 264.
Catechesis/Religious Programs—Tel: 860-521-8523.
Students 315.

2—St. Helena, (1966), Revs. Francis P. Johnson; Eugene M. Kilbride; Deacons Raymond Fugere; James Murphy. In res., Rev. Zigford J. Kriss.
Res., 30 Echo Ln., 06107-3698. Tel: 860-521-1921.
Catechesis/Religious Programs—Tel: 860-521-3661.
Students 288.

3—St. John the Evangelist, (1942) (Spanish), Revs. John P. Tracy, Admin.; Paul F. Kenefick; Deacon Thomas F. Breen, III.
Res., 251 Newfield Ave., 06106-3630. Tel: 860-953-3147.
Catechesis/Religious Programs—Students 80.

4—St. Mark the Evangelist, (1942), Team Ministry: Rev. Thomas J. Sas; Rev. Msgr. William J. Mullen; Deacon John J. Mylott.
Res., 467 S. Quaker Ln., 06110-1000. Tel: 860-233-1269.
Catechesis/Religious Programs—491 Quaker Ln., 06110. Tel: 860-236-3545. Agnes Allen, D.R.E.
Students 224.

5—St. Peter Claver, (1966), Revs. Joseph P. McGarry; James L. McKearney.
Res., 47 Pleasant St., 06107-1600. Tel: 860-561-4235.

Catechesis/Religious Programs—Tel: 860-521-2904.
Students 515.

6—ST. THOMAS THE APOSTLE CHURCH, (1921), Revs. Arthur J. Murphy; Patrick J. Curran (SLC); Edward M. Moran; Deacon Eugene Phaneuf. In res., Rev. John J. Stack.
Res., 872 Farmington Ave., 06119-1499. Tel: 860-233-8269; Fax: 860-523-8794.
School—25 Dover Rd., 06119. Tel: 860-236-6257; Fax: 860-236-8865.
Lay Teachers 27; Students 312.
Catechesis/Religious Programs—Tel: 860-523-4209.
Students 299.

7—ST. TIMOTHY'S, (1958), Rev. Henry P. Cody; Deacon George Brown. In res., Rev. Alphonse S. Labieniec.
Res., 1116 N. Main St., 06117-1209. Tel: 860-233-5131; Fax: 860-232-2189.
School—St. Timothy Middle School, 225 King Philip Dr., 06117. Tel: 860-236-0614; Fax: 860-236-0614.
Lay Teachers 14; Students 140.
Catechesis/Religious Programs—Tel: 860-232-3952.
Students 234.

West Haven, New Haven Co.,

1—OUR LADY OF VICTORY, (1935), Revs. Mark S. Suslenko; Mathew Kappalumakkel. In res., Rev. Gregory Altermatt, Pastor Emeritus.
Res., 600 Jones Hill Rd., 06516-6399. Tel: 203-934-6357; Fax: 203-932-3315.
School—Tel: 203-932-6457.
Lay Teachers 13; Students 251.
Catechesis/Religious Programs—Tel: 203-933-0044.
Students 657.

2—ST. JOHN VIANNEY, (1965), Rev. John F. Brinsmade; Deacons Frank J. Bevvino, Jr.; Charles W. Parlee, Jr.
Res., 300 Capt. Thomas Blvd., 06516-5974. Tel: 203-934-6000; Fax: 203-934-5677.
Catechesis/Religious Programs—Tel: 203-933-8471.
Students 255.

3—ST. LAWRENCE'S, (1886), Team Ministry: Rev. Thomas A. Sievel; Deacons Anthony P. Solli; John E. Wheeler. In res., Rev. Chacko K. Kumplamthanam (India).
Res., 207 Main St., 06516-4599. Tel: 203-934-8351; Fax: 203-937-7858.
School—233 Main St., 06516. Tel: 203-933-2518; Fax: 203-932-2058. Sr. Rosemarie Ryan, S.N.D., Dir.
Lay Teachers 11; Students 263.
Catechesis/Religious Programs—231 Main St., 06516. Tel: 203-933-2519.
Students 140.

4—ST. LOUIS, (1886) (French Territorial), Rev. Peter J. Pinto; Deacons Salvatore DeFilippo; Edward J. Mancini.
Res., 89 Bull Hill Ln., 06516-3998. Tel: 203-934-5249; Fax: 203-934-5240.

5—ST. PAUL'S, (1916), Rev. Lawrence Symolon; Deacons George Schiro; Richard Fournier.
Res., 41 Alling St., 06516-2799. Tel: 203-933-1024.
Catechesis/Religious Programs—Tel: 203-934-1357. Patricia Sastor, D.R.E.
Students 400.
Parish Center: 45 Alling St., 06516. Tel: 203-934-1357.
Mission—West Haven, Our Lady of Mt. Carmel Chapel, Fenwick St., 06516. Tel: 203-389-6384.

West Simsbury, Hartford Co., St. Catherine of Siena (1971), Rev. Richard R. Russell; Deacon Thomas F. Delehanty.
Res., Box 184, 06092. Tel: 203-658-1642.
Catechesis/Religious Programs—Students 266.

Wethersfield, Hartford Co., Corpus Christi (1941), Team Ministry: Revs. Thomas B. Campion, Co-Pastor; David W. Lonergan, Co-Pastor. In res., Rev. Bradford Colton, Pastor Emeritus.
Res., 84 Somerset St., 06109-3031. Tel: 860-529-2545.
School—Tel: 860-529-5487; Fax: 860-257-9106. Mrs. Eileen Sampiere, Prin.
Religious 1; Lay Teachers 23; Students 481.
Catechesis/Religious Programs—581 Silas Deane Hwy., 06109. Tel: 860-721-9419.
Students 545.

Incarnation (1963), Revs. John F. Edwards; Frederick M. Aniello; Deacons Robert J. D'Efemia; Carroll Violette.
Res., 544 Prospect St., 06109-3696. Tel: 860-529-2533.
Catechesis/Religious Programs—Tel: 860-529-6765. Noranne Wamester, D.R.E.
Students 444.

Sacred Heart (1876), Team Ministry: Revs. Thomas B. Campion, Co-Pastor; David W. Lonergan, Co-Pastor; Deacon Seth M. English.
Res., 56 Hartford Ave., 06109-1800. Tel: 860-529-1991.
Catechesis/Religious Programs—Tel: 860-529-0815.
Students 192.

Windsor, Hartford Co., St. Gabriel's (1894), Revs. James C. Rush; Richard J. Neumann; Michael F.X. Hinkley, S.T.D.; Deacons Joseph J. Cooke; Donald E. Norton; Ronald M. Biamomte.
Res., 379 Broad St., 06095-3004. Tel: 860-688-4905.
School—77 Bloomfield Ave., 06095. Tel: 860-688-6401.
Lay Teachers 12; Students 283.
Catechesis/Religious Programs—Students 288.

St. Gertrude's (1947), Rev. Maurice J. Barry; Deacons Francis J. Giunta; Vincent Thorney.
Res., 550 Matianuck Ave., 06095-3599. Tel: 860-522-6163.
Catechesis/Religious Programs—Students 164.

Windsor Locks, Hartford Co., St. Mary (1866), Revs. Robert A. O'Grady; Francis P. McDonnell.
Res., 42 Spring St., 06096-2311. Tel: 860-623-2524; Fax: 860-623-5684. [CEM]
Parish Center—45 Church St., 06096. Tel: 860-627-9469.
Catechesis/Religious Programs—Tel: 860-627-9469.
Students 507.

St. Robert Bellarmine (1962), Rev. Thomas F. Farrell.
Res., 52 S. Elm St., P.O. Box 315, 06096-0315. Tel: 860-623-0240; Fax: 860-623-0240.
Catechesis/Religious Programs—Students 151.

Winsted, Litchfield Co., St. Joseph's (1853), Revs. Anthony F. Moore, O.F.M.; Leon Ristuccia, O.F.M.; John W. Rudy, O.F.M.; Deacon William H. Wilcox.
Res., 31 Oak St., P.O. Box 808, 06098-0808. Tel: 860-379-3369; Fax: 860-379-4194. [CEM]
School—St. Anthony's, 55 Oak St., 06098. Tel: 860-379-7521. Sr. Fidelis Shepherd, F.M.D.M., Prin.
Lay Teachers 10; Students 253.
Catechesis/Religious Programs—Tel: 860-379-5968.
Students 312.

Wolcott, New Haven Co., St. Pius X (1955), Revs. Henry A. Balchunas; Vittorio Guerrera; Deacon Stephen J. Kelly.
Res., 525 Woodtick Rd., 06716-2898. Tel: 203-879-2544; Fax: 203-879-2545.
Catechesis/Religious Programs—Tel: 203-879-9030; Fax: 203-879-2545.
Students 619.

St. Maria Goretti (1973), Rev. William R. Sokolowski; Deacon Leonard R. Lewandoski.
Res., 1300 Woodtick Rd., P.O. Box 6291, 06716-0291. Tel: 203-879-4608; Fax: 203-879-4609.
Catechesis/Religious Programs—Tel: 203-879-5242.
Students 394.

Woodbridge, New Haven Co., Church of the Assumption (1924), Revs. Gene Gianelli; Robert J. Lord; Deacons Joseph P. Borland; Mario DiRienzo.
Res., 81 Center Rd., 06525-1699. Tel: 203-387-7119; Fax: 203-387-4281.
Catechesis/Religious Programs—Tel: 203-389-9863; Fax: 203-387-4281. Sr. Dorellen Sullivan, R.S.M., D.R.E.
Students 634.

Woodbury, Litchfield Co., St. Teresa's (1902), Rev. George G. Laliberte.
Res., P.O. Box A, 11 Washington Ave., 06798-0417. Tel: 203-263-2008.
Catechesis/Religious Programs—Students 294.

Woodmont, New Haven Co., St. Agnes (1906), Revs. Francis X. Callahan; George J. Raffaeta, Pastor Emeritus.
Res., 400 Merwin Ave., 06460-7198. Tel: 203-878-1617.
Catechesis/Religious Programs—Students 628.

Yalesville, New Haven Co., Our Lady of Fatima (1960), Revs. Salvatore F. Cavagnuolo; Thomas J. Cieslikowski. In res., Rev. Leo J. Daily, Pastor Emeritus.
Res., 382 Hope Hill Rd., 06492-2270. Tel: 203-265-0961; Fax: 203-269-9386.
Catechesis/Religious Programs—Tel: 203-265-6426; 265-6818 (Youth Minister); Fax: 203-269-9386. Linda O'Hara, D.R.E.
Students 742.

Chaplains of Public Institutions

HARTFORD. *Hartford Hospital*, 80 Seymour St., 06102-5037. Tel: 860-545-2251. Chaplains: Revs. Hudson R. Richard; Gerard Pelletier, S.M.; Ms. Diane L. Cardinal.

BRISTOL. *Bristol Hospital*, Brewster Rd., 06011-0977. Tel: 860-585-3431. Rev. Donald O. Rackliffe, Chap.

CHESHIRE. *Connecticut Correctional Institution*, 900 Milldale Rd., 06410. Tel: 203-272-2215. Rev. Daniel G. Keefe, Chap.
Manson Youth Institution, 42 Jarvis St., 06510. Tel: 203-272-5391. Rev. Alphonse S. Labieniec, Chap.

ENFIELD. *Carl Robinson Correctional Institution*, P.O. Box 1400, 06083-1400. Tel: 860-763-6200. Deacon Robert P. Gale, Chap.

NEW BRITAIN. *New Britain General Hospital*, 100 Grand St., 06050. Tel: 860-224-5011. Rev. Ronald T. Smith, Chap., Res., 396 Church St., 06051.

NEW HAVEN. *Community Correctional Institution*, 245 Whalley Ave., 06511. Tel: 203-789-7111. Rev. Steven H. Bzdyra, Chap.
Yale-New Haven Hospital, 20 York St., 06510-3202. Revs. Geoffrey C. Smith, Chap.; Ralph M. Colicchio, Coord. Catholic Apostolate, Tel: 203-785-2152.

NEWINGTON. *Department of Veteran Affairs Medical Center*, 555 Willard Ave., 06111. Tel: 860-666-6951. Rev. Francis M. Vella, Chap.

ROCKY HILL. *Veterans' Home and Hospital*, West St., 06067. Tel: 860-529-2571. Rev. James B. Quilty, M.S.

SUFFIELD. *Macdougall Correctional Institute*, 1153 E. St. S., 06080-0002. Tel: 860-627-2148; Fax: 860-627-2152. Rev. Anthony J. Bruno, Chap., Res., 90 Alden Ave., Enfield, 06082-2865. Tel: 860-745-9966.

WATERBURY. *Waterbury Hospital*, 64 Robbins St., 06708. Tel: 203-573-7213; Fax: 203-573-7326. Rev. Richard C. Bollea, Chap.

WEST HAVEN. *V.A. CT Health Care System*, 950 Campbell Ave., 06516. Tel: 203-932-5711. Rev. Daniel V. Scott, M.S.

Special and Other Archdiocesan Assignment:
Reverend Monsignors—
Ginty, Thomas M., Sec. to the Archbishop, Chancellor, Dir. Office for Divine Worship, 467 Bloomfield Ave., Bloomfield, CT 06002
Johnson, Charles B., Vicar for Priests, St. Thomas Seminary, 467 Bloomfield Ave., Bloomfield, CT 06002
Reverend Fathers—
Bergin, Robert D., Dir., Deaf Apostolate, Mercyknoll, 243 Steele Rd., West Hartford, CT 06117
Charman, Eugene J., Archdiocesan Computer Consultant, 50 Knowles Dr., Plantsville, CT 06479
Conte, John P., Min., Office of Ministry for Priests, 467 Bloomfield Ave., Bloomfield, CT 06002
Dietrich, John J., Vocations Dir., St. Thomas Seminary, 469 Bloomfield Ave., Bloomfield, CT 06002
Donohue, Aidan N., Rector & Pres., St. Thomas Seminary, 467 Bloomfield Ave., Bloomfield, CT 06002
Gatzak, John P., Dir., Office of Communications (Radio/Television), 785 Asylum Ave., Hartford, CT 06105
Kinnane, James F., J.C.L., Vicar for Religious, 134 Farmington Ave., Hartford, CT 06105-3784
Kriss, Zigford J., Supt. of Schools, 467 Bloomfield Ave., Bloomfield, CT 06002
LeBlanc, Alvin J., Adjutant Judicial Vicar (Vice Officialis), Chancery Tribunal, 134 Farmington Ave., Hartford, CT 06105
Liptak, David Q., Consulting Editor, "The Catholic Transcript", 785 Asylum Ave., Hartford, CT 06105
McCarthy, John J., Tribunal, Judicial Vicar (Officialis), Chancery, 134 Farmington Ave., Hartford, CT 06105-3784
McLean, Edward J., Dir., Catholic Library and Information Center, 125 Market St., Hartford, CT 06103
Motta, Michael J., Dir., Office of Religious Education, Newington, CT 06111
Murasso, Jeremiah N., Exec. Dir., Highland Heights, New Haven, CT
Tiano, Christopher M., Exec. Editor, "The Catholic Transcript", 785 Asylum Ave., Hartford, CT 06105
Vargo, Robert B., Vice Chancellor, 134 Farmington Ave., Hartford, CT 06105-3784
Wrenn, Lawrence G., Judicial Vicar for the Court of Appeals, Tribunal Office, 134 Farmington Ave., Hartford, CT 06105

On Duty Outside the Archdiocese:
Reverend Monsignors—
Sokolowski, Robert S., Catholic University of America, 401 Michigan Ave., N.E., Washington, DC 20064
Reverend Fathers—
Charbonneau, William R., 4900 Colonel Addison Pl., Upper Marlborough, MD 20772
Cwiekowski, Frederick J., S.S., St. Patrick Seminary, 320 Middlefield Rd., Menlo Park, CA 94025
Goekler, Thomas F., Maryknoll Technical School, 45 Choi Ha Rd., Jordan Valley, Kowloon, Hong China. Tel: 852-758-3539; Fax: 852-813-7221
Leavitt, Robert F., S.S., St. Mary Seminary, 5400 Roland Ave., Baltimore, MD 21210

Malave, Will-Roger, St. Boniface Rectory, Leading Creek, Rte. #2, Box 25, Camden, WV 26338-9737
Matera, Frank J., Catholic University of America, 401 Michigan Ave., N.E., Washington, DC 20017
McBrien, Richard P., University of Notre Dame, Notre Dame, IN 46556
Mitchell, Thomas R., Good Shepherd, (Buen Pastor Parish) Calle San Gerardo, A-1-A Terrace, Mayaguez, PR 00708
Morrison, Douglas A., 24 Courthouse Sq., Apt. 805, Rockville, MD 20850-2340
Novoa, Dominic E., Chap., St. Mary Hospital, West Palm Beach, FL 33407
Pfnausch, Edward G., Catholic University, 401 Michigan Ave., N.E., Washington, DC 20017
Thayer, David D., S.S., St. Mary Seminary & University, 5400 Roland Ave., Baltimore, MD 21210
Whalen, William C., 130 Springfield Ave., Ottawa, K1S OE5 Canada

Military Chaplains:
Reverend Fathers—
Cavanaugh, Kevin P., U.S. Army, 3147 Capstan Way, Colorado Springs, CO 80906
Hanley, Dennis P., U.S. Air Force, 90 MWG/HC, 7000 Randel Ave., F.E. Warren AFB, WY 82005
Hellwig, Lee W., U.S. Marines, 10315 E. Mathew Blvd., Albany, GA 31705

Retired:
Reverend Monsignors—
Connelly, James A., 182 Washington St., Norwich, CT 06360
Daly, Charles W., St. Luke Rectory, 66 Bolton St., Hartford, CT 06114-2698
Fries, Francis A., 42 Blakeslee St., Bristol, CT 06010
Kennedy, John S., 1213 N. Main St., West Hartford, CT 06117
Wodarski, John P., St. Stanislaus Rectory, 510 West St., Bristol, CT 06010
Reverend Fathers—
Archambault, James H., 2003 49th St. West, Bradenton, FL 34209
Barlowski, Joseph R., St. Mary Home, 2021 Albany Ave., West Hartford, CT 06117-2701
Bieluch, Chester A., St. Mary Home, 2021 Albany Ave., West Hartford, CT 06117-2701
Boyle, James M., St. Mary Rectory, 16 Bidwell Sq., Unionville, CT 06085-1116
Castellani, John J., 364 Lakeview Dr., Southington, CT 06489
Chagnon, Robert J., 19333 Summerlin Rd., Fort Myers, FL 33908
Colton, Bradford, Corpus Christi Rectory, 84 Somerset St., Wethersfield, CT 06109
Cook, John P., 45 Jefferson Rd., Bldg. 3, Apt. 15, Branford, CT 06082
Cretella, Biagio, 75 Washington Ave., Bldg. 4, #207, Hamden, CT 06518-3264
Cronin, W. Vincent, St. Mary Home, 2021 Albany Ave., West Hartford, CT 06117
Croteau, Francois A., Village Gate, 88 Scott Swamp Rd. #309, Farmington, CT 06032-2991
Crowley, Stephen L., 156 Circular Ave., Hamden, CT 06514
Curran, John F., Our Lady of Victory Rectory, 600 Jones Hill Rd., West Haven, CT 06516
Daily, Leo J., Our Lady of Fatima Rectory, 382 Hope Hill Rd., Yalesville, CT 06492
DeMuro, S. Patrick, 1229 Winsted Rd., #91, Torrington, CT 06790
Dery, Henry R., 45 Aldea Ave., Dudley, MA 01571
Dilion, Joseph A., 13 Leeway Dr., Westbrook, CT 06498
Donahue, Joseph P., St. Francis Rectory, 318 Church St., Naugatuck, CT 06770
Dyer, George A., St. Mary Home, 2021 Albany Ave., West Hartford, CT 06117
Ferrigno, Denis P., Our Lady of Good Counsel Rectory, 56 Center St., Folly Beach, NC 29439
Fiedorczyk, Henry P., Holy Cross Rectory, 31 Biruta St., New Britain, CT 06053
Flynn, Joseph A., 12 Yankee Peddler Path, Unit 2, Madison, CT 06443
Flynn, Vincent J., P.O. Box 651, Kent, CT 06757
Foran, Edward R., 52 Grove St., Yalesville, CT 06492
Gengras, Joseph C., St. Peter Claver Rectory, 47 Pleasant St., West Hartford, CT 06107-1600
Graziani, Joseph A., 380 Lake Plymouth Blvd., Plymouth, CT 06728
Guandalini, Julius S., 8 Sara Circle, North Haven, CT 06473
Hannon, John P., 21 Pleasant Rd., Enfield, CT 06082
Hastillo, Stanley E., 425 East Rd., Broad Brook, CT 06016
Hayes, William J., 47 Clark St., New Britain, CT 06051
Hewitt, Charles L., St. Joseph Manor, 6448 Main St., Trumbull, CT 06611
Horgan, John A., 1696 Litchfield Tpke., Woodbridge, CT 06525
Keane, Martin T., St. Mary Home, 2021 Albany Ave., West Hartford, CT 06117
Keeley, Alban F., St. Mary Home, 2021 Albany Ave., West Hartford, CT 06117
Kennedy, Charles T., St. Joseph Manor, 6448 Main St., Trumbull, CT 06117-2701
Killeen, John J., 40 Derbyshire St., Derby, CT 06418
LeClair, Lawrence J., Spring Lake Village, 661 Ledgeview Ct., Southington, CT 06489
Lescoe, Francis J., 196 Eddy Glover Blvd., New Britain, CT 06053
Maguire, Felix H., 688 Mulberry Rd., Guilford, CT 06437-3527
Malley, Michael A., St. Joseph Rectory, 4 Main St., Canaan, CT 06018
Matutis, Joseph J., 700 Maple Ave., Unit 209, Hartford, CT 06114
Maynard, Leo E., 123 Maple St., Somers, CT 06071
McGrath, Robert D., 873 Durham Rd., Madison, CT 06443
McGrath, William E., St. Christopher Rectory, 538 Brewer St., East Hartford, CT 06118-2399
Muha, Edward J., 236 Fairlawn Dr., Torrington, CT 06790
Murphy, Joseph G., Heritage Cove Condo, 85 River Rd., N1, Essex, CT 06426
Nazzaro, Stanley J., 135 West Ave., Great Barrington, MA 01230
Neveu, Armand A., 72 Castle Rock Rd., Woodstock, CT 06281
O'Connor, John R., St. Joseph Manor, 6448 Main St., Rm. A-310, Trumbull, CT 06611
O'Connor, John T., St. Dominic Rectory, 1050 Flanders Rd., Southington, CT 06489
O'Dea, James F., St. Michael Rectory, 25 Maple Ave., Beacon Falls, CT 06403
O'Leary, Donald J., St. Aloysius Rectory, 254 Burritt St., Plantsville, CT 06479
O'Neill, Francis S., 265 S.W. 14th Ct., Pompano, FL 33060
O'Neill, George T., 265 S.W 14th Ct., Pompano, FL 33060
Otero, Neil, 565 W. 169th St., Apt. 4C, New York, NY 10032
Paul, Raymond F., Holy Rosary Rectory, Fr. Salemi Dr., Ansonia, CT 06401
Perreault, Aurele R., 1884 Old Waterbury Rd., Cheshire, CT 06410
Pettit, Joseph H., 433 Lakeview Dr., Southington, CT 06489
Ptaszynski, Stephen F., 90 Wolcott St., Box 1271, Bristol, CT 06011-1271
Quinn, John J., 150 Pheasant Ln., Branford, CT 06405
Riccio, Alexis D., St. Mary Home, 2021 Albany Ave., West Hartford, CT 06117
Rush, James C., 161 Brunswick Ave., West Hartford, CT 06107
Sabulis, Paul P., St. Joseph Rectory, 46 Congress Ave., Waterbury, CT 06708-3845
Shamsher, Paul, Sacred Heart Rectory, 74 Liberty St., New Haven, CT 06519-2299
Shaw, Charles E., P.O. Box 10158, Phoenix, AZ 85064
Smith, William C., 82 W. Rocks Rd., Norwalk, CT 06851
Speer, Patrick J., St. Joseph Manor, 6448 Main St., Trumbull, CT 06611
Spodnik, A. Leo, P.O. Box 456, Higganum, CT 06441
Sullivan, James J., St. Mary Home, 2021 Albany Ave., West Hartford, CT 06117-2701
Sullivan, John L., The Canterbury, 45 Highland St., West Hartford, CT 06119
Testa, Genaro J., 5233 S.W. 11th Ct., Cape Coral, FL 33914
Thuer, William J., Visitation Plaza, 100 Jefferson Sq., Apt. 6-A, Waterbury, CT 06706
Toscano, Pasquale A., St. Joseph Residence, 1365 Enfield St., Enfield, CT 06082-4900
Tracy, John P., 140 Main St., B2, Hartford, CT 06106
Ventresca, A. Andrew, Spring Rd., P.O. Box 413, Bethlehem, CT 06751-0413
Ventura, Anthony C., Mother of Sorrows Chapel, 3050 Gap Knob Rd., New Hope, KY 40052
Vitka, Stephen G., Underhill Rd., P.O. Box 608, Sandy Hook, CT 06482-0608
Yuse, Raymond B., 3 Wongonk Tr., P.O. Box 1860, East Hampton, CT 06424
Zanavich, Albert J., Assumption Rectory, 61 N. Cliff St., Ansonia, CT 06401

Permanent Deacons:
Abdalla, John, St. Catherine, Broad Brook
Aconfora, Ralph A., Holy Rosary, Ansonia
Albert, Roger R., St. Gregory the Great, Bristol
Amat, Emiliano A., Unassigned
Angeloni, Carmine, St. Therese, North Haven
Anthony, Andrew, St. Bernard, Tariffville
Arena, Paul, St. Michael the Archangel, Terryville
Azzaro, Gabriel S., St. Bernadette, New Haven
Baldwin, Alan C., Good Shepherd, Seymour
Bandeira, Francis, St. Anne, Waterbury
Bartlett, William, Jr., St. Barnabas, North Haven
Battiston, Donald, (Retired)
Baxter, Wesley F., St. Bridget, Cheshire
Bergers, William, St. Monica, Northford
Bernd, Robert E., St. Martha, Enfield
Bertolini, Valentino H., Sacred Heart, Suffield
Bevvino, Frank J., Jr., St. John Vianney, West Haven
Biamonte, Ronald, St. Gabriel, Windsor
Bichi, Americo, Holy Infant, Orange
Blair, Robert N., St. Patrick, Collinsville
Borland, Joseph P., Assumption, Woodbridge
Brady, John F., Assumption, Ansonia
Breen, Thomas F., III, St. John the Evangelist, West Hartford
Brown, George S., St. Timothy, West Hartford
Brown, William J., St. Rose, East Hartford
Brunell, Robert J., St. Brendan, New Haven
Camden, Ronald P., St. Mary, New Britain
Camerota, Daniel A., St. John the Evangelist, Watertown
Campbell, Alan D., St. Ann, Avon
Cardona, Raul, St. Rose, Meriden
Carey, Edward J., (Retired)
Carrero, Adolfo G., Immaculate Conception, Hartford
Carroll, Michael E., SS. Peter & Paul, Waterbury
Casey, Francis J., Mary Our Queen, Plantsville
Cassidy, Vincent, Sacred Heart, Southbury
Cenci, Peter A., St. Mary, Newington
Chamberland, J. Fernand, Assumption, Manchester
Charles, John H., St. John the Evangelist, Watertown
Clifford, Thomas J., St. Mary, Union City
Colella, Charles, St. Leo the Great, Waterbury
Colella, Guy A., (Retired)
Conklin, Thomas J., St. Margaret Mary, South Windsor
Conte, John J.M., Jr., St. Lawrence, West Haven
Cooke, Joseph J., St. Gabriel, Windsor
Coppola, Angelo J., St. Thomas, Southington
Cote, Laurent L., St. Anthony, Bristol
Coyne, Joseph F., St. Elizabeth, Branford
Cretella, Joseph J., Jr., Holy Trinity, Wallingford
Croll, Calvin S., St. Gabriel, Milford
Crowley, John, St. Dominic, Southington
Cruess, Donald E., St. Francis Xavier, Waterbury
Culhane, Neil, St. John of the Cross, Middlebury
Cunniff, Charles E., Jr., St. Rose, Meriden
D'Efemia, Robert J., Incarnation, Wethersfield
Daigle, Ronald R., St. Mary, East Hartford
Dean, Henry A., (Retired)
DeFilippo, Salvatore A., St. Louis, West Haven
DeHippolytis, Albert J., Unassigned
DeJesus, Efrain, (Retired)
DeJesus, Isidiro, Sacred Heart, Hartford
DelCorte, Nicholas, Our Lady of Pompeii, East Haven
Delehanty, Thomas F., St. Catherine of Siena, West Simsbury
Delgado, Domingo, Our Lady of Sorrows, Hartford
Delmonte, Richard F., (Retired)
Dembishack, John L., Immaculate Heart of Mary, Harwinton
Dempsey, John F., St. Augustine, Hartford
Dickman, Arthur J., Holy Family, Enfield
Dickson, Edward, St. Francis of Assisi, Torrington
Dietsch, Charles C., Sacred Heart, Southbury
DiMauro, Joseph, Mary Our Queen, Plantsville
Dinkle, George J., St. Anthony, Prospect
Diorio, Nicholas J., St. Thomas, Goshen
DiPiro, Joseph L., Assumption, Ansonia
DiRienzo, Mario, Assumption, Woodbridge
Dlugokinski, Jose L., Immaculate Heart of Mary, Harwinton
DosSantos, Kenneth, St. Anthony of Padua, Litchfield
Doyle, Henry, St. Gabriel, Milford
Driscoll, Frank M., Unassigned
Dungan, Roy C., St. Gregory, Bristol
Dwyer, David F., St. Francis of Assisi, South Windsor
Elder, William A., St. Margaret, Madison
English, Seth M., Sacred Heart, Wethersfield
Eschrich, Paul C., (Retired)
Eyles, William H., St. Vincent de Paul, East Haven
Farrell, William A., St. Ann, Avon
Fiederlein, Frank H., (Retired)
Fitzgerald, Robert W., (Retired)
Flenke, Richard M., Unassigned
Florio, Louis J., St. Therese, North Haven
Fortier, James A., Holy Spirit, Newington

Fournier, Richard G., St. Paul, West Haven
Fracasso, Robert G., St. Donato, New Haven
Fugere, Raymond J., St. Helena, West Hartford
Fusco, Louis P., St. Monica, Northford
Gabriele, Joseph G., (Retired)
Gale, Robert P., Our Lady of Mt. Carmel, Meriden
Galiette, Andrew S., Immaculate Conception, Southington
Geraci, Gerald S., Our Lady of Mercy, Plainville
Giaimo, Thomas, Our Lady of Pompeii, East Haven
Giard, Edward J., St. James, Manchester
Gilles, William J., St. Christopher, East Hartford
Giordano, William D., (Retired)
Giunta, Francis J., (Retired)
Giusto, Oreste M., (Retired)
Godlewsky, Robert H., (Retired)
Gonzalez, Aquilino, St. Joseph, Meriden
Gordon, Robert D., Unassigned
Grant, Frederick M., St. Mary, Derby
Griffin, Wayne F., St. Mary, Lakeville
Gurr, Ronald, St. John the Baptist, New Haven
Guzzardi, Carmelo A., St. Paul, Kensington
Hajjar, George D., St. Margaret, Waterbury
Harla, Francis J., Jr., Unassigned
Hart, John L., St. Augustine, North Branford
Hayden, Bernard J., Holy Infant, Orange
Hernandez, Carmelo, Immaculate Conception, Hartford
Hickey, James E., Jr., St. Luke, Hartford
Hilliard, Robert J., St. Brigid, West Hartford
Hoffman, Harold, Holy Infant, Orange
Iadarola, Paul P., St. Anthony, Prospect
Iassogna, Nicholas J., Jr., St. Vincent Ferrer, Naugatuck
Impellitteri, Michael, Sr., (Retired)
Jacques, J. Martin, (Retired)
Johnson, Robert C., Assumption, Ansonia
Johnson, Thomas F., St. Patrick, Waterbury
Kane, Joseph E., St. Patrick, Farmington
Kelly, Stephen J., St. Pius X, Wolcott
Kieda, Rene J., St. Martha, Enfield
Kimball, Earle A., Sacred Heart, Waterbury
Klein, Peter J., Jr., St. John Fisher, Marlborough
Klimanowski, Peter J., Our Lady of Sorrows, Hartford
Klimas, Vincent A., (Retired)
Koch, Paul T., St. Joan of Arc, Hamden
Krasnicki, Frank J., St. Michael, Beacon Falls
Kraussman, George A., Holy Angels, South Meriden
Kristopik, Albert P., St. John the Evangelist, New Britain
Kulas, Michael J., Sacred Heart, Southbury
Kulas, Paul J., Mary Our Queen, Plantsville
Labagnara, Eugene A., St. Francis Cabrini, North Haven
Lambert, Robert E., St. Martha, Enfield
LaPierre, Joseph W., Our Lady of Pompeii, East Haven
LaRochelle, Robert R., St. Margaret Mary, South Windsor
LaRocque, Leo R., Assumption, Manchester
Lauer, Paul B., St. Mary, Milford
Lavoie, Joseph V., (Retired)
LeBlanc, Gaspard D., St. Anne, Waterbury
Lembo, Victor M., Holy Rosary, Ansonia
Lepkowski, Henry M., (Retired)
Levesque, Joseph J., St. Ann, Bristol
Lewandoski, Leonard R., St. Maria Goretti, Wolcott
Lickwar, R. Carl, St. Ann, New Britain
Linehan, F. Robert, Holy Family, Enfield
Locorotondo, Frank S., (Retired)
Loffredo, Eugene E., Unassigned
Lopatosky, Thomas J., (Retired)
Lopez, Alejandro, St. Cecilia, Waterbury
Lopez, Rafael, Our Lady of Sorrows, Hartford
Lotto, Henry, Our Lady of Pompeii, East Haven
Lovelace, William, St. Augustine, North Branford
Lowe, Burdon G., (Retired)
Lozier, Albert J., St. Ann, Bristol
Maffeo, John R., Good Shepherd, Seymour
Makara, John W., Immaculate Conception, Terryville
Mancini, Edward J., St. Louis, West Haven
Marcarelli, Julius R., St. Rose of Lima, New Haven
Masucci, Ernest J., (Retired)
McCusker, Kenneth F., Ascension, Hamden
McGivney, Raymond J., Jr., Holy Family, Enfield
McGrath, William M., Nativity, Bethlehem
McInnis, John P., Unassigned
McKaig, John W., St. Paul, Glastonbury
Michaele, Adam J., St. George, Guilford
Miller, Roland G., Sacred Heart, Kent
Mingrone, William F., St. Francis, Naugatuck
Mon, Joseph J.G., St. Bernard, Enfield
Monaco, Daniel G., (Retired)
Morales, Jose A., St. Augustine, Hartford
Motto, Vincent J., St. Catherine, Broad Brook
Muro, Robert E., Sr., Our Lady of the Lakes, New Milford
Murphy, James R., St. Helena, West Hartford
Mylott, John J., St. Mark the Evangelist, West Hartford
Navickas, Robert D., St. Therese, Granby
Nebiolo, Eugene, St. Dominic, Southington
Newbery, Robert D., St. Therese, Granby
Norton, Donald E., St. Gabriel, Windsor
O'Connell, Cornelius D., Corpus Christi, Wethersfield
O'Connor, Martin J., St. Mary Priory, New Haven
O'Day, Richard J., St. Matthew, Forestville
O'Donovan, John, Our Lady of Mt. Carmel, Hamden
O'Neill, James F., St. George, Guilford
O'Toole, Michael J., St. Mary, Newington
Ortiz, Edwin, Sacred Heart, Hartford
Ortiz, Jacinto, St. Rose of Lima, Meriden
Pahl, John E., St. Matthew, Forestville
Pallotti, Robert M., St. Joseph, Bristol
Pantalena, Edward J., Epiphany, Cheshire
Parenteau, Raymond A., St. John Fisher, Marlborough
Parlee, Charles, St. John Vianney, West Haven
Paturzo, Frank X., St. Therese, North Haven
Perez, Valentin, St. Michael, Hartford
Pettinico, George, Our Lady of Lourdes, Waterbury
Phaneuf, Eugene E., St. Thomas the Apostle, West Hartford
Poland, James K., (Retired)
Pond, Donald H., Jr., Holy Family, Enfield
Prete, Paul V., St. Mary, Branford
Probulis, Gerard J., Unassigned
Puskas, George A., St. Mary, Milford
Quinn, James P., St. Thomas, Southington
Ramos, Edmund J., Christ the Redeemer, Milford
Regan, Joseph M., Jr., St. Margaret, Madison
Renker, Richard E., St. John of the Cross, Middlebury
Rescildo, Ralph, St. Teresa, Woodbury
Rigely, John, (Retired)
Riotte, Eugene C., Holy Trinity, Wallingford
Rivera, Jose A., St. Peter, New Haven
Rivera, Pedro L., St. Lawrence O'Toole, Hartford
Rogers, Joseph K., (Retired)
Rogers, Thomas D., Unassigned
Rolando, Joseph E., St. Rita, Hamden
Roman, Chester J., (Retired)
Rosello, Modesto A., St. Leo the Great, Waterbury
Roy, Reginald, St. Jerome, New Britain
Ruiz, Candelario, (Retired)
Ryder, Donald A., Unassigned
Ryzewski, Joseph R., St. Aedan, New Haven
Sabo, Paul E., St. Mary, Milford
Saffo, John R., Sr., St. Augustine, Seymour
Sandford, Wayne E., St. Clare, East Haven
Santello, Richard L., Dir. Office Permanent Diaconate, St. Stephen, Hamden
Scanlon, Thomas P., St. Bernard, Tariffville
Schiro, George J., St. Paul, West Haven
Sennett, Richard M., St. Mary, Milford
Serafini, Ferdinand T., (Retired)
Shaffer, William B., Holy Infant, Orange
Shelto, Michael A., St. James, Rocky Hill
Shiels, James H., St. Rose, Meriden
Sill, Louis P., Jr., SS. Peter and Paul, Wallingford
Simonin, George A., St. John the Evangelist, Watertown
Singer, Norman H., St. Vincent de Paul, East Haven
Skipp, Barry T., St. Mary, Newington
Sloan, Daniel A., Our Lady of Mt. Carmel, Waterbury
Sloan, Joseph S., St. Joseph, Poquonock
Smith, Donald H., Jr., Holy Angels, South Meridan
Solli, Anthony P., St. Lawrence, West Haven
Sponzo, Michael T., (Retired)
St. Jean, Stephen E., Unassigned
Stadtlander, Hobart, St. Bernard, Enfield
Stanley, James H., St. Barnabas, North Haven
Stephens, George R., St. Francis Cabrini, North Haven
Stolfi, Domenic N., St. Michael, Waterbury
Streib, George H., St. Francis Xavier, New Milford
Sullivan, Joseph, Holy Infant, Orange
Suzio, John J., (Retired)
Sweeney, John M., St. Mary, Simsbury
Szewczyk, Edward J., St. Joseph, Suffield
Szumigala, Michael P., St. Hedwig, Union City
Taddei, Edward D., (Retired)
Talbot, Oral A., St. Paul, Kensington
Tartaris, Robert P., St. Mary, Branford
Taylor, James P., St. Barnabas, North Haven
Thayer, John E., St. Ann, Avon
Thompson, Bruce R., St. Peter, Hartford
Thorney, Vincent M., St. Gertrude, Windsor
Tomasiello, Frank R., (Retired)
Tripp, James A., Sr., Blessed Sacrament, Hamden
Twerago, John P., (Retired)
Vazquez, Julio, St. Rose of Lima, New Haven
Vecca, Carl M., Immaculate Conception, Waterbury
Violette, Carroll, Incarnation, Wethersfield
VonFeldt, Elmer, (Retired)
Wallin, Robert F., SS. Peter & Paul, Waterbury
Walton, Gilbert E., Jr., St. Therese, Branford
Weaver, Stephen L., St. Elizabeth Seton, Rocky Hill
Weir, John, Sacred Heart, Southbury
Wheeler, John E., St. Lawrence, West Haven
Whittel, Joseph B., Sacred Heart, Bloomfield
Wilber, Richard, St. Bridget, Cheshire
Wilcox, George, (Retired)
Wilcox, William H., St. Joseph, Winsted
Winiarski, Benedict L., Sacred Heart, Suffield
Wootton, Gerald R., St. Thomas, Thomaston

INSTITUTIONS LOCATED IN THE ARCHDIOCESE

[A] SEMINARIES, ARCHDIOCESAN

BLOOMFIELD. *St. Thomas Seminary*, 467 Bloomfield Ave., 06002-2999. Tel: 860-242-5573; Fax: 860-242-4886. Rev. Aidan N. Donahue, Rector & Contact; Mrs. Irene B. Ronan, Registrar. In res. Most Rev. Christie A. Macaluso, D.D.; Revs. Stephen C. Foley; Alvin J. LeBlanc; John P. Conte; Stanley J. Sikora. Fathers 4.

Pope Paul VI House of Formation, 469 Bloomfield Ave., 06002. Rev. John J. Dietrich, Dir. In res. Rev. Aidan N. Donahue. Students 5.

[B] SEMINARIES, RELIGIOUS OR SCHOLASTICATES

CHESHIRE. *Novitiate of the Legion of Christ*, 475 Oak Ave., 06410. Tel: 203-271-0805; Fax: 203-271-3845. Rectors: Revs. William Meade, L.C.; Julio Marti, L.C. Vice Rectors: Rev. Pedro Valdemar Garcia, L.C.; Bro. Scott Reilly, L.C.; Revs. Jose Felix Medina, L.C.; Anthony Bailleres, L.C., Asst. to the Natl. Dir. Instructors of Novices: Revs. Christopher Brackett, L.C.; Joseph Burtka, L.C. Studies: Revs. Owen Kearns, L.C.; Anthony Rodriguez, L.C.; Tarciscio Samaniego, L.C.; Jeffrey Bowker, L.C.; Walter Schuh, L.C. Priests 11; Religious 14; Juniors 60; Novices 85. (Center Harbor, N.H.).

[C] COLLEGES AND UNIVERSITIES

HAMDEN. *Mt. Sacred Heart College*, 265 Benham St., 06514-2801. Tel: 203-248-4225; Fax: 203-230-8341
For a complete listing, refer to the Colleges and Universities section.

NEW HAVEN. *Albertus Magnus College*, 700 Prospect St., 06511-1189. Tel: 203-773-8500; Fax: 203-785-8652.
E-mail: admissions@albertus.edu
Web site: www.albertus.edu
For a complete listing, refer to the Colleges and Universities section.

WEST HARTFORD. *Saint Joseph College*, 1678 Asylum Ave., 06117. Tel: 860-232-4571; Fax: 860-233-5695.
E-mail: info@mercy.sjc.edu
Web site: www.sjc.edu
For a complete listing, refer to the Colleges and Universities section.

[D] HIGH SCHOOLS, ARCHDIOCESAN

BRISTOL. *St. Paul Catholic High School*, 1001 Stafford Ave., 06010-3894. Tel: 860-584-0911. Sr. Joan A. O'Connor, C.S.J., Prin. & Contact. Asst. Principals: Craig R. Hill; Richard L. Marino. Faculty: Sisters 1; Lay Teachers 35; Students 430.

MANCHESTER. *East Catholic High School*, 115 New State Rd., 06040. Tel: 860-649-5336; Fax: 860-649-7191. Peggy Siegmund, Prin. Sisters of Notre Dame de Namur 7; Lay Teachers 42; Priests 1; Students 522.

WATERBURY. *Sacred Heart High School*, 142 S. Elm St., 06722. Tel: 203-753-1605.
E-mail: sacredhs@ct2.nai.net
Rev. John Meaney, M.M., Prin.; Mrs. Eileen Regan, Dir. Devel.; Mrs. Jacqueline Jennings, Vice Prin.; Rev. Joseph F. Gorman. Priests 1; Lay Teachers 39; Students 437.

WEST HARTFORD. *Northwest Catholic High School*, 29 Wampanoag Dr., 06117. Tel: 860-236-4221; Fax: 860-586-0911. Dr. Michael S. Griffin, Chief Admin. & Prin. & Contact; Mrs. Margaret R. Williamson, Vice. Prin.; Mr. Richard Callahan, Vice Prin. Priests 2; Lay Teachers 52; Students 565.

[E] HIGH SCHOOLS, PRIVATE

HAMDEN. *Sacred Heart Academy*, 265 Benham St., 06514-2833. Tel: 203-288-2309; Fax: 203-230-9680.
E-mail: Principal@SHA-Excelsior.org
Apostles of the Sacred Heart of Jesus. Sr. Claudia Calzetta, A.S.C.J., Prin. & Contact. Sisters 10; Lay Teachers 35; Students 480.

MILFORD. *Academy of Our Lady of Mercy*, Lauralton Hall, 200 High St., 06460. Tel: 203-877-2786; Fax: 203-876-9760. Sisters of Mercy. Mrs. Karen Yardley, Pres. & Contact. Sisters 5; Lay Teachers 47; Students 438.

NEW BRITAIN. *Mary Immaculate Academy*, Osgood and Corbin Aves., 06053. Tel: 860-229-1747. Daughters of Mary of the Immaculate Conception. Sr. Mary Felicitas, D.M., Prin. & Contact. Sisters 8; Lay Teachers 11; Students 114.

St. Thomas Aquinas High School, 74 Kelsey St., 06051. Tel: 860-225-7847; Fax: 860-224-4338.
E-mail: stahs.aquinas@juno.com
David P. McCreesh, Prin. & Contact; Rev. Joseph V. Napolitano, Dir. Spiritual Activities. Priests 1; Sisters 1; Lay Teachers 17; Students 150.

NEW MILFORD. *Canterbury School*, Aspetuck Ave., 06776. Tel: 860-355-3103. Coed. Boarding and day students. Thomas J. Sheehy, III, Headmaster; Rev. Sebastian Leonard, O.S.B., Chap. Priests 1; Lay Teachers 48; Students 330.

WATERBURY. *Holy Cross High School*, 587 Oronoke Rd., 06708. Tel: 203-757-9248. Brothers of the Congregation of Holy Cross. Bro. Jerome Donnelly, C.S.C., Chief Admin./Head of School & Contact; Mr. Timothy McDonald, Prin. Brothers 1; Sisters 2; Lay Teachers 61; Students 937.

WEST HAVEN. *Notre Dame High School*, 24 Ricardo St., 06516. Tel: 203-933-1673.
E-mail: ralph@notredamehs.com
Web site: www.notredamehs.com
Holy Cross Brothers. Bro. James Branigan, C.S.C., Headmaster; Mr. Ralph Proto, Prin.; Mr. Patrick Clifford, Asst. Prin.; Mr. Joseph Ramirez, Dir. of Guidance; Mrs. Gail Bellucci. Brothers 5; Sisters 1; Lay Teachers 44; Students 618.

Notre Dame Loyalty & Endowment Fund, Inc., 24 Ricardo St., 06516.

[F] ELEMENTARY SCHOOLS, PRIVATE

MADISON. *Our Lady of Mercy School, Incorporated*, 149 Neck Rd., 06443-2728. Tel: 203-245-4393.
E-mail: Our.Lady.mercy.sch@snet.net
Dr. Joan E. Venditto, Prin. & Contact. Sisters of Mercy 1; Lay Teachers 14; Students 220.

WEST HARTFORD. *Cedar Court School, Inc.*, 27 Park Rd., 06119. Tel: 860-523-0060. Sr. Vernice Molinari, Dir. & Contact. Sisters of St. Joseph of Chambery 4; Lay Teachers 4; Children 49.

[G] SPECIALIZED CHILD CARING HOME

NEW BRITAIN. *Marian Educational Clinic*, 314 Osgood Ave., 06053. Tel: 860-223-0501
For a complete listing, refer to the Special Care Facilities section.

NEW HAVEN. *St. Francis Home for Children, Inc.*, 651 Prospect St., 06511. Tel: 203-777-5513; Fax: 203-777-0644
For a complete listing, refer to the Special Care Facilities section.

[H] DAY CARE CENTER

HAMDEN. *Clelian Adult Day Center*, 261 Benham St., 06514. Tel: 203-288-0551; 288-4151. Sr. Shawn Lyons, A.S.C.J., Dir. & Contact. Apostles of the Sacred Heart of Jesus. A day health care facility for elderly and disabled adults. Total Assisted 86 per week; Total Staff 15.

Sacred Heart Manor Nursery and Kindergarten, 261 Benham St., 06514. Tel: 203-230-4889. Sr. Elaine Ann Lattanzi, Contact. Apostles of the Sacred Heart of Jesus 1; Lay Teachers 4; Students 105; Total Assisted 98.

NEW BRITAIN. *Our Lady of Rosehill Day Care Center*, 594 Burritt St., 06053. Tel: 860-223-4846. Sr. M. Terence, D.M., Contact. Daughters of Mary of the Immaculate Conception 3; Lay Teachers 8; Children 65.

WEST HARTFORD. *Park Village Child Development Center*, 27 Park Rd., 06119. Tel: 203-523-1482. Sisters of St. Joseph of Chambery 1; Children 30.

[I] GENERAL HOSPITALS

HARTFORD. *Saint Francis Hospital and Medical Center*, 114 Woodland St., 06105-1299. Tel: 860-714-4000; Fax: 860-714-7809
For a complete listing, refer to the Hospitals section.

NEW HAVEN. *Hospital of St. Raphael*, 1450 Chapel St., 06511. Tel: 203-789-3000; Fax: 203-789-3653
For a complete listing, refer to the Hospitals section.

Saint Regis Health Center, Inc., 1354 Chapel St., 06511. Tel: 203-867-8300
For a complete listing, refer to the Hospitals section.

WATERBURY. *St. Mary Hospital*, 56 Franklin St., 06706. Tel: 203-574-6000; Fax: 203-597-3238
For a complete listing, refer to the Hospitals section.

[J] SPECIAL HOSPITALS

WEST HARTFORD. *Saint Agnes Home, Inc.*, 104 Mayflower St., 06110. Tel: 860-521-7516; Fax: 860-521-6160.
E-mail: safc@aol.com
For a complete listing, refer to the Special Care Facilities section.

[K] HOMES FOR AGED

ENFIELD. *The Home for the Aged of the Little Sisters of the Poor*, 1365 Enfield St., 06082-4900. Tel: 860-741-0791
For a complete listing, refer to the Special Care Facilities section.

NEW BRITAIN. *Monsignor Bojnowski Manor, Inc.*, 50 Pulaski St., 06053 Fax: 860-229-3252
For a complete listing, refer to the Special Care Facilities section.

St. Lucian's Home for the Aged, 532 Burritt St., 06053. Tel: 860-223-2123
For a complete listing, refer to the Special Care Facilities section.

WEST HARTFORD. *Saint Mary Home*, 2021 Albany Ave., 06117. Tel: 860-236-1924
For a complete listing, refer to the Special Care Facilities section.

[L] HEALTH CARE CENTERS FOR AGED

WEST HARTFORD. *McAuley Center, Inc.*, 275 Steele Rd., 06117. Tel: 860-236-6300
For a complete listing, refer to the Hospitals section.

[M] MONASTERIES AND RESIDENCES OF PRIESTS AND BROTHERS

HARTFORD. *Missionaries of LaSalette Provincial Secretary*, 915 Maple Ave., 06114-2330. Tel: 860-956-8870.
E-mail: mlsadmin@aol.com
Province of Our Lady of Seven Dolors. Legal Title: *Missionaries of La Salette Corp.* Revs. James H. Kuczynski, M.S., Prov. Supr.; James A. Henault, M.S., Vicar & Prov. Sec. & Vocation Dir.; Joseph M. O'Neil, M.S., Asst. & Prov. Priests 3.
Religious Trust of the Missionaries of Our Lady of LaSalette. Legal Title: *Religious Trust of the Missionaries of Our Lady of LaSalette Province of Our Lady of Seven Dolors (MLS Trust).*

Missionaries of LaSalette, 85 New Park Ave., 06106-2184. Tel: 860-523-8275. Revs. Donald D. Simonds, M.S., Local Coord.; Richard R. Boucher, M.S., Treas.; Salvatore D. Altavista, M.S.; Michael J. Cox, M.S.; William H. Crane, M.S.; Joseph J. Horgan, M.S.; Stanley T. Kennedy, M.S.; William J. Kinney, M.S.; Joseph A. Markowicz, M.S.; William W. Mulcair, M.S.; John R. Nuelle, M.S.; James P. O'Reilly, M.S.; Louis M. Perpete, M.S.; James B. Quilty, M.S.; Daniel J. Scott, M.S.; John G. Toner, M.S.; Bros. Raymond J. Aubin, M.S.; Ronald R. Beaudoin, M.S.; David J. Cook, M.S.; Alexander J. Delaney, M.S.; Gabriel Frank, M.S.; Mark L. Gallant, M.S.; Andre J. Hamel, M.S.; Paul Maceyka, M.S.; Bonaventure Russell, M.S.; Francis X. Smith, M.S.; Peter Staskiewicz, M.S.; Alfred D. Tetrault, M.S.; Donald J. Wininski, M.S. Priests 16; Brothers 13.
Priests-Brothers of Province Serving Abroad: Missionaries in Argentina: Revs. Robert R. Butler, M.S.; Eugene P. Brennan, M.S.; John M. Garvey, M.S.; John F. Higgins, M.S., Region Supr.; James T. Lowery, M.S.; John J. McCarthy, M.S.; John P. Sullivan, M.S.
Bolivia: Rev. Norman H. Butler, M.S.

Immaculate Conception Rectory, 574 Park St., 06126-0610. Tel: 860-525-1522. Revs. Joseph J. Baxer, M.S.; James J. Aherne, M.S.

St. Anne, 820 Park St., 06106-2388. Tel: 860-728-7445. Revs. Joseph J. Baxer, M.S.; James J. Aherne, M.S.

Our Lady of Sorrows Rectory, 16 Greenwood St., 06106-2109. Tel: 860-233-4424. Co-Pastors: Revs. Joseph M. O'Neil, M.S.; Francis C. Cooney, M.S. In res. Rev. Stephen G. Dressell, M.S.

North American La Salette Mission Center, 85 New Park Ave., 06106-2184. Rev. John R. Nuelle, M.S., Dir.; Bro. Mark L. Gallant, M.S., Asst.

Sacred Heart Rectory, 49 Winthrop St., 06103-1030. Tel: 860-527-6459; Fax: 860-527-6450. Somascan Fathers. Total in Residence 3; Total Staff 3.

St. Patrick-St. Anthony Friary (Holy Name Prov.), 285 Church St., 06103-1196. Tel: 860-246-6874. Franciscan Friars.

St. Joseph Rectory, 31 Oak St., P.O. Box 808, Winsted, 06098-1715. Tel: 860-379-3369; Fax: 860-379-4194.

BLOOMFIELD. *Brothers of the Sacred Heart*, 1153 Blue Hills Ave., 06002-1901. Tel: 860-242-3342. Total in Residence 4.

CHESHIRE. *Legionaries of Christ*, 475 Oak Ave., 06410. Tel: 203-271-0805. 393 Derby Ave., Orange, 06477. Tel: 203-795-2800.

EAST HARTFORD. *Society of Our Lady of the Most Holy Trinity*, 15 Maplewood Ave., 06108. Tel: 860-289-7916.

ENFIELD. *St. Patrick Rectory*, 64 Pearl St., 06082. Tel: 860-745-2411. Redemptorist Fathers and Brothers. Total in Residence 2.

LITCHFIELD. *Montfort Missionaries*, Montfort Rd., P.O. Box 667, 06759. Tel: 860-567-8434; Fax: 860-567-9670. Revs. Thomas Poth, S.M.M., Supr. & Novice Dir.; Eugene Lynch, S.M.M., Contact; Donald Lasalle, S.M.M. Priests 3; Brothers 1.

Lourdes in Litchfield. Legal Title: *Lourdes Shrine Guild, Inc.*

Montfort House (Center for Spiritual Renewal).

Monfort Novitiate. Revs. Thomas Poth, S.M.M., Supr. & Novice Dir.; Eugene Lynch, S.M.M., Contact Person; Donald Lasalle, S.M.M. Priests 3; Brothers 1.

MANCHESTER. *DePaul Provincial Residence*. (Vincentian Fathers and Brothers), 234 Keeney St., 06040-7048. Tel: 860-643-2828; Fax: 860-533-9462. Congregation of the Mission, New England Province. Very Rev. John S. Sledziona, C.M., Prov. & Contact; Revs. George J. Dabrowski, C.M., Supr.; Chester R. Mrowka, C.M., Procurator; Casimir Kiczuk, C.M.; Henry Czekala, C.M.; Bros. Richard Glinski, C.M.; Henry Wojtkiewicz, C.M.; Joseph S. Zurowski, C.M. Legal Title: *The New England Province of the Congregation of the Mission Incorporated.*
Charitable Trust of the New England Province of the Congregation of the Mission.
Special Assignments: Revs. Martin Cymbrowski, C.M.; Edward Gicewicz, C.M.; Joseph C. Paciorek, C.M.; Stanley Staniszewski, C.M.

St. Joseph Rectory, 32 Jewett St., Ansonia, 06401-2499. Tel: 203-734-0402.

St. Michael the Archangel Rectory, 75 Derby Ave., Derby, 06418-2098. Tel: 203-734-0005.

St. Stanislaus Rectory, 82 Akron St., Meriden, 06450. Tel: 203-235-6341.

St. Stanislaus Rectory, 9 Eld St., New Haven, 06511-3899. Tel: 203-562-2828.

MILFORD. *The Augustinians*, 26 Shorefront, 06460. Tel: 203-878-9700. Bro. John N. Konwerski, O.S.A. Total in Residence 1.

Brothers of the Congregation of Holy Cross, 400 Merwin Ave., 06460. Tel: 203-816-9355.
E-mail: lar587@aol.com
Brothers of Holy Cross. Bro. Lawrence Lussier, C.S.C., Contact.
10 Ricardo St., West Haven, 06516. Bro. Thomas Gorman, C.S.C., Contact.
56 Brookwood Rd., Bethany, 06524. Tel: 203-393-0109. Bro. Jerome Donnelly, C.S.C., Contact.

NEW BRITAIN. *Conventual Franciscans*, 548 Burritt St., 06053-2869. Tel: 860-225-5786. Rev. Augustine Pilatowski, O.F.M.Conv., Supr.-Delegate & Contact. Chaplains: Revs. Walter Leon Mruk, O.F.M.Conv.; Gilbert Wdzieczyny, O.F.M.Conv. Daughters of Mary Motherhouse.

St. Paul Friary, 479 Alling St., Kensington, 06037-2100. Tel: 860-828-0331.

NEW HAVEN. *Priests of the Congregation of Holy Cross*, 203 Maple St., 06511. Tel: 203-776-2405.
E-mail: JLMYoung@poe.net

Sacred Heart Rectory, 74 Liberty St., 06519-2299. Tel: 203-562-7592. Sons of Charity.

St. Anthony Rectory, 25 Gold St., 06519. Tel: 203-624-1418. Missionaries of St. Charles-Scalabrinians.

St. Michael Rectory, 29 Wooster Pl., 06511. Tel: 203-562-7178.

St. Joseph Rectory, 129 Edwards St., 06511. Tel: 203-777-2548. Jesuit Fathers and Brothers. 700 Prospect St., 06511. Tel: 203-497-8672. Box 2160, 06520. Tel: 203-393-3193. 1365 Enfield St., Enfield, 06082-4900. Tel: 860-745-1381. 120 Retreat Ave., Apt. A-4, Hartford, 06106. Tel: 860-278-8900. 333 Christian St., Wallingford, 06492. Tel: 203-284-1402.

St. Joseph Rectory, 129 Edwards St., 06511. Tel: 203-777-2548. Marist Fathers. 1450 Chapel St., 06511. Tel: 203-789-3245.

St. Mary Priory, 5 Hillhouse Ave., 06505-1202. Tel: 203-562-6193; Fax: 203-562-1273.
Web site: http://www.connix/~mcs/stjos/stjoes.htm
Order of Preachers (Dominicans). Total in Residence 10.

NEW MILFORD. *Canterbury School*, Aspetuck Ave., 06776. Tel: 860-355-4891.
E-mail: admissions@canterbury.pvt.k12.ct.us
Web site: www.canterbury.pvt.k12.ct.us
Benedictine Monks.

NORTH GUILFORD. *Our Lady of Grace Monastery*, 11 Race Hill Rd., 06437. Tel: 203-457-1167. Order of Preachers (Dominicans). Total in Residence 45.

PLAINVILLE. *Our Lady of Mercy Rectory*, 15 S. Canal St., 06062. Tel: 860-793-1399. Missionhurst Congregation of the Immaculate Heart of Mary.

SUFFIELD. *Congregation of the Holy Redeemer*, St. Alphonsus College, 06078. Tel: 860-668-7393. Redemptorist Fathers and Brothers.

WATERBURY. *Immaculate Conception Rectory*, 74 W. Main St., 06702. Tel: 203-574-0017. Missionaries of the Holy Apostles; Oblates of Mary Immaculate.

St. Michael Rectory (Immaculate Conception Prov.), 62 St. Michael Dr., 06704-1295. Tel: 203-753-0689; Fax: 203-573-9101.

WEST HARTFORD. *Holy Family Monastery/Retreat*, 303 Tunxis Rd., 06107. Tel: 860-521-0440; Fax: 860-521-0883 (Community); 521-1929. Congregation of the Passion of Jesus Christ. Very Rev. Brice Edwards, C.P., Provincial Vicar; Rev. Ronan Callahan, C.P., Asst. Supr.

Monastery Staff: Revs. John Mark Aleckna, C.P.; Quentin Amrhein, C.P.; Cajetan Bendernagel, C.P.; Victor Donovan, C.P.; Jude Dowling; Kiernan Earley, C.P.; Robert Ehrne, C.P.; Joseph Leo Flynn, C.P.; Randall Gilette, C.P.; Alphonsus Grande, C.P.; Peter Hallisy, C.P.; Bennet Kelley, C.P.; Jeremiah Kennedy, C.P.; Stephen Kenny, C.P.; Cormac Kinkead, C.P.; Gerald Matejune, C.P.; John Francis McLoughlin, C.P.; Julian Morgan, C.P.; Florian Pekar, C.P.; John Baptist Pesce, C.P.; Linus Rottloff, C.P.; Owen Sharkey, C.P.; Basil Trahon, C.P.; Bros. Frederick Barton, C.P.; Gabriel Chilbert, C.P.; Charles Dell; William Drotar, C.P.; Edward Hall; John Jepson, C.P.; Joseph Rogers, C.P.

Retreat House. Revs. David Cinquegrani, C.P.; Earl Keating, C.P.; Terence Kristofak, C.P., Dir.

WEST HAVEN. *Franciscan Brothers of Brooklyn*, 233 Main St., 06516. Tel: 203-937-5103. Total in Residence 2.

WOLCOTT. *Maryknoll*, 8 S. View St., 06716. Tel: 203-879-3936.

[N] CONVENTS AND RESIDENCES FOR SISTERS

HARTFORD. *Dominican Oblates of Jesus*, 510 New Britain Ave., 06106. Tel: 203-249-2912. Sisters 4.

Medical Mission Sisters, 92 Sherman St., 06105. Tel: 860-233-0875.

St. Peter Convent, 11 Charter Oak Pl., 06106. Tel: 860-522-8428. Mercedarian Missionaries of Berriz, Sisters of Mercy of the Americas of Connecticut, Sisters of Notre Dame de Namur.

SS. Cyril & Methodius Convent, 45 Groton St., 06106. Tel: 860-527-3775. Felician Sisters of the Order of St. Francis of Connecticut. Rev. William P. Przybylo.

Sisters of Mercy of the Americas of Connecticut, 252 Laurel St. #296, 06105. Tel: 860-293-1764.

St. Joseph Convent, 35 Oxford St., 06105. Tel: 860-236-1494. 80 Girard Ave., 06105. Tel: 860-231-0252. 91 Mansfield St., 06112. Tel: 860-527-5079.

Sisters of Notre Dame de Namur, 305 Victoria Rd., 06114. Tel: 860-296-5400. Sisters 2.

Sisters of Notre Dame de Namur, One Gold St., Apt. 10, 06103. Tel: 860-246-7300. 18 Dover St., 06114. Tel: 860-296-1981. 191 Preston St., 06114. Tel: 860-956-8969. 217 Laurel St., 06105. Tel: 860-246-0678.

Sisters of St. Joseph, 338 Asylum St., 06103. Tel: 860-278-8389. Sisters of St. Joseph of Chambery. 46 Eastview St., 06114. Tel: 860-246-1316. 145 Elizabeth St., 06105. Tel: 860-523-5704. 149 Barker St., 06114. Tel: 860-296-2546.

Shalom Community, 33 Freeman St., 06114. Tel: 860-956-9247. 35B Freeman St., 06114. Tel: 860-956-9248. 35A Freeman St., 06114. Tel: 860-956-8157.

Sisters of the Cross and Passion, 391 Fairfield Ave., 06114. Tel: 860-956-5186.

Spirit of Mercy Community, 410 Campfield Ave., 06114. Tel: 860-956-3030. Daughters of the Holy Spirit, Sisters of Mercy of the Americas of Connecticut. 157 Kenyon St., 06105-2237. Tel: 860-232-6732.

Bethany Community/Formation Center, 7 Charter Oak Pl., 06106-1915. Tel: 860-728-0851.

ANSONIA. *Sisters of Holy Family of Nazareth*, 36 Jewett St., 06401. Tel: 203-736-9573.

BEACON FALLS. *Sisters of St. Joseph of the Third Order of St. Francis*, 68 Cambridge Ct., 06403. Tel: 203-729-9415.

BETHLEHEM. *Abbey of Regina Laudis*, 237 Flanders Rd., 06751. Tel: 203-266-7727. Bendictine Nuns of the Primitive Observance. Benedictine Nuns (Cloistered). Mothers Benedict Duss, O.S.B., Abbess; David Serna, O.S.B., Prioress & Mailing Contact. In res. Rev. Claude Peifer, O.S.B. Professed Nuns 29; In First Vows 4; Novices 3; Postulants 1.

St. Catherine's Convent of Mercy, 63 Crane Hollow Rd., 06751. Tel: 203-266-5411. Religious Sisters of Mercy (Alma, MI). Sisters 2.

BLOOMFIELD. *Sisters of Mercy of the Americas of Albany*, 467 Bloomfield Ave., 06002. Tel: 860-243-2374. Sr. Mary Costello, R.S.M.

Sisters of Mercy of the Americas of Connecticut, 5 Garrison Ter., 06002. Tel: 860-243-8524.

Sisters of Notre Dame de Namur. (Connecticut Province), 5 Garrison Ter., 06002. Tel: 860-243-8524.

Holy Innocents House, 546 Bloomfield Ave., 06002. Tel: 860-243-2542. Total in Residence 4.

BRISTOL. *Queen of Apostles Provincial House*, 474 East Rd., 06010. Tel: 860-584-2138; Fax: 860-582-1119.
E-mail: Ltflower@Erols.com
Religious Teachers Filippini. Sr. Christine Spirito, M.P.F., Prov. Supr.; Sr. Josephine Riccio, M.P.F., Community Archivist & Contact. Sisters in Diocese 17.

Sisters of Mercy of the Americas of Connecticut, 50 South St. Ext., 06010. Tel: 860-584-2418.

Sisters of St. Joseph of Chambery, 89 Putnam St., 06010. Tel: 860-582-3257.

CHESHIRE. *Sisters of St. Joseph of Chambery*, 1123 Waterbury Rd., #2A, 06410. Tel: 203-699-9421.

EAST HARTFORD. *Sisters of Notre Dame de Namur*, 21 Highview St., 06108. Tel: 860-289-5295. 37 Ridgeview Rd., 06118. Tel: 860-569-8794. 41 Applegate Ln., 06118. Tel: 860-569-7183. 50 Larrabee St. #F, 06108. Tel: 860-528-1024. 50 Larrabee St. #G, 06108. Tel: 860-289-2421. 52 Elms Village Rd., 06118. Tel: 860-569-0022. 8 Larrabee St., 06108. Tel: 860-290-8567. 908 Forbes St., 06118. Tel: 860-568-6958.

EAST HAVEN. *Dominican Sisters*. (Columbus, OH), 157 Short Beach Rd., 06512. Tel: 203-468-2280.

Missionary Franciscan Sisters of the Immaculate Conception, 157 Short Beach Rd., 06512. Tel: 203-468-2280.

Provincial House, 520 Thompson Ave., 06512. Tel: 203-469-7872; Fax: 203-469-8819. 87 Gerrish Ave., 06512. Tel: 203-468-9084.

Sisters of Notre Dame de Namur, 157 Short Beach Rd., 06512. Tel: 203-468-2280.

ENFIELD. *Felician Sisters - Our Lady of the Angels*, Provincial House, 1315 Enfield St., 06082-4929. Tel: 860-745-7791; 745-4946; Fax: 860-741-0819. Felician Sisters of the Order of St. Francis of Connecticut. Sr. Joan Marie Swierzb, C.S.S.F., Contact.

Provincial House and Novitiate. Sr. Mary Laureann Alexandrowicz, C.S.S.F., Prov. Min. Felician Sisters. Chaplains: Rev. Adolphe T. Renkiewicz.
In Province: Professed Sisters 147; Novices 2.

Felician Adult Day Care, 1333A Enfield St., 06082-4929. Tel: 860-745-2542; Fax: 860-745-2542. Total Assisted 22; Total Staff 12. Felician Sisters. Sr. Patricia Marie Iagrosso, C.S.S.F., Dir. A day respite health care facility for Caregivers of the Frail, elderly and Alzheimer Clients.

Felician Sisters Infirmary, 1315 Enfield St., 06082-4929. Tel: 860-745-0217.

Mother Angela Residence, 1333-B Enfield St., 06082-4929. Tel: 860-745-5705.

Child Jesus Convent, 1370 Enfield St., 06082-5526. Tel: 860-745-5847.

Enfield Montessori School, 1370 Enfield St., 06082-5526. Tel: 860-745-5847; Fax: 860-745-2010.
E-mail: Montessori@SNET.net
Sr. Mary Anastasia, C.S.S.F., Contact Person. Students 113.

St. Bernard Convent, 376 Hazard Ave., 06082-4709. Tel: 860-749-4214.

St. Adalbert Convent, 82 Alden Ave., 06082-2865. Tel: 860-745-4169.

Little Sisters of the Poor, 1365 Enfield St., 06082-4900. Tel: 860-741-0791.

St. Patrick Convent, 33 Spring St., 06082. Tel: 860-745-5174. Total in Residence 2. Sisters of Mercy of the Americas of Connecticut.

FARMINGTON. *St. Gabriel House*, 31 Colton St., 06032. Tel: 860-678-7274.

Sisters of Mercy of the Americas of Vermont, 33 Two Mile Rd., 06032. Tel: 860-677-0758.

Sisters of the Cross and Passion, St. Gabriel's House, 31 Colton St., 06032. Tel: 860-678-7274.

FORESTVILLE. *Daughters of Wisdom*, 45 Hawthorne St. D-2, 06010.

St. Matthew Convent, 119 Church Ave., 06010. Tel: 860-583-2004. Sisters, Servants of the Immaculate Heart of Mary.

Sisters of St. Joseph of the Third Order of St. Francis, 105 Kenney St., 06010. Tel: 860-582-1635. 82 Kenney St., 06010. Tel: 860-584-2985. Total in Residence 7; Total Staff 18.

GUILFORD. *Sisters of Mercy of the Americas of Connecticut*, 73A Church St., 06437. Tel: 203-453-3496.

HAMDEN. *Daughters of Wisdom*, 95 Kaye Vue Dr. Apt. 2E, 06514. Tel: 203-281-7800. Total in Residence 2.

Dominican Sisters of Hope, 1204 Whitney Ave., #217, 06517. Tel: 203-248-2601.

Mary, Mother of the Church Convent, 115 Denslow Hill Rd., 06514. Tel: 203-407-1042. Sisters 4.

Mount Sacred Heart Provincial House and Novitiate, 265 Benham St., 06514. Tel: 203-248-4225; Fax: 203-230-8341.
E-mail: srpascj@aol.com
Web site: http://www.ascj.org
Mothers Deborah Lopez, Prov. Supr.; Rosemary Zaffuto, Vicaress. Sisters in Province 190.
Residents in Convent: Sisters 22.

St. Rita Convent, 30 Gillies Rd., 06517. Tel: 203-288-4707. Dominican Sisters (Columbus, OH).

Sisters of Mercy of the Americas of Connecticut, 2809 Whitney Ave., 06518-2544. Tel: 203-287-9017.

St. Stephen Convent, 412 Ridge Rd., 06517. Tel: 203-288-7270. 77 Second St., 06514. Tel: 203-865-4821.

KENSINGTON. *St. Paul Convent*, 467 Alling St., 06037. Tel: 860-828-5223. Daughters of Mary of the Immaculate Conception. Sisters 3.

LITCHFIELD. *Daughters of Wisdom*, 229 E. Litchfield Rd., 06759. Tel: 860-567-3166.
E-mail: info@wisdomhouse.org
Web site: www.wisdomhouse.org

Dominican Sisters of Hope, 106 Clark Rd., 06759. Tel: 860-567-9487.

MADISON. *Sisters of Mercy of the Americas of Connecticut*, 149 Neck Rd., 06443. Tel: 203-245-4261. 167 Neck Rd., 06443. Tel: 203-245-7710.

Sisters of St. Joseph of Brentwood, 62 Kelsey Pl., 06443. Tel: 203-245-1329.

MANCHESTER. *Assumption Convent*, 21 S. Adams St., 06040. Tel: 860-643-0452. Sisters of Charity of Our Lady, Mother of the Church.

Daughters of the Holy Spirit, Case Dr. #44-D, 06040. Tel: 860-649-4755.

Dominican Sisters. (Columbus, OH), 69 Charter Oak St., 06040. Tel: 860-647-1699.

Sisters of Mercy of the Americas, 16 Lyndale St., 06040. Tel: 860-646-5902.

St. James Convent, 85 Park St., 06040. Tel: 860-649-5791.

Sisters of Notre Dame de Namur, 19 Moore St., 06040. Tel: 860-643-8761. 9 Plano Pl., 06040. Tel: 860-647-8544. 1198A Middle Tpke. W., 06040. Tel: 860-528-5091. 18 Winter St., 06040. Tel: 860-649-6891. Total in Residence 4.

Sisters of St. Joseph. (Springfield, MA), 82 Chestnut St., 06040. Tel: 860-647-7065.

Sisters of St. Joseph of Chambery, 241 E. New State Rd., 06040. Tel: 860-645-9750. 41 Florence St., 06040. Tel: 860-649-9791.

MERIDEN. *Generalate and Motherhouse of the Franciscan Sisters of the Eucharist*, 405 Allen Ave., 06451. Tel: 203-238-2243. The Institute of the Franciscan Sisters of the Eucharist. Sr. Suzanne Gross, F.S.E., Contact. Legal Title: *Franciscan Sisters of the Eucharist, Inc.* Mother Rosemae Pender, F.S.E., Mother General. Professed 20; Novices 2; Postulants 2. 275 Finch Ave., 06451. Tel: 203-238-2400. 269 Finch Ave., 06451. Tel: 203-630-1771.

Mt. Carmel Convent, 109 Goodwill Ave., 06451. Tel: 203-235-3622. Apostles of the Sacred Heart of Jesus.

St. Joseph Convent, 19 Goodwill Ave., 06451. Tel: 203-235-8551.

St. Stanislaus Convent, 70 Akron St., 06450. Tel: 203-237-1559. Sisters of St. Joseph of the Third Order of St. Francis, Sisters of Mercy.

Ursuline Sisters of the Congregation of Tildonk, Belgium, 125 Goodwell Ave., 06451. Tel: 203-686-1702.

MILFORD. *Franciscan Sisters of the Atonement*, 245 Orange Ave., 06460. Tel: 203-876-2902.

Sisters of Mercy of the Americas of Connecticut, 23 Jones Ct., 06460. Tel: 203-877-1170.

St. Mary Convent, 74 Gulf St., 06460. Tel: 203-874-8427.

NAUGATUCK. *Sisters of Mercy of the Americas of Connecticut*, 1006 New Haven Rd., 06770. Tel: 203-723-8735. 53 Clearview Cir., 06770. Tel: 203-729-2143.

NEW BRITAIN. *Cana*, 1190 Slater Rd., 06053. Tel: 860-826-1655. Total in Residence 3. Sisters of St. Joseph of Chambery. 1166 Slater Rd., 06053. Tel: 860-229-9291. Total in Residence 2.

Daughters of the Holy Spirit, 1222 Stanley St., Apt. 102, 06051-1514. Tel: 860-223-0445.

Dominican Sisters of Hope. (Ossining, NY), 597 Burritt St., 06053. Tel: 860-827-8511.

Holy Cross Convent, 225 Farmington Ave., 06053-2929. Tel: 860-229-0677. 40 Chestnut St. #307, 06052-2628. Tel: 860-827-1317.

Maryknoll Sisters of St. Dominic, 950 Farmington Ave. C30, 06053. Tel: 860-229-9912.

Motherhouse of Daughters of Mary of the Immaculate Conception, 314 Osgood Ave., 06053. Tel: 860-225-9406. Daughters of Mary of the Immaculate Conception. Mother Mary Mark Pizzotti, D.M., Supr. Gen.; Sr. Mary Christine, D.M., Sec. & Contact; Rev. Walter Mruk, O.F.M.Conv., Chap. Tel: 860-225-5786. Sisters in Community 57; Residence at the Motherhouse 33.

Sacred Heart Convent, 23 Orange St., 06053. Tel: 860-225-3989.

Msgr. Bojnowski Manor, 50 Pulaski St., 06053. Tel: 860-229-0336.

St. Lucian Home, 532 Burritt St., 06053. Tel: 860-223-2123.

Our Lady of Rose Hill Day Care Center, 594 Burritt St., 06053. Tel: 860-223-4846.

Marian Educational Clinic, 314 Osgood Ave., 06053. Tel: 860-223-0501.

St. Ann Convent, 112 North St., 06051. Tel: 860-229-1488. Religious Teachers Filippini. Sisters 5.

St. Francis of Assisi Convent, School Sisters of Notre Dame, 1757 Stanley St., 06053. Tel: 860-225-7143. E-mail: stfrancis@snet.net

Sisters of Mercy of the Americas, 1214 Stanley St. #203, 06051. Tel: 860-826-7328. 1218 Stanley St. #202, 06051. Tel: 860-225-3154. 37 Carlton St., 06053. Tel: 860-229-7575.

The Sisters of St. Francis of Philadelphia, 15 Wilcox St., 06051. Tel: 860-229-0463.

Sisters of the Cross and Passion, 25 Streamside Ln., 06052. Tel: 860-224-1193.

NEW HARTFORD. *Missionary Servants of the Most Blessed Trinity*, 595 Town Hill Rd., 06057. Tel: 860-379-4329.
E-mail: msbtphl@aol.com
Total in Residence 3.

NEW HAVEN. *Missionary Franciscan Sisters of the Immaculate Conception*, 904 Howard Ave., 06512. Tel: 203-468-2280.

St. Brendan Convent, 455 1/2 Whalley Ave., 06511. Tel: 203-787-4631. Sisters of Our Lady of the Garden.

St. Joseph Convent, 135 Edwards St., 06511. Tel: 203-562-9202. Sisters of Saint Anne. 15 Lincoln St., 06511. Tel: 203-865-7305. 1914 Chapel St., 06515. Tel: 203-389-9428.

Albertus Magnus College, 790 Prospect St., 06511. Tel: 203-777-7484.

Sisters of Charity of St. Elizabeth, Convent Station, 1450 Chapel St., 06511. Tel: 203-789-3377. 450 Central Ave., 06515. Tel: 203-397-5243. 80 Whittier Ave., 06515. Tel: 203-389-4400.

Sisters of Charity of St. Elizabeth, Convent Station, 1450 Chapel St., 06511. Tel: 203-789-5116.

Sisters of Mercy of the Americas, 355 Ferry St. #713, 06513. Tel: 203-773-1060. 510 Lombard St., 06513. Tel: 203-562-9361.

Sisters of Notre Dame de Namur, 180 Howard Ave., 06519. Tel: 203-782-2258. 311 Eastern St. #901E, 06513. Tel: 203-469-5093. 311 Eastern St. #917E, 06513. Tel: 203-469-8385. 311 Eastern St. #1704, 06513. Tel: 203-469-9934. 83 Porter St., 06519. Tel: 203-498-7011.

Sisters of St. Joseph of Chambery, 83 Porter St., 06519. Tel: 203-498-9569.

NEWINGTON. *Maryhouse*, 21 Hartford Ave. #9, 06111. Tel: 860-666-1085. Sisters of Mercy of the Americas.

St. Mary Convent, 168 Cedar St., 06111. Tel: 860-667-1790. Sisters of Charity of St. Elizabeth, Convent Station. Total in Residence 3.

Sisters of Notre Dame de Namur, 42 E. Robbins Ave., 06111.

NORTH BRANFORD. *Sisters of Mercy of the Americas of Detroit*, 1739 Foxon Rd., 06471-1566. Tel: 203-488-0692.

NORTH GUILFORD. *Monastery of Our Lady of Grace*, 11 Race Hill Rd., 06437. Tel: 203-457-0599. Dominican Nuns. A contemplative community with solemn vows and papal enclosure. Perpetual Adoration. Sr. Mary Ann, O.P., Prioress & Contact; Rev. Thomas B. Confer, O.P., Chap. Tel: 203-457-0595. Professed Sisters 44. Dominican Contemplative Nuns (Cloistered). Sr. Mary Ann, O.P., Prioress; Rev. Thomas B. Confer, O.P., Chap. Professed Sisters 44; Novices 1.

NORTH HAVEN. *St. Francis Cabrini Convent*, 94 Chapel Hill Rd., 06473. Tel: 203-239-8012. Sisters of the Sacred Heart of Jesus of Ragura. Total in Residence 3.

NORTHFORD. *Sisters of St. Joseph of Chambery*, 30 Mansfield Dr. #1603, 06472. Tel: 203-484-7018.

OXFORD. *Ursuline Sisters of the Congregation of Tildonk, Belgium*, 733 Oxford Rd., 06478. Tel: 203-888-4902.

SOUTHINGTON. *Congregation of Notre Dame*, 96 Summer St., 06489. Tel: 860-628-4506. Total in Residence 3.

SUFFIELD. *St. Joseph Convent*, 156 S. Main St., 06078. Tel: 860-668-2503.

TERRYVILLE. *Daughters of Wisdom*, 25 Allen St., 06786-6301. Tel: 860-583-8786. 41 Allen St., 06786-1503. Tel: 860-582-7676.

Maryknoll Sisters of St. Dominic, 10 Agney Ave. #2E, 06786. Tel: 860-589-4768.

TORRINGTON. *St. Francis of Assisi Convent*, 93 Marcia Dr., 06790. Tel: 860-489-7405. Sisters of Mercy of the Americas of Connecticut, Sisters of Notre Dame de Namur.

St. Peter Convent, 25 St. John Pl., 06790. Tel: 860-489-4035. Religious Teachers Filippini.

School Sisters of Notre Dame, 106 Mill Ln., 06790. Tel: 860-489-1741.

WALLINGFORD. *Holy Trinity Convent*, 25 N. Whittlesey Ave., 06492. Tel: 203-265-6999. Sisters of Mercy of the Americas of Connecticut, Sisters of Notre Dame de Namur.

Sisters of Mercy of the Americas of Connecticut, 1043 North Farms Rd., 06492. Tel: 203-265-6624.

WATERBURY. *Anawim Community*, 25 State St., 06702. Tel: 203-753-0867. Daughters of the Holy Spirit. 18 Hillview Ave., 06710. Tel: 203-756-2931. 27 State St., 06702. Tel: 203-754-0844. 44 Kramer Ave., 06705. Tel: 203-754-4825.

Franciscan Sisters of Allegheny, NY, 407 Robbinwood Rd., 06708. Tel: 203-753-1472.

Holy Land Convent, 60 Slocum St., 06706. Tel: 203-755-2456. Religious Teachers Filippini.

Maryknoll Sisters of St. Dominic, 55 Cole St., 06706. Tel: 203-754-2913. Total in Residence 8.

Notre Dame Convent, 119 Southmayd Rd., 06705. Tel: 203-753-4431; 753-1095. Sisters of the Congregation of Notre Dame. Sr. Rita Corley, C.N.D., Contact; Sr. Kathleen Reid, C.N.D.; Sr. Lena Mastroianni, C.N.D.; Sr. Edith Laflamme, C.N.D.; Sr. Pauline Dufresne, C.N.D.; Sr. Jewel Renna, C.N.D.; Sr. Marie Martin, C.N.D. Sisters 7. 587 Oronoke Rd., 06708. Tel: 203-755-8828. Sisters 6. 109 Highland Ave., 06708. Tel: 203-753-3073. Sisters 2.

St. Mary Hospital, 56 Franklin St., 06706. Tel: 203-574-6455. Sisters of St. Joseph of Chambery. 284 Windy Dr., 06705. Tel: 203-574-6374. 31 Marita Dr., 06705. Tel: 203-753-4503.

Sisters of Charity of St. Elizabeth, Convent Station, 100 Jefferson Sq. #31, 06706. Tel: 203-757-5685. 100 Jefferson Sq. #6H, 06706. Tel: 203-596-1331.

Sisters of Mercy of the Americas, 1054 Meriden Rd., 06705-3137. Tel: 203-753-3507.

Visitation Plaza, 100 Jefferson Sq. #7J, 06706. Tel: 203-755-7236. 36 Irving St. #2, 06710. Tel: 203-753-4503.

Sisters of Notre Dame de Namur, 131 Herschel Ave., 06708. Tel: 203-757-1444. 38 Summer St., 06704. Tel: 203-755-0012.

WATERTOWN. *St. John the Evangelist Convent*, 9 Academy Hill, 06795. Tel: 203-274-1820. School Sisters of Notre Dame. Sisters 5.

WEST HARTFORD. *Convent of Mary Immaculate, Provincial House of the Sisters of St. Joseph of Chambery.* (North American Province), 27 Park Rd., 06119. Tel: 860-233-5126; 232-8252. Sisters of St. Joseph of Chambery. Legal Title: *The Sisters of St. Joseph Corporation.* Sr. Mary Kelly, C.S.J., Prov. Supr.; Sr. Presentation Hoye, C.S.J., Contact. In Community: Professed Sisters 196.

Religious Trust of the Sisters of St. Joseph of Chambery (the "Trust").

Canticle Hall, 27 Park Rd., 06119. Tel: 860-232-2797.

Caritas, 27 Park Rd., 06119. Tel: 860-233-5126, Ext. 249.

Euphrasia Hall, 27 Park Rd., 06119. Tel: 860-233-1697.

Holy Family Monastery/Retreat, 303 Tunxis Rd., 06107. Tel: 860-521-1477. Feminine Congregation of the Passion.

Mercyknoll, Incorporated, 243 Steele Rd., 06117. Tel: 203-236-3503. Sisters of Mercy of the Americas of Connecticut. A retirement and health care facility of the Sisters of Mercy. Sr. Irene Holowesko, R.S.M., Admin. & Contact; Rev. Robert D. Bergin, Chap. Bed Capacity 82; Skilled Nursing 38; RHNS 10; HFA 34.

St. Mary Home, 2021 Albany Ave., 06117. Tel: 860-236-1924. Sisters of Mercy of the Americas of Connecticut.

Sisters of Mercy of the Americas of Albany, 2021 Albany Ave., 06117. Tel: 860-236-1924. Sisters of Mercy of the Americas.

Administrative Office, 249 Steele Rd., 06117. Tel: 860-232-8602. Sr. Judith A. Carey, R.S.M., Regl. Pres. Sisters in Community 289.

Sisters of Mercy of the Americas of Connecticut, 132 Milton St., 06119. Tel: 860-523-0707.

St. Joseph College, Lourdes Hall, 1678 Asylum Ave., 06117. Tel: 860-232-6730.

Convent of the Holy Spirit, 243 Steele Rd., 06117. Tel: 860-236-7805.

Catherine McAuley Unit, 243 Steele Rd., 06117. Tel: 860-236-3503.

St. Paul Convent, 243 Steele Rd., 06117. Tel: 860-232-7745.

Trocaire, 243 Steele Rd., 06117. Tel: 860-233-2195.

Sacred Heart Convent, 243 Steele Rd., 06117. Tel: 860-236-3503.

Maranatha, 243 Steele Rd., 06117. Tel: 860-236-9448. 25 Beechwood Rd., 06107. Tel: 860-561-5997. 27 Park Rd., 06119. Tel: 860-236-5626. 54 Boulanger Ave. #1, 06110. Tel: 860-231-8472. 54 Boulanger Ave. #2, 06110. Tel: 860-233-6679. 98 Caya Ave., 06110. Tel: 860-236-2051.

Sisters of Mercy of the Americas of Vermont, 25 Beechwood Ave., 06107. Tel: 860-561-5997.

Sisters of Notre Dame de Namur, 21 Prescott St., 06110. Tel: 860-231-7979.

Sisters of St. Joseph. (Springfield, MA), 50 Crescent St., 06119. Tel: 860-233-8708.

Vietnamese Dominican Sisters, 78 Westpoint Ter., 06107. Tel: 860-521-8296. Sr. Magdalene Nguyen, O.P., Supr. & Contact. Total in Residence 3.

WEST HAVEN. *Our Lady of Victory Convent*, 634 Jones Hill Rd., 06516. Tel: 203-934-8601. Ursuline Sisters of the Congregation of Tildonk, Belgium.

St. Paul Parish Center, 45 Alling St., 06516. Tel: 203-934-1357.

Sisters of the Assumption, 491 Washington Ave. #3W, 06516. Tel: 203-932-6449.
E-mail: morhous@pantheon.yale.edu

WETHERSFIELD. *Daughters of Wisdom*, 78 Fairlane Dr., 06109. Tel: 860-529-8419.

Maryknoll Sisters of St. Dominic, 547 Goff Rd., 06109. Tel: 860-529-1483. 96 Victoria Rd., Hartford, 06114. Tel: 860-296-1826.

Sisters of Notre Dame de Namur, 98-1 Folly Brook Blvd., 06109. Tel: 860-257-7091.

WINCHESTER CENTER. *Villa Ferretti, Religious Teachers Filippini*, 438 Winchester Rd., Box 55, 06094. Tel: 860-379-3279.

WINDSOR. *Sisters of Notre Dame de Namur*, Province Center, 468 Poquonock Ave., 06095-2473. Tel: 860-688-1832.
E-mail: sndct@aol.com
Administrative Team: Sr. Joan Farley, S.N.D. Tel: 860-285-0554; Sr. Elizabeth McLaughlin, S.N.D., Contact. Tel: 860-285-8901; Sr. Marilyn Pechillo, S.N.D. Tel: 860-285-8441.

Community, 468 Poquonock Ave., 06095. Tel: 860-285-0038.

Julie House, 425 Poquonock Ave., 06095. Tel: 860-298-8320. Assisted living home for S.N.D.'s only. Residents 19; Staff 3.

Sisters of St. Joseph of Chambery, 67 Bloomfield Ave., 06095. Tel: 860-285-0890.

WINDSOR LOCKS. *Sisters of Notre Dame de Namur*, 34 Ellis St., 06096-1704. Tel: 860-627-8002. Total in Residence 5.

WINSTED. *St. Anthony Convent*, 66 Oak St., 06098. Tel: 860-379-8375. Franciscan Missionaries of the Divine Motherhood. Sisters 2.

WOLCOTT. *Daughters of Wisdom*, 18 Munson Rd. #2, 06716. Tel: 203-879-3432.

[O] COUNSELING CENTERS

MERIDEN. *Franciscan Life Center*, 271 Finch Ave., 06451. Tel: 203-237-8084. Legal Title: *Franciscan Life Center Network, Inc.* Sr. Shaun Vergauwen, F.S.E., Dir. & Contact. Franciscan Sisters of the Eucharist 7; Total Assisted 1,200; Total Staff 17.

[P] ADOPTION SERVICES-HOME CARE

MERIDEN. *Franciscan Family Care Center*, 267 Finch Ave., 06450. Tel: 203-237-8084
For a complete listing, refer to the Special Care Facilities section.

[Q] RETREAT HOUSES-RENEWAL CENTERS

FARMINGTON. *Holy Family Retreat House*, 303 Tunxis Rd., 06107. Tel: 860-521-0440. For laymen and laywomen. Conducted by the Passionist Community. Very Rev. Terence Kristofak, C.P., Retreat Dir./Prov. Consultor. Assoc. Directors: Revs. David Cinquegrani, C.P.; Earl Keating, C.P.; Sr. Eileen Fucito, C.P.; Mr. William Walsh. Priests 2; Sisters 2; Lay Staff 2.

Our Lady of Calvary Retreat House. Conducted by the Sisters of the Cross and Passion for Religious and Lay Persons, 31 Colton St., 06032. Tel: 860-677-8519; Fax: 860-677-2873.
E-mail: olcret@juno.com
Retreat Team: Sr. Joanne Fahey, C.P., Admin. & Contact; Sr. Ann Rodgers, C.P., Prog. Dir.; Sr. Anna Marie Becker, C.P.; Joanne Ceccarelli-Egan; Marie D. Benedetto; Beverly Montana; Sr. Mary O'Brien, C.P.; Roberta Cote.

LITCHFIELD. *Wisdom House Retreat Center*, 229 E. Litchfield Rd., 06759-3002. Tel: 860-567-3163; Fax: 860-567-3166.
E-mail: info@wisdomhouse.com
Web site: www.wisdomhouse.org
A retreat center for spiritual and human development programs. Use of space is available for educational and spiritual programs and for non-profit organizations when their purpose corresponds to the Mission of Wisdom House. The Center is a ministry of the Daughters of Wisdom. Sr. Rosemarie Greco, D.W., Admin.

MADISON. *Mercy Center, Incorporated*, 167 Neck Rd., P.O. Box 191, 06443. Tel: 203-245-0401.
E-mail: mercymad@aol.com
Web site: www.mercyctrmadison.com
Sisters of Mercy. Sr. Eugenie Guterch, R.S.M., Admin. & Contact. Sisters 9; Total in Residence 6; Total Staff 25.

NEW HARTFORD. *Trinita*, 595 Town Hill Rd., Rte. 219, 06057. Tel: 860-379-4329. Total in Residence 3; Total Staff 5. Mailing Address: 3501 Solly Ave., Philadelphia, PA, 19136. Missionary Servants of the Most Blessed Trinity.

[R] NEWMAN CENTERS

HARTFORD. *University of Hartford Newman Center*, 200 Bloomfield Ave., 06117. Tel: 860-768-4899. Rev. Raymond S. Smialowski, Chap., Holy Spirit Rectory, 183 Church St., 06111. Trinity College Chapel, 300 Summit St., 06106. Tel: 860-297-2015. Rev. Raymond S. Smialowski, Chap.

HAMDEN. *Catholic Community at Quinnipac College*, P.O. Box 340, 06518. Rev. Louis Anthony Evangelisto, Chap. & Contact.

NEW BRITAIN. *Central Connecticut State University Newman House*, 145 Paul Manafort Dr., 06053-2552. Tel: 860-832-3795. Rev. Richard J. Donovan, O.F.M. Total Staff 1.

St. Francis of Assisi Friary, 1755 Stanley St., 06053.

NEW HAVEN. *Southern Connecticut State University Newman Center*, 129 Edwards St., 06511. Tel: 203-392-5331; 624-5297. Rev. John P. Sullivan.

Yale University-St. Thomas More Catholic Center and Chapel, 268 Park St., 06511. Tel: 203-777-5537; Fax: 203-777-0144. Rev. Robert L. Beloin, Ph.D., Chap. & Contact; Sr. Jo-Ann Veillette, S.A.S.V., Assoc. Chap.

[S] ORGANIZED CHARITIES

HARTFORD. *Catholic Charities-Catholic Family Services (Archdiocese of Hartford)*. Central Office. Archdiocesan Center, 467 Bloomfield Ave., Bloomfield, 06002-2999. Tel: 860-242-9577. Patrick J. Johnson, Jr., A.C.S.W., Dir. Charities & Exec. Dir.; Sr. Dorothy Strelchum, Assoc. Dir.; Linda S. Smith, C.I.S.W., Asst. Exec. Dir. Programs; Edgar Bernier, C.P.A., Controller; Francis Laffin, Dir. Group Home Svcs.

Hartford, 896 Asylum Ave., 06105. Tel: 860-522-8241. John R. Morrison, Regl. Dir.

Corpus Christi Child Development Center, 595 Silas Deane Hwy., 06109. Tel: 203-563-3747. Elizabeth Went, Contact Person.

Family Counseling Service, St. Bernard Church, 426 Hazard Ave., Enfield, 06082. Tel: 860-745-1727.

Institute for the Hispanic Family, 80 Jefferson St., 06105. Tel: 860-527-1124. Ramon Rojono, M.D., Dir.

The Hispanic Child Guidance Clinic, 80 Jefferson St., 06105. Tel: 860-524-8974. Peter Arroyo, Dir.

Travelers Aid, 896 Asylum Ave., 06105. Tel: 860-522-8241.

Lower Naugatuck Valley, 205 Wakelee Ave., P.O. Box 364, Ansonia, 06401. Tel: 203-735-7483. Patricia Nere, A.C.S.W., Regl. Dir.

Meriden, 220 Colony St., Meriden, 06450. Tel: 203-235-2707. Raymond S. Shocki, Jr., A.C.S.W., District Exec. Dir.

Outreach Office, 201 W. Main St., Plantsville, 06479.

Milford, 203 High St., P.O. Box 147, Milford, 06460. Tel: 203-874-6270. Wayne Crossman, M.S.W., District Exec. Dir.

New Britain, 90 Franklin Sq., New Britain, 06051. Tel: 860-225-3561. Gregory Paleologos, A.C.S.W., Regl. Dir.

New Haven, 478 Orange St., New Haven, 06502. Tel: 203-787-2207. Guilford Office, 57 Whitfield St., Guilford, 06437. Patricia Nere, A.C.S.W., Regl. Dir.

Torrington, 132 Grove St., Torrington, 06790. Tel: 860-482-5558. Jack Doyle, District Exec. Dir.

Waterbury, 56 Church St., Waterbury, 06702. Tel: 203-755-1196. Jack Doyle, A.C.S.W., District Exec. Dir.

Bristol Office, 300 Main St., Bristol, 06010. Tel: 860-589-8662.

Southbury Office, 88 Main St., Southbury, 06488.

Migration and Refugee Service, 125 Market St., 06103. Tel: 860-548-0059. Stephanie Morton, Dir.

[T] SOCIAL SERVICE CENTERS FOR SPANISH-SPEAKING AND BLACK PEOPLE

BLOOMFIELD. *Office for Hispanic Evangelization*, 467 Bloomfield Ave., 06002-2999. Tel: 860-243-0940. Most Rev. Peter A. Rosazza, Vicar Hispanics; Deacon Rafael Lopez, Dir.

NEW HAVEN. *Centro San Jose, Inc.*, 290 Grand Ave., 06513. Tel: 203-562-3135. Peter A. Noble, Exec. Dir.

WATERBURY. *Spanish-Speaking Center*, 83 Cherry St., 06702. Tel: 203-574-5156. Rev. John C. Blackall, Contact. Total Assisted 350; Total Staff 1.

[U] SOCIETY OF ST. VINCENT DE PAUL

HARTFORD. *Particular Council of the St. Vincent de Paul Society*. Greater Hartford, 134 Farmington Ave., 06105-3784. Tel: 860-541-6491. Legal Title: *Particular Council of the St. Vincent de Paul Society of the Archdiocese of Hartford.*

[V] MISCELLANEOUS

HARTFORD. *Mercy Housing & Shelter Corporation*, 45 Wyllys St., 06106. Lucy Callahan, Pres. & Exec. Dir.; Amy Lynn Silverman, Contact. Total Assisted 10,000; Total Staff 65.

North American La Salette Mission Center, Inc., 85 New Park Ave., 06106-2184. Tel: 860-523-4017. Rev. John R. Nuelle, M.S., Pres. & Exec. Dir.

Religious Trust of the Missionaries of Our Lady of LaSalette. Province of Our Lady of Seven Dolors, (MLS Trust), 915 Maple Ave., 06114-2330. Tel: 860-956-8870.
E-mail: mlsadmin@aol.com
Rev. Joseph M. O'Neil, M.S., Contact.

BLOOMFIELD. *Archdiocesan Spiritual Life Center*, 467 Bloomfield Ave., 06002-2903. Tel: 860-243-2374; Fax: 860-242-7914.
E-mail: spiritlifectr@juno.com
Sr. Barbara Flynn, S.S.A., Contact; Cathleen Murtha, D.W., Assoc. Dir.

Foundation for the Advancement of Catholic Schools, 467 Bloomfield Ave., 06002-2999. Tel: 860-242-4362. Christopher J. Rohrs, Pres.; Jeannine V. Dash, Exec. Dir. & Contact.

CHESHIRE. *Logos, Inc.*, 475 Oak Ave., 06410. Tel: 203-271-0805. Bro. Juan Sabadell, L.C., Contact.

HAMDEN. *Horizons Institute, Inc.*, 53 Rossotto Dr., 06514. Bro. Juan Sabadell, L.C., Sec. & Contact.

The Pastoral Theological Institute Inc., 2 Broadway, Ste. 6, 06518. Tel: 203-281-6593. Mr. William K. Larkin, Th.D., Pres. & Contact.

Rossotto, Inc., 53 Rossotto Dr., 06514. Tel: 203-281-4798. Bro. Juan Sabadell, L.C., Sec. & Contact.

LITCHFIELD. *Lourdes Shrine Guild, Inc.*, 83 Montfort Rd., 06759. Rev. Gerald Fitzsimmons, S.S.M., Prov. & Contact Person.

MERIDEN. *Franciscan Life Center Network, Incorporated*, 405 Allen Ave., 06450.

Franciscan Life Center, 271 Finch Ave., 06451.

Franciscan Life Process Center, 11650 Downes St., Lowell, MI, 49331.

Franciscan Montessori Earth School, 14750 S.E. Clinton St., Portland, OR, 97236.

Franciscan Northwoods Computer Center, 5601 Lilac Hill Rd., Duluth, MN, 55810.

John S. Duss Memorial Music Center, 2211 Greysolon Rd., Duluth, MN, 55812.

Franciscan Cre-Act School, 526 Grant St., P.O. Box 723, Pocatello, ID, 83204.

Franciscan Family Life Center, 1745 Pocatello Creek Rd., Pocatello, ID, 83201.

Creative Acting, 526 S. Grant St., Pocatello, ID, 83204.

NEW HAVEN. *Angelicum Fund*, L'Ecole Biblique et Archeologique Francaise de Jerusalem, 5 Hillhouse Ave., 06505. Tel: 203-562-6193; Fax: 203-562-1273. Rev. John P. McGuire, O.P., Dir.; Elaine Mello, Asst. Dir.

The Children's Foundation at St. Francis Home, Inc., 651 Prospect St., 06505. Tel: 203-777-5513. Rev. Jeremiah N. Murasso, Exec. Dir.

NEW MILFORD. *Our Lady of the Lakes Corporation*, 3 Old Town Park Rd., 06776-4212.

ORANGE. *Helping Hand Investments, Inc*, 393 Derby Ave., 06477. Tel: 203-795-2800. Bro. Juan Sabadell, L.C., Contact.

Horizons Institute, Inc., 393 Derby Ave., 06477. Bro. Juan Sabadell, L.C., Contact.

Legion of Christ, Inc., 393 Derby Ave., 06477. Tel: 203-795-2800; Fax: 203-795-2808. Revs. Anthony Bannon, L.C., Territorial Dir.; Patrick Langan, L.C., Devel.; Jeffrey Bowker, L.C., Devel.; John Curran, L.C., Secretary. Assistants: Revs. Emilio Diaz Torre, L.C.; Anthony Bailleres, L.C. Priests 6; Religious 16.

LUX ET VITA, INC., 393 Derby Ave., 06477. Tel: 203-795-2800. Bro. Juan Sabadell, L.C., Contact.

Racebrook, Inc., 393 Derby Ave., 06477. Tel: 203-281-4798. Bro. Juan Sabadell, L.C., Contact.

WEST HARTFORD. *Mercy Community Health, Inc.*, 249 Steele Rd., 06117-2796. Tel: 860-232-8602. Sr. Judith A. Carey, R.S.M., Bd. Chm.

Mercy Community Home Care Services, Inc., 275 Steele Rd., 06117. Tel: 860-232-8602. Mr. Jeff L. Lefkovich, Pres. & CEO.

Mercy Services, Inc., 249 Steele Rd., 06117-2796. Tel: 860-232-8602.
E-mail: JLCTMercy@aol.com
Mr. Jeff L. Lefkovich, Pres.

Project Hope, Inc. Business Office & Mailing Address, 27 Park Rd., 06119. Tel: 860-233-5126. Center Location, 873 New Britain Ave., Hartford, 06106. Tel: 860-953-2443. Sr. Helen Hart, C.S.J. Total Enrollment 72; Total Staff 3. Sisters of St. Joseph of Chambery.

WINDSOR. *The Connecticut Province of the Sisters of Notre Dame de Namur, Inc.*, 468 Poquonock Ave., 06095-2473. Tel: 860-688-1832.
E-mail: sndct@aol.com
Sr. Elizabeth McLaughlin, S.N.D.deN., Contact.

RELIGIOUS INSTITUTES OF MEN REPRESENTED IN THE ARCHDIOCESE

For further details refer to the corresponding bracketed number in the Religious Institutes of Men or Women section.

[0140]—*The Augustinians.*—O.S.A.
[0170]—*Basilian Fathers.*—C.S.B.
[0200]—*Benedictine Monks.*—O.S.B.
[0600]—*Brothers of the Congregation of Holy Cross.* (Notre Dame, IN).—C.S.C.
[1100]—*Brothers of the Sacred Heart.*—S.C.
[1330]—*Congregation of the Mission (Vincentian Fathers).*—C.M.
[1000]—*Congregation of the Passion.* (Prov. of St. Paul of the Cross).—C.P.
[0480]—*Conventual Franciscans.* (St. Anthony of Padua Prov.).—O.F.M.Conv.
[0515]—*Franciscan Brothers/Third Order.*—O.S.F.
[0520]—*Franciscan Friars.* (Immaculate Conception, Holy Name Provs.).—O.F.M.
[0690]—*Jesuit Fathers and Brothers.*—S.J.
[0730]—*Legionaries of Christ.*—L.C.
[0780]—*Marist Fathers.*—S.M.
[0800]—*Maryknoll.*—M.M.
[0720]—*The Missionaries of Our Lady of La Salette.* (Prov. O.L. of Seven Dolors).—M.S.
[1210]—*Missionaries of St. Charles-Scalabrinians.*—C.S.
[0590]—*Missionaries of the Holy Apostles.*—M.Ss.A.
[0860]—*Missionhurst Congregation of the Immaculate Heart of Mary.*—C.I.C.M.
[0870]—*Montfort Missionaries.*—S.M.M.
[0910]—*Oblates of Mary Immaculate.*—O.M.I.
[0430]—*Order of Preachers-Dominicans.* (Eastern Prov.).—O.P.
[0610]—*Priests of the Congregation of Holy Cross.*—C.S.C.
[1070]—*Redemptorist Fathers.* (Baltimore Prov.).—C.SS.R.
[1260]—*Society of Christ.*—S.Ch.
[0760]—*Society of Mary (Marianists).*—S.M.
[0975]—*Society of Our Lady of the Most Holy Trinity.*—S.O.L.T.
[1250]—*Somascan Fathers.*—C.R.S.
[]—*Sons of Charity.*—S.C.

RELIGIOUS INSTITUTES OF WOMEN REPRESENTED IN THE ARCHDIOCESE

[0130]—*Apostles of the Sacred Heart of Jesus.*—A.S.C.J.
[0180]—*Benedictine Nuns of the Primitive Observance.*—O.S.B.
[0860]—*Daughters of Mary of the Immaculate Conception.*—D.M.
[0820]—*Daughters of the Holy Spirit.*—D.H.S.
[0960]—*Daughters of Wisdom.*—D.W.
[1050]—*Dominican Contemplative Nuns.*—O.P.
[]—*Dominican Oblates of Jesus.* (Madrid, Spain).—J.S.O.P.
[1070-02]—*Dominican Sisters (Congregation of St. Mary of the Springs).*—O.P.
[]—*Dominican Sisters (Vietnamese Congregation of St. Catherine of Siena).*—O.P.
[1070-15]—*Dominican Sisters of Hope.*—O.P.
[1070-06]—*Dominican Sisters of Newburgh.*—O.P.
[1170]—*Felician Sisters.* (Our Lady of the Angels Province).—C.S.S.F.
[]—*Feminine Congregation of the Passion.*—C.F.P.
[]—*Franciscan Missionaries of the Divine Motherhood.*—F.M.D.M.
[1180]—*Franciscan Sisters of Alleghany, New York.*—O.S.F.
[1190]—*Franciscan Sisters of Atonement.*—S.A.
[1250]—*Institutes of the Franciscan Sisters of the Eucharist.*—F.S.E.
[2340]—*Little Sisters of the Poor.*—L.S.P.
[2470]—*Maryknoll Sisters of St. Dominic.*—M.M.
[2490]—*Medical Mission Sisters.*—M.M.S.
[2510]—*Mercedarian Missionaries of Berriz.*—M.M.B.
[1360]—*Missionary Franciscan Sisters of the Immaculate Conception.*—O.S.F.
[2790]—*Missionary Servants of the Most Blessed Trinity.*—M.S.B.T.
[3160]—*Parish Visitors of Mary Immaculate.*—P.V.M.I.
[2519]—*Religious Sisters of Mercy of Alma.* (MI).—R.S.M.
[3430]—*Religious Teachers Filippini.*—M.P.F.
[2970]—*School Sisters of Notre Dame.*—S.S.N.D.
[0520]—*Sisters of Charity of Our Lady, Mother of Mercy.*—S.C.M.M.
[0530]—*Sisters of Charity of Our Lady, Mother of the Church.*—S.C.M.C.
[0590]—*Sisters of Charity of Saint Elizabeth, Convent Station.*—S.C.

[2575]—*Sisters of Mercy of the Americas.* (Albany, Vermont, Detroit & Connecticut).—R.S.M.
[3000]—*Sisters of Notre Dame de Namur.* (Connecticut, Boston, California & Base Community).—S.N.D.deN.
[]—*Sisters of Our Lady of the Garden.*—O.L.G.
[3720]—Sisters of Saint Anne.—S.S.A.
[1650]—*Sisters of St. Francis of Philadelphia.*—O.S.F.
[3830-16]—*Sisters of St. Joseph.* (Springfield).—S.S.J.
[3830-05]—*Sisters of St. Joseph of Brentwood.*—C.S.J.
[3850]—*Sisters of St. Joseph of Chambery.*—C.S.J.
[3930]—*Sisters of St. Joseph of the Third Order of St. Francis.*—S.S.J.-T.O.S.F.
[0150]—*Sisters of the Assumption B.V.*—S.A.S.V.
[2980]—*Sisters of the Congregation de Notre Dame.*—C.N.D.
[3180]—*Sisters of the Cross and Passion.*—C.P.
[1970]—*Sisters of the Holy Family of Nazareth.*—C.S.F.N.
[]—*Sisters of the Sacred Heart of Jesus of Ragura.*—S.S.H.J.
[2170]—*Sisters, Servants of the Immaculate Heart of Mary.*—I.H.M.
[4130]—*Ursuline Sisters of The Congregation of Tildonk, Belgium.*—O.S.U.
[4190]—*Visitation Nuns.*—V.H.M.

ARCHDIOCESAN CEMETERIES

HARTFORD. *Catholic Cemeteries Association of the Archdiocese of Hartford, Inc.* 700 Middletown Ave., P.O. Box 517, North Haven, 06473-0517. Tel: 203-239-2557. Rev. Arthur J. DuPont, Dir.; Robert Marek, Exec. Dir.
Holy Trinity.
St. Patrick.
ANSONIA. *Old St. Mary.*
St. Mary.
BLOOMFIELD. *Mount Saint Benedict.*
DERBY. *Mount St. Peter.*
Old St. Mary.
EAST HARTFORD. *St. Mary.*
MANCHESTER. *St. Bridget.*
St. James.
MERIDEN. *Sacred Heart.*
St. Patrick.
NAUGATUCK. *St. Francis.* (New Haven Region).
St. James.
NEW BRITAIN. *Old St. Mary.*
St. Mary.
NEW HAVEN. *St. Bernard.*
St. Lawrence.
NORTH HAVEN. *All Saints.*
TORRINGTON. *Old St. Francis.*
St. Francis.
St. Peter.
WALLINGFORD. *Holy Trinity.*
St. John.
WATERBURY. *Calvary.*
Old St. Joseph.
St. Joseph.
WATERTOWN. *Mount Olivet.*

NECROLOGY

† Blaney, Philip L., (Retired). —Died May 21, 1997.
† Butler, Francis T., (Retired). —Died Sept. 29, 1997.
† D'Alonges, John P., (Retired). —Died Nov. 1, 1997.
† Geraghty, Walter F., Southington, CT, St. Dominic. —Died Feb. 23, 1997.
† Gradeck, A. Edward, (Retired). —Died Nov. 12, 1997.
† Hale, Francis A., (Retired). —Died March 30, 1997.
† Lyddy, Vincent E., (Retired). —Died Nov. 22, 1997.
† Lynch, Thomas J., Newington, CT, St. Mary. —Died Jan. 25, 1997.
† Otero, Neil, (Retired). —Died Jan. 15, 1998.
† Picher, Leo J., (Retired). —Died Aug. 13, 1997.
† Sanders, Robert E., (Retired). —Died April 14, 1997.
† Saunders, Robert E., (Retired). —Died April 20, 1997.
† Soucy, Maurice P., Meriden, CT, St. Laurent. —Died Nov. 14, 1997.
† Suppe, Joseph V., (Retired). —Died Sept. 28, 1997.
† Toohey, Thomas F., (Retired). —Died Feb. 12, 1997.

Diocese of Helena

(Dioecesis Helenensis)

ERECTED MARCH 7, 1884.

Square Miles 51,922.

Comprises the western part of the State of Montana, and is made up of the following Counties: Lewis and Clark, Glacier, Pondera, Flathead, Lake, Lincoln, Missoula, Mineral, Sanders, Powell, Granite, Ravalli, Deer Lodge, Silver Bow, Jefferson, Broadwater, Gallatin, Madison, Beaverhead, Meagher, Wheatland and parts of Teton and Toole.

Diocesan Legal Title—*Roman Catholic Bishop of Helena, Montana, a Corporation Sole.*

For legal titles of parishes and diocesan institutions, consult the Chancery Office.

Chancery and Diocesan Pastoral Office: 515 North Ewing, P.O. Box 1729, Helena, MT, 59624. Tel.: 406-442-5820; Fax: 406-442-5191.

STATISTICAL OVERVIEW

Personnel	
Priests: Diocesan Active in Diocese	51
Priests: Active Outside Diocese	11
Priests: Diocesan in Foreign Missions	1
Priests: Retired, Sick or Absent	26
Number of Diocesan Priests	89
Religious Priests in Diocese	9
Extern Priests in Diocese	4
Ordinations:	
Diocesan Priests	2
Transitional Deacons	1
Permanent Deacons in Diocese	27
Total Brothers	2
Total Sisters	63
Parishes	
Parishes	58
With Resident Pastor:	
Resident Diocesan Priests	43
Resident Religious Priests	3
Without Resident Pastor:	
Administered by Priests	8
Administered by Women Religious	4
Missions	39
Pastoral Centers	14
Professional Ministry Personnel:	
Brothers	2
Sisters	25
Lay Ministers	27
Welfare	
Catholic Hospitals	3
Total Assisted	181,351
Day Care and Extended Day Care Centers	2
Total Assisted	150
Educational	
Seminaries, Diocesan	1
Students from This Diocese	5
Students from Other Diocese	3
Diocesan Students in Other Seminaries	8
Total Seminarians	13
Colleges and Universities	1
Total Students	1,180
High Schools, Diocesan and Parish	2
Total Students	403
Elementary Schools, Diocesan and Parish	4
Total Students	852
Catechesis/Religious Education:	
High School Students	1,533
Elementary Students	5,948
Total Students Under Catholic Instruction	9,929
Teachers in the Diocese:	
Priests	10
Sisters	10
Lay Teachers	196
Vital Statistics	
Receptions into the Church:	
Infant Baptism Totals	952
Adult Baptism Totals	248
Received into Full Communion	115
First Communions	1,118
Confirmations	814
Marriages:	
Catholic	191
Interfaith	162
Total Marriages	353
Deaths	882
Total Catholic Population	66,500
Total Population	424,372

Former Bishops—Rt. Rev. JOHN B. BRONDEL, cons. Bishop of Victoria, V.I., Dec. 14, 1879; appt. Vicar Apostolic of Montana, April 17, 1883; Bishop of Helena, March 7, 1884; died Nov. 3, 1903.—Rt. Rev. JOHN P. CARROLL, D.D., cons. Bishop of Helena, Dec. 21, 1904; died Nov. 4, 1925.—Most Rev. GEORGE J. FINNIGAN, C.S.C., D.D., cons. Bishop of Helena, Aug. 1, 1927; died Aug. 14, 1932.—Most Rev. RALPH L. HAYES, D.D., cons. Bishop of Helena, Sept. 21, 1933; transferred to Rectorship North American College, Rome, Italy, September 11, 1935; transferred to Titular See of Hierapolis, Oct. 26, 1935; transferred to Davenport, Nov. 16, 1944; appt. Assistant at the Pontifical Throne, April 30, 1958; transferred to Titular See of Naraggara and retired, Oct. 20, 1966; died July 4, 1970.—Most Rev. JOSEPH M. GILMORE, S.T.D., cons. Bishop of Helena, Feb. 19, 1936; died April 2, 1962.—Most Rev. RAYMOND G. HUNTHAUSEN, ord. June 1, 1946; appt. July 8, 1962; cons. Bishop of Helena, Aug. 30, 1962; transferred to Archdiocese of Seattle, Feb. 25, 1975; installed Archbishop of Seattle, May 22, 1975; retired Aug. 21, 1991.—Most Rev. ELDEN F. CURTISS, D.D., ord. May 24, 1958; appt. March 4, 1976; cons. Bishop of Helena, April 28, 1976; transferred to Archdiocese of Omaha, May 4, 1993; installed Archbishop of Omaha, June 25, 1993.—Most Rev. ALEXANDER J. BRUNETT, Ph.D., ord. July 13, 1958; appt. April 19, 1994; cons. Bishop of Helena, July 6, 1994; transferred to Archdiocese of Seattle Oct. 28, 1997; installed Archbishop of Seattle Dec. 18, 1997.

Vicar General—Vacant.

Delegate for Carroll College—Rev. JOSEPH D. HARRINGTON, *Carroll College, Helena, 59625.* Tel: 406-447-4459.

Delegate for Senior Status Priests—Rev. BERNARD J. SULLIVAN, *311 9th Ave., Apt. 3, Helena, 59601.* Tel: 406-449-8839.

Chancery and Diocesan Pastoral Office—515 N. Ewing St., P.O. Box 1729, Helena, 59624. Tel: 406-442-5820; Fax: 406-442-5191.

Moderator of the Curia—Rev. JOHN W. ROBERTSON.

Chancellor—Rev. JOHN W. ROBERTSON.

Director of Pastoral Office—Sr. RITA MCGINNIS, S.C.L.

Archivist—Rev. WILLIAM DORNBOS.

Business Administration Office—PETER MCNAMEE, Diocesan Finance Officer, *515 N. Ewing St., P.O. Box 1729, Helena, 59624.* Tel: 406-442-5820.

Development Office—GERALD KUHL, Dir., *P.O. Box 1729, Helena, 59624.* Tel: 406-442-5820.

Western Montana Catholic Foundation—DONALD ST. PETER, Pres. GERALD KUHL, Contact Person, *P.O. Box 1729, Helena, 59624.* Tel: 406-442-5820.

Diocesan Tribunal—515 N. Ewing St., P.O. Box 1729, Helena, 59624. Tel: 406-442-5820.

Judicial Vicar—Rev. JOHN W. ROBERTSON.

Associate Judges—Revs. RAYMOND V. GILMORE; THOMAS HAFFEY; MATTHEW HUBER; PATRICK MCGURK.

Promoter of Justice—Rev. ROBERT GROSCH, J.C.L.

Defenders of the Bond—Revs. EMMETT KELLY; KEVIN O'NEILL; GARY RELLER.

Notaries—NADINE MCCURDY; GERALDINE ROBINSON.

Tribunal Consultant—Rev. JAMES PROVOST, J.C.D.

Diocesan Consultors—Revs. KEVIN CLARKE, S.J.; JOHN J. DARRAGH; WILLIAM J. GREYTAK; KEVIN S. O'NEILL; GARY W. RELLER; JOSEPH P. SULLIVAN.

Vicariates—Rev. ROBERT NOONAN, Conrad; Rev. WILLIAM J. GREYTAK, Helena; Rev. MATTHEW HUBER, Missoula; Rev. JOSEPH P. SULLIVAN, Kalispell; Rev. THOMAS HAFFEY, Butte.

Personnel Board—Revs. JOHN J. DARRAGH; THOMAS P. HAFFEY; JOHN F. HUNTHAUSEN, Chm. EDWARD G. KOHLER; JOHN MURRAY; DANIEL SHEA.

Inter-Diocesan Organizations

Montana Catholic Conference—SHARON HOFF, *P.O. Box 1708, Helena, 59624.* Tel: 406-442-5761; Fax: 406-442-9047.

Board of Directors—(Helena): Most Rev. ANTHONY MILONE, Admin.; (Great Falls): Sr. PAT CORMACK, S.C.S.C.; (Great Falls): JULIE FRENCH; (Great Falls): MYLES GROTBO; (Helena): Rev. EUGENE HRUSKA; (Great Falls): Rev. JEREMIAH LOWNEY; (Helena): Sr. MARY JOE MCDONALD; S.C.L.; (Butte): JOSEPH P. "PETE" MALIN; (Helena): EDWARD WAMBOLT.

Catholic Social Services for Montana, Inc.—MARILYN MCKIBBEN, Dir., *22 S. Ewing St., P.O. Box 907, Helena, 59601.* Tel: 406-442-4130; Fax: 406-442-4192. Coordinates and supervises all Catholic Social welfare in the State of Montana.

Board of Directors—(Helena): Most Rev. ANTHONY MILONE, Admin.; (Great Falls): Sr. PAT CORMACK, S.C.S.C.; (Great Falls): JULIE FRENCH; (Great Falls): MYLES GROTBO; (Helena): Rev. EUGENE HRUSKA; (Great Falls): Rev. JEREMIAH LOWNEY; (Helena): Sr. MARY JO MCDONALD, S.C.L.; (Butte): JOSEPH P. "PETE" MALIN; (Helena): EDWARD WAMBOLT.

Helena Office—MARILYN MCKIBBEN, Dir., Adoptions; Sr. MARY NOEL BRUCH, S.C.L., Social Worker, *22 S. Ewing, P.O. Box 907, Helena, 59624.* Tel: 406-442-4130.

Billings Office—Social Workers: BECKY HUBBERT, (Billings): SAM HUBBERT, (Columbus): *St. Vincent's Hospital, 2703 11th Ave. N., Billings, 59101.* Tel: 406-252-3399.

Great Falls Office—KYLA KALANICK, Social Worker, *1601 Second Ave. N., P.O. Box 7410, Great Falls, 59406.* Tel: 406-771-7805.

Missoula Office—BETSY ROBEL-GOMEZ, Social Worker, *St. Patrick Hospital, 554 W. Broadway, Missoula, 59801.* Tel: 406-329-5629.

Montana Association of Churches—MARGARET MACDONALD, Exec. Dir., *100 24th St. W., Suite G, Billings, 59102.* Tel: 406-656-9779. Rev. GARY W. RELLER, Diocesan Ecumenical Officer, *P.O. Box 1477, Polson, 59860.* Tel: 406-883-4607.

Diocesan Offices and Organizations

Borromeo Pre-Seminary Program—Rev. WILLIAM GREYTAK, *Carroll College, Helena, 59625.* Tel: 406-447-4350.

Campaign for Human Development—Sr. RITA MCGINNIS, S.C.L., *P.O. Box 1729, Helena, 59624.* Tel: 406-442-5820.

Catholic Committee on Scouting—JAMES TUCKER, Contact, *P.O. Box 1729, Helena, 59624.* Tel: 406-442-5820.

Catholic Youth Coalition—Deacon DAN MCGRATH, *P.O. Box 1729, Helena, 59624.* Tel: 406-442-5820.

Cemetery Director—SCOTT FITZPATRICK, *P.O. Box 1729, Helena, 59624.* Tel: 406-442-5820.

Charismatic Renewal—Diocesan Pastoral Office, P.O. Box 1729, Helena, 59624.

Christian Family Movement—Diocesan Pastoral Office, P.O. Box 1729, Helena, 59624.

Clergy Senior Status and Security Trust Board—Revs. ERNEST BURNS; JOSEPH HARRINGTON; EMMETT KELLY; PATRICK MCGURK; JOSEPH OBLINGER; KEVIN O'NEILL.

Continuing Formation of the Clergy—Rev. THOMAS P. HAFFEY, Dir., *2100 Farragut, Butte, 59701.* Tel: 406-723-4303.

Assembly of Women Religious—Sr. MARY JO MCDONALD, S.C.L., Pres., *2100 Farragut, Butte, 59701.* Tel: 406-723-4303.

Cursillo Movement, Journey and Search—Diocesan Pastoral Office, P.O. Box 1729, Helena, 59624. Tel: 406-442-5820.

Daughters of Isabella—CAROLYN SMITH, State Regent, *5128 Hwy. 200, Ovando, 59854.*

Diocesan Attorney—WARD SHANAHAN, *Gough, Shanahan, Johnson & Waterman, P.O. Box 1715, Helena, 59624.* Tel: 406-442-8560.

Diocesan Council of Catholic Women—DIONE ANDERSON, Pres., *P.O. Box 681, Cut Bank, 59427.* Tel: 406-873-5698.

Diocesan Ecumenical Officer—Rev. GARY W. RELLER, *PO Box 1477, Polson, 59860.* Tel: 406-883-4607.

Friends of The Catholic University—Rev. JOSEPH HARRINGTON, Chm., *Carroll College, Helena, 59625.* Tel: 406-447-4459.

Guatemala Missions—Rev. JOHN W. ROBERTSON, Dir., *P.O. Box 1729, Helena, 59624.* Tel: 406-442-5820.

Holy Childhood Association—Rev. JOSEPH L. BYRNE, Dir., *P.O. Box 610, Townsend, 59644.* Tel: 406-266-3973.

Legendary Lodge (Diocesan Summer Camp)—JAMES TUCKER, *P.O. Box 1729, Helena, 59624.* Tel: 406-442-5820.

Marriage Encounter—KRIS HEDSTROM; LEANN HEDSTROM, *1718 Buchanan St., Great Falls, 59404.*

Office of Due Process—Contact Judicial Vicar, *P.O. Box 1729, Helena, 59624.* Tel: 406-442-5820.

Program of Formation for Lay Ministry—JAMES TUCKER, *P.O. Box 1729, Helena, 59624.* Tel: 406-442-5820.

Program of Formation for the Permanent Diaconate—Deacon JAMES CURRY, Coord., *102 S. Washington, Butte, 59701.* Tel: 406-723-5407.

Office of Worship—Rev. EDWARD HISLOP, Liturgy Consultant; Sr. MARY JO QUINN, Liturgical Music Consultant, *1700 Missoula Ave., Helena, 59601.* Tel: 406-442-5268.

Priestly Formation—Rev. JOHN W. ROBERTSON, *P.O. Box 1729, Helena, 59624.* Tel: 406-442-5820.

Propagation of the Faith—Rev. JOSEPH L. BYRNE, Diocesan Dir., *P.O. Box 610, Townsend, 59644.* Tel: 406-266-3973.

Religious Education—JIM TUCKER, Dir., *515 N. Ewing St., P.O. Box 1729, Helena, 59624.* Tel: 406-442-5820.

Resource Center—KATHY WARD, Mgr., *515 N. Ewing St., P.O. Box 1729, Helena, 59624.* Tel: 406-442-5820.

Superintendent of Schools—Dr. THOMAS E. HART, *9 S. Idaho St., Butte, 59701.* Tel: 406-723-4770; Fax: 406-723-4759.

Third Order of St. Francis—KATHY POELMAN, S.F.O., *1702 Peosta, Helena, 59601.*

Vocations Office—*P.O. Box 1729, Helena, 59624.* Tel: 406-442-5820. Rev. THOMAS O'DONNELL, Dir., *P.O. Box 1110, East Helena, 59635.* Tel: 406-227-5334. Rev. VICTOR LANGHANS, Assoc. Dir., *P.O. Box 329, Frenchtown, 59834.* Tel: 406-626-4492. Rev. KEVIN O'NEILL, Assoc. Dir., *102 S. Washington, Butte, 59701.* Tel: 406-723-5407. Rev. LEO PROXELL, Assoc. Dir., *106 S. Maryland, Conrad, 59425.* Tel: 406-278-7517.

"Montana Catholic" (Diocesan Newspaper)—GERALD KORSON, Editor; M. CATHERINE TILZEY, Asst. Editor, *515 N. Ewing St., P.O. Box 1729, Helena, 59624.* Tel: 406-442-5820; Fax: 406-442-5191.

CLERGY, PARISHES, MISSIONS AND PAROCHIAL SCHOOLS

CITY OF HELENA
(Lewis and Clark County)

1—CATHEDRAL OF ST. HELENA (1866), Revs. John Darragh, Rector; Dougald J. McCallum; Herbert Pins (SEA); Deacon Fritz Roos. Pastoral Assocs.: Bro. Stephen Hale, C.F.C.; Sr. Nancy Svetlecic, S.C.L.; Lorraine Tucker.
Office: 530 N. Ewing St., 59601. Tel: 406-442-5825; 442-7094 (after hours); Fax: 406-449-5113.
Good Samaritan Thrift Store—(Assistance to those in need.) 1403 N. Cooke, 59601. Tel: 406-442-0780.

2—ST. MARY (1910), Rev. Edward J. Hislop. Pastoral Assocs.: Sr. Mary Agnes Hogan, S.C.L.; Sr. Mary Jo Quinn, S.C.L.; Helen Beausoleil; Janice Nankivel.
Office: 1700 Missoula Ave., 59601. Tel: 406-442-5268; Fax: 406-449-0860.

3—OUR LADY OF THE VALLEY, Rev. Daniel Shea; Deacon Richard Miller.
Office: 1502 Shirley Rd., 59601. Tel: 406-458-6114.
Missions—Wolf Creek, Lewis and Clark Co., Sacred Heart; Marysville, Lewis and Clark Co., Our Lady of Lourdes.

OUTSIDE THE CITY OF HELENA

Anaconda, Deer Lodge Co.,

1—ST. JOSEPH'S, (1957). Closed 1977. For inquiries for parish records contact Anaconda Catholic Community, Anaconda.

2—ST. PAUL'S, (1888). Closed 1980. For inquiries for parish records contact Anaconda Catholic Community, Anaconda.

3—ST. PETER'S, (1898). Closed 1980. For inquiries for parish records contact Anaconda Catholic Community, Anaconda.

4—ANACONDA CATHOLIC COMMUNITY, (1980). Serves the entire community of Anaconda. Revs. John E. Murray; Daniel Driscoll. Pastoral Assocs.: Sr. Eileen Johnson, S.C.L.; Sr. Constance Howe, R.S.M.; Mr. John McKenna, Admin.
Office: 217 W. Pennsylvania, 59711. Tel: 406-563-8406; Fax: 406-563-5912.
Res., 405 Alder St., 59711. Tel: 406-563-6633.
Churches—Holy Family, 217 W. Pennsylvania, 58711; St. Peter, 401 Alder St., 59711.
Station—Anaconda, Georgetown Lake.

Bigfork, Flathead Co., St. Catherine (1958), Rev. Richard H. Sodja.
Res., P.O. Box 277, 59911. Tel: 406-837-4846.
Church—105 Oliver Ln., 59911.
Mission—Somers, St. Ann.

Bonner, Missoula Co., St. Ann (1940), Rev. Michael Smith.
Res., P.O. Box 1008, 59823. Tel: 406-258-6815.
Mission—Seeley Lake, Missoula Co., Living Water Mission.

Boulder, Jefferson Co., St. Catherine (1894), Rev. William Greytak.
Res., Box 205, 59632. Tel: 406-225-3222.
Mission—Boulder Valley, Jefferson Co., St. John the Evangelist.

Bozeman, Gallatin Co., Holy Rosary (1885), Rev. Robert J. Beaulieu. Pastoral Assocs.: Sr. Patricia Toeckes, S.C.L.; Mary Fuller.
Office: 220 W. Main St., P.O. Box 96, 59771-0096. Tel: 406-587-4581; Fax: 406-582-0248.
Resurrection (1965). (Newman Parish). Rev. Robert Hall; Deacon Michael Certalic. Pastoral Assocs.: Marge O'Leary; Diane Dwyer.
Office: 1725 S. 11th, 59715. Tel: 406-586-9243; 406-587-8667 (Res.).
Mission—Big Sky.

Browning, Glacier Co., Church of the Little Flower (1904), Revs. Edward Kohler; Michael McHugh, S.J.; Sr. Edna Hunthausen, S.C.L., Pastoral Assoc.; Deacons Robert Bremner; Melvin Rutherford; John Gobert.
Office: P.O. Box 519, 59417. Tel: 406-338-5775.
Church—204 First St. N.E., 59417.
Missions—Babb, St. Mary, Queen of the World; Starr School, Sacred Heart; East Glacier, Church of the Ascension.

Butte, Silver Bow Co.,

1—BUTTE CATHOLIC COMMUNITY NORTH. Includes Immaculate Conception, St. Joseph, and St. Patrick Parishes. See individual listings. Revs. Joseph P. Moran, Moderator; Nathaniel Ndiokwere (Nigeria); Harry Butori; Deacons James Curry; Ronald Fournier.
Office and Res.: 102 S. Washington St., 59701. Tel: 406-723-5407; Fax: 406-782-8082.

2—HOLY SAVIOR, (1904). Closed 1974. For inquiries for parish records contact Butte Catholic Community North, Butte.

3—HOLY SPIRIT, (1978), Sr. Sharon Smith, S.C.L., Pastoral Admin.; Deacon Dan McGrath.
Office: 3930 East Lake, 59701. Tel: 406-494-5078.

4—IMMACULATE CONCEPTION, (1907). (Butte Catholic Community North). Rev. Joseph P. Moran.
Office and Res.: 102 S. Washington, 59701. Tel: 406-723-5407; Fax: 406-782-8082.
Church—Western & Caledonia St., 59701.

5—SACRED HEART PARISH, (1903). Closed 1970. For inquiries for parish records contact Butte Catholic Community North, Butte.

6—ST. ANN, (1917), Revs. Thomas P. Haffey; William F. Vernon; Sr. Mary Jo McDonald, S.C.L., Pastoral Assoc.; Deacon H. J. Johnson.
Res., 2100 Farragut, 59701. Tel: 406-723-4303.

7—ST. HELENA, (1921). Closed 1966. For inquiries for parish records contact Butte Catholic Community North, Butte.

8—ST. JOHN THE EVANGELIST, (1917), Rev. Edward Courtney. Pastoral Assocs.: John McPherson; Kathy Walter.
Office: 1500 Cobban Ave., 59701.
Res., 2040 Whitman, 59701. Tel: 406-782-8349.
Church—1500 Majors Ave., 59701.

9—ST. JOSEPH, (1905). (Butte Catholic Community North). Rev. Harry Butori.
Office and Res.: 102 S. Washington, 59701. Tel: 406-723-5407 (Office), 782-8668 (Res.); Fax: 406-723-5408.
Church—Utah & Second St., 59701.

10—ST. MARY, (1903). Closed 1986. For inquiries for parish records contact Butte Catholic Community North, Butte.

11—ST. PATRICK, (1881). (Butte Catholic Community North). Revs. Joseph P. Moran; Nathaniel Ndiokwere (Nigeria).
Office and Res.: 102 S. Washington St., 59701. Tel: 406-723-5407.
Church—Mercury & Washington St., 59701.

Choteau, Teton Co., St. Joseph (1898), Rev. Robert C. Noonan, Pastor.
Res., P.O. Box 640, 59422. Tel: 406-466-2961.
Church—320 Main St., 59422.

Columbia Falls, Flathead Co., St. Richard (1941), Rev. Joseph P. Sullivan; Sr. Lorane Coffin, O.S.B., Pastoral Assoc.; Deacon Robert Pearce.
Res., P.O. Box 2073, 59912. Tel: 406-892-5142.
Church—1210 Ninth St. W., 59912.
Mission—West Glacier, Flathead Co.
Station—Columbia Falls, Apgar.

Conrad, Pondera Co., St. Michael (1909), Rev. Leo Proxell; Sr. Mary Agnes Koenig, O.P., Pastoral Assoc.
Res., 106 S. Maryland St., 59425. Tel: 406-278-7517.
Station—Conrad, Stations Brady Ledger.

Cut Bank, Glacier Co., St. Margaret (1914), Rev. Stanley Popowski; Deacon James E. Hayes.
Res., 207 Second St., S.E., 59427. Tel: 406-873-4413.

Deer Lodge, Powell Co., Immaculate Conception (1911), Rev. Patrick McGurk.
Res., 605 Clark St., P.O. Box 786, 59722. Tel: 406-846-1444.
Mission—Avon, Powell Co., St. Theodore.

Dillon, Beaverhead Co., St. Rose of Lima (1901), Rev. Robert Porter (SFD).
Office: 226 S. Atlantic St., 59725. Tel: 406-683-4391; 683-6753 (Rectory).
Missions—Melrose, Silver Bow Co., St. John The Apostle; Wisdom, Beaverhead Co., Our Lady of Wisdom.

Drummond, Granite Co., St. Michael (1919), Rev. Kenneth E. Fortney.
Res., P.O. Box 329, 59832. Tel: 406-288-3847.
Mission—Goldcreek, Powell Co., St. Mary.

Dutton, Teton Co., St. William (1962), Rev. Leo Proxell, Sacramental Min.; Sr. Johanna Rickl, C.H.M., Pastoral Admin.
Res., 20 First Ave. N.E., Box 117, 59433. Tel: 406-476-3429.
Mission—Power, Guardian Angel.

East Helena, Lewis and Clark Co., SS. Cyril and Methodius (1907), Rev. Thomas M. O'Donnell; Deacon Gerald Kuhl.
Res., 214 W. Riggs St., P.O. Box 1110, 59635. Tel: 406-227-5334.
Missions—Canyon Ferry, Our Lady of the Lake; Clancy, St. John's.
Station—East Helena, Alhambra.

Eureka, Lincoln Co., Our Lady of Mercy (1916), Rev. Henry Steinhoff (B).
Res., 500 Dewey Ave., Box 626, 59917. Tel: 406-296-2118.

Fairfield, Teton Co., St. John (1941), Rev. Robert C. Noonan.
Res., 514 First Ave. S., P.O. Box 397, 59436. Tel: 406-467-2481.
Mission—Augusta, Lewis and Clark Co., St. Matthias.

Frenchtown, Missoula Co., St. John the Baptist (1884), Rev. Victor Langhans.
Res., P.O. Box 329, 59834. Tel: 406-626-4492. [CEM]
Missions—Superior, St. Mary Queen of Heaven; Alberton, Mineral Co., St. Albert the Great.

Hamilton, Ravalli Co., St. Francis (1896), Rev. Raymond Gilmore; Sr. Margaret Hogan, S.C.L., Pastoral Assoc.; Deacon Roland Peterson.
Res., 411 S. Fifth St., 59840. Tel: 406-363-1385.
Mission—Darby, Ravalli Co., St. Philip Benizi.

Harlowton, Wheatland Co., St. Joseph (1909), Rev. Jacob Vadakkekudy, (India), Admin.
Res., 26 Third St., N.W., Box 286, 59036. Tel: 406-632-5538.
Missions—Judith Gap, Wheatland Co., Immaculate Conception; Shawmut, Wheatland Co., Blessed Sacrament.

Heart Butte, Glacier Co., St. Anne (1911), Rev. Daniel Powers, S.J. Pastoral Assocs.: Sr. Marion McCrickard, O.S.U.; Bev Bullshoe; Deacon Melvin Rutherford.
Res., Blackfeet Reservation, P.O. Box 160, 59448. Tel: 406-338-2312.
Mission—Heart Butte, Glacier Co., Holy Family Mission. [CEM]

Helmville, Powell Co., St. Thomas (1889), Rev. Kevin Ryan, O.S.B.; Kathy Daniels, Pastoral Assoc.
Res., P.O. Box 90, 59843. Tel: 406-793-5697. [CEM]
Mission—Lincoln, Lewis and Clark Co., St. Jude's.

Kalispell, Flathead Co., St. Matthew (1895), Rev. Kevin S. O'Neill. Pastoral Assocs.: Deacon Fred Topp; Sr. Celine Regan, O.P.
Office: 602 S. Main St., 59901. Tel: 406-752-6788; Fax: 406-756-8248.
Res., 644 First Ave., W., 59901.

Risen Christ (1978), Rev. James Connor; Deacon Jack Pelowitz.
Res., 65 W. Evergreen Dr., 59901. Tel: 406-752-4219; 752-4226; Fax: 406-752-4226.

Libby, Lincoln Co., St. Joseph (1911), Rev. Raymond J. Hannigan.
Res., 719 Utah Ave., P.O. Box 1467, 59923. Tel: 406-293-4322; Fax: 406-293-7231.
Mission—Troy, Immaculate Conception.

Madison, Madison Co., Madison County Catholic Community. Comprised of St. Mary of the Assumption, Laurin; St. Joseph, Sheridan; and St. Patrick, Ennis. Rev. Edward L. Stupca. Pastoral Assocs.: Laurie Bartoletti; Kathy Miller; Roberta McKay.
Res., 105 Poppleton, P.O. Box 17, Sheridan, 59749. Tel: 406-842-5588.

Missoula, Missoula Co.,

1—CHRIST THE KING, (1966). (Newman Parish). Rev. James J. Hogan; Sr. Nancy Davis, C.S.J., Pastoral Assoc.; Dianne Peterson, Campus Min.
Office: 1400 Gerald Ave., 59801. Tel: 406-728-3845.

2—HOLY FAMILY, (1972), Rev. Matthew Huber; Deacon Thomas McCarthy; Sr. Ursula Keough, C.H.M, Pastoral Assoc.
Res., 4616 Gharrett St., 59803. Tel: 406-251-2692.
Mission—Lolo, Missoula Co., Spirit of Christ, 4200 Farm Ln., P.O. Box 743, Lolo, 59847. Tel: 406-273-2748.

3—POPE JOHN XXIII, (1971), Rev. Frank McCormick. Pastoral Assocs.: Beckie Hasse; Chris Kappes; Sr. Alice Ann Byrne, O.P.
Office: 1475 Eaton St., 59801. Tel: 406-721-2405.

4—ST. ANTHONY, (1921), Rev. John P. Miller. Pastoral Assocs.: Terry Jimmerson; Linda McKnight; Maggie Hommond.
Office: 217 Tremont St., 59801. Tel: 406-543-3129.

5—ST. FRANCIS XAVIER, (1881), Revs. Kevin T. Clarke, S.J.; Thomas F. Healy, S.J.; Deacon Carlton Quamme. In res., Rev. Roger E. Blanchette, S.J.; John S. Harrington, S.J.; Deacon Gregory Vance, S.J.
Res., 420 W. Pine St., 59802. Tel: 406-542-0321.

Philipsburg, Granite Co., St. Philip (1892), Rev. Kenneth E. Fortney.
Res., P.O. Box 329, Drummond, 59832. Tel: 406-288-3847.
Church—307 W. Kearney, P.O. Box 397, 59858. Tel: 406-859-3908.

Plains, Sanders Co., St. James (1889), Deacon Lynn F. McAtee.
Res., 107 Meany St., P.O. Box 745, 59859. Tel: 406-826-3668.
Mission—Hot Springs, Sacred Heart.

Polson, Lake Co., Immaculate Conception (1909), Rev. Gary W. Reller; Deacons Wesley Vert; Daniel Gullotta.
Res., 908 Fifth Ave. E., P.O. Box 1477, 59860. Tel: 406-883-4607; 883-2506 (Office). [CEM 3]
Church—1002 Fourth Ave. E., 59860.

Ronan, Lake Co., Sacred Heart (1911), Rev. Gary W. Keller.
Res., 325 Round Butte W., 59864. Tel: 406-676-4511.
Mission—Charlo, Mount Lake Co., St. Joseph's.

St. Ignatius, Lake Co., St. Ignatius (1854), Rev. Gustav H. Schmidt, S.J. Pastoral Assocs.: Sr. Dolores Shortal, O.P.; Sr. Joan Bartin, O.P.
Res., P.O. Box 667, 59865. Tel: 406-745-2768.
Missions—Arlee, Lake Co., Sacred Heart; Jocko, Lake Co., St. John Berchman's.

Shelby, Toole Co., St. William (1924), Rev. Carl Deitchman, Admin.
Res., 531 Main St., 59474. Tel: 406-434-2988.
Mission—Sunburst, St. Thomas Aquinas, (1917).

Stevensville, Ravalli Co., St. Mary (1842), Rev. Stephen Tallman.
Res., 333 Charlos St., 59870. Tel: 777-5574. [CEM]
Mission—Florence, Ravalli Co., St. Joseph.

Swan Valley, Lake Co., Swan Valley Catholic Community, Rev. Dusan A. Okorn, Admin.; Michelle Jenkins, Pastoral Assoc.
Res., The Sycamore Tree, Swan Lake, 59911. Tel: 406-754-2429.

Thompson Falls, Sanders Co., St. William (1955), Deacons Ronald Kazmierezak; Robert W. Kelley.
Res., Spruce & Preston St., P.O. Box 186, 59873. Tel: 406-827-4433.
Mission—Noxon.

Three Forks, Gallatin Co., Holy Family (1886), Rev. John F. Ward; Deacon Robert Lane.
Res., 104 Birch St., P.O. Box 99, 59752. Tel: 406-285-3592.
Mission—Belgrade, Valley of Flowers, 609 Quaw Blvd., Belgrade, 59714.

Townsend, Broadwater Co., Holy Cross (1903), Rev. Joseph L. Byrne; Deacon Donald Marks.
Res., 101 S. Walnut, P.O. Box 610, 59644. Tel: 406-266-3973.
Mission—Toston, Broadwater Co., Immaculate Conception.
St. Joseph's Historical Church—Canton.

Valier, Pondera Co., St. Francis (1909), Rev. Stanley Popowski; Sr. Anne Marie Burke, S.C.L., Pastoral Admin.
Res., 701-4th St., P.O. Box 338, 59486. Tel: 406-279-3327.
Mission—Dupuyer, Pondera Co., Holy Cross.

Walkerville, Silver Bow Co., St. Lawrence O'Toole (1896). Closed 1986. For inquiries for parish records contact Butte Catholic Community North, Butte.

West Yellowstone, Gallatin Co., Our Lady of the Pines, Rev. Joseph B. Oblinger, (Retired), Admin.
Res., Madison Ave. & Geyser St., P.O. Box 577, 59758. Tel: 406-646-7755.

Whitefish, Flathead Co., St. Charles (1890), Rev. Charles Roman.
Res., 230 Baker, Box 128, 59937. Tel: 406-862-2051.

Whitehall, Jefferson Co., St. Teresa (1911), Rev. Francis J. Wiegenstein; Al Feldsheim, Pastoral Assoc.
Res., 109 Second Ave. E., Box 430, 59759. Tel: 406-287-3893.
Mission—Twin Bridges, Jefferson Co., Notre Dame.

White Sulphur Springs, Meagher Co., St. Bartholomew (1916), Sr. Patricia Sullivan, S.C.L., Pastoral Admin.
Res., 407 Second Ave. S.E., P.O. Box 422, 59645. Tel: 406-547-3737.

DIOCESAN MISSIONS

Guatemala, Santo Tomas La Union,
10017 Departmento Suchitepequez. Rev. James Hazelton; Sr. Mary Waddell, B.V.M., Clinic Dir.; Sr. Anna Priester, B.V.M., D.R.E.

Helena, Guatemala Mission Medical Fund,
Supplies for needs of mission personnel, medicines, medical supplies, and health care needs to people in the mission area in Guatemala. Donations may be forwarded to the Fund at P.O. Box 1729, Helena, MT 59624. P.O. Box 1729, 59624.

Chaplains of Public Institutions

HELENA. *U.S. Veteran's Hospital*. Served by Helena Area Parishes. Fort Harrison.

BOULDER. *Boulder River School and Hospital*. Attended from St. Catherine, Boulder. Rev. William Greytak.

DEER LODGE. *Montana State Prison*. Vacant.

WARM SPRINGS. *Warm Springs State Hospital*. Vacant.

Special Assignments:
Reverend Fathers—
Dornbos, William, Diocesan Archivist, Mailing Address: P.O. Box 1729, Helena, MT 59624
Dumais, George J., S.J., Dir., Rochmont, Inc., 1700 Madeline, Missoula, MT 59801
Finnegan, Joseph, Mailing Address: P.O. Box 503, Whitehall, MT 59759
Malnar, Stan, 4220 W. Fremont Rd., Spokane, WA 99204
Robertson, John W., Chancellor & Moderator of the Curia, Mailing Address: P.O. Box 1729, Helena, MT 59624

On Duty Outside the Diocese:
Reverend Monsignors—
McCarthy, John F., Catholic Near East Association, Rome
Reverend Fathers—
Driscoll, Michael, Notre Dame University, Department of Theology, Notre Dame, IN 46556
Flynn, Thomas, Emory University, 1278 Oakdale Rd., N.E., Atlanta, GA 30307
Hazelton, James, Santo Tomas La Union, 10017 Departmento Suchitepequez, Guatemala
Provost, James H., Department of Canon Law, The Catholic University of America, Washington, DC 20064
Sullivan, James M., Creighton University, 2500 California St., Omaha, NE 68178

Graduate Studies:
Reverend Fathers—
Fleming, Jeffrey, 1025 Michigan Ave. N.E., Washington, DC 20017

On Leave of Absence:
Reverend Fathers—
Hunkler, Carl, P.O. Box 1729, Helena, MT 59624
Smith, Gregory D., P.O. Box 1729, Helena, MT 59624

Military Chaplains:
Reverend Monsignors—
Shea, Donald W., U.S. Army
Reverend Fathers—
Diphe, Juan, U.S. Air Force
Hightower, O. Lee., U.S. Army
Patton, Patrick G., U.S. Army

Retired:
Reverend Monsignors—
Brown, Anthony M., 30 Penny Ln., Butte, MT 59701
Harrington, D. B., 35 Wells St., Butte, MT 59701
Marsar, Joseph, P.O. Box 1110, East Helena, MT 59635
Reverend Fathers—
Burke, Gregory
Burns, Ernest, 100 E. Broadway #601, Butte, MT 59701
Chilton, Michael
Courtney, Humphrey J., Carroll College, Helena, MT 59625
Fenlon, Thomas J., 102 S. Washington St., Butte, MT 59701
Hunthausen, John F., Carroll College, Helena, MT 59625
Kaparich, Albert N., 100 E. Broadway, #701, Butte, MT 59701
Kelly, Emmett, 4309 Ghurrett, Missoula, MT 59801
Kirsch, John B., P.O. Box 893, Sheridon, MT 59749
Lynam, Gerald J., Carroll College, Helena, MT 59625
McCarthy, Bernard, 1325 W. Quartz, #306, Butte, MT 59701
Moran, Edward F., 410 Rosalie Manor, Butte, MT 59701
O'Sullivan, Sarsfield, 410 N. Western Ave., Butte, MT 59701

Oblinger, Joseph B., P.O. Box 577, West Yellowstone, MT 59758

Okorn, Dusan A., Sycamore Tree, Swan Lake, MT 59701

Plummer, J. Bruce, 261 Half Circle Way, Polson, MT 59860

Simons, Lawrence D., P.O. Box 696, Honaunau, HI 96726

Strom, Charles W., 341 Lupfer Ave., Whitefish, MT 59937

Sullivan, J. Bernard, 31 Ninth Ave., #3, Helena, MT 59601

Waggenor, William L., 3033 Busch St., #19, Whitehall, MT 59701

Wang, John, 425 Ford St., Missoula, MT 59801

Permanent Deacons:

Bremner, Robert, Sr., Little Flower, Browning

Britton, Michael, (Retired)

Certalic, Michael, Resurrection, Bozeman

Curry, James, Catholic Community North, Butte

Fournier, Ronald, Catholic Community North, Butte

Gobert, John, Little Flower, Browning

Gullotto, Daniel, Immaculate Conception, Polson

Hayes, James E., St. Margaret, Cut Bank

Johnson, H. J., St. Ann's, Butte

Kazmierczak, Ronald, St. William, Thompson Falls

Kelley, Robert, St. William, Thompson Falls

Kuhl, Gerald, Sts. Cyril and Methodius, East Helena

Lane, Robert, Holy Family, Three Forks

Marks, Donald, Holy Cross, Townsend

McAtee, Lynn F., St. James, Plains

McCarthy, Thomas, Holy Family, Missoula

McGrath, Daniel, Holy Spirit, Butte; Diocesan Youth Minister

Miller, Richard, Our Lady of the Valley, Helena

Pearce, Robert, St. Richard, Columbia Falls

Pelowitz, Jack, Risen Christ, Kalispell

Peterson, Roland, St. Francis Parish, Hamilton

Quamme, Carlton, St. Francis, Missoula

Roos, Fritz, Cathedral of St. Helena, Helena

Rutherford, Melvin, Little Flower, Browning

Topp, Frederick, St. Matthew, Kalispell

Vert, Wesley, Immaculate Conception, Polson

INSTITUTIONS LOCATED IN THE DIOCESE

[A] SEMINARIES, DIOCESAN

HELENA. *Carroll College*. Rev. William Greytak, Dir. Diocesan Pre-Seminary Program. Students 5.

[B] COLLEGES AND UNIVERSITIES

HELENA. *Carroll College*, (1909). Tel: 406-447-4300; Fax: 406-447-4533

For a complete listing, refer to the Colleges and Universities section.

[C] HIGH SCHOOLS, DIOCESAN

BUTTE. *Central High School*, 9 S. Idaho St., 59701. Tel: 406-782-6761; Fax: 406-723-3873. Patrick Prendergast, Prin.; Dr. Thomas E. Hart, Ph.D., Dir. Butte Central Schools. Lay Teachers 14; Students 174.

MISSOULA. *Loyola Sacred Heart High School*, 320 Edith St., 59801. Tel: 406-549-6101; Fax: 406-542-1432.
E-mail: lsh@montana.com
Web site: www.montana.com/loyola/index,html/loyola.htm
T. Daniel Gillen, Prin. Priests 1; Sisters 1; Lay Teachers 18; Students 229.

[D] SCHOOLS, ELEMENTARY

BUTTE. *Central Elementary School*. (Grades PreK-5), 1100 Delaware, 59701. Tel: 406-782-4500. Sr. Mary Jane Schmitz, S.C.L., Prin. Sisters 2; Lay Teachers 11; Students 284.

Central Junior High School. (Grades 6-8), 400 W. Park, 59701. Tel: 406-782-1233. Jacqueline M. Degel, Prin. Lay Teachers 11; Students 143.

KALISPELL. *St. Matthew School*, 602 S. Main St., 59901. Tel: 406-752-6303; Fax: 406-756-8249. Mary Grace Galvin, Administrative Assoc. Sisters 3; Lay Teachers 12; Students 185.

Day Care Center. (Ages 2-6). Ginger Jay, Dir. Students 50.

MISSOULA. *St. Joseph Elementary School*, 430 W. Pine St., 59802. Tel: 406-549-1290; Fax: 406-543-4034.
Web site: www.montana.com/stjoe
Tomas Anderson, Prin.

Child Care Center. (Ages 2-12). Evalie Hawkinson, Dir. Sisters 1; Lay Teachers 12; Students 240.

[E] GENERAL HOSPITALS

BUTTE. *St. James Community Hospital, Inc.*, 400 S. Clark St., 59701

For a complete listing, refer to the Hospitals section.

MISSOULA. *St. Patrick Hospital Corporation*, 500 W. Broadway, 59802.
Web site: www.saintpatrick.org

For a complete listing, refer to the Hospitals section.

POLSON. *St. Joseph Hospital Corporation*, Skyline Dr., P.O. Box 1010, 59860. Tel: 406-883-5377; Fax: 406-883-4388

For a complete listing, refer to the Hospitals section.

[F] CONVENTS AND RESIDENCES OF SISTERS

COLUMBIA FALLS. *Epiphany Monastery*, P.O. Box 8177, 59912. Tel: 406-892-4670. Monastery dependent upon St. Martin Monastery, Rapid City, SD. Sisters 3.

[G] HOUSES OF PRAYER

SWAN LAKE. *The Sycamore Tree Contemplative Prayer Center*, 59911. Tel: 406-754-2429. Rev. Dusan A. Okorn, Dir.; Michelle Jenkins, Asst.

[H] NEWMAN CHAPLAINS

BOZEMAN. *Montana State University*. (Resurrection Parish), Office: 1725 S. Eleventh, 59715-4218. Tel: 406-586-9243. Rev. Robert Hall; Deacon Michael Certalic, Campus Min., Res., 905 S. Fifth, 59715.

BUTTE. *Montana College of Mineral Science and Technology*, 102 S. Washington St., 59701. Tel: 406-723-5407; Fax: 406-723-8082. Rev. Nathaniel Ndiokwere (Nigeria), Chap.

DILLON. *Western Montana College*, 226 S. Atlantic St., 59725. Tel: 406-683-4391. Rev. Robert Porter; Jeannette Stewart, Campus Min.

MISSOULA. *University of Montana*. (Christ the King Parish), 1400 Gerald Ave., 59801-4230. Tel: 406-728-3845. Rev. James J. Hogan; Diane Peterson, Campus Min.

[I] MISCELLANEOUS

HELENA. *The St. Helena Cathedral Foundation, Inc.*, 530 N. Ewing St., 59601-4001. Tel: 406-442-5825; Fax: 406-449-5113. Marty Heller, Pres.

BUTTE. *Central Education Foundation*, P.O. Box 634, 59703-0634. Tel: 406-723-6706; Fax: 406-723-3873. Don Peoples, Jr., Exec. Dir.

St. Vincent de Paul Thrift Store, 123 E. Park St., 59701. Tel: 406-782-0233. Wayne Thomas, Mgr.

MISSOULA. *Loyola-Sacred Heart High School Foundation*, 300 Edith, 59801-3916. Tel: 406-728-2367; 728-2353; Fax: 406-542-9900. Sr. Rita Mudd, S.P., Alumni Dir.; Ted Bergsieker, Pres.; Bob Kelly, Dir. Devel.

STEVENSVILLE. *Historic St. Mary's Mission*, P.O. Box 211, 59870-0211. Tel: 406-777-5734. Lucylle H. Evans, Pres.

RELIGIOUS INSTITUTES OF MEN REPRESENTED IN THE DIOCESE

For further details refer to the corresponding bracketed number in the Religious Institutes of Men or Women sections.

[0200]—*Benedictine Monks (Swiss-American Congregation, St. Meinrad Archabbey)*.—O.S.B.

[0330]—*Brothers of the Christian Schools*. (Midwest Prov.).—F.S.C.

[0690]—*Jesuit Fathers and Brothers*. (Oregon Prov.).—S.J.

RELIGIOUS INSTITUTES OF WOMEN REPRESENTED IN THE DIOCESE

[0230]—*Benedictine Sisters of Pontifical Jurisdiction*. (Rapid City).—O.S.B.

[2100]—*Congregation of the Humility of Mary*.—C.H.M.

[1730]—*Congregation of the Sisters of the Third Order of St. Francis*. (Oldenburg, IN).—O.S.F.

[1780]—*Congregation of the Sisters of the Third Order of St. Francis of Perpetual Adoration*. (Western Prov.).—F.S.P.A.

[1070-03]—*Dominican Sisters*.—O.P.

[1070-11]—*Dominican Sisters*.—O.P.

[1070-13]—*Dominican Sisters*.—O.P.

[2575]—*Institute of the Sisters of Mercy of the Americas*. (Cedar Rapids, IA).—R.S.M.

[0440]—*Sisters of Charity of Cincinnati, Ohio*.—S.C.

[0480]—*Sisters of Charity of Leavenworth, Kansas*.—S.C.L.

[0430]—*Sisters of Charity of the Blessed Virgin Mary*.—B.V.M.

[3350]—*Sisters of Providence*.—S.P.

[3360]—*Sisters of Providence of Saint Mary-of-the-Woods, Indiana*.—S.P.

[3840]—*Sisters of St. Joseph of Carondelet*.—C.S.J.

[3960]—*Sisters of St. Mary of Oregon*.—S.S.M.O.

[1990]—*Sisters of the Holy Names of Jesus and Mary*.—S.N.J.M.

[1720]—*Sisters of the Third Order Regular of St. Francis of the Congregation of Our Lady of Lourdes*.—O.S.F.

[4110]—*Ursuline Nuns*.—O.S.U.

DIOCESAN CEMETERIES

HELENA. *Resurrection*, 515 N. Ewing St., P.O. Box 1729, 59624. Tel: 406-442-5820; Fax: 406-442-5191. Mr. Scott Fitzpatrick, Dir. Cemeteries; Laura Disney, Office Mgr.

BUTTE. *Holy Cross*. (St. Patrick's Cemetery), Office: 4700 Harrison Ave., 59701. Tel: 406-494-3812.

MISSOULA. *St. Mary*, Office: 641 Turner St., 59802. Tel: 406-543-7951.

NECROLOGY

† Cabaong, Henry, Helena, MT, Warm Springs Hospital & Montana State Prison. —Died Aug. 17, 1997.

† Fabing, Charles, (Retired). —Died May 15, 1997.

† O'Neill, Michael, (Special Assignment). —Died Sept. 27, 1997.

Diocese of Honolulu

(Dioecesis Honoluluensis)

Most Reverend

FRANCIS X. DILORENZO, D.D., S.T.D.

Bishop of Honolulu; ordained May 18, 1968; appointed Titular Bishop of Tigia and Auxiliary Bishop of Scranton January 26, 1988; consecrated March 8, 1988; appointed Apostolic Administrator October 12, 1993; succeeded to See November 29, 1994. *Mailing Address: Chancery Office, 1184 Bishop St., Honolulu, HI, 96813; Fax: 808-537-1860.*

Most Reverend

JOSEPH A. FERRARIO, D.D.

Retired Bishop of Honolulu; ordained May 19, 1951; appointed Titular Bishop of Cuse and Auxiliary November 8, 1977; ordained Bishop January 13, 1978; succeeded to See June 25, 1982; retired October 12, 1993. *Mailing Address: Catholic Chancery Office, 1184 Bishop St., Honolulu, HI, 96813-2858.*

Corporate Title: *The Roman Catholic Church In The State Of Hawaii.*

Comprises all of the Hawaiian Islands.

The Hawaiian Islands were annexed as a Territory of the United States in 1898. Hawaii became the 50th State of the Union on August 21, 1959.

Square Miles 6,435.

In 1826, a Prefecture-Apostolic was erected for the Hawaiian Islands, then called Sandwich Islands, and entrusted to the Fathers of the Sacred Hearts of Jesus and Mary (Picpus). The Very Rev. ALEXIS BACHELOT, SS.CC., was the first Prefect-Apostolic. He arrived with his companions at Honolulu on the 7th of July, 1827. In 1844, the Islands were erected a Vicariate. Diocese erected Sept. 10, 1941.

For legal titles of parishes and diocesan institutions, consult the Chancery Office.

Chancery Office: 1184 Bishop St., Honolulu, HI, 96813. Tel.: 808-533-1791; Fax: 808-521-8428.

Web site address: www.pono.net

E-mail address: bishop@pono.net

STATISTICAL OVERVIEW

Personnel	
Bishop	1
Retired Bishops	1
Priests: Diocesan Active in Diocese	40
Priests: Active Outside Diocese	14
Priests: Retired, Sick or Absent	16
Number of Diocesan Priests	70
Religious Priests in Diocese	79
Extern Priests in Diocese	4
Ordinations:	
Transitional Deacons	1
Permanent Deacons	39
Permanent Deacons in Diocese	33
Total Brothers	52
Total Sisters	152
Parishes	
Parishes	68
With Resident Pastor:	
Resident Diocesan Priests	37
Resident Religious Priests	28
Without Resident Pastor:	
Administered by Priests	2
Administered by Permanent Deacons	1
Professional Ministry Personnel:	
Brothers	3
Sisters	20
Lay Ministers	33
Welfare	
Catholic Hospitals	2
Total Assisted	394,015
Health Care Centers	3
Total Assisted	10,434
Homes for the Aged	2
Total Assisted	31,814
Day Care and Extended Day Care Centers	3
Total Assisted	195
Specialized Homes	1
Total Assisted	204
Special Centers for Social Services	2
Total Assisted	31,814
Residential Care of Disabled	1
Total Assisted	717
Other Institutions	82
Total Assisted	5,222
Educational	
Diocesan Students in Other Seminaries	4
Students Religious	2
Total Seminarians	6
Colleges and Universities	1
Total Students	2,592
High Schools, Diocesan and Parish	3
Total Students	1,171
High Schools, Private	4
Total Students	2,439
Elementary Schools, Diocesan and Parish	24
Total Students	6,923
Elementary Schools, Private	1
Total Students	363
Catechesis/Religious Education:	
High School Students	1,757
Elementary Students	5,295
Total Students Under Catholic Instruction	20,546
Teachers in the Diocese:	
Priests	6
Brothers	15
Sisters	57
Lay Teachers	390
Vital Statistics	
Receptions into the Church:	
Infant Baptism Totals	3,220
Adult Baptism Totals	391
Received into Full Communion	286
First Communions	2,162
Confirmations	1,278
Marriages:	
Catholic	724
Interfaith	357
Total Marriages	1,081
Deaths	1,572
Total Catholic Population	232,780
Total Population	1,178,600

Former Prelates—Very Rev. ALEXIS BACHELOT, SS.CC., Pref. Apost. died Dec. 5, 1837.—Very Rev. LOUIS MAIGRET, SS.CC., Pref. Apost. till 1844.—Rt. Rev. VINCENT FERRIER DUBOIZE, SS.CC., resigned before he was consecrated.—Rt. Rev. LOUIS MAIGRET, SS.CC., Titular Bishop of Arathia; cons. at Santiago, Oct. 31, 1847; died June 11, 1882.—Rt. Rev. HERMAN KOECKEMANN, SS.CC., Titular Bishop of Olba; cons. at San Francisco Aug. 21, 1881; died Feb. 18, 1892.—Rt. Rev. GULSTAN ROPERT, SS.CC., Titular Bishop of Panopolis; cons. at San Francisco, Sept. 25, 1892; died Jan. 3, 1903.—Rt. Rev. LIBERT H. BOEYNAEMS, SS.CC., Titular Bishop of Zeugma; cons. at San Francisco, July 25, 1903; died May 13, 1926.—Most Rev. STEPHEN P. ALENCASTRE, SS.CC., Titular Bishop of Arabissus; cons. at Los Angeles, Aug. 24, 1924; died Nov. 9, 1940.—Most Rev. JAMES J. SWEENEY, D.D., ord. June 20, 1925; appt. May 20, 1941; cons. at San Francisco, July 25, 1941; died June 19, 1968.—Most Rev. JOHN J. SCANLAN, D.D., Retired Bishop of Honolulu; ord. June 22, 1930; succeeded to see March 6, 1968; retired June 30, 1981; died Jan. 31, 1997.—Most Rev. JOSEPH A. FERRARIO, D.D., Retired Bishop of Honolulu; ord. May 19, 1951; succeeded to see June 25, 1982; retired Oct. 12, 1993.

Vicar General—Very Rev. JOHN F. BOLIN, S.M., V.G.

Moderator of the Curia—Very Rev. JOHN F. BOLIN, S.M.

Chancery Office—1184 Bishop St., Honolulu, 96813-2858. Tel: 808-533-1791; Fax: 808-521-8428. Office Hours: 8-4 Mon.-Fri.

Chancellor—Rev. Msgr. RAYMOND NISHIGAYA, J.C.L.

Administrative Council—Most Rev. FRANCIS X. DILORENZO, D.D., S.T.D.; Rev. Msgr. ALAN NAGAI; Rev. JOHN F. BOLIN, S.M., V.G.

Bishop's Administrative Advisory Council—Rev. JOHN F. BOLIN, S.M., V.G.; Rev. Msgr. TERRENCE WATANABE; WILLIAM BURTON; PATRICIA S. TOSSEY.

College of Consultors—Revs. JAMES BERRY; JOHN F. BOLIN, S.M., V.G.; GORDIAN CARVALHO; THOMAS GROSS; RAYMOND MALLEY, S.M.; GARY SECOR; HALBERT WEIDNER, C.O.; Rev. Msgr. TERRENCE WATANABE.

Finance Committee—Most Rev. FRANCIS X. DILORENZO, D.D.; Rev. JOHN F. BOLIN, S.M., V.G.; PHILIP CHING;

LAURA CHUN; GEORGE FREITAS; ROBERT BRUCE GRAHAM; ROBERT HASTINGS; JAMES SEVERSON; MANUEL SYLVESTER; EUGENE TIWANAK; JAMES VENTURA; LENORA WEE; Deacon RONALD CHOO, Auditor.

Planning and Building Commission—Rev. JOHN F. BOLIN, S.M., V.G., Chm. GARY BATCHELLER; WILLIAM BURTON; Revs. GORDIAN CARVALHO; GARY COLTON; MICHAEL DARCY; Rev. GEORGE DECOSTA; Sr. MARY LANGE, S.H.F.; RICHARD LEUNG; MARK LIVELY; WALTER YOSHIMITSU.

Vicar for Ethnic Ministries—Sr. GRACE DOROTHY LIM, M.M., J.C.L.

Chinese Ministry—Rev. ALOYSIUS LOU, M.A., Coord.

Japanese Ministry—Rev. FRANCIS NAKAGAWA, Coord.

Filipino Ministry—Sr. GRACE DOROTHY LIM, M.M., Dir.

Hispanic Ministry—Rev. JAMES MCFADDEN, M.M., Coord.

Korean Ministry—Rev. JOHN KANG, Coord.

Samoan Ministry—Sr. SEKOLASETIKA KENI, S.M.S.M., Coord.

Vietnamese Ministry—Rev. JOSEPH KY, S.S., Coord.

Tribunal—1184 Bishop St., Honolulu, 96813-2858. Tel: 808-533-1791; Fax: 808-521-8428. Office Hours: Mon.-Fri 8-4.

Judicial Vicar—Very Rev. JOSEPH BUKOSKI, III, SS.CC., J.C.L.

Adjutant Judicial Vicar—Rev. JOSEPH GRIMALDI, J.C.L.

Promoter of Justice—Rev. Msgr. RAYMOND NISHIGAYA, J.C.L.

Defender of the Bond—Rev. Msgr. RAYMOND NISHIGAYA, J.C.L.

Defender of the Bond Ad Hoc—Sr. GRACE DOROTHY LIM, M.M., J.C.L.

Judges—Very Rev. JOSEPH BUKOSKI, III, SS.CC., J.C.L.; Revs. ARTHUR DWYER, M.M., J.C.D.; JOSEPH GRIMALDI, J.C.L.; ROBERT PHELPS, O.F.M.Cap., J.D.; ROMEO RABUSA, S.T.B.; MATTHEW LOCHS, SS.CC., S.T.L.; Sr. GRACE DOROTHY LIM, M.M., J.C.L.

Notaries and Secretaries to the Tribunal—ANDREA L.V. SAYO; CATHERINE WONG.

Business Office—1184 Bishop St., Honolulu, 96813-2858. Tel: 808-533-1791; Fax: 808-521-8428. Office Hours: Mon.-Fri. 8-4.

Business Manager—WILLIAM L. BURTON, JR.

Diocesan Offices and Directors

Archivist—Rev. Msgr. RAYMOND NISHIGAYA, J.C.L.

Censor Liborum—Rev. MARC R. ALEXANDER, S.T.D.

Vicars Forane—Rev. HALBERT WEIDNER, C.O., East Honolulu; Rev. Msgr. TERRENCE WATANABE, West Honolulu; Rev. GARY SECOR, Leeward; Rev. THOMAS GROSS, Windward; Rev. JAMES BERRY, Hawaii Island; Rev. GORDIAN CARVALHO, Kauai; Rev. RAYMOND MALLEY, S.M., Maui.

Presbyteral Council—Revs. MARK ALEXANDER, S.T.D.; JAMES BERRY; ANTHONY BOLGER; JOHN F. BOLIN, S.M., V.G.; SCOTT BUSH; GORDIAN CARVALHO; ETUALE ETUALE; THOMAS GROSS; JOVEN JUNIO, M.S.; JOHN KUHN, SS.CC.; RAYMOND MALLEY S.M.; NATHAN MAMO; ROBERT PHELPS, O.F.M.Cap.; GARY SECOR; TERRENCE WATANABE; HALBERT WEIDNER, C.O.

Pastoral Council—CATHERINE WONG, Contact. Tel: 808-533-1791.

Delegate of the Bishop for Religious—Sr. BEATRICE TOM, O.S.F.

Associate Delegate of the Bishop for Religious—Bro. THOMAS SPRING, S.M.

Priest Retirement Board—Rev. JOHN F. BOLIN, S.M., V.G., Chm.; Revs. DANIEL DEVER; CLARENCE FISHER; Rev. Msgr. ALAN NAGAI; Rev. ROMEO RABUSA; Rev. Msgr. TERRENCE WATANABE.

Hawaii Catholic Herald—1184 Bishop St., Honolulu, 96813. Tel: 808-533-1791; Fax: 808-521-8428. Most Rev. FRANCIS X. DILORENZO, Publisher; PATRICK DOWNES, Editor.

Saint Stephen Diocesan Center—6301 Pali Hwy., Kaneohe, 96744-5298. Tel: 808-263-8844; Fax: 808-261-7022. Office Hours: Mon.-Fri, 8-4 (HST); GENE POLLOCK, Admin.

Religious Education—, Ext. 341. Sr. KATHLEEN MARIE SHIELDS, C.S.J., Dir.

Servant Leadership Education Program—Sr. KATHLEEN MARIE SHIELDS, C.S.J., Dir.

Hawaii Catholic Conference—, Ext. 342. Rev. MARC R. ALEXANDER, S.T.D., Exec. Dir. PATRICK DOWNES; WILLIAM GILARDY; JEROME E. RAUCKHORST; ANA ROSAL-SILVA; Sr. BEATRICE TOM, O.S.F.; Dr. SUE WESSELKAMPER.

Hawaii Catholic Schools—, Ext. 364. CARMEN HIMENES, Interim Supt. LOUISE WONG, Interim Assoc. Supt.

Oahu Social Ministry—, Ext. 334. LEELAMMA PALAZOTTO, Dir.

Office of Clergy—, Ext. 330. Rev. Msgr. ALAN NAGAI, Vicar for Priests; WALTER H. YOSHIMITSU, Episcopal Liaison to Deacon Community.

Personnel Board—Rev. Msgr. ALAN NAGAI, Chm. Members: Very Rev. JOHN F. BOLIN, S.M., V.G.; Revs. GEORGE DECOSTA; KONELIO FALETOI; CLARENCE FISHER; JOHN KUHN, SS.CC.; Rev. Msgr. RAYMOND NISHIGAYA.

Priestly Life and Ministry—Rev. HALBERT WEIDNER, C.O., Chm. Members: Revs. MARC ALEXANDER, S.T.D; GORDIAN CARVALHO; Rev. Msgr. BERNARD EIKMEIER; Revs. CLARENCE FISHER; HERMAN GOMES, SS.CC.; JOVEN JUNIO, M.S.; ANDREW MANETTA, O.F.M.Cap.; ROMEO RABUSA; ROBERT SCHWARZHAUPT.

Diocesan Screening Committee—Rev. Msgr. ALAN NAGAI, Chm. Members: Rev. MARC ALEXANDER, S.T.D; Dr. ALFRED ARENSDORF; Rev. JOSEPH BUKOSKI, SS.CC.; EVELYN CHAR; Sr. ALICIA DAMIEN LAU, O.S.F.; Sr. BRENDA LAU, C.S.J.; Deacon WALTER YOSHIMITSU.

Permanent Diaconate Advisory Board—Rev. MARC ALEXANDER, S.T.D., Chm. Members: BARBARA AKEO; Rev. JOHN F. BOLIN, S.M., V.G.; Deacon JOSEPH BORGES; SHARON CHIARUCCI; Bro. STEVE COFFEY; Rev. THOMAS GROSS; Deacon WILLIAM MCPEEK; FLORENCE MCPEEK; Deacon WALLY MITSUI; Rev. Msgr. ALAN NAGAI; MITSU PAPAYOANOU.

Permanent Deacon Formation—Coordinators: Deacon WILLIAM MCPEEK; FLORENCE MCPEEK,, Ext. 329. Members: Sr. DAVILYN AHCHICK, O.S.F.; Deacon ERNEST CARLBOM; DONNA CARLBOM; Deacon PATRICK CONSTANTINO; CORA CONSTANTINO; VIVIAN DECAIRES; Rev. CLARENCE FISHER; MARY HUGHES; Deacon WALLACE MITSUI; GWEN MITSUI; Deacons SIDNEY TOWNSLEY; WALTER YOSHIMITSU; FRANCES YOSHIMITSU.

Office of Development—Vacant,, Ext. 323.

Diocesan Development Committee—JOAN BICKSON; CHARLES BOCKEN; JOHN BROGAN, Chm. ROBERT BRUCE GRAHAM; STANLEY HONG; JON THOMAS HUNTER.

Office of the Diocesan Theologian—, Ext. 342. Rev. MARC R. ALEXANDER, S.T.D. Commission Members: Bro. JAMES CHRISTIANA, S.M., M.A., Ph.D.; DAVID COLEMAN, M.A.; Revs. NATHAN MAMO, S.T.L.; HALBERT WEIDNER, C.O., M.A., D.Phil.

Office for the Welcoming Parish—, Ext. 333. SHARON CHIARUCCI, Coord.

Office of Worship—, Ext. 328. Sr. MARY LANGE, S.H.F., Dir.

Diocesan Liturgical Commission—WENDELL APOSTOL; ROSE BRITO; BARBARA ISODA; Sr. MARY LANGE, S.H.F.; ROBERT MONDOY; MITSU PAPAYOANOU; FRANCIS PHILIPS; Sr. HELENE WOOD, SS.CC.

Respect Life Office—, Ext. 322. Deacon GEORGE THORP, Dir.

Natural Family Planning—TED BORN; HOLLY BORN.

Other Diocesan Offices—

Apostleship of the Sea—579-D Keolu Dr., Kailua, 96734. Tel: 808-262-5422. Rev. JOHN G. NEWTON, Port Chap.

Campaign for Human Development—3300 Ala Laulani St., Honolulu, 96818. Tel: 808-839-1876. Rev. Msgr. TERRENCE WATANABE, Mgr. Members: ROBERT AGRES; Sr. ROSITA ARANITA, C.S.J.; SHARON CHIARUCCI; ANNE CHIPCHASE; JUNE HASHIMOTO; ROBIN LEONG; KAREN TAGUCHI.

Catholic Charities—250 S. Vineyard St., Honolulu, 96813-2495. Tel: 808-537-6321; Fax: 808-523-8773. JEROME E. RAUCKHORST, Dir.,, Ext. 301.

Board of Trustees—Most Rev. FRANCIS X. DILORENZO, D.D., Pres.; Very Rev. JOHN F. BOLIN, S.M., V.G.; DAVID BELLO; WILLIAM BURTON; ROSE DOMONDON; GINO GABRIO; KATHLEEN HISHINUMA; Sr. ALICIA DAMIEN LAU, O.S.F.; WILLIAM POWELL; MICHAEL TIKNIS; ROBERT TONG; SHARON WEINER.

Board of Directors—Most Rev. FRANCIS X. DILORENZO, D.D., Pres. WILLIAM POWELL, Vice Pres. GINO L. GABRIO, Chm. CATHY SEKIGUCHI, Sec. MARY LOU BROGAN; Very Rev. JOHN F. BOLIN, S.M., V.G.; WILLIAM BURTON; CLIFF CISCO; ROSE DOMONDON; BRANDT FARIAS; Rev. CLARENCE L. FISHER; WILLIAM GILARDY; Rev. CLYDE GUERREIRO, SS.CC.; MARIANITA LOPEZ; Rev. RAYMOND MALLEY, S.M.; LILA MARANTZ; ALEXANDER MARRACK; SANDRA OHARA; MICHAEL PEARING; ALEX SANTIAGO; Rev. Msgr. TERRENCE WATANABE; ARTHUR YAMAMOTO; STEPHEN YI.

Catholic Charities Community Services—MORRIS MASUDA, Exec. Dir.,, Ext. 317.

Catholic Charities Elderly Services—2745 Pali Hwy., Honolulu, 96817. Tel: 808-595-0077; Fax: 808-595-0811. STELLA WONG, Exec. Dir.

Catholic Charities Family Services—200 N. Vineyard Blvd., Ste. 200, Honolulu, 96817. Tel: 808-536-1794; Fax: 808-599-8761. ANA ROSAL-SILVA, Exec. Dir.

Catholic Charities Immigration Services—712 N. School St., Honolulu, 96817. Tel: 808-531-5233; Fax: 808-531-1970. Sr. EARNEST CHUNG, M.M., Exec. Dir.,, Ext. 308.

Aina Kupaa 'O Maili—Most Rev. FRANCIS X. DILORENZO, D.D., Pres.

Hospital Ministry—1717 Ala Wai Blvd. #1806, Honolulu, 96815. Tel: 808-941-4979. Rev. PAUL SMITH, Dir.

Leadership Association of Religious Congregations—47-339-1 Hui Iwa St., Kaneohe, 96744. Tel: 808-239-1045. Sr. HILARIA DAWAL, S.H.F., Coord.

Office for Social Ministry—140 B Holomua St., Hilo, 96720. Tel: 808-935-3050; Fax: 808-935-3794. CAROL IGNACIO, Diocesan Dir.

Hoa 'Aina O Makaha—84-766 Lahaina St., Waianae, 96792. Tel: 808-695-9730. GIGI COCQUIO, Mgr.

Women's Prison Ministry—Vacant.

Oahu Branch—6301 Pali Hwy., Kaneohe, 96744-5298. LEELAMMA PALAZOTTO.

Maui County Branch—95 Mahalani St., Wailuku, 96793. Tel: 808-244-8106; Fax: 808-244-8106. Sr. ROSELANI ENOMOTO, C.S.J., Dir.

Hawaii Island Branch—CAROL IGNACIO, Dir.

Care-a-Van—CATHIE HAWKINS, Dir.

Catholic Relief Services—CAROL IGNACIO, Dir.

Hawaii Island Food Bank—CAROL IGNACIO, Dir.

Mobile Health Care Van—CAROL IGNACIO, Dir.

Bishop's Advisory Board for Persons with Disabilities—CAROL IGNACIO, Dir.

Boards and Commissions—

Bishop's Advisory Board for Persons with Disabilities—Members: Rev. MARC ALEXANDER, S.T.D.; LAVERNE CORPUZ-AYUDAN; SHARON CHIARUCCI; Sr. ROSELANI ENOMOTO, C.S.J.; PAUL JABER; Sr. MARY LANGE, S.H.F.; JOHN MAHER; LOURDES MUGAS; MAUREEN SATURNIO; Deacon JOHN SCHUSTER; IWIE TAMASHIRO; VALERIE YOSHIKAWA; CAROL IGNACIO, Staff Rep. PATRICIA TOSSEY, Bishop's Rep.

Diocesan Board of Conciliation—Sr. GRACE DOROTHY LIM, M.M., Dir.; Rev. Msgr. DANIEL DEVER, Ex Officio. Members: LUZ ABCEDE; Dr. PHIL BOHNERT; ROBERT GILKEY; RONALD LEE; Rev. ROBERT PHELPS, O.F.M.Cap.; ROBERT BRUCE GRAHAM, Counsel.

Diocesan Board of Education—Most Rev. FRANCIS X. DILORENZO, D.D., Pres.; Dr. LESLIE CORREA, Ed.D., Chm. Members: Sr. DAVILYN AHCHICK, O.S.F.; Dr. MARIANNE AU; Rev. JOHN F. BOLIN, S.M., V.G.; JOSEPH CARDOZA; MARLENE DECOSTA; Bro. JAMES DODS, S.M.; JEAN FLYNN; VICKI GAYNOR; Sr. JOHN JOSPEH GILLIGAN, C.S.J.; Revs. HERMAN GOMES, SS.CC.; CLYDE GUERREIRO, SS.CC.; Dr. EDWARD KLEIN; Rev. JOHN KUHN, SS.CC.; CAROL SOUZA; MEL VENTURA; MICHAEL WEAVER; CAROL WEST; BETTY WHITE; Dr. STEPHEN WOO.

Diocesan Justice and Peace Commission—DAVID COLEMAN, Chm. Members: MARTHA EVANS; Deacon RONALD GONSALVES; Rev. ALAPAKI KIM, C.S.P.; JOHN LAKE; Sr. BRENDA LAU, C.S.J.; STEVE QUEROBIN; HENRY TANCAYO; Rev. HALBERT WEIDNER, C.O.; FAYE YOSHIDA. Ex Officio: Rev. MARC ALEXANDER, S.T.D.; SHARON CHIARUCCI; Sr. ROSELANI ENOMOTO, C.S.J.; CAROL IGNACIO.

Maui Vicariate Catholic School Board—Bro. JAMES DODS, S.M., Pres. Members: JOSEPH ANDREWS; Dr. ALFRED ARENSDORF; Deacon JOSEPH BORGES; JOSEPH CARDOZA; Rev. GARY COLTON; JANICE DAVIS; LISA GLAMOYRIS; KATHERINE HUSKE; Rev. RAYMOND MALLEY, S.M.; JOSEPH RICKARD; DEBBIE WRIGHT. Associate Members: ISSAC BALICANTA; Sr. MATTHEW BRAZIL, O.P.; WINONA MARTINEZ; Sr. CHARLES MIRIAM WONG, O.S.F.

Women's Concerns Committee—Co-Chairs: KAREN GEBBIA-PENETTI; MARYLUCIA ARACE.

Lay Associations—

Apostleship of Prayer—91-1298 Renton Rd., Ewa, 96706. Tel: 808-681-3701; Fax: 808-681-5192. Rev. ELI CARTER, Dir.

Beginning Experience-Hawaii—1701 Wilder Ave., Honolulu, 96822. Tel: 808-973-2211; Fax: 808-973-2209. Rev. FRANCIS DIFFLEY, M.M., Spiritural Dir.

Catholic Committee on Scouting—130 Ohua Ave., Honolulu, 96815. Tel: 808-923-7024; Fax: 808-922-4086. Rev. THOMAS CHOO, SS.CC.

Catholic Daughters of America—2124 Pauoa Rd., Honolulu, 96813. Tel: 808-531-6980. Rev. MARK A. CONSALVI, SS.CC., Chap.

Catholic Women's Guild—1511 Nuuanu Ave, Prince Tower 30, Honolulu, 96817-3758. Tel: 808-524-4385. Rev. FRANCIS PETERSON, Chap.

Chinese Catholic Club—4470 Aliikoa St., Honolulu, 96821. Tel: 808-734-0396. Rev. ALOYSIUS LOU, Spiritual Dir.

Confraternity of Our Lady of Mt. Carmel—P.O. Box 219, Hana, 96813. Tel: 808-248-8030. Rev. PAUL ZEGERS, SS.CC.

Confraternity of the Most Holy Rosary—4524 Waikui St., Honolulu, 96821. Tel: 808-548-4613. Deacon ANDREW GERAKAS, Pres.

Cursillos of Hawaii—1124 7th Ave., Honolulu, 96816. Tel: 808-732-0281. Rev. GABRIEL VANDEN BROUCKE, SS.CC., Spiritual Dir.

Engaged Encounter—130 Ohua Ave., Honolulu, 96815. Tel: 808-923-7024. Rev. LANE AKIONA, SS.CC, Spiritual Dir.

Filipino Catholic Clubs, Diocesan Congress of—P.O. Box 787, Kaneohe, 96744. Tel: 808-247-3647. Rev. CLYDE GUERREIRO, SS.CC., Diocesan Dir.

Oahu—2124 Pauoa Rd., Honolulu, 96813. Tel: 808-531-6980. Rev. MARK CONSALVI, SS.CC., Spiritual Dir.

Kauai—P.O. Box 487, Kalaheo, 96741. Tel: 808-332-8011. Rev. GORDIAN CARVALHO.

Maui—3188 Kilani Pl., Pukalani, 96788. Tel: 808-572-8298. Deacon PATRICK CONSTANTINO, Spiritual Dir.

Hawaii Catholic Charismatic Renewal—6301 Pali Hwy., Kaneohe, 96744. Tel: 808-263-8844, Ext. 342. Rev. MARC ALEXANDER, S.T.D., Diocesan Liaison.

Holy Childhood Association—91-1298 Renton Rd., Ewa, 96706. Tel: 808-681-3701; Fax: 808-681-5192. Rev. ELI CARTER, Dir.

Holy Name Society, Diocesan Union of the—130 Ohua Ave., Honolulu, 96815. Tel: 808-923-7024. JAMES KAUHANE, Pres.

Knights of Columbus—Most Rev. FRANCIS X. DILORENZO, D.D., State Chap.; Most Rev. JOSEPH FERRARIO, State Chap. Emeritus. Assoc. State Chaplains: Rev. Msgr. BERNARD EIKMEIER; Rev. MARK CONSALVI, SS.CC.

Legion of Mary—

Oahu—1124 7th Ave., Honolulu, 96816. Tel: 808-732-0281. Rev. GERARD LEICHT, SS.CC., Spiritual Dir.

Hawaii Island—2159-A Awapuhi St., Hilo, 96720. Tel: 808-959-9782. Deacon HAVEY KAWAIHAE.

Maui—CARMEN GAZMEN.

Missionary Basic Christian Community of Hawaii—1184 Bishop St., Honolulu, 96813. Tel: 808-533-1791. Sr. GRACE DOROTHY LIM, M.M., Spiritual Dir.

Nocturnal Adoration Society—800 Kaheka St., Honolulu, 96814. Tel: 808-941-0675; Fax: 808-945-0689. Rev. Msgr. ROY PETERS, Spiritual Dir.

Reparation of the Immaculate Heart of Mary Association—1124 7th Ave., Honolulu, 96816. Tel: 808-732-0281. Rev. GABRIEL VANDEN BROUCKE, SS.CC., Spiritual Dir.

St. Francis Xavier Clubs—

Oahu—1184 Bishop St., Honolulu, 96813. Tel: 808-536-7036. Rev. FRANCIS NAKAGAWA, S.M.

Maui—1627-A Mill St., Wailuku, 96793-1999. Tel: 808-244-4148. Rev. CHARLES OYABU, S.M.

St. Vincent de Paul Society—2124 Pauoa Rd., Honolulu, 96813. Tel: 808-531-6980. Deacon RONALD CHOO.

Samoan Catholic in Hawaii, Diocesan Federation of—1614 Monte St., Honolulu, 96819. Tel: 808-845-0828. Rev. ETUALE ETUALE.

Secular Franciscan Order—99-312 Moanalua Rd., Honolulu, 96701. Tel: 808-487-2414. Rev. GORDON COMBS, O.F.M.Cap., Reg. Spiritual Asst.

Secular Order of Discalced Carmelites—1514 Keolu Dr., Kailua, 96734. Tel: 808-262-0362. GWENDOLYN B. LAW, O.C.D.S.

Serra Club of Honolulu—95-370 Kuahelani Ave., Mililani, 96789. Tel: 808-623-3332. Rev. GARY L. SECOR, Chap.

Society for the Propagation of the Faith—91-1298 Renton Rd., Ewa, 96706. Tel: 808-681-3701; Fax: 808-681-5192. Rev. ELI CARTER, Dir.

Third Order of Mary / Companions of Mary—91-1298 Renton Rd., Ewa, 96706. Tel: 808-681-3701; Fax: 808-681-5192. Rev. ELI CARTER.

Tongan Catholic Societies, Diocesan Federation of—P.O. Box 1680, Lahaina, 96761. Tel: 808-661-0552. Rev. MARISI PALEPALE, SS.CC.

Worldwide Marriage Encounter—1511 Nuuanu Ave., PT #30, Honolulu, 96817. Tel: 808-524-4385. Rev. FRANCIS PETERSON, Spiritual Dir.

Young Ladies' Institute—

Honolulu Institute No. 84—Rev. Msgr. RAYMOND NISHIGAYA, J.C.L., Spiritual Dir.

Ana Malia Institute No. 208—Rev. PATRICK FREITAS, Spiritual Dir.

Kailua Institute No. 213—Rev. GARY SECOR, Spiritual Dir.

Young Men's Institute—Rev. GARY SECOR, Chap.

CLERGY, PARISHES, MISSIONS AND PAROCHIAL SCHOOLS

ISLAND OF OAHU
CITY OF HONOLULU

1—CATHEDRAL OF OUR LADY OF PEACE (1843), Revs. Nathan Mamo, S.T.L., Rector; Michael Owens; Mrs. Ann Hannan, M.R.E., Pastoral Assoc. & D.R.E.
Res., 1184 Bishop St., 96813-2838. Tel: 808-536-7036; Fax: 808-536-7039.
School—Cathedral School, 1728 Nuuanu Ave., 96817. Tel: 808-533-2069; Fax: 808-533-2069. Mrs. Louise Wong, Prin.
Lay Teachers 15; Students 160.
Catechesis / Religious Programs—Students 75.

2—CO-CATHEDRAL OF ST. THERESA OF THE CHILD JESUS (1931) (Filipino), Revs. Michael W. Hill, O.F.M.; John J. Abts, O.F.M.
Res., 712 N. School St., 96817. Tel: 808-521-1700; Fax: 808-599-3629.
School—Tel: 808-536-4703; Fax: 808-524-6861. Sr. John Joseph Gilligan, C.S.J., Prin.
Sisters 10; Lay Teachers 14; Students 625.
Catechesis / Religious Programs—Students 100.
Convent—Tel: 808-533-3101. Sisters of St. Joseph of Carondelet

3—ST. ANTHONY (1916) (Filipino), Rev. Joven Junio, M.S. In res., Revs. Joseph Ky, S.S.; Edgar Serrano.
Res., 640 Puuhale Rd., 96819. Tel: 808-845-3255; Fax: 808-845-3664.
School—Tel: 808-845-2769. Sr. Concepcion Cambaya, R.V.M., Prin.
Sisters 3; Lay Teachers 8; Students 180.
Catechesis / Religious Programs—Students 139.
Convent—702 Puuhale Rd., 96819. Tel: 808-845-4888.
Religious of the Blessed Virgin Mary (R.V.M.) 4.

4—ST. AUGUSTINE (1854), Revs. Lane Akiona, SS.CC.; Thomas Choo, SS.CC.
Res., 130 Ohua Ave., 96815. Tel: 808-923-7024; Fax: 808-922-4086.

5—BLESSED SACRAMENT (1938), Rev. Mark Consalvi, SS.CC.; Deacon Ronald Choo.
Res., 2124 Pauoa Rd., 96813. Tel: 808-531-6980.
Catechesis / Religious Programs—Mr. Francis Aiu, D.R.E.
Students 42.

6—HOLY FAMILY (1950), Rev. Maurice McNeely.
Res., 830 Main St., 96818. Tel: 808-422-1135; Fax: 808-422-5030.
School—Tel: 808-422-9612; Fax: 808-422-5030. Antonio J. Boquer, Prin.
Lay Teachers 36; Students 460.
Catechesis / Religious Programs—D.R.E.: Ann Amrich; Deborah Naone.
Students 135.

7—NEWMAN CENTER-HOLY SPIRIT PARISH (1981), Revs. Randall H. Roche, S.J.; Daniel J. Sullivan, S.J.
Mailing Address: Newman Center, 1941 East West Center, 96822-2321. Tel: 808-988-6222; Fax: 808-988-7627.
Res., Jesuit House, 2727 Pamoa Rd., 96822-1838. Tel: 808-988-3464.

8—HOLY TRINITY (1939), Revs. Halbert Weidner, C.O.; Vincent P. Mainelli; Deacon Paul Lee. In res., Bro. Thomas Snyder.
Res., 5919 Kalanianaole Hwy., 96821. Tel: 808-396-0551; Fax: 808-396-1380.
School—Tel: 808-396-8466; Fax: 808-396-3310. Monica Des Jarlais, Prin.
Sisters 2; Lay Teachers 11; Students 99.
Catechesis / Religious Programs—Deacon Sam Taylor, D.R.E.
Students 185.
Oratory—Honolulu, The Oratory in Hawaii, Tel: 808-396-1147.

9—ST. JOHN THE BAPTIST (1844), Rev. Karl H. Krause; Sr. Hilaria Marie Dawal, S.H.F., Assoc. Admin. In res., Rev. James J. McFadden, M.M., Hispanic Ministry.
Res., 2324 Omilo Ln., 96819. Tel: 808-845-0984; Fax: 808-841-6643. [CEM]
School—Tel: 808-841-5551; Fax: 808-842-6104. Mary Lou Superio, Prin.
Dominican Sisters 6; Lay Teachers 9; Students 186.
Catechesis / Religious Programs—Tel: 808-845-3304.
Students 147.
Convent—2330 Omilo Ln., 96819. Tel: 808-845-2622.
Dominican Sisters of the Most Holy Rosary 6.

10—OUR LADY OF THE MOUNT (1870), Rev. Etuale Etuale. In res., Rev. Robert da Ponte.
Res., 1614 Monte St., 96819. Tel: 808-845-0828. [CEM]
Catechesis / Religious Programs—Tel: 808-845-0223.
Students 110.

11—ST. PATRICK (1929), Revs. John C. Kuhn, SS.CC.; Christopher Keahi; Bro. Richard Kupo, SS.CC. In res., Revs. Matthew Lochs, SS.CC.; Gerard Leicht, SS.CC.
Res., 1124 Seventh Ave., 96816. Tel: 808-732-5565; Fax: 808-737-2477. Please refer to the listing for St. Patrick Monastery under Monasteries and Residences for Priests and Brothers for additional residents.
School—Tel: 808-734-8979; Fax: 808-732-2851. Sr. Rose Miriam Schillinger, C.S.J., Prin.
Sisters 3; Lay Teachers 25; Students 530.
Catechesis / Religious Programs—Tel: 808-735-0252. Ms. Regina Pfeiffer, D.R.E.
Students 116.
Mission—Palolo, Honolulu Co., St. James, 2117 Palolo Ave., 96816.

12—ST. PHILOMENA (1942), Rev. Msgr. Terrence A.M. Watanabe. In res., Rev. Patrick Freitas.
Res., 3300 Ala Laulani St., 96818-2837. Tel: 808-839-1876; Fax: 808-834-6888.
School—Tel: 808-833-8080; Fax: 808-834-3438. Angeline A.V. Thomas, Prin.
Lay Teachers 8; Teacher Aids 4; Students 142.
Catechesis / Religious Programs—Erin Sauder, D.R.E.
Students 139.

13—SACRED HEART (1914), Revs. Francis A. Diffley, M.M.; Arthur J. Dwyer, M.M.; Deacon Dominic Kang; Sandra Campos, Pastoral Assoc. In res., Rev. John Kang, Korean Ministry.
Res., 1701 Wilder Ave., 96822. Tel: 808-973-2211; Fax: 808-973-2209.
School—Maryknoll Grade School, 1722 Dole St., 96822. Tel: 808-973-1777; Fax: 808-973-1799. Mr. James H. Gahler, Prin.
Teacher Aides 5; Lay Teachers 46; Students 816.
High School—1402 Punahou St., 96822. Tel: 808-973-1888; Fax: 808-973-1890. Mr. Andrew Corcoran, Prin.
Sisters 2; Lay Teachers 49; Students 542.
Catechesis / Religious Programs—Tel: 808-973-1780. Rose Anne Petro, D.R.E.
Students 106.

14—ST. STEPHEN (1932), Rev. Msgr. Raymond J. Nishigaya.
Res., 2747 Pali Hwy., 96817. Tel: 808-595-3105.
Catechesis / Religious Programs—Paula Kurashige, D.R.E.
Students 43.

15—STAR OF THE SEA (1946), Revs. John Sullivan, S.M.; Edward C. Blee, S.M.; Deacons Thomas Rienzi; Andrew Gerakas. In res., Revs. Edward McMonagle; Aloysius Lou, M.A.
Res., 4470 Aliikoa St., 96821. Tel: 808-734-0396; Fax: 808-735-6017.
School—Tel: 808-734-0208; Fax: 808-735-9790. Carola Souza, Prin.
Lay Teachers 22; Students 295.
Early Learning Center—Tel: 808-734-3840; Fax: 808-732-1738. Lisa Foster, Prin.
Lay Teachers 10; Assistants 13; Students 174.
Catechesis / Religious Programs—Tel: 808-735-0259. Darlene Ah Yo, D.R.E.
Students 209.

16—ST. PIUS X (1958), Rev. Louis H. Yim; Deacon Sidney J. Townsley.
Church—2821 Lowrey Ave., 96822-1644. Tel: 808-988-3308; 988-2651; Fax: 808-988-9313.
Res., 2949 Kahawai St., 96822-1699.
Catechesis / Religious Programs—Maria Minkel, D.R.E.
Students 14.

17—SAINTS PETER AND PAUL (1969), Rev. David O. Travers, S.J., Admin.; Rev. Msgr. Roy V. Peters; Deacon Richard Port.
Office: 800 Kaheka St., 96814. Tel: 808-941-0675; Fax: 808-945-0689.
Res., 1561 Kanunu St., #1006, 96814. Tel: 808-955-8830.
Catechesis / Religious Programs—Students 61.

OUTSIDE THE CITY OF HONOLULU
County of Honolulu

Aiea, St. Elizabeth (1926), Revs. Michel Dalton, O.F.M.Cap.; Robert Maher, O.F.M.Cap. In res., Rev. Gordon Combs, O.F.M.Cap.
Res., 99-312 Moanalua Rd., 96701. Tel: 808-487-2414; Fax: 808-487-2168.
School—Tel: 808-488-5322; Fax: 808-486-0856. Sr. M. Leonarda Montelto, O.P., Prin. Supr.
Sisters 5; Lay Teachers 7; Students 280.
Catechesis / Religious Programs—Tel: 808-487-7994. Vicky S. Llanos, D.R.E.
Students 206.
Convent—99-310 Moanalua Rd., 96701. Tel: 808-487-3131.
Dominican Sisters of the Most Holy Rosary 5.

Ewa, Immaculate Conception (1929), Rev. Eli K. Carter, Jr.
Res., 91-1298 Renton Rd., 96706. Tel: 808-681-3701; Fax: 808-681-3701.
Catechesis / Religious Programs—Tel: 808-681-6703.
Students 210.

Ewa Beach, Our Lady of Perpetual Help (1969), Rev. Robert Phelps, O.F.M.Cap. In res., Rev. Andrew Manetta, O.F.M.Cap.
Res., 91-1004 North Rd., 96706-2796. Tel: 808-689-8681; Fax: 808-689-4829.

School—91-1010 North Rd., 96706. Tel: 808-689-0474; Fax: 808-689-4847. Mr. Dennis Sasaki, Prin.
Lay Teachers 9; Students 177.
Catechesis/Religious Programs—Tel: 808-689-8563. Janese Akins, D.R.E.
Students 265.

Kahuku, St. Roch (1928), Rev. Sydney Fernandes, Pro tem.
Res., P.O. Box 295, 96731. Tel: 808-293-5026; Fax: 808-293-1737. [CEM]
Catechesis/Religious Programs—Students 83.
Mission—Punaluu, St. Joachim, (1917) P.O. Box 295, 96731.

Kailua, St. Anthony (1933), Revs. Dennis Koshko, Admin.; Paul Minchak, O.F.M. Cap.; Mrs. Maxine Pollock, Pastoral Assoc.; Deacons James Carroll; Jerome Weaver; Clarence DeCaires. In res., Rev. Msgr. Bernard J. Eikmeier.
Res., 114 Makawao St., 96734. Tel: 808-266-2222; Fax: 808-266-2229.
School—148 Makawao St., 96734. Tel: 808-261-3331; Fax: 808-263-3518. Mr. Gary Marr, Prin.
Sisters 1; Lay Teachers 22; Students 334.
Catechesis/Religious Programs—Tel: 808-266-2231. D.R.E.: Mrs. Kanani Asing; Mrs. Pam Aqui.
Students 250.

St. John Vianney (1962), Rev. Thomas L. Gross; Deacons Lauren S.F. Wong; Walter H. Yoshimitsu. In res., Rev. Msgr. Alan Nagai.
Res., 920 Keolu Dr., 96734. Tel: 808-262-8317.
School—940 Keolu Dr., 96734. Tel: 808-261-4651. Ms. Jean Flynn, Prin.
Lay Teachers 19; Staff 9; Students 280.
Catechesis/Religious Programs—Maria Brasher, D.R.E.
Students 178.

Kaneohe, St. Ann (1841), Revs. Clarence L. Guerreiro, SS.CC.; Bertram Lock, SS.CC.
Res., 46-129 Haiku Rd., 96744. Tel: 808-247-3092; Fax: 808-235-0717. [CEM]
School and Early Learning Center—46-125 Haiku Rd., 96744. Tel: 808-247-3492 (School); 247-3324 (Early Learning Center). Sr. Anne Clare DeCosta, SS.CC. Tel: 808-235-5682; Mrs. Daphne Kauhane, Prin. (School); Mrs. Frances Vasquez, Prin. (Early Learning Center).
Sisters 1; Lay Teachers 31; Students 436.
Catechesis/Religious Programs—Tel: 808-235-5682.
Students 331.

Makakilo, St. Jude (1988), Rev. Roland Pacudan.
Res., 92-104 Leipapa Way, Ewa Beach, 96707. Tel: 808-672-8669; Fax: 808-672-3779.
Catechesis/Religious Programs—Caren Argenzia, D.R.E.
Students 159.

Mililani Town, St. John Apostle and Evangelist (1969), Rev. Gary Secor; Karen L. Lee, Pastoral Assoc.; Deacon Wally Mitsui. In res., Rev. Thomas B. Killackey, M.M.
Res., 95-370 Kuahelani Ave., 96789. Tel: 808-623-3332; Fax: 808-623-3286.
St. John Catholic Preschool—Carmella Prose, Prin., Tel: 808-623-7331.
Catechesis/Religious Programs—Tel: 808-623-3661. Sandra Beltran, D.R.E.
Students 518.

Nanakuli, St. Rita (Hawaiian), Rev. Robert Schwarzhaupt.
Res., 89-318 Farrington Hwy., 96792. Tel: 808-668-7833; Fax: 808-668-7716.
Catechesis/Religious Programs—Tel: 808-682-5359. Cathy Agor, D.R.E.
Students 123.

Pearl City, Our Lady of Good Counsel (1958), Rev. Daniel J. McNichol; Deacon Thomas Miyashiro. In res., Rev. Paulo Tuugusamusu.
Res., 1525 Waimano Home Rd., 96782. Tel: 808-455-3012; Fax: 808-456-9443. [CEM]
School—1530 Hoolana St., 96782. Tel: 808-455-4533; Fax: 808-455-5587. Mrs. Cindy Olaso, Prin.
Lay Teachers 15; Students 297.
Catechesis/Religious Programs—Ms. Leilani Asuncion, D.R.E.
Students 376.
Convent—872 Hoomoana St., 96782. Tel: 808-455-2058.

Wahiawa, Our Lady of Sorrows (1939), Rev. Clarence L. Fisher; Deacons Benjamin A. Awana; George Kagehiro.
Res., 1403-A California Ave., 96786-2595. Tel: 808-621-5109; Fax: 808-622-5073.
School—Tel: 808-621-8951. Mrs. Deborah Bee, Prin.
Lay Teachers 11; Students 178.
Catechesis/Religious Programs—Mrs. Janice Vannatta, D.R.E.
Students 120.

Waialua, St. Michael (1853), Rev. Albert Garcia, SS.CC.
Res., 67-390 Goodale Ave., 96791. Tel: 808-637-4040; Fax: 808-637-4287.
School—67-340 Haona St., 96791. Tel: 808-637-7772; Fax: 808-637-7272. Sr. William Marie Eleniki, O.S.F., Prin. & D.R.E.
Sisters 3; Lay Teachers 19; Students 222.
Catechesis/Religious Programs—Students 149.
Convent—Tel: 808-637-7772; Fax: 808-637-7272.
Sisters 3.
Mission—Waimea Bay, SS. Peter and Paul, 67-390 Goodale, 96791. Tel: 808-638-7676.

Waianae, Sacred Heart (1838), Revs. Ralph Christman, M.M.; Elias J. Tederous, M.M.
Res., 85-786 Old Government Rd., 96792. Tel: 808-696-3773; Fax: 808-696-2242. [CEM]
Parish Outreach—Tel: 808-696-3746.
Catechesis/Religious Programs—Tel: 808-696-2242.
Students 156.

Waikane, Our Lady of Mt. Carmel (1850), Rev. Romeo Rabusa, Admin.
Res., 48-422 Kamehaineha Hwy., Kaneohe, 96744. Tel: 808-239-9269; Fax: 808-239-9269.
Catechesis/Religious Programs—Betty Kam, D.R.E.
Students 36.

Waimanalo, St. George (1960), Rev. William Mattimore, Admin.; Deacon Ernest Carlbom.
Res., 41-1323 Kalanianaole Hwy., 96795. Tel: 808-259-7188; Fax: 808-259-0169.
Catechesis/Religious Programs—Students 166.

Waipahu, Resurrection of the Lord (1986), Rev. Ronald J. Burke.
Mailing Address: 94-1260 Lumikula St., 96797. Tel: 808-676-4700; Fax: 808-676-4534.
Res., 94-1449 Waipio Uka, #K-106, 96797.
Catechesis/Religious Programs—Tel: 808-671-8498. Felicia K. Routon, D.R.E.
Students 212.

St. Joseph (1940), Revs. Alphonse Larochelle, M.S.; Rene Bisaillon; Antonio Quijano, M.S. In res., Rev. Erwin Dela Cruz, M.S.
Res., 94-675 Farrington Hwy., 96797. Tel: 808-677-4276; Fax: 808-671-3215. [CEM]
School—Tel: 808-677-4475; Fax: 808-677-8937. Miss Beverly Sandobal, Prin.
Sisters 2; Lay Teachers 19; Students 384.
Catechesis/Religious Programs—Al & Geraldine Simbahon, D.R.E.
Students 350.
Convent—91-807 Poowai Pl., Ewa Beach, 96706. Tel: 808-681-4610. Sisters of St. Joseph of Carondelet

ISLAND OF HAWAII
County of Hawaii

Hilo, St. Joseph (1919), Revs. Scott Bush; Marvin Samiano; Deacons LeRoy Andrews; Harvey Kawaihae; A. Jos. Schoemaker.
Res., 43 Kapiolani St., 96720. Tel: 808-935-1465; Fax: 808-969-1665. [CEM]
School—1000 Ululani St., 96720. Tel: 808-935-4935; Fax: 808-969-9019. Sr. Grace Michael Souza, O.S.F., Prin. (Elementary); Deacon Leroy Andrews, Prin. (Junior-Senior High School).
Franciscan Sisters of Third Order 4; Lay Teachers 42; Students 440.
Catechesis/Religious Programs—Tel: 808-935-1202. Barbara Austen, D.R.E.
Students 193.
Convent—440 Kapiolani St., 96720. Tel: 808-935-1388.

Hawi, Sacred Heart (1926), Rev. Thomas Donnelly, M.M.
Res., P.O. Box 220, 96719. Tel: 808-889-6436; Fax: 808-889-5698. [CEM]
Catechesis/Religious Programs—Tel: 808-889-5353. Carol Ching, D.R.E.
Students 155.
Mission—Halaula, Our Lady of Grace.

Holualoa, St. Michael The Archangel (1840), Revs. James A. Berry; Jack Ryan; Deacon John K. Shuster. In res., Rev. John B. Stawasz.
Res., 75 5769 Alii Dr., Kailua-Kona, 96740. Tel: 808-326-7771; Fax: 808-326-7096. [CEM 4]
Catechesis/Religious Programs—Rev. Jack Ryan, D.R.E.
Students 180.
Missions—Kalaoa, Holy Rosary; Holualoa, Immaculate Conception, P.O. Box 275, Holualoa, 96725; Kawanui, St. Paul; Kahaluu, St. Peter.

Honaunau, St. Benedict (1899), Rev. Robert Donnelly, M.M.
Res., Box 209, 96726. Tel: 808-328-2227. [CEM 5][JC 5]
Catechesis/Religious Programs—Marjorie Fujimoto, D.R.E.
Students 88.
Missions—Kealakekua, P.O. Box 209, 96726. Tel: 808-323-3711; Milolii, P.O. Box 209, 96726.

Honokaa, Our Lady of Lourdes (1870), Rev. Anastacio Postrano.
Mailing Address: P.O. Box 129, 96727.
Res., 45-5028 Plumeria St., 96727. Tel: 808-775-9591; Fax: 808-775-0591. [CEM 6]
Catechesis/Religious Programs—Students 159.
Mission—Paauilo, St. Joseph.

Kamuela, Church of the Annunciation (1965), Rev. Robert F. Wynne, M.M.; Deacon William McPeek.
Res., P.O. Box 301, 96743. Tel: 808-885-4196. [CEM]
Catechesis/Religious Programs—Students 110.
Mission—Kalikonani, Church of the Ascension, Puako, Puako, 96743.

Keaukaha, Hilo, Malia Puka'O Kalani (Mary Gate of Heaven) (1929) (Hawaiian), Rev. George De Costa.
Res., 326 Desha Ave., 96720. Tel: 808-935-9338; Fax: 808-935-3865.
Montessori Preschool—Coordinators: Marie Roberts, Prin. & D.R.E.; Joseph Camacho.
Catechesis/Religious Programs—Students 160.

Mountain View, St. Theresa, Rev. Edgardo C. Bonghanoy, Admin.; Sr. M. Yolanda DeFrancesco, S.H.F., Pastoral Assoc. & D.R.E.
Res., P.O. Box 37, 96771. Tel: 808-968-6233. [CEM 3]
Catechesis/Religious Programs—Students 144.
Mission—Keaau, Holy Rosary.

Naalehu, Sacred Heart (1846), Rev. Stephen A. Macedo.
Res., P.O. Box 150, 96772. Tel: 808-929-7474. [CEM]
Catechesis/Religious Programs—Tel: 808-929-7686. Margorie Pedra, D.R.E.
Students 59.

Pahala, Holy Rosary (1885), Rev. Stephen A. Macedo.
Res., P.O. Box 150, Naalehu, 96772. Tel: 808-929-7474; Fax: 808-929-7474. [CEM]
Catechesis/Religious Programs—Tel: 808-928-9054. Mary Ibarra, D.R.E.
Students 79.

Pahoa, Sacred Heart (1882), Rev. Alapaki K. Kim, C.S.P., Pro Tem. Pastoral Assoc.: Sr. Rosita Aranita, C.S.J.; Sr. Eva Joseph Mesina, C.S.J.
Res., P.O. Box 17, 96778. Tel: 808-965-8202. [CEM]
Catechesis/Religious Programs—Tel: 808-965-7866. Nathan Chang, D.R.E.
Students 105.

Papaaloa, St. Anthony (1926), Rev. George D. DeCosta; Deacon Lawrence J. Ignacio, Pastoral Admin.
Res., P.O. Box 339, Laupahoehoe, 96813. Tel: 808-962-6538. [CEM 2]
Catechesis/Religious Programs—D.R.E.: Kay Lundberg; Carol Mendes.
Students 20.
Mission—Ookala, St. James.

Papaikou, Immaculate Heart of Mary (1950), Rev. Konelio Faletoi.
Church—P.O. Box 79, 96781. Tel: 808-964-1240; 963-5434; Fax: 808-964-1240.
Catechesis/Religious Programs—Cheryl Udovic, D.R.E.
Students 104.
Mission—Honomu, Good Shepherd.

ISLAND OF KAUAI
County of Kauai

Kalaheo, Holy Cross (1909), Rev. Gordian J. Carvalho, Jr.; Deacon Dwight Larcomb.
Res., 2-2370 Kaumualii Hwy., 96741. Tel: 808-332-8011; Fax: 808-332-7749. [CEM]
Catechesis/Religious Programs—Students 202.
Mission—Eleele, Sacred Heart, P.O. Box 487, 96741.

Kapaa, St. Catherine (1887), Revs. Bruce Lery, S.M.; Francis Twiss, S.M.; Deacon Donald Waldemar.
Res., 5021-A Kawaihau Rd., 96746. Tel: 808-822-4804; Fax: 808-822-3014. [CEM 2]
School—Tel: 808-822-4212; Fax: 808-822-0991. Carol West, Prin.
Sisters 4; Lay Teachers 5; Students 137.

Catechesis/Religious Programs—Tel: 808-822-0665. Sr. Raymund Orquejo, D.R.E.
Students 210.
Convent—5021 Kawaihau Rd., 96746. Tel: 808-822-0665.
Dominican Sisters of The Most Holy Rosary 4.
Missions—Kilauea, St. Sylvester; Hanalei, St. William.

Kekaha, St. Theresa (1944), Rev. Francois A. Bourgeois, M.S. In res., Rev. Manuel J. Laviste.
Res., P.O. Box 159, 96752. Tel: 808-337-1784 (Rectory), 337-1548 (Office).
School—8311 Kaumualii Hwy, 96752. Tel: 808-337-1351. Sr. Valerie Lemansky, O.S.F., Prin.
Sisters 4; Lay Teachers 4; Students 100.
Catechesis/Religious Programs—Tel: 808-337-9992. Sr. Mary Jane Mertens, O.S.F., D.R.E.
Students 79.
Missions—Waimea, Sacred Hearts of Jesus & Mary, 9500 Kaumualii Hwy., Waimea, 96796.; Kaumakani, St. Joseph, Village Main St., Kaumakani, 96747.
Convent—P.O. Box 277, 96752. Tel: 808-337-9661. Sr. Janet Rose, Supr.
Franciscan Sisters of Christian Charity 5.

Koloa, St. Raphael (1841), Rev. Felix J. Vandebroek, SS.CC.; Abel Medeiros, Pastoral Assoc.
Res., 3011 Hapa Rd., 96756. Tel: 808-742-1955. [CEM 2]
Catechesis/Religious Programs—Students 83.

Lihue, Immaculate Conception (1884), Rev. Paul McLeod, SS.CC.
Res., 4453 Kapaia Rd., 96766. Tel: 808-245-2432; Fax: 808-245-5628. [CEM 2]
Catechesis/Religious Programs—Tel: 808-639-7195. Sr. Florence Remata, O.S.F., D.R.E.
Students 159.

ISLAND OF LANAI

Lanai City, Sacred Hearts (1930), Rev. Florencio B. Rebebes.
Res., P.O. Box 784, 96763. Tel: 808-565-6837.
Catechesis/Religious Programs—Tel: 808-565-6897. D.R.E.: Rosita Camero; Priscilla Felipe.
Students 106.

ISLAND OF MAUI
County of Maui

Haiku, St. Rita (1950), Rev. Gary Colton; Deacon Patrick Constantino.
Res., 655 Haiku Rd., 96708. Tel: 808-575-2601; Fax: 808-575-2063. [CEM]
Catechesis/Religious Programs—D.R.E.: Celia Fraser; Sandra Silva.
Students 81.
Mission—Keanae, St. Gabriel, 655 Haiku Rd., 96708. Tel: 808-248-8369.

Hana, St. Mary (1859), Rev. Paul A. Zegers, SS.CC.
Res., P.O. Box 219, 96713. Tel: 808-248-8030. [CEM]
Catechesis/Religious Programs—Stella Perry, D.R.E.
Students 55.
Missions—Puuiki, St. Peter; Kipahulu, St. Paul; Kaupo, St. Joseph.

Kahului, Christ the King (1932), Rev. William Shannon, Admin.; Deacon Frank R. Singson, Sr., Pastoral Assoc. In res., Rev. Gaudelio Donato.
Res., 20 W. Wakea Ave., 96732. Tel: 808-877-6098; Fax: 808-871-6296.
School—(Grades PreK-6). Tel: 808-877-6618. Dr. Debra Veit, Prin.
Sisters 5; Lay Teachers 9; Students 106.
Catechesis/Religious Programs—Tel: 808-877-7783. Sr. Angela Laurenzo, C.S.J, D.R.E.
Students 206.
Convent—211 S. Kaulawahine St., 96732. Tel: 808-877-0790. Sisters of St. Joseph of Carondelet

Kihei, St. Theresa (1908), Rev. Anthony Bolger. Pastoral Assocs.: Sr. Ann Gertrude Vierra, O.S.F.; Sr. Laura Abat, O.S.F.
Res., 25 W. Lipoa St., 96753. Tel: 808-879-2649; Fax: 808-879-0045. [CEM]
Catechesis/Religious Programs—Students 246.

Kula, Our Lady Queen of the Angels (1944) (Portuguese), Rev. Thomas R. Heinzel.
Res., R.R. 2, Box 211, 96790. Tel: 808-878-1261; Fax: 808-878-3105. [CEM 2]
Catechesis/Religious Programs—Mrs. Maureen Rompasky, D.R.E.
Students 69.
Missions—Waiakoa, Holy Ghost, 9 Lower Kula Rd., Waiakoa, 96790. Tel: 808-878-1091; Ulupalakua, St. James the Less.

Lahaina, Maria Lanakila (1846), Revs. Marisi Palepale, SS.CC.; Joseph Hendricks, SS.CC., Pastoral Assoc. In res., Rev. Raphael M. Smulders, SS.CC.
Res., P.O. Box 1680, 96767. Tel: 808-661-0552; Fax: 808-667-6963. [CEM]
School—Tel: 808-661-4720; Fax: 808-661-4720. Sr. Charles Miriam Wong, O.S.F., Prin.
Franciscan Sisters 3; Lay Teachers 8; Students 200.
Catechesis/Religious Programs—Tel: 808-661-6607. Sr. Susan Marie Alconcher, B.V.M., D.R.E.
Students 212.
Mission—Honokahua (Kapalua), Sacred Hearts of Jesus and Mary, Office Rd., Honokahua, 96761. Tel: 808-669-7022.

Makawao, St. Joseph (1851), Revs. Donald Macgregor; Alfred Rebuldelha; Deacon Albert Phillips, Jr.
Res., 1294 Makawao Ave., 96768. Tel: 808-572-7652; Fax: 808-573-2278. [CEM]
School—(Grades PreK-6). Tel: 808-572-8675; Fax: 808-572-0748. Sr. Mary Matthew Brasil, O.P., Prin.
Sisters 6; Lay Teachers 6; Students 140.
Catechesis/Religious Programs—Tina Andrade, D.R.E.
Students 120.
Convent—57 Dominican Ln., 96768. Tel: 808-572-8454.
Dominican Sisters of the Most Holy Rosary 5.

Paia, Holy Rosary (1915), Rev. Gary Colton; Deacon Patrick Constantino.
Church—954 Baldwin Ave., 96779-9605. Tel: 808-579-9551; Fax: 808-579-8714. [CEM]
Catechesis/Religious Programs—Mrs. Clara Pico, D.R.E.
Students 40.

Waihee, St. Ann (1935), Rev. Joseph C. Carrol, Pro Tem.
Res., 40 Kuhinia St., 96793-9216. Tel: 808-244-3284. [CEM][JC]
Missions—Waikapu, St. Joseph, 96793. [CEM][JC]
Kahakuloa, St. Francis Xavier, 96793. [CEM][JC]

Wailuku, St. Anthony (1846), Revs. Raymond E. Malley, S.M.; Charles Oyabu; Deacons Joseph Borges; James Ronald Gonsalves. In res., Rev. Thomas Hogan, S.M.
Res., 1627 B Mill St., 96793-1999. Tel: 808-244-4148; Fax: 808-242-9375. [CEM]
School—(Grades PreK-6). Tel: 808-244-4976; 242-9024 (PreK); Fax: 808-244-7950. Mrs. Winona Martinez, Prin.; Mrs. Carlene Santos, Dir. (PreK).
Lay Teachers 11; Students 208.
Catechesis/Religious Programs—Tel: 808-242-6040. Kay Stone, D.R.E.
Students 309.

ISLAND OF MOLOKAI

Kalaupapa, St. Francis (1873), Rev. Nobincio Fernandez.
Res., 96742. Tel: 808-567-6238.
Mission—Kalawao, St. Philomena, P.O. Box 9, 96742.

Kaunakakai, Molokai Catholic Community (1874). Attended by Our Lady of Sorrows, Kalua'aha; St. Joseph, Kamalo; St. Sophia, Kaunakakai; and St. Vincent, Maunaloa. Rev. James Orsini.
Mailing Address: P.O. Box 1948, 96748-1948. Tel: 808-553-5220. [CEM 2]
Office: 115 Ala Malama St., 96748.
Catechesis/Religious Programs—Students 144.

On Duty Outside the Diocese:
Reverend Fathers—
Butler, John
Coughlin, Thomas
DeRego, Frank
Drew, James F.
Farrell, Jeremiah
Guerrero, Robert
Lee, William, Chicago, IL
Rozycki, George

Military Chaplains:
Reverend Fathers—
Blazek, Eugene E., U.S. Air Force
Evers, Paul, U.S. Navy
Gervacio, Adrian R., U.S. Navy
Lanuevo, Victor, U.S. Navy
Santry, Robert, U.S. Army

Leave of Absence:
Reverend Fathers—
DeOtero, Roberto
Kaleikoa, Charles

Retired:
Reverend Monsignors—
Caraballo, Benito, 91-590 Farrington Hwy. #210-22, Kapolei, HI 96797
Dever, Daniel, 6301 Pali Hwy., Kaneohe, HI 96744
Eikmeier, Bernard J., 78 Kaikaina St, Kailua, HI 96734
Marzen, Francis A., P.O. Box 4935, Kaneohe, HI 96744
Reverend Fathers—
Carrol, Joseph, St. Ann, RR#1, Box 46, Wailuku, HI 96793
Ching, Herbert, 86-660 Lualualei Homestead, Maili, HI 96792
Churchill, Raymond, 1184 Bishop St., Honolulu, HI 96813
Duffy, Edwin J., Alexander Towers, 1226 Alexander St., Apt. 601, Honolulu, HI 96826
Halloran, John, Los Angeles, CA
Hannon, Robert E., 1184 Bishop St., Honolulu, HI 96813
Ky, Joseph, S.S., 640 Puuhale Rd., Honolulu, HI 96819
O'Brien, Arthur
O'Leary, Bartholomew J., Nazareth House, 245 Nova Albion Way, San Rafael, CA 94903
O'Mahony, James, One N. Golf View, Lakewood, FL 33460
Pascale, Anthony, 1778 Ala Moana Blvd., #2807, Honolulu, HI 96815
Peterson, Francis, 1511 Nuuanu Ave., PT 30, Honolulu, HI 96817
Sabog, Henry, 2909 Kalihi St., Honolulu, HI 96819
Siu, Robert K.C., P.O. Box 503, Lander, WY 82520
Smith, Paul, 1717 Ala Wai Blvd., #1806, Honolulu, HI 96851
Stawasz, James, 75-5769 Alii Dr., Kailua-Kona, HI 96740
Thomas, Donald, P.O. Box 0358, Haleiwa, HI 96812
Turner, Edward, 2723 Avenida De Anita, #102, Carlsbad, CA 92008

Permanent Deacons:
Aanavi, Don, On Leave of Absence
Andrews, LeRoy, St. Joseph, Hilo, 136 Ululani St., Hilo, HI 96720
Awana, Benjamin A., Our Lady of Sorrows, Wahiawa, 89-104 A Haleakala Ave., Nannakuli, HI 96792
Benet, Alphonse, On Leave of Absence
Borges, Joseph W., St. Anthony, Wailuku, Maui, 299 Liholiho St., Wailuku, HI 96793
Carlbom, Ernest F., St. George, Waimanalo, 41-865 Mahailua St., Waimanalo, HI 96795
Carroll, James L., (Retired), 323 Kuukama St., Kailua, HI 96734
Choo, Ronald T.Y., Blessed Sacrament, 46-144 Hilinama St., Kaneoha, HI 96744
Christiansen, George, On Leave of Absence
Constantino, Patrick R., Holy Rosary, Paia; St. Rita, Haiku, 3188 Kilani Pl., Pukalani, HI 96734
DeCaires, Clarence, Jr., St. John Vianney, 1131 Kupau St., Kailua, HI 96734
Gerakas, Andrew J., Star of the Sea, Honolulu, 4524 Waikui St., Honolulu, HI 96821
Gonsalves, James R., St. Anthony, Mailuku, Maui, 2534 Main St., Wailuku, HI 96793
Hart, Christopher L., On Leave
Hope, Jack M., On Leave
Ignacio, Lawrence, St. Anthony, Papaaloa, P.O. Box 317, Paauilo, HI 96776
Kawaihae, Harvey, St. Joseph, Hilo, 1838 Kilauea Ave., Hilo, HI 96720
Larcomb, Dwight, Holy Cross, Kalaheo, Kauai, HI 96741
Lee, Paul, Holy Trinity, Honolulu, Honolulu, HI 96821
Matsuo, Roy T., Sacred Hearts, Makiki (St. Louis High School/Kapiolani & Shriner's)
McPeek, William, Anunciation Parish, Kamuela, P.O. Box 278, Kapaau, HI 96755
Miller, Cletus J., (Retired), Holy Trinity, 5371 Opihi St., Honolulu, HI 96821
Mitsui, Wallace M., St. John Apostle & Evangelist, Mililani, 95-690 Lewanuu St., Mililani, HI 97689
Miyashiro, Thomas H., Our Lady of Good Counsel, Pearl City, 2054 Hoohai St, Pearl City, HI 96782
Phillips, Albert C., St. Joseph, Makawao, Maui, 3297 Haleakala Hwy., Pukalani, HI 96788
Port, Richard J., Sts. Peter and Paul, Honolulu, 1600 Ala Moana Blvd., #3100, Honolulu, HI 96815
Rienzi, Thomas M., Star of the Sea, Honolulu, 676 Elepaio St., Honolulu, HI 96819
Schoemaker, Andres J., St. Joseph, Hilo
Seagraves, Veral, On Leave
Shuster, St. Michael, Kailua-Kona, Kailua-Kona, HI 96725
Singson, Frank, Christ the King, Kahului, Kahului, HI 96732
Taylor, Sam, Holy Trinity, Honolulu, Honolulu, HI 96821
Thorp, George, Our Lady of Mount Carmel, Honolulu, 1459 Akamai St., Kailua, HI 96734
Townsley, Sidney J., St. Pius X, Honolulu, 2821 Lowrey Ave., Honolulu, HI 96822
Waldemar, St. Catherine, Kapaa, Kauai, HI 96746
Weaver, Jerome M., St. Anthony, Kaulua, 1031 Lunaai Pl., Kailua, HI 96734
Wong, Lauren H., St. John Vianney, Kailua, 1309 Kupau St., Kailua, HI 96734
Yoshimitsu, Walter H., St. John Vianney, Kailua, 681 Akoakoa St., Kailua, HI 96734

INSTITUTIONS LOCATED IN THE DIOCESE

[A] SEMINARIES, DIOCESAN

KANEOHE. *St. Stephen's Diocesan Center*, 6301 Pali Hwy., 96744. Tel: 808-263-8844. In res. Most Rev. Francis X. DiLorenzo, S.T.D., D.D.; Rev. Marc R. Alexander, S.T.D.; Rev. Msgr. Daniel J. Dever.

[B] COLLEGES AND UNIVERSITIES

*HONOLULU. *Chaminade University of Honolulu*, 3140 Waialae Ave., 96816. Tel: 808-735-4711.
E-mail: cuhadm@lava.net
Web site: www.chaminade.edu
For a complete listing, refer to the Colleges and Universities section.

[C] HIGH SCHOOLS, DIOCESAN AND PAROCHIAL

HONOLULU. *Maryknoll Schools*, 1701 Wilder Ave., 96822. Tel: 808-973-1770.
E-mail: baker@mhs.pvt.k12.HI.us
Michael E. Baker, Pres.; Kathleen W. Shimabukuro, Contact Person. Sisters 2; Lay Teachers 110; Students 1,357.

HILO. *St. Joseph Junior-Senior High School*, 1000 Ululani St., 96720; Fax: 808-969-9019.
E-mail: sjadmin@interpac.net
Deacon LeRoy M. Andrews, Prin. Sisters 1; Deacons 1; Lay Teachers 27; Students 233.

WAILUKU. *St. Anthony Junior-Senior High School*, 1618 Lower Main St., 96793.
E-mail: satrojan@poi.net
Web site: www.poi.net/~satrojan
Bro. James Dods, S.M., Prin. Brothers 2; Sisters 3; Lay Teachers 27; Students 375.

[D] HIGH SCHOOLS, PRIVATE

HONOLULU. *Damien Memorial High School*, 1401 Houghtailing St., 96817. Tel: 808-841-0195.
E-mail: odonnell@damien.edu
Web site: www.damien.edu
Congregation of Christian Brothers. Legal Title: *Congregation of Christian Brothers of Hawaii, Inc.* Bros. Gregory O'Donnell, C.F.C., Prin.; F. Louis Frick, C.F.C., Community Leader. Brothers 7; Sisters 1; Lay Teachers 27; Boys 456.

Sacred Hearts Academy. (Grades K-12), 3253 Waialae Ave., 96816. Tel: 808-734-5058.
Web site: www.sacred.pvt.k12.hi.us
Mrs. Betty White, Prin. Sisters 3; Lay Teachers 60; Girls 1,042; Support Staff, Counselors, Administrators 18.

St. Francis School. (Grades 6-12), 2707 Pamoa Rd., 96822. Tel: 808-988-4111.
Web site: www.hais.mhpcc.edu/st.francis/
Sr. Joan of Arc Souza, O.S.F., Prin.; Carol Caspillo, Contact Person.

St. Francis School. (Grades 9-10). (Kaua'i Campus). 3343 Kanakolu St., Lihue, 96766. Tel: 808-246-3802; Fax: 808-245-3680. Tom Ryan, Prin. Lay Teachers 5; Students 18. Sisters 11; Lay Teachers 41; Girls 444.

**St. Louis School*, 3142 Waialae Ave., 96816-1578. Tel: 808-739-7777; Fax: 808-739-4853.
E-mail: MJPariante@aol.com
Rev. Mario J. Pariante, S.M., Pres. Chaplains: Revs. John Bolin, S.M.; William O'Connell, S.M. Priests 3; Brothers 6; Sisters 1; Lay Teachers 60; Boys 860.

[E] PRESCHOOL CENTERS

HONOLULU. *St. Philomena Early Learning Center*, 3300 Ala Laulani St., 96818. Tel: 808-833-8080; Fax: 808-834-6888; 808-834-3438. Angie V. Thomas, Prin. Lay Teachers 20; Students 120.

HILO. *Hale O Kamalii Montessori Preschool*, 326 Desha Ave., 96720. Tel: 808-935-9338. Co-Directors: Marie Roberts; Joe Camacho. Students 15.

MILILANI TOWN. *St. John Catholic Preschool*, 95-370 Kuahelani Ave., 96789. Tel: 808-623-7331. Carmella Prose, Dir. Total Staff 10; Students 60.

[F] GENERAL HOSPITALS

HONOLULU. *St. Francis Healthcare System of Hawaii*, P.O. Box 30100, 96820. Tel: 808-566-4783.
Web site: www.sfhs.hi.org
For a complete listing, refer to the Hospitals section.

[G] SPECIAL HOSPITALS AND SANATORIA FOR INVALIDS

KALAUPAPA, MOLOKAI. *Kalaupapa Settlement*, 96742
For a complete listing, refer to the Special Care Facilities section.

[H] MONASTERIES AND RESIDENCES OF PRIESTS AND BROTHERS

HONOLULU. *Center Marianist Community*, 3140 Waialae Ave., 96816. Tel: 808-735-2711. Rev. John Bolin, S.M., Dir. Priests 1; Brothers 9; Total in Residence 10.

Chaminade Pohaku Marianist Community, 3140 Waialae Ave., 96816. Tel: 808-735-4857. Rev. Mario Pariante, S.M., Dir. Priests 1; Brothers 3.

Congregation of Christian Brothers, 1401 Houghtailing St., 96817. Tel: 808-845-2330. Bro. F. Louis Frick, C.F.C., Supr. Brothers 11.

Jesuit Fathers House, 2727 Pamoa Rd., 96822-1838. Tel: 808-988-3464. Revs. Randall H. Roche, S.J., Reg. Supr.; Bernard F. Cassidy, S.J.; Daniel J. Sullivan, S.J.

**Marianist Center of Hawaii*, 3140 Waialae Ave., 96816. Tel: 808-739-4738. Bro. Edward L.K. Gomez, S.M., Vice Pres. & Chm.

Marianist Hall Community, 3140 Waialae Ave., 96816. Tel: 808-739-8300; Fax: 808-739-8320. Rev. William O'Connell, S.M., Dir. Priests 2; Brothers 9.

Maryknoll Fathers House, Honolulu Society House, 1721 Dole St, 96822. Tel: 808-949-7737. Revs. Francis J. Taney, M.M.; Charles W. Schmidt, M.M.; Joseph Matheis, M.M.; Bro. Venard F. Ruane, M.M., Dir.; Rev. Arthur J. Dwyer, M.M., Unit Coord., Annunciation Church, P.O. Box 301, Kamuela, 96743. Rev. Robert F. Wynne, M.M., Sacred Heart Church, 1701 Wilder Ave., 96822. Revs. Francis A. Diffley, M.M.; Arthur Dwyer, M.M., Sacred Heart Church, 85-786 Old Government Rd., Waianae, 96792. Revs. Ralph Christman, M.M.; Elias J. Tederous, M.M., St. Benedict's Church, Box 209, 96726. Rev. Robert W. Donnelly, M.M., St. John Apostle and Evangelist, 95-370 Kuahelani Ave., Mililani, 96789. Rev. Thomas B. Killackey, M.M., St. John the Baptist, 2324 Omilo Ln., 96819. Rev. James J. McFadden, M.M. Priests 3; Brothers 1; Total in Residence 4; Total Staff 1.

St. Patrick's Monastery, 1124-A Seventh Ave., 96816. Revs. Joseph Bukosk, III, SS.CC.; Arsene Daenen, SS.CC.; Gerard Leicht, SS.CC.; Clement Geysen, SS.CC.; Timothy Jacobs, SS.CC.; Lawrence Mampaey, SS.CC.; Albert Miechielsen, SS.CC.; Anthony O'Brien, SS.CC.; Gabriel Vanden Brouke, SS.CC.; Alfred Vann, SS.CC.; Stephen Van den Eynde, SS.CC.; Christopher Keahi, SS.CC., Supr.; Ildephonse Kuntz, SS.CC.; Francis Schellemans, SS.CC.; Bros. James Dunn, SS.CC.; Leo Vendiola, SS.CC.; Patrick Hughes, SS.CC; Dominic Stone, SS.CC. Total in Residence 18; Total Staff 6.

Society of the Priests of St. Sulpice (Sulpicians) S.S., 640 Puuhale Rd., 96819. Tel: 808-842-0862. Vietnamese Catholic Community. Rev. Joseph Cao Ky, S.S.

KANEOHE. *Congregation of the Sacred Hearts of Jesus and Mary (Hawaii Province SS.CC.)*, P.O. Box 797, 96744. Tel: 808-247-5035. Very Rev. Clyde Guerreiro, SS.CC., Prov. Priests 35; Brothers 7.

Sacred Hearts Center, P.O. Box 787, 96744. Tel: 808-247-3647. Revs. Clyde Guerreiro, SS.CC., Prov.; Mark Consalvi, SS.CC.; Gaston Diels, SS.CC.; Nobincio Fernandez, SS.CC.; Herman Gomes, SS.CC.; Edward Popish, SS.CC.; Bros. Charles Kaahanui, SS.CC.; George Apo, SS.CC.

WAIALUA, OAHU. *Benedictine Monastery of Hawaii*, 67-290 Farrington Hwy., P.O. Box 490, 96791. Tel: 808-637-7887; Fax: 808-637-8601.
E-mail: benedicthi@aol.com
Benedictine Congregation of Our Lady of Mounte Oliveto, O.S.B. Revs. Michael Sawyer, O.S.B.; Timothy Ottman, O.S.B.; David Barfknecht, O.S.B., Supr.; Sr. Mary Jo McEnany, O.S.B.; Bro. Gregory Foret, O.S.B.

WAILUKU, MAUI. *Wailuku Marianist Community*, 1627 B Mill St., 96793. Tel: 808-244-3152. Revs. Raymond E. Malley, S.M.; Charles Oyabu, S.M.; Bro. James A. Dods, S.M.

Waiehu Marianist Community, 828 Analio St., 96793. Tel: 808-242-6874. Rev. Thomas W. Hogan, S.M., Supr.; Bros. Raymond L. Dotzler, S.M.; Charles J. Ehrenfeld, S.M.; Frank T. Spaeth, S.M.

[I] CONVENTS AND RESIDENCES FOR SISTERS

HONOLULU. *Congregation of the Sacred Hearts and of Perpetual Adoration*, 1120 Fifth Ave., 96816. Tel: 808-737-5822; Fax: 808-735-0878. Sisters of the Congregation of the Sacred Hearts of Jesus and Mary of Perpetual Adoration SS.CC. Sr. Regina Mary Jenkins, Pres. & Prov. Supr.; Sr. Katherine Francis Miller, SS.CC., Vice Pres.; Sr. Rose Kathleen Lenchanko, Sec.; Sr. Anne Clare DeCosta, Auditor; Sr. Mary Josephine Araki, Treas.; Sr. Regina M. Jenkins, Contact Person. Sisters 10.
The following are listings of residences and the number of sisters residing at each:

Paewalani Community, 45-901A Wailele Rd., 96744. Tel: 808-247-3688. Sr. Anne Clare DeCosta, SS.CC., Contact Person. Sisters 3.

Mali O Ka Malu Community, 1117 Fourth Ave., 96816. Tel: 808-734-2048. Sr. Helene Woods, SS.CC., Contact Person. Sisters 13.

Na Leo Ho'onani Community, 2151 Kauhana St., 96816. Tel: 808-739-5566. Sr. Katherine Francis Miller, SS.CC., Contact Person. Sisters 4.

Maryknoll Sisters of St. Dominic M.M. 125 Ainoni St., Kailua, 96734-2138. Tel: 808-261-0267. Sr. Earnest Chung, M.M., Contact Person.
The following are listings of residences and the number of sisters residing at each:

Maryknoll Sisters, 2880 Oahu Ave., 96822-1726. Tel: 808-988-6540. Sisters 6.

Maryknoll Sisters, 125 Ainoni St., Kailua, 96734-2138. Tel: 808-261-6356. Sisters 3.

Maryknoll Sisters, 1570 Mokulua Dr., Kailua, 96734-3254. Tel: 808-261-1674. Sisters 4.

Maryknoll Sisters, 87-204 Holomalia Pl., Nanakuli, 96792-3706. Tel: 808-668-1603. Sisters 3.

Maryknoll Sisters, St. Anthony Convent, 702 Puuhale Rd., 96819. Tel: 808-841-5652.

Maryknoll Sisters, P.O. Box 996, Pepeekeo, 96783. Tel: 808-964-3032. Sisters 2.

St. Anthony Home, 3351 Kalihi St., 96819. Tel: 808-845-4353; Fax: 808-848-2696. Sisters of the Sacred Hearts of Jesus and Mary and of Perpetual Adoration SS.CC. Sr. Rose Kathleen Lenchanko, SS.CC., Contact Person.

St. Anthony Retreat Center, 3351 Kalihi St., 96819. Tel: 808-845-0065. Sisters 8.

St. Francis Convent, 2715 Pamoa Rd., 96822-1885. Tel: 808-988-4432. Sisters 20.
The following are listings of residences and the number of sisters residing at each:

Marianne Cope Convent, 2102 Liliha St., 96817-1642. Tel: 808-538-1526. Sisters 7.

Sacred Hearts Convent, 239 Dickenson St., Lakaina, 96761-1204. Tel: 808-661-0163. Sisters 4.

Franciscan Sisters, 15 Kulanihakoi St., 10-C, Kihei, 96753-8128. Tel: 808-874-1029. Sisters 2.

St. Elizabeth Convent, Bishop Home and Hospital, Kalaupapa, 96742-0129. Tel: 808-567-6079. Sisters 3.

St. Joseph Convent, 440 Kapiolani St., Hilo, 96720-3937. Tel: 808-935-1388. Sr. Grace Michael Souza, O.S.F. Sisters 5.

St. Francis Medical Center - West, St. Clare Convent, 91-1048 A'awa Dr., Ewa Beach, 96706-3900. Tel: 808-687-3420. Sisters 7.

St. Michael Convent, 67-340 Haona St., Waialua, 96791. Tel: 808-637-5606; 637-7772.

Sisters of St. Joseph of Carondelet CSJ, Hawaii Vice-Province, 5311 Apo Dr., 96821-1829. Tel: 808-373-2096; Fax: 808-373-5341.
E-mail: palenacsj@juno.com
Sr. Brenda Lau, C.S.J., Vice Prov.
The following are listings of residences and the number of sisters residing at each:

Carondelet Community, 5311 Apo Dr., 96821-1829. Tel: 808-373-3850. Sisters 4.

Hale Medaille Community, 2220 E. Kalaiwa Way #19, 96819-2711. Tel: 808-847-7807. Sisters 2.

Holy Trinity Community, 5919 Kalanianaole Hwy., 96821-1112. Tel: 808-396-9182. Sisters 2.

Ho'omaluhia Community, 1635 Alaneo St., 96817-2915. Sisters 2.

Mana'olana Community, 1046 6th Ave., 96816-1644. Tel: 808-737-2130. Sisters 3.

St. Joseph the Worker Community, 17-202 Palula St., P.O. Box 609, Keaau, 96749-0609. Tel: 808-966-7754. Sisters 2.

St. Theresa Community, 712 N. School St., 96817-3098. Tel: 808-533-3101. Sisters 13.

Christ the King Community, 211 S. Kaulawahine St., 96732-2200. Tel: 808-877-0790. Sisters 7.

Hale Lokepa Community, 54 Kuhinia St., Waihe'e, 96793-9216. Tel: 808-244-8123. Sisters 4.

La'ialoha Community, 21 Craigside Pl., #6F, 96817-1759. Tel: 808-537-9223.

KANEOHE. *Carmel of the Holy Trinity (Carmelite Monastery)*, 6301 Pali Hwy., 96744-5224. Tel: 808-261-6542. Sr. Mary Agnes Tse, O.C.D., Prioress. Sisters 8.

MOUNTAIN VIEW. *Sisters of the Holy Family Residences*, P.O. Box 15, 96771. Tel: 808-968-6426.

WAIPAHU. *Dominican Center Hawaii*, 94-1249 Lumikula St., 96797. Tel: 808-676-1452; 845-2622.
E-mail: rpsadmin@damien.edu
Dominican Sisters of the Most Holy Rosary. Sr. M. Aurelia Sanchez, O.P., Reg. Supr.
Please refer to the following parish convents for additional residences: St. Elizabeth, Aiea; St. John, Honolulu; St. Catherine, Kapaa; St. Joseph, Makawao. Sisters 8.

Sisters of Charity of the Blessed Virgin Mary, 94-1031 Kauhahi Pl., Apt. G7, 96797. Tel: 808-676-4433. Sr. Joan Madden, Contact Person.

Sacred Hearts Convent, 239 Dickenson St., Lahaina, 96761. Tel: 808-661-0163.

[J] MISCELLANEOUS

HONOLULU. *Aina Kupaa O Maili*, 1184 Bishop St., 96813. Tel: 808-533-1791. Most Rev. Francis X. DiLorenzo, Pres.; Rev. John F. Bolin, S.M., V.G., Vice Pres.; Sr. Grace Dorothy Lim, M.M., Sec.; Jerome Rauckhorst, Treas. Total Assisted 1,368; Total Staff 25.

Leadership Association of Religious Congregation (LARC), 2712 Panmoa Rd., 96822. Tel: 808-988-7800. Rev. Halbert Weidner, C.O., Chm. Tel: 808-396-0551.

The Oratory. (Diocesan House), P.O. Box 26113, 96825. Total in Residence 2.

Our Lady of the Mystical Rose Chapel. (Oratory). Marianist Center of Hawaii, 3140 Waialae Ave., 96816; Fax: 808-737-5518.

People of Praise, c/o Chancery Office, 1184 Bishop St., 96813-2859. Lay Covenant Community (Charismatic group). Bob Linczer, Liaison & Branch Co-ord.

St. Paul Book and Media Center, 1143 Bishop St., 96813. Tel: 808-521-2731; Fax: 808-523-3685. E-mail: fsphi@aol.com
Daughters of St. Paul 4.

KANEOHE. *Augustine Educational Foundation*, St. Stephen Diocesan Center, 6301 Pali Hwy., 96744. Tel: 808-263-8844, Ext. 336; Fax: 808-261-7022. Most Revs. Francis X. DiLorenzo, Pres.; Joseph A. Ferrario, D.D., Chm.; Rev. Msgr. Daniel J. Dever, Sec.; Anna Ordenstein, Second Vice Pres.; Lawrence S.L. Ching, Treas.; Wendall K. Pang, Asst. Treas.; Tonya Story, Assoc. Admin.

RELIGIOUS INSTITUTES OF MEN REPRESENTED IN THE DIOCESE

For further details refer to the corresponding bracketed number in the Religious Institutes of Men or Women section.

[0200]—*Benedictine Monks*. (Olivetan).—O.S.B.
[0470]—*The Capuchin Friars*.—O.F.M.Cap.
[0310]—*Congregation of Christian Brothers*.—C.F.C.
[1140]—*Fathers of the Sacred Hearts*. (Hawaii Prov.).—SS.CC.
[0520]—*Franciscan Friars*.—O.F.M.
[0690]—*Jesuit Fathers and Brothers*.—S.J.
[0780]—*Marist Fathers*.—S.M.
[0800]—*Maryknoll*.—M.M.
[0720]—*The Missionaries of Our Lady of La Salette*. (Pacific Region).—M.S.
[0950]—*Oratorians*.—C.O.
[1030]—*Paulist Fathers*.—C.S.P.
[0760]—*Society of Mary*. (Prov. of the Pacific).—S.M.
[1290]—*Society of the Priest of Saint Sulpice*.—S.S.

RELIGIOUS INSTITUTES OF WOMEN REPRESENTED IN THE DIOCESE

[]—*Benedictine Congregation of Our Lady of Mounte Oliveto*.—O.S.B.
[]—*Congregation of Benedictine Sisters of the Eucharistic King*.—O.S.B.
[1070-01]—*Congregation of St. Catharine of Siena*.—O.P.
[0870]—*Congregation of the Daughters of Mary Immaculate (Marianist Sisters)*.—F.M.I.
[0420]—*Discalced Carmelite Nuns*.—O.C.D.
[1070-03]—*Dominican Sisters of the Most Holy Rosary*.—O.P.
[1230]—*Franciscan Sisters of Christian Charity*.—O.S.F.
[2420]—*Marist Missionary Sisters*.—S.M.S.M.
[2470]—*Maryknoll Sisters of St. Dominic*.—M.M.
[0950]—*Pious Society Daughters of St. Paul*.—D.S.P.
[]—*Religious of the Blessed Virgin Mary*.—R.V.M.
[]—*Servants of Holiness*.
[0430]—*Sisters of Charity of the Blessed Virgin Mary*.—B.V.M.
[3000]—*Sisters of Notre Dame de Namur*.—S.N.D.deN.
[1640]—*Sisters of St. Francis of Perpetual Adoration*.—O.S.F.
[1650]—*Sisters of St. Francis of Philadelphia*.—O.S.F.
[3840]—*Sisters of St. Joseph of Carondelet*.—C.S.J.
[1830]—*Sisters of the Good Shepherd*.—R.G.S.
[1960]—*Sisters of the Holy Family*.—S.H.F.
[3690]—*Sisters of the Sacred Hearts and of Perpetual Adoration*.—SS.CC.
[1490]—*Sisters of the Third Franciscan Order*. (Syracuse, NY).—O.S.F.

NECROLOGY

† Scanlan, Most Rev. John J., D.D., (Retired). —Died Jan. 31, 1997.
Churchill, Raymond, (Retired).—Died June 9, 1997.

Diocese of Houma-Thibodaux

(Dioecesis Humensis-Thibodensis)

Most Reverend

MICHAEL JARRELL, D.D.

Bishop of Houma-Thibodaux; ordained June 3, 1967; appointed December 29, 1992; consecrated and installed March 4, 1993. *Address: Chancery Office, 1801 Hwy. 311, Schriever, LA, 70395. Mailing Address: P.O. Box 9077, Houma, LA, 70361.* Tel.: 504-868-7720.

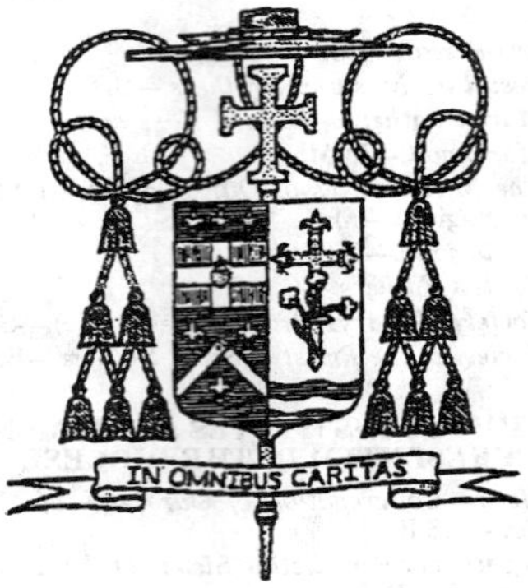

Address all Chancery correspondence to: P.O. Box 9077, Houma, LA, 70361. Tel.: 504-868-7720; Fax: 504-868-7727.

E-mail address: vght@cajun.net

ERECTED JUNE 5, 1977.

Square Miles 3,440.

Comprises the parishes of Lafourche, Terrebonne, parts of St. Mary and Jefferson.

For legal titles of parishes and diocesan institutions, consult the Chancery Office.

STATISTICAL OVERVIEW

Personnel	
Bishop	1
Priests: Diocesan Active in Diocese	45
Priests: Active Outside Diocese	1
Priests: Retired, Sick or Absent	27
Number of Diocesan Priests	73
Religious Priests in Diocese	7
Extern Priests in Diocese	1
Ordinations:	
Diocesan Priests	3
Permanent Deacons	3
Permanent Deacons in Diocese	25
Total Brothers	12
Total Sisters	34
Parishes	
Parishes	42
With Resident Pastor:	
Resident Diocesan Priests	32
Resident Religious Priests	1
Without Resident Pastor:	
Administered by Priests	6
Administered by Women Religious	3
Missions	6
Welfare	
Day Care and Extended Day Care Centers	1
Total Assisted	96
Specialized Homes	2
Total Assisted	65
Special Centers for Social Services	4
Total Assisted	9,506
Educational	
Diocesan Students in Other Seminaries	11
Total Seminarians	11
High Schools, Diocesan and Parish	3
Total Students	1,871
Elementary Schools, Diocesan and Parish	10
Total Students	4,186
Catechesis/Religious Education:	
High School Students	3,247
Elementary Students	6,382
Total Students Under Catholic Instruction	15,697
Teachers in the Diocese:	
Brothers	7
Lay Teachers	312
Vital Statistics	
Receptions into the Church:	
Infant Baptism Totals	1,768
Adult Baptism Totals	60
Received into Full Communion	159
First Communions	1,547
Confirmations	1,449
Marriages:	
Catholic	403
Interfaith	78
Total Marriages	481
Deaths	1,091
Total Catholic Population	97,993
Total Population	208,185

Former Bishops—Most Rev. WARREN L. BOUDREAUX, J.C.D., D.D., Retired Bishop of Houma-Thibodaux; ord. May 30, 1942; retired Dec. 29, 1992; died Oct. 6, 1997.

Chancery, *Address all correspondence to: P.O. Box 9077, Houma, 70361.* Office: *1801 Hwy. 311, Schriever, 70395.* Tel: 504-868-7720; Fax: 504-868-7727. Office Hours: Mon.-Fri. 8-5

Vicar General and Moderator of the Curia—Rev. Msgr. JAMES B. SONGY.

Chancellor—Rev. Msgr. JOSEPH N. LATINO.

Diocesan Tribunal, *Address all correspondence to: P.O. Box 9077, Houma, 70361.* Office: *1801 Hwy. 311, Schriever, 70395.* Tel: 504-850-3126

Judicial Vicar—Rev. VICENTE DELA CRUZ.

Judges—Rev. Msgr. WILLIAM KONINKX; Revs. BRENDAN FOLEY; JOHN A. GALLEN.

Defenders of the Bond—Rev. Msgr. JOSEPH N. LATINO; Revs. DANIEL M. POCHE; ROLANDO TIMBRE.

Counselor—Sr. KATERI BATTAGLIA, M.S.C.

Priests Council and College of Consultors—Rev. Msgr. JOSEPH N. LATINO; Rev. Msgr. JAMES B. SONGY; Revs. CARL COLLINS; ROCH NAQUIN; DANIEL POCHE; PATRICK KUJAWA; SHENAN BOQUET; PATRICK O'BRIEN; DEAN DANOS; Very Rev. OSCAR SOLIS, V.F., *Mailing Address: P.O. Box 9077, Houma, 70361. 1801 Hwy. 311, Schriever, 70395.*

Deans—Upper Lafourche Deanery: Very Rev. PATRICK O'BRIEN, *720 Talbot Ave., Thibodaux, 70301.* South Lafourche Deanery: Very Rev. OSCAR SOLIS, V.F., *Golden Meadow,* Terrebonne Deanery: Rev. Msgr. JOSEPH N. LATINO, V.F., *P.O. Box 4014, Houma, 70361.*

Diocesan Finance Council—Rev. WILFREDO DECAL; Rev. Msgr. FREDERIC J. BRUNET; Rev. Msgr. JOSEPH N. LATINO; A. J. CHAMPAGNE, JR.; ROBERT NAQUIN; Mr. LEE RINGEMAN; ANN BARKER.

Diocesan Pastoral Council—JAMES J. DANOS, Pres. RUSSELL DOMANGUE, Sec., *Mailing Address: P.O. Box 9077, Houma, 70361.*

Departments of the Diocesan Curia

Department of Administration Ministries:

Coordinator—DOUGLAS P. TOUPS, *1801 Hwy. 311, Schriever, 70395., Mailing Address: P.O. Box 9077, Houma, 70361.* Tel: 504-868-7720.

Accounting, Business Office, Finance, Insurance—DOUGLAS P. TOUPS, Business Mgr., *1801 Hwy. 311, Schriever, 70395., Mailing Address: P.O. Box 9077, Houma, 70361.* Tel: 504-868-7720.

Archives and Historical Research Center—Rev. Msgr. ROLAND J. BOUDREAUX, Dir., *205 Audubon St., Thibodaux, 70301.* Tel: 504-446-2383.

Building Commission—JAMES J. DANOS, Dir., *1801 Hwy. 311, Schriever, 70395., Mailing Address: P.O. Box 9077, Houma, 70361.* Tel: 504-868-7720.

Cemeteries—GEORGE COOKE, Dir., *949 Menard St., Thibodaux, 70301.* Tel: 504-446-0280.

Legal Services—Rev. Msgr. JAMES B. SONGY, Dir., *1801 Hwy. 311, Schriever, 70395., Mailing Address: P.O. Box 9077, Houma, 70361.* Tel: 504-868-7720. Attorneys: KENNETH WATKINS; DANIEL WALKER, *501 Roussell St., P.O. Box 5095, Houma, 70361.* Tel: 504-868-2333.

Stewardship and Development—Mr. J. C. CUNNINGHAM, Dir., *1801 Hwy. 311, Schriever, 70395., Mailing Address: P.O. Box 9077, Houma, 70361.* Tel: 504-868-7720.

Department for Clergy and Religious:

Coordinator—Rev. Msgr. JOSEPH N. LATINO, *1801 Hwy. 311, Schriever, 70395., Mailing Address: P.O. Box 9077, Houma, 70361.* Tel: 504-868-7720.

Clergy Personnel—Rev. Msgr. JOSEPH N. LATINO, *Mailing Address: P.O. Box 9077, Houma, 70361.* Tel: 504-868-7720.

Continuing Education of the Clergy-Ministry to Priests Program—Rev. GLENN LECOMPTE, Chm., *333 Twin Oaks, Raceland, 70394.* Rev. Msgr. FRANCIS LEGENDRE, Vicar for Priests, *15300 W. Main St., Cutoff, 70345.* Tel: 504-632-3858.

Permanent Diaconate—Deacon ROBERT DUSSE, *514 Gaynell Dr., Houma, 70364.* Tel: 504-876-5122., *1801 Hwy. 311, Schriever, 70395., Mailing Address: P.O. Box 9077, Houma, 70361.* Tel: 504-868-7720.

Vocations—Rev. JAY BAKER, *1801 Hwy. 311, Schriever, 70395., Mailing Address: P.O. Box 9077, Houma, 70361.* Tel: 504-868-7720.

Women Religious—Sr. BARBARA NELL LAPEROUSE, O.Carm., *902 Menard St., Thibodaux, 70301.* Tel: 504-447-9283.

Department of Formation Ministries:

Coordinator—LOUIS G. AGUIRRE, *1801 Hwy. 311, Schriever, 70395., Mailing Address: P.O. Box 9077, Houma, 70361.* Tel: 504-868-7720.

Campus Ministry—Rev. JAY BAKER, Dir., N.S.U., *Box 2051, Thibodaux, 70310.* Tel: 504-446-6201.

Catholic Schools—Sr. IMMACULATA PAISANT, M.S.C., Supt., *1801 Hwy. 311, Schriever, 70395., Mailing Address: P.O. Box 9077, Houma, 70361.* Tel: 504-868-7720.

Communications, Public Relations, Publications, Radio & Television—LOUIS G. AGUIRRE, Dir., *1801 Hwy. 311, Schriever, 70395., Mailing Address: P.O. Box 9077, Houma, 70361.* Tel: 504-868-7720.

Religious Education—Sr. FIONNUALA QUINN, O.P., Dir., *1801 Hwy. 311, Schriever, 70395., Mailing Address: P.O. Box 9077, Houma, 70361.* Tel: 504-868-7720.

Pastoral Staffing—Dr. MARIAN SCHWAB, Dir., *1801 Hwy. 311, Schriever, 70395., Mailing Address: P.O. Box 9077, Houma, 70361.* Tel: 504-868-7720.

"The Bayou Catholic"—(Diocesan Newspaper)—LOUIS G. AGUIRRE, Editor, *1801 Hwy. 311, Schriever, 70395., Mailing Address: P.O. Box 9077, Houma, 70361.* Tel: 504-868-7720.

Family Ministries—Sr. MARY KATERI BATTAGLIA, M.S.C., *1801 Hwy. 311, Schriever, 70395., Mailing Address: P.O. Box 9077, Houma, 70361.* Tel: 504-868-7720.

Worship—Rev. GLENN LECOMPTE, Dir., *1801 Hwy. 311, Schriever, 70395., Mailing Address: P.O. Box 9077, Houma, 70361.* Tel: 504-868-7720.

Youth Ministry—Bro. DOMINICK PUJIA, F.M.S., Dir., *1801 Hwy. 311, Schriever, 70395., Mailing Address: P.O. Box 9077, Houma, 70361.* Tel: 504-868-7720.

Department of Social Ministries:

Coordinator—Sr. MIRIAM MITCHELL, S.H.G., *1220 Aycock St., P.O. Box 883, Houma, 70361.* Tel: 504-876-0490.

Assisi Bridge House—Sr. MIRIAM MITCHELL, S.H.G., Dir., *Bull Run Rd., Schriever, 70395.* Tel: 504-872-5529. ROBERT GORMAN, Asst. Dir., *1220 Aycock St., P.O. Box 883, Houma, 70361.* Tel: 504-876-0490.

Campaign for Human Development—ROBERT GORMAN, Diocesan Dir., *1220 Aycock St., P.O. Box 3894, Houma, 70361.* Tel: 505-876-0490. Liaison for Catholic Relief Services, Respect Life, Justice and Peace.

Catholic Social Services—Sr. MIRIAM MITCHELL, S.H.G., Dir. ROBERT GORMAN, Asst. Dir., *1220 Aycock St., P.O. Box 3894, Houma, 70361.* Tel: 504-876-0490.

Disaster Relief—Sr. MIRIAM MITCHELL, S.H.G., Dir., *1220 Aycock St., P.O. Box 3894, Houma, 70361.* Tel: 504-876-0490.

St. Lucy's Day Care Center—BRENDA THOMAS, Admin., *1220 Aycock St., P.O. Box 3894, Houma, 70361.* Tel: 504-876-1246.

Other Offices and Commissions

Charismatic Renewal—Deacon ROBERT DUSSE, Dir., *1801 Hwy. 311, Schriever, 70394.* Tel: 504-868-7720.

Cursillo—Rev. ROCH R. NAQUIN, Dir., *5101 Grand Caillou Rd., Dulac, 70353.* Tel: 504-563-2325.

Ecumenism—Rev. WILMER TODD, Dir., *409 Funderburk Ave., Houma, 70364.* Tel: 504-879-1506.

Pontifical Societies for the Propagation of the Faith; Holy Childhood Association; Society of St. Peter the Apostle—Rev. NGUYEN VAN TY, Dir., *1027 Hwy. 308, Thibodaux, 70301.* Tel: 504-446-6663.

Scouting—Rev. SHENAN J. BOQUET, Dir., *1801 Hwy. 311, Schriever, 70395., Mailing Address: P.O. Box 9077, Houma, 70361.* Tel: 504-868-7720.

Organizations

Catholic Daughters of the Americas—Rev. Msgr. DONALD L. LEDET, Diocesan Advisor to State Court Officers, *3500 Hwy. 1, N., Raceland, 70394.* Tel: 504-537-3204.

Diocesan Council of St. Vincent de Paul Societies—AL JACKSON, Pres., *107 Point St., Houma, 70360.* Tel: 504-872-9373.

Knights of Columbus—Rev. Msgr. JOSEPH N. LATINO, Diocesan Chap., *P.O. Box 4014, Houma, 70361.* Tel: 504-876-6904.

Legion of Mary—ROSE M. MARCEAUX, Pres.; Rev. Msgr. JOSEPH N. LATINO, Spiritual Dir.

St. Vincent de Paul Store—Mr. PETER CAVALIER, Pres.; Mr. STERLING CHAISSON, Vice Pres. JAMES LEGARDE, Mgr., *107 Point St., Houma, 70360.* Tel: 504-872-9373.

Serra Club of Thibodaux—WILLIE ORGERON, Pres.

Serra Club of South Lafourche—Mr. BOBBY CHERAMIE, Pres.

Anawim—EVELYN RUCKSTUHL, Pres., *501 Grinage St., Houma, 70360.* Tel: 504-872-4761.

CLERGY, PARISHES, MISSIONS AND PAROCHIAL SCHOOLS

CITY OF HOUMA
(Parish Terrebonne)

1—CATHEDRAL OF ST. FRANCIS DE SALES (1847), Rev. Msgr. Joseph N. Latino; Rev. Lawrence A. Cavell. In res., Rev. Msgr. Emile Fossier.
Res., P.O. Box 4014, 70361. Tel: 504-876-6904; Fax: 504-851-4204. [CEM 2]
School—300 Verret St., 70361. Tel: 504-868-6646; Fax: 504-851-5896.
Lay Teachers 33; Students 828.
Catechesis/Religious Programs—Students 134.
Convent—501 Grinage St., 70361. Tel: 504-876-6904.

2—ANNUNZIATA (1963), Rev. James R. Morrison; Very Rev. Vincente Dela Cruz.
Res., 2323 Acadian Dr., 70363. Tel: 504-876-2971; Fax: 504-868-6414.
Catechesis/Religious Programs—Tel: 504-876-2865.
Students 345.

3—MARIA IMMACOLATA (1963), Rev. Caesar Silva; Deacon Douglas Authement.
Administration Office: 104 Corporate Dr., 70360. Tel: 504-876-3313; Fax: 504-879-2137.
Res., 326 Estate Dr., 70360. Tel: 504-868-4915.
School—324 Estate Dr., 70360. Tel: 504-876-1631; Fax: 504-876-1608.
Lay Teachers 19; Students 212.
Catechesis/Religious Programs—Students 370.

4—OUR LADY OF THE MOST HOLY ROSARY (1948). (Holy Rosary Church). Revs. Fred Link, O.F.M (Cincinnati); Paul Desch, O.F.M.; Louis Bartko. In res., Rev. Edwin Deane, O.F.M (Cincinnati); Deacons Raymond LeBouef; Harold Kurtz.
Res., 8594 Main St., 70363. Tel: 504-876-7652; Fax: 504-876-7647. [CEM]
Catechesis/Religious Programs—Tel: 504-876-7647. D.R.E.: Kathy Lirette; Debbie Hotard.
Students 360.

5—ST. BERNADETTE (1958), Revs. Wilmer Todd; Robert-Joel Cruz.
Res., 409 Funderburk Ave., 70364. Tel: 504-879-1506; Fax: 504-876-9654.
School—309 Funderburk Ave., 70364. Tel: 504-872-3854.
Lay Teachers 26; Students 470.
Catechesis/Religious Programs—Mrs. April Crochet, D.R.E.
Students 569.

6—ST. GREGORY BARBARIGO (1963), Rev. Wilfredo G. Decal.
Mailing Address: P.O. Box 1066, 70361.
Res., 439 Sixth St., 70364. Tel: 504-876-2003.
Administration Bldg.: 1005 Williams Ave., 70364. Tel: 504-876-2047; Fax: 504-876-0628.
School—441 Sixth St., 70364. Tel: 504-876-2038; Fax: 504-879-2789.
Lay Teachers 11; Students 226.
Catechesis/Religious Programs—Students 223.

7—ST. LOUIS (1965), Rev. Thomas R. Bouterie.
Res., 2226 Bayou Blue Rd., 70364. Tel: 504-876-3449; Fax: 504-876-6810. [CEM]
Catechesis/Religious Programs—Tel: 504-876-6810. Cheryl Griffin, D.R.E.
Students 475.

8—ST. LUCY, Rev. Fred J. Link, O.F.M.
Mailing Address: P.O. Box 3508, 70361. Tel: 504-879-2632; Fax: 504-876-4054.
Res., 1236 Aycock St., 70360.
Church—1222 Aycock St., 70360.
Catechesis/Religious Programs—Students 31.

CITY OF THIBODAUX
(Lafourche Parish)

1—ST. JOSEPH CO-CATHEDRAL (1817), Rev. Msgr. Francis J. Amedee; Revs. John Ruiz; Michael A. Bergeron; Deacon Willie R. Orgeron.
Res., 721 Canal Blvd., P.O. Box 966, 70302. Tel: 504-446-1387; Fax: 504-446-6571.
School—501 Cardinal Dr., 70301. Tel: 504-446-1346; Fax: 504-449-0760.
Lay Teachers 35; Students 725.
Catechesis/Religious Programs—Students 178.
Convent—212 Bayou Ln., 70301. Tel: 504-447-9283.

2—ST. CHARLES BORROMEO (1912), Rev. Nguyen Van Ty.
Res., 1027 Hwy. 308, 70301. Tel: 504-446-6663; Fax: 504-447-3348. [CEM]
Catechesis/Religious Programs—Students 194.

3—CHRIST THE REDEEMER (1983), Revs. Patrick O'Brien; Scott Dugas.
Res., 720 Talbot Ave., 70301. Tel: 504-447-2013; Fax: 504-447-4422. [CEM]
Catechesis/Religious Programs—Students 379.

4—ST. GENEVIEVE (1959), Revs. Joseph S. Pilola; Carlos S. Talavera.
Res., 815 Barbier Ave., 70301. Tel: 504-446-5571; Fax: 504-449-1939.
School—807 Barbier Ave., 70301. Tel: 504-447-9291.
Lay Teachers 26; Students 486.
Catechesis/Religious Programs—Tel: 504-446-5127.
Students 259.

5—ST. JOHN THE EVANGELIST (1919), Revs. Patrick O'Brien; Scott Dugas.
Res., 2085 Hwy. 1, 70301. Tel: 504-447-3995; Fax: 504-447-2092. [CEM]
Catechesis/Religious Programs—Students 310.

6—ST. LUKE, Rev. Msgr. Francis J. Amadee; Sr. Nancy McNemar, S.S.N.D., Pastoral Assoc.
Res., P.O. Box 1819, 70302. Tel: 504-446-0487; Fax: 504-446-4080.
Catechesis/Religious Programs—Students 65.

7—ST. THOMAS AQUINAS (1970), Rev. Jay L. Baker.
Res., Nicholls Sta., NSU Box 2051, 70310. Tel: 504-446-6201; Fax: 504-449-0710.

OUTSIDE THE CITIES OF HOUMA AND THIBODAUX

Amelia, St. Mary Parish, St. Andrew (1965), Rev. Charles J. Perkins.
Res., P.O. Box 310, 70340. Tel: 504-631-2333; Fax: 504-631-2334. [CEM]
Catechesis/Religious Programs—Students 100.
Thanh Gia (1981). Personal Parish for Vietnamese Community. Rev. Francis Bui.
Res., 711 Magnolia St., Morgan City, 70380. Tel: 504-631-3194; Fax: 504-631-2634.
Catechesis/Religious Programs—Students 110.
Domus Dei Institute, Inc.—Cypress St., Morgan City, 70380. Tel: 504-851-1351.

Bayou Black, Terrebonne Parish, St. Anthony (1876), Rev. Gerard C. Hayes.
Res., 3897 Bayou Black Dr., Houma, 70360. Tel: 504-872-0922; Fax: 504-872-2001.
Catechesis/Religious Programs—Students 215.

Bourg, Terrebonne Parish, St. Ann (1908), Rev. Guy P. Zeringue.
Res., 4355 Hwy. 24, P.O. Box 700, 70343. Tel: 504-594-3548; Fax: 504-594-3570. [CEM]
Catechesis/Religious Programs—Tel: 504-594-5088.
Students 471.

Chacahoula, Terrebonne Parish, St. Lawrence (1848), Sr. Fatima Robichaux, M.S.C., Pastoral Admin.
Res., 114 Carroll St., P.O. Box 229, Gibson, 70356. Tel: 504-575-3087; Fax: 504-575-8243. [CEM]

Chackbay, Lafourche Parish, Our Lady of Prompt Succor (1892), Rev. Roland Timbre.
Res., 529 Hwy. 20, Thibodaux, 70301. Tel: 504-633-2903; Fax: 504-633-9225. [CEM 2]
Catechesis/Religious Programs—Students 422.

Chauvin, Terrebonne Parish, St. Joseph (1948), Rev. Msgr. Frederic J. Brunet; Rev. Robert Sevigny.
Res., 5232 Hwy. 56, 70344. Tel: 504-594-5859; Fax: 504-594-2116. [CEM]
Catechesis/Religious Programs—Sharon Picou, D.R.E.
Students 650.
Missions—Cocodrie, Our Lady of the Gulf; Upper Little Caillou, Our Lady of Prompt Succor.

Cut-Off, Lafourche Parish, Sacred Heart (1923), Rev. Msgr. Francis J. Legendre; Rev. Sabino B. Rebosura, II.
Res., 15300 W. Main, 70345. Tel: 504-632-3858; Fax: 504-632-4452. [CEM]
Catechesis/Religious Programs—Tel: 504-632-6322.
Students 503.

Galliano, LaFourche Parish, St. Joseph (1958), Rev. Shenan J. Boquet.
Res., P.O. Box 516, 70354. Tel: 504-632-7321; Fax: 504-632-7345. [CEM]
Catechesis/Religious Programs—Students 302.

Gheens, LaFourche Parish, Community of St. Anthony. (Quasi Parish). Rev. Daniel M. Poche, Admin.
Res., P.O. Box 12, Mathews, 70375. Tel: 504-532-6497.
Catechesis/Religious Programs—Tel: 504-537-6002; Fax: 504-337-4408.
Students 134.

Gibson, Terrebonne Parish, St. Patrick (1920), Sr. Fatima Robichaux, M.S.C., Pastoral Admin.
Res., P.O. Box 229, 70356. Tel: 504-575-3087; Fax: 504-575-8243. [CEM]

Golden Meadow, LaFourche Parish, Our Lady of Prompt Succor (1916), Rev. Oscar A. Solis.
Res., 723 N. Bayou Dr., 70357. Tel: 504-475-5428; Fax: 504-475-7699.
Mission—Golden Meadow, Our Lady of La Salette. [CEM]
Catechesis/Religious Programs—Students 354.

Grand Caillou, Terrebonne Parish, Holy Family (1952), Rev. Jerome Webre.
Res., 5101 Grand Caillou Rd., Dulac, 70353. Tel: 504-563-2325; Fax: 504-563-4980. [CEM 2]
Catechesis/Religious Programs—Students 211.

Grand Isle, West Jefferson Parish, Our Lady of the Isle (1933), Rev. Warren F. Chassaniol.
Res., P.O. Box 885, 70358. Tel: 504-787-2385; Fax: 504-787-4530. [CEM]
Catechesis/Religious Programs—Students 116.

Kraemer, Lafourche Parish, St. Lawrence the Martyr (1962), Rev. Domingo Cruz.
Res., 1479 Hwy. 307, Thibodaux, 70301. Tel: 504-633-9431; Fax: 504-633-5706. [JC 2]
Mission—Choctaw, St. James, 1278 Choctaw Rd., Thibodaux, 70301. Tel: 504-633-9855. [CEM]
Catechesis/Religious Programs—Tel: 504-633-5714.
Students 170.

Larose, Lafourche Parish, Our Lady of the Rosary (1873), Revs. Dean F. Danos; Nghia Dink; Sr. Claire M. Rodrigue, C.I.C., Pastoral Assoc.
Res., Box 10, 70373. Tel: 504-693-3433; Fax: 504-693-7551. [CEM]
School—P.O. Box 40, 70373. Tel: 504-693-3342; Fax: 504-693-3348.
Sisters 1; Lay Teachers 12; Students 323.
Catechesis/Religious Programs—Tel: 504-693-3125. Camile Gautreaux, D.R.E.
Students 650.

Lockport, Lafourche Parish, Holy Savior (1850), Rev. Florentino Santiago.
Res., 612 Main St., 70374. Tel: 504-532-3533; Fax: 504-532-2010. [CEM]
School—201 Church St., 70374. Tel: 504-532-2536; Fax: 504-532-2269.
Lay Teachers 19; Students 296.
Catechesis/Religious Programs—Students 378.

Montegut, Terrebonne Parish, Sacred Heart (1864), Rev. Robert C. Rogers.
Res., P.O. Box 2, 70377. Tel: 504-594-5856; Fax: 504-594-8087. [CEM 2]
Catechesis/Religious Programs—Students 107.

Morgan City, St. Mary Parish, Sacred Heart of Jesus (1859), Rev. John A. Gallen.
Res., 415 Union St., P.O. Box 632, 70381. Tel: 504-385-0770; Fax: 504-384-7176.
Catechesis/Religious Programs—Tel: 504-384-8108.
Students 380.

Holy Cross (1964), Revs. Etienne LeBlanc; Patrick Kujawa; Deacon Andrew Dragna.
Res., P.O. Box 2623, 70381. Tel: 504-384-3551; Fax: 504-384-5790.
School—2100 Cedar St., Unit 2, 70381. Tel: 504-384-1933.
Lay Teachers 17; Students 405.
Catechesis/Religious Programs—Students 259.
Mission—Morgan City, St. Martin Parish, St. Rosalie, 1315 Stephensville Rd., 70380. Tel: 504-385-5713.

Pointe-Aux-Chenes, Terrebonne Parish, St. Charles Borromeo (1971), Rev. Robert C. Rogers.
Mailing Address: P.O. Box 54, Montegut, 70377.
Res., 531 Hwy. 665, Montegut, 70377. Tel: 504-594-6801; Fax: 504-594-6802. [CEM]
Catechesis/Religious Programs—Students 139.

Raceland, LaFourche Parish, St. Hilary of Poitiers (1965), Revs. Daniel M. Poche; Glenn D. LeCompte.
Res., 333 Twin Oaks, 70394. Tel: 504-537-6002; Fax: 504-537-4408.
Catechesis/Religious Programs—Students 527.

St. Mary's Nativity (1850), Rev. Msgr. Donald L. Ledet; Rev. Van L. Constant. In res., Very Rev. Stanislaus J. Manikowski.
Res., 3500 Hwy. 1, 70394. Tel: 504-537-3204; Fax: 504-537-3235. [CEM]
School—(Grades PreK-6) P.O. Box K, 70394. Tel: 504-537-7544; Fax: 504-537-4020.
Lay Teachers 8; Students 226.
Catechesis/Religious Programs—Students 233.

Schriever, Terrebonne Parish, St. Bridget (1912), Rev. Alexander M. Francisco.
Res., 100 Hwy. 311, 70395. Tel: 504-446-6801; Fax: 504-448-2764. [CEM]
Catechesis/Religious Programs—Students 275.

Theriot, Terrebonne Parish, St. Eloi (1875), Rev. Carl P. Collins; Deacons Glenn Porche; Daniel Bascle.
Res., 1335 Bayou Dularge Rd., 70397. Tel: 504-872-2946; Fax: 504-872-9961.
Catechesis/Religious Programs—Tel: 504-851-6893.
Students 164.

Chaplains of Public Institutions

HOUMA. *Terrebonne Parish General Hospital*. Rev. Loren Connell, O.F.M.

THIBODAUX. *Nicholls State University*. Rev. Jay Baker.
Thibodaux General Hospital. Rev. Toan Viet Vu.

Special and other Diocesan Assignment:
Reverend Monsignors—
Songy, James B., V.G.

On Duty Outside the Diocese:
Reverend Fathers—
Cao, John

On Leave:
Reverend Fathers—
Chaisson, Louis
Charpentier, Dale
Coyne, Joseph
Decell, Stephen
McCool, Malachy
Melancon, Robert
Prinz, Gerald
Violette, Tex

Retired:
Reverend Monsignors—
Boudreaux, Roland J., 142 Elmo Ln., Thibodaux, LA 70301
Koninkx, William, P.O. Box 1066, Houma, LA 70361
Reverend Fathers—
Bergeron, Albert G., Hollywood Park Apartments, 4000 West Bank Expwy., Apt. 65, Marrero, LA 70072
Brewerton, Peter H., P.O. Box 1404, Thibodaux, LA 70302
Broussard, Hubert C., Chateau Creole, 220 Monarch Dr., Apt. J13, Houma, LA 70360
Daigle, H.C. Paul, 1915 Branard St., Apt.16, Houston, TX 77098
Finnegan, Michael, Audubon Nursing Home
Foley, Brendan P., 182 E. 110th St., Galliano, LA 70354
Fossier, Emile, P.O. Box 4014, Houma, LA 70361
Landry, George A., 1016 France St., New Orleans, LA 70117
Luu, Joseph
Manikowski, Stanislaus J., P.O. Box 527, Raceland, LA 70394
Naquin, Roch, 539 Island Rd., Montegut, LA 70377
Newfield, John L., 2832 Burdette St., Apt. 428, New Orleans, LA 70125-2514
Pol, Dom Te, 3596 Friendswood, Apt.#6, Houma, LA 70363
Richardson, Albert, 3730 Fairfield Ave., Shreveport, LA 71104
Toth, Victor, 57 Marcus Mitchell Rd., Picayune, MS 39466
Whitney, Philip, 1201 Cardinal Dr., Thibodaux, LA 70302

Permanent Deacons:
Authement, Douglas, Maria Immacolata, Houma
Bascle, Daniel, St. Eloi, Theriot
Blanchard, Edward, St. Mary's Nativity, Raceland
Burregi, Sammy, Sacred Heart, Cut Off
Cantrelle, Michael, Holy Rosary, Larose
Didier, James V., St. Bridget Church, Schriever
Domangue, Kurt J., Holy Family Church, Grand Caillou
Dragna, Andrew J., Holy Cross, Morgan City
Dufrene, Roland, St. Hilary of Poitiers, Raceland
Dusse, Robert, St. Bernadette, Houma
Duthu, James, Annunziata, Houma
Fanguy, Bernard A. Harold, Holy Family, Grand Caillou
Giroir, Charles, Christ the Redeemer, Thibodaux
Hopkins, James, Holy Savior, Lockport
Kurtz, Harold, Our Lady of the Most Holy Rosary, Houma
Landry, Alduce, St. Charles, Thibodaux
LeBouef, Raymond, Holy Rosary, Houma
Legendre, Paul Joseph, Jr., St. Genevieve, Thibodaux
Marts, Melvin, St. Joseph, Galliano
Messina, Nick, St. Anthony, Bayou Black
Orgeron, Willie R., St. Joseph Co-Cathedral, Thibodaux
Porche, Glenn, St. Eloi, Theriot
Pujals, Pedro P., St. Thomas Aquinas, Thibodaux
Rabalais, Bertrand A., Annunziata, Houma
Uzee, Dickey, St. Mary's Nativity, Raceland

INSTITUTIONS LOCATED IN THE DIOCESE

[A] HIGH SCHOOLS, DIOCESAN

HOUMA. *Vandebilt Catholic High*, 209 S. Hollywood Rd., 70360. Tel: 504-876-2551; Fax: 504-868-9774.
E-mail: vchs@cajun.net
Web site: HTTP:11wwwz.cajun/~vchs/Index./HTML
Brothers of the Sacred Heart. Mr. David Keife, Prin.; Bro. Carl Evans, S.C., Chap. Brothers 3; Lay Teachers 58; Junior High Students 365; Senior High Students 530.

THIBODAUX. *Edward Douglas White Catholic High*. (Coed), 555 Cardinal Dr., 70301. Tel: 504-446-8486; Fax: 504-448-1275. Brothers of the Sacred Heart. Mr. Gary Phillips, Prin. Brothers 4; Lay Teachers 53; Students 787.
E.D. White Catholic High School Foundation, Inc.
E.D. White Catholic High School Alumni Association.

MORGAN CITY. *Central Catholic High*, 2100 Cedar St., 70380. Tel: 504-385-5372; Fax: 504-385-3444. Mr. Jordan Roy, Prin.; Patricia Roland, Guidance Counselor. Lay Teachers 19; Students 190.

[B] DAY CARE CENTERS

HOUMA. *St. Lucy's Day Care and Child Development Center*, P.O. Box 3894, 70361. Tel: 504-876-1246. Staff 10; Children 65.

[C] RETREAT CENTERS

SCHRIEVER. *Lumen Christi Retreat Center*, 100 Lumen Christi Ln., Hwy. 311, 70395. Tel: 504-868-1523; Fax: 504-868-1525. Rev. Duane R. Stenzel, O.F.M., Dir.

[D] CONVENTS

LOCKPORT. *Monastery of the Heart of Jesus*, 155 Church St., 70374. Dominican Contemplative Sisters of the Heart of Jesus of the Diocese of Houma-Thibodaux. Sr. Mary Henry McKanna, O.P., Prioress.

[E] MISCELLANEOUS

THIBODAUX. *Cemeteries Trust*, 949 Menard St., 70301. Tel: 504-446-0280; Fax: 504-446-1341.
The Diocese of Houma-Thibodaux Historical Research Center, 205 Audubon Ave., 70301. Tel: 504-446-2383; Fax: 504-449-0574. Rev. Msgr. Roland J. Boudreaux, Archivist.
Magnificat of the Houma-Thibodaux Diocese, 306 Cherokee Dr., 70301. Bonnie J. Bourg, Coord., Bayou River Chapter.
St. Joseph Manor. (Retirement Center), 1201 Cardinal Dr., 70301. Tel: 504-446-9050. Rev. Msgr. Francis J. Amedee, Exec. Dir.

RELIGIOUS INSTITUTES OF MEN REPRESENTED IN THE DIOCESE

For further details refer to the corresponding bracketed number in the Religious Institutes of Men or Women section.
[1100]—*Brothers of the Sacred Heart*.—S.C.
[0520]—*Franciscan Friars*.—O.F.M.
[1360]—*Xaverian Missionary Brothers*.—S.X.

RELIGIOUS INSTITUTES OF WOMEN REPRESENTED IN THE DIOCESE

[0400]—*Congregation of Our Lady of Mount Carmel*.—O.Carm.
[2550]—*Sisters of Mercy*.—R.S.M.
[2410]—*Congregation of the Marianites of Holy Cross*.—M.S.C.
[]—*Dominican Contemplative Sisters*.—O.P.
[]—*Dominican Sisters*. (Cabra, Ireland).—O.P.
[1140]—*Eucharistic Missionaries of St. Dominic*.—O.P.
[2970]—*School Sisters of Notre Dame*.—S.S.N.D.
[3830]—*Sisters of St. Joseph*.—C.S.J.
[2050]—*Sisters of the Holy Spirit and Mary Immaculate*.—S.H.Sp.
[2120]—*Sisters of the Immaculate Conception*.—C.I.C.

NECROLOGY

✠ Boudreaux, Most Rev. Warren Louis, (Retired). —Died Oct. 6, 1997.

Archdiocese of Indianapolis

(Archidioecesis Indianapolitana)

Most Reverend

DANIEL MARK BUECHLEIN, O.S.B., D.D.

Archbishop of Indianapolis; ordained May 3, 1964; appointed to Memphis January 20, 1987; consecrated Bishop March 2, 1987; installed March 2, 1987; appointed Archbishop of Indianapolis July 13, 1992; installed September 9, 1992.

The Archbishop Edward T. O'Meara Catholic Center: 1400 N. Meridian St., P.O. Box 1410, Indianapolis, IN, 46206. Tel.: 317-236-1400; Fax: 317-236-1401.

E-mail address: chancery@archindy.org

ESTABLISHED A DIOCESE IN 1834; ESTABLISHED AN ARCHDIOCESE DECEMBER 19, 1944. BY DECREE OF POPE PIUS XII

Square Miles 13,757.7.

Comprises the Counties of Bartholomew, Brown, Clark, Clay, Crawford, Dearborn, Decatur, Fayette, Floyd, Franklin, Hancock, Harrison, Hendricks, Henry, Jackson, Jefferson, Jennings, Johnson, Lawrence, Marion, Monroe, Morgan, Ohio, Orange, Owen, Parke, Perry, Putnam, Ripley, Rush, Scott, Shelby, Switzerland, Union, Vermillion, Vigo, Washington and Wayne, and the township of Harrison in Spencer County, in the southern part of Indiana.

For legal titles of parishes and archdiocesan institutions, consult the Chancery Office.

STATISTICAL OVERVIEW

Personnel	
Archbishop	1
Abbots	1
Retired Abbots	2
Priests: Diocesan Active in Diocese	120
Priests: Active Outside Diocese	5
Priests: Diocesan in Foreign Missions	1
Priests: Retired, Sick or Absent	38
Number of Diocesan Priests	164
Religious Priests in Diocese	115
Extern Priests in Diocese	12
Ordinations:	
Diocesan Priests	3
Religious Priests	2
Total Brothers	53
Total Sisters	780
Parishes	
Parishes	138
With Resident Pastor:	
Resident Diocesan Priests	100
Resident Religious Priests	23
Without Resident Pastor:	
Administered by Priests	6
Administered by Women Religious	9
Missions	13
Professional Ministry Personnel:	
Brothers	5
Sisters	35
Lay Ministers	152
Welfare	
Catholic Hospitals	2
Total Assisted	1,147,664
Homes for the Aged	5
Total Assisted	797
Day Care and Extended Day Care Centers	5
Total Assisted	348
Specialized Homes	3
Total Assisted	688
Special Centers for Social Services	9
Total Assisted	70,799
Educational	
Diocesan Students in Other Seminaries	26
Seminaries, Religious	1
Students Religious	122
Total Seminarians	148
Colleges and Universities	3
Total Students	2,675
High Schools, Diocesan and Parish	6
Total Students	3,173
High Schools, Private	3
Total Students	1,948
Elementary Schools, Diocesan and Parish	62
Total Students	19,854
Catechesis/Religious Education:	
High School Students	3,138
Elementary Students	14,479
Total Students Under Catholic Instruction	45,415
Teachers in the Diocese:	
Brothers	5
Sisters	53
Lay Teachers	1,425
Vital Statistics	
Receptions into the Church:	
Infant Baptism Totals	4,350
Adult Baptism Totals	684
Received into Full Communion	852
First Communions	3,557
Confirmations	2,276
Marriages:	
Catholic	672
Interfaith	743
Total Marriages	1,415
Deaths	1,979
Total Catholic Population	219,247
Total Population	2,201,503

The Diocese of Vincennes (now Indianapolis) was established by decree of Gregory XVI, May 6, 1834, and the See was fixed at Vincennes. The territory then comprised the entire State of Indiana and the eastern third of Illinois. By decree of Pius IX, January 8, 1857, the northern half of the State became the Diocese of Fort Wayne. The southern half of the State remained the Diocese of Vincennes.

The second Bishop of Vincennes, by Apostolic Brief, was permitted to establish his residence either at Vincennes, Madison, Lafayette or Indianapolis; the See city, however, was to remain at Vincennes. This permission was renewed to the fourth Bishop, with the exception of Lafayette. On the appointment of the fifth Bishop, he was directed to fix his residence at Indianapolis, but the Cathedral and title of the See were continued at Vincennes. By an Apostolic Brief dated March 28, 1898, the title of the Diocese was changed to that of "Diocese of Indianapolis" with the city of Indianapolis as the Episcopal See. By the same Brief the Patron Saint of the Diocese was to remain St. Francis Xavier, the title of the old Cathedral in Vincennes.

On December 19, 1944, Most Reverend Amleto Giovanni Cicognani, Apostolic Delegate to the United States, solemnly proclaimed the Papal Decree of Pope Pius XII in SS. Peter and Paul Cathedral, Indianapolis, elevating Indianapolis to the status of an Archdiocese, the State of Indiana being the Metropolitan Area. The Dioceses of Evansville and Lafayette-in-Indiana were created by the same decree and were made Suffragan Sees of Indianapolis. Upon the establishment of the Diocese of Gary on December 17, 1956, it too became a Suffragan See.

Former Bishops—Rt. Rev. SIMON GABRIEL BRUTE, S.S., D.D., cons. 1834; died 1839.—Rt. Rev. CELESTINE DE LA HAILANDIERE, D.D., cons. 1839; resigned 1847; died in France, 1882.—Rt. Rev. JOHN S. BAZIN, D.D., cons. 1847; died 1848.—Rt. Rev. MAURICE DE ST. PALAIS, D.D., cons. Jan. 14, 1849; died June 28, 1877.—Rt. Rev. FRANCIS SILAS CHATARD, D.D., cons. May 12, 1878; died Sept. 7, 1918.—Most Rev. JOSEPH CHARTRAND, D.D., cons. Titular Bishop of Flavias and Coadjutor Bishop, Sept. 15, 1910; succeeded to the See of Indianapolis, Sept. 7, 1918; died Dec. 8, 1933.—Most Rev. JOSEPH ELMER RITTER, S.T.D., cons. Titular Bishop of Hippo and Auxiliary Bishop, March 28, 1933; succeeded to the See March 24, 1934; installed as Archbishop Dec. 19, 1944; transferred to Metropolitan See of St. Louis, July 20, 1946; created Cardinal, Jan. 16, 1961; died June 10, 1967.—Most Rev. PAUL C. SCHULTE, D.D., cons. Bishop of Leavenworth, Sept. 21, 1937; appt. Archbishop of Indianapolis, July 20, 1946; installed Oct. 10, 1946; resigned Jan. 14, 1970; died Feb. 17, 1984.—Most Rev. GEORGE J. BISKUP, cons. Titular Bishop of Hermeria and Auxiliary of Dubuque, April 24, 1957; transferred to Des Moines Feb. 3, 1965 transferred to Indianapolis "cum jure successionis," July 26, 1967; succeeded to See Jan. 14, 1970; resigned March 20, 1979; died Oct. 17, 1979.—Most Rev. EDWARD T. O'MEARA, S.T.D., appt. Titular Bishop of Thisiduo and Auxiliary of St. Louis Feb. 1, 1972; cons. in the Basilica of St. Peter, Rome, Feb. 13, 1972; appt. Archbishop of Indianapolis Nov. 27, 1979; installed Jan. 10, 1980; died Jan. 10, 1992.

Archdiocesan Administration—Secretariats/Vicariates/Agencies and Office can be contacted through The Archbishop Edward T. O'Meara Catholic Center. *1400 N. Meridian St., Indianapolis, 46202., Address all mail unless otherwise indicated to:: P.O. Box 1410, Indianapolis, 46206-1410.* Tel: 317-236-1400; Fax: 317-236-1401.

Vicar General and Moderator of the Curia—Very Rev. JOSEPH F. SCHAEDEL, M.S., M.Div.

Chancellor—SUZANNE L. MAGNANT.

Assistant Chancellor—Rev. WILLIAM STUMPF.

Chief Financial Officer—JOSEPH B. HORNETT.

Board of Consultors—Most Rev. DANIEL M. BUECHLEIN, O.S.B., D.D., Chm.; Very Rev. JOSEPH F. SCHAEDEL, M.S., M.Div.; Rev. Msgr. FRANCIS R. TUOHY; Revs. J. PETER GALLAGHER; STANLEY HERBER; PAUL KOETTER; DANIEL MAHAN; DANIEL STAUBLIN; ANTHONY VOLZ.

Deaneries and Deans—Rev. PATRICK DOYLE, Indianapolis North; Rev. JOSEPH RIEDMAN, Indianapolis East; Rev. Msgr. RICHARD LAWLER, V.F., Indianapolis

South; Rev. JOHN RYAN, V.F., Indianapolis West; Rev. WILLIAM FARRIS, O.F.M., V.F., Batesville; Rev. CHARLES S. CHESEBROUGH, V.F., Bloomington; Rev. STANLEY J. HERBER, V.F., Connersville; Rev. JOHN BEITANS, V.F., New Albany; Rev. JOHN MEYER, Seymour; Rev. JEREMY KING, O.S.B., Tell City; Rev. JOSEPH KERN, Terre Haute.

Council of Priests—Most Rev. DANIEL M. BUECHLEIN, O.S.B., D.D., Pres. SUZANNE MAGNANT; Very Rev. JOSEPH F. SCHAEDEL, M.S., M.Div.; Revs. JAMES BYRNE; NOAH CASEY, O.S.B.; THOMAS CLEGG; FRANK ECKSTEIN; MICHAEL FRITSCH; J. PETER GALLAGHER; ROBERT GILDAY; JOHN HALL; PATRICK KELLY; JEREMY KING, O.S.B.; PAUL KOETTER; HERMAN LUTZ; DANIEL MAHAN; TODD RIEBE, M.C.C.J.; PAUL SHIKANY, Chm.; Rev. Msgr. FRANCIS R. TUOHY; Revs. CLIFFORD VOGELSANG; MICHAEL WELCH, Chm.

Finance Council—Most Rev. DANIEL M. BUECHLEIN, O.S.B., D.D., Chm.; Very Rev. JOSEPH F. SCHAEDEL, M.S., M.Div.; JOSEPH B. HORNETT, C.F.O. L. H. BAYLEY; MICHAEL BINDNER; JAY BREHM; MIKE DILTS; JOSEPH NAUGHTON; DENNIS SCHLICHTE; DONALD WILLIAMS. Tel: 317-236-1421.

Priests' Personnel Board—Most Rev. DANIEL M. BUECHLEIN, O.S.B., D.D.; Revs. PATRICK DOYLE; WILLIAM ERNSTES; GERALD KIRKHOFF; JOSEPH MCNALLY; RAYMOND SCHAFER; WILLIAM STUMPF; LARRY VOELKER; JAMES WILMOTH, Chm.

Secretariat for Catholic Charities and Family Ministries—THOMAS GAYBRICK, M.S.W., Sec. Tel: 317-236-1560.

Family Ministries—DAVID BATHURAM, Assoc. Sec. Tel: 317-236-1596.

Bloomington Catholic Social Services—KAREN BROSIUS, M.S.W., Dir., *511 S. Madison St., Bloomington, 47403*. Tel: 812-332-1262.

Campaign for Human Development—GRACE HAYES, Dir. Tel: 317-236-1559.

Catholic Social Services of Central Indiana—TOM COLBERT, Exec. Dir. Tel: 317-236-1500.

Deanery Counseling Services—

Batesville Deanery—RENEE RUST, M.A. Tel: 812-663-2113.

Seymour Deanery—CECILE BEAVIN. Tel: 812-342-1900.

Multicultural Ministry—Rev. KENNETH TAYLOR, Dir. Tel: 317-236-1596.

New Albany Deanery Catholic Charities—BARBARA WILLIAMS, M.S., Dir., *702 E. Market St., New Albany, 47150*. Tel: 812-948-0438.

Pro-Life Activities—Rev. VINCENT LAMPERT, Dir. Tel: 317-236-1569.

St. Elizabeth's—(Pregnancy Services); MARY ROSE NEVITT, Exec. Dir., *2500 Churchman Ave., Indianapolis, 46203*. Tel: 317-635-1491.

St. Elizabeth's Regional Maternity Center—(Pregnancy Services); KEITH E. STORMES, Exec. Dir., *601 E. Market St., New Albany, 47150*. Tel: 812-949-7305.

St. Mary's Child Center—Dr. PATRICIA WELCH, Exec. Dir., *901 Dr. Martin Luther King, Jr. St., Indianapolis, 46202*. Tel: 317-635-1491.

Tell City Catholic Charities—*802 Ninth St., Tell City, 47586*. Tel: 812-547-6414.

Terre Haute Catholic Charities—JOHN ETLING, M.S., Dir., *Corporate Square Annex, 2931 Ohio Blvd., Terre Haute, 47803*. Tel: 812-232-1447.

Youth and Family Ministries—DAVID BETHURAM, Exec. Dir. Tel: 317-236-1439.

Secretariat for Catholic Education and Faith Formation—DANIEL J. ELSENER, Sec. Tel: 317-236-1435.

Administration—G. JOSEPH PETERS, Assoc. Exec. Dir. Tel: 317-236-1437.

Faith Formation—JOSEPH M. KAPPEL, Assoc. Exec. Dir. Tel: 317-236-1431.

Catholic Youth Organization—EDWARD TINDER, Exec. Dir., *580 Stevens St., Indianapolis, 46203*. Tel: 317-632-9311.

Secretariat for Finance and Administrative Services—JOSEPH B. HORNETT, Sec. Tel: 317-236-1421.

Accounting Services—JEFF STUMPF, Controller. Tel: 317-236-1410.

Parish Financial Consultants—MIKE VOLK, Mgr. Tel: 317-236-3370.

Information Services—TOM O'DROBINAK, Dir. Tel: 317-236-1420.

Management Services—DAVID L. HODDE, Dir. Tel: 317-236-1452.

Catholic Cemeteries—GENE HARRIS, Dir., *9001 N. Haverstick Rd., Indianapolis, 46240*. Tel: 317-574-8898.

Roman Catholic Archdiocese of Indianapolis Properties—Most Rev. DANIEL M. BUECHLEIN, O.S.B., Pres.; Very Rev. JOSEPH F. SCHAEDEL, Vice Pres. Secretaries: SUZANNE L. MAGNANT; JOSEPH B. HORNETT. Tel: 317-236-1421.

Secretariat for Lay Ministry and Pastoral Services—SUZANNE L. MAGNANT, Sec. Tel: 317-236-7325.

Archives—JANET NEWLAND, Assoc. Archivist. Tel: 317-236-1429.

Archdiocesan Historian—Rev. JACK W. PORTER, Ph.D., Office in Archives:: Tel: 317-592-4073.

Human Resources—ED ISAKSON, Dir. Tel: 317-236-1594.

Lay Ministry—SUZANNE MAGNANT, Dir. Tel: 317-236-7325.

Parish Planning and Organizational Development—SUZANNE MAGNANT, Dir. Tel: 317-236-7325.

Secretariat for Spiritual Life and Worship—CHARLES GARDNER, Sec. Tel: 317-236-1483.

Archdiocesan Cathedral—Rev. RICHARD GINTHER, Pastor & Rector, *1347 N. Meridian St., Indianapolis, 46202-2396*. Tel: 317-634-4519.

Evangelization Commission—Rev. JOSEPH FOLZENLOGEN, S.J., Coord. Tel: 317-236-1489.

Office of Worship—CHARLES GARDNER, Dir. Tel: 317-236-1483.

Retreat & Renewal Ministries and Fatima Retreat House—KEVIN DEPREY, Dir., *5353 E. 56th St., Indianapolis, 46226*. Tel: 317-545-7681; Fax: 317-545-0095.

Secretariat for Stewardship and Communications—DANIEL CONWAY, Sec. Tel: 317-236-1407.

Archdiocesan Newspaper, "The Criterion"—Most Rev. DANIEL M. BUECHLEIN, O.S.B, D.D., Publisher; DANIEL CONWAY, Assoc. Publisher; WILLIAM BRUNS, Exec. Editor. Tel: 317-236-1507.

Mission Office—Sr. MARIAN T. KINNEY, S.P., Dir. Tel: 317-236-1485.

Catholic Communications Center—SUE ELLEN HETZLER, Dir. Tel: 317-236-1585.

Catholic Community Foundation, Inc.—Most Rev. DANIEL M. BUECHLEIN, O.S.B., D.D., Chm. SANDRA BEHRINGER, Dir. Endowment Devel. Tel: 317-236-1427.

Office of Stewardship and Development—MICHAEL HALLORAN, Exec. Dir. Tel: 317-236-1425.

Vicariate of Clergy and Parish Life Coordinators: Formation and Personnel—Rev. WILLIAM STUMPF, Vicar. Tel: 317-236-1495.

Ministry to Priests—Rev. NOAH CASEY, O.S.B., Dir. Tel: 317-236-1491.

Personnel: Priests and Parish life Corrdinators—Rev. WILLIAM STUMPF, Dir. Tel: 317-236-1449.

Priestly and Religious Vocations—Rev. PAUL ETIENNE, Dir. Tel: 317-236-1490.

Vicariate Judicial Metropolitan Tribunal—Rev. FREDERICK EASTON, J.C.L., Judicial Vicar. Tel: 317-236-1460.

Vice Vicars Judicial—Revs. ROBERT J. GILDAY, S.T.B.; PAUL M. SHIKANY, J.C.L.

Judge Instructor—JEAN GALANTI, B.A.

Advocates—REBECCA BARNES; KATHERINE LOZANO, B.A.; CATHERINE LOUGH, B.A.

Defender of the Bond—Rev. Msgr. CHARLES E. ROSS, J.C.L.; Revs. JAMES R. BONKE, J.C.L.; NATHANIAL REEVES, O.S.B.; JOSEPH W. DOOLEY, J.C.L.

Deputy Defender of the Bond—DIANE LIPTACK, J.D.

Archdiocesan Judges—Revs. CLEMENT DAVIS, M.Div.; JOHN DEDE, J.C.D.; BERNARD HEAD, M.A., S.T.L.; HERMAN LUTZ, S.T.L., J.C.L.; RICHARD MUELLER, S.T.L.; JOHN SCIARRA, Ad Hoc Archdiocesan Judge; Rev. Msgr. FRANCIS TUOHY, J.C.L., P.A.

Notaries—BARBARA ADAMS; CATHERINE FISLAR, B.S.; PEGGY FLECKER.

Indiana Provincial Tribunal of Second Instance—Rev. FREDERICK EASTON, J.C.L., Vicar Judicial.

Groups with Liaison to the Archdiocese

Activities for the National Shrine of the Immaculate Conception, Washington, D.C.—Rev. JOHN BEITANS, Archdiocesan Dir., *8310 St. John Rd., Floyds Knob, 47119*. Tel: 812-923-5785.

Archdiocesan Black Catholics Concerned—Bro. HOWARD P. STUDIVANT, O.S.B., *P.O. Box 88078, Indianapolis, 46208-0078*.

Archdiocesan Council of Catholic Women—Mrs. JOYCE SCHMITT, Pres.; Rev. ALBERT AJAMIE, Chap., *3423 Cartersburg Rd., Danville, 46122*. Tel: 317-539-5173.

Archdiocesan Deaf Apostolate—Rev. BERNARD COX, Dir., *1711 "I" St., Bedford, 47421*. Tel: 812-275-6539. Rev. JOSEPH W. DOOLEY, *8021 Guion Rd., Indianapolis, 46268*. Tel: 317-872-5485. Rev. JOSEPH PESOLA, *St. Pius X Parish*. Tel: 317-255-4534.

Beginning Experience—*Family Life Office, P.O. Box 1410, Indianapolis, 46206*. Tel: 317-236-1596.

Boy Scouts of America and Girl Scouts of America—Rev. THOMAS L. SCHLIESSMANN, Archdiocesan Chap., *270 S. Bond St., Scottsburg, 47170*. Tel: 812-752-3693. KERRY D. BLANFORD, Chm., Catholic Committee on Scouting, *456 E. Epler Ave., Indianapolis, 46227*. Tel: 317-782-0437.

Catholic Charismatic Renewal of Central Indiana—LEN BIELSKI, State Rep., *2960 N. Meridian St., Indianapolis, 46201*. Tel: 317-547-8100. Rev. PAUL LANDWERLEN, Liaison for Archdiocese, *4218 E. Michigan Rd., Shelbyville, 46176*. Tel: 317-398-4028.

Censor of Books—Very Rev. JOSEPH F. SCHAEDEL; Revs. MATTHIAS NEUMAN, O.S.B.; DANIEL MAHAN.

Catholic Widowed Organization—*Family Life Office, P.O. Box 1410, Indianapolis, 46206*. Tel: 317-236-1596.

Cursillo—DICK SHRIVER, Lay Dir., *8445 E. State Rd. 334, Zionsville, 46077*. Tel: 317-873-4443. Rev. GLENN O'CONNOR, Spiritual Dir.

Daughters of Isabella—ROSEMARY COX, *69 Stoneybrook Dr., Greenwood, 46142*.

Equiestrian Order of the Holy Sepulchre of Jerusalem—North Central Lieutenancy. GEORGE MALEY, State Rep., *4521 N. Meridian St., Indianapolis, 46208*.

Focolare - New Families Movement—JOHN WELCH; MARY WELCH. Tel: 317-845-8133.

Hibernians, Ancient Order of—PATRICK MILES, Pres.; Rev. GLENN O'CONNOR, Chap., *1911 Southern Ave., Beech Grove, 46107*. Tel: 317-783-9441.

Holy Childhood Association—Sr. MARIAN KINNEY, S.P., Dir.

Indiana Catholic Conference—Dr. M. DESMOND RYAN, Exec. Sec., *1400 N. Meridian St., P.O. Box 1410, Indianapolis, 46206*. Tel: 317-236-1455.

Indiana Interreligious Commission on Human Equality—*1100 W. 42nd St., Indianapolis, 46208*. Tel: 317-924-4226. Representatives: Rev. THOMAS MURPHY; LILLIAN STEVENSON.

Knights of Columbus—FREDERICK M. SCHRAMM, Pres., Indianapolis Chapter, *701 E. 700 N., Fortville, 46040*. Tel: 317-326-2593.

Knights and Ladies of Peter Claver—Indianapolis Central Committee. VIVIAN HILL THOMAS, Pres., *3688 Birchwood Ave., Indianapolis, 46205*.

Knights of St. John—DON SPRINGMEYER, Indiana Grand Commander, *214 W. 2nd St., Greensburg, 47240*. Tel: 812-663-3544.

Latvian Catholic Association—JANIS SVENTECKIS, Pres., *5849 Brouse Ave., Indianapolis, 46220*. Tel: 317-253-4684. Rev. JOHN BEITANS, Chap., *8310 St. John Rd., Floyds Knob, 47119*. Tel: 812-923-5785.

Legatus Society/Indiana—AL LANGSENKAMP, Pres., *Sigma/Micro Corp., 714 N. Senate, Indianapolis, 46202*. Tel: 317-631-0907. Very Rev. JOSEPH SCHAEDEL, Chap., *1400 N. Meridian, Indianapolis, 46202*.

Marriage Encounter of Central Indiana—*Family Life Office, P.O. Box 1410, Indianapolis, 46206*. Tel: 317-236-1596.

Oblates of St. Benedict of Our Lady of Grace Monastery—Sr. ANTOINETTE PURCELL, O.S.B., Dir., *1402 Southern Ave., Beech Grove, 46107*. Tel: 317-787-3287.

Oblates of St. Benedict of St. Meinrad—Rev. MEINRAD BRUNE, O.S.B., Dir., *St. Meinrad, 47577*. Tel: 812-357-6564; 357-6611.

St. Thomas More Society—PATRICIA MARSHALL, Pres., *One Indiana Sq., Indianapolis, 46204*. Tel: 317-634-9777. Rev. THOMAS J. MURPHY, Chap., *126 W. Georgia St., Indianapolis, 46225*. Tel: 317-635-2021.

Secular Franciscan Order—Holy Stigmata Fraternity and Sacred Heart Fraternity. Rev. ELIAS KOPPERT, O.F.M., Spiritual Asst., *Sacred Heart Church, 1530 Union St., Indianapolis, 46225*. Tel: 317-638-5551. People of Peace Fraternity. Sr. NORMA ROCKLAGE, O.S.F., Spiritual Asst., *Marion College, 3200 Cold Spring Rd., Indianapolis, 46222*. Tel: 317-929-0229.

Secular Order of Discalced Carmelites—Indianapolis: Sr. JEAN MARIE HESSBURG, Spiritual Advisor, *Monastery of the Resurrection, 2500 Cold Spring Rd., Indianapolis, 46222*. Tel: 317-926-5654. Terre Haute: Sr. THERESA HEWITT, Spiritual Advisor, *Monastery of St. Joseph, 59 Allendale, Terre Haute, 47802*. Tel: 812-299-1410.

Serra Club—Indianapolis: THOMAS SPENCER, Pres., *210 E. 82nd St., Indianapolis, 46240*. Tel: 317-255-1979. Rev. THOMAS MURPHY, Chap.; Terre Haute: ROD BOSLEY, Pres., *219 1/2 S. 19th St., Terre Haute, 47803*. Tel: 812-238-7411. Rev. LAWRENCE J. MORAN, Chap.

Society of St. Raphael - A Catholic Physician's Guild—Very Rev. JOSEPH F. SCHAEDEL, M.S., M.Div., Chap. Coordinators: Dr. PAUL MULLER; Dr. NICETA BRADBURN; Dr. DAMIAN EVERSMAN, *The O'Meara Catholic Center, P.O. Box 1410, Indianapolis, 46206*. Tel: 317-236-1585.

Sovereign Military Order of Malta—EUGENE WITCHGER, Archdiocesan Rep., *210 W. 77th St., Indianapolis, 46260*.

Teams of Our Lady—*Family Life Office, P.O. Box 1410, Indianapolis, 46206*. Tel: 317-236-1596. CARL WEBER. Tel: 317-353-8186. MARIE WEBER. Tel: 317-353-8186.

Tobit—GARY MEISTER, Council Pres., *Fatima Retreat House, 5353 E. 56th St., Indianapolis, 46226*. Tel: 317-545-7681.

Young Widowed Group—*Family Life Office, P.O. Box 1410, Indianapolis, 46206*. Tel: 317-236-1596.

CLERGY, PARISHES, MISSIONS AND PAROCHIAL SCHOOLS

CITY OF INDIANAPOLIS
(Marion County)

1—SS. PETER AND PAUL CATHEDRAL (1892), Rev. Richard M. Ginther. In res., Revs. James R. Bonke; William F. Stumpf.
Res., 1347 N. Meridian St., 46202. Tel: 317-634-4519; Fax: 317-634-0151. [JC]

2—CHRIST THE KING (1939), Rev. Msgr. Francis R. Tuohy; Rev. Christopher A. Craig.
Res., 5884 N. Crittenden, 46220. Tel: 317-475-6582.
Office: 5884 Crittenden Ave., 46220. Tel: 317-255-3666; Fax: 317-475-6579.
School—5858 Crittenden Ave., 46220. Tel: 317-257-9366.
Lay Teachers 26; Students 343.
Catechesis/Religious Programs—Tel: 317-255-3666; Fax: 317-475-6579.
Students 127.

3—GOOD SHEPHERD (1993). (St. Catherine, 1909, and St. James the Greater, 1951, were closed, merged, and renamed in 1993). Rev. Thomas Clegg; Thomas Meier, Pastoral Assoc.
Church & Parish Office: 1109 E. Cameron St., 46203. Tel: 317-783-3158; Fax: 317-781-5961. [JC]
School—Central Catholic School, 1155 E. Cameron St., 46203. Tel: 317-783-7759; Fax: 317-781-5964.
Students 227.
Catechesis/Religious Programs—Students 36.

4—HOLY ANGELS (1903) (African American), Rev. Clarence R. Waldon.
Res., 740 W. 28th St., 46208. Tel: 317-926-3324; Fax: 317-926-3325. [JC]
School—2822 Dr. Martin Luther King, Jr. St., 46208. Tel: 317-926-5211. Sr. Gerry O'Laughlin, Prin.
Sisters of St. Joseph 2; Lay Teachers 9; Students 185.
Catechesis/Religious Programs—Students 66.

5—HOLY CROSS (1895), Rev. Lawrence Voelker.
Church—125 N. Oriental St., 46202. Tel: 317-637-2620; Fax: 317-637-0112.
School—Tel: 317-638-9068; Fax: 317-638-0116.
Lay Teachers 17; Students 230.

6—HOLY ROSARY (1909) (Italian), Sr. Jean Marie Cleveland, O.S.F., Parish Life Coord.; Revs. Lawrence Voelker; Thomas Clegg, Priest Moderator.
Office: 520 Stevens St., 46203. Tel: 317-636-4478; Fax: 317-636-2522. [JC]

7—HOLY SPIRIT (1946), Revs. Joseph G. Riedman; Henry F. Tully. In res., Rev. Peter Gallagher.
Res., 7243 E. 10th St., 46219. Tel: 317-353-9404; Fax: 317-351-1707.
School—7241 E. 10th St., 46219. Tel: 317-352-1243.
Lay Teachers 23; Students 411.
Catechesis/Religious Programs—Tel: 317-357-6915.
Students 360.

8—HOLY TRINITY (1906), Rev. Kenneth E. Taylor; Sr. Anita Eberle, O.S.B., Pastoral Assoc.
Res., 2618 W. St. Clair St., 46222. Tel: 317-631-2939; Fax: 317-631-2921. [JC]
School—All Saints. Consolidated. See St. Anthony listing.

9—IMMACULATE HEART OF MARY (1946), Rev. Jeffery H. Godecker.
Parish Center: 5692 N. Central Ave., 46220. Tel: 317-257-2266; Fax: 317-475-7380. [JC]
Res., 5683 Washington Blvd., 46220. Tel: 317-252-5737.
School—317 E. 57th St., 46220. Tel: 317-255-5468; Fax: 317-475-7379.
Lay Teachers 30; Students 373.

10—NATIVITY OF OUR LORD JESUS CHRIST (1947), Rev. Steven Schwab.
7225 Southeastern Ave., 46239. Tel: 317-357-1200. [JC]
School—3310 S. Meadow Dr., 46239. Tel: 317-357-1459.
Sisters of Providence 2; Lay Teachers 8; Students 205.
Catechesis/Religious Programs—Tel: 317-359-6075.
Students 322.

11—OUR LADY OF LOURDES (1909), Rev. James Farrell.
Res., 5333 E. Washington St., 46219. Tel: 317-356-7291.
School—30 S. Downey St., 46219. Tel: 317-357-3316.
Lay Teachers 21; Students 454.

12—SACRED HEART OF JESUS (1875) (German), Revs. Robert Sieg, O.F.M.; Elias Koppert, O.F.M.; Justin Belitz, O.F.M.; Frank Jasper, O.F.M.
Res., 1530 S. Union St., 46225. Tel: 317-638-5551; Fax: 317-637-9741. [JC]
School—Central Catholic Consolidated. See Good Shepherd Listing. Tel: 317-783-7759.

13—ST. ANDREW THE APOSTLE (1946), Sr. Marilyn Herber, S.P., Parish Life Coord.; Revs. Pat Kelly; Mark A. Svarczkopf, Priest Moderator.
Parish Office: 3922 E. 38th St., 46218-1496. Tel: 317-546-1571; Fax: 317-549-6311. [JC]
School & Daycare: Tel: 317-549-6305; Fax: 317-549-6306.
Lay Teachers 20; Students 243.

14—ST. ANN (1917), Becky Gaynor, Pastoral Assoc.
Office: 2862 S. Holt Rd., 46241. Tel: 317-244-3750; Fax: 317-244-9841.
Res., 2850 S. Holt Rd., 46241. [JC]
Catechesis/Religious Programs—Laura Williams, D.R.E.
Students 90.

15—ST. ANTHONY (1891) (Irish-German), Rev. John T. Ryan, V.F. In res., Very Rev. Joseph F. Schaedel.
379 N. Warman Ave., 46222. Tel: 317-636-4828. [JC]
School—All Saints Consolidated, 337 N. Warman Ave, 46222. Tel: 317-636-3739.
Sisters of Providence 1; Lay Teachers 8; Students 166.
Catechesis/Religious Programs—Students 174.

16—ST. BARNABAS (1965), Revs. Joseph McNally; J. Patrick Mercier. In res., Rev. John N. Sciarra, (Retired).
Res., 8300 Rahke Rd., 46217. Tel: 317-882-0724; Fax: 317-887-8932.
School—Tel: 317-881-7422; Fax: 317-887-8933. Paulette Conner, Prin.
Lay Teachers 23; Students 585.
Catechesis/Religious Programs—Tel: 317-881-0631.
Students 390.

17—ST. BERNADETTE (1952), Rev. James Farrell. In res., Rev. Noah Casey, O.S.B.
Res., 4826 Fletcher Ave., 46203. Tel: 317-356-5867. [CEM]
Church & Parish Office: 4838 Fletcher Ave., 46203.

18—ST. CHRISTOPHER (Speedway City) (1937), Rev. D. Michael Welch. Pastoral Assocs.: Sr. Sue Bradshaw, O.S.F.; Sr. Marie Wolf, S.P.; Mr. Bill Szolek Van Valkenburgh; Nancy L. Meyer. In res., Rev. Robert J. Gilday.
Res., 5301 W. 16th St., 46224. Tel: 317-241-6314; Fax: 317-241-6587.
School—5335 W. 16th St., 46224. Fax: 317-244-6678. Mrs. Barbara Leek, Prin.
Lay Teachers 16; Students 226.
Catechesis/Religious Programs—Ms. Therese Brennan, D.R.E.
Students 311.

19—ST. GABRIEL THE ARCHANGEL (1963), Rev. William G. Marks; Sr. Mary Timothy Kavanaugh, O.S.F., Pastoral Assoc. In res., Rev. Frederick C. Easton.
Res., 6000 W. 34th St., 46224. Tel: 317-291-7014; Fax: 317-297-6453.
School—(Grades PreK-8). Tel: 317-297-1414.
Teachers 21; Students 375.
Catechesis/Religious Programs—Tel: 317-299-9924.
Students 60.

20—ST. JOAN OF ARC (1921), Revs. Patrick A. Doyle; James Chambers, S.J.
Res., 4217 Central Ave., 46205. Tel: 317-283-5508; Fax: 317-283-5511. [JC]
School—500 E. 42nd St., 46205. Tel: 317-283-1518.
Lay Teachers 14; Students 200.
Catechesis/Religious Programs—Tel: 317-283-5508; Fax: 317-283-5511.
Students 60.

21—ST. JOHN THE EVANGELIST (1837) (Irish), Rev. Thomas Murphy.
Res., 126 W. Georgia St., 46225. Tel: 317-635-2021; Fax: 317-635-2014. [JC]

22—ST. JOSEPH (1949), Rev. Glenn L. O'Connor. In res., Rev. Mark Tran-Xuan Thanh (Vietnam).
Res., 1375 S. Mickley Ave., 46241. Tel: 317-244-9002; Fax: 317-244-0278. [JC]
School—All Saints Consolidated. See St. Anthony Listing.

23—ST. JUDE (1959), Rev. Gerald J. Kirkhoff.
Res., 5353 McFarland Rd., 46227. Tel: 317-786-4371; 780-7588; Fax: 317-780-7592.
School—5375 McFarland Rd, 46227. Tel: 317-784-6828.
Sisters of Providence 2; Sisters of St. Joseph 1; Lay Teachers 20; Students 515.
Catechesis/Religious Programs—Tel: 317-780-7591.
Students 260.

24—ST. LAWRENCE (1949), Revs. Mark A. Svarczkopf; Thomas Stepanski, S.T.; Jeong Uk Kim, (Korean Community). In res., Rev. Henry Brown.
Office: 6944 E. 46th St., 46226. Tel: 317-546-4065; Fax: 317-543-4926.
Res., 4650 N. Shadeland Ave., 46226. Tel: 317-543-4921.
School—6950 E. 46th St., 46226. Tel: 317-543-4923; Fax: 317-543-4924.
Sisters of St. Francis 1; Lay Teachers 23; Students 385.
Catechesis/Religious Programs—Students 350.

25—ST. LUKE (1961), Rev. Daniel J. Mahan.
Res., 7575 Holliday Dr., E., 46260. Tel: 317-259-4373; Fax: 317-254-3210. [JC]
School—7650 N. Illinois St., 46260. Tel: 317-255-3912.
Lay Teachers 30; Students 477.
Catechesis/Religious Programs—Tel: 317-479-7373.
Students 315.

26—ST. MARK THE EVANGELIST (1946), Rev. Msgr. Richard C. Lawler. In res., Rev. Paul S. Petko, F.SS.P.
Res., 535 E. Edgewood, 46227. Tel: 317-787-8246; Fax: 317-781-6466.
School—541 E. Edgewood Ave., 46227. Tel: 317-786-4013.
Lay Teachers 24; Students 364.
Catechesis/Religious Programs—Tel: 317-784-7155.
Students 155.

27—ST. MARY/IMMACULATE CONCEPTION (1858), Rev. Mauro G. Rodas.
Res., 317 N. New Jersey St., 46204. Tel: 317-637-3983. [JC]
Catechesis/Religious Programs—The Marian Center, 311 N. New Jersey St., 46204. Tel: 317-237-9719.
Students 13.

28—ST. MATTHEW (1958), Rev. Donald L. Schmidlin. In res., Rev. Patrick J. Kelly; Bros. Joseph Umile, C.S.C.; Brian Guerrini, S.S.C.C.
Res., 4100 E. 56th St., 46220. Tel: 317-257-4297; 479-2382 (Rectory); Fax: 317-479-2381.
School—Tel: 317-251-3997.
Sisters 1; Lay Teachers 31; Students 545.
Catechesis/Religious Programs—Tel: 317-257-9733.
Students 110.

29—ST. MICHAEL THE ARCHANGEL (1948), Rev. Anthony Volz.
Res., 3354 W. 30th St., 46222. Tel: 317-926-7359; Fax: 317-921-3282.
School—3352 W. 30th St., 46222. Tel: 317-926-0516.
Lay Teachers 20; Students 362.
Catechesis/Religious Programs—Tel: 317-925-7597.
Students 124.

30—ST. MONICA (1956), Revs. Paul D. Koetter; Joseph B. Moriarty.
Res., 6131 N. Michigan Rd., 46228. Tel: 317-253-2193; Fax: 317-253-3342.
School—Tel: 317-255-7153; Fax: 317-259-5570.
Lay Teachers 29; Students 409.
Catechesis/Religious Programs—Tel: 317-257-3043.
Students 520.

31—ST. PATRICK (1865), Revs. Bruce Knox; Thomas Fox, O.F.M., (Hispanic Ministry); Paul S. Petko, F.SS.P.; Sr. Mary Slattery, S.P., Pastoral Assoc.; Sr. Jean Marie Cleveland, O.S.F., Parish Life Coord.
Church—950 Prospect St., 46203. Tel: 317-631-5824; Fax: 317-631-5828.
School—Consolidated. See Central Catholic Good Shepherd Parish.

32—ST. PHILIP NERI (1909), Rev. Herman G. Lutz; Mr. Tom Bogenschutz, Pastoral Assoc. In res., Rev. Carlton Beever.
Res., 550 N. Rural St., 46201. Tel: 317-631-8746; Fax: 317-632-8161. [JC]
School—545 Eastern Ave., 46201. Tel: 317-636-0134.
Lay Teachers 15; Students 265.
Catechesis/Religious Programs—Students 218.

33—ST. PIUS X (1955), Revs. Martin A. Peter; Joseph G. Pesola. In res., Rev. David F. Coons.
Res., 7200 Sarto Dr., 46240. Tel: 317-255-4534; Fax: 317-466-3354.
School—Tel: 317-466-3361.
Lay Teachers 25; Students 500.
Catechesis/Religious Programs—Tel: 317-257-1085.
Students 400.

34—ST. RITA (1919), Rev. Anthony Clark, S.V.D. In res., Revs. Charles Smith, S.V.D.; Kenneth Hamilton, S.V.D.; Chester Smith, S.V.D.
Res., 1733 Dr. Andrew J. Brown Ave., 46202. Tel: 317-632-9349; Fax: 317-687-0973. [JC]

School—1850 N. Arsenal Ave., 46218. Tel: 317-636-8580. Kathleen Sadlowski, Prin.
Lay Teachers 13; Students 181.

35—St. Roch (1922) (German), Rev. James R. Wilmoth.
Res., 3600 S. Pennsylvania St., 46227. Tel: 317-784-1763; Fax: 317-783-9617. [JC]
School—3603 S. Meridian St., 46217. Tel: 317-784-9144.
Lay Teachers 12; Students 250.

36—St. Simon (1961), Rev. Larry P. Crawford; Larry Hembree, Pastoral Assoc. In res., Rev. Peter Gallagher.
Res., 8155 Oaklandon Rd., 46236. Tel: 317-826-6000; Fax: 317-826-6020.
School—Lay Teachers 17; Students 239.
Catechesis/Religious Programs—Tel: 317-899-4997.
Students 155.

37—St. Therese of the Infant Jesus (Little Flower) (1925), Rev. Severin Messick, O.S.B., Admin.
Res., 4720 E. 13th St., 46201. Tel: 317-357-8352; Fax: 317-357-5316. [JC]
School—1401 N. Bosart Ave, 46202. Tel: 317-353-2282.
Lay Teachers 22; Students 513.
Catechesis/Religious Programs—Students 640.

38—St. Thomas Aquinas (1939), Rev. William G. Munshower.
Office: 4625 N. Kenwood Ave., 46208. Tel: 317-253-1461; Fax: 317-253-1461.
Res., 4650 N. Illinois St., 46208. Tel: 317-253-4112.
School—4600 N. Illinois St., 46208. Tel: 317-255-6244.
Lay Teachers 12; Students 213.

OUTSIDE THE CITY OF INDIANAPOLIS

Aurora, Dearborn Co., St. Mary of the Immaculate Conception (1857), Rev. Raymond E. Schafer.
203 Fourth St., 47001. Tel: 812-926-0060; Fax: 812-926-4439.
Res., 203 Fourth St., 47001. Tel: 812-926-0644.
School—211 Fourth St., 47001. Tel: 812-926-1558.
Lay Teachers 10; Students 174.
Catechesis/Religious Programs—Students 59.

Batesville, Ripley Co., St. Louis (1868), Revs. William J. Farris, O.F.M.; Al Hudepohl, O.F.M.; Alphonse Hoff, O.F.M., (Retired).
Res., 13 St. Louis Pl., 47006. Tel: 812-934-3204; Fax: 812-933-0667. [CEM]
School—17 St. Louis Pl., 47006. Tel: 812-934-3310; Fax: 812-934-6202.
Lay Teachers 26; Students 463.
Catechesis/Religious Programs—Students 290.

Bedford, Lawrence Co., St. Vincent de Paul (1864), Rev. Bernard Cox.
Res., 1711 I St., 47421. Tel: 812-275-6539; Fax: 812-275-3493.
School—913 18th St., 47421. Tel: 812-279-2540.
Lay Teachers 9; Students 181.
Catechesis/Religious Programs—Students 163.

Beech Grove, Marion Co., Holy Name (1908), Rev. Gerald F. Burkert. In res., Rev. Joseph F. Rautenberg.
Res., 89 N. 17th Ave., 46107. Tel: 317-784-5454; Fax: 317-784-1834. [JC]
School—21 N. 17th Ave., 46107. Tel: 317-784-9078. Jeanette Colburn, Prin.
Lay Teachers 17; Students 288.
Catechesis/Religious Programs—Students 129.

Bloomington, Monroe Co., St. Charles Borromeo (1864), Rev. Charles S. Chesebrough.
Res., 2222 E. Third St., 47401. Tel: 812-336-6846; Fax: 812-331-6732.
School—(Grades PreK-8) 2224 E. Third St., 47401. Tel: 812-336-5853; Fax: 812-349-0300.
Lay Teachers 30; Students 475.
Catechesis/Religious Programs—Tel: 812-334-1664.
Students 184.

St. John the Apostle (1970), Rev. Daniel B. Donohoo.
Res., 3410 W. Third St., 47404. Tel: 812-339-6006; Fax: 812-339-0400.
Catechesis/Religious Programs—Students 170.

St. Paul Catholic Center (1969), Revs. Daniel Atkins; Michael O'Mara.
Res., 1413 E. 17th St., 47408. Tel: 812-339-5561; Fax: 812-333-4846.
Catechesis/Religious Programs—Students 198.

Bradford, Harrison Co., St. Michael (1835), Rt. Rev. Bonaventure Knaebel.
Mailing Address: P.O. Box 22, 47107. Tel: 812-364-6646; Fax: 812-364-6614. [CEM]
Catechesis/Religious Programs—Tel: 812-364-6173.
Students 233.

Brazil, Clay Co., Annunciation of the Blessed Virgin Mary (1865), Rev. Anthony P. Spicuzza.
Res., 19 N. Alabama St., 47834. Tel: 812-448-1901. [CEM]
School—Tel: 812-448-1394.
Lay Teachers 4; Students 141.

Brookville, Franklin Co., St. Michael (1845), Rev. Louis E. Schumacher.
Res., 354 High St., P.O. Box J, 47012. Tel: 317-647-5462; Fax: 317-647-5462. [CEM]
School—145 Wallace St., P.O. Box J, 47012. Tel: 317-647-4961; Fax: 317-647-4961.
Sisters of the Third Order Regular of St. Francis 2; Lay Teachers 9; Students 235.

Brownsburg, Hendricks Co., St. Malachy (1869), Rev. Daniel J. Staublin; Very Rev. Joseph F. Schaedel, Vicar Gen.
Parish Center: 326 N. Green St., 46112. Tel: 317-852-3195; Fax: 317-852-8939. [CEM 2]
School—330 N. Green St., 46112. Tel: 317-852-2242; Fax: 317-852-3604.
Lay Teachers 22; Students 400.
Catechesis/Religious Programs—Tel: 317-852-8476.
Students 521.

Brownstown, Jackson Co., Our Lady of Providence (1934). Attended by St. Ambrose, Seymour. Rev. Joseph B. Sheets, Admin.
Mailing Address: c/o St. Ambrose Church, 325 S. Chestnut St., Seymour, 47274.
Res., Hwy. 50, 47220.

Cambridge City, Wayne Co., St. Elizabeth of Hungary (1852), Rev. John H. Luerman.
Res., 333 W. Maple St., 47327. Tel: 317-478-3242.
Catechesis/Religious Programs—Students 130.

Cannelton, Perry Co., St. Michael (1859), Revs. Severin Messick, O.S.B.; Benet Amato, O.S.B.
Parish Office: c/o Catholic Ministry Center, 802 Ninth St., Tell City, 47586. Tel: 812-547-7994; Fax: 812-547-6985.
Res., 814 Jefferson St., Tell City, 47586. Tel: 812-547-9901.
Church—Eighth St., 47520. [CEM]

Cedar Grove, Franklin Co., Holy Guardian Angels (1874) (German), Rev. Louis E. Schumacher, Admin.
Res., 405 U.S. Hwy. 52, 47016. Tel: 317-647-6981. [CEM]
Res., 354 High St., Brookville, 47012. Tel: 317-647-5462.
Catechesis/Religious Programs—Students 56.

Charlestown, Clark Co., St. Michael (1860), Rev. Stephen Donahue.
Res., 101 St. Michael Dr., 47111. Tel: 812-256-3200. [CEM]
Child Care Center—(Grades PreK-K) 102 St. Michael Dr., 47111. Tel: 812-256-3503.
Students 69.
Catechesis/Religious Programs—Students 52.
Mission—Henryville, Clark Co., St. Francis Xavier, (1869) Hwy. 31 & 160, P.O. Box 368, Henryville, 47126.

Clarksville, Clark Co., St. Anthony of Padua (1851), Rev. Dismas J. Veeneman, O.F.M.Conv. In res., Rev. Arnold Dearing, O.F.M.Conv.; Bro. Ray Ramos, O.F.M.Conv.
Res., 310 N. Sherwood Ave., 47129. Tel: 812-282-2290; Fax: 812-283-3924. [CEM]
School—320 N. Sherwood Ave., 47129. Tel: 812-282-2144.
Sisters of St. Benedict 1; Lay Teachers 22; Students 401.
Catechesis/Religious Programs—Students 53.

Clinton, Vermillion Co., Sacred Heart (1891), Rev. Micheal Kelley.
Office: 656 S. Sixth St., 47842. Tel: 317-832-8468; Fax: 317-832-2549.
Res., 558 Nebeker St., 47842.
School—610 S. Sixth St., 47842. Tel: 317-832-3228.
Lay Teachers 6; Students 63.
Mission—Universal, Vermillion Co., St. Joseph, (1920) Universal, 47884.

Columbus, Bartholomew Co., St. Bartholomew (1994). St Bartholomew (1841) and St. Columbas (1963) were closed, merged, and renamed St. Bartholomew. Revs. Clement T. Davis; Richard Hindel, O.S.B.
St. Bartholomew's Catholic Parish: 845 Eighth St., 47201. Tel: 812-379-9353; Fax: 812-375-0720.
Res., 1302 27th St., 47201. Tel: 812-372-1509.
Pre-School Center—845 8th st., 47201. Tel: 812-376-0468.
School—(Grades PreK-8) 1306 27th St., 47201. Tel: 812-372-6830; Fax: 812-376-0377.
Lay Teachers 22; Students 488.
Catechesis/Religious Programs—Tel: 812-372-2207.
Students 380.

Connersville, Fayette Co., St. Gabriel (1851), Rev. Stanley J. Herber, M.A.; Lynda Bell, Bus. Mgr.
Res., 232 W. Ninth St., 47331. Tel: 765-825-8578; Fax: 765-827-4347. [JC]
School—(Grades PreK-6) 224 W. Ninth St., 47331. Tel: 765-825-7951. Emily Lemming, Prin.
Lay Teachers 11; Students 228.
Catechesis/Religious Programs—220 W. Ninth St., 47331. Tel: 765-825-2944. Beth Luking, D.R.E.
Students 95.

Corydon, Harrison Co., St. Joseph (1896), Rev. Ernest Waechter, O.F.M.Conv.
Res., 312 E. High St., 47112. Tel: 812-738-2742; Fax: 812-738-2718. [CEM]
School—502 N. Mulberry St., 47112. Tel: 812-738-4549.
Lay Teachers 11; Students 162.
Catechesis/Religious Programs—Tel: 8112-738-2759.
Students 172.
Missions—New Middletown, Harrison Co., Most Precious Blood, (1880) 47112. [CEM]
Elizabeth, Harrison Co., St. Peter, (1849). [CEM]

Danville, Hendricks Co., Mary Queen of Peace (1939), Rev. Vincent P. Lampert.
Res., 1005 W. Main St., 46122. Tel: 317-745-4284; Fax: 317-745-7090.
Catechesis/Religious Programs—Students 242.

Dover, Dearborn Co., St. John the Baptist (1824), Rev. Louis Manna, O.F.M.Conv.
Res., 7525 Church Ln., West Harrison, 47060. Tel: 812-576-3593; Fax: 812-576-4302. [CEM]
Church—25743 State Rte. 1, Guilford, 47022. Tel: 812-576-4302.
Catechesis/Religious Programs—Students 178.

Edinburgh, Johnson Co., Holy Trinity (1851), Rev. Paul M. Shikany.
Res., P.O. Box 216, 46124. Tel: 812-526-9460.

Enochsburg, Decatur Co., St. John the Evangelist (1844) (German), Rev. Jonathan Stewart.
Res., 9995 E. Base Rd., Greensburg, 47240. Tel: 812-934-2880. [CEM]

Fortville, Hancock Co., St. Thomas (1869), Rev. Roger B. Gaudet.
Res., 523 S. Merrill St., 46040. Tel: 317-485-5101; Fax: 317-485-4373.
Catechesis/Religious Programs—Tel: 317-485-5103.
Students 146.

Franklin, Johnson Co., St. Rose of Lima (1868), Rev. Paul M. Shikany; Jean Martin, Pastoral Assoc., Tel: 317-738-2965.
Res., 114 Lancelot Dr., 46131. Tel: 317-738-3929; Fax: 317-738-3583.
School—(Grades PreK-3). Tel: 317-738-3451. Laura Riley, Prin.
Catechesis/Religious Programs—Tel: 317-736-6754.
Students 224.

French Lick, Orange Co., Our Lady of the Springs (1887), Rev. John M. Hall.
Res., 8796 W. State Rd. 56, 47432. Tel: 812-936-4568; Fax: 812-936-4568.
Mission—Paoli, Orange Co., Our Lord Jesus Christ the King, (1948) 47432.

Frenchtown, Harrison Co., St. Bernard (1849), Rev. Frederick J. Denison.
Res., 7600 Hwy. 337 N.W., Depauw, 47115. Tel: 812-347-2326. [CEM]
Mission—Frenchtown, Crawford Co., St. Joseph, (1855) 47115.

Fulda, Spencer Co., St. Boniface (1847), Revs. Jeremy King, O.S.B.; Adrian Burke, O.S.B.
Mailing Address: P.O. Box 1, 47536. Tel: 812-357-2483. [CEM]
Catechesis/Religious Programs—Students 107.

Greencastle, Putnam Co., St. Paul the Apostle (1853), Rev. Michael C. Fritsch.
Res., 202 E. Washington St., 46135. Tel: 765-653-5678; Fax: 765-653-4377.
Catechesis/Religious Programs—Students 77.

Greenfield, Hancock Co., St. Michael (1860), Rev. Robert E. Mazzola, S.T.B.
Res., 519 Jefferson Blvd., 46140. Tel: 317-462-4240.
School—515 Jefferson Blvd., 46140. Tel: 317-462-6380.
Lay Teachers 9; Students 186.
Catechesis/Religious Programs—Students 415.

Greensburg, Decatur Co., St. Mary (1858), Rev. Stephen Schaftlein.
Res., 302 E. McKee St., 47240. Tel: 812-663-8427; Fax: 812-663-6088. [CEM]
School—(Grades PreK-6) 210 S. East St., 47240. Tel: 812-663-2804.
Lay Teachers 16; Students 312.
Catechesis/Religious Programs—Students 234.

Greenwood, Johnson Co., Our Lady of the Greenwood (1948), Revs. Harold L. Knueven; Kenneth J. Ciano, M.Div.; James Bonke.
Res., 335 S. Meridian St., 46143. Tel: 317-888-2861; Fax: 317-885-5006. [JC]

School—399 S. Meridian St., 46143. Tel: 317-881-1300.
Lay Teachers 25; Students 513.
Catechesis/Religious Programs—Tel: 317-885-5007.
Students 408.

SS. Francis and Clare of Assisi (1993), Rev. Stephen Jarrell.
Church & Parish Office: 5901 Olive Branch Rd., 46143. Tel: 317-859-4673; Fax: 317-859-4678.
Catechesis/Religious Programs—Students 162.

Hamburg, Franklin Co., St. Anne (1869), Rev. Jonathan Stewart.
Res., 5267 N. Hamburg Rd., Oldenburg, 47036. Tel: 812-934-5854. [CEM]

Henryville, Clark Co., St. Francis Xavier (1869). Attended from St. Michael's, 101 St. Michael Dr., Charlestown, IN 47111. Tel: 812-256-3200. Rev. Stephen Donahue, Admin.
Church—Hwy 31 & Hwy 160, P.O. Box 368, 47126.

Jeffersonville, Clark Co., Sacred Heart (1953), Rev. David J. Groeller. In res., Rev. H. Michael Hilderbrand.
Church & Parish Office: 1840 E. 8th St., 47103. Tel: 812-282-0423; Fax: 812-284-6673.
School—1842 E. 8th St., 47130. Tel: 812-283-3123.
Lay Teachers 19; Students 346.
Catechesis/Religious Programs—Tel: 812-283-6914.
Students 59.

St. Augustine (1853), Rev. Clifford R. Vogelsang.
Res., 315 E. Chestnut St., P.O. Box 447, 47130. Tel: 812-282-2677; Fax: 812-282-8821. [CEM]
Catechesis/Religious Programs—316 E. Maple St., Tel: 812-282-1231.
Students 128.

Knightstown, Henry Co., St. Rose (1872), Revs. Joseph F. Rautenberg; Stanley J. Herber; Sr. Shirley Gerth, Parish Life Coord.
Mailing Address: P.O. Box 209, 46148. Tel: 765-345-5595.
Church—8144 W. U.S. Hwy. 40, 46148.

Lanesville, Harrison Co., St. Mary (1843) (German), Rev. Harold A. Ripperger.
Res., 2500 St. Mary's Dr., P.O. Box 144, 47136. Tel: 812-952-2853; Fax: 812-952-2852. [CEM]
Catechesis/Religious Programs—Tel: 812-952-2854.
Students 149.

Lawrenceburg, Dearborn Co., St. Lawrence (1842) (German), Rev. John Hartzer.
Res., 542 Walnut St., 47025. Tel: 812-537-3992. [CEM]
School—524 Walnut St., 47025. Tel: 812-537-3690.
Lay Teachers 9; Students 179.
Catechesis/Religious Programs—Tel: 812-537-1112.
Students 225.

Leopold, Perry Co., St. Augustine (1837), Rev. Sean Hoppe, O.S.B.
Res., 47551. Tel: 812-843-5143. [CEM]
Catechesis/Religious Programs—Students 180.

Liberty, Union Co., St. Bridget (1854), Rev. John O'Brien, O.S.B., Admin.
Res., 404 E. Vine St., 47353. Tel: 765-458-5412. [CEM]
Catechesis/Religious Programs—Students 82.

Madison, Jefferson Co., Prince of Peace (1993). St. Michael (1837), St. Mary (1851), St. Patrick (1853), Madison, and St. Anthony, China (1861), were closed, merged, and renamed, Prince of Peace. Rev. John A. Meyer.
Mailing Address: Catholic Community Center, 305 W. State St., 47250. Tel: 812-265-4166; Fax: 812-273-3427.
Res., 415 E. Second St., 47250. Tel: 812-265-4166. [CEM 2]
School—Pope John XXIII, (Grades K-6) 221 State St., 47250. Tel: 812-273-3957.
High School—Shawe Memorial Junior-Senior High School. See High Schools, Inter-Parochial, under Institutions Located in the Archdiocese. Tel: 812-273-2150; Fax: 812-273-6694.
Catechesis/Religious Programs—Students 139.

Martinsville, Morgan Co., St. Martin of Tours (1848), Rev. Mark Gottemoeller.
Res., 1709 E. Harrison St., 46151. Tel: 765-342-6379. [CEM]
Catechesis/Religious Programs—Tel: 765-342-8028.
Students 188.

Milan, Ripley Co., St. Charles Borromeo (1908), Rev. Msgr. Bernard R. Schmitz; Rev. Gregory Bramlage. In res., Rev. John J. Minta, (Retired).
Mailing Address: c/o St. Anthony, P.O. Box 3, Morris, 47033. Tel: 812-654-2009.
Church—213 Ripley St., 47031.
Mission—St. Pius, Ripley Co., St. Pius, (1859). [CEM]

Millhousen, Decatur Co., Immaculate Conception (1834), Revs. William G. Ripperger; Frank Eckstein; Sr. Christine Ernstes, O.S.F., Parish Life Coord.
Mailing Address: 2081 E. County Rd., 820 S., Greensburg, 47240. Tel: 812-591-2362.
Mission—St. Denis, Jennings Co., St. Denis, (1894) 12155 N. County Rd., 600 E., Westport, 47283. [CEM]
Catechesis/Religious Programs—Students 127.

Mitchell, Lawrence Co., St. Mary/Assumption (1869), Rev. Bernard Cox.
Res., 777 S. 11th St., 47446. Tel: 812-849-3570; Fax: 812-275-3493.
Catechesis/Religious Programs—Students 67.

Montezuma, Parke Co., Immaculate Conception (1867). Attended by St. Joseph's, 219 E. Ohio St., Rockville, IN. Tel: 765-569-5406. Rev. Joseph R. Kern, Admin.
Church—Madison & Sycamore St.

Mooresville, Morgan Co., St. Thomas More (1967), Rev. Edward J. Ripperger.
Res., 1200 N. Indiana St., 46158. Tel: 317-831-4142; Fax: 317-834-2947.
Catechesis/Religious Programs—Tel: 317-831-1431.
Students 323.

Morris, Ripley Co., St. Anthony of Padua (1856), Rev. Gregory Bramlage; Rev. Msgr. Bernard R. Schmitz.
Mailing Address: P.O. Box 3, 47033. Tel: 812-934-6218; Fax: 812-934-5936. [CEM]
Church—4781 E. Morris Church St., 47033.

Napoleon, Ripley Co., St. Maurice (1848), Rev. William G. Ripperger.
Mailing Address: 8874 Harrison St., P.O. Box 17, 47034. Tel: 812-852-4237. [CEM]
Catechesis/Religious Programs—Students 127.

Nashville, Brown Co., St. Agnes (1940), Rev. William-Paul Stumpf.
Mailing Address: 602 N. State Rd. 135, P.O. Box 577, 47448. Tel: 812-988-2778. [JC]
Catechesis/Religious Programs—Students 87.

Navilleton, Floyd Co., St. Mary (1845), Rev. Tony Hubler.
Res., 7500 Navilleton Rd., Floyds Knobs, 47119. Tel: 812-923-5419; Fax: 812-923-3430. [CEM]
Catechesis/Religious Programs—Students 288.

New Albany, Floyd Co., Holy Family (1954), Rev. Wilfred E. Day.
Res., 129 W. Daisy Ln., 47150. Tel: 812-944-8283; Fax: 812-945-0180.
School—217 W. Daisy Ln., 47150. Tel: 812-944-6090; Fax: 812-944-7299.
Lay Teachers 21; Students 395.
Catechesis/Religious Programs—Students 87.

Our Lady of Perpetual Help (1950), Rev. John L. Fink; Tom Yost, Pastoral Assoc.
Res., 1752 Scheller Ln., 47150. Tel: 812-944-1184.
School—Tel: 812-944-7676.
Lay Teachers 22; Students 450.
Catechesis/Religious Programs—Tel: 812-948-0185.
Students 74.

St. Mary (1858) (German), Rev. William W. Ernst, V.F.
Res., 415 E. Eighth St., 47150. Tel: 812-944-0417; Fax: 812-944-9557. [JC]
School—720 E. Elm St., 47150. Tel: 812-944-0888; Fax: 812-945-4770.
Sisters 1; Lay Teachers 8; Students 221.
Catechesis/Religious Programs—Students 81.

New Alsace, Dearborn Co., St. Paul (1833), Rev. William J. Turner; Mrs. Nancy Fahringer, Pastoral Assoc.
Mailing Address: 8044 Yorkridge Rd., Guilford, 47022. Tel: 812-623-3408; Fax: 812-623-4879.
Res., 8044 Yorkridge Rd., Guilford, 47022. Tel: 812-623-3408; 487-2096. [CEM]
School—(Grades K-6) 9775 N. Dearborn Rd., Guilford, 47022. Tel: 812-623-2631.
Lay Teachers 5; Students 90.
Catechesis/Religious Programs—Tel: 812-623-2662.
Students 60.

New Castle, Henry Co., St. Anne (1873), Revs. Joseph F. Rautenberg; Stanley J. Herber; Sr. Shirley Gerth, O.S.F., Parish Life Coord.
Parish Office: 102 N. 19th St., 47362. Tel: 765-529-0933; Fax: 765-529-8976. [CEM]
Church—1904 Broad St., 47362. Tel: 765-529-7413.
Catechesis/Religious Programs—Students 132.

New Marion, Ripley Co., St. Magdalen (1847). Attended from St. John, Osgood. Rev. Francis Eckstein.
Res., Tel: 812-689-4244.

New Middletown, Harrison Co., Most Precious Blood (1880). Attended from St. Joseph, 312 E. High St., Corydon, IN 47112. Tel: 812-738-2742. Rev. Ernest Waechter, O.F.M.Conv.

North Vernon, Jennings Co., St. Mary/Nativity of the Blessed Virgin Mary (1861), Rev. John B. Schoettelkotte.
212 Washington St., 47265. Tel: 812-346-3604. [CEM]
School—209 Washington St., 47265. Tel: 812-346-3445; Fax: 812-346-5930.
Lay Teachers 10; Students 213.

Oak Forest, Franklin Co., St. Cecilia of Rome/Formerly St. Philomena (1844). Attended by St. Mary-of-the-Rock, Franklin Co., where sacramental records are kept. Rev. Humbert Moster, O.S.B.
17440 St. Mary's Rd., Batesville, 47006. Tel: 812-934-4165.

Oldenburg, Franklin Co., Holy Family (1837), Rev. Sylvester Heppner, O.F.M. In res., Revs. Humbert Moster, O.F.M.; Raymar Middendorf, O.F.M.
Res., 3027 Pearl St., P.O. Box 98, 47036. Tel: 812-934-3013; Fax: 812-933-0728. [CEM]
Catechesis/Religious Programs—Students 210.

Osgood, Ripley Co., St. John (1867), Rev. Francis Eckstein.
Res., 331 S. Buckeye St., 47037. Tel: 812-689-4244. [CEM]
Mission—New Marion, Ripley Co., St. Mary Magdalen, (1847) 47037.
Catechesis/Religious Programs—349 S. Buckeye St., 47037. Tel: 812-689-6670.
Students 124.

Paoli, Orange Co., Our Lord Jesus Christ the King (1948). Attended from Our Lady of the Springs, French Lick. Rev. John M. Hall.
Church—Hwy. 150 E., 47454. Tel: 812-936-4568.

Plainfield, Hendricks Co., St. Susanna (1953), Rev. Richard I. Zore.
Res., 1210 E. Main St., 46168. Tel: 317-839-3333; Fax: 317-839-0732.
School—(Grades PreK-6) 1212 E. Main St., 46168. Tel: 317-839-3713; Fax: 317-838-7718.
Lay Teachers 13; Students 202.
Catechesis/Religious Programs—Tel: 317-838-7722.
Students 225.

Richmond, Wayne Co., Holy Family (1953), Revs. Todd M. Riebe, M.C.C.J., Admin.; Kevin J. Morris.
Mailing Address: 240 S. 6th St., 47374. Tel: 765-962-3902; Fax: 765-966-0820.
Res., 720 N. A St., 47374. Tel: 765-962-3569.
Church—815 W. Main St., 47374.
School—St. Elizabeth Ann Seton (West), (Grades 4-8) 801 W. Main St., 47374. Tel: 765-962-4877.
Lay Teachers 11; Students 153.

St. Andrew (1846), Revs. Todd M. Riebe, M.C.C.J., Admin.; Kevin J. Morris.
Mailing Address: 240 S. 6th St., 47374. Tel: 765-962-3902; Fax: 765-966-0820.
Res., 720 A North St., 47374. Tel: 765-962-3569. [JC]
Church—235 S. 5th St., 47374.
Parish Center—233 S. Fifth St., 47374. Tel: 765-966-0916.
Catechesis/Religious Programs—Tel: 765-966-0916.
Students 168.

St. Mary (1859), Revs. Todd M. Riebe, M.C.C.J., Admin.; Kevin J. Morris.
Mailing Address: 240 S. 6th St., 47374. Tel: 765-962-3902; Fax: 765-966-0820.
Church & Res.: 720 N. A St., 47374. Tel: 765-962-3569. [JC]
School—St. Elizabeth Ann Seton, (Grades K-3) 700 N. A St., 47374. Tel: 317-962-5010.
Lay Teachers 7; Students 155.

Rockville, Parke Co., St. Joseph (1867), Rev. Joseph R. Kern.
Res., 217 E. Ohio St., 47872. Tel: 765-569-5406.
Catechesis/Religious Programs—Students 60.
Mission—Montezuma, Parke Co., Immaculate Conception, (1867) Madison & Sycamore St., Montezuma, 47872. Tel: 765-245-0232. [CEM]

Rushville, Rush Co., Immaculate Conception/St. Mary (1857), Rev. Roger G. Rudolf.
Res., 512 N. Perkins St., 46173. Tel: 765-932-2588; Fax: 765-932-3639. [CEM]
School—(Grades PreK-6) 226 E. 5th St., 46173. Tel: 765-932-3639.
Lay Teachers 11; Students 263.
Catechesis/Religious Programs—Students 176.

St. Anne, Jennings Co., St. Anne (1841). Attended from St. Joseph, Jennings Co., 1875 S. County Rd. 700 W., North Vernon, IN 47265. Tel: 812-346-4783. Rev. John Schoettelkotte, Admin.

St. Croix, Perry Co., Holy Cross (1860), Rev. Isaac McDaniel, O.S.B.
Res., State Rd. 62, Gen. Delivery, 47576. Tel: 812-843-5701. [CEM]

St. Isidore the Farmer (1968). St. John, (1875), and St. Joseph, (1891), Perry Co., were closed, merged, and renamed, St. Isidore, in 1968. Rev. Isaac McDaniel, O.S.B.
Res., HC 64, Box 265, Bristow, 47515. Tel: 812-843-5713. [CEM]
Catechesis/Religious Programs—Students 93.

St. Denis, Jennings Co., St. Denis (1894). Attended by Immaculate Conception, Millhousen.
Church—12155 N. County Rd. 600E, Westport, 47283.
Mailing Address: 2081 E. County Rd. 820S, Greensburg, 47240. [CEM]

St. Joseph, Crawford Co., St. Joseph (1855). Attended by St. Bernard, Frenchtown. Rev. Fredrick J. Denison, Admin.
Mailing Address: 7600 Hwy. 337 N.W., Depauw, 47115. Tel: 812-347-2326.
Church—State Rd. 66, Marengo, 47140.

St. Joseph, Jennings Co., (1850), Rev. John B. Schoettelkotte, Admin.
Res., 1875 S. County Rd. 700 W., North Vernon, 47265. Tel: 812-346-4783. [CEM]
Mission—St. Anne, Jennings Co., St. Anne, (1841).

St. Joseph Hill, Clark Co., St. Joseph (1853), Rev. Richard Kaley, O.F.M.Conv., Admin. In res., Rev. Kent Biergans, O.F.M.Conv.
Res., 2605 St. Joe Rd., W., Sellersburg, 47172. Tel: 812-246-2512; Fax: 812-246-2671. [CEM]
Catechesis/Religious Programs—Tel: 812-246-3969.
Students 91.

St. Leon, Dearborn Co., St. Joseph (1841), Rev. Louis Manna.
Res., 7536 Church Ln., West Harrison, 47060. Tel: 812-576-3593. [CEM]
Catechesis/Religious Programs—29060 State Rte. 1, West Harrison, 47060. Tel: 812-576-3234.
Students 160.

St. Mark, Perry Co., St. Mark (1863) (German), Rev. Sean Hoppe, O.S.B.
Res., R.R. 1, Box 324, Tell City, 47586. Tel: 812-836-2481. [CEM][JC]
Catechesis/Religious Programs—Students 104.

St. Mary-of-the-Knobs, Floyd Co., St. Mary-of-the-Knobs (1823), Rev. John F. Geis.
Res., 3033 Martin Rd., Floyds Knobs, 47119. Tel: 812-923-3011; Fax: 812-923-9526. [CEM]
Catechesis/Religious Programs—Tel: 812-932-7258; Fax: 812-923-9526.
Students 466.

St. Mary-of-the-Rock, Franklin Co., St. Mary-of-the-Rock (1844) (German), Rev. Humbert Moster, O.F.M.
Office: 17440 St. Mary's Rd., Batesville, 47006. Tel: 812-934-4165. [CEM]
Res., Franciscans, Oldenburg, 47036.
Catechesis/Religious Programs—Students 50.
Mission—Oak Forest, Franklin Co., St. Cecilia of Rome, (1844).

St. Mary-of-the-Woods, Vigo Co., St. Mary (1837), Rev. Paul A. Evard, O.F.M.Conv.
Mailing Address: P.O. Box 155, 47876. Tel: 812-535-1240. [CEM]
Catechesis/Religious Programs—Tel: 812-535-3440. Mrs. Rhonda Maher, D.R.E.:
Students 66.

St. Maurice, Decatur Co., St. Maurice (1859), Rev. Jonathan Stewart.
Mailing Address: 1963 N. St. John St., Greensburg, 47240. Tel: 812-663-4754. [CEM]
Catechesis/Religious Programs—Students 136.

St. Meinrad, Spencer Co., St. Meinrad (1854), Revs. Jeremy King, O.S.B.; Adrian Burke, O.S.B.
Mailing Address: P.O. Box 8, 47577. Tel: 812-357-5533. [CEM]
Catechesis/Religious Programs—Students 182.

St. Nicholas, Ripley Co., St. Nicholas (1836), Rev. Msgr. Bernard R. Schmitz; Revs. Gregory Bramlage; William J. Engbers, (Retired).
Res., 6461 E. St. Nicholas Dr., Sunman, 47041. Tel: 812-623-2964; 934-6218; Fax: 812-623-2964. [CEM]
School—(Grades K-8) 6459 E. St. Nicholas Dr., Sunman, 47041. Tel: 812-623-2348.
Lay Teachers 11; Students 189.
Catechesis/Religious Programs—Students 72.

St. Peter, Franklin Co., St. Peter (1838), Revs. William J. Farris, O.F.M.; Humbert Moster, O.F.M.; Sr. Eileen Flavin, C.S.C., Parish Life Coord.
Res., 1207 East Rd., Brookville, 47012. Tel: 812-623-3670. [CEM]
Catechesis/Religious Programs—Students 91.
@PARISH2 =, Harrison Co., (1849). Attended from St. Joseph, Corydon, St. Peter, 312 E. High St., Corydon, Harrison Co., IN 47112. Rev. Ernest Waechter, O.F.M.Conv.
Church—Buena Vista Rd., Elizabeth, 47117.

St. Pius, Ripley Co., St. Pius (1859). Attended from St. Charles Borromeo, Milan. Rev. Msgr. Bernard Schmitz, Admin.; Rev. Gregory Bramlage.
Mailing Address: P.O. Box 3, Morris, 47033. Tel: 812-934-6218.

St. Vincent de Paul, Shelby Co., St. Vincent de Paul (1837), Rev. Paul Landwerlen.
Res., 4218 E. Michigan Rd., Shelbyville, 46176. Tel: 317-398-4028. [CEM]
Catechesis/Religious Programs—Tel: 317-392-3879.
Students 81.
Mission—. [CEM]

Salem, Washington Co., St. Patrick (1942), Rev. Thomas L. Schliessmann.
S. Shelby St., P.O. Box 273, 47167. Tel: 812-752-3693.

Scottsburg, Scott Co., American Martyrs (1938), Rev. Thomas Schliessmann.
270 S. Bond St., 47170. Tel: 812-752-3693.
Mission—Salem, Washington Co., St. Patrick, (1942).

Seelyville, Vigo Co., Holy Rosary (1908), Rev. Lawrence Moran, Admin.
Mailing Address: 2585 N. Main, P.O. Box 151, 47878. Tel: 812-877-1279.
Res., 1807 Poplar St., Terre Haute, 47803. Tel: 812-232-8518.

Sellersburg, Clark Co., St. Paul (1948), Rev. Paul F. Richart.
Res., 218 Scheller Ave., 47172. Tel: 812-246-3522.
School—(Grades K-6) 105 St. Paul St., 47172. Tel: 812-246-3266; Fax: 812-246-3397.
Lay Teachers 9; Students 224.
Catechesis/Religious Programs—216 Scheller Ave., 47172. Tel: 812-246-5088.
Students 47.

Seymour, Jackson Co., St. Ambrose (1860), Rev. Joseph B. Sheets.
Res., 325 S. Chestnut St., 47274. Tel: 812-522-5304; Fax: 812-522-8959. [CEM]
School—(Grades K-6) 301 S. Chestnut St., 47274. Tel: 812-522-3522.
Lay Teachers 8; Students 106.
Catechesis/Religious Programs—Tel: 812-522-2686.
Students 164.
Mission—Brownstown, Jackson Co., Our Lady of Providence, (1934) 47274.

Shelbyville, Shelby Co., St. Joseph (1868), Rev. John S. Maung.
Res., 125 E. Broadway, 46176. Tel: 317-398-8227; Fax: 317-392-7820. [CEM][JC]
School—(Grades PreK-8) 127 E. Broadway, 46176. Tel: 317-398-4202; Fax: 317-398-0270.
Sisters of the Third Order Regular of St. Francis 1; Lay Teachers 20; Students 324.
Catechesis/Religious Programs—Tel: 317-398-0530.
Students 185.

Siberia, Perry Co., St. Martin of Tours (1869), Revs. Jeremy King, O.S.B.; Adrian Burke, O.S.B.
Mailing Address: P.O. Box 1, Fulda, 47536. Tel: 812-357-2483. [CEM]

Spencer, Owen Co., St. Jude the Apostle (1951), Rev. Paul M. Dede.
300 W. Hillside Ave., P.O. Box 317, 47460. Tel: 812-829-3082; Fax: 812-829-0888.

Starlight, Clark Co., St. John the Baptist (1861) (German), Rev. John Beitans.
Res., 8310 St. John's Rd., Floyds Knobs, 47119. Tel: 812-923-5785; Fax: 812-923-2015. [CEM]
Catechesis/Religious Programs—Tel: 812-923-8406.
Students 82.

Tell City, Perry Co., St. Paul (1859), Rev. Benet Amato, O.S.B.
Parish Office: Catholic Ministry Center, 802 9th St., 47586. Tel: 812-547-7994; Fax: 812-547-6985.
Church—814 Jefferson St., 47586. [CEM]
Catechesis/Religious Programs—Tel: 812-547-7102.
Students 314.

Terre Haute, Vigo Co.,

1—Sacred Heart of Jesus, (1924), Rev. Stephen Giannini.
Res., 2322 N. 13 1/2 St., 47804. Tel: 812-466-1231; Fax: 812-466-9683. [JC]
School—1330 Lafayette Ave., 47804. Tel: 812-232-8901.
Sisters 4; Lay Teachers 5; Students 114.
Catechesis/Religious Programs—Students 138.

2—St. Ann, (1876), Sr. Constance Kramer, S.P., Parish Life Coord.; Rev. Stephen Giannini.
Res., 1440 Locust St., 47807. Tel: 812-232-6832; Fax: 812-232-2444. [JC]

3—St. Benedict, (1865) (German), Rev. Ron Borman, O.F.M.Conv.
Parish Office: 111 S. Ninth St., 47807. Tel: 812-235-3041; Fax: 812-238-9203. [JC]
Church—118 S. Ninth St., 47807.
Catechesis/Religious Programs—Tel: 812-232-8421.
Students 167.

4—St. Joseph, (1838), Revs. Martin Day, O.F.M.Conv.; Robert St. Martin, O.F.M.Conv.
Res., 113 S. Fifth St., 47807. Tel: 812-232-7011; Fax: 812-232-7012. [JC]
Catechesis/Religious Programs—Students 269.

5—St. Margaret Mary, (1920), Rev. John F. Dede.
Res., 2405 S. Seventh St., 47802. Tel: 812-232-3512. [JC]
Catechesis/Religious Programs—Students 115.

6—St. Patrick, (1881), Rev. Lawrence J. Moran; John Fuller, Pastoral Assoc.
Church—1807 Poplar St., 47803. Tel: 812-232-8518; Fax: 812-234-3312.
School—(Grades PreK-8) 449 S. 19th St., 47803. Tel: 812-232-2157. Sr. Theresa Boland, S.P., Prin.
Lay Teachers 15; Students 317.
Catechesis/Religious Programs—Tel: 812-232-2827. Barbara Black, D.R.E.
Students 205.

Troy, Perry Co., St. Pius (1849), Rev. Benet Amato, O.S.B.
Parish Office: Catholic Ministry Center, 802 9th St., Tell City, 47586. Tel: 812-547-7994; Fax: 812-547-6985. [CEM]
Church—State Rd. 66, 47588.

Universal, Vermillion Co., St. Joseph (1920). Attended from Sacred Heart, 656 S. Sixth St., Clinton, IN 47842. Tel: 317-832-8468. Rev. Micheal Kelley.
Church—270 E. Wood Ave., 47884.

Vevay, Switzerland Co., Most Sorrowful Mother of God (1876), Rev. John A. Meyer.
Mailing Address: Catholic Community Center, 305 W. State St., Madison, 47250. Tel: 812-265-4166; Fax: 812-273-3427.
Church—Ferry St., 47043.

West Terre Haute, Vigo Co., St. Leonard of Port Maurice (1912), Rev. Paul A. Evard.
Res., 126 N. Eighth St., 47885. Tel: 812-533-1240.

Yorkville, Dearborn Co., St. Martin (1852), Rev. William J. Turner; Mrs. Nancy Fahringer, Pastoral Assoc.
Res., 8044 Yorkridge Rd., Guilford, 47022. Tel: 812-487-2096; 623-3408; Fax: 812-623-4879. [CEM]
Catechesis/Religious Programs—Tel: 812-623-2662.
Students 60.

Chaplains of Public Institutions

Indianapolis. *Community Hospital North*. Rev. Henry Brown.
Indiana University Hospital/Riley Hospital for Children. Vacant.
Indiana Women's Prison. Rev. Lawrence Voelker.
Indianapolis Fire Department. Rev. James Wilmoth.
Indianapolis International Airport. Rev. Glenn L. O'Connor.
Larue D. Carter Hospital. Rev. Joseph S. Kos.
Marion County Sheriff Department. Rev. James R. Wilmoth.
Methodist Hospital. Rev. David Lawler.
Veterans' Administration Hospital. Revs. Joachim Keine, O.F.M.Conv.; Gordon P. Wagoner.
Winona Medical Center. Rev. Henry Brown.
Wishard Memorial Hospital. Rev. Joseph S. Kos.

Putnamville. *Indiana State Farm*. Rev. Michael C. Fritsch.

Richmond. *Richmond State Hospital*. Rev. Todd M. Riebe, M.C.C.J.

Terre Haute. *Regional Hospital/Union Hospital*. Rev. Maurice Hayes, O.F.M.Conv.
U.S. Penitentiary. Vacant.

On Duty Outside the Archdiocese:
Reverend Fathers—
Banet, Stephen J., Archdiocese of Mechelen-Brussels, Our Lady of Mercy Parish, Brussels, Belgium
Happel, Stephen P., Department of Religious Education, The Catholic University of America., Washington, DC 20064

On Special or Other Archdiocesan Assignment:
Reverend Fathers—
Porter, Jack W., Archdiocesan Historian. Tel: 317-592-4073

Military Chaplains:
Reverend Fathers—
Buchanan, Donald E.
Murphy, Kenneth J.

Graduate Studies:
Reverend Fathers—
Dant, Nicholas J.
Villa, Joseph L.

Leave of Absence:
Reverend Fathers—
Craig, Christopher
Miltz, Karl J.
Sims, Robert W.
Smith, Myles H.

On Disability Leave:
Reverend Fathers—
Mader, Joseph
Stahl, George

Retired:
Reverend Monsignors—
Kavanagh, Richard T., 6809 E. 77th St., Indianapolis, IN 46250
Ross, Charles E., St. Augustine Home, 2345 W. 86th St., Indianapolis, IN 46260
Sweeney, Kenny C., 8431 E. Fairmont Ave., Scottsdale, AZ 85251

Reverend Fathers—
Ajamie, Albert, Fatima Retreat House, 5353 E. 56th St., Indianapolis, IN 46226
Armstrong, Daniel F., Christian Brothers University, 650 E. Parkway, S., Memphis, TN 38104
Arneson, James E., 1868 Shore Dr. S., #114, South Pasadena, FL 33707
Beechem, Joseph, 6927 Atrium Boardwalk S., Indianapolis, IN 46250
Berkemeier, Charles A., 6268 Scottsville Navilleton Rd., Floyds Knobs, IN 47119
Burwinkel, Elmer J., M.Ed., M.Div., 3991 W.C.R. 925 S., Madison, IN 47250
Byrne, James F., S.T.L., 1670 1/2 W. 86th St., Indianapolis, IN 46260
Carey, Thomas P., St. Paul Hermitage, 501 N. 17th Ave., No. 107, Beech Grove, IN 46107
Cleary, William D., 874 W. Bauer Dr., Ninevah, IN 46164
Commons, Patrick M., 1868 Shore Dr. S., Apt. 114, South Pasadena, FL 33707
Dede, James R., 8499 W. U.S. Hwy. 150, Hardensburg, IN 47125
Dede, John F., 2421 S. Seventh St., Terre Haute, IN 47802
Diezeman, Andrew S., Star Rte., Box 37A, St. Croix, IN 47576
Dooley, Francis B., St. Paul Hermitage, 501 N. 17th Ave., Beech Grove, IN 46107
Dooley, Joseph W., 8021 Guion Rd., Indianapolis, IN 46268
Engbers, William J., 6457 St. Nicholas Dr., Sunman, IN 47041
Gayso, Edward V., 5235 E. Greenbriar Dr., Apt. 5A, Terre Haute, IN 47802
Herold, Carl A., 1650 Overlook Ln., Santa Barbara, CA 93103
Kraeszig, Charles J., 7901 Castle Dr., Lakewood Estates, New Port Richey, FL 34653
Marchino, Louis H., 127 Rossmore Dr., New Albany, IN 47150
Meny, Hilary G., P.O. Box 245, Haubstadt, IN 47639
Minta, John J., 213 Ripley, P.O. Box 336, Milan, IN 47031
Mueller, Richard J., 2722 B Marquette Manor W. Dr., Indianapolis, IN 46268
O'Riley, James K., 3388 Rothshire Cir., North Vernon, IN 47265
Sciarra, John N., 8300 Rahke Rd., Indianapolis, IN 46217
Sexton, Charles E., St. Paul Hermitage, 501 N. 17th St., Beach Grove, IN 46107
Stineman, William F., 7432-D Lions Head Dr., Indianapolis, IN 46260
Strahl, Ernest, St. Paul Hermitage, 501 N. 17th Ave., Beech Grove, IN 46107
Terrill, Richard F., 1391 Gardner Ave., Newago, MI 49337
Wright, John M., CHC,USN, 7972 Avenida Navidad, #86, San Diego, CA 92112

INSTITUTIONS LOCATED IN THE ARCHDIOCESE

[A] SEMINARIES, RELIGIOUS OR SCHOLASTICATES

ST. MEINRAD. *St. Meinrad Seminary*, 47577. Tel: 812-357-6611; Fax: 812-357-6964.
E-mail: @saintmeinrad.edu
Web site: www.saintmeinrad.edu
School of Theology. Revs. Mark O'Keefe, O.S.B., Pres. & Rector; Justin Duvall, O.S.B., Vice Rector & Provost; John J. Buckel; Patrick Cooney, O.S.B. (BEL); Simeon Daly, O.S.B.; Cyprian Davis, O.S.B.; Damian Dietlein, O.S.B.; Amador Garza (BWN); Harry Hagan, O.S.B.; Eugene Hensell, O.S.B.; Jeremy King, O.S.B.; J. Ronald Knott (L); Guy Mansini, O.S.B.; Noel Muller, O.S.B.; Jerome Neufelder (EVN); Nathaniel Reeves, O.S.B.; J. Lawrence Richardt (IND); Thomas Richstatter, O.F.M.; Denis Robinson, O.S.B. (MEM); Kurt Stasiak, O.S.B.; John Thomas (OWN); Cajetan White, O.S.B. Other Faculty and Staff 22; Students 89.

[B] COLLEGES AND UNIVERSITIES

INDIANAPOLIS. *Marian College*, 3200 Cold Spring Rd., 46222. Tel: 317-955-6000; Fax: 317-955-6048.
Web site: http://www.marian.edu
For a complete listing, refer to the Colleges and Universities section.

SAINT MARY-OF-THE-WOODS. *Saint Mary-of-the-Woods College*, 47876. Tel: 812-535-5151; Fax: 812-535-4613.
E-mail: smeier@woods.smwc.edu
Web site: http://woods.smwc.edu
For a complete listing, refer to the Colleges and Universities section.

ST. MEINRAD. *St. Meinrad Seminary-College of Liberal Arts*, 47577. Tel: 812-357-6611; Fax: 812-357-6964.
E-mail: @saintmeinrad.edu
Web site: www.saintmeinrad.edu
For a complete listing, refer to the Colleges and Universities section.

[C] HIGH SCHOOLS, INTER-PAROCHIAL

INDIANAPOLIS. *Bishop Chatard High School*, 5885 N. Crittenden Ave., 46220. Tel: 317-251-1451. Rev. David F. Coons. Priests 1; Sisters of St. Benedict 1; Brothers of the Holy Cross 1; Lay Teachers 44; Students 630.

Cardinal Ritter Junior-Senior High School, 3360 W. 30th St., 46222. Tel: 317-924-4333; Fax: 317-927-7822. Mr. Peter O'Rourke, Prin. Priests 2; Sisters 6; Lay Teachers 25; Students 401.

Father Thomas Scecina Memorial High School, 5000 Nowland Ave., 46201. Tel: 317-356-6377. Mr. Steve Papesh, Prin.; Rev. Peter Gallagher. Priests 1; Lay Teachers 36; Students 545.

Roncalli High School, 3300 Prague Rd., 46227. Tel: 317-787-8277.
E-mail: roncalli@indy.net
Web site: roncalli.org
Mr. Joseph D. Hollowell, Pres.; Rev. Steve Giannini. Priests 1; Sisters 3; Lay Teachers 65; Students 900.

CLARKSVILLE. *Our Lady of Providence*, 707 W. Hwy. 131, 47129. Tel: 812-945-2538. Mr. Cecil Mattingly, Prin.; Mr. Gerald Wilkinson, Pres.; Mr. Robert Casey, Asst. Prin.; Rev. H. Michael Hilderbrand, Chap. Priests 1; Sisters 1; Lay Teachers 52; Students (Grades 9-12) 642; Students (Grades 7-12) 720.

MADISON. *Shawe Memorial Junior-Senior High School*, 201 W. State St., 47250. Tel: 812-273-2150. Larry Truax, Pres.; Nancy McCabe, Prin. Lay Teachers 15; Priests 1; Sisters 1; Students 167.

[D] HIGH SCHOOLS, PRIVATE

INDIANAPOLIS. *Brebeuf Jesuit Preparatory School, Inc.*, 2801 W. 86th St., 46268-1925. Tel: 317-872-7050; Fax: 317-876-4732.
E-mail: brebeufl@iquest.net
Web site: www.brebeuf.indianapolis.in.us
Society of Jesus Community. 2823 W. 86 St., 46268-1926. Tel: 317-876-4700. Revs. Albert J. Bischoff, S.J., Rector; William P. O'Brien, S.J., Regent; Frederick J. Deters, S.J.; Joseph D. Folzenlogan, S.J.; Walter C. Deye, S.J.; J. Peter Carey, S.J.; George R. Menke, S.J.; Bro. John F. Buchman, S.J. Priests 6; Brothers 1; Regents 1; Lay Teachers 70; Students 729.

Cathedral High School (Cathedral Trustees, Inc.), 5225 E. 56th St., 46226.
E-mail: chsjtp@indy.net
Web site: www.cathedralirish.org
Julian Peebles, Pres.; Rev. Patrick J. Kelly, M.S., Prin. Sisters 5; Priests 2; Lay Teachers 72; Students 1,045.

OLDENBURG. *Oldenburg Academy of the Immaculate Conception*, 47036. Tel: 812-934-4440; Fax: 812-934-4838. Five-day boarding and day school. Martha J. Kollstedt, Prin. Sisters 3; Lay Teachers 17; Girls 180.

[E] RELIGIOUS EDUCATION CENTERS

CLARKSVILLE. *Aquinas Center for Continuing Religious Education*, 707 W. Hwy. 131, 47129. Tel: 812-945-0354.
E-mail: bobnadac@aol.com
Mr. Robert K. Leonard, Dir. Catechetical Ministry & Religious Education; Mr. D. Ray Lucas, Dir. Youth Ministries.
New Albany Deanery/Catholic Youth Ministry.

TERRE HAUTE. *Terre Haute Deanery Pastoral Center*, 2931 Ohio Blvd., 47803. Tel: 812-232-8400; Fax: 812-234-2665. Susan Butwin, Dir.; Marlene Mayfield, Staff Asst. Total Staff 2.

[F] GENERAL HOSPITALS

INDIANAPOLIS. *St. Vincent Hospital and Health Care Center, Inc.*, 2001 W. 86th St., 46260. Tel: 317-338-7000; Fax: 317-338-7005.
E-mail: jbford@stvincent.org
Web site: www.stvincent.org
For a complete listing, refer to the Hospitals section.

Seton Health Corporation of Central Indiana, 2001 W. 86th St., 46260. Tel: 317-338-7000; Fax: 317-338-7005.
E-mail: jbford@stvincent.org
Web site: www.stvincent.org
For a complete listing, refer to the Hospitals section.

BEECH GROVE. *St. Francis Hospital and Health Centers*, 1600 Albany St., 46107. Tel: 317-787-3311
For a complete listing, refer to the Hospitals section.

[G] PROTECTIVE INSTITUTIONS

TERRE HAUTE. *Gibault School for Boys*, 6301 S. U.S. Hwy. 41, P.O. Box 2316, 47802-0316. Tel: 812-299-1156
For a complete listing, refer to the Special Care Facilities section.

[H] HOMES FOR AGED

INDIANAPOLIS. *St. Augustine Home, Little Sisters of the Poor*, 2345 W. 86th St., 46260. Tel: 317-872-6420
For a complete listing, refer to the Special Care Facilities section.

BEECH GROVE. *St. Paul Hermitage*, 501 N. 17th Ave., 46107. Tel: 317-786-2261
For a complete listing, refer to the Special Care Facilities section.

NEW ALBANY. *Mercy Long Term Care Initiatives dba Providence Retirement Home*, 703 E. Spring St., 47150. Tel: 812-945-5221; Fax: 812-945-2614
For a complete listing, refer to the Special Care Facilities section.

[I] RETREAT HOUSES

INDIANAPOLIS. *Our Lady of Fatima Retreat House, Inc.*, 5353 E. 56th St., 46226. Tel: 317-545-7681; Fax: 317-545-0095. Mr. Kevin V. DePrey, Dir. Priests 1. Used by both clergy and laity.

BEECH GROVE. *Benedict Inn Retreat & Conference Center*, 1402 Southern Ave., 46107. Tel: 317-788-7581; Fax: 317-782-3142. Sr. Carol Falkner, O.S.B., Admin. Sisters 3. Retreats and workshops for clergy, religious, and laity.

MOUNT SAINT FRANCIS. *Mount Saint Francis Friary and Retreat Center*, 101 St. Anthony Dr., 47146-9999. Tel: 812-923-8817; Fax: 812-923-0177. Revs. Kevin Przybslki, O.F.M.Conv., Retreat Dir.; Ronald Bohl, O.F.M.Conv., Retreat Staff; Jim Van Dorn, O.F.M.Conv., Parish Missions; Eliot Comstock, O.F.M.Conv., Treasurer's Office. In res. Revs. Maximilian Korecki, O.F.M. Conv.; Robert Bayer, O.F.M.Conv.; Emmanuel Klump, O.F.M.Conv.; Dunstan Bryan, O.F.M.Conv., (Retired); Kenneth Gering, O.F.M.Conv., de familia; Ernest Waechter, O.F.M.Conv., de familia; Kevin Godfrey, O.F.M.Conv., de familia; Bros. Ambrose Eischens, O.F.M.Conv., Guardian; Robert Roddy, O.F.M.Conv., Retreat Staff; Angelo Catania, O.F.M.Conv., Retreat Staff; Lawrence Eberhardt, O.F.M.Conv., Archivist; Jeffry Hines, O.F.M.Conv., Sec. of the Province; Michael Austin, O.F.M.Conv., Vocation Promotion & Youth Min.; Bruno Nemcosky, O.F.M.Conv., Coord. of Medical Program & Mission Appeals; James Worchuck, O.F.M.Conv., Devel. Office Staff; Aloysius Wagener, O.F.M.Conv.

Province of Our Lady of Consolation, Inc. (Provincial Office). Tel: 812-923-8444; Fax: 812-923-8145. Revs. Kent Biergans, O.F.M.Conv., Min. Prov.; Richard Kaley, O.F.M.Conv., Vicar; Bro. Jeffrey Hines, O.F.M.Conv., Sec. of Province. Total Staff 4; Total in Residence 16.

ST. MEINRAD. *Archabbey Guest House*, 47577. Tel: 812-357-6585; 800-581-6905; Fax: 812-357-6325. Retreat House for Men, Women, Couples. Double Rooms 25.

[J] MONASTERIES AND RESIDENCES OF PRIESTS AND BROTHERS

INDIANAPOLIS. *St. Maur Priory*, 4615 N. Michigan Rd., 46208. Tel: 317-925-9095. Very Rev. Charles W. Henry, O.S.B., Prior; Rev. Bernardin Patterson, O.S.B. Priests 3; Brothers 4.

MOUNT SAINT FRANCIS. *Provincial Headquarters for the Conventual Franciscan Province*, 101 Anthony Dr., 47146. Tel: 812-923-8444; Fax: 812-923-8145. Very Rev. Kent Biergans, O.F.M.Conv., Minister Prov.; Rev. Richard Kaley, O.F.M.Conv., Vicar Prov.; Bro. Jeffrey Hines, O.F.M.Conv., Sec. of Province. Priests 3. Legal Title: *Provincial Headquarters for the Conventual Franciscan Province of Our Lady of Consolation.*

Vocation Office of the Province. St. Paul Friary, 6901 Dixie Hwy., Pleasure Ridge Park, KY, 40258. Tel: 502-933-4439. Rev. James Kent, O.F.M.Conv., Vocation Dir.

Priests of the Conventual Franciscan Province of Our Lady of Consolation Teaching or Studying at Universities: Rev. Duane Doherty, O.F.M.Conv., 3695 Lincoln, Birmingham, MI, 48010. Rev. Basil Heiser, O.F.M.Conv., Curia Generalizia, Piazza Ss. Apostoli, 51, Rome, Italy, 00187.

ST. MEINRAD. *St. Meinrad Archabbey*, 47577-1010. Tel: 812-357-6611; Fax: 812-357-6551.
E-mail: abbot@saintmeinrad.edu
Web site: www.saintmeinrad.edu
Archabbey of the Order of St. Benedict, including School of Theology and College of Liberal Arts, St. Meinrad Seminary. Rt. Rev. Lambert Reilly, O.S.B., Archabbot; Revs. Martin Dusseau, O.S.B., Prior; Harry Hagan, O.S.B., Master of Novices & Junior Master; Gavin Barnes, O.S.B.; Alban Berling, O.S.B.; Meinrad Brune, O.S.B.; Adrian Burke, O.S.B.; Adelbert Buscher, O.S.B.; Bede Cisco, O.S.B.; Aelred Cody, O.S.B.; Tobias Colgan, O.S.B.; Patrick Cooney, O.S.B. (BEL); John Cox, O.S.B. (PEO); Simeon Daly, O.S.B.; Augustine Davis, O.S.B.; Cyprian Davis, O.S.B.; Guerric DeBona, O.S.B.; Justin DuVall, O.S.B.; Gerard Ellspermann, O.S.B.; Jonathan Fassero, O.S.B.; Malachy Fulton, O.S.B.; Rembert Gehant, O.S.B.; Colman Grabert, O.S.B.; Theodore Heck, O.S.B.; Warren Heitz, O.S.B.; Eugene Hensell, O.S.B.; Columba Kelly, O.S.B.; Kilian Kerwin, O.S.B.; Micheas Langston, O.S.B.; Alcuin Leibold, O.S.B.; Mark Lewis, O.S.B. (SFD); Eric Lies, O.S.B.; Prosper Lindauer, O.S.B.; Conrad Louis, O.S.B.; Simon McTighe, O.S.B.; Guy Mansini, O.S.B.; Noel Mueller, O.S.B.; Louis Mulcahy, O.S.B.; Matthias Neuman, O.S.B.; Mark O'Keefe, O.S.B., Pres. & Rector, School of Theology & College; Rupert Ostdick, O.S.B.; Julian Peters, O.S.B.; David Rabenecker, O.S.B.; Nathaniel Reeves, O.S.B.; Denis Robinson, O.S.B. (MEM); Damian Schmelz, O.S.B.; Christopher Shappard, O.S.B.; Stephen Snoich, O.S.B.; Kurt Stasiak, O.S.B.; Germain Swisshelm, O.S.B.; Cyril Vrablic, O.S.B.; Donald Walpole, O.S.B.; Cajetan White, O.S.B. Priests 97; Brothers 37.

Priests of the Archabbey Teaching, Studying at Universities, or on Special Assignment: Rt. Rev. Bonaventure Knaebel, O.S.B., Resigned Archabbot, St. Michael Church, P.O. Box 22, Bradford, 47107. Rev. Benet Amato, O.S.B., St. Paul Parish, 814 Jefferson St., Tell City, 47586. Rev. Aurelius Boburek, O.S.B., The American College, Katholieke Universiteit Leuven, Naamsestraat 100, Leuven B-3000, Belgium. Rev. Theodore Brune, O.S.B., 1310 Broadway, Box 1750, Fargo, ND, 58107. Rev. Ephrem Carr, O.S.B., Collegio Sant' Anselmo, Piazza Cavalieri di Malta 5, Rome, Italy, I-00153. Rev. Noah Casey, O.S.B., 4826 Fletcher Ave., Indianapolis, 46203. Rev. Gregory D. Chamberlin, O.S.B., St. Benedict Church, 1328 Lincoln Ave., Evansville, 47714-1598. Rev. Camillus Ellspermann, O.S.B., St. Henry Rectory, 1311 W. 1100 S., Ferdinand, 47532. Rev. Cassian Folsom, O.S.B., Collegio Sant' Anselmo, Piazza Cavalieri di Malta 5, Rome, Italy, I-00153. Rev. Barnabas Gillespie, O.S.B., Guardian Angels Parish, 6531 Beechmont Avenue, Cincinnati, OH, 45230. Rev. Harold Hammerstein, O.S.B., 701 S. Boeke, Evansville, 47714. Rev. Boniface Hardin, O.S.B., 2171 Avondale Pl., P.O. Box 18567, Indianapolis, 46218. Rev. Richard Hindel, O.S.B., St. Bartholomew, 845 Eighth St., Columbus, 47201. Rev. Sean Hoppe, O.S.B., St. Augustine Church, General Delivery, Leopold, 47551. Rev. Aidan Kavanagh, O.S.B., 409 Prospect St., Hamden, CT, 06157. Rev. Michael Keene, O.S.B., St. John the Evangelist, 126 W. Georgia St., Indianapolis, 46225. Rev. Jeremy King, O.S.B., V.F., St. Meinrad Parish, 47577. Rev. Pius Klein, O.S.B., St. Mary Rectory, 313 Washington St., Huntingburg, 47532. Rev. Sebastian Leonard, O.S.B., Canterbury School, Aspetuck Ave., New Milford, CT, 06776. Rev. Edward Linton, O.S.B., 2106 Woodriver Dr., #8, Carbondale, IL, 62901. Rev. Ralph Lynch, O.S.B., St. Paul's Hermitage, 501 N. 17th Ave., Beech Grove, 46107. Rev. Keith McClellan, O.S.B., St. Mary of Celle Parish, 1428 S. Wesley, Berwyn, IL, 60402. Rev. Isaac McDaniel, O.S.B., St. Isidore Parish, Bristow, 47515. Rev. Alan R. McIntosh, O.S.B., 1500 S. St. James, Evansville, 47714. Rev. Severin Messick, O.S.B., St. Paul Parish, 814 Jefferson St., Tell City, 47586. Rev. Benedict Meyer, O.S.B., St. John the Baptist Parish, 203 W. Ash, Brinkley, AR, 72021. Rev. Godfrey Mullen, O.S.B., Catholic University of America, 311 Caldwell Hall, Washington, DC, 20064. Rev. Hilary Ottensmeyer, O.S.B., 1414 Southern Ave., Beech Grove, 46107. Rev. Mel Patton, O.S.B., Sacred Heart Monastery, 1005 W. Eighth St., Yankton, SD, 57078. Rev. Anselm Russell, O.S.B., St. Benedict Rectory, 1328 Lincoln Ave., Evansville, 47714-1598. Rev. Kevin Ryan, O.S.B., St. Thomas Church, P.O. Box 90, Helmville, MT, 59843. Rev. Raymond Studzinski, O.S.B., Curley Hall, Catholic University of America, Washington, DC, 20064. Rev. Timothy Sweeney, O.S.B., Parish of the Immaculate, 2516 Christie Place, Owensboro, KY, 42301. Rev. Vincent Tobin, O.S.B., Collegio di Sant'Anselmo, Piazza Cavalieri di Malta 5, Rome, Italy, I-00153. Rev. Frederick P. Walsh, O.S.B., Our Lady Queen Monastery, 50352 Antioch Rd., Tickfaw, LA, 70466. Rev. Joachim E. Walsh, O.S.B., Our Lady Queen Monastery, 50352 Antioch Rd., Tickfaw, LA, 70466. Rev. Marion Walsh, O.S.B., Our Lady Queen Monastery, 50352 Antioch Rd., Tickfaw, LA, 70466. Rev. Samuel Weber, O.S.B., St. Louis Church, 203 S. White Station Rd., Memphis, TN, 38117. Rev. Peter Yock, O.S.B., Collegio Sant'Anselmo, P. Cavalieri di Malta, 5, Rome, Italy, I-00153.

[K] CONVENTS AND RESIDENCES FOR SISTERS

INDIANAPOLIS. *Sisters of Our Lady of Mount Carmel Carmelite Monastery*, 2500 Cold Spring Rd., 46222. Tel: 317-926-5654; Fax: 317-926-1492. Sr. Joanne Dewald, O.C.D., Prioress. Professed Religious 14; Novices 3; Transfering from an Active Order 1.

BEECH GROVE. *Charitable Trust of the Monastery of Our Lady of Grace*, 1402 Southern Ave., 46107-1197. Legal Title: *Charitable Trust of the Monastery of Our Lady of Grace, Sisters of the Order of St. Benedict.*

Our Lady of Grace Monastery for Sisters of St. Benedict of Beech Grove, IN, Inc., 1402 Southern Ave., 46107-1197. Tel: 317-787-3287; Fax: 317-780-2368. Rev. Hilary Ottensmeyer, O.S.B., Chap., 1414 Southern Ave., 46107-1197. Tel: 317-786-0338. Sisters 89.

OLDENBURG. *Motherhouse of the Congregation of the Sisters of the Third Order of St. Francis*, 47036. Tel: 812-934-2475; Fax: 812-933-6403. Sr. Amy Kistner, O.S.F., Congregational Minister; Revs. Raymar Middendorf, O.F.M.; Sylvester Heppner, O.F.M., Assoc. Chap., Holy Family Friary. Professed Sisters in Congregation 372; Professed Sisters in Archdiocese 236; Total in Residence 139.

Sisters of St. Francis Community Support Trust.

SAINT MARY-OF-THE-WOODS. *Sisters of Providence General Administration*, 47876-1089. Tel: 812-535-4193; Fax: 812-535-4727.
Web site: www.spsmw.org
Sr. Diane Ris, S.P., Gen. Supr.; Rev. Bernard Head, Chap. Professed in Congregation 670; Professed Residing in Archdiocese 389; Novices 2; Postulants 1.

Sisters of Providence Community Support Trust.

Woods Day Care/Preschool, Inc. Total Staff 20; Children 58.

Providence Self-Sufficiency Ministries, Inc., 225 W. Daisy Ln., New Albany, 47150. Sr. Barbara Ann Zeller, Pres. Total Staff 36; Total Assisted 1,343.

St. Mary-of-the-Woods College. Total Staff 130; Total Assisted 1,267.

TERRE HAUTE. *Monastery of St. Joseph, Discalced Carmelites*, 59 Allendale, 47802-4751. Tel: 812-299-1410.
E-mail: carmelth@iquest.net
Mother Joseph of Jesus, Mary, O.C.D., Prioress. Solemnly Professed 14.

[L] ARCHDIOCESAN CHARITIES

INDIANAPOLIS. *Adult Day Services*, 1400 N. Meridian, P.O. Box 1410, 46201. Tel: 317-236-1500. Lula E. Baxter, Prog. Dir.

A Caring Place - Adult Day Care Center, c/o Fairview Presbyterian Church, 4609 N. Capital Ave., 46208. Tel: 317-466-0015; Fax: 317-261-3375. Sr. Susan Dinnin, Site Mgr.

Holy Trinity Place - Adult Day Care Center, 907 Holmes Ave., 46222. Tel: 317-638-8322. Joan Goote, Site Mgr.

St. Ann's Place - East, c/o Gethsemane Lutheran Church, 6810 E. 10th St., 46219. Tel: 317-261-3378. Susan Koehler, Program Coord.

St. Ann's Place - North, c/o Fairview Presbyterian Church, 4609 N. Capitol Ave., 46208. Susan Koehler, Program Coord.

Catholic Social Services of Central Indiana, The Catholic Center, 1400 N. Meridian St., P.O. Box 1410, 46206. Tel: 317-236-1500; Fax: 317-261-3375. Thomas Colbert, A.C.S.W., Exec. Dir. Total Staff 85; Total Assisted 3,848.

Holy Family Emergency Shelter, 30 E. Palmer St., 46225. Tel: 317-635-7830; Fax: 317-684-9702. Amy Moelhman, A.C.S.W., C.C.S.W., Dir. Total Staff 15; Total Assisted 1,437.

GREENSBURG. *Batesville Deanery Counseling & Family Mediations*, 420 E. Walnut St., 47240-1759. Tel: 812-663-2113.
E-mail: rrust@mail.gpbx.net
Dr. C. Renee Rust, D.Min., L.M.F.T., L.S.W., Counselor & Mediator.

NEW ALBANY. *Catholic Charities*, 702 E. Market St., 47150. Tel: 812-948-0438. Barbara K. Williams, M.S., C.S.W., Dir. Total Staff 3; Total Assisted 660.

St. Elizabeth's Regional Maternity Center, 601 E. Market St., 47150. Tel: 812-949-7305. Full-range maternity home and adoption agency offering residential and outreach services. Keith E. Stormes, Dir. Total Staff 15; Total in Residence 36.

TELL CITY. *Catholic Charities*, 802 Ninth St., 47586. Tel: 812-547-6414.

Rainbow Cottage Latch Key Program. Total Staff 4; Total Assisted 40.

TERRE HAUTE. *Catholic Charities of Terre Haute*, Corporate Square Annex, 2931 Ohio Blvd., 47803. Tel: 812-232-1447. John Etling, M.A., Dir. Total Staff 3.

Bethany House, 1402 Locust Ave., 47807. Tel: 812-232-4978. Marty Green, Mgr. Total Staff 3; Total Assisted 10,000.

Christmas House, 829 N. 14th St., 47808. Pat Armstrong, Dir. Total Staff 1; Total Assisted 3,600.

Household Exchange, 829 N. 14th St., 47807. John Etling, M.A., Dir. Total Staff 2; Total Assisted 960.

Ryves Hall Youth Center, 1356 Locust St., 47807. Tel: 812-235-1261. Jim Edwards, Youth Center Dir. Total Staff 4; Total Assisted 1,600.

Simeon House I (St. Patrick Parish), 1801 Poplar St., 47803. Tel: 812-232-6144. Delores Carbon, Dir. Total Staff 4; Total Assisted 175.

Anthony Square - Assisted Living, 400 College Ave., 47802. Tel: 812-232-6533. Harriett Johnson, Dir. Total Staff 4; Total Assisted 300.

Terre Haute Catholic Charities Foodbank, 1356 Locust St., 47807. Tel: 812-232-1447. Pat Etling, Dir. Total Staff 4; Total Assisted 80,000.

[M] CATHOLIC YOUTH ORGANIZATIONS

INDIANAPOLIS. *Catholic Youth Organization*, Related Ministries, 580 E. Stevens St., 46203. Tel: 317-632-9311. Mr. Edward J. Tinder, Exec. Dir.; Mr. Gerald R. Ross, Asst. Exec. Dir. Monsignor Downey Athletic Field. Perkins & Raymond St., 46203.

NASHVILLE. *C.Y.O. Camp Christina*, R.R. 2, Box 377, 47448. Mailing Address: 580 Stevens St., Indianapolis, 46203. Mr. Kevin Sullivan, Camp Mgr.

C.Y.O. Camp Rancho Framasa, 2230 N. Clay Lick Rd., 47448. Tel: 812-998-2839.
E-mail: cyocamp@aol.com
Mr. Kevin Sullivan, Camp Mgr.

[N] NEWMAN CENTERS

INDIANAPOLIS. *Butler University Newman Center*, 4615 Sunset Ave., 46208. Tel: 317-283-7651. Rev. Don Quinn, Dir. Total Staff 2; Total in Residence 1.

Indiana University-Purdue University, Indianapolis Newman Center, Catholic Student Center, 801 N. Dr. Martin Luther King Jr. St., 46202. Tel: 317-632-4378. Rev. Don Quinn, Dir. Total Staff 2; Total in Residence 1.

University of Indianapolis Newman Center, 4615 Sunset Ave., 46208. Tel: 317-283-7651. Rev. Don Quinn, Dir. Total Staff 2; Total in Residence 1.

BLOOMINGTON. *Indiana University, Bloomington Newman Center*, St. Paul's Catholic Center, 1413 E. 17th St., 47408. Tel: 812-339-5561.
E-mail: momara@indiana.edu
Web site: http://www.st-pauls.org
Revs. Michael O'Mara; Daniel Atkins. Total Staff 7; Total in Residence 9.

FRANKLIN. *Franklin College Newman Center*, 114 Lancelot Dr., 46131. Tel: 317-738-3929. Rev. Paul M. Shikany.

GREENCASTLE. *DePauw Catholic Campus Ministry*, c/o St. Paul Church, 202 E. Washington St., 46135. Tel: 317-653-5678. Rev. Michael C. Fritsch.

MADISON. *Hanover College Newman Center*, 305 W. State St., 47250. Tel: 812-265-4166; 273-1070. Rev. John A. Meyer.

RICHMOND. *Earlham College Newman Center*, 240 S. Sixth St., 47374. Tel: 317-962-3902. Revs. Todd M. Riebe, M.C.C.J., Admin.; Kevin J. Morris.

TERRE HAUTE. *Indiana State University, Rose Hulman Institute Newman Center*, St. Joseph Campus Center, 113 S. Fifth St., 47807-3577. Tel: 812-232-8088.

E-mail: slfmazzo@scifac.indstate.edu
Web site: http://mama.indstate.edu/users/sunmich
Janet R. Mazzoni, Pastoral Assoc. for Students.

[O] MISCELLANEOUS

INDIANAPOLIS. *Archdiocesan Black Catholics Concerned*, P.O. Box 88078, 46208-0078. Bro. Howard P. Studivant, O.S.B.

Association of Contemplative Sisters, c/o Carmelite Monastery, 2500 Cold Spring Rd., 46222. Tel: 317-926-5654. Ms. Barbara Scott, Pres. Membership 625.

**Holy Cross Chapter of St. Vincent De Paul Food Pantry, Inc.*, 125 N. Oriental St., 46202. Tel: 317-635-9560. Neal Mulligan, Coord. Total Assisted 5,000.

International Catholic Deaf Association (Chapter No. 38), c/o Metropolitan Tribunal, P.O. Box 1410, 46206. Tel: 317-236-1460; 872-5485; 800-855-2880 (TDD). Revs. Joseph W. Dooley, Chap.; Joseph G. Pesola.

St. Vincent De Paul Society Archdiocese Council of Indianapolis, Inc., P.O. Box 19133, 46219. Tel: 317-684-1009. Mr. Don Striegel, Pres. Total Assisted 25,000.

BEECH GROVE. *Alverno Administrative Services, Inc.*, 1300 Albany St., 46107. Tel: 317-783-9341; Fax: 317-781-2142. Mr. William G. Laker, Vice Pres. & CIO. Sponsored by Sisters of St. Francis Health Services, Inc.

Alverno-Beech Grove Corp., 1600 Albany St., 46107. Tel: 317-783-8133; Fax: 317-781-2142. Mr. Robert J. Brody, Pres. & CEO.

MADISON. *Prince of Peace Religious Education*, 305 W. State St., 47250. Tel: 812-265-4166. Sr. Alice Marie Gronotte, O.S.B., Pastoral Assoc. & D.R.E.

MOUNT SAINT FRANCIS. *Mount Saint Francis Sanctuary, Inc.*, 101 St. Anthony Dr., 47146-9999. Tel: 812-923-8817; Fax: 812-923-0177.
E-mail: thomasaZ@juno.com
Samuel L. Smith, Pres.; David Benedict, Vice Pres.; Thomas A. Smith, O.F.M.Conv., Treas.; Leopold Keffler, Sec.

NEW ALBANY. *New Albany Deanery-Catholic Youth Ministry*, 707 W. Hwy. 131, 47129. Tel: 812-945-0354; Fax: 812-945-2929.

[P] CLOSED PARISHES, SCHOOLS AND OTHER INSTITUTIONS

INDIANAPOLIS. *Archdiocese of Indianapolis Archives*, 1400 N. Meridian St., 46202. Tel: 317-236-1429.
Unless otherwise indicated, sacramental and other records may be found at the above address.
Closed Parishes and Missions:
Assumption (1894-1994). Merged with St. Anthony, where sacramental records are kept.
St. Bridget (1880-1994). Merged with SS. Peter & Paul, where sacramental records are kept.
St. Catherine of Siena (1909-1993). Merged with St. James and renamed Good Shephed, where sacramental records are kept.
St. Francis de Sales (1881-1983). Merged with four neighboring parishes.
St. James the Greater (1951-1993). Merged with St. Catherine and renamed Good Shepherd, where sacramental records are kept.
St. Joseph (1873-1949). Sacramental records kept at the new St. Joseph parish.
St. John the Evangelist (1855-1936), Acton.
St. Jude Thaddeus (1889-1898), Adyeville.
St. Patrick (1865-1973), Bainbridge.
Queen of the Most Holy Rosary (1917-1942), Blanford.
St. Patrick (1847-1902). Merged with St. Michael, Cannelton, where sacramental records are kept., Cannelton.
St. Joseph (1870-1970), Carbon.
St. Anthony (1917-1942), Centenary.
St. Anthony (1861-1993). Merged with Prince of Peace, Madison, where sacramental records are kept., China.
St. Columba (1963-1994). Merged with St. Bartholomew, Columbus, where sacramental records are kept., Columbus.
Sacred Heart (1868-1918), Cypress Dale.
St. Mary (1824-1973). Sacramental records kept at St. Augustine, Leopold., Derby.
St. John Baptist (Greek Uniate Catholic) (1897-1926), Diamond.
St. Mary (1897-1991), Diamond.
St. Michael (1820-1928), Dogwood.
Our Lady of Perpetual Help (1911-1982). Sacramental records kept at St. Mary, Sullivan Co., Diocese of Evansville., Dugger.
St. John (1910-1912), Ellsworth.
Mattingly Chapel (1874-1886), Eureka.
St. Augustine (1891-1980), Fontanet.
All Souls Chapel 1900-1915), Hovey.
St. Columban (1848-1868), Indian Creek.
St. Patrick (1868-1890), Knightsville.
Sacred Heart of Mary (1854-1922), Laconia.
St. Raphael (1869-1958). Sacramental records kept at St. Gabriel, Connersville., Laurel.
Mother of God (1854-1941), Lexington.
St. Joachim (1888-1930), Locust Point.
St. Mary (1851-1993). Merged with St. Patrick and renamed Prince of Peace, where sacramental records are kept., Madison.
St. Patrick (1853-1993). Merged with St. Mary and renamed Prince of Peace, where sacramental records are kept., Madison.
St. Patrick (1842-1881), McCutcheonville.
St. Mary (1905-1936), Mecca.
St. Joseph (1855-1974). Sacramental records kept at St. Joseph, Crawford Co., Milltown.
St. John Baptist (1852-1885), Mount Erin.
St. Rose (1821-1883), Mount Pleasant.
St. Bridget (1845-1936), Nebraska.
Holy Trinity (1836-1975). Merged with St. Mary, New Albany, where sacramental records are kept., New Albany.
St. Peter (1868-1885), Rome.
St. Catherine (1841-1871), St. Catherine.
St. James (1844-1850). Merged with St. Joseph, Perry Co. (1891-1968) and renamed St. Isidore, Perry Co., where sacramental records are kept., St. James.
St. Magdalen (1847-1941). Sacramental records kept at St. John, Osgood., St. Magdalen.
St. Paul (1859-1996). Sacramental records kept at St. Vincent, Shelby Co., St. Paul.
St. Peter, Perry Co.
St. Rose (1840-1903). Merged with St. Thomas, Knox Co., Diocese of Evansville, where sacramental records are kept., St. Rose.
St. Mary (1871-1902), Salem.
St. Patrick (1841-1958), Scipio.
St. Ann (1909-1978). Sacramental records kept at St. Mary, Sullivan, Diocese of Evansville., Shelburn.
Mother of God (1900-1920), Shirley.
St. Thomas (1845-1875), Taylorsville (Selvin).
St. John the Baptist (1855-1903), Valley Mills.
Our Lady of Lourdes (1900-1929), West Baden Springs.
St. Stephen (1906-1944), Willow Valley.
Closed Parish Grade Schools.
Assumption, All Saints Catholic School, 337 N. Warman Ave., 46222. Tel: 317-636-3739.
Cathedral, Holy Cross Central School, 125 N. Oriental St., 46201. Tel: 317-638-9068.
Holy Rosary, Holy Rosary Rectory, 520 Stevens St., 46203. Tel: 317-636-4478.
Holy Trinity, All Saints Catholic School, 337 N. Warman Ave., 46222. Tel: 317-636-3739.
Sacred Heart, Sacred Heart Rectory, 1530 Union St., 46225. Tel: 317-638-5551.
St. Ann, St. Ann Rectory, 2862 S. Holt Rd., 46241. Tel: 317-244-3750.
St. Anthony, All Saints Catholic School, 337 N. Warman Ave., 46222. Tel: 317-636-3739.
St. Bernadette.
St. Bridget.
St. Catherine, Central Catholic School, 1155 Cameron St., 46203. Tel: 317-783-7759.
St. Francis de Sales.
St. James the Greater, Central Catholic School, 1155 Cameron St., 46203. Tel: 317-783-7759.
St. Joseph, All Saints Catholic School, 337 N. Warman Ave., 46222. Tel: 317-636-3739.
St. Mary, Holy Cross Central School, 125 N. Oriental St., 46201. Tel: 317-638-9068.
St. Patrick, Central Catholic School, 1155 Cameron St., 46203. Tel: 317-783-7759.
St. Mary; St. Michael, Pope John XXIII Grade School, 221 State St., Madison, 47250. Tel: 812-273-3957.
St. Anthony, St. Anthony Rectory, P.O. Box 3, Morris, 47033. Tel: 812-934-6218.
St. Anne, St. Anne Rectory, 102 N. 19th St., New Castle, 47362. Tel: 765-529-0933.
Holy Family; St. Andrew; St. Mary, Elizabeth Ann Seton School, 801 W. Main St., Richmond, 47374. Tel: 765-962-4877.
St. Ann; St. Joseph, Student Services, Vigo County School Corp., P.O. Box 3703, Terre Haute, 47803. Tel: 812-462-4224.
St. Benedict, Terre Haute.
St. Margaret Mary, St. Margaret Mary Rectory, 2405 S. Seventh St., Terre Haute, 47802. Tel: 812-232-3512.
Closed High Schools and Academies.
Brute Latin School.
Chartrand; Kennedy; Sacred Heart, Roncalli High School, 3300 Prague Rd., 46227. Tel: 317-787-8277.
St. John; St. Agnes; Ladywood; Ladywood / St. Agnes Academies, Sisters of Providence, Records Office - Owens Hall, St. Mary-of-the-Woods, 47876. Tel: 812-535-3131.
St. Mary Academy, Registrar, Franciscan Motherhouse, Oldenburg, 47036. Tel: 812-934-2475.
Our Lady of Grace Academy, Our Lady of Grace Monastery, 1402 Southern Ave., Beech Grove, 46107. Tel: 317-787-3287.
Central Catholic High School for Girls, Terre Haute.
St. Patrick High School for Girls, Terre Haute.
St. Vincent Academy. Renamed St. Joseph Academy., Terre Haute.
Schulte High School, Student Services, Vigo County School Corp., P.O. Box 3703, Terre Haute, 47803. Tel: 812-462-4224.
Other Closed Institutions.
Sisters of the Good Shepherd Convent.
Angel Guardian School for Orphans. Entrance records, 1924-1937.
Marydale School For Girls. Sacramental records, 1875-1953. For other records contact Sisters of the Good Shepherd, 2849 Fischer Pl., Cincinnati, OH 45211. Tel:513-661-1833.
St. Edward Hospital, New Albany, Sisters of St. Francis of Perpetual Adoration (O.S.F.), Box 766, Mishawaka, 46546. Tel: 219-259-5427.
St. Ann Orphanage For Girls, Terre Haute.
St. Anthony Hospital, Terre Haute.

RELIGIOUS INSTITUTES OF MEN REPRESENTED IN THE ARCHDIOCESE

For further details refer to the corresponding bracketed number in the Religious Institutes of Men or Women section.

[0200]—*Benedictine Monks of St. Maur & St. Meinrad.*—O.S.B.
[0320]—*Brothers of Christian Instruction (Notre Dame Province).*—F.I.C.
[0600]—*Brothers of the Congregation of Holy Cross (Midwest & Eastern Provinces).*—C.S.C.
[0380]—*Camboni Missionaries of the Heart of Jesus.*—M.C.C.J.
[1140]—*Congregation of the Sacred Heart of Jesus & Mary.*—SS.CC.
[0480]—*Conventual Franciscans.* (Our Lady of Consolation Prov.).—O.F.M.Conv.
[0520]—*Franciscan Friars (St. John the Baptist & Sacred Heart Province).*—O.F.M.
[0690]—*Jesuit Fathers and Brothers.* (Chicago Prov.).—S.J.
[0840]—*Missionary Servants of the Most Holy Trinity.*—S.T.
[0420]—*Society of the Divine Word.* (Chicago Province).—S.V.D.

RELIGIOUS INSTITUTES OF WOMEN REPRESENTED IN THE ARCHDIOCESE

[0230]—*Benedictine Sisters of Pontifical Jurisdiction.* (Ferdinand, IN).—O.S.B.
[1920]—*Congregation of the Sisters of the Holy Cross.*—C.S.C.
[1730]—*Congregation of the Sisters of the Third Order of St. Francis, Oldenburg, IN.*—O.S.F.
[0760]—*Daughters of Charity of St. Vincent De Paul.* (Evansville, IN).—D.C.
[0420]—*Discalced Carmelite Nuns.*—O.C.D.
[1070-03]—*Dominican Sisters.*—O.P.
[2340]—*Little Sisters of the Poor.* (Baltimore, MD).—L.S.P.
[2820]—*Missionary Sisters of Our Lady of Africa.* (American Headquarters, Winooski, VT).—M.S.O.L.A.
[0440]—*Sisters of Charity of Cincinnati, Ohio.* (Central Region).—S.C.
[0500]—*Sisters of Charity of Nazareth.* (Nazareth, KY).—S.C.N.
[0430]—*Sisters of Charity of the Blessed Virgin Mary.* Dubuque, IA.—B.V.M.
[]—*Sisters of Loretto at the Foot of the Cross.* Nerinx, KY.—S.L.
[3360]—*Sisters of Providence of Saint Mary-of-the-Woods, IN.*—S.P.
[]—*Sisters of St. Benedict of Our Lady of Grace Monastery.* (Beech Grove, IN).—O.S.B.
[1640]—*Sisters of St. Francis of Perpetual Adoration.*—O.S.F.
[3840]—*Sisters of St. Joseph Carondelet.* (St. Louis, MO).—C.S.J.
[]—*Sisters of St. Joseph of Tipton.* (Tipton, IN).—C.S.J.
[3320]—*Sisters of the Presentation of the Blessed Virgin Mary.* (Dubuque, IA).—P.B.V.M.
[1720]—*Sisters of the Third Order Regular of St. Francis of the Congregation of Our Lady of Lourdes.*—O.S.F.
[2150]—*Sisters, Servants of the Immaculate Heart of Mary.* (Monroe, MI).—I.H.M.
[4120-03]—*Ursuline Nuns of the Congregation of Paris.*—O.S.U.

ARCHDIOCESAN CEMETERIES

INDIANAPOLIS. *Catholic Cemeteries*, 9001 Haverstick Rd., 46240.
Indianapolis Deanery.

Holy Cross.
St. Joseph.
Calvary.
Our Lady of Peace.
St. Malachy, Brownsburg.
St. Malachy, Pittsboro.

BATESVILLE. *Batesville Deanery.*
St. Mary, Greensburg.
St. John, Osgood.
St. Charles, Milan.
St. Maurice, Napoleon.

BLOOMINGTON. *Bloomington Deanery.*
Catholic, Martinsville.

CONNERSVILLE. *Connersville Deanery.*
St. Raphael, Laurel.
St. Michael, Brookville.
Holy Family, Oldenburg.
Holy Family Shrine, Oldenburg.
Cemetery North, Brookville.
Calvary, Rushville.
St. Bridget, Liberty.
St. Mary, Richmond.

NEW ALBANY. *New Albany Deanery.*
St. Joseph, Corydon.
St. Michael, Dogwood.
St. Peter, Taylor Two.
Cemetery South West, Bradford.
St. Bernard, Frenchtown.
St. Joachim, Locust Point.
St. Anthony, Jeffersonville.
Queen of Heaven.
St. Michael.

SEYMOUR. *Seymour Deanery.*
St. Ambrose.
St. Mary, North Vernon.
St. Catherine.
Old St. James.
St. Joseph.
St. Patrick.
St. Magdalen.

TELL CITY. *Tell City Deanery.*
St. Joseph, St. Croix.
St. Croix. (Cemetery on original parish site.), St. Croix.
St. Meinrad, St. Meinrad.
St. Paul.
St. Peter, Cannelton.

TERRE HAUTE. *Terre Haute Deanery.*
Catholic, Brazil.
Calvary.
St. Joseph.

NECROLOGY

† Courtney, Paul J., (Retired). —Died Feb. 2, 1997.
† Grogan, Richard, (Retired). —Died Oct. 4, 1997.
† Koopman, Bernard, Bradford, IN, St. Michael. —Died Feb. 26, 1997.

Diocese of Jackson

(Dioecesis Jacksoniensis)

Most Reverend

WILLIAM R. HOUCK, D.D.

Bishop of Jackson; ordained May 19, 1951; appointed Auxiliary Bishop of Jackson and Titular Bishop of Allessano on March 28, 1979; consecrated May 27, 1979; appointed Bishop of Jackson April 24, 1984; installed June 5, 1984. *Mailing Address: P.O. Box 2248, Jackson, MS, 39225-2248.*

Chancery Office: 237 E. Amite St., P.O. Box 2248, Jackson, MS, 39225-2248. Tel.: 601-969-1880; Fax: 601-960-8455.

Web site address: www.jacksondiocese.org

E-mail address: jxndio@netdoor.com

Legal Title: "Catholic Diocese of Jackson".

ESTABLISHED JULY 28, 1837 AS DIOCESE OF NATCHEZ. NAME CHANGED TO DIOCESE OF NATCHEZ-JACKSON, MARCH 7, 1957. NAME CHANGED TO DIOCESE OF JACKSON, JUNE 6, 1977

Square Miles 37,643.

Comprises 65 Counties in the State of Mississippi, namely: Adams, Alcorn, Amite, Attala, Benton, Bolivar, Calhoun, Carroll, Chickasaw, Choctaw, Claiborne, Clarke, Clay, Coahoma, Copiah, De Soto, Franklin, Grenada, Hinds, Holmes, Humphreys, Issaquena, Itawamba, Jasper, Jefferson, Kemper, Lafayette, Lauderdale, Leake, Lee, Leflore, Lincoln, Lowndes, Madison, Marshall, Monroe, Montgomery, Neshoba, Newton, Noxubee, Oktibbeha, Panola, Pike, Pontotoc, Prentiss, Quitman, Rankin, Scott, Sharkey, Simpson, Smith, Su.n-flower, Tallahatchie, Tate, Tippah, Tishomingo, Tunica, Union, Warren, Washington, Webster, Wilkinson, Winston, Yalobusha and Yazoo

STATISTICAL OVERVIEW

Personnel	
Bishop	1
Priests: Diocesan Active in Diocese	51
Priests: Active Outside Diocese	6
Priests: Diocesan in Foreign Missions	1
Priests: Retired, Sick or Absent	12
Number of Diocesan Priests	70
Religious Priests in Diocese	30
Permanent Deacons in Diocese	11
Total Brothers	9
Total Sisters	287
Parishes	
Parishes	74
With Resident Pastor:	
Resident Diocesan Priests	44
Resident Religious Priests	21
Without Resident Pastor:	
Administered by Priests	2
Administered by Professed Men Religious	1
Administered by Women Religious	4
Administered by Lay People	2
Missions	28
Pastoral Centers	3
Professional Ministry Personnel:	
Brothers	3
Sisters	23
Lay Ministers	15
Welfare	
Catholic Hospitals	1
Total Assisted	68,195
Health Care Centers	1
Total Assisted	7,655
Homes for the Aged	1
Total Assisted	225
Residential Care of Children	2
Total Assisted	168
Day Care and Extended Day Care Centers	2
Total Assisted	200
Specialized Homes	5
Total Assisted	2,000
Special Centers for Social Services	2
Total Assisted	8,050
Residential Care of Disabled	3
Total Assisted	60
Other Institutions	4
Total Assisted	150
Educational	
Diocesan Students in Other Seminaries	3
Total Seminarians	3
Colleges and Universities	1
Total Students	21
High Schools, Diocesan and Parish	4
Total Students	792
Elementary Schools, Diocesan and Parish	16
Total Students	3,200
Catechesis/Religious Education:	
High School Students	1,328
Elementary Students	4,543
Total Students Under Catholic Instruction	9,887
Teachers in the Diocese:	
Priests	2
Brothers	1
Sisters	22
Lay Teachers	313
Vital Statistics	
Receptions into the Church:	
Infant Baptism Totals	757
Adult Baptism Totals	167
Received into Full Communion	311
First Communions	740
Confirmations	474
Marriages:	
Catholic	98
Interfaith	228
Total Marriages	326
Deaths	459
Total Catholic Population	44,340
Total Population	1,980,025

Former Bishops—Rt. Rev. JOHN J. CHANCHE, S.S., D.D., cons. March 14, 1841; died July 22, 1852.—Rt. Rev. J. O. VAN DE VELDE, S.J., D.D., transferred from Chicago, July 29, 1853; died Nov. 13, 1855.—Most Rev. WILLIAM HENRY ELDER, D.D., cons. May 3, 1857; transferred to Cincinnati, 1880; died Oct. 31, 1904.—Most Rev. FRANCIS JANSSENS, D.D., cons. May 1, 1881; transferred to New Orleans, Aug. 7, 1888; died June 9, 1897.—Rt. Rev. THOMAS HESLIN, D.D., cons. June 18, 1889; died Feb. 22, 1911.—Rt. Rev. JOHN EDWARD GUNN, S.M., D.D., cons. Aug. 29, 1911; died Feb. 19, 1924.—Most Rev. RICHARD OLIVER GEROW, LL.D., S.T.D., ord. June 5, 1909; appt. June 25, 1924; cons. Oct. 15, 1924; retired Dec. 2, 1967; died Dec. 20, 1976.—Most Rev. JOSEPH B. BRUNINI, D.D., LL.D., J.C.D., ord. Dec. 5, 1933; cons. Jan. 29, 1957; appt. Bishop, Dec. 2, 1967; installed Jan. 29, 1968; retired Jan. 24, 1984; died Jan. 7, 1996.

Chancery Office—237 E. Amite St., P.O. Box 2248, Jackson, 39225-2248. Tel: 601-969-1880; Fax: 601-960-8455. The telephone number for all Diocesan Offices is 601-969-1880, unless otherwise listed. Office Hours: 8:30-4:30.

Office of the Bishop—Most Rev. WILLIAM R. HOUCK, D.D., *237 E. Amite St., P.O. Box 2248, Jackson, 39225-2248.*

Office of Vicar General—Revs. MICHAEL FLANNERY, J.C.L.; FRANCIS J. COSGROVE.

Department of Ecclesiastical Affairs—

Chancellor—Rev. MICHAEL FLANNERY, J.C.L., *237 E. Amite St., P.O. Box 2248, Jackson, 39225-2248.*

Vice Chancellor—Rev. AEDAN MANNING, S.T., J.C.L.

Director of Vocations—Rev. JOSEPH TONOS.

Director of Permanent Diaconate—Deacon FRANK AGOSTA.

Propagation of the Faith—Rev. Msgr. NOEL FOLEY, Dir., *P.O. Box 57, Jackson, 39205.* Tel: 601-969-3125.

Apostleship of Prayer—Rev. Msgr. NOEL FOLEY, Dir., *P.O. Box 57, Jackson, 39205.* Tel: 601-969-3125.

Archivist—JO ANN HAIEN.

Judicial Vicar—Rev. AEDAN MANNING, S.T., J.C.L.

Engaged Encounter—Rev. AEDAN MANNING, S.T., J.C.L., Dir.

Ecumenism—Rev. RICHARD SMITH, *St. Michael, P.O. Box 388, Forest, 39074-0388.* Tel: 601-469-1916.

Promoters of Justice—Revs. MICHAEL FLANNERY, J.C.L.; FRANCIS COSGROVE; THOMAS NIEMIRA.

Defenders of the Bond—Revs. MICHAEL FLANNERY, J.C.L.; FRANCIS COSGROVE; THOMAS NIEMIRA; WILLIAM CULLEN; DANIEL GALLAGHER; KEVIN SLATTERY.

Notaries—Rev. ROBERT OLIVIER; MARY BETH RABERT.

Diocesan Judges—Rev. Msgr. NOEL G. FOLEY, J.C.L.; Revs. PATRICK FARRELL; AEDAN MANNING, S.T., J.C.L.

Approved Advocate and Auditors—Revs. THOMAS DELANEY; CHARLES BUCCIANTINI; MEYRL SCHMIT; DON DERIVAUX, S.T.L.

Priests' Council—Most Rev. WILLIAM R. HOUCK, Pres.; Revs. ELVIN SUNDS, Chm. PATRICK FARRELL, Vice-Chm.; Rev. Msgr. NOEL FOLEY, Treas.; Revs. FRANCIS COSGROVE, Sec. GEORGE ARTIS, S.V.D.; CHARLES BUCCIANTINI; ALFRED CAMP; BRIAN CARROLL; MICHAEL FLANNERY, J.C.L.; SAMUEL MESSINA; MICHAEL O'BRIEN; ROBERT OLIVIER.

Diocesan Consultors—Revs. MICHAEL FLANNERY, J.C.L.; FRANCIS COSGROVE; Rev. Msgr. NOEL FOLEY; Revs. ROBERT OLIVIER; SAM MESSINA; PATRICK FARRELL.

Association of Priests—Most Rev. WILLIAM R. HOUCK, Co-Chm.; Most Rev. JOSEPH L. HOWZE, Co-Chm.; Rev. Msgr. NOEL FOLEY, Pres.; Rev. Msgr. RON HERZOG, Sec. & Treas. Trustees: Revs. KENT BOWLDS; THOMAS CONWAY; THOMAS MCGING; Rev. Msgr. MICHAEL THORNTON.

Personnel Board—Revs. MICHAEL FLANNERY, Personnel Dir. KENT BOWLDS; BRIAN CARROLL; JOSEPH DYER; ALFRED CAMP; PATRICK NOONAN.

Department of Administration & Finance—WILLIAM P. DUNNING, Dir., Admin. Affairs, *237 E. Amite St., P.O. Box 2248, Jackson, 39225-2248.*

Income Development—GEORGE ROMAN, Dir.
Department of Catholic Charities and Community Services—LINDA RAFF, Dir., *748 N. President St., P.O. Box 2248, Jackson, 39225-2248.* Tel: 601-355-8634; Fax: 601-960-8493.
Family Life—Sr. DOROTHY HEIDERSCHEIT, O.S.F., Dir. Tel: 601-355-8634.
Peace and Justice—LINDA RAFF, Dir., *P.O. Box 2248, Jackson, 39225-2248.*
Department of Educational Services—Rev. WILLIAM CULLEN, Dir., *237 E. Amite St., P.O. Box 2248, Jackson, 39225-2248.*
Superintendent of Schools—Sr. DEBORAH HUGHES, S.S.J.
Assistant Superintendent—Sr. MARY KAREN O'KELLY, O.P.
Early Child Development, Health and Education Projects—Sr. CYRENA HARKINS, R.S.M.
Director of Religious Education & Assistant of the Superintendant in School Administration—Sr. MAUREEN KENNEDY, O.P.
Director of Spring Hill Theology Program—Sr. MAUREEN KENNEDY, O.P.
Campus Ministry—Rev. WILLIAM CULLEN, Dir.
Department of Evangelization—Miss MARY WOODWARD, Dir.
Cursillo Movement—Rev. ANTHONY QUYET, Spiritual Dir.
Youth Ministry—Rev. JOSEPH TONOS, Diocesan Dir.
Pastoral Planning and Pastoral Councils—Miss MARY WOODWARD, Dir.
"Mississippi Today"—JANNA AVALON, Editor.
Intercultural Awareness/Diocesan Black Catholic Congress Board—Miss MARY WOODWARD, Dir.
Hispanic Ministry—Sr. PATRICIA BROWN, S.S.M.N., Dir.
Catholic Foundation-Diocese of Jackson—GEORGE ROMAN, Dir., *P.O. Box 2248, Jackson, 39225-2248.*
Friends of Catholic University—Rev. Msgr. NOEL FOLEY, Dir.
Holy Childhood, Pontifical Association—Sr. CYRENA HARKINS, R.S.M., Dir., *P.O. Box 2248, Jackson, 39225.*
The National Catholic Office for Motion Pictures—Rev. Msgr. NOEL FOLEY, Dir.

CLERGY, PARISHES, MISSIONS AND PAROCHIAL SCHOOLS

CITY OF JACKSON
(Hinds County)

1—ST. PETER CATHEDRAL, Rev. Patrick Farrell, Rector. In res., Revs. Michael Flannery; Daniel Gallagher.
Res., 123 N. West St., P.O. Box 57, 39205-0057. Tel: 601-969-3125; Fax: 601-969-3130.

2—ST. MARY, Revs. Richard P. Chiles, O.Praem., Admin.; Andrew Cribben, O.Praem.
Res., 653 Claiborne, 39209. Tel: 601-353-2292; Fax: 601-944-1606.
School—Tel: 601-353-7357. Sr. Mary Rose Meis, C.S.A., Prin.
Lay Teachers 6; Students 125.

3—ST. RICHARD, Rev. Msgr. Noel Foley; Rev. Jeffrey Waldrep. In res., Rev. Msgr. Michael Glynn; Rev. Aedan Manning, S.T.
Res., 1242 Lynnwood Dr., P.O. Box 16547, 39236. Tel: 601-366-2335; Fax: 601-366-0438.
School—Tel: 601-366-1157.
Sisters of Mercy 1; Lay Teachers 27; Students 450.

4—ST. THERESE, Rev. Thomas Lalor. Pastoral Assocs.: Mr. Nick L. Scheller; Mrs. Evelyn Thibeaux. In res., Rev. Brian Kaskie.
Res., 304 Fairhill Dr., 39204. Tel: 601-372-3441.
Church—309 McDowell Rd., P.O. Box 8642, 39284-8642. Tel: 601-372-4481.
School—Tel: 601-372-3323.
Lay Teachers 8; Students 154.

5—HOLY FAMILY, Rev. Edward Balser.
Res., 820 Forest Ave., 39206. Tel: 601-362-1888.

6—HOLY GHOST, Rev. George Artis, S.V.D.; Deacon Sam Baker.
Res., 1151 Cloister St., 39202. Tel: 601-353-1339.

7—CHRIST THE KING, Revs. Richard P. Chiles, O.Praem.; Andrew Cribben, O.Praem.
Res., 2303 J.R. Lynch St., 39209. Tel: 601-948-8867.
School—Preschool and Montessori, Tel: 601-352-5441. Mrs. Jocelyn Lyons, Dir.
Students 132.

OUTSIDE THE CITY OF JACKSON

Aberdeen, Monroe Co., St. Francis of Assisi, Rev. Timothy Murphy, Glmy.
Res., 104 S. James St., P.O. Box 134, 39730-0134. Tel: 601-369-2897.
Missions—Houston, Chickasaw Co., Immaculate Heart of Mary, P.O. Box 309, Houston, 38851. Tel: 601-456-5450; Okolona, Chickasaw Co., St. Theresa, 116 N. Fleming St., Okolona, 38860. Tel: 601-447-3008. Sr. Elizabeth Brown, C.S.J., Mission Coord.

Amory, Monroe Co., St. Helen, Sr. Marie Gilligan, S.C., Res. Pastoral Min.; Sr. Kathleen Quigley, S.C., Pastoral Assoc.
Res., 401 Eighth Ave. S., P.O. Box 97, 38821-0097. Tel: 601-256-8392.
Mission—Fulton, Itawamba Co., Christ the King, 100 E. Main St., Fulton, 38843-1207. Tel: 601-862-2239. Sr. Martha Werner, S.C., Mission Coord.

Batesville, Panola Co., St. Mary, Rev. Thomas Boyce.
Res., P.O. Box 569, 38606-0569. Tel: 601-563-2273.
Mission—Sardis, St. John the Baptist.

Belzoni, Humphreys Co., All Saints, Rev. Samuel Messina.
Res., 200 Bowles St., 39038-3602. Tel: 601-247-1408.
Mission—Anguilla, Our Mother of Mercy.

Booneville, Prentiss Co., St. Francis of Assisi, Rev. Thomas L. Burns, S.C.J.; Sr. Dorothy Pashuta, C.S.J., Pastoral Min.
Res., P.O. Box 654, 38829. Tel: 601-728-7509.
Mission—Iuka, Tishomingo Co., St. Mary, P.O. Box 651, Iuka, 38852. Tel: 601-423-9358. Sr. Dolores Partsch, C.S.J., Pastoral Min.

Brandon, Rankin Co., St. Paul, Rev. Brian Carroll; Deacon Frank Agosta.
Res., 115 Bellegrove Blvd., 39042. Tel: 601-992-9547; Fax: 601-992-9972.
Church—5971 Hwy. 25, 39042. Tel: 601-992-9547; Fax: 601-992-9972.
School—Learning Center, Tel: 601-992-2876; Fax: 601-992-9972. Sr. Terez Gonsoulin, S.S.N.D., Dir.
Students 100.

Brookhaven, Lincoln Co., St. Francis, Rev. Liam Pentony.
Res., 227 E. Cherokee St., P.O. Box 196, 39601. Tel: 601-833-1799.

Bruce, Calhoun Co., Calhoun County Catholic Community, Mrs. Amy Giorgio, Pastoral Coord.
Res., 204 E. Clay, P.O. Box 230, 38915. Tel: 601-983-2790; Fax: 601-983-2790.

Camden, Madison Co., Immaculate Conception, Rev. Joseph P. Keenan, S.T. In res., Rev. Celestine E. Pfannenstial, S.T.; Bro. Finbarr Ray, S.T.
Res., 1363 Hwy. 17, 39045. Tel: 601-468-2354.
School—Tel: 601-468-2324.
Sisters 3; Lay Teachers 5.

Canton, Madison Co., Sacred Heart, Rev. Patrick Noonan; Sr. Mary Ann Grausam, S.L.W., Pastoral Assoc. In res., Rev. Kevin Slattery.
Res., 238 E. Center St., P.O. Box 361, 39046. Tel: 601-859-3749.

Holy Child Jesus, Rev. Patrick Noonan, Admin.; Sr. Mary Ann Grausam, S.L.W., Pastoral Assoc.
Res., 315 Garrett St., P.O. Box 366, 39046. Tel: 601-859-2957.
School—Tel: 601-859-4168; Fax: 601-859-4168. Mrs. Doris Whigham, Prin.
Sisters 2; Lay Teachers 12; Students 184.

Carthage, Leake Co., St. Anne, Revs. Patrick Noonan, Admin.; Aedan Manning, S.T.; Sr. Patricia Godri, S.C., Res. Pastoral Min.
Res., 207 Red Dog Rd., 39051. Tel: 601-267-7190.

Charleston, Tallahatchie Co., St. John, Rev. Peter I. Machesky, O.F.M.
Res., 304 W. Cypress St., P.O. Box 30, 38921-0030. Tel: 601-647-3170.
Convent—402 N. Lafayette St., 38921. Tel: 601-647-8692. Daughters of Charity

Chatawa, Pike Co., St. Teresa, Rev. Robert Dore.
Res., P.O. Box 11, 39632-0011. Tel: 601-783-5931; Fax: 601-783-3984.
Mission—Magnolia, St. James.

Clarksdale, Coahoma Co., St. Elizabeth, Rev. Robert Kent Bowlds.
Res., 130 Florence Ave., 38614-2720. Tel: 601-624-4301.
School—109 Clark St., 38614-2720. Tel: 601-624-4239.
Lay Teachers 13; Students 137.

Immaculate Conception, Rev. Robert Kent Bowlds, Admin.; Sr. Agnes Zaroski, C.S.J., Pastoral Assoc.
Res., 510 Ritchie Ave., 38614. Tel: 601-624-4029; Fax: 601-627-4867.
Early Childhood Center—520 Ritchie Ave., 38614. Tel: 601-627-4823; Fax: 601-627-4867. Mrs. Catherine Fizer, Dir.
Lay Teachers 5; Students 65.

Cleveland, Bolivar Co., Our Lady of Victories, Rev. Charles Bucciantini.
Res., 215 Bishop Rd., P.O. Box 1450, 38732-1450. Tel: 601-846-6273.
Station—Cleveland, Delta State University.

Clinton, Hinds Co., Holy Savior, Rev. Noel Prendergast.
Res., 714 Lyndale St., P.O. Box 85, 39060. Tel: 601-924-6344.
Mission—Raymond, Immaculate Conception.

Columbus, Lowndes Co., Annunciation, Rev. Gerard Hurley; Sr. Josephine Fogarty, R.S.M., Pastoral Assoc.
Res., 808 College St., 39701. Tel: 601-328-2927; Fax: 601-329-8270.
School—223 N. Browder St., 39701. Tel: 601-328-4479; Fax: 601-328-0430.
Lay Teachers 14; Students 177.

Corinth, Alcorn Co., St. James, Rev. Thomas L. Burns, S.C.J.
Res., 3187 Harper Rd., P.O. Box 660, 38834-0660. Tel: 601-287-1385.
Church—3189 Harper Rd., 38834. Tel: 601-287-1051.

Crystal Springs, Copiah Co., St. John, Rev. Frank Corcoran.
Res., 217 E. Georgetown St., P.O. Box 167, 39059. Tel: 601-892-1717.
Mission—Hazlehurst, St. Martin.

Fayette, Jefferson Co., St. Anne, Rev. John Tyne, S.S.J.
Res., 195 New Harriston Rd., P.O. Box 159, 39069. Tel: 601-445-5700; Fax: 601-442-6030.

Forest, Scott Co., St. Michael, Rev. Richard Smith.
Res., P.O. Box 388, 39074. Tel: 601-469-1916.
Mission—Newton, St. Anne.

Greenville, Washington Co., St. Joseph, Revs. Richard Somers; John Joseph Bohn.
Res., 410 Main St., P.O. Box 1220, 38702-1220. Tel: 601-335-5251; Fax: 601-332-1178.
School—Our Lady of Lourdes, (Grades K-6). Tel: 601-334-3287; Fax: 601-332-9877. Sr. Marie Elizabeth Alspaugh, S.S.J., Prin.
Sisters 1; Lay Teachers 25; Students 345.
Junior & Senior High School—(Grades 7-12). Tel: 601-378-9711; Fax: 601-378-3496. Bro. Chris Kavanaugh, F.S.C., Prin.

Sacred Heart, Rev. August Langenkamp, S.V.D.; Bro. Matthew Connors, S.V.D., Pastoral Min.
Res., 560 E. Gloster St., 38701-3836. Tel: 601-332-0891.

Greenwood, LeFlore Co., Immaculate Heart of Mary, Rev. Thomas Delaney; Sr. Christiana Hofmann, S.C.N., Pastoral Min.; Deacon Leon S. Kitchin.
Res., 511 W. Washington St., P.O. Box 313, 38935-0313. Tel: 601-453-3980.
Parish Center—310 Henderson St., 38935-0313. Tel: 601-453-9535.

St. Francis of Assisi, Rev. Hilary Brzezinski, O.F.M.; Bros. Adrian Kolanczyk, O.F.M.; Paul West, O.F.M., Supr.; Donald Lucas, O.F.M.
Res., 2613 Hwy. 82 E., 38930-6070. Tel: 601-453-0623; Fax: 601-453-9060.
School—2607 Hwy. 82 E., 38930-6070. Tel: 601-453-9511; Fax: 601-453-9060.
Brothers 2; Sisters 4; Lay Teachers 6; Students 152.
Convent—2603 Hwy 82 E., 38930-6070. Tel: 601-453-1221; Fax: 601-453-9060.

Grenada, Grenada Co., St. Peter, Rev. Meyrl E. Schmit.
Res., 320 College Blvd., 38901. Tel: 601-226-2490.

Hernando, DeSoto Co., Holy Spirit, Revs. James A. Cunniffe, S.C.J.; Charles Yost, S.C.J.; Deacon Everell Van Tassel.
Res., P.O. Box 424, 38632. Tel: 601-429-7851; Fax: 601-429-7882.

Holly Springs, Marshall Co., St. Joseph, Revs. Paul Casper, S.C.J.; Lawrence Rucker, S.C.J., Assoc. Pastor.
Church—305 Van Dorn Ave., P.O. Box 430, 38635-0430. Tel: 601-252-3138; Fax: 601-252-1522.
School—Holy Family School, (Grades 1-8). Tel: 601-252-1612; Fax: 601-252-3694. Albert Langston, Jr., Prin.
Students 233.

Indianola, Sunflower Co., Immaculate Conception, Rev. Anthony Quyet.
Res., Hwy. 448, P.O. Box 944, 38751-9665. Tel: 601-887-4659.

St. Benedict the Moor, Rev. Anthony Quyet, Admin.
Res., 403 Church Ave., P.O. Box 407, 38751. Tel: 601-887-4608; 887-4659.

Kosciusko, Attala Co., St. Therese, Barbara A. Sturbaum, Ph.D., Pastoral Min.
Res., 108 Bell St., P.O. Box 628, 39090. Tel: 601-289-1193.

Leland, Washington Co., St. James, Rev. Sean Atkinson.
Res., 312 E. Third St., P.O. Box 352, 38756-0352. Tel: 601-686-7352; Fax: 601-686-7352.
Mission—Hollandale, Immaculate Conception.

Lexington, Holmes Co., St. Thomas, Rev. Hilary Brzezinski, O.F.M., Admin.
Res., 200 Boulevard St., P.O. Box 762, 39095. Tel: 601-834-4443.

Mission—Winona, Sacred Heart, 304 Jones St., Winona, 38967. Tel: 601-283-2808. Rev. John Rietti.

Louisville, Winston Co., Sacred Heart, Barbara A. Sturbaum, Ph.D., Res. Pastoral Min.
Res., 410 Spring Ave., 39339. Tel: 601-773-6062.

McComb, Pike Co., St. Alphonsus, Rev. William Henry.
Church—507 Delaware Ave., P.O. Box 1105, 39648-1105. Tel: 601-684-5648; Fax: 601-684-5290.
School—Elementary and Preschool, Tel: 601-684-1843. Mr. David Schommer, Dir.
Students 149.

Madison, Madison Co., St. Francis of Assisi, Revs. Francis J. Cosgrove; Jerry Alan Mattingly; Deacon Thomas Coffey.
Office: 4000 W. Tidewater Ln., 39110-8942. Tel: 601-856-5556; Fax: 601-856-2849.
Learning Center—Tel: 601-856-9494; Fax: 601-856-2849. Sr. Paula Blouin, S.S.N.D., Dir.
Students 155.
Mission—Gluckstadt, St. Joseph, Tel: 601-856-2054.

Magee, Simpson Co., St. Stephen, Rev. Robert Goodyear, S.T.
Res., 821 N. Jackson Drive, P.O. Box 427, 39111. Tel: 601-849-3237.
Mission—Raleigh, St. Paul.

Meridian, Lauderdale Co., St. Patrick, Rev. Elvin Sunds.
Church—2601 Davis St., P.O. Box 529, 39301. Tel: 601-693-1321; Fax: 601-484-8953. [CEM]
Res., 204-39th Ct., 39301.
School—Tel: 601-482-6044; Fax: 601-482-6044.
Lay Teachers 14; Students 240.
Mission—Quitman, Good Shepherd, Hwy. North, Quitman, 39355.
St. Joseph, Rev. Elvin Sunds, O.S.F., Admin.; Sr. Andre Burkhart, O.S.F., Pastoral Assoc.
Res., 1914 18th Ave., P.O. Box 532, 39302-0532. Tel: 601-485-5349.

Mound Bayou, Bolivar Co., St. Gabriel, Bro. Pius Kamphefner, F.S.C., Pastoral Min.
Res., P.O. Box 53, 38762-0053. Tel: 601-741-2439.
School—Tel: 601-741-2395.
Sisters 3; Lay Teachers 5; Students 70.

Natchez, Adams Co., Assumption of the B.V.M., Rev. John Brock.
Res., 10 Morgantown Rd., 39120-2788. Tel: 601-442-7250.
Mission—Meadville, St. Ann.
Holy Family, Rev. John J. Tyne, S.S.J.
Res., 16 Orange Ave., 39120. Tel: 601-445-5700; Fax: 601-442-6030.
School—Tel: 601-442-3947; Fax: 601-442-3947.
Sisters 3; Lay Teachers 12; Students 141.
Convent—8 Orange Ave., 39120. Tel: 601-445-4257. Sisters of the Holy Spirit
Mission—Cranfield, St. John the Baptist.
St. Mary, Revs. Alfred L. Camp; Walter W. Brown.
Res., 107 S. Union St., P.O. Box 1044, 39121-1044. Tel: 601-445-5616; Fax: 601-445-5616.
School—Cathedral Unit School. See High Schools, Inter-Parochial under Institutions Located in the Diocese. Tel: 601-442-2531.

New Albany, Union Co., St. Francis of Assisi, Rev. Steven P. Pawelk, Glmy.
Res., 1507 S. Central Ave., P.O. Box 887, 38652-0887. Tel: 601-534-9205.
Church—650 Hwy. 15 S., 38652-0887. Tel: 601-534-4654.
Mission—Pontotoc, Pontotoc Co., St. Christopher, S. Main St., P.O. Box 67, Pontotoc, 38863. Tel: 601-489-7749.

Olive Branch, DeSoto Co., Queen of Peace, Rev. John Young, S.C.J.; Deacon Henry Babin.
Res., 8680 Sandidge Rd., P.O. Box 65, 38654-0065. Tel: 601-895-5007; Fax: 601-895-5007.

Oxford, Lafayette Co., St. John, Rev. Joseph Dyer; Deacon Dr. Theodore Klingen.
Church: 403 University Ave., 38655-4329. Tel: 601-234-6073; 234-1940 (Res.); Fax: 601-234-6079.

Paulding, Jasper Co., St. Michael, Rev. Richard Smith, Admin.
Mailing Address: P.O. Box 388, Forest, 39074-0388.
Church—Star Rte., P.O. Box 15, 39348. Fax: 601-469-1916.

Pearl, Rankin Co., St. Jude, Rev. Martin Ruane. In res., Rev. William Cullen.
Res., 399 Barrow St., P.O. Box 5526, 39288-5526. Tel: 601-939-1863; 939-3181 (Office).
Station—Whitfield, Mississippi State Mental Hospital.

Philadelphia, Neshoba Co., Holy Cross, Rev. Kenan Ryan, S.T.
Res., 406 Wilson St., 39350-2906. Tel: 601-656-1841.
Holy Rosary (Tucker Community), Revs. David A. Hamm, S.T.; Raphael F. Toner, S.T.
Res., Hwy. 19, P.O. Box 37, 39350. Tel: 601-656-2880.
Missions—Conehatta, St. Catherine, Tel: 601-775-3900; Philadelphia, St. Theresa, Tel: 601-656-6411.

Port Gibson, Claiborne Co., St. Joseph, Rev. Msgr. Thaddeus Harkins.
Res., 411 Coffee St., P.O. Box 1012, 39150. Tel: 601-437-5790.

Ripley, Tippah Co., Tippah County Catholic Community, Mrs. Polly Duncan Collum, Pastoral Coord.
Res., 410 W. First St., 38663. Tel: 601-837-3529.

Rosedale, Bolivar Co., Sacred Heart, Pastoral Ministry Team: Sr. Marie Genevieve Love, O.P., Delta Dominican Ministries; Sr. Jeroma Day, B.V.M.; Sr. Catherine Leamy, S.N.J.M.; Revs. Charles Bucciantini; Donald F. Derivaux.
Res., P.O. Box 307, 38769. Tel: 601-759-6341.

Senatobia, Tate Co., St. Gregory the Great, Rev. James Schifano, S.C.J.
Res., 1360 Nesbit Rd., P.O. Box 38, Nesbit, 38651. Tel: 601-429-8266; Fax: 601-429-8369.
Church—P.O. Box 515, 707 Strayhorn St., 38668-0515. Tel: 601-562-5318 (Office).

Shaw, Bolivar Co., St. Francis of Assisi, In res., Rev. Donald F. Derivaux.
Res., 303 Dean Blvd., P.O. Box 239, 38773. Tel: 601-754-5561.

Shelby, Bolivar Co., St. Mary, Rev. James Carroll.
Res., 700 Second St., P.O. Box 208, 38774-0208. Tel: 601-398-7964.
Station—Shelby, Parchman State Penitentiary, Tel: 601-745-6611.

Southhaven, DeSoto Co., Christ the King, Revs. Brian McCullough, S.C.J.; Francis J. Burshnick, S.C.J.; Deacon Lawrence M. Campbell; Sr. Joann Mascari, O.P.
Office: 1090 Stateline Rd., W. Southhaven, 38671. Tel: 601-342-1073; Fax: 601-342-1074.

Starkville, Oktibbeha Co., St. Joseph, Rev. Michael O'Brien. In res., Rev. Francois Pellissier.
Res., 607 University Dr., 39759. Tel: 601-323-2257; Fax: 601-323-2258.
Mission—Macon, Corpus Christi.
Chaplaincy—Mississippi State University.

Tupelo, Lee Co., St. James, Rev. Henry Shelton.
Res., 820 Lakeshire Dr., P.O. Box 734, 38802-0734. Tel: 601-842-4881; Fax: 601-844-0327.
Mission—Saltillo, St. Thomas Aquinas.

Vicksburg, Warren Co., St. Paul, Rev. Thomas McGing.
Res., 713 Crawford St., P.O. Box 646, 39180-0646. Tel: 601-636-0140.
High School—Vicksburg Catholic School, (Grades K-12). See High Schools, Inter-Parochial under Institutions Located in the Diocese. Tel: 601-636-2256.
St. Mary, Rev. Charles Boykins.
Res., 1512 Main St., 39180. Tel: 601-636-0115.
St. Michael, Rev. James O'Riordan.
Res., 100 St. Michael Pl., 39180. Tel: 601-636-3445.

Walls, DeSoto Co., Sacred Heart, Revs. James Schifano, S.C.J., Pastoral Care; Francis J. Burshnick, S.C.J.
Office: P.O. Box 131, 38680. Tel: 601-781-0450.
School—Tel: 601-781-0650; Fax: 601-781-9225.
Sisters 2; Lay Teachers 25; Students 273.
Convent—P.O. Box 237, 38680. Tel: 601-781-9233. School Sisters of St. Francis
Mission—Tunica, Tunica Co., St. Anthony of Padua, E. Edwards St., Tunica, 38676. Rev. Dermot J. Twomey, S.C.J., Admin. Protem.

West Point, Clay Co., Immaculate Conception.Rev. John Vollor.
Res., 617 E. Main, 39773-3007. Tel: 601-494-3486.
Mission—Europa, Webster Co., St. John, 201 W. Roane St., Europa, 39744. Tel: 601-258-7539.

Woodville, Wilkinson Co., St. Joseph, Rev. Charles Loyacono.
Res., 338 Church St., P.O. Box 668, 39669. Tel: 601-888-3261.
Missions—Fort Adams, St. Patrick; Gloster, Amite Co., Holy Family, P.O. Box 548, Gloster, 39638. Tel: 601-225-4171.

Yazoo City, Yazoo Co., St. Mary, Rev. Patrick J. Curley.
Res., 129 N. Washington St., P.O. Box 27, 39194-0027. Tel: 601-746-1680.
St. Francis, Rev. Patrick J. Curley, Admin.
Res., 735 E. Powell St., 39194. Tel: 601-746-1680.

Chaplains of Public Institutions

JACKSON. *Institute for the Blind, Institute for the Deaf and Speech Impaired*. Rev. Msgr. Noel Foley.
University of Mississippi Medical Center. Rev. Patrick Farrell; Sr. Sharon Glumb, S.L.W., Campus Min.
Veterans Administration Hospital. Rev. Daniel Gallagher.

MERIDIAN. *East Mississippi State Hospital*. Rev. Elvin Sunds.

PARCHMAN. *Mississippi State Penitentiary*. Rev. James Carroll; Sr. Marie Genevieve Love, O.P., Chap.

PEARL. *Rankin County Prison*. Rev. Martin Ruane.

SANATORIUM. *Boswell Retardation Center*. Rev. Robert Goodyear, S.T.

WHITFIELD. *Mississippi State Hospital*. Rev. Martin Ruane.

On Duty Outside the Diocese:
Reverend Fathers—
Johnson, Howard
Lopez, Jose
Madden, Paul
Niemira, Thomas
O'Connor, David
Quinn, Peter
Spadini, Marian

Retired:
Reverend Monsignors—
Glynn, Michael, St. Richard Church, P.O. Box 16547, Jackson, MS 39236-6547
Koury, Joseph A., 105 Abby Oaks Dr., Clinton, MS 39056
Reverend Fathers—
Brett, James G., King's Daughters & Sons Rest Home, 6615 Poplar Spring Dr., Apt. #8, Meridian, MS 39305
Curley, Patrick J., 113 Sherri Ln., Oceanside, CA 92054
DeMeules, Donald H., 5500 Boone Ave. N., New Hope, MN 55428
Engelhart, William, 515 Laurel St., McComb, MS 39648
Green, Lacy, Miramar Lodge Nursing, 216 W. Beach Blvd., Pass Christian, MS 39571
Leonard, John, Vicksburg Apartments, 801 Clay St., Apt. #10-A, Vicksburg, MS 39180
Maloney, Walter, 200 Dominican Dr. #5108, Madison, MS 39110-8612
Pudenz, Anthony

Permanent Deacons:
Agosta, Frank, St. Paul, Brandon
Babin, Henry, Queen of Peace, Olive Branch
Baker, Sam, Holy Ghost, Jackson
Campbell, Lawrence M., Christ the King, Southhaven
Coffey, Thomas, St. Francis of Assisi, Madison
Kitchin, Leon S., Immaculate Heart of Mary, Greenwood
Klingen, Dr. Theodore, St. John, Oxford
McCarthy, Kevin J., St. Joseph Mission, Gluckstadt
Pancratz, Arnold, St. Richard, Jackson
Stasiulis, Stan, Unassigned
Van Tassel, Everell, Holy Spirit, Hernando

INSTITUTIONS LOCATED IN THE DIOCESE

[A] HIGH SCHOOLS, INTER-PAROCHIAL

JACKSON. *St. Joseph Catholic School*. (Grades 7-12). (Coed), 100 Holly Drive, 39206. Tel: 601-982-5000; Fax: 601-982-5001. Sr. Jackie Howard, R.S.M., Prin.; Rev. Msgr. Paul Canonici, Pres. Priests 3; Sisters 4; Lay Teachers 22; Students 293.

GREENVILLE. *St. Joseph Junior-Senior High School*. (Grades 7-12). (Coed), 700 Golf St., 38701. Tel: 601-378-9711; Fax: 601-378-3496. Bro. Chris Kavanaugh, F.S.C., Prin. Brothers 1; Lay Teachers 29; Students 370.

NATCHEZ. *Cathedral Unit School*. (Grades PreK-12). (Coed), 701 Martin Luther King, Jr. St., 39120. Tel: 601-442-2531; Fax: 601-445-9844.
E-mail: jaxchs@connectinc.com
Mr. Jules Michel, Prin. Sisters 2; Lay Teachers 41; Students 698.

VICKSBURG. *Vicksburg Catholic School*. (Grades K-12). (Coed), 1900 Grove St., 39180. Tel: 601-636-2256.
E-mail: jaxvcs@connectinc.com
Mr. George Valadie, Prin. Sisters 2; Lay Teachers 49; Students 655.

[B] SPECIAL SCHOOLS

JACKSON. *St. Richard's Special Kids Program*, P.O. Box 16172, 39236. John Tracy, Coord. Lay Teachers 2; Aides 2; Students 21.

[C] GENERAL HOSPITALS

JACKSON. *St. Dominic-Jackson Memorial Hospital*, 969 Lakeland Dr., 39216. Tel: 601-982-0121
For a complete listing, refer to the Hospitals section.

TUTWILER. *Tutwiler Clinic, Inc.*, 205 Alma St., P.O. Box 462, 38963-0462. Tel: 601-345-8334; Fax: 601-345-8336.
E-mail: sabrooks@pol.net
For a complete listing, refer to the Hospitals section.

[D] ORPHANAGES AND INFANT HOMES

JACKSON. *D'Evereaux Hall Home, Inc.*, P.O. Box 2248, 39225. Tel: 601-355-8634
For a complete listing, refer to the Special Care Facilities section.

St. Mary Orphan Home, Inc., P.O. Box 2248, 39225. Tel: 601-355-8634
For a complete listing, refer to the Special Care Facilities section.

[E] MONASTERIES AND RESIDENCES OF PRIESTS AND BROTHERS

JACKSON. *Priory of St. Moses the Black*, 653 Claiborne Ave., 39209. Tel: 601-354-3287. Canons Regular of Premontre (The Premonstratensian Fathers). Revs. Richard P. Chiles, O.Praem., Prior; Xavier G. Colavechio, O.Praem.; Martin Philipsen, O.Praem.; Andrew Cribben, O.Praem.; Norbert N'Zilamba, O.Praem.; Joseph Tonos; Bro. James Herring. Priests 6; Novices 1.

GREENVILLE. *Emmanuel House*, 710 Golf St., 38701. Tel: 601-335-4660. Bro. Chris Kavanaugh, F.S.C. Brothers 1.

NESBIT. *St. Michael Community House*, 1360 Nesbit Rd., P.O. Box 38, 38651. Tel: 601-429-8424. Revs. Charles Yost, S.C.J., Coord.; Francis J. Burshnick, S.C.J.; James A. Cunniffe, S.C.J.; Robert Hess, S.C.J.; Thomas Lind, S.C.J.; James Schifano, S.C.J.; Kenneth Stoll, S.C.J.; Dermot J. Twomey, S.C.J.

[F] CONVENTS AND RESIDENCES FOR SISTERS

JACKSON. *Our Lady of Mount Carmel and Little Flower Monastery*, 2155 Terry Rd., 39204. Tel: 601-373-1460.
E-mail: jm2155jt@aol.com
Sr. Dona Marie Degnan, O.C.D., Prioress. Discalced Carmelites. Nuns with Solemn Vows 3; Temporary Vows 1.

BROOKSVILLE. *The Dwelling Place*, 2824 Dwelling Place Rd., 39739-9537. Tel: 601-738-5348. Sr. Clare Van Lent, Dir.

CHATAWA. *St. Mary of the Pines*, 39632. Tel: 601-783-3494; Fax: 601-783-3984. Sr. Suzanne Pescay, S.S.N.D., Admin. Home for the Retired Sisters of the Dallas Province of the School Sisters of Notre Dame. Retreat Center for Lay and Religious Groups. Sisters in Residence 67.

PHILADELPHIA. *Holy Rosary Convent*, P.O. Box 496, 39350. Tel: 601-656-2949. Sister Servants of the Immaculate Heart of Mary 2.

VICKSBURG. *McAuley Home, Sisters of Mercy Retirement Home*, 102 McAuley Dr., 39180-2825. Tel: 601-636-0601. Sisters 13.

Sisters of Mercy, 1625 East Ave., 39180. Tel: 601-638-8636. Sisters of Mercy 3.

Sisters of Mercy Convent, 103 McAuley Dr., 39180-2824. Tel: 601-634-8845. Sisters 5.

[G] NEWMAN CENTERS

JACKSON. *Belhaven College Newman Center*, P.O. Box 57, 39205-0057.
E-mail: glumbs@okra.millsaps.edu
Rev. Msgr. Noel Foley; Sr. Sharon Glumb, S.L.W.

Jackson State University Newman Center, 2303 Lynch St., 32909. Revs. Richard P. Chiles, O.Praem.; Andrew Cribben, O.Praem.

Millsaps College Newman Center, P.O. Box 57, 39205-0057.
E-mail: glumbs@okra.millsaps.edu
Rev. Msgr. Noel Foley; Sr. Sharon Glumb, S.L.W.

Tougaloo College Newman Center, Holy Ghost Church, 1151 Cloister St., 39202. Rev. George Artis, S.V.D.

University of Mississippi Medical Center - Newman Center, P.O. Box 57, 39205-0057.
E-mail: glumbs@okra.millsaps.edu
Rev. Msgr. Noel Foley; Sr. Sharon Glumb, S.L.W.

AMORY. *Ittawamba Community College Newman Center*, St. Helen, P.O. Box 97, 38821-0097. Sr. Marie Gilligan, S.C.

BOONEVILLE. *Northeast Mississippi Community College Catholic Student Center*, St. Francis of Assisi, P.O. Box 654, 38829. Sr. Dorothy Pashuta, C.S.J.

BROOKHAVEN. *Lincoln Junior College Newman Center*, P.O. Box 196, 39601. Rev. Liam Pentony.

CLEVELAND. *Delta State University Newman Center*, Our Lady of Victories, 215 Bishop Rd., P.O. Box 1450, 38732-1450. Rev. Charles Bucciantini.

CLINTON. *Mississippi College Newman Center*, Holy Savior Church, P.O. Box 85, 39060. Rev. Noel Prendergast.

COLUMBUS. *Mississippi State University for Women Student Center*, Annunciation Church, 808 College St., 39701. Rev. Gerard Hurley.

FOREST. *East Central Community College Newman Center*, St. Michael's Church, P.O. Box 388, 39074. Rev. Richard Smith.

GREENWOOD. *Holmes Community College Newman Center*, St. Francis of Assisi, 2613 Hwy. 82 E., 38930-6070. Rev. Hilary Brzezinski, O.F.M.

HOLLY SPRINGS. *Rust College Newman Center*, St. Joseph's, P.O. Box 430, 38635. Rev. Lawrence Rucker, S.C.J., Chap.

OXFORD. *University of Mississippi Newman Center*, St. John Church, 403 University Ave., 38655; Fax: 601-234-6079. Rev. Joseph Dyer; Deacon Dr. Theodore Klingen; Ms. Lorraine Turgeon, Campus Min.

RAYMOND. *Hinds Community College Catholic Student Organization*, Immaculate Conception, 39154. Rev. Noel Prendergast; Mrs. Denise Scifres.

SENATOBIA. *Northwest Mississippi Community College Newman Center*, St. Gregory Church, P.O. Box 515, 38668. Rev. James Schifano, S.C.J.

STARKVILLE. *Mississippi State University Catholic Student Association*, St. Joseph Church, 607 University Dr., 39759. Rev. Michael O'Brien.

[H] MISCELLANEOUS

JACKSON. *Nuestra Senora Del Perpetuo Socorro*, P.O. Box 2248, 39225-2248. Rev. Msgr. Michael Thornton. Saltillo Mission Sponsored by Dioceses of Jackson and Biloxi. Apdo. 509 Suc. A, Saltillo, Mexico, C.P. 25000. Tel: 001-52-841-48516.

Pax Christi-Franciscan, LaVerna House, 2108 Alta Woods Blvd, 39204. Tel: 601-373-4463. Genevieve Feyen, Pres.; Rhoda Kalscheur, House Dir. A Public Association of the faithful, living a consecrated life, engaged in social and educational works. Consecrated Members 8.

ABERDEEN. *Catholic Committee of the South, Inc.*, St. Francis of Assisi, Box 134, 39730. Tel: 601-369-2897. Sr. Evelyn Dettling, O.S.B., Coord.

CANTON. *Notre Dame Education Center, Inc.* Mailing Address: P.O. Box 505, 39046. 153 E. Center St., 39046. Tel: 601-859-6826; Fax: 601-859-6898. Res., 519 E. Peace St., 39046. Tel: 601-859-7654.

GREENWOOD. *Pax Christi-Franciscan*, St. Francis Information Center, 708 Ave. I, 38930. Tel: 601-453-1465. Genevieve Feyen, Pres.; Bessie Willburn, Center Dir. A Public Association of the faithful, living a consecrated life, engaged in social and educational works. Consecrated Members 8.

MARKS. *DePorres Delta Ministries, Inc.*, 217 Locust St., P.O. Box 207, 38646. Tel: 601-326-2323.

DePorres Health Center, 411 Poplar St., P.O. Box 376, 38646. Tel: 601-326-9232. Sr. Andrea Balconis, O.P., M.D., Contact Person & Dir.

DePorres Social Services, 217 Locust St., P.O. Box 292, 38646. Tel: 601-326-2323. Sr. Selina Stanaway, O.P., Contact Person & Dir.

San Martin Center, 317 Locust St., P.O. Box 248, 38646. Tel: 601-326-5404. Sr. Joan Dunning, O.P., Contact Person & Dir.

WALLS. *Sacred Heart League*, 6050 Hwy. 61 N., P.O. Box 300, 38680-0300. Tel: 601-781-1360; Fax: 601-781-3340. Rev. Robert Hess, S.C.J., Pres. & Spiritual Dir.; Mr. Roger Courts, Dir. & CEO.

Sacred Heart Southern Missions Housing Corporation, P.O. Box 365, 38680-0365. Tel: 601-781-3298; Fax: 601-781-3534. Sr. Mary Anne Guthrie, Coord. of Housing; Mr. Paul Bauer, Pres.; Mr. Morgan Billingsley, Vice Pres. & Treas.; Mr. J. Martin Regan, Jr., Sec.

Sacred Heart Southern Missions, Inc., 6473 Hwy. 61 N., P.O. Box 190, 38680-0190. Tel: 601-781-1472; Fax: 601-781-0842. Sr. Maria V. Brocato, S.C.N., Exec. Dir.

RELIGIOUS INSTITUTES OF MEN REPRESENTED IN THE DIOCESE

For further details refer to the corresponding bracketed number in the Religious Institutes of Men or Women section.

[1350]—*Brothers of St. Francis Xavier.*—C.F.X.

[0330]—*Brothers of the Christian Schools.* (Prov. of St. Louis, MO).—F.S.C.

[0900]—*Canons Regular of Premontre.*—O.Praem.

[1130]—*Congregation of the Priests of the Sacred Heart.*—S.C.J.

[0520]—*Franciscan Friars.* (Pulaski, WI).—O.F.M.

[0570]—*Glenmary Home Missioners.*—Glmy.

[0840]—*Missionary Servants of the Most Holy Trinity.*—S.T.

[0700]—*St. Joseph's Society of the Sacred Heart.*—S.S.J.

[0420]—*Society of the Divine Word.*—S.V.D.

RELIGIOUS INSTITUTES OF WOMEN REPRESENTED IN THE DIOCESE

[]—*Congregation of Sisters of Charity of St. Charles Borromeo.*—C.B.

[2410]—*Congregation of the Marianites of the Holy Cross.*—M.S.C.

[3710]—*Congregation of the Sisters of Saint Agnes.*—C.S.A.

[1780]—*Congregation of the Sisters of the Third Order of St. Francis of Perpetual Adoration.*—F.S.P.A.

[0760]—*Daughters of Charity of St. Vincent de Paul.*—D.C.

[0420]—*Discalced Carmelite Nuns.*—O.C.D.

[1070-03]—*Dominican Sisters.* (Sinsinawa, WI).—O.P.

[1070-06]—*Dominican Sisters.* (Newburgh, NY).—O.P.

[1070-09]—*Dominican Sisters.* (Racine, WI).—O.P.

[1070-10]—*Dominican Sisters.* (Springfield, IL).—O.P.

[1070-13]—*Dominican Sisters.* (Adrian, MI).—O.P.

[1310]—*Franciscan Sisters of Little Falls, Minnesota.*—O.S.F.

[2575]—*Institute of the Sisters of Mercy of the Americas.* (Rochester, NY; St. Louis, MO).—R.S.M.

[]—*Literary Society of St. Catherine of Sienna Kentucky Dominican.*—O.P.

[2800]—*Missionary Sisters of the Most Sacred Heart of Jesus.*—M.S.C.

[2970]—*School Sisters of Notre Dame.* (Baltimore & Dallas Provs., Mankato).—S.S.N.D.

[1680]—*School Sisters of St. Francis.*—O.S.F.

[0500]—*Sisters of Charity of Nazareth.* (Kentucky).—S.C.N.

[0590]—*Sisters of Charity of Saint Elizabeth, Convent Station.*—S.C.

[0430]—*Sisters of Charity of the Blessed Virgin Mary.* (Dubuque, IA).—B.V.M.

[]—*Sisters of Christian Community.*—S.F.C.C.

[]—*Sisters of Humility of Mary.*—C.H.M.

[]—*Sisters of Mercy of Mississippi, Inc.*—R.S.M.

[3360]—*Sisters of Providence of Saint Mary-of-the-Woods, Indiana.*—S.P.

[1540]—*Sisters of Saint Francis, Clinton, Iowa.*—O.S.F.

[3893]—*Sisters of Saint Joseph of Chestnut Hill, Philadelphia.*—S.S.J.

[]—*Sisters of St. Francis of Sylvania, Ohio.*—O.S.F.

[1550]—*Sisters of St. Francis of the Holy Cross.* (Green Bay).—O.S.F.

[1570]—*Sisters of St. Francis of the Holy Family.* (Dubuque).—O.S.F.

[3830-02]—*Sisters of St. Joseph.* (La Grange Park, IL).—C.S.J.

[3830-15]—*Sisters of St. Joseph.* (Concordia, KS).—C.S.J.

[3840]—*Sisters of St. Joseph of Carondelet.* (St. Louis & St. Paul Provs.).—C.S.J.

[3930]—*Sisters of St. Joseph of the Third Order of St. Francis.* (Marymount Prov.).—S.S.J.-T.O.S.F.

[3950]—*Sisters of St. Mary of Namur.* (Belgium).—S.S.M.N.

[2980]—*Sisters of the Congregation de Notre Dame.* (Ridgefield, CT).—C.N.D.

[1030]—*Sisters of the Divine Savior.*—S.D.S.

[1990]—*Sisters of the Holy Names of Jesus and Mary.* (Albany, NY; Spokane, WA; Los Gatos, CA; Marylhurst, OR; Winnipeg, Canada).—S.N.J.M.

[2050]—*Sisters of the Holy Spirit and Mary Immaculate.*—S.H.Sp.

[2350]—*Sisters of the Living Word.*—S.L.W.

[1760]—*Sisters of the Third Order of St. Francis of Penance and Charity.*—O.S.F.

[2160]—*Sisters, Servants of the Immaculate Heart of Mary.*—I.H.M.

[4120-03]—*Ursuline Nuns, of the Congregation of Paris.*—O.S.U.

NECROLOGY

† Niemeyer, John, (Retired). —Died March 8, 1997.

† Quinn, Patrick, (On Duty Outside the Diocese). —Died Jan. 9, 1997.

Diocese of Jefferson City

(Dioecesis Civitatis Jeffersoniensis)

Most Reverend

JOHN RAYMOND GAYDOS, D.D.

Bishop of Jefferson City; ordained December 20, 1968; appointed June 25, 1997; consecrated August 27, 1997. *Res., Bishop's House, P.O. Box 417, Jefferson City, MO, 65102.*

ESTABLISHED JULY 2, 1956.

Square Miles 22,127.

Comprises the Counties of Adair, Audrain, Benton, Boone, Callaway, Camden, Chariton, Clark, Cole, Cooper, Crawford, Gasconade, Hickory, Howard, Knox, Lewis, Linn, Macon, Maries, Marion, Miller, Moniteau, Monroe, Montgomery, Morgan, Osage, Pettis, Phelps, Pike, Pulaski, Putnam, Ralls, Randolph, Saline, Schuyler, Scotland, Shelby and Sullivan in the State of Missouri.

For legal titles of parishes and diocesan institutions, consult the Chancery Office.

Chancery: 605 Clark Ave., P.O. Box 417, Jefferson City, MO, 65102. Tel.: 573-635-9127; Fax: 573-635-2286.

E-mail address: chance@sockets.net

STATISTICAL OVERVIEW

Personnel	
Bishop	1
Retired Bishops	1
Priests: Diocesan Active in Diocese	85
Priests: Active Outside Diocese	3
Priests: Diocesan in Foreign Missions	3
Priests: Retired, Sick or Absent	24
Number of Diocesan Priests	115
Religious Priests in Diocese	8
Extern Priests in Diocese	9
Ordinations:	
Diocesan Priests	1
Transitional Deacons	2
Permanent Deacons in Diocese	60
Total Brothers	7
Total Sisters	101
Parishes	
Parishes	95
With Resident Pastor:	
Resident Diocesan Priests	65
Resident Religious Priests	7
Without Resident Pastor:	
Administered by Priests	16
Administered by Professed Men Religious	1
Administered by Women Religious	5
Administered by Lay People	1
Missions	15
Closed Parishes	1
Professional Ministry Personnel:	
Brothers	1
Sisters	23
Lay Ministers	23
Welfare	
Catholic Hospitals	1
Total Assisted	117,463
Health Care Centers	15
Total Assisted	151,155
Homes for the Aged	2
Total Assisted	210
Day Care and Extended Day Care Centers	9
Total Assisted	1,062
Educational	
Seminaries, Diocesan	1
Students from This Diocese	20
Students from Other Diocese	4
Diocesan Students in Other Seminaries	10
Total Seminarians	30
High Schools, Diocesan and Parish	2
Total Students	985
Elementary Schools, Diocesan and Parish	37
Total Students	6,199
Catechesis/Religious Education:	
High School Students	2,733
Elementary Students	4,984
Total Students Under Catholic Instruction	14,931
Teachers in the Diocese:	
Priests	6
Brothers	5
Sisters	25
Lay Teachers	438
Vital Statistics	
Receptions into the Church:	
Infant Baptism Totals	1,392
Adult Baptism Totals	219
Received into Full Communion	284
First Communions	1,488
Confirmations	1,407
Marriages:	
Catholic	310
Interfaith	336
Total Marriages	646
Deaths	747
Total Catholic Population	81,122
Total Population	861,940

Former Bishops—Most Rev. JOSEPH M. MARLING, C.PP.S., D.D., ord. Feb. 21, 1929; appt. Auxiliary of Kansas City, June 9, 1947; cons. Aug. 6, 1947; appt. Bishop of Jefferson City, Aug. 24, 1956; retired July 2, 1969; died Oct. 2, 1979.—Most Rev. MICHAEL F. MCAULIFFE, S.T.D., ord. May 31, 1945; appt. July 2, 1969; cons. Aug. 18, 1969; retired August 27, 1997.

Vicar General—Rev. MICHAEL J. WILBERS, *P.O. Box 417, Jefferson City, 65102.*

Chancery Office—605 Clark Ave., P.O. Box 417, Jefferson City, 65102. Tel: 573-635-9127; Fax: 573-635-2286. All offices are at this address unless noted otherwise.

Chancellor—Sr. ETHEL-MARIE BIRI, S.S.N.D., M.R.Ed., M.A.

Vice-Chancellors—Revs. BRENDAN DOYLE; RICHARD CRONIN.

Moderator of the Curia—Rev. MICHAEL J. WILBERS, V.G.

Diocesan Tribunal—613 Clark Ave., Jefferson City, 65101.

Judicial Vicar—Rev. BRENDAN DOYLE.

Adjutant Judicial Vicar—Rev. GREGORY L. HIGLEY.

Defensors of the Bond—Revs. RICHARD CRONIN; ROBERT W. DUESDIEKER; LEONARD S. MISEY; PAUL M. HARTLEY.

Promoter of Justice—Rev. RICHARD CRONIN.

Judges—Revs. HUGH F. BEHAN; FRANCIS G. GILLGANNON; J. JAMES OFFUTT; MICHAEL F. QUINN.

Notaries—LORETTA NEUNER; CONNIE SCHEPERS.

Diocesan Consultors—Revs. FRED J. BARNETT; JAMES R. FUEMMELER; BRENDAN DOYLE; MICHAEL T. FLANAGAN; JOHN W. GRONER; GREGORY L. HIGLEY; ROBERT A. KURWICKI; J. DAVID MAHER; MICHAEL J. WILBERS, V.G.

Deans—I. Brookfield: Rev. PATRICK G. DOLAN, Dean: Brookfield, Brunswick, Clarence, Indian Grove, Macon (Bevier), Marceline (Hurricane Branch/ Mendon), Salisbury, Shelbina, Wien; II. Columbia: Rev. CHARLES D. PARDEE, Dean: Boonville, Columbia, Fayette, Moberly, Pilot Grove; III. Hannibal: Rev. KENNETH E. BROCKEL, Dean: Hannibal, Ilasco, Indian Creek (Hunnewell), Louisiana (Clarksville), Monroe City, Palmyra, Perry (Paris), St. Clement; IV. Jefferson City: Rev. EDWIN A. SCHMIDT, Dean: California, Holts Summit, Jefferson City, Osage Bend, Russelville, St. Martins, St. Thomas, Taos, Wardsville; V. Kirksville: Rev. J. DAVID MAHER, Dean: Baring, Canton (LaGrange), Edina, Ewing, Kahoka (Wayland), Kirksville (Novinger), Memphis, Milan (Unionville), St. Patrick; VI. Lake Ozark: Rev. JAMES R. FUEMMELER, Dean: Camdenton, Eldon, Laurie (Versailles), Hermitage (Climax Springs), Lake Ozark, Mary's Home, St. Anthony, St. Elizabeth; VII. Marshall: Rev. PHILLIP M. KANE, Dean: Glasgow, Marshall (Sweet Springs), Sedalia, Slater, Tipton, Warsaw (Cole Camp); VIII. Mexico: Rev. GERALD J. KAIMANN, Dean: Centralia, Fulton, Hermann, Jonesburg, Martinsburg, Mexico, Mokane, Montgomery City, Morrison, Rhineland, Vandalia (Laddonia), Wellsville; IX. Osage: Rev. ROBERT A. KURWICKI, Dean: Argyle (Koeltztown), Bonnots Mill, Chamois, Folk, Frankenstein, Freeburg, Linn, Loose Creek, Meta, Rich Fountain, Westphalia; X. Rolla: Rev. DONALD L. WALLACE, Dean: Belle, Bourbon, Brinktown, Crocker, Cuba, Dixon, Owensville, Richland, Rolla, Rosati, St. James, Steelville, Vienna, Waynesville.

Masters of Ceremonies—Revs. ROBERT A. KURWICKI; JOHN J. SCHUTTY; ROBERT W. DUESKIEKER; ROBERT H. FIELDS; JOSEPH HOI.

Personnel Board—Most Rev. JOHN RAYMOND GAYDOS; Revs. THOMAS J. DUGGAN; JOHN W. GRONER; CHARLES D. PARDEE; EDWIN A. SCHMIDT; MICHAEL J. WILBERS, V.G.

Priests Senate—Revs. FRED J. BARNETT; RICHARD A. COLBERT, C.PP.S.; PATRICK G. DOLAN; MICHAEL T. FLANAGAN; JAMES R. FUEMMELER; JOHN W. GRONER; GERALD J. KAIMANN; PHILLIP M. KANE; ROBERT A. KURWICKI; J. DAVID MAHER; MARION J. MAKAREWICZ; CHARLES D. PARDEE; Rev. Msgr. GERARD L. POELKER; Revs. EDWIN A. SCHMIDT; DONALD W. WALLACE; MICHAEL J. WILBERS, V.G.; J. JAMES OFFUTT, Consultant.

Diocesan Offices and Directors

Apostleship of Prayer—Rev. Msgr. RALPH G. KUTZ, Dir.

Campus Ministry—Rev. MICHAEL F. QUINN.

Catholic Relief Overseas Fund—ALICE J. WOLTERS.

Charismatic Renewal Program—Deacon ROBERT WATSON.

Communication—MARK D. SAUCIER, Dir.
Cursillo Movement—Rev. PATRICK J. SHORTT, Spiritual Dir. ART BOECKMAN, Dir.
Diocesan Pastoral Council—ANNETTE SMITH, Chm.
Diocesan Excellence in Education Fund, Inc.—Most Rev. JOHN RAYMOND GAYDOS, Chm.; Mr. LOUIS J. LEONATTI, Pres.; Sr. ETHEL-MARIE BIRI, S.S.N.D.; Sr. ANN MARIE BONVIE, S.S.N.D.; WILLIAM J. CARR; JOHN KOLB; GARY SHELL; LORETTA CLINE; Deacon DONALD W. ORSCHELN; Deacon GEORGE T. SPALDING; NORMAN P. STUCKENSCHNEIDER; Rev. MICHAEL J. WILBERS, V.G.
Diaconate Office—Rev. FRED J. ELSKAMP, Vicar; Deacon ROBERT RACKERS.
Ecumenical Commission—Rev. HUGH F. BEHAN, Dir.
Engaged Encounter—Coords.: RICHARD SPORLEDER; BERNICE SPORLEDER, *Rte. 3, Box 249, Moberly, 65270.* Rev. MICHAEL F. QUINN, Spiritual Dir.
Evangelization Office—Rev. HUGH F. BEHAN, Dir.
Family Life—MICHAEL A. VAN GUNDY.
Finance and Development—STEPHEN J. KOMAROMI, Dir.
Finance Committee—Most Rev. JOHN RAYMOND GAYDOS; Sr. ETHEL-MARIE BIRI, S.S.N.D.; OLIVIA BUERSMEYER; CHARLES CASSMEYER; Rev. MICHAEL T. FLANAGAN; Mr. CHRIS HERMANN; RICHARD KAMPETER; PAUL KANAGO; Rev. Msgr. RALPH G. KUTZ; Rev. Msgr. DONALD ORSCHELN; RONALD W. VESSEL; HELEN VOSSEN; Rev. MICHAEL J. WILBERS, V.G.
Historical Diocesan Archivist—Rev. ROBERT A. KURWICKI, *P.O. Box 116, Westphalia, 65085.* Tel: 573-455-2320.
Holy Childhood—(See Mission Office).
Human Development Campaign—BARBARA ROSS.
Information Office—MARK D. SAUCIER, Dir.
Leadership Services—Dr. STEPHANA J. LANDWEHR; Sr. ETHEL-MARIE BIRI, S.S.N.D.
Legion of Mary—Rev. WILLIAM KORTE, *Rte. 1, Eugene, 65032.* Tel: 573-498-3820.
Liturgical Commission—Rev. LOUIS E. DORN, Chm., *P.O. Box 220, Marshall, 65340.* Tel: 816-886-7960.
Mediation and Arbitration Board—Rev. LOUIS E. DORN, Vicar, *P.O. Box 220, Marshall, 65340.* Tel: 816-886-7960.
Ministry Formation—Rev. GEORGE KRAMER, Dir., *Bonnots Mill, 65016.* Tel: 573-897-2061.
Ministry to Priests—Rev. J. JAMES OFFUTT, Dir.; Most Rev. JOHN RAYMOND GAYDOS; Sr. ETHEL-MARIE BIRI, S.S.N.D.; Revs. DONALD J. ANTWEILER; KEVIN P. CLOHESSY; RICHARD CRONIN; FREDERICK J. ELSKAMP; JAMES L. FINDER; RICHARD W. FRANK; DONALD W. LAMMERS; IGNAZIO C. MEDINA; PATRICK L. PIERCEALL.
Mission Office (Peru Missions, Propagation of the Faith, Holy Childhood)—ALICE J. WOLTERS, Dir. MARK D. SAUCIER, *P.O. Box 551, Jefferson City, 65102.*
Newspaper—"Catholic Missourian"—Rev. HUGH BEHAN, Editor, *P.O. Box 1107, Jefferson City, 65102.*
Peruvian Development Foundation—Vacant, *P.O. Box 551, Jefferson City, 65102.*
Planning Commission—Rev. J. JAMES OFFUTT, Dir. & Exec. Sec.; Sr. ETHEL-MARIE BIRI, S.S.N.D.; Mr. LOUIS HOLROYD.
Priestly and Religious Vocations—Co-Directors: Sr. JEAN GREENWALD, S.C.C.; Rev. BRIAN DRISCOLL, *P.O. Box 417, Jefferson City, 65102.*
Priests' Eucharistic League—Rev. FRED J. ELSKAMP, Dir.
Priests' Mutual Benefit Society—Board of Trustees: Revs. RICHARD CRONIN; MICHAEL T. FLANAGAN; Rev. Msgr. RALPH G. KUTZ, Sec./Treas.; Rev. J. JAMES OFFUTT; Rev. Msgr. GERARD L. POELKER; Rev. Msgr. JOHN H. DREISOERNER, Consultant.
Priests' Purgatorial Society—Vacant.
Propagation of Faith & Holy Childhood—ALICE J. WOLTERS, Dir., *P.O. Box 551, Jefferson City, 65102.*
Religious Education Office—Mr. JAMES M. KEMNA, Dir. RANDY H. KOLLARS; CAROLYN A. SAUCIER; MICHAEL A. VAN GUNDY.
Research Assistant—Dr. STEPHANA LANDWEHR.
Resettlement Office—ALICE J. WOLTERS, Dir.
Residents Encounter Christ—BARBARA ROSS, Diocesan Liaison.
School Office—Sr. ANN MARIE BONVIE, S.S.N.D., Supt. BARBARA SWANSON, Assoc. Supt.
Scouting—Rev. GREGORY C. MEYSTRIK, Chap., *509 N. Main, Edina, 63537.* Tel: 816-397-2183.
Diocesan Sisters' Organization—Sr. MARY RUTH WAND, S.S.N.D., *Rte. 1, Box 3, Martinsburg, 65264.* Tel: 573-492-6283.
Social Concerns Dept.—BARBARA ROSS, Dir.; Sr. FRAN BUSHELL, S.S.N.D.; Dr. STEPHANA LANDWEHR; Sr. VIRGINIA GRUMICH, S.S.N.D.
Spiritual Renewal for the Laity—PEGGY VAN GUNDY, Dir.
Vigilance Council—The Rt. Rev. and Very Rev. Deans.
Youth Ministry—RANDY H. KOLLARS.

CLERGY, PARISHES, MISSIONS AND PAROCHIAL SCHOOLS

JEFFERSON CITY (Cole County)

1—ST. JOSEPH CATHEDRAL, Revs. Michael J. Wilbers, V.G., Rector; Christopher Cordes; Deacons Robert J. Rackers; Fred W. Weisel; Joseph Braddock.
Res., 2301 W. Main St., 65101. Tel: 573-635-7991; Fax: 573-635-7991. [JC]
School—2305 W. Main St., 65101. Tel: 573-635-5024; Fax: 573-635-5238.
Lay Teachers 25; Students 440.
Catechesis/Religious Programs—Students 93.

2—ST. PETER, Revs. Donald W. Lammers; Erwin R. Konrad; R. William Peckman; Deacons Harry M. Agniel; Robert L. Dulle; John C. O'Rourke; Thomas M. Whalen.
Res., 216 Broadway, 65101. Tel: 573-636-8159; Fax: 573-634-6079. [JC]
School—Tel: 573-636-8922; Fax: 573-634-6079.
Sisters 2; School Sisters of Notre Dame 1; Sisters of Charity of the Incarnate Word 1; Lay Teachers 27; Students 503.
Catechesis/Religious Programs—Students 95.

3—IMMACULATE CONCEPTION, Revs. J. James Offutt; Mark S. Smith; Deacons James R. Butler; Robert C. Osman.
Res., 1206 E. McCarty St., 65101. Tel: 573-635-6143; Fax: 573-635-6036. [JC]
School—Tel: 573-636-6289; Fax: 573-635-6036.
Sisters 1; Lay Teachers 32; Students 541.
Catechesis/Religious Programs—Students 118.

OUTSIDE JEFFERSON CITY

Argyle, Osage Co., St. Aloysius, Rev. Msgr. Ralph G. Kutz.
Res., 65001. Tel: 573-728-6212. [CEM]
Catechesis/Religious Programs—Students 113.
Mission—Koeltztown, St. Boniface, P.O. Box 36, 65001. Tel: 314-728-6919.

Baring, Knox Co., St. Aloysius. Attended by Edina. Rev. Gregory C. Meystrik.
Res., 509 N. Main St., Edina, 63537-1239. Tel: 660-397-2183. [CEM]

Belle, Maries Co., St. Alexander. Attended by Immaculate Conception, Owensville. Rev. Paul M. Hartley.
Mailing Address: 400 W. Third St., 65013. Tel: 573-859-6231.
Church—Tel: 573-859-6427. [CEM]

Bonnots Mill, Osage Co., St. Louis. Attended by Our Lady of Help, Frankenstein. Rev. Peter Walsh.
Res., 65016. Tel: 573-897-2587.
Mailing Address: Rte. 1, Box 201, 65016. [CEM]

Boonville, Cooper Co., SS. Peter and Paul, Rev. Charles D. Pardee; Deacons David Miller; John Tebbe.
Res., 322 7th St., 65233. Tel: 660-882-6468. [CEM]
School—Tel: 660-882-2589.
Sisters 1; Lay Teachers 10; Students 173.
Catechesis/Religious Programs—Students 145.

Bourbon, Crawford Co., St. Francis, Rev. Robert W. Duesdieker.
Res., P.O. Box 419, 65441. Tel: 573-732-4494. [CEM 2]
Sr. Carol Grawe, S.S.N.D., Pastoral Admin.
Res., 1098 Old Hwy. 66 W., 65441.

Brinktown, Maries Co., Guardian Angels. Attended by Visitation, Vienna. Rev. John J. Schmitz.
Res., General Delivery, 65443. Tel: 573-422-3105. [CEM]

Brookfield, Linn Co., Immaculate Conception, Rev. Thomas Duggan.
Res., 313 N. Livingston St., 64628. Tel: 660-258-2507. [CEM]
Catechesis/Religious Programs—Students 120.

Brunswick, Chariton Co., St. Boniface, Rev. Leonard S. Misey.
Res., 203 E. Vine St., P.O. Box 5, 65236. Tel: 660-548-3267. [CEM]
Catechesis/Religious Programs—Students 47.

California, Moniteau Co., Annunciation, Rev. Francis G. Gillgannon.
Res., 414 W. Patrick St., 65018. Tel: 573-796-4872. [CEM]
Catechesis/Religious Programs—Students 180.

Camdenton, Camden Co., St. Anthony, Rev. James R. Fuemmeler.
Res., Rte. 2, Box 344 E., 65020. Tel: 573-346-6652.
Rev. Donald E. Powers (KC).; Res., HCR 67, P.O. Box 777, Ruach, 65787. Tel: 573-346-2688.
Church—172 N. Hwy. 5, 65020. Tel: 573-346-2716; Fax: 573-346-2716.
Catechesis/Religious Programs—Tel: 573-346-7080; Fax: 573-346-2539.
Students 195.

Canton, Lewis Co., St. Joseph, Rev. David D. Cox; Bro. John Francis Tyrrell, F.F.S.C., Pastoral Admin.
Res., 812 Lewis St., 63435. Tel: 573-288-3198; Fax: 573-288-3198.
Catechesis/Religious Programs—Students 85.
Mission—La Grange, Lewis Co., Notre Dame, Rte. C, La Grange, 63448. Tel: 573-655-4296.

Centralia, Boone Co., Holy Spirit, Rev. Robert H. Fields.
Res., 404 S. Rollins St., 65240. Tel: 573-682-2815.
Catechesis/Religious Programs—Students 105.

Chamois, Osage Co., Most Pure Heart of Mary, Rev. Thomas J. Seifner.
Res., 65024. Tel: 573-763-5345. [CEM 2]
Catechesis/Religious Programs—Students 32.

Clarence, Shelby Co., St. Patrick, Rev. Patrick L. Pierceall.
Mailing Address: 32 Grand St., P.O. Box 177, 63437. Tel: 660-699-3805. [CEM]
Res., 307 E. Chestnut, Shelbina, 63468. Tel: 573-588-4458.

Columbia, Boone Co., Our Lady of Lourdes, Revs. Michael T. Flanagan; William D. Debo; Deacon Fred Fritsch.
Res., 903 Bernadette Dr., 65203. Tel: 573-445-7915; Fax: 573-446-7402.
School—817 Bernadette Dr., 65203. Tel: 573-445-6516; Fax: 573-446-7402.
Sisters 1; Lay Teachers 30; Students 462.
Catechesis/Religious Programs—Tel: 573-573-9602.
Students 530.

Sacred Heart, Rev. Edwin Cole; Deacons Bruce Cox; Michael Daly.
Res., 1115 Locust St., 65201. Tel: 573-443-2892; Fax: 573-875-3947.
Catechesis/Religious Programs—Students 129.

Columbia Newman Center, University of Missouri, Revs. Michael F. Quinn, Dir.; Dennis Schmidt.
Res., 701 Maryland, 65201. Tel: 314-445-8068.
Church—Tel: 573-449-5514; 449-5424; Fax: 573-874-2777.
Catechesis/Religious Programs—Students 380.

Crocker, Pulaski Co., St. Cornelius. Attended by Dixon. Rev. Walter J. Reisinger, C.M.
Res., P.O. Box 310, Dixon, 65459. Tel: 573-759-7521. [CEM]

Cuba, Crawford Co., Holy Cross, Rev. Robert W. Duesdieker; Deacons Earl Horsefield; Albert W. Wilmarth.
Res., 415 W. School St., 65453. Tel: 573-885-3520; 885-3291 (Rectory). [CEM]
School—407 W. School St., 65453. Tel: 573-885-4727. Mrs. Jeanne Heckmann, Prin.
Lay Teachers 3; Students 31.
Catechesis/Religious Programs—Teresa Leicht, D.R.E.
Students 67.

Dixon, Pulaski Co., St. Theresa, Rev. Walter J. Reisinger, C.M.
Res., P.O. Box 310, 65459. Tel: 573-759-7521. [CEM]

Edina, Knox Co., St. Joseph, Rev. Gregory C. Meystrik.
Res., 509 N. Main St., 63537-1239. Tel: 660-397-2183. [CEM 2]
Catechesis/Religious Programs—Tel: 660-397-3128.
Students 79.

Eldon, Miller Co., Sacred Heart, Rev. James J. O'Sullivan.
Res., 540 N. Mill St., 65026. Tel: 573-392-5334; Fax: 573-392-3493.
Catechesis/Religious Programs—Students 117.

Ewing, Lewis Co., Queen of Peace, Rev. Daniel I. Lueckenotte; Sr. Catherine Wellinghoff, A.S.C., Pastoral Admin.
Res., 307 N. Main, P.O. Box 347, 63440. Tel: 573-494-3343. [CEM 2]
Catechesis/Religious Programs—Students 50.

Fayette, Howard Co., St. Joseph, Rev. Richard A. Colbert, C.PP.S.
Res., 300 S. Cleveland, 65248. Tel: 660-248-2439; Fax: 660-248-2439. [CEM]
Catechesis/Religious Programs—Students 52.

Folk, Osage Co., St. Anthony of Padua, Rev. John H. Henderson.
Mailing Address: HCR 65, Box 91, Westphalia, 65085. Tel: 573-455-2888. [CEM]
Catechesis/Religious Programs—Students 52.

Frankenstein, Osage Co., Our Lady of Help, Rev. Peter Walsh.
Res., Rte. 1, Bonnots Mill, 65016. Tel: 573-897-2587. [CEM 2]

School—Tel: 573-897-2567.
Lay Teachers 4; Students 70.

Freeburg, Osage Co., Holy Family, Rev. Richard W. Frank.
Res., P.O. Box 97, 65035. Tel: 573-744-5254. [CEM]
School—Tel: 573-744-5200.
Sisters 1; Lay Teachers 3; Students 58.

Fulton, Callaway Co., St. Peter, Rev. Ignazio C. Medina.
Office: 700 Hwy. Z, 65251. Tel: 573-642-5562.
School—Tel: 573-642-2839.
Sisters 4; Lay Teachers 9; Students 156.
Catechesis/Religious Programs—Sisters of Christian Charity 4; Students 102.

Glasgow, Howard Co., St. Mary, Rev. Philip M. Kane; Deacons Jerome C. Brucks; Robert L. Himmelberg; Charles Nordmeyer.
Res., 421 Third St., 65254. Tel: 660-338-2053; Fax: 660-338-2589. [CEM]
School—Tel: 660-338-2258.
Sisters of Charity 1; Lay Teachers 10; Students 161.
Catechesis/Religious Programs—Students 15.

Hannibal, Marion Co., Holy Family, Revs. John W. Groner; Mark A. Porterfield; Deacons Lindell P. Shumake; Emmett E. Pierceall.
Res., 2100 Chestnut St., 63401. Tel: 573-221-1078; Fax: 573-221-1079. [JC]
School—Tel: 573-221-0456.
Brothers 1; Sisters of Notre Dame 1; Lay Teachers 8; Students 170.
Catechesis/Religious Programs—Students 120.

Hermann, Gasconade Co., St. George, Rev. Ambrose German, O.F.M.
Res., 128 W. 4th St., 65041-1099. Tel: 573-486-2723. [CEM]
School—Tel: 573-486-5914.
Lay Teachers 12; Students 200.
Catechesis/Religious Programs—Tel: 573-486-2157.
Students 82.

Hermitage, Hickory Co., St. Bernadette, Rev. Donald E. Powers (KC).
Church—Hwy. 254, P.O. Box 277, 65668. Tel: 417-745-6361.
Res., HCR 67, Ruach, 67787. Tel: 573-346-2688.
Mission—Climax Springs, Our Lady of the Snows.

Holts Summit, Callaway Co., St. Andrew, Rev. Frederick J. Elskamp.
Res., 400 St. Andrew Dr., 65043. Tel: 573-896-4309. [CEM]
Catechesis/Religious Programs—Students 110.

Ilasco, Ralls Co., Holy Cross. Closed. Records can be found at Holy Family Church, 2100 Chesnut, Hannibal, MO 63401.

Indian Creek, Monroe Co., St. Stephen, Rev. Charles A. Pfeiffer.
Res., Rte. 3, Box 29, Monroe City, 63456. Tel: 573-735-4033. [CEM 3]

Indian Grove, Chariton Co., St. Raphael. Attended by Brunswick. Rev. Leonard S. Misey.
Mailing Address: 203 E. Vine St., P.O. Box 5, Brunswick, 65236-0005. Tel: 660-548-3267. [CEM]

Jonesburg, Montgomery Co., St. Patrick, Rev. Gerald J. Kaimann; Ms. Kristin Roth, Pastoral Admin.
Res., 505 First St., 63351. Tel: 314-488-5623. [CEM]
Catechesis/Religious Programs—Students 69.

Kahoka, Clark Co., St. Michael the Archangel, Rev. Michael P. Murphy.
Res., P.O. Box 216, 622 W. Exchange St., 63445. Tel: 660-727-3472.
Catechesis/Religious Programs—Students 70.
Mission—Wayland, Clark Co., St. Martha, 202 S. Main St., Wayland, 63472.

Kirksville, Adair Co., Mary Immaculate, Revs. J. David Maher; William P. Kottenstette; Patricia Lehr, Pastoral Min.
716 E. Washington St., 63501. Tel: 660-665-2466; Fax: 660-665-8955. [CEM]
School—Tel: 660-665-1006; Fax: 660-665-1006.
Lay Teachers 11; Students 132.
Catechesis/Religious Programs—Tel: 660-665-2466.
Students 208.
Mission—Novinger, Adair Co., St. Rose of Lima, Hwy. 149, Novinger, 63559.

Lake Ozark, Miller Co., Our Lady of the Lake, Rev. John Long; Deacon Francis P. Zimmerman.
Res., 2411 Bagnell Dam Blvd., 65049. Tel: 573-365-2241; Fax: 573-365-4458.
Catechesis/Religious Programs—Students 116.

Laurie, Morgan Co., Shrine of St. Patrick, Rev. Fred J. Barnett.
Res., Hwy. 5, Box 17, 65038. Tel: 573-374-7855 (Office); Fax: 573-374-0627. [CEM]
Catechesis/Religious Programs—Tel: 573-372-2497.
Students 88.
Mission—Versailles, Morgan Co., St. Philip Benizi, Hwy. D, Versailles, 65084.
Shrine—Mary Mother of the Church, P.O. Box 1250, 65038. Tel: 573-374-6279.

Linn, Osage Co., St. George, Rev. Brendan Doyle.
Res., P.O. Box 49, 65051. Tel: 573-897-2293. [CEM]
School—Tel: 573-897-3645.
Lay Teachers 11; Students 191.
Catechesis/Religious Programs—Students 100.

Loose Creek, Osage Co., Immaculate Conception, Rev. Richard Cronin.
Res., 65054. Tel: 573-897-2922. [CEM 2]
School—Tel: 573-897-3516.
School Sisters of Notre Dame 2; Lay Teachers 5; Students 111.
Catechesis/Religious Programs—Students 75.

Louisiana, Pike Co., St. Joseph, Rev. Thomas L. Waickman.
Res., 508 N. 3rd St., 63353. Tel: 573-754-4757. [CEM]
Catechesis/Religious Programs—Students 56.
Mission—Clarksville, Pike Co., Mary Queen of Peace, South Second St., Clarksville, 63336. Tel: 573-242-3730.

Macon, Macon Co., Immaculate Conception, Rev. Russell R. Judge; Deacons Leo Prenger; Bernhard Toll.
Res., 402 N. Rollins St., 63552. Tel: 660-385-3792. [CEM]
School—Tel: 660-385-2711.
Sisters 2; Lay Teachers 2; Students 41.
Catechesis/Religious Programs—Students 56.
Mission—Bevier, Sacred Heart.

Marceline, Linn Co., St. Bonaventure, Rev. Manus P. Daly.
Res., 409 S. Kansas Ave., 64658-1301. Tel: 660-376-3239. [CEM 2]
School—Tel: 660-376-3580.
Lay Teachers 5; Students 67.
Catechesis/Religious Programs—Students 81.
Mission—Hurricane Branch, Chariton Co., St. Joseph.

Marshall, Saline Co., St. Peter, Rev. Louis E. Dorn.
Res., 1801 S. Miami Ave., P.O. Box 220, 65340. Tel: 660-886-7960.
School—Tel: 660-886-6390; Fax: 660-866-6606.
Lay Teachers 10; Students 113.
Catechesis/Religious Programs—Tel: 660-886-3112; Fax: 660-886-6606.
Students 135.
Mission—Sweet Springs, Saline Co., Holy Family, 200 Ruby St., Sweet Springs, 65351.

Martinsburg, Audrain Co., St. Joseph, Rev. Wayne M. Boyer.
Res., 408 E. Kellett, 65264. Tel: 573-492-6595. [CEM]
School—Tel: 573-492-6283. Sr. Mary Ruth Wood, S.S.N.D, Prin.
Lay Teachers 5; Students 91.

Mary's Home, Miller Co., Our Lady of the Snows, Rev. William L. Korte.
Res., Rte. 1, Eugene, 65032. Tel: 573-498-3820; Fax: 573-498-3820. [CEM]
School—Tel: 573-498-3574.
Lay Teachers 5; Students 78.
Catechesis/Religious Programs—Students 80.

Memphis, Scotland Co., St. John, Rev. William P. Kottenstette.
Rectory: Rte. 3, Box 274, 63555. Tel: 660-465-7130. [CEM]
Res., c/o Mary Immaculate Parish Newman Center, 716 E. Washington, Kirksville, 63501. Tel: 660-665-5269; 665-2466. [CEM]

Meta, Osage Co., St. Cecilia, Rev. John J. Schutty.
Res., P.O. Box 96, 65058-0096. Tel: 573-229-4811. [CEM]
Catechesis/Religious Programs—Students 145.

Mexico, Audrain Co., St. Brendan, Rev. Gregory L. Higley.
Res., 615 S. Washington St., 65265. Tel: 573-581-4720; Fax: 573-581-8801. [CEM]
School—Tel: 573-581-2443.
School Sisters of Notre Dame 1; Lay Teachers 10; Students 192.
Catechesis/Religious Programs—Mary Beardslee, D.R.E.
Students 89.

Milan, Sullivan Co., St. Mary, Rev. Thomas L. Alber; Deacon Terence L. Reibenspies.
Res., 101 W. Baker St., P.O. Box 147, 63556. Tel: 660-265-4110. [CEM 2]
Catechesis/Religious Programs—Tel: 660-265-4110.
Students 28.
Mission—Unionville, Putnam Co., St. Mary.

Moberly, Randolph Co., St. Pius X, Rev. Patrick J. Shortt; Deacon Donald W. Orscheln.
Res., 217 S. Williams St., P.O. Box 310, 65270. Tel: 660-263-5243; Fax: 660-263-0101. [CEM]
School—Tel: 660-263-5500.
Lay Teachers 14; Students 199.
Catechesis/Religious Programs—Tel: 660-263-0427; Fax: 660-263-0701.
Students 151.

Mokane, Callaway Co., St. Jude Thaddeus, Rev. Frederick J. Elskamp.
Mailing Address: P.O. Box 128, 65059. Tel: 573-676-3238.
Res., 400 St. Andrew Dr., Holts Summit, 65043. Tel: 573-896-4309.

Monroe City, Monroe Co., Holy Rosary, Rev. William Flanagan; Deacon Harold L. Parn.
Res., 405 S. Main St., 63456. Tel: 573-735-4718. [CEM]
School—Tel: 573-735-2422.
Sisters of St. Dominic 1; Lay Teachers 10; Students 173.
Catechesis/Religious Programs—Students 130.

Montgomery City, Montgomery Co., Immaculate Conception, Rev. Gerald J. Kaimann.
Res., 307 N. Walker, 63361. Tel: 573-564-2375. [CEM 2]
School—407 W. Third St., 63361. Tel: 573-564-2679.
Sisters 2; Lay Teachers 4; Students 54.
Catechesis/Religious Programs—Students 70.

Morrison, Gasconade Co., Assumption. Attended by Chamois. Rev. Thomas J. Seifner.
Mailing Address: P.O. Box 156, Chamois, 65024. Tel: 573-763-5345. [CEM 2]

Osage Bend, Cole Co., St. Margaret, Rev. Michael Coleman; Sr. Peggy Bonnot, C.C.V.I., Pastoral Admin.; Deacon Larry Hildebrand.
Mailing Address: 12025 Rte. W., Jefferson City, 65101. Tel: 573-496-3404. [CEM]
Catechesis/Religious Programs—Students 61.

Owensville, Gasconade Co., Immaculate Conception, Rev. Paul M. Hartley; Deacon Donald E. Warden.
Res., 404 S. First St., 65066. Tel: 573-437-2494. [CEM]
Catechesis/Religious Programs—Tel: 573-437-3086.
Students 185.

Palmyra, Marion Co., St. Joseph, Rev. Daniel I. Lueckenotte; Sr. Marlene Buese, S.S.N.D., Pastoral Min.
Res., 411 S. Lane St., P.O. Box 606, 63461. Tel: 573-769-3270.
Catechesis/Religious Programs—Tel: 573-769-2837.
Students 170.

Perry, Ralls Co., St. William, Rev. Kenneth E. Brockel.
Res., P.O. Box 339, 63462. Tel: 573-565-2852. [CEM]
Catechesis/Religious Programs—Students 49.
Missions—Perry, Monroe Co., St. Frances Cabrini, P.O. Box 339, Perry, 65275.; Center, Ralls Co., St. Paul (Historic Church).

Pilot Grove, Cooper Co., St. Joseph, Rev. Eric A. Schlachter; Deacon Ralph V. Reuter.
Res., 407 Harris St., 65276. Tel: 660-834-4251. [CEM 2]
School—Tel: 660-834-5600.
Lay Teachers 5; Students 67.
Catechesis/Religious Programs—Students 107.
Station—Clear Creek, St. John the Baptist. (Mass).

Rhineland, Montgomery Co., Church of the Risen Savior, Rev. Thomas J. Seifner; Deacons Joseph E. Horton; Gerald W. Korman.
Res., 65069. Tel: 573-236-4390. [CEM 2]
Catechesis/Religious Programs—Students 73.
Pilgrimage Site—Shrine of Our Lady of Sorrows, Starkenburg, Montgomery Co., Tel: 573-236-4390.

Rich Fountain, Osage Co., Sacred Heart, Rev. James L. Finder.
Res., Rte. 1, Box 118, 65035. Tel: 573-744-5987. [CEM]
School—Tel: 573-744-5898.
Sisters of Notre Dame 1; Lay Teachers 3; Students 93.

Richland, Pulaski Co., St. Jude, Rev. Brendan Lawless.
Res., 367 Old Hwy. 66, Waynesville, 65583. Tel: 573-336-3662.
Church—P.O. Box 8, 65556.

Rolla, Phelps Co., St. Patrick, Rev. Thomas McGrath, Temporary Admin.; Deacons Michael S. Brooks; William E. Louis; Thomas C. Manion.
Res., 17 St. Patrick Ln., 65401. Tel: 573-364-1435; 341-9004; Fax: 573-364-2073. [CEM]
School—Tel: 573-364-1162; Fax: 573-364-2073.
Lay Teachers 9; Students 168.
Catechesis/Religious Programs—Students 162.

Rosati, Phelps Co., St. Anthony, Rev. Joseph Hoi.
Res., 316 E. Scioto, St. James, 65559. Tel: 573-265-7247. [CEM]
Catechesis/Religious Programs—Students 6.

Russellville, Cole Co., St. Michael, Rev. Michael J. Wilbers, V.G.; Sr. Donna Eggering, O.S.F., Pastoral Admin.; Deacon Gary Christhoff.
Res., 13321 Railroad Ave., 65074-9447. Tel: 573-782-3171. [CEM]
Catechesis/Religious Programs—Tel: 573-782-4503.
Students 43.

St. Anthony, Miller Co., St. Anthony, Rev. Clarence E. Wiederholt.
Church—Rte. 2, Box 501, Iberia, 65486. Tel: 573-793-6550. [CEM]
Catechesis/Religious Programs—Students 97.

St. Clement, Pike Co., St. Clement, Rev. J. Patrick Quinn.
Res., 21509 Hwy. J, Bowling Green, 63334. Tel: 573-324-5545; Fax: 573-324-5155. [CEM]
School—Tel: 573-324-2166.
Lay Teachers 7; Students 89.
Catechesis/Religious Programs—Students 155.

St. Elizabeth, Miller Co., St. Lawrence, Rev. John F. Degnan.
Res., P.O. Box 128, 65075. Tel: 573-493-2301. [CEM]
Catechesis/Religious Programs—Tel: 573-493-2301.
Students 177.

St. James, Phelps Co., Immaculate Conception, Rev. Joseph Hoi.
Res., 316 E. Scioto, 65559. Tel: 573-265-7250. [CEM]
Catechesis/Religious Programs—Tel: 573-265-7269.
Students 97.

St. Martins, Cole Co., St. Martin, Rev. Edwin A. Schmidt; Sr. Bermita Wesinger, S.S.N.D., Pastoral Min.; Deacon Francis Butel.
Res., 7148 St. Martins Ave., Jefferson City, 65109. Tel: 573-893-2923. [CEM]
School—Tel: 573-893-3519.
Lay Teachers 12; Students 205.
Catechesis/Religious Programs—Tel: 573-893-2352.
Students 100.

St. Patrick, Clark Co., The Shrine of St. Patrick. Attended by Kahoka. Rev. Michael P. Murphy.
Church—P.O. Box 35, 63466. Tel: 660-727-3472. [CEM]

St. Thomas, Cole Co., St. Thomas the Apostle Church, Rev. Donald J. Antweiler.
Res., 14814 Rt. B, P.O. Box 146, 65076. Tel: 573-477-3315. [CEM]
School—P.O. Box 211, 65076. Tel: 573-477-3322. Mark D. Hoffman, Prin.
Lay Teachers 4; Students 78.
Catechesis/Religious Programs—Tel: 573-477-3398.
Students 57.

Salisbury, Chariton Co., St. Joseph, Rev. Patrick G. Dolan.
Res., 301 W. Williams, 65281. Tel: 660-388-5590. [CEM]
School—Tel: 660-388-5518.
Sisters of Charity of Leavenworth 1; Lay Teachers 9; Students 116.
Catechesis/Religious Programs—Students 136.

Sedalia, Pettis Co., St. Patrick, Rev. Thomas Albers, C.PP.S.; Deacons Peter K. Anderberg; Jerome Connery.
Res., 415 E. Fourth St., 65301. Tel: 660-826-2062.
Catechesis/Religious Programs—Students 51.
Station—Clifton City, St. Joseph. (Mass).

Sacred Heart, Revs. William Miller, C.PP.S.; John M. Behen, C.PP.S.; Deacons Peter K. Anderberg; G. Robert Watson; Jerome Connery.
Res., 421 W. Third St., 65301. Tel: 660-827-2311. [CEM]
School—Tel: 660-827-3800.
Sisters of Divine Providence 1; Lay Teachers 9; Students 198.
High School—Lay Teachers 12; Students 194.
Catechesis/Religious Programs—Students 168.
Mission—Bahner, Pettis Co., St. John.
Station—Spring Fork, St. Patrick. (Mass).

Shelbina, Shelby Co., St. Mary, Rev. Patrick L. Pierceall.
Res., 307 E. Chestnut St., 63468. Tel: 573-588-4498. [CEM]
Catechesis/Religious Programs—Students 82.

Slater, Saline Co., St. Joseph. Attended by Glasgow. Rev. Philip M. Kane.
Res., 325 W. Emma St., 65349. Tel: 660-529-2588.

Steelville, Crawford Co., St. Michael, Rev. Robert W. Duesdieker.
Res., P.O. Box 419, Bourbon, 65441. Tel: 573-732-4494. Sr. Carol Grawe, S.S.N.D., Pastoral Admin.; Res., 1098 Old Hwy. 66 W., Bourbon, 65441.

Taos, Cole Co., St. Francis Xavier, Rev. Kevin P. Clohessy.
Res., 7314 Rte. M, Jefferson City, 65101. Tel: 573-395-4401; Fax: 573-395-4302. [CEM]
School—Tel: 573-395-4612.
Lay Teachers 17; Students 225.
Catechesis/Religious Programs—Students 155.

Tipton, Moniteau Co., St. Andrew, Rev. Henry J. Reichert.
Res., 106 W. Cooper St., P.O. Box 598, 65081. Tel: 660-433-2162. [CEM]
School—Tel: 660-433-2232.
Lay Teachers 9; Students 142.
Catechesis/Religious Programs—Students 79.

Vandalia, Audrain Co., Sacred Heart, Rev. Donald E. Siciliano.
Res., 203 W. Home, 63382. Tel: 573-594-2717.
Catechesis/Religious Programs—Students 58.
Mission—Laddonia, Audrain Co., St. John, 7th and Elm, Laddonia, 63352. Tel: 573-373-5351.

Vienna, Maries Co., Visitation, Rev. John J. Schmitz.
Res., 105 N. Main St., P.O. Box 171, 65582. Tel: 573-422-3950. [CEM]
School—5th & Coffey St., P.O. Box 171, 65582. Tel: 573-422-3375.
Sisters of Notre Dame 1; Lay Teachers 5; Students 55.

Wardsville, Cole Co., St. Stanislaus, Rev. Michael Coleman.
Res., 6410 Rte. W., Jefferson City, 65101. Tel: 573-636-4925; Fax: 573-636-2534. [CEM]
School—Tel: 573-636-7802; Fax: 573-636-7802.
Lay Teachers 13; Students 248.
Catechesis/Religious Programs—Tel: 573-496-3404.
Students 12.

Warsaw, Benton Co., St. Ann, Rev. Dennis Schaab, C.PP.S.
Res., Rte. 2, Box 29-20, 65355. Tel: 660-438-3844 (Church); 438-5870 (Rectory). [CEM]
Catechesis/Religious Programs—Students 47.
Mission—Cole Camp, Benton Co., SS. Peter & Paul, Tel: 660-668-3952.

Waynesville, Pulaski Co., St. Robert Bellarmine, Rev. Brendan Lawless.
Res., 367 Old Hwy. 66, 65583. Tel: 573-336-3662. [CEM]
Catechesis/Religious Programs—Students 93.

Wellsville, Montgomery Co., Resurrection, Rev. Wayne M. Boyer; Deacon Vincent Garufi.
409 E. Bates, 63384.
Res., 408 E. Kellett, Martinsburg, 65264. [CEM]

Westphalia, Osage Co., St. Joseph, Rev. Robert A. Kurwicki.
Res., P.O. Box 116, 65085-0116. Tel: 573-455-2320. [CEM]
School—Tel: 573-455-2339.
Lay Teachers 9; Students 111.
Catechesis/Religious Programs—Students 80.

Wien, Chariton Co., St. Mary of the Angels, Rev. Philip M. Moriarty.
Res., Rte. 1, Box 65, New Cambria, 63558. Tel: 660-226-5243. [CEM]
Catechesis/Religious Programs—Students 80.
Station—Hamden, Immaculate Conception. (Mass).

Chaplains of Public Institutions

Prisons

JEFFERSON CITY. *Central Missouri Correctional Center* Hwy. 179, 65109. Rev. Hugh F. Behan, Chap.
Jefferson City Correctional Center P.O. Box 900, 65102. Tel: 573-751-3224. Rev. John H. Henderson, Chap., Tel: 573-455-2888; Sr. Ruth Heaney, O.S.B., Chap., Tel: 573-635-5393.
Missouri Intermediate Reformatory. (Algoa) Algoa Rd., 65101. Tel: 573-751-3911. Rev. Sylvester Bauer, Chap., Tel: 573-744-5913.
Renz Correctional Facility P.O. Box 3200, 65102. Tel: 573-751-4748. Rev. Hugh F. Behan, Chap., Tel: 573-635-9127.

BOONVILLE. *Boonville Correctional Center.* HCR 91, Westphalia, 65085. Tel: 573-455-2888. Rev. John H. Henderson, Chap., Tel: 573-455-2888.

FULTON. *Diagnostic and Reception Center* P.O. Box 581, 65251. Tel: 573-642-1707. Deacon Frederick Fritsch, Chap., Tel: 573-449-3307.

MOBERLY. *Missouri Training Center For Men* P.O. Box 7, 65270. Tel: 660-263-3778. Rev. Patrick J. Shortt, Chap., Tel: 816-263-5243.

TIPTON. *State Correctional Pre-Release Center* 65081. Tel: 660-433-2031. Rev. Henry J. Reichert, Chap., Tel: 660-433-2162.

Hospitals and Schools

JEFFERSON CITY. *Capital Region Medical Center, Memorial Campus* 1432 Southwest Blvd., 65109. Tel: 573-635-6811. Rev. David G. Buescher Tel: 573-636-9356.
Capital Region Medical Center, Still Campus 1125 Madison St., 65101. Tel: 573-635-7100. Rev. David G. Buescher, Chap., Tel: 573-635-9356.

COLUMBIA. *Boone Hospital Center* 1600 E. Broadway, 65201. Tel: 573-875-4545.
Charter Hillside Hospital 200 Portland, 65201. Tel: 573-876-8000.
Columbia Regional Hospital 404 Keene St., 65201. Tel: 573-875-9000.
Ellis Fischel State Cancer Hospital 115 Business Loop 70 W., 65201. Tel: 573-882-2100.
Mid-Missouri Mental Health Center 3 Hospital Dr., 65201. Tel: 573-449-2511.
Rusk Rehabilitation Center 315 Business Loop 70 W., 65203. Tel: 573-817-2703.
University Hospital & Clinics One Hospital Dr., 65201. Tel: 573-882-4141.
Chaplains for the Columbia Hospitals listed above: Revs. Edwin J. Cole, Dir., Tel: 578-443-2892; Robert H. Fields Tel: 573-682-2815; William D. Debo Tel: 573-445-7915; Eleanor Braddock, M.D. Tel: 573-445-6701; Sr. Florence Seib, A.S.C. Tel: 573-499-3810.
Veterans' Administration Medical Center. (Harry S. Truman Memorial) 800 Stadium Rd., 65201. Tel: 573-443-2511. Rev. Edwin J. Cole Tel: 573-443-2892.

FULTON. *Fulton State Hospital* Fifth St., 65251. Tel: 573-642-3311. Deacon Frederick Fritsch, Chap., Tel: 573-449-3307.
Missouri School for the Deaf E. Fifth St., 65251. Tel: 573-642-3301. Deacon Frederick Fritsch, Chap., Tel: 573-449-3307.

MARCELINE. *Pershing Regional Health Care Center.* Attended by St. Boniventure Rectory, 409 S. Kansas, Marceline, 64658. Tel.:660-376-3239. 225 W. Hayden, 64658. Tel: 660-376-3521.

MARSHALL. *Marshall State School-Hospital* E. Slater St., 65340. Tel: 660-886-2202. Rev. Louis E. Dorn, Chap., Tel: 660-886-7960.

ST. JAMES. *Missouri Veterans' Home* 620 N. Jefferson St., 65559. Tel: 573-265-3271. Rev. Joseph Hoi, Chap., Tel: 573-265-7250.

Special Assignments:
Reverend Fathers—
Behan, Hugh F., Editor, "Catholic Missourian"
Hunkins, Richard C., Dir. Columbia Nursing Home Ministry
Kramer, George J., Chancery, Ministry Formation

On Duty Outside the Diocese:
Reverend Fathers—
Hereford, Thomas D., 6305 N.W. Hogan, Parkville, MO 64152
Palmieri, Luigi, P.O. Box 5309, Trenton, NJ 08648
Stockman, Gerald, 1000 North Hills, St. Louis, MO 63121

Missionary Assignment in Peru:
Reverend Fathers—
Griffey, Brendan M.
Keyes, Raphael
Lawlor, Joseph

Absent on Leave:
Reverend Fathers—
Crosby, Donald W.
Doyle, Edward A.
Faletti, Stephen L.
Gormley, Kevin
Keogh, William
Linnebur, Vincent
McNally, James P.
Niemeyer, James J.
Smith, Mark C.
Starmann, Joseph W.
Wallace, Donald L.

Retired:
Reverend Monsignors—
Bugler, Joseph T., Salt River Nursing Home, Shelbina, MO 63468
Dreisoerner, John H., Santa Maria Apartments, Apt. 233, Hazelwood, MO 63042-1582. Tel: 314-291-7017
Poelker, Gerard L., P.O. Box 39, Holts Summit, MO 65043. Tel: 573-896-4748
Sommer, Jerome, Regina Cleri, 7850 Kenrick Rd., St. Louis, MO 63119. Tel: 314-961-0271
Reverend Fathers—
Boland, Joseph B., St. Joseph Home, Jefferson City, MO 65101
Bonn, Ferdinand C., Wyandott Apts., 2717 Wyandotte A5, Las Vegas, NV 89102
Buhman, Leo T., 5910 York St., St. Joseph, MO 64506. Tel: 816-233-7775
Chenoweth, Robert, 929 Country Club Dr., St.

Louis, MO 63121
Donohue, Edward J., St. Joseph Carmelite Home, 723 First Capital Dr., St. Charles, MO 63301
Forst, William, P.O. Box 5, Foristell, MO 63348-0005. Tel: 314-673-1052
Mersinger, Arthur, 7850 Kenrick Rd., Ste. 104, St. Louis, MO 63119-5004. Tel: 314-962-5894
Robl, Eugene J., 907 Clayton, Columbia, MO 65203. Tel: 573-443-0423
Stangl, Frank J., 151/331 Hammond St., Rocky Mount, NC 27804-5824
Wheeler, Clarence, M.S., 612 Norris Dr., Jefferson City, MO 65109. Tel: 573-635-0648

Permanent Deacons:
Agniel, Harry M.
Anderberg, Peter K.
Berry, Kenneth
Bilgrien, Kenneth D.
Bonnarens, Edwin C.
Braddock, Joseph
Breazile, James E.
Brooks, Michael
Brown, William J.
Brucks, Jerome C.
Butel, Francis J.
Butler, James R.
Capuano, Tom
Chaplin, Mark
Christoff, Gary
Connery, Jerome
Cox, Bruce
Daly, Michael M.
Davis, Howard E.
Dodds, Michael
Dulle, Robert L.
Fritsch, Frederick
Garufi, Vincent E.
Gerling, Thomas J.
Heidlage, Walter F.
Hildebrand, Larry
Himmelberg, Robert L.
Horsefield, Earl R.
Horton, Joseph E.
Houston, John D.
Kindle, Charles C.
Kinney, William J.
Korman, Gerald W.
Louis, William E.
Manion, Thomas C.
McEvoy, Tim
Miller, David
Nordmeyer, Charles
O'Rourke, John C.
Orscheln, Donald W.
Osman, Robert C.
Parn, Harold L.
Pierceall, Eugene E.
Prenger, Leo F.
Rackers, Robert J.
Reibenspies, Terence L.
Reuter, Ralph V.
Rockhold, Jess L.
Shumake, Lindell P.
Snooks, Richard W.
Spalding, George T.
Tebbe, John J.
Toll, Bernhard F.
Visot, Luis R.
Warden, Donald E.
Watson, G. Robert
Weisel, Fred M.
Whalen, Tom
Wilmarth, Albert W.
Zimmerman, Francis P.

INSTITUTIONS LOCATED IN THE DIOCESE

[A] SEMINARIES, DIOCESAN

HANNIBAL. *St. Thomas Aquinas Seminary*, P.O. Box 858, 245 N. Levering Ave., 63401. Tel: 573-221-4330.
E-mail: stasem@sockets.net
Web site: http://members.sockets.net/~stasem
Very Rev. Marion J. Makerewicz, Rector; Revs. James J. Wenting; Louis W. McCorkle; David D. Cox; Mark A. Porterfield; P. Gregory Oligschlaeger; Bro. Christian J. Guertin, F.F.S.C.; Mr. Robert Catalpa; Mr. Jeff Malone. Students 25.

[B] HIGH SCHOOLS, DIOCESAN

JEFFERSON CITY. *Helias High School*, 1305 Swift's Highway, 65109. Tel: 573-635-6139. Mr. Stan Ochsner, Student Support; Sr. Jean Dietrich, Prin.; Mr. Dennis Hughes, Admin.; Mr. Ron Vossen, Campus Ministry; Revs. Brendan Doyle; Mark S. Smith; R. William Peckman. Brothers of the Christian Schools 3; School Sisters of Notre Dame 1; Lay Teachers 38; Students 776.

[C] GENERAL HOSPITALS

JEFFERSON CITY. *St. Marys Health Center*, 100 St. Marys Medical Plaza, 65101. Tel: 573-761-7000
For a complete listing, refer to the Hospitals section.

[D] NURSING HOMES

JEFFERSON CITY. *St. Joseph's Home*, 1306 W. Main St., 65109. Tel: 573-635-0166
For a complete listing, refer to the Special Care Facilities section.
Villa Marie Skilled Nursing Facility, 1030 Edmonds St., 65109. Tel: 573-761-6700
For a complete listing, refer to the Special Care Facilities section.

STOUTSVILLE. *Columbia Nursing Home Ministry*, R.R. #1, P.O. Box 103-BC, 65283.
E-mail: rhunkins@trib.net
For a complete listing, refer to the Special Care Facilities section.

[E] CONVENTS AND RESIDENCES FOR SISTERS

JEFFERSON CITY. *Discalced Carmelite Monastery*, 2201 W. Main St., 65109. Mother Therese Dubois, O.C.D., Prioress. Professed of Solemn Vows 7; Professed of Temporary Vows 1; Novices 1.
Franciscan Sisters of Mary, Jericho Community, 202 Binder Dr., 65109-0815. Tel: 573-635-8123. Franciscan Sisters of Mary 4.

BRINKTOWN. *Guardian Angel Convent*, 65443. Tel: 573-422-3921. Franciscan Sisters of Mary.

COLUMBIA. *Our Lady of Peace Monastery*, 3410 W. Broadway St., 65203. Tel: 573-446-2300. Sr. JoAnn Schmidt, O.S.B., Prioress. Benedictine Sisters of Pontifical Jurisdiction 14.

MARCELINE. *Our Lady of the Rosary*, 200 W. Bigger St., 64658-1070. Tel: 660-376-3969. Franciscan Sisters of Mary 2.

[F] NEWMAN CENTERS

JEFFERSON CITY. *Lincoln University-Newman Center*, 708 Marshall St., 65101. Tel: 573-635-9356. Rev. David G. Buescher, Dir.

COLUMBIA. *University of Missouri-Columbia, Campus Ministry*, 701 Maryland, 65201. Tel: 573-449-5424.
E-mail: DenSchm@AOL.com
Web site: http://students.missouri.edu~newman
Revs. Michael F. Quinn, Dir.; Dennis Schmidt (STL).

FAYETTE. *Central Methodist College*, c/o St. Joseph Church, 300 Cleveland, 65248. Rev. Richard A. Colbert, C.PP.S., Dir.

KIRKSVILLE. *Catholic Newman Center, Truman State University*, 709 S. Davis, 63501. Tel: 660-665-4357. Mrs. Bettie Lesczynski, Dir.; Rev. William P. Kottenstette, Chap.

ROLLA. *University of Missouri-Rolla*, 2 Vichy Rd., 65401. Tel: 573-364-2133. Sr. Renita Brummer, O.S.F., Dir.

[G] MISCELLANEOUS

JEFFERSON CITY. *Diocesan Excellence in Education Fund, Inc.*, P.O. Box 417, 65102. Tel: 573-635-9127.
Missouri Catholic Conference, 600 Clark Ave., P.O. Box 1022, 65102. Tel: 573-635-7239; Fax: 573-635-7431.
St. Marys Health Center, Jefferson City, Missouri, Foundation, 100 St. Marys Medical Plaza, 65101. Tel: 573-761-7198. Member of the SSM Health Care. Ms. Jean Gruetzemacher, Dir.

ST. LOUIS. *Residents Encounter Christ*, Missouri State Board, 7522 Big Bend Blvd., 63119. Tel: 314-647-7060; Fax: 314-647-8380. Mr. Joseph Hedley, Exec. Dir.

RELIGIOUS INSTITUTES OF MEN REPRESENTED IN THE DIOCESE

For further details refer to the corresponding bracketed number in the Religious Institutes of Men or Women section.

[0330]—*Brothers of the Christian Schools.* (Midwest Prov.).—F.S.C.
[]—*Brothers of the Poor of St. Francis.* (Burlington, IA.)—C.F.P.
[1330]—*Congregation of the Mission.* (Midwest Prov.).—C.M.
[0510]—*Franciscan Brothers of the Holy Cross.*—F.F.S.C.
[0520]—*Franciscan Friars.* (Sacred Heart Prov.).—O.F.M.
[0720]—*The Missionaries of Our Lady of La Salette.* (Prov. of Mary Queen).—M.S.
[1060]—*Society of the Precious Blood.* (Kansas City Prov.).—C.PP.S.

RELIGIOUS INSTITUTES OF WOMEN REPRESENTED IN THE DIOCESE

[0100]—*Adorers of the Blood of Christ.* (Ruma, IL; Wichita, KS).—A.S.C.
[0230]—*Benedictine Sisters of Pontifical Jurisdiction.* (Columbia, MO).—O.S.B.
[0360]—*Carmelite Sisters of the Divine Heart of Jesus.*—Carmel.D.C.J.
[0460]—*Congregation of the Sisters of Charity of the Incarnate Word.*—C.C.V.I.
[1730]—*Congregation of the Sisters of the Third Order of St. Francis.* (Oldenburg, IN).—O.S.F.
[0420]—*Discalced Carmelite Nuns.*—O.C.D.
[1070-11]—*Dominican Sisters.* (Sparkill, NY).—O.P.
[1415]—*Franciscan Sisters of Mary.* (St. Louis Prov.).—F.S.M.
[1430]—*Franciscan Sisters of Our Lady of Perpetual Help.*—O.S.F.
[2970]—*School Sisters of Notre Dame.* (Milwaukee Prov.).—S.S.N.D.
[2970]—*School Sisters of Notre Dame.* (St. Louis Prov.).—S.S.N.D.
[1680]—*School Sisters of St. Francis.* (Milwaukee, WI).—O.S.F.
[0480]—*Sisters of Charity of Leavenworth, Kansas.* (Leavenworth, KS).—S.C.L.
[0660]—*Sisters of Christian Charity.* (Wilmette, IL).—S.C.C.
[0990]—*Sisters of Divine Providence.* (St. Louis Prov.).—C.D.P.
[2549]—*Sisters of Mercy.* (Co. Sligo, Ireland).—R.S.M.
[1670]—*Sisters of St. Francis of Savannah, MO.* (Savannah, MO).—O.S.F.
[3830-15]—*Sisters of St. Joseph.* (Concordia, KS).—C.S.J.
[3270]—*Sisters of the Most Precious Blood.* (O'Fallon, MO).—C.PP.S.

DIOCESAN CEMETERIES

JEFFERSON CITY. *St. Peter's Catholic Cemetery Association*, 427 Crystal View Terrace, 65109. Mr. Nelson Vincent, Pres.

NECROLOGY

† Owens, Edward M., (Retired). —Died Jan. 4, 1997.

Diocese of Joliet in Illinois

(Dioecesis Joliettensis in Illinois)

Most Reverend

JOSEPH L. IMESCH, D.D.

Bishop of Joliet; ordained December 16, 1956; ordained Auxiliary Bishop of Detroit April 3, 1973; appointed Bishop of Joliet June 30, 1979; installed August 28, 1979. *Res., 425 Summit St., Joliet, IL, 60435.*

Most Reverend

ROGER L. KAFFER, D.D.

Auxiliary Bishop of Joliet; Titular Bishop of Dusa; ordained May 1, 1954; appointed April 25, 1985; consecrated June 26, 1985. *Res., 425 Summit St., Joliet, IL, 60435.*

ESTABLISHED BY BULL DATED DECEMBER 11, 1948.

CANONICALLY ERECTED MARCH 24, 1949.

Square Miles 4,218.

Comprises the Counties of Du Page, Kankakee, Will, Grundy, Ford, Iroquois and Kendall in the State of Illinois.

PATRON OF DIOCESE: St. Francis Xavier.

For legal titles of parishes and diocesan institutions, consult the Chancery.

Chancery: 425 Summit St., Joliet, IL, 60435. Tel.: 815-722-6606; Fax: 815-722-6602.

STATISTICAL OVERVIEW

Personnel	
Bishop	1
Auxiliary Bishops	1
Abbots	1
Retired Abbots	2
Priests: Diocesan Active in Diocese	152
Priests: Active Outside Diocese	10
Priests: Diocesan in Foreign Missions	1
Priests: Retired, Sick or Absent	36
Number of Diocesan Priests	199
Religious Priests in Diocese	112
Extern Priests in Diocese	13
Ordinations:	
Diocesan Priests	2
Transitional Deacons	2
Permanent Deacons	26
Permanent Deacons in Diocese	138
Total Brothers	95
Total Sisters	766
Parishes	
Parishes	119
With Resident Pastor:	
Resident Diocesan Priests	99
Resident Religious Priests	17
Without Resident Pastor:	
Administered by Priests	3
Missions	10
New Parishes Created	1
Professional Ministry Personnel:	
Brothers	3
Sisters	69
Lay Ministers	167
Welfare	
Catholic Hospitals	3
Total Assisted	588,624
Homes for the Aged	10
Total Assisted	2,231
Day Care and Extended Day Care Centers	3
Total Assisted	1,126
Specialized Homes	1
Total Assisted	35
Special Centers for Social Services	5
Total Assisted	33,912
Residential Care of Disabled	1
Total Assisted	120
Educational	
Diocesan Students in Other Seminaries	21
Total Seminarians	21
Colleges and Universities	3
Total Students	12,530
High Schools, Diocesan and Parish	4
Total Students	2,515
High Schools, Private	4
Total Students	3,080
Elementary Schools, Diocesan and Parish	62
Total Students	19,311
Catechesis/Religious Education:	
High School Students	5,371
Elementary Students	48,682
Total Students Under Catholic Instruction	91,510
Teachers in the Diocese:	
Priests	34
Brothers	22
Sisters	44
Lay Teachers	1,485
Vital Statistics	
Receptions into the Church:	
Infant Baptism Totals	10,458
Adult Baptism Totals	332
Received into Full Communion	914
First Communions	9,335
Confirmations	6,789
Marriages:	
Catholic	1,724
Interfaith	812
Total Marriages	2,536
Deaths	3,534
Total Catholic Population	535,000
Total Population	1,494,978

Former Bishops—Most Rev. MARTIN D. MCNAMARA, D.D., first Bishop of Joliet; ord. Dec. 3, 1922; appt. Dec. 17, 1948; cons. March 7, 1949; died May 23, 1966.—Most Rev. ROMEO BLANCHETTE, D.D., appt. Auxiliary Bishop of Joliet and Titular Bishop of Maxita Feb. 8, 1965; cons. April 3, 1965; appt. Bishop of Joliet July 19, 1966; installed Aug. 31, 1966; resigned Jan. 30, 1979; died Jan. 10, 1982.

Chancery—425 Summit St., Joliet, 60435. Tel: 815-722-6606; Fax: 815-722-6602. Office Hours: Mon.-Fri. 8:30-4:30.

Vicar General—Most Rev. ROGER L. KAFFER, D.D., J.C.L.

Chancellor—Sr. JUDITH A. DAVIES, O.S.F.

Moderator of the Curia—Rev. JOSEPH TAPELLA.

Director of Administration—JAMES P. LYNCH.

Director of Finance—GUY A. SELL.

Matrimonial Tribunal—310 Bridge St., Joliet, 60435. Tel: 815-722-2256.

Judicial Vicar—Rev. JOSEPH TAPELLA, J.C.L.

Adjutant Judicial Vicar—Revs. MICHAEL GINTER, J.C.L.; ROBERT COLLOGAN, J.C.L.

Notaries—LORRAINE A'HEARN; SYLVIA CARBONI; MARIE SMEETS; BETTY JOUTRAS; HELEN MILCHERSKA.

Defender of the Bond—Sr. MARILYN PHILLIPS, O.S.F., Ph.D., J.C.D.

Judges—Revs. RICHARD L. SMITH, J.C.L.; JOSEPH TAPELLA, J.C.L.; MICHAEL W. GINTER, J.C.L.; ROBERT COLLOGAN, J.C.L.; Sr. MARILYN PHILLIPS, O.S.F., Ph.D., J.C.D.

Advocates—Mrs. VIRGINIA L. LANTZ; Mr. JAMES GILLIGAN.

Diocesan Offices and Directors

Board of Conciliation and Arbitration—425 Summit St., Joliet, 60435.

Campaign for Human Development—ELIZABETH FRANKLIN, *St. Charles Borromeo Pastoral Center, 402 S. Independence Blvd., Romeoville, 60441.* Tel: 815-834-4027.

Catholic Cemeteries—NORMAN SCHALL, Dir., *St. Charles Borromeo Pastoral Center, 402 S. Independence Blvd., Romeoville, 60441.* Tel: 815-838-0395.

Catholic Charities—Legal Title: *Catholic Charities of the Diocese of Joliet.* KATHLEEN MCGOWAN, Exec. Dir., *203 N. Ottawa St., Joliet, 60432.* Tel: 815-723-3405.

The Catholic Education Foundation of the Diocese of Joliet—MAME BYRNE, Foundation Dir., *St. Charles Borromeo Pastoral Center, 402 S. Independence Blvd., Romeoville, 60441.* Tel: 815-834-4033.

Catholic Relief Services—TOM GARLITZ, Dir., *St. Charles Center, 402 S. Independence Blvd., Romeoville, 60441.* Tel: 815-834-4026.

Catholic Women, Council of—Mrs. ANN BURDZINSKI, Dir., Office: *St. Charles Borromeo Pastoral Center, 402 S. Independence Blvd., Romeoville, 60441.* Tel: 815-834-4070.

Communications Office—St. Charles Borromeo Pastoral Center, 402 S. Independence Blvd., Romeoville, 60441. Tel: 815-834-4064.

Cursillo Movement—Rev. JOSEPH SHIMANEK, Moderator, *St. Charles Borromeo Pastoral Center, 405 S. Independence Blvd., Romeoville, 60441.* Tel: 815-838-8100.

Deans—Vacant, East Dupage; Rev. JOEL FORTIER, West Dupage Kendall; Rev. JAMES FITZGERALD, East Will; Rev. JAMES DOUGHERTY, West Will; Rev. CHARLES WHEELER, Kankakee-Grundy; Rev. F. LEE RYAN, Ford-Iroquois.

Diocesan Development Office—KEVIN DELABRE, Dir., *St. Charles Borromeo Pastoral Center, 402 S. Independence Blvd., Romeoville, 60441.* Tel: 815-838-8515.

Diocesan Coordinator for Health Affairs—Sr. JUDITH A. DAVIS, O.S.F., *Chancery, 425 Summit St., Joliet, 60435.* Tel: 815-722-6606.

Diocesan Vicar for Religious—Sr. MARY MEEGAN, O.P., *St. Charles Borromeo Pastoral Center, 402 S. Independence Blvd., Romeoville, 60441.* Tel: 815-834-4009.

Diaconate Program—Deacon WILL WORDEN, Dir., *St. Charles Borromeo Pastoral Center, 402 S. Independence Blvd., Romeoville, 60441.* Tel: 815-834-4091.

Divine Worship, Office of—Sr. SHARON MARIE STOLA, O.S.B., Dir., *St. Charles Borromeo Pastoral Center, 402 S. Independence Blvd., Romeoville, 60441.* Tel: 815-834-4010.

Ecumenism—Rev. STANLEY ORLIKIEWICZ, Dir., *St. Raymond Cathedral, 604 N. Raynor Ave., Joliet, 60435.* Tel: 815-722-6653.

Family Ministry, Office of—Dr. JAMES HEALY, Dir., *St. Charles Borromeo Pastoral Center, 402 S. Independence Blvd., Romeoville, 60441.* Tel: 815-838-5334.

Hispanic Ministry, Office of—Sr. JUDY CALLAHAN, B.V.M., Dir., *St. Charles Borromeo Center, 402 S. Independence Blvd., Romeoville, 60441.* Tel: 815-834-4037.

New Catholic Explorer—ALFRED DOBLIN, Editor, Office: *St. Charles Borromeo Pastoral Center, 402 S. Independence Blvd., Romeoville, 60441.* Tel: 815-838-6475; Fax: 815-834-4068.

Life Office—FRAN FORTIER, Dir.; Rev. DENIS WHITE, Moderator, *St. Charles Borromeo Pastoral Center, 402 S. Independence Blvd., Romeoville, 60441.* Tel: 815-834-4048.

Marriage Encounter—Rev. HUGH FULLMER, Diocesan Liaison, *Divine Savior Parish, 1200 67th St., Downers Grove, 60516.* Tel: 708-355-8980.

Marriage Preparation Office—Dr. JAMES HEALY, *St. Charles Borromeo Pastoral Center, 402 S. Independence Blvd., Romeoville, 60441.* Tel: 815-838-5334.

Ministry Formation—Dr. JEAN BOHR, Dir., *St. Charles Borromeo Pastoral Center, 402 S. Independence Blvd., Romeoville, 60441.* Tel: 815-834-4001.

Ministry to College Campuses and Young Adults—Bro. JOHN DORNBOS, C.F.C., *402 S. Independence Blvd., Romeoville, 60446-2264.* Tel: 815-834-4022.

Peace and Social Justice Ministry Office—THOMAS GARLITZ, *St. Charles Borromeo Pastoral Center, 402 S. Independence Blvd., Romeoville, 60441.* Tel: 815-834-4026.

Presbyteral Council—Rev. ERNEST NORBECK, Pres., *425 Summit, Joliet, 60435.* Tel: 815-722-6606.

Propagation of the Faith—Rev. DAMIEN GRAZIANO, Dir., *15314 Summit St., Oakbrook Terrace, 60181.* Tel: 708-629-5810.

Religious Education Office—Sr. MARILYN ELLERT, O.S.F., Supt., *430 N. Center St., Joliet, 60435.* Tel: 815-727-6411.

Rural Life—Rev. DENNIS WHITE, *St. Patrick, 119 N. Market St., Momeme, 60954.*

St. Vincent de Paul Society—*213 Main St., West Chicago, 60185.* Tel: 708-293-9420.

Schools—Sr. HELEN JEAN KORMELINK, O.S.B., Supt., *425 Summit St., Joliet, 60435.* Tel: 815-727-4674.

Scouts—Rev. JOHN DOYLE, Office: *St. Anne Parish, 1702 N. Dearborn, Joilet.* Tel: 815-722-3222.

Stewardship Office—MARIANNE MURPHY, Dir., *St. Charles Borromeo Pastoral Center, 402 S. Independence Blvd., Romeoville, 60441.* Tel: 815-834-4030.

Vocations—Rev. JOHN REGAN, Dir., *St. Charles Borromeo, 402 S. Independence Blvd., Romeoville, 60441.* Tel: 815-834-4002.

Youth Ministry—Mrs. HELEN JOHNSON, *Religious Education Office, 430 N. Center, Joliet, 60435.* Tel: 815-727-6411.

CLERGY, PARISHES, MISSIONS AND PAROCHIAL SCHOOLS

CITY OF JOLIET
(Will County)

1—THE CATHEDRAL OF ST. RAYMOND (1917), Revs. Stanley Orlikiewicz; Thomas Milota. In res., Rev. Joseph J. Tapella.
Res., 604 N. Raynor Ave., 60435. Tel: 815-722-6653; Fax: 815-722-6175.
School—713 Douglas St., 60435. Tel: 815-722-6626. Sisters 1; Lay Teachers 23; Students 500.
Catechesis/Religious Programs—Students 400.

2—HOLY CROSS, Rev. William Slikas.
Res., 901 Elizabeth St., 60435. Tel: 815-722-0785; Fax: 815-723-0679. [CEM]

3—HOLY FAMILY (1959), Rev. John L. Dennerlein; Deacon Richard M. Yarshen.
1205 N. Larkin Ave., 60435. Tel: 815-725-6880; Fax: 815-725-8649.
Res., 910 Westminster Rd., 60435. Tel: 815-725-6880.
School—1205 N. Larkin Ave., 60435. Tel: 815-725-8149.
Lay Teachers 14; Students 254.
Catechesis/Religious Programs—Tel: 815-729-2243.
Students 155.

4—MOUNT CARMEL (1939) (Mexican American), Rev. Raymond Corkery, O.Carm.
Res., 409 Irving St., 60432. Tel: 815-726-5208; Fax: 815-727-7225.
Catechesis/Religious Programs—Tel: 815-727-7187.
Students 270.

5—SACRED HEART (1886) (African American), Rev. Richard L. Bennett.
Res., 337 S. Ottawa St., 60436. Tel: 815-722-0295; Fax: 815-722-6088.
Catechesis/Religious Programs—Students 50.

6—ST. AMBROSE, Rev. Joseph F. Kilas.
Res., 1711 Burry Cir., Crest Hill, 60435. Tel: 815-722-3748.
Catechesis/Religious Programs—Tel: 815-722-9193.
Students 230.

7—ST. ANNE, Rev. John J. Doyle.
Res., 1702 N. Dearborn St., Crest Hill, 60435. Tel: 815-722-3222.
Catechesis/Religious Programs—Students 110.

8—ST. ANTHONY (Italian), Rev. Arthur LaPore.
Res., 100 Scott St., 60431-1210. Tel: 815-722-1057.

9—ST. BERNARD, Rev. Donald O'Connor.
Res., 1313 Ridgewood Ave., 60432. Tel: 815-726-4474.

10—SS. CYRIL AND METHODIUS (Slovak), Rev. Branislav Caniga, Admin.
Res., 704 Landau Ave., 60432. Tel: 815-722-3586; Fax: 815-722-7276.
Catechesis/Religious Programs—Students 62.

11—ST. JOHN THE BAPTIST, Revs. Edward Shea, O.F.M.; Medard Buvala, O.F.M.; Deacon Jose Lopez. In res., Rev. Louis Davino, O.F.M.; Bro. John Sweeney, O.F.M.
Res., 404 N. Hickory St., 60435. Tel: 815-727-4788; Fax: 815-740-1521. [CEM]
Catechesis/Religious Programs—403 N. Hickory St., 60435. Tel: 815-727-9077.
Students 109.

12—ST. JOSEPH (1891) (Slovenian), Rev. George F. Klepec.
Res., 416 N. Chicago St., 60432. Tel: 815-727-9378; Fax: 815-722-1213.
School—409 N. Scott St., 60432. Tel: 815-722-1005. Sisters 2; Lay Teachers 8; Students 230.
Catechesis/Religious Programs—Students 60.

13—ST. JUDE (1954), Rev. James A. Schwab; Deacons Raymond Clark; William Hetzel.
Res., 2212 McDonough St., 60436. Tel: 815-725-2209; Fax: 815-741-8844.
School—2204 McDonough St., 60436. Tel: 815-729-0288; Fax: 815-729-0344.
Sisters of St. Francis of Mary Immaculate 1; Lay Teachers 16; Students 308.
Catechesis/Religious Programs—Tel: 815-729-0288; Fax: 815-729-0344.
Students 363.

14—ST. MARY. Closed. For inquiries for parish records contact the Chancery.

15—ST. MARY MAGDALENE, Rev. Richard G. Ross.
Res., 127 S. Briggs St., 60433. Tel: 815-722-7653; Fax: 815-722-7680.
School—Tel: 815-727-9079; Fax: 815-727-2059.
Lay Teachers 9; Students 153.

16—ST. MARY NATIVITY (1906) (Croatian), Revs. David Stalzer; Christopher Groh; Michael Powell.
Res., 706 N. Broadway, 60435. Tel: 815-726-4031; Fax: 815-727-4393.
School—702 N. Broadway, 60435. Tel: 815-722-8518.
Sisters of St. Francis of Christ the King 4; Lay Teachers 14; Students 325.
Catechesis/Religious Programs—Students 160.

17—ST. PATRICK (1838), Rev. James M. Lennon; Deacons Paul Kolodziej; Charles Peterson. In res., Rev. Eugene Bucciferro.
Res., 710 W. Marion St., 60436. Tel: 815-727-4746; Fax: 815-727-4798.
School—110 Willow Ave., 60436. Tel: 815-726-2924; Fax: 815-726-9289.
Lay Teachers 15; Students 330.
Catechesis/Religious Programs—Tel: 815-727-4746.
Students 125.

18—ST. PAUL THE APOSTLE (1950), Revs. James Dougherty; Dennis Paul; Deacons James Bouldin; William Bevan; Alex Krostenko.
Res., 18 Woodlawn Ave., 60435. Tel: 815-725-1527; Fax: 815-725-3393.
School—130 N. Woodlawn Ave., 60435. Tel: 815-725-3390.
Lay Teachers 15; Students 405.
Catechesis/Religious Programs—120 Woodlawn Ave., 60435. Tel: 815-725-6927.
Students 215.

19—ST. THADDEUS, Rev. Edward P. Rowland.
Res., 501 Liberty St., 60432. Tel: 815-727-7212.
School—510 Columbia St., 60432. Tel: 815-727-7806.
Lay Teachers 6; Students 130.

OUTSIDE THE CITY OF JOLIET

Addison, Du Page Co., St. Joseph (1956), Revs. James T. Kempfer; Thomas McGivney; Deacons Dino J. Franch; Gabriel Gamboa.
Res., 330 E. Fullerton, 60101. Tel: 630-279-6553.
School—Tel: 630-279-4211; Fax: 630-279-4925. Mrs. Barbara Tatic, Prin.
Lay Teachers 11; Students 221.
Catechesis/Religious Programs—Tel: 630-832-5514. Sr. Suzanne D.R.E.
Students 530.

St. Philip The Apostle (1963), Revs. Raymond P. Garbin; Philip M. Danaher, S.V.D.; Raymond Stonich.
Res., 1223 W. Holtz Ave., 60101. Tel: 630-628-0900.
School—Tel: 630-543-4130.
Lay Teachers 16; Students 362.
Catechesis/Religious Programs—Tel: 630-543-1754.
Students 550.

Ashkum, Iroquois Co., Assumption of the Blessed Virgin Mary, Rev. James Holup.
Res., N. Second St., Box 218, 60911. Tel: 815-698-2262. [CEM]
Mission—L'Erable, Iroquois Co., St. John the Baptist, Box 218, 60911. Tel: 815-698-2262.
Catechesis/Religious Programs—Students 122.

Aurora, Du Page Co., Our Lady of Mercy (1988), Rev. Gerald Tivy. Pastoral Assocs.: Sr. Louise Staszewski, O.S.M.; Sr. Marianne Talian, O.S.M.
Res., 801 S. Eola Rd., 60504. Tel: 630-851-3444; Fax: 630-851-3468.
Catechesis/Religious Programs—Students 1,096.

Beaverville, Iroquois Co., St. Mary, Rev. Robert J. Coleman.
Res., 308 St. Charles St., P.O. Box 152, 60912. Tel: 815-435-2432. [CEM]
Catechesis/Religious Programs—Students 42.

Bensenville, Du Page Co., St. Alexis (1926), Revs. William Conway; Oswald S. Reimann; Sr. Laurina Kahne, C.S.J., Pastoral Assoc. In res., Rev. Raymond Davis.
Res., 400 W. Wood St., 60106. Tel: 708-766-3530; Fax: 708-766-3536.
Catechesis/Religious Programs—410 W. Wood St., 60106. Tel: 708-766-4417. Mrs. Trudy Anderson, D.R.E.
Students 443.

St. Charles Borromeo (1959), Rev. Don E. McLaughlin; Deacon Michael Principe.
Res., 1135 Daniel, 60106. Tel: 630-860-1120; Fax: 630-860-5029.
School—Tel: 630-766-0116; Fax: 630-766-0181.
Lay Teachers 9; Students 280.
Catechesis/Religious Programs—Tel: 630-766-8822; Fax: 630-766-0181.
Students 310.

Bloomingdale, DuPage Co., St. Isidore (1920), Revs. Joel F. Fortier; William Dewan; Raymond Guthrie; Sr. Helen Mantovani, O.P., Pastoral Assoc.; Deacons Ken Jackson; John Freund.
Res., 427 W. Army Trail Rd., 60108. Tel: 630-529-3045; Fax: 630-529-2940. [CEM]
School—Tel: 630-529-9323.
Religious 1; Lay Teachers 16; Students 290.
Catechesis/Religious Programs—Tel: 630-529-9191.
Students 1,850.

Bolingbrook, Will Co., St. Dominic (1964), Revs. James W. Antiporek; Agustin Ortega; Deacons Thomas Ross; John Knapstein; Robert Wallace; Paul Walen; Robert Erickson; Victor Ruiz; James Kelly.

Res., 440 E. Briarcliff Rd., 60440. Tel: 630-739-5703; Fax: 630-739-2036.
School—420 E. Briarcliff Rd., 60440. Tel: 630-739-1633.
Sisters of St. Francis of Christ the King 3; Lay Teachers 14; Students 300.
Catechesis/Religious Programs—Tel: 630-739-2102.
Students 585.

St. Francis of Assisi, Revs. David Hankus; Michael Pennock; Deacons Raymond Hamilton; Terrance Hanley, Sr.; Rudulfo Molano; Thomas Fricke.
Res., 325 Whitewater Dr., 60440. Tel: 630-759-7588; Fax: 630-759-5257.
Catechesis/Religious Programs—Tel: 630-759-7611. D.R.E.: Sr. Mary Jane Petzel, O.S.F.; Sr. Jeanette Pitts, O.S.F.
Students 500.

Bourbonnais, Kankakee Co., Maternity of the Blessed Virgin Mary (1847), Revs. Lawrence D. Lentz, C.S.V.; John N. Peeters, C.S.V.; Donald F. Lund, C.S.V.; Deacons Euchrist J. Marcotte; Francis Chamness.
Res., 308 E. Marsile St., 60914. Tel: 815-933-8285. [CEM]
School—Tel: 815-933-7758; Fax: 815-933-1884.
Sisters of the Congregation of Notre Dame 1; Lay Teachers 14; Students 256.
Catechesis/Religious Programs—Tel: 815-933-8226; Fax: 815-933-1884.
Students 500.

Bradley, Kankakee Co., St. Joseph (1904), Revs. John T. McGeean; Douglas Hauber; Deacons Bob LaMotte; Leon Fritz. In res., Rev. John Antczak.
Res., 211 N. Center Ave., 60915. Tel: 815-939-3573; Fax: 815-939-3138.
School—Tel: 815-933-8013; Fax: 815-933-2775.
Dominican Sisters 2; Lay Teachers 15; Students 289.
Catechesis/Religious Programs—283 N. Center Ave., 60915. Tel: 815-937-9340.
Students 250.
Convent—247 N. Center Ave., 60915. Tel: 815-932-0112.

Braidwood, Will Co., Immaculate Conception (1869), Rev. William M. White.
Res., 34060 S. School St., 60408. Tel: 815-458-2125. [CEM]
Catechesis/Religious Programs—Students 260.

Cabery, Ford Co., St. Joseph, Rev. Richard F. Kostelz.
Res., 112 W. Main St., P.O. Box 77, 60919. Tel: 815-949-1568. [CEM]
Mission—Reddick, St. Mary, 216 E. Lincoln, Reddick, 60961.

Carol Stream, Du Page Co., Corpus Christi (1989), Rev. Charles A. Gemskie; Sr. M. Laurentia Fenlon, O.P., Pastoral Assoc. In res., Rev. Henry Wilkening, (Retired).
Res., 1415 Lies St., 60188-0453. Tel: 630-483-4673; Fax: 630-483-4679.
Catechesis/Religious Programs—Tel: 630-483-4222.
Students 1,017.

St. Luke (1963), Rev. Thomas Schutter; Sr. Barbara Rowan, S.S.S.F., Pastoral Assoc.
Res., 421 Cochise Ct., 60188. Tel: 630-668-1325; Fax: 630-668-1356.
Catechesis/Religious Programs—Tel: 630-665-2322.
Students 700.

Channahon, Will Co., St. Ann Parish (1990), Rev. Richard Smith.
Res., 25050 W. Eames St., 60410. Tel: 815-467-6962; Fax: 815-467-2320.
Catechesis/Religious Programs—Tel: 815-467-6992.
Students 439.

Chebanse, Iroquois Co., SS. Mary and Joseph's (1869), Rev. Lee F. Bacchi.
Res., 525 S. Chestnut, P.O. Box 5, 60922. Tel: 815-697-2654. [CEM]
Catechesis/Religious Programs—Students 95.

Clarendon Hills, Du Page Co., Notre Dame (1954), Revs. Robert J. Schuler; Jess Testa; Venard Kommer, O.F.M.; Deacons Neill Carson; Frank Foys; David Lifka; Alan Symonanis.
Res., 64 Norfolk Ave., 60514. Tel: 708-654-3365; Fax: 708-654-8701.
School—Tel: 708-323-1642.
Lay Teachers 19; Students 287.
Catechesis/Religious Programs—Tel: 708-325-5387.
Students 361.

Clifton, Iroquois Co., St. Peter's, Rev. Lee F. Bacchi.
Res., 450 E. Third Ave., Box 25, 60927. Tel: 815-694-2027. [CEM]
Catechesis/Religious Programs—Students 132.

Coal City, Grundy Co., Assumption (1889), Rev. Mark Jendersyk; Sr. Mary Patricia Peacock, S.P., Pastoral Assoc.
Res., 245 S. Kankakee St., 60416. Tel: 815-634-4171; Fax: 815-634-4186.
Catechesis/Religious Programs—Tel: 815-634-8020.
Students 420.

Darien, Du Page Co., Our Lady of Peace (1970), Revs. Alphonse Micka, M.I.C.; Anthony Kelpsas, M.I.C.; William Hayward, M.I.C.; Deacons Frank Bina; Paul Brachle; Walter Schmidt; Dennis Stolarz.
Res., 701 Plainfield Rd., 60561. Tel: 630-323-4333; Fax: 630-323-4354.
School—709 Plainfield Rd., 60561. Tel: 630-325-9220; Fax: 630-325-1995.
Sisters of St. Casimir 1; Lay Teachers 29; Students 563.
Catechesis/Religious Programs—Tel: 630-986-8430; Fax: 630-986-1214.
Students 805.

Our Lady of Mount Carmel (1970), Revs. Gavin Quinn, O.Carm.; Michael O'Keefe, O.Carm.; Russell Gavin, O.Carm.; Deacons Marco Lovero; John Farrell.
Res., 8404 Cass Ave., 60561. Tel: 630-852-3303; Fax: 630-852-5227.
Catechesis/Religious Programs—Tel: 630-963-3053.
Students 1,268.

Downers Grove, Du Page Co., Divine Savior (1968), Revs. Robert E. Pietras; Leonard Guz.
Res., 1200 67th St., 60516. Tel: 630-969-1532; Fax: 630-969-1724.
Catechesis/Religious Programs—Tel: 630-969-1673.
Students 650.

St. Joseph (1907), Revs. Paul Hottinger; Edward Grotovsky.
Res., 4824 Highland, 60515. Tel: 630-964-0216; Fax: 630-964-0867.
School—Franklin & Highland, 60515. Tel: 630-969-4306; Fax: 630-969-3946.
Lay Teachers 32; Students 492.
Catechesis/Religious Programs—Tel: 630-971-1740; Fax: 630-964-0867.
Students 781.

St. Mary, Revs. Thomas Paul; Scott McCawley.
Res., 444 Wilson Ave., 60515. Tel: 630-969-1063; Fax: 630-969-1259.
School—444 Prairie Ave., 60515. Tel: 630-968-6155; Fax: 630-968-6205.
Felician Sisters 2; Lay Teachers 25; Students 587.
Catechesis/Religious Programs—Tel: 630-960-3565.
Students 641.

Elmhurst, Du Page Co., Immaculate Conception (1876), Revs. Gerald Riva; Robert Duda; John Balluff.
Res., 134 Arthur St., 60126. Tel: 630-530-8515; Fax: 630-530-9346.
School—Tel: 630-530-3490; Fax: 630-530-9787. Helen Kwasmiewski, Prin.
Sisters 1; Lay Teachers 21; Students 617.
High School—217 Cottage Hill Ave., 60126. Tel: 630-530-3460; Fax: 630-530-2290. Sr. Maureen Field, I.H.M.
Priests 1; Sisters 1; Lay Teachers 21; Students 254.
Catechesis/Religious Programs—Tel: 630-530-3480.
Students 531.

Mary, Queen of Heaven (1957), Rev. John Barrett. In res., Rev. Thomas Wolter; Deacons John Maloney; Charles Nunez.
Res., 426 N. West Ave., 60126. Tel: 630-279-5700; Fax: 630-279-4667.
Catechesis/Religious Programs—442 N. West Ave., 60126. Tel: 630-832-8962.
Students 340.

Visitation (1953), Revs. Michael Lane; William DeSalvo; Deacons Dominic Cuzzone; Jay Janousek; Anthony Spatafore.
Res., 779 S. York St., 60126. Tel: 630-834-6700; Fax: 630-834-6711.
School—Tel: 630-834-4931; Fax: 630-834-4936.
Sisters of St. Adrian Dominican 2; Lay Teachers 23; Students 500.
Catechesis/Religious Programs—851 S. York, 60126. Tel: 630-279-7058.
Students 667.

Frankfort, Will Co., St. Anthony, Revs. Vytas Memenas; John Ouger; Deacons Donald Berkey; Daniel Danahey; Richard Rosko. In res., Rev. John Regan.
Res., 7659 W. Sauk Trail, 60423. Tel: 815-469-3750; Fax: 815-469-6514.
Catechesis/Religious Programs—Tel: 815-469-6072; Fax: 815-469-6514.
Students 1,300.

Gibson City, Ford Co., Our Lady of Lourdes, Rev. William F. Smith.
Res., 534 N. Wood St., 60936. Tel: 217-784-4671.
Catechesis/Religious Programs—Students 69.
Mission—Melvin, St. George.

Gilman, Iroquois Co., Immaculate Conception, Rev. Robert F. Emerson.
Res., 224 N. Secor St., 60938. Tel: 815-265-7236. [CEM]
Catechesis/Religious Programs—Tel: 815-265-7315.
Students 98.
Mission—Onarga, Iroquois Co., Our Lady of Guadalupe, 504 W. Seminary Ave., P.O. Box 1, Onarga, 60955.

Glendale Heights, Du Page Co., St. Matthew, Revs. Franklin R. Tasker, O.Carm.; Norbert G. Piper, O.Carm.; David Dillon, O.Carm.; Deacons Ronald Darschewski; Richard A. Mangen; Vincent C. Rizzo.
Res., 1555 Glen Ellyn Rd., 60139. Tel: 630-469-6300; Fax: 630-469-6302.
School—Tel: 630-858-3112.
Lay Teachers 21; Students 408.
Catechesis/Religious Programs—Students 688.

Glen Ellyn, Du Page Co., Queenship of Mary, Rev. Nguyen Huy Quyen.
Res., 23W371 Armitage, 60137. Tel: 630-469-7494; Fax: 630-752-0332.
Catechesis/Religious Programs—Tel: 630-752-0332.
Students 120.

St. Petronille (1925), Revs. Michael A. O'Keefe; John Sullivan; Gerald Simonelli; Deacons Edward Schafer; Ronald Yurcus; Theodore Farrell; Mrs. Vinal Van Benthem, Pastoral Assoc. In res., Rev. Nguyen Huy Quyen.
Res., 420 Glenwood Ave., 60137. Tel: 630-469-0404; Fax: 630-469-0412.
School—Tel: 630-469-5041; Fax: 630-469-5071.
Lay Teachers 29; Students 513.
Catechesis/Religious Programs—458 Hillside, 60137. Tel: 630-858-3796; Fax: 630-858-6232.
Students 1,186.

St. James the Apostle (1965), Revs. John M. Sebahar; Jeff Stoneberg; Deacon Emmanuel Scavone.
Res., 480 S. Park Blvd., 60137. Tel: 630-469-7540; Fax: 630-469-7590.
School—Tel: 630-469-8060.
Lay Teachers 20; Students 296.
Catechesis/Religious Programs—490 S. Park Blvd., 60137. Tel: 630-858-5646; Fax: 630-858-5687.
Students 925.

Goodrich, Kankakee Co., Sacred Heart, Rev. Paul F. Jasinski, C.S.V.; Deacon John R. Reville.
Res., 588 S. 10000 W. Road, Bonfield, 60913-7019. Tel: 815-426-2221. [CEM]
Catechesis/Religious Programs—Students 60.

Herscher, Kankakee Co., St. Margaret Mary, Rev. Ronald Hart.
Res., 207 E. Fifth St., 60941. Tel: 815-426-2153; Fax: 815-426-2136. [CEM]
Catechesis/Religious Programs—Tel: 815-426-2550.
Students 115.

Hinsdale, Du Page Co., St. Isaac Jogues, Revs. Theodore Weitzel; Matthew Hughes.
Res., 306 W. Fourth St., 60521. Tel: 630-323-1248; Fax: 630-323-6373.
School—Tel: 630-323-3244.
Religious 2; Lay Teachers 29; Students 634.
Catechesis/Religious Programs—427 S. Clay St., 60521. Tel: 630-323-0265.
Students 746.

Hopkins Park, Kankakee Co., Sacred Heart, Rev. Denis E. White.
Res. & Mailing Address: 119 Market St., Momence, 60954. Tel: 815-944-5562.
Catechesis/Religious Programs—16485 E. Birch, P.O. Box 557, 60944.
Students 10.

Irwin, Kankakee Co., St. James The Apostle, Rev. Ronald Hart.
Res., 4372 Main St., Kankakee, 60901. Tel: 815-933-8807. [CEM]
Catechesis/Religious Programs—Students 75.

Itasca, Du Page Co., St. Andrew Kim, Rev. Simeon Je Chan-Kyu.
Res., 1275 Arlington Hts. Rd., 60143. Tel: 630-250-0576; Fax: 630-250-2502.

St. Peter the Apostle (1956), Revs. Donald P. Pock; Joseph Stalzer.
Res., 524 N. Rush St., 60143-1698. Tel: 630-773-1272; Fax: 630-773-1720.
School—500 N. Cherry St., 60143-1699. Tel: 630-773-1979; Fax: 630-773-2826.
Lay Teachers 10; Students 233.
Catechesis/Religious Programs—Tel: 630-773-1959; Fax: 630-773-2826.
Students 260.

Kankakee, Kankakee Co.,

1—ST. MARTIN OF TOURS, (1950), Rev. Dennis F. Settles.
Res., 953 S. Ninth Ave., 60901. Tel: 815-933-7177; Fax: 815-933-2171. [JC]
School—907 S. Ninth Ave., 60901. Tel: 815-932-7911.

Lay Teachers 9; Students 182.
Catechesis/Religious Programs—Students 230.

2—St. Patrick, (1893) (Irish), Revs. Richard Pighini, C.S.V.; Donald R. Wehnert; Sr. Mary Noel Plummer, O.P., Pastoral Min. Pastoral Assocs.: Marilyn Mulcahy; Deacon Joseph Cotugno. In res., Revs. Andrew A. Bialas, C.S.V.; Francis Cerwronka, C.S.V.
Res., 428 S. Indiana Ave., 60901. Tel: 815-932-6716; Fax: 815-932-6717.
School—Tel: 815-932-8124.
Lay Teachers 13; Students 230.
Catechesis/Religious Programs—Tel: 815-939-3879.
Students 115.

3—St. Rose of Lima, Rev. Charles Wheeler.
Res., 486 W. Merchant St., 60901. Tel: 815-933-9391; Fax: 815-933-9393.
Catechesis/Religious Programs—Students 80.

4—St. Stanislaus, (Polish). Closed. For inquiries for parish records contact the Chancery.

5—St. Teresa, Rev. Anthony Taschetta. Pastoral Assocs.: Barbara Staniszeski; Sr. Mary McElmeel, B.V.M.
Res., 361 N. St. Joseph Ave., 60901. Tel: 815-933-7683; Fax: 815-933-7692.
Lisieux Pastoral Center—371 St. Joseph Ave., 60901. Tel: 815-939-2913.
School—School and Religious Program combined with St. Patrick, Kankakee.

Kinsman, Grundy Co., Sacred Heart, Rev. Robert Maternoski, Admin.
Res., 219 Emmett St., 60437. Tel: 815-392-4245. [JC]

Lisle, Du Page Co., St. Joan of Arc (1924), Revs. Roman S. Galiardi, O.S.B.; Gabriel Baltes, O.S.B.; Kenneth Zigmond, O.S.B.; Deacons Denis Stucko; Joseph Dalpiaz.
Office: 820 Division St., 60532. Tel: 630-963-4500; Fax: 630-963-4568.
School—Tel: 630-969-1732; Fax: 630-963-9070.
Lay Teachers 20; Students 686.
Catechesis/Religious Programs—Students 473.

Lockport, Will Co.,

1—St. Bernard, (1978), Rev. Richard B. Prodehl; Sr. Mary Carr, O.P., Pastoral Assoc.
Res., 14135 Parker Rd., 60441. Tel: 708-301-3020; Fax: 708-301-0738.
Catechesis/Religious Programs—14724 S. Arboretum Dr., 60441. Tel: 708-301-6952; Fax: 708-301-8870.
Students 1,054.

2—St. Dennis, Revs. Jim Curtin; Thomson Panakal.
Res., 1214 Hamilton St., 60441. Tel: 815-838-0704; Fax: 815-838-2401.
School—1201 S. Washington St., 60441. Tel: 815-838-4494.
Lay Teachers 11; Students 248.
Catechesis/Religious Programs—Students 458.

3—St. John Vianney, Rev. Andrew L. Buezyna, Admin.
Res., 401 Brassel, 60441. Tel: 815-723-3291.

4—St. Joseph, Rev. Hugh Fullmer; Deacon Joe Urso; Dr. Jeanne M. Cosgrove, Pastoral Assoc.
Res., 410 S. Jefferson St., 60441. Tel: 815-838-0187; Fax: 815-838-5379.
School—529 Madison, 60441. Tel: 815-838-8173; Fax: 815-838-0504.
Franciscan Sisters of the Sacred Heart 2; Lay Teachers 8; Students 273.
Catechesis/Religious Programs—529 Madison St., 60441. Tel: 815-838-2112.
Students 145.
Convent—531 E. Fourth St., 60441. Tel: 815-838-0186.

5—Our Mother of Good Counsel, Revs. Thomas Osborne, O.S.A.; Donald Lewandowski, O.S.A.
Res., 15430 Sulky Dr., 60441. Tel: 708-301-6246; Fax: 708-301-6356.
Catechesis/Religious Programs—Students 185.

Lombard, Du Page Co., Christ the King, Rev. James Dvorscak; Deacon Philip Gavin.
Res., 1501 S. Main St., 60148. Tel: 630-629-1717.
School—Tel: 630-627-0640.
Lay Teachers 10; Students 123.
Catechesis/Religious Programs—Tel: 630-629-1719.
Students 329.

Sacred Heart (1912), Revs. Arno A. Dennerlein; John Zanoni; Deacon Thomas Bailey. In res., Rev. Raynor E. Richter, Pastor Emeritus.
Res., 114 S. Elizabeth St., 60148. Tel: 630-627-0687; Fax: 630-627-0688.
School—Tel: 630-629-0536; Fax: 630-629-4752.
Lay Teachers 15; Students 320.
Catechesis/Religious Programs—328 W. Maple St., 60148. Tel: 630-495-0843.
Students 457.

St. Pius X (1954), Revs. Herbert Essig; Lester Hochhalter; Sr. Pauline Schutz, O.S.F., Pastoral Assoc.; Deacons Thomas Goebel; Ron Knecht; William Crane; Larry Lissoh.
Res., 1025 E. Madison, 60148. Tel: 630-627-4526; Fax: 630-495-5926.
School—Tel: 630-627-2353; Fax: 630-627-1810. Ellen Herron, Prin.
Lay Teachers 24; Students 485.
Catechesis/Religious Programs—Tel: 630-627-1551. Sr. Helen Susan, D.R.E.
Students 492.

Manhattan, Will Co., St. Joseph (1891), Rev. Edward J. O'Malley.
Res., 235 W. North, P.O. Box 25, 60442. Tel: 815-478-3341; Fax: 815-478-5258. [CEM]
School—Tel: 815-478-3951.
Lay Teachers 8; Students 140.
Catechesis/Religious Programs—Tel: 815-478-4476.
Students 325.

Manteno, Kankakee Co., St. Joseph (1855), Rev. Mark Fracaro; Deacons Francis Henrisey; John Hindes; Richard Balgeman.
Res., 207 S. Main St., 60950. Tel: 815-468-3403; Fax: 815-468-7089. [CEM][JC]
Catechesis/Religious Programs—Tel: 815-468-8116.
Students 288.

Martinton, Iroquois Co., St. Martin, Rev. Robert J. Coleman.
Res., P.O. Box 152, Beaverville, 60912. Tel: 815-435-2432. [CEM]

Minooka, Grundy Co., St. Mary, Rev. Frank K. Vitus.
Res., 303 St. Mary St., P.O. Box 456, 60447. Tel: 815-467-2233; Fax: 815-467-1760. [CEM]
Catechesis/Religious Programs—Students 385.

Mokena, Will Co., St. Mary Church, Revs. James Fitzgerald; Robert Noesen; Sr. Marilyn Renninger, O.S.F., Pastoral Assoc.; Deacons Jim Fitzgerald; Donald Bernardini.
Res., 19517 S. 115th Ave., P.O. Box 2, 60448. Tel: 708-479-3380; Fax: 708-479-8403.
School—Tel: 708-479-3383; Fax: 708-479-4985.
Franciscan Sisters of the Sacred Heart 1; Lay Teachers 10; Students 316.
Catechesis/Religious Programs—11489 W. 195th St., 60448. Tel: 708-479-3385.
Students 1600.

Momence, Kankakee Co., St. Patrick (1859), Rev. Denis E. White; Deacons Jeffrey Jacob; Dan Hessling.
Res., 119 Market St., 60954. Tel: 815-472-2864; Fax: 815-472-3043. [CEM]
School—404 W. Second St., 60954. Tel: 815-472-2469.
Lay Teachers 5; Students 105.
Catechesis/Religious Programs—Students 276.
Vicariate—Sacred Heart, Hopkins Park, 60944. Tel: 815-944-5156.

Monee, Will Co., St. Boniface, Rev. Mark Menezes; Deacon Robert Jossey.
Res., 5301 W. Main St., P.O. Box 217, 60449. Tel: 708-534-9682; Fax: 708-534-9683.
Catechesis/Religious Programs—Tel: 708-534-9683.
Students 100.

Morris, Grundy Co., Immaculate Conception of the Blessed Virgin Mary (1852), Rev. Michael Foley.
Res., 516 E. Jackson St., 60450. Tel: 815-942-0620. [CEM]
School—Tel: 815-942-4111; Fax: 815-942-5094.
Lay Teachers 16; Students 257.
Catechesis/Religious Programs—505 E. North St., 60450. Tel: 815-942-4177.
Students 365.

Naperville, Will Co.,

1—St. Elizabeth Seton, (1986), Revs. Ernest Norbeck; James Radek; Deacons Thomas Sheridan; Bart Federici; William Murphy; Gregg Lawson.
Res., 2220 Lisson Rd., 60565. Tel: 630-416-3325; Fax: 630-416-3642.
Catechesis/Religious Programs—Tel: 630-416-1992.
Students 1,818.

2—Sts. Peter and Paul, DuPage Co., (1856), Revs. James Burnett; Gregor Gorsic; Gordon Mahoney; Gregory Rothfuchs. Pastoral Assocs.: Sr. Aniceta Skube, O.P.; Sr. Kathleen Hook, O.S.F.; Deacons William Girard; Manuel J. Solis.
Res., 26 N. Ellsworth St., 60540. Tel: 630-355-1081. [CEM]
School—201 E. Franklin, 60540. Tel: 630-355-0113; Fax: 630-355-9803. Mr. Frank Glowaty, Prin.
Sisters 2; Lay Teachers 25; Students 622.
Catechesis/Religious Programs—120 E. Franklin, 60540. Tel: 630-357-2436.
Students 1,250.

3—St. Raphael, DuPage Co., (1963), Revs. William E. Donnelly; Dennis Lewandowski; Deacons William Blessing; John McHugh; Andrew Repak.
Mailing Address: 1215 Modaff Rd., 60540-7818.
Res., 416 Gartner, 60540. Tel: 630-355-4545; Fax: 630-355-7470.
School—Lay Teachers 18; Students 326.
Catechesis/Religious Programs—Students 2,355.

4—St. Margaret Mary, DuPage Co., (1980), Revs. William J. O'Shea; Richard Dochstader; Sr. Madelyn Gould, S.S.S.F., Pastoral Assoc.; Deacons Kenneth J. Miles; Frederick E. Straub.
1450 Green Trails Dr., 60540. Tel: 630-369-0777; Fax: 630-369-1493.
Catechesis/Religious Programs—Tel: 630-369-0833.
Students 1,677.

5—St. Thomas the Apostle, DuPage Co., (1984), Revs. Donald Kenny; Richard Lundgren. Pastoral Assocs.: Sr. Ann James Murray, O.S.F.; Sr. Marlene Schemmel, C.S.J.; Deacons William Worden; Charles Lane.
Res., 1500 Brookdale Rd., 60563. Tel: 708-355-8980; Fax: 708-355-0521.
Catechesis/Religious Programs—Tel: 630-305-6318.
Students 1,983.

New Lenox, Will Co., St. Jude (1934), Revs. Richard T. Allen, O.S.A.; Raymond R. Ryan, O.S.A.; John P. Murphy, O.S.A.; Bro. Robert Fisher, O.S.A.; Deacon Robert Fitt. In res., Rev. John Paul Szura, O.S.A.
Res., 241 W. Second Ave., 60451. Tel: 815-485-8049; Fax: 815-485-7754.
School—Tel: 815-485-2549; Fax: 815-485-7754.
Lay Teachers 12; Students 259.
Catechesis/Religious Programs—Tel: 815-485-4852.
Students 1,035.

Oakbrook Terrace, DuPage Co., Ascension of Our Lord (1967), Rev. Damien Graziano; Jack Bartz, Pastoral Assoc.
Res., 1 S 314 Summit Ave., 60181. Tel: 630-629-5810; Fax: 630-953-8251.
Catechesis/Religious Programs—Tel: 630-629-5810, Ext. 215; 216.
Students 286.

Oswego, Kendall Co., St. Anne (1963), Revs. Daniel F. Stempora; Robert Collogan; Deacons David Brockman; William Dunn; Leslie Hancock.
Res., 551 Boulder Hill Pass, P.O. Box 670, 60543. Tel: 630-554-3331; Fax: 630-554-0530.
Catechesis/Religious Programs—(Grades K-8). Tel: 630-554-1425.
Students 1,138.

Park Forest, Will Co., St. Mary, Rev. John Ryan.
Res., 212 Monee Rd., 60466. Tel: 708-747-1600; Fax: 708-748-6907.
School—227 Monee Rd., 60466-2403. Tel: 708-748-6686.
Franciscan Sisters of the Sacred Heart 2; Lay Teachers 9; Students 216.

Paxton, Ford Co., St. Mary, Rev. James Heramb.
Res., 407 W. Pells, 60957. Tel: 217-379-4033.
Mission—Loda, Iroquois Co., St. Joseph, c/o St. Mary, 407 W. Pells, 60957.
Catechesis/Religious Programs—Students 140.

Peotone, Will Co., St. Paul the Apostle (1961), Rev. Michael Ginter.
Res., 501 N. Conrad St., P.O. Box 700, 60468-0700. Tel: 708-258-6917; Fax: 708-258-3031.
Catechesis/Religious Programs—Students 250.

Piper City, Ford Co., St. Peter, Rev. Ed Mumper.
Res. & Mailing Address: 212 Pine St., 60959. Tel: 815-686-2595.
Mission—Roberts, Immaculate Conception. [CEM]

Plainfield, Will Co., St. Mary Immaculate (1909), Revs. Anthony A. Nugent; Joseph Siegel; Deacons James Sossong; Terry Sakfo; James Walters; Jerry Krupowicz.
Mailing Address: 129 S. Division St. (Rte. 59), 60544.
Res., 116 Frederick, 60544. Tel: 815-436-2651; Fax: 815-436-5017. [CEM]
School—129 S. Division St., 60544-8806. Tel: 815-436-3953.
Lay Teachers 26; Students 438.
Catechesis/Religious Programs—Tel: 815-436-4501.
Students 1,402.

Plano, Kendall Co., St. Mary (1885), Revs. Jerome A. Zalonis, M.I.C.; Boniface Vaisnoras, M.I.C.; Deacons Dale Metcalf; Santos Martinez. In res., Rev. John Savukynas, M.I.C.
Res., 901 N. Center St., 60545. Tel: 630-552-3448; Fax: 630-552-3450.
School—817 N. Center Ave., 60545. Tel: 630-552-3345; Fax: 630-552-4385.
Sisters 1; Lay Teachers 8; Students 264.
Catechesis/Religious Programs—810 N. Center Ave., 60545. Tel: 630-552-1505. Sr. Kathryn Frankovich, O.S.F., D.R.E.
Students 468.

Mission—Bristol, Kendall Co., St. Patrick, 406 Walnut St., Yorkville, 60560. Tel: 708-553-6671; Fax: 708-553-6600. [CEM]

Rockdale, Will Co., St. Joseph (1914), Rev. Paul Wittosch.
Res., 1329 Belleview Ave., 60436. Tel: 815-725-4469.
Catechesis/Religious Programs—314 S. Midland Ave., 60436. Tel: 815-729-9149.
Students 65.

Romeoville, Will Co., St. Andrew the Apostle (1959), Rev. Richard Walsh; Deacons David Raskowski; Stephen Clancy.
Res., 219 Arlington Dr., 60446. Tel: 815-886-4165; Fax: 815-886-6119.
School—Tel: 815-886-5953.
Sisters 2; Lay Teachers 13; Students 270.
Catechesis/Religious Programs—505 Kingston Dr., 60446. Tel: 815-886-5962; Fax: 815-886-5962.
Students 340.

Roselle, Du Page Co., St. Walter (1946), Revs. Francis B. McDonald; John Guiney, S.M.A.; Peter Jarosz; Deacon Ron Searls.
Res., 130 W. Pine Ave., 60172. Tel: 630-894-2461; Fax: 630-582-4206.
School—201 W. Maple Ave., 60172. Tel: 630-529-1721; Fax: 630-529-9290.
Lay Teachers 29; Students 745.
Catechesis/Religious Programs—140 W. Pine, 60172. Tel: 630-894-5880; Fax: 630-582-4206. Ms. Barbara Ruments, D.R.E.
Students 1,106.

St. Anne, Kankakee Co., St. Anne, Rev. James Fanale, C.S.V.
Res., 230 N. Sixth Ave., 60964. Tel: 815-427-8265.

St. George, Kankakee Co., St. George, Rev. Kenneth Yarno, C.S.V.
Res., 5272 E. 5000 North Rd., Bourbonnais, 60914-9725. Tel: 815-939-1851. [JC]

South Wilmington, Grundy Co., St. Lawrence, Rev. Robert Maternoski; Deacon Joseph Riggi.
Res., 165 Rice St., Box 190, 60474. Tel: 815-237-2230.
Mission—Essex, Kankakee Co., St. Lawrence O'Toole, P.O. Box 190, 60474.

Steger, Will Co., St. Liborius (1901), Revs. Joseph Burns; Ron Neitzke; Thomas Vayalil.
Res., 71 W. 35th St., 60475. Tel: 708-754-1363; Fax: 708-754-0922.
School—(Steger Campus) 3436 Halsted Blvd., 60475. Tel: 708-754-0192.
Lay Teachers 15; Students 286.
Catechesis/Religious Programs—Tel: 708-754-3460.
Students 440.

Villa Park, Du Page Co., St. Alexander (1924), Revs. John M. Furdek; Tuan V. Nguyen; Deacon John Boyle.
Res., 300 S. Cornell Ave., 60181. Tel: 630-833-7730; Fax: 630-833-3127.
School—136 S. Cornell Ave., 60181. Tel: 630-834-3787; Fax: 630-834-1961.
Sisters of Notre Dame de Namur 2; Lay Teachers 15; Students 300.
Catechesis/Religious Programs—130 S. Cornell Ave., 60181. Tel: 630-832-0506.
Students 400.

St. John the Apostle (1959), Rev. James Duffy.
Res., 330 N. Westmore, 60181. Tel: 630-279-7404; Fax: 630-530-9918.
Catechesis/Religious Programs—Tel: 630-832-7588.
Students 217.

Warrenville, Du Page Co., St. Irene, Rev. Thomas A. Corbino; Sr. Roseann Eck, C.S.J., Pastoral Assoc.; Deacon Robert True.
Res., 28 W. 441 Warrenville Rd., 60555. Tel: 630-393-2400; Fax: 630-393-9680.
School—3S601 Warren Ave., 60555. Tel: 630-393-9303. Beverly Murphy, Prin.
Lay Teachers 13; Students 212.
Catechesis/Religious Programs—Students 212.

Watseka, Iroquois Co., St. Edmund, Rev. F. Lee Ryan; Deacon Lloyd Eastburn.
Res., 219 E. Locust St., 60970. Tel: 815-432-3274.
Catechesis/Religious Programs—Students 185.
Mission—Crescent City, St. Joseph.

Wayne, Du Page Co., Resurrection, Rev. Laurian Janicki, O.F.M.
Res., P.O. Box 626, 60184. Tel: 630-289-5400; Fax: 630-289-5407.
Catechesis/Religious Programs—Students 832.

West Chicago, Du Page Co., St. Mary (1894) (Hispanic), Revs. Vernon Arseneau; Andres Balvanera.
Res., 140 N. Oakwood Ave., 60185. Tel: 630-231-0013; Fax: 630-293-2671. [CEM]
School—147 Garden St., 60185. Tel: 630-231-1776.
Lay Teachers 12; Students 232.
Catechesis/Religious Programs—Tel: 630-231-5704; Fax: 630-293-6741.
Students 328.

Westmont, Du Page Co., Holy Trinity (1938), Revs. James A. Nowak; John Sponders.
Res., 111 S. Cass Ave., 60559. Tel: 630-968-1366; Fax: 630-968-7846.
School—25 E. Richmond, 60559. Tel: 630-971-0184; Fax: 630-971-1175.
Sisters 1; Lay Teachers 19; Students 375.
Catechesis/Religious Programs—Tel: 630-968-5978.
Students 428.

Wheaton, Du Page Co., St. Daniel the Prophet Church, Rev. Thomas J. White. Pastoral Assocs.: Sr. Josephine Sincak; Sr. Mary Potthast; Sr. Margaret Ivers, I.B.V.M.
Res., 231 Danada Dr., 60187. Tel: 630-682-5003; Fax: 630-682-5004.
Catechesis/Religious Programs—Students 810.

St. Mark, Rev. John Ducaji.
Res., 303 E. Parkway Dr., 60187. Tel: 630-665-0030.
Catechesis/Religious Programs—300 E. Cole St., 60187. Tel: 630-668-4614.
Students 137.

St. Michael (1884), Revs. Martin Gabel; Steven Bondi; Joseph A. Mundakal, C.M.I.; Deacons John Cozzens; William Stroner.
Res., 315 W. Illinois St., 60187. Tel: 630-665-2250; Fax: 630-665-6820. [CEM]
School—314 W. Willow Ave., 60187. Tel: 630-653-1454; Fax: 630-665-1491.
Notre Dame Sisters of Toledo 2; Lay Teachers 27; Students 594.
Catechesis/Religious Programs—Tel: 630-682-3650.
Students 1,142.

Wilmington, Will Co., St. Rose (1844), Rev. Francis Maher; Sr. Ann Ellen Quirk, B.V.M., Pastoral Assoc.; Deacon Don Dyer.
Res., 603 S. Main St., 60481. Tel: 815-476-7491; Fax: 815-476-1085. [CEM]
School—Tel: 815-476-6220.
Lay Teachers 12; Students 251.
Catechesis/Religious Programs—Students 150.

Wilton Center, Will Co., St. Patrick, Rev. S. C. Giunta.
Res., 14936 Wilmington Peotone Rd., Manhattan, 60442. Tel: 815-478-3440. [CEM]

Winfield, Du Page Co., St. John the Baptist (1867), Revs. Guy Vaccaro; John Bosco Panakal; Tony A. Stockinger; Deacons Don Mathieu; Andrew Nielo. In res., Rev. Michael Valente.
Res., O.S. 233 Church St., 60190. Tel: 630-668-0918; Fax: 630-668-1074. [CEM]
School—O.S. 259 Church St., 60190. Tel: 630-668-2625; Fax: 630-668-7176. Patricia Walther, Prin.
Lay Teachers 20; Students 340.
Catechesis/Religious Programs—Tel: 630-682-4400; Fax: 630-668-1074. Maureen Brennan, D.R.E.
Students 1,206.

Wood Dale, Du Page Co., Holy Ghost (1946), Revs. Kevin R. Farrell; Robert A. Hoffenkamp.
Res., 254 N. Wood Dale Rd., 60191. Tel: 630-860-2975; Fax: 630-860-9482.
School—Tel: 630-766-4508; Fax: 630-860-3693.
Lay Teachers 15; Students 223.
Catechesis/Religious Programs—Tel: 630-766-1045; Fax: 630-860-9482.
Students 635.

Woodridge, Du Page Co., Christ The Servant Parish (1990), Rev. James Ratigan.
Mailing Address: 2952 Harvest Pl., Darien, 60561. Tel: 630-910-0770; Fax: 630-910-6060 (call 0770 first).
Catechesis/Religious Programs—Students 89.

St. Scholastica (1962), Revs. Thomas Sularz; David Lawrence; Sr. Regina Ann Weissmann, O.S.B., Pastoral Assoc.; Deacons Roger Schmith; James Dixon.
Res., 7800 S. Janes Ave., 60517. Tel: 630-985-2351; Fax: 630-985-8770.
School—Tel: 630-985-2515; Fax: 630-985-2395. Mary Ann Deandt, Prin.
Lay Teachers 11; Students 290.
Catechesis/Religious Programs—7720 Janes Ave., 60517. Tel: 630-985-9255. Sr. Therese Kane, B.V.M., D.R.E.
Students 1,045.

Chaplains of Public Institutions

JOLIET. *Illinois State Penitentiary,* 404 N. Hickory St., P.O. Box 112, 60435. Jerry Bowman.
Illinois Youth Commission, Reception and Diagnostic Center, McDonough St., 60436. Deacon Joseph O'Connor.
Joliet Correctional Depot, Collins St. Revs. John Doyle; Joseph F. Kilas.
Silver Cross Hospital, 1200 Maple Rd., 60432. Rev. Andrew Buezyna.

ELMHURST. *Elmhurst Memorial Hospital,* 200 Berteau Ave., 60126. Rev. Thomas Wolter.

HINSDALE. *Hinsdale Hospital,* 120 N. Oak, 60521. Rev. James Walton, O.F.M.

KANKAKEE. *Riverside Medical Center,* 350 N. Wells, 60901. Rev. John Antczak.
Shapiro Development Center, 100 E. Jeffrey, 60901. Rev. Andrew A. Bialas, C.S.V.

NAPERVILLE. *Edward Hospital.* Vacant. S. Washington St., 60540.

WINFIELD. *Central DuPage Hospital,* 0N025 Winfield, 60190. Rev. Michael Valente.

On Duty Outside the Diocese:
Reverend Fathers—
Butters, Joseph, St. Patrick, 501 Fair Oaks Ave., Box 860, Arroyo Grande, CA 93421
Caruso, Carmen A., St. Isabel, 3559 Sanibel-Captiva Rd., Sanibel, FL 33957
Dieter, Thomas, St. Catherine of Siena, 1955 S. Belcher Rd., Clearwater, FL 34624
Hemrick, Eugene F., U.S.C.C., Department of Education, 1312 Massachusetts, N.W., Washington, DC 20005
Howlin, Carroll, Good Shepherd Catholic Services, P.O. Box 550, Whitley City, KS 42653
Moriarty, John, Society of St. James the Apostle, 24 Clark St., Boston, MA 02109
Murphy, James, St. Mary of the Lake Seminary, Mundelein, IL 60060
Schoenstene, Robert L., St. Mary of the Lake Seminary, Mundelein, IL 60060

Graduate Studies:
Reverend Fathers—
Martis, Douglas, L'Institut Catholique, Rome

Absent on Sick Leave:
Reverend Fathers—
Best, Richard
DeFilippis, Anthony
Joyce, Edwin
Massacavalo, Bruno

Absent on Leave:
Reverend Fathers—
Blanchette, Michael
Collins, Michael J.
Jankowski, Peter

Retired:
Reverend Monsignors—
Podesta, John F., 5555 N. Sheridan Rd., Apt. 1412, Chicago, IL 60640
Stenger, Frederick R., 3000 S. Ocean Blvd., Apt. 404, Boca Raton, FL 33432
Reverend Fathers—
Bowden, Lloyd, 115 N. May St., Joliet, IL 60435
Corley, Thomas, St. John Vianney Villa, 1464 Green Trails Dr., Naperville, IL 60450
Cullen, William, 6267 Trinity Dr., #2D, Lisle, IL 60532
Davis, Raymond, St. Alexis, 400 W. Wood St., Bensenville, IL 60106-2496
Doherty, Eugene, St. John Vianney Villa, 1464 Green Trails Dr., Naperville, IL 60540
Driscoll, John, St. Andrew the Apostle, 219 Arlington Dr., Romeoville, IL 60446
Fischer, Lowell, Motherhouse, 9201 W. St. Francis Rd., Frankfort, IL 60423
Fleming, Thomas, St. John Vianney Villa, 1464 Green Trails Dr., Naperville, IL 60450
Flynn, George, 2012E Lincoln, Apt. 210, Bloomington, IL 61701
Formusa, Salvatore, P.O. Box 46010, Chicago, IL 60046
Grasso, Raymond, St. John Vianney Villa, 1464 Green Trails Dr., Naperville, IL 60450
Hurley, George, 5 Oak Brook Dr., Oakbrook, IL 60521-1314
Kinzig, James J., 36 E. Naples, Chula Vista, CA 92011
Kloepfer, John S., Box 1742, Clarksville, VA 23927
Maher, Arthur, 1115 Lorraine Rd., #326, Wheaton, IL 60187
Morrissette, Dominic, Little Flower Haven, 8585 La Mesa Blvd., La Mesa, CA 91941-3998
Mulloy, Sylvester, St. Patrick Residence, 1400 Brookdale, Naperville, IL 60563-2126
Novak, John, Countryside Villas, Rte. 1, Box 7-1A, Clifton, IL 60927
Parnisari, Eugene, 23 Windwood Pass, Dana Point, CA 92629
Richter, Raynor E., Sacred Heart Parish, 114 E. Elizabeth, Lombard, IL 60148
Ryan, William, St. John Vianney Villa, 1464 Green Trails Dr., Naperville, IL 60540
Shimanek, Joseph, 438 N. LaGrange Rd., LaGrange Park, IL 60525

Stockinger, Tony, Community Health Care, 1136 Mill St., Room 119, Naperville, IL 60540
Thongamphai, Peter B., Thailand
Valentino, Dominic, 1230 E. East St., St. John Rd., Phoenix, AZ 85022
Wilkening, Henry, Corpus Christi, 1415 Lies Rd., Carol Stream, IL 60188-4841

Permanent Deacons:
Accardi, Rodger F., Wheaton Franciscan Service, Wheaton
Agurkis, Albert, St. Mary of Gostyn, Downers Grove
Anchor, Robert, On Duty Outside Diocese
Anderson, Roy D., Residing Outside Diocese
Bailey, Thomas, Sacred Heart, Lombard
Balgeman, Richard, St. Joseph, Manteno
Beabout, Norman, On Duty Outside Diocese
Beckley, Michael A., St. Margaret Mary, Naperville
Berkey, Donald, St. Anthony, Frankfort
Bernardin, Donald, St. Mary, Mokena
Bevan, William F., III, St. Paul the Apostle, Joliet
Bias, Ralph, Sacred Heart, Joliet
Bina, Frank, Our Lady of Peace, Darien
Blessing, William, St. Raphael, Naperville
Borkowicz, Leo M., On Duty Outside Diocese
Bouldin, James, St. Paul the Apostle, Joliet
Boyle, John R., St. Alexander, Villa Park
Brachle, Paul L., Jr., Our Lady of Peace, Darien
Brockman, David, St. Anne, Oswego
Carlson, Bruce, St. Mary, West Chicago
Carson, Neill, Notre Dame, Claredon Hills
Casey, William, Holy Trinity, Westmont
Chambers, Frank A., On Duty Outside Diocese
Chamness, Francis J., Maternity BVM, Bourbonnais
Christensen, Gerald G., Unassigned
Clancy, Steven, St. Andrew, Romeoville
Clark, Raymond, St. Jude, Joliet
Cole, John, Immaculate Conception, Elmhurst
Cook, Michael, Cathedral of St. Raymond, Joliet
Cooley, Stephen, Resurrection, Wayne
Cotugno, Joseph, St. Patrick, Kankakee
Cozzens, John, St. Michael, Wheaton
Crane, William H., St. Pius X, Lombard
Cuzzone, Dominic, Visitation, Elmhurst
Dalpiaz, Joseph C., St. Joan of Arc, Lisle
Danahey, Daniel, St. Anthony, Frankfort
Darschewski, Ronald, St. Matthew, Glendale Heights
Dixon, James A., St. Elizabeth Seton, Naperville
Donahue, James, St. Mary, Downers Grove
Dougherty, Michael, On Duty Outside Diocese
Dunn, William, St. Anne, Oswego
Dyer, Donald L., St. Rose, Wilmington
Eastburn, Lloyd D., St. Edmund, Watseka
Ellman, Edward, On Duty Outside Diocese
Erickson, Robert, St. Dominic, Bolingbrook
Farrell, John, Our Lady of Mt. Carmel, Darien
Farrell, Theodore, St. Petronelle, Glen Ellyn
Fitt, Robert, St. Jude, New Lenox
Fitzgerald, James P., Jr., St. Mary, Mokena
Foys, Frank F., Notre Dame, Clarendon Hills
Franch, Dino J., St. Joseph, Addison
Frederici, Bart, St. Elizabeth Seton, Naperville
Freund, John, St. Isidore, Bloomington
Fricke, Thomas E., St. Francis of Assisi, Bolingbrook
Fritz, Leon P., St. Joseph, Bradley
Gagnon, James, St. Joseph Medical Center, Joliet
Gamboa, Gabriel, St. Joseph, Addison
Gavin, Philip, Christ the King, Lombard
Girard, William, Sts. Peter and Paul, Naperville
Goebel, Thomas, St. Pius X, Lombard
Hamilton, Raymond, St. Francis of Assisi, Bolingbrook
Hamrlick, James, On Duty Outside Diocese
Hancock, Leslie E., St. Anne, Oswego
Hanley, Terrance R., St. Francis of Assisi, Bolingbrook
Henrissey, Francis R., St. Joseph, Manteno
Hessling, Danny E., St. Patrick, Momence
Hetzel, William, St. Jude, Joliet
Hindes, John T., St. Joseph, Manteno
Jackson, Kenneth, St. Isidore, Bloomingdale
Jacob, Jeffrey, St. Patrick, Momence
Janousek, Jay, Visitation, Elmhurst
Jazdzewski, Melvin J., On Duty Outside Diocese
Jossey, Robert, St. Boniface, Monee
Kelly, James, St. Dominic, Bolingbrook
Kelly, William, Immaculate Conception, Morris
Knapstein, John W., St. Dominic, Bolingbrook
Knecht, Ronald, St. Pius X, Lombard
Kolodziej, Paul, St. Patrick, Joliet
Krostenko, Alexander, St. Paul the Apostle, Joliet
Krupowicz, Jerome, St. Mary Immaculate, Plainfield
LaLonde, James A., St. Joseph, Downers Grove
Lamon, John D., On Duty Outside Diocese
LaMotte, Robert, St. Joseph, Bradley
Lane, Charles, St. Thomas, Naperville
Lawson, Gregg, St. Elizabeth Seton, Naperville
Lifka, David, Notre Dame, Clarendon Hills
Lissah, Lawrence, St. Pius X, Lombard
Lopez, Jose L., St. John the Baptist, Joliet
Lovero, Marco, Our Lady of Mount Carmel, Darien
Malloy, William, (Retired)
Maloney, John, Mary Queen of Heaven, Elmhurst
Mangen, Richard, St. Matthew, Glendale Heights
Marcotte, Euchrist, Maternity B.V.M., Bourbonnais
Marrow, Philip J., St. John the Apostle, Villa Park
Martinez, Santos H., St. Mary, Plano
Mathieu, Donulus, Sr., (Retired)
McHugh, John, St. Raphael, Naperville
Metcalfe, Dale R., St. Patrick, Bristol; St. Mary, Plano
Miles, Kenneth J., Jr., St. Margaret Mary, Naperville
Molano, Rodulfo N., St. Francis of Assisi, Bolingbrook
Murphy, William E., St. Elizabeth Seton, Naperville
Murray, John, St. Mary Magdalene, Joliet
Neher, Norman, Sacred Heart, Hopkins Park
Nielo, Andrew, Resurrection, Wayne
Nolan, Thomas J., On Duty Outside Diocese
Nowak, Richard, On Duty Outside Diocese
Nunez, Charles, Mary Queen of Heaven, Elmhurst
O'Connor, Joseph, Illinois Youth Commission, Joliet
Olszak, Leonard, St. Liborius, Steger
Pecka, Lawrence, St. Mary, Downers Grove
Pellack, Robert J., On Duty Outside Diocese
Petak, Edwin, Cathedral of St. Raymond, Joliet
Peterson, Charles M., St. Patrick, Joliet
Principe, Michael, St. Charles Borromeo, Bensenville
Raskowski, David, St. Andrew, Romeoville
Renville, John, Sacred Heart, Goodrich
Riggi, Joseph, St. Lawrence, South Wilimington
Rizzo, Vincent C., St. Matthew, Glendale Heights
Rosko, Richard, St. Anthony, Frankfort
Ross, Thomas, St. Dominic, Bolingbrook
Ruiz, Victor, St. Dominic, Bolingbrook
Safko, Terry L., St. Mary, Plainfield
Scavone, Emmanuel J., St. James, Glen Ellyn
Schlund, James, On Duty Outside Diocese
Schmidt, Walter F., Our Lady of Peace, Darien
Schmith, Roger, St. Scholastica, Woodridge
Schneider, Paul A., On Leave
Schubert, Anthony, St. Alexander, Villa Park
Schumacher, Carl N.J., St. Joseph, Downers Grove
Searls, Ronald, St. Walter, Roselle
Sheaffer, Harry, St. Mary, West Chicago
Sheridan, Thomas, St. Elizabeth Seton, Naperville
Siwek, Raymond, (Retired)
Solis, Joseph, Sts. Peter and Paul, Naperville
Sossong, James R., St. Mary Immaculate, Plainfield
Spatafor, Anthony, Visitation, Elmhurst
Stansberry, Robert T., Jr., Immaculate Conception, Morris
Stevens, Richard R., On Duty Outside Diocese
Stolarz, Dennis, Our Lady of Peace, Darien
Straub, Fred, St. Margaret Mary, Naperville
Stroner, William, St. Michael, Wheaton
Stucko, Denis, St. Joan of Arc, Lisle
Sullivan, Robert, On Leave
Symonanis, Alan, Notre Dame, Clarendon Hills
Tetrault, Robert L., On Duty Outside Diocese
True, Robert, St. Irene, Warrenville
Uffmann, William, St. Dennis, Lockport
Urso, Joseph, St. Joseph, Lockfort
Valdez, George, St. Mary, West Chicago
Van Dril, William, On Duty Outside Diocese
Walen, Paul J., Sr., St. Dominic, Bolingbrook
Wallace, Robert, St. Dominic, Bolingbrook
Walsh, Thomas, On Duty Outside Diocese
Walters, James C., St. Mary, Plainfield
Weierman, Robert, St. Dennis, Lockport
Wood, Charles, St. Raphael, Naperville
Worden, William, St. Thomas the Apostle, Naperville
Yarshen, Richard, Holy Family, Joliet
Yurcus, Ronald J., St. Petronille, Glen Ellyn

INSTITUTIONS LOCATED IN THE DIOCESE

[A] COLLEGES AND UNIVERSITIES

JOLIET. *College of St. Francis*, 500 N. Wilcox, 60435. Tel: 815-740-3360.
Web site: http://www.stfrancis.edu
For a complete listing, refer to the Colleges and Universities section.

LISLE. *Benedictine University*, 5700 College Rd., 60532-0900. Tel: 630-829-6000; Fax: 630-960-1126
For a complete listing, refer to the Colleges and Universities section.

ROMEOVILLE. *Lewis University*, Rt. 53, 60446. Tel: 815-838-0500.
Web site: http://www.lewisu.edu/
For a complete listing, refer to the Colleges and Universities section.

[B] HIGH SCHOOLS, DIOCESAN

KANKAKEE. *Bishop McNamara High School*, 550 W. Brookmont, 60901. Tel: 815-932-7413. Revs. Christopher Howe, O.S.A., Prin.; John Sotak, O.S.A.; Bro. Kenneth D. Mehn, O.S.A.; Sr. Madeleine LaMarre, C.N.D. Priests 3; Sisters 1; Brothers 2; Lay Teachers 32; Students 531; Total Staff 61.

[C] HIGH SCHOOLS, PRIVATE

JOLIET. *Joliet Catholic Academy*. (Coed), 1200 N. Larkin Ave., 60435. Tel: 815-741-0500. Carmelites & Joliet Franciscans. Sr. Faith Szambelanczyk, O.S.F., Pres. & CEO; Rev. Bernhard Bauerle, O.Carm., Prin. & COO; Dr. Robert Jenkins, Asst. Prin. Priests 6; Sisters 9; Brothers 2; Lay Teachers 43; Students 800.

ADDISON. *Driscoll Catholic High School*, 555 N. Lombard Rd., 60101. Tel: 630-543-6310. Bro. Thomas Hetland, F.S.C., Pres.; Mr. Bernard J. Kelly, Prin.; Mr. Tim Racki, Dean; Mrs. Loraine Parkers, Campus Minister. Brothers of Christian Schools 4; Lay Teachers 36; Students 472.

LISLE. *Benet Academy*, 2200 Maple Ave., 60532. Tel: 630-969-6550. Rt. Rev. Hugh R. Anderson, O.S.B., Chancellor; Rev. Jude D. Randall, Pres.; Mr. Ernest Stark, Prin.; Mr. James Brown, Asst. Prin.; Mr. William J. Maurer, Dir. Devel.; Rev. Anthony J. Jacob, O.S.B., Business Mgr. Priests 6; Sisters 2; Brothers 5; Lay Teachers 60; Students 1,265.

LOMBARD. *Montini Catholic High School*, 19 W. 070 16th St., 60148. Tel: 630-627-6930. Bro. Thomas A. Harding, F.S.C., Pres. Brothers of the Christian Schools 3; Sisters 1; Lay Teachers 41; Students 523.

NEW LENOX. *Providence Catholic High School*. (Coed), 1800 W. Lincoln Hwy., 60451. Tel: 815-485-2136. Revs. Richard J. McGrath, O.S.A., Pres.; John Merkelis, O.S.A., Prin.; Ms. Judith Legan, Asst. Prin.; Revs. Roland F. Follmann, O.S.A.; Donald Lewandowski, O.S.A.; Gerald A. Nicholas, O.S.A. In res. Rev. Gerald J. Theis, O.S.A. Priests 6; Brothers 1; Sisters 1; Lay Teachers 68; Students 1,182.

WHEATON. *St. Francis High School*, 2130 W. Roosevelt Rd., 60187. Tel: 630-668-5800. Mr. David Angerer, Prin. Sisters 1; Lay Teachers 39; Students 551.

[D] AGENCIES AND INSTITUTIONS OF THE CHARITIES OF THE DIOCESE

JOLIET. *Catholic Charities*, 203 N. Ottawa St., 60432. Tel: 815-723-3405. Kathleen McGowan, Exec. Dir. Diocesan Administrative Office and Regional Office for Will and Grundy Counties.

KANKAKEE. *Catholic Charities*, 657 E. Court St., 60901. Tel: 815-933-7791; Fax: 815-932-3030. Regional Office for Kankakee, Ford, and Iroquois Counties.

LOMBARD. *Catholic Charities*, 26 W. St. Charles Rd., 60148. Tel: 708-495-9850; Fax: 708-495-9854. Regional Office for DuPage and Kendall Counties.

[E] PROTECTIVE INSTITUTIONS

JOLIET. *Guardian Angel Home*, 1550 Plainfield Ave., 60435. Tel: 815-729-0930; Fax: 815-744-6087.
E-mail: sas726@aol.com
For a complete listing, refer to the Special Care Facilities section.

MOMENCE. *Good Shepherd Manor*, P.O. Box 260, 60954. Tel: 815-472-6492; Fax: 815-472-2160
For a complete listing, refer to the Special Care Facilities section.

[F] DAY CARE LEARNING CENTERS

JOLIET. *Franciscan Learning Center*, 1734 Theodore St., 60435. Tel: 815-744-7634. Sr. Margaret McGuckin, Dir. Students 84.
Vilaseca Day Care Center, 351 N. Chicago St., 60432. Tel: 815-727-1467. Students 82. Josephine Sisters.

BOURBONNAIS. *Alfred Fortin Villa and Day Care Learning Center*, 615 S. Main St., 60914. Tel: 815-932-8411. Sr. Joan Barbara, O.P., Dir. Day care for preschoolers. Sisters of St. Dominic 2; Staff 11; Students 54.

[G] GENERAL HOSPITALS

JOLIET. *St. Joseph Medical Center*, 333 N. Madison St., 60435. Tel: 815-725-7133
For a complete listing, refer to the Hospitals section.

KANKAKEE. *St. Mary's Hospital*, 500 West Court St., 60901. Tel: 815-937-2490
For a complete listing, refer to the Hospitals section.

[H] REHABILITATION CENTERS

WHEATON. *Marianjoy Rehabilitation Hospital & Clinics*, 26 W. 171 Roosevelt Rd., P.O. Box 795, 60189.

Tel: 630-462-4000. Franciscan Sisters, Daughters of the Sacred Hearts of Jesus and Mary (Wheaton, IL). Mr. Bruce A. Schurman, Pres.; Sr. Mariette Kalbac, Chap. Bed Capacity 110; Patients assisted annually 3,500. Legal Title: *Marianjoy, Inc.*

[I] HOMES FOR AGED

JOLIET. *Our Lady of Angels Retirement Home*, 1201 Wyoming, 60435. Tel: 815-725-6631
For a complete listing, refer to the Special Care Facilities section.

St. Elizabeth Home, 704 W. Marion St., 60436. Tel: 815-727-0125
For a complete listing, refer to the Special Care Facilities section.

Villa Franciscan, Franciscan Sisters Health Care Corp., 210 N. Springfield, 60435. Tel: 815-725-3400; Fax: 815-725-2160
For a complete listing, refer to the Special Care Facilities section.

BOURBONNAIS. *Our Lady of Victory Nursing Home*, 20 Briarcliff Ln., 60914. Tel: 815-937-2022; Fax: 815-936-3231
For a complete listing, refer to the Special Care Facilities section.

CLIFTON. *Merkle-Knipprath Countryside Home*, 1190 E. 2900 N Rd., 60927-9705. Tel: 815-694-2306
For a complete listing, refer to the Special Care Facilities section.

CRETE. *St. James Manor*, 1251 Richton Rd., 60417. Tel: 708-672-6700
For a complete listing, refer to the Special Care Facilities section.

DARIEN. *Carmelite Carefree Retirement Village*, 8419 Bailey Rd., 60561-5361. Tel: 630-960-4060
For a complete listing, refer to the Special Care Facilities section.

LISLE. *Queen of Peace Center*, 1910 Maple Ave., 60532. Tel: 630-852-5360
For a complete listing, refer to the Special Care Facilities section.

NAPERVILLE. *St. John Vianney Villa*, 1464 Green Trails Dr., 60540-8359. Tel: 630-983-0533
For a complete listing, refer to the Special Care Facilities section.

St. Patrick's Residence, 1400 Brookdale Rd., 60563-2125. Tel: 630-416-6565
For a complete listing, refer to the Special Care Facilities section.

OAK BROOK. *Mayslake Village*, 1801 35th St., 60521. Tel: 630-654-3280.
E-mail: mayslakvlg@aol.com
For a complete listing, refer to the Special Care Facilities section.

WHEATON. *Marian Park, Inc.*, 26 W. 171 Roosevelt Rd., P.O. Box 667, 60187. Tel: 630-665-9100
For a complete listing, refer to the Special Care Facilities section.

[J] MONASTERIES AND RESIDENCES OF PRIESTS AND BROTHERS

JOLIET. *Congregation of Christian Brothers, Brother Rice Provincialate*, 958 Western Ave., 60435. Tel: 815-723-5464; Fax: 815-723-5278. Legal Title: *The Christian Brothers of Ireland, Inc.* Bros. Charles J. Gattone, C.F.C., Prov. Leader; Robert N. Brouillette, C.F.C., Deputy Prov. Leader. Councillors: Bros. Charles D. McKenna, C.F.C.; Donald D. Murray, C.F.C.; Michael S. Segvich, C.F.C. In res. Bros. John Dornbos, C.F.C.; Karl J. Walczak, C.F.C.

St. Elias Carmelites, 3504 Lake Shore Dr., 60431-8819. Tel: 815-439-8246. Revs. Joseph Maisonneuve, O.Carm.; Bernhard Bauerle, O.Carm.; Emmet Gleeson, O.Carm.; Raymond Foster, O.Carm., Prior; Rocco DiLeonardi, O.Carm.; Louis Rogge, O.Carm.; Leopold Glueckert, O.Carm.; Timothy Andres, O.Carm.; Bros. Thomas Murphy, O.Carm.; Sean Keefe, O.Carm. Priests 8; Brothers 2.

St. John the Baptist Friary, 404 N. Hickory St., 60435. Tel: 815-727-9783; Fax: 815-740-1521. Revs. Edward Shea, O.F.M.; Louis Davino, O.F.M.; Medard Buvala, O.F.M.; Jason Kommer, O.F.M.; Gerold Schubert, O.F.M.; Jeffrey Donnelly, O.F.M., Chap.; Venard Kommer, O.F.M.; Bro. John Sweeney, O.F.M. Priests 7; Brothers 1.

BURR RIDGE. *Christian Brothers Provincial Office (Midwest Province)*, 200 S. Frontage Rd., Ste. 300, 60521-6953. Tel: 630-323-3725; Fax: 630-323-3779.
E-mail: midwest@lewisu.edu
Bros. Thomas Johnson, F.S.C., Prov.; Francis Carr, F.S.C., Auxiliary Prov.; Michael Fehrenbach, F.S.C., Auxiliary Prov.; Ms. Marge Beauvais, Dir. Lasallian Family; Bros. Edwin Dupre, F.S.C., Dir. Devel.; Joseph Saurbier, F.S.C., Dir. Finance; Thomas Sullivan, F.S.C., Dir. Vocations/Formation; Nicholas Schumer, F.S.C., Dir. St. La Salle Auxiliary.

DARIEN. *Carmelite Community*, St. Simon Stock Priory, 8501 Bailey Rd., 60561. Tel: 630-241-1802. Rev. Robert E. Colaresi, O.Carm., Prior; Bros. Robert Murphy, O.Carm.; Charles Kwiatkowski, O.Carm.; Revs. Gerald Williams, O.Carm.; Raymond J. Clennon, O.Carm., Midwest Commissary Prov.; Kevin Shanley, O.Carm.; Robert E. Lee, O.Carm.; Peter Byrth, O.Carm.; John Malley, O.Carm.; Leo McCarthy, O.Carm. Priests 7; Brothers 2.

Carmelite Provincial Office, 1317 Frontage Rd., 60561. Tel: 630-971-0050; Fax: 630-971-0195.
E-mail: provincial@carmelnet.org
Web site: http://carmelnet.org
Very Rev. Leo McCarthy, O.Carm., Prior Prov.; Rev. Daniel O'Neill, O.Carm., Prov. Procurator. Military Chaplains: Rev. Joseph Wallroth, O.Carm. Carmelites serving abroad: Rev. Craig Morrison, O.Carm., Basilica Parrocchiale, Rome, Italy, General Motherhouse, Via Giovanni Lanza, 138, Rome, Italy, 00184. Most Rev. John R. Malley, O.Carm., Prior Gen., International College of St. Albert, Rome, Italy; Rev. Joachim Smet, O.Carm. Carmelites serving in Canada: Very Rev. Malachy Smith, O.Carm.; Revs. Myles Colgan, O.Carm.; Gregory L. Klein, O.Carm.; Marcel Dube, O.Carm.; Leo Huard, O.Carm.; Felix Prior, O.Carm.; Benedict Hogan, O.Carm.; Murray Phelan, O.Carm.; Stanley Makacinas, O.Carm.; Robert Boley, O.Carm.; Thomas Hakala, O.Carm.; Jordon Rooney, O.Carm.; Leonard Broughan, O'Carm.; Bro. Gabriel Murray, O.Carm. Carmelites serving in Peru: Prelate Nullius, Sicuani, Peru. Most Rev. Alban Quinn, O.Carm.; Revs. Salvador Bartolo, O.Carm. (Malta); Joseph Cilia, O.Carm. (Malta); Herbert Jones, O.Carm.; Ferdinand Lansang, O.Carm.; Kevin Lafey, O.Carm.; Michael LaFay, O.Carm.; Gerald Payea, O.Carm.; Joseph Lucchesi, O.Carm.; Michael Sgarioto, O.Carm.; Enrique Laguna-Vargas, O.Carm.; Gregory Geaney, O.Carm.; Raul Maravic, O.Carm.; Edward Adelmann, O.Carm.; Bros. Miguel Macigalupo-Del Corrall, O.Carm.; Jorge Villegas, O.Carm.; Daniel Salazar, O.Carm.; Carlos Valdez, O.Carm.; Rodolfo Aznaran, O.Carm.; Paul Hensen, O.Carm.; Frank Sanchez, O.Carm. Carmelites serving elsewhere: Revs. Devin Griffin, O.Carm.; Kieran O'Hara, O.Carm.; Henry Ormond, O.Carm.; John F. Donohue, O.Carm.; Blaise McInerney, O.Carm.; Venard Poslusney, O.Carm.; Warren Carlin, O.Carm.; Barry Kremer, O.Carm.; Frank Weil, O.Carm.; Myron Judy, O.Carm.; Francis McCarthy, O.Carm.; David Murphy, O.Carm.; Rudolph Flanik, O.Carm.; Albert Koppes, O.Carm.; Matthew Sprouffske, O.Carm.; Charles Kurgan, O.Carm.; Anton Kollar, O.Carm.; David Fontaine, O.Carm.; Paul Robinson, O.Carm.; Guy McPartland, O.Carm.; Robert Primozic, O.Carm.; Michael Flynn, O.Carm.; Timothy Moore, O.Carm.; James Lewis, O.Carm. Carmelites serving in Mexico: Revs. Peter Hinde, O.Carm.; Joel Moelter, O.Carm.; John Hertel, O.Carm.; Thomas Jordon, O.Carm.; William Smith, O.Carm.; Frank Sanchez, O.Carm.

LISLE. *St. Procopius Abbey*, 5601 College Rd., 60532. Tel: 630-969-6410; Fax: 630-969-6426.
Web site: http://www.procopius.org
Benedictine Monks. Rt. Rev. Hugh R. Anderson, O.S.B., Abbot; Very Rev. Columban Trojan, O.S.B., Prior; Revs. James Flint, O.S.B., Subprior & Master of Novices & Juniors; Kevin J. Sheeran, O.S.B., Procurator & Business Mgr.; Gabriel Baltes, O.S.B.; Frederic J. Beller, O.S.B.; Christian W. Ceplecha, O.S.B.; Joseph Chang, O.S.B.; Thomas Chisholm, O.S.B.; Odilo Crkva, O.S.B.; Ivan Dobnikar, O.S.B.; Jerome Dobry, O.S.B.; Julian von Duerbeck, O.S.B.; Terence Fitzmaurice, O.S.B.; Becket Franks, O.S.B.; Roman Galiardi, O.S.B.; Rt. Rev. Thomas J. Havlik, O.S.B., Abbot, (Retired); Revs. Paschal D. Honner, O.S.B.; Alban Hrebic, O.S.B.; Zachary Hrisko, O.S.B.; Anthony J. Jacob, O.S.B.; Dismas Kalcic, O.S.B.; Michael E. Komechak, O.S.B.; Edward Kucera, O.S.B.; George Kuska, O.S.B.; Timothy R. Marceau, O.S.B.; Jude Randall, O.S.B., Pres., Benet Academy; Rt. Rev. Valentine Skluzacek, O.S.B., Abbot, (Retired); Revs. James Saul, O.S.B.; Clement Sobr, O.S.B.; Theodore D. Suchy, O.S.B.; Philip S. Timko, O.S.B.; David Turner, O.S.B.; Mel R. Uzdrowski, O.S.B.; Stanley G. Vesely, O.S.B.; Kenneth Zigmond, O.S.B.; Francis Lawrence; Most Rev. Daniel W. Kucera, O.S.B., (Retired) Archbishop of Dubuque, IA. Monks 54; Priests 36; Brothers 14; Bishops 1; Oblates 3.

Benedictine Chinese Mission, 2400 Maple Ave., 60532. Tel: 630-968-4264. Rev. James Saul, O.S.B., Dir.

Slav Missions, 5601 College Dr., 60532. Tel: 708-969-6410.

Benedictine University, 5700 College Rd., 60532. Tel: 630-960-1500.

Benet Academy, 2200 Maple Ave., 60532. Tel: 630-969-6550.

St. Scholastica Mission House. Missionary Oblates of St. Benedict, 24 W. 350 Maple Ave., Naperville, 60540. Tel: 630-969-6410.

St. Procopius Abbey Endowment, 5601 College Rd., 60532. Tel: 630-969-6410.

MOMENCE. *Brother Mathias Barrett Inc. of Illinois*, P.O. Box 260, 60954. Tel: 815-472-3131. Bro. Alphonsus Brown, Pres. Brothers 4.

NEW LENOX. *Augustinian Friary*, 1800 W. Lincoln Hwy., 60451.
(See separate listing for Providence High School). In res. Revs. Richard J. McGrath, O.S.A., Pres.; Roland F. Follmann, O.S.A.; John D. Merkelis, O.S.A., Prin.; Gerald A. Nicholas, O.S.A., Prior; Gerald J. Theis, O.S.A.; Bro. John E. Newton, O.S.A.

ROMEOVILLE. *Christian Brothers Center*, 200 De LaSalle Dr., 60446. Tel: 815-838-8903; Fax: 815-838-7089. Bro. Nick Schumer, F.S.C., Dir. Brothers 19.

De La Salle Hall, Lewis University Student Res., 200 De LaSalle Dr., 60441. Tel: 815-838-8902. Bro. Christopher Ford, F.S.C., Dir. Student Residents 55; Brothers 1.

La Salle House, Lewis University, Rte. 53, 60446. Tel: 815-838-0500, Ext. 5460; Fax: 815-838-9456. Bro. Tom Dupre, F.S.C., Dir. Brothers 19.

[K] CONVENTS AND RESIDENCES FOR SISTERS

JOLIET. *Josephine Sisters*, 351 N. Chicago St., 60431. Tel: 815-727-1467. Josephine Sisters of Mexico (Hermanas Josefinas). Sisters 7.

St. Francis Convent (Motherhouse), 520 Plainfield Ave., 60435. Tel: 815-727-3686; Fax: 815-727-9435. Congregation of the Third Order of St. Francis of Mary Immaculate, Joliet, IL. Sr. Mary Jean Morris, O.S.F., Pres.; Sr. Joan Clare Wisner, Building Admin. Sisters 66. Legal Title: *Retirement Plan Trust of the Congregation of the Third Order of St. Francis of Mary Immaculate.*

FRANKFORT. *Motherhouse, Novitiate, Sacred Heart Residence, Portiuncula, Center for Prayer*, St. Francis Woods, 9201 W. St. Francis Rd., 60423-8335. Tel: 815-469-4895; Fax: 815-469-4864.
Web site: http://www.fssh.com
Legal Title: *An Association of Franciscan Sisters of the Sacred Heart.* Sr. Karen Marie Lanigan, O.S.F., Gen. Supr.; Sr. Mary Mark Segvich, Admin.; Rev. Lowell Fischer, Chap. Sisters 80.

KANKAKEE. *St. Clare House of Prayer*, 2041 W. Rte. 113, 60901. Tel: 815-933-3945. Sisters of St. Francis of Mary Immaculate 6.

Servants of the Holy Heart of Mary, Provincial Administration, 145 S. Fourth Ave., 60901. Tel: 815-937-2380; Fax: 815-937-5520. Sr. Kathleen Mulchay, Prov. Supr. Professed Sisters 57. Legal Titles: *Servants of the Holy Heart of Mary Charitable Trust.; ServantCor—HealthCor—ServiceCor, Inc.—Servants United Foundation.*

LISLE. *Benedictine Sisters of the Sacred Heart, Sacred Heart Monastery*, 1910 Maple Ave., 60532.
E-mail: barbsuec@aol.com
Sr. Judith Ann Heble, O.S.B., Prioress; Rev. Philip S. Timko, O.S.B., Chap. Professed Sisters 52. Legal Title: *Benedictine Sisters of the Sacred Heart Charitable Trust.*

PLAINFIELD. *Mantellate Sisters Servants of Mary of Plainfield*, 16949 S. Drauden Rd., 60544-9219. Tel: 815-436-5796. Sr. Francis Gresser, O.S.M., Regional Supr. Sisters 12.
Ministry in the field of Academic Education, Parish Ministry, Social Work, Nursing, Homes for the Aged, and Foreign Missions. Homes for the Aged and Foreign Missions.

WHEATON. *Convent of Our Lady of the Angels Motherhouse and Novitiate.* Franciscan Sisters, Daughters of the Sacred Hearts of Jesus and Mary (Wheaton, IL), P.O. Box 667, 60189-0667. Tel: 630-462-7422; Fax: 630-462-7148. Sr. Mary Ellen McAleese, O.S.F., Prov. Dir. Sisters 65. Legal Title: *Wheaton Franciscan Sisters Corp.*

Loretto Convent, Religious of the Institute of the Blessed Virgin Mary, P.O. Box 508, 60189. Tel: 630-653-4740. Sr. Irene Howell, I.B.V.M. Sisters 25.

Loretto Conference Center.

Wheaton Franciscan Sisters Religious Charitable Trust, 26 W. 171 Roosevelt Rd., P.O. Box 667, 60189-0667. Tel: 630-462-7422; Fax: 630-462-7148.

[L] HOUSES OF RETREAT/PRAYER

DARIEN. *Carmelite Spiritual Center*, 8433 Bailey Rd., 60561. Tel: 630-969-4141; Fax: 630-969-3376. Revs. Kevin Shanley, O.Carm.; Robert E. Colaresi, O.Carm., Dir.; Bro. Lawrence Fidelus, O.Carm. Total Staff 16.

DOWNERS GROVE. *Mayslake Marmion Ministries, Inc.*, 4832 Main St., 60515. Tel: 630-719-1620. Rev. Jonathan D. Foster, O.F.M. Priests 1; Lay Staff 2.

FRANKFORT. *Portiuncula Center for Prayer*, 9263 W. St. Francis Rd., 60423. Tel: 815-464-3880.
E-mail: PORTCYP@aol.com

PLANO. *La Salle Manor Christian Brothers Retreat House*, 12480 Galena Rd., 60545. Tel: 630-552-3224. Robert Dressel, Pres.

WARRENVILLE. *Congregation of Our Lady of the Retreat in the Cenacle*, 29W012 Batavia Rd., P.O. Box 797, 60555-0797. Tel: 708-393-1231.
E-mail: cenacle@aol.com
Web site: http://www.cenacle.org
Sr. Lucille Kunz, R.C., Supr. Sisters 12.

[M] MISCELLANEOUS

JOLIET. *St. Vincent Thrift Shop*, 307 N. Chicago St., 60431. Tel: 815-722-1140. 211 Main St., West Chicago, 60185. Tel: 630-293-9420.

DARIEN. *Carmelite Mission Office*, 1317 Frontage Rd., 60561. Tel: 630-969-5220. Rev. John Malley, O.Carm., Dir.
Carmelite Visitor Center (National Shrine & Museum of St. Therese), 8501 Bailey Rd., 60561. Tel: 630-969-3311. Rev. Jerry Williams, O.Carm., Dir.
Office of the Carmelite Midwest Commissary Provincial, 8419 Bailey Rd., 60561-5361. Tel: 630-960-4934. Rev. Raymond J. Clennon, O.Carm., Commissary Prov.
Provincial Office of Lay Carmelites and Scapular Confraternity, 8501 Bailey Rd., 60561. Tel: 630-969-5050; Fax: 630-969-5536.
E-mail: laycarm@aol.com
Web site: carmelnet.org
Rev. Peter Byrth, O.Carm., Prov. Dir.; Sr. Christina Marie Griggs, O.Carm., Assoc. Dir.; Revs. Robert E. Lee, O.Carm., Assoc. Dir.; Aloysius Sierachi, O.Carm., (Retired).
Society of the Little Flower, 1313 Frontage Rd., 60561-5341. Tel: 630-968-9400; Fax: 630-968-9542.
E-mail: ltlflwr@ibm.net
Web site: littleflower.org
Rev. Robert E. Colaresi, O.Carm., Dir.

FRANKFORT. *Franciscan Sisters Health Care Corporation*, 9223 W. St. Francis Rd., 60423-8334. Tel: 815-469-4888; Fax: 815-469-4864.

KANKAKEE. *Lisieux Pastoral Center*, 371 N. St. Joseph Ave., 60901.

LISLE. *National Association of Catholic Nurses-U.S.A.*, P.O. Box 3016, 60532-3016. Tel: 630-852-1049. Marylee J. Meehan, Pres.

MOMENCE. *B.G.S. Charitable Trust*, P.O. Box 736, 60954-0736. Tel: 815-472-3131; Fax: 815-472-6914. Michael F. Mieszala, Esq.
Little Brothers of the Good Shepherd, Inc. of Illinois, 4129 N. Dixie Hwy., P.O. Box 736, 60954. Bro. Richard MacPhee, Treas. Gen.; Judy Brinkmann, Dir. of Finance.

NAPERVILLE. *Mercy Chicago Region Healthcare System*, 55 Shuman Blvd., Ste. 150, 60563-8469. Sr. Catherine C. Gallagher, R.S.M., Pres.

OAK BROOK. *Consolidated Catholic Health Care*, 1301 W. 22nd St., Ste. 202, 60523. Roger N. Butler, Exec. Dir.

ROMEOVILLE. *Charitable Trust of the Brothers of the Christian Schools*, 1205 Windham Pkwy., 60446-1697. Tel: 630-378-2900; Fax: 630-378-2501.
E-mail: info@cbservices.org
Christian Brothers Employee Benefit Trust, 1205 Windham Pkwy., 60446-1694. Tel: 630-378-2900; Fax: 630-378-2501.
E-mail: info@cbservices.org
Christian Brothers Employee Retirement Plan Trust, 1205 Windham Pkwy., 60446-1692. Tel: 630-378-2900; Fax: 630-378-2501.
E-mail: info@cbservices.org
Christian Brothers Fund, Inc., 200 De La Salle Dr., 60446-1899. Tel: 815-838-8903. Bro. Edwin Dupre.
Christian Brothers Religious Comprehensive Trust, 1205 Windham Pkwy., 60446-1695. Tel: 630-378-2900; Fax: 630-378-2501.
E-mail: info@cbservices.org
Christian Brothers Religious Deductible Trust, 1205 Windham Pkwy., 60446-1695. Tel: 630-378-2900; Fax: 630-378-2501.
E-mail: info@cbservices.org
**Christian Brothers Services*, 1205 Windham Pkwy., 60446-1691. Tel: 630-378-2900; Fax: 630-378-2501.
E-mail: info@cbservices.org
Bro. William Walz, F.S.C.
Religious & Charitable Risk Pooling Trust of the Brothers of the Christian Schools, 1205 Windham Pkwy., 60446-1693. Tel: 630-378-2900; Fax: 630-378-2501.
E-mail: info@cbservices.org

WEST CHICAGO. *Society of St. Vincent de Paul*, Diocesan Council of Joliet, 211 Main St., 60185. Tel: 708-293-9420; Fax: 708-293-9433.

WHEATON. *Assisi Homes - Aurora, Inc.*, 26 W. 171 Roosevelt Rd., 60187. Tel: 630-462-9271. Ray Wojcik, Pres.
Assisi Homes - Batavia Apartments, Inc., 26 W. 171 Roosevelt Rd., 60189. Tel: 708-462-9271. Ray Wojcik, Pres. Total in Residence 290; Total Staff 5.
Assisi Homes - Colony Park, Inc., 26 W. 171 Roosevelt Rd., 60187. Tel: 630-462-9271. Ray Wojcik, Pres.
Assisi Homes - Constitution House, Inc., 26 W. 171 Roosevelt Rd., 60187. Tel: 630-462-9271.
Assisi Homes - Downer Place, Inc., 26 W. 171 Roosevelt Rd., 60189. Tel: 630-462-9271. Garth R. Seehauer.
Assisi Homes of Gurnee, Inc., 26 W. 171 Roosevelt Rd., P.O. Box 667, 60189. Tel: 630-462-9271. Steve Kuklin, Pres.
Assisi Homes of Illinois, Inc., 26 W. 171 Roosevelt Rd., 60187. Tel: 630-462-9271. Ray Wojcik, Pres.; Garth R. Seehauer, Senior Vice Pres.
Canticle Place, Inc., 26 W. 105 Roosevelt Rd., #13, 60187. Tel: 630-588-9165; Fax: 630-588-9167. Garth Seehauer, Senior Vice Pres., Legal Services.
Clara Pfaender Fund, Inc., 26 W. 171 Roosevelt Rd., P.O. Box 667, 60189. Tel: 630-462-9271. Sr. Margaret Grampha, O.S.F., Pres.; Garth R. Seehauer, Senior Vice Pres. Franciscan Sisters, Daughters of the Sacred Hearts of Jesus and Mary (Wheaton, IL).
Franciscan Health & Education Corp., Inc., 26 W. 171 Roosevelt Rd., P.O. Box 667, 60189. Tel: 630-462-9271, Ext. 236.
Franciscan Ministries, Inc., P.O. Box 667, 26 W. 171 Roosevelt Rd., 60189. Tel: 630-462-9271. Rodger F. Accardi, Pres.; Garth R. Seehauer, Senior Vice Pres.
Institute of the Blessed Virgin Mary Charitable Trust, P.O. Box 508, 60189. Tel: 630-653-6113; Fax: 630-653-4886.
E-mail: ibvmbarb@aol.com
WFSI-Illinois, 26 W. 171 Roosevelt Rd., P.O. Box 667, 60189. Tel: 630-462-9271. John Oliverio, Pres.; Garth R. Seehauer, Senior Vice Pres.
Wheaton Franciscan Services, Inc., 26 W. 171 Roosevelt Rd., P.O. Box 667, 60189. Tel: 630-462-9271. Sr. Rose Mary Pint, O.S.F., Chm.; Mr. Wilfred F. Loebig, Jr., Pres. & CEO; Garth R. Seehauer, Senior Vice Pres.

RELIGIOUS INSTITUTES OF MEN REPRESENTED IN THE DIOCESE

For further details refer to the corresponding bracketed number in the Religious Institutes of Men or Women section.

[0140]—*The Augustinians.* (Mother of Good Counsel Prov.).—O.S.A.
[0200]—*Benedictine Monks.*—O.S.B.
[0330]—*Brothers of the Christian Schools.* (Midwest Prov.).—F.S.C.
[0580]—*Brothers of the Good Shepherd.*—B.G.S.
[0270]—*Carmelite Fathers & Brothers.* (Prov. of Pure Heart of Mary).—O.Carm.
[0275]—*Carmelites of Mary Immaculate.*—C.M.I.
[1320]—*Clerics of St. Viator.*—C.S.V.
[0310]—*Congregation of Christian Brothers.*—C.F.C.
[0430]—*Dominicans.* (Prov. of Albert the Great).—O.P.
[0520]—*Franciscan Friars.* (Sacred Heart, Assumption Provs.).—O.F.M.
[0540]—*Franciscan Missionary Brothers of the Sacred Heart of Jesus.*—O.S.F.
[0520]—*Franciscans.* (Order of Friars Minor, Sacred Heart Prov.).—O.F.M.
[0740]—*Marian Fathers.* (Prov. of St. Casimer).—M.I.C.
[0610]—*Priests of the Congregation of Holy Cross.*—C.S.C.
[0110]—*Society of African Missions.*—S.M.A.
[0690]—*Society of Jesus.* (Chicago and St. Louis Prov.).—S.J.

RELIGIOUS INSTITUTES OF WOMEN REPRESENTED IN THE DIOCESE

[0230]—*Benedictine Sisters of Pontifical Jurisdiction.* (Lisle, IL; Ferdinand, IN).—O.S.B.
[0330]—*Carmelite Sisters for the Aged and Infirm.* (Germantown, NY).—O.Carm.
[0400]—*Congregation of Our Lady of Mount Carmel.* (Lacombe, LA).—O.Carm.
[3110]—*Congregation of Our Lady of the Retreat in the Cenacle.*—R.C.
[2100]—*Congregation of the Humility of Mary.*—C.H.M.
[0460]—*Congregation of the Sisters of Charity of the Incarnate Word.*—C.C.V.I.
[3710]—*Congregation of the Sisters of Saint Agnes.*—C.S.A.
[1920]—*Congregation of the Sisters of the Holy Cross.*—C.S.C.
[1710]—*Congregation of the Third Order of St. Francis of Mary Immaculate, Joliet, IL.*—O.S.F.
[1070-01]—*Dominican Sisters.* (St. Catharine, KY).—O.P.
[1070-03]—*Dominican Sisters.* (Sinsinawa).—O.P.
[1070-10]—*Dominican Sisters.* (Springfield).—O.P.
[1070-13]—*Dominican Sisters.* (Adrian).—O.P.
[1170]—*Felician Sisters.*—C.S.S.F.
[1780]—*Franciscan Sisters of Perpetual Adoration.* (Woodruff, WI).—F.S.P.A.
[1450]—*Franciscan Sisters of the Sacred Heart.*—O.S.F.
[1240]—*Franciscan Sisters, Daughters of the Sacred Hearts of Jesus and Mary.*—O.S.F.
[1910]—*Hermanas Josefinas.*—H.J.
[2370]—*Institute of the Blessed Virgin Mary (Loretto Sisters).*—I.B.V.M.
[2575]—*Institute of the Sisters of Mercy of the Americas.* (Chicago, IL).—R.S.M.
[3570]—*Mantellate Sisters, Servants of Mary.* (Plainfield, IL).—O.S.M.
[]—*Missionary Sisters of the Holy Family.* (Komorrow-Warsaw, Poland).—M.S.H.F.
[3760]—*Order of St. Clare.*—P.C.C.
[2970]—*School Sisters of Notre Dame.* (Chicago Prov.).—S.S.N.D.
[1680]—*School Sisters of St. Francis.* (U.S. Prov.).—O.S.F.
[3590]—*Servants of Mary.* (Ladysmith, WI).—O.S.M.
[3520]—*Servants of the Holy Heart of Mary.*—S.S.C.M.
[0430]—*Sisters of Charity of the Blessed Virgin Mary.*—B.V.M.
[2990]—*Sisters of Notre Dame.* (Toledo, OH).—S.N.D.
[3000]—*Sisters of Notre Dame de Namur.* (Cincinnati Prov.).—S.N.D.deN.
[3360]—*Sisters of Providence of Saint Mary-of-the-Woods, IN.*—S.P.
[3740]—*Sisters of St. Casimir.*—S.S.C.
[1540]—*Sisters of St. Francis.* (Clinton, IA).—O.S.F.
[1705]—*The Sisters of St. Francis of Assisi.* (St. Francis).—O.S.F.
[1520]—*Sisters of St. Francis of Christ the King.*—O.S.F.
[1570]—*Sisters of St. Francis of Dubuque.* (Iowa).—O.S.F.
[1640]—*Sisters of St. Francis of Perpetual Adoration.* (Mishawaka).—O.S.F.
[1580]—*Sisters of St. Francis of the Immaculate Conception.*—O.S.F.
[3830-02]—*Sisters of St. Joseph.*—C.S.J.
[3930]—*Sisters of St. Joseph of the Third Order of St. Francis.* (Prov. of Immaculate Conception).—S.S.J.-T.O.S.F.
[2980]—*Sisters of the Congregation de Notre Dame.*—C.N.D.
[2350]—*Sisters of the Living Word.*—S.L.W.
[1720]—*Sisters of the Third Order Regular of St. Francis of the Congregation of Our Lady of Lourdes.* (Rochester, MN).—O.S.F.
[2150]—*Sisters Servants of the Immaculate Heart of Mary.*—I.H.M.

DIOCESAN CEMETERIES

JOLIET. *Holy Cross*, Theodore St. Tel: 815-838-0395.
Mount Olivet, 1320 E. Cass St. Tel: 815-838-0395.
St. John the Baptist, Ruby St. & Clemet St. Tel: 815-838-0395.
St. Mary Nativity, Caton Farm Rd. & Oakland Ave. Tel: 815-838-0395.
St. Patrick, Hunter St. & Jefferson St. Tel: 815-838-0395.
SS. Cyril and Methodius, Rte. 6 & Maple Rd. Tel: 815-838-0395.

BOURBONNAIS. *All Saints*, Rte. 102. Tel: 815-936-9378.
Maternity/BVM, Canberry Ln. Tel: 815-933-2342.

CAROL STREAM. *St. Stephen*, St. Charles Rd. Tel: 630-668-3313.

DOWNERS GROVE. *St. Bernard*, I 355 & Hobson Rd. Tel: 630-668-3313.
St. Mary, Finley Rd. Tel: 630-668-3313.

ELMHURST. *St. Mary*, Alexander Blvd. Tel: 630-668-3313.

KANKAKEE. *Mt. Calvary*, 2000 E. Court St. Tel: 815-933-2342.
St. Rose, Rte. 50. Tel: 815-933-2342.

LOCKPORT. *Calvary*, Rte. 171 & High Rd. Tel: 815-838-0395.

LOCKPORT SOUTH. *St. Dennis*, 16th St. & Washington St. Tel: 815-838-0395.

NAPERVILLE. *SS. Peter & Paul*, Columbia St. & North Ave. Tel: 630-668-3313.

ROMEOVILLE. *Resurrection*, 135th St. & Rte. 53. Tel: 815-838-0395.
St. Charles Borromeo, 402 S. Independence Blvd., 60446-2264. Tel: 815-838-0395.

WHEATON. *Assumption*, One S 510 Winfield Rd. Tel: 630-668-3313.

WINFIELD. *St. John the Baptist*, Summit Rd. & Gary Mill Rd. Tel: 630-668-3313.

NECROLOGY

† Dinan, Paul, (Retired). —Died Dec. 6, 1996.
† Gryga, Stanislaus, (Retired). —Died Nov. 15, 1996.
† Kosmal, John, (Retired). —Died Aug. 18, 1997.
† Ruffalo, Richard, Joliet, IL, Holy Cross. —Died Feb. 21, 1997.
† Van Duren, Charles, (Retired). —Died Aug. 30, 1997.

Diocese of Juneau

(Dioecesis Junellensis)

Most Reverend

MICHAEL W. WARFEL

Bishop of Juneau; ordained April 26, 1980; appointed November 19, 1996; installed December 17, 1996.

ESTABLISHED JUNE 23, 1951.

Square Miles 37,566.

Corporate Title: "Corporation of the Catholic Bishop of Juneau."

Comprises the entire southeastern part of the State of Alaska known legally as The First Judicial District.

For legal titles of parishes and diocesan institutions, consult the Chancery Office.

Chancery: 419 Sixth St., #200, Juneau, AK, 99801. Tel.: 907-586-2227; Fax: 907-463-3237.

STATISTICAL OVERVIEW

Personnel	
Bishop	1
Priests: Diocesan Active in Diocese	4
Priests: Active Outside Diocese	5
Priests: Retired, Sick or Absent	7
Number of Diocesan Priests	16
Religious Priests in Diocese	4
Permanent Deacons in Diocese	9
Total Sisters	10
Parishes	
Parishes	10
With Resident Pastor:	
Resident Diocesan Priests	3
Resident Religious Priests	4
Without Resident Pastor:	
Administered by Priests	3
Missions	15
Welfare	
Catholic Hospitals	1
Total Assisted	46,403
Homes for the Aged	1
Total Assisted	102
Day Care and Extended Day Care Centers	1
Total Assisted	100
Special Centers for Social Services	1
Total Assisted	6,047
Other Institutions	1
Total Assisted	7,850
Educational	
Diocesan Students in Other Seminaries	1
Total Seminarians	1
Elementary Schools, Diocesan and Parish	1
Total Students	105
Catechesis/Religious Education:	
High School Students	184
Elementary Students	610
Total Students Under Catholic Instruction	900
Teachers in the Diocese:	
Lay Teachers	9
Vital Statistics	
Receptions into the Church:	
Infant Baptism Totals	128
Adult Baptism Totals	36
Received into Full Communion	37
First Communions	110
Confirmations	33
Marriages:	
Catholic	16
Interfaith	27
Total Marriages	43
Deaths	26
Total Catholic Population	6,030
Total Population	74,217

Former Bishops—Most Rev. DERMOT O'FLANAGAN, D.D., ord. Aug. 27, 1929; appt. Bishop July 9, 1951; cons. Oct. 3, 1951; resigned June 19, 1968 and; appt. Titular Bishop of Trecalae; died Dec. 31, 1972.—Most Rev. FRANCIS T. HURLEY, D.D., ord. June 16, 1951; appt. Titular Bishop of Daimlaig and Auxiliary of Juneau, Feb. 4, 1970; cons. March 19, 1970; Ordinary of See, July 20, 1971; appt. Archbishop of Anchorage, May 4, 1976.—Most Rev. MICHAEL H. KENNY, D.D., ord. March 30, 1963; appt. March 20, 1979; cons. May 27, 1979; installed June 15, 1979; died Feb. 19, 1995.

Diocesan Pastoral Center

Chancery—419 Sixth St., #200, Juneau, 99801. Tel: 907-586-2227; Fax: 907-463-3237.

Chancellor—Rev. PATRICK J. TRAVERS, J.C.L., J.D.

Diocesan Consultors—Revs. PETER GORGES; Rev. Msgr. JAMES MILLER; Revs. BERNARD KONDA; PATRICK J. TRAVERS, J.C.L., J.D.; MICHAEL SCHWARTE; PAUL WIGHTMAN.

Tribunal—419 Sixth St., #200, Juneau, 99801. Tel: 907-586-2227.

Judicial Vicar—Rev. PATRICK J. TRAVERS, J.C.L., J.D.

Defender of the Bond—Rev. BERNARD KONDA, M.B.A., J.C.D.

Notary—ROBERTA IZZARD.

Administration—419 Sixth St., #200, Juneau, 99801. Tel: 907-586-2227; Fax: 907-463-3237.

Business Manager and Finance Officer—SKIP ELLIOTT.

Director of Administrative Services—ROBERTA IZZARD.

Assistant to the Finance Officer—DENISE GRANT.

Finance Council—Rev. PETER GORGES; SKIP ELLIOTT; HUGH GRANT; WIN GERMAIN; KATHY BARRETT; CHRIS MILLER; DENISE OLMSTEAD.

Diocesan Offices and Directors

Apostleship of the Sea—Port Chaplains: Revs. PETER GORGES, *416 Fifth St., Juneau, 99801.* BERNARD KONDA, *433 Jackson St., Ketchikan, 99801.* PAUL WIGHTMAN, *P.O. Box 495, Sitka, 99835.* ED MATTHEWS, *Box 469, Wrangell, 99929.* PAT TRAVERS, *P.O. Box 47, Petersburg, 99833.*

Catholic Community Service, Inc.—Rev. A. GORDON JOHNSON, Exec. Dir., *419 Sixth St., CCS Wing, Juneau, 99801.* Tel: 907-463-3933.

Board of Directors—Most Rev. MICHAEL W. WARFEL, Pres. NATALIE ALTON; ERROL CHAMPION; BILL CORBUS; MARY GORE; ROSEMARY HAGERIG; SHARON KELLY; MARJORIE MENZI; KEVIN SULLIVAN; MARIJO TONER; JOHN WILLIAMS.

Southeast Senior Services—PATRICIA JANIK, Program Dir., *419 Sixth St., CCS Wing, Juneau, 99801.* Tel: 907-586-6233.

Child Care & Family Resources—PATRICIA JANIK, Prog. Dir., *520 Harris St., Juneau, 99801.* Tel: 907-463-3933.

Diocesan Publication "Inside Passage"—LOUISE MILLER, Editor, *419 Sixth St., #200, Juneau, 99801.* Tel: 907-586-2237, Ext. 32.

Holy Childhood Association—Rev. PATRICK J. TRAVERS, J.C.L., J.D., Dir., *419 Sixth St., #200, Juneau, 99801.* Tel: 907-586-2227, Ext. 21.

Office of Ministries—Directors: Sr. JUDITH GOMILA, M.S.C.; Sr. CAROL CRATER, S.H.F.; Sr. ZITA SIMON, O.P., *419 Sixth St., #200, Juneau, 99801.* Tel: 907-586-2227.

Family Life Office—Vacant, *419 Sixth St., Juneau, 99801.* Tel: 907-586-2227, Ext. 29.

Permanent Deacon Program—Deacon CHARLES SESLAR, *4133 Columbia Blvd., Juneau, 99801.* Tel: 907-789-2262.

School—Rev. GARY CARR, Prin., *Holy Name School, 433 Jackson St., Ketchikan, 99901.* Tel: 907-225-2400.

Shrine of St. Therese—THOMAS FITTERER, *5933 Lund St., Juneau, 99801.* Tel: 907-780-6112. Caretakers: CHUCK GASPAREK; JOAN GASPAREK, *8695 Short Ct., Juneau, 99801.* Tel: 907-789-9815.

St. Vincent de Paul Society—STAN MILLER; JOANNE MILLER, *8617 Teal St., Juneau, 99801.* Tel: 907-789-5535.

Special Collections and Archivist—Deacon GARY HORTON, *419 6th St. #200, Juneau, 99801.* Tel: 907-586-2227, Ext. 36.

Vocations—Sr. ZITA SIMON, Dir., *419 6th St., #200, Juneau, 99801.* Tel: 907-586-2227, Ext. 34.

CLERGY, PARISHES, MISSIONS AND PAROCHIAL SCHOOLS

CITY AND BOROUGH OF JUNEAU

1—CATHEDRAL OF THE NATIVITY OF THE BLESSED VIRGIN MARY, Rev. Peter Gorges, Rector; Carol J. Crater, S.H.F., Pastoral Assoc.
Res., 416 Fifth St., 99801. Tel: 907-586-1513; Fax: 907-586-8091.
Mission—Pelican.

2—ST. PAUL THE APOSTLE, Rev. Jef Johnson.
Res., 9055 Atlin Ave., 99801. Tel: 907-789-2648; 789-7307 (Office); Fax: 907-790-3430.

OUTSIDE THE CITY AND BOROUGH OF JUNEAU

Craig, St. John by the Sea, Rev. Jim Blaney, O.M.I.; Sr. Laetitia Lariviere, I.H.M., Pastoral Assoc.
Res., P.O. Box 170, 99921. Tel: 907-755-2345; Fax: 907-755-2350.
Mission—Thorne Bay, P.O. Box 19150, Thorne Bay, 99919. Tel: 907-828-3324.
Stations—Coffman Cove; Hydaburg; Klawock; Thorne Bay; Kasaan; Whale Pass; Naukati.

Haines, Sacred Heart, Sr. Judith Gomila, M.S.C., Pastoral Assoc. In res., Rev. Msgr. James F. Miller, (Retired).

Res., Box 326, 99827. Tel: 907-766-2241.

Hoonah, Sacred Heart, Rev. Michael Schwarte; Sr. Carol J. Crater, S.H.F., Pastoral Admin.
Res., P.O. Box 368, 99289. Tel: 907-945-3323.

Ketchikan, Holy Name, Rev. Bernard A. Konda, J.C.D., Admin.
433 Jackson St., 99901. Tel: 907-225-2570; Fax: 907-247-0041; Rectory: Tel: 907-225-5352; Fax: 907-247-7585.
School—Lay Teachers 9; Students 100.
Mission—Metlakatla, Holy Family, P.O. Box 228, Metlakatla, 99926. Fax: 907-247-0041.

Petersburg, St. Catherine of Siena, Rev. Patrick J. Travers, O.M.I.
Res., P.O. Box 508, 99833. Tel: 907-772-3257; Fax: 907-772-3080.
Mission—Kake.

Sitka, St. Gregory of Nazianzen, Rev. Paul Wightman, O.M.I.; Sr. Maggie Butler, S.S.J., Pastoral Assoc.
Res., P.O. Box 495, 99835. Tel: 907-747-8371; 747-6997; Fax: 907-747-8051.
Mission—Angoon.

Skagway, St. Therese of the Child Jesus, Rev. Michael Schwarte; Sr. Judith Gomila, M.S.C., Pastoral Admin.
Res., Box 496, 99840. Tel: 907-983-2271.

Wrangell, St. Rose of Lima, Rev. Edward Matthews, O.M.I., Admin.
Res., Box 469, 99929. Tel: 907-874-3771; Fax: 907-874-3744.

Yakutat, St. Ann, Rev. Michael Schwarte; Sr. Judith Gomila, M.S.C., Pastoral Admin.
Res., P.O. Box 323, 99689. Tel: 907-784-3406.
Stations—Hobart Bay; Elfin Cove; Gustavus; Pelican; Tenakee Springs.

On Duty Outside the Diocese:
Reverend Fathers—
Finn, William, St. Louis Parish, 141 156th Ave., SE, Bellevue, WA 98007
Gutierrez, Javier, P.O. Box 6315, Chula Vista, CA 92011
Hayden, Michael, St. Mary Parish, 110 S. Conro St., Rhinelander, WI 54501
Saba, Joseph, 5660 W. Placita Del Risco, Tuscon, AZ 85745

Retired:
Reverend Monsignors—
Kekumano, Charles A., 700 Richards St., #2609, Honolulu, HI 96813
Miller, James F., Box 326, Haines, AK 99827
Reverend Fathers—
Cronin, James D., 1870-A Vista del Sur, Sante Fe, NM 87505
Frister, Jerome, 3621 Vista Campana S. #70, Oceanside, CA 92057
Manske, James J., P.O. Box 1672, Juneau, AK 99802
Melbourne, David, 3424 E. 15th Ave., Anchorage, AK 99508
Ryan, James, 2828 Sloat Rd., Pebble Beach, CA 93953

Permanent Deacons:
Benigno, Patrick, On Duty Outside the Diocese
Buck, Jack W., On Duty Outside the Diocese
Duvernay, Anthony, On Duty Outside the Diocese
Horton, Gary, Cathedral of the Nativity of the Blessed Virgin Mary, Juneau
Johnson, Charles, St. Gregory's, Sitka
Jones, Jerred, On Leave of Absence
Mackin, Francis, St. Gregory's, Sitka
Michaud, George, On Duty Outside the Diocese
Paradis, Paul, (Retired)
Seslar, Charles, Cathedral of the Nativity of the Blessed Virgin Mary, Juneau

INSTITUTIONS LOCATED IN THE DIOCESE

[A] NURSING HOMES

JUNEAU. *St. Ann's Care Center, Inc.*, 415 Sixth St., 99801. Tel: 907-586-3883
For a complete listing, refer to the Special Care Facilities section.

[B] HOSPITALS

KETCHIKAN. *Ketchikan General Hospital*, 3100 Tongass, 99901. Tel: 907-225-2173; Fax: 907-228-8322
For a complete listing, refer to the Hospitals section.

[C] CONVENTS AND RESIDENCES FOR SISTERS

JUNEAU. *St. Joseph Convent*, 2971 Douglas Hwy., 99801. Tel: 907-586-2085. Intercommunity residence of various religious orders of women. Sisters 3.

KETCHIKAN. *Sisters of St. Joseph of Peace*, 130 Bryant St., #108, 99901. Tel: 907-225-5171; Fax: 907-225-2173.

RELIGIOUS INSTITUTES OF WOMEN REPRESENTED IN THE DIOCESE

For further details refer to the corresponding bracketed number in the Religious Institutes of Women section.

[2410]—*Congregation of the Marianites of Holy Cross.*—M.S.C.

[1070]—*Dominican Sisters.*—O.P.

[]—*Sisters of St. Joseph.*—S.S.J.

[3890]—*Sisters of St. Joseph of Peace.*—C.S.J.P.

[]—*Sisters of the Holy Family.*—S.H.F.

[2150]—*Sisters, Servants of the Immaculate Heart of Mary.*—I.H.M.

NECROLOGY

(No Deaths)

Diocese of Kalamazoo

(Dioecesis Kalamazuensis)

Most Reverend

JAMES A. MURRAY

Bishop of Kalamazoo; ordained June 7, 1958; appointed Bishop of Kalamazoo November 18, 1997; ordained and installed January 27, 1998.

Most Reverend

PAUL V. DONOVAN, D.D.

Former Bishop of Kalamazoo; ordained May 20, 1950; appointed Bishop of Kalamazoo June 15, 1971; ordained and installed July 21, 1971; resigned November 22, 1994. *Mailing Address: 238 Falkirk Ct., Kalamazoo, MI, 49006.*

ESTABLISHED JULY 21, 1971.

Square Miles 5,337.

Comprises the following nine Counties in the State of Michigan: Allegan, Barry, Berrien, Branch, Calhoun, Cass, Kalamazoo, St. Joseph and Van Buren.

For legal titles of parishes and diocesan institutions, consult the Chancery.

Chancery: 215 N. Westnedge Ave., Kalamazoo, MI, 49007-3760. Tel.: 616-349-8714; Fax: 616-349-6440.

STATISTICAL OVERVIEW

Personnel	
Bishop	1
Retired Bishops	1
Priests: Diocesan Active in Diocese	36
Priests: Retired, Sick or Absent	21
Number of Diocesan Priests	57
Religious Priests in Diocese	10
Extern Priests in Diocese	10
Ordinations:	
Diocesan Priests	1
Permanent Deacons in Diocese	17
Total Brothers	5
Total Sisters	234
Parishes	
Parishes	46
With Resident Pastor:	
Resident Diocesan Priests	31
Resident Religious Priests	12
Without Resident Pastor:	
Administered by Permanent Deacons	1
Administered by Women Religious	2
Missions	13
Pastoral Centers	1
Professional Ministry Personnel:	
Brothers	4
Sisters	11
Lay Ministers	41
Welfare	
Catholic Hospitals	3
Total Assisted	565,960
Homes for the Aged	5
Total Assisted	423
Day Care and Extended Day Care Centers	2
Total Assisted	85
Specialized Homes	2
Total Assisted	820
Special Centers for Social Services	4
Total Assisted	27,730
Educational	
Diocesan Students in Other Seminaries	5
Total Seminarians	5
High Schools, Diocesan and Parish	3
Total Students	857
Elementary Schools, Diocesan and Parish	21
Total Students	4,474
Catechesis/Religious Education:	
High School Students	1,227
Elementary Students	6,773
Total Students Under Catholic Instruction	13,336
Teachers in the Diocese:	
Sisters	10
Lay Teachers	319
Vital Statistics	
Receptions into the Church:	
Infant Baptism Totals	1,587
Adult Baptism Totals	307
Received into Full Communion	252
First Communions	1,543
Confirmations	1,330
Marriages:	
Catholic	251
Interfaith	291
Total Marriages	542
Deaths	869
Total Catholic Population	109,328
Total Population	912,044

Former Bishops—Most Rev. PAUL V. DONOVAN, D.D., ord. May 20, 1950; appt. Bishop of Kalamazoo June 15, 1971; installed July 21, 1971; resigned Nov. 22, 1994.—Most Rev. ALFRED J. MARKIEWICZ, D.D., ord. June 6, 1953; appt. Titular Bishop of Afufenia and Auxiliary to the Bishop of Rockville Centre, July 7, 1986; ord. Bishop, Sept. 17, 1986; appt. Bishop of Kalamazoo, Nov. 22, 1994; installed Jan. 31, 1995; died Jan. 9, 1997.

Diocesan Administrator—Rev. EUGENE A. SEARS, *215 N. Westnedge Ave., Kalamazoo, 49007*. Tel: 616-349-6472; Fax: 616-349-6440.

Chancery—215 N. Westnedge Ave., Kalamazoo, 49007-3760. Tel: 616-349-8714; Fax: 616-349-6440. Office Hours: 9-5; Address all communications to this office.

Moderator of the Curia—Rev. ROBERT C. MORLINO, S.T.D., *542 W. Michigan Ave., Kalamazoo, 49007*. Tel: 616-349-6523.

Chancellor—Vacant.

Diocesan Tribunal—215 N. Westnedge Ave., Kalamazoo, 49007-3760. Tel: 616-349-7974; Fax: 616-349-6440.

Judicial Vicar—Rev. LEONARD A. BOGDAN, J.C.D.

Defenders of the Bond—Revs. MICHAEL A. HACK, J.C.D.; THOMAS A. MARTIN, J.C.D.

Promoter of Justice—Rev. THOMAS A. MARTIN, J.C.D.

Judges—Rev. Msgr. WALTER E. MEHM, J.C.D.; Revs. KENNETH W. SCHMIDT, J.C.D.; EDWARD A. HANKIEWICZ, J.C.L.; Sr. JOYCE HOBEN, S.N.D., J.C.L.

Advocates—Revs. THOMAS A. MARTIN, J.C.D.; MICHAEL A. OSBORN.

Chief Notary and Administrative Assistant—MARLENE J. PRANSKATIS.

Notaries—ANNA B. BOWMAN; AUDREY J. ARENDARSKI.

Archivist—Rev. ROBERT F. CREAGAN, *150 Taylor St., Coldwater, 49036*. Tel: 517-278-2650; Fax: 517-278-5800.

Diocesan Consultors—Revs. DAVID C. ADAMS; ROBERT E. CONSANI; WILLIAM J. FITZGERALD; MICHAEL D. HAZARD; JAMES S. O'LEARY; EUGENE A. SEARS.

Theological Consultant—Rev. ROBERT C. MORLINO, S.T.D.

Vicar for Religious—Sr. MARY JOAN WALSH, S.S.J., *215 N. Westnedge Ave., Kalamazoo, 49007-3760*. Tel: 616-349-8714; Fax: 616-349-6440.

Diocesan Offices and Directors

Campaign for Human Development—Sr. SUSAN RIDLEY, O.P., Dir., *215 N. Westnedge Ave., Kalamazoo, 49007-3760*. Tel: 616-349-7260.

Catholic Family Services—FRANCES H. DENNY, Exec. Dir., *1819 Gull Rd., Kalamazoo, 49001*. Tel: 616-381-9800; Fax: 616-381-2932.

Catholic Relief Services—Sr. SUSAN RIDLEY, O.P., Dir., *215 N. Westnedge Ave., Kalamazoo, 49007-3760*. Tel: 616-349-7260.

Cemeteries—Vacant, *215 N. Westnedge Ave., Kalamazoo, 49007*. Tel: 616-349-8714; Fax: 616-349-6440.

Children's Catechesis—Sr. MARY LOUISE MATT, C.S.J., Dir., *215 N. Westnedge Ave., Kalamazoo, 49007-3760*. Tel: 616-349-6404.

Christian Service—Sr. SUSAN RIDLEY, O.P., Dir., *215 N. Westnedge Ave., Kalamazoo, 49007-3760*. Tel: 616-349-7260.

Common Ministry—MARY JANE DOERR, Dir. BONNIE ROBINS, Coord., *215 N. Westnedge Ave., Kalamazoo, 49007-3760*. Tel: 616-349-1391; Fax: 616-349-6440.

Communications—SUSAN H. HAJEC, *215 N. Westnedge Ave., Kalamazoo, 49007-3760*. Tel: 616-349-6707.

Audio-Visual Resources—TERESA R.E. STUTZ, Coord., *215 N. Westnedge Ave., Kalamazoo, 49007-3760*. Tel: 616-349-6707.

Catholic Communications Campaign—Vacant, *215 N. Westnedge Ave., Kalamazoo, 49007-3760*. Tel: 616-349-1391.

Cursillo Movement—Vacant.

Diocesan Council of Catholic Women (D.C.C.W.)—Rev. DONALD P. KLINGER, Spiritual Dir.; Mrs. IRENE RUGA, Pres., *2648 116th Ave., Allegan, 49010*. Tel: 616-673-2850.

Diocesan Development Office—T. EDWARD CAREY, JR., Dir., *215 N. Westnedge Ave., Kalamazoo, 49007-3760.* Tel: 616-349-4677.

Diocesan Pastoral Council—Vacant, *215 N. Westnedge Ave., Kalamazoo, 49007-3760.* Tel: 616-349-7606.

Diocesan-Parish Council Ministry—Vacant, *215 N. Westnedge Ave., Kalamazoo, 49007-3760.* Tel: 616-349-7606.

Diocesan Pilgrimages—Rev. ROBERT F. CREAGAN, Diocesan Coord., *150 Taylor St., Coldwater, 49036.* Tel: 517-278-2650; Fax: 517-278-5800.

Education—FRANK C. WIPPEL, Ed.D., Supt. of Schools; Sr. CONSTANCE FIFELSKI, O.P., Assoc. Supt., *215 N. Westnedge Ave., Kalamazoo, 49007-3760.* Tel: 616-349-6427. Rev. WILLIAM J. FITZGERALD, Consultant-Resource Person on Educational Matters, *92 Capital Ave., N.E., Battle Creek, 49017.* Tel: 616-968-6645.

Evangelization—Vacant, *215 N. Westnedge Ave., Kalamazoo, 49007-3760.* Tel: 616-349-7606.

Finance Council—Revs. EUGENE A. SEARS; DAVID C. ADAMS; ROBERT C. MORLINO; T. EDWARD CAREY, JR.; ED EDWARDS; ED KOWIESKI; DANIEL KUNITZER; JERRY B. LOVE; JOHN A. PANFIL; LEO A. SWIAT.

Holy Childhood Association—Mrs. EDNA CARLSON, Acting Dir., *215 N. Westnedge Ave., Kalamazoo, 49007-3760.* Tel: 616-349-8316.

Indian Ministry—Vacant.

Inner City Ministry—Sr. RITA SCHAFER, S.S.J.; Sr. ROSE LAMBERTZ, S.S.J., *Catholic Community Center, 589 Pearl St., Benton Harbor, 49022.* Tel: 616-926-6424.

Jail Ministry—Sr. MARILYN SULLIVAN, S.S.J., Coord., *215 N. Westnedge Ave., Kalamazoo, 49007-3760.* Tel: 616-349-8714.

Knights of Columbus—Rev. LEONARD A. BOGDAN, Diocesan Chaplain, *215 N. Westnedge Ave., Kalamazoo, 49007-3760.* Tel: 616-349-7974.

Marriage and Family Ministry, Office of—JOE SCHMITT, Dir. MARCELLA V. KELEMEN, Admin. Dir., *215 N. Westnedge Ave., Kalamazoo, 49007-3760.* Tel: 616-349-8000.

Ministry Formation—Sr. MARLENE HALPIN, O.P., Dir., *215 N. Westnedge Ave., Kalamazoo, 49007-3760.* Tel: 616-349-1444.

Ministry with Persons with Disabilities—ANN SHERZER, Dir., *215 N. Westnedge Ave., Kalamazoo, 49007-3760.* Tel: 616-349-7276.

Missions—Mrs. EDNA CARLSON, Acting Dir., *215 N. Westnedge Ave., Kalamazoo, 49007-3760.* Tel: 616-349-8316.

Natural Family Planning Center of Southwestern Michigan—MARY CULP, Exec. Dir., *165 N. Washington St., Battle Creek, 49017.* Tel: 616-964-9474.

Permanent Diaconate—Deacon JOHN DESTAZIO, Chm., *211 Church St., St. Joseph, 49085.* Tel: 616-983-1575; Fax: 616-983-1576.

Presbyteral Council—Vacant.

Priestly Life and Ministry Office—Rev. JAMES S. O'LEARY, Dir., *61 N. 23rd St., Battle Creek, 49015.* Tel: 616-962-0165; Fax: 616-962-5937.

Respect Life—Sr. SUSAN RIDLEY, O.P., Dir., *215 N. Westnedge Ave., Kalamazoo, 49007-3760.* Tel: 616-349-7260.

St. Vincent DePaul Society—Rev. LAWRENCE W. KROLL, Spiritual Advisor, *534 W. Kilgore Rd., Kalamazoo, 49008.* Tel: 616-345-4389.

Scouting Apostolate—Deacon JERRY MIX, Chap., *62012 Bayshore Dr., Sturgis, 49091.* Tel: 616-467-8100.

Spanish-Speaking Apostolate—(Bishop's Committee for Migrant Workers), *215 N. Westnedge Ave., Kalamazoo, 49007-3760.* Tel: 616-349-7769.

Pastoral Team for Spanish-Speaking Residents-Migrants—Revs. ROBERT E. FLICKINGER; GERMAN PEREZ DIAZ, *St. Mary Church, 209 S. Brown St., Paw Paw, 49079.* Tel: 616-657-4459; Fax: 616-657-4260.

Vocations—Rev. MICHAEL A. OSBORN, Dir., *215 N. Westnedge Ave., Kalamazoo, 49007-3760.* Tel: 616-349-7722.

Worship, Office of—DAVID J. REILLY, Dir., *215 N. Westnedge Ave., Kalamazoo, 49007-3760.* Tel: 616-349-7721.

Youth and Young Adult Ministry—LISA IRWIN, Dir., *215 N. Westnedge Ave., Kalamazoo, 49007-3760.* Tel: 616-349-4947.

Address communications for all other offices to Chancery, Diocese of Kalamazoo. *215 N. Westnedge Ave., Kalamazoo, 49007-3760;* Fax: 616-349-6440.

CLERGY, PARISHES, MISSIONS AND PAROCHIAL SCHOOLS

CITY OF KALAMAZOO
(Kalamazoo County)

1—ST. AUGUSTINE CATHEDRAL, Revs. Robert C. Morlino; Thomas Seidel, C.S.C.; A. Thomas Fernando (India).
Res., 542 W. Michigan Ave., 49007. Tel: 616-345-5147; Fax: 616-349-0166.
School—600 W. Michigan Ave., 49007. Tel: 616-349-1945.
Lay Teachers 20; Students 359.

2—ST. JOSEPH, Rev. Michael D. Hazard.
Res., 936 Lake St., 49001. Tel: 616-343-6256.
School—930 Lake St., 49001. Tel: 616-342-9441; Fax: 616-343-1214.
Lay Teachers 13; Students 200.

3—ST. MARY, Rev. Stephen E. Naas.
Res., 939 Charlotte Ave., 49001. Tel: 616-342-0621; Fax: 616-342-0677.
School—929 Charlotte Ave., 49001. Tel: 616-342-2884.
Sisters 1; Lay Teachers 11; Students 188.
Convent—Tel: 616-342-8826.

4—ST. MONICA, Revs. Lawrence W. Kroll; Brian L. Stanley.
Res., 534 W. Kilgore Rd., 49008. Tel: 616-345-4389; Fax: 616-345-5211.
School—530 W. Kilgore Rd., 49008. Tel: 616-345-2444; Fax: 616-345-8534.
Sisters of St. Joseph 1; Lay Teachers 22; Students 530.

5—ST. THOMAS MORE STUDENT PARISH, Revs. Kenneth W. Schmidt; Robert Gerl (LAN).
Office: 421 Monroe St., 49006. Tel: 616-381-8917; Fax: 616-381-0195.

OUTSIDE THE CITY OF KALAMAZOO

Albion, Calhoun Co., St. John the Evangelist, Rev. Gordon L. Greene.
Office: 879 Finley Dr., 49224-9712. Tel: 517-629-4532; Fax: 517-629-9140. [CEM]
School—1020 Irwin Ave., 49224-1507. Tel: 517-629-6132.
Lay Teachers 8; Students 165.

Allegan, Allegan Co., Blessed Sacrament, Rev. Jerome M. Heyman, O.S.A.
Res., 422 Hubbard St., 49010-1246. Tel: 616-673-4455; Fax: 616-673-5869. [CEM]
Church—110 Cedar St., 49010-1244.

Bangor, Van Buren Co., Sacred Heart of Jesus, Rev. Michael A. Osborn.
Res., 201 S. Walnut St., 49013. Tel: 616-427-7514; Fax: 616-427-5558.
Chapel—Grand Junction, St. Cyril. (Summer).

Battle Creek, Calhoun Co., St. Jerome, Rev. Paul J. Cummings (LAN).
Res., 229 Collier Ave., 49017. Tel: 616-968-2218; Fax: 616-968-2233.

St. Joseph, Rev. James S. O'Leary; Rt. Rev. John Logan, O.Praem. In res., Revs. Stanislaus A. Nowakowski; Donn J. Taylor.
Res., 61 N. 23rd St., 49015. Tel: 616-962-0165; Fax: 616-962-5937.
School—63 N. 24th St., 49015. Tel: 616-965-7749; Fax: 616-965-0790.
Lay Teachers 17; Students 313.

St. Philip, Rev. William J. Fitzgerald.
Office: 126 Capital Ave., N.E., 49017. Tel: 616-968-6645; Fax: 616-968-0632.
Res., 92 Capital Ave., N.E., 49017. [CEM]
School—20 Cherry St., 49017. Tel: 616-963-4935; Fax: 616-963-5590.
Lay Teachers 11; Students 138.

Benton Harbor, Berrien Co., St. John-St. Bernard, Rev. David C. Adams.
Res., 600 Columbus Ave., 49022. Tel: 616-925-2425; Fax: 616-925-4678. [CEM]
Catechesis/Religious Programs—220 Church St., St. Joseph, 49085. Tel: 616-983-7797.
Students 61.

St. Bernard. Merged with St. John, Benton Harbor.

St. John the Evangelist. Merged with St. Bernard, Benton Harbor.

Bridgman, Berrien Co., Our Lady Queen of Peace, Rev. Raymond J. Barth.
Res., 3903 Lake St., P.O. Box 747, 49106-0747. Tel: 616-465-6252; Fax: 616-465-4930.

Bronson, Branch Co., St. Mary's, Rev. Richard A. Fritz.
Res., 602 W. Chicago, 49028. Tel: 517-369-2120; Fax: 517-369-5101. [CEM]
School—204 Albers Rd., 49028. Tel: 517-369-4625; Fax: 517-369-1652.
Lay Teachers 9; Students 126.
Mission—Colon, St. Barbara.

Buchanan, Berrien Co., St. Anthony, Rev. Charles T. Page.
Res., 509 W. 4th St., 49107. Tel: 616-695-3863; Fax: 616-695-3864.
Mission—Berrien Springs, St. Gabriel, Tel: 616-471-2424.

Byron Center, Kent Co., St. Mary's Visitation, Rev. Richard L. Altine.
Res., 2459 146th Ave., 49315. Tel: 616-681-9701; Fax: 616-681-9919. [CEM]
School—2455 146th Ave., 49315. Tel: 616-681-9607.
Lay Teachers 7; Students 160.

Cassopolis, Cass Co., St. Ann, Rev. Donald G. Potts.
Res., 313 N. Broadway, P.O. Box 247, 49031. Tel: 616-445-3140.
Church—421 N. Broadway, P.O. Box 247, 49031. Tel: 616-445-3000; Fax: 616-445-5787.

Coldwater, Branch Co., St. Charles, Rev. Robert F. Creagan.
Res., 150 Taylor St., 49036. Tel: 517-278-2650; Fax: 517-278-5800.
Mission—Union City, Our Lady of Fatima, Tel: 517-741-7275.

Decatur, Van Buren Co., Holy Family, Deacon Bartholomew E. Connelly.
Res., 500 W. St. Mary Blvd., 49045. Tel: 616-423-3151; Fax: 616-423-7755.

Delton, Barry Co., St. Ambrose, Rev. Richard G. Valls, Sch.P.
Res., 11252 Floria Rd., 49046. Tel: 616-623-2490; Fax: 616-623-2498.
Mission—Lacey, Our Lady of Great Oak, Tel: 616-758-3636.

Dorr, Allegan Co., St. Stanislaus, Rev. James Vinh Le.
Res., 1871 136th Ave., 49323. Tel: 616-793-7268. [CEM]
School—1861 136th Ave., 49323. Tel: 616-793-7204.
Lay Teachers 7; Students 130.
Mission—Watson, Allegan Co., Sacred Heart. [CEM]

Douglas, Allegan Co., St. Peter, Rev. Edward L. Hamel, O.S.A.
Res., St. Peter's Dr., 49406. Tel: 616-857-7951; 857-8175.

Dowagiac, Cass Co., Holy Maternity of Mary, Rev. Leo A. Taubitz.
Res., 210 N. Front St., 49047. Tel: 616-782-2808. [CEM]

Edwardsburg, Cass Co., Our Lady of the Lake, Rev. David C. Otto.
Res., 24832 U.S. 12 E., 49112. Tel: 616-699-5870; Fax: 616-699-5474.

Gobles, Van Buren Co., St. Jude, Sr. Theresa V. MacIntyre, S.S.J., Pastoral Min.
Res., 405 S. State, Apt. 2, 49055. Tel: 616-628-4424.
Church—13809 N. M-40, 49055. Tel: 616-628-2219.

Gull Lake, Kalamazoo Co., St. Ann, Rev. Mark J. Vyverman.
Res., 12648 E. D Ave., Augusta, 49012. Tel: 616-731-4721; Fax: 616-731-4147.

Hartford, Van Buren Co., Immaculate Conception, Rev. Stanley T. Staniszewski (Poland).
Res., 63559 60th Ave., P.O. Box 185, 49057. Tel: 616-621-4106; Fax: 616-621-2138.

Hastings, Barry Co., St. Rose of Lima, Rev. Charles H. Fischer.
Res., 805 S. Jefferson Ave., 49058. Tel: 616-945-4246. [CEM]
School—707 S. Jefferson St., 49058. Tel: 616-945-3164.
Sisters of St. Joseph 1; Lay Teachers 6; Students 130.
Mission—Nashville, St. Cyril.

Marshall, Calhoun Co., St. Mary, Rev. James L. Barrett.
Res., 212 Hanover St., 49068. Tel: 616-781-3949; 781-7341; Fax: 616-781-3632. [CEM]

Mattawan, Van Buren Co., St. John Bosco, Rev. Bogdan Werra (Poland).
Res., 23830 Front Ave., 49071. Tel: 616-668-3312; Fax: 616-668-3313.
Mission—Marcellus, Cass Co., St. Margaret Mary.

Mendon, St. Joseph Co., St. Edward, Rev. Thomas A. Martin.
Res., 332 W. State, P.O. Box 368, 49072. Tel: 616-496-3525; Fax: 616-496-8640. [CEM]

New Buffalo, Berrien Co., St. Mary of the Lake, Rev. Thomas F. DeVita.
Res., 718 W. Buffalo St., 49117. Tel: 616-469-2637; Fax: 616-469-7393.
School—704 W. Merchant St., 49117. Tel: 616-469-1515; Fax: 616-469-7393.
Lay Teachers 8; Students 189.

Niles, Berrien Co., St. Mark, Rev. Joseph W. Koma, C.S.C.
Res., 3 N. 19th St., 49120. Tel: 616-683-8650; Fax: 616-683-9314.

St. Mary, Rev. Marion M. Kencik (Poland).
Res., 211 S. Lincoln Ave., 49120. Tel: 616-683-5087; Fax: 616-683-5089. [CEM]
School—217 S. Lincoln Ave., 49120. Tel: 616-683-9191.
Sisters 2; Lay Teachers 7; Students 124.
Convent—219 S. State St., 49120. Tel: 616-683-8630.

Otsego, Allegan Co., St. Margaret, Rev. Donald P. Klingler.
Res., 245 Court St., 49078. Tel: 616-694-6311; Fax: 616-694-5415. [CEM]
School—736 S. Farmer, 49078. Tel: 616-694-2951; Fax: 616-694-4520.
Lay Teachers 10; Students 147.

Parchment, Kalamazoo Co., St. Ambrose, Rev. John M. Steffey.
Res., 1628 E. G Ave., 49004. Tel: 616-385-4152; Fax: 616-385-2527.

Paw Paw, Van Buren Co., St. Mary, Revs. Robert E. Flickinger; German Perez-Diaz.
Res., 209 S. Brown St., 49079. Tel: 616-657-4459; Fax: 616-657-4260. [CEM]
School—508 Paw Paw St., 49079. Tel: 616-657-3750; Fax: 616-657-4260.
Lay Teachers 9; Students 99.

Pearl, Allegan Co., San Felipe de Jesus, Mr. Ricardo Martinez, Pastoral Admin.
Mailing Address: P.O. Box 588, Fennville, 49408. Tel: 616-561-5029.

Portage, Kalamazoo Co., St. Catherine of Siena, Revs. John J. Klobuka, S.M.; Lawrence A. Schoettelkotte, S.M.
Res., 1150 W. Centre St., 49002. Tel: 616-327-5962; Fax: 616-327-7266.

St. Joseph, Berrien Co., St. Joseph, Revs. Eugene A. Sears; James A. Morris. In res., Rev. Carl F. Peltz (STU).
Res., 211 Church St., 49085. Tel: 616-983-1575; Fax: 616-983-1576. [CEM]
Annex: Stevensville, 5353 S. Roosevelt Rd., 49085. Tel: 616-489-1074.

Silver Creek, Cass Co., Sacred Heart of Mary, Sr. Monica Marie Ruoff, S.S.J., Pastoral Min.
Mailing Address: 51841 Leach Rd., Dowagiac, 49047. Tel: 616-782-5740; Fax: 616-782-5692. [CEM]

South Haven, Van Buren Co., St. Basil, Rev. John E. Young.
Res., 513 Monroe Blvd., 49090. Tel: 616-637-2404; Fax: 616-637-8374.
School—94 Superior St., 49090. Tel: 616-637-3529; Fax: 616-639-1242.
Lay Teachers 9; Students 196.

Sturgis, St. Joseph Co., Holy Angels, Rev. Leon H. Pohl.
Res., 402 S. Nottawa St., 49091. Tel: 616-651-5200; Fax: 616-659-8366.
School—Tel: 616-651-2088.
Lay Teachers 10; Students 160.

Three Oaks, Berrien Co., St. Mary of the Assumption, Rev. Wilfrid A. Menard, C.S.C.
Res., 28 W. Ash St., 49128. Tel: 616-756-2041; Fax: 616-756-2212.
Mission—Sawyer, St. Agnes.

Three Rivers, St. Joseph Co., Immaculate Conception, Rev. Mathew K. Illikattil.
Res., 645 S. Douglas Ave., 49093. Tel: 616-273-8953; Fax: 616-273-2114.
School—601 S. Douglas Ave., 49093. Tel: 616-273-2085.
Lay Teachers 9; Students 171.
Mission—Centreville, St. Clare.

Vicksburg, Kalamazoo Co., St. Martin, Sr. Marjorie Manning, C.S.C., Pastoral Min.
Res., 5855 E. W Ave., 49097. Tel: 616-649-1629; Fax: 616-649-2877.

Watervliet, Berrien Co., St. Joseph, Rev. Donald A. Wieber.
Res., 179 Lucinda Ln., Box 157, 49098. Tel: 616-463-5470; Fax: 616-463-4642. [CEM]
School—Tel: 616-463-3941; Fax: 616-463-4525.
Lay Teachers 8; Students 204.

Wayland, Allegan Co., St. Therese, Rev. Gary W. Pamment.
Res., 128 Cedar St., 49348. Tel: 616-792-2138; 792-9315; Fax: 616-792-2908.
School—Tel: 616-792-2016.
Felician Sisters 2; Lay Teachers 4; Students 71.
SS. Cyril and Methodius, Sr. Marie Beaulac, S.S.J., Pastoral Min.
Church—150-131st Ave., 49348. Tel: 616-792-2889; Fax: 616-792-6244. [CEM]

White Pigeon, St. Joseph Co., St. Joseph, Sr. Maxine McGee, S.S.J., Pastoral Min.
Res., 16603 E. U.S. 12, P.O. Box 344, 49099-0344. Tel: 616-483-7621; Fax: 616-483-7891.

Chaplains of Public Institutions

BATTLE CREEK. *Veteran's Administration Hospital* 49016. Tel: 616-966-5600. Rev. Michael Stafford, O.S.B (PRO) Chap.

COLDWATER. *Camp Branch.* Rev. Robert F. Creagan, Volunteer Chap., St. Charles Church, 150 Taylor St., 49036. Tel: 517-278-2650; Fax: 517-278-5800.
Florence Crane Correctional Facility for Women. Rev. Robert F. Creagan, Volunteer Chap.
Lakeland Correctional Facility for Men. Rev. Robert F. Creagan, Volunteer Chap.

Absent on Leave:
Reverend Fathers—
Snyder, Daniel L.

Retired:
Reverend Fathers—
Atchison, Donald W, 5021 Gilread Shores, Bronson, MI 49028
Burger, Frank J., P.O. Box 143, Grand Junction, MI 49506
Consani, Robert E., St. John Bosco, 23830 Front St., Mattawan, MI 49071
Crenner, William A., 465 Gladys, Apt. J, Kalamazoo, MI 49002
Crowley, Charles J., 1516 Vassar Dr., Kalamazoo, MI 49001
Flynn, Francis J., St. Ann's Home, 2161 Leonard St., Grand Rapids, MI 49504
Ginther, Benjamin H., 1328 E. V.W. Ave., Box 10, Vicksburg, MI 49097
Grathwohl, John M., 2065 Arrowhead, Traverse City, MI 49686
Hengesbach, Julius L., 13599 Jason Rd., Portland, MI 48875
Limbert, William G., 11859 Marquette Dr., New Buffalo, MI 49117
Nowakowski, Stanislaus A., St. Joseph Church, 61 N. 23rd St., Battle Creek, MI 49015
O'Meara, James J., 2469 Beech Dr., Kawkawlin, MI 48631
Sonefeld, Raymond G., 814 Engleman St., Manistee, MI 49660
Spillane, Walter J., 63 Centennial Dr., #17, Norwood, MA 02062
Taylor, Donn J., 61 N. 23rd St., Battle Creek, MI 49015
Thachet, Joseph, House 21, Skyline Park Villas, Cherukode, Peyad, TVM 695-573 Kerala, India
Weller, Joseph W., P.O. Box 231, New Buffalo, MI 49117
White, Leroy E., 311 W. Flint St., Davison, MI 48423-1053
Wieber, Elmer F., 3317 N. Stewart, Tucson, AZ 85716
Woods, Lawrence H., 560 Cosmopolitan, Marshall, MI 49068

Permanent Deacons:
Aleman, Eugenio, Immaculate Conception, Hartford
Barbosa, Juan, San Felipe de Jesus, Pearl
Cardosa, Abraham, (BWN)
Connelly, Bart, Holy Family, Decatur; Immaculate Conception, Three Rivers
DeStazio, John F. (TOL), St. Joseph, St. Joseph
Fleckenstein, Richard, Cincinnati, OH
Herrera, Manuel, Grand Rapids
Janowski, Victor (CHI), St. Mary of the Lake, New Buffalo
Karmon, Douglas, Kalamazoo
Lazaga, Alfred C. (MI), St. Joseph, St. Joseph
Middleton, Allan, Clare
Mix, Jerome (CHI), Holy Angels, Sturgis
Patrick, Albert W., St. Philip, Battle Creek
Pellack, Robert (JOL), Immaculate Conception, Three Rivers
Ponce, Julian, Fresno, CA
Prendergast, John (RCK), St. Catherine of Siena, Portage
Provot, Alvin (DET), St. Charles, Coldwater
Rauner, James D. (FTW), St. Joseph, Watervliet
Rodriguez, Maximino, San Felipe de Jesus, Pearl
Smoker, Gerald J., St. Mary, Bronson
Van Dril, William (JOL), Blessed Sacrament, Allegan
Whitehouse, Howard (DET), St. Mary, Niles
Wilcox, Harry V., West Melbourne, FL
Zientarski, Raymond S., St. Mary of the Lake, New Buffalo

INSTITUTIONS LOCATED IN THE DIOCESE

[A] HIGH SCHOOLS, DIOCESAN

KALAMAZOO. *Msgr. Hackett Catholic Central High School*, 1000 W. Kilgore Rd., 49008. Tel: 616-381-2646; Fax: 616-381-3919. Mr. Donald T. White, Prin. Lay Teachers 25; Students 505.

BATTLE CREEK. *St. Philip Catholic Central High School*, 20 Cherry St., 49017. Tel: 616-963-4503; Fax: 616-963-5590. Mr. Mike Low, Prin. Sisters 1; Lay Teachers 13; Students 138.

ST. JOSEPH. *Lake Michigan Catholic Junior High and High School.* (Grades 7-12), 915 Pleasant St., 49085. Tel: 616-983-2511; Fax: 616-983-0883. Mr. Philip Brooks, Prin. Adrian Dominican Sisters of Immaculate Conception Province 1; Lay Teachers 22; Students 310.

[B] GRADE SCHOOLS, INTERPAROCHIAL

ST. JOSEPH. *Lake Michighan Catholic Schools.* (Grades PreK-6), 3165 Washington Ave., 49085. Tel: 616-429-0227; Fax: 616-429-1461. Mrs. Karla J. Cook, Prin. Lay Teachers 21; Students 390.

[C] CATHOLIC SOCIAL AGENCIES

KALAMAZOO. *Catholic Family Services*, 1819 Gull Rd., 49001. Tel: 616-381-9800; Fax: 616-381-2932. Mrs. Frances H. Denny, A.C.S.W., Exec. Dir.

[D] GENERAL HOSPITALS

KALAMAZOO. *Borgess Medical Center*, 1521 Gull Rd., 49001. Tel: 616-226-7000; Fax: 616-226-7396
For a complete listing, refer to the Hospitals section.

BATTLE CREEK. *Battle Creek Health System*, 300 North Ave., 49016. Tel: 616-966-8000; Fax: 616-966-8010
For a complete listing, refer to the Hospitals section.

DOWAGIAC. *Lee Memorial Hospital*, 420 W. High St., 49047. Tel: 616-782-8681; Fax: 616-782-7611
For a complete listing, refer to the Hospitals section.

[E] RESIDENCES OF PRIESTS AND BROTHERS

DOUGLAS. *Order of St. Augustine.* (Chicago Prov.), St. Peter Dr., 49406. Tel: 616-857-8175. Rev. Edward L. Hamel, O.S.A. Brothers 2.

PORTAGE. *Society of Mary.* (Cincinnati Prov.), 1150 W. Centre St., 49024. Revs. Bernard L. Horst, S.M.; John J. Klobuka, S.M.; Lawrence A. Schoettelkotte. Brothers 3.

[F] HOMES FOR SENIOR CITIZENS

KALAMAZOO. *Borgess Nursing Home*, 537 Chicago Ave., 49001. Tel: 616-382-2392; Fax: 616-382-0843
For a complete listing, refer to the Special Care Facilities section.

BATTLE CREEK. *Mercy Pavilion Skilled Nursing Home and Senior Care Residence*, 80 N. 20 St., 49015. Tel: 616-964-5400; Fax: 616-964-5559
For a complete listing, refer to the Special Care Facilities section.

DOWAGIAC. *Dowagiac Nursing Home*, 610 Uneta St., 49047. Tel: 616-782-3471
For a complete listing, refer to the Special Care Facilities section.

NAZARETH. *Dillon Complex for Independent Living, Inc.*, 49074. Tel: 616-342-0263
For a complete listing, refer to the Special Care Facilities section.

OTSEGO. *Otsego Senior Apts., Inc.*, Baraga Manor, 301 Washington St., 49078. Tel: 616-694-9711
For a complete listing, refer to the Special Care Facilities section.

[G] CONVENTS AND RESIDENCES FOR SISTERS

NAZARETH. *Motherhouse and Novitiate of the Sisters of St. Joseph*, 49074. Tel: 616-381-6290; Fax: 616-381-4909. Sr. Janet Fleischhacker, S.S.J., Pres. Congregation; Rev. Michael J. Howell, Chap. Sisters in the Community 346.

[H] NEWMAN CENTERS

KALAMAZOO. *Western Michigan University, Kalamazoo College-Kalamazoo Valley Community College*, St. Thomas More Student Parish, 421 Monroe St., 49006. Tel: 616-381-8917; Fax: 616-381-0195. Revs. Kenneth W. Schmidt; Robert Gerl (LAN); Sr. Sue McCrery, S.S.J., Pastoral Assoc.

[I] MISCELLANEOUS LISTINGS

KALAMAZOO. *Borgess Health Alliance, Inc.*, 1521 Gull Rd., 49001. Tel: 616-226-7001; Fax: 616-226-7396. Integrated Health Care System sponsored by the

Sisters of St. Joseph which operates Borgess Ambulatory Care, Inc., Borgess Foundation, Borgess Medical Center, Borgess Nursing Home, Inc., Borgess-Pipp Health Center, Dowagiac Nursing Home, Lee Memorial Hospital Corp., ProMed Healthcare, Inc., and Western Nephrology Services, Inc. Incorporated in the State of Michigan. Mr. Timothy R. Stack, Pres.; Mr. Bryan Dunlop, M.D., Treas.; Sr. Judy A. Schroeder, S.S.J., Sec.

Diocesan Council of St. Vincent dePaul, 7959 Deerpath Rd., 49009. Tel: 616-375-3736. James Smolinski, Pres.

Kalamazoo Regional Catholic Schools Foundation, 1000 W. Kilgore Rd., 49008. Tel: 616-381-2646; Fax: 616-381-3919.

Secular Franciscan Order, 2903 E. Main St., 49001. Tel: 616-342-0989. Mr. Lawrence Verdon, Spiritual Asst.

BATTLE CREEK. *BCACS Foundation, Inc.*, 63 N. 24th St., 49015. Tel: 616-963-1131; Fax: 616-963-3917.

HASTINGS. *St. Rose Lima Trust Fund*, 805 S. Jefferson St., 49058. Tel: 616-945-4246.

ST. JOSEPH. *Twin-City Area Catholic School Fund, Inc.*, 220 Church St., 49085. Tel: 616-983-5529.

SOUTH HAVEN. *St. Basil Educational Endowment Fund*, 94 Superior St., 49090. Tel: 616-637-3529.

STURGIS.

**Holy Angels School Foundation, Inc.*, P.O. Box 24, 49091-0024. Tel: 616-467-8114.

RELIGIOUS INSTITUTES OF MEN REPRESENTED IN THE DIOCESE

For further details refer to the corresponding bracketed number in the Religious Institutes of Men or Women section.

[0140]—*The Augustinians.*—O.S.A.

[0200]—*Benedictine Monks.*—O.S.B.

[0900]—*Canons Regular of Premontre.*—O.Praem.

[1040]—*Piarist Fathers.*—Sch.P.

[0610]—*Priests of the Congregation of the Holy Cross.* (Indiana Prov.).—C.S.C.

[0760]—*Society of Mary.* (Cincinnati Prov.).—S.M.

RELIGIOUS INSTITUTES OF WOMEN REPRESENTED IN THE DIOCESE

[1920]—*Congregation of the Sisters of the Holy Cross.*—C.S.C.

[1070-05]—*Dominican Sisters.*—O.P.

[1070-13]—*Dominican Sisters.*—O.P.

[1070-14]—*Dominican Sisters.*—O.P.

[1170]—*Felician Sisters.* (Livonia, MI).—C.S.S.F.

[2575]—*Sisters of Mercy of the Americas.*—R.S.M.

[3830-11]—*Sisters of St. Joseph.* (Nazareth, MI).—S.S.J.

[3840]—*Sisters of St. Joseph of Carondelet.* (St. Paul, MN).—C.S.J.

[3930]—*Sisters of St. Joseph of the Third Order of St. Francis.*—S.S.J.-T.O.S.F.

[3260]—*Sisters of the Precious Blood.* (Dayton, Ohio).—C.PP.S.

[2150]—*Sisters, Servants of the Immaculate Heart of Mary.* (Monroe, MI).—I.H.M.

NECROLOGY

† Nadrach, Adolph W., (Retired). —Died June 15, 1997.

† Palmer, Edwin G., Battle Creek, MI, St. Jerome. —Died Feb. 13, 1997.

† Stewart, Rev. Msgr. Dell F., Kalamazoo, MI, Chancellor-Diocese of Kalamazoo. —Died Feb. 27, 1997.

† Sulka, Stanley E., (Absent on Sick Leave). —Died June 6, 1997.

Archdiocese of Kansas City in Kansas

(Archidioecesis Kansanopolitana in Kansas)

Most Reverend

JAMES P. KELEHER, S.T.D.

Archbishop of Kansas City in Kansas; ordained April 12, 1958; appointed Bishop of Belleville October 23, 1984; consecrated December 11, 1984; transferred to Kansas City in Kansas September 8, 1993. *Office: 12615 Parallel Pkwy., Kansas City, KS, 66109.* Tel.: 913-721-1570.

Most Reverend

IGNATIUS J. STRECKER, D.D., S.T.D.

Former Archbishop of Kansas City in Kansas; ordained December 19, 1942; appointed Bishop of Springfield-Cape Girardeau April 7, 1962; consecrated June 20, 1962; transferred to Kansas City September 10, 1969; retired September 8, 1993. *Res., 3408 Minnesota Ave., Kansas City, KS, 66101.*

Most Reverend

MARION F. FORST, D.D.

Former Auxiliary Bishop of Kansas City in Kansas; ordained June 10, 1934; consecrated Bishop of Dodge City, March 24, 1960; installed April 5, 1960; resigned from Dodge City; appointed Auxiliary October 16, 1976; retired December 23, 1986. *Res., 759 Vermont Ave., Kansas City, KS, 66101.*

ESTABLISHED VICARIATE APOSTOLIC JULY 19, 1850. DIOCESE OF LEAVENWORTH ESTABLISHED MAY 22, 1877. SEE CHANGED TO KANSAS CITY IN KANSAS MAY 10, 1947; CREATED ARCHDIOCESE AUGUST 9, 1952.

Square Miles 12,524.

Comprises the following 21 Counties of Kansas: Anderson, Atchison, Brown, Coffey, Doniphan, Douglas, Franklin, Jackson, Jefferson, Johnson, Leavenworth, Linn, Lyon, Marshall, Miami, Nemaha, Osage, Pottawatomie, Shawnee, Wabaunsee and Wyandotte.

PATRONS OF THE DIOCESE: I. Blessed Virgin Mary (Immaculate Conception); II. St. John Baptist Vianney.

Catholic Chancery Offices: 12615 Parallel Pkwy., Kansas City, KS, 66109. Tel.: 913-721-1570; Fax: 913-721-1577.

E-mail address: archkck@compuserve.com

STATISTICAL OVERVIEW

Personnel	
Archbishop	1
Retired Archbishops	1
Retired Bishops	1
Abbots	1
Retired Abbots	2
Priests: Diocesan Active in Diocese	79
Priests: Active Outside Diocese	2
Priests: Diocesan in Foreign Missions	1
Priests: Retired, Sick or Absent	14
Number of Diocesan Priests	96
Religious Priests in Diocese	77
Ordinations:	
Diocesan Priests	1
Transitional Deacons	2
Total Brothers	20
Total Sisters	830
Parishes	
Parishes	119
With Resident Pastor:	
Resident Diocesan Priests	59
Resident Religious Priests	18
Without Resident Pastor:	
Administered by Priests	42
Professional Ministry Personnel:	
Sisters	22
Lay Ministers	69
Welfare	
Catholic Hospitals	3
Total Assisted	327,154
Health Care Centers	2
Total Assisted	13,375
Homes for the Aged	4
Total Assisted	575
Special Centers for Social Services	10
Total Assisted	15,245
Residential Care of Disabled	1
Total Assisted	200
Educational	
Diocesan Students in Other Seminaries	11
Students Religious	2
Total Seminarians	13
Colleges and Universities	3
Total Students	2,430
High Schools, Diocesan and Parish	5
Total Students	3,085
High Schools, Private	2
Total Students	337
Elementary Schools, Diocesan and Parish	40
Total Students	11,672
Elementary Schools, Private	1
Total Students	40
Catechesis/Religious Education:	
High School Students	2,724
Elementary Students	14,396
Total Students Under Catholic Instruction	34,697
Teachers in the Diocese:	
Priests	1
Brothers	1
Sisters	59
Lay Teachers	977
Vital Statistics	
Receptions into the Church:	
Infant Baptism Totals	3,675
Adult Baptism Totals	429
Received into Full Communion	588
First Communions	3,568
Confirmations	2,877
Marriages:	
Catholic	713
Interfaith	511
Total Marriages	1,224
Deaths	1,337
Total Catholic Population	188,704
Total Population	952,000

Predecessors—Rt. Rev. J. B. MIEGE, S.J., cons. Bishop of Messenia, Vicar-Apostolic, March 25, 1851 resignation accepted by Pope Pius IX Nov. 8, 1874; died July 21, 1884.—Rt. Rev. LOUIS M. FINK, D.D., O.S.B., cons. Bishop of Eucarpia June 11, 1871; appt. first Bishop of Leavenworth May 22, 1877; died March 17, 1904.—Rt. Rev. THOMAS F. LILLIS, O.D., cons. Bishop of Leavenworth, Dec. 27, 1904; appt. Coadjutor Bishop of Kansas City, with right of succession March 14, 1910; succeeded to the See of Kansas City, Feb. 21, 1913.—Rt. Rev. JOHN WARD, D.D., ord. July 17, 1884; appt. Bishop of Leavenworth Nov. 25, 1910; cons. Feb. 22, 1911; died April 20, 1929.—Most Rev. FRANCIS JOHANNES, D.D., LL.D., cons. May 1, 1928; succeeded to the See, April 20, 1929; died March 13, 1937.—Most Rev. PAUL C. SCHULTE, D.D., ord. June 11, 1915; appt. Bishop of Leavenworth May 29, 1937; cons. Sept. 21, 1937; appt. Archbishop of Indianapolis July 20, 1946; installed Oct. 10, 1946.—Most Rev. GEORGE J. DONNELLY, S.T.D., ord. June 12, 1921; appt. Titular Bishop of Coela and Auxiliary of St. Louis March 19, 1940; cons. April 23, 1940; appt. Bishop of Leavenworth Nov. 9, 1946; died Dec. 13, 1950.—Most Rev. EDWARD J. HUNKELER, D.D., ord. June 14, 1919; appt. Bishop of Grand Island March 10, 1945; cons. May 1, 1945; transferred to Kansas City March 28, 1951; elevated to Archiepiscopal dignity Aug. 9, 1952; retired Sept. 10, 1969; died Oct. 1, 1970.—Most Rev. IGNATIUS J. STRECKER, D.D., S.T.D., ord. Dec. 19, 1942; appt. Bishop of Springfield-Cape Girardeau April 7, 1962; cons. June 20, 1962; transferred to Kansas City Sept. 10, 1969; retired Sept. 8, 1993.

Catholic Chancery Offices—12615 Parallel, Kansas City, 66109. Tel: 913-721-1570; Fax: 913-721-1577. Office Hours: 9-5.

Vicars General—Revs. CHARLES MCGLINN; THOMAS TANK.

Chancellor—Rev. THOMAS TANK.

Metropolitan Tribunal—12615 Parallel, Kansas City, 66109. Tel: 913-721-1570; Fax: 913-721-1577.

Judicial Vicar—Rev. PHILIP KENDALL, C.S.V., J.C.D.

Pro-Synodal Judges—Revs. PHILIP E. KENDALL, C.S.V., J.C.D.; GEORGE BERTELS, J.C.L.

Defenders of the Bond—Rev. GARY APPLEGATE, J.C.L.; Rev. Msgr. ROBERT BERGMAN, J.C.D.

Advocates—Selected priests, Sr. MARY ANN BARTOLAK, S.C.L.,selected Lay Advocates.

Director Notary—JOAN DEBAUGE.

Archdiocesan Consultors—Revs. RAYMOND DAVERN; THOMAS TANK; Rt. Rev. BARNABAS SENECAL, O.S.B.; Revs. FRANCIS KRISCHE; CHARLES MCGLINN; NORBERT LICKTEIG; TERRENCE CYR, O.Carm.

Archdiocesan Council on Finances—Rev. THOMAS TANK, Chancellor; Mr. RICHARD ANDERSON; Mr. JERRY MAYNE; Mr. FRANK SABATINI; Mr. JAMES J. OWENS; Mr. JOHN MEGHINI.

Archdiocesan Finance Officer—JAMES J. OWENS.

Regional Pastoral Leaders—Atchison: Rev. GERARD SENECAL, O.S.B., Emporia: Rev. MARK MERTES, Johnson Co.: Rev. CHARLES MCGINN, Lawrence: Rev. JAMES SHAUGHNESSY, Leavenworth: Rev. GARY APPLEGATE,

Nortonville: Rev. RONALD CORNISH, Topeka: Rev. PATRIC RILEY, Garnett: Rev. EARL DEKAT, Nemah-Marshall: Rev. RODERIC GILLER, O.S.B., St. Mary's: Rev. JOHN REYNOLDS, Wyandotte Co.: Rev. RAYMOND DAVERN.

Archdiocesan Administrative Team—Mrs. CATHERINE COGHLAN; Rev. CHARLES MCGLINN; Mr. BLAKE MULVANY; Mr. JAMES J. OWENS; Mr. DANIEL POPE; Rev. THOMAS TANK.

Catholic Foundation of Northeast Kansas—12615 Parallel, Kansas City, 66109.

Catholic Education Foundation—12615 Parallel, Kansas City, 66109.

Minister to Priests—Rev. JAMES WHITE, S.J., *12600 Hollingsworth Rd., Kansas City, 66109.* Tel: 913-721-3966.

Archdiocesan Archivist—Rev. LEO COOPER.

Archdiocesan Offices and Directors

Savior of the World Pastoral Center—12601 Parallel, Kansas City, 66109. Tel: 913-721-1097.

Black Catholics—REGINA BARGER, Dir., *2203 Parallel, Kansas City, 66104.* Tel: 913-321-1958.

Department of Parish Ministries—Rev. THOMAS TANK, Dir., *12615 Parallel Pkwy., Kansas City, 66109.* Tel: 913-721-1570.

Adult Spirituality/RCIA—Sr. ELEANOR SUTHER.

Deaf—Sr. ANN ALBRECHT.

Family Life—Mrs. JACKI CORRIGAN.

Liturgy—Rev. FRANCIS HUND; Mr. MICHAEL PODREBAREC.

Peace and Justice—Sr. BARBARA MCCRACKEN.

Religious Education—Mrs. JEANNE BRADY.

Youth—Mr. LAWRENCE LIVINGSTON.

Stewardship and Development Office—CATHERINE COGHLAN, Dir., *12615 Parallel, Kansas City, 66109.* Tel: 913-721-1570.

Apostleship of Prayer—Rev. FRANK SCHEPERS, *St. John the Baptist Parish, Greely, 66033.* Tel: 913-867-3120.

Catholic Youth Organization—DAVE NICK, Athletic Dir., *5041 Reinhardt Dr., P.O. Box 721, Shawnee Mission, 66201.* Tel: 913-384-7377.

Catholic Charities—DANIEL POPE, Dir., *2220 Central Ave., Kansas City, 66102.* Tel: 913-621-1504.

Council for Catholic Charismatic Renewal—Rev. MARK MERTES.

Catholic Community Service—2220 Central Ave., Kansas City, 66102. Tel: 913-621-1504.

Communications—12615 Parallel, Kansas City, 66109. Tel: 913-721-1570.

Catholic Scouts—Rev. JOHN REYNOLDS, Chap.

Hispanic Ministry—Revs. DANIEL GARDNER; MICHAEL HERMES; RAMON GAITAN, O.A.R.

Holy Childhood Association—Rev. NORBERT LICKTEIG, *12615 Parallel, Kansas City, 66109.* Tel: 913-721-1570.

Hospitals—Rev. JEREMIAS L. SPENCER, Dir., *16 S. Iowa, Kansas City, 66101.*

Kansas Catholic Conference—ROBERT RUNNELS, Exec. Dir., *6301 Antioch, Shawnee Mission, 66202.* Tel: 913-722-6633.

Legion of Mary—Rev. ROBERT BURGER, Dir., *8311 W. 93rd, Overland Park, 66212.*

Missions—Rev. NORBERT LICKTEIG, *12615 Parallel, Kansas City, 66109.*

Newspaper "The Leaven"—Rev. MARK GOLDASICH, Editor, *12615 Parallel, Kansas City, 66109.* Tel: 913-721-1570; Fax: 913-721-5276.

Nurses Association—Rev. JEREMIAS L. SPENCER, Dir., *16 S. Iowa, Kansas City, 66103.*

Priests' Council—Rev. NORBERT LICKTEIG, Chm.

Propagation of the Faith—Rev. NORBERT LICKTEIG, *12615 Parallel, Kansas City, 66109.*

Respect Life—DANIEL POPE, Coord. REBECCA MESSALL, Dir.

Schools—BLAKE MULVANY, Supt. VINCENT WEISS, Assoc. Supt., *12615 Parallel, Kansas City, 66109.* Tel: 913-721-1570.

Vocations Office—Directors: Revs. DENNIS SCHMITZ; MICHAEL MULLEN, *12615 Parallel, Kansas City, 66109.* Tel: 913-721-1570.

CLERGY, PARISHES, MISSIONS AND PAROCHIAL SCHOOLS

CITY OF KANSAS CITY
(Wyandotte County)

1—CATHEDRAL OF ST. PETER THE APOSTLE, Revs. Thomas Tank; Philip Kendall, C.S.V.; Steven Beseau.
Res., 409 N. 15th St., 66102. Tel: 913-371-2345.
Business Office: 431 N. 15th St., 66102. Tel: 913-371-0840.
School—422 N. 14th, 66102. Tel: 913-371-2151; Fax: 913-371-1014.
Lay Teachers 20; Students 265.
Child Care Center—424 N. 15th St., 66102. Tel: 913-342-5235.

2—BLESSED SACRAMENT, Rev. William McEvoy.
Res., 2203 Parallel Ave., 66104. Tel: 913-321-1958; Fax: 913-321-1997.

3—CHRIST THE KING, Rev. Raymond J. Davern.
Res., 3024 N. 53rd St., 66104. Tel: 913-287-8823; Fax: 913-287-8711.
School—3027 N. 54th St., 66104. Tel: 913-287-8883; Fax: 913-287-7409.
Lay Teachers 18; Students 264.

4—HOLY FAMILY (Slovene), Rev. Msgr. Heliodore Mejak.
Res., 274 Orchard Ave., 66101. Tel: 913-371-1561.
School—St. John and Holy Family. (Consolidated). See separate listing under St. John the Baptist. Tel: 913-371-3923.

5—HOLY NAME, Rev. Jeremiah L. Spencer.
Res., 16 S. Iowa St., 66103. Tel: 913-236-9219.
School—1007 S.W. Blvd., 66103. Tel: 913-722-1032; Fax: 913-722-4175.
Lay Teachers 8; Students 133.

6—SACRED HEART. Attended by St. John the Evangelist, Kansas City. Rev. Charles Andalikiewicz.
Res., 2910 Strong Ave., 66106. Tel: 913-677-4621.
School—Our Lady of Unity. See separate listing. Tel: 913-262-7022; Fax: 913-262-7836.

7—OUR LADY AND ST. ROSE. Attended by Blessed Sacrament, Kansas City.
Mailing Address: 2203 Parallel, 66104.
Church—2300 N. Eighth St., 66101. Tel: 913-321-1958; Fax: 913-321-1997.

8—ST. MARY-ST. ANTHONY, Rev. Matt J. Horvat. In res., Rev. Dennis Wait.
Res., 615 N. Seventh St., 66101. Tel: 913-371-1408.

9—SS. CYRIL AND METHODIUS (Slovak). Attended by St. Joseph-St. Benedict, Kansas City. Rev. Wilfred Fangman, O.S.B.
Res., 801 Vermont, 66101. Tel: 913-371-3549; Fax: 913-621-2709.

10—ST. JOHN THE BAPTIST (Croatian), Rev. Francis Horvat.
Res., 708 N. Fourth St., 66101. Tel: 913-371-0627.
School—St. John the Baptist and Holy Family. (Consolidated) 515 Ohio, 66101. Tel: 913-321-0649; 371-3923; Fax: 913-321-0649.
Lay Teachers 13; Students 164.

11—ST. JOHN THE DIVINE (Mexican). (Stational Church).

12—ST. JOHN THE EVANGELIST, Rev. Charles Andalikiewicz.
Res., 2910 Strong Ave., 66106. Tel: 913-677-4621.
School—Our Lady of Unity. Consolidated with Sacred Heart. See separate listing for further details.

13—ST. JOSEPH AND ST. BENEDICT, Revs. Wilfred Fangman, O.S.B.; Michael Hermes.
Res., 801 Vermont Ave., 66101. Tel: 913-371-1837; Fax: 913-621-2709.
School—All Saints. (Consolidated). See separate listing.

14—ST. PATRICK'S, Revs. Michael Mullen; Harold Wickey, Senior Assoc.
Res., 1086 N. 94th St., 66112. Tel: 913-299-3370.
School—1066 N. 94th, 66112. Tel: 913-299-8131; Fax: 913-299-2845.
Sisters 1; Lay Teachers 23; Students 350.

15—ST. THOMAS THE APOSTLE. Closed. For inquiries for parish records contact the Chancery.

OUTSIDE THE CITY OF KANSAS CITY

Alma, Wabaunsee Co., Holy Family. Attended by Paxico. Rev. John C. Reynolds.
Church—66401. Tel: 785-765-3545; Fax: 785-636-5538.

Atchison, Atchison Co., St. Benedict's, Rev. Donald Redmond, O.S.B.
Res., 1001 N. Second St., 66002. Tel: 913-367-0671; Fax: 913-367-0797. [JC]
School—Atchison Catholic Elementary. (Consolidated). See separate listing.
Sacred Heart, Rev. Donald Redmond, O.S.B.
Res., 1503 Kansas Ave., 66002. Tel: 913-367-0387. [JC]
School—Atchison Catholic Elementary. (Consolidated). See separate listing.
St. Joseph's, Rev. Gerard Senecal, O.S.B.
Res., 705 Spring Garden St., 66002. Tel: 913-367-4271. [JC]
School—Atchison Catholic Elementary. (Consolidated). See separate listing.

Axtell, Marshall Co., St. Michael's, Rev. Thomas H. Dolezal.
Mailing Address: P.O. Box K, 66403. Tel: 785-736-2220; Fax: 785-736-2230.
School—Tel: 785-736-2257.
Lay Teachers 3; Students 40.

Baileyville, Nemaha Co., Sacred Heart, Rev. Albert J. Fey, C.PP.S.
Church—Box 36, 66404. Tel: 785-336-6464.

Baldwin, Douglas Co., Annunciation. Attended by Assumption, Edgerton. Rev. Phillip Winkelbauer.
Church—P.O. Box 293, 66006. Tel: 913-594-3700. [CEM]

Basehor, Leavenworth Co., Holy Angels, Rev. Edwin P. Watson, O.S.B., Admin.
Res., 15440 Leavenworth Rd., Box 295, 66007. Tel: 913-724-3122 (Res.); 724-1665 (Church); Fax: 913-724-3122. [CEM]

Beattie, Marshall Co., St. Malachy's. Attended by St. Gregory, Marysville. Rev. George Bertels.
Church—1012 Main St., 66406. Tel: 785-353-2280.

Bendena, Doniphan Co., St. Benedict's. Attended by St. Joseph, Wathena. Rev. Daniel P. McCarthy, O.S.B.
Church—Rte. #1, Box 128, 66008. Tel: 913-359-6725; Fax: 913-989-2313. [CEM]

Blaine, Pottawatomie Co., St. Columbkille. Attended by St. Vincent de Paul, Onaga. Rev. Jude Burbach, O.S.B.
Church—66480.

Blue Rapids, Marshall Co., St. Elizabeth. Attended by Annunication, Frankfort. Rev. Bernard Mullen, C.PP.S.

Bonner Springs, Wyandotte Co., Sacred Heart, Rev. Patrick Jerome.
Res., 103 E. Insley, 66012. Tel: 913-422-5700; Fax: 913-422-5723.
School—216 Alcutt, 66012. Tel: 913-422-5520.
Lay Teachers 9; Students 160.

Burlington, Coffey Co., St. Francis Xavier's, Rev. Kenneth W. Kelly.
Res., 214 Juniatta, 66839. Tel: 316-364-2416; Fax: 316-364-2416. [CEM]

Corning, Nemaha Co., St. Patrick's. Attended by St. Mary's, St. Benedict. Rt. Rev. Owen Purcell, O.S.B. Tel: 785-336-3174.
Res., St. Mary, R.R. 1, Box 59, Seneca, 66538. Tel: 785-868-2790.

Delia, Jackson Co., Sacred Heart of Jesus. Unassigned. (Stational Church).

Doniphan, Doniphan Co., St. John's. Unassigned. (Stational Church).

Easton, Leavenworth Co., St. Lawrence's, Rev. David Rabe, Admin.
Res., P.O. Box 129, 66020. Tel: 913-773-5712.

Edgerton, Johnson Co., Assumption of the Blessed Virgin Mary, Rev. Phillip J. Winkelbauer.
Church—P.O. Box 74, 66021. Tel: 913-893-6272.

Effingham, Atchison Co., St. Ann's, Rt. Rev. Ralph Koehler, O.S.B.
Res., 301 William, Box 54, 66023. Tel: 913-833-5660.

Emerald, Anderson Co., St. Patrick's. Attended by St. Francis Xavier, Burlington. Rev. Kenneth W. Kelly.
Church—Williamsburg P.O., 66095. Tel: 316-364-2416; Fax: 316-364-2416.

Emmett, Pottawatomie Co., Holy Cross. Attended by Immaculate Conception, St. Marys. Rev. Carl M. Dekat.

Emporia, Lyon Co., Sacred Heart, Rev. Peter O'Sullivan.
Res., 101 Cottonwood St., 66801. Tel: 316-342-1061. [CEM]
School—102 Cottonwood St., 66801. Tel: 316-343-7394; Fax: 316-343-7394.
Lay Teachers 12; Students 196.
Rectory—123 Cottonwood St., 66801. Tel: 316-342-3328.
St. Catherine's. Attended by Sacred Heart, Paxico.
Church—205 S. Lawrence St., 66801. Tel: 316-342-1061. [CEM]

Eskridge, Wabaunsee Co., St. John Vianney's. Attended by Sacred Heart, Paxico. Rev. John C. Reynolds.

Eudora, Douglas Co., Holy Family, Rev. Paul W. Miller.
Res., P.O. Box H, 66025-0808. Tel: 785-542-2788. [CEM]

Fidelity, Brown Co., St. Augustine's. Attended by Sacred Heart, Sabetha. Rev. Emeric Fletcher, O.S.B.

Flush, Pottawatomie Co., St. Joseph's. Attended by St. Bernard, Wamego. Rev. Thomas N. Hesse Tel: 785-494-8234.

Fort Leavenworth, Leavenworth Co., St. Ignatius Chapel, Rev. Gregory Sykes, Military Services Army Chap. [Natl. CEM].
Res., 709 Bittersweet Ct., Lansing, 66043. Tel: 913-684-3000.
Church—66027.

Frankfort, Marshall Co., Annunciation, Rev. Bernard Mullen, C.PP.S.
Res., 213 E. Fifth St., 66427. Tel: 913-292-4462.

Gardner, Johnson Co., Sacred Heart, Rev. Gerald E. Sheeds.
Res., 122 E. Warren, 66030. Tel: 913-856-7781. [CEM]

Garnett, Anderson Co., Holy Angels, Rev. George A. Matz.
Res., 514 E. Fourth, 66032. Tel: 785-448-3846.
School—530 E. Fourth, 66032. Tel: 785-448-3423.
Sisters 2; Lay Teachers 4; Students 41.

Greeley, Anderson Co., St. John the Baptist's, In res., Rev. Frank Schepers.
Res., 66033. Tel: 785-867-3120. [CEM]
School—Tel: 785-867-2680.
Ursuline Sisters 1; Lay Teachers 4; Students 41.

Hartford, Lyon Co., St. Mary's. Attended by St. Joseph's, Olpe. Rev. Mark Mertes.

Hiawatha, Brown Co., St. Ann's, Rev. Terence Sullivan, O.S.B.
Res., 800 Hiawatha Ave., 66434. Tel: 785-742-3010.

Holton, Jackson Co., St. Dominic's, Rev. Ronald Cornish.
Res., 416 Ohio Ave., 66436. Tel: 913-364-3262. [CEM]

Horton, Brown Co., St. Leo's, Rev. Keith Lunsford.
Res., 1340 First Ave. E., 66439. Tel: 785-486-3971; Fax: 785-486-2402. [CEM 3]

Kelly, Nemaha Co., St. Bede's (1901). Attended by St. Mary, St. Benedict. Rt. Rev. Owen Purcell, O.S.B.
Tel: 785-336-3174. [CEM]
Catechesis/Religious Programs—Students 96.

LaCygne, Linn Co., Our Lady of Lourdes. Attended by St. Philip Neri, Osawatomie.
Church—66040.

Lansing, Leavenworth Co., St. Francis de Sales, Rev. Michael C. Stubbs.
Res., 119 Woodland Rd., 66043. Tel: 913-727-3768.
Church—900 Ida St., 66043. Tel: 913-727-3742; Fax: 913-727-3742.

Lapeer, Douglas Co., St. Francis. Attended by St. Patrick, Osage City. Rev. Michael Mulvany. [CEM]

Lawrence, Douglas Co., Corpus Christi, Rev. James E. Shaughnessy.
Church & Office: 1100 Kasold Dr., 66049. Tel: 785-843-6286; Fax: 785-865-3933.
Res., 3209 Harvard Rd., 66049. Tel: 785-749-4724.
St. John the Evangelist, Rev. Charles Polifka, O.F.M.Cap.
Res., 1229 Vermont St., 66044. Tel: 785-843-0109; Fax: 785-749-5064. [CEM]
School—Tel: 785-843-9511; Fax: 785-843-7143.
Sisters of Charity of Leavenworth 1; Lay Teachers 15; Students 303.

Leavenworth, Leavenworth Co.,

1—Immaculate Conception. (Old Cathedral). Revs. Terrence Cyr, O.Carm.; Fergus Lickteig, O.Carm.
Office: 747 Osage, 66048. Tel: 913-682-3953; Fax: 913-682-5599.
Church—Fifth & Kiowa St., 66048. Tel: 913-682-3953.
School—Xavier Elementary. (Consolidated). See separate listing.
Rectory, 300 N. Broadway, 66048. Tel: 913-682-0809.

2—Sacred Heart of Jesus, Rev. Gary Applegate.
Res., 1401 Second Ave., 66048. Tel: 913-772-1787.
School—Xavier Elementary. (Consolidated). See separate listing.

3—St. Casimir's, (Polish), Rev. Gary Applegate.
Res., 1401 Second Ave., 66048. Tel: 913-772-1787. [JC]
School—Xavier Elementary. (Consolidated). See separate listing.

4—St. Joseph's, Revs. Terrence Cyr, O.Carm; Fergus Lickteig, O.Carm.
Office: 747 Osage, 66048. Tel: 913-682-3953; 682-0809 (Res.); Fax: 913-682-5599.
School—Xavier Elementary. (Consolidated). See separate listing.

5—St. Joseph of the Valley. Attended by St. Lawrence, Easton. Rev. David Rabe, Admin.
Church—R.R. #3, 66048.

Leawood, Johnson Co., Church of the Nativity, Revs. Alfred Rockers; Michael Hawken.
Church—3800 W. 119th St., 66209. Tel: 913-491-5017; Fax: 913-491-5065.
School—3700 W. 119th St., 66209. Tel: 913-338-4330; Fax: 913-338-4331.
Lay Teachers 33; Students 624.
Cure of Ars, Revs. Charles McGlinn; Peter Jaramillo.
Res., 9401 Mission Rd., 66206. Tel: 913-649-1337; Fax: 913-649-1339.
School—9403 Mission Rd., 66206. Tel: 913-648-2620; Fax: 913-648-3810.
Lay Teachers 27; Students 587.
Vianney Center for Ministries—Tel: 913-649-8625; Fax: 913-649-1339.

Lenexa, Johnson Co., Holy Trinity, Revs. Raymond Burger; Robert Burger.
Office: 13520 W. 92nd St., 66215. Tel: 913-888-2770; Fax: 913-438-2572.
School—13600 W. 92nd St., 66215. Tel: 913-888-3250; Fax: 913-888-4403.
Lay Teachers 35; Students 715.

Lillis, Marshall Co., St. Joseph's (Frankfort). Attended by St. Vincent de Paul, Onaga. Rev. Jude Burbach, O.S.B.
Tel: 785-889-4896. [CEM]

Louisburg, Miami Co., Immaculate Conception, Rev. Stanley J. Loncarcic.
Res., Box 118, 66053. Tel: 913-837-2295. [CEM]

Marysville, Marshall Co., St. Gregory's, Rev. George Bertels.
Res., 204 N. 13th, 66508. Tel: 785-562-3302; Fax: 785-562-4039.
School—207 N. 14th, 66508. Tel: 785-562-2831; Fax: 785-562-4039.
Lay Teachers 7; Students 130.

Mayetta, Jackson Co., St. Francis Xavier. Attended by St. Dominic, Holton. Rev. Ronald Cornish.
Tel: 785-364-3262.

Meriden, Jefferson Co., St. Aloysius. Attended by St. Theresa, Perry. Rev. Francis Hund.
Res., P.O. Box 364, 66512. Tel: 785-484-3312. [CEM]

Mission, Johnson Co., St. Pius X, Rev. Robert Hasenkamp.
Res., 5601 Woodson Ave., 66202. Tel: 913-432-4808; Fax: 913-432-4855.
School—5500 Woodson, 66202. Tel: 913-432-9355; Fax: 913-432-2086.
Sisters of St. Benedict 1; Lay Teachers 12; Students 268.

Mooney Creek, Jefferson Co., Corpus Christi. Attended by St. Lawrence, Easton. Rev. David Rabe, Admin.
Mailing Address: P.O. Box 129, Easton, 66020. Tel: 913-773-5712.

Mound City, Linn Co., Sacred Heart Shrine to St. Philippine Duchesne. Attended by St. Philip Neri, Osawatomie. Rev. Joseph Cramer.
Res., 66056. Tel: 913-795-2724.

Nortonville, Jefferson Co., St. Joseph's, Rev. Thomas Cawley, C.M.
Res., 221 N. Sycamore St., 66060. Tel: 913-886-2030. [CEM]
School—Tel: 913-886-3510.
Sisters 1; Lay Teachers 1; Students 26.

Olathe, Johnson Co., St. Paul's, Rev. Charles T. McGinn. Office: 832 Larkspur, 66061. Tel: 913-764-0323.
Res., 840 Larkspur, 66061. Tel: 913-782-6062; Fax: 913-764-0323. [CEM]
School—Tel: 913-764-0619; Fax: 913-764-0619.
Lay Teachers 14; Students 196.
Prince of Peace, Revs. Frank Burger; Gerald Volz.
Res., 14229 Cottonwood Dr., 66062. Tel: 913-782-8864; Fax: 913-780-9658.
School—16000 W. 143rd St., 66062. Tel: 913-764-0650.
Sisters 4; Lay Teachers 22; Students 497.

Olpe, Lyon Co., St. Joseph's, Rev. Mark Mertes.
Res., P.O. Box 165, 66865. Tel: 316-475-3326. [CEM]
School—Tel: 316-475-3416.
Lay Teachers 6; Students 60.

Onaga, Pottawatomie Co., St. Vincent de Paul, Rev. Jude Burbach, O.S.B.
Res., Box 396, 66521. Tel: 785-889-4896.

Osage City, Osage Co., St. Patrick's, Rev. Michael Mulvany.
Res., 309 S. Sixth St., 66523. Tel: 785-528-3424; Fax: 785-528-3381. [CEM]

Osawatomie, Miami Co., St. Philip Neri, Rev. Joe Cramer.
Church—514 Parker Ave., 66064. Tel: 913-755-2652.
Chaplaincy—State Hospital for Mentally Ill, 66064.

Ottawa, Franklin Co., Sacred Heart, Rev. Tony Blaufuss.
Res., 409 S. Cedar St., 66067. Tel: 785-242-2174. [CEM]
School—426 S. Cedar, 66067. Tel: 785-242-4297.
Lay Teachers 7; Students 111.

Overland Park, Johnson Co.,

1—Church of the Ascension, Revs. Lawrence Albertson; Joseph Lopez.
Res., 9510 W. 127th St., 66213. Tel: 913-681-3348; Fax: 913-681-3517.
School—Tel: 913-851-2531; Fax: 913-851-2518.
Sisters 1; Lay Teachers 15; Students 251.

2—Holy Cross, Revs. Robert Pflumm; Timothy Haberkorn. In res., Rev. Msgr. Thomas Culhane.
Office: 8311 W. 93rd St., 66212. Tel: 913-381-2755; Fax: 913-381-2766.
Res., 8315 W. 93rd St., 66212. Tel: 913-341-5618.
School—8101 W. 95th, 66212. Tel: 913-381-7408; Fax: 913-381-1312.
Lay Teachers 25; Students 406.

3—Holy Spirit, Revs. Albert Hauser, O.S.B.; William A. Finnerty.
Res., 11300 W. 103rd St., 66214. Tel: 913-492-7318; Fax: 913-492-7370.
School—Tel: 913-492-2582.
Lay Teachers 25; Students 482.

4—Queen of the Holy Rosary, Rev. Ronald Livojevich.
Res., 7023 W. 71st St., 66204. Tel: 913-432-4616; Fax: 913-432-0620.
School—6915 W. 71st, 66204. Tel: 913-432-6350; Fax: 913-432-5081.
Lay Teachers 16; Students 202.

Paola, Miami Co., Holy Trinity, Rev. Earl Dekat.
Res., 505 E. Chippewa, 66071. Tel: 913-294-2067; Fax: 913-294-9286. [CEM]
School—Tel: 913-294-3286.
Lay Teachers 7; Students 111.

Paxico, Wabaunsee Co., Sacred Heart, Rev. John C. Reynolds.
Res., 66526. Tel: 785-636-5547; Fax: 785-636-5538. [CEM]

Perry, Jefferson Co., St. Theresa's, Rev. Francis Hund.
Res., 66073. Tel: 785-597-5656. [CEM]

Prairie Village, Johnson Co., St. Ann's, Rev. William M. Haegelin.
Res., 7231 Mission Rd., 66208. Tel: 913-362-2817; Fax: 913-362-2678.
School—7241 Mission Rd., 66208. Tel: 913-362-7008; Fax: 913-362-7059.
Lay Teachers 25; Students 536.

Purcell, Doniphan Co., St. Mary's (P.O. Huron, KS). Attended by St. Leo's, Horton. Rev. Keith Lunsford
Tel: 785-486-3971, Fax: 785-486-2402.

Reading, Lyon Co., Assumption. Closed. For inquiries for parish records contact the Chancery.

Richmond, Franklin Co., St. Therese. Attended by St. Boniface, Scipio. Rev. Clyde R. Ozminkowski, O.Carm.
Res., Rte. 1, Box 156, Garnett, 66032. Tel: 913-835-6273.

Roeland Park, Johnson Co., St. Agnes, Revs. Donald Cullen; John H. Wisner.
Res., 5250 Mission Rd., 66205. Tel: 913-262-2400; Fax: 913-262-1050.
School—5130 Mission Rd., 66205. Tel: 913-262-1686.
Lay Teachers 34; Students 468.

Rossville, Shawnee Co., St. Stanislaus. Attended by Immaculate Conception, St. Marys. Rev. Carl M. Dekat.

Sabetha, Nemaha Co., Sacred Heart, Rev. Emeric Fletcher, O.S.B.
Res., 1042 S. 14th, P.O. Box 244, 66534. Tel: 785-284-3068.

St. Benedict, Nemaha Co., St. Mary's, Rt. Rev. Owen Purcell, O.S.B.
Res., R.R. 1, Box 59, Seneca, 66538. Tel: 785-336-3174. [CEM]

St. Louis, Atchison Co., St. Louis. Attended by St. Ann's, Effingham. Rt. Rev. Ralph Koehler, O.S.B.
Mailing Address: c/o St. Ann's, 301 William, Box 54, Effingham, 66023. Tel: 913-833-5660.
Church—11321 Morton Rd., Atchison, 66002. Tel: 913-847-6849.

St. Marys, Pottawatomie Co., Immaculate Conception, Rev. Carl M. Dekat.
Res., 208 W. Bertrand, 66536. Tel: 785-437-2408. [CEM]

St. Patrick, Atchison Co., St. Patrick's. Attended by St. Joseph. Rev. Gerard Senecal, O.S.B. [CEM]

Scipio, Anderson Co., St. Boniface, Rev. Clyde R. Ozminkowsi, O.Carm. In res., Rev. Bernard Lickteig, O.Carm.
Res., R.R. No. 1, Box 156, Garnett, 66032. Tel: 913-835-6273.

Scranton, Osage Co., St. Patrick's. Attended by St. Patrick's, Osage City. Rev. Michael Mulvany.
Tel: 785-528-3424. [CEM]

Seneca, Nemaha Co., SS. Peter and Paul's, Revs. Roderic Giller, O.S.B.; Francis Broderick, O.S.B.
Res., 66538. Tel: 785-336-2208.

School—401 Pioneer, 66538. Tel: 785-336-2727. Benedictine Sisters 2; Lay Teachers 15; Students 189.

Shawnee, Johnson Co., Good Shepherd, Rev. George Seuferling.
Office: 7126 Bond, 66203. Tel: 913-631-7116; Fax: 913-631-7357.
Res., 7124 Bond, 66203. Tel: 913-631-5661.
Parish Center: 11411 W. 71st Ter., 66203.

St. Joseph's, Rev. Msgr. Robert Bergman; Rev. William Bruning.
Res., 5832 King St., 66203. Tel: 913-631-5983; Fax: 913-631-5973.
School—(Grades 1-8) 5901 Flint St., 66203. Tel: 913-631-7730; Fax: 913-631-3608.
Lay Teachers 41; Students 774.
Early Education Center—(Day Care, Preschool & Kindergarten) 5900 Bond St., 66203. Tel: 913-631-0004.
Auxiliary Teachers 39; Students 554.

Summerfield, Marshall Co., Holy Family. Attended by St. Michael's, Axtell. Rev. Thomas H. Dolezal.
Church—P.O. Box 136, 66541. Tel: 785-736-2220.

Tonganoxie, Leavenworth Co., Sacred Heart, Rev. Mark Goldasich.
Res., 703 E. River, P.O. Box 539, 66086. Tel: 913-369-2851.

Topeka, Shawnee Co.,

1—ASSUMPTION, Rev. John F. Rossiter.
Res., 204 S.W. Eighth Ave., 66603. Tel: 785-232-2907; Fax: 785-232-8147.
School—735 S.W. Jackson, 66603. Tel: 785-235-0953.
Sisters 2; Lay Teachers 10; Students 193.

2—CHRIST THE KING, Rev. Norbert Lickteig.
Res., 5972 W. 25th St., 66614. Tel: 785-273-0710; 273-0715; Fax: 785-273-4766.
School—5973 S.W. 25th St., 66614. Tel: 785-272-2220; Fax: 785-273-4766.
Lay Teachers 26; Students 310.

3—HOLY NAME, Rev. Phillip Winkelbauer.
Res., 1114 W. 10th Ave., 66604. Tel: 785-232-7744; Fax: 785-232-2341.
School—934 Clay St., 66606. Tel: 785-233-1727; Fax: 785-232-2341.
Sisters of Charity of Leavenworth 2; Lay Teachers 14; Students 228.

4—MOST PURE HEART OF MARY, Revs. Francis Krische; Kyle Haden; Thomas Melchior.
Church Office: 1800 S.W. Stone, 66604. Tel: 785-272-5590; Fax: 785-272-2801.
School—1750 S.W. Stone, 66604. Tel: 785-272-4313; Fax: 785-272-1138.
Lay Teachers 35; Students 522.

5—OUR LADY OF GUADALUPE, (Mexican), Revs. Daniel L. Gardner; Joseph E. Chontos.
Res., 1008 N.E. Atchison Ave., 66616. Tel: 785-232-5088; Fax: 785-232-5166.
School—210 N.E. Branner St., 66616. Tel: 785-233-9171.
Sisters of Charity of Leavenworth 2; Lay Teachers 11; Students 170.

6—SACRED HEART, Rev. John Erickson.
Res., 333 Freeman Ave., 66616. Tel: 785-234-3338.
School—1733 Seward Ave., 66616. Tel: 785-234-8980.
Lay Teachers 11; Students 145.

7—ST. JOSEPH'S, Rev. Arthur J. Trompeter.
Res., 227 Van Buren St., 66603. Tel: 785-232-2863.

8—ST. MATTHEW, Rev. Patric Riley.
Res., 2700 S.E. Virginia Ave., 66605. Tel: 785-232-5012; Fax: 785-232-0028.
School—Tel: 785-235-2188; Fax: 785-232-0028.
Lay Teachers 18; Students 229.

Troy, Doniphan Co., St. Charles. Attended by St. Joseph's, Wathena. Rev. Daniel P. McCarthy, O.S.B.
Church—133 S. Park, 66087.

Valley Falls, Jefferson Co., St. Mary's Immaculate Conception. Attended by St. Joseph's, Nortonville.
Church—Broadway at Linn, 66088. Tel: 913-945-3582.

Wamego, Pottawatomie Co., St. Bernard's, Rev. Thomas N. Hesse.
Res., 66547. Tel: 785-456-7869.

Waterville, Marshall Co., St. Monica's. Attended by Annunciation, Frankfort. Rev. Bernard Mullen, C.PP.S.

Wathena, Doniphan Co., St. Joseph's, Rev. Daniel McCarthy, O.S.B.
Res., P.O. Box 159, 66090. Tel: 913-989-4818; Fax: 913-989-2313. [CEM]

Waverly, Coffey Co., St. Joseph's. Attended by St. Francis Xavier, Burlington. Rev. Kenneth W. Kelly. Tel: 316-364-2416.

Wea, Miami Co., Holy Rosary (Bucyrus P.O.), Rev. Anthony J. Lickteig.
Res., 22779 Metcalf Rd., Bucyrus, 66013. Tel: 913-533-2285; Fax: 913-533-2285. [CEM]

Westphalia, Anderson Co., St. Teresa's. Attended by St. Francis Xavier, Burlington. Rev. Kenneth W. Kelly. Tel: 316-364-2416; Fax: 316-364-2416.

Wetmore, Nemaha Co., St. James, Rev. Alfred G. Koestner, O.S.B.
Res., 66550. Tel: 913-866-2780.

Wheaton, Pottawatomie Co., St. Michael's. Closed. For inquiries for parish records contact the Chancery.

Chaplains of Public Institutions

KANSAS CITY. *K.U. Medical Center and Chapel* Holy Name Church. Rev. Jeremiah L. Spencer, Chap.

LAWRENCE. *Haskell Institute*. (Government Indian School). Rev. Duane F. Reinert, O.F.M.Cap.

TOPEKA. *Kansas Neurological Institute and Kansas Reception and Diagnostic Center*. Rev. William Guthman (OM) Chap.
Topeka State Hospital. State Reform School attended from Holy Name Church. Menninger Clinic attended from Holy Name Church. Veterans Administration Hospital.

Special Assignment:
Reverend Fathers—
Cooper, Leo, Archdiocesan Archivist, 12615 Parallel, Kansas City, KS 66109
Hays, Edward, Prison Ministry, 251 Muncie Rd., Leavenworth, KS 66048

On Duty Outside the Archdiocese:
Reverend Fathers—
Schwalm, Donald, Minnesota
Tillia, Marc, Bahia, Brazil

Military Chaplains:
Reverend Fathers—
Ludwikoski, James E., U.S.A.F.
Williams, Anthony, U.S.A.F.

Sabbatical:
Reverend Fathers—
Hosler, Paul
Kearns, Thomas

Absent on Sick Leave:
Reverend Fathers—
Pecinovsky, Albert

Retired:
Reverend Monsignors—
Culhane, Thomas, Overland Park, KS
Reverend Fathers—
Burger, Robert, Lenexa, KS
Fitzgerald, Patrick, Kansas City, KS
Gardner, Maurice, Lenexa, KS
Klasinski, George, Topeka, KS
Nebiolo, Emilio, New York, NY
O'Grady, James, Lawrence, KS
Pool, Robert, LaCygne, KS
Stitz, John, Leavenworth, KS
Wempe, Richard C., Seneca, KS
Yadrich, John B., Kansas City, KS

INSTITUTIONS LOCATED IN THE ARCHDIOCESE

[A] COLLEGES AND UNIVERSITIES

KANSAS CITY. *Donnelly College*, 608 N. 18th St., 66102. Tel: 913-621-6070; Fax: 913-621-0354
For a complete listing, refer to the Colleges and Universities section.

ATCHISON. *Benedictine College*, 66002. Tel: 913-367-5340; Fax: 913-367-3673.
E-mail: peylar@raven.benedictine.edu
Web site: http:www.benedictine.edu
For a complete listing, refer to the Colleges and Universities section.

LEAVENWORTH. *Saint Mary College*, 66048. Tel: 913-682-5151; Fax: 913-758-6140
For a complete listing, refer to the Colleges and Universities section.

[B] HIGH SCHOOLS, INTERPAROCHIAL

KANSAS CITY. *Bishop Miege High School*. 5041 Reinhardt Dr., Shawnee-Mission, 66205. Tel: 913-262-2700; Fax: 913-262-3754. Joseph Passantino, Ed.D., Pres.; Stanley Herbic, Prin. Sisters 2; Lay Teachers 51; Students 890.
Bishop Miege High School Foundation.
Bishop Ward High School, 708 N. 18th St., 66102. Tel: 913-371-1201; Fax: 913-371-2145. Mr. Timothy Mulvany, Pres.; Mr. Robert Runnebaum, Prin.; Rev. Steven Beseau, Chap. Sisters of Charity of Leavenworth 2; Lay Teachers 29; Students 445.
Bishop Ward High School Foundation.

LEAVENWORTH. *Immaculata High School*, 66048. Tel: 913-682-3900. Dr. John L. Coakley, Prin. Lay Teachers 21; Students 214.

OVERLAND PARK. *Saint Thomas Aquinas High School, Inc.*, 11411 Pflumm Rd., 66215. Tel: 913-345-1411. Mr. Jerry Degan, Prin.; Sr. Kathleen Condry, Pres.; Rev. Gerald Volz, Chap. Sisters 3; Lay Teachers 75; Students 1,146.
St. Thomas Aquinas High School Foundation.

TOPEKA. *Hayden High School*, 401 Gage Blvd., 66606. Tel: 785-272-5210; Fax: 785-272-2975. Mr. Benno Schluterman, Pres.; Rev. Kyle Haden, Chap. Religious 2; Lay Teachers 39; Students 574.
Hayden High School Foundation.

[C] ELEMENTARY SCHOOLS, INTERPAROCHIAL

KANSAS CITY. *All Saints School*. Consolidated, 809 Vermont, 66101. Tel: 913-342-3669; Fax: 913-621-2709. Lay Teachers 14; Students 260.
Our Lady of Unity School, 2646 S. 34th, 66106. Sr. Delores Long, Prin. Sisters 1; Lay Teachers 12; Students 148.
St. John/Holy Family School. (Consolidated), 515 Ohio & 420 Barnett, 66101. Mary Staley, Prin. Sisters 1; Lay Teachers 11; Students 175.

ATCHISON. *Atchison Catholic Elementary*, 201 Division, 66002. Tel: 913-367-3503. Mrs. Donna McCloskey, Prin. Lay Teachers 23; Students 316.

LEAVENWORTH. *Xavier Elementary School*, Admin. Office, 721 Osage, 66048. Consolidation of the following parishes: St. Casimir (Grades PreK-K); Sacred Heart (Grades 1-3); St. Joseph (Grades 7-8); and Immaculate Conception (Grades 4-6), St. Ignatius, St. Francis de Sales, St. Lawrence, and St. Joseph of the Valley. Margaret O'Sullivan, Prin. Sisters 1; Lay Teachers 24; Students 491.

[D] ELEMENTARY AND SECONDARY SCHOOLS, PRIVATE

MAPLE HILL.. *Our Lady of Compassion*, P.O. Box 236, 66507. Tel: 913-256-4500. Rev. Peter Gee, F.S.S.P., Chap. Lay Teachers 3; Students 30.

[E] HIGH SCHOOLS, PRIVATE

ATCHISON. *Maur Hill Prep School*, 66002. Tel: 913-367-5482.
E-mail: head@maurhill.com
Web site: maurhill@maurhill.com
Mr. R. Mark Watson, Pres. & Headmaster; Mr. Rob Stevens, Resident Dir.; Rev. Camillus Wurtz, O.S.B. Profs. Religious 1; Lay Teachers 24; Students 202.
Domestic Department. Misioneras Guadalupanas de Cristo Rey, O.S.B. Sisters 12.
Mount St. Scholastica Academy, 810 R St., 66002. Tel: 913-367-1334.
E-mail: mssa@best.com
Web site: www.best.com/~mssa/
Sisters of St. Benedict. Girls boarding and day high school. Sr. Dorothy Wolters, O.S.B., Pres. Sisters 2; Lay Teachers 14; Students 125.

[F] GENERAL HOSPITALS

KANSAS CITY. *Providence Medical Center*, 8929 Parallel Pkwy., 66112 Fax: 913-596-4098
For a complete listing, refer to the Hospitals section.

LEAVENWORTH. *St. John Hospital*, 3500 S. 4th St., 66048. Tel: 913-680-6000
For a complete listing, refer to the Hospitals section.

TOPEKA. *St. Francis Hospital and Medical Center*, 1700 W. 7th St., 66606. Tel: 785-295-8000
For a complete listing, refer to the Hospitals section.

[G] NURSING AND REST HOMES

KANSAS CITY. *Marian Hall*, 1920 Tauromee, 66102. Tel: 913-621-4302
For a complete listing, refer to the Special Care Facilities section.
Providence Place, 8909 Parallel, 66112. Tel: 913-596-4200
For a complete listing, refer to the Special Care Facilities section.
St. Joseph Care Center, Inc., 759 Vermont Ave., 66101. Tel: 913-621-6800
For a complete listing, refer to the Special Care Facilities section.

OVERLAND PARK. *Villa St. Joseph Nursing Home*, 11901 Rosewood, 66209. Tel: 913-345-1745
For a complete listing, refer to the Special Care Facilities section.

[H] MONASTERIES AND RESIDENCES FOR PRIESTS AND BROTHERS

ATCHISON. *St. Benedict's Abbey*, 66002. Tel: 913-367-7853; Fax: 913-367-6230. Rt. Revs. Barnabus Senecal, O.S.B., Abbot; Owen Purcell, O.S.B., (Retired Abbot); Ralph Koehler, O.S.B., (Retired Abbot); Very Rev. Michael Santa, O.S.B., Prior; Revs. Meinrad Miller, O.S.B., Sub Prior; Maurice Haefling, O.S.B., Business Mgr.; Mark Broski, O.S.B.; Eugene Dehner, O.S.B.; James Downey, O.S.B.; Emeric Fletcher, O.S.B.; Thomas Flaherty, O.S.B.; Timothy Fry, O.S.B.; Matthew Habiger, O.S.B.; Hilary Heim, O.S.B.; Venard Helget, O.S.B.; Regis Hickey, O.S.B.; Hugh Keefer, O.S.B.; Bertrand LaNoue, O.S.B.; Benedict J. LaRocque, O.S.B.; Aaron Peters, O.S.B.; Blaine Schultz, O.S.B.; Paul Steingreaber, O.S.B.; Benjamin Tremmel, O.S.B.; Edwin P. Watson, O.S.B.; Gilbert Wolters, O.S.B.; Michael Zoellner, O.S.B.; Bros. James Albers, O.S.B.; Lawrence Bradford, O.S.B.; Martin Burkhard, O.S.B.; Boniface Butterworth, O.S.B.; Mark Cason, O.S.B.; Bede Healey, O.S.B.; Robert Heiman, O.S.B.; John Kaighin, O.S.B.; Walter Landwehr, O.S.B.; Michael Lyons, O.S.B.; Stephen McCann, O.S.B.; Francis Mutter, O.S.B.; John Peto, O.S.B.; Raymond Pfeiffer, O.S.B.; Brendan Rolling, O.S.B.; Joseph Ryan, O.S.B.; Nicholas Tockert, O.S.B.; Gregory Viscek, O.S.B.; Anthony Vorwerk, O.S.B. Bishops 1; Priests 49; Brothers 19.

LAWRENCE. *St. Conrad's Friary*. (Capuchins), 745 Tennessee, 66044. Tel: 913-843-0188.
E-mail: dfreinert@compuserve.com
In res. Revs. James Moster, O.F.M.Cap.; Duane F. Reinert, O.F.M.Cap.; Charles Polifka, O.F.M.Cap.; Bros. Benignus Scarry, O.F.M.Cap.; Francisco Ramirez, O.F.M.Cap.; Joseph McGlynn, O.F.M.Cap. Total in Residence 5.

[I] CONVENTS AND RESIDENCES FOR SISTERS

KANSAS CITY. *Convent of the Sisters, Servants of Mary*, 800 N. 18th St., 66102. Tel: 913-371-3423; Fax: 913-621-4962. Ministers to the Sick, Motherhouse of the Congregation for the United States. Nurses, private duty, and visiting nursing in the homes. Mother Alfonsa Bellido, S.M., Prov. Supr.; Rev. Mother Mercedes Rodriguez, S.M., Local Supr.; Rev. Philip Kendall, C.S.V., Chap., St. Peters Cathedral. Professed 40.

ATCHISON. *Dooley Center, Inc.*, 801 S. Eighth St., 66002. Tel: 913-367-6110; Fax: 913-367-3866. Benedictine Sisters of Mount St. Scholastica, Inc., Atchison, KS. Nursing care facility for the aged/infirmed members of this religious community.
Mount St. Scholastica, 801 S. 8th St., 66002. Tel: 913-367-6110; Fax: 913-367-3866.
Web site: http://www.benedictine.edu/mount.html
Motherhouse of the Sisters of St. Benedict. Sr. Mary Agnes Patterson, O.S.B., Prioress.
In community: Professed Sisters 234; Novices 1. Attended from St. Benedict's Abbey.

LEAVENWORTH. *Motherhouse of the Sisters of Charity of Leavenworth*, 66048-5054. Tel: 913-758-6501; Fax: 913-682-2128.
E-mail: kstefanintfs.net
Web site: http://www.smeks.edu/scl/sclweb.html
Sr. Mary Kathleen Stefani, Community Dir.; Sr. Jane Jackson, Local Coord.; Sr. Mary Kevin Hollow, Local Admin.; Revs. Daniel O'Shea, O.S.B., Chap.; Joseph Thoonkuzhy, Chap. Sisters 447; Total in Residence 143; Novices 1.

PAOLA. *Our Lady of Lourdes Convent*, 901 E. Miami St., 66071. Tel: 913-294-2349.
Motherhouse of the Ursuline Sisters. Sr. Patricia Lynch, O.S.U., Supr.; Rev. Aaron Peters, O.S.B., Chap. Sisters 38.

[J] CAMPUS MINISTRY

EMPORIA. *Didde Catholic Campus Center, Emporia State University*, Office: 1415 Merchant, 66801. Tel: 316-343-6765. Rev. William B. Porter, Chap., 1102 Neosho St., 66801. Tel: 316-342-8727.

LAWRENCE. *Haskell Catholic Campus Center*, 2301 Barker Ave., 66046-4813. Tel: 785-842-2401. Bro. Joseph McGlynn, O.F.M.Cap., Dir.; Rev. Duane F. Reinert, O.F.M.Cap., Chap. Total Staff 2.
St. Lawrence Center Foundation.
St. Lawrence Catholic Campus Center at the University of Kansas and Residence, 1631 Crescent Rd., 66044. Tel: 785-843-0357. Revs. Vincent E. Krische; Raymond May. Total Staff 14.

TOPEKA. *Catholic Campus Center of Washburn University*, 1633 Jewell, 66604. Tel: 785-233-2204.

[K] MISCELLANEOUS LISTINGS

KANSAS CITY. *Casa Juan Diego Centro de Evangelization*, 229 S. 8th, 66101. Tel: 913-342-1276. Rev. Ramon Gaitan, O.A.R.
Catholic Foundation of Northeast Kansas. (Formerly known as Archdiocesan Foundation), 12615 Parallel, 66109.
Duchesne Clinic, 636 Tauromee, 66101. Tel: 913-321-2626. A division of Caritas Clinics, Inc., Leavenworth, KS. Total Staff 6; Total Patients 5,490.
El Centro, Inc., 1333 S. 27th, 66106. Tel: 913-677-0100; Fax: 913-362-8250. Mr. Richard Ruiz, Dir. Sisters 4. 1330 S. 30th St., 66106. Tel: 913-677-1115.
Providence Medical Center Foundation, 8929 Parallel Pkwy., 66112. Tel: 913-596-4882.
Shalom Catholic Worker House, 2100 N. 13th, 66104. Tel: 913-321-2206. Total Staff 5; Total Assisted 2,000.

ATCHISON. *The Maur Hill Prep School Endowment Association, Inc.*, 1000 Green St., 66002. Tel: 913-367-5482. Rev. Edwin P. Watson, O.S.B., Contact Person.
The Mount Community Center, Inc., 751 S. 8th St., 66002. Tel: 913-367-6110. Sr. Noreen Hurter, O.S.B., Dir. of Programs.

EASTON. *Shantivanam Archdiocesan House of Prayer*, 22019 Meagher Rd., 66020. Tel: 913-773-8255.
E-mail: wnepps@lvnworth.com
Revs. Joseph F. Nassal, C.PP.S., Dir.; William A. Nordenbrock, C.PP.S. Total in Residence 5; Total Staff 8.

EMPORIA. *Community Service Center*, 116 W. 12th, 66801. Tel: 316-343-2296; Fax: 316-342-9517. Mr. Ron Scott, Dir.

LAWRENCE. *Community Service Center*, 320 Main St., P.O. Box 342, 66044. Tel: 785-841-0307; Fax: 785-832-1710.

LEAVENWORTH. *Caritas Clinics, Inc.*, 511 S. Fifth St., 66048. Tel: 913-651-8860. Sisters of Charity of Leavenworth. Ann Zimmerman, Pres.; Sr. Ann McGuire, Exec. Dir. Administrative structure for St. Vincent Clinic, Leavenworth and Duchesne Clinic, Kansas City. Total Staff 3.
Catholic School Foundation of the Leavenworth Region, Inc., 320 N. Broadway, 66048. Tel: 913-682-7801.
E-mail: joker@idir.net
Janice Ryan, Exec. Sec., Office of Devel.
Community Service Center, 716 N. 5th St., 66048. Tel: 913-651-8060. Sr. Jane Albert Mehrens, Dir.
Sisters of Charity of Leavenworth Health Services Corporation, 4200 S. 4th St., 66048. Tel: 913-682-1338.
E-mail: sclhsc@sclhsc.org
Web site: www.sclhsc.org
Sr. Marie Damian Glatt, S.C.L., Pres.

MAYETTA. *Our Lady of the Snows Catholic Shrine*, Potawatomi Reservation, 66509.

OLATHE. *Catholic Community Services*, 333 E. Poplar, 66061. Tel: 913-782-4077; Fax: 913-782-0983. Ms. Shirley Kelso, Dir.

PAOLA. *Lakemary Center, Inc.*, 100 Lakemary Dr., 66071-0449. Tel: 913-294-4361. Ursuline Sisters. Dr. William R. Craig, Pres. Serves children and adults with mental retardation. Total Staff 214; Total Assisted 205.
Ursuline Sisters Charitable Trust, 901 E. Miami, 66071. Tel: 913-294-2349.

TOPEKA. *Catholic Community Services Inc.*, 306 Van-Buren, 66603. Tel: 785-233-6300.
Catholic Health Association of Kansas, P.O. Box 2308, 66601. Tel: 913-233-7436.
El Centro de Servicios Para Hispanos, 216 N.E. Branner, 66616. Tel: 785-232-8207; Fax: 785-232-8834.
Marian Clinic, Inc., Medical Plaza Bldg., 1001 S.W. Garfield, 66604. Tel: 785-233-8081. Affiliate of Sisters of Charity of Leavenworth Health Services Corp. Sr. Marie Damian Glatt, S.C.L., Pres.; Marilyn Page, Exec. Dir. Total Patients 10,000.
St. Francis Hospital Foundation, 1700 W. 7th St., 66606. Tel: 913-295-5356; Fax: 913-295-5584.

RELIGIOUS INSTITUTES OF MEN REPRESENTED IN THE ARCHDIOCESE

For further details refer to the corresponding bracketed number in the Religious Institutes of Men or Women section.

[]—*Augustinian Recollects.*—O.A.R.
[0200]—*Benedictine Monks.*—O.S.B.
[0470]—*The Capuchin Friars.* (Holy Family).—O.F.M.Cap.
[0270]—*Carmelite Fathers & Brothers.* (American Prov.).—O.Carm.
[1320]—*Clerics of St. Viator.*—C.S.V.
[0520]—*Franciscan Friars.* (Cincinnati, OH.).—O.F.M.
[]—*Priestly Fraternity of St. Peter.*—F.S.S.P.
[]—*Society of Jesus.*—S.J.
[1060]—*Society of the Precious Blood.*—C.PP.S.
[]—*Vincentian Fathers.*—C.M.

RELIGIOUS INSTITUTES OF WOMEN REPRESENTED IN THE ARCHDIOCESE

[0100]—*Adorers of the Blood of Christ.*—A.S.C.
[0230]—*Benedictine Sisters of Pontifical Jurisdiction.*—O.S.B.
[1170]—*Felician Sisters.*—C.S.S.F.
[1430]—*Franciscan Sisters of Our Lady of Perpetual Help.*—O.S.F.
[3130]—*Our Lady of Victory Missionary Sisters.*—O.L.V.M.
[0480]—*Sisters of Charity of Leavenworth, Kansas.*—S.C.L.
[1520]—*Sisters of St. Francis of Christ the King.*—O.S.F.
[1570]—*Sisters of St. Francis of the Holy Family.*—O.S.F.
[3840]—*Sisters of St. Joseph of Carondelet.* (St. Louis, MO).—C.S.J.
[3830-18]—*Sisters of St. Joseph of Wichita.*—C.S.J.
[3600]—*Sisters, Servants of Mary.*—S.M.
[4120]—*Ursuline Nuns, of the Congregation of Paris.*—O.S.U.

ARCHDIOCESAN CEMETERIES

KANSAS CITY. *St. John's, Mount Calvary, Resurrection, St. Joseph's, Shawnee, and St. John, Lenexa.*
ATCHISON. *Mount Calvary.*
LEAVENWORTH. *Mount Calvary.*
LENEXA. *Holy Trinity.*
TOPEKA. *Mount Calvary.*

NECROLOGY

† DeRuntz, Clarence Maximillian, Worthington, KS, Pontifical College Josephinum. —Died May 5, 1997.
† Roberts, Edward Francis, (Retired). —Died Sept. 18, 1997.
† Yadrich, John Branko, (Retired). —Died Dec. 29, 1997.
† Zemites, Joseph Francis, (Retired). —Died May 23, 1997.

Diocese of Kansas City-St. Joseph

(Dioecesis Kansanopolitanae Sancti Josephi)

Most Reverend

RAYMOND J. BOLAND, D.D.

Bishop of Kansas City-St. Joseph; born February 8, 1932; ordained June 16, 1957; appointed Bishop of Birmingham February 2, 1988; consecrated March 25, 1988; appointed Bishop of Kansas City-St. Joseph June 22, 1993; installed September 9, 1993. *Mailing Address: P.O. Box 419037, Kansas City, MO, 64141-6037.*

Most Reverend

JOHN J. SULLIVAN, D.D.

Former Bishop of Kansas City-St. Joseph; born July 5, 1920; ordained September 23, 1944; appointed Bishop of Grand Island July 25, 1972; consecrated September 19, 1972; installed Grand Island September 21, 1972; appointed Bishop of Kansas City-St. Joseph June 27, 1977; installed August 17, 1977; retired September 9, 1993. *Res., 8745 James A. Reed Rd., Kansas City, MO, 64138.*

DIOCESE OF KANSAS CITY ESTABLISHED SEPTEMBER 10, 1880; DIOCESE OF ST. JOSEPH ESTABLISHED MARCH 3, 1868.

REDESIGNATED DIOCESE OF KANSAS CITY-ST. JOSEPH AUGUST 29, 1956.

Square Miles 15,429.

Comprises the Counties of Andrew, Atchison, Bates, Buchanan, Caldwell, Carroll, Cass, Clay, Clinton, Daviess, DeKalb, Gentry, Grundy, Harrison, Henry, Holt, Jackson, Johnson, Lafayette, Livingston, Mercer, Nodaway, Platte, Ray, Saint Clair, Vernon and Worth in the State of Missouri.

For legal titles of parishes and diocesan institutions, consult the Chancery Office.

Chancery: P.O. Box 419037, Kansas City, MO, 64141-6037. Tel.: 816-756-1850; Fax: 816-756-0878.

Web site address: http://www.diocese-kcsj.org

STATISTICAL OVERVIEW

Personnel	
Bishop	1
Retired Bishops	1
Abbots	1
Retired Abbots	1
Priests: Diocesan Active in Diocese	78
Priests: Active Outside Diocese	5
Priests: Diocesan in Foreign Missions	2
Priests: Retired, Sick or Absent	46
Number of Diocesan Priests	131
Religious Priests in Diocese	100
Ordinations:	
Diocesan Priests	3
Permanent Deacons in Diocese	60
Total Brothers	36
Total Sisters	327
Parishes	
Parishes	83
With Resident Pastor:	
Resident Diocesan Priests	60
Resident Religious Priests	20
Without Resident Pastor:	
Administered by Permanent Deacons	1
Administered by Women Religious	1
Administered by Lay People	1
Missions	14
Professional Ministry Personnel:	
Brothers	1
Sisters	22
Lay Ministers	160
Welfare	
Catholic Hospitals	3
Total Assisted	244,243
Homes for the Aged	14
Total Assisted	1,232
Day Care and Extended Day Care Centers	14
Total Assisted	303
Residential Care of Disabled	1
Total Assisted	26
Educational	
Diocesan Students in Other Seminaries	10
Seminaries, Religious	1
Students Religious	21
Total Seminarians	31
Colleges and Universities	2
Total Students	4,112
High Schools, Diocesan and Parish	5
Total Students	1,506
High Schools, Private	3
Total Students	1,669
Elementary Schools, Diocesan and Parish	33
Total Students	9,077
Elementary Schools, Private	1
Total Students	298
Catechesis/Religious Education:	
High School Students	930
Elementary Students	8,977
Total Students Under Catholic Instruction	26,600
Teachers in the Diocese:	
Priests	4
Brothers	2
Sisters	20
Lay Teachers	807
Vital Statistics	
Receptions into the Church:	
Infant Baptism Totals	2,437
Adult Baptism Totals	549
Received into Full Communion	389
First Communions	2,518
Confirmations	1,692
Marriages:	
Catholic	491
Interfaith	491
Total Marriages	982
Deaths	1,348
Total Catholic Population	161,043
Total Population	1,299,555

Former Bishops—Rt. Rev. JOHN JOSEPH HOGAN, D.D., ord. April 10, 1852; cons. Bishop of St. Joseph, MO, Sept. 13, 1868; transferred to Kansas City, Sept. 10, 1880; died Feb. 21, 1913.—Most Rev. THOMAS F. LILLIS, D.D., ord. Aug. 15, 1885; cons. Bishop of Leavenworth, Dec. 27, 1904; appt. Coadjutor to the Bishop of Kansas City, *"cum jure successionis,"* March 14, 1910 Bishop of Kansas City, Feb. 21, 1913; appt. assistant at the Pontifical Throne, Aug. 19, 1935; died Dec. 29, 1938.—Most Rev. EDWIN V. O'HARA, D.D., ord. June 10, 1905; appt. Bishop of Great Falls, MT, August 1, 1930; cons. Oct. 28, 1930; transferred to the See of Kansas City, April 15, 1939 made assistant at the Pontifical Throne, Jan. 5, 1949; appt. Archbishop "ad personam," June 29, 1954; died Sept. 11, 1956.—His Eminence JOHN CARDINAL CODY, S.T.D., ord. Dec. 8, 1931; appt. Titular Bishop of Appollonia and Auxiliary Bishop of St. Louis, May 14, 1947; cons. July 2, 1947; promoted to coadjutor of St. Joseph *"cum jure successionis," Jan. 27, 1954; appt. to Diocese of Kansas City-St. Joseph, Aug. 24, 1956; succeeded to Sept. 11, 1956; transferred to Archdiocese of New Orleans as Coadjutor Archbishop "cum jure successionis,"* Aug. 10, 1961; acceded the See of New Orleans, Nov. 8, 1964; transferred to the Archdiocese of Chicago, June 16, 1965; created Cardinal Priest, June 26, 1967; died April 25, 1982.—Most Rev. CHARLES H. HELMSING, D.D., ord. June 10, 1933; appt. Titular Bishop of Axomis and Auxiliary Bishop of St. Louis, March 17, 1949; cons. April 19, 1949; appt. Bishop of Springfield-Cape Girardeau, Aug. 24, 1956; transferred to Diocese of Kansas City-St. Joseph, Jan. 27, 1962; retired Aug. 17, 1977; died Dec. 20, 1993.—Most Rev. JOHN J. SULLIVAN, D.D., ord. Sept. 23, 1944; appt. Bishop of Grand Island, July 25, 1972; cons. Sept. 19, 1972; installed Grand Island, Sept. 21, 1972; appt. Bishop of Kansas City-St. Joseph, June 27, 1977; installed Aug. 17, 1977; retired Sept. 9, 1993.

Former Bishops of Diocese of St. Joseph, MO—Rt. Rev. JOHN J. HOGAN, D.D., ord. April 10, 1852; appt. first Bishop of St. Joseph, March 3, 1868; cons. Sept. 13, 1868; transferred to See of Kansas City, Sept. 10, 1880 administrator of St. Joseph until 1893; died Feb. 21, 1913.—Rt. Rev. MAURICE F. BURKE, D.D.,born May 5, 1844; ord. May 22, 1875; appt. first Bishop of Cheyenne, Wyoming, Aug. 9, 1887; cons. Oct. 28, 1887; transferred to St. Joseph, June 19, 1893; died March 17, 1923.—Most Rev. FRANCIS GILFILLAN, D.D.,born Feb. 16, 1872; ord. June 24, 1895; appt. titular Bishop of Spigas and Coadjutor with the right of succession to the See of St. Joseph, July 8, 1922; cons. Nov. 8, 1922; succeeded to the See of St. Joseph, March 17, 1923; died Jan. 13, 1933.—Most Rev. CHARLES H. LEBLOND, D.D., ord. Oct. 27, 1909; appt. Bishop of St. Joseph, July 21, 1933; cons. Sept. 21, 1933; resigned as Bishop of St. Joseph and appointed Titular Bishop of Orcistus, Aug. 24, 1956; died Dec. 30, 1958.

Vicar General—Rev. PATRICK R. RUSH.
Chancery—P.O. Box 419037, Kansas City, 64141-6037. Tel: 816-756-1850; Fax: 816-756-0878. All official matters should be sent to this address.
Chancellor—GEORGE M. NOONAN.
Vice Chancellor—Sr. JEAN BESTE, B.V.M.
Diocesan Finance Officer—DAVID A. MALANOWSKI.
Diocesan Tribunal—P.O. Box 419037, Kansas City, 64141-6037. Tel: 816-756-1850.
Judicial Vicar—Rev. C. MICHAEL COLEMAN, J.C.L.
Adjutant Judicial Vicar—Rev. JOSEPH H. MATT, J.C.L.
Canonical Consultant—Rev. RICHARD F. CARNEY, J.C.D.
Defender of the Bond—Sr. MARY HELEN MCINERNEY, S.C.L.
Procurators—Sr. MARY HELEN MCINERNEY, S.C.L.; DONNA EISENBARTH.
Secretary of the Tribunal—CAROLYN RAMM.
Diocesan Consultors—Rev. Msgr. HENRY G. BAUER; Revs. RICHARD CARNEY; C. MICHAEL COLEMAN; JAMES E. HEALY; ROBERT MURPHY; LLOYD E. OPOKA; ROBERT ROST; NORMAN ROTERT; PATRICK J. RUSH; JOHN C. SCHUELE; GERALD WARIS; THOMAS W. WIEDERHOLT.
Presbyteral Council—Rev. MICHAEL E. TIERNEY, Chm.; Rev. KEN RILEY, Vice Chm.; Rev. ANDREW MEINERS, C.Ss.R., Sec./Treas.
Deans—Rev. DONALD P. FARNAN, Deanery I; Rev. ANDREW MEINERS, C.SS.R., Deanery II; Rev. JOSEPH POWERS, Deanery III; Rev. JOHN WEISS, Deanery IV; Rev. MICHAEL TIERNEY, Deanery V; Rev. MICHAEL CLARY, Deanery VI; Rev. ROBERT STONE, Deanery VII; Rev. KENNETH CIRQUI, Deanery VIII; Rev. ROBERT CRIDER, Deanery IX; Rev. AUGUSTINE DREILING, O.S.B., Deanery X; Rev. ROBERT ROST, Deanery XI; Rev. THOMAS LUDWIG, Deanery XII; Rev. ROBERT STEWART, Deanery XIII; Rev. RONALD WILL, C.PP.S., Deanery XIV.

Diocesan Offices and Directors

Archivist—Rev. C. MICHAEL COLEMAN, J.C.L.
Building Commission—Revs. MICHAEL RICE; PATRICK J. RUSH, V.G.; DANIEL KENNALEY; Mr. BERNARD J. GRAM, Chm. WILLIAM TURNER; BERNARD JACQUINOT; DAVID GALLAGHER; STEPHEN F. OBARSKI; DAVID A. MALANOWSKI; Sr. JEAN BESTE, B.V.M.; WILLIAM MARKEY; THOMAS REDMOND; WILLIAM FAGAN; WAYNE ROY; ALLEN MILLER, (See Property Mgmt. Office).
The "Catholic Key" Diocesan Newspaper—ALBERT DE ZUTTER, Editor, *P.O. Box 419037, Kansas City, 64141-6037.* Tel: 816-756-1859.
Cemetery (Catholic Cemeteries Associated, Diocese of Kansas City-St. Joseph, Inc.)—Rev. ROBERT M. CAMERON, Diocesan Dir., *7601 Blue Ridge, Kansas City, 64138.* Diocesan Cemeteries: Kansas City, Mt. Olivet; Mt. St. Mary; Resurrection; St. Joseph, Mt. Olivet.
Censor Librorum—Rev. Msgr. WILLIAM J. BLACET, J.C.L.
Catholic Charities of Kansas City-St. Joseph, Inc.—1112 Broadway, Kansas City, 64105. Tel: 816-221-4377; Fax: 816-221-9116. *Executive Director:* NEAL D. COLBY, JR., L.I.C.S.W., A.C.S.W.,*Assistant Director:* DAVID G. HOWERY, M.A., L.I.C.S.W.,*Comptroller:* LEORY RAAB,*Community & Public Relations:* SINA BEIL. Tel: 816-363-8988. *Mental Health Services:* FLORA BOLDRIDGE, L.I.C.S.W., L.P.C., Supvr. *Child Welfare Services:* Mr. DAVID G. HOWERY, M.A., L.C.S.W.; Supvr. *In-Home Health Services:* DOLORES MOORE, M.A., Supvr. *Office of Quality Assurance:* RICK MALSICK, M.A.,*Parish Social Ministry:* VICKIE RIDDLE, A.C.S.W., L.S.C.S.W., Supvr. *Peace and Justice Office:* Sr. MARY ALICE GUILFOIL, O.S.B., Dir., *1310 Westport Rd., Kansas City, 64111.* Tel: 816-931-9744. *Northern Diocesan Branch Office:* KAREN S. HAUSER, Ed.D., L.P.C., Supvr., *1302 Faraon, St. Joseph, 64501.* Tel: 816-232-2885. *Southern Diocesan Branch Office:* SUSAN LOYD, A.C.S.W., L.I.C.S.W., Supvr., *123 E. Gay St., Ste. 2, Warrensburg, 64093.* Tel: 816-747-2241.
Center for Pastoral Life and Ministry—DENISE SIMEONE, Dir.
Ministry Formation—Catechetical Formation: TONY BUTEL; DENISE SIMEONE. Continuing Education: DENISE SIMEONE; CELE BREEN. Heartland Conference: CELE BREEN; TONY BUTEL. Loyola: CELE BREEN; DENISE SIMEONE. New Wine: CELE BREEN; DENISE SIMEONE. Parish Life Summer Institute: TONY BUTEL; DENISE SIMEONE.
Parish Life Development—Christian Initiation: ROSE MULLEN; BIAGIO MAZZA. Evangelization: DALE MOONEY; ROSE MULLEN. Hispanic Ministry: DALE MOONEY; BIAGIO MAZZA. Pastoral Leadership Councils: ROSE THERESE HUELSMAN; BIAGIO MAZZA. Pastoral Leadership Staff: ROSE MULLEN; DALE MOONEY. Religious Education: BIAGIO MAZZA; ROSE MULLEN. Small Christian Communities: ROSE THERESE HUELSMAN; ROSE MULLEN.
Central City School Fund Office—CAROLINE HENNESSY, Dir.
Diocesan Annual Appeal—THOMAS SEVERINO, Dir.
Diocesan Community Services, Inc.—NEAL D. COLBY, JR., A.C.S.W., L.I.C.S.W., Exec. Dir. RAY AGEE, M.B.A., Housing Coord., *616 E. 63rd St. #208, Kansas City, 64110.* Tel: 816-363-5140; Fax: 816-363-0868.
Diocesan Development—THOMAS SEVERINO, Dir.
Diocesan Ecumenical Officer—GEORGE M. NOONAN.
Diocesan Finance Council—Rev. GERALD R. WARIS; ROBERT AYLWARD; MICHAEL BROSNAHAN; JAMES STACY; JEANNINE STRANDJORD; MARYELLEN CONNOR; DAVID A. MALANOWSKI; JOHN DESTEFANO; JOHN HOULEHAN; THOMAS MCCULLOUGH; JAMES OLSON; THOMAS SEVERINO.
Diocesan Finance Office—DAVID A. MALANOWSKI, Finance Officer; MARYELLEN CONNOR, Internal Auditor; MONICA ADAMS, Accounting Mgr.
Diocesan Insurance Office—MARYELLEN CONNOR, Risk Mgr. PEGGY MCCARTHY, Benefits Coord.
Diocesan Ministry for Persons With Disabilities—JUDY SHUTE, Exec. Sec., *4101 E. 105th Ter., Kansas City, 64137.* Tel: 816-767-0058.
Education Office—Sr. ANNE SHEPARD, Ph.D., O.S.B., Supt., Schools; Sr. CAROL ANN PETERSON, O.S.B., Assoc. Supt. THOMAS BLAKE, Assoc. Supt. Tel: 816-753-6406; 756-1850.
Family Life Office—(Respect Life Activities)—Marriage and Parenting: KENNETH GREENE, Dir.
Holy Childhood Association—Rev. ROBERT M. CAMERON, Dir.
Legion of Mary—Rev. DONALD STURM, Dir.
Office of the Diaconate—Deacon ROSS BEAUDOIN, Dir. Assoc. Dirs.: Rev. MICHAEL COLEMAN; GEORGE NOONAN.
Office of Personnel and Planning—Sr. JEAN BESTE, B.V.M., Dir.
Priests' Purgatorial Society—Rev. ROBERT M. CAMERON, Sec.
Priests' Pension Plan—Administrative Committee: Rev. Msgr. HENRY G. BAUER; Rev. ROBERT M. CAMERON; DAVID A. MALANOWSKI.
Propagation of the Faith—(Pontifical Society for the Propagation of the Faith, Missionary Union of the Clergy and Religious, The Pontifical Society of St. Peter the Apostle for Native Clergy, and Daily World missionaries); Rev. ROBERT M. CAMERON, Dir.
Property Management—WAYNE ROY, Dir. JUDITH LISTON, Office Admin. Tel: 816-361-8108; Fax: 816-361-8921.
St. Vincent De Paul Particular Council—Sr. PATRICIA BACHMAN, D.C., Moderator.
Vocations—Revs. MICHAEL ROACH, Dir. JOSEPH CISETTI, Assoc. Dir.
Office of Worship—STEPHEN F. OBARSKI, Dir.
Youth Office—WILLIAM CORDARO, Dir.

CLERGY, PARISHES, MISSIONS AND PAROCHIAL SCHOOLS

KANSAS CITY
(Jackson County)

1—CATHEDRAL OF IMMACULATE CONCEPTION (1882). See listing for Old St. Patrick's. Rev. Msgr. Ernest J. Fiedler; Revs. Martin DeMeulenaere, O.S.B.; Jack McClure, C.P.P.S.
Res., 416 W. 12th St., 64105. Tel: 816-842-0416; Fax: 816-842-3849.

2—ST. MONICA PARISH (1995) (African American), Rev. Philip Egan.
Res., 1616 The Paseo, 64108. Tel: 816-471-3696; Fax: 816-471-1111.

3—ST. ALOYSIUS (1886) (Hispanic), Rev. John L. Hix.
Res., 2611 E. 11th St., 64127. Tel: 816-231-1886; Fax: 816-241-7010.
Catechesis/Religious Programs—Students 83.

4—ST. ANTHONY (1991), Rev. Joseph A. Mancuso.
Res., 318 Benton Blvd., 64124. Tel: 816-231-5445; Fax: 816-231-5446.

5—ST. BERNADETTE'S (1958), Rev. Kenneth A. Riley; Deacon Emory Corrigan.
Res., 9020 E. 51st Ter., 64133. Tel: 816-356-3700; Fax: 816-356-2874.
School—Tel: 816-356-3702.
Lay Teachers 14; Students 160.
Catechesis/Religious Programs—Tel: 816-356-2874.
Students 122.

6—BLESSED SACRAMENT. Closed. For inquiries for parish records contact the Chancery.

7—ST. CATHERINE OF SIENA (1926), Rev. John C. Schuele; Deacons William Markey; J. Mark Fountain; Veronica Ward, Pastoral Assoc. In res., Rev. John P. Coleman.
Res., 4101 E. 105th Ter., 64137-1649. Tel: 816-761-5483; Fax: 816-761-5489.
School—Our Lady of Peace Consolidated School, 10526 Grandview Rd., 64137-1699. Tel: 816-761-5605.
Catechesis/Religious Programs—Students 47.

8—ST. CHARLES BORROMEO (1947), Revs. John Wolf, C.PP.S.; Paul E. Sattler, C.PP.S.; Garry Richmeier, C.PP.S.; Bro. Robert Herman, C.PP.S.; Deacons Jerry Williams; Frank Peak; John Koch.
Res., 900 N.E. Shady Lane Dr., 64118. Tel: 816-436-0880; Fax: 816-436-0103.
School—804 N.E. Shady Lane Dr., 64118. Tel: 816-436-1009; Fax: 816-436-6293.
Lay Teachers 31; Students 450.
Catechesis/Religious Programs—Students 347.

9—CHRIST THE KING (1938), Revs. John C. Weiss; Thomas Holder.
Res., 8510 Wornall Rd., 64114. Tel: 816-363-4888; Fax: 816-363-2315.
School—425 W. 85th St., 64114. Tel: 816-363-1113; Fax: 816-363-2889.
Lay Teachers 37; Students 366.
Catechesis/Religious Programs—Students 85.

10—ST. ELIZABETH'S (1917), Revs. Robert S. Gregory; Joseph Hughes; Deacon Donald Schmit. In res., Rev. Martin DeMeulenaere, O.S.B.
Res., 7444 Main St., 64114. Tel: 816-523-2405; Fax: 816-444-9858.
School—Tel: 816-523-7100; Fax: 816-523-2566.
Lay Teachers 31; Students 430.
Catechesis/Religious Programs—Students 72.

11—ST. FRANCIS SERAPH. Closed. For inquiries for parish records contact the Chancery.

12—ST. FRANCIS XAVIER (1910), Revs. Timothy M. McMahon, S.J.; James F. Goeke, S.J.
Res., 1001 E. 52nd St., 64110. Tel: 816-523-5115; Fax: 816-333-0082.
School—5220 Troost Ave., 64110. Tel: 816-523-2258.
Lay Teachers 17; Students 226.
Catechesis/Religious Programs—Students 55.

13—ST. GABRIEL ARCHANGEL (1956), Rev. Denis Dougherty, O.S.B.
Res., 4737 N. Cleveland Ave., 64117. Tel: 816-453-1183; Fax: 816-453-6254.
School—Tel: 816-453-4443.
Lay Teachers 16; Students 204.
Early Childhood Learning Center—Tel: 816-453-4555.
Lay Teachers 29; Students 200.
Catechesis/Religious Programs—Students 287.

14—GUARDIAN ANGELS (1909), Margaret Lima, Pastoral Admin.; Rev. Glenn Mueller, S.J., Pastoral Assoc.
Parish Office: 1310 Westport Rd., 64111. Tel: 816-931-4351; Fax: 816-531-6396.
Schools—Our Lady of the Angels School, 211 W. Linwood, 64111. Tel: 816-931-1693; Fax: 816-753-3606.; Our Lady of Guadalupe School, 2310 Madison, 64111. Tel: 816-221-2539.
Catechesis/Religious Programs—Students 50.

15—HOLY CROSS (1902), Revs. Joseph B. Powers; Raymond Tu; Deacon Charles DiMartino.
Res., 5106 St. John Ave., 64123. Tel: 816-231-4845.

16—HOLY FAMILY (1981), Rev. Robert H. Stewart.
Res., 919 N.E. 96th St., 64155. Tel: 816-436-9200; Fax: 816-436-8049.
Catechesis/Religious Programs—Students 281.

17—CHURCH OF THE HOLY MARTYRS (1991) (Vietnamese), Revs. Joseph Phan Trong Hanh; Raymond Tu.
Res., 7801 Paseo, 64131. Tel: 816-333-3214.
Catechesis/Religious Programs—Tel: 816-333-5349.
Students 320.

18—HOLY ROSARY (1891) (Italian), Rev. Angelo Carbone, C.S.
Res., 911 Missouri Ave., 64106. Tel: 816-842-5440; Fax: 816-221-4264.

19—HOLY TRINITY. Closed. For inquiries for parish records contact the Chancery.

20—ST. JAMES (1906), Rev. William Hubmann, C.PP.S.
Res., 3909 Harrison St., 64110. Tel: 816-561-8512.
Catechesis/Religious Programs—Students 72.

21—ST. JOHN THE BAPTIST. Closed. For inquiries for parish records contact the Chancery.

22—ST. JOHN FRANCIS REGIS (1964), Rev. Paul Turner; Deacons Edwin Bonnarens; Marvin Mason.
Res., 8941 James A. Reed Rd., 64138. Tel: 816-761-1608; Fax: 816-966-1350.
School—Tel: 816-763-5837.
Sisters of Charity of the Blessed Virgin Mary 1; Lay Teachers 21; Students 361.
Catechesis/Religious Programs—Tel: 816-763-1366.
Students 459.

23—ST. MONICA, Rev. Philip Egan.
Res., 1616 The Paseo, 64108.

24—ST. LOUIS (1919) (African American), Rev. Donald Farnan.

Res., 5930 Swope Pkwy., 64130. Tel: 816-444-6535; Fax: 816-822-2615.
Catechesis/Religious Programs—Students 15.

25—ST. MATTHEW THE APOSTLE (1964), Rev. James Taranto; Deacon Joseph Ofenloch.
Res., 8001 Longview Rd., 64134. Tel: 816-763-0208; Fax: 816-763-4758.
School—Our Lady of Peace Consolidated School, 10526 Grandview Rd., 64134. Tel: 816-761-5605; Fax: 816-761-2797.
Catechesis/Religious Programs—Tel: 816-765-7381.
Students 90.

26—ST. MICHAEL ARCHANGEL. Closed. For inquiries for parish records contact the Chancery.

27—OLD ST. PATRICK'S (1869). Public Oratory associated with Cathedral of the Immaculate Conception. Rev. Msgr. Ernest J. Fiedler.
Res., The Cathedral House, 416 W. 12th St., 64105. Tel: 816-842-0416; Fax: 816-842-3849.

28—OUR LADY OF GOOD COUNSEL (1866), Rev. Msgr. William J. Blacet. In res., Rev. John VanGorder, (Retired).
Res., 3934 Washington, 64111-2904. Tel: 816-561-0400; Fax: 816-561-1551.

29—OUR LADY OF GUADALUPE. Closed. For inquiries for parish records contact the Chancery.

30—SACRED HEART-GUADALUPE (1887) (Hispanic), Rev. James G. Betzen, C.PP.S.
Res., 907 Cesar Chavez Ave., 64108. Tel: 816-842-6146; Fax: 816-471-7540.
Catechesis/Religious Programs—Students 34.

31—OUR LADY OF PEACE (1991), Rev. Donald Helfrey; Deacons Al Ohmes; Manuel Guerra.
Res., 1029 Bennington Ave., 64126-2299. Tel: 816-231-0953.
School—Consolidated School St. Stephen's Academy. See separate listing. Tel: 816-231-5227.

32—OUR LADY OF PERPETUAL HELP (1878), Revs. James Shea, C.Ss.R.; Andrew Meiners, C.Ss.R.; Joseph Curalli, C.Ss.R.; Bros. James Burke, C.Ss.R.; Charles Long, C.Ss.R. In res., Revs. James Springer, C.Ss.R.; Edward Kane, C.Ss.R.; Bernard Kramer, C.Ss.R.; Patrick Power, C.Ss.R.
Res., 3333 Broadway, 64111. Tel: 816-561-3771; Fax: 816-561-3704.
School—Our Lady of the Angels, 211 W. Linwood Blvd., 64111. Tel: 816-931-1693; Fax: 816-753-3606. Mary Kallman, Prin.
Sisters 3; Lay Teachers 12; Students 230.

33—OUR LADY OF SORROWS (1891), Revs. Richard F. Carney, J.C.D.; Ambrose G. Karels, Chap. of Latin Mass Community, Tel: 816-931-1030.
Res., 2552 Gillham Rd., 64108. Tel: 816-421-2112; Fax: 816-421-6037.

34—ST. PATRICK (1924), Rev. Michael G. Roach; Deacon Michael Lewis.
Res., 1357 N.E. 42nd Ter., 64116. Tel: 816-453-5510; Fax: 816-453-4458.
School—1401 N.E. 42nd Ter., 64116. Tel: 816-453-0971.
Lay Teachers 12; Students 240.
Catechesis/Religious Programs—Students 134.

35—ST. PETER'S (1927), Rev. Gerald R. Waris. In res., Rev. Patrick J. Rush, V.G.
Res., 6415 Holmes St., 64131. Tel: 816-363-2320; Fax: 816-363-2492; 363-8157.
School—6400 Charlotte St., 64131. Tel: 816-523-4899; Fax: 816-523-1248.
Sisters 2; Lay Teachers 25; Students 500.
Catechesis/Religious Programs—Students 50.

36—ST. RAPHAEL THE ARCHANGEL (1963), Rev. Alexander B. Sinclair.
Res., 7952 N.E. 54th St., 64119. Tel: 816-453-7449.
Catechesis/Religious Programs—Students 100.

37—ST. STANISLAUS. Closed. For inquiries for parish records contact the Chancery.

38—ST. THERESE LITTLE FLOWER (1925), Rev. Donald Farnan, Sac. Min.; Sr. Helen Flemington, C.S.J., Pastoral Admin.
Res., 5814 Euclid Ave., 64130. Tel: 816-444-5406; Fax: 816-444-9345.
Catechesis/Religious Programs—Students 50.

39—ST. THERESE PARISH (Kansas City North) (1949), Revs. James Hart; John McCormack; Philip Watanabe; Joseph Cisetti.
Res., 7207 Hwy. 9, N.W., 64152. Tel: 816-741-2800; Fax: 816-741-4959.
School—7277 Hwy. 9 N.W., 64152. Tel: 816-741-5400.
Lay Teachers 27; Students 613.
Catechesis/Religious Programs—Tel: 816-741-3957.
Students 584.

40—ST. THOMAS MORE (1964), Revs. William A. Bauman; J. Daniel Reardon.
Res., 11822 Holmes St., 64131. Tel: 816-942-2492; Fax: 816-942-8803.
School—Tel: 816-942-5581; Fax: 816-941-2450.
Lay Teachers 27; Students 569.
Catechesis/Religious Programs—Students 65.

41—VISITATION OF THE BLESSED VIRGIN (1915), Revs. Norman Rotert; Greg Haskamp. Pastoral Assocs.: Sr. Alice Smitherman, O.S.B.; Peg Ekerdt; Steve Engler; Anne Mcgwire.
Mailing Address: 5141 Main St., 64112. Tel: 816-753-7422; Fax: 816-753-5505.
Res., 2 E. 51st, 64112. Tel: 816-753-6968.
School—Tel: 816-531-6220; Fax: 816-531-2819.
Lay Teachers 24; Students 400.
Catechesis/Religious Programs—5134 Baltimore, 64118.
Students 400.

CITY OF ST. JOSEPH
(Buchanan County)

1—ST. JOSEPH'S CO-CATHEDRAL (1845), Rev. Richard Dierkes; Deacons William Dattilo; Richard W. Snooks.
Res., 519 N. 10th St., 64501. Tel: 816-232-7763; Fax: 816-232-2460.
School—518 N. 11th St., 65401. Tel: 816-232-8486; Fax: 816-232-8793.
Lay Teachers 14; Students 250.
Catechesis/Religious Programs—Students 75.

2—OUR LADY OF GUADALUPE (1981), Rev. Robert Murphy; Susan Tally, Office Mgr. Pastoral Assocs.: Kathryn Powers; Ellen Simon.
Church—4503 Frederick, 64506. Tel: 816-232-2847; Fax: 816-232-0269.
Catechesis/Religious Programs—Tel: 816-232-0112. Linda Powers, D.R.E.
Students 468.

3—ST. FRANCIS XAVIER (1890), Revs. Michael Volkmer, C.PP.S.; Joseph Bathke, C.PP.S. In res., Rev. Bernard Diekhoff, C.PP.S.
Res., 2618 Seneca St., 64507. Tel: 816-232-8449.
School—2614 Seneca St., 64507. Tel: 816-232-9411.
Lay Teachers 21; Students 427.
Catechesis/Religious Programs—Students 105.

4—ST. JAMES (1900), Rev. Vincent Rogers, Admin.; Deacon Robert Farris.
Res., 5814 King Hill Ave., 64504. Tel: 816-238-0853; Fax: 816-238-1758.
School—120 Michigan Ave., 64504. Tel: 816-238-0281.
Benedictine Sisters 1; Lay Teachers 8; Students 205.

5—ST. MARY'S (1891), Rev. Msgr. Victor G. Moser.
Res., 1606 N. 2nd St., 64505. Tel: 816-279-1154.
Catechesis/Religious Programs—Students 73.

6—ST. PATRICK'S (1869), Rev. Matthew Brumleve; Deacon Elmer Hoppins.
Office: 1723 S. 12th St., 64503. Tel: 816-279-2594.
School—1813 S. 12th St., 64503. Tel: 816-232-9001; Fax: 816-232-7904.
Lay Teachers 11; Students 149.
Catechesis/Religious Programs—Students 53.

7—QUEEN OF THE APOSTLES. Closed. For inquiries for parish records contact the Chancery.

OUTSIDE THE CITIES OF KANSAS CITY AND ST. JOSEPH

Belton, Cass Co., St. Sabina's (1944), Rev. Joseph H. Matt.
Res., 700 Trevis Ave., 64012. Tel: 816-331-4713; Fax: 816-322-6196.
Catechesis/Religious Programs—Students 285.

Bethany, Harrison Co., Blessed Sacrament (1945), Rev. Alexander Luetkemeyer, O.S.B.
Res., 1208 S. 25th St., 64424. Tel: 660-425-8160.
Mission—Cainsville, Harrison Co., St. Mary's, 1208 S. Hwy. 69, 64424.

Blue Springs, Jackson Co., St. John La Lande (1938), Revs. Michael O. Clary; John H. Wandless; Deacon John Maloney.
Res., 805 NW R.D. Mize Rd., 64015. Tel: 816-229-3378; Fax: 816-229-1362.
School—801 NW R.D. Mize Rd., 64015. Tel: 816-228-5895.
Lay Teachers 21; Students 344.
Catechesis/Religious Programs—Tel: 816-228-4511.
Students 412.

St. Robert Bellarmine (1983), Rev. Lloyd E. Opoka.
Res., 4313 S. Hwy. 7, 64014. Tel: 816-229-5168; Fax: 816-229-3981.
Catechesis/Religious Programs—Students 286.

Buckner, Jackson Co., Church of the Santa Fe (1965), Rev. Ralph L. Kaiser.
Res., P.O. Box 317, 64016. Tel: 816-650-9341.

Butler, Bates Co., St. Patrick's, Rev. Richard Ducate.
Res., 400 W. Nursery St., 64730. Tel: 660-679-4482.
Catechesis/Religious Programs—Students 40.
Mission—Rich Hill, Bates Co., St. Bridget's, 903 E. Walnut St., 64779.

Cameron, Clinton Co., St. Munchin (1867) (German-Irish), Rev. Alvin L. Herber, C.PP.S.; Deacon John Riead.
Res., 316 W. Third St., 64429. Tel: 816-632-2768. [CEM][JC 2]
Catechesis/Religious Programs—Tel: 816-632-6276.
Students 175.
Mission—Maysville, DeKalb Co., St. Aloysius.

Carrollton, Carroll Co., St. Mary's (1867), Rev. Kenneth Criqui.
Res., 211 E. Shanklin St., 64633. Tel: 660-542-1259. [CEM]
Catechesis/Religious Programs—Tel: 660-542-1681.
Students 75.

Chillicothe, Livingston Co., St. Columban's (1879), Rev. Reginald Sander, O.S.B.; Deacons Lawrence Schneider, (Retired); Joseph Crookshanks; Jerry Davis.
Res., 1111 Trenton St., 64601. Tel: 660-646-0190. [CEM]
School—Bishop Hogan Memorial School, 1112 Trenton St., 64601. Tel: 660-646-0705.
Lay Teachers 11; Students 143.
Catechesis/Religious Programs—Students 159.

Clinton, Henry Co., Holy Rosary (1875), Rev. Thomas W. Hermes.
Res., 610 S. 4th St., 64735. Tel: 660-885-4523.
School—400 E. Wilson, 64735. Tel: 660-885-4412.
Sisters 1; Lay Teachers 5; Students 94.
Catechesis/Religious Programs—Students 45.
Missions—Osceola, St. Clair Co., St. Catherine's, Hwy. WW, Osceola, 64776. Tel: 417-646-2217; Windsor, Henry Co., St. Bartholomew, 504 E. Benton, Windsor, 65360. Tel: 660-647-2613.

Conception Junction, Nodaway Co., St. Columba (1860), Rev. Augustine Dreiling, O.S.B.; Deacon Martin Goedken.
Res., One St. Columba Pl., 64434. Tel: 660-944-2301. [CEM]
Catechesis/Religious Programs—Students 159.

Easton, Buchanan Co., St. Joseph's (1830), Rev. Matthew Brumleve; Deacon Elmer E. Hoppins; Susan Christensen, Pastoral Assoc.
Res., P.O. Box 197, 64443. Tel: 816-473-2011. [CEM]
Catechesis/Religious Programs—Students 70.

Excelsior Springs, Clay Co., St. Ann (1889), Rev. William Caldwell, Admin.; Deacon John Lauhoff.
Res., 1503 Tracy, 64024. Tel: 816-630-6659.
Catechesis/Religious Programs—Connie Davis, D.R.E.
Students 213.

Gladstone, St. Andrew the Apostle (1964), Rev. Thomas W. Wiederholt.
Res., 6415 N.E. Antioch Rd., 64119. Tel: 816-453-2089; Fax: 816-453-2442.
Catechesis/Religious Programs—Tel: 816-454-7377.
Students 191.

Grandview, Jackson Co., Coronation of Our Lady (1958), Rev. Michael Tierney.
Res., 13000 Bennington, 64030. Tel: 816-761-8811; Fax: 816-761-8812.
Catechesis/Religious Programs—Students 165.

Hamilton, Caldwell Co., Sacred Heart (1921), Rev. Robert Kerr.
Res., 205 E. Middle St., 64644. Tel: 816-583-4413.
Catechesis/Religious Programs—Students 55.
Mission—Gallatin, Daviess Co., Mary Immaculate, Hwy. 13, Gallatin, 64640. Rev. Donald E. Sturm, Admin., Tel: 616-671-1510.

Harrisonville, Cass Co., Our Lady of Lourdes (1941), Rev. Bradley S. Offutt.
Res., 2700 N. Hwy. 7, 64701. Tel: 816-380-5744.
Catechesis/Religious Programs—Students 214.
Mission—Pleasant Hill, Cass Co., St. Bridget, (1884) P.O. Box 247, 64701.

Higginsville, Lafayette Co., St. Mary's (1879), Deacon Ron Elliott, Pastoral Admin.
Res., 400 W. 29th, 64037. Tel: 660-584-3038. [CEM]

Hirlingen, Buchanan Co., Seven Dolors (1872), Rev. Thomas Waterman.
Res., 12750 Hurlingen Rd., P.O. Box 115, Easton, 64443. Tel: 816-667-5645. [CEM]

Holden, Johnson Co., St. Patrick's (1896), Rev. Ernest L. Gauthier.
Res., 703 S. Olive St., 64040. Tel: 816-732-4516; Fax: 816-732-5595. [CEM]
Catechesis/Religious Programs—Tel: 816-850-4510.
Students 70.

Independence, Jackson Co.,

1—ST. ANN'S, (1917), Rev. Terry Bruce.
Res., 10113 Lexington Ave., 64053. Tel: 816-252-1160.

School—Tel: 816-252-1024; Fax: 816-252-3272.
Sisters of St. Francis of the Holy Eucharist 1; Lay Teachers 8; Students 188.
Catechesis/Religious Programs—Students 188.

2—St. Joseph the Worker, (1976), Rev. John E. Leitner.
Res., 2200 N. Blue Mills Rd., 64058. Tel: 816-796-6877; Fax: 816-796-6876.
Catechesis/Religious Programs—D.R.E.: Barbara Ganz; Sr. Joan Markley, S.L., (Adult Educ.).
Students 88.

3—St. Mark, (1965), Rev. James E. Healy; Deacon Philip R. Beaudoin.
Res., 3736 Lee's Summit Rd., 64055. Tel: 816-373-2600; Fax: 816-373-3816.
Catechesis/Religious Programs—Joyce Arthur, D.R.E.
Students 488.

4—St. Mary's, (1845), Revs. Charles F. Jones; Joseph Meisburger; Tom Borkowski; Deacon Thomas D. Powell.
Res., 611 N. Liberty St., 64050. Tel: 816-252-0121. [CEM]
Catechesis/Religious Programs—Students 150.

5—Nativity of the Blessed Virgin, (1938), Rev. Robert A. Rost, D.Min.
Res., 10017 E. 36th Ter., 64052. Tel: 816-353-2184; Fax: 816-358-5228.
School—10021 E. 36th Ter., 64052. Tel: 816-353-0284.
Lay Teachers 12; Students 245.
Catechesis/Religious Programs—Tel: 816-353-1638.
Students 38.

Kearney, Clay Co., Church of the Annunciation (1980), Rev. Thomas A. Conway, C.PP.S.
Mailing Address: P.O. Box 599, 64060-0599. Tel: 816-628-5030; Fax: 816-628-4279.
Catechesis/Religious Programs—Students 207.

Lee's Summit, Jackson Co., Our Lady of the Presentation (1896), Revs. Michael D. Rice; J. Martin Rotert; Deacons Joseph Stueve; Del Wilkinson.
Res., 130 N.W. Murray Rd., 64081. Tel: 816-524-3657; Fax: 816-525-8348.
School—Tel: 816-524-4121.
Lay Teachers 22; Students 347.
Catechesis/Religious Programs—Tel: 816-524-3690.
Students 786.
Holy Spirit (1979), Rev. Roger F. Miller.
Res., 616 S.W. 36th Ter., 64082. Tel: 816-537-7753.
Catechesis/Religious Programs—Tel: 816-537-6990.
Students 93.

Lexington, Lafayette Co., Immaculate Conception (1842), Rev. Terrell M. Finnell.
Res., 107 N. 18th St., 64067. Tel: 660-259-3043. [CEM]
Catechesis/Religious Programs—Sr. Joyce McNerney, O.S.B., D.R.E.
Students 89.
Chapel—Chapel of Ease, Lexington.

Liberty, Clay Co., St. James (1840), Revs. Ron Will, C.PP.S.; Dien Troung, C.PP.S.
Res., 309 S. Stewart Rd., 64068. Tel: 816-781-4343; Fax: 816-792-8691.
School—Tel: 816-781-4428; Fax: 816-781-0747.
Lay Teachers 21; Students 306.
Catechesis/Religious Programs—Students 309.

Maryville, Nodaway Co., St. Gregory Barbarigo (1860), Revs. Chuck Tobin; Donald S. Miller; Deacons Roy Seipel; Martin Schieber.
Res., 333 S. Davis St., 64468. Tel: 660-582-3833; Fax: 816-582-3832. [CEM 2]
School—315 S. Davis St., 64468. Tel: 660-582-2462; Fax: 816-582-2496.
Lay Teachers 13; Students 228.
Newman Center—606 College Ave., 64468. Tel: 660-582-7373. Rev. Xavier Nacke, O.S.B.
Catechesis/Religious Programs—Tel: 660-582-5914.
Students 223.

Montrose, Henry Co., Immaculate Conception (1876) (German), Rev. Robert Stone.
Res., 606 Kansas Ave., 64770-9601. Tel: 660-693-4651; Fax: 660-693-4713. [CEM][JC 2]
School—St. Mary School, Tel: 816-693-4502.
Lay Teachers 4; Students 51.
Mission—Urich, Henry Co., Holy Trinity, 1372 N.W. Grahm Rd., Urich, 64788. Tel: 660-638-4715.
Catechesis/Religious Programs—Students 69.

Nevada, Vernon Co., St. Mary's (1887), Rev. James H. Schrader, C.PP.S.
Res., 330 N. Main St., 64772. Tel: 417-667-5604. [CEM]
School—Tel: 417-67-7517.
Lay Teachers 3; Students 55.
Catechesis/Religious Programs—Students 90.

Odessa, Lafayette Co., St. George (1882), Rev. Peter M. Savage; Deacon Harry Rodman.
Res., 716 S. Third, 64076. Tel: 816-230-4127.
Mission—Oak Grove, Jackson Co., St. Jude the Apostle, 2001 S. Broadway, P.O. Box 590, Oak Grove, 64075. Tel: 816-625-3165.
Catechesis/Religious Programs—Students 116.

Parnell, Nodaway Co., St. Joseph's (1891), Rev. Roland Carbone, O.S.B.
Res., P.O. Box 78, 64475. Tel: 660-986-3305. [CEM]
Catechesis/Religious Programs—Students 99.

Plattsburg, Clinton Co., St. Ann's (1866) (Irish), Rev. Robert E. Crider.
Res., 700 Maple St., 64477. Tel: 816-539-2634. [CEM]
Catechesis/Religious Programs—Students 54.

Raytown, Jackson Co., Our Lady of Lourdes (1948), Rev. John Eldringhoff; Deacon Richard Muraski.
Res., 7009 Blue Ridge Blvd., 64133. Tel: 816-353-2380; Fax: 816-353-5737.
School—8812 E. Gregory Blvd., 64133. Tel: 816-353-7062; Fax: 816-353-7650.
Sisters of St. Joseph 2; Lay Teachers 16; Students 230.
Catechesis/Religious Programs—Tel: 816-356-5070.
Students 112.

Richmond, Ray Co., Immaculate Conception (1869), Rev. Mark A. Honhart.
Res., 602 S. Camden, 64085. Tel: 660-470-2268. [CEM]
Catechesis/Religious Programs—Students 46.
Mission—Norbone, Carroll Co., Sacred Heart, 201 E. Fifth St., Norbone, 64668. Tel: 816-594-3536.

Savannah, Andrew Co., St. Rose of Lima (1898), Rev. Thomas K. Ludwig.
Office: 707 Hall Ave., 64485. Tel: 816-324-5700.
Res., 101 E. Park Ave., 64485. Tel: 816-324-3231.
Catechesis/Religious Programs—Students 89.
Mission—Forest City, Holt Co., St. Patrick.

Smithville, Clay Co., Church of the Good Shepherd (1974), Rev. Bernard E. Branson.
Res., 109 Smith St., P.O. Box 653, 64089. Tel: 816-532-4344; 532-0522.
Catechesis/Religious Programs—Tel: 816-734-8925.
Students 162.

Stanberry, Gentry Co., St. Peter's (1880), Rev. Daniel Petsche, O.S.B.
Res., 614 N. Alanthus Ave., 64489. Tel: 660-783-2159. [CEM 2]
Catechesis/Religious Programs—Students 124.
Mission—Ford City, Gentry Co., St. Patrick's, King City, 64463.

Sugar Creek, Jackson Co., St. Cyril (1912) (Croatian-Slovak), Rev. Walter J. Pilecki.
Res., 11231 Chicago Ave., 64054. Tel: 816-252-9564.

Tarkio, Atchison Co., St. Paul the Apostle (1890), Rev. Quentin Kathol, O.S.B.
Res., 908 Elm St., 64491. Tel: 660-736-4342.
Catechesis/Religious Programs—Students 50.
Mission—Burlington Junction, Nodaway Co., St. Benedict Catholic Church, Burlington Junction, 64428. Tel: 660-725-4407.

Trenton, Grundy Co., St. Joseph's (1872), Rev. Edgar Probstfield, O.S.B.
Res., 1728 St. Joseph Ave., 64683. Tel: 660-359-2841. [CEM]
Mission—Trenton, Mercer Co., Immaculate Heart of Mary Church, 1728 St. Joseph Ave., 64683. [JC]
Catechesis/Religious Programs—Students 78.

Warrensburg, Johnson Co., Sacred Heart (1865), Rev. William P. Walter, C.PP.S.
Res., 200 Ming St., P.O. Box 926, 64093. Tel: 660-747-6154; Fax: 660-747-2387.
Catechesis/Religious Programs—Tel: 660-747-5965.
Students 140.

Weston, Platte Co., Holy Trinity (1842), Rev. Thomas Hawkins.
Res., 407 Cherry St., 64098. Tel: 816-640-2206. [JC]
Catechesis/Religious Programs—Students 124.

Special Assignment:
Reverend Fathers—
Cameron, Robert, 7601 Blue Ridge, Kansas City, MO 64138
Coleman, C. Michael, J.C.L., P.O. Box 419037, Kansas City, MO 64141-6037
Jankowski, Marcellus A., 6515 E. 7th St., Kansas City, MO 64612
Karels, Ambrose G., P.O. Box 410834, Kansas City, MO 64141
Mahoney, Robert J., Rockhurst College, Sociology Dept., 5225 Troost Ave., Kansas City, MO 64110
Moscaritdo, Mario, 4019 Warwick, Kansas City, MO 64111
Rush, Patrick J., V.G., P.O. Box 419037, Kansas City, MO 64141-6037
Schuele, Francis J., 8300 E. 88th Ter., #3002, Kansas City, MO 64138
Verhaeghe, Ronald, 1218 E. 49th Ter., Kansas City, MO 64110-2310

On Duty Outside the Diocese:
Reverend Fathers—
Blais, Roger
Cronin, Thomas
Holloway, David L.
Maxim, Craig

Mission Duty:
Reverend Fathers—
Gillgannon, Michael, Casilla 12162, La Paz, Bolivia
Walker, Michael, Santiago Atitlan 07019, Depto. Solola, Guatemala

---

On Educational Leave of Absence:
Reverend Fathers—
Cook, Steven, Pontifical North American College, Vatican City State, Rome, Italy

---

Leave of Absence:
Reverend Fathers—
Arciga, Michael
Evers, Paul K.
Monahan, Hugh F.
Townsend, C. Frederick
Turner, Thomas W.

Unassigned:
Reverend Fathers—
Deming, Robert N.

Retired:
Reverend Monsignors—
Bauer, Henry, 6425 Woodson, Kansas City, MO 64133
Froeschl, Martin H., P.O. Box 201, Oregon, MO 64473
Huhmann, John F., 10515 Bridlespur Dr., Kansas City, MO 64114-4712
Kearney, Vincent L., 12655 State Line, Kansas City, MO 64145
O'Brien, Thomas J., 11281 Oak, Apt. 101, Kansas City, MO 64114-5446
Summers, R. Emmett, 4114 N.E. Davidson Rd., Apt 314, Kansas City, MO 64116
Reverend Fathers—
Bachnak, Francis J., 705A Maple St., Plattsburg, MO 64477
Blaes, Paul, M.A., Ph.D., 1589 Carrollwood Rd., Sarasota, FL 34232
Boyle, Leo A., Marymount Place, 11960 McCracken Rd., Garfield Heights, OH 44125
Carson, Paul C., 1014 W. Main, Bethany, MO 64424
Cleary, Donald R., 411 E. 79th St., Kansas City, MO 64131
Coleman, John P., 4101 E. 105th Ter., Kansas City, MO 64137
Faller, Henry E., Jeanne Jugan Center, 8745 James A. Reed Rd., Kansas City, MO 64138
Giacopelli, John A., 494 Clinton St., Brooklyn, NY 11231
Hoppe, Sylvester J., 918 S. Noyes Blvd., St. Joseph, MO 64507
Jakubowski, Joseph J., 1131 Central, Apt. 1110, Kansas City, KS 66102
Lackamp, Franklin J., 31109 E. Old Major Rd., Grain Valley, MO 64029
Link, Linus F., 7030 N. Bales, Apt. 337, Gladstone, MO 64119
Lyons, James P., 9001 James A. Reed Rd., Kansas City, MO 64138
Mahoney, Jeremia W., Jeanne Jugan Center, 8745 James A. Reed Rd., Kansas City, MO 64138
McCarthy, Thomas H., 3303 Urban Crest Dr., San Antonio, TX 78209
McGlynn, Francis, 700 E. Eigth St., #910, Kansas City, MO 64106
McQuinn, Maurice, 115 W. 99th Terrace, No 102, Kansas City, MO 64114
Meisburger, Joseph C., 611 N. Liberty, Independence, MO 64050
Miller, Donald S., 333 S. Davis, Maryville, MO 64468
Mullin, Hugh J., 2100 Nursery Rd., Bldg. A-4, Clearwater, FL 34624
O'Connor, Patrick, Rte. 3, Box 32, Butler, MO 64730
Paa, Donald R., 1500 W. 23rd Ter., Apt. 3, Independence, MO 64050
Pecoraro, James A., 410 W. 104th St., Apt. A, Kansas City, MO 64114
Powell, Harold W., 333-A Front St., Grain Valley, MO 64029
Powers, Donald E., P.O Box 535, Roach, MO 65787

Russ, Francis J., 12900 E. 62nd, Kansas City, MO 64133
Ryan, C. Duane, Rte. 2, Box 335, Sunrise Beach, MO 65079
Ryan, Clarence R., 1901 Forrest Ave., Lexington, MO 64067
Saale, Richard T., 8800 Buckingham Ln., Apt. 14, Kansas City, MO 64138
Speichinger, Lawrence, Rte. 3 Box 22, Chillicothe, MO 64601
Van Gorder, John, 3934 Washington, Kansas City, MO 64111
Ward, Thomas, 3600 Poplar, Independence, MO 64052
Whelan, Thomas, 7801 Detroit Ave., Cleveland, OH 44102

Permanent Deacons:
Barry, James Timothy
Beaudoin, Phillip Ross
Bode, William
Bonnarens, Edwin
Browning, Melvin
Cathers, Calvin
Clark, Joseph P.
Corrigan, Emory S.
Crookshanks, Joseph V.
Dattilo, William
Davis, F. Jerry
DiMartino, Charles
Elliot, Ronald
Ernst, John H.
Falcon, Francis L.
Falcon, Louie P.
Farris, Robert E.
Fountain, Mark J.
Gach, Victor S.
Goedken, Martin J.
Guerra, Manuel P.
Henggeler, Francis J.
Hoppins, Elmer E.
Koch, John J.
Kopp, George C.
Kopp, Harold G., Sr.
Kratofil, Lawrence
Langdon, Harry
Lauhoff, John D.
Lewis, Michael
Lickteig, Wayne A.
Madden, Donald
Maloney, John J.
Markey, William R.
Mason, Marvin M.
McArdle, Paul
McCandless, Donald L.
McCoy, Warren W.
McKay, Clarence W.
McMenamy, Justin M.
Muraski, Richard J.
Ofenloch, Joseph C.
Ohmes, Albert J.
Peak, Francis L.
Powell, D. Thomas
Riead, John
Rodman, Harold M.
Sandoval, Antonio J.
Santellan, Alfred M.
Schieber, Martin L.
Schmit, Donald A.
Schneider, Lawrence
Seipel, Leroy
Snooks, Richard W.
Stoetzer, Jerome P.
Stueve, Joseph E.
Thompson, John R.
Wilkinson, Del
Williams, Garen R.
Williams, Jerry

INSTITUTIONS LOCATED IN THE DIOCESE

[A] SEMINARIES, RELIGIOUS OR SCHOLASTICATES

KANSAS CITY. *Precious Blood Mission House*, 5221 Rockhill Rd., 64110. Tel: 816-822-2596.
E-mail: KCProv@aol.com
Revs. Mark Miller, C.PP.S., Provincial Dir.; Alan Hartway, C.PP.S.; Jack McClure, C.PP.S.

CONCEPTION. *Conception Seminary College*, 64433. Tel: 660-944-2218.
E-mail: abbeys@netins.net
Web site: www.msc-net.com/~/cabbey/
Rt. Rev. Gregory Polan, O.S.B., Chancellor; Revs. Benedict Neenan, O.S.B., Pres.-Rector; Albert Bruecken, O.S.B.; Roland Carbone, O.S.B.; Patrick Caveglia, O.S.B.; Donald Grabner, O.S.B.; Thomas Greisen (OM); James Jones, O.S.B.; Quentin Kathol, O.S.B.; Xavier Nacke, O.S.B.; Daniel Petsche, O.S.B.; James Polich (Des Moines); Kenneth Reichert, O.S.B.; Duane F. Reinert, O.F.M.Cap.; Samuel Russell, O.S.B.; Alexis Saathoff, O.S.B.; Timothy Schoen, O.S.B.; Hugh Tasch, O.S.B.; Isaac True, O.S.B.; Peter Ullrich, O.S.B. Priests 20; Brothers 7; Lay Professors 6; Students 69.

LIBERTY. *Precious Blood Center.* (Kansas City Province), 2110-2140 Hughes Rd., 64068. Tel: 816-781-4344; Fax: 816-781-3639. Bro. Stephan Ohnmacht, C.PP.S., Local Dir. Priests 8; Brothers 2.
Society of the Precious Blood Provincial Offices, P.O. Box 339, 64069-0339. Tel: 816-781-4344; Fax: 816-781-3639.
E-mail: KCProv@aol.com
Revs. William P. Walter, C.PP.S., Prov. Vice; Mark Miller, C.PP.S., Prov. Dir.; Ronald Will, C.PP.S., Prov. Sec.; William Dineen, C.PP.S., Prov. Treas.

[B] COLLEGES AND UNIVERSITIES

KANSAS CITY. *Avila College*, 11901 Wornall Rd., 64145-1698. Tel: 816-942-8400; Fax: 816-942-3362.
Web site: www.avila.edu
For a complete listing, refer to the Colleges and Universities section.
Rockhurst College, 1100 Rockhurst Rd., 64110-2561. Tel: 816-501-4000; Fax: 816-501-4588
For a complete listing, refer to the Colleges and Universities section.

[C] HIGH SCHOOLS, DIOCESAN

KANSAS CITY. *Archbishop O'Hara High School.* (Coed), 9001 James A. Reed Rd., 64138. Tel: 816-763-4800. Mr. Walter Bowman, Prin. Christian Brothers 3; Lay Teachers 43; Students 550.
Bishop Hogan High School, 1221 E. Meyer Blvd., 64131. Tel: 816-444-3464. Ms. Mary Theresa (Terry) Macke, Prin. Lay Teachers 17; Students 182.
St. Pius X High School, 1500 N.E. 42nd Ter., 64116. Tel: 816-453-3450.
E-mail: NCARLIN@stpiusedu.com
Edward P. Carlin, Ph.D., Prin. Sisters of Charity of Leavenworth 1; Lay Teachers 23; Students 303.

ST. JOSEPH. *Bishop LeBlond High School*, 3529 Frederick Ave., 64506. Tel: 816-279-1629.
E-mail: leblond@ccp.com
Sr. Corrine Connelly, R.S.M., Prin.; Rev. Thomas K. Ludwig, Chap. Priests 1; Lay Teachers 25; Students 272.

INDEPENDENCE. *St. Mary's Diocesan High School-Bundschu Memorial*, 622 N. Main St., 64050. Tel: 816-252-8733. David Woolwine, Pres.; Judith Warren, Prin. Lay Teachers 20; Students 233.

[D] HIGH SCHOOLS, PRIVATE

KANSAS CITY. *De La Salle Academy*, 3732 Paseo, 64109. Tel: 816-531-6561. Special Educational Programs. Christian Brothers, F.S.C. and LaSallian Volunteers. Christian Brothers 4; LaSallian Volunteers 1.
Notre Dame de Sion High School, 10631 Wornall Rd., 64114. Tel: 816-942-3282; Fax: 816-942-4052.
E-mail: ndsion@worldnet.att.net
Web site: www.sion.edu
Affiliated with Sisters of Notre Dame de Sion. Alice Munninghoff, Head of School; Michelle Olson, Prin. Lay Teachers 29; Students 325.
Rockhurst High School, 9301 State Line Rd., 64114. Tel: 816-363-2036. Revs. Thomas A. Pesci, S.J., Pres.; Christopher P. Pinne, S.J., Superior; David J. Suwalsky, S.J.; Mark J. Daues, S.J.; Deacon R. Mark Michalski, S.J., Scholastic. Jesuit Priests 4; Lay Teachers 59; Students 877. RHS Jesuit Community, 3135 Karnes Blvd., 64111. Tel: 816-531-0806. Revs. Christopher P. Pinne, S.J., Superior; David J. Suwalsky, S.J.; Mark J. Daues, S.J.; Deacon R. Mark Michalski, S.J., Scholastic.
St. Teresa's Academy, 5600 Main St., 64113. Tel: 816-523-3522; Fax: 816-523-0232. Affiliated with Sisters of St. Joseph of Carondelet. Dr. Faith Wilson, Ph.D., Pres.; Mary Anne Hoecker, M.A., Assoc. Prin.; Nancy Hand, M.A., Assoc. Prin. Sisters 3; Lay Teachers 34; Students 467.

[E] ELEMENTARY SCHOOLS

KANSAS CITY. *Our Lady of Guadalupe School*, 2310 Madison, 64108. Tel: 816-221-2539. Connie Ginter, Prin. Lay Teachers 5; Students 88.
Our Lady of Peace School. (Grades PreK-8), 10526 Grandview Rd., 64137. Tel: 816-761-5605.
E-mail: ourladyofpeace@hotmail.com
Web site: http://www.kansascity.com/.schools
Mrs. Mary Ann Long, Prin. Consolidated with Coronation, St. Catherine's, St. Matthew's, and St. Sabina's to form Our Lady of Peace School. Lay Teachers 18; Students 388; Preschool Students 43.
St. Monica School. (Grades PreK-8), Elementary: 5809 Michigan, 64130. Tel: 816-444-6736. Mary Ann Kneib-Sadler, Prin. Consolidated with St. Monica of Africa, St Therese Little Flower, St. Louis, and St. James to form St. Monica's School. Sisters 1; Lay Teachers 22; Students 310.
St. Stephen's School, 1001 Bennington, 64126. Tel: 816-231-5227. Rev. Donald Helfrey; Sr. Leona Bax, O.S.F., Prin. Sisters 3; Lay Teachers 11; Students 176.

[F] ELEMENTARY SCHOOLS, PRIVATE

KANSAS CITY. *Notre Dame de Sion Elementary School*, 3823 Locust St., 64109. Tel: 816-753-3810; Fax: 816-753-0806.
E-mail: ndsion@worldnet.att.net
Web site: www.sion.edu
Affiliated with Sisters of Notre Dame de Sion. Alice Munninghoff, Head of School. Principals: Dr. Grace Ann Ancona, Ed.D.; Barbara Altergott. Lay Teachers 29; Students 308.

[G] GENERAL HOSPITALS

KANSAS CITY. *Saint Joseph Health Center*, 1000 Carondelet Dr., 64114. Tel: 816-942-4400
For a complete listing, refer to the Hospitals section.

BLUE SPRINGS. *St. Mary's Hospital of Blue Springs*, 201 W. R.D. Mize Rd., 64014. Tel: 816-228-5900; Fax: 816-228-7555
For a complete listing, refer to the Hospitals section.

MARYVILLE. *St. Francis Hospital & Health Services*, 2016 S. Main, 64468. Tel: 660-562-2600; Fax: 660-562-7911
For a complete listing, refer to the Hospitals section.

[H] SPECIAL CARE UNITS

BLUE SPRINGS. *St. Mary's Manor*, 111 Mock Ave., 64014. Tel: 816-228-5655
For a complete listing, refer to the Special Care Facilities section.

LIBERTY. *Immacolata Manor Foundation*, 2101 Hughes Rd., 64068-9397. Tel: 816-781-4332; Fax: 816-781-8820
For a complete listing, refer to the Special Care Facilities section.

[I] HOMES FOR THE ELDERLY

KANSAS CITY. *Brighton Place*, 2429 Brighton, 64127. Tel: 816-231-3211
For a complete listing, refer to the Special Care Facilities section.
Cathedral Square Towers, 444 W. 12th St., 64105. Tel: 816-471-6555
For a complete listing, refer to the Special Care Facilities section.
Columbus Park Plaza, 801 Pacific, 64106. Tel: 816-472-0887
For a complete listing, refer to the Special Care Facilities section.
Jeanne Jugan Center, 8745 James A. Reed Rd., 64138. Tel: 816-761-4744; Fax: 816-761-4724
For a complete listing, refer to the Special Care Facilities section.
Marlborough Manor, 1818 E. 79th St., 64132. Tel: 816-221-4377
For a complete listing, refer to the Special Care Facilities section.
Red Bridge Place, 11300 Colorado, 64137. Tel: 816-761-4667
For a complete listing, refer to the Special Care Facilities section.
Redemptorist Retirement Home, 207 W. Linwood, 64111-1327. Tel: 816-561-3025.
E-mail: solnnette@IX.netcom.com
For a complete listing, refer to the Special Care Facilities section.
Tremont Place, 6161 N. Chatham, 64151. Tel: 816-587-7707
For a complete listing, refer to the Special Care Facilities section.

LIBERTY. *Our Lady of Mercy Country Home*, 2205 Hughes Rd., 64068. Tel: 816-781-5711
For a complete listing, refer to the Special Care Facilities section.

SAVANNAH. *La Verna Heights Retirement Center, Inc.*, 104 E. Park Ave., P.O. Box 488, 64485-0488. Tel: 816-324-3179
For a complete listing, refer to the Special Care Facilities section.
La Verna Village Apartments, 1000-1005 Hall Ave., 64485. Tel: 816-324-3179
For a complete listing, refer to the Special Care Facilities section.
La Verna Village Nursing Home, 904 Hall Ave., P.O. Box 279, 64485. Tel: 816-324-3185; Fax: 816-324-4097
For a complete listing, refer to the Special Care Facilities section.

[J] MONASTERIES AND RESIDENCES OF PRIESTS

KANSAS CITY. *Redemptorists of Kansas City,* 3333 Broadway Blvd., 64111. Tel: 816-561-3771. Very Rev. James Shea, C.SS.R., Rector; Revs. Andrew Meiners, C.SS.R.; Joseph Curalli, C.SS.R.; Edward Kane, C.SS.R.; Bernard Kramer, C.SS.R.; Patrick Power, C.SS.R.; James Springer, C.SS.R.; Bros. James Burke, C.SS.R.; Charles Long, C.SS.R. Priests 7; Brothers 2.

Rockhurst College - Jesuit Community, 5133 Forest Ave., 64110. Tel: 816-926-0012. Revs. E. Edward Kinerk, S.J., Rector; Francis L. Pedrotti, S.J., Minister; E. Eugene Arthur, S.J.; Jules M. Brady, S.J.; Martin J. Bredeck, S.J.; Edward K. Burger, S.J.; Robert R. Burke, S.J.; Michael P. Caruso, S.J.; Thomas J. Casey, S.J.; Thomas F. Denzer, S.J.; Joseph M. Freeman, S.J.; Joseph E. Gough, S.J.; Wilfred L. LaCroix, S.J.; Keith P. McMillan, S.J.; Glenn P. Mueller, S.J.; Frank J. Murphy, S.J.; Walter G. Nesbit, S.J.; Louis J. Oldani, S.J.; Thomas A. Pesci, S.J., Pres. of High School; James D. Wheeler, S.J.; Bros. Glenn E. Kerfoot, S.J.; John R. Olson, S.J.; Gerard A. Schroeder, S.J. Total in Residence 24.

Rockhurst High School - Jesuit Community, 3135 Karnes Blvd., 64111. Tel: 816-531-0806, Ext. 294. Revs. Christopher P. Pinne, S.J., Sup.; David J. Suwalsky, S.J.; Mark J. Daues, S.J.

St. Francis Xavier - Jesuit Community, 1001 E. 52nd St., 64110. Tel: 816-523-5142. Rev. Timothy M. McMahon, S.J.

Vincentian Parish Mission Center, 2100 N. Noland Rd., 64050. Tel: 816-254-3000; Fax: 816-836-9922. Revs. Richard Gielow, C.M.; Ronald J. Hoye, C.M.; Francis Crowley, C.M.; Richard O'Brien, C.M.; Charles Prost, C.M.; Michael Mulhearn, C.M.; Thomas Cawley, C.M.; Carl G. Schulte, C.M., Supr.

CONCEPTION. *Conception Abbey,* 64433. Tel: 660-944-2211; Fax: 660-944-2800.
E-mail: abbeys@netins.net
Web site: www.msc-net.com/~/cabbey/
Rt. Rev. Gregory Polan, O.S.B., Abbot; Very Rev. Kenneth Reichert, O.S.B., Prior; Bro. Michael Marcotte, O.S.B., Subprior; Rt. Revs. Anselm Coppersmith, O.S.B., Retired Abbot; James Jones, O.S.B., Retired Abbot; Revs. Luke Becker, O.S.B.; Albert Bruecken, O.S.B.; Patrick Caveglia; Richard J. Cleary, O.S.B.; Martin DeMeulenaere, O.S.B.; Conrad Falk, O.S.B.; Lawrence Gidley, O.S.B.; Donald Grabner, O.S.B.; Placid Immegart, O.S.B.; Quentin Kathol, O.S.B.; Aidan McSorley, O.S.B.; Alfred Meyer, O.S.B.; Benedict Neenan, O.S.B.; Daniel Petsche, O.S.B.; Regis Probstfield, O.S.B.; Aelred Rosser, O.S.B.; Samuel Russell; Adam Ryan, O.S.B.; Alexis Saathoff; Norbert Schappler, O.S.B.; Timothy Schoen, O.S.B.; Gilbert Stack, O.S.B.; Augustine Stock, O.S.B.; Hugh Tasch, O.S.B.; Paschal Thomas, O.S.B.; Isaac True, O.S.B.; Peter Ullrich, O.S.B. Benedictine Monks. Priests 52; Brothers 25.

LIBERTY. *Precious Blood Center,* 2130 Hughes Rd., 64068. Tel: 816-781-4344. Bro. Stephen Ohnmacht, C.PP.S., Supr.; Revs. Ralph Bushell, C.PP.S.; Thomas A. Conway, C.PP.S.; Thomas Ozanne, C.PP.S.; David Dougherty, C.PP.S.; Edmund Weigel, C.PP.S.; Ronald Will, C.PP.S.; William Dineen, C.PP.S.; Dien Truong, C.PP.S.; Leonard Goettemoeller, C.PP.S.; Bro. Joseph Mary Hrezo.

Precious Blood Society Provincial Office, P.O. Box 339, 64069-0339. Tel: 816-781-4344; Fax: 816-781-3639.
E-mail: KCProv@aol.com
Very Rev. Mark Miller, C.PP.S., Prov. Dir.; Revs. Ronald Will, C.PP.S., Prov. Sec.; William Dineen, C.PP.S., Prov. Treas. Priests 8; Brothers 2.

[K] CONVENTS AND RESIDENCES FOR SISTERS

KANSAS CITY. *Mercederian Missionaries of Berriz,* U.S. Regional Headquarters, 1400 N.E. 42nd Ter., 64116. Tel: 816-454-1344; Fax: 816-454-6882. Sr. Betty Preston, M.M.B. Mercedarian Missionaries of Berriz 11.

Sisters of Notre Dame de Sion, 3627 Gillham Rd. #34, 64111. Tel: 816-531-1374. 3629 Gillham Rd., #57, 64111. Tel: 816-531-1374. Sisters 3.

Sisters of the Society of Our Lady of the Most Holy Trinity, 3738 Tracy, 64109. Tel: 816-561-8849. Society of Apostolic Life. Sisters 2.

BLUE SPRINGS. *Our Lady of the Springs Community,* 731 N. Sixth St., 64014-2404. Tel: 816-228-3739. Franciscan Sisters of Mary 3.

CLYDE. *Benedictine Convent of Perpetual Adoration,* 64432. Tel: 660-944-2221; Fax: 660-944-2133.
E-mail: srsean@netins.net
Sisters 45. Attended by Conception Abbey.

INDEPENDENCE. *St. Francis Convent Novitiate and Prayer Center,* 2100 N. Noland Rd., 64050. Tel: 816-252-1673; Fax: 816-252-5574. Motherhouse of the Sisters of St. Francis of the Holy Eucharist. Sr. M. Connie Boulch, O.S.F., Supr. Sisters 22.

LIBERTY. *Queen of Angels Monastery - Benedictine Sisters,* 23411 N.E. 100th St., 64068. Tel: 816-450-4631; Fax: 816-450-4641. Sr. Mary Imelda Koch, O.S.B., Prioress. Sisters 7; Total in Residence 10.

MARYVILLE. *St. Francis Convent,* 2022 S. Main St., 64468-2655. Tel: 660-582-4005. Franciscan Sisters of Mary. Franciscan Sisters of Mary 3.

PARKVILLE. *Sisters of the Third Franciscan Order,* 6108 B N.W. Hwy. 9, 64152.

SAVANNAH. *La Verna Heights Provincial House,* 104 E. Park, Box 488, 64485-0488. Tel: 816-324-3179; Fax: 816-324-6512. Sisters of St. Francis of Savannah, MO. Motherhouse and Novitiate. Rev. Walter Heeney, O.S.B., Chap. Sisters 29.

Maintenance and Custodial Care Trust of the Franciscan Sisters of Savannah, MO. Total Assisted 2,543; Total Staff 25.

[L] RETREAT ACTIVITY CENTERS

KANSAS CITY. *St. John's Diocesan Center,* 2015 E. 72nd St., 64132. Tel: 816-363-3585. Sr. Marion Renkens, C.S.J., Dir. Retreat and Conference Center for Groups of all Denominations.

[M] SERVICES

KANSAS CITY.
**Seton Center Family & Health Services,* 2816 E. 23 St., 64127. Tel: 816-231-3955.
E-mail: rasaro@pei.edu
Rachel A. Asaro, Dir. Total Assisted 6,000; Total Staff 21.

[N] NEWMAN CENTERS

KANSAS CITY. *Avila College Campus Ministry,* 11901 Wornall, 64145. Tel: 816-942-3362.
Web site: www.avila.edu
Rev. Daniel Torson, C.PP.S., Dir. of Campus Ministry.

MARYVILLE. *The Newman House at Northwest Missouri State University,* 606 College Ave., 64468. Tel: 660-582-7373.
E-mail: 0500052@acad.nwmissouri.edu
Web site: http://www.nwmissouri.edu/~0500052/index.html
Rev. Xavier Nacke, O.S.B.

WARRENSBURG. *Central Missouri State University Newman Center,* 106 Broad St., 64093. Tel: 660-747-6997. Mark S. Rush, Dir.

[O] MISCELLANEOUS

KANSAS CITY. *Benedictine Counseling and Consulting Institute,* 4737 N. Cleveland, 64117. Tel: 816-453-1183.
E-mail: denisosb@swbell.net
Rev. Denis Dougherty, O.S.B., Ph.D., Dir. Total Assisted 200.

**Bishop Sullivan Center,* 6435 Truman Rd., 64126. Tel: 816-231-0984; Fax: 816-231-3096. Rev. Thomas W. Turner, Dir. Total Assisted 10,000; Total Staff 11.

Camp Little Flower, 300 E. 36th St., P.O. Box 419037, 64141. Tel: 816-756-1850.

Catholic Woman's Club, 300 E. 36th St., P.O. Box 419037, 64141. Tel: 816-756-1850. Rev. Thomas Hernes, Diocesan Moderator.

Diocesan Council of Catholic Women, 300 E. 36th St., P.O. Box 419037, 64141. Tel: 816-756-1850. Rev. Joseph A. Mancuso, Diocesan Moderator.

Diocesan Education Endowment Trust Fund, 300 E. 36th St., P.O. Box 419037, 64111. Tel: 816-756-1850. Mr. Thomas Severino, Contact Person.

Friends, Inc., 300 E. 36th St., P.O. Box 419037, 64141-6037. Tel: 816-756-1850.

Immacolata Retreat Center, 300 E. 36th St., P.O. Box 419037, 64141-6037. Tel: 816-756-1850.

Knights of St. Peter Claver (K.P.C.). Ladies Auxiliary of St. Peter Claver. 1616 Paseo, St. Monica Parish, 64108. Tel: 816-471-3696.

Ladies of Charity of Metropolitan Kansas City, Seton Center, 2816 E. 23rd St., 64127. Tel: 816-942-5311. Mrs. Rita M. Rost, Pres. A group of volunteers who work and raise money to help the poor and those in need through Seton Center and other agencies.

Marillac Home for Children, P.O. Box 419037, 64141-6037.

Our Lady of Perpetual Help Charitable Trust, 3333 Broadway, 64111. Tel: 816-561-3771. Rev. James Shea, C.SS.R., Contact Person.

Red Bridge Place, 11300 Colorado, 64137.

St. Anthony's Home, 300 E. 36th St., P.O. Box 419037, 64141-6037. Tel: 816-756-1850.

St. John's Seminary, Inc., P.O. Box 419037, 64141-6037.

Siena Club, 300 E. 36th St., P.O. Box 419037, 64141. Tel: 816-756-1850.

Society of Our Lady of the Most Holy Trinity, 3704 Tracy, 64109. Tel: 816-931-9131. Rev. Eckley Macklin, S.O.L.T.

CONCEPTION. *Conception Benedictine Trust,* 64433. Tel: 660-944-2580; Fax: 660-944-2800.
E-mail: 0553007@acad.nwmissouri.edu
Rt. Rev. Gregory J. Polan, O.S.B., Pres.; Bro. Mark Kosiba, O.S.B., Vice Pres.; Rev. Albert Bruecken, O.S.B., Sec.-Treas.

Pontifical Institute of Liturgy Foundation, Conception Abbey, 64433. Tel: 660-944-2211; Fax: 660-944-2800. Rt. Rev. Marcel Rooney, O.S.B., Pres.

LEE'S SUMMIT. *Mercy Midwest Properties.* Mailing Address: Mercy Housing Midwest, 7262 Mercy Rd., Ste. 102, Omaha, NE, 68124-2348. Mercy Midwest Properties, 920 Northeast Ridgeview Dr., #A, 64086. Tel: 816-525-0990; Fax: 816-525-0078. Sr. Carolyn Coffey, R.S.M., Regional Pres. Affordable service enriched housing for individuals and families who are economically poor.

LIBERTY. *Our Lady of Mercy Home,* 2205 Hughes Rd., 64068-9469. Tel: 816-781-5711.

**St. Gaspar Society,* P.O. Box 339, 64069. Tel: 816-781-4344; Fax: 816-781-3639.

MARYVILLE. *St. Francis Hospital Foundation,* 2016 S. Main, 64468. Tel: 660-562-2600. Member of SSM Health Care.

RELIGIOUS INSTITUTES OF MEN REPRESENTED IN THE DIOCESE

For further details refer to the corresponding bracketed number in the Religious Institutes of Men or Women section.

[0200]—*Benedictine Monks.* (Conception Abbey).—O.S.B.

[0330]—*Brothers of the Christian Schools.* (St. Louis, MO).—F.S.C.

[]—*Christian Brothers of the Midwest, Burr Ridge.*—F.S.C.

[1330]—*Congregation of the Mission.* (Western Prov.).—C.M.

[1210]—*Congregation of the Missionaries of St. Charles.*—C.S.

[0690]—*Jesuit Fathers and Brothers.* (Missouri Prov.).—S.J.

[0800]—*Maryknoll.*—M.M.

[1070]—*Redemptorist Fathers.* (St. Louis Prov.).—C.SS.R.

[]—*Society of Our Lady of Most Holy Trinity.*—S.O.L.T.

[1060]—*Society of the Precious Blood.* (Kansas City Prov.).—C.PP.S.

RELIGIOUS INSTITUTES OF WOMEN REPRESENTED IN THE DIOCESE

[0100]—*Adorers of the Blood of Christ.*—A.S.C.

[0230]—*Benedictine Sisters of Pontifical Jurisdiction.* (Atchinson, KS; Columbia, MD; Liberty, MO).—O.S.B.

[]—*Congregation of Mary Queen,* (Springfield, MO).—CMR.

[2950]—*Congregation of Notre Dame de Sion.*—N.D.S.

[0220]—*Congregation of the Benedictine Sisters of Perpetual Adoration of Pontifical Jurisdiction.*—O.S.B.

[0760]—*Daughters of Charity of St. Vincent de Paul.*—D.C.

[]—*Dominican Sisters.* (Adrian, MI; Sinsinawa, WI).—O.P.

[1415]—*Franciscan Sisters of Mary.*—F.S.M.

[2575]—*Institute of the Sisters of Mercy of the Americas.* (Omaha, NE; Cedar Rapids, IA).—R.S.M.

[2340]—*Little Sisters of the Poor.*—L.S.P.

[2510]—*Mercedarian Missionaries of Berriz.*—M.M.B.

[]—*Notre Dame Sisters.* (Omaha, NE).—N.D.

[3130]—*Our Lady of Victory Missionary Sisters.*—O.L.V.M.

[]—*School Sisters of St. Francis.* (Milwaukee, WI).—O.S.F.

[]—*Sister Servants of Immaculate Heart of Mary.* (Monroe, MI).—I.H.M.

[0480]—*Sisters of Charity of Leavenworth, Kansas.*—S.C.L.

[0430]—*Sisters of Charity of the Blessed Virgin Mary.*—B.V.M.

[2360]—*Sisters of Loretto At the Foot of the Cross.*—S.L.

[1670]—*Sisters of St. Francis of Savannah, MO.*—O.S.F.

[1560]—*Sisters of St. Francis of the Holy Eucharist.* (Independence, MO).—O.S.F.

[]—*Sisters of St. Francis of the Holy Eucharist Foundation.*

[3830-15]—*Sisters of St. Joseph.*—C.S.J.

[3830-18]—*Sisters of St. Joseph.*—C.S.J.

[3840]—*Sisters of St. Joseph of Carondelet.*—C.S.J.

[3260]—*Sisters of the Precious Blood (Dayton, OH).*—C.PP.S.

[]—*Sisters of the Presentation.* (Dubuque, IA).—P.B.V.M.

[]—*Sisters of the Third Franciscan Order (Syracuse, NY).*

[]—*Society of Our Lady of the Most Holy Trinity.*—S.O.L.T.

[4120-02]—*Ursuline Nuns (Paola, KS; Cleveland, OH, Maple Mount, KY.*—O.S.U.

DIOCESAN CEMETERIES

KANSAS CITY. *Mount Olivet & Mount St. Mary.*

ST. JOSEPH. *Mount Olivet.*

KANSAS CITY NORTH. *Resurrection.*

NECROLOGY

† Byrne, Robert B., (Retired). —Died Oct. 13, 1997.

† Harper, Rev. Msgr. James J., (Retired). —Died Oct. 19, 1997.

† Mifkovic, Francis F., (Retired). —Died Aug. 7, 1997.

Diocese of Knoxville

Most Reverend

ANTHONY J. O'CONNELL, D.D.

Bishop of Knoxville; ordained 1963; appointed May 27, 1988; ordained and installed September 8, 1988. *Office: 805 Northshore Dr., P.O. Box 11127, Knoxville, TN, 37939-1127.*

ESTABLISHED SEPTEMBER 8, 1988.

Square Miles 14,242.

Comprises the Counties of Anderson, Bledsoe, Blount, Bradley, Campbell, Carter, Claiborne, Cocke, Cumberland, Fentress, Grainger, Greene, Hamblen, Hamilton, Hancock, Hawkins, Jefferson, Johnson, Knox, Loudon, McMinn, Marion, Meigs, Monroe, Morgan, Pickett, Polk, Rhea, Roane, Scott, Sequatchie, Sevier, Sullivan, Unicoi, Union and Washington in the State of Tennessee.

For legal titles of parishes and diocesan institutions, consult the Chancery Office.

Chancery Office: 805 Northshore Dr. S.W., P.O. Box 11127, Knoxville, TN, 37939-1127. Tel.: 423-584-3307.

STATISTICAL OVERVIEW

Personnel	
Bishop	1
Priests: Diocesan Active in Diocese	37
Priests: Active Outside Diocese	1
Priests: Retired, Sick or Absent	6
Number of Diocesan Priests	44
Religious Priests in Diocese	15
Extern Priests in Diocese	7
Ordinations:	
Transitional Deacons	1
Permanent Deacons in Diocese	23
Total Brothers	16
Total Sisters	52
Parishes	
Parishes	44
With Resident Pastor:	
Resident Diocesan Priests	29
Resident Religious Priests	6
Without Resident Pastor:	
Administered by Priests	8
Administered by Lay People	1
Missions	2
Pastoral Centers	2
New Parishes Created	1
Professional Ministry Personnel:	
Brothers	1
Sisters	7
Lay Ministers	22
Welfare	
Catholic Hospitals	2
Total Assisted	317,928
Health Care Centers	1
Total Assisted	103
Homes for the Aged	1
Total Assisted	277
Specialized Homes	1
Total Assisted	500
Special Centers for Social Services	6
Total Assisted	27,674
Educational	
Diocesan Students in Other Seminaries	19
Total Seminarians	19
High Schools, Diocesan and Parish	2
Total Students	945
Elementary Schools, Diocesan and Parish	8
Total Students	2,585
Catechesis/Religious Education:	
High School Students	1,142
Elementary Students	3,746
Total Students Under Catholic Instruction	8,437
Teachers in the Diocese:	
Priests	3
Brothers	1
Sisters	9
Lay Teachers	156
Vital Statistics	
Receptions into the Church:	
Infant Baptism Totals	786
Adult Baptism Totals	175
Received into Full Communion	284
First Communions	889
Confirmations	665
Marriages:	
Catholic	103
Interfaith	170
Total Marriages	273
Deaths	309
Total Catholic Population	45,482
Total Population	2,012,885

Vicar General (Moderator of the Curia)—Rev. F. XAVIER MANKEL, V.G.

Deans of the Diocese—Revs. WILLIAM H. GAHAGAN, Five Rivers Deanery; MICHAEL CRESON, Chattanooga Deanery; MICHAEL SWEENEY, Cumberland Mtn. Deanery; JOSEPH J. BRANDO, Smoky Mtn. Deanery.

Chancery Office—805 Northshore Dr. S.W., P.O. Box 11127, Knoxville, 37939-1127. Tel: 423-584-3307; Fax: 423-584-7538. Office Hours: Mon-Fri 9-4 All official business should be directed to this office.

Chancellor—Rev. J. VANN JOHNSTON, JR., J.C.L.

Auditors—All priests on assignment in the diocese.

Presbyteral Council—Revs. GEORGE E. SCHMIDT, JR., Chm. G. PATRICK GARRITY, Vice Chm. DAVID BOETTNER, Recording Sec. and all priests on assignment in the diocese.

Diocesan Consultors—Revs. JOSEPH J. BRANDO; WILLIAM C. CASEY; WILLIAM H. GAHAGAN; T. ALLEN HUMBRECHT; F. XAVIER MANKEL, V.G.; CHRIS MICHELSON; TOM VOS, O.F.M.

Diocesan Finance Council—DORMAN BLAINE; J. MICHAEL CONNOR; LARRY COOL, Ex-Officio, Diocesan Finance Officer; MARY ESBENSHADE; SHARON FOLK; TERRY TORRICELLI, Ex-Officio, Diocesan Dir. Stewardship & Devel.; Rev. F. XAVIER MANKEL, V.G., Ex-Officio; DUGAN MCLAUGHLIN; JOHN T. O'CONNOR, Ex-Officio, Diocesan Attorney; SOCRATES SABATER; DAVE SANTI; Revs. FRANCIS X. SCHILLING; GEORGE E. SCHMIDT, JR.; SUZANNE SCHRIVER; WILLIAM SWAIN; FRAN THIE; FRANK VARALLO; GEORGE WARNE.

Diocesan Offices and Directors

Adult Christian Living—Rev. EVAN ECKHOFF, O.F.M., Dir., *805 Northshore Dr., S.W., Knoxville, 37919.* Tel: 423-584-3307.

Appalachian Community Development—MARIE CIRILLO, Dir., *Rte. 1, Box 146-B, Clairfield, 37715.* Tel: 423-784-6832. Participants in CORE-Appalachian Ministries, a joint project of Dioceses of Covington, Knoxville, Lexington, Nashville, Richmond and Wheeling-Charleston.

Associated Catholic Charities of East Tennessee, Inc.—DAVID C. DOTSON, Exec. Dir., *119 Dameron Ave., Knoxville, 37917.* Tel: 423-524-9896. The umbrella agency for all Catholic charities of the diocese.

Campaign for Human Development—DAVID C. DOTSON, Dir., *119 Dameron Ave., Knoxville, 37917.* Tel: 423-524-9896.

Campus Ministries—

East Tennessee State University—Rev. WILLIAM H. GAHAGAN, Chap., *Catholic Center, 734 W. Locust St., Johnson City, 37604.* Tel: 423-926-7061.

University of Tennessee-Chattanooga—Rev. PATRICK BROWNELL, Dir., *514 Palmetto St., Chattanooga, 37403.* Tel: 423-267-3064.

University of Tennessee-Knoxville—Rev. TERRENCE RYAN, C.S.P., Dir., *1710 Melrose Pl., Knoxville, 37916.* Tel: 423-523-7931.

Catholic Schools Office—AURELIA MONTGOMERY, Supt., *805 Northshore Dr., S.W., Knoxville, 37919.* Tel: 423-584-3307.

Catholic Charities (Chattanooga Area)—LYNDA DIPRIMA, Admin., *859 McCallie Ave., Chattanooga, 37403.* Tel: 423-267-1297.

Catholic Charities (Knoxville Area)—VICKIE STOVALL, Admin., *119 Dameron Ave., Knoxville, 37917.* Tel: 423-524-9896.

Catholic Charities (Upper East Tennessee Area)—Sr. JEAN SONSALLA, S.S.J.-T.O.S.F., *703 East Jackson Blvd., P.O. Box 323, Jonesborough, 37659.* Tel: 423-753-3001.

Cemeteries—LARRY COOL, Dir., *805 Northshore Dr., S.W., Knoxville, 37919.* Tel: 423-584-3307. Rev. GEORGE E. SCHMIDT, JR., Contact, Mt. Olivet Cemetery in Chattanooga. Tel: 423-266-1618. Rev. THOMAS TAVELLA, C.S.P., Contact, Calvary Cemetery in Knoxville. Tel: 423-522-1508.

Chancellor—Rev. J. VANN JOHNSTON, JR., J.C.L., *805 Northshore Dr., S.W., Knoxville, 37919.* Tel: 423-584-3307.

Censor Librorum—Rev. ROBERT J. HOFSTETTER, *930 Ashland Ter., Chattanooga, 37415.* Tel: 423-870-2386.

Deaf Ministry—Rev. MICHAEL CUMMINS, Dir., *All Saints Church, 620 N. Cedar Bluff Rd., Knoxville, TN, 37923.* Tel: 423-531-0770.

Diocesan Council of Catholic Women—Rev. PAUL A. HOSTETTLER, Diocesan Spiritual Moderator, *P.O. Box 566, Copperhill, 37317.* Tel: 423-496-3498.

Ecumenism—Rev. WILLIAM CASEY, Dir., *225 Jamestowne Blvd., Knoxville, 37922.* Tel: 423-966-4540.

Evangelization—Sr. ALBERTINE PAULUS, R.S.M., Dir., *805 Northshore Dr., S.W., Knoxville, 37919.* Tel: 423-584-3307.

Finance Office—LARRY COOL, Diocesan Finance Officer, *805 Northshore Dr., S.W., Knoxville, 37919.* Tel: 423-584-3307.

Hispanic Ministry—JACK KRAMER, Dir., *119 Dameron Ave., Knoxville, 37917.* Tel: 423-637-4769.

Justice - Peace - Integrity of Creation—Co-Dirs.: MARCUS KEYES; GLENDA STRUSS-KEYES, *119 Dameron Ave., Knoxville, 37917.* Tel: 423-540-8348.

Marriage Tribunal—Rev. DEXTER BREWER, J.C.L. J.V., *2400 21st Ave. S., Nashville, 37212-5387.* Tel: 615-383-6393. Diocesan marriage tribunal is shared with the Diocese of Nashville.

Ministries of the Chattanooga Deanery—Rev. MICHAEL CRESON, Dean; PATRICIA APPLETON, Exec. Dir., *501 S. Moore Rd., Chattanooga, 37412.* Tel: 423-622-7232.

Ministries of the Five Rivers Deanery—Rev. WILLIAM H. GAHAGAN, Dean, *2211 E. Lakeview Dr., Johnson City, 37601.* Tel: 423-282-6367.

Ministries of the Cumberland Mt. Deanery—Rev. MICHAEL SWEENEY, Dean, *535 Margrave St., Harriman, 37748.* Tel: 423-882-9838.

Ministries of the Smoky Mtn. Deanery—Rev. JOSEPH J. BRANDO, Dean, *860 Louisville Rd., Alcoa, 37701.* Tel: 423-982-3672.

Diaconate—Co-Dirs.: Rev. GREGORY BOISVERT, A.A., *860 Louisville Rd., Alcoa, 37701.* Deacon CARL WUST. Tel: 423-982-3672; 483-8739.

Priestly Life and Ministry—Rev. ROBERT J. HOFSTETTER, Dir., *930 Ashland Ter., Chattanooga, 37415.* Tel: 423-870-2386.

Propagation of the Faith—Rev. J. VANN JOHNSTON, JR., J.C.L., Dir., *805 Northshore Dr., S.W., Knoxville, 37919.* Tel: 423-584-3307.

Religious Education—CATHY QUALLS, Dir., *212 Mt. Bethel Rd., Greeneville, 37745.* Tel: 800-553-0284.

Religious Education Resource Center—CATHY QUALLS, Dir., *212 Mt. Bethel Rd., Greeneville, 37745.* Tel: 800-553-0284.

Scouting—Deacon OTTO PRESKE, Scout Chap., *535 Buckhorn Rd., Gatlinburg, 37738.* Tel: 423-436-5339.

Stewardship and Development—TERRY TORRICELLI, Dir., *805 Northshore Dr., S.W., Knoxville, 37919.* Tel: 423-584-3307.

Strategic Pastoral Planning—PAUL TERHAAR, Dir., *805 Northshore Dr., S.W., Knoxville, 37919.* Tel: 423-584-3307.

"The East Tennessee Catholic"—(Diocesan Newspaper); EDGAR MILLER, Editor, *805 Northshore Dr., S.W., Knoxville, 37919.* Tel: 423-584-3307.

Vocations—Most Rev. ANTHONY J. O'CONNELL, D.D., Dir., *805 Northshore Dr., S.W., Knoxville, 37919.* Tel: 423-584-3307. Revs. MICHAEL CRESON, Diocesan Coord., Vocation Promotion; MICHAEL CUMMINS, Cumberland Mountain Deanery Vocation Coord. WILLIAM H. GAHAGAN, Five Rivers Deanery Vocation Coord. T. ALLEN HUMBRECHT, Smoky Mountain Deanery Vocation Coord. MICHAEL NOLAN, Chattanooga Deanery Vocation Coord. Assoc. Vocation Promoters: Revs. PETER IORIO; RAGAN SCHRIVER. Bishop O'Connell also serves as the Director of Seminarian Formation.

Worship and Liturgy—Rev. MICHAEL LINDER, Dir., *805 Northshore Dr., S.W., Knoxville, 37919.* Tel: 423-584-3307.

Youth Ministry—Rev. PETER IORIO, Diocesan Coord., *2701 Vermont Ave., Chattanooga, 37404.* Tel: 423-624-4618, Ext. 28. PAT RIECKE, Coord. Chattanooga Deanery, *501 S. Moore Rd., Chattanooga, 37412.* Tel: 423-629-6775. LINDA D. MURASKI, Coord., Five Rivers Deanery, *159 Carden Dr., Elizabethon, 37643.* Tel: 423-543-7449. ANNE MCGAUGH, Coord., Cumberland Mountain Deanery, *327 Vermont Ave., Oak Ridge, 37830.* Tel: 423-483-7519. PATRICK DONOVAN, Coord., Smoky Mountain Deanery, *711 Northshore Dr., Knoxville, 37919.* Tel: 423-558-8348.

CLERGY, PARISHES, MISSIONS AND PAROCHIAL SCHOOLS

CITY OF KNOXVILLE
(Knox County)

1—CATHEDRAL OF THE SACRED HEART OF JESUS (1956), Revs. T. Allen Humbrecht; David Boettner; Deacon James Lawson, Pastoral Assoc.
Res., 711 Northshore Dr., 37919. Tel: 423-588-5189; Fax: 423-558-9671. [JC]
School—Tel: 423-588-0415; Fax: 423-558-4139. Pamela Bernards, Prin.
Brothers 1; Sisters 1; Lay Teachers 54; Students 754.
Catechesis/Religious Programs—Tel: 423-584-4528; Fax: 423-558-9671. Joanne Romeo, D.R.E. Students 167.

2—ALL SAINTS CATHOLIC CHURCH (1994), Revs. Chris Michelson; Michael E. Cummins.
Mailing Address: 620 N. Cedar Bluff Rd., 37923. Tel: 423-531-0770; Fax: 423-531-1009.
Catechesis/Religious Programs—Tel: 423-531-0770; Fax: 423-531-1009.
Students 429.

3—IMMACULATE CONCEPTION (1852) (Irish), Revs. Thomas A. Tavella, C.S.P.; Broderick M. Walsh, C.S.P.
Res., 414 W. Vine Ave., 37902. Tel: 423-522-1508; Fax: 423-524-8514. [CEM]
Catechesis/Religious Programs—Betty Krusenklaus, D.R.E.
Students 138.

4—JOHN XXIII CATHOLIC CENTER (1968). (Non-territorial parish for the University of Tennessee at Knoxville). Revs. Terrence P. Ryan, C.S.P.; Robert E. Moran, C.S.P.
Res., 1710 Melrose Pl., 37916. Tel: 423-523-7931; Fax: 423-523-7979.
Catechesis/Religious Programs—Ruth Queen Smith, Pastoral Assoc.
Students 28.

5—HOLY GHOST (1908), Revs. F. Xavier Mankel, S.T.L., V.G.; J. Vann Johnston, Jr., J.C.L.
Res., 111 Hinton Ave., 37917. Tel: 423-522-2205; Fax: 423-525-6051. [JC]
School—St. Joseph, 1810 Howard Rd., 37918. Tel: 423-689-3424; Fax: 423-687-7885. Joan Turbyville, Prin.
Brothers 1; Sisters 1; Lay Teachers 19; Students 260.
Catechesis/Religious Programs—Betty Krusenklaus, D.R.E.
Students 118.

6—ST. JOHN NEUMANN (1977), Revs. John R. Dowling; Ragan Schriver; Deacons William Diesing; Donald Amelse; Marquis Syler.
Church—225 Jamestowne Blvd., 37922. Tel: 423-966-4540; Fax: 423-966-4541.
Res., 300 Dominion Cir., 37922. Tel: 423-966-8924.
School—625 St. John Ct., 37922. Tel: 423-777-0077; Fax: 423-675-0311. Sr. Mary Janice Brink, R.S.M., Prin.
Catechesis/Religious Programs—Tel: 423-966-4540; Fax: 423-966-4541. Margaret Fontenot, D.R.E. Students 636.

OUTSIDE THE CITY OF KNOXVILLE

Alcoa, Blount Co., Our Lady of Fatima (1950), Revs. Joseph J. Brando; Gregory L. Boisvert, A.A.; Deacon Michael G. Nestor.
Res., 860 Louisville Rd., 37701. Tel: 423-982-3672; Fax: 423-977-4183.
Catechesis/Religious Programs—Tel: 423-981-2676; Fax: 423-977-4183. LuAnne Zelasko, D.R.E.
Students 313.
Mission—Townsend, Blount Co., St. Francis of Assisi, 7717 River Rd., Townsend, 37882. Tel: 423-448-6070. Rev. Joseph W. Julius.
Catechesis/Religious Programs—Students 27.

Athens, McMinn Co., St. Mary (1968), Rev. Joseph Fiedorowicz.
Res., 2007 Congress Pkwy., 37303. Tel: 423-745-4277; Fax: 423-745-0904.
Catechesis/Religious Programs—Tel: 423-476-7869. Joyce Spurlin, D.R.E.
Students 136.

Chattanooga, Hamilton Co.,

1—SS. PETER AND PAUL, (1852), Rev. George E. Schmidt, Jr.; Deacons James Wilson; Andrew Wassick.
Res., 214 E. 8th St., 37402. Tel: 423-266-1618. [JC]
Catechesis/Religious Programs—Students 35.

2—OUR LADY OF PERPETUAL HELP, (1937), Revs. Michael F. Nolan; James P. Harvey, III; Deacons Mark Gang, Jr.; William Oleck.
Res., 501 S. Moore Rd., 37412. Tel: 423-622-7232; Fax: 423-624-2686. [CEM]
School—505 S. Moore Rd., 37412. Tel: 423-622-1481; Fax: 423-622-2016.
Sisters of Charity of the Blessed Virgin Mary 1; Lay Teachers 24; Students 437.
Catechesis/Religious Programs—Lois Colosia, D.R.E.
Students 93.
Convent—511 S. Moore Rd., 37412. Tel: 423-698-3274.

3—ST. JUDE, (1958), Revs. Robert J. Hofstetter; Patrick Brownell.
Res., 930 Ashland Ter., 37415. Tel: 423-870-2386. [JC]
School—Tel: 423-877-6022; Fax: 423-875-8920. JoAnne Bollman, Prin.
Lay Teachers 28; Students 456.
Catechesis/Religious Programs—Students 220.

4—ST. STEPHEN, (1961), Rev. P. J. McGinnity. In res., Rev. Peter Iorio.
Res., 7111 Lee Hwy., 37421. Tel: 423-892-1261; Fax: 423-892-3242.
Catechesis/Religious Programs—Tel: 423-892-2957.
Students 170.

Cleveland, Bradley Co., St. Therese of Lisieux (1914), Rev. Alex Waraska; Sr. Marian Ruede, Pastoral Assoc.
Res., 900 Clingan Ridge Dr., N.W., 37312. Tel: 423-476-8123; Fax: 423-479-3339.
Catechesis/Religious Programs—Tel: 423-476-8123; Fax: 423-479-3339. Darline Pullen, D.R.E.
Students 304.

Clinton, Anderson Co., St. Therese (1974), Rev. Dan G. Whitman; Sr. Yvette Gillen, R.S.M., Pastoral Assoc.
Church—701 S. Charles G. Seivers Blvd., 37716. Tel: 423-457-4073.
Res., 701 S. Charles G. Seivers Blvd., 37716. Tel: 423-457-1317.
Catechesis/Religious Programs—Students 85.

Copperhill, Polk Co., St. Catherine (1977). Attended by St. Mary, Athens. In res., Rev. Paul A. Hostettler.
Mailing Address: Box 566, 37317. Tel: 423-496-3498.
Catechesis/Religious Programs—Students 9.

Crossville, Cumberland Co., St. Alphonsus (1948), Rev. Michael B. Roark; Deacon Ralph Torrelli, Pastoral Assoc. & Business Mgr.
Res., 426 Sparta Dr., 38555. Tel: 931-456-5148; 484-2358 (Office).
Catechesis/Religious Programs—Tel: 931-456-5227. Terry Paradis, D.R.E.
Students 107.

Dayton, Rhea Co., St. Bridget (1969), Rev. John Milewski, K.H.S.; Deacon Tom Kiefer.
Res., 320 Walnut Grove Church Rd., 37321. Tel: 423-775-2664; 775-5542 (Rectory); Fax: 423-775-1545.
Catechesis/Religious Programs—Students 65.

Dunlap, Sequatchie Co., Shepherd of the Valley (1997). (Quasi Parish). Rev. Michael Creson.
Res., 110 Old York Hwy., P.O. Box 1747, 37327. Tel: 423-949-6903.

Elizabethton, Carter Co., St. Elizabeth (1982), Rev. Stephen K. Smith, O.P.
Res., 510 W. C St., 37643. Tel: 423-543-3412.
Catechesis/Religious Programs—Tel: 423-543-3412. Donna Townsend, D.R.E.
Students 41.

Fairfield Glade, Cumberland Co., St. Francis of Assisi (1983), Rev. Philip F. Thoni; Deacons Mark Frederick; Mark White.
Res., Peavine Rd., P.O. Box 1861, 38558. Tel: 931-484-3628. [CEM]
Catechesis/Religious Programs—Students 8.
Mission—Jamestown, Fentress Co., Fentress County Catholic Community, P.O. Box 1861 38558. Tel: 931-484-3628.
Catechesis/Religious Programs—Students 10.

Gatlinburg, Sevier Co., St. Mary (1935), Rev. Francis X. Schilling; Deacon Otto Preske.
Res., 304 Airport Rd., 37738. Tel: 423-436-4907.
Mission—Pigeon Forge, Sevier Co., Holy Cross, 144 Wears Valley Rd., Pigeon Forge, 37863. Tel: 423-429-5587; Fax: 423-453-8951. Rev. Jay Flaherty, Admin.
Catechesis/Religious Programs—Students 20.

Greeneville, Greene Co., Notre Dame (1955), Rev. William C. Casey.
Res., 212 Mt. Bethel Rd., 37745. Tel: 423-639-9381.
Catechesis/Religious Programs—D.R.E.: Diana Thompon, (Elementary); Maryann Connell, (Elementary); Cathy Qualls, (High School).
Students 84.

Harriman, Roane Co., Blessed Sacrament (1908), Rev. Michael Sweeney; Deacon James P. O'Connor.
Res., 535 Margrave St., 37748. Tel: 423-882-9838.
Catechesis/Religious Programs—Students 39.
Stations—Brushy Mountain Prison, Tel: 423-346-6641; Morgan County Regional Correctional Facility, Tel: 423-346-6641.

Helenwood, Scott Co., St. Jude Parish (1982). Attended by St. Therese, Clinton. Rev. Dan G. Whitman; Sr. Patricia Soete, R.S.M., Pastoral Assoc.
Mailing Address: Hwy. 27 S., P.O. Box 555, 37755. Tel: 423-569-3492; 569-9584 (Church).
Catechesis/Religious Programs—Students 10.

Jefferson City, Jefferson Co., Holy Trinity Catholic Church (1994), Rev. G. Patrick Garrity; Deacon G. James Fage.
475 N. Hwy. 92, P.O. Box 375, 37760. Tel: 423-471-0347.

Johnson City, Washington Co., St. Mary (1906), Revs. William H. Gahagan; Steve LaPrad.
Res., 2211 E. Lakeview Dr., 37601. Tel: 423-282-8696; Fax: 423-282-0224.
School—Tel: 423-282-8666; Fax: 423-282-0224. Sr. Beverly Reck, S.S.N.D., Prin.
Sisters 2; Lay Teachers 16; Students 207.
Catechesis/Religious Programs—Sr. Mary Jane Jansen, S.S.N.D., D.R.E.
Students 202.

Kingsport, Sullivan Co., St. Dominic (1941), Revs. Charles Burton; Tom Moser; Sr. Madeline MacDougall, Pastoral Assoc.; Deacon Milton Robelot.
Res., 2517 John B. Dennis Hwy., 37660. Tel: 423-288-2773; Fax: 423-288-7183.

School—Tel: 423-245-0362; Fax: 423-245-2907. Karen Barber, Prin.
Lay Teachers 11; Students 100.
Catechesis/Religious Programs—Tel: 423-288-8101; Fax: 423-288-7183. Shirley Parsons, D.R.E. Students 263.

LaFollette, Campbell Co., Our Lady of Perpetual Help (1905), Rev. Greg Neuzil.
Mailing Address: 923 E. Elm St., P.O. Box 1704, 37766. Tel: 423-562-0312; Fax: 423-562-0312.
Catechesis/Religious Programs—Students 32.

Lancing, Morgan Co., St. Ann (1982). Attended by Blessed Sacrament, Harriman. Rev. Michael Sweeney; Sr. Rita Bray, C.S.C., Pastoral Assoc.
Mailing Address: P.O. Box 77, 37770-0077. Tel: 423-346-6260.
Catechesis/Religious Programs—Students 7.

Lenoir City, Loudon Co., St. Thomas the Apostle (1973), Rev. George Dyer, O.P.; Deacon Jose Rivera.
Res., 2500 Harrison Rd., 37771. Tel: 423-986-9885.
Catechesis/Religious Programs—Students 59.

Madisonville, Monroe Co., Monroe County Catholic Church (1992). (Quasi Parish). Jay Gilchrist, Pastoral Coord.
Mailing Address: 737 Hwy. 411 N., 37354. Tel: 423-442-7273; 337-2714.
Catechesis/Religious Programs—Students 14.

Morristown, Hamblen Co., St. Patrick (1959), Rev. G. Patrick Garrity; Deacon Gerald Fage.
Res., 2518 W. Andrew Johnson Hwy., 37814. Tel: 423-586-9174; Fax: 423-318-7044.
Catechesis/Religious Programs—Tel: 423-586-4091. Patricia Holmes, D.R.E.
Students 92.

Mountain City, Johnson Co., St. Anthony of Padua Catholic Church (1995). (Quasi Parish). Rev. Thomas Vos, O.F.M.; Bro. Justin Huber, O.F.M.
Res., 513 Hickory St., 37683. Tel: 423-727-7870; Fax: 423-727-5156.
Catechesis/Religious Programs—Students 17.

Newport, Cocke Co., Good Shepherd (1982). Attended by Notre Dame, Greeneville. Rev. William C. Casey; Sr. Mary Ann Konieski, O.P., Pastoral Assoc.
Mailing Address: 659 E. Broadway, 37821. Tel: 423-623-5051.
School—Students 30.
Catechesis/Religious Programs—Students 29.

Norris, Anderson Co., St. Joseph (1949), Rev. Frank X. Brett.
Res., 3452 Andersonville Hwy. 61, P.O. Box 387, 37828. Tel: 423-494-7746; Fax: 423-426-8759.
Catechesis/Religious Programs—Tel: 423-494-7746. Sue Campbell, D.R.E.
Students 83.

Oak Ridge, Anderson Co., St. Mary (1943), Revs. Michael A. Woods; Gilbert Diaz; Deacons Frank Stoetzel; Carl Wust.
Res., 327 Vermont Ave., 37830. Tel: 423-482-2875.
School—323 Vermont Ave., 37830. Tel: 423-483-9700. Sr. Mary Reginald Lane, O.P., Prin.
Sisters of St. Cecilia Dominican Congregation 3; Lay Teachers 20; Students 234; Sisters 2.
Catechesis/Religious Programs—Tel: 423-481-8106.
Students 572.

Rogersville, Hawkins Co., St. Henry (1981), Rev. Michael T. Jennings.
Res., 112-114 Hwy. 70 N., 37857. Tel: 423-272-6897.
Catechesis/Religious Programs—Tel: 423-272-6897. Ellen McCoy, D.R.E.
Students 16.

Seymour, Sevier Co., Holy Family (1984), Rev. Thomas P. O'Connell.
Mailing Address: 307 Black Oak Ridge Rd., P.O. Box 817, 37865. Tel: 423-573-1203; Fax: 423-525-6236.
Catechesis/Religious Programs—Tel: 423-577-3881. Connie Bigelow, D.R.E.
Students 66.

Signal Mountain, Hamilton Co., St. Augustine (1938), Rev. Paul Valleroy; Deacon Gordon Kilburn.
Res., 1716 Anderson Pike, P.O. Box 10, 37377. Tel: 423-886-3424; Fax: 423-886-3451. [JC]
Catechesis/Religious Programs—Students 150.

Sneedville, Hancock Co., St. James the Apostle (1982). Attended by St. Henry, Rogersville. Rev. Mike Jennings.
Res., Hwy. 33, Rte. 2, Box 52, 37869. Tel: 423-272-6897.

South Pittsburg, Marion Co., Our Lady of Lourdes (1930), Rev. Michael Creson.
Res., P.O. Box 288, 37380. Tel: 423-837-7068.
School—Students 30.
Mission—Marian, Marian Co., Virgin of the Poor Shrine, P.O. Box 288, Marian, 37380. Tel: 423-837-7068.
Catechesis/Religious Programs—Students 30.

Tazewell, Claiborne Co., Christ the King (1990), Rev. Greg Neuzil.
Mailing Address: P.O. Box 404, 37879.
Res., 923 E. Elm St., LaFollette, 37766. Tel: 423-562-0312.
Catechesis/Religious Programs—Students 28.

Townsend, Blount Co., St. Francis of Assisi (1961). Attended by Our Lady of Fatima, Alcoa. In res., Rev. Joseph W. Julius (NSH).
Mailing Address: 7717 River Rd., 37882. Tel: 423-448-6070.
Catechesis/Religious Programs—Students 31.

Retired:
Reverend Monsignors—
Siener, Leo C., Alexian Village Health Care Center, 198 James Blvd., Rm. 711, Signal Mtn., TN 37377-1816
Reverend Fathers—
Bowes, David, P.O. Box 9325, Pensacola, FL 32513
Hostettler, Paul A., P.O. Box 566, Copperhill, TN 37317
Junod, Louis J., 1414 Continental Dr., Apt. 207, Chattanooga, TN 37405
Prescott, Herbert W., P.O. Box 4102, Chattanooga, TN 37405

Permanent Deacons:
Amelse, Donald, St. John Neumann, Knoxville
Diesing, William, St. John Neumann, Knoxville
Fage, Gerald J., II, St. Patrick, Morristown
Fischer, Robert W., St. Mary, Johnson City
Frederick, Mark A., St. Francis of Assisi, Fairfield Glade
Gang, Mark, Jr., Our Lady of Perpetual Help, Chattanooga
Kiefer, Thomas, St. Bridget, Dayton
Kilburn, Gordon, St. Augustine, Signal Mountain
Lawson, James, Sacred Heart Cathedral
McMahon, Joseph T., St. Mary, Johnson City
Nestor, Michael, St. Francis of Assisi, Townsend
O'Connor, James P., Blessed Sacrament, Harriman
Oleck, William A., Our Lady of Perpetual Help, Chattanooga
Preske, Otto F., St. Mary, Gatlinburg
Rivera, Jose, St. Thomas the Apostle, Lenoir City
Robelot, Milton P., St. Dominic, Kingsport
Stoetzel, Frank C., St. Mary, Oak Ridge
Syler, Marquis E., St. John Neumann, Knoxville
Torrelli, Ralph, St. Alphonsus, Crossville
Wassick, Andrew, SS. Peter and Paul, Chattanooga
White, Mark F., St. Francis of Assisi, Fairfield Glade
Wilson, James E., SS. Peter and Paul, Chattanooga
Wust, Carl J., St. Mary, Oak Ridge

INSTITUTIONS LOCATED IN THE DIOCESE

[A] HIGH SCHOOLS, DIOCESAN

KNOXVILLE. *Knoxville Catholic High School* (1932), 1610 E. Magnolia Ave., 37917. Tel: 423-525-0262; Fax: 423-525-6236.
E-mail: kchs@visit.net
Philip M. Dampf, III, Prin. Priests 2; Sisters 2; Lay Teachers 26; Students 383.
Knoxville Catholic High School Development Board of Trust.

CHATTANOOGA. *Notre Dame High School* (1876). (Grades 9-12), 2701 Vermont Ave., 37404. Tel: 423-624-4618; Fax: 423-624-4621. Mr. Perry Storey, Prin. Priests 1; Lay Teachers 51; Students 562.
Notre Dame High School Financial Board of Trustees.

[B] GENERAL HOSPITALS

KNOXVILLE. *St. Mary's Medical Center, Inc.*, (1930) 900 E. Oak Hill Ave., 37917. Tel: 423-545-8000
For a complete listing, refer to the Hospitals section.

CHATTANOOGA. *Memorial Hospital*, (1952) 2525 DeSales Ave., 37404. Tel: 423-495-2525
For a complete listing, refer to the Hospitals section.

[C] SPECIAL HOSPITALS

SIGNAL MOUNTAIN. *Alexian Village Health Care Center*, (1938) 100 James Blvd., 37377. Tel: 423-886-0100
For a complete listing, refer to the Special Care Facilities section.

[D] HOMES FOR THE AGED

SIGNAL MOUNTAIN. *Alexian Village of Tennessee, Inc.*, 100 James Blvd., 37377. Tel: 423-870-0101
For a complete listing, refer to the Special Care Facilities section.

[E] PROTECTIVE INSTITUTIONS

KNOXVILLE. *Columbus Home, Inc.*, 119 Dameron Ave., 37917. Tel: 423-971-3570; Fax: 423-546-0433
For a complete listing, refer to the Special Care Facilities section.

[F] MONASTERIES AND RESIDENCES OF PRIESTS AND BROTHERS

KNOXVILLE. *Brothers of Holy Cross*, 816 Creswell Ct., 37919. Bro. Roland Driscoll, C.S.C., (Retired). Total in Residence 1; Total Staff 1.
Presentation Brothers of Mary, 1409 Buxton Dr., 37922. Tel: 423-694-3135; Fax: 423-694-5080. Bros. Gerard Despathy, F.P.M.; Francis Schafer, F.P.M. Total in Residence 2.

LANCING. *Brothers of Holy Cross*, 297 Davidson Rd., 37770. Tel: 423-965-3392. Bro. Paul Bray, C.S.C.

MOUNTAIN CITY. *Franciscan Friars*, Alverna Friary, 513 Hickory St., 37683. Revs. Evan Eckhoff, O.F.M.; Thomas Vos, O.F.M.; Justin Huber, O.F.M.

SIGNAL MOUNTAIN. *Alexian Brothers*, 198 James Blvd., 37377. Tel: 423-886-0380. Bros. Lawrence Krueger, C.F.A., Asst. Dir.; Dominic Walsh, C.F.A., Supr. Gen.; Cajetan Gavranich, C.F.A.; Ewald Herb, C.F.A.; Polycarp Miller, C.F.A.; Francis Provasnik, C.F.A.; Simeon Pytel, C.F.A.; Eugene Ratley, C.F.A., Dir.; Eugene Gizzi, C.F.A.; Rupert Trudel, C.F.A.; Nolan Potch Webre, C.F.A.; Rev. Maro Cannon, C.F.A. Brothers 12.

[G] CONVENTS AND RESIDENCES FOR SISTERS

KNOXVILLE. *Sisters of Immaculate Heart of Mary*, 545 Mars Hill Rd., Apt. #114, 37923. Tel: 423-690-9601. Sr. Catherine Weibel, I.H.M.
Sisters of Mercy. (Cincinnati Region).
E-mail: SERiney@notes.mercy.com
St. Mary's Medical Center, 900 E. Oak Hill Ave., 37917. Tel: 423-545-8000. Sisters 11.
Sisters of the Divine Compassion, 601 Peters Rd., Apt. 8, 37922.

BUTLER. *Sisters of St. Joseph, Third Order of St. Francis*, 3466 Rte. 3, 37640.

CHATTANOOGA. *Missionary Sisters of the Sacred Heart of Jesus "Ad Gentes"*, 430 Glenwood Dr., 37404. Sisters 3.
Sisters of Charity of Nazareth, 425 Glenwood Dr., 37404. Sisters 3.
Sisters of Charity of Nazareth, 25 S. Germantown Rd., Apt. 244, 37411. Sisters 2.
Sisters of Charity of Nazareth, 25 S. Germantown Rd., Apt. #207, 37411. Tel: 423-629-5356; Fax: 423-495-7788. Sr. Margaret Spalding Wathen, S.C.N.
Sisters of Charity of the Blessed Virgin Mary, 511 S. Moore Rd., 37412-2949. Tel: 423-698-3274. Sr. Henkel, S.C.N.; Sr. Schaeffer, B.V.M.; Sr. Sherrard, B.V.M. Sisters 3.

CLAIRFIELD. *Sisters of the Presentation of the Blessed Virgin Mary*, 169 Kings Ln., 37715. Sr. Mary Dennis Lentsch, P.B.V.M.

CLEVELAND. *Sisters of Charity of Cincinnati*, 2701 Hilltop Dr., 37312. Tel: 423-476-5972.

CLINTON. *St. Therese Convent*, 701 S. Charles G. Seivers Blvd., 37716. Tel: 423-463-9734.

COPPERHILL. *Monastery of Our Lady of Little Citeaux*, Box 1799 McGee Rd., 37317. Tel: 423-496-7373. Sr. Veronica Sweeney; Sr. Angela Ferry. Sisters 2.

HARRIMAN. *Sisters of the Presentation, B.V.M.*, 582 Fairview Rd., 37748. Sr. Barrett; Sr. O'Neill; Sr. Sookov. Sisters 3.

HELENWOOD. *Sisters of Mercy*, P.O. Box 555, 13071 Scott Hwy., 37755. Tel: 423-569-3492.

HIXSON. *Sisters of Mercy (Cincinnati)*, 809-A Gadd Rd., 37343. Tel: 423-877-2453. Sr. Adamarie Kost, R.S.M.

JACKSBORO. *Presentation Sisters of B.V.M.*, 2151 W. Central Ave., 37757. Tel: 423-426-9289.
E-mail: socm@tdsnet.com

JELLICO. *Sisters of the Presentation of the Blessed Virgin Mary*, 133 Plank Ln., 37762. Tel: 423-784-9732. Total Assisted 1,450; Total Staff 4.

JOHNSON CITY. *School Sisters of Notre Dame*, 221 E. Tenth Ave., #2, 37601.

JONESBOROUGH. *Sisters of St. Joseph, Third Order of St. Francis*, 703 E. Jackson Blvd., 37659. Tel: 423-753-3963.

KINGSPORT. *Sisters of Notre Dame de Namur*, 2601 John B. Dennis Hwy. #1004, 37660. Tel: 423-288-8317; Fax: 423-288-7183.

LAKE CITY. *Sisters of Loretto*, 506 Old Lake City Hwy., 37769. Tel: 423-426-9435.

LANCING. *Sisters of Holy Cross*, 641 Island Ford Rd., 37770. Tel: 423-965-3923. Sr. Bray; Sr. Jacomet. Sisters 2.

NEWPORT. *Dominican Sisters.* (Congregation of The Holy Rosary), 659 E. Broadway, 37821. Tel: 423-623-5051.

OAK RIDGE. *Dominican Sisters (St. Cecilia Congregation)*, St. Mary's Convent, 323 Vermont Ave., 37830. Tel: 423-483-0720. Sisters 3. Sr. Lane; Sr. Lynch; Sr. Cummings.

RED BANK. *Sisters of Charity of Nazareth*, 4205 Oakland Terr., 37415. Sisters 2.

[H] RETREAT HOUSES

KNOXVILLE, TN. *The Mountaincrest*, 4902 Mountaincrest Dr., 37918. Tel: 423-687-6900. Johanna C. Humphrey.

[I] CAMPS AND COMMUNITY CENTERS

NEWCOMB. *Crazy Quilt Friendship Center*, 2967 Hwy. 297, 37819. Tel: 423-784-6022. Community center, crafts co-op and clothing store. Total Assisted 1,450; Total Staff 4.

[J] NEWMAN CENTERS

KNOXVILLE. *UT-Knoxville, Newman Foundation, Inc.*, John XXIII University Parish/Catholic Center, 1710 Melrose Pl., 37916. Tel: 423-523-7931. Revs. Terrence P. Ryan, C.S.P.; Robert E. Moran, C.S.P.

CHATTANOOGA. *Newman Foundation of Chattanooga, Inc.*, Catholic Student Center, 514 Palmetto St., 37403. Tel: 423-267-3064. Rev. Patrick Brownell; Marian Christiana, Assoc. Campus Min. Total Staff 5.

GREENEVILLE. *Tusculum College Newman Center.* Attended by Notre Dame Church, Greeneville. c/o Notre Dame Church, 212 Mt. Bethel Rd., 37745.

JOHNSON CITY. *ETSU-Catholic Center*, 734 W. Locust St., 37604. Tel: 423-926-7061. Rev. William H. Gahagan, Chap. Total Staff 1.

[K] MISCELLANEOUS

KNOXVILLE. *The Catholic Diocese of Knoxville Foundation, Inc.*, 805 Northshore Dr., S.W., 37919. Tel: 423-584-3307.

Catholic Foundation of East Tennessee, 805 Northshore Dr., S.W., 37919. Tel: 423-584-3307.

Diocesan Council of Catholic Women, 805 Northshore Dr., S.W., 37919. Rev. Paul A. Hostettler, Diocesan Spiritual Moderator. Deanery Spiritual Moderators: Revs. William H. Gahagan, Five Rivers; Robert J. Hofstetter, Chattanooga; Xavier Mankel, Smoky Mountain; Dan G. Whitman, Cumberland Mountain.

Ladies of Charity, 1031 Central Ave., 37917. Tel: 423-522-6341; 524-0538. Rev. Xavier Mankel, Spiritual Moderator. Total Assisted 17,674; Total Staff 5.

CHATTANOOGA. *Ladies of Charity*, 1800 E. Main St., 37404. Tel: 423-624-3222. Gives emergency assistance in the form of food, medicine, clothing, Lifeline, meals on wheels, layettes to new-born, payment on utilities, rent, glasses, dental work, etc.

RELIGIOUS INSTITUTES OF MEN REPRESENTED IN THE DIOCESE

For further details refer to the corresponding bracketed number in the Religious Institutes of Men or Women section.

[0120]—*Alexian Brothers.*—C.F.A.
[0130]—*Assumptionists.*—A.A.
[0600]—*Brothers of the Congregation of Holy Cross.*—C.S.C.
[0520]—*Franciscan Friars.*—O.F.M.
[0570]—*The Glenmary Home Missioners.*—Glmy.
[0430]—*Order of Preachers-Dominicans.*—O.P.
[1030]—*Paulist Fathers.*—C.S.P.
[]—*Presentation Brothers of Mary.*—F.P.M.

RELIGIOUS INSTITUTES OF WOMEN REPRESENTED IN THE DIOCESE

[1920]—*Congregation of the Sisters of Holy Cross.*—C.S.C.
[1070]—*Dominican Sisters (Congregation of the Holy Rosary).*—O.P.
[1070-07]—*Dominican Sisters (St. Cecilia Congregation).*—O.P.
[2575]—*Institute of the Sisters of Mercy of the Americas.* (Cincinnati Prov.).—R.S.M.
[]—*Missionary Sisters of the Sacred Heart of Jesus "Ad Gentes."*—M.A.G.
[2970]—*School Sisters of Notre Dame.*—S.S.N.D.
[0440]—*Sisters of Charity of Cincinnati, Ohio.*—S.C.
[0500]—*Sisters of Charity of Nazareth.*—S.C.N.
[0430]—*Sisters of Charity of the Blessed Virgin Mary.*—B.V.M.
[]—*Sisters of Immaculate Heart of Mary.*—I.H.M.
[2360]—*Sisters of Loretto at the Foot of the Cross.*—S.L.
[3000]—*Sisters of Notre Dame De Namur.*—S.N.D.deN.
[1510]—*Sisters of St. Francis.*—O.S.F.
[]—*Sisters of St. Joseph, Third Order of St. Francis.*—S.S.J.-T.O.S.F.
[0970]—*Sisters of the Divine Compassion.*—R.D.C.
[3320]—*Sisters of the Presentation of the B.V.M.*—P.B.V.M.

INTERPAROCHIAL CEMETERIES

KNOXVILLE. *Calvary*, Martin Luther King Blvd., 37915. Tel: 423-522-1508. Rev. Thomas Tavella, C.S.P.

CHATTANOOGA. *Mount Olivet*, Ringgold Rd., 37412. Tel: 423-266-1618. Rev. George Schmidt, Jr.

NECROLOGY

† Henkel, Albert J., Knoxville, TN, Holy Ghost. —Died Dec. 26, 1996.

Diocese of La Crosse

(Dioecesis Crossensis)

Most Reverend

RAYMOND L. BURKE, D.D., J.C.D.

Bishop of La Crosse; ordained June 29, 1975; appointed to the Residential See of La Crosse December 10, 1994; consecrated January 6, 1995; installed as Eighth Bishop of La Crosse February 22, 1995. *Res., 3720 East Ave., S., La Crosse, WI, 54602-4004. Mailing Address: P.O. Box 4004, La Crosse, WI, 54602-4004.* Tel.: 608-788-7700.

Chancery Office: 3710 East Ave. S., P.O. Box 4004, La Crosse, WI, 54602-4004. Tel.: 608-788-7700; Fax: 608-788-8413.

Web site address: www.dioceseoflacrosse.com

E-mail address: dioceselacrosse@compuserve.com

Most Reverend

JOHN J. PAUL, D.D.

Retired Bishop of La Crosse; ordained January 24, 1943; appointed Titular Bishop of Lambese and Auxiliary Bishop of La Crosse May 17, 1977; consecrated August 4, 1977; appointed to the Residential See of La Crosse October 18, 1983; installed as Seventh Bishop of La Crosse December 5, 1983; retired December 10, 1994. *Res., Holy Cross Diocesan Center, P.O. Box 4004, La Crosse, WI, 54602-4004.* Tel.: 608-788-8395; 788-7700.

Most Reverend

FREDERICK W. FREKING, D.D., J.C.D.

Retired Bishop of La Crosse; ordained July 31, 1938; appointed Bishop of Salina October 10, 1957; consecrated November 30, 1957; installed January 7, 1958; transferred to La Crosse December 30, 1964; installed February 24, 1965; retired May 10, 1983. *Res., Holy Cross Diocesan Center, P.O. Box 4004, La Crosse, WI, 54602-4004.* Tel.: 608-788-0668; 788-7700.

ERECTED MARCH 3, 1868. SUBDIVIDED MAY 3, 1905. SUBDIVIDED JANUARY 15, 1946.

Square Miles 15,078.

Comprises the following 19 Counties in the State of Wisconsin: Adams, Buffalo, Chippewa, Clark, Crawford, Dunn, Eau Claire, Jackson, Juneau, La Crosse, Marathon, Monroe, Pepin, Pierce, Portage, Richland, Trempealeau, Vernon and Wood.

For legal titles of parishes and diocesan institutions, consult the Chancery Office.

STATISTICAL OVERVIEW

Personnel	
Bishop	1
Retired Bishops	2
Retired Abbots	1
Priests: Diocesan Active in Diocese	124
Priests: Active Outside Diocese	7
Priests: Diocesan in Foreign Missions	3
Priests: Retired, Sick or Absent	62
Number of Diocesan Priests	196
Religious Priests in Diocese	24
Extern Priests in Diocese	7
Permanent Deacons in Diocese	22
Total Brothers	8
Total Sisters	542
Parishes	
Parishes	178
With Resident Pastor:	
Resident Diocesan Priests	105
Resident Religious Priests	6
Without Resident Pastor:	
Administered by Priests	53
Administered by Women Religious	11
Administered by Lay People	1
Completely Vacant	2
Pastoral Centers	2
Closed Parishes	3
Professional Ministry Personnel:	
Sisters	22
Lay Ministers	27
Welfare	
Catholic Hospitals	9
Total Assisted	313,632
Homes for the Aged	12
Total Assisted	1,038
Day Care and Extended Day Care Centers	1
Total Assisted	150
Specialized Homes	3
Total Assisted	6,500
Special Centers for Social Services	2
Total Assisted	1,000
Residential Care of Disabled	3
Total Assisted	185
Educational	
Seminaries, Diocesan	1
Students from This Diocese	2
Students from Other Diocese	6
Diocesan Students in Other Seminaries	36
Total Seminarians	38
Colleges and Universities	1
Total Students	1,637
High Schools, Diocesan and Parish	7
Total Students	1,897
Elementary Schools, Diocesan and Parish	78
Total Students	10,600
Catechesis/Religious Education:	
High School Students	8,749
Elementary Students	17,125
Total Students Under Catholic Instruction	40,046
Teachers in the Diocese:	
Priests	6
Sisters	21
Lay Teachers	594
Vital Statistics	
Receptions into the Church:	
Infant Baptism Totals	3,129
Adult Baptism Totals	140
Received into Full Communion	308
First Communions	3,345
Confirmations	3,318
Marriages:	
Catholic	928
Interfaith	497
Total Marriages	1,425
Deaths	2,248
Total Catholic Population	231,064
Total Population	882,036

Former Bishops—Most Rev. MICHAEL HEISS, D.D., cons. Sept. 6, 1868; appt. Titular Archbishop of Hadrianople, and coadjutor to the Metropolitan of Milwaukee March 14, 1880; promoted to Milwaukee, Sept. 1881; died March 26, 1890.—Rt. Rev. KILIAN CASPAR FLASCH, D.D., cons. Aug. 24, 1881; died Aug. 3, 1891.—Rt. Rev. JAMES SCHWEBACH, D.D., cons. Feb. 25, 1892; died June 6, 1921.—Most Rev. ALEXANDER J. MCGAVICK, D.D., LL.D., cons. Titular Bishop of Marcopolis and Auxiliary Bishop of Chicago, May 1, 1899; transferred to See of La Crosse, Nov. 21, 1921; died Aug. 25, 1948.—Most Rev. JOHN P. TREACY, S.T.D., cons. Titular Bishop of Metelis and Coadjutor of La Crosse "cum jure successionis," Oct. 2, 1945; succeeded to the See, July 23, 1946; died Oct. 11, 1964.—Most Rev. FREDERICK W. FREKING, D.D., J.C.D., cons. Bishop of Salina, KS, November 30, 1957; transferred to the See of La Crosse, Dec. 30, 1964; installed La Crosse, Feb. 24, 1965; retired May 10, 1983.—Most Rev. JOHN J. PAUL, D.D., appt. Titular Bishop of Lambese and Auxiliary Bishop of La Crosse, May 17, 1977; cons. Aug. 4, 1977; appt. to the Residential See of La Crosse, Oct. 18, 1983; installed as Bishop of La Crosse, Dec. 5, 1983; retired Dec. 10, 1994.

Vicar General—Very Rev. JOSEPH J. RAFACZ S.T.L., *St. Thomas More Parish, 2006 Weston St., La Crosse, 54601.*

Chancery Office—3710 East Ave. S., P.O. Box 4004, La Crosse, 54602-4004. Tel: 608-788-7700; Fax: 608-788-8413. Office Hours: Mon.-Fri. 8-4:30.

Chancellor—Sr. MARLENE WEISENBECK, F.S.P.A., J.C.L.

Vice-Chancellor—Rev. LEON A. POWELL.

Moderator of the Curia—Rev. MICHAEL J. GORMAN, J.C.L.

Secretary to the Bishop—Rev. MICHAEL J. GORMAN, J.C.L.

Archivist—Sr. MARLENE WEISENBECK, F.S.P.A., J.C.L.

Finance Officer—SONDRA RIEDER.

Ecclesiastical Notaries—Revs. MICHAEL J. GORMAN; LEON A. POWELL; Sr. MARLENE WEISENBECK, F.S.P.A.; KELLY MCCARTHY; SHERYL STAPLETON; SUSAN VLASAK, *P.O. Box 4004, La Crosse, 54602-4004.*

Diocesan Tribunal—3710 East Ave. S., P.O. Box 4004, La Crosse, 54602-4004. Tel: 608-788-7700. (Address all rogatory commissions to the Chancellor).

Judicial Vicar—Very Rev. ROBERT P. HUNDT, J.C.L.

Promoter of Justice—GEORGE E. NIX, J.C.L.

Defensores Vinculi—Sr. MARLENE WEISENBECK, F.S.P.A., J.C.L.; GEORGE E. NIX, J.C.L.
Auditors—GEORGE E. NIX, J.C.L.; SHERYL STAPLETON.
Diocesan Judge—Rev. MICHAEL J. GORMAN, J.C.L.
College of Consultors—Very Revs. JOSEPH J. RAFACZ, V.G.; ROBERT J. COOK; Revs. WILLIAM N. GREVATCH; EUGENE A. KLINK; JOHN L. PARR; MARK R. PIERCE; ROGER J. SCHECKEL; MICHAEL J. GORMAN, Sec.
Deans—Very Rev. LEONARD G. KAISER, Arcadia; Very Rev. THOMAS E. LANGER, Chippewa Falls; Very Rev. THOMAS J. DONALDSON, Durand; Very Rev. JOHN A. SCHULTZ, Eau Claire; Very Rev. ROBERT J. COOK, La Crosse; Very Rev. JAMES J. LOGAN, Marshfield; Very Rev. G. RICHARD ROBERTS, Mauston; Very Rev. EUGENE J. WOLF, Prairie du Chien; Very Rev. WAYNE R. KIDD, Richland Center; Very Rev. JAMES P. MCNAMEE, Sparta; Very Rev. DONALD L. PRZYBYLSKI, Stevens Point; Very Rev. ROMAN F. KAISER, Thorp; Very Rev. WILLIAM N. GREVATCH, Wausau; Very Rev. R. JOHN SWING, Wisconsin Rapids.

Diocesan Offices and Directors

Apostolate for the Indians—Vacant.
Boy Scouts—Rev. ANTHONY J. WOLF, *530 Main St., La Crosse, 54601.* Tel: 608-782-0322.
Building Commission—Very Rev. J. FLOYD DWYER; Revs. ALLAN L. SLOWIAK; MICHAEL J. GORMAN; Sr. MARLENE WEISENBECK, F.S.P.A.; SONDRA RIEDER; DONALD NOVOTNEY.
Catholic Women, Council of—Rev. DONALD M. BERG, Moderator, *St. Joachim Parish, P.O. Box 69, Pittsville, 54466-0069.* Tel: 715-884-6815.
Central Wisconsin Hispanic Ministry—*P.O. Box 4004, La Crosse, 54602-4004.* Tel: 608-788-7700.
Department of Catholic Education—ROBERT J. LECHELER, Dir., Catechetics; VIRGINIA HALBUR, Asst. Dir., Catechetics; DONALD F. NOVOTNEY, Dir., Schools; MARIANN HESIK, Asst. Dir., Schools; BOUA NENG YANG, LaCrosse Area Hmong Catechist, *3710 East Ave. S., P.O. Box 4004, La Crosse, 54602-4004.* Tel: 608-788-7707.
Office of Family Life—SUE GILBERT, Dir., *P.O. Box 4004, La Crosse, 54602-4004.* Tel: 608-788-7700.
Natural Family Planning—Coords.: JEFF HEINZEN; ALICE HEINZEN, *711 24th St. N.E., Menomonie, 54751.* Tel: 715-235-6226.
Holy Childhood Association—Very Rev. JOSEPH J. RAFACZ, Dir., *P.O. Box 4004, La Crosse, 54602-4004.* Tel: 608-788-7700.
Hospitals and Health Affairs—Co-Coords.: Rev. EDMUND J. KLIMEK, *Sacred Heart Hospital, 900 W. Clairemont Ave., Eau Claire, 54701.* Tel: 715-839-4121. Rev. LAWRENCE G. DUNKLEE, *St. Charles Borromeo Parish, P.O. Box 292, Genoa, 54632.* Tel: 608-689-2646.
Newman Campus Ministry—Rev. MARK R. PIERCE, Coord., *1732 State St., La Crosse, 54601.* Tel: 608-784-4994.
Office of Communications—ROSE A. HAMMES, Communications and Pub. Rels. Officer, *P.O. Box 4004, La Crosse, 54602-4004.* Tel: 608-788-7700.
Office of the Consecrated Life—Sr. MARLENE WEISENBECK, F.S.P.A., Dir., *P.O. Box 4004, La Crosse, 54602-4004.* Tel: 608-788-7700.
Office of Ecumenism—Rev. STEVEN J. BRICE, Diocesan Officer, Ecumenical Questions, *110 N. 6th St., Wausau, 54401.* Tel: 715-675-9749.
Office of Justice and Peace—MICHAEL R. BROWN, Dir., *P.O. Box 4004, La Crosse, 54602-4004.* Tel: 608-788-7700. Justice and Peace Commission-confer Office.
Office of Ministries—Rev. JOHN L. PARR, Dir., *P.O. Box 4004, La Crosse, 54602-4004.* Tel: 608-788-7700. Office of Ministries consists of Vocation Office, Permanent Diaconate, Lay Ministries & Clergy Continuing Education.
Office for Pastoral Planning—Vacant, *P.O. Box 4004, La Crosse, 54602-4004.* Tel: 608-788-7700.
Office of Sacred Worship—Vacant, *P.O. Box 4004, La Crosse, 54602-4004.* Tel: 608-788-7700. Sacred Worship Commission-confer Office.
Office of Youth Ministry—DENNIS KURTZ, Dir., *P.O. Box 1062, Eau Claire, 54702-1062.* Tel: 715-834-7079.
Pastoral Council—Most Rev. RAYMOND L. BURKE, Pres.; Very Rev. JOSEPH J. RAFACZ, V.G., Exec. Sec., *P.O. Box 4004, La Crosse, 54602-4004.* Tel: 608-788-7700.
Personnel Council—Most Rev. RAYMOND L. BURKE, Pres.; Rev. WILLIAM G. MENZEL, Chm.; Rev. LYLE L. SCHULTE, Sec.; Very Revs. THOMAS J. DONALDSON; JOSEPH J. RAFACZ, V.G.; Revs. DAVID C. KUNZ; JOHN L. PARR; T. MICHAEL SCHELBLE; CHARLES D. STOETZEL, *P.O. Box 4004, La Crosse, 54602-4004.* Tel: 608-788-7700.
Presbyteral Council—Most Rev. RAYMOND L. BURKE, Pres. Elected Members: Revs. BERNARD D. MCGARTY; ANDREW K. KAROBLIS; DANIEL J. KELLY; DELBERT J. MALIN; A. JOSEPH FOLLMAR; EUGENE A. KLINK; WILLIAM G. MENZEL; ROBERT A. STREVELER; MARK R. PIERCE; EDWARD J. SHUTTLEWORTH; CARL J. DOCKENDORFF; JOHN W. WAMBACH, S.J.
Ex-Officio Members—Very Rev. JOSEPH J. RAFACZ, V.G.; Rev. MICHAEL J. GORMAN, Moderator of the Curia. Consultors: Very Revs. ROBERT J. COOK; WILLIAM N. GREVATCH; Revs. JOHN L. PARR; ROGER J. SCHECKEL.
Propagation of the Faith—Very Rev. JOSEPH J. RAFACZ, V.G., Dir., *P.O. Box 4004, La Crosse, 54602-4004.* Tel: 608-788-7700.
Rural Life Conference and Community Development—*P.O. Box 4004, La Crosse, 54602-4004.* Tel: 608-788-7700.
St. Joseph's Priest Fund, Inc., (Benevolent Society)—Rev. MICHAEL J. GORMAN, Exec. Sec., *P.O. Box 4004, La Crosse, 54602-4004.* Tel: 608-788-7700.
"Times Review": Diocesan Newspaper—GERALD RUFF, Editor, *P.O. Box 4004, La Crosse, 54602-4004.* Tel: 608-788-1524.

CLERGY, PARISHES, MISSIONS AND PAROCHIAL SCHOOLS

CITY OF LA CROSSE
(La Crosse County)

1—ST. JOSEPH THE WORKMAN CATHEDRAL, Very Rev. Robert J. Cook, Rector; Rev. Anthony J. Wolf.
Res., 530 Main St., 54601. Tel: 608-782-0322; Fax: 608-782-8228. [CEM 2]
School—1319 Ferry St., 54601. Tel: 608-782-5998; Fax: 608-784-9933. John Stellflue, Prin.
Lay Teachers 10; Students 192.

2—BLESSED SACRAMENT, Rev. Bernard O. McGarty.
Res., 130 Losey Blvd. S., 54601. Tel: 608-782-2953; Fax: 608-785-1064. [CEM 2]
School—(Grades K-6) 225 S. 24th St., 54601. Tel: 608-782-5564. Kay Berra, Prin.
Lay Teachers 21; Students 290.

3—HOLY CROSS. Closed. For inquiries for parish records contact St. Joseph the Workman Cathedral, La Crosse.

4—HOLY TRINITY, Rev. Lawrence B. Berger.
Res., 1333 S. 13th St., 54601. Tel: 608-782-2028. [CEM 2]
School—1417 S. 13th, 54601. Tel: 608-782-1040.
Lay Teachers 8; Students 159.

5—ST. JAMES THE LESS, Rev. Roger J. Scheckel.
Res., 1032 Caledonia St., 54603. Tel: 608-782-7557; Fax: 608-796-0086. [CEM 2]
School—716 Windsor St., 54603. Tel: 608-784-6167.
Lay Teachers 10; Students 135.

6—ST. JOHN THE BAPTIST. Closed. For inquiries for parish records contact St. James, La Crosse.

7—ST. MARY. Closed. For inquiries for parish records contact St. Joseph the Workman Cathedral, La Crosse.

8—ST. PIUS X. Attended by St. Thomas More, La Crosse. Very Rev. Joseph J. Rafacz, V.G.; Deacon Richard Sage.
Res., 2006 Weston St., 54601. Tel: 608-788-5483. [CEM 2]
School—Tel: 608-788-6919.
Lay Teachers 9; Students 122.

9—RONCALLI NEWMAN PARISH, Rev. Mark R. Pierce.
Res., 1732 State St., 54601. Tel: 608-784-4994; Fax: 608-784-0230. [CEM 2]

10—ST. THOMAS MORE, Very Rev. Joseph J. Rafacz.
Res., 2006 Weston St., 54601. Tel: 608-788-5483; Fax: 608-788-4070. [CEM 2]
School—Tel: 608-788-5225.
Lay Teachers 10; Students 115.

11—ST. WENCESLAUS. Closed. For inquiries for parish records contact St. Joseph the Workman Cathedral, La Crosse.

OUTSIDE THE CITY OF LA CROSSE

Abbotsford, Clark Co., St. Bernard. Attended by Holy Rosary, Owen. Rev. Allen F. Jakubowski; Sr. Mary Jo Donaldson, O.S.B., Pastoral Assoc.
Res., 101 W. Cedar St., 54405-9558. Tel: 715-223-3331. [JC]

Adams, Adams Co., St. Joseph. Also serves St. Ann, Brooks. Rev. Dennis P. Stanchik; Deacon David Kennedy (MIL).
Res., Box 310, 53910. Tel: 608-339-3485. [CEM]

Alma, Buffalo Co., St. Lawrence. Attended by St. Boniface, Waumandee. Rev. Richard C. Dickman.
Mailing Address: P.O. Box 246, 54610. Tel: 608-685-3253; Fax: 608-685-3253.
Res., Box 962, Waumandee, 54622-0962. Tel: 608-626-2621. [CEM]

Alma Center, Jackson Co., Immaculate Conception. Attended by St. Joseph, Fairview. Rev. David A. Ziegelmaier.
Mailing Address: Box 188, 54611. Tel: 715-964-5201.
Res., N13740 Fairview Rd., Fairchild, 54741-8514. Tel: 715-334-2202. [CEM]

Almond, Portage Co., Holy Guardian Angels. Closed. For inquiries for parish records contact St. Maximilian Maria Kolbe, Southeastern Portage County.

Altdorf, Wood Co., St. Joseph, Rev. Joseph W. Hirsch.
Res., 530 10th Ave. N., Wisconsin Rapids, 54494. Tel: 715-421-5777. [CEM]

Altoona, Eau Claire Co., St. Mary, Rev. Norbert J. Wilger.
Res., 1827 Lynn Ave., 54720. Tel: 715-835-8813. [JC]
School—1828 Lynn Ave., 54720. Tel: 715-835-5334.
Lay Teachers 6; Students 75.

Amherst, Portage Co., St. James. Also serves St. Mary of Mount Carmel, Fancher. Rev. Robert F. Pedretti.
Res., 453 S Main, Box 280, 54406-0280. Tel: 715-824-3455. [CEM]

Arcadia, Trempealeau Co., Our Lady of Perpetual Help, Rev. Raymond J. Pedretti.
Office: 411 S. Washington St., 54612. Tel: 608-323-3178.
Res., 223 E. Maple St., 54612. Tel: 608-323-7116. [CEM 2]
School—Tel: 608-323-3676.
St. Stanislaus, Rev. Raymond J. Pedretti.
Res., 223 E. Maple St., 54612. Tel: 608-323-7116. [CEM]

Arkansaw, Pepin Co., St. Joseph, Rev. Matthew J. Molinaro.
Res., W. 7805 County Rd. Z, 54721. Tel: 715-285-5313. [CEM 2]

Arpin, Wood Co., St. Francis. Attended by St. James, Vesper. Rev. Chester J. Osowski.
Mailing Address: Box 68, Vesper, 54489. Tel: 715-569-4412. [CEM]

Athens, Marathon Co., St. Anthony de Padua. Also serves Holy Family, Poniatowski. Rev. Randy E. Olson.
Res., 417 Caroline St., Box 206, 54411-0206. Tel: 715-257-7684. [JC]
School—Tel: 715-257-7541.
Sisters 1; Lay Teachers 5; Students 90.

Auburndale, Wood Co., Nativity of the Blessed Virgin Mary. Also serves St. Michael, Hewitt. Rev. T. Michael Schelble.
Res., 5866 Main St., P.O. Box 177, 54412-0177. Tel: 715-652-2806; Fax: 715-652-8020. [CEM 2]
School—Tel: 715-652-2196; Fax: 715-652-8020.
Franciscan Sisters of Perpetual Adoration, F.S.P.A. 1; Lay Teachers 6; Students 73.

Augusta, Eau Claire Co., St. Anthony de Padua. Attended by Holy Guardian Angels, Brackett. Rev. Paul R. Gitter.
Mailing Address: 800 W. Brown St., P.O. Box 3, 54722. Tel: 715-286-2547.
Res., S10-444 U.S. Hwy. 53, Fall Creek, 54742. Tel: 715-878-4183.

Babcock, Wood Co., All Saints. Attended by Sacred Heart, Nekoosa. Very Rev. R. John Swing; Sr. Catherine Kaiser, F.S.P.A., Pastoral Assoc.
Mailing Address: 711 Prospect Ave., Nekoosa, 54457. Tel: 715-886-3422. [JC]

Bakerville, Wood Co., Corpus Christi. Attended by Sacred Heart, Marshfield. Rev. Robert A. Schaller. In res., Rev. Charles P. Schumacher Tel: 715-676-2824.
Mailing Address: 10075 Hwy. BB, Marshfield, 54449. Tel: 715-676-3658.
Res., 112 E. 11th St., Marshfield, 54449-4216. Tel: 715-384-3213. [CEM]

Bangor, La Crosse Co., St. Mary. Attended by St. Leo the Great, West Salem. Rev. Robert S. Hegenbarth. In res., Rev. Paul L. Sankoorikal.
Mailing Address: 210 W. Hamlin St., West Salem, 54669. Tel: 608-786-0610. [CEM]
Res., P.O. Box 290, 54614-0290. Tel: 608-486-2033.

Bear Valley, Richland Co., St. Kilian. Closed. For inquiries for parish records contact Nativity, B.V.M., Keyesville.

Bevent, Marathon Co., St. Ladislaus. Attended by St. Joseph, Galloway. Rev. Rex A. Zimmerman; Sr. Mary Ellen Diermeier, S.S.J.-T.O.S.F., Pastoral Assoc.
Mailing Address: 6455 State Hwy. 153, Hatley, 54440. Tel: 715-446-3060. [CEM]

Big River, Pierce Co., Nativity of the Blessed Virgin Mary, Rev. John W. Beckfelt.
Res., W10137 570th Ave., River Falls, 54022. Tel:

715-425-5806. [CEM 2]

Black River Falls, Jackson Co., St. Joseph, Rev. Michael C. Braun.
Res., 507 Main St., 54615-1699. Tel: 715-284-5613. [CEM]

Blair, Trempealeau Co., St. Ansgar. Attended by St. John the Apostle, Whitehall.
Mailing Address: P.O. Box 127, Whitehall, 54773-0127. Tel: 715-538-4607; Fax: 715-538-2224.

Blenker, Wood Co., St. Kilian. Attended by St. Wenceslaus, Milladore. Rev. John A. Wisneski.
Mailing Address: Box 100, Milladore, 54454. Tel: 715-457-2314. [CEM]

Bloomer, Chippewa Co., St. Paul. Also serves St. Jude, New Auburn. Very Rev. Thomas E. Langer.
Res., 1222 Main St., 54724. Tel: 715-568-3255; Fax: 715-568-3255. [CEM 3]
School—1210 Main St., 54724. Tel: 715-568-3233; Fax: 715-568-3255.
Sisters 2; Lay Teachers 11; Students 166.
Convent—1205 13th Ave., 54724. Tel: 715-568-3266.

Boyceville, Dunn Co., St. Luke. Attended by St. Joseph, Menomonie. Rev. Lyle L. Schulte; Sr. Judith Kramer, O.S.B., Min.
Mailing Address: 605 Center St., P.O. Box 136, 54725. Tel: 715-232-4922.
Res., St. Bede Priory, P.O. Box 66, Eau Claire, 54702-0066. Tel: 715-834-3176; Fax: 715-834-4292.

Boyd, Chippewa Co., Sacred Heart of Jesus-St. Joseph. Attended by Holy Family, Stanley. Rev. Robert W. Nelson. In res., Rev. Eugene P. Smith Tel: 714-667-3038.
Res., 719 Patten St., P.O. Box 10, 54726-0010. Tel: 715-667-3341. [CEM]
School—Tel: 715-667-3346.
Lay Teachers 4; Students 78.

Brackett, Eau Claire Co., Holy Guardian Angels. Also serves St. Anthony, Augusta; and St. John, Fall Creek. Rev. Paul R. Gitter.
Res., S10444 U.S. Hwy. 53, Fall Creek, 54742. Tel: 715-878-4183. [CEM]

Brooks, Adams Co., St. Ann. Attended by St. Joseph, Adams. Rev. Dennis P. Stanchik.
Mailing Address: P.O. Box 132, Oxford, 53952. Tel: 608-584-4900. [CEM]

Buena Vista, Portage Co., St. Martin. Closed. For inquiries for parish records contact St. Maximilian Maria Kolbe, Southeastern Portage County.

Cadott, Chippewa Co., St. Rose of Lima. Also serves St. Anthony, Drywood. Rev. Thomas F. Crowley.
Res., Box 160, 54727. Tel: 715-289-4551. [CEM]
School—Tel: 715-289-4985.
Lay Teachers 6; Students 54.

Camp Douglas, Juneau Co., St. James. Unassigned. Also serves St. Michael, Indian Creek.
Res., Box 289, 54618. Tel: 608-427-6762. [CEM]

Cashton, Monroe Co., Sacred Heart of Jesus. Attended by Nativity of the Blessed Virgin Mary, St, Mary's Ridge. Rev. Kevin C. Louis. In res., Rev. Aloysius Wozniak Tel: 608-654-7619.
Res., 26400 CTH U, 54619-9757. Tel: 608-823-7906; Fax: 608-823-7272. [CEM 3]
School—Sacred Heart of Jesus School, 1223 Front St., 54619. Tel: 608-654-7733; Fax: 608-654-7733.
Lay Teachers 8; Students 80.
Convent—Tel: 608-654-7413.

Cassel, Marathon Co., Sacred Heart. Attended by Nativity of the Blessed Virgin Mary, Marathon City. Revs. Joseph Diermeier, O.F.M.Cap.; Joseph B. Jeruzal, O.F.M.Cap.
Mailing Address: 3372 County Rd. S., P.O. Box 68, Marathon City, 54448-0068. Tel: 715-443-2045; Fax: 715-443-3045. [CEM]

Cazenovia, Richland Co., St. Anthony de Padua. Also serves Sacred Heart, Lone Rock; and St. Mary, Keyesville. Rev. Daniel J. Kiedinger.
Res., 32505 Co. Hwy. U, 53924. Tel: 608-983-2367. [CEM]
School—Tel: 608-983-2786.
Lay Teachers 4; Students 34.

Chili, Clark Co., St. Stephen. Attended by St. Mary, Neillsville. Rev. Joseph N. Henseler.
Mailing Address: P.O. Box 58, 54420-0058. Tel: 715-683-2418. [CEM]
Res., 1803 Black River Rd., Neillsville, 54456. Tel: 715-743-3840.

Chippewa Falls, Chippewa Co., Holy Ghost. Also serves St. Bridget, Springfield. Revs. Edmund J. Doerre; Charles J. Scherman, S.J.
Res., 412 S. Main St., 54729. Tel: 715-723-4890. [JC]
School—See Consolidated Elementary Schools, Chippewa Falls.

Notre Dame, Rev. Albert W. Sonnberger; Sr. Florence Domka, S.S.J.-T.O.S.F., Pastoral Assoc. In res., Rev. Eric R. Berns.
Res., 117 Allen St., 54729-2899. Tel: 715-723-7108; Fax: 715-723-7523.
School—See Consolidated Elementary Schools, Chippewa Falls.

St. Charles Borromeo. Also serves St. John the Baptist, Cooks Valley; St. Peter, Tilden. Revs. William P. Felix; Daniel B. DuChez, O.S.
Res., 810 Pearl St., 54729. Tel: 715-723-4088; Fax: 715-723-2195. [JC]
School—See Consolidated Elementary Schools, Chippewa Falls.

Colby, Clark Co., St. Mary Help of Christians, Rev. John E. Malik.
Res., 205 S. 2nd St., P.O. Box 436, 54421. Tel: 715-223-3048. [CEM]
School—Tel: 715-223-3033; Fax: 715-223-0223.
Lay Teachers 11; Students 162.

Cooks Valley, Chippewa Co., St. John the Baptist. Attended by St. Charles Borromeo, Chippewa Falls. Rev. William P. Felix.
Mailing Address: 4540 State Hwy. 40, Bloomer, 54724. Tel: 715-568-3778.
Res., 810 Pearl St., Chippewa Falls, 54729. Tel: 715-723-4088. [CEM]

Coon Valley, Vernon Co., St. Mary, Rev. Maryon C. Jordan, O.S.B.
Res., 904 Central Ave., 54623. Tel: 608-452-3841; Fax: 608-452-3841. [CEM]

Cornell, Chippewa Co., Holy Cross. Also serves Sacred Heart, Jim Falls. Rev. Jeremiah Cashman.
Res., 107 S. 8th St., P.O. Box 68, 54732. Tel: 715-239-6826. [CEM 2]

Custer, Portage Co., Immaculate Conception, Rev. Steven J. Kachel; Sr. Annette Marie Johnson, S.S.N.D., Pastoral Assoc.
Res., 3995 CTH K, Amherst, 54406. Tel: 715-824-2270. [CEM]

Czestochowa, Clark Co., St. Mary of Czestochowa. Closed. For inquiries for parish records contact Holy Family, Stanley.

De Soto, Crawford Co., Sacred Heart. Closed. For inquiries for parish records contact St. Charles Borromeo, Genoa.

Dilly, Vernon Co., St. John Nepomucene. Closed. For inquiries for parish records contact St. Aloysius, Hillsboro.

Dorchester, Clark Co., St. Louis, Rev. James F. Schaefer.
Res., 133 N. 3rd St., 54425-9577. Tel: 715-654-5089. [JC]
School—134 N. 4th St., 54425. Tel: 715-654-5467.
Lay Teachers 4; Students 29.

Drywood, Chippewa Co., St. Anthony. Attended by St. Rose of Lima, Cadott. Rev. Thomas F. Crowley.
Res., P.O. Box 68, Jim Falls, 54748. Tel: 715-382-4422. [CEM]

Durand, Pepin Co., St. Mary's Assumption. Also serves Holy Rosary, Lima. Rev. Edward J. Shuttleworth; Deacon James Weingart.
Res., 911 W. Prospect St., P.O. Box 188, 54736-1049. Tel: 715-672-5640; Fax: 715-672-4193. [CEM]
School—901 W. Prospect St., 54736. Tel: 715-672-5617; Fax: 715-672-3931.
Franciscan Sisters of Perpetual Adoration 2; Lay Teachers 12; Students 138.

Eastman, Crawford Co., St. Wenceslaus, Rev. John V. Cassidy.
Res., P.O. Box 109, 54626. Tel: 608-874-4151. [CEM]

Eau Claire, Eau Claire Co.,

1—Immaculate Conception, Rev. Eugene A. Klink.
Res., 1712 Highland Ave., 54701. Tel: 715-835-9935.
School—(Grades K-8) 1715 Sherwin Ave., 54701. Tel: 715-835-3500.
Sisters 4; Lay Teachers 16; Students 386.

2—Newman Community, Revs. George R. Szews; Edmund J. Klimek; Thomas J. Krieg.
Res., 110 Garfield Ave., 54701-4042. Tel: 715-834-3399. [JC]

3—Sacred Heart of Jesus, Rev. John W. Steiner.
Office: 416 N. Dewey St., 54703-3299. Tel: 715-835-9154.
Res., 318 Fulton St., 54703-5399. Tel: 715-832-0925; Fax: 715-835-4658. [CEM]
School—Eau Claire Coordinated Catholic Schools. See Consolidated Elementary Schools under Institutions Located in the Diocese. Tel: 715-835-1609.

4—St. James the Greater, Very Rev. John A. Schultz.
Res., 2502 Eleventh St., 54703-2700. Tel: 715-835-5887; Fax: 715-835-2032. [JC]
School—Eau Claire Coordinated Catholic Schools. See Consolidated Elementary Schools under Institutions Located in the Diocese. Tel: 715-832-8280.

5—St. Olaf, Rev. Frank Corradi, S.C.
Res., 2408 North Ln., 54703-0960. Tel: 715-832-2504; Fax: 715-832-0742. [JC]
School—Eau Claire Coordinated Catholic Schools. See Consolidated Elementary Schools under Institutions Located in the Diocese. Tel: 715-834-4959.

6—St. Patrick, Rev. John W. Steiner. In res., Rev. James F. Trempe.
Res., 318 Fulton St., 54703-5399. Tel: 715-832-0925. [CEM]
School—Eau Claire Coordinated Catholic Schools. See Consolidated Elementary Schools under Institutions Located in the Diocese. Tel: 715-835-8931; Fax: 715-835-4658.

Eau Galle, Dunn Co., St. Henry, Rev. Roy L. Mish.
Res., N. 460 CTH D, 54737. Tel: 715-283-4448. [CEM]

Edgar, Marathon Co., St. John the Baptist, Rev. Bernard L. Raschke; Deacon Herman Schulz.
Res., 103 N. Fourth Ave., P.O. Box 35, 54426. Tel: 715-352-3011; Fax: 715-352-3011. [CEM]
School—Tel: 715-352-3000.
Lay Teachers 9; Students 130.

Edson, Chippewa Co., Sacred Heart of Jesus. Attended by Sacred Heart of Jesus-St. Joseph, Boyd. Rev. Arthur S. Redmond.
Res., See Sacred Heart of Jesus-St. Joseph. R.R. 2, Box 284A, Boyd, 54726. Tel: 715-667-3341. [CEM]

Elk Mound, Dunn Co., St. Joseph, Rev. Henry R. Hoerburger.
Res., P.O. Box 275, 54739. Tel: 715-879-5332. [CEM]

Ellsworth, Pierce Co., St. Francis of Assisi, Very Rev. Thomas J. Donaldson.
Res., 264 S. Grant St., P.O. Box 839, 54011. Tel: 715-273-4774; Fax: 715-723-4774. [CEM]
School—Box 250, 54011. Tel: 715-273-4391.
Sisters of St. Benedict 1; Lay Teachers 8; Students 158.

Elmwood, Pierce Co., Sacred Heart. Also serves Sacred Heart of Jesus, Spring Valley. Rev. George A. Becker.
Res., 510 Wilson St., 54740. Tel: 715-639-2741. [CEM]

Elroy, Juneau Co., St. Patrick, Very Rev. G. Richard Roberts.
Res., 110 Spring St., 53929. Tel: 608-462-5875. [CEM]

Ettrick, Trempealeau Co., St. Bridget. Also serves St. Kevin, Melrose. Rev. Thomas J. McInnis.
Res., 22650 Washington St., 54627. Tel: 608-525-3811. [CEM]

Fairchild, Eau Claire Co., St. John Cantius. Attended by St. Joseph, Fairview. Rev. David A. Ziegelmaier.
Res., N13740 Fairview Rd., 54741-8514. Tel: 715-334-2202.

Fairview, Eau Claire Co., St. Joseph. Also serves Immaculate Conception, Alma Center; and St. John Cantius, Fairchild. Rev. David A. Ziegelmaier.
Res., N13740 Fairview Rd., Fairchild, 54741-8514. Tel: 715-334-2202.

Fall Creek, Eau Claire Co., St. John the Apostle. Attended by Holy Guardian Angels, Brackett. Rev. Paul R. Gitter.
Mailing Address: P.O. Box 322, 54742. Tel: 715-877-3400.
Res., S. 10444 U.S. Hwy. 53, 54742. Tel: 715-878-4183.

Fancher, Portage Co., St. Mary of Mount Carmel. Attended by St. James, Amherst. Rev. Robert F. Pedretti.
Res., P.O. Box 280, 453 S. Main St., Amherst, 54406. Tel: 715-824-3455. [CEM]

Fountain City, Buffalo Co., Immaculate Conception, Rev. J. Thomas Finucan.
Res., One Wall St., P.O. Box 218, 54629-0218. Tel: 608-687-3496. [CEM]

Galesville, Trempealeau Co., St. Mary. Attended by St. Bartholomew, Trempealeau.
Mailing Address: 20354 W. Ridge Ave., P.O. Box 68, 54630-0068. Tel: 608-582-2365.
Res., 11646 South St., Trempealeau, 54461-8238. Tel: 608-534-9760.

Galloway, Marathon Co., St. Joseph. Also serves St. Ladislaus, Bevent. Rev. Rex A. Zimmerman; Sr. Mary Ellen Diermeier, S.S.J.-T.O.S.F., Pastoral Assoc.
Res., 8846 CTH C, Wittenberg, 54499-8936. Tel: 715-454-6431. [CEM]

Gays Mills, Crawford Co., St. Mary. Also serves St. Philip, Rolling Ground. Rev. Leon S. Rausch, S.J.
Res., Box 36, 54631-0036. Tel: 608-735-4420. [JC]

Genoa, Vernon Co., St. Charles Borromeo, Rev. Lawrence G. Dunklee.
Res., P.O. Box 130, 54632. Tel: 608-689-2646. [CEM]
School—Tel: 608-689-2642.
Lay Teachers 6; Students 65.

Germantown, Juneau Co., Our Lady of the Lake. Attended by St. Paul, New Lisbon. Rev. Steven M. Baures.

Res., 408 W. River St., New Lisbon, 53950. Tel: 608-562-3125. [CEM]

Greenwood, Clark Co., St. Mary Help of Christians. Also serves Holy Family, Willard. Rev. A. Joseph Follmar.
Res., 123 N. Main St., P.O. Box 129, 54437. Tel: 715-267-6282. [CEM]
School—Tel: 715-267-6477.
Lay Teachers 3; Students 52.

Halder, Marathon Co., St. Patrick. Attended by Nativity of the Blessed Virgin Mary, Marathon City. Revs. Joseph Diermeier, O.F.M.Cap.; Joseph Jeruzal, O.F.M.Cap.
Mailing Address: 3158 Halder Dr., Mosinee, 54455. Tel: 715-693-2765. [CEM]

Hatley, Marathon Co., St. Florian, Rev. Thomas J. Abraham.
Res., 500 Church Ln., P.O. Box 110, 54440. Tel: 715-446-2252; 446-3085 (Office). [CEM]
School—Tel: 715-446-3950.
Lay Teachers 5; Students 78.

Heffron, Portage Co., St. John the Baptist. Closed. For inquiries for parish records contact St. Maximilian Maria Kolbe, Southeastern Portage County.

Hewitt, Wood Co., St. Michael. Attended by St. Mary, Auburndale. Rev. T. Michael Schelble.
Office: 11086 Main St., 54441. Tel: 715-384-7676.
Res., 5866 Main St., Box 177, Auburndale, 54412. Tel: 715-652-2806; Fax: 715-384-7675. [CEM]

Hillsboro, Vernon Co., St. Aloysius, Rev. James E. Ennis.
Res., 545 Prairie Ave., Box 466, 54634. Tel: 608-489-2580. [JC]

Holmen, La Crosse Co., St. Elizabeth Ann Seton, Rev. Delbert J. Malin; Sr. Bridget Donaldson, O.S.B., Pastoral Assoc.
Office: 515 N. Main St., 54636. Tel: 608-526-4424; Fax: 608-526-3177.
Res., 704 Hillcrest Dr., 54636.

Independence, Trempealeau Co., SS. Peter and Paul. Also serves St. Michael, North Creek. Very Rev. Leonard G. Kaiser.
Res., 36208 Osseo Rd., P.O. Box 428, 54747-0428. Tel: 715-985-2227. [CEM]
School—Tel: 715-985-3719.
Lay Teachers 10; Students 132.

Indian Creek, Juneau Co., St. Michael. Attended by St. James, Camp Douglas.
Mailing Address: P.O. Box 289, Camp Douglas, 54618. Tel: 608-427-6762. [CEM]

Jim Falls, Chippewa Co., Sacred Heart. Attended by Holy Cross, Cornell. Rev. Jeremiah Cashman.
Res., Box 68, 54748. Tel: 715-382-4422.

Junction City, Portage Co., St. Michael. Attended by St. Wenceslaus, Milladore. Rev. John A. Wisneski.
Res., P.O. Box 100, Milladore, 54454. Tel: 715-457-2314. [CEM]

Kendall, Monroe Co., St. Joseph. Also serves St. John the Baptist, Wilton. Very Rev. James P. McNamee.
Res., 307 Spring St., P.O. Box 155, 54638. Tel: 608-463-7120. [CEM]

Keyesville, Richland Co., Nativity of the Blessed Virgin Mary. Attended by St. Anthony, Cazenovia. Rev. Daniel J. Kiedinger.
Mailing Address: Rte. 2, Box 247, 53581. Tel: 608-585-4846. [CEM]
Res., R.R. 2, Box 175, Cazenovia, 53924. Tel: 608-983-2367.

Knowlton, Marathon Co., St. Francis Xavier. Also serves St. John the Baptist, Peplin. Rev. Joseph A. Grassl.
Res., 651 Mead Ln., Mosinee, 54455. Tel: 715-693-3120. [CEM]

Lanark, Portage Co., St. Patrick. Closed. For inquiries for parish records contact St. Maximilian Maria Kolbe, Southeastern Portage County.

Lima, Pepin Co., Holy Rosary. Attended by St. Mary, Durand. Rev. Edward J. Shuttleworth.
Office: N6235 CTH V, Durand, 54736. Tel: 715-672-5911; Fax: 715-672-4193.
Res., 911 W. Prospect St., Box 188, Durand, 54736-1048. Tel: 715-672-5640. [CEM]
School—Tel: 715-672-4276.
Lay Teachers 5; Students 74.

Lone Rock, Richland Co., Sacred Heart. Attended by St. Anthony, Cazenovia. Rev. Daniel J. Kiedinger.
Mailing Address: Rte. 2, Box 175, Cazenovia, 53924. Tel: 608-983-2367.

Loyal, Clark Co., St. Anthony of Padua, Very Rev. Roman F. Kaiser.
Res., 407 N. Division St., P.O. Box 69, 54446-0069. Tel: 715-255-8017. [CEM]
School—212 W. Spring St., Tel: 715-255-8636.
Lay Teachers 6; Students 81.

Lyndon Station, Juneau Co., St. Mary, Rev. Ronald T. Zinkle, S.J.
Res., 117 Juneau St. N., P.O. Box 303, 53944. Tel: 608-666-2421. [CEM]

Marathon City, Marathon Co., Nativity of the Blessed Virgin Mary. Also serves Sacred Heart, Cassel & St. Patrick, Halder. Revs. Joseph Diermeier, O.F.M.Cap.; Joseph B. Jeruzal, O.F.M.Cap.
Res., 712 Market St., Box 7, 54448-0007. Tel: 715-443-2045; Fax: 715-443-3045. [CEM]
School—Tel: 715-443-3430.
Franciscan Sisters of Perpetual Adoration 2; Lay Teachers 16; Students 255.

Marshfield, Wood Co., Our Lady of Peace, Very Rev. James J. Logan.
Res., 1414 W. 5th St., 54449. Tel: 715-384-9414. [JC]
School—1300 W. 5th St., 54449. Tel: 715-384-5474; Fax: 715-387-8697.
Sisters of Notre Dame 2; Lay Teachers 20; Students 261.

Sacred Heart of Jesus. Also serves Corpus Christi, Bakerville. Rev. Robert A. Schaller.
Res., 112 E. 11th St., 54449-4216. Tel: 715-384-3213. [JC]
School—School Sisters of Notre Dame, 1117 S. Central Ave., 54449. Tel: 715-384-3939.
Lay Teachers 6; Students 53.

St. John the Baptist. Also serves Christ the King, Spencer. Rev. Charles D. Stoetzel. In res., Rev. Douglas C. Robertson.
Res., 201 W. Blodgett St., P.O. Box 644, 54449-0644. Tel: 715-384-3252; Fax: 715-384-4989. [JC]
School—Tel: 715-384-4989.
Lay Teachers 15; Students 215.

Mauston, Juneau Co., St. Patrick, Rev. Thomas J. Reardon.
Res., 401 Mansion St., 53948-1393. Tel: 608-847-6054. [CEM 2]
School—325 Mansion St., 53948. Tel: 608-847-5844.
Lay Teachers 11; Students 198.

Melrose, Jackson Co., St. Kevin. Attended by St. Bridget, Ettrick. Rev. Thomas J. McInnis.
Mailing Address: St. Bridget, 22650 Washington, Ettrick, 54627. Tel: 608-525-3811. [JC]

Menomonie, Dunn Co., St. Joseph. Also serves St. Luke, Boyceville. Rev. Lyle L. Schulte. In res., Rev. Charles A. Blecha, (Retired).
Res., 910 Wilson Ave., 54751. Tel: 715-232-4922; Fax: 715-232-4923. [CEM]
School—Tel: 715-232-4920; Fax: 715-232-4923.
Lay Teachers 7; Students 190.

Middle Ridge, La Crosse Co., St. Peter. Also serves St. Joseph, St. Joseph Ridge. Very Rev. Robert P. Hundt.
Res., Box 101, W695 Hwy. 33, Rockland, 54653. Tel: 608-486-2180. [CEM]

Milan, Marathon Co., St. Thomas. Attended by St. John the Baptist, Wuerzburg. Rev. Leonard C. Stashek.
Mailing Address: 1506 Wuerzburg Rd., Athens, 54411. Tel: 715-257-7092. [CEM]

Mill Creek, Portage Co., St. Bartholomew. Attended by St. Stephen, Stevens Point. Very Rev. Dennis J. Lynch; Miss Laura J. Kaufmann, Pastoral Assoc.
Res., 2493 CTH M, Stevens Point, 54481. Tel: 715-344-3003. [CEM]

Milladore, Wood Co., St. Wenceslaus. Also serves St. Kilian, Blenker & St. Michael, Junction City. Rev. John A. Wisneski.
Res., 146 Main St., Box 100, 54454. Tel: 715-457-2314. [CEM]

Mondovi, Buffalo Co., Sacred Heart of Jesus, Rev. William J. Blazewicz.
Res., 503 W. Hudson St., 54755. Tel: 715-926-3619. [CEM 2]
School—227 S. State St., 54755. Tel: 715-926-4407.
Lay Teachers 3; Students 42.
Convent—Tel: 715-926-4418.

Mosinee, Marathon Co., St. Paul, Rev. Jerome G. Hoeser.
Res., 603 Fourth St., 54455. Tel: 715-693-2650; Fax: 715-693-1332. [CEM]
School—404 High St., 54455. Tel: 715-693-2675; Fax: 715-693-1332.
Sisters 1; Lay Teachers 11; Students 137.

Necedah, Juneau Co., St. Francis of Assisi, Rev. James J. Lesczynski.
Res., 202 W. 5th St., 54646-8142. Tel: 608-565-2488. [CEM]
Church—Main at Sixth, 54646.

Neillsville, Clark Co., St. Mary. Also serves St. Stephen, Chili. Rev. Joseph N. Henseler.
Res., 1803 Black River Rd., 54456. Tel: 715-743-3840. [CEM]

Nekoosa, Wood Co., Sacred Heart of Jesus. Also serves All Saints, Babcock; St. Alexander, Port Edwards. Very Rev. R. John Swing.
Res., 711 Prospect Ave., 54457. Tel: 715-886-3422; Fax: 715-886-3954.
School—710 Vilas Ave., 54457. Tel: 715-886-3761.
Lay Teachers 9; Students 148.

New Auburn, Chippewa Co., St. Jude. Attended by St. Paul, Bloomer. Very Rev. Thomas E. Langer.
Mailing Address: 1222 Main St., Bloomer, 54724. Tel: 715-568-3255; Fax: 715-568-3255. [JC]

New Lisbon, Juneau Co., St. Paul. Also serves Our Lady of the Lake, Germantown. Rev. Steven H. Baures.
Res., 408 W. River St., 53950. Tel: 608-562-3125. [CEM]

North Creek, Trempealeau Co., St. Michael. Attended by SS. Peter and Paul, Independence. Very Rev. Leonard G. Kaiser.
Mailing Address: 36028 Osseo Rd., Independence, 54747. Tel: 715-985-2227. [CEM]

Norwalk, Monroe Co., St. Augustine of Hippo. Attended by Nativity of the Blessed Virgin Mary, St. Mary's Ridge. Rev. Kevin C. Louis. In res., Rev. James W. Genovesi Tel: 608-823-7339.
Res., 26400 CTH U, Cashton, 54619-9757. Tel: 608-823-7906; Fax: 608-823-7272. [CEM]

Onalaska, La Crosse Co., St. Patrick, Rev. William J. Matzek; Deacon Frank Abnet. In res., Rev. Edwin J. Thome.
Res., 1031 Main St., 54650. Tel: 608-783-5535.
School—127 N. 11th Ave., 54650. Tel: 608-783-5483; Fax: 608-783-5483.
Lay Teachers 11; Students 228.

Owen, Clark Co., Holy Rosary. Also serves St. Bernard, Abbotsford. Rev. Allen F. Jakubowski.
Res., 415 W. 3rd St., P.O. Box 309, 54460-0309. Tel: 715-229-2747.
School—Tel: 715-229-2348.
Lay Teachers 5; Students 53.

Peplin, Marathon Co., St. John the Baptist. Attended by St. Francis Xavier, Knowlton. Rev. Joseph A. Grassl. In res., Rev. Wladyslaw J. Kowalski (SUP).
Mailing Address: 651 Mead Ln., Mosinee, 54455. Tel: 715-693-3120. [CEM]

Pine Creek, Trempealeau Co., Most Sacred Heart, Rev. Robert F. Polcyn, O.F.M.Cap., Parochial Admin.
Res., N20555 CTH G, Dodge, 54625-9721. Tel: 608-539-3704. [CEM]

Pittsville, Wood Co., St. Joachim. Also serves North American Martyrs, Spaulding. Rev. Donald M. Berg.
Res., 5312 Third Ave., P.O. Box 69, 54466-0069. Tel: 715-884-6815. [CEM]

Plover, Portage Co., St. Bronislava, Rev. Patrick A. Umberger.
Res., 3200 Plover Rd., P.O. Box 158, 54467-0158. Tel: 715-344-4326; Fax: 715-344-6121. [CEM]
School—3301 Willow Dr., 54467. Tel: 715-342-2015.

Plum City, Pierce Co., St. John the Baptist, Rev. Ambrose J. Blenker.
Res., 212 Church Rd., P.O. Box 206, 54761-0206. Tel: 715-647-2301. [CEM]
School—Tel: 715-647-2901.
Lay Teachers 5; Students 50.

Polonia, Portage Co., Sacred Heart. Attended by St. Adalbert, Rosholt. Rev. Joseph R. Konopacky.
Res., 7375 Church St., Custer, 54423. Tel: 715-592-4221. [CEM]
School—7379 Church St., Custer, 54423. Tel: 715-592-4902.
Lay Teachers 4; Students 47.
Convent—7381 Church St., Custer, 54423. Tel: 715-592-4213.

Poniatowski, Marathon Co., Holy Family. Attended by St. Anthony de Padua, Athens. Rev. Randy E. Olson; Deacon LeRoy Knauf.
Mailing Address: P.O. Box 206, Athens, 54411-0206. Tel: 715-257-7684. [CEM]

Port Edwards, Wood Co., St. Alexander, Very Rev. R. John Swing; Sr. Catherine Kaiser, F.S.P.A., Pastoral Assoc.
Office: 880 First St., 54469. Tel: 715-887-3012.
Res., 711 Prospect Ave., Nekoosa, 54457. Tel: 715-886-3422. [JC]

Prairie du Chien, Crawford Co., St. Gabriel, Revs. William F. Gerut, S.J.; Burton W. Pratt, S.J.; John W. Wambach, S.J.
Office: 506 N. Beaumont Rd., P.O. Box 176, 53821-0176. Tel: 608-326-2404. [JC]
School—515 N. Beaumont Rd., 53821. Tel: 608-326-8624.
Lay Teachers 16; Students 266.

St. John Nepomucene, Revs. William F. Gerut, S.J.; Burton W. Pratt, S.J.; John W. Wambach, S.J. In res., Rev. Raymond O. Burger, S.J.
Res., 710 S. Wacouta St., P.O. Box 28, 53821-0028. Tel: 608-326-6511; Fax: 608-326-4876.
School—Prairie Catholic Schools, 720 S. Wacouta St., 53821. Tel: 608-326-4400.
Lay Teachers 9; Students 79.

Prescott, Pierce Co., St. Joseph, Rev. Thomas J. Mannion.
Res., 269 Dakota St. S., P.O. Box 245, 54021-0245. Tel: 715-262-5310. [CEM]
School—281 Dakota St. S., 54021. Tel: 715-262-5912.
Franciscan Sisters of Perpetual Adoration 3; Lay Teachers 5; Students 116.
Convent—268 Dakota St. S., 54021. Tel: 715-262-5105.

Richland Center, Richland Co., St. Mary (Assumption of B.V.M.), Very Rev. Wayne R. Kidd.
Res., 160 W. 4th St., P.O. Box 456, 53581. Tel: 608-647-2621. [CEM]
School—155 W. 5th St., 53581. Tel: 608-647-2422.
Sisters 1; Lay Teachers 11; Students 114.
Convent—789 N. Central Ave., 53581. Tel: 608-647-4933.

Rising Sun, Crawford Co., St. James. Closed. For inquiries for parish records contact St. Mary, Viroqua.

Rock Falls, Dunn Co., St. Joseph, Rev. Anton L. Lecheler.
Res., E. 9265 STH 85, Mondovi, 54755-8857. Tel: 715-875-4539. [CEM]

Rolling Ground, Crawford Co., St. Philip. Attended by St. Mary, Gays Mills. Rev. Leon S. Rausch, S.J.
Mailing Address: P.O. Box 36, Gays Mills, 54631-0036. Tel: 608-735-4420. [CEM]

Rosholt, Portage Co., St. Adalbert. Also serves Sacred Heart, Polonia. Rev. Joseph R. Konopacky.
Res., 3315 St. Adalbert Rd., 54473. Tel: 715-677-4519. [CEM]
School—3314 St. Adalbert Rd., 54473. Tel: 715-677-4517.
Religious 1; Lay Teachers 5; Students 38.

Rothschild, Marathon Co., St. Mark, Rev. Allan L. Slowiak; Deacon Patrick McKeough.
Res., 602 Military Rd., 54474-1523. Tel: 715-359-5206.
School—Wausau Area Catholic Schools. See Consolidated Elementary Schools under Institutions Located in the Diocese.
St. Therese of the Child Jesus, Rev. Robert A. Streveler.
Res., 113 W. Kort St., 54474-1094. Tel: 715-359-2421. [CEM]
School—Wausau Area Catholic Schools. See Consolidated Elementary Schools under Institutions Located in the Diocese.

Rozellville, Marathon Co., St. Andrew. Attended by St. Joseph, Stratford. Rev. Thomas J. Rudolph. In res., Rev. Arthur S. Redmond Tel: 715-384-3859.
Res., Box 6, Stratford, 54484. Tel: 715-687-2404. [CEM]

Rudolph, Wood Co., St. Philip. Attended by St. Lawrence, Wisconsin Rapids. Rev. John P. Hogan.
Office: 6957 Grotto Ave., Box 165, 54475. Tel: 715-435-3286. [CEM]
Res., 530 Tenth Ave. N., Wisconsin Rapids, 54495. Tel: 715-421-5777.
School—Tel: 715-435-3386.
Lay Teachers 7; Students 69.

Saint Joseph Ridge, La Crosse Co., St. Joseph. Attended by St. Peter, Middle Ridge. Rev. Robert P. Hundt.
Res., W2601 Hwy. 33, La Crosse, 54601. Tel: 608-788-1646. [CEM]

Saint Mary's Ridge, Monroe Co., Nativity of the Blessed Virgin Mary. Also serves St. Augustine, Norwalk; St. John the Baptist, Summit; Sacred Heart of Jesus, Cashton. Rev. Kevin C. Louis.
Res., 26400 CTH U, Cashton, 54619-9157. Tel: 608-823-7906; Fax: 608-823-7272. [CEM]
School—Tel: 608-823-7577.
Lay Teachers 3; Students 33.

Seneca, Crawford Co., St. Patrick. Also serves Sacred Heart, Wauzeka. Very Rev. Eugene J. Wolf; Deacon Fredrick R. Skrade.
Res., Box 18, 54654. Tel: 608-734-3931. [CEM]

Sigel, Wood Co., Holy Rosary. Attended by St. James, Vesper. Rev. Chester J. Osowski.
Mailing Address: 6190 Chapel Rd., Wisconsin Rapids, 54495-9215. Tel: 715-569-4412. [CEM]

Southeastern Portage County, Portage Co., St. Maximilian Maria Kolbe, Rev. Charles J. Hiebl.
Res., 1632 Oak St., Box 66, Almond, 54909-0066. Tel: 715-366-2811; 824-3380. [CEM 4]

Sparta, Monroe Co., St. Patrick, Rev. Mark A. Walljasper.
Res., 319 W. Main St., 54656-2143. Tel: 608-269-2655. [CEM]
School—318 W. Oak St., 54654. Tel: 608-269-4748.
Lay Teachers 11; Students 168.

Spaulding-City Point, Jackson Co., North American Martyrs. Attended by St. Joachim, Pittsville. Rev. Donald M. Berg.
Mailing Address: Box 69, Pittsville, 54466-0069. Tel: 715-884-6815. [CEM 2]

Spencer, Marathon Co., Christ the King. Attended by St. John, Marshfield. Rev. Charles D. Stoetzel.
Res., 101 Wendell St., 54479-0156. Tel: 715-659-4480. [JC]

Spring Valley, Pierce Co., Sacred Heart of Jesus. Attended by Sacred Heart, Elmwood. Rev. George A. Becker; Sr. Karen Freund, O.P., Pastoral Assoc.
Res., S. 105 Sabin Ave., P.O. Box 456, 54767-0456. Tel: 715-778-5519. [CEM]

Springfield, Eau Claire Co., St. Bridget. Attended by Holy Ghost, Chippewa Falls. Revs. Edmund J. Doerre; Charles J. Scherman, S.J.
Office: 412 S. Main, Chippewa Falls, 54729. Tel: 715-723-4890. [CEM]

Stanley, Chippewa Co., Holy Family. Also serves Sacred Heart of Jesus-St. Joseph, Boyd. Rev. Robert W. Nelson.
Office: 226 E. 3rd Ave., P.O. Box 125, 54768. Tel: 715-644-5435.
Res., 239 S. Franklin St., P.O. Box 125, 54768. Tel: 715-644-5435. [CEM]
School—136 3rd Ave., 54768. Tel: 715-644-3602.
Lay Teachers 6; Students 75.
Convent—303 S. Franklin, 54768. Tel: 715-644-5953. Sisters of St. Joseph

Stevens Point, Portage Co.,

1—Newman University Parish, Rev. Thomas F. Lindner.
Office: 2108 Fourth Ave., 54481. Tel: 715-345-6500.
Res., 838 Fremont St., 54481. Tel: 715-344-9117. [JC]

2—St. Casimir. Also serves St. Mary, Torun. Rev. Donald J. Walczak; Sr. Catherine Kieliszewski, S.S.J.-T.O.S.F., Pastoral Assoc.
Res., 203 W. Casimir Rd., 54481. Tel: 715-344-9582. [CEM]

3—St. Joseph, Rev. Alan T. Burkhardt.
Res., 1709 Wyatt Ave., 54481-3699. Tel: 715-341-1617. [JC]
School—See Consolidated Elementary Schools, Stevens Point.

4—St. Peter, Rev. Gerald E. Fisher. In res., Rev. Dennis A. Worzalla (Diocese of Green Bay).
Res., 800 4th Ave., 54481-1627. Tel: 715-344-6115. [JC]
School—See Consolidated Elementary Schools, Stevens Point.

5—St. Stanislaus, Very Rev. Donald L. Przybylski; Deacon Hugh Walker.
Res., 838 N. Fremont St., 54481. Tel: 715-344-9117; Fax: 715-344-1771. [JC]
School—See Consolidated Elementary Schools, Stevens Point.

6—St. Stephen. Also serves St. Bartholomew, Mill Creek. Rev. Dennis J. Lynch; Deacon Robert Hensen.
Res., 1401 Clark St., 54481. Tel: 715-344-3319. [CEM]
School—See Consolidated Elementary Schools, Stevens Point.

Stratford, Marathon Co., St. Joseph. Also serves St. Andrew, Rozellville. Rev. Thomas J. Rudolph.
Res., 420 Larch St., Box 6, 54484. Tel: 715-687-2404. [CEM 3]
School—P.O. Box 6, 54484. Tel: 715-687-4145.
Lay Teachers 11; Students 110.

Summit, Monroe Co., St. John the Baptist. Attended by Nativity of the Blessed Virgin Mary, St. Mary's Ridge. Rev. Kevin C. Louis.
Mailing Address: 26400 CTH U, Cashton, 54619-9757. Tel: 608-823-7906; Fax: 608-823-7272. [CEM]

Thorp, Clark Co., St. Bernard-St. Hedwig Parish, Rev. John W. Puerner.
Res., Box 329, 54771. Tel: 715-669-5526. [CEM]
School—Box 369, 54771. Tel: 715-669-5530.
Sisters of St. Joseph 1; Lay Teachers 11; Students 130.

Tilden, Chippewa Co., St. Peter. Attended by St. Charles Borromeo, Chippewa Falls. Rev. William P. Felix.
Mailing Address: 11358 CTH Q, Chippewa Falls, 54729-6115. Tel: 715-288-6484; Fax: 715-228-6008.
Res., 11358 CTU Q, Chippewa Falls, 54729-6115. Tel: 715-723-4088; Fax: 715-723-2195. [CEM]
School—(Grades 1-8) 11370 CTH Q, 54729. Tel: 715-288-6250.
Lay Teachers 5; Students 78.

Tomah, Monroe Co., St. Mary (Immaculate Conception). Also serves St. Andrew, Warrens. Rev. Daniel E. Kozlowski.
Res., 303 W. Monroe St., 54660. Tel: 608-372-4516. [CEM]
School—315 W. Monroe St., 54660. Tel: 608-372-5765.
Lay Teachers 14; Students 223.

Torun, Portage Co., St. Mary. Attended by St. Casimir, Stevens Point. Rev. Donald J. Walczak; Sr. Catherine Kieliszewski, S.S.J.-T.O.S.F., Pres. & Pastoral Assoc.
Res., 5589 Dewey Dr., Stevens Point, 54481. Tel: 715-344-2599. [CEM]

Trempealeau, Trempealeau Co., St. Bartholomew. Also serves St. Mary, Galesville. Rev. Robert J. Wagner.
Res., 11646 South St., 54661-8238. Tel: 608-534-6652. [CEM 2]

Union Center, Juneau Co., St. Theresa of Avila. Closed. For inquiries for parish records contact St. Jerome, Wonewoc.

Vesper, Wood Co., St. James. Also serves St. Francis, Arpin; Holy Rosary, Sigel. Rev. Chester J. Osowski.
Res., 6623 N. Church St., Box 68, 54489. Tel: 715-569-4412. [CEM]

Viroqua, Vernon Co., Annunciation of the Blessed Virgin Mary, Rev. James H. Miller.
Res., 400 Congress Ave., 54665. Tel: 608-637-7711. [CEM]

Warrens, Monroe Co., St. Andrew. Attended by St. Mary (Immaculate Conception), Tomah. Rev. Daniel E. Kozlowski.
Mailing Address: 3365 Auger Rd., 54666. Tel: 608-378-4813.
Res., 303 W. Monroe St., Tomah, 54660. Tel: 608-372-4516.

Waumandee, Buffalo Co., St. Boniface. Also serves St. Lawrence, Alma.
Res., Box 962, 54622-0962. Tel: 608-626-2621; Fax: 608-685-3253. [CEM 2]
School—Tel: 608-626-2611.
Students 43.

Wausau, Marathon Co.,

1—Holy Name of Jesus, Rev. Norman D. Boneck; Mrs. Patricia Gaska, Pastoral Assoc.
Res., 1104 S. Ninth Ave., 54401. Tel: 715-842-4543; Fax: 715-845-5059.
School—Wausau Area Catholic Schools. See Consolidated Elementary Schools under Institutions Located in the Diocese. Tel: 715-848-3281.

2—St. Anne, Revs. Steven J. Brice; Woodrow H. Pace.
Res., 710 N. 6th Ave., 54401. Tel: 715-675-9749; Fax: 715-675-4718. [JC]
School—Wausau Area Catholic Schools. See Consolidated Elementary Schools under Institutions Located in the Diocese. Tel: 715-845-5754.

3—St. James the Greater, Rev. Stephen F. Gross.
Res., 621 Second St., 54403. Tel: 715-845-6715; Fax: 715-845-6715. [JC]
School—Wausau Area Catholic Schools. See Consolidated Elementary Schools under Institutions Located in the Diocese.

4—St. Mary (Immaculate Conception), Rev. Stephen F. Gross.
Office: 408 Seymour St., 54403-6266. Tel: 715-845-5379.
Res., 621 Second St., 54403. Tel: 715-845-6715; Fax: 715-845-6715. [JC]
School—Wausau Area Catholic Schools. See Consolidated Elementary Schools under Institutions Located in the Diocese.

5—St. Matthew, Rev. Robert T. Altmann; Deacon Garry Lee Jolliffe.
Res., 2700 Westwood Dr., 54401. Tel: 715-842-3148.
School—Wausau Area Catholic Schools. See Consolidated Elementary Schools under Institutions Located in the Diocese.
St. Matthew Parish Education Center—221 S. 28th Ave., 54401. Tel: 715-845-2938.

6—St. Michael, Very Rev. William N. Grevatch.
Res., 1315 6th St., 54403-3599. Tel: 715-842-4283; 842-2344; Fax: 715-849-2509. [CEM]
School—Wausau Area Catholic Schools. See Consolidated Elementary Schools under Institutions Located in the Diocese.
Convent—611 Stark, 54403. Tel: 715-845-6885.

Wauzeka, Crawford Co., Sacred Heart. Attended by St. Patrick, Seneca. Very Rev. Eugene J. Wolf; Sr. Donna Weber, F.S.P.A., Pastoral Assoc.
Res., 711 E. Main St., P.O. Box 237, 53826. Tel: 608-875-5401. [CEM]

West Salem, La Crosse Co., St. Leo the Great. Also serves St. Mary, Bangor. Rev. Robert S. Hegenbarth.
Res., 210 W. Hamlin St., 54669. Tel: 608-786-0610.

Weston, Marathon Co., St. Agnes, Rev. William J. Jablonske.
Res., 6101 Zinser St., 54476. Tel: 715-359-5675; Fax: 715-359-4392. [CEM]

Whitehall, Trempealeau Co., St. John the Apostle. Unassigned. Also serves St. Ansgar, Blair.
Res., 35900 Lee St., P.O. Box 127, 54773-0127. Tel: 715-538-4607; Fax: 715-538-2224.

Willard, Clark Co., Holy Family. Attended by St. Mary Help of Christians, Greenwood. Rev. A. Joseph Follmar.
Res., 123 N. Main St., Greenwood, 54437. Tel: 715-267-6282; 267-6760. [CEM]

Wilson, Eau Claire Co., St. Peter. Closed. For inquiries for parish records contact Sacred Heart-St. Joseph, Boyd.

Wilton, Monroe Co., St. John the Baptist. Attended by St. Joseph, Kendall. Very Rev. James P. McNamee.
Res., Box 155, Kendall, 54638. Tel: 608-463-7120. [CEM]

Wisconsin Rapids, Wood Co.,

1—Our Lady, Queen of Heaven, Rev. Mark A. Doyle.
Res., 750 10th Ave., S., 54494. Tel: 715-423-1251.
School—Tel: 715-423-9350.
Lay Teachers 12; Students 236.

2—St. Lawrence. Also serves St. Philip, Rudolph. Rev. John P. Hogan; Deacon James L. Landry. In res., Rev. Joseph W. Hirsch.
Res., 530 10th Ave., N., 54494. Tel: 715-421-5777; 424-2651. [JC]
School—551 10th Ave. N., 54494. Tel: 715-424-1112; Fax: 715-424-1124.
Lay Teachers 6; Students 64.

3—St. Vincent de Paul, Rev. William G. Menzel.
Res., 820 13 St. S., 54494-5336. Tel: 715-423-2111; Fax: 715-423-4227.
School—831 12th St. S., 54494. Tel: 715-423-6470.
Lay Teachers 13; Students 220.

4—SS. Peter and Paul, Rev. Andrew K. Karoblis.
Res., 1150 2nd St. N., 54494. Tel: 715-423-1351. [CEM]
School—1140 N. 2nd St., 54494. Tel: 715-423-4770.
Lay Teachers 10; Students 92.

Wonewoc, Juneau Co., St. Jerome. Attended by St. Patrick, Elroy. Rev. G. Richard Roberts.
Office: 528 N. Center St., R.R. 2, Box 87A, 53968. Tel: 608-464-7713.
Res., 110 Spring St., Elroy, 53929. Tel: 608-462-5875. [CEM]

Wuerzburg, Marathon Co., St. John the Baptist. Also serves St. Thomas, Milan. Rev. Leonard C. Stashek.
Res., 1506 Wuerzburg Rd., Athens, 54411. Tel: 715-257-7092. [CEM]

Yuba, Richland Co., St. Wenceslaus. Closed. For inquiries for parish records contact St. Aloysius, Hillsboro.

Chaplains of Public Institutions

Oxford. *Federal Correctional Institute* Tel: 608-584-5511. Rev. Richard Fliss, Chap.

Tomah. *Veterans Administration Medical Center.* Vacant. 54660. Tel: 608-372-3971.

Wausau. *Wausau Hospital Center* 333 Pine Ridge Blvd., 54401. Tel: 715-847-2121; 847-2840. Rev. Michael J. Lynch, Res., 4303 Lake Shore Dr., 54401. Tel: 715-355-4499.

Special Assignment:
Reverend Fathers—
Gorman, Michael J., Moderator of the Curia, P.O. Box 4004, La Crosse, WI 54602-4004
McHugh, John T., Dir. of Holy Cross Seminary House of Formation, P.O. Box 4004, Lacrosse, WI 54602-4004. Tel: 608-788-9095
Parr, John L., Dir. of Ministries, P.O. Box 4004, La Crosse, WI 54602-4004
Powell, Leon A., Vice Chancellor, P.O. Box 4004, La Crosse, WI 54602-4004. Tel: 608-788-7700; 788-4625
Rafacz, Joseph J., Vicar Gen. & Dir. Diocesan Mission Office, St. Thomas More Parish, 2006 Weston St., La Crosse, WI 54601. Tel: 608-788-5483

On Duty Outside the Diocese:
Reverend Fathers—
Faber, Emmett N., 77 Cynthia Dr., Bastrop, TX 78602-9530
Heagle, John L., Tara Center, 1037 S. 102nd St., Seattle, WA 98168. Tel: 206-763-8721
Mason, James E., 233 S. Kane St., Burlington, WI 53105
Monti, Robert M., 3003 Terramar St., Apt. 201, Fort Lauderdale, FL 33304-4037. Tel: 954-561-5908
O'Lenny, Patrick J., Pastor of Holy Family Chapel, N. Yorkshire, U.K., PSC 45, Box 1503, APO, APE, 09468 U.S.A.

Graduate Studies:
Reverend Fathers—
Gilles, Richard W., Casa Santa Maria, Via dell'Umita, 30, Rome 00187 Italy

Foreign Missions:
Reverend Fathers—
Flock, Robert H., Parroquia de la Santa Cruz, Casilla 713, Santa Cruz, Bolivia. Tel: 011-591-332-6302
Penchi, Edward J., Parroquia de la Santa Cruz, Casilla 713, Santa Cruz, Bolivia. Tel: 011-591-343-0302
Walijewski, Joseph A., Casa Hogar Juan Pablo II, Lurin 16, Peru. Tel: 011-5114-30-5646

Awaiting Assignment:
Reverend Fathers—
Fliss, Richard L.

Suspended:
Reverend Fathers—
Peters, Raymond W.

Retired:
Reverend Monsignors—
Dall, Norbert P., W5735 Timber Trail, New Lisbon, WI 53950. Tel: 608-565-7714
Finucan, James P., Holy Cross Diocesan Center, 3710 E. Ave. S., P.O. Box 4004, La Crosse, WI 54602-4004. Tel: 608-788-7151
Reverend Fathers—
Abts, Cletus, Box 402, Tomahawk, WI 54487. Tel: 715-453-3079
Blecha, Charles A., 420 Heller Rd., Apt. 322, Menomonie, WI 54751. Tel: 715-235-1860
Bofenkamp, Andrew H., 304 Second St., Apt. 5, Spencer, WI 54479. Tel: 715-659-2491
Bornbach, Raymond H., 215 W. Upham St., Marshfield, WI 54449. Tel: 715-384-7571;608-643-8361
Coke, James E., 209 Lake St., Elk Rapids, MI 49629
Connolly, Robert V., Holy Cross Diocesan Center, 3710 East Ave. S., P.O. Box 4004, La Crosse, WI 54602-4004. Tel: 608-788-1218
Cosgrove, J. Kelly, 4182 Mt. Vernon Ave., Titusville, FL 32780. Tel: 407-267-8601
Curtiss, John B., 207 Marlbank Dr., Yorktown, VA 23692-4233. Tel: 804-898-4459
Devine, Patrick T., Holy Cross Diocesan Center, 3710 East Ave. S., P.O. Box 4004, La Crosse, WI 54602-4004
Dockendorff, Carl J., 1092 Queensway, Nekoosa, WI 54457. Tel: 715-325-6125
Dwyer, J. Floyd, Holy Cross Diocesan Center, 3710 East Ave. S., P.O. Box 4004, La Crosse, WI 54602-4004. Tel: 608-788-6935
Eichman, Dominic P., Holy Cross Diocesan Center, 3710 East Ave. S., P.O. Box 4004, La Crosse, WI 54602-4004. Tel: 608-788-4174
Ferron, Joseph B., Longwood Building 5, #2C, 11811 Avenue of PGA, Palm Beach Gardens, FL 33418. Tel: 407-625-8714
Fischer, Anthony W., 408 W. Arnold St., Marshfield, WI 54449. Tel: 715-384-4997
Garthwaite, Thomas F., 163 Stanley St. E., West St. Paul, MN 55118. Tel: 612-552-9721
Geissler, Lloyd F., 309 Hwy. 107 N., Marathon, WI 54448. Tel: 715-443-3287
Geissler, Ralph J., 705 Munes St., Athens, WI 54411. Tel: 715-257-9212
Gerum, Jerome G., 1601 N. Palmetto Ave., P.O. Box 673, Marshfield, WI 54449-0673. Tel: 715-387-4783
Hansen, Robert H., St. Joseph Nursing Home, 2902 East Ave. S., La Crosse, WI 54601. Tel: 608-788-3918
Hemmersbach, Alfred F., Holy Cross Diocesan Center, 3710 East Ave. S., P.O. Box 4004, La Crosse, WI 54602-4004. Tel: 608-788-8326
Herrmann, Richard J., 309 W. Blodgett St., Marshfield, WI 54449. Tel: 715-384-5039
Kamla, Jerome J., 8316 E. Calypso Ave., Mesa, AZ 85208. Tel: 602-984-2344
Keating, Joseph R., P.O. Box 639, North East, MD 21901-0639. Tel: 301-287-9450
Kelly, Bernard T., W. 7407 CTH Z, R.R. 2, Box 284, Onalaska, WI 54650. Tel: 608-781-0281
King, Norbert E., 135 Charles St., Schofield, WI 54476-1202. Tel: 715-359-7367
Knauf, Edwin L., Loring Apartments, Apt. 3, 648 N. Main, River Falls, WI 54022. Tel: 715-425-9377
Kulovits, Fred A., 221 Scott St., Apt. 412, Wausau, WI 54403. Tel: 715-842-4823
Lee, Henry H., 817 Macomber St., Chippewa Falls, WI 54729. Tel: 715-723-1151
Leinfelder, Philip, Holy Cross Diocesan Center, 3710 East Ave. S., P.O. Box 4004, La Crosse, WI 54602-4004. Tel: 608-787-5833
Leisle, Charles E., 3141 Mayer Rd., Eau Claire, WI 54701. Tel: 715-831-0922
Leketas, Peter J., 109 North Oak Ave., Apt. M, Marshfield, WI 54449. Tel: 715-384-8331
Mauel, John N., 5533 Woodland St., Stevens Point, WI 54481. Tel: 715-342-0132
Mertens, Michael G., Holy Cross Diocesan Center, 3710 East Ave. S., P.O. Box 4004, La Crosse, WI 54602-4004. Tel: 608-788-0311
Moczarny, Chester B., Holy Cross Diocesan Center, 3710 East Ave. S., P.O. Box 4004, La Crosse, WI 54602-4004. Tel: 608-787-5834
Murphy, John T., Winter Residence, 1100 Ponce de Leon Cir., Apt. 208E, Vero Beach, FL 32960. Tel: 407-567-3547
Nikolai, William V., Holy Cross Diocesan Center, 3710 East Ave. S., P.O. Box 4004, La Crosse, WI 54602-4004. Tel: 608-787-1839
Nowak, Bernard J., Keeler Park Apartments, 601 Seneca Manor Dr., Apt. 14L, Rochester, NY 14621
Oberwinder, Robert J., Bethany-St. Joseph Care Center, 2501 Shelby Rd., La Crosse, WI 54601. Tel: 608-788-5700
Papiernik, Roman J., 3460 Woodbridge Ct., La Crosse, WI 54601. Tel: 608-787-6027
Redmond, Arthur S., St. Andrew Rectory, D1876 CTHC, P.O. Box 106, Stratford, WI 54484-0106
Reuter, Arnold F., Holy Cross Diocesan Center, 3710 East Ave. S., P.O. Box 4004, La Crosse, WI 54602-4004. Tel: 608-788-0717
Schreiber, Bernard G., Bethany-St. Joseph Care Center, 2501 Shelby Rd., La Crosse, WI 54601. Tel: 608-788-5399
Schulte, Oswald W., Holy Cross Diocesan Center, 3710 East Ave. S., P.O. Box 4004, La Crosse, WI 54602-4004. Tel: 608-788-1402
Schulz, Raymond B., Heritage Manor, 307 Royal Ave., Elroy, WI 53929. Tel: 608-462-8494; 847-2623
Schumacher, Charles P., Corpus Christi, 10775 Hwy. BB, Marshfield, WI 54449. Tel: 715-676-2824
Simmons, Hilary F., Winter Residence, 2731 S.W. 11th Ct., Fort Lauderdale, FL 33312. Tel: 305-583-8725
Smith, Eugene D., St. Joseph Rectory, P.O. Box 10, Boyd, WI 54726-0010. Tel: 715-667-3038
Szczerbicki, Thaddeus P., 5319 Greenview Ln., Stevens Point, WI 54481. Tel: 715-341-4616
Tetzlaff, Joseph W., 2327 Morningside Dr., Mosinee, WI 54455. Tel: 715-359-6504
Theisen, Donald J., 1025 Pine Beach Rd., Apt. 207, Marinette, WI 54143. Tel: 715-735-3199
Thome, Edwin J., St. Patrick Rectory, 1031 Main St., Onalaska, WI 54650. Tel: 608-783-5535
Wagner, Raymond J., 211 Rincon Loop, Tijeras, NM 87059. Tel: 505-281-9158; 612-535-9176
Wozniak, Aloysius A., Casilla 713, Santa Cruz, Bolivia. Tel: 011-591-343-0302
Zoromski, Herbert P., 409 Moonlite Rd., Wittenberg, WI 54499. Tel: 715-454-6994
Zvinklys, Antanas, Holy Cross Diocesan Center, 3710 East Ave. S., P.O. Box 4004, La Crosse, WI 54602-4004. Tel: 608-788-2539

Permanent Deacons:
Abnet, Frank, St. Patrick, Onalaska
Agema, Larry, Newman Community, Eau Claire
Barnum, John, St. Olaf, Eau Claire
Beck, Guy, Waverly, IA
Braski, Raymond, Retired
Delgado, Juan (Gary), Mauston
Ebben, Ronald, St. Anthony Retreat Center, Marathon
Hensen, Robert, St. Stephen, Stevens Point
Hite, James, Unassigned
Hurrish, Florian, (Retired)
Jolliffe, Garry, St. Matthew, Wausau
Kennedy, David (MIL), St. Joseph, Adams
Knauf, LeRoy, Holy Family, Poniatowski
Koza, J. Michael, Australia
Landry, James, St. Lawrence, Wisconsin Rapids
McKeough, Patrick, St. Mark, Rothschild
Proulx, Rahlf, Holy Family Medical Center, Manitowoc
Richard, Gordon, Winona, MN
Rueth, William, Menomonie
Sage, Richard, St. Pius X, La Crosse

Schulz, Herman, St. John the Baptist, Edgar
Skrade, Fredrick, St. Patrick, Seneca
Stack, William, Oregon
Walker, Hugh, St. Stanislaus, Stevens Point
Weingart, James, St. Mary's Assumption, Durand; Holy Rosary, Lima

INSTITUTIONS LOCATED IN THE DIOCESE

[A] SEMINARIES, DIOCESAN

LA CROSSE. *Holy Cross Seminary House of Formation*, 3710 East Ave. S., P.O. Box 4004, 54602-4004. Tel: 608-788-4925; Fax: 608-788-8413. Revs. John T. McHugh, Dir.; Michael J. Gorman, Asst. Dir.; Mr. Trevor M. Hall, Prefect. Tel: 608-788-4925. Students 8.

[B] COLLEGES AND UNIVERSITIES

LA CROSSE. *Viterbo College*, 815 S. 9th St., 54601-8802. Tel: 608-796-3000; Fax: 608-796-3050
For a complete listing, refer to the Colleges and Universities section.

[C] HIGH SCHOOLS, DIOCESAN

LA CROSSE. *Aquinas High School*, 315 S. 11th St., 54601. Tel: 608-784-0287; Fax: 608-782-8851. Mr. Jeffrey Brengman, Prin.; Rev. John T. McHugh, Chaplain Instructor. Central Catholic Secondary School for the La Crosse Area. Faculty: Priests 2; Lay Teachers 37; Students 498.

CHIPPEWA FALLS. *McDonell Central Catholic High School*, 1316 Bel Air Blvd., 54729. Tel: 715-723-9126; Fax: 715-723-1501. Mr. John Flanagan, Prin.; Rev. Eric R. Berns, Chap. Instructor. Central Secondary School for Catholics of Chippewa Falls and surrounding parishes. Priests 1; Lay Teachers 20; Students 273.

EAU CLAIRE. *Regis High School*, 2100 Fenwick Ave., 54701-4498. Tel: 715-835-5141. Mr. William Uelmen, Prin. Central Secondary School for Catholics of Eau Claire, Altoona and surrounding parishes. Priests 1; Lay Teachers 20; Students 241.

MARSHFIELD. *Columbus High School*, 710 Columbus Ave., 54449. Tel: 715-387-1177. Revs. Paul Lauzon, S.D.S., Prin.; Douglas C. Robertson, Chap. Instructor. Central Secondary School of Marshfield and surrounding area. Priests 2; Lay Teachers 19; Students 186.

STEVENS POINT. *Pacelli High School*, 1301 Maria Dr., 54481. Tel: 715-341-2442. Mrs. Rebecca Lindahl, Prin.; Rev. Steven J. Kachel, Chap., Instructor. Priests 1; Sisters 3; Lay Teachers 30; Students 301.

WAUSAU. *Newman High School*, 1130 W. Bridge St., 54401. Tel: 715-845-8274 Rev. Fax: 715-842-1302. Mr. Donald J. Sisler, Prin.; Rev. Woodrow H. Pace, Chap. Central Catholic Secondary School of Wausau, Marathon, Schofield, Rothschild and Mosinee. Priests 1; Lay Teachers 25; Students 234.

WISCONSIN RAPIDS. *Assumption High School*, 445 Chestnut St., 54494. Tel: 715-423-2920. Mr. James J. Dyer, Prin.; Rev. Joseph W. Hirsch, Chap., Instructor. Central Catholic Secondary School for Wisconsin Rapids and surrounding area. Priests 1; Lay Teachers 20; Students 180.

[D] CONSOLIDATED ELEMENTARY SCHOOLS

LA CROSSE. *Aquinas Middle School*. (Grades 7-8), 315 S. 11th St., 54601. Tel: 608-784-0287; Fax: 608-782-8851. Mrs. Kathleen Forslund, Prin.; Rev. John T. McHugh, Chap. Faculty 22; Students 260.

CHIPPEWA FALLS. *Chippewa Area Catholic Schools*, 1316 Bel Air Blvd., 54729. Tel: 715-723-0538; Fax: 715-723-1501. Mr. Michael Sullivan, Area Admin.
Holy Ghost. (Grades 3-5), 436 S. Main St., 54729. Tel: 715-723-6478. Margaret Glose, Prin. Lay Teachers 13; Students 175.
Notre Dame Middle School. (Grades 6-8), 22 S. Prairie, 54729. Tel: 715-723-4777. Sue Goslyn, Prin. Lay Teachers 13; Students 195.
St. Charles Borromeo. (Grades PreK-2), 429 W. Spruce St., 54729. Tel: 715-723-5827. Margaret Glose, Prin. Lay Teachers 13; Students 243.

EAU CLAIRE. *Eau Claire Coordinated Catholic Schools*, 322 Fulton St., 54703. Tel: 715-835-8931. Mr. Rob T. Fortener, Area Admin.
Sacred Heart. (Grades PreK-1), 418 N. Dewey St., 54703. Tel: 715-835-1609. Lay Teachers 4; Students 60.
St. James. (Grades 1-5), 2502 11th St., 54703-2700. Tel: 715-832-8280. Faculty 5; Students 91.
St. Olaf. (Grades 1-5), 2407 North Ln., 54703-0961. Tel: 715-834-4959. Faculty 5; Students 84.
St. Patrick Middle School. (Grades 6-8), 322 Fulton St., 54703. Tel: 715-835-8931. Rev. James F. Trempe, Chap. Faculty 7; Students 72.

MARSHFIELD. *Holy Family Middle School*. (Grades 7-8), 710 Columbus Ave., 54449. Tel: 715-384-7184. Revs. Paul Lauzon, S.D.S., Admin.; Douglas C. Robertson, Chap.; Scarlett K. Steinert, Head Teacher. Priests 2; Lay Teachers 8; Students 110.

STEVENS POINT. *Stevens Point Area Catholic Schools*, 1408 Ellis St., 54481. Tel: 715-341-2445. Mrs. Joanne Lodzinski, Area Admin.
St. Joseph. (Grades K-2), 1901 Lincoln Ave., 54481. Tel: 715-341-2878. Lay Teachers 6; Students 121.
St. Peter Middle School. (Grades 6-8), 708 First St., 54481. Tel: 715-344-1890. Anne Rogalski, Prin.; Rev. Steven J. Kachel, Chap. Lay Teachers 16; Students 210.
St. Stanislaus. (Grades K-5), 2150 High St., 54481. Tel: 715-344-3086. Lay Teachers 10; Students 185.
St. Stephen. (Grades PreK, 3-5), 1335 Clark St., 54481. Tel: 715-344-3751. Lay Teachers 8; Students 171.
St. Bronislava. (Grades K-3), 3301 Willow Dr., Plover, 54467. Tel: 715-342-2015. Lay Teachers 6; Students 138.

WAUSAU. *Wausau Area Catholic Schools*, 602 Second St., 54401. Tel: 715-845-5735; Fax: 715-848-3582. Marian Wolaver, Area Admin.
Holy Name. (Grades PreK-5), 1122 S. 9th Ave., 54401. Tel: 715-848-3281. Sisters of the Divine Saviour. Lay Teachers 11; Students 117.
St. Anne's. (Grades PreK-5), 604 N. 6th Ave., 54401. Tel: 715-845-5754. Lay Teachers 9; Students 270.
St. Matthew Middle School. (Grades 6-8), 225 S. 28th Ave., 54401. Tel: 715-845-5735. Rev. Woodrow H. Pace, Chap. Lay Teachers 19; Students 247.
St. Michael. (Grades PreK-5), 614 Steuben, 54403. Tel: 715-848-0206. Felician Sisters 1; Lay Teachers 14; Students 131.
St. Mark, Rothschild. (Grades K-3), 602 Military Rd., Rothschild, 54474-1523. Tel: 715-359-5206. Sisters of the Divine Savior. Lay Teachers 9; Students 111.
St. Therese, Schofield. (Grades PreK, 4-6), 113 W. Kort St., Schofield, 54476. Tel: 715-359-2131. Franciscan Sisters of St. Joseph. Lay Teachers 10; Students 104.

[E] GENERAL HOSPITALS

LA CROSSE. *Franciscan Skemp Healthcare, Mayo Health System, La Crosse Campus Medical Center*, 700 West Ave. S., 54601-4796. Tel: 608-785-0940; Fax: 608-791-9429
For a complete listing, refer to the Hospitals section.

ARCADIA. *Franciscan Skemp Healthcare, Mayo Health System, Arcadia Campus Hospital*, 464 S. St. Joseph Ave., 54612. Tel: 608-323-3341
For a complete listing, refer to the Hospitals section.

CHIPPEWA FALLS. *St. Joseph's Hospital*, 2661 County Hwy. I, 54729. Tel: 715-723-1811
For a complete listing, refer to the Hospitals section.

EAU CLAIRE. *Sacred Heart Hospital*, 900 W. Clairemont Ave., 54701-5105. Tel: 715-839-4121
For a complete listing, refer to the Hospitals section.

HILLSBORO. *St. Joseph's Memorial Hospital, Inc.*, 400 Water Ave., P.O. Box 527, 54634. Tel: 608-489-2211
For a complete listing, refer to the Hospitals section.

MARSHFIELD. *St. Joseph's Hospital*, 611 St. Joseph Ave., 54449. Tel: 715-387-1713
For a complete listing, refer to the Hospitals section.

SPARTA. *Franciscan Skemp Healthcare, Mayo Health System, Sparta Campus Hospital*, 310 W. Main St., 54656-2142. Tel: 608-269-2132
For a complete listing, refer to the Hospitals section.

*STANLEY. *Victory Medical Center, Inc.*, 230 E. Fourth Ave., 54768. Tel: 715-644-5571; Fax: 715-644-5665
For a complete listing, refer to the Hospitals section.

STEVENS POINT. *St. Michael's Hospital and School for Med. Technology*, 900 Illinois Ave., 54481. Tel: 715-346-5000; Fax: 715-346-5077
For a complete listing, refer to the Hospitals section.

[F] REHABILITATION FACILITIES

LA CROSSE. *St. Francis Community Programs, Inc.*, 700 West Ave. S., 54601-4796. Tel: 608-791-9582. Adult Day Care Center 82; Special Centers for Social Services & Assistance 350; Total Staff 44.
Gerard Hall. 14 bed home for single mothers.
St. Francis Community Housing, Inc. Apartment units for chronically mentally ill; 8 bed apartment unit in Dodgeville, WI; and 12 bed apartment unit in Prairie du Chien, WI.
St. Francis Housing Alternatives, Inc. Apartment units for the chronically mentally ill; 8 bed apartment unit in Arcadia, WI; 8 bed apartment unit in Black River Falls, WI; and 8 bed apartment unit in Mauston, WI.
Siena Hall. 20 bed home for mentally ill adults.
LAAR House. 24 bed home for chemically dependent adults.
Scarseth House. 8 bed home for chemically dependent adolescents.
Pinecrest Center. 32 bed home for chemically dependent adults.

CHIPPEWA FALLS. *Libertas-L.E. Phillips Treatment Center for the Chemically Dependent*, 2661 County Rd. I, 54729. Tel: 715-723-5585. Hospital Sisters Health System, Hospital Sisters of the Third Order of St. Francis. David B. Fish, Exec. Vice Pres.; Larry W. Monson, Program Coord. Bed Capacity 44; Patients assisted annually 11,072.
Transitus House, 1830 Wheaton St., 54729. Tel: 715-723-1155. Hospital Sisters of the Third Order of St. Francis. David B. Fish, Chm.; Susan J. Anderson, Ph.D., Program Coord. Transitional living facility for women recovering from chemical dependency. Legal Title: *Hospital Sisters HealthCare-West, Inc.* Beds 20; Assisted annually 90.

[G] HOMES FOR AGED

LA CROSSE. *Bethany-St. Joseph Care Center*, 2501 Shelby Rd., 54601. Tel: 608-788-5700
For a complete listing, refer to the Special Care Facilities section.
Elder Care of North La Crosse, Inc. (Village on St. James), 800 St. James St., 54603. Tel: 608-791-9784
For a complete listing, refer to the Special Care Facilities section.
Franciscan Elder Care, Inc., 800 West Avenue S., 54601-4796. Tel: 608-791-9774
For a complete listing, refer to the Special Care Facilities section.
Franciscan Skemp Healthcare, Mayo Health System, La Crosse Campus Nursing Home, 620 S. 11th St., 54601. Tel: 608-791-9787
For a complete listing, refer to the Special Care Facilities section.
St. Joseph's Nursing Home, 2902 East Ave., S., 54601. Tel: 608-788-9870
For a complete listing, refer to the Special Care Facilities section.

ARCADIA. *Franciscan Skemp Healthcare, Mayo Health System, Arcadia Campus Nursing Home*, 464 S. St. Joseph Ave., 54612. Tel: 608-323-3341
For a complete listing, refer to the Special Care Facilities section.

EAU CLAIRE. *St. Francis Apartment*, 851 University Dr., 54701. Tel: 715-834-1388
For a complete listing, refer to the Special Care Facilities section.

HILLSBORO. *St. Joseph's Nursing Home*, P.O. Box 527, 54634
For a complete listing, refer to the Special Care Facilities section.

ONALASKA. *Franciscan Skemp Healthcare, Mayo Health System, Onalaska Nursing Home*, 1600 Main St., 54650. Tel: 608-783-4681
For a complete listing, refer to the Special Care Facilities section.

SPARTA. *Elder Care of Sparta, Inc.*, 622 S. Court, 54656. Tel: 608-791-9774
For a complete listing, refer to the Special Care Facilities section.
Franciscan Skemp Healthcare, Mayo Health System, Sparta Campus Nursing Home, 310 W. Main St., P.O. Box 529, 54656-2142. Tel: 608-269-2132
For a complete listing, refer to the Special Care Facilities section.

WAUSAU. *Marywood Convalescent Center*, 1821 N. 4th Ave., 54401. Tel: 715-675-9451
For a complete listing, refer to the Special Care Facilities section.

[H] RETREAT HOUSES

LA CROSSE. *Franciscan Spirituality Center*, 920 Market St., 54601-8809. Tel: 608-791-5295. Sisters of the Third Order of St. Francis of Perpetual Adoration. Sr. Mary Kathryn Fogarty, F.S.P.A., Dir.

EAU CLAIRE. *Saint Bede Retreat and Conference Center*, 1190 Priory Rd., P.O. Box 66, 54702-0066. Tel: 715-834-8642. Benedictine Sisters. Sr. Hildegarde Geraets, O.S.B., Dir.; Mary Traynor, Asst. Dir.

MARATHON CITY. *St. Anthony Retreat Center*, 300 E. 4th St., 54448-9602. Tel: 715-443-2236. The Province of St. Joseph of the Capuchin Order, Inc. Rev. Gerald Kafer, O.F.M.Cap., Dir. Priests 5; Brothers 1.

POLONIA. *St. Clare Center for Spirituality*, 7381 Church St., 54423. Tel: 715-592-4099. Felician Sisters. Sr. Mary Therese Lukas, C.S.S.F., Dir.

[I] MONASTERIES AND RESIDENCES OF PRIESTS AND BROTHERS

LA CROSSE. *Holy Cross (Seminary) Diocesan Center*, 3710 East Ave. S., P.O. Box 4004, 54602-4004. Tel: 608-788-7700. Mr. John J. Newman, Dir. In res. Most Revs. Frederick W. Freking. Tel: 608-788-0668; John J. Paul. Tel: 608-788-8395; Rev. Msgr. James P. Finucan. Tel: 608-788-7151; Very Revs. J. Floyd Dwyer. Tel: 608-788-6935; Joseph J. Rafacz. Tel: 608-788-6594; Revs. James P. Binkowski. Tel: 608-788-2904; Robert V. Connolly. Tel: 608-788-1218; Patrick T. Devine; Dominic P. Eichman. Tel:

608-788-4714; Michael J. Gorman. Tel: 608-788-4578; Alfred F. Hemmersbach. Tel: 608-788-8326; Philip Leinfelder. Tel: 608-787-5833; John T. McHugh. Tel: 608-788-9095; Michael G. Mertens. Tel: 608-788-0311; Chester B. Moczarny. Tel: 608-787-5834; John T. Murphy. Tel: 608-788-9597; William V. Nikolai. Tel: 608-787-1839; John L. Parr. Tel: 608-788-4866; Leon A. Powell. Tel: 608-788-4625; Arnold F. Reuter. Tel: 608-788-0717; Oswald W. Schulte. Tel: 608-788-1402; Thomas J. Smith. Tel: 608-788-4555; Antanas Zvinklys. Tel: 608-788-2539.

DE SOTO. *Brothers of St. Pius X*, P.O. Box 217, 54624-0217. Tel: 608-648-2087. Bro. Charles Bisenius, C.S.P.X., Dir.

MARATHON CITY. *St. Anthony Retreat Center*, 300 E. Fourth St., 54448-9602. Tel: 715-443-2236. The Province of St. Joseph of the Capuchin Order, Inc. Revs. Kenneth W. Reinhart, O.F.M.Cap., Dir.; Peter Hesse, O.F.M.Cap.; John Guimond, O.F.M.Cap.; Loran Miller, O.F.M. Cap.; Jerry Kafer, O.F.M.Cap. Priests 5; Brothers 2.

ST. MARY'S RIDGE. *Immaculate Conception Priory*. 26384 CTH U, Cashton, 54619-9757. Tel: 608-823-7992; Fax: 608-823-7274. Institute of Christ the King-Sovereign Priest. Rev. Timothy E. Svea, Supr.

SPARTA. *Our Lady of Spring Bank, Cistercian Abbey*, 17304 Havenwood Rd., Rte. 3, Box 211, 54656-9536. Tel: 608-269-8138; Fax: 608-269-2800. Legal Office for Cistercian Monasteries Auxiliary. Very Rev. Gregory Norman, O.Cist., Admin.; Rev. Bernard McCoy, O.Cist., Supr.; Rt. Rev. Blaise Fuez, O.Cist., (Retired); Rev. Robert Keffer, O.Cist., Master of Novices & Vocation Dir. Solemnly Professed 4; Postulants 1; Novices 1.

[J] CONVENTS AND RESIDENCES FOR SISTERS

LA CROSSE. *St. Rose Convent*, 912 Market St., 54601. Tel: 608-782-5610; Fax: 608-782-6301. Motherhouse and Novitiate of the Congregation of the Franciscan Sisters of Perpetual Adoration. Sr. Marla Lang, F.S.P.A., Pres.
In community: Professed 510; Transfers 1.
In Motherhouse: Sisters 96.

Villa St. Joseph, W2658 State Rd. 33, 54601-2625. A Retirement home for aged and convalescent Sisters. Franciscan Sisters of Perpetual Adoration. Sr. Maris Kerwin, F.S.P.A., Admin. Sisters 15; Lay Staff 95; Under Care 108.

CHIPPEWA FALLS. *St. Francis Convent*, 2509 County Rd. I, 54729. Tel: 715-723-7476. Hospital Sisters of the Third Order of St. Francis. Sr. Frances E. Schmitz, O.S.F., Coord. Professed Sisters 5.

St. Joseph Convent, 5085 176th St., 54729. Tel: 715-723-7479. Hospital Sisters of the Third Order of St. Francis.

Sisters of St. Benedict - Lakeside North, 7490 156th St., 54729. Tel: 715-723-0005. Residence for Sisters of the Order of St. Benedict. Sr. Michaela Hedican, O.S.B., Health Care & House Coord. Sisters 15.

EAU CLAIRE. *Sacred Heart Hospital Franciscan Sisters Convent*, 901 University Ave., 54701. Tel: 715-839-8725. Hospital Sisters of the Third Order of St. Francis. Sr. Augusta Sperl, O.S.F., Coord. Professed Sisters 6.

St. Bede Priory, 1190 Priory Rd., P.O. Box 66, 54702-0066. Tel: 715-834-3176. Motherhouse of Sisters of the Order of St. Benedict. Retreat and Conference Center. Sr. Margaret Michaud, O.S.B., Prioress; Rev. Thomas J. Krieg, Chap. Professed 51.

POLONIA. *St. Clare Convent*, 7381 Church St., 54423. Tel: 715-592-4213. Sr. M. Ursula Myszka, Local Min. Felician Sisters 4.

STEVENS POINT. *St. Joseph Congregational Home*, 1300 Maria Dr., 54481. Tel: 715-344-2830. Residence of the Sisters of St. Joseph of the Third Order of St. Francis. Sr. Marise Zielinski, S.S.J.-T.O.S.F., Coord.; Sr. Janet Smolinski, S.S.J.-T.O.S.F., Coord.; Rev. Robert W. Greatorex, Chap. Tel: 715-344-8346. Sisters 71.

[K] SOCIAL SERVICE AGENCIES

LA CROSSE. *Catholic Charities of the Diocese of La Crosse, Inc.*, 128 S. 6th St., P.O. Box 266, 54601. Tel: 608-782-0704; Fax: 608-782-0702. Counseling and Mental Health Services, Family Financial Counseling, Adoption & Unwed Parent Services. Most Rev. Raymond Burke, J.C.D., Pres.; Rev. Michael Gorman, J.C.L., Vice Pres. & Treas.; Sr. Marlene Weisenbeck, F.S.P.A., J.C.L. Total Staff 18.

Catholic Residential Services, Inc., 505 King St., Ste. 010, P.O. Box 2394, 54602-2394. Tel: 608-784-5323; Fax: 608-784-7522. Mr. Robert Laubach, Pres.; Mrs. Barbara Smith, Vice Pres.; Mr. Bill Lundgren, Sec. Total Staff 171; Patients assisted annually 420.

WAUSAU. *Northland House*, 102 McClellan St., 54402-0231. Tel: 715-845-4898. Operated by Catholic Residential Services, Inc., Diocese of La Crosse. Residential Care of Children. Charles Wirtz, Admin.

[L] NEWMAN CAMPUS MINISTRY

LA CROSSE. *Roncalli Newman Parish*. Serving University of Wisconsin-La Crosse and Western Wisconsin Technical College. 1732 State St., 54601. Tel: 608-784-4994. Rev. Mark R. Pierce, Pastor.

EAU CLAIRE. *Newman Parish*. Serving University of Wisconsin-Eau Claire and Chippewa Valley Technical College. 110 Garfield Ave., 54701-4042. Tel: 715-834-3399. Revs. George R. Szews, Pastor; Edmund J. Klimek, Assoc.; Thomas J. Krieg, Assoc.

MENOMONIE. *The Ministry to the University of Wisconsin-Stout*, 108 3rd Ave. W., 54751. Tel: 715-235-4258. Rev. Thomas J. Krieg, Chap.; Dulcie Holtz, Campus Min.

STEVENS POINT. *Newman University Parish*. Serving University of Wisconsin-Stevens Point. 2108 Fourth Ave., 54481. Tel: 715-345-6500. Rev. Thomas F. Lindner, Pastor.

[M] FOUNDATIONS, FUNDS & TRUSTS

LA CROSSE. *Aquinas High School and Aquinas Schools Foundation*, 315 S. 11th St., 54601. Tel: 608-784-0287; Fax: 608-782-8851.

Bishop's Education Endowment Trust, P.O. Box 4004, 54602-4004. Tel: 608-788-7700.

Blessed Sacrament Parish Endowment Trust, 130 S. Losey Blvd., 54601. Tel: 608-782-2953; Fax: 608-782-2770.

Cathedral of St. Joseph the Workman Endowment Trust, 530 Main St., 54601.

Franciscan Skemp Foundation, Inc., 700 W. Ave. South, 54601-4796. Tel: 608-784-6449; Fax: 608-791-9799. Peter Grabow, Dir.

Holy Cross Seminary Education Fund Endowment Trust, P.O. Box 4004, 54602-4004. Tel: 608-788-7700; Fax: 608-788-8413.

Holy Trinity Catholic Church Endowment Trust, 1333 S. 13th St., 54601.

La Crosse Deanery Catholic Education Endowment Trust, P.O. Box 4004, 54602-4004.

Roncalli Newman Parish Student Endowment Trust, 1732 State St., 54601.

St. James Parish Endowment Trust, 1032 Caledonia St., 54603.

St. Pius X Parish Endowment Trust, P.O. Box 4004, 54602-4004.

St. Thomas More Parish Endowment Trust, 2006 Weston St., 54601.

ARCADIA. *Arcadia Catholic School Endowment Trust Fund*, 223 E. Maple St., 54612.

Franciscan Skemp Foundation of Arcadia, Inc., 464 S. St. Joseph Ave., 54612. Tel: 608-323-3341. Robert Tracey, Admin.

AUBURNDALE. *St. Mary Education Endowment Trust*, Box 177, 54412-0177.

BIG RIVER. *The St. Mary's-Big River Endowment Trust*. W10139 570th Ave., River Falls, 54022.

BLAIR. *The St. Ansgar Catholic Church Endowment Trust*. 35900 Lee St., P.O. Box 127, Whitehall, 54773-0127.

CADOTT. *St. Rose of Lima Catholic Church Endowment Trust*, Box 160, 54727.

CHIPPEWA FALLS. *The Chippewa Area Catholic Schools Endowment Trust*, 1316 Bel Air Blvd., 54729; Fax: 715-723-1501.

The Education/Sustaining Endowment Trust, 412 Main St., 54729.

Friends of St. Joseph's Foundation, St. Joseph's Hospital, 2661 County Hwy. I, 54729. Tel: 715-723-1811.

Notre Dame Children's Endowment Trust, 117 Allen St., 54729-2899.

Notre Dame Parish Endowment Trust, 117 Allen St., 54729-2899.

St. Charles Future Fund Trust, 810 Pearl St., 54729.

DURAND. *St. Mary Catholic School Endowment Trust*, 901 W. Prospect St., 54736-1049.

EAU CLAIRE. *Educational Endowment Trust of Eau Claire Coordinated Catholic Schools*, 322 Fulton St., 54703.

Friends of St. James the Greater Catholic School at Eau Claire Tuition Endowment Trust, 2502 11th St., 54703-2700.

The Newman Parish - Eau Claire Endowment Trust, 110 Garfield Ave., 54701-4042.

Regis High School Foundation, 2100 Fenwick Ave., 54701-4498.

The Sacred Heart Parish Endowment Trust, 416 N. Dewey St., 54701-3299. Tel: 715-835-3299.

The St. James the Greater Catholic Church Endowment Trust, 2502 11th St., 54703-2700.

St. Olaf Parish Endowment Trust, 2408 North Ln., 54703-0960.

St. Patrick Parish of Eau Claire Endowment Trust, 318 Fulton St., 54703-5399.

ELLSWORTH. *The St. Francis Parish Endowment Trust*, 264 S. Grant, Box 839, 54011.

HOLMEN. *St. Elizabeth Ann Seton Endowment Trust*, 515 N. Main St., 54636.

INDEPENDENCE. *The SS. Peter & Paul Parish-Independence Education Endowment Trust*, 36028 Osseo Rd., P.O. Box 428, 54747-0428.

LYNDON STATION. *Troy Quasi-Endowment Trust*, P.O. Box 303, 53944.

MARSHFIELD. *Columbus High School Foundation*, 710 S. Columbus Ave., 54449. Tel: 715-387-2444. Ms. Jodi Hansen, Dir. Devel.

Community Foundation of St. Joseph's Hospital of Marshfield, Inc., 611 St. Joseph Ave., 54449.

The Our Lady of Peace Endowment Trust, 1414 W. 5th St., 54449.

St. John the Baptist Educational Endowment Trust, 201 W. Blodgett, Box 644, 54449-0644.

St. John the Baptist Maintenance Endowment Trust, 201 W. Blodgett, Box 644, 54449.

MAUSTON. *St. Patrick's Congregation Trust*, 401 Mansion St., 53948-1393.

MENOMONIE. *The St. Joseph School at Menomonie Endowment Trust*, 910 Wilson Ave., 54747.

MOSINEE. *St. Paul Parish Endowment Trust*, 603 4th St., 54455.

NEILLSVILLE. *The St. Mary's Catholic Church Endowment Trust*, 1803 Black River Rd., 54456.

ONALASKA. *Father John Rossiter and Friends Endowment Trust of St. Patrick Parish*, 1031 Main St., 54650.

PITTSVILLE. *St. Joachim's Parish Endowment Trust*, P.O. Box 69, 54466-0069.

PRAIRIE DU CHIEN. *The St. Gabriel's Endowment Trust*, 506 N. Beaumont Rd., P.O. Box 176, 53821-0176.

The St. John's Endowment Trust, 710 S. Wacouta St., P.O. Box 28, 53821-0028.

RICHLAND CENTER. *The Assumption of the Blessed Virgin Mary Parish Endowment Trust*, 160 W. 4th St., Box 456, 53581.

ROTHSCHILD. *The St. Mark Catholic Parish Endowment Trust*, 602 Military Rd., 54474-1523.

St. Therese Catholic Church Endowment Fund, 113 Kort St., 54474.

ST. JOSEPH RIDGE. *St. Joseph Endowment Trust*. W2602 Hwy. 33, Rte. 1, La Crosse, 54601. Tel: 608-788-1646.

ST. MARY'S RIDGE. *Holy Family Endowment Trust Fund*. Rectory, 26400 CTH U, Cashton, 54619-9757.

SPARTA. *Endowment Trust of the Friends and Parishioners of St. Patrick Parish*, 319 W. Main St., 54656-2143.

Franciscan Skemp Foundation of Sparta, Inc., 310 W. Main St., 54656-2142. Tel: 608-269-2132. William P. Sexton, M.H.A., Exec. Dir.

STEVENS POINT. *Catholic Schools Endowment Trust in Portage County, Wisconsin*, 1408 Ellis St., 54481.

Community Foundation of Saint Michael's Hospital, 900 Illinois Ave., 54481. Phyllis A. Devlin, Dir.

Pacelli High School Foundation, 1301 Maria Dr., 54481. Tel: 715-341-2442.

St. Stephen Parish Endowment Trust, 1401 Clark St., 54481.

STRATFORD. *St. Joseph Parish Endowment Trust*, Box 6.

TILDEN. *St. Peter Parish Endowment Trust*, 11358 CTH Q. Chippewa Falls, 54729-6115.

TOMAH. *The St. Mary's Catholic Church Educational Endowment Trust*, 303 W. Monroe St., 54660. Tel: 608-372-4516.

WAUMANDEE. *St. Boniface Parish Catholic School Endowment Trust Fund*, Box 962, 54622-0962.

WAUSAU. *St. Michael Parish Endowment Trust*, 1315 6th St., 54403-3599.

**Wausau Area Catholic Schools Endowment Trust*, 602 Second St., 54403. Tel: 715-845-5735. Marian Wolaver, Admin.

WHITEHALL. *St. John Parish Endowment Trust*, 35900 Lee St., P.O. Box 127, 54773-0127.

WILLARD. *Holy Family Parish, Willard Endowment Trust*, 54493.

[N] ASSOCIATIONS OF THE FAITHFUL

PRESCOTT. *Franciscan Servants of Jesus*, Shekinah House of Prayer, 122 Court St., 54021. Tel: 715-262-3697. Sr. Julie Green, F.S.J., Prioress; Sr. Anne LeBlanc, F.S.J.

TILDEN. *Institute of St. Joseph*. 11358 CTH Q, Chippewa Falls, 54729-6115. Tel: 715-288-6272; Fax: 715-288-6008. Rev. William P. Felix, Moderator.

[O] SOCIETY FOR APOSTOLIC LIFE

CASHTON. *Institute of Christ the King-Sovereign Priest*, American Headquarters: Immaculate Conception Priory, 26384 CTHU, 54619-9757. Tel: 608-823-7992; Fax: 608-823-7274. Rev. Timothy E. Svea, Prior & U.S. Prior.

[P] MISCELLANEOUS LISTINGS

LA CROSSE. *Franciscan Skemp Healthcare, Inc., Mayo Health System, Corporate Office*, 700 West Ave. S., 54601-4796. Tel: 608-785-0940; Fax: 608-791-9429. Brian C. Campion, M.D., Pres. & CEO, Integrated

Healthcare Delivery System. Sponsored by the Congregation of the Sisters of the Third Order of St. Francis of Perpetual Adoration (Franciscan Sisters of Perpetual Adoration) and Mayo Foundation.

Franciscan Skemp Healthcare, Mayo Health System, La Crosse Campus Clinic, 800 West Ave. S., 54601. Tel: 608-782-9760. Brian C. Campion, M.D., Pres. & C.E.O. Total Staff 520; Patient Visits 298,200.

Franciscan Skemp Medical Center, Inc., 700 West Ave. S., 54601-4796. Tel: 608-785-0940. Brian C. Campion, M.D., Pres. & CEO.

ARCADIA. *Franciscan Skemp Healthcare, Mayo Health System, Arcadia Campus Clinic*, 464 St. Joseph Ave., 54612. Tel: 608-323-3341. Robert Tracey, Admin.

CHIPPEWA FALLS. *Northern Wisconsin Center for the Developmentally Disabled*. State Institution for the Developmentally Disabled, East Park Ave., 54729. Tel: 715-723-5542.

EAU CLAIRE. *Hospital Sisters Health Care-West, Inc.*, St. Francis Apartments, 851 University Dr., 54701. Tel: 715-834-1338.

SPARTA. *Franciscan Skemp Healthcare, Mayo Health System, Sparta Campus Clinic*, 310 W. Main St., 54656-2142. Tel: 608-269-2132. William P. Sexton, Admin.

STEVENS POINT. *Saint Michael's Associates*, 900 Illinois Ave., 54481.

RELIGIOUS INSTITUTES OF MEN REPRESENTED IN THE DIOCESE

For further details refer to the corresponding bracketed number in the Religious Institutes of Men or Women section.

[0200]—*Benedictine Monks, Corpus Christi Abbey*. (Sandia, TX).—O.S.B.

[1180]—*Brothers of Saint Pius X*. (La Crosse).—C.S.P.X.

[0240]—*Camillan Fathers and Brothers*.—O.S.Cam.

[0470]—*The Capuchin Friars*. (St. Joseph's Prov.).—O.F.M.Cap.

[0340]—*Cistercian Fathers*. (Sparta, WI).—O.Cist.

[1130]—*Congregation of the Priests of the Sacred Heart*. (Hales Corner, WI).—S.C.J.

[0690]—*Jesuit Fathers and Brothers*. (Missouri Prov. & Wisconsin Prov.).—S.J.

[0800]—*Maryknoll*.—M.M.

[0370]—*Society of St. Columban*.—S.S.C.

[1200]—*Society of the Divine Savior*. (Milwaukee).—S.D.S.

RELIGIOUS INSTITUTES OF WOMEN REPRESENTED IN THE DIOCESE

[0230]—*Benedictine Sisters of Pontifical Jurisdiction*. (Eau Claire, WI).—O.S.B.

[1070-09]—*Congregation of St. Catherine of Siena*. (Racine, WI).—O.P.

[1070-13]—*Congregation of the Most Holy Rosary*. (Adrian, WI).—O.P.

[1170]—*Congregation of the Sisters of St. Felix of Cantalice, of the III Order of St. Francis*. (Chicago, IL).—C.S.S.F.

[1780]—*Congregation of the Sisters of the Third Order of St. Francis of Perpetual Adoration*.—F.S.P.A.

[1310]—*Franciscan Sisters of Little Falls, Minnesota*.—O.S.F.

[1240]—*Franciscan Sisters, Daughters of the Sacred Hearts of Jesus and Mary*. (Wheaton, IL).—O.S.F.

[1820]—*Hospital Sisters of the Third Order of St. Francis*. (Springfield, IL).—O.S.F.

[2970]—*School Sisters of Notre Dame*. (Milwaukee Prov. & St. Louis Prov.).—S.S.N.D.

[1680]—*School Sisters of St. Francis*. (Milwaukee, WI).—O.S.F.

[3590]—*Servants of Mary*. (Ladysmith, WI).—O.S.M.

[1070-03]—*Sinsinawa Dominican Congregation of the Most Holy Rosary*.—O.P.

[2575]—*Sisters of Mercy of the Americas*. (Detroit Regional Community).—R.S.M.

[3360]—*Sisters of Providence of Saint Mary-of-the-Woods*. (Indiana).—S.P.

[1720]—*Sisters of St. Francis of the Third Order Regular of St. Francis of the Congregation of Our Lady of Lourdes*. (Rochester, MN).—O.S.F.

[3930]—*Sisters of St. Joseph - Third Order Regular*.—S.S.J.-T.O.S.F.

[1030]—*Sisters of the Divine Savior*.—S.D.S.

[3320]—*Sisters of the Presentation of the Blessed Virgin Mary*. (Dubuque, IA).—P.B.V.M.

[4100]—*Sisters of the Sorrowful Mother*.—S.S.M.

[1705]—*Sisters of the Third Order of St. Francis of Assisi of Penance and Charity*. (Milwaukee, WI).—O.S.F.

DIOCESAN CEMETERIES

LA CROSSE. *Catholic*, 519 Losey Blvd. S., 54601. Tel: 608-782-0238. Jeffrey Reinhart, Supt.

Gate of Heaven Cemetery; French Island Cemetery.

Woodlawn, 3636 Mormon Coulee Rd., 54601. Tel: 608-788-0980. John Reinhart, Supt.

CHIPPEWA FALLS. *Hope Cemetery and Mausoleum*, 418 N. State St., 54729. Tel: 715-723-0792. Walter Hurt, Supt.

EAU CLAIRE. *Calvary Cemetery and Mausoleum*, P.O. Box 755, 54702-0755. Tel: 715-832-1411. Harold Hunt.

MARSHFIELD. *Gate of Heaven*, 1803 S. Maple Ave., 54449. Tel: 715-384-3869. Monica Herman, Sec.

STEVENS POINT. *Stevens Point Area Catholic Cemetery Association, Inc.*, P.O. Box 497, 54481. Tel: 715-341-3236. Jack Hurrish, Supt.

NECROLOGY

† Hagmann, James J., Whitehall, WI, St. John the Apostle. —Died Oct. 3, 1997.

† Steinert, Thomas J., Camp Douglas, WI, St. James. —Died Aug. 27, 1997.

† Trant, John P., (Retired). —Died Aug. 28, 1997.

Diocese of Las Cruces

(Dioecesis Las Cruces)

Most Reverend

RICARDO RAMIREZ, C.S.B., D.D.

Bishop of Las Cruces; ordained December 10, 1966; appointed Titular Bishop of Vatarba and Auxiliary of San Antonio October 27, 1981; consecrated December 6, 1981; appointed First Bishop of Las Cruces August 31, 1982; installed October 18, 1982. *Res., 455 W. Palmer Rd., Las Cruces, NM, 88005.*

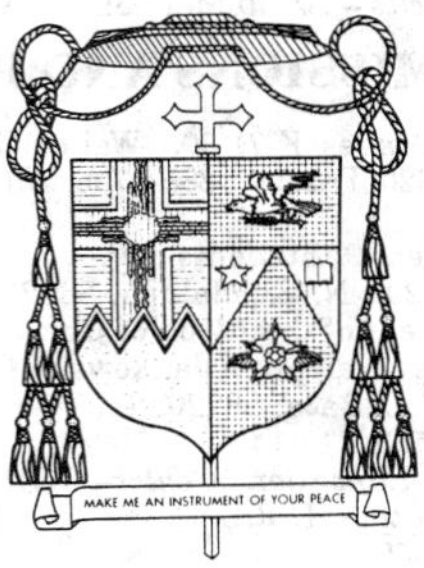

ESTABLISHED OCTOBER 18, 1982.

Square Miles 44,483.

Comprises the Counties of Dona Ana, Hidalgo, Grant, Luna, Sierra, Otero, Lincoln, Chaves, Eddy and Lea in the State of New Mexico.

For legal titles of parishes and diocesan institutions, consult The Pastoral Center.

The Pastoral Center: 1280 Med Park Dr., Las Cruces, NM, 88005. Tel.: 505-523-7577; Fax: 505-524-3874.

Web site address: http://www.zianet.com/diocese/

E-mail address: diocese@zianet.com

STATISTICAL OVERVIEW

Personnel	
Bishop	1
Priests: Diocesan Active in Diocese	19
Priests: Active Outside Diocese	1
Priests: Retired, Sick or Absent	7
Number of Diocesan Priests	27
Religious Priests in Diocese	50
Extern Priests in Diocese	6
Ordinations:	
Transitional Deacons	1
Permanent Deacons in Diocese	26
Total Brothers	4
Total Sisters	78
Parishes	
Parishes	44
With Resident Pastor:	
Resident Diocesan Priests	16
Resident Religious Priests	20
Without Resident Pastor:	
Administered by Priests	6
Administered by Permanent Deacons	1
Administered by Women Religious	1
Missions	45
Professional Ministry Personnel:	
Brothers	4
Sisters	17
Lay Ministers	20
Welfare	
Health Care Centers	3
Total Assisted	142,000
Day Care and Extended Day Care Centers	1
Total Assisted	40
Special Centers for Social Services	1
Total Assisted	3,000
Educational	
Diocesan Students in Other Seminaries	3
Total Seminarians	3
Elementary Schools, Diocesan and Parish	4
Total Students	635
Catechesis/Religious Education:	
High School Students	2,983
Elementary Students	8,344
Total Students Under Catholic Instruction	11,965
Teachers in the Diocese:	
Lay Teachers	41
Vital Statistics	
Receptions into the Church:	
Infant Baptism Totals	2,612
Adult Baptism Totals	72
Received into Full Communion	66
First Communions	2,346
Confirmations	1,231
Marriages:	
Catholic	419
Interfaith	83
Total Marriages	502
Deaths	946
Total Catholic Population	126,349
Total Population	463,500

The Pastoral Center—1280 Med Park Dr., Las Cruces, 88005. Tel: 505-523-7577; Fax: 505-524-3874. Office Hours: Mon.-Fri. 8:00-4:30.

Bishops Administrative Council—Most Rev. RICARDO RAMIREZ, C.S.B.; Very Rev. Msgr. JOHN E. ANDERSON; Revs. ROBERT POWER, C.S.B.; DENIS TEJADA; Sr. MARY ELLEN QUINN, R.S.M.

Vicar General—Very Rev. Msgr. JOHN E. ANDERSON.

Episcopal Vicar for Clergy and Personnel—Very Rev. Msgr. ROBERT L. GETZ.

Chancellor—Sr. MARY ELLEN QUINN, R.S.M.

Director of Clergy Personnel—Very Rev. Msgr. JOHN E. ANDERSON.

Diocesan Tribunal—Rev. JOHN S. WEBER, O.F.M.Conv., J.C.L., Judicial Vicar; Sr. CATHERINE C. DARCY, R.S.M., J.C.D., Admin. Dir., *1280 Med Park Dr., Las Cruces, 88005.*

Promoter of Justice—Very Rev. DANIEL R. BARFIELD, S.J.

Judges—Very Revs. GILES CARIE, O.F.M.Conv.; JOHN M. WILSON, C.S.B., J.C.L.; Revs. THOMAS P. BEGGANE, J.C.L.; ENRIQUE LOPEZ-ESCALERA, J.C.L.; Deacon ALPHONSO F. BOWERS; Sr. CATHERINE C. DARCY, R.S.M., J.C.D.

Defenders of the Bond—Very Rev. DANIEL R. BARFIELD, S.J.; Very Rev. Msgr. JOHN E. ANDERSON, V.G.; Revs. DAVID BERGS; RICHARD CATANACH; MICHAEL LINDSAY; NOEL KRAMER, O.F.M.Conv.

Assesors—JUDITH MONTES; ARTHUR E. JIRON; DANIEL MONTES.

Advocates—Sr. JANE KERNS, S.H.C.J.; JUDY MONTES; DAN MONTES; DELFINA AMEZAGA; LOUIS AMEZAGA.

Notaries—ARTHUR E. JIRON; IRENE V. PORTILLO; VELIA SALINAS.

Vicars—Revs. CONRADO PYTLIK; RICHARD CATANACH; VALENTINE JANKOWSKI, O.F.M.Conv.; DENNIS FOUNTAIN, O.F.M.Conv.; EDWARD HERRERA; Very Rev. ALFRED GALVAN.

Diocesan Consultors—Very Rev. Msgr. JOHN E. ANDERSON; Very Rev. Msgr. ROBERT L. GETZ; Revs. DENNIS FOUNTAIN, O.F.M.; VALENTINE JANKOWSKI, O.F.M.Conv.; CONRADO PYTLIK; DENIS TEJADA.

Presbyteral Council—Revs. EDWARD HERRERA, Pres. MICHAEL LINDSAY, Vice Pres. RICHARD CATANACH, Sec.; Very Rev. Msgr. ROBERT L. GETZ; Revs. ANDRES ALAVA, O.A.R.; WILLIAM MCCANN; RICHARD CATANACH; DAVID BERGS; FRANKLIN EICHHORST, O.F.M.Cap.; VALENTINE JANKOWSKI, O.F.M.Conv.; DENNIS FOUNTAIN, O.F.M.; MICHAEL LINDSAY; PAULUS KAO; CONRADO PYTLIK; ROBERT POWER, C.S.B.; JOHN WEBER, O.F.M.Conv., J.C.L.; DENIS TEJADA; Very Rev. Msgr. JOHN E. ANDERSON; Revs. MIGUEL ECHEVERRIA; ART ROBERTS, C.S.B.; ALFRED GALVAN.

Priests Personnel Board—Most Rev. RICARDO RAMIREZ, C.S.B.; Very Rev. Msgr. JOHN E. ANDERSON; Very Rev. Msgr. ROBERT L. GETZ; Revs. DENIS TEJADA; RODERICK NICHOLS; MICHAEL LINDSAY; Deacon DANIEL CHECK; Sr. MARY ELLEN QUINN, R.S.M.

Priestly Life and Ministry Committee—Rev. DAVID BERGS, Chm.; Most Rev. RICARDO RAMIREZ, C.S.B.; Very Rev. Msgr. ROBERT L. GETZ; Revs. FRANKLIN EICHHORST, O.F.M.Cap; VALENTINE JANKOWSKI, O.F.M.Conv.; MICHAEL LINDSAY; ROBERT POWER, C.S.B.; JOHN TICKLE; RICHARD CATANACH; RICARDO HINOJAL, O.A.R.

Lay Personnel Committee—Rev. ROBERT POWER, C.S.B.; MAGGIE CANDIA; DEBBIE ISHAM MOORE; Sr. MARY ELLEN QUINN, R.S.M.; MARGARET GARCIA; MANUEL LEYVA; ARTHUR E. JIRON.

Sisters Council—Sr. JANE MARIE KERNS, S.H.C.J., Chm.

Priests Retirement Fund Committee—Rev. MICHAEL LINDSAY; Very Rev. Msgr. ROBERT L. GETZ; Revs. WILLIAM MCCANN; DAVID BERGS; Mr. DANIEL DOLAN; FELIPE SALCIDO, JR.

Permanent Deacon Council—Deacons DANIEL CHECK, Pres. JOHNNIE PEREZ; PETE VELOTT; FRANK SCHRETLEN; JOHN LUCERO.

Comptroller—FELIPE SALCIDO, JR.

Finance Council—Most Rev. RICARDO RAMIREZ, C.S.B.; Very Rev. Msgr. JOHN E. ANDERSON; Revs. ROBERT POWER, C.S.B.; EDWARD HERRERA; Sr. MARY ELLEN QUINN, R.S.M.; FELIPE SALCIDO; DAN DOLAN; DON BEASLEY; EDDIE YBARRA; CHARLENE WARD; Mr. SAM ACOSTA; HAROLD GRANDI; EDWARD PILLAR.

Office of Stewardship and Development and United In Ministry Appeal—SUSAN ROBERTS, Exec. Dir.

Office of Insurance—MARTA ROMERO, Insurance Dir.

Office of Buildings and Properties—Rev. DENIS TEJADA, Dir. MANUEL LEYVA, Assoc. Dir.

Diocesan Ministries Offices and Directors

Vicar for Ministries—Rev. ROBERT POWER, C.S.B.

Office of Adult Catechesis and Ministerial Development—Rev. ROBERT POWER, C.S.B.

Art and Environment Committee—Sr. LUCY MEISSEN, C.PP.S.

Attorney—DANIEL DOLAN.

Campus Ministry—Revs. MITCHELL DOWALGO, C.S.B.; JON ALEXANDER, O.P.

Judicial Vicar—Rev. JOHN WEBER, O.F.M.Conv., J.C.L.
Office of Catholic Schools—Sr. JOAN BERNINGER, M.M., Supt.
Office of Catholic Social Ministry—ANTONIO LUJAN, Dir. CARLOS CORRAL, Assoc. Dir.
Office of Parish 2000—Rev. ROBERT POWER, C.S.B., Dir.
Cursillo Secretariat—VICTOR RODRIGUEZ, Pres. BLANCA LUNA, Treas. VICENTE LUNA, Sec.
Office of Elementary Catechesis—DAVID MCNAMARA, Dir.
Ecumenical Liaison—Sr. JANE KERNS, S.H.C.J.
Hispanic Ministry—Rev. ROBERT POWER, C.S.B.
Holy Childhood Association—Very Rev. Msgr. JOHN E. ANDERSON.
Hospital Ministry—Sr. FRANCIS ROYER, C.S.J.
Office of Liturgical Education—Sr. LUCY MEISSEN, C.PP.S.
Propogation of the Faith—Very Rev. Msgr. JOHN E. ANDERSON.
Order of Christian Initiation of Adults—Sr. LUCY MEISSEN, C.PP.S., Co-Chm. DAVID MCNAMARA, Co-Chm.; Sr. JANE MARIE KERNS, S.H.C.J.; NORMA SPINA.
Vocation Team—Sr. LUCY MEISSEN, C.PP.S.; Rev. RICHARD CATANACH.
Office of Adolescent Catechesis and Youth Ministry—KEVIN VIGIL.
Pastoral Councils—DAVID MCNAMARA; ANTONIO LUJAN.
Diocesan Resource Center—DAVID MCNAMARA, Coord. DOLORES DIAZ, Librarian.
Diocesan Archives—Rev. JOHN TICKLE, Archivist.
Charismatic Renewal Liaisons—LEO MARRUFO, (East); Mr. SAM TOME, (West); Mrs. SAM TOME, (West).
Agua Viva—CHRISTY ANCHONDO, Editor; DAVID MCNAMARA, Special Projects; LORETTA CHAVEZ, Advertising.
Agua Viva Editorial Advisory Board—Rev. ROBERT POWER, C.S.B.; Mr. ANTONIO LUJAN; PHILIP ALVAREZ; RUBEN ABEYTA; LALA GONZALEZ; MANUEL LEYVA; DAVID MCNAMARA; BETTY MORENO; Sr. MARY ELLEN QUINN, R.S.M.; CHRISTINA ANCHONDO.

CLERGY, PARISHES, MISSIONS AND PAROCHIAL SCHOOLS

CITY OF LAS CRUCES
(Dona Ana County)

1—CATHEDRAL OF IMMACULATE HEART OF MARY, Revs. Thomas P. Beggane; Louis D. Amezaga; Deacon Frank J. Lujan, (Retired).
Office: 1240 S. Espina St., 88001. Tel: 505-524-8563.
Campus—Las Cruces Area Catholic School, 1331 N. Miranda, 88001. Tel: 505-524-8563.
Lay Teachers 9; Students 139.

2—HOLY CROSS, Very Rev. Msgr. John E. Anderson; Rev. William Schmitt, S.S.C.
Office: 1327 N. Miranda St., 88005. Tel: 505-523-0167; Fax: 505-523-8023.
Campus—Las Cruces Area Catholic School, 1331 N. Miranda, 88001.
Lay Teachers 19; Students 192.

3—OUR LADY OF HEALTH, Revs. Narciso Rivera, O.A.R.; Antonio Martinez, O.A.R.
Res., 1178 N. Mesquite, 88001. Tel: 505-526-9545; Fax: 505-526-9545.

4—ST. ALBERT THE GREAT NEWMAN PARISH. Serving New Mexico State University. Revs. Mitchell G. Dowalgo, C.S.B.; Daryold Winkler, C.S.B.; Deacon Richard R. DeBlassie.
Res., 2615 S. Solano, 88001. Tel: 505-522-6202.

5—ST. GENEVIEVE, Revs. Denis Tejada; Juan Moreno; Roque Fernandes; Deacon LaRue Velott.
Res., 100 S. Espina, 88001. Tel: 505-524-9649. [CEM]

6—SANTA ROSA DE LIMA, Rev. Jesus Espinosa, O.A.R.
Church—5035 Holsome Rd., 88004. Tel: 505-382-9768.

OUTSIDE THE CITY OF LAS CRUCES

Alamogordo, Otero Co., Immaculate Conception, Revs. Bryant Hausfeld, O.F.M.; Gregg D. Petri; Bruce Hausfeld, O.F.M.
Res., 705 Delaware Ave., 88310. Tel: 505-437-3291; Fax: 505-437-3239. [CEM]
School—Rev. James B. Hay, 1000 E. Eighth St., 88310. Tel: 505-437-7821. Sr. Jean Berringer, M.M., Prin.
Lay Teachers 9; Students 120.
Missions—Boles Acres, Our Lady of the Desert; La Luz, Our Lady of the Light; Cloudcroft, Sacred Heart.
St. Jude, Very Rev. Daniel R. Barfield, S.J.
Office: 1404 College Ave., 88310. Tel: 505-437-0238; Fax: 505-437-0267.

Anthony, Dona Ana Co., St. Anthony's, Revs. Andres Alava, O.A.R.; Juan Almarza, O.A.R.
Res., P.O. Drawer C, 88021. Tel: 505-882-2239; Fax: 505-882-2239. [CEM]
Church—224 Lincoln St., 88021.
Convent—124 Tornillo Dr., Chaparral, 88021. Tel: 505-824-0508. Hermanas Dominicas de la Doctrina Cristiana
Missions—Chaparral, St. Thomas More, 528 E. Paseo, Chaparral, 88021. Tel: 505-824-4433. Rev. Miguel Echeverria, O.A.R.; La Union, Our Lady of Refuge, Rte. 1, Box 484A, La Union, 88021. Tel: 505-874-2967; Berino, Immaculate Conception, San Benito Rd., P.O. Box 155, Berino, 88024.

Artesia, Eddy Co., St. Anthony, Rev. Joseph P. Johnson, S.J.
Res., 502 S. Ninth St., 88210. Tel: 505-746-4471.
Our Lady of Grace, Rev. Vincent Petersen, O.F.M.Conv.
Res., 1111 N. Roselawn Ave., 88210. Tel: 505-748-1356.
Catechesis/Religious Programs—Martha Shoemaker, D.R.E.
Students 430.

Bayard, Grant Co., Our Lady of Fatima, Rev. Paulus Kao.
Res., P.O. Box 1425, 88023. Tel: 505-537-2421.
Missions—Fierro, St. Anthony; Hanover, Holy Family; San Lorenzo, San Lorenzo.

Carlsbad, Eddy Co., St. Edward, Rev. Noel R. Kramer, O.F.M.Conv. In res., Rev. Maurus Hauer, O.F.M. Conv.
Res., 610 W. Stevens, 88220. Tel: 505-885-6600.
School—(Grades K-7) 805 Walter St., 88220. Tel: 505-885-4620; Fax: 505-885-7706. William Threlkeld, Prin.
Lay Teachers 9; Students 110.
Convent—206 N. Guadalupe, 88220. Tel: 505-885-2480. Adorers of the Blood of Christ
San Jose, Rev. Valentine Jankowski, O.F.M. Conv.
Res., 1002 DeBaca, 88220. Tel: 505-885-5792; Fax: 505-887-3553.
Religious Education Center—Tel: 505-887-1346. Patsy Grantner, D.R.E.
Students 350.

Carrizozo, Lincoln Co., St. Rita, Rev. David J. Bergs.
Res., Box 727, 88301. Tel: 505-648-2853.
Missions—Capitan, Sacred Heart; Corona, St. Therese of the Little Flower.

Santa Clara, Grant Co., Santa Clara, Rev. Michael P. Lindsay.
Res., P.O. Box 215, 88026. Tel: 505-537-3713; Fax: 505-537-4929.

Chamberino, Dona Ana Co., San Luis Rey, Rev. Robert Villegas, C.S.C.
Res., P.O. Box 230, 88027. Tel: 505-882-2045.
Convent—275 San Pablo Rd., P.O. Box 149, 88027. Tel: 505-882-5811. Our Lady of Guadalupe Franciscan Missionaries of Mary 4.

Deming, Luna Co., Holy Family, Rev. Joseph K. Anderson, O.S.B.
Res., 612 S. Copper Ave., 88030. Tel: 505-546-9783; Fax: 505-544-3655.
St. Ann's, Rev. Alfred Galvan.
Res., 400 S. Ruby St., 88030. Tel: 505-546-3343.
Catechesis/Religious Programs—901 S. Pearl (Fr. Stangley Hall), 88030. Tel: 505-546-3905. Teresita D. Skully, D.R.E.
Students 261.
Mission—Columbus, Holy Family. In res., Rev. Aloys Ketteler, S.V.D.

Dexter, Chavez Co., Immaculate Conception, Deacon John S. Lucero, Admin.
Res., 400 W. Fifth, P.O. Box 189, 88230. Tel: 505-734-5478.
Missions—Lake Arthur, Our Lady of Guadalupe; Hagerman, St. Catherine.

Dona Ana, Dona Ana Co., Our Lady of the Purification, Rev. Miguel Macaya.
Mailing Address: P.O. Box 706, 88032. Tel: 505-526-2114. [JC]
Mission—San Isidro, San Isidro.

Garfield, Dona Ana Co., San Isidro, Sr. Marie Paule Willem, F.M.M., Parish Life Coord.
Res., H.C. 31, Box 43, 87936-9701. Tel: 505-267-5111.
Missions—San Jose, Arrey; Hillsboro, Our Lady of Guadalupe.

Hatch, Dona Ana Co., Our Lord of Mercy, Revs. Robert E. Power, C.S.B.; Bill McCann, Admin.
Res., Box 321, 87937. Tel: 505-267-4983.
Mission—Rincon, Our Lady of All Nations.

Hobbs, Lea Co., Our Lady of Guadalupe, Rev. Virgilio M. Flores; Deacon Samuel Navarrette.
Office: 914 S. Selman, 88240. Tel: 505-393-4991.
St. Helena, Revs. Donald J. Adamski, O.F.M.Conv.; Jose Reyes, O.F.M.Conv. Pastoral Assocs.: Sr. Margaret McTaggert, S.S.C.; Sr. Maurita Sharko, S.S.C.
Res., 100 E. Bender Blvd., 88240. Tel: 505-392-7551; 7552.
School—Tel: 505-392-5405; Fax: 505-392-0128. Mr. Larry Ebbens, Prin.
Lay Teachers 8; Students 123.
Convent—110 E. Bender, 88240. Tel: 505-392-8115.

Hurley, Grant Co., Infant Jesus, Rev. Daniel Porter.
Res., Box 97, 88043. Tel: 505-537-3691; 536-9405.
Missions—San Juan, San Juan; Faywood, San Jose.

Jal, Lea Co., St. Cecilia, Rev. Valentine Jankowski, O.F.M.Conv.
Res., P.O. Box 430, 300 N. Nevada St., 88252. Tel: 505-395-2431.
Mission—Eunice, St. Clare.

La Mesa, Dona Ana Co., San Jose, Rev. Jesus Perez-Recio, O.A.R.
Res., P.O. Box 278, 88044. Tel: 505-233-3191.
Mission—Vado, Dona Ana Co., San Pedro Del Cerro, P.O. Box 281, La Mesa, 88048.

Lordsburg, Hidalgo Co., St. Joseph, Rev. Tony Clark.
Res., 416 E. Second St., 88045. Tel: 505-542-3268.
Missions—Cotton City, St. Jude; Rodeo, San Felipe; Playas, St. Augustine; Hachita, St. Catherine.

Loving, Eddy Co., Our Lady of Grace, Rev. Dominic Manion, O.F.M.Conv.; Deacon Odie Saldivar.
Res., P.O. Box 428, 301 4th St., 88256. Tel: 505-745-3341.
Mission—Malaga, Cristo Rey.

Lovington, Lea Co., St. Thomas Aquinas, Rev. Franklin Eichhorst, O.F.M.Cap.
Res., 1301 N. Ninth St., 88260. Tel: 505-396-4206.
Mission—Tatum, Our Lady of the Holy Rosary.

Mescalero, Otero Co., St. Joseph (Apache Indian Mission), Rev. Paul Botenhagen, O.F.M.; Bro. Peter Boegel, O.F.M.; Sr. Robert Ann Hecker, O.S.F.
Res., Box 187, 88340. Tel: 505-671-4473.
Missions—Bent, Our Lady of Guadalupe; Three Rivers, St. Patrick.

Mesilla, Dona Ana Co., St. Albino, Rev. Conrad E. Pytlik.
Res., P.O. Box 26, 88046. Tel: 505-526-9349; Fax: 505-647-1619.

Mesilla Park, Dona Ana Co., Shrine and Parish of Our Lady of Guadalupe, Rev. John Weber, O.F.M.Conv.
Res., Box 296, 88047. Tel: 505-526-8171.

Roswell, Chaves Co., St. Peter, Revs. Dennis Fountain, O.F.M.; Richard Young, O.F.M. In res., Revs. Ramon Smith, O.F.M.; John Lanzrath, O.F.M.
Res., 105 E. Mathews, 88201. Tel: 505-622-5742; Fax: 505-623-9228.
St. John the Baptist, Revs. Dennis Fountain, O.F.M.; Richard Young, O.F.M.
Res., 105 E. Matthews, 88201. Tel: 505-622-7228; Fax: 505-623-8933.
Assumption of the Blessed Virgin Mary, Rev. Msgr. Robert Getz.
Res., 2808 N. Kentucky, 88201. Tel: 505-622-9895; Fax: 505-622-6845.

Ruidoso, Lincoln Co., St. Eleanor, Rev. Richard Catanach.
Res., P.O. Box 8300, 120 Junction Rd., 88355. Tel: 505-257-2330; Fax: 505-257-7062.
Missions—San Patricio, St. Jude Thaddeus; Lincoln, San Juan; Fort Stanton, Sacred Heart; Picacho, St. Joseph.

San Miguel, Dona Ana Co., San Miguel, Rev. Ricardo Hinojal, O.A.R.
Res., Drawer E, 88058. Tel: 505-233-2453; Fax: 505-233-2453.
Augustinian Recollects: P.O. Box 310, Mesilla, 88046. Tel: 505-523-7030; Fax: 505-233-7030.
Mission—Mesquite, Our Lady of Perpetual Help.

Silver City, Grant Co., St. Vincent de Paul, Rev. Rodrick Nichols; Deacons William Holguin; Johnnie Perez.
Res., 414 Bayard St., P.O. Box 1189, 88061. Tel: 505-538-9373; Fax: 505-388-0870.
Missions—Gila, St. Isidore; Pinos Altos, Holy Cross.
St. Francis Newman Center Parish. Serving Western New Mexico University. Rev. Jon Alexander, O.P.
Res., 914 W. 13th St., 88061. Tel: 505-538-3662; Fax: 505-534-1059.

Sunland Park, Dona Ana Co., St. Martin de Porres, Rev. Edward Herrera; Deacon Jesus Favela.
Res., P.O. Box 248, 88063. Tel: 505-589-2106.
Stations—El Naranjo, Shrine of Sierra de Cristo Rey; El Naranjo, Santo Nino de Atocha.

Tularosa, Otero Co., St. Francis de Paula, Rev. Robert Young, O.F.M.
Res., 303 Encino, 88352. Tel: 505-585-2793. [CEM]

Truth or Consequences, Sierra Co., Our Lady of Perpetual Help, Revs. Art Roberts, C.S.B.; Hugh Foley, C.S.B.
Res., 103 E. Sixth Ave., 87901. Tel: 505-894-7804; Fax: 505-894-0451.

Missions—Cuchillo, St. Joseph; Las Palomas, San Ysidro; Montecello, St. Ignatius; Placitas, San Lorenzo.
Chapels—St. Gregory, Chapels Chise.; San Miguel, Rancho de San Miguel.; Winston, St. Jude.

Special Assignment:
Reverend Fathers—
Lopez, Enrique
Morgan, Arthur

Retired:
Reverend Monsignors—
Lynch, Richard
Milano, James
VonderHaar, Roland
Reverend Fathers—
Griffith, Edwin
Lafrenz, James
Moynahan, Kevin

Permanent Deacons:
Alvarado, Alfonso, Blackrange Stations, San Lorenzo
Andis, John A., Leave of Absence
Bowers, Al, Our Lady of Guadalupe, Mesilla Park
Chavez, Rigoberto, Our Lady of Purification, Dona Ana
Check, Daniel, Our Lady of Purification, Dona Ana
Crowder, Richard, Holy Cross, Las Cruces
DeBlassie, Richard, Leave of Absence
Dickman, Donald, La Luz, Our Lady of the Light
Dougil, Edward, (Retired)
Favela, Jesus, Leave of Absence
Gale, Howard, (Retired), Immaculate Heart of Mary, Las Cruces
Holguin, William, St. Vincent de Paul, Silver City
Lehman, James, Leave of Absence
Lucero, John S., Immaculate Conception, Dexter
Lucero, Levy, Immaculate Conception, Alamogordo
Lujan, Frank, (Retired), Immaculate Heart of Mary, Las Cruces
Narvaez, Arthur, (Retired), St. Genevieve, Las Cruces
Navarrette, Sam, Our Lady of Guadalupe, Hobbs
Perez, Johnnie, Leave of Absence
Polson, Charles, Our Lady of Grace, Artesia
Roane, Tom, Our Lady of Guadalupe, Hobbs
Saldivar, Odie, Our Lady of Grace, Loving
Sanchez, Adam L., St. Jude, Alamogordo
Schretlen, Frank, (Retired), Our Lady of the Light, La Luz
Velott, Pete, St. Genevieve, Las Cruces
Vigil, Benjamin, St. Eleanors, Ruidoso

INSTITUTIONS LOCATED IN THE DIOCESE

[A] CLINICS

CARLSBAD. *St. Mary's Health Care Center*, 2330 West Pierce, 88220. Tel: 505-887-0516; Fax: 505-885-8239
For a complete listing, refer to the Special Care Facilities section.

HOBBS. *St. Mary Medical Center*, 2410 North Fowler, 88240. Tel: 505-392-5572; Fax: 505-392-4848
For a complete listing, refer to the Special Care Facilities section.

St. Mary's Family Health Care Center, 515 East Main, 88240. Tel: 505-393-1096; Fax: 505-393-3758
For a complete listing, refer to the Special Care Facilities section.

[B] MONASTERIES & RESIDENCES OF PRIESTS AND BROTHERS

LAS CRUCES. *Basilian Fathers*, 1682 Alta Vista Pl., 88011. Tel: 505-521-4269; Fax: 505-505-2042. Revs. Robert E. Power, C.S.B., Rector; Mitchell G. Dowalgo, C.S.B.; Daryold Winkler, C.S.B.

MESILLA. *Augustinian Recollects Fathers*. Province of St. Nicholas of Tolentine, Provincial Delegation in the South of U.S.A. San Alypius House, P.O. Box 310, 88046. Tel: 505-523-7030. Revs. Ricardo Hinojal, O.A.R. (Spain); Benito Suen, O.A.R; Jesus Perez-Recio, O.A.R.

[C] CONVENTS AND RESIDENCES FOR SISTERS

LAS CRUCES. *Fransiscan Sister*, 1700 Baldwin Dr., 88001. Tel: 505-522-7057.

Maryknoll Sisters, 700 California, Apt. 14, 88001. Tel: 505-525-0807.

Medical Mission Sisters, 3267 Executive Hills Rd., Apt. D, 88011. Tel: 505-521-4087.

Precious Blood Sisters, 1705 Montana, 88001. Tel: 505-522-3857. Sisters 2.

Sisters of St. Francis, 135 Roberts Dr., 88005. Tel: 505-526-3444.

Sisters of St. Joseph, Concordia, KS, 700 California, Apt. 16, 88001. Tel: 505-524-7223.

Society of the Holy Child Jesus, 1412 Gladys, 88001. Tel: 505-522-4873.

ANTHONY. *Sisters of Mercy of the Americas (Omaha Region & Vermont Region)*, 301 Lincoln St., P.O. Box 2411, 88021. Tel: 505-882-5553. Sisters 3.

CARLSBAD. *Adorers of the Blood of Christ*, St. Edwards Convent, 206 N. Guadalupe, 88220. Tel: 505-885-2480.

CHAMBERINO. *Franciscan Missionaries of Mary*, P.O. Box 149, 88027. Tel: 505-882-5811.

CHAPPARAL. *Dominicas De La Doctrina Cristiana*, 124 Tornillo, 88021. Tel: 505-824-0508. Sisters 6; Novices 8.

DEMING. *Daughters of the Heart of Mary*, P.O. Box 1531, 88030. Tel: 505-546-7599.

GARFIELD. *Franciscan Missionaries of Mary*, HC 31, Box 43, State Rd. 436, 87936-9701. Tel: 505-267-5111.

LAUNION. *Sisters of Mercy - New Jersey Region*, Rte. 1, Box 490 A, 88021. Tel: 505-589-0852. Sisters 2.

MESCALERO. *Franciscan Sisters of Our Lady of Perpetual Help*, P.O. Box 187, 88340. Tel: 505-671-4893. Sisters 2.

ROSWELL. *Poor Clare Monastery of Our Lady of Guadalupe*, 809 E. 19th St., 88201. Tel: 505-622-0868. Mothers M. Francis, P.C.C., Abbess; Mary Veronica, P.C.C., Vicaress. Professed Nuns 30; Novices 1; Postulants 3.

Sisters of St. Francis - Neumann Community, 4911 S. Pennsylvania Ave., 88201. Tel: 505-624-2475.

SILVER CITY. *Sisters of St. Joseph*, St. Mary's Center, 1801 N. Alabama, 88061. Tel: 505-538-3350. 1803 N. Alabama, 88061. Tel: 505-388-3684.

SUNLAND PARK. *Sister of Charity, Franciscan Sister, Sister of the Incarnate Word*, 115 Mesa Verde, P.O. Box 1768, 88063. Tel: 505-589-4412.

TRUTH OR CONSEQUENCES. *Sister of the Sorrowful Mother*, 216 Radium St., 87901.

[D] RETREAT CENTERS

MESILLA PARK. *Holy Cross Retreat and Friary*, P.O. Box 158, 88047. Tel: 505-524-3688; 524-3811 (Friary). Rev. Sebastian Cunningham, O.F.M.Conv.; Sr. Mary Kiely, O.S.F.

[E] MISCELLANEOUS

LAS CRUCES. *Catholic Diocese of Las Cruces Foundation, Inc.*, 1280 Med Park Dr., 80005. Susan Roberts, Exec. Dir.

Our Lady of Guadalupe Prayer Center, Inc., P.O. Box 6772, 88006. Tel: 505-522-5250.

The Priests' Retirement Plan of the Catholic Diocese of Las Cruces, Inc., 1280 Med Park Dr., 88005.

RELIGIOUS INSTITUTES OF MEN REPRESENTED IN THE DIOCESE

For further details refer to the corresponding bracketed numbers in the Religious Institutes of Men or Women section.

[0170]—*Basilian Fathers*.—C.S.B.
[0200]—*Benedictine Monks*.—O.S.B.
[0470]—*Capuchin Friars*. (St. Bonaventure).—O.F.M.Cap.
[0480]—*Conventual Franciscans*. (Our Lady of Guadalupe Custody).—O.F.M.Conv.
[0520]—*Franciscan Friars*. (St. John the Baptist, Our Lady of Guadalupe, St. Barbara Provs.).—O.F.M.
[0690]—*Jesuit Fathers and Brothers*. (New Orleans, Wisconsin Provs.).—S.J.
[0430]—*Order of Preachers*. (Province of St. Albert the Great, Chicago, IL).—O.P.
[0150]—*Order of the Augustinian Recollects*.—O.A.R.
[0610]—*Priests of the Congregation of Holy Cross*. (Southwest Prov.).—C.S.C.
[0370]—*Society of St. Columban*.—S.S.C.
[0420]—*Society of the Divine Word*.—S.V.D.

RELIGIOUS INSTITUTES OF WOMEN REPRESENTED IN THE DIOCESE

[0100]—*Adorers of the Blood of Christ*. (Wichita; Ruma, KS; Columbia, PA).—A.S.C.
[0460]—*Congregation of the Sisters of Charity of the Incarnate Word*.—C.C.V.I.
[0810]—*Daughters of the Heart of Mary*.—D.H.M.
[1110]—*Dominican Sisters of Our Lady of the Rosary and of Saint Catherine of Siena, Cabra*.—O.P.
[1070]—*Dominicas de la Doctrina Cristiana*.—O.P.
[1370]—*The Franciscan Missionaries of Mary*.—F.M.M.
[1430]—*Franciscan Sisters of Our Lady of Perpetual Help*.—O.S.F.
[2470]—*Maryknoll Sisters of St. Dominic*.—M.M.
[2490]—*Medical Mission Sisters*.—M.M.S.
[2690]—*Missionary Catechists of Divine Providence*.—M.C.D.P.
[3130]—*Our Lady of Victory Missionary Sisters*.—O.L.V.M.
[3760]—*Poor Clares Monastery of Our Lady of Guadalupe*.—P.C.C.
[]—*Sisters for Christian Community*.
[0440]—*Sisters of Charity of Cincinnati, Ohio*.—S.C.
[2575]—*Sisters of Mercy of the Americas*. (Omaha).—R.S.M.
[3740]—*Sisters of St. Casimir*.—S.S.C.
[1570]—*Sisters of St. Francis of the Holy Family*.—O.S.F.
[3830-15]—*Sisters of St. Joseph*.—C.S.J.
[2575]—*Sisters of the Americas (Omaha, Vermont and New Jersey)*.—R.S.M.
[3270]—*Sisters of the Most Precious Blood (O'Fallon, MO)*.—C.PP.S.
[4100]—*Sisters of the Sorrowful Mother (Third Order of St. Francis)*.—S.S.M.
[4060]—*Society of the Holy Child Jesus*.—S.H.C.J.

NECROLOGY

† Chavez, Very Rev. Msgr. Albert, (Retired). —Died Nov. 20, 1997.
† Viramontes, David Enriquez, Las Cruces, NM, St. Joseph Mission. —Died Aug. 13, 1997.

Diocese of Las Vegas

(Dioecesis Campensis)

Most Reverend

DANIEL F. WALSH, D.D.

Bishop of Las Vegas; ordained March 30, 1963; appointed Titular Bishop of Tigia and Auxiliary of San Francisco September 24, 1981; appointed Bishop of Reno-Las Vegas June 9, 1987; installed August 6, 1987. *Res., 2809 Cameo Cir., Las Vegas, NV, 89107.*

Chancery Office: 336 Cathedral Way, Las Vegas, NV, 89109. Mailing Address: P.O. Box 18316, Las Vegas, NV, 89114-8316. Tel.: 702-735-3500; Fax: 702-735-8941.

ERECTED BY HIS HOLINESS POPE PIUS XI MARCH 27, 1931.

REDESIGNATED DIOCESE OF RENO-LAS VEGAS BY POPE PAUL VI, OCTOBER 13, 1976.

REDESIGNATED DIOCESE OF LAS VEGAS BY HIS HOLINESS POPE JOHN PAUL II MARCH 21, 1995.

Square Miles 39,688.

For legal titles of parishes and diocesan institutions, consult the Chancery Office.

STATISTICAL OVERVIEW

Personnel	
Bishop	1
Priests: Diocesan Active in Diocese	24
Priests: Active Outside Diocese	1
Priests: Retired, Sick or Absent	20
Number of Diocesan Priests	45
Religious Priests in Diocese	19
Extern Priests in Diocese	29
Permanent Deacons in Diocese	8
Total Brothers	6
Total Sisters	51
Parishes	
Parishes	22
With Resident Pastor:	
Resident Diocesan Priests	17
Resident Religious Priests	5
Without Resident Pastor:	
Missions	7
Closed Parishes	1
Professional Ministry Personnel:	
Brothers	1
Sisters	6
Lay Ministers	29
Welfare	
Catholic Hospitals	1
Total Assisted	89,420
Special Centers for Social Services	10
Total Assisted	758,785
Educational	
High Schools, Diocesan and Parish	1
Total Students	1,098
Elementary Schools, Diocesan and Parish	6
Total Students	2,287
Catechesis/Religious Education:	
High School Students	1,787
Elementary Students	7,755
Total Students Under Catholic Instruction	12,927
Teachers in the Diocese:	
Priests	2
Brothers	3
Sisters	3
Lay Teachers	141
Vital Statistics	
Receptions into the Church:	
Infant Baptism Totals	4,503
Adult Baptism Totals	271
Received into Full Communion	243
First Communions	2,752
Confirmations	984
Marriages:	
Catholic	601
Interfaith	236
Total Marriages	837
Deaths	641
Total Catholic Population	377,000
Total Population	1,300,000

Chancery Office—336 Cathedral Way, Las Vegas, 89109. Tel: 702-735-3500; Fax: 702-735-8941. Office Hours: Mon.-Fri 8:30-12 & 1-4:30, *Mailing Address: P.O. Box 18316, Las Vegas, 89114-8316.*

Vicar General—Rev. PATRICK LEARY, V.G.

Chancellor—Rev. PATRICK R. LEARY. Tel: 702-735-9605.

Diocesan Tribunal Office-Judicial Vicar—Very Rev. FRANCIS M. VIVONA, S.T.M., J.C.L. Tel: 702-735-1210; Fax: 702-735-5146.

Auditor—CECELIA CAMMARANO.

Notary-Secretary—Mrs. SIDNEY MARSH; Mrs. CECELIA CAMMARANO.

Promoter of Justice—Rev. MARK ROBERTS, J.C.L.

Defender of the Bond—Rev. PETER ROMEO, J.C.L.

Diocesan Judges—Rev. Msgr. ADRIAN DWYER, J.C.D.; Rev. KEVIN MCAULIFFE, J.C.L.

Advocates—Revs. JOSEPH ANTHONY; ANTHONY VERCELLONE; MARY JO GRETZINGER, J.C.L.; Rev. PHILLIP ACQUARO, J.C.L.; RICHARD IMON.

Diocesan Offices and Directors

Building Committee—Most Rev. DANIEL F. WALSH, D.D., Chm.; Rev. PATRICK LEARY, V.G.; Bro. JOHN DODD, C.S.V.; Rev. DAVE CASALEGGIO.

Catholic Charities of Southern Nevada—808 S. Main St., Box 1926, Las Vegas, 89125. Tel: 702-385-2662. Mr. MIKE HUSTED, Exec. Dir.

Chief Financial Officer—Bro. JOHN DODD, C.S.V.

Development Office—Ms. PATSY VINCENT. Tel: 702-735-1109.

Education Department—

Superintendent of Schools—ELLEN AYOUB.

Office of Catechetical Ministries—Sr. MIRIAM MULLINS, O.P., Dir. Tel: 702-735-6044. Sr. KAREN CROUSE, O.S.F., Dir., Newman Apostolate. Tel: 702-736-0887.

Office of Peace and Social Justice—Rev. CAESAR J. CAVIGLIA.

Home and Foreign Missions—Rev. PATRICK LEARY, V.G. Tel: 702-735-9605.

Hospital Apostolate—Attended from St. Anne Parish. Tel: 702-735-0510.

Information, Communications and Media—Rev. BEDE WEVITA. Tel: 702-870-2767.

Italian Catholic Federation—Vacant.

Native American and Colored People Commission—Rev. PATRICK LEARY, V.G.

Newsletter—DESERT CLARION.

Pontifical Association of the Holy Childhood—Rev. PATRICK LEARY, V.G.

Priests' Pension Board—Revs. PHILIP O'DONNELL; FRANCIS VIVONA; GREGORY GORDON; Bro. JOHN DODD, C.S.V.

Priests' Personnel Board—Revs. DAVE CASALEGGIO; FRANCIS VIVONA; JOSEPH ANTHONY.

Property Management—Bro. JOHN DODD, C.S.V.

Vicar for Oriental Rites—Rev. FRANCIS VIVONA, S.T.M., J.C.L.

Vocations—Rev. ANTHONY VERCELLONE.

Diocesan Youth Council—Clergy Reps.: Revs. WILLIAM KENNY; BEDE WEVITA, *Diocese of Las Vegas: P.O. Box 18316, Las Vegas, 89114.* Tel: 702-735-9605.

CLERGY, PARISHES, MISSIONS AND PAROCHIAL SCHOOLS

CITY OF LAS VEGAS

(Clark County)

1—GUARDIAN ANGEL CATHEDRAL (1963), Revs. James Crilly, C.S.V., Rector; Francis P. White, C.S.V.; Daniel Reardon, C.S.V.; Stewart R. Schramko, C.S.V.; Sr. Timothy Malone, C.H.S., Pastoral Assoc.

302 Cathedral Way, 89109. Tel: 702-735-5241; Fax: 702-734-7086.

2—CHRIST THE KING (1978), Revs. William J.M. Kenny; Leo Coughlin; Robert Stoeckig.

Mailing Address: 4922 S. Torrey Pines, 89118.

Office & Res.: 5122 S. Torrey Pines, 89118. Tel: 702-871-1904; Fax: 702-251-4935.

Catechesis/Religious Programs—Beth Summers, D.R.E.

Students 675.

Mission—Sandy Valley, St. Catherine of Siena.

3—HOLY FAMILY (1975), Rev. John McShane.

Mailing Address: 4490 Mountain Vista, 89121.

Office & Res.: 4528 E. Harmon Ave., 89121-6548. Tel: 702-458-2211 (Office); 458-5997 (Res.); Fax: 702-458-0966 (Office).

Catechesis/Religious Programs—Tel: 702-458-3575.

Students 385.

4—OUR LADY OF LAS VEGAS (1957), Revs. Dave Casaleggio; Ray Schultz; Bede Wevita; Deacon Joshua Alves. In res., Rev. Bill Duff, (Retired).

Office: 3050 Alta Dr., 89107. Tel: 702-870-2767; Fax: 702-870-1267.

Res., 3104 Alta Dr., 89107.

School—3036 Alta Dr., 89107. Tel: 702-878-6841; Fax: 702-880-5758. Gerald Streit, Prin.

Lay Teachers 14; Students 341.

Catechesis/Religious Programs—Tel: 702-870-1882.
Students 600.

5—Prince of Peace (1981), Revs. Francis Timoney; J. Clarence Savial; Brian Stenson.
Office: 5485 E. Charleston Blvd., 89122. Tel: 702-431-2233; Fax: 702-431-2234.
Res., 653 Los Feliz, 89110.
Catechesis/Religious Programs—Tel: 702-431-2233; Fax: 702-431-2234.
Students 654.

6—St. Anne (1948), Revs. Robert Votta; Alberto Alzate (Colombia); Jesse Cortes (Philippines) Hospital Chap.
Office & Res.: 1901 S. Maryland Pkwy., 89104. Tel: 702-735-0510; Fax: 702-894-9237.
School—1813 S. Maryland Pkwy., 89104. Tel: 702-735-2586; Fax: 702-735-8357. Phyllis Joyce, Prin.
Lay Teachers 13; Students 343.
Catechesis/Religious Programs—Tel: 702-735-2985; Fax: 702-735-9237.
Students 415.

7—St. Bridget (1945), Rev. James L. Swenson.
Office: 220 N. 14th St., 89101-4312. Tel: 702-384-3382.
Res., 215 N. 14th St., 89101. Tel: 702-384-4264.
Catechesis/Religious Programs—Tel: 702-384-4264.
Students 77.

8—St. Elizabeth Ann Seton (1992), Revs. Kevin W. McAuliffe, J.C.L.; Raymond Rioux; Jerry Nadine; Deacons Joe Deegan; Frank Pemper; Howard Tigrath.
Office: 1811 Pueblo Vista Dr., 89128. Tel: 702-228-8311; Fax: 702-228-8310.
Res., 2109 Golden Lotus Dr., 89134.
Catechesis/Religious Programs—Tel: 702-228-8311.
Students 1101.

9—St. Francis de Sales (1964), Revs. James J. Bevan, Jr.; Frank S. Yncierto; John Andrew Sullivan, J.C.L.
Office: 1111 Michael Way, 89108. Tel: 702-647-3440; Fax: 702-646-3587.
Res., 1628 Desert Fort, 89128. Tel: 702-233-1010.
School—Tel: 702-647-2828. Mrs. Gloria Hagstrom, Prin.
Lay Teachers 11; Students 304.
Catechesis/Religious Programs—Tel: 702-646-2266.
Students 555.

10—St. James the Apostle (1942) (African American), Rev. Michael Blackburn, O.F.M.; Sr. Deborah Lockwood, O.S.F., Pastoral Assoc. & D.R.E.
Office: 820 N. H St., 89106. Tel: 702-648-6606; Fax: 702-648-0352.
Res., 1420 W. Bartlett, 89106. Tel: 702-648-2798; Fax: 702-648-2798.
Catechesis/Religious Programs—Tel: 702-648-6606; Fax: 702-648-0352.
Students 73.

11—St. Joan of Arc (1908), Rev. Philip O'Donnell.
Office & Res.: 315 S. Casino Center Blvd., 89101. Tel: 702-382-9909; Fax: 702-382-6655.
School—1300 Bridger Ave., 89101. Tel: 702-384-6909; Fax: 702-386-0249. Mrs. Lynda Ballard, Prin.
Lay Teachers 11; Students 285.

12—St. Joseph, Husband of Mary (1989), Revs. Joseph L. Anthony; Thomas E. Gallenbach; Gary Vollmer; Deacon Michael J. Heidenreich.
Mailing Address: Office, 7260 W. Sahara Ave., 89117. Tel: 702-363-1902; Fax: 702-363-7976.
Res., 3759 Barrelwood Dr., 89117.
Catechesis/Religious Programs—Tel: 702-363-3658; Fax: 702-363-0142. Dr. Joan Tansey, D.R.E.
Students 936.

13—St. Mary the Virgin (1983), Rev. Gregory Gordon, S.S.C. Tel: 702-453-9032.
Office: 5083 Judson Ave., 89115. Tel: 702-642-1154.

14—St. Paul Jung-Ha-Sang (1987) (Korean), Rev. Patrick R. Leary, Vicar Gen., Tel: 702-735-3500.
5225 Meikle Ln., 89115. Tel: 702-453-0033.

15—St. Viator (1954), Revs. Thomas Langenfeld, C.S.V.; Wayne Dupuis, C.S.V.; William Haesaert, C.S.V.; Bro. Dale Barth, C.S.V.
Office: 2461 E. Flamingo Rd., 89121. Tel: 702-733-8323; Fax: 702-733-8154.
School—Tel: 702-732-4477; Fax: 702-732-4418. Mr. William C. Langley, Prin.
Sisters 2; Lay Teachers 27; Students 697.
Catechesis/Religious Programs—Tel: 702-732-0459. Carol Russell, D.R.E.
Students 371.

16—Shrine of the Most Holy Redeemer (1991), Rev. Patrick R. Leary, Vicar Gen., Tel: 702-735-3500.
Office: 55 E. Reno Ave., 89119. Tel: 702-891-8600; Fax: 702-891-0339.

OUTSIDE THE CITY OF LAS VEGAS

Amargosa Valley, Nye Co., Christ of the Desert Catholic Church (1987), Sr. Jacinta Kaiser, Admin.
Office & Res.: P.O. Box 218, Amargosa, 89020. Tel: 702-372-5337. [JC]

Boulder City, Clark Co., St. Andrew's (1931), Rev. Joseph P. Annese.
1399 San Felipe Dr., 89005. Tel: 702-293-7500; Fax: 702-293-4419. [JC]
Catechesis/Religious Programs—Michael Willis, D.R.E.
Students 183.

Caliente, Lincoln Co., Holy Child (1870), Rev. Leo Slatterie.
Res., Culverwell St., 89008-0708. Tel: 702-726-3669. [CEM]

Henderson, Clark Co., St. Peter the Apostle (1943), Revs. Mark Roberts; Dionisio Besinga (Tagbilaran).
Res., 204 S. Boulder Hwy., 89015. Tel: 702-565-8406; Fax: 702-565-8731.
Catechesis/Religious Programs—Tel: 702-565-0284.
Students 740.

St. Thomas More (1986), Revs. Dan Nolan, C.S.V.; Michael Keliher, C.S.V.; Ken Morris, C.S.V.; Deacon George Flaherty.
Res., 130 N. Pecos Rd., 89014. Tel: 702-361-3022; Fax: 702-361-7784.
Catechesis/Religious Programs—Tel: 702-361-8840; Fax: 702-361-5992. Juliann Dwyer, D.R.E.
Students 1130.

Ely, White Pine Co., Sacred Heart (1907), Rev. Timothy C. Wehn, S.A.C.
Mailing Address: 501 Murry St., 89301. Tel: 702-289-2201; Fax: 702-289-2207.
Office & Res.: 515 Murry St., 89301.
School—(Catechetical Ministry Center) 1100 Park Ave., P.O. Box 278, 89301. Tel: 702-289-4302. Sr. Maura McGarry, R.S.M., Prin.
Sisters of Mercy 2.
Catechesis/Religious Programs—Students 156.
Convent—550 First St., 89301. Tel: 702-289-4733. Mercy Convent
Mission—McGill, St. Michael's, P.O. Box 26, Ely, 89301.

Laughlin, Clark Co., St. John the Baptist Catholic Mission (1992), Rev. Peter Romeo.
P.O. Box 31888, 89028. Tel: 702-298-0440.
Res., 3115 Terrace View, 89029.

North Las Vegas, Clark Co., St. Christopher (1953), Revs. Gregory Gordon; Manuel Quintero.
Mailing Address: 1800 N. Bruce, 89030. Tel: 702-642-1154; Fax: 702-642-0719.
Res., 1401 Flower Ave., NE 89030.
School—Tel: 702-657-8008; Fax: 702-642-2461. Mrs. Carol Haeberlin, Prin.
Lay Teachers 12; Students 317.
Catechesis/Religious Programs—Tel: 702-657-6779. Mrs. Sharon Pauli, D.R.E.
Students 1,365.

Overton, Clark Co., St. John, the Evangelist (1959), Rev. Gustavo Cruz.
Mailing Address: P.O. Box 493, 89040. Tel: 702-397-8096; Fax: 702-397-2846.
Office: 150 N. Moapa Valley Blvd., 89040. Fax: 807-397-2846.
Res., 425 W. Joan St., 89040.
Catechesis/Religious Programs—Students 155.
Mission—Bunkerville, Clark Co., La Virgen de Guadalupe, Corner of 1st W. & 1st S., P.O. Box 7309, Bunkerville, 89007. Tel: 702-346-7065.

Pahrump, Nye Co., Our Lady of the Valley (1985), Rev. John H. Lima.
Res., 781 E. Gamebird, 89041. Tel: 702-727-4044.
Mailing Address: P.O. Box 1506, 89041.
Catechesis/Religious Programs—Students 86.
Mission—Pahrump, Christ of the Desert.

Tonopah, Nye Co., St. Patrick (1902), Rev. James P McCauley, S.J.
P.O. Box 325, 89049. Tel: 702-482-6746.
Mailing Address: 144 South St., 89049.
Missions—Round Mountain & Fish Lake, St. Barbara/Our Lady of Guadalupe; Our Lady of Guadalupe.

Special Assignment:
Reverend Fathers—
Richard, Alain, O.F.M., PACE E BENE, 1420 W. Bartlett St., Las Vegas, NV 89106. Tel: 702-648-2798

Military Chaplains:
Reverend Fathers—
Grochowski, Bernard, Our Lady of the Skies, 4302 N. Washington Blvd., Nellis AFB, NV 89191. Tel: 702-652-2950
Hanrahan, William, Our Lady of the Skies, 4302 N. Washington Blvd., Nellis AFB, NV 89191
McNulty, Jerry, Dept. of Veterans Affairs, VAMC - 125, 1703 W. Charleston Blvd., Las Vegas, NV 89102. Tel: 702-426-2813

Retired:
Reverend Fathers—
Caviglia, Caesar
Duff, William
Fanning, Gerard F.
Franzinell, Benjamin
Lavoy, Elwood
McVeigh, John J.

Permanent Deacons:
Alves, Joshua
Deegan, Joseph
Flaherty, George
Heidenriech, Mike
Moffett, Steve
Pemper, Frank
Stoehr, George
Tirgrath, Howard

INSTITUTIONS LOCATED IN THE DIOCESE

[A] HIGH SCHOOLS, DIOCESAN

Las Vegas. *Bishop Gorman High School*, 1801 Maryland Pkwy., 89104. Tel: 702-732-1945; Fax: 702-732-2856.
E-mail: bghslv@wizard.com
Web site: http://members.aol.com/bghslv/
Rev. Thomas R. vonBehren, C.S.V., Pres.; David W. Erbach, Prin.; Rev. Norbert P. Bibeault, C.S.V. Priests 2; Brothers 3; Sisters 1; Lay Teachers 59; Students 1,098.

[B] GENERAL HOSPITALS

Henderson. *St. Rose Dominican Hospital*, 102 Lake Mead Dr., 89015. Tel: 702-564-2622
For a complete listing, refer to the Hospitals section.

[C] DAY NURSERIES

Las Vegas. *Holy Family Day Care Center*, 451 E. Twain, 89109. Tel: 702-735-4358. Connie Johnson, Dir.
Sponsor: Catholic Charities. Boys 62; Girls 68.

[D] MONASTERIES AND RESIDENCES OF PRIESTS AND BROTHERS

Las Vegas. *Clerics of St. Viator*, 1212 E. Oakey Blvd., 89104. Tel: 702-735-4637; Fax: 702-732-2856.
E-mail: bghslv@wizard.com
Rev. Thomas R. von Behren, C.S.V., Pres. Viatorian priests on facility of Gorman High School. In res. Bros. Corey D. Brost, C.S.V.; Robin L. Robertson, C.S.V.; Michael T. Gosch, C.S.V. Priests 1; Brothers 3.

Clerics of St. Viator Retirement Home, 4219 Pinecrest Cir. E., 89121. Tel: 702-456-8512. Revs. Robert F. Cooney, C.S.V., Dir.; Edward C. Anderson, C.S.V.; Norbert P. Bibeault, C.S.V.; Patrick J. Hayes, C.S.V. Priests 4.

[E] CONVENTS AND RESIDENCES FOR SISTERS

Las Vegas. *Carmelite Monastery of Jesus, Mary and Joseph (O.C.D.)*, 4835 Pearl Ave., 89121-6009. Mother Teresa, Prioress.

Convent of the Franciscan Sisters of Perpetual Adoration, 1304 E. St. Louis Ave., 89104-3466. Tel: 702-735-0640. Sisters 2.

Holy Family Convent, 5276 S. Lookout St., 89120. Tel: 702-435-1526.
E-mail: smd475@vegas.infinet
Sisters of the Holy Family 5.

Ely. *Mercy Convent*, 550 First St., P.O. Box 278, 89301. Tel: 702-289-4733. Sisters 2.

[F] RETREAT HOUSES

Caliente. *Monastery of Christ in the Mountains*, P.O. Box 708, 89008.

[G] MISCELLANEOUS

Las Vegas, NV. *Catholic Charities of Southern Nevada*, 808 S. Main St., P.O. Box 1926, 89125. Tel: 702-385-2662. Michael Husted, Exec. Dir.
Adoption Services.
Black Mountain Senior Nutrition Program & Meals-on-Wheels.
Crossroads Transitional Housing for Senior Men.

Deferred Giving Program.
Holy Family Day Care Center.
Immigration Services.
Marlan Transitional Housing for Senior Women.
Migration and Refugee Services.
Regina Hall.
Respite Care Referral Service.
RSVP (Retired & Senior Volunteer Program).
Senior Community Employment Service.
Senior Companion.
Senior Nutrition & Meals-on-Wheels.
Social Ministry.
Social Services.
St. Vincent Dining Room.
St. Vincent Shelter and Employment Services Center.
St. Vincent Thrift Stores.
NCWB Housing, Inc.
CCSN Mojave Project, Inc.
CCSN-CTS Annex, Inc.
CCSN McFarland Housing Development Corporation, Inc.

RELIGIOUS INSTITUTES OF MEN REPRESENTED IN THE DIOCESE

For further details refer to the corresponding bracketed number in the Religious Institutes of Men or Women section.

[0360]—*Claretian Missionaries.*—C.M.F.
[1320]—*Clerics of St. Viator.*—C.S.V.
[0520]—*Franciscan Friars.*—O.F.M.

RELIGIOUS INSTITUTES OF WOMEN REPRESENTED IN THE DIOCESE

[1780]—*Congregation of the Sisters of the Third Order of St. Francis of Perpetual Adoration.*—F.S.P.A.
[0420]—*Discalced Carmelite Nuns.*—O.C.D.
[1070-04]—*Dominican Sisters.*—O.P.
[1190]—*Franciscan Sisters of the Atonement.*—S.A.
[2690]—*Missionary Catechists of Divine Providence.*—M.C.D.P.
[1630]—*Sisters of St. Francis of the Penance and Christian Charity.* (St. Francis Prov.).—O.S.F.
[1960]—*Sisters of the Holy Family.*—S.H.F.

NECROLOGY
(No Deaths)

Diocese of Lafayette in Indiana

(Diocesis Lafayettenis in Indiana)

Most Reverend

WILLIAM L. HIGI, D.D.

Bishop of Lafayette in Indiana; ordained May 30, 1959; appointed Bishop of Lafayette in Indiana April 7, 1984; consecrated and installed June 6, 1984. *Res., 610 Lingle Ave., P.O. Box 260, Lafayette, IN, 47902.*

CANONICALLY ERECTED OCTOBER 21, 1944.

Square Miles 9,832.

Comprises the Counties of Benton, Blackford, Boone, Carroll, Cass, Clinton, Delaware, Fountain, Fulton, Grant, Hamilton, Howard, Jasper, Jay, Madison, Miami, Montgomery, Newton, Pulaski, Randolph, Tippecanoe, Tipton, Warren and White in the State of Indiana.

For legal titles of parishes and diocesan institutions, consult the Bishop's Office (Chancery).

Office of Bishop and Chancery: P.O. Box 260, Lafayette, IN, 47902. Tel.: 765-742-0275; Fax: 765-742-7513.

STATISTICAL OVERVIEW

Personnel	
Bishop	1
Priests: Diocesan Active in Diocese	81
Priests: Active Outside Diocese	19
Priests: Retired, Sick or Absent	21
Number of Diocesan Priests	121
Religious Priests in Diocese	22
Extern Priests in Diocese	2
Permanent Deacons in Diocese	5
Total Brothers	2
Total Sisters	92
Parishes	
Parishes	62
With Resident Pastor:	
Resident Diocesan Priests	51
Resident Religious Priests	4
Without Resident Pastor:	
Administered by Priests	7
Missions	1
Professional Ministry Personnel:	
Sisters	18
Lay Ministers	60
Welfare	
Catholic Hospitals	4
Total Assisted	207,767
Homes for the Aged	2
Total Assisted	385
Educational	
Diocesan Students in Other Seminaries	5
Total Seminarians	5
Colleges and Universities	3
Total Students	6,969
High Schools, Diocesan and Parish	1
Total Students	364
Elementary Schools, Diocesan and Parish	20
Total Students	3,934
Catechesis/Religious Education:	
High School Students	2,950
Elementary Students	9,271
Total Students Under Catholic Instruction	23,493
Teachers in the Diocese:	
Lay Teachers	235
Vital Statistics	
Receptions into the Church:	
Infant Baptism Totals	1,861
Adult Baptism Totals	292
Received into Full Communion	441
First Communions	1,842
Confirmations	1,252
Marriages:	
Catholic	296
Interfaith	326
Total Marriages	622
Deaths	780
Total Catholic Population	94,512
Total Population	1,115,156

Former Bishops—Most Rev. JOHN GEORGE BENNETT, D.D., LL.D., ord. June 27, 1914; appt. First Bishop of Lafayette Nov. 11, 1944; cons. Jan. 10, 1945; died Nov. 20, 1957.—His Eminence JOHN CARDINAL CARBERRY, D.D., ord. July 28, 1929; appt. Coadjutor with Right of Succession Aug. 22, 1956; appt. Bishop of Lafayette in Indiana Nov. 20, 1957; transferred to Diocese of Columbus, Jan. 20, 1965; transferred to the Archdiocese of St. Louis Mar. 24, 1968; created Cardinal April 28, 1969; retired July 31, 1979.—Most Rev. RAYMOND J. GALLAGHER, D.D., ord. March 25, 1939; appt. Bishop of Lafayette in Indiana June 23, 1965; cons. August 11, 1965; installed August 23, 1965; resigned October 26, 1982; retired April 13, 1983; died March 7, 1991.—Most Rev. GEORGE A. FULCHER, S.T.D., D.D., ord. Feb. 28, 1948; appt. Auxiliary Bishop of Columbus, OH and Titular Bishop of Morosbido May 24, 1976; cons. July 18, 1976; appt. Bishop of Lafayette in Indiana Feb. 8, 1983; installed April 14, 1983; died Jan. 25, 1984.

Vicar General—Rev. ROBERT L. SELL, III, J.C.L.

Chancellor and Moderator of the Curia—Rev. ROBERT L. SELL, III, J.C.L.

Office of Bishop and Chancery—P.O. Box 260, Lafayette, 47902. Tel: 765-742-0275; Fax: 765-742-7513.

Deans—Lafayette Deanery: Rev. DANIEL B. GARTLAND, Anderson Deanery: Rev. ROBERT L. WILLIAMS, Fowler Deanery: Rev. THOMAS E. FOX, Carmel Deanery: Rev. LEO A. PIQUET, Logansport Deanery: Rev. DONALD L. GROSS, Muncie Deanery: Rev. WILLIAM R. GRADY.

Diocesan Consultors—Revs. WILLIAM R. GRADY, V.F.; LEO A. PIGUET, V.F.; ROBERT L. SELL, III, J.C.L., V.G.; DONALD L. GROSS, V.F.; THEODORE D. ROTHROCK; MICHAEL J. MCKINNEY; DOMINIC G. YOUNG.

Diocesan Pastoral Office for Administration—ROBERT H. QUINN, Finance Officer, *P.O. Box 260, Lafayette, 47902.* Tel: 765-742-4852.

Diocesan Pastoral Office for Planning and Communication—THOMAS A. RUSSELL, Dir., *610 Lingle Ave., P.O. Box 1603, Lafayette, 47902.* Tel: 765-742-2050.

Publisher- "The Catholic Moment"—THOMAS A. RUSSELL, Editor; RUSSELL FLYNN, Editorial Asst. & Reporter; MARY MANCHA, Reporter; CAROLYN CASE, Sec.

Diocesan Pastoral Office for Social Ministry—DAVID R. WILSON, Dir., *836 S. Purdum, Kokomo, 46901-5533.* Tel: 765-457-1172. Assists parishes in developing parish social ministry; co-ordinates the work of the Campaign for Human Development and the Indiana Catholic Conference; liaison with St. Elizabeth Home (Indianapolis) relative to adoption services, Pro-Life Service Centers, St. Vincent dePaul and Ladies of Charity, and coordinates the Premarital Evaluation program.

Diocesan Pastoral Office for Formation—Sr. MARILYN WINTER, O.P., Dir., *Catholic Pastoral Center, 2300 S. Ninth St., Lafayette, 47905-2400.* Tel: 765-474-8072; Fax: 765-474-3403. Coordinates marriage preparation conferences and programs, Natural Family Planning, Separated-Divorced Catholic programs, Sacramental preparation with families, implementation of Family Perspective and Family Catechesis. Additional responsibilities include all programs (Catholic Schools, Religious Education, Youth Ministry, Preschools, Sacramental Preparation, Scouts, Athletics, etc.) for young people in the Local Church. That responsibility extends to the formation of those who minister to young people as catechists, teachers, coaches, youth leaders and administrators.

Diocesan Tribunal—Catholic Pastoral Center, 2300 S. Ninth St., Lafayette, 47905. Tel: 765-474-0506.

Judicial Vicar—Rev. DAVID L. RASNER, J.C.L.

Adjutant Judicial Vicar—Rev. WILLIAM R. VATH.

—First Instance:

Presiding Judges—Revs. DAVID L. RASNER, J.C.L.; WILLIAM R. VATH.

Defenders of the Bond—Revs. DAVID J. BUCKLES, J.C.L.; DONALD L. GROSS.

Deputy Defenders—Rev. PETER VANDERKOLK; Sr. KATHRYN KIRK.

Ecclesiastical Notary—VERNA S. MEEK.

Full-Time Advocates—BRIDGET O'BRIEN; MAREN SCHERF.

Periti—PHILLIP M. SUTTON, Ph.D.; MICHAEL MILLARD, Ph.D.

—Second Instance:

Presiding Judge—Rev. RICHARD E. MILLER, J.C.L.

Associate Judges—Rev. Msgr. JOHN C. DUNCAN; Rev. Msgr. FRED E. POTTHOFF; Revs. MELVIN BENNETT; GERALD J. BORAWSKI; JAMES R. GOODRUM; FRED H. GSCHWIND; DONALD B. VERNON; EDWARD F. DHONDT; THOMAS J. ZIMMER.

Defender of the Bond—Rev. JOSEPH W. DOOLEY.

Ecclesiastical Notary—PEGGY FLETCHER.

Advocates—Refer to Court of First Instance.

Lay Advocates—Refer to Court of First Instance.

Periti—Refer to Court of First Instance.

Administrative Causes—Rev. ROBERT L. SELL, III, J.C.L.

Diocesan Offices and Directors

Archivist—Vacant.

Building Commission—KEN MCGINITY, Chm.; Revs. THEODORE ROTHROCK; ROBERT SELL; Sr. MARILYN WINTER, O.P.; ROBERT GLOYESKE; ANN MCKEE; Dr. DOUGLAS SUTTON; WILL WRIGHT; ERIC ERNSTBERGER; ROBERT TURNER; DANIEL MADER.

Finance Officer—ROBERT H. QUINN, *P.O. Box 260, Lafayette, 47902.* Tel: 765-742-4852.

Administration—Refer to Diocesan Pastoral Office.

Corporation—Roman Catholic Diocese of Lafayette in Indiana, Inc.(Incorporated, March 21, 1958.); Most Rev. WILLIAM L. HIGI, Pres.; Revs. ROBERT L. SELL, III, J.C.L., Vice Pres.-Sec. RICHARD WEISENBERGER, Treas.

Director of Development—SHARON HUECKEL, *Bishop's Office, P.O. Box 1687, Lafayette, 47902.* Tel: 765-742-7000; Fax: 765-742-7513.

Director of Planned Giving—JOSEPH A. BONNER, *Bishop's Office, P.O. Box 1687, Lafayette, 47902.* Tel: 765-742-7000; Fax: 765-742-7513.

Fruitful Harvest Office—P.O. Box 1687, Lafayette, 47902. Tel: 765-742-4852.

Finance Council—Most Rev. WILLIAM L. HIGI; Rev. ROBERT L. SELL, III, J.C.L., V.G.; ROBERT H. QUINN, Dir. Pastoral Office for Admin. LEON CYR; MARGARET ANDREZJEWSKI; JOAN TRET; DON GOETZ; EDWARD LOPKE; JOHN F. BODLE, Legal Counsel.

Legal Council—JOHN DUFFEY, *Life Building, P.O. Box 1010, Lafayette, 47902.* Tel: 765-423-1561; Fax: 765-742-8175.

Presbyteral Council—Revs. DOMINIC G. YOUNG, Chm. MICHAEL J. MCKINLEY, Vice Chm.

Members—Revs. ROBERT L. SELL, III, J.C.L., V.G.; DENNIS J. GOTH; WILLIAM R. GRADY, V.F.; DONALD L. GROSS, V.F.; PHILIP S. HASLINGER; DOMINIC G. YOUNG; DANIEL B. GARTLAND, V.F.; LEO A. PIGUET, V.F.; THEODORE D. ROTHROCK; ROBERT L. WILLIAMS, V.F.; THOMAS E. FOX, V.F.; THOMAS H. METZGER; PATRICK R. CLICK.

Catholic Relief Services—Vacant.

Censor Librorum—Rev. DAVID L. RASNER, J.C.L., *Catholic Pastoral Center, 2300 S. Ninth St., Lafayette, 47905.* Tel: 765-474-0506.

Aquinas Educational Foundation, Inc.—Rev. PATRICK R. CLICK, Res. Agent, *535 State St., West Lafayette, 47906.* Tel: 765-743-4653.

Clergy Relief Association—Board of Directors: Revs. DAVID L. RASNER, J.C.L., Pres. RICHARD J. WEISENBERGER, Vice Pres. JERRY BORAWSKI, Sec. THOMAS FOX, Asst. Treas. ALEJANDRO PATERNOSTER, Treas.

Members—Revs. PHILIP T. BOWERS; THEODORE ROTHROCK; PAUL R. WICKLUM.

Catholic Charities Central Office—Refer to Diocesan Pastoral Office.

Social Ministry—DAVID R. WILSON, Diocesan Dir., *Diocesan Catholic Offices, 836 S. Purdum, Kokomo, 46901.* Tel: 765-457-1172.

Society of St. Vincent de Paul—DAVID R. WILSON, Diocesan Dir., *Diocesan Catholic Offices, 836 S. Purdum St., Kokomo, 46901.* Tel: 765-457-1172.

Association of Ladies of Charity—DAVID R. WILSON, Dir., *Diocesan Catholic Offices, 836 Purdum St., Kokomo, 46901.* Tel: 765-457-1172.

Liturgical Commission—Refer to Diocesan Pastoral Office.

Eucharistic League—The Chancery, P.O. Box 260, Lafayette, 47902.

Greater Lafayette Catholic School Board—DAVID WORLAND, Contact.

Greater Lafayette Catholic School Foundation, Inc.—JOSEPH BONNER, *2410 S. Ninth St., Lafayette, 47905.*

Holy Childhood Association—Vacant.

Diocesan Board of Education—In process of reorganization & formation.

D.C.C.W.—Vacant.

Ministry to Priests Program—Rev. DONALD L. GROSS, V.F., Dir., *All Saints Church, 112 E. Market St., Logansport, 46947.* Tel: 219-753-3020.

Newman Apostolate, Purdue University—Rev. PATRICK R. CLICK, Dir., *535 State St., West Lafayette, 47906.* Tel: 765-743-4652.

Newman Foundation, Ball State, Inc.—Rev. JOHN J. KEIFER, Dir., *800 Riverside Ave., Muncie, 47303.* Tel: 765-288-6180.

Newman Apostolate, Wabash College—Rev. LEROY KINNAMAN, Dir., *310 S. Grant Ave., Crawfordsville, 47933.* Tel: 765-362-6121.

Newspaper "The Catholic Moment"—THOMAS A. RUSSELL, Editor; RUSSELL FLYNN, Editorial Asst. & Reporter; MARY MANCHA, Reporter, Editorial Office, *P.O. Box 1603, Lafayette, 47902.* Tel: 765-742-2050.

Office of the Apostolate to the Spanish Speaking—Deacon DOMINGO CASTILLO, Assoc. Dir., *917 Branson St., Marion, 46952.* Tel: 317-662-3288., *Guadalupe Center.* Tel: 765-664-3710.

Propagation of the Faith—DAVID WILSON,Refer to Pastoral Office for Social Ministry.

Religious Education Dept.—Refer to Pastoral Office for Formation.

RENEW—Rev. THEODORE ROTHROCK, Dir., *St. Patrick Church, 502 S. Michigan St., Oxford, 47971-9731.* Tel: 765-385-2587.

Rural Life Program—Rev. FRED H. GSCHWIND, Dir., *340 N. Mill St., Tipton, 46072.* Tel: 765-675-2422.

Schools—Refer to Pastoral Office for Formation.

St. Joseph Memorial Hospital Foundation, Inc.—PEGGY CALDWELL, Exec. Dir., *1907 W. Sycamore St., Kokomo, 46901.* Tel: 765-456-5425.

Vicar for Clergy—Vacant.

Vicar for Religious—Vacant.

Vocation Director—Rev. THEODORE ROTHROCK, Dir., *St. Patrick, 502 S. Michigan St., Oxford, 47971-9731.* Tel: 765-385-2587.

CLERGY, PARISHES, MISSIONS AND PAROCHIAL SCHOOLS

CITY OF LAFAYETTE
(Tippecanoe County)

1—ST. MARY CATHEDRAL (1843), Revs. Richard J. Weisenberger; Alejandro Paternoster. In res., Rev. Joseph Bruetsch.
Res., 1207 Columbia St., 47901-1522. Tel: 765-742-4440; Fax: 765-742-8933. [JC]
School—(Grades PreK-3). Tel: 765-742-6302.
Lay Teachers 11; Students 209.
Catechesis/Religious Programs—Tel: 765-742-8336.
Students 130.

2—ST. ANN (1884), Revs. Michael J. McKinley; Maurice R. Miller.
Res., 612 Wabash Ave., 47905-1096. Tel: 765-742-7031. [JC]
Catechesis/Religious Programs—Tel: 765-423-4635.
Students 262.

3—ST. BONIFACE (1853) (German), Rev. Timothy M. Alkire; Deacon Ron Nevinger. In res., Rev. William R. Vath.
Res., 318 N. Ninth St., 47904-2597. Tel: 765-742-5063; Fax: 765-742-5018. [CEM]
School—Lafayette Catholic Middle School, (Grades 4-6). Tel: 765-742-7913; Fax: 765-423-4988. Sr. M. Lois DeLee, O.S.F., Prin.
Lay Teachers 7; Students 138.
Catechesis/Religious Programs—Tel: 765-742-1351.
Students 233.

4—ST. LAWRENCE (1895), Revs. Daniel B. Gartland; Christopher T. Miller. In res., Rev. Anthony Pogorelc (SAT).
Res., 1916 Meharry St., 47904-1442. Tel: 765-742-2107; Fax: 765-742-1347.
School—1902 Meharry St., 47904-1497. Tel: 765-742-4450. Mrs. Pam Peroutky, Prin.
Lay Teachers 11; Students 245.
Catechesis/Religious Programs—Tel: 765-423-2396. Susan Schmitz, D.R.E.
Students 273.

OUTSIDE THE CITY OF LAFAYETTE

Alexandria, Madison Co., St. Mary (1896), Rev. Philip S. Haslinger.
Res., 820 W. Madison St., 46001-1520. Tel: 765-724-2483; 724-4459.
School—Tel: 765-724-4459.
Sisters 3; Lay Teachers 4; Students 97.
Catechesis/Religious Programs—Students 64.

Anderson, Madison Co., St. Ambrose (1947), Rev. Edward F. Dhondt.
Res., 2801 Lincoln St., 46016-5067. Tel: 765-644-5956; Fax: 765-642-7348.
School—Tel: 765-642-8428; Fax: 765-642-7348.
Lay Teachers 13; Students 197.
Catechesis/Religious Programs—Tel: 765-644-5956.
Students 185.

St. Mary (1858), Rev. Robert L. Williams; Mrs. Mary Pat Marstall, Pastoral Assoc.
Res., 1115 Pearl St., 46016-1789. Tel: 765-644-8467.
School—Tel: 765-642-1848; Fax: 765-642-1828. Sr. Marge Ehlers, O.S.F., Prin.
Lay Teachers 13; Students 141.
Station—Anderson, St. John Medical Center Chapel, Tel: 765-649-2511.
Catechesis/Religious Programs—Tel: 765-642-5339.
Students 120.

Attica, Fountain Co., St. Francis Xavier (1890), Rev. Charles Kline.
Res., 407 S. Perry St., P.O. Box 55, 47918-0001. Tel: 765-762-3330; Fax: 765-762-1810. [CEM]
Catechesis/Religious Programs—Students 99.

Bryant, Jay Co., Holy Trinity (1860) (German), Rev. Robert C. Reinhart, C.PP.S.
Res., R.R. 1, P.O. Box 87, 47326-9724. Tel: 219-997-6450. [CEM]
Catechesis/Religious Programs—Tel: 219-997-6450.
Students 162.

Carmel, Hamilton Co., Our Lady of Mount Carmel (1955), Rev. Msgr. John C. Duncan; Revs. Kevin J. Haines; David J. Newton; Michael A. Ondo; Richard J. Doerr; Deacon William Rahill.
Office: 1045 W. 146th St., 46032-1198. Tel: 317-846-3475; Fax: 317-846-3477.
School—Tel: 317-846-1118.
Sisters of Notre Dame 4; Lay Teachers 34; Students 671.
Catechesis/Religious Programs—Tel: 317-846-3878.
Students 1,200.
Mission—Westfield, Hamilton Co., St. Maria Goretti, (1994) 17104 Springmill Rd., Westfield, 46074. Tel: 317-896-5582; Fax: 317-867-0783.

St. Elizabeth Ann Seton (1981), Revs. Leo A. Piguet; Robert W. Klemme; Fred A. Schroeder.
Res., 10655 Haverstick Rd., 46033-3800. Tel: 317-846-3850; 846-6073; 846-6945; Fax: 317-846-3710.
Catechesis/Religious Programs—Tel: 317-846-3850.
Students 699.

Cicero, Hamilton Co., Sacred Heart (1898) (German-Irish), Rev. W. Michael Kettron.
Res., 429 S. Main St., 46034-9680. Tel: 317-984-5117.
Catechesis/Religious Programs—Tel: 317-984-2115.
Students 91.

Covington, Fountain Co., St. Joseph (1861), Rev. Leroy G. Kinnaman.
Res., 308 Pearl St., 47932-1062. Tel: 765-793-3289. [CEM]
Catechesis/Religious Programs—Tel: 765-793-4961.
Students 53.

Crawfordsville, Montgomery Co., St. Bernard (1859), Rev. Melvin J. Bennett.
Res., 1306 E. Main St., P.O. Box 719, 47933-0719. Tel: 765-362-6121; Fax: 765-361-0796. [CEM]
Catechesis/Religious Programs—Tel: 765-362-5472.
Students 297.

Delphi, Carroll Co., St. Joseph (1859), Rev. Peter J. Vanderkolk.
Res., 207 N. Washington St., 46923-1297. Tel: 765-564-2407. [CEM]
Catechesis/Religious Programs—Tel: 765-564-3439.
Students 139.

De Motte, Jasper Co., St. Cecilia (1952), Rev. Paul R. Wicklum.
Res., 334 Fifteenth St., S.W., 46310-9705. Tel: 219-987-3511; Fax: 219-987-7755. [CEM]
Catechesis/Religious Programs—Tel: 219-987-3514.
Students 169.

Dunkirk, Jay Co., St. Mary (1896), Rev. Rick Tucker.
Res., 346 S. Broad St., 47336-1310. Tel: 765-768-6157.
Catechesis/Religious Programs—Students 42.

Dunnington, Benton Co., St. Mary (1876), Rev. Donald B. Vernon, Admin.
Mailing Address: 2961 South SR71, Ambia, 47917. Tel: 765-884-1818. [CEM]

Earl Park, Benton Co., St. John the Baptist (1888), Rev. Robert J. Bernotas, Admin.
Res., Chestnut St., 47944. Tel: 219-474-5514. [CEM]

Elwood, Madison Co., St. Joseph (1889) (Irish-German), Rev. Kenneth T. Raczek.
Res., 1306 S. A St., 46036-1941. Tel: 765-552-6753. [CEM][JC]
Catechesis/Religious Programs—Tel: 765-552-6753. Mary Pat Miller, D.R.E.
Students 196.

Fishers, Hamilton Co., Holy Spirit Church (1991), Revs. Phillip T. Bowers; T. Edward Kacena.
Mailing Address: 10350 Glaser Way, 46038. Tel: 317-849-9245; Fax: 317-849-9388.
Res., 10868 Geist Woods Ln., Indianapolis, 46256. Tel: 317-845-0992; Fax: 317-849-9388.
Catechesis/Religious Programs—Tel: 317-849-8016.
Students 919.

St. Louis de Montfort (1978), Rev. Donald J. Eder.
Res., 11441 Hague Rd., 46038-1876. Tel: 317-842-6778; 842-6358; 576-1932; Fax: 317-576-1932.
Catechesis/Religious Programs—Students 1,040.

Fowler, Benton Co., Sacred Heart of Jesus (1872), Rev. Donald B. Vernon.
Res., 107 E. Main St., 47944-1148. Tel: 317-884-1818. [CEM]
School—Tel: 317-884-0710. Sr. Helene Seculoff, Prin.
Sisters of St. Francis of Perpetual Adoration 2; Lay Teachers 7; Students 153.

Catechesis/Religious Programs—Students 100.

Francesville, Pulaski Co., St. Francis Solano (1867), Rev. Paul R. White, C.PP.S., Admin.
Res., St. Joseph's College, P.O. Box 852, Rensselaer, 47978. Tel: 219-866-6271.

Frankfort, Clinton Co., St. Mary (1875), Rev. Gerald J. Borawski.
Res., 600 St. Mary's Ave., P.O. Box 265, 46041-0181. Tel: 317-654-5796; Fax: 317-654-6589. [JC]
Preschool—Tel: 765-659-3914.
Catechesis/Religious Programs—Students 229.

Gas City, Grant Co., Holy Family (1908), Rev. A. Leonard Reemmer.
Res., 325 E. North A St., 46933-1431. Tel: 765-674-2605.
Catechesis/Religious Programs—Students 130.

Goodland, Newton, SS. Peter and Paul (1880), Rev. Robert J. Bernotas, Admin.
Res., South Newton St., 47948. [JC]
Church—419 S. Newton St., 47948.

Hartford City, Blackford Co., St. John the Evangelist (1865), Rev. Robert E. Moran.
Res., 209 S. Spring St., 47348-2551. Tel: 765-348-3123.
School—Tel: 765-348-3889; Fax: 765-348-4399.
Lay Teachers 5; Students 107.
Catechesis/Religious Programs—Students 41.

Kentland, Newton, St. Joseph (1864), Rev. Robert J. Bernotas.
Res., 409 E. Allen St., P.O. Box 131, 47951-1322. Tel: 219-474-5514. [CEM]
School—Tel: 219-474-5614.
Lay Teachers 6; Students 73.
St. Joseph School Foundation, Inc.—Tel: 219-474-5514.
Catechesis/Religious Programs—Tel: 219-474-5614.
Students 127.

Kewanna, Fulton Co., St. Ann (1857), Rev. John H. Zahn, Admin.
Res., P.O. Box 235, 46939-0181. Tel: 219-653-2520. [CEM]

Kokomo, Howard Co., St. Joan of Arc (1927), Revs. David E. Hellmann; Timothy D. Kroeger; Paul W. Cochran.
Res., 900 S. Purdum, 46901-5598. Tel: 765-457-9371; Fax: 765-454-7241.
School—SS. Joan of Arc & Patrick. (Consolidated School) 824 S. Purdum St., 46901-5500. Tel: 765-452-1610 (St. Joan); 459-4769 (St. Patrick).
Lay Teachers 21; Students 298.
Catechesis/Religious Programs—923 S. Jay St., 46901. Tel: 765-457-1375; Fax: 765-454-7241.
Students 412.

St. Patrick (1859), Revs. Francis I. Kilcline; Jack Trippel; Theodore C. Dudzinski, II.
Office and Mailing Address—1229 N. Washington St., 46901-2898.
Res., 320 W. Broadway, 46901-2898. Tel: 765-452-6021; Fax: 765-868-8384. [JC]
Schools—(Grades K-7). Tel: 765-459-4769.
Lay Teachers 22; Students 303; SS. Joan of Arc & Patrick. (South Campus) 824 S. Purdum St., 46901-5500. Tel: 765-452-1610.
(North Campus) 1230 N. Armstrong St., 46901.
Catechesis/Religious Programs—1229 N. Washington, 46901. Tel: 765-452-6021; Fax: 765-868-8384. Rita Ricci, D.R.E.
Students 175.

Lake Village, Newton, St. Augusta (1947), Rev. Ambrose M. Ziegler.
Res., 3228 W. St. Rd. 10, 46349-9706. Tel: 219-992-3220. [JC]
Catechesis/Religious Programs—Students 82.

Lebanon, Boone Co., St. Joseph (1862), Rev. Thomas H. Metzger.
Mailing Address: P.O. Box 309, 46052-0309. Tel: 765-482-5558.
Res., 319 E. South St., 46052-2684. Tel: 765-482-5558. [CEM]
Catechesis/Religious Programs—Tel: 765-482-1581.
Students 237.

Logansport, Cass Co., All Saints (1985). Consolidation of the following three parishes (Legal Titles): St. Bridget (1875); St. Joseph (1868); and St. Vincent de Paul (1838). Revs. Donald L. Gross; Leo J. Haigerty; Sr. Gemma Therese Harvey, S.S.N.D., Pastoral Assoc.
Parish Office: 111 E. Market St., 46947-2922. Tel: 219-722-4080; Fax: 219-722-5426.
Res., 112 E. Market St., 46947. Tel: 219-753-3020. [JC]
School—All Saints Elementary, 107 Eel River Ave., 46947-3188. Tel: 219-753-3714.
All Saints Middle School—620 Wilkinson St., 46947. Tel: 219-722-5622.
Lay Teachers 13; Students 274.
Catechesis/Religious Programs—Tel: 219-722-4080.
Students 200.
Convent—700 Wheatland Ave., 46947. Tel: 219-753-3684.

Lucerne, Cass Co., St. Elizabeth (1953), Rev. Donald L. Gross, Admin.
Mailing Address: 112 East Market, Logansport, 46947. Tel: 219-753-3020.
Office: P.O. Box 86, 46950. [CEM]

Marion, Grant Co., St. Paul (1868), Revs. Duane M. Craycraft; C. Alan Funk.
Res., 1031 Kem Rd., 46952-2098. Tel: 765-664-6345; Fax: 765-664-5953.
School—1009 Kem Rd., 46952. Tel: 765-662-2883. Mrs. Jackie Certain, Prin.
Lay Teachers 9; Students 184.
Catechesis/Religious Programs—Tel: 317-664-6345.
Students 201.

Our Lady of Guadalupe (Hispanic). Closed. For inquiries for parish records contact St. Paul, Marion.

Medaryville, Pulaski Co., St. Henry (1868), Rev. Paul R. White, C.PP.S., Admin.
Res., St. Joseph's College, P.O. Box 852, Rensselaer, 47978. Tel: 219-866-6271. [CEM]

Monterey, Pulaski Co., St. Anne (1851) (German), Rev. Dominic Young.
Res., Church St., P.O. Box 96, 46960-0096. Tel: 219-542-2061. [CEM]
School—Tel: 219-542-4711.
Lay Teachers 4; Students 40.
Catechesis/Religious Programs—Tel: 219-542-4711.
Students 15.

Monticello, White Co., Our Lady of the Lakes (1948), Rev. James R. Goodrum.
Res., 543 S. Main St., 47960-2948. Tel: 219-583-5724.
Catechesis/Religious Programs—Tel: 219-583-6790.
Students 215.

Montpelier, Blackford Co., St. Margaret of Scotland (1864), Rev. Frederick J. Perry.
Res., 207 W. Huntington St., P.O. Box 247, 47359. Tel: 765-728-5757. [CEM]

Muncie, Delaware Co., St. Francis of Assisi (1972). (Ball State University Parish). Revs. John D. Kiefer; Michael A. McKinney.
Res., 1200 W. Riverside Ave., 47303-3650. Tel: 765-288-6180.
Catechesis/Religious Programs—Students 176.

St. Lawrence (1869), Rev. Dennis J. O'Keeffe.
Res., 820 E. Charles St., 47305-2699. Tel: 765-288-9223; Fax: 765-289-9262.
School—2801 E. 16th St., 47302. Tel: 765-282-9353; Fax: 765-282-0457.
Lay Teachers 12; Students 158.
Catechesis/Religious Programs—Students 95.

St. Mary (1930), Revs. William R. Grady; Brian A. Dudzinski. In res., Revs. James T. Keane; Anthony J. Prosen.
Res., 2300 W. Jackson St., 47303-4797. Tel: 765-288-5308.
School—2301 W. Gilbert St., 47303-4797. Tel: 765-288-5878; Fax: 765-284-3685.
Lay Teachers 21; Students 274.
Catechesis/Religious Programs—Students 133.

Noblesville, Hamilton Co., Our Lady of Grace (1944), Revs. James R. Bates; Martin J. Sandhage.
Res., 9900 E. 191st St., 46060-1998. Tel: 317-773-4275; Fax: 317-773-9344.
Catechesis/Religious Programs—Tel: 317-773-0297.
Students 820.

Otterbein, Benton Co., St. Charles (1902), Rev. David L. Rasner.
Res., 108 N. Meadow St., Box 661, 47970-0661. Tel: 765-583-4641. [JC]
Catechesis/Religious Programs—Students 129.

Oxford, Benton Co., St. Patrick (1867) (Irish), Rev. Theodore D. Rothrock.
Res., 502 S. Michigan St., 47971-8562. Tel: 765-385-2587; Fax: 765-385-0225. [CEM]
Catechesis/Religious Programs—Students 104.

Peru, Miami Co., St. Charles Borromeo (1860), Rev. Virgil M. Barker.
Res., 58 W. Fifth St., 46970-2100. Tel: 765-473-5543. [CEM]
School—Tel: 765-473-5669.
Lay Teachers 7; Students 103.
Catechesis/Religious Programs—80 W. Fifth St., 46970. Tel: 765-472-2692.
Students 121.

Portland, Jay Co., Immaculate Conception (1876), Rev. Joseph W. Grace.
Res., 506 E. Walnut St., 47371-1599. Tel: 219-726-7341.
Catechesis/Religious Programs—Tel: 219-726-7055.
Students 242.

Remington, Jasper Co., Sacred Heart (1875), Rev. Thomas E. Fox.
Res., 124 New York St., P.O. Box 159, 47977-0159. Tel: 219-261-2302. [CEM]
Catechesis/Religious Programs—Tel: 317-279-2656.
Students 104.

Rensselaer, Jasper Co., St. Augustine (1883), Revs. Mark R. Peres, C.PP.S.; Leonard J. Kostka, C.PP.S., Pastoral Assoc.
Res., 318 N. McKinley St., 47978-2599. Tel: 219-866-5351. [CEM]
School—Tel: 219-866-5480; Fax: 219-866-5663.
Religious 2; Lay Teachers 5; Students 127.
Catechesis/Religious Programs—Tel: 219-866-5351.
Students 188.

Reynolds, White Co., St. Joseph (1866), Rev. Richard E. Miller.
Res., 601 South Kenton St., 47980-8098. Tel: 219-984-5401. [CEM]
Catechesis/Religious Programs—Students 110.

Rochester, Fulton Co., St. Joseph (1900), Revs. John H. Zahn; Alan B. Cox.
Res., 1310 S. Main St., 46975-2108. Tel: 219-223-2808; Fax: 219-224-2808. [JC]
Catechesis/Religious Programs—Tel: 219-223-3246.
Students 135.
Mission—Kewanna, Fulton Co., St. Ann, P.O. Box 235, Kewanna, 46939. Tel: 219-653-2520.

Star City, Pulaski Co., St. Joseph (1851), Rev. Ronald J. Schiml, C.PP.S.
Res., R.R. 2, P.O. Box 65, 46985-9517. Tel: 219-595-7198. [CEM 2]
Catechesis/Religious Programs—Students 82.

Tipton, Tipton Co., St. John the Baptist (1866), Rev. Fred H. Gschwind.
Res., 340 N. Mill St., 46072-1403. Tel: 765-675-2422. [CEM]
School—(Grades PreK-5). Tel: 765-675-4741; Fax: 765-675-2163.
Lay Teachers 12; Students 150.
Catechesis/Religious Programs—Students 155.

Union City, Randolph Co., St. Mary (1865) (Irish-German), Rev. Dennis J. Goth.
Res., 425 W. Hickory St., 47390-1301. Tel: 765-964-4202. [CEM]
Catechesis/Religious Programs—Students 79.

Westfield, Hamilton Co., St. Maria Goretti (1995),
Res., 17104 Springmill Rd., 46074. Tel: 317-896-5582; Fax: 317-867-0783.
School—Sisters of Notre Dame 1; Lay Teachers 9; Students 249.
Catechesis/Religious Programs—Students 105.

West Lafayette, Tippecanoe Co., Blessed Sacrament (1957), Rev. David M. Douglas.
Res., 2224 Sacramento Ave., 47906-1998. Tel: 765-463-5733; Fax: 765-497-7866.
Catechesis/Religious Programs—Students 290.
Stations—Indiana Veterans' Home, Tel: 765-463-1502; Mary Queen of the Universe Chapel.

St. Thomas Aquinas (1951). (Purdue University Parish). Revs. Patrick R. Click; Anthony J. Levi. Pastoral Assocs.: Mrs. Phyllis Scanlon; Mr. Christopher O'Neal.
Office: 535 State St., 47096-3592. Tel: 765-743-4652; Fax: 765-743-0426.
Catechesis/Religious Programs—Eileen Strater, D.R.E.
Students 466.

Wheatfield, Jasper Co., Sorrowful Mother (1887), Rev. Philip A. Mahalic.
Res., P.O. Box 248, 46392-0248. Tel: 219-956-3343. [CEM]
Church Hall: Tel: 219-956-4648.
Catechesis/Religious Programs—Students 137.

Winamac, Pulaski Co., St. Peter (1859), Rev. Herbert Woolson, C.PP.S.
Res., 401 N. Monticello St., 46996-1327. Tel: 219-946-4906. [CEM]
Catechesis/Religious Programs—424 N. Market St., 46996. Tel: 219-946-6804.
Students 196.

Winchester, Randolph Co., St. Joseph (1952), Rev. Louis S. Heitz.
Res., 425 W. North St., 47394-1502. Tel: 765-584-4391.

Zionsville, Boone Co., St. Alphonsus (1945), Rev. Douglas McCormack; Deacon Harold W. Cloud.
Res., 1870 W. Oak, 46077-1894. Tel: 317-873-2885; 873-2700; Fax: 317-873-8746.
Catechesis/Religious Programs—Tel: 317-873-9418.
Students 367.

Chaplains of Public Institutions

LAFAYETTE. *Indiana Veterans' Home, Queen of the Universe Chapel.* Attended from Blessed Sacrament Church, West Lafayette.

GRISSOM. *Grissom Air Force Base, St. Michael's Chapel* 46971. Tel: 765-688-2191. Rev. Richard E. Miller, Auxiliary Civilian Chap.

LOGANSPORT. *Logansport State Hospital.* Vacant.

MARION. *U.S. Veteran's Hospital.* Rev. James Rose (FTW) Chap., Auxiliary Chaplains: Revs. Joseph W. Grace; A. Leonard Reemmer.

PENDLETON. *Correctional Industrial Complex Ecumenical Chapel* P.O. Box 601, 46064. Tel: 765-778-8011. Rev. Anthony J. Prosen.

Indiana State Reformatory, St. Christopher Chapel P.O. Box 28, 46064. Tel: 765-778-2107. Rev. Anthony J. Prosen.

Special Assignment:
Reverend Fathers—
Buckles, David, J.C.L., Diocesan Tribunal, 2300 S. 9th St., Lafayette, IN 47905. Tel: 765-474-0506
Miller, Richard E., J.C.L., Diocesan Tribunal, 2300 S. 9th St., Lafayette, IN 47905. Tel: 765-474-0506
Prosen, Anthony J., 1315 W. University St., Muncie, IN 47303. Tel: 765-288-6180
Rasner, David L., J.C.L., Treas., Clergy Relief Association,.
Rothrock, Theodore D., Vocation Dir., 502 S. Michigan St., Oxford, IN 47971-9131. Tel: 765-385-2587
Sell, Robert L., III, J.C.L., Vicar Gen., Chancellor & Moderator of the Curia, 1128 E. State St., Lafayette, IN 47905. Tel: 765-742-3286
Vath, William R., Diocesan Tribunal, 2300 S. 9th St., Lafayette, IN 47905. Tel: 765-474-0506

On Duty Outside the Diocese:
Reverend Fathers—
Carr, Bernard, Sacred Heart Church, Box 118, Anza, CA 92306. Tel: 714-763-5636
Clegg, Timothy, 3635 Westchester Drive, Holiday, FL 34691
Comeau, Ronald R., 6 Johnson Rd., Aurora, Ontario L4C 2A2. Tel: 416-772-1965
Gross, Barry, 1601 Georgia Ave., Wheaton, MD 20902
Holbrook, William M., 6210 W. Bell Plaine, Chicago, IL 60634
Mannion, John H., St. Francis Hospital, Pastoral Care Department, 1600 Albany St., Beechgrove, IN 46107. Tel: 317-787-3311
Plaster, George, 1751 - 8436 Viburnum Ct., Indianapolis, IN 46260. Tel: 317-251-9249
Schultz, John C., P.O. Box 415, Danville, IL 61834. Tel: 217-443-3936
Westfall, Joseph B., P.O. Box 45715, Kansas City, MO 64171

Military Chaplains:
Reverend Fathers—
Kinney, John M., 2520 Crested Hills, Schertz, TX 78154. Tel: 210-658-6825

Leave of Absence:
Reverend Fathers—
Bohlinger, Kenneth
Cummings, John J.

Unassigned:
Reverend Fathers—
Colletti, Joseph A.
Courtney, Patrick E.
DiGeronimo, Richard
Hagan, Paul
Lutkenhoff, Bernard

Retired:
Reverend Monsignors—
Foley, Maurice D., Our Lady of the Lakes Parish, 543 S. Main St., Monticello, IN 47960. Tel: 219-583-5023
Foley, Maurice D., Albertine Home, 1501 Hoffman St., Hammond, IN 46327-1764. Tel: 219-937-9211
Klein, Sylvester P., St. Joseph Center, 1440 W. Division Rd., Tipton, IN 46072-8584. Tel: 765-675-4146
Potthoff, Fred E., 37 Wea Oaks St., Lafayette, IN 47905-3406. Tel: 765-474-7152
Sego, Arthur A., 6476 Eime Rd., Dittmer, MO 63023

Reverend Fathers—
Bruetsch, Joseph J., St. Mary Cathedral, 1212 South St., Lafayette, IN 47901-1576. Tel: 765-742-4440
Eckert, Carl E., Century Village Healthcare, 705 N. Meridan St., Rm. 501, Greentown, IN 46936-1246. Tel: 765-628-3377
Fosselman, Robert J., 3554 E. Bailey Rd., Monticello, IN 47960-7040. Tel: 219-253-7406
Funcheon, Gerald A., 1629 George Washington Way, Apt. 323, Richland, WA 99352. Tel: 509-946-4600
Hardebeck, Donald E., 5243 N. Crab Apple Loop, Monticello, IN 47960-7056. Tel: 219-583-6417
Heilman, Thomas O., 4511 Columbus Ave., Apt M89, Anderson, IN 46013-5118. Tel: 765-649-0777
Matuszak, Edward S., 619 1/2 E. 10th St., Erie, PA 16503-1315. Tel: 814-455-1166
Puetz, Richard W., St. Elizabeth Healthcare Center, 701 Armory Rd., Rm. 409, Delphi, IN 46923-1915. Tel: 765-564-2182
Remaklus, Charles W., 708 N. Mohee Dr., Hartford City, IN 47348-8603. Tel: 765-348-1998
Ruffing, Joseph R., 204 Cedar Creek Rd., Princeton, KY 42445-2341. Tel: 502-365-2932
Scheck, Francis M., 3920 E. 200 N., Lafayette, IN 47905-7855. Tel: 765-742-7488
Schiavone, Jeldo J., P.O. Box 13484, Tampa, FL 33681-3484. Tel: 813-835-0377
Schott, Victor P., 3706 E. Wilson Rd., Muncie, IN 47303-6203. Tel: 765-284-7355
Weller, Harold E., P.O. Box 235, Kewanna, IN 46939. Tel: 219-223-2305
Zimmer, Thomas J., 3814 Sunray Dr., Holiday, FL 34691-3239. Tel: 813-943-5112

Permanent Deacons:
Castillo, Domingo, St. Paul, Marion
Cloud, H. William, St. Alphonsus, Zionsville
Nevinger, Ronald, St. Boniface, Lafayette
Rahill, William, Our Lady of Mount Carmel, Carmel
Roscoe, John, Holy Spirit, Fishers

INSTITUTIONS LOCATED IN THE DIOCESE

[A] COLLEGES AND UNIVERSITIES

RENSSELAER *Saint Joseph's College*, 47978. Tel: 219-866-6000
For a complete listing, refer to the Colleges and Universities section.

[B] HIGH SCHOOLS, INTER-PAROCHIAL

LAFAYETTE. *Central Catholic Junior-Senior High School*, 2410 S. Ninth St., 47905. Tel: 765-474-2496. David L. Worland, Prin.; Miss Helen Klemme, Dir. Religious Studies. Lay Teachers 29; Students 364.

[C] GENERAL HOSPITALS

LAFAYETTE. *St. Elizabeth Medical Center*, 1501 Hartford St., P.O. Box 7501, 47903. Tel: 765-423-6011
For a complete listing, refer to the Hospitals section.

ANDERSON. *Saint John's Health System*, 2015 Jackson St., 46016. Tel: 765-649-2511
For a complete listing, refer to the Hospitals section.

ELWOOD. *St. Vincent Mercy Hospital, Inc.*, 1331 South A St., 46036-1942. Tel: 765-552-4600; Fax: 765-552-4700
For a complete listing, refer to the Hospitals section.

KOKOMO. *Saint Joseph Hospital & Health Center of Kokomo, Indiana, Inc.*, 1907 W. Sycamore St., 46901. Tel: 765-452-5611
For a complete listing, refer to the Hospitals section.

[D] NURSING HOMES

LAFAYETTE. *St. Anthony Health Care*, 1205 N. 14th St., 47904. Tel: 765-423-4861; Fax: 765-742-8790
For a complete listing, refer to the Special Care Facilities section.

DELPHI. *St. Elizabeth Healthcare Center*, 701 Armory Rd., 46923 Fax: 765-564-6384
For a complete listing, refer to the Special Care Facilities section.

[E] MONASTERIES AND RESIDENCES OF PRIESTS AND BROTHERS

LAFAYETTE. *Emmaus House*, 2500 S. Ninth St., 47905. Tel: 317-477-6441.

[F] CONVENTS AND RESIDENCES FOR SISTERS

LAFAYETTE. *Monastery of the Precious Blood*, 1106 State St., E., 47905-1219. Tel: 765-742-8227. Sr. Jacqueline Hayden, A.P.B., Supr.; Rev. John A. Bach, Chap., Res., 155 Durkee's Run Dr., 47905. Sisters Adorers of the Precious Blood. Professed 8.

ANDERSON. *Sisters of the Holy Cross*, 1007 Raible Ave., 46011. Tel: 765-642-6117. Sisters 2.
Additional addresses for Sisters of the Holy Cross: 2115 Meridian St., 46016. Tel: 765-642-2427. Sisters 3.
Sisters of the Holy Cross, Inc.

KOKOMO. *Maria Regina Mater Monastery*, 1175 N. County Rd. 300 W., 46901. Tel: 765-457-5743. Monastery of Poor Clares of the Reform of St. Colette. Mother Miriam, Abbess; Rev. Method Wilson, O.F.M., Chap. Solemnly Professed Nuns in Cloister 8; Perpetually Professed Extern Sister 1; Postulants 1.

TIPTON. *St. Joseph Center: Sisters of St. Joseph*, 1440 W. Division Rd., 46072-8584. Tel: 765-675-4146; Fax: 765-675-7471. Sr. Dorothy Gall, C.S.J., Pres. Sisters Resident at Motherhouse 30; Total in Residence 23; Total Staff 1. Tel: 765-675-6203. Friar Edmund Mundwiller, Chap.

[G] RETREAT HOUSES

HARTFORD CITY. *John XXIII Center*, 407 W. McDonald St., 47348. Tel: 317-348-4008. Rev. Keith P. Hosey, Dir.; Sr. Maureen Mangen, C.PP.S., Asst. Dir.

[H] NEWMAN CENTERS

CRAWFORDSVILLE. *Newman Center at Wabash College*, 310 S. Grant Ave., 47933. Tel: 765-362-8105. Rev. Leroy G. Kinnaman.

MUNCIE. *St. Francis of Assisi University Church*, Newman Center, 1200 W. Riverside Ave., 47303. Tel: 765-288-6180. Rev. Michael A. McKinney.

WEST LAFAYETTE. *St. Thomas Aquinas Parish and Foundation for Catholic Students Attending Purdue University*, 535 State St., 47906. Revs. Patrick R. Click, Pastor & Dir., Newman Apostolate; Tony Levi, Assoc. Pastor; Mrs. Phyllis Scanlon, Pastoral Assoc. & Admin. Dir.; Mr. Christopher O'Neal, Pastoral Assoc. In res. Revs. Frank DeRego (HON); David Buckles.

[I] MISCELLANEOUS

LAFAYETTE. *Catholic Foundation of Northcentral Indiana, Inc.*, P.O. Box 260, 47902-0260. Tel: 765-742-0275; Fax: 765-742-7513.

CARMEL. *Our Lady of Mount Carmel Parochial School*, 1047 W. 146 St., 46032. Tel: 317-846-3475. Rev. Msgr. John C. Duncan, Contact Person.

MISHAWAKA. *Alverno-Lafayette Corporation*, 1515 Dragoon Trail, P.O. Box 1290, 46546-1290.

RELIGIOUS INSTITUTES OF MEN REPRESENTED IN THE DIOCESE

For further details refer to the corresponding bracketed number in the Religious Institutes of Men or Women section.

[0520]—*Order of St. Francis Minors.*—O.F.M.
[1060]—*Society of the Precious Blood.*—C.PP.S.

RELIGIOUS INSTITUTES OF WOMEN REPRESENTED IN THE DIOCESE

[1920]—*Congregation of the Sisters of the Holy Cross.*—C.S.C.
[1070-09]—*Dominican Sisters.*—O.P.
[1780]—*Franciscan Sisters of Peace.*—F.S.P.A.
[4150]—*Irish Ursuline Union.*—O.S.U.
[0240]—*Olivetan Benedictine Sisters.*—O.S.B.
[3230]—*Poor Handmaids of Jesus Christ.*—P.H.J.C.
[2970]—*School Sisters of Notre Dame.*—S.S.N.D.
[0110]—*Sisters Adorers of the Precious Blood.*—A.P.B.
[0430]—*Sisters of Charity of the Blessed Virgin Mary.*—B.V.M.
[2990]—*Sisters of Notre Dame.* (Toledo Prov.).—S.N.D.
[3000]—*Sisters of Notre Dame de Namur.*—S.N.D.deN.
[3360]—*Sisters of Providence of Saint Mary-of-the-Woods, IN.*—S.P.
[]—*Sisters of St. Francis.* (Sylvania, OH).—O.S.F.
[1640]—*Sisters of St. Francis of Perpetual Adoration.*—O.S.F.
[3830-10]—*Sisters of St. Joseph.*—C.S.J.
[3260]—*Sisters of the Precious Blood.* (Dayton, Ohio).—C.PP.S.

NECROLOGY

† Craycraft, Duane M., Marion, IN, St. Paul. —Died Sept. 29, 1997.

Diocese of Lafayette

(Dioecesis Lafayettensis)

Most Reverend

EDWARD JOSEPH O'DONNELL, D.D.

Bishop of Lafayette; ordained April 6, 1957; appointed Titular Bishop of Britonia and Auxiliary Bishop of St. Louis December 6, 1983; consecrated February 10, 1984; appointed fifth Bishop of Lafayette November 8, 1994; installed December 16, 1994. *Mailing Address: P.O. Box 3387, Lafayette, LA, 70502.*

Most Reverend

GERARD LOUIS FREY, D.D.

Retired Bishop of Lafayette; ordained April 2, 1938; appointed Bishop of Savannah May 31, 1967; consecrated August 8, 1967; transferred to Lafayette November 7, 1972; installed January 7, 1973; retired May 13, 1989. *Office: 1408 Carmel Ave., Lafayette, LA, 70501.* Tel.: 318-261-5613.

ESTABLISHED JANUARY 11, 1918.

Square Miles 5,777.

Comprises the civil parishes (Counties) of Acadia, Evangeline, Iberia, Lafayette, St. Landry, St. Martin and St. Mary (west of Atchafalaya River) and Vermilion in the south central part of the State of Louisiana.

For legal titles of Diocese, parishes and diocesan institutions, consult the Chancery Office.

Administrative Offices: Diocesan Office Building, 1408 Carmel Ave., Lafayette, LA, 70501. Tel.: 318-261-5500; Fax: 318-261-5635.

STATISTICAL OVERVIEW

Personnel	
Bishop	1
Retired Bishops	2
Priests: Diocesan Active in Diocese	111
Priests: Active Outside Diocese	5
Priests: Diocesan in Foreign Missions	1
Priests: Retired, Sick or Absent	28
Number of Diocesan Priests	145
Religious Priests in Diocese	56
Extern Priests in Diocese	8
Ordinations:	
Diocesan Priests	6
Transitional Deacons	2
Permanent Deacons in Diocese	57
Total Brothers	32
Total Sisters	178
Parishes	
Parishes	121
With Resident Pastor:	
Resident Diocesan Priests	89
Resident Religious Priests	24
Without Resident Pastor:	
Administered by Priests	3
Administered by Permanent Deacons	1
Administered by Women Religious	3
Completely Vacant	1
Missions	35
Welfare	
Catholic Hospitals	1
Total Assisted	81,000
Health Care Centers	1
Total Assisted	16,000
Homes for the Aged	5
Total Assisted	1,200
Specialized Homes	2
Total Assisted	1,050
Special Centers for Social Services	6
Total Assisted	180,000
Educational	
Diocesan Students in Other Seminaries	28
Seminaries, Religious	1
Students Religious	15
Total Seminarians	43
High Schools, Diocesan and Parish	9
Total Students	3,755
High Schools, Private	1
Total Students	130
Elementary Schools, Diocesan and Parish	29
Total Students	11,000
Elementary Schools, Private	2
Total Students	670
Catechesis/Religious Education:	
High School Students	26,186
Elementary Students	10,571
Total Students Under Catholic Instruction	52,355
Teachers in the Diocese:	
Brothers	3
Sisters	23
Lay Teachers	820
Vital Statistics	
Receptions into the Church:	
Infant Baptism Totals	5,853
Adult Baptism Totals	173
Received into Full Communion	220
First Communions	5,396
Confirmations	4,325
Marriages:	
Catholic	1,525
Interfaith	306
Total Marriages	1,831
Deaths	3,587
Total Catholic Population	363,090
Total Population	545,000

Former Bishops—Most Rev. JULES B. JEANMARD D.D., LL.D., ord. June 11, 1903; appt. first Bishop of Lafayette, July 18, 1918; cons. Dec. 8, 1918; installed as first Bishop of Lafayette, Dec. 12, 1918; appt. Assistant at the Pontifical Throne, Dec. 8, 1943; resigned and named Titular Bishop of Bareta, March 13, 1956; died Feb. 23, 1957.—Most Rev. ROBERT E. TRACY, D.D., Auxiliary Bishop of Lafayette, March 18, 1959; appt. first Bishop of Baton Rouge, Aug. 10, 1961.—Most Rev. WARREN L. BOUDREAUX, D.D., J.C.D., Auxiliary Bishop of Lafayette, May 19, 1962; appt. second Bishop of Beaumont, Texas, June 4, 1971.—Most Rev. MAURICE SCHEXNAYDER, D.D., ord. April 11, 1925; appt. Titular Bishop of Tuscamia and Auxiliary of Lafayette, Dec. 11, 1950; cons. Feb. 22, 1951; appt. second Bishop of Lafayette, March 13, 1956; installed May 24, 1956; resigned Nov. 7, 1972; died Jan. 23, 1981.—Most Rev. GERARD L. FREY, D.D., appt. third Bishop of Lafayette, Nov. 7, 1972; installed Jan. 7, 1973; resigned May 13, 1989.—Most Rev. HARRY J. FLYNN, D.D., ord. May 28, 1960; appt. Coadjutor Bishop of Lafayette, April 19, 1986, fourth Bishop of Lafayette, May 13, 1989; appt. Coadjutor Archbishop of St. Paul, Minneapolis, Feb. 22, 1994.

Bishop's Office—Diocesan Office Building, P.O. Box 3387, Lafayette, 70502. Tel: 318-261-5614; Fax: 318-261-5603.

Administrative Offices—Diocesan Office Building, 1408 Carmel Ave., Lafayette, 70501. Tel: 318-261-5500; Fax: 318-261-5635.

Vicars General—Rev. Msgr. H. ALEXANDRE LARROQUE, J.C.D., *P.O. Box 3387, Lafayette, 70502.* Tel: 318-261-5613. Very Rev. RONALD BROUSSARD, *P.O. Box 3387, Lafayette, 70502.* Tel: 318-261-5536.

Chancellor and Director of Administration—Sr. JOANNA VALONI, S.S.N.D., *P.O. Box 3387, Lafayette, 70502.* Tel: 318-261-5611.

Deans—Rev. FRANCIS BORGIA AUBESPIN, S.V.D., East Lafayette Deanery; Rev. Msgr. GLEN J. PROVOST, West Lafayette Deanery; Very Rev. J. ROBERT ROMERO, Evangeline Deanery; Rev. MALCOLM O'LEARY, S.V.D., St. Landry Deanery; Rev. THOMAS JAMES, S.V.D., Iberia Deanery; Rev. RICHARD GREENE, St. Mary Deanery; Very Rev. RAYMOND CARIGNAN, S.S.J., Acadia Deanery; Rev. DONALD THERIOT, Vermilion Deanery.

Vicar for Religious—Sr. MILDRED LEONARDS, C.D.P., *1408 Carmel Ave., Lafayette, 70501.* Tel: 318-261-5634.

Vicar for Priests—Rev. RUSSELL HARRINGTON, *P.O. Drawer V, Lafayette, 70501.* Tel: 318-268-9677; Fax: 318-261-5545.

Tribunal—1408 Carmel Ave., Lafayette, 70501. Tel: 318-261-5623.

Officialis—Very Rev. KENNETH R. MORVANT, J.C.L.

Vice-Officiales—Revs. ROBIE ROBICHAUX, J.C.L.; ARTHUR M. WARREN.

Procurators-Advocates—Mrs. KAROL MEYNARD; Deacon EUGENE WAQUESPACK; Revs. A. REX BROUSSARD; BILL JOHN MELANCON; ROBERT COURVILLE.

Promoter of Justice—Rev. Msgr. H. A. LARROQUE, J.C.D., V.G.

Assessors—Mrs. KAROL MEYNARD; Deacon EUGENE WAGUESPACK.

Pro-Synodal Judges—Rev. Msgr. GLEN JOHN PROVOST; Revs. GRADY ESTILETTE; THOMAS FINLEY;

JUDE A. HALPHEN; ARTHUR WARREN; HERBERT MAY.
Defenders of the Bond—Revs. OVERTON JOSEPH BREAUX; J. DOUGLAS COURVILLE, J.C.L.
Coordinator of Cases—BERNARD BEYT, J.D.
Auditors—Mrs. KAROL MEYNARD; Deacon EUGENE WAGUESPACK.
Notaries—EULA B. LANDRY; BERNARD BEYT, J.D.
College of Consultors—Rev. Msgr. H. ALEXANDRE LARROQUE; Very Rev. RONALD BROUSSARD; Revs. LLOYD BENOIT; ANGELO CREMALDI; THOMAS FINLEY; AUSTIN LEGER.
Diocesan Consultors—Rev. Msgr. H. ALEXANDRE LARROQUE; Very Rev. RONALD BROUSSARD; Revs. LLOYD BENOIT; ANGELO CREMALDI; THOMAS FINLEY; L. MICHAEL HERPIN; AUSTIN LEGER.

Diocesan Offices and Directors

Adult Catechesis—GLORIA CLARK, *1408 Carmel Ave., Lafayette, 70501.* Tel: 318-261-5550.
Alcohol & Drug Abuse—PHYLLIS LUKE, *1408 Carmel Ave., Lafayette, 70501.* Tel: 318-261-5674.
Archives—ANNA JANE MARKS, *1408 Carmel Ave., Lafayette, 70501.* Tel: 318-261-5639; 261-5667.
Auxiliary Services—ELSIE HEBERT, *1408 Carmel Ave., Lafayette, 70501.* Tel: 318-261-5600.
Bishop's Services Appeal—CONNIE KLEINPETER, *1408 Carmel Ave., Lafayette, 70501.* Tel: 318-261-5641.
Black Catholics—Revs. CHESTER ARCENEAUX; RONALD BROUSSARD, V.G., *1408 Carmel Ave., Lafayette, 70501.* Tel: 318-261-5536.
Catholic Social Services—PAULA MILNER, *1408 Carmel Ave., Lafayette, 70501.* Tel: 318-261-5654.
Catholic Foundation of the Diocese of Lafayette—CONNIE KLEINPETER, *1408 Carmel Ave., Lafayette, 70501.* Tel: 318-261-5641.
Catholic Charismatic—Rev. ALBERT G. NUNEZ, *P.O. Box 40, Carencro, 70520.* Tel: 318-896-7732.
Christian Formation—Sr. LORRAINE LANDRY, S.S.N.D., *1408 Carmel Ave., Lafayette, 70501.* Tel: 318-261-5565.
Clergy Health Care & Retirement—BEVERLY BROUSSARD, *1408 Carmel Ave., Lafayette, 70501.* Tel: 318-261-5629.
Communications—Newspaper—*"Acadiana Catholic"*, THOMAS SUMMERS, Editor, *1408 Carmel Ave., Lafayette, 70501.* Tel: 318-261-5513; 261-5511; 261-5518.
Radio-TV—DAVID MERGIST, Producer/Dir., *1408 Carmel Ave., Lafayette, 70501.* Tel: 318-261-5626.
Community Services—J. BERNEL FONTENOT, *1408 Carmel Ave., Lafayette, 70501.* Tel: 318-261-5650.
Data Processing—ROBIN STEVENSON, *1408 Carmel Ave., Lafayette, 70501.* Tel: 318-261-5516.
Deaf Apostolate—MYRA MOUTON, *1408 Carmel Ave., Lafayette, 70501.* Tel: 318-261-5548.
Development—CONNIE KLEINPETER, *1408 Carmel Ave., Lafayette, 70501.* Tel: 318-261-5641.
Education / Communication—GERALD DILL, *1408 Carmel Ave., Lafayette, 70501.* Tel: 318-261-5526.
Family Life—BARBARA WALLEY, M.S.W., Mailing Address: *1408 Carmel Ave., Lafayette, 70501.* Tel: 318-261-5653.
Fiscal Administration—MARY PARKER, *P.O. Box 3387, Lafayette, 70502.* Tel: 318-261-5629.
Hispanic Ministry—Sr. VIVIAN COULON, M.S.C., *1408 Carmel Ave., Lafayette, 70501.* Tel: 318-261-5535; 261-5542.
Institutions—J. BERNEL FONTENOT, *1408 Carmel Ave., Lafayette, 70501.* Tel: 318-261-5650.
Justice and Peace—UNA HARGRAVE, *1408 Carmel Ave., Lafayette, 70501.* Tel: 318-261-5545.
Migration Refugee Services—TINA DAVIS, *1408 Carmel Ave., Lafayette, 70501.* Tel: 318-261-5535.
Office for Persons with Disabilities—MYRA MOUTON, *1404 Carmel Ave., Lafayette, 70501.* Tel: 318-261-5548.
Parish Services—Sr. LORRAINE LANDRY, S.S.N.D., *1408 Carmel Ave., Lafayette, 70501.* Tel: 318-261-5565.
Parish Finances—JEANNINE REYNOLDS, Mgr., *P.O. Box 3387, Lafayette, 70502.* Tel: 318-261-5632.
Permanent Diaconate—Deacon RONALD A. BOREL, *1408 Carmel Ave., Lafayette, 70501.* Tel: 318-261-5609.
Pro-Life Issues—BRENDA DESORMEAUX, *1408 Carmel Ave., Lafayette, 70501.* Tel: 318-261-5607.
Prison Ministry—1408 Carmel Ave., Lafayette, 70501. Tel: 318-261-5545.
Religious Education and Pastoral Ministry—Sr. CARMELITA LATIOLAIS, *1408 Carmel Ave., Lafayette, 70501.* Tel: 318-261-5674.
Religious Personnel—Sr. MILDRED LEONARDS, C.D.P., Vicar, *1408 Carmel Ave., Lafayette, 70501.* Tel: 318-261-5634.
Research & Information—A. JAMES BROUSSARD, *1408 Carmel Ave., Lafayette, 70501.* Tel: 318-261-5608.
Schools—RICHARD MEAUX, Supt., *1408 Carmel Ave., Lafayette, 70501.* Tel: 318-261-5529.
Seminarians—Rev. RUSSELL HARRINGTON, *1408 Carmel Ave., Lafayette, 70501.* Tel: 318-261-5690.
Vocations—Rev. THOMAS VOORHIES, *206 W. Church St., Delcambre, 70528.* Tel: 318-685-4426.
Youth Ministry—KATHY STELLY, *1408 Carmel Ave., Lafayette, 70501.* Tel: 318-261-5551.
Worship—Rev. JASON MOUTON, *1408 Carmel Ave., Lafayette, 70501.* Tel: 318-261-5536.

Diocesan Commissions and Boards

Building Review Board—Sr. JOANNA VALONI, S.S.N.D., *1408 Carmel Ave., Lafayette, 70501.* Tel: 318-261-5611.
Campus Ministry—Rev. W. CURTIS MALLET, Dir., *Our Lady of Wisdom Catholic Student Center, P.O. Box 43271, Lafayette, 70504.* Tel: 318-232-8742.
Catholic Daughters of America—Rev. DONALD PELOUS, *St. Bernard Church, 204 N. Main St., Breaux Bridge, 70517.* Tel: 318-332-2159.
Catholic Relief Services—UNA HARGRAVE, *1408 Carmel Ave., Lafayette, 70501.* Tel: 318-261-5545.
Clergy Personnel Advisory Board—Rev. LOUIS RICHARD, *St. Michael Church, P.O. Box 406, Crowley, 70527.* Tel: 318-783-7394.
Clergy Welfare Commission—Rev. Msgr. RICHARD MOUTON, Chm., *P.O. Box 80489, Lafayette, 70598.* Tel: 318-232-4656.
Continuing Formation of the Clergy—Rev. RUSSELL HARRINGTON, *1408 Carmel Dr., Lafayette, 70501.* Tel: 318-261-5690.
Credit Union—116 St. Jules St., Lafayette, 70506. Tel: 318-261-1151.
Cursillo—Rev. OVERTON JOSEPH BREAUX, *P.O. Box 8, Duson, 70529-0008.* Tel: 318-873-4962.
Diocesan Council of Catholic Women—Rev. Msgr. J. GUY LEMOINE, Diocesan Moderator, *St. Peter Church, P.O. Box 12507, New Iberia, 70562.* Tel: 318-369-3816.
Ecumenism—Rev. HERBERT DELAUNAY, *1112 Saturn Rd., Morgan City, 70380.* Tel: 504-395-2470.
Finance Advisory Board—LEON K. POCHE, K.S.G., *633 W. 17th St., Crowley, 70526.* Tel: 318-783-0650.
Holy Childhood—Sr. MILDRED LEONARDS, C.D.P., *1408 Carmel Ave., Lafayette, 70501.* Tel: 318-261-5634.
Holy Name Society—Vacant.
Hospitals—Vacant; Coord., Health Affairs, *P.O. Box 3387, Lafayette, 70502.* Tel: 318-261-5613.
Knights of Columbus—Rev. GEORGE SIMON, Diocesan Chap., *St. Martin de Porres, P.O. Box 728, Scott, 70583.* Tel: 318-232-1968.
Legion of Mary—Vacant.
Parish Boundaries and Future Parish Development Board—Sr. JOANNA VALONI, S.S.N.D., *1408 Carmel Ave., Lafayette, 70501.* Tel: 318-261-5611.
Retreats—Rev. JAMES C. BABB, S.J., *Our Lady of the Oaks Retreat House, P.O. Box D, Grand Coteau, 70541.* Tel: 318-662-5410. Rev. THOMAS MADDEN, S.J., Dir., *Jesuit Spirituality Center, P.O. Box C, Grand Coteau, 70541.* Tel: 318-662-5251.
Scouting—Rev. KENNETH DOMINGUE, Chap., *St. Augustine Church, P.O. Box 696, Basile, 70515.* Tel: 318-432-6817. ROBERT MARCEAUX, Lay Chm., *101 Bellridge Dr., Lafayette, 70506.* Tel: 318-984-1767.
Society for the Propagation of the Faith—Sr. MILDRED LEONARDS, C.D.P., *P.O. Box 3387, Lafayette, 70502.* Tel: 318-261-5634.

CLERGY, PARISHES, MISSIONS AND PAROCHIAL SCHOOLS

CITY OF LAFAYETTE
(Lafayette Parish)

1—ST. JOHN THE EVANGELIST CATHEDRAL, Revs. Keith Derouen, Rector; Cedric Sonnier; Russel J. Harrington; Deacon James Oliver. In res., Rev. Kurian Kanat (India).
Res., 515 Cathedral St., P.O. Drawer V, 70502. Tel: 318-232-1322; Fax: 318-232-1379.
School—Cathedral-Carmel Elementary, 848 St. John St., 70502. Tel: 318-235-5577; Fax: 318-261-9493. Mr. Linden Bercegeay, Prin.
Sisters of Mt. Carmel 5; Brothers of the Christian Schools 4; Lay Teachers 48; Students 815.

2—ST. PAUL THE APOSTLE, Rev. Dennet Jung, O.F.M.
Res., 326 S. Washington St., 70501. Tel: 318-235-0272; Fax: 318-235-3100.
Mission—Lafayette, Our Lady of Good Hope.

3—HOLY CROSS, Rev. Martin Borcherding; Deacons Michael Clark; Norbert Luke.
Res., 505 Broadmoor Blvd., 70503. Tel: 318-984-9636; Fax: 318-988-3790.

4—IMMACULATE HEART OF MARY, Revs. Francis Borgin Aubespin, S.V.D.; Stephan Brown, S.V.D.; Deacon Anthony Ozene. In res., Rev. Charles Heskamp, S.V.D.
Res., 818-12th St., P.O. Box 2398, 70502. Tel: 318-235-4618; Fax: 318-235-4775. [CEM]
School—800-12th St., 70502. Tel: 318-235-7843; 235-4775. Sr. Mary Joseph Charles, S.S.F., Prin.
Sisters of Holy Family 4; Lay Teachers 8; Students 191.

5—OUR LADY OF FATIMA, Rev. Msgr. Glen John Provost.
Res., 2319 Johnston St., 70503. Tel: 318-232-8945; Fax: 318-232-0323.
School—2315 Johnston St., 70503. Tel: 318-235-2464; Fax: 318-235-1320. Mr. Lloyd Guiberteau, Prin.
Lay Teachers 47; Students 900.

6—OUR LADY OF WISDOM, UNIVERSITY OF SOUTHWESTERN LOUISIANA, Rev. W. Curtis Mallet. In res., Rev. Thomas Finley.
Mailing Address: P.O. Box 42371, 70504. Tel: 318-232-8741; Fax: 318-236-6737.

7—OUR LADY QUEEN OF PEACE, Rev. Thomas Jason Mouton; Deacon Louis J. Lloyd.
Res., 145 Martin Luther King Jr. Dr., 70501. Tel: 318-233-1591; Fax: 318-232-5961.

8—ST. ANTHONY, Rev. Frank A. Charles, S.V.D.; Deacon Alvin Ray Dejean.
Res., 615 Edison St., 70501. Tel: 318-234-5855; Fax: 318-264-1507.

9—ST. EDMOND, Rev. Gary Schexnayder; Deacon Paul D. Matte.
Res., 4131 W. Congress St., 70506. Tel: 318-981-0874; Fax: 318-989-1417.

10—ST. ELIZABETH SETON, Rev. Harold Trahan.
Office: 610 Raintree Tr., 70507. Tel: 318-235-1483; Fax: 318-235-9645.
Res., 603 Raintree Tr., 70507. Tel: 318-232-7365.

11—ST. GENEVIEVE, Revs. Jody Simoneaux; Joseph Aaron Melancon.
Res., 417 E. Simcoe St., P.O. Box 90307, 70509. Tel: 318-234-5147; Fax: 318-234-8654. [CEM]
School—201 Elizabeth St., 70501. Tel: 318-234-5257; Fax: 318-237-6065. Mrs. Susan Stephen, Prin.
Lay Teachers 22; Students 374.
Mission—Lafayette, Gift of Mary Chapel.

12—ST. JULES, Rev. J. Douglas Courville.
Res., 116 St. Jules St., 70506. Tel: 318-234-2727; Fax: 318-261-1397.

13—ST. LEO, Rev. Michael J. Arnaud. In res., Rev. Richard Fabre.
Res., 300 W. Alexander St., 70501. Tel: 318-232-2404; Fax: 318-261-0801.
School—Sts. Leo-Seton, 502 St. Leo St., 70501. Tel: 318-234-5510. Mr. Lester Bourg, Prin.
Sisters 2; Lay Teachers 18; Students 483.

14—ST. MARY, MOTHER OF THE CHURCH, Rev. Msgr. Robert G. Angelle; Rev. Howard Blessing; Deacon Julian Judice.
Res., 419 Doucet Rd., 70503. Tel: 318-981-3379; Fax: 318-981-5445.
School—St. Mary Early Learning Center, (Grades Pre-K). Tel: 318-984-3750. Mrs. Renee McAlister, Prin.
Students 120.

15—ST. PATRICK, Rev. Robie E. Robichaux, J.C.L.
Res., 107 Petro St., 70501. Tel: 318-237-0988; Fax: 318-233-8868.

16—ST. PIUS X, Rev. Msgr. Richard von Phul Mouton.
Res., 200 E. Bayou Pkwy., P.O. Box 80489, 70598. Tel: 318-232-4656; Fax: 318-233-9468.
School—Our Lady of Life Preschool, 201 E. Bayou Pkwy., 70508. Tel: 318-237-3139. Mrs. Shirley Alexander, Dir.

OUTSIDE THE CITY OF LAFAYETTE

Abbeville, Vermilion Parish, St. Mary Magdalen, Revs. Donald C. Theriot; Kenneth Mayne; Mark Gerard Derise.
Mailing Address: P.O. Box D, 70511. Tel: 318-893-0244; 0245; Fax: 318-893-0427.
High School—Vermilion Catholic, 425 Park Ave., 70511. Tel: 318-893-6636; Fax: 318-893-8718. Mr. William Simon, Prin.
Sisters 1; Lay Teachers 20; Students 245.
St. Therese of the Child Jesus, Rev. Chester Arceneaux; Deacon Samuel Theriot.
Mailing Address: P.O. Box 609, 70511. Tel: 318-893-5631; Fax: 318-893-9168.

Arnaudville, St. Landry Parish, St. Francis Regis, Rev. William Ruskoski.
Mailing Address: P.O. Box 36, 70512. Tel: 318-754-5912. [CEM]
St. Catherine, Rev. William Ruskoski; Sr. Paula Derise, O.Carm., Pastoral Assoc.
Mailing Address: P.O. Box 53, 70512. Tel: 318-754-7754.

Baldwin, St. Mary Parish, Sacred Heart, Rev. Bill John Melancon; Deacons Harold Achee; Gerald Bourg.
Mailing Address: P.O. Box 308, 70514. Tel: 318-923-7781; Fax: 318-923-7781.

Basile, Evangeline Parish, St. Augustine, Rev. Kenneth Domingue.
Res., 2717 Third St., P.O. Box 696, 70515. Tel: 318-432-6817; Fax: 318-432-5203.
Mission—Basile, Assumption.

Bayou Vista, St. Mary Parish, St. Bernadette, Rev. Herbert C. deLaunay.
Res., 1112 Saturn Rd., Morgan City, 70380. Tel: 504-395-2470; Fax: 504-395-6514.

Berwick, St. Mary Parish, St. Stephen, Rev. Paul G. Bienvenu.
Res., 3217 Second St., 70342. Tel: 504-385-1280; Fax: 504-385-1279.

Breaux Bridge, St. Martin Parish, St. Bernard, Rev. Donald P. Pelous. In res., Rev. J. Wilson Matt; Deacons Harold Richard; Marcel P. Hebert, Jr.
Res., 204 N. Main St., 70517. Tel: 318-332-2159; Fax: 318-332-2276. [JC 2]
School—251 E. Bridge St., 70517. Tel: 318-332-5350; Fax: 318-332-5894. Keith Bartlett, Prin.
Sisters 1; Lay Teachers 23; Students 496.

St. Francis of Assisi, Rev. Richard F. Wagner, S.S.J.
Res., 610 N. Main St., 70517. Tel: 318-332-2250; Fax: 318-332-2052. [CEM]

Broussard, Lafayette Parish, Sacred Heart of Jesus, Rev. Msgr. L. Michael Herpin.
Mailing Address: P.O. Box 737, 70518. Tel: 318-837-1864; Fax: 318-837-1703.
School—St. Cecilia, P.O. Box 309, 70518. Tel: 318-837-6363; Fax: 318-837-3688. Mr. Russell Meyer, Prin.
Lay Teachers 23; Students 447.

St. Joseph, Rev. Brendan Murphy, S.V.D.
Mailing Address: P.O. Box 278, 70518. Tel: 318-837-6218; Fax: 318-837-6218.
Mission—Cade, St. Anthony.

Cankton, St. Landry Parish, St. John Berchmans, Rev. Jude A. Halphen.
Res., 552 Main St., 70584-9722. Tel: 318-668-4413; Fax: 318-668-4505.

Carencro, Lafayette Parish, St. Peter, Rev. Gregory Downs.
Mailing Address: P.O. Box 40, 70520. Tel: 318-896-9408; Fax: 318-896-9414.
School—Carencro Catholic, 200 W. St. Peter St., 70520. Tel: 318-896-8973. Mrs. Julie Breaux, Prin.
Lay Teachers 28; Students 529.

Our Lady of the Assumption, Rev. Paul J. LaFleur; Deacon John Thibodeaux.
Res., 410 N. Michaud St., 70520. Tel: 318-896-8304. [CEM]

Catahoula, St. Martin Parish, St. Rita, Rev. Louis Allen Breaux.
Res., 1006 St. Rita Hwy., St. Martinville, 70582. Tel: 318-394-4679.

Cecilia, St. Martin Parish, St. Joseph, Rev. Lloyd F. Benoit.
Mailing Address: P.O. Box 279, 70521. Tel: 318-667-6344; Fax: 318-667-7073. [JC]

St. Rose of Lima, Rev. Norbert W. Stein, S.S.J.
Mailing Address: P.O. Box 126, 70521. Tel: 318-667-6555; Fax: 318-667-6686. [CEM]

Centerville, St. Mary Parish, St. Joseph, Rev. Oneil A. Landry.
Res., 70522. Tel: 318-836-5659. [CEM]

Charenton, St. Mary Parish, Immaculate Conception, Rev. William Crumley, C.S.C.
Mailing Address: P.O. Box 278, 70523. Tel: 318-923-4281.

Chataignier, Evangeline Parish, Our Lady of Mount Carmel, Deacons Thomas J. Richard, Admin.; Charles Ortego. In res., Rev. T. Alcide Sonnier.
Mailing Address: P.O. Box 100, 70524. Tel: 318-885-3223; Fax: 318-885-3223.

Church Point, Acadia Parish, Our Lady of the Sacred Heart, Revs. Frederick O. Swenson; Donald N. Leger.
Res., 118 N. Rogers St., P.O. Box 403, 70525. Tel: 318-684-5494; Fax: 318-684-2133. [CEM 3][JC]
School—Our Mother of Peace, 218 N. Rogers St., 70525. Tel: 318-684-5780. Mr. Don Soucy, Prin.
Sisters 1; Lay Teachers 14; Students 292.
Chapel—Lewisburg, St. John.

Our Mother of Mercy, Rev. Francis Butler, S.S.J.
Res., 693 N. Main St., P.O. Box 237, 70525. Tel: 318-684-2319; Fax: 318-684-3086. [JC]

Coteau, Iberia Parish, Our Lady of Prompt Succor, Rev. Paul A. Thibodeaux.
Res., 2409 Coteau Rd., New Iberia, 70560. Tel: 318-369-6993. [CEM]

Coteau Holmes, St. Martin Parish, St. Elizabeth, Rev. Thomas Edapaddy, C.M.I. (India).
Office: 1006 St. Elizabeth St., St. Martinville, 70582. Tel: 318-394-6684; 394-7530.

Cow Island, Vermilion Parish, St. Anne, Rev. Lloyd Bordelon; Deacon Benedict M. Morello.
Res., 17315 Lionel Rd., Abbeville, 70510. Tel: 318-643-7714; Fax: 318-643-1021. [CEM]
Missions—Forked Island, Immaculate Conception; Pecan Island, Sacred Heart.

Crowley, Acadia Parish, St. Michael Archangel, Revs. Louis J. Richard; Rusty P. Richard.
Mailing Address: P.O. Box 406, 70527. Tel: 318-783-7394; Fax: 318-788-0237.
School—805 E. Northern Ave., 70527. Tel: 318-783-1410; Fax: 318-783-8547. Co-Principals: Mrs. Clementine Kirsh; Mrs. Myra Broussard.
Lay Teachers 27; Students 439.

Immaculate Heart of Mary, Revs. Joseph X. Steffes, C.SS.R.; Joseph Greenwell, C.SS.R. In res., Rev. Stephen Plei, C.SS.R.
Res., 901 E. Elm St., 70526. Tel: 318-783-3498; Fax: 318-783-7444.
School—Redemptorist Grade School, 606 South Ave. N., 70526. Tel: 318-783-4466. Mr. Dan Bouillion, Prin.
Lay Teachers 12; Students 301.

St. Theresa, Rev. Raymond P. Carignan, S.S.J.
Res., 417 W. 3rd St., 70526. Tel: 318-783-1880.

Delcambre, Vermilion Parish, Our Lady of the Lake, Rev. Thomas P. Voorhies. In res., Rev. Mario Romero.
Res., 206 W. Church St., 70528. Tel: 318-685-4426; Fax: 318-685-4426. [CEM]

Saint Martin de Porres, Rev. Thomas P. Voorhies.
Res., 206 W. Church St., 70528. Tel: 318-685-4426; Fax: 318-685-4426.

Duralde, Evangeline Parish, Annunciation of the B.V.M., Sr. Diane Hooley, O.P., Admin.
Res., 4476 Duralde Hwy., Eunice, 70535. Tel: 318-457-4849; Fax: 318-457-4502.

Duson, Lafayette Parish, St. Theresa of the Child Jesus, Rev. O. Joseph Breaux.
Mailing Address: P.O. Box 8, 70529. Tel: 318-873-4962; Fax: 318-873-3023.

St. Benedict the Moor, Very Rev. Ronald Broussard, V.G.
Mailing Address: P.O. Box 127, 70529. Tel: 318-873-6772.

Erath, Vermilion Parish, Our Lady of Lourdes, Rev. Wayne J. Duet.
Res., 700 S. Broadway, 70533. Tel: 318-937-6888. [CEM]

Eunice, St. Landry Parish, St. Anthony of Padua, Revs. Joseph J. Alexander; Mitchell Gregory Guidry.
Mailing Address: P.O. Box 31, 70535. Tel: 318-457-5285; Fax: 318-457-7904. [CEM][JC]
School—St. Edmund Elementary, 331 N. 3rd St., 70535. Tel: 318-457-5988. Sr. Stephanie Brignac, M.S.C., Prin.
High School—St. Edmund High, 351 W. Magnolia St., 70535. Tel: 318-457-2592. Mr. Harry Summerlin, Prin.
Lay Teachers 34; Students: Elementary 349; High 288.

St. Mathilda, Rev. Joseph V. Tyson, S.S.J.
Mailing Address: P.O. Box 346, 70535. Tel: 318-457-3286. [JC]

St. Thomas More, Rev. Jules M. Arceneaux; Deacon David Guillory.
Mailing Address: P.O. Box 1022, 70535. Tel: 318-457-8107; Fax: 318-457-1735.

Evangeline, Acadia Parish, St. Joseph, Rev. Donald Nicholas Leger.
Mailing Address: P.O. Box 183, 70537. Tel: 318-824-4995; Fax: 318-824-4995. [CEM]
Mission—Petit Mamou, St. Jules.

Four Corners, St. Mary Parish, St. Peter the Apostle, Rev. Barry Crochet.
Res., 1325 Big Four Corners Rd., Franklin, 70538. Tel: 318-276-5256; Fax: 318-276-5256.
Missions—Glencoe, St. Joan of Arc; Cypremort Point, St. Francis, (Independent Mission).

Franklin, St. Mary Parish, Assumption B.V.M., Rev. Michael Russo; Deacon Douglas Hebert.
Mailing Address: 913 Main St., 70538. Tel: 318-828-3869; Fax: 318-828-3872.
School—St. John Elementary, 924 Main St., 70538. Tel: 318-828-2648; Fax: 318-828-2112. Joseph Donald Doucet, Prin.
Lay Teachers 19; Students 344.
High School—Hanson High School, 903 Anderson St., 70538. Tel: 318-828-3487; Fax: 318-828-7431. Mr. Donald Dunbar, Prin.
Lay Teachers 28; Students 370.

St. Jules, Rev. George Thychery (India); Deacons Edward Bodin; Joseph Thomas.
Res., 601 Magnolia St., 70538. Tel: 318-828-1714.
Mission—Verdunville, Immaculate Conception.

Grand Coteau, St. Landry Parish, St. Charles Borromeo, Revs. Warren Broussard, S.J.; John Welsh, S.J.; Deacon Samuel Henry.
Mailing Address: P.O. Drawer A, 70541. Tel: 318-662-5279; Fax: 318-662-5270.
School—St. Ignatius, P.O. Drawer J, 70541. Tel: 318-662-3325. Mr. Ervin Fontenot, Prin.
Brothers 1; Sisters 1; Lay Teachers 14; Students 300.
Mission—Bellevue, Christ the King.

Grand Prairie, St. Landry Parish, St. Peter, Rev. Msgr. Louis J. Melancon.
Res., 1074 Hwy. 748, Washington, 70589. Tel: 318-826-3870; Fax: 318-826-5635.
Mission—Plaisance, St. Andrew.

Gueydan, Vermilion Parish, St. Peter, Rev. Grady J. Estilette.
Res., 603 Main St., P.O. Box 28, 70542. Tel: 318-536-9258.
School—513 6th St., 70542. Tel: 318-536-9460. Sr. Ann Louise Arno, M.S.C., Prin.
Sisters 3; Lay Teachers 8; Students 136.
Mission—Mulvey, St. David.

Henderson, St. Martin Parish, Our Lady of Mercy, Rev. Jefferson J. DeBlanc.
Res., Henderson Sta., P.O. Box 587, Breaux Bridge, 70517. Tel: 318-228-2352; Fax: 318-228-2352.
Mission—Butte La Rose, Sacred Heart.

Henry, Vermilion Parish, St. John, Rev. Charles F. Langlois.
Res., 18534 La. Hwy. 689, Erath, 70533. Tel: 318-937-5108; Fax: 318-937-0002. [CEM]
Mission—Esther, St. James.

Iota, Acadia Parish, St. Joseph, Revs. George Byers, C.P.M.; Albert J. Heidecke, C.P.M.
Mailing Address: P.O. Box 710, 70543. Tel: 318-779-2627.
School—St. Francis, P.O. Box 870, 70543. Tel: 318-779-2527. Mrs. Mary Ann Hadaway, Prin.
Lay Teachers 10; Students 198.
Mission—Egan, Acadia Parish, St. Michael, P.O. Box 298, Egan, 70531. Tel: 318-788-0529.

Jeanerette, Iberia Parish, St. John the Evangelist, Rev. Edward Degeyter; Deacon Theodule Landry.
Res., 1510 Church St., 70544. Tel: 318-276-4576; Fax: 318-276-5804.
School—St. Joseph, 10917 Old Jeanerette Rd., 70544. Tel: 318-276-3615; Fax: 318-276-3616. Mrs. Corinne Hebert, Prin.
Lay Teachers 19; Students 208.

Our Lady of the Rosary, Rev. Joseph E. Detig, S.V.D.
Res., 11200 Old Jeanerette Rd., 70544. Tel: 318-276-6900; Fax: 318-276-6900. [CEM][JC]

Judice, Lafayette Parish, St. Basil, Rev. Henry J. Broussard.
Res., 1803 Duhon Rd. (Judice), Duson, 70529. Tel: 318-984-2179; Fax: 318-988-3793. [CEM]

Kaplan, Vermilion Parish, Our Lady of the Holy Rosary, Revs. William C. Blanda; Donovan J. Labbe; Deacon Paul R. Eleazar.
Mailing Address: P.O. Box 429, 70548. Tel: 318-643-6472; Fax: 318-643-2516. [JC]
School—Maltrait Memorial, One Crusader Square, 70548. Tel: 318-643-7765; Fax: 318-643-2516. Mrs. Renee C. Meaux, Prin.
Lay Teachers 10; Students 140.
Mission—Kaplan, Vermilion Parish, St. Frances Xavier Cabrini.

Krotz Springs, St. Landry Parish, St. Anthony, Rev. Robert W. Courville.
Mailing Address: P.O. Box 425, 70750. Tel: 318-566-3527; Fax: 318-566-2803. [CEM]

Lawtell, St. Landry Parish, St. Bridget, Rev. Daniel Picard.
Mailing Address: P.O. Box 156, 70550. Tel: 318-543-7591; Fax: 318-543-7593. [CEM]
Mission—Prairie Ronde, Sacred Heart.

Holy Family, Rev. Andrew Peter John (India).
Mailing Address: P.O. Box 310, 70550. Tel: 318-543-2366; Fax: 318-543-8281.
Mission—Plaquemine Point, St. Agnes.

Lebeau, St. Landry Parish, Immaculate Conception. Unassigned.
Mailing Address: P.O. Box 415, 71345. Tel: 318-623-4783. [CEM]
Mission—Rideau Settlement, Sacred Heart.

Leonville, St. Landry Parish, St. Leo the Great, Rev. Daniel Schexnayder.
Mailing Address: P.O. Box 8, 70551. Tel: 318-879-2365; Fax: 318-879-3050. [JC]

St. Catherine, Rev. Raymond Hannah, S.V.D.
Mailing Address: P.O. Box 147, 70551. Tel: 318-879-2940.
Mission—Prairie Laurent, St. Jules.

Leroy, Vermilion Parish, Our Lady of Perpetual Help, Revs. A. Rex Broussard; Thomas Montelaro.
Res., 12995 Louisiana Hwy. 699, Maurice, 70555. Tel: 318-893-0610; Fax: 318-893-0694. [CEM]

Loreauville, Iberia Parish, St. Joseph, Rev. Charles Thevis.
Mailing Address: P.O. Box 365, 70552. Tel: 318-229-4254; Fax: 318-229-4255. [CEM]

Our Lady of Victory, Rev. John Vianney Choorackunnel, C.M.I. (India).
Mailing Address: P.O. Box 387, 70552. Tel: 318-229-8284; Fax: 318-229-4255. [JC]

Louisa, St. Mary Parish, St. Helen, Rev. Thomas Thanh Nguyen.
Res., 108 St. Helen Church Ln., Franklin, 70538. Tel: 318-276-5256.

Lydia, Iberia Parish, St. Nicholas, Rev. Emmanuel Fernandez; Deacon L. J. Freyou.
Mailing Address: P.O. Box 369, 70569. Tel: 318-364-5228.

Lyons Point, Acadia Parish, St. John the Baptist, Rev. Albert G. Nunez; Deacon Rodless Leleux.
Res., 8021 Lyons Point Highway, Crowley, 70526. Tel: 318-783-2457; Fax: 318-783-9015. [CEM]

Mallet, St. Landry Parish, St. Ann, Rev. Andrew Peter John (India); Deacon Jonas Mason.
Mailing Address: P.O. Box 310, Lawtell, 70550. Tel: 318-543-2385; Fax: 318-543-8281.

Mamou, Evangeline Parish, St. Ann, Revs. Timothy Richard; Pius Vallooram, C.M.I.
Parish Center: 716 Sixth St., 70554. Tel: 318-468-3159; Fax: 318-468-3427.
Mission—Vidrine, Holy Spirit.

Maurice, Vermilion Parish, St. Alphonsus, Rev. Martin C. Leonards.
Res., 8700 Maurice Ave., P.O. Box 190, 70555. Tel: 318-893-4099; Fax: 318-893-2474. [CEM]
St. Joseph, Rev. William R. Oliver, S.V.D.
Mailing Address: P.O. Box 250, 70555. Tel: 318-893-5428; Fax: 318-893-5428.

Melville, St. Landry Parish, St. John the Evangelist, Rev. Jose L.F. Padinjarepeedika, C.M.I. (India).
Mailing Address: 318 First St., P.O. Box 256, 71353-0256. Tel: 318-623-4957; Fax: 318-623-4970.
Mission—Palmetto, St. Thomas.

Mermentau, Acadia Parish, St. John the Evangelist, Rev. Msgr. Paul Metrejean; Deacon Leon Lejeune.
Mailing Address: P.O. Box 176, 70556. Tel: 318-824-2278; Fax: 318-824-9624. [CEM]
Mission—Estherwood, St. Margaret.

Milton, Lafayette Parish, St. Joseph, Rev. Louis J. Richard; Deacon Cody Miller.
Mailing Address: P.O. Box 299, 70558. Tel: 318-856-5997; Fax: 318-856-5955.

Mire, Acadia Parish, Assumption of the Blessed Virgin Mary, Rev. Donald J. Hebert; Deacon J. Douglas Melancon.
Res., 6080 Mire Hwy., Church Point, 70525. Tel: 318-873-6574.

Morrow, St. Landry Parish, St. Peter, Rev. George Thychary.
Mailing Address: P.O. Box 319, 71356. Tel: 318-346-7010.
Mission—Whiteville, Resurrection.

Morse, Acadia Parish, Immaculate Conception, Rev. Donald Pousson.
Mailing Address: P.O. Box 297, 70559. Tel: 318-783-2968.
Mission—Midland, St. Aloysius.

Mowata, Acadia Parish, St. Lawrence, Rev. George Heffner, S.V.D.
Res., 29031 Crowley-Eunice Hwy., Eunice, 70535. Tel: 318-457-2739; Fax: 318-457-2739. [CEM 2]

New Iberia, Iberia Parish,

1—St. Peter, Rev. Msgr. J. Guy Lemoine; Rev. William Rogalla; Deacons Carl Conrad; Ronald H. Broussard; James Wilson; Kenneth Waguespack. In res., Rev. Msgr. John H. Disch.
Mailing Address: P.O. Box 12507, 70562. Tel: 318-369-3816; Fax: 318-369-3192.

2—Nativity of Our Lady, Rev. Albert J. Boumans.
Res., Richelieu Circle, 70560. Tel: 318-364-8360; Fax: 318-364-1509. [CEM]

3—Our Lady of Perpetual Help, Rev. Michael Guidry; Deacons Ulysse J. Boudreaux; Ronald Borel; Albert A. Woodburn; George Sikes.
Res., 1303 St. Jude Ave., 70560. Tel: 318-365-5481; Fax: 318-365-5483.

4—St. Edward, Revs. Thomas James, S.V.D.; Ryszard Kalinowski, S.V.D. In res., Rev. Gerald Lewis, S.V.D.
Res., 175 Frere St., 70560. Tel: 318-369-3101; Fax: 318-369-3118. [CEM][JC]
School—720 Providence St., 70560. Tel: 318-369-6764. Sr. Michelle Callahan, S.B.S., Prin.
Sisters of the Blessed Sacrament 5; Lay Teachers 14; Students 360.
Mission—Olivier, St. Jude.

5—Sacred Heart of Jesus, Rev. Steven C. LeBlanc.
Res., 2514 Old Jeanerette Rd., 70560. Tel: 318-364-4439; Fax: 318-948-1295.

Opelousas, St. Landry Parish,

1—St. Landry, Rev. Charles Nicholas Trahan; Deacons Carlo Cannatella; John W. Miller. In res., Rev. Viateur Desilets.
Res., P.O. Box 232, 70570. Tel: 318-942-6552; Fax: 318-948-1295. [CEM][JC]

2—Our Lady of Mercy, Rev. F. David Broussard. In res., Rev. James Vellankal.
Res., 150 Camille St., 70570. Tel: 318-942-4174; Fax: 318-942-1476.

3—Our Lady Queen of Angels, Rev. Angelo Cremaldi.
Res., 2136 S. Union St., P.O. Box 508, 70570. Tel: 318-942-5628; Fax: 318-942-9708.

4—Holy Ghost, Revs. Malcolm O'Leary, S.V.D.; Raymond Guidry, S.V.D.
Res., 788 N. Union St., 70570. Tel: 318-942-2732; Fax: 318-948-4108. [JC]

Parks, St. Martin Parish, St. Joseph, Rev. Gregory P. Cormier.
Mailing Address: P.O. Box 2671, 70582. Tel: 318-845-4168; Fax: 318-845-5079.
Mission—Parks, St. Louis, Tel: 318-845-4681.

Patterson, St. Mary Parish, St. Joseph, Rev. Richard Greene.
Res., 1011-1st St., P.O. Box 219, 70392. Tel: 504-395-3616; Fax: 504-395-3616. [CEM]

Pine Prairie, Evangeline Parish, St. Peter, Rev. Leslie T.H. Prescott.
Mailing Address: P.O. Box 230, 70576. Tel: 318-599-2224. [CEM]
Mission—St. Landry, St. Theresa.

Plaisance, St. Landry Parish, St. Joseph, Rev. Michael Moody, S.V.D.
Res., 3283 Hwy. 167, Opelousas, 70570. Tel: 318-826-3395.
Mission—Frilot Cove, St. Ann.

Port Barre, St. Landry Parish, Sacred Heart of Jesus, Rev. Michael Herbert.
Mailing Address: P.O. Box 129, 70577. Tel: 318-585-2279; Fax: 318-585-2276. [CEM]
St. Mary, Sr. Maria Canez, O.P., Admin.
Mailing Address: P.O. Box 338, 70577. Tel: 318-585-2315; Fax: 318-585-2315. [JC]

Rayne, Acadia Parish, St. Joseph, Revs. Eugene R. Tremie; Mark Richard; Deacon Adam Sonnier.
Mailing Address: P.O. Box 199, 70578. Tel: 318-334-2193; Fax: 318-334-2199. [CEM][JC]
School—Rayne Catholic Elementary, 407 S. Polk St., 70578. Tel: 318-334-5657; 5658. Mrs. Sherry Cormier, Prin.
Lay Teachers 14; Students 304.
Shrine of Our Mother of Mercy, Rev. Joseph J. Campion, S.S.J.; Deacon Coley Bellamy.
Mailing Address: P.O. Box 468, 70578. Tel: 318-334-3516; Fax: 318-334-4416. [CEM]

Richard, Acadia Parish, St. Edward, Rev. J. Daniel Edwards.
Res., 1463 Charlene Hwy., Church Point, 70525. Tel: 318-684-5816. [CEM][JC]
Mission—Savoy, St. Thomas.

Robert's Cove, Acadia Parish, St. Leo IV, Rev. Francis L. Bourgeois.
Res., 7166 Roberts Cove Rd., Rayne, 70578-8912. Tel: 318-334-5056; 334-5950; Fax: 318-334-0832. [CEM]
Mission—Branch, St. Edmund.

Rynella, Iberia Parish, St. Marcellus, Rev. C. Conley Bertrand.
Res., 6100 Avery Island Rd., New Iberia, 70560. Tel: 318-364-0818; Fax: 318-364-0824.

St. Martinville, St. Martin Parish, St. Martin of Tours, Revs. P. Austin Leger; Kenneth Bienvenu. In res., Rev. Jean Marie Jammes.
Res., 133 S. Main St., P.O. Drawer 10, 70582. Tel: 318-394-6021; Fax: 318-394-6020. [CEM]
Notre Dame de Perpetuel Secours, Rev. Thomas A. Mullally, S.V.D.; Deacon Carlton Lee.
Res., 240 Gary St., 70582. Tel: 318-394-3084; Fax: 318-394-5380. [CEM][JC]

Scott, Lafayette Parish, SS. Peter and Paul, Rev. Gilbert J. Dutel.
Mailing Address: P.O. Box 458, 70583. Tel: 318-235-2433; Fax: 318-233-4868. [CEM]
Saint Martin de Porres, Rev. George H. Simon.
Mailing Address: P.O. Box 728, 70583. Tel: 318-232-1968; Fax: 318-232-1968.

Ville Platte, Evangeline Parish, Sacred Heart of Jesus, Revs. J. Robert Romero; Matthew Roussel; Deacon Harris Soileau.
Res., 708 E. Main St., 70586. Tel: 318-363-2989; Fax: 318-363-3500.
School—Sacred Heart Elementary, 532 E. Main St., 70586. Tel: 318-363-3322; Fax: 318-363-2318. Paula Landreneau, Prin.
High School—Sacred Heart High, 114 S. Trojan Ln., 70586. Tel: 318-363-1475; Fax: 318-363-0348. Larry Vidrine, Prin.
Lay Teachers 41; Students: Elementary 584; High 268.
Mission—Belaire Cove, Sacred Heart.
Our Lady Queen of All Saints, Rev. Gilbert J. Dutel; Deacons Paul N. Mayeux; Eugene Le Boeuf.
Res., 211 Parkview St., P.O. Drawer E, 70586. Tel: 318-363-5167; Fax: 318-363-5179.
St. Joseph. Unassigned.
Res., 1107 Martin L. King Dr., 70586. Tel: 318-363-1051.

Washington, St. Landry Parish, Immaculate Conception, Rev. Ralph J. Landry.
Mailing Address: P.O. Box 116, 70589. Tel: 318-826-7396.
Holy Trinity, Sr. Juliana Savoy, O.P., Admin.
Mailing Address: P.O. Box 186, 70589. Tel: 318-826-3376; Fax: 318-826-3376.

Youngsville, Lafayette Parish, St. Anne, Rev. Louis Lam Vu.
Mailing Address: P.O. Box 410, 70592. Tel: 318-856-8212; Fax: 318-856-8277. [CEM]

On Special Assignment:
Reverend Monsignors—
Larroque, H. Alexandre, Vicar General, 1408 Carmel Ave., Lafayette, LA 70501. Tel: 318-261-5613
Reverend Fathers—
Boyer, Millard G., Chap., Lafayette General Medical Center, 2104 Long Plantation Blvd., Lafayette, LA 70508. Tel: 318-988-4590
Dugas, Willard, 520 Dugas Rd., Lafayette, LA 70507
Dutra, Luiz C., Office for Persons with Disabilities, 1404 Carmel Ave., Lafayette, LA 70501. Tel: 318-261-5548
Morvant, Kenneth R., Office of the Tribunal, P.O. Box 3387, Lafayette, LA 70502-3387
Robichaux, Robie E., Office of the Tribunal, P.O. Box 3387, Lafayette, LA 70502-3387. Tel: 318-261-5623
Vellankal, James, Chap., Opelousas General Hospital and Doctors Hospital, P.O. Box 7067, Opelousas, LA 70570

On Duty Outside the Diocese:
Reverend Monsignors—
Mouton, C. Burton, Basilica of St. Mary Major, Vatican City State, 00120 Europe
Reverend Fathers—
Boudreaux, John S., Corpus Christi Church, 6300 McKenna Dr., Mobile, AL 36608
Meaux, Glenn, Haiti Mission, P.O. Box 46802, Gladstone, MO 64118
Rieboldt, Richard, 726 Kirk St., West Orange, NJ 07052. Tel: 973-669-8480
Voorhies, Bennett J., St. Anthony

Military Chaplains:
Reverend Fathers—
Ledoux, Louis V., Colonel, USAF, P.O. Box 4026, McCord A.F.B., WA 98438

Absent on Sick Leave:
Reverend Fathers—
Broussard, Paul, 112 Peg Ln., Lafayette, LA 70508. Tel: 318-237-5472
Montelaro, Thomas, P.O. Box 471, Eunice, LA 70535

Absent on Leave:
Reverend Fathers—
Broussard, Kenneth M.
Coupar, David A.
Ganucheau, William R.
Hebert, Lloyd P.

Retired:
Reverend Monsignors—
Barsen, Herman J., 130 N. Richelieu Circle, New Iberia, LA 70560. Tel: 318-365-0616
Benedict, Michael J., 2319 E. Main St., New Iberia, LA 70560
Benefiel, Harry E., 301 Eraste Landry Rd., Lafayette, LA 70506. Tel: 318-235-4373
Disch, John H., P.O. Box 12507, New Iberia, LA 70562
Martin, Ignatius, Rte. 2, Box 785, Maurice, LA 70555. Tel: 318-893-8931
Richard, Wayne R., 317 Guilbeau Rd., Apt. 202-B, Lafayette, LA 70506
Van Boxel, W. H., Apollolaan 454, NL-2324 CG Leiden, The Netherlands
Reverend Fathers—
Bourg, Edwin
Calais, Floyd J., 313 Rue Louis XIV, Apt. H, Lafayette, LA 70508. Tel: 318-988-6278
DeLeeuw, John, 526 Raintree Trail, Lafayette, LA 70507. Tel: 318-235-5706
Desilets, Viateur, 900 N. Union St., Opelousas, LA 70570. Tel: 318-942-6552

Edwards, Roy D., P.O. Box 280, Carencro, LA 70520
Fontaine, Edouard, Rt. 4, Box 317, Eunice, LA 70535
Hebert, T. J., 202 Stanford St., Apt. B, Lafayette, LA 70503. Tel: 318-981-8113
Jammes, Jean Marie, P.O. Drawer 10, St. Martinville, LA 70582. Tel: 318-394-6021
Larriviere, Marshall
LeBlanc, J. Whitney, P.O. Box 2576, Parks, LA 70582
Mau, Joseph, 3142 Lambert Dr., Baton Rouge, LA 70805
Robitaille, Raymond, 2319 Main St., New Iberia, LA 70560
Spekschate, John, Kapelaanspad, 24, NL-5801 BN Venray, B.N. 5801 The Netherlands
Speyrer, Jules, 105 White St., Basile, LA 70515-0212. Tel: 318-432-5054
Sylvester, J. Wilfred, 749 Prudhomme Ln., Apt. 215, Opelousa, LA 70570
Warren, Arthur

Permanent Deacons:
Achee, Harold L., Sr., Sacred Heart, Baldwin
Bellamy, Coley M., Our Lady of Wisdom, Lafayette
Benedetto, Joseph, Office for Persons with Disabilities, Lafayette
Bodin, Edward J., St. Jules Church, Franklin
Borel, Ronald, Our Lady of Perpetual Help, New Iberia
Boudreaux, Ulysse, Our Lady Perpetual Help, New Iberia
Bourg, Gerald J., Sacred Heart, Baldwin
Broussard, Ronald H., St. Peter, New Iberia
Cannatella, Carlo, St. Landry, Opelousas
Clark, Michael, Holy Cross, Lafayette
Conrad, Carl, St. Peter, New Iberia
Dejean, Alvin Ray, St. Anthony, Lafayette
Eleazar, Paul R., Holy Rosary, Kaplan
Freyou, Leonard J., St. Nicholas Church, Lydia
Guilbeau, James, St. John Cathedral, Lafayette
Guillory, David, St. Thomas More, Eunice
Hanemann, Louis, Fayetteville
Hebert, Douglas J., Assumption, Franklin
Hebert, Marcel, St. Bernard, Breaux Bridge
Henry, Samuel, St. Charles, Grand Coteau
Judice, Julian, St. Mary, Lafayette
Landry, Theodule, St. John, Jeanerette
Lebouef, Eugene J., Queen of All Saints, Ville Platte
Lee, Carlton J., Sr., Notre Dame, St. Martinville
Lejeune, Joseph L., St. John the Evangelist, Mermentau
Leleux, Rodless, St. John the Baptist, Lyons Point
Lloyd, Louis, Our Lady Queen of Peace, Lafayette
Luke, Norbert, Holy Cross, Lafayette
Mason, Jonas E., Holy Family, Lawtell; St. Ann, Mallet
Matte, Paul, St. Edmond, Lafayette
Mayeux, Paul N., Our Lady Queen of All Saints, Ville Platte
McDonner, Robert, Sts. Peter and Paul, Scott
Melancon, J. Douglas, Assumption, Mire
Melancon, Roy, Our Lady of Mercy, Henderson
Miller, Cody, St. Joseph, Milton
Miller, Ivy J., Our Lady of the Sacred Heart, Church Point
Miller, John W., St. Landry, Opelousas
Morello, Benedict, Sacred Heart Chapel, Pecan Island
Mouton, Melvin, Pasadena, TX
Oliver, James R., Cathedral of St. John the Evangelist, Lafayette
Ortego, Charles, Our Lady of Mount Carmel, Chataignier
Ozene, Anthony Leroy, Immaculate Heart of Mary, Lafayette
Perron, Roderick P., St. Joseph, Ville Platte
Richard, Harold, St. Bernard, Breaux Bridge
Richard, Thomas, Our Lady of Mount Carmel, Chataignier
Royston, John, Unassigned
Sikes, George, Our Lady of Perpetual Help, New Iberia
Soileau, Harris, Sacred Heart of Jesus, Ville Platte
Sonnier, Adam, St. Joseph, Rayne
Theriot, Samuel, St. Theresa of the Child Jesus, Abbeville
Thibodeaux, John, Assumption, Carencro
Thomas, Joseph, St. Jules, Franklin
Waguespack, Eugene, St. Jules, Lafayette
Waguespack, Kenneth, St. Elizabeth Mission, Coteau Holmes
Wilson, James, St. Peter, New Iberia
Woodburn, Albert A., M.D., Dauterive & Iberia General Hospitals, New Iberia

INSTITUTIONS LOCATED IN THE DIOCESE

[A] SEMINARIES, RELIGIOUS OR SCHOLASTICATES

GRAND COTEAU. *St. Charles College*, P.O. Box C, 70541-1003. Tel: 318-662-5251; Fax: 318-662-3187. Novitiate of New Orleans Province of the Society of Jesus. Revs. Francis W. Huete, S.J., Novice Dir.; David L. Andrus, S.J., Asst. Novice Dir. Priests 2; Novices 11.

[B] HIGH SCHOOLS, INTERPAROCHIAL

LAFAYETTE. *St. Thomas More*, 450 E. Farrel Rd., 70508. Tel: 318-988-3700.
Web site: www.stm.k12.la.us/index.html
Mr. Ray Simon, Prin. Brothers 1; Lay Teachers 58; Students 912.

Teurlings Catholic High, 139 Teurlings Dr., 70501. Tel: 318-235-5711; Fax: 318-234-0857. Mr. Michael H. Boyer, Prin. Lay Teachers 32; Students 580.

CROWLEY. *Notre Dame High School of Acadia Parish*, 910 N. Eastern Ave., 70526. Tel: 318-783-3519. Mr. John E. Dailey, Prin. Sisters 1; Lay Teachers 34; Students 501.

NEW IBERIA. *Catholic High School*. (Grades 4-12), 1301 DeLaSalle Dr., 70560. Tel: 318-364-5116.
E-mail: chs@aisp.net
Dave J. Cavalier, Jr., Prin. Lay Teachers 60; Students 908.

OPELOUSAS. *Opelousas Catholic School*. (Grades PreK-12), 415 E. Prudhomme Ln., 70570. Tel: 318-942-5404. Mrs. Karen Domengeaux, Prin. Elementary: Sisters of the Holy Family 1; Lay Teachers 24; Students 543. High School: Lay Teachers 24; Students 284.

[C] ELEMENTARY SCHOOLS, INTERPAROCHIAL

LAFAYETTE. *Holy Family School*, 200 St. John St., 70501. Tel: 318-235-0267. Sisters of the Holy Family. Sr. Frances Therese Remi, S.S.F., Prin. Sisters 3; Lay Teachers 12; Students 178.

ST. MARTINVILLE. *Trinity Catholic School*. (Grades PreK-8), P.O. Box 438. Miss Rosemary Pierre, Prin. Sisters 3; Lay Teachers 10; Students 279.

[D] ELEMENTARY SCHOOLS, PRIVATE

ABBEVILLE. *Mt. Carmel Elementary School*, 405 Park, 70510. Tel: 318-898-0859.
E-mail: carmel@acadian.net
Web site: www.acadian.net/~carmel
Sr. Janet LeBlanc, O.Carm., Prin. Sisters of Mt. Carmel 3; Lay Teachers 22; Students 500.

[E] HIGH AND ELEMENTARY SCHOOLS, PRIVATE

GRAND COTEAU. *Academy of the Sacred Heart*. (Grades PreK-12), P.O. Box 310, 70541. Tel: 318-662-5275.
E-mail: chaggarty@rscj.org
Web site: www.ash.lft.k12./a.us./
Day School for girls. Boarding facilities for girls 8th-12th grade. Sr. Carol Haggarty, R.S.C.J., Prin. Religious of the Sacred Heart 5; Lay Teachers 42; Students 373.

[F] GENERAL HOSPITALS

LAFAYETTE. *Our Lady of Lourdes Regional Medical Center, Inc.*, 611 St. Landry St., P.O. Box 4027, 70502. Tel: 318-289-2100.
E-mail: ololexec@popalexl.linknet.net
Web site: www.lourdes.net
For a complete listing, refer to the Hospitals section.

[G] HOMES FOR THE AGED INFIRM

LAFAYETTE. *Bethany M.H.S. Health Care Center*, P.O. Box 2308, 70502. Tel: 318-234-2459
For a complete listing, refer to the Special Care Facilities section.

Village du Lac, Inc., 1404 Carmel Ave., 70501. Tel: 318-234-5106
For a complete listing, refer to the Special Care Facilities section.

NEW IBERIA. *Consolata Home*, 2319 E. Main St., 70560. Tel: 318-365-8226
For a complete listing, refer to the Special Care Facilities section.

OPELOUSAS. *C'est La Vie Center of the Sisters Marianites of Holy Cross*, 749 E. Prudhomme Ln., 70570. Tel: 318-942-8154
For a complete listing, refer to the Special Care Facilities section.

Our Lady of Prompt Succor Home, 751 E. Prudhomme Ln., 70570. Tel: 318-948-3634
For a complete listing, refer to the Special Care Facilities section.

[H] MONASTERIES AND RESIDENCES PRIESTS AND BROTHERS

LAFAYETTE. *De La Salle Christian Brothers*, 1522 Carmel Dr., 70501. Tel: 318-235-3576. Retired Brothers Home. Bros. Louis Welker, F.S.C., Dir.; Jerry Vincent, F.S.C., Sub-Dir.; C. Daniel Duplantis, F.S.C., Coord.; Rev. Luiz C. Dutra, Chap. Brothers 22.

De La Salle Christian Brothers Provincialate, 1522 Carmel Dr., 70501. Tel: 318-234-1973; Fax: 318-261-1014. Headquarters for the New Orleans-Santa Fe District. Legal Title: *Brothers of the Christian Schools of Lafayette LA, Inc.* Bros. Clarence Fioke, F.S.C., Prov.; James Brown, F.S.C., Auxiliary Prov. and Finance Dir. Prov. Staff: Mrs. Clara Mouton, F.S.C., Sec. to the Provincial; Bro. Brendan Hayden, F.S.C., Prov. Bookkeeper.

OPELOUSAS. *Mother of the Redeemer Monastery*, 168 Monastery Ln., 70570. Tel: 318-543-2237. Priests 1; Brothers 2; Candidates 1.

[I] CONVENTS AND RESIDENCES FOR SISTERS

LAFAYETTE. *Discalced Carmelites*. Monastery of Mary, Mother of Grace. 1250 Carmel Ave., 70501. Tel: 318-232-4651. Mother Mary John Billeaud, O.C.D., Prioress; Rev. Msgr. H. Alexandre Larroque, Chap. Cloistered Nuns 17; Extern Sisters 4.

Dominican Sisters, P.O. Box 42371, 70504. Tel: 318-269-0324.

Eucharistic Missionaries of St. Dominic, 300 N. Chestnut St., 70501. Tel: 318-235-8345.

Franciscan Missionaries of Our Lady, Our Lady of Lourdes Hospital, P.O. Box 4027-C, 70502. Tel: 318-231-2110 (Convent); 237-7381 (Hospital). Sisters 3.

Marianites of Holy Cross, 1417 St. John St., 70506. Tel: 318-234-5454. Sisters 2.

Missionaries of Charity, 911 St. John St., 70501. Tel: 318-233-3929. Sisters 4.

School Sisters of Notre Dame, 1404 Carmel Ave., Apt. 40-C, 70501. Tel: 318-232-6975. Sisters 2.

Sisters of Divine Providence, 317 Guilbeau Rd., Apt. 101-E, 70506. Tel: 318-984-8520.
Other Addresses: 317 Guilbeau Rd., Apt. 202-H, 70506. Tel: 318-981-4215. 220 Wilkle St., Apt. 863, 70506. Tel: 318-234-4546.

Sisters of Mt. Carmel, 309 Evangeline Dr., 70501. Tel: 318-235-8687. Sisters 3.
Other Addresses: 506 Surrey St., 70501. Tel: 318-235-1837. Sisters 2. 317 Guilbeau Rd., Apt. 206A, 70506. Tel: 318-981-4378.

Sisters of St. Agnes, 609 Mudd Ave., 70501. Tel: 318-234-6768.

Sisters of St. Joseph of Carondelet, 317 Guilbeau Rd., No. 106-J, 70506. Tel: 318-988-0714.

Sisters of the Most Holy Sacrament, Convent Generalate, 313 Corona Dr., 70503-4757. Tel: 318-981-8475. Sr. Judine Theriot, M.H.S., Major Supr. Sisters 2. Administrative Offices, P.O. Box 90037, 70509-0727.
Other Addresses: 104 Beta Dr., 70506-3924. Tel: 318-984-4494. Sisters 2. 317 St. Patrick St., No. 1, 70506-4565. Tel: 318-234-6724. 317 St. Patrick St., No. 3, 70506-4565. Tel: 318-264-1948. Sisters 2. 317 St. Patrick St., No. 4, 70506-4565. Tel: 318-232-3443. 317 St. Patrick St., No. 5, 70506-4565. Tel: 318-264-1921. 317 St. Patrick St., No. 6, 70506-4565. Tel: 318-235-1755. 107 Wisteria Dr., 70506-6858. Tel: 318-989-9817. Sisters 3. St. Anne's Annex, P.O. Box 2308, 70502-2308. Tel: 318-233-8901. Sisters 4. Bethany MHS Health Care Center, P.O. Box 2308, 70502-2308. Sisters 11.

ABBEVILLE. *Sisters of Mt. Carmel*, 108 Petain St., 70510. Tel: 318-898-0140. Sisters 2.
Other Addresses: 2326 Camella, 70510. Tel: 318-898-1807. Sisters 3. 108 W. St. Victor St., 70510. Tel: 318-893-0138. Sisters 2.

ARNAUDVILLE. *Sisters of Mt. Carmel*, P.O. Box 53, 70512.

BREAUX BRIDGE. *Sisters of the Most Holy Sacrament*, 221 Berard St., 70517. Tel: 318-332-1951.

CHURCH POINT. *Sisters of the Blessed Sacrament*, 695 N. Main St., 70525. Tel: 318-684-2120. Sisters 2.

CROWLEY. *Marianites of the Holy Cross*, 516 N. Ave. E, 70526. Tel: 318-783-1550. Sisters 4.

Sisters of Divine Providence, 516 N. Ave. E, 70526. Tel: 318-783-1550.

Sisters of the Holy Spirit, 211 N. Avenue D, 70526. Tel: 318-783-6651.

Sisters of the Most Holy Sacrament, P.O. Box 695, 70527. Tel: 318-783-3675.

DUSON. *Eucharistic Missionaries of St. Dominic*, P.O. Box 725, 70529. Tel: 318-873-4159.

FRANKLIN. *Marianites of the Holy Cross*, 619 Iberia St., 70538. Tel: 318-828-5241.

GRAND COTEAU. *Religious of the Sacred Heart*, P.O. Box 292, 70541. Tel: 318-942-1551. Sisters 3.
Other Addresses: P.O. Box 446, 70541. Tel: 318-662-5526. Sisters 5. P.O. Box 308, 70541. Tel: 318-662-5453. Sisters 5.

Sisters of Mt. Carmel, P.O. Box 534, 70541. Tel: 318-662-7178.

IOTA. *Sisters of Divine Providence*, P.O. Box 870, 70543. Tel: 318-779-2228.

JEANERETTE. *School Sisters of Notre Dame*, 100 Beth St., 70544. Tel: 318-276-5640. Sisters 3.

LEBEAU. *Sisters of the Holy Spirit*, P.O. Box 40, 71345. Tel: 318-623-4405. Sisters 2.

NEW IBERIA. *Dominican Rural Missionaries*, 213 Oak Hill Rd., 70560. Tel: 318-364-3142.

Sisters of Providence, 213 Oak Hill Rd., 70560. Tel: 318-364-3142.

OPELOUSAS. *Sisters of the Holy Family*, 720 N. Union St., 70570. Tel: 318-942-2052. Sisters 3.

RAYNE. *Sisters of Mt. Carmel*, 411 S. Polk St., 70578. Tel: 318-334-3403. Sisters 6.

Sisters of the Blessed Sacrament, 710 Malvern St., 70578. Tel: 318-334-3606. Sisters 2.

ST. MARTINVILLE. *Sisters of Mercy of the Americas*, P.O. Box 674, 70582. Tel: 318-394-14486.

Sisters of the Blessed Sacrament, 201 Gary St., 70582. Tel: 318-394-3036. Sisters 3.

[J] RETREAT HOUSES

GRAND COTEAU. *Jesuit Spirituality Center*, P.O. Box C, 70541-1003. Tel: 318-662-5251; Fax: 318-662-3187.
E-mail: jespirtcen@aol.com
Year-round directed retreats of 3, 5, 8, or 30 days plus a variety of weekend retreats and/or programs open to men and women. Revs. Edmundo Rodriguez, S.J., Supr. & Dir.; Louis A. Arceneaux, C.M.; Thomas J. Jenniskens, S.J.; Albert P. Louapre, S.J.; Henry R. Montecino, S.J.; Austin N. Park, S.J.; Fred G. Reynolds, S.J.; Norman J. Rogge, S.J.; Bros. Raul A. Loya, S.J.; Michael J. Moore, S.J.; George A. Murphy, S.J.; Sr. Consuelo Champagne, M.S.C.; Sr. Patricia Willems, C.S.J. Priests 8; Brothers 3; Sisters 2.

Our Lady of the Oaks Retreat House, P.O. Box D, 70541. Tel: 318-662-5410. Preached retreats for men, women, and married couples. Jesuit Fathers. Rev. Kenneth Buddendorff, S.J., Dir. Assoc. Directors: Revs. Francis J. Coco, S.J.; John T. Condry, S.J.; Joseph P. McGill, S.J.; Louis A. Poche, S.J.

[K] CURSILLO CENTERS

OPELOUSAS. *Cursillo Center*, 3651 Hwy. 104, 70570. Tel: 318-873-4962; Fax: 318-873-3023. Rev. O. Joseph Breaux, Spiritual Dir.

[L] NEWMAN CENTERS

LAFAYETTE. *Our Lady of Wisdom Catholic Student Center*, University of Southwestern Louisiana, P.O. Box 43271, 70505. Tel: 318-232-8741; 232-8742. Rev. W. Curtis Mallet.

EUNICE. *Catholic Student Center-Louisiana State Univ.*, P.O. Box 1129, 70535. Tel: 318-457-8668.

[M] MISCELLANEOUS

LAFAYETTE. *Brothers of the Christian Schools of Lafayette - Retirement Trust*, 1522 Carmel Ave., 70501. Tel: 318-234-1973; Fax: 318-261-1014.

Community of Jesus Crucified, 421 1/2 Carmel Dr., 70501. Tel: 318-232-7491. Revs. Jerome Frey, Spiritual Dir.; Michael Champagne.

Holy Rosary Institute, P.O. Box 3387, 70501. 421 Carmel Ave., 70501.

St. Augustine Trust Fund, P.O. Box 90037, 70509. Sisters of the Most Holy Sacrament.

St. La Salle Auxiliary, 1522 Carmel Dr., 70501. Tel: 318-234-1973. Brothers of the Christian Schools.

Sisters of the Eucharistic Covenant, P.O. Box 80393, 70508. Sr. Camille Martinez, S.E.C., Pres.

[N] SOCIAL SERVICE CENTERS

LAFAYETTE. *Lafayette Catholic Service Centers, Inc.*, 409 St. John St., 70501. Tel: 318-235-4972.
Service Centers: Dr. Justin Green, Exec. Dir.
Msgr. A. O. Sigur Service Center.
St. Joseph Shelter for Men.
St. Joseph Diner.
Shalom House Family Shelter.
Emmanuel House Family Shelter.
St. Joseph Distribution Center.
The Bishop Harry J. Flynn Hospitality Center. Total Assisted Annually 235,196.

ABBEVILLE. *Christian Service Center*, 701 Chevis St., 70510. Tel: 318-893-9756; 893-3114. Elma B. Bourgeois, Dir.

St. Vincent de Paul Center, 507 N. Bailey St., 70510. Tel: 318-898-1830. Sr. Jeanette Bernhardt, Coord.

CROWLEY. *Crowley Christian Care Center*, 825 N. Ave. F, P.O. Box 686, 70527-0686. Tel: 318-783-5811.

NEW IBERIA. *Social Service Center*, 432 Bank Ave., 70560. Tel: 318-369-6384. Paul H. DeClouet, Dir.

OPELOUSAS. *Opelousas Housing Corporation*, P.O. Box 7045, 70571.
E-mail: newlife@1stnet.com
Web site: www.1stnet.com/newlife
dba New Life Center. Operated under the direction of the Lafayette Catholic Services Center, Inc.

VILLE PLATTE. *Christian Care and Share Center*, 129 W. Main St., P.O. Box 901, 70586. Tel: 318-363-8041. Mr. Eugene S. Fontenot, Chm.

RELIGIOUS INSTITUTES OF MEN REPRESENTED IN THE DIOCESE

For further details refer to the corresponding bracketed number in the Religious Institutes of Men or Women section.

[0200]—*Benedictines (Olivetan, Subiaco Congregation).* —O.S.B.

[0330]—*Brothers of the Christian Schools.* (New Orleans Prov.).—F.S.C.

[]—*Carmelites of Mary Immaculate.*—C.M.I.

[0360]—*Claretian Missionaries.*—C.M.F.

[0220]—*Congregation of the Blessed Sacrament.*—S.S.S.

[0520]—*Franciscan Friars.*—O.F.M.

[0690]—*Jesuit Fathers and Brothers.* (New Orleans Prov.).—S.J.

[]—*Missionaries of St. Paul.* (Nigeria).—M.S.P.

[0610]—*Priests of the Congregation of Holy Cross.*—C.S.C.

[1070]—*Redemptorist Fathers.*—C.SS.R.

[0700]—*St. Joseph's Society of the Sacred Heart.* (Baltimore Prov.).—S.S.J.

[0420]—*Society of the Divine Word.*—S.V.D.

RELIGIOUS INSTITUTES OF WOMEN REPRESENTED IN THE DIOCESE

[0400]—*Congregation of Our Lady of Mount Carmel.*—O.Carm.

[2410]—*Congregation of the Marianites of Holy Cross.*—M.S.C.

[1950]—*Congregation of the Sisters of the Holy Family.*—S.S.F.

[0420]—*Discalced Carmelite Nuns.*—O.C.D.

[1130]—*Dominican Rural Missionaries.*—O.P.

[1070-14]—*Dominican Sisters.*—O.P.

[]—*Dominican Sisters of Carondelet.*—O.P.

[1140]—*Eucharistic Missionaries of St. Dominic.*—O.P.

[1380]—*Franciscan Missionaries of Our Lady.*—O.S.F.

[2575]—*Institute of the Sisters of Mercy of the Americas.*—R.S.M.

[2710]—*Missionaries of Charity.* (Bronx, NY).—M.C.

[3530]—*Missionary Sisters Servants of the Holy Spirit.*—S.Sp.S.

[4070]—*Religious of the Sacred Heart.*—R.S.C.J.

[2970]—*School Sisters of Notre Dame.* (South Central).—S.S.N.D.

[0990]—*Sisters of Divine Providence.*—C.D.P.

[3360]—*Sisters of Providence of Saint Mary-of-the-Woods, Indiana.* (Prov. of St. Joseph).—S.P.

[3880]—*Sisters of St. Joseph of Medaille.*—C.S.J.

[0260]—*Sisters of the Blessed Sacrament for Indians and Colored People.*—S.B.S.

[2050]—*Sisters of the Holy Spirit and Mary Immaculate.*—S.H.Sp.

[2940]—*Sisters of the Most Holy Sacrament.*—M.H.S.

NECROLOGY

† Gremillion, Rev. Msgr. John Edward, (Retired). —Died Feb. 21, 1997.

† Ohlenforst, J. William, Morse, LA, Immaculate Conception. —Died Jan. 3, 1997.

† Sigur, Rev. Msgr. Alexander Octave, (Retired). —Died Aug. 13, 1997.

Diocese of Lake Charles

Most Reverend

JUDE SPEYRER, D.D.

Bishop of Lake Charles; ordained July 25, 1953; appointed First Bishop of Lake Charles January 29, 1980; ordained and installed April 25, 1980. *Mailing Address: P.O. Box 3223, Lake Charles, LA, 70602.*

ESTABLISHED APRIL 25, 1980.

Square Miles 5,313.

Comprises the civil parishes (or counties) of Allen, Beauregard, Calcasieu, Cameron and Jefferson Davis in the State of Louisiana.

For legal titles of parishes and diocesan institutions, consult the Chancery Office.

Chancery Office: 414 Iris St., P.O. Box 3223, Lake Charles, LA, 70602. Tel.: 318-439-7400; Fax: 318-439-7413.

Web site address: http://lcdiocese.laol.net

E-mail address: lcdiocese@laol.net

STATISTICAL OVERVIEW

Personnel	
Bishop	1
Priests: Diocesan Active in Diocese	44
Priests: Active Outside Diocese	6
Priests: Retired, Sick or Absent	6
Number of Diocesan Priests	56
Religious Priests in Diocese	18
Extern Priests in Diocese	8
Ordinations:	
Diocesan Priests	1
Permanent Deacons	3
Permanent Deacons in Diocese	25
Total Brothers	4
Total Sisters	28
Parishes	
Parishes	36
With Resident Pastor:	
Resident Diocesan Priests	24
Resident Religious Priests	12
Without Resident Pastor:	
Missions	25
Professional Ministry Personnel:	
Brothers	2
Sisters	7
Lay Ministers	39
Welfare	
Catholic Hospitals	1
Total Assisted	104,497
Day Care and Extended Day Care Centers	1
Total Assisted	57
Special Centers for Social Services	1
Total Assisted	2,166
Educational	
Diocesan Students in Other Seminaries	9
Total Seminarians	9
High Schools, Diocesan and Parish	1
Total Students	511
Elementary Schools, Diocesan and Parish	8
Total Students	2,386
Catechesis/Religious Education:	
High School Students	4,267
Elementary Students	5,817
Total Students Under Catholic Instruction	12,990
Teachers in the Diocese:	
Priests	1
Brothers	1
Lay Teachers	198
Vital Statistics	
Receptions into the Church:	
Infant Baptism Totals	1,772
Adult Baptism Totals	131
Received into Full Communion	225
First Communions	1,464
Confirmations	1,086
Marriages:	
Catholic	343
Interfaith	113
Total Marriages	456
Deaths	922
Total Catholic Population	82,414
Total Population	259,425

Diocesan Board of Administration (Legal Title - *Society of the Roman Catholic Church of the Diocese of Lake Charles, LA)*—Most Rev. JUDE SPEYRER; Rev. EGIDIO VECCHIO, M.S.; Rev. AUBREY GUILBEAU; Rev. Msgr. VINCENT A. SEDITA; Deacon HARRY E. WAGNER, JR.

Bishop's Office—414 Iris St., P.O. Box 3223, Lake Charles, 70602. Tel: 318-439-7400.

Chancery Office—414 Iris St., P.O. Box 3223, Lake Charles, 70602. Tel: 318-439-7400; Fax: 318-439-7413. Office Hours: Mon.-Fri. 8:30-4:30.

Chennault Office Complex—4029 Avenue G, Lake Charles, 70615. Tel: 318-439-7430; Fax: 318-439-7428. Office Hours: Mon.-Fri. 8:30-4:30.

Vicar General—Rev. Msgr. VINCENT SEDITA, V.G., *P.O. Box 3223, Lake Charles, 70602.* Tel: 318-439-7400.

Chancellor—Deacon GEORGE STEARNS, *P.O. Box 3223, Lake Charles, 70602.* Tel: 318-439-7400.

Assistant Chancellor—Deacon HARRY E. WAGNER, JR., *P.O. Box 3223, Lake Charles, 70602.* Tel: 318-439-7400.

Vicar Judicial—Rev. ANTONIO GARCIA, J.C.L., *P.O Box 3223, Lake Charles, 70607.* Tel: 318-439-7410.

Tribunal—414 Iris St., P.O. Box 3223, Lake Charles, 70602. Tel: 318-439-7410.

Judges—Rev. ANTONIO GARCIA, J.C.L.; Rev. Msgr. VINCENT SEDITA; Rev. Msgr. AMOS VINCENT; Rev. JOHN A. POERIO.

Advocates—Rev. Msgr. VINCENT SEDITA; Revs. JOHN POERIO; JOSEPH MCGRATH.

Defenders of the Bond—Rev. Msgr. HARRY GREIG; Rev. JAMES DOYLE.

Notary—PATRICIA SIGUR.

Episcopal Vicars—Rev. EGIDIO VECCHIO, M.S., West Deanery; Rev. AUBREY GUILBEAU, East Deanery; Rev. Msgr. A. J. VINCENT, Tribunal; Rev. Msgr. IRVING DEBLANC, Spec. Svcs.; Rev. Msgr. VINCENT SEDITA, Vicar Gen.; Rev. JOHN GILES, Christian Formation.

Vicars—Deacon EDWARD LAVINE, Black Catholics; Sr. ROSE ANN BLAIR, C.D.P., Religious.

Priest's Senate—Rev. HERBERT MAY, Chm.; Rev. Msgr. HARRY GREIG; Revs. KARL FUSELIER; RONALD GROTH; AUGUSTINE MULANJANANY.

Diocesan Consultors—Rev. Msgr. LOUIS MELANCON; Rev. Msgr. CHARLES J. DUBOIS; Rev. Msgr. A. J. VINCENT, Social Svcs.; Rev. Msgr. IRVING DEBLANC, Spec. Svcs.; Rev. Msgr. VINCENT SEDITA, Vicar Gen.; Rev. Msgr. HARRY GREIG; Rev. HENRY MANCUSO; Rt. Rev. HERBERT J. MAY, JR., J.C.L.; Revs. ALBERT BOREL; JUAN ALERS.

Offices, Boards, Commissions, Committees

Black Catholics—Deacon EDWARD LAVINE, *2043 11th St., Lake Charles, 70601.* Tel: 318-439-2646.

Calcasieu Center for Catholic Studies—Rev. JOHN GILES JR., *920 7th St., Lake Charles, 70601.* Tel: 318-439-7432.

Charismatic Renewal—Rev. ORIS BROUSSARD, *2409 2nd St., Lake Charles, 70601.* Tel: 318-439-1898.

Christian Formation—Rev. JOHN GILES, *4029 Avenue G, Lake Charles, 70601.* Tel: 318-439-7432.

Clergy Formation—Rev. DON PIRARO, *414 Iris St., Lake Charles, 70601.* Tel: 318-439-7400.

Communications—MORRIS LEBLEU, *4029 Avenue G, Lake Charles, 70601.* Tel: 318-439-7430.

Deaf Apostolate—Rev. AUBREY GUILBEAU, *418 Iris St., Lake Charles, 70601.* Tel: 318-439-4373.

Development Office—MORRIS LEBLEU, *P.O. Box 3223, Lake Charles, 70602.* Tel: 318-439-7434.

Diocesan Building Commission—Deacon GEORGE STEARNS, Chm., *P.O. Box 3223, Lake Charles, 70602.* Tel: 318-439-7400.

Diocesan Pastoral Council—Most Rev. JUDE SPEYRER, Chm., *P.O. Box 3223, Lake Charles, 70602.* Tel: 318-439-7400.

Diocesan Religious Council—Sr. ROSE ANN BLAIR, C.D.P., *P.O. Drawer P, Lake Arthur, 70549.* Tel: 318-774-2614.

Director of Seminarians—Rev. AUBREY GUILBEAU, *4029 Avenue G, Lake Charles, 70601.* Tel: 318-439-7430.

Education—Deacon MICHAEL MATHEWS, Supt., *4029 Avenue G, Lake Charles, 70601.* Tel: 318-439-7418.

Evangelization—GLENN HARMON. Tel: 318-439-7400.

Fiscal Administration—Deacon HARRY E. WAGNER, JR., *P.O. Box 3223, Lake Charles, 70602.* Tel: 318-439-7400.

Hispanic Ministry—Rev. Msgr. JUAN M. ALERS, *207 Meadow Dr., Oakdale, 71463.* Tel: 318-335-3780.

Office For Worship—Rev. JACE ESKIND, *221 Aqua Dr., Lake Charles, 70605.* Tel: 318-477-1434.

Parish Boundaries Commission—Deacon GEORGE STEARNS, Chm., *P.O. Box 3223, Lake Charles, 70602.* Tel: 318-439-7400.

Permanent Diaconate—Deacon EDWARD LAVINE, *P.O. Box 3223, Lake Charles, 70602.* Tel: 318-439-7400.

Personnel Board—P.O. Box 1029, Lake Charles, 70602. Tel: 318-439-7400.

Propagation of the Faith & Holy Childhood Association—Deacon HARRY E. WAGNER, JR., Dir., *P.O. Box 3223, Lake Charles, 70602.* Tel: 318-439-7400.

Religious Education—Mrs. SANDY GAY, *4029 Avenue G, Lake Charles, 70601.* Tel: 318-439-7429.

Relief Services Catholic—Deacon H. E. WAGNER, JR., *P.O. Box 3223, Lake Charles, 70602.* Tel: 318-439-7400.

St. Charles Retreat Center—Rev. DON PIRARO, Dir., *2151 Sam Houston Jones Pkwy., Lake Charles, 70611.* Tel: 318-855-1232.

Sea, Apostleship of the—PATRICK BROUSSARD, *160 Marine St., Lake Charles, 70601.* Tel: 318-436-1315.

Social Services, Catholic—Deacon EDWARD LAVINE, Dir., *4029 Ave. G, Lake Charles, 70615.* Tel: 318-439-7439.

Community Services, Catholic—Deacon EDWARD LAVINE, Vicar, *4029 Avenue G, Lake Charles, 70615.* Tel: 318-439-7439.

Scouting—Rev. MAURICE J. MARTINEAU, *11054 Hwy. 384, Lake Charles, 70607.* Tel: 318-598-3101.

Seminary Advisory Board—Rev. AUBREY GUILBEAU, *4029 Avenue G, Lake Charles, 70601.* Tel: 318-439-7430.

Vocation Director—Rev. TIMOTHY GOODLY, *4029 Avenue G, Lake Charles, 70601.* Tel: 318-439-7430.

CLERGY, PARISHES, MISSIONS AND PAROCHIAL SCHOOLS

LAKE CHARLES
(Calcasieu Parish)

1—IMMACULATE CONCEPTION CATHEDRAL (1869), Rev. Msgr. Harry D. Greig, II; Rev. Michael J. Barras; Deacons H. E. Wagner; Milton P. White; Michael Mathews.
Mailing Address: P.O. Box 1029, 70602. Tel: 318-436-7251; Fax: 318-436-7240.
Church—935 Bilbo, 70601. [CEM]
School—Tel: 318-433-3497; Fax: 318-436-8294. Mrs. Melanie Bradberry, Prin.
Lay Teachers 20; Students 275.

2—IMMACULATE HEART OF MARY (1953) (African American), Rev. Msgr. Ronald C. Groth; Rev. Karl Fuselier.
Res., 2031 Opelousas St., 70601. Tel: 318-436-8093; Fax: 318-436-8033.
Catechesis/Religious Programs—Tel: 318-436-8513.
Students 380.
Mission—Lake Charles, Calcasieu Parish, Our Lady of Fatima Chapel, 1500 Graham St., 70601.

3—SACRED HEART OF JESUS (1919) (African American), Rev. Raymond A. Jones, S.V.D.; Deacon Ed Lavine. In res., Rev. Alfredo Marco.
Res., 612 Louisiana Ave., 70601. Tel: 318-439-2646; Fax: 318-439-2650. [CEM]
School—Tel: 318-436-3588; Fax: 318-433-1761. Joseph W. Guillory, Prin.
Lay Teachers 13; Students 253.
Catechesis/Religious Programs—Tel: 318-439-9923. Willa Golden, D.R.E.
Students 164.

4—ST. HENRY (1942), Revs. Joseph Kariamadam, C.M.I.; Timothy Goodly; Deacon Ray Granger.
Res., 1021 Eighth Ave., 70601. Tel: 318-436-7223; Fax: 318-436-4614. [JC]
Catechesis/Religious Programs—Tel: 318-433-6119. Mrs. Cynthia Pitre, D.R.E.
Students 298.

5—ST. MARGARET (1940), Revs. Henry Mancuso; Alan P. Trouille; Deacon Dan Landry. In res., Rev. Scott DesOrmeaux.
Res., 2500 Enterprise Blvd., 70601. Tel: 318-439-4585; Fax: 318-433-3186.
School—Tel: 318-436-7959; Fax: 318-436-9932. Mrs. Priscilla Courville, Prin.
Sisters 1; Lay Teachers 29; Students 419.
Catechesis/Religious Programs—Tel: 318-436-6358. D.R.E.: Betty Timpa; Joanne Schwem.
Students 320.

6—ST. THEODORE'S (1974), Rev. Msgr. Charles J. Dubois; Deacon Jack Reynolds. In res., Revs. James Doyle; T.L. Herlong.
Res., 786 Sam Houston Jones Pkwy., 70611. Tel: 318-855-6662; Fax: 318-855-6663.
School—(Grades PreK-5). Tel: 318-855-9465. Mr. Franklin Foote, Prin.
Lay Teachers 11; Students 101.
Catechesis/Religious Programs—Tel: 318-855-6664. Victoria Hogan, D.R.E.
Students 500.

7—OUR LADY OF GOOD COUNSEL (1957), Rev. Whitney Miller; Sr. Claire Pellerin, S.E., Pastoral Assoc.
Res., 221 Aqua Dr., 70605. Tel: 318-477-1434; Fax: 318-479-2129.
Catechesis/Religious Programs—Gloria Taylor, D.R.E.
Students 112.

8—OUR LADY QUEEN OF HEAVEN (1957), Rev. Aubrey V. Guilbeau; Rev. Msgr. Irving A. DeBlanc, Vicar for Special Svcs.; Revs. John H. Giles, Jr.; Daniel A. Torres; Wayne LeBleu.
Mailing Address: P.O. Box 5940, 70606.
Res., 617 W. Claude St., 70605. Tel: 318-477-1236; Fax: 318-478-3451. [CEM]
School—(Grades K-8). Tel: 318-477-7349; Fax: 318-477-7384. Mrs. Mary Ann Moses, Prin.
Lay Teachers 41; Students 749.
Preschool and Day Care—Tel: 318-477-8438.
Students 57.
Catechesis/Religious Programs—3909 Creole St., 70605. Tel: 318-477-3937. D.R.E.: Mrs. Nancy Chehotsky, (Grades 7-12); Mrs. Robin Suire, (Grades 1-6).
Students 1,300.
Missions—Lake Charles, Calcasieu Parish, Christ the King, 7680 Gulf Hwy., 70605. Tel: 318-478-0213; Lake Charles, Calcasieu Parish, St. Martin de Porres, 5326 Elliot Rd., 70605. Tel: 318-478-3845.

OUTSIDE THE CITY OF LAKE CHARLES

Bell City, Calcasieu Parish, St. John Vianney (1939), Rev. John A. Poerio.
Res., Box 10, 70630. Tel: 318-622-3255; Fax: 318-622-3255. [CEM]
Catechesis/Religious Programs—Lisa Reber, D.R.E.
Students 200.
Mission—Hayes, Calcasieu Parish, St. Daniel Chapel, 70630.

Big Lake, Cameron Parish, St. Mary of the Lake, Rev. William M. Miller.
Res., 11054 Hwy. 384, 70607. Tel: 318-598-3101; Fax: 318-598-3101.
Mission—Sweet Lake, St. Patrick's.

Cameron, Cameron Parish, Our Lady Star of the Sea, Rev. Alphonse M. Volpe.
Res., P.O. Box L, 70631. Tel: 318-775-5342.
Catechesis/Religious Programs—Students 115.

Creole, Cameron Parish, Sacred Heart of Jesus (1890), Rev. E. Joseph McGrath.
Res., P.O. Drawer 9, 70632. Tel: 318-542-4795; Fax: 318-542-4641. [CEM 3]
Catechesis/Religious Programs—Tel: 318-542-4871. Stephanie Rodrique, D.R.E.
Students 238.
Mission—Cameron, Cameron Parish, St. Rose of Lima, 2267 Trosclair Rd., Cameron, 70631. Tel: 318-542-4795.

De Quincy, Calcasieu Parish, Our Lady of La Salette (1922) (African American), Rev. John L. Blumm, M.S.
Res., 203 S. Grand, P.O. Box 236, 70633. Tel: 318-786-3500; Fax: 318-786-3500.
Catechesis/Religious Programs—Tel: 318-786-3205.
Students 357.
Mission—Ragley, Beauregard Parish, St. Pius X, 16816 Hwy. 171, Ragley, 70657. Tel: 318-725-3719.

De Ridder, Beauregard Parish, St. Joseph's (1938), Revs. Roland Bernier, M.S.; Patrick McCarthy, M.S.; Deacon Sumner Kohlhund.
Res., 1125 Blankenship Dr., 70634. Tel: 318-463-6878; Fax: 318-463-6875.
Catechesis/Religious Programs—Sr. Rita Deschenes, S.S.J., D.R.E.
Students 235.
Missions—Merryville, Beauregard Parish, St. Bridget; De Ridder, Beauregard Parish, St. Jude, 5072 Hwy. 113, Tel: 318-328-8476. Rev. Thomas Panthalani.

Elton, Jefferson Davis Parish, St. Paul (1913), Rev. Marshall Boulet; Deacon John Eaves.
Res., P.O. Box 129, 70532. Tel: 318-584-2818; Fax: 318-584-2818. [CEM]
Catechesis/Religious Programs—Cathy Hollingsworth, D.R.E.
Students 153.

St. Joseph's (1950) (African American), Rev. Jose Vattakunnel; Deacon John Eaves.
Res., P.O. Box 789, 70532. Tel: 318-584-2038. [CEM]
Catechesis/Religious Programs—Tel: 318-584-2642. D.R.E.: Mary Jane Thomas; Carroll Sue Gobert.
Students 71.

Fenton, Jefferson Davis Parish, St. Charles Borromeo (1980), Rev. Augustine Mulanjanany.
Res., P.O. Box 309, 70640. Tel: 318-756-2529.
Catechesis/Religious Programs—Beverly Cornier, D.R.E.
Students 60.

Grand Chenier, Cameron Parish, St. Eugene (1962), Rev. Vincent Vadakkedath.
Res., 5035 Grand Chenier Hwy., 70643. Tel: 318-538-2245. [CEM]
Catechesis/Religious Programs—Students 83.
Mission—Grand Chenier, Cameron Parish, Immaculate Conception, 70643.

Hackberry, Cameron Parish, St. Peter Apostle (1955), Rev. Eugene F. McKenna, M.S.
Res., 1210 Main St., P.O. Box 236, 70645. Tel: 318-762-3365.
Catechesis/Religious Programs—Tel: 318-762-4255. Tamra Welch, D.R.E.
Students 170.
Mission—Holly Beach, Holy Trinity. Rev. Roland Vaughn.
Res., 6470 Gulf Beach Hwy., Holly Beach, 70631-9607. Tel: 318-569-2132.
Mission—Johnson Bayou, Our Lady of the Assumption.

Iowa, Calcasieu Parish, St. Raphael (1931), Rev. Carlos Garcia-Cardona (Columbia).
Res., P.O. Drawer 849, 70647. Tel: 318-582-3503; Fax: 318-582-6326. [CEM]
Catechesis/Religious Programs—Students 613.
Missions—Lacassine, Jefferson Davis Parish, St. John the Evangelist, 70647-0849. Tel: 318-588-4606; Le Bleu Settlement, Calcasieu Parish, St. Joseph, 70647-0849. Tel: 318-582-3483.

Jennings, Jefferson Davis Parish, Our Lady Help of Christians (1891), Rev. Msgr. Vincent A. Sedita; Deacon John P. Segura.
Res., 710 State St., P.O. Drawer 1170, 70546. Tel: 318-824-0168; Fax: 318-824-7597. [CEM]
School—600 Roberts Ave., 70546. Tel: 318-824-1743; Fax: 318-824-1743. Mrs. Octavie Koon, Prin.
Lay Teachers 19; Students 361.
Catechesis/Religious Programs—Tel: 318-824-0168. Janet Guidry, D.R.E.
Students 278.

Immaculate Conception (1956), Rev. Oris Broussard; Deacon Ed McNally.
Res., 515 Bryan St., P.O. Box 358, 70546. Tel: 318-824-1164; Fax: 318-824-1717.
Catechesis/Religious Programs—Bennett McNeal, D.R.E.
Students 177.

Our Lady of Perpetual Help (1941), Rev. Peter Nkedife.
Res., 920 S. Broadway, P.O. Box 1331, 70546. Tel: 318-824-3182; 824-3186. [CEM]
Catechesis/Religious Programs—Tel: 318-824-3703. Harriet Laudins, D.R.E.
Students 90.

Kinder, Allen Parish, St. Philip Neri (1937) (Acadian French), Rev. Msgr. James Gaddy. In res., Rev. Austin Park, S.J.
Res., P.O. Box 146, 70648. Tel: 318-738-5612. [CEM]
Catechesis/Religious Programs—Tel: 318-738-3353. Nancy Burleigh, D.R.E.
Students 388.
Missions—Indian Village, Sacred Heart Parish, Sacred Heart, 70648. Tel: 318-328-8476; Reeves, Sacred Heart Parish, St. Maurice, HC 64 Box 142 A, 70634.

Lake Arthur, Jefferson Davis Parish, Our Lady of the Lake (1922), Rev. Maurice J. Martineau.
Res., P.O. Drawer P, 70549. Tel: 318-774-2614; Fax: 318-774-3793. [CEM][JC 3]
Catechesis/Religious Programs—701 8th St., 70549. Tel: 318-774-3980.
Students 470.
Missions—Thornwell, Jefferson Davis Parish, St. Francis of Assisi Chapel; Andrus Cove, Jefferson Davis Parish, St. Gertrude Chapel.

Oakdale, Allen Parish, Sacred Heart (1948), Rev. Fred F. Russi. Pastoral Assocs.: Sr. Dora Ramirez, R.F.R.; Sr. Mercedes Lopez, R.F.R.
Mailing Address: P.O. Box 926, 71463-0926.
Res., 207 Meadow Dr., 71463. Tel: 318-335-3780; Fax: 318-335-0708. [CEM]
Catechesis/Religious Programs—Students 175.
Convent—1011 E. 7th Ave., 71463. Tel: 318-335-4390.
Mission—Elizabeth, Allen Parish, St. Frances, P.O. Box 926, 71463-0926.

Oberlin, Allen Parish, St. Joan of Arc (1920), Rev. Jude Brunnert, M.S.; Deacon Norris Chapman.
Res., 110 W. Fifth Ave., P.O. Box 479, 70655. Tel: 318-639-4399; 639-4798; Fax: 318-639-4799. [CEM]
Catechesis/Religious Programs—Sheryl Reed, D.R.E.
Students 273.
Mission—Soileau, Allen Parish, St. Joseph, P.O. Box 479, 70655.

Raymond, Jefferson Davis Parish, St. Lawrence (1957), Rev. Eappen Joseph.
Res., 5505 Pine Island Hwy., Jennings, 70546. Tel: 318-584-2700.
Catechesis/Religious Programs—Students 270.

Sulphur, Calcasieu Parish,

1—IMMACULATE CONCEPTION OF THE B.V.M., (1959), Revs. Egidio A. Vecchio, M.S.; Maurice Linehan, M.S.
Res., 2700 Maplewood Dr., 70663. Tel: 318-625-3364; Fax: 318-625-9547.
Catechesis/Religious Programs—Bro. Edmund Normantowicz, M.S., D.R.E.
Students 401.

2—OUR LADY OF LASALETTE, (1961), Revs. Joseph A. Decoteau, M.S.; Lawrence A. Kohler, M.S.
Res., 602 N. Claiborne St., 70663. Tel: 318-527-6722; Fax: 318-527-0909.
Catechesis/Religious Programs—Tel: 318-527-8307. Stella Barkate, D.R.E.
Students 502.

3—OUR LADY OF PROMPT SUCCOR, (1919), Revs. Donald Thomas, M.S.; George Repchick, M.S.; Charles A. Gendron, M.S.; William O'Brien, M.S.; Bro. Donald V. Smith, M.S.
Res., 1109 Cypress St., 70663. Tel: 318-527-5261; Fax: 318-528-2991.
School—Tel: 318-527-7828; Fax: 318-528-3778. Mrs. Sharon Tolin, Prin.
Lay Teachers 19; Students 225.
Catechesis/Religious Programs—1029 Lasalette Dr., 70663. Tel: 318-527-9964. D.R.E.: Theresa Cooper; Terry Sittig.
Students 423.
Mission—Sulphur, Calcasieu Parish, St. Peter Claver, 465 Maple St., 70663. Tel: 318-527-5987.

4—ST. THERESA, (1971), Rev. Francis Fitzsimmons, M.S.; Mary Little, Admin.
Res., 4822 Carlyss Dr., 70665. Tel: 318-583-4800; Fax: 318-583-4818.
Catechesis/Religious Programs—Tel: 318-583-4010. Charlotte Giese, D.R.E.
Students 335.

Vinton, Calcasieu Parish, St. Joseph (1920), Rev. Charles L. Soileau.
Res., 1502 Industrial, 70668. Tel: 318-589-7358; Fax: 318-589-7843.
Catechesis/Religious Programs—Tel: 318-589-2982.
Students 400.
Missions—Edgerly, St. John Evangelist; Starks, St. Michael.

Welsh, Jefferson Davis Parish, Our Lady of the Seven Dolors (1904), Rev. Herbert May.
Res., P.O. Box 515, 70591. Tel: 318-734-3446; Fax: 318-734-3697. [CEM][JC]
Catechesis/Religious Programs—Tel: 318-734-3848. Betty LaBouve, D.R.E.
Students 350.
St. Joseph (1941) (African American), Rev. William D. Hogan, S.S.J.
Res., P.O. Box 607, 70591. Tel: 318-734-3673. [JC]
Mission—Iowa, Calcasieu Parish, St. Peter Claver, 400 W. 2nd St., 70547.

Westlake, Calcasieu Parish, St. John Bosco (1955), Rev. Msgr. Joseph A. Bourque; Deacons Fred Reed, Jr.; Garrett Caraway, Jr. In res., Rev. Msgr. Amos J. Vincent; Rev. Cyprian Eze.
Res., P.O. Box 66, 70669. Tel: 318-433-2467; Fax: 318-436-7766.
Catechesis/Religious Programs—Tel: 318-439-6585; Fax: 318-436-9766. D.R.E.: Fred Reed; Judy Reed.
Students 518.

Chaplains of Public Institutions

LAKE CHARLES. *Lake Charles Memorial Hospital*. Rev. Scott DesOrmeaux.

DEQUINCY. *Phelps Correctional Center*. Rev. Jude Brunnert, M.S., Chap.

SULPHUR. *West Clacasieu Cameron Hospital*. Rev. William P. O'Brien, M.S., Chap.

On Special Assignment:
Reverend Fathers—
Harris, Whitney G., Dir. Ministry Relations, McNeese State University, Lake Charles, LA 70605. Tel: 318-475-5426

On Duty Outside the Diocese:
Reverend Monsignors—
Melancon, Louis, 1074 Hwy. 748, Washington, LA 70589
Reverend Fathers—
Lopez-Velez, Mauricio, 131 Bank St., San Antonio, TX 78204
Miles, James, 115 Gladys Ave., Lansdowne, MD 21227
Mullen, Thomas, 70 Nutwell Ct., Lothian, MD 20711

Graduate Studies:
Reverend Fathers—
Borel, Albert W., St. Paul University, Ottawa,Canada
Esbind, Jace, St. Paul University, Ottawa, Canada

Retired:
Reverend Monsignors—
Bernard, M.J., P.O. Drawer 358, Grand Chenier, LA 70643
Daigle, Jules O., Box 266, Welsh, LA 70591
DeBlanc, Irving A., 1505 Jeff Ln., Lake Charles, LA 70605
Vidrine, Curtis S., 185 Our Lady Rd., Cameron, LA 70631
Reverend Fathers—
Herlong, Theophilus L., 5635 B Welcome Rd., Lake Charles, LA 70611
Smit, Gerard C., 105 Justice Way, Elkton, MD 21921

Permanent Deacons:
Broussard, Gordon, St. Raphael, IA
Caraway, Julius G., Jr., St. John Bosco Church, Westlake
Chapman, Norris, St. Joan of Arc, Oberlin
Dronet, Manny, Immaculate Conception, Maplewood
Eaves, John, St. Paul, Elton
Granger, James R., St. Henry, Lake Charles
Hobert, Malone, St. Theresa, Carlyss
Kohlhund, Sumner, St. Joseph's, De Ridder
Landry, Dan, St. Margaret, Lake Charles
LaPoint, Frederick, St. Philip Neri, Kinder
Lavine, Edward, Sacred Heart, Lake Charles
Mathews, Michael, Supt. of Schools, Diocese of Lake Charles
McNally, Ed, Immaculate Conception, Jennings
Michaels, Richard, Immaculate Conception, Maplewood
Mounce, Johnny, Our Lady of LaSalette, Sulphur
Normantowicz, Edmund, Our Lady of the Lake, Lake Arthur
Reed, Frederick, St. John Bosco, Westlake
Reynolds, Jack J., St. Theodore's, Lake Charles
Segura, John, Our Lady Help of Christians, Jennings
Serice, Maurice, Our Lady of LaSalette, Sulphur
St. Mary, Harry, Jr., Immaculate Heart of Mary, Lake Charles
Stearns, George, Our Lady of Good Counsel, Lake Charles
Thompson, Paul, Holy City Community, Lake Charles
Wagner, Harry E., Jr., Immaculate Conception Cathedral, Lake Charles
White, Milton, Immaculate Conception Cathedral, Lake Charles

INSTITUTIONS LOCATED IN THE DIOCESE

[A] HIGH SCHOOLS, INTERPAROCHIAL

LAKE CHARLES. *St. Louis High School*, 1620 Bank St., 70601. Tel: 318-436-7275. Vic Bonnaffee, Prin. Lay Teachers 39; Students 511.
For Catholic Studies: 920 Seventh St. Tel: 318-439-7432. Very Rev. John H. Giles, Jr., Vicar of Christian Formation.

[B] GENERAL HOSPITALS

LAKE CHARLES. *St. Patrick Hospital of Lake Charles*, 524 S. Ryan St., 70601. Tel: 318-436-2511
For a complete listing, refer to the Hospitals section.

[C] RETREAT HOUSES

LAKE CHARLES. *Holy City Community*, 2409A Second St., 70601. Tel: 318-824-7122. Deacon Ed McNally, Moderator & Admin.; Rev. Oris Broussard, Chap.

MOSS BLUFF. *St. Charles Center*, 2151 Sam Houston Jones Pkwy., 70611. Tel: 318-855-1232; Fax: 318-855-9062. Rev. Don Piraro, Dir.

[D] MONASTERIES AND RESIDENCES OF PRIESTS AND BROTHERS

ELTON.
**Herald of Good News, Inc.*, P.O. Box 789, 70532. Tel: 318-584-2038.

[E] SPECIAL RESIDENCES

LAKE CHARLES. *Our Lady Queen of Heaven Manor*, Villa Maria, 3905 Kingston St., 70605. Tel: 318-478-4780. Rev. Msgr. Irving A. DeBlanc, Pres. Units 62.

[F] NEWMAN CENTERS

LAKE CHARLES. *Catholic Student Center*, McNeese State University, 221 Aqua Dr., 70605. Rev. Whitney Miller.

[G] SOCIAL SERVICE CENTERS

LAKE CHARLES. *Catholic Service Center*, 1938 E. Broad St., 70601. Kathryn Malveaux, Dir.

[H] MISCELLANEOUS

LAKE CHARLES. *School Food Services of Lake Charles, Inc.*, 4029 Ave. G, 70615.

RELIGIOUS INSTITUTES OF MEN REPRESENTED IN THE DIOCESE

For further details refer to the corresponding bracketed number in the Religious Institutes of Men or Women section.

[0600]—*Brothers of the Congregation of Holy Cross.*—C.S.C.
[0275]—*Carmelites of Mary Immaculate.*—C.M.I.
[]—*Heralds of Good News.*
[0690]—*Jesuit Fathers and Brothers.*—S.J.
[0720]—*The Missionaries of Our Lady of La Salette.* (Prov. of Mary Queen).—M.S.
[]—*Missionaries of St. Paul.*
[0700]—*St. Joseph's Society of the Sacred Heart.*—S.S.J.
[0420]—*Society of the Divine Word.*—S.V.D.

RELIGIOUS INSTITUTES OF WOMEN REPRESENTED IN THE DIOCESE

[1010]—*Congregation of Divine Providence of San Antonio, Texas.*—C.D.P.
[0470]—*Congregation of the Sisters of Charity of the Incarnate Word, Houston, Texas.*—C.C.V.I.
[]—*Daughters of Mary, Mother of Mercy.*
[1140]—*Eucharistic Missionaries of St. Dominic.*—O.P.
[]—*Franciscan Sisters of Our Lady of Refuge.*—R.F.R.
[]—*Sisters of Emanuel.*—S.E.
[3830-16]—*Sisters of St. Joseph.*—S.S.J.

NECROLOGY

(No Deaths)

Diocese of Lansing

(Dioecesis Lansingensis)

Most Reverend

CARL F. MENGELING, D.D., S.T.D.

Bishop of Lansing; ordained May 25, 1957; appointed Bishop of Lansing November 7, 1995; consecrated and installed January 25, 1996. *Address all communications to Chancery: 300 W. Ottawa St., Lansing, MI, 48933.* Tel.: 517-342-2452; Fax: 517-342-2505.

Most Reverend

KENNETH J. POVISH, D.D.

Retired Bishop of Lansing; ordained June 3, 1950; appointed Bishop of Crookston July 28, 1970; consecrated September 29, 1970; appointed Bishop of Lansing October 8, 1975; installed December 11, 1975; retired November 7, 1995. *Res., 401-A E. Madison, DeWitt, MI, 48820.*

ESTABLISHED MAY 22, 1937.

CANONICALLY ERECTED AUGUST 4, 1937.

Square Miles 6,218.

Comprises the Counties of Clinton, Eaton, Genesee, Hillsdale, Ingham, Jackson, Lenawee, Livingston, Shiawassee and Washtenaw, in the State of Michigan.

For legal titles of parishes and diocesan institutions, consult the Chancery Office.

Chancery: 300 W. Ottawa, Lansing, MI, 48933. Tel.: 517-342-2440; Fax: 517-342-2515.

E-mail address: chancery@dioceseoflansing.org

STATISTICAL OVERVIEW

Personnel	
Bishop	1
Retired Bishops	1
Priests: Diocesan Active in Diocese	104
Priests: Active Outside Diocese	7
Priests: Retired, Sick or Absent	41
Number of Diocesan Priests	152
Religious Priests in Diocese	28
Extern Priests in Diocese	11
Ordinations:	
Diocesan Priests	4
Transitional Deacons	3
Permanent Deacons in Diocese	62
Total Brothers	9
Total Sisters	441
Parishes	
Parishes	93
With Resident Pastor:	
Resident Diocesan Priests	77
Resident Religious Priests	8
Without Resident Pastor:	
Administered by Women Religious	7
Administered by Lay People	2
Missions	1
Pastoral Centers	2
New Parishes Created	1
Professional Ministry Personnel:	
Lay Ministers	400
Welfare	
Catholic Hospitals	9
Total Assisted	644,597
Health Care Centers	5
Total Assisted	8000
Homes for the Aged	2
Total Assisted	250
Residential Care of Children	3
Total Assisted	250
Day Care and Extended Day Care Centers	1
Total Assisted	150
Special Centers for Social Services	10
Residential Care of Disabled	1
Total Assisted	60
Educational	
Diocesan Students in Other Seminaries	28
Total Seminarians	28
Colleges and Universities	1
Total Students	2,000
High Schools, Diocesan and Parish	4
Total Students	2,397
Elementary Schools, Diocesan and Parish	38
Total Students	10,060
Elementary Schools, Private	1
Total Students	345
Catechesis/Religious Education:	
High School Students	3,027
Elementary Students	20,469
Total Students Under Catholic Instruction	38,326
Teachers in the Diocese:	
Priests	8
Brothers	1
Sisters	16
Lay Teachers	641
Vital Statistics	
Receptions into the Church:	
Infant Baptism Totals	596
Adult Baptism Totals	110
Received into Full Communion	1,061
First Communions	4,449
Confirmations	3,559
Marriages:	
Catholic	1,061
Interfaith	680
Total Marriages	1,741
Deaths	224
Total Catholic Population	210,460
Total Population	1,668,243

Former Bishops—Most Rev. JOSEPH H. ALBERS, D.D., J.C.D., appt. Titular Bishop of Lunda and Auxiliary to the Archbishop of Cincinnati, Dec. 16, 1929; cons. Dec. 27, 1929; appt. first Bishop of Lansing, Aug. 4, 1937; died Dec. 1, 1965.—Most Rev. ALEXANDER M. ZALESKI, D.D., S.S.L., appt. Titular Bishop of Lyrbe and Auxiliary of Detroit, March 28, 1950; cons. May 23, 1950; transferred to Lansing Oct. 7, 1964; acceded See Dec. 1, 1965; died May 16, 1975.—Most Rev. KENNETH J. POVISH, D.D., appt. Bishop of Crookston, July 28, 1970; cons. Sept. 29, 1970; appt. Bishop of Lansing, Oct. 8, 1975; installed Dec. 11, 1975; retired Nov. 7, 1995.

Chancery—300 W. Ottawa St., Lansing, 48933. Tel: 517-342-2440; Fax: 517-342-2519. Office Hours: Mon.-Fri. 8-12; 1-4:30 Address all communications to this office.

Bishop's Office—300 W. Ottawa St., Lansing, 48933. Tel: 517-342-2452; Fax: 517-342-2505. Rev. STEVEN J. RAICA, Chancellor and Bishop's Personal Sec. Tel: 517-342-2454. Rev. MICHAEL D. MURPHY, Moderator of the Curia. Tel: 517-342-2450. Rev. GEORGE C. MICHALEK, Vice Chancellor. Tel: 517-485-9902. Rev. J. THOMAS MUNLEY, Dir. of Seminarians. Tel: 517-342-2507; Fax: 517-342-2515.

Formation Houses—

Emmaus House—Rev. J. THOMAS MUNLEY, Dir. Tel: 320 M.A.C. Ave. *East Lansing, 48823.* Tel: 517-351-1543.

CHIRHO—Rev. ROGER PROKOP, Dir., *St. Thomas the Apostle Church, 517 E. Elizabeth St., Ann Arbor, 48104.* Tel: 313-761-8606.

Vicar-General—Very Rev. SYLVESTER L. FEDEWA, *St. Gerard Church, 4437 W. Willow, Lansing, 48917-2109.* Tel: 517-323-2379; Fax: 517-886-1394.

Regional Vicars—Lansing: Rev. BERNARD REILLY, Livingston: Rev. DAVID HOWELL, Genesee-Owosso: Rev. JOHN KLEIN, Jackson: Rev. JAMES SHAVER, Lenawee: Rev. DANIEL WHEELER, Washtenaw: Rev. CHARLES IRVIN.

College of Consultors—Revs. THOMAS BUTLER; SYLVESTER FEDEWA; PAUL GREHL; MARK INGLOT; ROBERT IRISH; JOHN KLEIN; DAN MCKEAN; ROGER PROKOP; DARIN ROBERT; DONALD RUSCH; ALFRED RUSSELL.

Vicar for Charismatic Communities—Rev. PHILIP DUPUIS, *St. Mary Church, 14200 Old U.S. 12, Chelsea, 48118.* Tel: 313-475-1697; Fax: 313-475-3207.

Vicar for Religious—Rev. MICHAEL D. MURPHY, *Chancery Office, 300 W. Ottawa St., Lansing, 48933.* Tel: 517-351-7215; 7216; Fax: 517-351-7271.

Vicar for Vietnamese Apostolate—Rev. JOSEPH TRAN, *St. Casimir Church, 815 Sparrow Ave., Lansing, 48910.* Tel: 517-482-1346.

Ecumenical Officer—Rev. ROBERT T. KERR, *St. Joseph Church, 9425 Whittaker Rd., Ypsilanti, 48197.* Tel: 313-461-6555; Fax: 313-461-1444.

Commissions and Councils—

Pastoral Council—Sr. RITA WENZLICK, O.P., Exec. Sec., *300 W. Ottawa St., Lansing, 48933.* Tel: 517-342-2502; Fax: 517-342-2468.

Presbyteral Council—Rev. MARK INGLOT, Chm., *Queen of the Miraculous Medal Church, 606 S. Wisner*

St., Jackson, 49203. Tel: 517-783-2748; Fax: 517-788-4528.

Board of Education—MARY MATTHEWS, Pres., *747 Beverly Park, Jackson, 49203.* Tel: 517-789-8798.

Building Commission—Rev. GILBERT O. RAHRIG, *St. Joseph Church, 440 E. Washington, Howell, 48843.* Tel: 517-546-0090.

Cursillo Movement—Vacant.

Conciliation/Arbitration—WILLIAM D. PARSLEY, *232 S. Capitol, Ste. 1000, Lansing, 48933.* Tel: 517-482-2400.

Finance Council—Rev. DAVID M. STOTENBUR, *St. Thomas Aquinas Church, 955 Alton Rd., East Lansing, 48823.* Tel: 517-351-7215; Fax: 517-351-7271.

Priest's Assignment Commission—Rev. JAMES SHAVER, *St. John the Evangelist Church, 711 Cooper St., Jackson, 49201.* Tel: 517-784-0553; Fax: 517-788-5381.

Diocesan Offices And Departments

Office of Moderator of the Curia—Rev. MICHAEL D. MURPHY. Tel: 517-342-2450; Fax: 517-342-2505.

Diocesan Archivist—Rev. GEORGE C. MICHALEK, *300 W. Ottawa St., Lansing, 48933.* Tel: 517-485-9902; Fax: 517-484-8880.

Joseph H. Albers Trust Fund for Diocesan Vocations—Rev. J. THOMAS MUNLEY, *300 W. Ottawa St., Lansing, 48933.* Tel: 517-342-2507; Fax: 517-342-2515.

Diocesan Mission Office—(Includes Propagation of the Faith, Holy Childhood Assoc., Inter-Parish Sharing) Rev. PHILIP P. GALLAGHER, Dir., *300 W. Ottawa St., Lansing, 48933.* Tel: 517-342-2451.

Legal Advisor—CAMILLE S. ABOOD, *300 W. Ottawa St., Lansing, 48933.* Tel: 517-342-2456; Fax: 517-342-2505.

Diocesan Tribunal—

Judicial Vicar—Very Rev. DAVID M. STOTENBUR, J.C.L., *300 W. Ottawa St., Lansing, 48933.* Tel: 517-484-8870; Fax: 517-484-9080. (Address all rogatory commissions to the Diocesan Tribunal.).

Tribunal Judges—Revs. STEVEN J. RAICA, J.C.D.; RAYMOND J. GOEHRING, J.C.L.; EILEEN JARAMILLO, J.C.D.

Defenders of the Bond—Revs. BENNETT P. CONSTANTINE, J.C.D.; DANIEL WUNDERLICH, J.C.L.

Court-Expert—RICHARD G. STRIFE, Ph.D.

Notaries—VIRGINIA A. DELUCA; WANDA D. MILLER.

Cemeteries—Vacant, *300 W. Ottawa St., Lansing, 48933.* Tel: 517-342-2440.

Communications—MICHAEL DIEBOLD, *300 W. Ottawa St., Lansing, 48933.* Tel: 517-342-2475.

Development—JAY JOHNSON, *300 W. Ottawa St., Lansing, 48933.* Tel: 517-342-2503.

Finance Officer—THOMAS PASTULA, *300 W. Ottawa St., Lansing, 48933.* Tel: 517-342-2448; Fax: 517-342-2519.

Real Estate/Environmental Issues—CHARLES BAKER, *300 W. Ottawa St., Lansing, 48933.* Tel: 517-342-2443.

Catholic Charities—ROBERT J. SMITH, A.C.S.W., Chm., *300 W. Ottawa St., Lansing, 48933.* Tel: 517-342-2462; Fax: 517-342-2446.

Aging Ministry—ELLEN MCKAY, A.C.S.W., Dir., *300 W. Ottawa St., Lansing, 48933.* Tel: 517-342-2467.

Bishop's Council on Alcoholism-Chemical Dependency—SANDRA MILLAR, Dir., *300 W. Ottawa St., Lansing, 48933.* Tel: 517-342-2471.

Campaign for Human Development—VIRGINIA SOVIS, Coord., *300 W. Ottawa St., Lansing, 48933.* Tel: 517-342-2470.

Catholic Relief Services—VIRGINIA SOVIS, Coord., *300 W. Ottawa St., Lansing, 48933.* Tel: 517-342-2470.

Family Ministry—SANDRA MILLAR. Tel: 517-342-2466.

Social Ministry—STEPHEN RALL, M.A., Dir., *300 W. Ottawa St., Lansing, 48933.* Tel: 517-342-2469.

Peace and Justice Ministry—C. MICHAEL, Ph.D., Dir. Tel: 517-342-2466.

Respect Life Ministry—C. MICHAEL, Ph.D., Dir. Tel: 517-342-2466.

Project Rachel (Post-Abortion Counseling)—TONI ROSSI, Dir., *1500 E. Saginaw, Lansing, 48906.* Tel: 517-484-4449; Fax: 517-484-8880.

Diocesan Council on Womens Concerns—JOHANNA VANDEN BERG, *300 W. Ottawa St., Lansing, 48933.* Tel: 517-342-2465.

Education and Formation—Sr. DORITA WOTISKA, O.P., Ph.D., Chm., *300 W. Ottawa St., Lansing, 48933.* Tel: 517-342-2481; Fax: 517-342-2515.

Superintendent of Schools—Sr. DORITA WOTISKA, O.P., *300 W. Ottawa St., Lansing, 48933.* Tel: 517-342-2481.

Director of Instructional Programs PreK-12—MARY OLIVE DION, *300 W. Ottawa St., Lansing, 48933.* Tel: 517-342-2483.

Director of Catechesis—PETER RIES, *300 W. Ottawa St., Lansing, 48933.* Tel: 517-342-2486.

Director of Youth Ministry—JAMES CORDER. Tel: 517-342-2485.

Director of Lay Ministry—MARY TARDIF, *300 W. Ottawa St., Lansing, 48933.* Tel: 517-342-2512.

Director of Permanent Diaconate—Deacon JOHN CAMERON, *300 W. Ottawa St., Lansing, 48933.* Tel: 517-342-2509.

Priestly Life and Ministry—Rev. LARRY DELANEY, Dir., *300 W. Ottawa St., Lansing, 48933.* Tel: 517-669-8321 or 669-8279; Fax: 517-669-2708.

Director of Vocation Services—Sr. CARLA MOEGGENBORG, O.P., *300 W. Ottawa St., Lansing, 48933.* Tel: 517-342-2506.

Diocesan Ministries—Sr. RITA WENZLICK, O.P., Chm., *300 W. Ottawa St., Lansing, 48933.* Tel: 517-342-2502; Fax: 517-342-2468.

Campus Ministries—Vacant, *St. Mary Student Parish, Ann Arbor, 48104-2295.* Tel: 313-663-0557.

Christian Initiation Steering Committee—Sr. RITA WENZLICK, O.P., Chm., *300 W. Ottawa St., Lansing, 48933.* Tel: 517-342-2502; Fax: 517-342-2468.

Ministry with Persons with Disabilities/Deaf Ministry/Catholic Inquiry for the Blind—RICHARD STRIFE, Ph.D., Dir.; Sr. MARLENE TAYLOR, A.D., Outreach Worker, *300 W. Ottawa St., Lansing, 48933.* Tel: 517-342-2497; 342-2500; Fax: 517-342-2468.

Hispanic/Migrant Ministry—SERAPIO C. HERNANDEZ, *300 W. Ottawa St., Lansing, 48933.* Tel: 517-342-2498; Fax: 517-342-2468.

Young Adult Ministry/Criminal Justice Ministry—GARY ASHBY, *300 W. Ottawa St., Lansing, 48933.* Tel: 517-342-2495; Fax: 517-342-2468.

Worship Office—Rev. PHILLIP D. SESSIONS, Dir. RITA THIRON, Assoc. Dir., *300 W. Ottawa St., Lansing, 48933.* Tel: 517-342-2480; Fax: 517-342-2468.

Worship Commission—Sr. LAURENA ALFLEN. Tel: 517-655-2520.

Music Consultant—Vacant. Tel: 517-484-5332.

Black Catholic Ministry—RONALD LANDFAIR, *300 W. Ottawa St., Lansing, 48933.* Tel: 517-342-2496; Fax: 517-342-2468.

CLERGY, PARISHES, MISSIONS AND PAROCHIAL SCHOOLS

CITY OF LANSING
(Ingham County)

1—ST. MARY CATHEDRAL (1866), Revs. Michael D. Murphy; George C. Michalek. In res., Rev. Steven J. Raica.
Res., 219 Seymour, 48933. Tel: 517-484-5332; Fax: 517-484-0475.

2—ST. CASIMIR (1921), Rev. William Lugger; Deacon Ronald Henderson. In res., Rev. Joseph Tran.
Res., 815 Sparrow Ave., 48910-8003. Tel: 517-482-1347; Fax: 517-482-1313.
Catechesis/Religious Programs—Tel: 517-482-1346.
Students 70.

3—HOLY CROSS (1924), Rev. Pius Poff, O.F.M.Conv.; Deacon David L. Purvis. In res., Rev. Timothy Byrnes.
Res., 1611 Oakland Ave., 48915. Tel: 517-484-7768; Fax: 517-484-5741.
School—1514 W. Saginaw St., 48915. Tel: 517-487-6079. Michael Marshall, Prin.
Dominican Sister 1; Lay Teachers 10; Students 120.
Catechesis/Religious Programs—Students 70.

4—IMMACULATE HEART OF MARY (1949), Rev. Patrick Cwik; Deacons William Fudge, III; John Cameron; Oliver G. Washington. In res., Rev. Raymond Goehring.
Office: 3815 S. Cedar, 48910. Tel: 517-393-3030; Fax: 517-393-0855.
School—Tel: 517-882-6631.
Lay Teachers 22; Students 405.
Catechesis/Religious Programs—Tel: 517-393-3033.
Students 432.

5—RESURRECTION (1922), Revs. William J. Koenigsknecht; Joseph Sy Kim.
Res., 1531 E. Michigan Ave., 48912. Tel: 517-482-4749; Fax: 517-484-4740.
School—Tel: 517-487-0439.
Lay Teachers 13; Students 192.
Catechesis/Religious Programs—1527 E. Michigan Ave., 48912. Tel: 517-482-2605.
Students 104.

6—ST. GERARD (Delta Township, Eaton Co.) (1958), Revs. Sylvester L. Fedewa; Brendan J. Walsh; Deacons Edwin Schneider; Robert McPhilamy; Richard Savage. In res., Rev. Michael Rejent, O.S.F.S.
Res., 4437 W. Willow, 48917. Tel: 517-323-2379; Fax: 517-886-1394. [JC]
School—4433 W. Willow, 48917. Tel: 517-323-6126.
Lay Teachers 25; Students 543.
Catechesis/Religious Programs—Tel: 517-321-4179.
Students 440.

7—ST. THERESE (1949), Rev. Michael W. Kuchar; Sr. Margaret Ann Roggenbuck, O.P., Pastoral Min.; Deacon David Borzenski.
Res., 102 W. Randolph St., 48906. Tel: 517-487-3749; Fax: 517-487-3755.
School—2620 N. Turner St., 48906. Tel: 517-482-1634. Mrs. Elissa Greenburg, Prin.
Lay Teachers 14; Students 154.
Catechesis/Religious Programs—Tel: 517-482-4152. Mrs. Joanne McGinnis, D.R.E.
Students 250.

8—CRISTO REY (1961) (Hispanic), Rev. Frederick L. Thelen; Sr. Mercedes Dominguez, C.F.P.; Deacon Rogelio Alfaro.
Office: 5430 S. Washington, 48911. Tel: 517-394-4639; Fax: 517-394-8090.
Res., 820 Mel Ave., 48911. Tel: 517-394-0676.
Catechesis/Religious Programs—Students 135.

OUTSIDE THE CITY OF LANSING

Adrian, Lenawee Co., St. Joseph (1864), Rev. James W. Lothamer, S.S.
Res., 415 Ormsby St., 49221. Tel: 517-265-8938; Fax: 517-265-1987. [CEM]
Catechesis/Religious Programs—Tel: 517-265-3732.
Students 200.
Convent—404 Finch St., 49221. Tel: 517-263-1973.

St. Mary of Good Counsel (1853), Rev. Thomas J. Helfrich, O.S.F.S.; Deacons Richard Bayes, Jr.; Calistro Torres; Sr. Regina Albers, C.P.P.S. In res., Rev. Louis A. Komorowski, O.S.F.S.
Office: 305 Division St., 49221. Tel: 517-263-4681; Fax: 517-263-4682.
Res., 320 Division St., 49221. Tel: 517-265-4160; Fax: 517-263-4682. [CEM]
Catechesis/Religious Programs—Tel: 517-265-4160.
Students 301.

Ann Arbor, Washtenaw Co.,

1—ST. FRANCIS OF ASSISI, (1950), Revs. James G. McDougall; John A. Byers.
Res., 2150 Frieze Ave., 48104. Tel: 313-769-2550; Fax: 313-769-2550.
School—(Grades K-8). Tel: 313-665-8082.
Lay Teachers 25; Students 540.
Catechesis/Religious Programs—Tel: 313-663-9663.
Students 747.

2—ST. PATRICK, (1831), Rev. Terrence J. Dumas.
Res., 5671 Whitmore Lake Rd., 48105. Tel: 313-662-8141; 663-1851; Fax: 313-662-8142. [CEM]
Catechesis/Religious Programs—Students 200.

3—ST. THOMAS THE APOSTLE, (1835), Revs. Roger Prokop; Dwight Ezop; Deacons James Miles; Warren Hecht. In res., Rev. Richard C. Lobert (BAL).
Res., 517 Elizabeth St., 48104. Tel: 313-761-8606; Fax: 313-997-8432. [CEM]
School—Tel: 313-769-0911; Fax: 313-769-9078.
Sisters 1; Lay Teachers 17; Students 296.
Catechesis/Religious Programs—Tel: 313-761-8606. Jude Fournier, D.R.E.
Students 404.

4—ST. MARY STUDENT PARISH, (1915), Rev. Thomas M. Firestone. Pastoral Assocs.: Rev. Cecilio C. Reyna; Nicole J. Smith; Anita M. Bohn; Grace M. Girvan.
Office: 331 Thompson St., 48104. Tel: 313-663-0557; 0558; Fax: 313-663-2756. (Serving students, faculty, and staff at the University of Michigan.).

Bellevue, Eaton Co., St. Ann (1923). (Quasi Parish). Revs. Stephen Raica; Patrick Cwik.
Res., 312 S. Main St., 49021. Tel: 616-763-9372; Fax: 616-763-0067.

Blissfield, Lenawee Co., St. Peter the Apostle (1910), Rev. Randall J. Miller; Deacon James Martinez.
Res., 309 S. Lane St., 49228. Tel: 517-486-2156.
Catechesis/Religious Programs—Students 115.

Brighton, Livingston Co., St. Mary Magdalen Church (1993),
Res., 2201 Old U.S. 23, 48116. Tel: 810-229-8624; Fax: 810-229-6471. Rev. David Howell; Deacon H. David Scharf.
Catechesis/Religious Programs—Students 500.

St. Patrick (1832) (Irish), Revs. Thomas W. Thompson; Keith L. Horstman; Deacon Patrick A. McDonald. Pastoral Ministers: Margaret Mullally-Henne; Winn Rhadigan. In res., Rev. William J. Carolin Tel: 810-229-8646.
Res., 711 Rickett Rd., 48116. Tel: 810-229-9863; Fax: 810-220-0730. [CEM]
School—710 Rickett Rd., 48116. Tel: 810-229-7946; Fax: 810-229-6206.

Lay Teachers 16; Students 266.
Catechesis/Religious Programs—Tel: 810-229-4221; Fax: 810-229-6206. Sr. Theresa M. Fifer, D.R.E.
Students 884.

Brooklyn, Lenawee Co., St. Joseph's Shrine (Irish Hills) (1845), Rev. Alfred Russell, O.S.F.S.
Res., 8743 U.S. 12, 49230. Tel: 517-467-2183; Fax: 517-467-4285. [CEM]
Catechesis/Religious Programs—Tel: 517-467-2106.
Students 277.

Burton, Genesee Co., Blessed Sacrament (1957) (Hungarian), Rev. Denis R. Spitzley; John Griffith, Pastoral Assoc.; Deacon Mike Barrett.
Res., 6340 Roberta, 48509. Tel: 810-742-3151; Fax: 810-742-1409.
Catechesis/Religious Programs—Tel: 810-742-3196. Paul Schlegelmilch, D.R.E.
Students 81.

Holy Redeemer 1940, Revs. Vincent DeLorenzo; Jeffery Robideau; Earl Matte, Pastoral Min.
Res., 1227 E. Bristol Rd., 48529. Tel: 810-743-3050; Fax: 810-743-4381.
School—3468 S. Grand Traverse, 48529. Tel: 810-743-2520; Fax: 810-743-9102. Carol Olson, Prin.
Lay Teachers 14; Students 235.
Catechesis/Religious Programs—Tel: 810-742-9460. Susan Kachel, D.R.E.
Students 408.

Charlotte, Eaton Co., St. Mary (1868), Rev. Thomas D. Nenneau.
Res., 812 St. Mary Blvd., 48813. Tel: 517-543-4319; Fax: 517-543-9078.
School—905 St. Mary Blvd., 48813. Tel: 517-543-3460.
Lay Teachers 6; Students 109.
Catechesis/Religious Programs—Tel: 517-543-3460.
Students 230.

Chelsea, Washtenaw Co., St. Mary (1845), Rev. Philip Dupuis; Deacon Richard Shaneyfelt.
Res., 14200 Old U.S. 12, 48118. Tel: 313-475-1697; Fax: 313-475-3207. [CEM]
Catechesis/Religious Programs—Tel: 313-475-8164; Fax: 313-475-3250.
Students 354.

Clarklake, Jackson Co., St. Rita (1916), Rev. Lehr Barkenquest, O.S.F.S.; Deacon Louis Weitzel.
Res., 10720 Hayes Rd., 49234. Tel: 517-592-5470; Fax: 517-592-4098.
Catechesis/Religious Programs—Tel: 517-592-5718.
Students 366.

Clinton, Lenawee Co., St. Dominic's (1853), Rev. Donald P. Rusch.
Res., 220 Brown St., 49236. Tel: 517-456-4559. [CEM]
Catechesis/Religious Programs—Students 82.

Clio, Genesee Co., SS. Charles and Helena (1953), Rev. Gerald J. Ploof. In res., Rev. Eoin Murphy (Ireland).
Res., 230 E. Vienna St., 48420-1423. Tel: 810-686-9861; Fax: 810-686-8070.
Catechesis/Religious Programs—Tel: 810-686-6720.
Students 441.

Concord, Jackson Co., St. Catherine Laboure (1953), Patricia Robertson, Pastoral Coord.
Res., 211 Harmon Ave., P.O. Box 188, 49237. Tel: 517-524-7578.
Catechesis/Religious Programs—Students 99.

Davison, Genesee Co., St. John (1871), Rev. Andrew A. Czajkowski; Deacons Robert Poulson; Neil Huiskens; Dan Fairweather. In res., Rev. Leroy E. White.
Res., 404 N. Dayton St., 48423-1397. Tel: 810-653-2377; 653-8015; Fax: 810-658-1123. [CEM]
Catechesis/Religious Programs—425 N. Genesee, 48423. Tel: 810-653-4056. D.R.E.: Elaine Davis; Marianne Muchmel.
Students 668.

Deerfield, Lenawee Co., St. Alphonsus (1864), Rev. James F. Eisele.
Church Office: 222 Carey St., 49238. Tel: 517-447-3500; Fax: 517-447-3210. [CEM]
Catechesis/Religious Programs—Students 152.

St. Augustine, Livingston Co., (1843). (Quasi Parish). Rev. Carl A. Simon; Deacon Bernard J. Endebrock.
Res., 6481 Fausset Rd., Howell, 48843. Tel: 517-546-9807. [CEM]
Parish House: Tel: 810-750-0354.
Catechesis/Religious Programs—Students 333.

De Witt, Clinton Co., St. Jude (1971), Rev. Bernard L. Reilly.
Res., 409 N. Wilson, P.O. Box 280, 48820. Tel: 517-669-8335; Fax: 517-669-8343.
Catechesis/Religious Programs—Tel: 517-669-8341.
Students 353.

Dexter, Washtenaw Co., St. Joseph (1840), Rev. Bernard L. Tyler; Deacon Romolo Leone.
Res., 3430 Dover St., 48130. Tel: 313-426-8483; Fax: 313-426-6451. [CEM]
Catechesis/Religious Programs—Tel: 313-426-2674; Fax: 313-426-6451.
Students 360.

Durand, Shiawassee Co., St. Mary (1900), Rev. Joseph Aubin.
Res., 700 Columbia Dr., 48429. Tel: 517-288-6704.
Catechesis/Religious Programs—Tel: 512-288-6704.
Students 240.

East Lansing, Ingham Co., St. John the Evangelist, Student Parish (1958), Rev. Thomas D. McDevitt. In res., Revs. Peter C. Dougherty; Richard Preston. Campus Ministers: Sr. Mary Ann Warner, H.M.; Sr. Kathleen Kurta; Liz Schweitzer; Al Weilbaecher.
Res., 327 MAC, 48823. Tel: 517-337-9778; Fax: 517-337-8358.

St. Thomas Aquinas (1940), Revs. David M. Stotenbur; Karl L. Pung; Deacon Stephen Hilker.
Res., 955 Alton Rd., 48823. Tel: 517-351-7215; Fax: 517-351-7271.
School—915 Alton Rd., 48823. Tel: 517-332-0813.
Lay Teachers 24; Religious 2; Students 500.
Catechesis/Religious Programs—Tel: 517-351-5460.
Students 570.

Eaton Rapids, Eaton Co., St. Peter (1881), Rev. Bennett Constantine.
Res., 515 E. Knight St., 48827. Tel: 517-663-4735; Fax: 517-663-7110.
Catechesis/Religious Programs—Tel: 517-665-2088. D.R.E.: Denise Clarke, (Adults); Cheryl Marks, (K-12).
Students 177.

Fenton, Genesee Co., St. John (1843), Revs. David W. Harvey; William J. Turner.
Res., 600 N. Adelaide St., 48430. Tel: 810-629-2251; Fax: 810-629-2302. [CEM 2]
School—514 Lincoln St., 48430. Tel: 810-629-6551; Fax: 810-629-2213. Sr. Patricia Fischer, O.P., Prin.
Lay Teachers 13; Students 254.
Catechesis/Religious Programs—512 N. Adelaide St., 48430. Tel: 810-629-1850. D.R.E.: Sr. Jeanine Boivin, O.P.; Ronald Kenney.
Students 819.

Flint, Genesee Co.,

1—St. Agnes, (1928), Rev. John P. Klein.
Res., 500 W. Pierson Rd., 48505. Tel: 810-785-3483; Fax: 810-785-0637.
Catechesis/Religious Programs—Students 60.

2—All Saints, (1910) (Polish), Rev. Anthony P. Majchrowski.
Res., G-4063 W. Pierson Rd., 48504. Tel: 810-787-0491. [CEM]

3—Christ the King, (1929) (African American), Sr. Joanne Fedewa, S.L.W., Pastoral Coord.
Res., 1832 Seymour St., 48503. Tel: 810-233-0402; Fax: 810-233-0402.

4—St. Francis of Assisi. Closed. For inquiries for parish records contact the Chancery.

5—Holy Rosary, (1951), Rev. Paul Schermer.
Res., 5199 Richfield Rd., 48506. Tel: 810-736-4040; Fax: 810-736-9129.
School—5191 Richfield Rd., 48506. Tel: 810-736-4220; Fax: 810-736-9129.
Lay Teachers 11; Students 260.
Catechesis/Religious Programs—Students 207.

6—Our Lady of Guadalupe, (1957) (Spanish), Rev. Eduardo Lorenzo.
Res., G-2316 W. Coldwater Rd., 48505. Tel: 810-787-5701; Fax: 810-787-3198.

7—St. John Vianney, (1941), Rev. Douglas Osborn.
Res., 2415 Bagley St., 48504. Tel: 810-235-1812; Fax: 810-235-4911.
Catechesis/Religious Programs—Students 386.

8—St. Leo the Great, (1957), Rev. James B. Bettendorf.
Res., 3632 Wyoming Ave., 48506. Tel: 810-736-2150; Fax: 810-736-0122.
Catechesis/Religious Programs—Tel: 810-736-7200.
Students 95.

9—St. Luke, (1951), Sr. Judith A. Blake, S.S.J., Pastoral Coord.
Res., 3202 Forest Hill, 48504. Tel: 810-239-5851; Fax: 810-239-9864.

10—St. Mary, (1919), Rev. Francis Faraci.
Res., 2500 N. Franklin Ave., 48506. Tel: 810-232-4012.
Catechesis/Religious Programs—Tel: 810-232-8784. Frances Pavelich, D.R.E.
Students 39.

11—St. Matthew, (1911), Rev. Frederick H. Taggart, O.S.A. In res., Rev. Edward M. Gorra.
Res., 706 Beach St., 48502. Tel: 810-232-0880; Fax: 810-232-4148.

12—St. Michael, (1843), Rev. William F. Wegher; Sue Meissner, Pastoral Assoc.
Res., 609 E. Fifth Ave., 48503. Tel: 810-238-2679; Fax: 810-232-6820.
Catechesis/Religious Programs—Tel: 810-238-7981; Fax: 810-232-6820.
Students 146.

13—St. Pius X, (1955), Rev. Richard J. Groshek; Deacon David Pigott.
Res., G-3139 Hogarth Ave., 48532. Tel: 810-235-8574; Fax: 810-235-8580.
School—Tel: 810-235-8572.
Sisters 1; Lay Teachers 11; Students 271.
Catechesis/Religious Programs—Tel: 810-235-8573.
Students 195.

14—Sacred Heart, (1928), Dr. Connie McClanahan, Pastoral Coord.; Deacon Anthony Verdun.
Res., 719 E. Moore St., 48505. Tel: 810-789-8579. [CEM]

Flushing, Genesee Co., St. Robert (1875), Revs. Steven F. Makranyi; Michael J. Williams; Deacon Michael Lynch.
Res., 310 N. Cherry St., 48433. Tel: 810-659-2501; Fax: 810-659-2564. [CEM]
School—Tel: 810-659-2503; Fax: 810-659-4002.
Lay Teachers 21; Students 450.
Catechesis/Religious Programs—Tel: 810-659-8556.
Students 439.

Fowler, Clinton Co., Most Holy Trinity (1881), Rev. Raymond M. Rademacher; Deacon Mark Simmon.
Res., 545 N. Maple St., 48835. Tel: 517-593-2162; Fax: 517-593-2801. [CEM]
School—11144 Kent St., 48835. Tel: 517-593-2616.
Lay Teachers 5; Students 122.
Catechesis/Religious Programs—Tel: 517-593-3774; Fax: 517-593-2801.
Students 217.

Fowlerville, Livingston Co., St. Agnes (1891) (Irish-German-Polish), Rev. Francis M. George.
Res., 855 E. Grand River Ave., 48836. Tel: 517-223-8684; Fax: 517-223-0813. [CEM]
Catechesis/Religious Programs—Tel: 517-223-8684.
Students 266.

Gaines, Genessee Co., St. Joseph (1871), Sr. Ann Marie Petri, O.P., Pastoral Coord.; Deacon Currie Cormier.
Res., 118 E. Lord St., 48436. Tel: 517-271-8434. [CEM]
Catechesis/Religious Programs—Tel: 517-271-8434.
Students 124.

Goodrich, Genesee Co., St. Mark the Evangelist (1979), Rev. Mark Dehetre; Sr. Joan M. May, S.S.J., Pastoral Coord.
Church—7296 Gale Rd. - P.O. Box 131, 48438. Tel: 810-636-2216; Fax: 810-636-7319.
Catechesis/Religious Programs—Students 282.

Grand Blanc, Genesee Co., Holy Family (1946), Revs. James R. Swiat; George R. Daisy, II.
Res., 11824 S. Saginaw, 48439. Tel: 810-694-4891; Fax: 810-694-1583.
School—(Grades PreK-8) 215 Orchard St., 48439. Tel: 810-694-9072; Fax: 810-694-9405.
Lay Teachers 34; Students 697.
Catechesis/Religious Programs—Tel: 810-694-3080.
Students 465.

Grand Ledge, Eaton Co., St. Michael (1902), Rev. Robert H. McGraw.
Res., 345 Edwards, 48837. Tel: 517-627-8493; 627-8494; Fax: 517-627-1289.
School—Tel: 517-627-2167; Fax: 517-627-0289.
Lay Teachers 7; Students 145.
Catechesis/Religious Programs—Tel: 517-627-8493.
Students 350.

Hamburg, Livingston Co., Holy Spirit (1979), Rev. Timothy D. Krzyzaniak.
Res., P.O. Box 610, 48139. Tel: 810-231-9199; Fax: 810-231-6129.
Catechesis/Religious Programs—Tel: 810-231-6780.
Students 220.

Hartland, Livingston Co., St. John The Baptist (1843), Rev. David Speicher.
Res., 2099 Hacker Rd., Howell, 48843. Tel: 517-546-7200; Fax: 517-546-0403. [CEM]
Catechesis/Religious Programs—Tel: 517-548-2540; Fax: 517-546-0403.
Students 443.

Hillsdale, Hillsdale Co., St. Anthony (1858), Rev. Thomas W. Butler; Deacon Michael Nunez.
Res., 11 N. Broad St., 49242. Tel: 517-437-3305; Fax: 517-437-0034. [CEM]
Catechesis/Religious Programs—Students 234.

Howell, Livingston Co., St. Joseph (1900), Rev. Gilbert O. Rahrig.
Res., 440 E. Washington, 48843. Tel: 517-546-0090; Fax: 517-546-0090. [CEM]
School—425 E. Washington, 48843. Tel: 517-546-1380; Fax: 517-546-8939.
Lay Teachers 19; Students 286.
Catechesis/Religious Programs—Tel: 517-546-3171.
Students 510.

Hudson, Lenawee Co., Sacred Heart (1846), Rev. H. Paul Ruddy, O.S.F.S.
Res., 207 S. Market St., 49247. Tel: 517-448-3811. [CEM]
School—Tel: 517-448-6405.
Lay Teachers 7; Students 104.
Catechesis/Religious Programs—Students 162.

Jackson, Jackson Co.,

1—ST. JOHN THE EVANGELIST, (1856), Revs. James R. Shaver; Gregg Pleiness; Deacon Joseph A. Kratofil. Pastoral Assocs.: Sr. Eileen Souva, O.P.; Patricia Willson.
Res., 711 Cooper St., 49201. Tel: 517-784-0553; Fax: 517-788-5381. [JC]
School—405 E. North St., 49202. Tel: 517-784-1714; Fax: 517-788-5382.
Lay Teachers 18; Students 360.
Catechesis/Religious Programs—Tel: 517-784-5716.
Students 360.

2—ST. JOSEPH, (1902) (Polish-Lithuanian), Rev. Marian J. Lesniak.
Res., 705 N. Waterloo Ave., 49202. Tel: 517-784-9716; Fax: 517-784-5411. [JC]
School—717 N. Waterloo Ave., 49202. Tel: 517-784-4660.
Felician Sisters 2; Lay Teachers 7; Students 130.

3—ST. MARY, STAR OF THE SEA, (1881), Rev. Phillip Schweda; Deacons William Everett; Vincent C. Genco.
Res., 301 S. Mechanic St., 49201. Tel: 517-784-7184; Fax: 517-783-2571.
School—116 E. Wesley St., 49201. Tel: 517-784-8811; Fax: 517-788-3425.
Lay Teachers 11; Students 191.
Catechesis/Religious Programs—Tel: 517-788-6153.
Students 109.

4—QUEEN OF THE MIRACULOUS MEDAL, (1934), Revs. Mark Inglot; Miguel Carlos (Mexico).
Res., 606 S. Wisner, 49203. Tel: 517-783-2748; Fax: 517-788-4528.
School—811 S. Wisner, 49203. Tel: 517-782-2664.
Lay Teachers 13; Students 456.
Catechesis/Religious Programs—Tel: 517-782-3609.
Students 237.

5—ST. STANISLAUS KOSTKA, (1920) (Polish), Rev. Canon Darius W. Wyszynski.
Res., 608 S. Elm Ave., 49203. Tel: 517-784-0551; Fax: 517-784-2639. [CEM]
School—614 S. Elm Ave., 49203. Tel: 517-782-6095.
Sr. Mary Thaddea Meyers, C.S.S.F., Prin.
Lay Teachers 4; Students 50.

Laingsburg, Shiawassee Co., St. Isidore (1902), Rev. Duaine H. Pamment.
Res., 310 Crum St., 48848. Tel: 517-651-6617; 651-6722 (Office). [CEM]
Catechesis/Religious Programs—Tel: 517-651-6722.
Students 126.

Leslie, Ingham Co., SS. Cornelius and Cyprian (Bunker Hill) (1863), Rev. Eugene J. Beiter.
Res., 1320 Catholic Church Rd., 49251. Tel: 517-589-8492. [CEM]
Catechesis/Religious Programs—Students 97.

Manitou Beach, Lenawee Co., St. Mary on the Lake (1959), Sr. Helen Walling, I.H.M., Pastoral Coord.
Res., 450 Manitou Rd., 49253. Tel: 517-547-7496.

Manchester, Washtenaw Co., St. Mary (1871), Rev. Charles E. Irvin.
Res., 210 W. Main St., P.O. Box 249, 48158. Tel: 313-428-8811; Fax: 313-428-1393. [CEM]
Catechesis/Religious Programs—Students 165.

Mason, Ingham Co., St. James (1942), Rev. Kenneth McDonald; Virginia M. Guarnaccia, Pastoral Assoc.
Res., 1010 S. Lansing St., 48854. Tel: 517-676-9111; Fax: 517-676-1343.
Catechesis/Religious Programs—Rose Robertson, D.R.E.
Students 357.

Michigan Center, Jackson Co., Our Lady of Fatima (1954), Revs. Andrew J. Dunne, O.S.F.S.; Thomas J. Smith, O.S.F.S.
Res., 913 Napoleon Rd., 49254. Tel: 517-764-2088; 764-2112; Fax: 517-764-0461.
School—911 Napoleon Rd., 49254. Tel: 517-764-2563.
Sisters of St. Joseph 1; Lay Teachers 7; Students 152.
Catechesis/Religious Programs—Tel: 517-764-1321.
Students 153.

Milan, Washtenaw Co., Immaculate Conception (1854), Rev. John M. Bosco. In res., Rev. Clair M. Dinger (STU).
Church—420 North St., 48160. Tel: 313-439-2667; Fax: 313-439-2030.
Catechesis/Religious Programs—Tel: 313-439-2030.
Students 167.

Montrose, Genesee Co., Good Shepherd (1979), Sr. Josephine McNamara, Pastoral Coord.
Res., 400 N. Saginaw, P.O. Box 3274, 48457. Tel: 810-639-7600.
Catechesis/Religious Programs—Students 131.

Morrice, Shiawassee Co., St. Mary (1892), Rev. Matthew J. Fedewa; Deacon Gary Edington.
Res., 509 N. Main St., P.O. Box K, 48857. Tel: 517-625-4260; Fax: 517-625-3050. [CEM]
Catechesis/Religious Programs—Tel: 517-625-6140.
Students 209.

Mount Morris, Genesee Co., St. Mary (1867), Rev. Robert F. McKeon.
Res., 11110 Saginaw St., 48458. Tel: 810-686-3920; Fax: 810-686-4790. [CEM]
School—Tel: 810-686-4790.
Sisters of the Immaculate Heart of Mary 2; Lay Teachers 9; Students 185.
Catechesis/Religious Programs—Fax: 810-686-7640.
Students 177.

Okemos, Ingham Co., St. Martha (1988), Rev. Jonathan Wehrle; Deacon Thomas Quasarano; Barbara McNicol, Pastoral Assoc.
Church—1100 W. Grand River, 48864. Tel: 517-349-1763.
School—Tel: 517-349-3322.
Sisters of Charity 4; Lay Teachers 8; Students 131.
Catechesis/Religious Programs—Students 622.

Otisville, Genesee Co., St. Francis Xavier (1947), Sr. Carol Weber, O.P. (Adrian, Dominican).
Res., 212 Center St., 48463. Tel: 810-631-6305. [JC]
Catechesis/Religious Programs—Tel: 810-631-4237. Rose Nixon, D.R.E.
Students 100.

Ovid, Shiawassee Co., Holy Family (1966). (Mission). Rev. Daniel F. Wunderlich.
Res., 620 N. Mabbitt Rd., P.O. Box 612, 48866. Tel: 517-834-5855.
Catechesis/Religious Programs—Tel: 517-834-2138.
Students 125.

Owosso, Shiawassee Co., St. Paul (1871), Rev. Robert D. Kolenski.
Res., 111 N. Howell St., 48867. Tel: 517-723-4277; Fax: 517-723-9503. [CEM 2]
School—738 W. Main St., 48867. Tel: 517-725-7766.
Lay Teachers 11; Students 185.
Catechesis/Religious Programs—718 W. Main St., 48867. Tel: 517-723-1400.
Students 305.

St. Joseph (1923) (Slavic), Rev. David E. Fisher; Mary Ann Dunn, Pastoral Min.
Res., 915 E. Oliver St., 48867. Tel: 517-725-5215; Fax: 517-725-1519.
School—811 E. Oliver St., 48867. Tel: 517-725-8067; Fax: 517-725-1802.
Students 83.
St. Joseph Child Care Services—Tel: 517-723-2030.
Child Care 171.
Catechesis/Religious Programs—811 E. Oliver St., 48867. Tel: 517-723-4765.
Students 211.

Pinckney, Livingston Co., St. Mary (1857), Rev. Kenneth F. Coughlin.
Res., 551 E. Hamburg St., 48169. Tel: 313-878-3161; Fax: 313-878-2383. [CEM]
School—Tel: 313-878-5616.
Lay Teachers 9; Students 200.
Catechesis/Religious Programs—Tel: 313-878-2217.
Students 285.

St. Johns, Clinton Co., St. Joseph (1874), Revs. Robert Sirico, C.S.P.; Robert D. Lunsford; Deacon Marvin Robertson.
Res., 109 Linden St., 48879. Tel: 517-224-8994; Fax: 517-224-3475.
School—Tel: 517-224-2421.
Lay Teachers 10; Students 311.
Catechesis/Religious Programs—Tel: 517-224-8537.
Students 298.

Saline, Washtenaw Co., St. Andrew (1968), Rev. William J. Stevenson; Deacon Paul Ellis.
Res., 910 Austin Dr., 48176. Tel: 313-429-5210; Fax: 313-429-0680.
Catechesis/Religious Programs—Tel: 313-429-7776.
Students 775.

Swartz Creek, Genesee Co., St. Mary (1912) (Czechoslovakian), Rev. Amos H. Wischmeyer.
Res., 7563 Mary St., 48473. Tel: 810-635-3240. [CEM]
School—4413 Morrish Rd., 48473. Tel: 810-635-4985.
Lay Teachers 8; Students 138; Kindergarten 24; PreK 32.
Catechesis/Religious Programs—Tel: 810-635-3989.
Students 221.

Tecumseh, Lenawee Co., St. Elizabeth (1947), Rev. Daniel Wheeler; Deacons James Nicholson; Ray Pizana.
Res., 506 N. Union St., 49286. Tel: 517-423-2447; Fax: 517-424-7706.
Catechesis/Religious Programs—512 N. Union St., 49286. Tel: 517-423-4501.
Students 377.

Westphalia, Clinton Co., St. Mary (1836) (German), Rev. William A. Ashbaugh.
Res., 201 N. Westphalia St., P.O. Box 267, 48894. Tel: 517-587-4201; Fax: 517-587-3838. [CEM]
School—Tel: 517-587-3702.
Sisters of Christian Charity 1; Lay Teachers 14; Students 223.
Catechesis/Religious Programs—Tel: 517-587-4201.
Students 272.

Williamston, Ingham Co., St. Mary (1869), Rev. Dan McKean.
Res., 157 High St., 48895. Tel: 517-655-2620; Fax: 517-655-3933. [CEM]
School—220 Cedar St., 48895. Tel: 517-655-4038. Deborah Walker, Prin.
Lay Teachers 6; Students 120.
Catechesis/Religious Programs—Tel: 517-655-2520. Bernadette Moline, D.R.E.
Students 332.

Ypsilanti, Washentaw Co.,

1—ST. ALEXIS. Closed. For inquiries for parish records contact the Chancery.

2—ST. JOHN, Washtenaw Co., (1858), Rev. Edmond L. Ertzbischoff; Deacons Wayne Charlton; Robert Chadwick.
Res., 410 W. Cross St., 48197. Tel: 313-483-3360; Fax: 313-483-0712. [CEM]
Catechesis/Religious Programs—Tel: 313-483-6378.
Students 214.
Convent—411 Florence St., 48197. Tel: 313-483-0742.

3—ST. JOSEPH, Washtenaw Co., (1889), Rev. Robert T. Kerr.
Res., 9425 Whittaker Rd., 48197. Tel: 313-461-6555; Fax: 313-461-1444. [CEM]
Catechesis/Religious Programs—Tel: 313-461-6321.
Students 276.

4—ST. URSULA, Washtenaw Co. Closed. For inquiries for parish records contact the Chancery.

5—HOLY TRINITY STUDENT CHAPEL, Washtenaw Co., (1965), Rev. Robert L. Irish.
Res., 511 W. Forest, 48197. Tel: 313-482-1400; 313-487-9756 (Rectory).
Catechesis/Religious Programs—Students 100.

6—TRANSFIGURATION CATHOLIC CHURCH, Washtenaw Co., (1994), Rev. David Franco, O.S.F.S.
Res., 1705 E. Forest Ave., 48198-4160. Tel: 313-482-6240; Fax: 313-482-1547.

Chaplains of Public Institutions

Hospitals

LANSING. *Michigan Capital Medical Center, Sparrow Hospital*. Alice Hill, Chap., Tel: 517-646-6850.

ANN ARBOR. *University of Michigan Hospitals/Pastoral Care Dept.* Revs. Darin Robert Tel: 734-936-4041; Ben Werner; Deacon Wayne Charlton.
Veterans' Hospital. Rev. Vincent Van Doan, Chap.

Prisons

JACKSON. *Southern Michigan Prison*. Vacant. Tel: 517-788-7560, Ext. 6594.

MILAN. *Federal Correctional Institution* 48160. Rev. Howard Stunek, O.F.M., Chap., Tel: 313-439-1511 Ext. 232.

Training Schools

CHELSEA. *Cassidy Lake Tech. School* Tel: 517-475-1697. Rev. Warren Paulson, Chap.

WHITMORE LAKE. *W.J. Maxey Boys Training School* P.O. Box 349, 48189. Tel: 313-662-8141. Toni McNamara, Chap.

YPSILANTI. *Huron Valley Womens Correctional Facility*

3511 Bemis Rd., 48197. Tel: 313-577-4003. Alberta Asmar, Chap.

Special Assignment:
Reverend Fathers—
Dougherty, C. Peter, 319 Charles St., East Lansing, MI 48823
Schmitter, Phillip, 2381 E. Carpenter, Flint, MI 48505

On Duty Outside the Diocese:
Reverend Fathers—
Bui, Vincent, Emmaus Sprituality Center, P.O. Box 32-0084 Woodlands, Lusaka Zambia, C. Africa
Crowley, Timothy
Gerl, Robert, P.O. Box 117, Bardstown, KY 40004
Kropf, Richard, Star Rte. 1, P.O. Box 629, Johannesburg, MI 49751
Madey, Louis, 219 18th Ave. S.W., Calgary, AB T2S 0C2 Canada
Taylor, Jon, The College of Great Falls, 1301-20th St. S., Great Falls, MT 59405
Thomsen, Stephen

Retired:
Reverend Monsignors—
Howard, Vincent, 1849 Pierce Rd., Chelsea, MI 48118
Mehm, Walter, 465 Ashley, Grand Blanc, MI 48439
Reverend Fathers—
Bednarski, Mitchell J., 14465 Levon, Apt. D, Livonia, MI 48154-5022
Bottazo, Alex, Senior Clergy Village, 14455D Levan St., Livonia, MI 48154
Brakora, Anthony, 2705 Ridgecliffe Dr., Flint, MI 48532
Brennan, Thomas, 460 Egan Hwy., Brooklyn, MI 49230
Bush, John H., 9787 Burning Tree Dr., Grand Blanc, MI 48439
Carolin, William, J., St. Patrick, 711 Rickett Rd., Brighton, MI 48116
Cornelli, Neil, 2501 Via Del Ray, Fernandina Beach, FL 32034
Cummings, Paul, 851 Bassett Lake Rd., Middleville, MI 49333
Eder, Donald, 6290 Oak Creek Dr., Swartz Creek, MI 48473
Foglio, John, P.O. Box 4098, East Lansing, MI 48826
Handley, Robert, P.O. Box 147, 4076 Beacon Hill, Port Hope, MI 48468
Immel, Joseph, 1971 Watkins Lake Rd., Waterford, MI 48328
Klauke, Raymond, 6636 Sherbourne, Inkster, MI 48141
Koenigsknecht, William J., 5300 W. Mall Dr., Apt. 2002, Lansing, MI 48917
Ledwidge, Brendan K., 7900 Lange Rd., Fowlerville, MI 48836
Martin, Francis T., St. Gerard Church, 4437 W. Willow, Lansing, MI 48917
McKeon, Robert, 10018 Lehring Rd., Byron, MI 48418-0132. Tel: 810-266-5674
McKeon, William J., St. Joseph Parish, Box 379, East Jordan, MI 49727
Murray, Frank, 2642 Walden Woods, Jackson, MI 49201. Tel: 517-768-9483
Novak, James, 14701 Colt Lane, Sun City West, AZ 85375. Tel: 602-214-5186
O'Grady, Edward F., St. Joseph Home, 1000 E. Porter, Jackson, MI 49202
Rademacher, William, 3842 Azalea Dr., Las Cruces, NM 88005-1027
Ramer, Leo, 235 Quebec St., Goderich, ON N7A 2H2 Canada
Schmitt, James, J., 215 Banberry N., Lansing, MI 48906
Sparks, Thomas J., Magdalen College, 511 Kearsage Mountain Rd., Warner, NH 03278
Srebernak, Francis, R.R. 1, Rural Box 82B, Hancock, MI 49930-9705
Stockwell, C. Robert, 335 Walnut St., Mount Morris, MI 48458
Werner, Benjamin, 620 Oakdale, Chelsea, MI 48118. Tel: 313-475-2157
Williams, Francis, 3621 Penbrook Ln., Apt. 12, Flint, MI 48507
Zipple, Frank

Permanent Deacons:
Alfaro, Rogelio R., Cristo Rey, Lansing
Barrett, David P., Queens, Jackson
Barrett, Michael, St. Mary, Williamston
Bayes, Richard B., Jr., St. Mary, Adrian.
Berger, Kenneth, Unassigned
Borzenski, David J., St. Therese, Lansing
Brown, James S., Holy Rosary, Flint
Butler, Gerald, St. Robert, Cleveland
Cameron, John, Immaculate Heart of Mary, Lansing
Ceballos, Santos R., Sr., Office of Hispanics, Lansing
Chadwick, Robert, St. John, Ypsilanti
Charlton, Wayne, St. John the Baptist, Ypsilanti
Cormier, Currie, St. Joseph, Gaines
Doran, Endre, St. Joseph, Howell
Eddington, Gary, St. Mary, Morrice
Ellis, Paul, St. Andrew, Saline
Endebrock, Bernard J., St. Augustine, Deerfield
Everett, William, St. Mary of the Sea, Jackson
Fairweather, Daniel, St. John, Davison
Foley, Daniel R. (BGP), Christ the King Catholic Association, Ann Arbor
Fudge, William H., III, Immaculate Heart, Lansing
Garber, J. Patrick, Senior Status
Genco, Vincent, St. Mary, Jackson
Guajardo, Arturo, Jr., Unassigned
Hecht, Warren Jay, St. Thomas, Ann Arbor
Henderson, Ronald D., St. Casimir, Lansing
Herzog, Robert, Baltimore
Hilker, Stephen, St. Thomas Aquinas, East Lansing
Hubbarth, John A., Kalamazoo
Huiskens, Neil F., St. John, Davison
Igoe, James Gerard, Criminal Justice Ministry, Lansing
Kilburn, Gordon P., Serving Knoxville
Kratofil, Joseph A., St. John, Jackson
Lackney, Robert, Unassigned
Leone, Romolo Joseph, St. Joseph, Dexter
Lynch, Michael T., St. Robert, Flushing
Martinez, James N., Office of Hispanics, Lansing
Mathias, James E., St. Ann, Bellevue
Mattox, William, Jr., Atlanta
Mc Philamy, Robert E., St. Gerard, Lansing
McCarthy, John L., St. Michael, Grand Ledge
McDonald, Patrick A., St. Patrick Church, Brighton
McPeek, Gwynn S., Senior Status
Miles, James J., St. Thomas, Ann Arbor
Nicholson, James R., St. Elizabeth, Tecumseh
Novak, Edwin, Blessed Sacrament, Burton
Nunez, Michael, St. Anthony, Hillsdale
O'Toole, Gerald D., Diocese of Phoenix, AZ
Pigott, David J., Jr., St. Pius, Flint
Pizana, Eulalio (Ray), St. Elizabeth, Tecumseh
Pohl, Bernard J., St. Mary's, Westphalia
Poulson, Robert R., St. John, Davison
Preston, Richard, Serving Charlotte, NC
Purvis, David L., Holy Cross, Lansing
Quasarano, Thomas (DET), St. Martha, Okemos
Robertson, Marvin, St. Joseph, St. Johns
Savage, Richard, St. Gerard, Lansing
Scharf, H. David, St. Mary Magdalene, Brighton
Schneider, Edwin J., St. Gerard, Lansing
Shaneyfelt, Richard, St. Mary, Chelsea
Simmon, Mark C., Most Holy Trinity, Fowler
Simon, Edward, Pago, Pago
Spaulding, Kenneth R., Queens, Jackson
Spencer, Claude S., St. John, Davison
Tardif, Joseph A., St. Michael, Grand Ledge
Torres, Calistro, St. Mary of Good Counsel, Adrian
Verdun, Anthony W., Sacred Heart, Flint
Washington, Oliver G., Immaculate Heart, Lansing
Weitzel, Louis U., St. Rita, Clarklake
Wendell, Max W., Serving Gaylord
Wines, Francis J., Pensacola, Tallahassee

INSTITUTIONS LOCATED IN THE DIOCESE

[A] COLLEGES AND UNIVERSITIES

ADRIAN. *Siena Heights College - President,* 1247 E. Siena Heights Dr., 49221-1796. Tel: 517-263-0731; Fax: 517-264-7702
For a complete listing, refer to the Colleges and Universities section.

[B] HIGH SCHOOLS, DIOCESAN

LANSING. *Lansing Catholic Central High School,* 501 N. Marshall St., 48912. Tel: 517-267-2100; Fax: 517-267-2135. James B. Olin, Interim Prin. Lansing Catholic Central Board of Education. Priests 1; Lay Teachers 33; Students 533.

ANN ARBOR. *Father Gabriel Richard High School,* 530 Elizabeth St., 48104. Tel: 313-662-0496. Mr. Richard Bayhan, Prin. Gabriel Richard Board of Education. Lay Teachers 21; Students 293.

CLINTON. *St. Thomas More High-Boysville,* 8744 Clinton-Macon Rd., 49236. Tel: 517-423-7451. Mr. Carl LaGore, Prin. Brothers 1; Total Staff 25.

FLINT. *Luke M. Powers Catholic High School,* G-2040 W. Carpenter Rd., 48505. Tel: 810-785-4741. Mr. Joseph Forlenza, Prin. Powers Catholic Board of Education. Priests 1; Sisters 2; Lay Teachers 51; Students 931; Total Staff 55.

JACKSON. *Lumen Christi High School,* 3483 Spring Arbor Rd., 49203. Tel: 517-787-0630; Fax: 517-787-1066. Oblates of St. Francis de Sales. Revs. Thomas W. Rieden, O.S.F.S., Prin.; Richard L. McLernan, O.S.F.S.; James Bradley, O.S.F.S.; Paul F. Grehl, O.S.F.S.; John W. Bailey, O.S.F.S. Priests 4; Sisters 2; Lay Teachers 35; Students 654.

[C] ELEMENTARY SCHOOLS, PRIVATE

ADRIAN. *St. Joseph Academy Montessori Children's House.* (Grades PreK-5), 1267 E. Siena Heights, 49221. Tel: 517-263-4898. Sisters of St. Dominic, Congregation of the Most Holy Rosary (Adrian, MI). Mrs. Deborah Keller, Prin. Sisters 1; Lay Teachers 48; Students 350.

BURTON. *St. Thomas More Academy.* (Grades K-12), 6456 E. Bristol Rd., 48519. Tel: 810-742-2411. Mr. Harry A. Plummer, Prin. Students 120.

FLINT. *Donovan-Mayotte Catholic School,* 2319 Bagley St., 48504. Tel: 810-235-5687. Mrs. Kathleen Slattery, Prin. Lay Teachers 20; Students 364.
Dukette Catholic School, 530 W. Pierson Rd., 48505. Tel: 810-785-4743. Dr. Janet Haffner, Prin. Lay Teachers 16; Total Staff 27; Students 226.

JACKSON. *Jackson Catholic Middle School,* 915 Cooper, 49202. Tel: 517-784-3385. Mrs. Pamela M. Sullivan, Prin. Lay Teachers 20; Students 334.

[D] CATHOLIC CHARITIES REGIONAL OFFICES

LANSING. *Catholic Social Services-St. Vincent Home, Inc.,* 913 W. Holmes Rd., Ste. 290, 48910. Tel: 517-272-1524. Donald Ballentine, A.C.S.W., Pres.
Family Mental Health Clinic, 300 N. Washington, Ste. 301, 48933. Tel: 517-372-4020.
Foster Grandparent Program, 6545 Mercantile Way, Suite 2B1, 48911. Tel: 517-272-9119.
Refugee Service, 2722 E. Michigan Ave., Ste. 100-B, 48912. Tel: 517-484-1010. St. Vincent Home for Children, 2800 W. Willow St., 48917. Tel: 517-323-4734.
Senior Companion Program, 5815 Wise Rd., 48911. Tel: 517-882-8777.
Intergenerational Daycare Center, 13060 U.S. 27, Dewitt, 48820. Tel: 517-669-1551.
Child Welfare Program, 2800 W. Willow St., 48917. Tel: 517-323-4734.
Ballentine Stepping Stones, 825 N. Pennsylvania, 48906. Tel: 517-485-4644.
Capital Area Interfaith Respite, 654 S. Mercantile Dr., Ste. 1A, 48911. Tel: 517-393-8520.
Parish Social Ministry, 300 N. Washington Ste. 301, 48933. Tel: 517-372-4020.
Retired and Senior Volunteer Program, 6545 Mercantile Way A1-A, 48911. Tel: 517-887-6116. Total Assisted 232; Total Staff 35.
Cristo Rey Community Center, 1717 N. High St., 48906. Tel: 517-372-4700. Tony Benavides, Dir. Total Assisted 59,916; Total Staff 54.
Migrant Clinic-Cristo Rey Community Center, 1717 N. High St., 48906. Tel: 517-372-4700. Tomasa Velasquez, Coord. Total Assisted 420; Total Staff 1.

ADRIAN. *Catholic Social Services of Lenawee County,* 307 E. Church St., 49221. Tel: 517-263-2191. Luanne Reaume, Dir.

ANN ARBOR. *C.S.S. of Washtenaw County,* 4925 Packard Rd., 48108. Tel: 313-971-9781. Lawrence J. Voight, A.C.S.W. Total Assisted 6,000; Total Staff 50.

BRIGHTON. *Livingston County Catholic Social Services,* 10291 E. Grand River, Suite D, 48116. Tel: 810-227-2151. Nancy A. Rosso, Dir. Total Assisted 2,000; Total Staff 17.

FLINT. *Catholic Outreach,* 509 N. Grand Traverse, P.O. Box 815, 48501. Tel: 810-234-4693. Sr. Claudia Burke, S.F.P., Dir. Total Assisted 27,001; Total Staff 12.
Catholic Social Services of Flint, 901 Chippewa St., 48503. Tel: 810-232-9950. Deborah J. McCormack, A.C.S.W., Pres.
North End Soup Kitchen. Catholic Social Services, Flint. P.O. Box 114, 48505. Tel: 810-785-6911. Deborah J. McCormack, A.C.S.W., Pres. Total Assisted Daily 750; Total Staff 9.
Shelter of Flint, Inc., 310 E. Third St., 48502. Tel: 810-238-4711; Fax: 810-238-6001. Patricia A. Motter, Exec. Dir.
Emergency Shelter for Women. 1917 Delaware St., 48506. Tel: 810-233-0689; Fax: 810-233-0850. Duane Elling, Assoc. Exec. Dir.

JACKSON. *Catholic Social Services of Jackson,* 407 S. Mechanic St., 49201. Tel: 517-782-2551. Mr. Keith Krusky, Dir. Total Assisted 7,300; Total Staff 12.

OWOSSO. *Catholic Social Services of Shiawassee County,* 120 W. Exchange, 48867. Tel: 517-723-8239. Harriet Johnson, Dir. Total Assisted 371; Total Staff 6.

[E] CHILD CARE FACILITIES

LANSING. *Boysville of Michigan, Inc., Grants Management Office*, Everett Plaza, 3400 S. Cedar St., Ste. 201, 48910. Tel: 517-887-3022. Bro. Francis Boylan, C.S.C., Exec. Dir.; Adolf Armbruster, Grants Mgr.

CHELSEA. *St. Louis Center for Exceptional Children & Adults*, 16195 Old U.S. 12, 48118. Tel: 313-475-8430. Revs. Enzo Addari, S.C.; Joseph Rinaldo, S.C., Prov. Admin.; Fortunato Turati, S.C.; Matthew Weber, S.C. Operated by the Servants of Charity. Priests 4; Staff 45; Students 70.

CLINTON. *Boysville of Michigan, Inc.*, 8744 Clinton-Macon Rd., 49236. Tel: 517-423-7451; Fax: 517-423-5442. Bro. Francis Boylan, C.S.C., Exec. Dir.; Mr. Eugene Hausmann, Pastoral Min.; Bro. Chester Freel, C.S.C., Regl. Dir. Brothers 7; Boys 140; Total Staff 158. Residential and community based treatment programs for troubled youth and families with facilities located throughout the state of Michigan and one in the state of Ohio under the auspices of the Brothers of Holy Cross & Notre Dame.

Boysville's Family & Community Support Program, 8744 Clinton-Macon Rd., 49236. Tel: 517-423-7451, Ext. 532. Bros. Francis Boylan, C.S.C., Exec. Dir.; Chester Freel, C.S.C., Reg. Dir. Specialized Foster Care Treatment and Supervised Independent Living. Total Staff 6; Total Assisted 43.

JACKSON. *St. Joseph Home for Children, Inc.*, 1000 E. Porter, 49202. Sr. Mary Concepta Mastey, C.S.S.F.; Rev. Edward F. O'Grady, Chap. Felician Sisters (C.S.S.F.). Day Care Center-Retreat-Conference Center and Kindergarten (ages 2 months-6 years). Children 100.

MOUNT MORRIS. *Corcoran House/Boysville of Michigan, Inc.*, 8212 N. Jennings Rd., 48458. Tel: 810-687-5100. Bro. Francis Boylan, C.S.C., Exec. Dir.; Mr. Rick Boone, Regional Dir. A day treatment program for 12 boys and girls. Total Assisted 33; Total Staff 14; Total in Residence 6.

[F] GENERAL HOSPITALS

LANSING. *St. Lawrence Hospital and Healthcare Services*, 1210 W. Saginaw St., 48915. Tel: 517-372-3610; Fax: 517-377-0382
For a complete listing, refer to the Hospitals section.

ANN ARBOR. *Catherine McAuley Health Services Corporation*, 5305 E. Huron River Dr., P.O. Box 992, 48106. Tel: 313-712-3789
For a complete listing, refer to the Hospitals section.

Catherine McAuley Health System, 5305 E. Huron River Dr., Box 992, 48106. Tel: 313-712-4025
For a complete listing, refer to the Hospitals section.

McAuley Clinic Corporation, 5333 McAuley Dr., Box 994, 48106. Tel: 313-712-3788
For a complete listing, refer to the Hospitals section.

St. Joseph Mercy Hospital, 5301 E. Huron River Dr., P.O. Box 995, 48106. Tel: 313-712-3456
For a complete listing, refer to the Hospitals section.

Sisters of St. Joseph Health Services Corp., 455 E. Eisenhower, Ste. 300, 48108. Tel: 313-741-1700
For a complete listing, refer to the Hospitals section.

Sisters of St. Joseph Health System, Inc., 455 E. Eisenhower, Ste. 300, 48108. Tel: 313-741-1700
For a complete listing, refer to the Hospitals section.

FLINT. *Center for Gerontology*, 303 W. Water St., Ste. 100, 48503. Tel: 810-767-7080
For a complete listing, refer to the Hospitals section.

Genesys Ambulatory Health Services, Inc., 302 Kensington Ave., 48503. Tel: 810-232-9900
For a complete listing, refer to the Hospitals section.

Genesys Home Health & Hospice, 100 S. Dort Hwy., 48503. Tel: 810-762-7500
For a complete listing, refer to the Hospitals section.

Genesys Regional Medical Center/Flint Osteopathic Campus, 3921 Beecher Rd., 48532-3699. Tel: 810-762-4000
For a complete listing, refer to the Hospitals section.

Genesys Regional Medical Center/St. Joseph Campus, 302 Kensington Ave., 48503-2000. Tel: 810-762-8000
For a complete listing, refer to the Hospitals section.

GOODRICH. *Genesys Hospice*, 7280 S. State Rd., 48438. Tel: 810-636-5000
For a complete listing, refer to the Hospitals section.

GRAND BLANC. *Genesys Convalescent Center, Grand Blanc, Inc.*, 8481 Holly Rd., 48439-1899. Tel: 810-694-1711
For a complete listing, refer to the Hospitals section.

Genesys Health System, One Genesys Pkwy., 48439. Tel: 810-606-6600
For a complete listing, refer to the Hospitals section.

Genesys Regional Medical Center, One Genesys Pkwy., 48439. Tel: 810-606-5000
For a complete listing, refer to the Hospitals section.

HOWELL. *McPherson Hospital*, 620 Bryon Rd., 48843-1093. Tel: 517-546-1410
For a complete listing, refer to the Hospitals section.

OKEMOS. *Majorie J. Gardner Wellness Center for Women*, 5100 Marsh Rd., 48864
For a complete listing, refer to the Hospitals section.

SALINE. *Saline Community Hospital*, 400 W. Russell, 48176. Tel: 313-429-1600
For a complete listing, refer to the Hospitals section.

[G] HOMES FOR THE AGED

DIMONDALE. *St. Lawrence Dimondale Center*, 4000 N. Michigan Rd. (M-99), 48821. Tel: 517-646-6258
For a complete listing, refer to the Special Care Facilities section.

FLINT. *Marian Hall*, 529 Martin Luther King Ave., 48502. Tel: 810-238-7646
For a complete listing, refer to the Special Care Facilities section.

[H] CONVENTS AND RESIDENCES FOR SISTERS

ADRIAN. *Motherhouse of the Sisters of St. Dominic. Congregation of the Most Holy Rosary*, 1257 Siena Heights Dr., 49221-1793. Tel: 517-266-3400; Fax: 517-266-3545. Sr. Patricia Walter, O.P., Prioress. Chaplains: Rev. Roland Calvert, O.S.F.S. Total Congregation 1,160.

Motherhouse Mission Chapter, 1257 Siena Heights Dr., 49221-1793. Tel: 517-266-4107. Sr. Celestine Dunne, O.P., Chap. Prioress.

Rosa de Lima Mission Chapter. (located in the Dominican Republic), c/o 1257 Siena Heights Dr., 49221-1793. Tel: 809-534-8017. Sr. Rose Ann Schlitt, O.P., Chapter Prioress.

Dominican Life Center, 1277 Siena Heights Dr., 49221-1755. Tel: 517-266-3650. Sr. Janet Capone, O.P., Admin.

ANN ARBOR. *Congregation of the Sisters of the Holy Cross*, 331 Thompson St., 48104-2213.

DE WITT. *St. Albert the Great House of Studies*, 217 Schavey Rd., P.O. Box 309, 48820. Tel: 517-669-2277. Religious Sisters of Mercy, Alma Michigan 5.

[I] RETREAT CENTERS

ADRIAN. *Weber Retreat Center*, 1257 Siena Heights Dr., 49221-1793. Tel: 517-266-4000; Fax: 517-266-4004. Sr. Kathleen Schanz, O.P., Dir.

DE WITT. *St. Francis Retreat Center*, 703 E. Main St., 48820. Tel: 517-669-8321. Revs. Lawrence Delaney, Dir.; Philip Gallagher, Assoc. Dir.; Sr. Suzanne Eichhorn, O.P., Assoc. Dir. Total in Residence 3; Total Staff 25.

FOWLERVILLE. *Divine Will House of Prayer*. (Affiliated with Homes of Providence), P.O. Box 1184, 48836. Rose Marie Garvie, Contact Person.

HOWELL.

**Emmaus Ministries*, Kennedy Center, 1875 Eager Rd., 48843. Tel: 517-546-4440. Valerie Catenacci, Admin.

[J] NEWMAN CENTERS

ADRIAN. *Siena Heights College Newman Center*, 1247 E. Siena Heights Dr., 49221. Tel: 517-263-0731. Sr. Marilyn Uline, O.P., Dir. Campus Ministry.

ANN ARBOR. *St. Mary Student Parish*, 331 Thompson St., 48104-2295. Tel: 313-663-0557. Rev. Thomas M. Firestone. Serving the University of Michigan. (Refer to the parish section for complete campus ministry staff). Total Staff 10.

EAST LANSING. *St. John Student Parish*. Serving Michigan State University, 327 M.A.C. Ave., 48823. Tel: 517-337-9778.
(Refer to the parish section for complete campus ministry staff).

HILLSDALE. *St. Anthony*. (Serving Hillsdale College), 11 Broad St., 49242. Tel: 517-437-3305. Total Assisted 300; Total Staff 1.

YPSILANTI. *Holy Trinity Student Chapel*, 511 W. Forest, 48197. Tel: 313-482-1400. Rev. Thomas Firestone; Sr. Maryanna Pratt, S.S.J., Campus Min.; Scott Wright, D.R.E. Serving Cleary College; Eastern Michigan University; Washtenaw Community College.

[K] ENDOWMENTS AND TRUSTS

LANSING. *Chancery Office*, 300 W. Ottawa, 48933. Tel: 517-342-2440.

Benefit Trust of the Adrian Dominican Congregation (Adrian).

Church of the Resurrection Educational Trust Fund (Church of the Resurrection, Lansing).

Father Al Miller Educational Trust Fund (St. Mary Parish, Westphalia).

Father Gabriel Richard High School Trust Fund (Fr. Gabriel Richard H.S., Ann Harbor).

Greater Lansing Catholic Education Foundation (Lansing).

Immaculate Heart of Mary St. Casimir School Mary Goeddeke Educational Trust Fund. (IHM-St. Casimir School, Lansing).

Luke M. Powers Educational Trust Fund (Flint).

Lumen Christi High School Endowment Fund (Lumen Christi H.S., Jackson).

Most Holy Trinity Educational Trust Fund (Most Holy Trinity Church, Fowler).

Msgr. Lawrence H. Soest Educational Trust Fund (St. Mary Parish, Flint).

Rev. Joseph R. Robb Educational Trust Fund (Holy Rosary Parish, Flint).

Sacred Heart Educational Fund (Sacred Heart Parish, Hudson).

St. Francis of Assisi Educational Trust Fund (St. Francis of Assisi Parish, Ann Harbor).

St. John the Evangelist Parish Educational Trust Fund (St. John the Evangelist Parish, Jackson).

St John School Educational Foundation, Inc. (St. John Parish, Fenton).

St. John Vianney Educational Trust Fund (St. John Vianney Parish, Flint).

St. Joseph Church of Howell Trust Fund (St. Joseph Church, Howell).

St. Joseph Educational Trust Fund (St. Joseph Church, Owosso).

St. Joseph Educational Trust Fund (St. Joseph Church, St Johns).

St. Louis Center for Exceptional Children & Adults Endowment Trust Agreement (St. Louis Center, Chelsea).

St. Mary Educational Trust Fund (St. Mary Parish, Mt. Morris).

St. Mary Parish Educational Trust Fund (St. Mary Parish, Charlotte).

St. Mary Star of the Sea Educational Trust Fund (St. Mary Star of the Sea Parish, Jackson).

St. Michael's School Endowment Fund Policy (St. Michael School, Grand Ledge).

St. Paul's School Education Trust Fund (St. Paul Parish, Owosso).

St. Pius X Church Educational Trust Fund (St. Pius X Church, Flint).

St. Robert Bellarmine/Fr. Charles Jacobs Educational Trust Fund (St, Robert Bellarmine Parish, Flushing). (St. Robert Bellarmine Parish, Flushing).

St. Therese Educational Trust Fund (St. Therese Parish, Lansing).

St. Thomas Aquinas Educational Foundation Trust (St. Thomas Aquinas Parish, East Lansing).

St. Thomas Grade School Trust Agreement (St. Thomas the Apostle Parish, Ann Arbor).

St. Patrick Parish Educational Trust Fund (St. Patrick Parish, Brighton). For further information regarding these listings contact the Chancery.

St. Gerard Educational Trust Fund (St. Gerard Parish, Lansing).

Holy Redeemer Educational Trust Fund (Holy Redemer Parish, Burton).

[L] MISCELLANEOUS LISTINGS

LANSING. *Catholic Lawyers Guild*, 300 W. Ottawa St., 48933. Tel: 517-342-2449.

Diocesan Service Committee. (Catholic Charismatic Renewal), 835 Maycroft Rd., 48917. Dr. Connie McClanahan, Chm.; Rev. Philip Dupuis, Bishop's Liaison, St. Mary Parish, Chelsea.

Michigan Catholic Conference, 505 N. Capitol Ave., 48933. Tel: 517-372-9310. Sr. Monica Kostielney, R.S.M., Pres. & CEO.

Priestly Life and Ministry, 300 W. Ottawa St., 48933.

St. Vincent de Paul Particular Council, St. Vincent de Paul Store, 1020 S. Washington, 48910. Tel: 517-484-5395. John Fiero, Pres.; Rhett Johnston, Store Mgr.

Society of St. Vincent de Paul. St. Thomas Conference. 517 Elizabeth St., Ann Arbor, 48104. Sr. Dolora Neumaier, I.H.M., Pres.

ADRIAN. *Adrian Dominican Office of Development*, 1257 E. Siena Hts. Dr., 49221-1793. Tel: 517-266-3417. Adrian Dominican Sisters.

ANN ARBOR. *Alma Redemptoris Mater*, 331 Thompson St., 48104-2295. Rev. Thomas Firestone, Contact Person.

Ann Arbor Catholic Forum, P.O. Box 2184, 48106-2184. Tel: 313-482-6619. Mr. Anthony Patti.

CHIRO, St. Thomas the Apostle Church, 517 Elizabeth St., 48104.

Christ the King Catholic Center, 2630 N. Earhart Pl., 48105. Tel: 313-665-5040. Rev. Edward O. Fride (LAN).

The Marnee and John DeVine Foundation, 4925 Packard, 48108. Tel: 313-971-9781. Lawrence J. Voight, Contact Person. Total Assisted 1,312; Total Staff 1.

Renewal Ministries Inc., 230 Collingwood Blvd., Ste. 250, 48103. Tel: 313-662-1730. Ralph Martin, Pres. Total Staff 10.

Servants of God's Love, 3208 Ravenwood, 48103. Ann Shields, Contact Person.

**The Catholic Evidence Guild*, 639 Barber Ave., 48103. Tel: 313-995-3125. Tom O'Brien, Pres. & Dir.

BROOKLYN. *Lake Vineyard Camps, Inc., (Camp de Sales)*, 1150 Ventura Dr., 49230-9078. Tel: 517-592-2074. Ronald Helfrich, Contact Person. Total in Residence 3; Total Staff 3.

Oblate Fathers of St. Francis De Sales, Inc., 150 N. Main St., 49230. Total in Residence 18.

DAVISON. *Outreach East*, 425 N. Genesee St. - P.O. Box 61, 48423. Tel: 810-653-7711. Rita Berby, S.S.J., Dir.; Total Assisted 1,050; Total Staff 1.

FLINT. *Dukette Intercultural Center for Black Catholic Ministry*, 609 E. Fifth Ave., 48503. Tel: 810-235-4950. Mrs. Peggy Cooper, Admin. Sec.

Particular Council of Flint, Society of St. Vincent DePaul Store 1912 N. Franklin, 48506. Gene R. Myers, Pres.; Richard Twomley, Store Dir.

GRASS LAKE. *The Pious Union of St. Joseph*, 971 E. Michigan Ave., 49240-9210. Tel: 517-522-8017 (Voice/TDD); Fax: 517-522-8387.

"Now and at the Hour" Magazine: Revs. Joseph Rinaldo, S.C., Editor in Chief; Germano Pegoraro, S.C., Dir./Mng. Editor; Estelle M. Humenay, Asst. Dir./Editor.

JACKSON. *Society of St. Vincent de Paul*, St. Vincent de Paul Store, 1509 E. Michigan Ave., 49202. Tel: 517-784-0609. Particular Council of Jackson. Alvin Glombowski, Particular Council Pres.

RELIGIOUS INSTITUTES OF MEN REPRESENTED IN THE DIOCESE

For further details refer to the corresponding bracketed number in the Religious Institutes of Men or Women section.

[0140]—*The Augustinians.*—O.S.A.

[0480]—*Conventual Franciscans.*—O.F.M.Conv.

[0920]—*Oblates of St. Francis de Sales.*—O.S.F.S.

[1220]—*Servants of Charity.*—S.C.

RELIGIOUS INSTITUTES OF WOMEN REPRESENTED IN THE DIOCESE

[1920]—*Congregation of Sisters of the Holy Cross.*—C.S.C.

[2110]—*Congregation of the Sisters of the Humility of Mary.*—H.M.

[1070-13]—*Dominican Sisters.*—O.P.

[1070-14]—*Dominican Sisters.* (Grand Rapids).—O.P.

[1170]—*Felician Sisters.*—C.S.S.F.

[1470]—*Franciscan Sisters of St. Joseph.*—F.S.S.J.

[1440]—*Franciscan Sisters of the Poor.*—S.F.P.

[2575]—*Institute of the Sisters of Mercy of the Americas.*—R.S.M.

[]—*Mexican Passionist Sisters.*—C.F.P.

[0440]—*Sisters of Charity of Cincinnati, Ohio.*—S.C.

[0660]—*Sisters of Christian Charity.*—S.C.C.

[1560]—*Sisters of St. Francis of the Holy Eucharist.*—O.S.F.

[3830-11]—*Sisters of St. Joseph.*—S.S.J.

[2110]—*Sisters of the Humility of Mary.*—H.M.

[2350]—*Sisters of the Living Word.*—S.L.W.

[3260]—*Sisters of the Precious Blood* (Dayton, OH).—C.PP.S.

[3320]—*Sisters of the Presentation of the Blessed Virgin Mary.*

[2150]—*Sisters Servants of the Immaculate Heart of Mary.*—I.H.M.

DIOCESAN CEMETERIES

LANSING. *St. Joseph.*

FLINT. *New Calvary.*

NECROLOGY

† Fitzgerald, James C., (Retired). —Died Oct. 18, 1997.

† Jacobs, Charles E., (Retired). —Died Dec. 12, 1996.

† Wieber, Joseph E., (Retired). —Died Feb. 9, 1997.

Diocese of Lexington

Most Reverend

JAMES KENDRICK WILLIAMS, D.D.

Bishop of Lexington; ordained May 25, 1963; appointed Titular Bishop of Catula and Auxiliary Bishop of Covington on April 15, 1984; consecrated June 19, 1984; transferred to Lexington March 2, 1988. *Res., 1310 Leestown Rd., P.O. Box 12350, Lexington, KY, 40582-2350.*

ESTABLISHED MARCH 2, 1988.

Square Miles 16,423.

Comprises the counties of Anderson, Bath, Bell, Bourbon, Boyd, Boyle, Breathitt, Carter, Clark, Clay, Elliott, Estill, Fayette, Floyd, Franklin, Garrard, Greenup, Harlan, Jackson, Jessamine, Johnson, Knott, Knox, Laurel, Lawrence, Lee, Leslie, Letcher, Lincoln, McCreary, Madison, Magoffin, Martin, Menifee, Mercer, Montgomery, Morgan, Nicholas, Owsley, Perry, Pike, Powell, Pulaski, Rockcastle, Rowan, Scott, Wayne, Whitley, Wolfe and Woodford.

For legal titles of parishes and diocesan institutions, consult the Chancellor.

The Catholic Center: 1310 Leestown Rd., P.O. Box 12350, Lexington, KY, 40582-2350. Tel.: 606-253-1993; Fax: 606-254-6284.

E-mail address: kseib@cdlex.org

STATISTICAL OVERVIEW

Personnel	
Bishop	1
Priests: Diocesan Active in Diocese	37
Priests: Active Outside Diocese	1
Priests: Retired, Sick or Absent	12
Number of Diocesan Priests	50
Religious Priests in Diocese	22
Extern Priests in Diocese	2
Ordinations:	
Diocesan Priests	1
Transitional Deacons	2
Permanent Deacons in Diocese	29
Total Brothers	3
Total Sisters	176
Parishes	
Parishes	60
With Resident Pastor:	
Resident Diocesan Priests	36
Resident Religious Priests	6
Without Resident Pastor:	
Administered by Priests	6
Administered by Permanent Deacons	1
Administered by Professed Men Religious	1
Administered by Lay People	1
Administered by Pastoral Teams, etc.	9
Missions	6
Closed Parishes	1
Professional Ministry Personnel:	
Brothers	4
Sisters	32
Lay Ministers	27
Welfare	
Catholic Hospitals	6
Total Assisted	410,631
Health Care Centers	4
Total Assisted	74,502
Homes for the Aged	1
Total Assisted	82
Day Care and Extended Day Care Centers	3
Total Assisted	150
Special Centers for Social Services	1
Total Assisted	8,179
Educational	
Diocesan Students in Other Seminaries	5
Total Seminarians	5
High Schools, Diocesan and Parish	1
Total Students	758
High Schools, Private	2
Total Students	89
Elementary Schools, Diocesan and Parish	14
Total Students	2,894
Elementary Schools, Private	1
Total Students	148
Catechesis/Religious Education:	
High School Students	753
Elementary Students	2,865
Total Students Under Catholic Instruction	7,512
Teachers in the Diocese:	
Priests	2
Sisters	22
Lay Teachers	215
Vital Statistics	
Receptions into the Church:	
Infant Baptism Totals	718
Adult Baptism Totals	142
Received into Full Communion	298
First Communions	1,027
Confirmations	720
Marriages:	
Catholic	112
Interfaith	182
Total Marriages	294
Deaths	212
Total Catholic Population	41,977
Total Population	1,444,148

The Catholic Center—1310 Leestown Rd., P.O. Box 12350, Lexington, 40582-2350. Tel: 606-253-1993; Fax: 606-254-6284. Office Hours: Mon.-Fri. 8:30-4:30.

Vicar General—Rev. ROBERT H. NIEBERDING.

Chancellor—Sr. MARY KEVAN SEIBERT, S.N.D.

Executive Secretary To The Bishop—SHEILA STEWART.

Finances—Dr. STUART DUBA, Dir., *1310 Leestown Rd., P.O. Box 12350, Lexington, 40582-2350.*

Diocesan Consultors—Rev. ROBERT H. NIEBERDING, V.G.; Revs. WILFRED FRAENZLE; FRANK OSBURG; MICHAEL RAMLER; JOHN CURTIS; STEPHEN GALLENSTEIN; MICHAEL CHOWNING, O.F.M., *1310 Leestown Rd., P.O. Box 12350, Lexington, 40582-2350.*

Regional Councillors—Fayette Region: Rev. WILFRED FRAENZLE, Bluegrass Region: Rev. MICHAEL RAMLER, Mt. West Region: Rev. JOHN CURTIS, Mt. East Region: Rev. MICHAEL CHOWNING, O.F.M., Big Sandy-Licking Region: Rev. STEPHEN GALLENSTEIN.

Diocesan Tribunal—1310 Leestown Rd., P.O. Box 12350, Lexington, 40582-2350. Tel: 606-253-1993. Rev. JAMES ZUSY, O.P., J.C.D., Dir.

Judicial Vicar—Rev. JOHN E. LIST, J.C.L.

Associate Judges—Rev. JAMES AARON, M.Div., M.Ed.; Sr. MARGARET STALLMEYER, C.D.P., J.C.L.; Mrs. LAURA LE FAVE, M.A., J.L.L.

Defenders Of The Bond—Revs. THOMAS THAI, Ph.D.; MICHAEL WEGLICKI; MAURICE RAJKOVICH, J.D.; Sr. GAYLE BRABEC, B.V.M.; WILLIAM DAVENPORT, J.D.

Case Instructor—CAROLYN SNOWDEN.

Promoter of Justice—Rev. PAUL PRABELL, M.S.

Notary—CAROLYN SNOWDEN.

Ministry Admissions Board—Most Rev. J. KENDRICK WILLIAMS.

Priests' Retirement Board—Revs. PATRICK STEWART; THEODORE KELLER; RAYMOND STRATMAN; GREGORY SCHULER; Mr. JOSEPH SAULINO; Mr. JOHN D. PRICE; WILLIAM TOZER; JOB D. TURNER; STUART DUBA.

Diocesan Offices And Directors

Archives—Sr. MARY KEVAN SEIBERT, S.N.D., Archivist, *1310 Leestown Rd., P.O. Box 12350, Lexington, 40582-2350.* Tel: 606-253-1993.

Campus Ministry—Newman Center Dir., Contact The Catholic Center, *P.O. Box 12350, Lexington, 40582-2350.* Tel: 606-253-1993.

Catholic Charismatic Prayer Groups—Rev. LOUIS LIPPS, S.J., Liaison.

Catholic Scouting—Rev. MICHAEL WEGLICKI, Diocesan Dir. Tel: 606-289-5502.

Catholic Social Service Bureau—Sr. FRANCES MOORE, C.D.P., Dir., Office: *1310 Leestown Rd., Lexington, 40508.* Tel: 606-253-1993.

Communications—Sr. M. KEVAN SEIBERT, S.N.D., Dir., *1310 Leestown Rd., P.O. Box 12350, Lexington, 40582-2350.* Tel: 606-253-1993.

Conciliation, Arbitration Board—CAROL JACKSON, Chm.

Continuing Formation of Priests—Rev. JOSEPH MUENCH.

Deaf Ministry—J. KEVIN MARTIN, Coord.; Rev. JOHN LIST, Chap., *1310 Leestown Rd., Lexington, 40582-2350.* Tel: 606-253-1993. Tel: TDD: 606-744-7876.

Development Office—J. GRANT CHAPLINE, *1310 Leestown Rd., P.O. Box 12350, Lexington, 40582-2350.* Tel: 606-253-1993.

Ecumenical Liaison—Mr. ARDEN WOLTERMAN, *3 Lansdowne Estates, Lexington, 40582.* Tel: 606-268-9067.

Education—

Secretary of Educational Ministries—Dr. MARGARET RALPH, *1310 Leestown Rd., Lexington, 40508.* Tel: 606-253-1993.

Director Of Instructional Services—Sr. RITA BRINK, O.S.B., *1310 Leestown Rd., Lexington, 40508.* Tel: 606-253-1993.

Director For Catechetical Services, Adult Faith Development—PATRICK GUENTERT, *1310 Leestown Rd., Lexington, 40508.* Tel: 606-253-1993.

Director R.C.I.A., And Evangelization—Dr. MARGARET RALPH, *1310 Leestown Rd., Lexington, 40508.* Tel: 606-253-1993.

Disciples in Mission—Sr. CHRISTEN SHUKWIT, O.S.F., Dir.

Family Ministry—Ms. KATHLEEN TOMAZIC, Diocesan Coord., *P.O. Box 12350, Lexington, 40582-2350.* Tel: 606-253-1993.

Healthcare—Sr. M. KEVAN SEIBERT, S.N.D., Diocesan Coord., *1310 Leestown Rd., Lexington, 40582-2350.* Tel: 606-253-1993.

Hispanic Ministry—Rev. JOSEPH VON HANDORF, Diocesan Dir., *1310 Leestown Rd., Lexington, 40582-2350.* Tel: 606-253-1993.

HIV/AIDS Ministry—Rev. JOHN C. CURTIS, Diocesan Coord.

Justice and Peace—Sr. CLARA FEHRINGER, O.S.U., Diocesan Coord.

Commission for African American Catholic Concerns—Dr. MARIAN SWOPE, Dir., *439 Bourbon Ave.,*

Lexington, 40508. Tel: 606-254-2154.

Rural Life—The Catholic Center, 1310 Leestown Rd., Lexington, 40508. Tel: 606-253-1993.

Liturgy—Sr. CLARA FEHRINGER, O.S.U., Dir., *1310 Leestown Rd., Lexington, 40582-2350.* Tel: 606-253-1993.

Ministry Formation—Sr. IRIS ANN LEDDEN, S.S.N.D., Dir., *P.O. Box 12350, Lexington, 40582-2350.*

Mission Office, Propagation Of The Faith And The Holy Childhood—Sr. MICHAEL LEO MULLANEY, S.C.N., Diocesan Dir., *1310 Leestown Rd., P.O. Box 12350, Lexington, 40582-2350.* Tel: 606-253-1993.

Newspaper "Cross Roads"—THOMAS F. SHAUGHNESSY, Editor, *1310 Leestown Rd., Lexington, 40508.* Tel: 606-253-1993; Fax: 606-259-0951.

Pastoral Services—Sr. HELEN MAHER GARVEY, B.V.M., Diocesan Dir., *1310 Leestown Rd., Lexington, 40582-2350.* Tel: 606-253-1993.

Permanent Diaconate—BILL REED, Dir., *3510 Danada Dr., Lexington, 40502.* Tel: 606-272-1546.

Persons with Disabilities—Mrs. MARY PETRY, *124 Rolling Hills, Danville, 40422.* Tel: 606-236-5017.

Presbyteral Council—Most Rev. J. KENDRICK WILLIAMS, Pres., Ex-officio; Revs. ROBERT H. NIEBERDING, V.G.; FRANK OSBURG, Chm. MICHAEL CHOWNING, O.F.M.; JOHN CURTIS; STEPHEN GALLENSTEIN; WILFRED FRAENZLE.

Priests' Personnel—Rev. LAWRENCE HEHMAN, Dir., *1310 Leestown Rd., P.O. Box 12350, Lexington, 40582-2350.*

Prison Ministry—Rev. JOHN NOE, Diocesan Coord., *Castlewood Apts. #19, Russell, 41169.* Tel: 606-928-6414.

Religious—Sr. HELEN MAHER GARVEY, B.V.M., Dir., *1310 Leestown Rd., Lexington, 40582-2350.* Tel: 606-253-1993.

Respect Life—Sr. MARY KEVAN SEIBERT, S.N.D., Diocesan Coord.

Vocations—Most Rev. J. KENDRICK WILLIAMS, Dir. Assoc. Dirs.: Revs. JOHN MORIARTY; MARK DREVES; Sr. AMINO BEJOS, S.C.N.; Sr. KATHLEEN WEIGAND, O.S.B, *P.O. Box 12350, Lexington, 40582-2350.*

Youth Ministry—BARBARA MURRAY, Dir., *The Catholic Center, P.O. Box 12350, Lexington, 40582-2350.*

CLERGY, PARISHES, MISSIONS AND PAROCHIAL SCHOOLS

CITY OF LEXINGTON
(Fayette County)

1—CATHEDRAL OF CHRIST THE KING (1945), Revs. Gregory Schuler, Rector; Robert J. Murphy, S.J.; Deacon Arden Wolterman. In res., Rev. Louis Lipps, S.J.
Res., 299 Colony Blvd., 40502. Tel: 606-268-2861; Fax: 606-268-2861.
School—(Grades K-8) 412 Cochran Rd., 40502. Tel: 606-266-5641.
Lay Teachers 29; Students 530.

2—THE NEWMAN CENTER, HOLY SPIRIT (1963). Parish for Students, Faculty and Staff of the University of Kentucky. Revs. Thomas Farrell; Walter Bado, S.J.
Res., 320 Rose Ln., 40508. Tel: 606-255-8566; Fax: 606-255-8567.

3—MARY, QUEEN OF THE HOLY ROSARY (1960), Revs. Robert H. Nieberding; Mark D. Dreves; Deacon Jeremiah Noe. In res., Rev. Louis R. Schmidt.
Res., 601 Hill'N Dale Rd., 40503. Tel: 606-278-7432; Fax: 606-278-2453.
Church—2501 Clays Mill Rd., 40503.
School—Fax: 606-277-1784.
Sisters of Notre Dame 2; Lay Teachers 25; Students 532.

4—PAX CHRISTI CATHOLIC CHURCH (1994), Rev. Lawrence W. Hehman.
Res., 1790 Viley Rd., 40504. Tel: 606-252-4259; Fax: 606-223-7960.

5—ST. ELIZABETH ANN SETON (1980), Rev. Wilfred J. Fraenzle; Sr. Eileen Golby, O.S.F., Pastoral Assoc.; Deacon James Horine. In res., Rev. Jay Van Handorf.
Res., 1750 Summerhill Dr., 40515. Tel: 606-273-0134.
Parish Center: Tel: 606-273-1318; Fax: 606-272-6988.; Education Office: Tel: 606-273-2318.

6—ST. PAUL (1865), Revs. Daniel Noll; Gino Donatelli, S.J.; Deacon Louis Fister; Sr. Joann Hayden, C.D.P., Pastoral Assoc. In res., Rev. James Zusy, O.P.
Res., 501 W. Short St., 40507-1254. Tel: 606-252-0738; Fax: 606-225-6127. [JC]
School—Inter-Parish Elementary - Sts. Peter and Paul School. See St. Peter for details.

7—ST. PETER (1812), Revs. Daniel Noll; Gino Donatelli, S.J.; Sr. Mary Margene Koester, S.N.D., Pastoral Assoc. In res., Rev. Theodore Keller, (Retired).
Res., 153 Barr St., 40507. Tel: 606-252-7551; Fax: 606-252-1853. [JC]
School—Inter-Parish Elementary - Sts. Peter and Paul School, Tel: 606-254-9257; Fax: 606-254-9050.
Lay Teachers 19; Students 312.

8—ST. PETER CLAVER (1887), Revs. Daniel Noll; Gino Donatelli, S.J. Pastoral Assocs.: Deacon Boyd Marshall; Sr. M. Lea Paolucci, S.N.D.
Res., 410 Jefferson St., 40508-1319. Tel: 606-254-0030; Fax: 606-253-6740.

OUTSIDE THE CITY OF LEXINGTON

Ashland, Boyd Co., Holy Family (1860), Rev. John J. Wordeman; Deacon Robert Barringer. In res., Revs. John Dane; Barry Burrus.
Res., 900 Winchester Ave., 41101-7497. Tel: 606-329-1607; Fax: 606-329-1806. [CEM]
School—932 Winchester Ave., 41101. Tel: 606-324-7040.
Lay Teachers 13; Students 233.
Mission—Greenup, St. Lawrence.

Barbourville, Knox Co., St. Gregory (1910), Rev. Stanley Tillman, S.J., Admin.
Church—329 N. Sycamore Dr., 40906. Tel: 606-546-4461.

Beattyville, Lee Co., Queen of All Saints (1965), Rev. Richard D. Edelen; Sr. Alice Retzner, O.S.F., Pastoral Assoc.
Mailing Address: P.O. Box 563, 41311. Tel: 606-464-3357.
Res., 90 Railroad St., 41311. Tel: 606-464-8695.
Missions—Booneville, Owsley Co., Booneville Catholic Church of the Holy Family, (1984) R.R. 2, Box 221, Booneville, 41314. Tel: 606-593-6948. Pastoral Assocs.: Sr. Marge Eilerman, O.S.F.; Sr. Karen Lindenberger, O.S.F.; Campton, Wolfe Co., Catholic Church of the Good Shepherd, (1987) P.O. Box 742, Campton, 41301. Tel: 606-668-3731. Sr. Margie Zurieck, C.PP.S., Pastoral Assoc.; Heidelberg, Lee Co., St. Therese, (1948) P.O.Box 563, Beattyville, KY 41311. Tel: 606-464-8695.

Berea, Madison Co., St. Clare (1950), Rev. John C. Curtis; Sr. Anne Regina Lannon, S.S.J., Pastoral Assoc.
Res., 622 Chestnut St., 40403. Tel: 606-986-4633.
Mission—McKee, Jackson Co., St. Paul, (1973) P.O. Box 189, McKee, 40447. Tel: 606-287-7601.

Carlisle, Nicholas Co., Shrine of Our Lady of Guadalupe (1962), Rev. Thomas Vu Minh Thai.
Church—617 E. Main St., 40311. Tel: 606-289-5502.
Res., 1007 Main St., Paris, 40361-1709. Tel: 606-987-1571.

Corbin, Knox Co., Sacred Heart (1902), Rev. Roger K. Arnsparger. In res., Rev. Thomas Imfeld, (Retired).
Res., 703 Masters St., P.O. Box 455, 40702. Tel: 606-528-5222; Fax: 606-523-9901.

Danville, Boyle Co., SS. Peter & Paul (1807), Revs. Paul Prabell; Carl J. Moell, S.J.
Res., 117 W. Main St., 40422. Tel: 606-236-2111; Fax: 606-236-2922.
Mission—Junction City, Boyle Co., St. Patrick, (1885).

Cumberland, Harlan Co., St. Stephen (1940), Rev. Edward H. Lammert, O.F.M.; Sr. Margaret Mary Mouch, S.N.D., Pastoral Assoc.; Deacon Michael Daukas. In res., Rev. Maynard Tetreault, O.F.M.
Res., 304 Central St., 40823. Tel: 606-589-5616; Fax: 606-589-4549.

Frankfort, Franklin Co., Good Shepherd (1848), Rev. Michael Ramler; Sr. Mary Clare Windholz, R.S.M., Pastoral Assoc.; Deacons James B. Barton; Joseph Alessio; Thomas Snyder.
Res., 310 Wapping St., 40601. Tel: 502-227-4511; Fax: 502-875-9854.
School—(Grades K-8) 316 Wapping St., 40601. Tel: 502-223-5041.
Lay Teachers 20; Students 302.

Georgetown, Scott Co., St. John's (1869), Rev. John E. List; Deacon John Calandrella.
Res., 604 E. Main St., 40324. Tel: 502-863-3404. [CEM]
School—(Grades K-5) 106 Military St., 40324. Tel: 502-863-2607.
Religious 2; Lay Teachers 4; Students 129.
Mission—White Sulphur, Scott Co., St. Francis de Sales, (1794) 4086 Frankfort Pike, 40324. Tel: 502-863-4516.

Grayson, Carter Co., Ss. John & Elizabeth (1964), Rev. Bruce C. Brylinski, Glmy.
Church—799 State Hwy. 1947, 41143. Tel: 606-474-9979.
Res., P.O. Box 841, 41143. Tel: 606-474-9897.

Harlan, Harlan Co., Holy Trinity (1948), Bro. Mark Ligett, O.F.M., Pastoral Dir.; Rev. Edward H. Lammert, O.F.M., Pastoral Coord.; Deacon Michael Daukas.
Res., 2536 S. U.S. Hwy. 421, 40831-1798. Tel: 606-573-6311; Fax: 606-574-0093.
School—Tel: 606-573-3570.
Sisters of Notre Dame 3; Lay Teachers 4; Students 100.

Harrodsburg, Mercer Co., St. Andrew (1858), Rev. Joseph Muench; Sr. Maria Goretti Browne, O.P., Pastoral Assoc.
Res., 334 S. Chiles, 40330. Tel: 606-734-4270; Fax: 606-733-9770.
Mission—Perryville, Boyle Co., St. Mary, (1949).

Hazard, Perry Co., Mother of Good Counsel (1913), Rev. Michael Chowning, O.F.M.; Ms. Patricia Riestenberg, Pastoral Assoc.
Res., 329 Poplar & Cedar Sts., 41701. Tel: 606-436-2533.

Jackson, Breathitt Co., Holy Cross (1923), Mrs. Joan Houk, M.Div., Pastoral Dir.; Rev. Michael Chowning, O.F.M.
Church—46 Brewers Dr., 41339-9616. Tel: 606-666-7871. [CEM]

Jellico, Whitley Co., KY & Campbell Co., TN, St. Boniface (1886), Rev. Robert Damron.
Res., 76 W. Sycamore St., Williamsburg, 40769. Tel: 606-549-2156. [CEM]

Jenkins, Letcher Co., St. George (1913), Rev. Edward L. Randall, O.M.I.
Res., P.O. Box 787, 41537. Tel: 606-832-2409.
Mission—McRoberts, Letcher Co., Holy Angels, (1960).

Lancaster, Garrard Co., St. William (1951), Rev. Michael Weglicki.
Res., 224 Lexington St., P.O. Box 261, 40444. Tel: 606-792-4009.

Lawrenceburg, Anderson Co., St. Lawrence (1873), Rev. Charles J. McDonald; Deacon Thomas Rohan.
Res., 105 Woodland Park Circle, 40342. Tel: 502-839-6381.

London, Laurel Co., St. William/St. Sylvester (1868), Rev. Jerome F. Stern.
Res., 525 W. 5th St., 40741. Tel: 606-864-7500; Fax: 606-864-8263. [CEM]

Louisa, Lawrence Co., St. Jude (1982), Rev. Msgr. Ralph Beiting.
Res., Rte. 5, Box 1083, 41230. Tel: 606-638-0219; Fax: 606-638-0220.
Mission—Hode, Martin Co., St. John Neumann, (1980) Rte. 292, Hode 41223. Tel: 606-395-5947.

Lynch, Harlan Co., Church of the Resurrection (1917), Rev. Edward H. Lammert, O.F.M.; Sr. Margaret Mary Mouch, S.N.D., Pastoral Assoc.
Res., 304 Central St., Cumberland, 40823. Tel: 606-589-5616; Fax: 606-589-4549.

Manchester, Clay Co., St. Ann (1952), Rev. Arturo Molina.
Res., 222 Town Branch Rd., P.O. Box 411, 40962. Tel: 606-598-2718.

Middlesboro, Bell Co., St. Julian (1890), Rev. Lee Francis Trimbur, Admin.; Deacon Donald Flowers.
Res., 118 E. Chester Ave., 40965-1256. Tel: 606-248-2068; Fax: 606-242-3290.
School—(Grades K-8) 116 E. Chester Ave., 40965. Tel: 606-248-8309.
Sisters 1; Lay Teachers 3; Students 70.
Mission—Pineville, Bell Co., St. Anthony, (1889) P.O. Box 628, Pineville 40977-0628. Tel: 606-337-2189.

Morehead, Rowan Co., Church of Jesus Our Savior (1961), Rev. William J. Fedders; Deacon William T. Buelterman.
Res., 315 Battson, Box 307, 40351. Tel: 606-784-4392.
Chapel—Morehead, St. Claire Medical Center, Tel: 606-783-6500.

Monticello, Wayne Co., St. Peter (1967), Deacon John Tohill, Pastoral Dir.; Rev. John Kieffer, S.J.
Office: P.O. Box 669, 42633. Tel: 606-348-9416.
Res., 109 Cooper Dr., Somerset, 42501. Tel: 606-678-4928.

Mt. Sterling, Montgomery Co., St. Patrick (1868), Rev. Msgr. John Rolf.
Res., 139 W. Main St., 40353. Tel: 606-498-0300; Fax: 606-498-2116. [CEM]

Mt. Vernon, Rockcastle Co., Our Lady of Mt. Vernon (1954), Rev. John C. Curtis. Pastoral Assocs.: Ed & Tricia Cortas.
Res., 622 Chestnut St., Berea, 40403. Tel: 606-256-4170.

Nicholasville, Jessamine Co., St. Luke (1867), Rev. William C. Bush; Deacon Carter Ross, Jr.
Res., 304 S. Main St., 40356. Tel: 606-885-4892.

Ottenheim, Lincoln Co., St. Sylvester (1885), Rev. Michael Weglicki.
Res., 224 Lexington St., P.O. Box 261, Lancaster, 40444. Tel: 606-792-4009. [CEM]

Paintsville, Johnson Co., St. Michael Catholic Church (1941), Rev. Terence E. Hoppenjans.
Res., 720 Washington Ave., 41240. Tel: 606-789-4455; Fax: 606-789-3661.
School—Our Lady of the Mountains, 405 Third St., 41240. Tel: 606-789-3661.
Sisters 2; Lay Teachers 7; Students 67.

Paris, Bourbon Co., Annunciation of the Blessed Virgin Mary (1856), Rev. Thomas Vu Minh Thai.
Res., 1007 Main St., 40361. Tel: 606-987-1571. [CEM]
School—St. Mary, 1121 Main St., 40361. Tel: 606-987-3815.
Sisters of Charity of Nazareth 1; Lay Teachers 5; Students 82.

Pikeville, Pike Co., St. Francis of Assisi (1949), Revs. Stephen Gallenstein; Linh Nguyen.
Res., 808 Bryan St.-Keel Addition, 41501. Tel: 606-437-6822.
Church—149 College St., 41501.
School—(Grades K-6) 809 Bryan St., 41501. Tel: 606-437-6117.
Sisters 1; Lay Teachers 3; Students 82.
Missions—Elkhorn City, Pike Co., St. Joseph the Worker, (1985) P.O. Box 55, Elkhorn City, 41522. Tel: 606-754-5225; Phelps, Pike Co., Jesus of the Mountains Catholic Church, (1988) 38 Birch Ct., Phelps, 41553. Tel: 606-456-7909. Sr. Grace Pasquarello, S.S.J., Pastoral Min.

Prestonsburg, Floyd Co., St. Martha (1984), Rev. John P. Moriarty.
Res., 75 Martha's Vineyard, 41653. Tel: 606-874-9526; Fax: 606-874-9526.
Mission—Salyersville, Magoffin Co., St. Luke's, (1982) 1221 Parkway Dr., 41240. Tel: 606-349-5320. Sr. Mary Catherine Vukmanic, O.S.U., Pastoral Assoc.
Chapel—Martin, Our Lady of the Way Hospital, Tel: 606-285-5181.

Ravenna, Estill Co., St. Elizabeth (1932), Rev. William G. Poole; Sr. Alice Rohe, O.S.F., Pastoral Assoc.
Res., 316 5th St., 40472. Tel: 606-723-4705.
Mission—Stanton, Powell Co., Our Lady of the Mountains, (1984) 1093 E. College, Stanton, 40380. Tel: 606-663-5919. Pastoral Assocs.: Sr. Kathleen McMullin, O.S.F.; Sr. Eileen Doherty.

Richmond, Madison Co., St. Mark (1867), Rev. Kenneth Waibel; Deacon Richard Jackson.
Res., 608 W. Main St., 40475. Tel: 606-623-2989.
School—Tel: 606-623-9112.
Lay Teachers 8; Students 176.
Mission—Richmond, St. Stephen the Martyr, (1977). (Eastern Kentucky University, Newman Center). Tel: 606-623-9400.

Somerset, Pulaski Co., St. Mildred (1887), Rev. Patrick F. Stewart; Deacons G. A. Weigel; Vincent E. Cheshire; John Borders; Larry Cranfill.
Res., 203 S. Central Ave., 42501. Tel: 606-678-5051.

Versailles, Woodford Co., St. Leo (1891), Rev. Frank C. Osburg; Deacon James Cox.
Res., 295 Huntertown Rd., 40383. Tel: 606-873-4573; Fax: 606-873-1495.
School—239 N. Main St., 40383. Tel: 606-873-4591.
Sisters of Notre Dame 1; Lay Teachers 10; Students 212.

West Liberty, Morgan Co., Prince of Peace (1963), Rev. Peter Richardson, Glmy.
Res., Pine Acres Dr., P.O. Box 393, 41472. Tel: 606-743-4817; Fax: 606-743-3266.
Mission—Owingsville, Bath Co., St. Julie Billiart, (1969). Deacon William R. Grimes.

Williamsburg, Whitley Co., Our Lady of Perpetual Help (1963), Rev. Robert Damron.
Res., 76 W. Sycamore St., 40769. Tel: 606-549-2156.

Winchester, Clark Co., St. Joseph (1872), Rev. Joseph A. Saulino.
Res., 254 S. Main St., 40391. Tel: 606-744-4917.
School—St. Agatha Academy, (Grades K-6). (Montessori) 244 S. Main St., 40391. Tel: 606-744-6484.
Sisters of Divine Providence of Kentucky 2; Lay Teachers 8; Students 178.

Whitley City, Mc Creaky Co., Good Shepherd Chapel (1974), Rev. Carroll Howlin (JOL) Admin.
Res., P.O. Box 350, 42653. Tel: 606-376-5815.

Chaplains of Public Institutions

LEXINGTON. *Federal Medical Center* 3301 Leestown Rd., 40507. Deacon Thaddeus Harbowy.
Veterans Administration Hospital Leestown Pk., 40511. Tel: 606-233-4511. Rev. George C. Maynard, S.J (DET) Chap.

ASHLAND. *Federal Correctional Institution*. Castlewood Apt., #19, Russell, 41169. Rev. John P. Noe, Chap.

MANCHESTER. *Federal Correctional Institution*. Rev. Arturo Molina, Chap.

Special Assignment:
Reverend Fathers—
Johnson, Carl, Federal Bureau of Prisons, Buckley, WV
Kenney, Henry, S.J., Spiritual Dir., Lexington, KY
Lipps, Louis, S.J., Spiritual Dir. for Women Religious

Retired:
Reverend Monsignors—
Nienaber, Leonard B., Vianney Renewal Center, 6476 Eime Rd., Dittmer, MD 63023
Reverend Fathers—
Blandford, James T., P.O. Box 367, Springfield, KY 40069
Brinker, Maurice J., Taylor Manor, P.O. Box 349, Versailles, KY 40383
Imfield, Thomas J., P.O. Box 455, Corbin, KY 40702
Keller, Theodore, 153 Barr St., Lexington, KY 40507
Moore, Elmer R., P.O. Box 1689, Lexington, KY 40592
Pilger, Joseph J., 1333 Gray Hawk Dr., Lexington, KY 40502
Schmidt, Louis R., 601 Hill'N Dale Rd., Lexington, KY 40503
Spalding, William, Nazareth Home, 2000 Newburg Rd., Louisville, KY 40205
Stratman, Raymond, 310 Wapping St., Frankfort, KY 40601. Tel: 502-227-4511
Wethington, Paul V., 551 Bob-O-Link, Lexington, KY 40503

Permanent Deacons:
Alessio, Joseph J.
Arnold, Paul J., Jr.
Barringer, Robert
Barton, James
Borders, John
Buelterman, William
Calandrella, John
Cheshire, Vincent
Cox, James H.
Cranfill, Larry
Daukas, Michael R.
Fister, Louis
Flowers, Don K.
Grimes, William R.
Harbowy, Thaddeus
Hohl, David (COL)
Horine, James
Jackson, Richard
Marshall, Boyd
Noe, Jeremiah, H.
O'Neil, Dennis J.
Pope, Michael
Rohan, Thomas
Ross, Carter, Jr.
Schueneman, Joseph T.
Snyder, Thomas
Tohill, John J.
Weigel, Gerard A.
Wolterman, Arden J.
Young, Melvin

PARISH PILGRIMAGE SHRINES

CARLISLE. *Our Lady of Guadalupe Shrine* 617 E. Main St., 40311.

INSTITUTIONS LOCATED IN THE DIOCESE

[A] HIGH SCHOOLS, DIOCESAN

LEXINGTON. *Lexington Catholic High School*, 2250 Clays Mill Rd., 40503. Tel: 606-277-7183. Rev. Robert J. Bueter, S.J., Pres.; Mrs. Sally Stevens, Prin. Priests 2; Sisters 1; Lay Teachers 53; Students 753.

[B] HIGH SCHOOLS, PRIVATE

LONDON. *All Saints High School*, 4870 S. Laurel, 40744. Tel: 606-528-7543. Mr. Robert C. Halcomb, Prin. Lay Teachers 5; Students 39.

MARTIN. *The Piarist School*. (Grades 9-12), Rte. 80, P.O. Box 870, 41649. Tel: 606-285-3950. College prep high school. Rev. Thomas R. Carroll, Sch.P., Prin. Priests 2; Lay Teachers 7; Students 52.

[C] ELEMENTARY SCHOOLS, PRIVATE

CORBIN. *St. Camillus Academy*. (Grades PreK-8), 709 E. Center St., 40701. Tel: 606-528-5077. Coed Day School. Sisters of Divine Providence of KY. Sisters 6; Lay Teachers 13; Students 180.

[D] GENERAL HOSPITALS

LEXINGTON. *St. Joseph Hospital*, 1 St. Joseph Dr., 40504. Tel: 606-278-3436
For a complete listing, refer to the Hospitals section.

ASHLAND. *Our Lady of Bellefonte Hospital, Inc.*, St. Christopher Dr., 41101. Tel: 606-833-3333; Fax: 606-833-3695
For a complete listing, refer to the Hospitals section.

IRVINE. *Marcum and Wallace Memorial Hospital*, 60 Mercy Ct., 40336. Tel: 606-723-2115; Fax: 606-723-2951
For a complete listing, refer to the Hospitals section.

LONDON. *London, Marymount dba Marymount Medical Center*, 310 E. Ninth St., 40741. Tel: 606-878-6520
For a complete listing, refer to the Hospitals section.

MARTIN. *Our Lady of the Way Hospital, Inc.*, Box 910, 41649. Tel: 606-285-5181
For a complete listing, refer to the Hospitals section.

MOREHEAD. *Saint Claire Medical Center*, 40351. Tel: 606-784-6661
For a complete listing, refer to the Hospitals section.

[E] PRIMARY HEALTH CARE SERVICES

FRENCHBURG. *Menifee Medical Center*, P.O. Box 49, 40322. Tel: 606-768-2191
For a complete listing, refer to the Hospitals section.

OLIVE HILL. *Carter County Medical Clinic*, P.O. Box 1268, U.S. 60 W., 41164. Tel: 606-286-4152
For a complete listing, refer to the Hospitals section.

OWINGSVILLE. *Bath County Medical Clinic*, 632 Slate Ave., 40360. Tel: 606-674-6386
For a complete listing, refer to the Hospitals section.

SANDY HOOK. *Elliot County Medical Clinic*, P.O. Box 748, 41171. Tel: 606-738-5155
For a complete listing, refer to the Hospitals section.

[F] NURSING HOMES

VERSAILLES. *Taylor Manor Nursing Home*, 300 Berry Ave., 40383. Tel: 606-873-4201
For a complete listing, refer to the Special Care Facilities section.

[G] RESIDENCES OF PRIESTS

PRESTONSBURG. *Piarist Fathers*, 99 Martha's Vineyard, 41653. Tel: 606-874-9594. Rev. Thomas R. Carroll, Sch.P. Priests 2.

[H] MONASTERIES FOR SISTERS

MARTIN. *Sisters of St. Benedict-The Dwelling Place Monastery*, 150 Mt. Tabor Rd., 41649. Tel: 606-886-9624. Sr. Judy Yunker, O.S.B., Supr. Total number in community 5.

[I] SECULAR INSTITUTES

LEXINGTON. *Society of St. Vincent de Paul*, 835 Glendover Rd., 40502. Tel: 606-269-4038. Thomas H. Nowack, Pres. District Council of Lexington; Deacon James Barton, Spiritual Dir.

ASHLAND. *Roman Catholic Daughters of the King*, 2801 Hackworth St., 41101. Tel: 606-329-1249. Mrs. Madonna Fisher, Pres. Chapters: Holy Family Chapter, Ashland; St. Augustine of Canterbury Chapter, Dunwoody, GA; Annunciation Chapter, Columbus, MS; Hannah Chapter, Houston, TX.

[J] SOCIAL SERVICES

MOUNT VERNON.
**Appalachia Science in the Public Interest*, 50 Lair St., 40456. Tel: 606-256-0077; Fax: 606-453-2105. Revs. Albert J. Fritsch, S.J.; John L. Kieffer, S.J.

[K] RENEWAL CENTERS

DANVILLE. *Cliffview Retreat Center*, P.O. Box 1505, 40423-1505. Tel: 606-792-3333.

HAZARD. *Father Farrell Spiritual Life Center*, 329 Poplar at Cedar, 41701. Tel: 606-436-2533. Rev. Michael Chowning, O.F.M., Dir.; Pat Riestenberg, Assoc. Dir.

MARTIN. *Sisters of St. Benedict, Mt. Tabor Retreat Center*, 150 Mt. Tabor Rd., 41649. Tel: 606-886-9624. Staff Sisters 5.

[L] NEWMAN CENTERS

LEXINGTON. *The Newman Center Holy Spirit Parish University of Kentucky*, 320 Rose Ln., 40508. Tel: 606-255-8566. Revs. Thomas Farrell; Walter Bado, S.J.

BARBOURVILLE. *St. Gregory Church-Union College*, 329 N. Sycamore St., 40906. Tel: 606-546-4461. Rev. Stanley Tillman, S.J.

BEREA. *St. Clare Church-Berea College*, 622 Chestnut St., 40403. Tel: 606-986-4633. Rev. John C. Curtis; Sr. Anne Regina Lannon, S.S.J.

MOREHEAD. *Catholic Student Center-Morehead State University*, P.O. Box 307, 40351. Tel: 606-784-4392. Rev. William Fedders, Campus Min.

RICHMOND. *Catholic Newman Center-St. Mark Church*, Eastern Kentucky University, 405 University Dr., P.O. Box 356, 40475. Tel: 606-623-7291; 623-9400 (Center). Rev. Kenneth Waibel, Pastor & Dir. Campus Ministry; Ms. Katherine A. Schmitt, Pastoral Assoc.

[M] MISCELLANEOUS

ASHLAND. *Franciscan Health System of Kentucky, Inc.*, St. Christopher Dr., 41101. Tel: 606-833-3333. Mr. Robert J. Maher, Pres.

RELIGIOUS INSTITUTES OF MEN REPRESENTED IN THE DIOCESE

For further details refer to the corresponding bracketed number in the Religious Institutes of Men or Women section.

[0520]—*Franciscan Friars*. (St. John Baptist Province).—O.F.M.

[0570]—*Glenmary Home Missioners*.—Glmy.

[0690]—*Jesuit Fathers and Brothers*. (Chicago & Detroit Provs.).—S.J.

[0910]—*Oblates of Mary Immaculate*. (Eastern American Prov.).—O.M.I.

[0430]—*Order of Preachers*.—O.P.

[1040]—*Piarist Fathers*. (U.S. Prov.).—Sch.P.

RELIGIOUS INSTITUTES OF WOMEN REPRESENTED IN THE DIOCESE

[0230]—*Benedictine Sisters of Pontifical Jurisdiction*. (Pittsburgh, PA; Covington, KY; Martin, KY).—O.S.B.

[1810]—*Bernardine Sisters of the Third Order of St. Francis*.—O.S.F.

[2980]—*Congregation de Notre Dame*. (Ridgefield, CT).—C.N.D.

[2100]—*Congregation of Humility of Mary*.—C.H.M.

[2230]—*Congregation of the Infant Jesus*.—C.I.J.

[3710]—*Congregation of the Sisters of St. Agnes*. (Bronx, NY).—C.S.A.

[1920]—*Congregation of the Sisters of the Holy Cross*.—C.S.C.

[1730]—*Congregation of the Sisters of the Third Order of St. Francis*. (Oldenburg, IN).—O.S.F.

[1780]—*Congregation of the Sisters of the Third Order of St. Francis of Perpetual Adoration*. (Eastern Region).—F.S.P.A.

[1710]—*Congregation of the Third Order Regular of St. Francis of Mary Immaculate, Joliet, IL*.—O.S.F.

[1070-03]—*Dominican Sisters*. (Sinsinawa, WI).—O.P.

[1070-09]—*Dominican Sisters*. (Racine, WI).—O.P.

[1070-13]—*Dominican Sisters*. (Adrian, MI).—O.P.

[1070-14]—*Dominican Sisters*. (Grand Rapids, MI).—O.P.

[1230]—*Franciscan Sisters of Christian Charity*.—O.S.F.

[1440]—*Franciscan Sisters of the Poor*.—S.F.P.

[2080]—*Home Mission Sisters of America (Glenmary)*.—G.H.M.S.

[2575]—*Institute of the Sisters of Mercy of the Americas*. (Charlotte, NC; Philadelphia, PA; West Hartford, CT).—R.S.M.

[2470]—*Maryknoll Sisters of St. Dominic*.—M.M.

[2710]—*Missionaries of Charity*.—M.C.

[2070]—*Religious of the Holy Union of the Sacred Hearts*.—S.U.S.C.

[2970]—*School Sisters of Notre Dame*. (Milwaukee; Baltimore).—S.S.N.D.

[1680]—*School Sisters of St. Francis*.—O.S.F.

[3580]—*Servants of Mary*.—O.S.M.

[0430]—*Sisters of Charity of Blessed Virgin Mary*. (Dubuque, IA).—B.V.M.

[0500]—*Sisters of Charity of Nazareth*.—S.C.N.

[0580]—*Sisters of Charity of St. Augustine*. (Rienfield, OH).—C.S.A.

[0590]—*Sisters of Charity of St. Elizabeth*. (Convent Station, NJ).—S.C.

[1000]—*The Sisters of Divine Providence of Kentucky*.—C.D.P.

[1010]—*Sisters of Divine Providence of San Antonio, Texas*.—C.D.P.

[2990]—*Sisters of Notre Dame*. (Covington Prov.; Chardon Prov.).—S.N.D.

[3000]—*Sisters of Notre Dame de Namur*. (Cincinnati Prov.).—S.N.D.deN.

[3360]—*Sisters of Providence of St. Mary-of-the-Woods, Indiana*.—S.P.

[3893]—*Sisters of Saint Joseph of Chestnut Hill, Philadelphia*.—S.S.J.

[1540]—*Sisters of St Francis*. (Clinton, IA).—O.S.F.

[3750]—*Sisters of St. Chretienne*. (Wrentham, MA).—S.S.Ch.

[1650]—*The Sisters of St. Francis of Philadelphia*.—O.S.F.

[3830-05]—*Sisters of St. Joseph*. (Baden, PA; Brentwood, NY).—C.S.J.

[3830-05]—*Sisters of St. Joseph*. (Brentwood, NY).—C.S.J.

[3850]—*Sisters of St. Joseph of Chambery*.—C.S.J.

[3920]—*Sisters of St. Joseph the Worker*.—S.J.W.

[1990]—*Sisters of the Holy Names of Jesus and Mary*.—S.N.J.M.

[3270]—*Sisters of the Most Precious Blood*. (O'Fallon, MO).—C.PP.S.

[3260]—*Sisters of the Precious Blood (Dayton, Ohio)*.—C.PP.S.

[3320]—*Sisters of the Presentation of the B.V.M.* (Fargo, ND; Dubuque, IA).—P.B.V.M.

[1760]—*Sisters of the Third Order of St. Francis of Penance and Charity*. (Tiffin, OH).—O.S.F.

[1720]—*Sisters of the Third Order Regular of St. Francis of the Congregation of Our Lady of Lourdes*.—O.S.F.

[2150]—*Sisters, Servants of the Immaculate Heart of Mary*.—I.H.M.

[4120-03]—*Ursuline Sisters of the Immaculate Conception*. (Louisville, KY).—O.S.U.

[4170]—*Vincentian Sisters of Charity*. (Bedford, OH).—V.S.C.

DIOCESAN CEMETERIES

LEXINGTON. *Calvary*.

ASHLAND. *Calvary*.

MT. STERLING. *St. Thomas*.

NECROLOGY

† Farmer, Matthew P., (Special Assignment). —Died Feb. 10, 1997.

Diocese of Lincoln

(Dioecesis Lincolnensis)

Most Reverend

FABIAN W. BRUSKEWITZ, D.D., S.T.D.

Bishop of Lincoln; ordained July 17, 1960; appointed Bishop of Lincoln March 24, 1992; consecrated May 13, 1992. *Mailing Address: Address all communications to P.O. Box 80328, Lincoln, NE, 68501-0328.*

ERECTED AUGUST 2, 1887.

Square Miles 23,844.

Comprises that part of the State of Nebraska south of the Platte River.

Legal Title: "The Catholic Bishop of Lincoln".

For legal titles of parishes and diocesan institutions, consult the Chancery.

Chancery: P.O. Box 80328, Lincoln, NE, 68501-0328. Tel.: 402-488-0921; Fax: 402-488-3569.

STATISTICAL OVERVIEW

Personnel	
Bishop	1
Priests: Diocesan Active in Diocese	113
Priests: Active Outside Diocese	7
Priests: Diocesan in Foreign Missions	2
Priests: Retired, Sick or Absent	22
Number of Diocesan Priests	144
Religious Priests in Diocese	11
Extern Priests in Diocese	2
Ordinations:	
Diocesan Priests	7
Transitional Deacons	5
Total Brothers	11
Total Sisters	113
Parishes	
Parishes	134
With Resident Pastor:	
Resident Diocesan Priests	85
Resident Religious Priests	3
Without Resident Pastor:	
Administered by Priests	46
Missions	1
Welfare	
Catholic Hospitals	3
Total Assisted	211,112
Homes for the Aged	3
Total Assisted	244
Special Centers for Social Services	4
Total Assisted	50,002
Residential Care of Disabled	1
Total Assisted	16
Other Institutions	2
Total Assisted	11,323
Educational	
Seminaries, Diocesan	1
Diocesan Students in Other Seminaries	36
Total Seminarians	36
High Schools, Diocesan and Parish	6
Total Students	1,727
Elementary Schools, Diocesan and Parish	24
Total Students	5,364
Non-residential Schools for the Disabled	1
Total Students	16
Catechesis/Religious Education:	
High School Students	2,253
Elementary Students	6,296
Total Students Under Catholic Instruction	15,692
Teachers in the Diocese:	
Priests	46
Sisters	56
Lay Teachers	426
Vital Statistics	
Receptions into the Church:	
Infant Baptism Totals	1,448
Adult Baptism Totals	168
Received into Full Communion	174
First Communions	1,497
Confirmations	2,243
Marriages:	
Catholic	235
Interfaith	205
Total Marriages	440
Deaths	633
Total Catholic Population	87,198
Total Population	516,662

Former Bishops—Most Rev. THOMAS BONACUM, D.D., Bishop of Lincoln; cons. Nov. 30, 1887; died Feb. 4, 1911.—Most Rev. J. HENRY TIHEN, D.D., cons. Bishop of Lincoln, July 6, 1911; transferred to the See of Denver, Sept. 21, 1917.—Most Rev. CHARLES J. O'REILLY, D.D., cons. Bishop of Baker City, Aug. 24, 1903; transferred to the See of Lincoln, March 20, 1918; died Feb. 4, 1923.—Most Rev. FRANCIS J. L. BECKMAN, S.T.D., cons. Bishop of Lincoln, May 1, 1924; elevated to the Metropolitan See of Dubuque, Jan. 17, 1930.—Most Rev. LOUIS B KUCERA, D.D., cons. Bishop of Lincoln, Oct. 28, 1930; died May 9, 1957.—Most Rev. JAMES V. CASEY, D.D., J.C.D., appt. Auxiliary of Lincoln April 5, 1957; cons. April 24, 1957; appt. Bishop of Lincoln June 14, 1957; promoted to Archbishop of Denver, Feb. 18, 1967; died March 14, 1986.—Most Rev. GLENNON P. FLAVIN, D.D., appt. Titular Bishop of Joannina and Auxiliary Bishop of St. Louis April 24, 1957; cons. May 30, 1957; promoted to See of Lincoln, May 29, 1967; retired March 24, 1992; died Aug. 27, 1995.

Chancery—3400 Sheridan Blvd., Lincoln, 68506., Mailing Address: P.O. Box 80328, Lincoln, 68501-0328. Tel: 402-488-0921; Fax: 402-488-3569. Office Hours: 9-5.

Moderator of the Curia—Rev. Msgr. ROBERT F. VASA, J.C.L.

Vicar General—Rev. Msgr. ROBERT F. VASA, J.C.L.

Chancellor—Rev. Msgr. TIMOTHY J. THORBURN, J.C.L.

Diocesan Tribunal—3400 Sheridan Blvd., Lincoln, 68506., Mailing Address: P.O. Box 80328, Lincoln, 68501-0328.

Officialis—Rev. DANIEL J. SEIKER, J.C.L.

Adjutant Judicial Vicars—Rev. Msgr. ROBERT F. VASA,J.C.L.; Rev. MAURICE H. CURRENT, J.C.L.

Promoter Justitiae—Rev. GAROLD L. GABEL, J.C.L.

Defensores Vinculi—Rev. Msgr. TIMOTHY J. THORBURN, J.C.L.

Judge—Rev. GAROLD L. GABEL, J.C.L.

Advocates—Revs. THOMAS Y. AU; DAVID F. BOUREK; MICHAEL K. HOULIHAN; JAMES W. COOPER; JOHN R. SULLIVAN; LORAS K. GRELL; THOMAS S. BROUILLETTE; DAVID F. BOUREK; Mr. DAVID A. BATTIATO.

Notaries—Revs. JOHN T. FOLDA; GAROLD L. GABEL, J.C.L.; Sr. COLLETTE BRUSKEWITZ, O.S.F.; MARY ANN T. BIGLIN; LOUANNE I. COOK; ROSE M. LE CORGNE.

Diocesan Consultors—Rev. Msgr. JAMES D. DAWSON; Rev. Msgr. LEONARD I. KALIN, M.A.; Very Rev. Msgr. DANIEL J. POHL, B.A.; Rev. Msgr. TIMOTHY J. THORBURN; Rev. Msgr. ROBERT F. VASA; Revs. M. JAMES DIVIS, S.T.L.; JOHN T. FOLDA, S.T.L.

Presbyteral Council—Rev. Msgr. ROBERT F. VASA; Rev. Msgr. TIMOTHY J. THORBURN; Rev Msgr. LEONARD I. KALIN; Rev. Msgr. MYRON J. PLESKAC; Revs. JOHN J. PERKINTON; CHARLES R. TOWNSEND; RUDOLF F. OBORNY; DAVID R. HINTZ; MICHAEL R. CHRISTENSEN; PETER J. GADIENT; Very Rev. JAMES G. MOEGLEIN, O.S.C.; Revs. LIAM M. BARR; ROBERT G. TUCKER; MICHAEL G. MCCABE.

Vicars For Religious—Rev. Msgr. TIMOTHY J. THORBURN; Rev. JOHN T. FOLDA.

Deaneries and Deans—Rev. Msgr. THOMAS L. HOLOMAN, Crete; Rev. Msgr. ADRIAN F. HERBEK, David City; Very Rev. PAUL E. SHEEHY, Fairbury; Very Rev. ROBERT A. ROH, Falls City; Very Rev. GREGORY P. PAWLOSKI, Grant; Rev. Msgr. JOHN J. MCCABE, Hastings; Rev. Msgr. DANIEL J. POHL, Indianola; Very Rev. STANLEY F. SCHIEFFER, Lawrence; Rev. Msgr. MYRON J. PLESKAC, Lincoln; Very Rev. JAMES M. O'CONNOR, Orleans; Very Rev. PAUL H. YORK, Plattsmouth; Very Rev. LAWRENCE J. GYHRA, Wahoo; Rev. Msgr. IVAN F. VAP, York.

Diocesan Offices and Directors

Apostleship of Prayer— Revs. JOHN W. KELLY, Dir. BERNARD V. KIMMINAU, Asst.

Apostolate to the Elderly—Rev. EDWIN L. STANDER.

Apostolate to the Spanish Speaking—Revs. JULIUS P. TVRDY, Dir. BERNARD A. LORENZ, Asst. Dir.

Apostolate of Suffering—Rev. STANLEY J. REDMERSKI, Dir.

Archivist—Sr. LORETTA GOSEN, C.PP.S.

Bishop's Lay Committee for Vocations—DOUGLAS C. CAREY, Pres.; Rev. Msgr. LEONARD KALIN, Chap.

Bishop's Pastoral Plan for Pro-Life Activities—GREG SCHLEPPENBACH, State Dir., *215 Centennial Mall S., Ste. 410, Lincoln, 68508.*

Building Commission—Rev. Msgr. ROBERT F. VASA, Chm.; Rev. Msgr. RAYMOND B. HAIN; Rev. Msgr. ADRIAN F. HERBEK; Rev. Msgr. IVAN F. VAP; Revs. JOHN J. PERKINTON; PETER J. GADIENT; Very Rev. STANLEY F. SCHIEFFER.

Catholic Relief Services—Rev. JOSEPH M. WALSH, Dir.

Cemeteries—Revs. RONALD PATTERSON, Dir. DAVID R. HINTZ, Asst. Dir.

Censores Librorum—Revs. M. JAMES DIVIS, S.T.L.; JOHN T. FOLDA; Rev. Msgr. TIMOTHY J. THORBURN.

Charities—Rev. JOSEPH M. WALSH, Dir. JOHN KOPETZKY, Vice Pres., Operations, *Catholic Social Services, 123 N. 25th St., Lincoln, 68503.* Tel: 402-474-1600., *Administrative Offices, 237 S. 70th St., Lincoln, 68510.* Tel: 402-489-1834., *Catholic Social Services, 518 East Side Blvd., Hastings, 68901.* Tel: 402-463-2112.

Clergy Relief Society—The Saint John Vianney

Association—Rev. Msgr. Robert F. Vasa, Sec.-Treas., *Mailing Address: P.O. Box 80328, Lincoln, 68501-0328.*

Commission on Alcohol and Drug Abuse—Rev. Msgr. Charles J. Keenan, Dir., *3301 Sheridan Blvd., Lincoln, 68506.* Tel: 402-483-1941.

Commission for Sacred Liturgy and Sacred Music—Rev. William D. Grant, Chm.; Sr. Mary Durr, O.S.U., Exec. Sec.; Revs. John T. Folda; Robert K. Barnhill; Maurice H. Current; M. James Divis; Joseph J. Nemec.

Office of Diocesan and Social Development—Rev. Liam M. Barr, Delegate, *P.O. Box 80328, Lincoln, 68501-0328.* Tel: 402-488-2040.

Catholic Planned Giving Office—Mr. Michael L. Henkenius, Dir., *6000 "A" St., Lincoln, 68510.* Tel: 402-488-2142.

Office of Religious Education (CCD)—Rev. John T. Folda, Diocesan Dir. Tel: 402-488-0921. Sr. Mary Durr, O.S.U., Asst. Dir. Diocesan Area CCD Directors: Revs. Thomas Y. Au; John L. Copenhaver, M.Div.; Douglas D. Dietrich; William D. Grant; Dennis M. Hunt; Philip L. Luther; Michael G. McCabe; Thomas L. Wiedel; James F. Benton, M.Div.; Thomas D. McGuire; Mark E. Seiker; Sean P. Redmond; Thomas Walsh, *P.O. Box 80328, Lincoln, 68501-0328.*

Cursillo—Rev. Mark E. Seiker, M.Div.

Diocesan Council of Catholic Women—Mrs. Jeanette Stengel, Pres.; Rev. Peter J. Gadient, Moderator, *P.O. Box 212, Osceola, 68651.*

Diocesan Director of Liturgy—Rev. William D. Grant.

Bishop Bruskewitz Charity and Stewardship Appeal (DDP)—Rev. Stanley Redmerski, Dir., *5401 South St., Lincoln, 68506.*

Diocesan Finance Council—Most Rev. Fabian W. Bruskewitz, D.D., S.T.D.; Rev. Msgr. Robert F. Vasa, Finance Officer; Rev. Msgr. Adrian F. Herbek; Revs. John T. Folda; Michael G. McCabe.

Diocesan Health Ministries, Inc.—Most Rev. Fabian W. Bruskewitz, D.D. S.T.D., Pres.; Rev. Msgr. Robert F. Vasa, Vice Pres.; Rev. John T. Folda, Sec., *P.O. Box 80328, Lincoln, 68501-0328.* Tel: 402-488-0921; Fax: 402-488-3569.

Diocesan Housing Ministries, Inc.—Most Rev. Fabian W. Bruskewitz, D.D., S.T.D., Pres.; Rev. Msgr. Robert F. Vasa; Revs. John T. Folda; Liam M. Barr; Joseph M. Walsh; Ms. Haton, *P.O. Box 80328, Lincoln, 68501-0328.* Tel: 402-488-2040.

Ecumenical Affairs, Commission for—Rev. M. James Divis, Chm.; Very. Rev. Msgr. Daniel J. Pohl; Revs. Paul K. Witt; Maurice H. Current.

Engaged Encounter—Rev. Robert K. Barnhill.

Family Life Office—Revs. Robert K. Barnhill, S.T.L., Dir. Christopher L. Barak, S.T.L., Asst. Dir., *P.O. Box 80328, Lincoln, 68501-0328.* Tel: 402-488-2040.

Holy Childhood, Pontifical Association—Rev. Ronald Patterson, Dir., *P.O. Box 80328, Lincoln, 68501-0328.*

Health Care Facilities—Revs. Stanley J. Redmerski, Dir. Paul J. Rutten, Assoc., *5401 South St., Lincoln, 68506.*

Office of Information and Media—Rev. Kenneth A. Borowiak, Dir., *P.O. Box 80329, Lincoln, 68501.* Tel: 402-488-0090.

Insurance—Rev. Msgr. Robert F. Vasa, Dir.; Mr. James F. McLaughlin, *P.O. Box 80328, Lincoln, 68501-0328.*

Legion of Mary—Rev. Peter J. Gadient, Spiritual Dir.; Rev. Leo V. Seiker, Asst. Spiritual Dir.; Mrs. Jackie Scott, Pres.

Liturgical Ministries—Revs. William D. Grant, Diocesan Dir. Maurice H. Current; Sr. Mary Durr, O.S.U.

Marriage Encounter—Rev. Robert K. Barnhill, Dir.

Missionary Union of the Clergy—Rev. Ronald Patterson.

Natural Family Planning—Rev. Robert K. Barnhill.

Nebraska Catholic Conference—James R. Cunningham, Exec. Dir., *215 Centennial Mall S., Ste. 410, Lincoln, 68508.* Tel: 402-477-7517; Fax: 402-477-1503.

Newman Center University of Nebraska—Rev. Msgr. Leonard I. Kalin, Chap.; Rev. Loras K. Grell, Asst. Chap., *320 N. 16th St., Lincoln, 68508.* Tel: 402-474-7914.

Newspaper—"The Southern Nebraska Register"; Rev. Kenneth A. Borowiak, Editor, *3336 High St., Lincoln, Mailing Address: P.O. Box 80329, Lincoln, 68501.* Tel: 402-488-0090.

Pre Cana—Rev. Robert K. Barnhill.

Priests' Continuing Education Committee—Rev. Msgr. James D. Dawson; Rev. Msgr. Thomas L. Holoman; Rev. Msgr. Leonard I. Kalin; Rev. Msgr. Myron J. Pleskac; Rev. Msgr. Timothy J. Thorburn, J.C.L.; Rev. Msgr. Robert F. Vasa, J.C.L.; Revs. Maurice H. Current, J.C.L.; John T. Folda; John J. Perkinton.

Pro Life—Rev. Msgr. Thomas L. Holoman.

Propagation of the Faith—Rev. Ronald Patterson, Dir., *P.O. Box 80328, Lincoln, 68501-0328.*

Rural Life Conference—Rev. David F. Bourek, *Saint Michael Church, P.O. Box 331, Hastings, 68902.* Tel: 402-463-1023.

Schools—Rev. John J. Perkinton, M.Div., M.A., Supt.; Sr. Collette, O.S.F., Asst. Supt., *3400 Sheridan Blvd., Lincoln, 68506., Mailing Address: P.O. Box 80328, Lincoln, 68501-0328.*

Scouting—Rev. Robert K. Barnhill.

Society of St. Vincent de Paul - Lincoln Council—Rev. Paul K. Witt, Spiritual Advisor; Thomas Safranek, M.D., Pres. Joyce Burgess, Council Sec./Resident Agent, *Blessed Sacrament Conference, 1720 Lake St., Lincoln, 68502.* Tel: 402-474-4249.

Teens Encounter Christ (TEC)—Rev. Robert K. Barnhill.

Vocations—Rev. Msgr. Leonard I. Kalin, Dir.; Rev. Loras K. Grell, Asst. Dir., *St. Thomas Aquinas Church, 320 North 16th St., Lincoln, 68508.* Tel: 402-474-7914.

CLERGY, PARISHES, MISSIONS AND PAROCHIAL SCHOOLS

CITY OF LINCOLN
(Lancaster County)

1—Cathedral of the Risen Christ (1932), Rev. Msgr. James D. Dawson; Revs. Robert A. Matya; David J. Davis. In res., Rev. John T. Folda.
Res., 3500 Sheridan Blvd., 68506. Tel: 402-488-0948; Fax: 402-488-7895. [JC]
School—Tel: 402-489-9621.
Benedictine Sisters (Yankton, SD) 1; Lay Teachers 28; Students 408.
Catechesis/Religious Programs—Tel: 402-489-9621.
Students 253.

2—Blessed Sacrament, Revs. Michael K. Houlihan; Finnian N. Waozer. In res., Rev. John J. Perkinton.
Res., 1720 Lake St., 68502. Tel: 402-474-4249. [JC]
School—Tel: 402-476-6202; Fax: 402-474-4258.
Priests 2; Sisters 4; Lay Teachers 18; Students 257.

3—Immaculate Heart of Mary (1979) (Vietnamese), Rev. Isidore D.T. Bac, C.M.C. (Vietnam).
Res., 2601 P St., 68503. Tel: 402-476-0133.
Catechesis/Religious Programs—Students 200.

4—North American Martyrs (1993), Revs. Garold L. Gabel; Jeffrey R. Eickhoff.
Res., 931 W. Harvest Dr., 68521. Tel: 402-476-8088. [JC]

5—Sacred Heart (1919), Rev. Ronald E. Patterson. In res., Revs. Edwin L. Stander; Julius Tvrdy.
Res., 3128 S St., 68503. Tel: 402-476-2610; Fax: 402-476-2369. [JC]
School—Tel: 402-476-1783; Fax: 402-476-3040.
Sisters 5; Lay Teachers 7; Students 135.
Catechesis/Religious Programs—Students 22.

6—St. John the Apostle (1959), Revs. Rudolf F. Oborny; Joseph S. Steele.
Res., 731 Sky Way Rd., 68505. Tel: 402-489-1946. [JC]
School—Tel: 402-486-1860.
Sisters 2; Lay Teachers 22; Students 384.
Catechesis/Religious Programs—Students 279.

7—St. Joseph (1976), Rev. Msgr. Myron J. Pleskac; Rev. Jeremy L. Hazuka.
Res., 7607 Trendwood Dr., 68506. Tel: 402-483-2288; Fax: 402-489-9729. [JC]
School—(Grades PreK-8). Tel: 402-489-0341.
Sisters 4; Lay Teachers 30; Students 442.
High School—Pius High School.
Students 189.
Catechesis/Religious Programs—Students 359.

8—St. Mary (1867), Revs. Paul K. Witt; John B. Birkel. In res., Rev. Robert K. Barnhill.
Res., 1420 K St., 68508. Tel: 402-435-2125. [JC]
School—Tel: 402-476-3987; Fax: 402-476-0838.
Sisters 1; Lay Teachers 10; Students 144.
Catechesis/Religious Programs—Students 14.

9—St. Patrick's (1893), Revs. David R. Hintz; Kenneth F. Hoesing.
Res., 6126 Morrill Ave., P.O. Box 29106, 68507. Tel: 402-466-2752; Fax: 402-466-3572. [JC]
School—Tel: 402-466-3710.
Benedictine Sisters (Yankton, SD) 1; Lay Teachers 12; Students 181.
Catechesis/Religious Programs—Students 396.

10—St. Peter (1990), Revs. Michael R. Christensen; Craig A. Doty.
Res., 4500 Duxhall Dr., 68516. Tel: 402-423-1239; Fax: 402-421-6507.
School—Tel: 402-421-6299.
Priests 2; School Sisters of Christ the King 3; Lay Teachers 23; Students 526.
Catechesis/Religious Programs—Students 298.

11—St. Teresa's (1926), Revs. Joseph J. Nemec; Thomas S. Brouillette. In res., Rev. Joseph M. Walsh.
Res., 735 S. 36th St., 68510. Tel: 402-477-3979. [JC]
School—616 S. 36th St., 68510. Tel: 402-477-3358.
Sisters 3; Lay Teachers 11; Students 280.
Catechesis/Religious Programs—Students 69.

12—St. Thomas Aquinas (1958), Rev. Msgr. Leonard I. Kalin; Rev. Loras K. Grell.
Res., 320 N. 16th St., 68508. Tel: 402-474-7914; Fax: 402-476-2620. [JC]

13—Bishop Bonacum Chancery, Rev. Msgr. Robert F. Vasa, V.G., Moderator of the Curia.
Res., 3400 Sheridan Blvd., P.O. Box 80328, 68501. Tel: 402-488-0921; Fax: 402-488-3569.

OUTSIDE THE CITY OF LINCOLN

Alma, Harlan Co., St. Joseph's (1909), Rev. Thomas L. Wiedel.
Res., 810 4th, P.O. Box 764, 68920. Tel: 308-928-2575.
Catechesis/Religious Programs—Students 59.
Missions—Bloomington, Franklin Co., Sacred Heart; Naponee, Franklin Co., St. Mary.

Ashland, Saunders Co., St. Mary's (1900), Rev. Francis J. Murphy.
Res., 1625 Adams St., 68003. Tel: 402-944-3554.
Catechesis/Religious Programs—Students 120.
Mission—Greenwood, Cass Co., St. Joseph's.

Auburn, Nemaha Co., St. Joseph's (1881), Rev. Philip J. Rauth.
Res., 1306 23rd St., P.O. Box 406, 68305. Tel: 402-274-3733. [CEM]
Catechesis/Religious Programs—Students 159.
Mission—Peru, St. Clara.

Aurora, Hamilton Co., St. Mary's (1888), Rev. John J. Keefe.
Res., 1419 10th St., P.O. Box 291, 68818. Tel: 402-694-3427.
Catechesis/Religious Programs—Students 154.
Mission—Giltner, Hamilton Co., St. Joseph's. [CEM]

Beatrice, Gage Co., St. Joseph's (1869), Rev. Mark E. Seiker.
Res., 612 High St., 68310. Tel: 402-223-2923. [CEM]
School—Tel: 402-223-5033.
Lay Teachers 9; Students 105.
Catechesis/Religious Programs—Students 121.

Beaver Crossing, Seward Co., Sacred Heart (1890), Rev. Maurice H. Current.
Res., P.O. Box 208, 68313. Tel: 402-532-2545.
Catechesis/Religious Programs—Students 26.
Mission—Utica, Seward Co., St. Patrick's. [CEM 2]

Bellwood, Butler Co., Presentation (1874), Rev. Leo D. Kosch.
Res., Rte. 1, Box 47, 68624. Tel: 402-367-3666. [JC]
Catechesis/Religious Programs—Students 40.
St. Peter's (1889), Rev. Leo V. Seiker.
Res., Rte. 1, Box 6, 68624. Tel: 402-538-3135. [JC]
Catechesis/Religious Programs—Students 128.
Mission—Bellwood, Butler Co., St. Joseph's.

Benkelman, Dundy Co., St. Joseph's (1911), Rev. Mark S. Pfeiffer.
Res., 817 Cheyenne St., P.O. Box 447, 69021. Tel: 308-423-2329. [CEM]
Catechesis/Religious Programs—Students 49.
Mission—Stratton, Hitchcock Co., St. Joseph's.

Brainard, Butler Co., Holy Trinity (1888), Rev. Stephen A. Cooney.
Res., P.O. Box 39, 68626. Tel: 402-545-2691; Fax: 402-545-2691. [CEM]
Catechesis/Religious Programs—Tel: 402-545-2003.
Students 123.

Bruno, Butler Co., St. Anthony (1899), Rev. Thomas J. Lux.
Res., P.O. Box 145, 68014. Tel: 402-543-2233. [CEM]
Catechesis/Religious Programs—Students 66.
Mission—Abie, Butler Co., SS. Peter and Paul.

Cambridge, Furnas Co., St. John's (1880), Rev. Melvin L. Rempe.
Res., 815 Nelson, P.O. Box F, 69022. Tel: 308-697-3722. [CEM]
Catechesis/Religious Programs—Students 106.
Mission—Arapahoe, Furnas Co., St. Germanus.

Campbell, Franklin Co., St. Ann's (1880), Rev. James C. Schrader, Jr.
Res., P.O. Box 156, 68932-0156. Tel: 402-756-8006. [CEM]
Catechesis/Religious Programs—Students 62.
Mission—Blue Hill, Webster Co., Holy Trinity.

Cheney, St. Michael (1909), Rev. Douglas J. Morin.
Res., 3230 S. 33rd St., Lincoln, 68506. Tel: 402-484-6341. [CEM]
Catechesis/Religious Programs—Students 63.

Colon, Saunders Co., St. Joseph's (1919), Rev. Patrick J. O'Byrne.
Res., 68018. Tel: 402-647-4901. [CEM]
Mission—Cedar Bluffs, Saunders Co., St. Mary. [CEM]

Cortland, Gage Co., St. James (1882), Rev. Michael J. Morin.
Res., 255 W. First, R.R. 1, Box 250, 68331. Tel: 402-798-7335; Fax: 402-798-7336. [CEM]
Catechesis/Religious Programs—Students 63.

Crete, Saline Co., Sacred Heart (1873), Rev. Nicholas J. Baker.
Res., 515 E. 14th St., 68333. Tel: 402-826-2044; Fax: 402-826-2318. [CEM]
School—(Grades K-6). Tel: 402-826-2318.
Lay Teachers 5; Students 76.
Catechesis/Religious Programs—Students 160.

Curtis, Frontier Co., St. James (1914), Rev. Gary G. Brethour. In res., Rev. Msgr. Jerome E. Murray.
Res., 313 E. 6th St., P.O. Box 144, 69025. Tel: 308-367-4280.
Catechesis/Religious Programs—Students 101.
Missions—Farnam, Dawson Co., St. Joseph's; Wellfleet, Lincoln Co., St. William's; North Platte, Lincoln Co., St. Elizabeth Ann Seton, (1994) P.O.Box 781, North Platte, 69103-0781. Tel: 308-534-5461.

Davey, Lancaster Co., St. Mary's (1876), Rev. Thomas P. Kuffel, O.S.
Res., 17630 N. 3rd St., P.O. Box 37, 68336. Tel: 402-785-3445. [CEM]
Catechesis/Religious Programs—Students 41.

David City, Butler Co., St. Mary's (1878), Rev. Msgr. Adrian F. Herbek, V.F.; Rev. Casey Porada, O.S.
Res., 580 I St., 68632. Tel: 402-367-3579. [CEM]
School—(Grades K-5). Tel: 402-367-3669.
Priests 1; Sisters 3; Lay Teachers 13; Students 225.
Catechesis/Religious Programs—Students 68.
Mission—David City, Butler Co., Assumption, (1878) 68632.

St. Francis (Center) (1878), Rev. Brian P. Connor.
Res., Rte. 1, Box 93, 68632. Tel: 402-367-4202. [CEM]
Catechesis/Religious Programs—Students 53.

Dawson, Richardson Co., St. Mary's, Rev. Michael G. McCabe.
Res., P.O. Box 96, 68337. Tel: 402-855-3595. [CEM]
Mission—Shubert, Richardson Co., St. Ann's. [CEM]

Denton, Lancaster Co., St. Mary's, Rev. Msgr. Thomas L. Holoman.
Res., 7105 Cass, P.O. Box 406, 68339. Tel: 402-797-2105.

Doniphan, Hall Co., St. Ann's (1888), Rev. John G. Hawkins, O.S.C.
Res., 5th & Cedar, P.O. Box 407, 68832. Tel: 402-845-2707. [CEM]
Catechesis/Religious Programs—Students 55.

Dwight, Butler Co., Assumption, Rev. Kenneth A. Borowiak.
Res., P.O. Box 70, 68635. Tel: 402-566-2765. [CEM]
Mission—Bee, Seward Co., St. Wenceslaus. [CEM]

Exeter, Fillmore Co., St. Stephen's (1871), Rev. John J. Glaves.
Res., P.O. Box 57, 68351. Tel: 402-266-5581.
Catechesis/Religious Programs—Students 85.

Fairbury, Jefferson Co., St. Michael's (1885), Rev. William David Grant.
Res., 807 F St., P.O. Box 406, 68352. Tel: 402-729-2058; Fax: 402-729-2058. [CEM]
School—(Grades PreK-6). Tel: 402-729-2151.
Lay Teachers 6; Students 68.
Catechesis/Religious Programs—Students 50.
Mission—Alexandria, Thayer Co., St. Mary's, 511 Amanda, Alexandria, 68303.

Falls City, Richardson Co., SS. Peter and Paul (1871), Very Rev. Robert A. Roh, V.F.
Res., 1820 Fulton St., 68355. Tel: 402-245-3002; Fax: 402-245-3002. [CEM 2]
School—(Grades PreK-12). Tel: 402-245-4151; Fax: 402-245-5217.
Lay Teachers 20; Students 285.
Catechesis/Religious Programs—Students 80.

Friend, Saline Co., St. Joseph's (1874), Rev. James W. Cooper.
Res., 405 S. Main St., 68359. Tel: 402-947-3651. [CEM]
Catechesis/Religious Programs—Students 80.
Mission—Milligan, Fillmore Co., St. Wenceslaus, (1874).

Geneva, Fillmore Co., St. Joseph's (1898), Rev. Msgr. Ivan F. Vap.
Res., 831 E St., 68361. Tel: 402-759-3225; Fax: 402-759-4405, Ext. 2. [CEM 2]
Catechesis/Religious Programs—Students 107.
Mission—Shickley, Fillmore Co., St. Mary, Tel: 402-627-7395.

Grafton, Fillmore Co., St. Helena's. (Administered from St. Mary Church, Sutton). Rev. Thaddeus Bryl.
Res., P.O. Box 65, 68365. Tel: 402-773-5346.

Grant, Perkins Co., Mother of Sorrows (1928), Rev. Valerian Bartek.
Res., 729 Garfield Ave., P.O. Box 536, 69140. Tel: 308-352-4803.
Catechesis/Religious Programs—Students 80.

Harvard, Clay Co., St. Joseph's (1878), Rev. Bernard A. Lorenz.
Res., 605 N. Kearney, P.O. Box 70, 68944. Tel: 402-772-3511.
Catechesis/Religious Programs—Students 61.

Hastings, Adams Co., St. Cecilia's (1878), Very Rev. Msgr. John J. McCabe, V.F.; Rev. Troy Schweiger. In res., Rev. James J. Meysenburg.
Res., 301 W. 7th St., 68901. Tel: 402-463-1336. [JC]
Catechesis/Religious Programs—Students 750.

St. Michael's (1945), Revs. David F. Bourek; K. William Holoubek.
Res., 715 Creighton Ave., P.O. Box 331, 68901. Tel: 402-463-1023.
Catechesis/Religious Programs—Hastings Catholic Schools, 521 N. Kansas, 68901. Tel: 402-462-2105; Fax: 402-462-2106.
Students 345.

Hebron, Thayer Co., Sacred Heart (1878), Rev. Paul E. Sheehy.
Res., 436 N. 3rd St., 68370. Tel: 402-768-6293. [CEM]
Catechesis/Religious Programs—Students 102.

Holdrege, Phelps Co., All Saints (1902), Rev. John A. Zastrow.
Res., 1202 Logan St., 68949. Tel: 308-995-4590.
Catechesis/Religious Programs—Students 175.
Mission—Smithfield, Gosper Co., St. John's.

Imperial, Chase Co., St. Patrick's (1903), Very Rev. Gregory P. Pawloski.
Res., 126 E. 7th St., P.O. Box 96, 69033. Tel: 308-882-4995.
Catechesis/Religious Programs—Students 128.
Mission—Wauneta, Chase Co., St. John's, Tel: 308-394-5440 (Church). [CEM]

Indianola, Red Willow Co., St. Catherine's (1888), Rev. Msgr. Daniel J. Pohl, V.F.
Res., P.O. Box 0, 69034. Tel: 308-364-2428. [CEM]
Catechesis/Religious Programs—Students 104.

Kenesaw, Adams Co., Sacred Heart (1908), Rev. John Hawkins, O.S.C.
Res., P.O. Box 789, Hastings, 68902. Tel: 402-461-3207; Fax: 402-463-5701.
Catechesis/Religious Programs—Tel: 402-752-8149.
Students 22.

Lawrence, Nuckolls Co., Sacred Heart (1893), Rev. Dennis Hunt.
Res., P.O. Box 247, 68957. Tel: 402-756-7393. [CEM]
School—(Grades 1-8). Tel: 402-756-7043.
Lay Teachers 4; Students 74.
Catechesis/Religious Programs—Students 159.
Missions—Deweese, Clay Co., Assumption; Lawrence, Nuckolls Co., St. Stephen's.

Loma, St. Luke's Czech Catholic Shrine (1912) (Czech), Mailing Address: c/o Rev. Msgr. Myron J. Pleskac, 7607 Trendwood Dr., Lincoln, 68506. Tel: 402-483-2288; Fax: 402-489-9729.

Manley, Cass Co., St. Patrick's (1881), Rev. Msgr. Raymond B. Hain.
Res., P.O. Box 27, 68403. Tel: 402-234-3595. [CEM]
Catechesis/Religious Programs—Students 163.
Mission—Elmwood, Cass Co., St. Mary's. [CEM]

McCook, Red Willow Co., St. Patrick (1886), Revs. Robert G. Tucker; Ferdinand J. Boehme.
Res., 612 E. 4th St., P.O. Box 216, 69001. Tel: 308-345-6734. [CEM]
School—(Grades PreK-8) 401 E. F St., 69001. Tel: 308-345-4546.
Priests 2; Lay Teachers 11; Students 117.
Catechesis/Religious Programs—Students 290.
Missions—McCook, Red Willow Co., Sacred Heart; McCook, Red Willow Co., St. Ann's. [CEM]

McCool Junction, York Co., St. Patrick's. (Administered from St. Joseph Church, York). Rev. James Divis.
Tel: 402-362-4595. [CEM]

Mead, Saunders Co., St. James (1882), Rev. Charles P. Townsend.
Res., 112 N. Elm, P.O. Box 91, 68041. Tel: 402-624-3555. [CEM]
Catechesis/Religious Programs—Students 49.

Minden, Kearney Co., St. John's (1882), Very Rev. James M. O'Connor, V.F.
Res., 624 N. Garber Ave., P.O. Box 245, 68959. Tel: 308-832-1245.
Catechesis/Religious Programs—Students 84.
Mission—Heartwell, Kearney Co., Holy Family.

Morse Bluff, Saunders Co., St. George (1945), Rev. Bernard F. Kimminau.
Res., P.O. Box 98, 68648. Tel: 402-666-5280.
Catechesis/Religious Programs—Students 60.
Mission—Cedar Hill, Saunders Co., Sacred Heart. [CEM]

Nebraska City, Otoe Co., St. Mary's (1869), Rev. Stephen P. Major. In res., Rev. Matthew F. Eickhoff.
Res., 218 N. 6th St., 68410. Tel: 402-873-3024. [CEM]
Catechesis/Religious Programs—Students 51.

St. Benedict's (1856), Rev. Mak A. Tasler.
Res., 411 5th Rue, 68410. Tel: 402-873-3047. [CEM]

Orleans, Harlan Co., St. Mary's (1878), Rev. Gerald F. Vap.
Res., P.O. Box 446, 68966. Tel: 308-473-3475. [CEM]
Catechesis/Religious Programs—Students 53.
Mission—Oxford, Furnas Co., St. Michael's.

Osceola, Polk Co., St. Vincent's (1946), Rev. Thomas D. McGuire.
Res., 751 S. Nance, P.O. Box 212, 68651. Tel: 402-747-3491.
Catechesis/Religious Programs—Students 26.
Mission—Osceola, Polk Co., St. Mary's, (1893).

Palmyra, Otoe Co., St. Leo's (1874), Rev. Christopher L. Barak.
Res., 330 W. 8th St., 68418-2537. Tel: 402-780-5535. [CEM]
Mission—Douglas, Otoe Co., St. Martin's.

Paul, Otoe Co., St. Joseph's (1871), Rev. Sean P. Redmond.
Res., Rte. 1, Box 243, Nebraska City, 68410. Tel: 402-873-4569. [CEM]
Catechesis/Religious Programs—Students 14.
Mission—Julian, Nemaha Co., St. Bernard's. [CEM]

Plattsmouth, Cass Co., Church of the Holy Spirit (1862), Very Rev. Paul H. York, V.F.
Res., 520 S. 18th St., P.O. Box C, 68048. Tel: 402-296-3139; Fax: 402-296-2408. [CEM]
School—(Grades K-8).
Lay Teachers 12; Students 182.
Catechesis/Religious Programs—Students 125.

Prague, Saunders Co., St. John's (1901), Rev. Ronald G. Homes.
Res., P.O. Box 96, 68050. Tel: 402-663-4615. [CEM]
Catechesis/Religious Programs—Students 58.
Mission—Plasi, Saunders Co., SS. Cyril and Methodius. [CEM]

Red Cloud, Webster Co., Sacred Heart (1893), Rev. Stanley F. Schieffer.
Res., 413 N. Seward St., 68970. Tel: 402-746-3750. [CEM]
Catechesis/Religious Programs—Students 38.
Mission—Riverton, Franklin Co., St. Catherine's.

Roseland, Adams Co., Sacred Heart (1921), Rev. Thomas Y. Au.
Res., P.O. Box 67, 68973. Tel: 402-756-6251.
Catechesis/Religious Programs—Students 66.
Mission—Juniata, Adams Co., Assumption. [CEM]

Rulo, Richardson Co., Immaculate Conception (1863), Rev. Lawrence J. Stoley.
Res., R.R. 1, Box 89C, 68431. Tel: 402-245-4731. [CEM]
Catechesis/Religious Programs—Students 37.
Mission—Arago, Richardson Co., St. Mary's.

Seward, Seward Co., St. Vincent de Paul (1878), Rev. James F. Benton.
Res., 152 Pinewood, 68434. Tel: 402-643-3421.
Catechesis/Religious Programs—Students 337.

Shelby, Polk Co., Sacred Heart, Rev. John L. Copenhaver.
Res., P.O. Box 340, 68662. Tel: 402-527-5425. [CEM]
Catechesis/Religious Programs—Students 125.

Steinauer, Pawnee Co., St. Anthony, Rev. Bradley J. Zitek.
Res., P.O. Box 98, 68441. Tel: 402-869-2256. [CEM]
Mission—Burchard, Pawnee Co., Sacred Heart. [CEM]

Superior, Nuckolls Co., St. Joseph's (1934), Rev. Frank J. Machovec.
Res., 1415 California, P.O. Box 366, 68978. Tel: 402-879-3735. [CEM]
Catechesis/Religious Programs—Students 87.
Mission—Nelson, Nuckolls Co., Sacred Heart, Tel: 402-225-3011.

Sutton, Clay Co., St. Mary's, Rev. Thaddeus Bryl, Admin.
Res., P.O. Box 406, 68979. Tel: 402-773-5346.

Syracuse, Otoe Co., St. Paulinus (1906), Rev. Michael S. Stec.
Mailing Address: P.O.Box C., 68446. Tel: 402-269-3382.
Catechesis/Religious Programs—Students 150.
Mission—Avoca, Cass Co., Holy Trinity. [CEM]

Tecumseh, Johnson Co., St. Andrew's (1866), Rev. John A. Cooper.
Res., 186 N. 5th St., P.O. Box 656, 68450. Tel: 402-335-3742. [CEM]
School—(Grades K-8). Tel: 402-335-2034.
Marian Sisters 2; Lay Teachers 3; Students 50.
Catechesis/Religious Programs—Students 64.
Mission—St. Mary, Johnson Co., St. Mary's. [CEM]

Trenton, Hitchcock Co., St. James (1894), Rev. Philip L. Luther.
Res., P.O. Box 488, 69044. Tel: 308-334-5328. [CEM]
Catechesis/Religious Programs—Students 54.
Mission—Palisade, Hitchcock Co., Holy Family.

Ulysses, Butler Co., Immaculate Conception (1915), Rev. John R. Sullivan.
Res., P.O. Box 128, 68669. Tel: 402-549-2437. [CEM]
Catechesis/Religious Programs—Students 84.

Valparaiso, Saunders Co., Sts. Mary and Joseph's, Rev. Liam M. Barr.
Res., P.O. Box 248, 68065. Tel: 402-784-2511. [CEM]

Wahoo, Saunders Co., St. Wenceslaus (1877), Very Rev. Lawrence J. Gyhra, V.F.; Rev. Anthony Stammitti. In res., Rev. Gary L. Gross.
Res., 214 E. 2nd St., 68066. Tel: 402-443-4235. [CEM]
School—(Grades K-6).
Sisters 2; Lay Teachers 10; Students 316.
Catechesis/Religious Programs—Students 37.

Wallace, Lincoln Co., St. Mary's, Rev. Thomas R. Walsh.
Res., P.O. Box 191, 69169. Tel: 308-387-4441.
Catechesis/Religious Programs—Students 73.
Mission—Elsie, Perkins Co., Resurrection of Our Lord.

Weston, Saunders Co., St. John Nepomucene (1885), Rev. Randall L. Langhorst.
Res., P.O. Box 10, 68070. Tel: 402-642-5245. [CEM]
School—(Grades K-6). Tel: 402-642-5234.
Notre Dame Sisters (Omaha, NE) 3; Lay Teachers 4; Students 115.
Mission—Touhy, Saunders Co., St. Vitus. [CEM]

Wilber, Saline Co., St. Wenceslaus (1878),
Res., 501 N. Wilson, P.O. Box 706, 68465. Tel: 402-821-2689.
Catechesis/Religious Programs—Students 113.
Mission—Tobias, Saline Co., St. Joseph's.

Wymore, Gage Co., St. Mary's (1881), Rev. Dennis W. Hotovy.
Res., 107 N. 11th St., P.O. Box 295, 68466. Tel: 402-645-3051. [CEM]
Catechesis/Religious Programs—Students 69.
Missions—Barneston, Gage Co., St. Joseph's; Odell, Gage Co., St. Mary's.

York, York Co., St. Joseph's (1878), Rev. James Divis. In res., Rev. Charles L. Gergen.
Res., 505 East Ave., 68467. Tel: 402-362-4595. [CEM]
School—(Grades K-8). Tel: 402-362-3021.
Franciscan Apostolic Sisters 4; Lay Teachers 11; Students 154.
Catechesis/Religious Programs—Students 171.

Shrines

Loma, St. Luke's Czech Catholic Shrine.

Chaplains of Public Institutions

LINCOLN. *Nebraska Penal Complex* 3128 S St., 68503. Tel: 402-435-0251. Rev. Edwin L. Stander, Chap.

DENTON. *U.S. Veterans' Hospital* 7105 Cass, P.O. Box 406, 68339. Tel: 402-797-2105. Rev. Msgr. Thomas L. Holoman, Chap.

On Duty Outside the Diocese:
Reverend Monsignors—
Jackels, Michael O., Villa Stritch, Via della Nocetta, 63, 00164 Rome, Italy
Olmsted, Thomas J., J.C.D., 7625 N. High St., Columbus, OH 43235-1498
Reverend Fathers—
Fucinaro, Thomas J., Villa Stritch, Via della Nocetta, 63, 00164 Rome, Italy
Johnson, Lyle M., Apartado 407, Barquisimeto, Venezuela, S.A.
Kalin, William A., Apartado 407, Barquisimeto, Venezuela, S.A.
Reinert, James M., 25 East 39th St., New York, NY 10016-0903

Graduate Studies:
Reverend Fathers—
Huber, Mark D., Casa Santa Maria, Via dell Umilta 30, 00187 Rome, Italy

---

Sick Leave:
Reverend Fathers—
Mika, John M., 5010 S. 41st Ave., Omaha, NE 68017

Retired:
Reverend Monsignors—
Barry, Denis L., Bonacum House, 3301 Sheridan Blvd., Lincoln, NE 68506
Keenan, Charles J., Bonacum House, 3301 Sheridan Blvd., Lincoln, NE 68506
Reisdorff, Clarence P., Bonacum House, 3301 Sheridan Blvd., Lincoln, NE 68506
Schuster, George J., Madonna Rehabilitation Hospital, 5401 South St., Lincoln, NE 68506
Reverend Fathers—
Banach, Walter F., P.O. Box 324, Geneva, NE 68361
Danko, Michael S., 201 N. Gregg Rd., Nixa, MO 65714
Derwinski, Victor A., 806 13th St., P.O. Box 281, Aurora, NE 68818
Gadient, Peter J., 380 Elm St., P.O. Box 4, Bee, NE 68314
Halligan, James, Choncaulfield, Moydow, Co. Longford, Republic of Ireland
Hebert, John M., 7323 Shirley, Apt. 102, Omaha, NE 68124
Kelly, John W., Bonacum House, 3301 Sheridan Blvd., Lincoln, NE 68506
Kotz, Anthony A., 28680 Aline Dr., Warren, MI 48093
Lyons, Patrick J., Bonacum House, 3301 Sheridan Blvd., Lincoln, NE 68506
Messman, Gerald C., Box 204, Duncan, NE 68634
Mroczkowski, Joseph A., Box 238, Cedar Creek, NE 68016
Rydz, Zygmund S., Marianna, Box 25R, Cedar Bluffs, NE 68015
Schnoebelen, Kenneth F., 143-21st St., S.W., Cedar Rapids, IA 52404
Sloup, Ernest O., Bonacum House, 3301 Sheridan Blvd., Lincoln, NE 68506
Smith, Robert H., Apartado Postal #54, Santa Ana Sonora, Mexico
Valasek, Edward A., 3322 Park Lane Dr., Apt. #201, Hastings, NE 68901

INSTITUTIONS LOCATED IN THE DIOCESE

[A] SEMINARIES, RELIGIOUS OR SCHOLASTICATES

HASTINGS. *Crosier Monastery*, Crosier Renewal Center, 223 E. 14th St., P.O. Box 789, 68902-0789. Tel: 402-463-3188; Fax: 402-463-5701. Very Rev. James G. Moeglein, O.S.C., Prior; Revs. Urban J. Schmitt, O.S.C.; Oscar C. Schoenberg, O.S.C.; John G. Hawkins, O.S.C.; Milton A. Thomas, O.S.C.; Ignatius Lempart, O.S.C.; John J. Vincent, O.S.C. Priests 7; Brothers 10.

SEWARD. *St. Gregory the Great Seminary*, 1301 280th Rd., 68434. Tel: 402-643-4052. Rev. John C. Rooney.

[B] ELEMENTARY SCHOOLS, INTERPAROCHIAL

HASTINGS. *St. Michael's Elementary, Hastings Catholic Schools*, 721 Creighton Ave., 68901. Tel: 402-462-6310; 462-6035. Priests 6; Lay Teachers 20; Students 375.

NEBRASKA CITY. *Lourdes Elementary*. (Grades K-6), 412 2nd Ave., 68410. Tel: 402-873-3253. Marian Sisters (Waverly, NE) 2; Ursuline Sisters (Maple Mount, KY) 1; Lay Teachers 6; Students 151.
Lourdes Primary. (Grades K-3), 411 5th Rue, 68410. Tel: 402-873-3739. Lay Teachers 4; Students 90.

[C] HIGH SCHOOLS, INTERPAROCHIAL

LINCOLN. *Pius X Central High School*, 6000 A St., 68510. Tel: 402-488-0931. Rev. Michael J. Morin, Supt.; Mr. Thomas Seib, Prin.; Mr. Kevin Wingard, Asst. Prin.; Mrs. Jan Frayser, Dir. of Guidance; Mr. George O'Boyle, Dir. Activities. Priests 13; Sisters 4; Lay Teachers 46; Students 990.

DAVID CITY. *Aquinas/St. Mary's Schools*. (Grades K-12), P.O. Box 149, 68632. Tel: 402-367-3175. Rev. Brian P. Connor, Supt.; Mr. David G. McMahon, Prin. (Aquinas High School); Mrs. JoAnn Havlovic, Prin. (St. Mary's); Rev. Thomas J. Lux, Guidance Dir. Priests 7; Sisters 6; Lay Teachers 34; Students 545.

FALLS CITY. *Sacred Heart School*, 1820 Fulton St., 68355. Tel: 402-245-4151. Revs. Robert A. Roh, Supt.; Lawrence J. Stoley, Prin.; Michael G. McCabe, Dir. Guidance.
High School. Priests 3; Lay Teachers 11; Students 79.
Elementary School. Priests 3; Lay Teachers 18; Students 188.

HASTINGS. *St. Cecilia's Middle School/High School*. (Grades 6-12), 521 N. Kansas, 68901. Tel: 402-462-2105. Rev. James Meysenberg, Supt. Priests 4; Sisters 2; Lay Teachers 26; Students 361.

NEBRASKA CITY. *Lourdes Junior-Senior High School*. (Grades 7-12), 412 2nd Ave., 68410. Tel: 402-873-6154. Rev. Matthew F. Eickhoff, Supt. Priests 5; Lay Teachers 9; Students 110.

WAHOO. *Neumann High School*, 202 S. Linden, 68066. Tel: 402-443-4151. Rev. Gary L. Gross, Supt.; Sr. Michelle Hayek, N.D., Prin.; Ms. Monica Flakus, Guidance Dir. Priests 5; Sisters 2; Lay Teachers 20; Students 328.

[D] GENERAL HOSPITALS

LINCOLN. *St. Elizabeth Community Health Center*, 555 S. 70th St., 68519. Tel: 402-489-7181
For a complete listing, refer to the Hospitals section.

NEBRASKA CITY. *St. Mary's Hospital*, 1314 3rd Ave., 68410. Tel: 402-873-3321
For a complete listing, refer to the Hospitals section.

[E] HOMES FOR AGED

LINCOLN. *Bonacum House*, 3301 Sheridan Blvd., 68506
For a complete listing, refer to the Special Care Facilities section.
Madonna Rehabilitation Hospital, 5401 South St., 68506. Tel: 402-489-7102
For a complete listing, refer to the Special Care Facilities section.

DAVID CITY. *St. Joseph's Villa, Inc.*, 927 7th St., 68632. Tel: 402-367-3045; Fax: 402-367-3730
For a complete listing, refer to the Special Care Facilities section.

[F] RETREAT HOUSES

WAVERLY. *Our Lady of Good Counsel Retreat House*, R.R. No. 1, Box 110, 68462. Tel: 402-786-2705. Rev. Msgr. Timothy J. Thorburn, Dir. Private Rooms 50. In res. Revs. Peter E. Cops, S.S.S.; Daniel Polzer, L.C.

[G] CONVENTS AND RESIDENCES FOR SISTERS

LINCOLN. *Adoration Convent and Church of Christ the King*, 1040 S. Cotner Blvd., 68510. Tel: 402-489-0765. Sister Servants of the Holy Spirit of Perpetual Adoration. Sr. Mary Catherine, Supr.; Rev. Joseph J. Nemec, Chap. Professed Sisters 9.
Congregation of Mary Queen (Vietnam), 6400 Nebraska Hwy. 2, 68516. Tel: 402-421-1704.
Daughters of the Holy Spirit, Nazareth of the Good Shepherd, Hispanic Apostolate, 110 W "E" St., 68508-3087. Tel: 402-477-7646. Sr. Margarita Iturbide, Supr.
School Sisters of Christ the King, Villa Regina Motherhouse & Novitiate, 4100 S.W. 56th St., 68522-9201. Tel: 402-477-5232. Mother Joan Paul, C.K., Supr. In res. Rev. Daniel J. Seiker. Tel: 402-477-1768.

WAVERLY. *Marian Sisters of the Diocese of Lincoln Motherhouse and Novitiate*. Mailing Address: Rte. 1, Box 108, 68462. Tel: 402-786-2750. Sr. Ann Divis, M.S. Professed 33.

[H] SPECIAL EDUCATION

LINCOLN. *Villa Marie School and Home for the Educable Mentally Handicapped*, P.O. Box 80328, 68501. Tel: 402-786-3625. Marian Sisters (Waverly, NE). Sr. Patricia Stoeckinger, M.S., Prin.; Rev. John J. Perkinton, Dir. Sisters 3; Students 16.

[I] NEWMAN CENTERS

LINCOLN. *University of Nebraska, Newman Club*, 320 N. 16th St., 68508. Tel: 402-474-7914. See also: St. Thomas Aquinas, Lincoln, NE. Rev. Msgr. Leonard I. Kalin, Chap., Vocation Dir.; Rev. Loras K. Grell, Asst. Chap. & Asst. Vocation Dir.

[J] FUNDS, FOUNDATIONS AND TRUSTS

LINCOLN. *Chancery*, P.O. Box 80328, 3400 Sheridan Blvd., 68501.
Seminary Burse Fund.
Mass Stipends.
Food for the Starving.
Latin America Fund.
Mission Office Fund.
Catholic Evangelization Fund.
St. Gregory the Great Seminary Fund.

[K] CATHOLIC SOCIAL SERVICES

LINCOLN. *Catholic Social Services*, Administrative Offices, 301 S. 70th St., Ste. 300, 68510. Tel: 402-489-1834. Rev. Joseph M. Walsh, Dir.; John Kopetzky, Vice Pres., Operations.
Other Addresses: 123 N. 25th St., 68503. Tel: 402-474-1600. 235 North St. Joseph Ave., Hastings, 68901. Tel: 402-463-2112.

[L] MISCELLANEOUS LISTINGS

LINCOLN. *Calvary Cemetery and Mausoleum Association*, 145 S. 40th St., 68510. Tel: 402-476-8787. Joint cemetery for Lincoln parishes. Revs. Ronald Patterson, Dir.; David R. Hintz, Asst. Dir.
Catholic Social Services, 301 S. 70th St., Ste. 300, 68510. Tel: 402-489-1834. Foster home care for children. Rev. Joseph M. Walsh, Dir.
Chancery Annex, 3325 Sheridan Blvd., 68506. Tel: 402-488-2040.
Cristo Rey Catholic Hispanic Center, 1335 N. 30th, 68503. Tel: 402-474-6201.
Kucera Hall, 5720 A St., 68510.
Pius X Foundation and Pius X Endowment Fund, 6000 A St., 68510. Tel: 402-488-0931. Rev. Michael J. Morin, Sec. & Treas.

DAVID CITY. *Aquinas High School Endowment Fund*, P.O. Box 149, 68632. Tel: 402-367-3175. Rev. Brian P. Connor, Sec. & Treas.

FALLS CITY. *Sacred Heart High School Endowment Fund*, 1820 Fulton St., 68355. Tel: 402-245-4151. Very Rev. Robert A. Roh, Sec. & Treas.

HASTINGS. *St. Cecilia High School Endowment Fund*, 521 N. Kansas, 68901. Revs. James J. Meysenberg, Sec.; David F. Bourek, Treas.

NEBRASKA CITY. *Lourdes Central High School Endowment Fund*, 412 Second Ave., 68410. Tel: 402-873-6154. Rev. Matthew F. Eickhoff, Sec. & Treas.

WAHOO. *Bishop Neumann High School Endowment Fund*, 202 S. Linden, 68066. Tel: 402-443-4151. Rev. Gary L. Gross, Sec. & Treas.

RELIGIOUS INSTITUTES OF MEN REPRESENTED IN THE DIOCESE

For further details refer to the corresponding bracketed number in the Religious Institutes of Men or Women section.

[0400]—*Canons Regular of the Order of the Holy Cross.* (Prov. of St. Odilia).—O.S.C.

[0220]—*Congregation of the Blessed Sacrament.*—S.S.S.

[]—*Congregation of the Mother Coredemptrix.* (Vietnamese).—C.M.C.

[]—*Oblates of Wisdom.*—O.S.

[0730]—Legionaries of Christ.—L.C.

RELIGIOUS INSTITUTES OF WOMEN REPRESENTED IN THE DIOCESE

[0100]—*Adorers of the Blood of Christ.*—A.S.C.
[]—*American Province of the Religious Order of Servants of Mary, Inc.*—O.S.M.
[0230]—*Benedictine Sisters of Pontifical Jurisdiction.*—O.S.B.
[]—*Congregation of Mary, Queen.* (Vietnam).
[]—*Daughters of the Holy Spirit, Nazareth of the Good Shepherd.*—H.Sp.S.
[1070-01]—*Dominican Sisters.*—O.P.
[]—*Franciscan Apostolic Sisters.*—F.A.S.
[2575]—*Institute of the Sisters of Mercy of the Americas.*—R.S.M.
[2400]—*Marian Sisters of the Diocese of Lincoln.*—M.S.
[2960]—*Notre Dame Sisters.*—N.D.
[]—*School Sisters of Christ the King.*—C.K.
[1680]—*School Sisters of St. Francis.*—O.S.F.
[3540]—*Sister Servants of the Holy Spirit of Perpetual Adoration.*—S.Sp.S.deA.P.
[0430]—*Sisters of Charity of the Blessed Virgin Mary.*—B.V.M.
[1600]—*Sisters of St. Francis of Martyr St. George.*—O.S.F.
[1640]—*Sisters of St. Francis of Perpetual Adoration.* (Prov. of St. Joseph).—O.S.F.
[3270]—*Sisters of the Most Precious Blood (O'Fallon, MO).*—C.PP.S.
[4120-05]—*Ursuline Nuns of the Congregation of Paris.*—O.S.U.

DIOCESAN CEMETERIES

LINCOLN. *Calvary.*

NECROLOGY

† Howe, John H., (Retired). —Died April 4, 1997.
† Leiblinger, Frank J., (Retired). —Died Feb. 4, 1997.
† Rezabek, Rev. Msgr. William J., (Retired). —Died Oct. 29, 1997.
† Wageman, Rev. Msgr. Raymond L., (Retired). —Died Dec. 27, 1996.

Diocese of Little Rock

(Dioecesis Petriculana)

Most Reverend

ANDREW J. MCDONALD, D.D., J.C.D.

Bishop of Little Rock; ordained May 8, 1948; appointed Bishop of Little Rock July 4, 1972; consecrated September 5, 1972; installed September 7, 1972. *Res., 30 Sherrill Rd., Little Rock, AR, 72202.* Tel.: 501-664-6738; 374-2794 (Cathedral); 664-0340 (Office). *Mailing Address: Diocese of Little Rock, 2415 N. Tyler, P.O. Box 7239, Little Rock, AR, 72217.*

Chancery: P.O. Box 7239, 2415 N. Tyler St., Little Rock, AR, 72217. Tel.: 501-664-0340.

ESTABLISHED NOVEMBER 28, 1843.

Square Miles 53,104.

Comprises the State of Arkansas.

For legal titles of parishes and diocesan institutions, consult the Chancery Office.

STATISTICAL OVERVIEW

Personnel	
Bishop	1
Abbots	1
Retired Abbots	1
Priests: Diocesan Active in Diocese	56
Priests: Active Outside Diocese	1
Priests: Retired, Sick or Absent	26
Number of Diocesan Priests	83
Religious Priests in Diocese	65
Extern Priests in Diocese	12
Permanent Deacons in Diocese	58
Total Brothers	47
Total Sisters	365
Parishes	
Parishes	90
With Resident Pastor:	
Resident Diocesan Priests	53
Resident Religious Priests	30
Without Resident Pastor:	
Administered by Priests	3
Administered by Permanent Deacons	2
Administered by Women Religious	2
Missions	44
Professional Ministry Personnel:	
Brothers	1
Sisters	39
Lay Ministers	38
Welfare	
Catholic Hospitals	10
Total Assisted	782,801
Health Care Centers	1
Total Assisted	3,000
Homes for the Aged	4
Total Assisted	279
Day Care and Extended Day Care Centers	8
Total Assisted	232
Specialized Homes	2
Total Assisted	93
Special Centers for Social Services	23
Total Assisted	14,982
Educational	
Diocesan Students in Other Seminaries	15
Total Seminarians	15
Total Students	15
High Schools, Diocesan and Parish	5
Total Students	1,416
High Schools, Private	2
Total Students	788
Elementary Schools, Diocesan and Parish	31
Total Students	6,601
Elementary Schools, Private	1
Total Students	66
Catechesis/Religious Education:	
High School Students	2,220
Elementary Students	4,589
Total Students Under Catholic Instruction	15,710
Teachers in the Diocese:	
Priests	10
Brothers	9
Sisters	46
Lay Teachers	544
Vital Statistics	
Receptions into the Church:	
Infant Baptism Totals	2,002
Adult Baptism Totals	248
Received into Full Communion	465
First Communions	1,643
Confirmations	1,206
Marriages:	
Catholic	271
Interfaith	370
Total Marriages	641
Deaths	891
Total Catholic Population	86,990
Total Population	2,509,791

Former Bishops—Rt. Rev. ANDREW BYRNE, D.D., cons. March 10, 1844; died in Helena, June 10, 1862.—Rt. Rev. EDWARD FITZGERALD, D.D., preconized June 22, 1866; cons. Feb. 3, 1867; died in Hot Springs, Feb. 21, 1907.—Most Rev. JOHN B. MORRIS, D.D., ord. June 11, 1892; cons. June 11, 1906; died in Little Rock, Oct. 22, 1946.—Most Rev. ALBERT L. FLETCHER, D.D., ord. June 4, 1920; cons. April 25, 1940; appt. Bishop of Little Rock Dec. 7, 1946; retired July 3, 1972; died Dec. 6, 1979.

Vicar General—Rev. Msgr. J. GASTON HEBERT, V.G.

Chancery—2415 N. Tyler St., P.O. Box 7239, Little Rock, 72217. Tel: 501-664-0340. Office Hours: Mon.-Fri. 8:30-4.

Chancellor for Canonical Affairs—Rev. FRANCIS I. MALONE, J.C.L.

Chancellor for Administration—Mr. GREGORY WOLFE.

Vice Chancellor—Rev. SCOTT L. MARCZUK, J.C.L.

Finance Officer—Mr. WILLIAM HARTMANN.

Diocesan Tribunal—2415 N. Tyler St., P.O. Box 7239, Little Rock, 72217. Tel: 501-664-0340.

Judicial Vicar—Rev. SCOTT L. MARCZUK, J.C.L.

Judges—Revs. JAMES M. DIXON, S.J.; GREGORY HART; GREGORY T. LUYET; FRANCIS I. MALONE, J.C.L.; SCOTT L. MARCZUK, J.C.L.

Defender of the Bond—Rev. JOHN KORDSMEIER; Mrs. BARBARA ANHALT.

Notaries—Mrs. JANICE BRASS; Mrs. SHAWN HALLMAN; Mrs. JEANNIE MOORE.

Vicar for Religious—Sr. MAXINE VOGAN, D.L.F., *621 S. Washington, Forrest City, 72335.* Tel: 501-663-1665.

Diocesan Consultors—Rev. Msgr. J. GASTON HEBERT, V.G.; Rev. Msgr. JOHN F. O'DONNELL; Rev. Msgr. BERNARD G. MALONE, V.F.; Revs. FRANCIS I. MALONE; SCOTT MARCZUK; JACK D. HARRIS.

Deans—Very Rev. Msgr. BERNARD G. MALONE, V.F.; Very Rev. Msgr. JOHN F. O'DONNELL, V.F.; Very Rev. Msgr. LEO RIEDMUELLER, V.F.; Very Revs. ROBERT T. DIENERT, V.F.; ERNEST HARDESTY, V.F.; DAVID JACOBS, V.F.; JOHN KORDSMEIER, V.F.; RICHARD OSWALD, V.F.; JOSEPH L. PALLO; W. ANDREW SMITH, V.F.; THOMAS MARKS, V.F.; Rt. Rev. JEROME KODELL, O.S.B., V.F.

Diocesan Offices and Directors

Adoption Services, Inc.—Ms. ANTJE HARRIS, Dir., *2415 N. Tyler St., P.O. Box 7239, Little Rock, 72217.* Tel: 501-664-0340.

Diocesan Council for Black Catholics—Rev. WARREN HARVEY, *1321 S. Van Buren St., Little Rock, 72204.* Tel: 501-666-5073.

Building Commission—Mr. JAMES DAVIS, Exec. Sec., *2415 N. Tyler St., P.O. Box 7239, Little Rock, 72217.* Tel: 501-664-0340.

Catholic Social Services—Mr. DENNIS LEE, Dir., *2415 N. Tyler St., P.O. Box 7239, Little Rock, 72217.* Tel: 501-664-0340. This office also handles: *Catholic Relief Services.*

Catholic Campus Ministries—See: *Catholic Youth Ministries.*

Catholic Women, Diocesan Council of—Rev. JAMES P. WEST, *589 W. Grand Ave., Hot Springs, 71901.* Tel: 501-623-6201.

Catholic Youth Ministries—PHYLLIS ENDERLIN, Dir., *2500 N. Tyler St., P.O. Box 7565, Little Rock, 72217.* Tel: 501-664-0340. This office also handles: Catholic Campus Ministries; Scouting; Catholic Youth Organization (CYO). Rev. JAMES P. WEST, CYO Moderator, *589 W. Grand Ave., Hot Springs, 71901.* Tel: 501-623-6201.

Cemetery, Greater Little Rock—BARBARA BAKER, Sec., Diocese of Little Rock, *2500 N. Tyler St., Little Rock, 72207.* Tel: 501-664-0340.

Charismatic Movement, Bishop's Liaison—Rev. JAMES E. MANCINI, *St. Patrick's Church, 211 W. 19th St., North Little Rock, 72114.* Tel: 501-758-1155.

Clergy Welfare Board—Rev. Msgr. J. GASTON HEBERT, V.G., Chm., *2415 N. Tyler St., P.O. Box 7239, Little Rock, 72217.* Tel: 501-664-0340.

Communications Department—Rev. FRANCIS I. MALONE, Dir., *P.O. Box 7417, Little Rock, 72217.* Tel: 501-664-0340.

Continuing Education for the Clergy—Rev. DAVID LESIEUR, Dir., *2500 N. Tyler St., P.O. Box 7565, Little Rock, 72217.* Tel: 501-664-0340.

Cursillo Movement—Rev. JOHN E. MARCONI, Moderator; Mrs. DEBBIE ECKERT, Exec. Dir., *2500 N. Tyler St., P.O. Box 7565, Little Rock, 72217.* Tel: 501-664-0340.

Data Processing—Rev. THOMAS SEBAUGH, Dir., *2500 N. Tyler St., P.O. Box 7565, Little Rock, 72217.* Tel: 501-664-0340.

Development Office—Mr. JOHN HEIRD, Dir., *P.O. Box 7239, Little Rock, 72217.* Tel: 501-664-0340.

Diaconate Program—Sr. YVONNE LERNER, O.S.B., Dir., *2500 N. Tyler St., P.O. Box 7565, Little Rock, 72217.* Tel: 501-664-0340.

Ecumenical and Inter-Religious Affairs Office—Mr. JOHN MARSCHEWSKI, Dir., *P.O. Box 7239, Little Rock, 72217*. Tel: 501-664-0340.

Family Life Office: (Beginning Experience, Pre-Cana, Marriage Encounter, Retrouvaille)—Ms. ELIZABETH REHA, Dir., *2500 N. Tyler St., P.O. Box 7565, Little Rock, 72217*. Tel: 501-664-0340.

Hispanic Ministry—Rev. JAMES BROCKMAN, S.J., Dir., *P.O. Box 7565, Little Rock, 72217*. Tel: 501-664-0340.

Hospitals—*2415 N. Tyler St., P.O. Box 7239, Little Rock, 72217*. Tel: 501-664-0340.

Catholic Immigration Services—Mrs. SHEILA GOMEZ, Dir., *2500 N. Tyler St., P.O. Box 7565, Little Rock, 72217*. Tel: 501-664-0340.

Lay Ministry and Parish Renewal—Deacon BO MCALLISTER, Dir., *2500 N. Tyler St., P.O. Box 7565, Little Rock, 72217*. Tel: 501-664-0340.

Liturgical Commission—Rev. FRANCIS I. MALONE, Dir., *2415 N. Tyler St., P.O. Box 7239, Little Rock, 72217*. Tel: 501-664-0340.

Minister to Priests—Rev. DAVID LESIEUR, *P.O. Box 7565, Little Rock, 72217*. Tel: 501-664-0340.

Newspaper "Arkansas Catholic"—Mr. DANNY STRAESSLE, Mng. Editor; Ms. MALEA WALTERS, Editor, *2500 N. Tyler St., P.O. Box 7565, Little Rock, 72217*. Tel: 501-664-0340.

Presbyteral Council—Rev. Msgr. J. GASTON HEBERT, V.G., Chm., *2415 N. Tyler St., P.O. Box 7239, Little Rock, 72217*. Tel: 501-664-0340.

Priests Personnel Board (Diocesan)—Rev. Msgr. J. GASTON HEBERT, V.G., Chm., *2415 N. Tyler St., P.O. Box 7239, Little Rock, 72217*. Tel: 501-664-0340.

Propagation of the Faith—Mr. DENNIS LEE, Dir., *2415 N. Tyler St., P.O. Box 7239, Little Rock, 72217*. Tel: 501-664-0340.

Refugee Resettlement Program—Col. DUTCH DORTCH, (Ret.) Dir., *2500 N. Tyler St., P.O. Box 7565, Little Rock, 72217*. Tel: 501-664-0340.

Religious Education Department—BARB MINCZEWSKI, Dir., *2500 N. Tyler St., P.O. Box 7565, Little Rock, 72217*. Tel: 501-664-0340.

Respect Life Office—Mrs. ANNE DIERKS, Dir., *2500 N. Tyler St., P.O. Box 7565, Little Rock, 72217*. Tel: 501-664-0340. This office also handles Project Rachel.

Rural Life Department—Vacant, *2500 N. Tyler St., P.O. Box 7565, Little Rock, 72217*. Tel: 501-664-0340.

St. John's Catholic Center—JOHN ROBINETTE, Mgr., *2500 N. Tyler St., P.O. Box 7565, Little Rock, 72217*. Tel: 501-664-0340.

Schools—Mr. MICHAEL ROCKERS, Supt., *2500 N. Tyler St., P.O. Box 7565, Little Rock, 72217*. Tel: 501-664-0340.

Scripture Study—Associate Directors: LILLY HESS; CACKIE UPCHURCH, *P.O. Box 7565, Little Rock, 72217*. Tel: 501-664-0340.

Seminary Endowment Fund (The Msgr. James E. O'Connell Seminary Burse)—Rev. Msgr. JAMES E. O'CONNELL, Dir., *2500 N. Tyler St., P.O. Box 7565, Little Rock, 72217*. Tel: 501-664-0340.

Social Action Office—Sr. JOAN PUTLIK, D.C., Dir., *2500 N. Tyler St., P.O. Box 7565, Little Rock, 72217*. Tel: 501-664-0340. This office also handles Parish Social Ministry.

Vocations—Rev. DAVID LESIEUR, Dir. JOHN HALL, Assoc. Dir., *2500 N. Tyler St., P.O. Box 7565, Little Rock, 72217*. Tel: 501-664-0340. Also serves as Director of Seminarians.

Westside Free Medical Clinic—Mrs. KAREN DIPIPPA, Dir., *2415 North Tyler St., P.O. Box 7239, Little Rock, 72217*. Tel: 501-664-0340; Fax: 501-664-9186.

CLERGY, PARISHES, MISSIONS AND PAROCHIAL SCHOOLS

GREATER LITTLE ROCK (Pulaski County)

1—CATHEDRAL OF ST. ANDREW (1845), Rev. Scott L. Marczuk, J.C.L., Rector; Deacon Gary Dollar.
Res., 617 Louisiana St., 72201. Tel: 501-374-2794; Fax: 501-375-3292. [JC]

2—ST. ANNE (North Little Rock) (1935), Revs. Francis I. Malone, J.C.L.; Clement Kalu.
Mailing Address: 6150 Remount Rd., North Little Rock, 72118. Tel: 501-753-3977.
Res., 7000 John F. Kennedy Blvd., North Little Rock, 72116. Tel: 501-835-4323; Fax: 501-834-5598. [JC]

3—ST. AUGUSTINE (1920) (African American), Rev. L. Warren Harvey, Admin.
Res., 1421 E. Second, North Little Rock, 72114. Tel: 501-375-9617; Fax: 501-375-9617. [JC]

4—ST. BARTHOLOMEW'S (1911) (African American), Rev. Donald Murrin, S.V.D.; Deacon Kirke Herman.
Res., 1622 Marshall St., 72202. Tel: 501-372-4682.

5—CHRIST THE KING, Rev. Msgr. J. Gaston Hebert, V.G.; Rev. John K. Antony; Deacons Bill Hartmann; Bo McAllister.
Res., 4000 N. Rodney Parham Rd., 72212. Tel: 501-225-6774; Fax: 501-225-8980. [JC]
School—Tel: 501-225-7883; Fax: 501-225-1315. Mrs. Kathy House, Prin.
Lay Teachers 31; Students 743.
Christ the King Endowment Trust Fund for Christ the King Catholic School—Tel: 501-225-7883; Fax: 501-225-1315.

6—ST. EDWARD (1884), Rev. Vincent Flusche; Deacon Ben Rodriquez.
Res., 815 Sherman St., 72202. Tel: 501-374-5767; Fax: 501-374-5839. [JC]
School—E. Ninth & Ferry St., 72202. Tel: 501-374-9166.
Lay Teachers 10; Students 180.
Educational Trust Fund for St. Edward School—.

7—IMMACULATE CONCEPTION (1948), Revs. Francis I. Malone, J.C.L.; Clement Kalu; Deacon William Nolan.
Res., 7000 John F. Kennedy Blvd., North Little Rock, 72116. Tel: 501-835-4323; Fax: 501-834-5598. [JC]
School—Tel: 501-835-0771.
Lay Teachers 23; Students 462.
Immaculate Conception School Endowment Fund—.
Mission—England, Lonoke Co., Holy Trinity, P.O. Box 243, England, 72046. Tel: 501-842-2460.

8—IMMACULATE HEART OF MARY (Marche) (Polish), Very Rev. Msgr. Bernard G. Malone, V.F.; Deacon Brunon Strozyk.
Res., 7006 Jasna Gora Dr., North Little Rock, 72118. Tel: 501-851-2763; Fax: 501-851-2763. [CEM]
School—Tel: 501-851-2760; Fax: 501-851-4769.
Lay Teachers 13; Students 187.
Immaculate Heart of Mary Educational Trust Fund for Immaculate Heart of Mary School—Tel: 501-851-2763.

9—ST. MARY (North Little Rock) (1897), Rev. Paul F. Worm.
Res., 1516 Parker St., North Little Rock, 72114. Tel: 501-374-7123; Fax: 501-372-2995.
School—1518 Parker St., North Little Rock, 72114. Tel: 501-374-5237; Fax: 501-374-5237.
Lay Teachers 10; Students 214.
St. Mary's School Endowment Fund—.

10—OUR LADY OF GOOD COUNSEL (1894), Revs. Thomas W. Keller; L. Warren Harvey. In res., Rev. Peter Le Quang.
Res., 1321 S. Van Buren St., 72204. Tel: 501-666-5073; Fax: 501-666-8246.
School—1204 S. Jackson St., 72204. Tel: 501-663-7426; Fax: 501-666-2239.
Lay Teachers 19; Students 241.
Msgr. Scheper Endowment Fund for Our Lady of Good Counsel Catholic School—.

11—OUR LADY OF THE HOLY SOULS (1947), Rev. David LeSieur; Deacon Larry Jegley. In res., Rev. Lawrence A. Frederick; Deacon Bill Cranford.
Res., 1003 N. Tyler St., 72205. Tel: 501-663-8632; Fax: 501-663-8699.
Mailing Address: P.O. Box 250202, 72225.
School—901 N. Tyler St., 72205. Tel: 501-663-4513; Fax: 501-663-1014.
Olivetan Benedictines 2; Lay Teachers 32; Students 526.
Msgr. Allen Trust Fund for Holy Souls School—Tel: 501-663-4512.

12—ST. PATRICK'S (1880), Rev. Paul F. Worm; Deacon George Siebenmorgan. In res., Rev. Do Duy Nho.
Res., 211 W. 19th St., North Little Rock, 72114. Tel: 501-758-1155. [JC]
School—1900 Orange St., North Little Rock, 72114. Tel: 501-758-1508.
Lay Teachers 17; Students 215.
St. Patrick's School Endowment Fund—.

13—ST. THERESA'S (1950), Rev. John M. Connell; Deacons Don Francis; Robert Maes; William R. Wrape, II.
Res., 6219 Baseline Rd., 72209. Tel: 501-565-9198; Fax: 501-565-3949. [JC]
School—Tel: 501-565-3855; Fax: 501-565-9522.
Lay Teachers 17; Students 300.
St. Theresa's Catholic School Endowment Fund—.

OUTSIDE THE CITY OF LITTLE ROCK

Adona, Conway Co., St. Elizabeth's (1884) (German). Attended by St. Boniface Church, New Dixie. Rev. Richard P. Davis.
Mailing Address: Rte. 1, Box 80 Dixie, Bigelow, 72016. Tel: 501-354-0631. [CEM]

Altus, Franklin Co., St. Mary (1879), Rev. Hilary Filiatreau, O.S.B.; Deacon Matthew Post.
Res., 72821. Tel: 501-468-2585. [CEM]

Arkadelphia, Clark Co., St. Mary's. Attended by St. John's Church, Malvern. Rev. Alan Rosenau; Sr. Teresa Daly, D.C., Admin.
Church—P.O. Box 26, 71923. Tel: 870-246-7575.

Atkins, Pope Co., Assumption B.V.M. (1878) (German), Rev. Edward G. Marley, C.S.Sp.; Deacon Veo J. Condley.
Res., P.O. Box 337, 72823. Tel: 501-641-7179. [CEM]

Barling, Sebastian Co., Sacred Heart of Mary, Rev. William Elser.
Res. and Office: 1301 Frank St., 72923. Tel: 501-452-1795. [CEM]

Batesville, Independence Co., St. Mary's, Rev. Clayton Gould.
Res., 3800 Harrison St., 72501. Tel: 870-793-7717; 793-7464.
Missions—Mountain View, Stone Co., St. Mary, Mabry St. & Luther St., Mountain View, 72560; Newport, Jackson Co., St. Cecilia, 2475 Galleria Dr., Newport, 72112. Tel: 870-523-6542.

Bella Vista, Benton Co., St. Bernard (1980), Rev. Joseph J. Enderlin.
Res., 1 St. Bernard Ln., 72715. Tel: 501-855-9060; 855-9069.

Benton, Saline Co., Our Lady of Fatima (1942), Rev. John Marconi; Deacon John Duke.
Res., 900 W. Cross St., 72015. Tel: 501-315-3398; Fax: 501-315-0927.
School—Olivetan Benedictine Sisters 1; Lay Teachers 8; Students 120.
Our Lady of Fatima School Endowment Fund—816 W. Cross St., 72015.
Station—Benton, Benton Services Center, Tel: 870-866-0500.

Bentonville, Benton Co., St. Stephen (1989), Rev. Michael D. Sinkler; Deacon Jerry Becker.
Mailing Address: P.O. Box 1396, 72712. Tel: 501-273-1240; Fax: 501-464-0969.
Res., 1300 N.E. J St., 72712. Tel: 501-273-1240.

Berryville, Carroll Co., St. Anne's, Rev. James M. Fanrak.
Mailing Address: Hwy. 62, P.O. Box 605, 72616. Tel: 870-423-3927.
Res., 30 Crescent Dr., Eureka Springs, 72632. Tel: 501-253-9853.

Bigelow, Perry Co., St. Boniface's (1879) (German), Rev. Richard P. Davis.
Res., Rte. 1, Box 80 Dixie, 72016. Tel: 501-759-2371. [CEM]
Missions—Little Italy, Pulaski Co., St. Francis; Adona, Conway Co., St. Elizabeth's.

Blytheville, Mississippi Co., Immaculate Conception (1894), Very Rev. Joseph L. Pallo, V.F.; Deacon William G. Brandon.
Res., 1301 W. Main St., 72315. Tel: 870-762-2506.
School—Tel: 870-763-9444.
Lay Teachers 9; Students 102.

Booneville, Logan Co., Church of Our Lady of the Assumption,
Mailing Address: E. 6th & Cherry St., 72923. Tel: 501-675-3371.
Res., Subiaco Abbey, Subiaco, 72865. Tel: 501-934-4295.

Brinkley, Monroe Co., St. John the Baptist (1875), Rev. Benedict Meyer, O.S.B.
Res., 203 W. Ash, 72021-3201. Tel: 870-734-1202. [CEM]

Camden, Ouachita Co., St. Louis (1923), Rev. Jon McDougal.
Mailing Address: 202 Adams N.W., 71701. Tel: 870-836-2426.
Res., 962 Ridgeview, 71701.
Mission—Magnolia, Columbia Co., Immaculate Heart of Mary, P.O. Box 365, Magnolia, 71753. Tel: 870-234-2710.

Carlisle, Lonoke Co., St. Rose of Lima Church, Rev. Charles J. Thessing; Deacon William Cunningham, Jr.
Res., Hwy. 70 E., P.O. Box M, 72024. Tel: 870-552-3601.

Center Ridge, Conway Co., St. Joseph's (1881) (Italian). Attended by Church of Assumption, Atkins. Rev. Edward G. Marley, C.S.Sp.
Mailing Address: 44 Valley Rd., 72027. Tel: 501-893-2887; Fax: 501-354-2711.
Church—Atkins, 72823. Tel: 501-893-2887; 641-7179; Fax: 501-354-2711. [CEM]

Charleston, Franklin Co., Sacred Heart (1879), Rev. Peter Sharum, O.S.B.
Res., Rte. 2, Box 500, 72933-9403. Tel: 501-965-2432. [CEM]

Cherokee Village, Sharp Co., St. Michael's (1939), Rev. James E. Mancini; Deacons Michael Cumnock; Anthony Ludloph.
Mailing Address: P.O. Box 970, 72525. Tel: 870-257-2850.
Res., 12 Micanopy Circle, 72529. Tel: 870-257-4456.
St. Michael Memorial Garden (Columbarium)—Hwy. 62/167, S. Tekakwitha Dr., 72529. Tel: 870-257-3840.

Clarksville, Johnson Co., Holy Redeemer (1879), Rev. Victor Gillespie, O.S.B.
Res., 103 E. Main St., 72830. Tel: 501-754-3610. [CEM]

Conway, Faulkner Co., St. Joseph's, Revs. Anthony McKay, C.S.Sp.; Joseph Deniger, C.S.Sp.; John Yates, C.S.Sp.; Edward T. Crowley, C.S.Sp., (Retired); Deacons David Westmoreland; Richard Bemrich, (Retired).
Res., 1115 College Ave., 72032. Tel: 501-327-6568; Fax: 501-329-6305. [CEM]
Parish Business Office: 375 Harkrider, 72032. Tel: 501-327-5528; Fax: 501-327-6607.
School—(Grades K-6). Tel: 501-327-1204; Fax: 501-327-8350. Daniel Fields, Prin.
Lay Teachers 18; Students 275.
High School—(Grades 7-12) 502 Front St., 72032. Tel: 501-329-5741; 329-5606; Fax: 501-327-8350.
Lay Teachers 17; Students 228.
St. Joseph School Endowment and Charitable Trust—P.O. Box 1709, 72032.

Crossett, Ashley Co., Holy Cross (1954), Rev. Victor Subb, Glmy.
Res., 808 Maple St., 71635. Tel: 870-364-4847; Fax: 870-364-4847. [JC]
Mission—Hamburg, Ashley Co., P.O. Box 188, Hamburg, 71646. Tel: 870-853-8991.

Dardanelle, Yell Co., St. Augustine. Attended by Russellville.
Mailing Address: 1900 Main St., P.O. Box 308, Russellville, 72801. Tel: 501-967-3699.

De Queen, Sevier Co., St. Barbara's (1911), Rev. R. Scott Friend.
Res., P.O. Box 86, 71832. Tel: 870-642-2256.
Missions—Foreman, Little River Co., Sacred Heart; Ashdown, Little River Co., St. Elizabeth Ann Seton, Hwy. 32 E., P.O. Box 966, Ashdown, 71822.

El Dorado, Union Co., Holy Redeemer (1923) (Spanish), Rev. Gregory A. Pilcher, O.S.B.
Res., 440 W. Main St., 71730-5757. Tel: 870-863-3620; Fax: 870-863-7537.
School—Ann Finch, Prin. Lay Teachers 10; Students 98.
El Dorado Holy Redeemer School Endowment Fund—1103 W. Cedar St., 71730. Tel: 870-863-8677; Fax: 870-863-7779.
Holy Redeemer Endowment Fund—.

Engelberg, Randolph Co., St. John the Baptist (Pocahontas P.O.) (1885) (German), Rev. Leslie A. Farley.
Res., 4650 Engelberg Rd., Pocahontas, 72455. Tel: 870-892-3780. [CEM]
Missions—Corning, Clay Co., St. Joseph, P.O. Box 385, Corning, 72422. Tel: 870-892-3780; Walnut Ridge, Lawrence Co., Immaculate Heart of Mary, 320 Free St., P.O. Box 70, Walnut Ridge, 72176. Tel: 870-886-2119.

Eureka Springs, Carroll Co., St. Elizabeth's (1909), Rev. James M. Fanrak; Deacons Samuel Hilburn; Bill Reuter.
Res., 30 Crescent Dr., 72632. Tel: 501-253-9853.
Mission—Berryville, Carroll Co., St. Anne's, Hwy. 62, P.O. Box 305, Berryville, 72616. Tel: 870-423-3927. Rev. James M. Fanrak.

Fairfield Bay, Van Buren Co., St. Francis Assisi, Rev. Francis D. Colavechio.
Res., 250 Woodlawn Dr., 72088. Tel: 501-884-3349.

Fayetteville, Washington Co., St. Joseph's, Rev. Mark Wood; Deacons Paul Cronan; Chuck Marino.
Office: 321 N. Leverett St., 72701-4308. Tel: 501-442-0890; Fax: 501-973-0150. [CEM]
Church—321 E. Lafayette St., 72701-4308.
School—Tel: 501-442-4554; Fax: 501-442-7887.
Lay Teachers 14; Students 286.
St. Joseph Endowment and Educational Trust Fund—313 E. Lafayette St., 72701. Tel: 501-442-4554.

St. Thomas Aquinas University Parish, Rev. Mark Wood, Sacramental Minister; Deacon Paul Cronan, Pastoral Admin.
Res., 603 N. Leverett Ave., 72701-3220. Tel: 501-444-0223; Fax: 501-444-0223.

Fordyce, Dallas Co., Good Shepherd (1977), Rev. Wilfred C. Okorochukwu.
Res., 410 Oak St., 71742. Tel: 870-352-2328; Fax: 870-352-5037. [CEM]
Mission—Sheridan, Grant Co., Holy Cross, 921 Vine St., Sheridan, 72150-0624. Tel: 870-942-4532.

Forrest City, St. Francis Co., St. Francis of Assisi (1876), Very Rev. Thomas Marks, V.F.; Sr. Maxine Vogan, D.L.F., Pastoral Admin.
Res., 621 S. Washington St., P.O. Box 786, 72336-0786. Tel: 870-633-1665; Fax: 870-633-1665.

Fort Smith, Sebastian Co., Immaculate Conception, Rev. Msgr. John F. O'Donnell, V.F.; Rev. Phillip A. Reaves.
Mailing Address: P.O. Box 1866, 72902-1866.
Res., 22 North 13th, 72901. Tel: 501-783-7963; Fax: 501-783-7865. [JC]
School—223 South 14th St., 72901. Tel: 501-783-6798; Fax: 501-783-0510.
Sisters of Mercy 1; Lay Teachers 24; Students 355.
Immaculate Conception School Educational Trust—.

St. Boniface (1886), Rev. Placidus Eckart, O.S.B.
Res., 1820 North B St., 72901. Tel: 501-783-6711. [JC]
School—201 N. 19th St., 72901. Tel: 501-783-6601; Fax: 501-783-6605.
Benedictine Sisters 1; Lay Teachers 12; Students 211.
Catholic Education Endowment Trust of Fort Smith, Arkansas—.

Christ the King (1928), Rev. Msgr. Royce R. Thomas.
Res., 1920 S. Greenwood Ave., 72901. Tel: 501-783-7745; Fax: 501-783-2025. [JC]
School—1918 S. Greenwood, 72901. Tel: 501-782-0614; Fax: 501-782-1098.
Lay Teachers 12; Students 191.
Catholic Education Endowment Trust of Fort Smith, Arkansas—.

Hamburg, Ashley Co., Holy Spirit. Attended by Holy Cross, Crossett.
P.O. Box 188, 71646. Tel: 870-853-8991.
Church—110 E. Franklin, 71646. [CEM]

Harrison, Boone Co., Mary, Mother of God (1919), Very Rev. John W. Kordsmeier, V.F.
Res., P.O. Box 2150, 72601. Tel: 870-741-5234.

Hartford, Sebastian Co., St. Leo's (1901), Rev. Phillip A. Reaves.
Mailing Address: P.O. Box 1866, Fort Smith, 72902. Tel: 501-783-7963; Fax: 501-783-7865.

Helena, Phillips Co., St. Mary's (1858), Rev. C. Edwin Graves, III.
Res., 123 Columbia St., 72342. Tel: 870-338-6990. [CEM]

Hope, Hempstead Co., Our Lady of Good Hope, Rev. Gregory T. Luyet; Deacon Robert V. Regan, (Retired).
Office: P.O. Box 517, 71801. Tel: 870-777-3202.
Res., 325 S. Walker St., 71801. Tel: 870-722-2921.
Mission—Nashville, Howard Co., St. Martin, 1011 W. Leslie St., Nashville, 71852. Tel: 870-845-1271.

Horseshoe Bend, Izard Co., St. Mary of the Mount (1974). Attended by Cherokee Village. Rev. Fredrick Schneider, O.F.M.
Mailing Address: P.O. Box 4012, 72512. Tel: 870-670-5896.
Res., 4th & Church St., 72512. Tel: 501-670-5896. [CEM]

Hot Springs National Park, Garland Co., St. Mary's of the Springs, Very Rev. Msgr. Leo A. Riedmueller, V.F.
Res., 100 Central Ave., 71901. Tel: 501-623-3233. [JC]

St. John the Baptist (1907), Rev. James P. West; Deacons David Briselden; Frank Sluppick; John Connell; Joe Harrison.
Res., 589 W. Grand Ave., 71901. Tel: 501-623-6201; Fax: 501-318-0328.
School—583 W. Grand Ave., 71901. Tel: 501-624-3141; Fax: 501-624-3141.
Sisters of Mercy 2; Lay Teachers 9; Students 185.
St. John's School Endowment—Tel: 501-624-3171.

Hot Springs Village, Garland Co., Sacred Heart of Jesus (1979), Very Rev. Raymond R. Rossi; Deacon Bernard Bauer.
Res., 22 Descollar, 71909. Tel: 501-922-2062.

Huntsville, Madison Co., St. John's (1963), Revs. Stanley Oleksy Salvaturian; Miles Heinen, C.M.; R. Rex Hays, C.M.
Church—Rte. 6, Box 99A, 72740. Tel: 501-738-2709.
Res., 1119 W. Poplar, Rogers, 72756. Tel: 501-636-2548. [JC]

Jacksonville, Pulaski Co., St. Jude the Apostle, Rev. Charles J. Thessing.
Res., 2403 McArthur Dr., P.O. Box 665, 72076. Tel: 501-982-4891; Fax: 501-982-0821.

Jonesboro, Craighead Co., Blessed Sacrament (1885), Rev. Jack D. Harris; Deacon Victor Stepka. In res., Rev. James Dixon, S.J.
Res., 614 S. Church St., P.O. Box 1735, 72401. Tel: 870-932-2529; Fax: 870-935-4444. [CEM]
School—Tel: 870-932-3684.
Olivetan Benedictine Sisters 3; Lay Teachers 9; Students 135.
Blessed Sacrament Educational Endowment Fund—.

Lake Village, Chicot Co., Our Lady of the Lake (1869), Rev. Henry B. Mischkowiuski.
Res., P.O. Box 272, 71653. Tel: 870-265-5439. [CEM]
School—Tel: 501-265-2921.
Lay Teachers 9; Students 110.
St. Mary's Educational Trust Fund—.

McGehee, Desha Co., St. Mary (1906), Rev. John Eaton, O.F.M.; Bro. Michel LeMier, O.F.M.
Res., 401 N. 3rd St., 71654. Tel: 870-222-3389. [CEM]
Missions—Dumas, Desha Co., Holy Child, E. Waterman St., Dumas, 71639; Dermott, Chicot Co., Nativity of the Blessed Virgin Mary, Gaines St., Dermott, 71638.

Malvern, Hot Spring Co., St. John the Baptist, Rev. John E. Marconi; Sr. Teresa Daly, D.C., Pastoral Admin.; Deacon Bud Daven.
Res., 1121 McBee St., P.O. Box 6, 72104. Tel: 501-332-6244.; Res., 249 N. 14th St., P.O. Box 26, Arkadelphia, 71923. Tel: 501-870-7575; Fax: 870-246-6836.
Mission—Arkadelphia, Clark Co., St. Mary's, P.O. Box 26, Arkadelphia, 71923. Rev. Alan Rosenau.

Mena, Polk Co., St. Agnes, Rev. Emmanuel Iheaka.
Res., 203 8th St., P.O. Box 1428, 71953. Tel: 501-394-1017. [CEM]
Missions—Waldron, Scott Co., St. Jude Thaddeus, P.O. Box 1688, Waldron, 72958. Tel: 501-637-2055; Mount Ida, Montgomery Co., All Saints, P.O. Box 724, Mount Ida, 71957. Tel: 870-326-4641.

Monticello, Drew Co., St. Mark (1975), Rev. Daniel Dorsey, Glmy.
Res., 452 W. Jefferson, 71655. Tel: 870-367-5974.
Church—1016 N. Hyatt St., 71655. Tel: 870-367-2848.
Res., 508 W. Pine, Warren, 71671. Tel: 870-226-5284.
Mission—Warren, Bradley Co., St. Luke, Warren, 71671.

Morrilton, Conway Co., Sacred Heart (1879), Rev. Joseph A. Seiter, C.S.Sp.; Deacon Oscar Rohlman.
Res., 506 E. Broadway, 72110. Tel: 501-354-4181. [CEM]
School—Tel: 501-354-8113.
Lay Teachers 9; Students 150.
High School—106 N. St. Joseph, 72110.
Lay Teachers 9; Students 114.
Sacred Heart School Endowment—.

Morrison Bluff, Logan Co., SS. Peter and Paul (1878), Rev. Victor Gillespie, O.S.B.
Res. & Mailing Address—c/o Holy Redeemer Church, 103 E. Main St., Clarksville, 72830. Tel: 501-754-3610 (Res.).

Mountain Home, Baxter Co., St. Peter the Fisherman (1959), Revs. Gregory G. Hart; Stan Swiderski, S.D.S; Deacons Bob Daye; John Krug; Richard Linstad.
Res., 249 Dyer St., P.O. Box 298, 72653-3515. Tel: 870-425-2832; Fax: 870-424-5172.
Mission—Yellville, Marion Co., St. Andrew's, P.O. Box 197, Yellville, 72687. Tel: 870-449-4850.

Newport, Jackson Co., St. Cecilia's, Rev. Clayton Gould.
Church—2475 Galeria Subdivision, 72112. Tel: 870-793-7464; 523-6542.
Res., St. Mary's Church, 3800 Harrison St., Batesville, 72501.

Osceola, Mississippi Co., St. Matthew's. Attended by Immaculate Conception, Blytheville. Very Rev. Joseph L. Pallo, V.F.
Church—P.O. Box 583, 72370.
Res., 1301 W. Main St., Blytheville, 72315. Tel: 870-762-2506.

Paragould, Greene Co., St. Mary's (1883), Rev. Joseph Kay, M.Afr., Admin.
Res., 301 W. Highland St., P.O. Box 861, 72450. Tel: 870-236-2568. [CEM]
School—Tel: 870-236-3681.
Lay Teachers 5; Students 54.
Mission—Rector, Clay Co., St. Henry's, 800 Ballard St., Rector, 72461.
St. Mary Educational Trust Fund—.

Paris, Logan Co., St. Joseph's (1879) (German), Rev. Sebastian Beshoner, O.S.B.
Res., 15 S. Spruce St., 72855. Tel: 501-963-2131. [CEM]
School—Tel: 501-963-2119; Fax: 501-963-8039.
Lay Teachers 6; Students 94.
St. Joseph Endowment Fund—.

Pine Bluff, Jefferson Co., St. Joseph's, Very Rev. W. Andrew Smith, V.F.; Deacons Wallace Gieringer; Tim Massanelli.
Res., 412 W. 6th Ave., P.O. Box 7434, 71611. Tel: 870-534-4701; Fax: 870-534-4703. [CEM]
School—St. Joseph's Junior High School, 422 W. 6th, 71601. Tel: 870-534-7545.
St. Joseph's Education Fund—Tel: 870-534-8393. Gertrude Schimmel, Pres.

Mission—Plum Bayou, Jefferson Co., St. Mary's, P.O. Box 7434, 71611.

St. Peter's, Rev. Bernard C. Keller, S.V.D.; Deacon Elton Harrison.
Res., 207 E. 16th Ave., 71601. Tel: 870-534-6418. [JC]
School—Tel: 870-535-4017; Fax: 870-535-4017.
Sisters of Notre Dame 3; Lay Teachers 6; Students 165.
Convent—Tel: 870-534-2316.
Mission—Pine Bluff, Jefferson Co., St. Raphael's, 71601.
St. Peter Catholic School Foundation—.

Pocahontas, Randolph Co., St. Paul the Apostle, Rev. Michael E. Bass; Deacon George Edwards.
Res., 1002 Convent St., 72455. Tel: 870-892-3319; Fax: 870-892-5199. [CEM]
School—Tel: 870-892-5639.
Olivetan Benedictine Sisters 2; Lay Teachers 7; Students 110.
St. Paul School Charitable Trust—311 Cedar St., 72455. Tel: 870-892-5199.

Ratcliff, Logan Co., St. Anthony (1879) (German), Rev. Harold Heiman, O.S.B.
Res., Subiaco Abbey, Subiaco, 72865. Tel: 501-934-4295. [CEM]

Rogers, Benton Co., St. Vincent de Paul (1941), Very Rev. Richard S. Oswald, V.F.; Rev. Michael D. Sinkler; Deacons Bruce Leach; Clarence Leis; Bill Cook.
Church—1305 W. Cypress St., 72758-4118. Tel: 501-636-4020; Fax: 501-631-2548. [CEM]
School—1315 W. Cypress St., 72758. Tel: 501-636-4421.
Lay Teachers 25; Students 258.
St. Vincent de Paul Endowment Fund—Tel: 501-621-1702; Fax: 501-621-1795. Rob Brothers.

Russellville, Pope Co., St. John's, Very Rev. Ernest L. Hardesty, V.F.
Res., 1900 W. Main St., P.O. Box 308, 72801. Tel: 501-967-3699.
School—Tel: 501-967-4644.
Benedictine Sisters 3; Lay Teachers 10; Students 128.
St. John's Educational Trust—1914 W. Main St., 72801.
Mission—Dardanelle, Yell Co., St. Augustine's, 1006 N. 2nd, Dardanelle, 72834. Tel: 501-229-3972.

St. Vincent, Conway Co., St. Mary (1880), Rev. Arthur B. Chiasson, M.Afr.
Res., 11 Kaufman Ln., Hattieville, 72063. Tel: 501-354-3206. [CEM]
Mission—Clinton, Van Buren Co., St. Jude, P.O. Box 526, Clinton, 72031. Tel: 501-745-5716.

Scranton, Logan Co., St. Ignatius (1913) (German), Rev. Raphael DeSalvo, O.S.B.
Church—P.O. Box 87, 72863. Tel: 501-938-2821. [CEM]
Mission—Prairie View, Logan Co., St. Meinrad, 72863.

Searcy, White Co., St. James, Very Rev. Robert T. Dienert, V.F.
Res., 1102 Pioneer Rd., P.O. Box 172, 72143. Tel: 501-268-2418.
Missions—Heber Springs, Cleburne Co., St. Albert, 21 Park Rd., Heber Springs, 72543. Tel: 501-362-2914; Bald Knob, White Co., St. Richard, 72143.

Sheridan, Grant Co., Holy Cross. Attended by Good Shepherd, Fordyce. Rev. Wilfred C. Okorochukwu.
Mailing Address: 921 Vine St., 72150. Tel: 870-942-4532. [CEM]

Shoal Creek, Logan Co., St. Scholastica's (New Blaine), Rev. Paul Hoedebeck, O.S.B.
288 St. Scholastica Rd., New Blaine, 72851. Tel: 501-938-7566.
Res., Subiaco Abbey, Subiaco, 72865. Tel: 501-934-4295. [CEM]

Siloam Springs, Benton Co., St. Mary's (1963), Rev. Richard M. Strock.
Res., P.O. Box 118, 72761. Tel: 501-524-8526.

Slovak, Prairie Co., SS. Cyril and Methodius. Attended by Holy Rosary, Stuttgart. Rev. John A. Janesko.
Res., Rte. 1, Box 117, Stuttgart, 72160. Tel: 870-241-3359. [CEM]

Springdale, Washington Co., St. Raphael's, Rev. Joseph M. Correnti.
Church—P.O. Box 6010, 72766-6010. Tel: 501-756-6711.
Res., P.O. Box 39, Tontitown, 72770.

Stamps, Lafayette Co., St. Vincent de Paul. Closed. For inquiries for parish records contact the Chancery.

Star City, Lincoln Co., St. Justin's. Unassigned.
Res., P.O. Box 128, 71667. Tel: 870-628-3092. [CEM]
Mission—Grady, Lincoln Co., Blessed Sacrament, 1207 S. Main, Grady, 71644.

Stuttgart, Arkansas Co., Holy Rosary (1887), Rev. John A. Janesko.
Res., 1815 S. Prairie St., 72160. Tel: 870-673-8351. [CEM]
School—Tel: 870-673-3211.
Benedictine Sisters 2; Lay Teachers 5; Students 52.
Mission—Gillett, Arkansas Co., St. Henry's.

Subiaco, Logan Co., St. Benedict (1878), Rev. Denis Soerries, O.S.B.
Res., 81 W. Parish Dr., 72865. Tel: 501-934-4321. [CEM]

Texarkana, Miller Co., St. Edward's (1903), Very Rev. David E. Jacobs, V.F.; Deacon Joe Bruick.
Res., 407 Beech St., P.O. Box 1186, 75504. Tel: 870-772-1115; Fax: 870-773-2890. [CEM]

Tontitown, Washington Co., St. Joseph's (1898) (Italian), Rev. Joseph M. Correnti.
Res., P.O. Box 39, 72770. Tel: 501-361-2612. [CEM]

Van Buren, Crawford Co., St. Michael's, Rev. Ralph Esposito; Deacon Al Genna.
Res., 1512 N. 11th, 72956. Tel: 501-474-6402.
Mission—Jenny Lind, Sebastian Co., Sts. Sabina and Mary's Church.

Walnut Ridge, Lawrence Co., Immaculate Heart of Mary. Attended by St. John the Baptist, Engelberg. Rev. Leslie A. Farley; Deacon Marlin Tate.
Res., P.O. Box 70, 72476. Tel: 870-886-2119. [JC]

Weiner, Poinsett Co., St. Anthony's (1902), Rev. James M. Dixon, S.J.
Mailing Address: P.O. Box 76, 72479. Tel: 870-684-2656.
Res., 415 Kings Hwy., 72479. [CEM]
Mission—Marked Tree, Poinsett Co., St. Norbert's, c/o Rev. Nicholas Fuhrmann, O.S.B., St. Bernard's Hospital, Jonesboro, 72401. Tel: 870-972-4270.

West Memphis, Crittenden Co., St. Michael's, Rev. William F. Thomas.
Res., 208 W. Cooper Ave., 72301. Tel: 870-733-1114.
Church—411 Missouri, P.O. Box 899, 72303. Tel: 870-733-1212; 735-7983; Fax: 870-732-4808.
School—405 Missouri, P.O. Box 899, 72303. Tel: 870-735-1730.
Olivetan Benedictine Sisters 2; Lay Teachers 6; Students 125.
St. Michael's School Endowment and Charitable Trust—.
Missions—Crawfordsville, Crittenden Co., Sacred Heart, Main St., Crawfordsville, 72327. Tel: 870-823-5313; Horseshoe Lake, Crittenden Co., St. Mary's of the Lake, Hwy. 131, Horseshoe Lake, 72348. Tel: 870-339-2404.

Winslow, Crawford Co., Our Lady of the Ozarks Shrine (1946), Deacon Dan Daily.
Mailing Address: 22741 N. Hwy. 71, 72959. Tel: 501-634-2181.
Res., 22741 N. Hwy. 71, 72959. Tel: 501-634-2181. [CEM]

Wynne, Cross Co., St. Peter's, Very Rev. Thomas C. Marks, V.F.
Res., P.O. Box 517, 72396. Tel: 870-238-2613.
Mission—McCrory, Woodruff Co., St. Mary's, Tel: 870-731-0048.

Chaplains of Public Institutions

LITTLE ROCK. *U.S. Veterans Administration Hospital* 4300 W. 7th St., 72205. Tel: 501-661-1202, Ext. 1121. Rev. Victor E. Bertrand, C.S.V., Chap.

FAYETTEVILLE. *U.S. Veterans Administration Hospital.* Attended from St. Joseph Church.

NORTH LITTLE ROCK. *U.S. Veterans Administration Hospital* North Little Rock Division, 72114. Tel: 501-661-1202, Ext. 1121. Rev. Victor E. Bertrand, C.S.V., Chap.

On Duty Outside the Diocese:
Reverend Fathers—
Gunti, Frederick W., Springhill College, Mobile, AL 33608

Retired:
Reverend Monsignors—
De Clerk, Rainer J., St. John Manor, 2414 N. Tyler, Apt. 309, Little Rock, AR 72205
Maus, Rudolph E., 210 N. Vancouver, Russellville, AR 72801
McKee, Francis J., Riley's Oak Manor, 8701 Riley Dr., Little Rock, AR 72205
Scheper, John B., Riley's Oak Hill Manor, 2501 John Ashley Dr., North Little Rock, AR 72114
Stemac, Louis V., St. John Manor, Apt. #307, 2414 N. Tyler St., Little Rock, AR 72207
Reverend Fathers—
Barnes, John E., St. John Manor, 2414 N. Tyler St., Apt. 308, Little Rock, AR 72207
Bauer, Ralph, P.O. Box 1172, Hot Springs, AR 71902
Booth, Earl J., St. John Manor, 2414 N. Tyler St., Apt. 202, Little Rock, AR 72207
Cheney, Jesse C., St. John Manor, Apt. #201, 2414 N. Tyler St., Little Rock, AR 72207
Donahue, Thomas J., St. John Manor, 2415 N. Tyler, Little Rock, AR 72267. Tel: 501-664-6486
Freyaldenhoven, George P., P.O. Box 123, Pottsville, AR 72858
Hlavacek, John F., St. John Manor, Apt. #306, 2414 N. Tyler St., Little Rock, AR 72207
Janesko, Francis J., P.O. Box 730, Rogers, AR 72757
Kepple, Robert, 107 Palm, Hot Springs, AR 71901
Manchino, John, St. Barbara's Nursing Home, P.O. Box 9066, Monogah, WV 26555
McGinnis, N. Charles, Benedictine Manor, P.O. Box 2249, Hot Springs, AR 71901
Oswald, John, St. John Manor, 2414 N. Tyler, Apt. 304, Little Rock, AR 72207
Preske, Venantius, P.O. Box 4018, Horseshoe Bend, AR 72512
Savary, James, 6720 Brentwood Rd., Little Rock, AR 72205
Strassle, Paul, P.O. Box 1545, Fairfield Bay, AR 72088
Torres, Robert A., 2000 Rebsamen Park Rd. #C-206, Little Rock, AR 72202. Tel: 501-664-8473; 664-9697
Turner, George F., 10631 Gulf Beach Hwy., Pensacola, FL 32507. Tel: 904-492-5741
Walters, James, 2505 S. 17th St., Paragould, AR 72450

INSTITUTIONS LOCATED IN THE DIOCESE

[A] SEMINARIES, RELIGIOUS OR SCHOLASTICATES

LITTLE ROCK. *Marylake - Carmelite Novitiate*, 5151 Marylake Dr., 72206. Tel: 501-888-3052. Discalced Carmelite Friars of the Province of St. Therese, Little Rock. Revs. Stephen Sanchez, O.C.D., Supr.; Raphael Kitz, O.C.D., Novice Master; Evarist V. Foix, O.C.D.; Felix Da Prato, O.C.D.; Aloysius Deeney, O.C.D., Prov.; Henry Bordeaux, O.C.D. Priests 6; Novices 4.

SEARCY. *St. Anthony Friary (Formerly Morris School for Boys)*, 285 Morris School Rd., 72143-9649. Tel: 501-268-8145. Bro. Maurus DiSabella.

SUBIACO. *Subiaco Monastery*, 72865. Tel: 501-934-4295; Fax: 501-934-4328.
E-mail: abbey@CSWNet.com
Rt. Rev. Jerome Kodell, O.S.B., Abbot; Revs. David Bellinghausen, O.S.B., Prior; Hugh Assenmacher, O.S.B.; Aaron Pirrera, O.S.B.; Andrew Wewer; Brendan Miller; Camillus Cooney; Columbian Kannitzer; Damian Wewers; David Flusche; David McKillin; Felix Fredeman; Harold Heiman; Herbert Vogelpohl; John Walbe; Leonard Wangler; Mark Stengel, Novice Master; Meinrad Marbaugh; Paul Hoedebeck; Timothy Donnelly, O.S.B.; William Wewers; Alcuin Kubis, O.S.B. Abbots 1; Monks 71.

[B] HIGH SCHOOLS, DIOCESAN

LITTLE ROCK. *Catholic High School*, 6300 Lee St., 72205. Tel: 501-664-3939. Revs. George W. Tribou, Rector; Lawrence A. Frederick. Priests 2; Brothers 1; Lay Teachers 33; Students 742. Legal Title: *Catholic High School of Little Rock, AR.*
Catholic High School Foundation, Inc.

CONWAY. *St. Joseph High School*, 502 Front St., 72032-5408. Tel: 501-329-5741. Daniel Fields, Prin.; Rita Strause, Asst. Prin. Lay Teachers 17; Students 228.

FORT SMITH. *Trinity Junior High*, 1205 S. Albert Pike, 72903. Tel: 501-782-2451. Rev. Msgr. Royce R. Thomas, J.C.L., Pastor Rep.; Eddie Haughey, Prin. Sisters of Mercy 3; Lay Teachers 14; Students 248.
Trinity Educational Trust Fund.

MORRILTON. *Sacred Heart Catholic School*, 106 N. St. Joseph St., 72110. Tel: 501-354-8113.
E-mail: SHCS@MEV.Net
Sr. Rachel Auringer, O.S.U., Prin.; Sr. Katherine Etris, Asst. Prin. Lay Teachers 10; Students 99.

[C] HIGH SCHOOLS, PRIVATE

LITTLE ROCK. *Mount St. Mary Academy.* (Girls), 3224 Kavanaugh Blvd., 72205. Tel: 501-664-8006; Fax: 501-666-4382.
E-mail: sdt@cei.Net
Sr. Deborah Raye Troillett, R.S.M., Pres.; Jeffrey T. Corrigan, Prin.; Sr. Joan Marie Pfauser, R.S.M., Asst. Prin. for Academics; Carolyn Chalmers, Asst. Prin. Student Life. Priests 1; Sisters of Mercy 7; Lay Teachers 35; Students 611.
Mount St. Mary Academy Endowment and Scholarship Fund.

SUBIACO. *Subiaco Academy.* (Boys), 72865. Tel: 501-934-4291.
E-mail: subiaco@CSWNET.COM

Web site: www.web-smiths.com/subiaco/
Rt. Rev. Jerome Kodell, O.S.B., Pres.; Rev. Timothy Donnelly, O.S.B., Headmaster. Priests 7; Brothers 8; Lay Teachers 16; Students 177.

[D] DAY CARE CENTERS

LITTLE ROCK. *Little Angel Day Care*, 9111 Auxer Rd., 72209. Sr. Philippa Wavrick, Dir. Olivetan Benedictine Sisters 2.

[E] GENERAL HOSPITALS

LITTLE ROCK. *St. Vincent Infirmary Medical Center*, No. 2 St. Vincent Circle, 72205. Tel: 501-660-3000; Fax: 501-671-4241
For a complete listing, refer to the Hospitals section.

FORT SMITH. *Northside Community Health Center*, 3202 North 6th, 72904. Tel: 501-782-1456
For a complete listing, refer to the Hospitals section.
St. Edward Mercy Medical Center, 7301 Rogers Ave., 72917. Tel: 501-484-6000; Fax: 501-452-1770
For a complete listing, refer to the Hospitals section.
St. Edward Mercy Medical Center, dba Harbor View Mercy Hospital and Counseling Center, 10301 Mayo Rd., P.O. Box 17000, 72917-7000. Tel: 501-484-5550
For a complete listing, refer to the Hospitals section.

HOT SPRINGS NATIONAL PARK. *St. Joseph's Regional Health Center*, 300 Werner St., 71913. Tel: 501-622-1000; Fax: 501-622-1199.
E-mail: tjmmcvey@htsp.smhs.com
For a complete listing, refer to the Hospitals section.

JONESBORO. *St. Bernard's Regional Medical Center*, 224 E. Matthews St., 72401. Tel: 870-972-4100
For a complete listing, refer to the Hospitals section.

MORRILTON. *Conway County Hospital*, #4 Hospital Dr., 72110-4510. Tel: 501-354-3512; Fax: 501-354-2830
For a complete listing, refer to the Hospitals section.

OZARK. *St. Edward Health Facilities of Franklin County, dba Mercy Hospital/Turner Memorial*, 801 W. River St., 72949. Tel: 501-667-4138; Fax: 501-667-4751
For a complete listing, refer to the Hospitals section.

PARIS. *St. Edward Health Facilities of Logan Co., dba North Logan Mercy Hospital*, 500 E. Academy, 72855
For a complete listing, refer to the Hospitals section.

ROGERS. *St. Mary-Rogers Memorial Hospital*, 72756. Tel: 501-636-0200, Ext. 705; Fax: 501-936-2906
For a complete listing, refer to the Hospitals section.

WALDRON. *St. Edward Health Facilities of Scott County dba Mercy Hospital*, Hwy. 71 & 80, Box 2230, 72958. Tel: 501-637-4135; Fax: 501-637-3523
For a complete listing, refer to the Hospitals section.

[F] PROTECTIVE INSTITUTIONS

LITTLE ROCK. *ABBA House, Missionaries of Charity*, 1014 S. Oak St., 72204. Tel: 501-666-9718
For a complete listing, refer to the Special Care Facilities section.
Catherine's House c/o Sisters of Mercy Health System, 1020 W. 14th St., 72202. Tel: 501-370-9100
For a complete listing, refer to the Special Care Facilities section.

HOT SPRINGS NATIONAL PARK. *Monastery of Our Lady of Charity of Refuge (Good Shepherd)*, 1125 Malvern Ave., 71901. Tel: 501-623-9651
For a complete listing, refer to the Special Care Facilities section.
St. Michael's School, 1125 Malvern Ave., 71901. Tel: 501-623-9651
For a complete listing, refer to the Special Care Facilities section.

[G] HOMES FOR AGED

BARLING. *Mercy Crest of Arkansas, Inc.*, 1300 Strozier Ln., 72923. Tel: 501-478-3000; Fax: 501-478-3006
For a complete listing, refer to the Special Care Facilities section.

[H] RESIDENCES FOR PRIESTS

LITTLE ROCK. *St. John Manor*, 2414 N. Tyler St., 72207. Bro. Blaise Betley, Mgr.; Rev. Msgr. Louis V. Stemac; Rev. Msgr. Rainer DeClerk; Revs. Jesse C. Cheney; John F. Hlavacek; John E. Barnes; Tom Donahue; Earl J. Booth; John Oswald. Priests 8.

[I] CONVENTS AND RESIDENCES FOR SISTERS

LITTLE ROCK. *Discalced Carmelite Nuns*, 7201 W. 32nd St., 72204-4716. Tel: 501-565-5121. Sr. Therese Stewart, Prioress. Legal Title: *Discalced Carmelite Nuns of Little Rock*. Sisters 13; Nuns with Solemn Vows 12; Externs 1.
Attended from Catholic High School, Little Rock.
Mt. St. Mary's Convent, 3508 Kavanaugh Blvd., 72205. Sr. Ann Hardcastle, R.S.M., Local Coord. Sisters of Mercy of Mount St. Mary Convent of Little Rock, Arkansas, Inc. 8.

BARLING. *Catherine McAuley Convent of Mercy*, 1300 Strozier Ln., 72923. Tel: 501-478-3002; Fax: 501-478-3006. Sisters of Mercy 18.

FORT SMITH. *St. Scholastica Monastery-Motherhouse*, 1301 S. Albert Pike, P.O. Box 3489, 72913. Tel: 501-783-4147.
E-mail: Scholast@ipa.Net
Sr. Elise Forst, Prioress; Sr. Catherine Markey, Archivist. Benedictine Professed Sisters 124; Novices 3; Candidate 1.
Sisters of Mercy, 7219 Rogers Ave., 72903. Tel: 501-484-6098; Fax: 501-452-1770. Sr. Judith Marie Keith, R.S.M., Local Coord.

HOT SPRINGS. *Monastery of Our Lady of Charity of Refuge*. (Good Shepherd), 1125 Malvern Ave., 71901. Tel: 501-623-9651. Sr. Theresa Marie Lalancette, Supr. Sisters 13; Novices 1.

JONESBORO. *Holy Angels Convent-Motherhouse*, 72403. Tel: 870-935-5810. Olivetan Benedictine Sisters. Rev. Nicholas Fuhrman, O.S.B. Sisters 53; Novices 1.

OZARK. *NAAS House of Mercy*, 1100 Bluff Dr., 72949. Tel: 501-667-4963. Sisters of Mercy 2.

WALDRON. *Waldron Convent of Mercy*, Rte. 2, Box 14A, 72958. Tel: 501-637-2287. Sisters of Mercy.

[J] NEWMAN CENTERS

LITTLE ROCK. *Catholic Campus Ministries*, 2500 N. Tyler St., P.O. Box 7565, 72217. Tel: 501-664-0340. Phyllis Enderlin, Dir.
Univ. of Arkansas at Little Rock Campus Ministry, Good Counsel Church, 1321 S. Van Buren, 72204. Mrs. Diane Hanley, Campus Min.
Henderson State Teachers College and Ouchita Baptist University Campus Ministry. (Arkadelphia), P.O. Box 26, Arkadelphia, 71923. Tel: 870-246-7575. Sr. Teresa Daly, D.C., Campus Min.
University of Central Arkansas & Hendrix College Campus Ministry. (Conway), #4 Briersprings, Conway, 72032. Tel: 501-327-4152. Mrs. Sherry Curran, Campus Min.
University of Arkansas, St. Thomas Aquinas University Parish. (Fayetteville), 603 N. Leverett, Fayetteville, 72701. Tel: 501-444-0223. Deacon Paul Cronan, Pastoral Admin.; Rev. Mark Wood, Sacramental Min.; Esther Breeding, Campus Min.
Blessed John Newman University Parish. (Jonesboro), 2800 E. Johnson Ave., Jonesboro, 72401. Tel: 870-972-1888. Rev. Jack D. Harris; Sr. Mary John Seyler, O.S.B., Campus Min.; Mary Ruth Standt, Dir. Campus Ministry.
Catholic University Parish at Arkansas Tech University. (Russellville), 501 W. L St., Russellville, 72801. Tel: 501-968-8249. Mrs. Pat Buford, Dir. Campus Ministry; Very Rev. Ernest Hardesty, V.F., Pastor.
Harding University (Searcy) Campus Ministry, 109 Campbell Dr., Beebe, 72012. Flo Fitch, Campus Min.; Denis Kimbrough, Campus Min.; Melodye Stickley, Campus Min.
University of Ozarks Campus Ministry (Clarksville), P.O. Box 111, Lamar, 72846. Tel: 501-885-3464. Campus Ministers: Denis Kimbrough; Melodye Stickley.

[K] RETREAT CENTERS

EUREKA SPRINGS. *Brothers and Sisters of Charity at Little Portion Hermitage*. (Integrated Monestary), Rte. 7, Box 608, 72631. Tel: 501-253-7710; Fax: 501-253-6640. Legal Title: *Brothers and Sisters of Charity at Little Portion, Inc.* John Michael Talbot, B.S.C., Gen. Min.; Viola Talbot, B.S.C., Vicar Gen. Min.
Little Flower Clinic for the Poor.
Little Portion Retreat and Training Center at More Mt., 171 Hummingbird Ln., 72632. Tel: 501-253-7379. John Michael Talbot, Exec. Dir.; Tom Fink, Admin. Dir.; Deacon Samuel Hilburn, Spiritual Dir. In Residence 4; Catholic Staff 7.

FORT SMITH. *St. Scholastica Center*, 1205 S. Albert Pike, P.O. Box 3489, 72913. Tel: 501-783-1135.
E-mail: Scholast@ipa.Net
Sr. Cabrini Schmitz, O.S.B., Dir. Center & Program Coord.; Sr. Gertrude Grabber, O.S.B., Dir. Maintenance and Hospitality; Sr. Macrina Wiederkehr, O.S.B., Retreats/Spiritual Dir. Conducted by Benedictine Sisters 23.

SHOAL CREEK. *Hesychia House of Prayer*. 204 St. Scholastica Rd., New Blaine, 72851. Sr. Louise Sharum, O.S.B., Dir. Benedictine Sisters 4. Attended from New Subiaco Abbey, Subiaco, AR.

[L] MISCELLANEOUS LISTINGS

LITTLE ROCK. *The "Arkansas Catholic"*. Published by Arkansas Catholic, Inc. of the Diocese of Little Rock. 2500 N. Tyler St., P.O. Box 7417, 72217. Tel: 501-664-0340; 664-0125; Fax: 501-664-9075. Mr. Danny Straessle, Mng. Editor; Ms. Malea Walters, Editor, P.O. Box 7417, 72217.
Christopher Homes of Arkansas, Inc., 2417 N. Tyler St., 72207. Tel: 501-664-1881. James T. Davis, Exec. Dir.
Christopher Homes of Augusta, Inc.
Christopher Homes of Brinkley, Inc.
Christopher Homes of Camden, Inc.
Christopher Homes of Clarendon, Inc.
Christopher Homes of Elaine, Inc.
Christopher Homes of El Dorado, Inc.
Christopher Homes of Forrest City, Inc.
Christopher Homes of Hot Springs, Inc.
Christopher Homes of Jonesboro, Inc.
Christopher Homes of Marianna, Inc.
Christopher Homes of Monette, Inc.
Christopher Homes of North Little Rock, Inc.
Christopher Homes of Palestine, Inc.
Christopher Homes of Paragould, Inc.
Christopher Homes of Parkin, Inc.
Christopher Homes of Searcy, Inc.
Christopher Homes of Strong, Inc.
Christopher Homes of West Helena, Inc.
Christopher Homes of Wynne, Inc. Total in Residence 510.
John Gazzola Trust Estate, P.O. Box 7239, 72217. Tel: 501-664-0340. Mr. William Hartmann, Dir.
Priestly Fraternity of St. Peter, 2414 N. Tyler St., #310, 72207-3735. Tel: 501-280-9155; Fax: 501-280-9225. Rev. Pablo D. Alvarez, F.S.S.P.
St. John's Home Missions Seminary, Inc., Endowment Fund, P.O. Box 7565, 72217. Tel: 501-664-0340, Ext. 380. Rev. Msgr. James E. O'Connell, Pres., Dir. of Endowment Funds.

BENTON. *Annunzitt, Inc.*, c/o Most Rev. Andrew J. McDonald, P.O. Box 105, 72018. Ms. Janice Sehgal, Dir.

BERRYVILLE. *St. Vincent de Paul Thrift Shop*, 204 S. Main, 72616. Tel: 870-423-3572. Ms. Margaret Duran, Pres.

BLYTHEVILLE. *Immaculate Conception Trust Fund*, 1301 W. Main St., 72315. Tel: 870-762-2506. Very Rev. Joseph L. Pallo, V.F., Contact Person.

EUREKA SPRINGS. *St. Vincent de Paul Society*, 1471 CR222, 72631. Ms. Beverly Anne Wright, Pres.

STUTTGART. *Holy Rosary Catholic School "Vision 2000" Educational Trust Fund*, 1815 S. Prairie St., 72160. Tel: 870-673-8351. Rev. John A. Janesko.

RELIGIOUS INSTITUTES OF MEN REPRESENTED IN THE DIOCESE

For further details refer to the corresponding bracketed number in the Religious Institutes of Men or Women section.

[0200]—*Benedictine Monks*. (New Subiaco Abbey).—O.S.B.
[0460]—*Brothers of the Poor of St. Francis*.—C.F.P.
[1330]—*Congregation of the Mission*.—C.M.
[0260]—*Discalced Carmelite Friars*. (St. Therese Prov.).—O.C.D.
[0510]—*Franciscan Brothers of the Holy Cross*.—F.F.S.C.
[0520]—*Franciscan Friars*. (St. John the Baptist Prov.).—O.F.M.
[0570]—*Glenmary Home Missioners*.—Glmy.
[0650]—*Holy Ghost Fathers*. (Western Vice Prov.).—C.S.Sp.
[0690]—*Jesuit Fathers and Brothers*.—S.J.
[0850]—*Missionaries of Africa*. (Prov. of Quebec, Canada).—M.Afr.
[0430]—*Order of Preachers (Dominicans)*. (Southern Prov.).—O.P.
[1065]—*Priestly Fraternity of St. Peter*.—F.S.S.P.
[]—*Public Association of the Faithful - Celibate Brotherhood of the Brothers and Sisters of Charity*.—B.S.C.
[0420]—*Society of the Divine Word*. (Techny, IL).—S.V.D.

RELIGIOUS INSTITUTES OF WOMEN REPRESENTED IN THE DIOCESE

[0230]—*Benedictine Sisters of Pontifical Jurisdiction*. (Fort Smith, AR).—O.S.B.
[0470]—*Congregation of the Sisters of Charity of the Incarnate Word, Houston, Texas*.—C.C.V.I.
[1780]—*Congregation of the Sisters of the Third Order of St. Francis of Perpetual Adoration*. (Central Region).—F.S.P.A.
[0760]—*Daughters of Charity of St. Vincent de Paul*. (West Central Prov.).—D.C.
[]—*Daughters of Our Lady of Fatima*.—D.L.F.
[0420]—*Discalced Carmelite Nuns*. (Little Rock, AR).—O.C.D.
[1070-10]—*Dominican Sisters*.—O.P.
[2575]—*Institute of the Sisters of Mercy of the Americas*. (St. Louis, MO).—R.S.M.
[2490]—*Medical Mission Sisters*.—S.C.M.M.
[2710]—*Missionaries of Charity*.—M.C.
[1360]—*Missionary Franciscan Sisters of the Immaculate Conception*.—O.S.F.

[3070]—*North American Union Sisters of Our Lady of Charity.* (Hot Springs, AR).—N.A.U.-O.L.C.

[0240]—*Olivetan Benedictine Sisters.* (Jonesboro, AR).—O.S.B.

[]—*Public Association of the Faithful - Celibate Sisterhood of the Brothers and Sisters of Charity.*—B.S.C.

[2940]—*School Sisters of Notre Dame.* (Prov. of Dallas).—S.S.N.D.

[0500]—*Sisters of Charity of Nazareth.*—S.C.N.

[4120-03]—*Ursuline Nuns of the Congregation of Paris.*—O.S.U.

CEMETERIES

LITTLE ROCK. *Calvary.*

FORT SMITH. *Calvary.*

NECROLOGY

† Bolds, Bernard L., (Retired). —Died Feb. 23, 1997.

† Dagwell, Robert A., (Retired). —Died Feb. 26, 1997.

† Murphy, Rev. Msgr. John E., (Retired). —Died May 14, 1997.

† Zarrilli, Very Rev. Frederick B., V.F., Forrest City, AR, St. Francis of Assisi. —Died June 6, 1997.

Archdiocese of Los Angeles

(Archidioecesis Angelorum in California)

His Eminence

ROGER CARDINAL MAHONY, D.D.

Archbishop of Los Angeles; ordained May 1, 1962; appointed Titular Bishop of Tamascani and Auxiliary Bishop of Fresno January 7, 1975; consecrated March 19, 1975; appointed Bishop of Stockton February 26, 1980; installed as the third Bishop of Stockton April 17, 1980; appointed Archbishop of Los Angeles July 16, 1985; installed as the fourth Archbishop of Los Angeles September 5, 1985; Created Cardinal June 28, 1991. *Res., 114 E. 2nd St., Los Angeles, CA, 90012. Office: 3424 Wilshire Blvd., Los Angeles, CA, 90015-1194.* Tel.: 213-637-7261; Fax: 213-637-6510.

Archdiocesan Catholic Center Office: 3424 Wilshire Blvd., Los Angeles, CA, 90010-2241. Tel.: 213-637-7000; Fax: 213-637-6607.

Web site address: http://www.LA-Archdiocese.org

Most Reverend

JOHN J. WARD, D.D., J.C.L., V.G.

Auxiliary Bishop and Vicar General; ordained May 4, 1946; appointed Titular Bishop of Bria and Auxiliary October 16, 1963; consecrated December 12, 1963; Assigned Titular Bishop of California, June 15, 1996; retired July 1, 1996. *Office: 3424 Wilshire Blvd., Los Angeles, CA, 90010-2248.*

Most Reverend

JUAN A. ARZUBE, D.D.

Retired Auxiliary Bishop and Vicar General; ordained May 5, 1954; appointed Titular Bishop of Civitate and Auxiliary Feb. 9, 1971; consecrated March 25, 1971; retired June 1, 1993. *Res., c/o Sacred Heart Church, 2889 N. Lincoln Ave., Altadena, CA, 91001-4598.*

Most Reverend

STEPHEN E. BLAIRE, D.D., V.G.

Auxiliary Bishop and Vicar General; ordained April 29, 1967; appointed Titular Bishop of Lamzella on February 17, 1990; ordained a Bishop on May 31, 1990. *Office: Regional Bishop, Our Lady of the Angels Pastoral Region, 2636 S. Mansfield Ave., Los Angeles, CA, 90016.*

Most Reverend

THOMAS J. CURRY, D.D., PH.D.

Auxiliary Bishop and Vicar General; ordained June 18, 1967; appointed Titular Bishop of Ceanannus Mor February 8, 1994. *Office: Regional Bishop, Santa Barbara Pastoral Region, 3240 Calle Pinon, Santa Barbara, CA, 93105.*

Most Reverend

JOSEPH M. SARTORIS, D.D., V.G.

Auxiliary Bishop and Vicar General; ordained May 30, 1953; appointed Titular Bishop of Oliva February 8, 1994; ordained a Bishop March 19, 1994. *Office: Regional Bishop, San Pedro Pastoral Region, 3555 St. Pancratius Pl., Lakewood, CA, 90712-1416.*

Most Reverend

GABINO ZAVALA, D.D., J.C.L., V.G.

Auxiliary Bishop and Vicar General; ordained May 28, 1977; appointed Titular Bishop of Tamascani February 8, 1994; ordained Bishop March 19, 1994. *Office: Regional Bishop, San Gabriel Pastoral Region, 16009 E. Cypress Ave., Irwindale, CA, 91706.*

Most Reverend

GERALD E. WILKERSON, D.D.

Auxiliary Bishop and Vicar General; ordained May 1, 1965; appointed Titular Bishop of Vincennes November 5, 1997; ordained Bishop January 21, 1998. *Office: San Fernando Pastoral Region, 15101 San Fernando Mission Blvd., Mission Hills, CA, 91316.*

DIOCESE ESTABLISHED 1840; AN ARCHBISHOPRIC JULY 11, 1936.

Square Miles 8,762.

Comprises the Counties of Los Angeles, Santa Barbara and Ventura in the State of California.

PATRONESS OF THE DIOCESE: ST. VIBIANA.

Legal Titles:

The Roman Catholic Archbishop of Los Angeles, a Corporation Sole.

Archdiocese of Los Angeles Education and Welfare Corporation.

Our Lady Queen of Angels Seminary.

St. John's Seminary College.

St. John's Seminary in California.

The Cardinal McIntyre Fund for Charity.

Catholic Charities of Los Angeles, Inc.

Catholic Charities Community Development Corporation.

The Tidings.

Vida Nueva.

For legal titles of parishes and archdiocesan institutions, consult the Chancery Office.

STATISTICAL OVERVIEW

Personnel	
Cardinal	1
Auxiliary Bishops	5
Retired Bishops	2
Abbots	1
Priests: Diocesan Active in Diocese	432
Priests: Active Outside Diocese	15
Priests: Retired, Sick or Absent	124
Number of Diocesan Priests	571
Religious Priests in Diocese	662
Extern Priests in Diocese	122
Ordinations:	
Diocesan Priests	5
Religious Priests	3
Permanent Deacons	9
Permanent Deacons in Diocese	153
Total Brothers	171
Total Sisters	1,944
Parishes	
Parishes	286
With Resident Pastor:	
Resident Diocesan Priests	210
Resident Religious Priests	65
Without Resident Pastor:	
Administered by Priests	10
Administered by Pastoral Teams, etc.	1
Missions	21
Pastoral Centers	1
New Parishes Created	1
Professional Ministry Personnel:	
Brothers	13
Sisters	165
Lay Ministers	444
Welfare	
Catholic Hospitals	20
Total Assisted	1,139,746
Health Care Centers	5
Total Assisted	12,000
Homes for the Aged	7
Total Assisted	2,256
Residential Care of Children	2
Total Assisted	500
Day Care and Extended Day Care Centers	81
Total Assisted	4,256
Specialized Homes	11
Total Assisted	938
Special Centers for Social Services	79
Total Assisted	259,248
Residential Care of Disabled	2
Total Assisted	315
Other Institutions	3
Total Assisted	106
Educational	
Seminaries, Diocesan	2
Students from This Diocese	74
Students from Other Diocese	72
Seminaries, Religious	15
Students Religious	24
Total Seminarians	98
Colleges and Universities	5
Total Students	10,009
High Schools, Diocesan and Parish	29
Total Students	17,352
High Schools, Private	22
Total Students	13,115
Elementary Schools, Diocesan and Parish	221
Total Students	69,903
Elementary Schools, Private	9
Total Students	2,718
Catechesis/Religious Education:	
High School Students	24,000
Elementary Students	200,000
Total Students Under Catholic Instruction	337,195
Teachers in the Diocese:	
Priests	76
Scholastics	24
Brothers	25
Sisters	381
Lay Teachers	4,379
Vital Statistics	
Receptions into the Church:	
Infant Baptism Totals	101,126
Adult Baptism Totals	1,956
Received into Full Communion	2,051
First Communions	46,861
Confirmations	15,494
Marriages:	
Catholic	10,646
Interfaith	1,448
Total Marriages	12,094
Deaths	13,395
Total Catholic Population	3,188,816
Total Population	10,603,000

Former Bishops—Rt. Rev. FRANCIS GARCIA DIEGO Y MORENO, O.F.M., D.D., cons. Oct. 4, 1840; Bishop of both Californias; died at Santa Barbara, April 30, 1846.—Rt. Rev. JOSEPH SADOC ALEMANY, O.P., D.D., cons. June 30, 1850; Bishop of Monterey; transferred to San Francisco, July 29, 1853; died in Valencia, Spain, April 14, 1888.—Rt. Rev. THADDEUS AMAT, C.M., D.D., cons. March 12, 1854; died May 12, 1878.—Rt. Rev. FRANCIS MORA, D.D., cons. Titular Bishop of Mosynopolis and Coadjutor to Bishop Amat, Aug. 3, 1873; resigned May 6, 1896; died Aug. 3, 1905 in Sarria, Barcelona, Spain.—Rt. Rev. GEORGE MONTGOMERY, D.D., cons. April 8, 1894, Bishop of Tmul and Coadjutor-Bishop of Monterey and Los Angeles *cum jure successionis* succeeded to May 6, 1896; appt. Coadjutor-Archbishop of San Francisco, Jan. 1, 1903; died in San Francisco, Jan. 10, 1907.—Rt. Rev. THOMAS JAMES CONATY, D.D., cons. Nov. 24, 1901, Titular-Bishop of Samos; appt. Bishop of Monterey and Los Angeles, March 27, 1903; died at Coronado, CA, Sept. 18, 1915.—Most Rev. JOHN J. CANTWELL, D.D., LL.D., appt. Bishop of Monterey-Los Angeles, Sept. 21, 1917; cons. Dec. 5, 1917; appt. Assistant to the Pontifical Throne, Sept. 30, 1929; transferred to Los Angeles, June 1, 1922; elevated to Archepiscopal dignity, July 11, 1936; installed Dec. 3, 1936; died Oct. 30, 1947, at Los Angeles, CA.—His Eminence JAMES FRANCIS CARDINAL MCINTYRE, D.D., appt. Auxiliary Bishop of New York, Nov. 16, 1940; cons. Jan. 8, 1941; promoted to Coadjutor Archbishop, July 20, 1946; appt. Archbishop of Los Angeles, Feb. 7, 1948; installed March 19, 1948; created Cardinal Priest, Jan. 12, 1953; resigned Jan. 21, 1970; died July 16, 1989.—His Eminence TIMOTHY CARDINAL MANNING, D.D., J.C.D., appt. Titular Bishop of Lesvi and Auxiliary Bishop of Los Angeles, Aug. 3, 1946; cons. Oct. 15, 1946; installed as first Bishop of Fresno, Dec. 15, 1967; appt. Titular Bishop of Capri and Coadjutor Archbishop of Los Angeles, May 26, 1969; appt. Archbishop of Los Angeles, Jan. 21, 1970; created a Cardinal Priest, March 5, 1973; retired Sept. 4, 1985; died June 23, 1989 at Los Angeles, CA.

Archdiocesan Catholic Center Office—3424 Wilshire Blvd., Los Angeles, 90010-2241. Tel: 213-637-7200; Fax: 213-637-6607.

Office of the Cardinal—His Eminence ROGER CARDINAL MAHONY, D.D., *3424 Wilshire Blvd., Los Angeles, 90010-2241.* Tel: 213-637-7288; Fax: 213-637-6510.
- *Priest Secretary*—Rev. Msgr. KEVIN KOSTELNIK. Tel: 213-637-7261.
- *Administrative Assistant*—Sr. MARY BRIGID FITZPATRICK, C.S.J. Tel: 213-637-7384.
- *Cardinal's Director of Special Services*—Sr. MARY JEAN MEIER, S.M. Tel: 213-637-7520.
- *General Counsel*—Sr. JUDY MURPHY, C.S.J. Tel: 213-637-7511.

Auxiliary Bishops-Vicars General—Most Rev. JOHN J. WARD, V.G., (Retired), *3424 Wilshire Blvd., Los Angeles, 90010-2241.* Tel: 213-637-7264; Fax: 213-637-6607. Most Rev. JUAN A. ARZUBE, (Retired), *Sacred Heart Church, 2889 N. Lincoln Ave., Altadena, 91001-4598.* Tel: 626-794-2046; Fax: 626-794-2046. Most Rev. STEPHEN E. BLAIR, Our Lady of the Angels of Region, *2636 S. Mansfield Ave., Los Angeles, 90016.* Tel: 213-936-2588; Fax: 213-938-1190. Most Rev. THOMAS J. CURRY, Santa Barbara Region, *3240 Calle Pinon, Santa Barbara, 93105.* Tel: 805-682-0442; Fax: 805-682-7509. Most Rev. JOSEPH M. SARTORIS, San Pedro Region, Office: *3555 Pancratius Pl., Lakewood, 90712.* Tel: 310-634-0456; Fax: 310-531-4783. Most Rev. GABINO ZAVALA, San Gabriel Region, Office: *16009 E. Cypress Ave., Irwindale, 91706.* Tel: 818-960-9344; Fax: 818-962-0455. Rev. Msgr. GERALD WILKERSON, Episcopal Vicar for San Fernando Region, *15101 San Fernando Mission Blvd., San Fernando, 91341.* Tel: 818-361-6009; Fax: 818-361-6270.

Moderator of the Curia-Chancellor—Rev. Msgr. TERRANCE L. FLEMING, S.T.D. Tel: 213-637-7255.

Vice Chancellor—Sr. CECILIA LOUISE MOORE, C.S.J. Tel: 213-637-7605.

Secretariat for Administrative Services—Bro. THOMAS FAHY, O.S.F. Tel: 213-251-7608.
- *Archival Center*—Tel: 818-365-1501.
- *Catholic Cemeteries*—Tel: 213-637-7801.
- *Chancery Operations*—Tel: 213-637-7000.
- *Communications*—Tel: 213-637-7312.
- *Construction Department*—Tel: 213-637-7850.
- *Human Resources/Insurance*—Tel: 213-637-7596.
- *Information Services Department*—Tel: 213-637-7271.
- *Media Relations Office*—Tel: 213-637-7215.
- *Purchasing/Mail Center*—Tel: 213-637-7535.
- *Real Estate*—Tel: 213-637-7270.
- *Tribunal*—Tel: 213-637-7245.
- *The Tidings*—Tel: 213-637-7251.
- *Vida Nueva*—Tel: 213-637-7310.

Secretariat for Educational and Formational Services—Sr. CECILIA LOUISE MOORE, C.S.J. Tel: 213-637-7605.
- *Campus Ministry*—Tel: 213-637-7527.
- *Catholic Schools*—Tel: 213-637-7300.
- *Diaconate Formation*—Tel: 213-637-7282.
- *Ministry with Persons with Disabilities*—Tel: 213-637-7252.
- *Mission Office*—Tel: 213-637-7223.
- *Cardinal Manning House of Prayer for Priests*—Tel: 213-662-0092.
- *Religious Brothers Council*—Tel: 213-637-7320.
- *Religious Education*—Tel: 213-637-7335.
- *Spirituality Center*—Tel: 213-747-6508.
- *Vicar for Clergy*—Tel: 213-637-7284.
- *Vicar for Women Religious*—Tel: 213-637-7592.
- *Vocations*—Tel: 213-637-7307.
- *Worship*—Tel: 213-637-7262.

Secretariat for Pastoral and Community Services—Sr. KATHLEEN REILLY, C.S.C. Tel: 213-637-7610.
- *African American Vicariate*—Tel: 213-637-7610.
- *Asian Pacific & Ethnic Ministries*—Tel: 213-637-7540.
- *Cardinal McIntyre Fund for Charity*—Tel: 213-251-3438.
- *Catholic Charities*—Tel: 213-251-3400.
- *Detention Ministries*—Tel: 213-637-7648.
- *Ecumenical/Interreligious Affairs Office*—Tel: 213-637-7555.
- *Family Life Office*—Tel: 213-637-7228.
- *Health Affairs Office*—Tel: 213-637-7531.
- *Hispanic Ministries*—Tel: 213-637-7287.
- *Justice and Peace Office*—Tel: 213-637-7690.
- *Lay Organizations*—
  - *Apostleship of Prayer*—Tel: 213-466-2406.
  - *Catholic Daughters*—Tel: 310-643-9411.
  - *Charismatic Renewal/SCRC*—Tel: 310-371-6433.
  - *Council of Catholic Women*—Tel: 213-637-7394.
  - *Cursillo*—Tel: 213-637-7268.
  - *Holy Name*—Tel: 213-637-7393.
  - *Ladies of Charity*—Tel: 213-382-3659.
  - *Marriage Encounter, Worldwide*—Tel: 805-496-0222.
  - *Ministry with Lesbian & Gay Catholics*—Tel: 213-637-7658.
  - *Pastoral & Parish Councils*—Tel: 213-637-7430.
  - *Respect Life*—Tel: 213-637-7621.

Chief Financial Officer—Mr. JOSE DEBASA. Tel: 213-637-7285.
- *Accounting*—Tel: 213-637-7593.
- *Audit, Internal*—Tel: 213-637-7622.
- *Budget*—Tel: 213-637-7623.
- *Investments*—Tel: 213-637-7292.
- *Payroll*—Tel: 213-637-7594.
- *Pension Plan*—Tel: 213-637-7286.

Archdiocesan Pastoral Regions

Santa Barbara Region—Most Rev. THOMAS J. CURRY, *3240 Calle Pinon, Santa Barbara, 93105-2760.* Tel: 805-682-0442; Fax: 805-682-7509.
- *Deanery 1*—Rev. Msgr. JOHN G. FITZGERALD, V.F. Tel: 805-733-2735.
- *Deanery 2*—Rev. Msgr. STEPHEN DOWNES, V.F. Tel: 805-967-5641.
- *Deanery 3*—Rev. Msgr. PETER D. NUGENT, V.F. Tel: 805-487-3891.
- *Deanery 4*—Rev. Msgr. MICHAEL BUNNY, V.F. Tel: 805-498-3602.

San Fernando Region—Most Rev. GERALD E. WILKERSON, *15101 San Fernando Mission Blvd., Mission Hills, 91345-2526.* Tel: 818-361-6009; Fax: 818-361-6270.
- *Deanery 5*—Most Rev. GERALD E. WILKERSON, V.F. Tel: 818-342-4686.
- *Deanery 6*—Rev. Msgr. FRANCIS T. WALLACE, V.F. Tel: 818-790-5155.
- *Deanery 7*—Rev. JOHN H. KEESE, V.F. Tel: 818-894-1176.
- *Deanery 8*—Rev. Msgr. TIMOTHY P. O'CONNELL, V.F. Tel: 805-942-7122.

San Gabriel Region—Most Rev. GABINO ZAVALA, V.F., *16009 E. Cypress Ave., Irwindale, 91706-2122.* Tel: 818-960-9344; Fax: 818-962-0455.
- *Deanery 9*—Rev. RICHARD SIEBENAND, V.F. Tel: 213-526-3800.
- *Deanery 10*—Rev. RICHARD PRINDLE, V.F. Tel: 818-797-1167.
- *Deanery 11*—Rev. Msgr. DAVID SORK, V.F. Tel: 818-918-8314.
- *Deanery 12*—Rev. Msgr. JAMES J. LOUGHNANE, V.F. Tel: 909-861-7106.

Our Lady of the Angels Pastoral Region—Most Rev. STEPHEN E. BLAIRE, *2636 S. Mansfield Ave., Los Angeles, 90016.* Tel: 213-936-2588; Fax: 213-938-1190.
- *Deanery 13*—Rev. Msgr. LLOYD A. TORGERSON, V.F. Tel: 310-393-9287.
- *Deanery 14*—Rev. Msgr. JOHN BEATTIE, V.F. Tel: 213-656-4433.
- *Deanery 15*—Rev. Msgr. DENNIS P. O'NEIL, V.F. Tel: 213-737-3325.
- *Deanery 16*—Rev. Msgr. PAUL M. MONTOYA, V.F. Tel: 310-677-2736.

San Pedro Region—Most Rev. JOSEPH M. SARTORIS, *3555 St. Pancratius Pl., Lakewood, 90712-1416.* Tel: 562-634-0456; Fax: 562-531-4783.
- *Deanery 17*—Rev. Msgr. ROBERT W. GIPSON, V.F. Tel: 562-923-4509.
- *Deanery 18*—Rev. Msgr. CHRISTIAN M. VAN LIEFDE, V.F. Tel: 562-942-7300.
- *Deanery 19*—Rev. Msgr. MICHAEL F. LENIHAN, V.F. Tel: 310-540-0329.
- *Deanery 20*—Rev. Msgr. DOUGLAS W. SAUNDERS, V.F. Tel: 562-594-4657.

Archdiocesan Catholic Center Offices

Unless otherwise listed, all ACC offices are located at: *3424 Wilshire Blvd., Los Angeles, CA 90010-2241.*

Accounting Department—Mr. ROBERT KEELER, Controller. Tel: 213-637-7593. Mr. HENRY NIERODZIK, Accounting Mgr. Tel: 213-637-7297.

African-American Vicariate—Rev. FISHER ROBINSON, S.V.D., Dir. Tel: 213-637-7435.

Alcohol and Substance Abuse—Rev. Msgr. T. TERRENCE RICHEY, Dir. Tel: 213-637-7644.

Annual Catholic Appeal—Mr. CHRISTOPHER MCLAUGHLIN, Dir. Tel: 213-637-7703; Fax: 213-637-6434.

Apostleship of Prayer—Rev. FRANCIS PARRISH, S.J., Dir., *5322 Franklin Ave., Los Angeles, 90027.* Tel: 213-466-2406.

Apostleship of the Sea—Rev. Msgr. PATRICK GALLAGHER, Port Chap.; Rev. SYLVESTER THOMAS, Maritime Chap., *870 W. Eighth St., San Pedro, 90731.* Tel: 310-833-3541.

Archives—Rev. Msgr. FRANCIS J. WEBER, Archivist, *15151 San Fernando Mission Blvd., Mission Hills, 91345.* Tel: 818-365-1501; Fax: 818-361-3276.

Asian Pacific and Ethnic Groups—Sr. LUCIA TU, S.D.S.H., Dir. Tel: 213-637-7540.

Audit Services—SANDRA SMITH. Tel: 213-637-7622.

Brothers Council, Religious—Bro. TIMOTHY MAYWORM, F.S.C., Chm. Tel: 213-637-7320. LUPE A. GARIBAY, Admin. Asst. Tel: 213-637-7320.

Budget—Mrs. JEANNE ZEIND. Tel: 213-637-7623.

Campaign for Human Development—THOMAS A. CHABOLIA, Diocesan Dir. Tel: 213-637-7610. MARIA ELENA BOBADILLA, Prog. Admin. Tel: 213-637-7560.

Campus Ministry (Newman Apostolate)—Mrs. LAURIE W. OESTER, Dir. Tel: 213-637-7527; Fax: 213-637-6527.

Canonical Services, Vicar for—Rev. MODESTO PEREZ, J.C.D. Tel: 213-637-6888.

Cardinal Manning House of Prayer for Priests—Revs. JOHN D. MCANULTY, S.J., Dir. Tel: 213-662-0044. JOHN CLARK, S.J., Assoc. Dir., *3441 Waverly Dr., Los Angeles, 90027-2597.* Tel: 213-662-7966; Fax: 213-953-4802. Staffed by: Little Brothers of the Good Shepherd; Bro. MALACHY CORBETT, B.G.S., Superior; Bro. MARK HARMUELLER, B.G.S. Tel: 213-662-0092., Residence: *3445 Waverly Dr., Los Angeles, 90027-2597.*

Cardinal McIntyre Fund for Charity—SUSAN V. WEIGHT, Assoc. Dir., *1531 W. Ninth St., Los Angeles, 90015-1194.* Tel: 213-251-3438.

Catholic Charities of Los Angeles—1531 W. Ninth St., Los Angeles, 90015-1194. Tel: 213-251-3400.
- *Chief Executive Officer*—Rev. Msgr. GREGORY A. COX, M.S.W. Tel: 213-251-3464.
- *Chief Administrative Officer*—RONALD LOPEZ, M.S.W. Tel: 213-251-3390.
- *Chief Financial Officer*—Mr. JAMES E. BATHKER. Tel: 213-251-3410.
- *Department of Human Resources*—MARILYN KAMERER, Dir. Tel: 213-251-3414.
- *Department of Resource Development*—ALEXANDRIA "SANDI" ARNOLD, Dir. Tel: 213-251-3495.
- *Deputy Assistant*—SUSAN VALERIE WEIGHT. Tel: 213-251-3438.
- *Adeste—Child Development Services*—ARMINE LALAIAN-SANJAR, Dir. Tel: 213-251-3468.
- *C.Y.O. Athletics*—BOB FITZPATRICK, Prog. Dir. Tel: 213-251-3453.
- *Hope in Youth*—MIKE CLEMENTS, Dir. Tel: 213-662-9636.
- *Regional Office Directors*—
  - *Our Lady of the Angels Pastoral Region*—Metro: GREG STUART. Tel: 213-662-4391. O.L.A. Western: JAMES STRATTON. Tel: 310-392-8701.
  - *San Fernando Pastoral Region*—MOEED KHAN. Tel: 818-883-6015.
  - *San Gabriel Pastoral Region*—MARY ROMERO. Tel: 213-266-3130.
  - *San Pedro Pastoral Region*—LUPE U. MACKER. Tel: 562-591-1351.
  - *Santa Barbara Pastoral Region*—DAVIDA WILLIS. Tel: 805-965-7045. Ventura Co.: A. DIANA MARTELL, M.F.C.C. Tel: 805-643-4694.

Catholic Charities Community Development Corporation, Inc.—His Eminence ROGER CARDINAL MAHONEY, D.D., Chm. Bd.; Rev. Msgr. GREGORY A. COX, M.S.W., C.E.O., *Central Office, 1531 W. Ninth St.,*

P.O. Box 15095, Los Angeles, 90015.
Operations—DAVID FOSTER. Tel: 213-251-3418.
Catholic Relief Services—THOMAS A. CHABOLLA, Diocesan Dir. Tel: 213-637-7610. MARIA ELENA BOBADILLA, Prog. Admin. Tel: 213-637-7560.
Cemeteries, Catholic—Tel: 213-637-7801; Fax: 213-637-6800. Mr. KEITH G. MYERS, Exec. Dir. & Gen. Mgr. Tel: 213-637-7805. SAM FRIAS, Pastoral Rels. Dir. Tel: 213-637-7809. LEWIS J. MCADAMS, Property Devel. - Long Range Planning Dir. Tel: 213-637-7809. Mr. JAMES M. TIXIER, Finance & Admin. Svcs. Dir. Tel: 213-637-7808. Mr. LEWIS J. MCADAMS, Oper. Dir. Region 1 (Acting). Tel: 213-637-7809. Mr. MICHAEL E. WESNER, Operations Dir. Region II. Tel: 213-637-7813.
Censor Liborum—Rev. Msgr. CRAIG A. COX. Tel: 213-637-7204.
Clergy, Vicar for—Rev. Msgr. RICHARD A. LOOMIS. Tel: 213-637-7284.
Personnel Board—Revs. GABRIEL GONZALES, Chm. DAVID J. AYOTTE; Rev. Msgr. JOHN KEESE, V.F.; Rev. Msgr. JAMES J. LOUGHNANE, V.F.; Rev. Msgr. PETER D. NUGENT, V.F.; Rev. Msgr. DENNIS P. O'NEIL, V.F.; Rev. Msgr. CHRISTIAN VAN LIEFDE, V.F.; Revs. JOHN W. LOVE; ALLAN ROBERTS; WILLIAM WOLFE.
Communications—DAVID MOORE, Exec. Dir. Tel: 213-637-6215; Fax: 213-637-6360. TERESA GARCIA, Office Mgr. Tel: 213-637-7581.
Media Relations—Rev. GREGORY CORIO, O.F.M.Cap., Dir. Tel: 213-637-7215; Fax: 213-385-6586.
Conciliation/Arbitration—Rev. Msgr. TERRANCE FLEMING, V.G. Tel: 213-637-7255.
Continuing Formation of Clergy—Rev. RICHARD KREKELBERG, Dir. Tel: 213-637-7571.
Construction—Bro. HILARION O'CONNOR, O.S.F., Dir. Tel: 213-637-7852. THOMAS HERWOOD, Construction Project Mgr. Tel: 213-637-7860. JAVIER RODRIGUEZ, Construction Project Supvr. Tel: 213-637-7853. CRAIG O. HEARN, Senior Construction Project Supvr. Tel: 213-637-7858. CECILIA URIBE, Construction Project Supvr. Tel: 213-637-7855. CHRISTOPHER TRAPP, Oper. Mgr. Tel: 213-637-7862. RUSS PITELKAU, Cathedral Project. Tel: 213-637-7859.
Council of Catholic Women—MARY PAT MAY, Pres. Tel: 213-637-7394; Fax: 213-637-6394.
Council of Priests—Rev. DAVID O'CONNELL, Chm. Tel: 213-637-7320.
Cursillo Movement—Revs. MODESTO PEREZ, J.C.D., Spanish Speaking Dir. Tel: 213-637-7482. Rev. ENRIQUE PARISI, O.F.M., English Speaking Spiritual Dir. Tel: 213-748-5394.
Deacons—Deacon JOSEPH ORTH, Dir. Deacons. Tel: 213-637-7734.
Detention Ministry—Sr. SUZANNE JABRO, C.S.J., Dir. Tel: 213-637-7648.
Development—KEVIN T. O'CONNOR, Chief Devel. Officer. Tel: 213-637-7617.
Annual Appeal—CHRISTOPHER C. MCLAUGHLIN, Dir. Tel: 213-637-7703.
Annual Appeal/Data Financial—JOSEPH HINDLEY, Mgr. Tel: 213-637-7673.
Cathedral Development Services and Systems—AMANDA MANSOUR. Tel: 213-637-7432.
Corporations & Foundations Programs—Tel: 213-637-7365.
Development Services and Systems—CHRISTOPHER C. MCLAUGHLIN, Dir. Tel: 213-637-7703.
Education Foundation—PHILLIP JORDAN, Exec. Dir. Tel: 213-637-7576. LINDA BAKER, Assoc. Exec. Dir. Tel: 213-637-7703. CAROLYN GAMBLE, Devel. Programs. Tel: 213-637-7452. BONNIE ONKEN, Data-Financial Coord. Tel: 213-637-7449.
Parish Stewardship Program—Vacant. Tel: 213-637-7617.
Trust and Estates Programs—Vacant. Tel: 213-637-7627.
Diaconate, Formation Office—Deacon JOHNNIE HAMMONDS, Dir. Tel: 213-637-7282; Fax: 213-637-6383. Assoc. Dirs.: Rev. FRANK FERRANTE, C.M.F. Tel: 213-637-7536. Sr. CHRIS MACHADO, S.S.S. Tel: 213-637-7747. Deacon CRIS VEGA. Tel: 213-637-7738. VICTOR STAFORELLI. Tel: 213-637-7755.
Earthquake—(See Construction).
Ecumenical and Interreligious Affairs—Vacant, Dir. Tel: 213-637-7556; Fax: 213-637-6555.
Ethnic Ministries—(See African-American, Hispanic, Asian Pacific).
Family Life Office—Mrs. JOAN VIENNA, Dir. Tel: 213-637-7227; Fax: 213-637-7681. Rev. Msgr. CHARLES B. FORTIER, Assoc. Dir. Tel: 213-637-7214.
Coordinator, Marriage Preparation Spanish-Speaking—GRACIELA VILLALOBOS. Tel: 213-637-7561.
Coordinator, Marriage Preparation English Speaking—CANDY METOYER. Tel: 213-637-7250.
Coordinator, Natural Family Planning—Rev. Msgr. CHARLES B. FORTIER. Tel: 213-637-7214.
Coordinator, Parent Education, English—GILDA SILVER. Tel: 213-637-7283.
Coordinator, Parent Education, Spanish—MICAELA REGALADO. Tel: 213-637-7504.
Divorce Recovery Ministry—Tel: 213-637-7283.
Gay and Lesbian Community, Ministry with—Rev. PETER LUIZZI, O.Carm., Dir. Tel: 213-637-7658.
Government Funded Programs—1543 W. Olympic Blvd., Ste. 424, Los Angeles, 90015-3807; Fax: 213-383-1529. LOU CASEY, Dir. Tel: 213-383-0199.
Pre-School Dir.—ETHEL ANTOINE. Tel: 213-388-1291.
Youth Employment Programs Dir.—ROBERT GUTIERREZ. Tel: 213-736-5456.
Health Affairs—Sr. M. CAROLITA HART, C.S.C., Dir. Tel: 213-637-7531.
Hispanic Ministry—Mr. LOUIS VELASQUEZ, Dir. Tel: 213-637-7280.
Pastoral Coordinator, Queen of Angels Region—Sr. ANTONEITA M. ZAPATA, M.G.Sp.S. Tel: 213-932-0998.
Pastoral Coordinator, San Fernando Region—Mr. VICTOR STAFORELLI. Tel: 818-361-9418.
Pastoral Coordinator, San Gabriel Region—Mr. HUMBERTO RAMOS. Tel: 818-960-2805.
Pastoral Coordinator, San Pedro Region—Vacant. Tel: 310-531-8155.
Pastoral Coordinator, Santa Barbara Region—Mr. JORGE RODRIGUEZ. Tel: 805-687-5422.
Holy Childhood Association—(See Missions Office).
Holy Name Association, Archdiocesan Union of Parish—Mr. VIC MARCELINO, Pres.; Mr. G. WILLIAM HENDERSON, Exec. Sec.; Rev. Msgr. PAUL MONTOYA, V.F., Moderator; Rev. RAMON MARTI, Sch.P., Assoc. Moderator. Tel: 213-637-7393.
House of Prayer for Priests—(See Cardinal Manning House of Prayer for Priests).
Human Resources/Insurance—WILLIAM HEINEN, Dir. Tel: 213-637-7596; Fax: 213-637-6116. MARGARET M. ANTCZAK, Senior Employee Rels./Training Specialist. Tel: 213-637-7625. Vacant, Senior Employment Relations/Training Specialist. Tel: 213-637-7371. SOFIA SANDRU, H.R. Assoc. Dir. Cemeteries Mgr. Tel: 213-637-7812.
Insurance—Mrs. LEVONTINE TOMACAN, Assoc. Dir. Tel: 213-637-7279. HOURIG DAKESSIAN, Insurance Specialist Disability. Tel: 213-637-7671. STEPHEN VAN BUREN, Insurance Risk Mgr. Tel: 213-637-7629. Sr. DILECTA PIERINI, S.S.S., Medical Benefits Consultant. Tel: 213-637-7680.
Information Services—Mr. JAMES R. CELONI, Dir. Tel: 213-637-7271. Rev. ANGUS C. COOPER, O.F.M., Asst. Dir. Tel: 213-637-7699.
Internal Audit—SANDRA SMITH, Dir. Tel: 213-637-7622.
Investments—EDNA CRISTOBAL, Dir. Tel: 213-637-7292.
Justice and Peace—THOMAS A. CHABOLLA, Exec. Dir. Tel: 213-637-7610. JEFF BONINO-BRITSCH, Assoc. Dir. Tel: 213-637-7690. MARIA ELENA BOBADILLA, Prog. Admin. Tel: 213-637-7560.
Knights of Columbus-California State Council Office—20280 S. Vermont Ave., Ste. 240, Torrance, 90502. Tel: 310-768-8593; Fax: 310-768-8596.
Ladies of Charity of St. Vincent de Paul—1531 W. Ninth St., Los Angeles, 90015. Tel: 213-382-3659.
Lay Mission Helpers—(See Mission Office).
Liturgy and Worship—(See Worship).
Marriage Encounter—Rev. JAMES GALVIN, C.M., Dir., *1964 Las Canoas Rd., Santa Barbara, 93105.* Tel: 805-882-1942.
Media Relations Office—Rev. GREGORY COIRO, O.F.M.Cap., Dir. Tel: 213-637-7215; Fax: 213-385-6586.
Ministry with Persons with Disabilities—VERONICA GRAY, Dir. Tel: 213-637-7236; 637-7252.
Mission Office—Rev. Msgr. MICHAEL MEYERS, Dir. Tel: 213-637-7223; Fax: 213-637-6223.
Holy Childhood Association—Tel: 213-637-7223.
Lay Mission Helpers—Tel: 213-637-7222.
Mission Circles—Tel: 213-637-7223.
Mission Doctors Assoc.—Dr. TIMOTHY LEFEVRE, Pres. Tel: 213-637-7222.
Propagation of the Faith—Tel: 213-637-7223.
Operations—EILEEN O'BRIEN. Tel: 213-637-7618. HUGO SANDOVAL. Tel: 213-637-7269.
Pastoral Councils—Tel: 213-637-7430; Fax: 213-637-7641. Mrs. MAGGIE STAPP, Reg. Dir. Santa Barbara. Tel: 805-682-0442.
Payroll—FRAN RUSHIE. Tel: 213-637-7594.
Pension Plan—SANDRA PULIDO LENZ. Tel: 213-637-7286.
Priest Pension Plan—LUPE A. GARIBAY. Tel: 213-637-7320.
Propagation of the Faith, Society for—(See Missions Office).
Purchasing/Mail Center—SANDY B. VILLAREAL, Purchasing Agent. Tel: 213-637-7535.
Real Estate—NEAL BLANEY, Dir. Tel: 213-637-7273; Fax: 213-637-6675.
Religious, Vicar for Women—Sr. MARY FAITH CLARKE, S.N.J.M. Tel: 213-637-7592.
Religious Education—Tel: 213-637-7335; Fax: 213-637-6574. Sr. EDITH PRENDERGAST, R.S.C., Dir. Tel: 213-637-7309. Assoc. Dirs.: Mrs. MONICA HUGHES. Tel: 213-637-7350. MARUJA SEDANO. Tel: 213-637-7345. GAIL KRAUSE, Office Coord. Tel: 213-637-7342.
Regional Offices—Our Lady of the Angels Region: Sr. ROSANNE BELPEDIO, C.S.J., *2636 Mansfield, Los Angeles, 90016-3512.* Tel: 213-931-2875; Fax: 213-938-1190. San Fernando Region: LYNN LANG, *15101 San Fernando Mission Blvd., San Fernando, 91345.* Tel: 818-365-5123; Fax: 818-361-6270. San Gabriel Region: EILEEN GATELEY, *San Gabriel Region Pastoral Center, 16009 E. Cypress Ave., Irwindale, 91706.* Tel: 626-962-7707; Fax: 626-962-0455. San Pedro Region: PATRICIA O'BRIEN, *San Pedro Regional Center, 3555 St. Pancratius Pl., Lakewood, 90712.* Tel: 562-630-6272; Fax: 562-531-4783. Santa Barbara Region: MARY BRAITMAN, *Bishop Garcia Diego Center, 4032 La Colina Rd., Santa Barbara, 93110.* Tel: 805-569-1135; Fax: 805-569-2746.
Adult Education—Rev. JAMES J. CLARKE. Tel: 213-637-7654. Sr. ANN DUNN, I.H.M., Santa Barbara Region: Tel: 805-569-2779. MARUJA SEDANO, Spanish Coord. Tel: 213-637-7345. MARY LOU MCGEE. Tel: 213-637-7704. MARIA EMILIA MAIRENA, Spanish. Tel: 213-637-7355. Sr. ALINA SPINCEMAILLE, I.C.M., Spanish. Tel: 213-637-7355.
Advanced Cathechetical Ministries and Cathechetical Formation—MONICA HUGHES. Tel: 213-637-7350. LOURDES GONZALES-RUBIO, Spanish. Tel: 213-637-7344.
Asian-Pacific Perspective—IRMA I. ISIP. Tel: 213-637-7669.
Catechesis in a Black Perspective—SHERYL LANGE. Tel: 213-637-7354.
Confirmation—JEAN ESSA. Tel: 213-637-7616. JUSTINA PIMENTEL, Spanish. Tel: 213-637-7343.
Early Childhood—NORMA THOMPSON HOLLIS. Tel: 213-637-7352.
Elementary—THELMA DELGADO, Spanish. Tel: 213-637-7351. STEVEN ELLAIR. Tel: 213-637-7410.
Junior High Ministry—RUBEN CASTORENA. Tel: 213-637-7305. JEAN ESSA, San Fernando. Tel: 213-637-7616.
Media—Reservations—YOLANDA ARANDA. Tel: 213-637-7340.
Religious Education Congress—Mrs. ADRIAN WHITAKER. Tel: 213-637-7332.
Young Adult Ministry (18-35)—LEILANI GOECKNER. Tel: 213-637-7498. CAROL SCHMIDT-CLAWSON. Tel: 213-637-7349. MARTHA NUNEZ, Spanish. Tel: 213-637-7705.
Youth Ministry—MICHAEL NORMAN. Tel: 213-637-7674. RUBEN CASTORENA. Tel: 213-637-7305. JEAN ESSA, San Fernando. Tel: 213-637-7616.
Respect Life Office—Mrs. LICIA NICASSIO, Dir. Tel: 213-637-7621.
St. Vincent de Paul Society—HILMAR ROSENAST, Pres., *210 N. Ave. 21, Los Angeles, 90031.* Tel: 213-224-6280. Mr. JOSE J. ROSSIER, Exec. Dir.; Mr. ANTHONY TERRAZAS, Dir., Los Angeles Main Store.
Schools, Dept. of Catholic—Tel: 213-637-7300; Fax: 213-637-6300. Mr. JEROME R. PORATH, Ph.D., Supt. Schools. Tel: 213-637-7313. Sr. MARY ELIZABETH GALT, B.V.M., Assoc. Supt. of Elementary Schools. Tel: 213-637-7315. Ms. BARBARA BROWN, Assoc. Supt. of Secondary Schools. Tel: 213-637-7539.
Elementary School Supervisors—Sr. JOANNE TIERNEY, C.H.F. Tel: 213-637-7318. Sr. JOAN FARAONE, R.J.M. Tel: 213-637-7584. Sr. JILL MARIE NAPIER, C.S.J. Tel: 213-637-7333. Mrs. PAT LIVINGSTON. Tel: 213-637-7323. Mrs. MARION FALCHI. Tel: 213-637-7314. Mrs. SANDRA RANDALL. Tel: 213-637-7322. FRANK MONTEJANO, Rel. Coord.; 213-637-7317.
Budget Director, Elementary Schools—Sr. JILL MARIE NAPIER, C.S.J. Tel: 213-637-7333.
Secondary School Supervisors—Sr. PATRICIA BUSSMAN, S.N.J.M. Tel: 213-637-7485. Mrs. DOROTHY PITTELKAU. Tel: 213-637-7325.
Consultant for Secondary School Finances/Director Technology—Sr. GINA MARIE BLUNCK, S.N.D. Tel: 213-637-7368; 7325.
Curriculum Director—Mrs. RINO NGO. Tel: 213-637-7311.
Coordinator for Projects & Programs—Sr. PATRICIA SUPPLE, C.S.J. Tel: 213-637-7537.
Director of Elementary Personnel—MARION FALCHI. Tel: 213-637-7314.
Director of Certification for High School Religion Teachers—Mrs. LINDA SCHULTZ. Tel: 213-637-7329.
Religion Coordinator Secondary—Rev. CRESCENCIO ROSALES. Tel: 213-637-7538. Sr. JOANNE WITTENBURG, S.N.D., Research Assoc. Tel: 213-637-7324. SANDRA BROSNAHAN, Special Resources Coord. Tel: 213-637-7325.
Scouting and Camp Fire Ministry—EILEEN GALLAGHER, Admin. Asst., *P.O. Box 91764, Long Beach, 90809-1764.* Tel: 310-427-2149.

Seminaries Development/Alumni Relations—Tel: 213-637-7434.

Sisters' Council—Tel: 213-637-7559.

Spirituality Center, Archdiocesan—Sr. THOMAS BERNARD MACCONNELL, C.S.J., Dir., *2 Chester Pl., Los Angeles, 90007*. Tel: 213-747-6508.

Telecommunication Services—DAVE MOORE, Dir. Tel: 213-637-7308. DAVID SCHMITT, Chief Engineer. Tel: 213-637-7526.

Theological Commission—Rev. Msgr. CRAIG A. COX, J.C.D. Tel: 213-637-7204. Sr. KAREN WILHELMY, C.S.J., Sec. Tel: 805-486-7301.

"The Tidings" (Archdiocesan Newspaper)—Tel: 213-637-7360; Fax: 213-637-6360. DAVID MOORE, Gen. Mgr. TOM GRIFFITHS, Exec. Publisher. Tel: 213-637-7312. TOD TAMBERG, Editor. Tel: 213-637-7493. EDUARDO ALVAREZ, Advertising Dir. Tel: 213-637-7232. MARY TRUDEAU MOTTOLA, Circulation Mgr. Tel: 213-637-7477. HERMINE LEES, Directory. Tel: 213-637-7392. Vacant; Creative Dir. Tel: 213-637-7380. Mr. POLO DIAS, Finance Officer. Tel: 213-637-7363. TERESA GARCIA PEREZ, Office Mgr. Tel: 213-637-7581.

Tribunal—Tel: 213-637-7245; Fax: 213-637-6245.

Judicial Vicar—Rev. Msgr. CRAIG A. COX, J.C.D. Tel: 213-637-7204., *Santa Barbara/Ventura Branch, P.O. Box 2215, Oxnard, 93034*. Tel: 805-486-6553; Fax: 805-486-3884.

Adjutant Judicial Vicar—Rev. GERALD B. FESSARD, J.C.L. Tel: 213-637-7397.

Canonical Staff—Rev. THOMAS C. ANSLOW, C.M., J.C.L. Tel: 805-486-6553. Rev. CHARLES J. CHAFFMAN, J.C.L. Tel: 213-637-7275. Sr. ANNE GIBLIN, R.S.C., J.C.L. Tel: 213-637-7211. Sr. PAULA K. MODAFF, S.P., J.C.L. Tel: 213-251-3203. Sr. MARGARET ANN MCCAULEY, O.P., J.C.L. Tel: 213-637-7205. Deacon HAROLD A. PARISH, J.C.D., Santa Barbara-Ventura Branch. Tel: 805-486-6553. Sr. ELISSA A. RINERE, C.P., J.C.D. Tel: 213-637-7397. Rev. LAURENCE J. SPITTERI, J.C.L. Tel: 213-637-7211.

Judges—Rev. THOMAS C. ANSLOW, C.M., J.C.L.; Revs. MICHAEL CARCERANO, J.C.L.; CHARLES J. CHAFFMAN, J.C.L.; JARLATH DOLAN; GERALD B. FESSARD, J.C.L.; Rev. Msgr. TERRANCE L. FLEMING, S.T.D.; Sr. ANNE GIBLIN, R.S.C., J.C.L.; Rev. Msgr. WILLIAM LESER, C.B., S.T.B.; Rev. Msgr. JAMES J. LOUGHNANE; Sr. MARGARET ANN MCCAULEY, O.P., J.C.L.; Sr. PAULA K. MODAFF, S.P., J.C.L.; Rev. Msgr. AUGUST MORETTI, J.C.D.; Rev. Msgr. DONAL MULCAHY; Deacon HAROLD A. PARISH, J.C.D.; Rev. MODESTO L. PEREZ, J.C.L.; Sr. ELISSA RINERE, C.P., J.C.D.; Revs. LAURENCE J. SPITTERI, J.C.L.; WILLIAM P. WOLFE, J.C.L.

Promotors of Justice—Rev. Msgr. HELMUT A. HEFNER, J.C.L.; Rev. Msgr. FRANCIS T. WALLACE, J.C.L.

Defenders of the Bond—Rev. Msgr. ARNOLD BIEDERMANN; Rev. JEROME A. BOUSKA, M.A.; Sr. ANNE GIBLIN, R.S.C., J.C.L.; Rev. ANSELM H. GOOSENS, C.J.; Rev. Msgr. HELMUT A. HEFNER, J.C.L.; Rev. NELSON TRINIDAD, J.C.L.; Rev. Msgr. FRANCIS T. WALLACE, J.C.L.

Advocates and Auditors—Rev. ROBERT BIROSCHAL; D. ANN CLABBY; FERNANDO ENGEL; Deacon JAMES HENRY; SANDRA HERRERA; Rev. PATRICK J. HILL; Deacon JOHN KUNSEMILLER; MARTHA ESTER LUNA; Rev. PETER T. NGO; JOAN SUTHERLAND; MARIA URANGA.

Notaries and Other Officials—Deacon EMILE ADAMS; LETICIA ASCENCIO; CESAR CASTRO; DESSIE DELOVINO; Deacon JOHN GAUDIN; RUTH GOMEZ; ALBA GUTIERREZ; BOBBIE LOPEZ; ANNA PARISH; SIOBHAN PRADO; MERCED SALCEDO; MARIA URANGA.

Trust and Estate Programs—Tel: 213-637-7472.

"Vida Nueva" (Archdiocesan Spanish Newspaper)—Tel: 213-637-7380; Fax: 213-637-6215. DAVID MOORE, Gen. Mgr. Tel: 213-637-7312. VICTOR ALEMAN, Editor. Tel: 213-637-7310. EDUARDO ALVAREZ, Advertising Dir. Tel: 213-637-7232. MARY TRUDEAU MOTTOLA, Circulation Mgr. Tel: 213-637-7477. Vacant; Creative Dir. Tel: 213-637-7380.

Vicar for Clergy—Rev. Msgr RICHARD A. LOOMIS. Tel: 213-637-7284. Rev. CURTIS BRYANT, S.J., Ph.D., Staff Consultant. Tel: 213-637-7668. Rev. RICHARD KREKELBERG, Continuing Formation Dir. Tel: 213-637-7571. Rev. Msgr. TERRENCE RICHEY, Alcohol/SA Ministry Dir. Tel: 213-637-7644. Rev. PAUL HRUBY, Ministry to Newly Ordained and Retired Priests. Tel: 213-759-1562. Deacon JOSEPH ORTH, Dir., Deacons. Tel: 213-637-7734. LUCILLE MILLER, Exec. Asst. Tel: 213-637-7204.

Vicar for Women Religious—Sr. MARY FAITH CLARKE, S.N.J.M. Tel: 213-637-7592.

Vocations—Revs. RICHARD MARTINI, Dir. Tel: 213-637-7248. Sr. KATHLEEN BRYANT, R.S.C., Sister Dir. Tel: 213-637-7517. Rev. DAVID M. VELAZQUEZ, M.Sp.S., Dir., Hispanic Vocations.

Vocations in Progress—Rev. ALEX ACLAN, Dir. Tel: 213-637-7356. JULIA RIVAS, Assoc. Dir.,VIP Program. Tel: 213-637-7356.

Worship—Rev. RICHARD ALBARANO, S.S.J., Dir. Tel: 213-637-7262. KATHY A. LINDELL, Assoc. Dir. Tel: 213-637-7513. Consultants—Christian Initiation (RCIA); DENI HAYES. Tel: 213-637-7591. Sr. MARILU COVANI, S.P., Hispanic Liturgy. Tel: 213-637-7588. CHRISTOPHER GREEN, Liturgy Certification. Tel: 213-637-7586. FRANK BROWNSTEAD, Music. Tel: 213-637-7587.

Women, Archdiocesan Council of Catholic—(See Council of Catholic Women).

Young Adult Ministry (18-35)—(See Religious Education).

Archdiocesan Advisory Boards

Archdiocesan Development Council—His Eminence ROGER CARDINAL MAHONEY, D.D.

Office of Development—Mr. CHARLES F. SMITH, Chm. Tel: 213-637-7434. Members: Rev. Msgr. MICHAEL BUNNY; Mr. LOUIS M. CASTRUCCIO; Rev. Msgr. TERRANCE L. FLEMING; Mr. WILLIAM T. HUSTON; Rev. Msgr. JOHN J. KANE; Rev. Msgr. MICHAEL LENIHAN; Mr. WILLIAM J. LYON; Mr. PETER W. MULLIN; Rev. Msgr. DENNIS P. O'NEIL.

Archdiocesan Finance Council—Mr. JOSE DEBASA, Chief Financial Officer. Tel: 213-637-7285. Members:: His Eminence ROGER CARDINAL MAHONY, D.D.; Mr. ROBERT ARRANGA, Robert Arrangea & Co.; Mrs. KAREN JUAREZ BOYD, Pres., Lumen Financial, Inc.; Mr. AVIS CHEUNG, Occidental Petroleum Co.; Rev. Msgr. STEPHEN DOWNES, Pastor, St. Raphael Church, Santa Barbara; Mr. ROBERT ERBURU, Time Mirror Co.; Mr. MARK S. GRANICH, C.E.O., Granich & Stromme; Mr. RUBEN JAUREGUI, Vargas & Co.; Mr. JOSEPH KEARNS, Vice Pres. & Treas., J. Paul Getty Trust; Mr. THOMAS LARKIN, Pres. & C.E.O, Trust Co. of the West; Rev. Msgr. MICHAEL LENIHAN, Regional Dean, Pastor, St. Lawrence Martyr Church, Redondo Beach; Mr. KENNETH OLSEN, Retired Pres. & C.E.O., Vons Grocery Co.; Mr. ROLAND SEIDLER, Chm. & C.E.O., the Seidler Companies, Inc.; Mr. WILLIAM SIART; Rev. Msgr. DAVID SORK, Regl. Dean, Pastor, St. Louis of France Church, La Puente; Rev. Msgr. LLOYD TORGERSON, Regl. Dean, Pastor, St. Monica Church, Santa Monica; Rev. Msgr. JOHN T. WHOLIHAN, Dean, College of Business, Loyola Marymount University; Rev. Msgr. GERALD WILKERSON, Regional Dean, Pastor, Our Lady of Grace Church, Encino.

Archdiocesan Commission for Catholic Life Issues—Mrs. LICIA NICASSIO, Dir., Office of Respect Life. Tel: 213-637-7621. Rev. LAWRENCE CARUSO, Co-Chm. Tel: 310-436-6481. Sr. PAULA VANDEGAER, S.S.S., Co-Chm. Tel: 213-382-2156. MARIAN BURMAN; THOMAS CHABOLLA; Rev. THOMAS CUSACK, S.S.C.; VINCENT FORTANASCE, M.D.; Rev. Msgr. CHARLES FORTIER; DAVID FREILINGER, M.D.; BONIFACIO GARCIA, ESQ.; GLORIA GRIFFIN; Sr. CAROLITA HART, C.S.C.; Rev. Msgr. JEREMIAH MCCARTHY; MARCELLA MELENDEZ; Ms. GLORIA MILLER, R.N.; Rev. Msgr. JOHN MORETTA; Mrs. BETTY ODELLO, R.N., M.S.N.; Ms. MARY SHERIDAN; ALAN SHEWMON, M.D.; MAGGIE STAPP; LOUIS VELASQUEZ; ENRIQUETA VILLAREAL, M.D.; Rev. STEPHEN WATSON, O.C.D.; Ms. GERMAINE WENSLEY, R.N.; Ms. MARLENE WILSON, M.S.W., L.C.S.W. Advisory Members: Rev. Msgr. GEORGE J. PARNASSUS, Ex Officio Chm. CARLA COTTI; MARTA M. FERNANDEZ, ESQ.; T. MURPHY GOODWIN, M.D.; Rev. JAMES MCNULTY, C.S.P.; Sr. JANE FRANCES POWER, C.S.J.; MERCEDES ROUX.

Archdiocesan Commission for Ecumenical and Interreligious Affairs—Tel: 213-637-7556. Members: Rev. Msgr. WILLIAM BARRY; MARY CASS; THOMAS CHABOLLA; Rev. GREGORY COIRO, O.F.M.Cap.; Sr. MOLUA CONHEADY, S.S.L.; Rev. JOHN FITZGERALD; MONICA HUGHES; Sr. EMILE ANN PALLADINO, S.N.D.; Rev. THOMAS RAUSCH, S.J.; KATHERINE ROUSSEAU; Rev. ALEXEI SMITH; Rev. EARL WALKER.

Archdiocesan Commission for Justice and Peace—Ms. JOAN HARPER, Chm.; Ms. SAUNDRA WILLINGHAM, Vice-Chm.; Mr. THOMAS CHABOLLA, Exec. Dir. Tel: 213-637-7690. Rev. Msgr. JACK BEATTIE; RAYMOND T. BENNETT; Ms. ELLIE CLARK; Mr. GEORGE COOK; ILLEGRA EVANS; Mr. TOM FRANKLIN; JAIME MENDOZA; Mr. FERNANDO MORENO; MARIE ALEXIS NAVARRO; Mr. BERNARDO PEREZ; PAMELA RECTOR. Ex Officios: His Eminence ROGER CARDINAL MAHONY, D.D.; Sr. KATHLEEN REILLY, C.S.C.; THOMAS A. CHABOLLA; Mr. JEFFREY BONINO-BRITSCH.

Archdiocesan Pastoral Councils—(See Pastoral Councils). Tel: 213-637-7430.

Archdiocesan Catholic School Board—Mrs. PATTY BALDWIN; Mr. MICHAEL BOTELLO; Dr. PAMELA BOURGEOIS; Mr. WILLIAM D. HAWKINS; Ms. CHRISTINE HANSON; Ms. JANICE M. HEXTALL; Ms. MICHAEL JACKMAN; Rev. Msgr. ANTHONY LEUER; Sr. CHERYL MILNER, S.N.J.M.; Mr. JOEY QUINTO; Mr. FRANK VILLALOBOS; Ms. CHRISTINE R. WHELAN; Ms. AGNES E. ZELUS.

College of Consultors—Most Rev. JOHN J. WARD; Most Rev. STEPHEN E. BLAIRE; Most Rev. THOMAS J. CURRY; Most Rev. JOSEPH M. SARTORIS; Most Rev. GABINO ZAVALA; Rev. Msgr. TERRANCE FLEMING, S.T.D.; Rev. Msgr. JOSEPH COKUS; Rev. Msgr. CHARLES E. HILL; Revs. WILLIAM BONNER, S.V.D.; MICHAEL JENNETT; ALEXANDER SALAZAR.

Council of Priests—His Eminence ROGER CARDINAL MAHONY, D.D., Pres.; Revs. DAVID O'CONNELL, Chm. Tel: 213-637-7320. WILLIAM BONNER, S.V.D., Vice Chm. JESUS A. PARRA, Sec. MARK V. TRUDEAU, Treas.

Members at Large—Revs. WILLIAM EASTERLING; PEDRO J. LOPEZ; ALEXANDER SALAZAR; DAVID J. AYOTTE, Recording Sec.

Age Group—Rev. Msgr. JAMES A. O'CALLAGHAN; Revs. JOHN B. FITZGERALD; FRANCIS R. COLBORN; TIMOTHY E. NICHOLS; LORENZO MIRANDA.

Appointees—Revs. RODEL BALAGATAS; WILLIAM BONNER, S.V.D.; JESUS PARRA; ALEXANDER SALAZAR; MARC V. TRUDEAU; ALBERT VASQUEZ, C.M.F.

Deanery Reps—Deanery 1 - 20: Revs. RICHARD VEGA; ANTONIO CACCIAPUOTI; MICHAEL J. JENNETT; JOSEPH COSGROVE; ROBERT J. MCNAMARA; LAWRENCE C. SIGNEY; KEVIN L. NOLAN; Rev. Msgr. PETER L. AMY; Revs. JESSE C. GALAZ; STEVEN GUITRON; PEDRO J. LOPEZ; WILLIAM T. EASTERLING; JAMES H. BARNES; HENRY L. HERNANDO; EMILLE BELLETTY; DAVID O'CONNELL; EDWARD J. DOBER; JOHN WOOLWAY; ALEXEI R. SMITH; JEROME C. ELDER.

Member at Large—Rev. Msgr. CHARLES E. HILL.

Ex Officios—Most Rev. JOHN J. WARD; Most Rev. JUAN ARZUBE; Most Rev. STEPHEN E. BLAIRE; Most Rev. THOMAS J. CURRY; Most Rev. JOSEPH M. SARTORIS; Most Rev. GERALD E. WILKERSON; Most Rev. GABINO ZAVALA; Rev. Msgr. TERRANCE L. FLEMING, S.T.D.; Rev. Msgr. RICHARD A. LOOMIS; Rev. Msgr. JEREMIAH J. MCCARTHY.

Consultants and Liaisons—Rev. Msgr. RICHARD A. LOOMIS; Rev. RICHARD G. KREKELBERG; Rev. Msgr. LAURENCE E. CLARK.

Sisters' Council—Tel: 213-637-7559.

Vicar for Women Religious—Sr. M. Faith Clark, S.N.J.M., Ex Officio.

Members—Sr. IMELDA ALCOBER, O.P.; Sr. PATRICIA ARNOLD, C.S.J.; Sr. GLORIA MARIE AVILA, R.S.M.; Sr. VIOLA BACA, F.M.I.; Sr. RENEE BAUERLY, D.M.J.; Sr. COLETTE BOYLAN, S.S.L.; Sr. PHILOMENA BREEMANS, I.C.M.; Sr. VIRGINIA BUCHHOLZ, S.C.R.H.; Sr. RITA CAMPOS, O.S.F.; Sr. MARGARET CLARE, P.S.N.; Sr. ANTOINETTE CLAY, O.S.F.; Sr. CHRISTINA MARIE CONROY, C.S.S.F.; Sr. ANNE JOSEPH CROOKSTON, S.S.J.-T.O.S.F.; Sr. CAMILLE CUADRA, D.C.; Sr. MARY ROSE CUNNINGHAM, C.S.C.; Sr. LUCILLE DEAN, S.P.; Sr. MARY EMILY DEMUTH, C.S.C.; Sr. JULIE DERMODY, O.S.F.; Sr. CARMEN MARIE DIAZ, O.S.F.; Sr. THERESE DOHERTY, R.S.C.; Sr. BARBARA DUGAN, C.S.J.; Sr. FRANCES MICHELE DUNAJ, O.S.F.; Sr. MARIE CELINE ENRIGHT, S.B.S.; Sr. JOAN MARIE FARAONE, R.J.M.; Sr. LORETTA FLOOD, C.S.J.; Sr. ESTHER FONSECA, S.M.; Sr. ELVIRA GONZALEZ, H.C.J.S.; Sr. MARY BRIDE GORMLEY, O.S.B.; Sr. JANET HARRIS, P.B.V.M.; Sr. MARGARET HOGARTY, L.S.P.; Sr. BARBARINE HOUDEK, O.S.F.; Sr. MILDRED INKS, R.S.H.M.; Sr. ANNE KELLEY, R.G.S.; Sr. PACHOMIA KIM, O.S.B.; Sr. CAROL KENNING, S.N.D.deN; Sr. MARIAN KOZLOWSKI, O.L.V.M.; Sr. RENE LANGENECKER, O.S.F.; Sr. ANGELA LEE, I.H.M.; Sr. BERNITA LINDSTROM, O.S.F.; Sr. ROSARIO LIZARDI, O.C.D.; Sr. GRACE LOPEZ, E.F.M.S.; Sr. DOLORES MADDEN, C.H.F.; Sr. CARMEN MALDONADO, S.S.C.; Sr. HELEN MARKOV, S.N.J.M.; Sr. M. DIANE MARTIN, O.S.F.; Sr. MILAGROS MARTIN, R.A.D.; Sr. MARY MCCLUSKEY, C.C.V.I.; Sr. ANNE MCMULLEN, C.S.J.; Sr. MARY JOSEPH MEI, M.J.M.J.; Sr. PATRICIA NOBLE, M.M.; Sr. M. PRISCA NWOGU, D.M.M.M.; Sr. GUADALUPE PARTIDA, S.H.F.; Sr. JEANNINE PERCY, O.S.M.; Sr. CESIRA PIEROTTI, F.M.A.; Sr. AGNES RADAY, S.D.S.H.; Sr. MARY MICHAEL RAY, O.C.D.; Sr. HILDA MARIA REYNOSO, S.J.S.; Sr. ELISSA RINERE, C.P.; Sr. FRANCIS ROSE RIVERS, S.S.N.D.; Sr. MARY ERNEST ROTHE, B.V.M.; Sr. FLORELIA SALAZAR, C.V.D.; Sr. IRENE SAN ROMAN, O.S.F.; Sr. TERESITA SAAVEDRA, S.S.S.; Sr. M. LETITA SENEGAL, S.S.F.; Sr. JUDITH SCHOMISCH, D.C.; Sr. DONNA SHANAHAN, C.S.J.; Sr. ELIZABETH ANNE SHEEHEY, C.S.J.P.; Sr. MARY JOHN SHIN, I.H.M.; Sr. MARY ELIZABETH STRECKER, S.C.L.; Sr. RITA STUCKEY, I.H.M.; Sr. GAIL TENNEY, O.S.F.; Sr. MIRIAM JOSEPH TERESI, O.S.F.; Sr. MARY LISETTE VALENZUELA, S.N.D.; Sr. ANNA MARIE VASQUEZ, S.N.D.; Sr. CATHERINE WHITE, S.P.; Sr. ROSE MARIE WILSON, O.S.F.; Sr. GIULII ZOBELEIN, O.P.; ELAINE HRITZ, Sec.

Spirituality Commission—Rev. JAMES CLARKE, Chm. Tel: 213-637-7654. Rev. AUSTIN DORAN; Sr. LAURA GORMLEY, S.S.L.; IRMA ISIP; Sr. THOMAS BERNARD

MACCONNELL, C.S.J. Tel: 213-747-6508. Rev. KENNETH MCGUIRE, C.S.P.; Dr. PATRICK MITCHELL.

Theological Commission—Rev. Msgr. CRAIG A. COX, J.C.D., Dir. Tel: 213-637-7204. Sr. KAREN WILHELMY, C.S.J., M.A., Sec. Tel: 805-486-7301.

Members:—Revs. RICHARD B. BENSON, C.M., S.T.D.; JOHN P. BRENNAN, S.M.A., D.D.; DOUGLAS BURTON-CHRISTIE, Ph.D.; Rev. Msgr. EDWARD WILLIAM CLARK, S.T.D.; Revs. FRANCIS R. COLBORN, S.T.D.; LUKE DYSINGER, O.S.B., M.D.; PAUL FORD, Ph.D.; JAMES G. HANICK, Ph.D.; Sr. MAUREEN KELLY, S.S.L., Ph.D.; KEITH LEWIS, Ph.D.; Rev. Msgr. JEREMIAH MCCARTHY, Ph.D.; JOHN R. POPIDEN, Ph.D.; Rev. THOMAS P. RAUSCH, S.J., Ph.D.; Sr. ELISSA A. RINERE, C.P., J.C.D.

CLERGY, PARISHES, MISSIONS AND PAROCHIAL SCHOOLS

CITY OF LOS ANGELES
(Los Angeles County)

1—CATHEDRAL OF OUR LADY OF THE ANGELS (1876). Closed. For inquiries for Sacramental Records contact the Chancery.

2—CATHEDRAL CHAPEL (1927), Revs. Earl G. Walker; Marcial D. Juan, Admin. In res., Most Rev. Stephen E. Blaire.
Church—927 S. La Brea Ave., 90036.
Res., 922 S. Detroit St., 90036. Tel: 213-935-1128; Fax: 213-935-7308.
School—755 S. Cochran Ave., 90036. Tel: 213-938-9976; Fax: 213-938-9930.
Lay Teachers 11; Students 272.
Catechesis/Religious Programs—Students 272.

3—ALL SAINTS (1926) (Hispanic), Revs. Jose L. Vega, O.M.; Gino Vanzillotta, O.M.; Constantino Mandarino, O.M.
Rectory—3431 Portola Ave., 90032. Tel: 213-223-1101; Fax: 213-223-9592.
School—3420 Portola Ave., 90032. Tel: 213-225-7264.
Sisters 1; Lay Teachers 8; Students 280.
Catechesis/Religious Programs—Tel: 213-225-5193.
Students 485.

4—ASCENSION (1923) (Hispanic-African American), Rev. Leo W. Albert, Admin. In res., Rev. Charles Chaffman.
Res., 517 W. 112th St., 90044. Tel: 213-754-2978; Fax: 213-754-3905.
School—500 W. 111th Pl., 90044. Tel: 213-756-4064; Fax: 213-756-1060. Mr. Michael Browning, Prin.
Lay Teachers 9; Students 330.
Catechesis/Religious Programs—Tel: 213-777-6356.
Students 344.

5—ASSUMPTION (1926) (Hispanic), Revs. Diosdado Martin; Anthoney Gonzalez.
Res., 2832 Blanchard St., 90033. Tel: 213-269-8171; Fax: 213-269-0106.
School—3016 Winter St., 90063. Tel: 213-269-4319; Fax: 213-269-2434. Ms. Lydia Ortega, Prin.
Lay Teachers 8; Students 250.
Catechesis/Religious Programs—Tel: 213-269-5920.
Students 300.
Mission—Los Angeles, Assumption, 414 N. Fresno St., 90063. Tel: 213-264-6363.

6—BLESSED SACRAMENT (1924), Revs. Anastacio Rivera, S.J.; John J. Brennan, S.J.; James A. Rude, S.J.; William J. Brennan, S.J.; James R. Gallas, S.J.; Deacon Richard Morgan.
Res., 6657 Sunset Blvd., 90028. Tel: 213-462-6311; Fax: 213-462-0113.
School—6641 Sunset Blvd., 90028. Tel: 213-467-4177.
Lay Teachers 11; Students 263.
Catechesis/Religious Programs—Tel: 213-463-9820. Sr. Maria del Socorro Cuevas, E.I.N., D.R.E.
Students 451.

7—CHRIST THE KING (1926), Revs. Alexander George; Roberto F. Jaranilla, Jr.
Res., 624 N. Rossmore Ave., 90004. Tel: 213-465-7605; Fax: 213-463-4895.
School—617 N. Arden Blvd., 90004. Tel: 213-462-4753; Fax: 213-462-8475.
Lay Teachers 9; Students 245.
Catechesis/Religious Programs—Tel: 213-465-7084; Fax: 213-463-4895.
Students 300.

8—CRISTO REY (1954) (Hispanic), Revs. Jose Luis Jimenez, O.A.R.; Juan J. Orobiourritia, O.A.R. In res., Rev. Anthony Iroz, O.A.R.
Res., 4343 Perlita Ave., 90039. Tel: 213-245-4585; Fax: 818-247-8831. [CEM]
Catechesis/Religious Programs—Students 220.

9—DIVINE SAVIOUR (1907) (Hispanic), Revs. Thomas Boudreau; Miguel Plascencia. In res., Rev. Msgr. Charles Fortier.
Res., 610 Cypress Ave., 90065. Tel: 213-225-9181; Fax: 213-225-1099.
School—Tel: 213-222-6077; Fax: 213-225-1099.
Lay Teachers 9; Students 246.
Catechesis/Religious Programs—Alice Perez, D.R.E.
Students 868.

10—DOLORES MISSION (1945) (Hispanic), Revs. Michael E. Kennedy, S.J.; Gregory R. Baumann, S.J.; Gregory R. Bonfiglio, S.J.; Gregory J. Boyle, S.J.; Mr. Eddy Martinez, Admin. In res., Rev. Robert Dolan, S.J.
Res., 171 S. Gless St., 90033. Tel: 213-881-0039 (Church); Fax: 213-881-0034.
School—Tel: 213-881-0001. Mrs. Angelita G. Trevizo, Prin.
Lay Teachers 12; Students 278.
Catechesis/Religious Programs—Sr. Givlii Zobelein, O.P., D.R.E.
Students 258.

11—HOLY CROSS (1906) (African American-Hispanic), Revs. Xavier Colleoni, M.C.C.J. (Italy); Bartholomew Battirossi, M.C.C.J. (Italy); Peter McGinley, M.C.C.J. (United Kingdom); Bro. Robert Strabla, M.C.C.J. (Italy).
Res., 4705 S. Main St., 90037. Tel: 213-234-5984; Fax: 213-234-0130.
Catechesis/Religious Programs—Students 733.

12—HOLY NAME OF JESUS (1921), Revs. Francis R. Colborn; Emile Belletty; Deacon John Gaudin.
Res., 2190 W. 31st St., 90018. Tel: 213-734-8888; Fax: 213-734-8430.
School—Tel: 213-731-2255. Ms. Christina R. Whelan, Prin.
Lay Teachers 9; Students 308.
Catechesis/Religious Programs—Tel: 213-731-5448.
Students 250.

13—HOLY SPIRIT (1926), Rev. Msgr. Anthony Leuer; Deacon Armando Garcia. In res., Rev. Msgr. Michael W. Meyers.
Res., 1421 S. Dunsmuir Ave., 90019-4031. Tel: 213-935-1333; Fax: 213-935-7741.
School—(Grades K-4) 1418 S. Burnside Ave., 90019. Tel: 213-933-7775.
Sisters of the Holy Faith 2; Lay Teachers 4; Students 138.
Catechesis/Religious Programs—Students 280.

14—HOLY TRINITY (1925), Revs. James E. McElroy; John Daly; Thomas Peacha; Mark H.S. Cheong.
Res., 3722 Boyce Ave., 90039. Tel: 213-664-4723; Fax: 213-664-2581.
School—3716 Boyce Ave., 90039. Tel: 213-663-2064; Fax: 213-663-0732.
Lay Teachers 9; Students 284.
Catechesis/Religious Programs—Students 145.

15—IMMACULATE CONCEPTION (1908) (Hispanic), Revs. Pedro E. Amezcua (Mexico); Jose Trinidad Rodriguez (Mexico); Ariel Munoz (Mexico); Rafael Ochoa (Mexico).
Res., 1433 W. Ninth St., 90015. Tel: 213-384-1019; Fax: 213-384-0437.
School—830 Green St., 90017. Tel: 213-382-5931. Ms. Mary Ann Murphy, Prin.
Lay Teachers 9; Students 326.
Catechesis/Religious Programs—832 Green St., 90017. Tel: 213-389-7277.
Students 650.

16—IMMACULATE HEART OF MARY (1910), Revs. Henry L. Hernando; Mateo Hicarte; Deacon George Asmar. In res., Rev. Alex Aclan.
Res., 4950 Santa Monica Blvd., 90029. Tel: 213-660-0034; 662-0564; Fax: 213-660-8127.
School—1055 N. Alexandria Ave., 90029. Tel: 213-663-4611.
Sisters 1; Lay Teachers 11; Students 319.
Catechesis/Religious Programs—4954 W. Santa Monica Blvd., 90029. Tel: 213-667-2675.
Students 345.

17—MOTHER OF SORROWS (1923) (Hispanic-African American), Revs. Perry D. Leiker; Gilbert J. Cruz.
Res., 114 W. 87th St., 90003. Tel: 213-758-7697; Fax: 213-758-7853.
School—Tel: 213-758-6204. Mr. Brian Tate, Prin.
Lay Teachers 6; Students 151.
Catechesis/Religious Programs—Tel: 213-789-6316.
Students 550.

18—NATIVITY (1920) (Hispanic-African American), Rev. Msgr. Timothy J. Dyer; Rev. Michael D. Gutierrez.
Res., 953 W. 57th St., 90037. Tel: 213-759-1562; Fax: 213-759-7716.
School—Tel: 213-752-0720.
Lay Teachers 8; Students 190.
Catechesis/Religious Programs—Tel: 213-752-1770.
Students 1,080.
Loretto Literary & Benevolent Institution—.

19—NATIVITY OF BLESSED VIRGIN MARY (Ukrainian-Byzantine), Rev. Oleh Romanenko.
Res., 5154 De Longpre Ave., 90027. Tel: 213-663-6307; Fax: 213-663-0369.

20—OUR LADY OF SOLITUDE (1925) (Hispanic), Revs. Arnold Gonzalez, C.M.F.; Manuel Marrufo, C.M.F.; Bro. Ernesto Bravo, C.M.F.; Deacon Fernando Aranda.
Res., 4561 Cesar Chavez Ave., 90022. Tel: 213-269-7248.
School—4545 Dozier St., 90022. Tel: 213-261-1083; Fax: 213-261-5300. Margaret Bestwick, Prin.
Lay Teachers 11; Students 236.
Catechesis/Religious Programs—Tel: 213-269-7248, Ext. 22.
Students 360.

21—OUR LADY HELP OF CHRISTIANS (MARIA AUXILIADORA) (1927), Rev. Juan Santillan, Sch.P. In res., Revs. Raul Palma, Sch.P.; Francis Boronat, Sch.P.
Res., 512 S. Ave. 20, 90031. Tel: 213-223-4153; Fax: 213-223-1427.
School—2024 Darwin Ave., 90031. Tel: 213-222-3913; Fax: 213-222-2561. Sr. Celia Martinez, M.C., Prin.
Poor Clare Missionary Sisters 5; Lay Teachers 6; Students 300.
Catechesis/Religious Programs—Tel: 213-225-2846.
Students 200.

22—OUR LADY OF THE BRIGHT MOUNT (1925) (Polish), Revs. Edward Mroczynski, S.Chr. (Poland); Rafal Dopierala, S.Chr. (Poland). In res., Rev. Wojciech M. Kania, S.Chr.
Res., 3424 W. Adams Blvd., 90018. Tel: 213-734-5249; Fax: 213-734-0046.
Catechesis/Religious Programs—Students 160.
Convent—Tel: 213-734-0899.
Missionary Sisters of Christ the King (Polonia) 3.

23—OUR LADY OF GUADALUPE (1923) (Hispanic), Revs. Robert Juarez; Pedro Antonio Esteban.
Res., 4018 Hammel St., 90063. Tel: 213-261-8051; Fax: 213-261-1259.
School—436 Hazard Ave., 90063. Tel: 213-269-4998; Fax: 213-261-1259.
Lay Teachers 9; Students 260.
Catechesis/Religious Programs—Tel: 213-262-7957.
Students 454.
Mission—Los Angeles, Los Angeles Co., San Felipe, 738 N. Geraghty Ave., 90063. Tel: 213-266-1433.

24—OUR LADY OF GUADALUPE (Rosehill) (1928) (Hispanic), Revs. Thomas E. Baker; Gustavo Lara; Stephen C. Hernandez, (Retired); Deacon Miguel Arroyo.
Res., 4509 Mercury Ave., 90032. Tel: 213-225-4201; Fax: 213-225-3668.
School—4504 Browne Ave., 90032. Tel: 213-221-8187.
Missionary Sisters of the Immaculate Heart of Mary 2; Lay Teachers 8; Students 284.
Catechesis/Religious Programs—Tel: 213-223-1777.
Students 425.

25—OUR LADY OF LORETTO (1905), Revs. Eamonn Donnelly, S.V.D.; Gerard O'Doherty, S.V.D.; Luc Trah, S.V.D.
Res., 250 N. Union Ave., 90026. Tel: 213-483-3013; Fax: 213-483-3017.
School—258 N. Union Ave., 90026. Tel: 213-483-5251; Fax: 213-463-6709.
Lay Teachers 8; Students 350.
Catechesis/Religious Programs—Students 295.

26—OUR LADY OF LOURDES (1910), Revs. Richard Siebenand; Alfred Hernandez. In res., Rev. Angel Mafezzini (Argentina).
Res., 3772 E. Third St., 90063. Tel: 213-526-3800; Fax: 213-526-3807.
School—315 S. Eastman Ave., 90063. Tel: 213-526-3813; Fax: 213-526-3814.
Lay Teachers 9; Students 259.
Catechesis/Religious Programs—Tel: 213-526-3804.
Students 680.

27—OUR LADY OF VICTORY (1966) (Spanish), Revs. Norbert Sharon, S.T.; Edward J. Sittinger, S.T.
Res., 1316 S. Herbert Ave., 90023. Tel: 213-268-9502; Fax: 213-780-3670.
Catechesis/Religious Programs—1317 S. Herbert Ave., 90023. Tel: 213-262-2101.
Students 650.

28—OUR LADY QUEEN OF THE ANGELS (1781) (Spanish), Revs. Albert M. Vazquez, C.M.F.; Joseph M. Gamm, C.M.F.; Domingo Zuniga, C.M.F.; Albert Domingo, C.M.F.
Res., 535 N. Main St., 90012. Tel: 213-629-3101; Fax: 213-629-1951.

Catechesis/Religious Programs—Students 899.

29—OUR LADY OF THE ROSARY OF TALPA (1928) (Mexican), Revs. Francisco Mateos, C.M.; Angel Oyanguren, C.M.; Helios del Cerro, C.M.; Felix Sarachaga, C.M.
Res., 2914 E. Fourth St., 90033. Tel: 213-268-9176; Fax: 213-268-4026.
School—411 S. Evergreen Ave., 90033. Tel: 213-261-0583; Fax: 213-261-0352.
Daughters of Charity of St. Vincent de Paul 2; Lay Teachers 8; Students 270.
Catechesis/Religious Programs—Tel: 213-264-3345.
Students 470.
Convent—427 S. Evergreen St., 90033. Tel: 213-268-7731.
Mission—Los Angeles, Los Angeles Co., La Purisima Chapel, 3236 Inez St., 90023.

30—OUR LADY QUEEN OF MARTYRS (Armenian), Revs. Raphael Minassian, P.I.A.; Basil Ferhatian, C.M.Vd.
Res., 1327 Pleasant Ave., 90033. Tel: 213-261-9898; Fax: 213-261-0522.

31—MOTHER OF GOOD COUNSEL (1925), Revs. Michael J. McFadden, O.S.A.; Anthony J. Wasko, O.S.A.; Gary C. Rye, O.S.A.
Res., 2060 N. Vermont Ave., 90027. Tel: 213-664-2111; Fax: 213-664-0556.
School—4622 Ambrose Ave., 90027. Tel: 213-664-2131; Fax: 213-664-1906. Miss Tina Katherine Kipp, Prin.
Sisters 1; Lay Teachers 8; Students 312.
Catechesis/Religious Programs—Students 312.

32—OUR SAVIOUR CATHOLIC CENTER (1957), Rev. William Messenger.
Res., 3207 University Ave., 90007. Tel: 213-749-5341; Fax: 213-749-3475.

33—PRECIOUS BLOOD (1923), Rev. Philip M. Kavanaugh. In res., Rev. Richard G. Krekelberg.
Res., 435 S. Occidental Blvd., 90057. Tel: 213-389-8439; Fax: 213-389-1951.
School—307 S. Occidental Blvd., 90057. Tel: 213-382-3345; Fax: 213-382-2078.
Lay Teachers 9; Students 200.
Catechesis/Religious Programs—Students 255.

34—PRESENTATION OF THE B.V.M. (1925) (Hispanic), Revs. Benigno A. Rodriguez; Antonio Garcia (Mexico).
Res., 6406 Parmelee Ave., 90001. Tel: 213-585-0570; Fax: 213-585-8148.
Catechesis/Religious Programs—Students 535.

35—RESURRECTION (1923) (Mexican), Rev. Msgr. John T. Moretta; Revs. Carl Tressler; Rafael Casillas; Deacons Richard Fajardo; Hernando Rodriguez.
Res., 3324 E. Opal St., 90023. Tel: 213-268-1141; Fax: 213-268-1143.
School—3360 E. Opal St., 90023. Tel: 213-261-5750. Mr. Daniel Vidal, Prin.
Franciscan Sisters of Mary Immaculate 2; Lay Teachers 8; Students 300.
Catechesis/Religious Programs—Students 1,073.

36—SACRED HEART (1887) (Hispanic), Revs. Gabriel Gonzales; Jesus A. Parra; Mr. Fred Flores, Admin. In res., Rev. George Horan.
Res., 2210 Sichel St., 90031. Tel: 213-221-3179; Fax: 213-221-3613.
School—2109 Sichel St., 90031. Tel: 213-225-4177; Fax: 213-225-2615.
Dominican Sisters of Mission San Jose 3; Lay Teachers 10; Students 316.
Catechesis/Religious Programs—Tel: 213-223-7571.
Students 510.
Convent—2108 Sichel St., 90031. Tel: 213-222-5157.

37—ST. AGATHA (1923), Rev. Ken Deasy; Deacon Hosea Alexander.
Res., 2610 S. Mansfield Ave., 90016. Tel: 213-935-8127; Fax: 213-939-3547.
Catechesis/Religious Programs—Tel: 213-933-0963.
Students 450.

38—ST. AGNES (1903) (Hispanic-Korean), Revs. William Delaney, C.PP.S.; John Franck, C.PP.S.; Sae Eul Kim.
Res., 2625 S. Vermont Ave., 90007. Tel: 213-731-2464; Fax: 213-731-6186.
School—Tel: 213-734-6441.
Sisters of the Holy Cross 2; Lay Teachers 8; Students 352.
Catechesis/Religious Programs—Tel: 213-731-0014. Sr. Iris Flores, C.PP.S., D.R.E.
Students 750.

39—ST. ALOYSIUS GONZAGA (1908) (Hispanic), Revs. George Aguilera; Ubaldo Chueca.
Res., 7814 Crocket Blvd., 90001. Tel: 213-585-4485; Fax: 213-589-8485.
School—Tel: 213-582-4965. Sr. Anna Marie Law, S.M., Prin.
Lay Teachers 8; Students 236.
Catechesis/Religious Programs—2023 E. Nadeau St., Tel: 213-582-7990.
Students 560.

40—ST. ALPHONSUS (1935) (Hispanic), Revs. Jesse C. Galaz; Joshua Peter Lee; Simon Orozco.
Res., 5223 Hastings St., 90022-2699. Tel: 213-264-3353; Fax: 213-264-4858.
School—Tel: 213-268-5165.
Lay Teachers 9; Students 315.
Catechesis/Religious Programs—552 South Amalia Ave., 90022. Tel: 213-266-0855.
Students 500.

41—ST. AMBROSE (1924), Rev. Michael Wakefield, Admin. In res., Revs. Bruno Massacavolo; Michael Wempe; Bede Warrington.
Res., 1281 N. Fairfax Ave., 90046. Tel: 213-656-4433; Fax: 213-656-6634.

42—ST. ANASTASIA (1953), Rev. Msgr. Royale M. Vadakin. In res., Rev. Msgr. Gregory A. Cox.
Res., 7390 W. Manchester Ave., 90045. Tel: 310-670-2243; Fax: 310-670-5052.
School—8631 S. Stanmoor Dr., 90045. Tel: 310-645-8816; Fax: 310-645-6923. Mrs. Rosemary Connolly, Prin.
Lay Teachers 20; Students 300.
Catechesis/Religious Programs—Tel: 310-215-9806.
Students 190.

43—ST. ANN (1937), Rev. Hugh Crowe; Rev. Msgr. John R. Brosnan, Pastor Emeritus.
Office: 1365 Blake Ave., 90031. Tel: 213-221-6368.
Res., 2302 Riverdale Ave., 90031. Tel: 213-221-6968; Fax: 213-276-9351.
Catechesis/Religious Programs—Sr. Eileen Collins, S.H.F., D.R.E.
Students 235.

44—ST. ANSELM (1924), Rev. Lawrence Shelton.
Res., 2222 W. 70th St., 90043. Tel: 213-758-6729; Fax: 213-758-8455.
School—7019 S. Van Ness Ave., 90043. Tel: 213-759-9371; Fax: 213-759-1131.
Lay Teachers 9; Students 280.

45—ST. ANTHONY (1910) (Croatian), Revs. John Segaric; Petar Vuletic (Croatia); Rev. Msgr. Felix S. Diomartich, Pastor Emeritus.
Res., 712 N. Grand Ave., 90012. Tel: 213-628-2938; Fax: 213-628-1635.

46—SAN ANTONIO DE PADUA (1926) (Hispanic), Rev. Msgr. Joseph W. Herres.
Res., 555 N. Fairview Ave., 90033. Tel: 213-225-1301; Fax: 213-225-2534.
School—1500 Bridge St., 90033. Tel: 213-221-6970; Fax: 213-343-3983.
Sisters of the Company of Mary 3; Lay Teachers 7; Students 287.
Catechesis/Religious Programs—Tel: 213-225-1086.
Students 180.

47—ST. BASIL'S (1920), Revs. M. Francis Meskill; Abelardo Luistro; Matthew Yoo.
Res., 637 S. Kingsley Dr., 90005. Tel: 213-381-6191; Fax: 213-382-5883. [CEM]
Catechesis/Religious Programs—Students 120.

48—ST. BERNADETTE (1947) (African American), Revs. Patrick J. Gorman; Emile Belletty; Deacon Emile Adams.
Res., 3825 Don Felipe Dr., 90008. Tel: 213-293-4877; Fax: 213-293-2838.
School—4196 Marlton Ave., 90008. Tel: 213-291-4284. Sr. Joan Mary O'Dwyer, C.S.J., Prin.
Sisters 3; Lay Teachers 9; Students 291.
Catechesis/Religious Programs—Students 89.

49—ST. BERNARD (1924), Rev. Msgr. Patrick McNulty, Pastor Emeritus; Rev. Gerald McSorley. In res., Rev. Patrick J. Hill.
Res., 2500 W. Ave. 33, 90065. Tel: 213-255-6142; Fax: 213-255-2351.
School—Tel: 213-256-4989.
Sisters of Charity of the Blessed Virgin Mary 2; Lay Teachers 9; Students 284.
Catechesis/Religious Programs—2515 W. Ave. 33, 90065. Tel: 213-256-6242.
Students 400.

50—ST. BRENDAN (1915), Rev. Msgr. Jeremiah T. Murphy. In res., Rev. Timothy Cahalane, M.S.C.
Res., 310 S. Van Ness Ave., 90020. Tel: 213-936-4656.
School—238 S. Manhatten Pl., 90004. Tel: 213-382-7401.
Sisters 2; Lay Teachers 10; Students 310.

51—ST. BRIGID'S (1920) (African American-Hispanic), Very Rev. Charles Andrus, S.S.J.; Rev. Fernando Arizti, S.J.; Deacons Gilbert Lanoix; William Hawkins, Jr.
Res., 5214 S. Western Ave., 90062. Tel: 213-292-0781; Fax: 213-290-1254.

52—ST. BRIDGET'S CHINESE CATHOLIC CENTER (1940) (Chinese), Rev. Joseph Cheng, S.D.B. (China).
Res., 445 1/2 Cottage Home St., 90012. Tel: 213-222-5518; Fax: 213-222-0814.
Church—510 Cottage Home, 90012. [JC]

53—ST. CAMILLUS DE LELLIS (1952). (Center for Pastoral Care). Revs. Christopher D. Ponnet, Dir.; Gustavo Lara, Chap.; Bob Jones, C.M., Chap.; Mike Baker, Chap.; Sr. Dora Hauchecorne, I.C.M., Chap.; Sr. Maria Perez, Chap.; Sr. Matilde Ortiz, Chap.; Sr. Mary Jean Ferry, B.V.M., Chap.; Deacon James Dillon; Mr. Jorge Manly-Gil, Chap. In res., Rev. Msgr. Terrence Richey.
Res., 1911 Zonal Ave., 90033-1032. Tel: 213-225-4461; Fax: 213-225-9096.

54—ST. CASIMIR (1946) (Lithuanian), Rev. Msgr. Algirdas Olsaukas; Rev. Msgr. John A. Kucingis; Rev. Stanislovas Anuzis.
Res., 2718 St. George St., 90027. Tel: 213-664-4660.
School—2716 St. George St., 90027. Tel: 213-661-9200; Fax: 213-668-1440.
Lay Teachers 9; Students 250.
Catechesis/Religious Programs—Students 110.

55—ST. CECILIA (1909), Revs. Luigi Zanotto, M.C.C.J.; Gerardo De Tomasi, M.C.C.J.; Sergio Contran, M.C.C.J.
Res., 4230 S. Normandie Ave., 90037. Tel: 213-294-6628; Fax: 213-294-3310.
School—4224 S. Normandie Ave., 90037. Tel: 213-293-4266.
Sisters of St. Joseph of Carondelet 2; Lay Teachers 8; Students 240.
Catechesis/Religious Programs—Tel: 213-295-5283.
Students 300.

56—ST. COLUMBAN (1945) (Filipino), Revs. Colm Rafferty; Sean McGrath.
Res., 125 S. Loma Dr., 90026. Tel: 213-250-8818; Fax: 213-250-9476.

57—ST. COLUMBKILLE (1921) (Hispanic-African American), Revs. Timothy J. Dyer; Michael Gutierrez. In res., Rev. Paul Hruby.
Res., 6315 S. Main St., 90003. Tel: 213-758-5540; Fax: 213-758-8108.
School—145 W. 64th St., 90003. Tel: 213-758-2284.
Sisters 2; Lay Teachers 6; Students 197.
Catechesis/Religious Programs—Students 460.

58—SAN CONRADO MISSION (1966). Unassigned.
Church & Mailing Address—1820 Bouett St., 90012. Tel: 213-223-6581.

59—ST. DOMINIC (1921), Revs. Anthony M. Patalano, O.P.; Martin Diaz, O.P.; Juan Carlos Diaz-Flores, O.P. In res., Rev. Aquinas Costello, O.P.; Bro. Frederick Narberes, O.P.
Res., 2002 Merton Ave., 90041. Tel: 213-254-2519; Fax: 213-255-3067.
School—Tel: 213-255-5803; Fax: 213-255-3067.
Dominican Sisters of San Rafael 1; Lay Teachers 18; Students 499.
Catechesis/Religious Programs—Tel: 213-255-6373.
Students 249.

60—ST. EUGENE (1942), Revs. Patrick J. Walsh; Paul F. Menke.
Res., 9505 Haas Ave., 90047. Tel: 213-757-3121; Fax: 213-757-8872.
School—9521 Haas Ave., 90047. Tel: 213-754-9536; Fax: 213-754-0913.
Lay Teachers 15; Students 260.

61—ST. FRANCES XAVIER CABRINI (1946), Rev. David O'Connell; Sr. Teresita Carrillo, R.S.H.M., Pastoral Assoc.
Res., 1440 W. Imperial Hwy., 90047. Tel: 213-757-0271; Fax: 213-757-9267.
School—1428 W. Imperial Hwy., 90047. Tel: 213-756-1354; Fax: 213-756-1157. Sr. Celeste Botello, O.P., Prin.
Dominican Sisters 2; Lay Teachers 7; Students 283.
Catechesis/Religious Programs—Tel: 213-756-8111.
Students 368.

62—SAN FRANCISCO CHURCH (1982) (Mexican), Rev. Severiano Castaneda; Deacon Benjamin Torres.
Res., 4800 E. Olympic Blvd., 90022. Tel: 213-262-4253; Fax: 213-268-8246. [CEM]
Catechesis/Religious Programs—Tel: 213-261-2447.
Students 413.

63—MARYKNOLL JAPANESE CATHOLIC CENTER (1921) (Japanese), Rev. Henry G. Mair, S.A., Admin. In res., Rev. David L. Doerner, S.A.
Res., 222 S. Hewitt St., 90012. Tel: 213-626-2279; Fax: 213-628-1757.
Catechesis/Religious Programs—Students 30.
Chapel—St. Francis Xavier.

64—ST. FRANCIS OF ASSISI (1921), Revs. Pasquale Vuoso, C.R.I.C.; Charles R. Lueras, C.R.I.C.; James G. Garceau, C.R.I.C.; Sergio E. Garcia, C.R.I.C.
Res., 1523 Golden Gate Ave., 90026. Tel: 213-664-1305; Fax: 213-664-4975.

School—1550 Maltman Ave., 90026. Tel: 213-665-3601.
Sisters of Notre Dame 4; Lay Teachers 8; Students 254.
Catechesis/Religious Programs—Tel: 213-664-9033.
Students 250.

65—ST. GERARD MAJELLA (1952), Revs. William J. Connor; Bernard Eatlin. In res., Revs. Emmanuel Osuji (Nigeria); Pius Itodo.
Res., 4439 Inglewood Blvd., 90066. Tel: 310-390-5034; Fax: 310-397-0964.
School—Tel: 310-397-9489.
Lay Teachers 13; Students 268.
Catechesis/Religious Programs—Tel: 310-391-9637.
Students 590.

66—ST. GREGORY NAZIANZEN (1923), Revs. Edward J. Johnson; Noel Ryan; Paul White, S.S.C.
Res., 900 S. Bronson Ave., 90019. Tel: 213-935-4224; Fax: 213-934-0016.
School—Tel: 213-936-2542; Fax: 213-936-1690. Ellinor Collins, Prin.
Religious 1; Lay Teachers 8; Students 260.
Catechesis/Religious Programs—Tel: 213-935-4701.
Students 200.

67—ST. IGNATIUS OF LOYOLA (1911), Revs. Arturo Velasco; Evaristus M. Eshiowu (Nigeria). In res., Rev. Nelson Trinidad.
Res., 322 N. Ave. 61, 90042. Tel: 213-256-3041; Fax: 213-256-0105.
School—6025 Monte Vista St., 90042. Tel: 213-255-6456; Fax: 213-255-0959.
Dominican Sisters, San Jose Mission 4; Lay Teachers 9; Students 316.
Catechesis/Religious Programs—Tel: 213-254-9073.
Students 600.

68—SANTA ISABEL (1915) (Hispanic), Revs. Luis Eduardo Larrea, M.F.E.; Rafael Alvarez, O.F.M.
Res., 918 S. Soto St., 90023. Tel: 213-268-4065; Fax: 213-268-4180.
School—2424 Whittier Blvd., 90023. Tel: 213-263-3716.
School Sisters of Notre Dame 5; Lay Teachers 7; Students 285.
Catechesis/Religious Programs—Tel: 213-268-3019.
Students 425.
Convent—943 S. Soto St., 90023. Tel: 213-262-1711; 264-6556; Fax: 213-526-1655.
Misioneras Eucaristicas Franciscanas 8.

69—ST. JEROME (1949), Revs. James F. Kavanagh; Michael Ume; Deacon Paul Weber.
Res., 5550 Thornburn St., 90045. Tel: 310-348-8212; Fax: 310-417-3577.
School—Tel: 310-670-1678.
Sisters of St. Joseph of Carondelet 3; Lay Teachers 9; Students 300.
Catechesis/Religious Programs—Tel: 310-645-8318.
Students 252.
Convent—5570 Thornburn St., 90045. Tel: 310-670-8838.

70—ST. JOAN OF ARC (1943) (Spanish), Revs. James H. Barnes; John F. Cunningham, Pastor Emeritus; John Higgins; Rev. Msgr. Robert F. Condon, Pastor Emeritus; Rev. Frederick Byaruhanga (Uganda).
Res., 11534 Gateway Blvd., 90064. Tel: 310-479-5111; Fax: 310-479-2513.
School—11561 Gateway Blvd., 90064. Tel: 310-479-3607.
Lay Teachers 8; Students 230.
Catechesis/Religious Programs—Students 145.

71—ST. JOHN, THE EVANGELIST (1909) (Mexican-African American), Revs. Melvin P. James, S.V.D.; Efrain Flores, S.V.D.; Deacon Willard Hall. In res., Revs. George Stephan, S.V.D.; Fisher Robinson, S.V.D.; Bro. Jeremiah M. Walsh, S.V.D.
Res., 6028 Victoria Ave., 90043. Tel: 213-758-9161; Fax: 213-758-0112.
School—Tel: 213-751-8545. Carla Cotton, Prin.
Lay Teachers 9; Students 240.
Catechesis/Religious Programs—Tel: 213-758-8735.
Students 200.

72—ST. JOSEPH (1888) (Hispanic), Revs. Raymond Tintle, O.F.M.; Alan McCoy, O.F.M.; Martial Luebke, O.F.M.; Enrique Parisi, O.F.M., Cursillo; Eugene David Burnett, O.F.M.; Angus C. Cooper, O.F.M.; Pedro Umana, O.F.M.; William Brand, O.F.M.; Emil Kyranon, O.F.M.; Kurt Schweiss, O.F.M.; Bros. Gerald Chumick, O.F.M.; Martin Soto, O.F.M.
Res., 218 E. 12th St., 90015. Tel: 213-748-5394; Fax: 213-748-4793.
School—Tel: 213-749-8894; Fax: 213-749-0424. Sr. Jean Marie Chavez, O.S.F., Prin.
Sisters 2; Brothers 1; Lay Teachers 7; Students 197.
Catechesis/Religious Programs—Students 130.
Mission—Los Angeles, St. Turibius, 1530 Essex, 90021.

73—ST. KEVIN (1923) (Hispanic-Filipino), Rev. Leo E. Steinbock. In res., Revs. Francis J. Cullen (Ireland); Ramon R. Andreu, S.J. (Spain).
Res., 4072 Beverly Blvd., 90004. Tel: 213-383-8206; Fax: 213-386-4390.
Catechesis/Religious Programs—Students 174.

74—ST. LAWRENCE OF BRINDISI (1908) (African American-Hispanic). Capuchin Franciscan Friary. Revs. Edward O'Keefe, O.F.M.Cap.; James L. Cleary, O.F.M.Cap.; Tony Marti, O.F.M.Cap.
Res., 10122 Compton Ave., 90002. Tel: 213-567-1439; Fax: 213-564-4050.
School—10044 Compton Ave., 90002. Tel: 213-564-3051.
Sisters of Notre Dame 3; Lay Teachers 8; Students 237.
Catechesis/Religious Programs—Tel: 213-567-4698.
Students 506.

75—ST. LUCY (1970) (Hispanic), Revs. Vicente Casaus, Sch.P.; Jose Maria Aguilar, Sch.P. In res., Rev. Romualdo M. Gonzalez, Sch.P.
Res., 1419 N. Hazard Ave., 90063. Tel: 213-266-0451; Fax: 213-266-4907. [CEM]

76—ST. MALACHY (1926) (Hispanic), Revs. William J. Bonner, S.V.D.; Enrique Huerta, S.V.D. In res., Rev. William Adams, S.V.D.
Res., 1221 E. 82nd St., 90001. Tel: 213-585-1437; Fax: 213-583-5391.
School—1220 E. 81st St., 90001. Tel: 213-582-3112.
Lay Teachers 8; Students 215.
Catechesis/Religious Programs—Tel: 213-582-0203. Sr. Magnolia, D.R.E.
Students 428.
Convent—St. Malachy Convent, 1228 E. 81st St., 90001. Tel: 213-582-0203. Missionaries of Jesus Crucified
Sisters 6.

77—ST. MARCELLINUS (1957), Rev. Jules A. Mayer.
Res., 2349 Strong Ave., 90040. Tel: 213-269-2733.
Catechesis/Religious Programs—Tel: 213-266-4938.
Students 160.

78—ST. MARTIN OF TOURS (1946), Rev. Msgr. Lawrence O'Leary; Rev. Donal Keohane (Ireland).
Res., 11967 Sunset Blvd., 90049. Tel: 310-476-7403; Fax: 310-440-0290.
Church—11967 Sunset Blvd., 90049.
School—Tel: 310-472-7419; Fax: 310-440-2298.
Sisters 2; Lay Teachers 13; Students 287.
Catechesis/Religious Programs—Tel: 310-472-1757.
Students 280.

79—ST. MARY (1886), Revs. James Nieblas, S.D.B.; Cresenciano Salcedo, S.D.B.; J. Francisco Munoz, S.D.B.; Lucian B. Lomello, S.D.B., Hospital Chap.
Res., 407 S. Chicago St., 90033. Tel: 213-268-7432; Fax: 213-268-8076.
School—(Grades PreK-8). Tel: 213-262-3395.
Daughters of Mary Help of Christians 2; Lay Teachers 12; Students 320.
Catechesis/Religious Programs—Tel: 213-268-7317.
Students 420.

80—ST. MARY MAGDALEN (1930), Revs. Patrick H. Sullivan; Patrick Adejoh.
Res., 1241 Corning St., LA, 90035. Tel: 213-655-7868.
School—Tel: 310-652-4723.
Sisters of the Holy Faith 1; Lay Teachers 6; Students 105.

81—ST. MICHAEL (1907) (Hispanic-African American), Revs. Bruce Correlo; Gilbert J. Cruz.
Res., 1016 W. Manchester Ave., 90044. Tel: 213-753-2696; Fax: 213-753-3475.
School—(Grades K-8) 1027 W. 87th St., 90044. Tel: 213-752-6101.
Dominican Sisters of Mission San Jose 3; Lay Teachers 6; Students 270.
Catechesis/Religious Programs—Tel: 213-753-2976.
Students 250.

82—SAN MIGUEL (1927) (Hispanic), Revs. Gabino Perez, O.A.R.; James McGuire, O.A.R.
Res., 2214 E. 108th St., 90059. Tel: 213-569-5951; Fax: 213-567-1850.
School—2270 E. 108th St., 90059. Tel: 213-567-6892.
Lay Teachers 11; Students 194.
Catechesis/Religious Programs—Students 425.

83—ST. ODILIA (1926) (African American-Hispanic), Revs. William F. Drobach, S.A.; Wilfred Tyrrell, S.A. In res., Bro. Marco Raposo, S.A.
Res., 5222 Hooper Ave., 90011. Tel: 213-231-5930; Fax: 213-231-9714.
School—5300 S. Hooper Ave., 90011. Tel: 213-232-5449. Ms. Helen Reneau-Martinez, Prin.
Lay Teachers 7; Students 230.
Catechesis/Religious Programs—Tel: 213-233-2651.
Students 440.
Mission—Los Angeles, Los Angeles Co., St. John Bosco, 5516 Duarte St., 90058.

84—ST. PATRICK (1904) (Hispanic), Rev. Francisco X. Ramirez.
Res., 1046 E. 34th St., 90011. Tel: 213-234-5963; Fax: 213-234-6725.
Catechesis/Religious Programs—Tel: 213-232-5460.
Students 283.

85—ST. PAUL (1917), Revs. Eugenio Romo, M.G.; Enrique Hernandez, M.G.
Office: 1920 S. Bronson Ave., 90018. Tel: 213-730-9490; Fax: 213-734-5266.
Res., 4112 W. Washington Blvd., 90018.
School—1908 S. Bronson Ave., 90018. Tel: 213-734-4022. Mrs. Iris Trouillier, Prin.
Lay Teachers 8; Students 285.
Catechesis/Religious Programs—Tel: 213-730-9492.
Students 342.

86—ST. PAUL THE APOSTLE (1928), Revs. William Edens, C.S.P., Supr.; William T. Kenney, C.S.P.; Ellwood E. Kieser, C.S.P.; Harold J. Powers, C.S.P.; James DiLuzio, C.S.P.; Paul A. Lannan; Theodore A. Vierra; Edward D. Wrobleski, C.S.P.; Jeremiah Sullivan, C.S.P.; Robert P. Curtis, C.S.P.; Mark A. Villano; John W. Mulhall, C.S.P.; James McNulty.
Res., 10750 Ohio Ave., 90024. Tel: 310-474-1527; Fax: 310-474-2897.
School—Tel: 310-474-1588; Fax: 310-474-4272.
Daughters of Mary and Joseph 2; Lay Teachers 27; Students 537.
Catechesis/Religious Programs—Students 220.

87—ST. PETER (1904) (Italian), Rev. Angelo Bordignon, C.S.
Res. & Mailing Address: 1039 N. Broadway, 90012-1429. Tel: 213-225-8119; Fax: 213-225-0085.

88—ST. RAPHAEL (1924) (Hispanic-African American), Revs. Tracy O'Sullivan, O.Carm.; Felix Rivera, O.Carm.; Mr. Jaime Morales, Pastoral Assoc.; Sr. Brigida Riveros, Dir. Hispanic Ministry; Mr. Harry Wiley, Dir. African American Ministry.
Res., 942 W. 70th St., 90044. Tel: 213-758-7100; Fax: 213-758-7134.
School—924 W. 70th St., 90044. Tel: 213-751-2774; Fax: 213-751-1244. Mrs. Anne Bouvet, Prin.
Sisters 1; Lay Teachers 8; Students 280.
Catechesis/Religious Programs—Tel: 213-752-5965.
Students 315.

89—ST. SEBASTIAN (1924), Rev. Aidan Comerford.
Res., 1453 Federal Ave., 90025-2301. Tel: 310-478-0136; Fax: 310-478-0137.
Parish Center—11607 Ohio Ave., 90025.
School—1430 Federal Ave. W., 90025. Tel: 310-473-3337; Fax: 310-473-3178.
Lay Teachers 12; Students 200.
Catechesis/Religious Programs—Tel: 310-478-4446.
Students 200.

90—ST. STEPHEN (1928) (Hungarian-German), Rev. Hermann-Joseph K. Rettig, O.Praem.
Res., 3705 Woodlawn Ave., 90011. Tel: 213-234-9246; Fax: 213-234-2455.
Catechesis/Religious Programs—Students 180.

91—ST. TERESA OF AVILA (1921), Revs. Alexander Salazar; Thomas W. McLaughlin, Pastor Emeritus.
Res., 2216 Fargo St., 90039. Tel: 213-664-8426; Fax: 213-665-3115.
School—(Grades K-8) 2215 Fargo St., 90039. Tel: 213-662-3777; Fax: 213-662-3420.
Lay Teachers 9; Students 291.
Catechesis/Religious Programs—Students 260.
Convent—2223 Fargo St., 90039. Tel: 213-661-4284.

92—SANTA TERESITA (1923) (Hispanic), Revs. Salvador Cudinach, Sch.P.; Manuel Sanahuja, Sch.P.
Res., 2645 Zonal Ave., 90033. Tel: 213-221-2446; Fax: 213-221-2216.
School—(Grades K-8) 2646 Zonal Ave., 90033. Tel: 213-221-1129; Fax: 213-221-6339.
Dominican Sisters 4; Lay Teachers 8; Students 275.
Catechesis/Religious Programs—Tel: 213-221-2511.
Students 429.

93—ST. THOMAS THE APOSTLE (1903) (Hispanic), Revs. Dennis O'Neil; J. Rigoberto Rodriguez; Juan Silva; Jose Perez (Venezuela).
Res., 1321 S. Mariposa Ave., 90006. Tel: 213-737-3325; Fax: 213-737-2665.
School—Tel: 213-737-4730; Fax: 213-737-6348.
Lay Teachers 10; Students 315.

Catechesis/Religious Programs—Tel: 213-737-5624.
Students 1,400.

94—ST. TIMOTHY (1943), Rev. William J. Brelsford.
Res., 10425 W. Pico Blvd., 90064. Tel: 310-474-1216; Fax: 310-475-6047.
School—Tel: 310-474-1811; Fax: 310-470-1391. Sr. Francis Marie DiNardo, S.N.D., Prin.
Lay Teachers 13; Students 260.

95—ST. VINCENT DE PAUL (1887), Revs. Antonio Ruiz, C.M.; Thomas H. Cargo, C.M.; Bro. Anthony B. Wiedemer, C.M., Admin. In res., Rev. Joseph L. Brennan, C.M.
Res., 621 W. Adams Blvd., 90007. Tel: 213-749-8950; Fax: 213-749-9137.
School—2333 S. Figueroa St., 90007. Tel: 213-748-5367.
Sisters 3; Lay Teachers 7; Students 330.
Catechesis/Religious Programs—Tel: 213-741-9347.
Students 420.
Mission—Santo Nino.

96—SANCTUARY OF OUR LADY OF GUADALUPE (1929) (Hispanic), Rev. Leslie N. Delgado (Panama).
Res., 4100 E. Second St., 90063. Tel: 213-261-4365; Fax: 213-261-2735.
Catechesis/Religious Programs—Students 351.

97—TRANSFIGURATION (1923) (African American), Rev. Msgr. Robert E. Howard; Revs. Emile Belletty; Michael Grieco.
Res., 2515 W. Martin Luther King Blvd., 90008. Tel: 213-291-1136; Fax: 213-291-8216.
School—4020 Roxton Ave., 90008. Tel: 213-292-3011; Fax: 213-292-1527.
Lay Teachers 11; Students 280.

98—VISITATION (1943), Rev. James F. O'Grady. In res., Rev. Msgr. Thomas Joseph O'Sullivan; Rev. Laurence Spiteri.
Res., 6561 W. 88th St., 90045. Tel: 310-216-1145; Fax: 310-216-1002.
School—8740 Emerson Ave., 90045. Tel: 310-645-6620; Fax: 310-645-4407.
Sisters 1; Lay Teachers 20; Students 293.
Catechesis/Religious Programs—Tel: 310-568-9085.
Students 130.

OUTSIDE THE CITY OF LOS ANGELES

Alhambra, Los Angeles Co., All Souls (1912), Rev. Msgr. William P. O'Toole; Rev. Steven J. Guitron; Deacon William Aust.
Res., 17 S. Electric Ave., 91801. Tel: 626-281-0466; Fax: 626-281-2163.
Catechesis/Religious Programs—29 S. Electric Ave., 91801. Tel: 626-284-7835.
Students 410.

St. Therese (1924). (Little Flower). Revs. Stephen Watson, O.C.D.; William Fenton, O.C.D.; Paul Keonig, O.C.D.; Deacon Gus Sebenius. In res., Rev. Jerome Lantry, O.C.D.
Res., 510 N. El Molino St., 91801. Tel: 626-282-2744; Fax: 626-282-7560.
School—Tel: 626-289-3364; Fax: 626-284-6700.
Lay Teachers 12; Students 325.
Catechesis/Religious Programs—Tel: 626-284-0020.
Students 160.

St. Thomas More (1948), Revs. Jeremiah O'Neill; Robert E. Butler, S.J.
Res., 2510 S. Fremont Ave., 91803. Tel: 626-284-8333; Fax: 626-282-4459.
School—Tel: 626-284-5778; Fax: 626-284-3303.
Sisters 1; Lay Teachers 10; Students 235.
Catechesis/Religious Programs—Tel: 626-457-5302.
Students 150.

Altadena, Los Angeles Co., St. Elizabeth of Hungary (1918), Revs. Richard G. Prindle; Humberto Bernabe; Bernard J. Jennings, (Retired).
Office: 1879 N. Lake Ave., 91001.
Res., 1849 N. Lake Ave., 91001. Tel: 626-797-1167; Fax: 626-797-9245.
School—Tel: 626-797-7727; Fax: 626-797-6541.
Lay Teachers 10; Students 292.
Catechesis/Religious Programs—Students 275.

Sacred Heart (1935), Rev. Jerome L. Schmit.
Church—2889 N. Lincoln Ave., 91001. Tel: 626-794-2046; Fax: 626-794-2046.
Catechesis/Religious Programs—Tel: 626-794-6961.
Students 356.

Arcadia, Los Angeles Co., Annunciation (1948), Rev. Jarlath Dolan; Rev. Msgr. Roland G. Zimmerman, Pastor Emeritus. In res., Rev. Ramon Marti.
Church Office & Mailing Address—2701 S. Peck Rd., Monrovia, 91016.
Res., 1307 E. Longden Ave., 91006. Tel: 626-447-6202; Fax: 626-447-9834.
School—Tel: 626-447-8262.
Sisters 2; Lay Teachers 10; Students 289.
Catechesis/Religious Programs—Tel: 626-446-1625.
Students 184.

Holy Angels (1935), Rev. Msgr. Norman F. Priebe; Rev. Mark A. Warnstedt; Rev. Msgr. Robert Walsh, Pastor Emeritus.
Res., 370 Campus Dr., 91007. Tel: 626-447-1671; Fax: 626-447-7617.
School—360 Campus Dr., 91007. Tel: 626-447-6312.
Lay Teachers 12; Students 300.
Catechesis/Religious Programs—Tel: 626-445-2967.
Students 380.

Artesia, Los Angeles Co., Holy Family (1931), Revs. Loreto Gonzales; Angelo Jaballa; Leonard Goswitz; Deacons Raul Viramontes; Guadalupe Mejia.
Res., 18708 S. Clarkdale Ave., 90701. Tel: 310-865-2185; Fax: 310-860-0718.
School—Our Lady of Fatima, 18626 S. Clarkdale Ave., 90701. Tel: 310-865-1621; Fax: 310-860-1091.
Lay Teachers 9; Students 325.
Catechesis/Religious Programs—Tel: 310-860-5973.
Students 1,157.

Avalon, Los Angeles Co., St. Catherine of Alexandria (1902), Rev. Paul Alcuin Siebenand.
Res., Box 735, 90704. Tel: 310-510-0192; Fax: 310-510-8360.

Azusa, Los Angeles Co., St. Frances of Rome (1908) (Hispanic), Revs. Edward J. Landreau; Edwin C. Duyshart; Rogue Fernandes.
Res., 501 E. Foothill Blvd., P.O. Box 637, 91702. Tel: 818-969-1829; Fax: 818-815-2755. [CEM]
School—734 N. Pasadena Ave., 91702. Tel: 818-334-2018; Fax: 818-815-2760.
Lay Teachers 10; Students 270.
Catechesis/Religious Programs—508 N. Soldano, 91702. Tel: 818-334-3500.
Students 970.

Baldwin Park, Los Angeles Co., St. John the Baptist (1946) (Hispanic-Filipino), Revs. James R. Forsen; Ramon Rojas; Michael Java; John Montejano.
Res., 3848 Stewart Ave., 91706. Tel: 626-960-2795; Fax: 626-960-5085.
School—3870 Stewart Ave., 91706. Tel: 626-337-1421.
Sisters of the Love of God 5; Lay Teachers 14; Students 479.
Catechesis/Religious Programs—Tel: 626-962-1004.
Students 1,400.
Convent—3963 Baldwin Park Blvd., 91706. Tel: 626-337-0527.

Bellflower, Los Angeles Co., St. Bernard (1923), Revs. Philip J. McGrath; Daniel Fox; Thomas F. Feltz, Admin.
Res., 9647 E. Beach St., Box 576, 90706. Tel: 310-867-2337; Fax: 310-867-4863.
School—9626 Park St., 90706. Tel: 310-867-9410; Fax: 310-866-2310. Ms. Kathleen M. Flynn, Prin.
Lay Teachers 11; Students 269.
Catechesis/Religious Programs—Tel: 310-925-9886.
Students 600.

St. Dominic Savio (1954), Revs. Gael Sullivan, S.D.B.; Paul M. Caporali, S.D.B.; Manuel Fernandez, S.D.B.
Res., 9720 Foster Rd., 90706. Tel: 310-920-7796; Fax: 310-920-0149.
School—9750 Foster Rd., 90706. Tel: 310-866-3617; Fax: 310-804-6738.
Salesian Sisters of St. John Bosco 3; Lay Teachers 10; Students 385.
Catechesis/Religious Programs—Tel: 310-866-6642; Fax: 310-920-0149.
Students 700.

Bell Gardens, Los Angeles Co., St. Gertrude (1938) (Hispanic), Rev. Msgr. Henry Gomez; Revs. Esteban Marquez; Jose Luis Ruiz (Guadalajara). In res., Deacon Chris Vega.
Res., 7025 Garfield Ave., 90201. Tel: 310-927-4495; Fax: 310-927-5826.
School—6824 Toler Ave., 90201. Tel: 310-927-1216.
Salesian Sisters of St. John Bosco 2; Lay Teachers 9; Students 287.
Catechesis/Religious Programs—Tel: 310-927-3185.
Students 1,209.

Beverly Hills, Los Angeles Co., Good Shepherd (1924), Rev. Colm O'Ryan. In res., Rev. George O'Brien; Rev. Msgr. Daniel F. Sullivan, Pastor Emeritus.
Res., 505 N. Bedford Dr., 90210. Tel: 310-285-5425; Fax: 310-285-5433.
School—Tel: 310-275-8601; Fax: 310-275-0366. Sr. Leonella Lynch, Prin.
Sisters 2; Lay Teachers 8; Students 270.
Catechesis/Religious Programs—Students 250.

Burbank, Los Angeles Co., St. Robert Bellarmine (1907), Rev. Msgr. Patrick Reilly; Rev. Msgr. Peter Healy; Rev. John Vogel.
Res., 133 N. Fifth St., 91501. Tel: 818-846-3443; Fax: 818-954-9441.
Church—Fifth St. and E. Orange Grove Ave., 91501.
School—154 N. Fifth St., 91501. Tel: 818-842-5033; Fax: 818-842-9789.
Sisters of Charity of the Blessed Virgin Mary 2; Lay Teachers 10; Students 334.
Catechesis/Religious Programs—Tel: 818-845-3521.
Students 300.

St. Finbar (1938), Revs. Jose R. Holguin; Thomas Cook; John Hoa Nguyen. In res., Rev. Michael Mc Cullough.
Res., 2010 W. Olive Ave., 91506. Tel: 818-846-6251; Fax: 818-846-1703.
School—2120 W. Olive Ave., 91506. Tel: 818-848-0191.
Lay Teachers 12; Students 292.
Catechesis/Religious Programs—Tel: 818-846-8715.
Students 1,014.

St. Francis Xavier (1954), Revs. Michael D. Couhig, C.S.C.; Ronald P. Raab, C.S.C.; William C. O'Connor, C.S.C.
Res., 3801 Scott Rd., 91504. Tel: 818-767-2445; Fax: 818-767-5096.
School—Tel: 818-767-2071, Ext. Z; Fax: 818-767-2661.
Lay Teachers 12; Students 309.
Catechesis/Religious Programs—Tel: 818-767-7000. Lee Jolly, D.R.E.
Students 245.

Camarillo, Ventura Co., Blessed Junipero Serra (1988). Liturgies celebrated at: Padre Serra Parish, 5205 Upland Rd., Camarilla, CA 93012. Rev. Liam J. Kidney; Deacons John Picard; Ludger Gueringer.
Office: 5205 Upland Rd., 93012. Tel: 805-482-6417; Fax: 805-987-8100.
Res., 5104 Hillridge Dr., 93012.
Catechesis/Religious Programs—Students 639.

St. Mary Magdalen (1940), Rev. Msgr. John C. Hughes; Rev. Marcos Gonzalez; Deacons George Bednar; Johnnie Hammonds; Larry Modugno.
Res., 2532 Ventura Blvd., 93010. Tel: 805-484-0532; Fax: 805-987-2941.
School—2534 Ventura Blvd., 93010. Tel: 805-482-2611; Fax: 805-987-8211.
Lay Teachers 13; Students 265.
Catechesis/Religious Programs—Tel: 805-482-1219.
Students 1,066.

Canoga Park, Los Angeles Co., Our Lady of the Valley (1921), Revs. Alden J. Sison; Olympio D'Mello; Samuel Rendon; Deacon Heriberto Vega.
Pastoral Center—22021 Gault St., 91303-1804. Tel: 818-592-2880; Fax: 818-592-0299.
School—Tel: 818-592-2894; Fax: 818-592-2896.
Lay Teachers 12; Students 262.
Catechesis/Religious Programs—22045 Gault St., 91303. Tel: 818-592-2892.
Students 650.

St. Joseph the Worker (1956) (Hispanic-Vietnamese), Revs. James C. Gehl; R. Dario Miranda; Deacon William S. Lacy; Raymonde Bennett, Admin.
Res., 19850 Cantlay St., 91306. Tel: 818-341-6634; Fax: 818-341-3875.
Parish Center—19808 Cantlay St., 91306.
School—19812 Cantlay St., 91306. Tel: 818-341-6616. Sr. Eva Bryan, R.S.C., Prin.
Lay Teachers 12; Students 323.
Catechesis/Religious Programs—Tel: 818-998-4166. Elizabeth Mattera Hise, D.R.E.
Students 315.

Canyon Country, Los Angeles Co., St. Clare (1977), Revs. Edmond M. Renehan; William Ustaski; Joseph Quattropane; Frank Purcell.
Res., 27341 Camp Plenty Rd., 91351. Tel: 805-252-3353; Fax: 805-252-1539.
Catechesis/Religious Programs—Tel: 805-252-6950. Peggy Pigors, D.R.E.
Students 829.
Mission—Saugus, Los Angeles Co., Blessed Kateri Tekakwitha Mission, P.O. Box 802200, Santa Clarita, 91380-2200. Tel: 805-296-3180; Fax: 805-296-7854.
Catechesis/Religious Programs—Renee Fields, D.R.E.
Students 731.

Carpinteria, Santa Barbara Co., St. Joseph (1933), Revs. David S. Herrera; Edward Donovan, C.S.P.; Rev. Msgr. Joseph V. Kearney, Pastor Emeritus.
Mailing Address: 5084 El Carro Lane, 93013. Tel: 805-684-2181; Fax: 805-684-0534.
Catechesis/Religious Programs—Tel: 805-684-2210.
Students 320.

Carson, Los Angeles Co., St. Philomena (1956), Revs. Riz. J. Carranza; Owen de Souza; Demetrio Bugayong; Cesar Raffo-Rivasplata (Peru); Sr. Teresa Kenny, S.J.C., Pastoral Assoc.
Res., 21900 S. Main St., 90745. Tel: 310-835-7161; Fax: 310-830-5494.
School—Tel: 310-835-4827; Fax: 310-835-1655.
Carmelite Sisters 6; Lay Teachers 7; Students 288.
Catechesis/Religious Programs—Students 323.
Convent—21832 1/2 S. Main St., 90745. Tel: 310-834-9180.

Chatsworth, Los Angeles Co., St. John Eudes (1963), Revs. Robert J. McNamara; Robert Folbrecht; Deacon Chet Holly, Admin.
Res., 10001 Mason Ave., 91311. Tel: 818-341-3680; Fax: 818-882-4326.
Church—9901 Mason Ave., 91311.
School—Tel: 818-341-1454.
Sisters of the Pious Schools 4; Lay Teachers 7; Students 272.
Catechesis/Religious Programs—9933 Mason Ave., Chatsworth, 91311. Tel: 818-882-9323.
Students 420.

Claremont, Los Angeles Co., Our Lady of the Assumption (1947), Revs. Thomas Welbers; Huy Nguyen; Benedict Agumanu; Anthony Sangwook Lee.
Res., 435 Berkeley Ave., 91711. Tel: 909-626-3596; Fax: 909-624-3680.
School—Tel: 909-626-7135; Fax: 909-398-1395.
Lay Teachers 25; Students 555.
Catechesis/Religious Programs—Tel: 909-624-1360.
Students 800.

Compton, Los Angeles Co., Our Lady of Victory (1920) Hispanic-African American, Revs. Stan Bosch, S.T.; Nicholas Barille, S.T.; Ermeregildo Saldana, S.T. In res., Revs. Anselm Deehr, S.T.; Gary Banks, S.T.
Res., 500 E. Palmer Ave., 90221. Tel: 310-631-3233; Fax: 310-886-5681.
School—Tel: 310-631-1320.
Sisters of the Holy Family 6.
Catechesis/Religious Programs—409 E. Palmer Ave., 90221. Tel: 310-631-1831.
Students 889.

Sagrado Corazon, Sacred Heart (1956) (Hispanic), Rev. Francisco Vitela.
Res., 1720 North Culver Ave., 90222. Tel: 310-635-5436; Fax: 310-635-2121.
Catechesis/Religious Programs—Tel: 310-635-8483.
Students 600.

St. Albert the Great (1949) (Hispanic-African American), Revs. Stephen Woodland; Lorenzo Miranda; Deacons Joseph H. Ledoux; Frank Millholland.
Res., 804 E. Compton Blvd., 90220. Tel: 213-321-0240; 310-329-7548; Fax: 310-329-8462.
School—Tel: 213-770-0984.
Sisters of the Holy Family 6; Lay Teachers 21; Students 739.
Catechesis/Religious Programs—Tel: 310-327-4199. Arturo Gallardo, D.R.E.
Students 260.

Covina, Los Angeles Co., Sacred Heart (1927), Revs. Brian Cavanagh; James Overend, C.M.G.; Mario Pacheco; Deacon Eliso Gutierrez.
Res., 314 W. Workman St., 91723. Tel: 818-332-3570; Fax: 818-967-4884.
School—360 W. Workman St., 91723. Tel: 818-332-7222; Fax: 818-967-8836.
Religious 3; Lay Teachers 11; Students 319.
Catechesis/Religious Programs—Tel: 818-331-7914.
Students 651.

St. Louise de Marillac (1963), Rev. Msgr. Robert T. Pierce; Revs. Eugene Herbert; Anthony Prem Raju; Deacon Joseph A. Rivet.
Mailing Address: 1720 E. Covina Blvd., 91724.
Res., 1770 E. Covina Blvd., 91724. Tel: 626-915-7873; Fax: 626-332-4431.
School—Tel: 626-966-2317.
Lay Teachers 9; Students 312.
Catechesis/Religious Programs—Tel: 626-332-5822.
Students 562.

Cudahy, Cudahy Mission, Revs. Javier Ochoa, M.S.C.; Juan Pineda, M.S.C.; Salvador Villaruel, M.S.C.; Onesimo Escobar, M.S.C.
4235 Clara St., 90201. Tel: 213-562-3356.

Culver City, Los Angeles Co., St. Augustine (1919), Rev. Alfred S. Burnham; Rev. Msgr. Ian E. Holland, Pastor Emeritus; Revs. John S. Schiavone; Andrew G. Encinas; Deacon Rafael Victorin. In res., Rev. Expedit Sserunjogi (Uganda).
Res., 3850 Jasmine Ave., 90232. Tel: 310-838-2477; Fax: 310-838-3070.
School—Tel: 310-838-3144; Fax: 310-838-7479.
Daughters of Mary and Joseph 1; Lay Teachers 8; Students 330.
Catechesis/Religious Programs—Tel: 310-836-6561.
Students 643.

Diamond Bar, Los Angeles Co., St. Denis (1971), Rev. Msgr. James J. Loughnane; Revs. James J. Kelly; Olin W. Mayfield. In res., Rev. Donald W. Potthoff, Pastor Emeritus.
Res., 2151 Diamond Bar Blvd., 91765-2981. Tel: 909-861-7106; Fax: 909-861-2697.
Catechesis/Religious Programs—Tel: 909-861-8018.
Students 1,510.

Downey, Los Angeles Co., Our Lady of Perpetual Help (1911), Rev. John Moloney; Deacons Charles Denisac; Richard Medina.
Res., 10727 S. Downey Ave., P.O. Box 280, 90241. Tel: 562-923-3246; Fax: 562-862-7020.
School—10441 S. Downey Ave., 90241. Tel: 562-869-9969; Fax: 562-923-0659.
Lay Teachers 12; Students 312.
Catechesis/Religious Programs—Tel: 562-862-7268. Lydia West, D.R.E.
Students 500.

St. Raymond (1956), Rev. Msgr. Robert W. Gipson, V.F.; Rev. Stephen V. Davoren; Deacon Joseph Ryan. In res., Rev. Msgr. John Fosselman; Rev. Richard Albarano.
Res., 12348 Paramount Blvd., P.O. Box 2085, 90242. Tel: 562-923-4509; Fax: 562-869-3359.
School—Tel: 562-862-3210; Fax: 562-862-6328.
Sisters of Holy Faith 4; Lay Teachers 11; Students 319.
Catechesis/Religious Programs—Tel: 562-862-6959. Sr. Nancy Hale, C.H.F., D.R.E.
Students 342.
Missions—Downey, Los Angeles Co., Rancho Los Amigos Hospital; Downey, Los Angeles Co., Los Padrinos Juvenile Hall.

El Monte, Los Angeles Co., Nativity (1923), Revs. Pedro J. Lopez; William Dowling; Francis Hoang Dang (Vietnamese).
Res., 3743 N. Tyler Ave., 91731. Tel: 818-444-2511; Fax: 818-443-1417.
School—10907 St. Louis Dr., 91731. Tel: 818-448-2414; Fax: 818-448-2763.
Sisters of St. Louis 4; Lay Teachers 7; Students 285.
Catechesis/Religious Programs—Tel: 818-448-8895.
Students 464.

Our Lady of Guadalupe (1973) (Hispanic), Revs. Pedro Ma. Ciordia; Jesus Castrillo (Spain).
Res., 11359 Coffield Ave., 91731. Tel: 626-448-1795; Fax: 626-448-7137.
Catechesis/Religious Programs—Tel: 626-448-7137.
Students 1,190.

El Segundo, Los Angeles Co., St. Anthony (1925), Revs. James F. O'Grady; Joseph G. Azadian, S.J.; Deacon Theodore A. Goodreau. In res., Rev. Augustine Kalemeera (Uganda).
Res., 710 E. Grand Ave., 90245. Tel: 310-322-4392; Fax: 310-322-0797.
School—233 Lomita St., 90245. Tel: 310-322-4218; Fax: 310-322-2659.
Sisters 2; Lay Teachers 7; Students 275.
Catechesis/Religious Programs—Tel: 310-615-0766.
Students 265.

St. Andrew (1936) (Russian-Greek Catholic), Rev. Alexei Smith.
Res., 538 Concord St., 90245. Tel: 310-322-1892; Fax: 310-322-1919.

Encino, Los Angeles Co., Our Lady of Grace (1945), Rev. Msgr. Gerald E. Wilkerson, V.F.; Revs. Michael J. Sears; Peter C. Ferrer. In res., Rev. Msgr. Francis M. Osborne, Pastor Emeritus; Rev. Msgr. Craig A. Cox.
Res., 5011 White Oak Ave., 91316. Tel: 818-342-4686; Fax: 818-342-6579.
School—Tel: 818-344-4126; Fax: 818-344-1736.
Sisters 5; Lay Teachers 15; Students 332.
Catechesis/Religious Programs—Tel: 818-342-4505.
Students 265.

St. Cyril (1949), Rev. Msgr. Carl F. Bell; Rev. Msgr. Cyril Navin, Pastor Emeritus.
Res., 4601 Firmament Ave., 91436. Tel: 818-986-8234; Fax: 818-986-3310.
School—4548 Haskell Ave., 91436. Tel: 818-501-4155; Fax: 818-501-8480.
Sisters 1; Lay Teachers 14; Students 301.
Catechesis/Religious Programs—Tel: 818-789-5947.
Students 54.

Fillmore, Ventura Co., St. Francis of Assisi (1926), Revs. Joseph Hernandez; Blas Alberto Hernandez; Deacon Gerald Fitzgerald.
Church—1048 West Ventura St., P.O. Box 757, 93016. Tel: 805-524-1306; Fax: 805-524-0784.
Mission—Piru, Ventura Co., San Salvador, 4039 E. Center St., P.O. Box 508, Piru, 93040. Tel: 805-521-1077; Fax: 805-521-1077.
Catechesis/Religious Programs—Tel: 805-524-2865.
Students 620.

Gardena, Los Angeles Co., St. Anthony of Padua (1910), Revs. Peter McGee; Samuel Orellana; Honesto Bismonte.
Res., 1050 W. 163rd St., 90247. Tel: 310-327-5830; Fax: 310-327-6440.
School—1003 W. 163rd St., 90247. Tel: 310-329-7170; Fax: 310-329-9843.
Sisters of Providence of St. Mary-of-the-Woods 3; Lay Teachers 11; Students 275.
Catechesis/Religious Programs—Tel: 310-323-0860.
Students 441.
Convent—St. Gardena, 1050 W. 161 St., 90247. Tel: 213-321-3820.

Maria Regina (1956), Rev. Thomas M. Acton; Deacon Phuoc Van Nguyen. In res., Rev. Theodore C. Ley, S.M.
Res., 2150 W. 135th St., 90249. Tel: 310-323-0030; Fax: 310-323-8081. [CEM]
School—Tel: 310-327-9133; Fax: 310-327-2636.
Lay Teachers 9; Students 311.
Catechesis/Religious Programs—13510 S. VanNess Ave., 90249. Tel: 310-327-4999.
Students 415.

Glendale, Los Angeles Co., Holy Family (1907) (Hispanic-Filipino), Rev. Joseph Shea; Rev. Msgr. Arthur J. Lirette, P.A., Pastor Emeritus; Revs. Glenn N. Sequeira; Charles Gard; Stanislaus Paul (India); Deacon Fred Pelletier.
Res., 209 E. Lomita Ave., 91205. Tel: 818-247-2222; Fax: 818-247-4780.
School—(Grades PreK-8). Tel: 818-243-9239; Fax: 818-243-0976.
Sisters 1; Lay Teachers 8; Students 327.
High School—(Girls) 400 E. Lomita Ave., 91205. Tel: 818-241-3178; Fax: 818-241-7753.
Sisters 4; Lay Teachers 18; Students 282.
Catechesis/Religious Programs—400 S. Louise, 91205. Tel: 818-240-6551.
Students 561.

Church of the Incarnation (1927), Rev. Msgr. Eugene Frilot; Rev. Robert Macchler; Deacon Restie Noriega. In res., Rev. Msgr. Laurence O'Brien, Pastor Emeritus.
Res., 1001 N. Brand Blvd., 91202. Tel: 818-242-2579; Fax: 818-507-4976.
School—Tel: 818-241-2269.
Lay Teachers 9; Students 312.
Catechesis/Religious Programs—Tel: 818-241-7045.
Students 190.

Glendora, Los Angeles Co., St. Dorothy (1958), Rev. Msgr. John Acton; Rev. Nestor Rebong (Philippines); Deacon Marv Estey.
Res., 241 S. Valley Center, 91741. Tel: 626-914-3941; Fax: 626-335-0059.
School—215 S. Valley Center, 91741. Tel: 626-335-0772.
Sisters 1; Lay Teachers 10; Students 306.
Catechesis/Religious Programs—Tel: 626-335-2811.
Students 673.

Goleta, Santa Barbara Co., St. Raphael (1896), Rev. Msgr. Stephen N. Downes; Revs. Alberto Ledesma; Antonio Cacciapuoti.
Res., 5444 Hollister Ave., Santa Barbara, 93111. Tel: 805-967-5641; Fax: 805-964-2988.
School—160 St. Joseph St., Santa Barbara, 93111. Tel: 805-967-2115; Fax: 805-683-9675. Ellen Manning, Prin.
Lay Teachers 10; Students 272.
Catechesis/Religious Programs—Tel: 805-967-1641.
Students 650.

St. Mark University Parish (1966), Revs. Ruben M. Patino, C.S.P.; Edward C. Nowak, C.S.P.; Mr. William Cork, Pastoral Assoc.
Res., 6550 Picasso Rd., 93117. Tel: 805-968-1078; Fax: 805-968-3965.

Granada Hills, Los Angeles Co., St. John Baptist de la Salle (1953), Rev. Michael J. Slattery; Rev. Msgr. Emmanuel G. Manahan; Rev. Msgr. Peter O'Sullivan, Pastor Emeritus.
Res., 16545 Chatsworth St., 91344. Tel: 818-363-2535; Fax: 818-360-7407.
School—Tel: 818-363-2270; Fax: 818-832-8950.
Lay Teachers 22; Students 579.
Catechesis/Religious Programs—Tel: 818-368-1514.
Students 622.

St. Euphrasia (1963), Deacon Joseph Orth.
Res., 11766 Shoshone Ave., 91344. Tel: 818-360-4611; Fax: 818-360-2755.
School—Tel: 818-363-5515.
Lay Teachers 10; Students 300.
Catechesis/Religious Programs—Tel: 818-368-4512.
Students 137.

Guadalupe, Santa Barbara Co., Our Lady of Guadalupe (1867) (Hispanic), Rev. Abel Suquilvide.
Res., 1164 Obispo St., P.O. Box 897, 93434. Tel: 805-343-2181; Fax: 805-343-6642. [JC]
Catechesis/Religious Programs—Tel: 805-343-4404.
Students 234.

Hacienda Heights, Los Angeles Co., St. John Vianney (1965), Rev. Msgr. John T. Kane; Rev. Gordon Chang; Rev. Msgr. James A. O'Callaghan, Pastor Emeritus; Deacon Eduardo Delgado.
Res., 1345 Turnbull Canyon Rd., 91745. Tel: 626-330-2269; Fax: 626-330-0220.
Catechesis/Religious Programs—Students 776.

Hawaiian Gardens, Los Angeles Co., St. Peter Chanel (1986) (Mexican-Filipino), Revs. Lawrence T. Darnell, O.M.V.; Edward Broom, O.M.V.; Alan Hall, O.M.V.
Res., 21611 Juan Ave., 90716-1117. Tel: 562-924-7591; Fax: 562-402-9411.
Church—12001 E. 214 St., 90716-1117.
Catechesis/Religious Programs—Tel: 562-860-3637.
Students 1,000.

Hawthorne, Los Angeles Co., St. Joseph (1915), Revs. Eugene Buhr; Joseph Moniz; Rev. Msgr. Patrick J. Redahan, Pastor Emeritus; Rev. Daniel G. Perez-Castaneda.
Res., 11854 Acacia Ave., 90250. Tel: 310-679-1139; Fax: 310-679-3034.
School—11886 Acacia Ave., 90250. Tel: 310-679-1014; Fax: 310-679-1310.
Lay Teachers 17; Students 542.
Catechesis/Religious Programs—Tel: 310-644-1234.
Students 1,125.

Hermosa Beach, Los Angeles Co., Our Lady of Guadalupe (1927), Revs. Gary Klauer, O.F.M.Conv.; John Farao, O.F.M.Conv.; Bro. Michael Zocholl, O.F.M.Conv., Admin. In res., Bro. John Cunningham, O.F.M.Conv.
Res., 320 Massey Ave., 90254. Tel: 310-372-7077; Fax: 310-798-4051.
School—340 Massey Ave., 90254. Tel: 310-372-7486. Mrs. Cheryl Hunt, Prin.
Religious 1; Lay Teachers 13; Students 275.
Catechesis/Religious Programs—Tel: 310-374-4649.
Students 320.

Huntington Park, Los Angeles Co., St. Martha (1913) (Hispanic), Revs. Vicente Gutierrez, M.Sp.S.; Jesus Arredondo, M.Sp.S.; Eugenio Cardenas, M.Sp.S.; David Mateo Velazquez, M.Sp.S.; Hilario Cisneros, M.Sp.S.
Res., 6019 Stafford Ave., 90255. Tel: 213-585-5776; Fax: 213-585-4560.
Catechesis/Religious Programs—Tel: 213-583-3678.
Students 950.

St. Matthias (1913) (Latino), Revs. Rody I. Gorman; Lucio Juarez; Abelardo Bailon; Mario A. Torres. In res., Rev. Samuel Villegas.
Res., 7125 Mission Pl., 90255. Tel: 213-588-2134; Fax: 213-588-4519.
School—Tel: 213-588-7253; Fax: 213-588-1136.
Sisters 3; Lay Teachers 8; Students 326.
Catechesis/Religious Programs—7105 Mission Pl., 90255. Tel: 213-587-3121; Fax: 213-588-4519.
Students 400.

Inglewood, Los Angeles Co., St. John Chrysostom (1923), Rev. Msgr. Paul Montoya; Rev. Msgr. Edward C. Maddox, Senior Priest; Revs. Javier Altuna, S.J.; Luciano Kamienski, S.D.B.; Deacon Roberto Vasquez.
Res., 546 E. Florence Ave., 90301. Tel: 310-677-2736; Fax: 310-677-0584.
School—Tel: 310-677-5868; Fax: 310-677-3429.
Sisters of St. Joseph of Carondelet 4; Lay Teachers 8; Students 300.
Catechesis/Religious Programs—Tel: 310-674-3733.
Students 765.

Irwindale, Los Angeles Co., Our Lady of Guadalupe (1964), Rev. Patrick M. Hughes. In res., Rev. Gerald Walker, Senior Priest.
Res., 16025 Cypress St., 91706. Tel: 818-962-3649; Fax: 818-337-3318.
Catechesis/Religious Programs—Tel: 818-960-1310.
Students 447.

La Canada Flintridge, Los Angeles Co., St. Bede the Venerable (1951), Rev. Msgr. Francis T. Wallace; Rev. Msgr. Leland Boyer, Pastor Emeritus; Revs. Lawrence Signey; Jerome Cummings; Sr. Kathleen McDonough, S.N.J.M, Pastoral Assoc.
Res., 215 Foothill Blvd., 91011. Tel: 818-790-5155; Fax: 818-790-9520.
School—(Grades K-8) 217 Foothill Blvd., 91011. Tel: 818-790-7884; Fax: 818-790-7887.
Lay Teachers 12; Students 275.
Catechesis/Religious Programs—Tel: 818-790-5094. Sr. Margaret Marso, B.V.M., D.R.E.
Students 400.

La Crescenta, Los Angeles Co., St. James the Less (1955), Rev. Msgr. Thomas Doyle; Rev. Gerard O'Brien.
Res., 4625 Dunsmore Ave., 91214. Tel: 818-248-3442; Fax: 818-248-9332.
School—4635 Dunsmore Ave., 91214. Tel: 818-248-7778; Fax: 818-248-5242.
Sisters 2; Lay Teachers 11; Students 270.
Catechesis/Religious Programs—Tel: 818-957-6168.
Students 177.

La Mirada, Los Angeles Co., Beatitudes of Our Lord (1964), Revs. James F. Williams; David Loftus.
Res., 13013 S. Santa Gertrudes Ave., 90638. Tel: 562-943-1521; Fax: 562-902-7627.
School—Tel: 562-943-3218.
Lay Teachers 9; Students 318.
Catechesis/Religious Programs—Tel: 562-943-5678.
Students 516.

St. Paul of the Cross (1955), Revs. Patrick J. Gannon; William P. Wolfe; Deacon Arthur Fitzpatrick.
Res., 14020 Foster Rd., 90638. Tel: 562-921-2914; Fax: 562-926-1514.
School—14030 Foster Rd., 90638. Tel: 562-921-2118; Fax: 562-802-2048.
Bernardine Sisters 1; Lay Teachers 9; Students 296.
Catechesis/Religious Programs—Tel: 562-921-4911.
Students 318.

La Puente, Los Angeles Co., St. Joseph (1919), Rev. Patrick J. Staunton; Rev. Msgr. Joseph W. Herres; Revs. Matthew T. Cumberland; William E. Ruther; Deacon Ruben Guerra.
Res., 550 N. Glendora Ave., 91744. Tel: 818-336-2001; Fax: 818-336-6010.
School—551 N. Glendora Ave., 91744. Tel: 818-336-2821; Fax: 818-369-8921.
Carmelite Sisters 5; Lay Teachers 6; Students 261.
Catechesis/Religious Programs—15650 E. Temple Ave., 91744. Tel: 818-336-1191.
Students 478.

St. Louis of France (1955), Rev. Msgr. David A. Sork; Revs. Arthur Guillen; Jose Luis Ochoa; Deacon Oscar Valeriano. In res., Rev. Msgr. James R. Mulcahy, Pastor Emeritus.
Res., 13935 E. Temple, 91746-2098. Tel: 626-918-8314; Fax: 626-917-8413.
School—Tel: 626-918-6210; Fax: 626-918-9549.
Sisters of St. Louis 1; Lay Teachers 13; Students 324.
Catechesis/Religious Programs—Tel: 626-918-7002.
Students 1,085.

Lakewood, St. Pancratius (1953), Rev. Msgr. Ronald E. Royer; Rev. Edward Fremgen. In res., Rev. Leo Miller, O.M.I.
Res., 3519 St. Pancratius Pl., 90712. Tel: 562-634-6111; Fax: 562-634-7817.
School—3601 St. Pancratius Pl., 90712. Tel: 562-634-6310.
Lay Teachers 10; Students 316.
Catechesis/Religious Programs—Tel: 562-634-1611.
Students 360.

Lancaster, Los Angeles Co., Blessed Junipero Serra (Quartz Hill) (1987), Revs. Mariano Biasio, C.S.J.; Ernest Candelaria, C.S.J. In res., Revs. Joseph Scalco, C.S.J.; Angelo Zonta, C.S.J.; Deacon Edward Caputo.
Res., 6122 W. Azalea Dr., 93536-3767. Tel: 805-943-4933.
Office: 42121 60th St. W., 93536-3767. Tel: 805-943-9314; Fax: 805-943-6863.
Catechesis/Religious Programs—Tel: 805-943-9314.
Students 584.
Mission—Quartz Hill, Los Angeles Co., St. Elizabeth, P.O. Box 3307, Quartz Hill, 93586-0307.

Sacred Heart (1886), Rev. Msgr. Timothy O'Connell; Rev. David J. Ayotte; Deacon Donald E. Simanski. In res., Rev. William J. Caffrey, S.V.D.
Res., 45007 N. Cedar Ave., 93534. Tel: 805-942-7122; Fax: 805-945-4255.
School—45002 N. Date Ave., 93534. Tel: 805-948-3613; Fax: 805-945-4235.
Lay Teachers 13; Students 318.
Catechesis/Religious Programs—45027 N. Cedar Ave., 93534. Tel: 805-948-3011.
Students 843.

Lomita, Los Angeles Co., St. Margaret Mary Alacoque (1937), Rev. Msgr. Patrick Thompson; Revs. Mark Choi; Marco T. Solis. In res., Rev. Sean Cronin; Deacon Dick Corwin.
Res., 25429 Eshelman Ave., 90717. Tel: 310-326-3364; Fax: 310-539-1570.
Parish Center—25511 Eshelman Ave., 90717.
Church—25505 Eshelman Ave., 90717.
School—(Grades K-8) 25515 Eshelman Ave., 90717. Tel: 310-326-9494.
Lay Teachers 12; Students 328.
Catechesis/Religious Programs—Tel: 310-326-3364, Ext. 14.
Students 994.

Lompoc, Santa Barbara Co., La Purisima Concepcion (1787), Rev. Msgr. Andrew McGrath, Pastor Emeritus; Rev. Richard Vega; Deacons John Burke; Charles Hays.
Res., 213 W. Olive Ave., 93436. Tel: 805-735-3068; Fax: 805-735-7649.
School—219 W. Olive Ave., 93436. Tel: 805-736-6210; Fax: 805-735-7649.
Lay Teachers 9; Students 220.
Catechesis/Religious Programs—Tel: 805-735-3068.
Students 635.

Our Lady Queen of Angels (1972), Rev. John G. Fitzgerald.
Res., 3495 Rucker Rd., 93436. Tel: 805-733-2735; Fax: 805-733-1235.
Catechesis/Religious Programs—Tel: 805-733-3155.
Students 262.

Long Beach, Los Angeles Co.,

1—St. Anthony, (1902), Rev. Lawrence Caruso; Rev. Msgr. Ernest J. Gualderon, Pastor Emeritus; Revs. Joseph Canna; Richard Patterson.
Res., 540 Olive Ave., 90802. Tel: 562-436-6481; Fax: 562-436-1631.
School—855 E. 5th St., 90802. Tel: 562-432-5946; Fax: 562-435-8606.
Students 290.
High School—620 Olive Ave., 90802. Tel: 562-432-3300; Fax: 562-437-5415.
Sisters 4; Lay Teachers 8; Students 325.
Catechesis/Religious Programs—Tel: 562-432-4266.
Students 520.
Mission—Long Beach, Los Angeles Co., Our Lady of Mt. Carmel, 1851 Cerritos Ave., 90806. Tel: 310-591-8477.

2—St. Athanasius, (1933), Rev. William McLean.
Res., 5390 Linden Ave., 90805. Tel: 310-423-7986; Fax: 310-422-0306.
School—5369 Linden Ave., 90805. Tel: 310-428-7422.
St. Francis Mission Community 2; Lay Teachers 6; Students 200.
Catechesis/Religious Programs—Tel: 310-428-3494.
Students 670.

3—St. Barnabas, (1939), Rev. Msgr. John P. Twomey; Rev. Lawrence Seyer; Rev. Msgr. Christopher J. Kennedy, Pastor Emeritus; Deacon Alden Bohlig.
Res., 3955 Orange Ave., 90807. Tel: 310-424-8595; Fax: 310-595-7875.
School—(Grades K-8). Tel: 310-424-7476; Fax: 310-981-3351.
Lay Teachers 12; Students 296.
Catechesis/Religious Programs—Tel: 310-427-7508.
Students 300.

4—St. Bartholomew, (1937), Rev. Jerome C. Elder. In res., Rev. Msgr. Peter C. Caslin, Pastor Emeritus.
Res., 252 Granada Ave., 90803. Tel: 562-438-3826; Fax: 562-438-2227.

5—St. Cornelius, (1951), Rev. Msgr. John Folliard, Pastor Emeritus; Rev. Michael Reardon; Deacon Alexander Lipski.
Res., 5500 Wardlow Rd., 90808. Tel: 562-421-8966; Fax: 562-421-5096.
School—3330 Bellflower Blvd., 90808. Tel: 562-425-7813; Fax: 562-425-2743.
Lay Teachers 9; Students 333.
Catechesis/Religious Programs—Tel: 562-420-7613.
Students 169.

6—St. Cyprian, (1945), Rev. Peter Foran.
Res., 4714 Clark Ave., 90808. Tel: 310-421-9487; Fax: 310-496-1024.
School—5133 Arbor Rd., 90808. Tel: 310-425-7341.
Sisters of St. Louis (Monaghan) 3; Lay Teachers 10; Students 305.
Catechesis/Religious Programs—Students 302.

7—Holy Innocents, (1926) (Spanish-Asian), Rev. Antonio P. Astudillo.
Res., 425 E. 20th St., 90806. Tel: 562-591-6924; Fax: 562-591-2164.
School—2556 Pacific Ave., 90806. Tel: 562-424-1018; Fax: 562-424-4162.
Carmelite Sisters of the Most Sacred Heart 6; Lay Teachers 7; Students 334.
Catechesis/Religious Programs—Tel: 562-427-8449.
Students 410.

8—ST. JOSEPH, (1955), Rev. Msgr. Douglas W. Saunders, V.F.; Rev. Michael W. Meyer; Rev. Msgr. John J. Reilly, Pastor Emeritus. In res., Rev. Harold L. Ford, Senior Priest.
Res., 6220 E. Willow St., 90815. Tel: 562-594-4657; Fax: 562-431-7424.
School—6200 E. Willow St., 90815. Tel: 562-596-6115; Fax: 562-596-6725.
Lay Teachers 12; Students 306.
Catechesis/Religious Programs—Tel: 562-598-0519.
Students 244.

9—ST. LUCY, (1944), Revs. Michael Roebert; Francis T. Bui; William Van Gastel, M.H.M.
Res., 2344 Cota Ave., 90810. Tel: 562-424-9051; Fax: 562-988-0376.
School—2320 Cota Ave., 90810. Tel: 562-424-9062.
Lay Teachers 13; Students 300.
Catechesis/Religious Programs—1731 W. 23rd St., 90810. Tel: 562-997-0511.
Students 280.

10—ST. MARIA GORETTI, (1955), Revs. John B. Fitzgerald; Allan Roberts.
Res., 3954 Palo Verde Ave., 90808-2298. Tel: 562-425-7459; Fax: 562-421-0475.
School—Tel: 562-425-5112; Fax: 562-425-5672.
Lay Teachers 14; Students 315.
Catechesis/Religious Programs—3950 Palo Verde Ave., 90808-2298. Tel: 562-420-1321.
Students 162.

11—ST. MATTHEW, (1920), Revs. Gerald Meisel; Guillermo Rodriguez (El Salvador).
Res., 672 Temple Ave., 90814. Tel: 562-439-0931; Fax: 562-434-7621.
Catechesis/Religious Programs—Tel: 562-434-6402; Fax: 562-434-7621.
Students 550.

12—OUR LADY OF REFUGE, (1948), Rev. William J. O'Keeffe. In res., Revs. Alfonso Scott; Ernest Montoya.
Res., 5195 Stearns St., 90815. Tel: 562-498-6641; Fax: 562-498-3344.
School—5210 Los Coyotes Diagonal, 90815. Tel: 562-597-0819; Fax: 562-597-1419.
Lay Teachers 11; Students 290.
Catechesis/Religious Programs—Tel: 562-597-3102.
Students 298.

Los Nietos, Los Angeles Co., Our Lady of Perpetual Help (1958), Revs. John S. Woolway; Josef Draugialis. In res., Rev. Jose Bellavista.
Res., 8545 S. Norwalk Blvd., 90606. Tel: 562-692-3758; Fax: 562-695-4068.
Catechesis/Religious Programs—Tel: 562-463-3389.
Students 900.

Lynwood, Los Angeles Co., St. Emydius (1924), Revs. Donal P. O'Connor; Jose G. Mejia; David Ochoa (Mexico); Luis Garcia (Mexico). In res., Rev. John C. O'Connor.
Res., 10900 California Ave., 90262-2094. Tel: 310-637-7095; Fax: 310-637-3319.
School—10990 California Ave., 90262. Tel: 310-635-7184; Fax: 310-605-3041.
Sisters of the Holy Faith 3; Lay Teachers 19; Students 516.
Catechesis/Religious Programs—Tel: 310-639-1249.
Students 1,243.
Convent—10950 California Ave., 90262. Tel: 310-635-3264.
Missionaries of Charity 6.

St. Philip Neri (1948) (Hispanic), Revs. Joseph G. Sanchez; Francisco Javier Trujillo; Deacon Joe T. Battle Tel: 310-632-4745.
Res., 4311 Olanda St., 90262. Tel: 310-632-7179; Fax: 310-632-5119.
Pastoral Center—12435 Cookacre Ave., 90262.
School—12522 Stoneacre Ave., 90262. Tel: 310-638-0341; Fax: 310-638-9805.
Lay Teachers 9; Students 308.
Catechesis/Religious Programs—Tel: 310-632-3698.
Students 1,086.

Malibu, Los Angeles Co., Our Lady of Malibu (1946), Rev. William F. Kerze; Rev. Msgr. John V. Sheridan, Pastor Emeritus.
Res., 3625 Winter Canyon Rd., 90265. Tel: 310-456-2361; Fax: 310-456-3942.
School—Tel: 310-456-8071; Fax: 310-456-7767.
Sisters of St. Louis 1; Lay Teachers 12; Students 215.
Catechesis/Religious Programs—Tel: 310-456-8813.
Students 210.

Manhattan Beach, Los Angeles Co., American Martyrs (1930), Rev. Msgr. John F. Barry; Revs. Michael J. Evans; Joseph S. Palumbo; Deacon Fred Rose.
Res., 624 15th St., P.O. Box 3639, 90266. Tel: 310-545-5651; Fax: 310-546-9209.
School—Tel: 310-545-8559; Fax: 310-546-7219.
Sisters 1; Lay Teachers 12; Students 408.
Catechesis/Religious Programs—1701 Laurel Ave., 90266. Tel: 310-546-4734.
Students 860.

Maywood, Los Angeles Co., St. Rose of Lima (1922) (Hispanic), Rev. Msgr. George Duran; Revs. Roberto Pirrone; Edward Soto.
Res., 4450 E. 60th St., 90270. Tel: 213-560-2381; Fax: 213-560-8537.
School—4422 E. 60th St., 90270. Tel: 213-560-3376.
Sisters of Notre Dame 3; Lay Teachers 10; Students 304.
Catechesis/Religious Programs—Tel: 213-560-0187.
Students 1,070.

Mission Hills, Los Angeles Co., San Fernando Rey Mission (1797), Rev. Msgr. Francis J. Weber, Admin.; Deacon Sam Frias.
Res., 15151 San Fernando Mission Blvd., 91345. Tel: 818-361-0186; Fax: 818-361-3276.

Monrovia, Los Angeles Co., Immaculate Conception (1904), Revs. Charles J. Ramirez; Francis Cassidy; Dennis A. Nobleza, Jr.; Deacon Fred Conrey.
Res., 740 S. Shamrock Ave., 91016. Tel: 818-358-1166; Fax: 818-358-6466.
School—726 S. Shamrock Ave., 91016. Tel: 818-358-5129; Fax: 818-358-3933.
Religious 1; Lay Teachers 10; Students 320.
Catechesis/Religious Programs—Tel: 818-357-3010.
Students 1,090.

Montebello, Los Angeles Co., St. Benedict (1906), Revs. Louis R. Vanderlay, O.S.B.; Manuel J. Magallanes, O.S.B.; Timothy P. Maloney, O.S.B.; Maurus P. Jaeb, O.S.B.; Gustavo Ramon; Bro. Dominic Ramirez, O.S.B.; Deacons Jose Lopez; James Dillon; David J. Estrada.
Res., 1022 W. Cleveland Ave., 90640. Tel: 310-721-1184; Fax: 213-721-5075.
School—Tel: 213-721-3348; Fax: 213-721-8698. Sr. Ann Lawrence Kolbeck, O.S.F., Prin.
Lay Teachers 20; Students 586.
Catechesis/Religious Programs—1009 W. Madison Ave., 90640. Tel: 213-722-6020, Ext. 10; Fax: 213-722-6006. Mrs. Helen Arvayo, D.R.E.
Students 750.

Our Lady of the Miraculous Medal (1950) (Hispanic), Rev. Msgr. Juan Matas; Rev. Lawrence J. Beck; Sr. Camille Cuadra, D.C., Pastoral Min.; Deacons Joseph Spada; Fred Rios. In res., Revs. Peter Ling; Brian Delaney.
Res., 820 N. Garfield Ave., 90640. Tel: 213-722-5866; Fax: 213-722-2654.
School—Tel: 213-728-5435; Fax: 213-728-8038.
Daughters of Charity of St. Vincent de Paul 4; Sisters of Providence 1; Lay Teachers 22; Students 580.
Catechesis/Religious Programs—Tel: 213-725-6962. Carol Lazar, D.R.E.
Students 374.
Convent—840 N. Garfield Ave., 90640. Tel: 213-721-4321.

Montecito, Santa Barbara Co., Our Lady of Mount Carmel (1856), Rev. Maurice O'Mahony; Rev. Msgr. Sylvester O'Byrne, Pastor Emeritus; Rev. Carrol O'Sullivan, (Retired).
Res., 1300 E. Valley Rd., Santa Barbara, 93108. Tel: 805-969-6868; Fax: 805-565-5959.
School—530 Hot Springs Rd., 93108. Tel: 805-969-5965; Fax: 805-565-9841.
Lay Teachers 15; Students 240.
Catechesis/Religious Programs—Tel: 805-969-4868.
Students 261.

Monterey Park, Los Angeles Co., St. Stephen (1921), Revs. Lawrence E. Estrada; Jose' J. Velasco, S.J.
Res., 320 W. Garvey Ave., 91754. Tel: 626-573-0427; Fax: 626-288-0260.
School—Tel: 626-573-1716; Fax: 626-573-3251.
Lay Teachers 19; Students 464.
Catechesis/Religious Programs—Tel: 626-573-4517.
Students 250.

St. Thomas Aquinas (1960) (Chinese), Revs. Edward R. Dover; Gabriel Lui; Deacon Jesse Martinez; Sr. Ellen Muldoon.
Res., 1501 S. Atlantic Blvd., 91754. Tel: 213-264-4447; Fax: 213-264-2524.
Catechesis/Religious Programs—Tel: 213-264-1338.
Students 286.

Montrose, Los Angeles Co., Holy Redeemer (1925), Revs. John K. Foley; Matthew Quinn, S.S.C.; Robert Rankin.
Res., 2411 Montrose Ave., 91020. Tel: 818-249-2008; Fax: 818-249-5642.
School—2361 Del Mar Rd., 91020. Tel: 818-541-9005; Fax: 818-541-9006.
Lay Teachers 13; Students 226.
Catechesis/Religious Programs—Tel: 818-249-8026.
Students 241.

Moorpark, Ventura Co., Holy Cross (1982), Revs. Joseph Cosgrove; John Love.
Res., 13539 Adlena Pl., 93021. Tel: 805-529-1397; Fax: 805-529-3939.
Parish Church & Administration Bldg.: 13955 Peach Hill Rd., 93021.
Catechesis/Religious Programs—Tel: 805-529-0283; Fax: 805-529-3939.
Students 920.

Newbury Park, Ventura Co., St. Julie Billiart (1969), Rev. Msgr. Michael Bunny; Rev. Cornelius Phelan.
Church—2475 Borchard Rd., 91320. Tel: 805-498-3602; Fax: 805-376-2332.
Catechesis/Religious Programs—Tel: 805-499-0979.
Students 441.

New Cuyama, Ventura and Santa Barbara Cos., Immaculate Conception (1969), Rev. Thomas Zagorski, O.F.M.Conv.
Res., 4793 Cebrian St., P.O. Box 257, 93254. Tel: 805-766-2741; Fax: 805-766-2919.

North Hollywood, Los Angeles Co.,

1—SACRED HEART SYRIAC CATHOLIC PARISH, (1996). (Jesus Sacred Heart Antiochene Syrian Catholic Mission, Antiochean Syriac Rite) Staffed by the Chancery.
10837 Collins St., 91601. Tel: 818-766-7001; Fax: 818-766-7254.

2—ST. CHARLES BORROMEO, (1921), Rev. Msgr. Thomas Kiefer; Revs. Vaughn Winters; Michael Wakefield. In res., Rev. Msgr. Richard Loomis.
Res., 10828 Moorpark St., 91602. Tel: 818-766-3838; Fax: 818-766-2855.
School—10850 Moorpark St., 91602. Tel: 818-508-5359.
Sisters 3; Lay Teachers 14; Students 326.
Catechesis/Religious Programs—Tel: 818-980-1826.
Students 465.

3—ST. JANE FRANCES DE CHANTAL, Revs. Michael Higgins, O.Carm.; Vicente Lopez, O.Carm.; Joseph Huh Tel: 818-755-0050.
Res., 13001 Victory Blvd., 91606. Tel: 818-985-8600; Fax: 818-985-0606.
School—Tel: 818-766-1714. Mrs. Catherine Doyle, Prin.
Lay Teachers 10; Students 340.
Catechesis/Religious Programs—Tel: 818-985-8272.
Students 365.

4—ST. PATRICK, (1948), Rev. Gregory C. King, Admin.
Office: 6153 Cahuenga Blvd., 91606. Tel: 818-752-3240; Fax: 818-769-6174.
Res., 10625 Erwin St., 91606. Tel: 818-752-3240; Fax: 818-769-6174.
School—10626 Erwin St., 91606. Tel: 818-761-7363; Fax: 818-761-6349.
Lay Teachers 13; Students 276.
Catechesis/Religious Programs—Tel: 818-769-0263.
Students 454.

5—ST. PAUL ASSYRIAN-CHALDEAN (1980), Rev. Emanuel Isho Shaleta (EST).
Res., 13050 Vanowen St., N. Hollywood, 91605. Tel: 818-765-3665; Fax: 818-765-0493.
Mission—Fullerton, Orange Co., St. George, 706 S. Lemon St., Fullerton, 92632.

Northridge, Los Angeles Co., Our Lady of Lourdes (1958), Rev. Msgr. Peter C. Moran; Revs. Andrew Diviney, S.J.; Charles P. Mayer; Deacon Juan Galido.
Church—18405 Superior St., 91325. Tel: 818-349-1500; Fax: 818-349-2516.
Res., 9800 Canby Ave., 91325.
School—Tel: 818-349-0245.
Sisters 2; Lay Teachers 9; Students 315.
Catechesis/Religious Programs—Tel: 818-349-1285.
Students 273.

Norwalk, Los Angeles Co., St. John of God (1950), Rev. Msgr. Bernard M. Leheny; Revs. Cesar A. Fernandez; Maurice D. Harrington. In res., Rev. Robert Gallagher.
Res., 13819 S. Pioneer Blvd., 90650. Tel: 562-863-5721; Fax: 562-406-3927.
School—13817 S. Pioneer Blvd., 90650. Tel: 562-863-5721, Ext. 228.
Sisters of the Holy Faith 2; Lay Teachers 10; Students 357.
Catechesis/Religious Programs—Tel: 562-863-5721, Ext. 231.
Students 927.

St. Linus (1961), Revs. Joseph V. Brennan; Michael Mikulski.
Res., 13915 Shoemaker Ave., 90650. Tel: 310-921-6649; Fax: 310-921-5150.

School—Tel: 310-921-0336; Fax: 310-921-1666.
Sisters of the Holy Faith 1; Lay Teachers 12; Students 323.
Catechesis/Religious Programs—Tel: 310-921-5179.
Students 450.

Oak Park, Ventura Co., St. Maximilian Kolbe (1992), Rev. Msgr. Peter A. O'Reilly.
Res., 638 Lindero Canyon Rd. #325, 91301. Tel: 818-991-3915; Fax: 818-991-7152.
Catechesis/Religious Programs—Tel: 818-991-5604.
Students 362.

Ojai, Ventura Co., St. Thomas Aquinas (1919), Revs. Patrick J. Keane, O.S.A.; William V. Olivas, O.S.A.; Deacon Allan Doane.
Res., 185 St. Thomas Dr., 93023. Tel: 805-646-4338; Fax: 805-646-5928.
Catechesis/Religious Programs—Tel: 805-646-0307.
Students 190.

Oxnard, Ventura Co.,

1—St. Anthony, (1959), Rev. George Sullivan; Rev. Msgr. Michael J. Condon, Pastor Emeritus; Revs. Angel Sagardoy; Joel Henson; Deacons James Henry; Jon McPheeters; Oscar Duke.
Res., 2511 S. C St., P.O. Box 2215, 93034. Tel: 805-486-7301; Fax: 805-486-3142.
School—Tel: 805-487-5317; Fax: 805-486-1537.
Sisters 1; Lay Teachers 9; Students 306.
Catechesis/Religious Programs—2421 S. C St., 93033. Tel: 805-486-0784.
Students 1,152.

2—Santa Clara, (1904), Rev. Msgr. Peter D. Nugent; Rev. Msgr. Charles F. O'Gorman, Senior Priest; Revs. John Higson; Valentine D. Zdilla; Deacons John H. Kunsemiller; John G. Castorena.
Res., 323 S. E St., 93030. Tel: 805-487-3891; Fax: 805-483-1734.
School—324 S. E St., 93030. Tel: 805-483-6935; Fax: 805-487-6686.
Lay Teachers 11; Students 337.
Catechesis/Religious Programs—Tel: 805-487-6742.
Students 855.
Mission—El Rio, Ventura Co., Santa Clara Chapel, 1333 Ventura Blvd., 93030. Tel: 805-485-7335; Fax: 805-981-1183.

3—Our Lady of Guadalupe Parish, (1958) (Hispanic), Revs. Ricardo de Alba, M.Sp.S.; Enrique Espinosa Ramirez, M.Sp.S.; Jose Natividad Vazquez, M.Sp.S.; Francisco Altamira, M.Sp.S.
Res., 500 N. Juanita Ave., P.O. Box 1091, 93030. Tel: 805-483-0987; 483-1481; Fax: 805-486-2434.
School—530 N. Juanita Ave., 93030. Tel: 805-483-5116; Fax: 805-385-7242.
Lay Teachers 9; Students 260.
Catechesis/Religious Programs—Tel: 805-487-4737; Fax: 805-486-2434.
Students 700.
Mission—Oxnard, Ventura Co., Christ the King, 535 Cooper Rd., 93030. Tel: 805-483-3499.

4—Mary Star of the Sea, (1963) (Filipino-Mexican), Revs. Paul Goni, O.A.R.; Francis de la Vega, O.A.R.; Deacons Harold A. Parish; Fidel Ramirez.
Res., 463 W. Pleasant Valley Rd., 93033. Tel: 805-486-6133; Fax: 805-483-6913.
Catechesis/Religious Programs—Tel: 805-483-9313.
Students 1,125.
Convent—4924 S. "F" St., 93033. Tel: 805-487-8008.

Pacific Palisades, Los Angeles Co., Corpus Christi (1950), Rev. Msgr. John A. Mihan; Rev. G. Neville Rucker, Pastor Emeritus; Deacon John P. Allen. In res., Revs. Joseph D. Burke, C.S.C.; Richard M. Martini.
Res., 887 Toyopa Dr., 90272. Tel: 310-454-1328; Fax: 310-454-3776.
School—Tel: 310-454-9411.
Sisters of St. Louis (Monaghan) 3; Lay Teachers 14; Students 325.
Convent—875 Toyopa Dr., 90272. Tel: 310-454-6262.

Pacoima, Los Angeles Co., Guardian Angel (1956), Rev. Juan Enriquez.
Res., 10886 Lehigh Ave., 91331. Tel: 818-899-2345; Fax: 818-899-2537.
School—Tel: 818-896-1113.
Religious of Jesus and Mary 4; Lay Teachers 6; Students 309.
Catechesis/Religious Programs—Tel: 818-899-8907.
Students 315.

Mary Immaculate (1957) (Spanish), Revs. Thomas Rush, O.M.I.; Luciano Anton, O.M.I.; Luis Valbuena, O.M.I.; Andrew Sensening, O.M.I.
Res., 10390 Remick Ave., 91331. Tel: 818-899-0278; Fax: 818-890-9878.
School—Tel: 818-834-8551; Fax: 818-896-7996.
Lay Teachers 9; Students 249.
Catechesis/Religious Programs—Tel: 818-899-2111.
Students 916.

Palmdale, Los Angeles Co., St. Mary (1890), Revs. Richard Miskella; James Gleason; Christopher Cunningham.
Res., 1600 E. Ave., R-4, 93550. Tel: 805-947-3306; Fax: 805-947-8687.
School—P.O. Box 902200, 93590-2200. Tel: 805-273-5555; Fax: 805-273-3845.
Salesian Sisters of St. John Bosco 4; Lay Teachers 9; Students 360.
Catechesis/Religious Programs—Students 310.

Panorama City, Los Angeles Co., St. Genevieve (1950), Rev. Msgr. Charles E. Hill; Revs. Vlatko Poljicak; Paul D. Wolkovits.
Res., 14061 Roscoe Blvd., 91402. Tel: 818-894-2261.
School—Tel: 818-892-3802; Fax: 818-893-8143.
Sisters 4; Lay Teachers 20; Students 660.
High School—13967 Roscoe Blvd., 91402. Tel: 818-894-6417; Fax: 818-892-9853.
Lay Teachers 24; Students 488.
Catechesis/Religious Programs—Tel: 818-892-7177.
Students 589.

Paramount, Los Angeles Co., Our Lady of the Rosary (1913) (Hispanic-Tongan), Rev. Msgr. Bernard O'Reilly, (Retired); Revs. Idelfonso Madrigal; Edward J. Dober; Larry Neumeier.
Res., 14815 S. Paramount Blvd., 90723. Tel: 310-633-1126; Fax: 310-633-3192.
School—Tel: 310-633-6360; Fax: 310-633-2641.
Sisters of the Daughters of Mary and Joseph 4; Lay Teachers 10; Students 334.
Catechesis/Religious Programs—Tel: 310-602-0086.
Students 1,370.
Mission—Paramount, Catholic Korean Community of St. Raphael (Downey & Alondra), 15946 Downey Ave., 90723. Tel: 310-630-6168. Rev. Alex Chung.

Pasadena, Los Angeles Co., St. Andrew (1886) (Hispanic), Rev. Msgr. Tobias P. English; Revs. Victor J. Ruvalcaba; Paul A. Sustatya.
Res., 311 N. Raymond Ave., 91103. Tel: 626-792-4183; Fax: 626-792-4456.
School—(Grades K-8). Tel: 626-796-7697.
Sisters of the Holy Names of Jesus and Mary 3; Lay Teachers 8; Students 288.
Catechesis/Religious Programs—42 Chestnut St., 91103. Tel: 626-577-1770.
Students 613.

Assumption of the Blessed Virgin Mary (1950), Rev. Msgr. August Moretti; Rev. Walter Fernando; Rev. Msgr. Timothy J. Crean, Pastor Emeritus; Deacon James J. Crowley.
Res., 2640 E. Orange Grove Blvd., 91107. Tel: 626-792-1343.
School—2660 E. Orange Grove Blvd., 91107. Tel: 626-793-2089; Fax: 626-793-4070. Lou Anne Insprucker, Prin.
Lay Teachers 18; Students 306.
Catechesis/Religious Programs—Tel: 626-792-6844. Elly Dunbar, D.R.E.
Students 223.

St. Philip the Apostle (1921), Rev. Msgr. Gary P. Bauler; Revs. Marc V. Trudeau; Mariano Tomaszewski; Deacon William Landa.
Res., 151 S. Hill Ave., 91106. Tel: 626-793-0693; Fax: 626-793-0733.
School—161 S. Hill Ave., 91106. Tel: 626-795-9691; Fax: 626-795-9946.
Lay Teachers 18; Students 419.
Catechesis/Religious Programs—Students 360.

Pico Rivera, Los Angeles Co., St. Hilary (1950), Rev. Msgr. Christian VanLiefde; Revs. Hugo Neyra; Frank Russo; Deacon Antonio Soto.
Res., 5465 Citronell Ave., 90660. Tel: 562-942-7300; Fax: 562-948-3760.
School—Tel: 562-942-7361.
School Sisters of Notre Dame 3; Lay Teachers 13; Students 360.
Catechesis/Religious Programs—5401 S. Citronell Ave., 90660. Tel: 562-942-7018.
Students 529.
Convent—5333 S. Citronell Ave., 90660. Tel: 562-942-7151.

St. Marianne de Paredes (1951) (Hispanic), Revs. Fernando Iglesias; Martin Slaughter; Manuel Pontones.
Res., 7922 S. Passons Blvd., 90660. Tel: 562-949-8240; Fax: 562-942-2405.
School—7911 Buhman Ave., 90660. Tel: 562-949-1234; Fax: 562-948-3855. Sr. Francis Rose Rivers, S.S.N.D.
School Sisters of Notre Dame 1; Lay Teachers 11; Students 290.
Catechesis/Religious Programs—Tel: 562-949-5653.
Students 450.

St. Francis Xavier (1939) (Hispanic), Rev. Jorge Penaloza.
Res., 4245 S. Acacia Ave., 90660. Tel: 562-699-7517; Fax: 562-699-5331.
Catechesis/Religious Programs—Students 660.

Pomona, Los Angeles Co., St. Joseph (1886), Rev. Richard Carey. In res., Rev. Labib Kobti.
Res., 1150 W. Holt Ave., 91768. Tel: 909-629-4101; Fax: 909-623-0265.
School—Tel: 909-622-3365; Fax: 909-469-5146.
Felician Sisters 5; Lay Teachers 10; Students 326.
Catechesis/Religious Programs—1200 W. Holt Ave., 91768. Tel: 909-629-1404; Fax: 909-469-5146.
Students 330.

Sacred Heart (1935), Rev. Msgr. Manuel O. Sanchez; Revs. Leland Wilson; Jose Ortiz.
Res., 1215 S. Hamilton Blvd., 91766. Tel: 909-622-4553; Fax: 909-623-0841.
School—1263 S. Hamilton Blvd., 91766. Tel: 909-622-7170.
Lay Teachers 12; Students 140.
Catechesis/Religious Programs—Tel: 909-622-4716. Victoria Duran, D.R.E.
Students 1,320.

St. Madeleine (1963), Rev. Msgr. Andrew Tseu.
Res., 931 E. Kingsley Ave., 91767. Tel: 909-629-9495; Fax: 909-623-7148.
Catechesis/Religious Programs—Tel: 909-620-1300.
Students 256.

Rancho Palos Verdes, Los Angeles Co., St. John Fisher (1961), Rev. Msgr. Eugene A. Gilb; Rev. John Nghi Tran. In res., Rev. John C. McNamee.
Res., 5448 Crest Rd., P.O. Box 2249, 90275. Tel: 310-377-5571; Fax: 310-377-6303.
School—Tel: 310-377-2800.
Immaculate Heart of Mary Sisters 2; Lay Teachers 11; Students 283.
Catechesis/Religious Programs—5400 Crest Rd., 90275. Tel: 310-377-4573. Eileen Loughran, D.R.E.
Students 718.

Redondo Beach, Los Angeles Co., St. James (1892), Revs. Timothy Nichols; Edward Berumen; Brendan Kearney, S.J.; Deacon Richard Shinkle. In res., Rev. Jim Clarke.
Res., 415 Vincent St., 90277. Tel: 310-372-5228; Fax: 310-379-5552.
School—4625 Garnet St., Torrance, 90503. Tel: 310-371-0416; Fax: 310-371-8377.
Sisters of St. Joseph of Carondelet 2; Lay Teachers 9; Students 322.
Catechesis/Religious Programs—Tel: 310-379-3221. Diana Holly, D.R.E.
Students 322.

St. Lawrence Martyr (1955), Rev. Msgr. Michael Lenihan; Revs. John W. Neiman; Paul Vigil; Deacon Frank Dieter.
Res., 1900 S. Prospect Ave., 90277-6099. Tel: 310-540-0329; Fax: 310-540-8999.
School—1950 Prospect Ave., 90277-6003. Tel: 310-540-3049; Fax: 310-316-0888.
Sisters of St. Joseph of Carondelet 1; Lay Teachers 21; Students 305.
Catechesis/Religious Programs—Tel: 310-316-4460.
Students 550.

Reseda, Los Angeles Co., St. Catherine of Siena (1949), Rev. Sean B. Flanagan. In res., Rev. Raul Cortes; Deacon Pedro Lira.
Res., 18115 Sherman Way, 91335. Tel: 818-343-2110.
School—7311 Lindley Ave., 91335. Tel: 818-343-9880; Fax: 818-343-1018.
Lay Teachers 9; Students 321.
Catechesis/Religious Programs—Tel: 818-996-4588.
Students 579.

Rowland Heights, Los Angeles Co., St. Elizabeth Ann Seton (1981), Rev. Msgr. Michael F. Killeen; Revs. Robert Victoria; Peter Tsang; Deacon Steven V. Hillman.
Church—1835 Larkvane Rd., 91748.
Res., 18090 Via Amorosa, 91748. Tel: 626-964-3629; Fax: 626-913-2209.
Catechesis/Religious Programs—Tel: 626-965-5792.
Students 789.

San Dimas, Los Angeles Co., Holy Name of Mary (1957), Rev. Richard Danyluk, SS.CC.; Deacon Jack Clinton.
Res., 724 E. Bonita Ave., 91773. Tel: 909-599-1243; Fax: 909-599-4230.
School—Tel: 909-599-1234, Ext. 24.
Sisters 1; Lay Teachers 18; Students 315.
Catechesis/Religious Programs—Tel: 909-599-1243, Ext. 32.
Students 854.

San Fernando, Los Angeles Co., St. Ferdinand (1902), Revs. Anthony Dummer, O.M.I.; Paul Ouellette, O.M.I.
Office: 1109 Coronel St., 91340. Tel: 818-365-3967; Fax: 818-365-0067.
School—1012 Coronel St., 91340. Tel: 818-361-3264; Fax: 818-361-5894.
Sisters of St. Joseph of Carondelet 3; Lay Teachers 10; Students 302.
Catechesis/Religious Programs—Tel: 818-361-1813.
Students 311.

Santa Rosa (1927) (Hispanic), Revs. Paul W. Wilhelm, O.M.I.; Patrick Thompson, O.M.I.; Edgar Garcia, O.M.I. (Peru).
Res., 668 S. Workman St., 91340. Tel: 818-361-4617; Fax: 818-365-8599.
School—1309 Mott St., 91340. Tel: 818-361-5096; Fax: 818-361-2259.
Franciscan Missionary Sisters of the Immaculate Conception 7; Lay Teachers 4; Students 304.
Catechesis/Religious Programs—Tel: 818-365-5161.
Students 500.

San Gabriel, Los Angeles Co., San Gabriel (1771). (Old Mission). Revs. Dennis Gallo, C.M.F.; Jose Sanchez, C.M.F.; Deacon Gil Chavez. In res., Rev. Jack Hencier, C.M.F.; Bro. Cruz Pettinato, C.M.F.
Res., 537 W. Mission Dr., 91776. Tel: 626-457-3035; Fax: 626-282-5308. [CEM]
School—547 W. Mission Dr., 91776. Tel: 626-281-2454; Fax: 626-281-4817.
Dominican Sisters 2; Lay Teachers 10; Students 290.
High School—254 S. Santa Anita St., 91776. Tel: 626-282-3181; Fax: 626-282-4209.
Sisters 6; Lay Teachers 21; Girls 365.
Catechesis/Religious Programs—Tel: 626-457-3041.
Students 751.
Convent—561 W. Mission Dr., 91776. Tel: 626-282-8475.

St. Anthony (1945) (Hispanic), Revs. Michael Gleeson (Ireland); Marco Reyes; Gaspar Bautista (Mexico); Deacon John Messer.
Res., 1901 S. San Gabriel Blvd., 91776. Tel: 626-288-8912; Fax: 626-288-3730.
School—1905 S. San Gabriel Blvd., 91776. Tel: 626-280-7255; Fax: 626-280-3870. Sr. Kathleen Callaway, S.N.J.M., Prin.
Sisters of the Holy Names of Jesus and Mary 3; Lay Teachers 30; Students 592.
Catechesis/Religious Programs—Tel: 626-288-5511. Margarita Flores, D.R.E.
Students 700.
Convent—626 E. Marshall St., 91726. Tel: 626-288-2200.

San Marino, Los Angeles Co., Saints Felicitas and Perpetua (1938), Rev. Msgr. Lawrence J. Gibson. In res., Rev. Msgr. Paul M. Konoske.
Res., 1190 Palomar Rd., 91108. Tel: 626-796-0432.
School—2955 Huntington Dr., 91108. Tel: 626-796-8223.
Sisters 6; Lay Teachers 7; Students 311.

San Pedro, Los Angeles Co., Mary, Star of the Sea (1889), Rev. Msgr. Patrick J. Gallagher; Revs. Lorenzo De Dominici, (Retired); Mate Bizaca (Croatia); Vivian Ben Lima; Raymond Perez, O.Praem.; Deacon Nino Crisafulli.
Res., 870 W. 8th St., 90731. Tel: 310-833-3541; Fax: 310-833-9254.
School—Tel: 310-831-0875; Fax: 310-831-0877.
Priests 1; Lay Teachers 15; Students 295.
High School—Tel: 310-547-1138; Fax: 310-547-1827.
Priests 6; Lay Teachers 11; Students 340.
Catechesis/Religious Programs—717 S. Cabrillo Ave., 90731. Tel: 310-833-3933.
Students 465.

Holy Trinity (1924), Revs. Thomas J. Glynn; Damian Fernando; Richard Hoynes.
Parish Center: 209 N. Hanford Ave., 90732. Tel: 310-548-6535; Fax: 310-833-1134.
Church—1292 W. Santa Cruz St., 90732.
School—1226 W. Santa Cruz St., 90732. Tel: 310-833-0703; Fax: 310-833-5219.
Lay Teachers 23; Students 617.
Catechesis/Religious Programs—Tel: 310-833-3500.
Students 490.

St. Peter (1965) (Hispanic), Revs. Claudio De Agostini, C.S.J.; Bruno De Santi, C.S.J. In res., Rev. John Trimaglio, C.S.J.
Res., 338 N. Grand Ave., 90731-2006. Tel: 310-831-5360; Fax: 310-831-0415.
Catechesis/Religious Programs—Tel: 310-832-6731.
Students 600.

Santa Barbara, Santa Barbara Co.,

1—Holy Cross, (1973), Rev. Ludo DeClippel, C.J., (Belgium) Admin.; Deacons Nicholas Curran; David Huff.
Res., 1740 Cliff Dr., 93109. Tel: 805-962-0411; Fax: 805-564-6921.

2—Our Lady of Sorrows, (1856), Revs. Martin L. Brewer, S.J.; Thomas P. Delaney, S.J.; P. Jeremiah Helfrich, S.J.; Robert McDevitt, S.J.; Deacons Enrique Sanchez; Manuel Martinez.
Res., 21 E. Sola St., 93101. Tel: 805-963-1734; Fax: 805-965-6461.
School—33 E. Micheltorena St., 93101. Tel: 805-965-1033. Carol Hoffer, Prin.
Lay Teachers 12; Students 235.
Catechesis/Religious Programs—Tel: 805-966-4941.
Students 310.
Convent—19 E. Micheltorena St., 93101. Tel: 805-966-3089.

3—Our Lady of Guadalupe, (1928) (Hispanic), Revs. Guillermo C. Garcia, C.J.; Timothy R. Lane, C.J.
Res., 801 Jennings Ave., 93103. Tel: 805-965-4060; Fax: 805-965-3386.
Catechesis/Religious Programs—Tel: 805-962-4441.
Students 360.

4—St. Barbara, (1786). (Old Mission). Revs. Vincent Mesi, O.F.M.; Howard Hall, O.F.M.; Deacons Jim Bret; Jack Ryan.
Res., Old Mission, 2201 Laguna St., 93105. Tel: 805-682-4713; Fax: 805-687-7841. [CEM]

5—San Roque, (1953), Rev. James M. Ford; Rev. Msgr. Philip Grill; Deacon William B. Sangster.
Res., 325 Argonne Circle, 93105. Tel: 805-687-5215; Fax: 805-682-9778. [JC]
School—314 Calle Cedro, 93105. Tel: 805-687-3717; Fax: 805-687-3581. Anne Marie Omweg, Prin.
Lay Teachers 13; Aides 1; Students 250.
Catechesis/Religious Programs—Tel: 805-682-1097.
Students 250.

Santa Clarita, Los Angeles Co., Our Lady of Perpetual Help (1944), Revs. Patrick A. Power; Jeffrey J. Deikel; Norm Supancheck; Sr. M. Jane Mast, S.H.F., Pastoral Min.; Deacon Richard Karl.
Res., 23233 Lyons Ave., 91321-2632. Tel: 805-259-2276; Fax: 805-259-1873.
School—Tel: 805-259-1141; Fax: 805-259-8254.
Franciscan Sisters of the Immaculate Conception 5; Lay Teachers 11; Students 330.
Catechesis/Religious Programs—Tel: 805-259-4266.
Students 985.
Convent—23719 Rotunda Rd., 91355. Tel: 805-259-5591.

Santa Fe Springs, Los Angeles Co., St. Pius X (1954) (Hispanic), Revs. John McHugh; Porfirio Alvarez; Antolin B. Torralba (Philippines); Peter Ha Son Le (Vietnamese); Rev. Msgr. Glen A. Rademacher, Pastor Emeritus.
Res., 10827 S. Pioneer Blvd., 90670. Tel: 562-863-8734; Fax: 562-868-0051.
School—Tel: 562-864-4818; Fax: 562-864-7120.
Lay Teachers 14; Students 361.
Catechesis/Religious Programs—Tel: 562-868-2389.
Students 774.

Santa Maria, Santa Barbara Co., St. Mary of the Assumption (1905), Rev. Msgr. James P. Colberg; Rev. Samuel Flores, O.F.M.Cap.
Res., 414 E. Church St., 93454. Tel: 805-922-5826; Fax: 805-922-1986.
School—P.O. Drawer 1965, 93454. Tel: 805-925-6713; Fax: 805-922-1986.
Sisters 1; Lay Teachers 11; Students 250.
Catechesis/Religious Programs—Tel: 805-925-1334.
Students 266.

St. Louis de Montfort (Santa Barbara) (1963), Revs. Mark L. Newman, C.J.; Campion W. Aspinall, C.J.; John A. Mayhew, C.J.; L. Bede Johnson, C.J., (Retired); Deacons Richard Carmody; Douglas Halvorsen.
Res., 5075 Harp Rd., 93455. Tel: 805-937-4555; Fax: 805-934-2805. [JC]
School—Tel: 805-937-5571; Fax: 805-937-3181.
Sisters 2; Lay Teachers 9; Students 292.
Catechesis/Religious Programs—Tel: 805-937-8363.
Students 700.
Mission—Los Alamos, Santa Barbara Co., St. Anthony's Church, 260 Helena St., Los Alamos, 93440.

St. John Neumann (Santa Barbara) (1986) (Hispanic), Revs. Emigdio Herrera; John Higson; Deacons Manuel Liendo; Lyle Goodspeed; Sr. Margaret Bannan, O.S.F., Pastoral Assoc.
Res., 966 W. Orchard, 93454. Tel: 805-922-7099; Fax: 805-346-1747.
Catechesis/Religious Programs—Tel: 805-922-5233.
Students 667.

Santa Monica, Los Angeles Co., St. Monica (1886), Rev. Msgr. Lloyd A. Torgerson; Revs. David Heney; Michael Rocha; Deacon Gene McNamara. In res., Revs. Jon Majarucon; Bernard O'Connor, C.M.F.; Robert A. Dowd, C.S.C (FTW).
Church—725 California Ave., 90403. Tel: 310-393-9287; Fax: 310-319-9758.
School—1039 Seventh St., 90403. Tel: 310-451-9801; Fax: 310-394-6001.
Lay Teachers 12; Students 290.
High School—1030 Lincoln Blvd., 90403. Tel: 310-394-3701; Fax: 310-458-1353.
Sisters 3; Lay Teachers 37; Students 620.
Catechesis/Religious Programs—Tel: 310-395-8903.
Students 300.

St. Anne (1951) (Hispanic), Rev. Adalberto Blanco.
Res., 2011 Colorado Ave., 90404. Tel: 310-829-4411; Fax: 310-829-9006.
School—2017 Colorado Ave., 90404. Tel: 310-829-2775.
Sisters of St. Louis 1; Lay Teachers 9; Students 213.
Catechesis/Religious Programs—Tel: 310-829-4040.
Students 231.

St. Clement (1904), Rev. Juan Romero. In res., Rev. Mark Strader.
Res., 3102 Third St., 90405. Tel: 310-396-2679; Fax: 310-396-4239.
Catechesis/Religious Programs—204 Hampton Dr., Venice, 90291. Tel: 310-392-5769.
Students 150.

Santa Paula, Ventura Co., St. Sebastian (1896), Rev. James A. Rothe.
Res., 235 N. Ninth St., 93060. Tel: 805-525-2149; Fax: 805-933-5520.
School—325 E. Santa Barbara St., 93060. Tel: 805-525-1575.
Lay Teachers 14; Students 250; Pre-School 32.
Catechesis/Religious Programs—Students 103.

Our Lady of Guadalupe (1929) (Hispanic), Rev. Rene Juarez, O.F.M.
Res., 427 N. Oak St., 93060. Tel: 909-622-4553; Fax: 909-623-0841. [CEM]
Catechesis/Religious Programs—423 N. Oak St., 93060. Tel: 909-525-2225.
Students 703.
Convent—432 N. Oak St., 93060. Tel: 805-525-9207.

Sepulveda, Los Angeles Co., Our Lady of Peace (1944), Revs. John Keese, Admin.; Sang V. Tran; David Granadino.
Res., 15444 Nordhoff St., 91343. Tel: 818-894-1176; Fax: 818-894-3838.
School—9022 Langdon Ave., 91343. Tel: 818-894-4059.
Lay Teachers 9; Students 286.
Catechesis/Religious Programs—Tel: 818-891-3578.
Students 577.

Sherman Oaks, Los Angeles Co., St. Francis de Sales (1938), Revs. Kevin J. Larkin; James M. Maher; Deacon John Coplen. In res., Rev. Jerome O'Mahony, M.S.C.
Res., 13360 Valleyheart Dr., 91423. Tel: 818-784-0105; Fax: 818-784-4807.
Church—Moorpark St. at Dixie Canyon Ave., 91423.
School—13368 Valleyheart Dr., 91423. Tel: 818-784-9573; Fax: 818-784-9649. Sr. Ellen Marie McGovern, Prin.
Sisters 2; Lay Teachers 12; Students 310.
Catechesis/Religious Programs—Students 150.

Sierra Madre, Los Angeles Co., St. Rita (1908), Rev. Msgr. Joseph J. Cokus; Rev. Msgr. Robert Gara, Pastor Emeritus; Deacon Ernest Nosari.
Res., 50 E. Alegria Ave., 91024. Tel: 818-355-1292; Fax: 818-355-2290.
School—Tel: 818-355-6114; Fax: 818-355-0713.
Lay Teachers 16; Students 306.
Catechesis/Religious Programs—Tel: 818-355-3841.
Students 245.

Simi Valley, Ventura Co., St. Peter Claver (1972), Revs. Gary P. Bauler; Rock Janowski; Deacon Richard Hamm.
Res., 5649 Pittman St., 93063. Tel: 805-526-6499; Fax: 805-526-7233.
Catechesis/Religious Programs—Tel: 805-526-0680; 526-3685.
Students 618.

St. Rose of Lima (1921), Revs. Michael J. Carcerano; John W. Sigler; Jerald W. Thompson; Deacon Peter Wilson.
Res., 1305 Royal Ave., 93065. Tel: 805-526-1732; Fax: 805-526-0067.

School—1325 Royal Ave., 93065. Tel: 805-526-5304; Fax: 805-526-0939.
Lay Teachers 19; Students 316.
Catechesis/Religious Programs—Tel: 805-526-5513.
Students 785.

Solvang, Santa Barbara Co., Old Mission Santa Ines (1804) (Spanish), Revs. Robert Barbato, O.F.M.Cap; Miguel Ortiz, O.F.M.Cap; Daniel Kabat, O.F.M.Cap. In res., Revs. Cyril Kelleher, O.F.M.Cap.; Timothy O'Sullivan, O.F.M.Cap.
Res., 1760 Mission Dr., P.O. Box 408, 93464. Tel: 805-688-4815; Fax: 805-686-4468.
Catechesis/Religious Programs—Tel: 805-688-4138.
Students 415.

South El Monte, Los Angeles Co., Epiphany (1956), Revs. Tomas A. Elis, Admin.; Benito Armenta.
Res., 10911 Michael Hunt Dr., 91733. Tel: 626-442-6262; Fax: 626-575-1738.
School—10915 Michael Hunt Dr., 91733. Tel: 626-442-6264; Fax: 626-442-6074.
Bernardine Sisters 4; Lay Teachers 7; Students 293.
Catechesis/Religious Programs—Tel: 626-448-3636.
Students 1,400.

South Gate, Los Angeles Co., St. Helen (1931), Revs. Jerome A. Bouska; Francisco Javier Perez.
Res., 8912 South Gate Ave., 90280. Tel: 213-563-3522; Fax: 213-563-0161.
School—Tel: 213-566-5491; Fax: 213-566-2810.
Sisters of Notre Dame 1; Lay Teachers 9; Students 339.
Catechesis/Religious Programs—Tel: 213-563-3536.
Students 525.

South Pasadena, Los Angeles Co., Holy Family (1910), Rev. Msgr. Clement J. Connolly; Revs. Finbarr Devine, SS.CC.; Michael J. Sezzi.
Res., 1301 Rollin St., 91030. Tel: 626-799-8908; Fax: 626-799-0423.
School—1519 Fremont Ave., 91030. Tel: 626-799-4354; Fax: 626-799-4530. Mrs. Anne Murphy, Prin.
Lay Teachers 9; Students 297.
Catechesis/Religious Programs—Tel: 626-403-5118.
Students 370.

Sun Valley, Los Angeles Co., Our Lady of the Holy Rosary (1937), Revs. Livio Stella, C.S. (Italy); Hily Gonzales, C.S. (Philippines); Rodolfo Lache (Colombia).
Res., 7800 Vineland Ave., 91352. Tel: 818-765-3350; Fax: 818-765-3170.
School—7802 Vineland Ave., 91352. Tel: 818-765-4897; Fax: 818-765-5791.
Servant Sisters of the Blessed Sacrament 5; Lay Teachers 8; Students 290.
Catechesis/Religious Programs—Tel: 818-982-4248. Claudia Marin, D.R.E.
Students 1,250.
Convent—7757 Cleon St., 91352. Tel: 818-764-9857.
Mission—North Hollywood, Los Angeles Co., Our Lady of Zapopan, 7824 Lankershim Blvd., North Hollywood, 91605. Tel: 818-503-8920.

Sylmar, Los Angeles Co., St. Didacus (1957), Rev. Msgr. Peter L. Amy; Rev. Julio Roman (Panama).
Res., 14339 Astoria St., 91342. Tel: 818-367-6181; Fax: 818-367-0604.
School—14325 Astoria St., 91342. Tel: 818-367-5886.
Lay Teachers 9; Students 326.
Catechesis/Religious Programs—Tel: 818-367-4155.
Students 900.

Temple City, Los Angeles Co., St. Luke the Evangelist (1946), Revs. Thomas King; Michael Carroll; Jeremiah O'Keeffe.
Parish Administrative Center—5605 Cloverly Ave., 91780.
Res., 9451 E. Broadway, P.O. Box 798, 91780. Tel: 626-291-5900; Fax: 626-287-2332.
School—Tel: 626-291-5959.
Lay Teachers 13; Students 311.
Catechesis/Religious Programs—Tel: 626-291-5925; Fax: 626-291-5925.
Students 436.

Thousand Oaks, Ventura Co., St. Paschal Baylon (1960), Rev. Msgr. Joseph S. George; Revs. Thomas O'Hanlon; Joseph Gaffney; Deacon James Robinson.
Res., 155 E. Janss Rd., 91360. Tel: 805-496-0222; Fax: 805-379-2506.
School—Tel: 805-495-9340.
Lay Teachers 15; Students 312.
Catechesis/Religious Programs—Tel: 805-497-2815.
Students 800.

Torrance, Los Angeles Co., Nativity (1924), Revs. Paul M. Albee; Miguel Amengual; Patrick J. McHugh, Pastor Emeritus. In res., Rev. Alexander Hoefler, S.V.D.
Res., 1447 Engracia Ave., 90501-3234. Tel: 310-328-2776; Fax: 310-328-0508.
School—2371 Carson, 90501. Tel: 310-328-5387; Fax: 310-328-5365.
Lay Teachers 13; Students 303.
Catechesis/Religious Programs—Tel: 310-320-6673.
Students 340.
Mission—Torrance, Los Angeles Co., St. Joseph, 2314 Del Amo, 90501.

St. Catherine Laboure (1949), Revs. John O'Byrne; Donald F. Grasha; J. Kim-Dang Nguyen; Deacon Matilde Magana. In res., Rev. Sabato Pilato.
Res., 3846 Redondo Beach Blvd., 90504. Tel: 310-323-8900; Fax: 213-321-0486.
School—Tel: 310-324-8732; Fax: 310-324-2471. Mrs. Kathleen Gorze, Prin.
Lay Teachers 19; Students 560.
Catechesis/Religious Programs—16831 Ainsworth, 90504. Tel: 310-515-6033. Elaine O'Keefe, D.R.E.
Students 508.

Tujunga, Los Angeles Co., Our Lady of Lourdes (1920), Revs. George R. Brincat; Blaise Brockman; Deacon Paul Chacon.
Res., 10321 Tujunga Canyon Blvd., 91042. Tel: 818-352-3218; Fax: 818-352-2738.
School—Tel: 818-353-1106.
Sisters of Charity of the Blessed Virgin Mary 1; Lay Teachers 8; Students 273.
Catechesis/Religious Programs—Tel: 818-353-3053.
Students 388.

Valinda, Los Angeles Co., St. Martha (1958) (Hispanic-Filipino), Revs. William T. Easterling; Rodel Balagtas; Matthias Berumen; Deacon Jacob Favela. In res., Rev. Msgr. Aidan M. Carroll.
Res., 444 N. Azusa Ave., 91744-4299. Tel: 626-964-4313; Fax: 626-913-2953.
School—Tel: 626-964-1093; Fax: 626-912-2014.
Sisters of the Love of God 5; Lay Teachers 4; Students 330.
Catechesis/Religious Programs—Tel: 626-912-2581.
Students 1,000.

Van Nuys, Los Angeles Co., St. Elisabeth (1919) (Hispanic), Revs. Kevin Nolan; Roger Labonte; John Brady; Deacon Wesley Balbuena.
Res., 6635 Tobias Ave., 91405. Tel: 818-779-1756; Fax: 818-785-4492.
School—Tel: 818-779-1766; Fax: 818-779-1768.
Lay Teachers 10; Students 327.
Catechesis/Religious Programs—Tel: 818-779-1772.
Students 750.

St. Bridget of Sweden (1955), Rev. Raymond Morales; Deacon Ramon Rivera. In res., Rev. Robert Milbauer.
Res., 16711 Gault St., 91406. Tel: 818-782-7180; Fax: 818-782-7184.
School—7120 Whitaker, 91406. Tel: 818-785-4422; Fax: 818-785-0490.
Lay Teachers 12; Students 270.
Catechesis/Religious Programs—Tel: 818-782-7711. Jacinta O'Connor, D.R.E.
Students 220.
Convent—16707 Gault St., 91406. Tel: 818-786-1401.

Venice, Los Angeles Co., St. Mark (1923), Revs. Roderic M. Guerrini; Mark A. Martinez. In res., Rev. Harry Cronin, C.S.C.
Res., 940 Coeur d'Alene Ave., 90291. Tel: 310-821-5058; Fax: 310-821-7031.
School—912 Coeur d'Alene, 90291. Tel: 310-821-6612; Fax: 310-822-6101.
Lay Teachers 9; Students 319.
Catechesis/Religious Programs—Tel: 310-822-1201.
Students 285.

Ventura, Ventura Co., San Buenaventura Mission (1782) (Hispanic), Rev. Msgr. Patrick J. O'Brien; Rev. Joseph D. Pina; Rev. Msgr. Michael Hughes, (Retired).
Res., 211 E. Main St., 93001. Tel: 805-643-4318; Fax: 805-643-7831.
School—183 E. Main St., 93001. Tel: 805-643-1500.
Lay Teachers 11; Students 207.
Catechesis/Religious Programs—Students 420.

Our Lady of the Assumption (1954), Revs. Michael Jennett; Lawrence J. Dowdel, Jr.; George L. Reynolds, II; Deacons James M. Farley; Rodger Adams.
Res., 3175 Telegraph Rd., 93003-3283. Tel: 805-642-7966; Fax: 805-642-7635.
School—3169 Telegraph Rd., 93003-3282. Tel: 805-642-7198; Fax: 805-642-7110.
Sisters 2; Lay Teachers 12; Students 319.
Catechesis/Religious Programs—Tel: 805-642-0568.
Students 530.

Sacred Heart (1966), Rev. Daniel O'Sullivan; Rev. Msgr. Arnold Biedermann, Pastor Emeritus; Deacon Braden McKinley, Admin.
Res., 10800 Henderson Rd., 93004. Tel: 805-647-3235; Fax: 805-647-8087.
School—(Grades K-8). Tel: 805-647-6174; Fax: 805-647-8087.
Sisters 1; Lay Teachers 9; Students 310.
Catechesis/Religious Programs—Tel: 805-647-6260.
Students 370.
Mission—Camarillo, Ventura Co., Cabrillo Chapel, 2361 Rose Ln., Camarillo, 93012. Tel: 805-491-3972. Rev. Ramon Farre.

Vernon, Los Angeles Co., Holy Angels Parish of the Deaf (1987), Revs. Brian Doran; Tom Schweitzer; Deacon James Dillon; Donald R. Rosenkjar, Admin.
Res., 4433 Santa Fe Ave., 90058. Tel: 213-587-0397 (TDD); Fax: 213-587-7193.

Walnut, Los Angeles Co., St. Lorenzo Ruiz (1991), Rev. Dennis C. Vellucci.
Res., 747 Meadowpass Rd., 91789. Tel: 909-595-9545; Fax: 909-594-3940.
Catechesis/Religious Programs—Tel: 909-468-1812.
Students 435.

West Covina, Los Angeles Co., St. Christopher (1954), Rev. Msgr. John P. Won; Rev. Charles Schwehr, Admin.; Deacon Douglas Maloney. In res., Rev. Eric A. Lewis.
Res., 629 S. Glendora Ave., 91790. Tel: 626-960-1805; Fax: 626-851-0595.
School—900 W. Christopher St., 91790. Tel: 626-960-3079. Ms. Gail Fernandez, Prin.
Lay Teachers 11; Students 311.
Catechesis/Religious Programs—Tel: 626-338-2937. Dolores Zavala, D.R.E.
Students 707.
Convent—840 W. Christopher St., 91790. Tel: 818-338-6056.
Mission—West Covina, St. Christopher Korean Catholic Community, 833-835 W. Christopher St., 91790.

West Hollywood, Los Angeles Co., St. Victor (1906), Rev. Msgr. George J. Parnassus; Rev. Frederick J. Heney, S.J.
Res., 8634 Holloway Dr., 90069. Tel: 310-652-6477; Fax: 310-652-6478.

Westlake Village, Los Angeles Co., St. Jude (1970), Rev. Msgr. William J. Leser, C.B.; Rev. Donald C. White; Deacons Aloysius Caffrey; Dick Dorman. In res., Rev. Msgr. Thomas O'Connell, Pastor Emeritus.
Res., 32032 W. Lindero Canyon Rd., 91361-4270. Tel: 818-889-1279; Fax: 818-889-3405.
School—32036 W. Lindero Canyon Rd., 91361-4270. Tel: 818-889-9483.
Lay Teachers 15; Students 303.
Catechesis/Religious Programs—32034 W. Lindero Canyon Rd., 91361-4270. Tel: 818-889-0612.
Students 735.

Whittier, Los Angeles Co., St. Mary of the Assumption (1803), Revs. Enrique A. Lopez, C.SS.R.; Joseph Tobin, C.SS.R.; Joseph Elliott, C.SS.R.; Donald Liberty, C.SS.R. In res., Revs. J. Timothy Watson, C.SS.R.; Lionel Sirois, C.SS.R. (Canada); Clarence Bodden, C.SS.R.; Arturo Uribe, C.SS.R.; Antonio Medina, C.SS.R.
Res., 7215 S. Newlin Ave., 90602. Tel: 310-698-0107; Fax: 310-696-1617.
School—Tel: 310-698-0253; Fax: 310-698-0206.
Sisters 1; Lay Teachers 25; Students 620.
Catechesis/Religious Programs—Tel: 310-693-3764.
Students 704.

St. Bruno (1955), Revs. Patrick O'Dwyer; James Bradley, S.D.S.; Deacon P. Michael Freeman. In res., Rev. Frank Mannion, S.S.C.
Res., 15740 Citrustree Rd., 90603. Tel: 310-947-5637; Fax: 310-943-3193.
School—15700 Citrustree Rd., 90603. Tel: 310-943-8812; Fax: 310-943-2172.
Lay Teachers 14; Students 345.
Catechesis/Religious Programs—Tel: 310-943-2510.
Students 550.
Convent—10734 S. Widener Ave., 90603. Tel: 310-947-1177. Sr. Theresa Thanh Hao Nguyen, L.H.C., Supr.

St. Gregory the Great (1951), Rev. Msgr. Donald J. Ruddy; Revs. Albert Bahhuth; Rolly Jardiniano; Deacon Servando Patlan.
Res., 13935 Telegraph Rd., 90604. Tel: 562-941-0115; Fax: 562-941-3785.
School—13925 Telegraph Rd., 90604. Tel: 562-941-0750.
Irish Presentation Sisters 2; Lay Teachers 8; Students 340.

Catechesis/Religious Programs—Tel: 256-944-8311.
Students 777.

Wilmington, Los Angeles Co., SS. Peter and Paul's (1866), Revs. Peter Irving; Joaquin Haefeli; Michael Perea, O.Praem.; Deacon Russell Harrison.
Res., 515 W. Opp St., 90744. Tel: 310-834-5215; Fax: 310-834-4685.
School—706 Bayview Ave., 90744. Tel: 310-834-5574.
Sisters 4; Lay Teachers 9; Students 275.
Catechesis/Religious Programs—Tel: 310-549-2048.
Students 550.

Holy Family (1929) (Hispanic), Revs. Esteban Marquez; Jesus Garay.
Res., 1220 N. Sanford Ave., P.O. Box 416, 90748. Tel: 310-834-6333; 834-2788; Fax: 310-834-9038.
School—1122 E. Robidoux St., 90748. Tel: 310-518-1440. Ms. Celia Campos, Prin.
Lay Teachers 6; Students 315.
Catechesis/Religious Programs—Students 193.

Woodland Hills, Los Angeles Co., St. Mel (1955), Rev. Msgr. Padraic Loftus; Revs. Matthew Di Maria, C.M.F.; Ramon Valera. Pastor Emeriti: Rev. Msgr. John T. Naughton; Rev. Msgr. Michael J. O'Connor.
Res., 20870 Ventura Blvd., 91364. Tel: 818-340-6020; Fax: 818-340-0261.
School—20874 Ventura Blvd., 91364. Tel: 818-340-1924; Fax: 818-347-4426.
Sisters of St. Louis 2; Lay Teachers 31; Students 601.
Catechesis/Religious Programs—Tel: 818-340-6250.
Students 285.

St. Bernardine of Siena (1962), Rev. Msgr. Paul T. Dotson; Rev. Msgr. Richard H. Murray, Pastor Emeritus; Revs. Timothy McGowan; Paul Brogan; Deacons Jerry Cellner; Dan McHugh; Dale Taufer.
Res., 24410 Calvert St., 91367. Tel: 818-888-8200; Fax: 818-888-5046.
School—Tel: 818-340-2130.
Lay Teachers 12; Students 320.
Catechesis/Religious Programs—6061 Valley Circle Blvd., 91367. Tel: 818-340-1440.
Students 282.

Chaplains of Public Institutions

Non-Catholic Hospitals/Institutions

LOS ANGELES. *Cedar Sinai Medical Center*. Rev. Michael Wempe, Chap., 8700 Beverly Blvd., Rm. 2508, 90048. Tel: 310-855-5550; Fax: 310-967-0643.
L.A. City Fire Dept. Rev. Msgr. Christian M. Van Liefde, Chap., Tel: 310-942-7300.
L.A. County Fire Dept. Rev. Robert Folbrecht Tel: 818-341-3680, 9901 Mason Ave., Chatsworth, 91311-4525. Fax: 818-882-4326 (St. John Eudes).
L.A. County/University of Southern California Hospital. St. Camillus Center for Pastoral Care, 1911 Zonal Ave., 90033. Tel: 213-225-4561; 223-9047 (Aids Center); Fax: 213-225-9096. Rev. Chris Ponnet, Chaplains: Rev. Steven Hernandez; Sr. Dora Hauchecorne, I.C.M.; Sr. Clara Kelkermans, I.C.M.; Ms. Lupe Guzman; Mr. Dennis Apel; Sr. Mary Jean Ferry, B.V.M.; Sr. Angeles Reyes, F.S.J.; Sr. Matilda Ortiz, C.M.S.T.; Sr. Maria Perez, C.M.S.T.; Mr. Jorge Manley-Gil; Mr. Eugene Kreider; Deacon James Dillon; Mr. Gregoria Alonso, Volunteer Coord., In res., Rev. Msgr. Terry Richey.
L.A. Police Department. Rev. Michael P. McCullough, Chap., Employee Assistance Unit, 150 N. Los Angeles St., 90012. Tel: 213-485-0703.

CAMARILLO. *Camarillo State Hospital-Development Center*. Rev. Hippolyte L. Goossens, C.J., Chap., Tel: 805-484-3661 Ext. 4459, P.O. Box 6022-250, 93011.
Ventura School, California Youth Authority 3100 Wright Rd., 93010-8307. Deacon Larry Modugno Tel: 805-278-3846.

DOWNEY. *Rancho Los Amigos Medical Center*. Rev. Msgr. John A. Fosselman Tel: 562-940-7257, 7601 E. Imperial Hwy., 90242.

DUARTE. *City of Hope Medical Center* 1500 E. Duarte Rd., 91010. Tel: 626-359-8911. Rev. Ramon Marti, Sch.P., Annunciation Parish, Arcadia. Tel: 626-447-6202.

LOMPOC. *Lompoc Federal Correctional Institution* 3600 Guard Rd., 93436. Tel: 805-736-4154, Ext. 725. Rev. Richard J. Vega, Chap.
US Penitentiary 3901 Klein Rd., 93436. Tel: 805-735-2771, Ext. 450 & 297. Chaplains: Rev. Michael Kirkness; Deacon John Burke.
Vandenberg Air Force Base. Rev. Thomas D. Kelly, Chap., 30SPW/HC Tel: 805-734-8232, 587 Utah St., Bldg. 16200, Vandenberg AFB, 93437-6309.

LONG BEACH. *Veterans Affairs Medical Center*. Rev. Leo M. Miller, O.M.I., Chap.; Rev. Msgr. Joseph F. Brennan, (Retired), USN; Rev. Anselm Deehr, S.T., 5901 E. 7th St., 90822. Tel: 562-494-5418.

NORWALK. *California Youth Authority*. Rev. Leo John Celano, O.Praem., Chap., Southern Reception Center and Clinic, 13200 S. Bloomfield Ave., 90650. Tel: 562-868-9979, Ext. 2467.
Metropolitan State Hospital. Rev. Jerome Stack, C.PP.S., Chap., Tel: 310-863-7011, 11400 S. Norwalk Blvd., 90650. Tel: 562-651-4311.

POINT MUGU. *Naval Air Station*. Rev. Donald Roy Moss, USNR, Code 83G000E NAWS, 521 Ninth St., Point Magu, 93042. Tel: 805-989-7967.

POMONA. *Frank D. Lanterman Development Center* 3035 W. Pomona Blvd., 91768. Tel: 909-595-1221, Ext. 7162. Mailing Address:Mailing Address: P.O. Box 100, 91759. Sr. Nuala Ryan, S.S.L., Chap., Tel: 909-869-0431.

PORT HUENEME. *Naval Construction Battalion Center*. Rev. James W. Anderson, 1000 23rd Ave. (Code 16), Bldg. 1433 Tel: 805-982-4358.

SAN PEDRO. *Fort MacArthur Annex*. Rev. Michael J. DiRenzo, 61-ABG/HC, Chaplain's Office, 325 Challenger Way, Ste, 1090, Los Angeles, 90245-5677. Tel: 310-363-1956.

SEPULVEDA. *Veterans Administration Medical Center*. Rev. Patrick O'Hagan, SS.CC. Tel: 818-895-9322, 16111 Plummer St.

TERMINAL ISLAND. *Federal Correctional Institution*. Rev. Lorenzo Miranda, Chap., 804 E. Compton, Compton, 90220-1198. Tel: 213-321-0420 (St. Albert the Great).

TORRENACE. *L.A. County-Harbor-U.C.L.A. Medical Center* 1000 W. Carson, 90509. Tel: 310-222-2345; 222-2167 (Catholic Chap. Office). Rev. Cesar Raffo-Rivasplata, 21900 S. Main St., Carson, 90745. Tel: 310-835-7161 (St. Philomena Parish).

WEST LOS ANGELES. *Veterans Administration Wadsworth Hospital Center*. Rev. Francis Kelly Tel: 310-824-4312, Chaplain Service, 11301 Willshire Blvd. 691/125, 90099-5786. Tel: 310-268-3391.

Detention Ministries

LOS ANGELES. *Department of Detention Ministries* 933 Grattan St., 90015-1194. Tel: 213-251-2648; Fax: 213-251-2675. Bro. Peter Donohue, C.F.X., Dir.; Sr. Suzanne Jabro, C.S.J., Parish Contact Coordinator.
L.A. Juvenile Detention Facilities Central Juvenile Hall, 1605 Eastlake Ave., 90033. Tel: 213-226-8530. Sr. Janet Harris, P.B.V.M.; Ms. Angelita Hurtado,
MacLaren Hall, Sr. Mary Allyn Ayres, O.P.,
Dorothy Kirby Center, Sr. Mary Allyn Ayres, O.P.
Los Angeles County Jails in the City of Los Angeles, Adult Facilities Biscailuz Center, 1060 Northeastern Ave., Tel: 213-267-2674.
L.A. Men's Central Jail, 441 Bauchet St., 90012. Tel: 213-974-8081. Rev. George Horan; Bros. Lawrence J. Moen, C.M.F.; Thomas P. Cunningham, C.S.C.; Mr. Pacifico Diaz,
Sybil Brand Institute, 4500 East City Terrace Drive, 90063. Tel: 213-267-2809. Mrs. Karen E. Brudney; Sr. Mary Leo Grijalva, S.N.J.M.; Sr. Rose Waldron, D.M.J.
Twin Towers Correctional Facility. (Men). 450 Bauchet St., 90063. Tel: 213-893-5241. Valentin Saucedo, Chap.
Twin Towers Correctional Facility. (Women). 450 Bauchet St., 90063. Tel: 213-893-5152. Chaplains: Sr. May Leo Grijalva, S.N.J.M; Karen E. Brudney.

DOWNEY. *Los Padrinos Juvenile Hall* 7285 Quali Dr., 90242. Tel: 562-940-8711; 8712. Sr. Teresa Doherty, R.S.C.

LANCASTER. *California State Prison, L.A. County* 44750 60th St. W., 93536-7620. Tel: 805-729-2000, Ext. 6129. Donald E. Simanski, Chap.
Challenger Youth Memorial Center 5300 West Ave. I, 93956. Tel: 805-940-4165; 4166. Mrs. Bertha Maldanado.

LYNWOOD. *Century Regional Detention Facility* 11705 S. Alameda St., 90262. Tel: 213-357-5114. Deacon Willard J. Hall.

OJAI. *Ojai Men's Honor Farm* 370 W. Baldwin Rd., 93023. Margaret Oberon, Chap., Tel: 805-988-0903.
Ojai Women's Jail Farm 370 W. Baldwin Rd., 93023. Margaret Oberon, Chap., Tel: 805-988-0903.

SANTA BARBARA. *Los Prietos Boy's Camp*. Vacant. Star Route, 93105-9722. Tel: 805-685-5326.
Santa Barbara County Jail 4436 Calle Real, 93110. Tel: 805-681-5334. Beth Morales.
Santa Barbara Juvenile Hall 4500 Hollister Avenue, 93111. Tel: 805-685-5326; 681-5334. Beth Morales.

SANTA MARIA. *Juvenile Hall* 812-B W. Foster Rd., 93454. Tel: 805-685-5326. Beth Morales.

SANTA PAULA. *Santa Paula Jail* 600 S. Todd Rd., 93060. Margaret Oberon, Chap., Tel: 805-988-0903.

SAUGUS. *North County Correctional Facility* 29340 The Old Road, 91350. Tel: 805-295-7800, Ext. 5217. William B. McKinley.
Pitchess Detention Center 29300 The Old Road, 91350. Medium South, Rev. John D. Murray Tel: 805-257-8853 Ext. 3020, Medium North, Gonzalo De Vivero Tel: 805-257-8840 Ext. 3445, Medium East, Sr. Rose M. Waldron, D.M.J. Tel: 805-257-8815 Ext. 3337.

SYLMAR. *Barry J. Nedorf Juvenile Hall* 16350 Filbert St., 91342. Tel: 818-364-2021. Ms. Doriscia Briceni.

THOUSAND OAKS. *East County Jail* 2101 E. Olsen Rd., 93162. Margaret Oberon, Chap., Tel: 805-988-0903.

VENTURA. *Colston Treatment Center*. Vacant. 315 N. Hillmont Ave., 93003. Tel: 805-988-0903.
Ventura County Jail 800 S. Victoria Ave., 93009. Margaret Oberon, Chap., Tel: 805-988-0903.
Ventura Juvenile Hall-Clifton Tatum Center. Vacant. 380 N. Hillmont Ave., 93003. Tel: 805-988-0903. Margaren Oberon, Chap.
Ventura Juvenile Restitution Project 381 Hospital Rd., 93003. Tel: 805-988-0903. Margaret Oberon, Chap.

WHITTIER. *Fred C. Nelles Correctional Facility* 11850 E. Whittier Blvd., 90601. Tel: 310-698-6781, Ext. 2532. John W. Hitchman, Chap.

Camps

LOS ANGELES. *Juvenile Probation Camps*.
Camp C.B. Afflerbaugh, Vacant. 6331 N. Stephens Ranch Rd., La Verne, 91750. Tel: 909-596-0686.
Camp Dorothy Kirby Center, Vacant. 1500 S. McDonnell Ave., 90022. Tel: 213-747-3542.
Camp David Gonzales, Vacant. 1301 N. Las Virgines Rd., Calabasas, 91302. Tel: 310-821-4126.
Camp Holton, Vacant. 12653 N. Little Tujunga Canyon Rd., San Fernando, 91342. Tel: 213-463-8133.
Camp Rockey, Vacant. 1900 N. Sycamore Canyon Rd., San Dimas, 91773. Tel: 818-966-5059.
Camp McLaren Hall, Vacant. 4024 Durfee Rd., El Monte, 91732. Tel: 310-393-7460.
Camp Miller, Vacant. 433 S. Encinal Canyon Rd., Malibu, 90265. Tel: 310-820-2191.
Camp John Munz, Vacant. 42220 Lake Hughes Rd., Lake Hughes, 93532. Tel: 805-942-1370.
Camp Paige, Vacant. 6601 N. Stephens Ranch Rd., La Verne, 91750. Tel: 909-593-7056.
Camp Kenyon J. Scudder, Vacant. 28750 N. Bouquet Canyon Rd., Saugus, 91350. Tel: 213-463-8133.
Camp Joseph Scott, Vacant. 28700 N. Bouquet Canyon Rd., Saugus, 91350. Tel: 805-527-2408.
Camp Kilpatrick, Vacant. 427 S. Encinal Canyon Rd., Malibu, 90265. Tel: 818-991-7878.
Camp Louis Routh, Vacant. 12500 Big Tujunga Rd., Tujunga, 91042. Tel: 213-663-1142.
Camp Wm. V. Mendenhall, Vacant. 42230 Lake Hughes Rd., Lake Hughes, 93532. Tel: 805-942-1370.
Sierra Conservation Camps, California Department of Correction.
#4 Fransciquito, Saugus. Tel: 805-296-4409.
#11 Acton, Tel: 805-268-0113.
#13 Malibu, Tel: 310-457-2253.
#16 Mount Gleason, Palmdale. Tel: 805-947-7784.
#19 Julius Klein, Azusa. Tel: 818-910-1213.

On Special or Other Archdiocesan Assignment:
Reverend Fathers—
Fessard, Gerald B., J.C.L., Judge, Tribunal Office, 340 Norumbega Dr., Monrovia, CA 91016

On Duty Outside the Archdiocese:
Reverend Fathers—
Brennan, Dennis J.
Cummins, Charles T.
Cunnane, Jarlath
Joy, Laurence
Kane, Brian E.
Murphy, John
O'Shea, Patrick
Palacios, Joseph M.
Tacderas, Joseph
Tucker, James S.
Young, Gerald A.
Zak, Steven B.

Military and VA Chaplains:
Reverend Fathers—
Collins, John M.
Kelly, Francis
Llanos, Philip S.
Marrell, Dennis P.
McNulty, Gerard J.

Graduate Studies:
Reverend Fathers—
Biroschak, Robert V.
Fahey, John P.
Mullen, Patrick

Sick Leave:
Reverend Fathers—
Atchely, Jonathan D.
Bebek, Dominic L.
Cullen, Francis J.
Dawson, John H.

Griffin, Noel
LaNier, Michael L.
Lee, Joseph P.
McDonnell, Anthony
Meskill, Thomas A.
Mongrain, Dennis P.
Nuanez, Anthony
O'Connor, John C.
Seymour, Francis J.
Warren, Thomas

Retired:
Most Rev.—
Arzube, Juan A., c/o Sacred Heart Church, 2889 N. Lincoln Ave., Altadena, CA 91001-4598
Ward, John J., 3424 Wilshire Blvd., Los Angeles, CA 90010-2241
Reverend Monsignors—
Atwill, William H., 24 Topsail St., Marina del Rey, CA 90292-7124
Biedermann, Arnold, Sacred Heart, 10800 Henderson Rd., Ventura, CA 93004-1895
Boyer, Leland J., St. Bede the Venerable, 215 Foothill, La Canada, CA 81001-0809
Brosnan, John R., St. Ann Church, 2302 Riverdale Ave., Los Angeles, CA 90031-1133
Caslin, Peter C., St. Bartholomew, 252 Granada Ave., Long Beach, CA 90803
Clark, Laurence E., 15322 Roselle Ave., Lawndale, CA 90260
Clyne, James B., Nazareth House, 3333 Manning Ave., Los Angeles, CA 90064-4804
Collins, Fachtna P., P.O. Box 535, Montrose, CA 91020
Condon, Michael J., St. Anthony, 2511 S. C St., P.O. Box 2215, Oxnard, CA 93034-2215
Condon, Robert F., Nazareth House, 3333 Manning Ave., Los Angeles, CA 90064-4804
Crean, Timothy J., Assumption of the B.V.M., 2640 E. Orange Grove Blvd., Pasadena, CA 91107
Dessert, James A., Nazareth House, 3333 Manning Ave., LA, CA 90064-4804
Diomartich, Felix S., St. Anthony, 712 N. Grand Ave., Los Angeles, CA 90012-2299
Doherty, John B., Dana Point Mobile Home Estates, 34202 Del Obispo, Space No. 85, Dana Point, CA 92629
Donnelly, Lawrence E., 1065 W. Lomita Rd., Harbor City, CA 90710
Foiliard, John P., St. Cornelius Church, 5500 E. Wardlow Rd., Long Beach, CA 90808-3698
Fosselman, John A., St. Raymond, 12348 Paramount Blvd., P.O. Box 2085, Downey, CA 90242-0285
Gara, Robert, St. Rita, 50 E. Alegria Ave., Sierra Madre, CA 91024
Grill, Philip L., San Roque, 325 Argonne Cir., Santa Barbara, CA 93105-2798
Gualderon, Ernest J., St. Anthony, 540 Olive Ave., Long Beach, CA 90802-2651
Hayes, Thomas G., Nazareth House, 3333 Manning Ave., Los Angeles, CA 90064-4804
Hernandez, Alfred, P.O. Box 777, Cedar Glen, CA 92321
Holland, Ian E., P.O. Box 11475, Marina Del Rey, CA 90295
Kearney, Joseph V., St. Joseph, 5048 El Carro Ln., Carpinteria, CA 93013-1450
Kelly, Matthew H., Pinyon Crest, P.O. Box 253, Mountain Center, CA 92361
Kennedy, Christopher J., 3938 Cerritos Ave., Long Beach, CA 90807-3799
Konoske, Paul M., SS. Felicitas and Perpetua, 1190 Palomar Rd., San Marino, CA 91108-2224
Kucingis, John A., St. Casimir, 2718 St. George St., Los Angeles, CA 90027
McCabe, Vincent, 1270 Franciscan Ct. #8, Carpenteria, CA 93013
McGrath, Andrew, 101 South "U" St. #5, Lompoc, CA 93436-7299
McNulty, Patrick, 2501 West Avenue 33, Los Angeles, CA 90065-2892
Mulcahy, Donal, Our Lady of the Assumption, 3175 Telegraph Rd., Ventura, CA 93003-3283
Mulcahy, James R., St. Louis of France, 13935 E. Temple Ave., La Puente, CA 91746
Murray, Richard H., St. Bernardine of Siena, 24410 Calvert St., Woodland Hills, CA 91367-1099
Naughton, John T., St. Mel Church, 20870 Ventura Blvd., Woodland Hills, CA 91364-2396
Navin, Cyril, St. Cyril of Jerusalem Church, 4601 Firmament Ave., Encino, CA 91436-3108
O'Brien, Kenneth R., St. John of God Nursing Home, 2035 W. Adams Blvd., Woodland Hills, CA 90018
O'Brien, Thomas L., St. John of God Nursing Home, 2035 W. Adams Blvd., Los Angeles, CA 90018
O'Byrne, Sylvester, Our Lady of Mt. Carmel, 1300 E. Valley Rd., Santa Barbara, CA 93108-1294
O'Callaghan, James A., St. John Vianney Church, 1345 Turnbull Canyon Rd., Hacienda Heights, CA 91745-2699
O'Connell, Thomas, St. Jude Church, 32032 W. Lindero Canyon Rd., Westlake Village, CA 91361-4270
O'Connor, Michael J., St. Mel, 20870 Ventura Blvd., Woodland Hills, CA 91364-2396
O'Reilly, Bernard, 15360 Virginia Ave., Paramount, CA 90723
O'Sullivan, Peter, St. John Baptist, 16545 Chatsworth St., Granada Hills, CA 91344
Osborne, Francis M., Our Lady of Grace, 5011 White Oak Ave., Encino, CA 91316-3799
Rademacher, Glen A., P.O. Box 230357, Encinitas, CA 92023-0357
Ravlic, Cornelius C., 239 Somerset Dr., Kalispell, MT 59901
Redahan, Patrick J., St. Joseph, 11854 Acacia Ave., Hawthorne, CA 90251-3083
Reilly, John J., 16222 Monterey Ln., Space 273, Huntington Beach, CA 92649
Sharpe, Joseph F., P.O. Box 240, Balboa Island, CA 92662
Sheridan, John V., Our Lady of Malibu, 3625 S. Winter Canyon Rd., Malibu, CA 90265
Sullivan, Daniel F., Nazareth House, 3333 Manning Ave., Los Angeles, CA 90064-4804
Valle, Fernando, 2nda Avenida A3-44, Zona #1, Guatemala 001, Guatemala
Von Son, Henry A., 11075 S.W. Muirwood, Portland, OR 97225
Walsh, Michael, Monea, Ardmore, Youghal, County Cork, Ireland
Walsh, Robert, Holy Angels, 370 Campus Dr., Arcadia, CA 91006-6917
Young, John M., 4142 Los Padres Dr., Fallbrook, CA 91006-92028
Zimmerman, Roland G., Annunciation, 1307 E. Longden Ave., Arcadia, CA 91006-5597
Reverend Fathers—
Barry, William J., Proto Notary Apostolic, 68 Balboa Coves, Newport Beach, CA 92663
Bellavista, Jose, 14334 Fallon Ave., P.O. Box 201, Norwalk, CA 90650
Bradley, Robert M., 202 Cole Rd., Sarver, PA 16055
Buckley, Michael, St. John of God Nursing Home, 2035 W. Adams Blvd., Los Angeles, CA 90018
Byrne, Robert P., Nazareth House, 3333 Manning Ave., Los Angeles, CA 90064-4804
Combs, Regis V., Ventura Marina Park, 1215 Anchor Way, Space 74, Ventura, CA 93001. Tel: 805-644-1026
Cooley, John E., 31402 Paseo del Mar, Laguna Niguel, CA 92677-2745
Coronado, Genero, 2505 W. Foothill Blvd., #145, San Bernardino, CA 92410
Cotter, Patrick John, 1854 Hanscom Dr., South Pasadena, CA 91030
Cunningham, John F., 1375 N.E. Elk Ct., Apt. #127, Bend, OR 97701-5318
Daly, John, Holy Trinity, 3722 Boyce Ave., Los Angeles, CA 90039-1810
DeDominici, Lorenzo, Mary Star of the Sea, 870 W. 8th St., San Pedro, CA 90731-3091
DeJonghe, Harold J., Nazareth House, 3333 Manning Ave., Los Angeles, CA 90064-4804
Delaney, Matthew S., P.O. Box 2007, Seal Beach, CA 90740
Duffy, Eugene J., Bridge St., Louisburgh, County Mayo, Ireland
Fallon, John J., Nazareth House, 3333 Manning Ave., Los Angeles, CA 90064-4804
Feeney, John J., Nazareth House, 3333 Manning, Los Angeles, CA 90064-4804
Gutting, John C., St. Athanasius, 5390 Linden Ave., Long Beach, CA 90805-6062
Han, Andrew, P.O. Box 1081, Encinitas, CA 92024
Hanly, John J., Nazareth House, 3333 Manning Ave., Los Angeles, CA 90064-4804
Harman, Charles W., 261 South Rodeo Dr., Beverly Hills, CA 90212
Hernandez, Stephen, Our Lady of Guadalupe, 4509 Mercury Ave., Los Angeles, CA 90032-1931
Infuhr, Frank J., St. John of God Nursing Home, 2035 W. Adams, Los Angeles, CA 90018
Jennings, Bernard J., St. Elizabeth, 1849 N. Lake Ave., Altadena, CA 91001-3097
Johnson, Henry J., 1211 N. Garden, Covina, CA 91724
Kass, George P., Nazareth House, 3333 Manning Ave., Los Angeles, CA 90064-4804
Kelly, Paul M.
Kennedy, John A., 5 Chester Square, County Glenageary, Dublin Ireland
Lee, Peter, 605 S. Sefton Ave., Monterey Park, CA 91754-1698
Lichtle, Thomas A., 658 Temple Ave., Long Beach, CA 90814
Lirette, Arthur J., Proto Notary Apostolic, Holy Family, 209 E. Lomita Ave., Glendale, CA 91205-1689
Luck, Robert O., 388 Thornhill Circle, Henderson, NV 89014
Maechler, Edmund F., 613 California St., Huntington Beach, CA 92648
Maechler, Gerald T., 18401 Delaware Ave., Huntington Beach, CA 92648
McGovern, Martin D., Mulranny, County Mayo, Ireland
McHugh, Patrick J., Nativity Church, 18401 Delaware Ave., Huntington Beach, CA 92648
McKeon, James F., St. John of God Nursing Home, 2035 W. Adams Blvd., Los Angeles, CA 90018
McLaughlin, Thomas W., St. Teresa of Avila, 2216 Fargo St., Los Angeles, CA 90039-3198
Meilak, John, 5 Grunju St., Nadur Gozo, Malta-Europe
Merino, Santiago, 959 LaDeney Dr., Ontario, CA 91762
Meskill, Patrick A., 63 Ilex Dr., Newbury Park, CA 91320
Murphy, Denis J., Our Lady of the Assumption, 3175 Telegraph Rd., Ventura, CA 93003-3283
Nagy, Joseph, 3756 Hellman Ave., Los Angeles, CA 90032
Nocero, Pascal F., P.O. Box 279, Oak View, CA 93022
O'Leary, Niall F.
O'Shea, Michael, P.O. Box 1803, Bellflower, CA 90706
O'Sullivan, Thomas C., Our Lady of Mt. Carmel Church, 1300 E. Valley Rd., Santa Barbara, CA 93108-1294
Pisano, Andrew, 6938 Grange Ave., Bell Gardens, CA 90201
Potthoff, Donald W., St. Denis Church, 2151 Diamond Bar Blvd., P.O. Box 4096, Diamond Bar, CA 91765-2860
Raymundo, Gregorio G., 419 Cameron Pl., Glendale, CA 91207
Rodriguez, Lawrence, Soto y Amio, Santoveniada San Marcos, C.P. 24125, (Leon) Spain
Rucker, Neville, Corpus Christi Church, 887 Toyopa Dr., P.O. Box 887, Pacific Palisades, CA 90272-0887
Sanchez, Eliseo, 13308 E. Loumont, North Whittier, CA 90601
Shimmaly, Edward F., P.O. Box 148, Eagle, ID 83616
Stehly, Thomas J., 9432 S. Bloomfield Ave., Cypress, CA 90630
Thomas, Sylvester J., Mary Star of the Sea, 870 W. Eighth St., San Pedro, CA 90731-3091
Thompson, Jerome H., 1330 Kenwood Rd., Apt. 157-F, Seal Beach, CA 90740
Vecsey, Stephen N., 1120 Northwood Rd., 186D, Seal Beach, CA 90740
Villa Gomez, Nemorio, Calle Durando 1208, S.H. Guadalajara, Jalisco, CP442-60 Mexico
Villegas, Samuel C., St. Matthias, 7125 Mission Pl., Huntington Park, CA 90255-5299
Weible, Thomas C., 4234 N. Main St. #508, Fall River, MA 02720
Wishard, John W., P.O. Box 6930, Santa Maria, CA 93456

Permanent Deacons:
Acquaviva, Dick, St. Clare, Canyon Country
Adams, Emile, Jr., St. Bernadette, Los Angeles
Adams, J. Rodger, Our Lady of the Assumption Church, Ventura
Adams, James V., Chaminade College Preparatory, Chatsworth
Alexander, Hosea, Sr., St. Agatha, Los Angeles
Allen, John P., Corpus Christi, Pacific Palisades
Aranda, Fernando, Jr., Our Lady of Solitude, Los Angeles
Arpaia, Frank, St. Elizabeth, Van Nuys
Arroyo, Miguel, Our Lady of Guadalupe, Los Angeles
Aust, William, All Souls, Alhambra
Baker, William, Ascension, Los Angeles
Balbuena, Wesley M., Jr., St. Elizabeth, Van Nuys
Battle, Joe T., St. Philip Neri, Lynwood
Bednar, George J., St. Mary Magdalen, Camarillo
Bohlig, Alden, St. Barnabas, Long Beach
Brandlin, Thomas E., Century Regional Detention Facility, Lynwood
Bravo, Anthony, St. Gerard Majela, Los Angeles
Burke, John, La Purisma Concepcion, Lompoc
Caffrey, Aloysius, St. Jude, Westlake Village
Caputo, Ed, Blessed Junipero Serra, Quartz Hill
Carmody, Richard, St. Louis de Montford, Santa Maria
Caro, Jose, St. Cecilia, Los Angeles
Castorena, John G., Santa Clara, Oxnard
Cellner, Jerry, St. Bernardine of Siena, Woodland Hills
Chacon, Paul, Our Lady of Lourdes, Tujunga

Chavez, Gilbert M., San Gabriel Mission, San Gabriel
Clinton, Jack, Holy Name of Mary, San Dimas
Collins, Oscar R., St. Patrick, North Hollywood
Conrey, Fred, Immaculate Conception, Monrovia
Corwin, Richard, St. Margaret Mary Alacoque, Lomita
Crisafulli, Nino D., Mary Star of the Sea, San Pedro
Curran, Nicholas P., Holy Cross, Santa Barbara
Delgado, Eduardo, St. John Vianney, Hacienda Heights
Denisac, Charles M., Jr., Our Lady of Perpetual Help, Downey
Dieter, Frank, St. Lawrence Martyr, Redondo Beach
Dillon, James, Holy Angels Church of the Deaf, Vernon
Doane, Allan E., St. Thomas Aquinas, Ojai
Dornan, Richard, St. Jude, Westlake Village
Duke, Oscar, St. Anthony, Oxnard
Dumlao, Felix, St. Anthony of Padua, Gardena
Escovedo, Arthur, Our Lady of the Assumption, Claremont
Estey, Marvin, St. Dorothy, Glendora
Fajardo, Richard, Resurrection, Los Angeles
Farley, James, Our Lady of the Assumption, Ventura
Favela, Jacobo M., Jr., St. Martha, Valinda
FitzGerald, Gerald M., St. Francis of Assisi, Fillmore
Fitzgerald, James, St. Mary of the Assumption, Whittier
Fitzpatrick, Arthur, St. Paul of the Cross, La Mirada
Freeman, Mike, St. Bruno, Whittier
Frias, Sam, San Fernando Mission, Mission Hills
Fry, Ralph M., Sacred Heart, Covina
Galido, Juan, Our Lady of Lourdes, Northridge
Garcia, Armando R., St. Joseph, Los Angeles
Gaudin, John, Holy Name of Jesus, Los Angeles
Goodreau, Theodore, St. Anthony, El Segundo
Goodspeed, Lyle, St. John Neumann, Santa Maria
Gueringer, Ludger A., Padre Serra, Camarillo
Guerra, Ruben, St. Joseph, La Puente
Gutierrez, Eliseo, Sacred Heart, Covina
Hall, Willard J., Sr., St. John the Evangelist, Los Angeles
Halley, James, St. Matthew, Long Beach
Halvorsen, Douglas A., St. Louis de Montfort, Santa Maria
Hamm, Richard S., St. Peter Claver, Simi Valley
Hammonds, Johnnie, St. Mary Magdalen, Camarillo
Harrison, Russell J., SS Peter and Paul, Wilmington
Hawkins, Bill, St. Brigid, Los Angeles
Hays, Charles D., La Purisima Concepcion, Lompoc
Henry, James J., St. Anthony, Oxnard
Hillman, Steven, St. Elizabeth Ann Seton, Rowland Heights
Holly, Chester N., St. John Eudes, Chatsworth
Huff, David W., Holy Cross, Santa Barbara
Karl, Richard J., Our Lady of Perpetual Help, Santa Clarita
Kunsemiller, John H., Santa Clara Church, Oxnard
Lacy, William S., St. Joseph the Worker, Canoga Park
Lambey, Alvin S., Mother of Sorrows, Los Angeles
Landa, William, St. Philip the Apostle, Pasadena
Lanoix, Gilbert, St. Brigid, Los Angeles
Ledoux, Joseph, St. Albert the Great, Compton
Lee, Paul D., St. Bruno, Whittier
Liendo, Manuel, St. Mary of the Assumption, Santa Maria
Lipski, Alexander, St. Cornelius, Long Beach
Lira, Pedro, St. Catherine of Siena, Reseda
Lopez, Jose, St. Benedict, Montebello
Magana, Matilde, St. Catherine Laboure, Torrance
Martinez, Jesse, St. Thomas Aquinas, Monterey Park
Martinez, Manuel J., Our Lady of Sorrows, Santa Barbara
Martinez, Randolph M., Santa Clara, Oxnard
McHugh, Daniel J., St. Bernardine of Siena, Woodland Hills
McKinley, Braden, Sacred Heart, Ventura
McPheeters, Jon C., St. Anthony, Oxnard
Medina, Richard J., Our Lady of Perpetual Help, Downey
Mejia, J. Guadalupe, Holy Family, Artesia
Messer, John, St. Anthony, San Gabriel
Millholland, Frank, St. Albert the Great, Compton
Mimiaga, Guillermo, St. Raphael, Los Angeles
Modugno, Larry, St. Mary Magdalen, Camarillo
Moloney, Doug, St. Christopher, West Covina
Morgan, Richard, Blessed Sacrament, Los Angeles
Nawrocik, Zenon L., Marian Medical Center, Santa Maria
Nguyen, Loc, St. Christopher, West Covina
Noriega, Restie, Incarnation, Glendale
Nosari, Ernest, St. Rita, Sierra Madre
Orth, Joseph, St. Euphrasia, Granada Hills
Parish, Harold A., J.C.D., Mary Star of the Sea, Oxnard
Patlan, Servando, Sr., St. Gregory the Great, Whittier
Patterson, Gary R., Our Lady of Guadalupe, Irwindale
Pelletier, Frederick H., Holy Family, Glendale
Pepe, Joseph, Office of the Catholic Chaplain, NCB, Oxnard
Picard, John B., Blessed Junipero Serra, Camarillo
Pina, Thomas, St. Anthony, Oxnard
Pruitt, Richard, Little Co. of Mary Hospital, Torrance
Ramirez, Fidel M., Mary Star of the Sea, Oxnard
Rascati, Wayne, St. Raphael, Santa Barbara
Rios, Fred, Our Lady of the Miraculous Medal, Montebello
Rivas, Manuel, Santa Clara, Oxnard
Rivera, Ramon, St. Bridget of Sweden, Van Nuys
Rivet, Joseph, St. Louise de Marillac, Covina
Robinson, James M., St. Paschal Baylon, Thousand Oaks
Rodriguez, Hernando, Resurrection, Los Angeles
Ryan, John E., Santa Barbara Mission, Santa Barbara
Ryan, Joseph M., St. Raymond, Downey
Sanchez, Enrique R., Holy Cross, Santa Barbara
Sangster, William B., San Roque, Santa Barbara
Saucedo, Valentin, St. Aloysius Gonzaga, Los Angeles
Schwerdt, Paul, Blessed Junipero Serra, Quartz Hill
Sebenius, Wayland, "Gus", St. Therese, Alhambra
Sevilla, Rodolfo, Our Lady Queen of Angels, (La Placita) Los Angeles
Shea, Clarke, St. Raphael, Goleta
Shinkle, Richard D., St. James, Redondo Beach
Simanski, Donald E., Sacred Heart, Lancaster
Skupnik, Raymond P., St. Cyprian, Long Beach
Soto, Antonio P., St. Hilary, Pico Rivera
Spada, Joseph D., Our Lady of the Miraculous Medal, Montebello
Suh, Ignatius Jin, Korean Catholic Center (St. Bridget of Sweden), Los Angeles
Taufer, Wm. Dale., St. Bernardine of Siena, Woodland Hills
Torres, Antonio B., San Francisco, Los Angeles
Torres, Pedro M., Our Lady of Loretto, Los Angeles
Ulibarri, Ralph, Holy Family, Wilmington
Valeriano, Oscar J., St. Louis of France, La Puente
Vazquez, Roberto L., St. John Chrysostom, Inglewood
Vega, Cris T., St. Gertrude, Bell Gardens
Vega, Heriberto (Ed), Our Lady of the Valley, Canoga Park
Victorin, Rafael, St. Augustine Church, Culver City
Viramontes, Raul, Holy Family, Artesia
Weber, Paul S., St. Jerome, Los Angeles
Wilson, Peter, St. Rose of Lima, Simi Valley

INSTITUTIONS LOCATED IN THE ARCHDIOCESE

[A] SEMINARIES, ARCHDIOCESAN

CAMARILLO. *St. John's Seminary*, 5012 Seminary Rd., 93012-2598. Tel: 805-482-2755; Fax: 805-484-4074. E-mail: jacque@vcnet.com
Major Seminary of the Archdiocese of Los Angeles. Rev. Msgr. Jeremiah J. McCarthy, Rector & Pres.; Revs. Richard Benson, C.M., Vice Rector; Austin Doran, Spiritual Dir.; Leon Hutton, Dir. of Students; Sr. M. Regina Robbins, S.N.D., Dir. of Field Education; Sr. Cecilia Canales, O.P., Dir. of Spiritual Formation; Rev. John D. Stoeger, Assoc. Dir. of Spiritual Formation; Ms. Jacquelein Rotter, Business Mgr.; Mr. Greg Julius, Facilities Mgr.; Dr. Mark F. Fischer, Ph.D., Dir. of Admissions; Mr. Ron Hastings, M.L.S., Librarian; Ms. Lois Marcus, Asst. Librarian; Ms. Rosa Coleman, Registrar; Revs. Richard Benson, C.M.; John P. Brennan, S.M.A.; Jorge Del Valle, M.Sp.S.; Austin Doran; Joseph Duc Minh; Daniel Harris, C.M.; Rev. Msgr. Helmut Heffner; Revs. Leon Hutton; Jeremiah McCarthy; Kevin McCracken, C.M.; Charles E. Miller, C.M.; Edward Owens, O.SS.T.; John Stoeger; Michael F. Walsh, C.M.; Sr. Cecilia Canales, O.P.; Sr. Sheila McNiff, S.H.C.J. Priests 14; Sisters 3; Lay Teachers 5; Students 101.

St. John's Seminary College of the Archdiocese of Los Angeles, 5118 Seminary Rd., 93012-2598. Tel: 805-482-2755; Fax: 805-987-5097.
E-mail: sjsc@west.net
Web site: http://www.west.net/~sjsc
Staffed by Archdiocesan, Vincentian and Sulpician Priests. Rev. Msgr. Edward Wm. Clark, President & Rector; Rev. Calixto Lopez, C.M., Vice Rector, Dean Formation; Dr. Lawrence Ryan, Vice Pres. & Academic Dean; Revs. James Stehly, Dir. Students; Lawrence Herrera, S.J., Dir. of Spiritual Formation; William Piletic, C.M., Dir. of Recruitment, Alumni Relations & Liturgy; Gary Landry, C.M., Dir. Admissions; Mr. Ron Hastings, Librarian; Ms. Lois Marcus, Asst. Librarian.
Additional Faculty: Revs. Richard MacDonough, S.S.; Joseph Duc-Minh; Ramon Farre, Sch.P.; Sr. Patrice Benson, S.S.L.; Sr. Catherine Foley, S.S.L., Dir. of Apostolic Work Program; Sr. Pegeen Connolly, S.C.R.H.; Sr. Tracey Sharp, S.C.R.H.; Sr. Rochelle Mitchell, S.S.S., L.C.S.W., B.C.D.; Mr. Jackson Schoos, Dir. of Music. Priests 9; Sisters 5; Lay Teachers 15; Students 85.

[B] SEMINARIES, RELIGIOUS OR SCHOLASTICATES

LOS ANGELES. *Canons Regular of the Immaculate Conception-Novitiate*, 1523 Golden Gate Ave., 90026. Revs. Pasquale Vuoso, C.R.I.C., Supr.; Charles R. Lueras, C.R.I.C.; James G. Garceau, C.R.I.C.; Sergio Garcia, C.R.I.C., St. Clare's, 19606 Calla Way Rd., c/o 27341 Camp Plenty, Canyon Country, 91351. Rev. William B. Ustaski, C.R.I.C., Nazareth House, 3333 Manning Ave., 90064. Rev. John Taggart, C.R.I.C.

St. Joseph's Novitiate, 2035 W. Adams Blvd., 90018; Fax: 213-731-5987. Hospitaller Brothers of St. John of God. Bros. Edward Francis McEnroe, O.H., Prov.; Stephen de la Rosa, O.H., Formation Dir. Brothers 2; Scholastics 2.

NORTH HILLS. *Carmel West Community*, 8936 Woodley Ave., 91343. Revs. Dominic Savino, O.Carm.; Peter J. Liuzzi, O.Carm.

SANTA MARIA. *St. Joseph Seminary (Josephite Fathers' Novitiate)*, 180 Patterson Rd., 93455. Tel: 805-937-5378. Revs. Thomas J. Elewaut, C.J.; Edward Jalbert, C.J.; John A. Mayhew, C.J.; Bede L. Johnson, C.J.; Anthony Runtz, C.J. Priests 5.

SANTA YNEZ. *San Lorenzo Novitiate and Seminary*, 1802 Sky Dr., P.O. Box 247, 93460. Tel: 805-688-5630. Capuchin Fransiscan Friars. Revs. Gerald Barron, O.F.M.Cap., Guardian; James Johnson, Vicar; Christopher Kearney, Postulant Dir.; Sebastian Ward, O.F.M.Cap., Chap.; Bros. Pius Higgins, O.F.M.Cap.; Joseph Slominski, O.F.M.Cap. Prayer Center: Priests 4; Brothers 2; Postulants 1.

[C] COLLEGES AND UNIVERSITIES

LOS ANGELES. *Loyola Marymount University*, 7900 Loyola Blvd., 90045-2699. Tel: 310-338-2700
For a complete listing, refer to the Colleges and Universities section.

Mount St. Mary's College.
E-mail: kkennelly@msmc.la.edu
Web site: www.msmc.la.edu
Chalon Campus, 12001 Chalon Rd., 90049-1599. Tel: 310-954-4000; Fax: 310-954-4379.
For a complete listing, refer to the Colleges and Universities section.

RANCHO PALOS VERDES. *Marymount College, Palos Verdes, California*, 30800 Palos Verdes Dr., E., 90275-6299. Tel: 310-377-5501.
E-mail: shart@marymountpv.edu
For a complete listing, refer to the Colleges and Universities section.

ROSEMEAD. *Don Bosco Technical Institute*, 1151 San Gabriel Blvd., 91770-4299. Tel: 626-307-6500; Fax: 626-280-9316
For a complete listing, refer to the Colleges and Universities section.

SANTA PAULA. *Thomas Aquinas College*, 10000 N. Ojai Rd., 93060. Tel: 805-525-4417
For a complete listing, refer to the Colleges and Universities section.

[D] HIGH SCHOOLS, ARCHDIOCESAN

LOS ANGELES. *Bishop Conaty-Our Lady of Loretto High School*. (Girls), 2900 W. Pico Blvd., 90006. Tel: 213-737-0012.
Sisters 6; Lay Teachers 13; Students 370.

Bishop Mora Salesian High School. (Boys), 960 S. Soto St., 90023. Tel: 213-261-7124; Fax: 213-261-9474. Salesians of Don Bosco. Mr. Manuel Villarreal, Prin.; Mr. Mark Johnson, Vice Prin.; Rev. Cris Rosales, S.D.B.; Bros. Robert Hennings, S.D.B.; John Kornak, S.D.B. Students 443.

Daniel Murphy Catholic High School. (Boys), 241 S. Detroit St., 90036. Tel: 213-935-1161; Fax: 213-935-1621. John T. Finn, Prin. Lay Teachers 21; Students 425.

Sacred Heart High School. (Girls), 2111 N. Griffin Ave., 90031. Tel: 213-225-2209; Fax: 213-225-5046. Sr. Patricia Ann Smith, O.P., Prin. Lay Teachers 22; Students 375.

Verbum Dei High School. (Boys), 11100 S. Central Ave., 90059-1199. Tel: 213-564-6651. Conducted by the Archdiocese of Los Angeles. Mrs. Wilma D. Elbouhnini, Prin.; Bro. Richard Morrill, S.V.D. Brothers 1; Sisters 2; Permanent Deacon 1; Lay Teachers 16; Students 259.

BURBANK. *Bellarmine Jefferson High School.* (Coed), 465 E. Olive Ave., 91501. Tel: 818-972-1400 (Main Office); 972-1401 (Athletic); 972-1402 (Attendance), Ext. 3. Sr. Cheryl Milner, Prin. Priests 1; Sisters 3; Brothers 1; Lay Teachers 23; Students 420.

COMPTON. *Queen of Angels Academy.* (Girls), 823 E. Compton Blvd., 90220. Tel: 310-515-3891; Fax: 310-515-3894. Conducted by the Archdiocese of Los Angeles. Staffed by the Sisters of the Holy Family. Sr. Henrietta Lazare, S.S.F., Prin. Sisters 5; Lay Teachers 13; Students 206.

DOWNEY. *Pius X - St. Matthias High School,* 7851 E. Gardendale St., 90242. Tel: 562-861-2271; Fax: 562-869-8652. Sisters 1; Lay Teachers 20; Students 421.

GARDENA. *Junipero Serra High School,* 14830 S. Van Ness Ave., 90249. Tel: 310-324-6675; Fax: 310-352-4953. Rev. Sabato Pilato, Prin.; Mrs. Margaret Shaukry, Vice Prin. Lay Teachers 20; Students 410.

LA PUENTE. *Bishop Amat Memorial High School.* (Coed), 14301 Fairgrove Ave., 91746. Tel: 818-962-2495. Conducted by the Archdiocese of Los Angeles. Rev. Msgr. Aidan M. Carroll, Prin.; Mrs. Kathleen Wiard, Vice Prin. Sisters 6; Lay Teachers 79; Students 1,675.

LA VERNE. *Damien Boys High School,* 2280 Damien Ave., 91750. Tel: 909-596-1946. Conducted by the Archdiocese of Los Angeles. Revs. Patrick Travers, SS.CC., Prin.; Peadar Cronin, SS.CC., Vice Prin.; Mr. Kenneth Kowalewski, Asst. Prin. & Campus Minister; Mr. Jeffrey Coray, Asst. Prin. Academic Affairs; Mr. Sam Pearsall, Asst. Prin. Summer Program; Mr. Timothy Carlson, Asst. Prin. Student Activities; Rev. Donal McCarthy, SS.CC., Asst. Prin. Guidance; Mr. Thomas Carroll, Asst. Prin. Athletic Activities. Legal Title: *Congregation of the Sacred Hearts, Inc.* Faculty Res., 2150 Damien Ave., 91750. Priests 3; Lay Teachers 55; Students 1,100.

LAKEWOOD. *Saint Joseph High School.* (Girls), 5825 N. Woodruff Ave., 90713. Tel: 562-925-5073; Fax: 562-925-3315.
E-mail: @mail.stjosephs.pvt.k12.ca.us
Web site: www.stjosephs.pvt.k12.ca.us
Conducted by Archdiocese of Los Angeles. Terri Mendoza, Ph.D., Prin.; Revs. Alfonso Scott; James Henry, S.V.D. Priests 2; Sisters 5; Lay Teachers 41; Students 844.

LANCASTER. *Paraclete High School.* (Coed), 42145 N. 30th St., W., 93536. Tel: 805-943-3255; Fax: 805-722-9455. Conducted by Archdiocese of Los Angeles. Staffed by Divine Word Missionaries and Fathers of St. Joseph. Revs. William J. Caffrey, S.V.D., Prin.; Joseph Scalco, C.S.J.; Angelo Zonta, C.S.J. Priests 3; Lay Teachers 40; Students 725.

MISSION HILLS. *Alemany High School,* 15101 San Fernando Mission Blvd., 91345. Tel: 818-365-3925. Revs. Robert Milbauer, Prin.; Alberto Villalobos; Patrick Argue, SS.CC. (Ireland), Priests' Res., 15201 Rinaldi St., 91345. Brothers' Res., 15201 Rinaldi St., 91345. Priests 3; Brothers 3; Sisters 6; Lay Teachers 63; Students 1,430.

MONTEBELLO. *Cantwell Sacred Heart of Mary High School.* (Coed), 329 N. Garfield Ave., 90640. Tel: 213-887-2066; Fax: 213-724-4332. Archdiocesan Institution. David Chambers, Prin. Sisters 2; Lay Teachers 24; Students 428.

OXNARD. *Santa Clara High School,* 2121 Saviers Rd., 93033. Tel: 805-483-9502. Mr. Keith Murphy, Prin.; Mrs. Helen Scovell, Vice Prin. and Dean of Studies; Mrs. Kay Brisslinger, Asst. Prin. & Dean of Discipline; Sr. Patrice McGee, C.S.C., Campus Minister; Mr. Matthew Crow, Dir. of Activities; Bro. Edward Gresnigt, C.F.M.M. Brothers 1; Sisters 3; Lay Teachers 14; Students 299.

PLAYA DEL REY. *St. Bernard High School.* (Coed), 9100 Falmouth Ave., 90293. Tel: 310-823-4651. Conducted by Archdiocese of Los Angeles. Revs. James Anguiano, Prin.; Mark Strader, Asst. Prin. Priests 2; Sisters 3; Lay Teachers 39; Students 750.

POMONA. *Pomona Catholic High School.* (Girls), 533 W. Holt Ave., 91768. Tel: 909-623-5297. Sr. Feliz Gil-Jimenez, C.S.S.F., Prin.; Mrs. Ann Hardman, Dean of Students. Sisters 5; Lay Teachers 22; Students 330.

ROSEMEAD. *Don Bosco Technical Institute.* (Boys), 1151 San Gabriel Blvd., 91770-4299. Tel: 626-307-6500; Fax: 626-280-9316. Secondary Section.
Staffed by Salesians of St. John Bosco. Rev. Carmine Vairo, S.D.B., Pres.; Mr. Michael Alvarez, Prin.; Rev. Marc Rougeau, S.D.B. Priests 2; Brothers 5; Lay Teachers 68; Students 780.

SANTA BARBARA. *Bishop Garcia Diego High School.* (Coed), 4000 La Colina Rd., 93110. Tel: 805-967-1266; Fax: 805-964-3178.
E-mail: bishop@bishopdiego.org
Web site: www.bishopdiego.org
Revs. Charles Hofschulte, C.J., Prin.; Alfred Verstreken, C.J. Priests 2; Sisters 1; Lay Teachers 24; Students 350.

SANTA FE SPRINGS. *St. Paul High School,* 9635 S. Greenleaf Ave., 90670. Tel: 562-698-6246; Fax: 562-696-8396. Conducted by Archdiocese of Los Angeles. Revs. Robert J. Gallagher, Prin.; John Provenza, Chap. Priests 2; Brothers 2; Sisters 4; Lay Teachers 54; Students 1,050.

SANTA MARIA. *St. Joseph High School.* (Coed), 4120 Bradley Rd., 93455. Tel: 805-937-2038. Conducted by Archdiocese of Los Angeles. Revs. Edward Jalbert, C.J.; Thomas J. Elewaut, C.J., 180 Patterson Rd., 93455. Priests 2; Lay Teachers 35; Students 650.

TORRANCE. *Bishop Montgomery High School.* (Coed), 5430 Torrance Blvd., 90503. Tel: 310-540-2021. Conducted by the Archdiocese of Los Angeles. Rosemary Libbon, Prin. Priests 4; Lay Teachers 71; Students 1,358.

VENTURA. *St. Bonaventure High School.* (Coed), 3167 Telegraph Rd., 93003-3281. Tel: 805-648-6836; Fax: 805-648-4903.
E-mail: seraph@aol.com
Conducted by Archdiocese of Los Angeles. Bro. Paulinus Horkan, O.S.F., Prin. Sisters 2; Brothers 1; Lay Teachers 32; Students 625.

[E] HIGH SCHOOLS, PAROCHIAL

LOS ANGELES. High Schools are maintained in the following parishes (for particulars refer to the individual parishes): Glendale: Holy Family; Long Beach: St. Anthony; San Gabriel: San Gabriel Mission; San Pedro: Mary Star of the Sea; Santa Monica: St. Monica; Van Nuys: St. Genevieve.

[F] HIGH SCHOOLS, PRIVATE

LOS ANGELES. *Cathedral High School of Los Angeles, Incorporated.* (Boys), 1253 Bishops Rd., 90012. Tel: 213-225-2438; 673-7328 (Voice Mail); Fax: 213-222-7223. Conducted by the Brothers of the Christian Schools. Bro. James Meegan, F.S.C. Brothers 6; Sisters 1; Lay Teachers 24; Students 448.

Immaculate Heart High School. (Girls), 5515 Franklin Ave., 90028. Tel: 213-461-3651.
E-mail: ihhs1@aol.com
Conducted by the Immaculate Heart Community. Sisters 4; Lay Teachers 37; Students 526.

Loyola High School, 1901 Venice Blvd., 90006. Tel: 213-381-5121; Fax: 213-387-0321. Jesuit Fathers. Revs. Gordon D. Bennett, S.J., Pres.; Patrick J. Cahalan, S.J.; Richard E. Cobb, S.J., Rector; J. Philip Conneally, S.J.; Robert T. Walsh, S.J., Prin.; Thomas H. O'Neill, S.J.; Lawrence B. Murphy, S.J.; Louis A. Peinado, S.J.; Kevin A. Leidich, S.J.; Thomas J. Carroll, S.J.; Mark K. Ciccone, S.J.; John I. Geiszel, S.J.; Thomas J. Reilley, S.J.; Thomas F. McCormick, S.J.; James V. Schaukowitch, S.J.; Rob Scholla, S.J.; William Thom, S.J. Priests 18; Brothers 2; Scholastics 3; Lay Teachers 68; Students 1,172.

Marymount High School. (Girls), 10643 Sunset Blvd., 90077. Tel: 310-472-1205.
E-mail: alumnae@marymounths.com
Web site: www.marymounths.com
Religious of the Sacred Heart of Mary. Dr. Mary Ellen Gozdecki, Head. Sisters 4; Lay Teachers 43; Students 355.

Notre Dame Academy. (Girls), 2851 Overland Ave., 90064. Tel: 310-839-5289. Sr. Marie Paul, S.N.D., Prin. Sisters of Notre Dame of Los Angeles 6; Lay Teachers 35; Students 477.

ALHAMBRA. *Ramona Convent Secondary School, Ramona Convent of the Holy Names.* (Girls Grades 7-12), 1701 W. Ramona Rd., 91803-3099. Tel: 626-282-4151. Sr. Margaret Spiller, S.N.J.M., Prin. Sisters of Holy Names of Jesus and Mary 8; Lay Teachers 37; Students 525.

BELLFLOWER. *St. John Bosco High School.* (Boys), 13640 S. Bellflower Blvd., 90706. Tel: 310-920-1734.
Web site: www.bosco.org
Revs. Richard R. Presenti, S.D.B., Pres.; Frank Ribotta, S.D.B.; Mario Mich, S.D.B.; Michael Baptista, S.D.B.; Joseph Ahn Le, S.D.B.; Bros. Frank Bracchi, S.D.B.; Noel DeBruton, S.D.B.; Barney Hagus, S.D.B.; John McLinden, S.D.B. Priests 5; Brothers 4; Lay Teachers 59; Students 1,065.

BURBANK. *Providence High School.* (Coed), 511 S. Buena Vista St., 91505. Tel: 818-846-8141; Fax: 818-843-8421.
E-mail: lucille@providencehigh.org
Sr. Lucille Dean, S.P., Prin.; Rafe Vega, Dir. Campus Ministry; C. Victor LeBreton, Vice Prin. Discipline & Student Affairs; Sr. Mary Hawkins, S.P., Vice Prin. Academics. Sisters 6; Lay Teachers 35; Students 526.

CHATSWORTH. *Chaminade College Preparatory,* Office of the President, 10210 Oakdale Ave., 91311-3533. Tel: 818-347-8300.
E-mail: jadams@chaminade.org
Web site: www.chaminade.org
19800 Devonshire St., 91311. Tel: 818-363-8127. (Coed Grades 6-12). James V. Adams, Pres.; Gary E. Murphy, Prin. West Hills; Ms. Christine Hunter, Prin. Chatsworth. Legal Title: *Chaminade College Preparatory.* Priests 3; Sisters 4; Brothers 2; Lay Teachers 113; Students 1,745.

Marianist Community. Bro. LeRoy Viera, S.M., Dir.; Revs. Lawrence Mann, S.M.; Allen DeLong, S.M.; Edwin Johnson. Priests 3; Brothers 4.

ENCINO. *Crespi Carmelite High School,* 5031 Alonzo Ave., 91316. Tel: 818-345-1672. Rev. Frederick Tillotson, O.Carm., Prin./Pres.; Ms. Judy Flaherty, Treas.; Revs. Dominic Savino, O.Carm.; Joseph Fitzgerald, O.Carm.; William Wert, O.Carm., Campus Min.; Bro. John Sprissler, O.Carm. In res. Revs. Augustine Carter, O.Carm.; John Coleman, O.Carm.; Mathias Ewing, O.Carm.; William Heery, O.Carm. Priests 4; Brothers 1; Lay Teachers 35; Students 492.

GLENDORA. *St. Lucy's Priory High School.* (Girls), 655 W. Sierra Madre Ave., 91741. Tel: 626-335-3322. Conducted by the Benedictine Sisters. Sr. Monica Collins, O.S.B., Prin. Sisters 3; Lay Teachers 39; Students 863.

INGLEWOOD. *St. Mary's Academy.* (Girls), 701 Grace Ave., 90301. Tel: 310-674-8470.
E-mail: nancymunro@aol.com
Sr. Nancy Munro, C.S.J., Prin. Sisters of St. Joseph of Carondelet 8; Lay Teachers 23; Students 430.

LA CANADA FLINTRIDGE. *Flintridge Sacred Heart Academy.* (Girls), 440 St. Katherine Dr., 91011. Tel: 818-356-1748. Legal Title: *Flintridge Sacred Heart Academy, A Corporation.* Sr. Ramona Bascom, O.P., Prin. Dominican Sisters of Mission San Jose 9; Lay Teachers 28; Students 392.

St. Francis High School. (Boys), 200 Foothill Blvd., 91011. Tel: 818-790-0325. Legal Title: *The Capuchin Franciscan Order of the Western American Province.* Revs. Matthew Elshoff, O.F.M.Cap., Pres. St. Francis High School; Gregory Coiro, O.F.M.Cap.; Chris Thiel, O.F.M.Cap.; Anthony Scannel, O.F.M.Cap.; Bros. Robert Edwards, O.F.M.Cap., Guardian of the Community; Bernard McAllister, Dir. of Vocations; Steven Tetreault, O.F.M.Cap., Dir. Campus Ministry; Sr. Barbarine Houdek, O.S.F. Priests 5; Brothers 3; Sisters 1; Lay Teachers 32; Total Teachers 41; Students 610.

OJAI. *Villanova Preparatory School,* 12096 Ventura Ave., 93023-3999. Tel: 805-646-1464; Fax: 805-646-4430.
E-mail: info@villanova.pvt.k12.ca.us
Web site: www.villanova.pvt.k12.ca.us
Legal Title: *Villanova Preparatory School of California.* Revs. John P. Pejza, O.S.A., Pres.; John F. Glynn, O.S.A. Conducted by Augustinian Fathers (Order of St. Augustine). Priests 2; Sisters 1; Brothers 1; Lay Teachers 27; Students 280.

PASADENA. *La Salle High School,* 3880 E. Sierra Madre Blvd., 91107. Tel: 626-351-8951; Fax: 626-351-0275.
E-mail: principal@lasallehs.org
Web site: lasallehs.org
Mr. Patrick Bonacci, Prin. Sisters 1; Lay Teachers 45; Students 731.

Mayfield Senior School of the Holy Child Jesus, 500 Bellefontaine St., 91105-2439. Tel: 818-799-9121; 213-682-2620; Fax: 818-799-8576.
E-mail: ahowell@wavenet.com
Mrs. Jeanne G. How, Registrar; Mrs. Edith Gardener, Business Mgr. Sisters 1; Lay Teachers 30; Students 264.

SHERMAN OAKS. *Notre Dame High School,* 13645 Riverside Dr., 91423. Tel: 818-501-2300; Fax: 818-501-0507.
Bro. William C. Nick, C.S.C., Pres.; Mrs. Stephanie Connelly, Prin. Brothers 6; Priests 1; Lay Teachers 63; Students 1,102.

SIERRA MADRE. *Alverno High School.* (Girls), 200 N. Michillinda Ave., 91024. Tel: 818-355-3463; Fax: 818-355-3153. Ann M. Gillick, M.S., Prin. Lay Teachers 18; Students 220.

THOUSAND OAKS. *La Reina High School.* (Girls Grades 7-12), 106 W. Janss Rd., 91360. Tel: 805-495-6494; Fax: 805-494-4966.
E-mail: lareina@adnetsol.com
Web site: www.lareina.com
Sr. Lisa Megaffin, S.N.D., Prin. Sisters of Notre Dame 4; Lay Teachers 38; Students 630.

WOODLAND HILLS. *Louisville High School.* (Girls), 22300 Mulholland Dr., 91364. Tel: 818-346-8812; Fax: 818-346-9483. Sr. Myra McPartland, S.S.L., Prin. Sisters 8; Lay Teachers 38; Students 483.

[G] MIDDLE SCHOOLS, ARCHDIOCESAN

LOS ANGELES. *Holy Cross Middle School,* 104 W. 47th Pl., 90037. Tel: 213-234-9023. Conducted by Archdiocese of Los Angeles. Sr. Daniel Therese, C.S.J.,

Prin. Sisters 3; Lay Teachers 8; Students 175.

[H] ELEMENTARY SCHOOLS, PRIVATE

LOS ANGELES. *Notre Dame Academy (Elementary)*, 2911 Overland Ave., 90064. Tel: 310-287-3895. Sr. Mary LaReina Kelly, S.N.D., Prin. Sisters of Notre Dame of Los Angeles 2; Lay Teachers 11; Students 313.

PASADENA. *Mayfield Junior School*, 405 S. Euclid Ave., 91101. Tel: 818-796-2774. Sisters of the Society of the Holy Child Jesus 1; Lay Teachers 45; Students 420.

SANTA BARBARA. *Marymount Academy*. (Grades K-8). (Coed), 2130 Mission Ridge Rd., 93103. Tel: 805-569-1811; Fax: 805-682-6892.
E-mail: mmountsbar@aol.com
Lay Teachers 21; Students 233.

[I] ORPHANAGES AND INFANT HOMES

ROSEMEAD. *Maryvale*, P.O. Box 1039, 91770-1003. Tel: 626-280-6510; 213-283-9311; Fax: 626-288-8903
For a complete listing, refer to the Special Care Facilities section.

[J] DAY NURSERIES

LOS ANGELES. *Divine Providence Pre-school and Kindergarten*, 2620 Monmouth St., 90007. Tel: 213-747-3074. Sr. Mary Pardo, O.D.M., Dir. Sisters of the Company of Mary 6; Lay Teachers 11; Children 140.

St. Jeanne de Lestonnac Kindergarten and Day Nursery, 4001 Venice Blvd., 90019. Tel: 213-737-1217. (Formerly Little Flower Kindergarten & Day Nursery). Sr. Charlotte Turritta, Supervisor. Lay Teachers 16; Children 200.

GARDENA. *St. Anthony's Day Nursery*, 1044 W. 163rd St., 90247. Tel: 310-329-8654. Sr. Rosa Lilia Arreola, M.C., Dir. Sisters 11; Children 90.

SAN FERNANDO. *Poverello of Assisi School*, 1519 Woodworth St., 91340. Tel: 818-361-5864. Franciscan Missionary Sisters of the Immaculate Conception. Sr. Irene San Roman. Sisters 7; Children 190.

[K] GENERAL HOSPITALS

LOS ANGELES. *Queen of Angels-Hollywood Presbyterian Medical Center*, 1300 N. Vermont Ave., 90027
For a complete listing, refer to the Hospitals section.

St. Vincent Medical Center, 2131 W. 3rd St., 90057. Tel: 213-484-7111
For a complete listing, refer to the Hospitals section.

Santa Marta Hospital, 319 N. Humphreys Ave., 90022. Tel: 213-266-6500; Fax: 213-260-8641 (Admin.)
For a complete listing, refer to the Hospitals section.

BURBANK. *Providence Health System*, 501 S. Buena Vista St., 91505. Tel: 818-365-8051; Fax: 818-898-4569
For a complete listing, refer to the Hospitals section.

Providence Saint Joseph Medical Center, 501 S. Buena Vista, 91505. Tel: 818-843-5111; Fax: 818-843-0641
For a complete listing, refer to the Hospitals section.

DUARTE. *Santa Teresita Hospital*, 819 Buena Vista St., 91010. Tel: 818-359-3243; Fax: 818-357-7166.
E-mail: sth@santa-teresita.org
Web site: www.santa-teresita.org
For a complete listing, refer to the Hospitals section.

*HAWTHORNE. *Hawthorne Community Hospital, Inc.*, 711 Grevilles Ave., 90250
For a complete listing, refer to the Hospitals section.

INGLEWOOD. *Daniel Freeman Memorial Hospital*, 333 N. Prairie Ave., 90301. Tel: 310-674-7050; 678-0361; Fax: 310-419-8273
For a complete listing, refer to the Hospitals section.

LONG BEACH. *St. Mary Medical Center*, 1050 Linden Ave., 90813
For a complete listing, refer to the Hospitals section.

St. Mary Medical Center Foundation, P.O. Box 887, 90801
For a complete listing, refer to the Hospitals section.

St. Mary Professional Building, Inc., 1045 Atlantic Ave., 90813
For a complete listing, refer to the Hospitals section.

LYNWOOD. *Catholic Health Care West-Southern California*, 3630 E. Imperial Hwy., 90262. Tel: 310-603-6000
For a complete listing, refer to the Hospitals section.

St. Francis Medical Center, 3630 E. Imperial Hwy., 90262. Tel: 310-603-6000
For a complete listing, refer to the Hospitals section.

MARINA DEL REY. *Daniel Freeman Marina Hospital*, 4650 Lincoln Blvd., 90292. Tel: 310-823-8911
For a complete listing, refer to the Hospitals section.

OXNARD. *St. John's Regional Medical Center*, 1600 N. Rose Ave., 93030. Tel: 805-988-2500
For a complete listing, refer to the Hospitals section.

SAN PEDRO. *San Pedro Peninsula Hospital*, 1700 W. Seventh St., 90732. Tel: 310-832-3311
For a complete listing, refer to the Hospitals section.

SANTA BARBARA. *St. Francis Medical Center of Santa Barbara*, 601 E. Micheltorena St., 93103. Tel: 805-962-7661; Fax: 805-966-5704
For a complete listing, refer to the Hospitals section.

SANTA MARIA. *Marian Medical Center*, 1400 E. Church St., 93454. Tel: 805-739-3000
For a complete listing, refer to the Hospitals section.

SANTA MONICA. *Saint John's Health Center*, 1328 22nd St., 90404. Tel: 310-829-5511; Fax: 310-315-6134
For a complete listing, refer to the Hospitals section.

TORRANCE. *Little Company of Mary Health Services*, 4101 Torrance Blvd., 90503. Tel: 310-543-5803; Fax: 310-540-7659
For a complete listing, refer to the Hospitals section.

WEST COVINA. *Citrus Valley Health Partners, Queen of the Valley Campus*, 1115 S. Sunset Ave., P.O. Box 1980, 91793. Tel: 818-962-4011; Fax: 818-814-2482.
E-mail: vip.pm@cvhp.org
Web site: www.cvhp.com
For a complete listing, refer to the Hospitals section.

[L] SPECIAL HOSPITALS AND SANATORIA FOR INVALIDS

LOS ANGELES. *Franciscan Health Center*, 2859 Glassell St., 90026. Tel: 213-413-1050
For a complete listing, refer to the Special Care Facilities section.

Knights of Malta Free Clinic, Inc., 2222 W. Ocean View #112, 90057. Tel: 213-384-4323; Fax: 213-384-4097
For a complete listing, refer to the Special Care Facilities section.

CULVER CITY. *Marycrest Manor, Convalescent Home*, 10664 St. James Dr., 90230-5498. Tel: 310-838-2778
For a complete listing, refer to the Special Care Facilities section.

NEWBURY PARK. *Mary Health of the Sick Convalescent and Nursing Hospital*, 2929 Theresa Dr., 91320. Tel: 805-498-3644; Fax: 805-498-5112
For a complete listing, refer to the Special Care Facilities section.

OJAI. *St. Joseph's Health and Retirement Center*, 2464 E. Ojai Ave., P.O. Box 760, 93024. Tel: 805-646-1466
For a complete listing, refer to the Special Care Facilities section.

[M] HANDICAPPED

LOS ANGELES. *Ministry with Persons with Disabilities*, 3424 Wilshire Blvd., Second Floor, 90010. Tel: 213-637-7236. Veronica Gray, Dir., Marian Homes for the Developmentally and Physically Disabled, Inc., Office of the Admin., 3424 Wilshire Blvd., 2nd Fl., 90010-2241. Tel: 213-637-7236. Katherine Boyet, Prog. Dir.

SANTA MONICA. *Saint John's Child Study Center, Saint John's Hospital & Health Center*, 1339 20th St., 90404. Tel: 310-829-8921; Fax: 310-829-8455. Conducted by Sisters of Charity of Leavenworth. Affiliated with Saint John's Hospital. Rebecca Refuerza, L.C.S.W., Dir. Children Treated Annually 1,800.

SUNLAND.
**Tierra del Sol Foundation*, 9919 Sunland Blvd., 91040. Tel: 818-352-1419; Fax: 818-353-0777. Community Program Supportive Employment for Adults with Disabilities. Stephen J. Miller, Exec. Dir.; Nancy Bissonette-Andrew, Assoc. Dir. Licensed Capacity 200.

VAN NUYS. *Tierra Del Sol West*, 14547 Gilmore St., 91411. Tel: 818-904-9164. Behavior Management Community Program for Adults with Developmental Disabilities. Stephen J. Miller, Exec. Dir.; Karen Alitz-Pelga, Program Dir. Capacity 50.

[N] CHILD ADOPTION SERVICES

PASADENA. *Holy Family Services, Adoption & Foster Care*, 402-A S. Marengo Ave., 91101-3113. Tel: 818-578-1156; Fax: 818-578-7321.
Branch Offices: 1403 South Main St., Los Angeles, 92707. Tel: 714-835-5551; Fax: 714-973-4971. YWCA, 8172 Magnolia Ave., Riverside, 92504. Tel: 800-464-2367. 80 E. Hillcrest #210, Thousand Oaks, 91360. Tel: 800-464-ADOPT.

Holy Family Adoption Foundation, Inc.
Auxiliaries of Holy Family Services: Holy Family's Adoptive Parents Organization, Inc., The Adoption Guild Regents, Adoption Guild of Southern Orange County, Angelique Guild, The 200 Associates. Birthparent unplanned pregnancy counseling 88; Foster care families recruited 10; Children placed in adoptive homes 64.

[O] VISITING NURSE SERVICES

LOS ANGELES. *Sisters Servants of Mary, Ministers of the Sick*, 2131 W. 27th St., 90018-3018. Tel: 213-731-5747. Sr. Esther Fonseca, S.M., Supr. Sisters 17; Total Assisted 92; Total Staff 7.

[P] PROTECTIVE INSTITUTIONS

LOS ANGELES. *Convent of the Good Shepherd-Good Shepherd Shelter*, 2561 Venice Blvd., 90019. Tel: 213-737-6111
For a complete listing, refer to the Special Care Facilities section.

Immaculate Conception Home for Girls, 1923 Micheltorena St., 90039. Tel: 213-664-7070
For a complete listing, refer to the Special Care Facilities section.

Little Flower Missionary House, 2434 Gates St., 90031. Tel: 213-221-9248.
E-mail: be629@lafn.org
Web site: www.geocities.com/athens/acropolis/7053/sst.html
For a complete listing, refer to the Special Care Facilities section.

Missionary Brothers of Charity, 1345 Alvarado Ter., 90006. Tel: 213-251-9707
For a complete listing, refer to the Special Care Facilities section.

St. Anne's, 155 N. Occidental Blvd., 90026. Tel: 213-381-2931; Fax: 213-381-7804.
E-mail: stannes@ix.netcom.com
Web site: www.stannes.org
For a complete listing, refer to the Special Care Facilities section.

CHATSWORTH. *Rancho San Antonio*, 21000 Plummer St., 91311. Tel: 818-882-6400
For a complete listing, refer to the Special Care Facilities section.

SANTA BARBARA. *St. Vincent Residence*, 4200 Calle Real, P.O. Box 669, 93102-0669. Tel: 805-683-6381; Fax: 805-967-7508
For a complete listing, refer to the Special Care Facilities section.

[Q] HOMES FOR AGED

LOS ANGELES. *Nazareth House*, 3333 Manning Ave., 90064. Tel: 310-839-2361; Fax: 310-839-4204
For a complete listing, refer to the Special Care Facilities section.

St. John of God Retirement and Care Center, 2035 W. Adams Blvd., 90018. Tel: 213-731-0641
For a complete listing, refer to the Special Care Facilities section.

SAN FERNANDO. *Mother Gertrude Home for Senior Citizens*, 11320 Laurel Canyon Blvd., 91340. Tel: 818-898-1546; Fax: 818-365-3159
For a complete listing, refer to the Special Care Facilities section.

SAN PEDRO. *Little Sisters of the Poor*, Jeanne Jugan Residence, 2100 S. Western Ave., 90732. Tel: 310-548-0625
For a complete listing, refer to the Special Care Facilities section.

SANTA MARIA. *Marian Residence*, 124 S. College Dr., 93454
For a complete listing, refer to the Special Care Facilities section.

SUN VALLEY. *Villa Scalabrini*, 10631 Vinedale St., 91352. Tel: 818-768-6500; Fax: 818-767-1410.
E-mail: mrainen@aol.com
For a complete listing, refer to the Special Care Facilities section.

[R] MONASTERIES AND RESIDENCES OF PRIESTS AND BROTHERS

LOS ANGELES. *Amat House*, 649 W. Adams Blvd., 90007-2596. Tel: 213-747-1227. Revs. Henry L. van Oudheusden, Supr.; Victor J. Sarrazin; Very Rev. Bernard J. Quinn, Prov.

De Paul Center, 1105 Bluff Rd., Montebello, 90640-6198. Revs. Patrick J. Mullin, Supr.; John J. Casey; Peter J. Diliberto; Robert J. Jones; Thomas J. McIntyre; Jacques J. Nouws; Terence M. O'Donnell, C.M.; Deacon John P. Kearney. Priests 7; Deacons 1.

St. Mary's Center, 1964 Las Canoas Rd., Santa Barbara, 93105-2351. Revs. James F. McOwen, Supr.; Roy A. Persich, C.M., Dir.; James M. Gavin. Priests 3. Priests 3.

Atonement Friars, 222 S. Hewitt St., 90012. Tel: 213-626-2279. Revs. David L. Doerner, S.A.; Henry Mair, S.A.

Brothers of John of God, Inc., The, 2425 S. Western Ave., 90018-2608. Tel: 213-734-0233; Fax: 213-731-5987.
Web site: www.hospitallers.org
Bro. Edward Francis McEnroe, O.H., Prov.
Women's League of St. John of God, Inc.
Helper's Club, Inc.
St. John of God Retirement and Care Center.
St. Joseph's Health and Retirement Center.
Hospitaller Foundation of California, Inc.
Women's League of St. Joseph's Health and Retirement Center.
Grande Apartments-Los Angeles.
Hospitaller Brothers Healthcare, Inc.
St. John of God Health Care Services.

Brothers of Our Lady, Mother of Mercy Inc., 7140 Ramsgate Ave., 90045. Tel: 310-649-3370. Bro. John H. Grever, C.F.M.M., Community Rep. Brothers 3.

Brothers of the Good Shepherd, Inc. of California, 3445 Waverly Dr., 90027. Tel: 213-662-3630. Bro. Malachy Corbett, B.G.S.

Canons Regular of the Immaculate Conception, 1523 Golden Gate Ave., 90026. Tel: 213-664-1305. Revs. James G. Garceau, C.R.I.C.; Charles R. Lueras, C.R.I.C.; Pasquale Vuoso, C.R.I.C., Pastor; Sergio Garcia, C.R.I.C. Priests 4.

Casa Guadalupe, Divine Word Missionaries, 807 N. Fresno, 90063. Tel: 213-263-7561. Revs. Lukas Bao Teluma, S.V.D.; Raymundus Bhia Wea, S.V.D.

Claretian Retreat Center Community, 1119 Westchester Pl., 90019. Tel: 213-731-9329; Fax: 213-733-6201. Very Rev. Ralph Berg, C.M.F., Provincial Superior; Revs. Carlos C. Castillo, C.M.F., Supr.; Frank J. Ferrante, C.M.F., Dir.; Bro. Rene LePage, C.M.F., Admin.; Revs. George Whedbee, C.M.F.; Gabriel Ruiz, C.M.F.; John Hampsch, C.M.F.; Robert Billett, C.M.F.; Roland Lozano, C.M.F.; John Raab, C.M.F.; Bro. Larry Moen, C.M.F.

Columban Fathers, Procure House, 2600 N. Vermont Ave., 90027. Tel: 213-665-4289. Revs. Thomas P. Parker, S.S.C., Supr.; Thomas Cusack, S.S.C.; Seamus Leddy, S.S.C.; Anthony Mortell, S.S.C.; Ernest L. Sullivan, S.C.S.; Denis Bartley, S.S.C.; Jim Shiffer, S.S.C.

Columbiere House. Formerly Connolly House. 5322 Franklin Ave., 90027. Tel: 213-466-3723; Fax: 213-466-3826. Jesuit Fathers. Revs. Francis J. Parrish, S.J.; John D. McAnulty, S.J.; George E. Krivanek, S.J.; John A. Houle, S.J. (China); Allan F. Deck, S.J., Supr.; Charles Prussing, S.J.; Peter Chu, S.J.; George R. Sullivan, S.J. (Wisconsin); John D. Dryden, S.J.; Robert Leonard, S.J.; Patrick Connolly, S.J. (Wisconsin); Frederick J. Heney, S.J. (Japan); Michael J. Mandala, S.J.; Felix A. Maiza, S.J.; Robert E. Griffin, S.J. Priests 15.

Congregation of St. Joseph Casa Nazareth, 2702 Abrigo Ave., 90031. Tel: 213-221-4809. Revs. Giampietro Gasparin, C.S.J.; John Trimaglio, C.S.J., Supr.

Dominic Savio Salesian Residence, 920 S. Soto St., 90023-1396. Tel: 213-266-1977; Fax: 213-266-0486.
E-mail: SDBinELA@aol.com
In res. Revs. Juan Francisco Munoz, S.D.B., St. Mary's; James Nieblas, S.D.B., Vicar for the Community, St. Mary's; Cresencio Rosales, S.D.B., Salesian High School; Crescenciano Salcedo, S.D.B., St. Mary's; William Schafer, S.D.B., Executive Director, Salesian Boys' & Girls' Club, Salesian Family Youth Center; Bros. Rudy Bertagnolli, S.D.B.; Robert Hennings, S.D.B., Community Treas., Salesian High, Salesian Clubs; Jesus Hinojosa, S.D.B., Program Dir., Salesian Family Youth Center; John Kornak, S.D.B., Salesian High School.
Salesians in Community but not in res.: Revs. Joseph Cheng, S.D.B., St. Bridget's Chinese Catholic Center; Lucian Lomello, S.D.B., Chap., Hospital.

Franciscan Brothers of the Third Order Regular, 4552 Gainsborough Ave., 90027. Tel: 213-644-2740. Bro. Hilarion O'Connor, O.S.F., Regl. Supr. Brothers 11.

Guadalupe Missioners Procure, 4714 W. 8th St., 90005. Tel: 213-937-2780. Revs. Santiago G. Lara, M.G., Local Supr.; Abraham R. Garcia, M.G., Asst.

Hospitaller Brothers of St. John of God, 2035 W. Adams Blvd., 90018. Tel: 213-731-0641; Fax: 213-731-5987.
Web site: www.hospitallers.org
Formation Community. Bro. Stephen de la Rosa, O.H., Novice Master & Prior. Brothers 14.

Maryknoll Fathers and Brothers. (Catholic Foreign Mission Society of America), 745 W. Adams Blvd., 90007. Tel: 213-747-9676; Fax: 213-747-8923. Revs. Richard R. Fries, M.M., Dir.; Richard P. Albertine, M.M.; Robert A. Hurteau, M.M.; Joseph A. Klecha, M.M. Priests 4.

Mill Hill Missionaries Procure. (St. Joseph Society for Foreign Missions), 1841 Camino Palmero, 90046. Tel: 213-876-0505; Fax: 213-876-0508. Revs. Theo M. Feldbrugge, M.H.M.; Henk Riesthuis, M.H.M. Priests 2.

Minim Fathers, 3431 Portola Ave., 90032. Tel: 213-223-1101; Fax: 213-223-9592. Revs. Constantino Mandarino, O.M., Supr.; Gino Vanzillotta, O.M., Supr.; Jose L. Vega, O.M. Priests 3.

Missionaries of Charity Brothers, Regional Office: 214 S. Witmer St., 90026. Tel: 213-481-8152; 8153.

House of Formation, 1325 S. Westlake Ave., 90006. Tel: 213-384-6116. Brothers 11.

Casa Teresa, 1316 S. Westlake Ave., 90006. Tel: 213-380-5225; 213-390-5356. Hospitality for men and boys.

Nuestro Hogar, 1345 Alvarado Terr., 90006. Tel: 213-251-9707. Daycenter for young adults. Total Assisted 60; Total Staff 5.

Missionary Sons of the Immaculate Heart of Mary. (Claretian Priests and Brothers). Prov. Headquarters of the Western Prov. of the USA, 1119 Westchecter Place, 90019. Tel: 213-734-1824; Fax: 213-737-0301. Legal Title: *Claretian Missionaries - Western Province, Inc.* Very Rev. Ralph Berg, C.M.F., Prov. Supr.; Rev. Roland Lozano, C.M.F., Prov. Treas.

Claretian Tape Ministry, Inc.

Dominguez Seminary, Inc., Compton.

Claretian Educational and Renewal Center, Inc. This is a non-profit corporation under the laws of the State of California having as its purpose the support of any Roman Catholic benevolent, charitable, educational or missionary undertakings of the Claretian Missionaries - Western Province, Inc.

Mount Carmel Priory, Carmelite Fathers and Brothers, 801 W. 70th St., 90044. Tel: 213-752-3972. Legal Title: *Fathers of the Order of Mount Carmel, Corporation*. Revs. Augustine W. Carter, O.Carm.; Matt J. Ewing, O.Carm., Prior; Bernard Kangley, O.Carm.; Bro. Stephen Diekemper, O.Carm. Priests 3.

Piarist Fathers, 512 S. Avenue 20, 90031. Tel: 213-223-4153. Revs. Raul Palma, Sch.P.; Francis Boronat, Sch.P., Rector of the Community; Juan Trenchs, Sch.P.; Miguel Campos, Sch.P. Priests 4.

St. John of God Retirement and Care Center, 2035 W. Adams Blvd., 90018. Tel: 213-731-0641. Bros. Edward F. McEnroe, O.H., Prov. & Chm.; Stephen de la Rosa, O.H., Local Supr. & Novice Master. Brothers 14.

Society of St. Paul. (Mexican Province), 112 Herbert St., 90063. Tel: 213-269-9814. Revs. Gonzalo Ponce, S.S.P., Supr.; Gilberto Martinez, S.S.P.; Tomas Martinez, S.S.P.; Valeriano Giachino, S.S.P.; Jesus Hernandez Vidal, S.S.P.; Francisco Manuel Rosas, S.S.P. Priests 6.

Society of the Divine Word Western Province, Office of the Provincial, 2181 W. 25th St., P.O. Box 77-F, 90007. Tel: 213-735-8130 (Provincial Office); 731-9982 (Community Phone); Fax: 213-735-8122 (Provincial Office). Revs. Eamonn Donnelly, S.V.D., Prov. Supr.; Gerard O'Doherty, S.V.D., Prov. Treas.; Bro. Jeremiah M. Walsh, S.V.D. In res. Rev. Francis L. Shigo, S.V.D.; Bro. Richard A. Morrill, S.V.D.

Vincentian Fathers and Brothers, Province of the West, Provincial Office, 650 W. 23rd St., 90007-2036. Tel: 213-748-9829. Vincentian Residence, 641 W. Adams Blvd., 90007. Legal Titles: *Congregation of the Mission in California, a Corporation.*; *Vincentian Community Charitable Trust.*; *Vincentian Foreign Mission Society.*; *DePaul Center Corporation.* (Formerly St. Vincent's Seminary Corporation). Revs. Pedro Villarroya, C.M., Supr.; Thomas C. Anslow, C.M.; Edward F. Danagher, C.M.; Stafford Poole, C.M.; Francis David Pansini, C.M.; Bro. Edward Graham, C.M. Brothers 1; Priests 5.

AZUSA. *Casa Comboni Mission Seminary*, 525 N. Pasadena Ave., 91702. Tel: 818-334-3531. Rev. Giovanni Esti, M.C.C.J. (Italy), Rector & Formation Dir. In res. Rev. Jose Luis Cuevas (Mexico). Priests 2; Students 5.

BALDWIN PARK. *Vietnamese Redemptorist Mission*, 3452 N. Big Dalton Ave., 91706. Revs. Vu Minh Nghiem, C.Ss.R.; Ngo Dinh Thoa, C.Ss.R.; Dinh Ngoc Que, C.Ss.R.; Nguyen Thanh Son, C.Ss.R.; Tran Quoc Bao, C.Ss.R.; Trinh Duc Hoa, C.Ss.R.; Pham Quoc Hung, C.Ss.R.; Bros. John M. Viet Hien, C.Ss.R.; Martin Nguyen Van Moi, C.Ss.R.
In Residence Elsewhere: 5404 N.E. Alameda Dr., Portland, OR, 97213. Rev. Hong Phuc, C.Ss.R., 8800 E. 22nd St., Tuscon, AZ, 85710. Rev. Tran Ngoc Bich, C.Ss.R., 22 Stone St., Salinas, 93901. Rev. Tran Dinh Phuc, C.Ss.R., 2458 Atlantic Ave., Long Beach, 90806. Revs. Nguyen Duc Mau, C.Ss.R.; Phan Phat Huon, C.Ss.R.; Ngo Van Dao, C.Ss.R.; Bui quang Tuan, C.Ss.R.; Bro. Vo Thanh Ha, C.Ss.R., 1907 E. Grauwyler Rd., Irving, TX, 75061. Revs. Nguyen Duc Thong, C.Ss.R.; Dinh Minh Hai, C.Ss.R.; Nguyen Duc Thanh, C.Ss.R., 600 Melwood W., Houston, TX, 77009. Revs. Chau Xuan Bau, C.Ss.R.; Le Quang Phung, C.Ss.R.; Tran Tu Nhan, C.Ss.R.; Le Huy Bang, C.Ss.R., 1011 Farm Rd., P.O. Box 1060, Rockport, TX, 78381. Rev. Nguyen Van Phan, C.Ss.R. Priests 23; Brothers 3; Student Clerics 20.

CAMARILLO. *Rogationist Fathers*, 2530 E. Ventura Blvd., 93010. Tel: 805-389-9910; Fax: 805-384-0189.
E-mail: RogVoc@aol.com
Revs. F. Antonio Carlucci, R.C.J., Supr., Dean of Studies; Loji Pilones, R.C.J., Treas., Vocation Dir., Vice Supr.

CULVER CITY. *Ignatius House, The Novitiate of the California Province, Society of Jesus*, P.O. Box 5166, 90231-5166. 10775 Deshire Pl., 90230-5017. Tel: 310-815-0166 (Staff); 815-0185 (Novices); Fax: 310-815-0170. Revs. Robert A. Fambrini, S.J., Supr. & Dir. of Novices; John W. Chandler, S.J., Socius, Min. & Asst. to Novice Dir.; George E. Schultze, S.J., Treas. In res. Rev. Steven E. Artiga, S.J.

FILLMORE. *Apostolate of Christian Renewal Holy Family*, 411 First St., P.O. Box 547, 93016-0547. Tel: 805-524-5890. Rev. Luke Zimmer, SS.CC.

LA VERNE. *Congregation of the Sacred Hearts*, 2150 Damien Ave., 91750. Revs. Donal McCarthy, SS.CC.; Patrick Travers, SS.CC.; Peadar Cronin, SS.CC.; Martin P. O'Loghlen, SS.CC. Priests 4.

MISSION HILLS. *Congregation of the Sacred Hearts*, 15201 Rinaldi St., 91345. Tel: 818-361-9152. Revs. Kenneth O. McCabe, SS.CC.; Patrick Argue, SS.CC. Priests 2.

NORTH HILLS. *Rogationist Fathers*, 9815 Columbus Ave., 91343. Tel: 818-894-2546; Fax: 818-895-8934.
Web site: http://informatique.1.0/.ie/rogusa
Revs. Vincenzo Buccheri, R.C.J.; Rodolfo D'Agostino, R.C.J., Rector. Legal Title: *Congregation of Rogationists, Inc.*

OXNARD. *Brothers of Our Lady, Mother of Mercy*, Mother of Mercy Novitiate, 2336 S. C St., 93033. Tel: 805-486-3692. Conducted by the Brothers of Our Lady, Mother of Mercy. Bros. Edward Gresnigt, Reg. Supr.; Edward Gresnigt, C.F.M.M., Local Supr. Brothers 8.

St. Augustine Priory, St. Augustine Priory, 400 Sherwood Way, 93033. Tel: 805-486-7433. Prepostulancy & Postulancy Vocation Center. Total in Residence 16.

St. Augustine Priory O.A.R., 400 Sherwood Way, 93033-7510. Tel: 805-486-7433; 486-9651 (Vocations). Prepostulancy and Postulancy Augustinian Recollects & Vocation Center. Revs. John Gruben, O.A.R., Prior; Francisco J. Legarra, O.A.R. (Spain), Prefect of Students & Subprior; Jose Luis Martinez, O.A.R., Dir. of Vocations; Albert Polt, O.A.R., (Retired); Bros. Raymond Fabrin, O.A.R.; Ramiro Munoz, O.A.R.

PASADENA. *Legionaries of Christ*, P.O. Box 61305, 91116. Tel: 626-305-5363.
E-mail: bwilson@cco.caltech.edu
Web site: http://www.legionaries.org
In res. Revs. Brian Wilson, L.C.; Juan Rivas, L.C.; Thomas White, L.C.; Thomas Maher, L.C.

Passionist Community, 651 N. Sierra Madre Blvd., 91107.

Passionist Retreat House, 700 N. Sunnyside Ave., Sierra Madre, 91024. Tel: 818-355-7188; Fax: 818-355-0485. Passionist Residence, 651 N. Sierra Madre Blvd., 91107. Tel: 818-564-1099; Fax: 818-564-1930. Congregation of the Passion, Mater Dolorosa Community. Very Rev. Peter Kumle, C.P., Local Supr.; Revs. Benedict Olson, C.P., Asst. Supr.; Damian McHale, C.P.; Patrick Brennan, C.P., Retreat Dir.; Godfrey Poage, C.P.; Benet Kieran, C.P.; Cyprian Towey, C.P.; Alan Phillip, C.P.; Philip Paxton, C.P., Assoc. Retreat Dir. & Vocational Dir.; Bros. John Rockenbach, C.P., Retreat House; Anthony Mimiaga, C.P. Priests 9; Brothers 2.

RANCHO DOMINGUEZ. *Dominguez Seminary Inc.*, 18127 S. Alameda St., 90220. Tel: 213-636-6030; 310-631-5981; 631-8484; Fax: 310-631-3518. Retirement Center, Ministries Community. Congregation of Missionaries, Sons of the Immaculate Heart of Mary (Claretian Missionaries). Revs. Robert Bishop, C.M.F., Supr.; Donald Lavelle, C.M.F., Admin.; Patrick McPolin, C.M.F.; Diego Barrios, C.M.F.; John Corominas, C.M.F.; Bernard Stacy, C.M.F.; Albert Connors, C.M.F.; Edward Widmer, C.M.F.; Basil Frison, C.M.F.; Francis X. Hogan, C.M.F.; Celestino de la Iglesia, C.M.F.; Walter Mischke, C.M.F.; Raymond Martinez, C.M.F.; Flavin Willathgamuwa, C.M.F.; Alberto M. Ruiz, C.M.F.; Salvatore Bonano, C.M.F., Vicar; Joseph Daries, C.M.F.; Bros. Paul Roy, C.M.F.; Franklin Stanford, C.M.F. Priests 17; Brothers 2.

SAN GABRIEL. *Claretian Missionaries (Missionary Sons of the Immaculate Heart of Mary)*, 537 W. Mission Dr., 91776. Tel: 626-457-3035. Claretians Old Mission. Revs. Dennis Gallo, C.M.F.; Jose Sanchez, C.M.F.; Jack Hencier, C.M.F. In res. Bro. Cruz Pettinato, C.M.F. Priests 3.

SANTA BARBARA. *Franciscan Friary, Order of Friars Minor (Old Mission)*, 2201 Laguna St., 93105. Tel: 805-682-4713. Revs. Clifford Herle, O.F.M., Guardian; Virgil Cordano, O.F.M., Theological Institute; David Carriere, O.F.M.; Nevin Ford, O.F.M.; Bertin Foxen, O.F.M.; Noel Moholy, O.F.M.; Frederick Bromham, O.F.M.; Benvenute Bavero, O.F.M.; Allan Wolter, O.F.M.; Adrian Erlenheim, O.F.M.; Virgilio Biasiol, O.F.M.; Maurus Kelly, O.F.M., Chap.; Vincent Mesi, O.F.M., St. Barbara's; John Flajole, O.F.M., Chap., Serra Wing; Francis Guest, O.F.M.; Howard Hall, O.F.M.; Paschal Morrisroe, O.F.M.; Andres Rivero, O.F.M.; Leo Sprietsma, O.F.M.; Bros. Timothy Arthur, O.F.M., Prov. Archivist; Damian Byrne, O.F.M.; Ernest Duplessis, O.F.M.; Adrian Furman, O.F.M.; Wenceslaus Farlow, O.F.M.; Joachim Grant, O.F.M.; Mateo Guerrero, O.F.M.; Augustine Hootka, O.F.M.; Philip Morales, O.F.M.; Peter Raferty, O.F.M.; William Siegler, O.F.M. Priests 19; Brothers 11.

St. Anthony's Seminary, 2300 Garden St., 93105-3696. Tel: 805-682-4720. Rev. Leo Sprietsma, O.F.M., Dir. In res. Rev. Nevin Ford, O.F.M.; Bros. Timothy Arthur, O.F.M.; Jan Honchosky, O.F.M.; Wenceslaus Farlow, O.F.M. Priests 2; Brothers 3.

TORRANCE. *Franciscan Friars, St. Bonaventure Friary*, 5432 Torrance Blvd., 90503. Tel: 310-540-1452. Conventual Franciscan Friars (St. Joseph Cupertino Province). Legal Title: *Conventual Franciscans of California, Inc.* Revs. Alexander J. Lewis, O.F.M.Conv., Supr.; Gary Klauer, O.F.M.Conv. In res. Revs. Ceaser Inserra, O.F.M.Conv.; Francisco Nahoe, O.F.M.Conv.; Bros. Casimir Roland, O.F.M.Conv.; Patrick Lytell, O.F.M.Conv.; Paul Gawlowski, O.F.M.Conv.; Anthony Tuyen Pham, O.F.M.Conv.

VALYERMO. *St. Andrew's Abbey*, 31001 N. Valyermo Rd., 93563-0040. Tel: 805-944-2178.
E-mail: standrab@ptw.com
Web site: www.ptw.com/~standrab
Benedictine Monks. Rt. Rev. Francis Benedict, O.S.B., Abbot; Very Revs. Luke Dysinger, O.S.B., Prior; Simon O'Donnell, O.S.B., Subprior; Revs. Eleutherius Winance, O.S.B.; Vincent Martin, O.S.B.; Werner Papeians de Morchoven, O.S.B.; Bro. Peter Zhou Bang-jiu, O.S.B.; Revs. Philip Edwards, O.S.B.; John Borgerding, O.S.B.; John Bosco Stoner, O.S.B.; Bro. Dominic Guillen, O.S.B.; Rev. Gregory Elmer, O.S.B.; Bros. Benedict Dull, O.S.B.; Joseph Iarrobino, O.S.B.; Revs. Isaac Kalina, O.S.B.; Martin Yslas, O.S.B.; Paul Pluth, O.S.B.; Bros. Anselmo Taborda, O.S.B.; Andrew Hayes, O.S.B.; Rev. Joseph (Dennis) Brennan, O.S.B.; Bros. Michael Weeks, O.S.B.; Thomas Babusis, O.S.B.; Carlos Lopez, O.S.B.; James Brennan, O.S.B. Priests 14; Brothers 10.

WHITTIER. *Redemptorist Fathers Mission House*, 7215 Newlin Ave., 40602. Tel: 310-698-0107. Revs. Enrique A. Lopez, C.SS.R., Supr.; Timothy Watson, C.SS.R.; Arturo Uribe, C.SS.R.; Joseph Elliott, C.SS.R.; Joseph Tobin, C.SS.R.; Lionel Sirois, C.SS.R.; Donald Liberty, C.SS.R.; Clarence Bodden, C.SS.R. (Chicago); Bro. Don E. O'Mara, C.SS.R. Priests 8; Brothers 1.

[S] CONVENTS AND RESIDENCES FOR SISTERS

LOS ANGELES. *California Institute of the Sisters of the Blessed Virgin Mary, I.H.M.*, Motherhouse, Novitiate, Retreat House: 3431 Waverly Dr., 90027. Tel: 213-664-1124. Legal Title: *California Institute of the Sisters of the Most Holy and Immaculate Heart of the Blessed Virgin Mary.* Sr. Eileen Doherty, I.H.M., Supr. Gen. Sisters 26.

Congregation of the Poor Sisters of Nazareth Motherhouse, U.S.A. and Novitiate, 3333 Manning Ave., 90064. Tel: 310-839-2361; 2362; Fax: 310-839-0648. Mother Margaret Clare, Reg. Supr.; Rev. Paul Peterson, S.S.C., Chap. Sisters 10.

Eucharistic Franciscan Missionary Sisters, Motherhouse: 943 S. Soto St., 90023. Tel: 213-264-6556; Fax: 213-526-1655. Rev. Mother Gemma de Jesus Aranda, E.F.M.S., Supr. Gen. Sisters 25.

Eucharistic Franciscan Missionary Sisters of Los Angeles, Nativity Convent: 1421 Cota Ave., Torrance, 90501. Tel: 310-328-6725; Fax: 310-328-5248.

Formation Community, Religious of the Sacred Heart of Mary, 2833 Sichel St., 90031. Sisters 4.

Guadalupanas Missionaries of the Holy Spirit. Novitiate. 758 S. Dunsmuir Ave., 90036. Tel: 213-936-0135.

Guadalupanas Missionaries of the Holy Spirit, 5467 W. 8th St., 90036. Tel: 213-936-6565. Formation House. Sisters 6.

Lovers of the Holy Cross Sisters. Mother House & Novitiate, 14700 S. Van Ness Ave., Gardena, 90249. Tel: 310-768-1406; 516-0271; Fax: 310-352-6435. Good Shepherd Center, 267 N. Belmont Ave., 90026. Tel: 213-250-5241. St. Bruno's Convent, 10734 S. Widener Ave., Whittier, 90603. Tel: 562-947-1177. Total Sisters & Novices 41.

Missionary Servants of the Most Blessed Trinity Ascension Missionary Cenacle, 518 W. 111th Pl., 90044. Tel: 213-754-0020.

Missionary Sisters of Christ the King (Poland), 3424 W. Adams Blvd., 90018. Tel: 213-734-6754. Sisters working in Archdiocese of Los Angeles 3.

Monastery of the Angels (Contemplative), 1977 Carmen Ave., 90068. Tel: 213-466-2186; Fax: 213-466-6645.
E-mail: mraym37819@aol.com
Sr. Mary Raymond, O.P., Prioress; Rev. Armando Ibanez, O.P., Chap. Tel: 213-463-6488. Nuns of the Order of Preachers. Professed Cloistered Nuns 24; Professed Extern Sisters 2.

Pious Disciples of the Divine Master, 215 S. Los Angeles St., 90012; Fax: 213-680-3466. Sr. Trinity Taricco. Sisters 7.

Provincial House of the Sisters of St. Joseph of Carondelet. (St. Mary's Provincialate, Carondelet Center), 11999 Chalon Rd., 90049-1524. Tel: 213-272-8016; 310-476-5253; Fax: 310-476-8735.
E-mail: lacsj@aol.com
Sr. Joyce Marie Gaspardo, Prov. Supr.; Sr. Cecilia Louise, Asst. Prov. Supr.; Sr. Maureen O'Connor, Asst. Prov. Supr. Superiors: Sr. Mary Adele St. Cyr; Sr. Paul Joseph Madden. Sisters 81.
Sisters of St. Joseph in California.
Sisters of St. Joseph Ministerial Services.
Sisters of St. Joseph in Arizona.

Religious Sisters of Charity Regional, 1206 N. Edgemont St., 90029. Sisters 31.

School Sisters of Notre Dame, 638 S. Irving Blvd., 90005. Sisters 6.

Sisters of Our Lady of Perpetual Help, S.O.L.P.H., St. Brendan Convent, 220 S. Manhattan Pl., 90004. Tel: 213-389-6398.

Sisters of Social Service of Los Angeles, General Motherhouse, 2303 S. Figueroa Way, 90007. Tel: 213-746-2117; Fax: 213-747-4499. Legal Titles: *Sisters of Social Service of Los Angeles, Inc.; Sisters of Social Service Support Trust Fund.* Sr. Simone Campbell, Gen. Dir. Sisters 104. Sisters of Social Service, Formation, 2303 S. Figeroa Way, 90007. Tel: 213-731-2117. Sr. Deborah Lorentz, S.S.S., Team Co-Chair; Sr. Sarah Nagle, S.S.S., Team Co-Chair. In Formation 6.

Sisters of St. Joseph of Orange, 8000 Regis Way, 90045. Tel: 310-645-2514; 645-0718. Sisters 2.

Sisters of the Company of Mary, 2634 Monmouth Ave., 90007. Tel: 213-747-3542. Sr. Teresa Zapata, O.D.N., Supr. Sisters 7.

Sisters of the Good Shepherd, 2561 Venice Blvd., 90019. Tel: 213-737-6111. Sisters 12.

Sisters of the Guardian Angel, 4529 New York St., 90022. Tel: 213-266-4431.

Sisters of the Immaculate Heart of Mary at Mirinae, I.H.M., P.O. Box 75867, 90075. Tel: 213-381-2481. Total in Residence 6.

Sisters of the Society Devoted to the Sacred Heart, Local Convent: 628 S. Irving Blvd., 90005. Tel: 213-936-8647. Sr. Lucia Tu, S.D.S.H., Supr. Sisters 6.

Sisters of the Society Devoted to the Sacred Heart, 869 S. Rimpau Blvd., 90005. Tel: 213-935-2372. Sisters 3.

ALHAMBRA. *Carmel of St. Teresa*, 215 E. Alhambra Rd., 91801. Tel: 626-282-2387; Fax: 626-282-2053. Discalced Nuns of the Order of Our Blessed Lady of Mt. Carmel. Mother Maria, Prioress. Sisters 15.

Carmelite Sisters of the Most Sacred Heart of Los Angeles, Generalate Motherhouse, Novitiate and Retreat House: 920 E. Alhambra Rd., 91801. Tel: 818-289-1353; Fax: 818-308-1913.
E-mail: CarmeliteSistersAlhambra@aol.com
Sr. Emma Luz Tresler, O.C.D., Dir. of Novices; Mother Vincent Marie Finnegan, O.C.D., Supr. General. Sisters 18; Postulants 3; Novices 5; Total Professed Sisters 121.

Carmelite Sisters of the Most Sacred Heart of Los Angeles.

ALTADENA. *Franciscan Sisters of the Sacred Heart*, 579 W. Mariposa St., 91001. Tel: 818-791-4359. Sisters 5.

BEVERLY HILLS. *Sisters of Mary Mother of the Church*, 504 N. Roxbury Dr., 90210.

CULVER CITY. *Daughters of St. Paul*, 3908 Sepulveda Blvd., 90230. Tel: 310-390-4699. Sr. Mary Assumpta, F.S.P., Supr. Sisters 5.

DOWNEY. *Sisters of the Holy Faith in California*, 12322 S. Paramount Blvd., P.O. Box 2085, 90242. Tel: 310-923-4013; Fax: 310-869-4609.
E-mail: shfaith@aol.com
Sisters 44.

EL SEGUNDO. *Sisters Servants of the Blessed Sacrament*, U.S. Vice Provincial House, 215 Lomita St., 90245. Tel: 310-615-0766. Sisters 8.

ENCINO. *Sisters of St. Louis*, 5001 White Oak Ave., 91316. Tel: 818-344-7825. Sisters 6. St. Joseph of Carondolet. Holy Names of Jesus and Mary. Ursuline Sisters.

GARDENA. *Poor Clare Missionary Sisters, Inc.*, 1103 W. 164th St., 90247. Tel: 310-323-9942. Sr. Maria S. Miranda, M.C., Supr. Sisters 12.

GLENDORA. *St. Lucy's Priory*, 19045 E. Sierra Madre Ave., 91741. Tel: 626-335-1682. Sr. Elizabeth Brown, Prioress. Legal Title: *St. Lucy's Priory of Glendora California, Inc.* Sisters 26.

LOMITA. *Sisters of the Korean Martyrs, S.K.M.*, 2263 W. 255th St., 90717. Tel: 310-835-3399.

LYNWOOD. *Daughters of Mary, Mother of Mercy, D.M.M.M.*, St. Francis Medical Center, 3630 E. Imperial Hwy., 90262. Tel: 310-603-6311. Mailing Address: D.M.M.M. Convent, Mother of Sorrows Parish, 100 W. 87th Pl., Los Angeles, 90003. Tel: 213-753-7805. St. Francis Medical Center, 3630 E. Imperial Hwy., 90262. Sisters 6.

MISSION HILLS. *Sisters of the Holy Cross*, 9933 Woodman Ave., 91345. Tel: 818-892-5611. Legal Title: *Sisters of the Holy Cross of California.*

MONROVIA. *Convent of the Maryknoll Sisters of St. Dominic*, 340 Norumbega Dr., 91016-2445. Tel: 626-358-1825; Fax: 626-358-1227. Sr. Andree Normandin, M.M., Coord. Sisters 42.

MONTEBELLO. *Religious of the Sacred Heart of Mary*, Provincial Center, 441 N. Garfield Ave., 90640-2901. Tel: 213-887-8821; Fax: 213-887-8952.

NORTH HOLLYWOOD. *School Sisters of St. Francis, O.S.F.*, St. Charles Borromeo, 10908 Moorpark St., 91602-8578. Tel: 818-509-8578.

NORTHRIDGE. *Mother of Mercy Convent*, 9329 Crebs Ave., 91324. Tel: 818-882-4095. Sister of Mercy Burlingame.

Sisters of the Society Devoted to the Sacred Heart, Motherhouse: 9814 Sylvia Ave., 91324. Tel: 818-772-9961. Sr. Jane Stafford, S.D.S.H., Supr. Gen. Sisters 3.

OXNARD. *Sisters Servants of Mary*, 428 S. F St., 93030. Tel: 805-486-5502. Sr. Felisa Ripa, S.M., Mistress of Novices. Professed Sisters 9; Novices 3.

PASADENA. *Convent of the Holy Child*, 500 Bellefontaine St., 91105. Tel: 818-799-5312. Sisters 3.

Convent of the Holy Child. Corporate Title: Society of the Holy Child Jesus, American Province, Inc. 443 S. Euclid Ave., 91101. Tel: 626-796-3924.
E-mail: uhpf31c@prodigy.com

RANCHO PALOS VERDES. *Daughters of Mary & Joseph, D.M.J.*, Provincial House: 5300 Crest Rd., 90275-5004. Tel: 213-377-9968; 541-0784; Fax: 310-544-0387. Sisters 7.

ROLLING HILLS. *Sisters of Charity of Rolling Hills*, 28600 Palos Verdes Dr. E., 90274. Tel: 310-831-4104. Sr. Dominica Buchholz, S.C.R.H., Supr. Gen. Sisters 10.

SAN FERNANDO. *Franciscan Sisters of the Immaculate Conception*, 11320 Laurel Canyon Blvd., 91340. Tel: 818-365-2582. Legal Title: *Franciscan Missionary Sisters of the Immaculate Conception, Province of St. Clare of Assisi Provincial House.* Sisters 102; Novices 6; Postulants 9.

Religious Sisters of Charity, 1608 Eighth St., 91340. Sisters 2.

SAN GABRIEL. *Sisters of the Cross & Passion, C.P.*, 401 E. Live Oak, #18, 91776. Tel: 626-285-5334.

SAN PEDRO. *Little Sisters of the Poor*, 2100 S. Western Ave., 90732. Tel: 310-548-0625. Sr. Margaret Charles, Supr. Sisters 12.

SANTA BARBARA. *Monastery of Poor Clares*, Cloistered Contemplative Monastery, 215 E. Los Olivos St., 93105. Tel: 805-682-7670. Mother Mary Clare of Jesus, Abbess. Professed 15. Attended by Franciscan Fathers of the Old Mission.

St. Francis Convent, 601 E. Micheltorena St., 93103. Tel: 805-962-7661.
E-mail: cbowman@sfmc.org
Web site: http://www.saintfrancis.org
Sr. Christine Bowman, O.S.F., Local Leader. Sisters 7.

SOLVANG. *Carmel of St. Joseph Discalced Carmelite Nuns*, 1883 Ringsted Dr., 93463. Tel: 805-686-4292. Legal Title: *Carmel of St. Joseph Discalced Carmelite Nuns of the Order of Our Blessed Lady of Mt. Carmel.* Mother Mary Veronica, O.C.D., Prioress. Sisters 12.

Sisters of the Society Devoted to the Sacred Heart, 1762 Mission Dr., 93463. Tel: 805-688-6158. Sr. Elizabeth Normanly, S.D.S.H., Supr. Sisters 3.

SYLMAR. *Poor Clare Missionary Sisters.* P.O. Box 227, San Fernando, 91340. Tel: 818-361-0591. Sr. Blanca G. Rivera, M.C., Supr.; Sr. Beatriz Aguilar, M.C. Sisters 7.

THOUSAND OAKS. *Sisters of Notre Dame*, Provincial House, Provincialate, 1776 Hendrix Ave., 91360. Tel: 805-496-3243; Fax: 805-379-3616.
E-mail: NDCTOCA@connectinc.com
Web site: http://www.sndl.org/ca.html
Sr. Mary Amy, S.N.D., Supr. Sisters 45.

TORRANCE. *Little Company of Mary Convent*, 20552 Mansel Ave., 90503. Tel: 310-214-3190; 514-5230 (Office); Fax: 310-514-5314. Sr. Mary Babcock, L.C.M. Sisters 4. 20562 Mansel Ave., 90503. Tel: 310-370-3992, 310-540-7676 (Office). Sr. Terrence, Landini, L.C.M. Sisters 3.

VENTURA. *Handmaids of the Sacred Heart of Jesus, Mary and Joseph*, P.O. Box 2957, 93002.
E-mail: jmj@anacapa.net
Web site: http://www.anacapa.net/~handmaids/

Sisters of the Holy Cross, Saint Catherine-by-the-Sea, 1931 Poli St., 93001. Tel: 805-652-1700. Residence for Retired Sisters. Legal Title: *Sisters of the Holy Cross of California.* Rev. James Gillis, C.S.C.; Sr. Patricia Ann Thompson, C.S.C., Supr. Sisters 37.

WHITTIER. *Sisters of the Sacred Heart of Jesus, H.C.J.S.*, 11506 Walnut St., 90606. Tel: 310-908-0618.

WOODLAND HILLS. *Sisters of St. Louis, Louisville Convent*, 22300 Mulholland Dr., 91364. Tel: 818-347-2115. Sr. Bernadette Murphy, S.S.L., Reg. Supr. Sisters 15.

[T] SECULAR INSTITUTES

LOS ANGELES. *Society of Our Lady of the Way*, 2339 N. Catalina St., 90027. Tel: 213-665-0333.
E-mail: elfr21a@prodigy.com
Legal Title: *Society of Our Lady of the Way of Southern California, Inc.*

WEST COVINA. *Fr. Kolbe Missionaries of the Immaculata*, 531 E. Merced Ave., 91790. Tel: 626-917-0040; Fax: 626-917-0900.

[U] ASSOCIATIONS OF THE FAITHFUL

LOS ANGELES. *Community of the Holy Spirit, C.H.S.*, Archdiocese of Los Angeles, 3424 Willshire Blvd., 90010-2241.
Handmaids of the Sacred Heart of Jesus, Mary and Joseph, J.M.J.
Trinitas.

[V] RESIDENCES FOR WOMEN

LOS ANGELES. *Bethany House*, 850 N. Hobart Blvd., 90029. Tel: 213-665-6937. Sisters 8; Residents 30.
Estrella del Mar, Inc. dba Regis House, 2303 S. Figueroa Way, 90025. Tel: 310-477-8168. Sr. Georgina Cahill, S.S.S., Dir.; Sr. Jennifer Gaeta, S.S.S., Dir. Sisters of Social Service 2.
Good Shepherd Center for Homeless Women, Languille Residence, 267 N. Belmont Ave., 90026. Tel: 213-250-5241; Fax: 213-250-5073.
(A Division of Catholic Charities). Women in Residence 30; Women Assisted Annually 2,444.
Mother-Child, Transitional Residence, 267 N. Belmont Ave., 90026. Tel: 213-469-6540; Fax: 213-469-0370. Mother-Children in Residence 30; Mother-Children Assisted Annually 150.
St. Anne's. For further details refer to listing in Special Care Facilities section. 155 N. Occidental Blvd., 90026. Tel: 213-381-2931; Fax: 213-381-7804.
E-mail: stannes@ix.netcom.com
Web site: www.stannes.org
Group Home for pregnant, parenting teens and their babies.
St. Joseph's Residence, 1124 W. Adams Blvd., 90007. Tel: 213-749-9577. Sisters of the Company of Mary. Women 62.

[W] RESIDENCES FOR MEN

LOS ANGELES. *"Casa Teresa," Missionary Brothers of Charity*, 1316 S. Westlake Ave., 90006. Tel: 213-380-5225; 380-5356. Temporary shelter for sick homeless men and home for Hispanic high school boys. Brothers 6; Novices 1.
"Nuestra Hogar" Missionaries of Charity Brothers, 1345 Alvarado Ter., 90006. Tel: 214-251-9707.
Catholic Kolping House, 1225 S. Union Ave., 90015. Tel: 213-388-9438. Rev. Richard Russell, Spiritual Dir.; Mr. Eddy Coronel, Mgr. Capacity 60.
The Little Brothers of the Good Shepherd, B.G.S., 3445 Waverly Dr., 90027. Tel: 213-662-0092 (Office); 662-3620 (Res.). Staff for Cardinal Manning House of Prayer.
Missionaries of Charity Brothers, House of Formation, 325 S. Westlake Blvd., 90006. Tel: 213-384-6116.
Missionaries of Charity Brothers, Regional Center and Novitiate, 214 S. Witmer St., 90026. Tel: 213-481-8152.

[X] RETREAT HOUSES

LOS ANGELES. *Claretian Retreat Center (All Groups)*, 1119 Westchester Pl., 90019. Tel: 213-737-8464; Fax: 213-733-6201. Revs. Robert Billett, C.M.F., Supr.; Frank J. Ferrante, C.M.F., Dir.; Bro. Rene Lepage, C.M.F., Admin.
Immaculate Heart Retreat House. (Days of Recollection Only), 3431 Waverly Dr., 90027. Tel: 213-664-1126. Conducted by the Sisters of the Immaculate Heart. Sr. Rita Callanan, I.H.M., Dir. Capacity 48; Sisters 10.

ALHAMBRA. *Retreat House of the Sacred Heart*, 920 E. Alhambra Rd., 91801.
E-mail: SrRosarioth@aol.com
Carmelite Sisters of the Most Sacred Heart of Los Angeles. Sr. Rosario Therese, O.C.D., Contact Person. Capacity 89; Sisters 12; Novices 5; Postulants 2.
(See Convents).

ENCINO. *Holy Spirit Retreat Center*, 4316 Lanai Rd., 91436. Tel: 818-784-4515. Sisters of Social Service.

MALIBU. *Serra Retreat*, 3401 Serra Rd., P.O. Box 127, 90265. Tel: 310-456-6631.
E-mail: warrenr480@aol.com
Web site: sbfranciscans.org
Franciscan Friars. Revs. Warren Rouse, O.F.M., Dir.; Michael Doherty, O.F.M., Guardian; Ralph Weishaar, O.F.M.; Bros. Samuel Cabot, O.F.M.; Pierre Despres, O.F.M. Priests 3; Brothers 2.

MONTEBELLO. *DePaul Center*, 1105 Bluff Rd., 90640-6198. Tel: 213-721-6060; Fax: 213-887-0765. (Formerly St. Vincent's Seminary). Congregation of the Mission (Vincentians). Retreat and Evangelization Center. Sr. Laura Gormley, S.S.L., Dir.; Rev. Patrick J. Mullin, C.M., Superior; Sr. Grace Briare, S.N.J.M.; Rev. Victor J. Sarrazin, C.M. In res. Revs. John J. Casey, C.M., (Retired); Peter J. Diliberto, C.M., (Retired); Robert J. Jones, C.M.; Thomas J. McIntyre, C.M., (Retired); James J. Nouws, C.M., (Retired); James V. Connors, C.M., (Retired); Bro. Edward D. Graham, C.M.; Deacon John P. Kearney, C.M.

RANCHO PALOS VERDES. *Mary and Joseph Retreat Center*, 5300 Crest Rd., 90275-5004. Tel: 310-377-4867. Daughters of Mary and Joseph. Retreat Center Capacity 64; Sisters 5.

ROSEMEAD. *St. Joseph's Salesian Youth Renewal Center.* (Boys and Girls), 8301 Arroyo Dr., P.O. Box 1639, 91770. Tel: 818-280-8622. Conducted by Salesians of St. John Bosco. Revs. Harry Rasmussen, S.D.B., Dir. & Dir. Novices; John Roche, S.D.B., Dir. Youth Ministry; Bill Bolton, S.D.B., Dir. Vocations; Mirko Flak, S.D.B., (Retired); Bros. George Ghiselli, S.D.B., Treas.; Larry King, S.D.B.; Robert Hennings, S.D.B.; Thien Nguyen; Steve Gomez; Rev. Teodoro Montemayor, S.D.B., Dir. Retreat Center. Priests 5; Brothers 2; Novices 5.

SAN FERNANDO. *Poverello of Assisi Retreat House*, 1519 Woodworth St., 91340. Tel: 818-365-1071. For men and women. Marriage Encounter in Korean. Engaged Encounter in English, Vietnamese and Spanish couples. Other Denominations workshops seminars, staff meetings. Franciscan Missionary Sisters of the Immaculate Conception. Sr. Mary Jesus, O.S.F., Dir. Capacity 112.

SANTA BARBARA. *St. Mary's Seminary Center*, 1964 Las Canoas Rd., 93105. Tel: 805-966-4829. Revs. James F. McOwen, C.M.; Roy A. Persich, C.M., Dir.; James Galvin, C.M.; Walter Housey, C.M. Priests 4.

SIERRA MADRE. *Mater Dolorosa Retreat Center*, 700 N. Sunnyside Ave., Box 68, 91025. Tel: 626-355-7188; Fax: 626-355-0485.
E-mail: Materdolorosa@compuserve.com
Web site: www.passionist.org
Conducted by the Passionist Community. Lay Retreat League for men and women. Specialized Retreats.
Retreat Team: Revs. Patrick Brennan, C.P., Retreat Dir.; Philip Paxton, C.P., Assoc. Retreat Dir.; Benedict Olson, C.P.; Sr. Judy Rinek, S.N.J.M.; Bros. John Rockenbach, C.P.; Anthony Mimiaga, C.P.; Mrs. Mary Lou Butler, Business Admin. Priests 3; Brothers 2.

VALYERMO. *St. Andrew's Abbey Retreat House (All Groups)*, 31001 N. Valyermo Rd., P.O. Box 40, 93563.
Web site: www.ptw.com/~standrab
Conducted by the Benedictine Monks. Revs. Francis Benedict, O.S.B., Retreat Dir. & Abbot. Tel: 805-944-2178; Philip Edwards, O.S.B., Guestmaster. Tel: 805-944-2178; Bro. Benedict Dull, O.S.B., Guestmaster; Rita Jones, Youth Center Contact Person. Tel: 805-944-2734.

[Y] PERSONAL PRELATURES

LOS ANGELES. *Opus Dei. Prelature of the Holy Cross and Opus Dei*, 655 Levering Ave., 90024. Tel: 310-208-0941. Revs. Rene J. Schatteman; John R. Waiss.

[Z] CATHOLIC CHARITIES OF CALIFORNIA

LOS ANGELES. *Catholic Charities of Los Angeles, Inc.* His Eminence Roger Cardinal Mahony, D.D.; Rev. Msgr. Gregory A. Cox, M.S.W., Exec. Dir. Tel: 213-251-3464.
Central Administrative Offices, 1531 W. 9th St., P.O. Box 15095, 90015-0095. Tel: 213-251-3400; Fax: 213-380-4603. Rev. Msgr. Gregory A. Cox, M.S.W., Exec. Dir.; Rev. G. Lopez, M.S.W., Chief Admin. Officer; James E. Bathker, Chief Financial Officer. Tel: 213-251-3410; Marilyn Kamerer, Dir. Dept. Human Resources. Tel: 213-251-3414; Alexandria "Sandi" Arnold, Dir. Dept. Resource Dev. Tel: 213-251-3495; Susan Valerie Weight, Deputy Asst. Tel: 213-251-3438.
ADESTE Child Care Services. Armine Lalaian-Sanjar, Quality Assurance Dir. Tel: 213-251-3468.
CYO Athletics. Bob Fitzpatrick, Prog. Dir. Tel: 213-251-3453.
Hope in Youth. Mike Clements, Dir. Tel: 213-662-9636.
Immigration & Refugee Services. Loc Nam Nguyen, Dir. Tel: 213-251-3489; Jo Marcel, Asst. Dir. Tel: 213-251-3471.
Immigration. Tel: 213-251-3459.
Refugee Resettlement. Tel: 213-251-3460.
Central Intake Project. Joe L. Le, Dir. Tel: 213-251-3445.
Psychological Services Department. Edward Nelson, Ph.D., Dir. Tel: 213-251-3459.
(see pastoral regions for other locations).
Spiritual Life Outreach Program. Sr. Marian Gallagher, C.S.J. Tel: 213-251-3476.
Regional Offices and Community Centers:
OUR LADY OF THE ANGELS METRO REGION. (Los Angeles Inner City), 4665 Willowbrook Ave., 90029. Greg Stuart, Regional Dir. Tel: 213-662-1462.
ADESTE Child Care, 601 E. 23rd St., 90011. Tel: 213-748-5246.
Central Intake Unit, 1530 W. Ninth St., 90015. Tel: 213-251-3481.
Community Service Centers: St. Mary's Center, 4665 Willowbrook Ave., 90029. Tel: 213-662-4391. St. Catherine of Alexandria Center, 934 W. 70th St., 90044. Tel: 213-752-3786. El Santo Nino Center, 601 E. 23rd St., 90011. Tel: 213-748-5246.
Education & Training, 1530 W. Ninth St., 90015. Tel: 213-251-3570. Richard Cadena, Dept. Dir.
Immigration & Refugee Services, 1530 W. Ninth St., 90015. Tel: 213-251-3471; 251-3460.
Psychological Services, 1530 W. Ninth St., 90015. Tel: 213-251-3572.
Shelters & Housing Services: Angels Flight - Runaway/Homeless Youth Shelter, 357 S. Westlake Ave., 90057. Tel: 213-413-2311; 800-833-2499 (Hotline). Outreach, 4665 Willowbrook Ave., 90029. Tel: 213-660-1942. Good Shepherd Center for Homeless Women, 267 N. Belmont Ave., 90026. Tel: 213-250-5241. Sr. Julia Mary Farley, C.S.J., Prog. Dir., Good Shepherd Mother & Child Center, 1719 N. Taft Ave., 90028. Tel: 213-469-6540. Hayward Hotel Social Services, 206 W. Sixth St., 90014. Tel: 213-622-0224. Marion Hotel, 642 S. Crocker St., 90021. Tel: 213-624-7205.
OUR LADY OF THE ANGELS WESTERN REGION. (Inglewood, Crenshaw District, Korea Town, West Los Angeles, Malibu & Los Angeles Airport region), 211 Third Ave., Venice, 90291. Tel: 310-392-8701. Jim Stratton, Regl. Dir.
ADESTE Child Care, 211 Third Ave., Venice, 90291. Tel: 310-392-8701.
Community Service Centers: St. Margaret's Center, 10505 Hawthorne Blvd., Lennox, 90304. Tel: 310-672-2208. St. Peter Claver Center, 4202 W. Jefferson Blvd., 90016. Tel: 213-737-6036. St. Robert's Center, 211 Third Ave., Venice, 90291. Tel: 310-392-8701.
Immigration & Refugee Services, St. Margaret's Center, 10505 Hawthorne Blvd., Lennox, 90304. Tel: 310-672-2208.
Psychological Services, 211 Third Ave., Venice, 90291. Tel: 310-392-8701.
Santa Monica Youth Employment & Training, 2013 Colorado Ave., Santa Monica, 90404. Tel: 310-829-5451.
SAN FERNANDO REGION. (Burbank, Glendale, Eagle Rock, Verdugo Hills, Antelope Valley, San Fernando Valley), 21600 Hart St., Canoga Park, 91303. Tel: 818-883-6105. Moeed Khan, Regl. Dir.
ADESTE Child Care, 511 Kalisher St., San Fernando, 91340. Tel: 818-883-6015.
Central Intake Unit, 217 E. Alameda Ave., #211, Burbank, 91502. Tel: 818-841-2430.
Community Service Centers: Glendale Community Services Center, 4322 San Fernando Rd., Glendale, 91204. Tel: 818-409-3080. Guadalupe Community Center, 21600 Hart St., Canoga Park, 91303. Tel: 818-365-3194. Loaves and Fishes I, 4322 San Fernando Rd., Glendale, 91204. Tel: 818-409-3080. Loaves and Fishes II, 14525 Delano St., #102, Van Nuys, 91411. Tel: 818-997-0943. Loaves and Fishes III, 511 Kalisher St., San Fernando, 91340. Tel: 818-365-3195. Loaves and Fishes IV, 21600 Hart St., Canoga Park, 91303. Tel: 818-340-2050. Santa Rosa Center, 511 Kalisher St., San Fernando, 91340. Tel: 818-365-3194.
Glendale Thrift Shop, 135 1/2 N. Brand Blvd., Glendale, 91204. Tel: 818-956-1857.
Immigration & Refugee Services, 511 Kalisher St., San Fernando, 91340. Tel: 818-365-3194; 3195.
Psychological Services, 7120 Hayvenhurst Ave., #200, Van Nuys, 91406. Tel: 818-988-2850.
Residential Youth Services, Rancho San Antonio, 21000 Plummer St., Chatsworth, 91311. Tel: 818-882-6400. Bro. John Crowe, C.S.C., Dir.
Shelter/Housing Services: Lancaster Community Shelter, 44611 Yucca Ave., Lancaster, 93534. Tel: 805-945-7524.
SAN GABRIEL REGION. (San Gabriel Valley, Mt. Baldy, Pomona Valley, East Los Angeles), 1307

Warren St., 90033. Tel: 213-266-3130. Mary Romero, Regl. Dir.
ADESTE Child Care, 1307 Warren Ave., 90033. Tel: 213-264-4981.
Central Intake Unit, 11100 Valley Blvd., Ste. 100, El Monte, 91731. Tel: 626-582-8073.
Community Service Centers: Brownson House Community Center, 1307 Warren Ave., 90033. Tel: 213-264-8700. Brother Miguel Center, 315 North Park Ave., Pomona, 91768. Tel: 909-622-3466. El Monte Center, 3017 Tyler Ave., #9, El Monte, 91733. Tel: 626-575-7652.
Immigration & Refugee Services, 3093 N. Tyler, Ste. 203, El Monte, 91731. Tel: 626-575-7652.
Psychologicl Services, 1028 N. Lake Ave., Pasadena, 91104. Tel: 626-398-7067.
San Gabriel Outreach, Irwindale Community Services, 16009 E. Cypress Ave., Irwindale, 91706. Tel: 626-338-5057.
SAN PEDRO REGION. (Long Beach, South Bay, Compton, Rio Hondo, Vernon, Huntington Park, Whittier, Pico Rivera), 123 E. 14th St., Long Beach, 90813. Tel: 310-591-1641. Lupe U. Macker, Regl. Dir.
ADESTE Child Care, 123 E. 14th St., Long Beach, 90813. Tel: 562-591-1351.
Central Intake Unit, 944 Pacific Ave., Ste. 1, Long Beach, 90813. Tel: 562-437-1399.
Community Service Centers: Long Beach Community Services, 123 E. 14th St., Long Beach, 90813. Tel: 562-591-1351. Mahar House Center, 1115 Mahar Ave., Wilmington, 90744. Tel: 310-834-7265. Pico Rivera Food Pantry, 9050 Washington Blvd., Pico Rivera, 90660. Tel: 562-988-2697.
Family Shelter for the Homeless, 123 E. 14th St., Long Beach, 90813. Tel: 562-591-1351.
OASIS - Older Adult Services, 1150 E. 4th St., Long Beach, 90802. Tel: 562-901-2977.
Psychological Services, 6505 Rosemead Blvd., Ste. 108, Pico Rivera, 90660. Tel: 562-949-2496.
TASC (Teens Assisting Seniors), 9200 Mines, P.O. Box 1016, Pico Rivera, 90660. Tel: 562-801-4304.
SANTA BARBARA REGION. (Lompoc, Santa Maria, Santa Barbara, Carpinteria), 609 E. Haley St., Santa Barbara, 93103. Tel: 805-965-7045. Davida Willis, Regl. Dir.
ADESTE Child Care. St. Raphael School, 160 St. Joseph St., Santa Barbara, 93111. Tel: 805-965-7045. Our Lady of Mt. Carmel School, 530 Hot Springs Rd., Santa Barbara, 93108. Tel: 805-965-7045.
Community Service Centers: Santa Barbara Community Services, 609 E. Haley St., Santa Barbara, 93103. Tel: 805-965-7045. Carpenteria Community Services, 941 Walnut St., Carpenteria, 93013. Tel: 805-684-8621. Lompoc Community Services, 1011 N. A St., Lompoc, 93436. Tel: 805-736-6226. Santa Maria Community Services, 607 W. Main, Santa Maria, 93454. Tel: 805-922-2059.
Thrift Stores: Lompoc Thrift Store, 1015 N. A St., Lompoc, 93436. Tel: 805-735-5236. St. Vincent de Paul/Catholic Charities Thrift Store, 609 E. Haley St., Santa Barbara, 93103. Tel: 805-966-9659. Santa Maria Thrift Store, 607 W. Main St., Santa Maria, 93454. Tel: 805-922-2059.
Immigration Services, 609 E. Haley St., Santa Barbara, 93103. Tel: 805-965-7045.
Psychological Services. 609 E. Haley St., Santa Barbara, 93103. Tel: 805-962-2028. 215 E. Fesler St., Santa Maria, 93454. Tel: 805-348-1627.
VENTURA COUNTY REGION. (Camarillo, Moorpark, Oxnard, Thousand Oaks, Simi Valley, Ventura, Conejo Valley), 303 N. Ventura Ave., Ventura, 93001. Tel: 805-643-4694. A. Diane, Martell, Regl. Dir.
ADESTE Child Care, 303 N. Ventura Ave., Ste. B, Ventura, 93001. Tel: 805-643-4760.
Community Service Centers: Ventura Community Services, 303 N. Ventura Ave., Ste. C, Ventura, 93001. Tel: 805-643-4694. Oxnard Community Services, 401 N. A St., Oxnard, 93030. Tel: 805-486-2900. Moorpark Community Services, 77 First St., Moorpark, 93021. Tel: 805-529-0720. Conejo Valley Community Services, 80 E. Hillcrest Dr., #216, Thousand Oaks, 91630. Tel: 805-496-1113.
BICS (Building Intergenerational Community Services), 80 E. Hillcrest, #203, Thousand Oaks, 91360. Tel: 805-495-9940.
Handicapables. Tel: 805-527-7806; 486-4437.
OASIS - Older Adult Services. 2532 Ventura Blvd., Camarillo, 93010. Tel: 805-987-2083. 5649 Pittman St., Simi Valley, 93063. Tel: 805-526-3009.
Psychological Services, 303 N. Ventura Ave., Ste. A, Ventura, 93001. Tel: 805-643-4780.

[AA] SUMMER CAMPS

LOS ANGELES. *Scouting and Camp Fire Ministry/ Catholic Youth Camps*, 1531 W. Ninth St., 90015. Tel: 310-427-2149. Eileen Gallagher, Contact Person; Al Garcia, Chm. Boy Scouts; Connie Hendry, Chm.; Rev. James J. Maher, Boy Scout Chap.; Sr. Lucille Coulihan, I.H.M., Girl Scout Chap.
St. Vincent dePaul Ranch Camp. (Boys), 210 N. Ave. 21st, 90031. Tel: 213-221-9886. Capacity 100. Sponsored by St. Vincent de Paul Society.
Camp Mariastella. (Girls). Coed Program for Developmentally Disabled, Ages 7-Adult. 1120 Manchester Pl., 90019. Tel: 213-733-1208.
Owned & Operated by Sisters of Social Service. Capacity 140.
Located in Wrightwood.
Sacred Heart Retreat Camp. Girls & Boys Sessions, Ages 8-17 years. 869 S. Rimpau Blvd., 90005. Tel: 213-935-2372.
Owned and operated by the Sisters of the Society Devoted to the Sacred Heart. Capacity 150.
Located at Big Bear Lake.
Camp Teresita Pines. (Girls), Ages 7-15 years. 1400 W. 9th St., P.O. Box 15095, 90015. Tel: 213-388-5126.
Owned & Operated by Catholic Daughters of the Americas. Capacity 125.
Located in Big Pines Area near Wrightwood.

[BB] ST. VINCENT DE PAUL SOCIETY

LOS ANGELES. *St. Vincent de Paul Society*, 210 N. Avenue 21, 90031. Tel: 213-224-6280. Jose J. Rossier, Exec. Dir.
Stores and Workshops, 210 N. Avenue 21, 90031. Tel: 213-224-6280. Anthony Terrazas, Store Dir.
St. Vincent de Paul Ranch Camp & Retreat Center, 210 N. Avenue 21, 90031. Tel: 213-224-6287. Olivia E. Reyes, Sec.
St. Vincent's Cardinal Manning Center, 231 Winston St., 90013. Tel: 213-229-9963; Fax: 213-620-9141. Joan Sotiros, Dir.
St. Vincent de Paul Stores, 210 N. Avenue 21, 90031. Tel: 213-224-6280.
For Pick Up: 213-224-6280; 800-974-3571.

[CC] NEWMAN CENTERS

LOS ANGELES. *Archdiocesan Office for Campus Ministry*, 3424 Wilshire Blvd., 90010-2248. Tel: 213-637-7527; Fax: 213-637-6527.
Web site: www.la-archdiocese.org
Laurie W. Oester, Archdiocesan Dir.
California State University, Los Angeles, 5151 State Univ. Dr. #220 Health Center, 90032. Tel: 213-343-2571; Fax: 213-343-6407. Rev. Gilbert Romero; Mr. Robert Warren.
Loyola Law School, 1441 W. Olympic Blvd., 90015. Tel: 213-736-1084; Fax: 213-380-3769. Rev. Jim Erps, S.J.
Loyola Marymount University, 7101 W. 80th St., 90045. Tel: 310-338-2860; Fax: 310-338-1805. Mr. Fernando Moreno, Dir.; Revs. John Boyle, S.J.; Thomas P. Higgins, S.J.; Keith Brehob, S.J.; Sr. Cecilia Magladry, C.S.J.; Sr. Peg Dolan, R.S.H.M.; Ms. Aimee Loth-Barton; Mr. Will Salvini; Mr. John Flaherty; Ms. Diane Bischetti Suggs; Rabbi Arthur Gross-Schaeffer; Ms. Debora Garza.
Mount St. Mary College, Chalon Campus, 12001 Chalon Rd., 90049. Tel: 310-471-9837; Fax: 310-476-9296. Ms. Gail Gresser, Dir.
Mount St. Mary College, Doheny Campus, 10 Chester Pl., 90007. Tel: 213-746-0450, Ext. 2152; Fax: 213-744-0833. Sr. Maria Angela Mesa, C.S.J.
Occidental College, Catholic Campus Ministry, 1600 Campus Rd., 90041. Tel: 213-341-4000, Ext. 3426. Rev. Martin Diaz, O.P.
University of California, Los Angeles, University Catholic Center, 840 Hilgard Ave., 90024. Tel: 310-208-5015; Fax: 310-208-6077. Revs. Theodore A. Vierra, C.S.P., Dir.; Mark A. Villano, C.S.P.; Ms. Cindy Yoshitomi; Ms. Heather Sheridan, University of Southern California, Our Saviour University Parish, 3207 University Ave., 90007. Tel: 213-749-5341; Fax: 213-749-3475. Rev. William Messenger, O.S.M.; Ms. Kay Tallmadge.
University of Southern California, Health Sciences Campus, Catholic Campus Ministry, MCH 160, 1333 San Pablo St., 90033. Tel: 626-305-5363; Fax: 626-305-5373. California Institute of Technology, Whinett 218-51, Pasadena, 91125. Tel: 626-395-6212. Revs. Thomas White, L.C.; Brian Wilson, L.C.
Claremont Colleges, McAllister Religious Center, 919 N. Columbia, 91711. Tel: 909-621-8825, Ext. 2937; Fax: 909-621-8304. Rev. Wayne Maro, C.P.P.S.
University of California Santa Barbara. St. Mark University Parish, 6550 Picasso Rd., Goleta, 93117. Tel: 805-968-1078; Fax: 805-968-3965. Revs. Ruben M. Patino, C.S.P.; Edward C. Nowak, C.S.P.; Mr. William Cork.
University of La Verne (La Verne). Catholic Campus Ministry, 1950 Third St., 91750. Tel: 909-593-3511, Ext. 4322; Fax: 909-593-0965. Ms. Maria Elena Cardena.
California State University - Long Beach. University Interfaith Center, 1250 Bellflower Blvd., USU-116, 90840. Tel: 562-985-7629; Fax: 562-985-5367. Ms. Laurie W. Oester.
California State University - Northridge. CSUN/ CNM, 1811 Nordhoff St., Northridge, 91330. Tel: 818-677-4850; Fax: 818-677-5815. Sr. Patricia Boroughs, S.N.J.M.
California State Polytechnic University (Pomona). Union Plaza Interfaith Center, 3801 West Temple Ave., 91768. Tel: 909-869-3608. Mrs. Jane Kirchner.
Marymount College (Rancho Palos Verdes). Campus Ministry, 30800 Palos Verdes Dr. E., 90274. Tel: 310-377-4240; Fax: 310-377-6223. Rev. Sean Cronin, Dir.
Don Bosco Technical Institute (Rosemead). Campus Ministry, 1151 San Gabriel Blvd., 91770. Tel: 626-307-6551; Fax: 626-280-9316. Rudy Herrera; Mr. Chris Trosclair.

[DD] MISCELLANEOUS LISTINGS

LOS ANGELES. Sponsored by Congregation of Holy Cross, Eastern Province. Revs. Hugh W. Cleary, C.S.C., Prov.; John P. Phalen, C.S.C., Interim Pres.; Fred Serraino, C.S.C., Natl. Dir.; Mr. Robert P. Klein, Vice Pres. Finance & Admin.
Archdiocesan Spirituality Center, 2 Chester Pl., 90007. Tel: 213-747-6508. Sr. Thomas Bernard, C.S.J., Dir.
Catholic Big Brothers, Inc., 3300 W. Temple St., 90026. Tel: 213-251-9800. Ken Martinet, Exec. Dir.; His Eminence Roger Cardinal Mahony, Honorary Chm.
Five branch offices in Los Angeles.
Catholic Charities Community Development Corporation, Inc., 1531 W. Ninth St., P.O. Box 15095, 90015-0095.
Catholic Healthcare West Southern California.
Robert F. Kennedy Medical Center.
St. Bernardine Medical Center.
St. Francis Medical Center.
St. Mary Medical Center.
St. Vincent Medical Center.
Charisma in Missions, La Porciuncula, 1059 S. Gage Ave., 90023; Fax: 213-260-7221. Catholic Center of Evangelization and renewal ministries. A service for hispanic people through ongoing affirmation and growth seminars and courses; Catholic evangelizers' formation courses; direct evangelization missions; social service programs; prayer hot-line services; television and radio ministries; and a bookstore providing Catholic books, audio and video cassettes.
Collaborative Project for Aging Religious, 2035 W. Adams Blvd., 90018. Tel: 213-735-3625.
Conrad N. Hilton Fund for Sisters, 10100 Santa Monica Blvd. #760, 90067. Tel: 310-785-0746; Fax: 310-785-0166.
E-mail: hltnsister@aol.com
Sr. Marcia Sichol, S.H.C.J.
Equestrian Order of the Holy Sepulcher of Jerusalem, 3424 Wilshire Blvd., 90010-2241. His Eminence Roger Cardinal Mahony, K.G.C.H.S., Grand Prior, 994 Rippey St., El Cajon, 92020. Sir George G. Zorn, K.G.C.H.S., Lieutenant.
Filipino Pastoral Ministry (Artesia), 18708 S. Clarkdale Ave., 90701. Tel: 562-402-9226; Fax: 310-860-0178.
E-mail: mac3exodus@aol.com
Rev. Msgr. Loreto Gonzales, Dir.
The Focolare Movement, Men's Branch (California) (Work of Mary), 8016 Cowan Ave., 90045. Tel: 310-670-6736; Fax: 310-670-8036. Formation in the Spirituality of Unity. Mr. Fritz Zuger, Dir. West Coast.
Friends of John Paul II Foundation of Southern California, 3424 W. Adams Blvd., 90018. Tel: 818-281-0516.
E-mail: kcybulski@earthlink.net
Stanislaw K. Cybulski, Pres.
Hospitaller Foundation of California, Inc., The, 2035 W. Adams Blvd., 90018. Tel: 213-731-7141. Bro. Patrick Corr, O.H., Pres., Dir. & Moderator. (Fund raising arm for St. John of God Retirement and Care Center).
Women's League of St. John of God.
Helpers Club of St. John of God.
Korean Catholic Renewal Movement of Southern California, 3422 W. 8th St., 90005.
Luz De Cristo USA. Member of Lumen 2000. 5953 W. 86th Pl., 90045. Tel: 310-641-2000; Fax: 310-641-1127.
National Catholic Council for Hispanic Ministry, Inc. (NCCHM), 2025 Chickasaw Ave., 90041. Tel: 213-344-9153; Fax: 213-344-9526.
E-mail: NCCHM@aol.com
Perpetual Eucharistic Adoration, Inc., 660 Club View Dr., 90024. Tel: 310-273-3856. L. Owen Traynor, Contact Person.
Queen of Angels Hospital, 155 N. Occidental Blvd., 90026. Tel: 213-381-2931. A California corporation sponsored by the Franciscan Sisters of the Sacred Heart. Tom Owenson, Admin. Mgr.
Rosary Hour Inc., The, 809 S. Flower St., 90017. Tel: 213-627-6863; Fax: 213-627-6864. Rev. James L. Kolling, Dir.
St. Francis Center, 1835 S. Hope St., 90015. Tel: 213-747-5347; Fax: 213-765-8915.

E-mail: stfrasisi@aol.com
His Eminence Roger M. Mahony, Honorary Pres.; Rev. Finian McGinn, O.F.M.Prov.

Provincial Definitors of the Province of Saint Barbara. Legal Title: *Provincial Definitors of the Province of Saint Barbara Franciscan Friars of California.* Mr. Phillip Cunliffe, Executive Dir.

St. Peter Claver Center, 4202 W. Jefferson Blvd., 90016-4113. Tel: 213-737-6036.

St. Vincent Senior Citizen Nutrition Program, Inc., 2131 W. Third St., 90057. Meals served daily 2,165.

Salesian Family Youth Center, 2228 E. 4th St., 90033. Tel: 213-266-1296. Christopher Westoff; Jeremy Wenokur, Esq. Tel: 510-874-4176.

Santa Marta Hospital Foundation, 319 N. Humphreys Ave., 90022. Tel: 213-260-8686. Mr. Michael A. O'Flaherty, Chm.; Mr. Ricardo Robles, Vice Chm.; Sr. Catherine Marie Kreta, C.S.J., Sec.; Mr. Michael J. Lightfoot, Treas.

Serra Ancillary Care, 3424 Wilshire Blvd., 90010. Tel: 213-637-7531; Fax: 213-637-6531. Sr. M. Carolita Hart, C.S.C., Pres.

Serra Institute, 2060 N. Vermont, 90002.

Servants of the Immaculate Child Mary, 5135 Dartsmouth Ave., 90032. Tel: 213-225-3279. Sr. Enedina Cuevas, Contact Person.

**South Central Los Angeles Ministry Project (LAMP),* 2303 S. Figueroa Way, 90007. Tel: 213-747-1444; Fax: 213-747-4499. Sr. Cathy White, S.P.

Vincentians Province of the West Support Trust Fund, 2131 W. Third St., 90057. Tel: 213-484-5559. Mr. Michael Garko, Contact Person.

BALDWIN PARK. *The Redemptorist Vietnamese Mission Corporation,* 3452 N. Big Dalton Ave., 91706. Revs. Vu Minh Nghiem, C.SS.R., Pres.; Nguyen Duc Thong, C.SS.R., Vice Pres.; Chau Xuan Bau, C.SS.R., Sec. & Treas.

BELLFLOWER. *St. John Bosco High School Alumni,* 13640 S. Bellflower Blvd., 90706. Tel: 310-920-1734. Rev. Richard Presenti.

World Apostolate of Fatima, Los Angeles Archdiocesan Division. Blue Army of Our Lady of Fatima. 15550 Bellflower Blvd., 90706-3819. Tel: 310-867-8661.

COVINA. *Comboni Missionaries,* 645 S. Aldenville Ave., 91723. Tel: 626-339-1914.

CULVER CITY. *Pauline Book and Media,* 3908 Sepulveda Blvd., 90230. Tel: 310-397-8676. Sr. Mary Assumpta, F.S.P., Supr.

EL MONTE. *Hombre Nuevo,* 12036 Ramona Blvd., 91732. Tel: 818-444-4442. Rev. Juan Rivas, L.C.

FILLMORE. *Apostolate of Christian Renewal / Holy Family Home of Peace,* 411 First St., P.O. Box 547, 93016-0547.

GRANADA HILLS. *Chinese Catholic Bishops Conference Vocations Center,* 11459 Hayvenhurst, 91344. Rev. Vincent Mao Men (Taiwan).

LA CRESCENTA. *Catholic Press Council,* 4919 Ramsdell, 91214. Tel: 818-957-0913. Ms. Sharon Benoit, Pres.

LA VERNE. *Picpus Charitable Trust,* 2150 Damien Ave., 91750.

LANCASTER. *Our Lady of Charity, Inc.,* P.O. Box 412. Tel: 805-942-3222. Ellen Butera. Tel: 805-948-8044.

LONG BEACH. *St. Mary Catholic Housing Corp.,* 1050 Linden Ave., P.O. Box 887, 90801.

St. Mary Medical Center Foundation. (Catholic Healthcare West), 1050 Linden Ave., P.O. Box 887, 90801. Tel: 562-491-9225; Fax: 562-491-9888. John T. Wagner, Pres.

MONTEREY PARK. *Congregation of St. John the Baptist,* 220 S. Ynez Ave., 91754. Tel: 818-280-1590; 213-261-3354. Very Rev. Stanislaus Su, C.S.J.B., Contact Person.

Theresian Sisters, 901 W. El Repetto Dr., 91754. Tel: 213-780-1965. Sr. Felicitas Hong, C.S.T., Contact Person.

OJAI.

**St. Joseph's Health and Retirement Center Foundation,* P.O. Box 760, 2464 E. Ojai Ave., 93024-0760. Ms. Rita Smith, Contact Person.

PACIFIC PALISADES. *Paulist Pictures,* P.O. Box 1057, 90272. Tel: 310-454-0688; Fax: 310-459-6549.
E-mail: Paulistpic@aol.com
Web site: http://www/members.aol.com/paulistpic

Paulist Productions, (Insight) 17575 Pacific Coast Hwy., 90272. Tel: 310-454-0688; Fax: 310-459-6549. Rev. Ellwood E. Kieser, C.S.P., Pres.

PASADENA.

**Journey House, Inc.,* 1232 N. Los Robles Ave., 91104-2814. Tel: 626-798-9478.
E-mail: maywormca@aol.com
Bro. Timothy Mayworm, F.S.C., Contact Person. Six bed group home for wards of the court helping young people finish high school. Clients have little or no family support.

PASADINA. *Franciscan Communications,* P.O. Box 463, 90602-0463. Tel: 213-251-9880, Ext. 202. Kenneth E. Martinet, Pres. & CEO. (St. Francis Theatre: Winston Press, TeleKETICS, AudioSPOTS, TeleSPOTS).

REDONDO BEACH. *SCRC (Southern California Renewal Communities),* 2850 Artesia Blvd., #207, 90278-3408. Tel: 310-371-6433; Fax: 310-371-8452.
Web site: http://scrc.comline.com
Dominic Berardino, Pres.; Donna Ross, Vice Pres.; Rev. William Delaney, S.J., Pastoral Coord.
Serving Catholic Charismatic Renewal through annual summer convention, pastoral teaching events, healing masses, retreats, book & tape ministry and a bi-monthly publication.

SAN FERNANDO. *Valley Family Center,* 302 S. Brand Blvd., 91340. Tel: 818-365-8588; Fax: 818-898-3382. Religious Sisters of Charity. Sr. Una Connolly, R.S.C., Exec. Dir.; Sr. Carmel Somers, R.S.C., Dir. of Learning Center. All Services are in English and Spanish. Counseling is available for individual, marriage, family, children/teen, chemical dependency, victims of sexual an physical abuse, and adults molested as children (AMAC). Special Programs include School Counseling; Parent Education; anger management; violence prevention; victims and perpatrators of domestic violence; at risk youth. Learning Center Programs include tutorials; basic skill building for children and adults, and opportunities for gifted students.

SAN PEDRO. *Apostleship of the Sea, Catholic Maritime Ministry,* Mary, Star of the Sea Parish, 870 W. 8th St., 90731. Tel: 310-833-3541. Rev. Msgr. Patrick J. Gallagher, Port Chap.; Rev. Sylvester J. Thomas, Dir. of Chap. Svcs., Center: Berth 93A, World Cruise Center, Port of Los Angeles, 90731. Tel: 310-521-1041.

SANTA BARBARA. *The Franciscan Sisters of the Sacred Heart in CA.* (A California non-profit corp.), 601 E. Micheltorena, 93103. Tel: 805-568-5816.
E-mail: cbowman@sfmc.org
Web site: http://www.saintfrancis.org
Franciscan Sisters of the Sacred Heart, (Frankfort). Sr. Karen Marie Lanigan, Gen. Supr.; Mr. Ron Biscaro, Admin.

World Wide Marriage Encounter, 1964 Las Canoas Rd., 93105-2351. Tel: 805-882-1942. Rev. James M. Galvin, C.M.

STUDIO CITY. *Association of Christian Therapists,* 3709 Laurel Canyon Blvd., 91604. Tel: 818-762-3329.

VENICE. *St. Joseph Center,* 204 Hampton Dr., 90219. Tel: 310-396-6468.
E-mail: stjosephctr@earthlink.net
Web site: home.earthlink.net/~stjosephctr
Sr. Mary Allen, Contact Person.

VENTURA. *CAREGIVERS: Volunteers Assisting the Elderly,* 261 N. Catalina St., 93001. Tel: 805-652-0566; Fax: 805-652-0568. 123 N. 10th St., Santa Paula, 93060. Tel: 805-525-5006.

WESTLAKE. *West San Fernando Valley Magnificat Chapter Ministry to Catholic Women,* 32149 Lake Meadow Ln., 91361. Tel: 818-889-8515.

WESTLAKE VILLAGE. *Veritas Communications, Inc.,* 3114 La Baya Dr., #200, 91362; Fax: 818-991-2024.
E-mail: youmag@earthlink.net
Web site: www.youmagazine.com

[EE] LEGAL TITLES

LOS ANGELES. *Chancery Office,* 3424 Wilshire Blvd., 90010-2241. Tel: 213-637-7000; Fax: 213-637-6000. For further information contact the Chancery. Also see Miscellaneous for additional listings.

Recollect Augustinian Fathers & Brothers, Province of St. Augustine, Inc.

Missionary Oblates of Mary Immaculate, Western Province, Inc.

School Sisters of Notre Dame de Namur of the California Province, Inc.

Congregation of the Sacred Heart of Jesus & Mary and of Perpetual Adoration, Inc.

Sisters of St. Louis Monaghan, Inc.

Ursulines of the Western Province, Inc.

RELIGIOUS INSTITUTES OF MEN REPRESENTED IN THE ARCHDIOCESE

For further details refer to the corresponding bracketed number in the Religious Institutes of Men or Women section.

[0140]—*The Augustinians.*—O.S.A.
[0200]—*Benedictine Monks (Congregation of the Annunciation).*—O.S.B.
[0980]—*Brothers of Our Lady Mother of Mercy.*—C.F.M.M.
[1350]—*Brothers of San Francis Xavier.*—C.F.X.
[1160]—*Brothers of St. Patrick.*—F.S.P.
[0330]—*Brothers of the Christian Schools.*—F.S.C.
[]—*Canons Regular of the Immaculate Conception.*—C.R.I.C.
[0470]—*The Capuchin Friars (St. Patrick's Custody).*—O.F.M.Cap.
[0270]—*Carmelite Fathers & Brothers.* (Prov. of the Most Pure Heart of Mary).—O.Carm.
[0360]—*Claretian Missionaries.* (Western Prov.).—C.M.F.
[0380]—*Comboni Missionaries of the Heart of Jesus.* (Verona).—M.C.C.J.
[0310]—*Congregation of Christian Brothers.*—C.F.C.
[]—*Congregation of St. John the Baptist.*—C.S.J.B.
[1150]—*Congregation of St. Joseph.*—C.S.J.
[1330]—*Congregation of the Mission.* (Prov. of the West).—C.M.
[1210]—*Congregation of the Missionaries of St. Charles.*—C.S.
[1000]—*Congregction of the Passion.* (Western Prov.).—C.P.
[1140]—*Congregation of the Sacred Hearts of Jesus and Mary.*—SS.CC.
[0480]—*Conventual Franciscans.* (St. Joseph Cupertino Prov.).—O.F.M.Conv.
[0520]—*Franciscan Friars.* (St. Barbara Prov.).—O.F.M.
[0530]—*Franciscan Friars of the Atonement.*—S.A.
[]—*Guadalupe Missioners.* (Mexico).—M.G.
[0650]—*Holy Ghost Fathers.*—C.S.Sp.
[0670]—*Hospitaller Brothers of St. John of God.*—O.H.
[0690]—*Jesuit Fathers and Brothers.* (Calif. Prov.).—S.J.
[0710]—*Josephite Fathers.*—C.J.
[0730]—*Legionaries of Christ.*—L.C.
[0580]—*Little Brothers of the Good Shepherd.*—B.G.S.
[0780]—*Marist Fathers.*—S.M.
[0800]—*Maryknoll.*—M.M.
[0830]—*Mill Hill Missionaries.*—M.H.M.
[]—*Missionaries of Charity Brothers.*—M.C.
[0660]—*Missionaries of the Holy Spirit.*—M.Sp.S.
[1110]—*Missionaries of the Sacred Heart.*—M.S.C.
[0840]—*Missionary Servants of the Most Holy Trinity.*—S.T.
[0910]—*Oblates of Mary Immaculate.* (Western Prov.).—O.M.I.
[0930]—*Oblates of St. Joseph.*—O.S.J.
[0940]—*Oblates of the Virgin Mary.*—O.M.V.
[]—*Operarios del Reino de Cristo.*—O.R.C.
[0835]—*Order of Minims.*—O.M.
[0430]—*Order of Preachers-Dominicans.* (Western Prov.).—O.P.
[0150]—*Order of the Augustinian Recollects.*—O.A.R.
[1020]—*Pauline Fathers and Brothers, Society of St. Paul.*—S.S.P.
[1030]—*Paulist Fathers.*—C.S.P.
[1040]—*Piarist Fathers.*—Sch.P.
[1050]—*Pontifical Institute for Foreign Missions.*—P.I.M.E.
[0610]—*Priests of the Congregation of Holy Cross.*—C.S.C.
[1070]—*Redemptorist Fathers.* (Oakland Prov.).—C.SS.R.
[1090]—*Rogationist Fathers.*—R.C.J.
[0700]—*St. Joseph's Society of the Sacred Heart.*—S.S.J.
[1190]—*Salesians of Don Bosco.*—S.D.B.
[1240]—*Servites.*—O.S.M.
[0110]—*Society of African Missions.*—S.M.A.
[1260]—*Society of Christ.*—S.Ch.
[0760]—*Society of Mary.*—S.M.
[0850]—*Society of Missionaries of Africa.*—M.Afr.
[0370]—*Society of St. Columban.*—S.S.C.
[0420]—*Society of the Divine Word.*—S.V.D.
[1060]—*Society of the Precious Blood.*—C.PP.S.
[1290]—*Society of the Priests of St. Sulpice.*—S.S.

RELIGIOUS INSTITUTES OF WOMEN REPRESENTED IN THE ARCHDIOCESE

[2120]—*Armenian Sisters of the Immaculate Conception.*—C.I.C.
[0230]—*Benedictine Sisters of Pontifical Jurisdiction.*—O.S.B.
[1810]—*Bernardine Sisters of the Third Order of St. Francis.*—O.S.F.
[2930]—*California Institute of the Sisters of the Most Holy and Immaculate Heart of the Blessed Virgin Mary.*—I.H.M.
[]—*Caritas Sisters of Miyazaki.*
[0370]—*Carmelite Sisters of the Most Sacred Heart of Los Angeles.*—O.C.D.
[2100]—*Congregation of the Humility of Mary.*—C.H.M.
[]—*Congregation of the Immaculate Heart of Mary Reparatrix.*—I.H.M.R.
[0470]—*Congregation of the Sisters of Charity for the Incarnate Word.*—C.C.V.I.
[3935]—*Congregation of the Sisters of St. Louis, Juilly Monaghan.*—S.S.L.
[1920]—*Congregation of the Sisters of the Holy Cross.*—C.S.C.
[1940]—*Congregation of the Sisters of the Holy Faith.*—C.H.F.

[1950]—*Congregation of the Sisters of the Holy Family.*—S.S.F.
[0760]—*Daughters of Charity of St. Vincent de Paul.* (Prov. of the West).—D.C.
[0880]—*Daughters of Mary and Joseph.*—D.M.J.
[0850]—*Daughters of Mary Help of Christians.*—F.M.A.
[]—*Daughters of Mary, Mother of Mercy.*—D.M.M.M.
[0420]—*Discalced Carmelite Nuns.*—O.C.D.
[1050]—*Dominican Comtemplative Nuns.*—O.P.
[1070-03]—*Dominican Sisters.*—O.P.
[1070-04]—*Dominican Sisters.*—O.P.
[1070-12]—*Dominican Sisters.*—O.P.
[1070-13]—*Dominican Sisters.*—O.P.
[1070-19]—*Dominican Sisters.*—O.P.
[1070-21]—*Dominican Sisters.*—O.P.
[]—*Dominican Sisters of Adrian (Pacific West Chapter).*—O.P.
[]—*Dominican Sisters of Adrian (Southwest Mission Chapter).*—O.P.
[1150]—*Eucharistic Franciscan Missionary Sisters.*—E.F.M.S.
[]—*Evangelizadores Eucaristicas de los Pobres.*—E.E.P.
[1170]—*Felician Sisters.*—C.S.S.F.
[1350]—*Franciscan Missionary Sisters of the Immaculate Conception.*—O.S.F.
[1230]—*Franciscan Sisters of Christian Charity.*—O.S.F.
[1310]—*Franciscan Sisters of Little Falls.*—O.S.F.
[1500]—*Franciscan Sisters of Mary Immaculate of the Third Order of St. Francis of Assisi.*—F.M.I.
[1780]—*Franciscan Sisters of Perpetual Adoration.*
[1450]—*Franciscan Sisters of the Sacred Heart.*—O.S.F.
[1845]—*Guadalupan Missionaries.*—M.G.Sp.S.
[]—*Handmaids of the Sacred Heart of Jesus, Mary & Joseph.*—J.M.J.
[]—*Hermanas Misioneras Servidoras de la Palabra.*—H.M.S.P.
[2575]—*Institute of the Sisters of Mercy of the Americas.* (Burlingame, CA).—R.S.M.
[2340]—*Little Sisters of the Poor.*—L.S.P.
[2390]—*Lovers of the Holy Cross Sisters.*—L.H.C.
[2470]—*Maryknoll Sisters of St. Dominic.*—M.M.
[2500]—*Medical Sisters of St. Joseph.*—M.S.J.
[2710]—*Missionaries of Charity.*—M.C.
[]—*Missionaries of Jesus Crucified.*—M.J.C.
[0210]—*Missionary Benedictine Sisters.*—O.S.B.
[0390]—*Missionary Carmelites of St. Theresa.*—C.M.S.T.
[2715]—*Missionary Sisters of Christ the King.*—M.S.C.K.
[2880]—*Missionary Sisters of St. Columban.*—S.S.C.
[2750]—*Missionary Sisters of the Immaculate Heart of Mary.*—I.C.M.
[3530]—*Missionary Sisters Servants of the Holy Spirit.*—S.Sp.S.
[3760]—*Order of St. Clare.*—P.C.C.
[3130]—*Our Lady of Victory Missionary Sisters.*—O.L.V.M.
[0980]—*Pious Disciples of the Divine Master.*—P.D.D.M.
[0950]—*Pious Society Daughters of St. Paul.*—F.S.P.
[2840]—*Poor Clare Missionary Sisters.*—M.C.
[3242]—*Poor Sisters of Nazareth.*—P.S.N.
[0930]—*Religious Daughters of St. Joseph.*—F.S.J.
[1145]—*Religious Missionaries of St. Dominic.*—O.P.
[3450]—*Religious of Jesus-Mary.*—R.J.M.
[3465]—*Religious of the Sacred Heart of Mary.*—R.S.H.M.
[3400]—*Religious Sisters of Charity.*—R.S.C.
[1505]—*St. Francis Mission Community.*—O.S.F.
[2970]—*School Sisters of Notre Dame.*—S.S.N.D.
[1680]—*School Sisters of St. Francis.*—O.S.F.
[3580]—*Servants of Mary (Servite Order).*—O.S.M.
[3499]—*Servants of the Blessed Sacrament.*—S.J.S.
[]—*Servants of the Immaculate Child Mary.*—E.I.N.
[0250]—*Sisters of Bethany.*—C.V.D.
[0480]—*Sisters of Charity of Leavenworth, Kansas.*—S.C.L.
[]—*Sisters of Charity of Rolling Hills.*—S.C.R.H.
[0570]—*Sisters of Charity of Seton Hill, Greensburg, Pennsylvania.*—S.C.
[0430]—*Sisters of Charity of the Blessed Virgin Mary.*—B.V.M.
[2360]—*Sisters of Loretto At the Foot of the Cross.* (Southern Prov.).—S.L.
[]—*Sisters of Mary, Mother of the Church.*—M.M.C.
[2575]—*Sisters of Mercy.* (New York).—R.S.M.
[2990]—*Sisters of Notre Dame.* (Prov. of Los Angeles).—S.N.D.
[3000]—*Sisters of Notre Dame de Namur.*—S.N.D.deN.
[]—*Sisters of Our Lady of Perpetual Help.*—S.O.L.P.H.
[3350]—*Sisters of Providence.*—S.P.
[3360]—*Sisters of Providence of Saint Mary-Of-The-Woods, Indiana.*—S.P.
[4080]—*Sisters of Social Service of Los Angeles, Inc.*—S.S.S.
[1705]—*Sisters of St. Francis of Assisi.*—O.S.F.
[1710]—*Sisters of St. Francis of Joliet.*—O.S.F.
[1620]—*Sisters of St. Francis of Millvale, Pennsylvania.*—O.S.F.
[1760]—*Sisters of St. Francis of Oldenburg.*—O.S.F.
[1630]—*Sisters of St. Francis of Penance and Christian Charity.*—O.S.F.
[1650]—*The Sisters of St. Francis of Philadelphia.*—O.S.F.
[1530]—*Sisters of St. Francis of Sylvania.*—O.S.F.
[1730]—*Sisters of St. Francis of Tiffin.*—O.S.F.
[3830-03]—*Sisters of St. Joseph.*—C.S.J.
[3830-18]—*Sisters of St. Joseph.*—C.S.J.
[3840]—*Sisters of St. Joseph of Carondelet.*—C.S.J.
[3860]—*Sisters of St. Joseph of Cluny.*—S.J.C.
[3830-11]—*Sisters of St. Joseph of Nazareth.*—S.S.J.
[3830]—*Sisters of St. Joseph of Orange.*
[3890]—*Sisters of St. Joseph of Peace.*—C.S.J.P.
[3930]—*Sisters of St. Joseph to the Third Order of St. Francis.*—S.S.J.-T.O.S.F.
[3960]—*Sisters of St. Mary of Oregon.*—S.S.M.O.
[0260]—*Sisters of the Blessed Sacrament for Indians and Colored People.*—S.B.S.
[0700]—*Sisters of the Company of Mary Our Lady.*—O.D.N.
[3180]—*Sisters of the Cross and Passion.*—C.P.
[1830]—*Sisters of the Good Shepherd.*—R.G.S.
[1850]—*Sisters of the Guardian Angel.*—S.A.C.
[]—*Sisters of the Heart of Jesus in the Blessed Sacrament.*—H.C.J.S.
[1960]—*Sisters of the Holy Family.*—S.H.F.
[1990]—*Sisters of the Holy Names of Jesus and Mary.*—S.N.J.M.
[]—*Sisters of the Immaculate Heart of Mary at Mirinac.*—I.H.M.M.
[2270]—*Sisters of the Little Company of Mary.*—L.C.M.
[]—*Sisters of the Love of God.*—R.A.D.
[3200]—*Sisters of the Pious Schools.*—Sch.P.
[]—*Sisters of the Poor of St. Catherine.*—S.D.P.
[3260]—*Sisters of the Precious Blood (Dayton, Ohio).*—C.PP.S.
[3320]—*Sisters of the Presentation of the B.V.M.* (San Francisco CA).—P.B.V.M.
[]—*Sisters of the Sacred Heart of Mary.*—C.S.C.M.
[4050]—*Sisters of the Society Devoted to the Sacred Heart.*—S.D.S.H.
[1490]—*Sisters of the Third Franciscan Order.*—O.S.F.
[3600]—*Sisters Servants of Mary.*—S.M.
[4060]—*Society of the Holy Child Jesus.*—S.H.C.J.
[]—*Theresian Sisters.*—C.S.T.
[3330]—*Union of Sisters of Presentation of the B.B.M.*—P.B.V.M.
[4110]—*Ursuline Nuns (Roman Union).*—O.S.U.

ARCHDIOCESAN CEMETERIES

LOS ANGELES. *Calvary Cemetery and Mausoleum.* Tel: 213-261-3106. Kevin Haynes, Mgr.

CULVER CITY. *Holy Cross Cemetery & Mausoleum & Columbarium.* Tel: 310-670-7697. Philip Birgel, Mgr.

LANCASTER. *Good Shepherd Cemetery & Mausoleum.* Tel: 805-722-0887. Daniel Rejniak, Mgr.

LONG BEACH. *All Souls Cemetery and Mausoleum.* Tel: 213-424-8601. Lillia Sanson, Mgr.

MISSION HILLS. *San Fernando Mission Cemetery & Mausoleum.* Tel: 818-361-7387. Michael Wesner, Mgr.

MONTEBELLO. *Resurrection Cemetery & Mausoleum.* Tel: 213-887-2024. Margaret Hunter, Mgr.

OXNARD. *Santa Clara Cemetery & Mausoleum.* Tel: 805-485-5757. Elizabeth Welsh, Mgr.

POMONA. *Holy Cross Cemetery.* Tel: 909-627-3602. Mary Ann McAdams, Mgr.

ROWLAND HEIGHTS. *Queen of Heaven Cemetery.* Tel: 818-964-1291. Norberta Orta, Mgr.

SANTA BARBARA. *Calvary Cemetery & Mausoleum.* Tel: 805-682-5793. Gwen Hueston, Mgr.

SIMI. *Assumption Cemetery.* Tel: 805-583-5825. Elizabeth Welsh, Mgr.

NECROLOGY

† Beattie, Rev. Msgr. John, Los Angeles, CA, St. Ambrose. —Died July 9, 1997.
† Coronel, Juan S., (Retired). —Died Dec. 17, 1996.
† Delaney, John J., (Retired). —Died Feb. 17, 1997.
† Fader, John J., (Retired). —Died Feb. 17, 1997.
† Hall, Finbar, (Retired). —Died March 16, 1997.
† Hourihan, Rev. Msgr. James, (Retired). —Died July 8, 1997.
† Kesterson, James, Van Nuys, CA, St. Bridget of Sweden. —Died July 7, 1997.
† Llanos, Theodore, Longbeach, CA, St. Lucy. —Died Dec. 30, 1996.
† Nicolas, Marcos, (Retired). —Died June 16, 1997.
† O'Sullivan, Rev. Msgr. Thomas J., Los Angeles, CA, Visitation. —Died Oct. 30, 1997.
† Shine, Cornelius, Silver Springs Shores, FL, Immaculate Heart of Mary. —Died Dec. 4, 1996.

Archdiocese of Louisville

(Archidioecesis Ludovicopolitana)

Most Reverend

THOMAS C. KELLY, O.P., D.D., J.C.D.

Archbishop of Louisville; ordained June 5, 1958; appointed Titular Bishop of Tusuro July 12, 1977; promoted Archbishop of Louisville December 29, 1981. *Office: 212 E. College St., P.O. Box 1073, Louisville, KY, 40201.*

Most Reverend

CHARLES G. MALONEY, D.D.

Auxiliary Bishop Emeritus of the Archdiocese of Louisville; born September 9, 1912; ordained December 8, 1937; appointed Auxiliary December 30, 1954; consecrated February 2, 1955; appointed Titular Bishop of Bardstown February 2, 1995. *Res., 212 E. College St., P.O. Box 1073, Louisville, KY, 40201.*

Most Reverend

THOMAS J. MCDONOUGH, D.D., J.C.D.

Retired Archbishop of Louisville; ordained May 26, 1938; appointed Titular Bishop of Thaenae March 10, 1947; consecrated April 30, 1947; transferred as Auxiliary from St. Augustine to Savannah, January 2, 1957; succeeded to See March 2, 1960; promoted Archbishop of Louisville March 1, 1967; resigned September 29, 1981.

ESTABLISHED AT BARDSTOWN APRIL 8, 1808.; TRANSFERRED TO LOUISVILLE FEB. 13, 1841; CREATED AN ARCHDIOCESE DEC. 10, 1937.

Square Miles 8,124.

Comprises the following twenty-four Counties in central Kentucky: Adair, Barren, Bullitt, Casey, Clinton, Cumberland, Green, Hardin, Hart, Henry, Jefferson, Larue, Marion, Meade, Metcalfe, Monroe, Nelson, Oldham, Russell, Shelby, Spencer, Taylor, Trimble and Washington.

For legal titles of parishes and archdiocesan institutions, consult the Chancery.

Chancery: 212 E. College St., P.O. Box 1073, Louisville, KY, 40201. Tel.: 502-585-3291.

Web site address: http://www.archlou.org

E-mail address: chancery@archlou.org

STATISTICAL OVERVIEW

Personnel	
Archbishop	1
Retired Archbishops	1
Retired Bishops	1
Abbots	1
Priests: Diocesan Active in Diocese	129
Priests: Active Outside Diocese	3
Priests: Diocesan in Foreign Missions	1
Priests: Retired, Sick or Absent	58
Number of Diocesan Priests	191
Religious Priests in Diocese	69
Ordinations:	
Diocesan Priests	2
Religious Priests	3
Permanent Deacons in Diocese	101
Total Brothers	87
Total Sisters	1,049
Parishes	
Parishes	112
With Resident Pastor:	
Resident Diocesan Priests	81
Resident Religious Priests	11
Without Resident Pastor:	
Administered by Priests	16
Administered by Permanent Deacons	1
Administered by Women Religious	2
Administered by Lay People	1
Missions	12
Pastoral Centers	3
New Parishes Created	1
Closed Parishes	2
Professional Ministry Personnel:	
Brothers	1
Sisters	45
Lay Ministers	119
Welfare	
Catholic Hospitals	2
Total Assisted	150,302
Health Care Centers	1
Total Assisted	2,300
Homes for the Aged	5
Total Assisted	796
Residential Care of Children	1
Total Assisted	62
Day Care and Extended Day Care Centers	1
Total Assisted	185
Specialized Homes	1
Total Assisted	223
Special Centers for Social Services	1
Total Assisted	3,521
Educational	
Diocesan Students in Other Seminaries	12
Total Seminarians	12
Colleges and Universities	3
Total Students	4,108
High Schools, Diocesan and Parish	4
Total Students	2,066
High Schools, Private	6
Total Students	4,023
Elementary Schools, Diocesan and Parish	57
Total Students	17,354
Elementary Schools, Private	3
Total Students	542
Non-residential Schools for the Disabled	1
Total Students	63
Catechesis/Religious Education:	
High School Students	1,212
Elementary Students	8,392
Total Students Under Catholic Instruction	37,772
Teachers in the Diocese:	
Priests	7
Brothers	15
Sisters	28
Lay Teachers	1,269
Vital Statistics	
Receptions into the Church:	
Infant Baptism Totals	3,101
Adult Baptism Totals	367
Received into Full Communion	627
First Communions	3,159
Confirmations	2,649
Marriages:	
Catholic	645
Interfaith	494
Total Marriages	1,139
Deaths	1,875
Total Catholic Population	181,896
Total Population	1,139,022

Former Bishops—Rt. Rev. BENEDICT JOSEPH FLAGET, S.S., D.D., cons. Bishop of Bardstown, Nov. 4, 1810; died Feb. 11, 1850.—Rt. Rev. JOHN B. DAVID, S.S., D.D., Coadjutor; cons. Aug. 15, 1819; died July 12, 1841.—Rt. Rev. GUY IGNATIUS CHABRAT, S.S., D.D., Coadjutor; cons. July 20, 1834; died Nov. 21, 1868.—Rt. Rev. MARTIN JOHN SPALDING, D.D., Coadjutor with right of succession; cons. Sept. 10, 1848; transferred to Baltimore, May 6, 1864; died Feb. 7, 1872.—Rt. Rev. PETER JOSEPH LAVIALLE, D.D., cons. Sept. 24, 1865; died May 11, 1867.—Rt. Rev. WILLIAM GEORGE MCCLOSKEY, D.D., cons. May 24, 1868; died Sept. 17, 1909.—Rt. Rev. DENIS O'DONAGHUE, D.D., ord. Sept. 6, 1874; cons. Titular Bishop of Pomario and Auxiliary of Indianapolis on April 25, 1900; transferred to Louisville, Feb. 7, 1910; transferred to the Titular See of Lebedus, July 26, 1924; died Nov. 7, 1925.—Most Rev. JOHN A. FLOERSH, D.D., ord. June 10, 1911; appt. Titular Bishop of Lycopolis and Coadjutor Bishop of Louisville with right of succession, Feb. 6, 1923; cons. April 8, 1923; succeeded to See July 26, 1924; elevated to Archiepiscopal dignity Dec. 10, 1937; resigned and named to Titular See of Sistroniana, March 1, 1967; died June 11, 1968.—Most Rev. THOMAS J. MCDONOUGH, D.D., resigned Sept. 29, 1981.

Vicars General—Very Rev. BERNARD J. BREEN; Most Rev. CHARLES G. MALONEY, D.D.

Chancery—212 E. College St., P.O. Box 1073, Louisville, 40201. Tel: 502-585-3291. Office Hours: 9-12:30 & 1:30-4:30 All applications for dispensations are to be sent to this office.

Archivist - Chancellor—Rev. ROBERT DALE CIESLIK.

Vice Chancellor—FLORENCE M. CRAWFORD.

Secretary to Archbishop—NORMA L. MERRICK.

Chief Administrative Officer—BRIAN B. REYNOLDS.

Chief Financial Officer—JEROME J. PAKENHAM.

Controller—PATRICIA J. MEYER.

Diocesan Tribunal—212 E. College St., P. O. Box 1073, Louisville, 40201. Tel: 502-585-3291.

Judicial Vicar and Director—Very Rev. CHARLES C. THOMPSON, J.C.L.

Adjutant Judicial Vicar—Rev. J. MARK SPALDING, J.C.L.

Associate Director of Tribunal—DONALD M. SWIFT J.C.D.

Promoter of Justice—Rev. JOHN W. HANRAHAN.

Defenders of the Bond—Revs. DONALD R. GOETZ; JOHN J. STOLTZ; ROBERT E. OSBORNE; ANTHONY L. CHANDLER; PATRICK J. DOLAN; ROBERT DALE CIESLIK; Dr. ROBERT L. STENGER; DONALD M. SWIFT.

Associate Judges—Revs. KENNETH R. FORTENER; THOMAS A. HOMMRICH; THOMAS P. CREAGH; T. MICHAEL TOBIN.

Assessor—PATRICIA A. NORRIS.

Notaries—CATHERINE M. MILLER; SHARON A. ARCHER; LINDA D. THOMAN.

College of Consultors—Most Rev. CHARLES G. MALONEY; Very Rev. BERNARD J. BREEN; Revs. KEVIN J. BRYAN; WILLIAM D. HAMMER; CLARENCE J. HOWARD; JOHN L. SCHINDLER; J. ROY STILES.

Deans—Rev. WILLIAM F. MEDLEY, Bardstown Deanery; Very Rev. CHARLES C. THOMPSON, Lebanon Deanery; Rev. J. RICHARD SULLIVAN, Elizabethtown Deanery.

Clergy Personnel Commission—Revs. ROY E. DENTINGER; JOHN R. BURKE; THOMAS L. BOLAND; CHARLES D. WALKER; VINCENT J. SCHWEIZER; J. WAYNE JENKINS, Dir.

Priests' Council—Most Rev. THOMAS C. KELLY, O.P., Presider; Revs. WILLIAM D. HAMMER, Pres., *5505 Hudson Ln., Louisville, 40291.* Mrs. ROSEMARIE BAUER, Sec. Ex Officio: Most Rev. CHARLES G. MALONEY; Very Rev. BERNARD J. BREEN; Revs. JOSEPH H. VOOR; ROBERT E. OSBORNE; THOMAS R. CLARK; JAMES W. GRAF; JOSEPH T. GRAFFIS; TRUMIE C. ELLIOTT; JOSEPH T. HERP; ANTHONY L. CHANDLER; THOMAS A. SMITH; Very Rev. CHARLES C. THOMPSON; Revs. J. ROY STILES; G. NICHOLAS RICE; GERALD L TIMMEL; CLARENCE J. HOWARD; MICHAEL D. LOTT; FRANK J. EIMER; JOHN J. STOLTZ; CARL LOUIS MASON, O.P.; JOHN LESOUSKY C.R.

Archdiocesan Examiners—Revs. JOHN HANRAHAN; VINCENT SCHWEIZER; WILLIAM WAGNER.

Archdiocesan Offices and Directors

Archdiocesan Communications Center—CECELIA PRICE, Chief Communications Officer, *Maloney Center, 1200 S. Shelby St., Louisville, 40203.* Tel: 502-636-0296.

Byzantine Rite Faithful—Rev. JOHN W. BIRK, Chap., *2914 S. Third St., Louisville, 40208.* Tel: 502-637-2058.

Catholic Cemeteries Office—KENNETH POPP, Dir. RICHARD E. STEINMETZ, Coord., *1600 Newburg Rd., P.O. Box 4096, Louisville, 40204.* Tel: 502-451-7710.

Catholic Deaf Office—Sr. THOMASINE DALEY, S.C.N., Dir., *Maloney Center, 1200 S. Shelby St., Louisville, 40203.* Tel: 502-636-0296; 634-8947 (TTY).

Catholic Services Appeal—ROSEMARY SMITH, Dir.; Rev. THOMAS E. GENTILE, General Chm., *212 E. College St., P.O. Box 1073, Louisville, 40201.* Tel: 502-585-3291.

Catholic Charities—Rev. TIMOTHY A. HOGAN, Exec. Dir., *2911 S. 4th St., Louisville, 40208.* Tel: 502-637-9786.

Office of Migration and Refugee Services—

Office for Ministry to the Sick and the Elderly—

Office of Parish Outreach—

Office of Parish Social Ministry—

Office of Catholic Rural Life—

Clergy Personnel Office—Rev. J. WAYNE JENKINS, Dir., *P.O. Box 1073, Louisville, 40201.* Tel: 502-585-3291.

Clerical Aid Society—*212 E. College St., P.O. Box 1073, Louisville, 40201.* Tel: 502-585-3291.

Continuing Education for Clergy-Ministry to Priests—Rev. WILLIAM S. GRINER, Dir., *P.O. Box 1073, Louisville, 40201.* Tel: 502-585-3291.

Cursillo Movement—Deacon BRUCE LINCOLN, Spiritual Dir., *Flaget Center, 1935 Lewiston Pl., Louisville, 40216.* Tel: 502-448-8581.

Due Process Board—JOHN LAUN, Chm., *Kentucky Home Life Building, 239 S. 5th St., Louisville, 40202.* Tel: 502-587-0330.

Ecumenism, Office of—Rev. JUDE WEISENBECK, S.D.S., Dir., *Maloney Center, 1200 S. Shelby St., Louisville, 40203.* Tel: 502-636-0296.

Family Ministries, Center for—BARBARA MACDONALD, Dir. THOMAS D. ROBBINS, Ph.D., Clinical Dir., *Maloney Center, 1200 S. Shelby St., Louisville, 40203.* Tel: 502-636-0296; Fax: 502-636-3381.

Respect Life—HELEN ROTHGERBER, Coord.

Holy Childhood Association—Rev. JAMES E. HARGADON, Dir., *212 E. College St., Box 1073, Louisville, 40201.* Tel: 502-585-3291.

Holy Name Society—MICHAEL HEEB, Pres., *2302 Bradford Dr., Louisville, 40218.* Tel: 502-454-7151.

L.A.M.P.—(Louisville Archdiocesan Mission Promoters), Most Revs. THOMAS C. KELLY, O.P.; CHARLES G. MALONEY; Very Rev. BERNARD J. BREEN, *212 E. College St., P.O. Box 1073, Louisville, 40201.* Tel: 502-585-3291.

Legion of Mary—Rev. ROGER A. BOEHMICKE, Spiritual Dir., *3521 Goldsmith Ln., Louisville, 40220.* Tel: 502-451-9300.

Mass of the Air—*1930 Bishop Ln., Ste. 1002, Louisville, 40218.* Tel: 502-459-5285; Fax: 502-459-5682.

Office of the Diaconate—Deacon BRIAN KARLEY, Dir., *Maloney Center, 1200 S. Shelby St., Louisville, 40203.* Tel: 502-636-0296.

Office of Lifelong Formation and Education—MATTHEW J. HAYES, Exec. Dir., *Flaget Center, 1935 Lewiston Pl., Louisville, 40216.* Tel: 502-448-8581.

Office of Ministry and Spirituality—Ms. MARTI JEWELL, Dir., *Maloney Center, 1200 S. Shelby St., Louisville, 40203.* Tel: 502-636-0296.

Office of Multicultural Ministry—M. ANNETTE TURNER, Dir., *Maloney Center, 1200 S. Shelby St., Louisville, 40203.* Tel: 502-636-0296.

Office of Worship—JUDY BULLOCK, Dir., *Maloney Center, 1200 S. Shelby St., Louisville, 40203.* Tel: 502-636-0296.

Opportunities for Life—JACKIE CARLSEN, Prog. Dir., *Maloney Center, 1200 S. Shelby St., Louisville, 40203.* Tel: 502-637-5949; 637-5968; 800-822-5824.

Parish Leadership Development Office—Sr. JUSTINA HENEGHAN, R.S.M., Dir., *212 E. College St., P.O. Box 1073, Louisville, 40201.* Tel: 502-585-3291.

Personnel and Planning—BRIAN B. REYNOLDS, Dir.; Ms. JUDY THOMAS, Svcs. Coord., *212 E. College, P.O. Box 1073, Louisville, 40201.* Tel: 502-585-3291.

Priests' Review for Growth in Ministry—Rev. ROBERT E. RAY, Dir., *903 Fairdale Rd., Fairdale, 40118.* Tel: 502-363-9929.

Propagation of the Faith—(Missions Office), Rev. JAMES E. HARGADON, Dir., *P.O. Box 1073, Louisville, 40201.* Tel: 502-538-4933; 955-5366.

Sacred Heart Enthronement Center—Rev. LAWRENCE H. LINDLE, Dir., *8191 New Haven Rd., New Haven, 40051.* Tel: 502-549-3751.

Stewardship and Development Office—ROSEMARY BISIG SMITH, Dir., *212 E. College St., P.O. Box 1073, Louisville, 40201.* Tel: 502-585-3291.

Vicar for Clergy—Rev. KENNETH L. KAMBER, *4029 Busath Ave., Louisville, 40218.* Tel: 502-491-1323.

Vocations—Rev. J. RONALD KNOTT, Dir., *Maloney Center, 1200 S. Shelby St., Louisville, 40203.* Tel: 502-636-0296.

CLERGY, PARISHES, MISSIONS AND PAROCHIAL SCHOOLS

CITY OF LOUISVILLE
(Jefferson County)

1—CATHEDRAL OF THE ASSUMPTION, Revs. William L. Fichteman; Martin A. Linebach; Deacon Joseph P. Wright. In res., Most Rev. Thomas C. Kelly, O.P.
Res., 443 S. 5th St., 40202. Tel: 502-582-2971; Fax: 502-582-3919.

2—ST. AGNES, Revs. John Baptist Ormechea, C.P.; Albert Schwer, C.P.
Res., 1920 Newburg Rd., 40205. Tel: 502-451-2220; Fax: 502-454-8483.
School—Tel: 502-458-2850. Beverly McAuliffe, Prin. Sisters of Charity of Nazareth 1; Lay Teachers 24; Students 436.

3—ST. ALBERT THE GREAT, Revs. Theodore R. Sans; Bertrand J. Rapp, Admin.; Deacons Kenneth M. Ward; Vincent G. Stanley.
Res., 1405 Techny Ln., 40222. Tel: 502-425-3940; Fax: 502-394-9896.
School—1301 Techny Ln., 40222. Tel: 502-425-1804. Jeanne Flowers, Prin.
Lay Teachers 43; Students 547.

4—ST. ALOYSIUS. Closed. For inquiries for parish records contact the Chancery.

5—ST. ANN. Merged with St. George, Louisville, to form St. Andrew, Louisville.

6—ST. ANDREW, Rev. Kenneth R. Fortener; Deacons C. Robert Markert; David L. Dalton.
Res., 1410 Dixie Hwy., 40210. Tel: 502-776-6020; Fax: 502-776-7434.

7—ST. ANTHONY, Rev. Leo Kennedy, O.F.M.Conv. In res., Revs. James Cantwell, O.F.M.Conv.; Simon Sauer, O.F.M.Conv.; Alexis Martini, O.F.M.Conv.; Bros. James Fields, O.F.M.Conv.; John Maurer, O.F.M.Conv.
Res., 2222 W. Market St., P.O. Box 11219, 40212. Tel: 502-778-7413; Fax: 502-776-3599.

8—ASCENSION OF OUR LORD, Rev. John B. Helm; Deacon Michael Edwards.
Res., 4600 Lynnbrook Dr., 40220. Tel: 502-451-3860; Fax: 502-459-9782.
School—Tel: 502-451-2535; Fax: 502-451-2535. Maureen Clerkin, Prin.

9—ST. ATHANASIUS, Revs. Robert L. Huber; James E. Wafzig; Sr. Jean Anne Zappa, O.S.U., Pastoral Assoc.; Deacon Donald Masterson.
Res., 5915 Outer Loop Dr., 40219. Tel: 502-969-3332; Fax: 502-966-8948.
School—(Grades K-8). Tel: 502-969-2345; Fax: 502-969-8974. Sr. Aidan Hogan, Prin.
Sisters 1; Lay Teachers 23; Students 431.

10—ST. AUGUSTINE, Revs. Joseph T. Graffis; Vernon W. Robertson; Deacon John Churchill.
Res., 1310 W. Broadway, 40203. Tel: 502-584-4602; Fax: 502-581-0893.
Stations—Blanton House, Tel: 502-587-1259; James Taylor Home, Tel: 502-589-0727.

11—ST. BARNABAS, Revs. Gary G. Davis; Mark M. Hamilton; Deacons James R. Plummer; Robert C. Bryant.
Parish Office: 3042 Hikes Ln., 40220. Tel: 502-459-4251; Fax: 502-459-9815.
Res., 3054 Hikes Ln., 40220. Tel: 502-451-0333.
School—Tel: 502-458-4038; Fax: 502-452-1117. Mary Helen Thompson, Prin.
Lay Teachers 31; Students 441.

12—ST. BARTHOLOMEW, Revs. Terry L. Bradshaw; R. Joseph Hemmerle; Bertrand J. Rapp; Deacon Thomas E. Box, Pastoral Assoc.
Res., 2040 Buechel Bank Rd., 40218. Tel: 502-499-0883; Fax: 502-499-0883.
School—Tel: 502-499-0421. Victoria Davis, Prin.
Ursuline Sisters 1; Lay Teachers 10; Students 194.

13—ST. BASIL, Rev. James P. Hendricks, Admin.
Res., 3901 Wayside Dr., 40216. Tel: 502-772-1017.

14—ST. BENEDICT. Consolidated with St. Charles Borromeo, Louisville, and Holy Cross, Louisville, to form St. Martin de Porres, Louisville.

15—ST. BERNARD, Rev. Joseph E. Vest; Deacon Michael Edwards; Sr. Katharine Hanrahan, S.C.N., Pastoral Assoc.
Res., 7500 Tangelo Dr., 40228. Tel: 502-239-9104; Fax: 502-239-5178.
School—Tel: 502-239-5178; Fax: 532-239-9025. Donald Matlock, Prin.
Sisters 1; Lay Teachers 22; Students 410.

16—ST. BONIFACE, Revs. Sergius H. Scherpenberg, O.F.M.; Stephen V. Schneider, O.F.M.; Edmund R. Moore, O.F.M.
Res., 531 E. Liberty St., 40202-1107. Tel: 502-584-4279; Fax: 502-584-8659.

17—ST. BRIGID, Revs. Donald R. Goetz; Joseph H. Voor; Sr. Helen McCarthy, Pastoral Assoc.
Res., 1520 Hepburn Ave., 40204. Tel: 502-584-5565; Fax: 502-451-1429.

18—ST. CECILIA, Revs. John Lesousky, C.R.; Charles Schoenbachler, C.R.; John Miles, C.R.; Deacons Paul Bissig; Philip Tremblay, C.R.
Res., 338 N. 25th St., 40212. Tel: 502-772-3694; Fax: 502-772-3695.
School—Tel: 502-778-1941; Fax: 502-778-9935. Sr. Barbara Van Bokern, Prin.
Lay Teachers 9; Students 130.

19—ST. CHARLES BORROMEO. Consolidated with St. Benedict, Louisville, and Holy Cross, Louisville, to form St. Martin de Porres, Louisville.

20—CHRIST THE KING, Rev. John R. Burke; Deacon Richard Dawson.
Res., 718 S. 44th St., 40211. Tel: 502-778-5055; Fax: 502-776-5120.

21—ST. COLUMBA. Closed. For inquiries for parish records contact the Chancery.

22—ST. DENIS, Rev. James P. Hendricks; Deacon Robert M. Kampschaefer.
Res., 4205 Cane Run Rd., 40216. Tel: 502-448-2961; Fax: 502-448-3656.
School—Tel: 502-447-5832. Ann Montgomery, Prin.
Lay Teachers 12; Students 242.

23—ST. ELIZABETH ANN SETON, Revs. Robert M. Abel, Admin.; Gerald L. Timmel; Deacon James C. Olrich; Sr. Alice Casper, S.C.N., Pastoral Assoc.
Res., 11501 Maple Way, 40229. Tel: 502-966-3164; 966-0661.

24—ST. ELIZABETH OF HUNGARY, Revs. H. Anthony Olges; Robert B. Gray. In res., Rev. Herman J. Naber.
Res., 1020 E. Burnett Ave., 40217. Tel: 502-636-3706; Fax: 502-634-5511.
School—St. Rose Catholic School, (Grades PreK-8) 1016 E. Burnett Ave., 40217. Tel: 502-634-1831; Fax: 502-634-0422. Eileen Soeder, Prin.
Lay Teachers 13; Aides 1; Students 192.

25—EPIPHANY, Rev. R. Cass Volpert; Sr. Josette Gocella, S.S.J., Pastoral Assoc.; Deacon Gary E. Becker.
Res., 914 Old Harrods Creek Rd., 40223. Tel: 502-245-9733; Fax: 502-245-7658.

26—St. Frances of Rome, Rev. John G. Eifler; Sr. Carmelita Dunn, S.C.N., Pastoral Assoc.; Deacon William Mullins.
Res., 2119 Payne St., 40206. Tel: 502-896-8401; Fax: 502-895-0310.

27—St. Francis of Assisi, Revs. Joseph M. Rankin; Donald M. Hill. In res., Rev. Joseph T. Merkt; Deacon Walton G. Jones.
Res., 1960 Bardstown Rd., 40205-1572. Tel: 502-456-6394; Fax: 502-456-9462.
School—1938 Alfresco Pl., 40205-1876. Tel: 502-459-3088. Katherine Schloemer, Prin.
Lay Teachers 15; Students 256.

28—St. Gabriel the Archangel, Revs. William D. Hammer; Jeffrey Patrick Leger; Deacon William Skeeters.
Res., 5505 Bardstown Rd., 40291. Tel: 502-239-5481; Fax: 502-239-7717.
School—Tel: 502-239-5535. Alan R. Huelsman, Prin.
Lay Teachers 34; Students 783.

29—St. George. Merged with St. Ann, Louisville, to form St. Andrew, Louisville.

30—Guardian Angels, Revs. Raymond Hofmann, C.R.; Norman Choate, C.R.; Deacon Cletus A. Ratterman.
Res., 6000 Preston Hwy., 40219. Tel: 502-968-5421; Fax: 502-962-1080.
School—Thomas Merton Academy. (Middle School). Tel: 502-969-5462. Ms. Ann Thompson, Prin.
Lay Teachers 12; Students 204.

31—St. Helen, Revs. Thomas E. Gentile; Charles J. Bindner; Deacon David McGinty.
Res., 4005 Dixie Hwy., 40216. Tel: 502-448-4008; Fax: 502-448-4045.
School—4007 Dixie Hwy., 40216. Tel: 502-447-9671. Diane Smith, Prin.
Lay Teachers 11; Students 202.

32—Holy Cross. Consolidated with St. Benedict, Louisville, and St. Charles Borromeo, Louisville, to form St. Martin de Porres, Louisville.

33—Holy Family, Rev. Anthony L. Chandler; Deacon Lamar Fante. In res., Rev. Michael L. Huggins.
Res., 3926 Poplar Level Rd., 40213. Tel: 502-459-6066; Fax: 502-459-6066.
School—Tel: 502-458-4531. Catherine Guizio, Prin.
Lay Teachers 13; Students 206.

34—Holy Name, Rev. John W. Birk.
Res., 2914 S. 3rd St., 40208. Tel: 502-637-2058.

35—Holy Spirit, Revs. Thomas L. Boland; J. Randall Hubbard; J. Wayne Jenkins; Frank B. Grauel.
Res., 3345 Lexington Rd., 40206. Tel: 502-893-3982; Fax: 502-893-8287.
School—322 Cannons Ln., 40206. Tel: 502-893-7700; Fax: 502-893-8018. Mrs. Janet Leitner, Prin.
Lay Teachers 23; Students 460.

36—Holy Trinity, Revs. Joseph M. Fowler; J. Wayne Jenkins; Deacon John Simpson.
Pastoral Center—501 Cherrywood Rd., 40207. Tel: 502-897-5207; Fax: 502-897-0962.
School—423 Cherrywood Rd., 40207. Tel: 502-897-2785; Fax: 502-896-0990. Mrs. Mary Alice Zettel, Prin.
Lay Teachers 22; Students 496.

37—St. Ignatius, Rev. Thomas P. Creagh; Deacon James R. Young.
Res., 1816 Rangeland Rd., 40219. Tel: 502-964-5904; Fax: 502-964-5905.
Thomas Merton Child Development Center—Tel: 502-969-2336. Ms. Mona Wilkerson, Dir.
Lay Teachers 18; Students 105.

38—Immaculate Heart of Mary, Rev. Louis J. Meiman.
Office: 1545 S. 34th St., 40211. Tel: 502-774-5772.

39—Incarnation, Rev. Joseph T. Herp.
Res., 2229 Lower Hunters Trace Rd., 40216. Tel: 502-447-2013; Fax: 502-448-3821.

40—St. James, Rev. Donald R. Goetz; Rev. Msgr. Alfred F. Horrigan; Rev. Joseph H. Voor; Deacon Jerome Fargen.
Res., 1826 Edenside Ave., 40204. Tel: 502-451-1420; Fax: 502-451-1429.
School—Tel: 502-454-0330. Colette Dumstorf, Prin.
Lay Teachers 6; Students 107.

41—St. John. Closed. For inquiries for parish records contact the Chancery.

42—St. John Vianney, Rev. J. Roy Stiles.
Res., 4839 Southside Dr., 40214. Tel: 502-366-5517.
School—Tel: 502-366-1266; Fax: 502-366-3257. Mrs. Dean Haueter, Prin.
Sisters 1; Lay Teachers 7; Students 155.

43—St. Joseph, Revs. Simeon Cleves, O.F.M.; Joachim Lux, O.F.M.
Res., 1406 E. Washington St., 40206. Tel: 502-583-7401; Fax: 502-589-7465.
School—Tel: 502-583-0892; Fax: 502-583-4607. Dottie Clarke, Prin.
Lay Teachers 8; Students 110.

44—St. Lawrence, Rev. Robert L. Stuempel; Sr. Ann Marie Howard, O.S.B., Pastoral Assoc.; Deacon James H. Abell.
Res., 1925 Lewiston Dr., 40216. Tel: 502-448-2122.
School—Tel: 502-447-3155; Fax: 502-447-3155. Judy Thomas, Prin.
Religious 1; Lay Teachers 21; Students 401.

45—St. Leo the Great. Closed. For inquiries for parish records contact St. John Vianney, Louisville.

46—St. Leonard, Rev. James F. Hackett; Mr. Robert G. Dever, Pastoral Assoc.
Res., 440 Zorn Ave., 40206. Tel: 502-897-2595; Fax: 502-896-8259.
School—Tel: 502-897-5265. Ms. Lynn Wilt, Prin.
Lay Teachers 13; Students 162.

47—St. Louis Bertrand, Revs. Charles H. O'Brien, O.P.; George G. Christian, O.P.; Daniel J. Kennedy, O.P.; Robert R. Blais, O.P.; Carl Louis Mason, O.P.; James Vincent Watson, O.P.
Res., 1104 S. 6th St., 40203. Tel: 502-583-4448; Fax: 502-583-6874.
Shrine—Lourdes Rosary Shrine, Inc., Tel: 502-583-1950.

48—St. Luke, Rev. Richard P. Berding.
Res., 4211 Jim Hawkins Dr., 40229. Tel: 502-969-3291.

49—St. Margaret Mary, Very Rev. Bernard J. Breen; Revs. T. Michael Tobin; William J. Brennan; Deacon John L. Simpson.
Res., 7813 Shelbyville Rd., P.O. Box 6387, 40206. Tel: 502-426-1588; Fax: 502-426-1503.
School—Tel: 502-426-2635. Ann Kalmey, Prin.
Lay Teachers 29; Students 492.

50—St. Martha, Rev. John D. Deatrick; Senior Deacon James D. Bennett, (Retired); Deacons Raymond G. Kramer, Pastoral Assoc.; Charles K. Brown; John P. Maher.
Res., 2825 Klondike Ln., 40218. Tel: 502-491-8535; Fax: 502-491-8536.
School—Tel: 502-491-3171. Sharon Dutton, Prin.
Lay Teachers 23; Students 524.

51—St. Martin, Rev. Dennis Cousens.
Res., 639 S. Shelby St., 40202. Tel: 502-582-2827; Fax: 502-582-1780.

52—St. Martin de Porres. Consolidated with St. Benedict, Louisville, St. Charles Borromeo, Louisville, and Holy Cross, Louisville, parishes. Rev. James Flynn; Deacon James Turner, Pastoral Admin.; Sr. Dorothy Jackson, S.C.N., Pastoral Assoc.; Deacon Frederick Higgins.
Mailing Address: 3112 W. Broadway, 40211. Tel: 502-778-1118.

53—St. Mary (Bullitt Co.), Rev. Robert M. Abel; Deacons Paul J. George; Kenneth J. Mitchell.
Res., 299 Crestwood Ln., 40229. Tel: 502-957-3385; Fax: 502-957-3385.

54—St. Mary Magdalen. See separate listing under Oratories.

55—St. Matthias, Gene Scheich; Sr. Joan Riedley, O.S.U., Pastoral Assoc.
Res., 2200 Dixie Hwy., 40210. Tel: 502-776-3250.

56—Most Blessed Sacrament, Rev. John U. Caskey; Deacon Harry Prestwood.
Res., 3509 Taylor Blvd., 40215. Tel: 502-361-0149; Fax: 502-375-1076.
School—1128 Berry Blvd., 40215. Tel: 502-361-7103; Fax: 502-367-1513. Michael Rouse, Prin.
Lay Teachers 12; Students 240.
Convent—1126 Berry Blvd., 40215. Tel: 502-368-6634.

57—Mother of Good Counsel, Rev. John T. Judie; Deacons Patrick Harris; Charles Voll; Joseph Raibert.
Res., 8509 Westport Rd., 40242. Tel: 502-425-2210; Fax: 502-425-0941.
School—Tel: 502-425-2637. Michael J. Doran, Prin.
Lay Teachers 25; Students 462.

58—Our Lady, Rev. Robert E. Reilly.
Res., 3511 Rudd Ave., 40212. Tel: 502-776-4666; Fax: 502-776-7746.

59—Our Lady of Lourdes, Revs. Robert E. Osborne; William Miller; Deacons Norbert Miller; Ben Thornbury, (Retired). In res., Rev. Robert Dale Cieslik.
Res., 512 Breckenridge Ln., 40207. Tel: 502-896-0241; Fax: 502-895-5435.
School—Tel: 502-895-5122; Fax: 502-893-5051. Bernadette Ritchey, Prin.
Lay Teachers 24; Students 480.

60—Our Lady of Mount Carmel, Revs. Niles J. Gillen, O.Carm.; Thomas Butler, O.Carm.; Bro. Thomas J. Conlon, O.Carm.
Res., 7333 Southside Dr., 40214. Tel: 502-366-5651; Fax: 502-368-9972.
School—Tel: 502-368-8506. Carol Nord, Prin.
Lay Teachers 25; Students 560.

61—Our Mother of Sorrows, Revs. John W. Hanrahan; Henry C. Stuecker; Deacon Richard E. Steinmetz.
Res., 747 Harrison Ave., 40217. Tel: 502-637-7442.
School—(Grades PreK-8) 770 Eastern Pkwy., 40217. Tel: 502-637-7814; Fax: 502-636-0260. Denise Stead, Prin.
Lay Teachers 14; Students (Grades K-8) 205; Students (Preschool) 24.

62—St. Patrick, Revs. John L. Schindler; James W. Graf.
Res., 1000 N. Beckley Station Rd., 40245-4550. Tel: 502-244-6083; Fax: 502-244-6083.

63—St. Paul. Closed. For inquiries for parish records contact the Chancery.

64—St. Peter Claver, Rev. Patrick D. Delahanty, Admin.
Res., 526 Lampton St., 40203. Tel: 502-585-3910.

65—St. Philip Neri. Closed. For inquiries for parish records contact St. Elizabeth of Hungary, Louisville.

66—St. Pius X, Revs. Charles D. Walker; Roger A. Boehmicke; William Martin Bowling; Sr. Mary Elaine Zehnder, S.C.N., Pastoral Assoc.
Res., 3521 Goldsmith Ln., 40220. Tel: 502-451-4124.
School—Tel: 502-452-1712; Fax: 502-451-2462. Patrice Super, Prin.
Lay Teachers 26; Students 456.

67—St. Raphael the Archangel, Revs. Kevin J. Bryan; Philip L. Erickson; John A. Dalton; Deacon Jim Sturgeon.
Res., 2141 Lancashire Ave., 40205. Tel: 502-451-2864.
Parish Offices: 2121 Lancashire Ave, 40205. Tel: 502-458-2500; Fax: 502-458-8049.
School—Tel: 502-456-1541. Paul DeZarn, Prin.
Lay Teachers 40; Students 589.

68—Resurrection D.N.J.C., Revs. Raymond Hofmann, C.R.; Norman Choate, C.R.
Res., 4601 Poplar Level Rd., 40213. Tel: 502-968-5483; Fax: 502-969-6375.

69—St. Rita, Revs. William J. Martin; Emmet Linden, C.P.; Deacon Charles "Mack" Nevitt, Pastoral Assoc.
Res., 8709 Preston Hwy., 40219. Tel: 502-969-4579.
School—Tel: 502-969-7067. Laura Glaser, Prin.
Lay Teachers 20; Students 421.

70—SS. Simon and Jude, Rev. William F. Wagner; Sr. Ann Carol Mann, S.C.N., Pastoral Assoc.
Res., 4335 Hazelwood Ave., 40215. Tel: 502-368-4887; Fax: 502-375-1988.
School—Tel: 502-366-2424. Sr. M. Michelle Duvall, Prin.
Lay Teachers 14; Students 226.

71—St. Stephen, Martyr, Rev. James J. Lichtefeld; Deacon Sylvester Nitzken.
Res., 1000 English Ave., 40217. Tel: 502-635-5813; 635-5888.
School—2931 Pindell, 40217. Tel: 502-635-7141.
Lay Teachers 23; Students 425.

72—St. Therese, Revs. H. Anthony Olges; Robert B. Gray; Herman J. Naber.
Res., 1010 Schiller Ave., 40204. Tel: 502-634-3671; Fax: 502-634-3672.

73—St. Thomas More, Revs. James Wayne Murphy, Admin.; Donald J. Fisher; Deacon Michael A. Tolbert.
Res., 6105 S. Third St., 40214. Tel: 502-366-1463; Fax: 502-363-3719.
School—226 Inverness Ave., 40214. Tel: 502-363-3719. Mrs. Donna Sansone, Prin.
Lay Teachers 11; Students 247.

74—St. Vincent de Paul. See separate listing under Oratories.

75—St. William, Mr. James J. Butler, Pastoral Admin.
Res., 2650 Six Mile Ln., 40220. Tel: 502-491-0052.
1226 W. Oak St., 40210.

OUTSIDE THE CITY OF LOUISVILLE

Albany, Clinton Co., Emmanuel Catholic, Rev. Lawrence J. Gelthaus.
Res., Hwy. 127 N., P.O. Box 126, 42602. Tel: 606-387-7251.
Mission—Burkesville, Cumberland Co., Holy Cross Catholic, 264 Glasgow Rd., P.O. Box 197, Burkesville, 42717. Tel: 502-864-4107.

Bardstown, Nelson Co., St. Joseph, Revs. William F. Medley; Terry Lee Langford; Deacons Richard J. Walsh; John Hamilton.
Res., P.O. Box 548, 310 W. Stephen Foster Ave., 40004. Tel: 502-348-3126; Fax: 502-349-0941. [CEM]

School—Tel: 502-348-5994; Fax: 502-348-5994.
Sisters of Charity of Nazareth 2; Lay Teachers 19; Students 450.
High School—Tel: 502-348-8594; Fax: 502-349-1247.
Sisters of Charity 4; Lay Teachers 21; Students 295.

St. Monica, Revs. Stephen A. Pohl; Joseph Irvin Mouser; Deacon Samuel R. Filiatreau, Pastoral Admin.
Res., 407 S. Third St., 40004. Tel: 502-348-5250.

Brandenburg, Meade Co., St. John the Apostle, Rev. John A. Barker; Deacon J. Michael Jones.
Res., P.O. Box 565, 40108. Tel: 502-422-2196; Fax: 502-422-2471. [CEM]
School—513 E. Broadway, 40108. Tel: 502-422-2088.
Augustinian Sisters, Servants of Jesus and Mary 4; Lay Teachers 4; Students 196.

Calvary, Marion Co., Holy Name of Mary, Rev. Joseph I. Dawson.
Res., 3265 Hwy. 208, Lebanon, 40033. Tel: 502-692-2298. [CEM]
Missions—Phillipsburg, Marion Co., Our Lady of Fatima; Spurlington, Taylor Co., St. Frances de Sales. [CEM 2]
Station—Lebanon, Parish Center, Tel: 502-692-6491.

Campbellsville, Taylor Co., Our Lady of Perpetual Help, Rev. John A. Caldwell; Deacon Joseph Ohnemus.
Office: 425 N. Central Ave., 42719. Tel: 502-465-4282. [CEM]

Cecilia, Hardin Co., St. Ambrose, Rev. Stanley L. Osborne, Admin.
Res., c/o 657 St. John Church Rd., Elizabethtown, 42701. Tel: 502-862-9816.

Clementsville, Casey Co., St. Bernard, Rev. Joseph S. Hall.
Res., Rte. 8, Box 244, Liberty, 42539. Tel: 606-787-7570.
Mission—Liberty, Casey Co., Sacred Heart, Tel: 606-787-7324.

Culvertown, Nelson Co., Immaculate Conception, Rev. Lawrence H. Lindle.
Res., 8191 New Haven Rd., New Haven, 40051-6030. Tel: 502-549-3757; Fax: 502-549-7258.
Mission—Bardstown, Nelson Co., St. Mark. Closed. For information contact Immaculate Conception, Culvertown.

Edmonton, Metcalfe Co., Christ the Healer, Rev. John J. Stoltz.
Res., 1610 W. Stockton St., 42129. Tel: 502-432-5024.
Mission—Tompkinsville, Monroe Co., Christ the King, P.O. Box 548, Tompkinsville, 42167. Tel: 502-487-8881.

Elizabethtown, Hardin Co., St. James, Revs. J. Richard Sullivan; Jeffrey S. Nicolas; Charles E. Reteneller; Deacons Jay Jenkins; Joseph Chathaparampil; William Clark.
Res., 307 W. Dixie Ave., 42701. Tel: 502-765-6268; Fax: 502-765-6268. [CEM]
School—114 N. Miles St., 42701. Tel: 502-765-7011; Fax: 502-769-5745.
Religious Teachers 1; Lay Teachers 17; Students 356.

Fairdale, Jefferson Co., St. Jerome, Revs. J. Roy Stiles, Admin.; Robert E. Ray.
Res., 903 Fairdale Rd., 40118. Tel: 502-363-9929.

Fairfield, Nelson Co., St. Michael, Revs. Donald L. Ryan; Albert J. Hartlage.
Res., P.O. Box 27, 40020. Tel: 502-252-8308. [CEM]
Mission—Taylorsville, Spencer Co., All Saints , 410 W. Main St., P.O. Box 531, 40071. Tel: 502-477-6676. [CEM]
Rev. Donald L. Ryan, Admin.

Finley, Taylor Co., Our Lady of the Hills, Rev. John A. Caldwell.
Office: 425 N. Central Ave., Campbellsville, 42718. Tel: 502-465-4282. [CEM]

Flaherty, Meade Co., St. Martin of Tours, Rev. Thomas A. Smith; Deacon John R. Whelan.
Res., 440 Saint Martin Rd., Vine Grove, 40175. Tel: 502-828-2552; Fax: 502-828-2562. [CEM]

Glasgow, Barren Co., St. Helen, Rev. Kenneth Frye, C.P.M.; Deacons Jack Hawkins; Lee Bidwell.
Res., 103 W. Brown St., 42141. Tel: 502-651-5263.
Mission—Horse Cave, Hart Co., Our Lady of the Caves Church, Rte. 31 W., Horse Cave, 42749.

Goshen, Oldham Co., Transfiguration of Our Lord, Rev. Herbert L. Lattis; Deacons Joseph F. Stuber; David Tomes.
Res., 1620 S. Hwy. 1793, 40026. Tel: 502-228-8665; Fax: 502-228-0355.

Greensburg, Green Co., Holy Redeemer, Rev. John A. Caldwell; Deacon Joseph Ohnemus.
Office: 425 N. Central Ave., Campbellsville, 42718-0484. Tel: 502-465-4282.
Church—110 Industrial Rd., 42743.

Hodgenville, Larue Co., Our Lady of Mercy, Rev. James T. Mudd; Deacon John Kromer.
Res., 208 Walters Ave., 42748. Tel: 502-358-4697. [CEM]

Holy Cross, Marion Co., Holy Cross, Sr. Mary Ellen Curl, R.S.M., Pastoral Admin.; Rev. James A. Covert.
Res., 3560 N. Saint Francis Rd., Loretto, 40037. Tel: 502-865-2521; Fax: 502-865-2521. [CEM]

Howardstown, Nelson Co., St. Ann, Rev. James T. Mudd, Admin. In res., Rev. Robert A. Brown.
Res., 7490 Howardstown Rd., 40051. Tel: 502-549-3285. [CEM]
School—(Grades 1-8). Tel: 502-549-7310.
Lay Teachers 3; Students 60.

Jamestown, Russell Co., Holy Spirit, Rev. Daniel L. Lincoln; Sr. Marietta Wethington, O.S.U., Pastoral Assoc.; Deacon Jerry Antle.
Res., 406 N. Main St., P.O. Box 247, 42629. Tel: 502-343-3346.
Mission—Columbia, Adair Co., Good Shepherd, P.O. Box 354, Columbia, 42728. Tel: 502-384-4528. Sr. Judith A. Prindiville, C.S.C., Pastoral Assoc.

Jeffersontown, Jefferson Co., St. Edward, Rev. Frank J. Eimer; Deacons Martin Brown; Peter Houck.
Res., 9608 Sue Helen Dr., 40299. Tel: 502-267-7494; Fax: 502-267-7495. [CEM]
School—Tel: 502-267-6633. Susan Jones, Prin.
Lay Teachers 26; Students 545.

St. Michael, Rev. William S. Griner; Agnes Tompkins, Pastoral Assoc.
Res., 12707 Taylorsville Rd., 40299. Tel: 502-266-5611 (Rectory & Parish Office); Fax: 502-267-9550.
Parish Activity Center & Church—Tel: 502-267-9550.

LaGrange, Oldham Co., Immaculate Conception, Rev. Michael D. Lott.
Res., 502 N. Fifth St., 40031. Tel: 502-222-0255; Fax: 502-222-0421.
School—Tel: 502-222-0671. Elizabeth Kenobbie, Prin.
Lay Teachers 9; Students 121.
Mission—Bedford, Trimble Co., St. Matthew, Rte. 2, Bedford, 40006. Tel: 502-255-7369.
Stations—LaGrange, Luther Luckett Correctional Center, Tel: 502-222-0363; Kentucky State Reformatory, Tel: 502-222-9441; Roederer Farm Prison, Tel: 502-222-0173; Cedar Lake Lodge, Tel: 502-222-7157; Tri-County Community Hospital, Tel: 502-222-5388.

Lebanon, Marion Co., St. Augustine, Very Revs. Charles C. Thompson; J. Mark Spalding; Deacon Tom Mattingly.
Res., 235 S. Spalding Ave., 40033. Tel: 502-692-4986; Fax: 502-692-5532. [CEM]
School—(Grades 1-8). Tel: 502-692-2063. Mary Gardner, Prin.
Lay Teachers 15; Students 252.

Lebanon Junction, Bullitt Co., St. Benedict, Rev. Gerald L. Bell.
Res., 139 N. Brook St., 40150. Tel: 502-833-4886; Fax: 502-833-4886.
School—227 W. Oak St., 40150. Tel: 502-833-4926. Iris Whitney, Prin.
Lay Teachers 4; Students 77.
Mission—St. Clare. See separate listing under Oratories. [CEM]

Mount Washington, Bullitt Co., St. Francis Xavier, Rev. James E. Hargadon.
Res., 155 Stringer Ln., 40047. Tel: 502-538-4933; Fax: 502-955-5366. [CEM]

New Haven, Nelson Co., St. Catherine, Rev. Clarence J. Howard; Deacon George B. Clark.
Res., P.O. Box 88, 40051. Tel: 502-549-3152; Fax: 502-549-5410. [CEM]
School—413 First St., P.O. Box 88, 40051. Tel: 502-549-3680.
Sisters 1; Lay Teachers 10; Students 186.

New Hope, Nelson Co., St. Vincent de Paul, Rev. Clarence J. Howard, Admin.; Deacon Edward J. Hutchins.
Res., 101 Church St., 40052. Tel: 502-549-3152; Fax: 502-549-5410. [CEM]

Payneville, Meade Co., St. Mary Magdalen of Pazzi, Rev. James R. Schook; Deacon Joseph Padgett.
Res., 110 Hwy. 376, 40157. Tel: 502-496-4333; Fax: 502-496-4790. [CEM]

Pewee Valley, Oldham Co., St. Aloysius, Revs. Vincent J. Schweizer; John W. Dickman; Frederick W. Klotter; Deacon Francis E. Klosterman.
Res., 202 Mount Mercy Dr., P.O. Box 468, 40056. Tel: 502-241-8452; Fax: 502-243-1740. [CEM]
School—Tel: 502-241-8516; Fax: 502-243-2241.
Lay Teachers 17; Students 288.
Stations—Pewee Valley, Kentucky Correctional Institute for Women; Friendship Manor Nursing Home, Tel: 502-241-8821.

Pleasure Ridge Park, Jefferson Co., St. Paul, Rev. Maurice Hayes, O.F.M.Conv. In res., Revs. James Kent, O.F.M.Conv.; Raymond Mallett, O.F.M.Conv.
Res., 6901 Dixie Hwy., 40258. Tel: 502-935-1223; Fax: 502-933-7747.
School—Tel: 502-935-5511; Fax: 502-935-5596.
Lay Teachers 11; Students 246.

St. Polycarp, Rev. William P. Burks; Deacons Jon Hosch; Tony Hasson.
Res., 7718 Columbine Dr., 40258. Tel: 502-935-4578; Fax: 502-933-1093.
School—Tel: 502-935-2022. Thomas Boone, Prin.
Lay Teachers 19; Students 374.

Radcliff, Hardin Co., St. Christopher, Rev. B. Leo Craycroft.
Res., 1138 Thomas St., 40160. Tel: 502-351-3706. [CEM]
School—1181 S. Wilson Rd., 40160. Tel: 502-351-3150.
Lay Teachers 8; Students 150.

Raywick, Marion Co., St. Francis Xavier Church, Revs. Vincent P. Dentinger, Admin.; Ernest Schumacher, C.R.
Res., 108 Main St., 40060. Tel: 502-692-2245. [CEM]

Rhodelia, Meade Co., St. Theresa, Rev. James R. Schook, Admin. Pastors Emeriti: Revs. Albert L. Wilson; James R. Meder.
Res., 9245 Rhodelia Rd., Payneville, 40157. Tel: 502-496-4343. [CEM]
Convent—Tel: 502-496-4314. Sisters of Charity of Nazareth

St. Francis, Marion Co., St. Francis of Assisi, Sr. Mary Ellen Curl, R.S.M., Pastoral Admin.; Rev. James A. Covert.
Res., 6785 Hwy. 52, 40062. Tel: 502-865-2521; Fax: 502-865-2521. [CEM]

St. John, Hardin Co., St. John the Baptist, Rev. Stanley L. Osborne; Deacon Michael Vessels.
Res., 657 St. John Church Rd., Elizabethtown, 42701. Tel: 502-862-9816. [CEM]

St. Joseph, Marion Co., St. Joseph. Closed. For inquiries for parish records contact St. Francis Xavier, Raywick.

St. Mary, Marion Co., St. Charles, Revs. Vincent P. Dentinger; Ernest Schumacher, C.R.; Deacon Joseph R. Dant.
Res., 675 Hwy. 327, Lebanon, 40033. Tel: 502-692-4513. [CEM]

St. Thomas, Nelson Co., St. Thomas, Revs. Stephen A. Pohl; J. Irvin Mouser; Deacon David Newton.
Res., 870 Saint Thomas Ln., Bardstown, 40004. Tel: 502-348-3717; Fax: 502-348-1905.
School—(Grades K-8).
Sisters 1; Lay Teachers 6; Students 89.

Samuels, Nelson Co., St. Gregory, Rev. Trumie Culpepper Elliott; Deacon Joseph E. Livers.
Parish Office: 330 Samuels Loop, Cox's Creek, 40013. Tel: 502-348-6337. [CEM]
School—Tel: 502-348-9583.
Lay Teachers 8; Students 139.

Shelbyville, Shelby Co., Annunciation of the Blessed Virgin Mary, Rev. C. Joseph Batcheldor.
Res., 105 W. Main St., 40065. Tel: 502-633-1547.
Mission—Eminence, Henry Co., St. John Chrysostom, 122 Penn St., Eminence, 40019.

Shepherdsville, Bullitt Co., St. Aloysius, Rev. Gerald L. Bell.
Res., 187 Plum St., 40165. Tel: 502-543-5918; 955-6370.
School—197 Plum St., 40165. Tel: 502-543-6721.
Lay Teachers 11; Students 239.

Springfield, Washington Co.,

1—St. Dominic, Rev. Leon C. Spalding.
Res., 303 W. Main St., 40069. Tel: 606-336-3569; Fax: 606-336-7169. [CEM]
School—Tel: 606-336-7165.
Lay Teachers 10; Students 244.

2—Holy Rosary, Rev. Patrick J. Dolan; Deacon Ernest Cooper.
Mailing Address: Box 146, 40069. Tel: 606-336-3898.

3—Holy Trinity, Rev. Christopher Allegra.
Res., 306 Fredericktown Rd., 40069. Tel: 606-284-5242. [CEM]
Mission—Manton, Washington Co., Holy Rosary. [CEM]

4—St. Rose, Rev. Thomas Bernard Smith, O.P. In res., Revs. Gerard Arthur Lessard, O.P.; William Brandon Tarrier, O.P.
Res., Hwy. 152, P.O. Box 71, 40069. Tel: 606-336-3121; Fax: 606-336-3841. [CEM]

Valley Station, Jefferson Co.,

1—ST. CLEMENT, Revs. Harry J. Gelthaus; Thomas Donohue.
Res., 5431 Johnsontown Rd., 40272-3400. Tel: 502-937-5920; Fax: 502-937-5927.
School—Tel: 502-937-1616; Fax: 502-995-3227.
Lay Teachers 14; Students 256.

2—OUR LADY HELP OF CHRISTIANS, Rev. Thomas R. Clark, Admin.; Deacon Robert L. Burns, Pastoral Assoc.
Res., 13512 Dixie Hwy., 40272. Tel: 502-937-1818.
Mission—West Point, Hardin Co., St. Patrick Church, 1216 Main St., West Point, 40177.

3—OUR LADY OF CONSOLATION, Rev. Donald W. Springman; Deacon Wayne Thieneman.
Res., 10801 Deering Rd., 40272. Tel: 502-937-2100.
School—Tel: 502-937-7400; Fax: 502-937-6588.
Lay Teachers 9; Students 193.

4—ST. TIMOTHY, Rev. Thomas R. Clark.
Res., 10300 Lower River Rd., 40272. Tel: 502-937-1238.

Vine Grove, Hardin Co., St. Brigid, Rev. Thomas A. Smith, Admin.; Deacon James Benton.
Res., 306 E. Main St., 40175. Tel: 502-877-2461; Fax: 502-828-2562. [CEM]
School—Tel: 502-877-2451; Fax: 502-877-6864.
Lay Teachers 7; Students 111.

White Mills, Hardin Co., St. Ignatius, Revs. J. Richard Sullivan; Jeffrey S. Nicolas; Charles E. Reteneller; Deacon Jay Jenkins.
Mailing Address: P.O. Box 64, 42788. Tel: 502-369-6279.
Res., 307 W. Dixie Ave., Elizabethtown, 42701. Tel: 502-765-6268; Fax: 502-765-6268. [CEM]

Oratories

1—ST. MARY MAGDALEN, Jefferson Co. Closed. For inquiries for parish records contact the Chancery.

2—ST. VINCENT DE PAUL, Jefferson Co. Closed. For inquiries for parish records contact St. Elizabeth of Hungary, Louisville.

3—ST. CLARE, Hardin Co. Closed. For inquiries for parish records contact St. Benedict, Lebanon Junction.

Chaplains of Public Institutions

LOUISVILLE. *Alliant Medical Pavillion*. Rev. C. Thomas Clark.
Audubon Regional Medical Center. Attended by St. Pius X. Rev. Roger A. Boehmicke.
Baptist Hospital East. Attended by Our Lady of Lourdes. Rev. Robert E. Osborne.
Caritas Medical Center. Rev. Joseph H. Stoltz.
Central State Hospital Lakeland Rd., 40223. Tel: 502-245-4121. Rev. James W. Graf, Chap.
Jewish Hospital. Rev. John B. Gephart.
Kosair-Children's Hospital. Rev. John B. Gephart.
Norton Hospital. Rev. John B. Gephart; Deacon Wheatley, Chap.
Southwest Hospital. Attended by Our Lady of Consolation.
Suburban Hospital. Attended by Ascension.
University Hospital. Rev. James E. Wafzig.
Vencor Hospital. Rev. Joseph H. Voor.

On Special Assignment:
Reverend Fathers—
Clark, Daniel C., Passionist Community, 1924 Newburg Rd., Louisville, KY 40205
Hayden, Joseph F., 7505 Westport Rd., Louisville, KY 40222
Hogan, Timothy A., Catholic Charities, 2911 S. Fourth St., Louisville, KY 40208
Hommrich, Thomas A., 2543 Ellsworth Ave., Louisville, KY 40217
Jones, John E., Taylor Wood Rd., Box 352, Finchville, KY 40022
Rice, George N., 214 Eline Ave., Louisville, KY 40207
Wimsett, Scott J., 10640 New Haven Rd., New Haven, KY 40051

On Duty Outside the Archdiocese:
Reverend Fathers—
Branch, Edward B., Office of Campus Ministry, Catholic Center at Atlanta University Complex, 1526 Westwood Ave. S.W., Atlanta, GA 30310. Tel: 404-775-9394
Brown, James J., St. Margaret Church, 122 W. Hawk Ave., Pharr, TX 78577
Dittmeier, Charles R., Bishop Ford Center, Tung Tau Tsuen, Kowloon, Hong Kong

---

Military Chaplains:
Reverend Fathers—
Brown, Benedict J., U.S. Navy

Retired:
Reverend Monsignors—
Horrigan, Alfred F., 1826 Edenside Ave., Louisville, KY 40204
O'Bryan, J. A., Rte. 1, Box 111, McDaniels, KY 40152
Reverend Fathers—
Birkel, Robert C., 7496 Stiles Rd., Howardstown, KY 40051
Boehmicke, Roger A., 3521 Goldsmith Ln., Louisville, KY 40220
Bowling, George K., 15 Audubon Plaza Dr., Louisville, KY 40217
Brennan, William J., St. Margaret Mary Church, P.O. Box 6387, Louisville, KY 40206
Brian, Bertrand J., Nazareth Village II, P.O. Box 2000, #22, Nazareth, KY 40048
Brown, Robert A., St. Ann Church, 7490 Howardstown Rd., Howardstown, KY 40051
Caldwell, William T., 3320 Bardstown Rd., No. 82, Louisville, KY 40218
Cecil, Ivo E., 1080 Optimist Rd., Lebanon Junction, KY 40150
Clark, C. Thomas, 1900 Bashford Manor Ln., Apt. G-77, Louisville, KY 40218
Craycroft, George P., 229 N. Main St., New Haven, KY 40051
Creed, C. Patrick, 122 Tom Vittitow Ln., Bardstown, KY 40004
Deddens, Norbert J., Our Lady Queen of the Universe Church, 121 Garrison St., San Benito, TX 78586
Dentinger, Roy E., 1664 Beechwood Ave., Louisville, KY 40204
Dickman, John W., 202 Mount Mercy Dr., Pewee Valley, KY 40056
Diersen, William M., 1695 County Line Rd., N.E., Palmyra, IN 47164
Dollinger, Robert J., P.O. Box 75, Georgetown, PEI C0A 1L0 Canada
Donohue, Thomas E., 9104 Mahoney Dr., Louisville, KY 40258
Gephart, John B., Bishop David Apartments, 5146 Dixie Hwy., Louisville, KY 40216
Giesler, Linus T., Nazareth Home, 2000 Newburg Rd., Louisville, KY 40205
Grauel, Frank B., Holy Spirit Church, 3345 Lexington Rd., Louisville, KY 40206
Hamilton, Joseph K., 4208 Browns Ln., #206, Louisville, KY 40220
Hannifin, Francis M., 1730 N. Stillwell Rd., Boston, KY 40107
Hartlage, William C., Bishop David Apartments, 5146 Dixie Hwy., Louisville, KY 40216
Hogan, William E., 3320 Bardstown Rd., Apt. 52, Louisville, KY 40218
Howard, Anthony, 6304 Southside Dr., Louisville, KY 40214
Kelty, Charles J., 800 S. Fourth St., Apt. 2001, Louisville, KY 40203
Kotheimer, Alex L., 2526 Hawthorne Ave., Louisville, KY 40205
Lenahan, John B., 3931 S. Third St., Louisville, KY 40214
Lyon, Joseph A., Doe Valley Park, 228 Pine Ridge Pk., Brandenburg, KY 40108
Magel, John E., Royal Arms Apartments, #F-67, 1900 Bashford Manor Ln., Louisville, KY 40218
Maloney, James C., 2301 Goldsmith Ln., Louisville, KY 40218
Meder, James R., 125 Meder Ln., Payneville, KY 40157
Mills, Robert N., Rte. 1, P.O. Box 115, Elizabeth, IN 47117
Moert, Jerome S., Bishop David Apartments, 5146 Dixie Hwy., Louisville, KY 40216
Morgan, John H., 4308 Rudy Ln., Louisville, KY 40207
Nord, Clarence C., 2820 Flora Ave., #15, Louisville, KY 40220
Oyler, George F., 1500 Hurricane Hills, #A3, Boston, KY 40107
Pank, Julian F., 2832 Pomeroy Dr., Louisville, KY 40218
Rapp, Bertrand J., 2040 Buechel Bank Rd., Louisville, KY 40218
Riede, Clifford A., 1516 Hepburn Ave., Apt. 4, Louisville, KY 40204
Robertson, Vernon W., 1352 S. 6th St., Louisville, KY 40208
Russell, Paul M., Bishop David Apartments, 5146 Dixie Hwy., Louisville, KY 40216
Scherzer, Edwin J., Bishop David Apartments, 5146 Dixie Hwy., Louisville, KY 40216
Smith, F. Harold, 908 Wilmington Ave., Apt. 601, Dayton, OH 45520
Stuecker, Henry C., 747 Harrison Ave., Louisville, KY 40217
Thompson, James W., Bishop David Apartments, 5146 Dixie Hwy., Louisville, KY 40216
Voor, Joseph H., St. James Church, 1826 Edenside Ave., Louisville, KY 40204
Weyhing, John, 340 Causeway Blvd., #116, Dunedin, FL 34698-1781
Wilson, Albert, 980 Ray Rd., Payneville, KY 40157
Zahner, William, Bishop David Apartments, 5146 Dixie Hwy., Louisville, KY 40216

Permanent Deacons:
Abell, James H., St. Lawrence, Louisville
Antle, Jerry L., Holy Spirit, Jamestown; Good Shepherd, Columbia
Becker, Gary E., Epiphany
Bennett, James D., (Retired), St. Martha Church, Louisville
Benton, James L., St. Brigid, Vine Grove
Bidwell, Lee G., St. Helen, Glasgow
Bishop, Joseph C., St. Dominic/Holy Rosary, Springfield
Bissig, Paul F., St. Cecilia Church
Box, Thomas E., Jr., St. Bartholomew, Louisville
Brown, Charles K., St. Martha, Louisville
Brown, Martin J., All Saints, Taylorsville; Hospice of Louisville
Bryant, Robert C., St. Barnabas, Louisville; Jefferson County Jail
Burns, Robert L., Our Lady Help of Christians, Valley Station
Carney, Edward P., Unassigned
Caspar, Robert J., St. Christopher, Radcliff
Chathaparampil, Joseph, St. James Church, Elizabethtown
Churchill, John R., St. Augustine, Louisville
Clark, George B., St. Catherine, New Haven
Clark, William V., Family Ministries, St. James, Elizabethtown
Collard, Paul J., (Retired), Immaculate Conception, La Grange
Cooper, Ernest A., Holy Rosary, Springfield
Dalton, David L., St. Andrew, Louisville
Dant, Joseph R., St. Charles, St. Mary; St. Francis Xavier, Raywick
Dawson, Richard L., Christ the King, Louisville
Dever, Robert Glen, St. Leonard
Dew, Joseph M., Military Parish of St. Patrick, Fort Knox
Downs, William A., Immaculate Conception, Culvertown
Ebert, John P., Transfiguration of Our Lord, Prospect
Edwards, Michael, Ascension, Louisville
Fante, Lamar W., Holy Family, Louisville; Vicar for Senior Deacons
Fargen, J. Jerome, (Retired), St. James Church, Louisville
Filiatreau, Joseph H., St. Gregory, Samuels
Filiatreau, Samuel R., St. Monica, Bardstown
George, Paul J., St. Mary, Louisville
Hamilton, John, St. Joseph, Bardstown
Harris, Patrick D., Mother of Good Counsel, Louisville
Hasson, Anthony P., St. Polycarp, Pleasure Ridge Park
Hawkins, Jack W., (Retired), St. Helen, Glasgow
Higgins, Frederick, St. Martin de Porres, Louisville
Hosch, Jon E., St. Polycarp, Pleasure Ridge Park
Houck, Peter L., Chap., Kentucky State Reformatory; St. Edward, Jeffersontown
Hutchins, Joseph E., St. Vincent De Paul, New Hope
Ishmael, Raymond L., On Leave
Jenkins, Jay R., St. James, Elizabethtown
Jones, James M., St. John the Apostle, Brandenburg
Jones, Walton G., St. Francis of Assisi, Louisville
Kampschaefer, Robert M., St. Denis, Louisville
Klosterman, Francis E., (Retired), St. Aloysius Church, Pewee Valley
Klump, William R., Church of Our Lady, Louisville
Kramer, Raymond G., St. Martha, Louisville
Kromer, Raymond G., Our Lady of Mercy, Hodgenville; St. Ann, Howardstown
Lincoln, James Bruce, Spiritual Advisor Cursillo; St. Barnabas, Louisville
Livers, Joseph E., St. Gregory, Samuels
Logsdon, Raymond L., (Retired), St. Michael, Jeffersontown
Maher, John P., St. Martha, Louisville
Markert, Clarence Robert, St. Andrew, Louisville
Masterson, Donald E., St. Athanasius, Louisville
Mattingly, Thomas, St. Augustine, Lebannon
McCulloch, Thomas B., (Retired)
McGinty, David L., St. Helen, Louisville
Miller, Norbert F., Our Lady of Lourdes, Louisville
Mitchell, James B., (Retired)
Mitchell, Kenneth J., St. Mary, Louisville
Mullins, William L., St. Francis of Rome, Louisville

Murphy, Howard J., (Retired)
Nevitt, Charles, St. Rita, Louisville
Nitzken, Syl J., St. Stephen Martyr, Louisville
Ohnemus, Joseph, Our Lady of Perpetual Help, Campbellsville
Olrich, James Charles, St. Elizabeth Ann Seton Church, Louisville
Osborne, Kenneth F., On Leave
Padgett, Joseph E., St. Mary Magdalen of Pazzi, Payneville; St. Theresa, Rhodelia
Patterson, Daniel Eugene, Leave of Absence
Plummer, James R., St. Barnabas, Louisville
Prestwood, Harry, Most Blessed Sacrament, Louisville
Raibert, Joseph A., Mother of Good Counsel, Louisville
Ratterman, Cletus A., Guardian Angels, Louisville
Ronald, Edward R., Jefferson County Department of Corrections, Louisville
Ryan, Thomas, Catholic Deaf Office
Shutts, John F., (Retired), Caritas Medical Center, Louisville
Siers, Ronald R., (Retired)
Simpson, John L., Holy Trinity & St. Margaret Mary, Louisville
Skeeters, William L., St. Gabriel, Louisville
Stanley, Vincent G., St. Albert, Louisville; Catholic Charities
Steinmetz, Richard Earl, Our Mother of Sorrows, Louisville
Stuber, Joseph F., Transfiguration, Goshen
Sturgeon, James C., Sr., St. Raphael, Louisville
Thieneman, C. Wayne, Our Lady of Consolation, Valley Station
Thomas, William A., (Retired), Church of the Resurrection, Louisville
Thornbury, Benjamin, Our Lady of Lourdes, Louisville
Tolbert, Michael A., St. Thomas More, Louisville
Tomes, David R., Transfiguration, Prospect
Turner, James R., St. Martin de Porres, Louisville
Vessels, Michael, St. John the Baptist, Rineyville; St. Ambrose, Cecilia
Voll, Charles Joseph, Mother of Good Counsel, Louisville
Walsh, Richard J., St. Joseph, Bardstown; Flaget Hospital
Walther, Charles F., St. Jerome, Fairdale
Ward, Kenneth M., St. Albert the Great, Louisville
Wheatley, Joseph P., Norton Hospital & Kosair Children's Hospital, Louisville
Whelan, John R., St. Martin of Tours, Flaherty
Wright, J. Patrick, Cathedral of the Assumption, Louisville
Young, R. James, St. Ignatius Martyr, Louisville

INSTITUTIONS LOCATED IN THE ARCHDIOCESE

[A] COLLEGES AND UNIVERSITIES

LOUISVILLE. *Bellarmine College*, 2001 Newburg Rd., 40205-0671. Tel: 502-452-8211
For a complete listing, refer to the Colleges and Universities section.

Spalding University, 851 S. 4th St., 40203. Tel: 502-585-9911; Fax: 502-585-7158
For a complete listing, refer to the Colleges and Universities section.

ST. CATHARINE. *St. Catharine College*, 2735 Bardstown Rd., 40061. Tel: 606-336-5082
For a complete listing, refer to the Colleges and Universities section.

[B] HIGH SCHOOLS, DIOCESAN

LOUISVILLE. *Holy Cross High School*, 5144 Dixie Hwy., 40216. Tel: 502-447-4363. Mr. George Pressey, Pres.; Mrs. Terry Crawley, Prin. Sisters 1; Lay Teachers 20; Students 340.

St. Francis DeSales High School, 425 Kenwood Dr., 40214. Tel: 502-368-6519. Mr. George Pressey, Pres.; Mr. Martin Minogue, Prin. Lay Teachers 24; Students 405.

The Carmelite Community of The St. Francis De-Sales Priory. Tel: 502-368-6553. Revs. Kyrin Caggiano, O.Carm., Faculty, DeSales High School; Nelson Belizario, O.Carm., Campus Min., Bellarmine College.

Trinity High School, 4011 Shelbyville Rd., 40207. Tel: 502-895-9427. Mr. Peter Flaig, Pres.; Mr. David Winkler, Prin.; Revs. Ronald J. Domhoff; R. Joseph Hemmerle; David H. Zettel. Priests 3; Lay Teachers 67; Students 1,043.

BARDSTOWN. *Bethlehem High School*, 40004. Tel: 502-348-8594. Sisters of Charity of Nazareth. William B. Hart, III, Prin. Sisters 3; Lay Teachers 21; Students 285.

[C] HIGH SCHOOLS, PRIVATE

LOUISVILLE. *Academy of Our Lady of Mercy*, 1176 E. Broadway, 40204. Tel: 502-584-4273. Mr. Michael C. Johnson, Prin.; Melinda C. Ernstberger, Asst. Prin. Sisters of Mercy 1; Lay Teachers 22; Students 286.

Assumption High School, 2170 Tyler Ln., 40205. Tel: 502-458-9551; Fax: 502-454-8411. Sisters of Mercy. Ms. Karen Russ, Prin. Lay Teachers 72; Students 918.

Holy Rosary Academy, 4801 Southside Dr., 40214. Tel: 502-366-4561. Dr. Karen M. Juliano, Prin. Sisters of St. Dominic (St. Catharine, KY) 2; Lay Teachers 18; Girls 201.

Presentation Academy, 861 S. 4th St., 40203. Tel: 502-583-5935; Fax: 502-583-1342.
Spalding University. Sisters 4; Lay Teachers 28; Students 401.

Sacred Heart Academy, 3175 Lexington Rd., 40206. Tel: 502-897-6097. Ursuline Sisters. Sr. Paula Kleine-Kracht, O.S.U., Prin. Sisters 2; Lay Teachers 45; Students 720.

St. Xavier High School, Xaverian Brothers, 1609 Poplar Level Rd., 40217. Tel: 502-637-4712. Bro. James M. Kelly, C.F.X., Pres.; Mr. Perry E. Sangalli, Prin. Priests 2; Brothers 8; Lay Teachers 85; Students 1,480.

[D] CONSOLIDATED SCHOOLS

LOUISVILLE. *Community Catholic School*, 2530 Slevin St., 40212. Tel: 502-778-1941. Sr. Barbara Von Bokern, S.C.N., Prin. Religious 1; Lay Teachers 8; Students 124. Children from St. Cecilia and Our Lady attend this school.

[E] ELEMENTARY SCHOOLS, PRIVATE

LOUISVILLE. *Holy Angels Academy, Inc.*, 1408 S. Second St., 40208. Tel: 502-634-3223. Principals: Joseph M. Norton, (Grade School); Marilyn G. Malone, (High School). Sisters 5; Lay Teachers 14; Students 174.

Mercy Montessori School, 2181 Tyler Ln., 40205. Tel: 502-459-6545. Sr. Mary Alicia McGinty, R.S.M., Dir. Students 80.

Sacred Heart Model School, 3121 Lexington Rd., 40206. Tel: 502-896-3959. Dr. Sarah Wannemuehler, Prin. Lay Teachers 39; Students 354.

Thomas Merton Academy, 4605 Poplar Level Rd., 40213. 6010 Preston Hwy., 40219. Rev. Raymond Hofmann, C.R.; Ann R. Thompson, Prin. Lay Teachers 12; Students 206.

Ursuline Montessori School, 3105 Lexington Rd., 40206. Tel: 502-896-3941. Sr. Delores Kemper, O.S.U., Admin. Students 96.

NAZARETH. *Nazareth Montessori Children's Center*, P.O. Box 44, 40048. Tel: 502-348-1540. Sr. Patricia Marie Hill, S.C.N., Dir. Sisters 2; Lay Teachers 5; Students 62.

[F] SPECIAL SCHOOLS

LOUISVILLE. *Pitt Academy*, 4605 Poplar Level Rd., 40213. Tel: 502-966-6979. Mrs. Doris Swenson, Prin. Sisters 1; Lay Teachers 8; Students 62.

St. Angela Education Center, 1731 Edenside Ave., 40204-1595. Tel: 502-459-9725. Sr. Jean Gertrude Mudd, O.S.U., Dir. Students 7.

St. Joseph Child Development Center, 2823 Frankfort Ave., 40206. Tel: 502-893-0241. Mimi Orr, Dir. Students 185.

Ursuline Child Development Center, 3105 Lexington Rd., 40206. Tel: 502-895-7798. Sr. Vera Del Grande, O.S.U., Dir. Students 150.

Ursuline School of Music and Drama, 3105 Lexington Rd., 40206. Tel: 502-897-1816. Anna Jo Paul, Dir. Students 336.

[G] ORPHANAGES AND INFANT HOMES

LOUISVILLE. *St. Joseph Catholic Orphan Society*, 2823 Frankfort Ave., 40206. Tel: 502-893-0241; Fax: 502-896-2394
For a complete listing, refer to the Special Care Facilities section.

St. Joseph Children's Home, 2823 Frankfort Ave., 40206. Tel: 502-893-0241; Fax: 502-896-2394
For a complete listing, refer to the Special Care Facilities section.

St. Thomas Orphan Society, Inc., P.O. Box 1073, 40201
For a complete listing, refer to the Special Care Facilities section.

St. Vincent's Orphan Society, Inc., P.O. Box 1073, 40201
For a complete listing, refer to the Special Care Facilities section.

[H] GENERAL HOSPITALS

LOUISVILLE. *Caritas Medical Center*, 1850 Bluegrass Ave., 40215. Tel: 502-361-6000
For a complete listing, refer to the Hospitals section.

BARDSTOWN. *Flaget Memorial Hospital*, 40004. Tel: 502-348-3923, Ext. 4641
For a complete listing, refer to the Hospitals section.

[I] SPECIAL HOSPITALS

LOUISVILLE. *Caritas Health Services, Inc. dba Caritas Peace Center*, 2020 Newburg Rd., 40205. Tel: 502-451-3330
For a complete listing, refer to the Special Care Facilities section.

[J] PROTECTIVE INSTITUTIONS

LOUISVILLE. *Boys' Haven*, 2301 Goldsmith Ln., 40205. Tel: 502-458-1171; Fax: 502-451-2161
For a complete listing, refer to the Special Care Facilities section.

Maryhurst, 1015 Dorsey Ln., 40223. Tel: 502-245-1576; Fax: 502-245-4737
For a complete listing, refer to the Special Care Facilities section.

[K] NURSING HOMES

LOUISVILLE. *Franciscan Health Care Center/Retirement Center*, 3625 Fern Valley Rd., 40219
For a complete listing, refer to the Special Care Facilities section.

Marian Home, 3105 Lexington Rd., 40206. Tel: 502-893-0121; Fax: 502-896-3925
For a complete listing, refer to the Special Care Facilities section.

Nazareth Home, 2000 Newburg Rd., 40205. Tel: 502-459-9681; Fax: 502-456-9077
For a complete listing, refer to the Special Care Facilities section.

St. Joseph Home for the Aged, 15 Audubon Plaza Dr., 40217 Fax: 502-636-2239
For a complete listing, refer to the Special Care Facilities section.

[L] MONASTERIES AND RESIDENCES OF PRIESTS AND BROTHERS

LOUISVILLE. *Bishop David Apartments*, 5146 Dixie Hwy., 40216. Tel: 502-447-8617. Revs. William C. Hartlage, Dir.; William Zahner; Jerome S. Moert; James W. Thompson; John B. Gephart; Edwin J. Scherzer. Priests 6; Sisters 2.

Sacred Heart Retreat. (Corporate Title: Congregation of the Passion, Sacred Heart Community), 1924 Newburg Rd., 40205. Tel: 502-451-2330. Very Rev. Richard L. Parks, C.P., Supr. In res. Revs. Francis W. Cusack, C.P.; Joachim Gemperline, C.P.; Forrest Macken, C.P.; Germain Legere, C.P. (Nova Scotia); Howard Ralenkotter, C.P.; Henry Kielty, C.P. (Ireland); Emmet Linden; Walter Kaelin, C.P.; James DeManuele, C.P.; William Browning, C.P.; John Baptist Ormechea, C.P.; Albert Schwer, C.P. Priests 13.

St. Boniface Friary, 531 E. Liberty St., 40202. Tel: 502-584-4279. Revs. Sergius H. Scherpenberg, O.F.M., Guardian & Pastor; Stephen Schneider, O.F.M.; Edmund R. Moore, O.F.M. Priests 3.

TRAPPIST. *Abbey of Our Lady of Gethsemani, of the Order of Cistercians of the Strict Observance*, 40051. Tel: 502-549-3117; Fax: 502-549-8281. Rt. Revs. Timothy Kelly, O.C.S.O., Abbot; Bernard Murray, O.C.S.O. (Chile); Linus Dodge (Austria); Herbert Seib, O.C.S.O.; Roman Ginn, O.C.S.O.; Paschal Phillips, O.C.S.O.; Chrysogonus Waddell, O.C.S.O.; Gregory Lambing, O.C.S.O.; Bede Kok, O.C.S.O.; Hilarion Schmock, O.C.S.O.; Alan Gilmore, O.C.S.O.; Matthew Kelty, O.C.S.O.; Damien Thompson, O.C.S.O.; Michael Casagram, O.C.S.O. (Venezuela); Jacob Raub, O.C.S.O.; Carlos Rodriguez, O.C.S.O.; Peter Tong, O.C.S.O. Priests 17; Brothers 54; Novices 1; Postulants 2.

[M] CONVENTS AND RESIDENCES FOR SISTERS

LOUISVILLE. *Monastery of the Discalced Carmelite Nuns*, 1740 Newburg Rd., 40205. Sr. Francis of the Mother of God, O.C.D., Prioress. Professed Nuns 11; Postulants 2.

St. Catherine Convent, 1172 E. Broadway, 40204. Tel: 502-583-7641. Sr. Mary Quentin Barth, R.S.M., Local Coord. Sisters of Mercy in residence 33.

Sisters of the Good Shepherd, 1015 Dorsey Ln., 40223. Sisters 3.

Ursuline Motherhouse of the Immaculate Conception, 3115 Lexington Rd., 40206. Tel: 502-893-0125. Sr. Sarah Stauble, O.S.U., Pres.; Rev. John J. Butler, Chap. Sisters in Motherhouse 57; Total in Congregation 228.

Ursuline Sisters. (Mount St. Joseph), 1731 Edenside Ave., 40204-1595. Tel: 502-451-8685. Sr. Amelia Stenger, Coord. Sisters 9. Attended from St. James.

BARDSTOWN. *Bethlehem Convent*, 40004. Tel: 502-348-3514. Sisters of Charity of Nazareth 3.

COLUMBIA. *Sisters of the Holy Cross*, 1221 Greensburg St., 42728.

NAZARETH. *Generalate, Motherhouse and Novitiate of the Sisters of Charity of Nazareth,* P.O. Box 172, 40048. Tel: 502-348-1555 (SCN Center & Generalate); 348-1500 (Motherhouse); Fax: 502-348-1502. Revs. Gary Young, C.R., Chap., Motherhouse; Robert A. DeWitt, Chap., Russell Hall. Sisters at Motherhouse 83; Sisters at Russell Hall 43; Sisters at David Hall 26; Sisters at SCN Center 2; Sisters at Guest House 3; Apt. 2 W, M.H. 4.

NERINX. *Motherhouse and Novitiate of the Sisters of Loretto at the Foot of the Cross,* 40049. Tel: 502-865-5811; Fax: 502-865-2200. Sr. Mary Ann Coyle, Pres.; Rev. J. Irvin Mouser, Chap. Sisters in the Motherhouse 119; Total in Congregation 425.

ST. CATHARINE. *St. Catharine of Siena Convent,* 2645 Bardstown Rd., 40061. Tel: 606-336-9303; Fax: 606-336-9306. Sr. Joan Scanlon, O.P., Pres. Tel: 606-336-9303; Rev. Charles E. Reteneller, Chap. Motherhouse of Dominican Sisters. Sisters in Motherhouse 47; Total in Congregation 302.

Sansbury Memorial Infirmary, 2645 Bardstown Rd., 40061. Tel: 606-336-3974. Sr. Susan Morris, O.P., Admin.; Revs. Charles E. Reteller, Chap.; Bertrand J. Brian; Lawrence A. Hardesty. Sisters in Infirmary 63.

TOMPKINSVILLE. *Sisters of the Holy Cross,* P.O. Box 548, 42167. Tel: 502-487-8881. Sr. Kathleen Moroney, C.S.C., Finance Councilor.

[N] HOMES FOR MEN AND WOMEN

LOUISVILLE. *Sacred Heart Home, Inc.,* 2120 Payne St., 40206. Tel: 502-895-9888; 895-9425; Fax: 502-894-9619
For a complete listing, refer to the Special Care Facilities section.

[O] RETREAT HOUSES

LOUISVILLE. *Catholic Charismatic Renewal,* Flaget Center, 1935 Lewiston Pl., 40216. Tel: 502-448-8581. Tony Doninger, Contact Person; Rev. James E. Wafzig, Spiritual Advisor.

Flaget Center for Spirituality and Ministry Formation, 1935 Lewiston Dr., 40216. Tel: 502-448-8581; Fax: 502-448-5518. Donna M. McHugh, Admin.

CRESTWOOD. *Lake St. Joseph Center,* 5800 Old LaGrange Rd., 40014. Tel: 502-241-4469.

NAZARETH. *Catherine Spalding Retreat and Conference Center,* 40048. Tel: 502-348-1515; Fax: 502-348-1518. Suzanne Gude, Dir. Staff Sisters 5; Lay Persons 3.

NERINX. *Knobs Haven,* 515 Nerinx Rd., 40049. Tel: 502-865-2621. Sr. Elaine Prevallet, S.L., Dir.

NEW HAVEN. *Bethany Spring,* 115 Dee Head Rd., 40051. Tel: 502-549-8277. Sr. Danielle Witt, S.S.N.D., Dir.

[P] ST. VINCENT DE PAUL SOCIETY

LOUISVILLE. *Society of St. Vincent de Paul, Council of Louisville,* P.O. Box 17126, 40217-0126. Tel: 502-584-2480; Fax: 502-587-1977. Dennis A. Shaw, Pres./CEO; Robert L. Dimke, Trustee/Board Chairman.

De Paul Apartments. (Transitional Shelter for Homeless Families).

De Paul Thrift Stores. 1029 S. Preston St., 40203. 248 E. Market St., 40202. 4443 Cane Run Rd., 40216. 9208 Dixie Hwy., 40272.

Open Hand Kitchen. (Community Kitchen), 9208 Dixie Hwy., 40272.

Ozanam Inn. (Men's Emergency & Transitional Shelter).

Parish Conferences.

Roberts Hall. (Women's Housing).

St. Jude House. (Women's Recovery).

Simon Hall. (Men's Recovery).

Tranquil House.

[Q] MISCELLANEOUS LISTINGS

LOUISVILLE. *Camp Tall Trees,* 2321 Carolina Ave., 40205.

Cathedral Heritage Foundation, Inc., 429 W. Muhammad Ali Blvd. #100, 40202-2334. Tel: 502-583-3100; Fax: 502-583-8524.

Cor Jesu Hermitage Foundation, Inc., P.O. Box 26522, 40250-6522.

Mass of the Air, 1930 Bishop Ln., Ste. 1002, 40218.

Our Lady's Rosary Makers, 4611 Poplar Level Rd., P.O. Box 37080, 40233. Tel: 502-968-1434. Deacon Harry Prestwood, Pres. & Gen. Mgr.; Rev. Edwin J. Scherzer, Chap.

Perpetual Eucharistic Adoration, P.O. Box 39191, 40233-9191. Tel: 502-637-5309; 583-7641. Rev. Lawrence H. Lindle, Spiritual Dir.

PROJECT AIMM, 1850 Bluegrass Ave., 40215. Sr. Anne Mary Lochner, O.S.U., Exec. Dir.

Publication: "The Record", Maloney Center, 1200 S. Shelby St., 40203-2600. Tel: 502-636-0296; Fax: 502-636-2379. Official newspaper of the Archdiocese of Louisville (Weekly).
Office: Archdiocesan Communications Center. Joseph E. Duerr, Editor & Gen. Mgr.

Ursuline Campus Schools, Inc., 3105 Lexington Rd., 40206. Tel: 502-896-3910; Fax: 502-895-0989. Sponsored by Ursuline Sisters.

Ursuline Society and Academy of Education, 3105 Lexington Rd., 40206. Tel: 502-897-1811; Fax: 502-896-3913.

BARDSTOWN. *Angeline Eder, HERMIT,* P.O. Box 762, 40004.

LEBANON. *The Laura,* 1995 Sam Browning Rd., 40033.

LORETTO. *Holy Cross Cemetery Trust, Inc.,* 7945 Loretto Rd., 40037.

NAZARETH. *Nazareth Arts For Life, Inc.,* O'Connell Hall, P.O. Box 14, 40048. Tel: 502-348-1554.

Office of Congregational Advancement, P.O. Box 9, 40048. Tel: 502-348-1520. Sisters of Charity of Nazareth.

Sisters of Charity of Nazareth Health System, P.O. Box 171, 40048. Tel: 502-349-6250; Fax: 502-349-6258. Mark W. Dundon, Pres.
Owns and operates 6 health care divisions in KY, AR, and TN, 2 of which are in the Louisville Archdiocese. Caritas Health Services and Flaget Memorial Hospital.

NERINX. *Sisters of Loretto Charitable Trust,* 515 Nerinx Rd., 40049-9999. Tel: 502-865-3414. Sr. Mary Swain, S.L., Treas.

NEW HAVEN. *Archdiocesan Marian Committee,* 8191 New Haven Rd., 40051-6030. Tel: 502-549-3757. Rev. Lawrence H. Lindle, Dir.

Via Escondida, 325 Dee Head Rd., 40051. Jacqueline D'Avy, Hermit.

World Apostolate of Fatima (Blue Army), 8191 New Haven Rd., 40051-6030. Tel: 502-549-3757. Rev. Lawrence H. Lindle, Spiritual Dir.

Sacred Heart Apostolate, 8191 New Haven Rd., 40051-6030. Tel: 502-549-3757. Rev. Lawrence H. Lindle, Dir.

NEW HOPE. *St. Martin De Porres Lay Dominican Community,* 40052. Tel: 502-325-3061; Fax: 502-325-3091. Hugh Pimentel, T.O.P., Prior.

PLEASURE RIDGE PARK. *The Franciscan Foundation, Inc.,* 6901 Dixie Hwy., 40258.

RELIGIOUS INSTITUTES OF MEN REPRESENTED IN THE ARCHDIOCESE

For further details refer to the corresponding bracketed number in the Religious Institutes of Men or Women section.

[1350]—*Brothers of St. Francis Xavier.* (American Central Prov.).—C.F.X.

[0600]—*Brothers of the Congregation of Holy Cross.* (Midwest Prov.).—C.S.C.

[0270]—*Carmelite Fathers & Brothers.* (Pure Heart of Mary Prov.).—O.Carm.

[0350]—*Cistercians Order of the Strict Observance-Trappists.*—O.C.S.O.

[0820]—*Congregation of the Fathers of Mercy.*—C.P.M.

[1000]—*Congregation of the Passion.* (Holy Cross Prov.).—C.P.

[1130]—*Congregation of the Priests of the Sacred Heart.*—S.C.J.

[1080]—*Congregation of the Resurrection.* (Rome, Italy).—C.R.

[0480]—*Conventual Franciscans.* (Prov. of Our Lady of Consolation).—O.F.M.Conv.

[0520]—*Franciscan Friars.* (St. John the Baptist Prov.).—O.F.M.

[0430]—*Order of Preachers-Dominicans.* (St. Joseph Prov.).—O.P.

[1070]—*Redemptorist Fathers.*—C.SS.R.

[1060]—*Society of the Precious Blood.*—C.PP.S.

RELIGIOUS INSTITUTES OF WOMEN REPRESENTED IN THE ARCHDIOCESE

[0100]—*Adorers of the Blood of Christ.*—A.S.C.

[2145]—*Congregation of Augustinian Sisters Servants of Jesus and Mary.*—O.S.A.

[1920]—*Congregation of the Sisters of the Holy Cross.*—C.S.C.

[0420]—*Discalced Carmelite Nuns.*—O.C.D.

[1070-01]—*Dominican Sisters.*—O.P.

[1070-13]—*Dominican Sisters.*—O.P.

[2575]—*Institute of the Sisters of Mercy of the Americas.*—R.S.M.

[2470]—*Maryknoll Sisters of St. Dominic.*—M.M.

[2490]—*Medical Mission Sisters.*—S.C.M.M.

[3130]—*Our Lady of Victory Missionary Sisters.*—O.L.V.M.

[0440]—*Sisters of Charity of Cincinnati, Ohio.*—S.C.

[0480]—*Sisters of Charity of Leavenworth, Kansas.*—S.C.L.

[0500]—*Sisters of Charity of Nazareth.*—S.C.N.

[1000]—*Sisters of Divine Providence of Kentucky.*—C.D.P.

[2360]—*Sisters of Loretto At the Foot of the Cross.*—S.L.

[3360]—*Sisters of Providence of Saint Mary-of-the-Woods, IN.* (St. Gabriel Prov.).—S.P.

[1640]—*Sisters of St. Francis of Perpetual Adoration.*—O.S.F.

[3830-16]—*Sisters of St. Joseph of Springfield, MA.*—S.S.J.

[1830]—*Sisters of the Good Shepherd.*—R.G.S.

[1720]—*Sisters of the Third Order Regular of St. Francis of the Congregation of Our Lady of Lourdes.*—O.S.F.

[2150]—*Sisters, Servants of the Immaculate Heart of Mary.*—I.H.M.

[4120-03]—*Ursuline Nuns, of the Congregation of Paris.*—O.S.U.

ARCHDIOCESAN CEMETERIES

Offices for all cemeteries: 1600 Newburg Rd., Louisville, KY 40205; Mailing Address: P.O. Box 4096, Louisville, KY 40204. Tel: 502-451-7710; Fax: 502-456-9270.

LOUISVILLE. *Calvary,* 1600 Newburg Rd., 40205.

St. John, 2601 Duncan St., 40205.

St. Louis, 1215 Barret Ave., 40205.

St. Michael, 1153 Charles St., 40205.

NECROLOGY

† Caster, Thomas Kevin, Louisville, KY, St. Albert the Great. —Died July 31, 1997.

† Pank, William H., (Retired). —Died Sept. 28, 1997.

† Prendiville, Joseph A., (Retired). —Died May 25, 1997.

† Schlich, James Lee, (Retired). —Died May 4, 1997.

† Schmidt, Stanley Andrew, (Retired). —Died May 2, 1997.

† Schwartz, Clarence Joseph, (Retired). —Died Aug. 26, 1997.

Diocese of Lubbock

Most Reverend

PLACIDO RODRIGUEZ, C.M.F.

Bishop of Lubbock; ordained May 23, 1968; consecrated December 13, 1983; installed Auxiliary Bishop of Chicago; appointed Second Bishop of Lubbock April 5, 1994; installed June 1, 1994. *Res., Catholic Center, P.O. Box 98700, Lubbock, TX, 79499-8700; Fax: 806-792-2953 (Bishop's Private Line).*

Legal Title: Roman Catholic Diocese of Lubbock.

ESTABLISHED AND CREATED A DIOCESE, JUNE 17, 1983.

Square Miles 23,382.

Comprises the Counties of Bailey, Lamb, Hale, Floyd, Motley, Cottle, Cochran, Hockley, Lubbock, Crosby, Dickens, King, Yoakum, Terry, Lynn, Garza, Kent, Stonewall, Haskell, Gaines, Dawson, Borden, Scurry, Fisher and Jones.

The Catholic Center: P.O. Box 98700, Lubbock, TX, 79499-8700. Tel.: 806-792-3943; Fax: 806-792-8109.

STATISTICAL OVERVIEW

Personnel	
Bishop	1
Priests: Diocesan Active in Diocese	31
Priests: Active Outside Diocese	1
Priests: Retired, Sick or Absent	2
Number of Diocesan Priests	34
Religious Priests in Diocese	10
Extern Priests in Diocese	6
Ordinations:	
Diocesan Priests	1
Permanent Deacons	24
Permanent Deacons in Diocese	47
Total Sisters	35
Parishes	
Parishes	36
With Resident Pastor:	
Resident Diocesan Priests	25
Resident Religious Priests	7
Without Resident Pastor:	
Administered by Priests	4
Missions	24
Pastoral Centers	1
Closed Parishes	3
Professional Ministry Personnel:	
Sisters	10
Lay Ministers	7
Welfare	
Catholic Hospitals	1
Total Assisted	97,399
Health Care Centers	35
Total Assisted	451,178
Special Centers for Social Services	1
Total Assisted	33,000
Educational	
Diocesan Students in Other Seminaries	12
Total Seminarians	12
High Schools, Diocesan and Parish	1
Total Students	92
Elementary Schools, Diocesan and Parish	2
Total Students	330
Catechesis/Religious Education:	
High School Students	3,136
Elementary Students	6,082
Total Students Under Catholic Instruction	9,652
Teachers in the Diocese:	
Lay Teachers	34
Vital Statistics	
Receptions into the Church:	
Infant Baptism Totals	1,526
Adult Baptism Totals	195
Received into Full Communion	91
First Communions	1,168
Confirmations	947
Marriages:	
Catholic	250
Interfaith	64
Total Marriages	314
Deaths	395
Total Catholic Population	53,035
Total Population	451,995

Former Bishops—Most Rev. MICHAEL J. SHEEHAN, S.T.L., J.C.D., ord. July 12, 1964; cons. and installed as the first Bishop of Lubbock, June 17, 1983; appt. Apostolic Administrator of Santa Fe, April 6, 1993; installed as the 11th Archbishop of Santa Fe, Sept. 21, 1993.

The Catholic Center—4620 Fourth, Lubbock, 79416. Mailing Address: P.O. Box 98700, Lubbock, 79499-8700. Tel: 806-792-3943; Fax: 806-792-8109; 792-2953 (Bishop's Office). Office Hours: Mon.-Fri. 8-5.

Chancellor—Rev. Msgr. ANTONIO G. GONZALEZ.

Moderator of the Curia—Rev. RONALD F. KRISMAN.

Bishop's Secretary—JESUSITA ALCORTA.

Diocesan Tribunal—P.O. Box 98700, Lubbock, 79499-8700. Tel: 806-792-3943.

Officialis—Rev. MALCOLM NEYLAND, M.C.L., J.C.L.

Advocates—Rev. Msgr. JOSEPH JAMES; Revs. CORNELIO RAMIREZ, S.A.C.; JOHN CASEY, S.A.C.; MARTIN PINA; GEORGE RONEY; MICHAEL MELCHER; JAMES MCCARTNEY; Deacon RICHARD WOOD.

Administrative Secretary—RITA ORTIZ.

Promoter of Justice—Rev. Msgr. ROLAND BUXKEMPER.

Defenders of the Bond—Rev. BEN KASTEEL, S.M.; Rev. Msgr. CURTIS T. HALFMANN; Rev. EUGENE J. DRISCOLL.

Defender of the Bond-Appeal—Rev. EUGENE J. DRISCOLL.

Notaries—RITA ORTIZ; JESUSITA ALCORTA.

Presbyteral Council & Diocesan Consultors—Very Rev. BEN KASTEEL, V.G.; Rev. Msgr. ANTONIO GONZALEZ; Revs. RONALD F. KRISMAN; EUGENE DRISCOLL; GERALD LEATHAM; ELBERT FADALLAN; MARTIN PINA; MICHAEL O'DWYER, S.A.C.; CHARLES HAMMOND, O.M.I.; JAMES O'CONNOR.

Priests Personnel Board—Rev. Msgr. TIMOTHY SCHWERTNER; Rev. Msgr. ANTONIO GONZALEZ; Most Rev. PLACIDO RODRIGUEZ; Very Rev. BEN KASTEEL, V.G.; Revs. JAMES O'CONNOR; EUGENE DRISCOLL.

Vicars Forane—Very Rev. BEN KASTEEL, V.G., Plainview Deanery, *Our Lady of Guadalupe Church, P.O. Box 1269, 400 W. 29th, Plainview, 79073.* Tel: 806-296-2753. Rev. ANDRES MENDOZA, Brownfield Deanery, *St. Williams Church, 401 Mustang Ave., Denver City, 79323.* Tel: 806-592-2063. Rev. MICHAEL J. MELCHER, Snyder Deanery, *St. Ann's Church, 104 New Braunfels St., Stamford, 79553.* Tel: 915-773-2659. Rev. EUGENE J. DRISCOLL, North Lubbock Deanery, *St. Elizabeth's Church, 2305 Main St., Lubbock, 79401.* Tel: 806-762-5225. Rev. MALCOLM NEYLAND, M.C.L., J.C.L., South Lubbock Deanery, *P.O. Box 98700, Lubbock, 79499.* Tel: 806-792-3943.

Superintendent of Schools—ROBERTA MEYER, *P.O. Box 98700, Lubbock, 79499.*

Director of Youth—PAUL FLOREZ, *P.O. Box 98700, Lubbock, 79499.*

Campus Ministry—Sr. DIANA AKROUSH, O.S.F., *2305 Main St., Lubbock, 79401.* Tel: 806-762-5225.

Director of Scouting—Rev. THOMAS DIEBEL, *P.O. Box 10753, Lubbock, 79408.* Tel: 806-792-3943.

Priests' Pension Fund—Rev. Msgr. JAMES COMISKEY; Revs. GEORGE RONEY; JAMES O'CONNOR; JAMES MCCARTNEY.

Diocesan Building Commission—Rev. BEN KASTEEL, V.G.; Rev. Msgr. JAMES COMISKEY; JOHN CONNORS; JOHN MOSSER; PAUL MEYER; MAX GARZA; BOB DAIKOWSKI; Rev. Msgr. ROLAND BUXKEMPER.

Diocesan Liturgical Commission—Rev. RONALD F. KRISMAN, *St. Michael's, 316 E. Washington St., Levelland, 79336-2611.* Tel: 806-894-2268.

Office of Christian Formation—Ms. ALICIA ALVAREZ, *P.O. Box 98700, Lubbock, 79499.* Tel: 806-792-3943.

Delegate of Religious—Sr. MARY GERRIOR, O.P., Pres., *3208-B 66th St., Lubbock, 79413-5701.* Tel: 806-792-7940.

Catholic Family Services, Inc.—STEVE HAY, Dir., *102 Avenue J, Lubbock, 79401.* Tel: 806-765-8475.

Director of Hispanic Affairs—Rev. Msgr. ANTONIO GONZALEZ, *Our Lady of Grace Church, 3111 Erskine, Lubbock, 79415.* Tel: 806-763-4156.

Ecumenical Affairs—Sr. MARY GERRIOR, O.P., *3208-B 66th St., Lubbock, 79413-5701.* Tel: 806-792-7940.

Diocesan Council of Catholic Women—Rev. GERARD KENNY, Moderator, *Christ the King Cathedral Church, 4011 54th St., Lubbock, 79413-4699.* Tel: 806-792-6168.

Director of Vocations—Revs. REYNALDO REYES, Seminarian Recruitment; EUGENE J. DRISCOLL, Seminarian Formation; RONALD F. KRISMAN, Continuing Education for Priests, *P.O. Box 98700, Lubbock, 79499.* Tel: 806-792-3943.

Diocesan Attorney—MADISON SOWDER, *1703 Ave. K, Lubbock, 79401.* Tel: 806-763-0409.

Diocesan Health Coordinator—Sr. CLAIRE OLIVIER, C.S.J., *St. Mary of the Plains Hospital, 4000 24th St., Lubbock, 79410.* Tel: 806-796-6000.

Propagation of the Faith—P.O. Box 98700, Lubbock, 79499-8100. Tel: 806-792-3943.

Office of Peace & Justice—Deacon DARIO RENDON, *Catholic Family Services, Inc., 102 Ave. J, Lubbock, 79401.* Tel: 806-765-8475.

Campaign for Human Development—Deacon DARIO RENDON, *Catholic Family Services, Inc., 102 Ave. J, Lubbock, 79401.* Tel: 806-765-8475.

Director of the Permanent Diaconate—Deacon CLARKE E. COCHRAN, *P.O. Box 98700, Lubbock, 79499.* Tel: 806-792-3943.

Director of Continuing Education of the Clergy—Rev. RONALD F. KRISMAN, *P.O. Box 98700, Lubbock, 79499.* Tel: 806-792-3943.

Cursillo Movement—Rev. Msgr. ANTONIO GONZALEZ, Dir. English & Spanish Cursillo, *P.O. Box 5238, Lubbock, 79217.* Tel: 806-792-4308.

Newspaper—"South Plains Catholic"; Deacon LEROY BEHNKE, Editor, *P.O. Box 98700, Lubbock, 79499.*

Director of Communications—Deacon LEROY BEHNKE.

Office of Evangelization—Mr. PAUL KEY, *P.O. Box 98700, Lubbock, 79499.* Tel: 806-792-3943.

Director of Family Life—Deacon JESSIE ESQUIVEL, *P.O. Box 98700, Lubbock, 79499.* Tel: 806-792-3943.

CLERGY, PARISHES, MISSIONS AND PAROCHIAL SCHOOLS

CITY OF LUBBOCK
(Lubbock County)

1—Cathedral Christ the King (1958), Rev. Msgr. James A. Comiskey; Rev. Gerard Kenney.
Res., 4011 54th St., 79413-4699. Tel: 806-792-6168; Fax: 806-792-1417.
School—Tel: 806-795-8283. Mrs. Roberta Meyer, Prin. & D.R.E.
Lay Teachers 16; Students 248.
Middle School—Tel: 806-795-6477.
Lay Teachers 9; Students 92.
Catechesis/Religious Programs—Tel: 806-792-6198.
Students 405.

2—Our Lady of Grace (1960) (Hispanic), Rev. Msgr. Antonio Gonzalez; Rev. Jorge Jimenez; Deacons Jesse Guerrero; Ernest Hernandez; Alfredo B. Jaime; Benny Brito.
Res., 3111 Erskine St., 79415-1623. Tel: 806-763-4156.
Catechesis/Religious Programs—Tel: 806-763-8727. Sr. Sandra Clark, O.S.F., D.R.E.
Students 575.

3—Our Lady of Guadalupe (1980) (Mexican), Rev. James O'Connor.
Res., 52nd & Ave. L, P.O. Box 3947, 79452-3947. Tel: 806-763-0710.
Catechesis/Religious Programs—Tel: 806-763-0732. Sr. Mechtilde Gogel, O.L.V.M., D.R.E.
Students 603.

4—St. Elizabeth University Parish (1935), Revs. Eugene Driscoll; Reynaldo Reyes; Deacon Sid Little; Sr. Diana A. Kroush, O.S.F., Campus Ministry.
Res., 2305 Main St., 79401-2924. Tel: 806-762-5225.
Catechesis/Religious Programs—Tel: 806-762-1672; Fax: 806-741-1962. Pat Key, D.R.E.
Students 450.

5—St. John Neumann (1979), Rev. Msgr. Curtis T. Halfmann; Deacons Thomas F. McCarthy, Pastoral Assoc.; Joe Richard; Richard Flores; Richard Wood; Kyle Broderson; Clarke Cochran.
Res., 5802 22nd, 79407-1721. Tel: 806-799-2649; Fax: 806-799-0037.
Catechesis/Religious Programs—Alisa Florez, D.R.E.
Students 369.

6—St. Joseph's (1924) (Hispanic), Rev. Michael O'Dwyer, S.A.C.
Res., 102 N. Ave. P, 79401-1199. Tel: 806-765-9935.
Catechesis/Religious Programs—Tel: 806-763-9695. Sr. Martha Molohon, O.L.V.M., D.R.E.
Students 435.

7—St. Patrick (1960) (Spanish), Rev. Cornelio C. Ramirez, S.A.C.
Res., 1603 Cherry Ave., 79403-6099. Tel: 806-765-5123.
Catechesis/Religious Programs—Tel: 806-765-6979. Sr. Vianney Martinez, O.S.F., D.R.E.
Students 295.
Mission—New Deal, Lubbock Co., Our Lady Queen of Apostles, Main St. N., 79401. Tel: 806-765-5123.

8—St. Theresa's (1961) (Mexican American), Rev. Msgr. Roland Buxkemper.
Res., Rte. 5, Box 285, 79407-9545. Tel: 806-795-2249.
Catechesis/Religious Programs—Tel: 806-866-4413. D.R.E.: Patricia Sprowls; Jimmy Sprowla.
Students 98.

OUTSIDE THE CITY OF LUBBOCK

Anson, Jones Co., St. Michael's (1960) (Mexican), Revs. Boniface Riedmann, S.A.; Oscar Del Rio.
Res., 2010 County Rd. 477, 79501-4732. Tel: 915-823-2777.
Catechesis/Religious Programs—D.R.E.: Sheri Hudson; Lupe Phillips; Mrs. Andrea Ramirez; Mrs. Sylvia Ruiz.
Students 99.
Mission—Hamlin, Jones Co., Holy Trinity.

Brownfield, Terry Co., St. Anthony's (1952) (Hispanic), Rev. John Casey, S.A.C., V.F.
Res., P.O. Box 671, 79316-0671. Tel: 806-637-6626.
Catechesis/Religious Programs—Jimmy Garza, D.R.E.
Students 288.
Mission—Ropesville, Hockley Co., San Francisco de Asis, P.O. Box 92, Ropesville, 79358.

Denver City, Yoakum Co., St. William (1955) (Hispanic), Rev. Andres Mendoza.
Res., 401 Mustang Ave., 79323-2749. Tel: 806-592-2063; Fax: 806-592-3943.
Catechesis/Religious Programs—D.R.E.: Martha DelaRosa; Alice Espinoza; Alice Gomez.
Students 485.
Mission—Plains, Yoakum Co., Sacred Heart, 1305 11th St., Plains, 79355. Tel: 806-456-7002.

Floydada, Floyd Co., St. Mary Magdalen (1928) (Hispanic), Rev. John Ohlig.
Res., 809 W. Ross, 79235. Tel: 806-983-5878; Fax: 806-983-2601. [JC]
Catechesis/Religious Programs—Ellen Enriquez, D.R.E.
Students 95.
Missions—Matador, Motley Co., Our Lady of Guadalupe, 701 Bundy St., Matador, 79244.; Paducah, Cottle Co., St. Elizabeth, Second St. & Clare St., Paducah, 79348. Tel: 806-492-3053.

Hale Center, Hale Co., St. Theresa's (1944) (Hispanic), Rev. Martin Pina.
Res., P.O. Box 528, 79041-0570. Tel: 806-839-2310.
Catechesis/Religious Programs—Tel: 806-839-9938.
Students 225.
Mission—Olton, Lamb Co., St. Peter Apostle, P.O. Box 655, Olton, 79064. Tel: 806-285-2140.

Idalou, Lubbock Co., St. Philip Benizi (1979) (Spanish), Rev. Msgr. Joseph W. James; Deacon Urbano Rodriguez.
Res., Box 1337, 79329-1337. Tel: 806-892-3042.
Mission—Lorenzo, San Lorenzo.

Lamesa, Dawson Co., St. Margaret Mary (1929) (Hispanic), Rev. Charles Hammond, O.M.I.
Res., 908 S. 2nd St, P.O. Box 599, 79331-6104. Tel: 806-872-7100. [CEM]
Catechesis/Religious Programs—Miss Delfina Luna, D.R.E.
Students 425.
Mission—Lamesa, Dawson Co., Our Lady of Guadalupe, P.O.Box 599, 79331.

Levelland, Hockley Co., St. Michael's (1956), Rev. Ronald F. Krisman.
Res., 316 E. Washington St., 79336-2611. Tel: 806-894-2268; Fax: 806-894-9348.
Catechesis/Religious Programs—Tel: 806-894-9880. Sr. Mildred Warminski, C.C.V.I., D.R.E.
Students 642.
Mission—Sundown, Hockley Co., San Isidro, 1306 S. Slaughter, P.O. Box 764, Sundown, 79372-0764.

Littlefield, Lamb Co., Sacred Heart (1921) (Hispanic), Rev. Clarence W. Huber.
Res., Eighth & Sunset, P.O. Box 1347, 79339-4234. Tel: 806-385-6043. [CEM]
Catechesis/Religious Programs—Mary Jane Aguirre, D.R.E.
Students 158.

Morton, Cochran Co., St. Ann (1955) (Hispanic), Rev. Ricardito P. Salditos (Philippines).
Res., 105 N.E. Eighth St., 79346-2719. Tel: 806-266-8693. [CEM]
Catechesis/Religious Programs—Tel: 806-266-5410. D.R.E.: Alfred Franco; Jane Dusterhaus.
Students 115.
Mission—Pep, Hockley Co., St. Philip Neri, Fm. Rd., #303, P.O. Box 395, Pep, 79353. Tel: 806-933-4355.

Muleshoe, Bailey Co., Immaculate Conception (1956) (Hispanic), Rev. Joseph Augustine Chorikavunkal (India).
Res., R.R. 3, Box 247, 79347-2460. Tel: 806-272-4384. [JC]
Catechesis/Religious Programs—Tel: 806-272-3896. Janie Balderas, D.R.E.
Students 165.
Mission—Earth, Lamb Co., St. Mary Magdalen, R.R.3 P.O. Box 247, Muleshoe, 79347.
Catechesis/Religious Programs—Tel: 806-257-3438. Janie Fuentes, D.R.E.
Students 35.

O'Donnell, Lynn Co., St. Pius X (1956) (Hispanic), Rev. Todd Arnberg.
Res., P.O. Box 579, 79351-0579. Tel: 806-428-3490. [CEM]
Catechesis/Religious Programs—Tel: 806-428-3497.
Students 50.
Mission—Tahoka, Lynn Co., St. Jude, P.O. Box 128, Tahoka, 79373-0128. Tel: 806-998-4436.

Petersburg, Hale Co., Sacred Heart (1959) (Mexican American), Rev. Louis Dussan, C.M.F.
Mailing Address: P.O. Box 330, 79250-0330. Tel: 806-667-3763.
Res., R.R. 2, Box 159-A, Abernathy, 79311-6921. Tel: 806-298-4278.
Catechesis/Religious Programs—Mary Esther, D.R.E.
Students 111.
Mission—Abernathy, Hale Co., St. Isidore, 510 S. Ave. D, 79311-6921.
Catechesis/Religious Programs—Nancy Olguin, D.R.E.
Students 143.

Plainview, Hale Co., St. Alice (1911), Rev. Msgr. Timothy Schwetner.
Res., 810 W. 11th, 79072-7124. Tel: 806-293-1903.
Catechesis/Religious Programs—1114 Houston, 79072. Tel: 806-293-2891. Sr. Mary Jane Alaniz, D.R.E.
Students 144.
Mission—Lockney, Floyd Co., San Jose, 303 S.E. Fourth, Lockney, 79241. Tel: 806-652-2321. Sr. Sophie Bonelli, O.S.F., Pastoral Assoc.

Our Lady of Guadalupe (1946) (Mexican), Rev. Ben Kasteel.
Mailing Address: P.O. Box 1269, 79073-1269. Tel: 806-291-0195.
Church—211 W. Seventh St., 79072-8013. Tel: 806-293-0085; Fax: 806-293-4507. [CEM]
Catechesis/Religious Programs—Tel: 806-293-0086. D.R.E.: Yolanda Gonzales, (Elementary); Armeldo Gonzales, (Junior High School & High School).
Students 486.

Sacred Heart (1964) (Hispanic), Rev. Elbert Fadallan.
Res. & Mailing Address—400 W. 29th St., 79072-2399. Tel: 806-296-2753.
Catechesis/Religious Programs—Tel: 806-296-6553.
Students 500.

Post, Garza Co., Holy Cross (1955), Rev. Lawrence A. Hemp.
Res., Box 190, 79356-0190. Tel: 806-495-2791. [JC]
Catechesis/Religious Programs—Paula Valdez, D.R.E.
Students 90.

Ralls, Crosby Co., St. Michael (1959) (Hispanic), Rev. Glenn Rosendale.
Mailing Address: P.O. Box 906, 79357-0906. Tel: 806-253-2008. [JC]
Catechesis/Religious Programs—Students 90.
Mission—Crosbyton, Crosby Co., St. Joseph, P.O. Box 906, Ralls, 79357. Tel: 806-675-7017.

Rotan, Fisher Co., St. Joseph (1923) (Hispanic), Rev. Johnrose H. Hayden.
Res., 301 E. Lee, 79546-3011. Tel: 915-735-3285; Fax: 915-735-2181. [CEM]
Catechesis/Religious Programs—Tel: 915-735-2935. D.R.E.: Rosemary Carrillo; Frances Zambrano.
Students 72.
Missions—Near Hamlin, Fisher Co., Sacred Heart Hwy. 92; Aspermont, Stonewall Co., St. Mary.

Seminole, Gaines Co., St. James (1958), Rev. William Sweeney, S.A.C. (Ireland).
Res., P.O. Box 898, 79360-0898. Tel: 915-758-2371.
Catechesis/Religious Programs—D.R.E.: Maria Hernandez; Susana Munoz.
Students 394.
Mission—Seagraves, Gaines Co., St. Paul's, P.O. Box 1321, Seagraves, 79359-1321. Tel: 806-546-2950.

Shallowater, Lubbock Co., St. Phillip Benizi (1967) (Mexican American), Rev. Nicholas Reudon, Admin.; Rev. Msgr. Antonio Gonzalez; Deacon Daniel Castro. Pastoral Assocs.: Deacons Isaac McDonald; Nash Revilla.
Res., P.O. Box 39, 79363-0039. Tel: 806-832-5915.
Catechesis/Religious Programs—Tel: 806-385-1123; 832-5576. D.R.E.: Teresa Juarez; Julia Escobedo.
Students 120.
Mission—Anton, Hockley Co., St. Anthony, (1966) P.O. Box 545, Anton, 79313. Tel: 806-997-5831.

Slaton, Lubbock Co., Our Lady of Guadalupe (1952), Rev. Lawrence A. Hemp.
Res., 705 S. Fourth, 79363-5406. Tel: 806-828-5108 (Office). [JC]
Catechesis/Religious Programs—Tel: 806-828-4573. Ernestina Perez, D.R.E.
Students 180.

St. Joseph's (1912) (German), Rev. Jim McCartney; Deacon Darris D. Linder.
Res., 205 S. 19th, 79364-3755. Tel: 806-828-3944.
School—20th W. Division, 79364. Tel: 806-828-6761; Fax: 806-828-5396. Mrs. Janet Kitten, Prin.
Lay Teachers 9; Students 82.
Catechesis/Religious Programs—Students 50.
Mission—Wilson, Lynn Co., Blessed Sacrament Church, P.O. Box 119, 79381. Tel: 806-828-6452.

Snyder, Scurry Co., St. Elizabeth's (1952), Rev. Gerald Leatham.
Res., 3005 Ave. A, 79549-3909. Tel: 915-573-2590; Fax: 915-573-1553. [CEM]
Catechesis/Religious Programs—Tel: 915-573-8824. Shirley Pavlik, D.R.E.
Students 104.
Mission—Hermeleigh, Scurry Co., St. John, Hwy. 84, 79549.

Our Lady of Guadalupe (1945), Rev. Patrick S. Maher (Ireland).

Res., 1311 Ave. K, 79549-9533. Tel: 915-573-3866.

Catechesis/Religious Programs—Tel: 915-573-7142. D.R.E.: Maria Ramirez; Roberto Ramirez.

Students 170.

Spur, Dickens Co., St. Mary (1948) (Hispanic), Rev. Glenn Rosendale.

Res., Box 189, 79370-0189.

Mission—Jayton, Kent Co., Epiphany.

Stamford, Jones Co., St. Ann (1955), Rev. Michael Melcher; Sr. M. Lalemant Pelikan, R.S.M., Pastoral Assoc.

Res., 104 New Braunfels, 79553-6415. Tel: 915-773-2659; Fax: 915-773-3622.

Catechesis/Religious Programs—Students 70.

Mission—Haskell, Haskell Co., St. George, 901 N. 16th St., Haskell, 79521-3340. Tel: 817-864-3171.

Catechesis/Religious Programs—Students 45.

Wolfforth, St. Francis of Assisi Mission. See San Ramon, Woodrow for details.

Woodrow, Lubbock Co., San Ramon (1974), Rev. George Roney.

Church—Rte. 6, Box 356, Lubbock, 79423. Tel: 806-863-2201.

Catechesis/Religious Programs—Tel: 806-863-3435.

Students 117.

Mission—Wolfforth, Lubbock Co., St. Francis of Assisi, P.O. Box 785, Wolfforth, 79382. Tel: 806-866-9007.

Special Assignment:

Reverend Fathers—

Diebel, Thomas, Dir. Scouting, P.O. Box 10753, Lubbock, TX 79408

Furlong, James, Pastoral Care, 1105 Genoa Ave., Lubbock, TX 79416

Thekkedam, George, Pastoral Care, St. Mary's Hospital, 4000 24th St., Lubbock, TX 79410

On Duty Outside the Diocese:

Reverend Fathers—

Cruz, David, The Assumption-St. John Seminary, 2600 W. Woodlawn, San Antonio, TX 78284

Luera, Ruben, 8000 Village Oak, Apt. K63, Live Oak, TX 78233

Military Chaplains:

Reverend Fathers—

Diab, Thomas (ALX), Reese Air Force Base, 64 ABG-HC, TX 79489. Tel: 806-885-3237

Retired:

Reverend Fathers—

Vaze Parampil, Thomas, Corpus Christi Abbey, HCR #2, Box 6300, San Dia, TX 78383-9949

Permanent Deacons:

Acevedo, Miguel, (Retired), St. Mary Magdalen, Earth
Barrera, Salome, Our Lady of Guadalupe, Snyder
Behnke, Leroy, St. Phillip Benizi, Shallowater
Brito, Benny, Our Lady of Grace, Lubbock
Cavazos, Jesus Z., On Duty Outside the Diocese
Cochran, Clarke E., St. John Neumann, Lubbock
DeLeon, Saragosa, (Retired), St. Joseph, Rotan
Flores, Antonio B., St. Michael's, Ralls
Garcia, Doroteo, Sacred Heart, Littlefield
Garcia, Pedro, St. Michael's, Ralls
Jaime, Alfredo B., Our Lady of Grace, Lubbock
King, Edward, St. Michael's, Levelland
Linder, Darris D., St. Joseph's, Slaton
Little, Sidney R., St. Elizabeth's, Lubbock
Martinez, Nasario, (Retired), St. Mary's, Sudan
Moreno, Jesse, (Retired), St. Ann, Stamford
Ortegon, Frank, Our Lady of Guadalupe, Snyder
Peralez, Catarino, (Retired), St. Philip Benizi, Idalou
Ramirez, Robert, Our Lady of Guadalupe, Snyder
Rendon, Dario, (Retired), St. Patrick's, Lubbock
Revilla, Nash, St. Phillip Benizi, Shallowater
Richard, Joseph N., St. John Newmann, Lubbock
Rodriguez, Urbano, St. Philip Benizi, Idalou
Thompson, Richard, Sacred Heart, Littlefield

INSTITUTIONS LOCATED IN THE DIOCESE

[A] CHRISTIAN RENEWAL CENTERS

LUBBOCK. *Christian Renewal Center*, P.O. Box 98296, 79499-8296. Tel: 806-792-1105. Paul Key, Exec. Dir.
Office of Evangelization, P.O. Box 98296, 79499-8296. Tel: 806-792-1105. Paul Key, Dir. Evangelization.
Office for Cursillo Movement, P.O. Box 98296, 79499-8296. Tel: 806-792-4308. Rev. Msgr. Antonio Gonzalez, Dir.

[B] GENERAL HOSPITALS

LUBBOCK. *St. Mary of the Plains Hospital*, 4000 24th St., 79410-1894. Tel: 806-796-6000; Fax: 806-796-6081
For a complete listing, refer to the Hospitals section.

[C] RETREAT HOUSES

SLATON. *Our Lady of Mercy Retreat Center*, P.O. Box 744, 19th & Division, 79364-0744. Tel: 806-828-6428. Rev. Msgr. Joseph W. James, Dir. Total in Residence 4; Total Staff 12.

[D] CONVENTS AND RESIDENCES FOR SISTERS

LUBBOCK. *Casa de San Jose*, 3817 23rd St., 79410. Tel: 806-796-6000; Fax: 806-796-6081. St. Mary of the Plains Hospital Convent. Sisters of St. Joseph of Orange, C.S.J. 3.
Casa Merced, Sisters of Mercy Convent, 4104 68th, 79413-5912. Tel: 806-791-4692. Sisters of Mercy of the Americas 4.
Dominican Sisters of St. Catharine, Kentucky, 3235-A 64th St., 79413-5701. Tel: 806-792-7940.
E-mail: mgerrior@juno.com
Our Lady of Grace Convent, 3101 Erskine, 79415. Tel: 806-747-7472. Missionary Catechists of the Sacred Hearts of Jesus and Mary 3.
St. Francis Mission Community Central House (1981), St. Francis Convent, 4305 54th St., 79413-4617. Tel: 806-793-9859. St. Francis Mission Community 6.
St. Joseph Convent, 1602 First St., 79401. Tel: 806-763-9695. Missionary Sisters of Our Lady of Victory 3.
St. Mary Convent, 3820 24th St., 79410. Tel: 806-796-6000.
E-mail: srclaire@pop3.cris.com
St. Mary of the Plains Hospital Convent. Sisters of St. Joseph of Orange, C.S.J. 3.
Sisters of St. Francis, Millvale, PA, 2706 Genoa Ave., K1, 79407. Tel: 806-793-0331. Sisters 2.

LEVELLAND. *Sisters of Charity of the Incarnate Word*, 320 E. Washington, 79336. Tel: 806-894-3424.

PLAINVIEW. *St. Alice Convent*, 1114 Houston, 79072. Tel: 806-296-5426. St. Francis Mission Community Sisters 3; Novices 1; Postulants 1.

SLATON. *Mercedarian Missionaries Convent*, 1035 W. Crosby, 79364. Tel: 806-828-3566. Sisters 3.

[E] MISCELLANEOUS LISTINGS

LUBBOCK. *Catholic Foundation, Diocese of Lubbock*, P.O. Box 98700, 79499-8700.
Christ the King Cathedral School Foundation, 4011 54th St., 79413.
E-mail: ctk9798@aol.com
Laurel S. Johnson, Chm. Total Staff 25.

RELIGIOUS INSTITUTES OF WOMEN REPRESENTED IN THE DIOCESE

For further details refer to the corresponding bracketed number in the Religious Institutes of Men or Women section.

[0460]—*Congregation of the Sisters of Charity of the Incarnate Word*.—C.C.V.I.

[]—*Dominican Sisters*.—O.P.

[]—*Mercedarian Missionaries of Berriz*.—M.M.B.

[2700]—*Missionary Cathechists of the Sacred Hearts of Jesus and Mary*.—M.C.SS.CC.J.M.

[3130]—*Our Lady of Victory Missionary Sisters*.—O.L.V.M.

[]—*St. Francis Mission Community*. (Amarillo, TX).—O.S.F.

[2575]—*Sisters of Mercy of the Americas*.—R.S.M.

[1620]—*Sisters of Saint Francis of Millvale, PA*.—O.S.F.

[3830]—*Sisters of St. Joseph of Orange*.—C.S.J.

NECROLOGY

(No Deaths)

Diocese of Madison

(Dioecesis Madisonensis)

Most Reverend

WILLIAM H. BULLOCK

Bishop of Madison; ordained June 7, 1952; appointed Auxiliary Bishop of St. Paul and Minneapolis and Titular Bishop of Natchez June 3, 1980; consecrated August 12, 1980; appointed Bishop of Des Moines February 10, 1987; installed April 2, 1987; appointed Bishop of Madison April 13, 1993; installed June 14, 1993.

Most Reverend

GEORGE O. WIRZ

Auxiliary Bishop of Madison and Titular Bishop of Municipa; ordained May 31, 1952; appointed December 20, 1977; consecrated March 9, 1978. *Mailing Address: Bishop O'Connor Center, 3577 S. High Point Rd., Madison, WI, 53719-4999.*

ESTABLISHED 1946.

Square Miles 8,070.

Corporate Title: "Roman Catholic Diocese of Madison."

Comprises the Counties of Columbia, Dane, Grant, Green, Green Lake, Iowa, Jefferson, Lafayette, Marquette, Rock and Sauk in the State of Wisconsin.

For legal titles of parishes and diocesan institutions, consult the Chancery.

Chancery: 15 E. Wilson St., P.O. Box 111, Madison, WI, 53701. Tel.: 608-256-2677; Fax: 608-256-1006.

Web site address: www.madisondiocese.org

E-mail address: diocese@madisondiocese.org

STATISTICAL OVERVIEW

Personnel	
Bishop	1
Auxiliary Bishops	1
Priests: Diocesan Active in Diocese	116
Priests: Active Outside Diocese	5
Priests: Retired, Sick or Absent	35
Number of Diocesan Priests	156
Religious Priests in Diocese	19
Permanent Deacons in Diocese	1
Total Brothers	10
Total Sisters	402
Parishes	
Parishes	137
With Resident Pastor:	
Resident Diocesan Priests	103
Resident Religious Priests	3
Without Resident Pastor:	
Administered by Priests	31
Professional Ministry Personnel:	
Brothers	1
Sisters	31
Lay Ministers	115
Welfare	
Catholic Hospitals	4
Total Assisted	241,348
Health Care Centers	2
Total Assisted	306
Homes for the Aged	6
Total Assisted	762
Day Care and Extended Day Care Centers	15
Total Assisted	688
Special Centers for Social Services	7
Total Assisted	47,154
Residential Care of Disabled	1
Total Assisted	400
Educational	
Diocesan Students in Other Seminaries	20
Total Seminarians	20
Colleges and Universities	1
Total Students	2,056
High Schools, Diocesan and Parish	1
Total Students	92
High Schools, Private	1
Total Students	584
Elementary Schools, Diocesan and Parish	44
Total Students	7,378
Elementary Schools, Private	1
Total Students	253
Catechesis/Religious Education:	
High School Students	11,254
Elementary Students	16,108
Total Students Under Catholic Instruction	37,745
Teachers in the Diocese:	
Brothers	2
Sisters	32
Lay Teachers	551
Vital Statistics	
Receptions into the Church:	
Infant Baptism Totals	3,278
Adult Baptism Totals	439
First Communions	3,181
Confirmations	2,580
Marriages:	
Catholic	799
Interfaith	515
Total Marriages	1,314
Deaths	1,650
Total Catholic Population	258,594
Total Population	876,469

Former Bishops—Most Rev. WILLIAM P. O'CONNOR, D.D., Ph.D., ord. March 10, 1912; appt. Bishop of Superior, Dec. 31, 1941; cons. March 7, 1942; transferred as first Bishop of Madison, Feb. 22, 1946; resigned Feb. 22, 1967; died July 13, 1973.—Most Rev. CLETUS F. O'DONNELL, D.D., J.C.D., ord. May 3, 1941; appt. Titular Bishop of Abrittum and Auxiliary of Chicago, Oct. 26, 1960; cons. Dec. 21, 1960; promoted to Bishop of Madison, Feb. 22, 1967; resigned April 18, 1992; died Aug. 31, 1992.

Vicar-General—Most Rev. GEORGE O. WIRZ, D.D., S.T.L.; Very Rev. PAUL J. SWAIN, J.D.

Chancery—15 E. Wilson St., P.O. Box 111, Madison, 53701. Tel: 608-256-2677; Fax: 608-256-1006. Office Hours: Mon.-Fri. 8-4.

Moderator of the Curia—Rev. PAUL J. SWAIN, J.D.

Chancellor—Rev. Msgr. JOSEPH P. HIGGINS, S.T.L.

Director of Finance—GREGORY J. KELLER.

Diocesan Tribunal—15 E. Wilson St., P.O. Box 111, Madison, 53701. Tel: 608-256-7810.

Judicial Vicar—Rev. MICHAEL E. HIPPEE, J.C.L.

Director of the Tribunal—J. MICHAEL RITTY, J.C.L., Ph.D.

Judges—Rev. JAMES W. HINNEN, J.C.L.

Defender of the Bond—RENATO F. AOANAN, J.C.L.

Auditor/Advocate—Rev. PATRICK R. SWENDROWSKI.

Notary—Rev. BERNARD H. DEITELHOFF; SUSAN STACK.

Diocesan Consultors—Most Rev. GEORGE O. WIRZ; Rev. Msgr. RAYMOND E. KLAAS, J.C.D.; Rev. Msgr. JOSEPH P. HIGGINS, Sec.; Revs. WILLIAM A. DEBOCK; DELBERT D. KLINK; JAMES J. UPPENA.

Presbyteral Council—Most Rev. GEORGE O. WIRZ, Ex-Officio. Elected: Revs. THOMAS R. DOHENY; DAVID H. RUNDE; JOHN H. HEDRICK; DOUGLAS DUSHACK; RAYMOND KERTZ; STEPHEN J. UMHOEFER; THOMAS F. BAXTER; JAMES L. GUNN; GARY L. KRAHENBUHL; ROGER G. NILLES; JOHN L. URBAN; STEVEN G. STEELE; KENNETH SMITS, O.F.M.Cap. Appointed: Rev. Msgr. RAYMOND E. KLAAS, P.A.; Revs. MICHAEL L. BURKE; DANIEL T. GANSHERT; Rev. Msgr. JOSEPH P. HIGGINS; THOMAS M. SEGERSON; PAUL J. SWAIN. Personnel Board: Revs. JOHN M. MEINHOLZ; ELMER J. DIETZEL; THOMAS R. DOHENY; LAWRENCE M. BAKKE; KENNETH FIEDLER; PATRICK SWENDROWSKI; PAUL J. SWAIN.

Vicars for Religious—Rev. DANIEL T. GANSHERT, *404 E. Main St., Madison, 53703-2891.* Tel: 608-257-5000. Sr. LUCILLE MARIE FROST, *855 Woodrow St., Madison, 53711.*

Deaneries—Rev. RAYMOND J. DISCHLER, Columbia Deanery; Rev. WILLIAM A. DEBOCK, East Dane Deanery; Rev. THOMAS F. BAXTER, Grant Deanery; Rev. HENRY N. KALSCHEVER, Iowa Deanery; Rev. THOMAS P. MARR, Jefferson Deanery; Rev. THOMAS J. COYLE, Lafayette Deanery; Rev. KENNETH J. FIEDLER, Madison Deanery; Rev. JEROME J. MAKSVYTIS, Marquette-Green Lake Deanery; Rev. EDWARD J. ERBE, Rock Deanery; Rev. DONALD J. WIECKI, Sauk Deanery; Rev. DELBERT L. SCHMELZER, West Dane Deanery.

Diocesan Offices and Directors

Apostleship of Prayer—Rev. JOSEPH L. HENRY, *432 Maxwell St., Baraboo, 53913.*

Apostolate to the Handicapped—Rev. THOMAS F. CAMPION, *P.O. Box 443, Monroe, 53566.* Tel: 608-324-1000.

Apostolate to the Deaf—Rev. GUY A. BLAIR, S.C.J., *St. Joseph Church, 1905 Beltline Hwy., Madison, 53713.* Tel: 608-278-1980.

Boy Scouts—Rev. BRUCE M. HENNINGTON, *209 South St., Waunakee, 53597-1396.* Tel: 608-849-5121.

Building Commission—Rev. DANIEL T. GANSHERT, Chm.; Revs. MICHAEL E. HIPPEE; DELBERT L. SCHMELZER; Mr. PATRICK GORMAN; Mrs. FRIEDIE CAREY; PAUL BROWN; ARTHUR MCCLURE.

Camp Gray—PHILIP C. DELONG, Dir., *E10213 Shady Lane Rd., Reedsburg, 53959.*

Catholic Relief Services—Rev. PAUL J. SWAIN, *P.O. Box 111, Madison, 53701.* Tel: 608-256-2677.

Cemeteries—THOMAS B. HANLON, JR., Diocesan Dir., Central Office: *2705 Regent St., Madison, 53705.* Tel: 608-238-5562.

Charities—Catholic Charities of the Diocese of Madison, Inc., 4905 Schofield St., Madison, 53716. Tel: 608-221-2000. BRIAN CAIN, Dir., *Administrative Office, 4905 Schofield St., Madison, 53716.* Tel: 608-221-2000., *Madison District Office, 30 S. Franklin St., Madison, 53703.* Tel: 608-256-2358., *Beloit District Office, 3311 Prairie Ave., Beloit, 53511.* Tel: 608-365-3665., *Janesville District Office, 2020 E. Milwaukee St., Janesville, 53545.* Tel: 608-752-4906.

Dir. of Clergy Development—Most Rev. GEORGE O. WIRZ, *15 E. Wilson St., Madison, 53701.* Tel: 608-256-2677.

Education—Rev. JAMES J. UPPENA, Dir., Religious Education, *142 W. Johnson St., Madison, 53703.* Tel: 608-255-5108. JACK MCBRIDE, Assoc. Dir., Adult & Special Education; KATHERINE KERKHOF, Assoc. Dir., Youth; JAMES R. SILVER, Supt., Schools, *P.O. Box 1606, Madison, 53701.* Tel: 608-256-0872. JUDY L. PEPPARD, Asst. Supt., *142 W. Johnson St., Madison, 53703.*

Saint Raphael Society Clergy Retirement Plan—Rev. PAUL J. SWAIN, *P.O. Box 111, Madison, 53701.* Tel: 608-256-2677.

Confraternity of the Blessed Sacrament—Rev. JOSEPH HENRY, Dir., *432 Maxwell St., Baraboo, 53913.* Tel: 608-356-4773.

Council of Catholic Women—Revs. DUANE R. MOELLENBERNDT, Moderator, *St. Joseph Parish, 11 N. 3rd St., Ft. Atkinson, 53538-1801.* Tel: 414-563-3029. LORIN M. BOWENS, Co-Moderator, *St. Boniface Parish, P.O. Box 60, Lime Ridge, 53942.* Tel: 608-986-2101.

Director of Communications—WILLIAM BROPHY. Tel: 608-256-2677.

Holy Childhood, Pontifical Association—Rev. DELBERT L. SCHMELZER, Dir., *301 N. Main St., Verona, 53593.* Tel: 608-845-7323.

Information—Rev. PAUL J. SWAIN, Dir., *P.O. Box 111, Madison, 53701.*

Office of Worship—Dr. PATRICK GORMAN, *Bishop O'Connor Catholic Pastoral Center, 3577 High Pt. Rd., Madison, 53719.* Tel: 608-833-6571.

Office of Family Ministry—Rev. JAMES J. UPPENA, Acting Dir., *142 W. Johnson St., Madison, 53703.* Tel: 608-251-7727.

Office for Justice and Peace—J. MARK BRINKMOELLER, Dir., *Bishop O'Connor Catholic Pastoral Center, 3577 High Pt. Rd., Madison, 53719.* Tel: 608-833-1010.

Newman Apostolate—Madison: Rev. STEVEN J. KORTENDICK, Dir., *St. Paul Univ. Catholic Center, 723 State St., Madison, 53703.* Tel: 608-256-2697. Platteville: Rev. JAMES H. MURPHY, *St. Augustine Newman Center, 135 S. Hickory, Platteville, 53818.* Tel: 608-348-7530.

Newspaper—"Catholic Herald, Madison Edition", MARY UHLER, Editor, *702 N. Blackhawk St., P.O. Box 5913, Madison, 53705.* Tel: 608-233-8060.

Priests' Eucharistic League—Rev. JOSEPH HENRY, Dir., *432 Maxwell St., Baraboo, 53913.* Tel: 608-356-4773.

Office of Hispanic Ministry—MARIO J. DELGADO, Dir., *Bishop O'Connor Catholic Pastoral Center, 3577 High Point Rd., Madison, 53719.* Tel: 608-833-8426.

Centro Pastoral Guadalupano—Sr. ROSEMARY EMPEN, O.P., Dir., *1862 Beld St., Madison, 53713.* Tel: 608-255-8471. *Our Lady of Guadalupe Migrant Center, Endeavor, and Queen of Americas Migrant Center, Cambria.*

Propagation of the Faith—Rev. DELBERT L. SCHMELZER, Dir., *St. Andrew, 301 N. Main St., Verona, 53593.* Tel: 608-845-7323.

Office of RENEW 2000—Sr. EDITH GORSKI, S.S.J-.T.O.S.F., *Bishop O'Connor Catholic Pastoral Center, 3577 High Point Rd., Madison, 53719.* Tel: 608-833-1306.

St. Vincent de Paul Society—Rev. FRANCIS J. STEFFEN, *222 W. Main St., Madison, 53703.* Tel: 608-256-5614.

Serra Clubs—Madison: Revs. JOHN R. AUBY, Janesville: Rev. RICHARD M. HEILMAN, Beloit: Rev. GARY L. KRAHENBUHL.

Vigilance Council—The Very Rev. Deans.

Vocations—Rev. JOHN R. AUBY, Dir., *Bishop O'Connor Catholic Pastoral Center, 3577 High Pt. Rd., Madison, 53719.* Tel: 608-833-6795.

Wisconsin Catholic Conference—JOHN HUEBSCHER, Exec. Sec., *30 W. Mifflin St., Room 302, Madison, 53703.* Tel: 608-257-0004.

CLERGY, PARISHES, MISSIONS AND PAROCHIAL SCHOOLS

CITY OF MADISON
(Dane County)

1—ST. RAPHAEL CATHEDRAL, Rev. Francis J. Steffen. In res., Revs. Steven J. Kortendick; Steven G. Steele.
Res., 222 W. Main St., 53703. Tel: 608-256-5614. [JC]

2—ST. BERNARD, Rev. Michael E. Hippee.
Res., 2450 Atwood Ave., 53704. Tel: 608-249-9256. [JC]

3—BLESSED SACRAMENT, Revs. Stanley Drongowski, O.P.; Jordan McGrath, O.P. In res., Revs. James Cornelius Hahn, O.P.; Hugh Wreisner, O.P.; Gregory J. Moore, O.P.
Res., 2131 Rowley Ave., 53705. Tel: 608-238-3471. [JC]
School—2112 Holister Ave., 53705.
Lay Teachers 19; Students 306.

4—HOLY REDEEMER, Rev. Kevin D. Holmes. In res., Revs. Lawrence J. Kieffer; Jesus Puentes. In res., St. Paul House, Rev. Kenneth Smits, O.F.M.Cap.
Res., 120 W. Johnson St., 53703. Tel: 608-255-1658.

5—IMMACULATE HEART OF MARY, Rev. John M. Meinholz.
Res., 5101 Schofield Ave., 53716. Tel: 608-221-1521. [JC]
School—4913 Schofield Ave., 53716.
Lay Teachers 13; Students 192.

6—OUR LADY, QUEEN OF PEACE, Revs. Kenneth J. Fiedler; Thomas L. Kelley.
Res. and Parish Center: 401 S. Owen Dr., 53711. Tel: 608-231-4600. [JC]
School—418 Holly Ave., 53711.
Lay Teachers 27; Students 486.

7—ST. DENNIS, Revs. Kent A. Schmitt; Randy J. Timmerman; Sr. Ginny Heldorfer, O.S.F., Pastoral Min.
Res., 313 Dempsey Rd., 53714. Tel: 608-246-5124. [JC]
School—Dominican Sisters Sinsinawa 3; Lay Teachers 14; Students 214.

8—ST. JAMES, Rev. Douglas L. Dushack. In res., Rev. John R. Auby.
Res., 1128 St. James Ct., 53715. Tel: 608-255-1656. [JC]
School—1204 St. James Ct., 53715. Tel: 608-256-3095.
Lay Teachers 16; Students 155.

9—SAINT JOSEPH, Rev. Bernard M. Brunette, O.Praem. In res., Rev. Guy A. Blair, S.C.J., Chap. for the Deaf Community.
Res., 1905 W. Beltline Hwy., 53713. Tel: 608-271-5771.

10—ST. MARIA GORETTI, Rev. Michael L. Burke. In res., Rev. Wilfred J. Schuster.
Res., 10 Maria Pl., 53711. Tel: 608-271-7421. [JC]
School—5405 Flad Ave., 53711. Tel: 608-271-7551.
Lay Teachers 12; Students 195.

11—ST. PATRICK, Rev. Daniel T. Ganshert. In res., Most Rev. George O. Wirz.
Res., 404 E. Main St., 53703. Tel: 608-257-5000. [JC]

12—ST. PAUL UNIVERSITY PARISH, Revs. Steven J. Kortendick; Steven G. Steele; Faye A. Darnall, M.Div., Pastoral Assoc.; Mary Gartland Rivera, M.M., Dir., Liturgy & Christian Formation.
Office: 723 State St., 53703. Tel: 608-258-3140. [JC]

13—ST. PETER, Rev. Roger G. Nilles.
Res., 5001 N. Sherman Ave., 53704. Tel: 608-249-6651. [JC]

14—ST. THOMAS AQUINAS, Rev. Donald J. Murray; Sr. Georgeann Roudebush, Pastoral Assoc.
Res., 602 Everglade Dr., 53717. Tel: 608-833-2600. [JC]

OUTSIDE THE CITY OF MADISON

Argyle, Lafayette Co., St. Joseph, Revs. George M. Hastrich; Bernard H. Deitelhoff.
Res., 313 N. Lafayette St., P.O. Box 76, 53504. Tel: 608-543-3631. [CEM]
Mission—Yellowstone, St. Michael.

Ashton, Dane Co., St. Peter's, Rev. Eugene F. Hollfelder.
Res., 7121 Co. Trunk K, Middleton, 53562. Tel: 608-831-4843. [CEM]
School—Tel: 608-831-4846.
Lay Teachers 4; Students 61.

Baraboo, Sauk Co., St. Joseph, Rev. Gerald P. Vosen.
Res., P.O. Box 70, 53913. Tel: 608-356-4773. [CEM]
School—Lay Teachers 11; Students 151.

Belleville, Dane Co., St. Mary of Lourdes, Rev. Kenneth J. Klink.
Res., 221 Frederick St., P.O. Box 220, 53508. Tel: 608-424-3681. [CEM]
Mission—Dayton, St. James. [CEM]

Belmont, LaFayette Co., St. Philomena, Rev. Monte E. Robinson.
Res., 338 Chestnut St., Box 345, 53510. Tel: 608-762-5446.
Missions—Calamine, St. Michael; Truman, Immaculate Conception. [CEM]

Beloit, Rock Co.,

1—OUR LADY OF THE ASSUMPTION, Rev. Gary L. Krahenbuhl.
Res., 2222 Shopiere Rd., 53511. Tel: 608-362-9066. [JC]
School—Lay Teachers 15; Students 197.

2—ST. JUDE, Rev. William R. Connell.
Res., 747 Hackett St., 53511. Tel: 608-364-2820. [JC]
School—Brother Dutton School.
Lay Teachers 13; Students 168.

3—ST. PAUL. Closed 1988. For inquiries for parish records contact St. Thomas the Apostle, Beloit.

4—ST. THOMAS THE APOSTLE, Rev. Thomas R. Doheny.
Res., 822 E. Grand Ave., P.O. Box 933, 53512. Tel: 608-362-1034.

Benton, Lafayette Co., St. Patrick, Rev. Richard J. Lenarz.
Res., 53803. Tel: 608-759-2131. [CEM]

Berlin, Green Lake Co., St. Joseph, Rev. Richard D. Lesniak.
Res., 320 S.W. Franklin St., 54923. Tel: 414-361-0940.
Church—246 E. Park Ave., 54923.
School—Consolidated School. See separate listing.
St. Michael, Rev. Richard D. Lesniak.
Res., 320 S.W. Franklin St., 54923. Tel: 414-361-0940. [CEM]
School—Consolidated School. See separate listing.
St. Stanislaus, Rev. Jerome J. Maksvytis.
Res., 167 N. Wisconsin St., 54923. Tel: 920-361-2354. [CEM]
School—Consolidated School. See separate listing.

Bloomington, Grant Co., St. Mary, Rev. David W. Timmerman.
Res., P.O. Box 35, 53804. Tel: 608-994-2526. [CEM 2]
School—Lay Teachers 7; Students 85.
Mission—Patch Grove, St. John.

Boscobel, Grant Co., Immaculate Conception, Rev. John L. Urban.
Res., 405 E. LeGrand St., 53805. Tel: 608-375-4257.

Briggsville, Marquette Co., St. Mary Help of Christians, Rev. August H. Buenzli.
Res., N565 Hwy. A, Box 127, 53920-0127. Tel: 608-981-2282.

Brodhead, Green Co., St. Rose, Rev. Elmer J. Dietzel.
Res., 1005 W. Second Ave., 53520. Tel: 608-897-2666.
Mission—Albany, St. Patrick's. [CEM]

Cambridge, Dane Co., St. Pius X, Rev. William A. Nolan.
Res., 701 W. Water St., P.O. Box 110, 53523. Tel: 608-423-3015.

Cassville, Grant Co., St. Charles Borromeo, Rev. John Norder.
Res., 605 E. Dewey St., 53806. Tel: 608-725-5595. [CEM 2]
School—521 E. Dewey St., 53806. Tel: 608-725-5173.
School Sisters of St. Francis 2; Lay Teachers 8; Students 97.
Mission—Glen Haven, St. Mary Help of Christians.

Clinton, Rock Co., St. Stephen, Rev. Patrick R. Swendrowski.
Res., Box 399, 53525. Tel: 608-676-2241.

Columbus, Columbia Co., St. Jerome, Rev. William J. Hower.

Parish Office—1550 Farnham St., 53925. Tel: 414-623-3753.
Res., 329 Folsom St., 53925. Tel: 414-623-2720. [CEM]
School—Sisters 1; Lay Teachers 11; Students 146.

Cottage Grove, Dane Co., St. Patrick, Rev. David H. Runde.
Res., P.O. Box 400, 53527-0400. Tel: 608-251-7857.

Cross Plains, Dane Co., St. Francis Xavier, Rev. D. Stephen Smith.
Res., 2947 Thinnes St., P.O. Box 35, 53528. Tel: 608-798-3491.
School—Lay Teachers 14; Students 210.

Cuba City, Grant Co., St. Rose of Lima, Rev. Richard A. Jiru.
Res., 53807. Tel: 608-744-2010. [CEM]
School—Dominican Sisters Sinsinawa, WI 1; Lay Teachers 9; Students 150.

Dane, Dane Co., St. Michael, Rev. Alfred J. Kunz.
Res., P.O. Box 170, 53529. Tel: 608-849-5619. [CEM]
School—Lay Teachers 5; Students 90.

Darlington, Lafayette Co., Holy Rosary, Rev. Thomas J. Coyle.
Res., 104 E. Harriet St., P.O. Box 208, 53530. Tel: 608-776-2251. [CEM 2]
School—Lay Teachers 7; Students 72.

De Forest, Dane Co., St. Olaf, Rev. Daniel P. Finnane.
Res., 623 Jefferson St., Box 446, 53532. Tel: 608-846-3812.

Dickeyville, Grant Co., Holy Ghost, Rev. David J. Flanagan.
Res., 305 W. Main St., 53808. Tel: 608-568-7519. [CEM]
School—Lay Teachers 7; Students 95.

Dodgeville, Iowa Co., St. Joseph, Rev. Henry N. Kalscheuer.
Res., 310 S. Ellwood St., 53533-1799. Tel: 608-935-3392. [CEM]
School—305 E. Walnut St., 53533.
Lay Teachers 11; Students 181.

Doylestown, Columbia Co., St. Patrick, Rev. George W. Fox.
Res., N4085 Bruce St., P.O. Box 40, 53928. Tel: 414-992-3343. [CEM]
Mission—Rio, St. Joseph's. [CEM]

Durward's Glen, Columbia Co., St. Camillus, Rev. Richard Korzinek, O.S.Cam.
Res., W. 11876 McLeish Rd., Baraboo, 53913. Tel: 608-356-4523. [CEM]
Mission—Merrimac, Sauk Co., St. Mary, Health of the Sick, P.O. Box 41, Merrimac, 53561.

East Bristol, Dane Co., St. Joseph, Rev. William A. DeBock.
Res., 1935 Co. Hwy. V, Sun Prairie, 53590. Tel: 608-837-6159. [CEM]

Edgerton, Rock Co., St. Joseph, Rev. James L. Gunn.
Res., St. Joseph's Cir., P.O. Box 147, 53534. Tel: 608-884-3038. [CEM 2]

Evansville, Rock Co., St. Paul, Rev. Edward J. Erbe.
Res., 35 Garfield Ave., 53536. Tel: 608-882-4138. [CEM]

Fennimore, Grant Co., St. Mary, Rev. George B. Horath.
Res., 930 Jefferson St., 53809. Tel: 608-822-6425. [CEM]
Mission—Mount Hope, St. Lawrence O'Toole.

Footville, Rock Co., St. Augustine, Rev. Bernard J. Pickarts.
Res., P.O. Box 325, 53537. Tel: 608-876-6251.

Fort Atkinson, Jefferson Co., St. Joseph, Rev. Duane R. Moellenberndt.
Res., 11 N. 3rd St., 53538. Tel: 920-563-3029. [CEM]
School—310 N. Main St., 53538. Mrs. Joan Meidl, Prin.
Lay Teachers 15; Students 148.

Gratiot, Lafayette Co., St. Joseph, Rev. Jerold F. Fitzpatrick.
Res., Box 37, 53541. Tel: 608-922-6456. [CEM]
Mission—South Wayne, St. John.

Green Lake, Green Lake Co., Our Lady of the Lake, Rev. John R. Dowd.
Res., 530 Ruth St., P.O. Box 215, 54941. Tel: 920-294-6440.

Hazel Green, Grant Co., St. Francis de Sales, Rev. Cyril O. Weisensel.
Res., 2630 N. Main St., P.O. Box 205, 53811-0205. Tel: 608-854-2392. [CEM]

Highland, Iowa Co., SS. Anthony and Philip, Rev. Kenneth J. Frisch.
Res., 1023 Dodgeville, P.O. Box 306, 53543. Tel: 608-929-7490. [CEM 2]

Hollandale, Iowa Co., St. Patrick, Rev. John Hedrick.
Res., P.O. Box 37, 53544. Tel: 608-967-2344. [CEM]
Mission—Blanchardville, Immaculate Conception. [CEM]

Janesville, Rock Co.,

1—NATIVITY OF ST. MARY, Rev. Raymond N. Kertz.
Res., 313 E. Wall St., 53545. Tel: 608-752-7861. [JC]
School—Sisters 1; Lay Teachers 13; Students 270.

2—ST. JOHN VIANNEY, Revs. Michael J. Doro; Richard M. Heilman.
Res., 1245 Clark St., 53545. Tel: 608-752-8708. [JC]
School—Lay Teachers 17; Students 219.

3—ST. PATRICK, Rev. J. Daryl Furlong.
Res., 315 Cherry St., 53545. Tel: 608-754-8193. [JC]
School—Sisters 1; Lay Teachers 9; Students 124.

4—ST. WILLIAM, Rev. Delbert D. Klink.
Res., 1815 Ravine St., 53545. Tel: 608-755-5180. [JC]
School—1822 Ravine St., 53545.
Lay Teachers 12; Students 136.

Jefferson, Jefferson Co., St. John the Baptist, Rev. Terrence L. Connors.
Res., 214 N. Sanborn Ave., 53549. Tel: 920-674-2025. [CEM]
School—Lay Teachers 11; Students 160.
St. Lawrence, Rev. Thomas E. Gillespie.
Res., W. 4926 Hwy. 18, 53549. Tel: 920-674-3217. [CEM]

Kieler, Grant Co., Immaculate Conception, Rev. Philip J. Krogman.
Res., Box 57, 53812. [CEM]
School—Lay Teachers 8; Students 106.

Lake Mills, Jefferson Co., St. Francis Xavier, Rev. John B. Walsh.
Res., 602 College St., P.O. Box 16, 53551. Tel: 414-648-2468.
Mission—Johnson Creek, St. Mary Magdalene. [CEM]

Lancaster, Grant Co., St. Clement, Rev. Thomas F. Baxter.
Res., 135 S. Washington St., 53813. Tel: 608-723-4990. [CEM 2]
School—Sisters 3; Lay Teachers 6; Students 122.

Lime Ridge, Sauk Co., St. Boniface, Rev. Lorin M. Bowens.
Res., 53942. Tel: 608-986-2101. [CEM]
Mission—La Valle, Holy Family. [CEM]

Lodi, Columbia Co., St. Patrick, Rev. Michael C. Richel.
Res., 515 Fair St., 53555. Tel: 608-592-4510. [CEM]

McFarland, Dane Co., Christ the King, Rev. Arthur R. Koth.
Res., 5211 Timber Ln., 53558-9661. Tel: 608-838-8776.

Markesan, Green Lake Co., St. Joseph, Rev. Timothy F. Gericke.
Res., Box 504, 53946-0504. Tel: 414-398-3146.
Mission—Kingston, St. Mary. [CEM]

Marshall, Dane Co., St. Mary's of the Nativity, Rev. Msgr. Raymond E. Klaas, P.A.
Res., P.O. Box 250, 53559-0250. Tel: 608-655-3708. [CEM]

Martinsville, Dane Co., St. Martin, Rev. Francis J. Schmidt.
Res., 5959 St. Martin Cir., Cross Plains, 53528-9312. Tel: 608-798-2815. [CEM]

Mazomanie, Dane Co., St. Barnabas, Rev. O. Charles Schluter.
Res., 113 E. Division St., P.O. Box 68, 53560. Tel: 608-767-3719. [CEM]
Mission—Mill Creek, St. John the Baptist.

Middleton, Dane Co., St. Bernard, Rev. Msgr. Joseph P. Higgins.
Res., 2015 Parmenter St., P.O. Box 620187, 53562-0187. Tel: 608-831-6531. [CEM]

Milton, Rock Co., St. Mary, Rev. James J. McEnery.
Res., 837 Parkview Dr., 53563. Tel: 608-868-3338. [CEM]

Mineral Point, Iowa Co., Congregation of St. Mary-St. Paul, Rev. Thomas M. Segerson.
Res., 224 Davis St., 53565. Tel: 608-987-2026. [JC 2]

Monroe, Green Co., St. Victor, Rev. Stephen J. Umhoefer.
Res., 1760 14th St., 53566. Tel: 608-325-9506. [CEM]
School—Sisters 1; Lay Teachers 9; Students 121.

Montello, Marquette Co., St. John the Baptist, Rev. Gary A. Wankerl.
Res., 277 E. Montello St., 53949. Tel: 608-297-2217. [CEM]
Mission—Westfield, Marquette Co., Good Shepherd, Westfield, 53964. [CEM]

Montfort, Grant Co., St. Thomas, Rev. Laverne G. Meier.
Res., Box 68, 53569. Tel: 608-943-6944. [CEM]
Mission—Castle Rock, St. John Nepomucene. [CEM]

Mount Horeb, Dane Co., St. Ignatius, Rev. Thomas J. Monaghan.
Res., 111 S. Sixth St., 53572. Tel: 608-437-5195. [CEM 2]
Mission—Perry, Holy Redeemer. [CEM]

Muscoda, Grant Co., St. John the Baptist, Rev. Roger H. Taylor.
Res., 341 N. Wisconsin Ave., P.O. Box 35, 53573. Tel: 608-739-3391. [CEM]
Mission—Avoca, St. Joseph. [CEM]

Neshkoro, Marquette Co., St. James, Rev. Joseph H. Schlaefer.
Res., Hwy. 73, P.O. Box 48, 54960. Tel: 920-293-4211. [CEM]

Oregon, Dane Co., Holy Mother of Consolation, Rev. Anthony J. Schumacher.
Res., 651 N. Main St., 53575. Tel: 608-835-5763. [CEM]

Palmyra, Jefferson Co., St. Mary, Rev. Robert E. Buholzer.
Res., 919 W. Main St., P.O. Box P, 53156. Tel: 414-495-2395. [CEM]

Pardeeville, Columbia Co., St. Mary, Rev. Thomas H. Schroeder.
Res., 318 S. Main St., 53954-0216. Tel: 608-429-3030. [CEM]
Education Center & Hall—Tel: 608-429-3129.
Mission—Buffalo, St. Andrew. [CEM]

Pine Bluff, Dane Co., St. Mary of Pine Bluff, Rev. Felix G. Oehrlein.
Res., 3673 Co. Trunk P, Cross Plains, 53528. Tel: 608-798-2111. [CEM]

Plain, Sauk Co., St. Luke, Rev. Michael A. Resop.
Res., 1240 Nachreiner Ave., 53577. Tel: 608-546-2482. [CEM 2]
School—Lay Teachers 8; Students 109.
Mission—Loreto, St. Patrick. [CEM 2]

Platteville, Grant Co., St. Mary, Rev. Kevin F. Dooley.
Res., 130 W. Cedar St., 53818. Tel: 608-348-9735. [CEM]
School—Lay Teachers 9; Students 167.
St. Augustine University Parish, Rev. James H. Murphy.
Res., 135 S. Hickory St., 53818. Tel: 608-348-7530.

Portage, Columbia Co., St. Mary, Rev. Thomas Fitzgerald.
Res., 307 W. Cook St., P.O. Box 216, 53901-0216. Tel: 608-742-6998. [CEM]
School—315 W. Cook St., 53901. Tel: 608-742-4998.
Lay Teachers 13; Students 173.
Convent—Tel: 608-742-2607.

Poynette, Columbia Co., St. Thomas, Rev. Raymond J. Dischler.
Res., 655 S. Main, P.O. Box 310, 53955-0310. Tel: 608-635-4326.

Princeton, Green Lake Co., St. John the Baptist, Rev. Dale W. Grubba.
Res., 1211 W. Main, 54968. Tel: 920-295-6209. [CEM]
School—Lay Teachers 6; Students 104.

Reedsburg, Sauk Co., Sacred Heart, Rev. Donald J. Wiecki.
Res., 624 N. Willow St., 53959. Tel: 608-524-2412. [CEM 3]
School—545 N. Oak St., 53959. Tel: 608-524-3611.
Lay Teachers 12; Students 208.

Ridgeway, Iowa Co., St. Bridget, Rev. Henry N. Kalscheuer.
Res., P.O. Box 127, 53582. Tel: 608-924-2441. [CEM]
Mission—Barneveld, Immaculate Conception.

Roxbury, Dane Co., St. Norbert, Rev. James G. Kuhn.
Res., 8944 County Rd. Y, Sauk City, 53583-9510. Tel: 608-643-3661. [CEM]

Sauk City, Sauk Co., St. Aloysius, Rev. William J. Seipp.
Res., 115 Madison St., 53583. Tel: 608-643-2449. [CEM 2]
School—Tel: 608-643-6868.
Lay Teachers 8; Students 111.

Seymour, Lafayette Co., Our Lady of Hope, Rev. James R. Lins.
Res., Rte. 1, Shullsburg, 53586. Tel: 608-776-2833. [CEM]
Mission—Elk Grove, St. Peter. [CEM]

Shullsburg, Lafayette Co., St. Matthew, Rev. James R. Lins.
Res., 344 Judgement St., 53586. Tel: 608-965-4518. [CEM 2]

Sinsinawa, Grant Co., St. Joseph, Rev. Donald F. Lange.
Res., 780 Hwy. Z, Hazel Green, 53811. Tel: 608-748-4528. [CEM 2]
School—Lay Teachers 5; Students 74.

Spring Green, Sauk Co., St. John the Evangelist, Rev. Kenneth E. Klubertanz.
Res., P.O. Box 628, 53588. Tel: 608-588-2028. [CEM]
School—Lay Teachers 6; Students 93.

Stoughton, Dane Co., St. Ann, Rev. Gerard M. Healy; Sr. Mary Ann Schroedl, O.S.F., Pastoral Assoc.
Res., 320 N. Harrison St., 53589. Tel: 608-873-7633. [CEM]
School—Poor Sisters of Nazareth 2; Students 189.

Sullivan, Jefferson Co., St. Mary Help of Christians, Rev. John H. Hebl.
Res., W. 856 Hwy. 18, 53178. Tel: 414-593-2250. [CEM]

Sun Prairie, Dane Co., Sacred Hearts of Jesus and Mary, Revs. James W. Hinnen; Randy J. Budnar. Pastoral Assocs.: Sr. Anne Raymond Gasser, S.S.N.D.
Res., 221 Columbus St., 53590. Tel: 608-837-7381. [CEM]
School—Lay Teachers 25; Students 435.
St. Albert the Great, Rev. Lawrence M. Bakke.
Res., 2420 St. Albert Dr., 53590. Tel: 608-837-3798.

Tennyson-Potosi, Grant Co., SS. Andrew-Thomas, Rev. Richard J. Leffler.
Res., 101 Church St., Potosi, 53820. Tel: 608-763-2671. [CEM]
School—100 Hwy. 61 N., P.O. Box 160, Potosi, 53820. Tel: 608-763-2120.
Lay Teachers 6; Students 61.

Verona, Dane Co., St. Andrew, Rev. Delbert L. Schmelzer.
Res., 301 N. Main St., 53593. Tel: 608-845-7323.
Mission—Paoli, St. William. [CEM]

Waterloo, Jefferson Co., St. Joseph, Rev. Ronald G. Rank.
Res., 205 W. Milwaukee Ave., 53594-1329. Tel: 414-478-2032. [CEM]
School—Lay Teachers 4; Students 70.

Watertown, Jefferson Co., St. Bernard, Rev. Thomas P. Marr.
Res., 114 S. Church St., 53094-4399. Tel: 414-261-5133. [CEM]
School—Sisters 2; Lay Teachers 12; Students 166.
St. Henry, Rev. Bernard E. Rott.
Res., 412 N. 4th St., 53094. Tel: 920-261-7273. [CEM]
School—300 Cady St., 53094.
Lay Teachers 9; Students 205.

Waunakee, Dane Co., St. John the Baptist, Revs. Bruce M. Hennington; Eric Nielsen.
Res., 209 South St., 53597. Tel: 608-849-5121. [CEM]
School—Lay Teachers 15; Students 258.

Westport, Dane Co., St. Mary of the Lake, Rev. James G. Kramer.
Res., 5460 Marylake Rd., Waunakee, 53597-9121. Tel: 608-849-4116. [CEM]

Wisconsin Dells, Columbia Co., St. Cecilia, Rev. Kevin W. Cassidy.
Res., 604 Oak St., P.O. Box 436, 53965. Tel: 608-254-8381. [CEM]

Chaplains of Public Institutions

MADISON. *Columbia County Institution*. Attended from St. Mary's Church, Portage.
Dane County Institution. Vacant.
Grant County Institution. Attended from St. Clement's Church, Lancaster.
Green County Institution. Attended from St. Victor's Church, Monroe.
Iowa County Institution. Attended from St. Joseph's Church, Dodgeville.
Madison-Meriter General Hospital. Vacant.
Mendota State Hospital. Vacant.
University Hospitals. Rev. Lawrence J. Kieffer, Chap., 120 W. Johnson, 53703.
Veterans' Administration Hospital. Rev. Lawrence R. Heitke, 8220 Raymond Rd., 53719. Tel: 608-256-1901, Ext. 327.

JANESVILLE. *Jefferson County Institution*. Attended from St. John the Baptist Church, Jefferson.
LaFayette County Institution. Attended from Holy Rosary Church, Darlington.
Mercy Hospital. Attended from Janesville Parishes, Janesville.
Rock County Institution. Attended from Janesville Parishes, Janesville.
Sauk County Institution. Attended from St. Boniface Church, Lime Ridge.
Wisconsin State School for the Blind. Attended from St. Patrick's Church, Janesville.

Military Chaplains:
Reverend Fathers—
Browne, Vincent T.
Hughes, Robert W.
Klarer, Michael E.
Turner, Jerome R.

Leave of Absence:
Reverend Fathers—
Clauder, J. Gibbs
McBride, William F.

Absent on Sick Leave:
Reverend Fathers—
Adams, Archie H.
Doherty, Patrick J.
Dutchoff, C. Robert
Runde, Raymond E.
Sosinski, Thomas P.

Retired:
Reverend Monsignors—
Doherty, Francis E., Rte. 3 W., 11031 Lakeview Dr., Lodi, WI 53555
Mack, Ferdinand A., Nazareth House, 814 Jackson St., Stoughton, WI 53589
O'Hara, Robert J., 317 N. VanBuren St., Stoughton, WI 53589
Reverend Fathers—
Bauhs, Eugene J., 6205 Mineral Point Rd., #216, Madison, WI 53705
Beck, Charles L., 502 St. Lawrence Ave., Janesville, WI 53545
Brechtl, Joseph A., 602 N. Segoe Rd., Madison, WI 53705
Brickl, Joseph M., 6130 Century Ave., Apt. 103D, Middleton, WI 53562
Brophy, Robert J., P.O. Box 44342, Madison, WI 53744-4342
Cieciorka, Josef, St. Anthony by the Sea Home, 1200 Surf Rd., Riviera Beach, FL 33404
Conlon, Philip J., 306 Michael Ave., P.O. Box 320, Hollister, MO 65672
Cox, Joseph C., 2515 Deerfield St., Portage, WI 53901-1081
Dominic, Francis J., 2029 Brenna Ct., Cuba City, WI 53807
Grasso, Philip A., 211 N. Lincoln, Cuba City, WI 53807
Heindl, Arthur W., N. 7157 Cottage Dr., Westboro, WI 54490
Henry, Joseph L., 432 Maxwell St., Baraboo, WI 53913
Holzer, Ambrose W., 130 N. Main St., Fall River, WI 53932
Marx, Lambert M., 1927 N. Pontiac, Janesville, WI 53545
Mattucci, James J., 47175 Burton, Utica, MI 48317
Meloy, Bernard F., 6817 Old Sauk Ct., Madison, WI 53717-1128
Mersberger, Jerome, Palmyra, WI 53156
Niglis, Joseph C., 1766 Fordem Ave., Madison, WI 53704
Pierick, Bernard E., P.O. Box 216, Portage, WI 53901
Reddington, Benjamin J., 201 Wallace Ave., Pottsville, PA 17901
Schubiger, Albert B., 424 Prospect Ave., Beloit, WI 53511
Schuster, Wilfred J., 10 Maria Pl., Madison, WI 53711
Stack, William E., 706 Jefferson, Sauk City, WI 53583
Turner, Wayne A., 502 St. Lawrence Ave., Janesville, WI 53545
Young, Anthony J., 2411 Tawhee Dr., Apt. 104, Madison, WI 53711

INSTITUTIONS LOCATED IN THE DIOCESE

[A] SEMINARIES, RELIGIOUS OR SCHOLASTICATES

DURWARD'S GLEN. *St. Camillus Monastery and Retreat Center*, P.O., Baraboo, W 11876 McLeish Rd., 53913. Tel: 608-356-4523. Rev. Richard Korzinek, O.S.Cam., Supr. Priests 1.

[B] COLLEGES

MADISON. *Edgewood College*, 855 Woodrow St., 53711. Tel: 608-257-4861
For a complete listing, refer to the Colleges and Universities section.

[C] HIGH SCHOOLS, DIOCESAN

BELOIT. *Catholic High School*, 1221 Henry Ave., 53511. Governed by the Board of Directors. Mr. Tim McKearn, Prin. Lay Teachers 12; Students 92.

[D] HIGH SCHOOLS, PRIVATE

MADISON. *Edgewood High School*, 2219 Monroe St., 53711. Tel: 608-257-1023. Dominican Sisters, Sinsinawa. Mr. Thomas E. Shipley, Pres.; Ms. Kathleen M. Hanlon, Prin. Priests 1; Lay Teachers 49; Students 584.

[E] CONSOLIDATED ELEMENTARY SCHOOLS

BERLIN. *Berlin Catholic School*, 151 S. Grove St., 54923. Tel: 414-361-1781. Jean Inda, Prin. Consolidation of the following parishes: St. Joseph; St. Michael; and St. Stanislaus. Lay Teachers 11; Students 151.

[F] ELEMENTARY SCHOOLS, PRIVATE

MADISON. *Edgewood Campus School*, 2324 Edgewood Dr., 53711. Tel: 608-257-7726. Dominican Sisters, Sinsinawa. Sr. Nancy Rae Reisdorf, O.P., Pres.; Mrs. Donna Jean Gifford, Prin. Sisters 1; Brothers 1; Lay Teachers 20; Students 253.

[G] GENERAL HOSPITALS

MADISON. *St. Marys Hospital Medical Center*, 707 S. Mills St., 53715. Tel: 608-251-6100
For a complete listing, refer to the Hospitals section.

BARABOO. *St. Clare Hospital and Health Services*, 707 14th St., 53913. Tel: 608-356-5561
For a complete listing, refer to the Hospitals section.

MONROE. *St. Clare Hospital of Monroe, Wisconsin, Inc., dba The Monroe Clinic, Inc.*, 515 22nd Ave., 53566. Tel: 608-324-1000
For a complete listing, refer to the Hospitals section.

PORTAGE. *Divine Savior Hospital & Nursing Home, Inc.*, 1015 W. Pleasant St., 53901. Tel: 608-742-4131; Fax: 608-742-6098
For a complete listing, refer to the Hospitals section.

[H] HOMES FOR THE AGED

MADISON. *St. Marys Care Center*, 1347 Fish Hatchery Rd., 53715. Tel: 608-257-0781
For a complete listing, refer to the Special Care Facilities section.

BARABOO. *St. Clare Meadows Care Center*, 1414 Jefferson St., 53913. Tel: 608-356-4838; Fax: 608-356-5441
For a complete listing, refer to the Special Care Facilities section.

JANESVILLE. *St. Elizabeth Home*, 502 St. Lawrence Ave., 53545. Tel: 608-752-6709
For a complete listing, refer to the Special Care Facilities section.

PORTAGE. *Divine Savior Nursing Home*, 715 W. Pleasant St., 53901. Tel: 608-742-4131
For a complete listing, refer to the Special Care Facilities section.

STOUGHTON. *Nazareth House*, 814 Jackson St., 53589. Tel: 608-873-6448; Fax: 608-873-0829
For a complete listing, refer to the Special Care Facilities section.

WATERTOWN. *St. Joseph's Home*, 705 Clyman St., 53094. Tel: 414-261-4283
For a complete listing, refer to the Special Care Facilities section.

[I] MONASTERIES AND RESIDENCES OF PRIESTS

MADISON. *Bishop O'Connor Catholic Pastoral Center*, 3577 High Point Rd., 53719. Tel: 608-833-1010. Revs. Paul J. Swain; James Uppena.

EDGERTON. *Legion of Christ, Inc.*, 432 Liquori Rd., P.O. Box 107, 53534. Tel: 608-884-3428; Fax: 608-884-8175. Revs. Thomas Moylan, L.C., Supr.; Juan Gabriel Guerra, L.C., Chap.; Matthew VanSmoorenburg, L.C., Promotion; Bros. Patrick Butler, L.C.; Alfonse Nazarro, L.C.; Michael Lee, L.C.; Alexander Kim, L.C.; Louis Judd, L.C.

[J] CONVENTS AND RESIDENCES FOR SISTERS

MADISON. *Franciscan Sisters of Mary*, 901 High St., 53715-1913. Tel: 608-255-1510. Sisters 4.
Monastery of Saint Benedict Center, P.O. Box 5070, 53705-0070. Tel: 608-836-1631; Fax: 608-831-9312. Monastery of the Sisters of Saint Benedict. Sr. Mary David Walgenbach, O.S.B., Prioress. Sisters 9.
Secular Institute of Schoenstatt Sisters of Mary, 5901 Cottage Grove Rd., 53718. Tel: 608-222-7208; Fax: 608-222-0430. Janice Heyl, Supr. Sisters 10.

BARABOO. *Community of Hope*, 1021 Ash St., 53913-2163. Tel: 608-356-8641. Franciscan Sisters of Mary. Sisters 3.
St. Marys Ringling Convent, 1208 Oak St., 53913-1698. Tel: 608-356-5577. Franciscan Sisters of Mary. Sr. Elizabeth Ruppert, F.S.M., Community Coord.; Rev. Leonard van-Ackeren, O.S.B. (Milwaukee), Chap. Sisters 14.

BELOIT. *Blessed Sacrament Convent*, 916 Bluff St., 53511. Tel: 608-362-3326.
Motherhouse of the Auxiliaries of the Blessed Sacrament. Mother Marie Dufresne, A.B.S., Supr. Gen. Sisters in Residence 5.

PRAIRIE DU SAC. *Valley of Our Lady Monastery*, 53578. Tel: 608-643-3520; 643-7986 (Altar Breads); Fax: 608-643-3520. Cistercian Nuns. Mother M. Paula Hannah, O.Cist., Prioress. Solemnly Professed 11; Simply Professed 3.

SINSINAWA. *Dominican Motherhouse*, 53824. Tel: 608-748-4411; Fax: 608-748-4491. Sinsinawa Dominican Congregation of the Most Holy Rosary. Sr. Jean McSweeney, O.P., Prioress of the Congregation. Provincials: Sr. Marise Barry, O.P., Eastern Prov.; Sr. Patricia Caraher, O.P., Southern Prov.; Sr. Carol Coenen, O.P., Western Prov.; Sr. Helen Martin, O.P., Prioress of the Motherhouse; Revs. Joseph Fogarty, O.P.; Brian Bricker, O.P. Sisters in the Congregation 923; Sisters 206.
Dominican Novitiate: Novices 4.

WISCONSIN DELLS. *North American Union of the Sisters of Our Lady of Charity, Inc.*, Administration Centre, P.O. Box 327, 53965-0327. Tel: 304-242-0042; Fax: 304-424-8981. Administration Office, 154 Edgington Ln., Wheeling, WV, 26003-1535. Tel: 304-242-0042; Fax: 303-242-8981. Sr. Deana Kohlman, Supr. Gen.; Sr. Ellen Patrick Stapleton, Bus. Mgr.

[K] CHARITABLE INSTITUTIONS

MADISON. *Catholic Charities, Inc.* Diocese of Madison, Administrative Center, 4905 Schofield St., 53716. Tel: 608-221-2000. Brian Cain, Dir.

Central City Counseling Services, 30 S. Franklin St., 53703. Tel: 608-256-2358.

Beloit District Office, 3311 Prairie Ave., Beloit, 53511. Tel: 608-365-3665.

Janesville District Office, 2020 E. Milwaukee St., Janesville, 53545. Tel: 608-752-4906.

Saint Martin House. (Interracial Center), 1862 Beld St., 53713. Tel: 608-255-1287. Rev. George M. Hastrich, Spiritual Dir. Volunteer Staff.

Society of St. Vincent de Paul. (District Council of Madison, Inc.), 1109 Jonathon Dr., 53713-3230. Tel: 608-278-2920. Rev. Francis J. Steffen, Spiritual Dir.; Mr. Jack W. Mussey, Council Pres.

JEFFERSON. *St. Coletta of Wisconsin, Inc.*, W. 4955 Hwy. 18, 53549. Tel: 920-674-4330. Sisters of St. Francis of Assisi. Dr. Henry C. Meece, Pres.; Sr. Verna Kayser, O.S.F., Coord.; Rev. Thomas E. Gillespie, Chap. Sisters 21; Brothers 1; Residents 400; Lay Staff 500.

[L] RETREAT HOUSES

MADISON. *Saint Benedict Center, Ecumenical Retreat and Conference Center*, P.O. Box 5070, 53705-0070. Tel: 608-836-1631; Fax: 608-831-9312. Sr. Mary David Walgenbach, O.S.B. Sisters 5.

[M] MISCELLANEOUS

MADISON. *Catholic Health Association of Wisconsin, Inc.*, 5721 Odana Rd., Ste. 204, 53719-1222. Tel: 608-274-5588; Fax: 608-274-6872. Sr. Rosemary Sabino, R.S.M., Pres. & CEO; Sr. Louis Bush, S.S.M., Chairperson of the Board.

Edgewood Incorporated, 855 Woodrow St., 53711. Dr. James A. Ebben, Pres. Sponsored by Sinsinawa Dominican Sisters of Sinsinawa, WI. Purpose: The education of individuals in such subjects as are usually taught in high schools, academies, and colleges.

Mid-America Catholic Colleges. (MACC), 15 E. Wilson St., P.O. Box 111, 53701. Membership consists of the following 9 colleges: Clarke College; College of St. Catherine; College of Saint Teresa; College of St. Thomas; Loras College; Mount Mercy College; Saint Mary's College; St. Norbert College; and Viterbo College.

San Damiano Friary, 4123 Monona Dr., 53716. Tel: 608-222-6238. Capuchin Order-Province of St. Joseph. House of Healing and Hospitality. Revs. Leo Petrimoulx, O.F.M.Cap.; Rupert Dorn, O.F.M.Cap; Benedict Adams, O.F.M.Cap.; Gary Keegstra, O.F.M.Cap., Local Min.; Bros. Leopold Gleissner, O.F.M.Cap.; Edward Hagman, O.F.M.Cap.

Wisconsin Association of Principals of Catholic Secondary Schools, 142 W. Johnson St., 53703-2298. Tel: 608-256-0872.

BARABOO. *Saint Vincent de Paul Society-Baraboo*, 100 S. Boulevard, P.O. Box 233, 53913. Tim Nolden, Contact Person. Sponsored by: Saint Vincent de Paul Society. Purpose: To help the poor and needy in a Vincentian spirit and manner.

EDGERTON. *Oaklawn Academy*, 432 Liguori Rd., 53534.

Oaklawn Incorporated, 432 Liguori Rd., R.R. P.O. Box 107, 53534. Chaplains: Thomas Moylan, L.C.; Rev. Juan Gabriel Guerra, L.C.; Mr. Eduardo Grandio, Prin.

PLATTEVILLE. *St. Augustine Newman Center*, 135 S. Hickory, 53818.
Please refer to St. Augustine University Parish, Platteville.

PRAIRIE DU SAC. *Society of Saint Vincent de Paul, Sauk-Prairie / Roxbury Area*, 815 19th St., 53578. Frank DiNovo, Contact Person. Sponsored by: Saint Vincent de Paul Society. Purpose: To help the poor and needy in a Vincentian spirit and manner.

SINSINAWA. *Sinsinawa Dominican Community Support Trust*, c/o General Delivery, 53824-9999. Sr. Jean McSweeney, O.P., Contact Person. Sponsored by: Sinsinawa Dominicans. Purpose: To provide financial support to retired and invalid vowed members of the Sinsinawa Dominicans.

RELIGIOUS INSTITUTES OF MEN REPRESENTED IN THE DIOCESE

For further details refer to the corresponding bracketed number in the Religious Institutes of Men or Women section.

[0200]—*Benedictine Monks.*—O.S.B.
[0900]—*Canons Regular of Premontre.*—O.Praem.
[0430]—*Order of Preachers-Dominicans.* (Prov. of St. Albert the Great).—O.P.
[0240]—*Order of St. Camillus.*—O.S.Cam.
[0990]—*Society of the Catholic Apostolate.* (Mater Dei Prov.).—S.A.C.

RELIGIOUS INSTITUTES OF WOMEN REPRESENTED IN THE DIOCESE

[]—*Auxiliaries of the Blessed Sacrament.*—A.B.S.
[0230]—*Benedictine Sisters of Pontifical Jurisdiction.*—O.S.B.
[0680]—*Cistercian Nuns.*—O.Cist.
[3735]—*Congregation of St. Brigid.*—C.S.B.
[3710]—*Congregation of the Sisters of Saint Agnes.*—C.S.A.
[1070-03]—*Dominican Sisters.*—O.P.
[1070-09]—*Dominican Sisters.*—O.P.
[1230]—*Franciscan Sisters of Christian Charity.*—O.S.F.
[1310]—*Franciscan Sisters of Little Falls, Minnesota.*—O.S.F.
[1415]—*Franciscan Sisters of Mary.*—F.S.M.
[2575]—*Institute of the Sisters of Mercy of the Americas.*—R.S.M.
[2970]—*School Sisters of Notre Dame.*—S.S.N.D.
[1680]—*School Sisters of St. Francis.*—O.S.F.
[]—*Secular Institute of Schoenstatt Sisters of Mary.*
[3020]—*Sisters Oblates to Divine Love.*—R.O.D.A.
[0530]—*Sisters of Charity of Our Lady, Mother of the Church.*—S.C.M.C.
[3930]—*Sisters of St. Joseph of the Third Order of St. Francis.* (Prov. of St. Joseph).—S.S.J.-T.O.S.F.
[1030]—*Sisters of the Divine Savior.*—S.D.S.
[1705]—*Sisters of the Third Order of St. Francis of Assisi.*—O.S.F.

DIOCESAN CEMETERIES

MADISON. *Resurrection*, 2705 Regent St., 53705. Tel: 608-238-5561.

BELOIT. *Calvary*. 1827 N. Washington, Janesville, 53545. Tel: 608-362-3092.

Mount Thabor. 1827 N. Washington, Janesville, 53545. Tel: 608-362-3092.

DOYLESTOWN. *Rocky Run*, P.O. Box 40, 53928. Tel: 414-992-3343.

JANESVILLE. *Mount Olivet*, 1827 N. Washington St., 53545. Tel: 608-754-3472.

NECROLOGY

† Moran, Donald V, Ridgeway, WI, St. Bridget. —Died Aug. 5, 1997.

Diocese of Manchester

(Dioecesis Manchesteriensis)

Most Reverend

ODORE J. GENDRON, D.D.

Retired Bishop of Manchester; ordained May 31, 1947; appointed December 12, 1974; consecrated February 3, 1975. *Res., St. Joseph Cathedral, 145 Lowell St., Manchester, NH, 03104-6135.*

Most Reverend

FRANCIS J. CHRISTIAN, PH.D.

Auxiliary Bishop of Manchester, Administrator of the Diocese of Manchester; ordained June 29, 1968; appointed April 2, 1996; consecrated May 14, 1996. *Res., St. Joseph Cathedral, 145 Lowell St., Manchester, NH, 03104-6135.*

Chancery Office: 153 Ash St., P.O. Box 310, Manchester, NH, 03105. Tel.: 603-669-3100; Fax: 603-669-0377.

Web site address: http://www.diocesemanch.org

E-mail address: mattmcsorley@grolen.com

ESTABLISHED 1884.

Square Miles 9,305.

Comprises the State of New Hampshire.

For legal titles of parishes and diocesan institutions, consult the Chancery Office.

STATISTICAL OVERVIEW

Personnel	
Bishop	1
Auxiliary Bishops	1
Retired Bishops	1
Abbots	1
Retired Abbots	1
Priests: Diocesan Active in Diocese	166
Priests: Active Outside Diocese	10
Priests: Retired, Sick or Absent	75
Number of Diocesan Priests	251
Religious Priests in Diocese	78
Ordinations:	
Diocesan Priests	4
Transitional Deacons	1
Permanent Deacons in Diocese	23
Total Brothers	46
Total Sisters	765
Parishes	
Parishes	131
With Resident Pastor:	
Resident Diocesan Priests	115
Resident Religious Priests	10
Without Resident Pastor:	
Administered by Priests	5
Missions	38
Professional Ministry Personnel:	
Brothers	1
Sisters	44
Lay Ministers	49
Welfare	
Catholic Hospitals	2
Total Assisted	15,182
Homes for the Aged	6
Total Assisted	433
Residential Care of Children	2
Total Assisted	62
Day Care and Extended Day Care Centers	1
Total Assisted	310
Educational	
Diocesan Students in Other Seminaries	15
Students Religious	1
Total Seminarians	16
Colleges and Universities	6
Total Students	6,439
High Schools, Diocesan and Parish	3
Total Students	1,569
High Schools, Private	1
Total Students	780
Elementary Schools, Diocesan and Parish	34
Total Students	6,850
Elementary Schools, Private	3
Total Students	837
Catechesis/Religious Education:	
High School Students	5,539
Elementary Students	28,591
Total Students Under Catholic Instruction	50,621
Teachers in the Diocese:	
Brothers	6
Sisters	58
Lay Teachers	622
Vital Statistics	
Receptions into the Church:	
Infant Baptism Totals	5,169
Adult Baptism Totals	178
First Communions	5,195
Confirmations	3,044
Marriages:	
Catholic	1,021
Interfaith	422
Total Marriages	1,443
Deaths	3,180
Total Catholic Population	326,870
Total Population	1,162,000

Former Bishops—Rt. Rev. DENIS M. BRADLEY, D.D., first Bishop of Manchester; cons. June 11, 1884; died Dec. 13, 1903.—Rt. Rev. JOHN B. DELANY, D.D., cons. Sept. 8, 1904; died June 11, 1906.—Most Rev. GEORGE ALBERT GUERTIN, D.D., cons. March 19, 1907; died Aug. 6, 1931.—Most Rev. JOHN B. PETERSON, D.D., cons. Auxiliary Bishop of Boston, Nov. 10, 1927; transferred to See, May 13, 1932; died March 15, 1944.—Most Rev. MATTHEW F. BRADY, D.D., cons. Oct. 26, 1938; transferred to See, Nov. 11, 1944; died Sept. 20, 1959.—Most Rev. ERNEST J. PRIMEAU, S.T.D., appt. Nov. 27, 1959; resigned Jan. 30, 1974; died June 15, 1989.—Most Rev. ODORE J. GENDRON, D.D., ord. May 31, 1947; appt. Dec. 12, 1974; cons. Feb. 3, 1975.—Most Rev. LEO E. O'NEIL, D.D., ord. June 4, 1955; appt. Coadjutor Oct. 17, 1989; succeeded to See June 12, 1990; died Nov. 30, 1997.

Vicars General—Rev. Msgr. JOHN E. MOLAN, V.G., P.A.; Rev. Msgr. ALBERT W. OLKOVIKAS, V.G., P.A., *153 Ash St., P.O. Box 310, Manchester, 03105.* Tel: 603-669-3100.

Secretary for Pastoral Services—Rev. Msgr. NORMAN P. BOLDUC, S.T.L., J.C.L., *153 Ash St., P.O. Box 310, Manchester, 03105.* Tel: 603-669-3100.

Co-Secretaries for Temporalities—Rev. Msgr. ALBERT W. OLKOVIKAS, S.T.L., J.C.D.; Rev. Msgr. JOHN E. MOLAN, *153 Ash St., P.O. Box 310, Manchester, 03105.* Tel: 603-669-3100.

Associate Secretary for Temporalities—Rev. EDWARD J. ARSENAULT, *153 Ash St., P.O. Box 310, Manchester, 03105.* Tel: 603-669-3100.

Secretary for Christian Formation—Sr. PAULINE LEBEL, C.S.C., *153 Ash St., P.O. Box 310, Manchester, 03105.* Tel: 603-669-3100.

Secretary for Community Services—Rev. Msgr. JOHN P. QUINN, *153 Ash St., P.O. Box 310, Manchester, 03105.* Tel: 603-669-3100.

Controller—Mr. DANA C. HIRST, *153 Ash St., P.O. Box 310, Manchester, 03105.* Tel: 603-669-3100.

Chancery Office—153 Ash St., P.O. Box 310, Manchester, 03105. Tel: 603-669-3100; Fax: 603-669-0377.

Chancellor—Rev. Msgr. NORMAN P. BOLDUC, S.T.L., J.C.L.

Vice Chancellor—Rev. Msgr. PAUL L. BOUCHARD, S.T.L., J.C.L.

Vicar for Clergy—Most Rev. FRANCIS J. CHRISTIAN, Ph.D.

Secretaries to Bishop—HELEN VOLLINGER; LUCILLE CONNOR.

Diocesan Tribunal—153 Ash St., P.O. Box 310, Manchester, 03105. Tel: 603-669-3100.

Judicial Vicar—Rev. Msgr. DONALD J. GILBERT, J.C.L.

Associate Judicial Vicar—Rev. JOHN J. MAHONEY, JR., J.C.L.

Promotor Justitiae—Rev. FRANCIS L. DEMERS, O.M.I., J.C.D.

Canonical Consultant and Judge—Rev. Msgr. RAYMOND O. BLAIR, J.C.D.

Advocates—Revs. KARL E. DOWD; RICHARD P. TETU.

Defensor Vinculi—Rev. FRANCIS DEMERS, O.M.I., J.C.D.; Rev. Msgr. PAUL L. BOUCHARD, S.T.L., J.C.L.; Rev. Msgr. NORMAN P. BOLDUC, S.T.L., J.C.L.; Sr. LOUISE TESSIER, P.M., J.C.L.

Associate Judges—Rev. Msgr. NORMAN P. BOLDUC, S.T.L., J.C.L.; Rev. Msgr. JOHN P. QUINN; Revs. GERALD R. DUNN; LEO L. FRECHETTE; DONALD E. LAFOND.

Notaries—JOAN FOX; DEBORAH HARRINGTON.

College of Consultors—Most Rev. FRANCIS J. CHRISTIAN, Ph.D.; Rev. Msgr. NORMAN P. BOLDUC, S.T.L., J.C.L.; Rev. Msgr. ALBERT W. OLKOVIKAS, S.T.L., J.C.D.; Rev. Msgr. JOHN E. MOLAN; Rev. Msgr. THOMAS J. HANNIGAN; Rev. Msgr. JOHN P. QUINN; Rev. Msgr. JOHN F. BURKE; Rev. Msgr. FERNAND L. PICHETTE; Revs. JOSEPH S. KLATKA; TIMOTHY R. O'DONNELL.

Diocesan Administrative Council—Rev. Msgr. ALBERT W. OLKOVIKAS, J.C.D.

Diocesan School Board—Bro. KENNETH HOGAN, Supt., Schools; JOSEPH HORTON; Sr. FRANCES LESSARD, C.S.C.; GUY CHAPDELAINE; JOAN DOBZANSKI; W. JAMES DOYLE; Revs. GEORGE E. HAM; A. STEPHEN MARCOUX, III; Ms. CHRIS MCMAHON; DAVID A. GABERT; CHARLES C. BURR; JOHN DOWD.

Diocesan Building and Real Estate Board—Rev. Msgr. JOHN E. MOLAN, Chm.; Rev. Msgr. NORMAN P. BOLDUC; Rev. Msgr. JOHN P. QUINN; Revs. DONALD GAUTHIER; BERNARD J. CAMPBELL, O.F.M.Cap.; Mr. JOSEPH W. FOBES; ROBERT L. LAFERRIERE; RUSSELL

GRADY; PAUL HOUGHTON; JOHN LYONS; THEODORE PAQUETTE, *153 Ash St., Manchester, 03105.* Tel: 603-669-3100.

Deans—Rev. JAMES W. HALLER, Manchester East; Rev. Msgr. PAUL L. BOUCHARD, Manchester West; Rev. WILFRED H. DESCHAMPS, Berlin; Rev. C. PETER DUMONT, Concord; Rev. PAUL D. MONTMINY, Dover; Rev. MAURICE R. LAROCHELLE, Franconia; Rev. RICHARD J. KELLEY, Keene; Rev. WILLIAM J. QUIRK, Laconia; Rev. RICHARD T. LOWER, Lebanon; Rev. ROBERT E. GORSKI, Nashua; Rev. MAURICE J. ROCHEFORT, Salem.

Council of Priests—Vacant; Pres.; Most Rev. FRANCIS J. CHRISTIAN; Rev. Msgr. ALBERT W. OLKOVIKAS; Rev. Msgr. JOHN E. MOLAN; Rev. Msgr. FERNAND L. PICHETTE; Rev. Msgr. JOHN P. QUINN; Rev. Msgr. JOHN F. BURKE; Rev. Msgr. THOMAS J. HANNIGAN; Rev. Msgr. COLIN E. MACDONALD; Rev. Msgr. NORMAN P. BOLDUC; Revs. RICHARD W. CONNORS; WILFRED H. DESCHAMPS; C. PETER DUMONT, Chm. JOSEPH S. KLATKA; THOMAS HORAN, O.M.I.; GEORGE E. HAM; ROBERT F. COLE; RICHARD T. LOWER; GERALD F. JOYAL; JOHN FORTIN, O.S.B.; ROBERT E. GORSKI; TIMOTHY R. O'DONNELL; W. PIERRE BAKER; ALBION F. BULGER; RICHARD F. CLAVELLE, O.S.B.; A. STEPHEN MARCOUX, III; MARK E. DOLLARD; AGAPIT H. JEAN; LEO A. LEBLANC.

Diocesan Pastoral Council—Vacant; Pres.; Most Rev. FRANCIS J. CHRISTIAN; Rev. Msgr. NORMAN P. BOLDUC; Bro. PAUL CRAWFORD; MATTHEW CARNEVALE; GERARD ROUTHIER; DAVID GAMACHE; DORIS BOUTIN-CYR; PATRICIA BOWERS; DEBORAH REINDERS; ANTHONY POEKERT; MARGARET PLUMER; FRANCIS KUSHI; JANICE STEENBEKE; PHYLLIS DIPRIZIO; ALBERT CORMIER; IRENE A. PLOURDE; RAMON ANDRADE; DE PHAM; MONICA JACOBS; Sr. RACHEL M. JETTE, C.S.C.; Sr. LOUISE TESSIER, P.M.; Sr. ROSINA BECHARD, F.C.S.C.J.; Sr. HARRIET CUTTING, S.N.D.deN.; Sr. MARIA ROSA, P.M.; Sr. FELICIA MCKONE, R.S.M.; Revs. DANIEL L. BERNIER; LEO A. LEBLANC; JOHN R. POIRIER; Deacon ALFRED A. LABONTE, JR.

Personnel Board—Rev. Msgr. THOMAS J. HANNIGAN; Rev. Msgr. NORMAN P. BOLDUC; Revs. MARC R. MONTMINY; ROBERT G. BOISVERT; WILLIAM L. QUIRK; PAUL L. GREGOIRE; DENIS F. HORAN; ROBERT F. COLE; GEORGE E. HAM; Rev. Msgr. JAMES P. WATSON.

Apostolate to the Deaf—Rev. BERNARD J. CAMPBELL, O.F.M.Cap., *St. Anne Church, 231 Merrimcack St., Manchester, 03103-5295.* Tel: 603-623-8809.

Campaign for Human Development—Sr. MARGARET CROSBY, S.N.D.deN., Dir., *153 Ash St., P.O. Box 310, Manchester, 03105.*

Camping—Rev. KARL E. DOWD, Dir., *153 Ash St., P.O. Box 310, Manchester, 03105.* Tel: 603-669-3100.

Censores Librorum—Rev. ROBERT G. BOISVERT, S.T.D.; Most Rev. FRANCIS J. CHRISTIAN, Ph.D.

Commission for Ecumenical Affairs—Rev. Msgr. NORMAN P. BOLDUC, S.T.L., J.C.L., Chm., *153 Ash St., P.O. Box 310, Manchester, 03105.* Tel: 603-669-3100.

Council of Catholic Women—Rev. ROGER A. FORTIER, *St. Peter Rectory, 90 Central St., P.O. Box 565, Farmington, 03835.*

Department of Spiritual Renewal Services—Rev. JOHN M. GRACE, Dir. GEORGE CURRAN, Assoc. Dir. RICHARD KIERNAN, Assoc. Dir.; Sr. MARY ANNE LAUGHLIN, S.N.D.deN., Assoc. Dir. CONNIE MCGRAW, Asst. Dir. MARILYN FREESE, Admin. Asst., *153 Ash St., Box 310, Manchester, 03105.* Tel: 603-669-3100.

Center for Spiritual Direction—Rev. JOHN M. GRACE.

Charismatic Renewal—GEORGE CURRAN.

Crown Ministry—RICHARD KIERNAN.

Cursillo Movement—Rev. JOHN M. GRACE.

Office of Evangelization—Rev. JOHN M. GRACE; GEORGE CURRAN; RICHARD KIERNAN.

Joseph House—Sr. MARY ANNE LAUGHLIN, S.N.D.deN.

La Rencontre—Rev. JOHN M. GRACE.

Marian Aposolate—Rev. JOHN M. GRACE.

Men of St. Joseph—RICHARD KIERNAN.

Young Adult Ministry—GEORGE CURRAN.

Department of Priestly Life and Ministry—Rev. Msgr. NORMAN P. BOLDUC, S.T.L., J.C.L., Dir., *153 Ash St., P.O. Box 310, Manchester, 03105.* Tel: 603-669-3100.

Department of Faith Development—Sr. BERNADETTE TURGEON S.N.D.deN., Dir.

Office of Adult Education—PATRICIA GABREE, Dir.

Office of Evangelization & Catechumenate—DIANE J. ALLEN, Dir.; Rev. MARC F. GUILLEMETTE, Pastoral Consultant.

Office of Catholic Scouting—Rev. RAYMOND A. BALL, Dir.

Catholic Youth Organization—THERESA ROOT, Dir.

Office of Youth Ministry—Directors: Sr. BERNADETTE TURGEON, S.N.D.deN.; MATTHEW GOODY; ANNE CAVANAUGH, Sec. JACQUELINE ST. HILAIRE, Sec.

Diocesan Bureau of Housing, DBH Shelter, DBH Shelter II, DBH Shelter III, DBH Management—Vacant; Pres.; Rev. JOHN P. QUINN, Vice Pres. JOSEPH W. FOBES, Treas. CAROL HAEBLER, Housing Coord., *323 Franklin St., Manchester, 03101.* Tel: 603-625-5422.

Diocesan Moderator for Marian Devotions—Rev. PAUL L. GREGOIRE, *St. Charles Borromeo Rectory, 577 Central Ave., Dover, 03820-3464.*

Diocesan Public Policy Committee—Sr. MARGARET CROSBY, S.N.D.deN., Coord., *153 Ash St., P.O.Box 310, Manchester, 03105.*

Displaced Persons Program—Rev. STANLEY J. PIWOWAR, Dir., *St. Joseph Rectory, Claremont, 03743.* Tel: 603-542-5732.

Holy Childhood, Pontifical Association—Rev. ANTHONY F. DIGIULIO, *153 Ash St., P.O. Box 310, Manchester, 03105.* Tel: 603-669-3100.

Hospitals—Rev. Msgr. JOHN P. QUINN, Diocesan Coord., Health Affairs, *215 Myrtle St., Manchester, 03104.* Tel: 603-669-3030.

Manchester Mission—CLARA BEAULE, *215 Myrtle St., Manchester, 03104.* Tel: 603-669-3030.

Masters of Ceremonies—Revs. MARC F. GUILLEMETTE; GERARD J. DION, *153 Ash St., P.O. Box 310, Manchester, 03105.* Tel: 603-669-3100.

Ministry for Persons with Disabilities—Rev. BERNARD J. CAMPBELL, O.F.M. Cap.; Sr. PAULINE LAFOND, P.M., *215 Myrtle St., P.O. Box 686, Manchester, 03105.* Tel: 603-668-4572; 669-3030.

Missionary Rosebushes of St. Theresa—Monastery of the Precious Blood—700 Bridge St., Manchester, 03104.

New Hampshire Catholic Charities, Inc.—Rev. Msgr. JOHN P. QUINN, Dir., *215 Myrtle St., Manchester, 03104.* Tel: 603-669-3030.

N.H. Council of Catholic Nurses—ALICE H. MANTEGANI, *160 Calef Rd., Manchester, 03103.* Tel: 603-623-3051.

Office of Communications—MATTHEW MCSORLEY, Dir. MARY BALON, Admin. Asst. JOHN HAYWOOD, TIDINGS Asst. Editor, *153 Ash St., Box 310, Manchester, 03105.* Tel: 603-669-3100.

Office of the Permanent Diaconate—Rev. MARC F. GUILLEMETTE, Dir., *153 Ash St., P.O. Box 310, Manchester, 03105.* Tel: 603-669-3100.

Office of Pastoral Planning—Most Rev. FRANCIS J. CHRISTIAN, *153 Ash St., P.O. Box 310, Manchester, 03105.*

Office of Worship—Rev. JOHN M. GRACE, Dir. BEVERLY DROLET, Environment & Art; MARY BAGNELL, Music; MARILYN FREESE, Admin. Asst., *153 Ash St., Box 310, Manchester, 03105.* Tel: 603-669-3100.

Priests' Eucharistic League—Rev. Msgr. JOHN F. BURKE, Dir., *153 Ash St., P.O. Box 310, Manchester, 03105.* Tel: 603-669-3100.

Propagation of the Faith—Rev. ANTHONY F. DIGIULIO, Dir., *153 Ash St., P.O. Box 310, Manchester, 03105.* Tel: 603-669-3100.

Rural Life Conference—Rev. GEORGE F. HARVEY, *Assumption Parish, 10 Chestnut St., Tilton, 03276.*

Sacred Liturgy, Art and Music—Rev. JOHN M. GRACE, Chm. MARY BAGNELL, Vice Chm.; Sr. ANITA MARCHESSEAULT, C.S.C., Sec./Treas., *153 Ash St., P.O, Box 310, Manchester, 03105.* Tel: 603-669-3100.

St. Vincent de Paul Society—Rev. Msgr. JOHN P. QUINN, *215 Myrtle St., Manchester, 03104.* Tel: 603-669-3030.

Schools—Bro. KENNETH HOGAN, Supt., Schools, *153 Ash St., P.O. Box 310, Manchester, 03105.* Tel: 603-669-3100.

Social Concerns Office—Sr. MARGARET CROSBY, S.N.D-.deN., Dir., *153 Ash St., P.O. Box 310, Manchester, 03105.*

Spanish Speaking Apostolate—Sr. MARIA LUZ CERVANTES, M.S.C., *St. Anne Church, 231 Merrimack St., Manchester, 03103-5295.* Tel: 603-625-4603. Sr. NANCY BRACELAND, C.S.J., *St. Francis Xavier Church, 41 Chandler St., Nashua, 03060.* Tel: 603-881-8065.

Vigilance Council—The Rt. Rev. Deans.

Vocation Directors—Revs. MARC R. MONTMINY; MARC F. GUILLEMETTE, *153 Ash St., P.O. Box 310, Manchester, 03105.* Tel: 603-669-3100.

Vocations, Diocesan Board—Vacant; Pres.; Rev. Msgr. NORMAN P. BOLDUC; Revs. DANIEL L. BERNIER; MARC GUILLEMETTE; ALBION F. BULGER; MARC B. DROUIN; DANIEL O. LAMOTHE; JOHN H. BRYSON; ANTHONY R. FRONTIERO, *153 Ash St., P.O. Box 310, Manchester, 03105.* Tel: 603-669-3100.

CLERGY, PARISHES, MISSIONS AND PAROCHIAL SCHOOLS

CITY OF MANCHESTER
(Hillsboro County)

1—ST. JOSEPH CATHEDRAL (1869), Rev. Humbert M. Oliveira, Rector. In res., Most Revs. Francis J. Christian; Odore J. Gendron; Rev. Msgr. Laurence R. Gardner; Rev. Msgr. Charles E. Crosby; Rev. Msgr. John P. Quinn.
Res., 145 Lowell St., 03104-6135. Tel: 603-622-6404; Fax: 603-626-4415. [CEM]
Chapels—Rectory.; Convent, Tel: 603-623-2411.
Stations—Kalivas Apartments.; Carpenter Center.; Gallen Apartments.; O'Malley Apartments.
Catechesis/Religious Programs—Students 120.

2—ST. ANNE (1848), Rev. John M. Gallagher, O.F.M.Cap. Pastoral Assocs.: Sr. Lorraine Cote, R.S.M.; Sr. Maria Luz Cervantes, M.S.C. In res., Revs. Bernard J. Campbell, O.F.M.Cap; Thomas Faiola, O.F.M.Cap.; Robert J. Densmore.
Res., 231 Merrimack St., 03103. Tel: 603-623-8809; Fax: 603-622-9382.

3—ST. ANTHONY OF PADUA (1899) (French), Rev. Charles E. DesRuisseaux; Dr. Elise B. Tougas, Pastoral Assoc. In res., Revs. Normand A. Fillion, O.M.I.; Raymond Laferriere; Andre J. Gagnon.
Res., 172 Belmont St., 03103-4452. Tel: 603-625-6409; Fax: 603-625-0099.
Catechesis/Religious Programs—Students 109.

4—ST. AUGUSTIN (1871) (French), Rev. Adrien R. Longchamps.
Res., 383 Beech St., 03103. Tel: 603-625-5655. [CEM]

5—BLESSED SACRAMENT (1907), Rev. Michael E. Sevigny, O.F.M.Cap. In res., Bro. Paul Crawford, O.F.M.Cap.; Revs. Joseph M. Cooper, O.F.M.Cap., D.R.E.; Anthony Donahue, O.F.M.Cap.
Res., 14 Elm St., 03103. Tel: 603-622-5445; Fax: 603-627-5983.
Catechesis/Religious Programs—Students 75.

6—ST. CATHERINE (1954), Very Rev. Msgr. Thomas J. Hannigan, V.F.; Revs. James P. Walsh; Anthony R. Frontiero.
Res., 207 Hemlock St., 03104. Tel: 603-622-4966.
Catechesis/Religious Programs—Tel: 603-622-2711. Sr. Janet Belcourt, D.R.E.
Students 950.

7—ST. EDMUND (1914) (French), Rev. Msgr. Paul L. Bouchard; Sr. Sally A. Howe, C.S.C., Pastoral Assoc. In res., Rev. John J. Mahoney, Jr.
Res., 55 Edmond St., 03102. Tel: 603-625-6025; Fax: 603-625-4067.
Catechesis/Religious Programs—Tel: 603-623-6820.
Students 190.

8—ST. FRANCIS OF ASSISI (1953), Rev. Paul F. Ruzzo. In res., Rev. Msgr. Colin A. MacDonald.
Res., 3221 Brown Ave., 03103. Tel: 603-623-7306; Fax: 603-623-5524.
School—(Grades K-6) 3223 Brown Ave., 03103. Tel: 603-669-2069.
Sisters of Mercy 1; Lay Teachers 9; Students 145.
Catechesis/Religious Programs—Students 500.

9—ST. GEORGE (1890) (French), Rev. George A. Desjardins. In res., Rev. Roland O. Blais.
Res., 517 Pine St., 03104. Tel: 603-623-6434; Fax: 603-645-1857.

10—ST. HEDWIG, Rev. Msgr. Alfred Daniszewski.
Res., 147 Walnut St., 03104. Tel: 603-623-4835. [CEM]
School—St. Casimir, (Grades K-8) 456 Union St., 03103. Tel: 603-623-6411. Sr. Mary Lawrence Lojko, C.S.S.F., Prin.
Felician Sisters 4; Students 231.

11—ST. JOHN THE BAPTIST (1914) (French), Revs. Leo A. LeBlanc; Raymond A. Ball. In res., Rev. Msgr. James Markham; Rev. Msgr. Roland Tancrede; Rev. Msgr. Wilfrid Paradis; Rev. Leonard R. Foisy.
Res., 107 Alsace St., 03102. Tel: 603-623-4715.
Catechesis/Religious Programs—Tel: 603-622-0504.
Students 250.

12—ST. MARIE (1880), Revs. Marc R. Montminy, V.F.; Michael E. Gendron; Deacon Frank Gallinaro. In res., Rev. John Grace.
Res., 378 Notre Dame Ave., 03102-3793. Tel: 603-622-4615; Fax: 603-666-4732. [CEM 2]
Chapels—Joseph House Chapel, 279 Cartier St., 03102.; Chapel of North American Martyrs.; St. Joan of Arc.
Catechesis/Religious Programs—Tel: 603-668-5863. D.R.E.: Sr. Doris Bernier, (Elementary); Sean Poza, (Junior & Senior High Schools); Jay Yvars, (Adult).
Students 209.
Convent—133 Wayne St., 03102-3793. Tel: 603-623-0815. Sisters of the Presentation of Mary

13—OUR LADY OF PERPETUAL HELP (1911) (English), Rev. Maurice D. Lavigne. In res., Rev. Msgr. John F. Burke.

Res., 266 Cypress St., 03103-3700. Tel: 603-622-2535; Fax: 603-668-0356.
Catechesis/Religious Programs—870 Hayward St., 03103-3700. Tel: 603-668-3985.
Students 180.

14—St. Patrick (1898) (Irish), Rev. Nicholas P. Rogers; Deacon Harry Kram. In res., Rev. Edward J. Arsenault.
Res., 138 Coolidge Ave., 03102. Tel: 603-624-4115; Fax: 603-624-4115. [CEM]
Catechesis/Religious Programs—100 Coolidge Ave., 03102. Tel: 603-624-0916.
Students 197.

15—St. Pius X (1955), Rev. Robert G. Boisvert.
Res., 575 Candia Rd., 03109. Tel: 603-622-6510; Fax: 603-626-1323.
Catechesis/Religious Programs—Tel: 603-669-4547.
Students 453.

16—St. Raphael (1888), Rev. Bede G. Camera, O.S.B.
Res., 103 Walker St., 03102. Tel: 603-623-2604; Fax: 603-645-9895. [CEM]
Catechesis/Religious Programs—Tel: 603-647-2283.
Students 231.

17—Sacred Heart of Jesus (1911) (French), Revs. Marc R. Montminy; Michael E. Gendron.
Res., 265 S. Main St., 03102. Tel: 603-625-9525.

18—St. Theresa, Rev. Jean Lemay.
Res., 140 Mitchell St., 03103. Tel: 603-623-5055.

OUTSIDE THE CITY OF MANCHESTER

Alton, Belknap Co., St. Joan of Arc (1961), Rev. Richard H. Wegman.
Res., 03809. Tel: 603-875-7191; Fax: 603-875-5747.
Catechesis/Religious Programs—Students 120.
Mission—Center Barnstead, Belknap Co., St. Paul, Rte. 28, Center Barnstead, 03225.

Ashland, Grafton Co., St. Agnes, Rev. George H. Robichaud.
Res., 6 Hill St., P.O. Box 556, 03217. Tel: 603-968-4433.

Auburn, Rockingham Co., St. Peter (1948), Rev. James W. Haller. In res., Rev. Msgr. Norman Bolduc, Jr.; Rev. Msgr. John E. Molan.
Res., 567 Manchester Rd., 03032-3123. Tel: 603-623-5429; Fax: 603-669-5598.
Catechesis/Religious Programs—Tel: 605-669-5134.
Students 312.

Bedford, Hillsborough Co., St. Elizabeth Seton (1964), Rev. Cornelius J. Goggin; Edward P. Munz, Pastoral Assoc. In res., Rev. Marc Guillemette.
Res., 190 Meetinghouse Rd., 03110-6027. Tel: 603-669-7444; Fax: 603-644-5371.
Catechesis/Religious Programs—Tel: 603-647-1940. James Whittaker, D.R.E.
Students 1,100.

Belmont, Belknap Co., St. Joseph (1899), Rev. Marc B. Drouin.
Res., One High St., P.O. Box 285, 03220. Tel: 603-267-8174; Fax: 603-267-1170.
Catechesis/Religious Programs—Students 147.

Bennington, Hillsborough Co., St. Patrick (1936), Rev. Andre L. Bedard.
Res., 10 Greenfield Rd., P.O. Box 147, 03442-0147. Tel: 603-588-2180; Fax: 603-588-2180. [CEM]
Catechesis/Religious Programs—Tel: 603-547-2670; Fax: 603-547-3623.
Students 157.

Berlin, Coos Co.,

1—St. Anne, (1885) (French), Rev. Gary F. Lord.
Res., 58 Church St., 03570-2493. Tel: 603-752-6654; Fax: 603-752-4115. [CEM 2]
Catechesis/Religious Programs—Tel: 603-752-5443.
Students 164.

2—St. Joseph, (1943) (French), Very Rev. Maurice R. Lacroix.
Res., 633 Third Ave., 03570. Tel: 603-752-4280; Fax: 603-752-4124. [JC]
Catechesis/Religious Programs—Tel: 603-752-4556.
Students 120.

3—St. Kieran, (1894), Rev. Richard A. Roberge.
Res., 162 Madison Ave., 03570. Tel: 603-752-2880; Fax: 603-752-1855. [CEM]
Catechesis/Religious Programs—140 Blanchard St., 03570. Tel: 603-752-5443.
Students 220.

4—Guardian Angel, (1917), Rev. William E. Babineau.
Res., 593 Sullivan St., 03570. Tel: 603-752-1421; Fax: 603-752-5287.
Catechesis/Religious Programs—140 Blanchard St., P.O. Box 518, 03570. Tel: 603-752-5443.
Students 309.

Bristol, Grafton Co., St. Timothy (1900), Rev. William L. Quirk.
Res., School St., P.O. Box 37, 03222. Tel: 603-744-2700.
Mission—Newfound Lake, Grafton Co., Our Lady of Grace, W. Shore Rd., 03222.

Candia, Rockingham Co., St. Paul (1971), Rev. Msgr. Donald J. Gilbert.
Res., 54 Main St., P.O. Box 276, 03034. Tel: 603-483-8481; Fax: 603-483-8481.
Catechesis/Religious Programs—Tel: 603-483-5516.
Students 305.
Station—Chester, St. Jerome.

Cascade, Coos Co., St. Benedict. Closed. For Sacramental records contact St. Kieran, Berlin.

Center Ossipee, Carroll Co., St. Joseph (1965), Rev. Timothy R. O'Donnell.
Res., P.O. Box 248, 03814. Tel: 603-539-5036.
Mission—Chocorua, Carroll Co., Our Lady of Perpetual Help.

Charlestown, Sullivan Co., St. Catherine, Rev. Shawn M. Therrien.
Res., 116 Main St., Box 332, 03603. Tel: 603-826-3359.
Station—Alstead, Holy Spirit.

Claremont, Sullivan Co., St. Joseph (1922) (Polish), Rev. Stanley J. Piwowar.
Res., 58 Elm St., P.O. Box 824, 03743. Tel: 603-542-5732; Fax: 603-543-3673.
Catechesis/Religious Programs—Students 246.

St. Mary (1823), Revs. Michael J. Ciullo; Gilmond Boucher, O.M.I.; Sr. Pauline Maurier, C.S.C., Pastoral Assoc.
Res., 32 Pearl St., 03743-2552. Tel: 603-542-9518; Fax: 603-542-9614. [CEM]
School—(Grades PreK-8) 18 Central St., 03743. Tel: 603-542-6341. Richard Lizotte, Prin. (Grades K-8).
Lay Teachers 13; Students 179.
Catechesis/Religious Programs—Students 244.

Colebrook, Coos Co., St. Brendan (1953), Rev. Albert A. Bellefeuille.
Res., 28 Pleasant St., P.O. Box 65, 03576. Tel: 603-237-4342. [CEM]
Catechesis/Religious Programs—Students 130.
Mission—Errol, Coos Co., St. Pius X. [CEM]
Station—Dixville, St. William of York.

Concord, Merrimack Co.,

1—St. John the Evangelist, (1886), Rev. Msgr. James P. Watson; Rev. Dennis A. Broussard.
Res., 72 S. Main St., 03301. Tel: 603-224-2328. [CEM]
Station—McKerley Home, Tel: 603-224-6561.

2—St. Peter, (1946), Revs. Mitchell J. Wanat, C.M.; Rafal Kopystynski, C.M.
Res., 135 N. State St., 03301. Tel: 603-225-2131; Fax: 603-228-4580.
Catechesis/Religious Programs—Students 223.

3—Sacred Heart, (1892) (French), Rev. Aime A. Boisselle.
Res., 52 Pleasant St., 03301. Tel: 603-225-6942.
Catechesis/Religious Programs—Tel: 603-225-6942.
Students 97.

4—Immaculate Heart of Mary, (1956), Rev. Donald E. Lafond; Deacon Peter J. Tumulty.
Res., 180 Loudon Rd., 03301. Tel: 603-224-4393; Fax: 603-224-4123.
Catechesis/Religious Programs—176 Loudon Rd., 03301. Tel: 603-225-2026.
Students 225.

Derry, Rockingham Co., Holy Cross (1989), Rev. James A. Riel.
Office: 187 Hampstead Rd., 03038. Tel: 603-437-7550.
Catechesis/Religious Programs—4 Belle Brook Ln.
Students 596.

St. Thomas Aquinas (1885), Revs. Joseph F. Lorenzo, O.F.M.; Thomas Garone, O.F.M.; Bro. Courtland Campbell, O.F.M.; Deacon Michael Ciryak.
Res., 26 Crystal Ave., 03038. Tel: 603-432-5000; Fax: 603-434-0518.
School—(Grades K-8) 3 Moody St., 03038. Tel: 603-432-2712; Fax: 603-432-2179. Sr. Jacqueline Brodeur, C.S.C., Prin.
Sisters 3; Lay Teachers 11; Students 304.
Catechesis/Religious Programs—16 Rollins St., 03038. Tel: 603-432-7530. Dr. Jane Dwyer, D.R.E.
Students 1,000.

Dover, Strafford Co., St. Charles (1893) (French), Rev. Paul L. Gregoire. In res., Rev. Armand J. Provost.
Res., 577 Central Ave., 03820. Tel: 603-742-1354. [CEM]
Catechesis/Religious Programs—150 Central Ave., Tel: 603-742-8838.
Students 68.

St. Joseph (1945), Very Rev. Daniel O. Lamothe, V.F.; Rev. John Poirier.
Res., 150 Central Ave., 03820. Tel: 603-742-4837; Fax: 603-749-6779.
Catechesis/Religious Programs—Students 445.
Mission—Barrington, Chapel of the Nativity, Rte. 9, P.O. Box 163, Barrington, 03825. Tel: 603-664-9336.

St. Mary (1833), Rev. Gerald R. Dunn.
Res., 25 Third St., 03820. Tel: 603-742-2619.
Catechesis/Religious Programs—Students 65.

Durham, Strafford Co., St. Thomas More, Rev. Daniel A. St. Laurent.
Res., 6 Madbury Rd., Box 620, 03824. Tel: 603-868-5252; 868-2666 (Office); Fax: 603-868-3765.

Enfield, Grafton Co., St. Helena (1899), Rev. Paul Rainville, M.S.; Deacon John St. George.
Res., South St., R.R. No. 2, Box 26, 03748. Tel: 603-632-4263; Fax: 603-632-7874.
Catechesis/Religious Programs—Tel: 603-632-7874.
Students 132.
Mission—Canaan, Grafton Co., St. Mary, 03748. Tel: 603-523-9955 (Hall).

Epping, Rockingham Co., St. Joseph (1898), Rev. Ronald E. Corriveau.
Res., 14 Church St., 03042-0337. Tel: 603-679-8805. [CEM]
Catechesis/Religious Programs—Tel: 603-679-5724.
Students 239.

Exeter, Rockingham Co., St. Michael (1859), Revs. Maurice J. Rochefort; Agapit H. Jean, Jr.
Res., 9 Lincoln St., 03833. Tel: 603-772-2494; Fax: 603-778-1629.
Catechesis/Religious Programs—Michael House, 11 Linden St., 03833. Tel: 603-772-3916. Julie Hayes, D.R.E.
Students 734.

Farmington, Strafford Co., St. Peter (1920), Rev. Roger A. Fortier.
Res., 90 Central St., P.O. Box 565, 03835. Tel: 603-755-2280; Fax: 603-755-9124.
Catechesis/Religious Programs—Tel: 603-755-3921.
Students 144.

Franklin, Merrimack Co., St. Paul (1884), Rev. Michael Kerper.
Res., 108 School St., P.O. Box 490, 03235. Tel: 603-934-5013; Fax: 603-934-6694. [CEM]
Catechesis/Religious Programs—Tel: 603-934-5739.
Students 220.

Goffstown, Hillsborough Co., St. Lawrence (1955), Rev. Donald F. Gauthier, Jr.
Res., 51 Main St., 03045. Tel: 603-497-2651; Fax: 603-497-3668.
Catechesis/Religious Programs—Tel: 603-497-4093.
Students 327.

Gonic, Strafford Co., St. Leo (1892), Rev. Paul D. Montminy.
Res., 59 Main St., 03839. Tel: 603-332-1624; Fax: 603-332-7623. [CEM]
Catechesis/Religious Programs—16 Bridge St., Rochester, 03867. Tel: 603-332-4803.
Students 54.

Gorham, Coos Co., Holy Family, Rev. Wilfred H. Deschamps, Admin.
Res., 5 Church St., 03581-1695. Tel: 603-466-2335. [CEM]

Groveton, Coos Co., St. Francis Xavier (1899) (French), Rev. Daniel R. Deveau.
Res., 10 State St., Box 72, 03582. Tel: 603-636-1047; Fax: 603-636-2549. [CEM]
Catechesis/Religious Programs—Students 80.

Hampstead, Rockingham Co., St. Anne, Rev. Florent R. Bilodeau.
Res., P.O. Box 339, 03841. Tel: 603-329-5886.
Station—Sandown, St. Michael.

Hampton, Rockingham Co., Our Lady of the Miraculous Medal (1948), Revs. George E. Ham; Stephen Marcoux; Michael J. Griffin; Deacon Paul Testa.
Res., 289 Lafayette Rd., 03842. Tel: 603-926-2206; Fax: 603-926-8602.
School—Sacred Heart School, (Grades PreK-8). Tel: 603-926-3254; Fax: 603-929-1109. Sr. Mary Joan Walsh, O.L.L., Prin.
Sisters 5; Lay Teachers 21; Students 348.
Catechesis/Religious Programs—(Grades K-12). Tel: 603-926-5573.
Students 530.
Mission—Seabrook Beach, Rockingham Co., St. Elizabeth's, Rte. 1-A, Seabrook Beach, 03874. Tel: 603-474-3839.

Hampton Beach, Rockingham Co., St. Patrick. Closed. Attended from Chancery. For all records contact O.L.M.M. Parish, Hampton.

Hanover, Grafton Co., St. Denis (1907), Rev. Arthur J. Kelliher.
Res., 8 Sanborn Rd., 03755. Tel: 603-643-2166.
Catechesis/Religious Programs—Students 235.

Harrisville, Cheshire Co., St. Denis. Attended by Sacred Heart, Marlborough.
Mission—Dublin, Our Lady of the Snows. [CEM]

Henniker, Merrimack Co., St. Theresa (1945), Rev. Andre M. Thibodeau.
Res., Rush Rd., P.O. Box 557, 03242. Tel: 603-428-3325.
Mission—Contoocook, Merrimack, St. Mary.
Catechesis/Religious Programs—Students 251.

Hillsborough, Hillsborough Co., St. Mary (1892), Rev. John A. Wright.
Res., 38 Church St., P.O. Box 907, 03244. Tel: 603-464-5565; Fax: 603-464-5565.
Parish Hall—Tel: 603-464-6021.

Hinsdale, Cheshire Co., St. Joseph (1884), Rev. Raymond J. Potvin.
Res., 12 Prospect St., P.O. Box 14, 03451. Tel: 603-336-5414; Fax: 603-336-7314. [CEM]
Mission—Chesterfield, Cheshire, Our Lady of the Lake.
Catechesis/Religious Programs—Students 127.

Hooksett, Merrimack Co., Holy Rosary, Rev. Fernand A. Croteau.
Res., 15 S. Main St., 03106. Tel: 603-485-3523. [CEM]

Hudson, Hillsborough Co., St. John the Evangelist (1949), Rev. John C. Horan. In res., Rev. Msgr. Joseph E. Desmond.
Res., 27 Library St., 03051. Tel: 603-882-3603.
Catechesis/Religious Programs—23 Library St., 03051. Tel: 603-882-6541. Mrs. Kathleen Cox, D.R.E.
Students 516.

St. Kathryn (1968), Rev. Gary J. Belliveau; Theresa Gagnon, Pastoral Assoc.
Res., 5 Wason Rd., 03051. Tel: 603-882-7793; Fax: 603-595-0143.
Catechesis/Religious Programs—Sr. Eleanor LaBranche, C.S.C., D.R.E.
Students 708.

Jaffrey, Cheshire Co., St. Patrick (1885), Rev. Richard J. Kelley; Deacon W. Carl Lefleur.
Res., 87 Main St., 03452. Tel: 603-532-6634; Fax: 603-532-6633. [CEM]
School—(Grades K-8) 70 Main St., 03452. Tel: 603-532-7676; Fax: 603-532-7476. David L. O'Connell, Prin.
Sisters 3; Lay Teachers 11; Students 180.
Catechesis/Religious Programs—Tel: 603-532-8831.
Students 260.

Keene, Cheshire Co., St. Bernard (1862), Very Rev. W. Pierre Baker, V.F.; Rev. Michael S. Taylor.
Res., 173 Main St., 03431. Tel: 603-352-3525; Fax: 603-352-7472. [CEM]
Catechesis/Religious Programs—St. Joseph School, 92 Wilson St., 03431. Tel: 603-357-4001.
Students 328.

St. Margaret Mary (1955), Rev. Richard M. Giroux.
Res., 35 Arch St., 03431-2297. Tel: 603-352-1311.
Catechesis/Religious Programs—Tel: 603-357-3781.
Students 152.

Laconia, Belknap Co., St. Joseph (1871), Rev. Gary J. Kosmowski.
Res., 30 Church St., 03246. Tel: 603-524-1442; Fax: 603-527-3534. [CEM]
Catechesis/Religious Programs—Tel: 603-524-4196.
Students 146.

Sacred Heart (1891) (French-Canadian), Rev. Eddy N. Bisson.
Res., 291 Union Ave., 03246. Tel: 603-524-9609; Fax: 603-527-2617. [CEM]
Catechesis/Religious Programs—Tel: 603-524-4155.
Students 116.

Lakeport, Belknap Co., Our Lady of the Lakes, Rev. George J. Soberick.
Res., 50 Washington St., 03246. Tel: 603-524-1357.
Catechesis/Religious Programs—Students 209.
Mission—Weirs Beach, Belknap, St. Helena.

Lancaster, Coos Co., All Saints (1856), Rev. Maurice R. Larochelle.
Res., 163 Main St., 03584. Tel: 603-788-2083; Fax: 603-788-3555. [CEM]
Mission—Jefferson, Coos, St. Agnes, Rt. 2, 03583.

Lebanon, Grafton Co., Sacred Heart (1875) (French), Revs. Henry Brodeur, M.S.; Giles Genest, M.S., Vicar. In res., Rev. John F. Mullin, S.J.
Res., 2 Hough St., P.O. Box 482, 03766. Tel: 603-448-1262.
Catechesis/Religious Programs—Tel: 603-448-1575.
Students 399.

Lincoln, Grafton Co., St. Joseph (1902), Rev. Roger Bilodeau.
Res., Church St., P.O. Box 128, 03251-0128. Tel: 603-745-2266; Fax: 603-745-2266.
Catechesis/Religious Programs—Students 52.

Lisbon, Grafton Co., St. Catherine of Siena (1957), Rev. Mark E. Dollard.
Res., c/o 21 Pine St., Woodsville, 03785.

Littleton, Grafton Co., St. Rose of Lima (1882), Very Rev. Joseph S. Klatka, V.F.
Res., 77 Clay St., 03561. Tel: 603-444-2593. [CEM]
Catechesis/Religious Programs—Students 271.
Missions—Bethlehem, Grafton Co., Christ the King, Main St., Bethlehem, 03574.; Franconia, Grafton, Our Lady of the Snows, Main St., 03580.

Londonderry, Rockingham Co., St. Jude (1962), Rev. W. Timothy Thibeault; Sr. Mary Elizabeth Whalen, S.N.D., Pastoral Assoc.
Res., 435 Mammoth Rd., 03053-2304. Tel: 603-432-3333; Fax: 603-432-1639.

St. Mark the Evangelist (1981), Rev. Thomas J. Bresnahan.
Res., One Griffin Rd., 03053. Tel: 603-432-8711; Fax: 603-434-6748.
Catechesis/Religious Programs—Tel: 603-434-5711.
Students 844.

Marlborough, Cheshire Co., Sacred Heart (1886), Rev. Thomas L. Duston; Sr. Lucie E. Ducas, C.S.C., Pastoral Assoc.
Res., 9 Ling St., 03455. Tel: 603-876-3804; Fax: 603-876-4327. [CEM]

Meredith, Belknap Co., St. Charles (1946), Rev. Msgr. Fernand L. Pichette.
Res., 281A Daniel Webster Hwy., P.O. Box 237, 03253-0237. Tel: 603-279-4403; Fax: 603-279-9924.
Catechesis/Religious Programs—Tel: 603-279-8691.
Students 254.
Mission—Center Harbor, Belknap Co., Our Lady of Victory. Bean Rd.

Merrimack, Hillsborough Co., Our Lady of Mercy (1950), Revs. Dennis J. Audet; Daniel J. Sinibaldi.
Res., 16 Baboosic Lake Rd., 03054. Tel: 603-424-3757; Fax: 603-424-1780.
Catechesis/Religious Programs—14 Baboosic Lake Rd., 03054. Tel: 603-424-4477. Elizabeth Lochman, D.R.E.
Students 834.

St. John Neumann (1982), Rev. Robert E. Gorski.
Res., 208 Naticook Rd., 03054. Tel: 603-880-4689; Fax: 603-881-9668.
Catechesis/Religious Programs—Tel: 603-880-0825.
Students 498.

Milford, Hillsborough Co., St. Patrick (1895), Rev. Andrew W. Cryans.
Res., 34 Amherst St., P.O. Box 27, 03055. Tel: 603-673-1311; Fax: 603-673-3687. [CEM]
Catechesis/Religious Programs—Tel: 603-673-4797.
Students 884.
Share Program—(A non-denominational outreach program for the local needy). Tel: 603-673-9898. Mrs. Mariette Facques, Dir.
Mission—Brookline, Hillsborough Co., Infant Jesus, 03055.

Nashua, Hillsborough Co.,

1—St. Aloysius, Rev. Roland P. Cote.
Res., 48 W. Hollis St., 03060. Tel: 603-882-4362. [CEM]

2—St. Casimir, Rev. Francis M. Spencer, M.S.
Res., 119 Temple St., 03060. Tel: 603-882-1313. [CEM]

3—St. Christopher, (1950), Revs. Karl E. Dowd, S.T.L.; John W. Fleming. In res., Rev. Bruce W. Collard.
Res., 62 Manchester St., 03060. Tel: 603-882-0632; Fax: 603-881-8728.
School—(Grades K-6) 20 Cushing Ave., 03060. Tel: 603-882-7442; Fax: 603-594-9523. Sr. Joan Marie Messier, R.S.M., Prin.
Students 369.
Catechesis/Religious Programs—Tel: 603-883-2572.
Students 496.

4—St. Francis Xavier, (1885), Rev. Marcel I. Martel; Sr. Nancy Braceland, C.S.J., Pastoral Assoc.
Res., 41 Chandler St., 03060. Tel: 603-882-2333; Fax: 603-594-9648. [CEM]
Catechesis/Religious Programs—Students 121.

5—Immaculate Conception, (1968), Revs. Mark R. Gagne; Robert Couto.
Res., 216 E. Dunstable Dr., 03062. Tel: 603-888-0321; Fax: 603-888-8407.
Parish Hall: Tel: 603-888-9841.
Catechesis/Religious Programs—Tel: 603-888-0608.
Students 1,092.

6—Infant Jesus, (1909) (French), Rev. Raymond E. Gagnon. In res., Rev. John E. Healey.
Res., 121 Allds St., 03060. Tel: 603-882-2462; Fax: 603-882-7104.
Catechesis/Religious Programs—Tel: 603-886-9725. Mr. Gerard Bergeron, D.R.E.
Students 250.

7—St. Joseph, (1955), Revs. Gerard R. Desmarais; Georges F. de Laire.
Res., 265 Lake St., 03060. Tel: 603-883-0757; Fax: 603-883-8057.
Catechesis/Religious Programs—Tel: 603-889-4372.
Students 478.

8—St. Patrick, Rev. Martin T. Kelly.
Res., 29 Spring St., 03060. Tel: 603-882-2262. [CEM]

9—Resurrection, (1970), Rev. Albion F. Bulger; Deacon E. Carl Hilston; Ms. Christine Patterson, Pastoral Min.
Pastoral Center: 449 Broad St., 03063-3412. Tel: 603-882-0925; Fax: 603-881-3561.
Catechesis/Religious Programs—Tel: 603-889-0012.
Students 530.

10—St. Stanislaus, (1908) (Polish), Rev. Daniel F. Szopa.
Res., 5 Green St., 03060. Tel: 603-882-0893; Fax: 603-881-7542. [CEM]

New London, Merrimack Co., Our Lady of Fatima (1952), Rev. Richard T. Lower.
Res., Main St., 03257. Tel: 603-526-4484; Fax: 603-526-8055.
Mission—Potter Place, Merrimack Co., Immaculate Conception, Church St., 03216. Tel: 603-735-5821.
Catechesis/Religious Programs—Students 140.

Newmarket, Rockingham Co., St. Mary (1878), Rev. John B. Finnigan. In res., Rev. Joseph E. Shields.
Res., 182 Main St., 03857. Tel: 603-659-3643; Fax: 603-659-8924. [CEM]
Catechesis/Religious Programs—Tel: 603-659-6474.
Students 142.
Mission—Newfields, Rockingham Co., Sacred Heart, 52 Main St., Newfields, 03856. Tel: 603-659-3246.

Newport, Sullivan Co., St. Patrick (1902), Rev. Daniel L. Bernier.
Res., 32 Beech St., 03773. Tel: 603-863-1422. [CEM]
Catechesis/Religious Programs—Tel: 603-863-7898.
Students 148.
Mission—Sunapee, Sullivan Co., St. Joachim, Rte. 11, Sunapee, 03782. Tel: 603-763-5940.

Newton, Rockingham Co., Mary, Mother of the Church (1967), Rev. Marcel M. Allard.
Res., 12 Amesbury Rd., 03858-0322. Tel: 603-382-6566; Fax: 603-382-5102.
Catechesis/Religious Programs—1 New Boston Rd., Kingston, 03848. Tel: 603-642-8885.
Students 428.
Mission—Kingston, Rockingham Co., St. Frederick, 3 New Boston Rd., Kingston, 03848. Tel: 603-642-8885.

North Conway, Carroll Co., Our Lady of the Mountains (1904), Revs. Edward J. Kelley; Louis A. Soucey.
Res., 28 Grove St., 03860. Tel: 603-356-2535; Fax: 603-356-2877. [CEM 2]
Catechesis/Religious Programs—P.O. Box 593, 03860. Tel: 603-356-3421.
Students 325.
Missions—Bartlett, Carroll, St. Joseph, P.O. Box 189, 03860.; North Conway, Carroll Co., St. Charles Borromeo, P.O. Box 189, 03860. Tel: 603-356-2535; Fax: 603-356-2877.

North Stratford, Coos Co., Sacred Heart (1888) (French), Rev. Daniel R. Deveau. Pastoral Assocs.: Sr. Marie Mansfield, S.G.M.; Sr. Helene Georges, S.G.M.
Church—121 Main St., P.O. Box C, 03590. Tel: 603-922-3360.
Res., St. Francis Xavier Rectory, Groveton, 03582. Tel: 603-636-1047; Fax: 603-636-2549. [CEM 2]

North Walpole, Cheshire Co., St. Peter (1877), Rev. Anthony DiRusso.
Res., 38 Church St., 03609. Tel: 603-445-5304; Fax: 603-445-2115. [CEM]
Catechesis/Religious Programs—Tel: 603-756-3444.
Students 88.
Mission—Walpole, Cheshire Co., St. Joseph, Elm St., 03608.

Pelham, Hillsborough Co., St. Patrick (1946), Rev. Edward D. Richard.
Res., 12 Main St., 03076. Tel: 603-635-3525; Fax: 603-635-3919.
School—(Grades K-8) 16 Main St., 03076. Tel: 603-635-2941; 635-9800. Jane A. Gaskell, Prin.
Lay Teachers 13; Students 226.

Catechesis/Religious Programs—Tel: 603-635-1447.
Students 714.

Penacook, Merrimack Co., Immaculate Conception (1880), Rev. Leo P. Lefebvre.
Res., 9 Pleasant St., 03303. Tel: 603-753-4413. [CEM]
Catechesis/Religious Programs—Tel: 603-753-6702.
Students 170.

Peterborough, Hillsborough Co., St. Peter (1900), Rev. William J. Kelley.
Res., 18 Vine St., 03458. Tel: 603-924-3819; Fax: 603-924-6166. [CEM]
Catechesis/Religious Programs—Students 189.

Pittsfield, Merrimack Co., Our Lady of Lourdes (1889), Rev. George Majka.
Res., 20 River Rd., 03263. Tel: 603-435-6242.
Catechesis/Religious Programs—25 Crescent St., 03263. Tel: 603-435-8840.
Students 255.
Mission—Northwood, Rockingham Co., St. Joseph. [CEM]

Plaistow, Rockingham Co., Holy Angels (1892), Rev. Richard B. Thompson. In res., Rev. Gerard A. Boucher.
Res., 8 Atkinson Depot Rd., Rte. 121, 03865. Tel: 603-382-8324; Fax: 603-382-8324. [CEM]
Catechesis/Religious Programs—Tel: 603-382-8824. Mrs. Beverly Fisher, D.R.E.
Students 457.

Plymouth, Grafton Co., St. Matthew (1916), Rev. Robert F. Cole.
Res., 46 Langdon St., 03264. Tel: 603-536-4700; Fax: 603-536-4709.
Catechesis/Religious Programs—Students 266.
Station—Campton, Waterville Valley.

Portsmouth, Rockingham Co., Immaculate Conception, Rev. Leo G. Gagnon; Deacon Charles Schladenhauffen.
Res., 98 Summer St., 03801. Tel: 603-436-0048. [CEM]

St. Catherine of Siena (1951), Rev. Msgr. Lawrence E. Burns.
Res., 845 Woodbury Ave., 03801-3294. Tel: 603-436-0344; Fax: 603-334-3393.
Catechesis/Religious Programs—Students 98.

St. James (1958), Rev. Gerald R. Belanger; Sr. Roberta O'Rourke, C.S.J., Pastoral Assoc.
Res., 2075 Lafayette Rd., 03801-5697. Tel: 603-436-4555; Fax: 603-433-4401.
Catechesis/Religious Programs—Students 203.

Rochester, Strafford Co., St. Mary (1868), Rev. Francis E. Kelso.
Res., 38 Charles St., 03867. Tel: 603-332-1869; Fax: 603-332-1869. [CEM]
Catechesis/Religious Programs—Students 276.

Holy Rosary (1883) (French), Revs. Paul D. Montminy; Albert J. Trembaly, Jr.
Res., 189 N. Main St., 03867. Tel: 603-332-1863; Fax: 603-330-0865. [CEM]
Catechesis/Religious Programs—16 Bridge St., 03867. Tel: 603-332-4803.
Students 305.

Rollinsford, Strafford Co., St. Mary (1856), Rev. Steven M. Kucharski.
Res., 404 High St., Somersworth, 03878. Tel: 603-692-4367; Fax: 603-692-4454. [CEM]
Catechesis/Religious Programs—Students 53.

Rye Beach, Rockingham Co., St. Theresa (1979), Rev. John V. Moran.
Res., 815 Central Rd., P.O. Box 482, 03871. Tel: 603-964-6440.
Catechesis/Religious Programs—Tel: 603-964-9878.
Students 285.

Salem, Rockingham Co., Mary, Queen of Peace (1966), Rev. Andrew M. Meehan, Admin.
Res., 200 Lawrence Rd., P.O. Box 685, 03079. Tel: 603-893-8661.
Catechesis/Religious Programs—Tel: 603-893-8662. Mrs. Marie Mullen, D.R.E.
Students 500.

St. Joseph (1910), Very Rev. Richard W. Connors; Revs. James A. MacCormack; Joseph Ryu, S.J., (Korean Community); Deacons David Costello; George Borkush.
Res., 33 Main St., P.O. Box 938, 03079. Tel: 603-898-4933; Fax: 603-893-9236.
Catechesis/Religious Programs—40 Main St., 03079. Tel: 603-893-9692. Sr. Lorraine LaPete, D.R.E.
Students 471.

Sanbornville, Carroll Co., St. Anthony (1908), Rev. Edmund A. Babicz.
Res., P.O. Box 490, 03872. Tel: 603-522-3304; Fax: 603-522-8273. [CEM]
Catechesis/Religious Programs—Students 153.
Mission—Milton, Strafford Co., Sacred Heart, P.O. Box 647, Milton, 03851. Tel: 603-652-9034.

Seabrook, Rockingham Co., St. Elizabeth. Attended by the Chancery. For all records contact Our Lady of the Miraculous Medal Parish, Hampton.

Somersworth, Strafford Co., Holy Trinity (1857), Rev. Steven M. Kucharski.
Res., 404 High St., P.O. Box 350, 03878. Tel: 603-692-4367. [CEM]
Catechesis/Religious Programs—Students 182.

St. Martin (1882) (French), Rev. Robert G. Biron.
Res., 120 Maple St. Ext., 03878-1999. Tel: 603-692-2172; Fax: 603-692-2172. [CEM]
Catechesis/Religious Programs—Tel: 603-692-5878.
Students 220.

Suncook, Merrimack Co., St. John the Baptist (1873), Rev. C. Peter Dumont.
Res., 10 School St., 03275-1917. Tel: 603-485-3113; Fax: 603-485-2113. [CEM 2]
Catechesis/Religious Programs—Tel: 603-485-3972.
Students 302.

Tilton, Belknap Co., St. Mary of the Assumption, Rev. George F. Harvey.
Res., 10 Chestnut St., 03276. Tel: 603-286-4445.

Troy, Cheshire Co., Immaculate Conception, Rev. Thomas Lierre Duston; Sr. Lucie Ducas, C.S.C., Pastoral Assoc.
Res., 33 School St., 03465. Tel: 603-242-6415; Fax: 603-876-4327. [CEM]
Mission—Fitzwilliam, St. Joseph.

West Lebanon, Grafton Co., Holy Redeemer (1953), Rev. Donald Jeffrey, M.S.
Res., 8 Prospect St. W., Box 5484, 03784. Tel: 603-298-8530.
Catechesis/Religious Programs—Tel: 603-298-5578.
Students 67.

West Stewartstown, Coos Co., St. Albert (1926), Rev. John B. Loughnane, Jr.
Mailing Address: P.O. Box 176, Beecher Falls, VT 05902.
Res., Church St., 03597. Tel: 603-246-8829; Fax: 603-246-7167. [CEM]
School—(Grades 1-8) P.O. Box 177, Beecher Falls, 05902. Tel: 603-246-8631. Sr. Lorraine Trottier, P.M., Prin.
Sisters of Presentation of Mary 4; Students 64.
Station—Coos County Institution.

West Swanzey, Cheshire Co., St. Anthony, Rev. John H. Bryson.
Res., 50 S. Winchester St., Box 117, 03469. Tel: 603-352-6246.
Mission—North Swanzey, St. Stephen.

Whitefield, Coos Co., St. Matthew (1886), Rev. Richard A. Smith.
Res., 9 Jefferson Rd., P.O. Box 246, 03598. Tel: 603-837-2558; Fax: 603-837-2831. [CEM 2]
Catechesis/Religious Programs—Students 60.
Mission—Carroll, St. Patrick, Rte. 3 & 302, Twin Mountain, 03595.
Shrine—Bretton Woods, Our Lady of the Mountain.

Wilton, Hillsborough Co., Sacred Heart, Rev. Donald E. Clinton.
Res. & Mailing Address—15 High St., Greenville, 03048. Tel: 603-654-6554.
Church—49 Maple St., 03086. [CEM]

Winchester, Cheshire Co., St. Stanislaus, Rev. Mark A. Rundzio.
Res., 80 Richmond St., 03470. Tel: 603-239-4312.
Mission—Ashuelot, St. Michael.

Windham, Rockingham Co., St. Matthew (1962), Rev. Wilfred G. Demers; Deacon Clarence R. Cummins.
Res., 2 Searles Rd., 03087-1298. Tel: 603-893-3336; Fax: 603-898-4008.
Catechesis/Religious Programs—Tel: 603-898-4818.
Students 901.

Wolfeboro, Carroll Co., St. Cecilia, Rev. Patrick F. Irwin.
Res., 205 S. Main St., 03894. Tel: 603-569-2548; Fax: 603-569-6659.

Woodsville, Grafton Co., St. Joseph (1896), Rev. Mark E. Dollard.
Res., 21 Pine St., 03785. Tel: 603-747-2038.
Mission—Warren, St. John Vianney.

Chaplains of Public Institutions

MANCHESTER. *Elliott Hospital*. Rev. Robert J. Densmore.
Nursing Homes. Revs. Albert L. Boulanger; Andre J. Gagnon; Gerard J. Dion.
V.A. Hospital. Rev. Francis A. Talbot.

BERLIN. *Androscoggin Valley Hospital*. Sr. Monique Theriault, R.S.M., Chap.

CONCORD. *N.H. State Hospital*. Rev. Normand G. Bordeleau.
N.H. State Prison. Russell Sweeney.

GOFFSTOWN. *Hillsborough County Nursing Home*. Rev. Gerard J. Dion.

HANOVER. *Mary Hitchcock Hospital*. Revs. John F. Mullin, S.J.; Roland S. Nadeau, M.S.

NASHUA. *Nursing Homes and Memorial Hospital*. Sr. Doris Gagnon, P.M., Chap.; Rev. John E. Healey.

On Duty Outside the Diocese:
Reverend Monsignors—
Blair, Raymond O., 1 Harbourside Dr., #4201, Delray Beach, FL 33438-5157
Reverend Fathers—
Barrett, Michael D., National Shrine of St. John Neumann (Church of St. Peter the Apostle), 1019 N. Fifth St., Philadelphia, PA 19123-1495
Connor, Kevin T., St. John Vianney Seminary, 2115 Summit Ave., Mail #5024, St. Paul, MN 55105-1095
Coyne, Emmett A., 490 M. St., SW, W307, Washington, D.C. 20024
Dauphinais, Gerard V., Holy Nativity Monastery, Bethlehem, SD 57708
Frontiero, Anthony R., St. Patrick Rectory, 619 Tenth St., NW, Washington, D.C. 20001-4587
Simoneau, Norman J., P.O. Box 430, Fortuna, CA 95540-0430

Military Chaplains:
Reverend Fathers—
Cody, Kevin W., 1225 Batson Dr., Charleston AFB, SC 29404
Crowley, Edmund G., 6025A Linden St., Fairchild AFB, WA 99011-2260
Decker, James D., 9204 A Ciarfeo St., Laughlin AFB, TX 78840
Glasgow, Robert K., USA, Staff Chaplain, Fort Huachuca, AZ 85613
Lamy, Raymond J., USAF, PSC 76, Box 7096, APO, AP 93619
Roma, Paul E., CHC, NSGA Winter Harbor, 10 Fabrigreen Ste. 10, Winter Harbor, ME 04693-0509

Absent on Sick Leave:
Reverend Fathers—
Daneault, Paul W.
Jannetta, Alfred L.
LaForest, Conrad V.
Lagueux, Maurice R.
Maguire, Joseph T.
Masterson, Clyde G.
Valliere, Romeo J.

Absent on Leave:
Reverend Fathers—
MacRae, Gordon J.
Memolo, Rocco C.
Pollitt, Michael J.

Sabbatical:
Reverend Fathers—
Aube, Paul L., P.O. Box 4602, Manchester, NH 03108-4602
Nolin, John W., 4604 Edwin Mechem Ave., NW, Albuquerque, NM 87114-5316

Retired:
Reverend Monsignors—
Burke, John F., Our Lady of Perpetual Help Rectory, 266 Cypress St., Manchester, NH 03103
Chicoine, George D., RFD 4 - 103, Village of Glen Falls, Goffstown, NH 03045-6214
Curran, Francis L., Bishop Peterson Residence, 221 Orange St., Manchester, NH 03104-4324
Desmond, Joseph E., St. John the Evangelist Rectory, 27 Library St., Hudson, NH 03051
Gardner, Laurence R., Cathedral Rectory, 145 Lowell St., Manchester, NH 03102. Tel: 603-622-6404
Hines, Leo F., St. Agnes Rectory, 1493 Cranston St., Cranston, RI 02920
Kenney, Philip J., 5 Thorndike St., Concord, NH 03301-3629
Lettre, Achille W., 21 Neptune Rd., Ormond Beach, FL 32176
MacDonald, Colin A., St. Francis of Assisi Rectory, 3221 Brown Ave., Manchester, NH 03103
Markham, James J., St. John the Baptist Rectory, 107 Alsace St., Manchester, NH 03102
McDonough, T. Joseph, St. Patrick Rectory, 29 Spring St., Nashua, NH 03060-3490
McGreal, James R., Courville at Manchester, 44 Webster St., Manchester, NH 03104-2912
Murphy, Eugene, Holy Angels, 8 Atkinson Depot Rd., Plaistow, NH 03865
Nolan, William L., Bishop Peterson Residence, 221 Orange St., Manchester, NH 03104-4324
Paradis, Wilfrid H., 107 Alsace St., Manchester, NH 03102

Tancrede, Roland, St. John the Baptist Rectory, 107 Alsace St., Manchester, NH 03102

Reverend Fathers—

Auger, Gerald E., 235 Alsace St., Manchester, NH 03102

Baillargeon, Albert G., 12 Jacobs Dr., Rochester, NH 03867

Blais, Roland O., St. George Rectory, 517 Pine St., Manchester, NH 03104

Bombardier, Wilfrid F., St. Kieran's Guest House, 158 Madison Ave., Berlin, NH 03570-2065

Boucher, Gerard A., Holy Angels Rectory, 8 Atkinson Depot Rd., Plaistow, NH 03865-3103

Boucher, Nelson, Sacred Heart Rectory, 291 Union Ave., Laconia, NH 03246

Bracq, Edward E., 14 Oldfield Rd., Nashau, NH 03060

Cameron, Albert S., Bishop Peterson Residence, 221 Orange St., P.O. Box 6623, Manchester, NH 03108-6623

Carty, Robert E., Bishop Peterson Residence, 221 Orange St., Manchester, NH 03104-4324

Chalifour, Gerald F., St. Augustine Rectory, 383 Beach St., P.O. Box 6272, Manchester, NH 03108-6272

Desjardins, Raymond S., 51 Partridge Green, Rochester, NH 03867

DiGiulio, Anthony F., 298 Water St., Keene, NH 03431-4246

Foisy, Leonard R., St. John the Baptist Rectory, 107 Alsace St., Manchester, NH 03102-3006

Frechette, Leo L., P.O. Box 68, West Nottingham, NH 03291

Gallant, Rodrigue J., P.O. Box 428, Belmont, NH 03220

Goodwin, Robert T., 4851 W. Gandy Blvd., #8-40, Tampa, FL 33611-3039

Griffin, Robert F., Bishop Peterson Residence, 221 Orange St., Manchester, NH 03104-4324

Horan, Denis F., 3 Oak Hill Ln., #309, Nashua, NH 03062

Houde, Arthur O., 5626 Marshfield Dr., Port Orange, FL 32127

Hughes, Lawrence J., P.O. Box 462, Rye, NH 03871

Joyal, Gerald F., 106 Mount Delight Rd., P.O. Box 166, Deerfield, NH 03037

Keenan, Thomas E., 39 Hough St., Dover, NH 03820

Kemmery, Robert J., 18 Gull Ln., Orleans, MA 02653

Knott, Edward J., Bishop Peterson Residence, 221 Orange St., Manchester, NH 03104-4324

Lampron, Maurice W., P.O. Box 717, Wolfeboro Falls, NH 03896-0717

MacDonald, Edward J., Bishop Peterson Residence, 221 Orange St., Manchester, NH 03104

Marchand, Robert A., 419 Coolidge Ave., Manchester, NH 03102-3214

McHugh, Paul F., 17 Picard Rd., Canterbury, NH 03824

Miller, A. Andrew, Bishop Peterson Residence, 221 Orange St., Manchester, NH 03104

Montplaisir, Roland A., 2950 Palm-Aire Dr., Apt. 502, Pompano Beach, FL 33069

O'Connor, Francis J., P.O. Box 704, Hampton, NH 03842

O'Connor, J. Kieran, St. Teresa's Manor, 519 Bridge St., Manchester, NH 03104

Pelletier, Eugene J., 19 S. Blueberry Ln., Box 84, Rochester, NH 03867

Polito, Victor J., 29 Knollwood Ave., Amsterdan, NY 12010

Provost, Armand J., St. Mary Rectory, 182 Main St., P.O. Box 337, Newmarket, NH 03857

Savage, Thomas J., P.O.Box 5531, Manchester, NH 03108

Shea, Leo A., P.O. Box 310, Manchester, NH 03105-0310

Shields, Joseph E., St. Mary Rectory, 182 Main St., P.O. Box 337, Newmarket, NH 03857

Soucey, Louis A., P.O. Box 222, Tamworth, NH 03886-0222

Tremblay, Donat E., Bishop Peterson Residence, 221 Orange St., Manchester, NH 03104-4324

Tremblay, Jean A., 110 Cilley Rd., Manchester, NH 03103-5638

Turgeon, Armand A., 111 Rochester Ter., Rochester, NH 03867

Vickery, Richard F., P.O. Box 984, Manchester, NH 03105

Permanent Deacons:

Borkush, George J., St. Joseph, Salem

Cloutier, Richard A., St. John Neumann, Merrimack

Costello, David T., St. Joseph, Salem

Cummins, Clarence R., St. Matthew, Windham

Ford, Thomas J.

Gallinaro, Frank, St. Mary, Manchester

Hilston, Edmund C., Resurrection Parish, Nashua

Kayser, Charles Douglas, St. Patrick, Milford

Kram, Harry A., St. Patrick, Manchester

LaBonte, Alfred A., Jr., St. Joseph, Nashua

LaFleur, William Carl, Jr., St. Patrick, Jaffrey

Martin, John J., St. Joseph Hospital, Nashua

Polcari, Joseph A., St. Matthew, Whitefield

Schladenhauffen, Charles D., Immaculate Conception, Portsmouth

St. George, John H., St. Helena, Enfield

St. Laurent, Lionel A., St. Joseph Cathedral, Manchester

Testa, Paul E., Our Lady of the Miraculous Medal, Hampton

Tumulty, Peter J., Immaculate Heart of Mary, Concord

INSTITUTIONS LOCATED IN THE DIOCESE

[A] SEMINARIES, RELIGIOUS OR SCHOLASTICATES

MANCHESTER. *St. Anselm Abbey Seminary*, 100 St. Anselm Dr., 03102. Tel: 603-641-7000; Fax: 603-641-7116.
E-mail: jdefelic@anselm.edu
Web site: www.anselm.edu
Order of St. Benedict. Rev. Jonathan P. DeFelice, O.S.B., Dir. Studies. Faculty 4; Students 2.

CENTER HARBOR. *Immaculate Conception Apostolic School*, Plymouth St., P.O. Box 936, 03226. Tel: 603-253-7728. Revs. David Steffy, L.C., Prin.; Kevin Meehan, L.C., Vice-Prin.; Patrick Walsh, L.C.; Victor Franco, L.C.; Bros. John Monette, L.C.; David Consoli, L.C.; Daren Weisbrod, L.C.; Thang Bui, L.C. Priests 4; Brothers 4; Lay Teachers 7; Students 120.

[B] COLLEGES AND UNIVERSITIES

MANCHESTER. *Notre Dame College*, 2321 Elm St., 03104. Tel: 603-669-4298; Fax: 603-644-8316
For a complete listing, refer to the Colleges and Universities section.

Saint Anselm College, 03102. Tel: 603-641-7000
For a complete listing, refer to the Colleges and Universities section.

MERRIMACK. *The Thomas More College of Liberal Arts*, 6 Manchester St., 03054. Tel: 603-880-8308; Fax: 603-880-9280
For a complete listing, refer to the Colleges and Universities section.

NASHUA. *Rivier College*, 03060. Tel: 603-888-1311.
E-mail: poneil@rivier.edu
Web site: www.rivier.edu
For a complete listing, refer to the Colleges and Universities section.

WARNER. *Magdalen College*, 511 Kearsarge Mountain Rd., 03278-9206. Tel: 603-456-2656
For a complete listing, refer to the Colleges and Universities section.

WINDHAM. *Castle College*, 23 Searles Rd., 03087-1200. Tel: 603-893-6111.
E-mail: ccadmin@ultranet.com
For a complete listing, refer to the Colleges and Universities section.

[C] HIGH SCHOOLS, DIOCESAN

MANCHESTER. *Trinity High School*, 581 Bridge St., 03104-3595. Tel: 603-668-2910; Fax: 603-668-2913. Mr. Denis Mailloux, Prin.; James Walker, Asst. Prin.; Rev. Raymond A. Ball, Chap. & Campus Min. Lay Teachers 27; Students 440.

CONCORD. *Bishop Brady High School*, 25 Columbus Ave., 03301. Tel: 603-224-7418.
E-mail: info@bishopbrady.org
Web site: www.bishopbrady.org
Jean Barker, Prin.; Joy Degnan, Asst. Prin. Sisters of Mercy. Sisters 2; Lay Teachers 36; Students 470.

DOVER. *St. Thomas Aquinas High School*, 197 Dover Point Rd., 03820. Tel: 603-742-3206.
E-mail: St.thomas@rscs.net
Web site: http://www.rscs.net/~kc2435/home.htm
Mr. Brian C. Newhall, Prin.; Rev. Albert Tremblay, Chap. Sisters 3; Lay Teachers 48; Students 660.

[D] HIGH SCHOOLS, PRIVATE

NASHUA. *Bishop Guertin High School*, 194 Lund Rd., 03060.
E-mail: bgl@tiac.net
Web site: www.bghs.org
Brothers of the Sacred Heart. (Coed). Bros. Leo Labbe, S.C., Headmaster; Paul Demers, S.C., Chap. Brothers 13; Lay Teachers 53; Students 782.

[E] REGIONAL ELEMENTARY SCHOOLS

MANCHESTER. *Mount Saint Mary Early Childhool Center*. (Grades PreK-3), 147 Laurel St., 03103. Tel: 603-623-3155. Sr. Gloria Morin, R.S.M., Prin. Sisters 2; Lay Teachers 8; Students 105.

St. Anthony School. (Grades K-6), 148 Belmont St., 03103. Tel: 603-622-0414. Mrs. Evelyn Bernier, Prin. Sisters 4; Lay Teachers 24; Boys 207; Girls 214.

St. Casimir School. (Grades K-8), 456 Union St., 03103. Tel: 603-623-6411. Sr. Mary Lawrence Lojko, C.S.S.F., Prin. Students 211.

St. Catherine School. (Grades K-6), 206 North St., 03104. Tel: 603-622-1711. Sr. Janet Belcourt, C.S.C., Prin. Sisters 5; Lay Teachers 19; Students 421.

St. Francis of Assisi School. (Grades K-6), 3223 Brown Ave., 03103. Tel: 603-669-2069.
E-mail: sfs@inc-net.com
Jude Chauvette, Prin. Sisters 1; Lay Teachers 7; Students 145.

St. Joseph Diocesan Regional Junior High Building. (Grades 7-8), 460 Pine St., 03104-6102. Tel: 603-624-4811; Fax: 603-624-6670.
Sr. Barbara McLean, R.S.M., Prin. Sisters 1; Lay Teachers 14; Students 250.

West Side Catholic Regional School. (Grades K-6), 85 Third St., 03102. Tel: 603-669-3932. Sr. Maria Rosa, P.M., Prin. Sisters 2; Lay Teachers 6; Students 145.

BERLIN. *St. Michael School*. (Berlin Regional Catholic School), 140 Blanchard St., 03570. Tel: 603-752-7413. Sr. Cecile Provost, C.S.C., Prin. Lay Teachers 12; Students 138.

CLAREMONT. *St. Mary School*. (Grades K-8), 18 Central St., 03743. Tel: 603-542-6341. Richard Lizotte, Prin. Lay Teachers 9; Students 165.

CONCORD. *St. John Regional School*, 61 S. State St., 03301. Tel: 603-225-3222. Sr. Irene Turgeon, S.N.D., Prin. Sisters 2; Lay Teachers 8; Students 264.

DERRY. *St. Thomas Aquinas School*. (Grades K-8), 3 Moody St., 03038. Tel: 603-432-2712; Fax: 603-432-2179. Sr. Jacqueline Brodeur, C.S.C., Prin. Students 292.

DOVER. *St. Mary Academy*, 222 Central Ave., 03820. Tel: 603-742-3299. Sr. Monica Markey, R.S.M., Prin. Sisters 5; Lay Teachers 26; Students 525.

HAMPTON. *Sacred Heart School*. (Grades P-8), 289 Lafayette Rd., 03842. Tel: 603-926-3254. Sr. Mary Joan Walsh, O.L.L., Prin. Sisters 5; Lay Teachers 25; Students 348.

JAFFREY. *St. Patrick School*. (Grades K-8), 70 Main St., 03452. Tel: 603-532-7676. David L. O'Connell, Prin. Students 164.

KEENE. *St. Joseph School*. (Grades PreK-8), 92 Wilson St., 03431. Tel: 603-352-2720. Carolyn O'Connell, Prin. Lay Teachers 14; Total Staff 25; Students 221.

LACONIA. *Holy Trinity*, 50 Church St., 03246. Tel: 603-524-3156. Mr. Jack Fortier, Prin. Lay Teachers 12; Total Staff 19; Students 177.

NASHUA. *Infant Jesus School*. (Grades K-6), 3 Crown St., 03060. Tel: 603-889-2649. Sr. Marie Henault, P.M., Prin. Sisters 3; Lay Teachers 17; Students 362.

Nashua Catholic Regional Junior High. (Grades 7-9), 6 Bartlett Ave., 03060. Tel: 603-883-6707; 882-7011. Mr. George R. LaVoice, Prin. Lay Teachers 22; Total Staff 31; Students 335.

St. Christopher School. (Grades K-6), 20 Cushing Ave., 03060. Tel: 603-882-7442. Sr. Joan Marie Messier, R.S.M., Prin. Sisters 3; Lay Teachers 11; Students 365.

PELHAM. *St. Patrick School*. (Grades K-8), 16 Main St., 03076. Tel: 603-635-2941; 635-9800.
E-mail: stpats@ultranet.com
Web site: ultranet.com/~stpats
Jane A. Gaskell, Prin. Lay Teachers 10; Students 230.

PORTSMOUTH. *St. Patrick*. (Grades PreK-8), 125 Austin St., 03801. Tel: 604-436-0739. Carol Davitt, Prin. Lay Teachers 14; Students 200.

ROCHESTER. *St. Elizabeth Seton School*. (Grades K-8), 16 Bridge St., 03867. Tel: 603-332-4803. Suzanne T. Boutin, Prin. Sisters 1; Lay Teachers 19; Students 318.

SALEM. *St. Joseph Regional School*. (Grades K-8), 40 Main St., 03079. Ms. Sandra A. Silvestro, Prin., Kindergarten. Rev. Richard Connors, Pastor. Lay Teachers 5; Students 72. Lay Teachers 16; Total Staff 38; Students 432.

WEST STEWARTSTOWN. *St. Albert School*. (Grades 1-8). P.O. Box 177, Beecher Falls, 05902. Tel: 603-246-8631. Sr. Lorraine Trottier, P.M., Prin. Sisters 3; Lay Teachers 2; Students 71.

[F] ELEMENTARY SCHOOLS, PRIVATE

MANCHESTER. *Holy Cross Kindergarten*, 357 Island Pond Rd., 03109-4811. Sr. Yvette M. Robert, C.S.C., Prin. & Admin. Sisters 3; Students 22.

St. Augustin Pre-School, 383 Beech St., 03103. Mrs. Mary Tremblay, Dir. Lay Teachers 21; Boys 21; Girls 27.

GOFFSTOWN. *Villa Augustina School.* (Grades K-8), 208 S. Mast St., 03045. Tel: 603-497-2361. Sr. Vivian Patenaude, R.J.M., Prin. Sisters 8; Lay Teachers 22; Students 322.

HUDSON. *Presentation of Mary Academy.* (Grades K-8), 182 Lowell Rd., 03051. Tel: 603-889-6054. Sisters of the Presentation of Mary. Sr. Rachel Morrisette, P.M., Prin. Sisters 5; Lay Teachers 16; Students 422.

[G] CATHOLIC CHARITIES

MANCHESTER. *Catholic Charities Administration,* 215 Myrtle St., 03104. Tel: 603-669-3030; Fax: 603-626-1252. Rev. Msgr. John P. Quinn, Diocesan Dir.; Mr. Robert L. Staniels, Dir. Admin. Svcs.; Mr. Raymond V. Mailloux, Dir. of Health Care Svcs.; Mr. Robert P. Clohosey, Dir. Family Svcs.; Mr. Timothy Kelly, Coord. of Immigration Svcs.; Mr. Richard J. Shannon, Dir. Parish Social Ministry; Mr. Denis J. Daigle, Assoc. Dir. Parish Social Ministry; Ms. Kathleen Crane, Dir. Devel.; Dominique A. Rust, Accounting Mgr.; Mr. Robert P. Clohosey, Supvr. Adoption & Maternity Svcs.; Mrs. Lan N. Truong, Coord. of Refugee Svcs. Total Staff 75; Total Assisted 35,000.

Consultation Services for Church Ministers, 282 Concord St., 03104. Tel: 603-668-0014. Dr. Michael A. Noonan; Sr. Patricia Schmidt, D.W.

New Hampshire Catholic Charities, Manchester District Office, 325 Franklin St., 03101. Tel: 603-624-4717. Joseph P. Naff, M.S.W., A.C.S.W., Supr.

New Hampshire Food Bank, 62 W. Brook St., 03101-1215. Tel: 603-669-9725. Albert J. Trembley, Sr., Admin. A program of New Hampshire Catholic Charities and a certified Second Harvest affiliate that provides food and personal care products to over 400 agencies statewide and distributes over 2 million pounds of food yearly to more than 30 programs.

Office of Family Ministries, 215 Myrtle St., 03104. Jane M. Cosmo, Dir.

BERLIN. *NH Catholic Charities,* 153 Grafton St., 03570. Tel: 603-752-1325.

CONCORD. *NH Catholic Charities.* Parish Social Ministries. Branch Office, 176 Loudon Rd., 03301. Tel: 603-228-1108. Sr. Rosemary Crowley, S.N.D.

KEENE. *NH Catholic Charities,* Monadnock Regional Office, 22 Middle St., 03431. Tel: 603-357-3093. April Geer Fitzgerald, M.S.W., J.D., Outreach Coord. Total Assisted for Outreach 304; Total Assisted for counselling 206; Staff 3.

LACONIA. *NH Catholic Charities,* Lakes Region Branch Office, 17 Gilford Ave., 03246. Tel: 603-528-3035. Janet O'Connell, A.C.S.W., Counseling Supvr.; Kay E. Smalley, Parish Social Ministry Coord.

LEBANON. *NH Catholic Charities,* Branch Office, 24 Hanover St., # 8, 03766-1334. Tel: 603-448-5151; Fax: 603-448-5155. Marc S. Cousineau, Dir.

LITTLETON. *NH Catholic Charities,* Regional Office, 41 Cottage St., P.O. Box 323, 03561. Tel: 603-444-7727. Anthony F. Poekert, M.S., Coord., Parish Social Min.; Janet O'Connell, A.C.S.W., Counselor (Part Time).

NASHUA. *NH Catholic Charities,* Nashua Regional Office, 261 Lake St., 03060. Tel: 603-889-9431. Mary A. Kenison, Supr.

ROCHESTER. *NH Catholic Charities,* Seacoast Regional Office, 23 Grant St., 03867. Tel: 603-332-7701. Joseph P. Naff, M.S.W., Supr.

SALEM. *NH Catholic Charities,* Branch Office, 130 Main St., Ste. 204, 03079. Tel: 603-893-1971. Mary A. Kenison, Supr.

[H] CHILD CARE INSTITUTIONS

MANCHESTER. *St. Peter's Home,* 03102-3093. Tel: 603-625-9313; Fax: 603-625-1910
For a complete listing, refer to the Special Care Facilities section.

ALLENSTOWN. *Pine Haven Boys Center,* River Rd., P.O. Suncook, 03275
For a complete listing, refer to the Special Care Facilities section.

ROCHESTER. *St. Charles Children's Home,* 19 Grant St., 03867
For a complete listing, refer to the Special Care Facilities section.

[I] GENERAL HOSPITALS

MANCHESTER. *Catholic Medical Center of Manchester, NH, Inc.,* 100 McGregor St., 03102. Tel: 603-668-3545
For a complete listing, refer to the Hospitals section.

NASHUA. *St. Joseph Hospital,* 172 Kinsley St., 03061. Tel: 603-882-3000
For a complete listing, refer to the Hospitals section.

[J] HOMES FOR THE AGED

MANCHESTER. *Carpenter Center, Inc.,* 323 Franklin St., 03101
For a complete listing, refer to the Special Care Facilities section.

Frances Warde House, Inc., 435 Union St., 03103
For a complete listing, refer to the Special Care Facilities section.

Mt. Carmel Nursing Home, 235 Myrtle St., 03104. Tel: 603-627-3811
For a complete listing, refer to the Special Care Facilities section.

St. Teresas Manor & Bishop Primeau Apartments, 519 Bridge St., 03104. Tel: 603-668-2373
For a complete listing, refer to the Special Care Facilities section.

BERLIN. *St. Vincent de Paul Nursing Home,* 29 Providence Ave., 03570. Tel: 603-752-1820
For a complete listing, refer to the Special Care Facilities section.

DOVER. *St. Ann Home,* 03820. Tel: 603-742-2612; Fax: 603-743-3055
For a complete listing, refer to the Special Care Facilities section.

JAFFREY. *Good Shepherd Nursing Home,* 20 Plantation Dr., 03452. Tel: 603-532-8762
For a complete listing, refer to the Special Care Facilities section.

LACONIA. *Bishop Bradley Apartments,* 406 Court St., 03246
For a complete listing, refer to the Special Care Facilities section.

St. Francis Home for the Aged, 03246. Tel: 603-524-0466; Fax: 603-527-0884
For a complete listing, refer to the Special Care Facilities section.

NASHUA. *Marguerite's Place,* 87 Palm St., 03060. Tel: 603-598-1582
For a complete listing, refer to the Special Care Facilities section.

WINDHAM. *Warde Health Center,* 21 Searles Rd., 03087 Fax: 603-890-1293
For a complete listing, refer to the Special Care Facilities section.

[K] MONASTERIES AND RESIDENCES OF PRIESTS AND BROTHERS

MANCHESTER. *St. Anselm Abbey.* of the Order of St. Benedict and St. Anselm College, including Seminary and Formation Program. 100 St. Anselm Dr., 03102-1310. Tel: 603-641-7000; Fax: 603-641-7116. Rt. Revs. Matthew K. Leavy, O.S.B., Abbot and Chancellor; Gerald McCarthy, O.S.B., Resigned Abbot; Very Revs. John R. Fortin, O.S.B., Prior; Peter J. Guerin, O.S.B., Subprior; Revs. Aquinas F. Cafarelli, O.S.B.; Bede G. Camera, O.S.B.; James G. Cassidy, O.S.B.; Richard F. Clavelle, O.S.B.; Mark A. Cooper, O.S.B.; David W. Cotter, O.S.B.; Michael H. Custer, O.S.B.; Jerome J. Day, O.S.B.; Jonathan P. DeFelice, O.S.B.; Daniel G. Dempski, O.S.B.; Cecil J. Donahue, O.S.B.; Brendan P. Donnelly, O.S.B.; Gerard J. Donnelly, O.S.B.; Mathias D. Durette, O.S.B.; Jude J. Gray, O.S.B.; Benedict M. Guevin, O.S.B.; Augustine G. Kelly, O.S.B.; Iain G. MacLellan, O.S.B.; Finbar P. O'Mahoney, O.S.B.; Benet C. Phillips, O.S.B.; Placidus H. Riley, O.S.B.; Lawrence Schlegel, O.S.B.; Christopher L. Senk, O.S.B.; Patrick M. Sullivan, O.S.B. Priests 28; Brothers 6; Novices 3; Joan of Arc Sisters 12; Benedictine Nuns 2.

COLEBROOK. *Shrine of Our Lady of Grace,* 03576. Tel: 603-237-5511. Oblates of Mary Immaculate (Northern U.S. Province). Revs. Adhemar S. Deveau, O.M.I., Supr.; Roland St. Pierre, O.M.I.; Roland M. Hamel, O.M.I.; Charles Moreau, O.M.I.; Robert M. Paradis, O.M.I.; Patrice Morel, O.M.I.; Bros. Onil Lauziere, O.M.I.; Maurice Violette, O.M.I. Priests 6; Brothers 2.

ENFIELD. *Shrine of Our Lady of La Salette,* P.O. Box 420, 03748. Tel: 603-632-4301 (Gift Shop); 632-7087 (Business). Revs. Robert Campbell, M.S., Supr.; Roland S. Nadeau, M.S., Chap.; Leo Mayfield, M.S., Chap.; Roger J. Plante, M.S.; Bros. Marc Gelinas, M.S.; Emile Morin, M.S.; Robert Roy, M.S.; Roger St. Germain, M.S.; Claude Rheaume, M.S.; Deacon David Carignan, M.S. Priests 4; Brothers 5; Deacons 1; Total Staff 13.

HUDSON. *Missionary Oblates of Mary Immaculate,* 61 Burns Hill Rd., 03051-4423. Tel: 603-883-3233; Fax: 603-883-6089. Provincial House of the Northern U.S. Province. Very Rev. Arthur T. Obin, O.M.I., Prov.; Revs. Charles Breault, O.M.I., Prov. Treas.; Robert Levesque, O.M.I.; Joseph Juaire, O.M.I., (Retired); Real Bourque, O.M.I.; Wilfred Harvey, O.M.I.; George Brown, O.M.I.; Bevil Bramwell, O.M.I.; Norman Comtois, O.M.I.; Joseph Horton, O.M.I. Priests 78; Brothers 10; Total Staff 2; Serving Abroad 6; Total in Residence 2; Total Membership 88.

NASHUA. *Brothers of the Sacred Heart,* 28 Berkeley St., 03060. Tel: 603-595-2712. Bro. Roland Champagne, S.C., Dir. Brothers 6. 194 Lund Rd., 03060. Tel: 603-883-3683. Bro. Donald Tardif, S.C., Dir. Brothers 9.

[L] CONVENTS AND RESIDENCES OF SISTERS

MANCHESTER. *Bishop's House,* 661 N. River Rd., 03104. Little Sisters of the Holy Family. Sr. Gabrielle Paille, P.S.S.F., Supr. Sisters 4.

Cathedral Rectory, 145 Lowell St., 03101-6135. Little Sisters of the Holy Family in charge of domestic department. Sr. Theresa Guillemette, P.S.S.F., Supr. Sisters 5.

Monastery of the Precious Blood, 700 Bridge St., 03104. Tel: 603-623-4264. Sisters Adorers of the Precious Blood. Sr. Mary Clare, Supr.; Rev. Msgr. Albert W. Olkovikas, Chap. Sisters 29; Novices 1.

Regional Office of the Sisters of Holy Cross, 377 Island Pond Rd., 03109; Fax: 603-622-9782. Sr. Lucille Cantin, C.S.C., Regional Rep. Total Staff 7.

St. Catherine Convent, 539 N. River Rd., 03104. Sisters of the Holy Cross 2.

St. George Manor, 357 Island Pond Rd., 03109. Tel: 603-624-4557. Sr. Lorraine Paille, C.S.C., Supr.; Rev. Andre J. Gagnon, Chap. (Non-residential). Sisters 82.

Sisters of Holy Cross, 133 Ashland St., 03104. Sisters 3.

Sisters of Holy Cross, 2298 Elm St., 03104. Sisters 3.

Sisters of Holy Cross, 969 Chestnut St., 03104. Sisters 5. 971 Chestnut St., 03104. Sisters 4.

Sisters of Holy Cross, 2264 Elm St., 03104. Sisters 2.

Sisters of Holy Cross, 454 Island Pond Rd., 03109-4812. Sisters 3.

Sisters of Holy Cross, 136 Lynwood Ln., 03109. Sr. Louise Audette, C.S.C., Supr. Sisters 2.

Sisters of Holy Cross. Queen of Angels Convent, 113 Wedgewood Ln., 03109-4825. Sisters 4.

Sisters of the Presentation of Mary Provincial House, 495 Mammoth Rd., 03104-5494. Tel: 603-669-1080; Fax: 603-622-4953. Sr. Mariette Plante, P.M., Prov. Supr. Sisters in the Diocese 216; Sisters of the Presentation of Mary 238. St. Joseph Residence, 495 Mammoth Rd., 03104-5494. Tel: 603-627-5831. St. Marie Residence, 495 Mammoth Rd., 03104-5494. Tel: 603-623-0671. Bethany House, 25 Garmon St., 03104. Tel: 603-625-1957. St. Marie Convent, 133 Wayne St., 03102. Tel: 603-623-0815. St. Bernard Convent, 161 Main St., Keene, 03431. Tel: 603-357-4472. Rivier College/Florence Hall, 429 Main St., Nashua, 03060. Tel: 603-888-1311, Ext. 8291. Presentation of Mary Academy, 182 Lowell Rd., Hudson, 03051-4987. Tel: 603-883-8192; 889-6362; Fax: 603-883-8054. Presentation of Mary Novitiate, 180 Lowell Rd., Hudson, 03051-4987. Tel: 603-880-8186; Fax: 603-880-0298. Trinity House, 186 Lowell Rd., Hudson, 03051-4908. Tel: 603-882-1347. Presentation of Mary Convent, 58 Church St., Berlin, 03570. Tel: 603-752-1176. St. Albert Covent, P.O. Box 177, Beecher Fall, VT, 05902. Tel: 603-246-3388. Our Lady of Hope House of Prayer, 400 Temple Rd., New Ipswich, 03071. Tel: 603-878-2346. Rivier College/Marywood-Gracewood, 4 Oldfield Rd., Nashua, 03060. Tel: 603-891-5737; 888-3668. Rivier College/St. Joseph Hall, 429 Main St., Nashua, 03060. Tel: 603-888-1311, Ext. 8299. Rivier College/Presentation Hall, 429 Main St., Nashua, 03060. Tel: 603-888-1311, Ext. 8296. Holy Angels Convent, 6 Atkinson Depot Rd., Rte 121, Plaistow, 03865. Tel: 603-382-2744.

BEDFORD. *Regina Pacis, Benedictine Srs.,* 333 Wallace Rd., 03110-4827. Tel: 603-472-3239. Benedictine Sisters. Sr. M. Raphaela, O.S.B., Supr. Sisters 2.

CONCORD. *Monastery of Discalced Carmelites,* 275 Pleasant St., 03301-2590. Tel: 603-225-5791. Sr. Thomas Aquinas, O.C.D., Prioress. Professed Sisters 11.

GOFFSTOWN. *Villa Augustina Convent,* 03045. Tel: 603-497-3636; 603-497-3445. Sr. Claire Lebreux, R.J.M., Supr. Religious of Jesus and Mary 24.

LITTLETON. *Provincial House of Daughters of the Charity of the Sacred Heart of Jesus,* Mount Sacred Heart, Grove St., P.O. Box 642, 03561. Tel: 603-444-5346; Fax: 603-444-5348. Local Superiors: Sr. Lucille Grandpre; Sr. Yvette Beloin; Sr. Rosina Bechard, Prov. Supr. Sisters 32.

LONDONDERRY. *Sisters of Holy Cross,* Londonderry House, 68 Mammoth Rd., 03053.

NEW IPSWICH. *Our Lady of Hope, House of Prayer,* 400 Temple Rd., 03071. Tel: 603-878-2346. Sr. Jeannette Levasseur, Supr. & Dir. Sisters 6.

PITTSFIELD. *Berakah.* A Place for Blessing, 96 Fairview Rd., 03263-3817. Sisters 6.

PORTSMOUTH. *Our Lady of Lourdes Convent,* 11 Fairview Dr., 03801. Tel: 603-436-6612. Sisters of Our Lady of Lourdes (O.L.L.). Sr. Mary Joan Walsh, O.L.L., Supr. Sisters 2.

WEST FRANKLIN. *Our Lady of the Sacred Heart Convent,* 21 Holy Cross Rd., 03235. Sr. Louise M. Tarpey, C.S.C., Supr.; Rev. Anthony DiGiulio, Chap. (Retired). Sisters 23.

Sisters of Holy Cross, 21 Holy Cross Rd., 03235. Sr. Louise M. Tarpey, C.S.C., Supr. Sisters 23.

WINDHAM. *Sisters of Mercy of the Americas.* Motherhouse of the Sisters of Mercy, Inc., Regional Community of New Hampshire, 21 Searles Rd., 03087-1297. Tel: 603-893-6550 (Admin. Office). Sisters of Mercy of New Hampshire. Sr. Patricia Sullivan, Reg. Community Pres. Sisters 46.

Mount Saint Mary Corporation of the Sisters of Mercy, Nashua.

Manchester Convent of the Sisters of Mercy, Manchester.

Warde Health Center.

Mount St. Mary Early Childhood Center, Manchester.

Frances Warde House, Manchester.

[M] RETREAT HOUSES

MANCHESTER. Discalced Carmelites. Revs. Bruno Cocuzzi, O.C.D., Acting Supr.; Terrence Dougherty, O.C.D.; Bro. Sebastian Reale, O.C.D.

Emmaus House, 286 Concord St., 03104. Tel: 603-624-1173. Sr. Bernadette Turgeon, S.N.D.deN., Dir.; Matthew Goody, Assoc. Dir. Total Staff 15.

ENFIELD. *La Salette Shrine and Center of Enfield,* Box 420, 03748. Tel: 603-632-7087 (Business); 632-4301 (Gift Shop). Revs. Robert Campbell, M.S., Supr.; Roland S. Nadeau, M.S.; Leo Maxfield, M.S., Chap.; Roger J. Plante, M.S. Priests 4; Deacons 1; Brothers 5; Total Staff 13.

HUDSON. *Oblates of Mary Immaculate Retreat House,* 200 Lowell Rd., 03051-4934. Tel: 603-882-8141. Revs. Thomas Horan, O.M.I., Dir.; Gerard Roux, O.M.I.; Bro. Paul Daly, O.M.I. Priests 2; Brothers 1.

NEW BOSTON. *Epiphany Monastery,* 96 Scobie Rd., Box 60, 03070. Tel: 603-487-3020; Fax: 603-487-3700. Rev. Romuald Duscher, O.S.B.Cam.; Bro. Jonah Kepfield, O.S.B.Cam.; Deacon Zacchaeus Naegele, O.S.B.Cam. Total Staff 3; Total in Residence 3.

[N] CAMPUS MINISTRY AND NEWMAN CENTERS

DURHAM. *Campus Ministries,* 6 Madbury Rd., P.O. Box 620, 03824-0620. Tel: 603-862-1310; Fax: 603-868-3765. Rev. Frederick J. Pennett, Dir., Aquinas House, P.O. Box 147, Hanover, 03755. Tel: 603-643-2154. Revs. Raynold J. Thibodeau; John McHugh, O.F.M.Cap., P.O. Box 557, Henniker, 03242. Tel: 603-428-3325. Rev. Andre M. Thibodeau, 2321 Elm St., Manchester, 03104. Tel: 603-669-4298, Ext. 100. Sr. Kathleen McInnis, R.S.M., 2500 N. River Rd., Manchester, 03104. Tel: 603-668-2211, Ext. 2139. Rev. Bruce W. Collard, 100 St. Anselm Dr., Manchester, 03102. Tel: 603-641-7130. Revs. Cecil J. Donahue, O.S.B.; Benet C. Phillips, O.S.B., Rivier College, 420 S. Main St., Nashua, 03060. Tel: 603-888-1311, Ext. 8577. Sr. Jacqueline LeBlanc, P.M.; Bro. Paul Demers, S.C. Tel: 603-888-1311 Ext. 8537, Box 200, New London, 03257. Tel: 603-526-2010. Rev. Richard T. Lower, 46 Langdon St., Plymouth, 03264. Tel: 603-535-2673. Sr. Helene Higgins, C.S.J., Catholic Student Center, P.O. Box 620, 03824. Tel: 603-862-1310. Rev. Frederick J. Pennett.

St. Thomas More Catholic Student Center at the University of New Hampshire, 6 Madbury Rd., P.O. Box 620, 03824-0620. Tel: 603-862-1310; Fax: 603-868-3765. Rev. Frederick J. Pennett, Chap; Amy E. Hickey, Assoc. Chap.; Venise T. Gonya, Assoc. Chap.

HANOVER. *The Catholic Student Center at Dartmouth, Aquinas House, Aquinas at Dartmouth, Inc.,* Occom Ridge & Webster Ave., P.O. Box 147, 03755. Tel: 603-643-2154; Fax: 603-643-9411.
Web site: http://www.dartmouth.edu/~aquinas
Revs. John P. McHugh, O.F.M.Cap., Dir.; Raynold P. Thibodeau, O.F.M.Cap., Assoc. Chap.; Anna Mae Mayer, Assoc. Chap. Total Staff 4; Total in Residence 2.

HENNIKER. *New England College Newman Center,* St. Theresa Rectory, 03242. Tel: 603-428-3325. Rev. Andre M. Thibodeau, Chap.

KEENE. *Keene State College, Catholic Newman Center,* 232 Main St., P.O. Box 491, 03431. Tel: 603-352-7785; 358-2100.

NEW LONDON. *Colby-Sawyer College Newman Center,* Our Lady of Fatima Rectory, 03257. Tel: 603-526-4484. Rev. Richard T. Lower, Chap.

PLYMOUTH. *Plymouth State College Campus Ministry,* Plymouth State College, Ste. A6, 03264.
E-mail: Heleneh@psc.edu
Sr. Helene Higgins, C.S.J., Catholic Campus Minister. Tel: 603-535-2673; Rev. Robert F. Cole, Chap.

RINDGE. *Franklin Pierce College Newman Center,* Keene State College, 232 Main St., P.O. Box 491, 03431. Tel: 603-352-7785. Mary Ann Damato, Chap.

[O] MISCELLANEOUS

MANCHESTER. *Crown Ministries —New Hampshire,* 25 Maybrook Ave., 03102. Tel: 603-627-8898. Geoff Ashman, Coord.

Diocesan Museum, 140 Laurel St., 03103. Tel: 603-624-1729; 623-8196. Judith Fosher, Coord.

Holy Cross Health Center, Inc., 357 Island Pond Rd., 03109-4811. Tel: 603-628-3550; Fax: 603-626-6270. Sr. Judith Langevin, C.S.C., N.H.A., Admin.

Sophia Institute Press, P.O. Box 5284, 03108. Tel: 603-641-9344; Fax: 603-641-8108.
E-mail: sipress@grolen.com
Web site: sophiainstitute.com
John L. Barger, Publisher.

CENTER HARBOR. *L.C. Center Harbor, Inc.,* Plymouth St., 03226.

FRANKLIN. *Holy Cross Associates of U.S. Region,* 33 Holy Cross Rd., 03235. Tel: 603-934-4874; 837-2835. Jan Rondeau, H.C.A., Pres. & Exec. Dir.; Lorraine Richard, H.C.A., Vice Pres.; Betty Poliquin, H.C.A., Treas.; Fran Miller, H.C.A., Sec.

GILFORD. *The Missionary Servants of Pope John Paul I,* 22 Boyd Hill Rd., 03246. Tel: 603-524-4740. The Missionary Servants of Pope John Paul I is a lay missionary association founded to aid established missionaries. Help is mainly given to Mother Teresa's missions in Haiti; however, shipments have also been made to Honduras, the Sudan, British Columbia, areas of the U.S. and to the local poor.

[P] SPECIAL APOSTOLATE CENTERS

BERLIN. *Christian Life Center,* Emery St., P.O. Box 354, 03570. Tel: 603-752-7883. Mrs. Judy J. Rheaume, Coord.

DURHAM. *Christian Life Center,* 6 Madbury Rd., P.O. Box 471, 03824. Tel: 603-868-5514. Sr. Claudette Carisse, S.A.S.V., Dir.

KEENE. *Christian Life Center,* 70 Island St., P.O. Box 293, 03431. Tel: 603-352-7662.

LACONIA. *Christian Life Center,* Box 306, 03247. Tel: 603-524-7503. Janet Leroux, Coord.

NASHUA. *Nashua Deanery Toward Marriage Program,* P.O. Box 3403, 03061-3403. Tel: 603-889-0707.

SALEM. *Christian Life Center,* P.O. Box 314, 03079. Tel: 603-893-5878. Paul J. Donovan, Dir.

[Q] CAMPS AND COMMUNITY CENTERS

CENTER OSSIPEE. *Camp Marist,* Rte. 25 E., 03814. Tel: 603-539-4552; Fax: 603-539-8318 (Summer Address). St. Mary's High School, 51 Clapham Ave., Manhasset, NY, 11030. Tel: 516-627-2711; Fax: 516-627-3209 (Winter Address). Bro. Ken Ward, F.M.S., Dir. Total Staff 90; Total Assisted 300.

GILMANTON IRON WORKS. *Camp Bernadette.* (Girls), Winter Business Office, P.O. Box 206, 03837-0206.
E-mail: Diocamps@InternetMCI.com
Web site: www.coolcamps.com/diocesancamps/
Summer Business Office, 83 Richards Rd., Wolfeboro, 03894. Mr. Gus Planchet, Dir. Total Staff 80; Total Assisted 800.

Camp Fatima. (Boys), Business Office, P.O. Box 206, 03837-0206.
E-mail: Diocamps@InternetMCI.com
Web site: www.coolcamps.com/diocesancamps/
Mr. Gus Planchet, Dir. Total Staff 80; Total Assisted 800.

RELIGIOUS INSTITUTES OF MEN REPRESENTED IN THE DIOCESE

For further details refer to the corresponding bracketed number in the Religious Institutes of Men or Women section.

[0140]—*The Augustinians.*—O.S.A.

[0190]—*Basilian Salvatorian Fathers.*—B.S.O.

[0200]—*Benedictine Monks.* (American Cassinese & Camaldolese Benedictine Congregations).—O.S.B.

[1350]—*Brothers of St. Francis Xavier.*—C.F.X.

[1100]—*Brothers of the Sacred Heart.* (New England Prov.).—S.C.

[0470]—*The Capuchin Friars.* (Prov. of St. Mary).—O.F.M.Cap.

[1320]—*Clerics of St. Viator.*—C.S.V.

[1330]—*Congregation of the Mission.* (New England Prov.).—C.M.

[1000]—*Congregation of the Passion.*—C.P.

[0260]—*Discalced Carmelite Fathers.* (Prov. of Immaculate Heart of Mary).—O.C.D.

[0520]—*Franciscan Friars.* (Prov. of Most Holy Name).—O.F.M.

[0520]—*Franciscan Friars.* (Province of the Immaculate Conception).—O.F.M.

[0690]—*Jesuit Fathers and Brothers.* (Maryland & New England Provinces).—S.J.

[0730]—*Legionaries of Christ.*—L.C.

[0770]—*The Marist Brothers.*—F.M.S.

[0720]—*The Missionaries of Our Lady of La Salette.* (Immaculate Heart of Mary & Our Lady of Seven Dolors Provinces).—M.S.

[0910]—*Oblates of Mary Immaculate.* (Prov. of St. John the Baptist).—O.M.I.

[0920]—*Oblates of St. Francis de Sales.*—O.S.F.S.

[0430]—*Order of Preachers (Dominicans).*—O.P.

[0610]—*Priests of the Congregation of Holy Cross.*—C.S.C.

[0760]—*Society of Mary (Marianists).*—S.M.

[1250]—*Somascan Fathers.*—C.R.S.

RELIGIOUS INSTITUTES OF WOMEN REPRESENTED IN THE DIOCESE

[0200]—*Benedictine Sisters.*—O.S.B.

[0230]—*Benedictine Sisters of Pontifical Jurisdiction.* (from Kaunas, Lithuania).—O.S.B.

[0330]—*Carmelite Sisters for the Aged and Infirm.*—O.Carm.

[2410]—*Congregation of the Marianites of Holy Cross.*—M.S.C.

[3815]—*Congregation of the Sisters of St. Joan of Arc.*—S.J.A.

[0750]—*Daughters of the Charity of the Sacred Heart of Jesus.*—F.C.S.C.J.

[0960]—*Daughters of Wisdom.*—D.W.

[0420]—*Discalced Carmelites Nuns.*—O.C.D.

[1110]—*Dominican Sisters of Our Lady of the Rosary and of Saint Catherine of Siena, Cabra.*—O.P.

[1170]—*Felician Sisters.*—C.S.S.F.

[1190]—*Franciscan Sisters of the Atonement.*—S.A.

[2575]—*Institute of the Sisters of Mercy of the Americas.* (Manchester, NH).—R.S.M.

[2320]—*The Little Sisters of the Holy Family.*—P.S.S.F.

[2420]—*Marist Missionary Sisters.*—S.M.S.M.

[2470]—*Maryknoll Sisters of St. Dominic.*—M.M.

[3450]—*Religious of Jesus and Mary.*—R.J.M.

[3465]—*Religious of the Sacred Heart of Mary.*—R.S.H.M.

[2970]—*School Sisters of Notre Dame.*—S.S.N.D.

[1680]—*School Sisters of St. Francis.*—O.S.F.

[3650]—*Servants of Our Lady, Queen of Clergy.*—S.R.C.

[0110]—*The Sisters Adorers of the Precious Blood.*—A.P.B.

[0490]—*Sisters of Charity of Montreal (Grey Nuns).*—S.G.M.

[0530]—*Sisters of Charity of Our Lady, Mother of the Church.*—S.C.M.C.

[0610]—*Sisters of Charity of St. Hyacinthe (Grey Nuns).*—S.C.S.H.

[0640]—*Sisters of Charity of St. Vincent De Paul, Halifax.*—S.C.

[1930]—*Sisters of Holy Cross.*—C.S.C.

[3000]—*Sisters of Notre Dame de Namur.*—S.N.D.deN.

[3080]—*Sisters of Our Lady of Christian Doctrine.*—R.C.D.

[]—*Sisters of Our Lady of Lourdes.*—O.L.L.

[3350]—*Sisters of Providence.* (Montreal).—S.P.

[3360]—*Sisters of Providence of Saint Mary-of-the-Woods, IN.*—S.P.

[3718]—*Sisters of St. Ann.*—S.S.A.

[3840]—*Sisters of St. Joseph of Carondelet.* (Prov. of Albany).—C.S.J.

[3850]—*Sisters of St. Joseph of Chambery.*—C.S.J.

[0150]—*Sisters of the Assumption.*—S.A.S.V.

[1990]—*Sisters of the Holy Names of Jesus and Mary.*—S.N.J.M.

[3310]—*Sisters of the Presentation of Mary.*—P.M.

[3320]—*Sisters of the Presentation of the B.V.M.*—P.B.V.M.

[4060]—*Society of the Holy Child Jesus.*—S.H.C.J.

NECROLOGY

† O'Neil, Leo E., Bishop of Manchester. —Died Nov. 30, 1997.

† Dumas, Alfred J., (Retired). —Died Dec. 1, 1996.

Diocese of Marquette

(Dioecesis Marquettensis)

Most Reverend

JAMES H. GARLAND, M.A., M.S.W., D.D.

Bishop of Marquette; ordained 1959; appointed Titular Bishop of Garriana and Auxiliary Bishop of Cincinnati June 2, 1984; consecrated July 25, 1984; appointed Bishop of Marquette October 6, 1992; installed November 11, 1992. *Res., 300 Rock St., P.O. Box 550, Marquette, MI, 49855.* Tel.: 906-225-1141.

Most Reverend

MARK F. SCHMITT, D.D.

Retired Bishop of Marquette; ordained May 22, 1948; appointed Titular Bishop of Kells and Auxiliary of Green Bay May 5, 1970; consecrated June 24, 1970; appointed to Marquette March 21, 1978; installed May 8, 1978; retired November 11, 1992. *Res., HCO1 Box 159, Marquette, MI, 49855.*

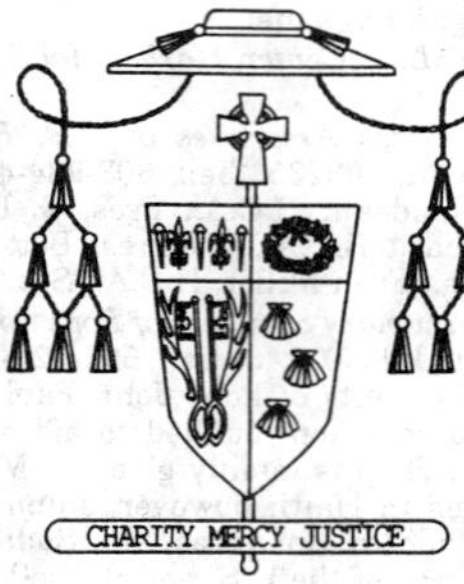

VICARIATE-APOSTOLIC JULY 29, 1853; DIOCESE 1857.

Square Miles 16,281.

Comprises the Upper Peninsula of the State of Michigan.

For legal titles of parishes and diocesan institutions, consult the Pastoral Office.

Chancery Office: 444 S. Fourth St., P.O. Box 550, Marquette, MI, 49855. Tel.: 906-225-1141; Fax: 906-225-0437.

E-mail address: asample@dioceseofmarquette.org

STATISTICAL OVERVIEW

Personnel	
Bishop	1
Retired Bishops	1
Priests: Diocesan Active in Diocese	58
Priests: Active Outside Diocese	7
Priests: Retired, Sick or Absent	43
Number of Diocesan Priests	108
Religious Priests in Diocese	12
Extern Priests in Diocese	5
Ordinations:	
Transitional Deacons	1
Permanent Deacons	3
Permanent Deacons in Diocese	18
Total Sisters	67
Parishes	
Parishes	74
With Resident Pastor:	
Resident Diocesan Priests	53
Resident Religious Priests	9
Without Resident Pastor:	
Administered by Priests	7
Administered by Permanent Deacons	1
Administered by Women Religious	4
Missions	24
Closed Parishes	1
Professional Ministry Personnel:	
Sisters	19
Lay Ministers	25
Welfare	
Catholic Hospitals	1
Total Assisted	66,670
Homes for the Aged	1
Total Assisted	123
Special Centers for Social Services	6
Total Assisted	1,393
Educational	
Diocesan Students in Other Seminaries	8
Total Seminarians	8
Elementary Schools, Diocesan and Parish	10
Total Students	1,695
Catechesis/Religious Education:	
High School Students	3,279
Elementary Students	6,346
Total Students Under Catholic Instruction	11,328
Teachers in the Diocese:	
Sisters	8
Lay Teachers	108
Vital Statistics	
Receptions into the Church:	
Infant Baptism Totals	1,071
Adult Baptism Totals	52
Received into Full Communion	159
First Communions	1,079
Confirmations	1,060
Marriages:	
Catholic	262
Interfaith	197
Total Marriages	459
Deaths	1,232
Total Catholic Population	71,706
Total Population	309,000

Former Bishops—Rt. Rev. FREDERIC BARAGA, D.D., first Bishop; cons. Nov. 1, 1853; died Jan. 19, 1868.—Rt. Rev. IGNATIUS MRAK, D.D., cons. Feb. 7, 1869; resigned 1878; transferred to Antinoe 1879; died Jan. 2, 1901.—Rt. Rev. JOHN VERTIN, D.D., cons. Sept. 14, 1879; died Feb. 26, 1899.—Rt. Rev. FREDERICK EIS, D.D., cons. Aug. 24, 1899 made Asst. at the Pontifical Throne July 13, 1922; resigned July 8, 1922; appt. Titular Bishop of Bita; died May 5, 1926.—Most Rev. PAUL JOSEPH NUSSBAUM, D.D., cons. Bishop of Corpus Christi May 20, 1913; resigned March 26, 1920; appt. Bishop of Marquette Nov. 14, 1922; died June 24, 1935.—Most Rev. JOSEPH CASIMIR PLAGENS, D.D., LL.D., cons. Sept. 30, 1924, Auxiliary Bishop of Detroit Titular Bishop of Rhodiopolis; appt. to See of Marquette Nov. 16, 1935; transferred to the See of Grand Rapids Dec. 16, 1940; died March 31, 1943.—Most Rev. FRANCIS J. MAGNER, D.D., appt. Dec. 21, 1940; cons. Feb. 24, 1941; died June 13, 1947.—Most Rev. THOMAS L. NOA, D.D., cons. March 19, 1946; Titular Bishop of Salona and Coadjutor Bishop of Sioux City; appt. Bishop of Marquette Aug. 20, 1947; retired March 25, 1968; died March 13, 1977.—Most Rev. CHARLES A. SALATKA, D.D., appt. Titular Bishop of Cariana and Auxiliary of Grand Rapids Dec. 9, 1961; cons. March 6, 1962; appt. Bishop of Marquette Jan. 10, 1968; installed March 25, 1968; appt. Archbishop of Oklahoma City Oct. 11, 1977.—Most. Rev. MARK F. SCHMITT, D.D., appt. Titular Bishop of Kells and Auxiliary of Green Bay May 5, 1970; cons. June 24, 1970; appt. Bishop of Marquette March 21, 1978; installed May 8, 1978; retired November 11, 1992.

Chancery Office—444 S. Fourth St., P.O. Box 550, Marquette, 49855. Tel: 906-225-1141; Fax: 906-225-0437. Office Hours: Mon.-Fri. 9-5.

Vicar General—Very Rev. PETER OBERTO, V.G., J.C.L.

Chancellor—Rev. ALEXANDER K. SAMPLE, J.C.L.

Diocesan Tribunal—444 S. Fourth St., P.O. Box 550, Marquette, 49855. Tel: 906-225-1141.

Judicial Vicar—Very Rev. PETER OBERTO, V.G., J.C.L.

Diocesan Judges—Revs. ALEXANDER K. SAMPLE, J.C.L.; JOSEPH NAGAROOR, J.C.D.

Defensor Vinculi—Rev. JOHN J. SHIVERSKI.

Advocates—Revs. FRANCIS J. DEGROOT; JOHN L. LONGBUCCO; BENEDETTO K. PARIS.

Notary—MARY C. JESKE.

Episcopal Vicar—West Region: Rev. NORMAN A. CLISCH.

Priests' Council—

Executive Board—Revs. MICHAEL J. STEBER, Chm. NORMAN A. CLISCH, Vice Chm. WAYNE E. MARCOTTE, Treas. JOHN E. PATRICK, Sec.

Deans—Rev. VINCENT L. OUELLETTE, Marquette; Rev. CHRISTOPHER B. GARDINER, Escanaba; Rev. THOMAS L. POISSON, Houghton; Rev. JOSEPH O. GOUIN, Iron Mountain; Rev. ALLAN J. MAYOTTE, Ironwood; Rev. PATRICK WISNESKE, Menominee; Rev. THEODORE J. BRODEUR, Sault Ste. Marie; Rev. NORMAN A. CLISCH, Iron River; Rev. TIMOTHY H. DESROCHERS, Manistique.

Consultors—Revs. RICK L. COURIER; JOHN J. SHIVERSKI; Very Rev. PETER OBERTO; Revs. NORMAN A. CLISCH; GEORGE C. GUSTAFSON; WAYNE E. MARCOTTE; JOHN E. PATRICK; ALEXANDER K. SAMPLE.

Diocesan Offices and Directors

Adiministration & Finance, Dept. of—RICHARD R. SCHAEFER, C.P.A., Dir. CAROL J. PARKER, Bookkeeper-Accountant, *444 S. Fourth St., P.O. Box 550, Marquette, 49855.* Tel: 906-225-1141; Fax: 906-225-0437.

Catholic Social Services, Dept. of—STEPHEN J. LYNOTT, M.S.W., Dir., *347 Rock St., Marquette, 49855.* Tel:

906-228-8630. Branch Offices: Houghton, Escanaba, Iron Mountain, Sault Ste., Marie, Ironwood.

Christian Education/Formation Services, Dept. of—Sr. JOYCE ROSE O.S.F., Dir. CLIFFORD LUFT, Supt. of Schools; DANIEL SPARAPANI, Coord. for Adult and Family Rel. Educ. JAMES GHIARDI, Pres., Board of Educ. ROBERT ST. LOUIS, Vice Pres., Board of Educ., *347 Rock St., P.O. Box 280, Marquette, 49855.* Tel: 906-226-3515.

Communication Services, Dept. of—LOREENE ZENO KOSKEY, Dir.

Newspaper "The Upper Peninsula Catholic"—JOSEPH ZYBLE, Editor, *347 Rock St., P.O. Box 548, Marquette, 49855.* Tel: 906-226-8821; Fax: 906-226-6941.

Ministry Personnel Services, Dept. of—Rev. ALEXANDER K. SAMPLE, Dir., *444 S. Fourth St., P.O. Box 550, Marquette, 49855.* Tel: 906-225-1141; Fax: 906-225-0437.

Spiritual Development Services, Dept. of—JAMES HANSEN, Dir., *444 S. Fourth St., P.O. Box 550, Marquette, 49855.* Tel: 906-225-1141; Fax: 906-225-4651.

Apostleship of the Sea—Rev. TED BRODEUR, Chap., *Holy Name of Mary Parish, 377 Maple St., Sault Ste. Marie, 49783.* Tel: 906-632-3381.

Bishop Baraga Association Inc.—615 S. Fourth St., P.O. Box 550, Marquette, 49855. Tel: 906-226-7024. An international organization to promote the Cause of the Beatification of the Most Rev. Frederic Baraga. Rev. ALEX K. SAMPLE, Exec. Dir., Treas., and Vice-Postulator; Rev. BRUNO KOROSAK, O.F.M., Postulator; ELIZABETH J. DELENE, Archivist.

Building Commission, Diocese of Marquette—RICHARD R. SCHAEFER, Sec., *P.O. Box 550, Marquette, 49855.* Tel: 906-225-1141.

Catholic Relief Services—Rev. Msgr. DAVID SPELGATTI, Dir., *P.O. Box 550, Marquette, 49855.*

Cemeteries—RICHARD R. SCHAEFER, Bishop's Rep. for Catholic Cemeteries, *444 S. Fourth St., Marquette, 49855.* Tel: 906-225-1141.

Charismatic Prayer Groups—Rev. RAYMOND J. ZEUGNER, Diocesan Liaison, *Guardian Angels Parish, Crystal Falls, 49920.* Tel: 906-875-3019.

Clergy Education—Rev. JAMES C. ZIMINSKI, *P.O. Box 550, Marquette, 49855.* Tel: 906-225-1141.

Council of Catholic Women—Rev. THOMAS L. POISSON, *St. Ignatius Loyola Parish, Houghton, 49931.*

Cursillo—Rev. TIMOTHY DESROCHERS, Diocesan Moderator, *Marygrove, P.O. Box 38, Garden, 49835.* Tel: 906-644-2771.

Ecumenical Officer—Deacon DONALD J. GIESEN, *W3747 Lake Louise Dr., North, Vulcan, 49892.*

Family Life Ministry—ROSALYN GROVES, Coord., *8260 23.3 Ln., Rapid River, 49878.* Tel: 906-474-6483.

Holy Childhood Association—Rev. LAWRENCE T. GAUTHIER, Dir., *P.O. Box 550, Marquette, 49855.* Tel: 906-225-1141.

Office of Stewardship—DAVID ADLER, Dir., *444 S. Fourth St., P.O. Box 550, Marquette, 49855.*

Panama Mission Fund—Rev. PAUL G. MANDERFIELD, *444 S. Fourth St., Marquette, 49855.* Tel: 906-225-1141.

Permanent Diaconate Program—Rev. JAMES C. ZIMINSKI, Dir., *P.O. Box 550, Marquette, 49855.* Tel: 906-225-1141.

Propagation of the Faith—Rev. LAWRENCE T. GAUTHIER, Diocesan Dir., *P.O. Box 550, Marquette, 49855.* Tel: 906-225-1141.

Retreats—Rev. TIMOTHY DESROCHERS, Dir., *Marygrove Retreat Center, Garden, 49835.* Tel: 906-644-2771.

St. Joseph Association—An Association of the Priests of the Diocese to provide Old Age Benefits. Rev. MICHAEL A. WOEMPNER, Pres., *St. Jude Parish, P.O. Box 427, White Pine, 49971.* Tel: 906-885-5763.

U.P. Catholic Services Appeal—RICHARD R. SCHAEFER, Coord., *444 S. Fourth St., P.O. Box 796, Marquette, 49855.* Tel: 906-225-1378.

Vocation Office—Rev. JAMES C. ZIMINSKI, Dir., *P.O. Box 550, Marquette, 49855.* Tel: 906-225-1141.

Women Religious—Sr. COLLEEN SWEETING, O.S.F., Dir., *P.O. Box 550, Marquette, 49855.* Tel: 906-225-1141.

CLERGY, PARISHES, MISSIONS AND PAROCHIAL SCHOOLS

CITY OF MARQUETTE
(Marquette County)

1—ST. PETER CATHEDRAL, Revs. Louis C. Cappo; Mariusz Makowski; Deacon Scott A. Jamieson. In res., Revs. Alfred Lopez, O.P.; Alex K. Sample.
Res., 311 Baraga Ave., 49855. Tel: 906-226-6548; Fax: 906-226-8683.
School—Father Marquette Catholic Central Schools System. See Elementary Inter-Parochial Schools under Institutions Located in the Diocese.

2—ST. CHRISTOPHER, Rev. Alexander K. Sample; Sr. Francis M. Mortola, S.P.C., Pastoral Coord.
Res., 2372 Badger St., 49855. Tel: 906-226-2265.

3—ST. JOHN THE BAPTIST. Closed. 1986. For inquiries for parish records, contact St. Peter's Cathedral.

4—ST. LOUIS (Harvey), Rev. Guy S. Thoren; Deacon David P. Adler.
Res., 264 Silver Creek Rd., 49855. Tel: 906-249-1438; Fax: 906-249-3428.
School—Father Marquette Catholic Central Schools System. See Elementary Inter-Parochial Schools under Institutions Located in the Diocese.

5—ST. MICHAEL, Revs. John E. Patrick; Timothy W. Hruska. In res., Rev. James C. Ziminski.
Res., 401 W. Kaye Ave., 49855. Tel: 906-228-8180; Fax: 906-228-5502.
School—Father Marquette Catholic Central Schools System. See Elementary Inter-Parochial Schools under Institutions Located in the Diocese.
Mission—Big Bay, Marquette Co., St. Mary.

OUTSIDE THE CITY OF MARQUETTE

Ahmeek, Keweenaw Co., Our Lady of Peace. (Keweenaw Catholic Missions). Rev. Miles Pfalzer, O.F.M.
Mailing Address: Box 517, Mohawk, 49950. Tel: 906-337-1966.
Missions—Eagle Harbor, Holy Redeemer; Copper Harbor, Our Lady of the Pines.

Alpha, Iron Co., St. Edward. Closed. For inquiries for parish records contact the Chancery.

Assinins, Baraga Co., The Most Holy Name of Jesus-Blessed Kateri Tekakwitha, Rev. John S. Hascall, O.F.M.Cap.
Res., Rte. 1, Box 47, Baraga, 49908. Tel: 906-353-6836; Fax: 906-353-6800.
Indian Mission—West & Central Diocese of Marquette.

Baraga, Baraga Co., St. Ann, Rev. Paul G. Manderfield.
Res., 318 Lyons St., P.O. Box 349, 49908. Tel: 906-353-6565.

Bark River, Delta Co., St. Elizabeth Ann Seton. Formerly St. George,Bark River; Sacred Heart of Jesus, Schaffer; & St. Michael, Perronville. Rev. Emmett M. Norden.
Res., 1216 12th Rd., P.O. Box 187, 49807. Tel: 906-466-9938.

Bessemer, Gogebic Co., St. Sebastian, Rev. Joseph D. Carne.
Res., 210 E. Iron St., 49911. Tel: 906-667-0952.
School—Tel: 906-667-0322.
Lay Teachers 8; Students 100.

Brimley, Chippewa Co., St. Francis Xavier, Rev. Jeff G. Johnson.
Mailing Address: P.O. Box 429, 49715. Tel: 906-248-3443.
Missions—Sugar Island, Chippewa Co., Sacred Heart; Sault Sainte Marie, Chippewa Co., St. Isaac Jogues; Bay Mills, Chippewa Co., Blessed Kateri Tekakwitha. (Formerly St. Catherine).

Calumet, Houghton Co., Sacred Heart, Rev. Marian Douglas, O.F.M.
Mailing Address: P.O. Box 546, 49913. Tel: 906-337-0810.

St. Paul the Apostle, Rev. Cyprian E. Berens, O.F.M. In res., Rev. Miles Pfalzer, O.F.M.
Res., 301 Eighth St., 49913. Tel: 906-337-2044.

Caspian, Iron Co., St. Cecilia, Rev. Otto J. Sartorelli; Deacon Robert J. Kostka.
Mailing Address: P.O. Box 517, 49915. Tel: 906-265-3777.

Champion, Marquette Co., Sacred Heart, Rev. Gilles Brault (STA); Sr. Margey Schmelzle, O.S.F., Pastoral Coord.
Mailing Address: P.O. Box 155, Republic, 49879. Tel: 906-376-8475.
Mission—Michigamme, Marquette Co., St. Agnes.

Channing, Dickinson Co., St. Rose, Rev. Michael Steber.
Mailing Address: P.O. Box 235, 49815. Tel: 906-542-3215; Fax: 906-542-3245.
Mission—Foster City, Dickinson Co., St. Joseph, Tel: 906-246-3490.

Chassell, Houghton Co., St. Anne, Rev. Bede G. Louzon, O.F.M.Cap.
Mailing Address: P.O. Box 407, 49916. Tel: 906-523-4912.
Missions—Painesdale, Houghton Co., Sacred Heart. Closed. For inquiries for mission records contact Holy Family, South Range; Donken, Houghton Co., Immaculate Heart of Mary. Closed. For inquiries for mission records contact Holy Family, South Range.

Cooks, Schoolcraft Co., St. Mary Magdalene, Rev. John E. Martignon.
Mailing Address: P.O. Box 68, Garden, 49835. Tel: 906-644-2626. [CEM]

Crystal Falls, Iron Co., Guardian Angels, Rev. Raymond J. Zeugner.
Res., 412 Crystal Ave., 49920. Tel: 906-875-3019; Fax: 906-875-1034.

Daggett, Menominee Co., St. Frederick. Closed. For inquiries for parish records contact Precious Blood Parish, Stephenson.

DeTour, Chippewa Co., Sacred Heart, Rev. Benedetto J. Paris. Pastoral Coordinators: Sr. Colleen Sweeting, O.S.F.; Sr. Lois Risch, O.S.F.
Mailing Address: P.O. Box 8, 49725. Tel: 906-297-3781.
Mission—Drummond Island, Chippewa Co., St. Florence.

Engadine, Mackinac Co., Our Lady of Lourdes, Rev. Jan Szczkowski (Poland).
Mailing Address: P.O. Box 123, 49827. Tel: 906-477-6223.
Missions—Naubinway, Mackinac Co., St. Stephen; Gulliver, Schoolcraft Co., Divine Infant of Prague. Deacon Gilbert G. Sablack.

Escanaba, Delta Co.,

1—ST. ANNE, Rev. Peter A. Minelli; Deacon Lewis Vailliencourt.
Res., 817 S. Lincoln Rd., 49829. Tel: 906-786-1421; Fax: 906-786-9346.
School—Holy Name Central Grade School. See Elementary Inter-Parochial Schools under Institutions Located in the Diocese.

2—ST. JOSEPH. Merged with St. Patrick, Escanaba to form St. Joseph & St. Patrick, Escanaba.

3—ST. PATRICK. Merged with St. Joseph, Escanaba to form St. Joseph & St. Patrick, Escanaba.

4—ST. JOSEPH & ST. PATRICK. (Formerly St. Joseph, Escanaba & St. Patrick, Escanaba). Rev. Ronald J. Skufca; Deacon Bill D. Hemes.
Res., 709 First Ave. S., 49829. Tel: 906-789-6244; Fax: 906-789-1213.
School—Holy Name Central Grade School. See Elementary Inter-Parochial Schools under Institutions Located in the Diocese.

5—ST. THOMAS THE APOSTLE, Rev. Joseph Nagaroor (India).
Res., 1820 Ninth Ave. N., 49829. Tel: 906-786-4627.
School—Holy Name Central Grade School. See Elementary Inter-Parochial Schools under Institutions Located in the Diocese.

Ewen, Ontonagon Co., Sacred Heart, Rev. Francis G. Dobrzenski.
Mailing Address: P.O. Box 169, 49925. Tel: 906-988-2310.
Mission—Sidnaw, Houghton Co., St. Francis Xavier.

Garden, Delta Co., St. John the Baptist, Rev. John E. Martignon.
Mailing Address: P.O. Box 68, 49835. Tel: 906-644-2626.

Gladstone, Delta Co., All Saints, Rev. Arnold J. Grambow.
Res., 715 Wisconsin Ave., P.O. Box 392, 49837. Tel: 906-428-3199.

Holy Family, Rev. Christopher B. Gardiner.
Res., 4011 CO 416-20th Rd., 49837. Tel: 906-786-1209; Fax: 906-786-0846.

Goetzville, Chippewa Co., St. Stanislaus Kostka, Rev. Benedetto J. Paris.
Mailing Address: P.O. Box 207, 49736. Tel: 906-297-5211; Fax: 906-297-5108. [CEM]
Mission—Hessel, Mackinac Co., Our Lady of the Snows, Tel: 906-484-3825.

Grand Marais, Alger Co., Holy Rosary Church, Rev. Joseph A. Plappallil (India).
Mailing Address: P.O. Box 424, 49839. Tel: 906-494-2589; Fax: 906-494-2589. [CEM]
Missions—Germfask, Schoolcraft Co., St. Therese; Curtis, Mackinac Co., St. Timothy.

Gwinn, Marquette Co., St. Anthony, Rev. David C. Jenner.
Res., 320 Iron St., P.O. Box 1358, 49841. Tel: 906-346-5312.
Mission—Northland, Marquette Co., St. Joseph.

Hancock, Houghton Co., Resurrection, Rev. Wayne E. Marcotte.
Res., 900 Quincy St., 49930. Tel: 906-482-0215; Fax: 906-482-5268. [CEM]
Mission—Dollar Bay, Houghton Co., St. Francis of Assisi.

Hermansville, Menominee Co., St. John Neumann. Formerly St. Mary, Hermansville; St. Francis Xavier, Spalding. Rev. Michael T. Vichich.
Res., P.O. Box 125, 49847. Tel: 906-498-7730; 497-5800 (Spalding).

Houghton, Houghton Co., St. Ignatius Loyola, Rev. Thomas L. Poisson.
Res., 305 Portage St., 49931. Tel: 906-482-0212.
Mission—Atlantic Mine, Houghton Co., St. Mary. Closed. For inquiries for parish records contact St. Ignatius Loyola, Houghton.
St. Albert the Great University Parish. (Michigan Technological University). Rev. Larry P. VanDamme.
Res., 411 MacInnes Dr., 49931. Tel: 906-482-5530; Fax: 906-482-5530.

Hubbell, Houghton Co., St. Cecilia, Rev. Eric E. Olson.
Mailing Address: c/o 701 Calumet St., Lake Linden, 49945. Tel: 906-296-6851.

Iron Mountain, Dickinson Co., Immaculate Conception of the Blessed Virgin Mary, Rev. Darryl J. Pepin; Deacon Donald R. Christy.
Res., 500 E. Blaine St., 49801-1840. Tel: 906-774-0511; Fax: 906-779-9953.
School—Dickinson Area Catholic School System. See Elementary Inter-Parochial Schools under Institutions Located in the Diocese.
St. Mary and St. Joseph, Rev. Daniel S. Zaloga.
Res., 411 W. B St., 49801. Tel: 906-774-2046.
School—Dickinson Area Catholic School System. See Elementary Inter-Parochial Schools under Institutions Located in the Diocese.

Iron River, Iron Co., St. Agnes, Rev. Norman A. Clisch.
Res., 702 N. Fourth St., 49935. Tel: 906-265-4557; Fax: 906-265-7155.

Ironwood, Gogebic Co., Our Lady of Peace. Combination of the following three parishes: Holy Trinity, St. Ambrose & St. Michael; 1986. Revs. Norbert B. Landreville; Hubby Mathew (India).
Res., 108 S. Marquette St., 49938. Tel: 906-932-0174; Fax: 906-932-1019.
School—Tel: 906-932-3200.
Sisters 1; Lay Teachers 8; Students 110.
St. Ambrose. Consolidated with Holy Trinity & St. Michael to form Our Lady of Peace Parish, 1986.
St. Michael. Consolidated with St. Ambrose & Holy Trinity to form Our Lady of Peace Parish, 1986.

Ishpeming, Marquette Co., St. John the Evangelist, Rev. Peter Oberto, V.G.
Res., 325 S. Pine, 49849. Tel: 906-486-6212.
Religious Education Center—335 S. Pine St., 49849. Tel: 906-486-9361. Sr. Catherine Gleason, C.S.J., Admin.
St. Joseph, Rev. Vincent L. Ouellette.
Office (All Mail): 1889 Prairie Avenue, 49849-1045.
Res., 1890 Prairie Ave., 49849-1044. Tel: 906-485-4200.
St. Pius X. Closed. For inquiries for parish records contact St. Joseph Church, 1889 Prairie Ave., Ishpeming, MI 49849.

Kingsford, Dickinson Co., American Martyrs, Rev. Joseph O. Gouin.
Res., 908 W. Sagola Ave., 49802. Tel: 906-774-0630.
St. Mary Queen of Peace, Rev. Paul J. Nomellini.
Res., 432 Edsel St., 49802. Tel: 906-774-6122.

Lake Linden, Houghton Co., St. Joseph, Rev. Eric E. Olson.
Res., 701 Calumet St., 49945. Tel: 906-296-6851.

L'Anse, Baraga Co., Sacred Heart, Rev. Gregory R. Heikkala.
Res., 16 S. Sixth St., 49946. Tel: 906-524-6424.
School—433 E. Baraga Ave., 49946. Tel: 906-524-5157.
Sisters 1; Lay Teachers 7; Students 99.

Mackinac Island, Mackinac Co., Ste. Anne de Michilimackinac (1695), Rev. James M. Williams.
Mailing Address: P.O. Box 537, 49757. Tel: 906-847-3507.

Manistique, Schoolcraft Co., St. Francis de Sales, Rev. George C. Gustafson; Deacon Gilbert Sablack.
Res., 330 Oak St., 49854. Tel: 906-341-5355.
School—Tel: 906-341-5512.
Sisters 5; Lay Teachers 6; Students 121.

Menominee, Menominee Co., Holy Redeemer (Birch Creek), Rev. Rick L. Courier; Deacon Roland Chaltry.
Res., W-5541 Birch Creek Rd. No. 6, 49858. Tel: 906-863-6920; Fax: 906-863-7303.
School—Menominee Catholic Central. See Elementary Inter-Parochial Schools under Institutions Located in the Diocese.
Holy Spirit, Rev. S. Patrick Wisneske.
Res., 1016 10th Ave., 49858. Tel: 906-863-5239; Fax: 906-863-2249.
School—Menominee Catholic Central. See Elementary Inter-Parochial Schools under Institutions Located in the Diocese.
Resurrection, Rev. Dino F. Silvestrini; Deacon Vincent W. Beckley.
Res., 2607 18th St., 49858. Tel: 906-863-3405; Fax: 906-863-9090.
School—Menominee Catholic Central. See Elementary Inter-Parochial Schools under Institutions Located in the Diocese.

Moran, Mackinac Co., Immaculate Conception, Rev. C. Michael Rhodes.
Res., 120 Church St., St. Ignace, 49781. Tel: 906-643-7671. [CEM]

Munising, Alger Co., Sacred Heart of Jesus, Rev. Dennis L. Borca; Deacon James E. Anderson.
Office: 110 W. Jewell St., P.O. Box 99, 49862. Tel: 906-387-4900; Fax: 906-387-4422.

Nadeau, Menominee Co., St. Bruno, Rev. Raymond J. Hoefgen; Deacon Donald Lobdell, Pastoral Coord.
Res., 49863. Tel: 906-639-2388.

Nahma, Delta Co., St. Andrew, Rev. John E. Martignon.
Mailing Address: P.O. Box 68, Garden, 49864. Tel: 906-644-2626.

Negaunee, Marquette Co., St. Paul, Rev. John J. Shiverski.
Res., 202 W. Case St., 49866. Tel: 906-475-9969.
Mission—Palmer, Marquette Co., Our Lady Perpetual Help, Tel: 906-475-4630.

Newberry, Luce Co., St. Gregory, Rev. George S. Maki; Deacon Dean Hermann.
Office: 212 W. Harrie St., 49868. Tel: 906-293-5511.
Res., 111 W. Harrie St., 49868. Tel: 906-293-5001.
Mission—Paradise, Chippewa Co., Our Lady of Victory.

Norway, Dickinson Co., St. Mary, Rev. Mark A. McQuesten.
Res., 401 Main St., 49870. Tel: 906-563-9845.
School—Holy Spirit Central Grade School. See Elementary Inter-Parochial Schools under Institutions Located in the Diocese.

Ontonagon, Ontonagon Co., Holy Family, Rev. John L. Longbucco.
Res., 515 Pine St., 49953. Tel: 906-884-2569; Fax: 906-884-6030. [CEM]

Perkins, Delta Co., St. Joseph, Rev. Antony Nirappel (India).
Res., 5803 Hwy. M-35, P.O. Box 99, 49872. Tel: 906-359-4701.

Perronville, Menominee Co., St. Elizabeth Ann Seton. (Formerly St. Michael). Rev. Emmett M. Norden.
Res., 1216 12th Rd., P.O. Box 187, Bark River, 49807. Tel: 906-466-9938.

Quinnesec, Dickinson Co., St. Mary. Closed. For inquiries for parish records contact St. Mary Parish, Norway,MI.

Ramsay, Gogebic Co., Christ the King. Closed. For inquiries for parish records contact St. Sebastian, Bessemer.

Rapid River, Delta Co., St. Charles Borromeo, Rev. David W. Sedlock; Deacon William Green.
Mailing Address: P.O. Box 247, 49878. Tel: 906-474-6741; Fax: 906-474-9087.

Republic, Marquette Co., St. Augustine, Rev. Gilles Brault (STA); Sr. Margey Schmelzle, O.S.F., Pastoral Coord.
Res., 49879.
Mailing Address: P.O. Box 155, 49879. Tel: 906-376-8475. [CEM]

Rockland, Ontonagon Co., St. Mary, Rev. John L. Longbucco; Deacon Karl L. Wadman.
Mailing Address: Holy Family Parish, 515 Pine St., Ontonagon, 49953. Tel: 906-884-2569.

Rudyard, Chippewa Co., St. Joseph, Revs. Francis J. DeGroot; Jerome A. Nowacki.
Mailing Address: P.O. Box 150, 49780. Tel: 906-478-4331.
Missions—Trout Lake, Chippewa Co., St. Mary; Barbeau, Holy Family.
Stations—Kinross Correctional Facility.; Chippewa Correctional Facility.; Chippewa Regional Facility.; Hiawatha Correctional Facility.

St. Ignace, Mackinac Co., St. Ignatius Loyola, Rev. C. Michael Rhoades; Deacon Donald F. Olmstead.
Res., 120 Church St., 49781. Tel: 906-643-7671. [CEM]

Sault Sainte Marie, Chippewa Co., Holy Name of Mary, Rev. Theodore J. Brodeur.
Res., 377 Maple St., 49783. Tel: 906-632-3381; Fax: 906-632-3390.
School—Tel: 906-635-6141.
Sisters 1; Lay Teachers 4; Students 104.
Nativity of Our Lord. Closed. For inquiries for parish records contact St. Joseph, Sault Sainte Marie.
St. Joseph, Rev. Pawel J. Mecwel; Deacon William J. Piche.
Res., 606 E. Fourth Ave., 49783. Tel: 906-632-9625.

Schaffer, Delta Co., St. Elizabeth Ann Seton. Formerly Sacred Heart of Jesus (See Perronville & Bark River). Rev. Emmett M. Norden.
Res., 1216 12th Rd. P.O. Box 187, Bark River, 49807. Tel: 906-466-9938. [CEM]

South Range, Houghton Co., Holy Family, Rev. Bede Louzon, O.F.M.Cap.; Deacon Paul D. Lucchesi.
Mailing Address: Box 369, 49963. Tel: 906-482-0684.

Spalding, Menominee Co., St. Francis Xavier. Closed. See St. John Neumann, P.O. Box 125, Hermansville, MI 49847.

Stephenson, Menominee Co., Precious Blood Church, Rev. Raymond J. Hoefgen.
Res., S304 Bluff St., 49887. Tel: 906-753-2562; Fax: 906-753-2811.

Trenary, Alger Co., St. Rita, Rev. Sebastian Kavumkal (India).
Mailing Address: P.O. Box 207, 49891. Tel: 906-446-3350; Fax: 906-446-3350.
Mission—Autrain, Alger Co., St. Therese.

Vulcan, Dickinson Co., St. Barbara, Rev. William P. Callari; Deacon Donald Giesen.
Mailing Address: P.O. Box 493, 49892. Tel: 906-563-9834.
School—Holy Spirit Central Grade School, Norway. See Elementary Inter-Parochial Schools under Institutions Located in the Diocese.

Wakefield, Gogebic Co., Immaculate Conception of the Blessed Virgin Mary, Rev. Allan J. Mayotte.
Res., 407 Ascherman St., 49968. Tel: 906-224-7851.
Mission—Marenisco, Gogebic Co., St. Catherine, Tel: 906-787-2353.

Watersmeet, Gogebic Co., Immaculate Conception, Rev. Francis G. Dobrzenski.
Mailing Address: Box 398, 49969. Tel: 906-358-4607.

Wells, Delta Co., St. Anthony, Rev. Richard C. Schaeffer.
Mailing Address: P.O. Box 280, 49894. Tel: 906-786-5002; Fax: 906-786-8992.
School—Holy Name Central Grade School, Escanaba. See Elementary Inter-Parochial Schools under Institutions Located in the Diocese.

White Pine, Ontonagon Co., St. Jude, Rev. Michael A. Woempner.
Mailing Address: P.O. Box 427, 49971. Tel: 906-885-5763.
Mission—Bergland, Ontonagon Co., St. Ann.

Indian Missions

Assinins, Baraga Co., The Most Holy Name of Jesus-Blessed Kateri Tekakwitha. Indian Missionaries, West & Central. Rev. John S. Hascall, O.F.M.Cap.
Res., Rte. 1, Box 47, Baraga, 49908.

Watersmeet, Gogebec Co., Lac Vieux Desert Reservation, Sr. Joyce Rybarczyk, O.P.
P.O. Box 78, 49969.

Bay Mills, Chippewa Co., Blessed Kateri Tekakwitha, Rev. Jeff G. Johnson.
P.O. Box 429, Brimley, 49715.

Sault Sainte Marie, Chippewa Co., St. Isaac Jogues, Rev. Jeff G. Johnson.
P.O. Box 429, Brimley, 49715.

Sugar Island, Chippewa Co., Sacred Heart. Indian Missionaries, East. Rev. Jeff Johnson.
P.O. Box 429, Brimley, 49715.

Chaplains of Public Institutions

MARQUETTE. *Marquette General Hospital* Tel: 906-228-9440; 225-3404. Revs. Frank M. Lenz; Gilles Brault (STA) Assoc. Chap.

IRON MOUNTAIN. *Veterans Administration Hospital* Tel: 906-774-3300; 563-7103. Rev. Patrick E. Murphy.

On Duty Outside the Diocese:
Reverend Fathers—
Challancin, James, St. Joseph College, P.O. Box 984, Rensselaer, IN 47978
Genovesi, James W., Our Lady of the Blessed Sacrament, Hermitage, P.O. Box 260, Norwalk, WI 54648
Timock, Ronald K., Byzantine Catholic Seminary of Sts. Cyril & Methodius, 3605 Perrysville Ave., Pittsburgh, PA 15214
Wantland, Thomas, Diocese of Venice, 164 Captain John Smith Loop, North Fort Myers, FL 33917

Graduate Studies:
Reverend Fathers—
Oniskiewicz, Mieczyslaw T., Canada

Special Assignment:
Reverend Fathers—
Sample, Alexander K., Dir., Dept. of Ministry Personnel Service
Schmied, Thomas, O.F.M.Cap., P.O. Box 368, Ahmeek, MI 49901
Ziminski, James C., Pastoral Office; Dir. of Vocations

Military Chaplains:
Reverend Fathers—
Kaczmarek, James, U.S.A.F., PSC 41, Box 607, APO, AE 09464

Leave of Absence:
Reverend Fathers—
Craig, Richard T.
Kurtz, Jeffrey A.
Rupp, Daniel N.

Sabbatical:
Reverend Fathers—
Sheedlo, Walter J.

Retired:
Reverend Monsignors—
Karol, Bernard A., 550 Warren Ave. #72, Spring Lake Heights, NJ 07762
LaViolette, Matt H., P.O. Box 497, Escanaba, MI 49829
McKevitt, Nolan B., Bishop Noa Home, 2900 Third St. S., Escanaba, MI 49829
Spelgatti, David P., (Winter), 21362 Walling Ct., Port Charlotte, FL 33954
Reverend Fathers—
Andary, Thomas M., 18515 Caminito Pasadero, Apt. 345, San Diego, CA 92128
Beyer, Emil J., Bishop Noa Home, 2900 Third St. S., Escanaba, MI 49829
Bracket, Louis P., 307 Eddy St., Wakefield, MI 49968
Brewer, Gervase, P.O. Box 158, Marquette, MI 49855
Dishaw, Conrad J., 2701 Fifth Ave. S., Apt. 102, Escanaba, MI 49829
Dunleavy, Thomas P., W8079 59, U.S. 2, Iron Mountain, MI 49801
Franczek, Walter J., 5062 S.E. 115th St., Belleview, FL 32620
Gauthier, Lawrence T., P.O. Box 550, Marquette, MI 49855
Goerner, Basil S., 2005 High Bluff Rd., Hilton Head, SC 29926
Gondek, Joseph A., P.O. Box 4, Iron River, MI 49935
Harris, David T., P.O. Box 88, Rockland, MI 49960
Hartman, Donald, 546 Main St., Apt. 529, Roosevelt Island, New York, NY 10044
Hasenberg, Aloysius J., P.O. Box 396, Watersmeet, MI 49969
Hebein, James M., Box 72 Hillside Apartments, #11, Vulcan, MI 49892
Hollenbach, Frank A., 9255 E. Pueblo A, Mesa, AZ 85208
Kichak, Joseph A., 301 W. Oak, Ironwood, MI 49938
LaCosse, Norbert R., 1534A W. Ridge St., Apt. 5, Marquette, MI 49855
LePine, Clement J., 2017 14th St., Menominee, MI 49858
Maloney, John, 917 Woodward Ave., Apt. 5, Kingsford, MI 49801
McArdle, John F., 4305 Sixth St., Menominee, MI 49858
Menapace, James L., Route 1, Box 56, Gulliver, MI 49840
Moncher, Raymond F., P.O. Box 175, Marenisco, MI 49947
Neurohr, Gilbert N., 5719 Pine 0-25 St., Gladstone, MI 49837
Olivier, John H., S.S., 2600 Hwy. 146, Paicines, CA 95043
Parrotta, Arthur J., St. Francis Hospital, 3401 Ludington St., Escanaba, MI 49829
Paulantonio, Joseph, 89-40 151st Ave., Howard Beach, NY 11414
Polakowski, Joseph, 5948 Country Club Ln., Lake Bluff, Gladstone, MI 49837
Ryan, John, 1600 N. 19th St., Escanaba, MI 49829
Schiska, Paul A., 6682 D Rd., Bark River, MI 49807
Shiroda, Daniel L., 807 W. 28th Ave., Apt. 4B, Sault Sainte Marie, MI 49783
Smith, Neil B., P.O. Box 452, Ramsay, MI 49959
Strelick, Charles J., 4420 Devonshire Ave., Spring Hill, FL 34609
Suda, Conrad P., 100 Pine St., Spalding, MI 49886
Valerio, Raymond A., 831 E. Grant, Iron Mountain, MI 49801
Vanitvelt, Milton H., 1524 Seventh St., Menominee, MI 49858
Wenzel, Edward J., Rte. 1, Box 491, Baraga, MI 49908

Permanent Deacons:
Adler, David, St. Louis the King, Marquette
Anderson, James, Sacred Heart of Jesus, Munising
Beckley, Vincent W., Resurrection, Menominee
Chaltry, Roland, Holy Redeemer, Menominee
Christy, Donald R., Immaculate Conception, Iron Mountain
Giesen, Donald, St. Barbara, Vulcan
Green, William, St. Charles Borromeo, Rapid River
Hemes, Dr. Bill D., St. Joseph & St. Patrick, Escanaba
Hermann, Dean, St. Gregory, Newberry
Jamieson, Scott A., St. Peter Cathedral, Marquette
Kostka, Robert J., St. Cecilia, Caspian
Lobdell, Donald, St. Bruno, Nadeau
Lucchessi, Paul, Holy Family, South Range
Olmstead, Donald F., St. Ignatius Loyola, St. Ignace
Piche, William J., St. Joseph, Sault Ste. Marie
Sablack, Gilbert G., Divine Infant of Prague, Gulliver & St. Francis de Sales, Manistique
Vailliencourt, Lewis, St. Anne, Escanaba
Wadman, Karl L., St. Mary, Rockland

INSTITUTIONS LOCATED IN THE DIOCESE

[A] ELEMENTARY INTER-PAROCHIAL SCHOOLS

MARQUETTE. *Fr. Marquette Catholic Central Schools System*, 500 S. Fourth St., 49855. Tel: 906-225-1129; Fax: 906-225-1987. James Ghiardi, Supt. Serving the following parishes: St. Peter's Cathedral; St. Louis; St. Michael. Lay Teachers 26; Students 302.

ESCANABA. *Holy Name Central Grade School*, 409 S. 22nd St., 49829. Tel: 906-786-7550. Barbara Mead, Prin. Lay Teachers 15; Students 349.

IRON MOUNTAIN. *Dickinson Area Catholic School System*, 406 W. B St., 49801. Tel: 906-774-2277. Mr. John Chandler, Prin. Lay Teachers 9; Students 207.

MENOMINEE. *Menominee Catholic Central*, 1406 10th Ave., 49858. Tel: 906-863-3190. Eric Weydt, Prin. Lay Teachers 13; Students 203.

NORWAY. *Holy Spirit Central School Educational Fund*, 201 Saginaw St., 49870. Tel: 906-563-8817. Mary Jo Kelly, Prin. Sisters 1; Lay Teachers 12; Students 96.

[B] CATHOLIC EDUCATION ENDOWMENT FUNDS

MARQUETTE. *Marquette Area Catholic Education Fund*, P.O. Box 550, 49855. Tel: 906-225-1141.
U.P. Catholic Education Endowment Fund, 444 S. Fourth St., P.O. Box 550, 49855. Tel: 906-225-1141. Mr. Richard R. Schaefer.

BESSEMER. *St. Sebastian School Endowment Fund*, 210 E. Iron St., 49911. Tel: 906-667-0952.

ESCANABA. *Holy Name Central Endowment Fund, Inc.*, 409 S. 22nd St., 49829. Tel: 906-786-7550.
Holy Name Scholarship Foundation, 409 S. 22nd St., 49829. Tel: 906-786-7550.

IRON MOUNTAIN. *Dickinson Area Catholic School Education Foundation*, 406 W. B St., 49801. Tel: 906-774-2277.

IRONWOOD. *Our Lady of Peace Catholic School Endowment Fund*, 106 S. Marquette St., 49938. Tel: 906-932-3200.

L'ANSE. *Sacred Heart School Endowment Fund*, 165 6th St., 49946.

MANISTIQUE. *St. Francis de Sales Education Foundation, Inc.*, 330 Oak St., 49854. Tel: 906-341-5355.

MENOMINEE.
**Menominee Catholic Education Fund, Inc.*, 1406 Tenth Ave., 49858-2604. Tel: 906-863-2723. Carrie Warren-Wandke, Office Mgr.

NEGAUNEE. *Negaunee St. Paul Endowment Fund*, 202 W. Case St., 49866.

NORWAY. *Holy Spirit Central School Educational Fund*, 201 Saginaw, 49870. Tel: 906-563-8817.

SAULT SAINTE MARIE. *Holy Family School Endowment Fund, Inc.*, 377 Maple St., 49783. Tel: 906-632-3381.

[C] GENERAL HOSPITALS

ESCANABA. *O.S.F. St. Francis Hospital*, 49829. Tel: 906-786-3311
For a complete listing, refer to the Hospitals section.

[D] HOMES FOR THE AGED

ESCANABA. *Bishop Noa Home for Senior Citizens*, 2900 3rd Ave., S., 49829. Tel: 906-786-5810; Fax: 906-786-5372
For a complete listing, refer to the Special Care Facilities section.

[E] CONVENTS AND RESIDENCES OF SISTERS

MARQUETTE. *Provincialate of the Sisters of St. Paul de Chartres*, 1300 County Rd. 492, 49855. Tel: 906-226-3932; Fax: 906-226-8734. Sr. Mary Ann Laurin, District Supr. Sisters 6.

IRON MOUNTAIN. *Monastery of the Holy Cross*, N4028 Hwy. U.S. 2, P.O. Box 397, 49801. Discalced Carmelite Nuns. Mother Pauline Marie, O.C.D., Prioress; Rev. Patrick E. Murphy, Chap. Cloistered Nuns: Professed 14; Extern Professed Sisters 2; Postulants 1; Novices 1.

[F] RETREAT HOUSES

GARDEN. *Marygrove Retreat Center*, 49835. Tel: 906-644-2771. Rev. Timothy H. Desrochers, Dir. Retreats and workshops for priests, religious and laity.

[G] NEWMAN CLUBS

MARQUETTE. *Catholic Campus Ministry-Northern Michigan University*, 1200 Hebard Ct., 49855. Tel: 906-228-3302; Fax: 906-225-0437. Sr. Catherine Mills, S.P.C., Dir.; Rev. James C. Ziminski, Sacramental Min.

HOUGHTON. *St. Albert the Great, University Parish*, 411 MacInnes Dr., 49931. Tel: 906-482-5530. Rev. Larry P. VanDamme.

SAULT SAINTE MARIE. *Lake Superior State University, Newman Center*, 517 W. Easterday, 49783. Tel: 906-635-5941. Enzo A. Tatasciore, Dir.

[H] MISCELLANEOUS

MARQUETTE. *St. Vincent De Paul Society*, 2118 Fitch Ave., Room #101, 49855. Tel: 906-226-2311.

RELIGIOUS INSTITUTES OF MEN REPRESENTED IN THE DIOCESE

For further details refer to the corresponding bracketed number in the Religious Institutes of Men or Women section.

[0470]—*The Capuchin Friars.* (Detroit, MI).—O.F.M.Cap.
[0520]—*Franciscan Friars.* (Cincinnati, OH).—O.F.M.

RELIGIOUS INSTITUTES OF WOMEN REPRESENTED IN THE DIOCESE

[3710]—*Congregation of the Sisters of Saint Agnes.*—C.S.A.
[0420]—*Discalced Carmelite Nuns.*—O.C.D.
[1070-09]—*Dominican Sisters.*—O.P.
[1070-13]—*Dominican Sisters.*—O.P.
[1630]—*Franciscan Sisters of Christian Charity.*—O.S.F.
[2380]—*Institute of the Blessed Virgin Mary (Sisters of Loretto).*—I.B.V.M.
[3130]—*Our Lady of Victory Missionary Sisters.*—O.L.V.M.
[2970]—*School Sisters of Notre Dame.*—S.S.N.D.
[3830-15]—*Sisters of St. Joseph.* (Concordia, Kansas).—C.S.J.
[3840]—*Sisters of St. Joseph of Carondelet.*—C.S.J.
[3980]—*Sisters of St. Paul of Chartres.*—S.P.C.
[2180]—*Sisters of the Immaculate Heart of Mary.*—I.H.M.
[3260]—*Sisters of the Precious Blood.*—C.PP.S.
[3320]—*Sisters of the Presentation of the B.V.M.*—P.B.V.M.
[1770]—*Sisters of the Third Order of St. Francis.* (Peoria, Illinois).—O.S.F.

DIOCESAN CEMETERIES

MARQUETTE. *Holy Cross.*
ESCANABA. *Holy Cross.*

NECROLOGY

† Cordy, Robert J., (Retired). —Died Jan. 14, 1997.
† Dunleavy, Rev. Msgr. Joseph J., (Retired). —Died Oct. 19, 1997.
† Ruppe, Thomas G., (Retired). —Died Nov. 20, 1997.

Diocese of Memphis

(Memphitana in Tennesia)

Most Reverend

J. TERRY STEIB, S.V.D., D.D.

Bishop of Memphis; ordained January 6, 1967; appointed Titular Bishop of Fallaba and Auxiliary Bishop of St. Louis December 6, 1983; consecrated February 10, 1984; appointed Bishop of Memphis May 5, 1993.

ESTABLISHED JANUARY 6, 1971.

Square Miles 10,682.

Comprises the Counties of Benton, Carroll, Chester, Crockett, Decatur, Dyer, Fayette, Gibson, Hardeman, Hardin, Haywood, Henderson, Henry, Lake, Lauderdale, McNairy, Madison, Obion, Shelby, Tipton and Weakley in the State of Tennessee.

For legal titles of parishes and diocesan institutions, consult the Chancery Office.

Catholic Center: P.O. Box 341669, Memphis, TN, 38184-1669. Tel.: 901-373-1200; Fax: 901-373-1269.

STATISTICAL OVERVIEW

Personnel	
Bishop	1
Priests: Diocesan Active in Diocese	48
Priests: Active Outside Diocese	4
Priests: Retired, Sick or Absent	14
Number of Diocesan Priests	66
Religious Priests in Diocese	11
Extern Priests in Diocese	7
Permanent Deacons in Diocese	21
Total Brothers	42
Total Sisters	107
Parishes	
Parishes	49
With Resident Pastor:	
Resident Diocesan Priests	34
Resident Religious Priests	5
Without Resident Pastor:	
Administered by Priests	8
Administered by Permanent Deacons	1
Administered by Women Religious	1
Missions	5
Pastoral Centers	1
Professional Ministry Personnel:	
Brothers	1
Sisters	9
Lay Ministers	23
Welfare	
Catholic Hospitals	1
Total Assisted	25,168
Health Care Centers	1
Total Assisted	335
Homes for the Aged	8
Total Assisted	1,076
Residential Care of Children	1
Total Assisted	236
Day Care and Extended Day Care Centers	9
Total Assisted	2,224
Specialized Homes	1
Total Assisted	564
Special Centers for Social Services	1
Total Assisted	7,046
Residential Care of Disabled	5
Total Assisted	78
Other Institutions	2
Total Assisted	318
Educational	
Diocesan Students in Other Seminaries	10
Total Seminarians	10
Colleges and Universities	1
Total Students	1,784
High Schools, Diocesan and Parish	4
Total Students	1,256
High Schools, Private	2
Total Students	1,132
Elementary Schools, Diocesan and Parish	11
Total Students	3,786
Elementary Schools, Private	2
Total Students	468
Non-residential Schools for the Disabled	1
Total Students	44
Catechesis/Religious Education:	
High School Students	709
Elementary Students	4,577
Total Students Under Catholic Instruction	13,766
Teachers in the Diocese:	
Priests	1
Brothers	10
Sisters	16
Lay Teachers	463
Vital Statistics	
Receptions into the Church:	
Infant Baptism Totals	1,075
Adult Baptism Totals	231
Received into Full Communion	363
First Communions	1,342
Confirmations	1,131
Marriages:	
Catholic	148
Interfaith	235
Total Marriages	383
Deaths	440
Total Catholic Population	59,138
Total Population	1,426,923

Former Bishops—Most Rev. CARROLL T. DOZIER, D.D., ord. March 19, 1937; appt. Nov. 17, 1970; cons. Jan. 6, 1971; retired July 27, 1982; died Dec. 7, 1985.—Most Rev. J. FRANCIS STAFFORD, D.D., ord. Dec. 15, 1957; cons. Bishop Feb. 29, 1976; appt. Nov. 16, 1982; appt. to Archdiocese of Denver, June 3, 1986.—Most Rev. DANIEL M. BUECHLEIN, O.S.B., D.D., ord. May 3, 1964; appt. Jan. 20, 1987; appt. to Archdiocese of Indianapolis, July 14, 1992.

Vicars General—Rev. J. PETER SARTAIN, V.G., *St. Louis, 203 S. White Station Rd., Memphis, 38117.* Tel: 901-682-6606. Rev. Msgr. PAUL W. CLUNAN, P.A., V.G., (Retired), *38 N. Idlewild #13, Memphis, 38104.*

Catholic Center Offices—Mailing Address: P.O. Box 341669, Memphis, 38184-1669. Tel: 901-373-1200; Fax: 901-373-1269. Office Hours: Mon.-Fri. 7:45-4:45, *5825 Shelby Oaks Dr., Memphis, 38134.*

Chancery

Office of Moderator of the Curia and Chancellor—Rev. ROBERT D. PONTICELLO, J.C.L., *P.O. Box 341669, Memphis, 38184-1669.* Tel: 901-373-1200.

Vice-Chancellor—VERDRUE DOMINIONI.

Notaries—MARIANNA RAMPERSAD; M. TERESA WILTCHER.

Catholic Public Policy Commission of Tennessee—P.O. Box 341669, Memphis, 38184-1669.

Office of Ecumenism—Rev. THOMAS D. KIRK, Dir., *1695 Central Ave., Memphis, 38104.* Tel: 901-725-2700. Rev. GREG SALATA, Assoc. Dir., *203 S. White Station Rd., Memphis, 38117.* Tel: 901-682-6606.

Clergy Personnel Board—Revs. MILTON J. GUTHRIE; WILLIAM R. KANTNER; DANIEL F. MOORE; J. PETER SARTAIN; ROBERT D. PONTICELLO.

Continuing Education for the Clergy—Rev. BRYAN P. TIMBY, Dir., *4851 Park Ave., Memphis, 38117.* Tel: 901-767-6949.

College of Consultors—Revs. J. EDWIN CREARY; J. PETER SARTAIN; Rev. Msgr. PETER P. BUCHIGNANI; Revs. MAURY SMITH, O.F.M.; VICTOR P. CIARAMITARO; Rev. Msgr. EDWARD O. HEYMER; Revs. RICHARD M. GANTERT; STEPHEN K. KENNY; ALBERT E. KIRK; DAN F. MOORE; ROBERT D. PONTICELLO; GABRIEL DiFEDERICO, Dir. Diaconal Formation. Tel: 901-767-6949.

Permanent Deacons Community—Deacon JOHN T. OATES, Dir., *5825 Shelby Oaks Dr., Memphis, 38134.* Tel: 901-373-1216.

Dean of the Jackson Deanery—Rev. VICTOR CIARAMITARO, *Holy Cross Church, 1210 E. Wood St., Paris, 38242.* Tel: 901-642-4681.

Director of Seminarians—Rev. R. BRUCE CINQUEGRANI.

Director of Vocations—Rev. DAVID GRAHAM.

Tribunal

Judicial Vicar—Rev. JOSEPH L. TAGG, III, J.D., J.C.L.

Defender of the Bond—Rev. ROBERT D. PONTICELLO, J.C.L.

Promoter of Justice—Rev. ROBERT D. PONTICELLO, J.C.L.

Auditor—Rev. GABRIEL DiFEDERICO.

Notary—M. TERESA WILTCHER.

Department of Financial Administration

Secretary—JAMES A. KLEISER, JR., *P.O. Box 341669, Memphis, 38184-1669.* Tel: 901-373-1200.

Calvary Cemeteries and All Saints Cemetery—RICHARD B. SMITH, Supt., *1663 Elvis Presley Blvd., Memphis, 38106.* Tel: 901-948-1529.

Controller—EDDIE WALDRUP.

Data Processing—BETTY FURR.

Employee Benefits—KATHY OWINGS.

Facilities and Risk Management—WILLIAM F. HERBERS.

Maintenance—ROBERT PELT.

Department of Catholic Schools

Secretary—Vacant, *P.O. Box 341669, Memphis, 38184-1669.* Tel: 901-373-1200.

Office of Catholic Schools—Vacant; JANET M. DONATO, Asst. Supt.

Department Of Associated Catholic Charities

Secretary—BRIAN J. O'MALLEY, Exec. Dir., *1325 Jefferson Ave., P.O. Box 41705, Memphis, 38174-1705.* Tel: 901-722-4777.

Catholic Charities, Inc.—KEVIN HICKEY, Dir. CHRISTI SHAW, Communication Dir. JAMES ABERNATHY, Finance Dir.

Community Outreach Services—JOSEPH PFEIFFER, Dir. ALICE HARDY, Parish Liaison.

Parish Social Ministry-Pallotti Center—DIANE McKINNA.

Ministry to the Sick and Elderly—

Ministry to the Imprisoned—Bro. TALBOT MCSHARRY.
Genesis House—GERALD BETTICE, Dir. Transitional shelter for homeless.
Refugee Resettlement Unit—CAROLYN TISDALE, Dir.
Day Care Services—VIRGINIA DAVENPORT, Dir.
Holy Names Center—LINDA STEED, Dir. TOMMIE HILL, Site Supvr.
St. Ann-Bartlett Extended Care Program—KAREN OTTS, Site Supvr.
St. Benedict at Auburndale Extended Care—PAMELA O'BRYAN, Site Supvr.
St. John Center—VELTEEN MCGHEE, Program Coord.
St. Louis Extended Care—LORI TUCKER, Site Supvr.
St. Peter Home Day Care Center—EVELYN HOWARD, Dir.
St. Michael Extended Care—DEBBIE KALLAHER, Site Supvr.
Extended Care Programs (After-School Care)—SUSAN FAUGHN, Supvr.
Diocese of Memphis Housing Corporation—DAVID FIELD, Exec. Dir.
St. Peter Villa Nursing Home—KAE WERK HOVEN, Admin.
St. Peter Home for Children—BRENT ADAMS, Admin.
St. Therese Little Flower Day Care Center—SHARON WEBB, Prog. Dir.
Mid South Caring, Inc.—BRIAN J. O'MALLEY, *1325 Jefferson Ave., P.O. Box 41705, Memphis, 38174-1705.*

Department for Worship and Spiritual Life

Secretary—Rev. R. BRUCE CINQUEGRANI, *P.O. Box 341669, Memphis, 38184-1669.* Tel: 901-373-1200.
Office of Worship—MARY MILLER, Assoc. Dir.; Sr. MAUREEN GRINER, O.S.U., Diocesan Dir. of Music.
Commission for Initiation Ministries—PAUL GRAY, Chm.; Rev. R. BRUCE CINQUEGRANI, Liaison.
Cursillo Movement—Rev. GABRIEL J. DIFEDERICO, Spiritual Advisor. Assoc. Spiritual Advisors: Rev. CHARLES BAUER; Mr. ERNIE ALBONETTI, Lay Dir.
Chrismatic Renewal—Rev. JAMES L. MARTELL, Diocesan Liaison; Rev. PAUL CASPER, Assoc. Diocesan Liaison.

Department for Development and Public Relations

Secretary—ANTONIO LOPEZ, *P.O.Box 341669, Memphis, 38184-1669.* Tel: 901-373-1200.
Planned Giving and Major Donors—LLOYD CROCKETT, Dir.
Communications and Public Relations—JOHN E. MORRIS, Dir.
Information Coordinator—PAIGE EMANUEL.

Department of Evangelization and Pastoral Services

Secretary—EILEEN C. HIVNER, *P.O. Box 341669, Memphis, 38184-1669.* Tel: 901-373-1200.
Diocesan Evangelization Commission—Vacant.
Office of Religious Education—CAROLYN TAMBOLI, Dir.
Resource Library—SARAH COLE.
Newspaper—*"West Tennessee Catholic", 5825 Shelby Oaks Dr., Memphis, 38134.*
Office of Christian Formation and Ministries—EILEEN HIVNER, Dir.
Institute for Pastoral Life Liaison—
Professional Ministry Enrichment Programs—
Parish Pastoral Councils—
Diocesan Ministries Training—
Office of Family Ministries—PATRICIA PERRY, Dir.
Diocesan Family Life Commission—JOHN HIVNER, Chm.
Committee for Separated, Divorced, Widowed—
Marriage Encounter—
Retrouvaille—Deacon JOHN HIVNER, Dir.
Natural Family Planning Center—MARY PAT VAN EPPS, Coord. Tel: 901-765-1757.
Programs for the Engaged—
Office of Youth and Young Adult Ministries—CATHERINE MENSI, Dir.; Rev. JAMES MCCARVER, Jackson Deanery.
Search Program—Rev. J. DAVID GRAHAM, JR., Dir.
Catholic Alumni Club—
Scouting—
Campus Ministry—Memphis, Deacon JOHN HIVNER; Sr. SUE RUSSELL, R.S.M.,Martin, Rev. JOSEPH PAOLOZZI, R.S.M.
Office of African American Catholic Ministry and Multi Cultural Ministries—Deacon CURTISS TALLEY, Dir.
African American Catholic Ministry—Deacon CURTISS TALLEY, Dir.
Comunidad Hispana Catolica de Memphis—GABRIEL PAEZ; Rev. DAVID KNIGHT, Chap.
Diocesan Commission for African American Catholics—O. C. PLEASANT, Chm.
Native American Ministry—RUTH ELLEN.
Polish Catholic Mission—BARBARA RYBINSKI; Deacon LARRY HOWELL, Chap.
Vietnamese Community—DOMINIC RAU VAN NGUYEN, Coord.; Sr. MARY PHUC, O.P., D.R.E.

CLERGY, PARISHES, MISSIONS AND PAROCHIAL SCHOOLS

CITY OF MEMPHIS
(Shelby County)

1—CATHEDRAL OF THE IMMACULATE CONCEPTION (1921), Revs. Thomas D. Kirk, Rector; Joseph Kerrigan; Deacon Dick Powelson.
Res., 1695 Central Ave., 38104. Tel: 901-725-2700; Fax: 901-725-2709.
School—1669 Central Ave., 38104. Tel: 901-725-2710; Fax: 901-725-2715. Dr. Maribeth Andereck, Prin.
Priests 2; Lay Teachers 20; Students 325.
High School—See separate category.

2—ST. ANN (Bartlett) (1950), Revs. R. Bruce Cinquegrani; J. David Graham; Edward K. Fisher; Deacon James Quinn.
Res., 6529 Stage Rd., Bartlett, 38134. Tel: 901-373-6011; 386-3377; Fax: 901-373-9030.
School—Tel: 901-386-3328.
Sisters 1; Lay Teachers 39; Students 691.

3—ST. ANNE'S (1933), Rev. James L. Pugh.
Res., 706 S. Highland St., 38111. Tel: 901-323-3817; Fax: 901-323-3151.
School—670 S. Highland St., 38111. Tel: 901-323-1344.
Sisters 2; Lay Teachers 10; Students 189.

4—CHURCH OF THE ASCENSION (1974), Rev. Richard L. Mickey; Deacons F. Joseph Mensi; John T. Oates.
Res., 3680 RaMill Rd., 38128. Tel: 901-372-1364; Fax: 901-373-9411.

5—ST. AUGUSTINE (1937), Rev. Frank Coens, O.F.M.; Deacon Curtiss Talley.
Church—1169 Kerr Ave., 38106. Tel: 901-774-2297; Fax: 901-774-3067.

6—ST. BRIGID (1992), Rev. Michael L. Stewart.
Church—7801 Lowrance Rd., 38125-2825. Tel: 901-758-0128; Fax: 901-758-8862.
Res., 4200 Thunderstone Cir. W., 38125-3108. Tel: 901-759-9628.

7—BLESSED SACRAMENT (1912), Rev. Michael A. Morgera.
Church—2564 Hale Ave., 38112. Tel: 901-452-1543.

8—ST. FRANCIS OF ASSISI (1985), Revs. Peter P. Buchignani; Ernie Deblasio; Deacon Max Saller.
Res., 8247 Chimneyrock Blvd., Cordova, 38018. Tel: 901-753-1494; Fax: 901-755-2168.
Church—8151 Chimneyrock Blvd., Cordova, 38018. Tel: 901-756-1213.

9—HOLY NAMES OF JESUS AND MARY (1939), Rev. Joseph L. Tagg, III, (Sacramental Ministry); Deacon Fred Brunner, Admin.
Res., 697 Keel Ave., 38107-2599. Tel: 901-525-9870.

10—HOLY ROSARY (1955), Revs. Bryan P. Timby; John A. Aiello; Gabriel DiFederico.
Church and Office: 4851 Park Ave., 38117. Tel: 901-767-6949; Fax: 901-767-8504.
School—4841 Park Ave., 38117. Tel: 901-685-1231.
Sisters 1; Lay Teachers 35; Students 609.

11—HOLY SPIRIT (1975), Revs. Albert E. Kirk; Edward M. Byrnes; Deacon Ned Turner.
Res., 2315 Hickory Crest, 38119.
Church—2300 Hickory Crest, 38119. Tel: 901-745-7146; Fax: 901-754-0102.

12—INCARNATION (1978), Rev. William R. Kantner; Deacon Charles Wells.
Res., 360 Bray Station Rd., Collierville, 38017. Tel: 901-853-7468; Fax: 901-854-0536.

13—ST. JAMES (1956), Rev. Patrick F. Heenan.
Res., 4180 LeRoy, 38108. Tel: 901-767-8672.

14—ST. JOHN'S (1947), Rev. Robert J. Holko, S.C.J.
Res., 2742 Lamar Ave., 38114. Tel: 901-743-4551.

15—ST. JOSEPH'S (1878), Rev. William F. Stelling.
Res., 3825 Neely Rd., 38109. Tel: 901-396-9996; Fax: 901-332-8691.

16—ST. LOUIS (1957), Revs. J. Peter Sartain; Richard Cortese; Gregory Salata; Cyril J. Wagner, O.F.M.; Samuel Weber, O.S.B.; Deacon Ralph Donati.
Res., 203 S. White Station Rd., 38117. Tel: 901-682-6606; Fax: 901-680-0571.
School—5192 Shady Grove Rd., 38117. Tel: 901-682-9692.
Lay Teachers 29; Aides 3; Students 519.

17—ST. MARY'S (1860), Rev. Maury Smith, O.F.M.; Deacon James Champion.
Church and Office: 155 Market St., 38105. Tel: 901-522-9420; Fax: 901-522-9452.
Res., Franciscan Friary, 1254 S. Lauderdale, 38106. Tel: 901-774-8191.

18—ST. MICHAEL'S (1951), Revs. John V. Atkinson; Alfred Graham.
Office: 3848 Forrest Ave., 38122. Tel: 901-323-0896; 324-6411; Fax: 901-323-3557.
Res., 3867 Summer Ave., 38122. Tel: 901-454-1349; 452-6036.
School—3880 Forrest Ave., 38122. Tel: 901-323-2162; Fax: 901-323-3557.
Lay Teachers 9; Students 150.

19—CHURCH OF THE NATIVITY (1979), Rev. Robert D. Ponticello.
Res., 5955 St. Elmo, Barlett, 38135. Tel: 901-382-2504; Fax: 901-382-3644.

20—ST. PATRICK'S (1866), Revs. Paul Dechant, C.S.P.; Gilbert Martinez, C.S.P.; James F. Fisher, C.S.P., (Retired).
Res., 277 S. Fourth St., 38126. Tel: 901-527-2542; Fax: 901-525-1147.

21—ST. PAUL THE APOSTLE (1944), Revs. John B. McArthur; Joseph Thinh Duc Nguyen; Deacon Richard Williams.
Res., 1425 E. Shelby Dr., 38116. Tel: 901-346-2380.
School—Tel: 901-346-0862.
Sisters 3; Lay Teachers 20; Students 330.

22—OUR LADY OF PERPETUAL HELP (1952), Revs. Milton J. Guthrie; J. Keith Zavelli; Marian Spadini; Deacon Walter Chandler.
Res., 8151 Poplar, Germantown, 38138. Tel: 901-754-1204; Fax: 901-754-0969.

23—ST. PETER'S (1840), Rev. Edward E. Everitt, O.P.
Res., 190 Adams Ave., 38103. Tel: 901-527-8282; Fax: 901-526-6882.

24—CHURCH OF THE RESURRECTION (1973), Rev. Daniel F. Moore.
Res., 5425 Newberry, 38115-3629. Tel: 901-794-8970; Fax: 901-794-8806.

25—SACRED HEART (1899), Rev. David B. Knight. In res., Rev. Berchmans Kodakal (Kerala).
Res., 1324 Jefferson Ave., 38104. Tel: 901-726-1891; Fax: 901-726-9272.

26—OUR LADY OF SORROWS (1926), Rev. William Burke, Admin.
Res., 3700 Thomas St., 38127. Tel: 901-353-1530; Fax: 901-353-1052.
School—3690 Thomas St., 38127. Tel: 901-358-7431.
Religious 1; Lay Teachers 7; Students 126.

27—ST. THERESE OF THE INFANT JESUS (1930), Rev. David M. Foley.
Res., 1644 Jackson Ave., 38107. Tel: 901-276-1412; Fax: 901-274-4476.

28—ST. WILLIAM (1951), Rev. J. Edwin Creary.
Res., 4932 Easley Ave., Millington, 38053. Tel: 901-872-4099; 872-2279; Fax: 901-872-4099.

OUTSIDE SHELBY COUNTY

Brownsville, Haywood Co., St. John (1952), Rev. William J. Parham.
Church—901 N. Washington Ave., Box 872, 38012.

Bolivar, Hardeman Co., St. Mary, Rev. Carl J. Hood.
Res., 223 Mecklinberg Dr., 38008-1736. Tel: 901-658-4627; Fax: 901-658-4627.

Camden, Benton Co., St. Mary Church (1981), Rev. Stephen K. Kenny.
Res., 220 W. Main St., 38320. Tel: 901-584-6459; Fax: 901-584-6446.
Mission—Huntingdon, Carroll Co., Holy Family Church, 265 Cotham Dr., Huntingdon, 38344. Tel: 901-986-2817.

Covington, Tipton Co., St. Alphonsus (1952), Rev. William J. DeVries.
Res., 1512 Evergreen, 38019. Tel: 901-476-0374; Fax: 901-476-9650.
Church—1225 Hwy. 51 S., P.O. Box 430, 38019. Tel: 901-476-8140.
Mission—Ripley, Lauderdale Co., Ave Maria, 664 S. Washington, Ripley, 38063. Tel: 901-635-8800.

Dyersburg, Dyer Co., Holy Angels (1940), Rev. Elbert Callis.
Res., 526 Charles St., P.O. Box 1929, 38025-1929. Tel: 901-287-8000; Fax: 901-287-7632.

Humboldt, Gibson Co., Sacred Heart (1872), Rev. Charles A. Bauer.
Res., 2877 E. Main, 38343. Tel: 901-784-3904; Fax: 901-784-5048.
Mission—Crockett Co.

Jackson, Madison Co., St. Mary's (1867), Revs. William J. Parham; J. Keith Stewart.
Res., 1665 Hwy. 45 Byp., 38305. Tel: 901-668-2596; Fax: 901-668-4387.
School—Tel: 901-668-2525; Fax: 901-668-0409.
Sisters 3; Lay Teachers 18; Students 295.
Mission—Brownsville, Haywood Co., St. John

Church, P.O. Box 872, Brownsville, 38012. Tel: 901-772-3514.

Lexington, Henderson Co., St. Andrew, Rev. Valentine Handwerker.
Church—311 Elizabeth Circle, 38351. Tel: 901-968-6393.
Res., 895 N. Broad, 38351. Tel: 901-968-7949; Fax: 901-967-1228.
Mission—Parsons, Decatur Co., St. Regina, 108 Skyline Ln., Parsons 38361. Tel: 901-847-2054.

Martin, Weakley Co., St. Jude's (1968), Rev. Joseph L. Paolozzi.
Res., 104 Hannings Ln., 38237. Tel: 901-587-9777; Fax: 901-587-9778.

Milan, Gibson Co., St. Matthew Mission, Rev. Charles A. Bauer.
Mailing Address: c/o Sacred Heart Church, 2881 E. Main St., Humboldt, 38343.
Church—9060 Telecom Dr., 38358. Tel: 901-686-8686.

Paris, Henry Co., Holy Cross (1921), Rev. Victor P. Ciaramitaro.
Res., 1210 E. Wood St., 38242. Tel: 901-642-4681; Fax: 901-644-9668.

Savannah, Hardin Co., St. Mary's (1948), Rev. James Joseph Martell.
Res., 1107 Clifton Rd., 38372. Tel: 901-925-4852; Fax: 901-925-4852.

Selmer, McNairy Co., St. Jude (1982), Rev. Carl J. Hood.
Res., P.O. Box 342, 38375. Tel: 901-645-4188.

Somerville, Fayette Co., St. Philip the Apostle (1981), Rev. Cyril J. Wagner, O.F.M.; Sr. Jeanne L. Dion, O.P., Pastoral Admin.
Church—11710 Hwy. 64, 38068. Tel: 901-465-8685; Fax: 901-466-1645.

Union City, Obion Co., Immaculate Conception (1891), Rev. Jim McCarver.
Res., 1303 E. Reelfoot Ave., 38261. Tel: 901-885-0963; Fax: 901-885-9960.

Chaplains of Public Institutions

MEMPHIS. *Federal Correctional Institute at Memphis.* Rev. Peter Literal, Chap.

On Duty Outside the Diocese:
Reverend Fathers—
Henkes, Donald E.
Kelly, Edward, St. Louis University, St. Louis, MO
Nobile, Angelo

Military Chaplains:
Reverend Fathers—
Danner, James L., COMNAVSURFPAC (N01G), 2841 Rendova Rd., San Diego, CA 92155-5490
Lamb, Gary E., Chap., U.S. Navy

Retired:
Reverend Monsignors—
Batson, John R., 2000 S. Ocean Dr. #508, Ft. Lauderdale, FL 33316. Tel: 954-467-1972
Clunan, Paul W., 38 N. Idlewild St., #13, Memphis, TN 38104
Davis, William F., 745 Loeb St., Memphis, TN 38111
Heymer, Edward D., 941 Ivy Rd., Memphis, TN 38117
Lynch, Patrick J., 141 N. McLean Blvd., #317, Memphis, TN 38104
Wiggs, Joel M., 4250 Main St., P.O. Box 306, Humboldt, TN 38343-0306. Tel: 901-784-3233
Reverend Fathers—
Cleary, Edward J., 4776 Childs Dr., Memphis, TN 38116. Tel: 901-397-5997
Elliott, Edward C., Kirby Pines Estates No. N-309, 3535 Kirby Rd., Memphis, TN 38115. Tel: 901-794-5256
Gaffney, James
Kelly, Edgar M., 38 N. Idlewild St., #3, Memphis, TN 38104
Murphy, James W., Mainstreet Lodge, 909 Main-street, N.E., #308, Minneapolis, MN 55413
Oglesby, J. Leonard, Rte. 1, Box 189, Pope, MS 38658
St. Charles, Paul W., 122 Tallwood Dr., Nashville, TN 37211-2711
Stritch, Morris G., Christian Brothers High School, 5900 Walnut Grove Rd., Memphis, TN 38120

Permanent Deacons:
Bass, George
Brunner, Fred
Champion, James
Chandler, Walter
Donati, Ralph
Finnegan, William
Hicks, Joseph
Hivner, John
Howell, Larry
Johnson, Eldon
McCarver, Kenneth
Mensi, Joseph
Messina, Joseph
Oates, John
Powelson, Richard
Quinn, Jim
Saller, Max
Schmall, James
Talley, Curtiss
Turner, Ned
Wells, Charles
Williams, Richard

INSTITUTIONS LOCATED IN THE DIOCESE

[A] COLLEGES AND UNIVERSITIES

*MEMPHIS. *Christian Brothers University,* (1871) 650 E. Parkway S., 38104. Tel: 901-321-3000
For a complete listing, refer to the Colleges and Universities section.

[B] DIOCESAN SCHOOLS

MEMPHIS. *Bishop Byrne High School* (1965), 1475 E. Shelby Dr., 38116. Tel: 901-346-3060; Fax: 901-346-3062. Mrs. Neddy Brookshaw, Prin. Sisters 2; Lay Teachers 25; Students 268.
Memphis Catholic High School and Middle School, 61 N. McLean Blvd., 38104. Tel: 901-276-1221. Mr. Donald Edwards, Prin. Sisters 1; Lay Teachers 26; Students 302.

CORDOVA. *St. Benedict at Auburndale School.* (Grades PreK-12), 2100 N. Germantown Pkwy., 38018. Tel: 901-388-7321. Special programs for gifted and learning disabled. Dr. Mary C. McDonald, Prin. Lay Teachers 57; Students 786.

[C] HIGH SCHOOLS, PRIVATE AND PAROCHIAL

MEMPHIS.
**Christian Brothers High School,* 5900 Walnut Grove Rd., 38120-2174. Tel: 901-682-7801; Fax: 901-682-7815.
Title of Incorporation: Christian Brothers (LaSalle) High School. Bros. Christopher Englert, F.S.C., Prin.; Michael Fugger, Co-Dir. Brothers' Community; Michael Livaudais, Co-Dir. Brothers' Community; Revs. Morris G. Stritch, (Retired); Eric Burdt, O.SS.T. Priests 2; Brothers 13; Lay Teachers 53; Students 862.
Immaculate Conception Cathedral Middle and High School (1950), 1725 Central Ave., 38104. Tel: 901-276-6341; Fax: 901-726-0141. Mrs. Cheri Kamler, Prin.; Rev. Thomas Kirk. Lay Teachers 28; Students 305.
St. Agnes Academy (1851), 4830 Walnut Grove Rd., 38117. Tel: 901-767-1377.
Title of Incorporation: St. Agnes Academy-St. Dominic School, Inc. Sisters of St. Dominic (St. Catharine, KY). Barbara Daush, Pres.; Marian Lehan Swicker, Dean. Lay Teachers 29; Students 243.

[D] ELEMENTARY SCHOOLS, PRIVATE

MEMPHIS. *St. Agnes Academy.* (Grades PreK-8), 4830 Walnut Grove Rd., 38117. Tel: 901-767-1377.
E-mail: bdaush@SAA-sds.org
Web site: www.saa-sds.org
Sisters of St. Dominic. (St. Catharine, KY). Barbara Daush, Pres. Lay Teachers 35; Students 233.
St. Dominic Boys School, 30 Avon Rd., 38117. Tel: 901-682-3011. Sisters of St. Dominic. (St. Catherine, KY). Mrs. Barbara Daush, Pres.; Mr. John Murphy, Dean. Lay Teachers 29; Students 226.

[E] CHILD-CARING INSTITUTIONS

MEMPHIS. *St. Peter Home for Children,* (1852) 3060 Baskin St., 38127-7799. Tel: 901-354-6300; Fax: 901-354-6343
For a complete listing, refer to the Special Care Facilities section.

GERMANTOWN. *Madonna Learning Center for Retarded Children,* 7007 Poplar Ave., 38138. Tel: 901-752-5767
For a complete listing, refer to the Special Care Facilities section.

[F] GENERAL HOSPITALS

MEMPHIS. *St. Joseph Hospital,* (1889) 220 Overton Ave., 38105. Tel: 901-577-2700; Fax: 901-577-3620
For a complete listing, refer to the Hospitals section.

[G] DAYCARE CENTERS

MEMPHIS. *Holy Names Preschool & After School Program,* 709 Keel, 38107. Tel: 901-525-8443. Legal Title: *Holy Names Center.* Ms. Linda Steed, Coord. & Prog. Dir.; Mr. Tommie Hill, Site Supvr. Children 300.
St. Louis Extended, 5192 Shady Grove Rd., 38117. Tel: 901-682-9692. Ms. Lori Tucker, Site Supvr. Children 100.
St. Michael Extended, 3880 Forrest Ave., 38122. Tel: 901-324-6662. Ms. Debbie Kallaher, Site Supvr. Children 100.
St. Therese Little Flower Day Care Center, 1666 Jackson Ave., 38107. Tel: 901-276-5111. Ms. Sharon Webb, Prog. Dir. Children 125.

CORDOVA. *St. Benedict at Auburndale Extended,* 2100 N. Germantown Rd., 38018. Tel: 901-381-2595. Ms. Pamela O'Bryan, Site Supvr. Children 112.

[H] ADULT RESIDENCES & HOMES FOR AGED

MEMPHIS. *Diocese of Memphis Housing Corp.,* P.O. Box 41705, 38174-1705. Tel: 901-722-4761; 722-4772
For a complete listing, refer to the Special Care Facilities section.
Northwood Park Apartments, 1130 N. Breedlove, 38107. Tel: 901-526-3964
For a complete listing, refer to the Special Care Facilities section.
St. Peter Manor, 108 N. Auburndale, 38104. Tel: 901-278-8200
For a complete listing, refer to the Special Care Facilities section.
St. Peter Villa, 141 N. McLean, 38104-2644. Tel: 901-276-2021
For a complete listing, refer to the Special Care Facilities section.

DYERSBURG. *St. Joseph Manor,* 885 Hwy. 51, Byp. W., P.O. Box 151, 38024. Tel: 901-285-8560
For a complete listing, refer to the Special Care Facilities section.
The Village Apartments, Box 151, Hwy. 51 Byp. W., 38024. Tel: 901-285-8560
For a complete listing, refer to the Special Care Facilities section.
Westgate Apartments, 1405-8 Meeks, 38024. Tel: 901-286-4874
For a complete listing, refer to the Special Care Facilities section.

HUMBOLDT. *St. Matthew Manor,* 2575 Viking Dr., 38343. Tel: 901-784-7229
For a complete listing, refer to the Special Care Facilities section.
St. Matthew Manor - West, 2575 Viking Dr., 38343. Tel: 901-824-3793
For a complete listing, refer to the Special Care Facilities section.

JACKSON. *St. Mary Manor,* 1771 Hwy. 45 By-Pass, 38305. Tel: 901-668-5633
For a complete listing, refer to the Special Care Facilities section.

MOSCOW. *St. Mark Village Apartments,* 85 St. Mark Cove, 38057. Tel: 901-877-3456
For a complete listing, refer to the Special Care Facilities section.

[I] CATHOLIC CHARITIES

MEMPHIS, TN. *St. Ann-Bartlett Extended Care,* 6529 Stage Rd., 38134. Tel: 901-382-3370. Ms. Karen Otts, Site Supvr.
St. John Center, 2718 Lamar Ave., 38114. Tel: 901-743-5925. Ms. Velteen McGhee, Prog. Dir.
St. Peter Day Care, 125 N. McLean Blvd., 38104. Tel: 901-725-8263. Ms. Evelyn Howard, Prog. Dir.

[J] RESIDENCES OF PRIESTS AND BROTHERS

MEMPHIS. *Brothers Of The Christian Schools (Prov. of St. Louis),* 650 E. Parkway, S., 38104. Tel: 901-321-3000; Fax: 901-321-3290. 5900 Walnut Grove Rd., 38119. Tel: 901-682-4704. Brothers 37.
Franciscan Friars (Sacred Heart Prov.) of Memphis, 1254 S. Lauderdale, 38106. Tel: 901-774-8191. Revs. Maury Smith, O.F.M.; Frank Coens, O.F.M.; Cyril J. Wagner, O.F.M.; Bro. Roch Pfeifer, O.F.M. Priests 3; Brothers 1.
Order Of Preachers (Southern Dominican Prov.), 190 Adams Ave., 38103. Tel: 901-527-8282. Revs. Terence Holachek, O.P.; Edward Everitt, O.P.; Bro. Michael Curtis, O.P.
Order Of The Holy Trinity, 5900 Walnut Grove Rd., 38120-2174. Rev. Eric T. Burdt, O.SS.T., Chap., Christian Brothers High School.

Paulist Fathers (New York), St. Patrick Church, 277 S. Fourth St., 38126. Tel: 901-527-2542; Fax: 901-525-1147. Revs. Paul Dechant, C.S.P., Pastor; Gilbert Martinez, C.S.P., Assoc. Pastor; James Fisher, C.S.P., (Retired). Priests 3.

JACKSON. *Brothers Of St. Francis Xavier (Xaverians, Sacred Heart Prov.)*, 611 Burkett St., 38301. Tel: 901-424-5003. Bro. Dan O'Brien, C.F.X.

[K] CONVENTS AND RESIDENCES FOR SISTERS

MEMPHIS. *Dominican Sisters, Congregation of St. Catharine of Siena, KY O.P.*, St. Agnes Convent, 4792 Walnut Grove Rd., 38117. Tel: 901-683-1333. Legal Title: *Dominican Sisters, Congregation of St. Cecilia (Nashville, TN), St. Paul Convent*. Sisters 6.

Dominican Sisters, Congregation of St. Cecila, 1488 Maurine Dr., 38116. Tel: 901-346-0251; Fax: 901-332-3983. Sisters 7.

Medical Mission Sisters of Philadelphia (PA) M.M.S. Mailing Address: 108 N. Auburndale, #1007, 38104. Tel: 901-726-1735.

Missionaries of Charity, 700 N. 7th St., 38107. Tel: 901-527-4947. Shelter. Tel: 901-526-5456. Sr. M. Janita, M.C., Superior. Sisters 4.

Missionary Sisters Of The Society Of Mary (Waltham, MA) S.M.S.M., 60 S. Auburndale, 38104. Tel: 901-272-2808. Sisters 5.

Monastery Of St. Clare O.S.C., 1310 Dellwood Ave., 38127. Tel: 901-357-6662. Sr. Mary Helen, O.S.C., Abbess. Sisters 8; Huehuetenango, Guatemala 3.

Sisters Of Charity Of Nazareth (KY) S.C.N., 904 Hawthorne, 38107. Tel: 901-276-7386.

Sisters Of Charity Of The Blessed Virgin Mary (Dubuque, IA) B.V.M., 437 N. Dickinson, 38112. Tel: 901-274-9015. Sr. Jacquelyn Cramer, B.V.M., Community Rep. Sisters 3.

Sisters of Our Lady of Charity of the Good Shepherd (St. Louis, MO) R.G.S., Convent of the Good Shepherd, 3911 Mallard Point Dr., 38128. Tel: 901-357-7316. Sr. Mary Rosalinda Sobremisana, R.G.S., Admin. Sisters 6.

Sisters Of St. Benedict (Ferdinand, IN) O.S.B., 5190 Normandy Ave., 38117. Tel: 901-767-7372. Sr. Mary Mark Graf. Sisters 2.

Sisters Of St. Francis (Rochester, MN) O.S.F., 695 S. Barksdale, 38104. Tel: 901-276-8756.

Sisters Of St. Francis Of Perpetual Adoration (Mishawaka, IN) O.S.F. Sr. Elizabeth Ann, O.S.F., St. Joseph Hospital Convent, 220 Overton Ave., 38105. Tel: 901-577-3879; Fax: 901-577-3620. Sisters 6.

Sisters Of St. Joseph Of Pennsylvania (Erie, PA) S.S.J., 931 Ivy, 38117. Tel: 901-821-9907. Sr. Marilyn Terwilliger, S.S.J.

HUNTINGDON. *Franciscan Sisters of Little Falls (Little Falls, MN)*, 257 Cotham Dr., 38344. Tel: 901-986-2817. Sr. Jeanette E. Martell, O.S.F.; Sr. Clara Schroedl, O.S.F.; Sr. Ruth Nistler, O.S.F. Sisters 3.

SOMERVILLE. *Sinsinawa Dominican Sisters*, 305 Charleston St. #6, 38068. Tel: 901-465-6371. Sr. Jeanne Dion, O.P.

[L] NEWMAN CENTERS

MEMPHIS. *Campus Ministry, University of Memphis, Rhodes College*, 3625 Mynders, 38111. Tel: 901-323-3051. UT Center for Health Sciences. Deacon John W. Hivner, Dir.

MARTIN. *Cooperative Ministries Interfaith Center*, 312 Lovelace Ave., 38237. Tel: 901-587-2603. Rev. Joseph L. Paolozzi.

[M] MISCELLANEOUS

MEMPHIS. *Catholic Hispanic Community of Memphis (Comunidad Catolica Hispana de Memphis)*, Sacred Heart Church, 1324 Jefferson, 38104. Tel: 901-726-1891. Suzanne Martin, Contact.

Cenacle Retreat League, 6763 Wild Berry Ln., 38119-5645. Tel: 901-754-6349. Mrs. Anita Fleming.

Diocesan Council of Catholic Women, 6659 Fossil Creek, 38120. Tel: 901-753-3751. Mrs. Mary Ann S. Brenner.

Knights of St. Peter Claver (St. Benedict the Black Council No. 188), 5600 Santa Barbara, 38116. Tel: 901-396-8315. Mr. Joseph Randolph, Grand Knight & Vice Pres. Metro Committee S.P.C.

Ladies of Charity of Memphis, 4046 Rhodes, 38111. Tel: 901-323-9076. Mrs. Barbara Singleton, Pres.

**Madonna Circle, Inc.* (Catholic Women's Service Organization), P.O. Box 172174, 38187-2174. Tel: 901-521-6652. Mrs. Raymond H. Moran, Pres.

Marriage Preparation Program, The Catholic Center, 5825 Shelby Oaks Dr., 38134. Tel: 901-373-1235. Mrs. Patricia A. Perry, Coord.

MCH, Inc. Court / Trezevant Apartments, 3418-2 Trezevant, 38127. Tel: 901-357-8831.

St. Patrick's Center, 277 S. Fourth St., 38126. Tel: 901-527-2542. Rev. Paul Dechant, C.S.P., Dir.

Saint Vincent Pallotti Center for Parish Social Ministry, 1325 Jefferson Ave., 38104-2097. Tel: 901-722-4758; Fax: 901-722-4791. P.O. Box 41705, 38174-1705. Diane McKinna, Dir.

Serra Club of Memphis, 5825 Shelby Oaks Dr., 38134. Tel: 901-755-3645. Mr. Stan Schulz, Pres.; Rev. J. David Graham, Chap.

SMS Community Housing, Inc., 3418-2 Trezevant, 38127. Tel: 901-357-8831.

Society of St. Vincent DePaul, P.O. Box 22651, 38122-0651. Mr. Kenny Bowen, District Council Pres. Tel: 901-365-4830; Rev. Carl J. Hood, Spiritual Advisor.

CAMDEN. *Good Samaritan Village*, 192A Post Oak Ave., 38320. Mrs. Francine Fitzgerald, Mgr. Tel: 901-584-1300.

JACKSON. *Jonah Inc.*, 416 E. Lafayette, 1st Floor, 38301. Tel: 901-427-1630. Mrs. Shirley Richmond, Exec. Dir.

SAVANNAH. *Charismatic Prayer Groups*, 1107 Clifton Rd., 38372. Tel: 901-925-4852. Rev. James Joseph Martell.

RELIGIOUS INSTITUTES OF MEN REPRESENTED IN THE DIOCESE

For further details refer to the corresponding bracketed number in the Religious Institutes of Men or Women section.

[1350]—*Brothers of St. Francix Xavier.*—C.F.X.
[0330]—*Brothers of the Christian Schools.* (St. Louis Prov.).—F.S.C.
[1130]—*Congregation of the Priests of the Sacred Heart.*—S.C.J.
[0520]—*Franciscan Friars.*—O.F.M.
[0430]—*Order of Preachers (Dominicans).*—O.P.
[1310]—*Order of the Holy Trinity.*—O.S.S.T.
[1030]—*Paulist Fathers.*—C.S.P.

RELIGIOUS INSTITUTES OF WOMEN REPRESENTED IN THE DIOCESE

[0230]—*Benedictine Sisters of the Pontifical Jurisdiction.*—O.S.B.
[1070-01]—*Dominican Sisters.*—O.P.
[1070-03]—*Dominican Sisters.*—O.P.
[1070-07]—*Dominican Sisters.*—O.P.
[1070-13]—*Dominican Sisters.*—O.P.
[1310]—*Franciscan Sisters of Little Falls, Minnesota.*—O.S.F.
[2420]—*Marist Missionary Sisters.*—S.M.S.M.
[2490]—*Medical Mission Sisters.*—S.C.M.M.
[2710]—*Missionaries of Charity.*—M.C.
[1360]—*Missionary Franciscan Sisters of the Immaculate Conception.*—O.S.F.
[3760]—*Order of St. Clare.* (Memphis, TN).—O.S.C.
[0440]—*Sisters of Charity of Cincinnati, Ohio.*—S.C.
[0500]—*Sisters of Charity of Nazareth.*—S.C.N.
[0430]—*Sisters of Charity of the Blessed Virgin Mary.*—B.V.M.
[1640]—*Sisters of St. Francis of Perpetual Adoration.* (Prov. of the Immaculate Heart of Mary).—O.S.F.
[3830-09]—*Sisters of St. Joseph.*—S.S.J.
[3830-13]—*Sisters of St. Joseph.*—C.S.J.
[1830]—*The Sisters of the Good Shepherd.* (St. Louis Prov.).—R.G.S.

DIOCESAN CEMETERIES

MEMPHIS. *All Saints*, c/o Calvary Cemetery, 1663 Elvis Presley Blvd., 38106. Tel: 901-948-1529.

Calvary, 1663 Elvis Presley Blvd., 38106. Tel: 901-948-1529.

JACKSON. *Calvary*.

NECROLOGY

(No Deaths)

Diocese of Metuchen

Most Reverend

VINCENT DE PAUL BREEN, D.D.

Bishop of Metuchen; ordained July 15, 1962; appointed Third Bishop of Metuchen July 8, 1997; consecrated September 8, 1997; installed September 8, 1997. *Res., 10 Library Pl., Metuchen, NJ, 08840.*

ESTABLISHED NOVEMBER 19, 1981.

Square Miles 1,424.55.

Comprises the Counties of Warren, Hunterdon, Somerset and Middlesex in the State of New Jersey.

Legal Corporate Title: The Diocese of Metuchen.

The Diocesan Center: P.O. Box 191, Metuchen, NJ, 08840. Tel.: 732-283-3800; Fax: 732-283-2012.

STATISTICAL OVERVIEW

Personnel	
Bishop	1
Retired Bishops	1
Priests: Diocesan Active in Diocese	163
Priests: Active Outside Diocese	17
Priests: Diocesan in Foreign Missions	1
Priests: Retired, Sick or Absent	29
Number of Diocesan Priests	210
Religious Priests in Diocese	46
Extern Priests in Diocese	21
Ordinations:	
Diocesan Priests	3
Transitional Deacons	2
Permanent Deacons in Diocese	103
Total Brothers	23
Total Sisters	492
Parishes	
Parishes	108
With Resident Pastor:	
Resident Diocesan Priests	97
Resident Religious Priests	5
Without Resident Pastor:	
Administered by Priests	6
Professional Ministry Personnel:	
Brothers	4
Sisters	40
Lay Ministers	64
Welfare	
Catholic Hospitals	1
Total Assisted	172,380
Health Care Centers	2
Total Assisted	2,500
Homes for the Aged	3
Total Assisted	273
Day Care and Extended Day Care Centers	7
Total Assisted	1,859
Specialized Homes	4
Total Assisted	219
Special Centers for Social Services	9
Total Assisted	21,147
Residential Care of Disabled	1
Total Assisted	10
Other Institutions	2
Total Assisted	42
Educational	
Diocesan Students in Other Seminaries	13
Total Seminarians	13
High Schools, Diocesan and Parish	4
Total Students	2,622
High Schools, Private	2
Total Students	1,132
Elementary Schools, Diocesan and Parish	42
Total Students	14,199
Elementary Schools, Private	1
Total Students	213
Non-residential Schools for the Disabled	1
Total Students	38
Catechesis/Religious Education:	
High School Students	1,208
Elementary Students	39,058
Total Students Under Catholic Instruction	58,483
Teachers in the Diocese:	
Priests	2
Brothers	9
Sisters	83
Lay Teachers	899
Vital Statistics	
Receptions into the Church:	
Infant Baptism Totals	7,311
Adult Baptism Totals	138
Received into Full Communion	293
First Communions	7,113
Confirmations	5,319
Marriages:	
Catholic	1,494
Interfaith	398
Total Marriages	1,892
Deaths	3,888
Total Catholic Population	483,500
Total Population	1,188,671

Former Bishops—Most Rev. THEODORE E. MCCARRICK, ord. May 31, 1958; appt. Titular Bishop of Rusibisir and Auxiliary to the Archbishop of New York, May 24, 1977; cons. June 29, 1977; appt. first Bishop of Metuchen, Nov. 19, 1981; installed Jan. 31, 1982; promoted to the Archdiocese of Newark, June 3, 1986; installed July 25, 1986.—Most Rev. EDWARD T. HUGHES, ord. May 31, 1947; appt. Titular Bishop of Segia and Auxiliary to the Archbishop of Philadelphia, June 14, 1976; cons. July 21, 1976; appt. second Bishop of Metuchen, Dec. 16, 1986; installed Feb. 5, 1987; retired Sept. 8, 1997.

The Diocesan Center—P.O. Box 191, Metuchen, 08840. Tel: 732-283-3800; Fax: 732-283-2012.

Vicar General—Rev. Msgr. JOHN B. SZYMANSKI.

Episcopal Vicars—Rev. Msgr. ANTHONY J. LUISINI; Rev. Msgr. ANTHONY J. GAMBINO; Rev. Msgr. JAMES P. MORAN.

Secretary to the Bishop—Rev. THOMAS J. SERAFIN.

The Diocesan Curia

Moderator—Rev. Msgr. JOHN B. SZYMANSKI, V.G.

The Secretariat for Canonical Affairs

Secretary—Rev. CHARLES T. O'CONNOR, J.C.L.

Delegates for Dispensations—Rev. THOMAS J. SERAFIN.

The Center for Counseling and Consultation Svcs.—29 Abeel St., New Brunswick, 08901. Rev. JOSEPH B. SZULWACH, Dir.

The Chancery

Chancellor—Sr. M. MICHAELITA WIECHETEK, C.S.S.F.

Vice Chancellor for Community Affairs—EILEEN A. TABERT, Office of Parish Leadership Services.

The Tribunal

The Diocesan Center—P.O. Box 191, Metuchen, 08840. Tel: 732-283-3800; Fax: 732-283-2012.

Judicial Vicar—Rev. Msgr. WILLIAM BENWELL, J.C.L.

Associate Judicial Vicar—Rev. RICHARD J. LYONS, J.C.L.

Staff—Revs. CHESTER H. CARINA, J.C.L.; NEIL W. DAVIN, C.P., J.C.L.; GEORGE KORYTKOWSKI, O.F.M.Cap., J.C.D.; ROBERT V. MEYERS, J.C.L.; GEORGE M. PISANELLO, J.C.L.; Rev. Msgr. JOHN R. TORNEY, P.A.; Sr. MARY A. KERWIN, R.S.M.; EUGENE F. HORAN; BARBARA J. REAVEY.

Psychological Consultant—FRED J. MCDONALD, Ph.D.

Notaries—MARY JEAN BELSKY; ZENORA LALA-OUTHMAN.

Vicariate for Administration

Vicar for Administration—Rev. Msgr. EUGENE PRUS.

Office of Resource Management—RICHARD P. GERRITY, Exec. Dir.

Department of Finance—RICHARD P. GERRITY, Dir.

Department of Insurance and Pensions—M. BARBARA FRANCFORT, Mgr.

Department of Cemeteries—THOMAS F. DOOLEY, Dir.; Very Rev. ANDREW L. SZAROLETA, Dir., Pastoral Care.

Department of Management Information Systems—MICHAEL L. GIRASOLI, Mgr.

Department of Property Management—ROGER A. STONE, Supvr., Building Maintenance.

Office of Stewardship—Rev. Msgr. MICHAEL J. CORONA, Dir.; Deacon WILLIAM C. VANZINO, Asst. Dir.; Deacon FRANK J. ENGEL, JR., Development Officer, Bishop's Appeal & Diocesan Projects.

Office of the Missions—Rev. Msgr. RICHARD A. BEHL, Dir.

Office of Personnel Management—JUDITH H. EICHMAN, Dir.

Commission on Building—Rev. Msgr. EUGENE PRUS, Chm.

Commission for Sites and Boundaries—Rev. STEPHEN H. CONGDON, Chm.

Vicariate for Education

Vicar for Education—Rev. Msgr. GEORGE M. BREMBOS, Ed.D.

Office of the Schools—LORRAINE P. AMENDOLARA, Ed.D., Supt. Assoc. Supts.: Sr. MARY ROSE WATKINS, O.S.F.; Sr. MARYANN JACOBS, S.C.C.; Sr. PATRICIA MCCLURE, S.S.J.; Bro. MICHAEL MULLIN, F.M.S.

Office of Religious Education—MARY KAY CULLINAN, Dir. DOLORES R. NANN, Assoc. Dir.

Office of Youth Ministry—Rev. DAVID J. NICGORSKI, O.M.V., Dir.

"The Catholic Spirit"—RAYANNE DAMIANO, Editor-in-Chief.

Commission for Young Adult Ministry—Rev. DAVID J. NICGORSKI, O.M.V., Dir.

Vicariate for Personnel in Ministry

Vicar for Personnel in Ministry—Rev. Msgr. SEAMUS F. BRENNAN.

Office of Ministry to Priests—Rev. CHARLES W. CICERALE, Dir.
Office of the Diaconate—Deacon LUKE J. HALLY, Dir.
Office for Religious—Sr. ALMA BLUME, M.P.F.
Office of Vocations—Revs. ROBERT W. MEDLEY, Dir. JOSEPH M. CURRY, Assoc. Dir. JOSEPH G. CELENO, Assoc. Dir., College Awareness.
Office of the Health Care Apostolate—Rev. JOSEPH L. DESMOND, Dir.
Commission for the Continuing Education of Priests—Rev. Msgr. WILLIAM BENWELL, Chm.
Board for Seminary Education—Rev. CHESTER H. CARINA.

Vicariate For Pastoral Life

Mailing Address: P.O. Box 6189, E. Brunswick, 08816. Tel: 732-651-8084
Vicar for Pastoral Life—Rev. Msgr. MICHAEL J. ALLIEGRO.
Office of Family Life Ministry—JUDITH A. PSOTA, Dir.
Office of Evangelization—ANNE MARIE WINTERS, Ph.D., Dir.
Office for Shared Ministry—DOROTHY S. HEITZ, Dir.
Office for Multi-Cultural Ministries—Rev. Msgr. ANTHONY J. GAMBINO, Dir.
Commission for African-American Catholic Ministry—JOSEPH J. POWELL, Chm.
Commission for Ecumenical Affairs—Rev. JEROME A. JOHNSON, Chm.
Commission for the Filipino Apostolate—Rev. EDGARDO D. ABANO, Chm.
Commission for Hispanic Ministry—Rev. Msgr. ANTHONY J. GAMBINO, Chm.
Chinese Apostolate—Rev. JOSEPH FU, Chap.
Korean Apostolate—Rev. PETER K. CHOI, Chap.
Portuguese Apostolate—Rev. LAURO C. SEDLMAYER, Chap.
Commission for Pro-Life Action—Rev. Msgr. RICHARD A. BEHL, Chm.
Commission for Ministry with People with Disabilities—Rev. ROBERT W. MEDLEY.
Vietnamese Apostolate—Rev. PETER PHONG VO, Chap.
Commission for Worship and Preaching—Rev. JOSEPH C. KORNOSKI, Chm.

Diocesan Organizations, Movements and Moderators

Campaign for Human Development—MARY E. NOWACKI, Diocesan Liaison.
Catholic Lawyers Guild—Rev. Msgr. MICHAEL J. ALLIEGRO, Moderator.
Catholic Scouting Movement—Rev. Msgr. MICHAEL J. CORONA, Moderator.
Catholic League for Religious and Civil Rights—Rev. Msgr. JAMES P. MORAN, Diocesan Liason.
Charismatic Movement—Co-Moderators: Rev. ROBERT L. SANTA BARBARA; DORIS BRENNAN.
Diocesan Council of Catholic Women—Rev. EDWARD M. O'NEILL, Moderator.
Diocesan Eucharistic League—Rev. CHARLES R. PRATS, Dir.
Diocesan Holy Name Society—Rev. THOMAS J. DZURENDA, Moderator.
Diocesan Home School Association—Rev. Msgr. GEORGE M. BREMBOS, Moderator.
Legion of Mary—Rev. Msgr. DOMINIC A. TURTORA, Moderator.
National Shrine of the Immaculate Conception—Rev. Msgr. DOMINIC A. TURTORA, Diocesan Liaison.
St. Vincent de Paul Societies—Mr. JOSEPH D. FLANNIGAN, Pres.

Vicariate For Charities and Social Ministry

Vicar for Charities and Social Ministry—Rev. Msgr. MICHAEL J. CASHMAN.
Catholic Charities—Sr. FLORENCE EDWARD KEARNEY, D.C., Exec. Dir. MICHAEL LESZCZUK, L.C.S.W., Assoc. Exec. Dir. Asst. Exec. Dirs.: MARY E. DAVEY, L.C.S.W.; MARIANNE MAJEWSKI, L.C.S.W., (See category for Catholic Charities under Institutions Located in the Diocese for the full listing).
HIV Services—DONALD STAGER.

Consultative Bodies

College of Consultors—Rev. Msgr. JOHN B. SZYMANSKI, V.G.; Rev. Msgr. ANTHONY J. LUISINI; Rev. Msgr. JAMES P. MORAN; Rev. Msgr. ANTHONY J. GAMBINO; Rev. Msgr. MICHAEL J. CORONA; Rev. Msgr. EUGENE PRUS; Rev. Msgr. MICHAEL J. CASHMAN; Revs. RAYMOND L. COLE; CHARLES T. O'CONNOR, Sec.
Deans—Very Rev. MICHAEL A. MCGUIRE, Cathedral Deanery; Very Rev. EDMUND J. SHALLOW, Arthur Kill Deanery; Very Rev. EDWARD J. STRUZIK, Forsgate Deanery; Very Rev. IGNATIUS H. KUZIEMSKI, Morris Canal Deanery; Very Rev. TERRANCE M. LAWLER, Raritan Bay Deanery; Very Rev. DANIEL SLOAN, County Seat Deanery; Very Rev. BLAISE R. BARAN, Somerset Hills Deanery; Very Rev. ANDREW L. SZAROLETA, Round Valley Deanery; Very Rev. JOSEPH M. CURRY, New Brunswick Deanery.
Presbyteral Council—Most Rev. VINCENT D. BREEN, Pres.
Theological Commission—Rev. GLENN J. COMANDINI, S.T.D., Chm.
Administrative Council—Rev. Msgr. JOHN B. SZYMANSKI, V.G., Chm.; Rev. Msgr. GEORGE M. BREMBOS; Rev. Msgr. SEAMUS F. BRENNAN; Rev. Msgr. EUGENE PRUS; Rev. Msgr. MICHAEL J. ALLIEGRO; Rev. Msgr. WILLIAM BENWELL; Rev. Msgr. MICHAEL J. CASHMAN; Rev. CHARLES T. O'CONNOR; Sr. FLORENCE EDWARD KEARNEY, D.C.; Sr. M. MICHAELITA WIECHETEK, C.S.S.F.; LORRAINE P. AMENDOLARA, Ed.D.; RAYANNE DAMIANO; RICHARD P. GERRITY.
Diocesan Pastoral Council—Most Rev. VINCENT D. BREEN; Rev. Msgr. JOHN B. SZYMANSKI, V.G.; JULES BORSHADEL; CHARLES CONVERY; MARGE CORONA; MARYANNE DAY; EDWARD DIJOSEPH; GRACE DOBROWOLSKI; DONNA FOJTLIN; Rev. Msgr. ANTHONY J. GAMBINO; JOHN GODOWSKI; Deacon LUKE J. HALLY; BILL KENNEDY; Sr. FRANCES LAURETTI, M.P.F.; CHARLES LINEK; MARIA MORALES; MICHAEL MYSZKA; DONNA PERK; FRANK P. QUINN, JR.; Bro. JOSEPH ROCCO, S.C.; Rev. JOSEPH V. ROMANOSKI; TINA SALVEMINI; CATHERINE SUTLIFF; EILEEN A. TABERT, Exec. Sec. KLARA TARSI.

CLERGY, PARISHES, MISSIONS AND PAROCHIAL SCHOOLS

BOROUGH OF METUCHEN
(Middlesex County)

1—CATHEDRAL OF ST. FRANCIS (1871), Rev. Msgr. Richard A. Behl, Rector; Rev. Msgr. Dominic A. Turtora, Rector Emeritus; Revs. Michael C. Saharic; Guy W. Selvester; Deacons Frank J. Cammarano; Robert P. Gellentien; Cornelius S. Smoyak; Paul G. Licameli.
Res., 32 Elm Ave., 08840. Tel: 732-548-0100; Fax: 732-549-1033.
School—45 Library Pl., 08840. Tel: 732-548-3107; Fax: 732-548-5760.
Sisters of Mercy 3; Lay Teachers 19; Students 452.

OUTSIDE THE BOROUGH OF METUCHEN

Alpha, Warren Co., St. Mary (1902), Rev. Msgr. Anthony J. Luisini; Rev. James A. Kyrpczak; Deacon George L. Bolash.
Res., 830 Fifth Ave., 08865. Tel: 908-454-0444; Fax: 908-454-7745.

Avenel, Middlesex Co., St. Andrew (1920), Revs. David B. Kosmoski, O.M.V.; S. Gregory Cleveland, O.M.V.; James A. Walther, O.M.V. In res., Rev. David J. Nicgorski, O.M.V.
Res., 244 Avenel St., 07001. Tel: 732-634-4355; Fax: 732-750-5905.
Stations—Avenel, Woodbridge State School.; Avenel, Woodbridge Emergency Reception Center, Tel: 732-636-4261.

Baptistown, Hunterdon Co., Our Lady of Victories (1973), Revs. David I. Fulton; Edward J. Nester, Pastor Emeritus; Deacon John T. Monahan.
Res., P.O. Box 127, 08803. Tel: 908-996-2068; Fax: 908-996-3525.

Basking Ridge, Somerset Co., St. James (1864), Rev. Msgr. William J. Capik; Rev. John F. Primich; Deacons James S. Bell; Luke J. Hally.
Res., 184 S. Finley Ave., P.O. Box 310, 07920. Tel: 908-766-0888; Fax: 908-766-1815.
School—200 S. Finley Ave., P.O. Box 310, 07920. Tel: 908-766-4774; Fax: 908-766-1815.
Felician Sisters 3; Lay Teachers 15; Students 400.

Belvidere, Warren Co., St. Patrick (1892), Rev. Michael A. Driscoll; Deacon John F. Dumschat.
Res., 327 Greenwich St., 07823. Tel: 908-475-2559.

Bernardsville, Somerset Co., Our Lady of Perpetual Help (1898), Rev. Chester H. Carina; Rev. Msgr. John R. Torney, P.A., Pastor Emeritus; Rev. Raniero C. Marincioni; Deacons Joseph E. O'Keefe; Joel R. Livingston.
Res., 111 Claremont Rd., 07924. Tel: 908-766-0079; Fax: 908-766-1185. [CEM]
School—School of St. Elizabeth, Seney Dr., 07924. Tel: 908-766-0244; Fax: 908-766-5372.
Sisters of Christian Charity 1; Lay Teachers 10; Students 249.
Chapel—Bernardsville, Sacred Heart (Chapel of Convenience).

Blairstown, Warren Co., St. Jude (1945), Rev. William J. Smith.
Res., Eisenhower Rd., P.O. Box N, 07825. Tel: 908-362-6444; Fax: 908-362-6862.

Bloomsbury, Hunterdon Co., Church of the Annunciation (1948), Rev. J. Philip Vadakkekara.
Res., 80 Main St., P.O. Box 136, 08804-0136. Tel: 908-479-4905.

Bound Brook, Somerset Co., St. Joseph (1876), Revs. Charles T. O'Connor; Louis A. Mattina; Deacon George D. Coleman.
Office: 124 E. Second St., P.O. Box 72, 08805. Tel: 732-356-0027; Fax: 732-356-8092.
Res., 304 John St., 08805. Tel: 732-356-8936. [CEM]
St. Mary of Czestochowa (1914) (Polish), Revs. Stanley J. Walega; Mieczyslaw Jarzabek.
Res., 193 W. High St., 08805. Tel: 732-356-0358; Fax: 732-356-1338.

Bridgewater, Somerset Co., Holy Trinity (1948), Revs. John R. Pringle; Sean G. Winters; Deacon Michael A. Forrestall.
Res., 60 Maple St., 08807. Tel: 908-526-2394.
St. Bernard (1843), Revs. John L. Brundage; James W. Hagerman; Deacons Patrick J. Cline; Paul L. Anderson; Gerard C. Sims.
Office: Tel: 908-725-0552; Fax: 908-725-4524.
Res., 500 Rte. 22, 08807. Tel: 908-526-6859. [CEM]

Califon, Hunterdon Co., St. John Neumann (1982), Rev. J. William Mickiewicz; Deacon Thomas J. Gilheany.
Res., P.O. Box 455, 07830. Tel: 908-832-2513; Fax: 908-832-7618.

Carteret, Middlesex Co.,

1—ST. JOSEPH, (1893), Rev. Edward C. Puleo. In res., Rev. Msgr. Donald M. Endebrock.
Res., 7 Locust St., 07008. Tel: 732-541-8946; Fax: 732-969-2282.
School—865 Roosevelt Ave., 07008. Tel: 732-541-7111.
Sisters 4; Lay Teachers 10; Students 247.

2—HOLY FAMILY, (1907) (Polish), Very Rev. Edmund J. Shallow.
Res., 213 Pershing Ave., 07008. Tel: 732-541-5768; Fax: 732-541-5871.
School—132 Emerson St., 07008. Tel: 732-541-2941.
Bernardine Sisters 1; Lay Teachers 9; Students 178.

3—SACRED HEART, (1910) (Slovak), Rev. Gerald Browne.
Res., 67 Fitch St., 07008. Tel: 732-541-5410.

4—ST. ELIZABETH OF HUNGARY, (1914) (Hungarian), Rev. Patrick H. Barrett.
Res., 119 Washington Ave., 07008. Tel: 732-541-5202.

Clinton, Hunterdon Co., Immaculate Conception (1864), Very Rev. Andrew L. Szaroleta; Rev. Alexander J. Carles; Deacons William R. Bauer; Dennis K. Webster.
Res., Rte. 633, Old Allerton Rd., P.O. Box 5400, 08809-0400. Tel: 908-735-7319; Fax: 908-735-4552. [CEM]
Mission—Pittstown, Hunterdon Co., St. Catherine of Siena, 08809.
Stations—Edna Mahan Correctional Facility for Women, Tel: 908-735-7111; Fax: 908-735-5246; Hunterdon Developmental Center, Tel: 908-735-4031; Fax: 908-730-1311.

Colonia, Middlesex Co., St. John Vianney (1959), Revs. Edward M. O'Neill; William F. Leonard; John R. Butler (RIC); Deacons Joseph A. Vivona; Joseph D. Ragucci. In res., Rev. John D. Murphy.
Res., 420 Inman Ave., 07067. Tel: 732-574-0150; Fax: 732-574-0050.
School—440 Inman Ave., 07067. Tel: 732-388-1662.
Bernardine Sisters 1; Lay Teachers 28; Students 658.

Cranbury, Middlesex Co., Nativity of Our Lord (1992), Rev. Stephen H. Congdon; Deacon Michel G. Morend. In res., Rev. Msgr. William J. Haughney.
Res., P.O. Box 583, 08512. Tel: 609-371-0499.

Dunellen, Middlesex Co., St. John the Evangelist (1879), Revs. Richard J. Lyons; Louis J. Eldridge.
Res., 317 First St., 08812. Tel: 732-968-2621; Fax: 732-968-2588.

East Brunswick, Middlesex Co., St. Bartholomew (1959), Rev. Msgr. Michael J. Alliegro; Rev. Msgr. J. Morgan Kelly, Pastor Emeritus; Revs. Peter R. Cebulka; Thomas J. Walsh; Deacons Richard R. Kaseta; John P. McShane; Anthony J. Gostkowski.
Res., 460 Ryders Ln., 08816. Tel: 732-257-7722; Fax: 732-257-7723.
School—470 Ryders Ln., 08816. Tel: 732-254-7105.
Lay Teachers 22; Students 505.

East Millstone, Somerset Co., St. Joseph (1883), Rev. Raymond L. Cole; Deacons George D. LaPolice; Leo F. Clementi; Joseph C. Moscinski; Warren C. Page.
Res., P.O. Box 2129, Livingston Ave., 08875. Tel: 908-874-3141; Fax: 908-874-7040.

Edison, Middlesex Co., Guardian Angels (1959), Revs. R. Kevin Crowley; Robert J. Miller.
Res., 37 Plainfield Ave., P.O. Box 1216, 08817. Tel: 732-985-7565.

Mission—Bonhamtown, Middlesex Co., St. Margaret Mary Alacoque, Woodbridge Ave., 08817.

St. Helena (1965), Rev. Msgr. Armando J. Perini; Revs. L. Roger Labonte; Salvatore J. Rossetti, O.P. Res., 950 Grove Ave., 08820. Tel: 732-494-3399; Fax: 732-494-2076.
School—930 Grove Ave., 08820. Tel: 732-549-6234. Felician Sisters 3; Lay Teachers 23; Students 403.
Convent—882 Grove Ave., 08820. Tel: 732-321-1462.

St. Matthew (1952), Rev. Msgr. Seamus F. Brennan; Revs. George A. Farrell; Thomas J. Serafin; Deacons Barry C. Demarest; Eric S. Massimei; Stephen F. Nemeth. In res., Rev. Neil W. Davin, C.P.
Res., 81 Seymour Ave., 08817. Tel: 732-985-5063; Fax: 732-985-9104.
School—Tel: 732-985-6633; Fax: 732-985-7748. Sisters of Mercy 3; Lay Teachers 20; Students 479.

Far Hills, Somerset Co., St. Elizabeth (1906), Rev. Msgr. George M. Brembos.
Res., Box 37, Peapack Rd., 07931. Tel: 908-234-0079; Fax: 908-234-2923.
Mission—Peapack, Somerset Co., St. Brigid, Main St., Peapack, 07977. Tel: 908-234-1265; Fax: 908-234-2923.

Flemington, Hunterdon Co., St. Magdalen de Pazzi (1864), Revs. John J. Barbella; Patrick C. Maccarone; Deacons John H. Purdy; Thaddeus Wislinski; Martin L. Koy; A. Shannon Trimmer.
Res., 105 Mine St., 08822. Tel: 908-782-2922; Fax: 908-782-0952. [CEM]

Fords, Middlesex Co., Our Lady of Peace (1919), Rev. Msgr. Robert J. Zamorski; Rev. Msgr. Joseph R. Brzozowski, Pastor Emeritus; Revs. Michael J. Bihuniak; Frank W. Fellrath; Deacons Joseph S. Petrovich; Salvatore J. Gagliano.
Res., 26 Maple Ave., P.O. Box 69, 08863. Tel: 732-738-7940; Fax: 732-738-3848.
School—Amboy Ave., 08863. Tel: 732-738-7464; Fax: 732-738-0026.
Dominican Sisters of Divine Providence 1; Lay Teachers 24; Students 375.

Great Meadows, Warren Co., SS. Peter and Paul (1921), Very Rev. Ignatius H. Kuziemski.
Res., Rte. 46, Box 156, 07838. Tel: 908-637-4269; Fax: 908-637-6896.

Hackettstown, Warren Co., Assumption of the Blessed Virgin Mary (1864), Rev. David J. Pekola; Rev. Msgr. Stephen A. Bielen, Pastor Emeritus.
Res., 305 High St., P.O. Box 547, 07840-0547. Tel: 908-852-3320; Fax: 908-852-3662.
School—Cook & Liberty Sts., 07840. Tel: 908-852-4791; Fax: 908-852-4180.
Sisters of Christian Charity 2; Lay Teachers 15; Students 370.

Hampton, Hunterdon Co., St. Ann (1859), Revs. William J. Hewitt; Garret J. Fitzgerald; Deacon Joseph J. Foldvary.
Res., 6 Church St., P.O. Box 405, 08827. Tel: 908-537-2221. [CEM]
Station—Glen Gardner, NJ State Hospital for Geriatrics.

Helmetta, Middlesex Co., Holy Trinity (1911) (Polish), Rev. Stanley Jarosz.
Res., 100 Main St., 08828. Tel: 732-521-0172; Fax: 732-521-0824. [CEM]

High Bridge, Hunterdon Co., St. Joseph (1880), Revs. Leonard F.A. Rusay; Richard A. Ewing, Pastor Emeritus; Deacon Charles A. Paolino.
Res., 59 Main St., 08829. Tel: 908-638-6211; Fax: 908-638-5802.

Highland Park, Middlesex Co., St. Paul the Apostle (1912), Rev. Sylvester J. Cronin.
Res., 504 Raritan Ave., 08904. Tel: 732-572-0977; Fax: 732-574-7497.
Convent—20 S. 6th Ave., 08904. Tel: 732-572-2485. Sisters of St. Joseph of Chesnut Hill, PA

Hillsborough, Somerset Co., Mary, Mother of God (1948), Revs. Liam A. Minogue; John M. Banko; Joseph F. Hogan.
Res., 157 S. Triangle Rd., 08876. Tel: 908-874-8220; Fax: 908-874-4183.

Iselin, Middlesex Co., St. Cecelia (1923), Rev. Msgr. James P. Moran; Revs. Daniel A. Gomez; Wayne M. Haddad; Deacon Belardino A. Lupini. In res., Rev. Raymond J. Leonard.
Res., 45 Wilus Way, 08830. Tel: 732-283-2300; Fax: 732-283-3326.
School—Tel: 732-283-2824.
Religious Teachers Filippini 4; Lay Teachers 13; Students 359.
Stations—NJ State Home for Disabled Veterans.; Roosevelt Hospital.

Jamesburg, Middlesex Co., St. James the Less (1878), Revs. Louis F. Stingel; Charles P. Scillieri.
Res., 36 Lincoln Ave., 08831. Tel: 732-521-0100; Fax: 732-521-8287. [CEM]
Station—State Home for Boys, Tel: 732-521-0030.

Kendall Park, Middlesex Co., St. Augustine of Canterbury (1952), Revs. Robert G. Lynam; Robert V. Meyers; Michael T. Kottar; Deacons William A. Beirne, (Retired); Richard McCarron.
Res., 51 Henderson Rd., 08824. Tel: 732-297-3000; Fax: 732-940-1746.
School—45 Henderson Rd., 08824. Tel: 732-297-6042.
Brothers of Sacred Heart 2; Lay Teachers 15; Students 353.

Lambertville, Hunterdon Co., St. John the Evangelist (1843), Revs. Leon J. Kasprzyk; John J. Szczepanik; Deacon Joseph J. Masterson.
Res., 44 Bridge St., 08530. Tel: 609-397-3350; Fax: 609-397-8713. [CEM]
Mission—Stockton, Hunterdon Co., St. Agnes, Main St., Stockton, 08559.

Laurence Harbor, Middlesex Co., St. Lawrence (1943), Rev. Raymond V. Attanasio; Deacon Stephen J. Gajewski.
Res., 109 Laurence Pkwy., 08879. Tel: 732-566-1093; Fax: 732-566-3252.

Manville, Somerset Co., Sacred Heart of Jesus (1919) (Polish), Revs. Peter G. Suhaka; Stanley G. Gromadzki; Hyacinth M. Dabrowski, O.F.M.Cap.
Res., 136 S. Main St., P.O. Box 924, 08835. Tel: 908-725-0072; Fax: 908-685-3029. [CEM]

Christ the King (1948), Very Rev. Daniel Sloan; Deacon Donald J. De Lorenzo.
Res., 211 Louis St., 08835. Tel: 908-231-1330; Fax: 908-231-1645.
School—99 N. 13th Ave., 08835. Tel: 908-526-1339. Lay Teachers 13; Students 300.

Martinsville, Somerset Co., Blessed Sacrament (1968), Rev. Msgr. Eugene Prus; Rev. Zenon A. Bochnak.
Res., 852 Newmans Ln., P.O. Box 563, 08836. Tel: 732-356-4442; Fax: 732-356-5172.

Middlesex, Middlesex Co., Our Lady of Mount Virgin (1943), Revs. Thomas G. Moore; Kenneth R. Kolibas; Deacon John R. Tietjen.
Res., 650 Harris Ave., 08846. Tel: 732-356-2149; Fax: 732-356-4961.
School—610 Harris Ave., 08846. Tel: 732-356-6560; Fax: 732-356-7860.
Sisters Apostles of the Sacred Heart 4; Lay Teachers 13; Students 270.

Milford, Hunterdon Co., St. Edward the Confessor (1944), Rev. Michael E. Crummy; Deacon James W. Hendrix.
Res., 61 Mill St., P.O. Box 522, 08848. Tel: 908-995-4723; Fax: 908-995-9353.

Milltown, Middlesex Co., Our Lady of Lourdes (1921), Revs. Thomas V. Perunilam; Edward A. Czarcinski.
Res., 233 N. Main St., 08850. Tel: 732-828-0011; Fax: 732-828-3133.
School—43 Cleveland Ave., 08850. Tel: 732-828-1951.
Little Servant Sisters of the Immaculate Conception 4; Lay Teachers 8; Students 251.

Monmouth Junction, Middlesex Co., St. Cecilia (1904), Revs. Joseph L. Desmond; Thomas A. Odorizzi.
Office: 10 Kingston Ln., 08852. Tel: 732-329-2893; Fax: 732-329-3866 (call first).
Res., 46 Kingston Ln., 08852. Tel: 732-274-1761.

New Brunswick, Middlesex Co.,

1—St. Peter Apostle, (1829), Very Rev. Joseph M. Curry; Rev. Timothy J. Lambert; Deacons Bernard A. Cribbin; Thaddeus C. Raczkowski. In res., Rev. Joseph G. Celano.
Res., 94 Somerset St., 08901. Tel: 732-545-6820; Fax: 732-545-4069. [CEM]
School—165 Somerset St., 08901. Tel: 732-545-1473; Fax: 732-545-2508.
Sisters 4; Lay Teachers 27; Students 390.
High School—175 Somerset St., 08901. Tel: 732-846-8046; Fax: 732-220-9560.
Sisters 2; Lay Teachers 28; Students 233.

2—St. John the Baptist, (1867) (German), Revs. Joseph B. Szulwach; Anthony Sirianni; Deacon Luis S. Moral. In res., Rev. Thomas F. Ryan.
Res., 29 Abeel St., 08901. Tel: 732-545-5267; Fax: 732-846-6594. [CEM]
Church—Neilson and Carman Sts., 08901.

3—Our Lady of Mt. Carmel, (1977) (Hispanic), Revs. Raymond L. Nacarino; Juan A. Albaladejo.
Res., 86 New St., 08901.
Church—75 Morris St., 08901. Tel: 732-846-5873; Fax: 732-846-5397.

4—St. Joseph, (1924) (Polish), Rev. George J. Korytkowski, O.F.M.Cap. In res., Revs. John F. Salwowski, O.F.M.Cap.; Joseph M. Kubiak, O.F.M.Cap.
Res., 15 Maple St., 08901. Tel: 732-545-2195.

5—Sacred Heart, (1883), Rev. Jerome A. Johnson; Deacon Thaddeus C. Raczkowski.
Res., 56 Throop Ave., 08901. Tel: 732-545-1681; Fax: 732-545-5059.

6—St. Ladislaus, (1904) (Hungarian), Revs. Paul Rotondi, O.F.M.; Capistran L. Polgar, O.F.M.; Stephen L. Galambos, O.F.M.
Res., 215 Somerset St., 08901. Tel: 732-545-1427; Fax: 732-545-8501.

7—St. Mary of Mount Virgin, (1905) (Italian), Rev. Msgr. Francis J. Crupi; Rev. Robert L. Santa Barbara.
Res., 190 Sandford St., 08901. Tel: 732-545-5090; Fax: 732-937-9290.
School—192 Sandford St., 08901. Tel: 732-249-7753.
Lay Teachers 9; Students 176.
Mission—Edison, Middlesex Co., St. Therese of the Infant Jesus, Fox Rd., Edison, 08817.

North Brunswick, Middlesex Co., Our Lady of Peace (1969), Rev. John V. Polyak.
Res., 277 Washington Pl., 08902. Tel: 732-297-9680; Fax: 732-297-1024.

North Plainfield, Somerset Co., St. Joseph (1882), Rev. John J. Casey.
Res., 41 Manning Ave., 07060. Tel: 908-756-3383; Fax: 908-756-1155.
School—101 Westervelt Ave., 07060. Tel: 908-756-9539.
Sisters of Mercy 3; Lay Teachers 14; Students 192.

St. Luke (1965), Rev. John C. Giordano; Deacons Albert C. Parenti; Dann C. Rossi.
Res., 300 Clinton Ave., 07063. Tel: 908-754-8811; Fax: 908-754-0120.

Old Bridge, Middlesex Co., St. Ambrose (1961), Revs. Charles F. Kelly; James W. McGuffey; James W. McLaughlin; Deacons Brian F. McIvor; Charles J. Damian; Andrew J. Strus.
Res., 96 Throckmorton Ln., 08857. Tel: 732-679-5666; Fax: 732-679-0853.
School—Tel: 732-679-4700; Fax: 732-679-6062.
Sisters of St. Joseph (Chestnut Hill) 2; Lay Teachers 30; Students 428.
Convent—94 Throckmorton Ln., 08857. Tel: 732-679-5509.

St. Thomas the Apostle (1921), Rev. Msgr. John B. Szymanski, V.G.; Revs. Edward G. Shaner; Kevin M. Casey, C.P.; Deacons John J. Fitzsimmons; Paul E. Featherman.
Res., One St. Thomas Plaza, 08857. Tel: 732-251-4000; Fax: 732-251-4946.
School—333 Hwy. 18, 08857. Tel: 732-251-4812.
Lay Teachers 22; Students 480.

Most Holy Redeemer (1983), Rev. Henry L. Hemmerling; Deacon Robert T. McGovern.
Res., P.O. Box 325, 08857. Tel: 732-566-9334; Fax: 732-566-2245.

Oxford, Warren Co., St. Rose of Lima (1864), Rev. Francis F. Vaz.
Res., Academy St., P.O. Box 88, 07863. Tel: 908-453-2034; Fax: 908-453-4425. [CEM]

Parlin, Middlesex Co., St. Bernadette (1956), Revs. L. Eugene Schellberg; Kenneth D. Brighenti; Deacon Nicholas J. Thornton.
Res., 20 Villanova Rd., 08859. Tel: 732-721-2772; Fax: 732-727-5188.

Perth Amboy, Middlesex Co.,

1—St. Mary, (1845), Rev. Michael P. Scott; Deacon Basilio D. Perez.
Res., 104 Center St., 08861. Tel: 732-442-0039.

2—St. Stephen, (1892) (Polish), Rev. John P. Stec; Deacon Joseph Kolasa, (Retired). In res., Rev. Jan P. Klich.
Res., 490 State St., 08861. Tel: 732-826-1395; Fax: 732-826-4217. [CEM]

3—Holy Trinity, (1899) (Slovak-Hispanic), Rev. John P. Alvarado.
Res., 474 Penn St., 08861. Tel: 732-826-0439. [CEM]

4—Our Lady of Fatima, (1960) (Hispanic), Revs. Leonard J. Brown, C.M.F.; Benjamin Martinez, C.M.F.; Deacons Angel P. Perez; Herminio Rivera; Daniel Torres.
Res., 380 Smith St., 08861. Tel: 732-442-6634; Fax: 732-826-0958.

5—Our Lady of Hungary, (1902) (Hungarian), Rev. John P. Alvarado, Admin.
Res., 697 Cortlandt St., 08861. Tel: 732-442-0512. [CEM]

6—Most Holy Rosary, (1904) (Italian), Rev. Msgr. Anthony J. Gambino; Deacon Edward Holowienka. In res., Rev. Robert J. Ascolese.
Res., 625 Florida Grove Rd., 08861. Tel: 732-826-2771; Fax: 732-826-0320.

7—Holy Spirit, (1944), Rev. Robert G. Gorman. In res., Rev. George M. Pisanello.
Res., 580 Hazel Ave., 08861. Tel: 732-826-4859; Fax: 732-697-9380.

8—La Asuncion, (1981) (Hispanic), Revs. Oran de Jesus Ramirez, C.SS.R., Admin.; Marco Antonio Caceras, C.SS.R.; Deacon Corpus V. Perez.
Mailing Address: 777 Cortlandt St., P.O. Box 1335, 08862. Tel: 732-826-4991; Fax: 732-826-6951.

9—Our Lady of the Rosary of Fatima, (1981) (Portuguese), Rev. Lauro C. Sedlmayer (Brazil) Admin.
Res., 188 Wayne St., 08861. Tel: 732-826-4350.

Phillipsburg, Warren Co., SS. Philip and James (1861), Rev. Msgr. Michael J. Corona; Revs. Richard M. Rusk; Vincent P. Chen (Taiwan); Deacons John F. Flynn; John T. Sheridan; William C. Vanzino.
Res., 430 S. Main St., 08865-3094. Tel: 908-454-0112; Fax: 908-454-0125. [CEM]
Mission—New Village, Warren Co., St. Christopher.

SS. Peter and Paul (1913) (Slovak). Closed. Records at St. Philip & St. James, Phillipsburg.

Piscataway, Middlesex Co., Our Lady of Fatima (1948), Revs. Herbert J. Stab; Thomas P. Ganley; Roberto D. Coruna (Philippines); Deacons Stanley J. Lorenc; Lawrence P. Reilly.
Res., 501 New Market Rd., 08854. Tel: 732-968-5555; Fax: 732-968-5959.
School—499 New Market Rd., 08854. Tel: 732-968-5017; Fax: 732-968-9259.
Sisters 2; Lay Teachers 15; Students 205.
Convent—50 Van Winkle Pl., 08854. Tel: 732-968-6136. Franciscan Sisters of Allegany

St. Frances Cabrini (1961), Revs. Edgardo D. Abano; Francis E. Grabowski, Pastor Emeritus; Deacon Michael P. Gleason.
Res., 208 Bound Brook Ave., 08854-4097. Tel: 732-885-5313; Fax: 732-885-9031.
School—2300 Cooper St., 08854. Tel: 732-885-1066; Fax: 732-885-5252.
Sisters of Mercy 1; Lay Teachers 16; Students 240.

Pittstown, Hunterdon Co., St. Catherine of Siena (1992). Closed. Mission parish of Immaculate Conception, Clinton.

Plainsboro, Middlesex Co., Queenship of Mary (1982), Very Rev. Edward J. Struzik.
Res., P.O. Box 759, 08536. Tel: 609-799-7511; Fax: 609-799-8904.

Port Murray, Warren Co., St. Theodore (1983), Rev. Albert L. Roca.
Res., P.O. Box 146, 07865. Tel: 908-689-8318.

Port Reading, Middlesex Co., St. Anthony of Padua (1906), Rev. Michael G. Krull; Deacon Joseph V. Szoke. In res., Rev. Peter Phong Vo.
Res., 436 Port Reading Ave., 07064. Tel: 732-634-1403; Fax: 732-602-0119.

Raritan, Somerset Co., St. Ann (1903) (Italian), Very Rev. Blaise R. Baran; Deacons John R. Pacifico; James Hewitt, III.
Res., 45 Anderson St., P.O. Box 86, 08869. Tel: 908-725-1008; Fax: 908-707-1915.
School—29 Second Ave., 08869. Tel: 908-725-7787.
Religious Teachers Filippini 4; Lay Teachers 13; Students 286.

St. Joseph (1912) (Slovak), Rev. Kevin A. Kaminski. In res., Rev. Charles W. Cicerale Tel: 908-253-0630.
Res., 16 E. Somerset St., 08869. Tel: 908-725-0163.

Sayreville, Middlesex Co., Our Lady of Victories (1885), Very Rev. Terrance M. Lawler; Revs. Ronald L. Jandernoa; Jeffrey R. Willingham; Deacon Michael P. Murtha.
Mailing Address: 42 Main St., 08872.
Res., 24 Main St., 08872. Tel: 732-257-0077; Fax: 732-651-1898.
School—36 Main St., 08872. Tel: 732-254-1676; Fax: 732-254-5066.
Sisters of Mercy 1; Lay Teachers 22; Students 480.

St. Stanislaus Kostka (1914), Rev. Leon S. Aniszczyk.
Res., 225 MacArthur Ave., 08872. Tel: 732-254-0212; Fax: 732-390-2989. [CEM]
School—MacArthur Ave., 08872. Tel: 732-254-5819; Fax: 732-257-2903.
Lay Teachers 11; Students 175.

Skillman, Somerset Co., St. Charles Borromeo (1982), Rev. Gregory E. S. Malovetz; Deacon Thomas J. Giacobbe.
Res., 376 Burnt Hill Rd., 08558. Tel: 609-466-0300; Fax: 609-466-0602.

Somerset, Somerset Co., St. Matthias (1962), Revs. Douglas J. Haefner; Timothy A. Christy; Deacon Stephen J. Holzinger, II.
Pastoral Center: 168 J.F. Kennedy Blvd., 08873. Tel: 732-828-1400; Fax: 732-828-0866.
Res., 166 J.F. Kennedy Blvd., 08873.
School—170 J.F. Kennedy Blvd., 08873.
Sisters 3; Lay Teachers 28; Students 589.

Somerville, Somerset Co., Immaculate Conception (1882), Rev. Msgr. J. Nevin Kennedy; Revs. Brian J. Nolan; Richard W. Palumbo; Deacons John B. Ivers; Arnold J. De Marco; Frank J. Quinn.
Res., 35 Mountain Ave., 08876. Tel: 908-725-1112; Fax: 908-725-6269. [CEM]
School—Tel: 908-725-6516; Fax: 908-725-3172.
Sisters 5; Lay Teachers 16; Students 556.
High School—Tel: 908-722-0200; Fax: 908-218-7765.
Sisters 13; Lay Teachers 58; Students 866.
Convent—230 Mountain Ave., 08876. Tel: 908-722-6894. Sisters, Servants of the Immaculate Heart of Mary

South Amboy, Middlesex Co., St. Mary (1864), Rev. Dennis R. Weezorak; Rev. Msgr. John L. Gerety, Pastor Emeritus; Deacon Stephen N. Laikowski.
Res., 256 Augusta St., 08879. Tel: 732-721-0179. [CEM]
School—Second St., 08879.
Sisters of Mercy 2; Lay Teachers 17; Students 234.

Sacred Heart (1895) (Polish), Revs. Joseph V. Romanoski; Joseph A. Krajewski; William M. Turowski (NY); Deacon Robert J. Klein.
Res., 531 Washington Ave., 08879. Tel: 732-721-0040; Fax: 732-721-4448. [CEM]
School—Tel: 732-721-0834; Fax: 732-316-0326.
Felician Sisters 1; Lay Teachers 14; Students 240.

South Bound Brook, Somerset Co., Our Lady of Mercy (1949), Rev. Daniel J. Herlihy.
Res., 122 High St., 08880. Tel: 732-356-1037; Fax: 732-356-1318.

South Plainfield, Middlesex Co., Sacred Heart (1906), Very Rev. Michael A. McGuire; Revs. Joseph C. Kornoski; Anthony M. Dandry; Deacon Joseph J. Stanczak.
Res., 149 S. Plainfield Ave., 07080. Tel: 908-756-0633; Fax: 908-757-5655. [CEM]
School—Tel: 908-756-0632.
Sisters 2; Lay Teachers 22; Students 373.

Our Lady of Czestochowa (1943) (Polish), Rev. John M. Skwara.
Mailing Address: P.O. Box 141, South Plainfield, 07080.
Res., 807 Hamilton Blvd., 07080. Tel: 908-756-1333.

South River, Middlesex Co., St. Mary of Ostrabrama (1903) (Polish), Revs. Robert L. Weil; J. Maciej Melaniuk.
Res., 30 Jackson St., 08882. Tel: 732-254-2220; Fax: 732-651-8182. [CEM]
School—22 Holmes Ave., 08882.
Bernardine Sisters 3; Lay Teachers 10; Students 178.

St. Stephen Protomartyr (1907) (Hungarian), Rev. Glenn J. Comandini.
Res., 20 William St., 08882. Tel: 732-257-0100; Fax: 732-257-4646.

Corpus Christi (1944), Revs. Kevin P. Duggan; August Neumann, Pastor Emeritus. In res., Rev. Maurice T. Carlton.
Res., 100 James St., 08882. Tel: 732-254-1800; Fax: 732-254-8063.
School—80 David St., 08882. Tel: 732-257-5200; Fax: 732-257-6390.
Lay Teachers 11; Students 175.

Spotswood, Middlesex Co., Immaculate Conception (1946), Revs. Harold L. Hirsch; Kenneth R. Murphy; Edward R. Flanagan; Deacon John H. McGuire.
Res., 18 South St., 08884. Tel: 732-251-3110; Fax: 732-251-2407.
School—23 Manalapan Rd., 08884. Tel: 732-251-3090; Fax: 732-251-8270.
Felician Sisters 2; Lay Teachers 18; Students 311.
Convent—Tel: 732-251-3446.

Three Bridges, Hunterdon Co., St. Elizabeth Ann Seton (1984), Rev. A. Gregory Uhrig; Deacon Martin B. Mulroy.
Res., 7 Forest Hill Dr., 08887. Tel: 908-782-1475; Fax: 908-782-6230.

Warren, Somerset Co., Our Lady of the Mount (1911), Rev. Msgr. William Benwell; Rev. Joseph M. Holup; Deacons Walter S. Maksimik; Thomas Sicola. In res., Rev. Robert W. Medley.
Res., 167 Mount Bethel Rd., 07059. Tel: 908-647-1075; Fax: 908-647-7885.

Washington, Warren Co., St. Joseph (1872), Rev. Michael A. Kochon.
Res., 200 W. Carlton Ave., 07882. Tel: 908-689-0058; Fax: 908-689-3436. [CEM]

Watchung, Somerset Co., St. Mary-Stony Hill (1847), Rev. Thomas J. Dzurenda; Deacons Henry F. Albert; Arthur J. Wise.
Res., 225 Mountain Blvd., 07060. Tel: 908-756-6524; Fax: 908-756-2111. [CEM]

Whitehouse Station, Hunterdon Co., Our Lady of Lourdes (1923), Revs. Florian J. Gall; John N. Fell; Deacons Samuel J. Damiano; John H. Hanna.
Res., 390 Rte. 523, 08889. Tel: 908-534-2319; Fax: 908-534-5670.

Woodbridge, Middlesex Co., St. James (1860), Rev. Msgr. Michael J. Cashman; Rev. Sean W. Kenney; Deacon Carl E. Psota.
Res., 145 Grove St., 07095. Tel: 732-634-0500; Fax: 732-602-1487. [CEM]
School—341 Amboy Ave., 07095. Tel: 732-634-2090.
Lay Teachers 15; Students 320.
Convent—Tel: 732-634-0176.
Sisters of Mercy 2.

Our Lady of Mt. Carmel (1921) (Hungarian), Revs. Vincent C. Cornejo; Michael M. Vincze.
Res., 267 Smith St., 07095. Tel: 732-634-1438; Fax: 732-634-1438 (call first).

Chaplains of Public Institutions

Annandale. *Mountainview Youth Correctional Facility* 08801. Tel: 732-741-6208. Rev. Robert G. Hoffman, Chap.

Avenel. *Woodbridge State School.* Attended by St. Andrew, the Apostle.

Belle Mead. *Carrier Clinic.* Rev. Norman R. St. John, S.V.D.

Belvidere. *Warren Correctional Center.* Attended by St. Patrick, Belvidere.

Clinton. *Edna Mahan Correctional Facility for Women.* Attended by Immaculate Conception, Clinton. Tel: 908-735-7319.

Hunterdon State School. Attended by Immaculate Conception. Very Rev. Andrew L. Szaroleta, Chap.

Edison. *John F. Kennedy Medical Center.* Chaplains: Revs. Laurence H. Smith; Anthonisamy Neethinathan.

Flemington. *Hunterdon Medical Center.* Attended by St. Magdalen de Pazzi.

Glen Gardner. *N.J. State Hospital for Geriatrics.* Attended by St. Ann, Hampton.

Hackettstown. *Hackettstown Community Hospital.* Attended by Assumption of the Blessed Virgin Mary.

Jamesburg. *N.J. State Training School for Boys.* Attended by St. James the Less.

Lyons. *U.S. Veterans Medical Center.* Revs. George F. Kelly, C.Ss.R.; William Warman (BAL); Joseph C. Chacko.

Menlo Park. *Roosevelt State Hospital.* Attended by St. Cecelia, Iselin.

New Brunswick. *Robert Wood Johnson University Hospital.* Revs. Anthony Sirianni; Joseph M. Kubiak, O.F.M.Cap.

North Brunswick. *Middlesex County Adult Detention Center.* Attended by Our Lady of Peace.

Old Bridge. *Old Bridge Regional Hospital.* Attended by St. Ambrose.

Perth Amboy. *Raritan Bay Medical Center* Tel: 732-826-2771. Revs. Robert J. Ascolese; John D. Murphy Tel: 732-826-0439.

Phillipsburg. *Warren Hospital* Tel: 908-454-0112. Rev. Vincent P. Chen (Taiwan).

Rahway. *East Jersey State Prison.* Attended from St. Andrew Church, Avenel. Tel: 732-634-4355.

Skillman. *NJ State Neuropsychiatric Institute.* Attended by St. Charles Borromeo.

Somerville. *Somerset Medical Center* Tel: 908-526-2394. Rev. Sean G. Winters.

South Amboy. *South Amboy Memorial Hospital.* Attended by St. Mary and Sacred Heart.

On Duty Outside the Diocese:
Reverend Fathers—
Alvarez, Anthony M., Society of Jesus Christ the Priest, Murcia, Spain
Carpena, Octavio R., Society of Jesus Christ the Priest, Murcia, Spain
Escribano, Peter E., Society of Jesus Christ the Priest, Murcia, Spain
Gordon, John B., Society of St. James the Apostle,Inc., Ecuador
Littleton, Gregory J., Diocese of Charlotte, NC
Marin, John L., Diocese of Arlington, VA
McCord, Kent G., USMC, Guam
Moya, Peter O., Society of Jesus Christ the Priest Murcia, Spain
Muccilli, Sebastian L., 618 Third St., Lake Park, FL 33403
Oterino, Francis L., Society of Jesus Christ the Priest, Ecuador
Pepel, Clement, Diocese of Phoenix, AZ
Ruiz, Faustino C., Society of Jesus Christ the Priest, Chili
Scarcella, Philip J., 6300 Woodbend Dr., Apt. N, Charlotte, NC 28212-2039
Venditti, J. Michael, Eparchy of Passaic, NJ

Retired:
Reverend Monsignors—
Brzozowski, Joseph R.
Endebrock, Donald M.
Gerety, John L.
Haughney, William J.
Kelly, J. Morgan
Krysztofik, Joseph M.
Torney, John R., P.A.
Turtora, Dominic A.

Reverend Fathers—
Abramowicz, Richard B.
Avery, Raymond
Banach, Joseph S.
Bielen, Stephen A.
Cashioli, Lawrence J.
Egierd, Henry A.
Ewing, Richard A.
Gonsorcik, Joseph S.
Grabowski, Francis E.
Kearns, Edward A.
Kramarz, Anthony M.
Laplante, Louis A.
Nebus, Vincent J.
Nester, Edward J.
Neumann, August
Przechacki, Casimir J.
Roos, William A.
Szulecki, Raymond L.
Thul, Joseph T.
Vielgus, Thaddeus A.
Vincze, Michael A.

Permanent Deacons:
Albert, Henry F.
Alexander, Russell C., (Retired)
Anderson, Paul L.
Bauer, William R.
Beirne, William A., (Retired)
Bell, James S.
Bolash, George L.
Cammarano, Frank J.
Clementi, Leo F.
Cline, Patrick J., Brooklyn
Coleman, George D.
Cribbin, Bernard A.
Czekaj, John R.
Daley, James M., (Retired)
Damian, Charles J.
Damiano, Samuel J.
De Blasio, Anthony A., On Leave
De Lorenzo, Donald J.
De Marco, Arnold J.
Demarest, Barry C.
Dumschat, John F.
Featherman, Paul E.
Fitzsimmons, John J.
Flynn, John T.
Foldvary, Joseph J.
Forrestall, Michael J.
Gagliano, Salvatore J.
Gajewski, Stephen J., Sr.
Gellentien, Robert P.
Gilheany, Thomas J., Newark
Gleason, Michael P.
Gostkowski, Anthony J.
Hally, Luke J.
Hanna, John H.
Heissenbuttel, Thomas A., On Leave
Hendrix, James W.
Hewitt, James, III
Holowienka, Edward
Holzinger, Stephen J., II
Ivers, John B.
Janthor, William G.
Kaseta, Richard R.
Klein, Robert J.
Kolasa, Joseph T., (Retired)
Koy, Martin L.
La Police, George D.
Laikowski, Stephen N.
Licameli, Paul G.
Livingston, Joel R.
Lorenc, Stanley J.
Lupini, Belardino A., M.D.
Maksimik, Walter S.
Marano, Francis J., (Retired)
Massimei, Eric S.
Masterson, Joseph J.
Maurer, Joseph S., (Retired)
McCarron, Richard
McGovern, Robert T.
McGrath, James G., On Leave
McGreevy, Robert A., On Leave
McGuire, John H.
McIvor, Brian F.
McShane, John P.
Monahan, John T.
Moral, Luis S.
Morend, Michel G., Newark
Moscinski, Joseph C.
Mulroy, Martin B., Brooklyn
Murtha, Michael P.
Nardi, Samuel, On Leave
Nemeth, Stephen F.
O'Keefe, Joseph E.
Pacifico, John R.
Page, Warren C., Syracuse
Paolino, Charles
Parenti, Albert C.
Perez, Angel P.
Perez, Basilio A., Dominican Republic
Perez, Corpus V.
Petrovich, Joseph S.
Psota, Carl E.
Purdy, John H., II
Quinn, Frank J.
Raczkowski, Thaddeus C.
Ragucci, Joseph D.
Reilly, Lawrence P.
Rivera, Herminio
Rooney, William R., (Retired)
Rossi, Dann P.
Sheridan, John T.
Sicola, Thomas
Sims, Gerard C.
Smoyak, Cornelius S.
Stanczak, Joseph J.
Strus, Andrew J.
Suswal, Carl S., (Retired)
Szoke, Joseph V.
Thornton, Nicholas J.
Tietjen, John R.
Torres, Daniel
Trimmer, A. Shannon
Vanzino, William C.
Vivona, Joseph A.
Webster, Dennis K.
Wise, Arthur J.
Wislinski, Thaddeus

INSTITUTIONS LOCATED IN THE DIOCESE

[A] HIGH SCHOOLS, DIOCESAN

EDISON. *Bishop Ahr High School*, One Tingley Ln., 08820. Tel: 732-549-1108. Sr. Donna Marie Trukowski, C.S.S.F., Prin.; Rev. Raymond J. Leonard, Chap. Felician Sisters 2; Lay Teachers 62; Students 1,005.

SOUTH AMBOY. *St. Mary Regional High School*, 310 Augusta St., 08879. Tel: 732-721-0748. John H. Gloss, Jr., Prin. Chaplains: Revs. Ronald J. Jandernoa; Jeffrey Willingham. Sisters 7; Lay Teachers 34; Students 540.

[B] HIGH SCHOOLS, PRIVATE

METUCHEN. *St. Joseph High School*, 145 Plainfield Ave., 08840-1099. Tel: 732-549-7600; Fax: 732-549-0664. Bros. Joseph Holthaus, S.C., Pres.; Dennis Wermert, S.C., Prin.; Peter Murphy, S.C., Chap. Brothers of the Sacred Heart 10; Lay Teachers 45; Boys 770.

NEW BRUNSWICK. *Shoreless Lake School*, 75 Morris St., 08901. Tel: 732-725-4879. Rev. Lope Pascual (Spain), Headmaster. Priests 5; Lay Teachers 11; Students 18.

WATCHUNG. *Mount St. Mary Academy*, 07060. Tel: 908-757-0108; Fax: 908-756-7528. Sr. M. Eloise Claire, R.S.M., Dir.; Rev. William T. Morris (NEW), Chap. Day school for girls. College preparatory only. Sisters of Mercy 15; Lay Teachers 38; Girls 365.

[C] INTER-PAROCHIAL ELEMENTARY SCHOOLS

BOUND BROOK. *Holy Family Academy*, St. Joseph Campus, 120 E. Second St., 08805. Tel: 732-356-1151. Mrs. Donna Kanowitz, Prin.

St. Mary Campus, 08805. Sr. Maryann Ronneburger, O.P., Prin., 333 W. Second St., 08805. Tel: 732-469-0055. Sisters 4; Students 417.

PERTH AMBOY. *Holy Spirit Campus*. (Grades PreK-4), Brace & Carlock Aves., 08861. Tel: 732-826-5747.

Perth Amboy Catholic School, 100 Fayette St., P.O. Box 651, 08862. Tel: 732-442-9533. Marie G. Acciani, Admin. Sisters 12; Students 690.

St. Mary Campus. (Grades 5-8), 351 Mechanic St., 08861. Tel: 732-442-1713.

St. Stephen Campus. (Grades K-4), 500 State St., 08861. Tel: 732-826-1598.

PHILLIPSBURG. *All Saints Regional School*, 137 Roseberry St., 08865. Tel: 908-859-1244; Fax: 908-859-1202. Mr. James A. Duris, Prin. Sisters 4; Lay Teachers 19; Students 407.

[D] SPECIAL SCHOOLS, PRIVATE

WATCHUNG. *McAuley School for Exceptional Children*, 1633 U.S. Hwy. 22, 07060. Tel: 908-754-4114. Sr. Lee Ann Amico, R.S.M., Dir. Students 38.

[E] CATHOLIC CHARITIES

BRIDGEWATER. *Family Service Office*, 540-550 U.S. Rte. 22, 08807. Tel: 908-772-1881. Mary Grace Billek, M.S.W., Prog. Dir.

Somerset County Services, 540-550 U.S. Rte. 22, 08807. Tel: 908-772-1881. Suzanne Siveris, L.C.S.W., Area Dir.

EAST BRUNSWICK. *Catholic Charities Central Office*, 288 Rues Ln., 08816. Tel: 732-257-6677; Fax: 732-651-2685. Sr. Florence Edward Kearney, D.C., M.A., Exec. Dir.; Michael Leszczuk, L.C.S.W., Assoc. Exec. Dir.; Mary E. Davey, L.C.S.W., Asst. Exec. Dir.; Marianne Majewski, L.C.S.W., Asst. Exec. Dir.

Mental Health Center, 288 Rues Ln., 08816. Tel: 732-257-6100; Fax: 732-257-6929. Mary Grace Billek, M.S.W., Admin.

EDISON. *Family Service Office*, 26 Safran Ave., 08863. Tel: 732-738-1323. Nelida Aranciba, Multi-Prog. Dir.

Middlesex County Office, 26 Safran Ave., 08837. Tel: 732-738-1323; Fax: 732-738-3896. Marilyn Wightman, M.A., Dir. Shelter Svcs.

FLEMINGTON. *Hunterdon County Services*, 6 Park Ave., 08822. Tel: 908-782-7905. Michael Gassaway, M.S.W., Dir.

MANVILLE. *Child Care Service Center*, 210 W. Camplain Rd., 08835. Tel: 908-725-1912. Linda Barood, Prog. Dir.

MILFORD. *Family Service Office*, 69 Water St., 08848. Tel: 908-782-7905. Michael Gassaway, Multi-Prog. Dir.

PERTH AMBOY. *Family Service Office*, 271 Smith St., 08861. Tel: 732-826-9160; Fax: 732-826-8342. Lu Ann Dias, L.C.S.W., Prog. Dir.

PHILLIPSBURG. *Family Service Office*, 700 Sayre Ave., 08865. Tel: 908-454-2074. Connie Citro.

Social Service Center, 309 S. Main St., 08865. Tel: 908-454-7986. Sr. M. Michaelita Popovice, R.S.M., Prog. Dir.

Warren County Office, 700 Sayre Ave., 08865. Tel: 908-454-2074. Joan Lorah, Service Area Dir.

WOODBRIDGE. *Social Service Center*, Bunns Ln., 07095. Tel: 732-738-1323. Suzanne Siverio, Dir. Youth Svc.

[F] GENERAL HOSPITALS

NEW BRUNSWICK. *St. Peter's Medical Center*, 254 Easton Ave., 08901. Tel: 732-745-8600; Fax: 732-745-9888
For a complete listing, refer to the Hospitals section.

[G] HOMES FOR AGED

NORTH PLAINFIELD. *Villa Maria Sanitarium*, 641 Somerset St., 07060-4909. Tel: 908-757-3050; Fax: 908-754-4939
For a complete listing, refer to the Special Care Facilities section.

SOMERSET. *McCarrick Care Center*, 15 Dellwood Ln., 08873. Tel: 732-545-4200
For a complete listing, refer to the Special Care Facilities section.

WOODBRIDGE. *St. Joseph Assisted Living Residence*, One St. Joseph Terr., 07095. Tel: 732-634-0004
For a complete listing, refer to the Special Care Facilities section.

[H] MONASTERIES AND RESIDENCES FOR PRIESTS AND BROTHERS

METUCHEN. *Brothers of the Sacred Heart*, 145 Plainfield Ave., 08840. Tel: 732-548-2292. Bro. Paul Joseph, S.C., Supr. Brothers 14.

Libermann House, 197 Middlesex Ave., 08840. Tel: 732-549-7598. Revs. Laurence H.F. Smith; Anthonysami Necthi-nathan.

ASBURY. *Lanteri House*, 668 Mountain View Rd., 08802. Tel: 908-689-5242. Revs. John Lyons, O.M.V.; Andrew Huhtanen, O.M.V.

NEW BRUNSWICK. *De Porres House*, 29 Mine St., 08901. Tel: 732-545-6663. Revs. Ronald A. Stanley, O.P.; Kieran Fergus, O.P.

NEW VILLAGE. *Society of Jesus Christ the Priest*, 70 Edison Rd., 08886. Tel: 908-213-1447. Rev. Lope Pascual, Dir.

PLAINSBORO. *Vincentian Residence*, 65 Mapleton Rd., Box 807, 08536-0807. Tel: 609-452-2144. Revs. Charles P. Strollo, C.M., Supr. & Dir.; Donald L. Doyle, C.M.; Walter F. Graham, C.M.; Charles A. Wolbang, C.M.; Charles F. Krieg, C.M.; Joseph P. McClain, C.M.; John G. Nugent, C.M.; Bros. Andrew Davis, C.M.; Frank Mallaghan, C.M.

RARITAN. *Clairvaux House*, 52 W. Somerset St., 08869. Tel: 908-526-6232. Revs. Lope Pascual; Charles V. Prats.

SOMERSET. *Consolata Society for Foreign Missions*, Provincial Headquarters, 2301 Rt. 27, P.O. Box 5550, 08875. Tel: 732-297-9191; Fax: 732-940-3121. Very Rev. Anthony Bellagamba, I.M.C., Prov. Supr.; Revs. Ivan Callone, I.M.C.; Charles Bonelli, I.M.C.; Robert Viscardi, I.M.C.; Jose Salgueiro da Costa, I.M.C.; Aventino Oliveira, I.M.C.; George J. Hickey, I.M.C.; Mario Lacchin, I.M.C.; Vincenzo Salemi, I.M.C.; Peter Mongiano, I.M.C.; Alphonsus Murariri Karinki, I.M.C.; Bro. Mario Petrino, I.M.C.

Maria Regina Residence, 5 Dellwood Ln., 08873. Tel: 732-828-6800. Rev. Msgr. John R. Torney; Rev. Msgr.

Dominic A. Turtora; Revs. Raymond Avery; Edward J. Nester; Francis E. Grabowski; Vincent T. Calderwood. Retirement home for Diocesan priests.

SOUTH RIVER. *Passionist Provincial Office*, 80 David St., 08882. Tel: 732-257-7177; Fax: 732-257-0042. Very Rev. Robert Joerger, C.P., Provincial Staff.
Consultors: Revs. Lucian Clark, C.P.; Paul Ruttle, C.P.; Richard Burke, C.P.; Terence Kristofak, C.P.; Victor Hoagland, C.P.; Paul Fagan, C.P.
Other Staff: Rev. Ambrose Cashman, C.P.; Bro. Jerome Cowan, C.P. Priests 9; Brothers 1. Rev. James A. Schiffer, Military Chap., USAF, PSC Box 826, Randolph Air Foce Base, TX, 78148.
Religious Service Outside the Province: Bro. Conrad Federspiel, C.P.
67 Lewis St., Toronto, Canada, M4M 2H2. Revs. Stephen Dunn, C.P.; John M. Lee, C.P., Holy Cross Center, R.R. 1, Port Burwell, Ontario, Canada, N0J 1T0. Revs. Gabriele Cingolani, C.P.; Paul Cusack, C.P.; John M. Lee, C.P.; Luigi Malorzo, C.P., 10 Red Maple Ct., Willowdale, Ontario, Canada, M2K 2T3.
Religious of the Province in Residences Not Listed Elsewhere: Rev. Michael Brennan, C.P., Mercy Medical Center, P.O. Box 6009, Redding, CA, 90099. Rev. Kevin Casey, C.P., St. Thomas the Apostle, One St. Thomas Plaza, Old Bridge, 08857. Rev. Neil W. Davin, C.P., St. Mathew's Rectory, 81 Seymour Ave., Edison, 08817. Rev. Norman Demeck, C.P., Georgian Institution, 391-D Picardy Court, Lakewood, 08701. Rev. Gerald Hynes, C.P., St. Ursula Rectory, 8801 Harford Rd., Baltimore, MD, 21234. Bro. Augustine Paul Lowe, C.P. (ORL), P.O. Box 1800, Orlando, FL, 32802-1800. Revs. Benedict Mawn, C.P.; Wilfred Scanlon, C.P., P.O. Box 946, Londonderry, NH, 03053. Rev. Gerard A. Orlando, C.P., St. Patrick Home, 66 Van Cortlandt Park, Bronx, NY, 10463. Rev. Theodore Vitali, C.P., 5859 Nottingham St., Saint Louis, MO, 63109. Rev. James McHugh, C.P., Military Chap., Dugway Proving Ground, 649B Pinyon Dr., Dugway, UT, 84022. 204 N. Church St., Dublin, GA, 31021. Rev. Salvatore Riccardi, C.P., Church of the Annunciation, 470 W. Chester Ave., Crestwood, NY, 10707. Rev. Paul Vaeth, C.P., P.O. Box 2605, Greenville, NC, 27836. Rev. Conan Conaboy, C.P., St. Joseph's Parish, 312 Davis St., Scranton, PA, 18505. Rev. Emmanuel Gordon, C.P., All Saints Church, 22824 Second St., Hayward, CA, 94541. Rev. Carrol Thorne, C.P., 316 N. 6th St., Apt. 101, Leavenworth, KS, 66048. Rev. Thomas Berry, C.P., 4301-A Four Farms Rd., Greensboro, NC, 27410.

[I] CONVENTS AND RESIDENCES FOR SISTERS

METUCHEN. *St. Francis R.C.I.A. Residence*, 44 Elm Ave., 08840.

BOUND BROOK. *Sisters of Jesus Our Hope*, 514 Church St., 08805. Tel: 732-271-5777. Sr. Julia Jamink, Supr. Sisters 5.

CARTERET. *Sisters of Jesus Our Hope*, 55 High St., 07008. Tel: 732-541-4678. Sr. Carlotta LaRocca. Sisters 5.

EAST BRUNSWICK. *DePaul House*, 528 Ryders Ln., 08816. Tel: 732-238-3638. Sisters 5.

EDISON. *St. Thomas Aquinas Convent*, 15 Wren Ct., 08820. Tel: 732-321-0137. Sisters 3.

FLEMINGTON. *The Carmel of Mary Immaculate and St. Mary Magdalen*, Harmony School Rd., P.O. Box 785, 08822. Mother Anne of Christ, O.C.D.; Rev. Sebastian Kaithackal, C.M.I., Chap. Nuns professed with solemn vows 11.

HACKETTSTOWN. *Villa Madonna*. Retirement Home, 1686 Rte. 517, 07840. Tel: 908-852-4551. Daughters of Divine Charity. Sisters 32.

HAMPTON. *Sisters of Jesus Our Hope*, 32 Main St., 08827. Tel: 908-537-6583. Sr. Claire Marie Lessard. Sisters 6.

NEW BRUNSWICK. *Sisters of St. Joseph of Peace*, 61 Jefferson Ave., 08901. Tel: 732-249-5644. Sr. Joanne Rusch, C.S.J.P. Sisters 3.

NORTH PLAINFIELD. *Congregation of the Holy Infancy of Jesus Regional House*, 641 Somerset St., 07060-4909. Tel: 908-757-3050; Fax: 908-754-9190.
Regional House for Congregation of the Servants of the Holy Child of Jesus. Sr. M. Dominic Ritter, O.S.F., Regl. Supr.; Rev. Severin Dietrich, O.F.M.Conv., Chap., Tel: 908-756-4186; 757-3050. Sisters 35.
St. Francis Convent, 450 Grove St., 07060-3606. Tel: 908-769-6498; 757-3050; Fax: 908-754-9190. Sr. Dominic Ritter, O.S.F., Regl. Supr. Sisters 4.

PISCATAWAY. *Divine Providence Convent*, 137 Metlars Ln., 08854. Tel: 732-572-3138. Sr. Maria Michele Armato, O.P., Supr. Sisters 4.

SKILLMAN. *Religious of the Sacred Heart*, 54 Robin Dr., 08558. Tel: 609-924-0180. Sr. Barbara Cooper, R.S.C.J.

SOMERSET. *St. Elizabeth Convent*, 13 Renfro Rd., 08873. Tel: 732-247-3697. Sr. M. Carista, O.S.F., Supr. Sisters 4.

SOUTH AMBOY. *Sacred Heart Convent*, P.O. Box 3005, 08879-3005. Tel: 908-727-2094. Sr. M. Anastasia, O.S.F., Supr. Sisters 5.

WASHINGTON. *Handmaids of Mary Immaculate*, Mountain View Rd., 07882. Tel: 908-689-7330. Sr. Mary Joseph Brech, A.M.I., Supr. Sisters 8.

WATCHUNG. *McAuley Hall Inc.*, Health Care Center, 1633 U.S. Hwy 22, 07060. Tel: 908-754-3663; Fax: 908-754-3502. Sr. Irene Gormley, R.S.M.; Revs. Edward Costello, O.F.M.Conv.; Otto Fouser, O.F.M.Conv. Retired Sisters 60.
Mount St. Mary, 1645 U.S. Hwy. 22 W., 07060-6587. Tel: 908-756-5348. Sisters of Mercy of the Americas, Regional Community of New Jersey. Sr. Diane Szubrowski, R.S.M., Pres., Regl. Com.; Rev. Edward M. Edwards, O.S.M., Chap. Professed Sisters 325.
Mt. St. Mary House of Prayer, 1651 U.S. Hwy. 22, 07060. Tel: 908-753-2091. Sr. Theresina Flannery, R.S.M., Supr. Sisters 2.

WOODBRIDGE. *St. Joseph Convent*, 184 Amboy Ave., 07095. Tel: 732-634-0807. Sr. Mary Lucy, L.S.I.C., Supr. Sisters 8.

[J] RETREAT HOUSES

BELVIDERE. *Sacred Heart Renewal Center*, P.O. Box 68, 07823. Tel: 908-475-4694. Bro. Thomas Woods, S.C., Dir. Brothers 4.

FLEMINGTON. *Our Lady of Providence*, 31 Britton Dr., 08822. Tel: 908-782-4495. Little Sisters of the Poor. Sr. Christine Marie de St. Joseph, L.S.P., Dir.

HIGHLAND PARK. *Cenacle Retreat House*, (Attn. Cenacle) 411 River Rd., 08904-1999. Tel: 732-249-8100; Fax: 732-249-8101. Sr. Barbara Whittemore. Sisters 6.

LITTLE YORK. *Bethany Ridge*, P.O. Box 241, 08834. Tel: 908-995-9758; Fax: 908-995-7299. Rev. Mark J. Dolak, Dir. Spirituality Center for Priests.

PERTH AMBOY. *Emmaus House*, 101 Center St., 08861. Tel: 732-442-7688. Sr. Susan McGrath, S.M.G., Dir. Sisters 2.

PLAINSBORO. *Vincentian Renewal Center*, 75 Mapleton Rd., P.O. Box 757, 08536. Tel: 609-520-9626; Fax: 609-452-2851. Revs. Charles P. Strollo, C.M., Dir.; Thomas D. Butler, C.M.; Charles F. Krieg, C.M.; Sr. Mary Francis Martin, D.C.

[K] SHRINES AND PUBLIC ORATORIES

BERNARDSVILLE. *Sacred Heart Chapel*. (Chapel of Convenience), 111 Claremont Rd., 07924; Fax: 766-1185. Rev. Chester H. Carina, Pastor.

RARITAN. *Shrine Chapel of the Blessed Sacrament*, 50 W. Somerset St., 08869. Tel: 908-722-1489. Rev. Charles V. Prats, Rector.

WASHINGTON. *Shrine of the Immaculate Heart of Mary*, Mountain View Rd., P.O. Box 976, 07882. Tel: 908-689-1700.

[L] PUBLIC ASSOCIATIONS OF THE FAITHFUL

BOUND BROOK. *Sisters of Jesus Our Hope*, 514 Church St., 08805. Sr. Julia Jamink, Supr. Sisters 15.

PHILLIPSBURG. *The Anawim Community*, 156 Broad St., 08865. Tel: 908-859-2049. Revs. Francis J. Marino, S.M. (BO), Dir.; Charles A. Sabella; Richard M. Rusk; Richard W. Palumbo.

PISCATAWAY. *Dominican Sisters of Divine Providence*, Divine Providence Convent, 137 Metlars Ln., 08854. Sr. Maria Michele Armato, O.P., Supr. Sisters 4.

WASHINGTON. *Handmaids of Mary Immaculate*, Holy House Convent, Mountain View Rd., 07882. Sr. Mary Joseph Brech, A.M.I., Supr. Sisters 8.

[M] CAMPUS MINISTRY

NEW BRUNSWICK. *Catholic Center at Rutgers University*, 17 Mine St., 08901. Tel: 732-545-6663; Fax: 732-545-3495. Chaplains: Revs. Ronald A. Stanley, O.P.; Kieran Fergus, O.P.; Joseph G. Celano; Sr. Jeanne Goyette, O.P., Pastoral Assoc.

[N] MISCELLANEOUS LISTINGS

METUCHEN. *The Catholic Lawyers Guild of the Diocese of Metuchen, Inc.*, 407 Main St., 08840. Rev. Msgr. Michael J. Alliegro, Moderator.
The Foundation for Catholic Education, P.O. Box 191, 08840. Most Rev. Vincent D. Breen, D.D., Pres.
The Fund for the Future, Inc., P.O. Box 191, 08840. Most Rev. Vincent D. Breen, Pres.
The Priestly Education Fund, Inc., P.O. Box 191, 08840. Most Rev. Vincent D. Breen, Pres.

EAST BRUNSWICK. *Community House at St. Thomas*, 288 Rues Ln., 08816. Tel: 732-257-6677; Fax: 732-651-2685. Mary E. Davey.
Metuchen Community Services Corporation, 288 Rues Ln., 08816. Tel: 732-257-6677; Fax: 732-651-2685. Michael Leszczuk, L.C.S.W.

EDISON. *The Ozanam Shelter for Families and Single Women*, 89 Truman Dr., 08817. Tel: 732-985-0327; Fax: 732-985-2449. Carmen Fernandez, Admin.
St. Paul and Media Center, Wick Plaza, 561 Rte. 1 S., 08817. Tel: 732-572-1200.

LAMBERTVILLE. *The Jesus School*, Church of St. John the Evangelist, 44 Bridge St., 08530. Tel: 609-397-0593. Sr. Marie Conaughton, Dir. Students 27.

NEW BRUNSWICK. *Catholic Charities Ozanam Men's Shelter*, 12 Neilson St., 08901. Tel: 732-745-5194; Fax: 732-545-0239. Wesley R. Moore, Prog. Dir.
St. John of God Community Health Center, 24 Abeel St., 08901. Tel: 732-745-9800. Steven J. Levin, M.D., Medical Dir.; Sharon Oshatz, M.T. (A.S.C.P.), Dir.

PEAPACK. *Everitt Academy*, Main St., P.O. Box 33, 07977. Tel: 908-234-1524; Fax: 908-234-2923. Rev. Msgr. George M. Brembos; Sr. Madeline Sarli, S.S.J., Dir.

PERTH AMBOY. *Nazareth House*, 156 Wayne St., 08861. Tel: 732-324-0437. Sabrina Myers, Program Dir.

PHILLIPSBURG. *St. Peter and Paul House*, 702 Sayre Ave., 08865. Tel: 908-454-0912. Dominic Romero, Coord.

SOMERSET. *Mission International, Inc.*, 2301 Hwy. 27, 08873. Tel: 732-297-9191; Fax: 732-940-3121. Rev. Charles Bonelli, I.M.C., Dir.

WASHINGTON. *Blue Army of Our Lady of Fatima, U.S.A., Inc.*, P.O. Box 976, 07882. Tel: 908-689-1700.

WATCHUNG. *McAuley Hall Foundation, Inc.*, 1633 U.S. Hwy. 22, 07060.

WOODBRIDGE. *Mt. Carmel Home Nursing Service*, 184 Amboy Ave., 07095. Tel: 732-634-0807. Sr. M. Lucy, L.S.I.C., Dir.

RELIGIOUS INSTITUTES OF MEN REPRESENTED IN THE DIOCESE

For further details refer to the corresponding bracketed number in the Religious Institutes of Men or Women section.

[1100]—*Brothers of the Sacred Heart*.—S.C.
[0470]—*The Capuchin Friars*.—O.F.M.Cap.
[0360]—*Claretian Missionaries*. (Eastern Prov.).—C.M.F.
[1330]—*Congregation of the Mission*.—C.M.
[1000]—*Congregation of the Passion*.—C.P.
[0390]—*Consolata Missionaries*.—I.M.C.
[0520]—*Franciscan Friars*. (Custody of St. John Capistran).—O.F.M.
[0940]—*Oblates of the Virgin Mary*.—O.M.V.
[0430]—*Order of Preachers (Dominicans)*. (Prov. of St. Joseph).—O.P.
[1070]—*Redemptorist Fathers*.—C.SS.R.

RELIGIOUS INSTITUTES OF WOMEN REPRESENTED IN THE DIOCESE

[0130]—*Apostles of the Sacred Heart of Jesus*.—A.S.C.J.
[1810]—*Bernardine Sisters of the Third Order of St. Francis*.—O.S.F.
[3110]—*Congregation of Our Lady of the Retreat in the Cenacle*. (Eastern Prov.).—R.C.
[0760]—*Daughters of Charity of St. Vincent De Paul*. (Albany Prov.).—D.C.
[0790]—*Daughters of Divine Charity*. (Prov. of St. Joseph).—F.D.C.
[0420]—*Discalced Carmelite Nuns*.—O.C.D.
[1070-18]—*Dominican Sisters*. (Caldwell).—O.P.
[1070-11]—*Dominican Sisters*. (Sparkill, N.Y.).—O.P.
[1070-06]—*Dominican Sisters of Hope*. (Ossining, N.Y.).—O.P.
[1170]—*Felician Sisters*. (Immaculate Conception Prov.).—C.S.S.F.
[1180]—*Franciscan Sisters of Allegany, New York*.—O.S.F.
[1650]—*Franciscan Sisters of Philadelphia*.—O.S.F.
[2575]—*Institute of the Sisters of Mercy of the Americas*. (New Jersey).—R.S.M.
[2300]—*Little Servant Sisters of the Immaculate Conception*.—L.S.I.C.
[2340]—*Little Sisters of the Poor*. (Brooklyn Prov.).—L.S.P.
[2700]—*Missionary Catechists of the Sacred Hearts of Jesus and Mary*.—M.C.
[0950]—*Pious Society Daughters of St. Paul*.—F.S.P.
[3640]—*Poor Servants of the Mother of God*.—S.M.G.
[3320]—*Presentation of the Blessed Virgin Mary*. (New Windsor, NY).—P.B.V.M.
[0970]—*Religious of Divine Compassion*. (White Plains, NY).—R.D.C.
[]—*Religious of the Blessed Virgin Mary*.—R.V.M.
[3430]—*Religious Teachers Filippini*. (St. Lucy Prov.).—M.P.F.

[3580]—*Servants of Mary.* (American Prov.).—O.S.M.
[1980]—*Servants of the Holy Child of Jesus.*—O.S.F.
[3630]—*Servants of the Most Sacred Heart of Jesus.*—S.S.C.J.
[0590]—*Sisters of Charity of Saint Elizabeth, Convent Station.*—S.C.
[0660]—*Sisters of Christian Charity.* (North American Eastern Prov.).—S.C.C.
[2970]—*Sisters of Notre Dame.* (Baltimore, MD).—S.N.D.
[3893]—*Sisters of Saint Joseph of Chestnut Hill, Philadelphia.*—S.S.J.
[1650]—*Sisters of St. Francis of Philadelphia.*—O.S.F.
[1600]—*Sisters of St. Francis of the Martyr St. George.*—O.S.F.
[3890]—*Sisters of St. Joseph of Peace.*—C.S.J.P.
[1190]—*Sisters of the Atonement.* (Graymoor).—S.A.
[2170]—*Sisters Servants of the Immaculate Heart of Mary.*—I.H.M.

DIOCESAN CEMETERIES

JAMESBURG. *Holy Cross Burial Park,* Cranbury Rd., Box 100, 08831. Tel: 732-521-0770.

PISCATAWAY. *Resurrection Burial Park,* 899 Lincoln Ave., 08854. Tel: 732-545-5966.

NECROLOGY

† Kapica, Francis A., (Retired). —Died March 5, 1997.

† McNulty, Michael A., Blairstown, NJ, St. Jude. —Died April 19, 1997.

† Molloy, William T., (Retired). —Died April 24, 1997.

† Piechocinski, Thomas A., Monmouth Junction, NJ, St. Cecilia. —Died March 25, 1997.

Archdiocese of Miami

(Archidioecesis Miamiensis)

Most Reverend

JOHN C. FAVALORA, D.D.

Archbishop of Miami; ordained December 20, 1961; appointed Bishop of Alexandria June 16, 1986; ordained and installed July 29, 1986; appointed Third Bishop of St. Petersburg March 7, 1989; installed May 16, 1989; appointed Third Archbishop of Miami November 3, 1994; installed December 20, 1994. *Office: 9401 Biscayne Blvd., Miami, FL, 33138.*

Most Reverend

AGUSTIN A. ROMAN, D.D., V.G.

Auxiliary Bishop of Miami; ordained July 5, 1959; appointed Titular Bishop of Sertei and Auxiliary of Miami February 6, 1979; consecrated March 24, 1979. *Res., 3605 S. Miami Ave., Miami, FL, 33133.*

Most Reverend

GILBERTO FERNANDEZ, D.D., V.G.

Auxiliary Bishop of Miami; ordained May 17, 1959; appointed Titular Bishop of Irina and Auxiliary of Miami June 24, 1997; consecrated September 3, 1997. *Office: 9401 Biscayne Blvd., Miami Shores, FL, 33138.*

Most Reverend

THOMAS G. WENSKI, D.D., V.G.

Auxiliary Bishop of Miami; ordained May 15, 1976; appointed Titular Bishop of Kearney and Auxiliary of Miami June 24, 1997; consecrated September 3, 1997. *Office: 9401 Biscayne Blvd., Miami Shores, FL, 33138.*

Pastoral Center: 9401 Biscayne Blvd., Miami Shores, FL, 33138. Tel.: 305-757-6241; Fax: 305-754-1897 (Chancery); 758-0356 (Communications Office).

Web site address: http://www.archdioceseofmiami~.org

E-mail address: miaarch@fitertown.com

Most Reverend

EDWARD A. MCCARTHY, D.D., S.T.D., J.C.D.

Retired Archbishop of Miami; ordained May 29, 1943; appointed Titular Bishop of Tamascani and Auxiliary of Cincinnati April 21, 1965; transferred to Phoenix August 25, 1969; installed December 2, 1969; appointed Coadjutor Archbishop of Miami *"cum jure successionis" September 17, 1976; Archbishop of Miami July 26, 1977; retired November 3, 1994. Office: 9401 Biscayne Blvd., Miami Shores, FL, 33138.*

ESTABLISHED AUGUST 13, 1958.

CREATED AN ARCHBISHOPRIC, JUNE 13, 1968.

Square Miles 4,958.

Comprises the Counties in the southern part of the State of Florida, namely, Broward, Dade and Monroe.

For legal titles of parishes and Archdiocesan institutions, consult the Pastoral Center.

STATISTICAL OVERVIEW

Personnel	
Archbishop	1
Retired Archbishops	1
Auxiliary Bishops	3
Priests: Diocesan Active in Diocese	213
Priests: Active Outside Diocese	8
Priests: Diocesan in Foreign Missions	1
Priests: Retired, Sick or Absent	43
Number of Diocesan Priests	265
Religious Priests in Diocese	122
Extern Priests in Diocese	56
Ordinations:	
Diocesan Priests	2
Transitional Deacons	1
Permanent Deacons in Diocese	128
Total Brothers	56
Total Sisters	345
Parishes	
Parishes	108
With Resident Pastor:	
Resident Diocesan Priests	99
Resident Religious Priests	9
Without Resident Pastor:	
Missions	5
Pastoral Centers	1
Professional Ministry Personnel:	
Brothers	2
Sisters	59
Lay Ministers	143
Welfare	
Catholic Hospitals	2
Total Assisted	573,198
Health Care Centers	3
Total Assisted	17,575
Homes for the Aged	4
Total Assisted	87,557
Residential Care of Children	2
Total Assisted	303
Day Care and Extended Day Care Centers	7
Total Assisted	3,345
Specialized Homes	5
Total Assisted	7,058
Special Centers for Social Services	38
Total Assisted	999,979
Residential Care of Disabled	1
Total Assisted	121
Other Institutions	11
Total Assisted	2,075
Educational	
Seminaries, Diocesan	1
Students from This Diocese	19
Students from Other Diocese	24
Diocesan Students in Other Seminaries	18
Total Seminarians	37
Colleges and Universities	2
Total Students	9,480
High Schools, Diocesan and Parish	7
Total Students	6,915
High Schools, Private	5
Total Students	2,949
Elementary Schools, Diocesan and Parish	54
Total Students	22,833
Elementary Schools, Private	3
Total Students	1,222
Non-residential Schools for the Disabled	2
Total Students	11,641
Catechesis/Religious Education:	
High School Students	2,935
Elementary Students	43,753
Total Students Under Catholic Instruction	101,765
Teachers in the Diocese:	
Priests	10
Brothers	21
Sisters	51
Lay Teachers	1,733
Vital Statistics	
Receptions into the Church:	
Infant Baptism Totals	16,788
Adult Baptism Totals	826
Received into Full Communion	1,019
First Communions	12,946
Confirmations	7,649
Marriages:	
Catholic	2,851
Interfaith	528
Total Marriages	3,379
Deaths	4,586
Total Catholic Population	774,125
Total Population	3,595,133

Former Archbishops—Most Rev. COLEMAN F. CARROLL, D.D., ord. June 15, 1930; appt. Titular Bishop of Pitanae and Auxiliary Bishop of Pittsburgh, Aug. 25, 1953; cons. Nov. 10, 1953; appt. first Bishop of Miami, Aug. 13, 1958; installed Oct. 7, 1958; appt. Archbishop of Miami, March 13, 1968; died July 26, 1977.—Most Rev. EDWARD A. MCCARTHY, D.D., S.T.D., J.C.D., ord. May 29, 1943; appt. Coadjutor Archbishop of Miami "cum jure successionis," Sept. 17, 1976; appt. Archbishop of Miami, July 26, 1977; retired November 3, 1994.

Pastoral Center—9401 Biscayne Blvd., Miami Shores, 33138. Tel: 305-757-6241; Fax: 305-754-1897 (Chancery Office); 754-1797 (Communications Office).

Vicars General—Most Rev. AGUSTIN A. ROMAN, V.G.; Most Rev. GILBERTO FERNANDEZ, V.G.; Most Rev. THOMAS G. WENSKI, V.G.; Rev. Msgr. WILLIAM J. HENNESSEY, V.G.

Chancellor—Very Rev. TOMAS M. MARIN, J.C.L.

Moderator of the Curia—Rev. Msgr. WILLIAM J. HENNESSEY, V.G.

Secretary to the Archbishop—Rev. MICHAEL CARRUTHERS.

Metropolitan Tribunal—Address all Rogatory commissions and matrimonial matters to the Tribunal (All Pastoral Center searches for information prior to October 7, 1958, should be directed to Diocese of St. Augustine, FL), *9401 Biscayne Blvd., Miami Shores, 33138.* Tel: 305-762-1161; Fax: 305-762-1178.

Judicial Vicar and Administrator—Very Rev. ANDREW L. ANDERSON, J.C.D.

Tribunal Secretary—Rev. CARL MORRISON, J.C.L.

Judges—Very Rev. TOMAS MARIN, J.C.L.; Sr. JEANNE-MARGARET MCNALLY, J.C.L., Ph.D.; Revs. JOSE BIAIN, O.F.M.; ERNESTO MOLANO, J.C.L.; GEORGE

PUTHUSSERIL, J.C.D.; KENNETH SCHWANGER, J.C.L.; MICHAEL THOMAS, J.C.D.; KENNETH WHITTAKER, J.C.L.

Promoters of Justice—Rev. KENNETH WHITTAKER, J.C.L.; J. MICHAEL FITZGERALD, J.C.L., Esq.

Defenders of the Bond—Rev. Msgr. ORLANDO FERNANDEZ; Revs. CARL MORRISON, J.C.L.; MANUEL ORTEGA, J.C.L.; RONALD PUSAK, J.C.L.; Mr. J. MICHAEL FITZGERALD, J.C.L., Esq.

Notaries—Ms. KATIA ARRIAZA; LILLIAN HUMARA; CONNIE LOFFREDO; KATHLEEN CHERRIS, C.P.S.

Assessors—Sr. ISABEL MAZARREDO, O.P.; ROSARIO BERGOUIGNAN.

Counsel-Assistant to the Tribunal—J. MICHAEL FITZGERALD, J.C.L., Esq.

Consultors—Most Rev. AGUSTIN ROMAN, V.G.; Most Rev. GILBERTO FERNANDEZ, V.G.; Most Rev. THOMAS G. WENSKI, V.G.; Rev. Msgr. WILLIAM J. HENNESSEY, V.G.; Very Rev. TOMAS M. MARIN; Revs. GUSTAVO MIYARES; VINCENT KELLY; ARTHUR DENNISON; ANTHONY MULDERRY.

Deans and Deaneries—Rev. Msgr. JOHN GLORIE, V.F., (Northeast Broward): Rev. Msgr. NOEL FOGARTY, V.F., (Northwest Broward): Very Rev. THOMAS O'DWYER, V.F., (South Broward): Very Rev. JOSE L. HERNANDO, V.F., (East Dade): Very Rev. SEAMUS DOYLE, V.F., (Northeast Dade): Very Rev. LUIS PEREZ, V.F., (Northwest Dade): Very Rev. JAMES FETSCHER, V.F., (South Dade): Very Rev. XAVIER MORRAS, V.F., (West Dade): Very Rev. GERALD MCGRATH, V.F., (Monroe):

Incardination Committee—Most Rev. JOHN C. FAVALORA; Most Rev. AGUSTIN A. ROMAN, V.G.; Most Rev. GILBERTO FERNANDEZ, V.G.; Most Rev. THOMAS G. WENSKI, V.G.; Rev. Msgr. PABLO A. NAVARRO; Rev. Msgr. WILLIAM J. HENNESSEY, V.G.; Very Rev. TOMAS M. MARIN; Revs. VINCENT KELLY; ARTHUR DENNISON; JAMES MURPHY.

Presbyteral Council—Most Rev. JOHN C. FAVALORA, Pres.; Revs. ARTHUR DENNISON, Vice Pres. MICHAEL HOYER, Sec.

Priests' Personnel Board—Rev. DANIEL KUBALA, Chm. Consultants: Most Rev. AGUSTIN ROMAN, V.G.; Most Rev. GILBERTO FERNANDEZ, V.G.; Most Rev. THOMAS G. WENSKI, V.G.; Rev. Msgr. WILLIAM J. HENNESSEY, V.G.; Very Rev. TOMAS M. MARIN. Members: Rev. ARTHUR DENNISON; JOSE LUIS HERNANDO; ANTHONY MULDERRY; THOMAS O'DWYER.

Ministry Of General Services

Executive Director—Very Rev. TOMAS M. MARIN.

Chancellor's Office—Very Rev. TOMAS M. MARIN, Chancellor/Exec. Dir.

Coordinator of Special Projects—Rev. PATRICK O'NEILL.

Pastoral Center Services—Mr. TERRY SUNDY.

Legal Services—PATRICK FITZGERALD, *110 Merrick Way, Ste. 3-B, Coral Gables, 33134.* Tel: 305-443-9162; Fax: 305-443-6613.

Communications Dept.—MARY ROSS AGOSTA, Dir. CYNTHIA GUTIERREZ, Coord. MIRIAM MIRANDA, Admin. Asst.

Public and Media Relations—MARY ROSS AGOSTA, Dir.

Community Information—MARY ROSS AGOSTA, Dir., Mailing Address: (for Communications, Public and Media Relations and: Community Information) *9401 Biscayne Blvd., Miami, 33138.* Tel: 305-762-1043; 1045; Fax: 305-762-1048.

Television and Radio Center—MARY ROSS AGOSTA, Dir. ERNESTO GONZALEZ, Oper. Mgr. CHRISTINE SLOAN, Producer; Revs. JOSE P. NICKSE, Producer & TV Mass Coord. (Spanish); FRANCISCO SANTANA, Producer & TV Mass Coord. (Spanish); CHRISTOPHER MARINO, TV Mass Producer (English), Mailing Address: *9920 N.E. 2nd Ave., Miami, 33138.* Tel: 305-751-0990.

Newspapers—MARY ROSS AGOSTA, Dir., *Mailing Address: for Newspapers: 9401 Biscayne Blvd., Miami, 33138.*

"The Florida Catholic"—ROBERT O'STEEN, Editor (English). Tel: 305-762-1131.

"La Voz Catolica"—Ms. ARACELI CANTERO, Exec. Editor (Spanish). Tel: 305-762-1125; Fax: 305-762-1130.

RADIO PEACE CATHOLIC BROADCASTING, INC.—Rev. FEDERICO CAPDEPON, Pres./Dir.; Deacon RAFAEL DE LOS REYES, V.P./Adm. Tel: 305-368-9729; Fax: 305-636-4571.

Radio Peace - WAXY, 790 AM—20450 N.W. 2nd Ave., Miami, 33169. Tel: 305-525-3193. JOE KEENER, Programming Dir.

Radio Paz - WACC, 830 AM—1779 N.W. 28 St., N. Miami, 33142. Tel: 305-638-9729. ISAUL GONZALEZ, Station Mgr.

Radio Ke Poze - WACC, 830 AM—1779 N.W. 28 St., Miami, 33142. Tel: 305-638-9729. Most Rev. THOMAS WENSKI, Programming Dir.

Catholic Office for Inter-Faith Activities and Catholic-Jewish Relations Commission—Rev. Dr. PATRICK H. O'NEILL, Exec. Dir., *9401 Biscayne Blvd., Miami Shores, 33138.* Tel: 305-762-1254; Fax: 305-754-1897.

Christian Unity Commission—Rev. Dr. PATRICK H. O'NEILL, Ecumenical Officer, *9401 Biscayne Blvd., Miami Shores, 33138.* Tel: 305-762-1254; Fax: 305-754-1897.

Ministry Of Christian Formation

Executive Director—Rev. VINCENT T. KELLY.

Department of Schools—Rev. VINCENT T. KELLY, Vicar, Christian Formation; Sr. M. NOREEN WERNER, C.S.F.N., Supt.; Mr. ALAN POWERS; Sr. CORINNE GMUER, S.S.N.D.; KRISTEN HUGHES; Sr. MARY TERZO, F.M.A., Assoc. Supt.; Sr. CONSTANCE CARRIGAN, S.S.N.D.

Department of Religious Education—Sr. ROSA MONIQUE PENA, O.P., Dir.

Archdiocesan Catechetical Center—Ms. INES EXPOSITO, Mgr.

Archdiocese of Miami Education Endowment Fund, Inc.—PATRICK J. HEFFERNAN, Ph.D., Exec. Dir.

Catholic Charities

Archdiocesan Director—Most Rev. THOMAS G. WENSKI, D.D., Auxiliary Bishop.

Catholic Relief Services—9401 Biscayne Blvd., Miami Shores, 33138. Tel: 305-754-2444; Fax: 305-754-6649.

Campaign for Human Development—9401 Biscayne Blvd., Miami Shores, 33138. Tel: 305-754-2444; Fax: 305-754-6649.

Pierre Toussaint Haitian Catholic Center, Human Services Division—EMILE VIARD, Exec. Dir., *110 NE 62 St., Miami, 33138.* Tel: 305-758-2462; Fax: 305-758-8216.

Catholic Charities Legal Services—

Little Haiti Office—RANDOLPH MCGRORTY, Supervising Attorney; MYRIAM MEZADIEU, Admin., *119 NE 62 St., Miami, 33138.* Tel: 305-758-3301; Fax: 305-756-6435.

Hialeah Office—MARISOL ZEQUEIRA, Supervising Attorney, *60 E. 3rd St., Ste. 206, Hialeah, 33010.* Tel: 305-887-8333; Fax: 305-887-8813.

Refugee Resettlement Services—ANITA GAWOR, Admin., *60 E. 3rd St., Ste. 206, Hialeah, 33010.* Tel: 305-883-4555; Fax: 305-883-4498.

Catholic Charities of the Archdiocese of Miami, Inc.—9401 Biscayne Blvd., Miami Shores, 33138. Tel: 305-754-2444; Fax: 305-754-6649. CARLOS BUSTABAD, Dir., Finance; Mr. RONALD A. HASSELL, Dir., Personnel & Mgmt. Information Svcs. RICARDO RIESGO, Dir., Accounting Svcs./Data Processing; LLOYDINE MCGUINN, Exec. Asst. LISA C. PINTO, Exec. Asst.

Dade Area Offices—

Miami Shores Office—ALBERT TRICOMI, A.C.S.W., Dir., *9999 N.E. 2nd Ave., Ste. 217, Miami Shores, 33138.* Tel: 305-758-0024; Fax: 305-757-6287.

South Dade Office—GRACIELA PEREZ, M.S.W., Admin., *18601 S.W. 97 Ave., Miami, 33157.* Tel: 305-378-6105; Fax: 305-233-3807.

Little Havana Office—ALICIA DEL TORO, M.S.W., Admin., *970 S.W. 1 St., Ste. 302, Miami, 33130.* Tel: 305-324-1104.

Services for the Elderly—MARY GREEN, Admin., *9900 N.E. 2nd Ave., Miami Shores, 33138.* Tel: 305-751-5203; Fax: 305-758-4972.

Broward Area Offices—VICKI KAUFMAN, M.A., Dir., *1505 N.E. 26 St., Wilton Manors, 33305.* Tel: 954-630-9404; Fax: 954-566-6026.

Catholic Family and Children's Services Trust of Broward County—PAUL A. GORE, Chm.; Most Rev. THOMAS G. WENSKI, Sec., *9401 Biscayne Blvd., Miami Shores, 33138.* Tel: 305-754-2444; 954-630-9404; Fax: 305-754-6649; 954-566-6026.

Child Welfare Services—MILDRED LUGO, L.C.S.W., Dir., *18601 S.W. 97 Ave., P.O. Box 970143, Miami, 33197.* Tel: 305-238-2381; Fax: 305-232-5421.

Boystown of Florida, Inc.—SALLY ABELLO, L.C.S.W., Admin., *11400 S.W. 137 Ave., Miami, 33186.* Tel: 305-385-1722; Fax: 305-385-8301.

Catholic Home for Children, Inc.—MILDRED LUGO, L.C.S.W., Admin., *18601 S.W. 97 Ave., P.O. Box 970143, Miami, 33197.* Tel: 305-238-2381; Fax: 305-232-5421.

Maternity and Foster Services—MILDRED LUGO, L.C.S.W., Admin., *18601 S.W. 97 Ave., P.O. Box 970143, Miami, 33197.* Tel: 305-238-1447; Fax: 305-232-5421.

Catholic Child Welfare Trust—JOSEPH W. MYRTETUS, Chm.; Most Rev. THOMAS G. WENSKI, Sec., *9401 Biscayne Blvd., Miami Shores, 33138.* Tel: 305-754-2444; Fax: 305-754-6649.

Substance Abuse Programs—

St. Luke's Addiction Recovery Programs (St. Luke Center, Inc.)—PATRICIA CARTER, Interim Dir. ANDREW CHERY, Clinical Dir., *7707 N.W. 2 Ave., Miami, 33150.* Tel: 305-795-0077; Fax: 305-795-0030.

Miami DARE Substance Abuse Prevention Prog.—7707 N.W. 2nd Ave., Miami, 33150. Tel: 305-795-0077; Fax: 305-795-0030.

Child Development Centers—LUCIA VICENCIO, Dir., *9401 Biscayne Blvd., Miami, 33138.* Tel: 305-754-2444; Fax: 305-754-6649.

Centro Hispano Child Care Center (Centro Hispano Catolico, Inc.)—FRANCISCO BRIZVELA, Admin., *144 N.W. 26 St., Miami, 33137.* Tel: 305-576-3461; Fax: 305-576-6446.

Centro Mater Child Care and Neighborhood Center (Centro Mater, Inc.)—ANA CRISTINA RODRIGUEZ, M.S.W., Admin., *418 S.W. 4 Ave., Miami, 33130.* Tel: 305-545-6049; 545-7720; Fax: 305-324-6162.

Centro Mater West Child Care Center—MIRIAM ROMAN, M.S.W., Admin., *8420 N.W. 103 St., Miami, 33016.* Tel: 305-827-1050; Fax: 305-827-1079.

Good Shepherd Day Care and Neighborhood Center—ALEIDA BARCENA-CAO, Admin., *18601 S.W. 97 Ave., Miami, 33157.* Tel: 305-235-1756; 235-1330; Fax: 305-255-2788.

Sagrada Familia Child Care Program—MARISABEL CAPOTE, Admin., *970 S.W. 1 St., Room 205, Miami, 33130.* Tel: 305-324-5424;326-8212; Fax: 305-325-0642.

Notre Dame Day Care and Neighborhood Center—AUDREY SEARS, Admin., *130 N.E. 62 St., Miami, 33138.* Tel: 305-751-6778; Fax: 305-751-6959.

Child Care Food Program—CHARIL FELDMAN, Admin., *9401 Biscayne Blvd., Miami Shores, 33138.* Tel: 305-754-2444; Fax: 305-754-6649.

Day Centers for the Elderly—

Miami-Senior Center—MARY GREEN, Admin., *9900 N.E. 2 Ave., Miami Shores, 33138.* Tel: 305-751-5203; Fax: 305-758-4972.

Broward Catholic Senior and Adult Day Care Centers—MIRANDA SGOUROS, Dir., *1505 N.E. 26 St., Wilton Manors, 33305.* Tel: 954-630-9404; Fax: 954-566-6026.

Broward-Central West Senior Day Center—SUSAN LANDAIS, Coord., *4644 S.W. 64 Ave., Davie, 33314.* Tel: 305-583-6446.

St. Elizabeth Senior Day Center—JOHN CAVOTO, Coord., *801 N.E. 33 St., Pompano Beach, 33064.* Tel: 954-781-0461.

Winton Manors Senior Day Center—KAY SWICORD, Coord., *1505 N.E. 26 St., Wilton Manors, 33305.* Tel: 954-581-7621.

Parish Social Ministry—

Dade-Monroe—ELVIRA GONZALEZ, Dir., *9999 N.E. 2nd Ave., Miami Shores, 33138.* Tel: 305-758-0024; Fax: 305-751-1660.

Broward—MURIEL KROLL, Coord., *1505 N.E. 26 St., Wilton Manors, 33305.* Tel: 954-630-9404; Fax: 954-566-6026.

Catholic Hospice, Inc.—Most Rev. THOMAS G. WENSKI; TONY PALUMBO, CEO, *14100 Palmetto Frontage Rd., Miami Lakes, 33016.* Tel: 305-822-2380; Fax: 305-827-0221.

Services to People with AIDS—

Dade, Genesis Programs, Inc.—Sr. B. EDITA ROJO, M.D., Dir.; Rev. PEDRO CORCES, Chap., *3675 S. Miami Ave., Miami, 33133.* Tel: 305-856-1043; Fax: 305-856-1633.

Broward, Ministry to People with AIDS—Rev. DENNIS RAUSCH, Admin., *1505 N.E. 26 St., Wilton Manors, 33305.* Tel: 954-630-9404; Fax: 954-566-6026.

Dade, Ministry to People with AIDS—ELIZABETH VERA, Coord., *9999 N.E. 2 Ave., #217, Miami Shores, 33138.* Tel: 305-758-0024; Fax: 305-757-6287.

Foreign Mission Board—ALICIA MARILL, Coord., *18601 S.W. 97 Ave., Miami, 33157.* Tel: 305-378-6306; Fax: 305-378-1660.

The Poverello Ctr., Inc.—Rev. WILLIAM COLLINS, O.F.M., Dir., *2292 Wilton Dr., Wilton Manors, 33305.* Tel: 954-561-3663; Fax: 954-566-7868.

Foundations—

Catholic Health and Rehabilitation Services Foundation—Most Rev. THOMAS G. WENSKI, Exec. Dir., *9401 Biscayne Blvd., Miami, 33138.* Tel: 305-754-2444; Fax: 305-754-6649.

Catholic Hospice Foundation, Inc.—14100 Palmetto Frontage Rd., Miami Lakes, 33016. Tel: 305-822-2380; Fax: 305-827-0221.

Catholic Commission for Social Advocacy—LEONA COOPER, Chm.; Most Rev. THOMAS G. WENSKI, Exec. Dir. PETER COATS, Assoc. Dir., *9401 Biscayne Blvd., Miami, 33138.* Tel: 305-754-2444; Fax: 305-754-6649.

Ministry of Catholic Health Services

Archdiocesan Director—Rev. THOMAS HONOLD.

Catholic Health Services, Inc.—Rev. THOMAS HONOLD, Dir. JOSEPH CATANIA, Exec. Dir. MICHAEL A. CASCIATO, Chief Oper. Officer; GLORIA HANSEN, Dir.,

Health Care Svcs., *4740 N. State Rd. 7, Bldg. C, Ste. 100, Lauderdale Lakes, 33319.* Tel: 954-484-1515.

Catholic Housing for the Elderly and Handicapped, Inc.

Catholic Housing Management—TERE SPRING, Admin., *4740 N. State Rd. 7, Bldg. C, Ste. 106, Lauderdale Lakes, 33319.* Tel: 954-677-8122.

Archbishop Carroll Manor—MARIO YANES, Mgr., *3667 S. Miami Ave., Miami, 33133.* Tel: 305-854-8953.

Archbishop Hurley Hall—LORETTA PALIS, Mgr., *632 N.W. 1st St., Hallandale, 33009.* Tel: 954-454-0855.

Marian Towers—FAUSTO FERNANDEZ, Mgr., *17505 N. Bay Rd., Miami Beach, 33160.* Tel: 305-932-1300.

Archbishop McCarthy Residence—ROSLYN WILLIAMS, Mgr., *13201 N.W. 28 Ave., Opa Locka, 33054.* Tel: 305-688-2700.

Palmer House—NOEMI DIAZ-MONTORO, Mgr., *1225 S.W. 107 Ave., Miami, 33174.* Tel: 305-221-9566.

St. Andrew Towers—ILBA I. DONNELLY, Mgr., *2700 N.W. 99 Ave., Coral Springs, 33065.* Tel: 954-752-3960.

St. Dominic Gardens—MARIO YANES, Mgr., *5849 N.W. 7th St., Miami, 33126.* Tel: 305-262-0962.

St. Elizabeth Gardens—JOHN CAMERON, Mgr., *801 N.E. 33rd St., Pompano Beach, 33064.* Tel: 954-941-4597.

St. Joseph Towers—DEBRA HAMELRATH, Mgr., *3475 N.W. 30th St., Lauderdale Lakes, 33311.* Tel: 954-485-5150.

St. Mary Towers—LORETA PALIS, Mgr., *7615 N.W. 2nd Ave., Miami, 33150.* Tel: 305-757-3190.

Stella Maris—ANN H. SMITH, Mgr., *8638 Harding Ave., Miami Beach, 33141.* Tel: 305-865-6841.

Nursing and Retirement Centers—

BROWARD:

St. Joseph Residence, Inc.—GLORIA HANSEN, Admin., *3485 N.W. 30 St., Lauderdale Lakes, 33311.* Tel: 954-739-1483.

St. John's Rehabilitation Hospital and Nursing Center, Inc.—DIANE DUBE, Admin., *3075 N.W. 35 Ave., Lauderdale Lakes, 33311.* Tel: 954-739-6233.

Catholic Hospice of Broward, Inc.—4740 N. State Rd. 7, Bldg. C, Ste. 100, Lauderdale Lakes, 33319. Tel: 954-484-1515.

Catholic Home Health Services of Broward, Inc.—BEVERLY IVES, Admin., *3075 N.W. 35 Ave., Lauderdale Lakes, 33311.* Tel: 954-486-3660.

DADE:

St. Anne's Catholic Nursing Center and St. Anne's Residence, Inc.—CHERYL HANSON RODRIGUEZ, Admin. LAVERNE KOONTZ, A.C.L.F., Admin., *11855 Quail Roost Dr., Miami, 33177.* Tel: 305-252-4000.

Villa Maria Nursing and Rehabilitation Center, Inc.—JACK RUTENBERG, Admin., *1050 N.E. 125 St., N. Miami, 33161.* Tel: 305-891-8850.

Villa Maria Health Care Services, Inc.—GLORIA HANSEN, Admin., *1050 N.E. 125 St., N. Miami, 33161.* Tel: 305-899-0400.

Villa Maria Adult Day Care—GWEN DUNCAN, Dir., *20855 N.W. 9 Ct., Box R-2, North Miami, 33169.* Tel: 305-651-0034.

Villa Maria Foundation, Inc.—1050 N.E. 125 St., N. Miami, 33161. Tel: 305-891-8850, Ext. 4315.

Special Education—(Developmentally handicapped and mentally retarded) Marian Center Services. MARIA CONSUEGRA, Dir., *15701 N.W. 37 Ave., Opa Locka, 33054.* Tel: 305-625-8354; Fax: 305-625-3696.

Catholic Cemeteries—MICHAEL TADROS, Dir. Cemetery Svcs., *11411 N.W. 25th St., Miami, 33172.* Tel: 305-592-0521.

Archdiocesan Cemeteries—Our Lady of Mercy Cemetery, 11411 N.W. 25th St., Miami, 33172. Tel: 305-592-0521., *Our Lady Queen of Heaven Cemetery, 1500 S. State Rd. 7, N. Lauderdale, 33068.* Tel: 954-972-1234.

Catholic Elderly Services, Inc.—4740 N. State Rd. 7, Bldg. C, Ste. 100, Lauderdale Lakes, 33319. Tel: 954-484-1515.

Ministry of Pastoral Services

Ministry of Pastoral Services—Most Rev. GILBERTO FERNANDEZ, Exec. Dir.

Campus Ministry—PATRICIA STOCKTON, Dir., *9401 Biscayne Blvd., Miami, 33138.* Tel: 305-762-1096.

Barry University—Sr. CORINNE SANDERS, O.P., Ed.D., Dir.; Rev. EMILIANO ZAPATA, O.P., Assoc. Dir.; Sr. MARY CAROL HURLEY, O.P.; ELSIE MIRANDA; FRANK VEGA, *11300 N.E. 2nd Ave., Miami Shores, 33161.* Tel: 305-899-3650.

FIU-North Miami—Revs. KENNETH SCHWANGER, J.C.L., Chap. LUIS PEREZ, Chap. ROLANDO CASTILLO, Chap. JOSE ESPINO, Chap. SILVIA TARAFA, Campus Min., *N.E. 151st St. & Biscayne Blvd., N. Miami, 33181.* Tel: 305-940-5609.

FIU-University Park—Revs. FELIPE ESTEVEZ; VICTOR BABIN, S.S.C.; Sr. SAGRARIO NUNEZ; Mr. GEORGE TINSLEY, *St. Agatha Church, 111 S.W. 107th Ave., Miami, 33174.* Tel: 305-222-1506; 348-3900.

Miami Dade CC-South—Rev. MICHAEL KISH; ANGEL ANTONIO RODRIGUEZ, *7270 S.W. 120 St., Miami, 33156.* Tel: 305-238-7562.

Florida Memorial College—Rev. JOHN MADIGAN, O.M.I., Chap., *15800 N.W. 42nd Ave., Miami, 33054.* Tel: 305-626-3714; 626-3719.

St. Thomas University—Rev. EDWARD BLACKWELL, JR., Ed.D., Dir.; Ms. KATIE MALONEY, Grad. Intern; Mr. LUIS DULZAIDES, Student Acting Dir., *16400 N.W. 32nd Ave., Miami, 33054.* Tel: 305-628-6525.

University of Miami—Dr. ARTHUR D. CANALES, Dir. JOHN KELLY, Assoc. Dir.; Rev. TERENCE E. HOGAN, S.L.D., Pastor, *St. Augustine Church, 1400 Miller Rd., Coral Gables, 33146.* Tel: 305-661-1648.

Miami Dade CC-North—Rev. JOHN V. KENNEDY, C.M., Chap. ANGEL ANTONIO RODRIGUEZ, *2000 N.W. 103rd St., Miami, 33147.*

Miami Dade CC-Downtown Wolfson Campus—Rev. THOMAS MADDEN, S.J.; ANGEL ANTONIO RODRIGUEZ, *Gesu Church, 118 N.E. 2 St., Miami, 33132.* Tel: 305-379-1424; 347-3000.

Broward CC-Central and NOVA University—SANDY BOUDEWYNS, *Pastoral Center, 9401 Biscayne Blvd., Miami, 33138.* Tel: 305-757-6241, Ext. 193 (Dade). Tel: 305-525-5157, Ext. 193 (Broward).

Catholic Daughters of America—Court 634, Vice-Regent: VIOLET PITA, *St. Mary Star of the Sea Church, 1010 Windsor Ln., Key West, 33040.* Tel: 305-294-1018. Local Chaplain: Very Rev. GERALD MCGRATH, V.F.

Evangelization—Vacant; Dir.; Ms. ROSA MARIA MONTENEGRO, Coord., Evangelization for Hispanics; Ms. GLORIA G. ALFONSO, Sec., *9401 Biscayne Blvd., Miami, 33138.* Tel: 305-762-1095; 1094; 1093; Fax: 305-758-2027.

Family Life Ministry—DAWNE M. FLERI, Dir. GLORIA MASMANN, Coord., Divorced & Separated; ELAINE M. SYFERT, Coord., Hispanic Ministry; GLADYS Z. GONZALEZ, Coord., Ministry to Engaged & Married Couples, *9401 Biscayne Blvd., Miami, 33138.* Tel: 305-762-1140; Fax: 305-762-1144.

Lay Apostolic Movements and Associations—

Agrupacion Catolica Universitaria (ACU)—Rev. AMANDO LLORENTE, S.J., Spiritual Dir., *720 N.E. 27 St., Miami, 33137.* Tel: 305-573-1418.

Archdiocesan Council of Catholic Women—Rev. LAURENCE J. CONWAY, Dir., *17775 N. Bay Rd., Miami Beach, 33160.* Tel: 305-931-0600. BERNICE KNOTHE, Pres. Spiritual Moderators: Rev. GERALD MORRIS, (Monroe Deanery): Revs. JOSEPH HUCK, (North Broward Deanery): FRANCIS MCCARTHY, (South Broward Deanery): MICHAEL GREER, (South Dade Deanery): Very Rev. ANDREW ANDERSON, (North East Dade Deanery):

Camino (Spanish)—Deacon JORGE GONZALEZ, Dir., *P.O. Box 524160, Miami, 33152-4160.* Tel: 305-226-4664.

Charismatic Renewal—Rev. Msgr. WILLIAM MCKEEVER, Archdiocesan Liaison; Rev. DANIEL DOYLE, S.M., Assoc. Archdiocesan Liaison Charismatic Services: *P.O. Box 816128, Hollywood, 33081.* Tel: 954-961-1856. *Spanish:* Rev. JORDI RIVERO, Spiritual Dir. CARLOS HERNANDEZ, Coord. *Centro Carismatico Catolico—500 N.W. 22 Ave., Miami, 33125.* Tel: 305-631-1007; Fax: 305-642-0006.

Christian Family Movement—Rev. JOSEPH CARNEY, Dir., *4020 Curtiss Pkwy., Miami Springs, 33166.* Tel: 305-871-5780. *Spanish:* Rev. ANGEL VILLARONGA, O.F.M., Spiritual Dir., *Casa Cana, 480 E. 8 St., Hialeah, 33010.* Tel: 305-888-4819.

Cofradia Nuestra Senora de la Caridad (Spanish)—Most Rev. AGUSTIN A. ROMAN, V.G., Dir., *3609 S. Miami Ave., 33133.* Tel: 305-854-2404; Fax: 305-854-8022.

Comunidad de Vida Cristiana (CVX) Regina Mundi—Rev. VICTOR HERNANDEZ, S.J., Ecclesiastical Asst., *Belen Jesuit Prep. School, 500 S.W. 127 Ave., Miami, 33184.* Tel: 305-223-8600.

Cursillo—Rev. DAVID SMITH, Spiritual Dir., *8670 S.W. 27 Ln., Miami, 33155.* Tel: 305-291-6611 (Beeper).; Deacon ROBERT BINDER, Assoc. Dir. *Spanish:* Rev. IGNACIO BLASCO, Dir., *12525 S.W. 42 St., Miami, 33175.* Tel: 305-223-0633.

Encuentros Familiares (Spanish)—Rev. FLORENTINO AZCOITIA, S.J., Dir., *Casa Manresa, P.O. Box 651512, Miami, 33265.* Tel: 305-596-0001; Fax: 305-596-9655.

Encuentros Juveniles (Spanish)—Rev. ANIBAL MORALES, Dir., *Youth Center, 3333 S. Miami Ave., Miami, 33133.* Tel: 305-856-3404.

Impacto (Spanish)—Deacon JORGE PRIETO, *P.O. Box 440973, Miami, 33144.* Tel: 305-829-9440.

Knights of Columbus (English and Spanish)—Rev. Msgr. XAVIER MORRAS, V.F., Archdiocesan Chap., *2711 Indian Mound Trail, Coral Gables, 33134.* Tel: 305-446-9950.

Legion of Mary (English Speaking)—Rev. RICHARD SOULLIERE, Dir., *2700 N.E. 36 St., Lighthouse Point, 33064.* Tel: 954-943-9154. (Spanish Speaking); ADOLFINA VAZQUEZ. Tel: 305-824-3060.

Marian Movements & Devotions—Rev. RICHARD SOULLIERE, Coord., *2700 N.E. 36th St., Lighthouse Point, 33064.* Tel: 954-943-9154.

Ministry to Cultural Groups—Most Rev. THOMAS WENSKI, Dir.

St. Martin de Porres Assoc.—LEONA COOPER, Pres., *P.O. Box 330102, Miami, 33133.* Tel: 305-324-3128; 443-9466; Fax: 305-324-3222.

Brazilian Apostolate(Portuguese)—

O.L. Aparecida Roman Catholic Mission—1618 Pierce St., Hollywood, 33020. Tel: 954-943-8898. Revs. SERGIO DALL'AGNESE, C.S., Coord. HORECIO CARLOS ANKLAN, C.S., Asst. Coord.

Filipino Apostolate—Ms. ROSA MARIA MONTENEGRO, *Evangelization Office, 9401 Biscayne Blvd., Miami Shores, 33138.* Tel: 305-762-1094, Ext. 189.

French-Canadians—Rev. LEO DIONNE, O.M.I., Coord., *Christ the King Church, 16000 S.W. 112 Ave., Miami, 33157.* Tel: 305-238-2485.

Haitians—Most Rev. THOMAS WENSKI, Dir., *Notre Dame d'Haiti Mission, 110 N.E. 62 St., Miami, 33138.* Tel: 305-751-6289., *St. Joseph Haitian Catholic Mission, 1210 N.W. 6th Ave., Pompano Beach, 33060.* Tel: 954-941-3095. Divine Mercy Haitian Catholic Mission; Rev. ROLAND LAMY, *1105 N.W. 6th Ave., Ft. Lauderdale, 33311.* Tel: 954-764-8519.

Hispanic—Most Rev. GILBERTO FERNANDEZ, V.G., Dir.

Native Americans—Most Rev. THOMAS WENSKI, Dir.

Indians—Rev. JAMES PARAPPALLY, (India), Chap., *St. Gabriel Church, 731 N. Ocean St., Pompano Beach, 33062.* Tel: 954-943-3684.

Korean—Rev. YEONG SIK KANG, *1051 W. Fairway Rd., Pembroke Pines, 33026.* Tel: 954-433-1824.

Polish - (Our Lady of Czestochowa)—Rev. JAN FIEDUREK, S.Ch., Dir., *2400 N.E. 12 St., Pompano Beach, 33062.* Tel: 954-946-6347; Fax: 954-946-0512.

Vietnamese—Rev. ISIDORE BAKY, Coord., *St. Helen Church, 3033 N.W. 33 Ave., Ft. Lauderdale, 33311.* Tel: 954-731-7314.

Ministry to the Deaf and Disabled—Rev. JAMES VITUCCI, Pastoral Dir. JACK GREEN, Exec. Dir.; Sr. CONLETH BRANNAN, C.S.J., Asst. Dir. NERY RODRIGUEZ, Pastoral Worker; IAN ROBERTSON, D.R.E. & Advocate Program Dir., *Schott Memorial Center, 6591 S.W. 124 Ave., Fort Lauderdale, 33330.* Tel: 954-434-3306.

Ministry to Sea—(serving Seafarers); Rev. JOSE M. PAZ, Dir./Chap., Port of Miami; Ms. ANGELA GREGORIO, Dir., *Stella Maris Seamen's Center, 1275 S. America Way, Miami, 33132.* Tel: 305-371-6272. Rev. ARMANDO PEREZ, Chap., *Stella Maris Seamen's Center, 2550 Eisenhower Blvd., Amman Bldg. No. 7, Port Everglades, 33316.* Tel: 954-527-0467.

Prison Ministry—FRANK VEGA, Dir.

Respect Life Office—Rev. JORDI RIVERO, Dir. JOAN CROWN, Assoc. Dir., *18340 N.W. 12 Ave., Miami, 33169.* Tel: 305-653-2921; Fax: 305-653-1001.

Respect Life Branch Offices-Emergency Pregnancy Services—

—N. Dade Central Office, 18340 N.W. 12 Ave., Miami, 33169. Tel: 305-653-2921.

—Coral Springs Office, 10141 W. Sample Rd., Ste. B, Coral Springs, 33065. Tel: 954-753-0770.

—Hialeah Office, 2024 E. 4th Ave., Hialeah, 33011. Tel: 305-883-2229.

—Hollywood Office (S. Broward), 6151 Washington St., Hollywood, 33023. Tel: 954-963-2229.

—Ft. Lauderdale Office, 2907 N. Andrews Ave., Wilton Manors, 33311. Tel: 954-565-8506.

—Coral Way Office, 2075 Coral Way, Miami, 33145. Tel: 305-856-5870.

Rural Life Ministry—Rev. PEDRO GARCIA, Dir.

Everglades Community Assoc.-Andrew Ctr.—19200 S.W. 380th St., Florida City, 33030.

Youth and Young Adult Ministry—Sr. ONDINA CORTES, R.M.I., Dir., *Pastoral Center, 9401 Biscayne Blvd., Miami Shores, 33138.* Tel: 305-762-1101.

Scouting—Rev. CURTIS KIDDY, Archdiocesan Scout Chap.

Ministry of Temporalities

Executive Director—Rev. Msgr. JOHN J. VAUGHAN.

Office of Temporalities—Rev. Msgr. JOHN J. VAUGHAN, Archdiocesan Finance Admin.

Management—Rev. Msgr. JOHN J. VAUGHAN, Archdiocesan Finance Admin.

Business Office—JOSEPH CATANIA, Treas.

Data Processing—CARLOS FERNANDEZ.

Building Commission—Most Rev. JOHN C. FAVALORA; GEORGE KAPLAN, Chm.; Rev. Msgr. JOHN J. VAUGHAN; Revs. FREDERICK J. BRICE; GABRIEL O'REILLY; EDMOND WHYTE; Rev. Msgr. XAVIER MORRAS; Rev. EMILIO MARTIN; Very Rev. GUSTAVO MIYARES; JAMES DETRICK.

Archdiocesan Fund-Raising & Assessments Committee—Rev. Msgr. JOHN J. VAUGHAN; Rev. Msgr. PATRICK MCDONNELL; Very Rev. SEAMUS DOYLE, V.F.; Very Rev. JAMES FETSCHER, V.F.; Revs. TIMOTHY HANON; EDMOND WHYTE; JOSE NICKSE; GEORGE GARCIA; DAVID RUSSELL; ARNALDO LOPEZ; WILLIAM CONROY; JOSEPH CATANIA.

Finance Council—Rev. Msgr. NOEL FOGARTY; Rev. Msgr. JOHN J. VAUGHAN; Revs. FREDERICK J. BRICE; IGNACIO MORRAS; JAMES CONNAUGHTON; Mr. J. PATRICK FITZGERALD; FRANK MCDONOUGH; RAUL MASVIDAL; THOMAS PENNEKAMP; JOSEPH CATANIA.

Lay Personnel—TERRY SUNDY.

Health and Welfare—Very Rev. TOMAS M. MARIN.

Pension—Most Rev. JOHN C. FAVALORA, Chm.; Rev. Msgr. NOEL FOGARTY, Vice Chm.

Real Estate Board—Rev. Msgr. JOHN J. VAUGHAN, Dir.; Revs. FREDERICK J. BRICE; ANTHONY MULDERRY; Mr. FRANK MCDONOUGH; HENRY BEZOLD.

Society for the Propagation of the Faith—Rev. FREDERICK J. BRICE.

Plant Operations—DAVID PYLE.

Ministry Of Worship And Spiritual Life

Executive Director—Rev. JUAN SOSA. Assoc. Directors: MICHAEL DERRICK; ROGELIO ZELADA.

Worship & Spiritual Life Commission—Chms.: Rev. MICHAEL GREER; MYRNA GALLAGHER.

Celebration and Rite Committee—Rev. JUAN SOSA, Chm.

Spiritual Life Committee—BARBARA RIETBERG.

Sacred Art & Architecture—Rev. PAUL VUTURO.

Liturgical Music—MICHAEL DERRICK.

Committee on Popular Piety—Most Rev. AGUSTIN A. ROMAN, V.G.; Revs. JUAN SOSA, Chm.; Mr. ROGELIO ZELADA.

Ministry of Persons

Ministry of Persons—Most Rev. AGUSTIN ROMAN, Exec. Dir.

Vocations—Rev. PEDRO CORCES, Dir., *9401 Biscayne Blvd., Miami, 33138.* Tel: 305-762-1137.

Archdiocesan Vocations Review Board—Very Rev. JOHN NOONAN, Rector, St. John Vianney College Seminary, Miami; Very Rev. GUSTAVO MIYARES, Chm.; Revs. FEDERICO CAPDEPON; NEIL DOHERTY; JAMES MURPHY; PEDRO CORCES; MICHAEL CARRUTHERS; Sr. ANN MCDERMOT, O.S.F.; Ms. PAT STOCKTON; Mr. BOB MORGAN; Rev. Msgr. PABLO NAVARRO, Consultant, Rector, St. Vincent de Paul Regional Seminary.

Seminary—St. John Vianney College Seminary, Miami, Very Rev. JOHN NOONAN, Rector.

Office for Religious—Vacant.

Priestly Life and Ministry—Rev. ARTHUR DENNISON, Dir., *9401 Biscayne Blvd., Miami, 33138.* Tel: 305-757-6241, Ext. 225.

Permanent Diaconate—Most Rev. JOHN C. FAVALORA, Dir.; Rev. ALFRED CIOFFI, Coord.; Deacons JOHN AVERY, Asst. Coord. ANTONIO MACEO, Dir. Selection; CARL CARIERI, Dir. Formation; IAN TAYLOR, Dir. Deacon Rels.

Lay Ministry—Sr. ANN E. MCDERMOTT, O.S.F., Dir. ADELE GONZALEZ, D.Min. (Cand.), Asst. Dir.; Sr. CLAUDIA STEGER, O.S.F., Prog. Coord. MARIA CANTON, Hispanic Ministry Outreach; MARY TERESA MORGAN, M.A., Educator; PAULA FLOR, Admin. Asst. MAYRA ROSSELL; MARILYN CANO, Staff.

Continuing Education for the Clergy—Rev. ARTHUR DENNISON, Dir., *9401 Biscayne Blvd., Miami, 33138.* Tel: 305-757-6241, Ext. 225.

Priests' Sabbaticals—Rev. ARTHUR DENNISON, Chm.

Retired Priests' Committee—Rev. SEAMUS DOYLE, Chm.; Rev. Msgr. GERARD T. LACERRA; Rev. Msgr. JOHN J. VAUGHAN; Rev. Msgr. BRYAN WALSH; Revs. MICHAEL HOYER; MARTIN CASSIDY; SEAMUS DOYLE; VINCENT KELLY; Very Rev. ANDREW ANDERSON; PATRICK FITZGERALD, (Legal).

Ministry to Professional Groups—

Catholic Educators' Guild—Rev. Msgr. WILLIAM MCKEEVER, Chap.

Catholic Funeral Directors' Guild—Very Rev. ANDREW ANDERSON, Chap.

Catholic Lawyers' Guild—Very Rev. ANDREW ANDERSON, Chap.

Catholic Physicians' and Dentists' Guild—Very Rev. TOMAS M. MARIN, Chap., DADE; Rev. WILLIAM MYLCHREEST, Chap., BROWARD.

Catholic Law Enforcement Ministry—Police Chaplains: Rev. PAUL EDWARDS, Coord. (Metro-Dade Police); Rev. Msgr. JOHN J. VAUGHAN, (Miami Beach Police); Rev. MICHAEL KISH, (City of Miami Police); Vacant; (Florida Highway Patrol, Troop K); Vacant; (FBI, Broward Co./City of Coral Springs).

Catholic Fire Service Ministry—Fire Chaplains: Revs. THOMAS ENGBERS, Coord. (City of Miami; Metro Dade); MICHAEL LYNCH, (City of Coral Gables/Margate).

Special Apostolates

Amor En Accion—(Love in Action)—P.O. Box 141523, Coral Gables, 33114. ALICIA MARRILL. Tel: 305-971-1535. LOURDES ROVIRA. Tel: 305-275-0919.

Archbishop Hurley Scholarship Fund—Rev. VINCENT T. KELLY, Vicar, Christian Formation, *9401 Biscayne Blvd., Miami, 33138.* Tel: 305-762-1076.

Campaign for Human Development—Most Rev. THOMAS G. WENSKI, Acting Archdiocesan Dir., *9401 Biscayne Blvd., Miami Shores, 33138.* Tel: 305-754-2444.

Catholic Alumni Club of South Florida—Vacant.

Catholic Relief Services—Most Rev. THOMAS G. WENSKI, Archdiocesan Dir.

Downtown Senior Citizens' Community Center at Gesu Church—Sr. MAURA PHILLIPS, O.P., *118 N.E. 2nd St., Miami, 33132.* Tel: 305-374-6099.

Food for the Poor, Inc.—FERDINAND G. MAHFOOD, *550 S.W. 12 Ave., Deerfield Beach, 33442.* Tel: 954-427-2222 (Broward).

Holy Childhood Association—Rev. FREDERICK BRICE, Dir.

Pilgrimages—Rev. RICHARD SOULLIERE, Archdiocesan Dir., Natl. Shrine of the Immaculate Conception, Washington, DC.

Priests' Purgatorial Society—Rev. FREDERICK BRICE.

Serra Club—Mrs. IDALIA LASTRA, Pres., *2498 S.W. 3rd. Ave., Miami, 33129.* Tel: 305-856-7180. Chaplains—Dade County: Rev. PEDRO CORCES,N. Broward Co.: Rev. Msgr. FRANCIS FAZZALARO; Rev. ALBERT CUTIE, Assoc.

The St. Vincent De Paul Society of Miami, Inc.—Revs. WILLIAM ELBERT, Dade Co. Chap. FREDERICK BRICE, Broward County Chap.

CLERGY, PARISHES, MISSIONS AND PAROCHIAL SCHOOLS

CITY OF MIAMI
(Dade County)

1—ST. MARY'S CATHEDRAL (1930), Very Rev. Andrew Anderson, Rector. Assoc. Rectors: Revs. Carlos Vega; Marc Presume. In res., Rev. Michael Grady.
Res., 7525 N.W. 2nd Ave., 33150. Tel: 305-759-4531; 4532; Fax: 305-757-7456.
School—Tel: 305-757-1993; Fax: 305-757-3050. Sr. Jane Stoecker, S.S.J., Prin.
Sisters of St. Joseph of St. Augustine 4; Lay Teachers 12; Students 321.
Catechesis/Religious Programs—Students 300.

2—CHRIST THE KING (1961), Revs. Leo Dionne, O.M.I.; Raymond Crowe, O.M.I. In res., Revs. Bernard Clancy, O.M.I.; Paul Frank, O.M.I.; Edwin Hayes, O.M.I.; Charles Clements.
Res., 16000 S.W. 112th Ave., 33157. Tel: 305-238-2485; Fax: 305-254-0330.
Catechesis/Religious Programs—Tel: 305-235-0293.
Students 127.

3—CORPUS CHRISTI (1941), Revs. Jose L. Menendez; Luis G. Garcia. In res., Rev. Sergio Carrillo.
Res., 3220 N.W. 7th Ave., 33127. Tel: 305-635-1331; Fax: 305-635-2031.
School—Tel: 305-635-8571; Fax: 305-633-7738. Sr. Gina Geraci, S.T.J., Prin.
Sisters 5; Lay Teachers 12; Students 252.
Catechesis/Religious Programs—Sr. Carmen Alvarez, M.R.I. Tel: 305-633-5824.
Students 800.
Missions—Miami, San Francisco y Santa Clara, 402 N.E. 29 St., 33137.; Miami, San Juan Bautista, 3116 N.W. 2nd Ave., 33127.; Miami, Nuestra Senora de Altagracia, 1779 N.W. 28th St., 33142.; Miami, La Milagrosa, 1860 N.W. 18th Ter., 33125.

4—EPIPHANY (1951), Rev. Msgr. Jude O'Doherty; Revs. Jan Malicki; Jesus Arias.
Res., 8235 S.W. 57th Ave., 33143. Tel: 305-667-4911; Fax: 305-667-8067.
School—Tel: 305-667-5251; Fax: 305-667-6828. Sr. Mary Henrich, I.H.M., Prin.
Sisters Servants of the Immaculate Heart of Mary 3; Lay Teachers 59; Students 1,026.
Catechesis/Religious Programs—Tel: 305-665-0037.
Students 349.

5—GESU (1896), Revs. Thomas J. Madden, S.J.; Sergio Figueredo, S.J.; Edwin Gros, S.J.; Fernando Lopez, S.J.; Thomas A. Griffin, S.J.; Michael J. Kossak, S.J.; William Kidwell, S.J.; Salvator J. San Marco, S.J.
Res., 118 N.E. 2nd St., 33132. Tel: 305-379-1424; Fax: 305-372-9544.

6—GOOD SHEPHERD (1977), Revs. Michael Greer; Miguel Gomez; Damian Flanagan.
Res., 6804 S.W. 139th Pl., 33183. Tel: 305-386-1580.
Church—14187 S.W. 72nd St., 33183. Tel: 305-385-4320; Fax: 305-386-2407.
School—(Grades PreK-1). Tel: 305-385-7002. Christine Valadez, Prin.
Lay Teachers 5; Students 100.
Catechesis/Religious Programs—Tel: 305-388-9877. Maria Changsut, D.R.E.
Students 1,130.

7—HOLY REDEEMER (1951), Rev. Richard Sudlik, O.M.I.
Church—1301 N.W. 71st St., 33147. Tel: 305-691-1701; Fax: 305-691-7074.
Catechesis/Religious Programs—Students 50.

8—MOTHER OF CHRIST (1983), Revs. Raul Angulo; Joaquin Perez-Pupo (Cuba).
Rectory: 2390 S.W. 139th Pl., 33175. Tel: 305-551-7046 (Office).
Church—14141 S.W. 26th St., 33175. Tel: 305-559-6111; Fax: 305-551-7047.
Catechesis/Religious Programs—Tel: 305-559-0163.
Students 700.

9—MOTHER OF OUR REDEEMER (1988), Rev. Fernando Compaired (Spain). In res., Rev. Federico Capdepon.
Res., 18928 N.W. 80th Ct., 33015. Tel: 305-829-6141; Fax: 305-829-3059.
Church—8445 N.W. 186 St., 33015.
Catechesis/Religious Programs—Students 410.

10—NOTRE DAME D'HAITI (1981), Revs. Gerard Darbouze; Lesly Jean.
Res., 110 N.E. 62nd St., 33138. Tel: 305-751-6289; Fax: 305-756-6470.
Catechesis/Religious Programs—Tel: 305-758-5560.
Students 1,050.
Missions—Fort Lauderdale, Broward Co., Divine Mercy, 1105 N.W. 6th Ave., Fort Lauderdale, 33311. Tel: 954-764-8519. Revs. Franky Jean; Roland Lamy.; Pompano Beach, Broward Co., St. Joseph, 1210 N.W. 6th Ave., Pompano Beach, 33060. Tel: 954-941-3095; Fax: 954-941-3115. Rev. Mary Kidney St-Jean.

11—OUR LADY OF DIVINE PROVIDENCE (1973), Revs. Luis Rivera; Reynaldo Terrero (Cuba); Fermin Solana (Cuba).
Church and Mailing Address—10205 W. Flagler St., 33172. Tel: 305-551-8113; 8114; Fax: 305-220-3164.
Res., 10420 S.W. 4th St., 33174. Tel: 305-226-7589.
Catechesis/Religious Programs—Tel: 305-225-0009.
Students 294.

12—OUR LADY OF THE HOLY ROSARY (1959), Revs. Sean J. Hyland; Michael J. Tabit (COL); Eduardo Jimenez; Adam F.X. Stromski.
Res., 9500 S.W. 184th St., 33157. Tel: 305-235-5135; Fax: 305-254-9045.
School—Tel: 305-235-5442; Fax: 305-235-5670. Sr. Carol Ann Ziecina, Prin.; Lyn Bimonte, Co-Prin.
Lay Teachers 30; Students 530.
Catechesis/Religious Programs—Students 375.

13—OUR LADY OF LOURDES (1985), Revs. Anthony Massi; Joaquin Rodriguez. In res., Rev. Kris Bartos.
Res., 14202 S.W. 111 Ln., 33186. Tel: 305-386-4121; Fax: 305-386-6881.
Church—11291 S.W. 142 Ave., 33186.
Catechesis/Religious Programs—Tel: 305-386-4894.
Students 1,005.

14—PRINCE OF PEACE (1987), Revs. Francisco G. Diaz; Pedro Corces.
Res., 275 N.W. 130 Ave., 33182. Tel: 305-559-3171; Fax: 305-559-3172.
Catechesis/Religious Programs—Students 290.

15—ST. AGATHA (1971), Revs. Felipe Estevez; Victor Babin; Samuel Muodiaju, C.S.Sp.
Res., 1111 S.W. 107th Ave., 33174. Tel: 305-222-1500; Fax: 305-222-1505.
School—Tel: 305-222-1500, Ext. 1040. Dr. Carlota Morales, Prin.
Sisters 1; Lay Teachers 42; Students 736.
Catechesis/Religious Programs—Tel: 305-222-1500, Ext. 1030. Mr. Efrain E. Sora, D.R.E.
Students 1,000.

16—ST. BRENDAN (1954), Revs. Jose P. Nickse; Raul Soutuyo; Francisco Calderon; Charles Peterman.
Res., 8725 S.W. 32 St., 33165. Tel: 305-221-0881; Fax: 305-226-6249.
School—Tel: 305-221-2722. Mrs. Emma A. Ventura.
Lay Teachers 34; Students 660.
Catechesis/Religious Programs—Tel: 305-226-2628; 221-2861. D.R.E.: Sr. Bertha Penabad; Rosmery Ortega.
Students 834.

17—ST. CATHERINE OF SIENA (1968), Revs. Juan J. Sosa; Francis Akwue, C.S.Sp.; Eliades Petit (Cuba).
Res., 9200 S.W. 107 Ave., 33176. Tel: 305-274-6333; Fax: 305-274-6337.

Catechesis/Religious Programs—Tel: 305-270-0830. Maria Mezquita, D.R.E.
Students 522.

18—ST. DOMINIC (1962), Revs. Jorge Presmanes, O.P.; Restituto Perez, O.P.; Desiderio Eguino, O.P.; Marcelo Solorzano, O.P. In res., Revs. Mark Wedig, O.P.; Henry B. Groover, O.P.; Emiliano Zapata, O.P. Res., 5909 N.W. 7th St., 33126. Tel: 305-264-0181; Fax: 305-262-4685.
Catechesis/Religious Programs—Tel: 305-264-3372.
Students 468.

19—ST. FRANCIS XAVIER (1927), Rev. John Raymond Lau, O.M.I.
Mailing Address: P.O. Box 01-1901, 33101-1901.
Res., 1698 N.W. 4th Ave., 33136. Tel: 305-576-2957; Fax: 305-576-3120.
School—Tel: 305-573-8532.
Lay Teachers 10; Students 163.
Catechesis/Religious Programs—Students 60.

20—ST. JAMES (1952), Rev. Jean Pierre.
Res., 540 N.W. 132nd St., 33168. Tel: 305-681-7428; Fax: 305-685-0631.
School—Tel: 305-681-3822.
Religious 1; Lay Teachers 14; Students 165.
Catechesis/Religious Programs—Tel: 305-681-2676.
Students 231.

21—ST. JOACHIM (1972), Rev. Jesus Saldana. In res., Rev. Ignacio Blasco.
Res., 11711 S.W. 193rd St., 33177. Tel: 305-233-1278; Fax: 305-233-2573.
Church—19150 S.W. 117th Ave., 33177.
Catechesis/Religious Programs—Students 778.

22—ST. JOHN BOSCO (1962), Rev. Msgr. Emilio Vallina; Rev. Roy Montealegre. In res., Rev. Msgr. Angel Gaztelu (Cuba); Rev. Msgr. William F. McKeever.
Mailing Address: P.O. Box 993, 33125.
Res., 1301 W. Flagler St., 33135. Tel: 305-649-5464; 5465; Fax: 305-541-0988.
Catechesis/Religious Programs—Tel: 305-649-5466. Angela Esparraguera, D.R.E.
Students 681.

23—ST. JOHN NEUMANN (1982), Revs. David Russell; Joseph Kottayil (India).
Res., 12125 S.W. 107th Ave., 33176. Tel: 305-255-6642; Fax: 305-233-3742.
School—Tel: 305-255-7315; 7316; Fax: 305-255-7316. Mrs. Maria M. Fernandez, Prin.
Lay Teachers 15; Aides 4; Students 335.
Catechesis/Religious Programs—Tel: 305-253-3081. Myrna E. Gallagher, D.R.E.
Students 1,351.

24—ST. KEVIN (1963), Revs. Alfred Cioffi; Jose Garcia (Cuba); Jose D. Lopez.
Res., 12525 S.W. 42 St., 33175. Tel: 305-223-0633; Fax: 305-554-9950.
School—4001 S.W. 127 Ave., 33175. Tel: 305-223-4015; Fax: 305-220-9048. Mrs. America Novas, Prin.
Lay Teachers 38; Students 658.
Catechesis/Religious Programs—Tel: 305-223-2469. Mrs. Maggie Enjamio, D.R.E.
Students 1,078.

25—ST. KIERAN (1967), Revs. James B. Curran, S.D.B.; Donald Zarkoski, S.D.B.; Richard Purnam, S.D.B.; Thomas Brennan, S.D.B.; Gumersindo Diaz, S.D.B. In res., Revs. Vincent Villar, S.D.B.; Innocent Clementi, S.D.B.
Res., 3605 S. Miami Ave., 33133. Tel: 305-854-1521; Fax: 305-854-5986.
Mission—Miami, La Purisima. 901 SW 3rd Ave.,#6.

26—ST. LOUIS (1963), Revs. James F. Fetscher; Michael A. Kish; Wallace A. McGowan; Jeffrey McCormick.
Res., 7270 S.W. 120 St., 33156. Tel: 305-238-7562; Fax: 305-238-6844.
Catechesis/Religious Programs—Tel: 305-238-7461. Peggy Santella, D.R.E.
Students 1,050.

27—ST. MICHAEL THE ARCHANGEL (1947), Revs. Jose M. Paz; Eduardo Pastor; Ronald Noguera. In res., Rev. Jordi Rivero.
Res., 2987 W. Flagler St., 33135. Tel: 305-649-1811; Fax: 305-642-6815.
School—300 N.W. 28 Ave., 33125. Tel: 305-642-6732. Sr. Florinda Bermudez, R.A., Prin.
Sisters 6; Lay Teachers 30; Students 600.
Catechesis/Religious Programs—Tel: 305-643-4661. George Briz, D.R.E.
Students 656.

28—SS. PETER AND PAUL (1938), Revs. Juan M. Lopez; Francisco Hernandez; Jose Berciano (Spain). In res., Rev. Juan Luis Sanchez.
Res., 900 S.W. 26th Rd., 33129. Tel: 305-858-2621; Fax: 305-858-8073.
School—Tel: 305-858-3722; Fax: 305-856-4322.
Sisters of St. Joseph of St. Augustine 3; Lay Teachers 34; Students 648.
Catechesis/Religious Programs—Students 375.

29—ST. RAYMOND (1969), Revs. Armando Balado; Sergio Cabrera.
Res., 3475 S.W. 17 St., 33145. Tel: 305-446-2427; Fax: 305-445-0472.
Catechesis/Religious Programs—Tel: 305-446-5108.
Students 265.

30—ST. RICHARD (1969), Rev. Ronald Pusak.
Res., 7500 S.W. 152 St., 33157. Tel: 305-233-8711; Fax: 305-254-2756.
Catechesis/Religious Programs—Tel: 305-233-8755.
Students 630.

31—ST. ROBERT BELLARMINE (1968), Rev. Omar A. Huesca.
Res., 3405 N.W. 27th Ave., 33142. Tel: 305-633-6009; Fax: 305-638-9480.
Catechesis/Religious Programs—Sr. Flor Maria Matamoros, O.P., D.R.E.
Students 321.

32—ST. THOMAS THE APOSTLE (1959), Revs. Daniel I. Kubala; Fernando Heria. In res., Rev. Anibal Morales.
Res., 7310 S.W. 62 St., 33143. Tel: 305-665-5600; Fax: 305-662-9034.
School—Tel: 305-661-8591; Fax: 305-661-7468. Sr. Marisa Ducore, O.C.D., Prin.
Lay Teachers 36; Students 567.
Catechesis/Religious Programs—Tel: 305-665-8591.
Students 270.

33—ST. TIMOTHY (1960), Rev. Msgr. Gerard T. LaCerra; Revs. Curtis Kiddy; Armando Alonso; Marcos Somarriba.
Office: 5300 S.W. 102 Ave., 33165. Tel: 305-274-8224; Fax: 305-598-1159.
School—Tel: 305-274-8229; Fax: 305-596-2952. Mrs. Jo-Ann Leskanic, Prin.
Sisters of St. Dominic of Newburgh 1; Lay Teachers 34; Students 675.
Catechesis/Religious Programs—Tel: 305-274-8225. Sr. Mary Carolyn Meehan, O.P., D.R.E.
Students 971.

34—ST. VINCENT DE PAUL (1962), Revs. Hector Gonzalez-Abreu; Martin Adu.
Res., 2000 N.W. 103rd St., 33147. Tel: 305-691-0771; Fax: 305-691-3352.
Catechesis/Religious Programs—Tel: 305-266-6485.
Students 220.

35—VISITATION (1956), Rev. Joseph Angelini.
Res., 19100 N. Miami Ave., 33169. Tel: 305-652-3624; Fax: 305-652-5207.
Catechesis/Religious Programs—100 N.E. 191 St., 33169. Tel: 305-651-7044.
Students 190.

METROPOLITAN DADE COUNTY

Coconut Grove, St. Hugh (1959), Revs. George Garcia; Rolando Castillo.
Res., 3460 Royal Rd., 33133. Tel: 305-444-8363; Fax: 305-444-4312.
School—Tel: 305-448-5602. Sr. Kathleen Donnelly, O.P., Prin.
Sisters 3; Lay Teachers 21; Students 332.
Catechesis/Religious Programs—Students 123.

Coral Gables, Little Flower (1926), Rev. Msgr. Xavier Morras; Revs. Hernando Villegas; Anthony O'Brien; Arnaldo Bazan. In res., Rev. Sean O'Sullivan.
Office: 2711 Indian Mound Tr., 33134. Tel: 305-446-9950; Fax: 305-446-7624.
Res., 1270 Anastasia Ave., 33134. Tel: 305-529-5475.
School—2701 Indian Mound Tr., 33134. Tel: 305-446-1738; Fax: 305-446-2877.
Sisters 5; Lay Teachers 46; Students 945.
Catechesis/Religious Programs—Tel: 305-446-5540.
Students 410.

St. Augustine (1969), Revs. Terence Hogan; Charles J. Powers, Jr.; James Suchocki (GAY).
Res., 1400 Miller Rd., 33146. Tel: 305-661-1648; Fax: 305-661-6392.
Catechesis/Religious Programs—Fax: 305-661-6293.
Students 348.

Hialeah

1—IMMACULATE CONCEPTION (1954), Revs. Gustavo J. Miyares; Jorge Noda (Cuba); Alberto Lahens; Enrique Boned.
Res., 4497 W. First Ave., 33012. Tel: 305-822-2011; Fax: 305-821-3481.
School—Tel: 305-822-6461; Fax: 305-822-0289. Sr. Theresita O'Sullivan, R.S.M., Prin.
Sisters of Mercy (Enniskillen, North Ireland) 1; Lay Teachers 46; Students 990.
Catechesis/Religious Programs—Tel: 305-823-9563. Nubia Stanley, D.R.E.
Students 775.

2—SAN LAZARO (1982), Revs. Pedro Luis Perez; Carlos Perez (Cuba). In res., Rev. Kenneth Schwanger.
Res., 4400 W. 18th Ave., 33012. Tel: 305-556-1717; Fax: 305-556-8918.
Catechesis/Religious Programs—Tel: 305-558-4078. Sr. Gloria Plasencia, D.R.E.
Students 700.

3—ST. BENEDICT (1973), Revs. Jose L. Paniagua (Spain); John M. Paszko; Jose Bardino (Cuba).
Res., 650 W. 80th St., 33014. Tel: 305-556-3278; Fax: 305-558-3705.
Church—701 W. 77th St., 33014. Tel: 305-558-2150.
Catechesis/Religious Programs—Tel: 305-557-2511. Maria de la Fe, D.R.E.
Students 730.

4—ST. CECILIA (1971), Revs. Emiliano Ordax; Isidro Perez.
Res., 1040 W. 29th St., P.O. Box 2931, 33012. Tel: 305-885-4614; 4615; Fax: 305-885-2327.
Catechesis/Religious Programs—Tel: 305-885-5504.
Students 305.

5—ST. JOHN THE APOSTLE (1945), Revs. Emilio Martin; William A. Elbert. In res., Revs. George Cardona, (Retired); Ignacio Morras, (Retired); Luis Casabon.
Res., 475 E. 4th St., 33010. Tel: 305-888-9769; Fax: 305-888-9341.
School—Tel: 305-888-6819; Fax: 305-887-1256. Ms. Elizabeth Furmanick, Prin.
Lay Teachers 28; Students 596.
Catechesis/Religious Programs—Students 620.

Hialeah Gardens, Santa Barbara (1987), Revs. Rafael Pedroso; Rolando Medina.
Res., 11960 N.W. 87 Ct., 33016. Tel: 305-556-4442; Fax: 305-558-7256.
Catechesis/Religious Programs—Students 473.

Homestead, Sacred Heart (1929), Revs. James McCreanor; Jose Sanchez, C.M.; Andre Tanguay, O.M.I.
Mailing Address: P.O. Box 901248, 33090-1248.
Res., 106 S.E. 1st Dr., 33030. Tel: 305-247-4405; Fax: 305-245-3002.
Church—208 S.E. 1st Dr., 33030.
School—300 S.E. 1st Dr., 33030. Tel: 305-245-2678. Mary Preston, Prin.
Lay Teachers 10; Students 212.
Catechesis/Religious Programs—Tel: 305-247-0760.
Students 212.

Key Biscayne, St. Agnes (1954), Revs. Jose L. Hernando; Enrique Delgado.
Res., 100 Harbor Dr., 33149. Tel: 305-361-2351; 361-2451; Fax: 305-361-8514.
Catechesis/Religious Programs—Students 302.

Leisure City, St. Martin de Porres Church (1990), Rev. Rolando Garcia.
Res., 28514 S.W. 147 Pl., 33033. Tel: 305-248-5355; Fax: 305-245-3047.
Church—14881 S.W. 288 St., 33033.
Catechesis/Religious Programs—Students 148.

Miami Beach

1—ST. FRANCIS DE SALES (1964), Revs. Alvaro Guichard; Manuel Martin (Venezuela); Francis J. Dunleavy.
Res., 621 Alton Rd., 33139. Tel: 305-672-0093; Fax: 305-673-8559.
Catechesis/Religious Programs—Students 115.

2—ST. JOSEPH (1942), Revs. Noel I. Bennett; Oscar Sarmiento; Edmund Gregory Fay, O.P.
Res., 8670 Byron Ave., 33141. Tel: 305-866-6567; Fax: 305-864-1069.
School—Tel: 305-866-1471; Fax: 305-866-3175. Mr. Richard S. Lynn, Prin.
Lay Teachers 17; Students 270.
Catechesis/Religious Programs—Students 205.

3—ST. MARY MAGDALEN (1955), Rev. Laurence J. Conway. In res., Rev. Manuel Ortega.
Res., 17775 N. Bay Rd., 33160. Tel: 305-931-0600; Fax: 305-931-0601.

4—ST. PATRICK (1926), Rev. Msgr. John J. Vaughan; Rev. Julio Solano. In res., Rev. George Puthusseril.
Office: 3716 Garden Ave., 33140.
Res., 3700 Meridian Ave., 33140. Tel: 305-531-1124; Fax: 305-538-3203.
School—Tel: 503-534-4616; Fax: 305-538-5463. Mrs. Josephine Kenna, Prin.
Lay Teachers 18; Students 231.
Catechesis/Religious Programs—Students 170.

Miami Lakes, Our Lady of the Lakes (1967), Revs. James Murphy; Francisco Martin. In res., Rev. Oscar Brantome.
Res., 15801 N.W. 67 Ave., 33014. Tel: 305-558-2202; Fax: 305-558-2631.
School—6600 Miami Lakeway N., 33014. Tel: 305-362-5315. Shelly Sweeney, Prin.
Lay Teachers 35; Students 615.
Catechesis/Religious Programs—Mary T. Tate, D.R.E.
Students 810.

Miami Shores, St. Martha (1970), Rev. Thomas J. Engbers. In res., Rev. Carl T. Morrison.
Res., 9301 Biscayne Blvd., 33138. Tel: 305-751-0005; Fax: 305-754-6930.
Catechesis/Religious Programs—Tel: 305-751-8759.
Students 90.

St. Rose of Lima (1946), Very Rev. Seamus Doyle; Rev. Pedro Lleo. In res., Rev. Raymond E. Brown, S.S.
Res., 415 N.E. 105 St., 33138. Tel: 305-758-0539; Fax: 305-751-8398.
School—Tel: 305-751-4257. Sr. Rita Murphy, I.H.M., Prin.
Sisters 4; Lay Teachers 38; Students 696.
Catechesis/Religious Programs—Tel: 305-757-6434.
Students 145.

Miami Springs, Blessed Trinity (1952), Revs. Joseph T. Carney; Anthony Mercieca (Malta); Joaquin Paret (Cuba).
Res., 4020 Curtiss Pkwy., 33166. Tel: 305-871-5780; Fax: 305-871-5781.
School—Tel: 305-871-5766. Mr. Pio Tei, Prin.
Lay Teachers 20; Students 278.
Catechesis/Religious Programs—Tel: 305-876-1753.
Students 225.

Naranja, St. Ann Mission (1960), Rev. Pedro Garcia.
Res., 13875 S.W. 264 St., P.O. Box 322205, 33032-1505. Tel: 305-258-3968; 258-9682; Fax: 305-258-3591.
Catechesis/Religious Programs—Students 500.

North Miami, Holy Family (1950), Revs. Jose Espino; Ferry Brutus.
Res., 14500 N.E. 11 Ave., 33161. Tel: 305-947-5043; 947-1471; Fax: 305-949-5591.
School—Tel: 305-947-6535; Fax: 305-949-5591. Mrs. Yolanda Minagorri, Prin.
Lay Teachers 17; Students 295.
Catechesis/Religious Programs—Tel: 305-947-7739.
Students 410.

North Miami Beach, St. Lawrence (1956), Revs. Roger Holoubek; Sergio Garcia-Miro.
Res., 2200 N.E. 191 St., 33180. Tel: 305-932-3560; Fax: 305-936-8050.
School—Tel: 305-932-4912; Fax: 305-932-4912. Ms. Dian Lopez, Prin.
Lay Teachers 14; Students 256.
Catechesis/Religious Programs—Tel: 305-931-6650.
Students 196.

Opa Locka, Our Lady of Perpetual Help Church (1954), Revs. Oscar Castaneda; Gregory Njoku, C.S.Sp.
Church & Res.: 13401 N.W. 28 Ave., 33054. Tel: 305-688-9663;688-9664; Fax: 305-685-8031.
Catechesis/Religious Programs—Tel: 305-685-5354.
Students 250.

St. Monica (1959), Revs. Alejandro Roque; Joseph Ferraioli, O.M.I.; John Curran, O.M.I.
Res., 3490 N.W. 191 St., 33056. Tel: 305-621-9846; Fax: 305-621-5608.
School—Tel: 305-621-2356.
Sisters 1; Lay Teachers 17; Students 202.
Catechesis/Religious Programs—Tel: 305-624-5132.
Students 240.

St. Philip (1953), Rev. John Madigan, O.M.I.
Res., 15700 N.W. 20 Ave. Rd., 33054. Tel: 305-624-6641.
Catechesis/Religious Programs—Students 80.

OUTSIDE METROPOLITAN DADE COUNTY

Big Pine Key, Monroe Co., St. Peter (1962), Rev. Thomas Mullane.
Res., U.S. 1, P.O. Box 430657, 33043. Tel: 305-872-2537; Fax: 305-872-0122.
Catechesis/Religious Programs—31300 Overseas Hwy., 33043.
Students 97.
Mission—Sugarloaf Shores, Sugarloaf Firehouse, Sugarloaf Shores, 33042.

Coconut Creek, Broward Co., St. Luke (1985), Rev. Stephen Hilley.
Res., 2370 Hammock Blvd., 33063. Tel: 954-977-0427; Fax: 954-978-1902.
Catechesis/Religious Programs—Tel: 954-974-1863.
Students 233.

Coral Springs, Broward Co., St. Andrew (1969), Revs. Arthur Dennison; Gabriel Vigues; John Peloso.
Res., 9950 N.W. 29 St., 33065. Tel: 954-752-3950; Fax: 954-752-3986.
School—Tel: 954-753-1280; Fax: 954-753-1933. Mrs. Mary Louise Balog, Prin.
Lay Teachers 58; Students 650.
Catechesis/Religious Programs—Tel: 954-752-3988. Deborah Andra, D.R.E.
Students 1,068.

St. Elizabeth Ann Seton (1985), Rev. Edward M. Kelly.
Res., 1401 Coral Ridge Dr., 33071. Tel: 954-753-3330; Fax: 954-753-8442.
Catechesis/Religious Programs—Tel: 305-345-7071.
Students 1,500.

Dania, Broward Co., Church of the Resurrection (1958), Revs. Michael J. Hughes, O.S.A.; James G. Glennon, O.S.A.
Res., 441 N.E. Second St., 33004. Tel: 954-923-2806; Fax: 954-923-1018.

Davie, Broward Co., St. David (1974), Rev. Gabriel O'Reilly; Rev. Msgr. Michael Conway (PAT).
Res., 3900 S. University Dr., 33328. Tel: 954-475-8046; Fax: 954-370-0819.
School—Tel: 954-472-7086; Fax: 954-452-8243. Mrs. Mariann Kiar, Prin.
Lay Teachers 45; Students 710.
Catechesis/Religious Programs—Tel: 954-475-1521. Pam McMillan, D.R.E.
Students 652.

Deerfield Beach, Broward Co., Our Lady of Mercy (1974), Rev. Michael Sullivan.
Parish Center and Office: 5201 N. Military Trail, Pompano Beach, 33064. Tel: 954-421-3246; Fax: 954-421-1973.

St. Ambrose (1962), Revs. John Bryan Dalton; James Connaughton, Pastor Emeritus; Kenneth Whittaker; John L. McCullen (TOL).
Res., 353 S.E. 12 Ave., P.O. Box 999, 33441. Tel: 954-427-2225; Fax: 954-421-1638.
School—Tel: 954-427-2226. Ms. Anita Gentile, Prin.
Lay Teachers 16; Students 400.
Catechesis/Religious Programs—Students 198.

Fort Lauderdale, Broward Co.,

1—BLESSED SACRAMENT, (1961), Rev. John P. McLaughlin.
Res., 1701 E. Oakland Park Blvd., 33334. Tel: 954-564-1010; Fax: 954-566-0301.

2—OUR LADY QUEEN OF MARTYRS, (1956), Revs. Michael Hoyer; Armando Perez; Roman J. Schaefer (NU); Rev. Dr. William Muniz.
Res., 2731 S.W. 11 Ct., 33312. Tel: 954-583-8725; Fax: 954-583-9315.
School—Tel: 954-583-8112; Fax: 954-797-4984. Mrs. Althea Mossop, Prin.
Lay Teachers 21; Students 340.
Catechesis/Religious Programs—Tel: 954-583-3307.
Students 225.

3—ST. ANTHONY, (1923), Revs. Timothy G. Hannon; John Donato, C.S.C.
Res., 901 N.E. 2nd St., 33301. Tel: 954-463-4614; Fax: 954-527-5411.
School—820 N.E. Third St., 33301. Tel: 954-467-7747; Fax: 954-467-9908. Mrs. Elaine L. Patterson, Prin.
Lay Teachers 18; Students 337.
Catechesis/Religious Programs—Tel: 954-467-7749.
Students 193.

4—ST. BONAVENTURE, (1985), Rev. Edmond Prendergast.
Res., 1301 S.W. 136th Ave., Davie, 33325-4300. Tel: 954-424-9504; 9505; Fax: 954-424-9505.
Catechesis/Religious Programs—Tel: 954-476-5204; Fax: 954-476-5203. Mariela Brink, D.R.E.
Students 1,900.

5—ST. CLEMENT, (1954), Revs. Peter Lambert; Albert R. Cutie; Henry Mullin, C.S.Sp. In res., Rev. Dennis Rausch.
Res., 2975 N. Andrews Ave., 33311. Tel: 954-563-1183; Fax: 954-564-6628.
School—Tel: 954-563-5608. Ms. Mary Ellen McKinney, Prin.
Sisters of St. Casimir 3; Lay Teachers 16; Students 265.
Catechesis/Religious Programs—Tel: 954-561-4641.
Students 335.

6—ST. GEORGE, (1964), Rev. Robert F. Tywoniak.
Res., 3640 N.W. 8th St., 33311. Tel: 954-583-5892; Fax: 954-583-0725.

7—ST. HELEN, (1968), Rev. Msgr. William Dever; Rev. Msgr. William E. Powers (GR); Revs. Joseph Kalariparampil; Isidore Baky.
Res., 3033 N.W. 33rd Ave., 33311. Tel: 954-731-7314; Fax: 954-739-9632.
School—Tel: 954-739-7094; Fax: 954-739-0797. Sr. Marie Colette Gerry, Prin.
Lay Teachers 17; Students 264.
Catechesis/Religious Programs—Tel: 954-484-3036.
Students 300.

8—ST. JEROME, (1960), Revs. Joseph Cinesi; Francis X. McCarthy, (Retired).
Res., 2533 S.W. 9th Ave., 33315. Tel: 954-525-4133; Fax: 954-525-0964.
School—Tel: 954-524-1990; Fax: 954-524-7439. Sr. Vivian Gomez, R.F., Prin.
Sisters of St. Philip Neri 4; Lay Teachers 19; Students 332.
Catechesis/Religious Programs—2601 S.W. 9th Ave., Ft. Lauderdale, 33315.
Students 60.

9—ST. JOHN THE BAPTIST, (1969), Revs. Vincent T. Kelly; James F. Daly, C.S.Sp.
Res., 4595 Bayview Dr., 33308. Tel: 954-771-8950; Fax: 954-771-4178.
Catechesis/Religious Programs—Students 176.

10—ST. MARK, (1985), Revs. Edmond F. Whyte; Paul Edwards; Thomas Mannix Stack.
Res., 5601 S. Flamingo Rd., 33330. Tel: 954-434-3777; Fax: 954-434-3125.
Catechesis/Religious Programs—Tel: 954-252-9899. Donna Villavisanis, D.R.E.
Students 1,117.

11—ST. MAURICE, (1970), Rev. Sean C. Mulcahy.
Res., 2851 Stirling Rd., 33312. Tel: 954-961-7777; Fax: 954-961-4358.
Catechesis/Religious Programs—Tel: 954-961-4358.
Students 178.

12—ST. PIUS X, (1959), Revs. Patrick C. Slevin; James J. Hampton; Harry Ringenberger.
Res., 2500 N.E. 33rd Ave., 33305. Tel: 954-564-1763.
Church—2511 N. Ocean Blvd. (A1A), 33308. Fax: 954-568-2212.

13—ST. SEBASTIAN, (1959), Rev. Msgr. Patrick McDonnell, V.F.; Rev. William F. Mylchreest.
Res., 2518 Barbara Dr., 33316. Tel: 954-524-9344; Fax: 954-524-9347.

Hallandale, Broward Co., St. Charles Borromeo (1968), Rev. Gary R. Steibel.
Res., 123 N.W. 6 Ave., 33009. Tel: 954-458-1914; Fax: 954-458-8770.

St. Matthew (1959), Revs. James A. Quinn; Paul Deyo, SS.CC.
Res., 542 Blue Heron Dr., 33009. Tel: 954-458-1590; Fax: 954-458-0612.
Catechesis/Religious Programs—Students 72.

Hollywood, Broward Co., Little Flower (1926), Revs. Thomas O'Dwyer; Paul Kane; Thomas Hanly; Patirck O'Shea.
Res., 1805 Pierce St., 33020. Tel: 954-922-3517; Fax: 954-922-6634.
School—Tel: 954-922-1217; Fax: 954-927-8962. Deacon William A. Watkins, Prin.
Lay Teachers 16; Students 275.
Catechesis/Religious Programs—Students 131.

Nativity (1960), Very Rev. Patrick J. Murnane; Revs. Andres Coucelo; James Russel, S.M.; Abraham Joseph Pallivathuckal (India).
Res., 5220 Johnson St., 33021. Tel: 954-987-3300; Fax: 954-987-3044.
School—Tel: 954-983-4981. Mrs. Elena Ortiz, Prin.
Sisters Servants of Immaculate Heart of Mary 1; Lay Teachers 31; Students 755.
Catechesis/Religious Programs—Students 471.

St. Bernadette (1959), Rev. Brendan Dalton; Rev. Msgr. Robert J. Yates, (Retired); Rev. Sean O'Dea, (Retired).
Res., 7450 Stirling Rd., 33024. Tel: 954-432-5313; Fax: 954-432-5344.
School—Tel: 954-432-7022. Mrs. Lynn Vander Wyde, Prin.
Sisters 1; Lay Teachers 19; Students 350.
Catechesis/Religious Programs—Tel: 954-432-6300.
Students 367.

Key Largo, Monroe Co., St. Justin Martyr (1973), Rev. Edward Olszewski.
Res., 105500 Overseas Hwy., 33037. Tel: 305-451-1316; Fax: 305-451-4633.

Key West, Monroe Co., St. Mary, Star of the Sea (1846), Revs. Gerald F. McGrath; Roberto Garza.
Res., 1010 Windsor Ln., 33040. Tel: 305-294-1018; Fax: 305-292-8096.
School—Tel: 305-294-1031; Fax: 305-294-2095.
Sisters 2; Brothers 1; Deacons 1; Lay Teachers 15; Students 198.
Catechesis/Religious Programs—Tel: 305-295-9615.
Students 185.

Lighthouse Point, Broward Co., St. Paul the Apostle (1968), Revs. Frederick J. Brice; John Richard Soulliere. In res., Revs. Sergio Dall'Agnese, C.S.; Horecio Carlos Anklan, C.S.
Res., 2700 N.E. 36th St., 33064. Tel: 954-943-9154; 9155; Fax: 954-943-9155.
Catechesis/Religious Programs—Students 153.

Marathon, Monroe Co., San Pablo (1958), Rev. Gerald R. Morris.
Res., 550 122nd St. Ocean, 33050. Tel: 305-289-0636; Fax: 305-743-8192.

Margate, Broward Co., St. Vincent (1960), Revs. Neil Doherty; Michael Lynch.
Res., 6350 N.W. 18th St., 33063. Tel: 954-972-0434; Fax: 954-971-9411.
Catechesis/Religious Programs—Tel: 954-972-7708.
Students 205.

Miramar, Broward Co., St. Bartholomew (1962), Rev. Paul Vuturo. In res., Rev. Edmund Ogbonna (Nigeria).
Res., 8005 Miramar Pkwy., 33025. Tel: 305-431-3600; Fax: 305-435-9591.
School—Tel: 305-431-5253. Maria Glass, Prin.
Lay Teachers 17; Students 315.
Catechesis/Religious Programs—Students 490.

St. Stephen (1956), Revs. James E. Taggart, O.M.I.; James Flavin, O.M.I.; Russell Nickerson, O.M.I.
Res., 6044 S.W. 19th St., 33023. Tel: 954-987-1100; Fax: 954-966-9881.
School—Tel: 954-983-2636; Fax: 954-986-8557.
Sisters of St. Joseph of St. Augustine 3; Lay Teachers 18; Students 255.
Catechesis/Religious Programs—Tel: 305-962-2112.
Students 887.

North Lauderdale, Broward Co., Our Lady Queen of Heaven (1974), Revs. Joseph Huck; Francis A. Lyons.
Res., 6771 Kimberly Blvd., 33068.
Church—1400 South St., Rd. 7, 33068. Tel: 954-971-5400; Fax: 954-972-4008.
Catechesis/Religious Programs—Tel: 954-973-3406.
Students 380.

Parkland, Mary Help of Christians Church (1989), Rev. Thomas Wisniewski.
Church—5980 University Dr., 33067. Tel: 954-340-6462; Fax: 954-340-6838.
Catechesis/Religious Programs—Tel: 954-340-2872.
Students 525.

Pembroke Pines, Broward Co., St. Boniface (1971), Revs. Antonio R. Silio; Timothy Sperber.
Res., 8330 Johnson St., 33024. Tel: 954-432-2750; Fax: 954-432-2756.
Catechesis/Religious Programs—Students 368.

St. Edward (1995), Rev. Michael Eivers.
Res., 1101 N.W. 184 Ter., 33029. Tel: 954-436-7944; Fax: 954-436-7506.
Catechesis/Religious Programs—Students 400.

St. Maximilian Kolbe (1983), Revs. James Vitucci; Ernest Biriruka (Ngozi).
Res., 11051 N.W. 16th St., 33026. Tel: 954-432-8289.
Church—701 N. Hiatus Rd., 33026. Tel: 954-432-0206; Fax: 954-432-0775.
Catechesis/Religious Programs—Tel: 954-435-3000.
Students 1,130.

Plantation, Broward Co., St. Gregory (1959), Rev. Msgr. Noel Fogarty, P.A.; Revs. Gary Wiesmann; Abel Barajas.
Res., 200 N. University Dr., 33324. Tel: 954-473-6261; Fax: 954-473-4599.
School—Tel: 954-473-8169; Fax: 954-472-1638. Ms. Barbara Rosini, O.S.F., Prin.; Mrs. Antoinette McNamara, Asst. Prin.
Sisters 1; Lay Teachers 34; Students 804.
Catechesis/Religious Programs—Tel: 954-473-8321.
Students 435.

Pompano Beach, Broward Co.,

1—Assumption, (1951), Revs. Martin J. Cassidy; John Handrahan, S.J.
Res., 2001 S. Ocean Blvd., 33062. Tel: 954-941-7647; Fax: 954-941-9620.

2—San Isidro, (1970), Revs. Ricardo C. Castellanos; Luis A. Perez; Hyacinth Edokwe, C.S.Sp.
Res., 2310 Martin Luther King Blvd., 33069-1591. Tel: 954-971-8780.
Dade: Tel: 954-940-8719.
Catechesis/Religious Programs—Students 375.

3—St. Coleman, (1959), Revs. Thomas F. Foudy; Joseph Maroor (India).
Res., 1200 S. Federal Hwy., 33062. Tel: 954-942-3533; Fax: 954-942-7869.
School—Tel: 954-942-3500; Fax: 954-785-0603.
Lay Teachers 28; Aides 5; Students 630.
Catechesis/Religious Programs—1285 S.E. 22nd Ave., 33062. Tel: 954-782-1461.
Students 400.

4—St. Elizabeth of Hungary Catholic Church, (1959), Rev. Msgr. John W. Glorie; Rev. Fernando Isern.
Res., 3331 N.E. 10 Ter., 33064-5298. Tel: 954-941-8117; Fax: 954-941-0999.
School—901 N.E. 33rd. St., 33064. Tel: 954-942-2161; Fax: 954-942-7551. Mrs. Rita A. O'Leary, Prin.
Sisters 1; Lay Teachers 24; Students 476.
Catechesis/Religious Programs—Tel: 954-943-6801.
Students 156.

5—St. Gabriel, (1967), Rev. Msgr. Francis J. Fazzalaro; Rev. James Parappally.
Res., 731 N. Ocean Blvd., P.O. Box 3044, 33062. Tel: 954-943-3684; Fax: 954-943-3656.

6—St. Henry, (1969), Rev. Msgr. James B. Reynolds; Rev. George Duffy.
Res., 1500 S.W. 12th Ave., 33069. Tel: 954-785-2450; Fax: 954-785-6958.
Catechesis/Religious Programs—Students 82.

Sunrise, Broward Co., All Saints (1982), Rev. Anthony J. Mulderry. In res., Rev. Guy Fenger.
Office: 10900 W. Oakland Park Blvd., 33351. Tel: 954-742-2666; Fax: 954-741-7238.
Catechesis/Religious Programs—Tel: 954-742-7742.
Students 1,207.

St. Bernard (1971), Very Rev. Michael Hourigan, V.F.
Res., 8279 Sunset Strip, 33322. Tel: 954-741-7800; Fax: 954-742-4558.
Catechesis/Religious Programs—Tel: 954-741-0275.
Students 158.

Tamarac, Broward Co., St. Malachy (1973), Revs. Dominick O'Dwyer; Daniel Cernauskas (Nassau).
Res., 6200 John Horan Terr., 33321. Tel: 954-726-1237; Fax: 954-726-0822.
Catechesis/Religious Programs—Tel: 954-721-5337; Fax: 954-726-0822. Lucille Moran, D.R.E.
Students 275.

Tavernier, Monroe Co., San Pedro (1954), Rev. John D. McGrath.
Res., Overseas Hwy., Plantation Key, P.O. Box 456, 33070. Tel: 305-852-5372; Fax: 305-852-3315.
Catechesis/Religious Programs—Students 119.

West Hollywood, Broward Co., Annunciation (1959), Rev. Michael Quilligan.
Res., 3781 S.W. 39th St., 33023. Tel: 954-989-0606; Fax: 954-989-0660.
School—Tel: 954-989-8287. Sr. Josephine Sherry, R.S.M., Prin.
Sisters 1; Lay Teachers 17; Students 303.
Catechesis/Religious Programs—Students 180.

Special Assignment:
Reverend Fathers—
Clements, Charles, Baptist Hospital & South Miami Hospital, Miami
Doyle, Dan F., S.M., 4921 Lincoln St., Hollywood, FL 33021. Tel: 954-964-1026
Fink, John, Broward General Hospital
Fishwick, Joseph, Baptist Hospital & South Miami Hospital, Miami
O'Neill, Patrick H., Coord. Spec. Projects, Ministry of General Services
Smith, David, Jackson Memorial Hospital

On Duty Outside the Archdiocese:
Reverend Monsignors—
Navarro, Pablo A.
Reverend Fathers—
Carbajales, Ignacio, Spain
O'Hala, Stephen, Boynton Beach (St. Vincent de Paul Seminary) (West Palm Beach)
O'Leary, John, Peru
Perales, Jorge, Mexico
Quijano, Jose Juan, Boynton Beach (St. Vincent de Paul Regional Seminary)
Scheiding, Philip, Mexico

Military Chaplains:
Reverend Fathers—
Gubbins, John
Melley, James

Higher Studies:
Reverend Fathers—
Estrada, Enrique, Rome, Italy
Rios, Juan Carlos, Rome, Italy
Souckar, Michael, Rome, Italy

Sabbatical:
Reverend Monsignors—
Delaney, John
Kirlin, Bernard

Absent on Sick Leave:
Reverend Fathers—
Brantome, Oscar
Montoya, Juan
Puerta, Jorge
Reiser, John

Absent on Leave:
Reverend Fathers—
Christman, Robert
Currid, Joseph
Fernandez, Fausto
Grogan, Brendan
Hayes, Joseph
Keener, Michael
Kudlo, Frank
Miyares, Carlos
Piano, Timothy
Reyes, Jose L.
Velie, Richard

Retired:
Most Rev.—
McCarthy, Edward A.
Reverend Monsignors—
Fernandez, Orlando
Walsh, Bryan O.
Reverend Fathers—
Biain, Jose
Brohammer, Ronald
Cahill, Frank
Cardona, George
Cliff, Joseph
Connaughton, James
Dennehy, Thomas
Dunleavy, Francis J.
Fernandez, Miguel A.
Fernandez, Nelson
Garcia-Fidalgo, Manuel
Gunther, William
Hanly, Thomas
Hudak, Cyril
Ireland, Donald
Jackson, Charles
Lucking, Aloysius
Lyons, Francis
Lyons, Lawrence
McKeever, William
Mitchell, Walter
Molano, Ernesto
Morras, Ignacio
Murray, Patrick
O'Sullivan, Sean
Perez, Maximiliano
Planas, Salvador
Puisis, Leonard
Punch, David
Quinlan, Eugene
Quinn, James E.
Rivas, Romeo
Scherer, Richard
Schlinkmann, John W.
Stadalnikas, Casimir J.
Valoret, Joseph
Vann, John C.

Permanent Deacons:
Abdallah, Mitchell C.
Aceto, Igino, Rockville Centre, NY
Aguayo, Orlando
Aguilu, Thomas
Alfonso, Manuel
Alonso, Jose P.
Asselin, Allen
Avery, John
Baez, Rodolfo, Santo Domingo, Dominican Republic
Bautista, Andres, Santo Domingo, Dominican Republic
Bechily, Antonio, Chicago
Benavides, Luis Pensacola
Binder, Robert
Blaha, Daniel C.
Blais, Robert, On Duty Outside the Archdiocese
Blanco, Eduardo
Bouker, Richard
Brizuela, Humberto
Buigas, Manuel
Calvo, Pedro P.
Camacho, Vidal, New York, NY
Canovaca, Manuel
Carieri, Carl
Carroll, Dr. Norman
Carroll, Richard A.
Chavez, Diego
Chinelly, John, Sr.
Colastin, Max
Coniglio, Philip, On Duty Outside the Archdiocese
Costea, Nicholas
Crawford, Jr. Frederick, On Duty Outside the Archdiocese

Cresswell, William H.
Cronin, Donald
Cuesta, Angel L.
Currier, Roger
DeCola, Joseph, Brooklyn, NY
DeLuca, Arnold J.
DeNunzio, Arthur
Diehl, William, On Duty Outside the Archdiocese
Dietsch, Charles, III, On Duty Outside the Archdiocese
DiLeonardo, Ignatius, On Duty Outside the Archdiocese
Dinsmore, Robert B.
Draughon, Woodworth R.
Dugan, Richard
Eberling, Vincent, Jr.
Estrada, Francisco
Fallon, Martin, On Duty Outside the Archdiocese
Farinato, Vincent
Fathauer, Ronald, On Duty Outside the Archdiocese
Fernandez, Pablo A.
Fiore, Charles
Friel, John
Fuentes, Rafael
Galard, John, On Duty Outside the Archdiocese
Garcia, Jose M., Sabbatical
Gazitua, Ralph
Gervasi, Angelo
Gibson, George
Gonzalez, Blas
Gonzalez, Jorge G.
Gonzalez, Luis
Gonzalez, Miguel
Goulet, Guy
Gouthro, Ronald
Green, John F.
Hanlon, Thomas F.
Harris, Willie
Hubbell, Carl
Hummel, John
Jordan, Dennis E.
Karrenberg, William H.
Knox, Terrence, On Duty Outside the Archdiocese
Kroll, John
Lam, Alex S.
Lang, Irving
Lannon, Billy, Jr.
Leon, Michael
Lezama, Jose V., On Duty Outside the Archdiocese
Livingstone, Donald
Llaneza, Oscar
Long, George H., Jr., On Duty Outside the Archdiocese
Lopez, Mario
Lopez, Pedro
Lopez, Victor
Loyola, Benito
Maceo, Antonio J.
Martinez, Jose
McClain, Kirby
McInerney, Vincent
Mickwee, George, On Duty Outside the Archdiocese
Mieyal, Denis
Mindel, Albert
Minetti, Bernard, On Duty Outside the Archdiocese
Moreno, Vicente
Moretti, Daniel
Munter, Paul H.
Murphy, Charles
Murray, Paul, On Duty Outside the Archdiocese
Musselman, Randall O.
Nerys, Jose A., San Juan, Puerto Rico
O'Malley, Robert F., Jr.
Ochoa, Roberto
Ortega, Ray
Padron, Rodolfo
Parlade, Miguel
Pearce, Joseph M.
Peremenis, John
Perez, Manuel
Perron, Charles
Phillips, Eugene
Pintado, Angel
Pita, Bernardo
Plummer, Joseph
Plummer, Michael
Polcari, Joseph A., On Duty Outside the Archdiocese
Prieto, Jorge
Raymond, Donald, On Duty Outside the Archdiocese
Renuart, Albert, On Duty Outside the Archdiocese
Reyes, Rafael de los
Rizo, Ornan, Jr., Sabbatical
Rodriguez, Jorge, On Duty Outside the Archdiocese
Rodriguez, Santos
Ruiz-Castaneda, Norman
Saavedra, Manuel
Scherrer, Thomas, Sabbatical
Shaw, Roger M.
Sierra, Feliciano
Sierra, Luis
Smith, David
Solorzano, Jose
Sommovigo, Joseph
Soucy, Joseph O.
Starzinski, Louis
Sutcavage, George P.
Taylor, Ian
Taylor, Timm
Teolis, Matthew, Chicago
Thesing, John
Tola, Vincent
Tomonto, James R.
Tosco, Jesus
Velez, Gregorio, On Duty Outside the Archdiocese
Venezia, Richard
Vitale, Perry
Waldman, Gerald
Watkins, William A.
White, James, On Duty Outside the Archdiocese
Zayas, Julio
Zayas, Luis

INSTITUTIONS LOCATED IN THE ARCHDIOCESE

[A] SEMINARIES, ARCHDIOCESAN

MIAMI. *St. John Vianney College Seminary*, 2900 S.W. 87th Ave., 33165. Tel: 305-223-4561; 4562; Fax: 305-223-0650. Very Rev. John Noonan, Rector; Ms. Zoila Diaz, D.Min., Academic Dean; Maria Rodriguez, Librarian; Revs. Oscar Mendez, S.J., Spiritual Dir.; Joseph Waters, Vice Rector, Dean of Students & Dir. Pre-Theology Programs; Michael Davis; Robert Vallee. In res. Revs. Manuel Garcia Fidalgo; Liam Quinn. Students 44.

[B] COLLEGES AND UNIVERSITIES

MIAMI. *Barry University*, 11300 N.E. 2nd Ave., 33161. Tel: 305-899-3000.
Web site: www.barry.edu
For a complete listing, refer to the Colleges and Universities section.

OPA LOCKA. *St. Thomas University*, 16400 N.W. 32nd Ave., 33054. Tel: 305-625-6000; Fax: 305-628-6511.
Web site: www.stu.edu
For a complete listing, refer to the Colleges and Universities section.

[C] HIGH SCHOOLS, ARCHDIOCESAN

MIAMI. *Archbishop Curley-Notre Dame High School*, 4949 N.E. 2nd Ave., 33137. Tel: 305-751-8367; Fax: 305-751-3517.
E-mail: rdemaria@curley.pvt.k12.fl.us
Web site: http://www.curley.pvt.k12.fl.us
Bro. Richard J. DeMaria, C.F.C., Prin.; Ms. Beatriz Rodriguez, Asst. Prin.; Rev. Christopher Marino, Chap. Priests 1; Brothers 6; Sisters 1; Lay Teachers 28; Students 490.

La Salle High School, 3601 S. Miami Ave., 33133. Tel: 305-854-2334.
E-mail: lashsmd@mailcity.com
Web site: www.lasallehighschool.com
Sr. Shermane Delgado, F.M.A., Prin.; Mr. Eric Shane, Asst. Prin. for Student Affairs; Ms. Antonia Ruiberriz, Asst. Prin. for Curriculum; Sr. Maryann Schaefer, F.M.A., Admin. Asst.; Rev. Richard Putnam, S.D.B., Coord. of Youth Ministry. Priests 2; Brothers 1; Sisters 5; Lay Teachers 30; Students 613.

Msgr. Edward Pace High School, 15600 Spartan Blvd., N.W. 32 Ave., 33054. Tel: 305-624-8534.
E-mail: pacetch@icanert.net
Bro. Anthony M. Iazzetti, F.M.S., Prin.; Revs. Gustavo J. Miyares, Supervising Prin.; Cyril J. Smith, O.S.A., Academic Dean; Michael Grady, Chap.; Mrs. Ginny Hutton, Asst. Prin. for Academics; Mr. Samuel Lilly, Dean of Students. Priests 3; Brothers 1; Lay Teachers 48; Students 850.

Our Lady of Lourdes Academy, 5525 S.W. 84th St., 33143. Tel: 305-667-1623. Sr. Susan Marie Kuk, I.H.M., Prin.; Rev. Marcos Somarriba. Servants of the Immaculate Heart of Mary 8; Lay Teachers 57; Students 829.

St. Brendan High School, 2950 S.W. 87 Ave., 33165. Tel: 305-223-5181; Fax: 305-220-7434.
E-mail: sabres@worldnet.att.net
Rev. Jose P. Nickse, Supervising Prin.; Bro. Felix A. Elardo, F.M.S., Prin.; Ms. Barbara Behnke, Dean of Students; Ms. Gloria Ramos, Dean Curriculum. Priests 2; Lay Teachers 66; Counselors 4; Students 1,255.

FORT LAUDERDALE. *Cardinal Gibbons High School*, 4601 Bayview Dr., 33308. Tel: 954-491-2900.
E-mail: cg-admin@ix.netcom.com
Web site: http://www.info-access.com/cardinalgibbons/
Very Rev. Joseph J. Kershner, Sch.P., Prin.; Sr. Marie Schramko, O.S.F., Asst. Prin.; Revs. Francis Pala, Sch.P., Asst. Prin.; Oscar Alonso, Sch.P.; Charles Newburn, Sch.P.; John Callan; Bro. Grant R. Ferris, O.S.F.S. Priests 3; Brothers 1; Sisters of St. Francis 1; Lay Teachers 48; Students 1,136.

St. Thomas Aquinas High School, 2801 S.W. 12 St., 33312. Tel: 954-581-2127; 581-0700.
E-mail: stahs@safari.net
Web site: http://www.safari.net/~stahs
Rev. Vincent T. Kelly, Supervising Prin.; Mr. William M. Heller, Prin.; Mrs. Tina Jones-Atkins, Asst. Prin.; Sr. Peggy Manning, O.P., Campus Min.; Mr. Paul Gomulinski, Dean of Students; Rev. Guy Fenger (OG). Priests 2; Sisters 4; Lay Teachers 92; Students 1,691.

[D] HIGH SCHOOLS, PRIVATE

MIAMI. *Belen Jesuit Preparatory School*, 500 S.W. 127 Ave., 33184. Tel: 305-223-8600. Very Rev. Benjamin Gonzalez-Buelta, Prov.; Revs. Marcelino Garcia, S.J., Pres, Prin., Contact; Pedro Cartaya, S.J.; Jorge Sardina, S.J.; Jose R. Tey, S.J.; Juan Manuel Dorta, S.J.; Eduardo Alvarez, S.J.; Jorge Munguia, S.J.; Francisco J. Lemus, S.J.; Francisco Perez-Lerena, S.J.; Victor M. Hernandez, S.J.; Bros. Pedro Estevez, S.J.; S. Martin Arias, S.J. Priests 10; Brothers 2; Sisters 1; Lay Teachers 64; Students 970.

Carrollton School of the Sacred Heart, 3747 Main Hwy., 33133. Tel: 305-446-5673.
E-mail: carrolad@netrunner.net
Sr. Ann Taylor, R.S.C.J., Headmistress. Religious of the Sacred Heart 3; Lay Teachers 72; Students 600.

Christopher Columbus High School, 3000 S.W. 87 Ave., 33165. Tel: 305-223-5650; Fax: 305-559-4306.
E-mail: mia_cchs@msn.com
Campus Ministers: Rev. Liam Quinn; Bros. Kenneth Curtin, F.M.S.; Angelo Palmieri, F.M.S., Prin.; Edmund Sheehan, F.M.S., Asst. Prin. (Scheduling); Michael Brady, F.M.S., Svc. Coord.; Mrs. Patricia Call, Asst. Prin. (Grades & Academic Credit); Mr. Christopher McKeon, Asst. Prin. (Discipline). Priests 1; Marist Brothers 14; Lay Teachers 64; Students 1,390.

HOLLYWOOD. *Chaminade-Madonna College Preparatory*, 500 Chaminade Dr., 33021-5800. Tel: 305-989-5150. Bro. John Campbell, S.M., Pres.; Anne McGrath, Prin. Marianist Brothers 4; Lay Teachers 52; Students 804.

[E] ELEMENTARY SCHOOLS, PRIVATE

KEY WEST. *Mary Immaculate Star of the Sea*, 700 Truman Ave., 33040. Tel: 305-294-1031. Brothers 1; Sisters 2; Lay Teachers 9; Students 198.

[F] SHELTERS

MIAMI. *Camillus House, Inc.*, P.O. Box 11829, 33101-1829
For a complete listing, refer to the Special Care Facilities section.

Gift of Hope, Missionaries of Charity, 724 N.W. 17 St., 33136. Tel: 305-326-0032
For a complete listing, refer to the Special Care Facilities section.

[G] GENERAL HOSPITALS

MIAMI. *Mercy Hospital*, 3663 S. Miami Ave., 33133. Tel: 305-854-4400
For a complete listing, refer to the Hospitals section.

FORT LAUDERDALE. *Holy Cross Hospital*, 4725 N. Federal Hwy., 33308. Tel: 954-771-8000; Fax: 954-492-5741
For a complete listing, refer to the Hospitals section.

[H] MONASTERIES AND RESIDENCES OF PRIESTS AND BROTHERS

MIAMI. *Casa San Lorenzo*, 16400 N.W. 32 Ave., 33054. Tel: 305-624-0775. Augustinian Fathers. Revs. Cyril J. Smith, O.S.A.; James L. MacDougall, O.S.A., Prior, Contact; Raymond E. Geisser, O.S.A.; Gary N. McCloskey, O.S.A.; John J. Kelly, O.S.A.; Thomas R. Cook, O.S.A. Total in Residence 6.

Franciscan Fathers' Residence, 2044 S.W. 22nd Ter., 33145. Tel: 305-856-5257. Revs. Jose Biain, O.F.M.; Angel Villaronga, O.F.M.

Marist Brothers Residences, 8230 S.W. 136th St., 33156. Bros. Charles Filiatraut, F.M.S., Contact; Damian Galligan, F.M.S.; Lawrence Poirier, F.M.S.; Daniel Andrew, F.M.S.; Norbert Rodriguez, F.M.S.; Simeon Ouellet, F.M.S.; Robert Ryan, F.M.S., 2790 S.W. 89 Ave., 33165. Bros. Bernard Nolan, F.M.S.; Thomas Edward, F.M.S.; Cornelius Russell, F.M.S.; Lucien Duguay, F.M.S.

Villa Arrieta. Belen Jesuit Fathers, Inc. 2928 S.W. 10 St., 33135. Tel: 305-541-6221. Revs. Pedro A. Suarez, S.J., (Superior) Contact; Pedro Cartaya, S.J.; Juan Manuel Dorta, S.J.; Gerardo Freire, S.J.; Francisco J. Lemus, S.J.; Otto Martinez, S.J.; Jorge Munguia, S.J.

Belen Jesuit Alumni Association, 911 N.W. 27 Ave., Ste. 5, 33125. Tel: 305-642-0433. Rev. Juan M. Dorta, S.J., Moderator.

Villa Javier. Belen Jesuit Fathers, Inc. 13339 S.W. 9 Ter., 33184. Tel: 305-559-9066; Fax: 305-222-1256.
E-mail: vjavier@aol.com
Revs. Eduardo Alvarez, S.J.; Florentino Azcoitia, S.J.; Eduardo Barrios; Marcelino Garcia, S.J.; Victor M. Hernandez, S.J., Supr., Contact; Tomas Macho, S.J.; Enrique Osle, S.J.; Francisco Perez-Lerena, S.J.; Jose R. Tey, S.J.; Jorge Sardina, S.J. Seminarians: Martin Arias, S.J.; Fulgencio Mayorga, S.J.; Bro. Pedro Estevez, S.J.

BAL HARBOUR. *Dominican Friars Residence*, The Plaza, No. 201, 10185 Collins Ave., 33154. Tel: 305-864-6593.
E-mail: madden@psca01.barry.edu
Web site: http://martin.barry.edu:80/artsci/theology/madden/danspg96.htm
Rev. Daniel P. Madden, O.P.

[I] CONVENTS AND RESIDENCES FOR SISTERS

MIAMI. *Congregation of the French-Cuban Dominican Sisters of Holy Rosary, Inc.*, 8900 S.W. 19th St., 33165. Tel: 305-221-0384. Sr. Olga Martinez, Contact; Sr. Mary Cecilia Alonso, Pres. & Treas. Houses of Religious Women 1; Total in Residence 6.

Daughters of Charity of St. Vincent de Paul. (Santurce, P.R.), Mision San Vicente de Paul. 500 N.W. 63rd Ave., 33126. Tel: 305-266-6485.
E-mail: caridad@netrunner.net
Web site: www.netrunner.net/~caridad
Ermita Nuestra Senora de la Caridad, 3609 S. Miami Ave., P.O. Box 330555, 33133. Tel: 305-854-2404.
Asociacion Hijas de la Caridad de San Vicente de Paul del Estado de la Florida, Inc. Sr. Eva Perez-Puelles, Contact.

Daughters of St. Paul, 11117 S.W. 2nd St., 33174. Tel: 305-554-0175.
E-mail: paulinas@icanect.net
Sr. Irene Mary Martineau, F.S.P., Supr., Contact. Houses of Religious Women 1; Total in Residence 6.

Guadalupan Missionaries of the Holy Spirit, 2483 S.W. 4 St., 33135. Tel: 305-642-9544. U.S. Delegation Headquarters. Other Address: 869 S.W. Third St., Florida City, 33034-4605. Tel: 305-248-3735. Legal Title: *Missionary Guadalupanas of the Holy Spirit, Inc.* Sr. Edith Lugo. House of Religious Women 1; House of Studies 1; Total in Residence 10.

Handmaids of the Sacred Heart of Jesus A.C.J. St. Rafaela's Faith Community, 1615 N.E. 108 St., 33161. Tel: 305-891-9161.
E-mail: acjmiami@dc.seflin.org
Sr. Sagrario Nunez, Contact. Sisters 5.

Missionaries of Charity, 727 N.W. 17th St., 33136. Tel: 305-545-5699. Sr. M. Ajaya, M.C., Supr. (Contact). Houses of Religious women 1; Total in Residence 6; Total Assisted 1,194.

FORT LAUDERDALE. *Sisters of Mercy Ministry Corporation*, 4841 N.E. 20th Ave., 33308. Tel: 954-776-3290; Fax: 954-776-3014. Sr. Genevra Baer, R.S.M., Contact Person.

MIAMI SHORES. *Franciscan Sisters of Allegany*.
Addresses: 138 N.E. 111 St., 33161. Tel: 305-751-3093. Total in Residence 3. St. Francis Convent, 99 N.W. 115 St., Miami, 33168. Tel: 305-751-1544. Total in Residence 3.

[J] RETREAT HOUSES

MIAMI. *Dominican Retreat House, Mary Queen of Apostles*, 7275 S.W. 124 St., 33156. Tel: 305-238-2711; Fax: 305-238-2717. Dominican Sisters of St. Catherine de Ricci (Motherhouse-Elkins Park, PA). Sr. Annette Lucero, O.P., Contact. Sisters 4; Capacity for Overnight Retreat Programs 60; Retreat Center 1; Total in Residence 3; Staff 7.

John Paul II Retreat House, 720 N.E. 27th St., 33137-4697. Tel: 305-576-2748; 573-1418; Fax: 305-576-2748.
E-mail: webmaster@acu-adsum.org
Web site: http://www.acu-adsum.org
Rev. Amando Llorente, S.J., Spiritual Dir., Contact. Total in Residence 2; Total Staff 8.
Agrupacion Catolica Universitaria, Inc.
Jesuit Fathers of the Province of the Antilles, Inc.

[K] CENTERS

MIAMI. *Family Life Ministry*. 9401 Biscayne Blvd., Miami Shores, 33138. Tel: 305-762-1140; Fax: 305-762-1144.
Web site: dfleri@aol.com
Mrs. Dawne M. Fleri.

Respect Life Office, 18340 N.W. 12 Ave., 33169. Tel: 305-653-2921; Fax: 305-653-1001. Rev. Jordi S. Rivero, Dir.; Ms. Joan Crown, Contact. Special Centers for Social Services 6; Total Assisted 8,702; Staff 7.

St. Paul Book and Media Center, 145 S.W. 107th Ave., 33174. Tel: 305-559-6715; 6716; Fax: 305-559-6717. Sr. Irene Mary Martineau, F.S.P., Supr. Daughters of St. Paul 6; Houses of Religious Women 1; Total in Residence 6; St. Paul Book & Media Center 1; Staff 13.

Shrine of Our Lady of Charity, 3609 S. Miami Ave., P.O. Box 330555, 33133. Tel: 305-854-2404. Most Rev. Agustin Roman, V.G., Dir. Associate Directors: Revs. Romeo Rivas; Francisco Santana. Sisters 5; Houses of Religious Women 1; Total in Residence 5.

Southeast Pastoral Institute, 7700 S.W. 56th St., 33155. Tel: 305-279-2333; Fax: 305-279-0925. Rev. Mario B. Vizcaino, Sch.P., Dir., Contact.

Southeast Regional Office for Hispanic Ministry, Inc., 7700 S.W. 56th St., 33155. Tel: 305-279-2333; Fax: 305-279-0925. Rev. Mario B. Vizcaino, Sch.P., Reg. Dir., Contact.

[L] MISCELLANEOUS LISTINGS

MIAMI. *Alumni Association of the Apostolate of Cuba (in Exile), Inc.*, P.O. Box 650721, 33265-0721. Tel: 305-271-4151. Maria Antonia Pena, Treas. (Contact.

Alumni of Apostolate Charity Foundation, Inc., P.O. Box 650721, 33265-0721. Maria Antonia Rodriguez, Pres. Tel: 305-226-8110; Maria Antonia D. Pena, Treas., Contact. Tel: 305-271-4151.

Claretian Missions, Inc., 7080 S.W. 99 Ave., 33173. Sr. Ondina Cortes, Superior (Contact). Sisters 5; Houses of Religous Women 3; Total in Residence 12.

Discalced Carmelite Friars of Miami, Inc. Our Lady of Mt. Carmel Spiritual Life Center. 18330 N.W. 12 Ave., 33169. Tel: 305-654-9760; Fax: 305-654-9345. Revs. Eusebio Gomez, O.C.D., Pres., Contact; Lucio del Burgo, O.C.D., Vice Pres.; Jose Francisco Rosario, O.C.D. Retreat Center 1; Total in Residence 3; Staff 6.

Dominican Fathers of Miami, Inc., 5909 N.W. 7th St., 33126-3199. Tel: 305-264-0181; Fax: 305-262-4685.
St. Dominic Priory. Houses of Religous Men 1; Total in Residence 8.
Southern Dominican Province Vocations Office, P.O. Box 431283, 33423.

Foundation of the Cuban Association of the S.M.O. of Malta, Inc., Grand Bay Plaza, Ste. 1100, 2665 S. Bayshore Dr., 33133. Tel: 305-285-0800; Fax: 305-285-0837. Fernando Garcia-Chacon, Pres.; Juan T. O'Naghten, Vice Pres.; Manuel Menendez, Treas.; Lodovico Blanc, Dir.

Human Services Division/Pierre Toussaint Haitian Catholic Center, Inc. (A Florida Not-for-Profit Corporation), 110 N.E. 62 St., 33138. Tel: 305-758-2462; Fax: 305-758-8216. Special Centers for Social Services & Assistance 1; Total Assisted 7,000; Total Staff 28.

Peruvian Mission, Inc (A Florida Not-for-Profit Corporation), P.O. Box 432745, 33143. Tel: 305-596-6738; Fax: 305-596-6738.
E-mail: perumision@aol.com

St. Luke's Center, Inc., 7707 N.W. 2nd Ave., 33150. Tel: 305-795-0077; Fax: 305-795-0030. Patricia Carter, Interim Dir. (Contact).

Addiction Recovery Center. Total in Residence 45; Total Staff 25.

SEPI Evangelization and Education Foundation, Inc., 7700 S.W. 56th St., 33155. Tel: 305-279-2333. Rev. Mario B. Vizcaino, Sch.P., Exec. Dir., Contact.

Teresian Institute, Inc. (Rome, Italy), Teresian Institute of Florida, Inc., 3400 S.W. 99 Ave., 33165. Tel: 305-553-8567; 226-3317. An International Association of the Faithful. Ana Mandiola, Contact. Total in Residence 3; Total Staff 5.
Center of Activities, National Headquarters.

CORAL GABLES. *Bahamas Mission of Florida, Inc.*, c/o J. Patrick Fitzgerald, Esq., 110 Merrick Way, Ste. 3-B, 33134. Tel: 305-443-9162; Fax: 305-443-6613.

Magnificat, Inc., 5031 Maggiore St., 33146. Board of Directors: Cristina Beato; Maria P. Vadia; Beatriz Harriman; Maria Horvath; Elsa Rodriguez.

FORT LAUDERDALE. *Schott Memorial Center Foundation, Inc.* (A Florida Not-for-Profit Corporation), 6591 S.W. 124th Ave., 33330. Tel: 305-434-3306; 434-7437; Fax: 305-434-3307.
E-mail: jrgschott@aol.com
John R. Green, Exec. Dir., Contact. Special Centers for Social Services & Assistance 1; Total Assisted 11,520; Total Staff 6.

HIALEAH. *Dominicas de la Inmaculada Concepcion*, 571 W. 33 Pl., 33012. Tel: 305-823-3282. Sr. Flor Maria Matamoros, Supr. Houses of Religous Women 1; Total in Residence 4.

KEY LARGO. *1-800-Mass-Times Trust*, 67 N. Bounty Lne, 33037. Tel: 305-852-4530.
E-mail: bhummel@aol.com
Robert A. Hummel, Chm.; Phyliss H. Hummel, Sec. Governing Board: Jerry Early; Rev. Jose P. Nickse. Toll-free telephone listing of local Catholic Churches with Mass times to assist travelers in finding Mass schedules.

MIAMI SHORES. *DOM, Inc.*, 9401 Biscayne Blvd., 33138. Tel: 305-757-6241.

Francis Realty Corporation, 9401 Biscayne Blvd., 33138. Tel: 305-757-6241.

Marbella Condominium 207 Association, Inc., 9401 Biscayne Blvd., 33138. Tel: 305-757-6241.

P.O.M., Inc., 9401 Biscayne Blvd., 33138. Tel: 305-757-6241.

Pooled Income Trust Fund, 9401 Biscayne Blvd., 33138. Tel: 305-757-6241.

Provincial Realty Associates, Inc. (A Florida Not-for-Profit Corporation), 9401 Biscayne Blvd., 33138. Tel: 305-757-6241.
Land Holding Corporation.

ST. PETERSBURG. *Franciscan Sisters of Allegany, NY*, Region III Office, 631-11 St. N., 33705. Tel: 813-824-0857. Sr. Gladys Sharkey, Reg. III Minister.

St. Francis Medical & Health Care Foundation, Inc.

St. Francis Medical & Health Care Services, Inc. Allegany Health System, 6200 Courtney Campbell Dr., Ste. 100, Tampa, 33607. Tel: 800-290-9098.

RELIGIOUS INSTITUTES OF MEN REPRESENTED IN THE ARCHDIOCESE

For further details refer to the corresponding bracketed number in the Religious Institutes of Men or Women section.

[0140]—*The Augustinians.* (St. Thomas of Villanova Prov.).—O.S.A.
[0200]—*Benedictine Monks.*—O.S.B.
[0810]—*Brothers of Mercy.*—M.M.
[0600]—*Brothers of the Congregation of Holy Cross.*—C.S.C.
[0580]—*Brothers of the Good Shepherd.*—B.G.S.
[0400]—Canons Regular of the Order of the Holy Cross.—O.S.C.
[0470]—*Capuchin Friars.*—O.F.M.Cap.
[0270]—*Carmelite Fathers & Brothers.*—O.Carm.
[1320]—*Clerics of St. Viator.*—C.S.V.
[0310]—*Congregation of Christian Brothers.* (Eastern Prov.).—C.F.C.
[1330]—*Congregation of the Mission.*—C.M.
[1080]—*Congregation of the Resurrection.*—C.R.
[1140]—*Congregation of the Sacred Hearts of Jesus and Mary.*—SS.CC.
[0260]—*Discalced Carmelite Friars.*—O.C.D.
[0520]—*Franciscan Friars.* (Most Holy Name & San Sebastion Provs.).—O.F.M.
[0650]—*Holy Ghost Fathers.*—C.S.Sp.
[0690]—*Jesuit Fathers and Brothers.* (Antilles & New Orleans Provs.).—S.J.
[0770]—*The Marist Brothers.* (Esopus & Poughkeepsie Provs.).—F.M.S.
[0800]—*Maryknoll.*—M.M.
[1210]—*Missionaries of St. Charles-Scalabrinians.*—C.S.
[0910]—*Oblates of Mary Immaculate.*—O.M.I.
[0920]—*Oblates of St. Francis de Sales.*—O.S.F.S.
[0950]—*Oratorians.*—C.O.
[0430]—*Order of Preachers (Dominican).* (St. Joseph & Southern Provs.).—O.P.
[1040]—*Piarist Fathers.*—Sch.P.
[0610]—*Priests of the Congregation of the Holy Cross.*—C.S.C.
[1070]—*Redemptorist Fathers.*—C.SS.R.
[1190]—*Salesians of Don Bosco.*—S.D.B.
[0760]—*Society of Mary (Marianists).*—S.M.
[1060]—*Society of the Precious Blood.*—C.PP.S.
[0560]—*Third Order Regular of St. Francis.*—T.O.R.

RELIGIOUS INSTITUTES OF WOMEN REPRESENTED IN THE ARCHDIOCESE

[0370]—*Carmelite Sisters of the Most Sacred Heart of Los Angeles.*—O.C.D.
[0685]—*Claretian Missionary Sisters.*—R.M.I.
[0270]—*Congregation of Bon Secours.*—C.B.S.
[3710]—*Congregation of the Sisters of St. Agnes.*—C.S.A.
[1710]—*Congregation of the Third Order of St. Francis of Mary Immaculate, Joliet, IL.*—O.S.F.
[0760]—*Daughters of Charity of St. Vincent de Paul.*—D.C.
[0790]—*Daughters of Divine Charity.*—F.D.C.
[0850]—*Daughters of Mary Help of Christians.*—F.M.A.
[]—*Daughters of Mary, Mother of Mercy (Nigeria).*—D.M.M.M.
[1070-13]—*Dominican Sisters (Adrian).*—O.P.
[1070-17]—*Dominican Sisters (Elkins Park).*—O.P.
[1070-06]—*Dominican Sisters (Newburgh).*—O.P.
[1070-03]—*Dominican Sisters (Sinsinawa).*—O.P.
[]—*Dominican Sisters of Bethany Congregation.*—O.P.
[]—*Dominican Sisters of Our Lady of the Most Holy Rosary (Columbia).*—O.P.
[]—*Dominicas de la Inmaculada Concepcion (Ecuador).*

[1180]—*Franciscan Sisters of Allegany, New York.*—O.S.F.
[1845]—*Guadalupan Missionaries of the Holy Spirit.* (Mexico).—M.G.Sp.S.
[]—*Handmaids of the Holy Child of Jesus.* (Nigeria).—H.H.C.J.
[1870]—*Handmaids of the Sacred Heart of Jesus.*—A.C.J.
[2575]—*Institute of the Sisters of Mercy of the Americas.* (Pittsburgh, PA; Cedar Rapids, IA; Rochester, NY; Merion, PA; North Carolina; Clogher, Ireland; Newfoundland, Canada).—R.S.M.
[]—*Marianitas.* (Santa Mariana de Jesus Institute, Inc.).—R.M.
[2710]—*Missionaries of Charity.*—M.C.
[3040]—*Oblate Sisters of Providence.*—O.S.P.
[]—*Oblates of the Sacred Heart of Jesus (El Salvador).*—O.C.J.
[3130]—*Our Lady of Victory Missionary Sisters.*—O.L.V.M.
[0950]—*Pious Society Daughters of St. Paul.*—F.S.P.
[3380]—*Religious of the Apostolate of the Sacred Heart.*—R.A.
[3390]—*Religious of the Assumption.*—R.A.
[2970]—*School Sisters of Notre Dame.* (Baltimore, MD; Chicago, IL; Wilton, CT; Mankato, MN).—S.S.N.D.
[0430]—*Sisters of Charity of the Blessed Virgin Mary.* (Davenport, IA).—B.V.M.
[]—*Sisters of Charity of the Sacred Heart of Jesus (Spain).*—S.C.S.H.J.
[]—*Sisters of Jesus the Saviour.* (Nigeria).—S.J.S.
[2540]—*Sisters of Mercy.* (Clogher, Northern Ireland).—R.S.M.
[3000]—*Sisters of Notre Dame de Namur (Baltimore, MA; Cincinnati, OH).*—S.N.D.deN.
[3350]—*Sisters of Providence.*—S.P.
[4080]—*Sisters of Social Service.*—S.S.S.
[3740]—*Sisters of St. Casimir.*—S.S.C.
[1620]—*Sisters of St. Francis of Millvale, Pennsylvania.*—O.S.F.
[1630]—*Sisters of St. Francis of Penance and Christian Charity.*—O.S.F.
[1650]—*Sisters of St. Francis of Philadelphia.*—O.S.F.
[3830-13]—*Sisters of St. Joseph (Baden, PA).*—C.S.J.
[3830-05]—*Sisters of St. Joseph (Brentwood, NY).*—C.S.J.
[3830-09]—*Sisters of St. Joseph (Erie, PA).*—S.S.J.
[3830-07]—*Sisters of St. Joseph (Rutland, VT).*—S.S.J.
[]—*Sisters of St. Joseph Benedict Cottolengo.*—S.S.J.C.
[3840]—*Sisters of St. Joseph of Carondelet.* (St. Louis, MO).—C.S.J.
[3850]—*Sisters of St. Joseph of Chambery.* (West Hartford, CT).—C.S.J.
[3900]—*Sisters of St. Joseph of St. Augustine, Florida.*—S.S.J.
[]—*Sisters of St. Philip Neri Missionary Teachers.*—R.F.
[1970]—*Sisters of the Holy Family of Nazareth.*—C.S.F.N.
[1990]—*Sisters of the Holy Names of Jesus and Mary.* (Longvevil, Quebec, Canada).—S.N.J.M.
[2070]—*Sisters of the Holy Union.*—S.U.S.C.
[2180]—*Sisters of the Immaculate Heart of Mary.*—I.H.M.
[2150]—*Sisters, Servants of the Immaculate Heart of Mary.*—I.H.M.
[2160]—*Sisters, Servants of the Immaculate Heart of Mary.*—I.H.M.
[2170]—*Sisters, Servants of the Immaculate Heart of Mary.*—I.H.M.
[2460]—*Society of Mary Reparatrix.*—S.M.R.
[4020]—*Society of St. Teresa of Jesus.*—S.T.J.
[4070]—*Society of the Sacred Heart.*—R.S.C.J.
[]—*Theatine Sisters of the Immaculate Conception (Religiosas Teatinas de la Inmaculada Concepcion).*—R.T.

NECROLOGY

† Dorrity, Daniel K., (Special Assignment). —Died March 16, 1997.

† Joseph, Karunei, Coral Springs, FL, St. Andrew. —Died Sept. 24, 1997.

Archdiocese for the Military Services, U.S.A.

Military Ordinariate

Most Reverend

JOSEPH T. RYAN, D.D.

Retired Ordinary of the Archdiocese for the Military Services, U.S.A.; ordained June 3, 1939; appointed First Archbishop of Anchorage February 7, 1966; consecrated March 25, 1966; appointed Titular Archbishop of Gabi and Coadjutor to the Military Vicar October 24, 1975; installed December 13, 1975; appointed Ordinary of the Archdiocese for the Military Services, U.S.A. March 16, 1985; installed March 25, 1985; retired May 13, 1991. *Res., 832 Varnum St., N.E., Washington, DC, 20017.*

Most Reverend

JOSEPH T. DIMINO, D.D.

Former Archbishop for the Military Services; ordained June 4, 1949; appointed Titular Bishop of Carini and Auxiliary Bishop to the Military Vicar March 29, 1983; consecrated May 10, 1983; appointed Ordinary to the Military Services May 13, 1991; resigned August 12, 1997.

Most Reverend

FRANCIS X. ROQUE, D.D.

Auxiliary Bishop; ordained September 19, 1953; appointed Titular Bishop of Bagai and Auxiliary Bishop to the Military Vicar March 29, 1983; consecrated May 10, 1983.

Most Reverend

EDWIN F. O'BRIEN, S.T.D.

Archbishop for the Military Services; ordained May 29, 1965; appointed Titular Bishop of Tizica and Auxiliary Bishop of New York March 25, 1996; appointed Coadjutor April 8, 1997; succeeded as Ordinary to the Military Services August 12, 1997.

Chancery: P.O. Box 4469, Washington, DC, 20017-0469. Tel.: 301-853-0400; Fax: 301-853-2246.

Most Reverend

JOSEPH J. MADERA, M.SP.S., D.D.

Auxiliary Bishop; ordained June 15, 1957; appointed Coadjutor Bishop of Fresno with the right of succession December 18, 1979; consecrated March 4, 1980; succeeded to See July 1, 1980; appointed Titular Bishop of Orte and Auxiliary Bishop of the Archdiocese of the Military Services May 28, 1991.

Most Reverend

JOHN J. GLYNN, D.D.

Auxiliary Bishop; ordained April 11, 1951; appointed Titular Bishop of Monteverde and Auxiliary Bishop of the Archdiocese for the Military Services December 10, 1991; ordained Bishop January 6, 1992.

ESTABLISHED AS MILITARY VICARIATE OF THE UNITED STATES SEPTEMBER 8, 1957.

Created Archdiocese For The Military Services, U.S.A. (Ordinariatus Castrensis) March 25, 1985.

Serving U.S. Catholics of the Army, Navy, Air Force, Marine Corps, Coast Guard, Department of Veterans Affairs and those in Government Service overseas.

STATISTICAL OVERVIEW

Personnel	
Archbishop	1
Retired Archbishops	2
Auxiliary Bishops	3
Priest chaplains are on loan from their diocese or religious community.	
Deacons who assist at chapels are volunteers from the local diocese.	
Educational	
Catechesis/Religious Education Programs:	
High School Students	21,000
Elementary Students	44,200
Total	65,200
Religious Education Teachers	5100
Sisters	12
Lay Teachers	220
Total	232
Vital Statistics	
Receptions into the Church:	
Infant Baptism Totals	5,896
Adult Baptism Totals	1,045
Received into Full Communion	493
First Communions	3,316
Confirmations	2,385
Marriages:	
Catholic	682
Interfaith	599
Total Marriages	1,281
Catholics, Active Duty Military	375,000
Family Members	520,000
Reserve/Guard Catholic personnel	204,000
Catholic residents, VA facilities	29,000
Civilian Catholics overseas	66,000
Total	1,194,000

Former Military Vicars—His Eminence PATRICK CARDINAL HAYES, cons. Titular Bishop of Tagaste, Oct. 28, 1914; appt. "Bishop Ordinary of U.S. Army and Navy Chaplains," Nov. 24, 1917; appt. Archbishop of New York, March 10, 1919; created Cardinal, March 24, 1924; died Sept. 4, 1938.—His Eminence FRANCIS CARDINAL SPELLMAN, cons. Auxiliary Bishop of Boston, Sept. 8, 1932; appt. Archbishop of New York, April 15, 1939; appt. "Military Vicar for the Armed Forces of U.S.," Dec. 11, 1939; created Cardinal, Feb. 18, 1946; died Dec. 2, 1967.—His Eminence TERENCE CARDINAL COOKE, cons. Auxiliary Bishop of New York, Dec. 13, 1965; appt. Archbishop of New York, March 2, 1968; appt. "Military Vicar of U.S. Armed Forces," April 4, 1968; created Cardinal, April 28, 1969; died Oct. 6, 1983.—Most Rev. JOSEPH T. RYAN, appt. first Archbishop of Anchorage, Feb. 7, 1966; cons. March 25, 1966; appt. Titular Archbishop of Gabi and Coadjutor Archbishop of the Military Vicar, Oct. 24, 1975; installed first Ordinary of the Archdiocese for the Military Services March, 25, 1985; retired May 13, 1991.—Most Rev. JOSEPH T. DIMINO, appt. Auxiliary Bishop of Military Vicar, March 29, 1983; cons. May 10, 1983; appt. Titular Bishop of Carini; appt. second Ordinary for the Military Services, May 13, 1991; retired Aug. 12, 1997.

Vicar General—Rev.Msgr. ALOYSIUS R. CALLAGHAN, S.T.L., J.C.D.

Regional Episcopal Vicars

Europe—Rev. JOSEPH GLATTS, Chap., *HQ USAFE/HCP Unit 3050, Box 50, APO AE, 09012.* Rev. PHILIP HILL, Chap., *HQ USAREUR & 7A CMR 420, Box 2977, APO AE, 09063.*

Japan—Rev. CAMPION LAYY, O.F.M., *St. Francis Friary, 14-20 Tsutsumi-Cho-3-Chome, Kiryu-Shi, Gumma-Ken, 376. Japan.*

Okinawa—Rev. CHARLES BANTLE, O.F.M.Cap., *Catholic Mission, 314 Asato, Naha, Okinawa, 902. Japan.*

Korea—Rev. Msgr. ROBERT H. SPIEGEL, Chap., *Office of the Chaplain Attn: FKCH, APO AP, 96205-0010.*

Oceana—Most Rev. ANTHONY SABIAN APURON, O.F.M.Cap., Archbishop of Agana, *Chancery Office, P.O. Box 126, Cuesta San Ramon, 26, Agana, Guam, M.I.*

Archdiocese Offices

Chancery—3311 Toledo Ter., Ste. A 201, Hyattsville, MD, 20782-4135. Tel: 301-853-0400; Fax: 301-853-2246.

Moderator of the Curia/Chancellor—Rev. Msgr. ALOYSIUS R. CALLAGHAN, S.T.L, J.C.D.

Office of Chaplain Personnel—

Vicar for Chaplains and Seminarians—Most Rev. JOHN J. GLYNN, D.D.

Director—Mrs. MARGARET SCUDERI.

Pastoral Support, Community Concerns and Vocations—Most Rev. JOSEPH J. MADERA, M.Sp.S., D.D.

Veterans Concerns—Most Rev. FRANCIS X. ROQUE, D.D.

Assistant to the Archbishop—Mrs. PATRICIA L. THACKER.

Director of Administration—Mr. JOHN SMITH.

Director of Sacramental Records—Mr. FRANK CALANDRA.

Director of Development—Mr. WILLIAM SHEPARD.

Tribunal—

Judicial Vicar—Rev. MICHAEL C. CONNOLLY, O.S.F.S., J.C.L.

Judges—Rev. Msgr. ALOYSIUS R. CALLAGHAN, J.C.D.; Rev.Msgr. GEORGE E. DOBES, J.C.L.; Revs. EDWARD G. PFNAUSCH, J.C.D.; RONNY E. JENKINS, J.C.L.; G. PAUL HERBERT, J.C.L.; ROBERT T. MORIARTY, J.C.L.; GEORGE BRUBAKER, J.C.L.; MARK MALLACK, J.C.L.; Mrs. DEBORAH BARTON, J.C.L.

Defenders of the Bond—Revs. DAVID F. O'CONNOR, S.T., J.C.D.; ALFRED A. SCHLERT, J.C.L.; STEVEN J. CRIBARI, J.C.L., J.D.; RODNEY COPP, J.C.L.

Procurator-Advocates—Most Rev. JOHN J. GLYNN, D.D.; Most Rev. FRANCIS X. ROQUE, D.D.

Notary—Mrs. MAY TOEPFER.

Presbyteral Council—Most Rev. EDWIN F. O'BRIEN, D.D.; Most Rev. JOHN J. GLYNN, D.D.; Most Rev. FRANCIS X. ROQUE, D.D.; Most Rev. JOSEPH J. MADERA, M.SP.S., D.D.; Rev. Msgr. ALOYSIUS R. CALLAGHAN, Exec. Sec.; Rev. Msgr. DONALD SHEA, (U.S.A.); Rev. Msgr. JOHN KAISING, (U.S.A.); Revs. CHARLES BOURKE, (U.S.N.); PATRICK FRYER, (U.S.N.); JAMES DIXON, (U.S.A.F.); Rev. Msgr. WILLIAM J. DENDINGER, (U.S.A.F.); Revs. AIDAN WALSH, (V.A.); FRANCIS CROWLEY, (V.A.).

Military Council of Catholic Women—Most Rev. FRANCIS X. ROQUE, Episcopal Moderator.

Areas of Service

Armed Forces, Active Duty

The Archdiocese for the Military Services is responsible for the pastoral care of the Catholic men and women who serve on active duty in the five branches of the U.S. Armed Forces. It is also responsible for the dependents of these persons. Included also are the cadets and resident personnel of the three military academies (West Point, the U.S. Air Force Academy at Colorado Springs, the U.S. Naval Academy at Annapolis) and the

U.S. Coast Guard Academy at New London as well as the U.S. Merchant Marine Academy at Kings Point, NY. Pastoral care is provided by priest chaplains on loan from their dioceses or religious communities to serve as chaplains for the Military and Department of Veterans Affairs. The pastor at West Point is a civilian priest of the Archdiocese of New York. Members of the Marines and Coast Guard are served by Navy Chaplains.

Armed Forces, Reserves, National Guard

In addition to the personnel on active duty in the Armed Forces, there is a considerable reserve component. Some of these personnel serve a number of days each year on active duty with a branch of the service; some serve on extended tours of active duty; all are subject to recall to active duty in a national emergency. In addition to the reserve components of the Army, Air Force, Navy and Coast Guard, which are organized on a state-by-state basis.

Department of Veterans Affairs

The Archdiocese for the Military Services is responsible for the spiritual care of Catholics at V.A. medical facilities. Chaplaincy services are provided by full- and part-time priests, many of whom are retired military chaplains.

U.S. Government Civilian Employees Abroad

U.S. citizens in government service abroad (and their family members living with them) are subjects of the Archdiocese for the Military Services.

There are only two full-time Catholic chaplains conducting pastoral programs for embassies: in Moscow and Bonn. The Embassy in Moscow has a program conducted by the Augustinians of the Assumption and is separate from the Archdiocese; it serves Catholics in the Foreign Service of other countries as well as Americans.

Civil Air Patrol

The Civil Air Patrol, as an auxiliary of the Air Force, is under the jurisdiction of the Archdiocese for the Military Services. The jurisdiction applies to its chaplains and members only when participating in exercises on a military installation.

UNITED STATES ARMY CHAPLAINS

REGULAR ARMY CHAPLAINS

Reverends

Amezcua, Mario M., *l.c.*
Arnoldt, David L. (WIN)
Bengco, Jose C. (Philippines)
Blickhan, Donald (SFD)
Bluett, James K. (PT)
Bolton, Paul (PRO)
Bomba, Paul (WOR)
Breaker, Donald J. (CIN)
Briganti, Phillip (PAT)
Burns, Vincent deP. (PH)
Carey, William F. (BGP)
Chilen, Michael D. (CC)
Coindreau, James M., *l.c.*
D'Emma, Gregory J. (NEW)
DiGregorio, Joseph (PH)
Drozd, Henry (DAL)
D'Silva, Joseph R. (India)
Ehrhart, Charles (RVC)
Flaska, John A., Jr. (SFE)
Gunti, Charles E., *o.f.m.*
Habarek, Jerome (PRO)
Hill, PHilip (NY)
Himmelsbach, James R. (STP)
Inghilterra, Vincent J. (TR)
Jones, James, *o.f.m.cap.*
Kaising, John J. (CIN)
Kenehan, David A., *o.s.f.s.*
Mandock, Patrick H. (GBG)
Marceaux, Sidney (BEA)
Mauricio, Clemente B., *m.s.c.*
Menz, Anthony, *o.c.s.o.*
Minch, Richard (SAV)
Morency, Raymond (PRT)
Mullen, Owen J. (WIL)
Mulvaney, Andrew (OG)
Niemeier, Dennis A. (CIN)
O'Keeffe, Joseph L., (ALB)
Prendergast, John (PEO)
Rappl, Joseph (BUF)
Rodriguez, Aloysius M. (BR)
Rutherford, Donald (ALB)
Sanner, James E. (E)
Santos, Elenito B. (Philippines)
Schmit, Louis L., *c.pp.s.*
Schroeder, Kenneth J., *c.pp.s.*
Seifried, Kenneth A. (SC)
Shea, Donald W. (HEL)
Sheil, James E. (CLV)
Spiegel, Robert H. (DAV)
Stahl, Allen M. (ORL)
Sykes, Gregory (OG)
Teahan, Timothy (BRK)
Tellez, Jairo, (SAT)
Travaglione, Michael, *o.f.m.*
Whalen, Frank J. (CIN)
Wilk, Mitchell S. (SPC)
Willett, William (OWN)
Wydeven, John L. (OAK)

ARMY RESERVE ON ACTIVE DUTY

Reverends

Albertson, Eric (ARL)
Betz, James (CAM)
Bleboo, Lawrence (Africa)
Borkowski, Frank J. (NY)
Borycz, Edmund S. (DET)
Bowman, James (RVC)
Castillo, Rolando C. (Philippines)
Cavanaugh, Kevin (HRT)
Cerrone, Michael J. (SAV)
Czech, Edward M. (CLV)
Deken, John C. (STL)
Denig, Philip (DEN)
Deponai, Joseph (NY)
Dormer, David J. (SCR)
Dynek, Wieslaw A. (Poland)
Fleury, Joseph, *s.m.*
Fuller, Orlando (Philippines)
Glasgow, Robert (MAN)
Goudreau, Joseph L. (PRT)
Hannon, Joseph, *s.d.b.*
Healy, Patrick, *s.s.j.*
Herrera, Jose (STV)
Herron, Jack B. (FAR)
Hightower, Oliver L. (HEL)
Hill, Donald W. (BIS)
Honor, Michael (Philippines)
Jagielski, James J. (DET)
Jaramillo, Peter (AMA)
Kelley, Edward (PRO)
Kirk, David R. (TOL)
Kopec, Rajmond (NEW)
Lagasse, Ronald (OAK)
Lanuevo, Victor (HON)
Madden, James J., *o.praem*
Martin, Edward C., *ss.cc.*
Mintegui, Marc (CHR)
O'Grady, John F. (PAT)
Patton, Patrick G. (HEL)
Pfeiffer, Carl, *o.ss.t.*
Ratigan, Patrick (OG)
Reyes, Armando (Philippines)
Roetzel, Robert E., *c.s.c.*
Rzasowski, Jerzy (Poland)
Saltysiak, Paul (WDC)
Santry, Robert (HON)
Serban, Ronald (SR)
Stevenson, R. Francis (SAC)
Sunberg, David (CIN)
Tadeo, Victor (Philippines)
Torm, Agustin (CHR)
Vakoc, Timothy (STP)

UNITED STATES AIR FORCE CHAPLAINS

REGULAR AIR FORCE

Reverends

Angelo, Thomas (NOR)
Bailey, James L. (SEA)
Barlow, James P. (SA)
Barmann, Karl W., *o.s.b.*
Berthlette, Ernest (PRO)
Biewind, Michael, *c.j.*
Blair, Stephen (East Anglia)
Booth, Stephen, *m.m.*
Bruno, Robert, *o.f.m.*
Burnet, Donald T., *o.m.i.*
Burnett, James (DAV)
Collins, John M. (LA)
Cote, David P. (PRT)
Crowley, Edmund G. (MAN)
Cusack, John J. (PAT)
Dendinger, William J. (OM)
Diab, Thomas P. (SAN)
Dillon, James P. (BRK)
Diphe, Juan (HEL)
Di Renzo, Michael J. (STU)
Dixon, James R. (NO)
Dunn, Richard B. (SY)
Fey, Thomas (ALX)
Figel, Terence, *o.m.i.*
Flood, Peter J. (TR)
Gallagher, Robert (STU)
Glatts, Joseph M. (PH)
Gosselin, Lawrence (NTN)
Grochowski, Bernard (WOR)
Guico, Manuel R. (Philippines)
Hall, Douglas (OM)
Hanley, Dennis (HRT)
Hanrahan, William P. (NEW)
Higginbotham, Robert (BLX)
Highfill, H. Brian (NO)
Ippolito, Robert, *m.s.*
Kaczmarek, James A. (MAR)
Kinney, John (LAF)
Koser, Rudolph J. (GBG)
Kovalcin, John (STL)
Kuan, Joseph (Philippines)
Lambert, Peter S. (DUL)
Lamy, Raymond (MAN)
Leurck, Raymond J. (CIN)
Lim, Joseph (Philippines)
Ludwikoski, James E. (KCK)
McCahon, Joseph (SP)
Malinsky, Gregory J. (PIT)
Mikalofsky, Hilarion (MIL)
Montecalvo, Carlo F. (PRO)
Moran, Edward C. (RIC)
Moreno, Antonio, *o.f.m.conv.*
Mueller, Jerome, *o.f.m.*
Mulnix, Gabriel R., *c.p.*
Mulvaney, Andrew R. (OG)
Munsell, Richard (GF)
Newland, Ronald A. (NEW)
Nguyen, Phillip D. (GR)
Nicholson, Patrick L. (MOB)
Nolan, John J. (SFD)
Novotny, Richard (RC)
Olszyk, Thomas P. (MIL)
O'Neill, Michael F. (NO)
Otto, Peter B. (AMA)
Regan, Richard (SAN)
Revello, James P. (DEN)
Ryan, Patrick J., *m.m.*
Saluta, Froilan (Philippines)
Sandi, Thomas P. (NY)
Schiffer, James A., *c.p.*
Schnipke, Eugene, *c.pp.s.*
Schueller, LaVerne L. (DUB)
Srode, John S., *c.pp.s.*
Supa, Joseph (Czechoslovakia)
Thomas, Arthur S. (NU)
Thomas, James (ALN)
Thompson, William D. (BGP)
Toledo, Nelson (Philippines)
Vella, Joseph C. (BRK)
Volmi, Dennis G. (WIL)
Wagner, Joseph (SFS)
Wallroth, Joseph R., *o.carm.*
White, Alan (NSH)
Williams, Anthony C. (KCK)
Zinzer, Walter W. (STL)

AIR FORCE RESERVE ON ACTIVE DUTY

Reverends

Abbott, Kerry, *o.f.m.conv.*
Adams, Walter (NY)
Angelo, Thomas (NOR)
Bailey, Lawrence (SEA)
Bartoul, William (SAM)
Beale, Kenneth (NEW)
Beck, R. Patrick (BEA)
Bell, Brian T. (TUC)
Benz, David H. (PH)
Bernadas, Rene (Philippines)
Blazek, Eugene E. (HON)
Breig, Gary (STL)
Brosk, Steven (NEW)
Butler, Timothy (BO)
Clegg, Timothy (LAF)
Cody, Kevin N. (MAN)
Czartorynski, David F. (ALN)
Decker, James D. (MAN)
Deichert, Joseph (BIS)
Demers, Richard D. (OG)
Doyle, Lawrence J., *o.s.m.*
Doyle, Thomas, *o.p.*
Fitzgerald, R. Martin (R)
Fitz-Patrick, David (WDC)
Fleta, Heraclio (Philippines)
Fletcher, Patrick (PCE)
Gaeta, David (SLC)
Gonia, Raymond (SUP)
Harbour, Linn (OM)
Hennessy, Joseph P. (PIT)
Higgins, Richard B. (SAC)
Hochreiter, Robert S. (SCR)
Humenay, Robert (E)
Ivey, David (Taiwan)
Kelly, Thomas (DEN)
Kowalik, Jacek (VEN)
Lee, Roy (MIL)
Llanos, Philip (LA)
Lowe, Francis (SB)
McKenna, Timothy (SEA)
McManus, Gerald (PH)
Marrell, Dennis (LA)
Motsay, Joseph R. (SCR)
O'Brien, Leo P., *o.praem.*
Omana, Max B.T. (Philippines)
Papp, Christopher (WIL)
Pieczara, Stanislaw, *s.d.s.*
Plourde, John G. (SP)
Raux, Redmond (BO)
Roberts, Randall, *o.f.m.*
Sanchez, Raul N. (GAL)
Sirianni, Klaus W. J. (WDC)
Sizelove, Dennis (NO)
Starbuck, James (OAK)
Swetnam, R. William (STL)
Tran, Joseph (RIC)
Tran, Luan Quach (P)
Underwood, Gary (TUC)
Voelker, David (BLX)
Voyt, Stephen (PT)
Vu, Joseph Minh (TUL)
Weber, Michael J., *o.praem.*
Zeller, Leonard H. (BAL)

UNITED STATES NAVY CHAPLAINS

REGULAR NAVY CHAPLAINS

Reverends

Anderson, James, *m.s.a.*
Banken, Robert (STL)
Barrett, Miles (SC)
Bourke, Charles E. (BO)
Brown, Michael (TOL)
Brzek, Jon (PIT)
Buchmiller, Ronald J. (SD)
Buenaventura, Cesar V. (Philippines)
Caiazzo, Gregory G. (RIC)
Carter, John T. (BAL)
Casimano, Santino A. (GLP)
Ceriello, Joseph A. (BRK)
Condon, Edwin D., Jr. (BO)
Coyle, Patrick, (DUL)
Creider, Philip B. (OKL)
Danner, James L. (MEM)
Dansak, Thomas E. (PIT)
Delis, Robert D., *s.d.b.*
Diaz, Michael, *s.c.j.*
Dillon, Jerome (OM)
Dillon, William P., *s.a.*
Dombrowski, Stanley, *o.s.f.*
Dory, Michael (GB)
Elkin, Frederic F. (SY)
Estabrook, Joseph W. (ALB)
Falkenthal, Thomas W. (CHI)
Ferraro, Joseph A. (OAK)
FitzGerald, John L. (BAL)
Fix, Donald (PIT)
Friel, John F., *o.s.f.s.*
Fryer, Patrick L. (WH)
Gallagher, Michael F. (NY)
Gomulka, Eugene T. (ALT)
Guarnieri, Leo J. (RIC)
Gubbins, John M. (MIA)
Gwudz, John S., Jr. (NOR)
Hall, Thomas P., *c.s.p.*
Hines, Joseph W. (WDC)
Holloway, David (KC)
Iasiello, Louis V., *o.f.m.*
Ignacio, Simon G. (Philippines)
Ingram, James A. (ORL)
Jennings, Thommie L. (SD)
Joslyn, James W. (CHI)
Kaul, John L. (DET)
Keane, Robert L., *s.j.*
Kelly, Brian (SCR)
Kennedy, William M. (BO)
Kienzle, Jerome (MIL)
Klarer, Michael (MAD)
Klepacki, Michael S. (CHL)
Krzywicki, Lance (PT)
Lamonde, Joseph (PIT)
Leibold, James C. (BRK)
Lesak, William (NEW)
McCord, Kent (MET)
McCormack, Patrick J. (ATL)
McGoery, Peter (NY)
McKenzie, John H., *o.s.b.*
McLaughlin, Paul (VEN)
Madden, John (SAV)
Malene, Robert (E)
Mandato, Kieran (NY)
Melley, James F. (MIA)
Mennis, James F. (SAC)
Murphy, Kenneth J. (IND)
Murphy, Thomas E. (WDC)
NGuyen, Joseph (Vietnam)
Nordhaus, Jeffrey J. (TOL)
Oddo, Peter A. (NEW)
Panec, Robert (NY)
Panes, Roy P. (Philippines)
Paris, Angel, *o.f.m.*
Parisi, Michael J. (PAT)
Pucciarelli, George W. (BO)
Remy, David P. (DUB)
Rocheford, Dennis J. (WOR)
Rodes, Kenneth, *s.d.b.*
Shuley, Keith J. (CC)
Sodano, Ralph H. (PAT)
Soto, Charles, *o.f.m.*
Targonski, Conrad
Trapani, Anthony (RVC)
Valko, Robert A. (PIT)
Vanden Boogard, Steven, *o.praem.*
Walsh, Michael A. (PAT)
Yagesh, Richard C. (PIT)
Young, David (CI)
Zuffoletto, Michael (BUF)

NAVY RESERVE CHAPLAINS ON ACTIVE DUTY

Reverends

Aguilera, Salvador (ELP)
Anson, Cesar R. (Philippines)
Barrett, Miles (SC)
Berchmanz, Antony (NEW)
Biala, Romeo (Philippines)
Bjorklund, Brian (DET)
Boisvert, Marc, *o.m.i.*
Borzych, Alexander (GI)
Boucher, Roger R. (WOR)
Bower, Alan Eugene (STA)
Boyle, Dennis (PH)
Brown, Benedict (L)
Brown, Lewis (ROC)
Brown, Shaun S. (NTN)
Buchanan, Donald (IND)
Carlos, Joseph, *o.f.m.*
Clark, Robert J., *s.s.c.*
Concha, Alfonso (PH)
Connolly, James (ALN)
Cuddy, William (BO)
Cummings, Carl (BAL)
Cunningham, Gerard M. (WDC)
Cusick, Kevin (WDC)
D'Aurora, Joseph (RIC)
DeAngelis, Mark J. (BO)
Deeley, Kevin J. (BO)
Devine, Joseph (HRT)
Devine, William (BO)
Domme, Edward, *o.m.v.*
Donohue, Stephen (BO)
D'Souza, Matthew (LUB)
Duesterhaus, Michael (ARL)
Dux, John H. (STA)
Egan, Brennan, *o.f.m.*
Erestain, Alfonso (Philippines)
Evers, Paul (HON)
Ferretti, Sam (SCR)
Finley, James F. (BRK)
Foley, Francis P. (PH)
Fry, James Q. (ORG)
Gardocki, Patrick, *o.f.m.*
Garvey, Michael P. (Y)
Gay, James (BGP)
Gegotek, Tadeusz (BEL)
Gergel, Stephen (ALT)
Gervacio, Adrian R. (HON)
Hall, Daniel, *c.s.v.*
Hellwig, Lee (HRT)
Hicks, Stephen (SAN)
Hogan, Timothy (DET)
Hoog, Eric, *c.ss.r.*
Hughes, Robert W. (MAD)
Hummer, Lawrence (COL)
Hussey, Daniel C. (GAL)
Janning, Timothy (CIN)
Johnson, Lawrence P. (DUL)
Johnson, Patrick, *c.s.p.*
Joslyn, James (CHI)
Kanicki, Phillip (RIC)
Kloak, David G. (CHI)
Koester, Timothy (BUF)
Kurilec, Robert E. (SB)
Kuss, Allen (BIS)
Labaro, Alfredo (Philippines)
Lamb, Gary (MEM)
Lee, Matthew (WDC)
Legarski, Anthony (ALT)
Leslie, Lawrence (COV)
Lindblad, Karl A. (NY)
Linehan, Stephen J. (BO)
Logan, Aidan, *o.s.c.o.*
Lopes, Richard, *o.f.m.cap*
Lott, Lawrence (MOB)
McClanahan, Robert (PT)
McLaughlin, Peter (CAM)
MacNew, James. J., *o.s.f.s.*
Madej, Paul (SY)
Madey, Louis (LAN)
Maxwell, Bruce, *o.s.c.*
Mensah, Gabriel (VIC)
Mikstay, Michael (Y)
Milewski, Robert F. (E)
Morris, John J. (NEW)
Moss, Donald (AUS)
Mudd, David (WDC)
Mueller, Michael (ORL)
Mulkerin, Terrence (BRK)
Neis, William P. (LC)
Nowak, Bernard U. (BUF)
Osendorf, James, *c.m.*
Panek, Robert M. (NY)
Petruska, William (SCR)
Pugliese, Frank (NY)
Quinn, John T. (SD)
Robinson, Jerome (MOB)
Rock, Stephen B. (BO)
Roma, Paul (MAN)
Russo, Lawrence J., Jr. (BO)
Salamoni, Vincent, *m.s.a.*
Scordo, Joseph, *o.p.*
Shaughnessy, Paul J., *s.j.*
Shimotsu, John M. (ORL)
Shuppert, William T. (TUC)
Simpson, Brian L. (CHI)
Smith, Lawrence, *s.j.*
Soutiere, Ronald A. (BUR)
Spangenberg, George, *c.s.sp.*
Stake, Ronald P. (CHI)
Stavoy, Stephen J. (SCR)
Steed, Donald, *m.m.*

St. George, Peter (CLV)
Sweeney, Kevin (ORG)
Tran, Quang Minh (SAV)
Vidrine, Richard (LAF)
Walsh, Francis (SPR)
Welch, Bernard (PRT)
Wheatley, R. Carroll (OWN)
Williams, Gary (Ecuador
Yossa, Kenneth (Canton)

AUXILIARY CHAPLAINS

Reverends

Ahern, John J. (CHI)
Amateis, Jacques (Saudi Arabia)
Ashkar, Dominic (SAM)
Balizan, Daniel M. (SFE)
Bauer, John J., *c.s.s.r.*
Bauer, Richard W. (SLC)
Betowski, E. Paul, *s.j.*
Boyle, Patrick J., *s.J.*
Bracken, John (BRK)
Brady, Jeremiah D. *s.s.j.*
Buckley, Charles, *o.s.b.*
Butler, Michael (COS)
Carlin, Bernard, *c.ss.r.*
Cavanaugh, Michael, *o.s.f.s.*
Chai, John (Taipei)
Chong, Young-Ku (Korea)
Cleary, William J., *o.s.a.*
Connolly, Leo L. (COL)
Crandall, Thomas A. (PT)
Creary, James (MEM)
Cuneo, James J.
Dentinger, Roy E. (L)
de Verteuil, Jack (FBK)
Devine, Kevin (BO)
Diniz, Felicio (Saudi Arabia)
Doody, Patrick, *c.s.sp.*
Dorney, James J. (NY)
Drury, Michael, *c.o.*
Dunn, Stephen (SD)
Effing, Myron (Agana)
Evanstock, Philip, *c.s.sp.*
Farias, Joseph (PAT)
Ferrer, Gonzalo, *t.o.r.*
Fewell, Michael, *c.m.f.*
Flannery, Michael (NY)
Fosselman, David, *c.s.c.*
Frank, Lawrence J., *o.m.i.*
Freeman, James (TUC)
Gillespie, Paul G., *o.s.f.s.*
Gitzen, Blase, *o.f.m.cap.*
Gnall, Julian, *o.s.b.*
Graves, Joseph A. (PEO)
Graves, William, *c.s.sp.*
Gribbon, Joseph, *c.ss.r.*
Habenight, James F., *m.m.*
Hacker, Louis, *o.s.b.*
Hamilton, Thomas M., *s.m.*
Hartgen, William, *s.s.*
Healy, Patrick, *o.m.i.*
Heathcote, Howard (AUS)
Hickey, Dennis W., *c.s.p.*
Hillyard, Matthew J., *o.s.f.s*
Hoffman, Louis, *s.f.*
Kelley, Thomas W., *o.s.f.s.*
Kelley, William J., *s.v.d.*
Kelly, James C., *o.s.b.*
Kelly, John R. (NY)
Keutzer, Walter (STL)
Kiczuk, Casimir, *c.m.*
Kieffer, Thomas (MRY)
Kita, Edward, *m.s.*
Klinger, Nevin (ALN)
Kneip, Paschal, *o.s.b.*
Kobza, John, *m.i.c.*
Kohler, Joseph (STL)
Kroker, Wolfgang (Germany)
Kucera, Edward J., *o.s.b.*
Kuchar, Matthew, *o.s.b.*
Kyzysteczko, Gothard, *c.m.*
Labo, Timothy (ORL)
Lenihan, Michael (CC)
Leveille, Andre (Japan)
Limon, Lidio
Listecki, Jerome E. (CHI)
Loftus, Conrad, *o.f.m.*
Loth, Alan J. (OKL)
McCormick, Thomas, *s.j.*
McGrath, John (BLX)
McHale, Damian, *c.p.*
McHugh, James, *c.p.*
McLoughlin, Patrick (United Kingdom)
McNally, Stephen (RIC)
McNicholas, Edward (BRK)
McQuilan, Cornelius, *c.s.sp.*
McSwigan, William, *c.s.sp.*
Macalintal, Dionisio R. (SD)
Madden, Paul J., *o.praem.*
Mages, Mark, *o.s.b.*
Majerus, Daniel (SCL)
Marsh, John, *c.ss.r.*
Martin, Michael, *o.s.b.*
Martinez, Anthony L. (SFE)
Mason, William (East Anglia)
Massoth, Charles, *o.s.b.*
Matson, Mark, *c.r.*
Merfeld, Vincent (DUB)
Messaro, Michael, *m.ss.cc.*
Metsy, Norman (PRO)
Metzbower, Francis X., *s.j.*
Middendorf, Cyril, *s.m.*
Mooney, Msgr. Robert M. (PRO)
Morley, John (NEW)
Mulhern, Joseph P., *o.p.*
Murphy, Dennis F., *s.a.*
Murphy, Msgr. Terrence J. (STP)
Nakireru, Omoviekobwa A. (Nigeria)
Nguyen, Huong Xuan (NO)
Nusbaum, Daniel C. (ALB)
O'Donnell, Brian, *s.j.*
O'Keeffe, Msgr. Richard W. (TUC)
O'Loughlin, Michael, *s.s.c.*
O'Neill, Joseph, *m.m.*
Olson, Benedict, *o.p.*
Perumpilly, Marcel (Bahrain)
Phillips, Christopher (SA)
Phillips, Randall (DET)
Picard, Norman, *c.i.c.m.*
Piskura, Joseph (CLV)
Power, Bernard, *c.ss.r.*
Quinlivan, Francis L., *c.s.c.*
Regan, John J. (BO)
Richardson, Edward, *s.m.a.*
Rimmele, Leo, *o.s.b.*
Roberson, Ronald G., *c.p.*
Rokusek, Robert (DET)
St. Pierre, Romeo A. (PRT)
Sanders, Peter, *c.o.*
Saucci, Robert R., *m.m.*
Scheller, John (OKL)
Schmidt, Raymond (BRK)
Schreiber, Gerard, *c.ss.r.*
Sego, Msgr. Arthur (LFT)
Shay, Michael, *s.d.s.*
Shay, Robert M., *s.t.*
Sierra, Frank (SD)
Simonelli, Bruno, *o.f.m.cap.*
Slater, Dennis (SY)
Smith, Ignatius E., *o.f.m.*
Smith, Msgr. Thomas (HBG)
Sousa, Peter, *c.ss.r.*
Spiteri, Joseph (Panama)
Stadmueller, Roman, *s.d.s.*
Stodola, Francis (CC)
Succi, Vincento, *o.f.m.cap.*
Sueper, Alban A., *s.s.c.*
Sullivan, Alan, *o.f.m.*
Thelen, Robert (BRK)
Thomas, Donald (HON)
Tomas, Francisco (Azores)
Valenti, Palmo, *s.j.*
Vaz, Rock I., *s.j.*
Waite, Patrick (SC)
Ward, Thomas, *s.f.*
Wood, Michael (SA)
Woster, Michael B. (RC)

DEPARTMENT OF VETERANS AFFAIRS HOSPITALS AND CHAPLAINS

Revs.

Richard Dunne (BRK), Chap. Mgr., Region I
Patrick Diffley (BRK), Prog. Mgr. for Continuing Educatio n

ALABAMA

Birmingham Vacant.

Montgomery

Rev.

David J. Tokarz (MOB)

Tuscaloosa Vacant.

Tuskegee Vacant.

ARIZONA

Phoenix

Revs.

Kenneth R. Kleiber (CHI)
Peter F. Morello (GLP)
Bernard L. Young (NO)

Prescott

Rev.

Gerald J. Caffrey, *c.m.f.*

Tucson Vacant.

ARKANSAS

Fayetteville Vacant.

North Little Rock

Rev.

Victor E. Bertrand, C.S.V.

CALIFORNIA

Fresno

Revs.

Richard F. Bevenour (DAV)
David LaPierre, *o.f.m.cap.*

Loma Linda

Rev.

Adolph Chavez (SB)

Long Beach

Revs.

Anselm T. Deehr, *s.t.*
Leo Miller, *o.m.i.*

Palo Alto

Revs.

John Kenneth Coleman (SFR)
Augustine Koilparampil (India)
John W. Murray (CHI)

Rev. Msgr.

William M. Roche (ROC)

San Diego

Revs.

Patrick J. Durkin, *c.s.v.*
Charles R. Eis (SPK)
Theodore Gryga (SY)
Jerry Hamperzonian (PSC)

San Francisco

Rev.

Francis P. Filice (SFR)

Sepulveda

Rev.

Patrick J. O'Hagan, *ss.cc.*

West Los Angeles

Revs.

Harry C. Cronin, *c.s.c.*
Francis Kelly (LA)

COLORADO

Denver

Rev.

Thomas J. Woerth (DEN)

Fort Lyon

Rev.

Philip J. Coury, *c.m.*

Grand Junction Vacant.

CONNECTICUT

Newington Vacant.

West Haven

Rev.
Daniel Scott, *m.s.*

DELAWARE

Wilmington

Revs.
Sean P. Connery, *o.s.f.s.*
William J. Dougherty, *o.s.f.s*

DISTRICT OF COLUMBIA

Revs.
John A. D'Antonio, *o.praem.*
John W. Kobza, *m.i.c.*
Luis Picazo, *s.f.*
John A. Welch, *m.s.*

FLORIDA

Bay Pines

Revs.
Daniel P. Greene (YAK)
Arthur D. Murray, *o.f.m.*
E. Matthew Turk, *s.j.*

Gainesville

Rev.
Francisco Revilla (STA)

Lake City

Revs.
Anthony Sebra (STA)
Patrick L. Murphy, *s.j.*

Miami

Revs.
Gerardo Freire, *s.j.*
Fred J. Nietfeld (TOL)

Tampa

Revs.
Carl A. Birarelli (CIN)
Robert Schindler (Mexico)

West Palm Beach

Rev.
Sebastian L. Muccilli (MET)

GEORGIA

Augusta

Revs.
P. James Costigan (SAV)
Thomas J. Peyton (SAV)

Decatur

Rev.
Thad B. Rudd (ATL)

Dublin Vacant.

IDAHO

Boise

Rev.
Donald J. Riffle (B)

ILLINOIS

Chicago—Lakeside

Rev.
Robert J. Borre (MAD)

Chicago—West Side

Rev.
Sebastian A. Ugochukwu (Nigeria)

Danville

Rev.
John Schultz (LFT)

Hines

Rev.
Max E.M. Saldua (Philippines)

Marion Vacant.

North Chicago

Revs.
Paul B. McDermott (PEO)
William Vander Heyden (GB)

INDIANA

Fort Wayne

Rev.
Daniel R. Leeuw (FTW)

Indianapolis

Revs.
Joseph Kiene, *o.f.m.conv.*
Gordon P. Wagoner (LFT)

Marion

Revs.
Joseph W. Grace (FTW)
Edward Narcowich (FTW)
August Reemmer (FTW)
James R. Rose (FTW)

IOWA

Des Moines

Rev.
Paul S. Holt (WDC)

Iowa City

Revs.
Andrew E. Kelly (DAV)
Louis J. Leonhart (DAV)

Knoxville Vacant.

KANSAS

Leavenworth

Rev.
Mario P. Moscaritolo (KC)

Topeka

Rev.
James E. Moster, *o.f.m.cap.*

Wichita

Rev.
H. Patrick Malone (WCH)

KENTUCKY

Lexington

Revs.
Wilton Henry Kenney, *s.j.*
George Maynard, *s.j.*

Louisville Vacant.

LOUISIANA

Alexandria

Revs.
Christudas A. Nayak (India)
Fred G. Reynolds, *s.j.*

New Orleans

Revs.
Lawrence A. DeMaria (NO)
Joseph Laboon (PIT)

Shreveport

Rev.
Philip Michiels (ALX)

MAINE

Togus

Rev.
Lazar David Mani (India)

MARYLAND

Baltimore

Rev.
Stephen E. Jeselnick (E)

Fort Howard

Rev.
Conan H. Timoney, *c.p.*

Perry Point

Revs.
John J. Abrahams (BAL)
Jeffrie S. Reynolds (BIR)

MASSACHUSETTS

Bedford

Revs.
Philip Cabasino, *c.ss.r.*
Ronald Lawson (Montreal)
Joseph P. Robinson (BO)
Aidan J. Walsh (BO)

Boston

Revs.
Philip Salois (FR)
Roger A. Sinclair (GBG)

Brockton

Revs.
Avelino R. Garcia (SP)
Austin Nagle, *ss.cc.*
Henry Nichols (BO)

Northampton

Rev.
Lionel E. Bonneville (SPR)

MICHIGAN

Ann Arbor

Rev.
Vincent VanDoan (LAN)

Battle Creek

Rev.
Michael Stafford, *o.s.b.*

Detroit

Revs.
John P. Melepuram (India)
Joseph Duc Vu (Vietnam)

Iron Mountain

Rev.
Patrick E. Murphy (MAR)

Saginaw

Revs.
Richard E. Jozwiak (SAG)
Joseph A. Schabel (SAG)

MINNESOTA

Minneapolis

Rev.
Joseph N. Safraniec (STU)

St. Cloud

Revs.
Lloyd Haupt (SCL)
Alfred E. Stangl (SCL)

MISSISSIPPI

Biloxi

Revs.
Joseph A. Dilettuso (BLX)
Frank X. Popeleski, *m.ss.a.*

Jackson

Rev.
Daniel N. Gallagher (JKS)

MISSOURI

Columbia

Rev.
Edwin J. Cole (JC)

Kansas City

Rev.
Ambrose Karels (KC)

Poplar Bluff

Rev.
Michael V. McDevitt (SPC)

St. Louis

Revs.
George P. Brennan (STL)
Patrick J. Christopher (STL)
Raymond Joyce (WCH)
John H. Schneider (STL)

MONTANA

Fort Harrison Vacant.

Miles City Vacant.

NEBRASKA

Grand Island

Revs.
Donald O'Brien (GI)
Walter M. Phelan (GI)
David L. Rykwalder (GI)

Lincoln

Revs.
Thomas Holoman (LIN)
Edwin L. Stander (LIN)

Omaha

Rev.
Richard Wolbach (OM)

NEVADA

Las Vegas

Rev.
Gerard J. McNulty (LA)

Reno Vacant.

NEW HAMPSHIRE

Manchester

Rev.
Francis A. Talbot (MAN)

NEW JERSEY

East Orange

Rev.
Thomas J. Davis, *o.f.m.cap.*

Lyons

Revs.
Joseph C. Chacko (India)
George F. Kelly, *c.ss.r.*
William Warman (BAL)

NEW MEXICO

Albuquerque

Revs.
Leonard L. Bayer (SFE)
Julian M. Rousseau, *s.s.s.*

NEW YORK

Albany

Revs.
Paul J. Antos (ALB)
Martin J. Fisher (ALB)
James R. McNerney (ALB)
John Minkler (ALB)
Dominick Ntsiful-Amissah (ALB)
Charles S. San Fratello, *o.f.m.*
Paul P. Tartaglia (ALB)
Gregory S. Weider (ALB)

Batavia

Revs.
Donald W. Becker (BUF)
John P. Bernard (CAM)

Bath

Revs.
David L. Carson (NY)
Paul R. Schnacky (ROC)

Bronx

Revs.
Roland P. LaFontant (France)
Gregory Lyttle (NY)
Rev. Msgr.
Joseph J. Zammit (NY)

Brooklyn

Revs.
Joseph M. Gleeson (NY)
Luke M. Karpil (Philippines)
Thomas J. Mullin (NY)
Vito Tiboni (NEW)

Buffalo

Revs.
Francis Chmielewski (BUF)
Clatus E. Snyder (BUF)

Canandaigua

Revs.
Mieczislaus Curzydlo, *s.a.c.*
Francis Vogt (ROC)

Castle Point

Revs.
Robert J. Brennan (NY)
Uldarico De la Pena (Philippines)
Donald B. Licata (NY)
Raymond A. Pavlick (PAT)

Montrose

Revs.
Daniel Lynch, *o.carm.*
Robert D. Tracy, *o.carm.*

New York City

Revs.
Bernardine P. Laghezza, *ss.cc.*
Frederick McCaffrey, *o.carm.*
Francis Morgan, *ss.cc.*

Northport

Rev.
Augustine Sheehan (RVC)

Syracuse

Revs.
Wilfred F. Evans (SY)
David J. James (SY)
Gregory C. LeStrange (SY)

NORTH CAROLINA

Asheville

Rev.
Andrew J. Latsko (CHL)

Durham Vacant.

Fayetteville

Rev.
Alexander O. Nakireru (Nigeria)

Salisbury

Rev.
Thomas P. Clements (CHL)

NORTH DAKOTA

Fargo Vacant.

OHIO

Chillicothe

Revs.
Richard F. Engle (COL)
Jonathan D. Lao (Philippines)

Cincinnati

Rev.
Warren Zeisler, *o.f.m.*

Cleveland

Revs.
John Bolan, *c.pp.s.*
Thomas J. Gallagher (CLV)

Dayton

Revs.
John J. Butler (HON)
J. Luis Fernandez (NO)

OKLAHOMA

Muskogee Vacant.

Oklahoma City Vacant.

OREGON

Portland

Rev.
William Wickham, *c.s.c.*

Roseburg Vacant.

White City

Revs.
Donald H. Salisbury, *o.p.*
Joseph Shirey, *s.j.*

PENNSYLVANIA

Altoona

Rev.
Edward Dabcosky (ALT)

Butler

Revs.
Henry Preneta (GBG)
William J. Ritzert (PIT)

Coatesville

Revs.
Joseph S. Hasieber (ALX)
McKinley E. Williams (RIC)

Erie

Revs.
Robert G. Craig (E)
Thomas M. Fialkowski (E)

Lebanon

Revs.
D. Gilbert Sweeney, *s.j.*
Dennis M. Young (STA)

Philadelphia

Revs.
Edward V. Griffin, *o.s.a.*
Joseph Griffin, *o.s.f.s.*

Pittsburgh—Highland Drive

Revs.
Frank A. Mitolo (PIT)
Pascall J. Schaller, *o.f.m.cap.*
Emett J. Schuler, *o.f.m.cap.*

Pittsburgh—University Drive

Revs.
Mark W. Glasgow (PIT)
John M. Jendzura, *c.s.sp.*
Ralph Zehe, *o.f.m.cap.*

Wilkes-Barre

Revs.
Benjamin Foerch, *o.f.m.*
Valentine R. Plevyak (SCR)

RHODE ISLAND

Providence

Rev.
Francis J. Crowley (BO)

SOUTH CAROLINA

Charleston

Rev.
William C. Burn (CHR)

Columbia Vacant.

SOUTH DAKOTA

Fort Meade

Rev.
Paul Dahms (RC)

Hot Springs

Rev.
Thomas Tierney, *s.j.*

Sioux Falls

Rev.
Kenneth J. Koster (SFS)

TENNESSEE

Memphis

Rev.
John J. Behnke, *c.s.p.*

Mountain Home Vacant.

Murfreesboro

Rev.
R. Orville Briscoe (NSH)

Nashville

Rev.
James Norman Miller (NSH)

TEXAS

Amarillo

Rev.
Francis Crowe, *o.p.*

Big Spring

Revs.
Jeremiah McCarthy, *m.s.c.*
Jeremiah Murphy, *m.s.c.*

Bonham Vacant.

Dallas

Rev.
Timothy Gollob (DAL)

Houston

Revs.
Peter Girardin (BO)
Clarito Z. Rara (Philippines)

Kerrville

Revs.
Michael J. Boulette (SAT)
Tony Vilano (SAT)

Marlin Vacant.

San Antonio

Revs.
Richard R. Benonis (PH)
Ralph Intranuovo, *s.c.j.*
Harry Martin (SAT)

Temple

Rev.
Harry Bilski (AUS)

Waco

Revs.
Richard J. Beyer (DAV)
Thomas Niemira (JKS)

UTAH

Salt Lake City

Revs.
Gebran Bou-Merhi (SAM)
Reyes Garcia Rodriguez (SLC)

VERMONT

White River Junction

Revs.
Adrien Pelletier, *s.m.*
Ronald Saunders, *s.m.*

VIRGINIA

Hampton

Revs.
Donald Cavey (RIC)
Lloyd F. Stephenson (RIC)

Richmond

Rev.
Benedict R. McDermott, *o.s.b.*

Salem

Rev.
Wayne L. Ball (RIC)

WASHINGTON

Seattle

Rev.
Thomas R. Park, *o.s.b.*

Spokane

Rev.
George H. McCabe (SPK)

Tacoma

Revs.
David Prebula, *o.s.b.*
Leo R. Rimmele, *o.s.b.*

Walla Walla

Rev.
Otto Koltzenburg (SPK)

WEST VIRGINIA

Beckley

Rev.
Frank A. O'Kruta (WH)

Clarksburg

Rev.
Peter A. Giannamore (WH)

Huntington

Rev.
Andrew G. Kranyc (WH)

Martinsburg

Revs.
William E. Coen, *s.t.*
William J. Nolte, Jr. (WH)
T. Matthew Rowgh (WH)

WISCONSIN

Madison

Rev.
Lawrence Heitke (MAD)

Milwaukee

Revs.
James F. Kovarik, *o.s.cam.*
Edward E. Lisowski (MIL)
Norman Oswald (MIL)

Tomah

Rev.
Timothy E. Svea (LC)

WYOMING

Cheyenne Vacant.

Sheridan

Revs.
John B. Norton, *o.p.*
Eugene P. Sullivan (CHY)

PUERTO RICO

San Juan

Revs.
Hector Diaz (SJN)
Luis A. Lopez-Alvarado (CGS)
Jose F. Quintero (SJN)

RESERVE CHAPLAINS

Reverends
Abreu, Felix, *c.s.s.p.*
Acosta, Humberto (BWN)
Albrecht, Louis (BAK)
Alexander, Marc R. (HON)
Almendras, Joel (MRY)
Ameling, Richard H. (GRY)
Amora, Edito (Philippines)
Anderson, Ronald C. (BWN)
Anderson, Terence R. (SF)
Arens, John F. (BO)
Arroyo, Brigido (Guam)
Augustyn, Boguslaw (Poland)
Austin, Walter (NO)
Baggetta, Joseph J. (BO)
Bailey, Douglas, *s.d.s.*
Bain, John K. (RNO)
Baratelli, David (NEW)
Barber, Michael, *s.j.*
Barch, Howard C., Jr. (PEO)
Barnhill, Robert K. (LIN)
Barry, Robert L., *o.p.*
Becker, Donald W. (BUF)
Beers, Michael (ALN)
Belanger, Gerald R.
Bendorf, Richard D., *o.f.m.*
Berberich, Thomas E. (HRT)
Bergbower, Daniel J. (SPC)
Bill, Ronald C. (SY)
Blais, Robert L. (PRO)
Blascovich, Joseph D. (HBG)
Blessin, Thomas C., *s.j.*
Bolduc, Norman P., Jr. (MAN)
Bonnot, Bernard R. (Y)
Bowe, John F. (PH)
Bower, Alan (STA)
Bower, Lawrence (BAK)
Brando, Joseph (KNX)
Bratko, Kenneth R., *c.r.*
Breaux, Duane (BR)
Brennan, Brian C. (NY)
Brinkmann, Frederick C., *c.ss.r.*
Broussard, Andre (NO)
Bruckner, Ronald L. (SFE)
Bryan, Allen K. (BUF)
Bucon, Raymond H. (DET)
Burns, Malcolm (GAL)
Butler, Michael (STL)
Butler, William L. (BO)
Cain, Robert (TLS)
Calderone, Joseph D., *o.s.a.*
Canez, Jorge A. (PHX)
Cannon, Richard (BO)
Cannon, Robert (VEN)
Caputo, Louis, *s.d.v.*
Carmody, James F. (WOR)
Caron, David (BO)
Carrington, Richard J.
Carter, Eli K., Jr. (HON)
Casaleggio, David (RNO)
Charbonneau, William R. (HRT)
Chavez, Filimon (SFE)
Chavez, Johnny Lee (SFE)
Chimiak, Karl A. (WDC)
Clark, John S., *s.s.s.*
Clarke, Thomas J., *c.s.c.*
Coby, Thomas W. (RVC)
Collogan, Robert E. (JOL)
Condron, Patrick
Connolly, Leo L. (COL)
Congro, Basil (CHR)
Connor, Kevin (MAN)
Coogan, Roch A., *o.f.m.*
Cordery, Robert (BO)
Corneille, Cecil C. (STV)
Coulthard, Gregory
Coyle, Robert J. (RVC)
Cregan, James A. (STA)
Crews, John S. (SR)
Cronin, Daniel (CGS)
Crosby, Msgr. Charles E. (MAN)
Crotty, Desmond (NO)
Cuevas, Randy M. (BR)
Cunningham, Douglas (SY)
Curcio, Ralph V. (NY)
Curley, Thomas J. (NY)
Dare, Glenn O. (PRT)
Darling, William G. (ROC)
Dawson, John H. (LA)
Decker, Douglas A. (OG)
DePorter, Arnold (WDC)
Dermott, William R. (ALN)
DeSanctis, Peter A. (BRK)
DeSocia, John (ROC)
Diacetis, Anthony (ALB)
Diegel, Ronald (FRS)
Diesta, Arwyn N. (Philippines)
DiLella, Mario (ATL)
Dinello, John E. (PIT)
Dolbec, Jacques D. (CC)
Donahue, Brian G. (FAR)
Donohoe, Richard (BIR)
Donohue, Michael T. (NOR)
Doran, John E. (WOR)
Dougherty, William J. (PH)
Dowds, James, *c.ss.r.*
Dowling, Joseph K. (NSH)
Doyle, Michael J. (BO)
Dura, Eduardo A. (SF)
Durbin, Samuel E. (COL)
Duzza, Donald (ALT)

Dziedzic, Gerald H. (HRT)
Echevia, Les Suberi (Philippines)
Emechete, Innocent A. (SAC; Nigeria)
Engelbrecht, Henry (NO)
Erikson, Richard M. (BOS)
Esquibel, Msgr. John L. (SFE)
Ethen, Jeffrey (SCL)
Everett, Willis E. (COL)
Farana, Mario P. (SFR)
Fawcett, Msgr. Henry F. (SD)
Feltis, Jerome (FAR)
Fernandes, Stephen (FR)
Fialkowski, Thomas M. (E)
Fischer, Richard O. (BAK)
Fitzgibbons, Peter (CHL)
Fitzpatrick, Robert M. (OM)
Flanigan, Thomas P. (PH)
Fleta, Heraclio (Philippines)
Flores, Jose (ARE)
Follett, John E. (CAM)
Folsom, Paul (SCL)
Foote, John, *o.s.b.*
Foster, Raymond, *o.carm.*
Fredericks, Michael (SB)
Fronk, Christopher, *s.j.*
Gaeta, Bernard N. (Y)
Gaglione, John R. (BUF)
Gale, Robert V. (BO)
Gallagher, John P. (DAV)
Gallagher, William (BUF)
Garcia, Millan J., *s.f.*
Gayton, John, *m.i.c.*
Gerres, Daniel (WIL)
Giese, Samuel (WDC)
Gills, Thomas (BAL)
Giordani, Mark J. (PAT)
Girardin, Peter T. (BO)
Glasgow, Thomas (NO)
Granadino, David F. (LA)
Greig, Harry D. (LAF)
Grice, Edward M. (NO)
Griffin, Thomas E., *o.s.a.*
Grizzelle-Reid, Paul, *s.c.j.*
Gross, Gary L. (LIN)
Guidry, Kevin James (ATL)
Hamaday, Ronald A., *o.s.a.*
Hannigan, John (CHI)
Hart, John B. (SLC)
Hays, Michael D. (SEA)
Healy, Stephen M. (BOS)
Hebert, Donald J. (SY)
Hendel, Lawrence M. (SJ)
Henke, James T. (SA)
Henson, Jerome M., *o.p.*
Herbert, G. Paul (WDC)
Herzog, Ronald P. (BLX)
Hewes, Robert (RVC)
Hoffman, Christopher (ORL)
Hogan, Michael J. (CHI)
Holland, William (SAC)
Honan, Eugene D. (SPR)
Howard, James (ALP)
Hower, William (MAD)
Hubbs, Timothy (SCR)
Hudak, Thomas R.
Hughes, Donald R. (BUF)
Hurley, Paul K. (BO)
Isopo, Dominic (ALB)
Jackson, James (WCH)
Jackson, Robert (CLV)
Jacques, Roger N. (BO)
Jaeger, James (ROC)
Jankowski, Daniel (CHI)
Janecek, James E. (CC)
Jaramillo, Peter (AMA)
Jeselnick, Stephen E. (E)
Jindra, Frank (OM)
Johannes, Nicholas A. (GB)
Johnson, James B. (SP)
Johnson, Lawrence (DUL)
Johnson, Patrick, *c.s.p.*
Jones, Michael (WDC)
Judge, Timothy M. (PH)
Kadera, Thomas (CHY)
Kahlich, Daniel (SA)
Kane, Edward R. (BRK)
Kasprzyk, James (BUF)
Kaszcak, Ivan (STF)
Kayatta, Francis P. (PRO)
Keenan, Patrick J. (NY)
Kehoe, James P. (CHI)
Keller, Robert J. (DET)
Keller, Thomas W. (LR)
Kelly, C. Richard, Jr. (DET)
Kiene, Joseph L., *o.f.m.conv.*
Kinnane, James F. (HRT)
Kinney, Thomas E. (NO)
Kiselica, John J., *s.m.*
Ko Suk, Joon (Seoul)
Koster, Kenneth J. (SF)
Kozen, Bert S. (SCR)
Krische, James (BR)
Krough, Jack Lee (WIN)
Kruse, David B. (BAL)
Kuczborski, Joseph (PEO)
Kukucka, Joseph (PBL)
Kurzak, John F. (SC)
Labo, Timothy (ORL)
Ladniak, Lawrence J. (CHI)
Laible, Jeffrey (PEO)
LaMorte, Joseph P. (NY)
Lane, Frank (COL)
Lang, James P. (Y)
Langan, William J.P. (SCR)
Langston, Micheas, *o.s.b.*
Larche, James (OG)
Laroche, Christopher (PRT)
Lavastida, Jose I. (NO)
Legaspi, Alex (SFR)
Leone, William B. (ROC)
Linsky, Gary S. (CHR)
Lioi, Phillip J. (ROC)
Listecki, Jerome E. (CHI)
Logan, Aidan, *o.c.s.o.*
Lomax, Mark (NO)
Lordemann, Francis W. (OM)
Lyle, John W., *o.s.f.s.*
McCabe, Kenneth O., *ss.cc.*
McCarthy, James C. (HEL)
McConville, James P. (STP)
McDonald, G. Malcolm (PIT)
McGinnis, James J. (PH)
McGrade, Kevin (BO)
McGuill, Martin F. (ARL)
McGuine, Peter (SD)
McHugh, Brian (BO)
McInnis, Francis L. (GF)
McLaughlin, Richard P. (BO)
McNalis, John P. (CHI)
McNamara, Brian J. (RVC)
McNulty, Gerard J.
Macek, Joseph S., *s.s.j.*
Mack, John (BUF)
Maguire, Stephen (NY)
Mahalic, Philip A. (LAF)
Maikowski, Thomas R. (GLP)
Malloy, Francis X. (MIL)
Manzo, Louis A., *c.s.c.*
Marcantonio, Robert (PRO)
Marcinano, Robert (PRO)
Martinez, Vidal (SFE)
Matheny, William K. (WH)
Mathis, Raymond P. (SY)
Matienzo, Ariel R. (Arecibo)
Maughan, Richard N. (NO)
Mazziotta, Richard, *c.s.c.*
Medairos, Anthony (BO)
Medve, Kenneth A. (ALN)
Merrell, Arthur (PIT)
Mescher, Michael (DUB)
Messier, Joseph H. (BUR)
Metzdorf, William C. (WDC)
Midura, Francis S. (RVC)
Miller, Robert A. (NEW)
Minder, Kevin W. (YAK)
Mink, John (WIL)
Mitolo, Frank A. (PIT)
Mizeur, Thomas R. (PEO)
Mockler, Patrick (BLX)
Molloy, Msgr. Thomas E. (RVC)
Mongale, Robert J. (BO)
Moore, William (STO)
Moran, Michael (MIL)
Morgan, Gerald (NY)
Morgan, Thomas T. (SP)
Moss, Robert D. (BUF)
Motta, Anthony (ALB)
Muhm, William J. (NY)
Mullin, Thomas (NY)
Murray, Gerald (NY)
Musni, Eduardo (Philippines)
Myers, Christopher (CC)
Naughton, William M. (PAT)
Neitzke, Ron (JOL)
Nenneau, Thomas D. (LAN)
Neuman, Eugene C. (MIL)
Nguyen, Van T. (NO)
Nishigaya, Raymond J. (HON)
Nolan, Kevin L. (LA)
Noone, Charles J. (PH)
O'Brien, Sean (SY)
O'Connor, John L. (ROC)
O'Donoghue, John J. (SA)
O'Grady, J. Frank (PAT)
O'Hara, Daniel (SY)
O'Hear, Daniel J. (SPR)
O'Leary, David M. (BO)
O'Malley, John J., *o.p.*
Oberts, David P. (SUP)
Ohm, Edward U. (PEO)
Oge, Raymond J. (STL)
Orlandi, Joseph (PAT)
Orzel, David (SY)
Ornelas, Angel, Jr. (CHY)
Padazinski, Michael (SFR)
Pagan, Alberto, *o.p.*
Parenti, Thomas M. (SFR)
Parker, Paul R. (BO)
Parker, Thomas (SR)
Parkinson, Forrest Todd (RVC)
Passamonti, Paul (WDC)
Pelletier, George C. (PRT)
Penkaul, Joseph H. (BUF)
Peoples, Joseph E. (HEL)
Perez, Gregory (AUS)
Perez, John C. (SJN)
Piekarczyk, Marian, *s.d.s.*.
Piontkowski, Richard (GI)
Pizza, Albert J. (CHI)
Plate, Brian (NEW)
Plaushin, Mark F., *o.s.f.s.*
Pleiness, Gregg A. (LAN)
Polk, Thomas T. (BAL)
Posey, Thaddeus J., *o.f.m.cap.*
Prez, Daniel J. (E)
Prinz, Gerald (HT)
Quinn, James A. (MIA)
Randall, Kevn S. (NOR)
Rapp, James F., *o.s.f.s.*
Reamer, Mark, *o.f.m.*
Reeson, David G. (OM)
Renard, John F. (NEW)
Reyes, Marco (LA)
Richtsteig, Eric J. (SLC)
Rigdon, Vincent J. (WDC)
Rimassa, Paul (TR)
Rivera-Saez, Adalin (PCE)
Robbins, Thomas (COV)
Roberson, Henry (OKL)
Robert, Darin Thomass (LAN)
Robichaud, Paul G., *c.s.p.*
Rogers, Francis J. (WIL)
Rogers, Patrick W. (COL)
Rowan, Mark (RVC)
Rowe, William (SAC)
Russo, Richardo, *o.f.m.*
Ryan, Kenneth (NO)
Sable, Robert (DET)
Sacus, Samuel S. (WH)
St. Martin, Robert J. (HRT)
Saldua, Max (Philippines)
Santana, Edward (CGS)
Santiago-Burgess, Felipe (SJN)
Sanchez-Munoz, Alejandro (STV)
Scalone, Jonathan (FWT)
Schaff, Tyrone J. (SP)
Schaub, Gregory P., *o.s.b.*
Scheer, John R., *s.a.c.*
Schindler, Carl A., *c.ss.r.*
Schultz, Charles F. (SB)
Seminack, Richard S. (PH)
Sera, Enrique J. (ORG)
Sewell, Jack K. (ORG)
Shannon, Richard (CHI)
Shea, Michael J. (SFE)
Sheehan, Joseph P. (PH)
Sickler, Robert, *m.ss.a.*
Siesle, John W., Jr. (STL)
Silva, Caesar (HT)
Silvestri, Anthony F., *o.s.f.s.*
Sippel, Bernard S. (MIL)
Sirianni, Richard D. (P)
Skufca, Ronald (MAR)
Slowinski, Thomas (DET)
Smith, Francis J. (ELP)
Smith, Gabriel (CHR)
Smith, Lawrence H. (BRK)
Sousa, Peter S., *c.ss.r.*
Spellman, John, *o.s.f.s.*
Spencer, F. Richard (BAL)
Spiegel, Thomas J. (DAV)
Spring, Mark S. (DAV)
Stakem, Ward G., *o.f.m.cap.*
Staley, Robert (R)
Stang, William, *c.pp.s.*
Sta.Maria, Nicanor (SJN)
Staszewski, Joseph P. (E)
Staszewski, Robert M. (PIT)
Stefula, Salvatore M., *t.o.r.*
Steiner, John W. (LC)
Stenson, Patrick J., *m.s.c.*
Stephenson, Alfonse (PAT)
Stewart, Paul (PT)

Sticco, Peter, *s.a.c.*
Stites, John F. (TOL)
Strittmatter, Lawrence R. (CIN)
Studniewski, Gary (WDC)
Sturn, Michael L. (SB)
Suellentrop, Anthony (DOD)
Sullivan, Robert J. (BIR)
Sutton, Stephen R. (BAL)
Sweeney, Daniel, *s.j.*
Szczesniak, Harry F. (BUF)
Tamalis, John J. (SCR)
Taylor, Samuel J. (NY)
Taylor, Thomas (LAN)
Tejada, Denis J. (LC)
Tero, Richard D. (ANC)
Tetreault, Raymond A. (PRO)
Theroux, Paul D. (PRO)
Thomas, Royce R. (LR)
Thompson, Richard B. (MAN)
Thorne, Thomas P. (BGP)
Toner, Patrick A. (COL)
Torsiello, Ralph C. (WDC)
Trabold, George R. (NEW)
Tracy, Robert D., *o.carm.*
Tran, Philip (NY)
Travers, Patrick (JUN)
Troutman, Richard E. (TUC)
Tuite, Thomas (RVC)
Tyrrell, Robert D. (BO)
Uhde, Peter M. (NEW)
Urnick, Charles B. (NEW)
Valenzano, Joseph A. (BRK)
Valko, George J. (ALT)
Van Alstyne, Donald, *m.i.c.*
Vavarek, Hayden (CHR)
Vandeberg, Joseph (SCL)
Ventura, John J. (BIR)
Verbrugghe, Albert E. (TUC)
Vialpando, Kenneth L. (SLC)
Vigil, Michael (GLP)
Vigilanti, John A. (NY)
Vucinovich, Albert P. (SFR)
Wagner, William C. (CIN)
Waibel, Philip, *o.s.b.*
Wallace, Richard J. (P)
Weber, Joseph A. (STL)
Wedeking, Patrick (GLP)
Weisner, Mark (OAK)
Welton, Arthur T. (NY)
Wendel, Alfred W. (CHY)
Wielunski, Gregory C. (BRK)
Willette, Donald (DEN)
Williams, John L. (HRT)
Williams, Ronald R. (DET)
Wilz, John C. (PH)
Wittouck, Frank, *s.c.j.*
Wojtasczyk, John S. (CC)
Woods, Curtis W. (ALX)
Worster, John (B)
Wulinski, Stanley (BRK)
Zeck, George F. (DUL)
Ziemkiewicz, Frank, *o.s.b.*
Zientek, Benedict J. (SAN)
Zizka, Peter J. (HRT)
Zygadlo, Mitchell (ROC)

CIVIL AIR PATROL CHAPLAINS

Reverends
Albrecht, Louis H. (BAK)
Allen, Joseph P. (CHI)
Ausperk, Michael D. (CLV)
Berean, Christopher H. (NY)
Birk, John G. (SPK)
Booth, Edward N. (STA)
Borkowski, Thomas (KC)
Brown, John T. (OWN)
Cameron, Albert S. (MAN)
Cantlow, Cronan (BAL)
Caron, Eduardo J., *c.s.sp.*
Churchill, Raymond (HON)
Coogan, Roch A. (SAV)
DeCrans, Joseph J. (CR)
DeMure, Salvatore Patrick (HRT)
Devaney, Michael, *o.m.i.*
Diener, John E. (CIN)
Donohue, Stephen S. (BO)
Dupuis, George H. (BUR)
Duran, Alphonsus M., *m.j.*
Ebner, Frank H. (SCL)
Elliott, Edward C. (MEM)
Emala, Walter (MEM)
Farland, David M. (SPR)
Feltz, John G. (BUR)
Fitzgerald, John P. (PIT)
Friederick, John J. (DUB)
Goeser, Peter J., *o.s.b.*
Greer, Michael G. (COV)
Guischard, John A. (BUR)
Hayden, Joseph M. (CAM)
Hennington, Bruce M. (MAD)
Hoffmaster, Harry E. (DET)
Hurley, Most Rev. Francis T. (ANC)
Kaszczak, Ivan (STF)
Kelley, James F. (ANC)
Kelly, George F., *c.ss.r.*
King, James E. (NTN)
Kost, Harold J. (SCL)
Kovarik, James, *o.s.cam.* (MIL)
Kremeier, James (GI)
Kukucka, Joseph G. (PBL)
LaBuda, David E., *m.m.*
Lamitie, Robert O. (OG)
LaPlante, Jean Paul (BUR)
LaPorte, Paul (PRO)
Lopez, Humberto (MGZ)
McGuire, Richard J. (E)
McQuillen, Thomas J. (TOL)
Maag, Ronald (BAK)
Maskell, Anthony J. (BAL)
Merrill, Arthur R. (PIT)
Michalski, Thaddeus (CLV)
Miller, Bruce (ALX)
Miller, James N. (NSH)
Nevins, Albert J., *m.m.*
Nollette, Neal P. (GI)
O'Connell, Msgr. James E. (LR)
O'Grady, Frank (PAT)
Ondik, Michael J. (CLV)
Orlando, Vincent, *s.j.*
Parker, James (CHR)
Phillips, George M. (OG)
Ratchford, Robert J., *s.j.*
Scanlan, Cornelius J. (JUN)
Scanlan, Francis G. (CHI)
Schaefer, Roman J. (MIA)
Sevigny, Robert, *o.m.i.*
Shamsher, Paul (HRT)
Shortt, David J. (PBR)
Smalley, William R. (NEW)
Smith, Lawrence C., *s.j.*
Sommer, Allan J. (MIL)
Strachota, Dennis J. (BAL)
Smith, Lawrence C., *s.j.*
Therrien, Shawn M. (MAN)
Vaughan, Richard F. (AMA)
Vogel, Walter J. (MIL)
Voity, Maurice J. (SAN)
Walters, James L. (LR)
Weber, Gabriel M., *o.s.m.*
Williams, John L. (HRT)
Wolesky, John A. (SAL)

PERMANENT DEACONS SERVING IN THE ARCHDIOCESE FOR THE MILITARY SERVICES

AMS Chancery

Deacon
Crowley, Ronald C.

Air Force

Deacons
Bonanno, Frederick R.
Ellis, Billy Joe
Jachimowicz, John J.
Kuntz, Edward E.
McAtee, Ralph H., Jr.
Moseley, Phil
Neville, Richard F.
Perry, Robert W.
Pfleger, James W.
Pinto, Richard A.
Prentiss, Richard C.
Richardson, Walter H.
Sarver, Richard H.
Scarbo, David
Sekinger, Eugene E.
Sheldon, Lawrence F.
Shields, Floyd M.
Yarawsky, William S.

Air National Guard

Deacon
Sloan, Joseph S.

Army

Deacons
Adam, Klaus M.
Dew, Joseph M.
Foster, George H.
Holbritter, Milton A.
Horne, Wilfred
Jones, Frederick, Jr.
Miller, Larry L.
Plowman, Kent M.
Rienzi, Thomas M.
Rowland, Robert D.
Schoebel, James G.
Shuffer, George M.

National Guard

Deacon
Salchert, John J.

Navy

Deacons
Gubatan, Nemsy, Jr.
Kaizen, Joseph C.
Ladouceur, Gerald J.
McGlade, Henry D.
McMahon, Anthony
Nartowicz, Edward C.
Pellosie, John C.
Pepe, Joseph
Ryan, Richard

Marines

Deacons
Hernandez, Nieves J.
Schmitt, Giles V.

State Department

Deacon
Perez, Julio

Veterans Administration

Deacons
Abler, Donald J.
Hare, Martin
Luft, Dennis M.
Menke, Richard A.
Rinkus, Louis
Salchert, John J.
Watson, John W.

Civil Air Patrol

Deacon
Schaible, John A.

DIOCESES WITH PRIESTS SERVING IN THE ARCHDIOCESE FOR THE MILITARY SERVICES

Albany
Alexandria
Allentown
Altoona-Johnstown
Amarillo
Arlington
Atlanta
Austin
Baltimore
Baton Rouge
Beaumont
Belleville
Bridgeport
Birmingham
Bismarck
Biloxi
Boise
Boston
Brooklyn
Buffalo
Burlington
Caguas, Puerto Rico
Camden
Canton (Romanian Catholic Diocese of St. George)
Caroline Islands
Charleston
Charlotte
Cheyenne
Chicago
Cincinnati
Cleveland
Columbus
Corpus Christi
Covington
Dallas
Davenport
Denver
Detroit
Dubuque
Duluth
El Paso
Erie
Fall River
Fargo
Fort Wayne-South Bend
Gallup
Grand Island
Grand Rapids
Great Falls-Billings
Green Bay
Greensburg
Hartford
Helena
Honolulu
Indianapolis
Jackson
Jefferson City
Kalamazoo
Kansas City
Kansas City-St. Joseph
Lafayette, IN
Lafayette, LA
Lansing
Lincoln
Los Angeles
Louisville
Lubbock
Madison
Manchester
Marquette
Memphis
Metuchen
Miami
Milwaukee
Mobile
Nashville
Newark
New Orleans
Newton (Melkite Rite)
New Ulm
New York
Norwich
Oakland
Ogdensburg
Oklahoma City
Omaha
Orange
Orlando
Owensboro
Passaic (Byzantine)
Paterson
Pensacola-Tallahassee
Peoria
Philadelphia
Pittsburgh
Ponce, Puerto Rico
Portland, ME
Providence
Rapid City
Richmond
Rochester
Rockville Centre
Sacramento
St. Augustine
St. Cloud
St. Louis
St. Maron
St. Paul-Minneapolis
St. Petersburg
St. Thomas, Virgin Islands
Salt Lake City
San Angelo
San Antonio
San Bernardino
San Diego
San Francisco
San Juan, Puerto Rico
Santa Fe
Santa Rosa
Savannah
Scranton
Seattle
Sioux City
Sioux Falls
Spokane
Springfield-Cape Girardeau
Springfield, IL
Springfield, MA
Steubenville
Superior
Syracuse
Toledo
Trenton
Tucson
Tulsa
Venice
Victoria
Washington, DC
Wheeling-Charleston
Wichita
Wilmington
Winona
Worcester
Yakima
Youngstown

COUNTRIES WITH PRIESTS SERVING IN THE ARCHDIOCESE FOR THE MILITARY SERVICES

Africa
Canada
Caroline Islands
Colombia
Czechoslovakia
East Anglia
Ecuador
France
Ghana
India
Mexico
Nigeria
Pakistan
Peru
Philippines
Poland
Spain
Taiwan
United Kingdom
Vietnam

RELIGIOUS INSTITUTES WITH PRIESTS SERVING IN THE ARCHDIOCESE FOR MILITARY SERVICES

A.A. Assumptionists
C.J. Josephite Fathers
C.M. Vincentian Fathers
C.M.F. Claretian Missionaries
C.P. Congregation of the Passion
C.PP.S. Society of the Precious Blood
C.S.C. Congregation of the Holy Cross
C.S.P. Paulist Fathers
C.S.Sp. Holy Ghost Fathers
C.SS.R. Redemptorist Fathers
C.S.V. Viatorian Fathers
L.C. Legionaries of Christ
M.I.C. Congregation of Marians of the Immaculate Conception
M.M. Maryknoll Missioners
M.S. Missionaries of Our Lady of LaSalette
M.S.C. Missionaries of the Sacred Heart
M.S.A. Missionaries of the Holy Apostles
O. Carm. Carmelite Fathers
O.C.S.O. Cistercians of the Strict Observance
O.F.M. Franciscan Fathers
O.F.M.Cap. Capuchins
O.F.M.Conv. Conventual Franciscans
O.M.I. Oblates of Mary Immaculate
O.M.V. Oblates of the Virgin Mary
O.P. Order of Preachers
O.Praem. Premonstratensian Fathers
O.S.A. The Augustinians
O.S.B. Benedictine Fathers
O.S.C. Crozier Fathers
O.S.Cam. Order of St. Camillus
O.S.F.S. Oblates of St. Francis de Sales
O.S.M. Servite Fathers
O.SS.T. Trinitarian Fathers
S.A. Atonement Fathers
S.A.C. Society of the Catholic Apostolate
S.Ch. Society of Christ
S.C.J. Sacred Heart Fathers
S.D.B. Salesian Fathers
S.D.S. Society of Divine Savior
S.F. Sons of the Holy Family
S.J. Jesuit Fathers
S.M. Marist Fathers
S.O.L.T. Society of Our Lady of the Most Holy Trinity
SS.CC. Fathers of the Sacred Hearts
S.S.J. St. Joseph's Society of the Sacred Heart
S.S.S. Congregation of the Blessed Sacrament
S.T. Missionary Servants of the Most Holy Trinity

ASSOCIATIONS SUPPORTING THE MISSION OF THE ARCHDIOCESE

The Centurions
The Chaplains Aid Association

Archdiocese of Milwaukee

(Archidioecesis Milvauchiensis)

Most Reverend

REMBERT G. WEAKLAND, O.S.B., D.D.

Archbishop of Milwaukee; ordained June 24, 1951; appointed Archbishop of Milwaukee September 20, 1977; consecrated and installed as Ninth Archbishop November 8, 1977. *Res., 3303 S. Lake Dr., St. Francis, WI, 53235-3703. All official communications to the Most Rev. Archbishop should be addressed to: Archbishop Cousins Catholic Center, 3501 S. Lake Dr., P.O. Box 07912, Milwaukee, WI, 53207-0912.*

Most Reverend

RICHARD J. SKLBA, D.D.

Auxiliary Bishop of Milwaukee; ordained December 20, 1959; appointed Titular Bishop of Castro November 6, 1979; consecrated December 19, 1979. *Res., 2491 N. Murray Ave., Milwaukee, WI, 53211.* Tel.: 414-962-3941.

ESTABLISHED NOVEMBER 28, 1843; CREATED ARCHBISHOPRIC FEBRUARY 12, 1875.

Square Miles 4,758.

Corporate Title: *"Archdiocese of Milwaukee."*

Comprises the Counties of Dodge, Fond du Lac, Kenosha, Milwaukee, Ozaukee, Racine, Sheboygan, Walworth, Washington and Waukesha in the State of Wisconsin.

For legal titles of parishes and archdiocesan institutions, consult the Chancery Office.

Chancery Office: Archbishop Cousins Catholic Center, 3501 S. Lake Dr., P.O. Box 07912, Milwaukee, WI, 53207-0912. Tel.: 414-769-3340; Fax: 414-769-3408.

Web site address: http:/ /www.archmil.org

E-mail address: archmil@execpc.com

STATISTICAL OVERVIEW

Personnel	
Archbishop	1
Auxiliary Bishops	1
Retired Bishops	1
Abbots	1
Retired Abbots	1
Priests: Diocesan Active in Diocese	287
Priests: Active Outside Diocese	27
Priests: Diocesan in Foreign Missions	3
Priests: Retired, Sick or Absent	157
Number of Diocesan Priests	474
Religious Priests in Diocese	290
Extern Priests in Diocese	18
Ordinations:	
Diocesan Priests	1
Religious Priests	4
Transitional Deacons	3
Permanent Deacons in Diocese	154
Total Brothers	31
Total Sisters	2,235
Parishes	
Parishes	274
With Resident Pastor:	
Resident Diocesan Priests	206
Resident Religious Priests	23
Without Resident Pastor:	
Administered by Priests	31
Administered by Women Religious	4
Administered by Lay People	7
Completely Vacant	3
Pastoral Centers	21
New Parishes Created	3
Closed Parishes	7
Professional Ministry Personnel:	
Brothers	5
Sisters	58
Lay Ministers	394
Welfare	
Catholic Hospitals	11
Total Assisted	1,912,592
Health Care Centers	1
Total Assisted	14,000
Homes for the Aged	27
Total Assisted	5,664
Day Care and Extended Day Care Centers	7
Total Assisted	1,132
Specialized Homes	6
Total Assisted	3,119
Special Centers for Social Services	45
Total Assisted	222,895
Educational	
Seminaries, Diocesan	1
Students from This Diocese	23
Seminaries, Religious	1
Students Religious	5
Total Seminarians	28
Colleges and Universities	5
Total Students	21,491
High Schools, Diocesan and Parish	7
Total Students	4,450
High Schools, Private	6
Total Students	3,213
Elementary Schools, Diocesan and Parish	143
Total Students	32,830
Elementary Schools, Private	2
Total Students	92
Non-residential Schools for the Disabled	2
Total Students	17
Catechesis/Religious Education:	
High School Students	14,556
Elementary Students	38,445
Total Students Under Catholic Instruction	115,122
Teachers in the Diocese:	
Priests	85
Brothers	10
Sisters	181
Lay Teachers	2,847
Vital Statistics	
Receptions into the Church:	
Infant Baptism Totals	9,466
Adult Baptism Totals	510
Received into Full Communion	611
First Communions	9,779
Confirmations	6,046
Marriages:	
Catholic	2,385
Interfaith	1,115
Total Marriages	3,500
Deaths	6,046
Total Catholic Population	680,170
Total Population	2,080,000

Former Bishops—Most Rev. JOHN MARTIN HENNI, D.D., cons. March 19, 1844; created Archbishop, Feb. 11, 1875; died Sept. 7, 1881.—Most Rev. MICHAEL HEISS, D.D., cons. Bishop of La Crosse, Sept. 6, 1868; appt. Coadjutor of Milwaukee and Titular Archbishop of Adrianople, March 14, 1880; succeeded to Archbishop Henni in 1881; died March 26, 1890.—Most Rev. FREDERICK XAVIER KATZER, D.D., cons. Sept. 21, 1886; Bishop of Green Bay; transferred to Milwaukee and raised to the Archiepiscopal Dignity, Jan. 30, 1891; died July 20, 1903.—Most Rev. SEBASTIAN GEBHARD MESSMER, D.D., D.C.L., ord. July 23, 1871; cons. March 27, 1892; Bishop of Green Bay, Wis. transferred to Milwaukee and raised to the Archiepiscopal dignity Dec. 10, 1903 made assistant at the Pontifical Throne, Nov. 16, 1906; died Aug. 4, 1930.—His Eminence SAMUEL ALPHONSUS STRITCH, D.D., ord. May 21, 1910; cons. Nov. 30, 1921; Bishop of Toledo, Ohio; transferred to Milwaukee and raised to the Archiepiscopal dignity, Aug. 26, 1930; transferred to Chicago, Dec. 27, 1939; created Cardinal, Feb. 18, 1946; died May 27, 1958.—Most Rev. MOSES E. KILEY, S.T.D., appt. Bishop of Trenton, Feb. 10, 1934; cons. March 17, 1934; appt. Archbishop of Milwaukee, Jan. 1, 1940; died April 15, 1953.—His Eminence ALBERT G. MEYER, S.T.D., S.S.L., ord. July 11, 1926; cons. Bishop of Superior, April 11. 1946; appt. Archbishop of Milwaukee, July 21, 1953; transferred to Chicago, Sept. 24, 1958; created Cardinal, Dec. 14, 1959; died Apr. 9, 1965.—Most Rev. WILLIAM E. COUSINS, D.D., ord. April 23, 1927; appt. Titular Bishop of Forma and Auxiliary Bishop of Chicago

Dec. 17, 1948; cons. March 7, 1949; appt. Bishop of Peoria, May 19, 1952; installed July 2, 1952; appt. Archbishop of Milwaukee, Dec. 18, 1958; installed Jan. 27, 1959; retired Sept. 20, 1977; died Sept. 14, 1988.

Chancery Office, Archbishop Cousins Catholic Center—3501 S. Lake Dr., P.O. Box 07912, Milwaukee, 53207-0912. Tel: 414-769-3340; Fax: 414-769-3408.

Vicars General—Most Rev. RICHARD J. SKLBA, D.D.; Very Rev. THOMAS F. KERSTEIN.

Deans—Very Revs. KENNETH J. METZ, District 1; JOSEPH F. HORNACEK, District 2; DENNIS E. VAN BEEK, District 3; EDWARD R. WIELAND, District 4; ROBERT D. GOSMA, District 5; BERNARD S. SIPPEL, District 6; CHARLES H. WESTER, District 7; PATRICK E. HEPPE, District 8; RICHARD J. CERPICH, District 9; Very Rev. Msgr. THOMAS J. GAJDOS, District 10; Very Revs. KENNETH P. KNIPPEL, District 11; DENNIS R. ACKERET, District 12; JOHN R. KERN, District 13; WILLIAM W. KEY, District 14; THOMAS P. EICHENBERGER, District 15; WILLIAM E. KOHLER, District 16.

Chancellor—BARBARA ANNE CUSACK, J.C.D.

Vice Chancellor—Rev. JAMES E. CONNELL, J.C.D.

Archivist—TIMOTHY D. CARY.

Secretary to Archbishop—Rev. LEONARD S. VAN VLAENDEREN, *Res., 3303 South Lake Dr., Milwaukee, 53207.* Tel: 414-769-7988.

Metropolitan Tribunal Archbishop Cousins Catholic Center—3501 S. Lake Dr., P.O. Box 07912, Milwaukee, 53207-0912. Tel: 414-769-3300. Please direct all Rogatory Commissions to; Rev. JOHN D. AIELLO, Defender of the Bond.

Judicial Vicar—Rev. THOMAS T. BRUNDAGE, M.Div., J.C.L.

Adjutant Judical Vicar—Rev. DENNIS C. KLEMME, J.C.D.

Executive Secretary—MAURICE C. THOMPSON.

Judges for First Instance—Revs. THOMAS T. BRUNDAGE, M.Div., J.C.L.; DENNIS C. KLEMME, J.C.D.; JOSEPH N. PERRY, M.Div., J.C.L.; JAMES J. JARUMBO, J.C.L.; JACK HOPKA, J.C.L.

Judges for Second Instance—Revs. DENNIS C. KLEMME, J.C.D.; FRANK ARESTA, S.C.J., J.C.L.; THOMAS T. BRUNDAGE, J.C.L.; JAMES E. CONNELL, J.C.D.; BARBARA ANNE CUSACK, J.C.D.; Revs. CURT J. FREDERICK, J.C.L.; JACK HOPKA, J.C.L.; JAMES J. JARUMBO, J.C.L.; JOSEPH A. JANICKI, J.C.L.; MICHAEL T. NEWMAN, J.C.L.; JOSEPH N. PERRY, M.Div., J.C.L.; BERNARD S. SIPPEL, M.Div.; PHILIP D. REIFENBERG, J.C.L.

Defender of the Bond Second Instance—Rev. JOHN D. AIELLO, M.Div.

Procurator Advocates—THOMAS DARROW, M.A.; ZABRINA DECKER; THOMAS R. BUDDE.

Promoters of Justice—Revs. ROBERT G. SAMPON, S.T.L., J.C.D.; PHILIP D. REIFENBERG, J.C.L.

Assessor / Due Process Coordinator—JOHN CARINI, J.D.

Notaries—Rev. JOHN D. AIELLO, M.Div.; MAURICE C. THOMPSON; MARY CHRIS ELLISON; NANCY DANIELS; JOYCE HRYNIEWICKI; ALICE PRIER.

Office for Marital Reconciliation-Separation—Rev. DENNIS C. KLEMME, J.C.D., Delegate.

Due Process Office—Rev. THOMAS T. BRUNDAGE, M.Div., J.C.L.

Archdiocesan Consultors—Most Rev. RICHARD J. SKLBA, D.D.; Very Rev. RICHARD J. CERPICH; Revs. ROLLAND T. GLASS; RALPH C. GROSS; JEFFREY R. HAINES; JOHN P. HANLEY; Very Rev. JOSEPH F. HORNACEK; Revs. DAVID H. REITH; DANIEL J. SANDERS.

Archdiocesan Council of Priests—Very Rev. RICHARD J. ROBINSON, Moderator, *3501 S. Lake Dr., P.O. Box 07912, Milwaukee, 53207-0912.* Tel: 414-769-3300.

Archdiocesan Pastoral Council—3501 S. Lake Dr., P.O. Box 07912, Milwaukee, 53207-0912. Tel: 414-769-3499.

Ministerial Formation - Saint Francis Seminary—Very Rev. ANDREW L. NELSON, S.T.L., Ph.D., Rector, *3257 S. Lake Dr., St. Francis, 53235.* Tel: 414-747-6400.

Continuing Formation of Clergy—Rev. STEPHEN V. DELEERS, Dir. Tel: 414-747-6417.

Vocations Office—Rev. ROBERT X. STIEFVATER, Dir., *3257 S. Lake Dr., St. Francis, 53235.* Tel: 414-747-6437.

Department for Clergy Personnel—Archbishop Cousins Catholic Center, 3501 S. Lake Dr., P.O. Box 07912, Milwaukee, 53207-0912. Tel: 414-769-3484.

Vicar for Clergy Personnel—Very Rev. THOMAS F. KERSTEIN.

Priests' Placement Board—Revs. LEONARD M. BARBIAN, Assoc. Vicar, Clergy; JAMES J. BRADY; JEROME P. MEYER; MICHAEL F. MORAN; ROBERT G. SAMPON; RICHARD J. STOFFEL; R. THOMAS VENNE. Tel: 414-769-3458.

St. Michael's Priest Fund—Rev. HERBERT B. SCHUBERT, Sec.

Priests' Pension Plan—Rev. GEORGE M. REBATZKI, Chm.

Deacon Services—Deacon KENNETH L. VERNON, Co-ord. Tel: 414-769-3409.

Archdiocesan Offices and Agencies

The following offices and agencies are located at the Archbishop Cousins Catholic Center unless otherwise indicated

Archbishop Cousins Catholic Center—3501 S. Lake Dr., P.O. Box 07912, Milwaukee, 53207-0912. Tel: 414-769-3300; Fax: 414-769-3408.

Department for Parishes

Archbishop's Delegate for Parishes—MAUREEN GALLAGHER, Ph.D. Tel: 414-769-3450.

Office for Multi-Cultural Services—Sr. SHAWNEE SYKES, S.S.N.D., Multi-Cultural Consultant/Dir., African-American Ministry. Tel: 414-769-3411. PEDRO MARTINEZ, Multi-Cultural Consultant/Dir., Hispanic Ministry. Tel: 414-769-3393. ROSINE L. SCHMITT, Dir. Multi-Cultural Consultant/Dir., Asian Ministry. Tel: 414-769-3376.

Parish Consultants—Districts 1, 2, 3: VALERIE KELLER-,Districts 4, 5, 7: NOREEN WELTE,Districts 6, 8, 9: PEG MUDROCH,Districts 10, 11, 12, 13: EVA J. DIAZ; CATHERINE O'NEILL,District 14: ROBERTO CORTES-,Districts 15 and 16: MARK PETERS. Tel: 414-769-3539.

Parish Council Leadership Formation—Vacant; Dir. Tel: 414-769-3378.

Office for Human Concerns / Respect Life—PEG FLAHIVE, Dir. Tel: 414-769-3426.

Office for Parish Finances—DAVID LAUER. Tel: 414-769-3377.

Office for Parish Planning & Collaboration—Sr. BARBARA DANNHAUSEN, O.P., Dir. Tel: 414-769-3379. ROBERT MELCHER, Assoc. Dir. Tel: 414-769-3381.

Office for Prayer and Worship—MICHAEL NOVAK, Dir. Tel: 414-769-3350. Vacant; Assoc. Dir. Tel: Tel: 414-769-3348.

Office for Adult and Family Ministry—THERESA JOHANEK, Dir. Tel: 414-769-3439.

Marriage and Family Ministry—RANDY NOHL, Assoc. Dir. Tel: 414-769-3440.

Singles, Separated, Divorced—PAT DOCKTOR, Assoc. Dir. Tel: 414-769-3445.

Bereavement Ministry—POLLY HORKY, Assoc. Dir. Tel: 414-769-3456.

Engaged Programs—MARIE GREVSMUEHL, Coord. Tel: 414-769-3441.

Campus Ministry—Milwaukee: CONSTANCE M. POPP; Rev. ROBERT J. LOTZ. Tel: 414-964-6640. Kenosha/Racine: EDITH PADGETT. Tel: 414-654-3630. Whitewater: Rev. JAMES M. GODIN. Tel: 414-473-5555.

Special Needs—THERESA JOHANEK. Tel: 414-769-3439.

Ministry to the Hearing Impaired—CYNTHIA DEEHRKOOB, Assoc. Dir. Tel: 414-769-3455 (V/TTY).

Adult Formation—ROSALIE HARTMANN, Assoc. Dir. Tel: 414-769-3447.

Office for Schools and Child-Youth Ministries—JOHN T. NORRIS, Supt. Schools/Dir. Schools, Child & Youth Ministries. Tel: 414-769-3366.

Student Activities & Services—W. SCOTT WEYDA, Assoc. Dir. Tel: 414-769-3359.

Staff Development—CAMILLE MORTIMORE, Assoc. Dir. Tel: 414-769-3358.

Curriculum & Instruction—DAVID PROTHERO, Assoc. Dir. Tel: 414-769-3357.

Youth & Young Adult Ministry—DONALD SCHWORZHOFF, Assoc. Dir. Tel: 414-769-3361.

Catechetics to Children—JEAN MARIE WEBER, Assoc. Dir. Tel: 414-769-3373.

Early Adolescent Ministry—LISA MARIE CALDERONE-STEWART, Assoc. Dir. Tel: 414-769-3360.

Technology and Communication—LOU WHITAKER, Assoc. Dir. Tel: 414-769-3313.

Department for Community Services

Archbishop's Delegate for Community Services—Deacon WARREN D. BRAUN. Tel: 414-769-3389.

Ecumenical and Interfaith Concerns—JUDITH A. LONGDIN, Dir. Tel: 414-769-3483.

Office for Social Concerns—WARREN BRAUN, Dir. Tel: 414-769-3389. MARJORIE MORGAN, Assoc. Dir. Tel: 414-769-3402.

Campaign for Human Development—MARY GROPPI, Co-ord. Tel: 414-769-3424.

Office for World Mission—Sr. FRANCIS CUNNINGHAM, O.S.F., Dir. Tel: 414-769-3404.

"Catholic Herald"—Official Publication of Archdiocese of Milwaukee. ETHEL M. GINTOFT, Assoc. Publisher/Exec. Editor, *3501 S. Lake Dr., P.O. Box 07913, Milwaukee, 53207-0913.* Tel: 414-769-3500.

Catholic Charities—THOMAS R. SCHNEIDER, Exec. Dir. Tel: 414-769-3419. (Legal Title: *Catholic Charities of the Archdiocese of Milwaukee, Inc.).*

Residential Programs for Developmentally Disabled—RONALD J. SPITZ, Dir. Tel: 414-769-3401.

Ministry on Aging—WILLIAM LEON, Dir. Tel: 414-769-3412.

Sexual Abuse Response Coordinator—ELIZABETH C. PIASECKI, Psy.D. Tel: 414-769-3436.

Department for Archdiocesan Finance and Administration

Archbishop's Delegate for Archdiocesan Finance and Administration—WAYNE A. SCHNEIDER. Tel: 414-769-3319.

Consultant for Legal Counsel—WAYNE A. SCHNEIDER. Tel: 414-769-3319.

Office for Archdiocesan Finance and Administrative Services—WAYNE A. SCHNEIDER, Dir./Controller; JOHN W. BOEHM, Dir. Computer Services/Asst. Controller. Tel: 414-769-3530.

Office for Cemeteries and Mausoleums—GREGG F. APOSTOLOFF, Dir., *7301 W. Nash St., Milwaukee, 53216.* Tel: 414-438-4430.

Office for Building Services—WILLIAM KREITZER, Dir. Tel: 414-769-3491.

Office for Printing Services—THOMAS WAL, Dir. Tel: 414-769-3487.

Department for Human Resources

Archbishop's Delegate for Human Resources—RICHARD TANK. Tel: 414-769-3370.

Office for Human Resources, Central Offices and Agencies—JUDITH A. MYERS, Dir. Tel: 414-769-3328.

Office for Parish and School Personnel—RICHARD J. TANK, Dir. Tel: 414-769-3370.

Archdiocesan Women's Commission—MARY JO RUNNOE. Tel: 414-769-3434.

Office for Religious—Rev. ALAN D. VEIK, O.F.M.Cap., Dir. Tel: 414-769-3375.

Department for Development

Archbishop's Delegate for Development—JOAN FEIEREISEN. Tel: 414-769-3457.

Annual Giving—BARBARA ANTHONY-CAPLIN, Dir. Tel: 414-769-3538.

Parish Stewardship—GERI DANIELS, Coord. Tel: 414-769-3331.

Donor Relations / Major & Planned Giving—DEBRA LETHLEAN, Dir. Tel: 414-769-3322.

Combined Collections—JOAN FEIEREISEN. Tel: 414-769-3457.

Department for Communication

JEAN MULLOOLY, Assoc. Dir. Tel: 414-769-3461. MARY CONARCHY, Coord. Publications. Tel: 414-769-3460

Archbishop's Delegate for Communication—JEROME TOPAZEWSKI. Tel: 414-769-3517. MARK BARTHEL, Webmaster/Coord. Electronic Communications. Tel: 414-769-3454.

CLERGY, PARISHES, MISSIONS AND PAROCHIAL SCHOOLS

CITY OF MILWAUKEE

(Milwaukee County)

1—ST. JOHN CATHEDRAL (1847), Very Rev. John H. Endejan. In res., Rev. James E. Connell.
Res., 802 N. Jackson St., 53202. Tel: 414-276-9814; Fax: 414-276-8285.

2—ST. ADALBERT (1908), Rev. John J. Wutscheck.
Res., 1923 W. Becher St., 53215-2611. Tel: 414-645-0413.
School—1913 W. Becher St., 53215-2688. Tel: 414-645-5450. Ms. Julia Hutchinson, Prin.
Lay Teachers 12; Students 172.

3—ST. AGNES. Closed. For sacramental records contact Archivist, Archdiocese of Milwaukee.

4—ST. ALBERT. Merged with Holy Redeemer and St. Nicholas to form Congregation of the Blessed Trinity. See listing for details.

5—ST. ALEXANDER (1926), Rev. Robert W. Nawrocki.
Res., 3373 S. 15th Pl., 53215. Tel: 414-645-9820.
School—3344 S. 16th St., 53215. Tel: 414-383-3453. Sr. Elmerine Acker, S.S.S.F., Prin.
Sisters 3; Lay Teachers 5; Students 210.

6—ST ANNE'S. Closed. For sacramental records contact Archivist, Archdiocese of Milwaukee.

7—ST. ANTHONY (1872), Revs. Lawrence V. Dulek; Edward Griesemer, S.C.J. In res., Revs. John B. Thanh Hung; Rafael Laiton; Robert F. Mueller.
Res., 1711 S. 9th St., 53204. Tel: 414-645-1455; Fax: 414-645-1456.
School—1747 S. 9th St., 53204. Tel: 414-384-1730. Richard Mason, Prin.
Sisters 6; Lay Teachers 3; Students 260.
Catechesis / Religious Programs—Tel: 414-347-4465. Dennis Hondel, D.R.E.
Students 268.

8—ST. ANTHONY OF PADUA (1923), Rev. James M. Heisler, S.A.C.

Res., 7622 W. Stevenson St., 53213. Tel: 414-453-5344; Fax: 414-453-4225.
School—7632 W. Stevenson St., 53213. Tel: 414-258-4165. Sr. Janet Neureuther, Prin.
Sisters 1; Lay Teachers 9; Students 177.

9—St. Augustine (1888) (German), Rev. Thomas F. Wittliff; Ms. Chiara Sainer, Pastoral Assoc.
Res., 2530 S. Howell Ave., 53207. Tel: 414-744-0808; Fax: 414-744-1231.
School—2523 S. Graham St., 53207. Tel: 414-481-5151. Mr. Gilbert Jaworski, Prin.
Lay Teachers 11; Students 141.

10—St. Barbara, Rev. James E. Kimla.
Res., 2059 S. 33rd St., 53215. Tel: 414-645-9172; Fax: 414-645-4732.
School—Grades K-4; in collaboration with Holy Spirit Parish, Milwaukee. 2075 S. 32nd St., 53215. Tel: 414-643-6090; Fax: 414-383-1836. Mrs. Carolyn Ettlie, Prin.
Sisters 1; Lay Teachers 4; Students 66.

11—St. Benedict the Moor (1908), Rev. Michael Sullivan, O.F.M.Cap.; Deacon John Champagne. In res., Rev. Michael Crosby, O.F.M.Cap.; Bros. Larry Ampe, O.F.M.Cap.; Kent Bauer, O.F.M.Cap.; Jerome Smith, O.F.M.Cap.; David Schwab, O.F.M.Cap.
Res., 1015 N. 9th St., 53233. Tel: 414-271-0135; Fax: 414-271-0637.

12—St. Bernadette (1958), Rev. William H. Whalen; Deacon John A. Ebel.
Res., 8200 W. Denver Ave., 53223. Tel: 414-358-4600.
School—8202 W. Denver Ave., 53223. Tel: 414-358-4603. Mary Lorusso, Prin.
Lay Teachers 10; Students 220.

13—Blessed Sacrament (1927) (Polish), Revs. Robert H. Katorski; Robert D. Turner; Sr. Sophie Banczak, S.S.J., Pastoral Assoc.; Deacon Richard Flynn.
Res., 3100 S. 41st St., 53215. Tel: 414-649-4720; Fax: 414-649-4726.
Church—S. 41st St. and W. Oklahoma Ave., 53215.
School—3126 S. 41st St., 53215. Tel: 414-649-4730. Sr. Rene Kuban, S.F.C.C., Prin.
Lay Teachers 16; Students 261.
Catechesis/Religious Programs—Tel: 414-649-4727.
Students 162.

14—Congregation of the Blessed Trinity (1991), Rev. Jerome P. Meyer, Admin.; Sheila Daly, Pastoral Assoc. & Lit. Coord.; Deacon Peter Gust, (Retired).
Pastoral Offices—4717 N. 38th St., 53209. Tel: 414-463-6921; Fax: 414-463-0349.
School—5375 N. Green Bay Ave., 53209. Tel: 414-228-9030; Fax: 414-228-7516. Linda Harrigan, Prin.
Lay Teachers 16; Students 145.

15—St. Boniface. Closed. For sacramental records contact Archivist, Archdiocese of Milwaukee.

16—St. Casimir (1894) (Polish-Spanish), Rev. James M. Flynt, Adm.; Patricia Beirne, Pastoral Assoc.
Mailing Address: 924 E. Clarke St., 53212-3009. Tel: 414-263-8220; Fax: 414-263-8233.
Res., 3055 N. Fratney St., 53212. Tel: 414-264-9814; 263-8228 (Office).
School—Catholic East Consolidated. See All Saints Catholic East School System, Inc., Listing in the Consolidated Elementary Schools section. Tel: 414-964-1770.

17—St. Catherine (1922), Darryl Olszewski, Parish Dir.; Rev. Paul Janette; Deacon Ralph W. Kornburger, Jr. In res., Revs. Charles A. Kleefisch; Wilson Paul Antony (India).
Res., 5101 W. Center St., 53210. Tel: 414-445-5115; Fax: 414-445-5198. [CEM]
School—2647 N. 51st St., 53210. Tel: 414-445-2846; Fax: 414-445-0448. Deborah Zabinski, Prin.
Lay Teachers 11; Students 155.

18—St. Catherine (Granville) (1855), Rev. Jeffery A. Prasser.
Office:—Tel: 414-365-2020; Fax: 414-365-2021.
Res., 8661 N. 76th Pl., 53223. Tel: 414-365-2039. [CEM]
School—8660 N. 76th Pl., 53223. Tel: 414-365-2030; Fax: 414-365-2021. Mr. Michael Howell, Prin.
Sisters 1; Lay Teachers 14; Students 215.
Catechesis/Religious Programs—Tel: 414-365-2025. Judith Jowalski, Ph.D., D.R.E.
Students 213.

19—St. Charles Borromeo (1960), Rev. Edward M. Safiejko.
Res., 5571 S. Marilyn Ave., 53221. Tel: 414-281-8115.
School—3100 W. Parnell Ave., 53221. Tel: 414-282-0767.
Lay Teachers 14; Students 220.
Catechesis/Religious Programs—Tel: 414-282-7010.
Students 200.

20—Corpus Christi (1958), Rev. Michael D. Strachota; Deacon James L. Aschenbrener; Judith Adrian, Pastoral Assoc.
Parish Center: 8607 W. Villard Ave., 53225. Tel: 414-464-5033; Fax: 414-464-0079.
School—8545 W. Villard Ave., 53225. Tel: 414-464-5775; Fax: 414-464-5775. Kagey Burdick, Prin.
Lay Teachers 13; Students 128.

21—SS. Cyril and Methodius (1893) (Polish), Rev. Paul L. Raczynski.
Office: 2427 S. 15th St., 53215. Tel: 414-383-3973; Fax: 414-383-3974.

22—St. Emeric (1919) (Hungarian), Rev. Bela Krigler, Sch.P.
Worship at Sacred Heart Church, Milwaukee. c/o 917 N. 49th St., 53208. Tel: 414-598-9231, 930-0844.

23—St. Elizabeth's. Closed. For sacramental records contact Archivist, Archdiocese of Milwaukee.

24—St. Florian (1911) (German), Revs. Leonard R. Copeland, O.C.D.; Timothy McGough, O.C.D. In res., Revs. Dominic T. Scheerer, O.C.D.; William Healy, O.C.D.; Philip Thomas, O.C.D.; Bros. Ralph Elias-Haddix, O.C.D.; Bernard Olk, O.C.D.; Bonaventure Potter, O.C.D.
Res., 1233 S. 45th St., 53214. Tel: 414-383-3565; Fax: 414-383-2708.
School—1215 S. 45th St., 53214. Tel: 414-383-4204.
Sisters 1; Lay Teachers 9; Students 123.

25—St. Francis of Assisi (1871), Revs. Niles Kauffman, O.F.M.Cap.; Robert Kose, O.F.M.Cap. In res., Revs. Ulric Buening, O.F.M.Cap.; Robert Wheelock, O.F.M.Cap.; Michael Sullivan, O.F.M.Cap.; Michael Zuelke, O.F.M.Cap.; Bro. Isidore Herriges, O.F.M.Cap.
Res., 327 W. Brown St., 53212. Tel: 414-374-5750; Fax: 414-374-5553.

26—St. Gabriel (1913) (Lithuanian). Closed. For parish records contact Congregation of the Great Spirit, Milwaukee.

27—St. Gall. Closed. For sacramental records contact Archivist, Archdiocese of Milwaukee.

28—St. Gerard (1925). Closed. For parish records contact Archivist, Archdiocese of Milwaukee.

29—Gesu Parish (1893), Revs. George E. Winzenburg, S.J.; John D. Campbell, S.J.; Michael G. Lee, S.J.; Patrick E. Walsh, S.J.; James Warosh, S.J.; Kenneth J. Herian, S.J.
Res., 1210 W. Michigan St., P.O. Box 495, 53201-0495. Tel: 414-288-7101; Fax: 414-288-5339.

30—Congregation of the Great Spirit (1989) (Native American), Rev. Edward J. Cook.
Mailing Address: 1050 W. Lapham St., 53204. Tel: 414-672-6989.
Res., 1575A S. 10th St., 53204.

31—St. Gregory the Great (1955), Revs. Kenneth E. Omernick; William Ericksen.
Office: 3160 S. 63rd St., 53219. Tel: 414-543-8292; Fax: 414-328-3881.
Res., 3129 S. 63rd St., 53219. Tel: 414-541-9059.
School—3132 S. 63rd St., 53219. Tel: 414-321-1350.
Lay Teachers 22; Students 494.
Catechesis/Religious Programs—Tel: 414-541-3720.
Students 228.

32—St. Hedwig (1871) (Polish), Rev. James N. Jablonowski.
Res., 1716 N. Humboldt Ave., 53202. Tel: 414-271-2165; Fax: 414-271-7988.
School—See All Saints Catholic East School System, Inc. in the Consolidated Elementary Schools section for further details. Tel: 414-964-1770 (Catholic East).

33—St. Helen (1925) (Polish), Rev. Michael A. Ignaszak; Sr. Helen Bronner, S.S.N.D., Pastoral Min.
Res., 3307 S. 10th St., 53215. Tel: 414-744-3695; 744-8292; Fax: 414-744-2874.
School—3329 S. 10th St., 53215. Tel: 414-744-7188. Sr. Kathleen Sowinski, S.S.S.F., Prin.
Sisters 5; Lay Teachers 6; Students 137.

34—Holy Angels. Closed. For sacramental records contact Archivist, Archdiocese of Milwaukee.

35—Holy Cross (1879), Revs. Robert J. Albers, S.A.C.; Paul Coutinha, S.A.C. (India).
Res., 5424 W. Bluemound Rd., 53208. Tel: 414-774-4420.
School—5522 W. Bluemound Rd., 53208. Tel: 414-258-0687. Ms. Barbara Kozleuchar, Prin.
Lay Teachers 10; Students 152.

36—Holy Redeemer. Merged with St. Albert and St. Nicholas to form Congregation of the Blessed Trinity. See listing for details.

37—Holy Rosary (1885) (Irish), Rev. Melvin P. Breit; Sr. Ellen Barrett, B.V.M., Admin. Assoc.
Res., 2003 N. Oakland Ave., 53202. Tel: 414-271-8605.
Church—E. Lafayette Pl. and N. Oakland Ave., 53202.
School—Catholic East Elementary. See All Saints Catholic East School System, Inc., Listing in the Consolidated Elementary Schools section. Tel: 414-964-1770.

38—Holy Spirit (1902) (German), Rev. Denis P. Weis; Deacons William A. Banach; David R. Pollak.
Res., 3132 W. Lincoln Ave., 53215-2497. Tel: 414-645-1742.
School—Holy Spirit School. Grades 5-8; in collaboration with St. Barbara Parish. 2251 S. 31st St., 53215. Tel: 414-645-1300.
Lay Teachers 8; Students 65.

39—Holy Trinity-Our Lady of Guadalupe (1849) (Hispanic), Rev. Michael F. Michalski; Deacon Jose H. Gutierrez.
Res., 613 S. 4th St., 53204. Tel: 414-271-6181; Fax: 414-271-3474.
Catechesis/Religious Programs—Tel: 414-271-6543.
Students 170.

40—St. Hyacinth (1883) (Polish-Hispanic), Rev. Ronald E. Kotecki.
Res., 1414 W. Becher St., 53215. Tel: 414-383-4010.

41—St. Ignatius Loyola. Merged with St. Barbara. For sacramental records see St. Barbara, Milwaukee.

42—Immaculate Conception (1870), Rev. Dennis M. Witz; Deacon John Wargin.
Res., 1023 E. Russell Ave., 53207. Tel: 414-769-2480.
School—1051 E. Russell Ave., 53207. Tel: 414-769-2485.
Lay Teachers 10; Students 179.
Catechesis/Religious Programs—Tel: 414-769-2488.
Students 37.

43—St. John Kanty (1907) (Polish), Rev. Carl M. Kazmierczak.
Res., 966 W. Dakota St., 53215. Tel: 414-744-5885.
School—2834 S. 10th St., 53215. Tel: 414-483-8780; 744-1846. Lois Maczuzak, Prin.
School Sisters of Notre Dame 2; Lay Teachers 8; Students 161.

44—St. John de Nepomuc. Closed. For sacramental records contact Archivist, Archdiocese of Milwaukee.

45—Basilica of St. Josaphat (1886) (Polish), Revs. William P. Callahan, O.F.M.Conv.; Robert Joseph Switanowski, O.F.M.Conv.; Deacon John C. Welnicki. In res., Bro. James M. Jankowski, O.F.M.Conv.
Res., 2333 S. 6th St., 53215. Tel: 414-645-5623; Fax: 414-645-1174.
School—801 W. Lincoln Ave., 53215. Tel: 414-645-4378. Mrs. Carolyn Trawitzki.
Lay Teachers 9; Students 162; School Sisters of St. Francis 1.

46—St. Lawrence (1888), Very Rev. William W. Key.
Res., 2604 W. Orchard St., 53204. Tel: 414-645-2088.
School—1418 S. Layton Blvd., 53215. Tel: 414-645-4922.
Sisters 3; Lay Teachers 6; Students 143.

47—St. Leo's. Closed. For sacramental records contact Archivist, Archdiocese of Milwaukee.

48—St. Margaret Mary (1955), Revs. Ralph C. Gross; Allen Bratkowski; Deacon Michael R. Rooney.
Res., 3930 N. 92nd St., 53222-2588. Tel: 414-461-6073; Fax: 414-463-2373.
School—3950 N. 92nd St., 53222-2587. Tel: 414-463-8760; Fax: 414-463-2373. Susan Nelson, Prin.
Sisters of St. Agnes 1; Lay Teachers 24; Students 438.
Catechesis/Religious Programs—Tel: 414-462-9660.
Students 211.

49—Old St. Mary (1846) (Bavarian/German), Rev. George M. Rebatzki; Deacon Claude Kennedy.
Res., 836 N. Broadway, 53202. Tel: 414-271-6180; Fax: 414-271-7782.

50—St. Mary of Czestochowa (1907) (Polish), Rev. James M. Flynt.
Res., 3055 N. Fratney St., 53212. Tel: 414-264-0049; Fax: 414-264-7177.
School—All Saints Catholic Elementary. See All Saints Catholic East School System, Inc., Listing in the Consolidated Elementary Schools section. Tel: 414-964-1770.

51—St. Mary Magdalen (1925) (Polish), Rev. Frank J. Yaniak.
Res., 1854 W. Windlake Ave., 53215. Tel: 414-645-4773.

52—St. Matthew (1892), Rev. James L. Dammeir; Sr. Leora Leon, S.S.S.F., Pastoral Assoc.; Michael P. Mernagh, Pastoral Assoc., Dir. of Lit.
Office: 1138 S. 25th St., 53204. Tel: 414-645-8786.
School—Consolidated with St. Lawrence. 1114 S. 25th St., 53204. Tel: 414-383-2157. Sr. Marilyn Winkel, C.S.A., Prin.

Sisters of St. Agnes, Fond du Lac, WI 1; Lay Teachers 11; Students 106.

53—ST. MATTHIAS (1851), Revs. Carl A. Last; Scott R. Leannah; Brian G. Mason.
9306 W. Beloit Rd., 53227. Tel: 414-321-0893; Fax: 414-321-1330. [CEM]
School—Tel: 414-321-0894.
Sisters 2; Lay Teachers 22; Students 472.
Catechesis/Religious Programs—Tel: 414-321-8680.
Students 347.

54—ST. MICHAEL (1883), Rev. Dennis J. Lewis, Admin. Pastoral Associates: Sr. Alice Thephouthay, Laotian Pastoral Ministry; Sr. Carmelita DeAnda, Hispanic Pastoral Ministry; Deacons Blong Yang, Hmong Pastoral Ministry; Juan Molina, Hispanic Pastoral Ministry.
Res., 1445 N. 24th St., 53205. Tel: 414-933-3143; Fax: 414-933-1956.
Catechesis/Religious Programs—Students 400.

55—MOTHER OF GOOD COUNSEL (1925), Rev. Daniel T. Pekarske, S.D.S.; Deacon Dean J. Collins. Pastoral Associates: Sr. Diane Goetzinger, S.D.S.; Sr. Anne Koszarek, S.S.J.-T.O.S.F.
Res., 6924 W. Lisbon Ave., 53210-1259. Tel: 414-442-7600; Fax: 414-444-0408.
School—3001 N. 68th St., 53210. Regina Shaw, Prin.
Sisters 1; Lay Teachers 24; Students 440.

56—MOTHER OF PERPETUAL HELP (1941), Rev. Richard J. Robinson; Deacon Thomas J. Schimmels.
Res., 5409 W. Villard Ave., 53218. Tel: 414-438-0669.
School—Merged with St. Stephen Martyr and is now called Resurrection Catholic Academy. 5135 N. 54th St., 53218. Tel: 414-438-4783; Fax: 414-463-8721. Thomas Hage, Prin.; Judy Rivas, Asst. Prin.
Sisters 2; Lay Teachers 12; Students 247.

57—ST. NICHOLAS. Merged with St. Albert and Holy Redeemer to form Congregation of the Blessed Trinity. See listing for details.

58—OUR LADY OF GOOD HOPE (1952), Revs. Paul A. Stanosz; Joseph A. Wolf; Deacons Michael Cesarec; Joseph H. Kastenholz; Robert M. Schieffer; Bryan Martin, Bus. Mgr. In res., Rev. John R. Kolanko.
Office: 7152 N. 41st St., 53209. Tel: 414-352-1148; Fax: 414-352-3042.
School—7120 N. 41st St., 53209. Tel: 414-352-7980. Nancy Behr, Prin.
Lay Teachers 12; Students 181.
Catechesis/Religious Programs—Tel: 414-352-8140. Barbara Krieger, D.R.E.
Students 215.

59—OUR LADY OF LOURDES (1958), Revs. Thomas M. Suriano; Michael G. Savio; Deacon John Monday; Mrs. Judith Bialk, Pastoral Assoc.
Office: 3722 S. 58th St., 53220. Tel: 414-545-4316; Fax: 414-541-2251.
Catechesis/Religious Programs—Tel: 414-541-9470.
Students 314.

60—OUR LADY, QUEEN OF PEACE (1948), Rev. Gilbert G. Arciszewski.
Res., 3222 S. 29th St., 53215. Tel: 414-672-0313; Fax: 414-672-0441.
School—2733 W. Euclid Ave., 53215. Tel: 414-672-6660. Christopher Multhauf, Prin.
Sisters 2; Lay Teachers 12; Students 217.

61—OUR LADY OF SORROWS (1955), Rev. Gregory A. Chycinski.
Res., 4063 N. 64th St., 53216. Tel: 414-463-3180.
School—4059 N. 64th St., 53216. Tel: 414-463-3878. Miss Patricia Wilkum, Prin.
Lay Teachers 10; Students 148.

62—ST. MARTIN DE PORRES (1994) (African American), Rev. Philip D. Reifenberg, Admin.
Office: 128 W. Burleigh St., 53212-2046. Tel: 414-372-3090; Fax: 414-372-0356.

63—ALL SAINTS (1994) (African American), Rev. Joseph N. Perry; Deacons Kenneth Vernon; Edward Blaze.
Office: 4060 N. 26th St., 53209-6695. Tel: 414-444-5610; Fax: 414-444-5709.

64—ST. PATRICK (1876), Revs. Richard P. Abert, S.J.; David M. Shields, S.J.
Res., 723 W. Washington St., 53204. Tel: 414-645-7624; Fax: 414-645-3733.
Catechesis/Religious Programs—Tel: 414-645-7624.
Students 185.

65—ST. PAUL (1920), Revs. James Winiarski, M.S.; Frank Kula, M.S.
Res., 1720 E. Norwich Ave., 53207. Tel: 414-482-3510.
School—3945 S. Kansas Ave., 53207. Tel: 414-482-4790; Fax: 414-482-2703.
Lay Teachers 9; Students 143.

66—SS. PETER AND PAUL (1889) (German), Very Rev. John R. Kern. Pastoral Assocs.: Rita Kuhnen; Monica Meagher; Thomas Koester Tel: 414-962-8103. In res., Most Rev. Richard J. Sklba.
Res., 2491 N. Murray Ave., 53211. Tel: 414-962-2443; Fax: 414-962-8183.
School—Catholic East Elementary, Tel: 414-964-1770; Fax: 414-962-8183.
See All Saints Catholic East School System, Inc. listing in the Consolidated Elementary Schools section.
Day Care Center—2480 N. Cramer St., 53211. Tel: 414-964-6638.
Children 94.
Catechesis/Religious Programs—East Side Child & Youth Ministry. Consolidated from the following parishes: SS. Peter & Paul, St. Casimir, St. Mary Czestochowa, St. Hedwig, Holy Rosary, Cathedral of St. John the Evangelist. 924 E. Clarke St., 53212. Tel: 414-263-8230.
Students 32.

67—ST. PHILIP NERI (1956), Rev. John L. Brophy, Admin.
Res., 5566 N. 69th St., 53218. Tel: 414-464-6721.
School—5501 N. 68th St., 53218. Tel: 414-466-0470. Sr. Suzanne Zinda, Prin.
Schoenstatt Sisters of Mary 1; Lay Teachers 8; Students 138.
Catechesis/Religious Programs—Tel: 414-466-4481. Mrs. Rita Leren, D.R.E.
Students 53.

68—ST. RITA (1936) (Italian), Rev. Melvin P. Breit; Sr. Marie Louise Balistrieri, S.C.S.J.A., Pastoral Assoc.
Res., 1603 N. Cass St., 53202. Tel: 414-276-1157.
School—Catholic East Elementary. See All Saints Catholic East School System, Inc., Listing in the Consolidated Elementary Schools section. Tel: 414-964-1770.

69—ST. ROBERT (1912), Revs. John J. Pulice; Roman S. Stikel.
Res., 4019 N. Farwell Ave., 53211. Tel: 414-332-0117; Fax: 414-332-2599.
School—2200 E. Capital Dr., 53211. Tel: 414-963-9540; Fax: 414-332-7355. Larry Patterson, Prin.; Sr. Ruth Brings, Pastoral Assoc.; Eileen Ambrose Steckbauer, Pastoral Min.
Sisters 1; Lay Teachers 25; Students 374.
Catechesis/Religious Programs—Tel: 414-332-2230.
Students 225.

70—ST. ROMAN (1956) (Polish), Revs. Robert L. Betz; Larry Sepich; Deacon William J. Lukacevich.
Res., 1710 W. Bolivar Ave., 53221. Tel: 414-282-9063; Fax: 414-282-6464.
School—1810 W. Bolivar Ave., 53221. Tel: 414-282-7970; Fax: 414-282-5140.
Lay Teachers 20; Students 465.
Catechesis/Religious Programs—Students 220.

71—ST. ROSE (1888), Rev. Dennis J. Lewis; Deacon Juan Molina.
Res., 544 N. 31st St., 53208. Tel: 414-342-1778; Fax: 414-342-7510.
School—See Elementary Schools, Archdiocesan, Catholic Urban Academies. Tel: 414-933-6070; Fax: 414-933-6071.

72—SACRED HEART (1917) (Croatian), Rev. Stephen Bedenikovic, O.F.M. (Croatia).
Res., 917 N. 49th St., 53208. Tel: 414-774-9418; Fax: 414-774-7406.

73—ST. SEBASTIAN (1911), Rev. Charles H. Schramm; Deacons James J. Peterson; Warren D. Braun.
Res., 5400 W. Washington Blvd., 53208. Tel: 414-453-1061; Fax: 414-453-9449.
School—1747 N. 54th St., 53208. Tel: 414-453-5830.
Sisters 1; Lay Teachers 23; Students 393.
Catechesis/Religious Programs—Tel: 414-453-7150.
Students 230.

74—ST. STANISLAUS (1866). Unassigned.
Res., 524 W. Mitchell St., 53204. Tel: 414-645-8170.

75—ST. STEPHEN (1847) (German). (Airport). Rev. Joseph A. Aufdermauer; Anita H. Kowalski, Pastoral Assoc.
Office: 5880 S. Howell Ave., 53207. Tel: 414-483-2685. [CEM 2]
Catechesis/Religious Programs—Tel: 414-483-2658.
Lay Teachers 10; Students 222.

76—ST. STEPHEN, MARTYR (1907) (Slovak), Rev. Richard J. Robinson.
Res., 5409 W. Villard Ave., 53218. Tel: 414-438-4780.
School—Merged with Mother of Perpetual Help to form Resurrection Catholic Academy. 5140 N. 55th St., 53218. Tel: 414-438-4783; Fax: 414-463-8721. Thomas Hage, Prin.; Sr. Judy Rivas, Assoc. Prin.
Sisters 2; Lay Teachers 12; Students 202.

77—ST. THERESE (1954), Rev. Roger C. Heck.
Res., 9525 W. Bluemound Rd., 53226. Tel: 414-771-2500.
Catechesis/Religious Programs—Tel: 414-476-5580. D.R.E.: Ralph Robers; Barbara Searing.
Students 200.

78—ST. THOMAS AQUINAS. Closed. For sacramental records contact Archivist, Archdiocese of Milwaukee.

79—ST. VERONICA (1926), Revs. Joseph B. Frederick; Gary D. Nowicki; Deacons John R. Burns; John Dziennik.
Res., 4017 S. Whitnall Ave., 53207. Tel: 414-482-2920; Fax: 414-482-3025.
School—341 E. Norwich St., 53207. Tel: 414-744-1214; Fax: 414-482-3025. Sr. Marie Estelle Kuczynski, Prin.
Sisters 1; Lay Teachers 21; Students 413.
Catechesis/Religious Programs—Tel: 414-481-0777.
Students 232.

80—ST. VINCENT DE PAUL (1888) (Polish), Rev. Stephen J. Lampe; Deacon John Martinez.
Res., 2114 W. Michell St., 53204. Tel: 414-645-3400; Fax: 414-645-3450.

81—ST. WENCESLAUS (1883) (Hispanic), Rev. Julio E. Miralbes-Drago.
Res., 1410 W. Scott St., 53204. Tel: 414-645-6497.

OUTSIDE THE CITY OF MILWAUKEE

Adell, Sheboygan Co., St. Patrick (1853) (Irish). Also serves St. Mary, Cascade; St. Nicholas, Dacada; St. Michael, Mitchell; & St. Mary, Random Lake. Very Rev. Richard J. Cerpich.
Mailing Address: St. Mary, 230 Butler St., Random Lake, 53075-9435. Tel: 920-994-4380; Fax: 920-994-2605. [CEM]
Church—W4960 S. Hwy. A, 53001.

Allenton, Washington Co., Resurrection (1997). Consolidation of Sacred Heart, Allenton; St. Anthony, Allenton; and Ss. Peter and Paul, Nenno. Rev. Michael L. Wild.
Parish Office:—215 Main St., P.O. Box 96, 53002. Tel: 414-629-5240.
Church—209 Main St., 53002. [CEM 3]
Catechesis/Religious Programs—Tel: 414-629-1500. Kathleen A. Ritger, D.R.E.
Students 214.
Convent—632 Church St., P.O. Box 356, 53002. Tel: 414-629-5342. School Sisters of Notre Dame
Sacred Heart (1917). Closed. For sacramental records contact Resurrection, Allenton.
St. Anthony (1851). Closed. For sacramental records contact Resurrection, Allenton.

Armstrong, Fond du Lac Co., Our Lady of Angels (1856) (Irish). Also serves St. Michael, Dotyville. Rev. Kevin J. Wester.
Res., W762 Armstrong Rd., Campbellsport, 53010-1400. Tel: 920-477-3201. [CEM]
School—W771 Armstrong Rd., Campbellsport, 53010. Tel: 920-477-2081. Roselyn Baker, Prin.
Lay Teachers 5; Students 46. Also serves St. Michael, Dotyville.

Ashford, Fond du Lac Co., St. Martin (1847). Also serves St. Kilian, St. Kilian. Rev. Wayne J. Barta, Admin.
1271 Minnie Ln., Campbellsport, 53010. Tel: 920-533-8644. [CEM]

Auburn, Fond du Lac Co., St. Matthias (1863) (German). Unassigned.
Res., Campbellsport, 53010. Tel: 414-533-8351. [CEM]

Beaver Dam, Dodge Co., St. Michael (1893) (Polish), Rev. John J. Radetski; Deacon Randal S. Wells.
Res., 835 Madison St., 53916. Tel: 920-885-3885. [CEM]
Catechesis/Religious Programs—344 Rosendale St., 53916. Tel: 920-887-7082.
Students 190.
St. Patrick (1860) (Irish), Rev. Charles A. Scheuerell; Deacon Robert A. Truttschel.
Res., 131 W. Maple Ave., 53916. Tel: 920-887-2082. [CEM]
School—Unified Catholic Parish Schools of Beaver Dam. See St. Peter. Tel: 920-885-5558.
St. Peter (1855), Rev. John L. Simon.
Res., 101 E. South St., 53916-2599. Tel: 920-885-5525; Fax: 920-885-4999. [CEM]
School—Consolidated with St. Patrick and St. Michael to form Unified Catholic Parish Schools of Beaver Dam. 503 S. Spring St., 53916-2598. Tel: 920-885-5558; Fax: 920-885-5510.
Lay Teachers 23; Students 179.
Catechesis/Religious Programs—Christian Formation, 503 S. Spring St., 53196-2598. Tel: 920-885-6023.
Students 274.

Belgium, Ozaukee Co., St. Mary (1848) (German-Luxembourg), Rev. Donald A. Schmidt.
Res., 6092 Lake Church Rd., 53004. Tel: 414-285-3040. [CEM]
School—Tel: 414-285-3532. Sr. Suzanne Dietz, S.S.J., Prin.
Sisters 1; Lay Teachers 4; Students 68.
Catechesis/Religious Programs—675 Hwy. D, 53004. Students 166.

Big Bend, Waukesha Co., St. Joseph (1920), Rev. Robert F. Surges.
Res., S89 W22650 Milwaukee Ave., 53103. Tel: 414-662-2832; Fax: 414-662-0783.
School—W227 S8930 St. Joseph Dr., 53103. Tel: 414-662-2737; Fax: 414-662-0783. Bill Bass, Prin.
Lay Teachers 14; Students 229.
Catechesis/Religious Programs—Tel: 414-662-3317. D.R.E.: Mary L. Kozlik; Barb Gawlik.
Students 400.

Brandon, Fond Du Lac Co., St. Brendan (1921). Also serves St. Joseph, Waupun and St. Mary, Springvale. Revs. John Elmer, O.F.M.Conv.; Russan Cole, O.F.M.Conv.
Mailing Address: 118 W. Main St., Waupun, 53963. Tel: 920-324-5400.

Brighton, Kenosha Co., St. Francis Xavier (1839) (German), Rev. James T. Volkert.
Res., 1704 240th Ave., Kansasville, 53139. Tel: 414-878-2267. [CEM]
School—Providence Catholic School. Consolidated with St. John the Baptist, 1481-172 N. Ave., Paris, Union Grove, WI 53182, Tel.: 414-859-2007. 1714 240th Ave., Kansasville, 53139. Tel: 414-878-2713.
Lay Teachers 10; Students 145.

Bristol, Kenosha Co., St. Scholastica (1945), Rev. Andrew V. Garber, O.S.B.
Res., 18700 116th St., 53104. Tel: 414-857-2068. [CEM]
Catechesis/Religious Programs—Tel: 414-857-9032.
Students 152.

Brookfield, Waukesha Co., St. Dominic (1886), Revs. Curt J. Frederick; Mark R. Jones; Deacons John Libecki; Larry LaFond; Diane Diederich, Pastoral Assoc.
Res., 18255 W. Capitol Dr., 53045-1422. Tel: 414-781-3480; Fax: 414-781-3283. [CEM]
School—18105 W. Capitol Dr., 53045-1425. Tel: 414-783-7565. Ms. Joyce Steffan, Prin.
Lay Teachers 22; Students 457.
Catechesis/Religious Programs—Tel: 414-783-4248. D.R.E.: Kathleen Beuscher; Debbie Olla.
Students 560.

St. John Vianney (1956), Rev. Dennis M. Andrews; William C. Burkert, S.T.
Office: 1755 N. Calhoun Rd., 53045-5036. Tel: 414-796-3940; Fax: 414-782-0372.
School—17500 W. Gebhardt Rd., 53045-5096. Tel: 414-796-3942. Colleen Terry, Prin.
Lay Teachers 25; Students 480.
Catechesis/Religious Programs—Tel: 414-796-3944.
Students 1,100.

St. Luke (1956), Rev. Harvey W. Brahm.
Res., 1300 San Lucas Dr., 53045. Tel: 414-782-0032; Fax: 414-782-6057.
School—Tel: 414-782-4892. Ronald Andryk, Prin.
Lay Teachers 17; Students 247.
Catechesis/Religious Programs—Tel: 414-782-0892. Sr. Virgena Clark, R.S.M., D.R.E.
Students 185.
Convent—1305 Davidson Rd., 53045. Tel: 414-782-8148.

Burlington, Racine Co., Immaculate Conception (1838), Revs. David H. Reith; Michael C. Petersen.
Res., 108 McHenry St., 53105. Tel: 414-763-1500; Fax: 414-763-1680. [CEM]
School—225 W. State St., 53105. Tel: 414-763-1515; Fax: 414-763-1508.
Priests 2; Lay Teachers 19; Students 419.
Catechesis/Religious Programs—Tel: 414-763-1505. Mary Spiegelhoff, D.R.E.
Students 218.
Chapel—Powers Lake, St. Theresa.

St. Charles (1910) (Irish), Rev. Michael C. Benham.
Res., 456 Kendall St., 53105. Tel: 414-763-2260. [CEM]
School—449 Conkey St., 53105. Tel: 414-763-2848; 762-2637 (Grade School); Fax: 414-763-3818. Kris M. Tibbetts, Prin.
Lay Teachers 15; Students 265.
Catechesis/Religious Programs—Tel: 414-763-1505.
Students 205.

Butler, Waukesha Co., St. Agnes (1915), Rev. Richard A. Liska.
Office:—12801 W. Fairmount Ave., 53007. Tel: 414-781-9521; Fax: 414-781-3512.
School—Tel: 414-781-4996; Fax: 414-781-3512. Sr. Mary Alice Walters, C.S.A., Prin.
Sisters 2; Lay Teachers 13; Students 264.
Catechesis/Religious Programs—Tel: 414-781-6998. Robert Thibault, D.R.E.
Students 211.

Byron, Fond du Lac Co., St. John (1847). Also serves St. James, Oakfield. Rev. Donald F. Zerkel.
Res., W5882 Church Rd., Fond du Lac, 54937. Tel: 920-922-1167. [CEM]
Catechesis/Religious Programs—Tel: 920-921-5807.
Students 175.

Caledonia, Racine Co., St. Louis (1846), Rev. Gerald J. Hessel.
Parish Office: 13207 Hwy. G, 53108. Tel: 414-835-4533; Fax: 414-835-0421. [CEM]
School—13125 Hwy. G, 53108. Tel: 414-835-2166. Mrs. Beth Eichman, Prin.
Lay Teachers 8; Students 90.
Catechesis/Religious Programs—Students 167.

Campbellsport, Fond du Lac Co., St. Matthew (1864), Rev. Edwin M. Kornath; Deacon Robert Fazen.
Parish Center: P.O. Box 740, 419 Mill St., 53010. Tel: 920-533-4441; Fax: 920-533-4688. [CEM]
School—Tel: 920-533-4103. Joan M. Wuest, Prin.
Lay Teachers 13; Students 158.
Catechesis/Religious Programs—Students 297.

Cascade, Sheboygan Co., St. Mary- Cascade (1852). Also serves St. Mary, Random Lake; St. Patrick, Adell; St. Nicholas, Dacada; & St. Michael, Mitchell. Very Rev. Richard J. Cerpich.
Mailing Address: 230 Butler St., Random Lake, 53075. Tel: 920-994-4380; Fax: 920-994-2605. [CEM]

Cedarburg, Ozaukee Co., Divine Word (1970), Very Rev. Msgr. Thomas Gajdos.
Res., 1375 Covered Bridge Rd., 53012. Tel: 414-377-1070; Fax: 414-377-6898.
Catechesis/Religious Programs—Tel: 414-377-7371.
Students 400.

St. Francis Borgia (1844), Rev. Edward J. Wawrzyniakowski.
Res., N44 W6055 Hamilton Rd., 53012. Tel: 414-377-1968. [CEM]
School—N43 W6005 Hamilton Rd., 53012. Tel: 414-377-2050; Fax: 414-377-4099. Sue Brandley, Prin.
Lay Teachers 30; Students 409.
Catechesis/Religious Programs—Tel: 414-377-4891. D.R.E.: Janet Sprink; Helen Jackson; Chris Dunst.
Students 300.

Clyman, Dodge Co., St. John (1900), Rev. Guy J. Gurath.
Res., Box 190, 53016. Tel: 414-696-3430. [CEM 2][JC]

Cudahy, Milwaukee Co., St. Frederick (1896), Rev. Jan M. Kieliszewski.
Res., 4611 S. Kirkwood Ave., 53110. Tel: 414-744-6622. [JC]
Catechesis/Religious Programs—Tel: 414-481-6880. Susan Kinane Kirch, D.R.E.
Students 180.

Holy Family (1900), Very Rev. Thomas P. Eichenberger; Deacon Gerald Ponec.
Res., 3767 E. Underwood Ave., 53110. Tel: 414-744-6892; Fax: 414-744-6694. [JC]
School—3776 E. Hammond Ave., 53110. Tel: 414-481-0930.
Sisters 3; Lay Teachers 10; Students 154.

St. Joseph (1909) (Slovak and Moravian), Patricia B. Knuth, Parish Dir.
Res., 4970 S. Swift Ave., 53110. Tel: 414-744-7565; Fax: 414-744-1025. [JC]
Catechesis/Religious Programs—Tel: 414-483-8370.
Students 125.

Dacada, Sheboygan Co., St. Nicholas (1848) (Luxembourg), Very Rev. Richard J. Cerpich.
Mailing Address: Also serves St. Mary, Random Lake; St. Patrick, Adell; St. Mary, Cascade; & St. Michael, Mitchell. 230 Butler St., Random Lake, 53075-9435. Tel: 920-994-4380; Fax: 920-994-2605.
Church—W4270 Hwy. K, Random Lake, 53075. [CEM]

Delafield, Waukesha Co., St. Joan of Arc (1923), Rev. James P. Loehr.
Res., N41 W33557 Nashotah Rd., Nashotah, 53058. Tel: 414-567-3466; Fax: 414-567-0213. [CEM]
School—N50 W34835 Wisconsin Ave., P.O. Box 116, Okauchee, 53069. Tel: 414-567-5775; Fax: 414-567-5786. Sr. Julie Wambach, S.S.N.D., Prin.
School Sisters of Notre Dame 1; Lay Teachers 6; Students 72.
Catechesis/Religious Programs—Colleen Sasso, D.R.E.
Students 139.

Delavan, Walworth Co., St. Andrew (1848), Rev. Joseph E. Debski.
Res., 714 E. Walworth Ave., 53115. Tel: 414-728-5922. [CEM]
School—Tel: 414-728-6211. Julie Supernaw, Prin.
Lay Teachers 9; Students 210.
Catechesis/Religious Programs—Tel: 414-728-2792. Mrs. Kathy Zambito, D.R.E.
Students 232.

Dotyville, Fond du Lac Co., St. Michael (1853) (German), Rev. Kevin J. Wester.
Parish Address: N5730 County Rd., W., Mount Calvary, 53057-9620. Tel: 920-922-6179.
Res., Also serves Our Lady of Angels, Armstrong. W762 Armstrong Rd., Campbellsport, 53010-1400. Tel: 920-477-3201. [CEM]

Dousman, Waukesha Co., St. Bruno (1850), Rev. John P. Schreiter; Deacon Thomas Filipiak.
Res., 266 W. Ottawa Ave., 53118. Tel: 414-965-2332; Fax: 414-965-4749. [CEM]
School—Tel: 414-965-2291. David Lesczynski, Prin.
Lay Teachers 9; Students 129.
Catechesis/Religious Programs—Tel: 414-965-4200.
Students 297.

Eagle, Waukesha Co., St. Theresa (1852) (German), Mariangela Pledl, Parish Dir.
Res., 136 Waukesha Rd., 53119. Tel: 414-594-5200. [CEM]
Catechesis/Religious Programs—Tel: 414-594-5201.
Students 155.

East Troy, Walworth Co., St. Peter (1854) (Irish-German), Rev. Kenneth J. Derfus.
Res., 1975 Beulah Ave., 53120. Tel: 414-642-7225; Fax: 414-642-7228. [CEM]
School—3001 Elm St., 53120. Tel: 414-642-5533. Ms. Linda Cooney, Prin.
Lay Teachers 11; Students 155.
Catechesis/Religious Programs—Tel: 414-642-3634.
Students 247.

Eden, Fond du Lac Co., St. Mary (1888), Rev. Robert G. Braun.
Res., Box 128, 53019. Tel: 920-477-3741. [CEM][JC]
School—Tel: 920-477-3551.
Lay Teachers 5; Students 72.

Eldorado, Fond Du Lac Co., St. Mary. Also serves St. John the Baptist, Woodhull. Rev. Roger A. Savage.
Mailing Address: W8272 Forest Ave. Rd., 54932-8901. Tel: 920-922-2412. [CEM]

Elba, Dodge Co., St. Columbkille (Irish). Also serves Holy Family, Reeseville. Rev. Edward J. Hussli.
Mailing Address: P.O. Box 277, Reeseville, 53579. Tel: 920-623-3989. [CEM]

Elkhart Lake, Sheboygan Co., St. George (1896). Also serves St. Fridolin, Glenbeulah. Rev. Daniel J. Lasecki.
Res., 94 N. Lincoln, 53020-0396. Tel: 920-876-2457. [CEM]
Catechesis/Religious Programs—Tel: 920-876-2360. Lori Nielsen, D.R.E.
Students 115.

Elkhorn, Walworth Co., St. Patrick (1878) (Irish-German), Rev. Terrance J. Huebner; Sr. Mary Lou Fischbach, Pastoral Assoc.
Res., 107 W. Walworth St., 53121. Tel: 414-723-5565; Fax: 414-723-7856. [CEM]
School—534 Sunset Dr., 53121. Tel: 414-734-4258. Mrs. Mary Steele, Prin.
Lay Teachers 14; Students 211.
Catechesis/Religious Programs—Students 206.

Elm Grove, Waukesha Co., St. Mary (1848), Revs. Daniel J. Pakenham; Romanus Nwaru; Deacons Charles J. Kustner; Richard Piontek.
Res., 1260 Church St., 53122. Tel: 414-782-4575; Fax: 414-782-0677. [CEM]
School—Tel: 414-782-7057. Sr. Elizabeth Uchytil, S.S.N.D., Prin.
Sisters 2; Lay Teachers 19; Students 407.
Catechesis/Religious Programs—13000 Juneau Blvd., 53122. Tel: 414-782-9470.
Students 204.

Farmington, Washington Co., St. John of God (1859) (Irish). Also serves St. Michael's, St. Michael. Sr. Carol Ann Jaeger, S.S.S.F., Parish Dir.
Mailing Address: 8877 Forestview Rd., Kewaskum, 53040. Tel: 414-334-5270. [CEM]

Fond du Lac, Fond du Lac Co.,

1—St. Joseph, (1871), Rev. Patrick E. Heppe.
Res., 83 E. Second St., 54935. Tel: 920-921-0454; Fax: 920-921-5494.
School—Consolidated into the F.A.C.E.S. School System St. Joseph Parishioners, (Grades K-8). Tel: 920-921-5300. Sr. Collean Walsh, Coord.
Students 181.

Catechesis/Religious Programs—Tel: 920-922-8229. Ray Mrozinski, D.R.E.
Students 502.

2—ST. LOUIS, (1847) (French), Rev. Jerome A. Wagner; Deacon Ricardo Munoz.
Rectory: 209 N. Macy St., 54935. Tel: 920-921-0580; Fax: 920-922-4866. [JC]
Catechesis/Religious Programs—Tel: 920-922-8868. Beverly Sabel, D.R.E.
Students 206.

3—ST. MARY, (1866) (German), Rev. Peter C. Drenzek.
Res., 93 Marquette St., 54935. Tel: 920-921-1311; Fax: 920-921-7576.
School—Fond du Lac Area Catholic Education System (FACES), (Grades 6-8) 63 E. Merrill St., 54935. Tel: 920-922-3364; Fax: 920-922-7849.
St. Mary Campus Middle School—Tel: 920-921-9610; Fax: 920-921-0457.
Catechesis/Religious Programs—Tel: 920-923-4353. Rick Voell, D.R.E.
Students 390.

4—ST. PATRICK, (1855), Rev. Michael O. Sturm; Sr. Roberta Meis, C.S.A., Pastoral Assoc.
Res., 41 E. Follett St., 54935. Tel: 920-921-0347; Fax: 920-921-6708. [JC]
School—Fond du Lac Area Catholic Education System (FACES), (Grades 3-5). Tel: 920-922-3364.
Catechesis/Religious Programs—Tel: 920-921-6214.
Students 259.

5—SACRED HEART, (1957) (German), Rev. Eugene C. Neuman.
Res., 232 S. Peters Ave., 54935. Tel: 920-921-8831; Fax: 920-921-9344. [JC]
School—Fond du Lac Area Catholic Education System (FACES), Tel: 920-921-5873.
Catechesis/Religious Programs—Tel: 920-922-7690. Barbara Kratz, D.R.E.
Students 280.

Fontana, Walworth Co., St. Benedict (1912), Rev. Stephen J. Stradinger.
Res., Box 110, 53125. Tel: 414-275-2480; Fax: 414-275-6426.
Catechesis/Religious Programs—Tel: 414-275-2993. D.R.E.: Barbara Obligato; Linda Gullo.
Students 302.

Fox Lake, Dodge Co., Immaculate Conception - St. Mary (1850) (Irish), Rev. Donald B. Braun.
Res., Also serves St. Mary, Lost Lake; & St. Gabriel, Randolph. 305 W. Green St., P.O. Box 85, 53933-0085. Tel: 920-928-3513; Fax: 920-928-6334. [CEM]

Fox Point, Milwaukee Co., St. Eugene (1957), Very Rev. Kenneth P. Knippel; Mrs. Pat Quinn-Casper, Pastoral Assoc.
Res., 7600 N. Port Washington Rd., 53217. Tel: 414-241-6002; Fax: 414-241-6011.
School—Tel: 414-241-6020; Fax: 414-241-6022. Mr. K. James Colle, Prin.
Lay Teachers 19; Students 222.
Catechesis/Religious Programs—Tel: 414-241-6030. D.R.E.: Miss Mary Joy Dick, (Children's Ministry); Mrs. Rita Capriolo, (Young Adult Ministry).
Students 359.

Franklin, Milwaukee Co., St. James (1857), Rev. Kenneth J. Augustine; Judy Brooks, Pastoral Assoc.
Office: 7219 S. 27th St., 53132. Tel: 414-761-0480; Fax: 414-761-2208. [CEM]
Catechesis/Religious Programs—Students 260.

Sacred Hearts of Jesus and Mary (1858). Also serves Holy Assumption, St. Martins. Revs. Charles Bisgrove, S.C.J.; Anthony P. Russo, S.C.J. In res., Rev. John Nitzki, S.C.J.
Res., 7963 S. 116th St., 53132. Tel: 414-425-1114; Fax: 414-425-2527. [CEM]
School—7933 S. 116th St., 53132. Tel: 414-425-9200. Deacon A. Ronald Colaianni, Prin.
Lay Teachers 8; Students 155.
Catechesis/Religious Programs—Students 495.

Fredonia, Ozaukee Co., St. Rose of Lima (1909). Also serves Mother of Sorrows, Little Kohler & Holy Cross, Holy Cross. Rev. Neil G. Zinthefer; Deacon Gerald Malueg.
Res., 305 Fredonia Ave., P.O. Box 250, 53021. Tel: 414-692-9994. [CEM]
School—Rosemary Catholic, 53021. Tel: 414-692-2141; Fax: 414-692-9994. Mrs. Catherine Leannah, Prin.
Lay Teachers 6; Students 63.
Catechesis/Religious Programs—Students 78.

Genesee Depot, Waukesha Co., St. Paul (1863), Very Rev. Robert D. Gosma; Deacon Larry Normann; Len Grassman, Pastoral Assoc.
Res., 53127. Tel: 414-968-3865; Fax: 414-968-5546. [CEM]
School—Tel: 414-968-3175. Ms. Jeanne Karl, Prin.
Lay Teachers 11; Students 190.
Catechesis/Religious Programs—Tel: 414-968-2276. D.R.E.: Bob Graf, (Grades K-12); Marion Lopina, (Adult).
Students 422.

Germantown, Washington Co., St. Boniface (1845), Very Rev. Bernard S. Sippel.
Res., W204 N11940 Goldendale Rd., 53022. Tel: 414-628-2040; Fax: 414-628-2076. [CEM]
School—W204 N11968 Goldendale Rd., 53022. Tel: 414-628-1955.
Lay Teachers 12; Students 194.
Catechesis/Religious Programs—William Farrell, D.R.E.
Students 392.

Glenbeulah, Sheboygan Co., St. Fridolin (1878). Also serves St. George, Elkhart Lake. Rev. Daniel J. Lasecki.
Mailing Address: Box T, Elkhart Lake, 53020. Tel: 920-876-2437. [CEM]

Grafton, Ozaukee Co., St. Joseph (1849), Rev. Michael G. Barrett; Deacons Richard J. Govek; Donald F. Kabara.
Pastoral Center: 1619 Washington St., 53024. Tel: 414-375-6500; Fax: 414-375-6509. [CEM]
School—1206 16th Ave., 53024. Tel: 414-375-6505.
Lay Teachers 13; Students 234.
Catechesis/Religious Programs—Tel: 414-375-6510.
Students 528.

Greendale, Milwaukee Co., St. Alphonsus (1938), Revs. Richard J. Aiken, Admin.; Aurelio Perez; Deacon Theodore A. Gurzynski. In res., Rev. Hugh G. Birdsall, S.D.S., M.A., M.S.
Res., 5960 W. Loomis Rd., 53129. Tel: 414-421-2442; Fax: 414-421-8744.
School—6000 W. Loomis Rd., 53129. Tel: 414-421-1760. Margaret Roushar, Prin.
Sisters 1; Lay Teachers 29; Students 508.
Catechesis/Religious Programs—Tel: 414-421-0690.
Students 688.

Greenfield, Milwaukee Co., St. John the Evangelist (1916), Revs. Richard J. Talaska; Richard R. Verberg; Deacon Peter L. LoCoco.
Res., 8500 W. Cold Spring Rd., 53228. Tel: 414-321-1965.
School—53228. Tel: 414-321-8540. Sr. Francine Hribar, O.S.F., Prin.
Sisters of St. Francis of Christ the King 3; Lay Teachers 9; Students 255.
Catechesis/Religious Programs—Tel: 414-321-4450. D.R.E.: Debbie Melian; Jennifer Eaton Tel: 414-321-8922.
Students 250.

Hales Corners, Milwaukee Co., St. Mary (1842), Revs. Arthur G. Heinze; Gregory J. Greiten; Mary Matestic, Pastoral Assoc.
Res., 9520 W. Forest Home Ave., 53130. Tel: 414-425-2174; Fax: 414-425-9432. [CEM]
School—9553 W. Edgerton Ave., 53130. Tel: 414-425-3100; Fax: 414-425-6270. Mary Ann Rudella, Prin.; Mary Kopp, Vice Prin.
Lay Teachers 26; Students 456.
Catechesis/Religious Programs—Tel: 414-425-3101; Fax: 414-425-9432. D.R.E.: Barbara Schwartz, (Children); Timothy Winters, (Young Adult).
Students 893.

Hartford, Washington Co., St. Kilian (1863), Rev. Michael J. Petrie Tel: 414-673-4831, Ext. 401; Sr. Helen Hurley, Pastoral Assoc. Tel: 414-673-4831, Ext. 402.
Res., 264 W. State St., 53027. Tel: 414-673-4831; Fax: 414-673-4872. [CEM 2]
School—245 High St., 53027. Tel: 414-673-3081. Joseph Bellante, Prin. Tel: 414-673-3081, Ext. 116.
Lay Teachers 17; Students 270.
Catechesis/Religious Programs—Tel: 414-673-3746. June Strobel, D.R.E. Tel: 414-673-4831, Ext. 406.
Students 342.

Hartland, Waukesha Co., St. Charles (1906), Rev. Thomas P. Demse.
Office: 313 Circle Dr., 53029-1899. Tel: 414-367-0800; Fax: 414-367-6960.
Res., 521 Renson Rd., 53029. Tel: 414-367-9936. [CEM]
School—Tel: 414-367-2040. Sr. Rosemary Rombalski, S.S.S.F., Prin.
Lay Teachers 9; Students 234.
Catechesis/Religious Programs—Tel: 414-367-3277.
Students 844.

Holy Cross, Ozaukee Co., Holy Cross (1845) (Luxemburg). Also serves St. Rose of Lima, Fredonia & Mother of Sorrows, Little Kohler. Rev. Neil G. Zinthefer.
Mailing Address: 305 Fredonia Ave., P.O. Box 250, Fredonia, 53021.
Res., 5330 Hwy. B, Belgium, 53004. Tel: 414-692-9994. [CEM]

Holy Hill, Washington Co., St. Mary of the Hill (1860), Rev. Fred Alexander, O.C.D.
Res., P.O. Box 38, Hubertus, 53033. Tel: 414-628-3606; 673-7505. [CEM]
Catechesis/Religious Programs—Mrs. Connie Massingale, D.R.E.
Students 173.

Horicon, Dodge Co., St. Malachy (1856), Rev. M. Eugene Kinney.
Parish Center: 113 Valley St., 53032. Tel: 920-485-2427.
Res., 109 Valley St., 53032. Tel: 920-485-2937. [CEM]
Catechesis/Religious Programs—Tel: 920-485-2708. David Froemming, D.R.E.
Students 180.

Hubertus, Washington Co., St. Hubert (1846), Rev. Charles T. Hanel.
Res., 3727 Hubertus Rd., 53033. Tel: 414-628-1141. [CEM]
School—3733 Hubertus Rd., 53033. Tel: 414-628-1711; Fax: 414-628-0280.
Lay Teachers 13; Students 168.
Catechesis/Religious Programs—Tel: 414-628-2840.
Students 227.

Johnsburg, Fond du Lac Co., St. John the Baptist (1840), Rev. Donald T. Musinski.
Res., N9288 County W, Fond du Lac, 54935. Tel: 920-795-4316. [CEM]
Schools—(Grades 4-6). Tel: 920-795-4222. Sharon Allen, Coord.; Consolidated Parochial Elementary School. See Holy Cross, Mount Calvary. Tel: 920-753-4811.

Juneau, Dodge Co., Immaculate Conception (1870), Rev. Guy G. Gurath.
Res., 319 N. Main St., 53039. Tel: 414-386-4964. [CEM]
Catechesis/Religious Programs—Tel: 414-386-4964. Teresa Anderson, D.R.E.
Students 167.

Kansasville, Racine Co., St. Mary-Dover (1869), Rev. James B. Cera.
Mailing Address: P.O. Box 126, 53139.
Res., 23211 Church Rd., 53139. Tel: 414-878-1762. [CEM]

Kenosha, Kenosha Co.,

1—ST. ANTHONY, (1910) (Slovak), Rev. Ray W. Wawiorka.
Mailing Address: 2223 51st St., 53140. Tel: 414-652-1844. [JC]

2—ST. CASIMIR, (1901), Rev. Robert T. McDermott.
Res., 1009 Washington Rd., 53140. Tel: 414-657-6544; Fax: 414-657-9955. [CEM]
High School—St. Joseph Interparish Jr. High School, 2401 69th St., 53143. Tel: 414-654-8651. Mr. Richard Ruhl, Prin.
Lay Teachers 6; Students 140. Sponsored by St. Casimir, St. Mark, St. Therese and St. Thomas Aquinas, Kenosha.

3—ST. GEORGE, (1851), Rev. Gerald P. Schmitz.
Res., 4804 7th Ave., 53140. Tel: 414-657-6875; Fax: 414-657-1495. [CEM]

4—ST. JAMES, (1845) (Irish), Rev. Frederick A. Heuser.
Res., 5804 Sheridan Rd., 53140. Tel: 414-658-8071; Fax: 414-658-2490. [CEM]

5—ST. MARK, (1924), Very Rev. Kenneth J. Metz; Rev. Pere Cane-Gombau; Karen Metallo, Pastoral Assoc.; Deacons Patrick H. Frye; Gregorio M. Lebron; Patricia L. Andrews, Bus. Mgr.
Res., 7117 14th Ave., 53143. Tel: 414-652-1972; Fax: 414-656-7375.
School—7202 14th Ave., 53143. Tel: 414-652-4022. Miss Shirley A. Boss, Prin.
School Sisters of St. Francis 1; Lay Teachers 14; Students 256.
Junior Academy—(Preschool). Tel: 414-652-8556.
Lay Teachers 12; Students 158.
Catechesis/Religious Programs—Tel: 414-652-3226. Colleen A. Reddy, D.R.E.
Students 304.
Latin American Center—1320 73rd St., 53143-5459. Tel: 414-657-7222. Revs. Pere Cane, Dir.; Luis Bulto, Assoc. Dir.

6—ST. MARY, (1929), Revs. Howard G. Haase; Mark J. Danczyk; Deacons Ronald F. Lesjak; James S. Francois; Wilson Shierk.
Res., 7307 40th Ave., 53142. Tel: 414-694-6018; Fax: 414-694-6048.
School—7400 39th Ave., 53142. Tel: 414-694-6650; Fax: 414-694-6740. Bradley Norcross, Prin.
Lay Teachers 24; Students 420.
Catechesis/Religious Programs—Tel: 414-694-5474. D.R.E.: Jane Delfield; Sandy Slivon.
Students 955.

7—OUR LADY OF MOUNT CARMEL, (1904) (Italian), Rev. John J. Richetta.
Res., 1919 54th St., 53140. Tel: 414-652-7660; 652-7683; Fax: 414-652-2542.

School—5400 19th Ave., 53140. Tel: 414-652-7660. Paul Cera, Prin.
Lay Teachers 7; Students 152.
Catechesis/Religious Programs—Tel: 414-652-5057.
Students 104.

8—OUR LADY OF THE HOLY ROSARY, (1904) (Italian), Revs. John J. Molnar, O.S.A.; Henry B. Maibusch, O.S.A.; Bro. Robert Schurman, O.S.A.
Res., 2224 45th St., 53140. Tel: 414-652-2771; Fax: 414-652-0183.
School—4400 22nd Ave., 53140. Tel: 414-652-5950. Sr. M. Bertina, F.S.S.J., Prin.
Franciscan Sisters of St. Joseph (Hamburg, NY) 7; Lay Teachers 14; Students 418.
Catechesis/Religious Programs—Bro. Fred Kaiser, O.S.A., D.R.E.
Students 252.

9—ST. PETER, (1903), Revs. Dan Cambra, M.I.C.; Pete Cibulskis, M.I.C.; Deacon Terrance A. Maack.
Res., 2224 30th Ave., 53144. Tel: 414-551-9004.
School—Tel: 414-551-8383. Mr. Sigmund Kolano, Prin.
Lay Teachers 6; Students 118.
Catechesis/Religious Programs—Tel: 414-897-2602.
Students 325.

10—ST. THERESE, (1953), Rev. Brian T. Holbus.
Res., 9005 22nd Ave., 53143-6699. Tel: 414-694-4695; Fax: 414-694-7284.
School—2020 91st St., 53143. Tel: 414-694-8080. Mrs. Jean Kuklenski, Prin.
Lay Teachers 9; Students 140.
Catechesis/Religious Programs—Students 161.

11—ST. THOMAS AQUINAS, (1911), Rev. Thomas A. LeMieux.
Res., 6202 25th Ave., 53143-4370. Tel: 414-658-8662.
School—St. Joseph Interparish Jr. High School, 2401 69th St., 53143. Tel: 414-654-8651. Rick Ruhl, Prin.
Lay Teachers 10; Students 141. Sponsored by St. Casimir, St. Mark, St. Therese, St. Thomas Aquinas, and Our Lady of Mt. Carmel, Kenosha.

Kewaskum, Washington Co., Holy Trinity (1861). Unassigned.
Res., 331 Main St., P.O. Box 461, 53040. Tel: 414-626-2860. [CEM 2]
School—305 Main St., 53040. Tel: 414-626-2603. Mrs. June Gauvin, Prin.
Lay Teachers 13; Students 179.
Catechesis/Religious Programs—Tel: 414-334-4195. Sr. Eileen Curran, S.S.N.D., D.R.E.
Students 253.

Kohler, Sheboygan Co., St. John Evangelist (1927), Rev. Louis J. Wilimek.
Res., 600 Green Tree Rd., 53044. Tel: 920-452-9623; Fax: 920-452-9633.
Catechesis/Religious Programs—Tel: 920-458-9931.
Students 156.

Lake Five, Washington Co., St. Columba (1843). Also serves St. John, Monches. Rev. Richard L. Grebasch.
Mailing Address: 106 Hwy. J, Colgate, 53017. Tel: 414-628-9089. [CEM]

Lake Geneva, Walworth Co., St. Francis de Sales (1842), Revs. David J. Braun; David J. Meinholz.
Res., 148 W. Main St., 53147. Tel: 414-248-8524; Fax: 414-248-5302. [CEM]
School—130 Main St., 53147. Tel: 414-248-2778; Fax: 414-248-7860.
Lay Teachers 9; Students 222.
Catechesis/Religious Programs—Tel: 414-248-8526. Sr. Evelyn Trapp, S.S.S.F., D.R.E.
Students 255.

Le Roy, Dodge Co., St. Andrew (1849), Rev. Robert J. Berghammer.
Res., W3081 County Tr. Y, Lomira, 53048. Tel: 920-583-4125; 387-4321. [CEM]

Lima, Sheboygan Co., St. Rose (1860). Also serves St. George, St. George. Rev. Eugene D. Winkler; Deacon William T. Jens.
Mailing Address: N3589 County Rd., A.E., Sheboygan Falls, 53085. Tel: 920-467-4576. [CEM]

Little Kohler, Ozaukee Co., Mother of Sorrows. Also serves St. Rose of Lima, Fredonia and Holy Cross, Holy Cross. Rev. Neil G. Zinthefer.
Mailing Address: 305 Fredonia Ave., P.O. Box 250, Fredonia, 53021. Tel: 414-692-9994. [CEM]

Lomira, Dodge Co., St. Mary (1870), Rev. Vincent B. Holubowicz; David C. Gilles, Pastoral Assoc.
Res., 645 Milwaukee St., 53048. Tel: 414-269-4429. [CEM]
School—(Grades 1-8) 705 Milwaukee, 53048. Tel: 414-269-4326. Sr. Rosemary Herriges, O.S.F., Prin.
Sisters 1; Lay Teachers 8; Students 119. Consolidated with St. Theresa to form Consolidated Catholic School of Lomira-Theresa. Tel: 414-488-4543.

Catechesis/Religious Programs—Tel: 920-269-7273.
Students 180.

Lost Lake, Dodge Co., St. Mary (1893). Also serves St. Gabriel, Randolph; & St. Mary, Fox Lake. Rev. Donald B. Braun.
Res., W11821 Concord Rd., Randolph, 53956. Tel: 920-326-3585. [CEM]

Lyons, Walworth N Co., St. Kilian. Also serves St. Joseph, Lyons. Mr. Daniel L. Hull, Parish Dir.
Mailing Address: P.O. Box 60, 53148-0060. Tel: 414-763-2050. [CEM]

St. Joseph, Walworth Co., (1870). Also serves St. Kilian, Lyons. Daniel L. Hull, Parish Dir.
Res., 1540 Mill St., Box 60, 53148-0060. Tel: 414-763-2050. [CEM]
Mission—St. Kilian's.

Mapleton, Waukesha Co., St. Catherine (1847) (Irish), Rev. David A. Verhasselt.
Res., W359 N8512 Brown St., Oconomowoc, 53066. Tel: 920-474-7000; Fax: 920-474-4661. [CEM]
Catechesis/Religious Programs—Students 161.

Marytown, Fond du Lac Co., St. Mary (1849), Rev. Joseph H. Coerber.
Res., N10232 Hwy. 149, New Holstein, 53061. Tel: 920-898-4040; Fax: 920-898-9002. [CEM]
School—See Holy Cross, Mt. Calvary for details. Tel: 920-753-4811.

Mayville, Dodge Co., St. Mary (1856), Very Rev. Charles H. Wester.
Res., 112 S. German St., P.O. Box 22, 53050-0022. Tel: 920-387-2470; 387-3130 (Parish Center). [CEM]
School—28 Naber St., 53050. Tel: 920-387-2920.
Lay Teachers 7; Students 145.
Catechesis/Religious Programs—Tel: 920-387-3130.
Students 223.

Menomonee Falls, Waukesha Co.,

1—ST. ANTHONY, (1846), Revs. Anthony G. Klink; Robert S. Kroeger; Deacons David L. Zimprich; Robert Wodushek.
Res., N74 W13604 Appleton Ave., 53051. Tel: 414-251-5910; Fax: 414-251-6564. [CEM]
School—N74 W13646 Appleton Ave., 53051. Tel: 414-251-4390; Fax: 414-251-2412. Jacob J. Jilling, Prin.
Lay Teachers 10; Students 235.
Catechesis/Religious Programs—Tel: 414-251-8868. Lisa M. Boehm, D.R.E.
Students 373.

2—GOOD SHEPHERD, (1957), Rev. Paul A. Daniels; Deacon Gene Christensen; Joseph Strazishar, Dir. of Admin. Svcs.
Church—N88 W17658 Christman Rd., 53051-2630. Tel: 414-255-2035; Fax: 414-255-2020.
Res., W177 N8916 St. Thomas Dr., 53051-2023. Tel: 414-255-1341.
Catechesis/Religious Programs—Tel: 414-255-2210. D.R.E.: Matthew Hakes; Jean Newman; Richard Harter.
Students 651.

3—ST. JAMES, (1847), Rev. Eugene J. Doda, Jr.; Sr. Cyndi Nienhaus, Social & Service Dir.
Res., W 220-N 6588 Town Line Rd., 53051. Tel: 414-251-3944; Fax: 414-250-2679. [CEM]
Catechesis/Religious Programs—Tel: 414-251-0891; Fax: 414-250-2679. D.R.E.: Margie Lang; Jane Clare Ishiguro.
Students 585.

4—ST. MARY, (1904), Rev. Joseph A. Janicki; Deacons Robert H. Buth; Thomas H. Wuchterl; Thomas Monday.
Res., N 89 W 16297 Cleveland Ave., 53051. Tel: 414-251-0220; Fax: 414-251-6948. [CEM]
School—N 89 W 16215 Cleveland Ave., 53051. Tel: 414-251-1050; Fax: 414-502-1671. Barbara A. Heil, Prin.
Lay Teachers 24; Students 433.
Catechesis/Religious Programs—Tel: 414-251-1154. D.R.E.: Margaret Geyer; Nancy Dubord.
Students 428.

Mequon, Ozaukee Co., St. James (1851) (German), Revs. Gregory M. Spitz; George Ssebadduka (Uganda) Tel: 414-242-3541. In res., Rev. William H. Wallaik Tel: 414-242-3750.
Res., 11300 N. St. James Ln., 28W, 53092. Tel: 414-242-7967; Fax: 414-242-7970. [CEM]
School—(Grades K & 4-8). Tel: 414-242-7960; Fax: 414-512-8986. Mr. Richard Goeden, Prin.
Lay Teachers 24; Students 508. Consolidated with St. Cecilia, Thiensville to form SS. Cecilia and James.
Catechesis/Religious Programs—Tel: 414-242-7963; Fax: 414-242-7970. Ms. Pat Roehrig, D.R.E.
Students 589.

Mitchell, Sheboygan Co., St. Michael (1852). Also serves St. Mary, Random Lake; St. Patrick, Adell; St. Mary, Cascade; St. Nicholas, Dacada. Very Rev. Richard J. Cerpich.
Mailing Address: 230 Butler St., Random Lake, 53075. Tel: 920-994-4380; Fax: 920-994-2605. [CEM]

Monches, Waukesha Co., St. John (1843). Also serves St. Columba, Lake Five. Rev. Richard L. Grebasch.
Res., W302 N9583 O'Neil Rd., Hartland, 53029. Tel: 414-966-2777; Fax: 414-966-3731. [CEM]
Catechesis/Religious Programs—Tel: 414-628-3939. Mrs. Cathy Twiford, D.R.E.
Students 44.

Mount Calvary, Fond du Lac Co., Holy Cross (1849), Rev. Peter P. Kutch, O.F.M.Cap.
Res., P.O. Box 176, 53057. Tel: 920-753-3311; Fax: 920-2130. [CEM]
School—(Grades 1-8) 100 Notre Dame St., 53057. Tel: 920-753-4811.
Lay Teachers 15; Students 78. Consolidated Parochial Elementary School of Mount Calvary (CPES): St. John the Baptist, Johnsburg; St. Mary, Marytown; Holy Cross, Mount Calvary; St. Cloud, St. Cloud.
Catechesis/Religious Programs—Students 141.

Mukwonago, Waukesha Co., St. James (1896), Rev. Robert J. Drutowski.
Res., 830 Hwy. NN East, 53149. Tel: 414-363-7615; Fax: 414-363-2416.
School—Tel: 414-363-8152. Sharon Warsh, Prin.
Lay Teachers 8; Students 176.
Catechesis/Religious Programs—Tel: 414-363-5529.
Students 665.

Muskego, Waukesha Co., St. Leonard Congregation (1957), Revs. Jerome A. Rinzel; Loyola Amalraj; Deacon Ralph Wisniewski; Carlene S. Larson, Pastoral Assoc.
Res., W173 S7743 Westwood Dr., 53150. Tel: 414-679-1773; Fax: 414-679-4210.
School—Tel: 414-679-0451. Mr. Robert Radomski, Prin.
Lay Teachers 16; Students 262.
Catechesis/Religious Programs—Tel: 414-679-0880. Judee Weber, D.R.E.
Students 889.

Nabob, Washington Co., St. Matthias (1848), Rev. Alois R. Van Beek.
Mailing Address: 4886 Hwy. 175, Hartford, 53027. Tel: 414-644-5701. [CEM]

Nenno, Washington Co., SS. Peter and Paul (1848). Closed. For sacramental records contact Resurrection, Allenton.

Neosho, Dodge Co., St. Matthew (1857) (German). Also serves St. Mary, Woodland & St. John, Rubicon. Rev. Russel J. Stommel.
Res., 148 W. Lehman St., P.O. Box 45, 53059. Tel: 920-625-3144. [CEM]
Catechesis/Religious Programs—Tel: 414-625-3290.
Students 172.

New Berlin, Waukesha Co., Holy Apostles (1855), Very Rev. Edward R. Wieland; Rev. Timothy C. Bickel.
Res., 16000 W. National Ave., 53151. Tel: 414-786-7330; Fax: 414-786-0425. [CEM]
School—Tel: 414-786-7331. Brenda Sue White, Prin.
Sisters 2; Lay Teachers 19; Students 502.
Catechesis/Religious Programs—Tel: 414-786-2035.
Students 598.

St. Elizabeth Ann Seton (1981), Rev. Steven J. Amann; Deacon Eugene Brah; Marni Geissler, Pastoral Assoc.
Church & Office—12700 W. Howard Ave., 53151. Tel: 414-782-6760; Fax: 414-782-4763.
Catechesis/Religious Programs—Tel: 414-782-8982. Joanne Prei, D.R.E.
Students 666.

Newburg, Washington Co., Holy Trinity (1859), Rev. Robert G. Sampon.
Res., Box 16, 53060-0016. Tel: 414-675-6256. [CEM 3]
Stations—Trenton, St. Augustine, (1857); Farmington, St. Peter, (1855).

New Munster, Kenosha Co., St. Alphonsus (1851) (German), Rev. Thomas E. Biersack.
Res., 6301 344th Ave., P.O. Box 767, 53152. Tel: 414-537-4370; Fax: 414-537-4370. [CEM]
School—Tel: 414-537-4379.
Lay Teachers 4; Students 70.

North Fond du Lac, Fond du Lac Co., Presentation of the Blessed Virgin (1902), Rev. John A. O'Brien, Ph.D.; Deacon Paul S. Monzel.
Res., 705 Michigan Ave., 54937. Tel: 920-921-9383; Fax: 920-921-1309. [JC]

Catechesis/Religious Programs—Tel: 920-921-5873. Jean Sheely, D.R.E.
Students 313.

North Lake, Waukesha Co., St. Clare (1916), Rev. Anthony T. McCarthy.
Res., Box 68, 53064. Tel: 414-966-2191; Fax: 414-966-1829. [CEM]
Catechesis/Religious Programs—Tel: 414-966-7010.
Students 483.

Oak Creek, Milwaukee Co., St. Matthew (1841), Rev. Joseph G. Sukup; Alice Hatzenbeller, Pastoral Assoc.
Res., 9303 S. Chicago Rd., 53154. Tel: 414-762-4200; Fax: 414-571-9973. [CEM]
School—9329 S. Chicago Rd., 53154. Tel: 414-762-6820; Fax: 414-762-3686.
Franciscan Sisters of Our Lady of Perpetual Help 1; Sisters of St. Francis of Assisi 1; Lay Teachers 9; Students 241.
Catechesis/Religious Programs—Tel: 414-762-6847.
Students 468.

Oakfield, Fond Du Lac Co., St. James (1909). Also serves St. John, Bryon. Rev. Donald F. Zerkel.
Mailing Address: W5882 Church Rd., Fond Du Lac, 54937. Tel: 920-583-4376.
Res., 101 N. Main, 53065.

Oconomowoc, Waukesha Co., St. Jerome (1860), Rev. John G. Yockey.
Res., 211 S. Main St., 53066. Tel: 414-569-3020; Fax: 414-569-3022. [CEM]
School—110 Third St., 53066. Tel: 414-569-3030.
Franciscan Sisters of Perpetual Adoration 1; Lay Teachers 21; Students 295.
Catechesis/Religious Programs—Tel: 414-569-3025.
Students 481.

Paris, Kenosha Co., St. John the Baptist (1859), Rev. Thomas G. Fait.
Parish Office: 1501 172nd Ave., Union Grove, 53182. Tel: 414-859-2484. [CEM]
School—Providence Catholic School. Consolidated with St. Francis Xavier, Brighton. 1481 172nd Ave., Union Grove, 53182. Tel: 414-859-2007; 414-878-2713. Sr. Kathryn Dean Strandell, O.S.F., Prin.
Lay Teachers 9; Students 162; Religious 3.
Catechesis/Religious Programs—Students 42.

Pell Lake, Walworth Co., St. Mary (1928), Rev. Dennis D. Callahan; Deacon Anthony Martino; Marilyn Kingston, Pastoral Assoc.
Res., Box 34, 53157. Tel: 414-279-6295. [JC]

Pewaukee, Waukesha Co.,

1—QUEEN OF APOSTLES, (1997). Consolidation of St. Mary's, Pewaukee and Ss. Peter and Paul, Pewaukee. Revs. Carl P. Alberte; R. Michael Grellinger.
Mailing Address: P.O. Box 220, 53072. Tel: 414-691-1535. [CEM]
School—449 W. Wisconsin Ave. Kathleen Rempe, Prin., Tel: 414-691-2120.
Notre Dame Sisters 1; Lay Teachers 7; Students 135.
Catechesis/Religious Programs—D.R.E.: Jackie Schulz; Ree Kogh; Bill Eder.
Students 275.

2—ST. ANTHONY, (1918), Revs. R. Thomas Venne; Michael G. Krejci; Deacon Dennis Anderson.
Res., W 280 N 2101 Hwy. SS., 53072. Tel: 414-691-2326; Fax: 414-691-7376.
School—Tel: 414-691-0460; 691-1173 (Parish Center).
Lay Teachers 11; Students 149.
Catechesis/Religious Programs—Kathleen Amidei, D.R.E.
Students 515.

3—ST. MARY'S, (1858). Closed. For sacramental records contact Queen of Apostles, Pewaukee.

4—SS. PETER AND PAUL, (1848). Closed. For sacramental records contact Queen of Apostles, Pewaukee.

Pleasant Prairie, St. Anne, Rev. Donald H. Thimm.
Mailing Address: c/o Archdiocese of Milwaukee, 3501 S. Lake Dr., P.O. Box 07912, Milwaukee, 53207-0912. Tel: 414-769-3422.

Plymouth, Sheboygan Co., St. John the Baptist (1861), Rev. Wayne W. Bittner.
Res., 115 Plymouth St., 53073. Tel: 920-892-4006; Fax: 920-893-8444. [CEM]
School—116 Pleasant St., 53073. Tel: 920-893-5961. Mary Jo Sizonen, Prin.
Lay Teachers 19; Students 281.
Catechesis/Religious Programs—Tel: 414-892-6015.
Students 371.

Port Washington, Ozaukee Co., St. Mary (1853), Rev. Allan J. Sommer.
Office: 430 N. Johnson St., 53074. Tel: 414-284-5771; Fax: 414-284-4112. [CEM]
School—Consolidated with St. Peter of Alcantara to form Port Washington Catholic School, Inc. 1802 N. Wisconsin St., 53074. Tel: 414-284-2441 (K-4); 284-2682 (5-8).
School Sisters of Notre Dame 1; Lay Teachers 21; Students 308.
Catechesis/Religious Programs—Consolidated with St. Peter of Alcontara. Tel: 414-284-6472. D.R.E.: Patricia Gibes, (Grades K, 4-6); Kathy Gordon, (Grades 7-11), Tel: 414-284-2102.
Students 339.

St. Peter of Alcantara (1966), Rev. Joseph H. Haas; Deacon Thomas J. Surges.
Res., 1800 N. Wisconsin St., 53074. Tel: 414-284-4266; Fax: 414-284-4216.
School—Port Washington Catholic School. See St. Mary for details. Tel: 414-284-2682.
Catechesis/Religious Programs—Tel: 414-284-6472. D.R.E.: Patricia Gibes, (Grades K-6); Kathleen Gordon, (Grades 7-12), Tel: 414-284-2102.
Students 250.

Racine, Racine Co.,

1—ST. CASIMIR, (1913) (Lithuanian), Rev. Russell G. Roetzer.
Res., 715 11th St., 53403. Tel: 414-634-2811. [JC]

2—CRISTO REY, (1980) (Hispanic), Rev. Robert J. McGlinn (CHI) Admin.
Res., 800 Wisconsin Ave., 53403. Tel: 414-632-3151.

3—HOLY NAME, (1884) (German), Rev. Edward A. Vogel.
Res., 1509 Grand Ave., 53403. Tel: 414-637-8374; Fax: 414-637-4230.
School—1510 Villa St., 53403. Tel: 414-637-7673. Susan Chenoweth, Prin.
Lay Teachers 12; Students 238.
Catechesis/Religious Programs—Students 170.

4—HOLY TRINITY, (1914) (Slovak). Also serves St. Stanislaus, Racine. Rev. Louis P. Luljak.
Mailing Address: 815 21st St., 53403-2699. Tel: 414-634-6926. [JC]

5—ST. EDWARD, (1919), Rev. Richard J. Molter.
Office: 1430 Grove Ave., 53405. Tel: 414-636-8040; Fax: 414-636-8052.
Res., 1401 Grove Ave., 53405. Tel: 414-636-8049.
School—1435 Grove Ave., 53405. Tel: 414-636-8044. Joseph Majowski, Prin.
Dominican Sisters (Racine) 1; Lay Teachers 22; Students 426.
Catechesis/Religious Programs—Tel: 414-636-8042.
Students 200.

6—ST. JOHN NEPOMUK, (1896), Rev. Thomas F. Lijewski.
Res., 700 English St., 53402. Tel: 414-634-5647; Fax: 414-637-1436. [JC]
School—1923 Green St., 53402. Tel: 414-637-9349; Fax: 414-637-0711.
School Sisters of St. Francis 2; Lay Teachers 11; Students 145.

7—ST. JOSEPH, (1875) (German), Rev. Richard J. Stoffel.
Office: 1532 N. Wisconsin St., 53402. Tel: 414-633-8284; Fax: 414-633-8285.
Res., 1712 Chatham St., 53402. Tel: 414-632-6487. [JC 4]
School—1525 Erie St., 53402. Tel: 414-633-2403. Charles T. Cooper, Prin.
Lay Teachers 14; Students 247.
Catechesis/Religious Programs—Tel: 414-633-9005. Susan Gehrig, D.R.E.
Students 194.

8—ST. LUCY, (1958), Rev. Jeffrey M. Thielen.
Res., 3101 Drexel Ave., 53403. Tel: 414-554-1801; Fax: 414-554-2009.
School—3035 Drexel, 53403. Tel: 414-554-1091; Fax: 414-554-7618.
Lay Teachers 12; Students 286.
Catechesis/Religious Programs—Tel: 414-554-1801. Sandra Gottfredsen, D.R.E.
Students 337.

9—ST. MARY BY THE LAKE, (1852), Rev. Leon J. Schneider, Admin.; Deacon James Devona.
Mailing Address: Box 1782, 53401-1782. Tel: 414-633-2336.
Res., 1440 Main, 53403. Tel: 414-633-2336. [JC]
Church—7605 Lakeshore Dr., 53402. Tel: 414-639-3616.

10—ST. PATRICK, (1856) (Hispanic), Sr. Carol Kottewitz, R.C., Parish Dir.; Deacon Emilio Coca.
Res., 1100 Erie St., 53402. Tel: 414-632-8808. [JC 4]

11—ST. PAUL THE APOSTLE, (1965), Rev. Paul M. Esser; Deacon Willard Widmar.
Res., 5700 Washington Ave., 53406-4082. Tel: 414-886-0530; Fax: 414-886-0737. [JC]
Catechesis/Religious Programs—Tel: 414-886-0531. D.R.E.: Christine H. Mueller; James Beuscher.
Students 242.

12—ST. RITA, (1925), Revs. Joseph G. Stobba, O.S.A.; John T. Shirley, O.S.A.; Deacon Bro. Christopher Steinle, O.S.A.
Res., 4339 Douglas Ave., 53402. Tel: 414-639-3223; Fax: 414-681-0628. [CEM]
School—Tel: 414-639-3333.
Lay Teachers 11; Students 275.
Catechesis/Religious Programs—Tel: 414-639-6280.
Students 256.

13—ST. ROSE, (1886), Rev. Russell G. Roetzer; Deacon Russell Missureli.
Res., 715 Eleventh St., 53403. Tel: 414-633-1796.

14—SACRED HEART, (1916), Very Rev. Joseph F. Hornacek.
Res., 2201 Northwestern Ave., 53404. Tel: 414-634-5526; Fax: 414-634-5767. [JC]
School—2023 Northwestern Ave., 53404. Tel: 414-637-2012; Fax: 414-637-5130. Mr. Robert Hesse, Prin.
Lay Teachers 10; Students 256.
Catechesis/Religious Programs—Tel: 414-634-3607. Mrs. Donna Joas, D.R.E.
Students 183.

15—ST. STANISLAUS, (1904) (Polish). Also serves Holy Trinity, Racine. Rev. Louis P. Luljak.
Res., 1754 Grand Ave., 53403. Tel: 414-634-6926. [JC]

Randolph, Columbia C Co., St. Gabriel. Also serves St. Mary, Lost Lake and St. Mary, Fox Lake. Rev. Donald B. Braun.
Mailing Address: W11821 Concord Rd., 53956. Tel: 920-326-3585. [CEM]

Random Lake, Sheboygan Co., St. Mary- Random Lake (1855). Also serves St. Patrick, Adell; St. Mary, Cascade; St. Nicholas, Dacada; & St. Michael, Mitchell. Very Rev. Richard J. Cerpich.
Res., 230 Butler St., 53075. Tel: 920-994-4380; Fax: 920-994-2605. [CEM]
School—Also serves St. Nicholas, Dacada & St. Patrick, Adell. 306 Butler St., 53075. Tel: 920-994-9962; 994-2499.
Lay Teachers 8; Students 171.
Catechesis/Religious Programs—Tel: 920-994-8033.
Students 126.

Reeseville, Dodge Co., Holy Family (1901). Also serves St. Columbkille, Elba. Rev. Edward J. Hussli.
Res., 302 Prairie St., P.O. Box 277, 53579. Tel: 920-927-3102. [CEM 2]

Richfield, Washington Co., St. Mary (1854) (German), Rev. Walter J. Vogel.
Res., 2414 Hillside Rd., 53076. Tel: 414-628-3533; Fax: 414-628-3533. [CEM]

Ripon, Fond du Lac Co., St. Patrick (1858), Rev. John A. Schmitz.
Res., 218 Blossom St., 54971-1560. Tel: 414-748-2345. [CEM]
School—222 Blossom St., 54971. Tel: 414-748-3760. Dorothy Tessmann, Prin.
Lay Teachers 5; Students 63.
Catechesis/Religious Programs—Students 259.

St. Wenceslaus (1896) (Polish), Rev. William L. Toelle.
Res., 411 E. Fond du Lac St., 54971-1591. Tel: 920-748-2325.
Catechesis/Religious Programs—Tel: 920-748-3826.
Students 165.

Rubicon, Dodge Co., St. John (1870) (German). Also serves St. Matthew, Neosho; & St. Mary, Woodland. Rev. Russell J. Stommel.
Mailing Address: W1170 Rome Rd., 53078.
Res., 148 W. Lehman, Neosho, 53059. Tel: 920-625-3144. [CEM][JC]
Church—W1170 Rome Rd., P.O. Box 17, 53078. Tel: 414-673-3380.
Catechesis/Religious Programs—Tel: 414-673-3380.
Students 197.

St. Cloud, Fond du Lac Co., St. Cloud (1870) (German), Rev. Peter P. Kutch, O.F.M.Cap.
Res., 924 Main St., P.O. Box 138, 53079. Tel: 920-999-2011; Fax: 920-753-2130. [CEM]
School—(Grades 6-8) 920 Main St., Box 89, 53079-0138. Tel: 920-999-2411. Mrs. Jeanette Jankowski, Bldg. Coord. Consolidated Parochial Elementary School. See Holy Cross, Mount Calvary.

St. Francis, Milwaukee Co., Sacred Heart of Jesus (1868), Alexandra Guliano, Parish Dir.
Office: 3635 S. Kinnickinnic Ave., 53235. Tel: 414-481-2330; Fax: 414-744-7222. [CEM]
School—Tel: 414-744-2483. Shirley Hubbard, Prin.
Sisters 1; Lay Teachers 15; Students 214.
Catechesis/Religious Programs—Tel: 414-486-3945.
Students 91.

St. George, Sheboygan Co., St. George (1860). Also serves St. Rose, Lima. Rev. Eugene D. Winkler; Deacon William T. Jens.
Res., N3589 County Rd. A E., Sheboygan Falls, 53085. Tel: 920-467-4576. [CEM]

St. Joe, Fond du Lac, Co., St. Joseph (1858) (German), Rev. Peter P. Kutch, O.F.M.Cap.
Res., W620 County G, P.O. Box 138, St. Cloud, 53079-0138. Tel: 920-999-3131; Fax: 920-753-2130. [CEM]

St. Kilian, Fond du Lac Co., St. Kilian (1848), Rev. Wayne J. Barta, Admin. In res., Rev. Victor A. Kemmer.
Res., 188 Hwy. W South, Rte. 4, Campbellsport, 53010. Tel: 414-626-2636. [CEM]

St. Lawrence, Washington Co., St. Lawrence (1846) (German), Rev. Alois R. Van Beek.
Res., 4886 Hwy. 175, Hartford, 53027. Tel: 414-644-5701. [CEM]
Catechesis/Religious Programs—Tel: 414-644-0011.
Students 202. Also serves St. Matthias, Nabob.

St. Martins, Milwaukee Co., Holy Assumption. Also serves Sacred Hearts of Jesus and Mary, Franklin. Revs. Charles Bisgrove, S.C.J.; Anthony P. Russo, S.C.J.
Mailing Address: 7963 S. 116th St., Franklin, 53132. Tel: 414-529-1202; Fax: 414-425-1114.
Res., 1132 W. St. Martins Rd.

St. Michael, Washington Co., St. Michael (1846) (German). Also serves St. John of God, Farmington. Sr. Carol Ann Jaeger, S.S.S.F., Parish Dir.; Deacon Ralph Horner.
Res., 8877 Forestview Rd., Kewaskum, 53040. Tel: 414-334-5270. [CEM]
Catechesis/Religious Programs—Tel: 414-334-4195. Sr. Eileen Curran, S.S.N.D., D.R.E.
Students 182.

St. Peter, Fond du Lac Co., St. Peter (1867) (German), Rev. Jerome A. Wagner.
Res., N8079 Church Rd., Malone, 53049. Tel: 920-921-3583; Fax: 920-922-4866. [CEM]
Catechesis/Religious Programs—W. 3880 Evergreen Ct., Malone, 53049. Tel: 920-922-3914.
Students 168.

Saukville, Ozaukee Co., Immaculate Conception (1858), Rev. Karl H. Acker.
Res., 145 W. Church St., 53080. Tel: 414-284-0276. [CEM]
School—341 S. Dries St., 53080. Tel: 414-284-0277. Sr. Jean Hassenberg, S.S.N.D., Prin.
Sisters 1; Lay Teachers 5; Students 46.
Catechesis/Religious Programs—Students 224.

Sharon, Walworth Co., St. Catherine (1854), Thomas McKenna, Parish Dir.
Mailing Address: P.O.Box 502, 53585. Tel: 414-736-4615.
Res., Tel: 815-569-2530. [CEM]

Sheboygan, Sheboygan Co.,

1—St. Clement, (1914), Rev. James Vojtik; Deacon Baleriano Gonzales.
Res., 522 New York Ave., 53081. Tel: 920-457-4629. [JC]
Catechesis/Religious Programs—Tel: 920-452-5256.
Students 158.

2—SS. Cyril and Methodius, (1910) (Slovenian), Rev. Richard J. Fleischman.
Res., 822 New Jersey Ave., 53081. Tel: 920-457-7110. [CEM]

3—St. Dominic, (1927) (German-Dutch), Rev. James J. Jarumbo.
Res., 2133 N. 22nd St., 53081. Tel: 920-458-8787; Fax: 920-458-3280. [JC]
School—2100 N. 21st St., 53081. Tel: 920-452-8747. Peggy Henseler, Prin.
Lay Teachers 11; Students 145.
Catechesis/Religious Programs—Tel: 920-458-5390. D.R.E.: Brian Reindl; Jean Puls; Sharon Pentek, (Preschool).
Students 600.

4—Holy Name, (1845) (German), Rev. Daniel J. Sanders.
Res., 807 Superior Ave., 53081. Tel: 920-458-7721; Fax: 920-459-9108. [CEM]
School—814 Superior Ave., 53081. Tel: 920-452-1571. Valerie Black, Prin.
Lay Teachers 19; Students 312.
Catechesis/Religious Programs—Tel: 920-452-0129. D.R.E.: Mary Ann Zoch; Sue Seymour.
Students 222.

5—Immaculate Conception, (1903) (Lithuanian), Rev. Glenn E. Powers.
Res., 2705 S. 14 St., 53081. Tel: 920-457-3967; Fax: 920-457-5885. [CEM]
School—Christ Child Academy.
(Grades K-5): 1449 S. 12th St., 53081. Tel: 920-459-2663.; (Grades 6-8): 2722 Henry St., 53081. Tel: 920-459-2660. Marilyn Burns, Prin.
Lay Teachers 16; Students 203.
Catechesis/Religious Programs—Tel: 414-459-2665. Donald Wright, D.R.E.
Students 178.

6—St. Peter Claver, (1888) (German), Revs. Brian J. Szyszko; Paul J. Fliss.
Res., 1444 S. Eleventh St., 53081. Tel: 920-457-9408; Fax: 920-457-5290. [CEM]
School—Christ Child Academy, (Grades PreK-5). See Immaculate Conception for Details. Tel: 920-459-2663.
Catechesis/Religious Programs—Tel: 920-452-2759. D.R.E.: Judy Stalter; Barbara Leonhardt.
Students 320.

Sheboygan Falls, Sheboygan Co., St. Mary (1896) (German), Rev. Michael F. Moran.
Rectory: 327 Giddings Ave., 53085. Tel: 920-467-4616; Fax: 920-467-4290. [CEM]
School—Tel: 920-467-6291. Sr. Marcia Vogl, Prin.
Sisters 1; Lay Teachers 13; Students 171.
Catechesis/Religious Programs—Sally Schenk, D.R.E., Tel: 920-467-4616.
Students 277.

Slinger, Washington Co., St. Peter (1856) (German), Rev. Robert J. Bales; Deacon Bernard J. Wendt.
Res., 202 E. Washington St., 53086. Tel: 414-644-8083. [CEM 2][JC]
School—Tel: 414-644-8325; Fax: 414-644-5203. Virginia Miller, Prin.
Lay Teachers 14; Students 130.
Catechesis/Religious Programs—Tel: 414-644-7333. William Thimm, D.R.E.
Students 552.

South Milwaukee, Milwaukee Co.,

1—St. Adalbert, (1898) (Polish), Rev. Herbert B. Schubert; Deacon Leon Zalewski, Pastoral Assoc.
Res., 1611 Manitoba Ave., 53172. Tel: 414-762-0291. [JC]
School—1800 16th Ave., 53172. Tel: 414-762-0064. Felician Sisters 2; Lay Teachers 8; Students 214.
Catechesis/Religious Programs—Students 175.
Convent—1610 Minnesota Ave., 53172. Tel: 414-762-2885.

2—St. John, (1893) (Irish), Rev. Joseph G. Anderson.
Res., 800 Marquette Ave., 53172. Tel: 414-762-2440. [JC]
School—Holy Cross. Consolidated with St. Mary. 805 Marquette Ave., 53172. Tel: 414-762-4670.
Lay Teachers 8; Students 135.
Catechesis/Religious Programs—Tel: 414-762-8600. Kristine Schell, D.R.E.
Students 250.

3—St. Mary, (1893), Rev. Ronald G. Engel.
Res., 1304 Manitoba Ave., 53172. Tel: 414-762-6810; Fax: 414-762-8326. [JC]
School—Consolidated with St. John's, Holy Cross School. Tel: 414-762-4670.
Catechesis/Religious Programs—1310 Manitoba Ave., 53172. Tel: 414-764-3350; Fax: 414-764-3575.
Students 181.

4—St. Sylvester, (1962), Rev. Thomas A. Trepanier; Deacon A. James Leggett.
Res., 675 College Ave., 53172. Tel: 414-762-6800.
School—695 College Ave., 53172. Tel: 414-764-4360; Fax: 414-764-7078.
Lay Teachers 12; Students 204.
Catechesis/Religious Programs—Tel: 414-764-5488. Patricia Walsh, D.R.E.
Students 199.

Springvale, St. Mary (1858) (Irish). Also serves St. Joseph, Waupun and St. Brendan, Brandon. Revs. John Elmer, O.F.M.Conv.; Russan Cole, O.F.M.Conv.
Mailing Address: 118 W. Main St., Waupun, 53963-1453. Tel: 920-324-5400. [CEM]

Sturtevant, Racine Co., St. Sebastian (1906), Rev. James Kendzierski, O.F.M.; Deacon DeSales Wisniewski, O.F.M., Pastoral Assoc.
Res., 3126 95th St., 53177. Tel: 414-886-4398; Fax: 414-886-4396.
School—3030 95th St., 53177. Tel: 414-886-2806. Diane Davis, Prin.
Lay Teachers 10; Students 190.
Catechesis/Religious Programs—Tel: 414-886-4420.
Students 161.

Theresa, Dodge Co., St. Theresa (1849) (German), Rev. Vincent B. Holubowicz, Admin.
102 Church St., 53091.
Mailing Address: P.O. Box 330, 53091-0330. Tel: 920-269-4429. [CEM]
School—(Grades 1-4). Consolidated with St. Mary, Lomira to form Consolidated Catholic School of Lomira-Theresa. 105 W. Rock River St., 53091. Tel: 414-488-4543. Sr. Rosemary Herriges, S.S.S.F., Prin.

Thiensville, Ozaukee Co., St. Cecilia (1919), Rev. Gerald J. Dominiak; Deacon Joseph P. Wenzler.
Res., 101 Ellenbecker Rd., 53092. Tel: 414-512-8980; Fax: 414-242-7976.
School—(Grades K4-3). Consolidated with St. James, Mequon to form SS. Cecilia and James. 116 N. Orchard, 53092. Mr. Richard Goeden, Prin.
Lay Teachers 13; Students 286.
Catechesis/Religious Programs—Program consolidated with St. James, Mequon. Tel: 414-512-8984. Patricia Roehrig, D.R.E.
Students 589.

Thompson, Washington Co., St. Patrick (Tn. Erin) (1855) (Irish), Rev. Walter J. Vogel.
Res., 1908 Hwy. 83 S., Hartford, 53027. Tel: 414-673-2988. [CEM 2]

Twin Lakes, Kenosha Co., St. John (1932), Rev. Ronald C. Kowalski.
Res., 701 N. Lake Ave., 53181. Tel: 414-877-2557; Fax: 414-877-2431. [CEM]
Catechesis/Religious Programs—Tel: 414-877-3033. Diane Baltazar, D.R.E.
Students 207.

Union Grove, Racine Co., St. Robert Bellarmine (1965), Rev. Charles E. Conley.
Res., 3320 S. Colony Ave., P.O. Box 107, 53182. Tel: 414-878-3476. [JC]
Catechesis/Religious Programs—Tel: 414-878-2009. Ms. Kris Seifert, D.R.E.
Students 312.

Waterford, Racine Co., St. Thomas Aquinas (1851), Very Rev. Dennis E. Van Beek; Deacon Carl A. Mahnke.
Res., 305 First St., 53185. Tel: 414-534-2255; Fax: 414-534-2929. [CEM]
School—Tel: 414-534-2265.
Lay Teachers 12; Students 257.
Catechesis/Religious Programs—Students 370.

Waukesha, Waukesha Co.,

1—St. Joseph, (1844), Revs. Ronald J. Gramza; John C. Lukaszewicz; Deacons Gene Kempka; Mike Erwin.
Res., 822 N. East Ave., 53186. Tel: 414-542-2589; Fax: 414-542-2570.
School—Waukesha Catholic School System, (Grades 6-8) 841 Martin St., 53186. Tel: 414-896-2930; Fax: 414-896-2930. Mrs. Pat McGrane, Prin.
Franciscan Sisters of Christian Charity Sisters 2; Lay Teachers 18; Students 290.
Catechesis/Religious Programs—Tel: 414-542-9392; Fax: 414-542-2570. Ruth Weiss, D.R.E.
Students 355.

2—St. Mary, (1950), Revs. Michael T. Newman; Gordon A. Weber.
Res., 225 S. Hartwell Ave., 53186. Tel: 414-547-6555; Fax: 414-547-6714.
School—Tel: 414-896-2932; Fax: 414-896-2931. Sr. Kathleen Swain, Prin.
Sisters 4; Lay Teachers 11; Students 356.
Catechesis/Religious Programs—Tel: 414-547-6326. Lisa Floch Gilvary, D.R.E.
Students 326.

3—St. John Neumann, (1981), Revs. Glen G. Graczyk; Dennis G. Budka; Deacon Thomas McGuine.
Mailing Address: 2400 W. STH 59, 53188-6323. Tel: 414-549-0223; 549-0898; Fax: 414-549-0444. [CEM]
School—Waukesha Catholic School System, (Grades PreK-8). Tel: 414-547-3020.
Students 149.
Catechesis/Religious Programs—D.R.E.: Sr. Dolores Pertzborn; Sr. Virginia Azqueta; Shelly McGuine.
Students 810.

4—St. William, (1957), Rev. David C. Filut.
Res., 440 N. Moreland Blvd., 53188. Tel: 414-542-0456; Fax: 414-547-3616. [JC]
School—Waukesha Catholic School System, (Grades PreK-5) 444 N. Moreland Blvd., 53188. Tel: 414-896-2920; Fax: 414-896-2925. Sr. Toni Gradisnik, O.S.F., Campus Prin.
Students 200.
Catechesis/Religious Programs—D.R.E.: Kay Curty Tel: 414-547-3216; Mary Osep Tel: 414-547-3375.
Students 688.

Waupun, Fond du Lac Co., St. Joseph (1866) (Irish). Also serves St. Brendan, Brandon & St. Mary, Springvale. Revs. John Elmer, O.F.M.Conv.; Russan Cole, O.F.M.Conv.
Res., 118 W. Main St., 53963. Tel: 920-324-5400; Fax: 920-324-1040. [CEM]
Catechesis/Religious Programs—Tel: 920-324-3891. D.R.E.: Maureen Flynn; Karen Schmidt.
Students 273.

Wauwatosa, Milwaukee Co.,

1—St. Bernard, (1911) (Irish), Rev. Victor R. Capriolo. In res., Revs. Robert E. Massey; Donald F. Quartana.
Res., 1500 Wauwatosa Ave., 53213. Tel: 414-258-4320; Fax: 414-258-7866.

School—7440 Harwood Ave., 53213. Tel: 414-258-9977. Consuelo Roybal, Prin.
Religious 2; Lay Teachers 14; Students 236.
Catechesis/Religious Programs—Tel: 414-476-5968.
Students 220.

2—CHRIST KING, (1939), Very Rev. Dennis R. Ackeret; Rev. Michael E. Nowak; Deacon Arthur C. Dallman.
Res., 2604 Swan Blvd., 53226. Tel: 414-258-2604; Fax: 414-258-1993.
School—2646 N. Swan Blvd., 53226. Tel: 414-258-4160. Sr. Martha Meyer, S.S.N.D., Prin.
School Sisters of Notre Dame 1; Lay Teachers 24; Students 449.
Catechesis/Religious Programs—Tel: 414-258-0916. Barbara Schveidler, D.R.E.
Students 219.

3—ST. JOSEPH CONGREGATION, (1855), Revs. Jerome M. Hudziak; Robert Fictum, S.D.S.; Deacon Jose Gonzales.
Mailing Address: Office, 12130 W. Center St., 53222-4096. Tel: 414-771-4626; Fax: 414-771-4311.
Res., 12130 W. Hadley St., 53222-4097. Tel: 414-771-4627.
School—2750 N. 122nd St., 53222. Tel: 414-771-5577; Fax: 414-771-9826. Jane Uebelher, Prin.
Lay Teachers 18; Students 280.
Catechesis/Religious Programs—Tel: 212-771-6096.
Students 478.

4—ST. JUDE THE APOSTLE, (1928), Rev. Peter P. Carek; Sr. Mary La Von Lauer, O.S.F., Pastoral Min. to Senior Citizens; Deacon Donald Borkowski; Gary Heun, Pastoral Assoc. In res., Rev. Emmanuel Udo (Nigeria).
Res., 734 Glenview Ave., 53213. Tel: 414-258-8821; Fax: 414-258-0165.
School—8042 St. Jude Ct., 53213. Tel: 414-771-1520; Fax: 414-771-3748. Roger Baehr, Prin.
Sisters 1; Lay Teachers 22; Students 464.
Catechesis/Religious Programs—Tel: 414-259-0950. D.R.E.: Gary Heun; Dave Baudry.
Students 163.

5—ST. PIUS X, (1952), Rev. Keith Brennan, S.D.S.
Res., 2506 Wauwatosa Ave., 53213. Tel: 414-453-3875; Fax: 414-453-7570.
School—2520 Wauwatosa Ave., 53213. Tel: 441-778-0880.
Lay Teachers 13; Students 144.
Catechesis/Religious Programs—Tel: 414-453-1153. Mary Jane Duffey, D.R.E.
Students 222.

Wayne, Washington Co., St. Bridget. Unassigned. Also serves Holy Trinity, Kewaskum.
Mailing Address: 331 Main St., P.O. Box 461, Kewaskum, 53040. Tel: 414-626-2603.

West Allis, Milwaukee Co.,

1—ST. ALOYSIUS, (1920), Revs. John N. Baumgartner; Daniel J. Massie; Deacon John A. Fricano.
Res., 1414 S. 93rd St., 53214. Tel: 414-476-3803.
School—1435 S. 92nd St., 53214. Tel: 414-476-0751. Richard Bagemihl, Prin.
Lay Teachers 14; Students 261.
Catechesis/Religious Programs—Tel: 414-257-3088. Martha Van Duser, D.R.E.
Students 171.

2—ST. AUGUSTINE, (1928) (Croatian), Rev. Lawrence Frankovich, O.F.M.
Res., 6762 W. Rogers St., 53219. Tel: 414-541-5207; Fax: 414-541-0273.
School—6763 W. Rogers St., 53219. Tel: 414-545-2120.
Sisters 3; Lay Teachers 5; Students 160.

3—HOLY ASSUMPTION, (1902), Rev. David E. Cooper; Deacon George P. Sherman.
Res., 1525 S. 71st St., 53214. Tel: 414-774-3010.
School—1532 S. 72nd St., 53214. Tel: 414-476-0508. Mary Kathleen Tate, Prin.
School Sisters of Notre Dame 2; Lay Teachers 10; Students 135.

4—IMMACULATE HEART OF MARY, (1948), Rev. Karl J. Schneider; Deacons Dennis E. Fietz; Walter Henry.
Res., 1121 S. 116th St., 53214. Tel: 414-453-5192; Fax: 414-453-0137.
Catechesis/Religious Programs—Tel: 414-453-0300.
Students 139.

5—ST. JOSEPH, (1909) (Polish), Rev. James B. Pozanski.
Res., 1642 S. 65th St., 53214. Tel: 414-543-8310.

6—MARY, QUEEN OF HEAVEN, (1958), Very Rev. William E. Kohler; Rev. Michael F. Merkt.
Office: 2322 S. 106th St., 53227. Tel: 414-328-5566; Fax: 414-328-5561.
School—2360 S. 106th St., 53227. Tel: 414-328-5577; Fax: 414-328-5573. Mrs. Marilyn Marzolf, Prin.
Lay Teachers 10; Students 163.
Catechesis/Religious Programs—Tel: 414-328-5570. Nicholas Balducci, D.R.E.
Students 287.

7—ST. MARY, HELP OF CHRISTIANS, (1907) (Slovenian), Rev. Joseph L. Cunningham.
Res., 1210 S. 61st St., 53214. Tel: 414-771-8313.

8—OUR LADY OF MT. CARMEL, (1938) (Italian), Rev. James B. Posanski, Admin.
Res., 6625 W. Beloit Rd., 53219. Tel: 414-543-9210; Fax: 414-543-6919.

9—ST. RITA, (1924), Revs. Richard E. Mirsberger; Kevin J. Kowalske; Deacons Sam Lupo; Richard Brown.
Res., 2318 S. 61st St., 53219. Tel: 414-541-7515; Fax: 414-541-7568.
School—6021 W. Lincoln Ave., 53219. Tel: 414-327-5020. Sr. Joyce Wagner, S.S.S.F., Prin.
School Sisters of St. Francis 4; Lay Teachers 15; Students 277.
Catechesis/Religious Programs—Tel: 414-541-7515. Sr. Mary Theiss, S.S.S.F., D.R.E.
Students 268.

West Bend, Washington Co., Holy Angels (1855), Revs. Gerald W. Brittain; Jerome V. Repenshek.
Res., 138 N. 8th Ave., 53095. Tel: 414-334-3038; Fax: 414-334-1334. [CEM]
School—230 N. 8th Ave., 53095. Tel: 414-338-1148; Fax: 414-334-1334. Mike Sternig, Prin.
Lay Teachers 21; Students 460.
Catechesis/Religious Programs—Tel: 414-334-9393. Nan Jacoby, D.R.E.
Students 508.

Immaculate Conception (1857), Rev. Patrick R. Wendt.
Res., 406 Jefferson St., 53090. Tel: 414-338-5600. [CEM]
School—Tel: 414-338-5602.
Lay Teachers 8; Students 204.
Catechesis/Religious Programs—Tel: 414-338-5605. D.R.E.: Dolores Ecker; Marge Schinker.
Students 344.

St. Frances Cabrini (1955), Revs. Jeffrey R. Haines; Kenneth A. Mich; Deacons Michael Koebel; Steven Przedpelski; Mike Sepersky, Dir. of Admin. Svcs.
Res., 1025 S. 7th Ave., 53095. Tel: 414-338-2366; Fax: 414-338-2348. [JC]
School—529 Hawthorn Dr., 53095. Tel: 414-334-7142; Fax: 414-334-8168. Janice Stauske, Prin.
Lay Teachers 24; Students 442.
Catechesis/Religious Programs—Tel: 414-334-9511. Judy Schroeder, D.R.E.
Students 610.

Whitefish Bay, Milwaukee Co., St. Monica (1923), Rev. Alan F. Jurkus; Deacon Eugene Van Garsse. In res., Revs. John R. Paczesny; Richard C. Brietbach.
Res., 160 E. Silver Spring Dr., 53217. Tel: 414-332-1576; 332-1577; Fax: 414-332-2462.
School—Tel: 414-332-3660; Fax: 414-332-8649. Dr. Maureen Polczynski, Prin.
School Sisters of St. Francis 2; Lay Teachers 29; Students 426.
Catechesis/Religious Programs—Tel: 414-964-8780. Sr. Fran Buschell, D.R.E.
Students 225.

Holy Family (1949), Revs. Laurin J. Wenig; Timothy L. Kitzke; Deacon Daniel T. Zozakiewicz.
Office: 4825 N. Wildwood Ave., 53217. Tel: 414-332-9220; Fax: 414-961-7396.
School—4849 N. Wildwood Ave., 53217. Tel: 414-332-8175. Rebecca Jones, Prin.
Lay Teachers 17; Students 216.
Catechesis/Religious Programs—Tel: 414-332-8156. Barbara O'Neil, D.R.E.
Students 461.

Whitewater, Walworth Co., St. Patrick (1853), Revs. Ronald O. Crewe; James M. Godin.
Office: 1225 W. Main St., 53190-1620. Tel: 414-473-3143; Fax: 414-473-7010.
Res., 126 S. Elizabeth St., 53190-1628. [CEM]
Catechesis/Religious Programs—Tel: 414-473-8834. Sr. Therese Rekowski, S.S.N.D., D.R.E.
Students 208.

Wilmot, Kenosha Co., Holy Name of Jesus (1856), Sr. Kathleen Hurley, O.S.F., Parish Dir.
Res., P.O. Box 188, 53192. Tel: 414-862-6466; Fax: 414-862-6466. [CEM]
Catechesis/Religious Programs—Tel: 414-862-2361.
Students 229.

Wind Lake, Racine Co., St. Clare (1965), Rev. John D. Hemsing; Deacon Richard E. Milbauer.
Mailing Address: Parish Office, 7616 Fritz St., 53185. Tel: 414-895-2729; Fax: 414-895-3601.
Res., 7616 Fritz St., 53185.
Catechesis/Religious Programs—Mrs. Millie Luhmann, D.R.E.
Students 250.

Woodhull, Fond du Lac Co., St. John the Baptist. Also serves St. Mary, Eldorado. Rev. Roger A. Savage.
Res., W8272 Forest Ave. Rd., Eldorado, 54932-9801. Tel: 920-922-2412. [CEM]
Catechesis/Religious Programs—Carol Huck, D.R.E.
Students 137.

Woodland, Dodge N Co., St. Mary. Also serves St. Matthew, Neosho & St. John, Rubicon. Rev. Russel J. Stommel.
Mailing Address: 148 W. Lehman St, P.O. Box 45, Neosho, 53059. Tel: 414-625-3144. [CEM]

Chaplains of Public Institutions

MILWAUKEE. *Milwaukee County House of Correction*. Attended by St. James, Franklin.
Milwaukee County Jail. Bro. Jerome Smith, O.F.M.Cap., Chap.
St. Luke's Medical Center Box 21677, 53221. Rev. Donald E. Sass, Chap.

JUNEAU. *Dodge County Center*. Attended by Immaculate Conception.

KENOSHA. *Kenosha Hospital and Medical Center* 6308 8th Ave., 53143-5082. Rev. Michael P. Dineen, Chap.

WALES. *Ethan Allen School for Boys* P.O. Box 900, 53183-0900. Tel: 414-646-3341. Rev. Mark L. Molling, Chap.

WAUWATOSA. *Froedtert Memorial Lutheran Hospital*. Rev. Robert J. Gloudeman, Chap., 9200 W. Wisconsin Ave., Milwaukee, 53226.

WEST ALLIS. *West Allis Memorial Hospital* 8901 W. Lincoln Ave., 53227. Tel: 414-328-6000. Rev. Charles G. Zabler, Chap.

WOOD. *Veterans Administration Medical Center* P.O., 53193. Tel: 414-384-2000. Chaplains: Revs. James Kovarik, O.S.Cam.; Edward E. Lisowski; Norman R. Oswald.

Special Assignment:
Most Rev.—
Sklba, Richard J., Auxiliary Bishop, 3501 S. Lake Dr., P.O. Box 07912, Milwaukee, WI 53207-0912
Reverend Fathers—
Aiello, John D., Metropolitan Tribunal, 3501 S. Lake Dr., P.O. Box 07912, Milwaukee, WI 53207-0912
Avella, Steven M., Marquette University Faculty, 422 E. Fremont Pl., Milwaukee, WI 53207
Bandle, Ronald J., Nursing Home Ministry, 5937 N. 35th St., #2, Milwaukee, WI 53209
Barbian, Leonard M., Assoc. Vicar of Clergy, Priests' Placement Bd., 3501 S. Lake Dr., P.O. Box 07912, Milwaukee, WI 53207-0912
Breitbach, Richard C., Cardinal Stritch University Faculty, 160 E. Silver Spring Dr., Whitefish Bay, WI 53217-4701
Brundage, Thomas T., Judicial Vicar, Metropolitan Tribunal, 3501 S. Lake Dr., P.O. Box 07912, Milwaukee, WI 53207-0912
Connell, James E., Vice Chancellor, Archdiocese of Milwaukee, 3501 S. Lake Dr., P.O. Box 07912, Milwaukee, WI 53207-0912
Duffy, James H., Madonna House, Combermere, Ontario KOJ 1LO Canada
Hammer, Michael J., Coord. Catholic AIDS Ministry, 802 N. Jackson St., Milwaukee, WI 53202-3879
Janette, Paul D., Service for Senior Priests, 3501 S. Lake Dr., P.O. Box 07912, Milwaukee, WI 53207-0912. Tel: 414-769-3345
Klemme, Dennis C., Metropolitan Tribunal, P.O. Box 07912, Milwaukee, WI 53207-0912. Tel: 414-769-3330
Knoebel, Thomas L., Sacred Heart School of Theology Faculty, P.O. Box 429, Hales Corner, WI 53130-0429
Massey, Robert E., Marquette Univ. Faculty, 1500 Wauwatosa Ave., Wauwatosa, WI 53213
O'Brien, Timothy J., Faculty, Marquette University, 8521 Kenyon Ave., Wauwatosa, WI 53226
Santo, Mark C., Federal Prison Chap.
Schlenkler, Richard J., Sacred Heart School of Theology Faculty, 3729 S. Packard, #38, St. Francis, WI 53235
Stiefvater, Robert X., Dir. Office of Vocations, 3257 S. Lake Dr., St. Francis, WI 53235. Tel: 414-747-6437
Stoll, Jerome L., Nursing Home Ministry, Archdiocese of Milwaukee, P.O. Box 207, Waterford, WI 53185-0207
Thimm, Donald H., Archbishop's Delegate for Human Resources, 3501 S. Lake Dr., P.O. Box 07912, Milwaukee, WI 53207-0912
Van Vlaenderen, Leonard S., Sec. to the Archbishop, 3501 S. Lake Dr., P.O. Box 07912, Milwaukee, WI 53207-0912
Wheatley, Charles J., Chap., Archdiocesan Cemetery System, 4463 S. Taylor Ave., Milwaukee, WI 53207
Very Rev.—
Kerstein, Thomas F., Vicar Gen. & Vicar for Clergy Personnel, 3501 S. Lake Dr., P.O. Box 07912, Milwaukee, WI 53207-0912. Tel: 414-769-3490

On Duty Outside the Archdiocese:
Reverend Monsignors—
Harvey, James M., Diplomatic Corps, Villa Stritch, Via Della Nocetta, 63, Rome, 00164 Italy
Malloy, David J., Diplomatic Corps, Permanent Observer Mission of the Holy See to the United Nations, 20 E. 72nd St., New York, NY 10021-4196
Reverend Fathers—
Bryl, Thaddeus J., St. Mary, 312 S. Saunders, P.O. Box 406, Sutton, NE 68979
Clapp, Kenneth A., Holy Family Parish, Apartado 53, Azua, Dominican Republic
DeVries, Thomas D., NCCB Office for the Catechism, 3211 4th St., N.E., Washington, D.C. 20017-1194
Dolezal, Richard R., 5053 N. Ridgeway, Chicago, IL 60625-6021
Kobida, Vincent F., Diocese of San Juan De La Maguana, D.R., c/o Lynx Air-SDQ, Box 407052, Fort Lauderdale, FL 33340
Konkel, Eugene J., S.S., Vatican II Institute, 320 Middlefield Rd., Menlo Park, CA 94025
Lamb, Matthew L., Faculty, Boston College, Horizon East 411, 125 Coolidge Ave., Watertown, MA 02172
Marek, Dean V., Box 1332, Rochester, MN 55903-1332
Palermo, Albert A., St. Albert the Great, 1104 Huntridge Cir., Austin, TX 78758-3909
Shmauz, Donald A., 5570 Woodland Dr., Waunakee, WI 53597
Skeris, Robert A., Christendom College, 2101 Shenandoah Shores Rd., Front Royal, VA 22630
Thompson, Jerome F., St. Anne, P.O. Box 19079, 91190 Jerusalem, Israel
Tino, Robert F., Western State Hospital, 9601 Steilacoom Blvd., S.W., Tacoma, WA 98498-7213

Military Chaplains:
Reverend Fathers—
Kienzle, Jerome C.
Lee, Roy A.
Malloy, Francis X., Catholic Memorial High School, 601 E. College Ave., Waukesha, WI 53186-5538. Tel: 414-542-7101
Mikalofsky, Hilarion A.
Olszyk, Thomas P.
Richter, Robert J.

Graduate Studies:
Reverend Fathers—
Hartman, Paul B., 595 Third St., N.W., Washington, D.C. 20001
Schuerman, James T., Faculty, Saint Francis Seminary, 3257 S. Lake Dr., St. Francis, WI 53235
Shecterle, Ross A., St. Mary's Seminary, 5400 Roland Ave., Baltimore, MD 21210-1994

On Leave:
Reverend Fathers—
Becker, Franklyn W.
Collova, S. Joseph
Lanser, Jerome E.
Neuberger, Michael T.
Sosa, Carlos
Wagner, John C.

Sick Leave:
Reverend Fathers—
Cane-Gombau, Pere
Walker, Thomas J.
Walter, Charles W.

Awaiting Assignment:
Reverend Fathers—
Beno, Brian M.
Gaberle, Jiri P.
Hying, Donald J.
Knighton, Marvin T.
Lazarski, Marvin I.
Pocernich, Eugene S.
Stanfield, William L.

Retired:
Reverend Monsignors—
Donovan, John T., 3501 S. Lake Dr., St. Francis, WI 53235
Emmenegger, Joseph E., 3501 S. Lake Dr., St. Francis, WI 53235
Gass, Sylvester F., 3501 S. Lake Dr., St. Francis, WI 53235
Kapalczynski, Eugene J., 3501 S. Lake Dr., St. Francis, WI 53235
Murphy, John F., 5510 N. Lake Dr., Oconomowoc, WI 53066
Prudell, Harold O., 2462 N. Prospect Ave., Milwaukee, WI 53211-4462
Schmit, Ralph R., 3253 S. Lake Dr., St. Francis, WI 53235
Reverend Fathers—
Adamsky, Raymond J., 3253 S. Lake Dr., St. Francis, WI 53235
Amrhein, Peter T., 530 N. 103rd St., #22, Milwaukee, WI 53226
Andre, Leonard J., 11926 W. Mill Rd., #1, Milwaukee, WI 53225
Badem, Wendel J., 3253 S. Lake Dr., #206, St. Francis, WI 53235
Baran, Joseph L., 2022 N. 86th St., Wauwatosa, WI 53226-2745
Baranowski, Stanley A., W782 County Rd. A, Randolph, WI 53956
Beck, Richard P., 5606 Cynthia Ln., Sarasota, FL 34235
Beitzinger, George J., 4139 Los Altos Ct., Naples, FL 34109
Belda, Leo W., 3253 S. Lake Dr., #101, St. Francis, WI 53235-3704
Bistricky, Frederick J., 5171 N. 64th St., Milwaukee, WI 53218
Brady, James J., 3501 S. Lake Dr., St. Francis, WI 53235
Braun, Edgar F., W6895 Lost Lake Rd., Pearson, WI 54462-8009
Brey, Lawrence S., 109 Military Rd., P. O. Box 170, Dane, WI 58529
Brielmaier, Leon J., 422 Fox Isle Pk., Waterford, WI 53185
Briske, Larry F., 12753 Caminito Cancion, Unit 128, San Diego, CA 92128
Budzynski, Daniel A., 3253 S. Lake Dr., #305, St. Francis, WI 53235
Callahan, Raymond J., 10101 W. Wisconsin Ave., Wauwatosa, WI 53226
Carroll, Edward E., 15000 W. Cleveland Ave., #226, New Berlin, WI 53151-3766
Clark, Gerard J., 3508 5th Ave., South Milwaukee, WI 53172
Cox, William E., 4816 Westway Ave., Racine, WI 53406-3634
Darnieder, Donald A., 3253 S. Lake Dr., St. Francis, WI 53235
Dionne, Earl J., 3501 S. Lake Dr., St. Francis, WI 53235
Dougherty, Matthew C., 3540 S. 43rd St., Milwaukee, WI 53220
Dreher, Ernest O., 310 E. 11th St., Fond du Lac, WI 54935
Elverman, Donald A., 3501 S. Lake Dr., St. Francis, WI 53235
Enders, Robert F., 238 S. Hartwell Ave., Waukesha, WI 53186-6403
Ernster, James M., 570 Highway D, Belgium, WI 53004
Eschweiler, Edward R., 3501 S. Lake Dr., St. Francis, WI 53235
Etzel, George A., 365 Gillett St., Fond du Lac, WI 54935
Farrell, William J., 10100 W. Bluemound Rd., Wauwatosa, WI 53226
Fetterer, Raymond A., 930 N. 6th St., Sheboygan, WI 53081-4162
Fleischmann, George R., 3501 S. Lake Dr., St. Francis, WI 53235
Furtmann, John A., N110 W16906 Ashbury Ln., #7, Germantown, WI 53022
Garity, Linus J., Dammert Geriatrics, 9500 W. State, Rte. 15, Belleville, IL 62223
Gehl, Walter N., Rte. 2, Box 250, Hiles, WI 54511
Gibbons, George J., 10100 W. Bluemound Rd., Wauwatosa, WI 53226
Glass, Rolland T., 531 W. 11th St., Fond du Lac, WI 54935
Goebel, Nicholas L., N9628 Winnebago Park Rd., Fond du Lac, WI 54935
Hanauska, Joseph F., 31068 Timber Lane, Burlington, WI 53105-9738
Hanley, John P., 3501 S. Lake Dr., St. Francis, WI 53235
Hauser, Gerald B., 3501 S. Lake Dr., St. Francis, WI 53235
Heffron, William M., 200 Southtowne Dr., #308, South Milwaukee, WI 53172
Hentzner, John T., 3501 S. Lake Dr., St. Francis, WI 53235
Herkowski, Arthur M., 1299 Flora Glen Dr., Sparks, NV 89434-0742
Hess, James W., 1607A N. 8th St., Sheboygan, WI 53081-2733
Hickey, Thomas D., 3253 S. Lake Dr., #303, St. Francis, WI 53235
Hmircik, Donald A., 104 St. Franciscus St., Mount Calvary, WI 53057
Hopf, George S., 80 W. Northwest Hwy., Palatine, IL 60067
Huber, George L., 3253 S. Lake Dr., St. Francis, WI 53235
Ide, Harold J., 3501 S. Lake Dr., St. Francis, WI 53235
Jautz, Martin L., 10100 W. Bluemound Rd., Wauwatosa, WI 53226
Johnson, Howard J., W6332 Lake Ellen Dr., Cascade, WI 53011
Jordan, Francis W., 2527 Ole Davidson Rd., Racine, WI 53405-1442
Kaiser, Cletus H., 239 Terrace Dr., West Bend, WI 53095-4748
Kasten, Edward F., 7979 W. Glenbrook Rd., Milwaukee, WI 53223
Kemmer, Victor A., 188 Hwy. W S., Rte. 4, Campbellsport, WI 53010
Klauck, Stanley B., 12621 E. Laurel Ln., Scottsdale, AZ 85259
Kleefisch, Charles A., 5101 W. Center St., Milwaukee, WI 53210-2361
Knoernschild, William F., 10101 W. Wisconsin Ave., Wauwatosa, WI 53226
Knotek, John T., 5116 22nd Ave., Kenosha, WI 53140-5925
Kolanda, George A., 10101 W. Wisconsin Ave., Wauwatosa, WI 53226
Kolanko, John R., 7164 N. 42nd St., #2, Milwaukee, WI 53209
Kowalski, Leo S., 3441 S. 10th St., Milwaukee, WI 53215-5117
Kreuzer, Eugene T., 21618 Plank Rd., Kansasville, WI 53139
Kurkiewicz, Raymond J., 3501 S. Lake Dr., St. Francis, WI 53235
Labaj, Stephen V., 1439 Ohio St., Racine, WI 53405-3119
Lambert, Leo M., 3501 S. Lake Dr., St. Francis, WI 53235
Leack, Lawrence J., 1845 N. 60th St., Milwaukee, WI 53208-1637
Lippert, Paul R., Box 238, Plainfield, WI 54966-0238
Loehr, Charles D., W1452 Hwy. T, Mount Calvary, WI 53057
Lyons, Mark J., 10100 W. Bluemound Rd., Wauwatosa, WI 53226
Mackin, William H., 3501 S. Lake Dr., St. Francis, WI 53235
Macoskie, Melvin H., 3501 S. Lake Dr., St. Francis, WI 53235
Maney, Robert L., 9431 W. Beloit Rd., #308, Milwaukee, WI 53227
Matt, Erwin H., 3253 S. Lake Dr., St. Francis, WI 53235
McCormick, Robert J., 11274 Pineapple Rd., Punta Gorda, FL 33955-1238
McLaughlin, Owen F., 400 Sunnyslope Dr., Apt. 119, Hartland, WI 53029-1416
Mogilka, Erwin E., 4321 Marine Dr., Burlington, WI 53105
Morgan, Walter N., 523 W. 11th St., Fond du Lac, WI 54935
Mueller, Joseph J., 10100 W. Bluemound Rd., Wauwatosa, WI 53226
Mueller, Robert F., 1711 S. 9th St., Milwaukee, WI 53204-3586
Murphy, John M., 3501 S. Lake Dr., St. Francis, WI 53235
Murphy, Lawrence C., P.O. Box 50, Boulder Junction, WI 54512-0050
Murray, William F., 3253 S. Lake Dr., St. Francis, WI 53235-3705
Myszel, George G., 26503 Angelica Rd., Punta Gorda, FL 33955-1408
Nickolai, Arthur A., 6100 Hwy. 73N., Rte. 2, Marshall, WI 53559-9423
Novotny, Robert J., 3253 S. Lake Dr., St. Francis, WI 53235
O'Brien, Eugene C., 1193 Masterpiece Dr., Oceanside, CA 92057
O'Rourke, Francis J., 10101 W. Wisconsin Ave., Wauwatosa, WI 53226
Okopinski, Louis S., 3253 S. Lake Dr., St. Francis, WI 53235
Orzechowski, Walter B., N8180 Lakeview Rd., Fond du Lac, WI 54935
Parr, Raymond A., 4031 E. Van Norman Ave., Cudahy, WI 53110-1231
Peters, Donald R., P.O. Box 91245, Lakeland, FL 33804-1245
Piechowski, Leonard E., 5761 Lakeview Dr., Greendale, WI 53129
Podolak, William S., 3501 S. Lake Dr., St. Francis, WI 53235
Quartana, Donald F., 1500 Wauwatosa Ave., Wauwatosa, WI 53213-2623
Rausch, John W., Box 475, Eagle, WI 53119
Rodriguez, Robert, 502 Amber Horizon St., Henderson, NV 89015
Roensch, Frederick J., P.O. Box 25578, Milwaukee, WI 53225-0578
Roscioli, Dominic J., 5412 23rd Ave., Kenosha, WI 53140-3505

Rykowski, Valerian J., 3503 Silver Lake Dr., Traverse City, MI 49684
Sanfelippo, Frank J., P.O. Box 1504, Milwaukee, WI 53201-1504
Schaefer, Verne B., 412 Oak Lodge Rd., Waterford, WI 53185
Schlaffer, James J., 9244 29th Ave., #206, Kenosha, WI 53143
Schmelzer, Linus L., 3501 S. Lake Dr., St. Francis, WI 53235
Schmidt, Frederick N., Rte. 3, Box 96, Pardeeville, WI 53954
Schmitt, Warren J., 9115 S. Cactus Ln., Sun Lakes, AZ 85248-6903
Schmitz, Gerald T., 365 Gillett St., Campbellsport, WI 53010
Schneider, Vincent N., 33108 80th St., Rte. 5, Burlington, WI 53105-8816
Schuster, Valery P., 199 Vine St., Sun Prairie, WI 53590
Schwinn, Joseph F., 3253 S. Lake Dr., St. Francis, WI 53235
Seramur, Leo J., 3253 S. Lake Dr., St. Francis, WI 53235
Silvestri, Vincent A., 10100 W. Bluemound Rd., Wauwatosa, WI 53226
Simon, Martin M., 1401 Grove Ave., Racine, WI 53405-3453
Sippel, Edward F., 519 W. 11th St., Fond du Lac, WI 54935
Smith, Fred A., 3916 S. Tara Hill Dr., Greenfield, WI 53220-2520
Sowinski, Albin F., 20295C Independence Dr., Brookfield, WI 53045
Stangel, Mark J., 3501 S. Lake Dr., St. Francis, WI 53235
Strenski, Joseph A., 3501 S. Lake Dr., St. Francis, WI 53235
Strupp, James A., 580 S. 18th Ave., West Bend, WI 53095-3755
Sutschek, Francis C., 111 S. Maple Ave. #2, Slinger, WI 53086-9414
Theisen, John J., 536 Lake Dr., Random Lake, WI 53075
Trenier, Anthony S., 1154 N. 45th St., Milwaukee, WI 53208-2733
Twomey, John E., 2885 Klovar Ln., #3, East Troy, WI 53120
Uhen, Cletus V., 1100 Fountain Dr. #208A, Racine, WI 53406-3767
Valdez, Jose R., 3126 S. 21st St., Milwaukee, WI 53215
Van Beck, Alfred F., 2009 Elevada St., Oceanside, CA 92054
Verhalen, Charles J., 3253 S. Lake Dr., St. Francis, WI 53235
Wallaik, William H., 11300 N. St. James Ln., 28W, Mequon, WI 53092-3047
Walter, John F., 10100 W. Bluemound Rd., Wauwatosa, WI 53226
Weber, Donald N., Brookfield Highlands #1006, 20950 George Hunt Cir., Waukesha, WI 53186
Weishar, Paul M., N110 W16973 Ashbury Cir., #6, Germantown, WI 53022
Wilbur, David F., 530 N. 103rd St., Wauwatosa, WI 53226
Witkowski, Raymond A., 3939 S. 92nd St., Greenfield, WI 53228
Wittemann, Paul J., 104 St. Franciscus St., Mount Calvary, WI 53057
Wolf, Robert J., 3501 S. Lake Dr., St. Francis, WI 53235
Wollet, George H., 10101 W. Wisconsin Ave., Wauwatosa, WI 53226
Zeihen, Joseph N., 3501 S. Lake Dr., St. Francis, WI 53235
Zens, Roger A., 2620 S. 30th St., Milwaukee, WI 53215
Zwaska, Victor L., 1201 Hughitt Ave., Box 969, Superior, WI 54880

Permanent Deacons:
Acosta, Carlos R., St. Lawrence, Milwaukee
Anderberg, Russell F. (CHI), St. Benedict, Fontana
Anderson, Dennis D., St. Anthony, Pewaukee
Aschenbrener, James L., Corpus Christi, Milwaukee
Banach, William A., Holy Spirit, Milwaukee
Beck, Lawrence E., (Retired)
Blaze, Edward, All Saints, Milwaukee
Borkowski, Donald A., St. Jude the Apostle, Wauwatosa
Brah, Eugene D., St. Elizabeth Ann Seton, New Berlin
Braun, Warren D., St. Sebastian, Milwaukee
Brousseau, Gerald A., Out of Archdiocese
Brown, Richard J., St. Rita, West Allis
Burns, John R., St. Veronica, Milwaukee
Buth, Robert H., St. Mary's, Menomonee Falls
Buyck, Gerald W., Out of Archdiocese
Castaneda, Claudio C., Leave of Absence
Cebrzynski, Stanly J., (Retired)
Cesarec, Michael E., Our Lady of Good Hope, Milwaukee
Champagne, John I., St. Benedict the Moor, Milwaukee
Christensen, Eugene M., Good Shepherd, Menomonee Falls
Coca, Emilio, St. Patrick, Racine
Colainni, Arthur R., Awaiting Assignment
Collins, Dean J., Mother of Good Counsel, Milwaukee
Corsten, Dale, Leave of Absence
Dahlen, Clarence J., (Retired)
Dallman, Arthur C., Christ King, Wauwatosa
Devona, James E., St. Mary, Racine
Doerr, George J., Out of Archdiocese
Dziennik, John R., St. Veronica, Milwaukee
Ebel, John A., St. Bernadette, Milwaukee
Fazen, Robert J., St. Matthew, Campbellsport
Ference, Dennis H., Leave of Absence
Fietz, Dennis E., Immaculate Heart of Mary, West Allis
Filipiak, Thomas P., St. Bruno, Dousman
Flynn, Richard M., Unassigned
Francois, James S., St. Mary, Kenosha
Fricano, John A., St. Aloysius, West Allis
Frye, Patrick H., St. Mark, Kenosha
Gamez, Antonio U., Leave of Absence
Gliniecki, Harry F., Unassigned
Gonzales, Jose U., St. Joseph, Wauwatosa
Gonzalez, Baleriano O., St. Clement, Sheboygan
Goodman, Robert E., Sacred Heart of Jesus, St. Francis
Govek, Richard J., St. Joseph, Grafton
Gramza, Richard G., (Retired)
Griffiths, Joseph J., Out of Archdiocese
Grimyser, Peter G., Leave of Absence
Gurzynski, Theodore A., St. Alphonsus, Greendale
Gust, Peter L., (Retired)
Guttierrez, Jose H., Holy Trinity-Guadalupe, Milwaukee
Guzman, Armindo, Out of Archdiocese
Hammond, Eugene R., (Retired)
Henry, Walter, Immaculate Heart of Mary, West Allis
Hiller, Richard D., (Retired)
Horner, Ralph E., St. Michael, St. Michael; St. John of God, Farmington
Hughes, Larry L., St. Joseph, Fond du Lac
Hughes, Wayne W., Leave of Absence
Hying, Joseph H., Personal Leave
Janasik, Ralph R., Personal Leave
Jens, William T., St. George, St. George; St. Rose of Lima, Lima
Kabara, Donald F., St. Joseph, Grafton
Kaczmarek, Raymond J., Sick Leave
Kastenholz, Joseph H., Our Lady of Good Hope, Milwaukee
Kehrer, Daniel F., St. Casimir, Kenosha
Kempka, Eugene A., St. Joseph, Waukesha
Kennedy, Claude V., Old St. Mary's, Milwaukee
Kennedy, David L., Out of Archdiocese
Klinkhammer, Phillip H., (Retired)
Koebel, Michael S., St. Frances Cabrini, West Bend
Kornburger, Ralph W., Jr., St. Catherine, Milwaukee
Kuban, Donald J. (PHX), St. Peter, East Troy
Kustner, Charles J., St. Mary, Elm Grove
La Fond, M. Larry, Jr., St. Dominic, Brookfield
Lazaga, Alfred C., Out of Archdiocese
Lebron, Gregorio, Latin Amerian Center, Kenosha and St. Mark
Leggett, A. James, St. Sylvester, South Milwaukee
Lesjak, Ronald F., St. Mary, Kenosha
Libecki, John K., (Retired)
Lo Coco, Peter L., St. John the Evangelist, Greenfield
Losiniecki, Thomas, Leave of Absence
Lukacevich, William J., St. Roman, Milwaukee
Lupo, Samuel J., St. Rita, West Allis
Lydolph, Donald J., St. Dominic, Sheboygan
Maack, Terrance A., St. Peter, Kenosha
Mahnke, Carl A., St. Thomas Aquinas, Waterford
Maier, Louis A., Jr., Out of Archdiocese
Majewski, Edward H., (Retired)
Malischke, Carl J., Leave of Absence
Malueg, Gerald D., St. Rose of Lima, Fredonia; St. Mary, Little Kohler
Mandujano, J. Eufemio, Leave of Absence
Martinez, John S., St. Vincent de Paul, Milwaukee
Martino, Anthony, St. Mary, Pell Lake
McGuine, Thomas W., St. John Neumann, Waukesha
Mensah, Anthony J., St. Martin de Porres, Milwaukee
Merten, Arthur H., (Retired)
Meyer, August M., (Retired)
Milbauer, Richard E., St. Clare, Wind Lake
Miller, Kenneth J., Sick Leave
Missureli, Russell A., St. Rose and St. Casimir, Racine
Moczydlowski, Chester A., (Retired)
Molina, Juan A., St. Rose of Lime, St. Michael, St. Francis of Assisi, Milwaukee
Monday, John P., Our Lady of Lourdes, Milwaukee
Monday, Thomas C., St. Mary, Menomonee Falls
Monzel, Paul S., Presentation, North Fond du Lac
Moser, Arnet L., (Retired)
Mueller, Arthur W., Sick Leave
Munoz, Ricardo, St. Louis, Fond du Lac
Nawrocik, Zenon L., Out of Archdiocese
Nicholas, Keith P., Leave of Absence
Normann, Larry E., St. Paul, Genesee Depot
Nowicki, Edward J., (Retired)
Ode, LeRoy, Sacred Heart of Jesus, St. Francis
Oelke, Gordon R., Leave of Absence
Pemper, Frank, Out of Archdiocese
Peterson, James J., St. Sebastian, Milwaukee
Petre, Harvey A., (Retired)
Pettey, Lawrence C., (Retired)
Piontek, Richard T., St. Mary, Elm Grove
Pollak, David R., Holy Spirit, Milwaukee
Ponec, Gerald R., Holy Family, Cudahy
Poulin, Edwin D., Leave of Absence
Przedpelski, Steven J., St. Francis Cabrini, West Bend
Regan, Sylvester R., (Retired)
Rick, Wayne W., Leave of Absence
Rodriguez, Virgilio, Out of Archdiocese
Rooney, Michael R., St. Margaret Mary, Milwaukee
Schieffer, Robert M., Our Lady of Good Hope, Milwaukee
Schimmels, Thomas J., Mother of Perpetual Help, Milwaukee
Schopper, Eugene E., Out of Archdiocese
Sherman, George, Holy Assumption, West Allis
Shierk, Wilson A., St. Mary, Kenosha
Sinden, Carroll J., Sick Leave
Spoke, Chester R., (Retired)
Surges, Thomas J., St. Peter of Alcantara, Port Washington
Thoresen, Norman, Out of Archdiocese
Treichel, Robert B., Out of Archdiocese
Truttschel, Robert A., St. Patrick, Beaver Dam
Van Garsse, Eugene E., St. Monica, Whitefish Bay
Vernon, Kenneth L., All Saints, Milwaukee
Wargin, John R., Immaculate Conception, Milwaukee
Weber, C. Edward, Leave of Absence
Wells, Randal S., St. Michael, Beaver Dam
Welnicki, John C., (Retired)
Wendt, Bernard J., St. Peter, Slinger
Wenzel, Donald P., Personal Leave
Wenzler, Joseph P., St. Cecilia, Thiensville
Widmar, Willard M., St. Paul the Apostle, Racine
Wisniewski, DeSales, O.F.M., St. Sebastian, Sturtevant
Wisniewski, Ralph, St. Leonard, Muskego
Wodushek, Robert A., St. Anthony, Menomonee Falls
Wolf, Kenneth W., (Retired)
Wuchterl, Thomas H., St. Mary, Menomonee Falls
Yang, Blong P., St. Michael (Hmong Community), Milwaukee
Zalewski, Leon J., St. Adalbert, South Milwaukee
Zimprich, David L., St. Anthony, Menomonee Falls
Zozakiewicz, Daniel T., Holy Family, Whitefish Bay

INSTITUTIONS LOCATED IN THE ARCHDIOCESE

[A] SEMINARIES, ARCHDIOCESAN

MILWAUKEE. *St. Francis Seminary*, 3257 S. Lake Dr., 53235. Tel: 414-747-6400.
E-mail: bjanczak@sfs.edu
Web site: www.sfs.edu
Very Rev. Andrew L. Nelson, S.T.L., Ph.D., Rector; Rev. Michael G. Witczak, M.Div., S.L.L., S.L.D., Vice Rector & Dir. Worship; Dr. David A. Stosur, Ph.D., Academic Dean; Rev. James T. Schuerman, Mag.Theol., Spiritual Dir.; Mr. Gary Pokorny, M.Div., Dir. Lay Formation; Dr. Nancy A. Sell, M.T.S., D.Min., Dir. Pastoral Formation; Sr. Mary Jane Wagner, S.S.S.F., M.A., Assoc. Dir. Worship; Sr. Mary Ellen Collins, O.S.F., M.A., Assoc. Dir. Worship for Music; Ms. Mary Burgett, B.S., Dir. Salzmann Library; Ms. Meredith Curtis, M.L.I.S., Technical/Public Service Librarian; Mr. Timothy Charek, M.Div., Dir. Certificate Division; Ms. Barbara V. Schauer, M.T.S., Assoc. Dir. Certificate Division; Ms. Maria Borda-Wiesner, B.A., M.A.P.S., C.N.A., Coord., Spanish-Speaking Certificate Formation Programs; Ms. DeAnn Cortez, B.A., Coord., Pastoral Form. Certificate Programs; Mr. Paul A. Hudec, M.B.A., Treas. & Business Dir.; Ms. Patricia Young, B.A., Advancement Dir.; Revs. Joseph J. Juknialis, B.A., M.A., Dir. Preaching Institute;

Stephen V. DeLeers, B.A., M.Div., M.A., D.Min; Stephen J. Lampe, S.T.D., M.A., M.Div., S.S.L.; Bryan N. Massingale, M.Div., S.T.L., S.T.D.; Melvin E. Michalski, M.Ph., Ph.L., D.Theo.; Dr. Dennis D. Sylva, Ph.D.; Dr. Barbara G. Turner, Ph.D. Administration & Faculty 23; Priests 8; Sisters 2; Lay Staff 13; Seminary Students 104.

College Formation Program, SS. Peter and Paul Residence, 2479 N. Murray Ave., 53211. Tel: 414-964-6982. Rev. Joseph J. Juknialis, Dir. Tel: 414-964-6970. Priests 1; Students 8.

Casa San Antonio, 1711 S. 9th St., 53204-3519. Tel: 414-645-1455. Rev. Lawrence V. Dulek, Dir. Casa Program. Priests 1; Students 5.

[B] SEMINARIES, RELIGIOUS OR SCHOLASTICATES

FRANKLIN. *Xaverian Missionary Fathers College Seminary*, 4500 Xavier Dr., 53132. Tel: 414-421-0831.
E-mail: xavmissionswi@juno.com
Very Rev. Vasco J. Milani, S.X.; Revs. Alfredo Turco, S.X. (Italy); Euan Garcia Jesus Robigue (Mexico); Dominic Caldognetto, S.X. (Italy). Priests 4; Religious Seminarians 3.

HALES CORNERS. *Sacred Heart School of Theology*, 7335 S. Highway 100, P.O. Box 429, 53130-0429. Tel: 414-425-8300; Fax: 414-529-6999.
E-mail: shst@msn.com
Web site: www.execpc.com/~rakirsch/SHST/SHST.html
Very Rev. James D. Brackin, S.C.J., M.Div., J.D., Pres.-Rector; Revs. Otto N. Bucher, O.F.M.Cap., S.T.L., S.S.L., Vice Rector, Dir. of Recruitment; Thomas L. Knoebel, Ph.D., Academic Dean & Dir. M.A. Programs, Dir. of Admissions; Robert Schiavone, M.A., Dir. Field Education; Peter Schuessler, S.D.S., M.A., Dir. Spiritual Formation; Ms. Margaret E. Boyles, M.E.P.D., Dir. Public Relations; Ms. Kathleen M. Harty, M.R., M.A.L.S., Dir. of Library; Mr. Richard Kirsch, M.S., Dir. Continuing Education; Ms. Sally Smits, M.B.A., Vice Pres. Finance/Personnel; Mr. Gary Talsky, Ph.B., Ph.L., Registrar & Asst. to Academic Dean; Revs. Matthias P. Cremer, S.C.J., S.T.L., Professor Emeritus; John T. O'Connor, S.C.J., J.C.L., S.T.D., Professor Emeritus; Joseph Gole, S.T.D. (Slovenia), Professor Emeritus; Sr. Martine Hundelt, S.S.S.F., Ph.D., Professor Emerita; Sr. Agnese Jasko, P.H.J.C., M.A.L.S., Professor Emerita.
Full-Time Faculty: Revs. Martin Barnum, M.A., M.Div.; Hugh G. Birdsall, S.D.S., M.A., M.S.; Vincent McNally, Ph.D. (Canada); Raul Gomez, S.D.S., M.Div., M.P.A.; Paul Grizzelle-Reid, S.C.J., M.S., M.Div.; Jerome Higgins, O.F.M.Cap., M.Ed., M.A.S.; Paul Kelly, S.C.J., M.Div., M.A.; Andre Papineau, S.D.S., M.A.; Richard Schlenker, Ph.D.; Sr. Mary C. Carroll, S.S.S.F., M.A.; Sr. Elizabeth M. Hoell, S.S.N.D., M.M., M.Chr.Sp.; Sr. Joan Koehler, S.S.S.F., M.Ed., M.A.; Sr. Christine Morkovsky, C.D.P., Ph.D.; Sr. Roseann Wagner, S.S.S.F., B.M., M.T.S.; Dr. John Gallam, Ph.D.; Dr. Richard Lux, Ph.D.; Dr. Bruce Malchow, Ph.D.; Dr. Steven Shippee, Ph.D.; Mr. C. Christian Rich, B.A., M.M.; Ms. Linda Gonzales, M.L.I.S.
Part-Time Faculty: Revs. Thomas T. Brundage, J.C.L.; Joseph N. Perry, M.Div., J.C.L.; John G. Yockey, Ph.D.; Dr. Mark Kemmeter, M.T.S., D.Min.; Ms. Glenna Gustin, B.A., M.F.A.; Ms. Mary Quirk, B.A.; Ms. Barbara Scherrer, B.A., M.S.T. Priests 18; Sisters 5; Lay Staff 18; Non-Catholic Clergymen 1; Rabbis 1; Religious Candidates 5; Diocesan Candidates 88; M.A. Candidates 21; Students 145; Total Staff 43.

MOUNT CALVARY. *St. Felix Friary*, W1754 State Hwy. 149, 53057. Tel: 414-753-3111. Novitiate House of the Capuchin Province of St. Joseph and St. Mary. Revs. Paul Koenig, O.F.M.Cap., Vocation Dir.; Michael Marigliano, O.F.M.Cap., Novitiate Team, Supr.; Kenneth R. Casper, O.F.M.Cap., Novice Dir. Priests 3; Novices 4.

St. Lawrence Seminary, 53057. Tel: 920-753-3911; Fax: 920-753-2907. High School Seminary and Ministry Program. Revs. Dennis Druggan, O.F.M.Cap., Rector & Pres.; Edwin F. Dziedziejko, O.F.M.Cap., Dean of Students; Kenan Siegel, O.F.M.Cap., Dir. Devel.; Campion Baer, O.F.M.Cap., Academic Dean; Oliver Bambenek, O.F.M.Cap., Supr.; Gary Wegner, O.F.M.Cap.; Randall Knauf, O.F.M.Cap.; Elroy Pesch, O.F.M.Cap.; Bros. Douglas Bode, O.F.M.Cap.; John Freienstein, O.F.M.Cap.; Dismas Seward, O.F.M.Cap.; Neal Plale, O.F.M.Cap.; Carl Schaefer, O.F.M.Cap.; John Willger, O.F.M.Cap.; Larry Groeschel, O.F.M.Cap.; Jerome Campbell, O.F.M.Cap.; John Scherer, O.F.M.Cap.; Mr. Harlan Swift, Business Mgr.; Mr. Kenneth Holehouse, Guidance Dir. Priests 8; Brothers 9; Sisters 1; Lay Teachers 12; Students 212; Total Staff 32.

[C] COLLEGES AND UNIVERSITIES

MILWAUKEE. *Alverno College*, 3401 S. 39th St., P.O. Box 343922, 53234-3922. Tel: 414-382-6000; Fax: 414-362-6354
For a complete listing, refer to the Colleges and Universities section.

Cardinal Stritch University, 6801 N. Yates Rd., 53217. Tel: 414-352-5400.
Web site: www.ocs.stritch.edu
For a complete listing, refer to the Colleges and Universities section.

**Marquette University*, P.O. Box 1881, 53201-1881. Tel: 414-288-7250.
Web site: www.mu.edu
For a complete listing, refer to the Colleges and Universities section.

Mount Mary College, 2900 N. Menomonee River Pkwy., 53222-4545. Tel: 414-258-4810.
Web site: www.mtmary.edu
For a complete listing, refer to the Colleges and Universities section.

FOND DU LAC. *Marian College of Fond du Lac*, 45 S. National Ave., 54935. Tel: 414-923-7600
For a complete listing, refer to the Colleges and Universities section.

[D] HIGH SCHOOLS, ARCHDIOCESAN AND PAROCHIAL

MILWAUKEE. *Pius XI High School*, 135 N. 76th St., 53213. Tel: 414-290-7000; Fax: 414-290-7001.
E-mail: piusxi@execpc.com
Revs. Robert V. Carney, S.A.C.; Richard J. Gunderman, S.A.C.; Anthony S. Zimmer, Chap. School Sisters of St. Francis 6; Sisters of Mercy 2; Lay Teachers 81; Students 1,580.

Thomas More High School, 2601 E. Morgan Ave., 53207. Tel: 414-481-8370; Fax: 414-481-3382. (Coed). Mr. Joel Eul, Prin. Sisters 2; Lay Teachers 34; Students 735; Total Staff 53.

BURLINGTON. *Catholic Central High School*, 148 McHenry St., 53105. Tel: 414-763-1510. Mr. Kenneth D. Kortens, M.Ed., Prin.; Rev. Lawrence J. Chapman, Chap. Priests 1; Sisters 1; Lay Teachers 14; Students 230.

FOND DU LAC. *St. Mary's Springs High School*, 255 County Rd. K, 54935. Tel: 920-921-4870. Thomas J. Borek, Prin. Sisters 1; Lay Teachers 18; Students 350; Total Staff 19.

KENOSHA. *St. Joseph High School*, 2401 69th St., 53143. Tel: 414-654-8651. Mr. Rick J. Ruhl, Prin. Sisters 2; Lay Teachers 20; Students 412; Total Staff 22.

WAUKESHA. *Catholic Memorial High School*, 601 E. College Ave., 53186. Tel: 414-542-7101; Fax: 414-542-1633. Mr. Paul Stauffacher, Pres. & Prin.; Rev. Frank Malloy, Chap. Franciscan Sisters of Christian Charity 7; Priests 1; Lay Teachers 59; Students 1,002; Total Staff 88.

[E] HIGH SCHOOLS, PRIVATE

MILWAUKEE. *Divine Savior Holy Angels High School*. (Girls). 4257 N. 100th St., 53222. Tel: 414-466-3706; Fax: 414-466-4778.
E-mail: dsha@dsha.k12.wi.us
Web site: www.dsha.k12.wi.us
Sponsored by the Sisters of the Divine Savior. Sr. Virginia Honish, S.D.S., Prin.; Rev. Jerome G. Herda. Priests 1; Sisters 3; Lay Teachers 42; Students 529; Total Staff 69.

Marquette University High School. (Boys). 3401 W. Wisconsin Ave., 53208. Tel: 414-933-7220.
Web site: www.muhs.edu
(See separate listing for resident information). Revs. Douglas J. Leonhardt, S.J., Pres.; John M. Belmonte, S.J.; Terrence M. Brennan, S.J.; Thomas M. Doyle, S.J.; Michael R. Kolb, S.J.; Charles L. Stang, S.J.; Edward G. Witt, S.J. Priests 7; Scholastics 2; Lay Teachers 55; Students 960; Total Staff 64.

St. Joan Antida High School, Inc. (Girls). 1341 N. Cass St., 53202. Tel: 414-272-8423; Fax: 414-272-3135. Sr. Monica Fumo, S.C.S.J.A., Prin. Sisters of Charity of St. Joan Antida 6; Lay Teachers 26; Students 415; Total Staff 42.

RACINE. *St. Catherine's High School*, 1200 Park Ave., 53403. Tel: 414-632-2785; Fax: 414-632-5144. Ms. Marilyn J. McGoldrick, Prin.; Sr. Jane Weiss, Asst. Prin.; Rev. Russell G. Roetzer. Dominican Sisters (Racine) 4; Lay Teachers 42; Students 631.

WHITEFISH BAY. *Dominican High School*, 120 E. Silver Spring Dr., 53217. Tel: 414-332-1170. Sponsored by Sinsinawa Dominicans. Paul M. McInerny, Ph.D., Pres.; Michael Maguire, Prin.; Judy Down, Assoc. Prin.; Sr. Margaret Ann Brennan, O.P., Chm. Religion Dept. Dominican Sisters of the Congregation of the Most Holy Rosary, Sinsinawa, WI 2; Lay Teachers 35; Students 466.

[F] ELEMENTARY SCHOOLS, ARCHDIOCESAN

MILWAUKEE. *St. Leo School, Inc.* St. Leo Catholic Urban Academy, 2458 W. Locust St., 53209. Tel: 414-442-1100. Sponsored and accredited by the Archdiocese of Milwaukee. Sisters 1; Lay Teachers 11; Students 210; Total Staff 13.

St. Rose Catholic Urban Academy, 514 N. 31st St., 53208. Tel: 414-933-6070. Sponsored and accredited by the Archdiocese of Milwaukee. Sisters 1; Lay Teachers 15; Students 240; Total Staff 20.

[G] ELEMENTARY SCHOOLS, PRIVATE

MILWAUKEE. *Nativity Jesuit Middle School, Inc.* (Boys). 1115 S. Seventh St., 53204. Tel: 414-645-1060.
E-mail: nativity@marquette.edu
Web site: www.homeboyz.com/nativity
Wisconsin Province of the Society of Jesus. Rev. William T. Johnson, S.J., Pres.; Mr. Lawrence H. Siewert, Prin. Priests 1; Sisters 1; Lay Teachers 8; Students 49; Total Staff 11.

Notre Dame Middle School, Inc., 1420 W. Scott St., 53204. Tel: 414-671-3000.
E-mail: akilkelly@aol.com
Sr. Ann Kilkelly, S.S.N.D., Admin.; Sr. Lucille Conghlin, S.S.N.D., Prin. Sisters 4; Lay Teachers 2; Volunteers 2; Students 43. Sponsored by: School Sisters of Notre Dame. Purpose: To educate at-risk girls for college preparatory high schools and for community service and leadership.

St. Coletta Day School of Milwaukee, 1740 N. 55th St., 53208. Tel: 414-453-1850. For Exceptional Children. William A. Koehn, Prin. & Admin. Lay Teachers 2; Students 12.

[H] CONSOLIDATED ELEMENTARY SCHOOLS

MILWAUKEE. *All Saints Catholic East School System, Inc.*, 1716 N. Humboldt Ave., 53202. Tel: 414-276-9814. Sponsored by the following Milwaukee parishes: Cathedral of St. John the Evangelist; St. Casimir; St. Hedwig; Holy Rosary; Old St. Mary's; St. Mary Czestochowa; Ss. Peter and Paul; St. Rita. Rev. John H. Endejan, Chm., Pastor Liaison. Students 221.

Catholic East Elementary. (Grades K-8), 2461 N. Murray Ave., 53211. Tel: 414-964-1770. Members: St. Hedwig, SS. Peter and Paul, St. Mary of Czestochowa, Old St. Mary, Holy Rosary, St. Casimir, Cathedral of St. John the Evangelist. Mr. Christopher Montezon, Prin. Sisters 2; Lay Teachers 11; Students 223.

Resurrection Catholic Academy, 5135 N. 54th St., 53218. Tel: 414-438-2745; Fax: 414-438-2990. Thomas Hage, Prin.; Judy Rivas, Asst. Prin. Sisters 2; Lay Teachers 12; Students 247. Members: St. Stephen Martyr and Mother of Perpetual Help, Milwaukee.

BEAVER DAM. *Unified Catholic Parish Schools of Beaver Dam*, 503 S. Spring St., 53916-2598. Tel: 920-885-5558; Fax: 920-885-5510. Barbara M. Haase, Prin. Lay Teachers 23; Students 333. Members: St. Michael, St. Patrick, St. Peter.

FOND DU LAC. *Fond du Lac Area Catholic Education System (FACES)*, 706 Minnesota Ave., 54937. Tel: 414-924-0993.
E-mail: srgolias@thesurf.com
Members: St. Joseph; St. Louis; St. Mary; St. Patrick; Sacred Heart; Presentation of the Blessed Virgin, North Fond du Lac. Sr. Deborah Golias, C.S.A., Ph.D., System Admin.

Faces Primary Campus, 95 E. Second St., 54935. Tel: 414-923-5300. Sr. Colleen Walsh, Coord. Lay Teachers 14; Students 282.

Faces Middle School Campus, 63 E. Merrill St., 54935. Tel: 414-921-9610. Mrs. Susan Zacherl, Coord. Lay Teachers 14; Students 214.

Faces Intermediate Campus, 37 E. Follett St., 54935. Tel: 414-921-6710. Mrs. Jane McGovern, Coord. Lay Teachers 10; Students 208.

LOMIRA. *Consolidated Catholic School, Lomira-Theresa*, 705 Milwaukee St., 53048-9520. Tel: 920-269-4326. Sr. Rosemary Herriges, O.S.F., Prin. Sisters 1; Lay Teachers 8; Students 119. Members: St. Mary, Lomira; St. Theresa, Theresa.

MEQUON. *Ss. Cecilia and James School*, 11300 N. St. James Ln., #28 W, 53092. Mr. Richard Goeden, Prin., St. Cecilia Campus: (Grades K-3), 116 W. Orchard St., Thiensville, 53092. Tel: 414-242-7965. St. James Campus: (Grades 4-8), 11300 N. St. James Ln., 53092. Tel: 414-242-7960. Members: St. Cecilia, Thiensville; St. James, Mequon. Lay Teachers 28; Students 510.

MOUNT CALVARY. *Consolidated Parochial Elementary School*, 100 Notre Dame St., 53057. Tel: 920-753-4811. Sr. Alicia Collins, Prin. Sisters 2; Lay Teachers 16; Students 230. Members: St. John the Baptist, Johnsburg; St. Mary, Marytown; Holy Cross, Mount Calvary; St. Cloud, St. Cloud.

SOUTH MILWAUKEE. *Holy Cross School.* (Catholic Centennial School System), 805 Marquette Ave., 53172. Tel: 414-762-4670. Carol J. Makholm, Prin. Lay Teachers 15; Students 135. Members: St. John, St. Mary.

WAUKESHA. *Waukesha Catholic School System, Inc.*, 440 N. Moreland Blvd., 53188. Rev. Glen G. Graczyk, Pastor Liaison. Tel: 414-549-0223. Members: St. Joseph, St. Mary, St. John Neumann, St. William.

St. Joseph Campus, 822 N. East Ave., 53186. Tel: 414-896-2930. Patricia McGrane, Prin. Sisters 4; Lay Teachers 13; Students 251.

St. Mary Campus, 520 N. Newhall Ave., 53186. Tel: 414-896-2932. Sr. Kathleen Swain, O.S.F., Prin. Sisters 3; Lay Teachers 15; Students 354.

St. William Campus, 444 N. Moreland Blvd., 53188. Tel: 414-896-2920. Sr. Toni Gradisnik, O.S.F., Prin. Sisters 1; Lay Teachers 11; Students 193.

[I] SPECIAL SCHOOLS

WEST ALLIS. *Holy Assumption School for the Blind*, 1526 S. 72nd St., 53214. Tel: 414-774-8783. Sr. Melmarie Stoll, S.S.N.D., Dir. School Sisters of Notre Dame 1; Lay Teachers 1; Students 5.

[J] CHILD CARE CENTERS

MILWAUKEE. *Guardian Angel Learning Center, Inc.*, 1540 N. Jefferson, 53202. Tel: 414-277-9474; Fax: 414-277-9482. Sisters of Charity of St. Joan Antida. Sr. Marie Louise Balistrieri, S.C.S.J.A., Admin. Sisters of Charity of St. Joan Antida 1; Lay Teachers 22; Students 101. The center is licensed for ages 6 weeks to 11 years with a school age program.

Seton Children's School, Inc., 8677 N. Port Washington Rd., 53217. Tel: 414-352-6115. Operated by the Daughters of Charity of St. Vincent de Paul. A licensed center for comprehensive early childhood educational programs and day care. Children 187. Other Locations: 2330 N. Prospect Ave., 53211. Tel: 414-220-8494. Children 115. 13133 N. Port Washington Rd., Mequon, 53097. Tel: 414-243-7318. Children 57.

South Day Care Center of St. Joseph, 3249 S. 18th St., 53215. Tel: 414-645-5337. Sr. M. Carolita Turzin, C.S.S.F., Admin. Felician Sisters 10; Lay Teachers 26; Children 610; Total Staff 48.

SOUTH MILWAUKEE. *Franciscan Villa Child Day Care Center*, 3601 S. Chicago Ave., 53172. Tel: 414-764-4100. Judy Greene, Supervisor. Lay Teachers 5; Children 50. Affiliate of Catholic Health Initiatives.

WAUWATOSA. *Carmelite Home, Inc.*, 1214 Kavanaugh Pl., 53213. Tel: 414-258-4791. Residential Treatment Center for Adolescent Boys. Sr. M. Regina, Admin.; James E. Lewis, Treatment Dir. Residents 40; Lay Teachers 4.

WEST ALLIS. *St. Joan Antida Day Care Center, Inc.*, 6640 W. Beloit Rd., 53219. Tel: 414-541-6575; 541-9840; Fax: 414-541-8040. Day Care for children ages 3-5. Sr. Maria Augustine Giannini, S.C.S.J.A., Admin. Sisters of Charity of St. Joan Antida 3; Lay Teachers 4; Children 76.

[K] GENERAL HOSPITALS

MILWAUKEE. *St. Francis Hospital*, 3237 S. 16th St., 53215. Tel: 414-647-5000
For a complete listing, refer to the Hospitals section.

St. Joseph's Hospital of Franciscan Sisters, Milwaukee, Inc., 5000 W. Chambers St., 53210. Tel: 414-447-2000
For a complete listing, refer to the Hospitals section.

St. Mary's Hospital of Milwaukee, 2323 N. Lake Dr., P.O. Box 503, 53201-0503. Tel: 414-291-1000; Fax: 414-291-1444
For a complete listing, refer to the Hospitals section.

St. Michael Hospital of Franciscan Sisters of Milwaukee, Inc., 2400 W. Villard Ave., 53209. Tel: 414-527-8000
For a complete listing, refer to the Hospitals section.

BROOKFIELD. *Elmbrook Memorial Hospital, Inc.*, 19333 W. North Ave., 53045. Tel: 414-785-2000
For a complete listing, refer to the Hospitals section.

FOND DU LAC. *Agnesian HealthCare, Inc.*, 430 E. Division St., 54935. Tel: 414-929-2300; Fax: 414-929-1866
For a complete listing, refer to the Hospitals section.

KENOSHA. *St. Catherine's Hospital*, 3556 Seventh Ave., 53140. Tel: 414-656-3011
For a complete listing, refer to the Hospitals section.

MEQUON. *St. Mary's Hospital Ozaukee, Inc.*, 13111 N. Port Washington Rd., 53097. Tel: 414-243-7300; 800-848-2844; Fax: 414-243-7416
For a complete listing, refer to the Hospitals section.

RACINE. *St. Mary's Medical Center, Inc.*, 3801 Spring St., 53405. Tel: 414-636-4011; Fax: 414-636-4540
For a complete listing, refer to the Hospitals section.

SHEBOYGAN. *St. Nicholas Hospital*, 1601 N. Taylor Dr., 53081. Tel: 920-459-8300
For a complete listing, refer to the Hospitals section.

WAUPUN. *Waupun Memorial Hospital*, 53963. Tel: 414-324-5581
For a complete listing, refer to the Hospitals section.

[L] SPECIAL HOSPITALS AND SANATORIA

MILWAUKEE. *Sacred Heart Rehabilitation Institute, Inc.*, 2350 N. Lake Dr., 53211. Tel: 414-298-6700
For a complete listing, refer to the Special Care Facilities section.

[M] PROTECTIVE INSTITUTIONS

MILWAUKEE. *Daystar, Inc.*, P.O. Box 11709, 53217. Tel: 414-228-8887
For a complete listing, refer to the Special Care Facilities section.

Rosalie Manor, Inc., 4803 W. Burleigh St., 53210. Tel: 414-449-2868.
E-mail: rosaliemanor@aeronet
For a complete listing, refer to the Special Care Facilities section.

St. Charles Youth and Family Services, 151 S. 84th St., P.O. Box 14005, 53214. Tel: 414-476-3710.
E-mail: jamesms@aol.com
For a complete listing, refer to the Special Care Facilities section.

MOUNT CALVARY. *Cristo Rey Ranch, Inc.*, N8102 Calvary St., 53057. Tel: 920-753-2026; 753-3211; Fax: 920-753-3100
For a complete listing, refer to the Special Care Facilities section.

[N] HOMES FOR AGED AND NURSING HOMES

MILWAUKEE. *Adult Day Services and Resource Center*, 1919 N. 60th St., 53208. Tel: 414-464-8004
For a complete listing, refer to the Special Care Facilities section.

Alexian Village of Milwaukee, Inc., 9301 N. 76th St., 53223. Tel: 414-355-9300
For a complete listing, refer to the Special Care Facilities section.

Marian Catholic Center, Inc., 3333 W. Highland Blvd., 53208. Tel: 414-344-8100
For a complete listing, refer to the Special Care Facilities section.

Marian Franciscan Center, Inc., 9632 W. Appleton Ave., 53225. Tel: 414-461-8850
For a complete listing, refer to the Special Care Facilities section.

**Milwaukee Catholic Home*, 2462 N. Prospect Ave., 53211-4462. Tel: 414-224-9700
For a complete listing, refer to the Special Care Facilities section.

St. Ann Rest Home, 2020 S. Muskego Ave., 53204. Tel: 414-383-2630
For a complete listing, refer to the Special Care Facilities section.

St. Anne's Home for the Elderly, 3800 N. 92nd St., 53222. Tel: 414-463-7570; Fax: 414-463-2311.
E-mail: mah@execpc.com
Web site: www.wahsa.org/st.anne/index.html
For a complete listing, refer to the Special Care Facilities section.

St. Mary's Nursing Home, 3515 W. Hadley St., 53210. Tel: 414-873-9250; Fax: 414-873-6876
For a complete listing, refer to the Special Care Facilities section.

The Terrace at St. Francis, Inc., 3200 S. 20th St., 53215 Fax: 414-389-3300
For a complete listing, refer to the Special Care Facilities section.

Villa St. Francis, Inc., 1910 W. Ohio Ave., 53215 Fax: 414-649-2880
For a complete listing, refer to the Special Care Facilities section.

FOND DU LAC. *St. Francis Home for Aged*, 365 Gillett St., 54935. Tel: 920-923-7980; Fax: 920-923-7995
For a complete listing, refer to the Special Care Facilities section.

GREENFIELD. *Clement Manor Health Center*, 3939 S. 92nd St., 53228. Tel: 414-321-1800
For a complete listing, refer to the Special Care Facilities section.

Clement Manor Retirement Community, 9339-9405 W. Howard Ave., 53228. Tel: 414-546-7375
For a complete listing, refer to the Special Care Facilities section.

KENOSHA. *St. Joseph's Adult Day Care Center, Inc.*, 9244 29th Ave., 53144. Tel: 414-694-6000
For a complete listing, refer to the Special Care Facilities section.

St. Joseph's Home for the Aged, 9244 29th Ave., 53143. Tel: 414-694-0080.
E-mail: apanites@ix.netcom.com
For a complete listing, refer to the Special Care Facilities section.

LOMIRA. *Hope Nursing Home, Inc.*, 438 Ashford Ave., P.O. Box 280, 53048-0280. Tel: 414-269-4386; Fax: 414-269-4616
For a complete listing, refer to the Special Care Facilities section.

MOUNT CALVARY. *Villa Loretto Nursing Home*, N8114 Calvary St., 53057. Tel: 920-753-3211; Fax: 920-753-3100.
E-mail: sister@thesurf.com
For a complete listing, refer to the Special Care Facilities section.

RACINE. *Marian Housing Center, Inc*, 4105 Spring St., 53405. Tel: 414-633-5807
For a complete listing, refer to the Special Care Facilities section.

St. Monica's Senior Citizens Home, Inc., 3920 N. Green Bay Rd., 53404. Tel: 414-639-5050
For a complete listing, refer to the Special Care Facilities section.

ST. FRANCIS. *Canticle Court, Inc.*, 3201 S. Lake Dr., 53235. Tel: 414-744-9959; Fax: 414-744-7636.
E-mail: junipe29@mail.idt.net
For a complete listing, refer to the Special Care Facilities section.

Juniper Court, Inc., 3209 S. Lake Dr., 53235-3702. Tel: 414-744-5878; Fax: 414-744-7636.
E-mail: junipe29@mail.idt.net
For a complete listing, refer to the Special Care Facilities section.

St. Ann Center for Intergenerational Care, Inc., 3221 S. Lake Dr., 53235. Tel: 414-482-1340; Fax: 414-482-9351
For a complete listing, refer to the Special Care Facilities section.

SOUTH MILWAUKEE. *Franciscan Villa of South Milwaukee, Inc.*, 3601 S. Chicago Ave., 53172. Tel: 414-764-4100
For a complete listing, refer to the Special Care Facilities section.

WAUWATOSA. *St. Camillus Health Center, Inc.*, 10101 W. Wisconsin Ave., 53226. Tel: 414-258-1814
For a complete listing, refer to the Special Care Facilities section.

San Camillo, Inc., 10200 W. Bluemound Rd., 53226. Tel: 414-259-6300
For a complete listing, refer to the Special Care Facilities section.

WEST ALLIS. *St. Joan Antida Home, Inc.*, 6700 W. Beloit Rd., 53219. Tel: 414-541-6575; 541-9840; Fax: 414-541-8040
For a complete listing, refer to the Special Care Facilities section.

Villa Clement Health Center, 9047 W. Greenfield Ave., 53214. Tel: 414-453-9290
For a complete listing, refer to the Special Care Facilities section.

[O] PERSONAL PRELATURES

BROOKFIELD. *Opus Dei-Prelature of the Holy Cross and Opus Dei.*, 12900 W. North Ave., 53005. Tel: 414-784-1523.
E-mail: laytonsc@execpc.com
Layton Study Center for men. Revs. Robert P. Bucciarelli; John C. Kubeck.

[P] MONASTERIES AND RESIDENCES FOR PRIESTS AND BROTHERS

MILWAUKEE. *Alexian Brothers Community*. Immaculate Conception Province, 7979 W. Glenbrook Rd., 53223. Tel: 414-355-9300. Bros. Anthony Ragucci, C.F.A., Dir.; Robert Peterson, C.F.A.; Theodore Loucks, C.F.A. Brothers 3.

Arrupe House Jesuit Community, 831 N. 13th St., 53233. Tel: 414-274-7460. Society of Jesus, Wisconsin Province. Revs. John L. Treloar, S.J., Supr.; Thomas N. Brennan, S.J.; Eugene M. Dutkiewicz, S.J.; Peter J. Etzel, S.J.; Michael A. Fahey, S.J.; J. Robert Hilbert, S.J.; D. Thomas Hughson, S.J.; Lawrence D. Kelly, S.J.; Michael R. Kolb, S.J.; Michael G. Lee, S.J.; Philip J. Rossi, S.J.; Charles L. Stang, S.J. Priests 12.

Francis and Clare House, 1648 S. 37th St., 53215-1724. Tel: 414-383-7934. Revs. Eliot Bacia, O.F.M.; Stephen Malkiewicz, O.F.M.; Jerome Zawada, O.F.M.; Cantius J. Kobak, O.F.M.; Roch Niemier, O.F.M.; Hugh Zurat, O.F.M. Priests 6.

Jesuit Community at Marquette University, 1404 W. Wisconsin Ave., 53233. Tel: 414-288-5000. Marquette Jesuit Associates, Inc. Very Rev. Eugene F. Merz, S.J., Rector; Revs. Robert W. Leiweke, S.J., Asst. Rector; Thomas A. Caldwell, S.J., Min.; Richard P. Abert, S.J.; Richard H. Ahler, S.J.; Frank A. Arcuri, S.J.; Francis Xavier Baskara Tulus Wardaya, S.J. (Indonesia); Charles R. Baumann, S.J.; Ronald R. Bieganowski, S.J.; Thaddeus J. Burch, S.J.; Patrick J. Burns, S.J.; Michael D. Class, S.J.; John P. Donnelly, S.J.; William E. Dooley, S.J.; Patrick J. Dorsey, S.J.; James M. Ewens, S.J.; James E. Fitzgerald, S.J.; Grant S. Garinger, S.J.; Raymond T. Gawronski, S.J.; James E. Grummer, S.J.; Mr. James D. Holub, S.J.; Revs. Robert J. Joda, S.J.; William T. Johnson, S.J.; William J. Kelly, S.J.; William J. Kidd, S.J.; James M. Kubicki, S.J.; Cyprianus Kuntoro Adi, S.J. (Indonesia); Michael D. Kurimay, S.J.; William S. Kurz, S.J.; Robert W. Lambeck, S.J.; Wendell E. Langley,

S.J.; John D. Laurance, S.J.; Jeffrey R. Loebl, S.J.; Frank A. Majka, S.J.; Albert William Manuel (Madurai); D. Edward Mathie, S.J.; Donald R. Matthys, S.J.; James E. Mauel, S.J.; Richard A. McGarrity, S.J.; T. Michael McNulty, S.J.; Charles J. Mehok, S.J.; Alexius Minj, S.J. (Darjeeling); John E. Naus, S.J.; Mr. Gregory J. O'Meara, S.J.; Revs. Francis Paul Prucha, S.J.; Robert F. Purcell, S.J.; Charles Isaac Puthota, S.J. (Andhra); Gregory A. Schissel, S.J.; Mount Joseph Selvan, S.J. (Madurai); Richard F. Sherburne, S.J.; David M. Shields, S.J.; Walter J. Stohrer, S.J.; Reginald J. Tauro, S.J. (Bombay); Roland J. Teske, S.J.; Joachim Thainese, S.J. (Andhra); Andrew J. Thon, S.J.; George Sebastian Vallocheril (Kerala); William A. Van Roo, S.J.; Kenneth T. Walleman, S.J.; Robert A. Wild, S.J.; Edward Yarnold, S.J. (Britain); Michael J. Zeps, S.J. Priests 61; Scholastics 1.

Jesuit Provincial Office, Wisconsin Province, P.O. Box 08277, 53208-0277. Tel: 414-937-6949; Fax: 414-937-6950.
E-mail: wisprov@vms.csd.mu.edu
Web site: www.mu.edu/dept/wip/wisprov.html
Very Rev. D. Edward Mathie, S.J., Prov. and Coord. for Higher Education; Revs. James E. Grummer, S.J., Asst. Prov., Asst. Intl. Ministries & Coord. Province Planning & Communication; James M. Kubicki, S.J., Asst. for Formation; Eugene M. Dutkiewicz, S.J., Asst. for Finance; J. Robert Hilbert, S.J., Asst. for Pastoral and Retreat Min.; Warren J. Sazama, S.J., Dir. of Devel. Priests 6.
Corporate Title: Wisconsin Province of the Society of Jesus.
Priests of the Province Serving Abroad: Rev. Robert L. Faricy, S.J., Gregoriana University, Piazza della Pilotta 4, Rome, Italy, 00187. Revs. Frederick E. Brenk, S.J.; Donald F. Rauscher, S.J.; Robert G. North, S.J., Via della Pilotta 25., Rome, Italy, 00187. Rev. John P. Egan, S.J., Regis College, 15 St. Mary St., Toronto, Canada, M4Y 2R5. Rev. Eugene C. Kollasch, S.J., Sogang University Jesuit Residence, CPO Box 1142, Seoul, Korea, 100-611. Rev. John D. Mace, S.J., Arrupe International Residence, P.O. Box 216, U.P. Campus, 1144 Quezon City, Philippines. Rev. Francis E. Hogan, S.J., (Yoro), Iglesia El Carmen, El Negrito, Honduras. Rev. Philip E. Pick, S.J., Casa Cural, Yoro, Honduras, 23101. Rev. Nicholas E. Schiel, S.J., AP 676, Tegucigalpa, Honduras. Rev. John R. Schak, S.J., Iglesia San Jose Obrero, J. Larrea 1161, Salta Ciudad, Argentina, 4440. Rev. Robert P. Raszkowski, S.J., St. John's College, Landivar, P.O. Box 548, Belize City, Belize. Rev. Francis J. Ring, S.J., Box 25, Punta Gorda, Belize. Revs. Anthony J. Wach, S.J.; William J. Callahan, S.J., P.O. Box 7300, Kampala, Uganda. Rev. Jonathan Haschka, S.J., P.O. Box 21399, Nairobi, Kenya. Rev. Robert W. Dundon, S.J., P.O. Box MP 320, Harrare, Zimbabwe. Rev. Charles C. Murphy, S.J., P.O. Box 21399, Nairobi, Kenya. Rev. Daniel J. Kenney, S.J., Holy Family Minor Basilica, P.O. Box 40891, Nairobi, Kenya.
Priests of the Province Not Otherwise Listed: Rev. Joseph A. Brown, S.J., Southern Illinois University, Black American Studies Dept., Mail Code 4529, Carbondale, IL, 62901-4529. Rev. Thomas P. Sweetser, S.J., 4849 W. Hutchinson, Chicago, IL, 60641. Rev. James F. Hanley, S.J., 5110 S. 49th St., Apt. 609, Omaha, NE, 68117. Rev. Joseph F. Eagan, S.J., St. Patrick's Parish, 114 King St., Larkspur, CA, 94939. Rev. William R. Duffey, S.J., 9455 Watertown Plank Rd., 53226. Rev. William M. Kegel, S.J., 30 Mandalay Rd., Oakland, CA, 94618. Rev. Edward J. McCarthy, S.J., 1320 Padre Dr., Salinas, CA, 93901. Rev. John E. Bernbrock, S.J., Our Lady of Perpetual Help, 7655 Main St., Scottsdale, AZ, 85252. Rev. Oscar L. Benzinger, S.J., Presentation Heights, 1500 N. Main, Aberdeen, SD, 57401. Rev. William J. Mehok, S.J., 5320 12th St. S., Apt. 218E, Fargo, ND, 58104. Rev. George A. Maloney, S.J., St. Patrick Novitiate, 7820 Bolsa Ave., Midway City, CA, 92655. Rev. Cletus H. Pfab, S.J., 1325 N. Jefferson, #814, 53202-2614. Rev. Paul B. Steinmetz, S.J., Santa Maria Church, 20 Santa Maria Way, Orinda, CA, 94563-2677. Rev. Lawrence A. Jonas, S.J., St. Dominic's Parish, 800 E. Walnut, Canton, SD, 57013. Rev. Hubert G. Boschert, S.J., St. Joseph Church, 512 Elm St., Owatonna, MN, 55060. Rev. Benno G. Kornely, S.J., Manresa Jesuit Retreat House, 1390 Quarton Rd., Bloomfield Hills, MI, 48304-3554. Rev. Richard A. Tomasek, S.J., Pontifical College Josephinum, 7625 N. High St., Columbus, OH, 43225-1498. Rev. William J. Ellos, S.J., 7626 Callaghan, Apt. 2201, San Antonio, TX, 78229-2722. Rev. James L. Empereur, S.J., Cathedral of San Fernando, 115 Main Plaza, San Antonio, TX, 78205-2787. Rev. Theodore M. Kalamaja, S.J., Loyola University, 6363 St. Charles Ave., New Orleans, LA, 70118-6195. Rev. James T. Bretzke, S.J., 2535 LeConte Ave., Berkeley, CA, 94709-1133. Rev. Theodore F. Zuern, S.J., Leonard Neale House, 1726 New Hampshire Ave., NW, Washington, DC, 20009-2526. Rev. James M. Radde, S.J., Georgetown Court, #211, 5820 E. River Rd., Minneapolis, MN, 55432. Rev. Richard C. Burbach, S.J., Leonard Neale House, 1726 New Hampshire Ave., N.W., Washington, DC, 20009-2526. Rev. Daniel C. McDonald, S.J., Leonard Neale House, 1726 New Hampshire Ave., Washington, DC, 20009-2526. Rev. James E. Hug, S.J., Center of Concern, 320 K. St., N.W., Washington, DC, 20002-3522. Rev. Eugene F. Shaw, S.J., Loyola Center, St. Joseph's University, 5600 City Ave., Philadelphia, PA, 19131-1395. Rev. John E. Blewett, S.J., Jesuit Hall, 3601 Lindell Blvd., St. Louis, MO, 63108-3393. Rev. Leon S. Rausch, S.J., P.O. Box 36, Gays Mills, 54631. Rev. James P. Scull, S.J., 120 Retreat Ave., Apt. A4, Hartford, CT, 06106-2539. Rev. John H. Rainaldo, S.J., Apostleship of Prayer, 3 Stephen Ave., New Hyde Park, NY, 11040. Rev. John F. Snyder, S.J., Jesuit Hall, 3601 Lindell Blvd., St. Louis, MO, 63108-3393. Rev. Timothy J. Howard, S.J., 5808 N. Placita Esplendora, Tucson, AZ, 85718. Rev. James E. O'Hearn, S.J., 4530 58th Ave. N. Apt. 330, Brooklyn Center, MN, 55429. Rev. Charles J. Scherman, S.J., 412 S. Main St., Chippewa Falls, 54729. Rev. J. Roger Lucey, S.J., Santa Maria Parish, 20 Santa Maria Way, Orinda, CA, 94563-2677. Rev. Kevin T. Fitzgerald, S.J., Zeitler Jesuit Community, 315 N. Grove Ave., Oak Park, IL, 60302-2023. Rev. Patrick L. Murphy, S.J., Epiphany Church, Rte. 10, Box 161-B, Lake City, FL, 32025. Rev. George R. Sullivan, S.J., 5322 Franklin Ave., Los Angeles, CA, 90027. Rev. Ned H. Cassem, S.J., Campion Center, 319 Concord Rd., Weston, MA, 02193-1310. Rev. Edward V. Vacek, S.J., Hopkins House, 40 Kirkland St., Cambridge, MA, 02138-2031.
Priests of the Province Engaged in Higher Studies: Rev. George W. Drance, S.J., Notre Dame Parish, 405 W. 114th St., New York, NY, 10025. Rev. Thomas P. Sherman, S.J., University of Toronto, 94 Kendal Ave., Toronto, Ontario, Canada, M5R 1L9. Rev. James P. Flaherty, S.J., Xavier High School Jesuit Community, 30 W. 16th St., New York, NY, 10011-6302. Rev. Stephen R. Schloesser, S.J., Nobili Hall, Santa Clara University, Santa Clara, CA, 95053. Rev. Timothy R. Lannon, S.J., 6 Sumner Rd., Cambridge, MA, 02138-3015. Rev. John F. Montag, S.J., St. Edmund's College, Cambridge, United Kingdom, CB3 OBN. Rev. Thomas J. Hansen, S.J., Jesuit Community, Creighton University, 2500 California Plaza, Omaha, NE, 68178-0522. Rev. Thomas D. Stegman, S.J., Immaculate Heart of Mary Rectory, 2855 Briarcliff Rd., N.E., Atlanta, GA, 30329.

La Salette Fathers. Missionaries of Our Lady of La Salette. 1607 E. Howard Ave., 53207. Tel: 414-769-7113. Revs. Frances Kula, M.S.; Anthony Dudek, M.S.; James Winiarski, M.S.; Bro. Gerald Buraczewski, M.S. Priests 4; Brothers 1; Total in Residence 5.

Pallotti House, 5424 W. Bluemound Rd., 53208. Tel: 414-258-0653; 259-0688 (Provincial Offices). Residence of Fathers and Brothers and Offices of Mother of God Province of the Society of the Catholic Apostolate. Very Rev. Robert V. Carney, S.A.C., Prov. Supr.; Revs. Jerome A. Hapka, S.A.C.; Leon J. Martin, S.A.C.; William E. Lemanski, S.A.C.; Eugene H. Jarosch, S.A.C.; Richard J. Lorenz, S.A.C.; Richard F. Storch, S.A.C.; Bruce J. Schute, S.A.C.; Paul Coutinha, S.A.C.; Bro. Donald Wagner, S.A.C. Priests 9; Brothers 1.

Pere Marquette House Jesuit Community, 726 N. 34th. St., 53208-3301. Society of Jesus, Wisconsin Province. Revs. Edward G. Witt, S.J., Supr.; John M. Belmonte, S.J.; Terrence M. Brennan, S.J.; Thomas M. Doyle, S.J.; Douglas J. Leonhardt, S.J.; Warren J. Sazama, S.J.; Mr. Michael R. Johnson, S.J.; Mr. Patrick J. Malone, S.J. Priests 6; Scholastics 2.

Provincial Offices - Discalced Carmelites, 1233 S. 45th St., 53214-3693. Tel: 414-672-7212; Fax: 414-672-3138.
E-mail: prthomas@execpc.com
Very Rev. Philip Thomas, O.C.D., Prov.; Sr. Beth Lyman, S.S.S.F., Prov. Admin. Asst.
Serving abroad: Revs. Thomas Martin, O.C.D., Philippines; Alan J. Rieger, O.C.D., Philippines; Ignacio Read, O.C.D., Philippines; Arnold Boehme, O.C.D., Philippines; Reginald Foster, O.C.D., Rome; Lawrence Daniels, O.C.D. (Nairobi); Dennis Geng, O.C.D. (Nairobi); Daniel Chowning, O.C.D. (Spain); George Mangiaracina, O.C.D (Rome).
Priests of the Province not otherwise listed: Revs. Michael Ciullo, O.C.D.; Guy Lofy, O.C.D.; Daniel McCauley, O.C.D.; William McNamara, O.C.D.; James Meldrum, O.C.D.; Vincent Bowes, O.C.D. Total in Residence 29; Total Staff 8.

St. Conrad House, 3138 N. 2nd St., 53212. Tel: 414-372-3620. Capuchin Friars, Province of St. Joseph. Revs. Myron Kowalsky, O.F.M.Cap, Supr.; Otto N. Bucher, O.F.M.Cap.; Richard Hart, O.F.M.Cap.; Jerome Higgins, O.F.M.Cap.; Adrian Staehler, O.F.M.Cap.; Claude Pulvermacher, O.F.M.Cap.; Reynold Rynda, O.F.M.Cap.; Bros. Robert Smith, O.F.M.Cap.; Michael Auman, O.F.M.Cap. Priests 7; Brothers 1; Total in Residence 8.

St. Joseph House of Formation, 937 N. 37th St., 53208. Tel: 414-344-0710. Priests of the Sacred Heart. Revs. Charles Brown, S.C.J.; Paul Kelly, S.C.J., Supr.; Jack Kurps, S.C.J.; Steve Wiese, S.C.J.; Bro. Michael Fette, S.C.J. Priests 4; Brothers 1.

St. Vincent Community, 145 S. 76th St., 53214. Tel: 414-476-3211. Very Rev. Robert Carney, S.A.C., Rector; Revs. Richard J. Gunderman, S.A.C.; Francis Hueller, S.A.C.; Harold J. Liebl, S.A.C.

Salvatorian Formation Community, 1039 E. Russell Ave., 53207-1898. Tel: 414-482-1144. Society of the Divine Savior. Rev. Donald Loskot, S.D.S., Dir. Formation & Dir. Novices; Bros. Wayne Madala, S.D.S., Dir. Candidates; John Rice, S.D.S. Priests 1; Brothers 2; Candidates 3.

Salvatorian Provincial Residence, 1735 Hi-Mount Blvd., 53208-1720. Tel: 414-258-1735; Fax: 414-258-1934.
E-mail: salvatorians@sdsusa.org
Web site: www.execpc.com/~mhoffman/sds
Society of the Divine Savior.
USA Provincial Team: Very Rev. Dennis D. Thiessen, S.D.S., Prov.; Revs. Michael Shay, S.D.S., Vicar; Jean Blais, S.D.S., Dir. Personnel; Joseph Rodrigues, S.D.S., Dir. Planning & Communications.
1735 Hi-Mount Blvd.: Revs. Joseph Henn, S.D.S.; Michael Hoffman, S.D.S., Dir. Vocations; Bruce Brentrup, S.D.S.; Joseph Lubrano, S.D.S., Assoc. Dir. Vocations; C. Robert Nugent, S.D.S.; Joseph Turner, S.D.S.; Luke McArthur, S.D.S.; Roman Pikula, S.D.S.; Bros. Fidelis Rausch, S.D.S.; Arthur Studt, S.D.S.; Paul Sullivan, S.D.S.; Maurus Ellery, S.D.S.
Priests at Residences Not Listed Elsewhere: Revs. Raphael Birringer, S.D.S. Tel: 414-476-9261; Neil Durham, S.D.S. Tel: 414-453-6786, 7811 W. Center St., 53222-4920. Rev. Julian Guzman, S.D.S., Box 129, Ulster Park, NY, 12487-0129. Tel: 914-338-7357. Rev. Raymond Schrimpf, S.D.S., Box 142, Francis Creek, 54214-0142. Tel: 414-684-5384. Rev. Scott Wallenfelsz, S.D.S., 7100 W. Old Loomis Rd., Greendale, 53129-2761. Tel: 414-427-8117. Rev. Jude Weisenbeck, S.D.S., 1903 Lynn Lea Rd., Louisville, KY, 40216-2836. Tel: 502-448-4359. Rev. Bruce Clanton, S.D.S., P.O. Box 574, Racine, 53401-0574. Tel: 414-633-4032. Rev. Leonard Walker, S.D.S., 4410 N. Longview Ave., Phoenix, AZ, 85014-4579. Tel: 602-234-1342. Rev. Barry Griffin, S.D.S., 1703 Hoover St., New Holstein, 53061-1662. Tel: 414-898-5790. Revs. Peter Schuessler, S.D.S.; Donald Skwor, S.D.S., 124 Union Ave., Clifton, NJ, 07011-2630. Tel: 201-546-8983. Rev. Cyril Dickrell, S.D.S., W2754 St. Charles Rd., Chilton, 53014-9625.
Priests and Brothers of the USA Province Serving at the Generalate in Rome, Italy: Revs. Richard Driscoll, S.D.S.; Michael Henseler, S.D.S.; Thomas Novak, S.D.S.; Bro. Van Todd, S.D.S.

Salvatorians - Jordan Hall, 3800 N. 92nd St., 53222-2589. Tel: 414-463-6733. Fathers & Brothers of the Society of the Divine Savior. Bro. John Hauenstein, S.D.S., Local Coord.; Revs. Edward DeBruin, S.D.S.; Claude Klotz, S.D.S.; Gary McGinnis, S.D.S.; Eric Middlecamp, S.D.S.; George Sheehan, S.D.S.; Donald Verhagen, S.D.S.; Bros. Joseph Kreutzer, S.D.S.; Nilus Taddy, S.D.S.; Virgil Mertzlufft, S.D.S.; Ladislaus Markoski, S.D.S.; Reimar Noerz, S.D.S.; Julian Landolf, S.D.S.; Alex Peserik, S.D.S.; Cornelius Pope, S.D.S.; Camillus Becker, S.D.S.; Charles Kubat, S.D.S. Priests 6; Brothers 11.

St. Mary's Home for the Aged, 2005 Division St., Manitowoc, 54220-5699. Revs. Robert Casper; Romuald Dibble; Reginald Schrimpf.

BENET LAKE. *St. Benedict's Abbey*, 12605 224th Ave., 53102. Tel: 414-396-4311.
E-mail: benetlake@aol.com
Web site: www.osb.org/osb/benlake/index.html
Rt. Revs. Leo M. Ryska, O.S.B., Abbot; Andrew V. Garber, O.S.B., Resigned Abbot; Very Rev. Edmund J. Boyce, O.S.B., Prior; Bro. Richard J. Aplington, O.S.B., Subprior; Revs. Henry V. Nurre, O.S.B.; Francis C. Reedy, O.S.B.; Quentin S. Koplinka, O.S.B.; Kevin J. Murphy, O.S.B.; Leonard J. van Ackeren, O.S.B., St. Mary's Ringling Convent, 1208 Oak St., Baraboo, 53913. Rev. Basil J. Anderson, O.S.B., Holy Family Church, 612 S. Copper Ave., Deming, NM, 88030. Dependent Priory: San Benito Abad, Apdo. 296, 58000 Morelia, Michoacan, Mexico. Rev. Jaime Velasco Rivera, O.S.B.; Rt. Rev. Robert C. Schoofs, O.S.B., Prior. Priests 11; Brothers 16.

BURLINGTON. *Queen of Peace Friary*, 523 S. Brown's Lake Dr., P.O. Box 40, 53104-0040. Tel: 414-763-3241. Franciscan Friars of the Assumption B.V.M. Province. Retirement Home for Franciscan Friars. Revs. Robert Konkol, O.F.M., Guardian; Albin

Miklaszewski, O.F.M.; Alexius Lukasik, O.F.M.; Basil Janasik, O.F.M.; Dacian Bluma, O.F.M.; Edmund Czech, O.F.M.; Herbert Silko, O.F.M.; Humphrey Tobias; James Verdick, O.F.M.; Joachim Studwell, O.F.M.; Mark Szych, O.F.M.; Reginald Maslinski, O.F.M.; Reynold Jarecki, O.F.M.; Sante De Angelis, O.F.M.; Sereno Baiardi, O.F.M. Priests 15; Brothers 9.

EAST TROY. *Divine Word Seminary*, Box 107, 53120. Tel: 414-642-3300; Fax: 414-642-7754. Society of the Divine Word. Revs. John F. Fincutter, S.V.D.; John Beemster, S.V.D.; Bernard Fisher, S.V.D.; Thomas Lavin, S.V.D.; Raymond Weisenberger, S.V.D.; Ralph Wiltgen, S.V.D.; Joseph Kallanchira, S.V.D.; Bros. Bernard Scherger, S.V.D.; Raymond Albers, S.V.D. Priests 7; Brothers 2; Total in Residence 9.

FRANKLIN. *Dehon House*, 10731 W. Rawson Ave., 53132. Tel: 414-425-3768.
E-mail: mcguirescj@aol.com
Priests of the Sacred Heart. Rev. Paul J. McGuire, S.C.J.
Priests of the Province Living Outside the Community: Rev. Edward Kilianski, S.C.J., P.O. Box 960, Occidental, CA, 95465. Rev. James Schroeder, S.C.J., 5375 Kenrick Parke Dr. N. #305, St. Louis, MO, 63119. Priests 3.

St. Francis Residence, 12001 W. Woods Rd., 53132. Tel: 414-529-0332. Provincial Residence, Priests of the Sacred Heart. Revs. John Czyzynski, S.C.J.; Anthony P. Russo, S.C.J., Supr. Priests 2.

Villa Maria, 7330 S. Lovers Lane Rd., 53132. Tel: 414-425-5968; 425-5981. Revs. Jim Alexander, S.C.J.; Frank Aresta, S.C.J.; Donald Barnd, S.C.J.; Patrick M. Cremer, S.C.J.; John Dalbec, S.C.J.; Wm. Denis Devine; Justin Gross, S.C.J.; Peter Miller, S.C.J.; Bros. Raymond Kozuch, S.C.J.; Benedict Humpfer, S.C.J., Supr.; Steve Cyr, S.C.J.; Matthew Miles, S.C.J.; Frank Miller, S.C.J.; Conrad Thelen, S.C.J.; Deacon Marion Quagliariello, S.C.J.; Rev. Thomas Hunt, S.C.J., 3553 S. 41st St., Milwaukee, 53221. Priests 8; Brothers 6; Deacons 1.

HALES CORNERS. *Priests of the Sacred Heart*, 6871 S. Lovers Lane Rd., P.O. Box 289, 53130-0289. Tel: 414-425-6910; Fax: 414-425-2938.
E-mail: scjuspro@cathtel.com
Rev. John Czyzynski, S.C.J., Prov. Supr.; Bro. Raymond Kozuch, S.C.J., Prov. Sec.; Revs. Jerome Schaad, S.C.J., Prov. Treas.; Frank Arresta, S.C.J., Dir. Foreign Missions; Robert Bossie, S.C.J., Dir. J&P; Michael Burke, S.C.J., Dir. Formation; Richard Johnston, S.C.J., Dir. Apostolates; Jack Kurps, S.C.J., Dir. Vocations; Anthony Russo, S.C.J., Dir. Admissions & Dir. Denonian Affiliates.
Priests of the Province Serving Abroad: Most Rev. Evert Baaij, S.C.J., 10 Park Ln., 6001 Port Elizabeth, Rep. of S. Africa. Rev. Bernard Rosinski, S.C.J., Sacerdoti del S. Cuore, Via Casale S. Pio V, 20, 00165 Rome, Italy.
Provincialate Residence: Priests of the Sacred Heart, 12001 W. Woods Rd., 53132. Revs. John Czyzynski, S.C.J., Prov. Supr.; Anthony P. Russo, S.C.J.
Attached to the Province but Living Elsewhere: Rev. Bryan Benoit, S.C.J., 1841 Benecia Ave., Los Aneles, CA, 90025. Rev. Jerome Clifford, S.C.J., 300 S. Grand Blvd., #701, St. Louis, MO, 63103. Rev. David Emerick, S.C.J., 16802 Springhaven Ct., Humble, TX, 77396-1364. Rev. Pat Gonsorcik, S.C.J., Ontario, 130 Springhurst, #203, Ottawa, Canada, K1S OE5. Rev. John Kasparek, S.C.J., 1200 E. 10th St., Stuart, FL, 34996. Rev. Terence Langley, S.C.J., St. Irene Rectory, 187 East St., Carlisle, MA, 01741. Rev. Robert Markunas, S.C.J., 412 Noya Ln., Apopka, FL, 32712. Rev. Michael Ortiz, S.C.J., 10404 Cheviot Ct., San Diego, CA, 92126. Rev. Douglas Watson, S.C.J., 11800 Braesview, #2203, San Antonio, TX, 78213. Bro. Thomas Bridges, S.C.J., 1403 N. St. Mary's St., San Antonio, TX, 78215. Bro. Steven Roy, 2345 S. 107th St., #310, West Allis, 53227. Bro. Bernard Taube, S.C.J., 2833 Moland St., #3, Madison, 53704.

Sacred Heart Monastery. Priests of the Sacred Heart, 7335 S. Lovers Ln., P.O. Box 566, 53130. Tel: 414-425-5323. Revs. George Balderrama, S.C.J.; James Brackin, S.C.J.; Joseph Gole, S.T.D. (Ljubljana); Justin Guiltnane, S.C.J., Supr.; Wayne Jenkins, S.C.J.; Patrick Lloyd, S.C.J.; Kevin McInnis, S.C.J.; John T. O'Connor, S.C.J.; Paul Reid, S.C.J.; Jerome Schaad, S.C.J.; Bro. James Willis, S.C.J.
Attached to the Province but Living Elsewhere: Rev. Guy Blair, S.C.J., St. Joseph, 1905 Belt Line Hwy., Madison, 53713. Rev. Thomas Garvey, S.C.J., House Number IV/145, W. Veliyathunadu P.O., Via Alangadu, Kerala, India, 683511. Rev. Edward Griesemer, S.C.J., 1711 S. 9th St., Milwaukee, 53204. Rev. Richard Zelonis, S.C.J., 3920 N. Green Bay Rd., Racine, 53404. Total in Residence 11.

HOLY HILL. *Discalced Carmelite Monastery*, 1525 Carmel Rd., Hubertus, 53033. Tel: 414-628-1838; 673-3540; Fax: 414-628-4294. Revs. Jude Peters, O.C.D., Prior; Matthias Montgomery, O.C.D., Subprior & Dir. Novices; Paul Fohlin, O.C.D.; Daniel Chowning, O.C.D.; Francis Xavier Cotter, O.C.D.; Patrick J. Farrel, O.C.D.; Joseph-Mary Flanery, O.C.D.; Michael Griffin, O.C.D.; Cyril Guise, O.C.D., Shrine Dir.; Denis Read, O.C.D.; Ernest Unverdorben, O.C.D.; Redemptus Short, O.C.D.; Fred Alexander, O.C.D.; John Grennon, O.C.D.; Bros. Martin Murphy, O.C.D.; Augustine Wharf, O.C.D.; Robert Sentman, O.C.D. Priests 14; Brothers 3; Novices 2.

Holy Hill National Shrine of Mary Help of Christians, 1525 Carmel Rd., Hubertus, 53033.

Retreat Center, 1525 Carmel Rd., Hubertus, 53033.

MOUNT CALVARY. *St. Lawrence Friary*, 301 Church St., 53057. Tel: 920-753-3911. Revs. Edwin F. Dziedziejko, O.F.M.Cap.; Oliver Bambenek, O.F.M.Cap., Supr.; Gary Wegner, O.F.M.Cap.; Campion Baer, O.F.M.Cap.; Philip Casper, O.F.M.Cap.; Joachim Strupp, O.F.M.Cap.; Dennis Druggan, O.F.M.Cap.; Ronald Jansch, O.F.M.Cap.; Randall Knauf, O.F.M.Cap.; Elroy Pesch, O.F.M.Cap.; Emil F. Schneweis, O.F.M.Cap.; Kenan Siegel, O.F.M.Cap.; Luis Sonntag, O.F.M.Cap.; Eugene Tuller, O.F.M.Cap.; Anthony Will, O.F.M.Cap.; Eugene Wolf, O.F.M.Cap.; Paul Yaroch, O.F.M.Cap.; Bros. Douglas Bode, O.F.M.Cap.; Jerry Campbell, O.F.M.Cap.; John Freienstein, O.F.M.Cap.; Larry Groeschel, O.F.M.Cap.; Neal Plale, O.F.M.Cap.; Mark Rehlinger, O.F.M.Cap.; Arnold Sauter, O.F.M.Cap.; Carl Schaefer, O.F.M.Cap.; John Scherer, O.F.M.Cap., Vicar; Dismas Seward, O.F.M.Cap.; John Willger, O.F.M.Cap. Priests 15; Brothers 11.

OCONOMOWOC. *Austin Hall*, 954 Dousman Rd., 53066. Augustinians/Province of Our Mother of Good Counsel, Olympia Fields, IL. Bro. Bruce A. Jendraszak, O.S.A., Contact Person, Tolentine Center, 20300 Governors Hwy., Olympia Fields, IL, 60461-1081. Tel: 708-748-9500.

RACINE. *Augustinian Novitiate*, 4335 Douglas Ave., 53402-2956. Tel: 414-681-3221. Rev. Alvin P. Metzger, O.S.A., Prior, Treas. Priests 1.

ST. FRANCIS. *St. Camillus Formation Community*, 3661 S. Kinnickinnic Ave., 53235. Tel: 414-481-3696. Rev. Louis Lussier, O.S.Cam., Supr.; Bro. Mario Crivello, O.S.Cam. Priests 1; Brothers 1.

TWIN LAKES. *La Salette Missionaries Shrine*, Box 777, 53181. Tel: 414-877-3111.
E-mail: lasalette@techeadnet.com
Web site: www.members.techeadnet.com/lasalette
Revs. James Stajkowski, M.S., Prov.; Thaddeus Galuszka, M.S.; Terrence Niziolek, M.S., Dir.; John Gabriel, M.S.; Henry Wojtunik, M.S.; Bros. Adam Mateja, M.S.; Anthony Such, M.S., Oblate. Priests 5; Brothers 1; Oblate Brothers 1.

WAUWATOSA. *Jesuit Community at St. Camillus*, 10100 W. Bluemound Rd., 53226-4386. Tel: 414-259-3784 (Court East); 258-1814 (Skilled Care). Society of Jesus, Wisconsin Province. Revs. Luis Rodriguez, S.J., Supr.; Anthony L. Dagelen, S.J., Asst. Supr.; Robert R. Boyle, S.J.; Leo J. Burns, S.J.; James B. Corrigan, S.J.; M. Joseph Costelloe, S.J.; Norbert C. Eberhardt, S.J.; Edwin F. Falteisek, S.J.; Robert J. Flahavan, S.J.; Robert M. Frommelt, S.J.; Joseph F. Gregory, S.J.; George J. Guenther, S.J.; Bro. Henry J. Guenther, S.J.; Rev. Cletus J. Healy, S.J.; Bro. Gerald E. McKeever, S.J.; Revs. Robert C. Ostertag, S.J.; Richard L. Porter, S.J.; Perry J. Roets, S.J.; Jerome E. Rohrer, S.J.; Joseph D. Scallon, S.J.; Joseph D. Sheehan, S.J.; Charles T. Shinners, S.J.; Paul G. Stockhausen, S.J. Priests 21; Brothers 2.

St. Camillus Community House, 600 N. 103rd St., 53226. Tel: 414-259-3789.
E-mail: jimcamk@execpc.com
Revs. James Kovarik, O.S.Cam., Supr.; Raoul Thibeault, O.S.Cam.; Vitaliano Turci, O.S.Cam.; Joseph L. Bisoffi, O.S.Cam.; Carlo Notaro, O.S.Cam.; Bros. Nelson DeLoria, O.S.Cam.; Herman Moellenhoff, O.S.Cam.; Alfred Weber, O.S.Cam.; Roland Wild, O.S.Cam. In res. Rev. Claude Pulvermacher, O.F.M.Cap. Priests 6; Brothers 4.

St. Camillus Provincialate, 10101 W. Wisconsin Ave., 53226. Tel: 414-259-4511. Provincial offices for the North American Province of the Order of the Servants of the Sick (Order of Saint Camillus). Very Rev. William F. Cronin, O.S.Cam., M.S.W., Prov. & Pres. Prov. Counselors: Revs. Louis Lussier, O.S-.Cam., First Counselor/Vicar; James Kovarik, O.S-.Cam.; Bros. Nelson Deloria, O.S.Cam.; Thomas Farrell, O.S.Cam. Total in Residence 25; Total Staff 3.

[Q] CONVENTS AND RESIDENCES FOR SISTERS

MILWAUKEE. *Ancilla Convent*. Inter-Community, hospitality for religious women. 3601 S. 41st St., 53221. Tel: 414-384-6535. Sr. Agnese Jasko, P.H.J.C., Dir.; Rev. Patrick M. Cremer, S.C.J., Chap. Sisters 27.

Marian Hall, 2925 W. Orchard St., 53215. Tel: 414-384-0995. Retired School Sisters of St. Francis. Sr. Cecilia Zachman, O.S.F., Admin. Sisters 53.

Mercedes Molina - Instituto Santa Mariana de Jesus, 1234 N. 24th Pl., 53205. Tel: 414-931-7163. Sr. Gloria Piedad Garzon, Supr. Sisters 4.
Corporate Title: Mercedes Molina, Inc.

Monastery of the Perpetual Rosary, 217 N. 68th St., 53213. Tel: 414-258-0579.
E-mail: joannaop@execpc.com
Cloistered Dominican Sisters of the Perpetual Rosary. Mother Miriam Leonard, O.P., Prioress. Professed Sisters 12.

Sacred Heart Center, 1545 S. Layton Blvd., 53215. Tel: 414-383-4490. Home for retired and infirm School Sisters of St. Francis. S. Joann Riesterer, Coord. of Health and Housing Services; Sr. Rosalia Zachman, O.S.F., Coord. Sisters Living Group. Sisters 60.

St. Clare Convent, 3276 S. 16th St., 53215. Tel: 414-647-5812; 647-2437. Felician Sisters. Sr. M. Laurentine Zygmuntowicz, Local Min. Sisters 4.

St. Dominic Center, 1727 S. 9th St., 53204. Tel: 384-4873. Vietnamese Dominican Sisters. Sr. Clara Nguyen, O.P., Supr. Sisters 4; Postulants 23.

St. Felix Convent, 3159 S. 17th St., 53215. Tel: 414-389-9803. Felician Sisters. Sr. Lisa Marie Drover, C.S.S.F., Local Minister. Sisters 3.

St. Francis Convent, 3170 S. 17th St., 53215. Tel: 414-643-6387. Felician Sisters. Sr. M. Gemma Franczak, C.S.S.F., Local Minister. Sisters 5.

St. Joseph Convent, General Motherhouse of the School Sisters of St. Francis, 1501 S. Layton Blvd., 53215. Tel: 414-384-4105; Fax: 414-645-7198.
E-mail: sssfgen@execpc.com
Web site: www.schoolsistersstfrancis.org
Sr. Frances Brenner, O.S.F., Pres.; Sr. Phyllis Vater, 1st Vice Pres.; Sr. Raphaela Muench, Vice Pres.; Sr. Alida Lopez, Vice Pres.; Sr. Celestine Schall, Prov.; Rev. James E. Mauel, S.J., Chap. Sisters 63; Total in Congregation 1,590. Legal Titles: *Generalate-School Sisters of St. Francis, Inc.*; *School Sisters of St. Francis of St. Joseph's Convent, New Castle, Inc.*

Sisters of Charity of St. Joan Antida. St. Rita Convent, 1621 N. Cass St., 53202. Tel: 414-276-5153. Sr. Elizabeth Anne Weber, S.C.S.J.A. Sisters 5.

Sisters of Charity of St. Joan Antida Convent (Emmanuel), 1522 N. Astor St., 53202. Tel: 414-289-0774. Sr. Monica Fumo, S.C.S.J.A., Supr. Sisters 4.

Sisters of Charity of St. Joan Antida Convent (Maranatha), 3044 N. 25th St., 53206. Tel: 414-444-3994. Sr. Andrea Christine Peters, S.C.S.J.A. Sisters 2.

Sisters of Charity of St. Joan Antida Convent (Presentation), 1329 N. Cass St., 53202. Tel: 414-276-4173. Sr. Anne Marie Baemmert, S.C.S.J.A., Supr. Sisters 10.

Sisters of Charity of St. Joan Antida Regina Mundi Provincial House and Novitiate, 8560 N. 76th Pl., 53223. Tel: 414-354-9233; Fax: 414-355-6463. Sr. Jennifer L. Daul, S.C.S.J.A., Prov. Sisters 4; Total in Community 48.

Sisters of the Divine Savior, 4311 N. 100th St., 53222-1393. Tel: 414-466-0810; Fax: 414-466-4335.
E-mail: sdswomen@execpc.com
Provincial Administration. Prov. Team: Sr. Sheila Novak, S.D.S., Prov. Leader; Sr. Mary Lee Grady, S.D.S., Vicaress; Sr. Jane Eschweiler, Vice Pres.; Sr. Pauline Feiner, Vice Pres. Total Sisters in Province 130.
Corporate Title: Sisters of the Divine Savior.

Salvatorian Heights Assisted Living Unit, 2720 N. 36th St., 53210. Tel: 414-445-8485. Sr. Deanna Schroeder, S.D.S., Coord.; Patricia Smith, Health Care Coord. Sisters 22.

United States Province, 1515 S. Layton Blvd., 53215. Tel: 414-384-1515; Fax: 414-384-1950.
E-mail: sssf@earth.execpc.com
Web site: www.schoolsistersstfrancis.org
School Sisters of St. Francis. Provincial Team: Sr. Celestine Schall, O.S.F.; Sr. Therese Thoenen, O.S.F.; Sr. Jane Elyse Russell, O.S.F. Total in U.S. Province 1,040.
Corporate title: The School Sisters of St. Francis of St. Joseph's Convent, Milwaukee, Wisconsin.
Corporate Title: Congregational Support Charitable Trust.

BROWN DEER. *Sisters of the Sorrowful Mother-Generalate, Inc.*, 9056 N. Deerbrook Tr., 53223. Tel: 414-357-8940. Sr. M. Helen Malolepsy, Gen. Supr.

CAMPBELLSPORT. *St. Joseph Convent*, 526 Mill St., 53010. Tel: 920-533-8351; Fax: 920-533-5394. School Sisters of St. Francis. Retirement Home/Health Care Center. Sr. Phyllis Wirtz, S.S.S.F., Facility Dir.; Sr. Dorothy McKeague, S.S.S.F., Living Group Coord.; Sr. Theresa Marie Jarvis, S.S.S.F., R.N., Dir. Nursing; Sr. Anita Wolf, S.C.S.C., Dir. Pastoral Svcs.; Rev. Nicholas L. Goebel, Chap. Sisters 184; Total Staff 150.

CEDAR GROVE. *Sacred Heart of the Lake Chalet*, Box 46A, 53013. Tel: 414-285-3084. Recreation Home for Sisters of St. Mary's Home for Aged, Manitowoc, WI & Felician Sisters of the Mother of Good Counsel Province.

DELAVAN. *Villa Celine*, 3127 S. Shore Dr., 53115. Tel: 773-792-6363; Fax: 773-792-9590. Summer Rest Home for Sisters of the Resurrection. Sr. Virginia Ann Wanzek, C.R., Prov. Supr. & Contact Person, Mailing Address: 7432 W. Talcatt Ave., Chicago, IL, 60631.

ELM GROVE. *Notre Dame of Elm Grove*, 13105 Watertown Plank Rd., 53122-2291. Tel: 414-782-1450; Fax: 414-782-2349.
S.S.N.D. Assisted Care, Independent Living. School Sisters of Notre Dame. Total in Residence 164; Total Staff 83.

School Sisters of Notre Dame, 13105 Watertown Plank Rd., 53122-2291. Tel: 414-782-9850; Fax: 414-782-5725. Sr. Marilyn Kesler, S.S.N.D., Prov. Leader. Total in Milwaukee Province 620; Total Staff 34. Legal Titles: *School Sisters of Notre Dame at Milwaukee, Wisconsin, Inc.; School Sisters of Notre Dame at Milwaukee, Wisconsin, Inc. Charitable Trust.*

ERIE, PA. *Mount St. Benedict Monastery*, 6101 E. Lake Rd., 16511.

FOND DU LAC. *Convent of the Sisters of St. Agnes.* Motherhouse. 475 Gillett St., 54935. Tel: 920-923-2121. Legal Title: *Congregation of Sisters of St. Agnes of Fond du Lac, Wisconsin, Inc.* Sr. Mary Mollison, C.S.A., General Superior; Rev. Tony Will, O.F.M.Cap., Chap. Sisters 44; Total Religious in Community 411.

Nazareth Heights, Inc., 1755 E. Johnson St., 54935. Tel: 920-921-5826. Retirement Home sponsored by the Congregation of the Sisters of St. Agnes. Sr. Irene Kohne, C.S.A., Admin. Sisters 94.

KENOSHA. *Kenosha Dominicans*, P.O. Box 1288, 53141-1288. Tel: 414-694-2067; Fax: 414-694-6542. Congregation of the Dominican Sisters of St. Catherine of Siena of Kenosha. Sr. Susan Anne Snyder, O.P., Prioress. Total Religious in Community 30.

MANITOWOC. *Sisters of Saint Elizabeth, Inc.*, 2005 Division St., 53005. Tel: 920-684-7171 (St. Mary's Home). Sisters of St. Elizabeth. Mother Mary Rita Amrhein, S.S.E., Mother General. Sisters 5.

MEQUON. *Sisters of the Sorrowful Mother, Novitiate House*, 4823 Bonniwell Rd., 53092. Tel: 414-242-5770. Sisters 4.

MOUNT CALVARY. *Loretto Convent*, N8114 Calvary St., 53057. Tel: 920-753-3211; Fax: 920-753-3100. General Motherhouse of Sister-Servants of Christ the King. Sr. Mary Rose, Supr. Sisters 9.
Corporate Title: Congregation of Sister Servants of Christ the King, Inc.

Our Lady of Mt. Carmel Convent, 53057. Tel: 920-753-2131; 753-2036; Fax: 920-753-2116. Leadership Team: Sr. Muriel Glodosky, S.S.N.D.; Sr. Mary Dora Kipp, S.S.N.D.
Home for Retired Sisters. School Sisters of Notre Dame 50.

OCONOMOWOC. *Villa St. Joseph Summer Day Camp*, 2653 Mill Rd., 53066. Tel: 414-646-2185. Sponsored by Felician Sisters. Sr. M. Carolita Turzin, C.S.S.F., Admin. Total Assisted 175; Total Staff 18.

PEWAUKEE. *Carmel of the Mother of God*, W267 N2517 Meadowbrook Rd., 53072. Tel: 414-691-0336. Discalced Carmelite Nuns. Sr. Mary Agnes Kramer, O.C.D., Prioress; Rev. Dennis C. Klemme, Chap. Professed Sisters 6; Novices 3.

RACINE. *Convent of St. Catherine of Siena.* Siena Center, 5635 Erie St., 53402. Tel: 414-639-4100. Motherhouse of the Sisters of St. Dominic (Congregation of St. Catherine of Siena). Sr. Evelyn Lins, O.P., Pres. Sisters 138; Total Religious in Community 266.
Corporate title: Sisters of St. Dominic.

ST. FRANCIS. *St. Francis Convent, Motherhouse of the Sisters of St. Francis of Assisi*, 3221 S. Lake Dr., 53235-3799. Tel: 414-744-1160; Fax: 414-744-7193. Web site: www.geocities.com/wellesley/3221LAKEFRANCISCANS
Sr. Marita Maschmann, O.S.F., Dir. of the Congregation. Assoc. Directors: Sr. Joanne Schatzlein, O.S.F.; Sr. Charlotte Roost, O.S.F. Total in Community 369.
Corporate title: The Sisters of St. Francis of Assisi, Milwaukee, Wis. Legal Titles: *The Sisters of St. Francis of Assisi.; The Ongoing Community Support Fund of the Sisters of St. Francis of Assisi.*

SHEBOYGAN. *Hospital Sisters of the Third Order of St. Francis*, 1724 N. 29th St., 53081. Tel: 920-459-8785. Hospital Sisters of the Third Order of St. Francis 3.

SLINGER. *Franciscan Sisters of Christian Charity (O.S.F.).* San Damiano Convent, 4270 Cedar Creek Rd., 53086-9795. Tel: 414-644-8916. Sr. Jukiana Weber, O.S.F., Supr. Sisters 26; Total Staff 2.

WAUWATOSA. *Provincial Motherhouse of the Carmelite Sisters of the Divine Heart of Jesus*, 1230 Kavanaugh Pl., 53213. Tel: 414-453-4040; Fax: 414-453-5603. Sr. M. Immaculata, Prov. Supr. Sisters 5; Total Religious in Province 28; Total Assisted 185; Total Staff 93.
Corporate title: Carmelite Sisters of the Divine Heart of Jesus, Milwaukee, Wisconsin.

WEST ALLIS. *Missionary Sisters of the Holy Family.* (Poland). 1665 S. 64th St., 53214. Tel: 414-327-4068. Sr. Maria Sarafin, M.S.F., Supr.; Sr. Danuta Kujalowicz, M.S.F., Supr. Asst. Sisters 6.

Sisters of Charity of St. Joan Antida Convent, 6640 W. Beloit Rd., 53219. Tel: 414-541-6575. Sr. Theresa Lucibello, S.C.S.J.A., Supr. Sisters 8.

[R] HERMITAGES

CAMPBELLSPORT. *Carmelite Hermit of the Trinity, Mount Carmel Hermitage*, N3493 Chapel Heights, 53010. Sr. Joseph Marie, Carmelite Hermit of the Trinity (Solitary).

[S] RETREAT HOUSES

MILWAUKEE. *Archdiocesan Retreat Center at Archbishop Cousins Catholic Center*, 3501 S. Lake Dr., P.O. Box 07912, 53207-0912. Tel: 414-769-3491. William Kreitzer, Dir. Bldg. Svcs. Total Staff 2.

Cardoner Retreat Center, 1501 S. Layton Blvd., 53215. Tel: 414-384-2120. Rev. James E. Mauel, S.J., Dir.

The Dwelling Place, 528 N. 31st St., 53208. Tel: 414-933-1100. Revs. Francis J. Dombrowski, O.F.M.Cap.; Jerome Schroeder, O.F.M.Cap.; Mary Klotz, Team Member. Priests 2; Total in Residence 3; Total Staff 3.

BURLINGTON. *Franciscan Retreat Center, Inc.*, 503 S. Browns Lake Dr., 53105. Tel: 414-763-3600.
Web site: www.sfran@015-inc.com
Mr. Frederick Stoltz, Pres.; Ms. Eloise Samano-Williamson, Admin. Total in Residence 5; Total Staff 17.

ELKHORN. *St. Vincent Pallotti Center.* Pallottine Fathers, N. 6409 Bowers Rd., 53121. Tel: 414-723-2108.
E-mail: gpserwa@elknet.net
Web site: www.elknet.net/gpserwa/
Retreat and Christian formation Center. Rev. Gregory P. Serwa, S.A.C., Dir. Priests 1; Lay Staff 8.

OCONOMOWOC. *Our Mother of Perpetual Help Retreat Center*, 1800 N. Timber Trail Ln., 53066-4897. Tel: 414-567-6900. Revs. Peter Connolly, C.Ss.R., Supr.; John A. Broker, C.Ss.R.; William Broker, C.Ss.R.; Bro. John Matthys, C.Ss.R.; Rev. James White, C.Ss.R.; Sr. Olga Neft, O.S.F. Priests 4; Total in Residence 6; Sisters 1; Brothers 1.

WAUKESHA. *Schoenstatt Retreat Center*, W284 N698 Cherry Ln., 53188-9402. Tel: 414-547-7733. Sr. M. Darlene Jankiewicz, Supr. Sisters 10; Total Staff 2.

[T] SECULAR INSTITUTES

MILWAUKEE. *Secular Institute of the Schoenstatt Sisters of Mary*, 5310 W. Wisconsin Ave., 53208. Tel: 414-774-0520. Sr. M. Michelle Mindham, Supr. Sisters 8.

WAUKESHA. *Secular Institute of Schoenstatt Fathers.* Schoenstatt Fathers, W284 N746 Cherry Ln., 53188. Tel: 414-548-9061; Fax: 414-548-9593. Revs. Gerold M. Langsch, Supr.; Dietrich A. Haas; Jonathan J. Niehaus. Priests 7; Total in Residence 4.
Attached to the house but living elsewhere: Revs. Robert DeCock, C.C.; Antonio Rodriguez, C.C.; Hector R. Vega, C.C.

Secular Institute of the Schoenstatt Sisters of Mary, W284 N404 Cherry Ln., 53188-9416. Tel: 414-542-4384; 542-1544. Sr. M. Jacoba Kesselheim, Prov. Supr.; Sr. M. Jacinta Brunner, Supr. Sisters 32.

[U] ASSOCIATIONS OF THE FAITHFUL

MILWAUKEE. *The Christian Sisters*, 1927 S. 7th St., 53204. Tel: 414-643-1188. Sr. M. Corona Kroes, C.S., Pres. Sisters 5.

BELOIT. *Franciscan Sisters of Our Lady*, 2110 Bootmaker Dr., 53511. Tel: 608-365-7257. Sr. Mary Timothy Geenen, F.S.O.L., Supr. Sisters 4.

FRANKLIN. *Franciscan Sisters of Saint Clare, Inc.*, 7732 S. 51st St., 53132. Tel: 414-421-8257. Non-Cloistered Contemplative Community. Sr. Mary Celine Stein, F.S.S.C., Supr. Gen. Professed Sisters 3; Associate Sisters 2; Lay Affiliates 49; Postulant Candidates 1.

KENOSHA. *Franciscans of the Sorrowful Mother*, 935 Washington Rd., 53140. Tel: 414-605-9480. Ana Maria Solis, Moderator. Members 3.

[V] MISSIONARY ACTIVITIES

MILWAUKEE. *Milwaukee Archdiocesan Office for World Mission.* (Formerly Latin American Office), 3501 S. Lake Dr., P.O. Box 07912, 53207-0912. Tel: 414-769-3406. Sr. Frances Cunningham, O.S.F., Dir. Sends priests and supports laity in overseas mission. Educates and raises funds for worldwide mission.

Missionary Association of Catholic Women, 3501 S. Lake Dr., 53235. Tel: 414-769-3406. Sr. Frances Cunningham, O.S.F., Rep. Provides aid to home and foreign missions.

Our Blessed Lady of Victory Mission, Inc., 5430 W. Vliet St., 53208-2175. Tel: 414-774-3128. Rev. Lawrence J. Leack, Chap.; Agnes J. Ryan, Pres.

St. Boniface Mission League, Inc., 3501 S. Lake Dr., P.O. Box 07912, 53207-0912. Tel: 414-769-3406. Sr. Frances Cunningham, O.S.F., Pres.
Partners in World Mission formerly known as St. Boniface Mission League, Inc. Furnishes aid to home and foreign missions since 1913, with a special focus on the archdiocesan sister parish in the Dominican Republic.

Society for the Propagation of the Faith, Holy Childhood Association. (Pontifical Mission Aid Societies). 3501 S. Lake Dr., P.O. Box 07912, 53207-0912. Tel: 414-769-3406. Sr. Frances Cunningham, O.S.F., Dir. Raises funds and educates for worldwide mission, under papal auspices.

ELM GROVE. *Family Unity International, Inc.*, 12750 Stephen Pl., 53122. Tel: 414-784-7448. Patricia J. Parks, Pres. Raises and distributes funds to the missions of the Working Boys' Center. Organization is under the supervision of the Director of the Milwaukee Archdiocesan Office for World Mission.

[W] SOCIETIES

MILWAUKEE. *Council of Catholic Women*, 3501 South Lake Dr., P.O. Box 07912, 53207-0912. Tel: 414-695-1406. Mrs. Betty Kurtzweil, Pres.; Rev. Eugene D. Winkler, Moderator.

Cursillos in Christianity, P.O. Box 07033, 53207. Revs. William Key, Spiritual Dir.; Denis Read, O.C.D., Dir. Spanish Speaking Cursillo; Sr. Anne Mary Rischar, O.S.F., Dir. English Speaking Secretariat. Total in Residence 4; Total Staff 6.

Priests' Purgatorial Society, 3501 S. Lake Dr., P.O. Box 07912, 53207-0912. Tel: 414-769-3300. Barbara Anne Cusack, Sec.

St. Vincent de Paul Society, 9601 W. Silver Spring Dr., 53225. Tel: 414-462-7837; Fax: 414-462-5458.
E-mail: svdp@execpc.com
Web site: www.execpc.com/~svdp
Mr. Gerald H. Felsecker, Exec. Dir., Milwaukee Archdiocesan Council, Council of Racine, 926 LaSalle St., Racine, 53404. Council of Kenosha, 6201 14th Ave., Kenosha, 53143. Council of Fond du Lac, 401 N. Hickory, Fond du Lac, 54935. Council of Sheboygan, 4215 Hwy. 42 N., Sheboygan, 53083. Council of Waukesha, 305 E. Main St., Waukesha, 53186. Council of Beaver Dam, 316 S. Spring St., Beaver Dam, 53916. Council of Washington County, 420 River Rd., West Bend, 53095. Council of Ozaukee County, P.O. Box 59, Port Washington, 53074. Total Assisted 30,000; Total Staff 5,200.

HORICON. *Legion of Mary*, 109 Valley St., 53032. Tel: 920-485-2937; Fax: 920-485-2427. Rev. M. Eugene Kinney, Spiritual Dir.; Ms. Dolores Wanta, Pres.

WAUWATOSA. *Apostolate of Suffering.* A Pious Union of the Sick. 7452 Harwood Ave., 53213. Tel: 414-771-7466. Mrs. Lorayne Hall, Pres.

Milwaukee Archdiocesan Holy Name Society, 2431 N. 63rd St., 53213. Mr. John Lando, Pres.; Deacon Samuel J. Lupo, Spiritual Dir.

[X] NEWMAN CENTERS

MILWAUKEE. *Marquette University Ministry.*
Web site: www.mu.edu
Alumni Memorial Union 236, P.O. Box 1881, 53201. Tel: 414-288-6873; Fax: 414-288-3696. Dr. Mary Feeley, Dir.; Dr. Susan Mountin, Assoc. Dir.

Milwaukee Archdiocesan Campus Ministry, P.O. Box 07912, 53207-0912. Tel: 414-769-3439. Legal Title: *Campus Ministry of the Archdiocese of Milwaukee.*

University of Wisconsin - Milwaukee, Newman Center, 3001 N. Downer Ave., 53211. Tel: 414-964-6640. Constance M. Popp; Rev. Robert J. Lotz.

U.W. Parkside and Carthage College, 6203 54th. Ave., Kenosha, 53142. Tel: 414-694-5526. Edith Padgett.

Whitewater Campus Ministry (Whitewater), 344 N. Prairie St., Whitewater, 53190. Tel: 414-473-5555. Rev. James M. Godin.

[Y] MISCELLANEOUS

MILWAUKEE. *Agape Community Center of Milwaukee, Inc.*, 3400 W. Silver Spring Dr., 53209. Tel: 414-464-4440. A subsidiary corporation of the Sisters of the Sorrowful Mother-Ministry Corporation. Sr. Myra Smith, Exec. Dir.

Alternative Residential Arrangements, Inc., P.O. Box 07912, 53207-0912; Fax: 414-769-3428. Group Homes for Developmentally disabled adults.
Other Locations: 6609 N. 53rd St., 53223. 5255 S. 18th St., 53221. Sponsored by Catholic Charities of the Archdiocese of Milwaukee, Inc.

Apostleship of the Sea, 3501 S. Lake Dr., P.O. Box 07912, 53207-0912.

Archdiocesan Marian Shrine. 141 N. 68th St., 53213. Tel: 414-257-0155. Rev. Anthony S. Trenier, Dir.

Assisi Community Organization, Inc., 5325 W. Burleigh, 53210. Tel: 414-449-3960. Sponsored by Franciscan Sisters, Daughters of the Sacred Hearts of Jesus and Mary (Wheaton, Illinois). Robert J. Makowski, Pres. Total Staff 6.

Assisi Homes - Eldr Manor, Inc., 5325 W. Burleigh St., 53210. Tel: 630-462-9271. Rodger F. Accardi, Chm.; Garth Seehawer, Contact Person. Franciscan Sisters, Daughters of the Sacred Heart of Jesus and Mary of Wheaton, Illinois.

Assisi Homes - Gateway, Inc., 5325 W. Burleigh St., 53210. Rodger F. Accardi, Chm. Tel: 630-462-9271; Garth Seehawer, Contact Person. Franciscan Sisters, Daughters of the Sacred Hearts of Jesus and Mary of Wheaton, IL. To acquire or develop and operate housing projects for low income families and elderly persons; and to provide for human and other charitable/benevolent services required by the residents.

Assisi Homes - Howard Woods, Inc., 5325 W. Burleigh St., 53210. Tel: 630-462-9271. Rodger F. Accardi, Chm.; Garth Seehawer, Contact Person. Franciscan Sisters, Daughters of the Sacred Hearts of Jesus and Mary of Wheaton, Illinois. Purpose: To acquire, or develop, and operate housing projects for low income families and elderly persons; and to provide for human and other charitable/benevolent services required by the residents.

Assisi Homes - Jefferson Court, Inc., 415 E. Knapp St., 53202. Tel: 630-462-9271. Rodger F. Accardi, Chm. Franciscan Sisters, Daughters of the Sacred Hearts of Jesus and Mary of Wheaton, Illinois.

Assisi Homes - Kenosha, Inc., 5325 W. Burleigh St., 53210. Tel: 414-449-3960. Steve Kuklin, Pres. Franciscan Sisters, Daughters of the Sacred Hearts of Jesus and Mary of Wheaton, IL. Independent Housing for Low Income Elderly.

Assisi Homes - Mabess Manor, Inc., 5325 W. Burleigh St., 53210. Tel: 630-462-9271. Rodger F. Accardi, Chm.; Garth Seehawer, Contact Person. Franciscan Sisters, Daughters of the Sacred Hearts of Jesus and Mary of Wheaton, IL. Purpose: To acquire or develop, and operate housing projects for low income families and elderly persons.

Assisi Homes - Rock View, Inc., 5325 W. Burleigh St., 53210. Tel: 630-462-9271. Rodger F. Accardi, Chm.; Garth Seehawer, Contact Person. Franciscan Sisters, Daughters of the Sacred Hearts of Jesus and Mary of Wheaton, Illinois. Housing Projects for Low Income Families.

Assisi Homes - Saxony, Inc., 5325 W. Burleigh St., 53210. Tel: 630-462-9271. Steve Kuklin, Pres.; Garth Seehawer, Contact Person. Franciscan Sisters, Daughters of the Sacred Heart of Jesus and Mary of Wheaton, Illinois. Independent Housing for Low Income Elderly.

Assisi Homes of Milwaukee, Inc., 5325 W. Burleigh St., 53210. Tel: 630-462-9271. Rodger F. Accardi, Chm.; Garth Seehawer, Contact Person. Franciscan Sisters, Daughters of the Sacred Hearts of Jesus and Mary of Wheaton, Illinois. Purpose: To acquire, or develop and operate housing projects for low income families and elderly persons and to provide for human and other charitable services required by the residents.

Assisi Homes of Wisconsin, Inc., 5325 W. Burleigh St., 53210. Tel: 630-462-9271. Franciscan Sisters, Daughters of the Sacred Hearts of Jesus and Mary, Wheaton, IL. Rodger F. Accardi, Chm. Total in Residence 148; Total Staff 6.

Capuchin Franciscan Tertiary Province of St. Joseph of Wisconsin, Inc., 327 W. Brown St., 53212. Tel: 414-374-5750. Rev. Ulric Buening, O.F.M.Cap., Prov. Asst.

Capuchin Franciscan Volunteer Corps, Inc., 1015 N. 9th St., 53233-1468. Tel: 414-271-0135.
E-mail: stbens@execpc.com
Purpose: To serve as a religious organization which recruits, places, and supports Christian volunteers in service to people in need. Bro. David Schwab, O.F.M.Cap., Dir. Total Assisted 180,000; Total Staff 2.

Cathedral Preservation, Inc., 802 N. Jackson St., 53202. Tel: 414-276-9814. Rev. John H. Endejan, Pres.

The Catholic Charismatic Renewal Office of Southeastern Wisconsin, Inc., P.O. Box 07912, 53207-0912. Tel: 414-482-1727. Deacon Robert E. Goodman, Liaison; Mary Goodman, Admin.

Catholic Charities Child Care, Inc., 3501 S. Lake Dr., P.O. Box 07912, 53207-0912. Tel: 414-769-3400. Thomas R. Schneider, Pres.

Catholic Charities Foundation, Inc., 3501 S. Lake Dr., P.O. Box 07912, 53207-0912. Tel: 414-769-3400. Thomas R. Schneider, Registered Agent.

Catholic Charities of the Archdiocese of Milwaukee, Inc., 3501 S. Lake Dr., P.O. Box 07912, 53207-0912. Tel: 414-769-3400; Fax: 414-769-3428. Mr. Thomas R. Schneider, Exec. Dir.
Regional Offices: 2021 N. 60th St., 53208. Tel: 414-771-2881. 2711 19th St., Racine, 53403. Tel: 414-637-8888. 503 Wisconsin Ave., Sheboygan, 53081. Tel: 920-458-5726. 741 N. Grand Ave., Suite 210, Waukesha, 53186. Tel: 414-547-2463.
Area Offices: 5820 3rd Ave., Kenosha, 53140. Tel: 414-658-2088. 191 S. Main St., Fond du Lac, 54935. Tel: 414-923-2550.
Other Offices: Beaver Dam, Brookfield, Burlington, Germantown, Menomonee Falls, Milwaukee North, Milwaukee South, Milwaukee Southwest, North Lake, Port Washington, West Bend. Total Assisted Annually 33,500.

Catholic Information Center, 633 W. Wisconsin Ave., Suite 1008, 53203. Tel: 414-272-8285. Rev. Charles J. Mehok, S.J., Dir. Total in Residence 4; Total Staff 4.

Clare Towers II, Inc. dba Clare Woods, 3576 S. 43rd St., 53220. Tel: 414-643-6501. Sponsored by School Sisters of St. Francis. Housing Facility for physically disabled to live independently. Apartments 32.

Clare Towers, Inc., 1546 S. 29th St., 53215. Tel: 414-643-6501. Sponsored by School Sisters of St. Francis. Housing facility for physically disabled to live independently. Apartments 25.

Convergence, Inc., 1501 S. Layton Blvd., 53215. Tel: 414-384-4105. Sr. Jeanne Schweickert, S.S.S.F., Pres. & Exec. Dir.; Sr. Anne Beitzinger, Vice Pres. Board Members: Sr. Charlita Foxhoven; Sr. Alphonsa Puls.

Covenant Community Foundation, Inc., 1126 S. 70th St., Ste. S306, P.O. Box 14970, 53214-0970. E. Thomas Sheahan, Pres. Sponsored by Franciscan Sisters, Daughters of the Sacred Hearts of Jesus and Mary, Wheaton, IL.

Covenant Healthcare System, Inc., 1126 S. 70th St., Ste. S306, P.O. Box 14970, 53214-0970. Tel: 414-456-2300; Fax: 414-456-2363. E. Thomas Sheahan, Pres. & CEO. Franciscan Sisters, Daughters of the Sacred Hearts of Jesus and Mary, Wheaton, IL. Congregation of the Sisters of St. Felix of Cantalice (Felician Sisters), Chicago, IL.

Covenant Home Health Services, Inc., 10010 W. Bluemound Rd., 53223. Tel: 414-259-7412; Fax: 414-453-3187. Franciscan Sisters, Daughters of the Sacred Hearts of Jesus and Mary, Wheaton, IL. Total Served 243; Total Staff 36.

Divine Savior Holy Angels High School Endowment Foundation, Inc., 4311 N. 100th St., 53222. Tel: 414-466-0810.
E-mail: dsha@dsha.k12.wi.us

East Side Service for Senior Citizens, 2727 E. Hampshire, 53211. Tel: 414-961-0661. Marylou Parthum, Dir.
Corporate Title: East Side Service for Senior Citizens, Inc. - an Interfaith Outreach Program. Sponsored by St. Hedwig, Holy Rosary, SS. Peter and Paul, St. Rita, Lake Park Lutheran Church, Plymouth and United Church of Christ, St. Casmir's and St. Mary Czestochowa, Milwaukee. Total Assisted 475; Total Staff 3.

Franciscan Peacemakers, Inc., Milwaukee, 2470 W. Locust St., 53206. Tel: 414-873-5078.
E-mail: franpax@execpc.com
Web site: www.execpc.com~/franpax
Rev. Robert Wheelock, O.F.M.Cap., Pres.; Jan Parrott, Exec. Dir. Total Assisted 16,250; Total Staff 2.

Franciscan Pilgrimage Programs, Inc., 1648 S. 37th St., 53215-1724. Tel: 414-383-9870. Rev. Roch Niemier, O.F.M., Pres. Operate a Catholic Franciscan Pilgrimage Program for religious men and women, leaders in Franciscan based institutions, members of the Secular Franciscan Order and others who desire to deepen their Franciscan values and spirituality.

Franciscan Seniors, Kenosha, Inc., 5325 W. Burleigh St., 53210. Tel: 630-462-9271. Steve Kuklin, Pres.; Garth Seehawer, Contact Person. Franciscan Sisters, Daughters of the Sacred Hearts of Jesus and Mary of Wheaton, IL.

House of Peace, 1702 W. Walnut St., 53205-1616. Tel: 414-933-1300. Charles Holton, Dir.; Rev. Matthew Gottschalk, O.F.M.Cap., Spiritual Dir. In res. Revs. Martin Pable, O.F.M.Cap.; Al Veik, O.F.M.Cap.; Bro. Booker T. Ashe, O.F.M.Cap., Dir. Emeritus. Total Assisted 5,000; Total in Residence 3; Total Staff 4.

International Institute of the Heart of Jesus, 7236 Wellauer Dr., 53213-3666. Tel: 414-475-2694. Dennis J. Brand (USA), Exec. Vice Pres. & Treas.; Rev. Roger Vekemans, S.J. (Chile), Pres.; Rev. Msgr. Walter O. Kern (USA), Vice Pres. & Sec.

The Jesuit Partnership, 3400 W. Wisconsin Ave., 53208. Tel: 414-937-6955. Revs. Eugene M. Dutkiewicz, S.J., Treas.; Warren J. Sazama, S.J., Pres.; Robert M. Frommeht, S.J., Asst. to Pres.

Korean Catholic Community, 1842 W. Windlake Ave., 53215. Tel: 414-672-6416. Rev. Augustine Park.

**LaFarge Lifelong Learning Institute, Inc.*, 1501 S. Layton Blvd., 53215. Tel: 414-383-2550. Continuing Education Program for older adults. Marion K. Hook, Exec. Dir.; Sr. Celia Schulte, Admin. Asst.

M.F.S.I., Inc., 3301 W. Highland Blvd., 53208. Wilfred F. Loebig, Jr., Pres. Sponsored by Franciscan Sisters, Daughters of the Sacred Hearts of Jesus and Mary, Wheaton, IL.

Milwaukee Achiever Program, Inc., 1506 W. Pierce St., 53204. Tel: 414-643-5108. Dennis J. Purtell, Esq., Legal Counsel. Sponsored by the School Sisters of St. Francis; Sisters of St. Francis of Assisi; School Sisters of Notre Dame.
Purpose: To provide adult literacy education to economically and educationally disadvantaged adults in the Greater Milwaukee area. Total Assisted 400; Total Staff 13.

Milwaukee Archdiocesan Council of Deacons. P.O. Box 07912, 53207-0912. Advisory/Governing Board of Deacons. Deacon Gerald R. Ponec, Pres.

Milwaukee Archdiocesan Elementary Principal's Association, 3501 S. Lake Dr., P.O. Box 07912, 53201-0912. Tel: 414-284-2682. Ms. Sandra Duffy, Coord. & Contact Person.

National Association of Catholic Chaplains, 3501 S. Lake Dr., P.O. Box 07473, 53207-0473. Tel: 414-483-4898; Fax: 414-483-6712.
E-mail: nacc@nacc.org
Web site: www.nacc.org
Rev. Joseph J. Driscoll (BO), Exec. Dir.

National Office of Post-Abortion Reconciliation and Healing, Inc., 3501 S. Lake Dr., P.O. Box 07477, 53207-0477. Tel: 414-483-4141; Fax: 414-483-7376.
E-mail: noparh@juno.com
Web site: www.marquette.edu/rachel
Victoria M. Thorn, Pres. Total Assisted 3,600; Total Staff 3.

O.S.F. Services, Inc., 1126 S. 70th St., Ste. S306, P.O. Box 14970, 53214-0970. Tel: 414-456-2300. Mr. Wilfred F. Loebig, Jr., Pres. Sponsored by Franciscan Sisters, Daughters of the Sacred Hearts of Jesus and Mary, Wheaton, IL.

Pallottine Fathers and Brothers, Inc., Disability Trust, 5424 W. Bluemound Rd., 53208. Very Rev. Robert V. Carney, S.A.C., Pres.; Rev. Harold J. Liebl, S.A.C., Treas.

Pallottine Fathers and Brothers, Inc., Educational and Apostolic Ministry Trust, 5424 W. Bluemound Rd., 53208. Tel: 414-259-0688. Very Rev. Robert V. Carney, S.A.C., Prov.; Rev. Harold J. Liebl, S.A.C., Sec. & Treas.

S.E.T. Ministry, Inc., 2977 N. 50th St., 53210. Tel: 414-449-2680. Sr. Lucina Halbur, C.S.A., Pres. & C.E.O. Wheaton Franciscan Services, Inc., Corporate Sponsor, Joint Sponsored by 17 Religious Congregations. Health and Human Services Outreach Programs. Total Assisted 3,500.

S.F.A. of Racine, Inc., 1126 S. 70th St., Ste. S306, 53214-0970. Mr. Wilfred F. Loebig, Jr., Pres. Sponsored by Franciscan Sisters, Daughters of the Sacred Hearts of Jesus and Mary, Wheaton, IL.

S.I.S. (Sisters Interacting with Seniors), 1720 S. 29th St., #420, 53215. Tel: 414-643-4529. Sr. Irene Kay, R.S.M., Coord. Total Assisted 600; Total Staff 3.

St. Benedict Community Meal. (Province of St. Joseph of the Capuchin Order, Inc.). 1015 North 9th St., 53233. Tel: 414-271-0135. Mr. Tom Plakut, Dir. Provides a free evening meal Sunday through Friday to those in need. Total Assisted 130,000 Meals Served; Total Staff 4.

St. Catherine Residence, Inc., 1032 E. Knapp St., 53202. Tel: 414-272-8470. A housing facility serving disadvantaged women in transition, with onsite programs advocating self-sufficiency. Includes a Right Start Program for first-time, single, pregnant women over the age of 18. Sr. Ruth Mutchler, R.S.M., Admin. Sisters 3; Residents 150. Legal Title: *St. Catherine Residence, Inc.*

St. Clare Management, Inc., 1545 S. Layton Blvd., 53215. Tel: 414-643-6501. Philip Aggen, Pres. & CEO. Sponsored by the School Sisters of St. Francis.

St. Francis Corporation, 3237 S. 16th St., 53215; Fax: 414-647-5565. Gregory A. Banaszynski. Total Staff 37.

St. Mary's Hospital, Milwaukee Foundation, Inc., 2320 N. Lake Dr., 53202. Tel: 414-291-1425; Fax: 414-291-1441. Mr. Mark D. Langer, Chm.; Sr. Renee Rose, D.C., Pres. Sponsored by the Daughters of Charity of St. Vincent de Paul.

St. Michael Hospital Community Foundation, Inc., 2400 W. Villard Ave., 53209. Tel: 414-527-8205. John H. Kopmeier, Jr., Pres. Franciscan Sisters, Daughters of the Sacred Hearts of Jesus and Mary, Wheaton, IL.

St. Stephen's League. (of the Archdiocesan Council of Deacons). P.O. Box 07912, 53207-0912. Deacon Juan A. Molina, Pres.

St. Thomas More Lawyers Society, 4060 N. 26th St., 53209. Tel: 414-444-5610. Rev. Joseph N. Perry, Chap.

Santa Fe Communications, Inc., 1126 S. 70th. St., Ste. S216A, 53214. Tel: 414-475-4444. Dr. William Thorn, Pres.; Rev. Anthony Scannell, O.F.M.Cap., Treas. Total Staff 3.

The School Sisters of Saint Francis of St. Joseph's Convent Congregational Support Charitable Trust, 1515 S. Layton Blvd., 53215. Tel: 414-384-1515. Sr. Helen Butzler, Trustee.

Seton Health Care Services, Inc., 4545 N. Port Washington Rd., 53212. Tel: 414-291-1300; Fax: 414-291-1319. Operated by the Daughters of Charity of St. Vincent de Paul.

Seton Health Corporation of Wisconsin, 2320 N. Lake Dr., 53211. Sr. Veronica Ann Brown, D.C., Chm. Operated by the Daughters of Charity of St. Vincent de Paul.

Shade Tree Family Resource Center, Inc., 2661 N. Teutonia Ave., 53206. Tel: 414-562-7934. Celia Jackson, Pres.; Valerie Nash, Contact Person. Sponsored by: School Sisters of Notre Dame. Operation of a community-based family center committed to the preservation of families and the prevention of violence; conducts programs, education, support groups and self awareness. Total Assisted 1,027; Total Staff 3.

Sisters of the Sorrowful Mother Ministry Health Care, 11925 W. Lake Park Dr., 53224. Tel: 414-359-1060. Sr. M. Lois Bush, S.S.M., CEO; Nicholas Desien, Pres. & COO.

Society of the Divine Savior Ongoing Community Support Trust, 1735 Hi Mount Blvd., 53208.

**St. Francis Foundation of Milwaukee, Inc.*, 3237 S. 16th St., 53215. Tel: 414-647-5515. Sponsored by the Felician Sisters. Fund development for St. Francis Hospital, Villa St. Francis, and The Terrace at St. Francis. Sr. Julie Weckwerth.

**St. Joan Antida High School Foundation, Ltd.*, 1341 N. Cass St., 53202. Tel: 414-354-9233. Sr. Kathy Lundwall, S.C.S.J.A., Contact Person.

**St. Josaphat Basilica Foundation, Inc.*, 573 W. Lincoln Ave., 53207. Tel: 414-385-3263; Fax: 414-385-3270. Mr. Michael J. Murry, Chm.; Mr. Richard C. Thomas, Admin.

Telos, Inc. dba Clare Heights, Clare Meadows, Clare Lakes, Clare Court, Clare Place and Clare Central. 1545 S. Layton Blvd., 53215. Tel: 414-643-6501. Sponsored by the School Sisters of St. Francis. Housing for physically disabled to live independently. Sr. Regina Pacis, Pres. Apartments 107.

Villa St. Joseph, Inc., 8526 W. Mill Rd., 53225. Tel: 630-462-9271. Steve Kuklin, Pres.; Garth Seehawer, Contact Person. Franciscan Sisters, Daughters of the Sacred Hearts of Jesus and Mary of Wheaton, IL. To acquire or develop and operate housing projects for low income families and elderly persons.

Villa St. Theresa, Inc., 5325 W. Burleigh St., 53210. Tel: 630-462-9271. Rodger F. Accardi, Chm.; Garth Seehawer, Contact Person. Franciscan Sisters, Daughters of the Sacred Hearts of Jesus and Mary of Wheaton, IL. To acquire or develop and operate housing projects for low income families and elderly persons.

VISION Ministries, Inc., 1515 S. Layton Blvd., 53215. Tel: 414-384-1515.
E-mail: sssf@earth.execpc.com
Web site: www.schoolsistersstfrancis.org
Sr. Regina Pacis Meservey, Exec. Dir. Sponsored by The School Sisters of St. Francis of St. Joseph's Convent, Milwaukee, WI, Inc.
Purpose: To further the mission of the congregation and to manage, promote support and engage in related ministries.

BRISTOL. *Mercy Retreat Center*, 12009 221st Ave., 53104. Tel: 414-862-6648. Sisters of Mercy of the Americas, Regional Community of Chicago. Sr. Lois Graver, R.S.M., Contact Person.

BROWN DEER. *Sisters of the Sorrowful Mother Charitable Trust*, 9056 N. Deerbrook Rd., 53223. Sr. M. Helen Malolepsy. Provides for the needs of the aged and infirm members of the Sisters of the Sorrowful Mother.

Sisters of the Sorrowful Mother International Finance, Inc., 9056 N. Deerbrook Terr., 53223. Tel: 414-357-8940.
Sr. M. Helen Malolepsy.

FOND DU LAC. *Hazotte Ministries, Inc.*, 475 Gillett St., 54935. Tel: 920-923-2121. Sponsored by the Congregation of the Sisters of St. Agnes. Sr. Hertha Longo, C.S.A., Pres.

St. Francis Home Foundation Inc., 365 Gillett St., 54935. Mary Weber, Pres. Sponsored by the Congregation of the Sisters of St. Agnes.

FRANKLIN. *Congregation of the Priests of the Sacred Heart Support and Maintenance Trust*, 6871 S. Lovers Lane Rd., 53132. Trustees: Revs. Justin Guiltnane, S.C.J.; Patrick Lloyd, S.C.J.; Bro. Benedict Humpfer, S.C.J.

Friends of Theophane, P.O. Box 32101, 53132. Mr. Ronald Zeilinger, Contact Person. To collect information and promote knowledge of the reputation for holiness of the late Frater Theophane Prenderville, S.C.J.

GREENDALE. *Volunteer Missionary Movement (VMM)*, 5980 W. Loomis Rd., 53129. Tel: 414-423-8660; Fax: 414-423-8964.
E-mail: vmm@execpc.com
Donald J. Mueller, Dir. Recruits, trains and sends Christian men and women to areas of need in the world.

HALES CORNERS. *Development Office*. Sacred Heart Monastery-Priests of the Sacred Heart-Reign of the Sacred Heart, Inc. 6889 S. Lovers Lane Rd., P.O. Box 900, 53130. Tel: 414-425-3383. Mr. Patrick R. Thompson, Pres. U.S. Province of the Priests of the Sacred Heart.

KENOSHA. *Dominican Fund of Kenosha, Inc.*, P.O. Box 1288, 53141-1288. Tel: 402-393-7661. James R. Kaskie, Contact Person. Sponsored by: Dominican Sisters of St. Catherine of Siena of Kenosha, Inc.

St. Mark Latin American Center, 1320 73rd St., 53143-5459. Tel: 414-657-7222. Revs. Pere Cane, Dir.; Luis Bulto, Assoc. Dir.; Deacon Gregorio Lebron. Total Assisted 1,800; Total Staff 4.

The Women's Health Center Foundation, Inc., 3556 Seventh Ave., 53140.
E-mail: stcath@acronet.net
Web site: www.acronet.net/~stcath
Susan Dyke, Chap. Sponsored by the Wheaton Franciscan Services, Inc.

MANITOWOC. *Sisters of St. Elizabeth, Inc., Congregational Support Charitable Trust*, 2005 Division St., 54220-5699. Tel: 920-684-7171, Ext. 291; 303. Mother M. Rita Amrhein, S.S.E., Trustee.

MEQUON. *St. Mary's Foundation Ozaukee, Inc.*, 13133 N. Port Washington Rd., Ste. G01, 53097. Tel: 414-243-7472; Fax: 414-243-7416. Ms. Jean Ansay, Chm. Sponsored by Daughters of Charity of St. Vincent DePaul.

OMAHA, NE. *Dominican Health Care, Inc.* c/o Catholic Health Initiatives, Central Midwest Region, 920 S. 107th Ave., Ste. 200, 68114. Tel: 402-393-7661. Eleanor G. Claus, Pres. Sponsored by the Congregation of the Dominican Sisters of St. Catherine of Siena of Kenosha, WI.

RACINE. *All Saints Healthcare Foundation, Inc.*, 3801 Spring St., 53405. Edward DeMeuLenaere, Pres. Franciscan Sisters, Daughters of the Sacred Hearts of Jesus and Mary, Wheaton, IL.

All Saints Healthcare System, Inc., 3801 Spring St., 53405. Tel: 414-636-4860; Fax: 414-636-4540. Edward DeMeulenaere, Pres. Franciscan Sisters, Daughters of the Sacred Hearts of Jesus and Mary, Wheaton, IL.

All Saints Visiting Nurse Association and Hospice of Racine, Inc., 4000 Spring St., P.O. Box 4045, 53404-0045. Tel: 414-635-7580. Debra A. Ostroski, Pres. Franciscan Sisters, Daughters of the Sacred Hearts of Jesus and Mary of Wheaton, IL. Home Care 60,992; Hospice Days 5,839.

Catherine Marian Housing, Inc., 5635 Erie St., 53402. Tel: 414-639-4100. Racine Dominican Ministries, Inc. and Franciscan Ministries, Inc.

Dominican College of Racine, Inc., 5635 Erie St., 53402. Tel: 414-639-4100. Sr. Evelyn Lins, O.P., Pres.

Marian Center of Racine, Inc., 3801 Spring St., 53405. Tel: 414-636-4011; Fax: 414-636-4540. Mr. Edward P. DeMeulenaere, Pres. Franciscan Sisters, Daughters of the Sacred Hearts of Jesus and Mary, Wheaton, IL.

Missionary Community of St. Paul the Apostle and Mary, Mother of the Church, Inc., 2512 Westwood Dr., 53404. Tel: 414-634-2666; Fax: 414-635-1910.
E-mail: 0mcsp@aol.com
Rev. Pere Cane, Pres. A private Association of Christian Faithful, comprised of clergy and laity, with missions in Africa and South America, while promoting mission awareness internationally.

Racine Dominican Ministries, Inc., 5635 Erie St., 53402. Tel: 414-639-4100. Sr. Evelyn Lins, O.P., Pres.

St. Catherine's High School Corporation, 1200 Park Ave., 53403. Tel: 414-632-2785; Fax: 414-632-5144. John Crimmings, Chpn.

St. Catherine's High School of Racine, Inc., 5635 Erie St, 53402. Tel: 414-639-4100. Sr. Evelyn Lins, O.P., Pres.

St. Catherine's Infirmary, Inc., 5635 Erie St., 53402. Tel: 414-639-4100. Sr. Evelyn Lins, O.P., Pres.

St. Francis Health Care Corporation of Racine, 3801 Spring St., 53405. Tel: 414-636-4011; Fax: 414-636-4540. Edward DeMeulenaere, Pres. Franciscan Sisters, Daughters of the Sacred Hearts of Jesus and Mary, Wheaton, IL.

Senior Companion Program. (Racine Dominican Ministries, Inc.). 5365 Erie St., 53402. Tel: 414-639-4100. Sr. Brenda Walsh, O.P., Dir.

Villa St. Anna, Inc., 5737 Erie St., 53402. Tel: 414-639-9757. Sponsored by Franciscan Sister, Daughters of the Sacred Hearts of Jesus and Mary of Wheaton, Illinois and the Sisters of St. Dominic of Racine, Wisconsin. To provide assisted living for the elderly of low and moderated income. Steve Kuklin, Pres. Residents 71.

ST. FRANCIS. *Foundation for Religious Retirement, Inc.*, 3221 S. Lake Dr., 53235. Tel: 414-483-9128; Fax: 414-744-7193. Jan Parrott, Exec. Dir. Raises funds to fulfill the needs of retired women religious in the Milwaukee Archdiocese.

SHEBOYGAN. *St. Thomas High School, Inc.*, 822 New Jersey Ave., 53081. Tel: 414-457-7110. Rev. Richard J. Fleischman, Sec. & Treas. A fund to provide youth and adult religious education programs within the county.

STONE BANK.

**Tyme Out Youth Ministry Center, Inc.* Mailing Address: W332 N6786 County Rd. C, Nashotah, 53058-9737. Tel: 414-966-1800. Sr. Kieran Sawyer, S.S.N.D., Dir. Total in Residence 2; Total Staff 16.

TAYCHEEDAH. *St. Charles Cemetery*. See St. Patrick Parish. Fond du Lac, 54935. Tel: 920-921-0347.

WATERFORD. *General Secretariat of the Franciscan Missions, Inc.*, P.O. Box 130, 53185. Tel: 414-534-5470; Fax: 414-534-4342. Revs. Sereno Baiardi, O.F.M., Dir.; Sante De Angelis, O.F.M., Assoc. Dir. General Secretariat of the Franciscan Missions, Inc. Missionaries 5,400.

WAUWATOSA. *Franciscan Shared Laboratory, Inc.*, 11020 W. Plank Ct., Ste. 100, 53226. Sponsored by Franciscan Sisters, Daughters of the Sacred Hearts of Jesus and Mary, Wheaton, IL. James Fantus, Pres. Medical Laboratory Serving Healthcare Institutions.

Friends of Calvary Cemetery, Inc., 2554 N. 66th St., 53213. Tel: 414-778-1187. Mr. Keith Schultz, Pres. Purpose: To raise funds in connection with the restoration of Calvary Chapel located at Calvary Cemetery, 5503 West Bluemound Rd., Milwaukee, Wisconsin, and overseeing such restoration.

St. Camillus Communities, Inc., 10101 W. Wisconsin Ave., 53226. Tel: 414-259-4511. Very Rev. William F. Cronin, O.S.Cam., M.S.W., Pres. & Prov. Supr. Total in Residence 25; Total Staff 3.

St. Camillus Institute, Inc., 10100 W. Bluemound Rd., 53226. Very Rev. William F. Cronin, O.S.Cam., M.S.W., Pres. & Prov. Supr.; Revs. Louis Lussier, O.S.Cam., Vice Pres.; James Kovarik, O.S.Cam., Vice Pres. & Treas. Management Corporation. Order of the Servants of the Sick (Order of St. Camillus). Total Assisted 128.

St. Camillus Ministries, Inc., 10101 W. Wisconsin Ave., 53226. Tel: 414-259-4511; 259-4664; Fax: 414-259-7702. Very Rev. William F. Cronin, O.S.Cam., M.S.W., Pres. & Prov. Supr.; Bro. Stephen E. Braddock, O.S.Cam., Ph.D., Vice Pres. & Exec. Dir. St. Camillus Ministries, Inc. operates under the auspices of the Order of St. Camillus and sponsors HIV/AIDS Ministry, Raphael House, Emmaus House and Magdalene House; Durward's Glen Retreat and Conference Center; Clinical Pastoral Education; and all social concerns ministry of the Order. Total Served 1,435; Total Staff 14.

WEST ALLIS.

**Archdiocese of Milwaukee Supporting Fund, Inc.*, 1126 S. 70th St., Suite S-506, 53214-3151. Tel: 414-475-2673. Erica P. John, CEO.

**Region 6 Development Association*, 6753 W. Rogers, 53219. Tel: 414-545-2120. Sr. Mary Coffelt, F.D.C., Vice Pres.
Purpose: To build a community of educators with new resiliency in Catholic education, emphasize the critical importance of on-going professional development.

WHITEFISH BAY. *Association of Ladies of Charity of Milwaukee, Wisconsin*, 4849 N. Wildwood Ave., 53217. Rev. Timothy L. Kitzke, Archdiocesan Spiritual Advisor; Dorotht A. Domer, Co-Pres.; Mary Reuter, Co-Pres. Children 900; Total Staff 15.

RELIGIOUS INSTITUTES OF MEN REPRESENTED IN THE ARCHDIOCESE

For further details refer to the corresponding bracketed number in the Religious Institutes of Men or Women section.

[0120]—*Alexian Brothers.* (Immaculate Conception Prov.).—C.F.A.

[0140]—*The Augustinians.* (Mother of Good Counsel Prov.).—O.S.A.

[0200]—*Benedictine Monks.*—O.S.B.

[0600]—*Brothers of the Congregation of Holy Cross.* (Midwest Prov.).—C.S.C.

[0470]—*The Capuchin Friars.* (Prov. of St. Joseph).—O.F.M.Cap.

[0740]—*Congregation of Marians of the Immaculate Conception.*—M.I.C.

[1130]—*Congregation of the Priests of the Sacred Heart.*—S.C.J.

[0480]—*Conventual Franciscans.* (St. Bonaventure, Prov. of Our Lady of Consolation).—O.F.M.Conv.

[0260]—*Discalced Carmelite Friars.* (Prov. of the Immaculate Heart of Mary).—O.C.D.
[0520]—*Franciscan Friars.*—O.F.M.
[0690]—*Jesuit Fathers and Brothers.*—S.J.
[0720]—*The Missionaries of Our Lady of La Salette.* (Prov. of Mary, Queen of Peace).—M.S.
[0240]—*Order of St. Camillus-Camillian Fathers.*—O.S.Cam.
[1070]—*Redemptorist Fathers.* (St. Louis Prov.).—C.SS.R.
[0990]—*Society of the Catholic Apostolate.* (Mater Dei Prov.).—S.A.C.
[1200]—*Society of the Divine Savior.* (American Prov.).—S.D.S.
[0420]—*Society of the Divine Word.* (Northern Prov.).—S.V.D.
[1360]—*Xaverian Missionary Fathers.*—S.X.

RELIGIOUS INSTITUTES OF WOMEN REPRESENTED IN THE ARCHDIOCESE

[0230]—*Benedictine Sisters of Pontifical Jurisdiction.* (Erie, PA).—O.S.B.
[0360]—*Carmelite Sisters of the Divine Heart of Jesus.*—Carmel.D.C.J.
[]—*The Christian Sisters (Pious Union).*—C.S.
[]—*Congregation of Institutio Santa Mariana de Jesus.*
[3710]—*Congregation of the Sisters of Saint Agnes.*—C.S.A.
[1780]—*Congregation of the Sisters of the Third Order of St. Francis of Perpetual Adoration.* (Eastern Region).—F.S.P.A.
[0760]—*Daughters of Charity of St. Vincent De Paul.*—D.C.
[0790]—*Daughters of Divine Charity.*—F.D.C.
[0420]—*Discalced Carmelite Nuns.*—O.C.D.
[1060]—*Dominican Contemplative Sisters.*—O.P.
[1070-03]—*Dominican Sisters.*—O.P.
[1070-09]—*Dominican Sisters.*—O.P.
[1070-25]—*Dominican Sisters.*—O.P.
[1070-27]—*Dominican Sisters.*—O.P.
[]—*Dominican Sisters.* (Vietnam).
[1170]—*Felician Sisters.*—C.S.S.F.
[1230]—*Franciscan Sisters of Christian Charity.*—O.S.F.
[1310]—*Franciscan Sisters of Little Falls, MN.*—O.S.F.
[1415]—*Franciscan Sisters of Mary.*—F.S.M.
[]—*Franciscan Sisters of Our Lady (Pious Union).*—F.S.O.L.
[1430]—*Franciscan Sisters of Our Lady of Perpetual Help.*—O.S.F.
[]—*Franciscan Sisters of St. Clare (Pious Union).*—F.S.S.C.
[1470]—*Franciscan Sisters of St. Joseph.*—F.S.S.J.
[1240]—*Franciscan Sisters, Daughters of the Sacred Hearts of Jesus and Mary.*—O.S.F.
[]—*Hermitage of the Trinity.*
[1820]—*Hospital Sisters of the Third Order of St. Francis.*—O.S.F.
[]—*Missionary Sisters of the Holy Family.*—M.S.F.
[3230]—*Poor Handmaids of Jesus Christ.*—P.H.J.C.
[2970]—*School Sisters of Notre Dame.*—S.S.N.D.
[1680]—*School Sisters of St. Francis.*—O.S.F.
[]—*Secular Institute of Schoenstatt Sisters of Mary.*—I.S.S.M.
[0600]—*Sisters of Charity of St. Joan Antida.*—S.C.S.J.A.
[0430]—*Sisters of Charity of the Blessed Virgin Mary.*—B.V.M.
[2575]—*Sisters of Mercy of the Americas.*—R.S.M.
[3800]—*Sisters of St. Elizabeth.*—S.S.E.
[1705]—*The Sisters of St. Francis of Assisi.*—O.S.F.
[1520]—*Sisters of St. Francis of Christ the King.*—O.S.F.
[3930]—*Sisters of St. Joseph of the Third Order of St. Francis.*—S.S.J.-T.O.S.F.
[4020]—*Sisters of St. Rita.*—O.S.A.
[1030]—*Sisters of the Divine Savior.*—S.D.S.
[4100]—*Sisters of the Sorrowful Mother (Third Order of St. Francis).*—S.S.M.
[3510]—*Sisters Servants of Christ the King.*—S.S.C.K.

ARCHDIOCESAN CEMETERIES

MILWAUKEE. *Calvary.*
Holy Cross.
Holy Trinity.
Mount Olivet.
St. Adalbert.
FRANKLIN. *All Souls.*
KENOSHA. *All Saints.*
MEQUON. *Resurrection.*
WAUKESHA. *St. Joseph.*

NECROLOGY

† Bier, Joseph V., (Retired). —Died Oct. 31, 1997.
† Boskamp, Charles, Waukesha, WI, Secular Institute of Schoenstatt Fathers. —Died Feb. 28, 1997.
† Brochtrup, Eugene, Milwaukee, WI, Salvatorians-Jordan Hall. —Died Jan. 10, 1997.
† Conley, Joseph J., (Retired). —Died March 5, 1997.
† Dowd, Patrick A., (Retired). —Died March 5, 1997.
† Eschweiler, Francis L., (Retired). —Died Dec. 27, 1997.
† Fechhelm, Richard A., (Retired). —Died March 26, 1997.
† Fischer, Joseph A., (Retired). —Died May 4, 1997.
† Haen, Edmund H., (Retired). —Died Oct. 23, 1997.
† Halmo, John F., (Retired). —Died May 10, 1997.
† Koren, Louis F., (Retired). —Died March 13, 1997.
† Litzau, John B., (Retired). —Died June 8, 1997.
† Petta, LeRoy A., Milwaukee, WI, St. Stanislaus. —Died Oct. 19, 1997.
† Sablica, Michael J., (Retired). —Died June 15, 1997.
† Schneider, Robert W., (Retired). —Died June 25, 1997.
† Stier, Joseph S., (Retired). —Died May 24, 1997.
† Straub, Very Rev. Carrol C., Vicar for Priest Personnel. —Died May 7, 1997.
† Tearney, Thomas A., Oconomowoc, WI, St. Jerome. —Died Feb. 16, 1997.
† Urban, Matthew J., (Retired). —Died Dec. 16, 1997.
† Wagner, Ralph J., (Retired). —Died July 31, 1997.

Archdiocese of Mobile

(Archidioecesis Mobiliensis)

Most Reverend

OSCAR H. LIPSCOMB, D.D., PH.D.

Archbishop of Mobile; ordained July 15, 1956; appointed July 29, 1980; consecrated November 16, 1980. *Res., 400 Government St., P.O. Box 1966, Mobile, AL, 36633.* Tel.: 334-434-1585.

Chancery Office: 400 Government St., P.O. Box 1966, Mobile, AL, 36633. Tel.: 334-434-1585; Fax: 334-434-1588.

ESTABLISHED AS VICARIATE-APOSTOLIC OF ALABAMA AND THE FLORIDAS, 1825; DIOCESE OF MOBILE, MAY 15, 1829; NAME CHANGED TO DIOCESE OF MOBILE-BIRMINGHAM, JULY 9, 1954; REDESIGNATED, JUNE 28, 1969. RAISED TO RANK OF ARCHDIOCESE NOVEMBER 16, 1980

Square Miles 22,969.

Comprises the lower 28 Counties of the State of Alabama, namely: Choctaw, Clarke, Wilcox, Dallas, Autauga, Elmore, Lee, Russell, Macon, Montgomery, Lowndes, Barbour, Bullock, Pike, Crenshaw, Butler, Monroe, Conecuh, Escambia, Covington, Coffee, Geneva, Dale, Henry, Houston, Washington, Baldwin and Mobile.

For legal titles of parishes and archdiocesan institutions consult the Chancery Office.

STATISTICAL OVERVIEW

Personnel	
Archbishop	1
Priests: Diocesan Active in Diocese	75
Priests: Active Outside Diocese	5
Priests: Diocesan in Foreign Missions	2
Priests: Retired, Sick or Absent	23
Number of Diocesan Priests	105
Religious Priests in Diocese	47
Extern Priests in Diocese	8
Ordinations:	
Diocesan Priests	1
Religious Priests	1
Transitional Deacons	1
Permanent Deacons in Diocese	41
Total Brothers	16
Total Sisters	221
Parishes	
Parishes	76
With Resident Pastor:	
Resident Diocesan Priests	52
Resident Religious Priests	19
Without Resident Pastor:	
Administered by Priests	4
Administered by Professed Men Religious	1
Missions	15
Pastoral Centers	3
Closed Parishes	1
Professional Ministry Personnel:	
Brothers	2
Sisters	13
Lay Ministers	37
Welfare	
Catholic Hospitals	1
Total Assisted	182,750
Health Care Centers	4
Total Assisted	4,211
Homes for the Aged	3
Total Assisted	375
Residential Care of Children	1
Total Assisted	200
Day Care and Extended Day Care Centers	4
Total Assisted	234
Specialized Homes	2
Total Assisted	63
Special Centers for Social Services	9
Total Assisted	94,632
Residential Care of Disabled	3
Total Assisted	176
Other Institutions	3
Total Assisted	260
Educational	
Diocesan Students in Other Seminaries	14
Students Religious	4
Total Seminarians	18
Colleges and Universities	1
Total Students	960
High Schools, Diocesan and Parish	3
Total Students	1,602
Elementary Schools, Diocesan and Parish	21
Total Students	5,942
Catechesis/Religious Education:	
High School Students	810
Elementary Students	3,516
Total Students Under Catholic Instruction	12,848
Teachers in the Diocese:	
Priests	1
Brothers	2
Sisters	21
Lay Teachers	510
Vital Statistics	
Receptions into the Church:	
Infant Baptism Totals	1,215
Adult Baptism Totals	221
Received into Full Communion	353
First Communions	1,230
Confirmations	1,232
Marriages:	
Catholic	185
Interfaith	295
Total Marriages	480
Deaths	660
Total Catholic Population	68,838
Total Population	1,452,506

Former Prelates—Rt. Rev. MICHAEL PORTIER, D.D., First Bishop; cons. Nov. 5, 1826; died May 14, 1859.—Rt. Rev. JOHN QUINLAN, D.D., cons. Dec. 4, 1859; died March 9, 1883.—Rt. Rev. DOMINIC MANUCY, D.D., appt. Vicar Apostolic of Brownsville and cons. Bishop of Dulma Dec. 8, 1874; transferred to Mobile March 9, 1884, but resigned in the same year; died at Mobile, Dec. 4, 1885.—Rt. Rev. JEREMIAH O'SULLIVAN, D.D., cons. Sept. 20, 1885; died Aug. 10, 1896.—Rt. Rev. E. P. ALLEN, cons. May 16, 1897; died Oct. 21, 1926.—Most Rev. THOMAS J. TOOLEN, D.D., cons. May 4, 1927; appt. Archbishop "ad personam," May 27, 1954; resigned Oct. 8, 1969; died Dec. 4, 1976.—Most Rev. JOHN L. MAY, D.D., ord. May 3, 1947; appt. Titular Bishop of Tagarbala and Auxiliary Bishop of Chicago, June 21, 1967; cons. Aug. 24, 1967; transferred to Mobile, Oct. 8, 1969; installed Dec. 10, 1969; appt. to Saint Louis, Jan. 29, 1980; died March 24, 1994.

Vicar General—Very Rev. JOHN AHERNE, V.G., *Holy Name of Jesus Church, P.O. Box 557, Semmes, 36575.* Tel: 334-694-4794.

Regional Episcopal Vicars—Very Rev. F. CHARLES TRONCALE, *St. Joseph Church, 511 Memorial Pkwy. N., Prattville, 36067.* Tel: 334-365-8680. Rev. Msgr. TIMOTHY DEASY, *Christ the King Church, P.O. Box 549, Daphne, 36526.* Tel: 334-626-2343. Very Rev. PATRICK GALLAGHER, *St. Columba Church, 2700 W. Main St., Dothan, 36301.*

Archivist—BERNADETTE MATHEWS.

Chancery Office—400 Government St., P.O. Box 1966, Mobile, 36633. Tel: 334-434-1589; Fax: 334-434-1588.

Chancellor—Very Rev. G. WARREN WALL, S.T.L., M.S.W.

Vice Chancellor—Rev. WILLIAM F. FIELDS, S.S.L.

Metropolitan Tribunal—14 S. Franklin St., P.O. Drawer D, Mobile, 36601. Tel: 334-432-4609. Please address all rogatory commissions and matrimonial matters to the Office of the Tribunal.

Judicial Vicar—Rev. Msgr. ANTHONY MCDEVITT, J.C.D., S.T.L.

Adjutant Judicial Vicar—Rev. Msgr. JOHN R. AMOS, J.C.D., M.Div.

Associate Judge—Rev. Msgr. KENNETH J. KLEPAC, J.C.L.

Defenders of the Bond—Rev. Msgr. JOHN R. AMOS; Sr. MARY ELIZABETH BUTLER, M.S.B.T.

Advocate—VICTOR WHELAN.

Court Clerk For 1st Instance—DANICE ENTREKIN.

Court Clerk For Appeal Court—JEAN MCGOWAN.

Notaries—DOROTHY BARRETT.

Archdiocesan Consultors—Very Rev. JOHN AHERNE, V.G.; Rev. Msgr. JOHN R. AMOS; Revs. PETER J. CUNNINGHAM; FRANCIS V. CUSACK; PATRICK MAHER; Rev. Msgr. PATRICK C. O'CONNOR; Rev. WILLIAM J. SKONEKI; Very Rev. G. WARREN WALL.

Vicars for Religious—Mobile District-Baldwin Escambia Deanery: Rev. ROBERT B. RIMES, S.J., *Spring Hill College, 4000 Dauphin St., Mobile, 36608.* Tel: 334-460-2175. Montgomery-Dothan Deaneries: Rev. Msgr. WILLIAM R. JAMES, *P.O. Drawer 1367, Robertsdale, 36567.* Tel: 334-947-5054.

Acting Vicar for Education—THOMAS L. DOYLE, Ph.D., *P.O. Box 129, Mobile, 36601.* Tel: 334-438-4611.

Vicar for Ministry to Persons with Disabilities and the Deaf—Rev. PATRICK J. MADDEN, *4350 Moffett Rd., Mobile, 36618.* Tel: 334-342-6449.

Vicar for Vietnamese Affairs—c/o Chancery, P.O. Box 1966, Mobile, 36633.

Archdiocesan Offices and Directors

Apostleship of Prayer—Rev. Msgr. J. EDWIN STUARDI, *Mercy Medical, P.O. Box 1090, Daphne, 36526.* Tel: 334-626-2694.

Apostleship of the Sea—Very Rev. G. WARREN WALL, Port Chap. JOSEPH V. CONNICK, III, Dir., *Catholic Maritime Club, 261 Dauphin St., Mobile, 36602.* Tel: 334-432-7339; Fax: 334-433-4618.

Apostolate for Aging—Rev. Msgr. GEORGE C. ROYER, *Sacred Heart Residence, P.O. Box 6805, Mobile, 36660.*

Archdiocese of Mobile Cursillo Center—Tel: 334-887-5540. Rev. JAMES DANE, Spiritual Dir., *1001 Hand Ave., Bay Minette, 36507.* Tel: 334-937-2026. ELLIE

SHOOK, *4940 C. Vaughn Pointe Dr., Montgomery, 36116.*

Archdiocesan Council of Catholic Women (ACCW)—Mrs. PAT SHRAND, Pres. MARIE D. MARTIN, Pres., *Priests Burse Club, 400 Government St., Mobile, 36602.*

Boy Scouts—Rev. STEVEN WILLIAMS, *St. Mary Church, 1453 Old Shell Rd., Mobile, 36604.* Tel: 334-432-8678.

Campaign for Human Development—Rev. WILLIAM J. SKONEKI, Dir. Funding Office for charitable and other works of Archdiocese, *356 Government St., P.O. Box 230, Mobile, 36601.* Tel: 334-438-9668; Fax: 334-434-1547.

Catholic Charities Appeal Office—Rev. PAUL G. ZOGHBY, Dir. Funding Office for charitable and other works of Archdiocese, *356 Government St., P.O. Box 230, Mobile, 36601.* Tel: 334-438-9668; Fax: 334-434-1547.

Catholic Housing of Mobile, Inc.—Most Rev. OSCAR H. LIPSCOMB, Pres.; Very Rev. G. WARREN WALL, Vice Pres.; Rev. Msgr. JOHN R. AMOS, Sec./Treas. Nonprofit Corp. of the State of Alabama, *Office: P.O. Box 1966, Mobile, 36633.* Tel: 334-434-1585.

Queen's Court I Apartments—W. Clark Ave., Prichard, 36610.

Catholic Housing Authority of Montgomery, Inc.—Very Rev. CHARLES TRONCALE, Pres. BILL PEARSON, Vice Pres.

Catholic Publishing Co., Inc.—Publisher of the Archdiocesan Newspaper *"The Catholic Week"*; LARRY WAHL, Editor, *P.O. Box 349, Mobile, 36601.* Tel: 334-432-3529.

Catholic University, Friends of—Rev. RUSSELL BIVEN, *Our Savior Church, 1801 Cody Rd., Mobile, 36695.* Tel: 334-633-6762.

Catholic Youth Organization—PAUL CRANE, Exec. Dir., *P.O. Box 6955, Mobile, 36660.* Tel: 334-471-0062.

Catholic Youth Ministry—GREG S. THOMPSON, Dir., *2518 Forbes Rd., Montgomery, 36110.* Tel: 334-265-2722. WARREN DAZZIO, Assoc. Dir., *1413 Old Shell Rd., Seton Center, Mobile, 36604.* Tel: 334-433-4138.

Cemeteries—Very Rev. G. WARREN WALL, *P.O. Box 1966, Mobile, 36633.* Tel: 334-434-1585. Deacon ROBERT L. NOUWEN, Dir., *1700 Dr. Martin Luther King Jr. Ave., Mobile, 36617.* Tel: 334-479-5305., *P.O. Box 190634, Mobile, 36619.*

Censor Librorum—Rev. J. ALEX SHERLOCK, S.T.M., M.A., *St. Peter Church, P.O. Box 114, Montgomery, 36101.* Tel: 334-262-7304; Fax: 334-262-9735.

Charismatic Movement—Liaisons: Deacon EUGENE STAKER; Mrs. STAKER, *Our Lady Queen of Mercy Parish, 4421 Narrow Lane Rd., Montgomery, 36116.* Tel: 334-288-2850; Fax: 334-281-7884.

Charities—(Listing under Catholic Social Services).

Clergy Retirement Association—Very Rev. JOHN AHERNE, Chm., *Holy Name of Jesus Church, P.O. Box 557, Semmes, 36575.* Tel: 334-649-4794.

Archdiocesan Coordinator of Health Affairs—Sr. ELISE BOUDREAUX, D.C., Pres., *Providence Hospital, 6801 Airport Blvd., P.O. Box 850429, Mobile, 36685.* Tel: 334-633-1000.

Ecumenical Commission—Rev. W. BRY SHIELDS, Chm., *St. Ignatius Church, 3704 Spring Hill Ave., Mobile, 36608.* Tel: 334-342-9221.

Family Life Director—Vacant.

Handicapped, Apostolate to the—Rev. PATRICK MADDEN, Dir., *4350 Moffett Rd., Mobile, 36618.* Tel: 334-342-6449.

Hispanic Apostolate—Rev. CHRISTOPHER VISCARDI, S.J., Dir., *Spring Hill College, 4000 Dauphin St., Mobile, 36608.* Tel: 334-380-3085.

Hispanic Pastoral Ministry—712 Dauphin Island Pkwy., Mobile, 36606. Tel: 334-478-3737.

Holy Childhood Association—Rev. JOHN C. ROBINSON, Dir., *Holy Family Church, 1304 Garland St., Mobile, 36618.* Tel: 334-344-0271.

Holy Name Society—Vacant.

Liturgical Commission—Very Rev. G. WARREN WALL, Chm., *P.O. Box 1966, Mobile, 36633.*

McGill Institute, A Corporation—P.O. Box 1966, Mobile, 36633.

McGill-Toolen Foundation, The—BEVERLY FINKBOHNER, Dir., Devel., *1501 Old Shell Rd., Mobile, 36604.* Tel: 334-432-0788, Ext. 48.

Office of Ministry to the Deaf—4350 Moffett Rd., Mobile, 36618.

Mobile Provincial Conference of Bishops and Priests' Councils—P.O. Box 1966, Mobile, 36633. Tel: 334-434-1585.

Newspaper "The Catholic Week"—LARRY WAHL, Editor, *356 Government St., P.O. Box 349, Mobile, 36601.* Tel: 334-432-3529; 432-3520.

Pastoral Council—GEORGE VELLA, Chm., *6657 Hounds Run N., Mobile, 36608.* Tel: 334-344-9839.

Permanent Diaconate Program—Very Rev. JOHN AHERNE, Dir.; Deacon JOSEPH MCGONAGIE, Assoc. Dir., *Holy Name of Jesus Church, P.O. Box 557, Semmes, 36575.* Tel: 334-649-4794.

Planned Giving—Deacon WILLIAM R. DOLAN, Dir., *P.O. Box 230, Mobile, 36601.* Tel: 334-432-1369.

Priests' Council—Most Rev. OSCAR H. LIPSCOMB, Pres. Officers: Rev. Msgr. PATRICK O'CONNOR, Chm.; Very Rev. PATRICK GALLAGHER, Vice Chm.; Rev. PAUL G. ZOGHBY, Treas.; Rev. MICHAEL KELLY, Record. Sec. DAVID CARUCCI, Corresponding Sec.

Ex-Officio Members—Vacant; Baldwin Dean; Vacant; Montgomery Dean; Very Rev. JOHN P. AHERNE, V.G. Consultors: Rev. Msgr. JOHN R. AMOS; Very Rev. G. WARREN WALL; Rev. PATRICK MAHER; Rev. PETER CUNNINGHAM; Very Rev. JOHN AHERNE; Rev. FRANCIS CUSACK; Rev. Msgr. PATRICK O'CONNOR.

Appointed Members & Consultors—Rev. Msgr. JOHN R. AMOS; Very Rev. G. WARREN WALL.

Elected Members—Group I: Rev. Msgr. WILLIAM R. JAMES; Rev. Msgr. PATRICK C. O'CONNOR; Rev. FRANK CUSACK. Group II: Very Rev. JOHN AHERNE, V.G.; Rev. F. CHARLES TRONCALE; Rev. Msgr. TIMOTHY DEASY. Group III: Rev. ADRIAN L. COOK; Rev. Msgr. JOHN R. AMOS; Rev. MATTHEW O'CONNOR. Group IV: Rev. JOSEPH S. WADAS; Revs. WILLIAM F. FIELDS; WILLIAM SKONEKI.

Religious—Revs. ROBERT MCCOWN, S.J.; CHARLES MOFFATT, S.S.J.

Priests' Eucharistic League—Rev. Msgr. J. EDWIN STUARDI, *Mercy Medical, P.O. Box 1090, Daphne, 36526.* Tel: 334-626-2694.

Priests' Personnel Board—St. Catherine of Siena Church, 2605 Springhill Ave., Mobile, 36607. Tel: 334-473-1415.

Priests' Retirement Fund—Very Rev. JOHN AHERNE, Pres., *P.O. Box 1966, Mobile, 36633.* Tel: 334-434-1585.

Propagation of the Faith—Rev. JOHN C. ROBINSON, *Holy Family Church, 1304 Garland St., Mobile, 36618.* Tel: 334-344-0271.

Radio and Television Communications—c/o Chancery Office, P.O. Box 1966, Mobile, 36633. Tel: 334-434-1585.

School Education Department—GWEN BYRD, Supt., *P.O. Box 129, Mobile, 36601.* Tel: 334-438-4611.

Office of Religious Education—14 S. Franklin St., P.O. Drawer D, Mobile, 36601. Tel: 334-433-6991. Ms. LORIE CREPEAU, Dir., *533 S. Union St., Montgomery, 36104.* Tel: 334-269-2389. Sr. FRANCIS ASSISI PIELMEIER, C.S.A., Dir., *P.O. Box A, Ozark, 36360.* Tel: 334-774-3214. Sr. PENNY SMITH, O.P., Dir.

Serra Club of Mobile—Dr. ADRIEN BODET, Pres.

Seton Haven Management Corporation—Col. DALE SCOTT, Pres., *3721 Wares Ferry Rd., Montgomery, 36193.* Tel: 334-272-4000.

Toolen Institute for Parish Services (TIPS)—Dr. AIDAN LICARI, Dir., *Drawer D, Mobile, 36601.* Tel: 334-438-6121.

Vocations—Rev. MARK I. NESKE, Dir., *Little Flower Church, 2053 Government St., Mobile, 36606.* Tel: 334-478-3381. Rev. ARTHUR SCHRENGER, Assoc. Dir., *Holy Spirit Church, 1150 Vaughn Rd., Pike Rd., 36064.* Tel: 334-277-5631.

CLERGY, PARISHES, MISSIONS AND PAROCHIAL SCHOOLS

CITY OF MOBILE
(Mobile County)

1—CATHEDRAL OF THE IMMACULATE CONCEPTION (1704), Most Rev. Oscar H. Lipscomb, D.D., Ph.D.; Rev. Msgr. James W. Oberkirch, Rector; Rev. William F. Fields. In res., Rev. James F. Dorrill.
Cathedral & Rectory—400 Government St., P.O. Box 1966, 36633. Tel: 334-434-1565; Fax: 334-434-1588.

2—ST. CATHERINE OF SIENA (1913), Rev. Edwin P. Beachum, Admin.
Res., 2605 Springhill Ave., 36607. Tel: 334-473-1415; 473-1427.
Catechesis/Religious Programs—Students 90.
Convent—2609 Spring Hill Ave., 36607. Tel: 334-473-5130.

3—CORPUS CHRISTI (1958), Revs. James F. Zoghby; John S. Boudreaux (LAF); Deacon Arthur W. Robbins.
Res., 6300 McKenna Dr., 36608. Tel: 334-342-1852; Fax: 334-342-6313.
School—Tel: 334-342-5474. Mrs. Brenda C. Elsevier, Prin.
Lay Teachers 23; Students 500; Aides 9.
Catechesis/Religious Programs—Tel: 334-342-7686.
Students 170.

4—ST. DOMINIC (1958), Revs. William J. Skoneki; Johnny S. Savoie; Deacon Edward Connick. In res., Rev. Msgr. Francis C. Murphy (Ireland).
Res., 4156 Burma Rd., 36693. Tel: 334-661-5130; Fax: 334-661-0469.
School—4160 Burma Rd., 36693. Tel: 334-661-5226. Mrs. Ann Zimlich, Prin.
Sisters of Mercy 2; Lay Teachers 22; Students 554.
Catechesis/Religious Programs—Students 98.
Convent—Tel: 334-661-3229.

5—ST. FRANCIS XAVIER (1867) (African American), Bro. Ricardo Gourrier, S.S.J., Admin.; Rev. Armand J. Manuel, S.S.J.; Deacon Alexander Moore, Pastoral Assoc.
Res., 2034 St. Stephens Rd., 36617. Tel: 334-473-4975; Fax: 334-473-4940.

6—HOLY FAMILY (1959), Revs. John C. Robinson; Ernest R. Hyndman, Jr.; Deacon Patrick Kelly.
Res., 1304 Garland St., 36618. Tel: 334-344-0271; Fax: 334-344-0296.
School—Tel: 334-344-1781. Mr. Thomas Al-Greene, Prin.
Lay Teachers 16; Students 277.

7—ST. IGNATIUS (Spring Hill) (1947), Very Rev. G. Warren Wall; Revs. J. Frank Sofie, Jr.; W. Bry Shields; Deacons Joseph P. McGonagle; J. Carleton Wilkins; Charles J. Fontana; Marvin C. Johns; Abraham Lopez.
Res., 3704 Spring Hill Ave., 36608. Tel: 334-342-9221; Fax: 334-341-1481.
School—Tel: 334-342-5442; Fax: 334-344-0944. Miss Janet Murray, Prin.
Lay Teachers 38; Students 664.
Child Care Programs—Jeannie Harris, Child Care; Janice Kerstin, Mother's Day Out.
Preschool—Jan Murray, Dir.
Catechesis/Religious Programs—Tel: 334-342-0516.
Students 106.

8—ST. JOAN OF ARC (1920), Rev. Msgr. Kenneth J. Klepac.
Res., 1260 Elmira St., 36604. Tel: 334-432-3505; Fax: 334-432-4422.

9—ST. JOSEPH (1857), Rev. E. J. Jacques, S.J.
Res., 808 Springhill Ave., 36602. Tel: 334-432-4218.

10—ST. JOSEPH (Maysville) (1944) (African American), Rev. Cornelius Sexton, S.S.J.
Res., 1703 Dublin St., 36605. Tel: 334-473-3761.
Convent—1701 Dublin St., 36605. Tel: 334-478-3292.

11—LITTLE FLOWER (1928), Rev. Mark I. Neske; Rev. Msgr. Maurice L. Shields, Pastor Emeritus; Rev. Vincent Phan; Deacons Wallace McKinney; Fenwick Walsh; Hank Pouliot. In res., Rev. Austin Conry.
Res., 2053 Government St., 36606. Tel: 334-478-3381; Fax: 334-476-4064.
School—2103 Government St., 36606. Tel: 334-479-5761. Sr. Mary Joyce Bringer, C.S.J., Prin.
Lay Teachers 14; Students 263; Aides 3.
Catechesis/Religious Programs—Students 34.
Convent—411 Little Flower Ave., 36606. Tel: 334-479-1198.

12—ST. MARY (1867), Rev. Peter J. Cunningham; Rev. Msgr. Cordell J. Lang; Rev. Paul G. Zoghby; Sr. M. Magdalena Langlois, C.S.A., Pastoral Assoc.; Deacons Ernest J. Johnson, Jr.; William Dolan. In res., Rev. Steven T. Williams.
Res., 1453 Old Shell Rd., 36604. Tel: 334-432-8678.
School—Tel: 344-433-9904. Miss Angela R. Ostmann, Prin.
Lay Teachers 12; Students 238.
Catechesis/Religious Programs—Tel: 344-432-0929.
Students 51.

13—ST. MATTHEW (1904), Rev. Joseph M. Bolling, Admin.
Res., 906 Garrity St., 36605-4699. Tel: 334-432-4784.

14—ST. MONICA (1950), Rev. Cu Minh Duong; Deacon James C. Burns.
Res., 1131 Dauphin Island Pkwy., 36605. Tel: 334-479-7360.
Convent—1950 St. Monica Dr., 36605. Tel: 334-479-1239.

15—MOST PURE HEART OF MARY (1901) (African American), Rev. Charles P. Moffatt, S.S.J. In res., Rev. William McKenna, S.S.J.
Res. and Mailing Address—304 Sengstak St., 36603. Tel: 334-432-3344.
School—Most Pure Heart of Mary, Tel: 334-432-5270. Sr. Nancy Crossen, O.S.F., Prin.
Religious 6; Lay Teachers 10; Students 175.
Catechesis/Religious Programs—Students 40.
Convent—310 Sengstak St., 36603. Tel: 334-433-6519.

16—OUR LADY OF LOURDES, Rev. Patrick Maher; Deacon Gordon Kenny.
Res., 1621 Boykin Blvd., 36605. Tel: 334-479-9885.
School—Tel: 334-479-4007; 479-2367. Mrs. Carol Dupree, Prin.
Lay Teachers 12; Students 183.
Catechesis/Religious Programs—Students 33.

17—OUR SAVIOR, Rev. Louis Russell Biven. In res., Rev. Msgr. Anthony McDevitt.
Office: 1801 Cody Rd., 36695. Tel: 334-633-6762; Fax: 334-633-7790.
Catechesis/Religious Programs—Students 168.

18—PRINCE OF PEACE (1970) (African American), Rev. Alfred A. Dean, S.S.J.
Res., 454 Charleston St., 36603. Tel: 334-432-2364.
Catechesis/Religious Programs—Tel: 334-433-1494.
Students 61.

19—ST. PIUS X (1954), Revs. Michael D. Kelly; James S. Kee; Charles J. McCabe; Deacons William L. Tew; Gerald F. Kingman.
Res., 217 S. Sage Ave., 36606. Tel: 334-471-2449; Fax: 334-471-2441.
School—Tel: 334-473-5004; Fax: 334-473-5008. Mrs. Alice S. Tibbetts, Prin.
Sisters 1; Lay Teachers 27; Students 521.
Catechesis/Religious Programs—Tel: 334-473-4381.
Students 16.

OUTSIDE THE CITY OF MOBILE

Andalusia, Covington Co., Christ the King, Rev. Robert W. Fulton.
Res., 504 Sanford Rd., P.O. Drawer 1546, 36420. Tel: 334-222-4808.
Catechesis/Religious Programs—Students 70.

Atmore, Escambia Co., St. Robert Bellarmine (1943), Rev. Michael J. Sreboth.
Res., 600 S. Main St., 36502-2825. Tel: 334-368-3615.

Auburn, Lee Co., St. Michael (1965), Revs. Stephen M. Staff, C.M.; James N. Dean, Campus Min.
Res., 302 E. Magnolia Ave., 36830. Tel: 334-887-5540; 887-5573; Fax: 334-887-5572.
Catechesis/Religious Programs—Students 220.
Joyland Child Development Center—Tel: 334-821-7624; Fax: 334-821-5583.
Chaplaincy—Auburn University, Auburn University Chapel, Catholic Student's Association. Tel: 334-887-5380; Fax: 334-887-1889.
Convent—Tel: 334-821-0588.

Bay Minette, Baldwin Co., St. Agatha Church, Rev. James E. Dane.
Church—1001 Hand Ave., 36507. Tel: 334-937-2026; 580-3194 (Res.).

Bayou LaBatre, Mobile Co., St. Margaret (1880), Revs. Patrick Madden; Trung John Nguyen.
Res., P.O. Box 365, 36509. Tel: 334-824-2415; Fax: 334-824-4114. [CEM]
Catechesis/Religious Programs—Students 120.

Belle Fontaine, Mobile Co., St. Philip Neri (1908), Rev. John R. La Brake, S.S.E.
Res., 9101 Dauphin Island Pkwy., 36582. Tel: 334-973-2096.

Brewton, Escambia Co., St. Maurice (1948), Rev. Adrian L. Cook.
Res., 202 E. Jackson St., P.O. Box 206, 36427-0206. Tel: 334-867-5189; Fax: 334-867-7993.

Butler, Choctaw Co., St. John (1958), Rev. Robert Kieltyka.
Res., 401 E. Pushmataha St., P.O. Box 456, 36904. Tel: 205-459-3129.
Mission—Chatom, Washington Co., St. Paul, 36904.

Camden, Wilcox Co., St. Joseph, Rev. John Barbernitz.
Res., P.O. Box 248, Orrville, 36737. Tel: 205-996-8850.
Mission—Orrville, Dallas Co., Mission of Immaculate Conception, Orrville, 36767.

Chastang, Mobile Co., St. Peter the Apostle (1860), Revs. James P. Fallon, S.S.J., Admin.; Joseph Calamari, S.S.J.
Mailing Address: P.O. Box 456, Mount Vernon, 36560. Tel: 334-829-6263. [CEM]
Catechesis/Religious Programs—Students 75.
Missions—West Mount Vernon, Mobile Co., St. Theresa; Fairford, Washington Co., Our Lady of Sorrows.

Chickasaw, Mobile Co., St. Thomas the Apostle, Rev. John Lynes; Sr. Anne Matisek, C.S.A., Pastoral Assoc.
Res., 251 N. Craft Hwy., P.O. Box 11061, 36611. Tel: 334-456-7931; Fax: 334-452-9837.
Parish Center—253 N. Craft Hwy., 36611. Tel: 334-452-9837.

Citronelle, Mobile Co., St. Thomas (1919), Rev. John Coghlan.
Res., 8025 State St., P.O. Box 61, 36522. Tel: 334-866-7505.

Daphne, Baldwin Co., Christ the King (1896), Rev. Msgr. Timothy Deasy; Rev. Timothy Evans; Deacons Malcolm Zellner; Leo Ollinger; Sr. Joan O'Donovan, Pastoral Assoc.
Res., 715 College Ave., P.O. Box 549, 36526. Tel: 334-626-2343; 626-3740; Fax: 334-626-3740. [CEM]
School—Tel: 334-626-1692; Fax: 334-626-9976. Sr. Maureen Nolan, Prin.
Presentation Sisters 2; Lay Teachers 26; Students 477.
Catechesis/Religious Programs—Tel: 334-626-5963.
Students 210.
Convent—713 College Ave., P.O. Box 901, 36526. Tel: 334-626-2431.
Presentation Sisters 3.
Shrine of the Holy Cross (1900), Rev. Robert M. McCown, S.J.
Res., P.O. Box 1497, 36526. Tel: 334-626-1447.
Mission—Bromley, St. John.

Dauphin Island, Mobile Co., St. Edmund-by-the-Sea, Rev. Eamon Miley.
Res., P.O. Box 6, 36528. Tel: 334-861-2352. [CEM]
Church—Cadillac Ave.

Dothan, Houston Co., St. Columba, Very Rev. Patrick J. Gallagher; Rev. Cecil Reeves Spotswood; Deacon Ron Moore. In res., Rev. Jose Joffre Paillacho, Hispanic Min.; Deacon Harold Grant.
Res., 2700 W. Main St., 36301. Tel: 334-793-5802; Fax: 334-792-2816. [JC]
Catechesis/Religious Programs—Tel: 334-792-3065.
Students 304.
Mission—Columbia, Houston Co., Good Shepherd, Columbia, 36319.

Elberta, Baldwin Co., St. Bartholomew (1911) (German), Rev. Howard R. Moussier, O.S.B.
Res., P.O. Drawer A, 36530. Tel: 334-986-8142; Fax: 334-987-5251. [CEM]
School—Tel: 334-986-8143. Mrs. Claudia Adam, Prin.
Lay Teachers 15; Students 230; Aides 4.
Catechesis/Religious Programs—St. Benedict's School.
Students 175.

Enterprise, Coffee Co., St. John (1959), Rev. Hugh Maguire; Deacon Gary Rasponi.
Church—123 Heath St. P.O. Box 311066, 36331-1066. Tel: 334-347-6751.
Res., 614 Alberta, 36331. Tel: 334-347-7345.
Catechesis/Religious Programs—Students 193.
Mission—Geneva, Geneva Co., St. Mary, 100 S. Commerce, Geneva, 36340.

Eufaula, Barbour Co., Holy Redeemer (1859), Rev. Joseph S. Wadas, Admin.
Res., 515 W. Broad St., 36027. Tel: 334-687-3716; Fax: 334-687-3766.
Catechesis/Religious Programs—Students 50.
Missions—Union Springs, Bullock Co., St. Piux X, 308 Kennon St., Union Springs, 36089.; Union Springs, Bullock Co., Bullock County Correctional Facility, P.O. Box 5107, Union Springs, 36089. Tel: 334-738-5625; Clayton, Barbour Co., Ventress Correctional Facility, P.O. Box 769, Clayton, 36016. Tel: 334-775-3331.

Fairhope, Baldwin Co., St. Lawrence (1961), Revs. Gordon Milsted; Primitivo Maravilla (Philippines); Deacon Henry O'Brien.
Res., 370 S. Section St., 36532. Tel: 334-928-5931; Fax: 334-928-5938.
Church—Sacred Heart, Battles Wharf, 36532.
Catechesis/Religious Programs—Students 259.
Chapel—Battles Wharf, Baldwin Co., Sacred Heart.

Foley, Baldwin Co., St. Margaret (1951), Rev. Charles J. Reiner, O.S.B.
Res., 601 Laurel St., 36535. Tel: 334-943-4009. [CEM]

Grand Bay, Mobile Co., St. John Baptist (1924), Rev. John J. Stryjewski.
Res., P.O. Box 417, 36541. Tel: 334-865-6902.

Greenville, Butler Co., St. Elizabeth (1894), Rev. Robert Fulton, Admin.
Res., 407 E. Walnut St., 36037. Tel: 334-382-6203.

Grove Hill, Clarke Co., Sacred Heart (1944), Rev. James Havens. In res., Rev. Francis Messing.
Res., Hwy. 43 N., P.O. Box 70, 36451. Tel: 334-275-3665.
Missions—Jackson, Clarke Co., Visitation, 135 W. Clinton St., Jackson, 36545.; Thomasville, Clarke Co., St. Joseph, W. Front St., Thomasville, 36784.

Gulf Shores, Baldwin Co., Our Lady of the Gulf (1952), Rev. Msgr. Patrick C. O'Connor; Rev. Lee O'Neil.
Res., 308 E. 22nd Ave., P.O. Box 515, 36547-0515. Tel: 334-968-7062.
Catechesis/Religious Programs—P.O. Box 2288, 36547-2288. Tel: 334-968-4133. John Baas, D.R.E.
Students 104.

Heron Bay, Mobile Co., St. Michael the Archangel (1880), Rev. William N. Gorman.
Mailing Address: 15872 Heron Bay Loop Rd. E., Coden, 36523. Tel: 334-873-4719.

Holy Trinity, Russell Co., St. Joseph, Rev. Thaddeus Searles, S.T. In res., Rev. Maurice Haiss; Bros. Pascal Haas, S.T.; Christopher Ilg, S.T.; Boris Farrah, S.T.; Rene Martin, S.T.; Matthew Rezmer, S.T.; Michael Lobo, S.T.
Church—1444 Hwy. 165, 36859. Tel: 334-855-3148; Fax: 334-855-3256.

Lillian, Baldwin Co., St. Joseph, Rt. Rev. Edward Markley, O.S.B.
Res., 34290 U.S. Hwy. 98, 36549. Tel: 334-962-2049; Fax: 334-962-3649. [JC]

Magnolia Springs, Baldwin Co., St. John the Baptist (1881), Rev. Msgr. Guido Calleja.
Res., 10797 St. John's Ln., P.O. Box 206, 36555. Tel: 334-965-7719. [CEM][JC 2]
Mission—Bon Secour, Baldwin Co., Our Lady of Bon Secour.

Millbrook, Elmore Co., St. Elizabeth Ann Seton (1978), Rev. Albert P. Kelly; Deacon A. B. King.
Church—4831 Hwy. 14, 36054-0585. Tel: 334-285-7000.
Res., 109 Crossgate Dr., Elmore, 36025.
Mission—Wetumpka, Elmore Co., St. Mark's, P.O. Box 765, Wetumpka, 36092.

Mon Luis Island, Mobile Co., St. Rose of Lima (1853), Rev. Msgr. John R. Amos.
Res., 2951 Durette Ave. (Mon Luis Island), Coden, 36523. Tel: 334-973-2592. [CEM]

Monroeville, Monroe Co., Annunciation, Rev. Sean Horgan, C.Ss.R.
Res., Whetstone St., P.O. Box 883, 36460. Tel: 334-575-2644.
Catechesis/Religious Programs—Students 32.
Missions—Uriah, Monroe Co., Our Lady of Mount Carmel, Hwy. 21 N., Uriah, 36480.; Vredenburgh, Monroe Co., St. Martin de Porres, Beech St., Vredenburgh, 36481. Tel: 334-337-4671.

Montgomery, Montgomery Co.,

1—ST. PETER, (1834), Rev. Alexander Sherlock.
Res., 219 Adams Ave., P.O. Box 114, 36101. Tel: 334-262-7304; Fax: 334-262-9735. [CEM]

2—CHURCH OF ST. ANDREW THE APOSTLE, Rev. Wilbur Kissell.
Mailing Address: P.O. Box 241303, 36124.
Res., 433 Clayton St., 36124. Tel: 334-262-3241.

3—ST. BEDE, (1925), Revs. David J. Tokarz; Michael Farmer; Fergus Prendergast; Deacons Eugene Wadas; Charles Gulley.
Office: 3870 Atlanta Hwy., 36109. Tel: 334-272-3463; Fax: 334-272-3492.
School—3850 Atlanta Hwy., 36109. Tel: 334-272-3033; Fax: 334-272-9394. Mr. Gerald Shook, Prin.
Lay Teachers 26; Students 425.
Catechesis/Religious Programs—Students 120.
Children's Center—3840 Atlanta Hwy., 36109. Tel: 334-277-8551. Eleanor McCormack, Dir.

4—CHURCH OF THE HOLY SPIRIT, (1977), Rev. Arthur C. Schrenger.
Res., 8570 Vaughn Rd., Pike Road, 36064. Tel: 334-277-5631; Fax: 334-277-2895.
Catechesis/Religious Programs—Tel: 334-277-1989.
Students 240.

5—ST. JOHN THE BAPTIST, (1908), Rev. David Carucci.
Res., 553 S. Union St., 36104. Tel: 334-264-6274; Fax: 334-262-3012.

6—ST. JUDE, (1934) (African American), Rev. Matthew A. Sindik. In res., Rev. James Holden.
Res., 2048 W. Fairview Ave., St. Jude, 36108. Tel: 334-265-1390.
School—Tel: 334-263-6121. Miss Mildred Lewis, Prin.
Sisters 2; Lay Teachers 16; Students 208.
High School—Tel: 334-264-5376; Fax: 334-264-6669. Sr. Mary Beth, D.C., Prin.
Lay Teachers 17; Students 162.
Catechesis/Religious Programs—Students 75.

7—OUR LADY, QUEEN OF MERCY, (1954), Rev. William P. Folsom, Jr.; Deacons Gene Staker; James LaBadie.
Res., 4427 Narrow Lane Rd., 36116. Tel: 334-288-2850; Fax: 334-281-7884.
School—Tel: 334-288-5334; Fax: 334-288-5395. Mrs. Mary Kaye McCooey, Prin.
Lay Teachers 14; Students 190.
Catechesis/Religious Programs—Tel: 334-288-5342. Mary Lou Staker, D.R.E.
Students 40.
Child Development Center—Tel: 334-613-0340.

8—RESURRECTION CATHOLIC CHURCH, (1943), Rev. Manuel Williams, C.R. In res., Revs. Casimir J. Wilczynski, C.R.; Henryk Licznerski, C.R. (Poland); John J. Krozser, C.M., Retired USAF Chap.
Res., 2815 Forbes Rd., 36110. Tel: 334-269-1770; Fax: 334-265-8081.

School—St. John/Resurrection School, Tel: 334-265-4615; Fax: 334-263-4999. Mrs. Mary Deas-Mears, Prin.
Religious 7; Lay Teachers 14; Students 130.
Mission—Montgomery, Montgomery Co., Resurrection Catholic Mission, 2815 Forbes Rd., 36110. Tel: 334-263-4221; 269-1770. Rev. Manuel Williams, C.R., Dir.

Mount Vernon, Mobile Co., St. Cecilia (1929), Rev. John Coghlan.
Res., 1305 Military Rd., P.O. Box 847, 36560. Tel: 334-829-9531. [CEM]

Opelika, Lee Co., St. Mary of the Mission (1910), Rev. William M. Allegretto, C.M.; Deacons Donald Canonica; John Taylor. In res., Rev. Bruce Krause, C.M.
Res., 1000 4th Ave., 36801. Tel: 334-749-8359; Fax: 334-749-6312.
Catechesis/Religious Programs—Tel: 334-745-3432.
Students 64.

Orange Beach, Baldwin Co., St. Thomas by the Sea, Rev. Francis V. Cusack; Deacon Raymond Basoco.
Mailing Address: P.O. Box 1190, 36561. Tel: 334-981-8138; 981-8132.

Orrville, Dallas Co., Immaculate Conception, Rev. John Barbernitz.
Church—13663 Alabama Hwy. 22 W., 36767.
Res., P.O. Box 248, 36767. Tel: 334-996-8850.
Mission—Camden, Wilcox Co., St. Joseph, 300 Whiskey Run Rd., 36726.

Ozark, Dale Co., St. John (1963), Rev. Brendan J. Keller.
Res., 709 Camilla Ave., P.O. Box 1008, 36360. Tel: 334-774-6826; Fax: 334-774-3923. [JC]
Catechesis/Religious Programs—Students 89.

Phenix City, Russell Co., St. Patrick (1911), Rev. Thomas D. Weise.
Res., 1502 Broad St., P.O. Box 147, 36868-0147. Tel: 334-298-9025.
Catechesis/Religious Programs—Students 101.
Convent—St. Patrick's Missionary Cenacle, 2701 40th St., 36867. Tel: 334-298-0708.
Missionary Servants of the Most Blessed Trinity 6.
Mother Mary Parish (1941), Rev. James McKenna, S.D.S.
Res., 318 Seale Rd., 36869. Tel: 334-298-2343.
School—Tel: 334-298-6371. Sr. M. Cecelia Harrison, F.M.S., Prin.
Sisters 2; Lay Teachers 8; Students 166.
Catechesis/Religious Programs—Students 160.

Plateau, Mobile Co., Our Mother of Mercy (1926) (African American), Rev. Charles E. McMahon, S.S.J.
Mailing Address: P.O. Box 10306, Prichard, 36610.
Res., 805 East St., 36610. Tel: 334-456-3551.

Prattville, Autauga Co., St. Joseph Church (1963), Very Rev. F. Charles Troncale; Deacon Samuel Shippen.
Res., 511 N. Memorial Dr., 36067-2133. Tel: 334-365-8680; Fax: 334-365-2267.
Catechesis/Religious Programs—Students 198.

Prichard, Mobile Co., Our Lady of Fatima (1949). Closed. For inquiries for parish records contact the Chancery.
St. James Major (1911) (African American), Rev. Henry E. Dickson, S.S.J.
Res., 714 S. College St., 36610. Tel: 334-456-6842; Fax: 334-456-6843.
School—Tel: 334-452-1883. Sr. Mary Stella Aquilina, D.C., Prin.
Daughters of Charity 3; Lay Teachers 8; Students 191.
Catechesis/Religious Programs—Students 67.
Convent—927 W. Prichard Ave., 36610. Tel: 334-457-9396.

Robertsdale, Baldwin Co., St. Patrick (1974), Rev. Msgr. William R. James.
Res., P.O. Box 1367, 36567. Tel: 334-947-5054; Fax: 334-947-7395.
School—(Grades K-8) P.O. Drawer 609, 36567. Tel: 334-947-7395. Sr. Margaret Harte, P.B.V.M., Prin.
Presentation Sisters 1; Lay Teachers 11; Students 185.
Catechesis/Religious Programs—Students 80.
Convent—P.O. Box 609, 36567. Tel: 334-947-7396.

Selma, Dallas Co., Our Lady Queen of Peace (1850), Rev. Carroll W. Plourde, S.S.E.
Office: 309 Washington St., 36701. Tel: 334-874-8931.
Res., 2511 Summer Field Rd., 36701. Tel: 334-874-8475.
Catechesis/Religious Programs—Students 98.

Semmes, Mobile Co., Holy Name of Jesus (1977), Very Rev. John Aherne, V.G.
Res., 2275 Snow Rd., P.O. Box 557, 36575. Tel: 334-649-4794.
Catechesis/Religious Programs—Students 70.

Tallassee, Elmore Co., St. Vincent De Paul (1955), Rev. Francis A. Lynch, C.M.
Res., 620 Gilmer Ave., P.O. Box 780487, 36078-0487. Tel: 334-283-2169. [JC]

Tillman's Corner, Mobile Co., St. Vincent de Paul (1971), Rev. Matthew O'Connor; Deacon Robert Nouwen.
Res., 5023 Camelot Dr., Mobile, 36619. Tel: 334-661-3908; Fax: 334-661-3908.
School—Tel: 334-666-8022; Fax: 334-666-8022. Kendall F. McKee, Prin.
Lay Teachers 10; Students 187.
Catechesis/Religious Programs—Tel: 334-666-4066.
Students 80.

Troy, Pike Co., St. Martin, Rev. David I. McGuinness.
Res., Elba Hwy., P.O. Box 313, 36081. Tel: 334-566-2630; Fax: 334-566-9105.
Catechesis/Religious Programs—Students 55.
Station—Luverne.

Tuskegee Institute, Macon Co., St. Joseph (1940), Rev. Charles E. McNeice, S.S.E.
Res., 2007 Montgomery Rd., 36088. Tel: 334-727-2710.
School—(Grades K-8) 2009 Montgomery Rd., 36088. Tel: 334-727-0620; 727-0642. Miss Jacqueline Grant, Prin.
Sinsinawa Dominicans 1; Lay Teachers 8; Students 117.

Whistler, Mobile Co., St. Bridget (1864), Rev. Leo Blanchet; Deacon Raymond Vrazel.
Res., 3625 W. Main St., P.O. Box 13357, 36613. Tel: 334-452-3676.

Chaplains of Public Institutions

CLAYTON. *Ventress Correctional Institution* 36016. Rev. Joseph S. Wadas.

UNION SPRINGS. *Bullock County Correctional Facility* 36089. Rev. Joseph S. Wadas.

On Duty Outside the Archdiocese:
Reverend Fathers—
Becherer, David, Parroquia, Del Santisimo, Sacramento, Apartado #324, Piura, Peru
McKenna, Philip A., Casa Parroquial, Zorritos, Tumbes, Peru

On Leave from the Archdiocese:
Reverend Monsignors—
Cullen, Thomas J.
Reverend Fathers—
Dahmen, Vernon
Dalton, Peadar
Kinane, James G.
Lemming, Patrick W.
Lott, Lawrence
Nicholson, Patrick
Reskey, George
Robinson, Jerome
Smith, Edward E.
Stauter, Andrew
Trosch, David

Retired:
Reverend Monsignors—
Aucoin, Charles
Jennings, Joseph
Madigan, James
McArdle, Joseph G.
McGuinness, Michael
Murphy, Francis
O'Connor, Francis
Royer, George C.
Stuardi, J. Edwin
Reverend Fathers—
Desmond, Barry
Hay, Theodore H., S.T.L.
McDonnell, Vincent
Rogers, Furman

Permanent Deacons:
Ba Soco, Raymond
Burns, James C.
Canonica, Donald A.
Connick, Edward G.
Dolan, William R.
Fontana, Charles J.
Grant, Harold
Gulley, Charles
Hamilton, John B.
Hicks, George, (Retired)
Johns, Marvin C.
Johnson, Ernest
Kelly, Patrick
Kenny, Gordon
King, A. B.
Kingman, Gerald
LaBadie, James
Lopez, Abraham
May, Frank J.
McGonagle, Joseph P.
McKinney, Wallace R.
McMeans, Leo
Moore, Alexander
Nouwen, Robert
O'Brien, Henry F.
Ollinger, H. Leo, Jr.
Pouliot, Henry
Pry, Jackie T.
Rasponi, Gary A.
Robbins, Arthur
Sheldon, Paul
Shippen, Samuel
Staker, Gene
Taylor, John E.
Tew, William L., Jr.
Vrazel, Raymond
Wadas, Eugene
Walsh, Fenwick
Wilkins, J. Carleton
Zellner, Malcolm

INSTITUTIONS LOCATED IN THE ARCHDIOCESE

[A] SEMINARIES, RELIGIOUS OR SCHOLASTICATES

SELMA. *Edmundite House of Formation*, Ujima House, 1423 Broad St., 36701-4314. Tel: 334-875-6089; Fax: 334-872-3777.
E-mail: myhalyk@aol.com
Web site: http://www.sse.org
Revs. Richard M. Myhalyk, S.S.E., Dir., Novices and Post-Novitiate Formation; Stephen W. Hornat, S.S.E., Dir., Edmundite Mission Corps.
Perpetually Professed: Bro. Francis J. Hagerty, S.S.E., Nurse Practitioner.
Temporary Professed: Bros. Christopher Daignault, S.S.E., Seminarian, Weston School of Theology, Cambridge, MA.; Daniel Manzano, S.S.E., Collegian, St. Michael's College, Colchester, VT.; Kenneth D. White, S.S.E., Brother-in-Training, Bishop Perry Middle School, New Orleans, LA; Brian T. Dwyer, S.S.E., Pre-Theology, St. Michael's College, Colchester, VT. Priests 2; Brothers 1; Total Staff 3.

[B] COLLEGES AND UNIVERSITIES

MOBILE. *Spring Hill College*, (1830) 4000 Dauphin St., 36608. Tel: 334-380-4000; Fax: 334-460-2195.
Web site: www.shc.edu
For a complete listing, refer to the Colleges and Universities section.

[C] HIGH SCHOOLS, ARCHDIOCESAN

MOBILE. *McGill-Toolen High School*, 1501 Old Shell Rd., 36604. Tel: 334-432-0784.
E-mail: shieldsb@mcgill.put.k12.dl.us
Revs. W. Bry Shields, Pres.; O. William Lee, Prin.; Steven T. Williams. Priests 2; Brothers of the Sacred Heart 2; Sisters of Loretto 1; Lay Teachers 84; Students 1,185.

MONTGOMERY. *Montgomery Catholic High School*, 5350 Vaughn Rd., 36116. Tel: 334-272-7220.
Web site: http://www.knights.put.k12.al.us
Mr. Faustin N. Weber, Prin. Lay Teachers 20; Students 250.

St. Jude High School, 2048 W. Fairview Ave., 36108. Tel: 334-264-5377. Sr. Marybeth Kubera, D.C., Prin. Lay Teachers 15; Students 162.

[D] CHILDREN'S HOMES

MOBILE. *St. Mary's Home*, 4350 Moffat Rd., 36618. Tel: 334-344-7733
For a complete listing, refer to the Special Care Facilities section.

[E] GENERAL HOSPITALS

MOBILE. *Providence Foundation*, 6701 Airport Blvd., Ste. C-130, P.O. Box 850429, 36608. Tel: 334-639-2050
For a complete listing, refer to the Hospitals section.
Providence Healthcare Services, 6801 Airport Blvd., P.O. Box 850429, 36608. Tel: 334-633-1000; Fax: 334-633-1679
For a complete listing, refer to the Hospitals section.

Providence Hospital, 6801 Airport Blvd., P.O. Box 850429, 36608. Tel: 334-633-1000; Fax: 334-633-1679
For a complete listing, refer to the Hospitals section.
Seton Health Corp. of South Alabama, 6801 Airport Blvd., P.O. Box 850429, 36608. Tel: 334-633-1660; Fax: 334-633-1679
For a complete listing, refer to the Hospitals section.
Seton Medical Management, Inc., 6801 Airport Blvd., P.O. Box 850429, 36608. Tel: 334-633-1000
For a complete listing, refer to the Hospitals section.

[F] SPECIAL HOSPITALS, SCHOOLS AND HOMES FOR THE AGED

MOBILE. *Allen Memorial Home Skilled Nursing Facility*, 735 S. Washington Ave., 36603. Tel: 334-433-2642
For a complete listing, refer to the Special Care Facilities section.
Little Sisters of the Poor, Home For the Aged, Inc., Sacred Heart Residence, 1655 McGill Ave., 36604. Tel: 334-476-6335; Fax: 334-478-6519
For a complete listing, refer to the Special Care Facilities section.

DAPHNE. *Mercy Medical*, P.O. Box 1090, 36526. Tel: 334-626-2694.
E-mail: info@mercymedical.com
Web site: www.mercymedical.com
For a complete listing, refer to the Special Care Facilities section.

MARBURY. *Resurrection Catholic Nursing Home*, 165 County Rd. 20 E., P.O. Box 89, 36051-0089
For a complete listing, refer to the Special Care Facilities section.

MONTGOMERY. *City of St. Jude, Inc., The*, 2048 W. Fairview Ave., 36108. Tel: 334-265-6791
For a complete listing, refer to the Special Care Facilities section.
Father Purcell Memorial Exceptional Children Center, 2048 W. Fairview Ave., 36108. Tel: 334-834-5590; Fax: 334-834-5592
For a complete listing, refer to the Special Care Facilities section.
Father Walter Memorial Center for Handicapped Children, 2815 Forbes Dr., 36199. Tel: 334-262-6421; Fax: 334-262-2265
For a complete listing, refer to the Special Care Facilities section.
St. Bede's Children's Center, 3840 Atlanta Hwy., 36109
For a complete listing, refer to the Special Care Facilities section.
St. John Resurrection Early Childhood Center, 2815 Forbes Dr., 36110
For a complete listing, refer to the Special Care Facilities section.

[G] HOUSING FOR THE ELDERLY

MOBILE. *Cathedral Place*, 351 Conti St., 36602. Tel: 334-434-1590
For a complete listing, refer to the Special Care Facilities section.

MONTGOMERY. *Laboure Complex Foundation*, P.O. Box 3074, 36109. Tel: 334-277-5213
For a complete listing, refer to the Special Care Facilities section.
Seton Haven, 3721 Wares Ferry Rd., 36109. Tel: 334-272-4000
For a complete listing, refer to the Special Care Facilities section.

PRICHARD. *Queen's Court I Apartments*, W. Clark Ave., 36610
For a complete listing, refer to the Special Care Facilities section.

[H] MONASTERIES AND RESIDENCES OF PRIESTS AND BROTHERS

MOBILE. *Brothers of the Sacred Heart*, 60 N. Catherine St., 36604. Tel: 334-438-3812.
E-mail: mulliganp@email.msn.com
Bros. Paul Mulligan, S.C., Dir.; Victor Bendillo, S.C., Sub.Dir.; Flavian Udinsky, S.C.; Alcuin Kelly, S.C.; Celestine Algero, S.C.; John Moore, S.C. Brothers 6.

SELMA. *Edmundite Fathers*, Edmundite Missions House, 1401 Broad St., 36701. Tel: 334-872-6221.
E-mail: RogerLac@aol.com
Web site: http://www.EdmunditeMissions.com
Legal Title: *Fathers of St. Edmund Southern Missions, Inc.* Revs. Carroll W. Plourde, S.S.E., Supr.; Roger J. LaCharite, S.S.E., Missions Dir.; Richard M. Myhalyk, S.S.E., Programs Dir.; Stephen W. Hornat, S.S.E., Missions Corp. Dir.; Edward F. Conlin, S.S.E.; Francis A. Donnellan, S.S.E.; Robert J. Sheehey, S.S.E.; James F. Ryan, S.S.E.; Nelson B. Ziter, S.S.E.; Bro. Francis J. Hagerty, S.S.E. Priests 9; Brothers 1; Total Assisted 166,050; Total Staff 42.

[I] CONVENTS AND RESIDENCES OF SISTERS

MOBILE. *Blessed Trinity Missionary Cenacle*, 604 Barksdale Dr. W., 36606. Tel: 334-476-4803. Missionary Servants 3.
Convent of the Sisters of Mercy of the Americas Baltimore Regional Community, 101 Wimbledon Dr., W., 36608. Tel: 334-344-1377. Sr. Carolyn Oberkirch, R.S.M., Admin. Sisters 19; Total Staff 10.
Other Residences: 4301 Bit & Spur Rd., 36608. Tel: 334-344-1377. 606 Bay Bluff East, Daphne, 36526. Tel: 334-626-0130. 2902 Brierwood Dr., 36606. Tel: 334-476-4605. 172 N. Lafayette St., 36604. Tel: 334-432-3178. Portier Place, 4363 Old Shell Rd., 36608. Sr. Ruth Handren, Admin., Huntleigh Woods, Apt. N-205, 375 Hillcrest Rd., 36608. Tel: 334-344-9388. 3700 Whispering Pines, Apt. 47C, 36608-1149. Tel: 334-343-4435.
Convent of the Sisters of St. Agnes, 1701 Dublin St., 36605. Tel: 334-478-3292. Sisters 6.
Monastery of Discalced Carmelite Nuns, 716 Dauphin Island Pkwy., 36606. Rev. Mother Agnes, O.C.D., Prioress. Solemnly Professed 7.
Sisters of Loretto, 1408 Old Shell Rd., 36604-2244. Tel: 334-431-6735.
E-mail: ardoyns@mcgill.pvt.k12.al.us
Sr. Sandra Ardoyno, S.L.
Sisters of Mercy of the Americas, St. Louis Regional Community, 4009 Old Shell Rd., Apt. C-23, 36608. Tel: 334-460-0478. Sr. Mary Giles Peresich, R.S.M.
Visitation Monastery and Retreat House, 2300 Spring Hill Ave., 36607. Tel: 334-473-2321. Mother Rose Marie Kinsella, Supr. Sisters 13; Total Staff 3.

ALBERTA. *Alberta Health Center*, P.O. Box 97, 36720. Tel: 334-573-2493.

AUBURN. *St. Louise Missionary Cenacle*, 302 E. Magnolia Ave., 36830. Tel: 334-821-0588. Missionary Servants of the Most Blessed Trinity 1.

CAMDEN. *Sisters of St. Joseph*, 490 Whiskey Run Rd., 36726. Tel: 334-682-4144.
E-mail: rcookmd@juno.com
Sisters 2; Total Staff 6.
Sisters of St. Joseph of Philadelphia, 15 Cherokee Dr., 36726. Tel: 334-682-4474.
E-mail: jgriff71@juno.com
Sr. Donna Jo Loeper, S.S.J.; Sr. Jacqueline Griffith, S.S.J.

DOTHAN. *Holy Spirit Missionary Cenacle*, 3205 Redmond Rd., 36303. Tel: 334-983-3116.

HAYNEVILLE. *Daughters of the Holy Spirit*, 1016 Hwy. 12, 36040. Tel: 334-563-7382. Sisters 2.

HOLY TRINITY. *Blessed Trinity Shrine Retreat and Cenacle*, 36859. Tel: 334-855-4474.
E-mail: msbtphl@aol.com
Sr. Ann Maura O'Keefe, M.S.B.T., Dir. Missionary Servants of the Most Blessed Trinity 4; Lay Volunteers 2; Retreat House Capacity 40.

HURTSBORO. *Spirit of Peace Missionary Cenacle*, P.O. Box 117, 38660. Tel: 334-667-6536. Sr. Zelie Therese Pendergast, M.S.B.T.

MARBURY. *Dominican Monastery of St. Jude (St. Jude Monastery)*, P.O. Box 170, 36051. Mother Mary Aimee, O.P., Prioress. Cloistered Dominican Nuns of Perpetual Adoration and Rosary. Professed Sisters 9.

MONTGOMERY. *Daughters of Charity*, 577-579 Eastdale Rd., S., 36117. Tel: 334-272-3354. Sisters 6.
Mater Dei Missionary Cenacle, 784 Spring Valley Rd., 36116. Tel: 334-288-4544. Missionary Servants of the Most Blessed Trinity 3.

OZARK. *Sinsinawa Dominican Sisters*, Rte. 3, Box 50, 36360. Tel: 334-299-6671.
E-mail: psmith8037@aol.com
Sr. Penny Smith, O.P.

PHENIX CITY. *St. Patrick's Missionary Cenacle*, 2701 Fortieth St., 36867. Tel: 334-298-0708. Missionary Servants of the Most Blessed Trinity 6.

PINE APPLE. *Sisters of St. Joseph*, Rte. 2, P.O. Box 9-A, 36768. Tel: 334-746-2584. Sisters 4.

SELMA. *Sisters Residence*, 911 Mabry St., 36701. Tel: 334-874-6536. Sisters 3.

VREDENBURGH. *Emmanuel Community*, P.O. Box 365, 36481. Tel: 334-337-4484.

[J] ARCHDIOCESAN SOCIAL SERVICE

MOBILE. *Catholic Social Services, Archdiocese of Mobile*. Mailing Address: P.O. Box 759, 36601. 400 Government St., 36602. Tel: 334-434-1550; Fax: 334-434-1549. Sr. Frances Louise Sheridan, M.S.B.T., Archdiocesan Dir.; Marilyn Davis King, Dir.
Branch Offices: 4455 Narrow Lane Rd., Montgomery, 36116. Tel: 334-793-3601; Fax: 334-702-0825. Sr. Patricia Louise Langan, M.S.B.T., Dir., P.O. Box 870, Robertsdale, 36567. Tel: 334-947-2293. Mrs. Michele Prockup, Dir., P.O. Box 1105, Chatom, 36518. Tel: 334-847-2708. Mrs. Joyce Yocum, Dir., P.O. Box 6184, Dothan, 36302. Tel: 334-793-3601. Sr. Florence Young, M.S.B.T., Dir., P.O. Box 70, Hwy. 43 N., Grove Hill, 36451. Tel: 334-275-4893. Mrs. Martha Coaker, Dir.
Service Center of Catholic Social Services, 555 Dauphin St., 36602. Tel: 334-434-1500. Sr. Judith Vander Grinten, C.S.A., M.S.W., Dir. Total Assisted 23,441; Total Staff 25.

CHATOM. *Chatom Office of Catholic Social Services*, P.O. Box 1105, 36518. Tel: 334-847-2708. Joyce Yocum, Supvr. Total Assisted 6,899; Total Staff 2.

DOTHAN. *Dothan Office of Catholic Social Services*, P.O. Box 6184, 36302. Tel: 334-793-3601.

MONTGOMERY. *Catholic Social Services of Montgomery*, 4455 Narrow Lane Rd., 36116. Tel: 334-288-8890; Fax: 334-288-9322. Sr. Patricia Langan, M.S.B.T., Dir. Total Assisted 7,696; Total Staff 12.

ROBERTSDALE. *Robertsdale Office of Catholic Social Services*, P.O. Box 870, 36567. Tel: 334-947-2293; Fax: 334-947-4058. Ms. Michele Prockup, Dir. Total Assisted 7,956; Total Staff 5.

[K] NEWMAN CENTERS

MOBILE. *Spring Hill College Newman Center*, 4000 Dauphin St., 36608. Tel: 334-380-4000; Fax: 334-460-2195. Rev. John R. Payne, S.J.
University of South Alabama Newman Center, Catholic Student Center, 6051 Old Shell Rd., 36608. Tel: 334-343-3662. Rev. James F. Dorrill, Ph.D., Chap.; Sonia Moulard, Dir. & Asst. Campus Min.

AUBURN. *Auburn University Newman Center*, 302 E. Magnolia Ave., 36830. Tel: 334-887-5380.
E-mail: deanjam@mail.auburn.edu
Web site: http://www.auburn.edu/~stmcsol
Rev. James N. Dean; Victoria Bolling, Asst. Campus Min.

DOTHAN. *George C. Wallace Jr. Community College Newman Center*, 2700 W. Main St., 36301. Tel: 334-793-5802. Very Rev. Patrick J. Gallagher.

MONROEVILLE. *Alabama Southern Community College Newman Center*, P.O. Box 883, 36460-0883. Tel: 334-275-3665. Rev. Sean Horgan, C.Ss.R.

MONTGOMERY. *Alabama State University Newman Center*, 553 S. Union St., 36104. Tel: 334-264-6274. Rev. David Carucci.
Huntington College Newman Center, 4421 Narrow Lane Rd., 36116. Tel: 334-288-2850. Rev. William P. Folsom, Jr.

SELMA. *Marion Institute Newman Center*, 309 Washington St., 36703. Tel: 334-874-8931. Rev. Carroll W. Plourde, S.S.E.

TROY. *Troy State University Newman Center*, P.O. Box 313, 36081. Tel: 334-566-2630. Rev. David I. McGuinness.

TUSKEGEE INSTITUTE. *Tuskegee University Newman Center*, 2007 Montgomery Rd., 36088. Tel: 334-727-2710. Rev. Charles McNeice, S.S.E. Total Staff 1.

[L] MISCELLANEOUS LISTINGS

MOBILE. *Catholic High Schools Alumni Association of Mobile*, 1501 Old Shell Rd., 36604. Tel: 334-432-0784. Eleanor Woolsey, Alumni Dir.
L'Arche, 151 S. Ann St., 36604. Tel: 334-438-2094.
E-mail: larchmob@acan.net
Christian non-profit organization-community where handicapped and non-handicapped people live. Marty O'Malley, Dir. Handicapped People 19; Assistants 14.
Ladies of Charity, 207 So. Florida St., 36606. Tel: 334-479-0089. Mrs. P. J. Cooney, Pres.
**Providence Building Corporation*, P.O. Box 850429, 36685. 6801 Airport Blvd., 36608. John R. Roeder, Pres.; Sr. Marilyn Moore, D.C., Chm.; Sr. Betty Gunselman, D.C., Sec.
St. Ignatius Day Care - Mobile, 3704 Springhill Ave., 36608. Tel: 334-342-3322. Mrs. Jeanne Harris, Dir.
Society of St. Vincent de Paul, 411 S. Broad St., 36603. Tel: 334-432-5173. Wes Chiniche, Pres., 411 S. Broad St., 36603.

DAPHNE. *Apostleship of Prayer*, P.O. Box 1090, 36532. Tel: 334-626-2694. Rev. Msgr. J. Edwin Stuardi.

DOTHAN. *St. Columba Preschool*, 2700 W. Main St., 36301. Tel: 334-793-6742. Mrs. Cathy Dedmon, Dir.

HAYNEVILLE. *Lowndes County Catholic Center*, 1016 Hwy. 12, 36040. Tel: 334-563-9139.

HURTSBORO. *John XXIII Center*, P.O. Box 117, 36860. Tel: 334-667-7770. Sr. Zelie Therese Pendergast, M.S.B.T., Admin.

MONTGOMERY. *The City of St. Jude, Inc.*, 2048 W. Fairview Ave., 36108. Tel: 334-265-6791. Mr. Thomas C. Logan, Exec. Dir.; Rev. Msgr. Matthew A. Sindik, Dir.
St. John's Soup Kitchen, Inc., 553 S. Union St., 36104. Tel: 334-264-6274; Fax: 334-262-3012. P.O. Box 230512, 36123-0512. Tel: 334-264-6204. Rev. David Carucci.
St. Margaret's Foundation, 818 S. Perry St., Ste. 2, 36104. Tel: 334-262-0785. Susan Meehan, Pres.; Dr. Ray Furlong, Chm.; Haywood M. Sport, Vice Chm.; Mary Francis J. Moore, Sec. & Treas.

St. Margaret's Services, 818 S. Perry St., Ste. 2, 36104. Tel: 334-262-0784. Susan Meehan, Pres.; Sr. Mary Ann O'Brien, D.C., Chm.; Sr. Virginia Delaney, D.C., Vice Chm.; Harold Parrish, Sec. & Treas. Daughters of Charity of St. Vincent de Paul 5. Care for the poor, frail elderly and homebound disabled through Elderly Outreach and Interfaith Volunteer Caregivers.

PRICHARD. *Ladies of Charity*, 1013 N. College St., 36610. Tel: 334-456-1142. Mrs. Jean Lewis, Pres.

RELIGIOUS INSTITUTES OF MEN REPRESENTED IN THE ARCHDIOCESE

For further details refer to the corresponding bracketed number in the Religious Institute of Men or Women section.

[0200]—*Benedictine Monks.*—O.S.B.

[1100]—*Brothers of the Sacred Heart.* (New Orleans Prov.).—S.C.

[1330]—*Congregation of the Mission.* (Eastern Prov.).—C.M.

[1080]—*Congregation of the Resurrection.* (Chicago Prov.).—C.R.

[0690]—*Jesuit Fathers and Brothers.* (New Orleans Prov.).—S.J.

[0840]—*Missionary Servants of the Most Holy Trinity.*—S.T.

[0700]—*St. Joseph's Society of the Sacred Heart.* (Baltimore, MD).—S.S.J.

[0440]—*Society of Saint Edmund.* (Selma, AL).—S.S.E.

RELIGIOUS INSTITUTES OF WOMEN REPRESENTED IN THE ARCHDIOCESE

[0200]—*Benedictine Sisters of Pontifical Jurisdiction.* (Cullman, AL; Ferdinand, IN).—O.S.B.

[3710]—*Congregation of the Sisters of Saint Agnes.*—C.S.A.

[1780]—*Congregation of the Sisters of the Third Order of St. Francis of Perpetual Adoration.*—F.S.P.A.

[0760]—*Daughters of Charity of St. Vincent de Paul.*—D.C.

[0820]—*Daughters of the Holy Spirit.*—D.H.S.

[0420]—*Discalced Carmelite Nuns.*—O.C.D.

[1050]—*Dominican Contemplative Nuns.*—O.P.

[1070-03]—*Dominican Sisters.*—O.P.

[1070-13]—*Dominican Sisters.*—O.P.

[1070-18]—*Dominican Sisters.*—O.P.

[2575]—*Institute of the Sisters of Mercy of the Americas.*—R.S.M.

[2340]—*Little Sisters of the Poor.*—L.S.P.

[2790]—*Missionary Servants of the Most Blessed Trinity.*—M.S.B.T.

[0430]—*Sisters of Charity of the Blessed Virgin Mary.*—B.V.M.

[2360]—*Sisters of Loretto At the Foot of the Cross.*—S.L.

[2550]—*Sisters of Mercy.*—R.S.M.

[3360]—*Sisters of Providence of Saint Mary-of-the-Woods, Indiana.*—S.P.

[1650]—*Sisters of St. Francis of Philadelphia.*—O.S.F.

[3830-14]—*Sisters of St. Joseph.*—S.S.J.

[3830-15]—*Sisters of St. Joseph.*—C.S.J.

[3840]—*Sisters of St. Joseph of Carondelet.*—C.S.J.

[3850]—*Sisters of St. Joseph of Chambery.*—C.S.J.

[1970]—*Sisters of the Holy Family of Nazareth.*—C.S.F.N.

[2150]—*Sisters, Servants of the Immaculate Heart of Mary.*—I.H.M.

[3330]—*Union of the Sisters of the Presentation of the Blessed Virgin Mary.*—P.B.V.M.

[4170]—*Vincentian Sisters of Charity.* (Perryville, PA).—V.S.C.

[4190]—*Visitation Nuns.*—V.H.M.

NECROLOGY

† Adams, Rev. Msgr. Oliver Edward, Mobile, AL, St. Catherine of Siena. —Died July 21, 1997.

† Duignan, Rev. Msgr. Kevin Francis, Montgomery, AL, St. Peter's. —Died Sept. 19, 1997.

† Gill, Joseph Cecil, (Retired). —Died Dec. 7, 1996.

Diocese of Monterey in California

(Montereyensis in California)

Most Reverend

SYLVESTER D. RYAN, D.D.

Bishop of Monterey; ordained May 3, 1957; appointed Auxiliary Bishop of Los Angeles and Titular Bishop of Remesiana February 17, 1990; ordained Bishop on May 31, 1990; appointed Bishop of Monterey January 28, 1992; installed March 19, 1992.

Most Reverend

HARRY ANSELM CLINCH, D.D.

Retired Bishop of Monterey; ordained June 6, 1936; appointed Titular Bishop of Badiae and Auxiliary to the Bishop of Monterey-Fresno December 5, 1956; consecrated February 27, 1957; installed as Third Bishop of Monterey in California December 14, 1967; retired January 19, 1982. *Res., 3400 Paul Sweet Rd., C-119, Santa Cruz, CA, 95065.* Tel.: 408-476-5847.

Pastoral Office: 580 Fremont St., P.O. Box 2048, Monterey, CA, 93942-2048. Tel.: 408-373-4345; Fax: 408-373-1175.

E-mail address: ammdom@aol.com

E-mail address: diocese@dioceseofmonterey.org

ESTABLISHED NOVEMBER 20, 1849. RE-ESTABLISHED DECEMBER 14, 1967. FORMERLY. DIOCESE OF MONTEREY-FRESNO.

Square Miles 8,475.

Legal Titles:

Diocese of Monterey in California.

The Diocese of Monterey Education and Welfare Corporation.

The Roman Catholic Bishop of Monterey, California, a Corporation Sole.

The Bishop Harry A. Clinch Endowment Fund of the Diocese of Monterey.

Catholic Charities of the Diocese of Monterey (Corporation).

Villa Serra Corporation.

Comprises the Counties of Monterey, San Benito, San Luis Obispo and Santa Cruz in the State of California.

For legal titles of parishes and diocesan institutions, consult the Pastoral Office.

STATISTICAL OVERVIEW

Personnel	
Bishop	1
Retired Bishops	2
Abbots	1
Priests: Diocesan Active in Diocese	55
Priests: Active Outside Diocese	4
Priests: Retired, Sick or Absent	32
Number of Diocesan Priests	91
Religious Priests in Diocese	24
Extern Priests in Diocese	7
Ordinations:	
Diocesan Priests	1
Transitional Deacons	1
Permanent Deacons in Diocese	4
Total Brothers	26
Total Sisters	151
Parishes	
Parishes	46
With Resident Pastor:	
Resident Diocesan Priests	38
Resident Religious Priests	7
Without Resident Pastor:	
Administered by Priests	1
Missions	9
Welfare	
Catholic Hospitals	1
Total Assisted	116,693
Health Care Centers	1
Total Assisted	46
Homes for the Aged	3
Total Assisted	422
Educational	
Diocesan Students in Other Seminaries	12
Students Religious	1
Total Seminarians	13
High Schools, Diocesan and Parish	2
Total Students	607
High Schools, Private	2
Total Students	776
Elementary Schools, Diocesan and Parish	12
Total Students	3,426
Elementary Schools, Private	3
Total Students	627
Catechesis/Religious Education:	
High School Students	1,524
Elementary Students	10,763
Total Students Under Catholic Instruction	17,736
Teachers in the Diocese:	
Priests	1
Brothers	6
Sisters	21
Lay Teachers	268
Vital Statistics	
Receptions into the Church:	
Infant Baptism Totals	5,757
Adult Baptism Totals	195
Received into Full Communion	193
First Communions	3,577
Confirmations	1,072
Marriages:	
Catholic	763
Interfaith	202
Total Marriages	965
Deaths	1,073
Total Catholic Population	176,650
Total Population	883,250

Former Prelates of the Diocese of Monterey—Rt. Rev. FRANCISCO GARCIA DIEGO Y MORENO, O.F.M., cons. Bishop of Both Californias, Oct. 1840; died April 30, 1846.—Most Rev. JOSEPH SADOC ALEMANY, O.P., cons. Bishop of Monterey, June 30, 1850; appt. first Archbishop of San Francisco, July 29, 1853; resigned and appointed Titular Archbishop of Pelusium, Dec. 28, 1884; died April 14, 1888.—Rt. Rev. THADDEUS AMAT, C.M., cons. Bishop of Monterey March 12, 1854 became Bishop of Monterey-Los Angeles, 1859; died May 12, 1878.—Rt. Rev. FRANCIS MORA, cons. Titular Bishop of Mosynopolis and Coadjutor to Bishop Amat, August 3, 1873 became Bishop of Monterey-Los Angeles, 1878; resigned May 6, 1896; named Titular Bishop Hierapolis; died August 3, 1905.—Rt. Rev. GEORGE MONTGOMERY, D.D., cons. April 8, 1894; Bishop of Tmul and Coadjutor-Bishop of Monterey-Los Angeles (cum jure successionis); succeeded to May 6, 1896; appt. Coadjutor-Archbishop of San Francisco, Titular Bishop of Auxum, January 1, 1903; died Jan. 10, 1907.—Rt. Rev. THOMAS JAMES CONATY, cons. Nov. 24, 1901; Titular Bishop of Samos; appt. Bishop of Monterey-Los Angeles, March 27, 1903; died Sept. 18, 1915.—Most Rev. JOHN J. CANTWELL, D.D., LL.D., appt. Bishop of Monterey-Los Angeles, September 21, 1917; cons. December 5, 1917 assumed the title Bishop of Los Angeles-San Diego June 1, 1922; appt. Assistant to the Pontifical Throne, Sept. 30, 1929; elevated to Archepiscopal Dignity, June 11, 1936; installed Dec. 3, 1936; died Oct. 30, 1947.—Most Rev. JOHN B. MACGINLEY, D.D., cons. May 10, 1910; Bishop of Nueva Caceres; transferred to Monterey-Fresno as first Bishop, March 24, 1924; resigned Sept. 30, 1932; named Titular Bishop of Croae; died Oct. 18, 1969.—Most Rev. PHILIP G. SCHER, D.D., ord. June 6, 1903; appt. April 28, 1933; cons. June 29, 1933; died Jan. 3, 1953.—Most Rev. ALOYSIUS J. WILLINGER, C.SS.R., ord. July 2, 1911; appt. Bishop of Ponce, March 8, 1919; cons. October 28, 1929; appt. Titular Bishop of Bida and Coadjutor of Monterey-Fresno (cum jure successionis), December 12, 1946; installed Bishop of Monterey-Fresno, Jan. 3, 1953; appt. Assistant to the Pontifical Throne, Nov. 13, 1953; resigned Oct. 25, 1967; died July 25, 1973.—Most Rev. HARRY ANSELM CLINCH, D.D., ord. June 6, 1936; appt. Titular Bishop of Badiae and Auxiliary to the Bishop of Monterey-Fresno, Dec. 5, 1956; cons. Feb. 27, 1957; installed as Third Bishop of Monterey in California, Dec. 14, 1967; retired Jan. 19, 1982.—Most Rev. THADDEUS SHUBSDA, D.D., Fourth Bishop of Monterey; ord. April 26, 1950; Titular Bishop of Trau and Auxiliary Bishop of Los Angeles; Episcopal Ordination; appt. Feb. 19, 1977; named Bishop of Monterey in California, June 1, 1982; installed as fourth Bishop of Monterey, July 1, 1982; died April 26, 1991.—Rev. CHARLES G. FATOOH, appt. Administrator of the Diocese of Monterey, April 26, 1991 - March 19, 1992.

Moderator of the Curia / Chancellor—Rev. Msgr. CHARLES G. FATOOH.

Vice Chancellor—Bro. Sir JOHN F. O'BRIEN, C.F.X., K.H.S.

Vicar General—Rev. Msgr. D. DECLAN MURPHY.

Pastoral Office—580 Fremont St., P.O. Box 2048,

Monterey, 93942-2048. Tel: 408-373-4345; Fax: 408-373-1175.

Pastoral Office, Ecclesiastical Notaries—DONA LOGEMAN ACUFF; PATRICIA FITZPATRICK.

Deans—Monterey: Very Rev. JERRY MCCORMICK, V.U., Santa Cruz: Very Rev. JOHN GRIFFIN, V.F., Salinas: Very Rev. MANUAL CANAL, V.F., San Luis Obispo: Very Rev. JOSEPH R. HERCEK, V.F.

Diocesan Departments, Directors and Offices

Archivist—Bro. Sir JOHN F. O'BRIEN, C.F.X., K.H.S., *485 Church St., Monterey, 93940.* Tel: 408-373-2127; Fax: 408-373-3534.

Attorney—ALBERT S. HAM, ESQ., *470 Camino El Estero, Monterey, 93940.* Tel: 408-649-3111; Fax: 408-649-3043.

Business Manager & Diocesan Finance Officer—THOMAS H. RIORDAN, *580 Fremont St., P.O. Box 2048, Monterey, 93942-2048.* Tel: 408-373-4345; Fax: 408-373-1175.

Communication—"The Observer"; Rev. EDWARD J. KAMINSKI, C.S.C., Dir.; Most Rev. SYLVESTER D. RYAN, Publisher, *485 Church St., P.O.Box 2079, Monterey, 93942-2079.* Tel: 408-373-2919; Fax: 408-373-4510.

Curator—Sir RICHARD MENN, K.C.S.G., K.H.S., K.M., *3080 Rio Rd., Carmel, 93923.* Tel: 408-624-3600; Fax: 408-624-0658.

Finance Office—WILLIAM J. COAKER, III, Controller; ANNE M. MCGUIRE, Business Outreach Coord., *580 Fremont St., P.O.Box 2048, Monterey, 93942-2048.* Tel: 408-373-4666; Fax: 408-373-1175.

Health Care Coordinator—Sr. JEANNE BURNS, O.P., *Dominican Santa Cruz Hospital, 1555 Soquel Dr., Santa Cruz, 95060.* Tel: 408-462-7670; Fax: 408-462-7555.

Human Resources—MOLLY A. MCDONALD, ESQ., *580 Fremont St., P.O. Box 2048, Monterey, 93942-2048.* Tel: 408-373-4345; Fax: 408-373-4765.

Stewardship—Most Rev. SYLVESTER D. RYAN; Rev. Msgr. CHARLES G. FATOOH; THOMAS H. RIORDAN, *580 Fremont St., P.O.Box 2048, Monterey, 93942-2048.* Tel: 408-373-4345; Fax: 408-373-1175.

Campus Ministry Department—Sr. CHRISTINA HELTSLEY, O.P., Ed.D., Diocesan Dir.; Sr. THERESA HARPIN, C.S.J., Dir., Campus Ministry San Luis Obispo; Rev. ROLAND BUNDA, S.M., Dir., Campus Ministry Santa Cruz, *485 Church St., P.O. Box 350, Monterey, 93942-0350.* Tel: 408-373-1608; Fax: 408-373-0173.

Catechetical Ministries Department—530 Ramona Ave., Monterey, 93940. Tel: 408-373-1607; Fax: 408-373-1601. Sr. DOLORES FENZEL, S.A., Dir. LORRAINE BUONOCORE, Admin. Asst. MARGARET COREY, Audio Visual Coord. Tel: 408-373-3506. SALLY EQUINOA, Consultant, San Luis Obispo Deanery, *221 Daly Ave., San Luis Obispo, 93405.* Tel: 805-541-1441.

Catholic Schools Department—485 Church St., P.O.Box 350, Monterey, 93942-0350. Tel: 408-373-1608; Fax: 408-373-0173. Sr. CHRISTINA HELTSLEY, O.P., Ed.D., Supt. JAMES GENTILUCCI, Ph.D., Asst. Supt. MIRIAM "MIMI" SCHWERTFEGER, Admin. Asst.

Diocese of Monterey Department of Catholic Schools—774 Palm St., San Luis Obispo, 93401. Tel: 805-543-0509; Fax: 805-543-0524.

Cemeteries—CLANCY D'ANGELO, Dir. REX HILL, Operations Mgr., *Cemeteries Administrative Office, 792 Fremont St., Monterey, 93940.* Tel: 408-372-0327; Fax: 408-372-8726., *Mailing Address: P.O.Box 2048, Monterey, 93942-2048.*

Diocesan Tribunal—485 Church St., P.O. Box 350, Monterey, 93942-0350. Tel: 408-373-1833; Fax: 408-373-6761.

Judicial Vicar—Rev. KENNETH J. LAVERONE, M.A.

Administrator—FRAYLNE SAN FILIPPO.

Judges—Revs. KENNETH J. LAVERONE; DAVID SCHUYLER, S.M., J.C.D.

Defenders of the Bond—Sr. LILIANA BONELLO, I.M., J.C.L.; Revs. PATRICK DOOLING; THOMAS KIEFFER, Orat. PAUL R. VALDEZ.

Advocates—Revs. JOHN C. GRIFFIN; MICHAEL MARINI.

Promotor of Justice—Rev. THOMAS KIEFFER, Orat.

Notaries—DONA LOGEMAN ACUFF; PATRICIA FITZPATRICK; FRAYLNE SAN FILIPPO.

Divine Worship Department—Sr. BARBARA ANN LONG, O.P., Dir. ANN KREYCHE, Admin. Asst., *126 High St., Santa Cruz, 95060.* Tel: 408-423-4797; Fax: 408-423-1043.

Hispanic Ministry Department—Sr. PATRICIA MURTAGH, I.M., Dir.; Sr. LYDIA SCHNEIDER, I.M., Assoc. Dir. JUANITA ZEPEDA, Exec. Sec. BEATRIZ MUNOZ, Sec., *22 Stone St., P.O. Box 1684, Salinas, 93902-1684.* Tel: 408-424-4076; Fax: 408-424-5221.

Migrant Ministry Coord.—MARINA O'CAMPO, *22 Stone St., P.O. Box 1684, Salinas, 93902-1684.* Tel: 408-424-4076; Fax: 408-424-5221.

Respect Life Department—DORA LEE RARAS, Dir., *405 Palma Dr., Salinas, 93901-1822.* Tel: 408-796-0136; Fax: 408-796-0138.

Certified Natural Family Planning Practitioner—SHEILA ST. JOHN, C.N.F.P.P., *1217 Tyler St., Salinas, 93906.* Tel: 408-433-3743.

Youth and Young Adult Ministry—JOSE LUIS MEDINA, Dir., *22 Stone St., P.O. Box 1684, Salinas, 93902-1684.* Tel: 408-424-5512; Fax: 408-424-5221.

Scouting—Rev. CARL M.D. FARIA, Chap., *303 Hillcrest Ave., Marina, 93933.* Tel: 408-384-5434; Fax: 408-384-7011.

Vicar for Clergy and Diocesan Director for RENEW—Rev. MICHAEL MILLER, *530 Ramona Ave., Monterey, 93940.*

Vicars for Religious—Sr. ADRIENNE PIENNETTE, O.P., *St. Angela's Church, 146 8th St., Pacific Grove, 93950.* Tel: 408-655-4162; Fax: 408-372-5026.

Vocations—Rev. ANTONIO SANCHEZ, Dir., *Our Lady of the Assumption Church, 100 Salinas Rd., Watsonville, 95076.* Tel: 408-722-1104; Fax: 408-722-1254. Rev. MICHAEL VOLK, Assoc. Dir., *St. Theodore's Church, P.O. Drawer B, Gonzales, 93926.* Tel: 408-675-8648; Fax: 408-675-8360.

Charismatics—Rev. GERONIMO CUEVAS, Diocesan Dir., *St. Mary of the Nativity Church, 1702 Second Ave., Salinas, 93905.* Tel: 408-758-1669; Fax: 408-758-4715.

Cursillo—Rev. PETER CRIVELLO, Spiritual Dir., *Resurrection Church, P.O. Box 87, Aptos, 95001-0087.* Tel: 408-688-4300; Fax: 408-688-6921. Rev. MICHAEL VOLK, Spiritual Dir., *St. Theodore's Church, Drawer B, Gonzales, 93926.* Tel: 408-675-3648; Fax: 408-675-8360.

Ecumenism—Rev. JOHN KEANE, S.A., Dir., *St. Francis Xavier Church, 1475 LaSalle Ave., P.O. Box 247, Seaside, 93955-0247.* Tel: 408-394-8546; Fax: 408-394-5414.

Holy Childhood Association—Rev. FELIX MIGLIAZZO, Dir., *P.O. Box 88, Monterey, 93942-0088.* Tel: 408-372-9120; Fax: 408-372-9120.

Propagation of the Faith—Rev. FELIX MIGLIAZZO, Dir., *P.O. Box 88, Monterey, 93942-0088.* Tel: 408-372-9120.

RENEW Department—Rev. MICHAEL MILLER, Dir., *530 Ramona Ave., Monterey, 93940.* Tel: 408-373-8707; Fax: 408-373-1601.

St. Joseph's Archive and Conference Center—485 Church St., Monterey, 93940.

St. Vincent de Paul—Rev. RICHARD BONJEAN, Dir., *490 Elizabeth Ct., Templeton, 93465.* Tel: 805-434-2449.

Catholic Charities of the Diocese of Monterey—

Central Office—MARTINA S. O'SULLIVAN, Exec. Dir., *530 Ramona Ave., Monterey, 93940.* Tel: 408-375-1577; Fax: 408-373-3416.

Counseling Program—Tel: 408-375-3165.

Direct Material Aid—Tel: 408-375-1577.

Campaign for Human Development—MARTINA S. O'SULLIVAN, Dir., *530 Ramona Ave., Monterey, 93940.* Tel: 408-375-1577; Fax: 408-373-3416.

Catholic Relief Services—MARTINA S. O'SULLIVAN, Dir., *530 Ramona Ave., Monterey, 93940.* Tel: 408-375-1577; Fax: 408-373-3416.

Salinas Office—Buckley Hall, St.Mary of the Nativity Church, 1705 2nd Ave., Salinas, 93905. Tel: 408-422-0602; Fax: 408-422-0759.

Counseling—Tel: 408-422-0609.

Direct Material Aid—Tel: 408-375-1577.

Immigration—Tel: 408-422-0602.

Watsonville Office—406 Main St., #308, Watsonville, 95076. Tel: 408-722-2675; Fax: 408-722-9921.

Direct Material Aid—Tel: 408-722-2675.

Counseling—Tel: 408-772-2791.

Immigration—Tel: 408-722-2675.

Boards, Commissions, Committees and Councils

Administrative Committee Priest's Pension Plan—Revs. EUGENIO ARAMBURO; GARY BYRNE; PETER CRIVELLO; MICHAEL L. CROSS, Chm. PAUL R. VALDEZ.

Bishop Harry A. Clinch Endowment Fund, The Bishop Sylvester D. Ryan Continuing Education Fund, The Bishop Shubsda Memorial Seminary Endowment Burse and The Cemetery Endowment Burse—Mr. RAYMOND AMRHEIN; Mr. CHARLES J. BRIGGS; Rev. Msgr. CHARLES G. FATOOH; Mrs. ELIZABETH HELFRICH; Mr. BOB HOUGARDY; Mr. MICHAEL MORRIS, Chm.; Mr. RONALD PASQUINELLI; Mr. LARRY SAGE; Rev. Msgr. ROBERT TRUPIA; Mr. RICHARD UCCELLI; Mr. JOHN WECKER; THOMAS H. RIORDAN, Ex Officio, Diocesan Business Mgr.

Building Commission—Contact Persons: Rev. JOHN GRIFFIN, *Holy Eucharist Church, 527 Corralitos Rd., Corralitos, 95076.* Tel: 408-722-5490; Fax: 408-722-8157. THOMAS H. RIORDAN, *Diocese of Monterey, 580 Fremont St., P.O. Box 2048, Monterey, 93942-2048.* Tel: 408-373-4345; Fax: 408-373-1175.

Catholic Charities—Mr. ROBERT BANKS; Mrs. ROBIN L. COURTNEY; Rev. Msgr. CHARLES G. FATOOH; Mr. RUBEN GARCIA; Mrs. ANNE KEYES; Mr. JACK KILMARTIN; Very Rev. JERRY MCCORMICK, V.F.; Most Rev. SYLVESTER D. RYAN; Mr. LARRY SAGE; Mr. BILL SLEZAK; Mr. FRANK ST. DENIS. Ex Officio: Mrs. MARTINA S. O'SULLIVAN, Exec. Dir.; Mr. THOMAS H. RIORDAN, Diocesan Business Mgr. DONA LOGEMAN ACUFF, Recording Sec.

Ecumenical Commission—Ms. KAREN ALBERTUS; Rev. JOEL ALMENDRAS; Mr. DICK GORMAN; Rev. JOHN KEANE, S.A., Chm.; Sr. MARY KELLY, S.A.; Rev. SCOTT MCCARTHY; Ms. SUSAN PETERSON; Rev. RUDY RUIZ; Bro. TONY YOUNG.

Emergency Preparedness Task Force—Mr. VIC COLLINS; Rev. Msgr. CHARLES G. FATOOH; Chief JAMES GARDINER; Sr. CHRISTINA HELTSLEY, O.P.; MOLLY MCDONALD; Mr. JACK MCGILVRAY, Chm.; Chief TERRY MEDINA; MARTINA O'SULLIVAN; THOMAS H. RIORDAN; Most Rev. SYLVESTER D. RYAN; Mr. TOM TREANOR.

Finance Council—Rev. EUGENIO ARAMBURO; Rev. Msgr. CHARLES G. FATOOH; Mrs. PEGGY HARRAY, Chm.; Mr. MCKENZIE MOSS; Rev. Msgr. D. DECLAN MURPHY; Mr. RONALD PASQUINELLI; Mr. JOHN PETERSDOFF; Most Rev. SYLVESTER D. RYAN; Rev. PAUL R. VALDEZ. Ex Officio: THOMAS H. RIORDAN, Diocesan Business Mgr. DONA LOGEMAN ACUFF, Recording Sec.

Historical Review Committee—Sir RICHARD MENN, K.C.S.G., K.H.S., K.M., Diocesan Curator; Bro. Sir JOHN F. O'BRIEN, C.F.X., Diocesan Archivist; Mrs. ELIZABETH HILLEARY; Sir LEWIS CHARLES SCOTT; Rev. Msgr. FRANCIS J. WEBER.

Insurance Committee—Mr. GREG CAMPBELL; Mr. MICHAEL KELLY, Chm. MOLLY MCDONALD; THOMAS H. RIORDAN; Rev. PAUL R. VALDEZ.

Lay Employees Non-Qualified Pension Committee—Rev. Msgr. CHARLES G. FATOOH; Rev. Msgr. D. DECLAN MURPHY; Mr. THOMAS H. RIORDAN, Chm. Consultants: Mr. ALBERT S. HAM; Mr. TONY KARACHALE; GINA M. RUIZ, Recording Sec.

Lay Employee Pension Plan Committee—Rev. Msgr. CHARLES G. FATOOH; Mr. RONALD PASQUINELLI; Mr. THOMAS H. RIORDAN, Chm.; Mr. TOD D. SANCHEZ. Consultants: Mr. ALBERT S. HAM; Mr. TONY KARACHALE; GINA M. RUIZ, Recording Sec.

Presbyteral Council—Very Rev. MANUEL CANAL, V.F.; Revs. SIRO DAL DEGAN, O.S.J.; PATRICK DOOLING; Rev. Msgr. CHARLES G. FATOOH; Revs. JAMES FRERKES; JOHN GRIFFIN, V.F.; Very Rev. JOSEPH R. HERCEK, V.F.; Revs. LARY KAMBITSCH, Treas. JERRY MAHER, Sec. MICHAEL A. MARINI, Pres.; Very Rev. JERRY MCCORMICK, V.U., Vice Pres.; Rev. Msgr. D. DECLAN MURPHY; Rev. MATTHEW PENNINGTON; Most Rev. SYLVESTER D. RYAN; Rev. GREGORY L. SANDMAN; Ms. PATRICIA FITZPATRICK, Recording Sec.

Priestly Life and Ministry—Mr. ANDY ANDERSON; Sr. RITA EILEEN DEAN, O.P., Co-Chm.; Sr. JOAN DOYLE, S.N.J.M.; Mrs. ROSEMARY MATZERATH; Rev. SCOTT MCCARTHY; Very Rev. JERRY MCCORMICK, V.U.; Revs. MICHAEL MILLER; MATTHEW PENNINGTON, Co-Chm.; Most Rev. SYLVESTER D. RYAN; Revs. DENNIS STEIK, S.M.; MIKE VOLK.

Priest's Personnel Board—Rev. Msgr. CHARLES G. FATOOH; Revs. JOHN GRIFFIN, V.F.; MICHAEL A. MARINI; Very Rev. JERRY MCCORMICK, V.U.; Most Rev. SYLVESTER D. RYAN; Rev. ANTONIO SANCHEZ.

Real Estate Committee—Mr. RICK KENNIFER; Mr. DAVID KENT, Chm.; Mr. THOMAS H. RIORDAN; Mr. RICHARD SELDOW; Mr. SAM WRIGHT.

Renew Committee—Sr. DOLORES FENZEL, S.A.; Ms. CAROL KAPLAN; Rev. MICHAEL MILLER, Dir.; Sr. PATRICIA MURTAGH, I.M.; Mrs. JONDELL DEVEAUX WRIGHT.

Stewardship Board—Mrs. MARY AGEE; Mr. WILLIAM AGEE; Mr. DON CHAPIN; Mrs. DON CHAPIN; Mrs. JOAN CLARK; Judge WILLIAM CLARK; Mr. PETER CONIGLIO; Sr. JULIE HYER, O.P.; Mr. JACK KILMARTIN; Mrs. JACK KILMARTIN; Mr. JOSEPH KORDSMEIER; Mr. ALEX MADONNA; Mrs. PHYLLIS MADONNA; Mr. ROGER MAIROSE; Mrs. WENDY MAIROSE; Mr. CLEM RICHARDSON; Mrs. CLEM RICHARDSON, JR.; Most Rev. SYLVESTER D. RYAN. Ex Officios: Rev. Msgr. CHARLES G. FATOOH; THOMAS H. RIORDAN.

Villa Serra Board—Rev. Msgr. CHARLES G. FATOOH; Mr. ROGER HITE; Sr. JULIE HYER, O.P., Pres.; Mr. MCKENZIE MOSS; Mr. JOHN PETERSDORF; Mr. THOMAS H. RIORDAN; Most Rev. SYLVESTER D. RYAN.

Vocation Board—Revs. EUGENIO ARAMBURO; ROLAND BUNDA, S.M.; PETER CRIVELLO; Sr. PATRICIA MURTAGH, I.M.; Sr. ADRIENNE PIENNETTE, O.P.; Revs. ANTONIO SANCHEZ, Dir. GREGORY L. SANDMAN, V.F.; FRANCIS THOME; MICHAEL A. VOLK; PATRICIA FITZPATRICK, Recording Sec.

CLERGY, PARISHES, MISSIONS AND PAROCHIAL SCHOOLS

CITY OF MONTEREY
(Monterey County)

1—CATHEDRAL OF SAN CARLOS BORROMEO (1770), Revs. Joseph L. Occhiuto, Rector; Gerald John Maher (Ireland); Deacon Harold Miller, Pastoral Assoc.
Mailing Address: 500 Church St., 93940.
Res., 550 Church St., 93940. Tel: 408-373-2628; Fax: 408-373-0518.
Preschool—450 Church St., 93940. Tel: 408-375-1324; Fax: 408-375-9736. Sr. Mary Jane Clark, O.P., Prin.
Dominican Sisters (Adrian, MI) 2; Lay Teachers 25; Students 300.
Catechesis/Religious Programs—Tel: 408-373-4101; Fax: 408-373-1175.
Students 220.

OUTSIDE THE CITY OF MONTEREY

Aptos, Santa Cruz Co., Resurrection (1968), Rev. Peter A. Crivello.
Res., 7600 Soquel Dr., P.O. Box 87, 95001. Tel: 408-688-4300; Fax: 408-688-6921.
School—Good Shepherd School (Inter-Parish), (Grades PreK-8). See Star of the Sea Parish, Santa Cruz.
Catechesis/Religious Programs—Tel: 408-688-4300; Fax: 408-688-6921.
Students 100.

Arroyo Grande, San Luis Obispo Co., St. Patrick (1886), Revs. James Henry, Pastor; Joseph Butters.
Res., 501 Fair Oaks Ave., P.O. Box 860, 93421. Tel: 805-489-2680; Fax: 805-489-1316.
School—(Grades K-8) 900 W. Branch St., 93420. Tel: 805-489-1210; Fax: 805-489-7662. Kathy Tyree, Prin.
Sisters of Mercy 5; Lay Teachers 7; Students 332.
Catechesis/Religious Programs—Tel: 805-481-2990.
Students 332.
Mission—Oceano, San Luis Obispo Co., St. Francis of Assisi. 17th & Beach.
Shamrock Thrift Shop—924 Grand Ave., Grover City, 93433. Tel: 805-481-0612. Andy Tellez.

Atascadero, San Luis Obispo Co., St. William's (1948), Very Rev. Joseph R. Hercek, V.F.
Mailing Address: P.O. Box 2230, 93423. Tel: 805-466-0849; Fax: 805-461-0743.
Res., 6410 Santa Lucia Rd., 93422.
Catechesis/Religious Programs—Students 317.

Boulder Creek, Santa Cruz Co., St. Michael (1921), Rev. Martin McDonald.
Res., 13005 Pine St., 95006. Tel: 408-338-6112; Fax: 408-338-6112.
Catechesis/Religious Programs—Students 54.

Cambria, San Luis Obispo Co., Santa Rosa (1961), Rev. Dennis Gilbert.
Res., 1174 Main St., 93428. Tel: 805-927-4816; Fax: 805-927-2880. [CEM]
Catechesis/Religious Programs—Students 80.

Capitola, Santa Cruz Co., St. Joseph (1904), Revs. Patrick Dooling; Tom Foster, S.J.; Sr. Marie Wiedner, O.P., Pastoral Assoc.
Res., 435 Monterey Ave., 95010. Tel: 408-475-8211; Fax: 408-475-2601.
School—Good Shepherd School (Inter-Parish), (Grades K-8). See Star of the Sea Parish, Santa Cruz and Resurrection Church, Aptos. Tel: 408-476-4000; Fax: 408-476-0948.
Catechesis/Religious Programs—Tel: 408-475-8213; Fax: 408-475-2601.
Students 213.

Carmel, Monterey Co., San Carlos Borromeo Basilica (1771). (Carmel Mission). Rev. Msgr. D. Declan Murphy; Rev. Richard D. Clark.
Res., Rio Rd. and Lasuen Dr., P.O. Box 2235, 93921. Tel: 408-624-1271; Fax: 408-624-8050.
School—Junipero Serra School, (Grades K-8) 2992 Lasuen Dr., 93923. Tel: 408-624-8322; Fax: 408-624-8050. Mary V. Marchi, Prin.
Lay Teachers 9; Students 242.
Catechesis/Religious Programs—Tel: 408-624-6846.
Students 141.
Mission—Big Sur, Monterey Co., St. Francis of the Redwoods, Hwy. 1, Big Sur, 93920.
Chapel—Blessed Sacrament.

Carmel Valley, Monterey Co., Our Lady of Mt. Carmel (1953), Rev. Cornelius Scott McCarthy.
Res., 9 El Caminito, P.O. Box 195, 93924. Tel: 408-659-2224; Fax: 408-659-9186.
Catechesis/Religious Programs—Students 85.

Castroville, Monterey Co., Our Lady of Refuge (1869), Rev. Rudy Ruiz.
Res., 11140 Preston St., 95012. Tel: 408-633-4015; Fax: 408-633-4653.
Catechesis/Religious Programs—Tel: 408-633-4016.
Students 452.

Cayucos, San Luis Obispo Co., St. Joseph (1907), Rev. Anthony Gurnell.
Res., 360 Park Ave., P.O. Box 437, 93430. Tel: 805-995-3243; Fax: 805-995-2838.

Corralitos, Santa Cruz Co., Holy Eucharist (1969), Rev. John Cullen Griffin.
Res., 527 Corralitos Rd., 95076. Tel: 408-722-5490; Fax: 408-722-8157.
Catechesis/Religious Programs—Students 145.

Davenport, Santa Cruz Co., St. Vincent De Paul (1935), Rev. Siro Dal Degan, O.S.J.
Res., 544 W. Cliff Drive, Santa Cruz, 95060. Tel: 408-471-1702; 429-1426; Fax: 408-457-1317.

Felton, Santa Cruz Co., St. John's (1952), Rev. Michael L. Cross.
Res., Russell at Hwy. 9, P.O. Box M-1, 95018. Tel: 408-335-4657; Fax: 408-335-4648.
Catechesis/Religious Programs—Students 156.

Gonzales, Monterey Co., St. Theodore (1892), Rev. Michael Volk.
Res., 120 First St., P.O. Drawer B, 93926. Tel: 408-675-3648; Fax: 408-675-8360.
Catechesis/Religious Programs—Tel: 408-675-2100; Fax: 408-675-2975.
Students 733.

Greenfield, Monterey Co., Holy Trinity (1951) (Mexican-Swiss-Italian), Rev. Eugenio Aramburo.
Res., 803 Elm Ave., Box 276, 93927. Tel: 408-674-5428; Fax: 408-674-5285.
Catechesis/Religious Programs—Tel: 408-674-3695. Rosa Garcia, D.R.E.
Students 470.

Hollister, San Benito Co., Sacred Heart (1877), Revs. Gary Byrne; Ronald Green; Fabian Vela.
Res., 540 College St., P.O. Box 1040, 95024. Tel: 408-637-9212; Fax: 408-637-7299. [CEM]
Pastoral Center—680 College St., P.O. Box 1040, 95023. Tel: 408-637-9212; Fax: 408-637-7299.
School—(Grades K-8) 670 College St., 95023. Tel: 408-637-4157; Fax: 408-637-4164. Mrs. Mary White, Prin.
Lay Teachers 16; Students 410.
Catechesis/Religious Programs—Tel: 408-637-8291. D.R.E.: Tish Scargill; Lety Perez; Eileen McCullough.
Students 533.

Jolon, Monterey Co., San Antonio Mission (1771), Rev. John E. Gini, O.F.M. In res., Bros. Chris Rogan, O.F.M.; Anthony F. Lavorin, O.F.M.
Res., Box 803, 93928. Tel: 408-385-4478; Fax: 408-386-9332.
Mission—Jolon, Monterey Co., South Shore of Lake San Antonio.

King City, Monterey Co., St. John the Baptist (1891) (Hispanic), Rev. Lawrence J. Kambitsch. Pastoral Assocs.: Sr. Loretta Guevarra, S.A.; Sr. Maria Del Rey Perezchica, S.A.
Res., 504 N. Third St., 93930. Tel: 408-385-3377; Fax: 408-385-3317.
Catechesis/Religious Programs—Tel: 408-385-3464; Fax: 408-385-3317. D.R.E.: Cindy LaFont; Claudia Zuniga.
Students 390.
Mission—San Lucas, Monterey Co., St. Luke, Main St., 93954.

Los Gatos, Santa Cruz Co., Christ Child (1983), Rev. Marvin J. Steffes, C.PP.S.
Res., 23230 Summit Rd., 95033. Tel: 408-353-2210; Fax: 408-353-8680.

Los Osos, San Luis Obispo Co., St. Elizabeth Ann Seton (1984), Rev. Mark Stetz.
Res., 2050 Palisades Ave., 93402. Tel: 805-528-5319; Fax: 805-528-8893.
Catechesis/Religious Programs—Students 150.

Marina, Monterey Co., St. Jude Parish Community (1963), Rev. Carl M.D. Faria.
Res., 303 Hillcrest Ave., 93933-3599. Tel: 408-384-5434; Fax: 408-384-7011.
Catechesis/Religious Programs—Tel: 408-384-8268; Fax: 408-384-7011.
Students 170.

Morro Bay, San Luis Obispo Co., St. Timothy (1950), Rev. Msgr. Cornelius Sweeney.
Res., 962 Piney Way, 93442. Tel: 805-772-2840.
Catechesis/Religious Programs—951 Pacific, 93442. Tel: 805-772-3032; Fax: 805-772-3184. Elizabeth Olson, D.R.E.
Students 85.

Nipomo, San Luis Obispo Co., St. Joseph (1968), Revs. James J. Frerkes; Jose Chavez.
Res., 298 S. Thompson, 93444. Tel: 805-929-1922; Fax: 805-929-2662.
Catechesis/Religious Programs—Tel: 805-929-3730.
Students 179.

Pacific Grove, Monterey Co., St. Angela (1928), Revs. Anthony Phuc, C.SS.R., Assoc. Pastor; Jerry McCormick.
Res., 161 Ninth St., 93950. Tel: 408-655-4160; Fax: 408-372-5026.
Office: 146 Eighth St., 93950.
Preschool—136 Eighth St., 93950. Tel: 408-372-3555. Virginia Ziomek, Prin.
Catechesis/Religious Programs—Tel: 408-373-6311.
Students 125.

Paso Robles, San Luis Obispo Co., St. Rose (1922), Rev. Derek Hughes; Sr. Maris Stella O'Loghl'en, Pastoral Assoc.; Deacon Jack Copelen.
Office: 642 Trigo Ln., P.O. Box 790, 93447. Tel: 805-238-2218; Fax: 805-238-2762.
Res., 820 Creston Rd., P.O. Box 790, 93447. Tel: 805-238-2218; Fax: 805-238-2762. [CEM][JC]
School—(Grades PreK-8) 900 Tucker Ave., 93446. Tel: 805-238-0304; Fax: 805-238-7393. James Brescia, Prin.
Lay Teachers 14; Students 313.
Catechesis/Religious Programs—Students 205.

Pismo Beach, San Luis Obispo Co., St. Paul the Apostle (1930), Rev. Charles Kozanecki, O.F.M.Conv. In res., Revs. Alphonse Van Guilder, O.F.M.Conv.; Peter Parchem, O.F.M.Conv., Pastor Emeritus.
Res., 800 Bello St., 93449. Tel: 805-773-2219; Fax: 805-773-8617. [JC]

Salinas, Monterey Co.,

1—CHRIST THE KING, (1995), Rev. Manuel Canal.
Res., 240 Calle Cebu, 93901. Tel: 408-422-6543; Fax: 408-422-7218.
Religious Education Office: Tel: 408-422-6722.
Catechesis/Religious Programs—Students 500.

2—SACRED HEART, (1877), Revs. Paul R. Valdez; James L. Plastino; Antonio Cortes.
Res., 22 Stone St., 93901. Tel: 408-424-1959; Fax: 408-424-0788.
School—(Grades K-8) 123 W. Market St., 93901. Tel: 408-771-1310; Fax: 408-771-1314. Sr. Paulette Tiefenbrunn, S.S.N.D., Prin.
Sisters 3; Lay Teachers 10; Students 307.
Catechesis/Religious Programs—Tel: 408-772-8232. Sr. Cristina Bortolotti, I.M., D.R.E.
Students 600.

3—ST. MARY OF THE NATIVITY, (1947), Revs. Geronimo Cuevas; Sergio Valdivia.
Res., 1702 Second Ave., 93905. Tel: 408-758-1669; Fax: 408-758-4715.
Catechesis/Religious Programs—Tel: 408-422-9964.
Students 700.

4—MADONNA DEL SASSO, (1960), Revs. Ronald R. Shirley; John Burns; Mrs. Gail Branner, Pastoral Assoc.; Rev. Michael Miller.
Res., 320 E. Laurel Dr., 93906. Tel: 408-422-5323; Fax: 408-422-0536.
School—(Grades K-8) 20 Santa Teresa Way, 93906. Tel: 408-424-7813; Fax: 408-424-3359.
Sisters of Notre Dame 1; Lay Teachers 10; Students 294.
Catechesis/Religious Programs—Tel: 408-422-1439.
Students 305.

San Juan Bautista, San Benito Co., San Juan Bautista (1797). (Old Mission). Rev. Edward Fitz-Henry.
Res., 2nd & Mariposa St., P.O. Box 400, 95045. Tel: 408-623-2127; Fax: 408-623-2433. [CEM]
Catechesis/Religious Programs—Tel: 408-623-4178.
Students 170.

San Luis Obispo, San Luis Obispo Co., San Luis Obispo (1772). (Old Mission). Revs. Francis E. Thome; Charles J. Tilley, S.J. Pastoral Assocs.: Revs. John Arul; Miguel A. Grajeda.
Res., 751 Palm St., 93401. Tel: 805-781-8220; Fax: 805-781-8214.
Preschool—221 Daly Ave., 93401. Tel: 805-549-8819. Jim Gentilucci, Prin.
School—(Grades 1-8) 761 Broad St., 93401. Tel: 805-543-6019; Fax: 805-543-6246. Valerie Ratto, Prin.
Lay Teachers 12; Students 272.
Catechesis/Religious Programs—Students 200.

Nativity of Our Lady (1964), Rev. Michael Cicinato; Deacon David Leach.
Res., 221 Daly Ave., 93405-1099. Tel: 805-544-2357; Fax: 805-544-6756.
Catechesis/Religious Programs—Students 70.

San Miguel, San Luis Obispo Co., San Miguel (1797). (Old Mission). Rev. James Kyrie, O.F.M. Pastoral Assocs.: Sr. Loretta Guevarra, S.A.; Sr. Maria Del Rey Perezchica, S.A.
Res., 775 Mission St., P.O. Box 69, 93451. Tel: 805-467-3256; Fax: 805-467-2448. [CEM]

Catechesis/Religious Programs—Fax: 805-467-3448.
Students 66.
Missions—San Ardo, Monterey Co., Our Lady of Ransom; Bradley, Monterey Co., Our Lady of Guadalupe.
Station—Heritage Ranch.

Santa Cruz, Santa Cruz Co., Holy Cross (1791), Revs. Michael A. Marini; Ignacio Martinez.
Res., 126 High St., 95060. Tel: 408-423-4182; Fax: 408-423-1043. [CEM]
School—(Grades K-8) 150 Emmet St., 95060. Tel: 408-423-4447; Fax: 408-423-0752. Marlene Canzano, Prin.
Lay Teachers 14; Students 265.
Catechesis/Religious Programs—Tel: 408-458-3041; Fax: 408-458-1043.
Students 367.

Star of the Sea (1947), Rev. Rene Iturbe, S.M.; Deacon Ken Johnson, S.M.
Res., 515 Frederick St., 95062. Tel: 408-429-1018; Fax: 408-429-5832.
Good Shepherd Preschool—(Inter-Parish) 2727 Mattison Ln., 95062. Tel: 408-476-4000; Fax: 408-476-0948. Celeste Kathleen O'Donnel, Prin.
Students 140.
Catechesis/Religious Programs—Students 485.
Chapel—Villa Maria del Mar, Tel: 408-475-1236; Fax: 408-475-8867.

Santa Margarita, San Luis Obispo Co., Santa Margarita de Cortona (1934), Rev. Joseph Grech, Admin.
Res., 22515 H St., P.O. Box 350, 93453-0350. Tel: 805-438-5383; Fax: 805-438-4313. [JC]
Mission—Carrissa Plains, San Luis Obispo Co., St. James Mission, P.O. Box 3055, 93453. Tel: 805-475-2222.

Scotts Valley, Santa Cruz Co., San Agustin (1969), Rev. Matthew Pennington.
Res., 257 Glenwood Dr., 95066. Tel: 408-438-3633; Fax: 408-438-0973.
Catechesis/Religious Programs—Students 170.

Seaside, Monterey Co., St. Francis Xavier (1950), Revs. John J. Keane, S.A.; Henry Mair, S.A. In res., Revs. Michael Daniel, S.A.; Charles G. Fatooh.
Res., 1475 LaSalle Ave., P.O. Box 247, 93955. Tel: 408-394-8546; Fax: 408-394-5414.
Catechesis/Religious Programs—Tel: 408-394-8546; Fax: 408-394-5414.
Students 323.

Soledad, Monterey Co., Our Lady of Solitude (1933) (Spanish), Rev. Eleutherio Sanz.
Res., 235 Main St., 93960. Tel: 408-678-2731; Fax: 408-678-2731.
Catechesis/Religious Programs—Tel: 408-678-1277; 675-2975. Sr. Alicia Pereira, D.R.E.
Students 800.
Mission—Soledad, Monterey Co., Nuestra Senora de la Soledad, Rte. 1, Box 72, 93960. Tel: 408-678-2586.

Spreckels, Monterey Co., St. Joseph (1969), Rev. Jim Nisbet.
Res., One Railroad Ave., P.O. Box 7158, 93962. Tel: 408-455-2249; Fax: 408-455-9357.
Catechesis/Religious Programs—St. Joseph's Religion Center, 15 First St., P.O. Box 7158, 93962. Tel: 408-455-8720; Fax: 408-455-9357. Sr. Liliana Bonello, I.M., J.C.L., D.R.E.
Students 272.

Tres Pinos, San Benito Co., Immaculate Conception (1904), Rev. Larry Betrozoff.
Res., 7290 Airline Hwy., P.O. Box 247, 95075. Tel: 408-628-3216; Fax: 408-628-3602.
Catechesis/Religious Programs—Sr. Carol Pesce, S.H.F., D.R.E.
Students 97.

Watsonville, Santa Cruz Co., Our Lady Help of Christians (1854), Rev. Bernardo Soares.
Res., 2401 E. Lake Ave., 95076. Tel: 408-722-2665; Fax: 408-722-8305. [CEM]
Catechesis/Religious Programs—Students 63.

St. Patrick (1861), Revs. Gregory Sandman; Jesus Enrique Herrera; Heiber Castaneda.
Res., 721 Main St., 95076. Tel: 408-724-1317; Fax: 408-724-1627.
Catechesis/Religious Programs—Tel: 408-724-2141. Gregoria Alvarez, D.R.E. (English & Spanish).
Students 785.

Assumption (1953) (Hispanic), Rev. J. Antonio Sanchez.
Res., 100 Salinas Rd., Pajaro, 95076. Tel: 408-722-1104; Fax: 408-722-1931. [CEM]
Catechesis/Religious Programs—Tel: 408-722-9938. Sr. Rosa Dolores Rodriguez, D.C., D.R.E.
Students 370.

Shrines

Santa Cruz, Santa Cruz Co., Shrine of St. Joseph Guardian of the Redeemer,
Res., 544 W. Cliff Dr., 95060-6147. Tel: 408-471-0442; Fax: 408-457-1317. Rev. Philip Massetti, O.S.J.
Guardian of the Redeemer Bookstore—Tel: 408-471-1700; Fax: 408-457-1317.

Chaplains of Public Institutions

ATASCADERO. *Atascadero State Hospital*. Vacant.
BOULDER CREEK. *Ben Lomond Youth Authority Camp*. Rev. Martin McDonald.
PASO ROBLES. *El Paso de Robles School*. Dept. of the Youth Authority. Sr. Mary E. McKay, S.N.J.M.
SAN LUIS OBISPO. *California Men's Colony East*. Rev. Alphonse Van Guilder, O.F.M.Conv.
California Men's Colony West. Rev. Michael T. Bell.
SOLEDAD. *Correctional Training Facility*. Rev. Joel Almendras.
Salinas Valley State Prison. Rev. Michael A. Bethancourt.

On Duty Outside the Diocese:
Reverend Fathers—
Adams, Michael T., Archdiocese of Samoa, APIA, Fetuolemoana, P.O. Box 532 APIA, Western Samoa. Tel: 685-20-400 20-401
Cadera, James R., 601-C Washington, Coalinga, CA 93210. Tel: 209-934-1450

Special Assignment:
Reverend Monsignors—
Fatooh, Charles G., Chancellor & Moderator of the Curia, Diocese of Monterey, P.O. Box 2048, Monterey, CA 93940. Tel: 408-373-4345
Reverend Fathers—
Hill, Scott, O.M.I., Catholic Chap., Dominican Santa Cruz Hospital, 1555 Soquel Ave., Santa Cruz, CA 95065. Tel: 408-462-7707; Fax: 408-462-7558
Laverone, Kenneth J., Judicial Vicar, P.O. Box 69, San Miguel, CA 93451. Tel: 805-467-3256; Fax: 805-467-2248
Miller, Michael, Vicar for Clergy & Diocesan Dir. for RENEW, 530 Ramona Ave., Monterey, CA 93940. Tel: 408-373-8707; Fax: 408-373-1601
Sanchez, Antonio, Dir. of Vocations, Our Lady of the Assumption, 100 Salinas Rd., Watsonville, CA 95076. Tel: 408-722-1104; Fax: 408-722-1254

Absent on Sick Leave:
Reverend Fathers—
Enciso, Herman, Our Lady of Guadalupe, 39100 Orchard Ave., Cherry Valley, CA 92223-3797
Mai, Emmanuel K., P.O. Box 85, Mt. View, CA 94042

Retired:
Reverend Monsignors—
Kennedy, John, P.O. Box 4023, Felton, CA 95018. Tel: 408-335-3119
Lane, William, 3400 Paul Sweet Rd., C-130, Santa Cruz, CA 95065. Tel: 408-479-3775
MacMahon, Eamon, 24631 Guadalupe St., Carmel, CA 93923. Tel: 408-624-2275
Marron, James, 246 Ridge Rd., Pismo Beach, CA 93449. Tel: 805-773-3549
McGuinness, Brendan, P.O. Box 789, Monterey, CA 93942-0789. Tel: 408-375-7301
Morgan, Thomas, 1118 Victoria St., Hollister, CA 95023. Tel: 408-637-1084
Stieger, Joseph, c/o 161 Broad St., San Luis Obispo, CA 93405. Tel: 805-543-3284
Reverend Fathers—
Bonjean, Richard, 490 Elizabeth Ct., Templeton, CA 93465. Tel: 805-434-2449
Carvajal, Raul H.
Cowan, Vincent, P.O. Box 3186, Fremont, CA 94539-3186. Tel: 415-656-7175
Freiermuth, Harry, P.O. Box 6923, Salinas, CA 93912-6923. Tel: 408-757-6656
Hall, Henry, P.O. Box 462312, Escondido, CA 92046-2312. Tel: 760-737-9001
Keating, Douglas, P.O. Box 2284, Avila Beach, CA 93424. Tel: 805-595-9415
Kelly, James, c/o Valley Heights, 925 Freedom Blvd., A-114, Watsonville, CA 95076. Tel: 408-728-6565
Leonard, Joseph, 18430 Vista Granada Way, Los Gatos, CA 95030
Markey, Francis, 375 Coastview Dr., Santa Cruz, CA 95065. Tel: 408-475-7436
Matz, Leo, Mount Angel Towers, One Tower Ln., Mount Angel, OR 97362. Tel: 503-845-7568
McEvoy, John, 14 Herrmann Dr., Monterey, CA 93940. Tel: 408-375-3828
McSweeney, John, 1320 Padre Dr., Salinas, CA 93901. Tel: 408-422-4584
Migliazzo, Felix, 1249 Josselyn Canyon Rd., P.O. Box 88, Monterey, CA 93942. Tel: 408-373-9120
Murphy, John, c/o St. Clare's Retreat, 2381 Laurel Glen Rd., Soquel, CA 95073. Tel: 408-423-8093
O'Halloran, Richard, 1335 Byron Dr., Salinas, CA 93901. Tel: 408-758-6285
O'Sullivan, Michael, 2247 Idylwild Pl., Arroyo Grande, CA 93420. Tel: 805-489-9160
Rodrigues, Antonio, 143 Swift St., Santa Cruz, CA 95060. Tel: 408-423-0650
Santamaria, Max, Cr. de Arizala 7, 31178 Abaruza, Navarra, Spain. Tel: 011-344-452-0021
Schwarz, Robert, Golden Oaks #4103, 30 Monte Vista Dr., Monterey, CA 93940. Tel: 408-372-8848
Sweeney, James, 194 Island St., Morro Bay, CA 93442. Tel: 805-773-4108
Toan, Francis, 2034 N. Main St., Salinas, CA 93906. Tel: 408-449-0449
Watt, Joseph, 2010 Pleasant Valley Rd., Aptos, CA 95001. Tel: 408-724-2829

Permanent Deacons:
Copelen, Jack, St. Rose Church, P.O. Box 790, Paso Robles, CA 93447. Tel: 805-238-2218; Fax: 805-238-2762
Leach, David, Nativity of Our Lady, 221 Daly Ave., San Luis Obispo, CA 93401. Tel: 805-544-2357
Miller, Harold, 121 Robin Dr., Marina, CA 93933. Tel: 408-883-2601

INSTITUTIONS LOCATED IN THE DIOCESE

[A] SEMINARIES, RELIGIOUS OR SCHOLASTICATES

BIG SUR. *New Camaldoli*. (See Monasteries). Priests 4; Brothers 1; Seminary Students 7.

[B] HIGH SCHOOLS, PRIVATE

MONTEREY. *Santa Catalina Upper School*. (Girls), 1500 Mark Thomas Dr., 93940. Tel: 408-655-9372; Fax: 408-649-3056. Sr. Carlotta, Head of School. Lay Teachers 65; Total Enrollment (Grades 9-12) 302.

SALINAS. *Christian Brothers Institute of California, Inc. dba Palma High School*. (Boys). (Grades 7-12), 919 Iverson St., 93901-1816. Tel: 408-422-6391; Fax: 408-422-5065. Congregation of Christian Brothers. Bro. Patrick D. Dunne, C.F.C., Prin. Brothers 8; Lay Teachers 31; Boys (Jr. High) 160; Boys (Total) 634. Congregation of Christian Brothers Residence, 935 Iverson St., 93901-1898. Tel: 408-758-2127. Bro. Frank L. Dalton, C.F.C., Dir. Brothers 10.

[C] HIGH SCHOOLS, DIOCESAN

SALINAS. *Notre Dame High School*, 455 Palma Dr., 93901. Tel: 408-751-1850; Fax: 408-757-5749.
E-mail: ndhsal@connectinc.com
Web site: www.notredame.salinas.ca.us
Dr. Roger D. Richter, Prin. Sisters 1; Lay Teachers 36; Girls 430.

SAN LUIS OBISPO. *Mission College Preparatory Catholic High School*, 682 Palm St., 93401. Tel: 805-543-2131; Fax: 805-543-4359.
E-mail: missionprepi@connectinc.com
Rev. Charles J. Tilley, S.J., Prin. Lay Teachers 14; Students 176.

[D] ELEMENTARY SCHOOLS, PRIVATE

MONTEREY. *Santa Catalina Lower School*. (Grades PreK-8). (Coed), 1500 Mark Thomas Dr., 93940. Tel: 408-655-9324; Fax: 408-649-3056. Dr. Nancy Diamonti, Dir.; Jane Stile, Sec. Lay Teachers 30; Students 254.

CORRALITOS. *Salesian Sisters' School: Mary Help of Christians Youth Center*. (Grades K-8), 605 Enos Ln., 95076. Tel: 408-728-4700; 728-5518; Fax: 408-728-5802. Sr. Phyllis Neves, F.M.A., Prin. Sisters 7; Lay Teachers 9; Students 220.

WATSONVILLE. *Moreland Notre Dame School*, 133 Brennan St., 95076. Tel: 408-728-2051; Fax: 408-728-2052.
E-mail: morelandwat@connect.com
Sisters of Notre Dame de Namur. Sr. Teresa Ann Leahy, S.N.D., Prin. Lay Teachers 8; Students 320.

St. Francis Youth Center, 2400 E. Lake Ave., 95076. Tel: 408-763-4484.
E-mail: salesian@msn.com
Conducted by the Salesians of St. John Bosco. Revs. John Itzaina, S.D.B., Exec. Dir.; Jesse Montes, S.D.B., Prog. Dir.; Bros. Abel Zanella, S.D.B.; William Regner, S.D.B.; Michael Herbers, S.D.B. Lay Staff 8; Total Enrollment 800.

St. Francis Youth Center includes drama, dance, band, athletics and recreation, religious instruction, a tattoo removal program, prayer groups, and a food distribution site.

[E] GENERAL HOSPITALS

SANTA CRUZ. *Dominican Santa Cruz Hospital*, 1555 Soquel Dr., 95065. Tel: 408-462-7700; Fax: 408-462-7555
For a complete listing, refer to the Hospitals section.

[F] SPECIAL HOSPITALS AND SANATORIA ACUTE CARE HOSPITAL

MONTEREY. *Ave Maria Convalescent Hospital*, 1249 Josselyn Canyon Rd., P.O. Box 1977, 93940. Tel: 408-373-1216
For a complete listing, refer to the Special Care Facilities section.

SANTA CRUZ. *Dominican Health Services*, 1555 Soquel Dr., 95065. Tel: 408-462-7700; Fax: 408-462-7555
For a complete listing, refer to the Special Care Facilities section.

[G] MONASTERIES AND RESIDENCES OF PRIESTS AND BROTHERS

MONTEREY. *Oratorian Community-Congregation of the Oratory of Pontifical Right*, 302 High St., P.O. Box 1688, 93942. Tel: 408-373-0476. Very Rev. Peter C. Sanders, C.O., Provost. Tel: 408-375-9769; Revs. Michael P. Drury, C.O., Vicar. Tel: 408-646-8278; Lidio Limon, C.O., Sec. Tel: 408-372-6094; Thomas A. Kieffer, C.O., Treas. Tel: 408-372-1325. Priests 4.

ARROYO GRANDE. *St. Joseph Cupertino Province, Provincial Center*, P.O. Box 820, 93421. Tel: 805-489-1012.
E-mail: allenram@aol.com
Revs. Allen A. Ramirez, O.F.M.Conv., Minister Prov.; Victor Abegg, O.F.M.Conv., Vicar Prov.; Bros. James Reiter, O.F.M.Conv., Province Sec.; Casimir Roland, O.F.M.Conv., Prov. Econom; George Cherrie, O.F.M.Conv., Prov. Exactor.
Attached to the Province but outside friaries: Revs. Kerry Abbott, O.F.M.Conv., Chap. Captain, (U.S.A.F.); Juniper Schneider, O.F.M.Conv.; Gregory Gilroy, O.F.M.Conv.; Bro. Robert Ouellette, O.F.M.Conv.; Rev. Christopher Lucas, O.F.M.Conv. Total in Residence 20.
St. Joseph's Cupertino Novitiate, 1352 Dale Ave., P.O. Box 820, 93421. Tel: 805-473-2256. Bro. James M. Reiter, O.F.M.Conv., Dir. Novices & Guardian; Rev. Roch Bartman, O.F.M.Conv., (Retired). Priests 1; Brothers 1; Novices 16.

BIG SUR. *New Camaldoli Hermitage*, 93920. Tel: 408-667-2456; Fax: 408-667-0480.
E-mail: monks@contemplation.com
Web site: www.contemplation.com
Very Rev. Robert Hale, O.S.B.Cam., Prior; Revs. Bruno Barnhardt, O.S.B.Cam.; John Powell, O.S.B-.Cam.; Joseph Diemer, O.S.B.Cam.; Bernard Massicotte, O.S.B.Cam.; Isaiah Teichert, O.S.B.Cam.; Raniero Hoffman, O.S.B.Cam.
On Special Assignment: Rev. Andrew Colnaghi, O.S.B.Cam., Prior, Incarnation Priory, 2208 Cedar, 94709. Rev. Romuald Duscher, O.S.B.Cam., Prior, Epiphany Monastery, 96 Scobie Rd.
On Leave: Rev. Louis Coddaire, O.S.B.Cam. Professed Monks (including 9 priests) 23; Brothers 13.

SALINAS. *Palma Community*, 935 Iverson St., 93901. Tel: 408-758-2127. Congregation of Christian Brothers. Bros. B. Sebastian Samp, C.F.C.; F. L. Dalton, C.F.C.; Patrick D. Dunne, C.F.C.; Anthony C. O'Grady, C.F.C.; Benjamin L. Favero, C.F.C.; John O'Brien, C.F.X.; Dennis J. Peterson, C.F.C.; Daniel L. Oehrle, C.F.C.; Charles J. Avendano, C.F.C.; Kevin J. Reilly, C.F.C. Brothers 10.

SAN LUIS OBISPO. *Monastery of the Risen Christ*, P.O. Box 3931, 93403. Tel: 805-544-1810. Men's Residence, 2308 O'Connor Way, 93405. Tel: 805-544-1810. Rt. Rev. David Geraets, O.S.B., Supr.; Revs. Raymond V. Roh, O.S.B., Prior; Stephen Odenbrett, O.S.B.; Albert Meyer, O.S.B.; Raymond Greco, O.S.B., (Retired).

SAN MIGUEL. *Franciscan Friars, O.F.M.* (Province of St. Barbara, Old Mission), P.O. Box 69, 93451. Tel: 805-467-3256; Fax: 805-467-2248.
E-mail: johnvaug@juno.com
Revs. John Vaughn, O.F.M., Guardian; Jerry Ahles, O.F.M.; James Kyrie, O.F.M.; Thomas Messner, O.F.M.; Rodrigo Ortiz, O.F.M.; Bros. Bartholomew Mitchell, O.F.M.; Quentin Watson, O.F.M.; Marion Alfonso, O.F.M.; Victor Hunter, O.F.M.
Novitiate House for the Franciscan Friars, O.F.M. (Province of St. Barabara), P.O. Box 69, 93451. Tel: 805-467-2801; Fax: 805-467-2448.
E-mail: johnvaug@juno.com
Revs. John Vaughn, O.F.M., Master of Novices; Thomas Messner, O.F.M.; Bro. Marion Alfonso, O.F.M. Novices 3.

SANTA CRUZ. *Oblates of St. Joseph Provincial House and Shrine*, 544 W. Cliff Dr., 95060.
Religious Community. Tel: 408-471-1702.
Provincial. Tel: 408-457-1868; Fax: 408-457-1317.
Shrine of St. Joseph. Tel: 408-471-0442. Revs. Siro Dal Degan, O.S.J. (Italy), Rector; Aldo Grasso, O.S.J. (Italy); Bronius Kaunas, O.S.J. (Lithuania); Philip Massetti, O.S.J., Prov. Supr.; Thomas Russo, O.S.J.; Bro. Duain O'Mara. Priests 5; Total in Residence 6.
Religious Community. Tel: 408-471-1702. Legal Title: *Oblates of St. Joseph, Provincial House and Shrine of St. Joseph, Guardian of the Redeemer*.
Society of Mary, Marianists, 285 Meder St., 95060. Tel: 408-423-9400; Fax: 408-423-8163.
E-mail: RolBunda@aol.com
Rev. Roland Bunda, S.M., Dir.; Bro. Anthony Young, S.M. Total Staff 2; Total in Residence 2.
Society of Mary, Marists, Marist Community, 436 Effey St., 95062-2640. Tel: 408-425-5202; Fax: 408-429-5832. Revs. Rene Iturbe, S.M.; Dennis Steik, S.M.; George Fahey, S.M.; Deacon Ken Johnson, S.M. Total in Residence 5.

[H] CONVENTS AND RESIDENCES FOR SISTERS

MONTEREY. *Ave Maria Convent*, 1249 Josselyn Canyon Rd., P.O. Box 1977, 93942-1977. Tel: 408-373-1216. Motherhouse of the Franciscan Sisters of the Immaculate Conception and St. Joseph for the Dying. Sr. Constance, Supr.; Rev. Filex Migliazzo, Chap. Sisters 7.

APTOS. *St. Joseph's Monastery of the Poor Clares (Colettines)*, 1671 Pleasant Valley Rd., P.O. Box 160, 95001-0160. Tel: 408-761-9659; 761-9481. Mother Mary Clare, P.C.C., Abbess. Professed Sisters (Cloistered) 11; Postulants 1; Extern 2; Novices 2.

CARMEL. *Carmelite Monastery of Our Lady and St. Therese*, 27601 Hwy. 1, 93923. Tel: 408-624-3043; Fax: 408-624-5495. Mother Francisca of the Holy Spirit, O.C.D., Prioress. Professed Nuns 13; Postulants 1.

CORRALITOS. *Daughters of Mary Help of Christians*, 605 Enos Ln., 95076. Tel: 408-728-4700; Fax: 408-728-5802. Sr. Phyllis Neves, F.M.A., Supr. Sisters 7; Candidates in Formation 4.

GONZALES. *Sisters of Charity of the Infant Mary Community of Formation*, 512 Fairview Dr., Box 178, 93926. Tel: 408-675-2975. Sr. Rosangela Filippini, I.M., Supr. Residents 5.

SALINAS. *Bethany*, 15785 Alto Way, 93907. Tel: 408-663-3675. Sisters of Charity of the Infant Mary. Sr. Gabriela Covi-Maffei, Supr. Residents 4.
Congregation of the Sisters of the Holy Cross, 1335 Byron Dr., 93901. Tel: 408-754-0786. Madonna Manor Convent. Sr. Sebastian Adza, C.S.C., Admin.; Rev. Richard O'Halloran, Chap. Sisters 6.
Madonna Del Sasso Convent, 163 Rosarita Dr., 93906. Tel: 408-424-4370. Sisters of Notre Dame. Residents 3.

SAN JUAN BAUTISTA. *Franciscan Sisters of the Atonement*, P.O. Box 1094, 95045. Tel: 408-623-4267. Franciscan Sisters of Atonement 6.

SAN LUIS OBISPO. *Monastery of the Risen Christ*. (Women's Residence), P.O. Box 3931, 93403-3931. 2304 O'Connor Way, 93405. Tel: 805-544-7808. Sr. Marie DiSciullo, O.S.B., O.B.L.
Sisters of St Joseph of Carondelet, 3335 Broad St., #7, 93401. Tel: 805-544-9020. Sr. Miriam Therese Larkin, C.S.J.; Sr. Janet Husung, C.S.J.; Sr. Theresa Harpin, C.S.J., 1991 Hays St., 93401. Tel: 805-782-9028.

SANTA CRUZ. *Adrian Dominican Sisters*, Pacific West Mission Chapter, P.O. Box 2235, 95063-2235. Tel: 408-457-7117; Fax: 408-457-7139.
E-mail: PacificADS@aol.com
Web site: http://www.op.org/adrian/
Sr. Jane Robert Stuckel, O.P., Chapter Prioress.
Franciscan Hospitaller Sisters of the Immaculate Conception, 1522 W. Cliff Dr., 95060. Tel: 408-426-5035. Sr. Maria dos Anjos Francisco, Local Supr. Total Residents; 3.
Villa Maria del Mar, 2-1918 East Cliff Dr., 95062. Tel: 408-475-1236; Fax: 408-475-8867.
E-mail: 103006.627@compuserve.com
Sr. Geraldine Will, S.N.J.M., Dir. Sisters of the Holy Names of Jesus and Mary 6.

SOQUEL. *St. Clare's Retreat*, 2381 Laurel Glen Rd., 95073. Tel: 408-423-8093.
E-mail: stclares@retreat.juno.com
Sr. Mary Francis Coleman, O.S.F., Supr.; Rev. John Murphy, Chap. Total Staff 18; Total Residents 9.

WATSONVILLE. *Moreland Notre Dame Convent*, 656 Main St., 95076. Tel: 408-724-7696; 724-3670. Sisters of Notre Dame de Namur. Sr. Denis Marie Harney, S.N.D., Coord. Residents 6.

[I] RETREAT HOUSES

APTOS. *Camp St. Francis*, 2320 Sumner Ave., 95003. Tel: 408-684-0300. Office: 2400 E. Lake Ave., Watsonville, 95076. Tel: 408-763-4486.
Conducted by Salesians of St. John Bosco. Summer Camp for Boys 8-14, Meeting Center for large groups, and Retreat Center for large groups of youth or adults.

BIG SUR. *New Camaldoli Hermitage*, 93920. Tel: 408-667-2456; Fax: 408-667-0480.
E-mail: monks@contemplation.com
Web site: www.contemplation.com
Very Rev. Robert Hale, O.S.B.Cam., Prior. Camaldolese Hermitage and retreat house. Total in Residence 32.

SAN JUAN BAUTISTA. *St. Francis Retreat Center*, P.O. Box 970, 95045. Tel: 408-623-4234; Fax: 408-623-9046.
E-mail: stfranret@aol.com
Web site: www.sbfranciscans.org
Conducted by Franciscan Friars. Province of St. Barbara. Revs. Godfrey D. McSweeney, O.F.M.; Richard McManus, O.F.M., Dir. and Local Guardian; Bart Welsh, O.F.M. Priests 3; Brothers 1; Total in Residence 10; Total Staff 18. Retreats for men, women, singles, married couples, A.A. and 12-step. Programs include Spiritual Growth, Ecumenical, Spanish.

SAN MIGUEL. *San Miguel Retreat House*, P.O. Box 69, 93451. Tel: 805-467-3256.
E-mail: johnvaug@juno.com
Rev. John Vaughn, O.F.M., Supr.

SANTA CRUZ. *Villa Maria del Mar*, 2-1918 E. Cliff Dr., 95062. Tel: 408-475-1236; Fax: 408-475-8867.
E-mail: 103006.627@compuserve.com
Sr. Geraldine Will, S.N.J.M., Contact. Sisters of the Holy Names of Jesus and Mary 6.

SOQUEL. *St. Clare's Retreat House*, 2381 Laurel Glen Rd., 95073. Tel: 408-423-8093; Fax: 408-423-1541. Sr. Mary Francis Coleman, O.S.F., Retreat Dir.; Rev. Enda Heffernan, O.F.M.Cap., Retreat Master. Franciscan Missionary Sisters of Our Lady of Sorrows 9; Total Staff 18.

[J] NEWMAN CHAPLAINS AND CENTERS

MONTEREY. *Department of Campus Ministry*, 485 Church St., P.O. Box 350, 93942. Tel: 408-373-1608; Fax: 408-373-0173.
E-mail: schools@dioceseofmonterey.org
Sr. Christina Heltsley, O.P., Dir.; Miriam "Mimi" Schwertfeger, Admin. Asst. Total in Residence 2; Total Staff 13.
California State Polytechnic Institute/Cuesta College, Newman Catholic Center, 1472 Foothill Blvd., San Luis Obispo, 93405-1416. Sr. Theresa Harpin, C.S.J., Dir.; Sr. Mary Pat White, R.S.C.J., Assoc. Dir.; Nancy Sanchez, Admin. Asst.; Sr. Moira Lyons, I.H.M., Receptionist & Sec.; Ryan Alaniz, Custodian. Student Assistants: Kevin Goodwin; Heather Perhach; Emily Ramos; Gabriel Rivas; Kelly Youker.
Cabrillo College, Santa Cruz, 95064. Revs. Roland Bunda, S.M., Dir. Campus Ministry, Newman Catholic Community, (Marianist); Dennis Steik, S.M., Asst. Dir., (Marist); Bro. Anthony Young, S.M., Outreach & Ecumenical Min.
University of California at Santa Cruz, 285 Meder St., Santa Cruz, 95060. Revs. Roland Bunda, S.M., Chap. & Dir. Campus Ministry, Newman Catholic Community, (Marianist); Dennis Steik, S.M., Asst. Dir., (Marist); Bro. Anthony Young, S.M., Outreach & Ecumenical Min.
California State University of Monterey Bay. Revs. Roland Bunda, S.M., Dir. Campus Ministry, Newman Catholic Community, (Marianist); Dennis Steik, S.M., Asst. Dir., (Marist); Bro. Anthony Young, S.M., Outreach & Ecumenical Min., 285 Meder St., Santa Cruz, 95060.

[K] SENIOR RESIDENCES

SALINAS, CA. *Madonna Manor Retirement Home*, 1335 Byron Dr., 93901. Tel: 408-758-0931. Owned and operated by Catholic Daughters of America Home, Inc. Administered and Managed by the Sisters of the Holy Cross. Sr. Sebastian Adza, C.S.C., Admin.; Rev. Richard O'Halloran, Chap. Total Residents 65.
Villa Serra Corporation, 1320 Padre Dr., 93901. Tel: 408-754-5532; Fax: 408-754-5609. Clyde Vaughn, Mgr. Sponsored by the Diocese of Monterey and Dominican Santa Cruz Hospital. Total in Residence 135; Total Staff 50.

SANTA CRUZ, CA. *Dominican Oaks Corporation*, 3400 Paul Sweet Rd., 95065. Tel: 408-462-6257; Fax: 408-462-6742. Jack Baskin, Pres.; Roger Stevens, Mgr. Sponsored by the Dominican Santa Cruz Hospital. Total Staff 73; Total Residents 222.

[L] MISCELLANEOUS

MONTEREY. *Newman Institute for Historical and Religious Studies*, Domus Patris Foundation, P.O. Box 748, 93942. Tel: 408-373-0477. Rev. Thomas A. Kieffer, C.O., Admin.

SALINAS. *Villa Serra Corporation*, 1320 Padre Dr., 93901. Tel: 408-754-5532; Fax: 408-754-5609. Total in Residence 135; Total Staff 50.

WATSONVILLE. *Magnificat the Monterey Bay Chapter*, 120 Enos Ln., 95076. Tel: 408-724-6933. Maureen Roach, Coord.

St. Thomas More Society, c/o 262 E. Lake Ave., 95076. Tel: 408-722-2456; Fax: 408-722-0414. Raymond A. AmRhein, Pres.

RELIGIOUS INSTITUTES OF MEN REPRESENTED IN THE DIOCESE

For further details refer to the corresponding bracketed number in the Religious Institutes of Men or Women section.

[1350]—*Brothers of St. Francis Xavier.*—C.F.X.
[]—*Camaldolesi Hermits.*—O.S.B.Cam.
[0310]—*Congregation of Christian Brothers.* (San Francisco Prov.; Western U.S.).—C.F.C.
[]—*Congregation of the Holy Cross.*—C.S.C.
[0480]—*Conventual Franciscans.*—O.F.M.Conv.
[]—*DeLaSalle Christian Brothers.*—F.S.C.
[0520]—*Franciscan Friars.* (Santa Barbara Prov.).—O.F.M.
[0530]—*Franciscan Friars of the Atonement.* (Graymoor, Garrison, NY).—S.A.
[0910]—*Oblates of Mary Immaculate.*—O.M.I.
[0930]—*Oblates of St. Joseph.* (Asti, Italy).—O.S.J.
[0950]—*Oratorians.*—C.O.
[0200]—*Order of St. Benedict.* Monastery of the Risen Christ.—O.S.B.
[1070]—*Redemptorist Fathers.*—C.SS.R.
[1190]—*Salesians of Don Bosco (Turin, Italy).*—S.D.B.
[0690]—*Society of Jesus.*—S.J.
[0760]—*Society of Mary, Marianists.*—S.M.
[]—*Society of Mary, Marist.*—S.M.
[1060]—*Society of the Precious Blood.*—C.PP.S.

RELIGIOUS INSTITUTES OF WOMEN REPRESENTED IN THE DIOCESE

[1070-13]—*Congregation of the Most Holy Rosary-Adrian Dominican Sisters.*—O.P.
[1070-03]—*Congregation of the Most Holy Rosary - Sinsinawa Dominican Sisters.*—O.P.
[1920]—*Congregation of the Sisters of the Holy Cross.* (Western Region).—C.S.C.
[0760]—*Daughters of Charity of St. Vincent de Paul.*—D.C.
[0880]—*Daughters of Mary & Joseph.*—D.M.J.
[0850]—*Daughters of Mary of Help of Christians.*—F.M.A.
[0420]—*Discalced Carmelite Nuns.*—O.C.D.
[1270]—*Franciscan Hospitaller Sisters of the Immaculate Conception.*—F.H.I.C.
[1390]—*Franciscan Missionary Sisters of Our Lady of Sorrows.*—O.S.F.
[1190]—*Franciscan Sisters of the Atonement.*—S.A.
[1300]—*Franciscan Sisters of the Immaculate Conception and St. Joseph for the Dying.*—O.S.F.
[]—*Immaculate Heart of Mary.*—I.H.M.
[2575]—*Institute of the Sisters of Mercy of the Americas.*—R.S.M.
[]—*Maryknoll Missioners.*—M.M.
[3760]—*Order of St. Clare.*—P.C.C.
[2970]—*School Sisters of Notre Dame.*—S.S.N.D.
[1960]—*Sister of the Holy Family.*—S.H.F.
[]—*Sisters of Charity of the Infant Mary.*—I.M.
[2990]—*Sisters of Notre Dame.*—S.N.D.
[3000]—*Sisters of Notre Dame de Namur.*—S.N.D.deN.
[]—*Sisters of St. Benedict.* Monastery of the Risen Christ.—O.S.B.
[3840]—*Sisters of St. Joseph of Carondolet.*—C.S.J.
[1990]—*Sisters of the Holy Name of Jesus and Mary.*—S.N.J.M.

DIOCESAN CEMETERIES

MONTEREY. *Diocesan Cemeteries Office.* Mailing Address: P.O. Box 2048, 93942-2048. 792 Fremont St., 93940. Tel: 408-372-0327; Fax: 408-372-8276. E-mail: cemeteries@dioceseofmonterey.org
Mr. Clancy D'Angelo, Dir.
San Carlos. Tel: 408-372-0327.

CAMBRIA. *Old Santa Rosa.* Tel: 805-541-0584.
HOLLISTER. *Sacred Heart / Calvary.* Tel: 408-637-0131.
SALINAS. *Queen of Heaven.* Tel: 408-449-5890.
SAN LUIS OBISPO. *Old Mission.* Tel: 805-541-0584.
SANTA CRUZ. *Holy Cross.* Tel: 408-475-3222.

NECROLOGY

† O'Sullivan, Laurence, (Retired). —Died Feb. 18, 1997.

Diocese of Nashville

(Dioecesis Nashvillensis)

Most Reverend

EDWARD U. KMIEC, D.D., S.T.L.

Bishop of Nashville; ordained December 20, 1961; appointed Titular Bishop of Simidicca and Auxiliary Bishop of Trenton August 26, 1982; consecrated November 3, 1982; appointed Bishop of Nashville October 13, 1992; installed December 3, 1992. *Office: The Catholic Center, 2400 21st Ave., S., Nashville, TN, 37212.* Tel.: 615-383-6393.

Most Reverend

JAMES D. NIEDERGESES, D.D.

Retired Bishop of Nashville; ordained May 20, 1944; appointed April 8, 1975; consecrated May 20, 1975; retired October 13, 1992. *Res., 239 Cana Cir., Nashville, TN, 37205.*

ESTABLISHED JULY 28, 1837.

Square Miles 16,302.

Comprises the Counties of Bedford, Cannon, Cheatham, Clay, Coffee, Davidson, DeKalb, Dickson, Franklin, Giles, Grundy, Hickman, Houston, Humphreys, Jackson, Lawrence, Lewis, Lincoln, Macon, Marshall, Maury, Montgomery, Moore, Overton, Perry, Putnam, Robertson, Rutherford, Smith, Stewart, Sumner, Trousdale, VanBuren, Warren, Wayne, White, Williamson and Wilson in the State of Tennessee.

For legal titles of parishes and diocesan institutions, consult the Chancery Office.

Chancery Office: 2400 21st Ave., S., Nashville, TN, 37212. Tel.: 615-383-6393; Fax: 615-292-8411.

Web site address: http://www.serve.com/diocnash

E-mail address: nashdio@aol.com

STATISTICAL OVERVIEW

Personnel	
Bishop	1
Retired Bishops	1
Priests: Diocesan Active in Diocese	35
Priests: Active Outside Diocese	6
Priests: Retired, Sick or Absent	12
Number of Diocesan Priests	53
Religious Priests in Diocese	20
Extern Priests in Diocese	4
Ordinations:	
Diocesan Priests	2
Transitional Deacons	1
Permanent Deacons in Diocese	28
Total Brothers	2
Total Sisters	137
Parishes	
Parishes	50
With Resident Pastor:	
Resident Diocesan Priests	30
Resident Religious Priests	8
Without Resident Pastor:	
Administered by Priests	11
Administered by Lay People	1
Missions	3
Professional Ministry Personnel:	
Sisters	9
Lay Ministers	30
Welfare	
Catholic Hospitals	1
Total Assisted	153,760
Homes for the Aged	3
Total Assisted	451
Day Care and Extended Day Care Centers	2
Total Assisted	300
Specialized Homes	1
Total Assisted	246
Special Centers for Social Services	6
Total Assisted	34,069
Other Institutions	2
Total Assisted	774
Educational	
Diocesan Students in Other Seminaries	5
Total Seminarians	5
Colleges and Universities	1
Total Students	385
High Schools, Diocesan and Parish	1
Total Students	1,000
High Schools, Private	1
Total Students	200
Elementary Schools, Diocesan and Parish	13
Total Students	3,436
Elementary Schools, Private	2
Total Students	724
Catechesis/Religious Education:	
High School Students	1,675
Elementary Students	6,401
Total Students Under Catholic Instruction	13,826
Teachers in the Diocese:	
Priests	1
Sisters	44
Lay Teachers	391
Vital Statistics	
Receptions into the Church:	
Infant Baptism Totals	1,670
Adult Baptism Totals	204
Received into Full Communion	439
First Communions	1,331
Confirmations	1,204
Marriages:	
Catholic	216
Interfaith	230
Total Marriages	446
Deaths	456
Total Catholic Population	60,405
Total Population	1,803,687

Former Bishops—Rt. Rev. RICHARD PIUS MILES, O.P., D.D., cons. Sept. 16, 1838; died Feb. 21, 1860.—Rt. Rev. JAMES WHELAN, O.P., D.D., cons. May, 1859; resigned May, 1863; died Feb. 18, 1878.—Rt. Rev. P. A. FEEHAN, cons. Nov. 1, 1865; created first Archbishop of Chicago, Sept. 10, 1880; died July 12, 1902.—Rt. Rev. JOSEPH RADEMACHER, D.D., cons. June 24, 1883; transferred to Ft. Wayne, July 13, 1893; died Jan. 12, 1900.—Rt. Rev. THOMAS S. BYRNE, D.D., cons. July 25, 1894; died Sept. 4, 1923.—Most Rev. ALPHONSE J. SMITH, D.D., cons. March 25, 1924; died Dec. 16, 1935.—Most Rev. WILLIAM L. ADRIAN, D.D., cons. April 16, 1936; died Feb. 13, 1972.—Most Rev. JOSEPH A. DURICK, D.D., cons. March 24, 1955; retired April 8, 1975; died June 26, 1994.—Most Rev. JAMES D. NIEDERGESES, D.D., cons. May 20, 1975; retired Oct. 13, 1992.

Vicar General—Rev. J. PATRICK CONNOR, *3019 Cayce Ln., Columbia, 38401.*

Vicar General—Rev. Msgr. GEORGE W. ROHLING, *237 Cana Cir., Nashville, 37205.*

Vicar General Emeritus—Rev. Msgr. CHARLES M. WILLIAMS, P.A., *100 James Blvd., Apt. 13, Signal Mountain, 37377.*

Moderator of the Curia—Rev. DAVID R. PERKIN, J.C.L.

Deans—Rev. W. BERNARD NIEDERGESES, Central Deanery; Rev. DAVID R. CHOBY, Northeast Deanery; Rev. CHARLEY GIACOSA, Northwest Deanery; Rev. JOHN L. KIRK, Southeast Deanery; Rev. RICHARD G. BUCHIGNANI, Southwest Deanery.

Vicar for Catholic Charities—Rev. WILLIAM J. FLEMING.

Chancery Office—2400 21st Ave. S., Nashville, 37212. Tel: 615-383-6393; Fax: 615-292-8411. Office Hours: Mon.-Fri. 8:30-4:30 All Official business should be directed to this office.

Chancellor—ANN K. KRENSON.

Assistant Chancellors—BETTY L. SALZMAN; RAMONA F. STEJSKAL.

Accounting Systems—MICHAEL F. NOLAN, Chief Financial Officer; TERESA OSBORNE, Mgr., Central Accounting.

General Counsel—Rev. JAMES K. MALLETT.

Diocesan Tribunal—2400 21st Ave. S., Nashville, 37212. Tel: 615-383-6393; Fax: 615-292-8411.

Judicial Vicar—Rev. DEXTER S. BREWER, J.C.L.

Defenders of the Bond—Revs. JOHN C. HENRICK; JOSEPH A. SANCHES.

Advocates—Revs. EDWARD F. STEINER; ERIC FOWLKES; MARK R. FULLER; Mrs. PATRICIA BURNS; Mrs. JULIE CONNOLLY; Mrs. LINDA NELSON.

Judges—Revs. DEXTER S. BREWER; DAVID R. CHOBY; RICHARD G. BUCHIGNANI.

Assessors—Mrs. LINDA NELSON; Sr. MARY CARL WHITE, R.S.M.; Mrs. PATRICIA BURNS.

Formal Case Instructor—Mrs. JULIE CONNOLLY.

Documentary Case Instructor—Mrs. LINDA NELSON.

Auditors—All priests and deacons assigned in the Nashville and Knoxville dioceses.

Secretary-Notaries—Mrs. PATRICIA BURNS; Mrs. JULIE CONNOLLY; Mrs. LINDA NELSON; Mrs. ANN H. KANENGIETER.

Presbyteral Council and College of Consultors—Most Rev. EDWARD U. KMIEC; Revs. MARK BECKMAN, Vice Chm. MICHAEL BIGLEY, S.D.S.; PHILIP M. BREEN; MATTHEW CHEERAMKUZHY, C.M.I.; DAVID R. CHOBY; J. PATRICK CONNOR, V.G.; MARK R. FULLER; WIATT A. FUNK; JOHN C. HENRICK, Chm. PATRICK J. KIBBY; STEPHEN A. KLASEK.

The Diocesan Finance Board—Most Rev. EDWARD U. KMIEC; Mr. JOHN C. FOX, Chm.; Rev. Msgr. GEORGE W. ROHLING; Revs. J. PATRICK CONNOR; STEPHEN A. KLASEK; JAMES K. MALLETT; DAVID R. PERKIN; Mr. MICHAEL F. NOLAN; Mr. RICHARD D. TAYLOR; Mr. PAUL HEER; Mr. KEVIN MARCHETTI; Mr. STEVE FRIDRICH; Mr. WILLIAM J. DICKSON; Mr. L. GINO MARCHETTI; Mr. TOM CONNOR; Mr. J. TERRY HUNTER.

DIONASH—A Partnership acting as Nominee for marketable securities for the Diocese of Nashville.

Diocesan Offices and Directors

The following offices and agencies are located at the Chancery unless otherwise indicated

Archives and Records—ANN K. KRENSON.

Campaign for Human Development—Mr. WILLIAM P. SINCLAIR, Dir., *St. Mary Villa, 30 White Bridge Rd., Nashville, 37205.*

Campus Ministries—Rev. JAMES F.X. PRATT, S.J., Diocesan Coord.

Vanderbilt—Rev. JAMES F.X. PRATT, S.J., *Vanderbilt Catholic Community, Box 6311, Station B, Nashville, 37235.* Tel: 615-322-2457.

MTSU-Murfreesboro—Rev. WIATT A. FUNK, *St. Rose of Lima Church, 1601 N. Tennessee Blvd., Murfreesboro, 37130.* Tel: 615-893-1843.

Austin Peay-Clarksville—Rev. ERIC FOWLKES, *Immaculate Conception, 716 Franklin St., Clarksville, 37040.* Tel: 931-645-6275.

Tenn. Tech-Cookeville—Rev. GLEN SAYERS, S.D.S., *St. Thomas Aquinas Church, 401 N. Washington Ave., Cookeville, 38501.* Tel: 931-565-2575.

Fisk-Meharry-Tennessee State University Campus Ministries—Rev. DERRAN COMBS, O.F.M., *St. Vincent de Paul Church, 1700 Heiman St., Nashville, 37208.* Tel: 615-320-0695.

Univ. of South-Sewanee—Rev. DEXTER S. BREWER, *Good Shepherd Church, 200 Tammy Dr., Decherd, 37324.* Tel: 931-967-0961.

Catholic Charismatic Renewal—Rev. JOHN KIRK, Bishop's Liaison; Mrs. TERESA SEIBERT, Assoc. Liaison.

Catholic Charities of Tennessee, Inc.—WILLIAM P. SINCLAIR, A.C.S.W., Dir., *St. Mary Villa, 30 White Bridge Rd., Nashville, 37205.* Tel: 615-352-3087; Fax: 615-352-8591.

Catholic Public Policy Commission of TN—JOSEPH SWEAT, Exec. Sec.

Catholic Social Services of Nashville—Ms. EILEEN BEEHAN, Dept. Dir., *St. Mary Villa, 30 White Bridge Rd., Nashville, 37205.* Tel: 615-352-3087.

Catholic Youth Office and Search Program—Rev. MARK BECKMAN, *2011 West End Ave., Nashville, 37203.* Tel: 615-327-0674.

Cemeteries—MICHAEL F. NOLAN, Dir.

Censor Librorum—Rev. JAMES K. MALLETT.

Clergy Benefit Foundation—Most Rev. EDWARD U. KMIEC, Pres.; Revs. CHARLEY GIACOSA; ERIC FOWLKES; JOHN SIMS BAKER; ALBERT SIENER; JAMES K. MALLETT; JOSEPH MCMAHON; EDWARD F. STEINER, Chm. J. PATRICK CONNOR; Mr. MICHAEL F. NOLAN.

Clergy Personnel Board—Most Rev. EDWARD U. KMIEC; Revs. WILLIAM J. FLEMING, Chm. MICHAEL O. JOHNSTON; STEPHEN A. KLASEK; MARK BECKMAN.

Continuing Education of Clergy—Rev. MARK FULLER, Dir.

Cursillo—JAMES CORBY, Lay Dir.; Rev. MATTHEW CHEERAMKUZHY, C.M.I., Spiritual Advisor; Deacon MARTIN DESCHENES, Assoc. Spiritual Advisor.

Permanent Diaconate Office—Rev. MARK FULLER, Dir.

Diocesan Planning—Rev. STEPHEN A. KLASEK.

Ecumenical and Interreligious Relations—Deacon WILLIAM J. DICKSON.

Hispanic Ministry—Rev. RICHARD GAGNON, Dir.; Mrs. ANABELL C. TREVINO, Asst. Dir., *30 White Bridge Rd., Nashville, 37205.* Tel: 615-356-2708.

Holy Childhood Association—Mr. STEPHEN J. HAMMOND, Dir.

Lay Retirement Administrative Board—ANN K. KRENSON; MICHAEL F. NOLAN; GLENN SEAGRAVES; JACK SMITHWICK, Chm. ROBERT TRUE.

Liturgical Life—Rev. PATRICK J. KIBBY, Dir.

Ministry Formation Services—Sr. ADRIAN MULLOY, R.S.M., Dir. Contact this office for the following concerns: Religious Education, Family Ministry, Youth Ministry, Pastoral Services, Liturgy, Parish Councils, Leadership Training, Lay Ministry, Rite of Christian Initiation of Adults, Pro-Life Education Evangelization, Peace & Justice.

Newspaper—*"The Tennessee Register"*, ANTHONY J. SPENCE, Editor.

Prison Ministry—TERRANCE HORGAN, Ph.D., Criminal Justice Advocacy.

Propagation of the Faith—ANN K. KRENSON, Dir.

Catholic Charities Refugee Resettlement Program—WILLIAM TOWLE, Dir., *10 S. 6th St., Nashville, 37206.* Tel: 615-259-3567; Fax: 615-259-2851.

Schools Office—STEPHEN J. HAMMOND, Supr.

Office of Stewardship and Development—ANDY GAERTNER, Dir.

Vocations—Rev. JOSEPH V. MCMAHON, Dir., *6401 Harding Rd., Nashville, 37205.* Tel: 615-352-2259.

CLERGY, PARISHES, MISSIONS AND PAROCHIAL SCHOOLS

CITY OF NASHVILLE
(Davidson County)

1—CATHEDRAL OF THE INCARNATION (1909), Revs. William J. Fleming; Stephen J. Wolf. In res., Most Rev. Edward U. Kmiec; Revs. David R. Perkin; James F.X. Pratt, S.J.
Res., 2001 West End Ave., 37203. Tel: 615-327-2330; Fax: 615-320-5650.
Catechesis/Religious Programs—Barbara Dodd, D.R.E.
Students 236.

2—ST. ANN (1921), Rev. Philip M. Breen.
Res., 5101 Charlotte Ave., 37209. Tel: 615-298-1782; Fax: 615-297-4326.
School—Tel: 615-269-0568. Betty Krogman, Prin.
Lay Teachers 13; Students 202.
Catechesis/Religious Programs—Stephanie Keller, D.R.E.
Students 51.

3—ASSUMPTION (1859). Attended by St. Pius X Church, Nashville. Rev. W. Bernard Niedergeses.
Church—1227 Seventh Ave. N., 37208. Tel: 615-256-2729; Fax: 615-256-0987.

4—CHURCH OF CHRIST THE KING (1937), Rev. James K. Mallett.
Res., 3001 Belmont Blvd., 37212. Tel: 615-292-2884; Fax: 615-383-0026.
School—Tel: 615-292-9465. Mrs. Alice Valiquette, Prin.
Lay Teachers 17; Students 240.
Catechesis/Religious Programs—Christine Caron, D.R.E.
Students 90.

5—ST. EDWARD'S (1952), Rev. Joseph P. Breen.
Res., 188 Thompson Ln., 37211. Tel: 615-833-5520; Fax: 615-833-9739.
School—Tel: 615-833-5770. Jerry B. Beckman, Prin.
Lay Teachers 24; Students 449.
Catechesis/Religious Programs—Sr. Louise Shoulta, R.S.M., D.R.E.
Students 338.

6—ST. HENRY (1958), Revs. Michael O. Johnston; Stephen G. Gideon; Deacons Jack Srouji; Martin Deschenes. In res., Rev. Joseph V. McMahon.
Res., 6401 Harding Rd., 37205. Tel: 615-352-2259; Fax: 615-356-6321.
School—Tel: 615-352-1328. Sr. John Mary Fleming, O.P., Prin.
Dominican Sisters of St. Cecilia Congregation 4; Lay Teachers 38; Students 660.
Catechesis/Religious Programs—Sr. Suzanne Stalm, R.S.M., D.R.E.
Students 264.

7—HOLY ROSARY (1954), Rev. Stephen A. Klasek; Deacons Jonathan P. Borgerding; Joseph Coen, Sr.; Gilbert P. Huhlein; Kenneth Steinbrecher.
Res., 190 Graylynn Dr., 37214. Tel: 615-889-4065; Fax: 615-885-5100.
School—Tel: 615-883-1108. Peggy Walker, Prin.
Lay Teachers 30; Students 553.
Catechesis/Religious Programs—Students 125.

8—ST. MARY VILLA PARISH COMMUNITY (1982), Rev. Msgr. George W. Rohling.
Church—30 White Bridge Rd., 37205.
Res., 237 Cana Cir., 37205. Tel: 615-352-3087.

9—ST. MARY'S OF THE SEVEN SORROWS (1838), Rev. James Norman Miller.
Mailing Address: P.O. Box 190606, 37219.
Res., 2823 Hazelwood Dr., #4, 37212.
Church—330 Fifth Ave. N., 37219. Tel: 615-256-1704; Fax: 615-256-7307.

10—CHURCH OF THE MOST HOLY NAME (1857), Rev. Joseph A. Sanches (ATL) Admin.
Res., 521 Woodland St., 37206. Tel: 615-254-8847; Fax: 615-254-1106.
Catechesis/Religious Programs—Students 59.

11—ST. PATRICK'S (1891), Rev. Joseph A. Sanches (ATL) Admin.; Deacon William J. Dickson.
Res., 1219 2nd Ave. S., 37210. Tel: 615-256-6498.
Catechesis/Religious Programs—Gerald Farris, D.R.E.
Students 27.

12—ST. PIUS X (1958), Rev. W. Bernard Niedergeses.
Res., 2800 Tucker Rd., 37218. Tel: 615-244-4093; Fax: 615-256-0987.
School—Tel: 615-255-2049. Sr. Robert Ann Britton, O.P., Prin.
Dominican Sisters of St. Cecilia Congregation 5; Lay Teachers 11; Students 150.
Catechesis/Religious Programs—Allison Bernhardt, D.R.E.
Students 9.

13—ST. VINCENT DE PAUL (1932), Revs. Fernand J. Cheri, III, O.F.M.; J. Derran Combs, O.F.M.; Bro. Joseph Manning, O.F.M.
Church—1700 Heiman St., 37208. Tel: 615-320-0695; Fax: 615-320-0698.
School—Tel: 615-320-1374.
Lay Teachers 11; Students 190.

OUTSIDE THE CITY OF NASHVILLE

Antioch, Davidson Co., St. Ignatius of Antioch (1976), Rev. John C. Henrick; Deacons Jack Nulty; P. J. Hoefler.
Res., 601 Bell Rd., 37013. Tel: 615-367-0085; Fax: 615-367-1712.
Catechesis/Religious Programs—Sandra Roberts, D.R.E.
Students 266.

Ashland City, Cheatham Co., St. Martha (1975), Rev. Peter Do Quang Chau.
Church—Bell St., P.O. Box 306, 37015. Tel: 615-792-4255.
Catechesis/Religious Programs—Carol Twork, D.R.E.
Students 55.

Brentwood, Williamson Co., Holy Family (1989), Rev. Edward T. Alberts.
Res., 9108 Demery Ct., 37027.
Church—9100 Crockett Rd., 37027. Tel: 615-373-4696; Fax: 615-377-3823.
Catechesis/Religious Programs—Patricia Gaines, D.R.E.
Students 950.

Centerville, Hickman Co., Christ the Redeemer (1983). Attended by Holy Trinity, Hohenwald. Rev. Joseph Kevin Dowling.
Mailing Address: Holy Trinity, 610 Kimmins St., Hohenwald, 38462.
Church—1515 Woodland Dr., 37033. Tel: 931-729-4669.

Clarksville, Montgomery Co., Immaculate Conception (1845), Revs. Eric L. Fowlkes; Wieslaw Burakowski (Poland).
Res., 716 Franklin St., 37040. Tel: 931-645-6275; Fax: 931-552-0331.
Catechesis/Religious Programs—Dominick Azzara, D.R.E.
Students 720.

Columbia, Maury Co., St. Catherine (1843), Rev. J. Patrick Connor.
Res., 5018 Hays Dr., 38401.
Church—3019 Cayce Ln., 38401. Tel: 931-388-3803; Fax: 931-381-8837.
Catechesis/Religious Programs—Candice Barton, D.R.E.
Students 390.

Cookeville, Putnam Co., St. Thomas Aquinas (1951), Revs. Peter Coffey, S.D.S.; Glen Sayers, S.D.S.
Res., 421 N. Washington Ave., 38501. Tel: 931-526-2575; Fax: 931-526-5869.
Catechesis/Religious Programs—Kay Herman, D.R.E.
Students 185.
Mission—Celina, Clay Co., Divine Savior.

Decherd, Franklin Co., Good Shepherd (1900), Rev. Dexter S. Brewer.
Res., 2021 Decherd Blvd., 37324. Tel: 931-967-0961; Fax: 931-967-3569.

School—2037 Dechard Blvd., 37324. Tel: 931-967-5673. Christopher Burns, Prin.
Lay Teachers 13; Students 107.
Catechesis/Religious Programs—Jan Johnson, D.R.E.
Students 88.
Mission—Alto, Franklin Co., St. Margaret Mary.

Dickson, Dickson Co., St. Christopher (1951), Rev. Charley Giacosa.
Res., 713 W. College St., 37055. Tel: 615-446-3927; Fax: 615-446-7339.
Catechesis/Religious Programs—Peggy Laws, D.R.E.
Students 153.

Dover, Stewart Co., St. Francis of Assisi (1982), Rev. Thomas Maurer, S.D.S.
Mailing Address: P.O. Box 307, 37058-0307.
Church—417 Spring St., Tel: 931-232-6982.
Catechesis/Religious Programs—Norma Smith, D.R.E.
Students 24.

Fayetteville, Lincoln Co., St. Anthony (1983), Rev. Thomas McElhinney, Glmy.
Res., 1900 Huntsville Hwy., 37334. Tel: 931-433-6525.
Catechesis/Religious Programs—Students 66.

Franklin, Williamson Co., St. Matthew (1979), Rev. Luzerne A. Schnupp; Deacons Sam Francescon; James Walsh; James Henry.
Res., 535 Sneed Rd., 37069. Tel: 615-646-0378; Fax: 615-646-5230.
Catechesis/Religious Programs—Sr. Thomasetta Mogan, R.S.M., D.R.E.
Students 220.

St. Philip (1843), Rev. Edward C. Arnold; Deacon Alphonse Toppeto (CHI).
Res., 113 2nd Ave. S., 37064. Tel: 615-794-4236.
Catechesis/Religious Programs—Kimberlie Leisinger, D.R.E.
Students 830.

Gallatin, Sumner Co., St. John Vianney (1929), Rev. David R. Choby.
Res., 449 N. Water St., 37066. Tel: 615-452-2977; Fax: 615-452-0323.
Catechesis/Religious Programs—Students 133.

Hendersonville, Sumner Co., Our Lady of the Lake (1969), Rev. William S. Bevington; Sr. Maria Edwards, R.S.M., Pastoral Assoc.; Deacon Thomas E. Bomkamp.
Mailing Address: Box 279, 37077.
Church—New Shackle Island Rd., 37075. Tel: 615-824-3276; Fax: 615-824-7989.
Catechesis/Religious Programs—C. Edward Ryckeley, D.R.E.
Students 338.

Hohenwald, Lewis Co., Holy Trinity (1983), Rev. Joseph Kevin Dowling.
Church—610 Kimmins St., 38462. Tel: 931-796-3738.
Catechesis/Religious Programs—Carol Sharp, D.R.E.
Students 26.

Joelton, Davidson Co., St. Lawrence's (1885), Rev. Msgr. James R. Hitchcock.
Church—5655 Clarksville Hwy., 37080. Tel: 615-876-2127; Fax: 615-876-7923. [CEM]

Lafayette, Macon Co., Holy Family (1982). Attended by St. Frances Cabrini, Lebanon. Revs. Mark Fuller; Zacharias Payikat, C.M.I.
Church—901 Vinson Rd., 37083. Tel: 615-666-6466.
Catechesis/Religious Programs—Students 17.

Lawrenceburg, Lawrence Co., Sacred Heart (1870), Rev. Richard G. Buchignani.
Res., 206 Berger St., P.O. Box 708, 38464. Tel: 931-762-3183; Fax: 931-762-5128. [CEM]
School—Tel: 931-762-6125. Sr. Mary Janice, R.S.M., Prin.
Catechesis/Religious Programs—Connie Hollman, D.R.E.
Students 41.
Convent—220 Berger St., Tel: 931-762-5207.
Sisters of Mercy 1; Lay Teachers 10; Students 115.

Lebanon, Wilson Co., St. Frances Cabrini (1953), Revs. Mark Fuller; Zacharias Payikat, C.M.I.
Res., 300 S. Tarver Ave., 37087. Tel: 615-444-0524; Fax: 615-444-3704.
Catechesis/Religious Programs—Dottie Climer, D.R.E.
Students 161.
Station—Smith & Trousdale counties.

Lewisburg, Marshall Co., St. John the Evangelist (1982). Attended by St. William, Shelbyville. Rev. Michael J. Bigley, S.D.S.; Sr. Cathryn Kever, O.S.F., Pastoral Assoc.
Church—1061 S. Ellington, 37091. Tel: 931-359-5017.
Catechesis/Religious Programs—Lisa Jackson, D.R.E.
Students 83.

Loretto, Lawrence Co., Sacred Heart (1872), Rev. Matthew Cheeramkuzhy, C.M.I.; Deacon Samuel Beckman.
Mailing Address: P.O. Box 86, 38469.
Res., 305 Church St., 38469. Tel: 931-853-4370; Fax: 931-853-4373. [CEM]
School—Tel: 931-853-4388. Mrs. Catherine N. Bradley, Prin.
Lay Teachers 6; Students 87.
Catechesis/Religious Programs—Students 34.

McEwen, Humphreys Co., St. Patrick (1855), Rev. John Sims Baker.
Res., 123 St. Patrick St., 37101. Tel: 931-582-3417; Fax: 931-582-6386. [CEM]
School—Tel: 931-582-3493. Sr. Mary Aquinas Halbmaier, O.P., Prin.
Dominican Sisters of St. Cecilia Congregation 3; Lay Teachers 5; Students 87.
Station—Humphreys Co.

McMinnville, Warren Co., St. Catherine (1958), Rev. James J. Bretl, S.D.S.
Res., Faulkner Spring Rd., 37110. Tel: 931-473-4932; Fax: 931-473-0799.
Catechesis/Religious Programs—Judy Davis, D.R.E.
Students 86.
Station—Van Buren Co.

Madison, Davidson Co., St. Joseph's (1953), Revs. Edward F. Steiner, III; Mathai J. Thonikuzhiyil, C.M.I.
Res., 1225 Gallatin Rd. S., 37115. Tel: 615-865-1071; Fax: 615-868-4900.
School—Tel: 615-865-1491; Fax: 615-612-0228. Sr. Bernadette O.P., Prin.
Dominican Sisters of St. Cecilia Congregation 3; Lay Teachers 23; Students 445.
Catechesis/Religious Programs—Rose M. Nicholson, D.R.E.
Students 160.

Murfreesboro, Rutherford Co., St. Rose of Lima (1929), Rev. Wiatt A. Funk.
Mailing Address: P.O. Box 4169, 37133-4169.
Res., 1601 N. Tennessee Blvd., 37130. Tel: 615-893-1843; Fax: 615-895-9787.
Catechesis/Religious Programs—Robert Carney, D.R.E.
Students 654.

Old Hickory, Wilson Co., St. Stephen (1952), Rev. Patrick J. Kibby; Deacon James M. Batcheldor.
Res., 14544 Lebanon Rd., 37138. Tel: 615-758-2424; 754-4454; Fax: 615-754-0043.
Catechesis/Religious Programs—Donna Young, D.R.E.
Students 315.

Pulaski, Giles Co., Immaculate Conception (1941). Attended by St. Anthony, Fayetteville. Rev. Thomas McElhinney, Glmy.; Kathleen M. O'Brien, Parish Coord.
Mailing Address: Box 363, 38478.
Church—Elkton Hwy. South, Tel: 931-363-5776; Fax: 931-363-6953.
Catechesis/Religious Programs—Students 27.

Saint Joseph, Lawrence Co., St. Joseph (1872). Attended by Sacred Heart, Loretto. Rev. Matthew Cheeramkuzhy, C.M.I.
Mailing Address: P.O. Box 86, Loretto, 38469. Tel: 931-853-4570; Fax: 931-853-4373.
Church—American Rd., 38481.

Shelbyville, Bedford Co., St. William (1941), Rev. Michael J. Bigley, S.D.S.
Res., 719 N. Main St., 37160. Tel: 931-684-8745; Fax: 931-684-6154.
Catechesis/Religious Programs—Mary Jo Johnson, D.R.E.
Students 67.

Smithville, DeKalb Co., St. Gregory (1982). Attended by St. Catherine, McMinnville. Rev. James J. Bretl, S.D.S.
Mailing Address: P.O. Box 712, 37166.
Church—1024 Faulkner Spring Rd., McMinnville, 37110. Tel: 931-473-4932.
Catechesis/Religious Programs—Jan Trahan, D.R.E.
Students 27.

Smyrna, Rutherford Co., St. Luke (1982), Revs. Richard Gagnon, S.D.S.; Augustine Lucca, S.D.S. In res., Rev. Lorenzo Martinez (Mexico); Deacon Ken Levinson.
Mailing Address: P.O. Box 907, 37167-0907.
Res., 10682 Nashville Hwy., 37167. Tel: 615-459-9672; 459-3046; Fax: 615-459-3989.
Catechesis/Religious Programs—Denise M. Leaver, D.R.E.
Students 216.

Sparta, White Co., St. Andrew (1982). Attended by St. Thomas Aquinas, Cookeville. Revs. Peter Coffey, S.D.S.; Glen Sayers.
Mailing Address: 401 N. Washington Ave., Cookeville, 38501.
Church—Hwy. 111, 38583. Tel: 931-526-2575; Fax: 931-526-5869.
Catechesis/Religious Programs—Students 21.

Springfield, Robertson Co., Our Lady of Lourdes (1946), Rev. Mark Beckman.
Res., 103 Golf Club Ln., 37172. Tel: 615-384-6200; Fax: 615-384-5837. [CEM]
Catechesis/Religious Programs—Jan Hennessy, D.R.E.
Students 120.
Mission—Cedar Hill, Robertson Co., St. Michael. [CEM]

Tennessee Ridge, Houston Co., St. Elizabeth Ann Seton (1977). Attended by St. Patrick, McEwen. Rev. John Sims Baker. Pastoral Assocs: Sr. Marlene Huck, C.PP.S.; Sr. Darlene Huck, C.PP.S.
Res., Rte. 3, Box 161, Erin, 37061. Tel: 931-289-5401.
Mailing Address: P.O. Box 85, 37178.
Church—Hwy. 49.
Catechesis/Religious Programs—Students 12.

Tullahoma, Coffee Co., St. Paul the Apostle (1954), Rev. John L. Kirk.
Res., 304 W. Grizzard St., 37388. Tel: 931-455-3050; Fax: 931-455-8298.
School—Tel: 931-455-4221. Suzanne Miller, Prin.
Lay Teachers 12; Students 151.
Catechesis/Religious Programs—Lisa Anderson, D.R.E.
Students 140.
Station—Manchester, Coffee Co.

Waynesboro, Wayne Co., St. Cecilia (1982). Attended by Holy Trinity, Hohenwald. Rev. Joseph Kevin Dowling.
Mailing Address: Holy Trinity Church, 610 Kimmins St., Hohenwald, 38462.
Church—526 Hwy. 64 E., 38485. Tel: 931-796-3738.
Catechesis/Religious Programs—Students 11.

On Duty Outside the Diocese:
Reverend Fathers—
Campion, Owen F., Our Sunday Visitor, 200 Noll Plaza, Huntington, IN 46750
Flaherty, Jay M., Holy Cross Church, 144 Wears Valley Rd., Pigeon Forge, TN 37863
McMurry, John E., S.S., St. Mary's Spiritual Center, 600 N. Paca St., Baltimore, MD 21201-1995
McMurry, Vincent deP., S.S., St. Mary's Seminary, 5400 Roland Ave., Baltimore, MD 21210
Miller, Brendan, New Subiaco Abbey, Subiaco, AR 72865
Ney, Charles, Dennehotso Health Clinic, Dennehotso, AZ 86535

Absent on Leave:
Reverend Fathers—
Strobel, Charles

Retired:
Reverend Monsignors—
Williams, Charles M., 100 James Blvd., Apt. 13, Signal Mountain, TN 37377
Reverend Fathers—
Ballentine, Edgar S., 702 Nichol St., Pulaski, TN 38478
Baltz, John P., Jr., 2146 Oakland St., Nashville, TN 37210
Briscoe, Orville, P.O. Box 3118, Murfreesboro, TN 37133
Cain, John N., 305 Davidson Rd., Nashville, TN 37205
Clements, Daniel A., 924 Rose Petal Ln., Knoxville, TN 37938
Julius, Joseph W., St. Francis of Assisi, 7715 River Rd., Townsend, TN 37882
Murray, James B., 25720 Hickory Blvd. S.W., Apt. 414-B, Bonita Springs, FL 33923
Nolan, William N, P.O. Box 210781, Nashville, TN 37221
Rudisill, James A., 3216 S. Waynoka Cir., Memphis, TN 38111-3615
Siener, Albert, Chowning Square #22, 4141 Woodlawn Dr., Nashville, TN 37205

Permanent Deacons:
Bainbridge, Frank, Prison Ministry, Nashville; St. Christopher, Dickson
Batcheldor, James M., Jr., St. Stephen, Old Hickory
Bauman, Frank, St. Mary Villa Parish Community, Nashville
Beckman, Samuel C., Sacred Heart, Loretto
Bomkamp, Thomas E., Our Lady of the Lake, Hendersonville
Borgerding, Jonathan P., Holy Rosary, Nashville
Carroll, John B., (Retired)
Coen, Joseph, Sr., Holy Rosary, Nashville
Deschenes, Martin, St. Henry, Cursillo, Nashville

Dickson, William J., St. Patrick, Nashville; Diocesan Ecumenical Dir.
Francescon, Samuel A., St. Matthew, Franklin
Henry, James R., St. Matthew, Franklin
Hoefler, Paul J., St. Ignatius, Antioch
Hooper, Hugh C., (Retired)
Huhlein, Gilbert P., Holy Rosary, Nashville
Levinson, Ken, St. Luke, Smyrna
McBrayer, J. Harold, Jr., (Retired)
McBride, Gordon W., Sr., St. Joseph, Madison
McGinn, George P., Hospital Ministry, Nashville
Nulty, Jack, St. Ignatius, Antioch
Randall, Ralph, St. Christopher, Dickson
Srouji, Jack, St. Henry, Nashville
Steinbrecher, Kenneth, Holy Rosary, Nashville
Steltemeier, William, Jr., Unassigned
Toppeto, Alphonse A. (CHI), St. Philip, Franklin
Von Mann, Milton, Prison Ministry, St. Edward, Nashville
Walsh, James F., Jr., St. Matthew, Franklin
Welsh, Theodore B., St. Joseph, Madison

INSTITUTIONS LOCATED IN THE DIOCESE

[A] COLLEGES

NASHVILLE. *Aquinas College*, 4210 Harding Rd., 37205. Tel: 615-297-7545.
Web site: www.aquinas-TN.edu
For a complete listing, refer to the Colleges and Universities section.

[B] HIGH SCHOOLS, DIOCESAN

NASHVILLE. *Father Ryan High School* (1925), 700 Norwood Dr., 37204. Tel: 615-383-4200; Fax: 615-383-9056.
Web site: www.serve.com/nashfrhs
Corporate Title: Father Ryan High School, Inc. Mr. M. Edward Krenson, Prin.; Rev. Joseph V. McMahon, Assoc. Prin. Pastoral Affairs. Priests 1; Sisters 1; Lay Teachers 75; Students 1000.
Father Ryan Board of Trust, Devel. & Alumni Office, 770 Norwood Dr., 37204. Tel: 615-269-7926.

[C] HIGH SCHOOLS, PRIVATE

NASHVILLE. *St. Cecilia Academy* (1860), Dominican Campus, 4210 Harding Rd., 37205. Tel: 615-298-4525; Fax: 615-297-9128.
Web site: www.stcecilia.edu/sca
Legal Title: *St. Cecilia Academy*. Conducted by the St. Cecilia Congregation of Dominican Sisters. Rev. William M. Fitzgerald, O.Praem, Chap.; Sr. Mary Elizabeth, O.P., Prin. Sisters 7; Lay Teachers 18; Students 200.

[D] ELEMENTARY SCHOOLS, PRIVATE

NASHVILLE. *Overbrook School*, 4210 Harding Rd., 37205. Tel: 615-292-5134; Fax: 615-783-0560.
Web site: www.overbrook.edu
The St. Cecilia Congregation of Dominican Sisters. Sr. Catherine Marie, O.P., Prin. Sisters 7; Lay Teachers 28; Students 367.
**St. Bernard Academy*, 2020 24th Ave. S., 37212-4202. Tel: 615-385-0440; Fax: 615-783-0241.
Web site: www.stbernard.org
Legal Title: *Saint Bernard Academy Corporation*. Dr. Margaret Isabell, Dir. Sisters 4; Lay Teachers 24; Students 357.

[E] CHILD-CARING INSTITUTIONS

NASHVILLE. *St. Mary Orphanage, Inc. dba St. Mary Villa*, 30 White Bridge Rd., 37205
For a complete listing, refer to the Special Care Facilities section.
St. Mary Villa Child Development Center, 30 White Bridge Rd., 37205. Tel: 615-356-6336
For a complete listing, refer to the Special Care Facilities section.
**St. Bernard After School Program*, 2020 24th Ave. S., 37212. Tel: 615-298-1298
For a complete listing, refer to the Special Care Facilities section.

[F] GENERAL HOSPITALS

NASHVILLE. *St. Thomas Hospital*, (1898) 4220 Harding Rd., 37205. Tel: 615-222-2111
For a complete listing, refer to the Hospitals section.

[G] HOMES FOR THE AGED

NASHVILLE. *St. Mary Villa Retirement Community, Inc.*, 2400 21st Ave., 37212
For a complete listing, refer to the Special Care Facilities section.
Villa Maria Manor, Inc. dba Villa Maria Manor, 32 White Bridge Rd., 37205. Tel: 615-352-3084
For a complete listing, refer to the Special Care Facilities section.

[H] MONASTERIES AND RESIDENCES OF PRIESTS AND BROTHERS

NASHVILLE. *Franciscan Friars*, 1608 Tynewood Dr., 37215. Tel: 615-665-7313. Revs. Fernand Cheri; Derran Combs.
Glenmary Home Missioners, 1307 6th Ave., N., 37208. Tel: 615-242-1885. Revs. Robert Hare; Dennis Holly; Bro. William D. Wright.

[I] CONVENTS AND RESIDENCES FOR SISTERS

NASHVILLE. *Mercy Convent*, 2629 Pennington Bend Rd., 37214. Tel: 615-885-1863. Legal Title: *Sisters of Mercy of Nashville, TN, Inc.* Sr. Mary Judith Coode, R.S.M., Dir.; Rev. Stephen Stolowski, Chap. Sisters 31.
St. Cecilia Convent, 801 Dominican Dr., 37228-1909. Tel: 615-256-5486. Motherhouse and Novitiate of St. Cecilia Congregation of Dominican Sisters. Mother Christine Born, O.P., Prioress Gen.; Sr. Anne Therese Moats, O.P., Prioress; Rev. Joseph Angers, O.P., Chap. Sisters in Residence 80; Novices 10; Postulants 9.

[J] CAMPS AND COMMUNITY CENTERS

FAIRVIEW. *Camp Marymount*, 1639 Fairview Blvd. E., 37062. Tel: 615-799-0410.
Web site: www.serve.com/campmmnt
Catholic summer camp for boys and girls. Tommy Hagey, Dir.

[K] RENEWAL CENTERS

LIBERTY. *Carmelites of Mary Immaculate Center of Spirituality*, 610 Bluff Rd., 37095. Tel: 615-536-5177; Fax: 615-536-5499. P.O. Box 117, 37095. Rev. Matthew Cheeramkuzhy, C.M.I., Dir.

[L] MISCELLANEOUS

NASHVILLE. *Catholic Foundation of Tennessee, Inc.*, 2400 21st Ave. S., 37212. William J. Dunigan, Dir.
**Catholic Media Productions*, 700 Harpeth Knoll Ct., 37221. James F. Walsh, Jr., Pres.
Diocesan Council of Catholic Women, 2400 21st Ave. S., 37212. Rev. Richard G. Buchignani, Dir.
Diocesan Properties, Inc. dba Marina Manor East Apartments, 2400 21st Ave. S., 37212. Tel: 615-383-6393. Michael F. Nolan, Sec./Treas.
**Dismas, Inc.*, 30 White Bridge Rd., 37205. Tel: 615-352-6807. Francis McCaffrey, Pres.; Terrence Horgan, Ph.D., Exec. Dir. Homes in which former prisoners and college students live. Mentoring women prisoners by volunteers.
Glenmary Department of Pastoral Services, 1312 5th Ave. N., 37208. Tel: 615-256-1900. A national center serving parishes and other ministries staffed by Glenmary Home Missioners. Rev. Dennis Leo Holly, Dir. Pastoral Svcs.; Bro. William D. Wright.
Glenmary Co-Missioners, 1312 5th Ave. N., 37208. Tel: 615-248-6325. A Lay Missionary Association working in the rural South among struggling communities. Muzaffar Fazaluddin, Coord.
Glenmary Personnel Office, 1312 5th Ave. N., 37208. Tel: 615-259-1235. Resource for Glenmary Member's Personnel. Rev. Robert Hare, Personnel Dir.
Establishing Mission Churches with Lay Leaders, 1312 5th Ave. N., 37208. Tel: 615-256-4384. A project for establishing new missions with lay persons. Rev. Frank Ruff, Dir.
Haitian Office, 2400 21st Ave. S., 37212. Mr. Harry Hosey, Diocesan Dir.
Holy Name Loaves and Fishes Community Meal, 521 Woodland St., 37206. Margaret Emsweller, Exec. Dir.
Ladies of Charity Center, Inc., 2216 State St., 37203. Tel: 615-327-3453; 327-3430. Affiliated with the Ladies of Charity of the United States of America, LCUSA, and the Association of International Charities, AIC.
Ladies of Charity Welfare Agency, Inc., 2212 State St., 37203. Tel: 615-327-3430. Mrs. Terri Puma, Exec. Dir.; Rev. Msgr. George W. Rohling, V.G., Moderator.
Mid-Tennessee Rural Outreach Association, 30 White Bridge Rd., 37205. Tel: 615-352-3087. Legal Title: *Mid-Tennessee Rural Outreach Association; Assumption-St. Vincent North Nashville Outreach Association.*
St. Patrick Ecumenical Shelter for the Homeless, 30 White Bridge Rd., 37205.
**St. Henry Property Development, Inc. dba The Cloister*, 30 White Bridge Rd., 37205.
HENDERSONVILLE. *Legion of Mary*, P.O. Box 279, 37077-0279. Rev. William S. Bevington, Dir.
Priests Eucharistic League, P.O. Box 279, 37077-0279. Rev. William S. Bevington, Dir.

RELIGIOUS INSTITUTES OF MEN REPRESENTED IN THE DIOCESE

For further details refer to the corresponding bracketed number in the Religious Institutes of Men or Women section.
[0900]—*Canons Regular of Premontre*.—O.Praem.
[0275]—*Carmelites of Mary Immaculate*.—C.M.I.
[0520]—*Franciscan Friars*. (Prov. of Sacred Heart).—O.F.M.
[0570]—*Glenmary Home Missioners*.—Glmy.
[0690]—Jesuit Fathers and Brothers.—S.J.
[0430]—*Order of Preachers-Dominicans*. (Southern Prov.).—O.P.
[1200]—*Society of the Divine Savior*. (Milwaukee, WI).—S.D.S.

RELIGIOUS INSTITUTES OF WOMEN REPRESENTED IN THE DIOCESE

[0760]—*Daughters of Charity of St. Vincent de Paul*. (East Central Prov., Evansville, IN).—D.C.
[1070-03]—*Dominican Sisters*.—O.P.
[1070-07]—*Dominican Sisters*.—O.P.
[1070-09]—*Dominican Sisters*.—O.P.
[2575]—*Institute of the Sisters of Mercy of the Americas*. (Baltimore, MD; Cincinnati, OH).—R.S.M.
[]—*Sacred Heart Congregation (India)*.—S.H.
[1680]—*School Sisters of St. Francis*.—S.S.S.F. - O.S.F.
[]—*Sisters for Christian Community*. (St. Louis).—S.F.C.C.
[0990]—*Sisters of Divine Providence*. (St. Louis Prov.).—C.D.P.
[3840]—*Sisters of St. Joseph of Carondolet*.—C.S.J.
[3270]—*Sisters of the Most Precious Blood*.—C.PP.S.

DIOCESAN CEMETERIES

NASHVILLE. *Calvary Cemetery*, 1001 Lebanon Rd., 37210.

NECROLOGY

(No Deaths)

Archdiocese of Newark

(Archidioecesis Novarcensis)

Most Reverend

PETER LEO GERETY, D.D.

Archbishop Emeritus of Newark; ordained June 29, 1939; appointed Coadjutor Bishop of Portland March 4, 1966; Episcopal ordination June 1, 1966; appointed Apostolic Administrator February 18, 1967; succeeded to See September 15, 1969; appointed Archbishop of Newark April 2, 1974; installed June 28, 1974; Pallium conferred December 12, 1974; retired June 1, 1986. *Res., 60 Home Ave., Rutherford, NJ, 07070.* Tel.: 201-460-1369; Fax: 201-842-0724.

Most Reverend

ROBERT F. GARNER, D.D.

Retired Auxiliary Bishop of Newark; ordained June 15, 1946; appointed Titular Bishop of Blera and Auxiliary Bishop of Newark May 3, 1976; Episcopal ordination June 25, 1976; retired August 1, 1995. *Res., St. Joseph's House, 140 Shepherd Lane, Totowa, NJ, 07512.*

Most Reverend

NICHOLAS A. DIMARZIO, PH.D., D.D.

Auxiliary Bishop of Newark; ordained May 30, 1970; appointed Titular Bishop of Mauriana and Auxiliary Bishop of Newark September 10, 1996; Episcopal ordination October 31, 1996. *Res., Our Lady of Mt. Carmel Rectory, 259 Oliver St., Newark, NJ, 07105.* Tel.: 973-589-2090; Fax: 973-589-2662. *Mailing Address: 1160 Raymond Blvd., Newark, NJ, 07105.*

Most Reverend

THEODORE E. MCCARRICK, PH.D., D.D.

Archbishop of Newark; ordained May 31, 1958; appointed Auxiliary Bishop of New York and Titular Bishop of Rusibisir May 24, 1977; Episcopal ordination June 29, 1977; appointed First Bishop of Metuchen November 19, 1981; installed January 31, 1982; appointed Archbishop of Newark May 30, 1986; Pallium conferred June 29, 1986; installed July 25, 1986. *Office: 171 Clifton Ave., P.O. Box 9500, Newark, NJ, 07104-9500.* Tel.: 973-497-4011; Fax: 973-497-4018 (Office); 482-4793 (Cathedral).

Archdiocesan Center: 171 Clifton Ave., P.O. Box 9500, Newark, NJ, 07104-9500. Tel.: 973-497-4000; Fax: 973-497-4033.

Web site address: www.rcan.org

E-mail address: webmaster@rcan.org

Most Reverend

PAUL G. BOOTKOSKI, D.D., V.G.

Auxiliary Bishop of Newark; ordained May 28, 1966; appointed Titular Bishop of Zarna and Auxiliary Bishop of Newark July 14, 1997; Episcopal ordination September 5, 1997. *Res., Cathedral Basilica of the Sacred Heart, 89 Ridge St., Newark, NJ, 07104.* Tel.: 973-484-4600; Fax: 973-497-4018.

Most Reverend

DOMINIC A. MARCONI, D.D.

Auxiliary Bishop of Newark; ordained May 30, 1953; appointed Titular Bishop of Bure and Auxiliary Bishop of Newark May 3, 1976; Episcopal ordination June 25, 1976. *Res., 238 E. Blancke St., Linden, NJ, 07036.* Tel.: 908-486-1022; Fax: 908-486-7701.

Most Reverend

DAVID ARIAS, O.A.R., D.D.

Auxiliary Bishop of Newark; ordained May 31, 1952; appointed Titular Bishop of Badie and Auxiliary Bishop of Newark January 25, 1983; Episcopal ordination April 7, 1983. *Res., St. Joseph of the Palisades Rectory, 6401 Palisade Ave., West New York, NJ, 07093.* Tel.: 201-861-6644; Fax: 201-861-7799.

Most Reverend

CHARLES J. MCDONNELL, D.D.

Auxiliary Bishop of Newark; ordained May 29, 1954; appointed Titular Bishop of Pocofelto and Auxiliary Bishop of Newark March 15, 1994; Episcopal ordination May 12, 1994. *Res., Holy Trinity Rectory, 34 Maple Ave., Hackensack, NJ, 07601.* Tel.: 201-343-5170; Fax: 201-343-5067.

DIOCESE ESTABLISHED, 1853; ERECTED AN ARCHDIOCESE, DECEMBER 10, 1937.

Square Miles 513.

Comprises Four Counties in the State of New Jersey, viz.: Bergen, Hudson, Essex and Union.

For legal titles of parishes and archdiocesan institutions, consult the Chancery Office.

STATISTICAL OVERVIEW

Personnel	
Archbishop	1
Retired Archbishops	1
Auxiliary Bishops	5
Retired Bishops	1
Abbots	1
Priests: Diocesan Active in Diocese	560
Priests: Active Outside Diocese	42
Priests: Diocesan in Foreign Missions	5
Priests: Retired, Sick or Absent	157
Number of Diocesan Priests	764
Religious Priests in Diocese	250
Extern Priests in Diocese	77
Ordinations:	
Diocesan Priests	14
Transitional Deacons	17
Permanent Deacons in Diocese	228
Total Brothers	124
Total Sisters	1,757
Parishes	
Parishes	233
With Resident Pastor:	
Resident Diocesan Priests	203
Resident Religious Priests	30
Without Resident Pastor:	
Pastoral Centers	172
New Parishes Created	1
Closed Parishes	5
Professional Ministry Personnel:	
Brothers	18
Sisters	172
Lay Ministers	193
Welfare	
Catholic Hospitals	7
Total Assisted	866,365
Health Care Centers	90
Total Assisted	24,665
Homes for the Aged	7
Total Assisted	498
Day Care and Extended Day Care Centers	126
Total Assisted	3,000
Specialized Homes	4
Total Assisted	167
Special Centers for Social Services	240
Total Assisted	125,377
Residential Care of Disabled	2
Total Assisted	48
Other Institutions	7
Total Assisted	16,355
Educational	
Seminaries, Diocesan	3
Students from This Diocese	109
Students from Other Diocese	22
Diocesan Students in Other Seminaries	2
Seminaries, Religious	1
Students Religious	20
Total Seminarians	131
Colleges and Universities	4
Total Students	16,283
High Schools, Diocesan and Parish	18
Total Students	8,530
High Schools, Private	19
Total Students	7,343
Elementary Schools, Diocesan and Parish	140
Total Students	43,571
Elementary Schools, Private	6
Total Students	1,632
Non-residential Schools for the Disabled	5
Total Students	265
Catechesis/Religious Education:	
High School Students	4,571
Elementary Students	57,094
Total Students Under Catholic Instruction	139,420
Teachers in the Diocese:	
Priests	133
Brothers	39
Sisters	382
Lay Teachers	3,773
Vital Statistics	
Receptions into the Church:	
Infant Baptism Totals	18,425
Adult Baptism Totals	577
Received into Full Communion	712
First Communions	14,344
Confirmations	10,643
Marriages:	
Catholic	4,711
Interfaith	794
Total Marriages	5,505
Deaths	11,918
Total Catholic Population	1,346,185
Total Population	2,649,657

Former Bishops—Most Rev. JAMES ROOSEVELT BAYLEY, D.D., cons. Oct. 30, 1853; promoted to the Archiepiscopal See of Baltimore, July 30, 1872; died Oct. 3, 1877.—Most Rev. MICHAEL AUGUSTINE CORRIGAN, D.D., cons. May 4, 1873; promoted to the Archiepiscopal See of Petra, Oct. 1, 1880; succeeded to the Archiepiscopal See of New York, Oct. 10, 1885; died May 5, 1902.—Most Rev. WINAND MICHAEL WIGGER, D.D., cons. Oct. 18, 1881; died Jan. 5, 1901.—Most Rev. JOHN JOSEPH O'CONNOR, D.D., ord. Dec. 22, 1877; cons. July 25, 1901; died May 20, 1927.—Most Rev. THOMAS J. WALSH, S.T.D., J.C.D., ord. Jan. 27, 1900; appt. Bishop of Trenton, May 10, 1918; cons. July 25, 1918 made Assistant at the Pontifical Throne March 13, 1922; transferred to the See of Newark, March 2, 1928; appt. Archbishop of Newark, Dec. 10, 1937 Pallium conferred, Dec. 18, 1937; installed April 27, 1938; died June 6, 1952.—Most Rev. THOMAS A. BOLAND, S.T.D., LL.D., ord. Dec. 23, 1922; appt. Titular Bishop of Hirina and Auxiliary to the Archbishop of Newark, May 21, 1940; cons. July 25, 1940; transferred to Paterson, June 21, 1947; appt. Archbishop of Newark, Nov. 15, 1952; installed Jan. 14, 1953 Assistant at the Pontifical Throne, May 6, 1965; retired April 2, 1974; died March 16, 1979.—Most Rev. PETER LEO GERETY, D.D., ord. June 29, 1939; appt. Coadjutor Bishop of Portland, March 4, 1966; cons. June 1, 1966; succeeded to See, Sept. 15, 1969; appt. Archbishop of Newark, April 2, 1974; installed June 28, 1974; retired June 1, 1986.

Chancery—Archdiocesan Center, 171 Clifton Ave., P.O. Box 9500, Newark, 07104-9500. Tel: 973-497-4000; Fax: 973-497-4033. Open Mon.-Fri. 8:45-4:45. (Dispensation Requests or Questions regarding Canonical Matters can be directed to: Rev. Msgr. Frank G. Del Prete, J.C.D., Judical Vicar, at P.O. Box 9500, Newark, NJ 07104-9500. Tel: 973-497-4145; Fax 973-497-4138.).

Vicar General and Moderator of Curia—Most Rev. PAUL G. BOOTKOSKI, D.D., V.G. Tel: 973-497-4002; Fax: 973-497-4018.

Vicar General for the Apostolates—Rev. Msgr. JOSEPH T. SLINGER, Ph.D. V.G. Tel: 973-497-4318; Fax: 973-497-4249.

Vicar General for Planning and Public Affairs—Rev. Msgr. RONALD J. ROZNIAK, V.G. Tel: 973-497-4015; Fax: 973-497-4018.

Chancellor / Delegate for Religious—Sr. THOMAS MARY SALERNO, S.C., M.A. Tel: 973-497-4010; Fax: 973-497-4018.

Vice Chancellor for Archdiocesan Archives—Rev. Msgr. FRANCIS R. SEYMOUR. Tel: 973-497-4012; Fax: 973-497-4018.

Secretaries to the Archbishop—Revs. THOMAS A. DENTE; CHRISTOPHER M. CICCARINO. Tel: 973-497-4005; 4006; Fax: 973-497-4018.

Secretrary to the Archbishop for Development—Rev. JAMES S. CHOMA. Tel: 973-497-4134; Fax: 973-497-4031.

Judicial Vicar Archdiocesan Metropolitan Tribunal—Rev. Msgr. FRANK G. DELPRETE, J.C.D. Tel: 973-497-4145; Fax: 973-497-4138.

Vicar for Priests—Rev. Msgr. JAMES J. FINNERTY, *St. John Rectory, 22 Mulberry St., Newark, 07102.* Tel: 973-623-0822; Fax: 973-623-6804.

Vicar for Permanent Deacons—Rev. Msgr. THOMAS M. O'LEARY, *700 Wyckoff Ave., Wyckoff, 07481.* Tel: 201-891-1122; Fax: 201-847-8518.

Director of Vocations—Rev. THOMAS P. NYDEGGER. Tel: 973-497-4365; Fax: 973-497-4369.

Secretary for Education—Sr. DOMINICA ROCCHIO, S.C., Ed.D. Tel: 973-497-4250; Fax: 973-497-4249.

Vicar for Evangelization—Rev. Msgr. WILLIAM J. KOPLIK. Tel: 973-497-4360; Fax: 973-497-4033.

Vicar for Pastoral Life—Rev. Msgr. LOUIS F. FIMIANI. Tel: 973-497-4322; Fax: 973-497-4317.

Vicar for Human Services—Most Rev. NICHOLAS A. DIMARZIO, D.D. Tel: 973-596-4050; Fax: 973-596-3807.

Secretary for Temporal Admin.—Mr. JOSEPH C. NEHILA. Tel: 973-497-4051; Fax: 973-497-4033.

Regional Bishops—Most Rev. CHARLES J. MCDONNELL, D.D., Regional Bishop - Bergen Co.; Most Rev. NICHOLAS A. DIMARZIO, D.D., Regional Bishop - Essex Co.; Most Rev. DAVID ARIAS, O.A.R., D.D., Regional Bishop, Hudson Co./Vicar, Hispanic Affairs; Most Rev. DOMINIC A. MARCONI, D.D., Regional Bishop, Union Co.

Episcopal Vicars—

Bergen County—Northwest (Deaneries 1, 4): Rev. Msgr. THOMAS DONATO, V.E., *St. Paul, 200 Wyckoff Ave., Ramsey, 07446.* Tel: 201-327-0976. South Bergen (Deaneries 5, 7): Rev. Msgr. THOMAS G. MADDEN, V.E., *Queen of Peace, 10 Franklin Pl., N. Arlington, 07031.* Tel: 201-997-0700. East Bergen (Deaneries 2, 3, 6): Very Rev. JOSEPH O'BRIEN, O.Carm., V.E., *St. Cecilia, 55 Demarest Ave., Englewood, 07631.* Tel: 201-568-0364.

Hudson County—North Hudson (Deaneries 8, 9, 14): Rev. Msgr. MICHAEL J. DESMOND, V.E., *St. Stephen, 141 Washington Ave., Kearney, 07032.* Tel: 201-998-3314. South Hudson (Deaneries 10-13): Rev. Msgr. CHARLES G. STENGEL, V.E., *St. John the Baptist, 3026 J.F.K. Blvd., Jersey City, 07306.* Tel: 201-653-8814.

Essex County—West Essex (Deaneries 15-18): Rev. Msgr. CHARLES W. GUSMER, V.E., *St. Catherine of Siena, 339 Pompton Ave., Cedar Grove, 07009.* Tel: 201-239-7960. City of Newark: Very Rev. LUKE EDELEN, O.S.B., V.E., *Newark Abbey, 528 Martin Luther King Blvd., Newark, 07102.* Tel: 201-643-4800.

Deans—

BERGEN COUNTY—Northwest Bergen Region Deanery 1: Rev. Msgr. OWEN J. HENDRY, V.F., *Blessed Sacrament Rectory, 787 Franklin Lake Rd., Franklin Lakes, 07417.* Tel: 201-891-4200. Northeast Bergen Region Deanery 2: Rev. Msgr. PHILIP D. MORRIS, V.F., *St. John the Baptist, 69 Valley St., P.O. Box 308, Hillsdale, 07642.* Tel: 201-664-3131. Central Bergen Region Deanery 3: Very Rev. ROBERT H. SLIPE, V.F., *St. Peter the Apostle, 445 Fifth Ave., River Edge, 07661.* Tel: 201-261-3366. Southwest Bergen Region Deanery 4: Very Rev. PAUL L. BOCHICCHIO, V.F., *Our Lady of Mt. Virgin Rectory, 188 MacArthur Ave., Garfield, 07026.* Tel: 973-772-2295. South Central Bergen Deanery 5: Very Rev. JOSEPH C. DOYLE, V.F., *St. Francis Rectory, 114 Mt. Vernon St., Ridgefield Park, 07660.* Tel: 201-641-6464. Southeast Bergen Region Deanery 6: Very Rev. GERALD F. GREAVES, V.F., *Holy Rosary Rectory, 365 Undercliff Ave., Edgewater, 07020.* Tel: 201-945-0135. South Bergen Region Deanery 7: Very Rev. CHARLES J. MILLER, V.F., *Sacred Heart Rectory, 324 Ridge Rd., Lyndhurst, 07071.* Tel: 201-438-2200.

HUDSON COUNTY—North Hudson Deanery 8: Very Rev. JOHN F. RENARD, V.F., *St. John Nepomucene, 7007 Polk St., Guttenberg, 07093.* Tel: 201-869-6834. Central Hudson Region Deanery 9: Very Rev. ANDREW JAMIESON, O.F.M.Cap., V.F., *St. Ann, 704 Jefferson St., Hoboken, 07030.* Tel: 201-659-1114. Jersey City North Region Deanery 10: Very Rev. VICTOR P. KENNEDY, V.F., *St. Anne Rectory, 3545 Kennedy Blvd., Jersey City, 07037.* Tel: 201-656-2490. Jersey City Downtown Deanery 11: Very Rev. GREGORY J. STUDERUS, V.F., *St. Bridget Rectory, 372 Montgomery St., Jersey City, 07302.* Tel: 201-434-8500. Jersey City South Deanery 12: Very Rev. JOHN J. CRYAN, V.F., *Our Lady of Mercy Rectory, 40 Sullivan Dr., Jersey City, 07305.* Tel: 201-434-7500. Bayonne Deanery 13: Rev. Msgr. EDWARD J. HAJDUK, V.F., *St. Henry Rectory, 82 W. 29th St., Bayonne, 07002.* Tel: 201-436-0857. West Hudson Region Deanery 14: Very Rev. NORBERT T. LASKOWSKI, V.F., *St. Cecilia Rectory, 120 Kearny Ave., Kearny, 07032.* Tel: 201-991-1116.

ESSEX COUNTY—West Essex Deanery 15: Very Rev. ANDREW M. PRACHAR, *St. Raphael, 346 E. Mt. Pleasant Ave., Livingston, 07039.* Tel: 973-992-9490. North Essex Deanery 16: Very Rev. DENNIS COCOZZA, V.F., *St. Anthony Rectory, 750 N. 7th St., Newark, 07107.* Tel: 973-481-1991. Central Essex Deanery 17: Very Rev. THOMAS P. LIPNICKI, V.F., *Holy Spirit / Help of Christians, 17 N. Clinton St., E. Orange, 07017.* Tel: 973-673-1077. South Essex Deanery 18: Very Rev. RICHARD J. KELLY, V.F., *Our Lady of Sorrows Rectory, 217 Prospect St., South Orange, 07079.* Tel: 973-763-5454. North Newark Essex Deanery 19: Very Rev. ANTHONY J. LIONELLI, V.F., *Immaculate Conception Rectory, 390 Woodside Ave., Newark, 07104.* Tel: 973-482-0619. Central Newark Deanery 20: Very Rev. PAUL D. SCHETELICK, V.F., *Blessed Sacrament, 15 Van Ness Pl., Newark, 07108.* Tel: 973-824-6548. Ironbound Deanery 21: Very Rev. GEORGE C. LUTZ, *St. James, 143 Madison St., Newark, 07105.* Tel: 973-344-8322.

UNION COUNTY—Union Northwest Deanery 22: Very Rev. ROBERT B. STAGG V.F., *St. James Rectory, 45 S. Springfield Ave., Springfield, 07081.* Tel: 201-376-3044. Union North Deanery 23: Very Rev. JOSPEH S. BEJGROWICZ, V.F., *St. Theresa Rectory, 541 Washington Ave., Kenilworth, 07033.* Tel: 908-272-4444. Union County Southeast Deanery 24: Rev. KARL J. ROESCH, O.S.B., *St. Elizabeth of Hungary, 179 Hussa St., Linden, 07036.* Tel: 908-486-2514. Elizabeth Deanery 25: Very Rev. ROBERT J. HARRINGTON, V.F., *St. Mary of the Assumption Rectory, 155 Washington St., Elizabeth, 07202.* Tel: 908-352-5154. Union County Southwest Deanery 26: Very Rev. JOHN F. KENNEDY, V.F., *Immaculate Heart of Mary Rectory, 1571 S. Martine Ave., Scotch Plains, 07076.* Tel: 908-889-2100.

Advisory Bodies

College of Consultors—Most Rev. THEODORE E. MCCARRICK, Pres.; Rev. Msgr. WILLIAM C. HATCHER, Sec.; Most Rev. DAVID ARIAS, O.A.R.; Most Rev. PAUL G. BOOTKOSKI, D.D., V.G.; Most Rev. NICHOLAS A. DIMARZIO; Most Rev. DOMINIC A. MARCONI; Most Rev. CHARLES J. MCDONNELL; Rev. Msgr. EDWARD J. CIUBA; Rev. Msgr. RICHARD J. ARNHOLS; Rev. Msgr. PETER S. CHEPLIC; Rev. Msgr. RONALD J. ROZNICK, V.G.; Rev. Msgr. OWEN J. HENDRY; Rev. Msgr. JOHN GILCHRIST; Rev. Msgr. THOMAS P. IVORY.

Presbyteral Council—Most Rev. THEODORE E. MCCARRICK, Pres.; Rev. Msgr. EDWARD CIUBA, Exec. Sec. Members: Most Rev. DAVID ARIAS, O.A.R.; Most Rev. PAUL G. BOOTKOSKI, D.D., V.G.; Most Rev. DOMINIC A. MARCONI; Most Rev. CHARLES J. MCDONNELL; Most Rev. NICHOLAS A. DIMARZIO; Rev. Msgr. PETER S. CHEPLIC; Rev. Msgr. JOHN GILCHRIST; Rev. Msgr. OWEN J. HENDRY; Rev. Msgr. THOMAS IVORY; Rev. Msgr. EDWARD KAVIN; Rev. Msgr. PHILIP MORRIS; Rev. Msgr. RAYMOND POLLARD; Rev. Msgr. RONALD J. ROZNIAK, V.G.; Revs. ROBERT ANTCZAK; PETER BALDACCHINO; JOSEPH BEJGROWICZ; GEORGE GILLEN; KENNETH JENNINGS; GERARD H. MCCARREN; MICHAEL MERLUCCI; JOHN PALADINO; ANTHONY RANDAZZO; Rev. Msgr. TIMOTHY SHUGRUE; Rev. ACHILLES CASSIERE, O.F.M.Cap.

Priest Personnel Policy Board—Rev. Msgr. JOSEPH P. MASIELLO; Rev. Msgr. THOMAS M. O'LEARY; Rev. Msgr. EDWARD G. PRICE; Revs. ROBERT B. STAGG; ROBERT M. CHABAK, Archbishop's Delegate; FRANK J. MCNULTY; MICHAEL A. HANLY.

Diaconate Executive Committee—Deacons ROBERT V. THOMANN, Chm. CHARLES F. KILEY, Vice Chm. Tel: 973-497-4223.

Archdiocesan Incardination Board—Most Rev. PAUL G. BOOTKOSKI, D.D., V.G.; Most Rev. CHARLES J. MCDONNELL, D.D.; Rev. Msgr. FRANK G. DEL PRETE, J.C.D.; Rev. WILLIAM J. FADROWSKI.

Archdiocesan Development Committee—Rev. Msgr. GEORGE R. TRABOLD, Chm. Tel: 201-384-0101; Fax: 201-384-2055.

Priestly Vocation Board—Rev. Msgr. ROBERT FUHRMAN; Rev. Msgr. THOMAS MADDEN, V.E.; Rev. Msgr. MICHAEL DESMOND, V.E.; Revs. JOSEPH BEJGROWICZ; THOMAS M. CEMBOR; Rev. Msgr. THOMAS O'LEARY; Revs. JORGE CHACON; ROBERT EMERY; C. ANTHONY ZICCARDI; Rev. Msgr. WILLIAM DALY.

Archdiocesan Pro-Life Commission—DANIEL KRAFT, Chm. Members: Most Rev. PAUL G. BOOTKOSKI, D.D., V.G.; Rev. Msgr. RICHARD M. MCGUINNESS; Rev. Msgr. JOSEPH T. SLINGER, V.G.; TRAUDE BARBIERO; LOUISE FIGUEIRO; ESTELE FRESE; BONNIE LUDWIG; BRIAN LUDWIG; KEVIN MORGAN; CESAR ORTEGA; THOMAS RUSSO; JUAN RYAN, Esq.; JAMES SONDY; Dr. LEONIE WATSON; Dr. RICHARD WATSON.

Women & Men Religious Council—

Chairman—Sr. THOMAS MARY SALERNO, S.C., Chancellor/Delegate for Religious. Members: Sr. ALMA BLUME, M.P.F.; Sr. ELIZABETH CAHILL, S.C.; Sr. MARY FEEHAN, O.S.B.; Rev. ASHLEY HARRINGTON, O. Carm.; Sr. ELAINE KEENAN, O.P.; Rev. EDWIN LEAHY, O.S.B.; Sr. MARILYN MINTER, C.S.S.F.; Bros. STEPHEN OVERT, F.S.C.; MICHAEL STECHMANN, O.A.R.

Archdiocesan Finance Council—RICHARD J. BOYLE; CHARLES C. CARELLA; LAWRENCE R. CODEY; JOHN W. CULLIGAN; DONALD M. DANIELS; ANNE EVANS ESTABROOK; ADRIAN M. FOLEY, JR.; ALBERT R. GAMPER, JR.; LESLIE A. HYNES; ARTHUR E. IMPERATORE; MILTON F. LEWIS; BRIAN D. MCAULEY; W. PETER MCBRIDE; JOSEPH L. MUSCARELLE, JR.; FRANK A. OLSON; ARTHUR F. RYAN; EDWARD F. RYAN; GARRY J. SCHEURING; ANTHONY P. TERRACCIANO; JOSEPH A. UNANUE.

Archdiocesan Women's Commission—Sr. THOMAS MARY SALERNO, Chm. ANN BURGNEGER; MARY ELAINE CONNELL; LINDA ENGLISH; LUCILLE FOREMAN; Dr. ZENI FOX; ANNA GROVES; ADELAIDE JACKSON; ANA LOPO; Sr. MARGART T. MCGOVERN, O.P.; SHARON MUSCARELLE.

Medical-Moral Committee—Rev. Msgr. HAROLD P. DARCY, S.T.L., J.C.D., Chm. Tel: 201-768-7565; 973-497-4145.

Archdiocesan Pastoral Council—JOSEPH DUFF, Chm. ALBERTA PHILLIPS, Vice Chm. CATHERINE JACKSON, Sec.; Sr. VIRGINIA STANTON, S.S.J., Staff. Tel: 973-497-4350.

Archdiocesan Commission for Christain Unity—Rev. Msgr. PHILIP D. MORRIS, S.T.D., Chm.; Rev. PHILIP F.A. LATRONICO, Exec. Sec., *69 Valley St., P.O. Box 308, Hillsdale, 07642.* Tel: 973-497-4338.

Archdiocesan Commission for Interreligious Affairs—Rev. Msgr. JOHN GILCHRIST, Chm.; Rev. PHILIP F.A. LATRONICO, Exec. Sec. Tel: 973-497-4338.

Metropolitan Tribunal of the Archdiocese of Newark

Archdiocesan Center, 171 Clifton Ave., Newark, 07104. Tel: 973-497-4145; Fax: 973-497-4138

Judicial Vicar—Rev. Msgr. FRANK DEL PRETE, J.C.D.

Associate Judicial Vicar—Rev. Msgr. JAMES P. MCMENEMIE, S.T.L.

Archdiocesan Staff—Sr. CATHERINE MARY RAYMOND, J.C.L.; Bro. LEONARD VOEGTLE, J.C.D.; Rev. JOHN F. CONNOR, S.T.B.

Part-time Staff—Revs. EVAN BANKS, O.F.M.; FERNANDO CARRANZA; Rev. Msgr. VINCENT P. COBURN, J.C.D.; Rev. Msgr. HAROLD P. DARCY, J.C.D.; Rev. Msgr. FRANCIS HOUGHTON; Rev. Msgr. VINCENT J. DOYLE, J.C.D.; Rev. Msgr. GEORGE R. TRABOLD, J.C.L.; Revs. WILLIAM A. MAHON; GABRIEL B. COSTA, Ph.D.; JOHN J. CRYAN, M.Div.; EDWARD DONOHUE, O.F.M.; ROBERT E. EMERY, J.C.L.; RICHARD G. FRANCESCO, J.C.L.; Rev. Msgr. ROBERT HARRINGTON; Revs. NORBERT LASKOWSKI, B.A.; ROBERT G. MCBRIDE, J.C.L.; JEREMIAH MCGINLEY, O.F.M.; Deacon VINCENT E. MESSINA, M.Div.; Revs. BERNARD N. MOHAN, B.S.; JOHN S. OLSZEWSKI, S.T.L.; ROBERT S. MEYER, J.C.L.; Sr. RUTHE MORGAN, R.S.M.; Rev. MICHAEL M. WALTERS, J.C.L.

Promotor of Justice—Rev. Msgr. ROBERT F. COLEMAN, J.C.D.

Notaries—MARGARET RUSSO; SANDRA PERRINI; BETSY TRUNZO; JOHN WALSH.

Vicar General for Planning and Public Affairs

Rev. Msgr. RONALD J. ROZNIAK, V.G. Tel: 973-497-4015; Fax: 973-497-4018

Office of Development—Rev. JAMES S. CHOMA, Sec. to the Archbishop for Devel. Tel: 973-497-4135; Fax: 973-497-4031.

Archbishop's Annual Appeal—JOHN F. WALSH, Exec.Dir. Tel: 973-497-4124.

Special Events Office—JOHN NEVINS, Dir. Tel: 973-497-4130.

Planned Giving—BARBARA WARNER, Assoc Dir. Tel: 973-497-4125.

Vicar General and Moderator of the Curia

Most Rev. PAUL G. BOOTKOSKI, D.D., V.G., *Archdiocesan Center, 171 Clifton Ave., Newark, 07104.* Tel: 973-497-4002; Fax: 973-497-4018

Office of Counsel—WILLIAM A. CAMBRIA, ESQ. Tel: 973-497-4302; Fax: 973-497-4310.

Office of Archdiocesan Internal Audit—ANDREW T. SUKALA, C.P.A., Dir. Tel: 973-497-4085; Fax: 973-497-4033.

Office of Communications and Public Relations—MICHAEL HURLEY, Dir. Tel: 973-497-4190; Fax: 973-497-4185.

Chancellor/Delegate for Religious—Sr. THOMAS MARY SALERNO, S.C., M.A. Tel: 973-497-4010; Fax: 973-497-4018.

Vice Chancellor for Archives—Rev. Msgr. FRANCIS R. SEYMOUR. Tel: 973-497-4012; Fax: 973-497-4018.

Office of Research and Planning—JOSEPH A. VANCIO, M.A., Dir. Tel: 973-497-4025; Fax: 973-497-4028.

Health Care Personnel—Sr. THOMAS MARY SALERNO, S.C., M.A. Tel: 973-497-4009; Fax: 973-497-4018.

Pastoral Associates—Sr. THOMAS MARY SALERNO, S.C., M.A. Tel: 973-497-4009; Fax: 973-497-4018.

St. John Vianney Priests' Residence—Rev. Msgr. EDWARD F. KAVIN, Dir.; Mrs. JOAN D'GEROLAMO, Admin., *60 Home Ave., Rutherford, 07070.* Tel: 201-933-5155.

Propagation of the Faith—Rev. Msgr. ROBERT J. FUHRMAN, Dir. Tel: 973-497-4375.

Office of Clergy Personnel—Rev. WILLIAM J. FADROWSKI, Exec. Dir., *171 Clifton Ave., P.O. Box 9500, Newark, 07104-9500.* Tel: 973-497-4222; Fax: 973-497-4219.

Diocesan Priest Personnel—Rev. WILLIAM J. FADROWSKI, Dir.; Ms. JOSEPHINE CHOKRAN, Admin. Asst. Tel: 973-497-4222; Fax: 973-497-4219.

Adjunct Clergy Personnel—Rev. WILLIAM J. FADROWSKI, Dir.; Ms. FRANCES DOWNING, Admin. Asst. Tel: 973-497-4222.

Ministry to Retired Priest—Rev. Msgr. EDWARD F. KAVIN, Dir. Tel: 973-497-4224.

Continuing Education of Priests—Rev. Msgr. THOMAS A. MCCARTHY, Dir. Tel: 973-497-4221.

Continuing Formation of Priests—Rev. STEVEN FEEHAN, Dir. Tel: 973-497-4221.

Permanent Diaconate—Deacon EDWARD W. PORTER, Dir. Tel: 973-497-4223. Deacon DANIEL RAVELO, Assoc. Dir.- Hispanic Deacons; Rev. Msgr. RICARDO GONZALEZ, Spiritual Dir.- Hispanic Deacons.

Secretary For Temporal Administration—JOSEPH C. NEHILA, C.P.A., Sec. Tel: 973-497-4051; Fax: 973-497-4031.

Office of Business Administration—JOSEPH A. FRANK, Dir. Tel: 973-497-4040; Fax: 973-497-4031.

Accounting—GEORGE PERALTA, Dir. Tel: 973-497-4055; Fax: 973-497-4031.

Office of Banking and Investments—GEORGE PERALTA, Dir. MATTHEW J. PHELAN, Mgr. Tel: 973-497-4070; Fax: 973-497-4031.

Office of Plant Services—JOHN P. MINIERI, Dir. Tel: 973-497-4110; Fax: 973-497-4033.

Office of Catholic Cemeteries—Rev. Msgr. WILLIAM NAEDELE, Dir.; Mr. JAMES T. FAHEY, Exec. Dir., *340 Ridge Rd., N. Arlington, 07032.* Tel: 201-991-7404; Fax: 201-997-9560.

Office of Parish Services—ROBERT KENNA, Dir. Tel: 973-497-4080; Fax: 973-497-4033.

Office of Parish Internal Audit—JEROME JARECKI, Dir. Tel: 973-497-4074; Fax: 973-497-4031.

Office of Personnel and Benefits—WILLIAM E. MULLIS, III, Dir. Tel: 973-497-4104; Fax: 973-497-4103.

Cooperative Supply Services—STEPHEN MIHALIK, Dir., *171 Clifton Ave., Newark, 07104.* Tel: 973-497-4170; Fax: 973-497-4174. ERICA PHINN, Customer Svc. Rep. Tel: 973-497-4166.

Vicar General and Moderator of the Curia is the Archbishop's liaison to the following:

Archdiocesan Commission for Christian Unity—Rev. Msgr. PHILIP D. MORRIS, S.T.D., Chm.; Rev. PHILIP F.A. LATRONICO, Exec. Sec. Tel: 973-497-4338.

Archdiocesan Commission for Interreligious Affairs—Rev. Msgr. JOHN J. GILCHRIST, M.A., Chm.; Rev. PHILIP LATRONICO, Exec. Sec. Tel: 973-497-4338.

Archdiocesan Commission on Justice and Peace—Dr. WILLIAM TOTH, Chm. THOMAS MCCANN, Exec. Sec. Tel: 973-497-4341.

Archdiocesan Liturgical Commission—Sr. SANDRA DEMASI, S.S.J., Chm. Tel: 973-497-4347.

Archdiocesan Pro-Life Commission—DAN KRAFT, Chm., *1805 Penbrook Ter., Union, 07036.* Tel: 908-925-6442.

Vicar General for the Apostolates

Rev. Msgr. JOSEPH T. SLINGER, Ph.D., *Archdiocesan Center, 171 Clifton Ave., P.O. Box 9500, Newark, 07104-9500.* Tel: 973-497-4319; Fax: 973-497-4249

"The Catholic Advocate", Archdiocesan Newspaper—Mr. ROBERT DYLAK, Publisher, *171 Clifton Ave., Newark, 07104-9500.* Tel: 973-497-4200; Fax: 973-497-4192.

Secretariat For Education—Sr. DOMINICA ROCCHIO, S.C., Ed.D., Sec. Tel: 973-497-4250; Fax: 973-497-4249.

Catechetical Office—Mr. RONALD L. PIHOKKER, M.A., Dir. Tel: 973-497-4285. Sr. ELIZABETH CAHILL, S.C., M.A., Catechist Certification. Tel: 973-497-4293. Sr. ALICIA CAVANAUGH, C.S.J.P., Ph.D., Union Co.-Catechetical Leaders. Tel: 973-497-4289. ANITA HERNANDEZ, M.A., Catechesis for Hispanics. Tel: 973-497-4290. CHRISTINE MAGGIO, Educational Technology. Tel: 973-497-4292. JOAN ROVERE, M.A., Bergen Co.-Adult Catechesis. Tel: 973-497-4295. Sr. FRANCES SCARFONE, S.C., M.Div., Hudson Co.-Catechist Formation. Tel: 973-497-4296. PATRICIA VAILLANCOURT, M.A., Catechesis with Families. Tel: 973-497-4297.

Scholarship Fund for Inner City Children—KEVIN P. MORIARTY, Dir. Tel: 973-497-4281; Fax: 973-497-4279.

Office of the Superintendent of Schools—Sr. DOMINICA ROCCHIO, S.C., Ed.D., Supt. Tel: 973-497-4260. Mr. JOHN O'NEIL, M.A., Deputy Supt.- Secondary Schools; Sr. PATRICIA BUTLER, S.C., Deputy Supt.- Elementary Schools; Sr. CATHERINE ROCHE, S.S.J., M.A., Admin. Asst.; Bro. JAMES A. FINNEGAN, C.F.C., M.A., Planning; Bro. RALPH DARMENTO, F.S.C., M.A., Secondary Schools; Sr. ELIZABETH SCULLY, C.N.D., M.A., Christian Formation; Sr. SUZANNE BELLENOIT, S.S.J., M.A., Govt. Programs; Sr. MURIEL SMITHWICK, C.S.J., M.A., Asst. Supt. Essex Co.-Elementary; Sr. MARIE GAGLIANO, M.P.F., M.A., Asst. Supt. Hudson Co.-Elementary; Sr. JOAN AMELIA FERRUGGIARO, S.S.J., M.A., Asst. Supt. Union Co.-Elementary; Sr. MARIE LALANDE, C.S.J., M.S., Asst. Supt. Bergen Co.-Elementary; Rev. JOHN CONNOLLY, S.D.B., M.A., Dir.- Education Technology; Mrs. ESTELLE FRESE, M.A., Dir. Personnel; Mrs. GRACE PIETROPINTO, B.A., Dir. Finance; Deacon RONALD R. WICKS, B.S., LL.B., Dir. Marketing; GLORIA CASTUCCI, M.A., Dir. Early Childhood; Sr. LOUISE CABABE, O.P., Ph.D., Dir. Corriculum & Testing; MARVIN N. BROWN, B.S., Dir.- Data Systems Operator & Technician.

Vicar for Evangelization—Rev. Msgr. WILLIAM J. KOPLIK, *34 Maple Ave., Hackensack, 07601.* Tel: 201-343-5170.

Vicar for Pastoral Life—Rev. Msgr. LOUIS F. FIMIANI. Tel: 973-497-4322; Fax: 973-497-4317.

Hispanic Apostolate—Rev. JORGE E. CHACON, Dir. Tel: 201-497-4335. Rev. JOSE M. JUANGO, Dir., *Centro Guadalupe Hispanic Pastoral Center;* Rev. JOSE M. JUANGO, O.A.R., Dir., *547 35 St., Union City, 07087.* Tel: 973-497-4335.

Office of Black Catholic Affairs—Mrs. LUCILLE E. FOREMAN, Dir. Tel: 973-497-4340.

African-American and African Ethnic Apostolate Ministry—Deacon MARSHALL S. ANDREWS, Coord. Tel: 973-497-4304.

Black Catholic Coordinating Team—Tel: 973-497-4340.

Council for Multi-Cultural Concerns—Rev. Msgr. LOUIS F. FIMIANI, Chm., *171 N. Clifton St. - P.O. Box 9500, Newark, 07104-9500.* Tel: 973-497-4321.

Brazilian Apostolate—Rev. GEORGE C. LUTZ, Coord., *143 Madison St., Newark, 07105.* Tel: 973-344-8322.

Chinese Apostolate—Rev. JOSEPH FU, Coord., *188 MacArthur Ave., Garfield, 07026.* Tel: 201-772-2295.

Asian-Indian Apostolate—Rev. THOMAS THOTTUNGAL, Coord., *691 West Side Ave., Jersey City, 07304.* Tel: 201-433-6365.

Filipino Apostolate—Rev. JEREMIAS REBANAL, Coord., *800 Bergen Ave., Jersey City, 07306.* Tel: 201-433-6800.

Haitian Apostolate—Rev. JEAN-MARIE FRITZ LIGONDE, Coord., *492 Bramhall Ave., Jersey City, 07304.* Tel: 201-332-8600.

Liaison to the Irish Community—Rev. Msgr. MICHAEL E. KELLY, *120 Northfield Ave., W. Orange, 07052.* Tel: 973-325-6624.

Italian Apostolate—Rev. JOSEPH F. AMBROSIO, Coord., *Our Lady of Mt. Carmel, 259 Oliver St., Newark, 07105.* Tel: 973-589-2090.

Korean Apostolate—Rev. AUGUSTIN PARK, Coord., *St. Andrew Kim Parish, 257 Central Ave., Orange, 07050.* Tel: 973-673-1366.

Polish Apostolate—Rev. FELIZ R. MARCINIAK, Coord., *St. Theresa of the Child Jesus, 131 East Edgar Rd., Linden, 07036.* Tel: 908-862-1166.

Portugese Apostolate—Rev. Msgr. JOHN S. ANTAO, Coord., *403 Spring St., Elizabeth, 07201.* Tel: 908-355-3810.

Vietnamese Apostolate—Rev. JOSEPH TRI MINH NGUYEN, Coord., *St. Michael, 252 Ninth St., Jersey City, 07302.* Tel: 201-653-2147; 7328.

Department of Human Concerns—Vacant. Tel: 973-497-4341.

Department of Shared Responsibility—Sr. REGINA SUPLICK, S.C., Dir. Tel: 973-497-4353.

Ministerial Development Center—Sr. VIRGINIA STANTON, S.S.J., Dir. Tel: 973-497-4350.

Worship Office—Sr. SANDRA DE MASI, S.S.J., Dir. Tel: 973-497-4345; Fax: 973-497-4348. Rev. MICHAEL J. SHEEHAN, Dir.- RCIA; Rev. THOMAS B. IWANOWSKI, Assoc Dir.- Liturgical Formation; Rev. ROBERT G. LAFERRERA, Assoc Dir.- Parish Liturgical Services; Rev. Msgr. RICHARD F. GRONCKI, Archdiocesan Ceremonies.

Respect Life Office—Rev. Msgr. RICHARD M. MCGUINNESS, S.T.L., Ph.D., *1805 Penbrook Ter., Linden, 07036.* Tel: 908-925-6442.

Campus Ministry—Vacant; Dir., *Newman Center, 45 Bleeker St., Newark, 07112.* Tel: 973-642-1613; Fax: 973-642-1613.

Family Life Ministries—Ms. JUDITH MILLER, M.A., Dir. BARBARA KATULKA, Admin. Asst., *Archdiocesan Center, 171 Clifton Ave., P.O. Box 9500, Newark, 07104-9500.* Tel: 973-497-4325.

Family Life Center—*256 Franklin Ave., Maplewood, 07040.* Tel: 201-763-7659.

Pre-Cana Reservations—NANCY DELLISANTI. Tel: 201-497-4328.

Ministry with Separated, Divorced and Widowed Catholics—Revs. JOSEPH GIRONE, Chap., Separated and Divorced; THOMAS ARMINIO, Chap., Widows and Widowers. Tel: 201-497-4327.

Hispanic Family Life Ministries—REINA BASUALDO, Assoc. Dir. Tel: 201-497-4326.

Catholic One Parent Organization—Rev. JOSEPH M. DOYLE, Chap. Tel: 201-433-0950.

Engaged Encounter—Rev. PHILIP F. LATRONICO, Chap., *70 W. Passaic Ave., Rutherford, 07070.* Tel: 201-935-0344. Chaircouple: HARRY KUHLES; TERRY KUHLES.

Marriage Encounter Resources—Coordinators: Rev. Msgr. FRANCIS J. HOUGHTON. Tel: 732-899-1507. Couple: MICHAEL MUCCIA; PENNY MUCCIA, *248 Manning Ave., River Edge, 07661.* Tel: 201-265-0915. Registration/Information: STEPHANIE MURTHA; TOM MURTHA. Tel: 800-823-LOVE.

Pastoral & Matrimonial Renewal Center—Rev. CHARLES GALLAGHER, Dir., *67 Prince St., Elizabeth, 07208.* Tel: 908-353-8640.

Natural Family Planning—Rev. RICHARD CARRINGTON, Chap./Coord. Chaircouple: KAREN DOYLE; KEVIN DOYLE, *31 Hill St., Haworth, 07641.* Tel: 201-384-9458.

CYO Youth Ministries—Rev. RONALD J. MARCZEWSKI, Acting-Exec. Dir., *171 Clifton Ave., P.O. Box 9500, Newark, 07104-9500.* Tel: 973-497-4500; Fax: 973-497-4505. FRANK MAHENO, Finance Mgr. JUAN PAVLOWSKI, Acctg. Mgr. MARC CREGAN, Dir. in Young Adult Ministry. Tel: 973-497-4502. Directors in Youth Ministry: ABRAHAM ALARCON. Tel:

973-497-4519. DELIA CHAMORRO. Tel: 973-497-4503. ALBERT FORSYTHE. Tel: 973-497-4516. JOANNE TRAINA, *973-497-4506.*

CYO Retreat Center—499 Belgrove Dr., Kearny, 07032. GLORIA WIERZALIS, Dir., Retreats. Tel: 201-998-0088, Ext. 111. GLORIA O'NEILL, Facility Coord. Tel: 201-998-0088, Ext. 114. BETTY WHITE, Receptionist. Tel: 201-998-0088, Ext. 110. ROBERT GARRITY, Dir. Food Services. Tel: 201-998-9607.

Boy Scouts of America/Catholic Committee on Scouting—499 Belgrove Dr., Kearney, 07032. GABRIEL FELTZ, Coord. Tel: 201-998-0088, Ext. 135. Rev. VICTOR P. KENNEDY, Chap. Tel: 201-656-2490. RON VERHEYEN, Committee Chm. Tel: 201-433-0128. Bergen Council: EDWARD ROSE, *244 Ottawa Ave., Hasbrouck Heights, 07604.* Tel: 201-288-2355. Rev. MICHAEL M. WALTERS, Chap.; Essex Council: VICTOR M. SANCHEZ, JR., *P.O. Box 365, Bloomfield, 07003-0365.* Tel: 973-743-5306. Rev. KEVIN A. GUGLIOTTA, Chap.; Hudson Liberty Council: JUDY VERHEYEN, *20 Gray St., Jersey City, 07302.* Tel: 201-433-0128. Rev. EUGENE J. FIELD, Chap.; Watchung Council: JOSEPH A. MANCINI, *Immaculate Conception Seminary, Seton Hall University, South Orange, 07079.* Tel: 973-763-5204. Rev. MANUEL D. RIOS, Chap.

Archdiocesan Girl Scouts of America—171 Clifton Ave., P.O. Box 9500, Newark, 07104-9500. MAUREEN COLEMAN, Archdiocesan Coord. Tel: 973-497-4512. Rev. DONALD K. HUMMEL, Chap.

Archdiocesan Council of Catholic Women—MARY LOFTUS, Pres.; Rev. Msgr. WALTER GORSKI, Moderator, *171 Clifton Ave., Newark, 07104.* Tel: 973-497-4356. District Moderators: Bergen-Paramus: Vacant Bergen-Hackensack: Deacon NICHOLAS SIMONELLI-,North Hudson: Vacant South Hudson: Vacant Essex-Suburban: Vacant Union-Westfield: Vacant Union-Elizabeth: Rev. DANIEL A. DANIK.

Charismatic Renewal—Rev. PHILIP J. ROTUNNO, Coord., *5808 Kennedy Blvd., W. New York, 07093.* Tel: 201-867-2642.

The Community of God's Love—70 W. Passaic Ave., Rutherford, 07070. Tel: 201-935-0344. THOMAS RICHARD, Dir.; Rev. PHILIP LATRONICO, Chap.

Cursillo Movement—Rev. JAMES F. REILLY, Archdiocesan Coord. Tel: 201-944-1061.

RENEW International, Office of—Rev. Msgr. THOMAS A. KLEISSLER, Dir., *1232 George St., Plainfield, 07062-1717.* Tel: 908-769-5400; Fax: 908-769-5660. Sr. CECILIA KING, C.S.J.P., Coord.-International RENEW; MARGO LEBERT, Coord.- RENEW 2000; Sr. KATHY WARREN, O.S.F., Coord.-American RENEW; Sr. MARY MCGUINNESS, O.P., Coord.- Small Christian Communities; Sr. MARIA LOUISE IGLESIAS, S.C., Coord.- Hispanic RENEW. International Service Team: Sr. LOUISE ALF, F.M.D.C.; BOB BURSLEY; Sr. MAUREEN COLLEARY, F.S.P.; Sr. PAT CROWLEY, O.P.; Sr. CHERYL ERB, R.S.M.; Rev. JACK FARLEY, S.V.D.; ROBERT HOWLETT; SCOTT LEET; Rev. J. FRANCISCO MONTERROSA; Sr. CARMEN OLIVERA, O.P.; C. WILLIAM REILLY; Sr. BETH TAYLOR, C.S.J.P.; CARLOS TORRADO; Sr. DOROTHY URBAN, S.S.J.; Sr. ALICE YOHE, S.S.J., Admin. Asst. JOHN LANDVATER, Fin. Asst. ROSANNE BARONE, Office Mgr.

Medical-Moral Committee—Rev. HAROLD P. DARCY, Chm., *Seton Hall University School of Law, 1111 Raymond Blvd., Newark, 07102.* Tel: 973-642-8859.

Sacred Heart Institute—P.O. Box 985, West Caldwell, 07007-0985. Tel: 973-226-7077; Fax: 973-226-0818. Rev. GERALD P. RUANE, Dir. JULIE A. JAHN, Admin.

Vicariate for Human Services

Most Rev. NICHOLAS A. DIMARZIO, Ph.D., D.D., L.S.W., Vicar, *1160 Raymond Blvd., Newark, 07102.* Tel: 973-596-4050; Fax: 973-596-3807. Rev. Msgr. DENNIS J. MAHON, Ph.D., Exec. Dir., *1160 Raymond Blvd., Newark, 07102.* Tel: 973-596-4050; Fax: 973-596-3807. THOMAS J. CATLAW, M.A., COO. Tel: 973-596-4054. All offices at above address unless otherwise indicated

General and Administative Offices—BARBARA BRANDE-DESMOND, L.C.S.W., Dir.- Program Devel. Tel: 973-596-4038; Fax: 973-596-3819. CHRIS MARICS, M.S.W., Grant & New Program Specialist. Tel: 973-596-4058. ELAINE V. COHEN, Ph.D., Dir.- Evaluation & Planning. Tel: 973-596-4057. DANIEL DEAN, J.D., Dir.- Public Affairs. Tel: 973-596-4046. TIMOTHY SULLIVAN, M.A., Dir.- Communications. Tel: 973-596-4086. Finance Office:Tel: 973-596-3952; Fax: 973-596-3949. JOHN CARDILLO, Controller. Tel: 973-596-3945. Human Resources; JOSEPH M. TURCO, M.S., Dir. Tel: 973-596-4071; Fax: 973-596-3822. ANTHONY BIUNNO, Dir.- General Services. Tel: 973-596-4092. DONALD GAROFALO, M.B.A., Dir.- Information Systems. Tel: 973-693-6637. DANIEL A. CORDASCO, Dir.- Special Events. Tel: 973-596-4063; Fax: 973-596-3819. Legal Depatment: JACQUELINE I. HEATH, General Counsel. Tel: 973-596-4120; Fax: 973-242-0791. Bro. BENEDICT LO BALBO, Dir.- Board Affairs. Tel: 973-596-4180; Fax: 973-596-3819.

Detailed list of services and staff:—

VICARIATE FOR HUMAN SERVICES—CATHERINE L'INSALATA, M.S., C.S.W., Special Asst. for Vicarate Services. Tel: 973-596-4060.

Apostolate for the Developmentally Disabled—Sr. EILEEN BYRNE, O.P., M.A. Tel: 973-226-9402.

Apostolate with the Deaf—Sr. JOAN WALTERS, S.C. Ed.D. Tel: 973-348-0527; TTY: 596-3893.

Ministry with the Deaf—THOMAS SMITH, B.A., C.S.W. Tel: 973-596-3962; TTY: 596-3893.

New Day Community—VINCENT MCMAHON, M.A. Tel: 973-596-4060; 763-7999.

Emergency Food & Nutrition Network—SHARON REILLY-TOBIN. Tel: 973-596-4060; Fax: 973-596-3735.

Parish Access Center - Central Office—Sr. ROSE PHILIP, M.S.B.T., A.C.S.W. Tel: 1-800-CCS-7413.

HIV/AIDS—ROBERT HANSON. Tel: 973-596-3932.

Bergen County—W. 50 Midland Ave., Paramus, 07652. Tel: 201-967-4177. Rev. JOHN MCCRONE, Coord.

Hudson County—Sr. RENEE ZINCIUK. Tel: 201-792-6161.

Essex County—56 Elmwood Ave., Montclair, 07042. Tel: 973-783-4852. Rev. JOHN P. NICKAS, Coord.

Union County—280 Parker Ave., Maplewood, 07040. Tel: 973-763-5019. Rev. DOMINIC G. FUCCILE, Coord.

Hispanic Community—3900 New York Ave., Union City, 07087. Tel: 201-863-5116. Rev. Msgr. THOMAS W. HECK, Coord.

AIDS Support Center—(See Catholic Community Services Essex).

Franciska House—(See Catholic Community Services Hudson).

Prison Ministry—66 Fleming Ave., Newark, 07105. Tel: 973-491-6090. Rev. WILLIAM GYURE.

Ministry to the People on the Move—

Apostleship of the Air—Rev. DAVID J. BARATELLI, Dir., *Newark International Airport Chaplaincy, P.O. Box 2220, Newark, 07114.* Tel: 973-961-0260.

Apostleship of the Sea—Rev. SALVATORE MALANGA, *Newark International Seaport Chaplaincy - Stella Maris Chapel, 114 Corbin St., Newark, 07101.* Tel: 973-483-0356.

Office of the Consultant for Health Affairs—Bro. BENEDICT LO BALBO. Tel: 973-596-4180; Fax: 973-596-3819. Rev. Msgr. ROBERT MOREL, Spec. Asst. to the Vicar. Tel: 973-639-6643.

Campaign for Human Development—Sr. CATHERINE DALY, O.P., M.S. Tel: 973-596-3890; Fax: 973-596-3933.

Quest Essex Youth Services—St. Charles Center, 85 Custer St., Newark, 07112. Tel: 973-926-9895; Fax: 973-926-0448. Dr. REGINA ADESANYA, Div. Dir. JOYCE SMITH CARTER, Program Dir.

Office of Volunteer Services—CATHERINE L'INSALATA, M.S., Dir. Tel: 973-596-4060.

Archdiocesan Housing Office (Domus Corporation)—CHRIS GARLIN, Dir. Tel: 973-639-6647. The Vicar for Human Services is the Archbishop's Liaison to the Archdiocesan Housing Commission: General Secretary for Archdiocesan Housing Commission.

Catholic Community Services—Affiliated Agencies: Associated Catholic Charities; Mount Carmel Guild; New Jersey Boystown; The Guild Social Service Center.

BERGEN COUNTY Division—MICHAEL MATTHEWS, L.S.W., Div. Dir., *425 Paramus Rd., Paramus, 07652.* Tel: 201-444-3883. Tel: 201-444-3172. Programs: Outreach/Case Management for HIV Hispanics; One Stop Case Management; MICHELLE GROSSO, M.A.,Eldercare Consultation & Referral; MARY ELLEN MERTZ, M.S.,Parish Access Center; JANE SCERBO.

MT. CARMEL GUILD BEHAVIORAL HEALTHCARE DIVISION—LEONARD S. ALTAMURA, D.S.W., Div. Dir. Tel: 973-639-6597; Fax: 973-639-6663. Dr. AMBROSE MGBAKO, M.D., Medical Dir. Tel: 973-596-4043; Fax: 973-596-3701.

Behavioral Healthcare - Essex County—JULIE WILLIS, L.C.S.W., Regl. Mgr. Tel: 973-596-4099; Fax: 973-242-0563.

Addictions Treatment Services—Tel: 973-596-3858. GAIL PHILLIPS, L.C.S.W., CADC. Tel: 973-596-3789.

Admissions—Tel: 973-596-4190. TAMIKA CARTER-RICE, M.A. Tel: 973-596-3964.

Day Treatment Center—Tel: 973-596-3998.

Patient Support Services—Tel: 973-596-4089.

MICA/Spanish MICA—NUZHAT IQBAL, M.A. Tel: 973-596-3971.

Mt. Carmel Guild Inpatient Unit—Tel: 973-596-4084. ALEX KUSMA, M.A., R.N. Tel: 973-596-3855.

Outpatient Department—Tel: 973-596-4042. MARC GROSSMAN, L.C.S.W.

Medical Records—LOUISE SCHACHTER, A.R.T. Tel: 973-596-4035.

Integrated Case Management (ICMS)—273 Oliver St., Newark, 07105. ROMAN Z. MYTYTA, L.C.S.W. Tel: 973-522-2100.

PACT Program—Tel: 888-MCG-PACT., *269 Oliver St., Newark, 07105.* Tel: 973-466-1659., *37 Evergreen Pl., East Orange, 07017.* THOMAS PATITUCCI, M.S.W.

Behavioral Healthcare - Bergen County—425 Paramus Rd., Paramus, 07652. Tel: 201-444-3883. RICCA ANN HAIM, L.C.S.W., Regional Mgr., . Fax: 201-444-3172.

Family and Community Services—425 Paramus Rd., Paramus, 07652. FELICIA POLCARI, M.A. Tel: 201-444-3883.

Family Counseling Services—499 Belgrove Dr., Kearny, 07032. Rev. FRANCIS MAIONE, Ed.S., LMFT. Tel: 201-991-2850; Fax: 201-991-7306.

Couseling Center—18 Cottage Pl., Montclair, 07042. Tel: 973-744-1790; Fax: 973-744-7350. Rev. JOHN MORLEY, D.Min.

Behavioral Healthcare - Union County—108 Alden St., Cranford, 07016. Tel: 908-497-3968. WILLIAM HODGDON, L.C.S.W., Regl. Mgr., . Fax: 908-272-9268.

Family Services-Union County Addiction Treatment Services—505 South Ave. E., Cranford, 07016. Tel: 908-497-3968. COLLEEN RUSH-SZEFINSKI, M.A., CADC.

Outpatient Department—505 South Ave. E., Cranford, 07016. Tel: 908-497-3968. CONSTANCE H. SCHMALZ, L.C.S.W.

Community Mental Health Center—108 Alden St., Cranford, 07016. Tel: 908-497-3968; Fax: 908-272-9268.

Day Treatment Center, Extended Day Treatment Center, Project Care 450 Program—MARGERY GRIMM, M.A.

Integrated Case Management (ICMS)—654 East Jersey St., Elizabeth, 07206., 108 Alden St., Cranford, 07016. WILLIAM MERRIT, L.C.S.W. Tel: 908-497-3968; Fax: 888-624-2678.

Behavioral Healthcare - Hudson County—249 Virginia Ave., Jersey City, 07304. ROSE MARIE PRATT, L.C.S.W., Regl. Mgr. Tel: 201-332-4365; Fax: 201-434-4386.

Community Mental Health Center—249 Virginia Ave., Jersey City, 07304. Tel: 201-332-4365; Fax: 201-434-4386.

Hispanic Outreach Program Outpatient Department—EUGENIA KAFES, L.C.S.W.

Project Home (Transitional Residence)—SANDRA POWELL, L.C.S.W.

Day Treatment Center—LINDA COLOSIMO, L.C.S.W.

Addictions Treatment Services MICA Drop In Center (Mentally ILL Chemical Abusers)—285 Magnolia Ave., Jersey City, 07306. ANTHONY WINTERS, CADC. Tel: 201-435-4030; Fax: 201-435-9580.

Supportive Employment—1009 Kennedy Blvd., North Bergen, 07047. HARRY FRAZIER. Tel: 201-271-2758.

Mt. Carmel Guild Day Treatment Center—285 Magnolia Ave., Jersey City, 07306. Tel: 201-435-4030. *201-435-9580.*

Community Mental Health Center—3201 Central Ave., Union City, 07087. MICHAEL ZAVADA, L.C.S.W. Tel: 201-864-0270; Fax: 201-864-1899.

Day Treatment Center—CHRISTINE MUSCADIN, M.A.

Outpatient Department—LAUREN BALKAN, L.C.S.W.

Project Hudson House (Transitional Res.)—REGINA DEMARCO, M.A.

ESSEX COUNTY Division—REGINA ADESANYA, Psy.D., Div. Dir. Tel: 973-596-4040; Fax: 973-596-4037. VIRGILIO ALOMAR, L.C.S.W., Asst. Div. Dir. Tel: 973-639-6656.

AmeriCorps Volunteer Program—MIRNA LARUE. Tel: 973-639-6649.

Catholic School Social Service Program—Tel: 201-596-4147.

Parish Access Center—160 E. Passaic St., Bloomfield, 07003. Tel: 973-639-6541.

Eric J. Feldman Child & Family Development Center—.

Communication Disorders—Tel: 973-596-3925; Fax: 973-596-3869.

Child Development Center—(Includes Child Study Teams; Speech/Language Pathology; Therapeutic Nursery).

Industrial Audiology,—Tel: 973-596-3925.

St. Bridget's Residence & Aids/HIV Support Center—404 University Ave., Newark, 07102. Tel: 973-799-0484; Fax: 973-799-0486.

Department of Special Education—MARIAN KUGELMASS, M.Ed., Dir. Tel: 973-596-4065; Fax: 973-596-4037.

Mt. Carmel Guild School—60 Kingsland Ave., Kearny, 07032. Tel: 201-991-7733; Fax: 201-991-7776. THEODORE KORNEGAY, Ed.D., Prin.

Mt. Carmel Guild Pre-school—10 Commerce Ct., Newark, 07102. Tel: 973-639-6622; Fax: 973-639-6626. KATHARINE THORNTON, M.P.A., Prin.
St. Anthony's School—25 N. 7th St., Belleville, 07109. Tel: 973-751-2550; Fax: 973-751-5725. Sr. ANNE ROSALIE, Prin.
St. Patrick's School—72 Central Ave., Newark, 07102. Tel: 973-643-6772; Fax: 973-643-7625. PHIL K. REYNOLDS, M.Ed., Prin.
The Guild Social Service Center—56 Freeman St., Newark, 07105. Tel: 973-344-0067; Fax: 973-344-6750. ROBERT ROBINSON.
Halfway House for Alcoholic Men—Tel: 973-344-0514.
Senior Day Care for the Frail and Elderly—
Visually Handicapped Socialization Program.—494 Broad St., Newark, 07102. Tel: 973-642-6367. PAULINE ZIOMEK, R.N.
St. Ann's Family Emergency Residence (SAFER) Youth Chance.—368 S. 7th St., Newark, 07103. Tel: 973-242-6646; Fax: 973-242-2864. DWAYNE KEELING.
St. Rocco's Family Residence (Women & Children)—355 S. 6th St., Newark, 07103. Tel: 973-242-7242; Fax: 973-242-4854. TREVA YOUNG.
Mt. Carmel Guild Children's Center—39 Bleeker St., Newark, 07102. Tel: 973-643-4956. KATHLEEN O'PRAY, M.A.
St. Rocco's Outreach Center (Men)—712 Springfield Ave., Newark, 07103. Tel: 973-371-5266; Fax: 973-371-5850. NOEL HICKS, B.A.
HUDSON COUNTY Division—249 Virginia Ave., Jersey City, 07304. Tel: 201-332-4365; Fax: 201-332-6585. MARGARET M. MURTHA, L.C.S.W., C.A.D.C., Div. Dir. LESLEY MOORE, L.C.S.W., Asst. Div. Dir.
Parish Access Center—3201 Central Ave., Union City, 07087. Tel: 201-863-8085. Tel: 201-863-8320. CARMEL GALASSO, M.A.
New Jersey Boystown-New Beginnings Counseling & Adoption/Search Services—499 Belgrove Dr., Kearny, 07032. Tel: 201-991-3770; Fax: 201-991-7306. PATRICIA CHIARELLO.
Project Rachel—Sr. MONICA VINGES, M.A.
Foster Grandparents—249 Virginia Ave., Jersey City, 07304. Tel: 201-332-2175. MELINDA ACEVEDO.
Edna McLaughlin Residence at Carmel House—162 Bidwell Ave., Jersey City, 07305. Tel: 201-413-1556. Sr. BRIDGET KAPIN.
Coming Home Hospice—3040 Kennedy Blvd., Jersey City, 07306. Tel: 201-656-3557; Fax: 201-656-1707. ELIZABETH PATTERSON, B.S.N., J.D.
MICA Outreach (Mentally Ill Chemical Abuser)—308 Academy St., Jersey City, 07306. Tel: 201-217-9665; Fax: 201-219-1902. MICHAEL BACON.
Mt. Carmel Guild Family Resource Centers-Intensive Family Support Services—
Intensive Family Counseling Program—3040 Kennedy Blvd., Jersey City, 07306. Tel: 201-656-3557; Fax: 201-656-1707. ELIZABETH MCCLENDON, L.C.S.W.; ROSA JONES, M.A.; DIANE JORDAN, M.A.; SHARON BIRCH, M.S.W.
Malta Providence Residence—114 Clifton Pl., Jersey City, 07365. Tel: 201-915-1202. Tel: 201-985-2343. THOMAS LYNCH, L.C.S.W.
Hudson County Correctional Program-PAYBACC Program-Providence Malta Prep—75 Greenville Ave., Jersey City, 07305. Tel: 201-946-1007; Fax: 201-451-5198. VIRGINIA HART, L.C.S.W.
PRIDE Mentoring Program—3040 Kennedy Blvd., Jersey City, 07306. Tel: 201-798-1006; Fax: 201-798-2644. GILMA GARCIA.
Family Crisis Intervention—114 Clifton Ave., Jersey City, 07304. Tel: 201-915-1202; Fax: 201-985-2343. DOLORES WESTBROOKS, M.A.
St. Lucy's Homeless Programs—619 Grove St., Jersey City, 07310. Tel: 201-656-7201; Fax: 201-656-0412. ROBERT MACK, M.A.,Programs: Counseling and Outreach; Single Residence (Men & Women); Neuville Family Residence; Project Link.
Franciska House—615 Grove St., Jersey City, 07310. Tel: 201-653-5395. JANE NASH.
Anthony House—246 2nd St., Jersey City, 07302. Tel: 201-420-1070. NANCY PINEDA.
UNION COUNTY Division—505 South Ave. E.: *Cranford, 07016.* Tel: 908-497-3900; Fax: 908-709-9580. JOSEPH P. BORDO, L.C.S.W.; CLARE ELTON, L.S.W., Asst. Div. Dir.
Employee Assistance Program (CARE),—Tel: 908-497-3900. RUTH MOORE, C.N.S., CADC.
Catholic School Social Service Program,—Tel: 908-497-3900. MARY LOU SHERRY, M.S.W.
Older Adult Services—Tel: 908-497-3900; Fax: 908-709-4583. SUSAN CRANK, L.C.S.W.
Adult Protective Services,—Tel: 908-497-3900.
Retired Senior Volunteer Program (RSVP),—Tel: 908-497-3900. JOANN CROTEAU.
Family Resource Center—Tel: 908-497-3900. Programs: In-Home Hispanic Services, Child Protective Services, Correctional Program.
New Jersey EASE—Tel: 908-497-3900.
Hispanic Seniors Multi-Service Center,—Tel: 908-497-3900.
The Engel Center (Senior Day Care)—Tel: 908-497-3900.
Visually Impaired Seniors Program,—Tel: 908-497-3900.
Parish Access Center—215 Court St., Elizabeth, 07206. Tel: 908-289-8043. Sr. MARY STEWART, M.A.
Raphael Life House—231 Court St., Elizabeth, 07206. Tel: 908-354-4750. PATRICIA EADDY.
Work Force Development Resource Center—220 Msgr. Kemezis Pl., Elizabeth, 07206.
Early Childhood Education Program—220 Msgr. Kemezis Pl., Elizabeth, 07206. Tel: 908-289-6843. ELIZABETH DRISCOLL.
Special Services Division—494 Broad St., Newark, 07102. Tel: 973-242-1999; Fax: 973-242-3755. GEORGE PIEGARO, M.A., Div. Dir. BARBARA LONEGRO, L.C.S.W., Asst. Div. Dir.
Citizenship Program—PEDRO PACAJA, C.S.W.
Employment Services—THOMAS HENKEL.
Education & Training Programs—MARIA BIANCHERI-THOMPSON, M.A.
Citizenship/Immigration Assistance—CINDI DRESDNER.
Refugee Resettlement & Employment Services—GIZELLA MENDLOVICH.
Project Haven—BARBARA LONEGRO, L.C.S.W.
Office of Migration—972 Broad St., Newark, 07102. Tel: 973-733-3516; Fax: 973-733-9631. CINDI DRESDNER-,Programs: Immigration Assistance; Citizenship.
Hispanic Women's Resource Center—533 35th St., Union City, 07087. Tel: 201-866-3208; Fax: 201-866-5854. MARTA SAN MARTIN, M.A.,Programs: Employment Services; Citizenship/Immigration Assistance; Refugee Resettlement; Drug/Alcohol Counseling and Education; Education & Training.
Italian Social Service Center—380 Monmouth St., Jersey City, 07302. Tel: 201-653-6515; Fax: 201-653-1301. Programs: Employment Services; Citizenship/Immigration Assistance; Refugee Resettlement; Education & Training.
Office of Migration—505 South Ave., East Cranford, 07016. Tel: 908-497-3900. Programs: Citizenship/Immigration Assistance.
Haitian Outreach Center—37 Evergreen Pl., East Orange, 07017. Tel: 973-672-6607. PIERRE MOREAU, B.A.,Programs: Employment Services; Citizenship/Immigration Assistance; Refugee Resettlement; Education & Training.
Vocational Rehabilitation Services & Skills Training—101 University Ave., Newark, 07102. Tel: 973-242-1999. Tel: 973-242-3755. MICHAEL MYERS, M.A.
Sheltered Workshop—101 Universtiy Ave., Newark, 07102. FRED SIMON. Tel: 973-242-1999; Fax: 973-242-3755.
Work Force Development—494 Broad St., Newark, 07102. Tel: 973-242-1999; Fax: 973-242-3755. GARY DI NARDO.

Miscellaneous

Affirmative Action Council—Most Rev. JOSEPH A. FRANCIS, S.V.D., Chm. WILLIAM A. CAMBRIA, Officer, *Archdiocesan Center, 171 Clifton Ave., Newark, 07104.* Tel: 973-497-4300.
Blue Army—Vacant; Natl. & Archdiocesan Dir. Tel: 973-497-4011.
Catholic Relief Services—171 Clifton Ave., Newark, 07104. Tel: 973-497-4000.
Censores Librorum—Rev. Msgr. EDWARD J. CIUBA, S.T.L., S.S.L.; Rev. Msgr. JOSEPH F. FLUSK, Music; Rev. Msgr. CARL D. HINRICHSEN, S.T.L., Ph.D.; Rev. Msgr. THOMAS P. IVORY, S.T.D.; Rev. Msgr. JOHN H. KOENIG, S.T.L.; Rev. Msgr. RICHARD M. LIDDY, S.T.D.; Revs. JAMES M. CAFONE, S.T.D.; FRANCIS A. DEDOMENICO, S.T.L.; CHARLES W. GUSMER, S.T.D.; GEORGE M. KEATING; FRANK MCNULTY, S.T.D.; JOHN RUSSELL, O.Carm.; ARTHUR J. SERRATELLI, S.T.D., S.S.L.; JAMES B. SULLIVAN, S.T.L., Ph.D.
Confraternity of the Blessed Sacrament—Rev. Msgr. WALTER J. JARVAIS, Dir., *60 Home Ave., Rutherford, 07111.* Tel: 201-933-8138.
Archdiocesan School Advisory Board—Mr. FRANCIS X. FALCICCHIO, Pres.; Mr. JOHN CRUITT, Vice Pres.; Mrs. KATHLEEN MASKER, Sec.; Mrs. FRANCINE M. ASTER; Mrs. DONNA J. BABOULIS; Mrs. MARY D. BAIER; Ms. KAY GRUSENSKI; SUSAN D. GUARNIERI; Mr. DAVID KIENAST; Mrs. BRENDA LEAHY; ELIZABETH MADARA; MICHAEL SCILINGO; Sr. LILLIAN SHARROCK, S.C.; Bro. MICHAEL STECHMANN, O.A.R.
Scholarship Fund for Inner-City Children—DAVID C. FARRAND, Pres., Board of Trustees; DIEGO R. VISCEGLIA, ESQ., Treas. JOHN C. WALCOTT, Sec. KEVIN P. MORIARTY, Exec. Dir., *Archdiocesan Center, 171 Clifton Ave., Newark, 07104.* Tel: 973-497-4279.
New Jersey Alliance of Catholic School Families—Sr. SUZANNE BELLENOIT, S.S.J., Coord. Tel: 973-497-4274.
Holy Name Federation—Rev. Msgr. RICHARD M. MCGUINNESS, Archdiocesan Dir. County Dirs.: Revs. JOHN LAFERRARA, Essex-West Hudson; RICHARD J. CARRINGTON, Hudson; MARTIN J. SILVER, Bergen; JOSEPH G. SHEEHAN, Union, *1805 Penbrook Ter., Linden, 07036.* Tel: 908-486-6363.
Lawyers Guild—Rev. Msgr. HAROLD P. D'ARCY, Dir., *Seton Hall University, School of Law, 1111 Raymond Blvd., Newark, 07102.* Tel: 973-642-8859.
Legion of Mary—Newark Comitum: Rev. CHARLES H. MCTAGUE, Dir. Tel: 973-497-4011. Bergen Curia: Vacant Hudson County Curia: Rev. JAMES W. MCFARLAND, Dir., *21 Skillman Ave., Jersey City, 07306.* Tel: 201-963-7640. Hudson Hispanic Curia: Rev. NAZARENO ORLANDI, *4206 Kennedy Blvd., Union City, 07107.* Tel: 201-863-1427. Essex and Union Hispanic Curia: Rev. MICHAEL A. FUINO, Dir., *243 Abington Ave., Newark, 07107.* Tel: 973-482-8410. Essex Korean Curia: Rev. AUGUSTIN PARK, *257 Central Ave., Orange, 07050.* Tel: 973-673-1366. Korean/Mary Most Humble Curia: Rev. GABRIEL LEE, *280 County Rd., Demarest, 07627.* Tel: 201-767-1954. Bergen-Korean/Mother of God Curia: Rev. JOHN JO, *1252 Abbott Blvd., Fort Lee, 07024.* Tel: 201-224-4452.
New Jersey Catholic Historical Records Commission—JOSEPH F. MAHONEY, Dir., *Seton Hall University Archives, South Orange, 07079.* Tel: 973-761-9476.
Our Lady of Fatima First Saturday Club—Rev. PAUL BOCHICCHIO, Chap., *188 MacArthur Ave., Garfield, 07026.* Tel: 201-772-2295.
Propagation of the Faith; Society of St. Peter the Apostle Missionary Union of Priests/Religious—Rev. Msgr. ROBERT J. FUHRMAN, Dir., *Archdiocesan Center, 171 Clifton Ave., Newark, 07104.* Tel: 973-497-4375.
Priests' Eucharistic League—Rev. Msgr. WALTER G. JARVAIS, *60 Home Ave., Rutherford, 07070.* Tel: 201-939-8138.
Serra Clubs—JAMES P. BARRY, Governor-District 22. Tel: 201-945-1194; Fax: 201-224-8721.

CLERGY, PARISHES, MISSIONS AND PAROCHIAL SCHOOLS

CITY OF NEWARK

1—CATHEDRAL BASILICA OF THE SACRED HEART (1889), Rev. Msgr. Richard Groncki, Rector; Rev. Fernando Carranza. In res., Most Revs. Theodore E. McCarrick; Paul G. Bootkoski, D.D.; Rev. Msgr. Joseph T. Slinger, V.G.; Revs. Manuel Cruz; Christopher Ciccarino; Thomas A. Dente.
Res., 89 Ridge St., 07104. Tel: 973-484-4600; Fax: 973-483-8253; 482-4793.

2—ST. PATRICK'S PRO-CATHEDRAL (1848), Rev. Neil J. Mahoney. In res., Rev. Msgr. Horton Raught; Revs. Guillermo Arias-Hurtado; Khai Vu.
Res., 91 Washington St., 07102. Tel: 973-623-0497; Fax: 973-623-2030.

3—BLESSED SACRAMENT (1905) (African American), Very Rev. Paul D. Schetelick, V.F.; Rev. Joseph A. Barrow.
Res., 15 Van Ness Pl., 07108. Tel: 973-824-6548; Fax: 973-624-6030.
School—600 Clinton Ave., 07108. Tel: 973-824-5859.
Sisters of St. Joseph 2; Lay Teachers 14; Students 300.
Convent—Tel: 201-824-8475.

4—ST. ALOYSIUS (1877), Rev. Javier Losarcos, V.F. In res., Rev. William L. Gyure.
Res., 66 Fleming Ave., 07105. Tel: 973-344-4736.

5—ST. ANTONINUS (1875), Revs. Paul J. Lehman; Eustace Edomobi.
Res., 337 South Orange Ave., 07103. Tel: 973-623-0258; Fax: 973-623-0694.

6—ST. ANN (1886), Rev. Paul Lehman, Admin.; Deacon Cesar A. Ortega Escobar.
Church Office: 337 South Orange Ave., 07103.
Res., Tel: 973-642-4217; Fax: 973-623-0694.

7—ST. AUGUSTINE'S (1874) (German), Rev. Paul A. Viale, Admin.; Deacons Vicente Rodriquez; Daniel Mendez.
Church Office: P.O. Box 1390, 07101-1390.
Res., Tel: 973-482-1817; Fax: 973-482-5475.
Convent—168 Sussex Ave., 07103. Tel: 973-483-0165. Sisters Missionaries of Charity
Women's Shelter Queen of Peace—170 Sussex Ave., 07103. Tel: 973-481-9056.

8—ST. BENEDICT'S (1854), Revs. Richard G. Francesco; Paulo dos Santos Frade. Pastoral Associates: Sr. Philomena McCartney; Sr. Ann Jerome Kociolek.

Res., 65 Barbara St., 07105. Tel: 973-589-7930; Fax: 973-589-3665.
School—124 Niagara St., 07105. Tel: 973-589-7295. Mrs. Susan Wilson, Prin.
Lay Teachers 23; Students 380.
Catechesis/Religious Programs—Students 330.

9—St. Bridget's (1887). Merged with St. Patrick's Pro-Cathedral. Records located at St. Patrick's, Newark. Tel: 973-623-0497.

10—St. Casimir's (1908) (Polish), Revs. Joseph Uraban; Zbigniew Choromanski (Poland).
Res., 164 Nichols St., 07105-2596. Tel: 973-344-2743; Fax: 973-344-5629.
School—(1910), 366 E. Kinney St., 07105. Tel: 973-589-0108; Fax: 973-589-0239. Sr. Mary Lourdes, C.S.S.F., Prin.
Felician Sisters 3; Lay Teachers 14; Students 303.
Catechesis/Religious Programs—Tel: 973-596-4500, Ext. 3674.
Students 303.
Convent—Tel: 973-589-5737.

11—St. Charles Borromeo's (1910), Rev. Paul D. Schetelick, Admin.
Res., 84 Custer Ave., 07112. Tel: 973-923-6798; Fax: 973-923-6799.

12—St. Columba's (1869) (Hispanic), Rev. Decimo Crevani, C.S.
Res., 25 Thomas St., 07114. Tel: 973-622-7712; Fax: 973-621-2021.
School—(1882), 25 Pennsylvania Ave., 07114. Tel: 973-623-8859.
Lay Teachers 17; Students 340.
Convent—Tel: 973-622-7325.

13—Epiphany (1992) (Portuguese), Rev. Peter M. Uhde, Admin.
Res., Holy Trinity Rectory, 207 Adams St., 07105. Tel: 973-491-9761; Fax: 973-344-5641.

14—Queen of Angels (1930) (African American), Rev. James J. McConnell, S.M.A.; Deacons Robert Botts, (Retired); Edward Botts, (Retired). In res., Rev. Chris Anyanwu (Nigeria).
Res., 44 Irvine Turner Blvd., 07103. Tel: 973-642-1610; Fax: 973-642-0755.
School—28 Irvine Turner Blvd., 07103. Tel: 973-642-1531; Fax: 973-622-0472. Bro. Stephen Schlitte, F.M.S., Prin.
Brothers 3; Lay Teachers 9; Students 250.
Catechesis/Religious Programs—Tel: 973-642-0857.
Students 250.

15—St. Francis Xavier (1914), Revs. Arthur Frank Humphrey, S.T.M., M.A.; James J. Redstone; Frederick A. Pfeifer; Deacon Paul R. Daniele, J.D. In res., Rev. Michael A. Fuino.
Res., 243 Abington Ave., 07107-2598. Tel: 973-482-8410; Fax: 973-485-7471.
School—(1924), 594 N. Seventh St., 07107. Tel: 973-482-9410.
Maestre Pie Filippini (Religious Teachers Filippini) 4; Lay Teachers 9; Students 277.
Catechesis/Religious Programs—Students 275.
Convent—Tel: 973-484-5200.

16—Holy Trinity (1901) (Lithuanian), Rev. Peter M. Uhde, Admin.
Res., 207 Adams St., 07105. Tel: 973-344-6847; Fax: 973-344-5641.

17—St. James (1854) (Brazilian-Portuguese), Revs. George Lutz; Angelo Amaral, Pastoral Assoc. In res., Revs. Charles H. McTague; Raymond McKeon.
Res., 143 Madison St., 07105. Tel: 973-344-8322; Fax: 973-344-6158.
Catechesis/Religious Programs—Students 36.

18—St. John's (1826), Rev. Msgr. James J. Finnerty.
Res., 22 Mulberry St., 07102. Tel: 973-623-0822; Fax: 973-623-6804.

19—St. Joseph's (1850). Closed. Records located at Seton Hall University Archives, South Orange, 07079. Tel: 973-761-9476; Fax: 973-761-9550.

20—Immaculate Heart of Mary (1926) (Spanish), Revs. Antonio Terrassa, T.O.R. (Spain); John Riera, T.O.R. (Spain).
Res., 114 Prospect St., 07105. Tel: 973-589-8249; Fax: 973-589-1858.
Catechesis/Religious Programs—Tel: 973-589-5794.
Students 388.
Convent—121 Congress St., 07105.
Missionary Sisters of the Blessed Sacrament and Mary Immaculate 4.

21—Immaculate Conception (1925), Rev. Anthony J. Lionelli. In res., Rev. John F. O'Connor, S.T.B.
Res., 390 Woodside Ave., 07104. Tel: 973-482-0619.

22—St. Lucy's (1891) (Italian), Rev. Msgr. Joseph J. Granato; Revs. Joseph S. Nativo; Anthony Forte.
Res., 118 Seventh Ave., 07104. Tel: 973-482-6663; Fax: 973-483-7569.
School—(1904), 12 Amity Pl., 07104. Tel: 973-482-4756; Fax: 973-482-7363.
Sisters 4; Lay Teachers 8; Students 215.
Catechesis/Religious Programs—Students 262.
Convent—Tel: 973-482-5750.

23—St. Mary's, Essex Co., (1842). (Newark Abbey Church). Revs. Philip J. Waters, O.S.B.; Linus V. Edogwo (Nigeria); Sr. Linda Klaiss, S.S.J., Pastoral Assoc.
Res., 528 Martin Luther King, Jr. Blvd., 07102. Tel: 973-643-4800, Ext. 202; Fax: 973-643-6922.
School—(1842), Tel: 973-643-4800, Ext. 300.
Sisters of St. Joseph of Chestnut Hill 3; Lay Teachers 15; Students 260.
Convent—Tel: 973-824-8475.

24—St. Mary Magdalene (1893). Closed. Records located at Seton Hall University Archives, South Orange, 07079. Tel: 973-761-9476; Fax: 973-761-9550.

25—St. Michael's (1878), Revs. Louis Caputo, S.D.V.; Angelito Rosales, S.D.V.; Anthony Basso, S.D.V.; Giosue Scotto DiCesare, S.D.V.; Deacons Alberto Gomez; Daniel Ravelo; Restituto Quintana.
Res., 25 Crittenden St., 07104. Tel: 973-484-7100; Fax: 973-482-7209.
School—(1881), 27 Crittenden St., 07104. Tel: 973-482-7400; Fax: 973-482-1833.
Sisters of Charity 2; Sisters of Charity of Ottawa 3; Lay Teachers 21; Students 642.
Perpetual Help Day Nursery—170 Broad St., 07104. Tel: 973-484-3535.
Vocationist Sisters 5; Lay Teachers 10; Children 170.
Catechesis/Religious Programs—Students 395.
Convent—Tel: 973-484-5261.

26—Our Lady of Fatima (1956) (Portuguese), Revs. Mario Nunes; Carlos C. Mamede.
Res., 82 Congress St., 07105. Tel: 973-589-8433; Fax: 973-589-2611.
Day Nursery—79 Jefferson St., 07105. Tel: 973-589-1639.
Catechesis/Religious Programs—Students 1,080.

27—Our Lady of Good Counsel (1902), Revs. Robert Tooman; John E. Rodriguez Gamboa.
Res., 654 Summer Ave., 07104. Tel: 973-482-1274.
School—(1913), 239 Woodside Ave., 07104. Tel: 973-482-1241; Fax: 973-482-8257.
Sisters of St. Joseph, Chestnut Hill 4; Lay Teachers 24; Students 594.
High School—(1922), Tel: 973-482-1209.
Sisters of St. Joseph, Chestnut Hill 9; Marist Brothers 1; Lay Teachers 24; Students 411.
Catechesis/Religious Programs—Students 150.
Convent—Tel: 973-483-4256.

28—Our Lady of Mt. Carmel (1889) (Italian), Most Rev. Nicholas A. DiMarzio; Rev. Joseph Ambrosio, Admin. In res., Rev. Msgr. Eugene A. Fanelli.
Res., 259 Oliver St., 07105. Tel: 973-589-2090; Fax: 973-589-2662.

29—Our Lady of the Rosary (1918) (Italian). Closed. For inquiries for parish records contact Our Lady of Mt. Carmel, Newark. Tel: 973-589-2090.

30—St. Peter's (1864). Closed. For inquiries for parish records contact Seton Hall University Archives, South Orange. Tel: 973-761-9476; Fax 973-761-9550.

31—St. Philip Neri (1887). Closed. For inquiries for parish records contact Seton Hall University Archives, South Orange. Tel: 973-761-9476; 973-761-9550.

32—St. Rocco's (1899). (National Historic Landmark). Rev. Josephat Kato Kalema, O.C.S.O., Admin.
Res., 208 Hunterdon St., 07103. Tel: 973-824-1652.
School—21 Ashland St., 07103. Tel: 201-622-0428. Sr. Eileen Jude Wust, S.S.J., Prin.
Lay Teachers 18; Students 453.

33—St. Rose of Lima (1888), Rev. Msgr. William J. Linder; Rev. Robert Cormier.
Res., 11 Gray St., 07107. Tel: 973-482-0682; Fax: 973-482-2137.
School—(1892), 540 Orange St., 07107. Tel: 973-481-5582. Arthur L. Wilson, Prin.
Sisters 2; Lay Teachers 12; Students 320.
Convent—Tel: 973-481-6566.

34—Sacred Heart (Vailsburg) (1892), Very Rev. Patrick W. Donohue, V.F.; Rev. G. Arokiasamy (India).
Res., 481 Sandford Ave., 07106. Tel: 973-373-9790; Fax: 973-374-4047.
School—(Grades PreK-8) 24 Hazelwood Ave., 07106. Tel: 973-372-4441; Fax: 973-372-4157. Bro. Patrick Byrne, O.A.R., Prin.
Religious 22; Lay Teachers 53; Students 850.
Convent—Tel: 973-374-2730; Fax: 973-374-4656.

35—St. Stanislaus (1889) (Polish), Rev. Bogumil Chrusciel.
Res., 146 Irvine Turner Blvd., 07103. Tel: 973-642-7961; Fax: 973-642-2295.

36—St. Stephen's (1902). Closed. For inquiries for parish records contact Seton Hall University Archives, South Orange. Tel: 973-761-9476; Fax: 973-761-9550.

37—St. Thomas Aquinas (1957), Rev. Ray A. Francis; Mary C. Tighe, Pastoral Assoc.; Deacon Jose A. Rodriguez.
Res., 40 Ludlow St., 07114. Tel: 973-242-6703.

OUTSIDE THE CITY OF NEWARK

Allendale, Bergen Co., Guardian Angel (1954), Rev. Msgr. Cajetan P. Salemi.
Res., 320 Franklin Turnpike, 07401. Tel: 201-327-4359; Fax: 201-327-6478.
School—St. Thomas More Interparochial School. See Nativity Parish, Midland Park for details.
Catechesis/Religious Programs—Tel: 201-327-0352.
Students 320.

Bayonne, Hudson Co.,

1—St. Mary Star of the Sea, (1861), Revs. Lawrence J. Miller; Thomas P. Conheeney; Gerard T. Prindiville; Sr. Jane Veronica Walsh, S.S.J., Pastoral Assoc.
Res., 326 Avenue C, 07002. Tel: 201-437-4090; Fax: 201-437-0388.
School—(1879), 19 W. 13th St., 07002. Tel: 201-437-2888.
Sisters of St. Joseph 1; Lay Teachers 11; Students 250.
Catechesis/Religious Programs—Tel: 201-437-0010.
Students 260.
Convent—Tel: 201-436-0870.

2—St. Andrew's, (1914), Rev. John R. Doherty; Rev. Msgr. Edward F. Wojtycha, Pastor Emeritus; Rev. Robert M. Hoatson; Deacon Raymond Sanderson.
Res., 125 Broadway, 07002. Tel: 201-437-0833; Fax: 201-858-3477.
School—124 Broadway, 07002. Tel: 973-437-0139.
Sisters of St. Joseph 1; Lay Teachers 9; Students 218.
Catechesis/Religious Programs—Tel: 201-437-9062.
Students 400.

3—St. Henry's, (1889), Rev. Msgr. Edward J. Hajduk, S.T.L., M.S.S.; Rev. Thomas M. Foye.
Res., 82 W. 29th St., 07002. Tel: 201-436-0857; Fax: 201-823-4611.
Catechesis/Religious Programs—Avenue C & 28 St., 07002. Tel: 201-339-0319. Sr. Beatrice Doria, M.P.F.
Students 390.

4—St. Joseph's, (1888) (Slovak), Rev. Msgr. Edward M. Matash.
Res., 317 Ave. E, 07002. Tel: 201-339-1122; Fax: 201-339-1009.

5—St. Vincent de Paul, (1894), Revs. Michael J. O'Grady; Michael A. Patete; Joseph Murray. In res., Rev. Carl Arico.
Res., 979 Ave. C., 07002. Tel: 201-436-2222; Fax: 201-437-5235.
School—(1920), 80 W. 47th St., 07002. Tel: 201-339-4438.
Lay Teachers 12; Students 227.
Catechesis/Religious Programs—Tel: 201-823-0184.
Students 450.

6—Mt. Carmel, (1898) (Polish), Rev. Msgr. Joseph A. Marjanczyk, Pastor Emeritus; Revs. Anthony J. Kulig; Kazimierz Kuczynski; William G. Cook; Deacon Robert Zywicki.
Res., 39 E. Twenty-second St., 07002. Tel: 201-339-2070; Fax: 201-339-3676.
School—(1902), 19 E. Twenty-second St., 07002. Tel: 201-339-1839.
Felician Sisters 4; Lay Teachers 10; Students 258.
Catechesis/Religious Programs—Students 150.
Convent—Tel: 201-436-5820.

7—Our Lady of the Assumption, (1902) (Italian), Revs. Donald Di Pasquale; Paul Pesenti, O.M.I.; Gabriel Francesco Vargas; Deacon William Giordano.
Res., 531 Ave. C, 07002. Tel: 201-436-8160.
Church—91 W. Twenty-third St., 07002.
School—101 W. Twenty-third St., 07002. Tel: 201-339-0249.
Religious Teachers Filippini 4; Lay Teachers 9; Students 154.
Catechesis/Religious Programs—Tel: 201-437-1867.
Students 263.
Convent—95 W. Twenty-third St., 07002. Tel: 201-858-0202.

8—St. Michael's, (1907) (Lithuanian), Revs. Albert J. Matulis; James F. Tortora, Ph.D. In res., Rev. J. M. Patricius.
Res., 15 E. Twenty-third St., 07002. Tel: 201-436-1412.

Catechesis/Religious Programs—Students 165.

Belleville, Essex Co., St. Anthony's (1901) (Italian), Revs. Dennis Cocozza; Joseph J. Cestaro, Pastor Emeritus; Neil J. Collins; Eugene Bernas (Philippines). In res., Rev. Salvatore T. Malanga.
Res., 750 N. Seventh St., Newark, 07107. Tel: 973-481-1991; Fax: 973-481-1993.
Church—63 Franklin Ave., Newark, 07107.

St. Peter's (1837), Revs. Joseph D. Girone; Mark A. O'Connell; Robert E. Emery; Deacon William Valladares.
Res., 155 William St., 07109. Tel: 973-751-2002; Fax: 973-751-6201. [CEM]
School—(1854), 152 William St., 07109. Tel: 973-759-3143.
Sisters of Charity 4; Lay Teachers 12; Students 240.
Catechesis/Religious Programs—Students 240.
Convent—Tel: 973-759-2432.

Bergenfield, Bergen Co., St. John the Evangelist (1909), Rev. Msgr. George R. Trabold; Rev. Msgr. Joseph J. Donovan, Pastor Emeritus, (Retired); Revs. Ernesto Tibay; Raymond R. Filipski; Francesco Carraro; Deacon Patrick Miney.
Res., 29 N. Washington Ave., 07621. Tel: 201-384-0101; Fax: 201-384-2055.
School—(1921), 17 Bradley Ave., 07621. Tel: 201-384-3627.
Sisters 3; Lay Teachers 24; Students 264.
Catechesis/Religious Programs—35 N. William St., 07621. Tel: 201-384-3601.
Students 887.
Convent—Tel: 201-384-2675.

Berkeley Heights, Union Co., Church of the Little Flower (1955), Very Rev. John P. McGovern; Revs. David Milliken; Alfred Burke.
Res., 110 Roosevelt Ave., 07922. Tel: 908-464-1585; Fax: 908-464-6342.
Church—310 Plainfield Ave., 07922.
Catechesis/Religious Programs—Tel: 908-464-7444.
Students 553.

Bloomfield, Essex Co., Sacred Heart (1878), Revs. Richard P. Kwiatkowski; Peter West; Theodore Osbahr.
Res., 76 Broad St., 07003. Tel: 973-748-1800; Fax: 973-748-2028. [CEM]
School—(1879), 683 Bloomfield, 07003. Tel: 973-743-4015; Fax: 973-743-0723.
Sisters of Charity 3; Lay Teachers 17; Students 345.
Convent—Tel: 973-743-0838.
Catechesis/Religious Programs—Tel: 973-743-4061.
Students 234.

St. Valentine (1899) (Polish), Revs. Robert M. Chabak; Michael C. Santoro. In res., Rev. John J. Donohue.
Res., 125 N. Spring St., 07003. Tel: 973-743-0220; Fax: 973-743-2041.
Catechesis/Religious Programs—Tel: 973-743-6122. Mrs. Joyce Bowen, D.R.E.
Students 181.

Church of St. Thomas the Apostle (1939), Rev. Msgr. William C. Hatcher; Revs. Matthew Pawlikowski; Peter K. Funesti; Rev. Msgr. Vincent P. Coburn, Pastor Emeritus. Pastoral Assocs.: Sr. Antoinette Munafo, S.S.J.; Sr. Anita Sibilia, M.P.F.; Sr. Patricia Michael, S.C. In res., Revs. Stephen S. Feehan; John Connolly, S.D.B.
Res., 60 Byrd Ave., 07003. Tel: 973-338-9190; Fax: 973-338-4224.
School—(1940), 50 Byrd Ave., 07003. Tel: 973-338-8505; Fax: 973-338-9565.
Sisters of Charity 4; Lay Teachers 23; Students 473.
Catechesis/Religious Programs—Tel: 973-338-7400.
Students 905.
Convent—Tel: 973-338-9118.

Bogota, Bergen Co., St. Joseph's (1929), Revs. Paul Schweizer, O.Carm.; Edward Ward, O.Carm.; Deacons Walter Lynn; Michael Fitzgerald. In res., Revs. Robert Wolfe, O.Carm.; John Lord, O. Carm.
Res., 115 E. Fort Lee Rd., 07603. Tel: 201-342-6300; Fax: 201-883-9392.
School—(1925), 131 E. Fort Lee Rd., 07603. Tel: 201-487-8641; Fax: 201-487-7405. Sr. Regina Miriam, F.S.P., Prin.
Franciscan Sisters of Peace 1; Lay Teachers 9; Students 249.
Catechesis/Religious Programs—Tel: 201-343-4316.
Students 554.
Convent—Tel: 201-342-4684.

Caldwell, Essex Co., St. Aloysius (1892), Revs. John J. Laferrera; Robert D. Jacunski; Mark Francis O'Malley. In res., Rev. Lester A. McGuinness; Rev. Msgr. Benjamin Piazza, (Retired).
Res., 219 Bloomfield Ave., 07006. Tel: 973-226-0221; Fax: 973-226-2204.
School—(1991). (Co-Sponsored) Trinity Academy 235 Bloomfield Ave., 07006. Tel: 973-226-3386; Fax: 973-226-6548.
Sisters 6; Lay Teachers 36; (PreK-8) 480.
Catechesis/Religious Programs—Tel: 973-226-0209.
Students 600.

Cedar Grove, Essex Co., St. Catherine of Siena (1949), Rev. Msgr. Charles W. Gusmer, V.E.; Revs. Kevin J. Schott; John Chadwick.
Res., 339 Pompton Ave., 07009. Tel: 973-239-7960; Fax: 973-239-1008.
School—(1958), 39 E. Bradford Ave., 07009. Tel: 973-239-6968.
Sisters of St. Dominic 1; Lay Teachers 19; Students 276; Franciscan Sister of Peace 2.
Catechesis/Religious Programs—Tel: 973-239-3332.
Students 400.
Convent—Tel: 973-239-3362.

Clark, Union Co., St. Agnes (1961), Revs. Eugene F. Marcone; Steven C. Conner.
Res., 332 Madison Hill Rd., 07066. Tel: 732-388-7852; Fax: 732-388-7064.
School—(1963), 342 Madison Hill Rd., 07066. Tel: 732-381-0850.
Lay Teachers 12; Students 204.
Catechesis/Religious Programs—Students 400.

Cliffside Park, Bergen Co., Epiphany (1916), Revs. Thomas F. Olsen; Robert P. Cozzini; Joseph A. Scarangella.
Res., 247 Knox Ave., 07010. Tel: 201-943-7320; Fax: 201-943-1779.
School—(1930), 263 Lafayette Ave., 07010. Tel: 201-945-1194.
Lay Teachers 12; Students 246; Religious 3.
Catechesis/Religious Programs—Tel: 201-945-1164.
Students 295.
Convent—228 Knox Ave., 07010. Tel: 201-943-2660.

Closter, Bergen Co., St. Mary's (1912), Rev. James T. McKenna. In res., Rev. Gerald Bajek.
Res., 20 Legion Pl., 07624. Tel: 201-768-7565; Fax: 201-784-5814.
School—300 High St., 07624. Tel: 201-768-2627; Fax: 201-768-6660.
Sisters 3; Lay Teachers 13; Students 121.
Catechesis/Religious Programs—Tel: 201-767-8247.
Students 215.

Cranford, Union Co., St. Michael's (1872), Revs. Lawrence W. Cull; Sebastian Kunnath; Krzysztof Maslowski; Sr. Arleen D. Crimmins, O.P., Pastoral Assoc.; Deacon Daniel Wilverding.
Res., 40 Alden St., 07016. Tel: 908-276-0360; Fax: 908-272-0273.
School—(1929), Alden and Miln Sts., 07016. Tel: 908-276-9425.
Lay Teachers 26; Students 399.
Catechesis/Religious Programs—100 Alden St., 07016. Tel: 908-276-2050. Mr. Martin Arsenault.
Students 793.

Cresskill, Bergen Co., St. Therese of Lisieux (1924), Revs. James J. Boyce, O.Carm.; Michael M. Mulhall, O.Carm.; Bro. Richard Supple, O.Carm.; Sr. Rosalie O'Connor, O.S.F., Pastoral Assoc. In res., Rev. Paul T. Hoban, O.Carm.
Res., 120 Monroe Ave., 07626. Tel: 201-567-2528; Fax: 201-567-6759.
School—220 Jefferson Ave., 07626. Tel: 201-568-4296; Fax: 201-568-3179.
Lay Teachers 14; Students 229.
Catechesis/Religious Programs—200 Jefferson Ave., 07627. Tel: 201-567-4781; Fax: 201-541-1269.
Students 520.

Demarest, Bergen Co., St. Joseph's (1931), Revs. William O'Malley, O.Carm.; Eugene Bettinger, O.Carm.
Res., 280 County Rd., 07627. Tel: 201-768-2371; Fax: 201-768-2466.
School—St. Joseph, Sacred Heart Interparochial School, 573 Piermont Rd., 07627. Tel: 201-768-5534; Fax: 201-768-2620.
Lay Teachers 10; Students 183.
Catechesis/Religious Programs—Tel: 201-768-6886; Fax: 201-768-4128.
Students 173.
Mission—Demarest, Bergen Co., St. Joseph Korean Catholic Community, 274 County Rd., 07627. Tel: 201-767-1854.

Dumont, Bergen Co., St. Mary's (1914), Revs. Donald P. Sheehan; Edward C, Thompson; Donald McLaughlin; Sr. Elizabeth Mullen, C.S.J., Pastoral Assoc. In res., Revs. Mathew Chandrankunnel (India); Theodore A. Szelest, (Retired).
Res., 280 Washington Ave., 07628. Tel: 201-384-0557; Fax: 201-384-4986.
School—(1951), 21-31 New Milford Ave., 07628. Tel: 201-384-0512.
Sisters 5; Lay Teachers 17; Students 304.
Catechesis/Religious Programs—Tel: 201-384-3062.
Students 619.

East Newark, Hudson Co., St. Anthony's (1901) (Italian), Rev. Anthony F. Granato. In res., Rev. Francis T. Maione.
Res., 409 N. Second St., 07029. Tel: 973-483-4680; Fax: 973-483-2396.
Catechesis/Religious Programs—Students 150.

East Orange, Essex Co.,

1—Holy Name of Jesus, (1910), Revs. Robert J. Rischmann, Admin.; Jerome S. Arthasseril; Edward Heavey; Deacon Leo Woodruff. In res., Rev. Joseph L. Affanoso.
Res., 184 Midland Ave., 07017.
Parish Center—200 Midland Ave., P.O. Box 5244, 07017-1855. Tel: 973-675-4444; Fax: 973-674-1767.

2—Holy Spirit-Our Lady Help of Christians, (1882), Very Rev. Thomas Paul Lipnicki, V.F.; Rev. Nerva W. Dugue. In res., Rev. George Kelly, C.SS.R.
Res., 17 N. Clinton St., 07017. Tel: 973-673-1077; Fax: 973-676-6494.
School—(1883), 23 N. Clinton St., 07017. Tel: 973-677-1546.
Lay Teachers 17; Students 535.

3—St. Joseph's, (1916), Rev. William M. Giblin; Deacons Joseph Fiore, (Retired); Alonzo C. Jackson.
Res., 110 Telford St., 07018. Tel: 973-678-4030; Fax: 973-677-7875.
School—115 Telford St., 07018. Tel: 973-674-2326; Fax: 973-674-7718.
Religious Teachers Filippini 3; Lay Teachers 16; Students 429.
Catechesis/Religious Programs—Students 417.
Convent—Tel: 201-677-0812.

4—Our Lady of All Souls, (1914). Closed. For inquiries for parish records contact Seton Hall University Archives, South Orange. Tel: 973-761-9476; Fax: 973-761-9550.

5—Our Lady of the Most Blessed Sacrament, (1916). Closed. For inquiries for parish records contact Seton Hall University Archives, South Orange. Tel: 973-761-9476; Fax: 973-761-9550.

East Rutherford, Bergen Co., St. Joseph's (1872), Revs. Richard S. Husted, O.F.M.; Edward J. Donahue, O.F.M.; Brian Linehan, O.F.M.; Paul Sinnema, O.F.M.; Sr. Agnes Morrisseey, S.C., Pastoral Min., Tel: 201-507-8842.
Res., 120 Hoboken Rd., 07073. Tel: 201-939-0457; Fax: 201-939-4196. [CEM]
School—(1879), 20 Hackensack St., 07073. Tel: 201-939-3193; Fax: 201-939-1913. Mrs. Frances Alberta, Prin.
Lay Teachers 11; Students 209.
Catechesis/Religious Programs—Tel: 201-939-3441.
Students 562.
Convent—Tel: 201-460-4961.

Edgewater, Bergen Co., Holy Rosary (1906), Rev. Gerald F. Greaves; Deacon Robert E. Thomson.
Res., 365 Undercliff Ave., 07020. Tel: 201-945-6329 (Parish Center); Fax: 201-945-6599.

Elizabeth, Union Co.,

1—St. Mary of the Assumption, (1844), Rev. Msgr. Robert J. Harrington; Revs. William Crum; Manuel D. Rios. Pastoral Assocs.: Sr. Ruth Morgan, R.S.M.; Sr. Elaine Maguire, F.S.P.; Maria Castillo; Colleen Reynolds. In res., Revs. Robert Becerra; Robert Haber.
Res., 155 Washington Ave., 07202. Tel: 908-352-5154; Fax: 908-352-0350. [CEM]
School—(1868), 237 S. Broad St., 07202. Tel: 908-352-0717.
Lay Teachers 10; Students 221.
High School—Tel: 908-352-4350; Fax: 908-352-2359.
Sisters 3; Lay Teachers 26; Students 335.
Child Care Center—Tel: 908-355-8723.
Sisters 1; Students 68.
Catechesis/Religious Programs—Tel: 908-352-0296.
Students 414.
Convent—Tel: 908-352-1455.

2—St. Adalbert's, (1905) (Polish), Revs. Ronald J. Marczewski; Marek Wysocki; Deacon Joseph J. Lubas.
Res., 250 E. Jersey St., 07206. Tel: 908-352-2791; Fax: 908-354-2828. [CEM]
School—(1905), Tel: 908-353-3160.
Felician Sisters 2; Lay Teachers 9; Students 167.

3—St. Anthony's, (1895) (Italian), Revs. Vincent Zuliani, S.D.B.; Johon Masiello, S.D.B.; Vincent Paczkowski; Teofilo Revilla. In res., Rev. Mario Balbi-Port.
Res., 853 Third Ave., 07202. Tel: 908-351-3300; Fax: 908-351-3609.
School—229 Centre St., 07202. Tel: 908-352-7419.
Sisters of Charity of Convent Station 5; Lay Teachers 12; Students 350.

Catechesis/Religious Programs—Students 415.
Convent—Tel: 908-354-0825.

4—BLESSED SACRAMENT, (1922), Rev. Msgr. Joseph P. Plunkett; Rev. John Stanley Gomes.
Res., 1096 North Ave., 07201. Tel: 908-352-0338; Fax: 908-352-4553.
School—(1926), 1086 North Ave., 07201. Tel: 908-352-8629; Fax: 908-352-7934.
Lay Teachers 9; Students 201.

5—IMMACULATE CONCEPTION, (1907), Revs. Alfred J. Kowalski; Fabio R. Brenes-Chaves; Deacon Jose Rosado.
Res., 425 Union Ave., 07208. Tel: 908-352-6662; Fax: 908-352-8484.
School—(1913), 417 Union Ave., 07208. Tel: 908-351-4242.
Sisters of St. John the Baptist 4; Lay Teachers 6; Students 168.
Convent—424 Westminister Ave., 07208. Tel: 908-353-8463.

6—ST. GENEVIEVE'S, (1920), Rev. Msgr. Hugh A. O'Donnell; Rev. Msgr. Edward G. Price, Pastor Emeritus; Revs. Roy James DeLeo; John G. Netta.
Res., 200 Monmouth Rd., 07208. Tel: 908-351-4444; Fax: 908-351-5454.
School—(1929), 209 Princeton Rd., 07208. Tel: 908-355-3355.
Benedictine Sisters 4; Lay Teachers 20; Students 440.
Catechesis/Religious Programs—Tel: 908-355-1584.
Students 350.
Convent—Tel: 908-353-0736.

7—ST. HEDWIG'S, (1926) (Polish), Rev. Msgr. Bronislaw Wielgus. In res., Rev. Thomas J. Lewczak.
Res., 716 Clarkson Ave., 07202. Tel: 908-352-1448; Fax: 908-352-8389.
School—(1928), Clarkson Ave. and Myrtle St., 07202. Tel: 908-354-5653.
Little Servant Sisters of the Immaculate Conception 3; Lay Teachers 12; Students 220.
Catechesis/Religious Programs—Tel: 908-354-5650.
Students 278.
Convent—717 Polonia Ave., 07202. Tel: 908-355-8409.

8—ST. JOSEPH'S, (1911) (Slovak). Closed. Records at Holy Family, Linden. Tel: 908-862-1060.

9—OUR LADY OF MOST HOLY ROSARY/ST. MICHAEL, (1886/1852), Rev. Jan Sasin. In res., Rev. William C. Reed.
Res., 52 Smith St., 07201. Tel: 908-354-2454; Fax: 908-354-3207. [JC]

10—ST. PATRICK'S, (1858) (Hispanic), Rev. Msgr. Richard J. Arnhols; Rev. Gerard M. Lombardo; Deacon Nestor Charriez.
Res., 215 Court St., 07206. Tel: 908-354-0023; Fax: 908-355-0926. [CEM]
School—(1863). See Elizabethport Catholic School. 227 Court St., 07206. Tel: 908-351-2188; Fax: 908-351-6086.
High School—(1863), 221 Court St., 07206. Tel: 908-353-5220; Fax: 908-629-1123.
Brothers 1; Sisters 1; Lay Teachers 15; Students 233.

11—SACRED HEART, (1871). Merged Records at Our Lady of Fatima Parish, Elizabeth. Tel: 908-355-3810.

12—HOLY ROSARY, (1886). Merged Records at Our Lady of Most Holy Rosary/St. Michael, Elizabeth. Tel: 908-354-2454; Fax: 908-354-3207.

13—SS. PETER AND PAUL'S, (1895) (Lithuanian), Revs. Alfred Zemeikis; Peter M. Aquino; Deacon Henry Keturwitis.
Res., 211 Ripley Pl., 07206. Tel: 908-352-2271; Fax: 908-353-2851.

14—IMMACULATE HEART OF MARY, (1947) (Spanish), Revs. Francisco Dols, T.O.R. (Spain); Jorge Oliver, T.O.R.
Res., 205 E. Jersey St., 07206. Tel: 908-355-0807; Fax: 908-355-0526.
Convent—Tel: 908-354-8388.

15—OUR LADY OF FATIMA, (1973) (Portuguese), Rev. Msgr. John S. Antao; Revs. Anthony Bico; Jose Manuel Fernandes.
Res., 403 Spring St., 07201. Tel: 908-355-3810.
Catechesis/Religious Programs—Students 750.

Elmwood Park, Bergen Co., St. Leo's (1912), Revs. Brian P. Cullinane, O.F.M.; Roland A. Fregault, O.F.M.; Theodore F. Lehr, O.F.M.; Robert J. Norton, O.F.M.
Res., 324 Market St., 07407. Tel: 201-796-3521; Fax: 201-703-8408.
School—(1912), 300 Market St., 07407. Tel: 201-796-5156.
Franciscan Sisters of Peace 3; Lay Teachers 15; Students 417.
Catechesis/Religious Programs—Students 200.
Convent—Tel: 201-797-6993.

Emerson, Bergen Co., Church of the Assumption (1947), Rev. Eugene J. Hazewski; Rev. Msgr. Caesar G. Orrico, Pastor Emeritus; Revs. Mathew Aymanathil (India); Bryan F.J. Adamcik.
Res., 29 Jefferson Ave., 07630. Tel: 201-262-1122; Fax: 201-262-7855.
School—35 Jefferson Ave., 07630. Tel: 201-262-0300; Fax: 201-262-5910.
Sisters 3; Lay Teachers 19; Students 310.
Catechesis/Religious Programs—Tel: 201-986-0970.
Students 320.

Englewood, Bergen Co., St. Cecilia's (1866), Very Rev. Joseph O'Brien, O.Carm., V.E., Pastor & Prior; Revs. Emil Agostino, O.Carm.; Sean O'Leary, O.Carm. In res., Revs. Noel Ahrens, O.Carm.; Brendan Gilmore, O.Carm.; Very Rev. Timothy Moore, O.Carm.; Revs. Ellis Reinert, O.Carm.; Anthony Palo, O.Carm.; Carl Pfister, O.Carm.
Res., 55 Demarest Ave., 07631. Tel: 201-568-0364; Fax: 201-568-0654.
School—St. Cecilia Interparochial School, (1874), 85 W. Demarest Ave., 07631. Tel: 201-568-2615.
Lay Teachers 10; Students 200.
Catechesis/Religious Programs—Students 88.

Fairfield, Essex Co., St. Thomas More (1962), Revs. Charles P. O'Connor; Santos Bertiz; George Ruane; Sr. Agnes Bernard, O.P., Pastoral Assoc.
Res., 210 Horseneck Rd., 07004. Tel: 973-227-0055; Fax: 973-227-2495.
Catechesis/Religious Programs—(Grades 1-8) 12 Hollywood Ave., 07004. Tel: 973-227-3607; Fax: 973-808-9032. Mary Rogers, D.R.E.
Students 388.

Fair Lawn, Bergen Co., St. Anne's (1909), Revs. James Nero, O.F.M.; Jack Kull, O.F.M.; Jeremiah V. McGinley, O.F.M.; John Alderson, O.F.M.; Evan Banks, O.F.M.; Deacons Joseph Marcom; Richard Titmas; Richard McGarry. In res., Revs. Brennan Connelly, O.F.M.; Felican Foy, O.F.M.
Res., 15-05 Saint Anne St., 07410. Tel: 201-791-1616; Fax: 201-791-1871.
School—(1950), 1-30 Summit Ave., 07410. Tel: 201-796-3353; Fax: 201-791-1871.
Sisters of St. Joseph of Peace 1; Lay Teachers 21; Students 352.
Catechesis/Religious Programs—Tel: 201-791-1618.
Students 544.
Convent—Tel: 201-796-1899.

Fairview, Bergen Co., St. John the Baptist (1873), Revs. John J. Gibbons; James J. Carroll; Deacon Anton Tarabokija. In res., Revs. Giordano Belanich (PAT); Gildardo Garcia.
Res., 239 Anderson Ave., 07022. Tel: 201-945-4865; Fax: 201-945-8171.
School—St. Elizabeth Seton Interparochial School, (1991). Co-Sponsored. Fourth & Walker, 07022. Tel: 201-945-2212.
Lay Teachers 9; Students 230.
Catechesis/Religious Programs—Students 300.

Our Lady of Grace (1922) (Italian), Revs. Francis Gaetano, S.A.C.; Pompeo Luciani, S.A.C.
Res., 395 Delano Pl., 07022. Tel: 201-943-0904.
School—400 Kamena St., 07022. Tel: 201-945-8300.
Lay Teachers 15; Students 342.
Catechesis/Religious Programs—Tel: 201-945-1201.
Students 225.

Fort Lee, Bergen Co., Holy Trinity (1906), Revs. James B. Sullivan; Michael T. Mickelson.
Res., 2367 Lemoine Ave., 07024-6269. Tel: 201-947-1216; Fax: 201-947-1217.
School—Christ the Teacher Interparochial School. Co-Sponsored. (See Madonna Parish, Fort Lee). Tel: 201-944-0421.
Catechesis/Religious Programs—Tel: 201-585-0381.
Students 205.
Convent—Tel: 201-944-2911.

Madonna (1858), Revs. John P. Ryan, Admin.; John L. Paprocki; Robert H. Langdon; Camilo L. Lopez.
Res., 340 Main St., 07024. Tel: 201-944-2727; Fax: 201-944-5986. [CEM]
School—(1991). Christ the Teacher Interparochial School 359 Whiteman St., 07024. Tel: 201-944-0421.
Sisters 1; Lay Teachers 19; Students 260.
Catechesis/Religious Programs—Madonna Religious Education Center.
Students 174.

Franklin Lakes, Bergen Co., Most Blessed Sacrament (1961), Rev. Msgr. Owen J. Hendry; Rev. Msgr. Carl D. Hinrichsen, Pastor Emeritus; Rev. Brian G. Plate.
Res., 787 Franklin Lake Rd., 07417. Tel: 201-891-4200; Fax: 201-891-4243.
School—(1963), 785 Franklin Lake Rd., 07417. Tel: 201-891-4250; Fax: 201-847-9227.
Sisters of St. Joseph of Chestnut Hill 2; Lay Teachers 15; Students 267.
Catechesis/Religious Programs—Tel: 201-891-8390.
Students 690.
Convent—Tel: 201-891-4292.

Garfield, Bergen Co.,

1—OUR LADY OF MT. VIRGIN, (1901) (Italian), Revs. Paul L. Bochicchio; Joseph Fu (China); James Muntz; Deacon Dominic Riccio.
Res., 188 MacArthur Ave., 07026. Tel: 973-772-2295; Fax: 973-478-4389.
School—Garfield Catholic Academy, (1951) (Grades PreK-8). (Mt. Virgin Campus) 200 MacArthur Ave., 07026. Tel: 973-772-0416; Fax: 973-772-3301. Sr. Mary Lou Shulas, M.P.F., Prin.
Religious Teachers Filippini 2; Lay Teachers 10.
Catechesis/Religious Programs—Tel: 973-253-1399. Sr. Jo Ann Jankowski, M.P.F., D.R.E.
Students 175.
Convent—410 Maywood Ave., Maywood, 07607. Tel: 201-845-9568.

2—HOLY NAME, (1911), Rev. Benedict P. Militello.
Res., 99 Marsellus Pl., 07026. Tel: 973-340-0032; Fax: 973-340-1618.
School—Garfield Catholic Academy, (Grades PreK-8) 200 MacArthur Ave., 07026.

3—CHURCH OF OUR LADY OF SORROWS, (1917), Revs. John K. Gurski; Michael Guba.
Res., 69 Market St., 07026. Tel: 973-772-7889.
School—Garfield Catholic Academy, (Grades PreK-8) 200 MacArthur Ave., 07026.

4—ST. STANISLAUS KOSTKA, (1917) (Polish), Revs. Edward P. Szpiech; Marian Spanier; Eugene S. Kowalski, Pastor Emeritus.
Res., 184 Ray St., 07026. Tel: 973-772-7922; Fax: 973-772-4178.
School—Garfield Catholic Academy, (1919) (Grades K-8). (St. Stanislaus Kostka Campus) 210 Lanza Ave., 07026. Tel: 973-772-0345; Fax: 973-772-8393.
Felician Sisters 1; Lay Teachers 9; Students 162.
Catechesis/Religious Programs—Tel: 973-794-0620.
Students 270.
Convent—Tel: 973-772-4644.

Garwood, Union Co., Church of St. Anne (1925), Rev. Msgr. John Philip O'Connor; Rev. William A. Mahon. In res., Rev. Joseph V. Derbyshire.
Res., 325 Second Ave., 07027. Tel: 908-789-0280; Fax: 908-789-3099.
Catechesis/Religious Programs—Tel: 908-789-4745.
Students 325.

Glen Rock, Bergen Co., St. Catharine (1953), Rev. Dennis Cohan; Rev. Msgr. Richard J. Holmes, Pastor Emeritus; Revs. Jose Agan; James J. Weiner. Pastoral Assocs.: John Forsman; Catherine Furlani; Roberta Maguire; Vicki Peluse; Deacons Leonard A. Minichino; Paul Schnieder; James Mueller. In res., Rev. John A. Merity.
Res., 905 S. Maple Ave., 07452. Tel: 201-445-3703; Fax: 201-670-7149.
School—St. Catharine Interparochial School, 180 Rodney St., 07452. Tel: 201-445-0622; Fax: 201-445-8345. Sr. Mary Elizabeth DeBoer, O.P., Prin.
Sisters 1; Lay Teachers 25; Students 505.
Catechesis/Religious Programs—Tel: 201-444-5690.
Students 779.
Convent—Tel: 201-447-4342.

Guttenberg, Hudson Co., St. John Nepomucene (1910) (Slovak), Rev. John F. Renard.
Res., 7007 Polk St., 07093. Tel: 201-869-6834; Fax: 201-869-2408.
School—7111 Polk St., North Bergen, 07047. Tel: 201-869-5404.
School Sisters of St. Francis 4; Lay Teachers 12; Students 295.
Convent—Tel: 201-869-2099.

Hackensack, Bergen Co.,

1—HOLY TRINITY, (1861), Most Rev. Charles J. McDonnell, D.D.; Revs. Robert M. Brennan; J. Orlando Rengifo; Alfonso DeCondorpusa; Deacon Vincent Messina; Sr. Emily Marie Walsh, Parish Min.
Res., 34 Maple Ave., 07601. Tel: 201-343-5170; Fax: 201-343-5067. [CEM]
School—(1869), 43 Maple Ave., 07601. Tel: 201-489-6870; Fax: 201-489-2981.
Sisters of Charity 4; Lay Teachers 11; Students 198.
Catechesis/Religious Programs—Mrs. Carol Thee, D.R.E.
Students 209.
Convent—Tel: 201-342-1996.

2—IMMACULATE CONCEPTION, (1891), Rev. Gerard J. Graziano.
Res., 49 Vreeland Ave., 07601. Tel: 201-440-2798.

3—ST. JOSEPH'S, (1909) (Polish), Rev. Martin J. Silver.
Res., 460 Hudson St., 07601. Tel: 201-440-3224.

4—ST. FRANCIS, (1917) (Italian), Revs. Peter Nicosia, O.F.M.Cap.; Paschal Caccavalle, O.F.M.Cap.; Deacon Arthur Cauceglia.

Res., 50 Lodi St., 07601. Tel: 201-343-6243; Fax: 201-343-0854.
School—100 S. Main St., 07601. Tel: 201-488-8862.
Lay Teachers 11; Students 283.

Harrington Park, Bergen Co., Our Lady of Victories (1910), Rev. Edward V. Duffy. In res., Rev. Msgr. Roger A. Reynolds; Rev. Bernard L. Keitz, O.P.
Res., 81 Lynn St., 07640-1831. Tel: 201-768-1706; Fax: 201-768-3962.
School—Holy Family Interparochial School, Norwood. (See Immaculate Conception, Norwood.) Tel: 201-768-1605). Tel: 201-768-1605; Fax: 201-768-0796.
Catechesis/Religious Programs—(Grades K-8) 155 The Parkway, 07640-1820. Tel: 201-768-1400. Miss Elizabeth Foer, D.R.E.
Students 334.
Convent—145 The Parkway, 07640-1820. Tel: 201-768-1705.

Harrison, Hudson Co., Holy Cross (1865), Rev. Msgr. John J. Gilchrist; Rev. Anthony DaSilva. In res., Revs. Carlos A. Bracci (Brazil); James J. Reilly; Sr. Doris DeLotto, S.S.C., Pastoral Assoc.
Res., 16 Church Sq., 07029. Tel: 973-484-5678; Fax: 973-484-0906.
School—(1871), 14 S. F.E. Rodgers Blvd., 07029. Tel: 973-485-0340.
Lay Teachers 15; Students 232.
Catechesis/Religious Programs—Students 272.
Convent—Tel: 973-485-2632. Holy Cross Convent

Our Lady of Czestochowa (1908) (Polish), Revs. Rudolf Zubik; Henry P. Marciniak.
Res., 115 S. Third St., 07029. Tel: 973-483-2255; Fax: 973-483-4688.

Hasbrouck Heights, Bergen Co., Corpus Christi (1897), Rev. Msgr. Francis A. DeDomenico; Revs. Raymond M. Holmes; Andrew Zmerlicki.
Parish Offices & Center: 218 Washington Pl., 07604. Tel: 201-288-4844; Fax: 201-288-0237.
School—(1928), 215 Kipp Ave., 07604. Tel: 201-288-0614; Fax: 201-288-5956.
Lay Teachers 24; Students 432.
Catechesis/Religious Programs—Tel: 201-288-5133.
Students 510.

Haworth, Bergen Co., Sacred Heart (1914), Rev. Msgr. James F. Bouffard; Rev. Joseph W. Nealon, Pastor Emeritus.
Res., 123 Maple St., P.O. Box S, 07641. Tel: 201-387-0080; Fax: 201-439-1395.
School—St. Joseph's Interparochial School. (See St. Joseph, Demarest. Tel: 201-768-5534).
Catechesis/Religious Programs—400 St. Nicholas Ave., 07641. Tel: 201-384-6454.
Students 175.

Hillsdale, Bergen Co., St. John the Baptist (1925), Rev. Msgr. Philip D. Morris, S.T.D., V.F.; Rev. Michael J. Moran. Pastoral Assocs.: Margaret M. Keenan, M.A.; Sr. Kathryn A. Malone, S.S.J., M.A.; Sr. Thomas Therese, S.S.J.; Catherine Wollyung. In res., Rev. John J. Paladino, M.Div.
Res., 69 Valley St., 07642. Tel: 201-664-3131; Fax: 201-664-0772.
School—St. John's Academy, (1955), 460 Hillsdale Ave., 07642. Tel: 201-664-6364; Fax: 201-664-8096.
Sisters of St. Joseph, Chestnut Hill, PA 2; Lay Teachers 23; Students 360.
Catechesis/Religious Programs—The Duffy Center, Tel: 201-666-2707.
Students 476.
Convent—Tel: 201-664-3800.

Hillside, Union Co., St. Catherine of Siena (1912), Revs. Richard A. Villanova; Robert L. Daly, Pastor Emeritus. In res., Rev. Thomas R. McLaughlin.
Res., 19 King St., 07205. Tel: 908-351-1515; Fax: 908-351-2139.
School—(1920), 1003 N. Broad St., Elizabeth, 07205. Tel: 908-352-8029.
Lay Teachers 15; Students 240.
Catechesis/Religious Programs—Elizabeth, Tel: 908-352-8068.
Students 170.

Christ the King (1948), Revs. Richard D. Carlson; Valentine C. Ugwuanya.
Res., 411 Rutgers Ave., 07205. Tel: 908-686-0722; Fax: 908-686-2504.
School—(1953), 397 Columbia Ave., 07205. Tel: 908-686-6740; Fax: 908-686-3819.
Sisters 2; Lay Teachers 17; Students 225.
Catechesis/Religious Programs—Tel: 908-686-0234.
Students 116.
Convent—Tel: 908-686-2560.

Hoboken, Hudson Co.,

1—Our Lady of Grace, (1851), Revs. Richard J. Carrington; Arcadio Munoz. In res., Rev. Frederick M. Eid.
Res., 400 Willow Ave., 07030. Tel: 201-659-0369; Fax: 201-659-5833.
School—(1864), Fifth St. & Willow Ave., 07030. Tel: 201-659-3025.
Lay Teachers 14; Students 208.
Convent—Tel: 201-659-1216.
Catechesis/Religious Programs—Students 143.

2—St. Joseph's, (1871), Rev. Michael Gugliemelli, O.F.M.Conv., Admin.; Deacons Luis Montanez; Pedro Rivera.
Res., 61 Monroe St., 07030. Tel: 201-659-0221.
School—John Paul II Interparochial School. (See St. Ann, Hoboken). Tel: 201-963-9535.

3—St. Francis, (1888) (Italian), Revs. Michael V. Guglielmelli, O.F.M.Conv.; Rodrigo Archangel Restrepo-Restrepo.
Res., 308 Jefferson St., 07030. Tel: 201-659-1772; Fax: 201-222-7975.
School—John Paul II Interparochial School. (See St. Ann, Hoboken. Tel: 201-963-9535).

4—SS. Peter and Paul's, (1889), Rev. Msgr. Frank G. Del Prete, J.C.D.; Revs. George Faour; Charles W.A. Herr; Deacon Primitivo Cruz.
Res., 404 Hudson St., 07030. Tel: 201-659-2276; Fax: 201-659-5062.
School—(1889), 410 Hudson St., 07030. Tel: 201-659-7158; Fax: 201-656-8135.
Caldwell Dominicans 3; Lay Teachers 8; Students 240.
Convent—Tel: 201-659-1784.

5—St. Ann's, (1900) (Italian), Revs. Andrew Jamieson, O.F.M.Cap.; Joseph Mezzanote, O.F.M.Cap.; Philip Volpe, O.F.M.Cap.
Res., 704 Jefferson St., 07030. Tel: 201-659-1114; Fax: 201-659-1416.
School—John Paul II Interparochial School, (1955), 555 Seventh St., 07030. Tel: 201-963-9535.
Sisters 3; Lay Teachers 11; Students 235.

Hohokus, Bergen Co., St. Luke's (1864), Rev. William J. Dowd; Rev. Msgr. Joseph F. Flusk; Deacon Edwin J. Alsing. In res., Rev. Msgr. Richard J. Holmes, Pastor Emeritus.
Res., 340 N. Franklin Tpke., 07423. Tel: 201-444-0272; Fax: 201-652-7044. [CEM]
School—St. Thomas More Interparochial School. Serving the Parish Communities of St. Luke's, Nativity and Guardian Angel. (See Nativity Parish, Midland Park).
Catechesis/Religious Programs—Tel: 201-447-2779. Sr. Regina Chassar, S.S.J., D.R.E.
Students 527.

Irvington, Essex Co.,

1—Assumption of the Blessed Virgin Mary, (1907) (Hungarian). Closed. For inquiries for parish records contact Seton Hall University Archives, South Orange. Tel: 973-596-9476.

2—St. Leo's, (1878), Revs. Thomas M. Cembor; Eugene E. Geiger; Frederick C. Koerner; John Wassell; Dennis McKenna, Pastor Emeritus; Deacon Victor Reyes.
Res., 103 Myrtle Ave., 07111. Tel: 973-372-1272; Fax: 973-416-8819.
School—(1892), 123 Myrtle Ave., 07111. Tel: 973-372-7555. Ms. Debra Brower, Prin.
Lay Teachers 16; Students 302.
Convent—Tel: 973-374-6397.

3—Sacred Heart of Jesus, (1925) (Polish), Revs. Robert T. Ulak; Jordan Mysliwiec, S.D.S.
Res., 537 Grove St., 07111. Tel: 973-373-2232; Fax: 973-373-5935.
School—(1929), 15 Smalley Ter., 07111. Tel: 973-372-6372.
Felician Sisters 1; Lay Teachers 9; Students 190.
Convent—Tel: 973-372-6528.

4—St. Paul the Apostle, (1948), Revs. William R. Smalley; Venantius M. Fernando.
Res., 954 Stuyvesant Ave., 07111. Tel: 973-375-8568; Fax: 973-375-7040.
School—(1950), 285 Nesbit Ter., 07111. Tel: 973-375-0659; Fax: 973-375-7040.
Sisters of St. Dominic 4; Lay Teachers 9; Students 230.
Convent—972 Stuyvesant Ave., 07111. Tel: 973-374-2277.
Catechesis/Religious Programs—Tel: 973-375-2688.
Students 238.

Jersey City, Hudson Co.,

1—St. Aedan's, (1912), Revs. Jeremias R. Rebanal, J.C.D., Ph.D.; Robert L. Quigley; Edito Gamallo, S.T.B. In res., Rev. Thomas Kunnath.
Res., 800 Bergen Ave., 07306. Tel: 201-433-6800; Fax: 201-433-1222.
School—(1913), 41 Tuers Ave., 07306. Tel: 201-435-6528; Fax: 201-985-8975.
Sisters 5; Lay Teachers 18; Students 394.
Convent—Tel: 201-451-8109.

2—St. Aloysius, (1897), Rev. Msgr. Peter A. Cheplic; Rev. Msgr. Martin Kelly; Revs. Thomas Thottungal; Kenneth E. Jennings; Deacon Stephen Liptak. In res., Revs. Edward Malkiewicz, (Retired); Joseph A. Petrillo.
Res., 691 West Side Ave., 07304. Tel: 201-433-6365; Fax: 201-451-6438.
Schools—(1897), 721 West Side Ave., 07306. Tel: 201-433-4270; Fax: 201-433-6916.
Sisters of Charity 3; Lay Teachers 27; Students 455; High School Sisters of Charity, Tel: 201-435-9240; Fax: 201-435-2115.
Sisters 3; Lay Teachers 18; Students 250.
Catechesis/Religious Programs—Students 209.
Convent—Tel: 201-433-5759.

3—St. Anne's, (1903), Very Rev. Victor P. Kennedy, V.F.; Revs. Juan Perez De Mesa; Arnelo A. Galeon. In res., Revs. Gerard J. Sudol; Kevin P. Ashe.
Res., 3545 J.F. Kennedy Blvd., 07307. Tel: 201-656-2490; Fax: 201-795-3817.
School—(1904), 255 Congress St., 07307. Tel: 201-659-0450. Mrs. Marlene Bartram, Prin.
Lay Teachers 16; Students 330.
Catechesis/Religious Programs—Tel: 201-659-1794. Sr. Alberta Manzo, F.S.R., D.R.E.
Students 172.
Convent—Tel: 201-963-0998.

4—St. Ann's, (1910) (Lithuanian). Closed. For inquiries for parish records contact Seton Hall University Archives, South Orange. Tel: 201-761-9476, Fax: 201-761-9550.

5—St. Ann's, (1911) (Polish), Revs. Thaddeus Stasik; George Idzik.
Res., 291 St. Paul's Ave., 07306-5008. Tel: 201-656-4018; Fax: 201-656-0741.

6—St. Anthony of Padua, (1884) (Polish), Revs. Michael E. Gubernat, Admin.; Stanley Kostrzomb.
Res., 330 Sixth St., 07302. Tel: 201-653-0343.

7—Assumption/All Saints, (1896), Revs. Eugene P. Squeo, J.D.; Jean-Marie Fritz Ligonde; Francis E. Schiller; Sr. Manuela Villaroel, Pastoral Assoc.; Deacon Joseph Del Monte.
Res., 344 Pacific Ave., 07304. Tel: 201-333-1971.
School—301 Whiton St., 07304. Tel: 201-433-6087.
Sisters of Charity 5; Lay Teachers 21; Students 260.
Catechesis/Religious Programs—Students 265.
Convent—Tel: 201-451-2765.

8—St. Boniface's, (1863). Merged with St. Bridget, St. Mary, St. Michael and St. Peter to form Parish of the Resurrection, June 1997. For inquiries for parish records call Tel: 201-434-8500.

9—St. Bridget's, (1869). Merged with St. Boniface, St. Mary, St. Michael and St. Peter to form Parish of the Resurrection, June 1997. For inquiries for parish records call Tel: 201-434-8500.

10—Christ, the King, (1930) (African American), Rev. John Edmunds, S.T.; Deacon Leon Johnson.
Res., 768 Ocean Ave., 07304. Tel: 201-333-4862; Fax: 201-433-6352.

11—Holy Rosary, (1885) (Italian), Rev. Robert G. Laferrera; Rev. Msgr. Gerard M. Santora, Pastor Emeritus; Rev. Rino Lavaroni. In res., Rev. Robert M. Iaquinto.
Res., 344 Sixth St., 07302. Tel: 201-795-0120; Fax: 201-610-1389.
School—189 Brunswick St., 07302. Tel: 201-653-1699; Fax: 201-418-9019. Sr. Dolores Jensen, Prin.
Religious Teachers Filippini 4; Lay Teachers 11; Students 189.
Catechesis/Religious Programs—Tel: 201-792-7959.
Students 23.
Convent—Tel: 201-653-0697.

12—St. John the Baptist, (1884), Rev. Msgr. Charles G. Stengel; Revs. Paul A. Cannariato; Joseph Kallepallil, S.J. (India); Rev. Msgr. Joseph A. Beggans, Pastor Emeritus.
Res., 3026 John F. Kennedy Blvd., 07306. Tel: 201-653-8814; Fax: 201-653-3771.
School—(1886) (Grades PreK-8). Co-Sponsored. Saints John and Ann School. 3044 John F. Kennedy Blvd., 07306. Tel: 201-653-4416; Fax: 201-653-7452.
Lay Teachers 13; Students 340.

13—St. Joseph's, (1856), Rev. James V. Pagnotta.
Res., 511 Pavonia Ave., 07306. Tel: 201-653-0392.
Church—Baldwin Ave., 07306. Fax: 201-222-6481.
School—(1876), 509 Pavonia Ave., 07306. Tel: 201-653-0128; Fax: 201-222-5324.
Sisters of Charity 1; Lay Teachers 10; Students 200.
Convent—Tel: 201-963-1428.
Catechesis/Religious Programs—Tel: 201-659-5929.
Students 168.

14—St. Lucy's, (1884). Closed. For inquiries for parish records contact Parish of the Resurrection. Tel: 201-434-8500.

15—St. Mary's, (1854) (Hispanic-Filipino). Merged with St. Boniface, St. Bridget, St. Michael, and St. Peter, to form Parish of the Resurrection, June 1997. For inquiries for parish records call Tel: 201-434-8500.

16—ST. MICHAEL'S, (1867). Merged with St. Boniface, St. Bridget, St. Mary and St. Peter to form Parish of the Resurrection, June 1997. For inquiries for parish records call Tel: 201-434-8500.

17—MT. CARMEL, (1905) (Italian), Rev. Robert G. Marotta. In res., Rev. Walter L. Genzlinger.
Res., 99 Broadway, 07306. Tel: 201-435-7080; Fax: 201-432-4476.
School—(1955), 95 Broadway, 07306. Tel: 201-435-0209; Fax: 201-435-0298.
Religious Teachers Filippini 1; Lay Teachers 11; Students 200.

18—ST. NICHOLAS, (1886) (German), Revs. Peter P. Galdon; Jose Saltarin; Rev. Msgr. Joseph C. Manz, Pastor Emeritus. In res., Rev. Msgr. Jose M. Alba; Rev. Mamerto Cordero (Philippines).
Res., 122 Ferry St., 07307. Tel: 201-659-5354; Fax: 201-798-6868.
School—(1884), 118 Ferry St., 07307. Tel: 201-659-5948.
Sisters of Christian Charity 4; Lay Teachers 14; Students 331.
Catechesis/Religious Programs—Students 145.
Convent—Tel: 201-659-5644.

19—OUR LADY OF CZESTOCHOWA, (1911) (Polish), Revs. Thomas B. Iwanowski; Tadeusz Trela (Poland). In res., Rev. Alexander M. Santora.
Res., 120 Sussex St., 07302. Tel: 201-434-0798; Fax: 201-985-0918.
School—(1911), Marin Blvd. & York St., 07302. Tel: 201-434-2405.
Lay Teachers 11; Students 185.
Convent—Tel: 201-434-5579.

20—OUR LADY OF MERCY, (1963), Revs. John J. Cryan; Bartley P. Baker; Victor E. Paloma; Deacon Nicholas Fargo.
Res., 40 Sullivan Dr., 07305. Tel: 201-434-7500; Fax: 201-432-2885.
School—254 Bartholdi Ave., 07305. Tel: 201-434-4091; Fax: 201-434-8405.
Lay Teachers 30; Students 646.
Convent—Tel: 201-451-4615.
Catechesis/Religious Programs—Students 156.

21—CHURCH OF OUR LADY OF SORROWS, (1914), Rev. James F. O'Brien; Sr. Alice McCoy, O.P., Pastoral Assoc.
Res., 93-95 Clerk St., 07305. Tel: 201-433-0626; Fax: 201-433-2928.

22—OUR LADY OF VICTORIES, (1917), Revs. John E. Basil, M.Div., Admin.; Walter J.F. Swenson, Pastor Emeritus; Seamus Clements, C.S.Sp.; John Nadura.
Res., 2217 John F. Kennedy Memorial Blvd., 07304-1497. Tel: 201-433-4152.
School—(1930), Tel: 201-434-4040; Fax: 201-434-5356.
Lay Teachers 21; Students 525.

23—ST. PATRICK'S, (1869), Revs. Eugene P. Squeo, J.D.; Francis E. Schiller, J.D.; Edward J. Kearney; Jean-Marie Fritz Ligonde.
Res., 492 Bramhall Ave., 07304. Tel: 201-332-8600; Fax: 201-324-3919.
School—(1909), Tel: 201-433-4664.
Sisters of Charity of St. Elizabeth 4; Lay Teachers 32; Students 500.
Convent—345 Pacific Ave., 07304. Tel: 201-451-2765.

24—PARISH OF THE RESURRECTION, (1997). (Formerly Parishes of St. Boniface, St. Bridget, St. Mary, St. Michael and St. Peter). Very Rev. Gregory J. Studerus, V.F.; Rev. Msgr. William J. Reilly; Revs. Richard J. Caplice, S.J.; Hugh V. Fitzgerald; John Martin; Vincent Sullivan, S.J.; Bro. Louis N. Mauro, S.J.; Deacons Pedro Gonzalez; Jaime Ortiz; Leopoldo Polanco. Pastoral Assocs.: Sr. Grace Reape, S.C.; Sr. Mercedes Salinas, S.C.; Sr. Jean Young, S.C.
Parish Office: 370 Montgomery St., 07302. Tel: 201-434-8500; Fax: 201-333-1816.
Churches—St. Boniface, 262 First St., 07302.; St. Bridget, 372 Montgomery St., 07302.; St. Michael. (Shrine of St. Jude Pepetual Novena) 252 Ninth St., 07302.; St. Mary, 219 Third St., 07302.; St. Peter, 144 Grand Street, 07302.
Schools—St. Bridget Elementary, (1873), Tel: 201-432-3588.; St. Mary Elementary, (1868), 209 Third St., 07302. Tel: 201-653-3333.; St. Peter's Elementary, (1864), 153 York St., 07302. Tel: 201-434-8154; Fax: 201-434-1613.
High School—St. Mary, 209 Third St., 07302. Tel: 201-656-8008; Fax: 201-653-4818.

25—ST. PAUL OF THE CROSS, (1868), Revs. George A. Ligos; Andres J. Reyes, Admin.; Stanley M. Lobo. In res., Rev. Msgr. Robert E. Duffy.
Res., 156 Hancock Ave., 07307. Tel: 201-798-7900.
School—(1869), 211 Sherman Ave., 07307. Tel: 201-659-6919.
Sisters of Charity 4; Lay Teachers 10; Students 252.
Catechesis/Religious Programs—Students 315.
Convent—Tel: 201-659-1414.

26—ST. PAUL'S, (1861), Revs. Robert Antczak; Jose Gamba; John F. Bauman.
Res., 14 Greenville Ave., 07305. Tel: 201-433-8500; Fax: 201-433-9886.
School—(1872), 193 Old Bergen Rd., 07305. Tel: 201-435-8204; Fax: 210-435-8205.
Sisters of St. Dominic 1; Lay Teachers 19; Students 313.
Catechesis/Religious Programs—Tel: 201-433-1054.
Students 155.
Convent—Tel: 201-333-2443.

27—ST. PETER'S, (1831) (Hispanic). Merged with St. Boniface, St. Bridget, St. Mary and St. Michael to form Parish of the Resurrection, June 1997. For parish inquiries call Tel: 201-434-8500.

28—SACRED HEART, (1905), Rev. Charles T. Quinn, O.P., Pastor; Sr. Elaine Keenan, O.P., Pastoral Assoc.
Res., 183 Bayview Ave., 07305. Tel: 201-332-6771 (Parish); 332-6773 (Priory); Fax: 201-332-8375.
School—(1913), 183 Bayview Ave., 07305. Tel: 201-332-7111; Fax: 201-332-7160. Sr. Maureen Killough, S.C., Prin.
Sisters of Charity 5; Sisters of St. Joseph 2; Lay Teachers 15; Students 411.
Sacred Heart Priory—Tel: 201-332-8667; Fax: 201-332-8375. Revs. Gerard Maley, O.P., Prior; Hugh D. Burns, O.P.; Edward L. Martin, O.P.; Henry Camacho, O.P.; Val La France, O.P.; Bro. John Jude Locchetto, O.P.

Kearny, Hudson Co., St. Cecilia's (1893), Revs. Norbert Laskowski; Michael Ward; Brendan H. Quinn. In res., Rev. Msgr. Francis R. Seymour; Rev. Patrick R.C. Wilhelm.
Res., 120 Kearny Ave., 07032. Tel: 201-991-1116; Fax: 201-998-4437.
School—(1896), 114 Chestnut St., 07032. Tel: 201-991-9142.
Lay Teachers 11; Students 220.
Catechesis/Religious Programs—Students 310.

Our Lady of Sorrows (1915) (Lithuanian), Rev. Michael J. O'Brien, Admin.; Rev. Msgr. Dominick A. Pocus, Pastor Emeritus; Rev. Henry M. Naddeo; Deacon Leonard J. Mackesy.
Res., 136 Davis Ave., 07032. Tel: 201-998-4616; Fax: 201-997-8659.
Catechesis/Religious Programs—Students 150.
Convent—Tel: 201-991-7983.

St. Stephen's (1904), Very Rev. Msgr. Michael J. Desmond, V.E.; Revs. Scott F. Attanasio; David S. McLaughlin.
Res., 141 Washington Ave., 07032. Tel: 201-998-3314; Fax: 201-998-4924.
School—(1904), 131 Midland Ave., 07032. Tel: 201-991-3217; Fax: 201-998-4924.
Sisters of Charity 2; Lay Teachers 15; Students 260.
Catechesis/Religious Programs—Tel: 201-991-0236. D.R.E.: Sr. Rita Kearney, S.S.J.; Dorothy Reid.
Students 560.
Convent—Tel: 201-991-1422.

Kenilworth, Union Co., St. Theresa's (1949), Revs. Joseph S. Bejgrowicz; Charles Kern, (Retired); Dominick Lenoci; Louis Scarpa, Pastoral Assoc. In res., Rev. George M. Keating.
Res., 541 Washington Ave., 07033. Tel: 908-272-4444; Fax: 908-272-2252.
School—540 Washington Ave., 07033. Tel: 908-276-7220. Sr. Mary Louise Aguirre, F.M.A.
Salesian Sisters 3; Lay Teachers 14; Students 275.
Catechesis/Religious Programs—Tel: 908-276-4881. Sr. Monique Huart D.R.E.
Students 435.
Convent—Tel: 908-276-5028.

Leonia, Bergen Co., St. John the Evangelist's (1912), Revs. Robert Traudt, O.Carm.; Ronald Gray, O.Carm.; Bradley Peterson, O.Carm.
Res., 235 Harrison St., 07605. Tel: 201-947-4545.
School—260 Harrison St., 07605. Tel: 201-944-4361; Fax: 201-944-2195.
School Sisters of Notre Dame 1; Lay Teachers 9; Students 235.
Catechesis/Religious Programs—Tel: 201-944-4346.
Students 325.
Convent—Tel: 201-944-4362.

Linden, Union Co.,

1—ST. ELIZABETH'S, (1909), Revs. Karl J. Roesch, O.S.B.; Benedict Worry, O.S.B.; Patrick M. Hurley, O.S.B.; Wilfred Schulz, O.S.B.; Deacon Donald P. Niles.
Res., 179 Hussa St., 07036. Tel: 908-486-2514; Fax: 908-486-1757.
School—(1927), 170 Hussa St., 07036. Tel: 908-486-2507; Fax: 908-486-1757.
Dominican Sisters of Caldwell 6; Lay Teachers 20; Students 500.
Convent—Tel: 908-486-2737.
Catechesis/Religious Programs—170 Hussa St., Tel: 908-486-2509.
Students 500.

2—HOLY FAMILY, (Tremley Point) (1955) (Slovak), Rev. Pierce D. Byrne; Rev. Msgr. Michael A. Komar, Pastor Emeritus; Rev. Eugene Diurczak.
Res., 210 Monroe St., 07036. Tel: 908-862-1060; Fax: 908-862-7331.
Church—2709 Parkway Ave., 07036.

3—ST. JOHN THE APOSTLE, (1948), Rev. Msgr. Richard M. McGuinness; Revs. Brian McFadden; Joseph A. Meagher; Deacons Guy Paredes, (Retired); George Ross. In res., Rev. Joseph Sheehan, (Retired).
Res., 1805 Penbrook Ter., 07036. Tel: 908-486-6363; Fax: 908-486-5345.
Catechesis/Religious Programs—Tel: 732-388-1253. Sr. Cynthia Johnson, D.R.E.
Students 450.
Convent—Tel: 732-388-3768.

4—ST. THERESA OF THE CHILD JESUS, (1925) (Polish), Revs. Felix R. Marciniak; Marek Chachlowski (Poland); Gene R. Mixtacki. Pastoral Associates: Sr. Mary Andrew Borys, C.S.S.F.; Sr. Maria Emilia Zdeb, S.S.N.D.; Deacon Alexander Czerepka.
Res., 122 Liberty St., 07036. Tel: 908-862-1116; Fax: 908-862-2930.
Church—131 E. Edgar Rd., 07036.
School—(1930), 705 Clinton St., 07036. Tel: 908-862-7551.
Lay Teachers 13; Students 200.
Catechesis/Religious Programs—Tel: 908-862-1388.
Students 351.
Convent—18 Liberty Ave., 07036. Tel: 908-862-4820.

Little Ferry, Bergen Co., St. Margaret of Cortona (1941), Revs. James O. Sheerin; William A. Lusik.
Res., 31 Chamberlain Ave., 07643. Tel: 201-641-2988; Fax: 201-641-0664.
Catechesis/Religious Programs—Tel: 201-641-3937. Sr. Dorothy A. Donovan, S.S.J., D.R.E.
Students 435.

Livingston, Essex Co., St. Philomena (1927), Rev. Msgr. Edward J. Eilert; Rev. Msgr. William J. Daly, Pastor Emeritus; Rev. Stephen A. Kopacz; Rev. Msgr. Robert T. Lennon; Rev. Lawrence J. Fama; Deacon Joseph Francione; Anita Foley, Pastoral Assoc.
Res., 386 S. Livingston Ave., 07039. Tel: 973-992-0994; Fax: 973-992-0970.
Schools—Aquinas Academy, (1952), 388 S. Livingston Ave., 07039. Tel: 973-992-1587; Fax: 973-992-1742. Sr. Patricia Tavis, Prin.
Dominican Sisters of Caldwell 2; Lay Teachers 29; Students 299; Early Childhood Center, Tel: 973-992-5181; Fax: 973-992-2652.
Lay Teachers 16; Students 109.
Catechesis/Religious Programs—Tel: 973-992-4466.
Students 392.
Convent—Tel: 973-992-1581.

St. Raphael (1961), Rev. Msgr. G. Thomas Burns; Revs. Andrew Prachar; Anthony Ciorra, Weekend Assoc. In res., Rev. John E. O'Brien.
Res., 346 E. Mt. Pleasant Ave., 07039. Tel: 973-992-9490; Fax: 973-740-0236.
Catechesis/Religious Programs—Students 550.

Lodi, Bergen Co., St. Francis de Sales (1854), Revs. Charles F. Theobald; Jesus A. Encisco; Yesudasan Choondassery (India). In res., Rev. John B. Baron.
Res., 125 Union St., 07644. Tel: 973-779-4330; Fax: 973-779-8842. [CEM]
School—Mother Cabrini Interparochial, (1991), 123 Union St., 07644. Tel: 973-777-4635.
Felician Sisters 2; Lay Teachers 12; Students 218.
Catechesis/Religious Programs—Tel: 973-779-3949.
Students 140.
Convent—Tel: 973-773-4366.

St. Joseph's (1913) (Italian), Revs. Hector DiNardo, C.R.M.; Americo Salvi, C.R.M., Pastoral Assoc. In res., Rev. Gabriel M. Lucarelli, C.R.M.
Res., 40 Spring St., 07644. Tel: 973-779-0643; Fax: 973-447-1442.
School—Mother Cabrini Interparochial School, (1991), 123 Union St., 07644. Tel: 973-777-4635.
Lay Teachers 12; Students 218.
Catechesis/Religious Programs—Tel: 973-779-8275.
Students 314.

Lyndhurst, Bergen Co., Sacred Heart (1905), Revs. Charles J. Miller; Steven Conner; Juancho De Leon; Raymond Rodriguez. In res., Rev. Alan Guglielmo.
Res., 324 Ridge Rd., 07071. Tel: 201-438-1147; Fax: 201-507-5861. [CEM]
School—620 Valley Brook Ave., 07071. Tel: 201-939-4277; Fax: 201-896-1016.
Sisters 1; Lay Teachers 28; Students 561.

Catechesis/Religious Programs—Tel: 201-935-3094.
Students 355.

Our Lady of Mount Carmel (1966) (Italian), Revs. Nazareno Orandi; Thomas J. Kenna.
Res., 197 Kingsland Ave., 07071. Tel: 201-935-1177; Fax: 201-935-5675.
Catechesis/Religious Programs—146 Copeland Ave., 07071. Tel: 201-935-5467.
Students 250.

St. Michael's (1912) (Polish), Revs. Richard S. Czachorowski; Joseph Szklarski; John Borowik; Deacon Vincent Serzan. In res., Rev. Msgr. James Mc Menemie.
Res., 624 Page Ave., 07071. Tel: 201-939-1161; Fax: 201-939-7571.
School—(1951), 622 Page Ave., 07071. Tel: 201-939-0350.
Felician Sisters 3; Lay Teachers 8; Students 149.
Convent—Tel: 201-438-0430.

Mahwah, Bergen Co., Immaculate Heart of Mary (1915) (Polish), Revs. Joseph Tyminski, S.D.B.; Alfred J. Sokol, S.D.B.; Joseph S. Bajorek, S.D.B.
Res., 47 Island Rd., 07430. Tel: 201-529-3517; Fax: 201-529-4401.
School—St. Paul's Interparochial School, (1991). (See St. Paul's, Ramsey. Tel: 201-327-1108; Fax: 201-327-6197).
Sisters of Charity 2; Lay Teachers 12; Students 255.

Immaculate Conception (1929), Rev. M. Christen Beirne; S. Geraldine Muller, Pastoral Assoc. In res., Rev. James R. White.
Res., 900 Darlington Ave., 07430. Tel: 201-327-1276; Fax: 201-327-0185.
School—St. Paul's Interparochial School, Tel: 201-327-1108; Fax: 201-327-6197.
Catechesis/Religious Programs—Tel: 201-825-0333. Mrs. Roberta Medalis, D.R.E.
Students 214.

Maplewood, Essex Co., Immaculate Heart of Mary (1955), Revs. Dominic G. Fuccile; Frank J. Rocchi.
Res., 280 Parker Ave., 07040. Tel: 973-763-5019; Fax: 973-763-3622.
School—(1957), 276 Parker Ave., 07040. Tel: 973-763-0031.
Lay Teachers 14; Students 206.

St. Joseph's (1914), Revs. Thomas Wisniewski; Joseph Ferraro; John T. Browne, O.S.B.
Res., 767 Prospect St., 07040. Tel: 973-761-5933; Fax: 973-761-6705.
School—(1930), 240 Franklin Ave., 07040. Tel: 973-761-4033.
Lay Teachers 14; Students 164.
Catechesis/Religious Programs—Students 205.

Maywood, Bergen Co., Our Lady Queen of Peace (1950), Revs. Joseph P. Pietropinto; Stephen J. Cinque; James A. Hamel; Deacon Anthony Balistieri; Sr. Louise DelCarpine, Pastoral Assoc. In res., Rev. Paul Nolan.
Res., 400 Maywood Ave., 07607. Tel: 201-845-9566; Fax: 201-845-3742.
Catechesis/Religious Programs—Tel: 201-845-9545.
Students 358.
Convent—Tel: 201-845-9568.

Midland Park, Bergen Co., Nativity (1955), Revs. John R. O'Connell; James P. Whelan. In res., Rev. Kurt Holderied, O.Carm.
Res., 315 Prospect St., 07432. Tel: 201-444-6362; Fax: 201-444-5056.
School—St. Thomas More Interparochial School, 321 Prospect St., 07432. Tel: 201-447-3088; Fax: 201-447-4145.
Lay Teachers 17; Students 221.
Catechesis/Religious Programs—Tel: 201-447-1776.
Students 443.

Montclair, Essex Co., Immaculate Conception (1864), Rev. Msgr. Timothy J. Shugrue; Revs. Frank J. Burla; Donald P. Gleeson. Pastoral Assocs.: Sr. Margaret Tierney, S.C.; Sr. Cora Marie McGuire, M.S.B.T. In res., Rev. Louis Pambello.
Res., 30 N. Fullerton Ave., 07042. Tel: 973-744-5650; Fax: 973-744-7936. [CEM]
Pre-School—(1997), Tegakwita Academy, 17-19 Munn St., 07042. Tel: 973-744-5282.
Sisters 1; Lay Teachers 2; Students 15.
High School—(1919), 33 Cottage Pl., 07042. Tel: 973-744-7445; Fax: 973-744-3926.
Sisters 5; Lay Teachers 22; Students 250.
Catechesis/Religious Programs—Tel: 973-744-6672.
Students 235.

Our Lady of Mt. Carmel (1907) (Italian), Revs. Thomas J. Petrillo; Donald Cialene; Deacon Henry Haas.
Res., 94 Pine St., 07042. Tel: 973-744-1074; Fax: 973-744-0205.

St. Peter Claver (1932), Rev. John P. Nickas; Deacons John Coffey; Wilfred Leconte.
Res., 56 Elmwood Ave., 07042. Tel: 973-783-4852; Fax: 973-783-3261.

Moonachie, Bergen Co., St. Anthony (1931). Closed. For inquiries for parish records contact Seton Hall University Archives: South Orange. Tel.: 973-761-9476; Fax: 973-761-9550.

Mountainside, Union Co., Our Lady of Lourdes (1958), Revs. Patrick J. Leonard, Admin.; Piotr Michota; Paul J. Prevosto; Gerard J. McGarry, Pastor Emeritus.
Res., 300 Central Ave., 07092. Tel: 908-232-1162; Fax: 908-232-0776.
School—Holy Trinity Interparochial School, (1991). (See Holy Trinity, Westfield. Tel: 908-233-0484).
Lay Teachers 15; Students 312.
Catechesis/Religious Programs—Tel: 908-233-1777. Sr. Brenda E. Rowe, M.P.F., D.R.E.
Students 300.

New Milford, Bergen Co., Ascension (1953), Rev. Msgr. Thomas P. Ivory; Revs. Joy Alappat (India); James Brown; Deacon Harold Bates.
Res., 256 Azalea Dr., 07646. Tel: 201-836-8961; Fax: 201-836-5896.
School—1092 Carnation Dr., 07646. Tel: 201-836-7074.
Sisters of St. Dominic 2; Students 241.
Catechesis/Religious Programs—Tel: 201-836-3085.
Students 350.

New Providence, Union Co., Our Lady of Peace (1942), Rev. Sean Cunneen; Rev. Msgr. Paul J. Hayes, Pastor Emeritus; Rev. Robert Cio. In res., Rev. Thomas Hart.
Res., 111 South St., 07974. Tel: 908-464-7600; Fax: 908-508-1845.
School—99 South St., 07974. Tel: 908-464-8657.
Sisters of St. Joseph 1; Lay Teachers 15; Students 228.
Catechesis/Religious Programs—Tel: 908-464-8156.
Students 400.
Convent—Tel: 908-464-8223.

North Arlington, Bergen Co., Queen of Peace (1922), Rev. Msgr. Thomas G. Madden; Revs. Samuel Monaco; Peter Smutelovic; Stephen D. D'Andrea; Deacons William R. Benedetto; William H. Myers. In res., Rev. William J. Fadrowski.
Res., 10 Franklin Pl., 07031. Tel: 201-997-0700; Fax: 201-997-6214.
School—(1925), 21 Church Pl., 07031. Tel: 201-998-8222.
Sisters of St. Joseph of Chestnut Hill 4; Lay Teachers 19; Students 460.
High School—(1930), 191 Rutherford Pl., 07031. Tel: 201-998-8227; Fax: 201-998-3040.
Brothers of the Christian School 7; Sisters 6; Lay Teachers 49; Students 807.
Catechesis/Religious Programs—Tel: 201-998-0901.
Students 475.
Convent—Tel: 201-997-2141.

North Bergen, Hudson Co., Sacred Heart (Hudson Heights Station) (1917) (Polish), Rev. Anthony G. Robak.
Mailing Address: Box 9007, 07047.
Res., 246 Hudson Pl., Cliffside Park, 07010. Tel: 201-943-0305; Fax: 201-943-2676.
School—St. Elizabeth Seton Interparochial School, (1991). Co-Sponsored. (See St. John's Parish, Fairview. Tel: 201-945-2212).

St. Brigid (1900), Revs. Jorge Chacon; Luis C. Sanchez.
Res., 4501 Liberty Ave., 07047. Tel: 201-863-0160; Fax: 201-863-0173.

Our Lady of Fatima (1963), Rev. John J. Korbelak; Rev. Msgr. George O'Gorman, Pastor Emeritus; Rev. Eric Kowalski.
Res., 8016 Kennedy Blvd., 07047. Tel: 201-869-7244; Fax: 201-869-0940.
Catechesis/Religious Programs—Tel: 201-869-0506.
Students 307.

North Caldwell, Essex Co., Notre Dame (1962), Rev. Msgr. Edward J. Ciuba; Rev. Anthony J. Randazzo; Sr. Carol Jaruszewski, R.S.M., Pastoral Assoc.
Res., 358 Central Ave., 07006. Tel: 973-226-0979; Fax: 973-226-4118.
Catechesis/Religious Programs—Tel: 973-228-3338.
Students 494.

Northvale, Bergen Co., St. Anthony's (1890) (Italian), Rev. Msgr. William J. Koplik; Rev. Robert J. Halliwell. In res., Rev. Thomas Norton.
Res., 199 Walnut St., 07647. Tel: 201-768-1177; Fax: 201-768-2522.
School—Holy Family School. (See Immaculate Conception, Norwood). Tel: 201-768-1605; Fax: 201-768-8006.
Catechesis/Religious Programs—Tel: 201-768-5945.
Students 265.

Norwood, Bergen Co., Immaculate Conception (1921), Rev. Charles B. Urnick; Deacon James Puliatte.
Res., 211 Summit St., 07648. Tel: 201-768-1600; Fax: 201-768-8006.
School—Holy Family Interparochial School, (1991), 200 Summit St., 07648. Tel: 201-768-1605; Fax: 201-768-0796. Miss Patricia Bliss., Prin.
Sisters 2; Lay Teachers 19; Students 330.
Catechesis/Religious Programs—Tel: 201-768-1771; Fax: 201-768-8006. Sr. Susanne Reynolds, S.S.J.
Students 300.

Nutley, Essex Co., St. Mary's (1876), Revs. Leonard Dembow; Matthew Kunnath; George Sharp.
Res., 17 Msgr. Owens Pl., 07110. Tel: 973-235-1100; Fax: 973-661-0233.
School—Good Shepherd Academy. (See Holy Family, Nutley. Tel: 973-667-2049). Tel: 973-667-0026; Fax: 973-661-1714.
Catechesis/Religious Programs—Tel: 973-667-8239; Fax: 973-661-0233.
Students 700.
Convent—Tel: 973-667-0611.

Holy Family (1909) (Italian), Revs. Peter J. Zaccardo; Francis A. Heinen; Albert Malgeri.
Res., 28 Brookline Ave., 07110. Tel: 973-667-0026; Fax: 973-661-1714.
School—Good Shepherd Academy, (1992). Co-sponsored by 3 area churches. 24 Brookline Ave., 07110. Tel: 973-667-2049; Fax: 973-661-9259.
Religious Teachers Filippini 5; Lay Teachers 19; Students 455.
Catechesis/Religious Programs—Tel: 973-667-6018.
Students 789.
Convent—Tel: 973-667-2050.

Our Lady of Mount Carmel (1925) (Polish), Thomas J. Ciba, M.P.A.; Rev. Richard Odoemela.
Res., 120 Prospect St., 07110. Tel: 973-667-2580; Fax: 973-667-0648.
School—Good Shepherd Academy. (See Holy Family, Nutley). Tel: 973-667-2049.
Catechesis/Religious Programs—Students 194.

Oakland, Bergen Co., Our Lady of Perpetual Help (1960), Rev. Robert A. Connors. In res., Rev. George L. Mader.
Res., 25 Purdue Ave., 07436. Tel: 201-337-7596; Fax: 201-337-7810.
Catechesis/Religious Programs—Tel: 201-337-7596, Ext. 21.
Students 453.
Convent—Tel: 201-337-5364.

Old Tappan, Bergen Co., St. Pius X (1954), Rev. Joseph H. Murphy; Deacon Richard G. Hodges.
Res., 5 Charles Pl., 07675. Tel: 201-664-0913; Fax: 201-664-1013.
School—Holy Family Interparochial School. (See Immaculate Conception, Norwood. Tel: 201-768-1605). Fax: 201-768-0796.
Catechesis/Religious Programs—Tel: 201-664-0927.
Students 325.

Oradell, Bergen Co., St. Joseph's (1903), Revs. George M. Reilly; Peter J. Palmisano; Joseph Duykim Tran; Joseph F. Coda, Weekend Asst.
Res., 105 Harrison St., New Milford, 07646. Tel: 201-261-0148; Fax: 201-261-0369.
School—(1939), 305 Elm St., 07649. Tel: 201-261-2388; Fax: 201-261-0830.
Sisters 7; Lay Teachers 23; Students 515.
Catechesis/Religious Programs—300 Elm St., 07649. Tel: 201-265-8880; Fax: 201-634-0640. Annette Ziegler, D.R.E.
Students 698.
Convent—Tel: 201-265-0289.

Orange, Essex Co.,

1—St. John's, (1851) (Hispanic), Rev. Msgr. Ricardo Gonzalez; Rev. Msgr. John J. Fahy, Pastor Emeritus; Revs. Manuel Revuelto; Edward G. Bradley, Weekend Asst.
Res., 94 Ridge St., 07050. Tel: 973-674-0110. [CEM]
School—(1855), 455 White St., 07050. Tel: 973-674-8951; Fax: 973-674-6126.
Sisters of Charity 5; Lay Teachers 10; Students 387.
Convent—Tel: 973-673-1263.

2—Our Lady of the Valley, (1873), Revs. Floyd Rotunno; Dennis E. Reiff. In res., Rev. Dioscoro P. Bocod.
Res., 510 Valley St., 07050. Tel: 973-674-7500; Fax: 973-672-8341.

3—St. Venantius, (1886). Merged For inquiries for parish records contact St. Andrew Kim Parish, Orange. Tel: 201-673-1366.

4—MT. CARMEL, (1896) (Italian), Revs. Achilles Cassiere, O.F.M.Cap.; Edward Henning, O.F.M.Cap. In res., Rev. Alexander Davis, O.F.M.Cap.
Res., 103 S. Center St., 07050. Tel: 973-674-2052; Fax: 973-675-1342.
School—(1939), 268 Capuchin Way, 07050. Tel: 973-673-5933; Fax: 973-677-2166. Sr. Margaret Mary Hanlon, M.P.F., Prin.
Religious Teachers Filippini 1; Lay Teachers 10; Students 235.
Convent—264 Capuchin Way, 07050. Tel: 973-678-7720.

5—HOLY SPIRIT, (1931). Merged For inquiries for parish records contact Holy Spirit-Our Lady Help of Christians, East Orange. Tel: 201-673-1077.

6—ST. ANDREW KIM, (1972) (Korean), Rev. Augustin C. Park. In res., Revs. Paul Kang; Luis Kim; Daniel Suh; David Yang.
Res., 257 Central Ave., 07050. Tel: 973-673-1366; 672-6650; Fax: 973-673-2030.
Catechesis/Religious Programs—Students 245.
Convent—Tel: 973-674-1618.

Palisades Park, Bergen Co., St. Michael's (1912), Revs. James F. Reilly; Vincent J. Quinn, Pastor Emeritus; David C. Hubba.
Res., 19 Central Blvd., E., 07650. Tel: 201-944-1061; Fax: 201-947-1798.
Schools—Notre Dame Interparochial, Elementary Division, (1991) (Grades 2-8) 312 First St., 07650. Tel: 201-947-5262; Fax: 201-945-3796.; Primary Division, (1991) (Grades PreK-1) 555 Prospect Ave., Ridgefield, 07657. Tel: 201-943-5757. Sr. Ellen McMahon, Prin.
Catechesis/Religious Programs—324 First St., 07650. Tel: 201-944-0070; Fax: 201-947-1798. Mary Fleischbein, D.R.E.
Students 190.

St. Nicholas (1923) (Italian), Rev. Antonio L. da Silva, S.D.V. (Brazil).
Res., 442 Brinkerhoff Ave., 07650. Tel: 201-944-1154; 944-1138; Fax: 201-944-9510.
School—Notre Dame Interparochial School, (1991). (See St. Matthew, Ridgefield for Primary Division. Tel: 201-943-5757) (See St. Michael Palisades Park for Elementary Division. Tel: 201-947-5262).

Paramus, Bergen Co., Our Lady of the Visitation (1952), Rev. Msgr. Francis R. Lo Bianco; Revs. Patrick R. Flannery; Ulysses L. Ubalde. In res., Rev. Joseph S. Chiang.
Res., 234 Farview Ave., 07652. Tel: 201-261-6080; Fax: 201-261-2995.
School—Visitation Academy, (1991). Co-Sponsored. 222 Farview Ave., 07652. Tel: 201-262-6067; Fax: 201-261-4613. Sr. Louise Parisot, S.C., Prin.
Sisters 3; Lay Teachers 17; Students 346.
Catechesis/Religious Programs—Tel: 201-265-3812. Mrs. Barbara D'Arrigo, D.R.E.
Students 518.

Annunciation (1953), Revs. Michael J. Sheehan; Charles Pinyan; Deacons Joseph Niland; William D. Joyce; Sr. Rita Dermody, S.C., Pastoral Assoc. In res., Rev. John M. McCrone.
Res., 50 W. Midland Ave., 07652. Tel: 201-261-6322; Fax: 201-261-6227.
School—(1991). (See Visitation Academy, Our Lady of the Visitation Parish, Paramus). Tel: 201-262-6067.
Catechesis/Religious Programs—Tel: 201-265-5677.
Students 362.

Carmelite Chapel of St. Therese (1970), Revs. Brice E. Riordan, O.Carm., Dir.; Norman G. Werling, O.Carm.; Zachary Monet, O.Carm.; Daniel Smith, O.Carm.; Richard W. Bradley, O.Carm.
Res., 135 Gertrude St., 07652. Tel: 201-845-6392.
Church—Bergen Mall, 07652. Tel: 201-845-6115.

Park Ridge, Bergen Co., Our Lady of Mercy (1902), Revs. Charles P. Granstrand; Eugene P. Heyndricks; Rev. Msgr. James C. Turro, S.T.L., S.S.L., A.M., Weekend Asst. In res., Rev. Msgr. Carl D. Hinrichsen.
Res., 2 Fremont Ave., 07656. Tel: 201-391-5315; Fax: 201-391-5614.
School—Our Lady of Mercy Interparochial School, (1950), 25 Fremont Ave., 07656. Tel: 201-391-3838; Fax: 201-391-5614.
Lay Teachers 28; Students 422.
Catechesis/Religious Programs—50 Pascack Rd., 07656. Tel: 201-391-3590.
Students 625.
Convent—Tel: 201-391-7788.

Plainfield, Union Co., St. Mary (1851), Revs. Kenneth Jones; Francisco R. Ponce; Renzo L. Scaramella; Deacon Martin P. Macaluso. In res., Revs. Aloysius S. Carney; Henry T. Kaminski.
Res., 516 W. Sixth St., 07060. Tel: 908-756-0085; Fax: 908-756-1658. [CEM]
Catechesis/Religious Programs—Tel: 908-561-7143.
Students 306.
Convents—524 W. Sixth St., 07060. Missionary Sisters of the Most Blessed Sacrament & Mary Immaculate
Sisters 3; 513 Liberty St., 07060. Tel: 908-754-1978. Missionaries of Charity, (Contemplative)
Sisters 21.

St. Bernard's (1921), Revs. Joseph F. Barbone; Thomas C. Roberts.
Office: 368 Sumner Ave., P.O. Box 2844, 07062. Tel: 908-756-3393; Fax: 908-756-3059.
Rectory—1235 George St., 07062.

St. Stanislaus Kostka (1919), Rev. Henry T. Kaminski.
Res., St. Mary's Rectory, 516 W. Sixth St., 07060. Tel: 201-756-9178.
Church—1020 W. Seventh St., 07063. (For Churches in North and South Plainfield see Diocese of Metuchen).

Rahway, Union Co., St. Mary's (1854), Revs. Michael J. Feketie; Edward J. Myers; J. Rico Madrilejos; Joseph Mukalel; Deacons J. William Courtney; James O'Neill.
Res., 232 Central Ave., 07065. Tel: 732-388-0082. [CEM]
School—(1873), 244 Central Ave., 07065. Tel: 732-382-0011; Fax: 732-382-4784.
Lay Teachers 18; Students 267.
Catechesis/Religious Programs—Tel: 201-382-0004.
Students 308.

St. Mark's (1871) (German), Rev. Eugene J. Kasper.
Res., 287 Hamilton St., 07065. Tel: 732-499-9230.
Catechesis/Religious Programs—Tel: 732-388-7036.
Students 100.

Ramsey, Bergen Co., St. Paul (1904), Rev. Msgr. Thomas A. Donato; Revs. James R. O'Neill, Pastor Emeritus; Richard J. Kelly.
Res., 200 Wyckoff Ave., 07446. Tel: 201-327-0976; Fax: 201-327-6197.
School—St. Paul's Interparochial School, 187 Wyckoff Ave., 07446. Tel: 201-327-1108.
Dominican Sisters of Sparkill 1; Lay Teachers 20; Students 255.
Catechesis/Religious Programs—Tel: 201-327-8010.
Students 825.

Ridgefield, Bergen Co., St. Matthew's (1899), Revs. Timothy J. Horgan; Michael M. Walters; Deacon Gustave Grieder. In res., Rev. Msgr. James Johnson; Rev. John E. Komar.
Res., 555 Prospect Ave., 07657. Tel: 201-945-3500; Fax: 201-945-3796.
School—Notre Dame Interparochial Primary Division, (1991) (Grades PreK-1) Edgewater Ave., 07657. Tel: 201-943-5757; Fax: 201-943-4209; 947-8319.
Sisters 2; Lay Teachers 23; Students 538.
Catechesis/Religious Programs—Students 250.

Ridgefield Park, Bergen Co., St. Francis of Assisi (1890), Revs. Joseph C. Doyle; James Teti; Sr. Catherine Higgins, S.C., Pastoral Assoc.; Deacon Nicholas Simonelli; Brenda McWeeney, Pastoral Assoc.
Res., 114 Mt. Vernon St., 07660. Tel: 201-641-6464; Fax: 201-641-2282.
School—(1915), 110 Mt. Vernon St., 07660. Tel: 201-641-9159; Fax: 201-641-4091. Sr. Patricia Meidhof, Prin.
Sisters 3; Lay Teachers 19; Students 320.
Catechesis/Religious Programs—Tel: 201-641-9467.
Students 330.

Ridgewood, Bergen Co., Our Lady of Mount Carmel (1889), Rev. Msgr. Ronald J. Rozniak, V.G.; Revs. Robert G. Gibney, Pastor Emeritus; Peter Baldacchino; Anthony R. Lipari; Patrick M. Mulewski; Sr. Lucy Sullivan, S.C., Pastoral Assoc.; Deacon Robert V. Thomann. In res., Rev. Joseph A. Stulb.
Res., 1 Passaic St., 07450-4309. Tel: 201-444-2000; Fax: 201-444-2002.
School—St. Catharine's Interparochial School. (See St. Catharine, Glen Rock). Tel: 201-445-0622.
Catechesis/Religious Programs—Tel: 201-444-0211; Fax: 201-444-4421. Sr. Bernard Mary Herlihy, M.S.B.T., D.R.E.
Students 999.
Convent—Tel: 201-445-2077.

River Edge, Bergen Co., St. Peter the Apostle (1948), Revs. Robert H. Slipe; Michael J. German; Rev. Msgr. David J. Casazza, Pastor Emeritus; Rev. Michael A. Saporito; Deacon Edward Bowen.
Res., 445 Fifth Ave., 07661. Tel: 201-261-3366; Fax: 201-261-0117.
School—St. Peter Academy, (1952), 431 Fifth Ave., 07661. Tel: 201-261-3468; Fax: 201-261-4316.
Sisters 2; Lay Teachers 17; Students 279.
Catechesis/Religious Programs—Tel: 201-265-6019.
Students 424.
Convent—Tel: 201-845-9568.

Rochelle Park, Bergen Co., Sacred Heart (1917), Very Rev. Lewis V. Papera, V.F.; Rev. William O'Brien.
Res., 12 Terrace Ave., 07662. Tel: 201-843-1722; Fax: 201-843-3542.
School—(1991). Co-Sponsored. (See Visitation Academy, Our Lady of Visitation Parish, Paramus). Tel: 201-262-6067.
Catechesis/Religious Programs—Tel: 201-843-1077. Mary Ann Cassidy, D.R.E.
Students 251.

Roseland, Essex Co., Our Lady of the Blessed Sacrament (1955), Rev. Msgr. Louis F. Fimiani; Revs. Richard J. Chilmark; Edward R. Bognacki. Pastoral Assocs.: Sr. Rie Crowley, S.S.J., (Youth); Sr. Mary Ganly, S.S.J., (Sick & Homebound); Maurica Twaddell, (Sacramental Programs); Philip Mealey, (Liturgical Music).
Res., 28 Livingston Ave., 07068. Tel: 201-226-7288; Fax: 201-226-4893.
Catechesis/Religious Programs—Tel: 201-226-5251. Kathleen A. Detlet, Ph.D., D.R.E.
Students 567.

Roselle, Union Co., Church of St. Joseph the Carpenter (1895), Revs. George D. Gillen; Beaubrun Ardouin; John Spino.
Res., 157 E. Fourth Ave., 07203. Tel: 908-241-1250; Fax: 908-241-6311.
School—(1913), 150 E. Third Ave., 07203. Tel: 908-245-6560.
Sisters 3; Lay Teachers 17; Students 475.
Convent—135 E. Fourth Ave., 07203. Tel: 908-245-1594. Sisters of St. Joseph, Chestnut Hill.

Roselle Park, Union Co., The Assumption (1907), In res., Rev. Armand Mantia; Rev. Msgr. Edward G. Price, (Retired).
Res., 113 Chiego Pl., 07204. Tel: 908-245-1107.
Catechesis/Religious Programs—110 Chiego Pl., 07204. Tel: 908-245-6572.
Students 541.

Rutherford, Bergen Co., St. Mary's (1908), Revs. Michael J. Kreder, Admin.; John Gordon.
Res., 91 Home Ave., 07070. Tel: 201-438-2200; Fax: 201-438-1098.
School—(1916), 72 Chestnut St., 07070. Tel: 201-933-8410.
Lay Teachers 16; Students 330.
High School—(1928), 64 Chestnut St., 07070. Tel: 201-933-5220; Fax: 201-933-0834.
Lay Teachers 23; Students 342.
Catechesis/Religious Programs—Students 550.
Convent—Tel: 201-933-2910.

Saddle Brook, Bergen Co., St. Philip the Apostle (1953), Revs. Robert G. McBride; Matthew Fonseka; Richard J. Mroz; Deacons Paul Magarelli; Philip Salerno.
Res., 488 Saddle River Rd., 07663. Tel: 201-843-1888; Fax: 201-368-9161.
School—492 Saddle River Rd., 07663-4634. Tel: 201-843-2240; Fax: 201-843-3150.
Sisters 3; Lay Teachers 10; Students 245.
Catechesis/Religious Programs—Students 400.

Saddle River Borough, Bergen Co., St. Gabriel the Archangel (1952), Rev. Msgr. Robert J. Fuhrman; Revs. John J. O'Brien, S.J.; Timothy G. Graff.
Res., 3 W. Church Rd., 07458. Tel: 201-327-5663; Fax: 201-327-7063.
School—St. John's Academy. (See St. John's Parish, Hillsdale). Tel: 201-664-6364; Fax: 201-664-8096.
Catechesis/Religious Programs—Tel: 201-825-0275.
Students 235.

Scotch Plains, Union Co., St. Bartholomew (1948), Rev. Michael A. Merlucci; Rev. Msgr. Francis A. Reinbold, Pastor Emeritus; Revs. John J. Lester; Thomas A. Grogan. In res., Joy Alookaran (India).
Res., 2032 Westfield Ave., 07076. Tel: 908-322-5192; Fax: 908-322-2598.
School—St. Bartholomew Interparochial, (1950), Tel: 908-322-4265; Fax: 908-322-2598.
Religious Teachers Filippini 4; Lay Teachers 7; Students 239.
Catechesis/Religious Programs—Tel: 908-322-2359.
Students 430.
Convent—Tel: 908-322-5619.

Immaculate Heart of Mary (1964), Revs. John F. Kennedy; Ken Evans; Robert Paterson.
Res., 1571 S. Martine Ave., 07076. Tel: 908-889-2100; Fax: 908-889-9477.
Catechesis/Religious Programs—Tel: 908-889-6263; Fax: 908-889-6263.
Students 595.

Secaucus, Hudson Co., Immaculate Conception (1908), Rev. Msgr. Donald E. Guenther; Revs. Raymond T. Lukenda; Richard Corbett.
Res., 1219 Paterson Plank Rd., 07094. Tel: 201-863-4840; Fax: 201-863-3537.
School—(1949), 760 Post Pl., 07094. Tel: 201-864-9346.

School Sisters of Notre Dame 4; Lay Teachers 7; Students 242.
Catechesis / Religious Programs—Students 560.
Convent—Tel: 201-866-4752.

Short Hills, Essex Co., St. Rose of Lima (1852), Rev. Msgr. William P. Devine; Revs. Michael Charles Fugee; Kevin A. Gugliotta; Stanley E. Ortyl; Deacons Joseph M. Persinger; Daniel G. McCarren. In res., Rev. Msgr. Vincent P. Coburn.
Res., 50 Short Hills Ave., 07078. Tel: 973-379-3912; Fax: 973-379-6157. [CEM]
School—(1869), 52 Short Hills Ave., 07078. Tel: 973-379-3973; Fax: 973-379-3722.
Lay Teachers 27; Students 298.
Catechesis / Religious Programs—61 Short Hills Ave., 07078. Tel: 973-376-1960.
Students 484.

South Orange, Essex Co., Our Lady of Sorrows (1887), Rev. Msgr. John E. Doran; Revs. Marc A. Vicari; John A. Palasits.
Res., 217 Prospect St., 07079. Tel: 973-763-5454; Fax: 973-763-9506.
School—(1890), 172 Academy St., 07079. Tel: 973-763-5169; Fax: 973-378-9781.
Lay Teachers 27; Religious 1; Students 415.
Catechesis / Religious Programs—Students 465.

Springfield, Union Co., St. James (1923), Revs. Robert B. Stagg; Robert J. Piatkowski; Anthony J. Nardo; Deacons John M. Baltus; Jerry Bongiavanni; Sr. Roseann M. Treston, S.S.J., Pastoral Assoc.
Res., 45 S. Springfield Ave., 07081. Tel: 973-376-3044; Fax: 973-376-0560.
School—41 S. Springfield Ave., 07081. Tel: 973-376-5194. Sr. Mary Elizabeth Guyer, S.S.J., Prin.
Sisters of St. Joseph 2; Lay Teachers 10; Students 210.
Catechesis / Religious Programs—Tel: 973-376-2061. D.R.E.: Sr. Alice Neef, S.C.; Lynne A. Haley.
Students 275.

Summit, Union Co., St. Teresa's (1863), Rev. Msgr. Robert E. Harahan; Rev. Msgr. Anthony F. Bogdziewicz, Pastor Emeritus; Revs. Thomas Blind; John Gabriel. Pastoral Associates: Sr. Margaret Regan, S.S.N.J.; Sr. Winifred Tormey, S.S.J.; Mrs. Catherine Hansen; Deacons Charles Cederroth; Frank Gisoldi; Joseph Wall. In res., Rev. Msgr. John H. Koenig; Rev. Frank McNulty.
Res., 306 Morris Ave., 07901. Tel: 908-277-3700; Fax: 908-273-5909. [CEM]
Catechesis / Religious Programs—Tel: 908-273-6975.
Students 950.

Teaneck, Bergen Co., St. Anastasia's (1908), Revs. Hilary Milton, O.Carm.; Gerald Heinen, O.Carm.; Deacon Roland Bianchi. In res., Rev. Emeric Carmody, O.Carm.
Res., 1095 Teaneck Rd., 07666. Tel: 201-837-3354.
School—St. Cecilia's Interparochial School. (See St. Cecilia, Englewood. Tel: 201-568-2615).
Catechesis / Religious Programs—Tel: 201-837-3356. Sr. Adrienne Bradley, S.S.J., D.R.E.
Students 230.
Convent—Tel: 201-837-3153.

Tenafly, Bergen Co., Our Lady of Mount Carmel (1873), Revs. Ashley Harrington, O.Carm.; Joseph Atcher, O.Carm.
Res., 10 County Rd., 07670. Tel: 201-568-0545; Fax: 201-568-3215.
School—(1879), Tel: 201-567-6491.
Franciscan Sisters 1; Lay Teachers 16; Students 227.
Catechesis / Religious Programs—Tel: 201-871-4662.
Students 320.

Union, Union Co., St. Michael's (1928), Revs. Matthias T. Conva; Charles B. McDermott; Anselm I. Nwaorgu; W. Gerard Sogiuzzo; Sr. Ann Dominic, O.P., Pastoral Assoc. for Social Concerns.
Res., 1212 Kelly St., 07083. Tel: 908-688-1232; Fax: 908-810-1076.
School—(1931), 1211 Orange Ave., 07083. Tel: 908-688-1063; Fax: 908-687-7927. Sr. Margaret William, Prin.
Sisters of St. Dominic 3; Lay Teachers 18; Students 328.
Catechesis / Religious Programs—Tel: 908-964-0965; Fax: 908-810-1076. Marie Sellers, D.R.E.
Students 700.
Convent—Tel: 908-686-3839.

Holy Spirit (1963), Rev. Msgr. Vincent J. Doyle; Rev. Msgr. John H. Koenig, Pastor Emeritus; Revs. Edward G. Furrevig; Stanley E. Ortyl; John M. Ballweg, Weekend Asst.
Res., 971 Suburban Rd., 07083. Tel: 908-687-3327; Fax: 908-687-1312.
School—Morris Ave. & Suburban Rd., 07083. Tel: 908-687-8415.
Lay Teachers 10; Students 216.
Catechesis / Religious Programs—984 Suburban Rd., 07083. Tel: 908-964-7533.
Students 600.

Union City, Hudson Co.,

1—HOLY FAMILY, (1857), Rev. Antonio Lasheras, O.A.R. In res., Rev. Jose Maria Juango, O.A.R.
Res., 530 35th St., 07087. Tel: 201-867-6535.
Catechesis / Religious Programs—Tel: 201-866-9214; Fax: 201-867-1357.
Students 150.

2—ST. AUGUSTINE'S, (1886), Rev. Msgr. Thomas W. Heck; Revs. Pedro Navarro; Felipe Lopez; Deacon John McCarthy. In res., Rev. Paul J. Nolan.
Res., 3900 New York Ave., 07087. Tel: 201-863-0233.
School—(1891), 3920 New York Ave., 07087. Tel: 201-865-5319; Fax: 201-865-2567.
Sisters of Charity 6; Lay Teachers 15; Students 460.
Catechesis / Religious Programs—Students 550.
Convent—312 39th St., Union, 07083. Tel: 201-348-0527.

3—SS. JOSEPH AND MICHAEL, (1887; 1851), Revs. William J. Habling; Carlos Flor.
Res., 1314 Central Ave., 07087. Tel: 201-865-2325; Fax: 201-348-4412.
School—Mother Seton Grammar School, 1501 New York Ave., 07087. Tel: 201-863-8433.
Lay Teachers 14; Students 330.
Catechesis / Religious Programs—Tel: 201-863-8145.
Students 290.

4—ST. ANTHONY OF PADUA, (1899) (Italian), Revs. Ilario Crepaz (Italy); Randy A. Guillen; Leone Donini.
Res., 615 Eighth St., 07087. Tel: 201-867-3818; Fax: 201-867-8859.
School—700 Central Ave., 07087. Tel: 201-864-5605.
Religious Teachers Filippini 1; Lay Teachers 13; Students 260.
Catechesis / Religious Programs—Students 200.

5—ST. ROCCO'S, (1912) (Italian), Rev. Robert E. Templeton.
Res., 4206 Kennedy Blvd., 07087. Tel: 201-863-1427.
Mission House—4214 Kennedy Blvd., 07087. Tel: 201-863-5727.
Religious Teachers Filippini 2.

Upper Montclair, Essex Co., St. Cassian (1896), Revs. John G. Judge; Eugene G. Gniewyk; Deacon Thomas J. Nilan.
Res., 187 Bellevue Ave., 07043. Tel: 973-744-2850; Fax: 973-744-6187.
School—190 Lorraine Ave., 07043. Tel: 973-746-1636; Fax: 973-746-3271.
Lay Teachers 15; Students 238.
Catechesis / Religious Programs—Students 400.

Upper Saddle River, Bergen Co., Church of the Presentation (1961), Rev. Msgr. John F. McDermott; Rev. Gerald Hahn.
Office: 271 W. Saddle River Rd., 07458. Tel: 201-327-1313; Fax: 201-818-0722.
Res., 41 Riverview Ter., 07458.
School—St. Paul's Interparochial School, (1990). (See St. Paul, Ramsey). Tel: 201-327-1108.
Catechesis / Religious Programs—Tel: 201-327-3055.
Students 1,400.

Verona, Essex Co., Our Lady of the Lake (1923), Revs. Michael A. Hanly; Joseph A. D'Amico; Deacons Pat Vuolo; David Garcia. In res., Rev. John D. Dennehy; Sr. Anne Marie Lennon, O.P., Pastoral Assoc.
Res., 32 Lakeside Ave., 07044. Tel: 973-239-5696; Fax: 973-239-7190.
School—(1924), 22 Lakeside Ave., 07044. Tel: 973-239-1160; Fax: 973-239-6496. Sr. Mary Agnes Sullivan, O.P., Prin.
Sisters 1; Lay Teachers 13; Students 252.
Catechesis / Religious Programs—Tel: 201-239-7643.
Students 615.

Wallington, Bergen Co., Most Sacred Heart of Jesus (1942) (Polish), Rev. Msgr. Walter J. Gorski; Revs. Jan Krzysztof Lebdowicz; Marek Bokota.
Res., 127 Paterson Ave., 07057. Tel: 973-778-7405; Fax: 973-778-7750.
School—(1943), 6 Bond St., 07057. Tel: 973-777-4817.
Sisters 2; Lay Teachers 10; Students 230.
Catechesis / Religious Programs—Students 373.

Washington Township, Bergen Co., Our Lady of Good Counsel (1959), Rev. Msgr. Thomas A. McCarthy; Revs. Donald A. Cooper; Stephen J. Duffe; Sr. Joseph Miriam Blackwell, M.S.B.T., Pastoral Assoc. In res., Rev. Robert G. Gibney.
Res., 668 Ridgewood Rd., Westwood P.O., 07675. Tel: 201-664-6624; Fax: 201-664-0095.
School—Our Lady of Mercy Interparochial School. (See Our Lady of Mercy, Park Ridge. Tel: 201-391-3838; Fax: 201-391-5614).
Catechesis / Religious Programs—Tel: 201-664-1679. Catherine Russo, D.R.E.
Students 490.

Weehawken, Hudson Co., St. Lawrence's (1887), Rev. Charles F. Noble.
Res., 22 Hackensack Ave., 07087. Tel: 201-863-6464; Fax: 201-863-6656.
School—John Paul II Interparochial School. (See St. Francis, Hoboken).

Westfield, Union Co., St. Helen (1968), Rev. Msgr. James A. Burke; Revs. Donald K. Hummel; Peter K. O'Brien.
Res., 1600 Rahway Ave., 07090. Tel: 908-232-1214; Fax: 908-232-1867.
School—Holy Trinity Interparochial School, (1991). Co-Sponsored. (See Holy Trinity Parish, Westfield). Tel: 908-233-0484; Fax: 908-233-6204.
Catechesis / Religious Programs—Tel: 908-233-8757.
Students 2,055.

Holy Trinity (1872), Rev. Msgr. Joseph P. Masiello; Revs. Matthew D. Looney; Nicholas G. Figurelli; Sr. Catherine Looker, S.S.J., Pastoral Assoc.; Deacons Charles F. Kiley; Thomas A. Pluta.
Res., 315 First St., 07090. Tel: 908-232-8137; Fax: 908-654-8780.
School—(1991) (Grades PreK-8). Co-Sponsored, Holy Trinity Interparochial School. 336 First St., 07090. Tel: 908-233-0484; Fax: 908-233-6204.
Lay Teachers 19; Students 310.
Catechesis / Religious Programs—Tel: 908-233-7455. Sr. Kathleen J. Burton, S.S.J., D.R.E.
Students 451.

West New York, Hudson Co., St. Mary Help of Christians (1895), Rev. Carlo Fortunio, O.P., (Italy) Admin.; Deacon Ewald Randl.
Res., 6502 Jackson St., 07093. Tel: 201-868-9444; Fax: 201-868-6451.
Catechesis / Religious Programs—Students 200.

St. Joseph of the Palisades (1875), Most Rev. David Arias, O.A.R., D.D.; Revs. Frank Rose, Admin.; Agustin Pedrosa, S.M. (Spain); Minh Hai Nguyen; Leonardo Jaramillo (Colombia); Gioacchino Basile.
Res., 6401 Palisade Ave., 07093. Tel: 201-854-7006; Fax: 201-861-7799.
School—(1872), 6408 Palisade Ave., 07093. Tel: 201-861-3327; Fax: 201-861-5744.
Franciscan Missionary Sisters of the Sacred Heart 5; Lay Teachers 20; Students 510.
High School—5400 Broadway, 07093. Tel: 201-864-9700.
Priests 2; Sisters 5; Lay Teachers 13; Students 220.
Catechesis / Religious Programs—Students 905.
Chapels—North Bergen, Immaculate Heart of Mary.; Cor Jesu.
Convent—Tel: 201-861-3337.

Our Lady of Libera (1902) (Italian), Rev. Philip J. Rotunno.
Res., 5808 John F. Kennedy Memorial Blvd., 07093. Tel: 201-867-2642.
School—5800 John F. Kennedy Memorial Blvd., 07093. Tel: 201-864-5557.
Sisters 2; Lay Teachers 13; Students 375.
Convent—Tel: 201-868-6113. Religious Teachers Filippini

West Orange, Essex Co., Our Lady of Lourdes (1914), Revs. Gerald A. Marchand; Michael H. Hansen.
Res., 1 Eagle Rock Ave., 07052. Tel: 973-325-0110; Fax: 973-243-1480.
School—(1925), 100 Valley Way, 07052. Tel: 973-325-0555. Mary Cassels, Prin.
Sisters of Charity 1; Lay Teachers 20; Students 314.
Catechesis / Religious Programs—Tel: 973-325-0029. Sr. Ann Sweeney, O.P., D.R.E.
Students 158.
Convent—Tel: 973-325-0318.

St. Joseph's (1932), Revs. Bernard N. Mohan; John D. Sweeney; Deacon Joseph F.X. Cunningham. In res., Rev. Msgr. William J. Daly.
Res., 44 Benvenue Ave., 07052. Tel: 973-669-3221; Fax: 973-669-0385.
School—(1956), 8 St. Cloud Pl., 07052. Tel: 973-731-3503.
Lay Teachers 10; Students 237.
Catechesis / Religious Programs—Students 310.

Westwood, Bergen Co., St. Andrew's (1889), Revs. Ward P. Moore; Rocco F. Provinzano; Deacon Joseph J. Paulillo. Pastoral Assocs.: Joan M. Rovere, Parish Catechesis; Mary Jean Conroy, Child Catechesis; Alan Pitman, Teens.
Res., 124 Washington Ave., 07675. Tel: 201-666-1100; Fax: 201-722-1432. [CEM]
School—St. John's Academy. (See St. John the Baptist, Hillsdale. Tel: 201-664-6364; Fax: 201-664-8096).

Catechesis/Religious Programs—Tel: 201-664-6777.
Students 436.

Woodcliff Lake, Bergen Co., Our Lady Mother of the Church (1967), Rev. Thomas G. Arminio; Sr. Frances Schier, O.P., Pastoral Assoc. In res., Rev. Msgr. Joseph C. Manz; Rev. Edward J. Kearney.
Church—209 Woodcliff Ave., 07675.
Rectory: 130 Apple Ridge, 07675. Tel: 201-391-2826; Fax: 201-391-7101.
School—St. John the Baptist Interparochial School. (See St. John the Baptist, Hillsdale). Tel: 201-664-3131; Fax: 201-664-0772.
Catechesis/Religious Programs—Tel: 201-391-7400.
Students 250.

Wood-Ridge, Bergen Co., Our Lady of the Assumption (1926), Revs. James W. Czerwinski, O.F.M.; Richard Trezza, O.F.M.; Paul Sinnema, O.F.M.; Thomas Kelly, O.F.M.
Res., 143 First St., 07075. Tel: 201-438-5555; Fax: 201-438-6747.
School—151 First St., 07075. Tel: 201-933-0239; Fax: 201-438-6408.
Lay Teachers 19; Students 250.
Catechesis/Religious Programs—Hayes Center, 152 Second St., Tel: 201-933-6118.
Students 375.
Convent—Tel: 201-939-4274.

Wyckoff, Bergen Co., St. Elizabeth (1902), Rev. Msgr. Thomas M. O'Leary; Rev. Charles W. Hartling; Deacons Robert Kratchman; Joseph De Maria.
Res., 700 Wyckoff Ave., 07481. Tel: 201-891-1122; Fax: 201-847-8518.
School—Greenwood Ave., 07481. Tel: 201-891-1481. Sisters of St. Joseph of Peace; Lay Teachers 15; Students 290.
Catechesis/Religious Programs—Tel: 201-891-3262. Marlene Malenda, D.R.E.
Students 850.
Convent—Tel: 201-891-1495.

Chaplains of Public Institutions

Hospital Chaplaincy

NEWARK. *Office of Health Care Personnel* 171 Clifton Ave., 07102. Tel: 201-497-4009. Sr. Thomas Mary Salerno, S.C., Chancellor.

Bergen County

ENGLEWOOD. *Englewood Hospital* 350 Engle St., 07631. Tel: 201-894-3000. Chaplains: Revs. Mathew Chandrankunnel; John E. Komar.

HACKENSACK. *Hackensack Medical Center* 22 Hospital Pl., 07601. Tel: 201-996-2000; 996-2345. Chaplains: Revs. William Yeo; Bernard Fernando; Deacon Nicholas Simonelli.

PARAMUS. *Bergen Pines County Hospital* E. Ridgewood Ave., 07652. Tel: 201-967-4177; Fax: 201-967-4277. Chaplains: Revs. John McCrone; Joseph P. Rice; Gerald Bajek; Deacons Michael Morend; Edward Moran.

RIDGEWOOD. *Valley Hospital* Linwood Ave. & N. Van Dien Ave., 07451. Tel: 201-447-8160. Chaplains: Revs. Kurt Holdereid, O.Carm.; Joseph A. Stulb; Anne Devine, Dir.

TEANECK. *Holy Name Hospital* 718 Teaneck Rd., 07666. Tel: 201-833-3000. Chaplains: Sr. Lois Jablonski, S.S.J., Dir.; Rev. Jose Puthenparambil; Deacons Willy Malarcher; Martin Hemberger.

WESTWOOD. *Pascack Valley Hospital* Old Hook Rd., 07675. Tel: 201-358-3000. Chaplains: Revs. Thomas Norton; Kurt Holdereid, O.Carm.

Essex County

NEWARK. *Beth Israel Hospital* 201 Lyons Ave., 07112. Tel: 201-926-7000. Rev. Thomas R. McLaughlin, Chap.
St. James Hospital 155 Jefferson St., 07015. Tel: 201-489-1300. Chaplains: Rev. Kenneth Martin; Sr. Josephine Cervi.
St. Michael Medical Center 306 Martin Luther King Blvd., 07102. Tel: 201-877-5467. Chaplains: Revs. Chris Anyanwu; Manuel Cruz; Joseph Khai Vu.
University of Medicine & Dentistry 100 Bergen St., 07103. Tel: 201-982-5658. Rev. Eustace Edomobi, Chap.

BELLEVILLE. *Clara Maass Hospital* I-A Franklin Ave., 07109. Tel: 201-450-2000. Chaplains: Revs. John Donahue; Alan Guglielmo; Deacon Ralph Cordasco.

CEDAR GROVE. *Essex County Hospital Center* 125 Fairview Ave., 07009. Tel: 201-456-4300. Rev. Ronald R. Regula, Chap.

EAST ORANGE. *East Orange Hospital* 300 Central Ave., 07019. Tel: 201-672-8400. Rev. Deo Bocad, Chap.
Veterans Administration Hospital Tremont Ave. & Center St., 07019. Tel: 201-676-1000. Rev. Alexander Davis, O.F.M.Cap.

LIVINGSTON. *St. Barnabas Medical Center* 94 Old Short Hills Rd., 07039. Tel: 201-533-5015. Chaplains: Revs. Leo O. Farley; Peter Vinh Q. Nguyen; Sr. Adele Solari, S.S.J., Dir.

MONTCLAIR. *Mountainside Hospital* Bay Ave. & Highland Ave., 07042. Tel: 201-429-6000. Chaplains: Revs. Alan Guglielmo; Louis Pambello.
St. Vincent Nursing Home 45 Elm St., 07102. Tel: 201-746-4000. Sr. Anita William O'Neil, S.C., Chap.; Deacon Henry Stark.

ORANGE. *Hospital Center at Orange* 188 S. Essex St., 07051. Tel: 201-266-2000. Rev. Deo Bocad, Chap.

Hudson County

BAYONNE. *Bayonne Hospital* 29 E. 29th St., 07002. Tel: 201-858-5000. Rev. J. M. Patricius.

HOBOKEN. *St. Mary's Hospital* 308 Willow Ave., 07030. Tel: 201-714-8900. Rev. Dennis Kaelin.

JERSEY CITY. *B.S. Pollak Hospital* 100 Clifton St., 07304. Tel: 201-434-5883. Rev. John Corbett.
Christ Hospital 176 Palisades Ave., 07304. Tel: 201-795-8200. Sr. Marie Tansey, S.C.; Rev. Mamerto Cordero.
Jersey City Medical Center 50 Baldwin Ave., 07304. Tel: 201-915-2000. Rev. Edmundo A. Surban.
St. Francis Health Center 25 McWilliams Pl., 07302. Tel: 201-792-8314. Rev. Gerard J. Sudol; Sr. Mary Meehan, S.S.N.D.; Rev. Thomas Kunnath.

KEARNY. *West Hudson Hospital* 206 Bergen Ave., 07032. Tel: 201-955-7000. Rev. Patrick R.C. Wilhelm.

NORTH BERGEN. *Palisades General Hospital*. Vacant. 7600 River Rd., 07047. Tel: 201-854-5000.

Union County

BERKELEY HEIGHTS. *Runnells County Hospital* 07922. Tel: 908-771-5700. Rev. William T. Hart.

ELIZABETH. *Elizabeth General Medical Center* Chaplain's Office: 655 E. Jersey St., 07206. Tel: 908-351-9000. Revs. William C. Reed; Robert Becerra.
St. Elizabeth Hospital 225 Williamson St., 07202. Tel: 908-527-5000. Revs. Edward Haber; Virgilio P. Chagas; Sr. Dorothy Apprich, Dir.

PLAINFIELD. *Muhlenberg Medical Center* Park Ave. & Randolph Rd., 07061. Tel: 908-668-2007. Revs. Aloysius S. Carney; Joy Alappat.

RAHWAY. *Rahway Hospital* 865 Stone St., 07065. Tel: 908-381-4200. Deacons J. William Courtney; James O'Neill.

ROSELLE. *Center for Hope Hospice* 219 E. Fourth Ave., 07203. Tel: 908-241-1132. Sr. Mary McGrath; Deacon Cyril Massar.

SUMMIT. *Overlook Hospital* 99 Beauvoir Ave., 07902. Tel: 908-522-2000; 522-2108. Revs. John Quill; John P. Holian; Sr. Patricia Murphy, S.S.J., Dir.

UNION. *Union Hospital* 1000 Galloping Hill Rd., 07083. Tel: 908-687-1900. Rev. George M. Keating.

Prison Chaplaincy

NEWARK. *Office of Prison Ministry* P.O. Box 9500, 07104. Tel: 973-497-4022. Rev. William Louis Gyure, Dir.

Bergen County

HACKENSACK. *Bergen County Jail* 160 S. River St., 07601. Tel: 201-488-1190, Ext. 407. Rev. Joseph Buzzerio.

PARAMUS. *Bergen County Juvenile Detention Center* 296 Ridgewood Ave., 07652. Deacon Robert Kratchman.

Essex County

NEWARK. *Essex County Jail* 60 Nelson Pl., 07102. Tel: 973-621-5154. Rev. Paul Nolan.
Essex County Youth Detention Center 203 Sussex Ave., 07102. Tel: 973-482-5510. Revs. Anthony Bico; Paul Viale.
Northern State Prison 168 Frontage Rd., 07114. Tel: 973-497-4022. Revs. William Gyure; Robert Cormier; Deacons Sam Ventola; David Loman.

CALDWELL. *Essex County Jail Annex* P.O. Box 349, 07006. Tel: 973-364-5347. Rev. Paul Nolan.

Hudson County

SECAUCUS. *Hudson County Juvenile Detention Center* 635 County Ave., 07094. Tel: 201-319-3750. Rev. Giordano Belanich.

SOUTH KEARNY. *Hudson County Correctional Center* 35 Hackensack Rd., 07032. Tel: 973-497-4022. Deacon Joseph Del Monte.

Union County

ELIZABETH. *Elizabeth Detention Center* 625 Evans St., 07201. Tel: 973-497-4022. Revs. William Gyure; George Sharp; Deacon Stephen Liptak.
Union County Jail 15 Elizabeth Town Plaza, 07207. Tel: 973-497-4022. Rev. William Gyure.

Special Assignment:
Reverend Fathers—
Ashe, Kevin P., Exec. Dir. Park Theatre Performing Arts Ctr., Inc.
Lebranche, Raymond, Dir. Eucharistic Shrine of the Adorable Face of Jesus

---

On Duty Outside the Archdiocese:
Reverend Monsignors—
Casale, Franklyn M., St. Thomas University, 16400 N.W. 32nd Ave., Miami, FL 33054
McDade, Thomas J., 4001 14th St. N.E., Washington, DC 20017
Radano, John A., Villa Stritch, Via Della Nocetta 63, Rome, 00164 Italy
Reverend Fathers—
Arata, Miguel A., Tartu P Neitsi Maarja Kogudus, Veski TN 1-1A EE 2400, Tartu, EESTI NI Estonia
Arvay, Alfred S., 5128 Mentmore Ave., Spring Hill, FL 34606
Ballance, Harvey J., Obispado de San Martin, San Lorenzo 2416 (1650), Buenos Aires, Argentina
Batista, George L., Church of St. Luke, 2892 S. Congress Ave., Lake Worth, FL 33461
DiGiovanni, Alfonso, Apostlite Peetruse Ja., Pauluse, Kogudus Tallinas, Vene Tn. 18, Tallin, EE001 Estonia
Figueiredo, Anthony Jesus, Casa Santa Maria, Via dell'Ulmita, Rome, 30, 00187 Italy
Kirchner, James A., Our Divine Savior Church, 1205 Love Ave., P.O. Box 212, Tifton, GA 31793
Krozser, John J., C.M., Church of the Resurrection, 2815 Forbes Dr., Montgomery, AL 36110
Kukura, Joseph W., Via Caritas, 57 Willowbrook Blvd., Wayne, NJ 07470
Kunze, Robert W., Church of St. Augustine, 45 Henderson Rd., Kendall Park, NJ 08824
Leahy, Robert T., St. Pius X Church, 203 W. Lacey Rd., Forked River, NJ 08731
Lintz, Christoph, Internationaler Seminar - Kurs, Koenigsberger Str. 34, Berlin, Germany
Livolsi, Sylvester J., Sanctuary of Mary, 252 Wantage Ave., Branchville, NJ 07826
Merdinger, Philip E., Brotherhood of Hope, 194 Summer Ave., Sumerville, MA 02143
Miller, Frederick L., St. Charles Borromeo Seminary, 1000 E. Wynnewood Rd., Overbrook, PA 19096
Montes de Oca, Jose, Tartu P. Neitsi Maarja Kogudus, Veski TN 1-1A EE 2400, Tartu, (EESTI) Estonia
Mulvey, John J., M.Div., Church of St. Charles Borromeo, 21505 Augusta Ave., Port Charlotte, FL 33952
Papalia, Pasquale A., Sts. Peter & Paul, 285 Hamilton St., Somerset, NJ 08873
Perricone, John A., St. Agnes, 143 E. 43rd St., New York, NY 10017
Reinbold, Charles, Mt. St. Francis, 250 South St., Peekskill, NY 10566
Russo, Michael A., St. Mary College, Box 5166, Moraga, CA 94575
Scheip, Michael, 4515 Linwood St., Sarasota, FL
Schute, Arthur B., 1113 Fleetwood Dr., Port Charlotte, FL 33952
Smith, Paul H., 1717 Ala Wai Blvd., Apt. 1806, Honolulu, HI 96815
Sypko, Tadeusz Marek, St. Rose of Lima Parish, 311 Central Ave., Safford, AZ 85546
Tiboni, Vito, Veteran's Hospital, 800 Poly Pl., Apt. 15 W., Brooklyn, NY 11209
Vaccaro, Joseph V., Carmel Blessed Virgin Mary, 8251 De Montreville Tr. N., Lake Elmo, MN 55042
Wegg, Mark, St.Peter's Parish, P.O. Box 3700, Deland, FL 32723
Wilson, William P., Nativity of Blessed Virgin Mary, 99 E. Tioga St., Tunkhannock, PA 18657

Military Chaplains:
Reverend Fathers—
Arminio, Alfonse M., Wharfside MNR Condo, Apt. 17, 172 Park Rd., Monmouth Beach, NJ 07750
Beale, Kenneth R., Capt., PSC2, P.O. Box 9137, APO AE, 09012
Berchmanz, Anthony, Vista Pacifica, Apt. 1405, 1066 Calle del Gerro, San Clemente, CA 92672
Brosk, Steven J., 11020 Huebner Oaks #2235, San Antonio, TX 78230
D'Emma, Gregory J., CMR 427, Box 284, APO AE, 09630
Hanrahan, William P., Chap., 2411 Postal Service Center, Nellis AFB, NV 89191
Kopec, Rajmund, Capt., West Meadow Dr., Colorado Springs, CO 80906
Lesak, William P., US Sixth Fleet, Code 014, Unit 50148, FPO, AE 09501
Morris, John J., CHC USNR, 5424 Keystone Pl., Virginia Beach, VA 23464
Newland, Ronald A., Chap. Lt. Col., PSC 41, Box 4431, APO AE
Oddo, Peter A., 421 Westminster Pl., Lodi, NJ 07644
Pinho, Antonio M., 417 BSB, Unit 26410, CMR 408-Box 125, APO, AE 09182

Higher Studies:
Reverend Fathers—
Figueiredo, Anthony J., Casa Santa Maria, Via dell'Umilta, 30, Rome, 00187 Italy

Retired:
Reverend Monsignors—
Abramowicz, Sylvester, 893 Westfield Ave., Elizabeth, NJ 07208
Alba, Jose M., St. Nicholas, 122 Ferry St., Jersey City, NJ 07307
Beggans, Joseph A., Pope John Paul II Pavilion, 135 S. Center St., Orange, NJ 07050
Bogdziewicz, Anthony F., St. John Vianney Residence, 60 Home Ave., Rutherford, NJ 07070
Bonelli, Theodore V., Clearbrook Village, 120B Ironwood Plaza, Cranbury, NJ 08512
Capozzelli, Emmanuel, 632 Bayside Ave., Beachwood, NJ 08722
Carey, Thomas, 29 Park Rd., Maplewood, NJ 07040
Casazza, David J., 426 Jefferson Ave., Avon-by-the-Sea, NJ 07717
Coburn, Vincent P., 1802 Ravine Dr., Forked River, NJ 08731
Daly, William J., St. Joseph's Rectory, 44 Benvenue Ave., West Orange, NJ 07052
Donovan, Joseph J., 13 Cruiser Ct., Toms River, NJ 08753
Duffy, Robert E., St. Paul of the Cross Rectory, 156 Hancock Ave., Jersey City, NJ 07307
Egan, Robert P., P.O. Box 476, Convent Station, NJ 07961
Fahy, John J., 60 Home Ave., Rutherford, NJ 07070
Fanelli, Eugene A., Our Lady of Mt. Carmel, 259 Oliver St., Newark, NJ 07105
Fleming, Edward J., Immaculate Conception Seminary, Seton Hall University, South Orange, NJ 07079
Hayes, Paul J., 197 Riverside Dr. N., Bricktown, NJ 08724
Hinrichsen, Carl D., Our Lady of Mercy Rectory, 2 Freemont Ave., Park Ridge, NJ 07656
Hogan, William F., St. John Vianney Res., 60 Home Ave., Rutherford, NJ 07070
Holmes, Richard J., St. Luke, 430 N. Franklin Tpke., Ho-Ho-Kus, NJ 07423
Houghton, Francis J., 2316 Blue Jay Tr., Point Pleasant, NJ 08742
Jarvais, Walter G., 60 Home Ave., Rutherford, NJ 07070
Johnson, James, 555 Prospect Ave., Ridgefield, NJ 07657
Koenig, John H., St. Teresa of Avila, 306 Morris Ave., Summit, NJ 07901
Komar, Michael A., 188 W. 31st Street, Bayonne, NJ 07002
Manz, Joseph C., Our Lady Mother of the Church, 130 Apple Ridge, Woodcliff Lake, NJ 07675
Marjanczyk, Joseph A., P.O. Box 456, Point Pleasant, NJ 08742
Murray, Harold A., 50 Willow Way, Manasquan, NJ 08736
O'Gorman, George A., 60 Home Ave., Rutherford, NJ 07070
Orrico, Caeser G., 20 Locust Ave., Emerson, NJ 07630
Piazza, Benjamin A., P.O. Box 696, Toms River, NJ 08754
Pocus, Dominick A., Clara Maass Continuing Care Center, 195 Belgrove Dr., Kearny, NJ 07032
Pollard, Raymond J., 2316 Blue Jay Tr., Point Pleasant, NJ 08742
Price, Edward G., Church of the Assumption, 113 Chiego Pl., Roselle Park, NJ 07204
Reinbold, Francis A., 250 South St., Peekskill, NJ 10566
Reynolds, Roger A., Our Lady of Victories Rectory, 81 Lynn St., Harrington Park, NJ 07640
Santora, Gerard M., St. John Vianney Residence, 60 Home Ave., Rutherford, NJ 07070
Sullivan, Edwin V., Seton Hall University, South Orange Ave., South Orange, NJ 07079
Turro, James C., S.T.L., S.S.L., A.M., Immaculate Conception Seminary, Seton Hall University, South Orange, NJ 07079
Walsh, Gerard W., 2940 Bowspirit Ln., St. James City, FL 33956
Welsh, Aloysius J., The Rev. Msgr. James F. Kelley Residence for Retired Priests, 247 Bloomfield Ave., Caldwell, NJ 07006
Wojtycha, Edward F., 1800 S.E. St. Lucie Blvd., 2-202, Stuart, FL 34996

Reverend Fathers—
Adamczyk, Stanley J., St. John Vianney Res., 60 Home Ave., Rutherford, NJ 07070
Affanoso, Joseph L., Holy Name of Jesus Rectory, 184 Midland Ave., East Orange, NJ 07017
Anta, Antonio, c/o Maria Rodriguez, 716 Dennis Pl., Linden, NJ 07036
Babulski, Robert E., 28 E. Stimpson Ave., Linden, NJ 07036
Bergeur, John X., St. John Vianney Res., 60 Home Ave., Rutherford, NJ 07070
Byrne, W. Gordon, 37 Atlantic Ave., Ocean Grove, NJ 07756
Callahan, James, Post Chaplains Office, 1821 Dora Dr., Cardiff, CA 92007
Carey, Thomas, One Upper Mountain Ave., Montclair, NJ 07042
Cassidy, Joseph L., St. John Vianney Annex, 64 Home Ave., Rutherford, NJ 07070
Cestaro, Joseph J., St. John Vianney Residence, 60 Home Ave., Rutherford, NJ 07070
Clyde, George A., 2121 Butternut Rd., Sea Girt, NJ 08750
Coda, Joseph F., 60 Home Ave., Rutherford, NJ 07070
Cooper, Donald A., 3220 Keith Ln., P.O. Box 3, Lavallette, NJ 08735
Daly, Robert L., 387-0 Newport Way, Jamesburg, NJ 08831
Danik, Daniel A., 2046 Ingalls Ave., Linden, NJ 07036
Davis, Thomas E., 367 Stiles Ct., West Orange, NJ 07052
Debold, Walter A., Seton Hall University, South Orange Ave., South Orange, NJ 07079
Derbyshire, Joseph V., St. Anne Rectory, 325 Second Ave., Garwood, NJ 07027
DiGirolamo, Dante, Eucharistic Shrine of the Adorable Face of Jesus, P.O. Box 455, Kearny, NJ 07032
DiPeri, Joseph B., Leisure Ridge, 303 Devon St., Lakehurst, NJ 08733
Doherty, George E., 133 S. Second St., Harrison, NJ 07029
Dowling, John C., c/ Mrs. H. Battles, 585 Bloomfield Ave., Apt. 35, West Caldwell, NJ 07006
Dowling, Michael J., 4 Brookline Ct., Middletown, NJ 07748
Doyle, John F., 1724 Lockhart St. R.D. #3, Toms River, NJ 08757
Doyle, Joseph M., 145 Pearsall Ave., Jersey City, NJ 07305
Drexler, George D., Box 316, Sea Girt, NJ 08750
Driscoll, James J., P.O. Box 541, Spring Lake, NJ 07762
Egan, John J., 31 Fitzroy Dr., Charleston, SC 29414
Eid, Frederick M., 400 Willow Ave., Hoboken, NJ 07030
Fagan, Joseph P., P.O. Box 545, Spring Lake, NJ 07762
Ferrazoli, Henry R., 149 Orlando Blvd., Toms River, NJ 08757
Finn, Francis J., 26 Kent Dr., Bricktown, NJ 08723
Fiorino, Joseph, 1006 Sailor Dr., Manahawkin, NJ 08050
Fitzpatrick, Patrick F.X., Allendale Nursing Home, 85 Harreton Ave., Allendale, NJ 07401
Foley, James F., St. Mary's Life Care Center, 135 S. Center St., Orange, NJ 07050
Foran, Martin J., Seton Hall Prep, 11 Beverly Rd., West Orange, NJ 07052
Frank, Joseph A., 44 Saltspray Dr., P.O. Box 779, Forked River, NJ 08731
French, Walter V., 26 Rogerene Way, Landing, NJ 07850
Fuino, Michael A., St. John Vianney Residence, 60 Home Ave., Rutherford, NJ 07070
Galdon, Richard M., P.O. Box 10, Jemez Springs, NM 87025
Garoffolo, Vincent, 71 Market St., Garfield, NJ 07026. Tel: 201-340-9029
Gavin, Francis T., Seton Hall University, South Orange Ave., South Orange, NJ 07079
Geiger, Eugene E., Pope John Paul II Pavilion, 135 S. Center St., Orange, NJ 07050
Genzlinger, Walter L., Mt. Carmel, 99 Broadway, Jersey City, NJ 07306
Gibney, Robert G., The Rev. Msgr. James F. Kelley Residence for Retired Priests, 247 Bloomfield Ave., Caldwell, NJ 07006
Hanley, John G., Pope John Paul II Pavilion, 135 S. Center St., Orange, NJ 07050
Hayes, Edward J., St. Joseph's Home, 140 Shepherd Ln., Totowa, NJ 07512
Hearns, Joseph A., St. Joseph Home, 140 Shepherd Ln., Totowa, NJ 07512
Henry, Thomas J., The Rev. Msgr. James F. Kelley Residence for Retired Priests, 247 Bloomfield Ave., Caldwell, NJ 07006
Hermanns, Harold T., St. John Vianney Residence, 60 Home Ave., Rutherford, NJ 07070
Kenny, Thomas A., 24 Chesapeake St., Barnegat, NJ 08005
Kern, Charles P., 183 Evergreen Rd., Apt. 7A, Edison, NJ 08817
Koerner, Frederick C., St. John Vianney Residence, 60 Home Ave., Rutherdford, NJ 07070
Kowalski, Eugene S., 15 E. Eighth St., Clifton, NJ 07011
Laudati, Joseph J., 36 Milton Ave., Nutley, NJ 07110
Loughlin, James F., 1943 Ship Ct., Toms River, NJ 08753
Ludlum, William, St. Francis Life Care Corp., 21 Pocono Rd., Denville, NJ 07834
Lynch, Charles M., St. Francis Life Care Corp., 21 Pocono Rd., Denville, NJ 07834
Lynch, Thomas F., 2065 Lakeside Dr. W., Highland Lakes, NJ 07422
Macho, George S., 1825 Buttonwood Ave., Toms River, NJ 08755
Madden, John J., 60 Home Ave., Rutherford, NJ 07070
Mader, George L., The Rev. Msgr. James F. Kelley Residence for Retired Priests, 247 Bloomfield Ave., Caldwell, NJ 07006
Mahoney, Daniel F., 7450 Dundee Way, Brooksville, FL 34613
Malkiewicz, Edward S., St. Aloysius Rectory, 691 West Side Ave., Jersey City, NJ 07304
McFarland, James W., 21 Skillman Ave., Jersey City, NJ 07306
McGuinness, Lester A., St. Aloysius, 219 Bloomfield Ave., Caldwell, NJ 07006
McKenna, Denis R., 149 Meisel Ave., Springfield, NJ 07081
McKeon, Raymond T., St. James Rectory, 143 Madison St., Newark, NJ 07105
McNulty, Francis J., St. Teresa of Avila Rectory, 306 Morris Ave., Summit, NJ 07901
McTague, Charles H., St. James Rectory, 143 Madison St., Newark, NJ 07105
Merity, John A., 905 S. Maple Ave., Glen Rock, NJ 07452
Merzena, Carl J., 60 Home Ave., Rutherford, NJ 07070
Miller, Ferdinand B., 309 Downer St., Mantoloking, NJ 08738
Mills, James Leo, 6131 Grand Ave., Apt. 7C, North Bergen, NJ 07047
Miodowski, Chester A., Richmond Rd., Lake Lackawanna, Stanhope, NJ 07874
Miodowski, Leonard A., St. John Vianney Res., 60 Home Ave., Rutherford, NJ 07070
Morel, John J. Q, 44 Lincoln Pl., North Plainfield, NJ 08753
Murphy, Daniel A., Seton Hall University, South Orange Ave., South Orange, NJ 07079
Nealon, Joseph W., 3360 Canoe Creek Tr., Palm City, FL 34990
O'Brien, John E., 346 Mt. Pleasant Ave., Livingston, NJ 07039
O'Keefe, Maurice L., 60 Home Ave., Rutherford, NJ 07070
O'Leary, Robert A., 252 Genes Dr., Toms River, NJ 08753
O'Neill, James R., St. Paul's, 200 Wyckoff Ave., Ramsey, NJ 07446
Olszewski, John S., St. Mark's Rectory, 287 Hamilton St., Rahway, NJ 07065
Osorio, Rudolfo B., 2438 Fruit Ave., S.E., Port Lucie, FL 34952
Pikula, Zygmunt, Holy Trinity Church, 207 Adams St., Newark, NJ 07105
Prestera, Vincent J., 1015 Aoloa Pl. #450, Kailua, HI 96734
Quinlan, Joseph M., 18 Ellsworth Ct., Red Bank, NJ 07701
Quinn, Vincent J., The Rev. Msgr. James F. Kelley Residence for Retired Priests, 247 Bloomfield Ave., Caldwell, NJ 07006
Rischmann, Edward, 146 Skyline Drive, Brick, NJ 08724

Rock, John J., 200 Springfield Ave., Apt. 5023, Springfield, NJ 07081
Rutkowski, Stephen C., 1730 NE 63rd Ct., Ft. Lauderdale, FL 33334
Salomon, Jean Francois, St. Anthony of Padua Rectory, 615 Eighth Ave., Union City, NJ 07087
Sapeta, Joseph S., St. Hedwig, 1062 Dewey Pl., Elizabeth, NJ 07202
Scanlan, Charles V., 60 Home Ave., Rutherford, NJ 07070
Scherer, Donald R., P.O. Box 764, Robert, LA 70455
Schulte, William P., Brester's Guest House, 477 Mt. Prospect Ave., Newark, NJ 07104
Sheehan, Joseph G., St. John the Apostle, 1805 Penbrook Ter., Linden, NJ 07036
Shih, John M., St. John Vianney Annex, 60 Home Ave., Rutherford, NJ 07070
Simko, Michael S., 380 Avenue E, Bayonne, NJ 07002
Swenson, Walter, J.F., 72 Windsor Pl., Kenilworth, NJ 07033
Swierzbinski, Edward, P.O. Box 342, Normandy Beach, NJ 08739
Szelest, Theodore A., Church of St. Mary, 280 Washington Ave., Dumont, NJ 07628
Tracy, John A., 17 Third Ave., Hawthorne, NJ 07506
Urbanik, Stanley J., 122 Park St., Roselle, NJ 07203
Waldron, John R., Troy Towers, 40 Conger St., Apt.302A, Bloomfield, NJ 07003
Wightman, John H., 1215 Windlass Dr., Manahawkin, NJ 08050
Young, Carl A., 1738 Certainty Dr., Point Pleasant, NJ 08742
Zuber, Thaddeus F., 60 Home Ave., Rutherford, NJ 07070

Permanent Deacons:
Acocella, Louis, St. Anthony, Belleville
Allgaier, John, On Duty Outside the Archdiocese
Alsing, Edwin J., (Retired)
Alvarez, Juan, On Duty Outside the Archdiocese
Amaro, Claudino, On Duty Outside the Archdiocese
Anders, Joseph L., On Duty Outside the Archdiocese
Andrews, Marshall, Our Lady of the Valley, Orange
Antola, Aldo P., St. Thomas the Apostle, Bloomfield
Araya, Alfonso, On Duty Outside the Archdiocese
Balestrieri, Anthony A., Our Lady of Peace, Maywood
Baltus, John M., St. James, Springfield
Barrett, Thomas J., St. Joseph's and St. Michael's, Union City
Basch, Peter J.
Bates, Harold L., Ascension, New Milford
Behringer, Charles, (Retired)
Benedetto, William R., Queen of Peace, North Arlington
Berkise, John, On Duty Outside the Archdiocese
Besida, Dennis J., St. Thomas, Bloomfield
Bond, Charles H., Holy Family, Nutley
Bongiovanni, Jerome C., St. James, Springfield
Bonilla, Benjamin, On Duty Outside the Archdiocese
Botts, Edward, Leave of Absence
Botts, Robert, Leave of Absence
Bowen, Edmund, (Retired)
Bowen, Edward J., St. Peter the Apostle, River Edge
Brennan, Vishno H., On Duty Outside the Archdiocese
Byrnes, Richard, Our Lady of Good Counsel, Washington Township
Campione, Frank J., St. Thomas More, Fairfield
Carr, Patrick V., Community Hospital, Montclair
Cata, David, Leave of Absence
Cauceglia, Arthur J., St. Francis of Assisi, Hackensack
Charriez, Nestor, On Duty Outside the Archdiocese
Coffey, John J., St. Peter Claver, Montclair
Collins, Thomas F., Bergen Pines Hospital
Colon, German, On Duty Outside the Archdiocese
Colon, Hector, On Duty Outside the Archdiocese
Concepcion, Asuncion, On Duty Outside the Archdiocese
Cook, William R., On Duty Outside the Archdiocese
Cordasco, Ralph J., On Duty Outside the Archdiocese
Courtney, J. William, St. Mary's, Rahway
Coyle, Thomas J., St. Thomas, Bloomfield
Cruz, Primitivo, Sts. Peter & Paul, Hoboken
Cullinane, John, On Duty Outside the Archdiocese
Cunningham, Joseph, St. Joseph, West Orange
Czerepka, Alexander J., St. Theresa, Linden
Daniele, Paul, St. Francis Xavier, Newark
Davignon, Paul M., On Duty Outside the Archdiocese
DeBenedictis, Thomas, SS. Joseph and Michael, Union City
Degnon, Robert F., On Duty Outside the Archdiocese
Del Monte, Joseph J., Assumption-All Saints, Jersey City
Delgado, Carlos, On Duty Outside the Archdiocese
DeLucca, Nicholas J., Our Lady, Mother of the Church, Woodcliff Lake
DeMaria, Joseph, Jr., St. Elizabeth, Wyckoff
Dempsey, John J., Leave of Absence
Diaz-Rojas, Andres, (Retired)
DiMeo, John J., St. Mary's, Rutherford
Dove, Winston, On Duty Outside the Archdiocese
Downey, John L., St. Cecilia's, Kearny
Fargo, Nicholas C., Our Lady of Mercy, Jersey City
Fernandez, Jose R., Blessed Sacrament, Elizabeth
Ferraiuola, Lex, Our Lady of Mt. Carmel, Tenafly
Fiore, Joseph, (Retired)
Fischer, Robert, On Duty Outside the Archdiocese
Fitzgerald, Michael J., St. Joseph, Bogota
Francione, Joseph, St. Philomena, Livingston
Freeman, Gerald, St. Paul, Irvington
Fuentes, Julio, Leave of Absence
Garcia, David, Our Lady of the Lake, Verona
Gilheany, Thomas J., On Duty Outside the Archdiocese
Giordano, William J., Our Lady of Assumption, Bayonne
Gisoldi, Frank A., St. Teresa of Avila, Summit
Glogoza, Theodore J., Sacred Heart, Bloomfield
Gomez, Alberto, St. Michael's, Newark
Gonzalez, Faustino (NY), Leave of Absence
Gonzalez, Pedro, St. Boniface, Jersey City
Gorini, Joseph, On Duty Outside the Archdiocese
Gray, Brandon, On Duty Outside the Archdiocese
Grieder, Gustave, St. Matthew, Ridgefield
Haas, Henry W., Our Lady of Mt. Carmel, Montclair
Hall, J. Bruce, On Duty Outside the Archdiocese
Heinrich, Joseph R., On Duty Outside the Archdiocese
Hemberger, Martin R., Holy Name Hospital, Teaneck; St. Michael, Palisades Park
Higgins, Leonard F., Our Lady of Mercy, Park Ridge
Hildebrandt, Edward J., Leave of Absence
Hodges, Richard G., St. Pius X, Old Tappan
Hoefling, Edward J., On Duty Outside the Archdiocese
Hrdina, Joseph, (Retired)
Huff, Sidney E., Holy Spirit-Help of Christians, East Orange
Inguaggiato, John M., Our Lady of Sorrows, South Orange
Jackson, Alonzo, St. Joseph, East Orange
Johnson, Leon, Christ the King, Jersey City
Joyce, William, Annunciation, Paramus
Jurjevic, Svetko, On Duty Outside the Archdiocese
Kelly, Walter, On Duty Outside the Archdiocese
Keturwitis, Henry J., Sts. Peter & Paul, Elizabeth
Kiley, Charles F., Permanent Diaconate Office, Holy Trinity, Westfield
King, Aidan P., St. Thomas More, Fairfield
Kirkham, Donald F., On Duty Outside the Archdiocese
Kramer, Richard D., On Duty Outside the Archdiocese
Kratchman, Robert M., St. Elizabeth, Wyckoff
Lawless, Timothy, (Outside Archdiocese)
Leary, Gerald, St. Mary, Closter
LeConte, Wilfrid, St. Peter Claver, Montclair
Liptak, Stephen J., St. Aloysius, Jersey City
Llanza, Oscar, On Duty Outside the Archdiocese
Loman, David B., Northern State Prison, Newark; Our Lady of Mt. Carmel, Tenafly
Lopez, George, On Duty Outside the Archdiocese
Lopez, Sixto, University Hospital, Newark
Lubas, Joseph, St. Adalbert, Elizabeth
Lynn, Walter, St. Joseph, Bogota
Macaluso, Martin P., St. Mary, Plainfield
Mackesy, Leonard J., Our Lady of Sorrows, Kearny
Magarelli, Paul S., St. Philip the Apostle, Saddle Brook
Mainero, Frank A., On Duty Outside the Archdiocese
Malanga, Joseph J., St. Valentine, Bloomfield
Malarcher, Willy J., Holy Name Hospital, Teaneck
Marcom, Joseph E., Permanent Diaconate Preparation Program; St. Anne's, Fair Lawn
Maron, Edward, Bergen Pines Hospital
Martinez, Jose, St. Columba, Newark
Massar, Cyril J., Leave of Absence
Matos, William, Jr., St. Columba, Newark
Matthews, Michael, Catholic Community Services
McAulay, John R., Leave of Absence
McCarren, Daniel G., Jr., St. Rose of Lima, Short Hills
McCarthy, John T., St. Augustine's, Union City
McComb, David, On Duty Outside the Archdiocese
McFadden, Edward, St. Michael's Hospital, Newark
McGarry, Richard M. (SA), St. Anne's, Fairlawn
McNulty, James, On Duty Outside the Archdiocese
Mendez, Daniel, St. Augustine's, Newark
Messina, Dominic S., St. Thomas More, Fairfield
Messina, Vincent, Holy Trinity, Hackensack
Meyers, Vincent J., (Retired)
Miney, Patrick F., St. John's, Bergenfield
Minichino, Leonard A., St. Catharine's, Glen Rock
Mistretta, Alfonso G., Leave of Absence
Montanez, Luis A., St. Joseph, Hoboken
Montemurro, Michael V., Leave of Absence
Montini, Leo, On Duty Outside the Archdiocese
Moore, Brett O., Sacred Heart, Lyndhurst
Morend, Michel, On Duty Outside the Archdiocese
Mueller, James A., St. Catherine, Glen Rock
Myers, William, Queen of Peace, North Arlington
Nazzaro, Joseph J., On Duty Outside the Archdiocese
Negron, Victor, On Duty Outside the Archdiocese
Nilan, Thomas, St. Cassian's, Upper Montclair
Niland, Joseph, Annunciation, Paramus
Niles, Donald P., St. Elizabeth of Hungary, Linden
Noone, Thomas H., On Duty Outside the Archdiocese
O'Connell, Brian, On Duty Outside the Archdiocese
O'Neill, James, St. Mary's, Rahway
Ortega, Cesar, St. Ann, Newark
Ortiz, Jaime, St. Michael's, Jersey City
Osborne, Charles E., St. Rocco, Newark
Paredes, Guy, (Retired)
Paulillo, Joseph J., St. Andrew's, Westwood
Perez, Buenaventura, On Duty Outside the Archdiocese
Perez, Prudencio, On Duty Outside the Archdiocese
Persinger, Joseph M., St. Rose of Lima, Short Hills
Peterson, Victor, Bergen County Institutions
Pluta, Thomas A, Holy Trinity, Westfield
Polanco, Leopoldo, St. Boniface, Jersey City
Porter, Edward W., Jr., Cathedral Basilica of the Sacred Heart-Permanent Diaconate Office
Postadan, Romulo D., On Duty Outside the Archdiocese
Puglisi, Robert, On Duty Outside the Archdiocese
Puliatte, James, Immaculate Conception, Norwood
Quintana, Restituto, St. Michael's, Newark
Ramos-Villeda, Ramon, Our Lady of Good Counsel, Newark
Ravelo, Daniel, St. Michael's, Newark
Raymundo, Ranulfo, Sacred Heart, Bloomfield
Restivo, Louis, On Duty Outside the Archdiocese
Reyes, Jose, On Duty Outside the Archdiocese
Reyes, Modesto, On Duty Outside the Archdiocese
Reyes, Victor, St. Leo, Irvington
Riccio, Dominick, O.L. of Mt. Virgin, Garfield
Rice, George F., Our Lady of Mercy, Park Ridge
Riche, Philip, (Retired)
Rivera, Pedro, Leave of Absence
Roccanova, Rocco, Inactive
Rodack, Stephen, Inactive
Rodriguez, Gustavo, (Outside Archdiocese)
Rodriguez, Jose A., St. Thomas Aquinas, Newark
Rodriguez, Justo, St. Rocco, Newark
Rodriguez, Vicente, St. Augustine's, Newark
Rolon, Cristobal, On Duty Outside the Archdiocese
Romero, Alberto, St. Joseph of the Palisades, West New York
Rosado, Jose F., Immaculate Conception, Elizabeth
Ross, George A., St. John the Apostle, Linden
Salerno, Philip, St. Philip, Saddle Brook
Sanderson, Raymond, St. Andrew's, Bayonne
Schneider, Paul, (Retired)
Serzan, Vincent C., St. Michael's, Lyndhurst
Shea, Raymond, On Duty Outside the Archdiocese
Shelhamer, William, On Duty Outside the Archdiocese
Simonelli, Nicholas, St. Francis, Ridgefield Park
Somma, Alfred P., On Duty Outside the Archdiocese
Soto, Anibal, Bergen County Jail
Stanecki, Walter J., On Duty Outside the Archdiocese
Stark, Henry A., (Retired)
Stoehr, George, On Duty Outside the Archdiocese
Stumbar, James P., Little Flower, Berkeley Heights
Suarez, Ibrahim, (Outside Archdiocese)
Suarez, Juan B., St. Cecilia, Kearny
Swider, Charles P., Inactive
Tarabokija, Anton, St. John's, Fairview
Taylor, Michael A., On Duty Outside the Archdiocese
Thomann, Robert V., Mt. Carmel, Ridgewood
Thomson, Robert E., Holy Rosary, Edgewater
Titmas, Richard C., St. Anne's, Fair Lawn
Tizzano, Albert H., St. Thomas, Bloomfield
Torres, Antonio, On Duty Outside the Archdiocese
Tynan, Charles, Sacred Heart, Lyndhurst
Valladares, Guillermo, St. Peter's, Belleville
Vargas, Rafael, St. Michael's Medical Center, Newark
Ventola, Samuel, Northern State Prison, Newark
Vitale, Incoronato M., On Duty Outside the Archdiocese

Vrindten, Joseph G., Ramapo College, Mahwah
Vuolo, Pasquale, Our Lady of the Lake, Verona
Walker, George, On Duty Outside the Archdiocese
Wall, Joseph J., St. Teresa, Summit
Wandell, Raymond A., St. Joseph's and St. Michael's, Union City
White, Thomas, On Duty Outside the Archdiocese
Wicks, Ronald, On Duty Outside the Archdiocese
Wilverding, Daniel J., St. Michael, Cranford
Woodruff, Leo A., Holy Name, East Orange
Yannazzone, Robert, Assumption, Roselle Park
Zywicki, Robert S., Mount Carmel, Bayonne

INSTITUTIONS LOCATED IN THE ARCHDIOCESE

[A] SEMINARIES, ARCHDIOCESAN

KEARNY. *Redemptoris Mater.* Archdiocesan Missionary Seminary, 672 Passaic Ave., 07032. Tel: 201-997-3220; Fax: 201-997-5552. Revs. Jose Matias Diaz, Rector; Luis P. Gonzalez, Asst. to the Rector; Renato Grasselli, Asst. to the Rector; Raymond LaBranche, Spiritual Dir. Priests 4.

SOUTH ORANGE. *Immaculate Conception Seminary*, 400 South Orange Ave., 07079. Tel: 973-761-9575.
E-mail: theology@shu.edu
Web site: http://www.shu.edu
Officers of Admin.: Very Rev. Thomas R. Peterson, O.P., S.T.D., Ph.D., Chancellor; Rev. Msgr. Robert Sheeran, S.T.D., Pres.; Rev. Msgr. John W. Flesey, S.T.D., Rector & Dean; Dr. John M. Grondelski, Ph.D., Assoc. Dean; Rev. Msgr. Robert F. Coleman, J.C.D., Vice Rector & Business Mgr.; Rev. Msgr. Andrew T. Cusack, M.A., M.Div., Ph.D. (BGP), Dir. of Formation; Rev. John F. Russell, O.Carm., M.A., S.T.L., S.T.D., Spiritual Dir.; Rev. Msgr. James C. Turro, M.A., S.T.L., S.S.L., Ph.D., Acting Spiritual Dir. & Dir. of Library Svcs.; Patricia Feoranz, Registrar; Dr. Zeni Fox, Ph.D., Dir. of Lay Ministry; Rev. Martin F. O'Brien, Dir. Field Education. Full-Time Faculty: Rev. W. Jerome Bracken, C.P., Ph.D.; David R. Foster, Ph.D.; Zeni V. Fox, Ph.D.; Revs. Thomas G. Guarino, S.T.L., S.T.D.; Lawrence B. Porter, S.T.B., S.T.L., M.A., Ph.D.; Boniface Ramsey, O.P., S.T.D.; Arthur J. Serratelli, S.S.L., S.T.D.; William J. Toth, Ph.D.; Rev. Msgr. Robert J. Wister, S.T.B., S.T.M., D.Eccl.Hist.; Rev. C. Anthony Ziccardi, S.S.L.

Darlington Fund. Development Agency for Immaculate Conception Seminary. Priests 13; Lay Teachers 4; Total Enrollment 211.

Seton Hall University College Seminary, St. Andrew Hall, 07079. Tel: 973-761-9420. Rev. Thomas R. Peterson, O.P., Chancellor; Rev. Msgr. Robert T. Sheeran, Pres.; Revs. Arthur Serratelli, S.S.L., S.T.D., Rector; William P. Sheridan, Spiritual Dir. Priests 2; Total Enrollment 18.

[B] COLLEGES AND UNIVERSITIES

CALDWELL. *Caldwell College*, 9 Ryerson Ave., 07006. Tel: 973-228-4424
For a complete listing, refer to the Colleges and Universities section.

JERSEY CITY. *Saint Peter's College*, 2641 Kennedy Blvd., 07306-5997. Tel: 201-915-9000; Fax: 201-451-0036
For a complete listing, refer to the Colleges and Universities section.

LODI. *Felician College*, 262 S. Main St., 07644. Tel: 201-778-1190; Fax: 201-778-4111.
E-mail: petersen@inet.felician.edu
Web site: www.felician.edu
For a complete listing, refer to the Colleges and Universities section.

SOUTH ORANGE. *Seton Hall University*, (1856) 400 South Orange Ave., 07079. Tel: 973-761-9000; Fax: 973-275-2361
For a complete listing, refer to the Colleges and Universities section.

[C] HIGH SCHOOLS, PRIVATE

NEWARK. *St. Benedict's Preparatory School.* (Grades 7-12), 520 Dr. Martin Luther King, Jr. Blvd., 07102-1314. Tel: 973-643-4800.
E-mail: nwkabbey@connectinc.com
Web site: www.sbp.org
Rev. Edwin D. Leahy, O.S.B., Headmaster. Benedictine Monks of Newark Abbey 1; Priests 13; Brothers 2; Sisters 1; Lay Teachers 40; Boys 545.

St. Vincent Academy. (Girls), 228 W. Market St., 07103. Tel: 973-622-1613. Sr. June Favata, Admin. Dir. Sisters 7; Lay Teachers 21; Students 305.

BAYONNE. *Holy Family Academy*, 239 Ave. A, 07002. Tel: 201-339-7341; Fax: 201-339-9295.
E-mail: arnew32100@connectinc.com
Web site: http://www.hfa.bayonne.net
Sisters of St. Joseph of Chestnut Hill, Philadelphia, PA. Sr. Joan Immaculate O'Donnell, S.S.J., Pres.; Sr. Mary Ellen Ford, S.S.J., Prin. Sisters 9; Lay Teachers 21; Girls 300.

Marist High Schoool. (Coed), 1241 Kennedy Blvd., 07002. Tel: 201-437-4544; Fax: 201-437-6013. Marist Brothers. Bro. Kevin Handibode, F.M.S., Prin. Brothers 7; Sisters 2; Lay Teachers 24; Students 453.

CALDWELL. *Mount St. Dominic Academy.* (Girls), 3 Ryerson Ave., 07006-6196. Tel: 973-226-0660; Fax: 973-226-2693.
E-mail: msd73@hotmail.com
Web site: http://infolink.org/msd
Sisters of St. Dominic of Caldwell. Sr. Doris Ann Bowles, O.P., Prin. Sisters 10; Lay Teachers 27; Girls 268.

DEMAREST. *Academy of the Holy Angels.* (Girls), 315 Hillside Ave., 07627. Tel: 201-768-7822.
E-mail: arnew12100@connectinc.com
Web site: www.holyangels.org
Conducted by School Sisters of Notre Dame. Sr. Claire Bonneau, S.S.N.D., Pres. Brothers 1; Sisters 6; Lay Teachers 52; Girls 562.

ELIZABETH. *Benedictine Academy*, 840 N. Broad St., 07208-2599. Tel: 908-352-0670; Fax: 908-352-0698. Benedictine Sisters of Elizabeth, NJ. Adele Kosinski, Prin. Sisters 2; Lay Teachers 18; Girls 190. College Preparatory High School (Girls).

HOBOKEN. *Academy of the Sacred Heart.* (Girls), 713 Washington St., 07030. Tel: 201-659-7139.
E-mail: arnew32102@connectinc.com
Sisters of Charity of St. Elizabeth. Sr. Diane Collesano, S.C., Prin. Sisters 4; Lay Teachers 18; Girls 153.

JERSEY CITY. *Academy of St. Aloysius.* (Girls: Grades 9-12), 2495 John F. Kennedy Memorial Blvd., 07304. Tel: 201-433-8877; Fax: 201-433-8839.
E-mail: arnew32103@connectinc.com
Sisters of Charity of St. Elizabeth. Mrs. Tara Brunt, Prin. Sisters 4; Lay Teachers 18; Students 166.

St. Anthony High School, 175 Eighth St., 07302. Tel: 201-653-5143. Conducted by Felician Sisters. Sr. Mary Felicia, C.S.S.F., Prin. Brothers 1; Sisters 4; Lay Teachers 24; Students 330.

St. Dominic Academy. (Girls), 2572 John F. Kennedy Memorial Blvd., 07304. Tel: 201-434-5938. Dominican Sisters of Caldwell. Sr. Bettyanne Schultz, O.P., Prin. Sisters 9; Lay Teachers 39; Students 538.

St. Peter's Preparatory School, 144 Grand St., 07302. Tel: 201-434-4400; Fax: 210-547-6421. Revs. D. James French, S.J., Rector; James F. Keenan, S.J., Pres.; Mr. John R. Raslowsky, Prin.; Mr. Patrick Reidy, Vice Prin.; Mr. James Horan, Vice Pres. External Affairs; Mr. James Collins, Dean of Students; Revs. Charles F.X. Dolan, S.J., Vice Pres. Alumni Affairs; Anthony J. Azzarto, S.J., Chap.; Raymond J. Balduf, S.J., College Admissions; Erwin G. Beck, S.J.; John E. Browning, S.J.; Bro. Ralph Cilia, S.J.; Revs. Robert G. Cregan, S.J.; Daniel A. Degnan, S.J.; James S. Foley, S.J.; Francis J. Hamill, S.J.; Mr. Michael Guzik, S.J.; Bro. Paul J. Harrison, S.J.; Revs. Michael R. Hoag, S.J.; Thomas V. O'Connor, S.J.; Harold J. Oppido, S.J.; Enrico Raulli, S.J., Res., 220 W. 98th St., Apt. 4E, New York, NY, 10025. In res. Revs. Michael E. Browne, S.J.; John J. Rohr, S.J.; Bro. Frank Turnbull, S.J.; Mr. Jose Luiz Salazar, S.J.; Revs. Edward J. Snyder, S.J.; Francis P. Valentino, S.J.; Joseph T. Watson, S.J.; Bro. Joseph J. Griffin, S.J. Priests 21; Brothers 4; Scholastics 2; Sisters 1; Lay Teachers 60; Students 793.

LODI. *Immaculate Conception High School*, 258 S. Main St., 07644. Tel: 201-773-2400. Sr. Anelle Velivis, Ph.D., Prin. Sisters 6; Lay Teachers 20; Girls 216.

ORADELL. *Bergen Catholic.* (Boys), 1040 Oradell Ave., 07649. Tel: 201-261-1844; Fax: 201-599-9507.
E-mail: brosullo@idt.net
Congregation of Christian Brothers. Rev. James R. White, Chap.; Bro. J.G. Sullo, C.F.C., Pres.; Mr. Joseph S. Fusco, Prin. Priests 1; Brothers 12; Lay Teachers 48; Boys 875.

RAMSEY. *Don Bosco Preparatory High School for Boys*, 492 N. Franklin Tpke., 07446. Tel: 201-327-8003. Salesians of St. John Bosco. Revs. John Grinsell, S.D.B., Dir.; Louis Molinelli, S.D.B., Coord. of Youth Ministry; Brendan K. Kilroy, S.P.S., Guidance Dir.; Peter Sella, S.D.B.; Jerzy Schneider, S.D.B.; Paul Chuong Nguyen, S.D.B.; Anthony Luongo, S.D.B.; Bro. Gerald Warner, S.D.B. Priests 7; Brothers 1; Sisters 1; Lay Teachers 51; Students 750.

SOUTH ORANGE. *Marylawn of the Oranges, High School for Girls*, 445 Scotland Rd., 07079. Tel: 973-762-9222. Sisters 9; Lay Teachers 14; Girls 160.

SUMMIT. *Oak Knoll School of the Holy Child Upper School.* (Grades 7-12). (Girls), 44 Blackburn Rd., 07901. Tel: 908-522-8100. Conducted by the Sisters of the Holy Child Jesus. Sr. Cynthia Vives, S.H.C.J., Ed.D., Headmistress; Mary Ellen Ryan, Prin. Sisters 1; Lay Teachers 36; Students 276.

UPPER MONTCLAIR. *Lacordaire Academy, Secondary Division*, 155 Lorraine Ave., 07043. Tel: 973-744-1156; Fax: 973-783-9521.
Web site: http://home.earthlink.net/~lacordaire/index.html
Sisters of St. Dominic. Sr. Suzanne McCaffrey, O.P. Priests 1; Sisters 3; Lay Teachers 15; Girls 120.

WEST ORANGE. *Seton Hall Preparatory School*, 120 Northfield Ave., 07052. Tel: 973-325-6624; Fax: 973-325-6652.
Web site: www.shp.org
Rev. Msgr. Michael E. Kelly, M.A., Headmaster. Resident Faculty: Revs. Edward G. Bradley, S.T.L., M.A.; Martin J. Foran, S.T.B., M.A.; Bruce G. Janiga, M.A.; Stephen M. Kilcarr, B.A.; William J. Melillo, M.A., M.Div.; Joseph R. Reilly, S.T.B., S.T.L., B.A.; Joseph F. Wortmann, M.A., S.T.L. Priests 8; Lay Instructors 65; Students 800.

[D] HIGH SCHOOLS, DIOCESAN

CLARK. *Mother Seton (Girls) Regional High School*, Valley Rd., 07066. Tel: 908-382-1952.
E-mail: arnew42100@connectinc.com
Sisters of Charity of St. Elizabeth. Sr. Regina Martin, S.C., Prin. Sisters 12; Lay Teachers 25; Girls 400.

EAST ORANGE. *Bishop Joseph Francis Catholic High School*, 135 Glenwood Ave., 07017. Tel: 973-674-4200; Fax: 973-674-9121. Congregation of Christian Brothers. Bro. James A. DePiro, C.F.C. Priests 1; Sisters 1; Brothers 6; Lay Teachers 25; Boys 400.

JERSEY CITY. *Hudson Catholic High School*, 790 Bergen Ave., 07306. Tel: 201-332-5970.
E-mail: hudsoncath@aol.com
Web site: http://members.aol.com/hudsoncath/ppl.htm
Brothers of Christian Schools. Bro. Charles Barbush, F.S.C., Prin. Brothers 7; Sisters 1; Lay Teachers 30; Boys 585.

MONTVALE. *St. Joseph Regional High School.* (Boys), 40 Chestnut Ridge Rd., 07645. Tel: 201-391-3300; Fax: 201-391-8073. Rev. John Paladino, Chap.; John R. Job, Prin. Priests 1; Brothers 2; Sisters 1; Lay Teachers 31; Boys 451.

PARAMUS. *Paramus Catholic High School.* (Coed), 425 Paramus Rd., 07652. Tel: 201-445-6465; Fax: 201-445-6440. James P. Vail, Pres.; Mrs. Barbara C. Griffin, Prin. Sisters of Charity of St. Elizabeth. Priests 1; Sisters 4; Lay Teachers 58; Boys 356; Girls 501.

ROSELLE. *Roselle Catholic High School.* (Coed), Raritan Rd., 07203. Tel: 908-245-2350; Fax: 908-241-3869.
E-mail: rchs3@injersey.com
Web site: www.rosellecatholichs.org
Marist Brothers. Bro. Vincent Damian, F.M.S., Prin. Brothers 7; Sisters 1; Lay Teachers 44; Students 793.

SCOTCH PLAINS. *Union Catholic Regional High School.* (Coed), 1600 Martine Ave., 07076. Tel: 908-889-1600; Fax: 908-889-7867.
E-mail: ucrhs@idt.net
Web site: www.unioncatholic.org
Sr. Percylee Hart, R.S.M., Prin. Sisters 5; Lay Teachers 39; Students 701.

SUMMIT. *The Oratory Catholic Preparatory School.* (Grades 7-12), 1 Beverly Rd., 07901. Tel: 908-273-1084. Revs. F. Kevin Murphy, Headmaster; Stephen F. Duffy; John F. Johnston (BRK); Paul R. Manning, Res., 14 Bedford Rd. Tel: 908-273-7563. Priests 4; Lay Teachers 20; Students 224.

WASHINGTON TOWNSHIP. *Immaculate Heart Academy.* (Girls), 500 Van Emburgh Ave., 07675. Tel: 201-445-6800.
E-mail: arnew12190@connectinc.com
Web site: www.ihahs.com
Apostles of the Sacred Heart. Sr. Ellen Cronan, A.S.C.J., Prin. Sisters 7; Lay Teachers 46; Girls 744.

[E] ELEMENTARY SCHOOLS, PRIVATE

NEWARK. *Link Community School, Inc.*, 139 Livingston St., 07103. Tel: 201-642-0529; 642-8510. Dominican Sisters of Caldwell. Sr. Patricia McKearney, Prin. Sisters 4; Lay Teachers 10; Students 115.

St. Lucy Filippini Academy, 142 Jefferson St., 07105. Tel: 973-344-4806.
E-mail: arnew21118@connectinc.com
Sr. Mary Valitzski, M.P.F., Prin. Sisters 3; Lay Teachers 23; Students 400.

ELIZABETH. *Bender Memorial Academy*, 416 Linden Ave., 07202. Tel: 908-352-4406. Sisters of St. Benedict. Sr. Marie Therese Hayes, O.S.B., Prin. Sisters 5; Lay Teachers 8; Students 209.

Elizabethport Catholic School. (Central Office), 214 Ripley Pl., 07206. Tel: 908-352-9391; Fax: 908-352-4794. Ms. JoAnn Mathews, Dir.

Catholic Community Services, Early Childhood Center, 220 Msgr. Kemezis Pl., 07206. Tel: 908-289-6843; Fax: 908-289-1042. Students 25. Grade Levels include: Infants, Toddlers, PK3 and PK4.

Lower Campus. (Grades K-5), 261 Fulton St., 07206. Tel: 908-353-3160; Fax: 908-352-3878. Students 150.

Upper Campus. (Grades 6-8), 227 Court St., 07206. Tel: 908-351-2188; Fax: 908-351-6086. Students 150.

JERSEY CITY. *St. Joseph's School for the Blind,* 253 Baldwin Ave., 07306. Tel: 201-653-0578; Fax: 201-653-4087. Mr. Herbert Miller, Admin.; Dennis Cruz, Prin. School for visually impaired, multi-disabled children; non-graded; Early Intervention Program, 5-day Residential Program, Outreach Services. Lay Teachers 10; Students 80.

KEARNY. *Sacred Heart School,* 22 Wilson Ave., 07032. Tel: 201-991-0628. Sisters of the Catholic Apostolate. Sr. M. Leonore Parlati, C.S.A.C., Prin. Sisters 9; Lay Teachers 17; Students 390.

Day Care Center. Mrs. Nora Munoz, Head Teacher. Lay Teachers 10; Students 84.

LODI. *The Felician School for Exceptional Children,* 260 S. Main St., P.O. Box 530, 07644. Tel: 201-777-5355; Fax: 201-777-0725. Sr. Mary Ramona, C.S.S.F., Dir.

Day Program. Capacity 145. Sisters 4; Lay Teachers 16; Children 130.

SUMMIT. *Oak Knoll School of The Holy Child, Lower School.* (Grades K-6). (Coed), 44 Blackburn Rd., 07901. Tel: 908-522-8120. Sr. Cynthia Vives, S.H.C.J., Headmistress; Mrs. Joanne L. Ainsworth, Prin.; Mrs. Elisabeth Barclay, Guidance Counselor. Lay Teachers 28; Students 235.

UNION CITY. *Holy Rosary Academy,* 501 15th St., 07087. Tel: 201-864-0332. Sr. M. Gertrude Schiavone, C.S.A.C., Prin. Sisters of the Catholic Apostolate (Pallottine) 8; Lay Teachers 6; Students 230.

St. Francis Academy, 1601 Central Ave., 07087. Tel: 201-863-4112. Missionary Franciscan Sisters of the Immaculate Conception. Sr. Dora Sartino, O.S.F., Prin. Sisters 1; Lay Teachers 8; Students 238.

UPPER MONTCLAIR. *Lacordaire Academy-Elementary Division,* 155 Lorraine Ave., 07043. Tel: 973-746-2660. Dominican Sisters of Caldwell. Mrs. Mary Anne Ford, Prin. Lay Teachers 10; Students 100.

[F] CATHEDRAL HEALTHCARE SYSTEM OF ARCHDIOCESE OF NEWARK

NEWARK. *Cathedral Healthcare System, Inc.,* 219 Chestnut St., 07105. Tel: 973-690-3600; Fax: 973-690-3601. Mr. Frank L. Fumai, Pres. & CEO.

Cathedral Health Services, Inc.

St. Michael's Medical Center Division, Newark.

St. James Hospital Division, Newark.

St. Mary's Life Center Inc.-Pope John Paul II Pavilion.

[G] GENERAL HOSPITALS

NEWARK. *Catholic Community Services (C.C.S.) Mt. Carmel Guild Hospital,* 1160 Raymond Blvd., 07102. Tel: 973-596-4084

For a complete listing, refer to the Hospitals section.

St. James Hospital, 155 Jefferson St., 07105. Tel: 973-589-1300

For a complete listing, refer to the Hospitals section.

Saint Michael's Medical Center, 268 Dr. Martin Luther King. Jr. Blvd., 07102-9880. Tel: 973-877-5411; Fax: 973-877-2714

For a complete listing, refer to the Hospitals section.

ELIZABETH. *St. Elizabeth Hospital,* 225 Williamson St., 07207. Tel: 908-527-5000; Fax: 908-820-0554. E-mail: seam5122@aol.com

For a complete listing, refer to the Hospitals section.

ORANGE. *Saint Mary Life Center, Inc. - Pope John Paul II Pavilion,* 135 S. Center St., 07050. Tel: 973-266-3000

For a complete listing, refer to the Hospitals section.

TEANECK. *Holy Name Hospital,* 718 Teaneck Rd., 07666. Tel: 201-833-3000; Fax: 201-833-3230

For a complete listing, refer to the Hospitals section.

[H] HOMES FOR AGED

JERSEY CITY. *St. Ann's Home for the Aged,* 198 Old Bergen Rd., 07305. Tel: 201-433-0950

For a complete listing, refer to the Special Care Facilities section.

MONTCLAIR. *Mother Seton Residence,* 51 Washington St., 07042. Tel: 973-783-1400

For a complete listing, refer to the Special Care Facilities section.

St. Vincent's Nursing Home, 45 Elm St., 07042. Tel: 973-754-4800; Fax: 973-746-2362

For a complete listing, refer to the Special Care Facilities section.

PARAMUS. *Mount St. Andrew Villa,* 55 W. Midland Ave., 07652. Tel: 201-261-5950

For a complete listing, refer to the Special Care Facilities section.

SADDLE RIVER. *Villa Marie Claire,* 12 W. Saddle River Rd., 07458

For a complete listing, refer to the Special Care Facilities section.

[I] HOMES FOR THE BLIND

JERSEY CITY. *St. Joseph's Home for the Blind,* 537 Pavonia Ave., 07306. Tel: 201-653-8300

For a complete listing, refer to the Special Care Facilities section.

[J] DAY NURSERIES

NEWARK. *Our Lady of Perpetual Help Day Nursery,* 170 Broad St., 07104. Tel: 973-484-3535. Vocationist Sisters. Sisters 5; Lay Teachers 12; Children 180.

ELIZABETH. *Immaculate Heart of Mary Nursery, School & Kindergarten,* 205 E. Jersey St., 07206. Tel: 201-354-8388. Sr. Marianna Perrella, M.P.F., Prin. Religious Teachers Filippini 4; Children 111.

JERSEY CITY. *St. Elizabeth's Child Care Center,* 129 Garrison Ave., 07306. Tel: 201-795-1443; Fax: 201-795-4121. Franciscan Sisters of St. Elizabeth. Mother Rose Cosenza, Supr. Sisters 13; Total Staff 32; Children 270.

NUTLEY. *Holy Family Day Nursery and Convent,* 174 Franklin Ave., 07110. Tel: 201-235-1170. Franciscan Sisters of St. Elizabeth. Mother Romilda Chiga, F.S.S.E., Supr. Sisters 7; Children 80.

RAMSEY. *St. Joseph Pre-School,* 372 Wyckoff Ave., 07430. Tel: 201-825-8386. Franciscan Sisters of St. Elizabeth. Sr. Rosemary DiLauro, Supr. Sisters 4; Children 25.

[K] PROTECTIVE INSTITUTIONS

NEWARK. *Queen of Peace,* 60 Jay St., 07103. Tel: 973-481-9056

For a complete listing, refer to the Special Care Facilities section.

HOBOKEN. *Good Counsel, Inc. (St. Francis Home),* 303 Madison St., 07030. Tel: 201-798-9059; 795-0637; 800-723-8331 (Hotline); Fax: 201-795-0809

For a complete listing, refer to the Special Care Facilities section.

JERSEY CITY. *St. Joseph's Home,* 81 York St., 07302. Tel: 201-413-9280

For a complete listing, refer to the Special Care Facilities section.

KEARNY. *New Jersey Boystown,* 499 Belgrove Dr., 07032. Tel: 201-991-3770

For a complete listing, refer to the Special Care Facilities section.

[L] HOMES FOR WOMEN

JERSEY CITY. *St. Mary's Residence for Business and Professional Women,* 240 Washington St., 07302. Tel: 201-432-6289

For a complete listing, refer to the Special Care Facilities section.

[M] PERSONAL PRELATURES

SOUTH ORANGE. *Opus Dei.* (Prelature of the Holy Cross and Opus Dei), 170 Montrose Ave., 07079. Tel: 973-763-8397; Fax: 973-762-1794. Revs. James W. Albrecht; Thomas J. Lamb. Legal Title: *The Work of God, Inc.*

[N] MONASTERIES AND RESIDENCES OF PRIESTS AND BROTHERS

NEWARK. *Marist Brothers,* Queen of Angels Brothers' Residence, 28 Irvine Turner Blvd., 07103. Tel: 201-642-4820. Bros. Luke Reddington, Dir.; John Klein; Stephen Schlitte. Brothers 3.

Newark Abbey, 528 Dr. Martin Luther King, Jr. Blvd., 07102. Tel: 973-643-4800; Fax: 973-643-6922. E-mail: nwkabbey@connectinc.com

Rt. Rev. Melvin J. Valvano, O.S.B., Abbot & Pres. American Cassinese Congregation, O.S.B.; Very Revs. Mark M. Payne, O.S.B., Prior; Boniface J. Treanor, O.S.B., Subprior; Revs. John T. Browne, O.S.B.; Declan J. Cunniff, O.S.B.; Augustine J. Curley, O.S.B.; Lucien R. Donnelly, O.S.B.; Luke A. Edelen, O.S.B.; Albert T. Holtz, O.S.B., Novice Master; Theodore J. Howarth, O.S.B.; Edwin D. Leahy, O.S.B.; Bro. Thomas R. Lee, O.S.B.; Revs. Malachy M. McPadden, O.S.B.; Emilian Muschette, O.S.B.; Maynard G. Nagengast, O.S.B.; Bro. Gereon J. Reuter, O.S.B.; Revs. Benedict E. Tyler, O.S.B.; Philip J. Waters, O.S.B.; Bro. Francis M. Woodruff, O.S.B.; Rev. Matthew S. Wotelko, O.S.B., St. Maur Priory, 4615 N. Michigan Rd., Indianapolis, IN, 46208. Very Rev. Charles W. Henry, O.S.B., Prior; Revs. Robert McElaney, O.S.B.; Bernardin J. Patterson, O.S.B.; Bros. Francis Dachs, O.S.B.; Mark Hayden, O.S.B.; Jerome Rice, O.S.B.; Anthony Streit, O.S.B. Priests 20; Non-Clerical Brothers 7.

BAYONNE. *Marist Brothers,* Champagnat Residence, 1241 Kennedy Blvd., 07002. Tel: 201-437-4115. Bro. Ralph Dinielli, F.M.S., Dir. Brothers 8.

CALDWELL. *The Rev. Msgr. James F. Kelley Residence for Retired Priests,* 247 Bloomfield Ave., 07006. Tel: 973-364-1121. Mrs. Joan Stevens, Admin.; Rev. Msgr. Aloysius J. Welsh; Revs. Robert G. Gibney; Thomas J. Henry; George L. Mader; Vincent J. Quinn; Leo O. Farley; Vincent J. Prestera.

CLIFFSIDE PARK. *St. Patrick's Missionary Society,* 70 Edgewater Rd., 07010. Tel: 201-943-6575. E-mail: mission@stpatrickfathers.com
Web site: www.stpatrickfathers.com
Revs. Stephen Donohue; Brendan K. Kilroy, S.P.S.; Donald McDonagh, S.P.S.; Michael Moore, S.P.S.; James Barry. Total Staff 5; Total in Residence 5.

EAST ORANGE. *Congregation of Christian Brothers,* Essex Catholic Brothers' Residence, 135 Glenwood Ave., 07017. Tel: 973-676-3334. In res. Bros. H. A. McKenzie, Local Leader; P. R. Duffy; D. F. McCulloch; S. J. Johnsen; J. A. DePiro; J. J. Fagan. Brothers 6.

EAST RUTHERFORD. *Sacred Heart Friary,* 4 Jersey St., 07073. Tel: 973-778-1915.

HOBOKEN. *F.A.I.T.H. Services,* 307 Willow Ave., 07030. Tel: 201-792-6161; (Brothers Residence) 420-1554. Brothers of the Poor of St. Francis (C.F.P.). Bro. Robert J. Reinke, C.F.P. Total Staff 22; Total Assisted 2,188.

HOHOKUS. *St. Anthony of Padua,* 67 Arbor Dr., P.O. Box 40, 07423. Tel: 201-612-9763; Fax: 201-612-9869. Revs. Daniel Lanahan, O.F.M., Guardian; Kevin Cronin, O.F.M.; John Kelleher, O.F.M.; Emmet Murphy, O.F.M.; Francis N. Smith, O.F.M.

JERSEY CITY. *Brothers of the Christian Schools.* Hudson Catholic Brothers' Residence, 790 Bergen Ave., 07306-4535. Tel: 201-332-0971. Bro. Raymond Murphy, F.S.C. Brothers 9.

Jesuits of Saint Peter's College, Inc., 50 Glenwood Ave., 07306-4606. Tel: 201-433-2527. Revs. John F. Wrynn, S.J., Rector; William M. Abbott, S.J.; Thomas C. Blessin, S.J.; Edward W. Brande, S.J.; John M. Buckley, S.J.; Claudio M. Burgaleta, S.J.; Laurence L. Cassidy, S.J.; James H. Dahlinger, S.J.; Mark T. DeStephano, S.J.; Eugene J. Devlin, S.J.; J. Juan Diaz Vilar, S.J. (Spain); James F. Dolan, S.J.; Bro. Patrick T. Flanagan, S.J.; Revs. Charles A. Gallagher, S.J.; Edward B. Gillen, S.J.; Jerome H. Gruszczyk, S.J.; Edward J. Heavey, S.J.; Jose Kadankavil, S.J. (India); Joseph Kallipollil, S.J. (India); Joseph A. Kelly, S.J. (Ireland); Robert E. Kennedy, S.J.; James N. Loughran, S.J.; Joseph W. Lux, S.J.; T. Patrick Lynch, S.J.; Donal T. MacVeigh, S.J.; Oscar G. Magnan, S.J.; William F.X. Maher, S.J.; Edmund W. Majewski, S.J.; Carsten P. Martensen, S.J.; Robert E. McCarty, S.J.; William A. McKenna, S.J.; Aidan C. McMullen, S.J.; John J. O'Brien, S.J.; John P. Ruane, S.J.; John P. St. George, S.J.; Thomas L. Sheridan, S.J.; David X. Stump, S.J. Total Staff 34; Total in Residence 37.

MONTCLAIR. *Comboni Missionaries of the Heart of Jesus (Verona Fathers),* 88 High St., P.O. Box 138, 07042-0138. Tel: 973-744-8080; Fax: 973-744-8919. E-mail: combonimj@igc.apc.org
Revs. Pasquino Panato, M.C.C.J., Supr.; Paul Ewers, M.C.C.J., Bursar; Remus A. Catellani, M.C.C.J.; J.M. Carillo, M.C.C.J. Total Staff 7; Total in Residence 4.

MONTVALE. *Xaverian Brothers,* Xaverian Brothers' Residence, 40 Chestnut Ridge Rd., 07645. Tel: 201-391-8071; Fax: 201-391-8073. Brothers 2.

NORTH ARLINGTON. *Brothers of the Christian Schools,* Christian Brothers' Residence, 200 Ridge Rd., 07031. Tel: 973-991-0235.
E-mail: arnew12103@connectinc.com
Web site: www.qphs.org
Brothers 10.

ORADELL. *Congregation of Christian Brothers,* Bergen Catholic Brothers' Residence, 1040 Oradell Ave., 07649. Tel: 201-261-1816. Brothers 14.

ORANGE. *St. Veronica Giuliani Friary, Capuchin Franciscan Friars,* Province of St. Mary, 518-B Valley St., 07050-1231. Tel: 201-672-8080. Bro. John Shento, O.F.M.Cap., Guardian; Rev. John Gallagher, O.F.M.Cap., Vicar; Bros. Terrence Taffe, O.F.M.Cap.; John Conway, O.F.M.Cap.; Celestino Arias, O.F.M.Cap.; Maurice Moreau, O.F.M.Cap.; Larry Evans, O.F.M.Cap.; Luis Ramos, O.F.M.Cap.; Richard Crawley, O.F.M.Cap.; Oliver Anastacio, O.F.M.Cap.; Scott Leet, O.F.M.Cap.

ROSELLE. *Marist Brothers Residence,* Roselle Catholic High School, 1 Raritan Rd., 07203. Tel: 908-245-3574. Brothers 12.

RUTHERFORD. *St. John Vianney Residence for Priests,* 60 Home Ave., 07070. Tel: 201-933-5155; Fax: 201-933-4467. Mrs. Joan D'Gerolamo, Admin.; Rev. Msgr. Edward F. Kavin, Dir. In res. Most Rev. Peter L. Gerety, Archbishop Emeritus; Rev. Msgr. John J. Fahy; Rev. Msgr. Walter G. Jarvais, P.A.; Rev. Msgr. Anthony F. Bogdziewicz; Revs. Joseph Coda; Harold T. Hermanns; Rev. Msgr. William F. Hogan; Rev. Carl J. Merzena; Rev. Msgr. George O'Gorman; Rev. Maurice L. O'Keefe; Rev. Msgr. Gerard M. Santora; Rev. Msgr. Aloysius Welch; Revs. Charles V. Scanlan; John Bergeur; Leonard Midowski; John Madden; Thaddeus F. Zuber; Joseph J. Cestaro; Joseph Cassidy; Michael Fumo; Frederick Kaliner; John Shih. Resident Priests 1; Total in Residence 24; Total Staff 14.

SOUTH ORANGE. *The Salesian Community*. Don Bosco Residence. 315 Self Pl., 07079. Tel: 973-761-0201; Fax: 973-761-1032.
E-mail: sosdb@aol.com
Revs. James Heuser, S.D.B., Dir. & Vice Prov. Tel: 973-761-0153; James Berning, S.D.B., Vice Dir.; Clement Cardillo, S.D.B.; William Ferruzzi, S.D.B.; Francis Klauder, S.D.B.; Bro. Benjamin Natoli, S.D.B.; Rev. Frank Nugent, S.D.B.; Bros. John Zito, S.D.B.; Tho Bui, S.D.B.; Gilbert Michael Gonzales, S.D.B.; Alberto Hernandez Calle, S.D.B.; Khoa Luong, S.D.B.; Paul Long Mai, S.D.B.; Thien Nguyen, S.D.B.; Armando Pacheco, S.D.B.; Gerardo Rodriguez, S.D.B.; Van Tran, S.D.B.; Alphonse Vu, S.D.B.; Steven Way, S.D.B. Total in Residence 19.

Salesian Residence. House of Discernment, 9 Kingman Rd., 07079. Tel: 973-763-5350.
E-mail: salres@aol.com
Revs. William Ferruzzi; Frank Nugent. Total Staff 3; Total in Residence 9.

TENAFLY. *Society of African Missions, Provincialate, S.M.A. Fathers*, 23 Bliss Ave., 07670. Tel: 201-567-0450; Fax: 201-541-1280.
E-mail: SMAUSA-C@ix.netcom.com
Web site: http://www.smafathers.org
Very Rev. Douglas B. Gilbert, S.M.A., Prov. Supr. Tel: 201-567-9085 (Prov. Office); 567-7156 (Fax); Revs. Ulick Bourke, S.M.A., Local Supr.; Daniel Cullen, S.M.A.; Francis Gilfether, S.M.A.; Albert James, S.M.A.; George Landry, S.M.A.; John Francis Murray, S.M.A.; Kevin Scanlan, S.M.A.; James McConnell, S.M.A.; James H. Sullivan, S.M.A.; Thomas M. Wright, S.M.A.

UNION CITY. *Capuchin Friars - Province of the Sacred Stigmata of St. Francis*, P.O. Box 809, 07087. Tel: 201-865-0611; Fax: 201-866-7035. Very Rev. Robert Grix, O.F.M.Cap., Prov. Min.; Rev. Cyprian Rosen, O.F.M.Cap., Vicar Prov.; Bro. Kellen Mears, O.F.M.Cap., Councillor & Vocation Dir.; Revs. Vincent Fortunato, O.F.M.Cap., Councillor & Dir. Formation; Achilles Cassiere, O.F.M.Cap., Councillor; Francis Sariego, O.F.M.Cap., Prov. Sec. & Dir. Missionary Activity; Paul Daleo, O.F.M.Cap., Dir. Devel.

Congregation of the Passion (Passionists)-St. Michael's Residence, 526 Monastery Pl., 07087. Tel: 201-864-0018.
E-mail: hoaglan@mail.idt.com
Web site: www.cptryon.org

Center of Social Concerns. Rev. Kilian McGowan, C.P., Dir. Tel: 201-864-0018.

Passionist Missionaries, Inc. Tel: 201-867-6400; 867-6404. Revs. Sebastian Kolinovsky, C.P., Pass. Missionaries, Dir. Tel: 201-867-6400; Morgan Hanlon, C.P., Prov. Archivist. Tel: 201-617-0110; Victor Hoagland, C.P., Dir. Passionist Press & Supr. Tel: 201-864-0018; Paul Zilonka, C.P. Tel: 201-864-0018; Mr. James Fitzgerald, Lay Assoc. Tel: 201-864-0018; Rev. Darrell J. Mell, Dir. Devel. Tel: 201-867-0236.

VERONA. *The Salvatorian Fathers*. (Polish Mission House), 23 Crestmont Rd., 07044. Tel: 201-746-8770. Revs. Edward A. Toman, S.D.S., Supr. & Treas.; John L. Kozuch, S.D.S.; Wlodzimierz R. Las, S.D.S., Consultor; Andrzej Kielkowski, S.D.S.; Andrew J. Pitlok, S.D.S.; Andrzej Waszczenko, S.D.S.; Jan J. Mysliwiec, S.D.S.; Krzysztof Bugno, S.D.S., Vice Supr.; Grzegorz Szewczyk, S.D.S.; Strzadala Wieslaw, S.D.S.; Palka Bogdan, S.D.S.; Majcher Tadeusz, S.D.S., Consultor; Bro. Damian Marek, S.D.S.

WEST ORANGE. *Augustinian Recollects*. Prov. Res., Monastery of St. Cloud, 29 Ridgeway Ave., 07052. Tel: 973-731-0616; Fax: 973-731-1033. Very Rev. Francis E. Peluso, O.A.R., Prior Prov.; Revs. Jose Arias, O.A.R. (Mexico); Placido Lanz, O.A.R. (Mexico); Jose Luis Domaica, O.A.R. (Mexico); Marlon Beof, O.A.R. (Mexico); Bros. Anthony Torretti, O.A.R.; Michael Stechmann, O.A.R. Priests 5; Brothers 2.

[O] CONVENTS AND RESIDENCES FOR SISTERS

NEWARK. *Hermanas Misioneras del Corazon de Jesus (HMCJ)*. Parish Ministry. Sacred Heart Convent, 109 Parker St., 07104. Tel: 973-484-1516. Sr. Josefina Rosario, Supr. Sisters 4.

Missionary Sisters of the Most Blessed Sacrament and Mary Immaculate. Day Care Center. 121 Congress St., 07105. Tel: 973-589-5794. Sr. Guadalupe Grande, Supr. Sisters 4.

Monastery of St. Dominic, 375 13th Ave., 07103-2124. Tel: 973-622-6622. Dominican Nuns of the Order of Preachers (Cloistered). Sisters 20.

St. Michael's Convent, 182 Broadway, 07104. Tel: 201-482-7400 (School). Confraternity School of Religion; Lay Apostolate; Home Visiting. Sisters 6.

Sister Servants of the Merciful Redeemer, 5 Reynolds Pl., 07106. Tel: 973-761-9570. Sr. Andrea D'Angiolillo.

Sisters of Our Lady of Mercy. Mercederian Missionaries from Barcelona (Spain), 16 Longfellow Ave., 07106. Tel: 201-399-7322. Sisters of Our Lady of Mercy.

Sisters of St. Joseph of Chestnut Hill, Thea House, 39 Bleeker St., 07102. Tel: 201-622-7056. Total in Residence 4.

Vocationist Sisters, 172 Broad St., 07104. (Our Lady of Perpetual Help Center). Perpetual Help Day Nursery. Sisters 5; Total Assisted 200; Total Staff 21.

CALDWELL. *Motherhouse and Novitiate of Sisters of St. Dominic*, 1 Ryerson Ave., 07006. Tel: 973-403-3331; Fax: 973-228-9611.
E-mail: jeanneak@hotmail.com
Sr. Joan Doyle, Prioress. Sisters in Community 223; Sisters in Diocese 190.

ELIZABETH. *Little Servant Sisters of the Immaculate Conception (L.S.I.C.)*, St. Hedwig's School, 717 Polonia Ave., 07202. Tel: 908-355-8409. Sisters 4.

St. Walburga Monastery, 851 N. Broad St., 07208. Tel: 908-352-4278.
E-mail: Bensisnj@aol.com
Benedictine Sisters of Elizabeth, NJ. Sr. Louise Garley, O.S.B., Prioress. In Archdiocese 58; Professed Sisters 70.

Servants of St. Joseph Convent, 49 Smith St., 07201. Tel: 201-351-5749. Sr. Fabiola Ospina, Supr. Sisters 4; Total Staff 1; Total in Residence 4.

ENGLEWOOD CLIFFS. *St. Joseph Province Shalom Center*, 399 Hudson Terrace, 07632. Tel: 201-568-6348; Fax: 201-568-3764. Congregation of Sisters of St. Joseph of Peace. Sr. Mary Rattigan, C.S.J.P., Prov. Leader; Sr. Nora Molyneux, C.S.J.P., Asst. Province Leader; Sr. Theresette Hunting, C.S.J.P., Archivist. Sisters in Community 163. Provincial Office for St. Joseph's Province of the Sisters of St. Joseph of Peace.

St. Ann's Home for the Aged. Total Staff 166; Total in Residence 106.

St. Ann Day Care. Staff 6; Children 35.

St. Joseph Home for the Blind. Total Staff 95; Total in Residence 129.

St. Joseph School for the Blind. Total Staff 100; Total in Residence 47.

St. Joseph Home. Total Staff 13; Total in Residence 102.

St. Mary's Residence. Total Staff 7; Total in Residence 38.

Villa Marie Claire. Total Staff 8; Total in Residence 19.

Nurturing Place Day Care. Child Development Center. Staff 15; Children 50.

St. Michael Villa, 399 Hudson Ter., 07632. Tel: 201-871-1620; Fax: 201-871-7313. Sisters of St. Joseph of Peace. Sr. Clare McNerney, C.S.J.P., Admin.; Rev. Walter Cron, Chap. Sisters 46; Total Staff 42; Total in Residence 42. Senior Sisters Residence and Infirmary for St. Joseph Province.

FORT LEE. *Holy Trinity Convent*, 199 Myrtle Ave., 07024. Sisters 2.

IRVINGTON. *Immaculate Conception Convent*, 121 Myrtie Ave., 07111. Tel: 201-374-6397. Augustinian Recollect Sisters (Cloistered) 10.

JERSEY CITY. *Holy Rosary Convent*, 189 Brunswick St., 07302. Religious Teachers of St. Lucy Filippini 9.

Religious Institute of Our Lady of Mercy of Barcelona (Spain), 320 Whiton St., 07304. Tel: 201-451-0453. Sr. Maria Luz Palomino, R.M.M.

St. Nicholas Convent, 115 Ferry St., 07307. Tel: 201-659-5644. Sr. Mary Mark Smith, S.C.C., Supr.

Servants of the Gospel of Life, S.G.L., 20 Greenville Ave., 07305. Tel: 201-333-2443. Sr. Diane Carollo.

Sisters of Charity of St. Elizabeth (Convent, NJ) Northern Provincial House, 41 Emory St., 07301. Tel: 201-435-0868; Fax: 201-435-3134. Sr. Mary Morley, S.C., Prov. Supr. Sisters 5.

Sisters of St. Joseph of Peace, 25 Reservoir Ave., 07307. Tel: 201-656-7928.

KEARNY. *Our Lady of Sorrows Convent*, 55 Ivy St., 07032. Tel: 973-991-7983. Sisters of St. Francis of the Providence of God. Sr. Alma Pukel, O.S.F. Total in Residence 4.

LODI. *Immaculate Conception Convent*, 260 S. Main St., 07644-2196. Tel: 973-473-7447.
E-mail: CSSF@inet.felician.edu
Web site: http://www.felician.edu/CSSF.htm
Sr. Mary Antonelle Chunka, C.S.S.F. Chaplains: Revs. Harold Niedzwiecki, O.F.M.; Sebastian Kus, O.F.M.; Damian Colicchio, O.F.M.Cap. Sisters in Community 241; Professed Sisters 239.
Provincial House, Novitiate and Infirmary of the Felician Sisters.

PLAINFIELD. *Contemplative Convent of the Missionaries of Charity*, 513 Liberty St., 07060. Tel: 908-754-1978. Total in Residence 18.

SCOTCH PLAINS. *Union Catholic Convent*, 1600 Martine Ave., 07076. Sisters of Mercy of New Jersey (R.S.M.). Total in Residence 9.

SOUTH ORANGE. *Marylawn of the Oranges Convent*, 425 Scotland Rd., 07079. Sisters 11.

SPRINGFIELD. *St. James Convent*, 35 S. Springfield Ave., 07081. Tel: 973-376-7596. Sisters of St. Joseph, Chestnut Hill, Philadelphia. Total in Residence 10.

SUMMIT. *Monastery of Our Lady of the Rosary*, Morris Ave. & Springfield Ave., 07901. Tel: 908-273-1228. Sr. Mary Martin de Porres of Jesus, O.P., Prioress; Rev. Mathew V. Reilly, O.P., Chap. Tel: 908-277-6472. Legal Title: *Monastery of Our Lady of the Rosary, Dominican Nuns of the Perpetual Adoration and Perpetual Rosary*. Professed Sisters 19; Novices 1.

TENAFLY. *Convent of Our Lady of the Angels*, 253 Knickerbocker Rd., 07670. Tel: 201-568-2171; Fax: 201-568-2352. Missionary Franciscan Sisters of the Immaculate Conception. Sr. Marion Morrissey, O.S.F., Supr. Sisters 62.
Attended by Carmelite Fathers from Tenafly.

UNION CITY. *Holy Rosary Convent*, 1514 Central Ave., 07087. Tel: 201-617-4638. Sisters of the Catholic Apostolate (Pallotines). Sr. Patricia Gatti, C.S.A.C. Sisters 7.

Monastery of the Dominican Nuns of the Perpetual Rosary. (Contemplative), 14th St. and West St., 07087-3199. Mother Mary Jordan, O.P., Prioress. Professed Sisters 9; Novices 1; Aspirants 2; Total Staff 2; Total in Residence 10.

WEST ORANGE. *Provincialate, Southern Province, Sisters of Charity of St. Elizabeth*, 139 Gregory Ave., 07052; Fax: 973-669-2844. Sisters in Provincial House 4; Sisters in Province 257.

[P] RETREAT HOUSES

MAHWAH. *Carmel Retreat House*, 1071 Ramapo Valley Rd., 07430. Tel: 201-327-7090; Fax: 201-327-9133. Carmelite Community and House of Prayer. Retreats (groups, directed, private), Days of prayer, recollection for priests, religious and laity. Revs. David Simpson, O.Carm., Dir.; Paul Kirchner, O.Carm., (Retired); Ivan Cormac Marsh, O.Carm., Prior; Michael Wastag, O.Carm. Priests 4; Sisters 1; Total Staff 9; Total in Residence 4.

[Q] CAMPUS MINISTRY

NEWARK. *Archdiocesan Campus Ministry*, 45 Bleeker St., 07102. Tel: 973-642-1613.
E-mail: newmanctr@aol.com
Web site: www.catholiccampusministry.org
Mrs. Noel B. Wicks, Dir. Campus Ministry.

Essex County College, Rutgers University/Newark, NJIT, 45 Bleeker St., 07102. Tel: 973-642-1613.
E-mail: newmanctr@aol.com
Web site: www.catholiccampusministry.org
Mrs. Noel Wicks, Dir.; Rev. John D. Dennehy, Campus Min. & Chap. Legal Title: *Essex County College, Rutgers University/Newark Campus, New Jersey Institute of Technology*.

BLOOMFIELD. *Bloomfield College*, 12 Austin Pl., 07003. Tel: 201-748-9000, Ext. 250. Rev. James J. Reilly, Chap. & Campus Min.

CRANFORD. *Union County College*, 1033 Springfield Ave., 07016. Tel: 908-709-7092. Rev. James J. Reilly, Campus Min.

HOBOKEN. *Stevens Institute of Technology*, Castle Point on the Hudson, 07030. Tel: 201-963-4324. Rev. John J.F. Paladino, Campus Min. & Chap.

JERSEY CITY. *Jersey City State College*, 2039 Kennedy Blvd., 07305. Tel: 201-963-4324. Rev. John J.F. Paladino, Campus Min. & Chap.

MAHWAH. *Ramapo College*, 505 Ramapo Valley Rd., Room SC207, 07430. Tel: 201-825-9693. Rev. William T. Morris; Deacon Joseph Vrindten, Campus Min. Total Staff 2; Students 4,700.

TEANECK. *Fairleigh Dickinson Univ.-Teaneck Campus*, 1000 River Rd., 07666. Tel: 201-692-2406. Rev. John B. Baron, Campus Min. Total Staff 1.

UNION. *Kean College*, Catholic Campus Ministry, Green Ln., 1000 Morris Ave., 07083-7131. Tel: 908-629-7106; Fax: 201-985-0918. Rev. Alexander M. Santora, Campus Min.

UPPER MONTCLAIR. *Montclair State University*, Newman Catholic Center, 894 Valley Rd., 07043-2116. Tel: 973-746-2323; Fax: 973-783-3313.
E-mail: bernera@saturn.montclair.edu
Rev. Albert J. Berner, B.A., S.T.D., M.A., Campus Min. & Chap.; Mrs. Mary Lou Vinges, Admin. Asst. Total Staff 2.

[R] SHRINES

KEARNY. *Eucharistic Shrine of the Adorable Face of Jesus*, 672 Passaic Ave., 07032-1305. Tel: 201-997-6173; Fax: 201-997-1270. Rev. Raymond LaBranche, Dir.

[S] MISCELLANEOUS LISTINGS

NEWARK. *CatholiCare, Inc.*, 171 Clifton Ave., P.O. Box 9500, 07104-9500. Tel: 973-497-4007. Most Rev. Paul G. Bootkoski, D.D.

Deacon St. Lawrence Welfare Fund, Office of Permanent Diaconate, 171 Clifton Ave., P.O. Box 9500, 07104-9500. Tel: 973-497-4223.

Diaconate Executive Committee, Archdiocesan Center, 171 Clifton Ave., P.O. Box 9500, 07104-9500. Tel: 973-497-4223. Deacon Edward Porter.

New Jersey Caritas Corporation, Inc., 171 Clifton Ave., P.O. Box 9500, 07104-9500. Tel: 973-497-4007. Most Rev. Paul G. Bootkoski, D.D.

CCS Holding Corporation, Inc. Catholic Community Services (See Curia Section, Vicariate for Human Services).

Domus Corporation, Inc.

Canaan House, Inc., 1160 Raymond Blvd., 07102.

Sunrise House, 1160 Raymond Blvd., 07102. Tel: 973-596-4050. Most Rev. Nicholas A. DiMarzio, Ph.D., L.S.W., Dir.

Carmel House of Jersey City, Inc., 1160 Raymond Blvd., 07102. Tel: 973-596-4050. Most Rev. Nicholas A. DiMarzio, Ph.D., L.S.W., Dir.

BAYONNE. *Marist Brothers Support Trust*, 1241 Kennedy Blvd., 07002. Tel: 201-823-1115. Bros. Stephen Martin, F.M.S.; Benedict Lo Balbo, F.M.S. Congregation of the Marist Brothers, Province of Esopus.

ELIZABETH. *Alexian Brothers of Elizabeth, Inc.*, 655 E. Jersey St., 07206. Tel: 201-351-9000. Congregation of Alexian Brothers, Immaculate Conception Province. Bruce Fisher, Pres. & CEO.

Alexian Brothers of New Jersey, Inc., 655 E. Jersey St., 07206. Parent Corporation of Alexian Brothers of Elizabeth, Inc.

St. Joseph's Social Service Center, 118 Division St., 07201. Tel: 201-352-2989; 352-2966. Sr. Jacinta Fernandes, O.S.B., Dir. Total Staff 5; Total Assisted 4,052.

HOBOKEN. *F.A.I.T.H. Services, Inc.*, 307 Willow Ave., 07030. Tel: 201-792-6161. Bro. Robert J. Reinke, C.F.P., Admin.; Sr. Renee Zinciuk, C.S.W., L.C.S.W., Dir. Clinical Svcs. & Referrals for Svcs. Total Staff 22; Total Assisted 2,188. Extends the religious apostolate of charitable services of the Franciscan Sisters of the Poor, a religious congregation of the Roman Catholic Church by fulfilling the specific purposes set forth as follows: To provide community-based case management, education, counseling and other social support services for HIV/AIDS persons, their significant others and caregivers.

JERSEY CITY. *Franciscan Health System of New Jersey, Inc.*, One McWilliams Pl., 07332. Tel: 201-418-1000. Joan Quigley, Vice Pres. External Affairs & Contact Person.

St. Francis Hospital, 25 McWilliams Pl., 07302. Tel: 201-418-1000; Fax: 201-418-2011. Robert Chaloner, Pres.; Sr. Mary Meehan, S.S.N.D., Corp. Vice Pres., Mission; Sr. Jo-Ann Jackowski, S.F.P., Project Coord., Mission; Sr. Loretta Kirby, S.F.P., Pastoral Care; Revs. Gerard J. Sudol, Chap.; Thomas Kunnath. Franciscan Sisters of the Poor 2; Bed Capacity 254; Patients assisted annually 32,000.

St. Mary Hospital. (Sub. of Franciscan Health System of New Jersey, Inc.), 308 Willow Ave., Hoboken, 07030. Tel: 201-418-1000; Fax: 201-418-1013. Franciscan Sisters of the Poor. Ulrich J. Rosa, Pres. & CEO; Sr. Mary Meehan, S.S.N.D., Corporate Vice Pres., Mission; Sr. Rita Marie Donnelly, S.F.P., Pastoral Care; Sr. Maria Teresa Romeo, S.F.P., Pastoral Care; Sr. Jo-Ann Jackowski, S.F.P., Project Coord., Mission; Revs. Allen Guglielmo, Chap.; Thomas Kunnath. Franciscan Sisters of the Poor 3; Bed Capacity 328; Patients assisted annually 121,722.

KEARNY. *The Family of Nazareth, Inc.*, 672 Passaic Ave., 07032. Tel: 201-997-3220; Fax: 201-997-5552. Fred Canlas, Pres. A foundation to support the work of the Redemptoris Mater Mission Seminary and for new evangelization.

LODI.

**The Promise Outreach, Inc.*, 260 S. Main St., 07644. We visit, correspond with, and provide opportunity to teens in programs, institutions and centers for spirituality and other basic needs.

MAHWAH. *Paulist Press*, 997 MacArthur Blvd., 07430. Tel: 201-825-7300.
E-mail: paulistp@pipeline.com
Web site: www.paulistpress.com
Revs. Kevin A. Lynch, C.S.P.; Lawrence Boadt, C.S.P.

RUTHERFORD. *The Community of God's Love*, 70 W. Passaic Ave., 07070. Tel: 201-935-0344. Catholic Charismatic Community. Rev. P. Latronico, Chap.; Thomas C. Richard, Dir.

SCOTCH PLAINS. *Ministry Resource Center for Women Religious*, 1600 Martine Ave., 07076. Tel: 908-889-6425.
E-mail: ministrc@webspan.net
Web site: www.ministryconnect.org.
Sr. Bernadette Dougherty, S.S.J., Dir. Total Staff 1; Total Assisted 180.

**The Mercy Conservatory of Music*, 1600 Martine Ave., 07076. Tel: 908-889-8356. Sr. Mary Sharon Gross, R.S.M., Dir.

SOUTH ORANGE. *The Pallottines of South Orange, Inc.*, 204 Raymond Ave., 07079-2305. Tel: 973-763-5591. Bro. Francis Meo, S.A.C., Supr.

Salesians of Don Bosco, S.D.B., Don Bosco Annex, 361 Irving Ave., 07079. Tel: 201-761-0345.
E-mail: joeydba@aol.com
Rev. Timothy Zak, S.D.B., Coord. of Community Activities. Total in Residence 5.

U.S. Catholic China Bureau, Seton Hall University, 07079-2689. Tel: 973-761-9785; Fax: 973-275-2223.
E-mail: chinabur@shu.edu
Eugene Theroux, Esq., Chm., Bd. Trustees; Janet Carroll, M.M., Exec. Dir.; John P. Daly, S.J., Assoc. Dir. Promotes understanding among Catholics in America about the reality of the Chinese Catholic Church and fosters mutuality in relations between the Sister-Churches, publishes quarterly newsletter, sponsors National Catholic China Conference, religious study tours to China and other activities to sustain a shared commitment to mission with the Catholic Church in China. Total Staff 3.

TEANECK. *Holy Name Health Care Foundation*, 721 Teaneck Rd., 07666. Tel: 201-833-3187.
Web site: www.holyname.org
Sisters of St. Joseph of Peace. Michael Maron, Pres.

UNION CITY. *Park Performing Arts, Inc.* (Home of the Passion Play), 560 32nd St., 07087. Tel: 201-865-6980; Fax: 201-865-5339. Rev. Kevin P. Ashe, Exec. Dir. Total Staff 7.

RELIGIOUS INSTITUTES OF MEN REPRESENTED IN THE ARCHDIOCESE

For further details refer to the corresponding bracketed number in the Religious Institutes of Men or Women section.

[0100]—*Adorno Fathers.*—C.R.M.
[0200]—*Benedictine Monks.* (Newark Abbey; St. Mary Abbey).—O.S.B.
[0330]—*Brothers of Christian Schools.* (Baltimore Prov.; New York Prov.).—F.S.C.
[1350]—*Brothers of St. Francis Xavier.*—C.F.X.
[0460]—*Brothers of the Poor of St. Francis.*—C.F.P.
[0470]—*The Capuchin Friars.* (Prov. of the Stigmata; Prov. of St. Mary).—O.F.M.Cap.
[0270]—*Carmelite Fathers & Brothers.* (American Prov.).—O.Carm.
[0380]—*Comboni Missionaries of the Heart of Jesus (Verona).*—M.C.C.J.
[0310]—*Congregation of Christian Brothers.*—C.F.C.
[1000]—*Congregation of the Passion.* (Eastern Prov.).—C.P.
[0480]—*Conventual Franciscans.*—O.F.M.Conv.
[0520]—*Franciscan Friars.* (Prov. of Most Holy Name; Prov. of the Assumption).—O.F.M.
[0530]—*Franciscan Friars of the Atonement.*—S.A.
[0690]—*Jesuit Fathers and Brothers.* (Prov. of New York).—S.J.
[0770]—*The Marist Brothers.*—F.M.S.
[1210]—*Missionaries of St. Charles (Scalabrinians).*—C.S.
[0840]—*Missionary Servants of the Most Holy Trinity.*—S.T.
[0430]—*Order of Preachers-Dominicans.* (Prov. of St. Joseph, Eastern Dominican Prov.).—O.P.
[0150]—*Order of the Augustinian Recollects.*—O.A.R.
[1030]—*Paulist Fathers.*—C.S.P.
[]—*Province of the Immaculate Conception.*
[1070]—*Redemptorist Fathers*(Byzantine Ukrainians).—C.Ss.R.
[1170]—*St. Patrick Missionary Society.*—S.P.S.
[1190]—*Salesians of Don Bosco.*—S.D.B.
[0110]—*Society of African Missions.*—S.M.A.
[0990]—*Society of the Catholic Apostolate.* (Prov. of the Immaculate Conception).—S.A.C.
[1200]—*Society of the Divine Savior.*—S.D.S.
[0560]—*Third Order Regular of Saint Francis.* (U.S.A. Commissarate of the Spanish Prov.).—T.O.R.
[]—*Union Lumen Dei.*—L.D.
[1340]—*Vocationist Fathers.*—S.D.V.

RELIGIOUS INSTITUTES OF WOMEN REPRESENTED IN THE ARCHDIOCESE

[0100]—*Adorers of the Blood of Christ.*—A.S.C.
[0130]—*Apostles of the Sacred Heart of Jesus.*—A.S.C.J.
[]—*Augustinian Recollect Sisters.*—O.A.R.
[0230]—*Benedictine Sisters of Pontifical Jurisdiction-Newark.* (Benedictine Sisters of Baltimore; Benedictine Sisters of Elizabeth).—O.S.B.
[0760]—*Daughters of Charity of St. Vincent de Paul.* (North East Prov.).—D.C.
[0790]—*Daughters of Divine Charity.*—F.D.C.
[0850]—*Daughters of Mary Help of Christians.*—F.M.A.
[]—*Daughters of Mary, Mothers of Mercy.* (Nigeria).—D.M.M.M.
[1050]—*Dominican Contemplative Nuns (Cloistered).*—O.P.
[1070-11]—*Dominican Sisters.* (Sparkill, NY).—O.P.
[1070-15]—*Dominican Sisters.* (Blauvelt, NY).—O.P.
[1070-18]—*Dominican Sisters.* (Caldwell, NJ).—O.P.
[1070-06]—*Dominican Sisters of Hope.* (Newburgh, NY).—O.P.
[1070-09]—*Dominican Sisters of St. Catherine of Siena (Philippines).*
[1170]—*Felician Sisters.*—C.S.S.F.
[1400]—*Franciscan Missionary Sister of the Sacred Heart.*—F.M.S.C.
[1180]—*Franciscan Sisters of Allegany, New York.*—O.S.F.
[1425]—*Franciscan Sisters of Peace.*—F.S.P.
[1420]—*Franciscan Sisters of Ringwood.*—F.S.R.
[1460]—*Franciscan Sisters of St. Elizabeth.*—F.S.S.E.
[1190]—*Franciscan Sisters of the Atonement.*—S.A.
[]—*Franciscan Sisters of the Immaculate Heart of Mary (India).*—F.I.H.M.
[1440]—*Franciscan Sisters of the Poor.*—S.F.P.
[1240]—*Grey Nuns of the Sacred Heart.*—G.N.S.H.
[]—*Hermanas Missionaras del Corazon de Jesus.* (Dominican Republic).—H.M.C.J.
[3790]—*Institute of the Sisters of St. Dorothy.*—S.S.D.
[2300]—*Little Servant Sisters of the Immaculate Conception.*—L.S.I.C.
[2470]—*Maryknoll Sisters of St. Dominic.*—M.M.
[]—*Mercedarian Sisters (Missionary Sisters of Our Lady of Mercy).*—R.M.M.
[2710]—*Missionaries of Charity.*—M.C.
[1360]—*Missionary Franciscan Sisters of the Immaculate Conception.*—M.F.I.C.
[2790]—*Missionary Servants of the Most Blessed Trinity.*—M.S.B.T.
[2760]—*Missionary Sisters of the Immaculate Conception of the Mother of God.*—S.M.I.C.
[2780]—*Missionary Sisters of the Most Blessed Sacrament and Mary Immaculate.*—M.SS.M.I.
[]—*Religious of the Virgin Mary (Philippines).*—R.V.M.
[3430]—*Religious Teachers Filippini.*—M.P.F.
[2970]—*School Sisters of Notre Dame.*—S.S.N.D.
[1700]—*School Sisters of the Third Order of St. Francis.* (Bethlehem, PA).—O.S.F.
[]—*Servants of the Gospel of Life.*—S.G.L.
[]—*Sister Servants of the Merciful Redeemer.*
[0540]—*Sisters of Charity of Ottawa.*—S.C.O.
[0590]—*Sisters of Charity of Saint Elizabeth, Convent Station.*—S.C.
[0660]—*Sisters of Christian Charity.*—S.C.C.
[2575]—*Sisters of Mercy of the Americas.* (New Jersey).—R.S.M.
[]—*Sisters of Our Lady of Perpetual Help (Korea).*—S.O.L.P.H.
[1620]—*Sisters of Saint Francis of Millvale, Pennsylvania.*—O.S.F.
[3893]—*Sisters of Saint Joseph of Chestnut Hill, Philadelphia.*—S.S.J.
[3730]—*Sisters of St. Basil the Great.*—O.S.B.M.
[1650]—*The Sisters of St. Francis of Philadelphia.*—O.S.F.
[3820]—*Sisters of St. John the Baptist.*—C.S.J.B.
[3890]—*Sisters of St. Joseph of Peace.*—C.S.J.P.
[3930]—*Sisters of St. Joseph of the Third Order of St. Francis.*—S.S.J.-T.O.S.F.
[3140]—*Sisters of the Catholic Apostolate (Pallottine).*—C.S.A.C.
[2980]—*Sisters of the Congregation of Notre Dame.*—C.N.D.
[1490]—*Sisters of the Third Franciscan Order.*—O.S.F.
[3610]—*Sisters Servants of Mary Immaculate.*—S.S.M.I.
[3595]—*Sisters, Servants of St. Joseph.*—S.S.J.
[2160]—*Sisters, Servants of the Immaculate Heart of Mary (Scranton).*—I.H.M.
[4060]—*Society of the Holy Child Jesus.*—S.H.C.J.
[]—*Union Lumen Dei.*—L.D.
[4210]—*Vocationist Sisters.*—S.D.V.

ARCHDIOCESAN CEMETERIES

COLONIA. *St. Gertrude.*
DARLINGTON. *Maryrest.*
EAST HANOVER. *Gate of Heaven.*
EAST ORANGE. *Holy Sepulchre.*
St. Mary.
FRANKLIN LAKES. *Christ the King.*
JERSEY CITY. *Holy Name.*
Saint Peter.
NORTH ARLINGTON. *Holy Cross.*
RIVER VALE. *St. Andrew.*

PAROCHIAL CEMETERIES

NEWARK. *Mount Olivet.*

BELLEVILLE. *St. Peter's.*
BLOOMFIELD. *Mount Olivet.*
CLARK. *St. Mary's.*
FORT LEE. *Madonna.*
HACKENSACK. *St. Joseph's.*
HO-HO-KUS. *St. Luke's.*
LINDEN. *Mount Calvary.*
LYNDHURST. *St. Joseph's.*
ORANGE. *St. John's.*
PLAINFIELD. *St. Mary's.*
RIVER VALE. *St. Andrew's.*
SHORT HILLS. *St. Rose of Lima.*
SUMMIT. *St. Teresa's.*
TENAFLY. *Mount Carmel.*
UPPER MONTCLAIR. *Immaculate Conception.*

NECROLOGY

✠ Francis, Most Rev. Joseph A., Retired Auxiliary Bishop of Newark. —Died Sept. 1, 1997.

† Bukowski, Vincent J., (Retired). —Died May 9, 1997.

† Cassidy, Joseph L., (Retired). —Died June 1, 1997.

† Darcy, Rev. Msgr. Harold P., Closter, NJ, St. Mary. —Died Dec. 24, 1997.

† Doyle, Robert A., Jersey City, NJ, Our Lady of Mercy. —Died July 18, 1997.

† Foley, James F., (Retired). —Died Oct. 29, 1997.

† Gillick, Thomas A., Rutherford, NJ, St. John Vianney. —Died June 19, 1997.

† Hanly, John G., (Retired). —Died Oct. 16, 1997.

† Hudson, Charles J., Westfield, NJ, St. Helen's. —Died Jan. 21, 1997.

† Loreti, Rev. Msgr. Joseph F., Roselle Park, NJ, Assumption. —Died Nov. 22, 1997.

† McCloskey, James F., (Retired). —Died Feb. 22, 1997.

† O'Brien, Rev. Msgr. John F., (Retired). —Died Feb. 6, 1997.

† Reilly, Peter J., Rutherford, NJ, St. Mary. —Died Feb. 21, 1997.

† Synan, Rev. Msgr. Edward A., (Retired). —Died Aug. 2, 1997.

† Zaorski, Thaddeus L., (Retired). —Died June 22, 1997.

Archdiocese of New Orleans

(Archidioecesis Novae Aureliae)

Most Reverend

FRANCIS B. SCHULTE, D.D.

Archbishop of New Orleans; ordained May 10, 1952; appointed Titular Bishop of Afufenia and Auxiliary Bishop of Philadelphia June 27, 1981; ordained to the episcopacy August 12, 1981; appointed Sixth Bishop of Wheeling-Charleston June 4, 1985; promoted to Metropolitan See of New Orleans December 13, 1988; installed February 14, 1989. *Office: 7887 Walmsley Ave., New Orleans, LA, 70125-3496.* Tel.: 504-861-9521.

Archdiocesan Administration Building: 7887 Walmsley Ave., New Orleans, LA, 70125-3496. Tel.: 504-861-9521; Fax: 504-866-2906.

Web site address: http://www.catholic.org/neworleans/

Most Reverend

PHILIP M. HANNAN, D.D., J.C.D., S.T.L.

Former Archbishop of New Orleans; ordained December 8, 1939; appointed Titular Bishop of Hieropolis and Auxiliary Bishop of Washington June 16, 1956; consecrated August 28, 1956; promoted to Archbishop of New Orleans September 29, 1965; installed October 13, 1965; retired February 14, 1989. *Address correspondence to: 2929 S. Carrollton Ave., New Orleans, LA, 70118-4301.* Tel.: 504-866-7411.

Most Reverend

NICHOLAS D'ANTONIO, O.F.M., D.D.

Retired; ordained June 7, 1942; appointed Prelate Nullius, Ordinary of Olancho, Honduras, C.A. December 31, 1963; consecrated July 25, 1966; appointed Vicar for Spanish-Speaking, New Orleans August 22, 1977; retired July 10, 1991. *Res., 1221 Mandeville St., New Orleans, LA, 70117-8498.* Tel.: 504-943-5561.

Most Reverend

DOMINIC CARMON, S.V.D., D.D., V.G.

Auxiliary Bishop of New Orleans and Titular Bishop of Rusicade; ordained February 2, 1960; appointed December 16, 1992; consecrated February 11, 1993. *Office: 4111 St. Blase Dr., Kenner, LA, 70065-1656.* Tel.: 504-468-1441; Fax: 504-468-3305.

Most Reverend

GREGORY M. AYMOND, D.D., V.G.

Auxiliary Bishop of New Orleans and Titular Bishop of Acolla; ordained May 10, 1975; appointed November 19, 1996; consecrated January 10, 1997. *Office: 2901 S. Carrollton Ave., New Orleans, LA, 70118-4391.* Tel.: 504-866-7426.

CREATED A DIOCESE APRIL 25, 1793; ARCHDIOCESE JULY 19, 1850.

Square Miles 4,208.

Comprises the following Parishes of Louisiana: Orleans, St. Bernard, Plaquemines, Jefferson, St. Charles, St. John the Baptist, St. Tammany and Washington.

For legal titles of parishes and archdiocesan institutions, consult the Chancery Office.

STATISTICAL OVERVIEW

Personnel	
Archbishop	1
Retired Archbishops	1
Auxiliary Bishops	2
Retired Bishops	1
Abbots	1
Priests: Diocesan Active in Diocese	168
Priests: Active Outside Diocese	19
Priests: Retired, Sick or Absent	42
Number of Diocesan Priests	229
Religious Priests in Diocese	217
Extern Priests in Diocese	16
Ordinations:	
Diocesan Priests	1
Transitional Deacons	3
Permanent Deacons in Diocese	194
Total Brothers	141
Total Sisters	870
Parishes	
Parishes	146
With Resident Pastor:	
Resident Diocesan Priests	108
Resident Religious Priests	34
Without Resident Pastor:	
Administered by Priests	4
Missions	8
Pastoral Centers	1
Closed Parishes	1
Welfare	
Health Care Centers	3
Total Assisted	5,180
Homes for the Aged	17
Total Assisted	3,051
Residential Care of Children	2
Total Assisted	201
Day Care and Extended Day Care Centers	17
Total Assisted	1,136
Specialized Homes	4
Total Assisted	3,660
Special Centers for Social Services	55
Total Assisted	158,562
Residential Care of Disabled	9
Total Assisted	93
Other Institutions	14
Total Assisted	2,266
Educational	
Seminaries, Diocesan	2
Students from This Diocese	23
Students from Other Diocese	132
Diocesan Students in Other Seminaries	1
Seminaries, Religious	3
Students Religious	17
Total Seminarians	41
Colleges and Universities	3
Total Students	10,311
High Schools, Diocesan and Parish	10
Total Students	6,627
High Schools, Private	13
Total Students	9,810
Elementary Schools, Diocesan and Parish	74
Total Students	32,742
Elementary Schools, Private	6
Total Students	1,441
Non-residential Schools for the Disabled	1
Total Students	192
Catechesis/Religious Education:	
High School Students	4,148
Elementary Students	18,072
Total Students Under Catholic Instruction	83,384
Teachers in the Diocese:	
Priests	95
Brothers	40
Sisters	155
Lay Teachers	3,515
Vital Statistics	
Receptions into the Church:	
Infant Baptism Totals	7,060
Adult Baptism Totals	408
Received into Full Communion	365
First Communions	6,754
Confirmations	5,984
Marriages:	
Catholic	1,809
Interfaith	591
Total Marriages	2,400
Deaths	4,580
Total Catholic Population	471,107
Total Population	1,335,563

Former Bishops and Archbishops—Rt. Rev. LUIS PENALVER Y CARDENAS, D.D., cons. in 1793; transferred to Guatemala, in 1801; resigned in 1806; retired to Havana, Cuba; died in Havana, July 17, 1810. Under the administration of the Archbishop of Baltimore from 1805-1815.—Rt. Rev. FRANCIS PORRO, Bishop-elect.—Rt. Rev. LOUIS WILLIAM DUBOURG, S.S., D.D., cons. Sept. 24, 1815; died Archbishop of Besancon, Dec. 1833.—Rt. Rev. JOSEPH ROSATI, D.D., C.M., cons. March 25, 1824; Bishop of Tanagre and coadjutor; transferred to St. Louis, March 20, 1827; died Sept. 25, 1843.—Rt. Rev. LEO DE NECKERE, C.M., D.D., cons. Aug. 4, 1829; died Sept. 4, 1833.—Most Rev. ANTOINE BLANC, first Archbishop; cons. Nov. 22, 1835; Archbishop, July 19, 1850; died June 20, 1860.—Most Rev. JEAN MARIE ODIN, C.M., D.D., cons. Bishop of Claudiopolis and Vicar-Apostolic of Texas, March 6, 1842; transferred to Galveston, 1847; promoted to New Orleans in 1861; died at Ambierle, France, May 25, 1870.—Most Rev. NAPOLEON J. PERCHE, cons. Bishop of Abdera and coadjutor, March 21, 1870; promoted to the See of New Orleans, May 25, 1870; died Dec. 1883.—Most Rev. F. X. LERAY, D.D., cons. Bishop of Natchitoches, April 22, 1877; appt. coadjutor of New Orleans, and Bishop of Janopolis, Oct. 23, 1879; promoted to the See of New Orleans, Dec., 1883; died at Chateaugiron, France, Sept. 23, 1887.—Most Rev. FRANCIS JANSSENS, D.D., cons. Bishop of Natchez, MS, May 1, 1881; promoted to the Archiepiscopal See of New Orleans, Aug. 7, 1888; died June 9, 1897.—Most Rev. PLACIDE LOUIS CHAPELLE, D.D., Apostolic Delegate Extraordinary for Cuba and Puerto Rico; Archbishop of New Orleans; appt. Bishop of Arabissus and Coadjutor of Santa Fe *cum jure successionis,* Aug. 21, 1891; cons. Nov. 1, 1891; promoted to the Titular Archiepiscopal See of Sebaste May 10, 1893; Archbishop of Santa Fe, Jan. 9, 1894; appt. to New Orleans, Dec. 1, 1897; died Aug. 9, 1905.—Most

Rev. JAMES H. BLENK, S.M., D.D., appt. Bishop of Puerto Rico, June 12, 1899; cons. July 2, 1899; promoted to the See of New Orleans, April 20, 1906; died April 20, 1917.—Most Rev. JOHN W. SHAW, D.D., appt. Coadjutor Bishop of San Antonio, Feb. 7, 1910; cons. Titular Bishop of Castabala, April 14, 1910; succeeded to the See of San Antonio, March 11, 1911 made assistant at the Pontifical Throne, Sept., 1916; promoted to the See of New Orleans, Jan. 25, 1918; died Nov. 2, 1934.—Most Rev. JOSEPH FRANCIS RUMMEL, D.D., ord. May 24, 1902; appt. Bishop of Omaha, March 30, 1928; cons. May 29, 1928; appt. Archbishop of New Orleans, Mar. 9, 1935; died Nov. 8, 1964.—His Eminence JOHN CARDINAL CODY, D.D., cons. July 2, 1947; promoted to Coadjutor *cum jure successionis* of New Orleans, Aug. 10, 1961; acceded See, Nov. 8, 1964; transferred to Chicago, June 16, 1965; created Cardinal, June 26, 1967; died April 25, 1982.—Most Rev. PHILIP M. HANNAN, D.D., Archbishop of New Orleans; ord. Dec. 8, 1939; appt. Titular Bishop of Hieropolis and Auxiliary Bishop of Washington, June 16, 1956; cons. Aug. 28, 1956; promoted to Archbishop of New Orleans, Sept. 29, 1965; retired Feb. 14, 1989.

Vicars General—Most Rev. DOMINIC CARMON, S.V.D., *4111 St. Blase Dr., Kenner, 70065-1565.* Tel: 504-468-1441; Fax: 504-468-3305. Most Rev. GREGORY M. AYMOND, V.G., *2901 S. Carrollton Ave., New Orleans, 70118-4391.* Tel: 504-866-7426; Fax: 504-866-3119. Rev. Msgr. THOMAS J. RODI, V.G., *7887 Walmsley Ave., New Orleans, 70118-3496.* Tel: 504-861-6262; Fax: 504-866-2906.

Chancellor and Moderator of the Curia—Rev. Msgr. THOMAS J. RODI, V.G. Tel: 504-861-6262; 861-9521; Fax: 504-866-2906.

Controller—Mr. JOSEPH E. INGRAHAM.

Archdiocesan Administration Building—7887 Walmsley Ave., New Orleans, 70125-3496. Office Hours: Mon.-Fri. 9-5. Tel: 504-861-9521; Fax: 504-866-2906.

Metropolitan Tribunal—7887 Walmsley Ave., New Orleans, 70125-3496. All rogatorial commissions should be sent to this address: c/o Very Rev. VIEN THE NGUYEN, J.C.L.

Judicial Vicar—Very Rev. VIEN THE NGUYEN, J.C.L.

Adjutant Judicial Vicars—Rev. Msgr. CLINTON J. DOSKEY, J.C.L.; Rev. JOSEPH P. MULLIN, S.M., S.T.L.

Judges—Rev. Msgr. THOMAS C. DOWLING, M.A.; Rev. Msgr. LOUIS P. LEBOURGEOIS; Rev. Msgr. THOMAS J. RODI, V.G.; Rev. Msgr. L. EARL GAUTHREAUX, J.C.L.; Revs. THOMAS E. KINNEY, J.C.L.; GERARD LAPORTE, C.SS.R., J.C.L.; PETER O'GRADY; ANDREW TAORMINA, J.D.

Associate Judges—Mr. PETER E. DUFFY, J.D.; Mr. FRANS LABRANCHE, JR., J.D.; Mr. PAUL A. NALTY, J.D.; Mr. PETER C. RIZZO, J.D.

Defensores Vinculi—Very Rev. GERALD L. SEILER, J.C.L.; Revs. WILLIAM J. O'DONNELL, J.C.L.; RAMON MARTINEZ, M.Div.; BENJAMIN PIOVAN, M.A.; LEE J. SALOY, M.Div.; Sr. WALDIA A. WARDEN, O.P., J.C.L.

Executive Secretary—Sr. WALDIA A. WARDEN, O.P., J.C.L.

Archdiocesan Consultors—Most Rev. DOMINIC CARMON, S.V.D., D.D., V.G.; Most Rev. GREGORY M. AYMOND, V.G.; Rev. Msgr. FRANCIS G. BOESHANS; Rev. Msgr. CLINTON J. DOSKEY; Rev. Msgr. RAY P. HEBERT; Rev. Msgr. CROSBY W. KERN; Rev. Msgr. JOHN P. REYNOLDS; Rev. Msgr. THOMAS J. RODI, V.G.

Deans—Very Rev. FRANCIS M. HULL, S.S.J., V.F., Cathedral Deanery I; Rev. NEAL W. MCDERMOTT, O.P., V.F., City Park-Gentilly Deanery II; Very Rev. HENRY H. ENGELBRECHT, V.F., Uptown Deanery III; Very Rev. KENNETH BORGESEN, O.SS.T., V.F., Inner City Deanery IV; Rev. Msgr. CROSBY W. KERN, V.F., East Jefferson Deanery V; Very Rev. ROBERT G. VINCENT, V.F., St. John-St. Charles Deanery VI; Very Rev. MICHAEL B. FRASER, V.F., West Bank Deanery VII; Rev. Msgr. ALLEN J. ROY, V.F., Algiers-Plaquemines Deanery VIII; Very Rev. WALTER J. AUSTIN, V.F., St. Bernard Deanery IX; Rev. Msgr. FRANCIS G. BOESHANS, V.F., St. Tammany-Washington Deanery X.

Archdiocesan Administrative Council—Most Rev. FRANCIS B. SCHULTE, D.D., Chm.; Rev. Msgr. THOMAS J. RODI, V.G., Vice Chm.; Very Rev. GERALD L. SEILER, Sec. Members of the Board: Most Rev. DOMINIC CARMON, S.V.D., V.G.; Most Rev. GREGORY M. AYMOND, V.G.; Sr. SUELLEN TENNYSON, M.S.C.; Rev. Msgr. RAY P. HEBERT; Mr. JOSEPH E. INGRAHAM; Rev. Msgr. ROGER P. MORIN.

Archdiocesan Pastoral Council—Sr. MARJORIE HEBERT, M.S.C., Pres.

Priests Council—Most Rev. FRANCIS B. SCHULTE, D.D., Pres.; Rev. Msgr. LANAUX J. RARESHIDE, Chm.

Archdiocesan Finance Council—Most Rev. FRANCIS B. SCHULTE, Chm.; Rev. Msgr. THOMAS J. RODI, V.G., Vice Chm.

Censores Librorum—Very Rev. GERALD L. SEILER, Co-ord.

Louisiana Catholic Conference—Mr. KIRBY J. DUCOTE, Dir., *3423 Hundred Oaks Ave., Baton Rouge, 70808-1548.* Tel: 504-344-7120; Fax: 504-383-9591.

Office of the Vicar General and Moderator of the Curia

Rev. Msgr. THOMAS J. RODI, V.G., Vicar General, *7887 Walmsley Ave., New Orleans, 70125-3496.* Tel: 504-861-6262; Fax: 504-866-2906

Catholic Foundation for the Archdiocese of New Orleans, Inc.—Mr. JOSEPH L. LANGENDERFER, Exec. Dir., *1000 Howard Ave., Ste. 700, New Orleans, 70113-1903.* Tel: 504-596-3045; Fax: 504-596-3068.

Communications—Mr. THOMAS M. FINNEY, Dir., *7887 Walmsley Ave., New Orleans, 70125-3496.* Tel: 504-861-6239; 861-9521; Fax: 504-866-2906.

Development Office—Mr. JOSEPH L. LANGENDERFER, Exec. Dir., *1000 Howard Ave., New Orleans, 70113-1903.* Tel: 504-596-3045; Fax: 504-596-3068.

Legal Services—Rev. Msgr. THOMAS J. RODI, V.G., Dir. CHARLES I. DENECHAUD, JR.; THOMAS A. RAYER; CHARLES I. DENECHAUD, III; OTTO SCHOENFELD; EDWARD DENECHAUD; DON M. RICHARD, *1207 First NBC Bldg., New Orleans, 70112-4100.* Tel: 504-522-4756; Fax: 504-568-0783.

Newspaper—"Clarion Herald", Newspaper of the Archdiocese of New Orleans. Published by Clarion Herald Publishing Co., Inc., PETER P. FINNEY, JR., Gen. Mgr. & Exec. Editor, *1000 Howard Ave., Ste. 400, New Orleans, 70113-1903.* Tel: 504-596-3030; Fax: 504-596-3020.

Department of Christian Formation

Executive Director—Most Rev. GREGORY M. AYMOND, D.D., *7887 Walmsley Ave., New Orleans, 70125-3496.* Tel: 504-861-6253; 861-9521; Fax: 504-866-2906.

Campus Ministry—Most Rev. GREGORY M. AYMOND, D.D., *2901 S. Carrollton Ave., New Orleans, 70118-4391.* Tel: 504-866-7426; Fax: 504-866-3119.

Catholic Schools Office—Mr. HOWARD J. JENKINS, Supt. Assoc. Supts.: Mrs. JANE O'CONNELL BAKER; Dr. MARIAN O'NEIL; Mr. JOSEPH R. ROSOLINO; Dr. MYLES SEGHERS; Mr. THOMAS BECKER. Asst. Supts.: Mr. THOMAS E. MCLAUGHLIN; Mr. JOSEPH PEYCHAUD; VINCENT SCOZZARI; Mr. RODNEY J. THOULION, Dir., Mktg. & Pub. Rels.; Dr. MILES M. SEGHERS, Coord., Personnel Svcs.; Sr. MARY HILARY SIMPSON, O.P., Dir., Instrumental Music; Sr. LILLIAN MCCORMACK, S.S.N.D., Dir., Special Education, *7887 Walmsley Ave., New Orleans, 70125-3496.* Tel: 504-861-6223; 861-9521; Fax: 504-866-2906.

Catholic Youth Organization and Youth Ministry Office—MICHAEL PATIN, Dir., *3801 Monroe St., New Orleans, 70118-3499.* Tel: 504-486-6289; Fax: 504-486-4087.

Lay Retreats—Rev. H. WILLIAM REED, Coord., Adult Programs, *2545 Bayou Rd., New Orleans, 70119-2398.* Tel: 504-945-3591; Fax: 504-945-3216. Youth Retreats: Contact CYO-Youth Ministry Office, *3801 Monroe St., New Orleans, 70118-3499.* Tel: 504-486-6289; Fax: 504-486-4087.

Ministry of Evangelization & Spiritual Renewal—Rev. Msgr. ROBERT I. GUSTE, *4423 LaSalle St., New Orleans, 70115-5909.* Tel: 504-891-4401; Fax: 504-891-4402.

Religious Education—Bro. EDWARD KIEFER, S.M., Dir., *7887 Walmsley Ave., New Orleans, 70125-3496.* Tel: 504-861-6270; 861-9521; Fax: 504-866-2906.

Department of Clergy

Executive Director—Rev. Msgr. RAY P. HEBERT, *4401 7th St., Marrero, 70072-2099.* Tel: 504-341-9516; Fax: 504-341-9517.

Continuing Formation for Priests—Rev. JOSE I. LAVASTIDA, *2901 S. Carrollton Ave., New Orleans, 70118-4391.* Tel: 504-866-7426; Fax: 504-866-3119.

Jesus Caritas Fraternity of Priests—Rev. Msgr. ROBERT I. GUSTE, *4423 LaSalle St., New Orleans, 70115-5909.* Tel: 504-891-4401; Fax: 504-891-4402.

Permanent Diaconate—Mr. JAMES W. SWILER, Dir., *7887 Walmsley Ave., New Orleans, 70125-3496.* Tel: 504-861-6265; 861-9521; Fax: 504-866-2906.

Priest Personnel Office—Rev. JOHN C. SAX, *7887 Walmsley Ave., New Orleans, 70125-3496.* Tel: 504-861-6269; 861-9521; Fax: 504-866-2906.

Priests for Life (Organization of Priests Dedicated to the Protection of All Human Life)—Rev. ROGER A. SWENSON, Coord., *2916 Paris Ave., New Orleans, 70119-1840.* Tel: 504-945-8754; Fax: 504-949-8899.

Retired Priests—Rev. Msgr. W. WENDELL SONTHEIMER, Coord., *1029 N. Atlanta St., Metairie, 70003-5803.* Tel: 504-467-2193; Fax: 504-466-4858.

Vocation Office—Rev. HENRY J. BUGLER, Dir., *7887 Walmsley Ave., New Orleans, 70125-3496.* Tel: 504-861-6298; 861-9521; Fax: 504-866-2906.

Liaison with Conference of Major Superiors of Men and Retired Priests—.

Department of Community Services

Executive Director—Rev. Msgr. ROGER P. MORIN, *1000 Howard Ave., New Orleans, 70113-1900.* Tel: 504-596-3090; Fax: 504-596-3098.

Archdiocesan Alcoholism Counseling Ministry—Rev. ANTHONY J. WHITE, Dir., *724 Camp St., New Orleans, 70130-3757.* Tel: 504-525-4413; Fax: 504-568-1324.

Apostleship of the Sea—Deacon GILBERT W. SMITH, JR., Port Chap. & Dir., *Stella Maris Maritime Center, 4219 Constance, New Orleans, 70115-1440.* Tel: 501-891-6677; Fax: 504-891-1237.

Archbishop's Community Appeal (Philmat, Inc.)—Sr. ADELE LAMBERT, C.S.J., Dir., *1000 Howard Ave., Ste. 800, New Orleans, 70113-1900.* Tel: 504-596-3083; Fax: 504-596-3098.

Campaign for Human Development—Sr. ADELE LAMBERT, C.S.J., *1000 Howard Ave., New Orleans, 70113-1900.* Tel: 504-596-3085; Fax: 504-596-3098.

Catholic Human Relations Commission—Rev. Msgr. ROGER P. MORIN, Dir., *1000 Howard Ave., Ste. 800, New Orleans, 70113-1900.* Tel: 504-596-3090; Fax: 504-596-3098.

Charities—Catholic Charities Archdiocese of New Orleans—Mr. MICHAEL ECKSTEIN, Pres., Board of Advisors; Sr. ANTHONY BARCZYKOWSKI, D.C., Chief Exec. Dir., *1000 Howard Ave., Ste. 1200, New Orleans, 70113-1916.* Tel: 504-523-3755; Fax: 504-523-2789. Mr. DAVID J. LOGSDON, Chief Financial Officer;Mr. ORVILLE DUGGAN, Chief Admin. Officer. Div. Dirs.: Ms. JANE BREWER; Dr. REBECCA LOMAX.

AIDS Housing/Shelter:—Ms. LOIS FALK.

Beyond Shelter—Ms. VALLERIE BURRISS.

Ciara Community Services—Ms. MONETTA CLARK, Ciara House, Ciara Independent Living Program.

Health Education Department—Ms. JANET DILEO.

Hope Haven Center—Mr. ROBERT GUASCO,Hope Haven-Madonna Manor; St. Elizabeth's; Independent Living Skills Program.

AIDS Transportation Service—.

Regional AIDS Interfaith Network (RAIN)—Ms. ANITA TIRCUIT.

Padua Community Services—Mr. ELTON BATISTE-,Padua Adult Residential Program, Ocean Avenue Community Home, St. Catherine of Siena Supervised Apartment, St. Jude the Apostle, Sts. Mary and Elizabeth, St. Peter the Fisherman, St. Rosalie, Supervised Apartments.

Padua Pediatric Residential Program—Ms. PASHENA CASIMIRE.

Adult Day Health Care Centers—Ms. ELLEN SOMERS,Alpha House, Kenner, New Directions, Greenwalt Center for Alzheimer's Day Care & Research.

Children's Day Care Centers—Ms. ELLEN SOMERS,Cabrini Head Start, El Yo Yo, Flint Goodridge, Florida Head Start, Leslie Center, Louise, St. Anthony Head Start, St. Jude Baby Village.

Maternity and Adoption Services—Ms. JANE BREWER-,ACCESS Pregnancy/Referral Centers; Adoption Services; St. Vincent Maternity Clinic.

Immigration and Refugee Services—Ms. SUSAN WEISHAR,Refugee Health Screening; Refugee Resettlement Services; Refugee Social Services; Targeted Assistance for Refugees.

Social Adjustment—Ms. SHARON ALEXIS.

CARE Centers—Ms. CONNIE ANDRY,CARE Center, New Orleans; Jefferson Parish CARE Center.

Clinical Counseling Programs—Ms. JANE BREWER, Metairie & New Orleans Office, *433 Metairie Rd., Ste. 206, Metairie, 70005-4324.* Tel: 504-835-5007.

St. Tammany Branch Office—Ms. ANN LABAUVE, *1925-C Corporate Sq., Slidell, 70458-3165.* Tel: 504-641-8120.

St. Charles Branch Office—Mr. PETER YUSLUM, *P.O. Box 60, Hahnville, 70057-6000.* Tel: 504-783-2906.

St. John The Baptist Branch Office—Ms. DIANE LEONARD, *1706 Cannes Dr., LaPlace, 70068-2407.* Tel: 504-652-4330.

St. Bernard Branch Office—Ms. BARBARA LAUGHLIN, *2626 Charles Dr., Chalmette, 70043-3773.* Tel: 504-279-7636.

Westbank Office—Ms. ANDREA KENT-READ, *732 Berhman Hwy., Ste. C, Gretna, 70056.* Tel: 504-391-0370.

Crescent House—Ms. LYNN HOLLAND.

Deaf Action Center of Greater New Orleans—Ms. KATHY TREUBIG.

Information and Referral—Ms. YOLANDA BOWRIE.

Family Preservation—Ms. MAMIE HALL-LANDRY.

Job Search—Ms. NELLIE STOKES-PERRY.

Parish Social Ministry—Sr. JANINE BENIGER, C.S.J.; Mr. VINCENT LIBERTO.

Senior Citizens Groups—Mr. RAPHAEL FOLEY.

Project S.A.V.E.—Ms. JANE WOODARD-ROBSON.

Therapeutic Family Services—Ms. ARTHEA LARSON.

Foster Grandparents—Ms. DORIS LALA.

Volunteer Department—Ms. AUDREY FONTANA.

Christopher Homes, Inc.—Mr. THOMAS P. PERKINS, Exec. Dir., *1000 Howard Ave., Ste. 100, New Orleans, 70113-1903.* Tel: 504-596-3460; Fax: 504-596-3466.

Disaster Relief—Rev. Msgr. ROGER P. MORIN, Dir., *1000 Howard Ave., Ste. 800, New Orleans, 70113-1900.* Tel: 504-596-3090; Fax: 504-596-3098.

Social Apostolate Office (PHILMAT, Inc.)—Most Rev. FRANCIS B. SCHULTE, Pres.; Sr. ADELE LAMBERT, C.S.J., Dir. GORDON R. WADGE, Assoc. Dir., *1000 Howard Ave., Ste. 800, New Orleans, 70113-1900.* Tel: 504-596-3080; Fax: 504-596-3098.

Food for Families/Food for Seniors—Mr. TIMOTHY ROBERTSON, Dir., *8326 Apricot St., New Orleans, 70118-3198.* Tel: 504-861-3555; Fax: 504-861-1435.

**Second Harvesters Food Bank of Greater New Orleans, Inc.*—Mr. S. BRIAN GREENE, Dir., *1201 Sams Ave., Harahan, 70123-2236.* Tel: 504-734-1322; 733-8336; Fax: 504-733-8336.

Summer Social Action Program (Witness)—*1000 Howard Ave., New Orleans, 70113-1903.* Tel: 504-596-3080; Fax: 504-596-3098.

Social Action Centers.

Incarnate Word Center—Mrs. CAROLYN POTTS, Dir., *8326 Apricot St., New Orleans, 70118-3198.* Tel: 504-866-8918; Fax: 504-864-9922.

Our Lady of Lourdes Center—Mrs. JANET M. ROUSSO, Dir., *2401 Jena St., New Orleans, 70115-5998.* Tel: 504-895-0216; Fax: 504-895-0629.

St. John the Baptist—Sr. MARION BRETT, D.C., Dir., *1920 Clio St., New Orleans, 70113-1214.* Tel: 504-581-4987; Fax: 504-581-4991.

St. Louis Community Center—Ms. SHIRLEY A. LACHMANN, *1022 Barracks St., New Orleans, 70116-2526.* Tel: 504-524-7023; Fax: 504-524-2881.

St. Mary of the Angels—Sr. ELIZABETH PAWLICKI, O.P., *2301 Gallier St., New Orleans, 70117-5833.* Tel: 504-949-1506; Fax: 504-945-9115.

St. Philip Community Center—Mrs. DOMINIQUE B. WHEELER, Dir., *3333 Clouet St., New Orleans, 70126-5700.* Tel: 504-944-8848; Fax: 504-944-8853.

Spur-Senior Advocacy Program—Mr. JOHN GRAHAM, Acting Dir., *7100 St. Charles Ave., New Orleans, 70118-3595.* Tel: 504-861-4951; Fax: 504-861-3395.

Department of Financial Services

Executive Director—Mr. JOSEPH E. INGRAHAM, *7887 Walmsley Ave., New Orleans, 70125-3496.* Tel: 504-861-6252; 861-9521; Fax: 504-866-2906.

Accounting and Financial Review Office—Mrs. KIM O. RAMSEY, Controller, *7887 Walmsley Ave., New Orleans, 70125-3496.* Tel: 504-861-6236; 861-9521; Fax: 504-866-2906.

Assessment Committee—Mr. JOSEPH E. INGRAHAM, Coord., *7887 Walmsley Ave., New Orleans, 70125-3496.* Tel: 504-861-6252; 861-9521; Fax: 504-866-2906.

Building Office—Most Rev. FRANCIS B. SCHULTE, Pres.; Mr. JOSEPH E. INGRAHAM, Exec. Dir.; Mr. AUGUST J. BARBIER, JR., Dir., *7887 Walmsley Ave., New Orleans, 70125-3496.* Tel: 504-861-6210; 861-9521; Fax: 504-866-2906.

Employee Benefits Committee—Mr. JOSEPH E. INGRAHAM, Chm., *7887 Walmsley Ave., New Orleans, 70125-3496.* Tel: 504-861-6252; 861-9521; Fax: 504-866-2906.

Insurance Office—Mr. JOSEPH E. INGRAHAM, Exec. Dir. Claim Mgrs.: Mrs. CHERYL HARPER; Mr. TRAVIS BOURGEOIS, *7887 Walmsley Ave., New Orleans, 70125-3496.* Tel: 504-861-6259; 861-9521; Fax: 504-866-2906.

Missions Office—Society for the Propagation of the Faith, Holy Childhood Pontifical Assn., Missionaries of St. Therese—Most Rev. GREGORY M. AYMOND, V.G., Dir., *7887 Walmsley Ave., New Orleans, 70125-3496.* Tel: 504-866-7410; Fax: 504-866-3119.

New Orleans Archdiocesan Cemeteries and New Orleans Cemeteries Trust—Mr. MICHAEL D. BOUDREAUX, Dir., *1000 Howard Ave., New Orleans, 70113-1903.* Tel: 504-596-3050; Fax: 504-596-3055.

Parish Sites & Boundaries Committee—Rev. Msgr. MARTIN VAN DER WERFF, Chm.; Rev. Msgr. THOMAS J. RODI, V.G., Coord., *7887 Walmsley Ave., New Orleans, 70125-3496.* Tel: 504-861-6262; 861-9521; Fax: 504-866-2906.

Personnel Office—Mr. JOSEPH E. INGRAHAM, Dir., *7887 Walmsley Ave., New Orleans, 70125-3496.* Tel: 504-861-6252; 861-9521; Fax: 504-866-2906.

Property Committee—Most Rev. FRANCIS B. SCHULTE, D.D., Pres.; Rev. Msgr. CHARLES E. DUKE, Chm., *4845 Meadowdale St., Metairie, 70006-4037.* Tel: 504-889-0850; Fax: 504-888-4934.

Retired Priests' Pension Commission—Mr. JOSEPH E. INGRAHAM, Coord., *7887 Walmsley Ave., New Orleans, 70125-3496.* Tel: 504-861-6252; 861-9521; Fax: 504-866-2906.

School Food Services—Rev. Msgr. JOHN P. REYNOLDS, Supt.; Mrs. PATRICIA H. FARRIS, Dir., *1000 Howard Ave., Ste. 300, New Orleans, 70113-1919.* Tel: 504-596-3434; Fax: 504-596-3459.

Department of Pastoral Services

Executive Director—Very Rev. GERALD L. SEILER, *7887 Walmsley Ave., New Orleans, 70125-3496.* Tel: 504-861-6294; 861-9521; Fax: 504-866-2906.

Archbishop Antoine Blanc Memorial—Rev. Msgr. ALVIN J. O'REILLY, Admin., *1100 Chartres St., New Orleans, 70116-2596.* Tel: 504-529-2001; Fax: 504-529-2001.

Archives (Archdiocesan)—Dr. CHARLES E. NOLAN, *1100 Chartres St., New Orleans, 70116-2596.* Tel: 504-529-2651; Fax: 504-529-2001.

Black Catholics Office—Deacon DAN VINCENT, *7887 Walmsley Ave., New Orleans, 70125-3496.* Tel: 504-861-6207; 861-9521; Fax: 504-866-2906.

Canonical Permissions and Dispensations—Very Rev. GERALD L. SEILER; Rev. JOSEPH P. MULLIN, S.M., *7887 Walmsley Ave., New Orleans, 70125-3496.* Tel: 504-861-6294; 861-9521; Fax: 504-866-2906.

Charismatic Renewal—Liaisons: Mr. AL MANSFIELD; Mrs. AL MANSFIELD, *3000 26th St., Ste. 200, Metairie, 70002-6002.* Tel: 504-828-1368; Fax: 504-828-2133.

Ecumenical Commission—Rev. EARL F. NIEHAUS, S.M., Chm., *448 Metairie Rd., Metairie, 70005-4371.* Tel: 504-834-0340; 483-7408.

Family Life Apostolate—Mrs. PAULA D'ALBOR STUCKART, Dir., *7887 Walmsley Ave., New Orleans, 70125-3496.* Tel: 504-861-6243; 861-9521; Fax: 504-866-2906.

Commission for Persons with Disabilities—Mrs. PAULA D'ALBOR STUCKART, *7887 Walmsley Ave., New Orleans, 70125-3496.* Tel: 504-861-6243; Fax: 504-866-2906.

Hispanic Apostolate—Mr. MARTIN GUTIERREZ, Exec. Dir., *3368 Esplanade Ave., New Orleans, 70119-3132.* Tel: 504-486-1983; Fax: 504-486-3985.

Mensaje, Inc.—Rev. PEDRO NUNEZ, *3368 Esplanade Ave., New Orleans, 70119-3132.* Tel: 504-482-8803; Fax: 504-943-9461.

Holy Name Societies—Mr. BEN RAPHAEL, Exec. Dir., *7887 Walmsley Ave., New Orleans, 70125-3496.* Tel: 504-283-5427; Fax: 504-866-2906.

Pastoral Planning—Sr. MYRA BANQUER M.S.C., Coord., *7887 Walmsley Ave., New Orleans, 70125-3496.* Tel: 504-861-6222; Fax: 504-861-2906.

Prisons Apostolate—Deacon LOUIS STALL, Archdiocesan Dir., *P.O. Box 388, Gretna, 70054-0388.* Tel: 504-374-7700, Ext. 3109.

Renovacion Carismatica Catolica Hispana—Deacon RODOLFO J. MARTINEZ, *4401 Seventh St., Marrero, 70072-2099.* Tel: 504-341-9516; Fax: 504-341-9517. Mr. JULIO MOLINA, *2953 Mt. Kennedy Dr., Marrero, 70072-5210.* Tel: 504-348-2959.

Vietnamese Catholics Office—Rev. Msgr. DOMINIC LUONG, Dir., *5069 Willowbrook Dr., New Orleans, 70129-0745.* Tel: 504-254-5660; Fax: 504-254-9250.

Worship Office—Rev. Msgr. KENNETH J. HEDRICK, Dir.; Deacon RONALD GUIDRY, Assoc. Dir., *7887 Walmsley Ave., New Orleans, 70125-3496.* Tel: 504-861-6300; 861-9521; Fax: 504-866-2906.

Liturgical Commission—Rev. Msgr. KENNETH J. HEDRICK, Coord., *7887 Walmsley Ave., New Orleans, 70125-3496.* Tel: 504-861-6300; 861-9521; Fax: 504-866-2906.

Master of Ceremonies—Rev. Msgr. KENNETH J. HEDRICK; Deacon RONALD GUIDRY, *7887 Walmsley Ave., New Orleans, 70125-3496.* Tel: 504-861-6300; 861-9521; Fax: 504-866-2906.

Department of Religious

Executive Director—Sr. SUELLEN TENNYSON, M.S.C., *7887 Walmsley Ave., New Orleans, 70125-3496.* Tel: 504-861-6281; 861-9521; Fax: 504-866-2906.

Liaison with Leadership Conference of Women Religious, Religious Institutes of Brothers and Sisters and Secular Institutes—.

Archdiocesan Offices and Corporations

Archdiocesan Horizons Fund for the Aged, Inc.—Most Rev. FRANCIS B. SCHULTE, Pres., *7887 Walmsley Ave., New Orleans, 70125-3496.* Tel: 504-861-9521.

Bernard A. Grehan Trust—*7887 Walmsley Ave., New Orleans, 70125-3496.* Tel: 504-861-9521.

Catholic Charities Children's Day Care Centers—Registered Office: *1000 Howard Ave., Ste. 1200, New Orleans, 70113-1916.*

Community Host Campaign—Most Rev. FRANCIS B. SCHULTE, Pres., *7887 Walmsley Ave., New Orleans, 70125-3496.* Tel: 504-861-9521.

Mental Health Association Development Corporation—*7887 Walmsley Ave., New Orleans, 70125-3496.* Tel: 504-861-9521.

St. Elizabeth's Home Registered Office—*1000 Howard Ave., Ste. 1200, New Orleans, 70113-1916.*

St. Gertrude's Retirement Center—Most Rev. FRANCIS B. SCHULTE, D.D., Pres., *7887 Walmsley Ave., New Orleans, 70125-3496.*

St. Mary's Catholic Orphan Boys Asylum Board—*1000 Howard Ave., Ste. 1200, New Orleans, 70113-1916.*

St. Vincent's Infant and Maternity Home Registered Office—*1000 Howard Ave., Ste. 1200, New Orleans, 70113-1916.*

Lay Organizations

Apostleship of Prayer—Rev. JOSEPH REISING, S.J., Dir., *500 S. Jefferson Davis Pkwy., New Orleans, 70119-7192.* Tel: 504-821-0334; Fax: 504-822-5322.

Archdiocesan Federation of Christian Life Communities—Rev. H. WILLIAM REED, Spiritual Dir., *2545 Bayou Rd., New Orleans, 70119-2398.* Tel: 504-945-3591; Fax: 504-945-3216.

Archconfraternity of St. Ann—Rev. Msgr. JOSEPH E. BOURGEOIS, Spiritual Dir., *4920 Loveland St., Metairie, 70006-4099.* Tel: 504-455-7071; Fax: 504-455-7076.

Blessed Brother Andre Acadians Prayer Group—Deacon IRVING J. DAIGLE, Spiritual Moderator, *529 S. Telemachus, New Orleans, 70119-7043.* Tel: 504-486-7190.

Blue Army of Our Lady of Fatima—Rev. DENZIL M. PERERA, Spiritual Dir., *1342 Moss St., New Orleans, 70119-2998.* Tel: 504-488-2659; Fax: 504-488-6741.

Catholic Alumni Club—Miss MARIE SPICUZZA, Pres., *668 Spartan Ln., Kenner, 70065-2644.* Tel: 504-466-1552.

Catholic Charities Association Inc.—Mr. CRAIG SILVA, Pres., *1000 Howard Ave., Ste. 1200, New Orleans, 70113-1916.* Tel: 504-581-BALL.

Catholic Knights of America—Rev. BENJAMIN PIOVAN, Spiritual Dir., *799 Fairway Dr., LaPlace, 70068-2007.* Tel: 504-652-2615; Fax: 504-652-7291.

Catholic Order of Foresters—Mr. EDWIN HADLEY, State Chief Ranger, *4701 Stephen Girard, New Orleans, 70126-4757.* Tel: 504-282-5432.

Catholic Physicians Guild of New Orleans—Rev. Msgr. ELMO L. ROMAGOSA, Chap., *700 Maple St., Harvey, 70058-4008.* Tel: 504-368-1397; Fax: 504-368-0662.

Chateau de Notre Dame Guild—Rev. JOSEPH J. LAWLOR, S.S.J., Spiritual Dir., *2832 Burdette St., New Orleans, 70125-2596.* Tel: 504-866-2741; Fax: 504-866-6769.

Closer Walk Ministries—Rev. HAROLD F. COHEN, S.J., Dir., *P.O. Box 50860, New Orleans, 70150-0860.* Tel: 504-834-4200; Fax: 504-834-4204.

Come, Lord Jesus Program of Prayer and Scripture—Ms. MARIE WOJDAC, Coord., *1728 Pine St., New Orleans, 70118-5322.* Tel: 504-861-4189.

Community of St. John the Evangelist—Mr. DAN DEMERS, Chm., *3342 Hyman Pl., New Orleans, 70131-7040.* Tel: 504-394-1795.

Confraternity of the Holy Face—Rev. Msgr. LANAUX J. RARESHIDE, Dir., *2327 S. Galvez St., New Orleans, 70125-3198.* Tel: 504-821-9500; Fax: 504-821-9500.

Council of Catholic Men—Mr. BEN RAPHAEL, Dir., *7887 Walmsley Ave., New Orleans, 70125-3496.* Tel: 504-283-5427.

Council of Catholic School Cooperative Clubs—Rev. H. WILLIAM REED, Spiritual Moderator, *2545 Bayou Rd., New Orleans, 70119-2398.* Tel: 504-945-3591; Fax: 504-945-3216.

Council of Catholic Women—Rev. H. WILLIAM REED, Spiritual Dir., *2545 Bayou Rd., New Orleans, 70119-2398.* Tel: 504-945-3591. Mrs. BERNICE BONZANT, Pres.

Courage (Catholic Ministry to Homosexual Persons)—*P.O. Box 8074, New Orleans, 70182-8074.* Tel: 504-288-6877.

Engaged Encounter—GARY LEVY; CLAUDIA LEVY. Tel: 504-837-9121.

Eucharistic Adoration Society—Mrs. NOVA LACOMBE, Pres., *6232 Milne Blvd., New Orleans, 70124-2016.* Tel: 504-482-9632.

Knights of Columbus—Rev. FRANCIS J. CARABELLO, Archdiocesan Chap., *610 6th St., Gretna, 70053-6098.* Tel: 504-368-1313; Fax: 504-368-6841.

Knights of Peter Claver—Mr. W. CHARLES KEYES, JR., Exec. Sec., *1825 Orleans Ave., New Orleans, 70116-2894.* Tel: 504-821-4225; Fax: 504-821-4253.

Korean Catholic Community Center—Rev. JOANNES JAE-SANG HAN, *140 27th St., Kenner, 70062-4906.* Tel: 504-469-3956.

Ladies of Charity of the Archdiocese—Rev. HAROLD DICHARRY, Spiritual Dir., *1025 Napoleon Ave., New Orleans, 70115-2898.* Tel: 504-899-1378; Fax: 504-899-0480.

Ladies of Madonna—Mrs. E. J. DEVERGES, Pres., *2818 Palmer Ave., New Orleans, 70118-5620.* Tel: 504-866-5809.

Lay Carmelites of Our Lady of Mount Carmel—*420 R.E. Lee Blvd., New Orleans, 70124-2596.* Tel: 504-288-8553.

Legion of Mary—Rev. HAROLD DICHARRY, Spiritual Dir., New Orleans Comitium, *1025 Napoleon Ave., New Orleans, 70115-2898.* Tel: 504-899-1378; Fax: 504-899-0480.

Living Waters Program (Radio Ministry)—Rev. Msgr. ROBERT I. GUSTE, Dir., *4423 LaSalle St., New Orleans, 70115-5909.* Tel: 504-891-4401; Fax: 504-891-4402.

Magnificat, Ministry to Catholic Women—Mrs. PETER QUIRK, Pres. Central Svc. Team, *1201 Beverly Gardens Dr., Metairie, 70002.* Tel: 504-834-0057.

Marians of New Orleans—Mrs. HELEN W. DELAHOUSSAYE, Pres., *2716 Whitney Pl., #417, Metairie, 70002-6232.* Tel: 504-838-9145.

Marians of Metairie—Mrs. ELIZABETH BERTUCCI, Pres., *4708 Kent Ave., Metairie, 70006-2014.* Tel: 504-887-4342.

Marriage Encounter—GARY DAIGLE; MARCIA DAIGLE. Tel: 504-649-0999.

Maryknoll Education Center (Promotions of Missionary Work)—Mr. MATT ROUSSO, Education Asst., *7214 St. Charles Ave., New Orleans, 70118.* Tel: 504-866-8516.

Mary's Children—Ms. NORA LAMBERT, Pres., *631 St. Charles Ave., New Orleans, 70130-3411.* Tel: 504-288-4408.

Mary's Helpers (Medjugorje Information)—Mrs. MARGARET TROSCLAIR, Dir., *P.O. Box 1853, Marrero, 70072-1853.* Tel: 504-348-7729.

Medjugorje Star—Rev. CHARLES SELLARS, O.M.I., Spiritual Dir. Dirs.: HUBIE MULE; KAY MULE, *2627 David Dr., Metairie, 70003-4599.* Tel: 504-889-1708; Fax: 504-889-1714.

MIR Group (Medjugorje Information Center)—Ms. GERI FAIA, *1 Galleria Blvd., Ste. 907, Metairie, 70001-2081.* Tel: 504-849-2570; Fax: 504-849-2574.

Missionaries of St. Theresa—Most Rev. GREGORY M. AYMOND, V.G., Spiritual Moderator, *2901 S. Carrollton Ave., New Orleans, 70118-4391.* Tel: 504-866-7410; Fax: 504-866-3119.

Naim Conference—Mr. JOSEPH A. BARRECA, Pres. Elect, *774 Crystal St., New Orleans, 70124-3608.* Tel: 504-283-5397.

National Council of Catholic Men—Mr. BEN RAPHAEL, Dir., *7887 Walmsley Ave., New Orleans, 70125-3496.* Tel: 504-283-5427.

National Council of Catholic Women—Rev. H. WILLIAM REED, Spiritual Dir., *2545 Bayou Rd., New Orleans, 70119-2398.* Tel: 504-945-3591.

Pax Christi New Orleans—Co-Chm.: Mrs. JEAN EGAN; Ms. JUDY YUSLUM, *916 St. Andrew St., New Orleans, 70130-5020.* Tel: 504-522-3751; Fax: 504-525-0011.

St. Elizabeth's Guild—Mrs. WILLIAM B. MARTIN, JR., Pres., *1101 Barataria Blvd., Marrero, 70072.*

St. Margaret's Daughters—Mrs. AUGUSTINE MOLL, Pres., *926 Charbonnet St., New Orleans, 70117-2655.* Tel: 504-943-0706.

St. Thomas More Catholic Lawyers Association—Rev. JOSEPH S. PALERMO, JR., *5500 Paris Ave., New Orleans, 70122-2699.* Tel: 504-288-4224; Fax: 504-288-2152.

St. Vincent de Paul Society—Mrs. TOBY CHARBONNET, Pres.; Mr. ARMAND H. BERTIN, SR., Exec. Sec., *2601 Canal St., New Orleans, 70119-6498.* Tel: 504-822-9288; Fax: 504-822-1964.

St. Vincent Infant and Maternity Home Guild—*1000 Howard Ave., Ste. 1200, New Orleans, 70112-1916.* Tel: 504-523-3755.

Scouting—Deacon DANIEL FLYNN, Chap., Boy Scouts, *251 Halsey Dr., Harahan, 70123-4401.* Tel: 504-737-8370. Mrs. COLLEEN R. LAROCCA, Chm., Girl Scouts, *25 Brentwood Dr., Metairie, 70003-3831.* Tel: 504-734-8527.

Serra Clubs—Serra Club of New Orleans; Rev. HENRY J. BUGLER, Chap., *7887 Walmsley Ave., New Orleans, 70125-3496.* Tel: 504-861-6298; Fax: 504-866-2906. Serra Club of Downtown New Orleans; Rev. ANDREW C. TAORMINA, Chap., *448 Metairie Rd., Metairie, 70005-4371.* Tel: 504-834-0340. Serra Club of East Jefferson; Rev. JAMES LOHAN, Chap., *105 Bonnabel Blvd., Metairie, 70005-3798.* Tel: 504-835-9343. Serra Club of St. Bernard; Rev. WAYNE C. PAYSSE, Chap., *58203 Hwy. 433, Slidell, 70460-3121.* Tel: 504-643-3832; 800-641-6771.

The Theresians—Mrs. ELIZABETH RARESHIDE, Pres., *3840 Napoleon Ave., New Orleans, 70125-4444.* Tel: 504-861-8673.

Victorious Missionaries—Deacon ALBERT LEVY, III, Chap., *621 Lebeau St., Arabi, 70032.* Tel: 504-277-5053.

CLERGY, PARISHES, MISSIONS AND PAROCHIAL SCHOOLS

CITY OF NEW ORLEANS
(Orleans Civil Parish)

1—ST. LOUIS CATHEDRAL (1720). (A Minor Basilica). Rev. Msgr. Kenneth J. Hedrick, Rector; Revs. Frank Montalbano, O.M.I.; John C. Sax; John Sokolski, O.M.I.; Deacon Ron Guidry.
Res., 615 Pere Antoine Alley, 70116-3291. Tel: 504-525-9585; Fax: 504-525-9583.
School—820 Dauphine St., 70116-3089. Tel: 504-525-3860; Fax: 504-525-3193. Sr. Maria Luisa Aldape, Prin.
Sisters of the Society of St. Teresa of Jesus 3; Brother of the Sacred Heart 1; Lay Teachers 10; Students 173.
Mission—New Orleans, Orleans Civil Parish, Our Lady of Guadalupe, Tel: 504-525-1551; Fax: 504-525-1827.
Shrine—International Shrine of St. Jude. Revs. Raymond A. Lebrun, O.M.I.; George E. Knab, O.M.I.; Mr. Michael W. Thomas, Pastoral Assoc. & Asst. Admin.
Res., 411 N. Rampart St., 70112-3594. Tel: 504-525-1551; 525-1557; Fax: 504-525-1827.
St. Jude Community Center—400 N. Rampart St., 70112-3594. Tel: 504-522-8290; Fax: 504-522-8830.

2—ALL SAINTS (1919), Rev. Joseph J. Campion, S.S.J.
Res., 1441 Teche St., 70114-5899. Tel: 504-361-8835; Fax: 504-361-9802.
School—1415 Teche St., 70114-5898.
Sisters of the Holy Family 4; Lay Teachers 12; Students 289.

3—ANNUNCIATION (1844), Most Rev. Nicholas D'Antonio, O.F.M., D.D.
Res., 1221 Mandeville St., 70117-8498. Tel: 504-943-5561; Fax: 504-943-5562.

4—BLESSED SACRAMENT (1915) (African American), Very Rev. John E. O'Hallaran, S.S.J.; Deacon Raymond J. Guillot. In res., Revs. Howard W. Byrd, S.S.J.; Joseph E. Okoro, C.M.F. (Nigeria).
Res., 5018 Constance St., 70115-1798. Tel: 504-897-0955; Fax: 504-897-0950.

5—CORPUS CHRISTI (1916) (African American), Revs. John E. O'Hallaran, S.S.J.; Emmanuel Madu (Nigeria); Bro. Louis Tomasso, S.S.J.; Deacon Alfred D. White, Jr.
Res., 2022 St. Bernard Ave., 70116-1388. Tel: 504-945-8931; Fax: 504-947-5347.
School—Tel: 504-943-6131; Fax: 504-947-7736. Sr. Elizabeth Ann Holmes, S.S.F., Prin.
Sisters 7; Lay Teachers 41; Students 395.
Catechesis/Religious Programs—Students 125.

6—EPIPHANY (1948), Revs. Joseph M. Doyle, S.S.J., Admin.; Oliver Obele, M.S.P.; Ashley J. Perry, S.S.J.
Res., 1949 Duels St., 70119-1198. Tel: 504-944-2646; Fax: 504-945-5251.

7—HOLY GHOST (1915) (African American), Revs. Michel Boutot, C.S.Sp.; Alphonce Kimathy, C.S.Sp. In res., Rev. O. Hugh Stout.
Res., 2015 Louisiana Ave., 70115-5294. Tel: 504-891-3172; Fax: 504-891-9284.
School—2035 Toledano St., 70115-5295. Tel: 504-899-6782. Sr. Angela Smith, S.S.F., Prin.
Sisters 4; Lay Teachers 6; Students 290.

8—HOLY NAME OF JESUS (1892), Revs. Paul Patin, S.J.; Paul Schott, S.J.; Deacon Philip De Verges. In res., Rev. Donald Pearce, S.J.
Res., 6220 LaSalle Pl., 70118-6236. Tel: 504-865-7430; Fax: 504-866-3391.
School—6325 Cromwell Pl., 70118-6299. Tel: 504-861-1466; Fax: 504-861-1480. Sr. Mary Nicholas Schiro, R.S.M., Prin.
Sisters of Mercy 6; Lay Teachers 42; Students 545.
Catechesis/Religious Programs—Tel: 504-572-2469.
Students 90.

9—HOLY NAME OF MARY (ALGIERS) (1848), Rev. Raymond Carr, S.M.
Res., 500 Eliza St., 70114-1098. Tel: 504-362-5511; Fax: 504-367-3504. [CEM 2]
School—502 Oliver St., 70114-1099. Tel: 504-361-4004. Sr. Doris Daigle, M.S.C., Prin.
Sisters 5; Lay Teachers 7; Students 224.

10—HOLY SPIRIT (1972), Rev. Msgr. Allen J. Roy, V.F.; Deacon Raphael Duplechan, Jr.
Res., 6201 Stratford Pl., 70131-7397. Tel: 504-394-5492; Fax: 504-398-0901.
Catechesis/Religious Programs—Tel: 504-392-0927; Fax: 504-398-0901. Beverly Baldwin, D.R.E. Students 155.

11—IMMACULATE CONCEPTION (1851), Revs. Harry W. Tompson, S.J.; Thomas J. Hidding, S.J.; J. Emile Pfister, S.J.
Res., 130 Baronne St., 70112-2304. Tel: 504-529-1477; 1478; Fax: 504-524-0155.

12—IMMACULATE HEART OF MARY (1954), Rev. Joseph M. de Water; Deacon Paul Mumme.
Res., 6300 Pines Blvd., 70126-2697. Tel: 504-242-6900; Fax: 507-243-6655.
School—6360 Pines Blvd., 70126-2699. Dr. Geralyn Dell, Prin.
Lay Teachers 4; Students 10.

13—INCARNATE WORD (1922), Rev. Msgr. Roger P. Morin; Rev. Francis Ferrie.
Res., 8316 Apricot St., 70118-3199. Tel: 504-866-3679; Fax: 504-866-0722.

14—MARY, QUEEN OF VIETNAM (1983) (Vietnamese), Rev. Msgr. Dominic Mai Thanh Luong; Deacon Pham Sy Hiep. In res., Rev. Peter Neuman, I.C.
Res., 5069 Willowbrook Dr., P.O. Box 29745, 70129-1047. Tel: 504-254-5560; Fax: 504-254-9250. [JC]
Catechesis/Religious Programs—Tel: 504-254-5247.
Students 855.
Mission—New Orleans, Orleans Civil Parish, Our Lady of La Vang, 6054 Vermillion Blvd., 70122-4296. Tel: 504-283-0559; Fax: 504-286-1937. Rev. Dominic Huyen Duc Nguyen.
Chapel—Vietnamese Martyrs, 14400 Peltier Dr., New Orleans East, 70129-1713. Tel: 504-254-5660; Fax: 504-254-9250.

15—MATER DOLOROSA (1848), Rev. John T. Hinton; Deacons Donald Walsh; Walter Beyer. In res., Rev. David A. Boileau.
Res., 8128 Plum St., 70118-2012. Tel: 504-866-3669; Fax: 504-866-2349.
Catechesis/Religious Programs—Tel: 504-866-3660.
Students 120.

16—OUR LADY OF GOOD COUNSEL (1887), Revs. Kenneth Borgesen, O.SS.T.; Francis Whatley, O.SS.T.; Vincent Bechamps, O.SS.T.; Deacon Ray Richardson.
Res., 1307 Louisiana Ave., 70115-2494. Tel: 504-891-1906; Fax: 504-895-5871.

17—OUR LADY OF GUADALUPE /INTERNATIONAL SHRINE OF ST. JUDE. (Quasi Parish). Revs. John Sokolski, O.M.I.; George E. Knab, O.M.I.; Raymond A. Labrun, O.M.I.; Mr. Michael W. Thomas, Pastoral Assoc. & Asst. Admin.
Res., 411 N. Rampart St., 70112. Tel: 504-525-1551; Fax: 504-525-1827.

18—OUR LADY OF LOURDES (1905), Rev. Msgr. Robert I. Guste; Deacon Everett Williams.
Res., 4423 La Salle St., 70115-5909. Tel: 504-891-4401; Fax: 504-891-4402.
School—2437 Jena St., 70115-5998. Tel: 504-897-0154; Fax: 504-897-0155.
Lay Teachers 10; Students 212.

19—OUR LADY OF THE ROSARY (1907), Revs. James A. Tarantino; Denzil M. Perera; Deacons Ralph Schonacher, (Retired); Richard Gaiennie; John David Hamm; Henry Nuss.
Res., 1342 Moss St., 70119-2998. Tel: 504-488-2659; Fax: 504-448-6741.

20—OUR LADY STAR OF THE SEA (1911), Rev. Eugene F. Jacques; Deacons John Blanchard; Tony Peres.
Res., 1835 St. Roch Ave., 70117-8199. Tel: 504-944-0166; Fax: 504-948-9555.

21—THE RESURRECTION OF OUR LORD (1963), Revs. Cyprian Devold; Patrick Collum; Deacon William P. Curry, Jr.
Res., 9701 Hammond St., 70127-3519. Tel: 504-242-8669; Fax: 504-242-8767.
School—4861 Rosalia Dr., 70127-3598. Tel: 504-242-6222; Fax: 504-241-7363. Ms. Angela Francis, Prin.
Lay Teachers 25; Students 446.
Catechesis/Religious Programs—Students 97.

22—SACRED HEART OF JESUS (1879), Revs. C. Richard Nowery, C.S.C.; Joseph M. Moyer, C.S.C.; Deacon Irving J. Daigle. In res., Rev. Thomas E. Chambers, C.S.C.; Bros. Shawn Priggel, C.S.C.; Richard Kelly, C.S.C.
Res., 139 S. Lopez St., 70119-6284. Tel: 504-827-1481; Fax: 504-821-5109.

23—ST. ALPHONSUS (1847) (Irish), Revs. Gerard B. LaPorte, C.SS.R.; Binh Thanh Ta, C.SS.R.; Luong Uong, C.SS.R.; Sr. Jane Briseno, R.S.M., Pastoral Assoc.; Bro. Andrew Lawson, C.SS.R.; Deacon Maurice J. Hartson, III.
Res., 2030 Constance St., 70130-5099. Tel: 504-522-6748; Fax: 504-523-3734.
School—2001 Constance St., 70130-5094. Tel: 504-523-6594. Sr. Monica Ellerbusch, R.S.M., Prin.
Sisters 2; Lay Teachers 14; Students 258.

24—ST. ANDREW THE APOSTLE (1952), Rev. Msgr. John A. Tomasovich; Rev. Joel P. Cantones; Deacon Chris J. DiGrado.
Res., 3101 Eton St., 70131-5399. Tel: 504-393-2334; Fax: 504-392-0635.
School—Tel: 504-394-4171; Fax: 504-391-3627.
Sisters 3; Lay Teachers 43; Students 780.
Catechesis/Religious Programs—Tel: 504-394-4010.
Students 112.

25—ST. ANTHONY OF PADUA (1915), Rev. Donald T. Dvorak, O.P.; Very Revs. Thomas A. Clifford, O.P., Prior; Alberto Rodriguez, O.P., Prov.; Revs. Wayne Cavalier, O.P.; Carl B. Trutter, O.P.; John J. Boll,

O.P.; Bryan J. Fontenot, O.P.; John N. Morgenthaler, O.P.; Robert L. Every, O.P.; John A. Powers, O.P.; Bruce Schultz, O.P.; Angel Vizcarra, O.P.; Bros. Timothy Wrinn, O.P.; Herman Johnson; Sr. M. Aimee Haulard, O.P., Pastoral Min.; Sr. Diane McOsker, O.P., Pastoral Assoc.
Res., 4640 Canal St., 70119-5892. Tel: 504-488-2651; Fax: 504-488-1842.
School—4601 Cleveland Ave., 70119-5893. Tel: 504-488-4426; 482-3672; Fax: 504-488-5373. Sr. Ruth Angelette, O.P., Prin.
Sisters of St. Dominic 2; Lay Teachers 28; Students 415.
Catechesis/Religious Programs—Students 46.

26—ST. AUGUSTINE (1841), Rev. Jerome LeDoux, S.V.D.; Deacon Lloyd St. Clair Glapion.
Res., 1210 Gov. Nicholls St., 70116-2324. Tel: 504-525-5934; Fax: 504-523-2473.

27—ST. BRIGID (1977), Rev. Thomas G. Glasgow.
Res., 13435 Granville St., P.O. Box 29626, 70129-1210. Tel: 504-254-3538; Fax: 504-254-3520.
Catechesis/Religious Programs—Tel: 504-254-5115. Mary Kittles, D.R.E.
Students 80.

28—ST. CECILIA (1897), Rev. Ronald F. Whitlow. In res., Rev. Gerard P. Kinane.
Res., 1015 France St., 70117-5398. Tel: 504-945-1597; 945-6622; Fax: 504-945-0188.

29—ST. DAVID (1937), Very Rev. Francis M. Hull, S.S.J., V.F.; Rev. John E. Hardman, S.S.J.; Deacon Irvin Williams.
Res., 5617 St. Claude Ave., 70117-2533. Tel: 504-947-2853; Fax: 504-948-7852.
School—Tel: 504-943-1523. Sr. Teresa Rooney, C.H.F., Prin.
Sisters 4; Lay Teachers 7; Students 230.
Catechesis/Religious Programs—Iris Labeaud, D.R.E.
Students 105.

30—ST. DOMINIC (1924), Revs. Neal McDermott, O.P.; Edward W. Conley, O.P., Prior; Victor Brown, O.P.; Richard Murphy, O.P., (Retired); William J. Brady, O.P., (Retired); Val A. McInnes, O.P., Dir. Devel.; John I. Reardon, O.P., (Retired); Dominic J. Tamburello, O.P.; Albert J. Coburn, O.P.; Bros. Roger Shondel, O.P.; Richard Bontempo, O.P.; Deacons Chris J. Weber; John Pippinger.
Res., 775 Harrison Ave., 70124-3192. Tel: 504-482-4156; Fax: 504-488-0906.
School—Tel: 504-482-4123; Fax: 504-486-3870.
Sisters 2; Lay Teachers 39; Students 670.
Catechesis/Religious Programs—Tel: 504-486-9731.
Students 145.

31—ST. FRANCES XAVIER CABRINI (1952), Revs. Joseph S. Palermo, Jr., Temp. Admin.; Joseph Thang Dinh Tran; Deacons John Paul Muhleisen; Norbert Gubert; Peter C. Rizzo.
Res., 5500 Paris Ave., 70122-2699. Tel: 504-288-4224; Fax: 504-288-2152.
School—1500 Prentiss Ave., 70122-2098. Tel: 504-288-4249; Fax: 504-283-8161.
Lay Teachers 21; Students 333.

32—ST. FRANCIS OF ASSISI (1890), Rev. Desmond G. Crotty.
Res., 631 State St., 70118-5899. Tel: 504-891-4479; Fax: 504-891-4470.

33—ST. FRANCIS DE SALES (1870) (African American), Rev. Victor H. Cohea; Deacon Raymond Lewis.
Res., 2203 Second St., 70113-2545. Tel: 504-895-7749; Fax: 504-899-0434.
Catechesis/Religious Programs—Tel: 504-891-9544.
Students 60.

34—ST. GABRIEL THE ARCHANGEL (1954) (African American), Rev. Msgr. Douglas A. Doussan, Admin.; Rev. Bernard W. Schmaltz.
Office: 4700 Pineda St., 70126-3599. Tel: 504-282-0296; Fax: 504-288-8585.
Catechesis/Religious Programs—Tel: 504-288-7914.
Students 100.

35—ST. GERARD (1971), Rev. Pedro F. Nunez.
Res., 3037 Dauphine St., 70117-6724. Tel: 504-943-2456; Fax: 504-945-7200.

36—ST. HENRY (1856), Very Rev. Henry H. Engelbrecht, V.F.; Deacon Henry A. Garon.
Res., 812 General Pershing St., 70115-2797. Tel: 504-891-6359; Fax: 504-895-0486.

37—HOLY TRINITY. Closed. For inquiries for parish records contact the Chancery.

38—ST. JAMES MAJOR (1920), Rev. Leo A. Meyer. In res., Rev. Douglas C. Brougher.
Res., 3736 Gentilly Blvd., 70122-6199. Tel: 504-945-2165; Fax: 504-945-9899.
School—3774 Gentilly Blvd., 70122-3198. Tel: 504-945-1015; Fax: 504-945-1050.
Sisters 2; Lay Teachers 11; Students 238.

39—ST. JOAN OF ARC (1909) (African American), Rev. Peter C. Weiss, S.S.J. In res., Deacon Irvin Stewart, Sr.
Res., 8321 Burthe St., 70118-1195. Tel: 504-866-7330; Fax: 504-866-1319.
School—Tel: 504-861-2887; Fax: 504-866-9588.
Sisters of Holy Family 4; Lay Teachers 9; Students 212.

40—ST. JOHN THE BAPTIST (1851) (Irish), Rev. Matthias Moore, C.S.Sp.
Res., 1139 Oretha Castle Haley Blvd., 70113-1215. Tel: 504-525-1726; Fax: 504-524-4090.

41—ST. JOSEPH (1844). (Legal Title: St. Joseph Roman Catholic). Rev. Perry F. Henry, C.M.
Res., 1802 Tulane Ave., 70112-2246. Tel: 504-522-3186; Fax: 504-522-3171.

42—ST. JULIAN EYMARD (1952) (African American-Hispanic), Revs. Salvador Galvez; John Asare-Dankwah; Deacon Harold Vincent.
Res., 2701 Lawrence St., 70114-3099. Tel: 504-367-7730; Fax: 504-367-2603.

43—ST. LEO THE GREAT (1920), Rev. Roger A. Swenson.
Res., 2916 Paris Ave., 70119-1840. Tel: 504-945-8750; Fax: 504-949-8899.
School—1501 Abundance St., 70119-2098. Tel: 504-943-1482; Fax: 504-944-5895.
Dominican Sisters (Cabra, Ireland) 2; Lay Teachers 20; Students 405.
Catechesis/Religious Programs—Tel: 504-945-8750; Fax: 504-949-8899.
Students 70.

44—ST. MARIA GORETTI (1965), Rev. Msgr. L. Earl Gauthreaux; Rev. Jaime G. Apolinares (Philippines); Deacons Peter E. Duffy; Ildefonso R. DeLeon.
Mailing Address: 7300 Crowder Blvd., 70127-1599. Tel: 504-242-7554; Fax: 504-242-0755.
School—(Nursery-PreK). Tel: 504-242-1313.
Lay Teachers 2; Students 14.
Catechesis/Religious Programs—Students 225.

45—ST. MARY OF THE ANGELS (1925) (African American), Rev. Bart Pax, O.F.M. In res., Rev. Robert C. Seay, O.F.M.; Bro. Gordon Boykins, O.F.M. Pastoral Assocs.: Bros. Mark Gehret, O.F.M.; Martin Humphreys, O.F.M.; Valerie Shields.
Res., 3501 N. Miro St., 70117-5899. Tel: 504-945-3186; Fax: 504-945-9115.
School—2225 Congress St., 70117-5898. Tel: 504-943-5687; Fax: 504-943-6673. Sr. Carmelita Mulry, S.H.Sp., Prin.
Lay Teachers 10; Students 238.

46—ST. MATTHIAS (1920) (African American), Rev. John Cisewski. In res., Rev. Edmund Akordor (Ghana); Deacon Jose A. Sierra.
Res., 4230 S. Broad St., 70125-3699. Tel: 504-822-3394; Fax: 504-822-3395.
Catechesis/Religious Programs—Students 37.

47—ST. MAURICE (1852), Rev. Urbano Gracias.
Res., 605 St. Maurice Ave., 70117-1598. Tel: 504-279-5231; Fax: 504-279-5232.

48—ST. MONICA (1924) (African American), Rev. Msgr. Lanaux J. Rareshide; Deacon Herman Williams.
Res., 2327 S. Galvez St., 70125-3198. Tel: 504-821-9500; Fax: 504-821-9500.
School—2323 Galvez St., 70125-3199. Tel: 504-821-3321; Fax: 504-821-5631.
Lay Teachers 10; Students 140.
Catechesis/Religious Programs—Students 35.

49—ST. NICHOLAS OF MYRA (1971), Rev. Arthur J. Ginart.
Res., Rte. 6, Box 146-BE, 70129-9799. Tel: 504-662-5339; Fax: 504-662-5339.

50—ST. PATRICK (1833), Rev. Msgr. John P. Reynolds; Rev. Anthony J. White.
Res., 724 Camp St., 70130-3757. Tel: 504-525-4413; Fax: 504-568-1324.

51—ST. PAUL THE APOSTLE (1947) (African American), Rev. Francis A. Dixon, S.V.D.; Deacon Daniel P. Vincent.
Res., 6828 Chef Menteur Hwy., 70126-5297. Tel: 504-242-7934; Fax: 504-242-1777. [CEM]
School—Tel: 504-242-5962; Fax: 504-242-0584.
Lay Teachers 9; Students 205.
Catechesis/Religious Programs—Students 95.

52—ST. PETER CLAVER (1920) (African American), Rev. Michael P. Jacques, S.S.E.; Deacon Rudolph Rayfield. Pastoral Assocs.: Sr. Mary Anne Hebert, C.S.J., Dir. Social Apostulate; Pearl Dupart, Assoc. Dir. Social Apostulate; Patrice Bell, Dir. Devel.; Rosie Papion.
Office: 1923 St. Philip St., 70116-2199. Tel: 504-822-8059; Fax: 504-822-9251.
School—1020 N. Prieur St., 70116-2194. Tel: 504-822-8191. Mr. Don Boucree, Prin.
Lay Teachers 15; Students 260.
Catechesis/Religious Programs—Tel: 504-822-8176. Alena Boucree, D.R.E.
Students 255.

53—SS. PETER AND PAUL (1848), Rev. Michael Roberson; Rev. Msgr. Arthur W. Hauth, Pastor Emeritus.
Res., 2317 Burgundy St., 70117-8587. Tel: 504-945-1531; Fax: 504-945-1537.

54—ST. PHILIP THE APOSTLE (1949) (African American), Rev. Michael P. Jacques, S.S.E.; Deacon Raymond Rayfield, Sr.
Res., 3304 Metropolitan St., 70126-5799. Tel: 504-945-2122; Fax: 504-945-2128.
Catechesis/Religious Programs—Students 60.

55—ST. PIUS X (1953), Rev. Msgr. Clinton J. Doskey; Deacons Chris T. Weber; William A. Glennon.
Res., 6666 Spanish Fort Blvd., 70124-4398. Tel: 504-282-3332; Fax: 504-283-8984.
School—Tel: 504-282-2811.
Lay Teachers 26; Students 482.
Catechesis/Religious Programs—Students 110.

56—ST. RAPHAEL THE ARCHANGEL (1947), Rev. Horace L. Brignac, Jr.; Rev. Msgr. Vernon P. Aleman, Pastor Emeritus.
Res., 2212 Prentiss Ave., 70122-5399. Tel: 504-282-6494; Fax: 504-282-2955.
School—5601 Elysian Fields Ave., 70122-4286. Tel: 504-288-1474. Sr. Jean Held, S.C.C., Prin.
Sisters of Christian Charity 2; Lay Teachers 5; Students 168.

57—ST. RAYMOND (1927), Revs. Richard T. Sadlier, S.S.J.; Henry J. Davis, S.S.J.; Deacons John B. Williams; Dwight Alexander.
Res., 3738 Paris Ave., 70122-2399. Tel: 504-288-1272; Fax: 504-283-3069.
School—Tel: 504-282-5563; Fax: 504-282-2344. Sr. Patricia Ann Williams, S.S.F., Prin.
Sisters of the Holy Family 4; Lay Teachers 12; Students 296.
Catechesis/Religious Programs—Students 90.

58—ST. RITA (1921), Revs. Henry J. Bugler; Rodney Anthony Ricard; Deacon Wilbur A. Toups. In res., Rev. Wilfred F. Meridier.
Res., 2729 Lowerline St., 70125-3599. Tel: 504-866-3621; Fax: 504-861-0338.
School—65 Fontainebleau Dr., 70125-3495. Tel: 504-866-1777; Fax: 504-861-8512.
Marianites of Holy Cross 8; Lay Teachers 10; Students 265.

59—ST. ROSE OF LIMA (1857), Rev. H. William Reed.
Res., 2545 Bayou Rd., 70119-2398. Tel: 504-945-3591; Fax: 504-945-3216.

60—ST. SIMON PETER (1986), Rev. Martin J. Smullen; Deacons Peter C. Rizzo; Daniel Haggerty, Jr.; Jesse A. Watley.
Office: 7600 Gannon Rd., 70128-1402. Tel: 504-243-9214; Fax: 504-243-9251.
School—Tel: 504-243-9241. Mrs. Camille Treaudo, Prin.

61—ST. STEPHEN (1849), Revs. James Garcia Ward, C.M.; Harold E. Dicharry, C.M.; Deacon Charles J. Smith, Jr. In res., Revs. James Schott; Joseph Maniangat; Perry F. Henry, C.M.; Bro. James Steinbach, C.M.
Res., 1025 Napoleon St., 70115-2898. Tel: 504-899-1378; Fax: 504-899-0480.
School—4310 Chestnut St., 70115-2790. Tel: 504-891-1927; Fax: 504-891-1928. Sr. Juanita Chenevert, D.C., Prin.
Daughters of Charity of St. Vincent de Paul 2; Lay Teachers 14; Students 266.

62—ST. THERESA OF AVILA (1848), Revs. Teodoro Agudo, O.F.M.Cap. (Spain); Eutiquiano Miguel, O.F.M.Cap.; Deacon Francis J. Fleischer.
Res., 1404 Erato St., 70130-4387. Tel: 504-525-4226; Fax: 504-525-6014.

63—ST. THERESA OF THE CHILD JESUS (1927) (African American), Rev. Quentin Moody.
Res., 3810 Leonidas St., 70118-4698. Tel: 504-482-1668; Fax: 504-486-8179.

64—ST. THOMAS THE APOSTLE. (University of New Orleans). Rev. Francis Berner; Deacon Eric Gamble.
Res., UNO Newman Center, 70148-0001. Tel: 504-288-6336; Fax: 504-288-6344.

65—ST. THOMAS MORE (1970). (The Community of St. Thomas More for Tulane Univ.). Rev. John J. Boll, O.P.; Deacon Joseph R. Rosato.
Res., 1037 Audubon St., 70118-5294. Tel: 504-866-0984; Fax: 504-865-1914.
Catechesis/Religious Programs—Students 105.

66—ST. VINCENT DE PAUL (1838), Rev. Pedro F. Nunez; Deacon Lawrence Keller.
Res., 3053 Dauphine St., 70117-6794. Tel: 504-943-5566; Fax: 504-943-5501.

OUTSIDE THE CITY OF NEW ORLEANS

Abita Springs, St. Tammany Parish, St. Jane de Chantal (1887), Rev. William J. MacCandless, O.S.B.; Deacons Frans Labranche, Jr.; Don Bourgeois.
Res., 22122 Main St., P.O. Box 187, 70420-0187. Tel: 504-892-1439; Fax: 504-871-9547. [JC]

Catechesis/Religious Programs—72049 Hickory St., 70420-3931. Tel: 504-893-3914.
Students 264.
Mission—Bush, St. Tammany Civil Parish, St. Michael the Archangel, Hwy. 41, 70431. Tel: 504-886-3868.

Ama, St. Charles Parish, St. Mark (1974), Rev. John M. Perino.
Res., P.O. Box 556, 70031-0556. Tel: 504-431-8505; Fax: 504-431-8506.
Catechesis/Religious Programs—Tel: 504-431-8507. Keith Kravet, D.R.E.
Students 91.

Arabi, St. Bernard Parish, St. Louise De Marillac (1954), Revs. Edward M. Grice; James Nguyen Bach, Pastoral Assoc.; Deacons Alvin C. Miester, Jr.; Alex J. Seruntine, Jr.
Res., 6800 Patricia St., 70032-1496. Tel: 504-271-4671; Fax: 504-271-7727.
School—Tel: 504-271-1677; Fax: 504-271-1678. Constance Thorn, Prin.
Congregation of the Most Holy Sacrament Sister 1; Lay Teachers 25; Students 455.
Catechesis/Religious Programs—Tel: 504-277-4215.
Students 154.

St. Robert Bellarmine (1964), Rev. Lich Van Nguyen; Deacon Curles P. Reeson.
Res., 408 Cougar Dr., 70032-2098. Tel: 504-279-8215; Fax: 504-277-7656.
School—815 Badger Dr., 70032-1996. Tel: 504-279-6466.
Lay Teachers 22; Students 514.
Catechesis/Religious Programs—Tel: 504-271-9112.
Students 75.

Avondale, Jefferson Parish, St. Bonaventure (1965), Rev. Dennis J. Hayes, III.
Res., 329 S. Jamie Blvd., 70094-2821. Tel: 504-436-1279; Fax: 504-436-1300.
Catechesis/Religious Programs—Tel: 504-436-0744. Trudy Cook, D.R.E.
Students 125.

Belle Chasse, Plaquemines Parish, Our Lady of Perpetual Help (1928), Rev. Michael J. Schneller; Deacon Charles P. Moore; Sr. Cynthia Sabathier, C.S.J., Pastoral Assoc.
Res., 8968 Hwy. 23, 70037-2296. Tel: 504-394-0314; Fax: 504-394-0376. [CEM]
School—Tel: 504-394-0757. Sr. Elizabeth Hebert, S.L.W., Prin.
Sisters 2; Lay Teachers 23; Students 269.
Catechesis/Religious Programs—Nanette Carpenter, D.R.E.
Students 255.

Bogalusa, Washington Parish, Annunciation B.V.M. (1907), Rev. Kevin Clark, O.S.B.; Deacon Charles Hartman, III.
Res., 517 Avenue B, 70427-3723. Tel: 504-732-4280; Fax: 504-735-1042. [JC]
School—511 Avenue C, 70427-3797. Tel: 504-735-6643; Fax: 504-735-6119.
Lay Teachers 15; Students 256.
Catechesis/Religious Programs—Students 256.

Bridge City, Jefferson Parish, Holy Guardian Angels (1963), Rev. Msgr. J. Anthony Luminais.
Res., 1701 Bridge City Ave., P.O. Box 9069, 70094-9069. Tel: 504-436-4712; Fax: 504-436-4070.
Catechesis/Religious Programs—Students 109.

Buras, Plaquemines Parish, Our Lady of Good Harbor (1864), Rev. Msgr. Terry B. Becnel.
Mailing Address: 240 Buras River Rd., 70041-9188. Tel: 504-657-9873; Fax: 504-657-9878.
Catechesis/Religious Programs—Students 159.
Missions—Empire, Plaquemines Parish, St. Ann; Venice, Plaquemines Parish, St. Anthony. [CEM]

Chalmette, St. Bernard Parish, Our Lady of Prompt Succor (1951), Revs. Warren L. Cooper; Joseph Duc Dzien; Deacons Henry A. Cassou, Jr.; Julius Zimmer.
Res., 2320 Paris Rd., 70043-5098. Tel: 504-271-3441; Fax: 504-271-2927.
School—2305 Fenelon St., 70043-4951. Tel: 504-271-2953; Fax: 504-271-1470. Evelyn Kingston, Prin.
School Sisters of Notre Dame 2; Lay Teachers 38; Students 698.
Catechesis/Religious Programs—Tel: 504-271-1217. Brenda Tromatore, D.R.E.
Students 393.

Prince of Peace (1977), Rev. Walter J. Austin; Deacon Frank W. Rhodes, Jr.
Res., 3700 Jean Lafitte Pkwy., 70043-1199. Tel: 504-271-1664; Fax: 504-279-8023.
Catechesis/Religious Programs—Tel: 504-277-6070; Fax: 504-279-8023. Tricia Hanzo, D.R.E.
Students 225.

St. Mark (1964), Revs. Mark Lomax; Joseph Man Tran; Deacons Raymond Rivere; Albert A. Levy, III; Kenneth Madere.
Res., 3024 Charles Dr., 70043-3798. Tel: 504-279-6073; Fax: 504-279-9403.
School—Tel: 504-271-1694; Fax: 504-277-7195. Pam Truxillo, Prin.
Daughters of Divine Providence 2; Lay Teachers 28; Students 608.
Catechesis/Religious Programs—Tel: 504-277-2584. Sr. Pier Carla, F.D.P., D.R.E.
Students 695.
Convent—3100 Mumphrey Rd., 70043-3735. Tel: 504-279-4619; Fax: 504-279-4619. Daughters of Divine Providence

Covington, St. Tammany Parish, St. Peter (1843), Revs. William J. McGough; Herbert J. Kiff, Jr.; Deacons Carmelo Graffagnini; Charles Heine; Charles Read.
Res., 128 E. 19th St., 70433-3195. Tel: 504-892-2422; Fax: 504-898-1998.
School—Tel: 504-892-1831; Fax: 504-898-2185. Mrs. Sharon Coll, Prin.
Lay Teachers 31; Students 594.
Catechesis/Religious Programs—Tel: 504-893-2446.
Students 594.

Crown Point, Jefferson Parish, St. Pius X (1971), Rev. Terence Hayden.
Res., Rte. 1, Box 368, Marrero, 70072-9704. Tel: 504-689-2381; Fax: 504-689-7417.
Catechesis/Religious Programs—Students 89.

Des Allemands, St. Charles Parish, St. Gertrude (1955), Rev. William J. O'Donnell; Deacon Landry Matherne.
Res., P.O. Box 767, 70030-0767. Tel: 504-758-7542; Fax: 504-758-7591. [CEM]
Catechesis/Religious Programs—Tel: 504-758-1332. Sr. Bernadette Nguyen, D.R.E.
Students 165.

Destrehan, St. Charles Parish, St. Charles Borromeo (1723), Revs. John Phuc; Ray Hymel; Deacons Harry Schexnayder; Theodore Roussel.
Res., 13396 River Rd., P.O. Box 428, 70047-0428. Tel: 504-764-6383; Fax: 504-764-3948. [CEM]
School—Lay Teachers 31; Students 445.

Diamond, Plaquemines Parish, St. Jude (1981), Rev. John C. Hegarty, C.S.Sp.
Res., P.O. Box 36, Port Sulphur, 70083-0036. Tel: 504-564-2182; Fax: 504-564-2077.
School—Tel: 504-564-3773. Sr. Suzanne Clark, O.S.F., Prin.
Sisters of St. Francis of Perpetual Adoration 4; Lay Teachers 5; Students 174.

Edgard, St. John the Baptist Parish, St. John the Baptist (1770), Rev. Donald Duffy.
Res., 2361 Hwy. 18, 70049-9101. Tel: 504-497-3412; 497-8470; Fax: 504-497-3965. [CEM]
Catechesis/Religious Programs—Students 263.

Florissant, St. Bernard Parish, San Pedro Pescador (1966) (Islenos), Rev. John Patrick Grenham.
Church—P.O. Box 457, St. Bernard, 70085-0457. Tel: 504-676-3719; Fax: 504-676-9996.
Res., 205 Florissant Hwy., St. Bernard, 70085-9703.
Catechesis/Religious Programs—Tel: 504-676-3565. D.R.E.: Mrs. Kristie Vollentine; Mrs. Carla Lee, (Youth).
Students 150.

Folsom, St. Tammany Parish, St. John the Baptist (1921), Rev. Jonathan M. DeFrange, O.S.B.; Deacon Clayton J. Guitterrez.
Res., 11345 St. John Church Rd., 70437-7155. Tel: 504-796-3806; Fax: 504-796-9554.
Catechesis/Religious Programs—Tel: 504-796-5507.
Students 165.

Franklinton, Washington Parish, Holy Family (1982), Rev. William H. Blank.
Res., 1213 14th Ave., P.O. Box 471, 70438-0471. Tel: 504-839-4040; Fax: 504-839-2429.

Garyville, St. John the Baptist Parish, St. Hubert, Rev. Charles J. Caluda; Deacon Joseph Mamou.
Res., P.O. Box K, 70051-0851. Tel: 504-535-2828; Fax: 504-535-1849.

Gretna, Jefferson Parish, St. Anthony (1920), Rev. Msgr. Gerard W. Poche; Rev. Louis A. Persac, (Retired). In res., Very Rev. Gerald L. Seiler, J.C.L.
Res., 924 Monroe St., 70053-2299. Tel: 504-368-6161; Fax: 504-362-7811.
School—Tel: 504-367-0689; Fax: 504-361-0054. Mrs. Marie K. Cannon, Prin.
Sisters of the Living Word 2; Lay Teachers 10; Students 275.
Catechesis/Religious Programs—Students 54.

St. Cletus (1965), Revs. Adrian B. Hall; Quang Nguyen; Sr. Mary Estelle Foucheaux, Pastoral Assoc.; Deacons Louis W. Stall; Peter B. Schlette; Elliott Arendt, Sr.
Res., 3600 Claire Ave., 70053-7699. Tel: 504-367-7951; Fax: 504-367-7928.
School—Tel: 504-366-3538; Fax: 504-366-0011. Mrs. Joan Fischer, Prin.
Lay Teachers 38; Students 587.
Catechesis/Religious Programs—Tel: 504-361-4805. Mrs. Ruth Susslin, D.R.E.
Students 330.

St. Joseph (1857), Revs. Francis J. Carabello; Ronald J. Braud.
Res., 610 Sixth St., 70053-6098. Tel: 504-368-1313; Fax: 504-368-6841.

Hahnville, St. Charles Parish, Our Lady of the Holy Rosary (1877), Rev. Bernard C. Francis.
Res., #1 Rectory Ln., 70057. Tel: 504-783-1199; Fax: 504-783-1974. [CEM]

Harahan, Jefferson Parish, St. Rita (1950), Revs. Frank J. Giroir; Minh Cong Phan; Mr. Al Martin, Pastoral Assoc. & D.R.E.; Deacons Nolen J. LeBlanc; Nicholas L. Mistretta; Danny Flynn.
Res., 160 Imperial Woods Dr., 70123-4998. Tel: 504-737-2915; Fax: 504-737-2921.
School—194 Ravan Ave., 70123-4999. Tel: 504-737-0744; Fax: 504-738-2184. Mrs. Barbara Hollier, Prin.
Lay Teachers 26; Students 459.
Catechesis/Religious Programs—Students 148.

Harvey, Jefferson Parish,

1—Infant Jesus of Prague, (1969), Rev. Msgr. Elmo L. Romagosa; Deacon Ferris Duet.
Res., 700 Maple St., 70058-4008. Tel: 504-368-1397; Fax: 504-368-0662.
Catechesis/Religious Programs—Students 80.

2—St. John Bosco, (1983), Revs. Sidney Figlia, S.D.B.; Ernest Faggioni, S.D.B.
Res., 2114 Oakmere Dr., 70058-2275. Tel: 504-340-0444; Fax: 504-340-9521.
Catechesis/Religious Programs—Brenda C. Baker, D.R.E.
Students 120.

3—St. Martha, (1973), Rev. William O'Riordan; Deacon Leslie D. Vincent.
Res., 2555 Apollo Dr., 70058-5813. Tel: 504-366-1604; Fax: 504-366-1100.

4—St. Rosalie, (1949), Revs. Thomas E. Ruekert, S.D.B.; Gregory Fishel, S.D.B. In res., Rev. Jonathan Parks, S.D.B.
Parish Offices:—600 2nd Ave., 70058-2728. Tel: 504-340-1962; Fax: 504-340-1546.
Res., 608 1st Ave., 70058-2799. Tel: 504-341-5656.
School—617 Second Ave., 70058-2798. Tel: 504-341-4342; Fax: 504-347-0271.
Middle School—2115 Oakmere Dr., 70058-2276. Tel: 504-348-9330; Fax: 504-348-9331.
Dominican Sisters (Cabra, Ireland) 3; Lay Teachers 50; Students 1,200.

Jefferson, Jefferson Parish, St. Agnes (1931), Revs. Peter O'Grady; Robustiano D. Morgia (Philippines); Deacons Piero Caserta; Nelvin Luke; Rev. Msgr. Louis P. LeBourgeois, Admin.
Res., 3310 Jefferson Hwy., 70121-2699. Tel: 504-833-3366; Fax: 504-834-1532.
School—Lay Teachers 22; Students 409.

Kenner, Jefferson Parish,

1—Nativity of Our Lord, (1977) (Spanish), Rev. Danilo C. Digal; Deacons John LeDoux; Eddy Beckendorf; Roberto Mendieta.
Office: 3325 Loyola Dr., 70065-2567. Tel: 504-466-5016; Fax: 504-467-8575.
Catechesis/Religious Programs—Tel: 504-464-9664. Mrs. Donna Johnsen, D.R.E.
Students 254.

2—Our Lady of Perpetual Help, (1869), Rev. Richard M. Miles.
Res., 1908 Short St., 70062-7599. Tel: 504-464-0361; Fax: 504-465-0930.
School—Tel: 504-464-0531; Fax: 504-464-0725. Sr. Mary Henry Simoneaux, R.S.M., Prin.
Sisters of Mercy 3; Lay Teachers 26; Students 447.

3—St. Elizabeth Ann Seton, (1981), Most Rev. Dominic Carmon, S.V.D.; Rev. Peter Nam Van Tran; Deacons Andrea Capaci; Noel W. Martinsen; Garland Bourgeois.
Res., 4111 St. Blase Dr., P.O. Box 641000, 70065-1656. Tel: 504-468-1441; Fax: 504-468-3305.
School—Lay Teachers 13; Students 506.

4—St. Jerome, (1963), Rev. Robert C. Cavalier; Deacons Daniel Cordes; Edgar Dragon; Luis Campuzano, Sr.; Ernesto Morales. In res., Rev. Donald M. Byrnes, (Retired).
Res., 2400 33rd St., 70065-3899. Tel: 504-443-3174; Fax: 504-443-5499.
Catechesis/Religious Programs—Gail Bordelon, D.R.E.
Students 237.

Lacombe, St. Tammany Parish, Sacred Heart (1890), Rev. Paul H. Desrosiers; Deacon James Biales.
Res., P.O. Box 1080, 70445-1080. Tel: 504-882-5229; Fax: 504-882-9034.
Catechesis/Religious Programs—Students 195.

St. John of the Cross (1984), Rev. Msgr. Francis G. Boeshans; Deacon Joseph LeRose. In res., Rev. Kieran O'Hara, (Retired).
Res., 61051 Brier Lake Dr., 70445-2911. Tel: 504-882-3779; Fax: 504-882-9282.
Catechesis/Religious Programs—Tel: 504-882-6225.
Students 149.

Lafitte, Jefferson Parish, St. Anthony (1936), Rev. John Ryan.
Res., Rte. 1, Box 499A, 70067-9714. Tel: 504-689-4101; Fax: 504-689-4102. [CEM]
Catechesis/Religious Programs—Tel: 504-689-2451. Esther Belsome, D.R.E.
Students 320.

La Place, St. John the Baptist Parish, Ascension of Our Lord (1979), Rev. Benjamin Piovan; Deacons Arthur Sandman, Sr.; Percy Vicknair; Paul H. Dupuy, Jr.
Res., 799 Fairway Dr., 70068-2007. Tel: 504-652-2615; Fax: 504-652-7291.
School—1809 Greenwood Dr., 70068-2098. Tel: 504-652-4532; Fax: 504-651-5151.
Lay Teachers 27; Students 405.
Catechesis/Religious Programs—Fax: 504-652-2791.
Students 170.

St. Joan of Arc (1947), Very Rev. Robert G. Vincent, V.F.; Rev. Philip Landry.
Res., P.O. Box 490, 70069-0490. Tel: 504-652-9100; Fax: 504-651-2920. [JC]
School—412 Fir St., 70068-4310. Tel: 504-652-6310; Fax: 504-652-6390. Sr. Mary Germaine, O.P., Prin.
Sisters of St. Dominic 2; Lay Teachers 44; Students 786.
Catechesis/Religious Programs—Tel: 504-651-0894. Mrs. Connie Cambre, D.R.E.
Students 279.

Luling, St. Charles Parish, Holy Family (1980), Rev. John P. Finn; Deacon Coy Landry.
Res., 155 Holy Family Ln., 70070-6103. Tel: 504-785-8585; Fax: 504-785-1167.
Catechesis/Religious Programs—D.R.E.: Diane Faucheux, (High School); Sasha Sevin, (Grade School).
Students 564.

St. Anthony of Padua (1961), Rev. Patrick Gannon; Deacon Paul J. Donnaud. In res., Rev. Patrick J. R. Kennedy.
Res., 234 Angus Dr., 70070-9513. Tel: 504-785-8885; Fax: 504-785-8882.
Catechesis/Religious Programs—Tel: 504-785-0050.
Students 169.

Madisonville, St. Tammany Parish, St. Anselm (1962), Rev. Alan R. Weseman; Deacon John Glover.
Res., P.O. Box 40, 70447-0040. Tel: 504-845-7342; Fax: 504-845-3076.
Catechesis/Religious Programs—Tel: 504-845-7912. Celie Clark, D.R.E.
Students 354.

Mandeville, St. Tammany Parish, Mary Queen of Peace (1988), Rev. Ronald L. Calkins; Deacon Anthony J. Ferretti.
Res., 1501 W. Causeway Approach, 70471-3047. Tel: 504-626-6977; Fax: 504-626-6971.
School—Tel: 504-674-2466. Mrs. Rhonda Parenton, Prin.
Students 93.
Catechesis/Religious Programs—Students 644.

Our Lady of the Lake (1850), Rev. Msgr. Joseph L. Chotin; Rev. Dean Robins; Deacons Dwight Johnson; Joseph Lazo; Philip Baham; Louis N. Mire.
Res., 2115 Jefferson St., 70448-5820. Tel: 504-626-5671; Fax: 504-626-5422.
School—Tel: 504-626-5678; Fax: 504-626-4337. Joseph Miller, Prin.
Lay Teachers 45; Students 762.
Catechesis/Religious Programs—Tel: 504-626-7901. Richard Beben, D.R.E.
Students 1081.

Marrero, Jefferson Parish,

1—IMMACULATE CONCEPTION, (1924) (Hispanic), Rev. Msgr. Ray P. Hebert; Revs. Nicholas Pericone; Alberto Bermudez; Deacons Wilfred Robichaux, Jr.; Rodolfo Martinez. In res., Rev. Denver B. Pentecost.
Res., 4401 7th St., 70072-2099. Tel: 504-341-9516; Fax: 504-341-9517.
School—601 Avenue C, 70072-2098. Tel: 504-347-4409; Fax: 504-341-2766. Sr. Fernanda Rossi, F.M.A., Prin.
Salesian Sisters 3; Lay Teachers 43; Students 871.
High School—Immaculata, 537 Avenue D, 70072-2027. Tel: 504-341-6217; Fax: 504-341-6229. Sr. Rosann Ruiz, F.M.A., Prin.
Sisters 2; Lay Teachers 36; Students 509.
Catechesis/Religious Programs—Tel: 504-347-8449.
Students 169.

2—ST. AGNES LE THI THANH (1995) (Vietnamese). (Personal Parish for Southeast Asians). Rev. John Baptist Vu Han.
Res., 1000 Westwood Dr., 70072-2415. Tel: 504-347-4725; Fax: 504-340-2476.
Church—6851 8th St., 70072-2556. Rev. John Baptist Vu Han.
Missions—Avondale, Jefferson Civil Parish, Assumption of Mary, 172 Noel Dr., Avondale, 70094-2900. Rev. Andrew Tran Cao Tuong, Admin.; New Orleans, Jefferson Civil Parish, St. Joseph, 6450 Kathy Ct., New Orleans, 70131-7515. Rev. Joseph Pham Van Tue, Admin.
Catechesis/Religious Programs—1216 Ave. G, 70072-3750. Tel: 504-348-8206.
Students 940.

3—ST. JOACHIM, (1985), Rev. Burnick J. Terrebonne; Deacon Charles Duhe.
Res., 5505 Barataria Blvd., 70072-6660. Tel: 504-341-9226; Fax: 504-340-8829.
Catechesis/Religious Programs—Tel: 504-347-6829. Mrs. Peggy Toyne, D.R.E.
Students 223.

4—ST. JOSEPH THE WORKER, (1955) (African American), Rev. Paul G. McQuillen, S.S.E.
Res., 455 Ames Blvd., 70072-1599. Tel: 504-347-8438; Fax: 504-340-9538.
School—Tel: 504-347-3704; Fax: 504-347-0852. Rev. Paul G. McQuillen, S.S.E., Prin.
Lay Teachers 12; Students 235.
Catechesis/Religious Programs—Students 168.

5—THE VISITATION OF OUR LADY, (1963), Very Rev. Michael B. Fraser, V.F.; Rev. Patrick B. Wattigny; Deacons Larry Murphy; Francis Minor.
Res., 3500 Ames Blvd., 70072-5699. Tel: 504-347-2203; Fax: 504-347-2223.
School—3520 Ames Blvd., 70072-5698. Tel: 504-347-3377; Fax: 504-341-5378. Mary Kitterman, Prin.
Lay Teachers 42; Students 802.
Catechesis/Religious Programs—Tel: 504-341-4499. Cheryl Tourelle, D.R.E.
Students 213.

Metairie, Jefferson Parish,

1—OUR LADY OF DIVINE PROVIDENCE, (1965), Revs. Milton L. Reisch; Lance J. Campo; Deacons Fred C. Memleb, Jr.; Barry Campeaux. In res., Rev. W. Wendell Sontheimer.
Res., 1000 N. Starrett Rd., 70003-5899. Tel: 504-466-4511; Fax: 504-466-4858.
School—917 N. Atlanta St., 70003-5898. Tel: 504-466-0591; Fax: 504-466-0671. Mrs. Shirley Bertucci, Prin.
Lay Teachers 35; Students 585.
Catechesis/Religious Programs—Mrs. Nancy Campeaux, D.R.E.
Students 270.

2—ST. ANGELA MERICI, (1964), Rev. Msgr. Crosby W. Kern, V.F.; Rev. John Nhan Van Tran; Deacons Gilbert R. Schmidt; Nicholas Chetta.
Res., 901 Beverly Gardens Dr., 70002-5085. Tel: 504-835-0324; Fax: 504-834-9709.
School—835 Melody Dr., 70002-5095. Tel: 504-835-8491; Fax: 504-835-4463. Jim Campbell, Prin.
Lay Teachers 28; Students 611.
Catechesis/Religious Programs—Tel: 504-837-9347.
Students 80.

3—ST. ANN CHURCH AND SHRINE, (1971), Rev. Msgr. Joseph E. Bourgeois; Rev. Jose Roel G. Lungay (Philippines); Deacons Phillip E. Doolen; Chris Bertucci.
Res., 4920 Loveland St., 70006-4099. Tel: 504-455-7071; Fax: 504-455-7076.
School—4921 Meadowdale St., 70006-4098. Tel: 504-455-8383; Fax: 504-455-9572.
Lay Teachers 52; Students 1150.
Catechesis/Religious Programs—Tel: 504-455-7071, Ext. 125.
Students 188.

4—ST. BENILDE, (1964), Revs. Carroll E. Heffner; Joseph Dau Van Nguyen; Deacons Biaggio DiGiovanni; Clifford S. Wright; Richard Brady.
Res., 1901 Division St., 70001-2798. Tel: 504-834-4980; Fax: 504-831-5810.
School—1801 Division St., 70001-2799. Tel: 504-833-9894; Fax: 504-834-4380. Mrs. Cheryl Orillion, Prin.
Lay Teachers 40; Students 668.
Catechesis/Religious Programs—Students 95.

5—ST. CATHERINE OF SIENA, (1921), Revs. James Lohan; James J. Jeanfreau, Jr.; Curtis R. Thomas; Deacons Michael Coney; Jere Crago; Sr. Rose Mary Wessel, M.S.C., Pastoral Assoc.
Res., 105 Bonnabel Blvd., 70005-3798. Tel: 504-835-9343; 835-5491; Fax: 504-835-1525.
School—400 Codifer Blvd., 70005-3797. Tel: 504-831-1166; Fax: 504-833-8982. Sr. Imelda Moriarty, Prin.
Sisters of Charity of the Incarnate Word 4; Lay Teachers 63; Students 1,160.
Catechesis/Religious Programs—Students 41.

6—ST. CHRISTOPHER THE MARTYR, (1947), Revs. H. J. Adams, Jr.; Kenneth Harney; Charles L. Mueller; Deacons Charles Duke; S. J. Calamia.
Res., 309 Manson Ave., 70001-4898. Tel: 504-837-8214; Fax: 504-837-8303.
School—(Grades PreK-8) 3900 Derbigny St., 70001-4999. Tel: 504-837-6871; Fax: 504-834-0522. Ruth Meche, Prin.
Lay Teachers 35; Students 842.
Catechesis/Religious Programs—Tel: 504-831-7691. Doris Marse, D.R.E.
Students 100.

7—ST. CLEMENT OF ROME, (1965), Rev. Msgr. Ralph E. Carroll; Rev. David Dufour; Deacons Kenneth Boe; Ed Dorvin; Jerry Martinez; Jeff Fariss.
Res., 4317 Richland Ave., 70002-3097. Tel: 504-887-7821; Fax: 504-454-3906.
School—3978 W. Esplanade Ave., 70002-3099. Tel: 504-888-0386; Fax: 504-885-8273. Glenn Gennaro, Prin.
Lay Teachers 28; Students 562.
Catechesis/Religious Programs—Students 160.

8—ST. EDWARD THE CONFESSOR, (1964), Revs. Gilmer J. Martin; G. Amaldoss; Vien The Nguyen; Deacons A. David Warriner, Jr.; Gerard J. Fasullo, Sr.; August Mendel. Parish Office: 4921 W. Metairie Ave., 70001-4466. Tel: 504-888-0703; Fax: 504-455-5443.
School—Tel: 504-888-6353. Sr. Mary de Lourdes, S.L.W., Prin. & D.R.E.
Sisters of the Living Word 2; Lay Teachers 26; Students 591.
Catechesis/Religious Programs—Students 90.

9—ST. FRANCIS XAVIER, (1924), Revs. Andrew C. Taormina; Thomas Kinney; Deacons Paul Nalty; Charles E. Coudrain, Jr. In res., Rev. Earl F. Niehaus, S.M.
Res., 448 Metairie Rd., 70005-4371. Tel: 504-834-0340; 837-4733; Fax: 504-837-8735.
School—215 Betz Ave., 70005-4167. Tel: 504-833-1471; Fax: 504-833-1498. Steve Labranche, Prin.
Lay Teachers 25; Students 460.
Catechesis/Religious Programs—444 Metairie Rd., 70005-4307. Tel: 504-834-0348.
Students 120.

10—ST. LAWRENCE THE MARTYR, (1958), Rev. Richard N. Maughan; Deacons Randall L. Engel; Sterling Ohlmeyer; Alfred Zeringue.
Res., 2525 Maine Ave., 70003-5446. Tel: 504-466-6236; Fax: 504-467-4945.
School—2505 Maine Ave., 70003-5498. Tel: 504-469-5262; Fax: 504-469-5293. Louise A. Olsen, Ed.D., Prin.
Lay Teachers 12; Students 209.
Catechesis/Religious Programs—Tel: 504-466-8344.
Students 64.

11—ST. LOUIS KING OF FRANCE, (1947), Rev. Msgr. Joseph O. Lorio; Rev. Gerard Stapleton; Deacon Wilbur Martinez. In res., Rev. Lawrence A. deMaria.
Res., 1609 Carrollton Ave., 70005-1498. Tel: 504-834-9977; Fax: 504-834-9979.
School—1600 Lake Ave., 70005-1499. Tel: 504-833-8224; Fax: 504-838-9938.
Lay Teachers 31; Students 537.

12—ST. MARY MAGDALEN, (1955), Rev. Msgr. Robert D. Massett; Rev. Nghiem Vinh Nguyen; Deacons Charles Nunez; Angeles Robin; Susan Sullivan, Pastoral Assoc.
Res., 6425 W. Metairie Ave., 70003-4395. Tel: 504-733-0922; Fax: 504-733-0869.
School—6421 W. Metairie Ave., 70003-4395. Tel: 504-733-1433; Fax: 504-736-0727. Sr. Amelia Ibarra, Prin.
Teresians Sisters 2; Lay Teachers 28; Students 655.
Catechesis/Religious Programs—Students 275.

13—ST. PHILIP NERI, (1960), Revs. Lee John Saloy; James Richard Day; Deacons Jerry L. Harrison; Thomas E. Caffery, Jr.; Edward R. Cannon; Paul A. Cimino.
Res., 6500 Kawanee Ave., 70003-3298. Tel: 504-887-5535; Fax: 504-885-6259.
School—6600 Kawanee Ave., 70003-3199. Tel: 504-887-5600; Fax: 504-456-6857.
Lay Teachers 30; Students 629.
Catechesis/Religious Programs—Tel: 504-889-0089. Mrs. E. Seton Jenkins, D.R.E.
Students 182.

Norco, St. Charles Parish, Sacred Heart of Jesus (1959), Rev. John J. Marse.
Res., 401 Spruce St., P.O. Box 515, 70079-2197. Tel: 504-764-6503; Fax: 504-725-0512.
School—Tel: 504-764-9958; Fax: 504-764-0041. Colleen S. Remont, Prin.
Lay Teachers 13; Students 234.
Catechesis/Religious Programs—Students 237.

Paradis, St. Charles Parish, St. John the Baptist (1971), Rev. Msgr. James C. Moragne.
Res., P.O. Box 1498, 70080-1498. Tel: 504-758-2668; Fax: 504-758-2901.
Catechesis/Religious Programs—Students 205.

Pearl River, St. Tammany Parish, SS. Peter and Paul (1970), Rev. Bac-Hai Viet Tran; Deacon John F. Howard.
Res., 66009 St. Mary Dr., 70452-5705. Tel: 504-863-7935; Fax: 504-863-5431.
Catechesis/Religious Programs—Students 141.

Pointe a la Hache, Plaquemines Parish, St. Thomas (1844) (African American), Rev. Thomas J. Miller, C.S.Sp.
Res., P.O. Box 98, 70082-0098. Tel: 504-333-4465; Fax: 504-333-9933.
Mission—Braithwaite, Plaquemines Parish, Assumption of the Blessed Virgin, 6951 Hwy. 39, Braithwaite, 70040-0063. Tel: 504-682-5607. [CEM]

Port Sulphur, Plaquemines Parish, St. Patrick (1956), Rev. Ramon P. Martinez.
Res., 28698 Hwy. 23, 70083-9623. Tel: 504-564-3284; Fax: 504-564-3108. [CEM]
Catechesis/Religious Programs—Tel: 504-564-2803.
Students 126.
Mission—Potash, Plaquemines Parish, St. Joseph.

Reserve, St. John the Baptist Parish, Our Lady of Grace (1937), Rev. George W. Burden, S.S.J.; Bro. Peter J. McLaughlin, S.S.J.
Mailing Address: P.O. Box 464, 70084-0464.
Res., 772 Hwy. 44, 70084-0464. Tel: 504-536-2613; Fax: 504-536-1819.
School—Ms. Wilhelmina Armour, Admin.; Ms. Olivia French. Lay Teachers 9; Students 163.
Catechesis/Religious Programs—Myrtle Ann Lucas, D.R.E.
Students 139.

St. Peter (1864), Rev. Patrick B. Sanders; Deacon David W. Farinelli.
Res., 1550 Hwy. 44, P.O. Box 435, 70084-0435. Tel: 504-536-2887; Fax: 504-536-7078. [CEM]
School—Tel: 504-536-4296. Helena Cupit, Prin.
Lay Teachers 14; Students 213.
Catechesis/Religious Programs—Students 200.

River Ridge, Jefferson Parish, St. Matthew the Apostle (1959), Rev. Brendan Morgan; Deacons Russell LeBlanc; Dan Dorsey; Roland Bienvenu.
Res., 10021 Jefferson Hwy., 70123-2498. Tel: 504-737-4537; Fax: 504-737-4033.
School—Tel: 504-737-4604; Fax: 504-738-7985.
Lay Teachers 32; Students 613.
Catechesis/Religious Programs—Students 85.

St. Benedict, St. Tammany Parish, St. Benedict (1970), Rev. Marian E. Larmann, O.S.B.
Res., Smith-Stafford Rd., 70457-9999. Tel: 504-892-1216; Fax: 504-892-4211.
Catechesis/Religious Programs—Tel: 504-892-0784.
Students 184.

St. Bernard, St. Bernard Parish, St. Bernard (1787), Rev. John P. Grenham.
Res., 2805 Bayou Rd., P.O. Box 70085-0220, 70085-9748. Tel: 504-682-5493; 682-3709; Fax: 504-682-8915. [CEM]

Slidell, St. Tammany Parish,

1—Our Lady of Lourdes, (1890), Rev. Msgr. Howard H. Hotard; Deacon Charles B. Faler, Jr.
Res., 3924 Berkley Ave., 70458-5198. Tel: 504-643-4137; Fax: 504-643-1675. [CEM]
School—345 Westchester Pl., 70458-5299. Tel: 504-643-3230; Fax: 504-645-0648. Mr. Robert V. Kiefer, Jr., Prin.
Sisters 1; Lay Teachers 25; Students 535.
Catechesis/Religious Programs—Tel: 504-643-1742. Mrs. Patricia S. Andrews, D.R.E.
Students 425.

2—St. Genevieve, (1968), Rev. Wayne C. Paysse; Deacon George Menges.
Res. and Mailing Address: 58203 Hwy. 433, 70460-3121. Tel: 504-643-3832; Fax: 504-649-5294.
Catechesis/Religious Programs—Tel: 504-641-5220. Claire Campbell, D.R.E.
Students 347.

3—St. Luke the Evangelist, (1982), Revs. Rodney P. Bourg; Rhenne A. Cervantes (Philippines); Deacons Harold J. Burke; Robert Trainor.
Office: 910 Cross Gates Blvd., 70461-8414. Tel: 504-641-6429; Fax: 504-847-0742.
Catechesis/Religious Programs—Tel: 504-641-2570.
Students 800.

4—St. Margaret Mary, (1965), Rev. Msgr. Richard L. Carroll; Revs. Joseph A. Benson; Thomas Gallagher, S.P.S.; Deacons Clarence Vicroy; John C. Weber; Robert Binney.
Res., 1050 Robert Blvd., 70458-2098. Tel: 504-643-6124; Fax: 504-643-6126.
School—Tel: 504-643-4612; Fax: 504-643-4659. Mr. Bobby Ohler, Prin.
Sisters 2; Lay Teachers 36; Students 763.
Catechesis/Religious Programs—Tel: 504-649-3055.
Students 601.

Terrytown, Jefferson Parish, Christ the King (1963), Revs. Lawrence A. Hecker; Jose Ladra; Deacons Cornelius Armshaw; James Swiler; Robert G. Beaumont, Sr.
Res., 535 Deerfield Rd., 70056-2899. Tel: 504-361-1500; Fax: 504-361-0632.
School—Tel: 504-367-3601; Fax: 504-367-3679.
Lay Teachers 27; Students 511.

Violet, St. Bernard Parish, Our Lady of Lourdes (1916), Revs. Frank J. Lipps; Mauro Raul Venust Lobo (India); Sr. Kathy Broussard, O.P., Pastoral Assoc.; Deacon William Chiappetta.
Res., 6305 E. St. Bernard Hwy., 70092-9506. Tel: 504-682-3046; Fax: 504-682-4470.
Catechesis/Religious Programs—6413 E. St. Bernard Hwy., 70092-9508. Tel: 504-682-0919.
Students 403.

Waggaman, Jefferson Parish, Our Lady of the Angels (1978), Rev. Paul Nguyen Van Tung; Deacon Gilbert Smith.
Res., 139 Herman St., 70094-2404. Tel: 504-436-4459; Fax: 504-436-4459. [CEM]
Catechesis/Religious Programs—Tel: 504-437-0514. Mr. & Mrs. Augustus Alby, D.R.E.
Students 162.

Westwego, Jefferson Parish, Our Lady of Prompt Succor (1920), Rev. Anthony M. Serio; Deacon Ernest F. Elfer, Jr.
Res., 146 Fourth St., 70094-4297. Tel: 504-341-9522; Fax: 504-341-5957. [CEM][JC]
School—531 Avenue A, 70094-4294. Tel: 504-341-9505; Fax: 504-341-9508. Sr. Rose Zanella, F.M.A., Supr.; Sr. Amparo Uribe, F.M.A., Prin.
Sisters 3; Lay Teachers 19; Students 300.
Catechesis/Religious Programs—Students 270.

Non-Parochial Churches & Chapels

New Orleans, Orleans Parish,

1—Our Lady of Prompt Succor National Shrine Church, Deacon Charles E. Coudrain, Jr.
Church—2635 State St., 70118-6339. Tel: 504-866-1472.

2—St. Mary Church, (1845). (Shrine of St. Lazarus of Jerusalem). Rev. Msgr. Alvin J. O'Reilly, Rector.
Church—1116 Chartres St., 70116-2596. Tel: 504-529-3040; Fax: 504-529-2001.

3—St. Mary's Assumption, (1858) (German), Rev. Gerard LaPorte, C.Ss.R.
Church—2030 Constance St., 70130-5099. Tel: 504-522-6748; Fax: 504-523-3734.

4—Chapel of the Vietnamese Martyrs, (1978) (Vietnamese), Rev. Msgr. Dominic Mai Thanh Luong.
Church—14400 Peltier Dr., 70129-1713. Tel: 504-254-5660; Fax: 504-254-9250.

Pilgrimage Shrines

New Orleans, Orleans Parish, Our Lady of Prompt Succor National Shrine (1810), Deacon Charles E. Coudrain, Jr.
Res., 2635 State St., 70118-6339. Tel: 504-866-1472; Fax: 504-866-8300.
St. Roch's Chapel in St. Roch's Cemetery,
Res., 1725 St. Roch Ave., 70117-8223. Tel: 504-596-3050; Fax: 504-596-3055.
Shrine of St. Lazarus of Jerusalem, Rev. Msgr. Alvin J. O'Reilly, Rector.
Church—1116 Chartres St., 70116-2596. Tel: 504-529-2651; Fax: 504-529-2001.

Metairie, Jefferson Parish, St. Ann Shrine, Rev. Joseph E. Bourgeois.
Church—4920 Loveland, 70002-4099. Tel: 504-455-7071; Fax: 504-455-7076.

Non-Parochial Community

New Orleans, Orleans Parish, Byzantine Catholic Mission (1978). Ruthenian Rite Jurisdiction. Rev. Ellis L. DePriest, S.M.
Church—3801 Monroe St., 70118-3490. Tel: 504-524-5192.

Chaplains of Public Institutions

Hospitals

New Orleans. *Charity Hospital* 1532 Tulane Ave., 70140-1015. Tel: 504-568-3262. Rev. Eutiquiano Miguel, O.F.M.Cap., Chap.
Children's Hospital 200 Henry Clay Ave., 70118-5799. Tel: 504-899-9511; Fax: 504-896-9707. Chaplains: Deacons Roland Bienvenu Tel: 504-737-8166; Charles J. Smith, Jr. Tel: 504-271-5124.
F. Edward Herbert Hospital. Vacant. No. 1 Sanctuary Dr., 70114-1500. Tel: 504-363-2200.
Jo Ellen Smith Convalescent Center 4502 General Meyer Ave., 70114-3531. Tel: 504-361-7923. Deacon Robert G. Beaumont, S.R.
Memorial Medical Center. Mid-City Campus 301 N. Jefferson Davis Pkwy., 70119-5397. Tel: 504-483-5000. Revs. Clement Monroe, C.SS.R., Chap.; Nicholas F. Husain.
Memorial Medical Center. Uptown Campus 2700 Napoleon Ave., 70115-6996. Tel: 504-899-9311. Revs. Nicholas F. Husain, Chap., Tel: 504-891-8369; Thomas J. Sheehan, S.J.
Methodist Hospital 5620 Read Rd., 70127-0103. Tel: 504-244-5100. Deacon John P. Muhleisen, Chap., Tel: 504-282-5114.
Touro Infirmary 1401 Foucher St., 70115-3593. Tel: 504-897-7011. Rev. Douglas C. Brougher, Chap., Tel: 504-897-7011; 945-5878.
Transitional Hospital Corporation Facility 3601 Coliseum St., 70115-3687. Tel: 504-899-1555; Fax: 504-899-1509. Chaplains: Deacons Richard E. Deichmann; William A. Glennon.
United Medical Center. Attended from St. Vincent de Paul Parish. 3419 St. Claude Ave., 70117-6198. Tel: 504-948-8200.
University Hospital 2021 Perdido St., 70112-1396. Tel: 504-588-3000. Rev. Vincent Bechamps, O.SS.T., Chap., Tel: 504-588-3175.
Veterans Affairs Medical Center 1601 Perdido St., 70146-2000. Tel: 504-568-0811. Chaplains: Revs. Joseph D. Laboon; Lawrence DeMaria.

Chalmette. *Chalmette Medical Centers* 9001 Patricia St., 70043-1799. Tel: 504-277-8011. 801 Virtue St., 70043-1298. Tel: 504-277-7711. Deacon Raymond H. Rivere, Chap.

Covington. *Lakeview Regional Medical Center* 95 E. Fairway Dr., 70433. Tel: 504-867-3800. Deacon Louis N. Mire, Chap.

Gretna. *Meadowcrest Hospital* 2500 Belle Chasse Hwy., 70056-7127. Tel: 504-392-3131. Deacon Leslie D. Vincent, Dir. Pastoral Care.

Jefferson. *Elmwood Medical Center* 1221 S. Clearview Pkwy., 70121-1029. Tel: 504-734-1900; Fax: 504-736-4901. Rev. Lawrence Pandolfo, O.P., Chap.
Ochsner Foundation Hospital 1516 S. Clearview Pkwy., 70121-2484. Tel: 504-842-3000. Rev. Wilfred F. Meridier, Chap., Tel: 504-866-7713.

Mandeville. *Southeast Louisiana Hospital* P.O. Box 3850, 70470-3850. Tel: 504-626-6317; Fax: 504-626-6658. Rev. Msgr. Marion Schutten, Chap., Tel: 504-892-9493; Deacon Robert Binney, Assoc.

Marrero. *West Jefferson General Hospital* 4500 11th St., 70072-3191. Tel: 504-347-5511. Rev. Denver B. Pentecost, Chap.
Wynhoven Health Care Center 1050 Medical Center Blvd., 70072-3170. Tel: 504-347-0777. Rev. Denver B. Pentecost, Chap.

Metairie. *Columbia Lakeside Hospital* 4700 S. I-10 Service Rd., 70001. Tel: 504-885-3342. Deacon August B. Mendel, Chap.
Doctors Hospital of Jefferson 4320 Houma Blvd., 70002-2973. Tel: 504-456-5555. Deacon Charles Duke, Chap.
East Jefferson General Hospital 4200 Houma Blvd., 70002-2970. Tel: 504-454-4000. Rev. Charles L. Mueller, Chap.; Deacon Raymond E. Heap, Assoc. Chap.

Slidell. *Greenbriar Nursing & Convalescent Home* 505 Robert Rd., 70458-1699. Tel: 504-643-6900. Chaplains: Rev. Msgr. Richard L. Carroll Tel: 504-643-6124; Revs. Joseph A. Benson; Thomas Gallagher, S.P.S.
Greenery Neurologic Rehabilitation Center at Slidell 1400 W. Lindberg Dr., 70458-3193. Tel: 504-641-4985. Chaplains: Rev. Msgr. Richard L. Carroll Tel: 504-643-6124; Revs. Joseph A. Benson; Thomas Gallagher, S.P.S.
Guest House of Slidell Nursing Home 1051 Robert Rd., 70458-2011. Tel: 504-643-5630. Chaplains: Rev. Msgr. Richard L. Carroll Tel: 504-643-6124; Revs. Joseph A. Benson; Thomas Gallagher, S.P.S.
North Shore Living Center. Attended by St. Luke the Evangelist, Slidell. 106 Medical Center Dr., 70461-7833. Tel: 504-643-0307.
North Shore Regional Medical Center. Attended by St. Luke the Evangelist, Slidell. 100 Medical Center Dr., 70461-7833. Tel: 504-649-7070.
Slidell Memorial Hospital. Attended by St. Margaret Mary, Slidell. 1001 Gause Blvd., 70458-2987. Tel: 504-643-2200.

Colleges and Universities

New Orleans. *Delgado College* 615 City Park Ave., 70119. Tel: 504-288-6336. Rev. Francis Berner, Chap.; Deacon Eric Gamble, Assoc. Chap.
Delgado Community College, School of Nursing 4133 Banks St., 70119-6883. Tel: 504-568-6282. Rev. Louis E. Meyers, S.J., Chap.
Louisiana State University Medical Center 4133 Banks St., 70119-6883. Tel: 504-568-6282. Rev. Louis E. Meyers, S.J., Chap.

Southern University in New Orleans UNO Newman Center, 70148-0001. Tel: 504-288-6336. Rev. Francis Berner, Chap.; Bro. Thomas Ward, F.S.C., Assoc. Chap.
Tulane-Newcomb 1037 Audubon St., 70118-5294. Tel: 504-866-0984. Rev. John J. Boll, O.P.
University of New Orleans UNO Newman Center, 70148-0001. Tel: 504-288-6336. Rev. Francis Berner, Chap.

Prisons

NEW ORLEANS. *Orleans Parish Correctional Center* 521 S. Broad St., 70119-7490. Tel: 504-822-8000. Chaplains: Rev. Theodore M. Kalamaja, S.J.; Deacons Randolph J. Crochet, Jr.; Jeffrey Fariss; Jose A. Sierra.
Orleans Parish House of Detention 2735 Perdido St., 70119-7390. Tel: 504-822-8000. Pastoral Ministers: Sr. Lilianne Flavin, O.P.; Sr. Victor Allain, R.S.M.
ANGIE. *Washington Correctional Institute* 27268 Hwy. 21, 70426-3030. Tel: 504-848-5232. Deacon Charles Hartman, Chap.
CHALMETTE. *St. Bernard Parish Prison* St. Bernard Courthouse, 70043-4793. Tel: 504-279-8823. Deacon Alex J. Seruntine, Jr., Chap.
GRETNA. *Jefferson Parish Correctional Center* P.O. Box 388, 70054-0388. Tel: 504-368-5360, Ext. 109. Chaplains: Rev. Robert J. Ratchford, S.J.; Deacons Louis Stall; Ralph Fray.
HARVEY. *Rivarde Juvenile Detention Home* 1525 Manhattan Blvd., 70058-3405. Tel: 504-392-2097. Deacon Ralph Fray, Chap.
MANDEVILLE. *St. Tammany Parish Prison.* c/o St. Joseph Abbey, St. Benedict, 70457-9999. Tel: 504-892-1800. Chaplains: Rev. Daniel Cobb, O.S.B.; Deacon Charles Read, Jr. Tel: 504-892-8324.

On Special or Other Archiocesan Assignment:
Reverend Monsignors—
Rodi, Thomas J., Vicar General

On Duty Outside the Archdiocese:
Reverend Fathers—
Calamari, Paul, St. Mary of the Assumption, Hockessin, DE 19797
Calkins, Arthur B., Villa Stritch, Via della Nocetta, 63, 00164, Rome, Italy
Fernandez, Luis J., VA Medical Center, 4165 D Indian Runn Dr., Dayton, OH 45415
Henao, Luis, Medellia, Colombia
Mongeon, Peter M., 1410 West St., Wrentham, MA 02093
Nguyen, Michael Nam Hoang, Philippines
Picado, Rodrigo, 50 Vs, E. Cortel, Curridabat, San Jose, Costa Rica
Planea, John, Philippines

Graduate Studies:
Reverend Fathers—
Nguyen, Michael Joseph Vinh N., North American College, Casa Santa Maria, Via Dell'Umilta, 30, Rome 00187 Italy. Tel: 06.69001.260; Fax: 06.69001.823

Military Chaplains:
Reverend Fathers—
Dixon, James R., U.S.A.F., Headquarters, USAF/HCX, 112 Luke Ave., Bolling AFB, DC 20332-9050
Highfill, H. Brian, U.S.A.F., PSC 80, Box 12349, APO AP, 96367-2349
O'Neill, Michael F., U.S.A.F., 100 ARW/HC, Unit 4905, Box 230, APO-AE, 09459-5230
Sizelove, Dennis M., PSC 94, Box 73, APO-AE, 09824
Young, Bernard L., VA Medical Center, 6205 N. 21st Dr., Phoenix, AZ 85015

Unassigned:
Reverend Fathers—
Duffy, Stephen
Gilbride, Thomas

Absent on Leave:
Reverend Fathers—
Keane, Patrick
Manko, Rodney A.
Schmaltz, Bernard W., (Administrative Leave)

Retired:
Reverend Monsignors—
Aleman, Vernon P., Chateau de Notre Dame, 2832 Burdette St., New Orleans, LA 70125
Bane, Raymond T., P.O. Box 1550, Paradis, LA 70080-1550
Brynes, Donald M., St. Jerome, 2400 33rd St., Kenner, LA 70065
Dowling, Thomas C., 303 Jeff Davis, Waveland, MS 39576
Duke, Charles J., 4845 Meadowdale St., Metairie, LA 70006
Hauth, Arthur W., Wynhoven Health Care Center, Marrero, LA 70072
Iverson, Stanley J., 5501 Tullis Dr., Bldg. 13-108, New Orleans, LA 70131
Landry, Michael, 36405 Old Bayou Liberty Rd., Slidell, LA 70460
Martin, Harrison A., 349 Bonnabel Blvd., Metairie, LA 70005
O'Reilly, Alvin J., 1116 Chartres St., New Orleans, LA 70116
Roeten, Winus, 9512 Kuepferle Ct., River Ridge, LA 70123
Sontheimer, W. Wendell, 1029 N. Atlanta St., Metairie, LA 70003
Woods, Earl C., 1438 Verna St., New Orleans, LA 70119
Reverend Fathers—
Arbizu, Juventino, 41 Calle, 12-29 Villasol, Zona 12, Guatemala City, Guatemala
Barattini, John H., Casella Postale 79, 16043, Chiavari, Italy
Dabria, Jerry J., 401 S. Gatehouse Dr., Apt. G, Metairie, LA 70001-2039
De La Pinera, Fernando, Casa Sacerdotal, Plaza Bendicho, 9, Almeria, 14001 Spain
Ernst, Albert C., P.O. Box 640400, Kenner, LA 70064-0400
Gonzales, Gabriel, 4011 Gen. Pershing St., New Orleans, LA 70125
Grennan, Thomas J., Pope John XXIII Priests' Residence, 2403 Holcombe Blvd., Houston, TX 77021
Hajtas, Francis, Karlsruherstrasse 9, Heidelberg, Germany
Kennedy, Patrick J.R., 234 Angus Dr., Luling, LA 70070
Lamendola, Francis S., 2820 Burdette St., New Orleans, LA 70125
Mele, Rudolph, 2832 Burdette St., New Orleans, LA 70125
Mitchell, Royce, 1512 Gardena Dr., New Orleans, LA 70122
Monzillo, Oneil, 532 Indian Bluff, Las Vegas, NV 89128
Ngo, Joseph Linh Duy, 2711 Barrington St., Arlington, TX 76014-2101
Perera, Denzil M., 1342 Moss St., New Orleans, LA 70119-2998
Perkovic, Anton, 446 Adair St., Mandeville, LA 70448
Persac, Louis A., 924 Monroe St., Gretna, LA 70053
Pieris, Timothy, 6564 Fleur de Lis St., Apt. 9, New Orleans, LA 70124
Pijoan, L. Adrian M. Figuerola, St. Augustine Home, 2345 W. 86th St., Indianapolis, IN 46260
Qui, Vincent, 421 Pat Dr., Avondale, LA 70094
Texada, David Ker, 1923 Salem St., Alexandria, LA 71301-3840
Tranchina, Joseph, 2832 Burdette St., New Orleans, LA 70125
Trinchard, Paul, 446 Crystal St., New Orleans, LA 70124
Vitte, Jules, 38 Grande Rue, 25300, Les Fourges, France
Walsh, Laurence, 8035 S. Quebec St., Englewood, CO 80112

Permanent Deacons:
Alexander, Dwight, St. Raymond, New Orleans
Arendt, Elliott, Sr., St. Cletus, Gretna
Armshaw, Cornelius, Christ the King, Terrytown
Attaway, Charles, On Leave
Baham, Philip C., Our Lady of the Lake, Mandeville
Balderas, Robert, Sr., National Dir., U.S. Apostleship of the Sea, Washington DC
Bastian, Herman, (Retired)
Beaumont, Robert G., Christ the King, Terrytown
Beckendorf, Edward, Nativity of Our Lord, Kenner
Bertucci, Chris, St. Ann, Metairie
Beyer, Walter L., Mater Dolorosa, DePaul Hospital, New Orleans
Bialas, James, Sacred Heart, Lacombe; Lazarus House, New Orleans
Bienvenu, Roland, St. Matthew the Apostle, River Ridge; Children's Hospital, New Orleans
Binney, Robert, St. Margaret Mary, Slidell; Southeast LA Hospital, Mandeville
Blanchard, John, Our Lady Star of the Sea, New Orleans
Boe, Kenneth, St. Clement of Rome, Metairie
Bourgeois, Don, St. Jane de Chantal, Abita Springs
Bourgeois, Garland, St. Elizabeth Ann Seton, Kenner
Brady, Richard, St. Benilde, Metairie
Burke, Harold J., St. Luke the Evangelist, Slidell
Caffery, Thomas E., Jr., Assoc. Dir. Archdiocesan Spirituality Ctr., St. Philip Neri, Metairie
Calamia, S.J., St. Christopher the Martyr, Metairie
Campeaux, Barry G., Our Lady of Divine Providence, Metairie
Campuzano, Luis A., St. Jerome, Kenner
Cannon, Edward, St. Philip Neri, Metairie
Capaci, Andrea, St. Elizabeth Ann Seton, Kenner; Assoc. Dir., Family Life Apostolate
Caserta, Piero, St. Agnes, Jefferson; Covenant House, New Orleans
Cassou, Henry A., Jr., Our Lady of Prompt Succor, Chalmette
Chetta, Nick, St. Angela Merici, Metairie
Chiappetta, William, Our Lady of Lourdes, Violet
Cimino, Paul, St. Philip Neri, Metairie; Ozanam Inn, New Orleans
Cleveland, Carl, On Leave
Coney, Michael, St. Catherine of Siena, Metairie
Cordes, Daniel J., St. Jerome, Kenner
Coudrain, Charles E., Jr., Our Lady of Prompt Succor Shrine, New Orleans; St. Francis Xavier, Metairie
Crago, Jere, St. Catherine of Siena, Metairie
Crochet, Randolph J., Orleans Parish Correctional Ctr. and Ozanam Inn, New Orleans
Curry, William P., Jr., Resurrection of Our Lord, New Orleans
Daigle, Irving J., Sacred Heart of Jesus, New Orleans
Daly, Edward, (Retired)
Deichmann, Richard, Transitional Hospital, New Orleans
DeLeon, Ildefonso R., St. Maria Goretti, New Orleans
DeVerges, Philip, Holy Name of Jesus, New Orleans
DiGiovanni, Biaggio, St. Benilde, Metairie
DiGrado, Chris, St. Andrew the Apostle, New Orleans
DiMaggio, John, On Leave
Donnaud, Paul J., St. Anthony of Padua, Luling
Doolen, Philip E., St. Ann, Metairie
Dorsey, Dan, St. Matthew the Apostle, River Ridge
Dorvin, Edwin, St. Clement of Rome, Metairie
Dragon, Edgar P., St. Jerome, Kenner
Duet, Ferris J., Jr., Infant Jesus of Prague, Harvey
Duffy, Peter E., St. Maria Goretti, New Orleans
Duhe, Charles J., St. Joachim, Marrero
Duke, Charles, St. Christopher the Martyr, Metairie
Duplechain, Raphael, Jr., Holy Spirit, New Orleans
Dupuy, Paul H., Jr., Ascension of Our Lord, La Place
Durbin, Oscar A., Jefferson Parish Sheriff's Office
Elfer, Ernest C., Jr., Stella Maris Maritime Center, New Orleans; Our Lady of Prompt Succor, Westwego
Engel, Randall L., St. Lawrence the Martyr, Metairie
Faler, Charles Pete, Our Lady of Lourdes, Slidell
Fandal, Wendolen, Jr., (Retired)
Farinelli, David W., St. Peter, Reserve; Assoc. Dir., Family Life Apostolate
Fariss, Jeffrey, St. Clement of Rome, Metairie; Chap. of Orleans Parish Correctional Center
Fasullo, Gerard, Sr., St. Edward the Confessor, Metairie
Ferretti, Anthony J., Mary Queen of Peace, Mandeville
Fleischer, Francis J., St. Theresa of Avila, New Orleans
Flynn, Dan, St. Rita, Harahan, Catholic Committee on Scouting
Foret, Clarence, Jr., (Retired)
Fray, Ralph, Jefferson Parish Correctional Ctr., Gretna; Rivarde Juvenile Detention Home, Harvey
Gaiennie, Richard M., Our Lady of the Rosary, New Orleans
Gamble, Eric, St. Thomas the Apostle, UNO, and Covenant House, New Orleans
Garon, Henry A., St. Henry & Ozanam Inn, New Orleans
Genna, Al, On Duty Outside the Archdiocese
Glapion, Lloyd St. Clair, St. Augustine, New Orleans
Glennon, William A., Jr., St. Pius X, Transitional Hospital Corporation Facility, New Orleans
Glover, John A., St. Anselm, Madisonville
Graffagnini, Carmelo, St. Peter, Covington
Gubert, Norbert, St. Frances Xavier Cabrini, New Orleans
Guidry, Ronald, Assoc. Dir., Office of Worship, St. Louis Cathedral, New Orleans
Guillot, Raymond J., Stella Maris Maritime Ctr.; Blessed Sacrament, New Orleans
Guitterrez, Clayton J., St. John the Baptist, Folsom
Haggerty, Daniel, Jr., St. Simon Peter, New Orleans; Chap., Slidell Police Dept.
Hamm, John David, Our Lady of the Rosary, New Orleans
Harrison, Jerry, St. Philip Neri, Metairie

Hartman, Charles, Annunciation, Bogalusa; Washington Correctional Institute, Angie
Hartson, Maurice, III, St. Alphonsus & Project Lazarus, New Orleans
Heap, Raymond E., East Jefferson Hospital, Metairie
Heine, Charles, St. Peter, Covington
Hooper, Edward B., (Retired)
Howard, John, Sts. Peter & Paul, Pearl River
Insley, J. Vernon, On Leave
Jeansonne, Bennie, (Retired)
Johnson, Dwight J., Our Lady of the Lake, Mandeville
Jones, Melvin C., Sr., On Leave
Keller, Lawrence, St. Vincent de Paul, New Orleans
Labranche, Frans, Jr., St. Jane de Chantal, Abita Springs
Landry, Coy, Holy Family, Luling
Lazo, Joseph, Our Lady of the Lake (Northshore Hospice Prog.), Mandeville
LeBlanc, Ames P., Jr., On Leave
LeBlanc, Nolen J., St. Rita, Harahan
LeBlanc, Russell T., (Retired), St. Matthew the Apostle, River Ridge
LeDoux, John, Nativity of Our Lord, Kenner
LeRose, Joseph R., St. John of the Cross, Lacombe
Levy, Albert A., III, St. Mark, Chalmette
Lewis, Raymond, St. Francis de Sales, New Orleans
Luke, Nelvin, St. Agnes, Jefferson
Madere, Kenneth P., St. Mark, Chalmette; Chap., Covenant House, New Orleans
Mallerich, Walton J., On Leave
Mamou, Joseph, St. Hubert, Garyville; Chap., Louisiana State Penitentiary
Martinez, Gerald J., St. Clement of Rome, Metairie
Martinez, Rodolfo J., Immaculate Conception, Marrero
Martinez, Wilbur, St. Louis King of France, Metairie
Martinsen, Noel W., St. Elizabeth Ann Seton, Kenner
Matherne, Landry, St. Gertrude, Des Allemands
Mathews, Michael Schmid, On Duty Outside the Archdiocese
Memleb, Fred C., Jr., Our Lady of Divine Providence, Metairie
Mendel, August B., St. Edward the Confessor; Chap., Columbia Lakeside Hospital, Metairie
Mendieta, Roberto, Nativity of Our Lord, Kenner
Menges, George, St. Genevieve, Slidell
Miester, Alvin C., Jr., St. Louise de Marillac, Arabi
Minor, Francis M., Visitation of Our Lady, Marrero; Chap., Ozanam Inn
Mire, Louis N., Our Lady of the Lake, Mandeville; St. Tammany Parish & Highland Park Hospitals, Covington
Mistretta, Nicholas L., St. Rita, Harahan
Moore, Charles R., Our Lady of Perpetual Help, Belle Chasse
Moragas, Lucien, On Duty Outside the Archdiocese
Morales, G. Ernesto, St. Jerome, Kenner
Muhleisen, John P., St. Frances Xavier Cabrini, New Orleans
Mumme, Paul, Sr., Immaculate Heart of Mary, New Orleans
Murphy, Larry, Visitation of Our Lady, Marrero
Nalty, Paul A., St. Francis Xavier, Metairie; Chap, Malta Park Assisted Living Residence, New Orleans
Nestor, Mike, On Duty Outside the Archdiocese
Nunez, Charles R., Sr., St. Mary Magdalen, Metairie
Nuss, Henry, Our Lady of the Rosary, New Orleans
O'Connor, Gerard R., Center of Jesus the Lord, New Orleans
O'Regan, William D., (Retired)
Ohlmeyer, Sterling, St. Lawrence the Martyr, Metairie
Peres, Anthony W., Our Lady Star of the Sea, New Orleans
Pham, Hup, Mary Queen of Vietnam, New Orleans
Pippenger, John, St. Dominic, New Orleans
Rayfield, Rudolph J., Sr., St. Peter Claver & St. Philip the Apostle, New Orleans
Read, Charles, Jr., St. Peter, Covington; St. Tammany Prison, Mandeville
Reeson, Curles P., Jr., St. Robert Bellarmine, Arabi; Chap., Ozanam Inn
Rhodes, Frank W., Jr., Prince of Peace, Chalmette
Richard, Don Michael, Administrative Leave
Richardson, Ray, Our Lady of Good Counsel, New Orleans
Rivere, Raymond H., St. Mark, Chalmette; Chap., Chalmette Medical Facility
Rizzo, Peter C., St. Frances Xavier Cabrini & St. Simon Peter, New Orleans
Robichaux, Wilfred, Jr., Immaculate Conception, Marrero
Robicheaux, Dalferes F., Jr., (Retired)
Robin, Angelas, St. Mary Magdalen, New Orleans
Rosato, Joseph R., St. Thomas More, Christ the Healer Prog., New Orleans
Rougelot, Sidney, (Retired)
Roussel, Theodore, St. Charles Borromeo, Destrehan
Sandman, Arthur, Sr., Ascension of Our Lord, La Place
Schaubhut, Anthony L., On Leave
Schexnayder, Harry, St. Charles Borromeo, Destrehan
Schlette, Peter B., St. Cletus, Gretna; Chap., Ozanam Inn
Schmidt, Gilbert R., St. Angela Merici, Metairie
Schonacher, Ralph, (Retired)
Seruntine, Alex J., Jr., St. Louise de Marillac, Arabi
Shelly, Ceaser, On Leave
Sherman, Lynn, On Duty Outside the Archdiocese
Sierra, Jose A., St. Matthias, New Orleans; Chap., Orleans Parish Correctional Center
Smith, Charles J., Children's Hospital and St. Stephen, New Orleans
Smith, Gilbert, Our Lady of Angels, Waggaman; Port Chap., Stella Maris Ctr., New Orleans
Sorensen, George A., Jr., On Duty Outside the Archdiocese
Stall, Louis W., St. Cletus, Prisons Apostolate, Dir. Jefferson Parish Correctional Ctr., Gretna
Stewart, Irvin, Sr., St. Joan of Arc, New Orleans
Strahan, Douglas H., On Leave
Swiler, James W., Dir. Office of Permanent Diaconate, Christ the King, Terrytown
Toups, Wilbur A., St. Rita, New Orleans
Trainor, Robert, St. Luke the Evangelist, Slidell
Vicknair, Percy, Ascension of Our Lord, La Place
Vicroy, Clarence, (Retired), St. Margaret Mary, Slidell
Vincent, Dan, St. Paul the Apostle, Dir. Black Catholics Office, New Orleans
Vincent, Harold, St. Julian Eymard, New Orleans
Vincent, Leslie D., St. Martha, Harvey; Chap., Meadowcrest Hospital, Gretna
Walsh, Donald, Mater Dolorosa, Ozanam Inn, New Orleans
Warriner, David, St. Edward the Confessor, Metairie
Watley, Jesse A., St. Simon Peter, New Orleans
Weber, Chris J., St. Pius X, New Orleans
Weber, John C., St. Margaret Mary, Slidell
White, Alfred, Corpus Christi, New Orleans
Williams, Everett, Our Lady of Lourdes, New Orleans
Williams, Herman, St. Monica, New Orleans
Williams, Irvin, St. David, New Orleans
Williams, John B., St. Raymond, New Orleans
Wilson, Earl McMahon, Jr., On Leave
Wong, Peter, On Duty Outside the Archdiocese
Wright, Clifford S., St. Benilde, Metairie
Zeringue, Alfred, St. Lawrence the Martyr, Metairie
Zimmer, Julius T., Our Lady of Prompt Succor, Chalmette
Zornman, Raymond L., On Leave

INSTITUTIONS LOCATED IN THE ARCHDIOCESE

[A] SEMINARIES, ARCHDIOCESAN

NEW ORLEANS. *Notre Dame Seminary Graduate School of Theology* (1923), 2901 S. Carrollton Ave., 70118-4391. Tel: 504-866-7426; Fax: 504-866-3119. Administration: Most Rev. Gregory M. Aymond, M.Div., V.G., Pres. & Rector; Revs. Jose I. Lavastida, M.A., S.T.D., S.T.L., Academic Dean; Geoffrey Graystone, S.M., S.T.D., S.S.D., Asst. Dean; Clarence C. Menard, O.M.I., H.E.L., H.E.D., Spiritual Dir.; Carl J. Davidson, M.Mu., Dir. Spiritual Formation; Stanley J. Klores, M.A. M.Div. S.T.L. S.T.D., Dir. Student Guidance & Welfare; Sr. Barbara Dupuis, M.S.C., M.S.L.S., Dir. Library; Sr. Joycelin Staempfli, M.S.C., M.A., Dir. Finances; Revs. F. Hampton Davis, M.Div., Dir. Field Education; Patrick J. Williams, M.Div., M.S., Asst. to the Rector; Mrs. Margaret Ann Breaux, Registrar; Dr. John A. Brun, Ph.D., Psychological Counselor. Faculty: Rev. Glenn D. LeCompte, M.Div., S.T.L.; Rev. Msgr. Franz Graef, M.A., S.T.L., S.T.D.; Rev. Msgr. Ignatius M. Roppolo, M.Div.; Revs. Terry T. Tekippe, M.A., S.T.L., Ph.D.; Vien The Nguyen, M.Div., J.C.L.; J. Emile Pfister, S.J., S.T.L., S.T.D.; Gerald L. Seiler, Jr., M.Div., J.C.L.; Frank Montalbano, O.M.I., S.T.L., S.S.L.; Dennis J. Hayes, III, M.Div., S.T.L.; Dau Nguyen, M.Div., S.T.L.; Ellis L. Depriest, S.M., M.A.; Sr. Elizabeth Willems, S.S.N.D., M.A., Ph.D.; Sr. Elizabeth Fitzpatrick, O.Carm., M.A.; Dr. Gregory Vall, M.A., Ph.D.; Sr. Janet Bodin, M.S.C., M.A., Ph.D.; Dr. Charles Nolan, H.E.D., M.Ed.; Bro. Philip Murphy, F.S.C.; Sr. Noel Toomey, O.P., M.A.; Revs. Roger A. Swenson, M.A.Ed., M.Ed., M.A.; David Boileau, Ph.D.; Mrs. Paula D'Albor-Stuckart, M.R.E. Priests 21; Laymen 3; Laywoman 2; Men Religious 1; Women Religious 6; Seminarians 144.

ST. BENEDICT. *St. Joseph's Seminary College* (1890), 70457-9999. Tel: 504-892-1800; Fax: 504-867-2270.
E-mail: rectorsec@stjosephabbey.org
Web site: www.stjosephabbey.org
Benedictine Monks. Conducted by Provinces of New Orleans and Mobile and Monks of St. Joseph's Abbey. Very Rev. Scott J. Underwood, O.S.B., M.Ed., M.T.S., Rector-Pres.; Rev. Matthew R. Clark, O.S.B., M.A., Vice Rector & Dean of Students; Sr. Jeanne d'Arc Kernion, O.S.B., M.A., Dir. of Admin.; Bro. Brian Harrington, O.S.B., Asst. Dean of Students; Revs. Sean B. Duggan, O.S.B., M.F.A., M.A., Dir. Spiritual Formation; Aelred M. Kavanagh, O.S.B., S.S.L., S.T.D., Academic Dean; Mr. Leslie R. Lavergne, Dir. Fin. Aid; Mr. Thomas A. Siegrist, M.Ed., Ed.S., Registrar & Dir. Admissions. Faculty: Revs. Lawrence J. Phelps, O.S.B., M.Ed.; William J. MacCandless, O.S.B., S.S.L.; Dominic R. Braud, O.S.B., M.Mus.; Gregory M. Boquet, O.S.B., M.A.; Timothy J. Burnett, O.S.B., M.S.L.S., M.A.Th.; Peter E. Hammett, O.S.B., Th.M., M.T.S., M.A.Th.; Adam Begnaud, O.S.B., M.S.; Marian E. Larmann, O.S.B., M.A.; Jonathan M. DeFrange, O.S.B., Ph.D.; Augustine E. Foley, O.S.B., M.A., M.A.Th.; William F. Maestri, M.A.; Thomas E. Perrier, O.S.B., M.A.; Rt. Rev. Patrick J. Regan, O.S.B., S.T.D.; Rev. Ambrose G. Wathen, O.S.B., S.T.D., Ph.D.; John E. Hebert, Ph.D.; Ann K. Nauman, Ph.D.; Sarah D. Spence, Ph.D.; Peter M. Emerson, Ph.D.; Aileen Mootoo, M.A.; Ms. Jan M. Fluitt-Dupuy, M.A.; Ms. Clara V. Muller, M.A.; Dr. Edward J. Dupuy, M.A., Ph.D.; Mr. John V. Tower; Mr. Michael Greene; Dr. J. E. Trowbridge, Jr., M.A., Ph.D.; Russell Pottle, Ph.D. Priests 18; Brothers 1; Sisters 1; Lay Teachers 14; Seminarians 54; Lay People 8.

[B] SEMINARIES, RELIGIOUS OR SCHOLASTICATES

NEW ORLEANS. *Josephite House of Studies*, 2000 St. Bernard Ave., 70116-1390. Tel: 504-945-1359; Fax: 504-948-3049. Very Rev. Thomas R. Frank, S.S.J., Rector. Priest Candidates 2.

St. John of the Cross, Discalced Carmelite House of Studies, 2925 S. Carrollton Ave., 70118-4301. Tel: 504-861-9102; Fax: 504-865-1751. Rev. Jerome Earley, O.C.D. Priests 2; Brothers 3; Religious Seminarians 3.

METAIRIE. *Congregation of the Mother Coredemptrix Formation House*, 112 Lilac St., 70005-1817. Tel: 504-835-9746. Rev. Joseph M. Phan Nam, C.M.C., Dir. Priests 1; Brothers 10.

[C] COLLEGES AND UNIVERSITIES

NEW ORLEANS. *Loyola University*, (1912) 6363 St. Charles Ave., 70118-6195. Tel: 504-865-2011; Fax: 504-865-3851
For a complete listing, refer to the Colleges and Universities section.

Our Lady of Holy Cross College, 4123 Woodland Dr., 70131-7399. Tel: 504-394-7744; Fax: 504-391-2421
For a complete listing, refer to the Colleges and Universities section.

Xavier University of Louisiana, Palmetto and Pine Sts., 70125-1098. Tel: 504-486-7411; Fax: 504-485-7904.
Web site: www.xavier.xula.edu
For a complete listing, refer to the Colleges and Universities section.

[D] HIGH SCHOOLS, ARCHDIOCESAN

NEW ORLEANS. *Redeemer-Seton High School*, 1453 Crescent St., 70122-2099. Tel: 504-288-1494; Fax: 504-288-1499. Mr. Arthur L. Schmitt, Pres.; Joan G. Johnson, Prin. School Sisters of Notre Dame 1; Daughters of Charity 1; Lay Teachers 36; Students 465.

COVINGTON. *St. Scholastica Academy*, P.O. Box 1210, 70434-1210. Tel: 504-892-2540; Fax: 504-893-5256.
E-mail: ssa@nternet.com
Web site: www.ssacad.com
Mrs. Marguerite S. Celestin, Prin. Priests 1; Lay Teachers 39; Girls 512.

GRETNA. *Archbishop Blenk High School*, 17 Gretna Blvd., 70053-4989. Tel: 504-367-2626; Fax: 504-367-7128.
E-mail: arnoblenk@connectinc.com
Web site: www.gnofn.org/~blenk
Mr. David Pooley, Prin. Priests 1; Lay Teachers 45; Girls 602.

LA PLACE. *St. Charles Catholic High School*, 100 Dominican Dr., 70068-3499. Tel: 504-652-3809; Fax: 504-652-2609.
Web site: www.scc-comets.com
Mr. Andrew C. Cupit, Prin. Priests 1; Lay Teachers 27; Students 459.

MARRERO. *Archbishop Shaw High School*, 1000 Salesian Ln., 70072-2950. Tel: 504-340-6727; Fax: 504-347-9883. Salesians of St. John Bosco. Rev. Steven Dumais, S.D.B., Dir. & Prin.; Mr. John Corb, Financial Admin.; Revs. John DiFiore; Serges Lamaute, S.D.B.; Joseph Vien Hoang, S.D.B.; Eric T. Wyckoff, S.D.B., Coord. Youth Ministry. Priests 4; Brothers 1; Lay Teachers 44; Boys 465.

MERAUX. *Archbishop Hannan High School*, 2501 Archbishop Philip M. Hannan Blvd., 70075-2630. Tel: 504-279-1921; Fax: 504-279-0200.
E-mail: ARNOHannan@connectinc.com
Mr. John Serio, Prin. Priests 1; Brothers 1; Lay Teachers 44; Students 560.

METAIRIE. *Archbishop Chapelle High School*, 8800 Veterans Blvd., 70003-5235. Tel: 504-467-3105; Fax: 504-466-3191.
E-mail: arnochapel@connectinc.com
Web site: www.achs.chapelle.k12.la.us
Miss Beth Johnson, Pres.; Mrs. Susan Gutierrez, Prin.; Ms. Mary Beth Drez, Asst. Prin.; Revs. Lance Campo; Rick Day. Priests 2; Sisters 2; Lay Teachers 72; Girls 1,110.

Archbishop Rummel High School, P.O. Box 663, 70004-0663. Tel: 504-834-5592; Fax: 504-832-4016.
E-mail: arnorummel@idsno.com
Web site: www.rummel.idsno.com
1901 Severn Ave., 70001-2893. Mr. David J. Hardin, Prin. Brothers 2; Lay Teachers 86; Boys 1,350.
Rummel Alumni Association, Inc.

SLIDELL. *Pope John Paul II High School*, 1901 Jaguar Dr., 70461-9098. Tel: 504-649-0914; Fax: 504-649-5494.
E-mail: PJP@Communique.net
Ms. Carmen Schexnaildre, Prin. Lay Teachers 28; Students 396.

[E] HIGH SCHOOLS, PAROCHIAL

MARRERO. *Immaculata High School*, 537 Avenue D, 70072-2027. Tel: 504-341-6217; Fax: 504-341-6229. Sr. Rosann Ruiz, F.M.A., Prin. Sisters 2; Lay Teachers 38; Girls 510.

[F] HIGH SCHOOLS, PRIVATE

NEW ORLEANS. *Academy of the Sacred Heart "The Rosary"* (1887). (Grades 9-12), 4521 St. Charles Ave., 70115-9990. Tel: 504-891-1943; Fax: 504-891-9939. Sr. Shirley Miller, Headmistress. Religious of the Sacred Heart 2; Carmelite 1; Lay Teachers 29; Girls 261.

Brother Martin High School (1869), 4401 Elysian Fields Ave., 70122-3898. Tel: 504-283-1561; Fax: 504-286-8462. Bro. Ivy LeBlanc, S.C., Pres.; Mr. John J. Devlin, III, Prin. Sisters 3; Brothers of the Sacred Heart 13; Lay Teachers 80; Boys 1,480.

Cabrini High School, 1400 Moss St., 70119-2997. Tel: 504-482-1193; Fax: 504-483-8671. Mrs. Frances Dee Tarantino, Pres./Prin. Missionary Sisters of the Sacred Heart 4; Lay Teachers 33; Girls 420.
Cabrini High School, Inc.

De La Salle Senior High School (1949). (Grades 10-12), 5300 St. Charles Ave., 70115-4999. Tel: 504-895-5717; Fax: 504-895-1300.
E-mail: arnodelasa@connectinc.com
Web site: www.gnofn.org/~dlsalle
(Coed). Mrs. Yvonne Gelpi, Pres.; Bro. Jeffrey Calligan, F.S.C., Prin. Brothers of the Christian Schools 4; Sisters 2; Lay Teachers 68; Students 862.

Holy Cross School (1879), 4950 Dauphine St., 70117-4399. Tel: 504-942-3100; Fax: 504-943-7676.
E-mail: arnohlycro@connectinc.com
Web site: adele@america.net
Bro. Stephen Walsh, C.S.C., Headmaster. Brothers of the Congregation of Holy Cross, Southwest Province 5; Lay Teachers 39; Boys 538.

Jesuit High School (1847), 4133 Banks St., 70119-6883. Tel: 504-486-6631; Fax: 504-483-3816.
E-mail: alumni@jesuithigh.org
Web site: www.jesuithigh.org
(Boys). Revs. Raymond R. Fitzgerald, S.J., Rector; Anthony F. McGinn, S.J., Pres.; Mr. Barry J. Neuberger, Prin.; Revs. Peter Callery, S.J.; John J. Capelle, S.J.; Raymond R. Fitzgerald, S.J.; Thomas W. Hoffman, S.J.; Donald A. Hawkins, S.J.; Martin V. Jarreau, S.J.; Norman B. O'Neal, S.J.; Nicholas T. Schiro, S.J.; Joseph H. Reising. Priests 6; Scholastics 2; Brothers 1; Lay Teachers 89; Boys 1,113.

Mount Carmel Academy, 7027 Milne Blvd., 70124-2395. Tel: 504-288-7626; Fax: 504-288-7629.
E-mail: arnomtcarm@connectinc.com
Congregation of Our Lady of Mount Carmel. Sr. Camille Anne Campbell, O.Carm., Pres./Prin. Sisters 8; Lay Teachers 91; Girls 1,034.

St. Augustine High School (1951), 2600 A.P. Tureaud Ave., 70119-1299. Tel: 504-944-2424; Fax: 504-947-7712. Josephite Community. Rev. Joseph M. Doyle, S.S.J., Pres.; Mr. Carl A. Blouin, Sr., Prin.
(See Separate Listing for Residence.). Priests 8; Brothers 1; Lay Teachers 34; Boys 723.

St. Mary's Academy of the Holy Family. (Grades 7-12), 6905 Chef Menteur Hwy., 70126-5291. Tel: 504-245-0200; Fax: 504-245-8732. Sr. Mary Leona Bruner, S.S.F., Prin. Priests 1; Sisters of the Holy Family 16; Lay Teachers 27; Girls 621.

St. Mary's Dominican High School, 7701 Walmsley Ave., 70125-3494. Tel: 504-865-9401; Fax: 504-866-5958. Ms. Cynthia A. Thomas, Pres.; Mrs. Melanie B. Verges, Prin. Sisters 10; Brothers 1; Lay Teachers 63; Students 1,017.

Ursuline Academy, 2635 State St., 70118-6399. Tel: 504-866-2725; Fax: 504-861-7392. Secondary Dept. Day School College Prep. Sr. Ann Barrett, O.S.U., Prin. Sisters 1; Lay Teachers 29; Girls 382.

Xavier Prep School, 5116 Magazine St., 70115-1899. Tel: 504-899-6061; Fax: 504-891-0347. Mrs. Ann Zanders, Pres.; Mr. Alvarez A. Peychaud, Prin. Priests 1; Sisters 7; Lay Teachers 31; Girls 507.

COVINGTON. *The St. Paul's School* (1911). (Grades 8-12), P.O. Box 928, 70434-0928. Tel: 504-892-3200; Fax: 504-892-4048.
E-mail: arnostpaul@connectinc.com
Web site: www.stpauls.com
Bro. Raymond Bulliard, F.S.C., Prin.; Rev. Peter Blanchard, S.M., Chap. Boarding and Day School for Young Men. Brothers of the Christian Schools of the New Orleans-Santa Fe Province 5; Lay Teachers 45; Boys 600.

[G] ELEMENTARY SCHOOLS, ARCHDIOCESAN

NEW ORLEANS. *Marian Central Catholic Middle School*, 2221 Mendez St., 70122-5267. Tel: 504-288-1411; Fax: 504-286-0209. Sr. Maeve McMahon, O.P., Pres.; Sr. Jennie Jones, S.S.F., Prin. Sisters 5; Lay Teachers 19; Students 400.

MARRERO. *Archbishop Shaw Junior High School*. (Grades 8-9), 1000 Salesian Ln., 70072-2950. Tel: 504-340-6727; Fax: 504-347-9883.
E-mail: arnoshaw@connectinc.com
Mr. Dennis R. Coulon, Prin.; Rev. Steven Dumais, S.D.B., Dir. Priests 3; Brothers 1; Lay Teachers 35; Students 253.

METAIRIE. *Archbishop Rummel Junior High School*. (Grades 8-9), 1901 Severn Ave., 70001-2893. Tel: 504-834-5592; Fax: 504-832-4016. Mr. Steven Barton, Asst. Prin. Brothers 2; Lay Teachers 48; Boys 500.

[H] ELEMENTARY SCHOOLS, PRIVATE

NEW ORLEANS. *Academy of the Sacred Heart*. (Grades PreK-8), 4521 St. Charles Ave., 70115-9990. Tel: 504-891-1943; Fax: 504-891-9939. Sr. Shirley Miller, R.S.C.J., Headmistress. Religious of the Sacred Heart 2; Lay Teachers 53; Girls 524.

Brother Martin High School. (Grade 8), 4401 Elysian Fields Ave., 70122-3898. Tel: 504-283-1561; Fax: 504-286-8462. Mr. John J. Devlin, III, Prin. Brothers of the Sacred Heart 5; Lay Teachers 22; Boys 224.

Cabrini High School. (Grades 8-12), 1400 Moss St., 70119-2997. Tel: 504-482-1193; Fax: 504-483-8671. Mrs. Frances Dee Tarantino, Pres. & Prin.

Christian Brothers School. (Grades 5-7), City Park, #8 Frederichs Ave., 70124-4602. Tel: 504-486-6770; Fax: 504-486-1053. Bro. Andre P. Lacoste, F.S.C., Prin. Brothers 7; Lay Teachers 8; Boys 245.

De La Salle Junior High School. (Grades 8-9), 5300 St. Charles Ave., 70115-4999. Tel: 504-895-5717; Fax: 504-895-1300.
E-mail: arnodelasa@connectinc.com
Web site: www.gnofn.org/~dlsalle
(Coed). Mrs. Yvonne Gelpi, Pres.; Ms. Gina F. Hall, Prin. Lay Teachers 29; Students 274.

Holy Cross School. (Grades 5-8), 4950 Dauphine St., 70117-4399. Tel: 504-942-3100; Fax: 504-943-7676.
E-mail: arnohlycro@connectinc.com
Web site: www.adele@iamerica.net
Bro. Stephen Walsh, C.S.C., Headmaster. Brothers of the Congregation of Holy Cross 5; Lay Teachers 26; Boys 242.

Jesuit High School. (Grade 8), 4133 Banks St., 70119-6883. Tel: 504-486-6631; Fax: 504-483-3816.
E-mail: alumni@jesuithigh.org
Web site: www.jesuithigh.org
Rev. Anthony F. McGinn, S.J., Pres.; Mr. Barry J. Neuberger, Prin. Priests 3; Lay Teachers 17; Boys 246.

St. Augustine High School. (Grade 8), 2600 A.P. Tureaud Ave., 70119-1299. Tel: 504-944-2424; Fax: 504-947-7712. Rev. Joseph M. Doyle, S.S.J., Pres.; Mr. Carl A. Blouin, Sr., Prin. Priests 3; Lay Teachers 6; Boys 60.

St. Mary's Academy. (Grades 7-8), 6905 Chef Menteur Hwy., 70126-5291. Tel: 504-245-0200; Fax: 504-245-8732. Sr. M. Leona Bruner, S.S.F., Prin. Priests 1; Sisters of the Holy Family 16; Lay Teachers 23; Girls 621.

St. Mary's Dominican High School, 7701 Walmsley Ave., 70125-3494. Tel: 504-865-9401; Fax: 504-866-5958. Ms. Cynthia A. Thomas, Pres.; Mrs. Melanie B. Verges, Prin. Brothers 1; Sisters 4; Lay Teachers 65; Girls 987.

Ursuline Academy. (Grades Toddler-8), 2635 State St., 70118-6399. Tel: 504-866-5260; Fax: 504-861-7392. Mrs. Elizabeth LaForge, Prin. Sisters 2; Lay Teachers 35; Students 358.

COVINGTON. *The St. Paul's School*. (Grades 8-12), P.O. Box 928, 70434-0928. Tel: 504-892-3200; Fax: 504-892-4048.
E-mail: arnostpaul@connectinc.com
Web site: www.stpauls.com
Brothers of the Christian Schools. Bro. Raymond Bulliard, F.S.C., Prin.; John Morvant, Asst. Prin. Brothers 5; Lay Teachers 45; Boys 600.
(See St. Paul's School Under High Schools, Private).

[I] SPECIAL EDUCATION

NEW ORLEANS. *Archdiocesan Department of Special Education*. St. Michael Special School, 1522 Chippewa St., 70130-4513. Tel: 504-524-7285; Fax: 504-524-5883. Sr. M. Lillian McCormack, S.S.N.D., Dir. Religious 4; Lay Teachers 21; Students 193.

Bishop Perry Middle School. (Grades 5-8), 1941 Dauphine St., 70116-1609. Tel: 504-943-3734.
E-mail: arnobperry@connectinc.com
Web site: www.sse.org/bpmstc.html
(Boys). Revs. David G. Cray, S.S.E., Pres.; David J. Theroux, S.S.E., Prin.; Dr. Rudolph Detiege, Devel. Dir. Society of St. Edmund Fathers 2; Priests 1; Brothers 1; Lay Teachers 6; Boys 66.

Holy Rosary Academy, 3368 Esplanade Ave., 70119. Tel: 504-482-7173; Fax: 504-482-7229. Mrs. Rose Howrilla, Prin. Sisters 3; Lay Teachers 6; Students 44.

House of the Holy Family School. (Grades 1-3), 7100 Chef Menteur Hwy., 70126-5220. Tel: 504-242-1810. Sr. Mary Louisette DeSalle, S.S.F., Admin. Children 56.

St. Gerard Majella Alternative School, 3774 Gentilly Blvd., 70122-0198. Tel: 504-947-9360. Sr. Rose Elaine Kessler, S.S.N.D., Prin.

MARRERO. *Hope Haven Center*, 1101 Barataria Blvd., 70072-3085. Tel: 504-347-5581; Fax: 504-340-2075. Mrs. Barbara Garland, M.Ed., Prin. Lay Teachers 16; Students 92.

[J] DAY CARE CENTERS AND PRESCHOOLS

NEW ORLEANS. *Cabrini Head Start*, 817 St. Philip St., 70116-2419. Tel: 504-523-4020; Fax: 504-943-6813. Ms. Irma Williams, M.S., Prog. Dir. Total Staff 10; Total Assisted 42.

El Yo Yo Bilingual Day Care Center, 735 Gen. Pershing St., 70115-1448. Tel: 504-899-6165; Fax: 504-895-3129. Ms. Gaynell Anderson, Prog. Dir. Total Assisted 100; Total Staff 14.

Flint-Goodridge Day Care Center, 3306 Freret St., 70115-6029. Tel: 504-895-3487; Fax: 504-895-3129. Susie Foucher, Prog. Dir.

Florida Head Start, 2631 Alvar St., 70117-3364. Tel: 504-945-8115; Fax: 504-943-6813. Mrs. Liz Bailey, Prog. Dir. Total Assisted 66; Total Staff 11.

Incarnate Word Preschool Program, 8326 Apricot St., 70118-3198. Tel: 504-866-2309; Fax: 504-861-1435. Ms. Doris Williams, Spvr. Lay Staff 12; Children 70.

Lafon Child Development Center, 7024 Chef Menteur Hwy., 70126-5295. Tel: 504-242-2431. Sr. M. Francella Jackson, S.S.F., Admin. Sisters 2; Children (Daily Average) 130.

Leslie Day Care Center, 2126 Constance St., 70130-5044. Tel: 504-522-2725. Ms. Amauunet Ashe, Prog. Dir. Total Staff 5.

Louise Day Care Center, 1205 Louisiana Ave., 70115-2488. Tel: 504-891-2871; Fax: 504-895-3129. Ms. Irma Cavalier, Prog. Dir. Total Assisted 85; Total Staff 17.

Mary Queen of Peace Child Development Center, 5075 Willow Brook Dr., 70129-1047. P.O. Box 29073, 70189-9073. Tel: 504-254-1528; Fax: 504-254-9250. Sr. Mary Francis Dang, F.M.S.R., Dir. Staff 12; Children (Daily Average) 65.

St. Anthony Head Start, 5407 Dauphine St., 70117-3023. Tel: 504-943-6952; Fax: 504-943-6813. Ms. Melba Hart, Program Dir.

St. John Berchmans Child Development Center, 2710 Gentilly Blvd., P.O. Box 8623, 70182-3098. Tel: 504-943-5060. P.O. Box 8623, 70182-8623. Sr. Mary Laurita Oliver, S.S.F., Admin. Sisters 2; Lay Staff 13; Children 130; Total Assisted 1,125.

St. John the Baptist Pre-School Program, 1920 Clio St., 70113-1214. Tel: 504-529-2557; 581-4987 (Center); 581-2569 (Preschool); Fax: 504-581-2028 (Center). Lay Staff 11; Children 57.

St. Jude Baby Village (1972), 1723 S. White St., 70125-2937. Tel: 504-821-4686; Fax: 504-895-3129. Mrs. Esperanza L. Martinez, Prog. Dir. Total Assisted 75; Total Staff 8.

St. Philip Preschool, 3333 Clouet St., 70126-5700. Tel: 504-944-2640; Fax: 504-944-8853. Mrs. Betty Lavigne, Supvr. Staff 13; Children (Daily Average) 77.

CHALMETTE. *Our Lady of Prompt Succor Child Care Center*, 2217 Fenelon St., 70043-4991. Tel: 504-271-3491. Mrs. Cynthia Dazet, Dir.

METAIRIE. *St. Lawrence the Martyr Child Care Center*, 2525 Maine Ave., 70003-5446. Tel: 504-469-3988. Ms. Jayne Parkhurst, Lead Teacher. Staff 5; Children (Daily Average) 20.

St. Mary Magdalen Early Childhood Development Center, 1005 Airline Park Blvd., 70003-4395. Tel: 504-736-0863. Ms. Dina L. Castille, M.Ed., Dir. Staff 16; Children (Daily Average) 55.

[K] HOMES FOR CHILDREN AND YOUTH

NEW ORLEANS. *Boys Hope*, 4128 Baudin St., 70119-6815. Tel: 504-486-6030.
E-mail: boyshope-girlshope@charitiesusa.com
Web site: www.boyshopegirlshope.org
For a complete listing, refer to the Special Care Facilities section.

**Covenant House*, 611 N. Rampart St., 70112-3540. Tel: 504-584-1111; 800-999-9999 (Hotline); Fax: 504-584-1171
For a complete listing, refer to the Special Care Facilities section.

BELLE CHASSE. *Padua Community Services Pediatric Residential Program*, 200 Beta St., 70037-1499. Tel: 504-392-0502; Fax: 504-392-5411
For a complete listing, refer to the Special Care Facilities section.

MARRERO. *Hope Haven Center*, (1925) 1101 Barataria Blvd., 70072-3085. Tel: 504-347-5581; Fax: 504-340-2075
For a complete listing, refer to the Special Care Facilities section.

[L] RESIDENCES, ADULT

NEW ORLEANS. *CARE CENTER*, 4222 S. Broad St., 70125-3660. Tel: 504-822-3751; Fax: 504-822-3761. Mrs. Connie Andry, Admin. Temporary Residence for Homeless Women and their Children.

Ciara House, 1131 St. Andrew St., 70130-5124. Tel: 504-524-8394; Fax: 504-524-0224. Ms. Monetta Clark, Admin.

Crescent House. Office, 1000 Howard Ave., 70113-1928. Tel: 504-523-3755; Fax: 504-523-0007. Temporary residence for abused women and their children. Ms. Lynn Holland, Prog. Dir.

Marie's Family Home, 2118 Martin Luther King Blvd., 70113-2315. Tel: 504-523-3716. Sponsored by St. Vincent de Paul Society. Shelter for Women and Children. Ms. Shirley Collins, Coord.

Ozanam Inn, 843 Camp St., 70130-3751. Tel: 504-523-1184; Fax: 504-523-1187. Sponsored by Society of St. Vincent de Paul. Shelter for Homeless Men. Roy R. Allain, Admin. Sisters 1; Lay Staff 12.

Project Lazarus, P.O. Box 3906, 70177-3906. Tel: 504-949-3609; Fax: 504-944-7944. Residential Program for Persons with AIDS. Ms. Susan Banks, Exec. Dir. Total in Residence 75; Total Staff 32.

GRETNA. *Ocean Avenue Community Home*, 361 Ocean Ave., 70053-4726. Tel: 504-361-0674; Fax: 504-367-6952. Residential Facility for Developmentally Disabled Adults. Total Assisted 6; Total Staff 7.

St. Jude the Apostle, 1430 Claire Ave., 70053-7436. Tel: 504-361-8457; Fax: 504-367-6952. Residential Facility for Developmentally Disabled Adults.

St. Rosalie, 119 Kass St., 70053-3828. Tel: 504-361-8320; Fax: 504-367-6952. Padua Adult Residential Program for Developmentally Disabled Adults.

Supervised Apartments, 1430 Claire Ave., 70053-7436. Tel: 504-367-1465; Fax: 504-367-6952. Supervised Apartments for Developmentally Disabled Adults. Total in Residence 4; Total Staff 4.

HARVEY. *St. Catherine of Siena Supervised Apartment*, 3021 Sienna Dr., 70058-2180. Tel: 504-347-6069; Fax: 504-367-6952. Residential Program for Developmentally Disabled Adults.

MARRERO. *Jefferson Care Center*, 1108 Barataria Blvd., 70072-3085. Tel: 504-347-0772. Ms. Earline Perique, Prog. Dir. Temporary Residence for Homeless Families.

METAIRIE. *Sts. Mary & Elizabeth*, 720 N. Elm St., 70003-6022. Tel: 504-738-6959; Fax: 504-738-8320. Residential Facility for Developmentally Disabled Adults. Total Assisted 6; Total Staff 11.

SLIDELL. *St. Peter the Fisherman*, 62269 Airport Rd., 70460-5242. Tel: 504-641-4914; Fax: 504-367-6952. Residential Facility for Developmentally Disabled Adults.

[M] DAY CARE CENTERS (ADULT)

NEW ORLEANS. *Carmel in the Business District*. (Ministry to Women and Child Care Center), 246 Loyola Ave., 70112-2002. Tel: 504-529-8856; Fax: 504-529-8861. Sr. Gwen Grillot, O.Carm., Exec. Dir.; Sr. Brenda Lege, O.Carm., Prog. Dir. Total Assisted 26; Total Staff 9.

New Directions Adult Day Health Care Center, 1523 N. Dorgenois St., 70119-2419. Tel: 504-943-9418; Fax: 504-948-3633. Total Assisted 43; Total Staff 10.

People Program, 1200 Mirabeau Ave., 70122-1886. Tel: 504-288-3171; Fax: 504-288-3503. Ms. Mary Catherine Lombard, Prog. Dir.; Ms. Barbara McCurdy, Devel. Dir.

COVINGTON. *Alpha House Adult Day Health Care Center*, 20115 Hwy. 36, 70433-8658. Tel: 504-892-7074; Fax: 504-893-1962. Ms. Steve Ryan, Prog. Dir.

KENNER. *The Greenwalt Center for Alzheimer's Day Care and Research*, 1926 18th St., 70062-6208. Tel: 504-461-5889; Fax: 504-461-5795. Ms. Linda Greenwalt, Asst. Admin.

Kenner Adult Day Health Care Center, 1000 Clay St., 70062-6715. Tel: 504-469-9492; Fax: 504-465-0632. Ms. Kathy C. Fitzhugh, Prog. Dir. Total Assisted 40; Total Staff 6.

NORCO. *Norco Adult Day Care*, 425 Spruce St., 70079-2355. Tel: 504-764-9084; Fax: 504-764-0041. Ms. Kathleen Landry, R.N., Dir.

[N] HOMES AND RESIDENCES FOR FAMILIES AND SENIOR CITIZENS

NEW ORLEANS. *The 1540 House*, 1540 N. Johnson St., 70116-1721. Tel: 504-945-0253
For a complete listing, refer to the Special Care Facilities section.

Annunciation Inn, 1220 Spain St., 70117-8369. Tel: 504-944-0512; Fax: 504-944-0514
For a complete listing, refer to the Special Care Facilities section.

Carriage House Apartments, Pontchartrain Housing Corp. I, 10151 Curran Blvd., 70127-1390
For a complete listing, refer to the Special Care Facilities section.

Chateau de Notre Dame, 2832 Burdette St., 70125-2596. Tel: 504-866-2741; Fax: 504-866-6769
For a complete listing, refer to the Special Care Facilities section.

Christopher Inn Apts., 2110 Royal St., 70116-1693. Tel: 504-949-0312; Fax: 504-945-2634
For a complete listing, refer to the Special Care Facilities section.

DeLille Inn, 6924 Chef Menteur Hwy., 70126-5260. Tel: 504-241-4877; Fax: 504-241-1828
For a complete listing, refer to the Special Care Facilities section.

Haydel Heights Apartments, 4402 Reynes St., 70126. Tel: 504-242-4438; Fax: 504-242-4061
For a complete listing, refer to the Special Care Facilities section.

Josephine Apartments, 1410 St. Andrew St., Apt. #6, 70130-5344. Tel: 504-522-5425; Fax: 504-522-5446
For a complete listing, refer to the Special Care Facilities section.

Lafon Nursing Home of the Holy Family, 6900 Chef Menteur Hwy., 70126-5296. Tel: 504-246-1100; Fax: 504-241-6672
For a complete listing, refer to the Special Care Facilities section.

Mary-Joseph Residence for the Elderly, (1868) 4201 Woodland Dr., 70131-7398. Tel: 504-394-2200; Fax: 504-391-3347
For a complete listing, refer to the Special Care Facilities section.

Nazareth II, 9640 Hayne Blvd., 70127-4725. Tel: 504-246-9640; Fax: 504-241-9631
For a complete listing, refer to the Special Care Facilities section.

Nazareth Inn, 9630 Hayne Blvd., 70127-1260. Tel: 504-241-9630; Fax: 504-241-9631
For a complete listing, refer to the Special Care Facilities section.

St. John Berchmans Manor, 3400 St. Anthony St., 70122-3098. Tel: 504-943-9343; Fax: 504-947-6090
For a complete listing, refer to the Special Care Facilities section.

St. Margaret's Daughters' Home, 6220 Chartres St., 70117-1595. Tel: 504-279-6414; Fax: 504-277-1834
For a complete listing, refer to the Special Care Facilities section.

St. Martin Manor, 1501 N. Johnson St., 70116-1720. Tel: 504-945-7728; Fax: 504-945-1645
For a complete listing, refer to the Special Care Facilities section.

Timber Ridge Apartments Pontchartrain Housing Corp. III, 6364 Woodland Hwy., 70131-7474. Tel: 504-391-9841; Fax: 504-391-9996
For a complete listing, refer to the Special Care Facilities section.

Villa St. Maurice, 500 St. Maurice Ave., 70117-1568. Tel: 504-277-8477; Fax: 504-277-8493
For a complete listing, refer to the Special Care Facilities section.

Villa St. Maurice II (Villa Additions), 6101 Douglas St., 70117-2100. Tel: 504-277-8731; Fax: 504-277-8493
For a complete listing, refer to the Special Care Facilities section.

LA PLACE. *Place Dubourg, Inc.*, 201 Rue Dubourg, 70068-2433. Tel: 504-652-1981; Fax: 504-651-6147
For a complete listing, refer to the Special Care Facilities section.

MANDEVILLE. *Rouquette Lodge*, 4300 Hwy. 22, 70448-2824. Tel: 504-626-5217; Fax: 504-626-9226
For a complete listing, refer to the Special Care Facilities section.

MARRERO. *Villa D'Ames Apartments*, 6305 Fourth St., 70072-1513. Tel: 504-347-0474; Fax: 504-347-0476
For a complete listing, refer to the Special Care Facilities section.

Wynhoven Apartments and Wynhoven II, 4600-10th St., 70072-3048. Tel: 504-347-8443; Fax: 504-340-6076
For a complete listing, refer to the Special Care Facilities section.

Wynhoven Health Care Center, 1050 Medical Center Blvd., 70072-3170. Tel: 504-347-0777; 347-3443 (Convent); Fax: 504-341-7240
For a complete listing, refer to the Special Care Facilities section.

MERAUX. *St. Bernard Manor, St. Bernard II, and St. Bernard III*, 2400 Archbishop Hannan Blvd., 70075-2640. Tel: 504-277-2441; Fax: 504-277-6300
For a complete listing, refer to the Special Care Facilities section.

METAIRIE. *Cascades Apartments, Walmsley Housing Corp.*, 2212 N. Arnoult Rd., 70001-1807. Tel: 504-835-2998; Fax: 504-835-3647
For a complete listing, refer to the Special Care Facilities section.

Metairie Manor, Metairie II, and Metairie III, 4929 York St., 70001-1013. Tel: 504-456-1467; Fax: 504-887-3718
For a complete listing, refer to the Special Care Facilities section.

Rock Creek Apartments, Walmsley Housing Corp., 4817 York St., 70001-1168. Tel: 504-455-3886; Fax: 504-455-3888
For a complete listing, refer to the Special Care Facilities section.

ST. ROSE. *River Road Apartments, Pontchartrain Housing Corp. II*, 100 A East Club Dr., 70087-9411. Tel: 504-464-0326; Fax: 504-466-1987
For a complete listing, refer to the Special Care Facilities section.

[O] CATHOLIC HEALTH SERVICES

NEW ORLEANS. *Daughters of Charity Services of New Orleans*, 3900 S. Carrollton Ave., 70118-4712. Tel: 504-482-2080; Fax: 504-483-6016
For a complete listing, refer to the Hospitals section.

Inter-Community Health Care, Inc., 1011 Gallier St., 70117-6111. Tel: 504-945-1620; Fax: 504-944-0756
For a complete listing, refer to the Hospitals section.

St. John's Place of New Orleans, Inc. dba Mercy Family Center, 3816 Bienville St., 70119-5206. Tel: 504-482-6600; Fax: 504-482-6125
For a complete listing, refer to the Hospitals section.

[P] MONASTERIES AND RESIDENCES OF PRIESTS AND BROTHERS

NEW ORLEANS. *Brothers of the Sacred Heart*.
E-mail: pom01@gnofn.org
Provincial Office, New Orleans Province, 4540 Elysian Fields Ave., 70122-3826. Tel: 504-282-5693; Fax: 504-288-9920. Bro. Ray Hebert, S.C., Vocation Dir. Tel: 504-383-5060, Hospitality Center/ Volunteer Service Community, 4600 Elysian Fields Ave., 70122-3938. Tel: 504-282-5631. Bro. Jean Sobert, S.C., Dir., 4601 Elysian Fields Ave., 70122-3937. Tel: 504-288-8301. Bro. Warren Laudumiey, S.C., Dir., 2150 Brutus St., 70122-3958. Tel: 504-282-1995. Bro. Neal Golden, S.C., Dir., Novitiate House, 1156 City Park Ave., 70119-3736. Tel: 504-488-1353. Bro. Matthias Amos, S.C., Dir., 4671 Painters St., Pre-Novitiate, 70122-5001. Tel: 504-283-6448. Bro. Barry Landry, S.C., Dir. Total Brothers 25. Ordained Brothers: Bro. Louis Couvillon, S.C., 4671 Painters St., 70122. Bro. Carl Evans, S.C., 209 S. Hollywood Rd., Houma, 70360. Bro. Albert Guarino, S.C., 4601 Elysian Fields Ave., 70122-3937. Bro. Farrel Lorio, S.C., 175 St. Joseph St., Thibodaux, 70301. Bro. William McCue, S.C., 855 Hearthstone Dr., Baton Rouge, 70806. Bro. Vincent Bono, S.C., 1236 N. Rampart St., 70116-2497. Bro. Ray Hebert, S.C., 855 Hearthstone Dr., Baton Rouge, 70806.

Dominican Fathers & Brothers, Southern Dominican Province. Provincial Headquarters, 1421 N. Causeway Blvd., Ste. 200, Metairie, 70001-4144. Tel: 504-837-2129; Fax: 504-837-6604.
E-mail: frprov@aol.com
Very Revs. Alberto Rodriguez, O.P., Prov.; Carl B.

Trutter, O.P., Socius & Vicar Prov.; James A. McDonough, O.P. (AUS), Treas.; Wayne Cavalier, O.P., Promoter of Permanent Formation and Community Life; Rev. Henry B. Groover, O.P. (MIA), Promoter of Vocations. Priests in the Archdiocese 24; Brothers in the Archdiocese 4.

Assigned but working elsewhere: Revs. Emiliano Alamo, O.P., (On Leave); Gerald Fath, O.P., On Leave; Paul D. Watkins, O.P., On Leave; Richard Paul MacLeay, O.P.; Brian J. Pierce, O.P.; Bro. Francis Dinet (SB).

Working Abroad: Rev. Emanuel M. Camilleri, O.P., Home for the Clergy, Fleur de Lys, Malta, BRK 09. Rev. James Linus Dolan, O.P., Provincia Dominicana de San Juan Bautista del Peru, Apartado 4169, Lima 1, Peru. Rev. Juan Carlos Duran, O.P., Casa de San Martin de Porres, Apartado 337, David, Chiriqui, Panama. Rev. Raymond C. Finn, O.P., Curia Generalizia Domenicani, Convento Santa Sabina, Piazza Pietro d'Illiria, 1 (Aventino), Rome, Italy, 00153. Rev. Jesus de Vianney Guerra, O.P., Parroquia de Santiago Apostol, Av. Varsovia Malta-California Sur, Apdo. 76176, Caracas, Venezuela, 1070. Rev. Carmen Mele, O.P., Casa de Santo Tomas de Aquino, Apartado 96-2400, Desamparados, San Jose, Costa Rica. Rev. Bertrand E. Ebben, O.P., Dominican Friars, P.O. Box 2760, Arusha, Tanzania. Rev. Alfred W. Wilder, O.P., Universita San Tommaso, Largo Angelicum 1, Rome, Italy, 00184.

Dominican Vocation Sponsors, 1421 N. Causeway Blvd., Ste. 200, Metairie, 70001-4144.

Southern Dominican Foundation, 1421 N. Causeway Blvd., Ste. 200, Metairie, 70001-4144. Revs. Alberto Rodriguez, O.P., Pres.; Carl B. Trutter, O.P., Vice Pres./Sec.; Val A. McInnes, O.P., Promoter of Devel.; Nora P. Fine, Dir. of Devel.

Southern Dominican Global Missions, 1421 N. Causeway Blvd., Ste. 200, Metairie, 70001-4144. Rev. John Raymond Corr, O.P. (SA), Dir., St. Martin de Porres Shrine, 1421 N. Causeway Blvd., Ste. 200, Metairie, 70001-4144. Rev. Carl B. Trutter, O.P. (NO), Acting Dir.

University San Tommaso, Largo Angelicum 1, Rome, Italy, 00184. Rev. Michael J. O'Rourke, O.P.

Franciscan Fraternity. Tau House, 1029 Gov. Nicholls St., 70116-2432. Tel: 504-529-3569; Fax: 504-558-0429. Revs. Ralph R. Parthie, O.F.M.; Michael J. Jennrich, O.F.M.; Bro. Edward-Marc Arambasich, O.F.M. Center for the Spiritual Empowerment of those infected with or affected by the HIV/AIDS.

Ignatius Residence, 6321 Stratford Pl., 70131-7325. Tel: 504-394-2411. Revs. Clair M. Cazayoux, S.J., Supr.; Emmett M. Bienvenu, S.J.; Joseph E. Browning, S.J.; Thomas D. Culley, S.J.; Bro. C. Robert Doherty, S.J.; Revs. Russell L. Dornier, S.J.; John P. Driscoll, S.J.; Lawrence J. Luettgen, S.J.; Warren S. Martin, S.J.; John H. Millet, S.J.; John Q. Minvielle, S.J.; William H. Moran, S.J.; Laurence M. O'Neill, S.J.; Herve P. Racivitch, S.J.; Roy W. Vollenweider, S.J.; Bros. Lloyd A. Barry, S.J.; H. Francis Hinze, S.J.; Dennis P. Lonergan, S.J.; Alfred M. Nowak, S.J.; Hilliard F. Stiegler, S.J. Priests 14; Brothers 6.

Jesuit Provincial Office. (Prov. of New Orleans), 500 S. Jefferson Davis Pkwy., 70119-7192. Tel: 504-821-0334; Fax: 504-822-5322.
E-mail: noprovsj@loynd.edu
Legal Title: *Catholic Society of Religious and Literary Education*. Very Rev. James P. Bradley, S.J., Prov.; Revs. John F. Armstrong, S.J., Socius & Prov. Asst. Education; Donald J. Martin, S.J., Prov. Asst. Parishes & Retreat Ministry; Robert J. Ratchford, S.J., Staff Asst.; Bro. Lawrence J. Lundin, S.J., Treas. Priests 4; Brothers 1.

Priests of the Province Abroad: Rev. Charles B. Thibodeaux, S.J., Casa Parroquial, Santa Rosa (Misiones), Paraguay. Rev. John F. Schroder, S.J., P.O. Box 34, Corozal Town, Belize. Rev. Edward J. Dougherty, S.J., Ave. Rio de Janiero 327, Campinas, SP, Brazil, 13031-340. Rev. Edward G. Benya, S.J., CP 521, Teresina, PI, Brazil, 64010. Rev. A. Gerard Fineran, S.J., R. Ricardo Tim, 183, Campinas, SP, Brazil, 13041-460. Cx. P. 2452, Manaus-AM, Brazil, 69001-970. Rev. Mark Lewis, S.J., C.P. 6139 Prati, Rome, Italy, 00195. Rev. Patrick S. Madigan, S.J., POB MP 320, Mt. Pleasant, Harare, Zimbabwe. Rev. Anthony J. Corcoran, S.J., P/Box Inigo, ue. Levitana 38, Novosibirsk, Russia. Rev. Stephen C. Rowntree, S.J., POB MP 320, Mt. Pleasant, Harare, Zimbabwe. Rev. John R. Stacer, S.J., P Bag A6109, Avondale, Harare, Zimbabwe. Rev. Earl C. Muller, S.J., Pontifical Univ. Gregoriana, Piazza della Pilotta, 4, Rome, Italy, 00187. Rev. Joseph A. Tetlow, S.J., Curia, Society of Jesus, CP 6139, Prati, Rome, Italy, 00195. Rev. Joseph A. Carola, S.J., Collegio S. Roberto Bellarmino, Via del Seminario 120, Rome, Italy, 00186. Rev. Reynaldo Garcia, S.J., Cx. P. 2452, Manaus-AM, Brazil, 69001-970. Rev. Thomas H. Stahel, S.J., Jesuit Novitiate, P.O. Box 854, Benin City, Nigeria. Rev. Leo V. Leise, S.J., Casa Parroquial, Iturbe 870, San Ignacio (Misiones), Paraguay. Rev. O. Kenneth Johnson, S.J., P.O. Box 660195, Monze, Zambia. Rev. Roland J. Lesseps, S.J., P.O. Box 30652, Lusaka, Zambia.

Jesuit Health Trust. Rev. Eugene M. Dutkiewicz, S.J., Chm.; Bro. Lawrence J. Lundin, S.J., Sec.

Josephite Fathers and Brothers. St. Augustine High School Faculty House, 1911 Law St., 70119-1397. Tel: 504-943-6593; Fax: 504-947-7712. Very Rev. Nelson A. Moreira, S.S.J., Rector; Rev. Robert P. Pavlak, S.S.J., Vice Rector; Bro. Laurence E. Price, S.S.J.; Revs. Robert Bowen, S.S.J.; Wilbur J. Atwood, S.S.J.; Vincent Keenan, S.S.J.
(See Separate Listing for School).

Society of the Divine Word Augustine Tolton House, 2236 D'Abadie St., 70119-2639. Tel: 504-943-4917. Rev. Antoine Leason, S.V.D., Dir. Vocation Recruitment Office.

Vincentian Fathers. DePaul Residence, 812 Constantinople St., 70115-2726. Tel: 504-897-3976; Fax: 504-899-7603. Very Rev. Robert E. Lamy, C.M., Supr.; Revs. Anthony D. Fassbender, C.M.; Ignatius L. Foley, C.M.; Lee B. Zimmerman, C.M.; P. Francis Zimmermann, C.M.; Bernard P. Degan, C.M.

ST. BENEDICT. *St. Joseph Abbey* (1890), 70457-9999. Tel: 504-892-1800; Fax: 504-867-2270.
Web site: www.stjosephabbey.org
Rt. Rev. Patrick Regan, O.S.B., Abbot; Revs. Raphael Barousse, O.S.B.; Hugh Baumann, O.S.B.; Adam Begnaud, O.S.B., M.S.; Gregory M. Boquet, O.S.B.; Dominic Braud, O.S.B.; Justin Brown, O.S.B.; Timothy J. Burnett, O.S.B.; Kevin Clark, O.S.B.; Matthew R. Clark, O.S.B.; Daniel Cobb, O.S.B.; Jonathan M. DeFrange, O.S.B.; Sean B. Duggan, O.S.B.; Augustine E. Foley, O.S.B.; Ignatius Fossier, O.S.B.; Peter Hammett, O.S.B.; Gerald Hindman, O.S.B.; Adrian Hovey, O.S.B.; Michael Jung, O.S.B.; Aelred Kavanagh, O.S.B.; Marian E. Larmann, O.S.B.; William J. MacCandless, O.S.B.; Paul Miranne, O.S.B.; Stan Moseley, O.S.B.; Thomas E. Perrier, O.S.B.; Lawrence J. Phelps, O.S.B.; Francis Sander, O.S.B.; Albert Terrillion, O.S.B.; Scott J. Underwood, O.S.B.; Ambrose Wathen, O.S.B. Priests 30; Brothers 17; Novices 1.

[Q] CONVENTS AND RESIDENCES FOR SISTERS

NEW ORLEANS. *Congregation of Divine Providence, C.D.P.*, 504 Fern, 70118-3830. Tel: 504-861-0284. Total Sisters in Archdiocese 2.

Congregation of the Sisters of the Holy Faith, C.H.F., 2741 St. Anthony St., 70119-1298. Tel: 504-945-7743; Fax: 504-949-5969. Total Sisters in Archdiocese 4.

Daughters of Charity of St. Vincent de Paul, D.C. Sisters' Residence, 1040 Calhoun St., Helis #2, 70118-5999. Tel: 504-899-8228. Sr. Catherine Chernick, D.C., Supr. Total Sisters in Archdiocese 31.

Daughters of Our Lady of the Holy Rosary Provincial House, F.M.S.R., 1492 Moss St., 70119-2904. Tel: 504-486-0039. Sr. Mary James Hang Nga, F.M.S.R., Prov. Supr. Total Sisters in Archdiocese 41.

Dominican Sisters (Cabra, Ireland) O.P., 1930 Robert E. Lee Blvd., 70122-3518. Tel: 504-288-1593. Sr. Elizabeth Ferguson, O.P., Reg. Supr. Total Sisters in Archdiocese 10.

Eucharistic Missionaries of St. Dominic, O.P., 3801 Canal St., Ste. 400, 70119-6049. Tel: 504-486-1133; Fax: 504-486-6547. Total Sisters in Archdiocese 23.

Regina Coeli Retreat Center, 17225 Regina Coeli Rd., Covington, 70435-9156. Tel: 504-892-4110.

Generalate of the Dominican Sisters, O.P., Congregation of St. Mary, 580 Broadway, 70118-3593. Tel: 504-861-8183; Fax: 504-861-8184.
E-mail: Rosebwn@aol.com
Web site: www. op.org/stmarys/
Sr. Therese Leckert, O.P., Prioress. Generalate Staff Sisters 5; Total Sisters in Archdiocese 72.

Little Sisters of the Poor, L.S.P., 4201 Woodland Dr., 70131-7398. Tel: 504-394-2200. Sisters 12.

Marianites of Holy Cross, M.S.C. (1848), 1011 Gallier St., 70117-6111. Tel: 504-945-1620; Fax: 504-944-0756. Sr. Mary Kay Kinberger, Congregational Leader. Total Sisters in Archdiocese 97.

Missionary Sisters of the Sacred Heart (Cabrini) M.S.C., 3400 Esplanade Ave., 70119-2993. Tel: 504-488-4174; Fax: 504-483-4180. Total Sisters in Archdiocese 4.

Presentation Sisters of the Blessed Virgin Mary, 1920 Robert E. Lee Blvd., 70122-3512. Tel: 504-283-3352.
E-mail: presis@gnofn.org
Web site: www.gnofn.org/~presis
Legal Title: *Union of Sisters of the Presentation of the Blessed Virgin Mary (United States Prov.)*. Sr. Vera Butler, P.B.V.M., Devel. Dir. Total Sisters in Archdiocese 3.

Religious of the Good Shepherd, R.G.S., 4934 Hauk Dr., 70127; Fax: 504-899-1335. Total Sisters in Archdiocese 4.

Religious of the Sacred Heart, R.S.C.J., 1837 Milan St., 70115-9990. Tel: 504-899-3037. Sisters 5. 4600 Carondelet St., 70115-4822. Tel: 504-891-0412. Sisters 4. 1719 Napoleon Ave., 70115-4809. Tel: 504-899-6027; Fax: 504-899-6210. Sr. Sharon O'Grady, R.S.C.J., Dir. Sisters 5. Total Sisters in Archdiocese 14.

St. Clare's Monastery of the Blessed Sacrament, O.S.C. (1885), 720 Henry Clay Ave., 70118-5891. Tel: 504-895-2019. Nuns of the Order of St. Clare. Sr. Elizabeth Mortell, O.S.C., Abbess. Solemn Professed Nuns 11.

School Sisters of Notre Dame (Dallas, TX), S.S.N.D., Redeemer Convent, 7010 Milne Blvd., 70124-2343. Tel: 504-288-5002. Total Sisters in Archdiocese 21.

Sisters of Mercy of the Americas, R.S.M. (St. Louis Regional Community), 6024 Freret St., 70118. Tel: 504-891-4639; Fax: 504-482-6125. Mercy Family Center, 3816 Bienville St., 70119. Tel: 504-482-6600.

Mercy Hospital Convent, 301 N. Jefferson Davis Pkwy., 70119-5397. Tel: 504-483-5000. Total Sisters in Archdiocese 46.

Sisters of St. Joseph of Medaille, New Orleans, C.S.J., 1200 Mirabeau Ave., 70122-1997. Tel: 504-283-9493; Fax: 504-288-4044.
E-mail: annecsj@juno.com
Sr. Anne Meridier, C.S.J., Coord. of Complex. Total Sisters in Archdiocese 69.

People Program, Inc., 1200 Mirabeau Ave., 70122-1997. Tel: 504-288-3171; Fax: 504-288-3503. Sr. Carolyn Brady, C.S.J., Pres.; Mrs. Mary Catherine Lombard, Dir.

Sisters of the Blessed Sacrament, S.B.S., 947 S. Cortez St., 70125-1105. Tel: 504-488-5325. 5116 Magazine St., 70115. Tel: 504-897-0235. 5014 Howard Ave., New Orleans, 70125. Tel: 504-486-2474. 3812 Pine St., 70125. Tel: 504-482-0917. Total Sisters in the Archdiocese 36.

Sisters of the Holy Family Motherhouse and Novitiate, S.S.F. (1842), 6901 Chef Menteur Hwy., 70126-5290. Tel: 504-242-8315; 504-241-5400; Fax: 504-241-3957.
E-mail: holshf@juno.com
Mother M. de Chantal St. Julien, S.S.F., Supr. Gen. Total Sisters in Archdiocese 139.

Sisters of the Holy Family Development Office, 2710 Gentilly Blvd., 70122-3098. Tel: 504-949-4572; Fax: 504-241-3957.

Sisters, Servants of Mary, S.M., 5001 Perlita St., 70122-1999. Tel: 504-282-5549. Sr. Auxilio Corrales, S.M., Supr. Total Home Nursing Sisters in Archdiocese 21.

Ursuline Sisters of the Roman Union, O.S.U. (1727), 2734 Nashville Ave., 70115-7008. Tel: 504-866-1472. Sr. Susan Kienzler, O.S.U., Prioress. Total Sisters in Archdiocese 19.

CHALMETTE. *Daughters of Divine Providence, F.D.P.*, 3100 Mumphrey Rd., 70043-3735. Tel: 504-279-4617. Total Sisters in Archdiocese 3.

COVINGTON. *Carmelite Nuns, Discalced, O.C.D., Monastery of St. Joseph and St. Theresa* (1877), 73530 River Rd., 70435-2206. Tel: 504-898-0923; Fax: 504-871-9333. Professed Nuns 9.

Teresian Sisters (Society of St. Teresa of Jesus), S.T.J., Provincial House, 18080 St. Joseph's Way, 70435-5623. Tel: 504-893-1470; Fax: 504-893-2476. Sr. Carmen Gloria Plasencia, S.T.J., Prov. Sisters 20.

Formation House, 18158 St. Joseph's Way, 70435-5624. Tel: 504-893-1557. Sr. Marina Aranzabal, S.T.J., Dir. Novices.

GRETNA. *Sisters of the Living Word, S.L.W.*, 901 Hancock St., 70053-2227. Tel: 504-366-5358. Sisters 2; Total Sisters in Archdiocese 12.

HARVEY. *Sinsinawa Dominican Congregation of the Most Holy Rosary, O.P.*, 2824 Keith Way Dr., 70058-1921. Tel: 504-340-6822.
E-mail: arterywood@aol.com; eapawlicki@aol.com
Sr. Carol Artery, O.P.; Sr. Priscilla Wood, O.P.; Sr. Elizabeth Pawlicki, O.P. Sisters 3.

LACOMBE. *Congregation of Our Lady of Mount Carmel, O.Carm.* (1833), Generalate P.O. Box 476, 70445-0476. Tel: 504-882-7577; 524-2398; Fax: 504-524-5011.
E-mail: mountcarmel@mindspring.com
Sr. Rose Marie Penouilh, O.Carm., Pres. Sisters 65. Mount Carmel Development Office, P.O. Box 1160, 70445-1160. Tel: 504-882-7577; 524-2398; Fax: 504-524-5011. Sr. Andree Marie Bindewald, O.Carm., Dir.

MANDEVILLE. *St. Gertrude's Convent, Benedictine Sisters*, c/o Prieto & Prieto, Attorneys, 2900 E. Causeway Approach, Ste. D, 70448-3597.

MARRERO. *Lovers of the Holy Cross, L.H.C.*, 1216 Avenue G, 70072-3750. Tel: 504-348-8206. Sr. Martha Ann Nguyen, L.H.C., Supr. Total Sisters in Archdiocese 5.

Salesian Sisters (Daughters of Mary Help of Christians) F.M.A., Immaculate Conception Convent, 612 Avenue B, 70072-2016. Tel: 504-347-8449; Fax: 504-347-8044. Sisters in Archdiocese 8.

METAIRIE. *Daughters of St. Paul Convent, F.S.P.*, St. Paul Book & Media Center, 4403 Veterans Memorial Blvd., 70006-5321. Tel: 504-887-7631; Fax: 504-888-4745.
E-mail: skatie1@aol.com
Total Sisters in Archdiocese 4.
Incarnate Word Sisters, C.C.V.I., 2904 Houma Blvd., Apt. D, 70006-1422. Tel: 504-888-1410. Total Sisters in Archdiocese 6.
Religious of Our Lady of the Retreat in the Cenacle, R.C., The Cenacle Retreat House, 5500 St. Mary St., P.O. Box 8115, 70011-8115. Tel: 504-887-1420; Fax: 504-887-6624. Sr. JoAnn Viviano, R.C., Supr. Sisters 7.
Sisters of the Most Holy Sacrament, M.H.S., 420 Bonnabel Blvd., 70005-3240. Tel: 504-831-5786. Total Sisters in Archdiocese 7.

PORT SULPHUR. *Sisters of St. Francis of Perpetual Adoration, O.S.F.*, St. Jude Convent, P.O. Box 36, 70083-0036. Tel: 504-564-3234. Sr. M. Louise Pfeifer, Supr. Sisters 4.

SLIDELL. *Dominican Sisters (Adrian), O.P.*, 952 Asheville Dr., 70458-2145. Tel: 504-643-7007. Total Sisters in Archdiocese 4.

[R] RETREAT HOUSES

NEW ORLEANS. *Archdiocesan Spirituality Center*, 2901 S. Carrollton Ave., 70118-4391. Tel: 504-861-3254. Sr. Noel Toomey, O.P., Dir.
Center of Jesus the Lord, 1236 N. Rampart St., 70116-2497. Tel: 504-529-1636; Fax: 504-529-5003.
E-mail: CCRCNO@aol.com
Web site: www.members.aol.com/CCRCNO
Rev. Vincent Bono, S.C., Dir. Total Assisted 314; Total Staff 11.
Dominican Conference Center, 540 Broadway, 70118-3593. Tel: 504-861-8711; Fax: 504-861-8718. Ms. Charlotte Fenerty Ewing, Admin. Total in Residence 6; Total Staff 7.
Sophie Barat House, 1719 Napoleon Ave., 70115-4809. Tel: 504-899-6027; Fax: 504-899-6210.
E-mail: jmckinlay@rscj.org
Sr. Mary Blish, R.S.C.J.; Sr. Jane McKinlay, R.S.C.J.; Sr. Anne Sturges, R.S.C.J. Total Staff 3; Total in Residence 4.

COVINGTON. *Regina Coeli Retreat Center*, 17225 Regina Coeli Rd., 70435-9156. Tel: 504-892-4110. Managers: Earl Magner; June Magner.

LACOMBE. *Blessing Place*, P.O. Box 130, 70445-0130. Tel: 504-882-7579; Fax: 504-882-3619.
E-mail: BlessingPlace@worldnet.att.net
Web site: www.worldnet.att.net
Sr. Barbara Breaud, O.Carm., Dir. Personal growth and development community for women and men religious and clergy.

MARRERO. *Ave Maria Retreat House*, HC 62, Box 368 AB, 70072-9704. Tel: 504-689-3837; Fax: 504-689-2785. Rev. Gerald J. Fogarty, O.M.I., Dir.; Bro. Danna J. Gauthreaux, O.M.I., Assoc. Dir. Total Staff 7; Total in Residence 2.

METAIRIE. *Cenacle Retreat House*, 5500 St. Mary St., P.O. Box 8115, 70011-8115. Tel: 504-887-1420; Fax: 504-887-6624. Sr. JoAnn Viviano, R.C., Retreat House Admin.; Sr. Mary C. Daniel, O.P., Ministry Coord.; Rev. John L. Hein, S.J., Chap. Religious 8; Total Staff 32.

PONCHATOULA. *Magnificat Center of the Holy Spirit*, 23629 Faith Rd., 70454. Tel: 504-362-4356; 800-531-9710. Rev. Vincent Bono, S.C., Dir. Total in Residence 90; Total Staff 4.

ST. BENEDICT. *Abbey Christian Life Center*, St. Joseph Abbey, 70457-9999. Tel: 504-892-3473; 892-1800. Conducted by Benedictine Monks. Rev. Thomas Perrier, O.S.B., Dir.

[S] MISCELLANEOUS

NEW ORLEANS. *Christian Brothers Foundation*, #8 Friederichs Ave., 70124-4602. Tel: 504-482-3349.
Equestrian Order of the Holy Sepulchre. (of Jerusalem, Southeastern Lieutenancy of the U.S.), 5614 Marcia Ave., 70124-1006. Lt. George H. Toye, K.G.C.H.S.
**Focus Syndicate, Inc.*, 2929 S. Carrollton Ave., 70118. Tel: 504-866-7411; Fax: 504-861-5186. Most Rev. Philip M. Hannan, Pres. & Board of Trustees.
Foundation for Christian Education, S.T.J., 1611 Mirabeau Ave., 70112-2511. Tel: 504-288-1289; Fax: 504-288-9946.
E-mail: fce@gnofn.org
Sr. Carmen Gloria Plasencia, S.T.J., Pres.
Jesuit Program for Living and Learning of New Orleans, Inc., 4128 Baudin St., 70119-6815. Rev. Robert C. Allanach, O.M.I., Ph.D., Exec. Dir.
Jesuit Seminary and Mission Fund, 500 S. Jefferson Davis Pkwy., 70119-7192. Tel: 504-827-4043; Fax: 504-827-9931. Revs. Thomas Clancy, S.J., Dir.; Martin V. Jarreau, S.J., Assoc. Dir.
MCA Foundation, 420 Robert E. Lee Blvd., 70124-2596. Tel: 504-524-2398.
E-mail: mountcarmel@mindspring.com
Sr. Rose Marie Penouilh, O.Carm., Pres.
The Patrons of the Vatican Museums in the South, Inc., 775 Harrison Ave., 70124-3192. Very Rev. Val A. McInnes, O.P., Founder & Pres. Emeritus; Mr. Paul A. Nalty, Pres.
Pierre Toussaint Foundation of New Orleans, Inc., 2600 A.P. Tereaud Ave., 70119-1299. Tel: 504-949-3113. Rev. Joseph M. Doyle, S.S.J., Pres.
Stella Roman Foundation, Inc., 1207 First NBC Bldg., 70112-4100. Rev. Msgr. John P. Reynolds, Pres.
**WLAE-TV, Educational Broadcasting Foundation, Inc.*, 2929 S. Carrollton Ave., 70118-4301. Tel: 504-866-7411; Fax: 504-861-5186. Most Rev. Philip M. Hannan, Pres., Bd. of Trustees.

HARAHAN.
**Second Harvesters Food Bank of Greater New Orleans*, 1201 Sams Ave., 70123-2236.

METAIRIE. *Southern Dominican Foundation*, 1421 N. Causeway Blvd., Ste. 200, 70001-4144. Tel: 504-837-2129; Fax: 504-837-6604. Revs. Alberto Rodriguez, O.P., Pres.; Carl B. Trutter, O.P., Vice Pres./Sec.; Val A. McInnes, O.P., Promoter of Development; Nora P. Fine, Dir. of Development.
Southern Dominican Global Missions, 1421 N. Causeway Blvd., Ste. 200, 70001-4144. Rev. John Raymond Corr, O.P. (SA), Dir.

SLIDELL.
**S.A.V.E., Inc. (Suffering Abortion Victims Embraced)*, P.O. Box 1594, 70459. Tel: 504-847-0133. Mrs. Linda Jefferson, Pres.

SECULAR INSTITUTES

NEW ORLEANS. *Society of Our Lady of the Way*, 6044 Louis XIV St., 70124-2919. Tel: 504-486-2506.

ABITA SPRINGS. *Caritas*, Administration Center, P.O. Box 308, 70420-0308. Tel: 504-892-4345.
Daraja House, 810 N. Madison St., Covington, 70433-2130. Tel: 504-893-2261.

RELIGIOUS INSTITUTES OF MEN REPRESENTED IN THE ARCHDIOCESE

For further details refer to the corresponding bracketed number in the Religious Institutes of Men or Women section.

[0200]—*Benedictine Monks.*—O.S.B.
[1350]—*Brothers of St. Francis Xavier.*—C.F.X.
[0330]—*Brothers of the Christian Schools.* (New Orleans Prov.).—F.S.C.
[0600]—*Brothers of the Congregation of Holy Cross.* (Midwest; Southwest Provs.).—C.S.C.
[0470]—*The Capuchin Friars.*—O.F.M.Cap.
[0270]—*Carmelite Fathers.*—O.Carm.
[0360]—*Claretian Missionaries.*—C.M.F.
[0220]—*Congregation of the Blessed Sacrament.*—S.S.S.
[1330]—*Congregation of the Mission of St. Vincent de Paul Fathers & Brothers.* (Southern Prov.).—C.M.
[]—*Congregation of the Mother Coredemptrix.*—C.M.C.
[0260]—*Discalced Carmelite Friars.*—O.C.D.
[0520]—*Franciscan Friars.*—O.F.M.
[0650]—*Holy Ghost Fathers.* (Western Vice Prov.; Ireland).—C.S.Sp.
[]—*Incarnational Consecration.*—I.C.
[0690]—*Jesuit Fathers and Brothers.* (New Orleans).—S.J.
[0780]—*Marist Fathers and Brothers.* (Washington Prov.).—S.M.
[0840]—*Missionary Servants of the Most Holy Trinity.*—S.T.
[0910]—*Oblates of Mary Immaculate.* (Southern American Prov.).—O.M.I.
[0430]—*Order of Preacher-Dominicans.* (Southern Prov.).—O.P.
[1310]—*Order of the Most Holy Trinity.*—O.SS.T.
[1100]—*Priests and Brothers of the Sacred Heart.* (Metuchen, NJ).—S.C.
[0610]—*Priests of the Congregation of Holy Cross.* (Southern Prov.).—C.S.C.
[1070]—*Redemptorist Fathers and Brothers.* (New Orleans).—C.SS.R.
[0700]—*St. Joseph's Society of the Sacred Heart.* (Baltimore, MD).—S.S.J.
[1170]—*St. Patrick Missionary Society.*—S.P.S.
[1190]—*Salesians of Don Bosco.*—S.D.B.
[0760]—*Society of Mary.* St. Louis Province.—S.M.
[0440]—*Society of St. Edmund.*—S.S.E.
[0420]—*Society of the Divine Word.* (St. Augustine Prov.).—S.V.D.

RELIGIOUS INSTITUTES OF WOMEN REPRESENTED IN THE ARCHDIOCESE

[0230]—*Benedictine Sisters of Pontifical Jurisdiction.* (Colorado; Atchison, KS).—O.S.B.
[0400]—*Congregation of Our Lady of Mount Carmel.*—O.Carm.
[3110]—*Congregation of Our Lady of the Retreat in the Cenacle.*—R.C.
[1940]—*Congregation of Sisters of the Holy Faith.*—C.H.F.
[2410]—*Congregation of the Marianites of Holy Cross.*—M.S.C.
[0460]—*Congregation of the Sisters of Charity of the Incarnate Word.*—C.C.V.I.
[1950]—*Congregation of the Sisters of the Holy Family.*—S.S.F.
[0800]—*Daughters of Divine Providence.*—F.D.P.
[0850]—*Daughters of Mary Help of Christians.*—F.M.A.
[]—*Daughters of Our Lady of the Holy Rosary.*—F.M.S.R.
[0760]—*Daughters of St. Vincent de Paul.*—D.C.
[0420]—*Discalced Carmelite Nuns.*—O.C.D.
[1110]—*Dominican Sisters of Our Lady of the Rosary and of Saint Catherine of Siena, Cabra, Ireland.*—O.P.
[1070-08]—*Dominican Sisters, Congregation of St. Mary.*—O.P.
[1070-02]—*Dominican Sisters, Congregation of St. Mary of the Springs.*—O.P.
[1070-13]—*Dominican Sisters, Congregation of the Most Holy Rosary.*—O.P.
[1070-03]—*Dominican Sisters, Sinsinawa Dominican Congregation of the Most Holy Rosary.*—O.P.
[1140]—*Eucharistic Missionaries of St. Dominic.*—O.P.
[1430]—*Franciscan Sisters of Our Lady of Perpetual Help.*—O.S.F.
[]—*Handmaids of the Holy Child of Jesus.*—H.H.C.J.
[2340]—*Little Sisters of the Poor.*—L.S.P.
[2390]—*Lovers of the Holy Cross Sisters.*—L.H.C.
[2490]—*Medical Mission Sisters.*—M.M.S.
[2790]—*Missionary Sisters of the Most Blessed Trinity.*—M.S.B.T.
[2860]—*Missionary Sisters of the Sacred Heart.*—M.S.C.
[0950]—*Pious Society Daughters of St. Paul.*—F.S.P.
[3760]—*Poor Clare Nuns, Order of St. Clare.*—O.S.C.
[2970]—*School Sisters of Notre Dame.* (Dallas & Mankato, South Central Prov.).—S.S.N.D.
[]—*Sisters for Christian Community.*—S.F.C.C.
[0660]—*Sisters of Christian Charity.* (Wilmette, IL).—S.C.C.
[1010]—*Sisters of Divine Providence of San Antonio, Texas.*—C.D.P.
[2575]—*Sisters of Mercy of the Americas.* (Brooklyn; St. Louis).—R.S.M.
[2630]—*Sisters of Mercy of the Holy Cross.*—S.C.S.C.
[]—*Sisters of St. Francis.* (Glen Riddle, PA).—O.S.F.
[1640]—*Sisters of St. Francis of Perpetual Adoration.*—O.S.F.
[1670]—*Sisters of St. Francis of Savannah.*—O.S.F.
[1530]—*Sisters of St. Francis of the Congregation of Our Lady of Lourdes, Sylvania, Ohio.*—O.S.F.
[3840]—*Sisters of St. Joseph of Carondelet.*—C.S.J.
[3880]—*Sisters of St. Joseph of Medaille.*—C.S.J.
[3830-11]—*Sisters of St. Joseph, Kalamazoo.*—S.S.J.
[0260]—*Sisters of the Blessed Sacrament for Indians and Colored People.*—S.B.S.
[1830]—*Sisters of the Good Shepherd.*—R.G.S.
[2050]—*Sisters of the Holy Spirit and Mary Immaculate.*—S.H.Sp.
[2120]—*Sisters of the Immaculate Conception.*—C.I.C.
[2350]—*Sisters of the Living Word.*—S.L.W.
[2940]—*Sisters of the Most Holy Sacrament.*—M.H.S.
[3320]—*Sisters of the Presentation of the B.V.M.* (Aberdeen, SD; Newburgh, NY).—P.B.V.M.
[3600]—*Sisters Servants of Mary.*—S.M.
[4020]—*Society of St. Teresa of Jesus.*—S.T.J.
[4060]—*Society of the Holy Child Jesus.*—S.H.C.J.
[4070]—*Society of the Sacred Heart.*—R.S.C.J.
[4110]—*Ursuline Nuns.*—O.S.U.
[4120]—*Ursuline Nuns, of the Congregation of Paris.* (Paola, KS).—O.S.U.
[]—*West Indian Franciscans.*—W.I.F.

NECROLOGY

† Boudreaux, Rev. Msgr. Edward L., New Orleans, LA, Our Lady of the Rosary. —Died Sept. 4, 1997.

† Bruns, J. Edgar, New Orleans, LA, Notre Dame Seminary. —Died May 29, 1997.

† Reid, Rev. Msgr. Marion M., (Retired). —Died Oct. 26, 1997.

Diocese of New Ulm

(Dioecesis Novae Ulmae)

Most Reverend

RAYMOND A. LUCKER, S.T.D.

Bishop of New Ulm; ordained June 7, 1952; appointed Titular Bishop of Meta July 12, 1971; consecrated September 8, 1971; appointed to New Ulm December 23, 1975; installed February 19, 1976. *Res., Catholic Pastoral Center, 1400 6th St. N., New Ulm, MN, 56073-2099.* Tel.: 507-359-2966; Fax: 507-354-3667.

ESTABLISHED NOVEMBER 18, 1957.

Square Miles 9,863.

Comprises the Counties of Big Stone, Brown, Chippewa, Kandiyohi, Lac Qui Parle, Lincoln, Lyon, McLeod, Meeker, Nicollet, Redwood, Renville, Sibley, Swift and Yellow Medicine in the State of Minnesota.

For legal titles of parishes and diocesan institutions, consult the Catholic Pastoral Center.

Catholic Pastoral Center: 1400 6th St. N., New Ulm, MN, 56073-2099. Tel.: 507-359-2966; Fax: 507-354-3667.

E-mail address: dnucomm@ic.new-ulm.mn.us

STATISTICAL OVERVIEW

Personnel	
Bishop	1
Priests: Diocesan Active in Diocese	54
Priests: Active Outside Diocese	9
Priests: Diocesan in Foreign Missions	2
Priests: Retired, Sick or Absent	28
Number of Diocesan Priests	93
Religious Priests in Diocese	1
Extern Priests in Diocese	3
Permanent Deacons in Diocese	3
Total Sisters	91
Parishes	
Parishes	80
With Resident Pastor:	
Resident Diocesan Priests	46
Without Resident Pastor:	
Administered by Priests	15
Administered by Women Religious	16
Administered by Lay People	3
Missions	2
Professional Ministry Personnel:	
Sisters	8
Lay Ministers	52
Welfare	
Catholic Hospitals	1
Total Assisted	7,750
Health Care Centers	2
Total Assisted	7,435
Homes for the Aged	6
Total Assisted	460
Other Institutions	1
Total Assisted	1,200
Educational	
Diocesan Students in Other Seminaries	7
Total Seminarians	7
High Schools, Diocesan and Parish	3
Total Students	554
Elementary Schools, Diocesan and Parish	19
Total Students	3,049
Catechesis/Religious Education:	
High School Students	3,883
Elementary Students	8,807
Total Students Under Catholic Instruction	16,300
Teachers in the Diocese:	
Priests	1
Sisters	11
Lay Teachers	211
Vital Statistics	
Receptions into the Church:	
Infant Baptism Totals	1,124
Adult Baptism Totals	66
Received into Full Communion	103
First Communions	1,282
Confirmations	1,269
Marriages:	
Catholic	245
Interfaith	226
Total Marriages	471
Deaths	736
Total Catholic Population	73,202
Total Population	283,229

Former Bishop—Most Rev. ALPHONSE J. SCHLADWEILER, D.D., ord. June 9, 1929; appt. Nov. 28, 1957; cons. Jan. 29, 1958; retired Dec. 23, 1975; died April 3,1996.

Diocesan Officials

Catholic Pastoral Center—Most Rev. RAYMOND A. LUCKER, S.T.D., *1400 6th St. N., New Ulm, 56073-2099.* Tel: 507-359-2966; Fax: 507-354-3667.

Vicar General—Rev. DENNIS C. LABAT, *Catholic Pastoral Center, 1400 6th St. N., New Ulm, 56073-2099.* Tel: 507-359-2966.

Chancellor—EUGENE E. BURKE, *Catholic Pastoral Center, 1400 6th St. N., New Ulm, 56073-2099.* Tel: 507-233-5322; 359-2966.

Vice-Chancellor—Rev. JOHN G. BERGER, *Church of St. Willibrord, 1032 Ash Ave., Gibbon, 55335-9998.* Tel: 507-834-6461.

Diocesan Tribunal—

Officialis—Rev. JOHN G. BERGER, *Church of St. Willibrord, 1032 Ash Ave., Gibbon, 55335-9998.* Tel: 507-834-6461.

Associate Judges—Revs. EUGENE L. LOZINSKI; MARK S. MALLAK; PAUL L. WOLF; DOUGLAS L. GRAMS.

Defenders of the Bond—Rev. EUGENE L. LOZINSKI.

Auditor—EUGENE E. BURKE.

Advocates—Rev. MICHAEL L. SUMMERFIELD; EUGENE E. BURKE.

Notaries—ROSEMARY SCHUELLER; JANELLE DREXLER; SHERI JOHNSON.

Diocesan Boards and Councils

Building Committee—Revs. STEVEN J. VERHELST, Chm., *Church of St. Francis, 412 12th St. N., Benson, 56215-1228.* Tel: 320-843-2342. EUGENE C. HACKERT; RAY MCCLELLAN; RICHARD GREENE; LUCILLE O'DONNELL; JANE BERNARD; GREG WALSH; JOE EIKMEIER; RAYMOND MARTIN.

College of Consultors—Revs. GEORGE V. SCHMIT; PATRICK L. CASEY; RICHARD C. GROSS; BRIAN L. MANDEL; WILLIAM A. SPRIGLER; DENNIS C. LABAT; DAROLD R. LEHMAN.

Committee on Parishes—Sr. KATHRYN SCHOOLMEESTERS, S.S.N.D., Chm. EUGENE E. BURKE, Staff; Revs. ANTHONY J. STUBEDA; DENNIS C. LABAT; GERALD S. MEIDL; MICHAEL L. SUMMERFIELD; JOSEPH EIKMEIER; JUDI WEBER; DONALD A. CLASEMANN; ROSE JONCAS; WILLIAM HENDRICKSON; Sr. JEANETTE HOMAN, O.S.F.

Corporate Board—Most Rev. RAYMOND A. LUCKER; Rev. DENNIS C. LABAT; Mr. EUGENE E. BURKE; Mr. WILLIAM T. O'CONNOR; Mr. PAUL ZINS.

Diocesan Pastoral Council—ANDREW RHODE, Chm., *P.O. Box 453, Clara City, 56222.* Tel: 320-847-3675(Office); 847-2148(Home). DONALD PALS, Vice Chm. AGNES MEIUM, Sec. EUGENE E. BURKE, Staff. Members: MARY ANN BLANCHETTE; MARY BOLEK; DARRELL BREYFOGLE; SHERRY DREITZ; DONNA HANLON; Sr. JEANETTE HOMAN, O.S.F.; MARY ANN KRAMER; ANDREW KUBAT; LEO MCTIGHE; MARION MONNENS; WALLY MAUS; ARNIE NIMPS; JOAN NIMPS; KEITH SALISBURY; Revs. RICHARD C. GROSS; GEORGE V. SCHMIT, JR.

Finance Council—Revs. GERMAIN P. RADEMACHER; BERNARD J. STEINER; ANTHONY J. STUBEDA; GERI BURESH; DANIEL BERANEK; RAY MCCLELLAN; NANCY O'LEARY; THOMAS SENDEN; SANDY REDDING.

Priests' Council—Rev. GEORGE V. SCHMIT, JR., Chm., *Cathedral of the Holy Trinity, 605 N. State St., New Ulm, 56073-1898.* Tel: 507-354-4158. Rev. WILLIAM A. SPRIGLER, Vice Chm. PATRICK L. CASEY, Treas.; Revs. DENNIS C. LABAT; RICHARD C. GROSS; BRIAN L. MANDEL.

Sisters' Council—Executive Committee: Sr. KATHRYN SCHOOLMEESTERS, S.S.N.D.; Sr. JOANNE BACKES, O.S.B.; Sr. GLADYS MEINDL, O.S.F.; Sr. BETTY LARSON, O.S.B., Staff Liaison.

Catholic Pastoral Center

Coordinator of Diocesan Staff—EUGENE E. BURKE, *Catholic Pastoral Center, 1400 6th St. N., New Ulm, 56073-2099.* Tel: 507-359-2966; 233-5322.

Office of Finance—Mr. RAY MCCLELLAN, Dir., *Catholic Pastoral Center, 1400 6th St. N., New Ulm, 56073-2099.* Tel: 507-359-2966.

Office of Development—Rev. ANTHONY J. STUBEDA, Dir., *Catholic Pastoral Center, 1400 6th St. N., New Ulm, 56073-2099.* Tel: 507-359-2966; 233-5327.

Evangelization and Catechesis—

Religious Education/Adult Religious Education—JOANN BORCHERT, Dir., *Catholic Pastoral Center, 1400 6th St. N., New Ulm, 56073-2099.* Tel: 507-359-2966.

Catholic Schools/Ministry Formation—Sr. BETTY LARSON, O.S.B., Dir., Schools, *Catholic Pastoral Center, 1400 6th St. N., New Ulm, 56073-2099.* Tel: 507-359-2966.

Youth & Young Adult Ministry—BILL CASEY, Dir., *Catholic Pastoral Center, 1400 6th St. N., New Ulm, 56073-2099.* Tel: 507-359-2966.

A-TEC (Adult/Teens Encounter Christ)—Rev. DENNIS C. LABAT, Coord., *Catholic Pastoral Center, 1400*

6th St. N., New Ulm, 56073-2099. Tel: 507-359-2966.

Communications—PAULA MARTI, Dir., *Catholic Pastoral Center, 1400 6th St. N., New Ulm, 56073-2099.* Tel: 507-359-2966; Fax: 507-354-3667.

"Prairie Catholic"—PAULA MARTI, Editor, *Catholic Pastoral Center, 1400 6th St. N., New Ulm, 56073-2099.* Tel: 507-359-2966.

Committee for Evangelization & Catechesis—SUE FLEEGEL; Chm. Revs. PATRICK L. CASEY; PHILIP M. SCHOTZKO; ANNA MARIE REITER; MARIANNE PAFFEL; JUDITH SCHINDLER; KAREN ECKSTEIN; LORI CARSTONS; Sr. MARY WEIDNER, O.S.B.

Office of Worship and Spiritual Life—JANE BERNARD, Dir., *1400 6th St. N., New Ulm, 56073-2099.* Tel: 507-359-2966.

Worship Committee—JANE BERNARD, Staff, *1400 6th St. N., New Ulm, 56073-2099.* Tel: 507-359-2966. Members: Rev. JEFFREY P. HOREJSI, Chm.; Revs. GERALD S. MEIDL; RONALD V. HUBERTY; Sr. MONICA WAGNER, S.S.N.D.; Sr. BETTY LARSON, O.S.B.; JOANN BORCHERT; MARY BETH HAUSER; KATIE HENRICH; KAY OSBORNE; TERESA GUILLEMETTE; MARY BOLEK; GEORGE BLACKNEY; BEV SULLIVAN; KEVIN KALKFOFF.

RCIA Network—JANE BERNARD, *1400 6th St. N., New Ulm, 56073-2099.* Tel: 507-359-2966.

Charismatic Renewal—JAN CROWE, Diocesan Liaison, *21907 705th Ave., Dassel, 55325.* Tel: 320-275-2424.

Retreat Team—JAN CROWE, Coord., *21907 705th Ave., Dassel, 55325.* Tel: 320-275-2424.

Center for Spiritual Development—Co-Dirs.: Sr. JANET MALLAK, S.S.N.D.; Sr. MARJORIE KLEIN, S.S.N.D., *211 10th St., P.O. Box 538, Bird Island, 55310-0538.* Tel: 320-365-3644.

Ecumenical Director—Vacant.

Members—Sr. CAROLYN PUCCIO, C.S.J.; TOM CROWE; JAN CROWE; JUDITH SCHINDLER; TOM CHRISTOFFER.

Office of Social Concerns and Family Life—CHRISTOPHER A. LOETSCHER, Dir., *1400 6th St. N., New Ulm, 56073-2099.* Tel: 507-359-2966.

Social Concerns Committee—CHRISTOPHER A. LOETSCHER; Rev. JOHN A. NORDICK; ARNOLD NIMPS; JOAN NIMPS; CLIFF SCHLOSSER; KAY FINNEMAN; MIKE MONNENS.

Family Life—CHRISTOPHER A. LOETSCHER, Dir., *1400 6th St. N., New Ulm, 56073-2099.* Tel: 507-359-2966. Marriage Preparation, Natural Family Planning, Resources & Referral for Marriage & Family Concerns, Divorced/Separated.

Retrouvaille—BOB PLAETZ; JULIE PLAETZ, *P.O. Box 52, Lucan, 56255.* Tel: 507-747-2345.

AIDS Ministry—Rev. PAUL A. SCHUMACHER, *Church of St. Patrick, P.O. Box 164, Kandiyohi, 56251-0164.* Tel: 320-382-6424.

Caritas Family Services: Pregnancy Counselor & Pro-Life Activities—Vacant, *1400 6th St. N., New Ulm, 56073-2099.* Tel: 507-359-2966.

Propagation of the Faith/Holy Childhood Association—Rev. WILLIAM H. BOWLES, *1400 6th St. N., New Ulm, 56073-2099.* Tel: 507-359-2966. San Lucas Mission Office; Rev. Msgr. GREGORY T. SCHAFFER; KATHY HUEBERT, *1400 6th St. N., New Ulm, 56073-2099.* Tel: 507-359-2966.

Hispanic Ministry—Rev. ANTHONY J. STUBEDA, Dir., *1400 6th St. N., New Ulm, 56073-2099.* Tel: 507-359-2966.

Office of Personnel—

Priest Personnel—Rev. DENNIS C. LABAT, Dir., *1400 6th St. N., New Ulm, 56073-2099.* Tel: 507-359-2966.

Priest Personnel Board—Revs. DENNIS C. LABAT, Dir. ROBERT J. MRAZ; GERMAIN P. RADEMACHER; FREDERICK T. FINK; BRIAN W. OESTREICH; MERLE MONNENS; PAUL VAN DE CROMMERT.

Pastoral Administrators—Rev. DENNIS C. LABAT; Supvr., *1400 6th St. N., New Ulm, 56073-2099.* Tel: 507-359-2966.

Bishop's Delegate in Matters Pertaining to Sexual Misconduct—EUGENE E. BURKE, *Catholic Pastoral Center, 1400 6th St. N., New Ulm, 56073-2099.* Tel: 507-359-2966; 233-5322.

New Ulm Diocesan Review Board on Sexual Misconduct—LILA SCHMIDT, Chm. STEVE SCHNEIDER; Vice Chm. EUGENE E. BURKE; MARY BOHLMANN; Rev. PAUL A. SCHUMACHER; WILLIAM F. WAGNER Ph.D.; MARY LINDSTROM.

Office of Conciliation—EUGENE E. BURKE, Interim Dir., *1400 6th St. N., New Ulm, 56073-2099.* Tel: 507-359-2966; 233-5322.

Vocations—Rev. BRIAN W. OESTREICH, Dir., *Cathedral of the Holy Trinity, 605 N. State St., New Ulm, 56073-1898.* Tel: 507-354-4158; Fax: 507-354-2563. Sr. SUE TORGERSEN C.S.J., Assoc. Dir., *1400 6th St. N., New Ulm, 56073-2099.* Tel: 507-359-2966; 233-5328.

Continuing Education of Clergy—Sr. SUE TORGERSEN C.S.J., Dir., *1400 6th St. N., New Ulm, 56073-2099.* Tel: 507-359-2966; 233-5328.

Committee for Continuing Education of Clergy—Rev. Msgr. ANTONY J. LEIFELD; Revs. EUGENE C. HACKERT; RONALD V. HUBERTY; MICHAEL M. DOYLE; ANDREW J. MICHELS; JOSEPH A. STEINBEISSER; Sr. SUE TORGERSEN, C.S.J.; Rev. DENNIS C. LABAT; Sr. VIVIAN PETERSEN, O.S.B.; Sr. JOVANN IRRGANG, S.S.N.D.

Board of Trustees for Pension Plan for Priests—Revs. DENNIS C. LABAT; JOHN H. BRUNNER; FREDERICK T. FINK; WILLIAM A. SPRIGLER; DONALD GUGGEMOS; MICHAEL G. REYNOLDS; KENNETH W. KUEHNER; RAY MCCLELLAN.

Vicar for Retired Priests—Rev. Msgr. ANTONY J. LEIFELD, *717 6th St. N., New Ulm, 56073-1853.* Tel: 507-359-9848.

Organizations in the Diocese of New Ulm

Diocesan Council of Catholic Women—JUNE BRUST, Pres., *Box 208, 203 Maye St., Tyler, 56178.* Tel: 507-247-5862. Rev. EUGENE L. LOZINSKI, Diocesan Moderator.

Girl Scouts—Mrs. MARJORIE NELSON, *720 Bonham Blvd., Willmar, 56201-2953.* Tel: 320-235-1566.

Boy Scouts—Rev. ANDREW J. MICHELS, *Church of St. John, 421 Madison Ave., P.O. Box 205, Ortonville, 56278-0205.* Tel: 320-839-2772.

Marriage Encounter—BARB WETTER; CRAIG WETTER, *P.O. Box 302, Lamberton, 56152.* Tel: 507-752-6118.

Minnesota Pax Christi—Most Rev. RAYMOND A. LUCKER, Pres., *1400 6th St. N., New Ulm, 56073-2099.* Tel: 507-359-2966.

CLERGY, PARISHES, MISSIONS AND PAROCHIAL SCHOOLS

CITY OF NEW ULM
(Brown County)

1—CATHEDRAL OF THE HOLY TRINITY (1856). Clustered with Searles. Revs. George V. Schmit, Jr.; Brian W. Oestreich; Eugene M. Brown; Rev. Msgr. Antony J. Leifeld, (Retired).
Res., 605 N. State St., 56073-1898. Tel: 507-354-4158; Fax: 507-354-2563. [CEM][JC]
School—New Ulm Area Catholic Schools. See separate listing under the Institutions for further explanation and statistics. Tel: 507-354-2719; Fax: 507-354-5711.
Catechesis/Religious Programs—Students 355.

2—ST. MARY (1911), Revs. Michael L. Summerfield; Eugene M. Brown.
Res., 417 S. Minnesota St., 56073-2120. Tel: 507-354-4043. [CEM 2][JC 2]
School—New Ulm Area Catholic Schools. See separate listing under the Institutions for further explanation and statistics.
Catechesis/Religious Programs—Tel: 507-354-6497.
Students 456.

OUTSIDE THE CITY OF NEW ULM

Appleton, Swift Co., St. John (1880), Rev. Paul J. Hadusek.
Mailing Address: 450 S. Gaulke St., P.O. Box 122, 56208-1516. Tel: 320-289-1211; Fax: 320-289-1146. [CEM 2][JC 2]
Church—350 S. Edquist St., 56208. Tel: 320-289-1146.
Catechesis/Religious Programs—Tel: 320-289-1146.
Students 94.

Arlington, Sibley Co., St. Mary (1864). Clustered with Faxon Township, Green Isle, Henderson & Jessenland. Rev. James D. Barry.
Res., 504 7th Ave., N.W., P.O. Box 392, 55307-0392. Tel: 507-964-5413; Fax: 507-964-5425. [CEM]
Catechesis/Religious Programs—Students 180.

Barry, Big Stone Co., St. Barnabas. Closed. For sacramental records contact Holy Rosary, Graceville.

Beardsley, Big Stone Co., St. Mary (1884). Clustered with Graceville. Sr. Kathleen Henneberry, C.H.M., Pastoral Admin.; Rev. John A. Nordick, (Graceville), Tel: 320-748-7313.
Res., 101 Church St., P.O. Box 299, 56211-0299. Tel: 320-265-6916 (Church); 265-6113 (Rectory). [CEM]
Catechesis/Religious Programs—Students 68.

Bechyn, Renville Co., St. Mary. Closed. For sacramental records contact St. Aloysius, Olivia.

Belgrade, Nicollet Co., St. Michael. Closed. For sacramental records contact St. Paul, Nicollet.

Benson, Swift Co., St. Francis (1881). Clustered with Clontarf, Danvers, De Graff & Murdock. Rev. Steven J. Verhelst Tel: 320-843-2342. Area Pastoral Leaders: Rev. Ronald V. Huberty, (Murdock), Tel: 320-875-2451; Sr. Clara M. Stang, O.S.F., Pastoral Admin. (Danvers), Tel: 320-567-2278; Sr. Darlene Gutenkauf, P.B.V.M., Pastoral Admin. (De Graff), Tel: 320-843-3883.
Area Office—Tel: 320-842-4271; Fax: 320-843-2264.
Church—508 13th St. N., 56215-1228. [CEM]
Catechesis/Religious Programs—Students 241.

Birch Coolie, Renville Co., St. Patrick. Closed. For sacramental records contact Sacred Heart, Franklin.

Bird Island, Renville Co., St. Mary (1879). Clustered with Hector. Rev. Philip M. Schotzko.
Res., 220 S. 10th St., P.O. Box 500, 55310-0500. Tel: 320-365-3593; Fax: 320-365-3142. [CEM]
School—(Grades K-8). Tel: 320-365-3693. Sr. Patricia McCusker, S.S.N.D., Prin.
Sisters 1; Lay Teachers 12; Students 199.
Catechesis/Religious Programs—Students 79.

Canby, Yellow Medicine Co., St. Peter (1897). Clustered with St. Leo. Rev. Paul H. van de Crommert.
Res., 307 W. 4th St., 56220-1211. Tel: 507-223-7304. [CEM]
School—(Grades K-6). Tel: 507-223-7729. Mary Kontz, Prin.
Sisters 1; Lay Teachers 6; Students 96.
Catechesis/Religious Programs—(Grades PreK-10). Tel: 507-223-7304.
Students 189.

Clara City, Chippewa Co., St. Clara (1890). Clustered with Granite Falls. Rev. William A. Sprigler, (Granite Falls), Tel: 320-564-2335; Sr. Ruth Ann Takes, P.B.V.M., Pastoral Admin.
Church—414 N. Main St., P.O. Box 310, 56222-0310. Tel: 320-847-2256. [CEM 2]
Catechesis/Religious Programs—Tel: 320-847-2445.
Students 142.

Clarkfield, Yellow Medicine Co., St. Isidore. Closed. For sacramental records contact St. Joseph, Montevideo.

Clements, Redwood Co., St. Joseph (1902). Clustered with Morgan. Sr. Kathryn Schoolmeesters, S.S.N.D., Pastoral Admin.; Rev. Eugene C. Hackert, (Morgan), Tel: 507-249-3643.
120 Ash St., P.O. Box 56, 56224-0056. Tel: 507-692-2181. [CEM]

Clontarf, Swift Co., St. Malachy (1878). Clustered with Benson, Danvers, De Graff & Murdock. Rev. Steven J. Verhelst, (Benson), Tel: 320-843-2342. Area Pastoral Leaders: Rev. Ronald V. Huberty, (Murdock), Tel: 320-875-2451; Sr. Clara M. Stang, O.S.F., Pastoral Admin. (Danvers), Tel: 320-567-2278; Sr. Darlene Gutenkauf, P.B.V.M., Pastoral Admin. (De Graff), Tel: 320-843-3883.
Area Office—Tel: 320-842-4271.
Church—P.O. Box 218, 56226-0218. Tel: 320-843-2026; 843-2514 (Parish Hall); Fax: 320-843-2264. [CEM]
Catechesis/Religious Programs—Students 85.

Comfrey, Brown Co., St. Paul (1900). Clustered with Leavenworth. Thomas R. Christoffer, Pastoral Admin.; Rev. Mark S. Mallak, (Leavenworth), Tel: 507-794-6974.
Res., 209 N. Field St., P.O. Box 277, 56019-0277. Tel: 507-877-2361. [CEM]
Catechesis/Religious Programs—Students 84.

Cottonwood, Lyon Co., St. Mary (1902). Clustered with Green Valley. Rev. John A. Pearson.
Res., 225 W. 4th St., R.R. 1 Box 17A, 56229-9702. Tel: 507-423-5220; Fax: 507-423-5220. [CEM]
Catechesis/Religious Programs—Students 157.

Danvers, Swift Co., Church of the Visitation (1885). Clustered with Benson, Clontarf, De Graff & Murdock. Sr. Clara M. Stang, O.S.F., Pastoral Admin., Tel: 320-567-2278; Revs. Ronald V. Huberty, (Murdock), Tel: 320-875-2451; Steven J. Verhelst, (Benson), Tel: 320-843-2342; Sr. Darlene Gutenhauf, P.B.V.M., Area Pastoral Leader & Pastoral Admin. (De Graff), Tel: 320-843-3883.
Church—201 County Rd. 14, P.O. Box 18, 56231-0018. Tel: 320-567-2278. [CEM]
Rectory: 201 Washington Ave., 56231.
Area Office—Tel: 320-842-4271; Fax: 320-843-2264.

Darwin, Meeker Co., St. John (1861). Clustered with Forest City. Rev. Frederick T. Fink.
Res., 106 N. 4th St., 55324-9998. Tel: 320-693-6878; 275-2915. [CEM]
Catechesis/Religious Programs—Tel: 320-286-2800.
Students 235.

Dawson, Lac Qui Parle Co., St. James (1898). Clustered with Madison. Sr. Vivian Petersen, O.S.B., Pastoral Admin.; Rev. Robert P. Goblirsch, (Madison), Tel: 320-598-3690.
Res., 10th & Locust, P.O. Box 270, 56232-0270. Tel: 320-769-4465. [CEM]
Catechesis/Religious Programs—Students 109.

De Graff, Swift Co., St. Bridget (1876). Clustered with Benson, Clontarf, Danvers & Murdock. Rev. Ronald V. Huberty, (Murdock), Tel: 320-843-2026; Sr. Darlene Gutenkauf, P.B.V.M., Pastoral Admin. (De Graff), Tel: 320-843-3883. Area Pastoral Leaders: Revs. Ronald V. Huberty, (Murdock), Tel: 320-875-2451; Steven J. Verhelst, (Benson), Tel: 320-843-2342; Sr. Clara M. Stang, O.S.F., Pastoral Admin. (Danvers), Tel: 320-567-2278; Sr. Darlene Gutenkauf, P.B.V.M., Pastoral Admin.
Church—501 3rd St. S., 56271. Tel: 320-843-3883. [CEM]
Area Office—Tel: 320-842-4271; Fax: 320-843-2264.
Catechesis/Religious Programs—St. Bridget Activity Center, 405 5th St. S., DeGraff, 56233. Tel: 320-843-2005.
Students 37.

Eden Valley, Meeker Co., St. Peter (1903). Clustered with Eden Valley - St. Cloud Diocese. Rev. Virgil R. Braun (SCL).
Church—349 State St. S., P.O. Box 9, 55329-0009. Tel: 320-453-2788. [CEM]
Catechesis/Religious Programs—Tel: 320-453-5765.
Students 77.

Fairfax, Renville Co., St. Andrew (1871). Clustered with Franklin. Rev. John H. Brunner, Prin.
Res., 15 S.E. First St., P.O. Box C, 55332-0903. Tel: 507-426-7125; Fax: 507-426-7125. [CEM]
School—(Grades 1-6). Tel: 507-426-7739.
Lay Teachers 4; Students 34.
Catechesis/Religious Programs—Students 140.

Faxon Township, Sibley Co., St. John-Assumption (1859). Clustered with Arlington, Green Isle, Henderson & Jessenland. Sr. Marian Kemper, O.S.B., Pastoral Admin., Tel: 612-873-4390; Rev. Dennis Labat, (Green Isle), Tel: 507-326-5111.
Res., R.R. 2, Box 183, Belle Plaine, 56011-9302. Tel: 320-873-4390. [CEM 2]
Catechesis/Religious Programs—Students 72.

Forest City, Meeker Co., St. Gertrude (1857). Clustered with Darwin. Thomas E. Johnson, Pastoral Admin.; Rev. Frederick T. Fink, (Darwin), Tel: 320-693-6878.
Res., 31626 650th Ave., Litchfield, 55355-9998. Tel: 320-693-7801. [CEM]
Catechesis/Religious Programs—Students 70.

Franklin, Renville Co., Sacred Heart (1898). Clustered with Fairfax. Rev. John H. Brunner, (Fairfax).
Res. & Mailing Address—15 S.E. First St., P.O. Box C, Fairfax, 55332-0903. Tel: 507-426-7125; 557-2413; Fax: 507-426-7125.
Church—P.O. Box 175, 55333-0175. [CEM 2]
Catechesis/Religious Programs—Students 66.

Gaylord, Sibley Co., St. Michael (1882). Clustered with Winthrop. Rev. Richard G. Bonin.
Res., 361 4th St., P.O. Box 357, 55334-0357. Tel: 507-237-2851.
Catechesis/Religious Programs—Tel: 507-237-2888.
Students 104.

Ghent, Lyon Co., St. Eloi (1883). Clustered with Minneota & Taunton. Sr. Carol Quinn, P.B.V.M., Pastoral Admin.; Rev. Gerald A. Hillesheim, (Minneota), Tel: 507-872-6346.
Church—306 W. McQuestion, 56239. Tel: 507-428-3285; Fax: 507-872-5263. [CEM]
Catechesis/Religious Programs—Students 85.

Gibbon, Sibley Co., St. Willibrord (1886), Rev. John G. Berger.
Res., 1032 Ash Ave., 55335-9998. Tel: 507-834-6461. [CEM]
Catechesis/Religious Programs—Students 98.

Glencoe, McLeod Co., St. George. Closed. For sacramental records, contact St. Pius X, Glencoe.
Ss. Peter and Paul. Closed. For sacramental records, contact St. Pius X, Glencoe.
St. Pius X (1983), Rev. Eugene L. Lozinski.
Res., 1014 Knight Ave., 55336-2300. Tel: 320-864-5162; 864-2963 (Rectory). [CEM]
School—(Grades PreK-4). Tel: 320-864-3214; Fax: 320-864-5163. Bill Dingwall, Prin.
Lay Teachers 4; Students 45.
Catechesis/Religious Programs—Students 206.

Graceville, Big Stone Co., Holy Rosary (1878). Clustered with Beardsley. Rev. John A. Nordick; Deacon Art D. Abel Tel: 320-748-7573.
Res., 511 Studdart Ave., P.O. Box 7, 56240-0007. Tel: 320-748-7313.
Catechesis/Religious Programs—517 Studdart Ave., 56240. Tel: 320-748-7501.
Students 198.

Granite Falls, Yellow Medicine Co., St. Andrew (1885). Clustered with Clara City. Rev. William A. Sprigler.
Res., 1094 Granite St., 56241-1355. Tel: 320-564-2335; Fax: 320-564-2336. [CEM]
Catechesis/Religious Programs—1056 Fourth St., 56241. Tel: 320-564-2336.
Students 183.

Green Isle, Sibley Co., St. Brendan (1854). Clustered with Arlington, Faxon Township, Henderson & Jessenland. Rev. Dennis C. Labat, Parochial Admin.
Res., 221 McGrann St. S., P.O. Box 85, 55338-0085. Tel: 507-326-5111. [CEM]
Catechesis/Religious Programs—Students 92.

Green Valley, Lyon Co., St. Clotilde (1912). Clustered with Cottonwood. Rev. John A. Pearson, (Cottonwood).
Church—R.R. 3, Marshall, 56258-8903. Tel: 507-532-2841.
Res., 225 W. 4th St., R.R. 1, P.O. Box 17A, Cottonwood, 56229-9702. Tel: 507-423-5220; Fax: 507-423-5220. [CEM]
Catechesis/Religious Programs—Students 71.

Greenleaf, Meeker Co., St. Columban. Closed. For inquiries for sacramental records contact St. Philip, Litchfield.

Hector, Renville Co., Church of St. John (1878). Clustered with Bird Island. Sr. Sharon Nohner, O.S.B., Pastoral Admin.; Rev. Philip M. Schotzko, (Bird Island), Tel: 320-365-3593.
Church—301 Cedar Ave., E., P.O. Box 295, 55342-0295. Tel: 320-848-6437. [CEM]
Catechesis/Religious Programs—Students 104.

Hegbert, Swift Co., St. Agnes. Closed. For sacramental records, contact St. John, Appleton.

Henderson, Sibley Co., St. Joseph (1859). Clustered with Arlington, Faxon Township, Green Isle & Jessenland. Sr. Jovann Irrgang, S.S.N.D., Pastoral Admin.; Rev. James D. Barry, (Arlington), Tel: 507-964-5413.
Res., 213 S. 6th St., P.O. Box 427, 56044-0427. Tel: 507-248-3550. [CEM]
Catechesis/Religious Programs—Students 89.
Mission—Jessenland, St. Thomas.

Holloway, Swift Co., St. Joseph. Closed. For sacramental records, contact St. John, Appleton.

Hutchinson, McLeod Co., Church of St. Anastasia (1866). Clustered with Stewart. Revs. Dennis E. Becker; James W. Devorak.
Res., 460 Lake St., S.W., 55350-2349. Tel: 320-587-6507; Fax: 320-234-6756. [CEM]
School—(Grades PreK-6). Tel: 320-587-2490. Sr. Joyce Willenbring, O.S.B., Prin.
Sisters 1; Lay Teachers 14; Students 245.
Catechesis/Religious Programs—Students 411.

Ivanhoe, Lincoln Co., SS. Peter & Paul (1900). Clustered with Wilmo. Rev. David L. Breu.
Res., 111 N. Sherwood, P.O. Box 49, 56142-0049. Tel: 507-694-1402; Fax: 507-694-1437. [CEM]
Catechesis/Religious Programs—Rte. 1, Box 59, 56142. Tel: 507-694-1225; Fax: 507-694-1548. Sr. M. Ellen Hoemberg, I.S.S.M.
Students 125.

Jessenland, Sibley Co., St. Thomas (Mission) (1856). Clustered with Arlington, Faxon Township, Green Isle, & Henderson. Sr. Jovann Irrgang, S.S.N.D., Pastoral Admin.; Rev. James D. Barry, (Arlington), Tel: 507-964-5413.
Res., 213 S. Sixth St., P.O. Box 427, Henderson, 56044-0427. Tel: 507-248-3550. [CEM]

Kandiyohi, Kandiyohi Co., St. Patrick (1868). Clustered with Lake Lillian. Rev. Paul A. Schumacher, Parochial Admin.
Res., 245 3rd St. E., P.O. Box 164, 56251-0164. Tel: 320-382-6424. [CEM 2]
Catechesis/Religious Programs—Students 216.

Lafayette, Nicollet Co., St. Gregory the Great (1942). Clustered with West Newton Township. Rev. James E. Moran.
Res., 440 6th St., P.O. Box 5, 56054-0005. Tel: 507-228-8298. [CEM]
Catechesis/Religious Programs—Students 114.

Lake Benton, Lincoln Co., St. Genevieve (1897). Clustered with Tyler. Rev. Michael M. Doyle, (Tyler), Tel: 507-247-3464.
Res., 513 E. Hughes St., P.O. 310, Tyler, 56178-0310. Tel: 507-247-5167.
Mailing Address: 119 S. Sherman St., P.O. Box 348, 56149-0348. Tel: 507-368-4232. [CEM]
Catechesis/Religious Programs—Tel: 507-368-4232.
Students 80.

Lake Lillian, Kandiyohi Co., St. Thomas More (1934). Clustered with Kandiyohi. Rev. Paul A. Schumacher, Parochial Admin., (Kandiyohi) Tel: 320-382-6424.
Res., 245 3rd St. E., P.O. Box 164, Kandiyohi, 56251-0164. Tel: 320-382-6424.
Church—840 Second St. E., P.O. Box 57, 56253-0057. Tel: 320-664-4810.
Catechesis/Religious Programs—Students 55.

Lamberton, Redwood Co., St. Joseph (1895). Clustered with Sanborn and Wanda. Sr. Pauline Micke, O.S.B., Pastoral Admin.; Rev. Bernard J. Steiner, Sacramental Min. (Wanda), Tel: 507-752-7523; 342-5451.
Res., 400 W. 2nd Ave., P.O. Box 458, 56152-0458. Tel: 507-752-7269. [CEM]
Catechesis/Religious Programs—Students 84.

Leavenworth, Brown Co., Church of the Japanese Martyrs (1867) (German). Clustered with Comfrey. Rev. Mark S. Mallak.
Res., R.R. 2, Box 93 (Leavenworth), Sleepy Eye, 56085-9624. Tel: 507-794-6974; Fax: 507-794-6972. [CEM]
Catechesis/Religious Programs—Tel: 507-794-6460.
Students 69.

Lester Prairie, McLeod Co., St. Conrad. Closed. Incorporated but never organized. No sacramental records.

Litchfield, Meeker Co., St. Philip (1859), Rev. Peter C. Nosbush.
Res., 306 N. Holcombe Ave., 55355-2223. Tel: 320-693-3313. [CEM]
School—(Grades K-4). Tel: 320-693-6283. Teresa Hankins, Prin.
Lay Teachers 8; Students 84.
Catechesis/Religious Programs—225 E. Third St., 55355.
Students 339.

Lucan, Redwood Co., Our Lady of Victory (1889). Clustered with Milroy. Rev. Merle W. Monnens, Parochial Admin.
Res., P.O. Box 96, 56255-0096. Tel: 507-747-2231. [CEM]
School—(Grades 1-6) 301 3rd St, 56255-0096. Tel: 507-747-2233; Fax: 507-747-2160. Mary Ann Kramer, Prin.
Lay Teachers 3; Students 19.

Madison, Lac Qui Parle Co., St. Michael (1884). Clustered with Dawson. Rev. Robert P. Goblirsch.
Res., 412 3rd St., 56256-1494. Tel: 320-598-3690. [CEM]
Catechesis/Religious Programs—Tel: 320-598-3690.
Students 149.

Manannah, Meeker Co., Church of Our Lady (1876), Rev. Francis J. Garvey.
Res., 57382 CSAH 3, Grove City, 56243-9786. Tel: 320-693-8900; 453-7526. [CEM]
Catechesis/Religious Programs—Students 73.

Marshall, Lyon Co., Holy Redeemer (1883), Revs. Gerald S. Meidl; Celestine C. Pistulka; Brian L. Mandel.
Res., 503 W. Lyon St., 56258-1390. Tel: 507-532-5711; Fax: 507-532-5712. [CEM]
School—(Grades K-8). Tel: 507-532-6642. Barbara Wood, Prin.
Lay Teachers 23; Students 394.
Catechesis/Religious Programs—503 S. Whitney St., 56258. Tel: 507-532-3602. D.R.E.: Patti Watkins, (Grades K-6); Mary Beth Johnson, (Grades 7-12).
Students 488.

Middle Lake, Nicollet Co., St. Nicholas. Closed. For sacramental records, contact St. Paul's, Nicollet.

Milroy, Redwood Co., St. Michael (1904). Clustered with Lucan. Sr. Justin Wirth, S.S.N.D., Pastoral Admin.; Rev. Merle W. Monnens, (Lucan), Tel: 507-747-2231.
Res., P.O. Box 117, 56263-0117. Tel: 507-336-2505. [CEM]
Catechesis/Religious Programs—Students 148.

Minneota, Lyon Co., St. Edward (1880). Clustered with Ghent & Taunton. Rev. Gerald A. Hillesheim.
Res., R.R. 1, Box 431, 56264-9801. Tel: 507-872-6346; Fax: 507-872-5263. [CEM]
Church—409 N. Adams St., 56264-9801.
School—(Grades 1-8). Tel: 507-872-6391. Mrs. Carol J. DeSmet, Prin.
Lay Teachers 9; Students 123.
Catechesis/Religious Programs—Students 210.

Montevideo, Chippewa Co., St. Joseph (1882), Rev. Jerome E. Paulson.
Res., 521 Eureka Ave., 56265-1899. Tel: 320-269-8623; Fax: 320-269-7555. [CEM]
Church—512 Black Oak Ave., 56265-1874. Tel: 320-269-5954.
Catechesis/Religious Programs—Students 241.

Morgan, Redwood Co., St. Michael (1887). Clustered with Clements. Rev. Eugene C. Hackert.
Res., 514 W. 3rd St., P.O. Box 443, 56266-0443. Tel: 507-249-3643. [CEM]
School—(Grades 1-6) 612 W. 3rd St., P.O. Box 443, 56266-0443. Tel: 507-249-3192. Sr. Gladys Meindl, O.S.F., Prin.
Sisters 1; Lay Teachers 5; Students 68.
Catechesis/Religious Programs—Tel: 507-692-2181.
Students 110.

Morton, Renville Co., St. John (1873). Clustered with Redwood Falls. Sr. Jo Anne Backes, O.S.B., Pastoral Admin.; Rev. Germain P. Rademacher, (Redwood Falls), Tel: 507-637-8114.

Res., 341 W. 3rd St, P.O. Box 88, 56270-0088. Tel: 507-697-6120. [CEM]
Catechesis/Religious Programs—Students 66.

Murdock, Swift Co., Church of the Sacred Heart (1879). Clustered with Benson, Clontarf, Danvers & De Graff. Rev. Ronald V. Huberty, (Murdock). Area Pastoral Leaders: Rev. Steven J. Verhelst, (Benson), Tel: 320-843-2342; Sr. Clara M. Stang, O.S.F., (Danvers), Tel: 320-567-2278; Sr. Darlene Gutenkauf, P.B.V.M., (De Graff), Tel: 320-843-3883.
Res., 201 Orleans, P.O. Box 9, 56271-0009. Tel: 320-875-2451; 842-4271 (Area Office); Fax: 320-843-2264. [CEM]
Catechesis/Religious Programs—Students 127.

Nassau, Lac Qui Parle Co., St. James (1902). Clustered with Ortonville and Rosen. Rev. Andrew J. Michels, (Ortonville).
Res. & Mailing Address: 421 Madison Ave., P.O. Box 205, Ortonville, 56278-0205. Tel: 320-839-2772. [CEM]

Nicollet, Nicollet Co., St. Paul (1907), Rev. William H. Bowles.
Res., 411 5th St., P.O. Box 248, 56074-0248. Tel: 507-225-3857. [CEM 4]
Catechesis/Religious Programs—Students 135.

Swan Lake, Nicollet Co., The Church of the Visitation. Closed. For sacramental records, contact St. Paul, Nicollet.

North Mankato, Nicollet Co., Holy Rosary (1924), Rev. Edward J. Ardolf.
Res., 525 Grant Ave., 56003-2939. Tel: 507-387-6501; Fax: 507-388-2017.
School—546 Grant Ave., 56003-0698. Tel: 507-345-6765. Jim Rouse, Supt.
School is part of Mankato Area Catholic Schools, Diocese of Winona. Numbers are reported by Winona Diocese.
Catechesis/Religious Programs—Students 398.

Olivia, Renville Co., St. Aloysius (1888). Clustered with Renville. Rev. Patrick L. Casey.
Res., 302 S. 10th St., 56277-1288. Tel: 320-523-2030. [CEM 2]
Catechesis/Religious Programs—Tel: 320-523-2030.
Students 290.

Ortonville, Big Stone Co., St. John (1879). Clustered with Nassau & Rosen. Rev. Andrew J. Michels.
Res., P.O. Box 205, 421 Madison Ave., 56278-0205. Tel: 320-839-2772.
Catechesis/Religious Programs—Tel: 320-839-2873.
Students 151.

Raymond, Kandiyohi Co., Sacred Heart. Closed. For sacramental records, contact St. Clara, Clara City.

Redwood Falls, Redwood Co., St. Catherine (1870). Clustered with Morton. Rev. Germain P. Rademacher.
Church—900 E. Flynn St., P.O. Box 383, 56283-0383. Tel: 507-637-2278; Fax: 507-637-2643. [CEM]
Res., 904 E. Flynn St., P.O. Box 383, 56283-0383. Tel: 507-637-8114.
Catechesis/Religious Programs—Students 385.

Regal, Kandiyohi Co., St. Anthony (Mission) (1933). Clustered with Spicer. Rev. Felix J. Fasching, (Spicer).
Res., 13722 Hwy. 23 N.E., Spicer, 56288-9659. Tel: 320-796-5664. [CEM]
Catechesis/Religious Programs—Students 34.

Renville, Renville Co., Holy Redeemer (1891). Clustered with Olivia. Donald A. Clasemann, Pastoral Admin.; Rev. Patrick L. Casey, (Olivia), Tel: 320-523-2030.
Church—106 S.E. 3rd St., P.O. Box 401, 56284-0401. Tel: 320-329-3884. [CEM]
Catechesis/Religious Programs—Tel: 320-329-8219.
Students 173.

Rosen, Lac Qui Parle Co., St. Joseph (1885). Clustered with Nassau & Ortonville. Rev. Andrew J. Michels, (Ortonville).
Res. & Mailing Address: 421 Madison Ave., P.O. Box 205, Ortonville, 56278-0205. Tel: 320-839-2772. [CEM]
Catechesis/Religious Programs—Tel: 320-568-2428.
Students 60.

St. Leo, Yellow Medicine Co., St. Leo (1881). Clustered with Canby. Rev. Paul H. van de Crommert, (Canby), Tel: 507-223-7304.
Church—202 W. Church St., 56286-0114. Tel: 507-224-2289. [CEM]

St. Peter, Nicollet Co., St. Peter (1856), Rev. Harry P. Behan; Kay Osborne, Pastoral Assoc.
Res., 524 W. Myrtle St., P.O. Box 522, 56082-0522. Tel: 507-931-1628; Fax: 507-931-2977. [CEM]
School—John Ireland School, (Grades K-6) 618 S. 5th, 56082-1412. Tel: 507-931-2810. Ms. Brenda Lenertz, Prin.
Lay Teachers 10; Students 127.
Catechesis/Religious Programs—Tel: 507-931-4162. D.R.E.: Sr. Thomasin Sergot; Sr. Donna Walerius Tel: 507-931-3662.
Students 388.

Immaculate Conception. Closed. For sacramental records, contact St. Peter's, St. Peter.

Sanborn, Redwood Co., St. Thomas (1902). Clustered with Lamberton & Wanda. Sr. Jeanette Homan, O.S.F., Pastoral Admin.; Rev. Bernard J. Steiner, (Wanda), Tel: 507-752-7523; 342-5451.
Res., 311 E. Winona St., P.O. Box 176, 56083-0176. Tel: 507-648-3754.
Catechesis/Religious Programs—Students 58.

Seaforth, Redwood Co., St. Mary (1880). Clustered with Wabasso. Rev. Paul L. Wolf, (Wabasso).
Res., P.O. Box 239, Wabasso, 56293-0239. Tel: 507-342-5190; 984-5411 (Church); 342-5155 (Rectory). [CEM 2]

Searles, Brown Co., St. John the Baptist (1905) (German). Clustered with Cathedral, New Ulm. Sr. Monica Wagner, S.S.N.D., Pastoral Admin.; Rev. George V. Schmit, Jr., (New Ulm, Cathedral), Tel: 507-354-4158.
113 First Ave. S., P.O. Box 113, 56084-0113. Tel: 507-359-4244. [CEM]
School—New Ulm Area Catholic Schools. See separate listing for details. Tel: 507-354-2719; Fax: 507-354-5711.
Catechesis/Religious Programs—Tel: 507-354-4158; Fax: 507-354-2563.
Students 29.

Silver Lake, McLeod Co., St. Adalbert. Closed. For sacramental records, contact Holy Family, Silver Lake.

St. Joseph. Closed. For sacramental records, contact Holy Family, Silver Lake.

Church of the Holy Family (1993), Rev. Robert J. Mraz.
Res., 720 W. Main St., P.O. Box 326, 55381-0326. Tel: 320-327-2261; Fax: 320-327-2261. [CEM 4]
School—Silver Lake Catholic School, (Grades PreK-6) 700 Main St., P.O. Box 346, 55381-0346. Tel: 320-327-2356.
Lay Teachers 7; Students 94.
Catechesis/Religious Programs—Tel: 320-327-2931; 327-2930.
Students 208.

Sleepy Eye, Brown Co., St. Mary (1876), Rev. John A. Richter.
Res., 636 First Ave. N., 56085-1004. Tel: 507-794-4171; Fax: 507-794-5871. [CEM]
School—(Grades PreK-6). Tel: 507-794-6141; Fax: 507-794-4841. Mr. Wayne Pelzel, Prin.
Sisters 1; Lay Teachers 20; Students 386.
High School—(Grades 7-12). Tel: 507-794-4121. Mr. Jerry Neubauer, Prin.
Sisters 1; Lay Teachers 20; Students 287.
Catechesis/Religious Programs—Tel: 507-794-4067.
Students 183.

Spicer, Kandiyohi Co., Our Lady of the Lakes (1962). Clustered with Regal. Rev. Felix J. Fasching.
Res., 13722 Hwy. 23 N.E., 56288-9659. Tel: 320-796-5664. [CEM]
Catechesis/Religious Programs—Tel: 320-796-5968.
Students 327.

Springfield, Brown Co., St. Raphael (1874) (German & Irish), Rev. Darold R. Lehman.
Res., 112 W. Van Dusen St., 56087-1396. Tel: 507-723-4727; Fax: 507-723-4290. [CEM]
School—(Grades K-6). Tel: 507-723-4291; Fax: 507-723-5409. Sr. Therese Colison, S.S.N.D., Prin.
Sisters 2; Lay Teachers 7; Students 93.
Catechesis/Religious Programs—Tel: 507-723-4293.
Students 266.

Stewart, McLeod Co., Church of St. Boniface (1877). Clustered with Hutchinson. Sr. Idamarie Primus, O.S.B., Pastoral Admin.; Rev. James W. Devorak, (Hutchinson), Tel: 320-587-6507.
Res., 551 Main St., P.O. Box 202, 55385-0202. Tel: 320-562-2344. [CEM]
Catechesis/Religious Programs—Students 78.

Swan Lake, Nicollet Co., Visitation. Closed. For sacramental records, contact St. Paul, Nicollet.

Taunton, Lyon Co., SS. Cyril and Methodius (1895) (Polish-Belgian-German). Clustered with Ghent & Minneota. Sr. Roselle Zollar, S.S.N.D., Pastoral Admin.; Rev. Gerald A. Hillesheim, (Minneota), Tel: 507-872-6346.
Res., Lincoln St., P.O. Box 368, 56291-0368. Tel: 507-872-5150. [CEM 2][JC 2]
Catechesis/Religious Programs—Students 37.

Tracy, Lyon Co., St. Mary (1880). Clustered with Walnut Grove. Rev. Douglas L. Grams.
Res., 249 6th St., 56175-1114. Tel: 507-629-3227; Fax: 507-629-4075. [CEM]
Church—285 6th St., 56175. Tel: 507-629-3841 (Church Hall).
School—(Grades K-6). Tel: 507-629-3270. Mrs. Irene Palzer, Prin.
Lay Teachers 8; Students 71.
Catechesis/Religious Programs—Tel: 507-629-3667.
Students 149.

Tyler, Lincoln Co., St. Dionysius (1880). Clustered with Lake Benton. Rev. Michael M. Doyle.
Res., 513 E. Hughes St., P.O. Box 310, 56178-0310. Tel: 507-247-5167; 247-3464 (Office). [CEM]
Church—213 Linwood St., 56178. Tel: 507-247-5807.
Catechesis/Religious Programs—Tel: 507-247-5807; 368-4232.
Students 148.

Vesta, Redwood Co., Holy Name. Closed. For sacramental records, contact St. Catherine's, Redwood Falls.

Wabasso, Redwood Co., St. Anne (1900). Clustered with Seaforth. Rev. Paul L. Wolf.
Res., P.O. Box 239, 1021 Cedar St., 56293-0239. Tel: 507-342-5155; 342-5190 (Office). [CEM]
School—(Grades K-6). Tel: 507-345-5389. Rev. Paul L. Wolf, Prin.
Lay Teachers 7; Students 136.
Catechesis/Religious Programs—Tel: 507-342-5190.
Students 141.

Walnut Grove, Redwood Co., St. Paul (1902) (German). Clustered with Tracy. Rev. Douglas L. Grams, (Tracy), Tel: 507-629-3227.
Res., 600 3rd St., P.O. Box 236, 56180-0236. Tel: 507-859-2164. [CEM]

Wanda, Redwood Co., St. Mathias (1871). Clustered with Lamberton & Sanborn. Rev. Bernard J. Steiner.
Res., 308 St. Mathias Blvd., P.O. Box 308, 56294-0308. Tel: 507-342-5451; 752-7523. [CEM]
Catechesis/Religious Programs—Students 61.

Watkins, Meeker Co., Church of St. Anthony (1889) (German), Rev. Richard C. Gross.
Res., 171 Central Ave. S., P.O. Box 439, 55389-0439. Tel: 320-764-2755. [CEM]
Catechesis/Religious Programs—Tel: 320-764-5722.
Students 221.

West Newton Township, Nicollet Co., St. George (1857) (German). Clustered with Lafayette. Rev. James E. Moran, (Lafayette).
Church—Tel: 507-228-8298.
Res., P.O. Box 5, 440 6th St., Lafayette, 56054-0005. Tel: 507-228-8298; 359-9013. [CEM]
Catechesis/Religious Programs—Students 10.

Willmar, Kandiyohi Co., St. Mary (1871), Revs. Joseph A. Steinbeisser; Jeffrey P. Horejsi; Deacon Jack Herzog Tel: 612-235-5535.
Church—713 12th St., S.W., 56201-3099. Tel: 320-235-0118; Fax: 320-235-0153. [CEM]
Res., 56201-3025. Tel: 320-235-6365.
Catechesis/Religious Programs—Tel: 320-235-3982.
Students 759.

Wilno, Lincoln Co., St. John Cantius (1883). Clustered with Ivanhoe. Rev. David L. Breu, (Ivanhoe).
Res., R.R. 1, Box 59, Ivanhoe, 56142. Tel: 507-694-1225; 694-1402; Fax: 507-694-1548. [CEM]
Catechesis/Religious Programs—Sr. Ellen M. Hoemberg, I.S.S.M.
Students 180.

Winsted, McLeod Co., Holy Trinity (1869) (German), Rev. Robert J. Wyffels.
Res., 111 Winsted Ave., W., P.O. Box 9, 55395-0009. Tel: 320-485-4421; Fax: 320-485-4283. [CEM 2]
School—(Grades PreK-6). Tel: 320-485-2314. Mrs. Ann Brown, Prin.
Lay Teachers 11; Students 215.
High School—(Grades 7-12). Tel: 320-485-2182. Rev. Robert J. Wyffels, Supt.; Mr. Stephen Byrne, Prin.
Lay Teachers 12; Students 164.
Catechesis/Religious Programs—Students 157.

Winthrop, Sibley Co., St. Francis de Sales (1906). Clustered with St. Michael's, Gaylord. Rev. Richard G. Bonin.
Res., 361 4th St., P.O. Box 357, Gaylord, 55334-0357. Tel: 507-237-2851.
Church—P.O. Box 447, 55396-0447. Tel: 507-647-5334.
Catechesis/Religious Programs—P.O. Box F, 55396. Tel: 507-647-5894. Pam Osborne, D.R.E.
Students 63.

Chaplains of Public Institutions

IVANHOE. *Divine Providence Hospital & Home.* Rev. Marion G. Casey, Chap.

WILLMAR. *Regional Treatment Center.* Rev. Francis J. Garvey, Chap.

WINSTED. *St. Mary's Care Center.* Rev. Martin Rath, O.S.B., Chap.

On Special or Other Diocesan Assignment:

Reverend Fathers—

Labat, Dennis C.

Stubeda, Anthony J.

On Duty Outside the Diocese:

Reverend Monsignors—

Schaffer, Gregory T., Parroquia San Lucas Toliman, Depto. Solola 07013, Guatemala. Tel: 011-502-722-0112; Fax: 011-502-722-0112

Reverend Fathers—

Goggin, John T., Parroquia San Lucas Toliman, Depto. Solola, 07013 Guatemala. Tel: 011-502-722-0112; Fax: 011-502-722-0112

Hansen, Lawrence H., Mercy Catholic Medical Center, Lansdowne Ave. & Baily Rd., Darby, PA 19023. Tel: 215-237-4000

Martinka, Stanley V., San Alfonso Mission, 1218 Lonewood, El Paso, TX 79925. Tel: 915-598-0900

Mead, Leland C., R.R. 1, Box 47, Madison Lake, MN 56063-9706. Tel: 507-243-3868

Plathe, Anthony H., 9501 McIntosh Dr., El Paso, TX 79925. Tel: 915-591-0939; Fax: 915-595-0734

Military Chaplains:

Reverend Monsignors—

Thomas, Arthur S., Chap. Maj. Gen. & Chief of Air Force Chap. Svc., HQ USAF/HC Bldg. 5683, Washington, DC 20332-5000. Tel: 202-767-4577

Reverend Fathers—

Wagener, John M., Lt. Col. (Retired), 117 E. Summit Ave., San Antonio, TX 78212-2953

Absent on Leave:

Reverend Fathers—

Berg, John Leonard, 960 Stonebridge Rd., Apt. 5, Platteville, WI 53818. Tel: 608-348-9447

Clark, Robert P., Jr., 548 Lafond Ave., St. Paul, MN 55103-1672. Tel: 612-293-1710

Retired:

Reverend Monsignors—

Berg, Arnold J., 107 W. Lincoln, Springfield, MN 56087-1302. Tel: 507-723-6316

Leifeld, Antony J., 717 6th St. N., New Ulm, MN 56073-1853. Tel: 507-359-9848

Ward, John C., Leo C. Byrne Residence, 60 S. Mississippi Blvd., Apt. 225, St. Paul, MN 55105-1052. Tel: 612-698-8175

Reverend Fathers—

Adrian, Stephen J., 10410 E. Twilight Dr., Sun Lakes, AZ 85248. Tel: 602-895-0465

Brandes, John F. (STP), Parroquia San Lucas Toliman, Depto. Solola 07013, Guatemala. Tel: 011-502-722-0112; Fax: 011-502-722-0112

Casey, Marion G., Divine Providence Health Center, 312 E. George, Box G, Ivanhoe, MN 56142-0136. Tel: 507-694-1414

Cepress, Adalbert J., Woodbury Health Care Center, 7012 Lake Rd., Woodbury, MN 55125-2499. Tel: 612-735-6000

Exley, Thomas G., 1128 Iowa Ave. W., St. Paul, MN 55108-2242. Tel: 612-489-3562

Fleming, John R., Gallery Towers Apt. 801, 26 W. 10th St., St. Paul, MN 55102-1038. Tel: 612-228-1717

Gleason, John L., 43601 Florida Ave., Lot 13, Hemet, CA 92544-5259. Tel: 909-927-2729

Gorman, Paul J., P.O. Box 983, Winnebago, MN 56098-0983. Tel: 507-854-3103

Guetter, Michael A., R.R. 2, Box 2A4B, Wabasso, MN 56293-9998. Tel: 507-342-5201

Guillemette, Arthur T., Oak Terrace Senior Apartments, Apt. 11, 640 Third St., P.O. Box 386, Gaylord, MN 55334-0386. Tel: 507-237-5586

Hayden, Ralph W., R.R.3, Box 110, Le Sueur, MN 56058-9428. Tel: 507-665-4143

Irrgang, Kenneth E., 740 14th St. S., Apt. 13, St. Cloud, MN 56301-5518. Tel: 320-654-1008

Jenniges, Leonard J. (STP), R.R. 2 Box 142, Sanborn, MN 56083. Tel: 507-342-5134

Karels, Agdus S. (STP), 513 4th St. N.W., Ortonville, MN 56278-1305. Tel: 320-839-3766

Kasel, Joseph M., 701 Madison St., Apt. A-1, Minneota, MN 56264-9801. Tel: 507-872-6289

Krystosek, Robert H. (GI), P.O. Box 425, Clara City, MN 56222-0425. Tel: 320-847-2615

McGowan, Myles P., Leo C. Byrne Residence, 60 S. Mississippi River Blvd., Apt. 223, St. Paul, MN 55105. Tel: 612-690-9002

Merth, Robert J., 19414 Cedar Island Ct., Richmond, MN 56368-8300. Tel: 320-597-3788

Murphy, John M., 390 Cottage Ave. W., Apt. 33, St. Paul, MN 55117-4251. Tel: 612-487-9821

O'Connor, Michael F., Church of St. Joseph, 23945 Nicolai Ave. E., Hastings, MN 55033-9650. Tel: 612-437-3526

O'Connor, Richard T., 2001 Stanford Ave., St. Paul, MN 55105-1657. Tel: 612-699-1966

Penzimas, Joseph A., 3746 3rd St. N.E., Columbia Heights, MN 55421-3736. Tel: 612-781-6499

Roney, David A., Parroquia San Lucas Toliman, Depto. Solola 07013, Guatemala. Tel: 011-502-722-0112; Fax: 011-502-722-0112

Schaefer, Roman J., Church of Our Lady Queen of Martyrs, 2731 S.W. 11th Ct., Ft. Lauderdale, FL 33312-2901. Tel: 305-583-8725

Schreiner, Bernard P., Watkins Retirement Center, 341 4th St. N., P.O. Box 246, Watkins, MN 55389-0246. Tel: 320-764-2894

Schwinn, Alexander L., Leo C. Byrne Residence, 60 S. Mississippi River Blvd., Apt. 319, St. Paul, MN 55105-1000. Tel: 612-690-4111

Siebenand, Ambrose F., Benedict Village, 2000 15th Ave., S.E., Apt. 314, St. Cloud, MN 56304-2423. Tel: 320-253-2655

Siebenand, John N., Benedict Village, 2000 15th Ave., S.E., Apt. 313, St. Cloud, MN 56304-2423. Tel: 320-253-2655

Wojtowicz, Edward L., Leo C. Byrne Residence, 60 S. Mississippi River Blvd., Apt. 310, St. Paul, MN 55105. Tel: 612-698-6926

INSTITUTIONS LOCATED IN THE DIOCESE

[A] NEW ULM AREA CATHOLIC SCHOOLS

NEW ULM. *New Ulm Area Catholic Schools,* 515 N. State St., 56073-1897. Tel: 507-354-2719; Fax: 507-354-5711. David Schieffert, Supt. Consolidated: The five schools consolidated under the above title are as follows:

Edu Care Pre-School and Daycare, 527 S. Minnesota, 56073. Tel: 507-359-7331. Jean Nielsen, Dir.

St. John's Elementary School, P.O. Box 198, Searles, 56084-0198. Tel: 507-359-4511. Kris Hodapp, Head Teacher.

St. Mary's Elementary School, 519 S. Minnesota St., 56073-2199. Tel: 507-354-2928. Paul Schieffert, Head Teacher.

Holy Trinity Middle School, 515 N. State St., 56073-1897. Tel: 507-354-4311. Sr. Sharon Waldoch, S.S.N.D., Elementary Prin.

Cathedral High School, 600 N. Washington St., 56073-1897. Tel: 507-354-4511. Paul Klinkhammer, Prin.
High School: Sisters 1; Lay Teachers 18; Students 225.
Elementary: Sisters 1; Lay Teachers 32; Students 495.

[B] GENERAL HOSPITALS

GRACEVILLE. *Graceville Health Center dba Holy Trinity Hospital and Grace Home,* 115 W. 2nd St., 56240-0157. Tel: 320-748-7223
For a complete listing, refer to the Hospitals section.

IVANHOE. *Divine Providence Health Center,* 312 E. George St., P.O. Box G, 56142-0136. Tel: 507-694-1414; Fax: 507-694-1191
For a complete listing, refer to the Hospitals section.

WINSTED. *St. Mary's Care Center,* 551 4th St. N., P.O. Box 750, 55395-0750. Tel: 320-485-2151; Fax: 320-485-4241
For a complete listing, refer to the Hospitals section.

[C] HOMES FOR AGED

SLEEPY EYE. *Divine Providence Community Home & Lake Villa Maria Senior Apts.,* 700 3rd Ave. N.W., 56085-1099. Tel: 507-794-3011; 794-5333.
E-mail: divine@prairie.lake.com
For a complete listing, refer to the Special Care Facilities section.

[D] RETREAT HOUSES

BIRD ISLAND. *Center for Spiritual Development,* P.O. Box 538, 211 S. 10th St., 55310-0538. Tel: 320-365-3644; Fax: 320-365-4042.
E-mail: ctrbl@aol.com
Co-Directors: Sr. Marjorie Klein, S.S.N.D.; Sr. Janet Mallak, S.S.N.D. Total in Residence 5; Total Staff 6.

SLEEPY EYE. *Schoenstatt Sisters of Mary,* R.R. 1, Box 247, 56085-9436. Tel: 507-794-7727; 794-5622. Sr. Marie Day, I.S.S.M., Dir.; Sr. M. Donna Krzmarzick, Maintenance; Sr. M. Alice Kunz, I.S.S.M., Librarian; Sr. Rita Marie Otto, I.S.S.M., Supr.; Sr. M. Danielle Peters, I.S.S.M., Coord.

[E] YOUTH CENTERS

NEW ULM. *Center for Youth Ministry,* c/o Catholic Pastoral Center, 1400 6th St. N., 56073-2099. Tel: 507-359-2966. Bill Casey, Dir. Youth Ministry.

[F] HEALTH CARE CENTERS

ST. PETER. *St. Peter Regional Treatment Center,* 100 Freeman Dr., 56082-1599. Tel: 507-931-7104
For a complete listing, refer to the Hospitals section.

[G] MISCELLANEOUS

GRACEVILLE. *Graceville Missionary Benedictine Sisters, Inc.,* 116 W. 3rd St., P.O. Box 276, 56240-0276. Tel: 320-748-7223; 748-7128 (Convent); Fax: 320-748-7225. Sisters 4.

WILLMAR. *Willmar Regional Treatment Center,* 1550 Hwy. 71 N.E., 56201-1128. Tel: 320-231-5100; Fax: 320-231-5329. Rev. Francis J. Garvey, Chap.; Sr. Cecile Schueller, S.S.N.D., Chap. Patients assisted annually 1,200; Total Staff 400.

RELIGIOUS INSTITUTES OF MEN REPRESENTED IN THE DIOCESE

For further details refer to the corresponding bracketed number in the Religious Institutes of Men or Women Section.

[0200]—*Benedictine Monks.* (Collegeville, MN).—O.S.B.

RELIGIOUS INSTITUTES OF WOMEN REPRESENTED IN THE DIOCESE

[0230]—*Benedictine Sisters of Pontifical Jurisdiction.* (St. Joseph, MN; Federation of St. Benedict, Duluth, MN; Crookston, MN).—O.S.B.

[2100]—*Congregation of the Humility of Mary.* (Davenport, IA).—C.H.M.

[0940]—*Daughters of St. Mary of Providence.* (Chicago, IL).—D.S.M.P.

[1310]—*Francisan Sisters of Little Falls, Minnesota.* (Little Falls, MN).—O.S.F.

[0210]—*Missionary Benedictine Sisters.* (Norfolk, NE).—O.S.B.

[]—*Schoenstatt Sisters of Mary.* (Waukesha, WI).

[2970]—*School Sisters of Notre Dame.* (Mankato, MN).—S.S.N.D.

[1680]—*School Sisters of St. Francis.* (Milwaukee, WI).—O.S.F.

[1070-03]—*Sinsinawa Dominicans.* (Sinsinawa, WI).—O.P.

[1570]—*Sisters of St. Francis of the Holy Family.* (Dubuque, IA).—O.S.F.

[3840]—*Sisters of St. Joseph of Carondelet.* (St. Paul, MN).—C.S.J.

[]—*Sisters of St. Joseph of La Grange.* (La Grange Park, IL).—C.S.J.

[3320]—*Sisters of the Presentation of the B.V.M.* (Aberdeen, SD).—P.B.V.M.

[1720]—*Sisters of the Third Order Regular of St. Francis of the Congregation of Our Lady of Lourdes.* (Rochester, MN).—O.S.F.

[]—*Sisters of St. Francis of Assisi.* (Milwaukee, WI).—O.S.F.

NECROLOGY

† Hesse, Harold W., (Retired). —Died Sept. 20, 1997.

† Zwicky, Richard C., (Retired). —Died Dec. 7, 1996.

IUBILAEUM
CHRISTUS HERI
HODIE SEMPER
A.D. 2000

Archdiocese of New York

(Archidioecesis Neo-Eboracensis)

His Eminence

JOHN CARDINAL O'CONNOR, D.D., PH.D.

Archbishop of New York; ordained December 15, 1945; appointed Titular Bishop of Curzola and Auxiliary Bishop to the Military Vicar April 24, 1979; consecrated May 27, 1979; appointed Bishop of Scranton May 10, 1983; installed June 29, 1983; appointed Archbishop of New York January 31, 1984; installed March 19, 1984. Created Cardinal Priest May 25, 1985. *Res., 452 Madison Ave., New York, NY, 10022.*

Chancery: 1011 First Ave., New York, NY, 10022. Tel.: 212-371-1000; Fax: 212-826-6020.

Most Reverend

PATRICK V. AHERN, D.D.

Auxiliary Bishop of New York; Titular Bishop of Najiera; ordained January 27, 1945; appointed February 3, 1970; consecrated March 19, 1970. *Res., St. Thomas More, 65 E. 89th St., New York, NY, 10128.*

Most Reverend

JAMES P. MAHONEY, D.D.

Retired Auxiliary Bishop of New York; Titular Bishop of Ipagro; ordained May 19, 1951; appointed July 25, 1972; consecrated September 15, 1972; retired December 1997. *Res., Assumption Parish, 131 Union Ave., Peekskill, NY, 10566.*

Most Reverend

ANTHONY F. MESTICE, D.D.

Auxiliary Bishop of New York; Titular Bishop of Villanova; ordained June 4, 1949; appointed March 5, 1973; consecrated April 27, 1973. *Res., Resurrection, 910 Post Rd., Rye, NY, 10580.*

Most Reverend

FRANCISCO GARMENDIA, D.D.

Auxiliary Bishop of New York; Titular Bishop of Limisa; ordained June 28, 1947; appointed May 24, 1977; consecrated June 29, 1977. *Res., St. Thomas Aquinas, 1900 Crotona Pkwy., Bronx, NY, 10460.*

Most Reverend

AUSTIN B. VAUGHAN, D.D.

Auxiliary Bishop of New York; Titular Bishop of Cluain Iraird; ordained December 8, 1951; appointed May 24, 1977; consecrated June 29, 1977. *Res., Our Lady of Consolation, 3103 Arlington Ave., Bronx, NY, 10463.*

Most Reverend

WILLIAM J. McCORMACK, D.D.

Auxiliary Bishop of New York, Titular Bishop of Nicives; ordained February 21, 1959; appointed December 23, 1986; consecrated January 6, 1987. *Res., 142 E. 29th St., New York, NY, 10016.*

Most Reverend

PATRICK J. SHERIDAN, D.D.

Auxiliary Bishop of New York; Titular Bishop of Curzola; ordained March 1, 1947; appointed October 30, 1990; consecrated December 12, 1990. *Res., 452 Madison Ave., New York, NY, 10022.*

Most Reverend

ROBERT A. BRUCATO, D.D.

Auxiliary Bishop of New York; Titular Bishop of Temuniana; ordained June 1, 1957; appointed July 1, 1997; consecrated August 25, 1997. *Res., St. Joseph's Seminary, Yonkers, NY, 10704.*

SEE ERECTED APRIL 8, 1808.

CREATED AN ARCHDIOCESE JULY 19, 1850.

Square Miles 4,683.

(Legal title: Archdiocese of New York).

Comprises the Boroughs of Manhattan, Bronx, and Richmond of the City of New York, and the Counties of Dutchess, Orange, Putnam, Rockland, Sullivan, Ulster and Westchester in the State of New York.

STATISTICAL OVERVIEW

Personnel	
Cardinal	1
Auxiliary Bishops	8
Retired Bishops	2
Priests: Diocesan Active in Diocese	588
Priests: Active Outside Diocese	55
Priests: Retired, Sick or Absent	252
Number of Diocesan Priests	895
Religious Priests in Diocese	1,021
Extern Priests in Diocese	246
Ordinations:	
Diocesan Priests	8
Permanent Deacons	9
Permanent Deacons in Diocese	310
Total Brothers	414
Total Sisters	3,849
Parishes	
Parishes	413
With Resident Pastor:	
Resident Diocesan Priests	314
Resident Religious Priests	80
Without Resident Pastor:	
Administered by Priests	19
Welfare	
Catholic Hospitals	17
Total Assisted	1,969,157
Health Care Centers	3
Total Assisted	157,310
Homes for the Aged	17
Total Assisted	20,800
Residential Care of Children	14
Total Assisted	40,456
Day Care and Extended Day Care Centers	15
Total Assisted	1,744
Specialized Homes	5
Total Assisted	624
Special Centers for Social Services	148
Total Assisted	685,800
Educational	
Seminaries, Diocesan	2
Students from This Diocese	75
Students from Other Diocese	8
Diocesan Students in Other Seminaries	2
Seminaries, Religious	2
Students Religious	6
Total Seminarians	83
Colleges and Universities	12
Total Students	60,700
High Schools, Diocesan and Parish	25
Total Students	13,824
High Schools, Private	30
Total Students	14,597
Elementary Schools, Diocesan and Parish	223
Total Students	76,021
Elementary Schools, Private	15
Total Students	3,913
Non-residential Schools for the Disabled	4
Total Students	200
Catechesis/Religious Education:	
High School Students	13,050
Elementary Students	99,700
Total Students Under Catholic Instruction	282,088
Teachers in the Diocese:	
Priests	50
Brothers	49
Sisters	260
Lay Teachers	4,200
Vital Statistics	
Receptions into the Church:	
Infant Baptism Totals	35,883
Adult Baptism Totals	1,038
Received into Full Communion	541
First Communions	26,947
Confirmations	19,990
Marriages:	
Catholic	8,062
Interfaith	1,145
Total Marriages	9,207
Deaths	16,413
Total Catholic Population	2,347,100
Total Population	5,213,513

Succession of Prelates—Rev. R. LUKE CONCANEN, O.P., D.D., first Bishop; cons. April 24, 1808; died June 19, 1810.—Rt. Rev. JOHN CONNOLLY, O.P., D.D., second Bishop; cons. Nov. 6, 1814; died Feb. 6, 1825.—Rt. Rev. JOHN DUBOIS, S.S., D.D., third Bishop; cons. Oct. 29, 1826; died Dec. 20, 1842.—Most Rev. JOHN HUGHES, D.D., cons. Titular Bishop of Basileopolis and coadjutor to the Bishop of New York, Jan. 7, 1838; succeeded to the See of New York, Dec. 20, 1842; created first Archbishop, July 19, 1850; died Jan. 3, 1864.—His Eminence JOHN CARDINAL MCCLOSKEY, second Archbishop; cons. Titular Bishop of Axiere, and coadjutor to the Bishop of New York, March 10, 1844 translated to the See of Albany, May 21, 1847; promoted to New York, May 6, 1864; created Cardinal Priest of the Holy Roman Church, March 15, 1875 under the title of Sancta Maria Supra Minervam; died Oct. 10, 1885.—

Most Rev. MICHAEL AUGUSTINE CORRIGAN, D.D., third Archbishop; cons. Bishop of Newark, NJ May 4, 1873; promoted to the Archiepiscopal See of Petra and made coadjutor to His Eminence CARDINAL MCCLOSKEY, Archbishop of New York, with the right of succession, Oct. 1, 1880; succeeded to the See of New York, Oct. 10, 1885 made Assistant at the Pontifical Throne, April 19, 1887; died May 5, 1902.—His Eminence JOHN CARDINAL FARLEY, fourth Archbishop of New York; ord. June 11, 1870; cons. Titular Bishop of Zeugma and Auxiliary to the Archbishop of New York, Dec. 21, 1895; promoted to this See, Sept. 15, 1902; preconized June 22, 1903 made Assistant at the Pontifical Throne, Dec. 4, 1904; created Cardinal Priest of the Holy Roman Church under the Title of Sancta Maria Supra Minervam, Nov. 27, 1911; died Sept. 17, 1918.—His Eminence PATRICK CARDINAL HAYES, fifth Archbishop of New York; ord. Sept. 8, 1892; appt. Auxiliary to the Archbishop of New York, July 3, 1914; cons. Titular Bishop of Tagaste, Oct. 28, 1914; appt. Bishop Ordinary of U.S. Army and Navy Chaplains by the Holy See, Nov. 24, 1917; promoted to the See of New York, March 10, 1919; created Cardinal Priest of the Holy Roman Church under the title of Sancta Maria in Via, March 24, 1924; died Sept. 4, 1938.—His Eminence FRANCIS CARDINAL SPELLMAN, sixth Archbishop of New York; ord. May 14, 1916; appt. Auxiliary Bishop of Boston, July 30, 1932; cons. Sept. 8, 1932; appt. to the See of New York, April 15, 1939; appt. Military Vicar for the Armed Forces of the United States, Dec. 11, 1939; created and proclaimed Cardinal under the title of SS. John and Paul in the Consistory, Feb. 18, 1946; died Dec. 2, 1967.—His Eminence TERENCE CARDINAL COOKE, seventh Archbishop of New York; ord. Dec. 1, 1945; appt. Auxiliary Bishop of New York, Sept. 15, 1965; cons. Dec. 13, 1965; appt. to the See of New York, March 8, 1968; installed and appt. Military Vicar of the United States Armed Forces, April 4, 1968; created and proclaimed Cardinal under the title of SS. John and Paul in the Consistory, April 28, 1969; died Oct. 6, 1983.

Vicar General—Most Rev. PATRICK J. SHERIDAN, D.D., V.G.

Episcopal Vicars of the Archdiocese—

Vicar for Pastoral Guidance—Most Rev. ROBERT A. BRUCATO, *201 Seminary Ave., Yonkers, 10704.*

Manhattan (West)—Rev. Msgr. THOMAS P. LEONARD, *Holy Trinity, 213 W. 82nd St., New York, 10024.* Tel: 212-787-0634.

Manhattan (North)—Rev. Msgr. JOACHIM B. BEAUMONT, *St. Elizabeth, 268 Wadsworth Ave., New York, 10033.* Tel: 212-568-8803.

Manhattan (South)—Rev. Msgr. KEVIN P. O'BRIEN, *Immaculate Conception, 414 E. 14th St., New York, 10009.* Tel: 212-254-0200.

Manhattan (East)—Rev. Msgr. JOHN G. WOOLSEY, *St. John the Martyr, 259 E. 71st St., New York, 10021.* Tel: 212-744-4880. Rev. Msgr. THOMAS A. MODUGNO, *St. Monica, 413 E. 79th St., New York, 10021.* Tel: 212-288-6250.

Bronx (Northwest)—Rev. Msgr. PATRICK J. BOYLE, *St. Brendan's, 333 E. 260th St., Bronx, 10467.* Tel: 718-547-6655.

Bronx (Northeast)—Rev. Msgr. FRANCIS X. TONER, *St. Barnabas, 409 E. 241st St., Bronx, 10470.* Tel: 718-324-1478.

Bronx (East)—Rev. Msgr. CHARLES M. KAVANAGH, *St. Raymond, 1759 Castle Hill Ave., Bronx, 10462. 718-792-4044.*

Bronx (South)—Most Rev. FRANCISCO GARMENDIA, *St. Thomas Aquinas, 1900 Crotona Pkwy., Bronx, 10460.* Tel: 718-589-5235.

Richmond—Rev. Msgr. JOSEPH C. ANSALDI, *St. Joseph-by-the-Sea High School, 5150 Hylan Blvd., Huguenot, Staten Island, 10312.* Tel: 718-984-6500.

Westchester (Central)—Most Rev. ANTHONY F. MESTICE, D.D., *Resurrection, 910 Post Rd., Rye, 10580.* Tel: 914-967-0142.

Westchester (Yonkers)—Rev. Msgr. HUGH CORRIGAN, *Immaculate Conception, 103 S. Broadway, Yonkers, 10701.* Tel: 914-963-0156.

Westchester (South Shore)—Rev. Msgr. HOWARD W. CALKINS, *Sacred Heart, 115 Sharp Blvd., Mt. Vernon, 10550.* Tel: 914-668-7440.

Westchester (North) and Putnam—Rev. Msgr. DERMOT R. BRENNAN, *St. Patrick, 137 Moseman Rd., Yorktown Heights, 10598.* Tel: 914-962-5050.

Dutchess—Rev. Msgr. DOMINICK J. LAGONEGRO, *Church of St. Columbia, P.O. Box 428, Hopewell Junction, 12533.* Tel: 914-227-8380.

Orange—Most Rev. AUSTIN B. VAUGHAN, D.D., *Res., Our Lady of Consolation Residence, 3103 Arlington Ave., Bronx, 10463.* Rev. Msgr. GEORGE J. VALASTRO, *St. Joseph, 149 Cottage St., Middletown, 10940.* Tel: 914-343-6013.

Rockland—Rev. Msgr. WILLIAM J. BELFORD, *St. Catharine, 523 Western Hwy., Blauvelt, 10913.* Tel: 914-359-0542.

Ulster—Rev. Msgr. WILLIAM E. WILLIAMS, *St. Joseph, 242 Wall St., Kingston, 12401.* Tel: 914-338-1554.

Sullivan—Rev. EDWARD GREENE, O.F.M., *St. George's, Jeffersonville, 12748.* Tel: 914-482-4640.

Archbishopric of New York—1011 First Ave., New York, 10022. (Cable Address: Curia New York). Tel: 212-371-1000.

Chancery—1011 First Ave., New York, 10022. Tel: 212-371-1000; Fax: 212-826-6020.

Chancellor—Rev. Msgr. JEREMIAH P. MONAHAN; VINCENT T. EUK, Admin. Asst. to the Chancellor.

Vice-Chancellors—Rev. Msgr. EDWARD O'DONNELL; Rev. Msgr. GEORGE THOMPSON; Revs. JOHN D. FLANAGAN; DOUGLAS J. MATHERS, J.D., J.C.L.; Miss DOLORES BERNADETTE GRIER, M.A.

Secretary to the Archbishop—Rev. Msgr. GERALD T. WALSH.

Metropolitan Tribunal—1011 First Ave., New York, 10022. Tel: 212-371-1000.

Judicial Vicar—Rev. Msgr. DESMOND J. VELLA, J.C.D., S.T.L.

Vice Judicial Vicars—Revs. JOHN DELANEY, J.D.; JOHN VIGILANTI, J.C.L., Ph.D.

Judges—Revs. FRANCIS J. MULLER, O.F.M., J.C.D.; DOUGLAS J. MATHERS, J.D., J.C.L.; VINCENT GROGAN, O.F.M., J.C.D.; ALBERT DELUCA, M.S.; WILLIAM S. ELDER, J.C.D.; PETER THUMMA, J.C.D.; KENNETH SMITH, M.A., S.T.B.; GERARD MURRAY, J.C.D.; JOHN KOCHUTHUNCIL, J.C.O.D.; Sr. AMADEUS MCKEVITT, O.S.U., J.C.L.

Defenders of the Bond—Revs. ROBERT J. HOSPODAR, J.C.L.; MAREK SUCKOCKI, J.C.L.

Promoter of Justice—Rev. JOHN A. VIGILANTI, J.C.L.

Canonical Consultants—Sr. DORIS HEINLEIN, S.C., M.S.; Mrs. ROSEMARY P. DOHERTY; Revs. RAFAEL CORNIEL; SHAWN G. DE MUNNIK, M.A.; Mrs. INGRID PENA.

Mt. Kisco Office—Rev. JOHN VIGILANTI, J.C.L., Ph.D., *12 Green St., Mt. Kisco, 10549.* Tel: 914-666-2583.

Poughkeepsie Office—Revs. JOHN A. BIDA, J.C.L.; GERARD J. COLACICCO, J.C.L., *240 Church St., Poughkeepsie, 12601.* Tel: 914-452-1400.

Interdiocesan Tribunal of New York State—201 Seminary Ave., Yonkers, 10704. Tel: 914-968-4301.

Judicial Vicar—Rev. Msgr. WALTER F. KENNY, S.T.D.

Vicar for the Religious—Rev. BARTHOLOMEW DALY, M.H.M., *1011 First Ave., New York, 10022.* Tel: 212-371-1000, Ext. 2575. Sr. CATHERINE QUINN, P.V.B.M. , Ext. 2576.

Archdiocesan Offices and Directors

Catholic Health Care Network in the Archdiocese of New York—MARY HEALEY-SEDUTTO, Ph.D., Exec. Dir., *1011 First Ave., New York, 10022.* Tel: 212-371-1000.

Apostleship of Prayer—Rev. Msgr. JAMES G. WILDERS, Archdiocesan Dir. Tel: 212-628-2800.

Apostleship of the Sea—Rev. KEVIN J. NELAN, Dir., *Stella Maris Maritime Center for Seamen, Pier 52, New York, 10019.* Tel: 212-265-5020.

Archdiocesan Consultors—Rev. Msgr. EDWARD CONNORS; Rev. Msgr. JOSEPH MURPHY; Most Rev. PATRICK SHERIDAN; Rev. Msgr. JEREMIAH P. MONAHAN; Rev. Msgr. LAWRENCE CONNAUGHTON; Rev. Msgr. THOMAS J. BERGIN; Most Rev. ROBERT A. BRUCATO, *1011 First Ave., New York, 10022.* Tel: 212-371-1000.

Archives—Sr. MARGUERITA SMITH, Archivist, *St. Joseph's Seminary, 201 Seminary Ave., Yonkers, 10704.* Tel: 914-476-6333.

Bishops' Resettlement Committee for Refugees—Mr. PAUL MARTIN, Dir., *1011 First Ave., New York, 10022.* Tel: 212-371-1000.

Black Ministry, Office of—Bro. TYRONE DAVIS, C.F.C., Dir., *1011 First Ave., New York, 10022.* Tel: 212-371-1000.

Building Commission—St. Joseph's Seminary, Yonkers, 10704. Tel: 914-476-1058.

Director—Mr. WILLIAM J. O'CONNOR.

Business Manager—Mr. STEVEN BELLOISE.

Consultants—Mr. ANDREW J. CRYAN; HOWARD R. EVANS; DANIEL M. HARRIGAN; Deacon JOHN LARKIN; JOHN J. MASTRONARDI; LAURENCE J. RICE; PHILIP J. WHALEN.

Cardinal's Archdiocesan Appeal—CAROLINE HENNESSY, Dir., *1011 First Ave., New York, 10022.* Tel: 212-371-1000.

Cardinal's Committee of the Laity—Mr. JACK DUNNE, Dir., *1011 First Ave., New York, 10022.* Tel: 212-371-1000.

Catechumenate, Office of—Srs. ROSE VERMETTE, R.C.D.; ONELLYS VILLEGAS, M.H.S.H. Tel: 212-371-1000, Ext. 2690.

Catholic High School Association—1011 First Ave., New York, 10022.

Center for Catholic Lay Leadership Formation—Mr. RUDY VARGAS, IV, Exec. Dir., *1345 Grand Concourse, Bronx, 10452.* Tel: 718-588-4100.

Catholic New York—(See Ecclesiastical Communications Corp.), ANNE BUCKLEY, Editor; ARTHUR L. MCKENNA, Gen. Mgr., *1011 First Ave., New York, 10022.* Tel: 212-688-2399.

Cemeteries—(The Trustees of St. Patrick's Cathedral in the City of New York, Inc.); Mr. ANTHONY V. ROINA, Exec. Dir., *1011 First Ave., New York, 10022.* Tel: 212-753-4883.

Censors—Board of Diocesan Censors of Books, Rev. Msgr. DANIEL V. FLYNN, J.C.D., Chm., *215 Halsted Ave., Harrison, 10528.*

Center for Spiritual Development—ANN MARIE WALLACE, Ph.D., Dir.; Sr. MARY FRANCES MILLS, O.S.F., Assoc. Dir., *96 Milton Rd., Rye, 10580.* Tel: 914-967-7328.

Central Services—Archdiocese of New York, 1011 First Ave., New York, 10022. Tel: 212-371-1000.

Catholic Charities—Rev. Msgr. JAMES J. MURRAY; Rev. Msgr. WILLIAM J. TOOHY, *1011 First Ave., New York, 10022.* Tel: 212-371-1000. (Consult separate listing.).

Chinese Apostolate—Rev. PETER MA, *1011 First Ave., New York, 10022.* Tel: 212-371-1000.

Commission on Church Music—Mr. JOHN MICHAEL CAPRIO, Dir., *1011 First Ave., New York, 10022.* Tel: 212-371-1000, Ext. 2290.

Committee on Housing—Mr. ROBERT PAUL, Coord., *1011 First Ave., New York, 10022.* Tel: 212-371-1000, Ext. 2536-2537.

Communications Office (Bureau of Information for the Media)—Mr. JOSEPH ZWILLING, Dir.; Mrs. HOLLY M. GONZALEZ, Asst. Dir.; Rev. PAUL KEENAN, Asst. Dir., Radio Min.; Mrs. TANIA RIOS, Asst. Dir. Spanish Communications, *1011 First Ave., New York, 10022.* Tel: 212-371-1000, Ext. 2990.

Conciliation and Arbitration, Office of—Rev. DOUGLAS J. MATHERS, J.D., J.C.L, Dir., *1011 First Ave., New York, 10022.* Tel: 212-371-1000.

Coordinating Committee of Catholic Lay Organizations—Rev. Msgr. WILLIAM J. TOOHY, Moderator, *1011 First Ave., New York, 10022.* Tel: 212-371-1000.

Criminal Justice, Office of—Mr. KENNETH HOFFARTH, Dir., *1011 First Ave., New York, 10022.* Tel: 212-371-1000, Ext. 3166.

The Data Systems Center—Mr. ANDREW J. DONNELLY, Dir., *1011 First Ave., New York, 10022.* Tel: 212-371-1000. Mr. JAMES F. MAHER, D.P. Oper. Mgr.; Mr. BRENDAN J. RYAN, Programming & Systems Mgr., *201 Seminary Ave., Yonkers, 10704.* Tel: 914-968-2303.

Telecommunications Office—Mr. ANDREW J. DONNELLY, Dir.; Telecommunications Dir. Vacant.

Deaf, Catholic Center for—Rev. Msgr. PATRICK P. MCCAHILL, Dir., *1011 First Ave., New York, 10022.* Tel: 212-988-8563.

Development, Archdiocesan Office of—Rev. Msgr. CHARLES M. KAVANAGH, Vicar; HELEN T. LOWE, Exec. Dir., *1011 First Ave., New York, 10022.* Tel: 212-371-1000.

Ecclesiastical Assistance Corporation—1011 First Ave., New York, 10022. Tel: 212-371-1000.

Ecclesiastical Communications Corp.—1011 First Ave., New York, 10022. Tel: 212-371-1000.

Ecclesiastical Maintenance Services, Inc.—Mr. EDWARD WOODS, Gen. Mgr. Area Supvrs.: Mr. STEVEN MILISITS; Mr. FRANK ORTIZ; Mr. ROBERT SCULLY, *1011 First Ave., New York, 10022.* Tel: 212-371-1000.

Ecclesiastical Properties Corporation—1011 First Ave., New York, 10022.

Ecumenical and Interreligious Affairs, Commission on—Rev. Msgr. EDWARD D. O'DONNELL, Chm.; Rev. Msgr. FERDINANDO D. BERARDI, M.A., S.T.L., Vice Chm.; Rev. JAMES LOUGHRAN, S.A., Dir., *1011 First Ave., New York, 10022.*

Educational Services of the Archdiocese of New York, Inc.—1011 First Ave., New York, 10022.

Education, Dept. of, Archdiocese of New York—1011 First Ave., New York, 10022. Tel: 212-371-1000. (Consult separate listing.).

Education, Vicar for—Rev. Msgr. THOMAS J. BERGIN, Vicar; Sr. EILEEN CLIFFORD, O.P., Assoc. Vicar, *1011 First Ave., New York, 10022.* (Consult separate listing.).

Ethnic Affairs, Office of—Rev. DOUGLAS J. MATHERS, J.D., J.C.L., Dir., *1011 First Ave., New York, 10022.* Tel: 212-371-1000.

Evangelization, Office of—Rev. Msgr. FRANCIS OLIVERIO, Coord., *1011 First Ave., New York, 10022.* Tel: 212-371-1000.

Family Consultation Service—Rev. GEORGE E. REINHEIMER, Ph.D., Dir. FRANK CATALANO, Ph.D., Supervising Psychologist, *1011 First Ave., New York, 10022.* Tel: 212-371-1000.

Family Life / Respect Life Office—Rev. JOHN BONNICI S.T.D., Dir., *1011 First Ave., New York, 10022.* Tel: 212-371-1000. (Consult separate listing.).

Hispanic Affairs, Vicar—(Vicario, Asuntos Hispanos), Rev. JOSU IRIONDO, C.R.L., *1011 First Ave., New York, 10022.* Tel: 212-371-1000, Ext. 2982.

Catholic Charismatic Center—(Centro Carismatico Catolico); Rev. JOSU IRIONDO, C.R.L., Center Dir., *826 E. 166th St., Bronx, 10460.* Tel: 212-378-1734.

Hispanic Institute of Pastoral Formation—(Instituto Hispano de Formacion Pastoral); Deacon GUILLERMO ROMAGOSA, Dir.; Sr. MARIA TRANSITO SANCHEZ, Exec. Sec. Tel: 212-371-1000, Ext. 8270.

Permanent Diaconate Formation Program—(Programa de Formacion para Diaconos); Deacon ANTHONY CASSANETO, Dir., *St. Joseph's Seminary, Dunwoodie, 10704.* Tel: 914-968-6200, Ext. 8269.

Intercultural Institute—Rev. JOSU IRIONDO, C.R.L., Dir. ANGELA MARTINEZ, Sec. Tel: 212-371-1000, Ext. 2982.

Intercultural Council—Most Rev. PATRICK J. SHERIDAN, Chm.; Dr. RUTH DOYLE, Facilitator. Tel: 212-371-1000, Ext. 3250.

Language Institute—Class Schedule: Wed. 4-7 pm Cardinal Hayes High School. Mr. EDWARD CRESPO, Supvr., *1011 First Ave., New York, 10022.* Tel: 212-371-1000, Ext. 2982.

Light and Life Evangelization Program—(Luz y Vida), *St. Joseph's Cursillo Center, 523 W. 142nd St., New York, 10031.* Tel: 212-926-7433.

St. Joseph's Cursillo Center—Rev. FRANK PELUSO, O.A.R., Dir., *275 West 230th St., Bronx, 10463.* Tel: 718-796-4340.

Palante-Con-Cristo Evangelization and Prayer Movement—Rev. JOHN OLDFIELD, O.A.R., Spiritual Dir.; Deacon LUIS FONTANEZ, Asst. Spiritual Dir., *Tagaste Monastery, Suffern, 10901.* Tel: 914-357-0067. Deacon EDMUNDO RAMOS. Tel: 718-204-0816.

Mary Help of Christians Ev. Community—(Auxiliadora); Rev. KENNETH SMITH, Spiritual Dir.; Deacon LUIS FONTANEZ, Asst. Dir., *328 W. 14th St., New York, 10014.*

Holy Childhood, Pontifical Association—Rev. Msgr. FERDINANDO D. BERARDI, Dir.; Sr. PAULINE CHURCHIRILLO, P.B.V.M., Mission Education Dir., *1011 First Ave., New York, 10022.* Tel: 212-371-1000.

Holy Name Society Archdiocesan Union of New York—Rev. JAMES P. CONNOLLY, Dir.; Mr. ANTHONY J. MEROLLA, Exec. Sec., *1011 First Ave., New York, 10022.* Tel: 212-931-9239.

Hospital Apostolate—Rev. Msgr. MARC J. FILACCHIONE, *1011 First Ave., New York, 10022.* Tel: 212-371-1000.

Information, Bureau of and Radio-T.V. Communications—See Communications.

Inner City Scholarship Fund, Inc.—Mr. WILLIAM GOODLOE, Dir., *1011 First Ave., New York, 10022.* Tel: 212-371-1000.

Institutional Commodity Services Corporation—Mr. RICHARD COSTELLO, Dir.; Mr. VINCENT HEINTZ, Gen. Mgr. Dept. Mgrs.: RICHARD HESSION; ROBERT MCGRATH; PHYLLIS PALUMBO; ROBERT SCHIAVI; NANETTE MELERA, Food Serv. Dir., *1011 First Ave., New York, 10022.* Tel: 212-371-1000.

Instructional T.V. Communications Center—Mr. MICHAEL LAVERY, Dir., *St. Joseph's Seminary, 201 Seminary Ave., Yonkers, 10704.* Tel: 914-968-7800.

Insurance Division—Vacant; Dir., *1011 First Ave., New York, 10022.* Tel: 212-371-1000, Ext. 3024.

Inter-Parish Financing, Commission for—Rev. DENNIS P. KEANE, Chm.; Rev. Msgr. GEORGE F. BARDES, Exec. Sec., *1011 First Ave., New York, 10022.* Tel: 212-371-1000.

Italian Apostolate—Rev. Msgr. GEORGE J. CASCELLI, Dir., *1011 First Ave., New York, 10022.* Tel: 212-371-1000.

Justice and Peace, Archdiocesan Office of—1011 First Ave., New York, 10022. Tel: 212-371-1000.

Legion of Mary—Rev. LAWRENCE M. PAOLICELLI, Dir., *1011 First Ave., New York, 10022.*

Liturgical Commission, Archdiocesan—Sr. JANET BAXENDALE, S.C., Exec. Sec., *Liturgical Resource Center, 1011 First Ave., New York, 10022.* Tel: 212-371-1000, Ext. 2692; 2685.

Parish Councils, Archdiocesan Office for—Rev. ROBERT J. AUFIERI, Dir.; Sr. ROSALIE KALEY, S.C., Assoc. Dir., *1011 First Ave., New York, 10022.* Tel: 212-371-1000.

Parish Mission Team—Rev. THOMAS DEVERY, Dir., *38 Montebello Rd., Suffern, 10901.* Tel: 914-357-1300.

Pastoral Council, Archdiocesan—MADELEINE MORRISSEY, Chm.; Rev. ROBERT J. AUFIERI, Exec. Sec.

Pastoral Guidance, Office of—Most Rev. ROBERT A. BRUCATO, Vicar, *201 Seminary Ave., Yonkers, 10704.*

Pastoral Life Conference—1011 First Ave., New York, 10022. Tel: 212-371-1000.

Pastoral Research and Planning Office—Dr. RUTH T. DOYLE, Dir., *1011 First Ave., New York, 10022.* Tel: 212-371-1000.

Pastoral Services, Archdiocese of New York—1011 First Ave., New York, 10022. Tel: 212-371-1000.

Pension Office, Archdiocesan—Mr. WILLIAM J. DALY, Exec. Sec., *1011 First Ave., New York, 10022.* Tel: 212-371-1000.

Personnel Board, Archdiocesan—Rev. Msgr. EDWARD D. O'DONNELL, Dir.; Rev. Msgr. GEORGE THOMPSON, Vice-Chancellor, Priest Personnel. Members of the Board: Rev. Msgr. FRANCIS BOYLE; Rev. ROBERT VERRIGNI; Rev. Msgr. DANIEL PEAKE; Rev. Msgr. RICHARD GUASTELLA; Rev. ANTHONY SORGIE, *1011 First Ave., New York, 10022.* Tel: 212-371-1000.

Preaching and Liturgy, Institute for—Vacant.

Priests Council of the Archdiocese of New York—His Eminence JOHN J. O'CONNOR, Pres.; Rev. Msgr. WALLACE A. HARRIS, Chm.; Rev. Msgr. DANIEL V. FLYNN, Vice Chm.; Rev. ANTHONY SORGIE, Sec./Treas., *1011 First Ave., New York, 10022.* Tel: 212-371-1000.

Prison Apostolate—Rev. Msgr. LESLIE J. IVERS, Dir., *1011 First Ave., New York, 10022.* Tel: 212-371-1000.

Propagation of the Faith—Archdiocesan Office, Rev. Msgr. FERDINAND O. BERARDI, Archdiocesan Dir.; Sr. PAULINE CHURCHIRILLO, P.B.V.M., Mission Education Coord., *1011 First Ave., New York, 10022.* Tel: 212-371-1000.

Propagation of the Faith—National Office, Most Rev. WILLIAM J. MCCORMACK, Natl. Dir., *366 Fifth Ave., New York, 10001.* Tel: 212-563-8700.

Real Estate Division—Mr. DAVID BROWN, Dir., *1011 First Ave., New York, 10022.* Tel: 212-371-1000.

Retirement Plan for Priests—Rev. Msgr. ROBERT A. FORD, Chm., *1011 First Ave., New York, 10022.* Tel: 212-371-1000, Ext. 2935.

Schools, Superintendent of—Dr. CATHERINE HICKEY, Supt., *1011 First Ave., New York, 10022.* Tel: 212-371-1000. (Consult separate listing.).

Sodalities, Federation—1011 First Ave., New York, 10022. Tel: 212-371-1000.

Spiritual Development, Office of—Rev. EUGENE J. FULTON, Dir., *One Pryer Manor Rd., Larchmont, 10538.* Tel: 914-235-6839.

Trustees of St. Patrick's Cathedral in the City of New York, Inc.—Rev. Msgr. JAMES K. VAUGHEY, Exec. Dir., Cemeteries; Mr. ANTHONY V. ROINA, Asst. Exec. Dir., Cemeteries.

University Apostolate—Rev. MICHAEL CRIMMINS, Coord., *1011 First Ave., New York, 10022.* Tel: 212-371-1000.

Vocations—Rev. ROBERT MCKEON, Special Asst. to the Archbishop, *St. Joseph's Seminary, Yonkers, 10704.* Tel: 914-968-1340. Sr. DEANNA SABETTA, Dir., Women's Vocations, *1011 First Ave., New York, 10022.* Tel: 212-371-1000.

Women Religious, Archdiocesan Council of—Sr. MARGARET KELLY, S.C., Pres.; Sr. ROSALIE KALEY, S.C., Exec. Sec., *1011 First Ave., New York, 10022.* Tel: 212-371-1000.

CLERGY, PARISHES, MISSIONS AND PAROCHIAL SCHOOLS

NEW YORK CITY
BOROUGH OF MANHATTAN

1—CATHEDRAL OF ST. PATRICK (Old, 1809; New, 1879), Rev. Msgr. Anthony Dalla Villa, Rector; Revs. Thomas A. Nielson; Brian C. Brennan; Eugene G. Connolly; William Scafidi, M.Ss.A.; Marion Cascino, O.F.M.
Rectory: 460 Madison Ave., 10022. Tel: 212-753-2261; Fax: 212-755-4128.
Res., 452 Madison Ave., 10022. Most Revs. Patrick J. Sheridan; Henry Mansell; Rev. Gregory Mustaciuolo; Rev. Msgr. James McCarthy.
Chapel—New York, Sts. Faith, Hope and Charity. Records at St. Patrick Cathedral.

2—ST. AGNES (1873), Rev. Msgr. Eugene V. Clark; Revs. William M. Shelley; Matthew Farrelly, C.S.Sp.; Venant LeLonde, O.F.M.; Kasimierz A. Kowalski. In res., Rev. Msgr. Florence Cohalan; Rev. Msgr. Carl J. Marucci (CAM); Revs. John A. Perricone; Thomas Donlan, O.P.; James M. Reinert (LIN); George W. Rutler.
Res., 143 E. 43rd St., 10017. Tel: 212-682-5722; Fax: 212-370-5791.
High School—High School for Boys, 555 West End Ave., 10024. Tel: 212-873-9100. Bro. Thomas Potenza, F.M.S., Prin.
Brothers 6; Lay Teachers 16; Students 300.

3—ST. ALBERT (1916). Closed. Parochial records at Sacred Heart.

4—ALL SAINTS (1879) (African American), Rev. Theodore K. Parker, O.S.C.; Bro. Timothy T. Tomczak, O.S.C., Pastoral Assoc.; Deacon Joseph Price. In res., Revs. William C. Graham (DUL); Francis Kelly Scheets, O.S.C.; Timothy C. Conlon, O.S.C.
Res., 47 E. 129th St., 10035. Tel: 212-534-3535; Fax: 212-987-1930.
School—(1900), 52 E. 130th St., 10037. Tel: 212-534-0558; Fax: 212-831-6343. Sr. Marguerite Lewis, S.B.S., Prin.
Sisters of the Blessed Sacrament 6; Lay Teachers 11; Students 235.
Convent—14 E. 129 St., 10035. Tel: 212-410-3197.
Chapels—St. Benedict's Day Nursery, 34 W. 134th St., 10035. Tel: 212-283-3350; Rice High School Christian Brothers, 124 St. & Lenox Ave., 10035. Tel: 212-369-4100; Fax: 212-348-4631; Franciscan Handmaids of Mary Convent, 15 W. 124th St., 10035. Tel: 212-289-5655; Fax: 212-987-5447.
Catechesis/Religious Programs—Students 225.

5—ST. ALOYSIUS (1899), Revs. Thomas P. Green, S.J.; Edward J. Durkin, S.J. In res., Rev. Joseph F. Burke, S.J.
Res., 219 W. 132nd St., 10027. Tel: 212-234-2848; Fax: 212-234-4198.
School—(1940), 223 W. 132nd St., 10027. Tel: 212-283-0921. Ms. Laurel D. Senger, Prin.
Priests 2; Lay Teachers 15; Students 270.

6—ST. ALPHONSUS (1847). Closed. Records at St. Anthony of Padua.

7—ST. AMBROSE (CHAPEL CENTRO MARIA) (1897). Closed. Records at Sacred Heart Church.

8—ST. ANDREW (1842). Blessed Sacrament Fathers and Brothers. Revs. Roger Pageot, S.S.S.; James Hayes, S.S.S.; Lionel Lavigne, S.S.S.; Thomas E. Waldie, S.S.S., Chap.; Thomas McKeon, S.S.S., New York Infirmary Beekman Downtown Hospital; James P. Hayes, Pace University. In res., Bros. Stanley Kolwaski, S.S.S.; Thomas Morrissey, S.S.S.; Thomas Mella, S.S.S.
Res., 20 Cardinal Hayes Pl., 10007. Tel: 212-962-3972; 3973.
Stations—New York Infirmary Beekman Downtown Hospital, 170 William St., 10007.; St. Margaret's House, 49 Fulton St., 10007.; Pace University, Pace Plaza, 10007.

9—ST. ANN'S ARMENIAN CATHOLIC CHURCH (1852) (Armenian), Most Rev. Hovhannes Tertzakian.
Res., 110 E. 12th St., 10003. Tel: 212-477-2030; Fax: 212-477-2185.

10—ST. ANN'S ROMAN CATHOLIC CHURCH (1852), Rev. Msgr. Kevin P. O'Brien, Admin.
Res., 110 E. 12th St., 10003. Tel: 212-254-0200; Fax: 212-477-2185.

11—ST. ANN (1911) (Spanish), Revs. Victor Muzzin, F.D.P. (Italy); Pasquale Ruggieri, F.D.P. (Italy).
Res., 312 E. 110th St., 10029. Tel: 212-534-3856.
School—(1926), 314-318 E. 110th St., 10029. Tel: 212-722-1295. Sr. Josephine Cioffi, Prin.
Priests 1; Sisters, Servants of the Immaculate Heart of Mary 4; Lay Teachers 12; Students 320.
Chapel—St. Ann's Convent, 319 E. 109 St., 10029. Tel: 212-534-8321.

12—ANNUNCIATION (1853), Revs. Felix Jimenez (Spain); Jose M. Clavero, Sch.P. (Spain); Aroldo Guerra, Sch.P. (Cuba); Felix Ganuza (Spain).
Res., 88 Convent Ave., 10027. Tel: 212-234-1919; Fax: 212-281-7205.
School—(1858), 461 W. 131st St., 10027. Tel: 212-281-7174. Oscar Aviles, Prin.
Lay Teachers 16; Students 411.
Catechesis/Religious Programs—Students 500.

13—ST. ANTHONY OF PADUA (Org. 1859; Re-org. 1866), Revs. Daniel Morey, O.F.M.; Dennis Baum, O.F.M.; Bro. Vincent Ciaravino.
Res. & Chapel—154 Sullivan St., 10012. Tel: 212-777-2755; Fax: 212-673-6684.
School—(1874), 60 MacDougal St., 10012. Tel: 212-477-1297.
Franciscan Sisters of Allegany 1; Lay Teachers 10; Students 210.
Catechesis/Religious Programs—Tel: 212-477-5792. Sr. Agenesine M.H.S.H., D.R.E. Students 20.

14—ASCENSION (1895), Revs. John P. Duffell; Sixto Quezada (Dominican Republic); Deacon Constancio Soto.
Res., 221 W. 107th St., 10025. Tel: 212-222-0666; Fax: 212-961-1086.
School—(1912), 220 W. 108th St., 10025. Tel: 212-222-5161.
Lay Teachers 11; Students 202.
Catechesis/Religious Programs—Tel: 212-749-5938.
Students 285.
Chapels—C.Y.O. Grace Ministry, 218 W. 108th St., 10025. Tel: 212-666-6598; Riverside Study Center. (Opus Dei) 330 Riverside Dr., 10025. Tel: 212-222-3285; Fax: 212-316-3629.

15—ASSUMPTION (1858). Closed. Records at Sacred Heart Church.

16—ST. BENEDICT THE MOOR (1883) (Spanish). Attended by Sacred Heart of Jesus, 212-265-5020,

457 W. 51st St., New York, NY 10019. Rev. Kevin J. Nelan.
Res., 457 W. 51st St., 10019. Tel: 212-265-5020.

17—St. Bernard (1868), Rev. Kenneth J. Smith. In res., Revs. George Hill (WOR); Cesar Ching Espineda, S.V.D.
Res., 328 W. 14th St., 10014. Tel: 212-243-0265; Fax: 212-255-8466.
School—(1916), 327 W. 13th St., 10014. Tel: 212-243-6368; Fax: 212-99-7363. Ms. Imelda David, Prin.
Sisters of Charity of St. Vincent de Paul 1; Lay Teachers 9; Students 172.
Chapel—Crosier Fathers Priory, 326 W. 14th St., 10014. Tel: 212-255-5431.

18—Blessed Sacrament (1887), Revs. Robert B. O'Connor; Kevin V. Madigan; Alfredo Balinong, S.J. (Philippines); Alexis Bastides (Venezuela). In res., Rev. Msgr. William J. Toohy.
Res., 152 W. 71st St., 10023. Tel: 212-877-3111; Fax: 212-799-6233.
School—(1902), 147-152 W. 70th St., 10023. Tel: 212-724-7561. Janice Desmond, Prin.
Lay Teachers 10; Students 250.
Chapels—Convent of Blessed Sacrament, 133 W. 70th St., 10023. Tel: 212-877-8076; St. Agnes' Home, 237 W. 74th St., 10023. Tel: 212-874-9203; Archdiocese Teachers Residence, 22 W. 70th St., 10023.

19—St. Boniface (1858). Closed. Records at Holy Family Church.

20—St. Brigid (1848; 1955), Revs. Michael J. Conway, O.SS.T., Admin.; Joseph C. Gidaro, O.SS.T. In res., Rev. Aaron M. Dowdell, O.SS.T.
Res., 119 Avenue B, 10009. Tel: 212-228-5400.
School—185 E. Seventh St., 10009. Tel: 212-677-5210; Fax: 212-260-2262.
Lay Teachers 9; Students 100.

21—St. Catherine of Genoa (1887), Rev. Robert T. Ritchie.
Res., 506 W. 153rd St., 10031. Tel: 212-862-6130; Fax: 212-491-6272.
School—(1910), 508-510 W. 153rd St., 10031. Tel: 212-926-0252.
Lay Teachers 10; Students 330.
Catechesis/Religious Programs—Students 240.

22—St. Catherine of Siena (1897), Very Rev. Christopher Johnson, O.P., Prior; Revs. Vincent Ferrer McHenry, O.P., Sub-Prior; George Lawrence Concordia, O.P.; John Jerome Conroy, O.P.; Paul B. Fu, O.P.; Patrick Francis Connolly, O.P.; Frank Bede Shipps, O.P.; Robert Philip Fitzsimmons, O.P.; John Thaddeus Murphy, O.P.
Res., 411 E. 68th St., 10021. Tel: 212-988-8300; Fax: 212-988-6918.

23—St. Cecilia (1873), Revs. James P. Brennan, C.SS.R.; Daniel Francis, C.SS.R.; Thomas Maceda, C.SS.R.; William Jacob, C.SS.R.; Rev. Msgr. John K. Graham, C.SS.R.; Rev. Bruce Lewandowski, C.SS.R.; Bros. Francis Alfone, C.SS.R.; Christopher Colarossi, C.SS.R.
Res., 125 E. 105th St., 10029. Tel: 212-534-1350; Fax: 212-410-6177.
Day Nursery—118 E. 106 St., 10029. Tel: 212-534-8423. Sisters of the Atonement.

24—St. Charles Borromeo (1888), Rev. Msgr. Wallace A. Harris.
Res., 211 W. 141st St., 10030. Tel: 212-281-2100; Fax: 212-862-1881.
School—(1904), 214 W. 142 St., 10030. Tel: 212-368-6666. Sr. Marianne Poole, Prin.
Sisters of the Blessed Sacrament 7; Lay Teachers 17; Students 520.

25—St. Clare (1903). Closed. Records at St. Raphael's Church.

26—St. Clemens Mary (1909). Closed. Records at Holy Cross Church, Manhattan.

27—St. Columba (1845), Rev. Frank Scanlon, Admin. In res., Rev. Joseph Hien.
Res., 343 W. 25th St., 10001. Tel: 212-807-8876.
School—(1847), 331-333 W. 25th St., 10001.
Sisters of Congregation of Notre Dame 2; Lay Teachers 9; Students 243.
Chapel—Sisters of Congregation of Notre Dame, 329 W. 25 St., 10001.

28—Corpus Christi (1906), Rev. Msgr. Patrick J. Carney; Rev. Msgr. Myles M. Bourke, Pastor Emeritus; Revs. James P. Flaherty, S.J.; Roberto J. Ricci, S.J. (Argentina). In res., Rev. Linus Inwanyanwu (Nigeria).
Res., 529 W. 121st St., 10027. Tel: 212-666-9350.
School—(1907), 535 W. 121st St., 10027. Tel: 212-662-9344; Fax: 212-662-2725. Ms. Niki Montalro, Prin.
Lay Teachers 11; Students 271.
Catechesis/Religious Programs—Students 271.

29—SS. Cyril and Methodius - St. Raphael (1913; 1886) (Croatian), Revs. Marko Puljic, O.F.M.; Stephen Raich, O.F.M.; Valentin Vukoja, O.F.M.
Res., 502 W. 41st St., 10036. Tel: 212-563-3395; Fax: 212-868-1203.

30—St. Cyril (1916) (Slovenian). Unassigned. Rev. Krizolog Cimerman, O.F.M.
Res., 62 St. Mark's Pl., 10003. Tel: 212-674-3442; Fax: 212-674-3442.

31—St. Elizabeth (1869), Rev. Msgr. Joachim B. Beaumont; Revs. Rudolph F. Gonzalez; Jose Serrano; Carlos Perez (Puerto Rico); Deacon Odalis R. Rosado.
Res., 268 Wadsworth Ave., 10033. Tel: 212-568-8803; Fax: 212-781-2754.
School—(1936), 612 W. 187th St., 10033. Tel: 212-568-7291; Fax: 212-928-2515.
Sisters 2; Lay Teachers 19; Students 696.
Catechesis/Religious Programs—Tel: 212-923-4900.
Students 600.
Chapels—Sisters Residence, 612 W. 187th St., 10033.; Cabrini Chapel, 701 Ft. Washington Ave., 10040.
Isabella Geriatric Center—515 Audubon Ave., 10040.

32—St. Elizabeth of Hungary (1891) (Slovak), Rev. Msgr. Patrick P. McCahill.
Res., 211 E. 83rd St., 10028-2854. Tel: 212-734-5747; 988-1903 (TTY); Fax: 212-988-1903.
Catechesis/Religious Programs—Students 25.

33—St. Emeric (1949), Revs. Peter K. Meehan; Luis M. Dolan, C.P. (Argentina).
Res., 185 Avenue D, 10009. Tel: 212-228-4494.
Catechesis/Religious Programs—Students 251.

34—Epiphany (1868) (Irish), Rev. Msgr. Walter J. Niebrzydowski; Revs. Belevendiram Rathhinam (India); Erno B. Diaz (Archdiocese of Manila); Sr. Doris Sayhonne, R.C.D., Pastoral Assoc.; Sr. Christine Gates, R.G.S., Social Worker. In res., Revs. Edmond J. Nixon, C.SS.R. (Australia); John S. Bonnici.
Res., 239 E. 21st St., 10010. Tel: 212-475-1966; Fax: 212-477-0537.
School—(1869), 234 E. 22nd St., 10010. Tel: 212-473-4128; Fax: 212-473-4392.
141 E. 28th St., 10016. Tel: 212-473-4496; Fax: 212-473-4537.
Sisters 1; Lay Teachers 35; Students 520.
Catechesis/Religious Programs—Students 140.

35—St. Francis of Assisi (1844) (Franciscan), Revs. Ronald P. Stark, O.F.M., Guardian & Pastor; Thomas J. Walters, O.F.M., Vicar; Peter Brophy, O.F.M.; Christian F. Camadella, O.F.M.; Eric Carpine, O.F.M.; Gerald F. Carr, O.F.M.; Brian Carroll, O.F.M.; Bros. Denis Gordon Clark, O.F.M.; F. Edward Coughlin, O.F.M.; Revs. Alcuin Coyle, O.F.M.; Anthony Fedell, O.F.M.; John M. Felice, O.F.M.; Brennan Fitzgerald, O.F.M.; Robert A. Gavin, O.F.M.; Bro. Charles Gilmartin, O.F.M.; Revs. Vincent B. Grogan, O.F.M.; Joseph M. Hertel, O.F.M.; Michael Judge, O.F.M.; Joseph Juracek, O.F.M.; Francis de Paul Kealy, O.F.M.; Christopher Keenan, O.F.M.; Francis Kim, O.F.M.; Vincent A. Laviano, O.F.M.; Miguel A. Loredo, O.F.M.; Bro. William Mann, O.F.M.; Revs. Francis Matthews, O.F.M.; Vincent McCann, O.F.M.; Marcellus A. McCartney, O.F.M.; Michael McDonnell, O.F.M.; John W. McDowell, O.F.M.; Felix P. McGrath, O.F.M.; Cassian Miles, O.F.M.; Bro. Timothy Miskowski, O.F.M.; Revs. John J. McVean, O.F.M.; Francis J. Muller, O.F.M.; Bro. Nathanael Necaster, O.F.M.; Revs. Robert Nee, O.F.M.; Quintin A. Neyland, O.F.M.; James R. O'Connell, O.F.M.; Miguel A. Sepulveda, O.F.M.; Timothy J. Shreenan, O.F.M.; Bro. Sebastian Tobin, O.F.M.; Revs. Kevin Tortorelli, O.F.M.; Lambert F. Valentine, O.F.M.; Allan G. Von Kobs, O.F.M.; Rayner F. Williams, O.F.M.; Dennis M. Wilson, O.F.M. (For priests and brothers not listed here see St. Francis Monastery under Monasteries and Residences of Priests and Brothers.).
Res., 135 W. 31 St., 10001. Tel: 212-736-8500; Fax: 212-736-8545.

36—St. Francis de Sales (1894), Rev. Robert V. Lott, S.T.M.; Rev. Msgr. Oscar Aquino, J.C.D.; Joseph M. McLafferty, Pastoral Assoc.
Res., 135 A E. 96th St., 10128. Tel: 212-289-0425; Fax: 212-996-2028.
School—St. Francis de Sales & St. Lucy Academy, (1993), 116-120 E. 97th St. & 340 E. 104th St., 10029. Tel: 212-289-0680; 534-4021; Fax: 212-534-4130. Bro. Paul Beaudin, C.F.C., Prin.
Congregation of Christian Brothers 4; Lay Teachers 18; Students 600.

37—St. Francis Xavier (1847), Revs. Louis S. Sogliuzzo, S.J.; John P. Bucki, S.J. Pastoral Assocs.: Sr. Honora Nicholson, R.S.M.; Mr. Thomas Sanger; Ms. Kathleen Duffy.
Office: 55 W. 15th St., 10011. Tel: 212-627-2100; Fax: 212-675-6997.

38—St. Frances Xavier Cabrini (1973), Rev. Joseph P. Gorman.
Res., 555 Main St., Roosevelt Island, 10044. Tel: 212-832-6778.

39—The Church of St. Gabriel (1867). Closed. Records at Church of Sacred Hearts of Jesus and Mary.

40—St. Gregory (1907), Revs. Raymond M. Rafferty; Arturo Motolinia, O.S.A. (Mexico). In res., Rev. Kevin L. Sullivan.
Res., 144 W. 90th St., 10024. Tel: 212-724-9766; 9767.
School—(1913), 138 W. 90th St., 10024. Ms. Deborah Hurd, Prin.
Lay Teachers 9; Students 210.

41—Good Shepherd (1912), Revs. Patrick Traynor, C.S.P.; Lionel A. de Silva, C.S.P.; Kevin A. Devine, C.S.P.; Gerard Tully, C.S.P.; Marcos Zamora, C.S.P.; Sr. Acela Rodriguez, H.C.C.S.; Deacon Rafael Then. In res., Rev. Lawrence E. Boadt, C.S.P.
Res., 608 Isham St., 10034. Tel: 212-567-1300; Fax: 212-567-1476.
School—(1925), Cooper & Isham Sts., 10034. Tel: 212-567-5800; Fax: 212-567-5839.
Sisters of Mercy of the Union 3; Lay Teachers 29; Students 600.
Catechesis/Religious Programs—Mrs. Jacqueline Martin, D.R.E., Pastoral Assoc.
Students 275.
Chapel—Convent of Sisters of Mercy. (Private) 630 Isham St., 10034. Tel: 212-567-1600.

42—Guardian Angel (1888), Revs. Philip Phan; John Martin, C.S.S.R.
Res., 193 Tenth Ave., 10011. Tel: 212-929-5966.
School—(1911). Maureen McElduff, Prin.
Sisters of St. Dominic 2; Lay Teachers 8; Students 247.
Chapel—Sisters of St. Dominic & Franciscan Sisters, 407 W. 21st St., 10011. Tel: 212-243-2266.

43—St. Hedwig (1934). Closed. Parochial records at St. Stanislaus Church.

44—Holy Agony (1930) (Spanish), Revs. Victor Elia, C.M.; Candido Arrizurieta, C.M.; Santiago Lluch, C.M.
Res., 1834 Third Ave., 10029. Tel: 212-289-5589; Fax: 212-289-8321.

45—Holy Cross (1852), Revs. Peter M. Colapietro; Gary Seibert, S.J.; Deacon Lawrence C. McNeill. In res., Rev. Angel Cruces.
Res., 329 W. 42nd St., 10036. Tel: 212-246-4732; Fax: 212-307-5033.
School—(1864), 332 W. 43rd St., 10036. Tel: 212-246-0923. Sr. Mary Theresa Dixon, O.P., Prin.
Sisters of St. Dominic of Blauvelt 1; Lay Teachers 15; Students 340.
Convent—460 W. 44th St., 10036. Tel: 212-246-9768. Dominican Convent
Chapels—St. Joseph's Home, 425 W. 44th St., 10036. Tel: 212-246-5363; Covenant House, 692 Eighth Ave., 10036. Tel: 212-613-0300.

46—Holy Family (1924), Revs. Robert J. Robbins; Robert E. O'Brien, S.J. In res., Rev. John J. McAuley, M.M.
Res., 315 E. 47th St., 10017-2318. Tel: 212-753-3401; Fax: 212-753-3428.

47—Holy Innocents (1866), Rev. Msgr. Donald Sakano; Rev. William J. Delaney.
Res., 128 W. 37th St., 10018. Tel: 212-279-5861; Fax: 212-714-9313.

48—Holy Name of Jesus (1868), Revs. James F. Hynes, O.F.M.; Charles Miller, O.F.M.; Robert J. Kennedy, O.F.M.; Paul Lostritto, O.F.M.; Bros. Bill Herbst, O.F.M.; William Margraf, O.F.M.
Res., 207 W. 96th St., 10025. Tel: 212-749-0276; Fax: 212-749-2045.
School—(1905), Amsterdam Ave. & 97th St., 10025. Tel: 212-749-1240; Fax: 212-663-1939. Bro. Richard Grieco, F.S.C., Prin.
Brothers 2; Lay Teachers 20; Students 632.
Catechesis/Religious Programs—Tel: 212-655-1888. Jayne Porcelli, D.R.E.
Students 240.

49—Holy Rosary (1884) (Augustinian), Revs. Angel Dulanto, O.S.A.; Abel Alvarez, O.S.A.; Juan Manuel Chaguaceda, O.S.A.
Res., 444 E. 119th St., 10035. Tel: 212-534-0740; Fax: 212-534-7572.
School—(1949), 371 Pleasant Ave., 10035. Tel: 212-876-7555; Fax: 212-876-0152.
Sisters 1; Lay Teachers 9; Students 220.
Catechesis/Religious Programs—Students 220.

50—Holy Trinity (1898), Rev. Msgr. Thomas P. Leonard; Rev. Gerardo Bengochea, S.J. In res., Rev. Michael Lanning, O.F.M.
Res., 213 W. 82 St., 10024. Tel: 212-787-0634; Fax: 212-787-4917.
Chapel—Chinese Catholic Information Center, 86 Riverside Dr., 10024. Tel: 212-787-6969; Fax: 212-787-0351.

51—ST. IGNATIUS LOYOLA (1851), Revs. Walter F. Modrys, S.J.; William J. Bergen, S.J.; Mark C. Hallinan, S.J.; Deacon Stephen N. Katsouros; Ms. Mary Christine O'Connor, M.Div., Pastoral Assoc.
Res., 980 Park Ave., 10028. Tel: 212-288-3588; Fax: 212-734-3671.
School—(1854), 50 E. 84th St., 10028. Tel: 212-861-3820; Fax: 212-879-8248.
Sisters of Charity of St. Vincent de Paul 3; Lay Teachers 21; Students 567.
Day Nursery—240 E. 84th St., 10028. Tel: 212-734-6427; Fax: 212-734-6972.
Lay Assistants 15; Capacity 107.
Catechesis/Religious Programs—Tel: 212-861-4764. Ms. Joanne Cunneen M.A., D.R.E.
Students 450.
Convent—Tel: 212-288-5544. St. Ignatius Loyola
High School—Regis High School, 55 E. 84th St., 10028. Tel: 212-288-1100; Fax: 212-794-1221.
Schools—Loyola School, Tel: 212-288-3522; Fax: 212-861-1021.; Marymount School, 1028 Fifth Ave., 10028. Tel: 212-744-4486; Fax: 212-744-0163.

52—IMMACULATE CONCEPTION (1855), Rev. Msgr. Kevin P. O'Brien; Revs. Francis X. Buu; John P. Moore; Richard J. Neuhaus; Misael Bacleon (Philippines). In res., Rev. Msgr. Desmond J. Vella; Revs. Edwin J. Conlin; John J. Delaney; John Gibson.
Res., 414 E. 14th St., 10009. Tel: 212-254-0200; Fax: 212-505-7610.
School—(1864), 419 E. 13th St., 10009. Tel: 212-475-2590; Fax: 212-475-7413.
Sisters 1; Lay Teachers 13; Students 398.
Catechesis/Religious Programs—Students 398.

53—INCARNATION (1908), Revs. Gabriel La Paz; John N. Paddack; Fernando Fernandez; Antonio Almonte; Aroldo Guerra.
Res., 1290 St. Nicholas Ave., 10033. Tel: 212-927-7474; Fax: 212-928-0315.
School—(1910), 568-570 W. 175th St., 10033. Tel: 212-795-1030; Fax: 212-795-1564.
Lay Teachers 22; Students 596.
Catechesis/Religious Programs—Sr. Teresa Sheehan, D.R.E.
Students 1,803.

54—ST. JAMES (1827), Revs. Robert J. Poveromo; Jesus P. Enojo; Joseph Chao.
Res., 23 Oliver St., 10038. Tel: 212-233-0161.
School—(1854), 37 St. James Place, 10038. Tel: 212-267-9289. Sr. Josefa Marie Curcio, C.S.J.B., Prin.
Sisters of St. John the Baptist 4; Lay Teachers 8; Students 210.
Chapel—St. James Convent, 21 Oliver St., 10038. Tel: 212-962-0840.

55—ST. JEAN BAPTISTE (1882), Revs. John Kamas, S.S.S.; Bernard J. Camire, S.S.S.; Edmund Slattery, S.S.S.; Donald Brouillard, S.S.S. In res., Revs. William O'Halloran, S.S.S.; Eugene LaVerdiere, S.S.S.; Williams Dahms, S.S.S.
Res., 184 E. 76th St., 10021. Tel: 212-288-5082.
High School—173 E. 75th St., 10021. Tel: 212-288-1645; Fax: 212-288-6540.
Sisters of the Congregation of Notre Dame 11; Religious 2; Lay Teachers 34; Students 490.
Chapel—Sisters' Convent, Tel: 212-472-1230 (Apt. A); 472-8821 (Apt. B).

56—ST. JOACHIM (1888) (Italian). Closed. Parochial records are at Church of St. Joseph.

57—ST. JOHN THE BAPTIST (1840). (Capuchin-Franciscan Friars). Revs. Francis Gasparik, O.F.M.Cap., Guardian & Pastor; Gerard Mulvey, O.F.M.Cap. In res., Revs. Armand Dasseville, O.F.M.Cap., Spiritual Asst. of Secular Order of St. Francis; John Clermont, O.F.M.Cap.; Peter Kaseta, O.F.M.Cap., Dir. of Devel./Capuchin Mission Assn.; John Conner, O.F.M.Cap.; Thomas Houle, O.F.M.Cap., Chap.; Leonard Glavin, O.F.M.Cap., (Retired); Ramon Frias, O.F.M.Cap.; Joseph Mullen, O.F.M.Cap.; Philip Romano, O.F.M.Cap.; Matthias Wesnofske, O.F.M.Cap., Spiritual Asst. of Secular Order of St. Francis; Bros. Luke Benbrook, O.F.M.Cap., Pastoral Assoc.; John Conway, O.F.M.Cap., Chap.; George McCloskey, O.F.M.Cap., Dir. Communications.
Res., 210 W. 31st St., 10001-2876. Tel: 212-564-9070; Fax: 212-564-3964.

58—ST. JOHN THE EVANGELIST (1840), Rev. Msgr. Michael J. Wrenn; Rev. James P. Connolly; Rev. Msgr. George A. Kelly; Rev. Msgr. Thomas J. Bergin.
Res., 348 E. 55th St., 10022. Tel: 212-753-8418; Fax: 212-826-1848.

59—ST. JOHN NEPOMUCENE (1895) (Slovak), Revs. Robert J. Tomlian; Marian Kacir (Slovakia). In res., Rev. Msgr. George J. Cascelli.
Res., 411 E. 66th St., 10021. Tel: 212-734-4613; 734-4370.
Chapel—Sisters' Convent, 320 E. 66th St., 10021. Tel: 212-734-6640.

60—ST. JOHN THE MARTYR (1903), Rev. Msgr. John G. Woolsey; Rev. Joseph W. Baker. In res., Rev. Msgr. George P. Thompson.
Res., 259 E. 71st St., 10021-4596. Tel: 212-744-4880; 4881; Fax: 212-628-6662.

61—ST. JOSEPH (1829), Revs. Aldo J. Tos; Michael K. Holleran; Sr. Anne Tahaney, O.P., Pastoral Assoc.; Deacon Thomas Johnson; Carol M. Reina, Parish Mgr.
Res., 371 Sixth Ave., 10014. Tel: 212-741-1274; Fax: 212-741-2147.
School—111 Washington Pl., 10014. Tel: 212-929-5134; Fax: 212-929-5105.
Lay Teachers 9; Students 196.

62—ST. JOSEPH (1873) (German), Rev. Msgr. Lawrence M. Connaughton; Revs. Charles T. Murr; John Walsh, S.J. In res., Rev. William S. Elder.
Res., 404 E. 87th St., 10128. Tel: 212-289-6030; Fax: 212-831-4043.
School—(1880), 420 E. 87th St., 10128. Tel: 212-289-3057; Fax: 212-289-7239.
Sisters 2; Lay Teachers 9; Students 270.

63—ST. JOSEPH OF THE HOLY FAMILY (1860), Revs. Philip J. Kelly, Admin.; Victor Emuwen; Jose Mesa, S.J.; Deacon Domingo Lopez.
Res., 405 W. 125th St., 10027. Tel: 212-662-9125.
School—(1862), 168 Morningside Ave., 10027. Tel: 212-662-1736; Fax: 212-662-1490.
Daughters of Charity of St. Vincent de Paul 4; Lay Teachers 7; Students 250.
Catechesis/Religious Programs—Students 170.
Convent—400 W. 126th St., 10027. Tel: 212-678-0585.

64—ST. JOSEPH (1924), Revs. Andrew Brizzolara, C.S.; Peter Tsoi, (Chinese Apostolate).
Res., 5 Monroe St., 10002. Tel: 212-267-8376; Fax: 212-267-8379.
School—(1926), One Monroe St., 10002. Tel: 212-233-5152; Fax: 212-267-8379.
Apostles of the Sacred Heart of Jesus 6; Lay Teachers 7; Students 243.
Convent—83 Madison St., 10002. Tel: 212-233-5670.
Apostles of the Sacred Heart of Jesus 6.

65—ST. JUDE (1949), Revs. Elias Isla, Sch.P.; Jose M. Aguilar; Ricardo Fajardo; Deacon Porfirio Rodriguez.
Res., 431 W. 204th St., 10034. Tel: 212-569-3000.
School—(1953), 433 W. 204th St., 10034.
Lay Teachers 17; Students 588.
Chapel—New York, St. Jude Convent.

66—ST. LEO (1880). Closed. Parochial records at St. Stephen's Church.

67—ST. LUCY (1900) (Hispanic), Revs. Esviardo Palomino; Jose Herrero, O.S.A.
Res., 344 E. 104th St., 10029. Tel: 212-534-1470.
School—(1942). Consolidated with St. Francis de Sales School to form St. Francis de Sales-St. Lucy Academy (1993). 340 E. 104th St., 10029. Tel: 212-534-4021; Fax: 212-354-4130. Bro. Paul Beaudin, C.F.C., Prin.

68—ST. MALACHY'S (1902). (The Actors' Chapel). Revs. Michael C. Crimmins; Joseph A. Kelly, S.J.; Sr. Maureen Gibbons, O.P.
Res., 239 W. 49th St., 10019. Tel: 212-489-1340; Fax: 212-262-6224.
Encore Community Services—Fax: 212-757-0244. Sr. Elizabeth Hasselt, O.P., Exec. Dir., Tel: 212-489-1341; Sr. Bernadette Gayor, S.H.C.J., Finance Dir., Tel: 212-489-1943.
Encore Community Center & Programs—Tel: 212-581-2910. Sr. Lillian McNamara, O.P., Dir.
Encore 49 Residence—Tel: 212-246-0880; 581-3490. Mrs. Mary Noone, R.N., Housing Dir.

69—ST. MARK THE EVANGELIST (1907) (African American), Revs. Leonard Tuozzolo, C.S.Sp.; Daniel McCarthy, C.S.Sp.
Res., 65 W. 138th St., 10037. Tel: 212-281-4931; Fax: 212-491-6803.
School—(1912), 55 W. 138th St., 10037. Tel: 212-283-4848; Fax: 212-926-0419. Sr. Lu Ann Carmon, D.C., Prin.
Daughters of Charity of St. Vincent de Paul 5; Lay Teachers 10; Students 385.
Chapel—St. Mark's Convent, Tel: 212-283-4966.

70—ST. MARY (1826), Rev. Msgr. Neil A. Connolly; Rev. Msgr. Thomas J. Keogh, Pastor Emeritus; Revs. Peter Ma, (Chinese Apostolate); Andrew O'Connor.
Res., 28 Attorney St., 10002. Tel: 212-674-3266.

71—ST. MARY MAGDALEN (1873) (German). Closed. Parochial records at Immaculate Conception Church.

72—MARY HELP OF CHRISTIANS (1908) (Spanish), Revs. Patrick Diver, S.D.B.; George Atuk, S.D.B.; Jose Berrueta, S.D.B.; Edward Frizzell, S.D.B.; Denis Kelleher, S.D.B.; Bro. Adelard La Bonte, S.D.B.
Res., 440 E. 12th St., 10009. Tel: 212-254-0058; Fax: 212-505-3769.
School—435-437 E. 11th St., 10009. Tel: 212-254-3596.
Daughters of Mary Help of Christians 5; Lay Teachers 8; Students 200.
Catechesis/Religious Programs—Students 230.
Convent—429 E. 12 St., 10009.

73—ST. MATTHEW (1902). Closed. Parochial records at Blessed Sacrament Church.

74—ST. MICHAEL (1857), Rev. Msgr. Marc A. Filacchione; Rev. John F. Harvey, O.S.F.S.
Res., 424 W. 34th St., 10001. Tel: 212-563-2575.
High School—(1866-1874), 425 W. 33 St., 10001. Tel: 212-563-2547. Sr. Kathleen Cusak, P.B.V.M., Prin.
Sisters of the Presentation 7; Lay Teachers 28; Girls 445.
Chapel—Sacred Heart, 419 W. 33rd St., 10001.

75—ST. MICHAEL CHAPEL (1936) (Russian), Rev. John Soles; Deacon Christopher LiGreci.
Res., 266 Mulberry St., 10012. Tel: 212-226-2644.

76—ST. MONICA (1879), Rev. Msgr. Thomas A. Modugno; Revs. Lazarus Sequeira (India); William M. Leydon. In res., Rev. George E. Baker; Rev. Msgr. Ferdinando D. Berardi.
Res., 413 E. 79th St., 10021. Tel: 212-288-6250; Fax: 212-570-1562.
Chapel—St. Monica Convent, 404 E. 80th St., 10021. Tel: 212-288-5016.

77—MOST HOLY CRUCIFIX (1925) (Italian), Rev. Christopher Hartley, Admin.
Res., 378 Broome St., 10013. Tel: 212-226-2556.

78—MOST HOLY REDEEMER (1844), Revs. Joseph Tizio, C.SS.R.; Jerome Holland, C.SS.R. In res., Rev. Terrance Moran, C.SS.R.
Res., 173 E. Third St., 10009. Tel: 212-673-4224; Fax: 212-472-4097.
Catechesis/Religious Programs—Students 162.

79—MOST PRECIOUS BLOOD (1891) (Italian), Revs. Fabian Grifone, O.F.M.; Louis Troiano, O.F.M.; Albin Fusco, O.F.M.
Res., 109 Mulberry St., 10013. Tel: 212-226-6427.

80—NATIVITY (1842) (Hispanic). (Jesuit). Revs. Anthony S. Aracich, S.J.; Joseph J. Kavanagh, S.J. In res., Revs. Michael J. Sala, S.J.; George M. Anderson, S.J.; James F. Joyce, S.J.
Res., 44 Second Ave., 10003. Tel: 212-674-8590; 8591; Fax: 212-674-8789.
Nativity Mission Center—204 Forsyth St., 10002. Tel: 212-477-2472.

81—ST. NICHOLAS (1833) (German). Closed. Parochial records at Most Holy Redeemer Church.

82—NOTRE DAME (1910), Rev. Msgr. Christopher Maloney; Rev. Thomas Valenti (ROC). In res., Revs. Timothy Valentine, S.J.; Ngozi Osuji (Nigeria); George Drance, S.J.
Res., 405 W. 114th St., 10025. Tel: 212-866-1500; Fax: 212-222-5704.
Station—New York, St. Luke's Hospital Amsterdam House.

83—OUR LADY QUEEN OF ANGELS (1886) (German), Revs. Philip F. Bohan, O.F.M.Cap.; Martin Curtin, O.F.M.Cap., Guardian & Pastoral Assoc.; Bros. Pius Blandino, O.F.M.Cap.; Christopher Varley, O.F.M.Cap.; George Tucker, O.F.M.Cap.; Deacon Luis Martinez.
Res., 226 E. 113th St., 10029. Tel: 212-534-6218; Fax: 212-534-6285.
School—(1886 and 1955), 229-231 E. 112th St., 10029. Tel: 212-722-9277. Bro. Louis J. Esposito, O.F.M.Cap., Prin. & Vicar.
Priests 1; Brothers 1; Sisters 1; Lay Teachers 18; Students 546.
Chapel—Convent of Sisters of St. Agnes, 232 E. 113th St., 10029. Tel: 212-369-5291.

84—OUR LADY OF ESPERANZA (1912) (Spanish), Rev. Msgr. Peter C. O'Donnell.
Res., 624 W. 156th St., 10032. Tel: 212-283-4340.
Catechesis/Religious Programs—Students 300.

85—OUR LADY OF GOOD COUNSEL (1886), Revs. Dennis P. Keane, Ph.D.; Arthur Leone; Richard Terga.
Res., 230 E. 90th St., 10128. Tel: 212-289-1742; Fax: 212-427-5643.
School—(1904), 323-329 E. 91st St., 10128. Tel: 212-289-6730. Mr. Donald Kramer, Prin.
Lay Teachers 10; Students 228.

86—OUR LADY OF GRACE (Stanton St.) (1907). Closed. Parochial records at Church of the Nativity.

87—OUR LADY OF GUADALUPE (1902) (Spanish), Revs. Peter R. Precourt, A.A.; Philip Bonvouloir, A.A.; Deacons Rafael Bello; Henry Bernal; Rene Garcia. In res., Rev. Albert E. Brochu, A.A.
Res., Priests of the Assumption, Inc., 229 W. 14th St., 10011. Tel: 212-243-5317; Fax: 212-675-0637.

88—OUR LADY OF LORETO (1891) (Sicilian), Rev. Msgr. John B. Ahern; Rev. Patrick J. Carroll; Rev. Msgr. Philip J. Murnion.
Res., 309 Elizabeth St., 10012. Tel: 212-431-9840.
Holy Name Centre for Homeless Men—Tel: 212-226-5848.

89—Our Lady of Lourdes (1901), Revs. Thomas B. Fenlon; Fabio E. Jaramillo (Quibdo). In res., Revs. Lawrence E. Lucas; Alphonsus Anumudu (Orlu).
Res., 472 W. 142nd St., 10031. Tel: 212-862-4380; Fax: 212-862-4126.
School—(1903), 462-468 W. 143rd St., 10031. Tel: 212-926-5820; Fax: 212-491-6034. Ms. Cathryn Rivera, Prin.
Lay Teachers 22; Students 640.
Catechesis / Religious Programs—Students 695.
Chapel—Convent of Our Lady of Lourdes, 463 W. 142nd St., 10031. Tel: 212-926-1150; Fax: 212-862-4126.

90—Our Lady of the Miraculous Medal (1926). Closed. Records at Holy Agony.

91—Our Lady of Mt. Carmel (1884) (Italian), Revs. Peter J. Rofrano, S.A.C.; Severino Dominicis, S.A.C.; Anthony Kelly, S.A.C.; Girolamo D'Ambrosi, S.A.C.
Res., 448 E. 116th St., 10029-0614. Tel: 212-534-0681; Fax: 212-534-0629.
School—Mt. Carmel-Holy Rosary, 371 Pleasant Ave., 10035. Tel: 212-876-7555.
Sisters 1; Lay Teachers 8; Students 175.
Convent—456 E. 116th St., 10029-0614. Tel: 212-427-2381.
Sisters of Charity 10.

92—Our Lady of Perpetual Help (1887), Revs. Frank J. Freel, C.SS.R.; James May, C.SS.R.; William Heanue, C.SS.R. In res., Revs. Thomas O'Connell, C.SS.R.; Joseph Noll, C.SS.R.; Thomas McPartland, C.SS.R.; Raymond McCarthy, C.SS.R.; James Ferris, C.SS.R.
Church—328 E. 62nd St., 10021. Tel: 212-832-9087.
High School—Commercial High School. Sr. Anthony Mary, S.S.N.D., Prin.
Sisters of Notre Dame 1; Lay Teachers 8; Girls 170.
Chapel—New York, National Shrine of the Infant of Prague.

93—Our Lady of Peace (1918) (Italian), Rev. Bartholomew Daly, M.H.M., Admin. In res., Rev. Paul A. Keenan.
Res., 237 E. 62nd St., 10021. Tel: 212-838-3189; Fax: 212-308-4819.

94—Our Lady of Pompeii (1892) (Italian), Revs. Ralph A. Bove, C.S.; Bernabe Sison; Bro. Michael La Mantia, C.S. In res., Rev. Giulivo Tessarolo, C.S.
Res., 25 Carmine St., 10014. Tel: 212-989-6805; Fax: 212-727-3139.
School—(1930), 240 Bleecker St., 10014. Tel: 212-242-4147; Fax: 212-691-2361.
Apostles of the Sacred Heart of Jesus 4; Lay Teachers 10; Students 264.

95—Our Lady Queen of Martyrs (1927), Revs. Daniel S. Kearney; Ambiorix Rodriguez; Jose del Carmen Arroyo (Dominican Republic); Deacon Narciso Hernandez. In res., Rev. Donald Johnston, Chap., Columbia Presbyterian Hospital.
Res., 91 Arden St., 10040. Tel: 212-567-2637; Fax: 212-567-1305.
School—(1932), 71 Arden St., 10040. Tel: 212-567-3190; Fax: 212-304-8587. Andrew Woods, Prin.
Lay Teachers 18; Students 536.
Catechesis / Religious Programs—Students 795.

96—Our Lady of the Rosary (1883). Shrine of St. Elizabeth Ann Seton. Rev. Msgr. Timothy S. Collins; Rev. Msgr. James G. Wilders, Pastor Emeritus; Rev. Martin Betances Torres. In res., Rev. John D. Flanagan.
Res., 7 State St., 10004. Tel: 212-269-6865.

97—Our Lady of the Scapular/St. Stephen (1889; 1848) (Spanish), Revs. Matthew Faulkner, O.Carm.; Francis Amodio, O.Carm.; John Canning, O.Carm. In res., Most Rev. William J. McCormack; Rev. Msgr. Andrew P. Landi (BRK); Rev. Christopher Byrnes, O.Carm.
Res., 142 E. 29th St., 10016. Tel: 212-683-1675; 532-2232; Fax: 212-683-7921.
Catechesis / Religious Programs—Students 163.
Chapels—Bellevue Hospital, Chapel of Our Lady Helper of the Sick, Tel: 212-561-4440. Revs. John Logan, O.Carm.; Robert Greco, O.Carm.; Philip Marani, O.Carm.; Veterans Administration Hospital, Tel: 212-686-7500. Rev. Edmund McCaffrey, O.Carm.

98—Our Lady of Sorrows (1867) (English-Spanish), Revs. Joseph Gurdak, O.F.M.Cap.; John Mellitt, O.F.M.Cap.; Javier Sebastian Donazar; Bro. Robert Gerdin, O.F.M.Cap.; Deacon Eusebio Maldonado. In res., Bros. John Shento, O.F.M.Cap., Guardian; James Wieland, O.F.M.Cap; Larry Evans, O.F.M.Cap.; Richard Crawley, O.F.M.Cap.; Celestino Arias, O.F.M.Cap.
Res., 213 Stanton St., 10002-1898. Tel: 212-673-0900; Fax: 212-982-0166.
Church—103 Pitt St., 10002.
School—(1867), 219 Stanton St., 10002. Tel: 212-473-0320; Fax: 212-420-0285.
Lay Teachers 13; Students 274.
Catechesis / Religious Programs—Students 226.

99—Our Lady of Victory (1944), Rev. Msgr. Edward J. Mitty; Revs. Jan Deptula (Poland); Andrew M. Cieszkowski (Poland); Raian A. Thommai, S.D.B. (India); Sebastian Ousepparampil (India); Lucian Cybruch (Poland). In res., Rev. John E. Fanning.
Res., 60 William St., 10005. Tel: 212-422-5535; Fax: 212-509-5336.

100—Our Lady of Vilna (1905) (Lithuanian), Rev. Dr. Eugene A. Sawicki, R.N., J.C.L., Admin.
Res., 32 Dominick St., 10013. Tel: 212-255-2648; Fax: 212-924-6210.
Church—570 Broome St., 10013.

101—Our Saviour (1955), Revs. Jeremiah P. O'Neill; John T. Mulligan; Koshy George Chirayath (India). In res., Rev. Douglas J. Mathers.
Res., Park Ave. at 38th St., 10016. Tel: 212-679-8166; Fax: 212-213-0352.

102—St. Patrick Old Cathedral (1809), Rev. Msgr. Guy S. Vinci; Rev. Msgr. Nicholas Marinacci, Pastor Emeritus; Revs. Andrew Thi; Carlos A. Mullins.
Res., 263 Mulberry St., 10012. Tel: 212-226-8075.
School—Boys & Girls Depts., (1817), 233-239 Mott St., 10012.
32-38 Prince St., 10012.
Sisters of Charity of St. Vincent de Paul 7; Lay Teachers 17; Students 832.
Chapels—Immaculate Conception, 32 Prince St., 10012.; St. Michael, 266 Mulberry St., 10012.

103—St. Paul (1834), Revs. Rafael G. Corniel, Temp. Admin.; Jose Otero (Argentina).
Res., 113 E. 117th St., 10035. Tel: 212-534-4422.
School—(1870), 114-122 E. 118th St., 10035.
Sisters of Charity of St. Vincent de Paul 5; Lay Teachers 9; Students 204.
Convent—149 E. 117th St., 10035.

104—St. Paul the Apostle (1858), Revs. Donald C. Campbell, C.S.P., Supr.; John B. Ardis, C.S.P., Dir. of Vocations; Robert M. Cary, C.S.P., Gen. Treas.; Joseph F. Mahon, C.S.P., Dir. of Missions; Rudolph T. Vorisek, C.S.P., Hospital Chap.; James F. McQuade, C.S.P., Hospital Chap.; Charles Kullmann, C.S.P.; James B. Lloyd, C.S.P.; John C. Reynolds, C.S.P.; Richard J. Walsh, C.S.P.; Joseph P. Flynn, C.S.P.; Francis X. Diskin, C.S.P.; John E. Collins, C.S.P.; Donal F. Forrester, C.S.P.; Kevin A. Lynch, C.S.P.; Michael J. Hunt, C.S.P.; Charles S. White, C.S.P.; Timothy P. Tighe, C.S.P.; Joseph F. Troy, C.S.P.; Robert A. O'Donnell, C.S.P. Pastoral Assocs.: Revs. Brett Hoover, C.S.P.; Eric Andrews, C.S.P.
Mailing Address: 415 W. 59th, 10019. Tel: 212-265-3495; Fax: 212-262-9239.
Chapel—Oblates of Jesus the Priest, Tel: 212-265-3209; Fax: 212-265-4154.

105—St. Peter (1785), Rev. Msgr. Robert M. O'Connell; Revs. Michael B. Dibble; Donald T. Fussner; James J. Halligan.
Res., 16 Barclay St., 10007. Tel: 212-233-8355; Fax: 212-285-0497.
Chapel—St. Joseph's Chapel, 385 South End Ave., 10280. Tel: 212-466-0131. In res., Rev. Msgr. Joseph J. Zammit, Chap., N.Y.C. Police Dept.

106—St. Raphael (1886). See Sts. Cyril and Methodius.

107—Resurrection (1907) (African American-Hispanic), Revs. Michael P. Sepp, Admin.; Samuel Taylor; Deacon Kenneth Radcliff.
Res., 276 W. 151st St., 10039. Tel: 212-690-7555; Fax: 212-690-6590.
School—(1910), 282 W. 151 St., 10039. Tel: 212-690-7524.
Lay Teachers 8; Students 197.

108—St. Rose (1868). Closed. Parochial records at St. Mary Church.

109—St. Rose of Lima (1901), Revs. Manuel Machado; Richard T. Adams; Ralph V. Curcio.
Res., 510 W. 165th St., 10032. Tel: 212-568-0091.
School—(1924), 517 W. 164th St., 10032.
Dominican Nuns (Sparkill, NY) 2; Lay Teachers 16; Students 483.
Chapel—St. Rose of Lima Convent, 509 W. 164th St., 10032. Medical Centre.

110—Sacred Heart of Jesus (1876), Rev. Kevin J. Nelan; Sr. Ana Ospina, Pastoral Assoc.; Rev. Tomas DelValle. In res., Rev. Msgr. Edward D. O'Donnell.
Res., 457 W. 51st, 10019. Tel: 212-265-5020; Fax: 212-977-4116.
School—(1892), 456 52nd St., 10019. Tel: 212-246-3264.
Congregation of Christian Brothers 2; Lay Teachers 10; Students 260.
Chapels—Centro Maria, 539 W. 54th St., 10019.; Convent of Sacred Heart, 450 W. 51st St., 10019.
Catechesis / Religious Programs—Students 210.

111—Sacred Hearts of Jesus and Mary (1914), Rev. Albert J. DeLuca; Rev. Msgr. William J. Rinschler, Pastor Emeritus.
Res., 307 E. 33rd St., 10016. Tel: 212-889-2133; Fax: 212-889-2133.
Chapel—Convent of the Sacred Heart of Jesus and Mary, 325 E. 33rd St., 10016. Tel: 212-889-3886.
Station—N.Y.U. Rehabilitation Hospital, Tel: 212-889-3886.

112—St. Sebastian (1915). Closed. Parochial records at Epiphany Church.

113—St. Stanislaus (1872) (Polish), Revs. Christopher Wieliczko, O.S.P.; Bogdan Kolmaga, O.S.P.
Res., 101 E. Seventh St., 10009. Tel: 212-475-4576.

114—St. Stephen (1848). Consolidated in 1990. See Our Lady of Scapular/St. Stephen for details.

115—St. Stephen of Hungary (1902) (Hungarian), Revs. Neil J. O'Connell, O.F.M., Guardian Franciscan Community; Dominic Csorba, O.F.M. (Hungary); Vianney M. Devlin, O.F.M. In res., Revs. Leo Clifford, O.F.M. (Ireland); Reginald A. Redlon, O.F.M.; Bro. Glenn Humphrey, O.F.M.
Res., 414 E. 82nd St., 10028. Tel: 212-861-8500; Fax: 212-535-9221.
School—(1918), 408 E. 82nd St., 10028. Tel: 212-288-1989. Carol O'Connor, Prin.
Lay Teachers 9; Students 160.

116—St. Teresa (1863), Revs. Dennis J. Sullivan; John B. Chiang (China); Alfredo Monteiro (India).
Res., 141 Henry St., 10002. Tel: 212-233-0233; Fax: 212-233-1306.
Church—16 & 18 Rutgers St., 10002.
Catechesis / Religious Programs—Students 210.

117—St. Thomas the Apostle (1889), Revs. Paul Grauls, S.D.B.; George Hanna, S.D.B.; Bro. Anthony Ambrogio, S.D.B.
Res., 262 W. 118th St., 10026. Tel: 212-662-2693; Fax: 212-662-4560. [CEM]
Don Bosco Harlem Association, Inc.—262 W. 118th St., 10026. Tel: 212-662-9228.

118—St. Thomas More (1950), Revs. John A. Boehning; John E. Halborg; Stanley Moseley. In res., Most Rev. Patrick V. Ahern; Rev. Thomas Shelley.
Res., 65 E. 89th St., 10128. Tel: 212-876-7718; Fax: 212-831-5756.
Catechesis / Religious Programs—Narnia Clubs, 20 Sutton Pl. S., 10022. Tel: 212-593-4879.
Students 185.
Chapel—Convent of Sacred Heart and Academy, 1 E. 91st St., 10022. Tel: 212-722-4745.

119—Transfiguration (1827) (Chinese-English), Rev. Raymond J. Nobiletti, M.M.
Res., 29 Mott St., 10013. Tel: 212-962-5157; Fax: 212-962-5217.
School—(1853), Tel: 212-962-5265; Fax: 212-964-8965. Suzanne O'Reilly, Prin.
Lay Teachers 9; Students 278.

120—St. Veronica (1887), Rev. Kenneth J. Smith, Admin.
Res., 328 W. 14th St., 10014. Tel: 212-243-0265; Fax: 212-255-8466.
Church—149-155 Christopher St., 10014. Tel: 212-924-5628.
Mission—New York, New York Co., Gift of Love, 657 Washington St., 10014. Tel: 212-645-0587.

121—St. Vincent Ferrer (1867), Very Rev. James Boniface Ramsey, O.P., Prior; Rev. John P. Gerhard, O.P., Subprior; Bros. Christopher McCabe, O.P.; Damian McCarthy, O.P.
Res., 869 Lexington Ave., 10021-6680. Tel: 212-744-2080; Fax: 212-327-3011.
High School—151 E. 65th St., 10021. Tel: 212-535-4680; Fax: 212-988-3455. Ms. Margaret Quinn, Prin.
Sisters of St. Dominic, Columbus, OH 6; Lay Teachers 26; Girls 439.
Chapels—Sisters of St. Dominic, 152 E. 66th St., 10021. Tel: 212-744-2375; Dominican Academy, 44 E. 68th St., 10021. Tel: 212-744-0195; Fax: 212-744-0375; Grace Institute, 1233 Second Ave., 10021. Tel: 212-832-7605; Fax: 212-486-2869.

122—St. Vincent de Paul (1840) (French), Rev. Maurice E. Carroll. In res., Rev. Robert Poveromo.
Res., 116 W. 24th St., 10011. Tel: 212-243-4727.
Church—123 W. 23rd St., 10011.

BOROUGH OF BRONX

123—St. Adalbert (1898) (Polish). Closed. For inquiries for parish records contact the Chancery.

124—St. Angela Merici (1899), Revs. Carlos A. Mullins; Michael O'Kere.
Res., 917 Morris Ave., 10451. Tel: 718-293-0984; Fax: 718-293-6617.
Church—E. 163rd St., 10451.
School—(1917), Morris Ave. & 163rd St., 10451. Tel: 718-293-3365. Patrick Kelly, Prin.
Lay Teachers 19; Students 586.

125—St. Ann (1927), Rev. Msgr. Robert M. Trainor; Rev. Michael Lipareli. In res., Rev. Varghese Chethipuzha (India).
Res., 3519 Bainbridge Ave., 10467. Tel: 718-547-9350.

School—(1928), Bainbridge Ave. & Gun Hill Rd., 10467. Tel: 718-655-3449; Fax: 718-547-4020. Miss L. DiJusto, Prin.
Students 275.
Catechesis/Religious Programs—Students 154.

126—ST. ANSELM (1892), Revs. Blas Montenegro, O.A.R.; Jose Luis Duenas, O.A.R.; Dionisio Gutierrez, O.A.R.
Res., 685 Tinton Ave., 10455. Tel: 718-585-8666.
School—(1908), Tel: 718-993-9464. Sr. Peter Brigid Smith, O.P., Prin.
Sisters of St. Dominic of Blauvelt 2; Lay Teachers 22; Students 680.

127—ST. ANTHONY (1908) (Hispanic), Revs. Joseph J. Kelly; John Tran. In res., Rev. Michael J. Allessandro.
Res., 1496 Commonwealth Ave., 10460. Tel: 718-931-4040; 4041; Fax: 718-792-4622.
School—(1931), St. Lawrence Ave. & Mansion St., 10460. Tel: 718-892-1244; Fax: 718-863-0202.
Sisters of Charity of St. Vincent de Paul of NY 1; Lay Teachers 9; Students 230.
Catechesis/Religious Programs—Students 110.
Chapel—Sisters of Charity, 1492 Commonwealth Ave., 10460.

128—ST. ANTHONY (1919) (Italian), Rev. Nicholas F. Milazzo.
Res., 4505 Richardson Ave., 10470. Tel: 718-324-8787; Fax: 718-324-6354.
School—(1953), 4520 Matilda Ave., 10470. Tel: 718-324-5104. Mrs. Roma Barone, Prin.
Lay Teachers 12; Students 202.
Convent—4500 Matilda Ave., 10470.

129—ST. ANTHONY OF PADUA (1903) (African American & Hispanic), Revs. Josu Iriondo, Admin.; Francis Reginald John (St. Lucia).
Res., 832 E. 166th St., 10459. Tel: 718-542-7293.

130—ST. ATHANASIUS (1907), Rev. Msgr. William J. Smith; Rev. Pompilio Alvarez (Spain); Deacon Alejandro Rosado. In res., Rev. Louis R. Gigante.
Res., 878 Tiffany St., 10459. Tel: 718-328-2558.
School—(1913), 830 Southern Blvd., 10459. Tel: 718-542-5161. Marianne Kraft, Prin.
Sisters 2; Lay Teachers 12; Students 370.
Catechesis/Religious Programs—Tel: 718-328-3121.
Students 350.

131—ST. AUGUSTINE (1849), Revs. S. Keith Outlaw, Admin.; Miguel Zentner (Argentina). In res., Revs. Ruben Cammayo (PH); Gregory Lyttle.
Res., 1183 Franklin Ave., 10456. Tel: 718-893-0072; Fax: 718-861-3080.
Church—E. 167th St., 10456.
School—(1887), 1176 Franklin Ave., 10456. Tel: 718-542-3633; Fax: 718-542-7871. J. Kent Horton, Prin.
Lay Teachers 10; Students 300.

132—ST. BARNABAS (1910), Rev. Msgr. Francis X. Toner; Rev. Rees W. Doughty; Deacons John Hennessy; Vincent Laurato; Cornelius Manning. In res., Rev. Msgr. John J. Considine, Pastor Emeritus; Revs. Thomas P. Flynn (Ireland); Cyprian I. Onyeihe (Nigeria).
Res., 409 E. 241st St., 10470. Tel: 718-324-1478; Fax: 718-324-1479.
School—(1912), 415 E. 241st St., 10470. Tel: 718-324-1088.
Sisters 1; Lay Teachers 22; Students 635.
High School—High School for Girls, (1924), 425 E. 240th St., 10470. Tel: 718-325-8800.
Sisters 12; Lay Teachers 20; Students 325.
Catechesis/Religious Programs—Tel: 718-324-0865.
Students 275.
Chapel—Annunciation, 1033 McLean Ave., Yonkers, 10704.

133—ST. BENEDICT (1923), Revs. Kenneth L. Marks; David K. Clifford; Thomas Kottoor; Rev. Msgr. Thoephilus Nwalo; Deacon John Simpson.
Res., 2969 Otis Ave., 10465-2198. Tel: 718-828-3403; Fax: 718-829-1304.
School—(1923), 1016 Edison Ave., 10465. Tel: 718-829-9557.
Sisters 3; Lay Teachers 25; Students 451.
Catechesis/Religious Programs—Tel: 718-829-1200.
Students 386.
Chapel—St. John, 1082 Edison Ave., 10465.

134—BLESSED SACRAMENT (1927), Revs. Thomas Farrelly; Carlos M. Rodriguez; Deacon Epi Portalatin.
Res., 1170 Beach Ave., 10472. Tel: 718-892-3214; Fax: 718-892-3907.
School—(1929), 1160 Beach Ave. & 1141 Taylor Ave., 10472. Tel: 718-892-0433. Mary Fallon, Prin.
Lay Teachers 19; Students 506.
Catechesis/Religious Programs—Tel: 718-863-4620.
Students 210.

135—ST. BRENDAN (1908), Rev. Msgr. Patrick J. Boyle; Rev. Msgr. William B. O'Brien; Revs. Michael J. Morrow; David F. Nolan.
Res., 333 E. 206th St., 10467. Tel: 718-547-6655; Fax: 718-547-6579.
School—(1912), 268 E. 207th St., 10467. Tel: 718-653-2293. Mrs. Patricia Gatti, Prin.
Sisters of St. Dominic (Sparkill, NY) 1; Lay Teachers 19; Students 629.
Catechesis/Religious Programs—Students 510.
Chapel—Dominican Sisters, 260 E. 207th St., 10467. Tel: 718-798-2460.

136—ST. CLARE OF ASSISI (1929) (Italian), Revs. Richard Guarnieri; John Voglio, S.D.B.; Deacon Bernie Moran.
Res., 1918 Paulding Ave., 10462. Tel: 718-863-8974; Fax: 718-863-8975.
Church—1027 Rhinelander Ave., 10462.
School—(1951), 1911 Hone Ave., 10461. Tel: 718-892-4080. Sr. Josephine Stabile, Prin.
Sisters 4; Lay Teachers 20; Students 615.
Catechesis/Religious Programs—Tel: 718-829-9624.
Students 194.
Chapel—Bronx, Morningside House Chapel, Tel: 718-409-8200.

137—CHRIST THE KING (1926), Revs. Patrick Hennessy; Guillermo Velez Lopez.
Res., 141 Marcy Pl., 10452. Tel: 718-538-5546; Fax: 718-538-3081.
School—Tel: 718-538-5959.
Lay Teachers 13; Students 535.
Catechesis/Religious Programs—Students 689.

138—ST. DOMINIC (1924) (Italian), Revs. Thomas K. Dicks; S. Anthony Samy (India).
Res., 1739 Unionport Rd., 10462. Tel: 718-828-2424; Fax: 718-823-4450.
School—(1953), 1684 White Plains Rd., 10462. Tel: 718-829-4837; Fax: 718-792-6912. Sr. Josefa Curcio, C.S.J.B., Prin.
Sisters of St. John Baptist 8; Lay Teachers 18; Students 525.
Convent—1710 Unionport Rd., 10462. Tel: 718-824-2580.
Sisters 12.

139—ST. FRANCIS OF ASSISI (1928), Rev. Carlos Lopez Acosta.
Mailing Address: P.O. Box 520013, 10452.
Res., 1544 Shakespeare Ave., 10452. Tel: 718-731-6840; 6841.

140—ST. FRANCIS OF ASSISI (1949), Revs. Anthony J. Giuliano; Thomas P. D'Angelo; James P. Clark.
Res., 4343 Baychester Ave., 10466. Tel: 718-994-8736; Fax: 718-994-6990.
Church—4300 Baychester Ave., 10466.
School—Tel: 718-994-4650. Dr. Patrick Taharally, Prin.
Sisters 1; Lay Teachers 12; Students 317.
Chapel—S. 10th Ave & W. 7th St., Mt. Vernon, 10550.

141—ST. FRANCES DE CHANTAL (1927), Rev. Msgr. Leslie J. Ivers; Rev. Msgr. Joseph M. Devlin, Pastor Emeritus; Revs. Donald C. Baker; Anthony Osuagwu (Nigeria).
Res., 190 Hollywood Ave., 10465. Tel: 718-792-5500; Fax: 718-792-1824.
School—(1929), 2962 Harding Ave., 10465. Tel: 718-892-5359; Fax: 718-892-6937. Marie McCarrick, Prin.
Lay Teachers 31; Students 820.
Catechesis/Religious Programs—Students 225.
Convent—198 Hollywood Ave., 10465. Tel: 718-863-2264. Convent of Sisters of Life
Chapels—Monastery of the Poor Clares, 142 Hollywood Ave., 10465. Tel: 718-822-7271; House of the Holy Family, 2780 Schurz Ave., 10465. Tel: 718-863-9134.

142—ST. FRANCES OF ROME (1898), Revs. Karl A. Bauer; Sebastian Buccellato, O.F.M.; Michael Martine. In res., Rev. Bernard Iheoha.
Res., 4307 Barnes Ave., 10466. Tel: 718-324-5340; 5341; Fax: 718-324-5373.
Church—Moore Plaza & E. 236 St., 10466.
School—(1926), 4321 Barnes Ave., 10466. Tel: 718-324-7360; Fax: 718-994-3694. Dina Monti, Prin.
Sisters of the Presentation 2; Lay Teachers 14; Students 260.

143—ST. FRANCIS XAVIER (1928), Revs. Joseph W. Hickey; Kenneth A. Jesselli; Robert Holick, M.H.M.; Sancho E. Garrote (Philippines).
Res., 1703 Lurting Ave., 10461. Tel: 718-892-3330; Fax: 718-931-6890.
School—(1930), 1711 Haight Ave., 10461. Tel: 718-863-0531. Mrs. Angela Deegan, Prin.
Lay Teachers 25; Students 530.
Chapel—St. Francis Xavier Convent, 1661 Haight Ave., 10461. Tel: 718-892-9466.

144—ST. GABRIEL (1939), Rev. Thomas R. Kelly; Rev. Msgr. Charles McManus, Senior Priest; Rev. Msgr. John T. Doherty, Pastor Emeritus; Rev. Myles P. Murphy; Deacon Eugene Burke.
Res., 3250 Arlington Ave., 10463. Tel: 718-548-4470; Fax: 718-548-6451.
Church—235th & Netherland Ave., 10463.
School—590 W. 235th St., 10463. Tel: 718-548-0444. Sr. Claire Dandeneau, R.J.M., Prin.
Lay Teachers 9; Students 265.
Catechesis/Religious Programs—Tel: 718-548-6585. Mr. Glenn A. McCarthy, D.R.E.
Students 125.

145—ST. HELENA (1940), Revs. Thomas B. Derivan; Joseph J. O'Shea; John J. Haggerty; Edmundo Gomez; Albert P. Bartlett, S.J.; Joseph Ligory (Sri Lanka); Jerome Ofoegbu (Nigeria).
Res., 1315 Olmstead Ave., 10462. Tel: 718-892-3232; Fax: 718-892-3078.
School—(1941), 2050 Benedict Ave., 10462. Tel: 718-892-3234; Fax: 718-892-3924. Richard Heller, Prin.
Sisters of St. Dominic (Sparkill, NY) 2; Lay Teachers 19; Students 535.
High School—Msgr. Scanlan High School, (1949). (Coed) 915 Hutchinson River Pkwy., 10465. Tel: 718-430-0100; Fax: 718-892-8845.
Sisters of St. Dominic (Sparkill, NY) 12; Lay Teachers 32; Students 625.
School—Commercial School, St. Helena's, (1957). (Coed) 955 Hutchinson River Pkwy., 10465. Tel: 718-792-1395; Fax: 718-824-7392.
Sisters of St. Dominic (Sparkill, NY) 6; Lay Teachers 10; Students 250.

146—HOLY CROSS (1921), Revs. Aubrey McNeil, O.F.M.; Joseph G. Rozansky, O.F.M., Guardian & Dir. of Franciscan Formation; Matthew A. Pravetz, O.F.M.; Anthony Schneider, O.F.M.; Thadeus M. Sapio, O.F.M.; Bro. Peter Alheim, O.F.M.; Deacons Luis Fontanez; Juan Rodriguez.
Res., 600 Soundview Ave., 10473. Tel: 718-893-5550; Fax: 718-893-9267.
School—(1923 and 1955), Randall & Thieriot Aves., 10473. Tel: 718-842-4492; Fax: 718-842-4052.
Franciscan Sisters of Allegany, NY 4; Lay Teachers 15; Students 503.
Catechesis/Religious Programs—Tel: 718-328-1054.
Students 503.
Chapel—Franciscan Sisters of Allegany, Thieriot Ave., 10473. Tel: 718-842-2615.

147—HOLY FAMILY (1896), Revs. James D. Flanagan; Joseph P. McAndrew; Deacon Dhoel Canals.
Res., 2158 Watson Ave., 10472. Tel: 718-863-9156; Fax: 718-597-5560.
School—(1913), 2169 Blackrock Ave., 10472. Tel: 718-863-7280; Fax: 718-931-8690.
Sisters of St. Agnes 1; Lay Teachers 32; Students 766.
Catechesis/Religious Programs—2169 Black Rock Ave., 10472. Tel: 718-822-8030.
Students 214.
Chapel—Sisters of St. Agnes, 2155 Blackrock Ave., 10472. Tel: 718-828-4488.

148—HOLY ROSARY (1925), Revs. Lamont R. Hamilton; John J. Higgins; Deacons Joseph D'Aiello; Joseph Solanto. In res., Revs. Thomas F. Petrillo; Eric A. Dadson (Ghana).
Res., 1510 Adee Ave., 10469. Tel: 718-379-4432; 379-4654; Fax: 718-379-9028.
School—(1927; 1955), 1500 Arnow Ave., 10469. Tel: 718-652-1838. Edward Beglane, Prin.
Sisters 2; Lay Teachers 21; Students 650.
Chapel—Holy Rosary Convent, 2755 Woodhull Ave., 10469. Tel: 718-798-6435.

149—HOLY SPIRIT (1901), Rev. Pascual Cervera, Admin.; Deacon Felix Morillo.
Res., 1940 University Ave., 10453. Tel: 718-583-0120; Fax: 718-583-1444.
School—(1913), 1960 University Ave., 10453. Tel: 718-583-1570.
Lay Teachers 14; Students 357.
Catechesis/Religious Programs—Students 305.

150—IMMACULATE CONCEPTION (1853) (German), Very Rev. Francis Skelly, C.Ss.R.; Revs. John McTighe, C.Ss.R.; Dennis Walsh, C.Ss.R.; William Gaffney, C.S.s.R.; Yoshi Akano, C.S.s.R.; Daniel Francis, C.S.s.R.; Bro. Stephen Lendvay, C.Ss.R.; Deacon Cristobal Rodriguez.
Res., 389 E. 150th St., 10455. Tel: 718-292-6970; Fax: 718-292-4603.
Perpetual Help Center—294 E. 150th St., 10455. Tel: 718-585-3678; Fax: 718-993-5870.
School—(1854), 378 E. 151st St., 10455. Tel: 718-585-4843; Fax: 718-585-6846.
Sisters of Christian Charity 9; Lay Teachers 18; Students 712.
Catechesis/Religious Programs—Oscar Cruz, D.R.E.
Students 210.
Chapel—Sisters of Christian Charity, 371 E. 150th St., 10455. Tel: 718-585-8981.

151—IMMACULATE CONCEPTION (1903), Revs. Michael Ristori, O.F.M.Cap.; Paschal Caccavalle, O.F.M.Cap.; Robert Calabrese, O.F.M.Cap.; Camillus Protomastro, O.F.M.Cap.; Francis Sariego; Bro. Matthew DeFamio, O.F.M.Cap.; Deacon Carlos Mercado.
Res., Capuchin Friary, 754 Gun Hill Rd., 10467. Tel: 718-653-2200.
School—Tel: 718-547-3346.
Priests 5; Brothers 2; Lay Teachers 13; Students 601.
Chapel—Immaculate Conception Convent, 3305 Wallace Ave., 10467.

152—ST. JEROME'S (1869), Revs. John Grange; Carmelo Amantegui, S.J.
Res., 230 Alexander Ave., 10454. Tel: 718-665-5533.
School—(1871), 222 Alexander Ave., 10454.
Lay Teachers 10; Students 267.
Catechesis/Religious Programs—D.R.E.: Sr. Josephin Stabile; Dina Monti.
Students 150.

153—ST. JOAN OF ARC (1949), Revs. Edward Bader; Julius Mwau; Deacon Ismael Camacho.
Res., 1372 Stratford Ave., 10472. Tel: 718-842-2233.
Catechesis/Religious Programs—Students 150.

154—ST. JOHN'S (1886), Revs. Edward J. Fagan, O.A.R.; Robert Huse, O.A.R.; Deacon Andrew Rivera. In res., Very Rev. Francis E. Peluso, O.A.R.; Revs. Gregorio Arista, O.A.R.; Domingos Machado, O.A.R.; Bro. Mario Alvarez, O.A.R.
Res., 3021 Kingsbridge Ave., 10463. Tel: 718-548-1221; Fax: 718-548-7774.
School—(1903), 3143 Kingsbridge Ave., 10463. Tel: 718-548-0255; Fax: 718-548-0864. Sr. Patricia Brito, R.J.M., Prin.
Sisters 3; Lay Teachers 13; Students 350.
Catechesis/Religious Programs—Tel: 718-884-2627.
Students 350.
Convent—3029 Godwin Ter., 10463. Tel: 718-548-4902; 543-2454. Religious of Jesus and Mary

155—ST. JOHN CHRYSOSTOM'S (1899), Revs. Joseph P. O'Meara; John P. Sheehan; Deacon Victor Pino.
Res., 985 E. 167th St., 10459. Tel: 718-542-6164.
School—(1914), 1144 Hoe Ave., 10459. Tel: 718-328-7226; Fax: 718-378-5368. Sr. Mary Elizabeth Mooney, O.P., Prin.
Sisters of St. Dominic (Sparkill, NY) 13; Lay Teachers 18; Students 649.
Catechesis/Religious Programs—Tel: 718-328-3580.
Students 367.

156—ST JOHN NAM (1989) (Korean), Rev. Simon Nam.
Res., 3663 White Plains Rd., 10467. Tel: 718-231-2414; Fax: 718-405-0053.

157—ST. JOHN VIANNEY, CURE OF ARS (1960), Revs. Antonio Lasheras, O.A.R.; Jesus Sobejano, O.A.R.; Blas Montenegro, O.A.R.; Deacons Rafael Martinez; Al Leasiolagi; Rafael A. Ramos; Ismael Camacho.
Res., 715 Castle Hill Ave., 10473. Tel: 212-863-4411.
School—2141 Seward Ave., 10473. Tel: 718-892-4400.
Lay Teachers 9; Students 270.

158—ST. JOSEPH (1873), Rev. Rufino Lecumberri.
Res., 1949 Bathgate Ave., 10457. Tel: 718-731-2504.
School—(1905), 1946 Bathgate Ave., 10457. Tel: 718-583-9432; Fax: 718-299-0780. Janine A. Duffy, Prin.
Lay Teachers 13; Students 280.

159—ST. LUCY (1927), Revs. Robert J. Norris; Neil Kelly; Alexander Iheonunekwa (Nigeria); Deacons Wilfredo Miranda; William Bebert. In res., Rev. Frederick J. Becker.
Church—833 Mace Ave., 10467. Tel: 718-882-0710; Fax: 718-882-8876.
School—(1955), 830 Mace Ave., 10467. Tel: 718-882-2203; Fax: 718-547-8351. Dr. Peter A. Mutarelli, Prin.
Lay Teachers 24; Students 602.
Catechesis/Religious Programs—Tel: 718-652-0295.
Students 318.

160—ST. LUKE (1897) (Hispanic-African American), Rev. Msgr. Gerald J. Ryan; Rev. Jose Aguilar. Pastoral Assocs.: Mary Kay Louchart; Sharon Joslyn.
Res., 623 E. 138th St., 10454. Tel: 718-665-6677; Fax: 718-665-0898.
School—(1910), 604-616 E. 139th St., 10454. Tel: 718-585-0380.
Sisters of St. Dominic (Blauvelt) 2; Lay Teachers 13; Students 367.
Catechesis/Religious Programs—Tel: 718-665-8956.
Students 350.
Chapel—St. Luke Convent, 621 E. 138th St., 10454. Tel: 718-292-3016.

161—ST. MARGARET OF CORTONA (1887), Revs. William E. Warren; Robert A. Quarato; Thomas Murphy, S.J. In res., Rev. Robert J. Aufieri.
Res., 6000 Riverdale Ave., 10471. Tel: 718-549-8053; Fax: 718-543-3432.
School—(1926), 452 W. 260th St., 10471. Tel: 718-549-8580. Sr. Dorothy DeYoung, Prin.
Sisters 2; Lay Teachers 12; Students 335.
Catechesis/Religious Programs—Tel: 718-884-9777.
Students 160.
Chapel—Bronx, Our Lady of Grace.

162—ST. MARGARET MARY (1923), Rev. Robert P. Arce. In res., Revs. Robert A. Jeffers; Hyacinth Njoku (Nigeria).
Res., 1914 Morris Ave., 10453-5904. Tel: 718-299-4233; Fax: 718-583-3726.
School—(1923), 121 E. 177th St., 10453. Tel: 718-731-5905; Fax: 718-731-8924.
Sisters of Mercy of the Americas 4; Lay Teachers 11; Students 350.
Catechesis/Religious Programs—Students 368.

163—ST. MARTIN OF TOURS (1897), Revs. John C. Flynn; Vicente Florido; Sr. Peggy Gannon, O.P., Pastoral Min.; Deacons Frankie Vazques; Reynaldo Rosado.
Res., 664 Grote St., 10457. Tel: 718-295-0913.
School—(1926), E. 182nd St. & Crotona Ave., 10457. Tel: 718-733-0347. Sr. M. Cecilia, Prin.
Dominican Sisters (Sparkill, NY) 2; Lay Teachers 16; Students 288.
Catechesis/Religious Programs—Students 350.
Chapel—Dominican Convent, 695 E. 182nd St., 10457.

164—ST. MARY (1866), Rev. John B. Sullivan. In res., Rev. James Cunningham.
Res., 650 E. 226th St., 10466. Tel: 718-547-8000; Fax: 718-547-8001.
Church—White Plains Rd., 10466.
School—(1950), 3956 Carpenter Ave., 10466. Tel: 718-547-0500; Fax: 718-547-0530.
Lay Teachers 13; Students 292.
Chapel—Convent, 3961 Carpenter Ave., 10466. Tel: 718-652-2873. School Chapel, E. 224th St., 10466.

165—ST. MARY STAR OF THE SEA (1887), Revs. Robert J. Moore; Donald F. Partridge; Thomas Myladil, O.C.D. (India); Deacon William J. Mueller.
Res., 595 Minneford Ave., 10464-1118. Tel: 718-885-1440.
Church—600 City Island Ave., 10464.
School—(1931), 580 Minneford Ave., 10464. Tel: 718-885-1527.
Dominican Sisters of Blauvelt 2; Lay Teachers 9; Students 270.
Chapel—Dominican Sisters, 176 Kilroe St., 10464. Tel: 718-885-0849.

166—ST. MICHAEL (1969), Revs. William J. Luciano; Benedict C. Varghese, C.M.I. (India).
Res., 765 Co-Op City Boulevard, 10475-1601. Tel: 718-671-8050; Fax: 718-320-3776.

167—NATIVITY OF OUR BLESSED LADY (1924), Rev. Jaime H. Duenas.
Res., Rectory, 1531 E. 233rd St., 10466. Tel: 718-324-3531; Fax: 718-324-3531.
School—(1953), 3893 Dyre Ave., 10466. Tel: 718-324-2188; Fax: 718-324-3531.
Lay Teachers 20; Students 326.
Convent—1534 E. 233rd St., 10466.

168—ST. NICHOLAS OF TOLENTINE (1906), Revs. John F. Dello Russo, O.S.A.; Christopher Nowak, O.S.A.; Russell Ortega, O.S.A.; Thomas Wilhelm, O.S.A.; Joseph Tran; Sr. Susan McCarthy, R.D.C., Pastoral Assoc. In res., Rev. William J. Wallace, O.S.A.; Bro. Michael Duffy, O.S.A.
Res., 2345 University Ave., 10468. Tel: 718-295-6800; Fax: 718-367-7411.
School—(1907), 2336 Andrews Ave., 10468. Tel: 718-364-5110; Fax: 718-561-3964.
Sisters of St. Dominic of Blauvelt 1; Lay Teachers 13; Students 399.
Catechesis/Religious Programs—Tel: 718-295-6770. Mr. Oscar Aviles, D.R.E.
Students 542.
Chapels—Convent of St. Nicholas of Tolentine, 2341 University Ave., 10468. Tel: 718-367-3102; St. Nicholas of Tolentine School Chapel, Tel: 718-364-5110.

169—OUR LADY OF ANGELS (1924), Revs. David P. Casella; Antonio Aldana (Mexico); Kevin O'Reilly; Deacon Luis Delgado.
Res., 2860 Webb Ave., 10468. Tel: 718-548-3005; Fax: 718-884-2450.
Church—2860 Sedgwick Ave., 10468.
School—(1928), 2865 Claflin Ave., 10468. Tel: 718-549-3503. Sr. Mary Ann Cleary, Prin.
Sisters of Charity of St. Vincent de Paul 3; Lay Teachers 18; Students 470.
Catechesis/Religious Programs—Students 310.

170—OUR LADY OF THE ASSUMPTION (1923), Revs. Donald M. Dwyer; Jarlath Quinn; Deacon Howard Banker. In res., Rev. Peter Thumma, J.C.D.
Res., 1634 Mahan Ave., 10461. Tel: 718-824-5454; Fax: 718-824-5456.
School—(1928), 1617 Parkview Ave., 10461. Tel: 718-829-1706.
Sisters 1; Lay Teachers 20; Students 527.
Catechesis/Religious Programs—Tel: 718-904-8464.
Students 504.
Chapel—Convent, 1639 Parkview Ave., 10461. Tel: 718-829-7980.

171—OUR LADY OF GOOD COUNSEL (1969) (Albanian), Revs. Peter Popovich, Admin.; Andrew Nargaj, O.F.M.
Res., Albanian Roman Catholic Center, 4221 Park Ave., 10457. Tel: 718-294-6981. [CEM]

172—OUR LADY OF GRACE (1924), Revs. Walter A. Birkle; Philip J. Caruso; Felix J. Gonzalez (Venezuela).
Res., 3985 Bronxwood Ave., 10466. Tel: 718-652-4817.
School—Denise Rigano, Prin. Lay Teachers 1; Students 410.

173—OUR LADY OF MERCY (Fordham) (1852-1892), Revs. Lawrence J. Quinn; John Rueda (Colombia); Pablo Rentino (Philippines).
Res., 2496 Marion Ave., 10458. Tel: 718-933-4400.
School—(1907), 2512 Marion Ave., 10458. Tel: 718-367-0237.
Sisters 5; Lay Teachers 14; Students 530.
Catechesis/Religious Programs—Students 210.
Chapel—Convent, 2473 Valentine Ave., 10458. Tel: 718-367-5558.

174—OUR LADY OF MT. CARMEL (1906) (Italian), Rev. Msgr. John A. Ruvo; Rev. Msgr. Thomas F. Heneghan. In res., Revs. Nicholas F. Basile; Anthony D'Antonio; Anthony Giampietro, C.S.B.
Res., 627 E. 187th St., 10458. Tel: 718-295-3770.
School—(1925), 189th St. & Bathgate Ave., 10458. Tel: 718-295-6080. James E. Irwin, Prin.
Lay Teachers 11; Students 281.
Catechesis/Religious Programs—Students 150.
Convent—2410 Hughes Ave., 10458. Tel: 718-329-0390. Suore Missionarie del Catechismo
Sisters 4.
Chapel—Brothers of Holy Cross, Tel: 718-733-8036.

175—OUR LADY OF PITY (1908) (Italian-Hispanic), Rev. Peter Damian Nuzzo, O.F.M., Guardian & Pastor; Deacon James Francis.
Res., 276 E. 151st St., 10451. Tel: 718-665-3880.

176—OUR LADY OF REFUGE (1923), Rev. Msgr. John J. Jenik.
Res., 290 E. 196th St., 10458. Tel: 718-367-4690; Fax: 718-365-7644. [JC]
School—(1923), 2708 Briggs Ave., 10458. Tel: 718-367-3081; Fax: 718-365-7644.
Lay Teachers 10; Students 310.
Catechesis/Religious Programs—Tel: 718-367-3384.
Students 315.

177—OUR LADY OF SOLACE (1902), Revs. John M. Knapp; Francisco Imperial (Philippines); Thomas Seraphin Parambi, C.S.T. (India).
Res., 731 Morris Park Ave., 10462. Tel: 718-863-3282; Fax: 718-792-4950.
School—(1916), 1804 Holland Ave., 10462. Tel: 718-792-9947.
Religious of the Presentation 2; Lay Teachers 8; Students 324.

178—OUR LADY OF VICTORY (1909), Rev. Peter Gavigan.
Res., 1512 Webster Ave., 10457. Tel: 718-583-4044; Fax: 718-583-4044.

179—OUR SAVIOUR (1912) (Hispanic), Revs. Jose Gabriel Piedrahita, M.X.Y.; Julio Ramirez, M.X.Y.
Res., 2317 Washington Ave., 10458. Tel: 718-295-9600; Fax: 718-295-9601.

180—SANTA MARIA (1926) (Italian), Revs. Fernando Real, M.ID., Admin.; Antimo Fiorillo, Pastor Emeritus; Robert Badillo, M.ID.; Eduardo Rodriguez, M.ID.
Res., 2352 St. Raymond Ave., 10462. Tel: 718-828-2380; Fax: 718-828-3412.
School—(1951), 1510 Zerega Ave., 10462. Tel: 718-823-3636. Sr. Christian Price, Prin.
Sisters Apostles of the Sacred Heart 3; Lay Teachers 9; Students 230.
Chapel—Santa Maria Convent, 1460 Zerega Ave., 10462.

181—ST. PETER AND ST. PAUL (1897), Rev. Vincent A. Resta.
Res., 833 St. Ann's Ave., 10456. Tel: 718-665-3924.
School—(1911), 838 Brook Ave., 10456. Tel: 718-665-2056.
Sisters 5; Lay Teachers 14; Students 485.
Chapel—Sisters of Charity, 839 St. Ann's Ave., 10456. Tel: 718-292-7057.

182—SS. PHILIP AND JAMES (1949), Sr. Sharon Donohue, R.S.M., Pastoral Assoc.; Deacons Albert V. Welhous; Robert Santana. In res., Revs. Bededict Paul; Pat F. Rossi, Ph.D.

Res., 1160 E. 213th St., 10469. Tel: 718-547-2203; Fax: 718-231-8160.
School—(1953), 1160 E. 213th St., 10469. Tel: 718-882-4576.
Sisters of St. Dominic (Blauvelt) 1; Lay Teachers 9; Students 300.
Chapel—Dominican Sisters Convent, 1180 E. 214th St., 10469.

183—ST. PHILIP NERI (1898), Rev. Msgr. Kevin J. Colleran; Revs. Sean Horrigan, C.S.Sp. (Ireland); Stephen Ryan; Deacon Hector Rodriguez. In res., Revs. Paul Miki Gyamfi; Martin Onyebuchi (Nigeria).
Res., 3025 Grand Concourse, 10468. Tel: 718-733-3200.
School—(1913), 3031 Grand Concourse, 10468. Tel: 718-365-8806. Bro. Brian Johnston.
Irish Franciscan Brothers 1; Ursuline Sisters 2; Lay Teachers 23; Students 690.
Catechesis/Religious Programs—Students 240.
Chapels—Convent of Mount St. Ursula, Marion Ave. & 200th St., 10468. Tel: 718-365-7410; Kolping Residence, Kolping Society, 2916 Grand Concourse, 10468. Tel: 718-733-6119; Ursuline Residence, 2850 Marion Ave., 10468. Tel: 718-295-6094. Irish Franciscan Brothers, 260 E. 201 St., 10468. Tel: 718-365-5694. St. Mary's Hall. (Ursuline) 323 E. 198th St., 10468. Tel: 718-933-9894.

184—ST. PIUS V (1907), Revs. Edward Russell; Adolfo Romero-Rios (Argentina); Deacons Raul Padron; Luis Torres.
Res., 420 E. 145th St., 10454. Tel: 718-665-6642.
School—(1913), 413 E. 144th St., 10454. Tel: 718-665-5075; Fax: 718-665-2987.
Lay Teachers 9; Students 230.
High School—500 Courtlandt Ave., 10454. Tel: 718-292-3636; Fax: 718-402-1704.
Lay Teachers 13; Students 210.
Catechesis/Religious Programs—Students 160.

185—ST. RAYMOND (1842), Rev. Msgr. Charles M. Kavanagh; Rev. Msgr. Henry J. Vier, Pastor Emeritus; Rev. Msgr. George A. Cocuzzi (ROC); Revs. Edward M. Conroy; Joseph Tyrrell; Anthony P. Settle; Deacons Aldo Preti; Roberto Fernandez.
Res., 1759 Castle Hill Ave., 10462. Tel: 718-792-4044; Fax: 718-863-8509. [CEM 2]
School—(1909), 2380 E. Tremont Ave., 10462. Tel: 718-597-3232. Victor J. Presto, Prin.
Sisters 1; Lay Teachers 20; Students 630.
High Schools—(Boys) 2151 St. Raymond Ave., 10462. Tel: 718-824-5050. Bro. Frank Byrne, F.S.C., Prin.
Sisters 1; Brothers of the Christian Schools 8; Lay Teachers 42; Students 770; (Girls). Tel: 718-824-4220. Sr. Marian Jude, S.C., Prin.
Sisters of Charity 10; Sisters 1; Lay Teachers 14; Students 300.
Catechesis/Religious Programs—Mrs. Ann O'Keefe, D.R.E.
Students 406.
Family Outreach Program—1720 Metropolitan Ave., 10462. Tel: 718-792-2087. Bro. Raymond Meagher, F.S.C., Dir.
Chapel—Brothers Residence, 1754 Castle Hill Ave., 10462.
Brothers of the Christian Schools 10.

186—ST. RITA OF CASCIA SHRINE CHURCH (1900), Rev. Jesus Perez Recio, O.A.R.
Res., 448 College Ave., 10451. Tel: 718-585-5900; Fax: 718-585-5901.
Catechesis/Religious Programs—Students 165.

187—ST. ROCH (1899) (Spanish), Rev. Francisco Oviedo, O.A.R., Admin.
Res., 525 Wales Ave., 10455. Tel: 718-292-3834.

188—SACRED HEART (1875), Revs. Mark T. Cregan, C.S.C.; Robert R. Baker, C.S.C.; Ms. Yolanda Torres, Pastoral Assoc.
Res., 1253 Shakespeare Ave., 10452. Tel: 718-293-2766; Fax: 718-293-1581.
Schools—Primary Division, (1950), 95 W. 168th St., 10452. Tel: 718-293-4288; Fax: 718-293-4886. Joanne Walsh, Prin.
Lay Teachers 15; Students 452; Middle School, (1926), 1248 Nelson Ave., 10452. Tel: 718-293-6040. Bro. Stephen Milan, F.M.S., Prin.
Lay Teachers 16; Students 442.
Catechesis/Religious Programs—Sr. Christina Dougherty, P.B.V.M., D.R.E.
Students 340.
Chapel—St. Eugene, 979 Ogden Ave., 10452. Tel: 718-681-2222.

189—ST. SIMON STOCK (1919) (Hispanic), Revs. Ruben Rodriguez, O.Carm.; Estebon Rodriguez, O.Carm.
Res., 2191 Valentine Ave., 10457. Tel: 718-367-1251.
Church—East 182nd St. & Ryer Ave., 10457.
School—182nd St. & Valentine Ave., 10457. Tel: 718-367-0453; Fax: 718-933-8822.
Lay Teachers 20; Students 700.
Catechesis/Religious Programs—Students 350.

190—ST. THERESA OF THE INFANT JESUS (1927) (Italian), Revs. Robert F. Grippo; Robert F. Ashman; Rev. Msgr. John L. Guido, Pastor Emeritus; Deacon Anthony P. Cassaneto; Christopher A. Buonocore, Parish Mgr. In res., Rev. Msgr. John G. Woolsey.
Res., 2855 St. Theresa Ave., 10461. Tel: 718-892-1900.
School—(1954), 2872 St. Theresa Ave., 10461. Tel: 718-792-3688; Fax: 718-892-9441. Mr. Malachy Cleary, Prin.
Lay Teachers 19; Students 387.

191—ST. THOMAS AQUINAS (1890), Most Rev. Francisco Garmendia, D.D.; Revs. Peter J. Byrne, Admin.; Fernando A. Hernandez. In res., Rev. Paul Adogamhe (Nigeria).
Res., 1900 Crotona Pkwy., 10460. Tel: 718-589-5235.
School—(1907), 1909 Daly Ave., 10460. Tel: 718-893-7600.
Lay Teachers 21; Students 510.
Convent—1899 Daly Ave., 10460.

192—ST. VALENTINE (1891) (Polish), Rev. Msgr. Stanislaus Jablonski.
Res., 810 E. 221st St., 10467. Tel: 718-652-3197.

193—VISITATION (1928), Rev. Msgr. Robert W. Larkin; Revs. Arthur T. Welton; John Horan, C.S.Sp.; Deacon George McGowan. In res., Rev. Francis P. O'Malley.
Res., 160 Van Cortlandt Park S., 10463. Tel: 718-548-1455.
School—(1932), Putnam Ave. & W. 239th St., 10463. Tel: 718-543-2250; Fax: 718-543-3665.
Priests 3; Sisters 6; Lay Teachers 4; Students 256.

BOROUGH OF RICHMOND
STATEN ISLAND

194—ST. ADALBERT (Elm Park) (1901) (Polish), Revs. John J. Hynes; John J. Wroblewski; Deacon Joseph J. Rentkowski.
Res., 30 St. Adalbert Pl., Elm Park, 10303. Tel: 718-442-8476.
School—(1905), 355 Morningstar Rd., Elm Park, 10303. Tel: 718-442-2020; Fax: 718-447-2012.
Priests 2; Lay Teachers 9; Students 325.
Catechesis/Religious Programs—Tel: 718-442-5446.
Students 200.

195—ST. ANN (1914), Rev. Lawrence T. Quinn; Rev. Msgr. Vincent F. Clyne, Pastor Emeritus; Revs. Sylvester P. McGinn; Matthew Iraly (India); Terence O'Rourke, O.S.A.
Res., 101 Cromwell Ave., 10304. Tel: 718-351-0270; Fax: 718-980-4731.
School—(1955), 125 Cromwell Ave., 10304. Tel: 718-351-4343.
Presentation Nuns 1; Lay Teachers 12; Students 329.
Catechesis/Religious Programs—Michael Mazella, D.R.E.
Students 485.

196—ST. ANTHONY (1908), Rev. Msgr. Raphael F. Pakulniewicz.
Res., 24 Shelly Ave., 10314. Tel: 718-761-6660.
Church—Victory Blvd., 10314.

197—ASSUMPTION (1922) (Italian), Rev. John A. Pinterbone, K.H.S.
Res., 15 Webster Ave., 10301. Tel: 718-727-4594.

198—ST. BENEDICTA (1925). Closed. For inquiries for parish records contact Our Lady of Mount Carmel.

199—BLESSED SACRAMENT (1910), Rev. Msgr. Francis V. Boyle; Rev. Joseph Victor Arenas (Philippines). In res., Rev. Francis A. Naccarato; Rev. Msgr. Daniel L. Sullivan.
Res., 30 Manor Rd., 10310. Tel: 718-442-1581; Fax: 718-442-1398.
Church—Manor Rd. & Forest Ave., 10310.
School—(1917), 830 Delafield Ave., 10310. Tel: 718-442-3090; Fax: 718-442-9654. Sr. Ann McLaughlin, I.H.M., Prin.
Sisters, Servants of the Immaculate Heart of Mary 6; Lay Teachers 20; Students 692.
Catechesis/Religious Programs—Tel: 718-448-0378.
Students 300.

200—ST. CHARLES (1960), Rev. Msgr. Thomas J. Gaffney; Rev. Msgr. Robert J. Kelly, Pastor Emeritus; Rev. Mark G. Vaillancourt; Deacons Vincent Brigande; Michael Calafiore.
Res., 644 Clawson St., 10306. Tel: 718-987-2670; Fax: 718-987-7950.
School—Tel: 718-987-0200.
Sisters of St. Dominic (Blauvelt) 1; Lay Teachers 21; Students 817.
Catechesis/Religious Programs—Tel: 718-979-6800.
Students 525.

201—ST. CHRISTOPHER (1926) (Italian-Irish), Rev. Msgr. Kenneth A. Gerathy; Revs. George Mikolajczyk, M.M.; Michael A. Arputham.
Res., 130 Midland Ave., 10306. Tel: 718-351-2452; Fax: 718-351-1174.
School—(1930), 15 Lisbon Pl., 10306. Tel: 718-351-0902; Fax: 718-351-0975. Catherine Mizzi-Gili, Prin.
Lay Teachers 11; Students 322.
Catechesis/Religious Programs—Students 218.

202—ST. CLARE (1921), Rev. Msgr. Joseph P. Murphy; Revs. Michael W. Cichon; Edward Tissera; Andrew King; Deacon Richard Mitchell.
Res., 110 Nelson Ave., 10308. Tel: 718-984-7873; Fax: 718-966-8420.
School—151 Lindenwood Rd., 10308. Tel: 718-984-7091. Sr. Rosemary Ward, Prin.
Sisters Religious of the Presentation 1; Lay Teachers 20; Students 688.
Catechesis/Religious Programs—Tel: 718-948-4829.
Students 1,895.

203—ST. CLEMENT (1910), Rev. Msgr. Nicholas J. Soares; Rev. Manuel I. Rojas (Peru).
Res., 207 Harbor Rd., 10303. Tel: 718-442-1688; Fax: 718-442-4689.
Church—126 Van Pelt Ave., 10303.
Catechesis/Religious Programs—Tel: 718-727-6442.
Students 342.

204—HOLY CHILD (1966), Rev. Msgr. John D. Burke; Rev. Msgr. Francis M. Brennan, Pastor Emeritus; Revs. Morgan J. Kuhl; Emmanuel Nwogwugwu; Renato B. Cruz.
Res., 4747 Amboy Rd., 10312. Tel: 718-356-5890; Fax: 718-356-5995.
Preschool Office—4747 Amboy Rd., 10312. Tel: 718-356-5159; Fax: 718-356-1933.
School—School of Religion, Tel: 718-356-5277; Fax: 718-227-0898.
Lay Teachers 116; Students 1,200.

205—HOLY FAMILY (1966), Rev. Msgr. Daniel J. Keehan; Rev. Msgr. Francis J. Glynn, Pastor Emeritus; Revs. Henry S. Gentile, C.S.; William Muhm.
Mailing Address: 366 Watchogue Rd., 10314. Tel: 718-761-6663; Fax: 718-982-0287.
School—School of Religion, (1967). (Elementary & High School) 330 Watchogue Rd., 10314. Tel: 718-761-1598.
Sisters 2; Lay Teachers 54; Students 540.
Catechesis/Religious Programs—Students 550.
Convent—85 Delmore St., 10314. Tel: 718-698-3118.

206—HOLY ROSARY (1927), Rev. Msgr. Richard J. Guastella; Revs. Joy Mampilly, C.M.I. (India); Stephen G. Challman; Robert Dillon; Deacon Rosario Tirella. In res., Rev. Percy Joseph Raj, O.F.M., Chap.
Res., 80 Jerome Ave., 10305. Tel: 718-727-3360; Fax: 718-448-6819.
School—(1955), 100 Jerome Ave., 10305. Tel: 718-447-1195. Florence M. Bricker, Prin.
Lay Teachers 21; Students 621.
Catechesis/Religious Programs—Tel: 718-273-6695. Sr. Catherine Shanahan, D.R.E.
Students 421.

207—IMMACULATE CONCEPTION (1887), Rev. Peter J. Byrne.
Res., 128 Targee St., 10304. Tel: 718-447-2165.
School—(1908), 104 Gordon St., 10304. Tel: 718-447-7018; Fax: 718-447-7018. Sr. Mary Timothy, Prin.
Sisters 2; Lay Staff 8; Students 201.
Catechesis/Religious Programs—Students 89.
Chapel—Bayley Seton Hospital, Bay St., 10304. Tel: 718-390-6000. Rev. Edward Datty, S.A.

208—ST. JOHN THE BAPTIST DE LA SALLE (1900), Rev. Peter J. Byrne, Admin.
Res., 128 Targee St., 10304. Tel: 718-447-2165.
Church—76 Jackson St., 10304.

209—ST. JOHN NEUMANN (1982), Revs. James Malley; Julius Rodulfa; James Bolger.
Res., 1380 Arthur Kill Rd., 10312. Tel: 718-984-8535; Fax: 718-984-8840.
Catechesis/Religious Programs—Tel: 718-966-7327.
Students 408.

210—ST. JOSEPH (1902) (Italian), Rev. Msgr. John T. Servodidio.
Parish Office: 463 Tompkins Ave., 10305. Tel: 718-816-0047; Fax: 718-816-4529.
Res., 171 St. Mary's Ave., 10305.
Church—466 Tompkins Ave., 10305.
School—139 St. Mary's Ave., 10305. Tel: 718-447-7686. Linda Bilotti, Prin.
Lay Teachers 12; Students 336.

211—ST. JOSEPH, ST. THOMAS (1848), Rev. Msgr. Peter G. Finn; Rev. Msgr. John J. Gordon, Pastor Emeritus; Revs. Richard Veras; Evangelio R. Suaybagio (Philippines); Francisco H. Lanzaderas (Philippines); Deacon Arthur Fama.
Res., 6135 Amboy Rd., 10309. Tel: 718-984-4572. [CEM]

School—Tel: 718-356-3344; Fax: 718-227-9531. Theresa Simmonds, Prin.
Lay Teachers 10; Students 350.
Catechesis/Religious Programs—Tel: 718-984-1156.
Students 892.

212—ST. MARGARET MARY (1926), Rev. Robert J. Navins; Deacon Joseph Graf. In res., Rev. Msgr. John Gordan.
Res., 560 Lincoln Ave., 10306. Tel: 718-351-2612.
School—(1925), 556 Lincoln Ave., 10306. Tel: 718-351-4778. Sr. Kathryn Anderson, Prin.
Sisters, Religious of the Presentation 2; Lay Teachers 7; Students 191.
Catechesis/Religious Programs—Students 190.

213—ST. MARY (1852), Revs. Victor J. Buebendorf; Peter Selvaraj.
Res., 1101 Bay St., 10305. Tel: 718-727-0671. [CEM]
School—(1853), 1124 Bay St., 10305. Tel: 718-447-1842. Virginia Savarese, Prin.
Lay Teachers 10; Students 295.

214—ST. MARY OF THE ASSUMPTION (1853), Rev. William Harder, Admin.
Res., 2230 Richmond Ter., 10302. Tel: 718-442-6372; Fax: 718-442-3299. [CEM]
Mission—New York, Richmond Co., Christ the King, 182 Park Ave., 10302.

215—ST. MICHAEL (1922), Rev. Msgr. Nicholas J. Soares; Rev. Manuel I. Rojas (Peru).
Res., 207 Harbor Rd., 10303. Tel: 718-442-1688; Fax: 718-442-4689.
Church—211-213 Harbor Rd., 10303.
Catechesis/Religious Programs—Tel: 718-727-6442.
Students 342.

216—OUR LADY OF GOOD COUNSEL (1898), Revs. Joseph S. Mostardi, O.S.A., Pastor/Prior; Robert T. Drummond, O.S.A.; Augustus C. Sandmann, O.S.A.; Robert F. Andrews, O.S.A.; Luis A. Vera, O.S.A.; Deacons Arthur W. Eccleston; Walter Sweeney; Alfred Thompson.
Res., 10 Austin Pl., 10304. Tel: 718-447-1503; Fax: 718-447-7361.
School—(1923), 42 Austin Pl., 10304. Tel: 718-447-7260. Mrs. Frances Santangelo, Prin.
Lay Teachers 11; Students 270.
Catechesis/Religious Programs—Sr. Patricia Flattery, D.R.E.
Students 150.

217—OUR LADY HELP OF CHRISTIANS (1898), Revs. Edmund P. Connors; Abraham B. Dominic (Sri Lanka); Deacons Edward J. Wetherall; John Singler.
Res., 7396 Amboy Rd., 10307. Tel: 718-317-9772.
School—(1910 and 1955), 23 Summit St., 10307. Tel: 718-984-1360; Fax: 718-966-9356. Mrs. Nancy Lucas, Prin.
Lay Teachers 10; Students 260.
Catechesis/Religious Programs—Tel: 718-356-3888.
Students 600.

218—OUR LADY OF MT. CARMEL-ST. BENEDICTA (1913), Rev. Philip Cordisco, O.SS.T. In res., Rev. Joseph F. Lupo, O.SS.T.
Res., 1265 Castleton Ave., 10310. Tel: 718-442-3411; Fax: 718-442-3997.
School—285 Clove Rd., 10310. Tel: 718-981-5131.
Catechesis/Religious Programs—Students 285.

219—OUR LADY, QUEEN OF PEACE (1922), Revs. Robert I. Gannon; John A. DeBellis; John J. Sheehan; Deacon Ross Calimano. In res., Rev. James Garisto.
Res., 90 Third St., 10306. Tel: 718-351-1093.
School—(1924), 22 Steele Ave., 10306. Tel: 718-351-0370. Sr. Mary Regina Gibbons, Prin.
Sisters of the Presentation 1; Lay Teachers 17; Students 600.
Catechesis/Religious Programs—Tel: 718-979-0989.
Students 570.
Mission—New Dorp Beach, Richmond Co., Our Lady of Lourdes, Cedar Grove Ave., 10306.
Chapel—St. Therese of the Child Jesus, 62 Cloister Pl., 10306. Tel: 718-351-0209.

220—OUR LADY OF PITY (1923) (Italian), Rev. Msgr. Philip J. Franceschini; Rev. Msgr. Robert R. Mazziotta, Pastor Emeritus; Revs. John E. Mercer; Eugene E. Azorji.
Res., 1616 Richmond Ave., 10314. Tel: 718-761-5421; Fax: 718-983-6225.
Catechesis/Religious Programs—Tel: 718-761-5463.
Students 730.

221—OUR LADY STAR OF THE SEA (1935), Rev. Msgr. Jeffrey Conway; Revs. Robert Porpora; Angelo Palermo, S.A.C.; Dr. Patrick Del Zoppo, Pastoral Assoc.
Res., 5371 Amboy Rd., Huguenot Park, 10312. Tel: 718-984-0593; Fax: 718-984-5203.
School—(1958), 5411 Amboy Rd., 10312. Tel: 718-984-5750.
Sisters 1; Lay Teachers 26; Students 960.
Catechesis/Religious Programs—5411 Amboy Rd., 10312. Tel: 718-984-1885.
Students 1,150.

222—ST. PATRICK (1862), Rev. Msgr. John M. McCarthy; Revs. John G. Pedulla; Sekar Sagayaraj; Deacon Joseph Hooghuis.
Res., 53 St. Patrick's Pl., 10306. Tel: 718-351-0044.
School—(1919), 3560 Richmond Rd., 10306. Tel: 718-979-8815; 979-4227 (Parish). Sr. Mary Ferro, S.S.D., Prin.
Sisters 3; Lay Teachers 23; Students 602.
Catechesis/Religious Programs—Tel: 718-979-1272.
Students 486.

223—ST. PAUL (1924), Rev. Vincent Bartley; Sr. Jean Conaty, I.H.M.
Mailing Address: 148 Cassidy Pl., 10301.
Res., 145 Clinton Ave., 10301. Tel: 718-447-6362; Fax: 718-720-0106.
School—(1924), 129 Clinton Ave., 10301. Tel: 718-447-5774; Fax: 718-447-5881. Ms. Fran Jorin, Prin.
Lay Teachers 9; Students 200.
Catechesis/Religious Programs—Students 208.
Christian Brothers Residence: 148 Cassidy Pl., 10301.

224—ST. PETER (1839), Rev. Msgr. James J. Dorney; Revs. John T. Thenen; Matthias Ndulaka (Nigeria).
Res., 53 St. Mark's Pl., 10301. Tel: 718-727-2672; Fax: 718-720-9269. [CEM]
School—300-310 Richmond Ter., 10301. Tel: 718-447-1796; Fax: 718-447-4240.
Lay Teachers 12; Students 303.
High Schools—Boys High School, 200 Clinton Ave., 10301. Tel: 718-447-1676; Fax: 718-447-4027. Mr. John Fodera, Prin.; Bro. James Kelly, F.S.C., Pres. Brothers of the Christian Schools 6; Lay Teachers 29; Students 679; Girls High School, Tel: 718-447-0304. Dr. Susan Siefert, Prin.
Lay Teachers 9; Students 137.
Chapel—Sacred Heart Convent of Sisters of Charity, 280 Richmond Ter., 10301. St. Joseph, Brothers' House, Tel: 718-447-2815.

225—ST. RITA (1921), Revs. John F. Reardon; Austin E. Titus.
Res., 281 Bradley Ave., 10314. Tel: 718-698-3746.
School—(1922), 30 Wellbrook Ave., 10314. Tel: 718-961-2504.
Dominican Sisters 1; Lay Teachers 16; Students 535.
Catechesis/Religious Programs—Students 443.
Chapel—Dominican Sisters. (Roman Congregation of St. Dominic) 61 Wellbrook Ave., 10314. Tel: 718-761-1171.

226—ST. ROCH (1922), Revs. Alfred J. Pucci; John Boyle. In res., Rev. G. David Sears (SY).
Res., 602 Richmond Ave., 10302. Tel: 718-442-4755; 448-2424. [CEM]
School—465 Villa Ave., 10302. Sr. Mary Patricia, Prin.
Sisters of St. John the Baptist 3; Lay Teachers 8; Students 285.
Catechesis/Religious Programs—Students 160.

227—SACRED HEART (1875), Rev. James E. Burke; Rev. Msgr. Andrew F. Quinn, Pastor Emeritus; Revs. Selvaraj Manickam (India); Thomas Kallumady.
Res., 981 Castleton Ave., 10310. Tel: 718-442-0058; Fax: 718-816-8006.
School—(1875), 301 N. Burgher Ave., 10310. Tel: 718-442-0347. Mrs. Zoilita M. Herrera, Prin.
Lay Teachers 20; Students 558.
Catechesis/Religious Programs—Tel: 718-448-1536.
Students 285.

228—ST. STANISLAUS KOSTKA (1923) (Polish), Revs. John A. Pinterbone, M.Th., M.A., Admin.; Marek Suchocki, J.C.L., M.Th (Poland).
Res., 109 York Ave., 10301. Tel: 718-447-3937.

229—ST. SYLVESTER (1921), Rev. Arthur A. Golino; Rev. Msgr. Daniel L. Sullivan, Pastor Emeritus; Rev. Msgr. Anthony O. Erhueh (Nigeria); Revs. Dennis M. Dinan; Sebastian Thozhuthumparambil, C.M. (India).
Res., 854 Targee St., 10304-4517. Tel: 718-727-4639; Fax: 718-273-2950.
School—(1930), 884 Targee St., 10304. Tel: 718-442-4938; Fax: 718-442-8177. Nancy Bushman, Prin.
Lay Teachers 10; Students 279.
Catechesis/Religious Programs—Tel: 718-442-4949.
Students 279.

230—ST. TERESA (1926), Revs. William J. Boldt; John J. O'Hara.
Res., 1634 Victory Blvd., 10314. Tel: 718-442-5412; Fax: 718-442-9041.
School—(1955), 1632 Victory Blvd., 10314. Tel: 718-448-9650.
Sisters of the Presentation 2; Lay Teachers 18; Students 600.
Catechesis/Religious Programs—Tel: 718-981-2632.
Students 425.
Mission—Staten Island, St. Nicholas.
Chapel—St. Nicholas, La Bau Ave. & Northern Blvd., 10314.

OUTSIDE THE CITY OF NEW YORK

Amenia, Dutchess Co., Immaculate Conception (1868), Rev. John L. Durkin; Deacon David Weinstein.
Res., 4 Lavelle Rd., 12501. Tel: 914-373-8193. [CEM]
Catechesis/Religious Programs—Students 200.
Mission—Millerton, Dutchess Co., St. Patrick, Church St., Millerton, 12546. [CEM]

Ardsley, Westchester Co., Our Lady of Perpetual Help (1929), Revs. Robert J. Duane; Emeka Godfrey Amanchukwu (Nigeria).
Res., One Cross Rd., 10502. Tel: 914-693-0030; Fax: 914-674-9020.
Catechesis/Religious Programs—Tel: 914-693-3831.
Students 351.

Armonk, Westchester Co., St. Patrick (1966), Rev. John F. Quinn; Rev. Msgr. Walter L. Schroeder, Pastor Emeritus; Rev. Daniel J. Brady.
Res., 29 Cox Ave., P.O. Box 6, 10504. Tel: 914-273-9724.
Catechesis/Religious Programs—Tel: 914-273-8226. Mrs. Ann O'Sullivan, D.R.E.
Students 420.

Bangall, Dutchess Co., Immaculate Conception (1919), Rev. Msgr. John G. Shevlin, Pastor Emeritus; Rev. Richard O'Gorman.
Res., Hunns Lake Rd., 12506. Tel: 914-868-1923; Fax: 914-868-1593. [CEM]
Mission—Clinton Corners, Dutchess Co., St. Joseph, (1883) Clinton Corners, 12514.

Barrytown, Dutchess Co., Sacred Heart. Closed. Parochial records at St. Christopher, Red Hook.

Beacon, Dutchess Co., St. Joachim (1853), Revs. Donald J. Poulin; Ronald P. Altrui. In res., Rev. Donald B. Licata.
Res., 61 Leonard St., 12508. Tel: 914-831-0377; Fax: 914-831-9504. [CEM 2]
Church—57 Leonard St., 12508.
School—(1861). School is now consolidated with St. John the Evangelist School. All school reports emanate from the school office there. 60 Liberty St., 12508.

St. John Evangelist (1887), Revs. Joseph J. Bisignano; Matthew M. Jelenek; Nimal Mendis.
Res., 35 Willow St., 12508. Tel: 914-831-0422; Fax: 914-831-1009.
School—St. Joachim - St. John School, (1908) (Grades PreK-8) 31 Willow St., 12508. Tel: 914-831-1358.
Lay Teachers 10; Students 232.
Catechesis/Religious Programs—Tel: 914-831-3638; Fax: 914-831-1009.
Students 146.

Bedford, Westchester Co., St. Patrick (1928), Rev. Msgr. Thomas A. Gartland; Rev. John B. Kauta (Uganda).
Res., State Rd., 10506. Tel: 914-234-3668.
School—(1956), State Rd., 10506. Tel: 914-234-7914. Mrs. Catherine Mendrzycki, Prin.
Lay Teachers 9; Students 205.
Catechesis/Religious Programs—Tel: 914-234-3775.
Students 366.

Blauvelt, Rockland Co., St. Catharine (1868), Rev. Msgr. William J. Belford; Rev. Abraham Orapankal; Deacon John C. Kelleher.
Res., 523 Western Hwy., 10913. Tel: 914-359-0542; Fax: 914-365-2387. [CEM]
School—(1957), 517 Western Hwy., 10913. Tel: 914-359-4330. Mr. Philip Gorrasi, Prin.
Sisters of St. Dominic of Blauvelt 1; Lay Teachers 10; Students 225.
Catechesis/Religious Programs—Tel: 914-359-4014. Sr. Marie Murphy, O.P., D.R.E.
Students 545.

Brewster, Putnam Co., St. Lawrence O'Toole (1878), Revs. Robert J. DeJulio; John A. Bida; Deacons Benjamin Wallace; Mark Shkreli.
Res., 31 Prospect St., 10509. Tel: 914-279-2021; Fax: 914-279-7441. [CEM]
School—(1928), Eastview Ave., 10509. Tel: 914-279-5164; Fax: 914-279-8165. Mrs. Sharyn O'Leary, Prin.
Lay Teachers 13; Students 340.
Catechesis/Religious Programs—Tel: 914-279-6098. Sr. Catherine Murphy, S.H.C.J., D.R.E.
Students 585.

Briarcliff Manor, Westchester Co., St. Theresa (1926), Rev. Msgr. James K. Vaughey; Rev. Thomas P. Kiely.

Res., 1394 Pleasantville Rd., 10510. Tel: 914-941-1646; Fax: 914-944-9503.
School—Tel: 914-762-1050.
Sisters 2; Lay Teachers 8; Students 170.
Catechesis/Religious Programs—Tel: 914-923-3286.
Students 435.
Mission—Millwood, Westchester Co., Our Lady of the Wayside.

Bronxville, Westchester Co., St. Joseph (1906), Rev. Msgr. James F. Doyle; Revs. William A. Kelleher; Carmine J. Rita. In res., Revs. Dawson Ambosta; Paul Vezhaparambil, C.M.I.
Res., 15 Cedar St., 10708. Tel: 914-337-1660; Fax: 914-337-1342.
School—(1951), 30 Meadow Ave., 10708. Tel: 914-337-0261; Fax: 914-395-1192. Mauro Durso, Prin.
Lay Teachers 19; Students 261.
Catechesis/Religious Programs—28 Meadow Ave., 10708. Tel: 914-337-6383.
Students 261.

Buchanan, Westchester Co., St. Christopher (1929), Rev. Msgr. Donald W. Hendricks; Rev. Leonard J. DiNola; Deacon Ronald J. Schlitt.
Res., 94 Albany Post Rd., 10511. Tel: 914-737-1046.

Callicoon, Sullivan Co., Holy Cross (1870), Rev. Ignatius E. Smith, O.F.M.
Res., 12723. Tel: 914-887-5450. [CEM]
Mission—Long Eddy, Sullivan Co., St. Patrick, Long Eddy, 12760.
Chapel—Callicoon, Holy Cross Rectory.

Carmel, Putnam Co., St. James the Apostle (1913), Revs. Joseph J. Faraone; Vincent Howley; Americo Savoca; Anthony Marchitelli; Deacons James Attridge; Charles T. Borsavage; Tony Gruerio. In res., Rev. Samuel Asantey.
Res., 14 Gleneida Ave., 10512. Tel: 914-225-2079; Fax: 914-225-5566.
School—(1954), Tel: 914-225-9365.
Lay Teachers 15; Students 387.
Catechesis/Religious Programs—Tel: 914-225-6504.
Students 1,528.
Mission—Lake Carmel, Putnam Co., Our Lady of the Lake, Noonan Dr., 10512.

Centerville, Ulster Co., St. John the Evangelist (1886), Rev. Msgr. William E. Williams; Deacon Edwin R. Topple. In res., Rev. James W. Derrenbacher.
Res., 915 Rte. 212, Saugerties, 12477. Tel: 914-246-9581; Fax: 914-246-9582.
Office: Tel: 914-246-9581.
Catechesis/Religious Programs—Students 250.

Chappaqua, Westchester Co., St. John and St. Mary (1922), Rev. Msgr. Timothy A. McDonnell; Rev. Kenneth O'Toole, Senior Priest. In res., Rev. John A. Vigilanti.
Res., 15 St. John's Pl., 10514. Tel: 914-238-3260; Fax: 914-238-3354.
Catechesis/Religious Programs—30 Poillon Rd., 10514. Tel: 914-238-3696.
Students 437.

Chester, Orange Co., St. Columba (1875), Rev. Thomas J. Curley; Sr. Anna Roche, S.C., Sacramental Min.; Deacon Frank Carlino.
Res., 27 High St., 10918. Tel: 914-469-2108; Fax: 914-469-2109. [CEM]
Catechesis/Religious Programs—Tel: 914-469-9503.
Students 270.
Station—Greycourt, Camp La Guardia. (NYC Homeless Shelter). Tel: 914-469-6200.

Cold Spring-on-Hudson, Putnam Co., Our Lady of Loretto (1834), Rev. Frederick Sullivan; Deacon John O'Reilly.
Res., 24 Fair St., Cold Spring, 10516. Tel: 914-265-3718; Fax: 914-265-4309.
Catechesis/Religious Programs—Tel: 914-265-2594. Sr. Ann Teresa Nagy, S.A., D.R.E.
Students 280.
Mission—Garrison, Putnam Co., St. Joseph, Garrison, 10524.

Congers, Rockland Co., St. Paul (1896), Rev. Msgr. Thomas E. Gilleece; Rev. Daniel J. Spalthoff; Deacons Dominic Buonocore; John W. McSherry; James Gorman.
Res., 82 Lake Rd. W., 10920. Tel: 914-268-4464; Fax: 914-268-6790. [CEM]
School—365 Kings Hwy., Valley Cottage, 10989. Tel: 914-268-6506; Fax: 914-268-1809. Sr. Stephen Gerard, O.P., Prin.
Sisters 3; Lay Teachers 13; Students 375.
Catechesis/Religious Programs—Tel: 914-268-5442.
Students 739.
Chapel—Congers, Sisters' Convent and School.

Cornwall-on-Hudson, Orange Co., St. Thomas of Canterbury (1870), Revs. John F.X. Smith; Bernard P. Heter.
Res., 10 Second St., 12520. Tel: 914-534-2547. [CEM]
School—(1913), Hudson St., 12520. Tel: 914-534-2019. Sr. Ann Cecilia Regan, O.P., Prin.
Sisters 2; Lay Teachers 8; Students 253.
Catechesis/Religious Programs—Tel: 914-534-9393.
Students 520.
Chapel—St. Thomas' Convent, 336 Hudson St., 12520. Tel: 914-534-4215.

Cortlandt Manor, Westchester Co., St. Columbanus (Van Cortlandtville) (1950), Rev. Msgr. Patrick J. Keenan; Rev. Joseph A. Blenkle; Deacon John J. Coppola. In res., Rev. Augustine Ansu Damoah (Ghana).
Res., 122 Oregon Rd., 10566. Tel: 914-737-4705; Fax: 914-736-7476.
School—122 Oregon Rd., 10566. Tel: 914-739-1200.
Sisters 3; Lay Teachers 8; Students 248.
Catechesis/Religious Programs—Tel: 914-739-2441.
Students 858.
Mission—Lake Peekskill, Putnam Co., North American Martyrs, 55 Oscawana Lake Rd., Putnam Valley, 10579. Tel: 914-528-6433.

Holy Spirit (1966), Rev. Msgr. James P. Cassidy, Ph.D.; Rev. Msgr. William J. McMahon, Ph.D.; Rev. Anthony Afful-Broni (Africa); Deacon Raymond Parchen.
Res., 1969 Crompond Rd., 10566-4113. Tel: 914-737-2316; Fax: 914-737-6882.
Catechesis/Religious Programs—Tel: 914-734-9243.
Students 517.
Chapel—Cortlandt Manor.

Crestwood, Westchester Co., Church of the Annunciation (1931), Rev. Msgr. James R. Moore; Revs. Eugene J. Carrella; Salvatore Riccardi, C.P.; Deacon Albert Conner.
Res., 470 Westchester Ave., 10707. Tel: 914-779-7345; 779-7542; Fax: 914-337-8878.
School—(1943), 465 Westchester Ave., 10707. Tel: 914-337-8760. Sr. Anne Massell, P.B.V.M., Prin.
Sisters 4; Lay Teachers 18; Students 437.

Croton Falls, Westchester Co., St. Joseph (1845), Revs. James E. Borstelmann; Jude Aquwa; Sr. Mary L. Mazza, C.N.D., Pastoral Assoc.
Res., 10 Croton Falls Rd., 10519. Tel: 914-277-3765; 277-3877; Fax: 914-277-1823.
School—(1949), Tel: 914-277-3783.
Lay Teachers 9; Students 152.
Catechesis/Religious Programs—14 Croton Falls Rd., 10519. Tel: 914-276-1067.
Students 825.
Missions—Goldens Bridge, Westchester Co., St. Michael, Park Ave., Goldens Bridge, 10526.; North Salem, Westchester Co., St. John, Rte. 116, North Salem, 10560. [CEM]

Croton-on-Hudson, Westchester Co., Holy Name of Mary (1874), Revs. Gennaro L. Gentile; Matthew Yatkauskas; Deacons Richard Santana; Albert Mazza.
Res., 110 Grand St., 10520. Tel: 914-271-4797; Fax: 914-271-6841.
Catechesis/Religious Programs—114 Grand St., 10520. Tel: 914-271-4254.
Students 360.
Mission—Harmon, Westchester Co., Church of the Good Shepherd, 10520.

Dobbs Ferry, Westchester Co., Sacred Heart (1862), Rev. Terry Attridge; Sr. Connie Koch, O.P., Pastoral Assoc.; Deacons Patrick D. Troy; John J. Kollar.
Res., 18 Bellewood Ave., 10522. Tel: 914-693-0119; Fax: 914-693-3408.
Church—Broadway and Ashford Ave., 10522.
Catechesis/Religious Programs—Students 245.

Our Lady of Pompeii (1922) (Italian), Rev. Carmelo Glavina, Admin.; Deacon N. Anthony Barbieri.
Res., 95 Palisade St., 10522. Tel: 914-693-1839.

Dover Plains, Dutchess Co., St. Charles Borromeo (1859), Rev. Edward Barry.
Res., P.O. Box 9, Mill St., 12522. Tel: 914-877-9934; Fax: 914-877-9936. [CEM]
Catechesis/Religious Programs—Tel: 914-832-6989.
Students 351.
Mission—Wingdale, Dutchess Co., Our Lady of Solace Mission, P.O. Box 329, Wingdale, 12594. Tel: 914-832-6989.

East Kingston, Ulster Co., St. Colman (1904), Rev. John C. McGuire, Admin.
Res., 18 Brigham St., Kingston, 12401. Tel: 914-336-8237.

Ellenville, Ulster Co., St. Mary and St. Andrew (1850), Rev. Msgr. Robert P. Hickey; Rev. Robert J. Ginel.
Res., 137 S. Main St., 12428. Tel: 914-647-6080.
Mission—Kerhonkson, Ulster Co., Our Lady of Lourdes, Kerhonkson, 12446.

Elmsford, Westchester Co., Our Lady of Mt. Carmel (1904), Rev. Vincent A. Lancellotti; Deacon Peter E. Reynolds.
Res., 59 E. Main St., 10523. Tel: 914-592-6789; Fax: 914-592-7526.
School—(1929), E. Main St., 10523. Tel: 914-592-7575; Fax: 914-592-7526.
Sisters of Divine Compassion 4; Lay Teachers 7; Students 237.
Catechesis/Religious Programs—Tel: 914-592-4280.
Students 216.

Fishkill, Dutchess Co., Church of St. Mary, Mother of the Church (1953), Rev. Msgr. Joseph A. Martin; Revs. Kent Wilson; Rick De La Pena; Deacon Martin Kazimir.
Res., 103 Jackson St., P.O. Box L, 12524-0499. Tel: 914-896-6400; Fax: 914-896-4575.
School—(1955), Tel: 914-896-9561. Mrs. Elizabeth Carufe.
Lay Teachers 9; Students 260.
Catechesis/Religious Programs—Tel: 914-896-6430.
Students 950.

Florida, Orange Co., St. Joseph (1895) (Polish), Rev. Joseph Tokarczyk, Admin.
Res., 14 Glenmere Ave., 10921. Tel: 914-651-7792; Fax: 914-651-7793. [CEM]
School—(1915), 21 Glenmere Ave., 10921. Tel: 914-651-7873.
Sisters 1; Lay Teachers 10; Students 150.
Catechesis/Religious Programs—Students 125.
Mission—Pellets Island (New Hampton), Orange Co., St. Andrew Bobola, Maple Ave., Pellets Island, 10958.
Chapel—St. Joseph Convent, 19 Glenmere Ave., 10921. Tel: 914-651-4213.

Forestburgh, Sullivan Co., St. Thomas Aquinas (1900), Rev. Msgr. Robert J. McCabe; Deacon Paul A. Rausch.
Res., 5 Forestburgh Rd., 12777. Tel: 914-791-7400; Fax: 914-791-7978. [CEM]

Gardiner, Ulster Co., St. Charles Borromeo (Irish-Italian) (1883), Rev. Eugene A. Kosnick; Deacon Harold N. Carroll.
Res., 12525. Tel: 914-255-1374; Fax: 914-256-9050. [CEM]
Catechesis/Religious Programs—Students 246.

Garnerville, Rockland Co., St. Gregory Barbarigo (1961), Revs. John J. Backes; Herbert P. De Garis; Deacon Augustine A. Pappalardo.
Res., 21 Cinder Rd., 10923. Tel: 914-947-1873.
School—Tel: 914-947-1330; Fax: 914-947-4392. Sr. Kathleen Gorres, O.P., Prin.
Sisters of St. Dominic (Sparkill) 2; Lay Teachers 10; Students 270.
Catechesis/Religious Programs—Tel: 914-429-2775. Marie Kiely, D.R.E.
Students 840.

Glasco, Ulster Co., St. Joseph (1921) (Italian-Irish), Rev. Charles F. Zanotti.
Res., Glasco Turnpike, Box 208, 12432. Tel: 914-246-5453.
A-Villa St. Dominic—Rest House for Ladies. Dominican Sisters (Sparkill). Also Known as Corazon Center. Tel: 914-246-8941.
Catechesis/Religious Programs—Tel: 914-246-6644.
Students 180.

Goshen, Orange Co., St. John the Evangelist (1837), Revs. Richard T. Adams; Robert G. Hilfiker.
Res., 71 Murray Ave., 10924. Tel: 914-294-5328; Fax: 914-294-2577. [CEM]
School—77 Murray Ave., 10924. Tel: 914-294-6434. Sr. M. Paracleta, O.P., Prin.
Sisters 2; Lay Teachers 8; Students 260.
Catechesis/Religious Programs—Tel: 914-294-6847.
Students 1,250.
Chapels—Immaculate Conception Convent, 73 Murray Ave., 10924.; Presentation Sisters Convent, Fletcher St., 10924.; John S. Burke H. S. Chapel; Our Lady of the Blessed Sacrament, Broadlea, 10924. Tel: 914-294-5481.
Stations—Orange County Home and Infirmary, Tel: 914-294-7971; Orange County Jail, Tel: 914-294-6166; Campbell Hall Nursing Facility, Tel: 914-294-8154; Arden Hill Life-Care Center, Tel: 914-294-9797.

Greenburgh, Westchester Co., Church of Our Lady of Shkodra (1989) (Albanian), Rev. Peter Popovich.
Res., 361 W. Hartsdale Ave., Hartsdale, 10530. Tel: 914-761-3523; Fax: 914-949-2690.

Greenwood Lake, Orange Co., Holy Rosary (1954), Revs. Robert J. Sweeney; Robert Dahlke, S.J.; Deacon Ralph D. Longo.
Res., 41 Windemere Ave., 10925-2105. Tel: 914-477-8378; Fax: 914-477-0984.

Catechesis/Religious Programs—Tel: 918-477-0906.
Students 298.

Harriman, Orange Co., St. Anastasia (1899), Rev. Joseph F. Reynolds; Deacon Eugene E. Bormann. In res., Rev. Lawrence X. McCaffrey, S.J.
Res., 21 N. Main St., 10926. Tel: 914-783-3571. [CEM]
Catechesis/Religious Programs—Tel: 914-782-5099.
Students 380.

Harrison, Westchester Co., St. Gregory the Great (1900), Rev. Msgr. Daniel V. Flynn, J.C.D.; Rev. Msgr. Guy S. Vinci; Rev. Msgr. Joseph J. Raimondo, Senior Priest; Rev. Philip J. Gagliano.
Res., 215 Halstead Ave., 10528. Tel: 914-835-0677; Fax: 914-835-0796.
School—(1953), 94 Broadway, 10528. Tel: 914-835-1278; Fax: 914-835-2070. Debra A. Trignani, Prin.
Lay Teachers 10; Students 170.
Catechesis/Religious Programs—189 Fremont St., 10528. Tel: 914-835-4291.
Students 604.

Hartsdale, Westchester Co., Sacred Heart (1926), Rev. Msgr. John V. Wilkinson; Rev. Richard Seagraves; Deacon Benjamin D'Arconte.
Res., 10 Lawton Ave., 10530. Tel: 914-949-0028; Fax: 914-289-0398.
School—(1953), 59 Wilson St., 10530. Tel: 914-946-7242. Sr. Margaret Smith, S.C., Prin.
Sisters 4; Lay Teachers 16; Students 235.
Catechesis/Religious Programs—Tel: 914-428-5043.
Students 215.
Convent—11 Lawton Ave., 10530. Tel: 914-946-2581.

Hastings-on-Hudson, Westchester Co., St. Matthew (1892), Rev. Msgr. Edward J. McCorry; Rev. James Smyth.
Res., 616 Warburton Ave., 10706. Tel: 914-478-2822; Fax: 914-478-3681.
School—(1911), Tel: 914-478-3343. Sr. Margaret Patricia, O.P., Prin.
Sisters 2; Lay Teachers 8; Students 150.
Catechesis/Religious Programs—Students 275.
Mission—Hastings-on-Hudson, Westchester Co., Andras Nursing Home.

St. Stanislaus Kostka (1912) (Polish), Rev. Msgr. Edward J. McCorry.
Res., 616 Warburton Ave., 10706. Tel: 914-478-2822; Fax: 914-478-3681.
Church—52 Main St., 10706.

Haverstraw, Rockland Co., St. Peter (1848), Revs. Charles S. Kelly; Richard Smith; Tomas Bobadilla.
Res., 115 Broadway, 10927. Tel: 914-429-2196; Fax: 914-947-4564. [CEM][JC]
School—(1884), Ridge St., 10927. Tel: 914-429-5311. Miss Kathleen Dunn, Prin.
Lay Teachers 10; Students 230.
Catechesis/Religious Programs—21 Ridge St., 10927. Tel: 914-429-8824.
Students 194.
Stations—West Haverstraw, Helen Hayes Hospital, Tel: 914-947-3000; Walnut Hill, Senior Citizen Apts., Tel: 914-429-3033; Haverstraw, Green Hills Home, Tel: 914-429-8411; Haverstraw, Northern Riverview Health Care Center, Tel: 914-429-5381.

St. Mary (1899) (Slovak), Rev. Mario Zicarelli.
Res., 46 Conklin Ave., 10927. Tel: 914-429-2245.

Hawthorne, Westchester Co., Holy Rosary (1901), Revs. Daniel T. Davies, O.P.; James A. Nicolicchia, O.P.; James B. Muller, O.P.
Res., 170 Bradhurst, 10532. Tel: 914-769-0030; Fax: 914-769-3326.
School—(1955), 180 Bradhurst Ave., 10532. Tel: 914-769-4549; Fax: 914-769-2768.
Lay Teachers 10; Students 246.
Catechesis/Religious Programs—Tel: 914-769-3338. Sr. June Quinian, O.P., D.R.E.
Students 586.

Highland, Ulster Co., St. Augustine (1899), Revs. Eugene Keane; Thomas Lutz.
Res., 55 Main St., 12528. Tel: 914-691-7673.
School—(1958), Phillips Ave. and Elting Pl., 12528. Tel: 914-691-2338. Mrs. Laurette McKercher, Prin.
Lay Teachers 9; Students 204.
Catechesis/Religious Programs—Students 296.

Highland Falls, Orange Co., Sacred Heart of Jesus (1870). Unassigned.
Res., 353 Main St., 10928. Tel: 914-446-4609; Fax: 914-446-2343. [CEM]
School—(1930), 7 Cozzens Ave., 10928. Tel: 914-446-2674.
Lay Teachers 7; Students 190.
Catechesis/Religious Programs—Maryann Brigham, D.R.E.
Students 205.
Chapel—Fort Montgomery, Blessed Sacrament. Rev. Michael P. McLoughlin.

Highland Mills, Orange Co., St. Patrick (1957), Revs. Gerard P. Travers; Sebastian Pandarathikudiyil, V.C. (India); Deacon Paul Weireter.
Res., 18 Hunter St., 10930. Tel: 914-928-6027.
Catechesis/Religious Programs—Tel: 914-928-6688.
Students 600.

Hopewell Junction, Dutchess Co., St. Columba (1992), Rev. Msgr. Dominick J. Lagonegro; Revs. Michael L. Palazzo; Martin J. Mahoney; Deacons William Alvarado; John Reilly; George Stewart; Warren Testa; Stanley Wyke.
Res., 601 Rte. 82, P.O. Box 428, 12533. Tel: 914-227-8380; Fax: 914-227-8390.
School—St. Denis-St. Columba, Tel: 914-227-7777. Sr. Ann Daniels, Prin.
Sisters 2; Lay Teachers 15; Students 519.
Catechesis/Religious Programs—P.O. Box 368, Hopewell Jct., 12533. Tel: 914-221-4900. Rev. Bruce O. Bowes, D.R.E.
Students 1,688.

St. Denis (1899), Rev. William B. Cosgrove; Deacons Walter Dauerer; Stanley Aviles.
Res. & Office: 325 Beekman Rd., P.O. Box 10, 12533. Tel: 914-227-8382; Fax: 914-227-3951. [CEM]
School—St. Denis-St. Columba. See St. Columba for details. Tel: 914-227-7777; Fax: 914-227-8390.
Catechesis/Religious Programs—P.O. Box 368, 12533. Tel: 914-221-4900.
Students 771.

Hyde Park, Dutchess Co., Regina Coeli (1863), Rev. Peter J. Vianney; Deacons William E. Biskup; Frank J. Gohl; Joseph M. Bonanno. In res., Rev. James J. LeBar.
Res., 2 Harvey St., 12538. Tel: 914-229-2134; Fax: 914-229-8423.
School—(1955), Albany Post Rd., 12538. Tel: 914-229-8589.
Lay Teachers 16; Students 275.
Catechesis/Religious Programs—Tel: 914-229-9139.
Students 350.
Mission—Staatsburg, Dutchess Co., St. Paul, (1851) Mulford Ave., Staatsburg, 12580.

Irvington-on-the-Hudson, Westchester Co., Immaculate Conception (1873), Revs. Raymond J. Byrne; Timothy J. Scannell; Abraham Vettiyankal, C.M.I.
Res., 16 N. Broadway, 10533. Tel: 914-591-7480; Fax: 914-591-7806.
School—(1908), Tel: 914-591-9330.
Lay Teachers 16; Students 222.
Catechesis/Religious Programs—Tel: 914-591-7740.
Students 275.

Jeffersonville, Sullivan Co., St. George, Rev. Edward Greene, O.F.M.
Res., 12748. Tel: 914-482-4640.

Katonah, Westchester Co., St. Mary of the Assumption (1908), Revs. William P. Dalton; Adrian C. Piotrowski, O.S.C.
Res., 117 Valley Rd., 10536. Tel: 914-232-3356.
Catechesis/Religious Programs—99 Valley Rd., 10536. Tel: 914-232-4648.
Students 685.
Missions—Bedford Hills, Westchester Co., St. Matthias, (1909) Babbitt Rd., Bedford Hills, 10507; South Salem, Westchester Co., South Salem Presbyterian Church, Spring St., South Salem, 10590.

Kingston, Ulster Co.,

1—Holy Name of Jesus, (1884), Rev. Edmund M. Burke; Deacon Robert B. Sheeley.
Res., 11 Fitch St., 12401. Tel: 914-331-1606.

2—Immaculate Conception, (1896) (Polish), Rev. John W. Borzuchowski (Poland).
Res., 467 Delaware Ave., 12401. Tel: 914-331-0846; Fax: 914-331-7647. [CEM]

3—St. Joseph, (1868), Rev. Msgr. Charles McDonagh; Revs. Frank J. Damis; Alfred Glancy; Deacons Donald Droulette; Richard Frohmiller; Robert Winrow; John Peters; Joseph Doherty. In res., Rev. Msgr. James V. Keating.
Res., 242 Wall St., 12401. Tel: 914-338-1554.
School—(1869), Wall & Pearl Sts., 12401. Tel: 914-339-4390.
Sisters, Society of St. Ursula 1; Lay Teachers 13; Students 149.
Chapel—St. Joseph Mission, Zandhoeck Rd., Hurley, 12443.

4—St. Mary, (1842), Rev. Edmund M. Burke. In res., Rev. Cornelius C. Woulfe, C.S.Sp., Chaplain Kingston Hospital.
Res., 160 Broadway, 12401. Tel: 914-331-0301. [CEM]
School—Kingston Catholic School, (1867), 159 Broadway, 12401. Tel: 914-331-9318. Sr. Esther Fazione, S.C.C., Prin.
Sisters of Christian Charity 2; Lay Teachers 9; Students 215.
Catechesis/Religious Programs—Students 175.

5—St. Peter, (1858) (German), Rev. Msgr. William J. Collins.
Res., 93 Wurts St., 12401. Tel: 914-331-0436. [CEM]
Chapel—Kingston, Sisters of Christian Charity Convent, Tel: 914-338-7319.

Lake Katrine, Ulster Co., St. Catherine Laboure (1957), Rev. John T. Kearney.
Res., Tuytenbridge Rd., P.O. Box 271, 12449. Tel: 914-382-1133.

Larchmont, Westchester Co., St. Augustine (1892), Rev. Msgr. Walter F. Kenny. In res., Rev. Joseph A. DeSanto.
Res., 18 Cherry Ave., 10538. Tel: 914-834-1220; Fax: 914-833-2130.
Catechesis/Religious Programs—Tel: 914-834-9523.
Students 340.

SS. John and Paul (1949), Revs. Joseph Boyd; Robert J. Verrigni; Deacon James Brown.
Res., 280 Weaver St., 10538. Tel: 914-834-5458; Fax: 914-833-5081.
School—(1952), Tel: 914-834-6332. Anne A. Menno, Prin.
Lay Teachers 13; Students 260.
Catechesis/Religious Programs—Tel: 914-834-4597.
Students 411.

Liberty, Sullivan Co., St. Peter (1894), Rev. Edward F. Straub; Deacon John Riley.
Res., 264 N. Main St., 12754. Tel: 914-292-4525. [CEM]
Catechesis/Religious Programs—Students 200.

Livingston Manor, Sullivan Co., St. Aloysius (1899), Rev. Alfred M. Croke.
Res., Church St., Box 206, 12758. Tel: 914-439-5625. [CEM]
Missions—De Bruce, Sullivan Co., Sacred Heart, P.O. Box 206, 12758.; Roscoe, Sullivan Co., Gate of Heaven, Highland Ave., Roscoe, 12776.
Catechesis/Religious Programs—Students 125.

Mahopac, Putnam Co., St. John the Evangelist (1889), Rev. Msgr. Raymond T. Powers, S.T.D.; Revs. Andrew P. Carrozza; William F. Woodruff; Deacons John Armo; Robert Esposito.
Res., 235 Msgr. O'Brien Blvd., 10541. Tel: 914-628-2006; Fax: 914-628-5970.
School—(1955), Tel: 914-628-6464.
Religious of the Divine Compassion 2; Lay Teachers 8; Students 200.
Catechesis/Religious Programs—Tel: 914-628-5222.
Students 1,712.
Chapel—Convent of Religious of the Divine Compassion, Tel: 914-628-6497.

Mamaroneck, Westchester Co., Holy Trinity (1874), Revs. Joseph F. Irwin; William A. Rooney; Gabriel Muteru (Kenya).
Res., 320 E. Post Rd., 10543. Tel: 914-698-5944; Fax: 914-698-5274.

St. Vito (1911) (Italian), Revs. James F. Healy; Edward O'Neil; C. Ambrose (India); Sr. Catherine Duignan, O.P., Pastoral Assoc.
Res., 816 Underhill Ave., 10543. Tel: 914-698-2648; Fax: 914-698-6081.
Catechesis/Religious Programs—826 Underhill Ave., Mamaronek, 10543. Tel: 914-698-2949.
Students 443.

Marlboro, Ulster Co., St. Mary (1900), Rev. Alfred R. Pizzuto; Rev. Msgr. Edward T. Dugan, Pastor Emeritus. Pastoral Team: Tel: 914-236-4340. Sr. Norma Carney, P.B.V.M.; Sr. Mary O'Neill, P.B.V.M.; Deacons John T. Repke; Thomas Cornell.
Res., Bloom St., P.O. Box 730, 12542. Tel: 914-236-4340. [CEM]
Catechesis/Religious Programs—Students 450.
Mission—Roseton, Orange Co., Our Lady of Mercy, River Rd., 12550.

Maybrook, Orange Co., Assumption (1907), Revs. Daniel M. O'Hare; Andrew T. Magee, Pastor Emeritus; Deacon Edward M. Grosso.
Res., 211 Homestead Ave., 12543. Tel: 914-427-2046; Fax: 914-427-7005.
Catechesis/Religious Programs—Tel: 914-427-5318.
Students 243.

Middletown, Orange Co., St. Joseph (1865), Rev. Msgr. George J. Valastro; Revs. Joseph P. Fallon; Ludovico Angella (Italy); Gerald Blom (Sri Lanka) Hospital Chap.; Deacon Richard Trapani.
Res., 149 Cottage St., 10940. Tel: 914-343-6013; Fax: 914-344-4735. [CEM]
School—(1889), 113 Cottage St., 10940. Tel: 914-343-3139. Deborah Scofield, Prin.
Lay Teachers 14; Students 235.

Catechesis/Religious Programs—Tel: 914-343-4415.
Students 617.

Our Lady of Mt. Carmel (1912), Rev. Lucian W. Beltzner, O.Carm. Pastoral Assocs.: Revs. Edward Duffy, O.Carm.; Raymond Bagdonis, O.Carm.; Very Rev. Mario Esposito, O.Carm.; Revs. David Kearns, O.Carm.; Patrick McGuigan, O.Carm.; Deacons Edward Woods; John Frohbose.
Res., 90 Euclid Ave., 10940. Tel: 914-343-4121; Fax: 914-343-4433.
School—205 Wawayanda Ave., 10940. Tel: 914-343-8836.
Lay Teachers 13; Students 286.
Catechesis/Religious Programs—Tel: 914-342-1510.
Students 411.
Missions—Bloomingburgh, Sullivan Co., Our Lady of the Assumption, P.O. Box 216, Bloomingburgh, 12721. Tel: 914-733-1477; Fax: 914-733-6691; Bullville, Orange Co., St. Paul, Rte. 17K, Bullville, 10915. Tel: 914-361-3107; Fax: 914-361-4201; South Centerville, Orange Co., Holy Cross, 626 County Rte. 22, South Centerville, 10973. Tel: 914-355-4439; Unionville, Orange Co., Our Lady of the Scapular, 125 Main St., Unionville, 10988. Tel: 914-726-3222.

Millbrook, Dutchess Co., St. Joseph (1890), Revs. James T. O'Connor; John F. Antony.
Res., North Ave., 12545. Tel: 914-677-3422; Fax: 914-679-3423. [CEM]
School—(1957), Tel: 914-677-3670.
Lay Teachers 9; Students 230.
Catechesis/Religious Programs—Tel: 914-677-3273.
Students 330.
Chapel—Millbrook, Cardinal Hayes Home for Children.
Stations—Millbrook, County Infirmary.; Millbrook, Green Briar Home.

Milton, Ulster Co., St. James (1874) (Italian), Rev. Fred Kempfirl. In res., Rev. Eugene Daniels.
Res., State Rd., 12547. Tel: 914-795-2255.

Monroe, Orange Co., Sacred Heart Church (1957), Revs. Carl D. Johnson; Vernon Wickrematunge (Sri Lanka); Thomas L. Kreiser; Deacons Peter Brockmann; James Burns; Richard McCarthy.
Res., 26 Still Rd., 10950. Tel: 914-782-8510; Fax: 914-782-3593.
School—(1965), Tel: 914-783-0365; Fax: 914-782-0354. Teresita Fajardo, Prin.
Sisters 1; Lay Teachers 11; Students 285.
Catechesis/Religious Programs—(Grades PreK-8). Tel: 914-782-7420. Sr. Rose O'Rourke, D.R.E.
Students 1,122.
Convent—Still Rd., 10950.
Chapel—Stage Rd., 10950.

Montgomery, Orange Co., Holy Name of Mary (1868), Rev. Joseph D. Sullivan.
Res., 89 Union St., 12549. Tel: 914-457-5276. [CEM]
Catechesis/Religious Programs—Tel: 914-457-1738. Sr. Grace Mary McGuire, D.R.E.
Students 330.

Monticello, Sullivan Co., St. Peter (1874),
Res., 10 Liberty St., 12701. Tel: 914-794-5577. [CEM]
Catechesis/Religious Programs—Tel: 914-791-7172.
Students 389.
Missions—Mongaup Valley, Sullivan Co., St. Joseph, 12701.; White Lake, Sullivan Co., St. Anne, 12701.

Mt. Kisco, Westchester Co., St. Francis of Assisi (1871), Rev. Ralph A. Villani. In res., Rev. Michael M. Burke (CC).
Res., 2 Green St., 10549. Tel: 914-666-5986; Fax: 914-666-3859. [CEM]
Catechesis/Religious Programs—Tel: 914-666-3161; Fax: 914-666-5474.
Students 350.

Mt. Vernon, Westchester Co.,

1—Sacred Heart, (1872), Rev. Owen J. Lafferty.
Res., 115 S. Fifth Ave., 10550. Tel: 914-668-7440.
School—(1895), Second St. & S. Fifth Ave., 10550.
Lay Teachers 8; Students 243.
Chapel—Sacred Heart Convent, 67 S. Fifth Ave., 10550.

2—Our Lady of Victory, (1871), Rev. Msgr. Thomas F. Scanlon; Rev. Vincent O. Ajayi (Nigeria).
Res., 28 W. Sidney Ave., 10550. Tel: 914-668-5861; Fax: 914-668-0161.
School—(1898), 38 N. Fifth Ave., 10550. Tel: 914-667-4063. Margaret Balfe, Prin.
Lay Teachers 11; Students 260.
Chapel—Dominican Convent, Tel: 914-667-2564.

3—St. Mary, (1894), Rev. John T. Meehan.
Res., 23 S. High St., 10550. Tel: 914-664-5855.

4—Our Lady of Mount Carmel, (1897) (Italian), Revs. Octavio Jose Salinas, O.F.M.; James Villa, O.F.M.; Benedict D'Alessandro, O.F.M.; Bro. Dominic Poirier, O.F.M.; Deacon Vincent T. Piro.
Res., 10550. Tel: 914-668-3540; Fax: 914-668-4393.

5—SS. Peter and Paul, (1929) (Italian), Rev. Msgr. Patrick J. Barry; Revs. Leonard Da Custa; Augustine Matthew, C.M.I.
Res., 129 Birch St., 10552. Tel: 914-668-9815; Fax: 914-668-6052.
School—Tel: 914-664-1321; Fax: 914-664-2951.
Sisters 1; Lay Teachers 12; Students 240.
Catechesis/Religious Programs—Tel 914-668-9880.
Students 150.

6—St. Ursula, (1908), Revs. John T. McLoughlin; Sabbas J. Kilian, O.F.M.; Deacons Thomas J. Abbamont; Pasquale Giglio; Carl Degenhardt.
Res., 214 E. Lincoln Ave., 10552. Tel: 914-668-0085; Fax: 914-668-4228.
Saint Ursula's Learning Center For the Learning Disabled—183 Rich Ave., 10552. Tel: 914-664-6656; Fax: 914-668-0592.
Catechesis/Religious Programs—Tel: 914-699-7964. Sr. Roberta Smith, O.S.F., D.R.E.
Students 225.
Convent—29 Clinton Pl., 10552. Tel: 914-668-4031.

Nanuet, Rockland Co., St. Anthony (1897), Revs. William V. Reynolds; Peter Tran Van Phat; Christopher Pliaplis; Deacon John Maloney. In res., Rev. Joseph Anyimaduwireko.
Res., 36 West Nyack Rd., 10954. Tel: 914-623-2138; Fax: 914-623-5556. [CEM]
School—(1953), 32-34 West Nyack Rd., 10954. Tel: 914-623-2311; Fax: 914-623-2406. Barbara Casey, Prin.
Sisters 4; Lay Teachers 19; Students 572.
Catechesis/Religious Programs—Tel: 914-624-2230. Ms. Ann Malloy, D.R.E.
Students 798.

Narrowsburg, Sullivan Co., St. Francis Xavier (1862), Rev. Thomas Jones, O.F.M.
Res., 151 Bridge St., 12764. Tel: 914-252-6681; Fax: 914-252-6519. [CEM]
Mission—Lake Huntington, Sullivan Co., Our Lady of the Lake, Lake Huntington, 12752. Tel: 914-252-6681.

Newburgh, Orange Co.,

1—St. Patrick, (1836), Rev. Msgr. John J. Budwick; Revs. Louis Van Thanh; Alfonso Henao (Colombia); Deacons Fred Steup; Frank Russell; William Glover. Spanish Apostolates: Sr. Yliana Hernandez; Sr. Paula Cormier.
Res., 55 Grand St., 12550. Tel: 914-561-0885; Fax: 914-561-0888. [CEM]
Catechesis/Religious Programs—Tel: 914-561-6470. D.R.E.: Sr. Francis Morley; Ms. Mary Jane Newman.
Students 600.
Mission—Orange Lake, Orange Co., Our Lady of the Lake, Lakeside & Rte. 52, 12550.

2—St. Francis of Assisi, (1909) (Polish), Rev. John J. Vondras; Deacon Jack Seymour.
Res., 145 Benkard Ave., 12550. Tel: 914-561-1317; Fax: 914-561-1337. [CEM]
School—Now Sacred Heart-St. Francis of Assisi School. Merged in Sept. 1992. 24 S. Robinson Ave., 12550. Tel: 914-561-1433.
Catechesis/Religious Programs—Tel: 914-561-6697. Louise Pisano, D.R.E.
Students 475.
Chapel—St. Francis Convent, (1955), 153 Benkard Ave., 12550. Tel: 914-561-5914; Fax: 914-561-1123.

3—St. Mary, (1875), Rev. William A. Scafidi; Deacon John J. Buckley.
Res., 180 South St., 12550. Tel: 914-562-0862; Fax: 914-562-0876.

4—Sacred Heart, (1912) (Italian), Revs. Gerardo J. Colacicco; William J. Damroth; Deacons Dominick Casadone; Peter Haight; Lawrence Kawula. In res., Rev. Donald Timone.
Res., 301 Ann St., 12550. Tel: 914-561-2264; Fax: 914-562-7144.
School—(1951), 24 S. Robinson Ave., 12550. Tel: 914-561-1433.
Religious 1; Lay Teachers 15; Students 260.
Catechesis/Religious Programs—Tel: 914-561-2589.
Students 598.

New City, Rockland Co., St. Augustine (1957), Rev. Msgr. William J. Foley; Revs. James B. Hynes; George T. Vadakel (India); Deacons Michael G. McCabe; Lawrence O'Toole.
Res., 140 Maple Ave., 10956. Tel: 914-634-3641; Fax: 914-639-6118.
School—Tel: 914-634-7060; Fax: 914-634-8725. Sr. Helen Doychak, O.P., Prin.
Sisters 1; Lay Teachers 14; Students 304.
Catechesis/Religious Programs—Tel: 914-634-8462.
Students 837.

New Paltz, Ulster Co., St. Joseph (1894), Revs. Michael Banks, O.F.M.Cap.; Barnabas Keck, O.F.M.Cap.; Knute Kenlon, O.F.M.Cap., Chap.; Bro. Timothy Jones, O.F.M.Cap., Univ. Chap.
Res., 34 S. Chestnut St., 12561. Tel: 914-255-5635; Fax: 914-255-5679.
Catechesis/Religious Programs—Tel: 914-255-0237; Fax: 914-256-0687.
Students 490.
Station—Lake Mohonk.

New Rochelle, Westchester Co.,

1—Blessed Sacrament, (1848), Rev. Msgr. William J. Bradley; Revs. Charles Imokhai (Nigeria); Salagunla Xavier Anul; Samuel Savio (India); Deacons Charles Rizzo; Frank Orlando; Charles Wendelken.
Res., 15 Shea Pl., 10801. Tel: 914-632-2300; Fax: 914-632-0732. [CEM]
School—New Rochelle Catholic Elementary, (1866), 24 Maple Ave., 10801. Tel: 914-632-0511. Joan Woods, Prin.
Lay Teachers 16; Students 230.
High School—(Coed) 24 Shea Pl., 10801. Tel: 914-632-2595; Fax: 914-632-3321. Bro. Brendan Ramos, C.F.C., Prin.
Congregation of Christian Brothers 3; Sisters 5; Lay Teachers 19; Students 260.
Catechesis/Religious Programs—Tel: 914-235-7311. Mrs. Judith Anastacio, D.R.E.
Students 600.

2—St. Gabriel, (1893), Revs. Patrick V. McNamara; Jude Paulraj (India); John Muscat, Chap.
Res., 120 Division St., 10801. Tel: 914-632-0211.
Chapel—Sisters of Charity of St. Vincent de Paul, 13 Washington Ave., 10801.

3—St. Joseph, (1901) (Italian-Portuguese), Revs. Cosimo Fazio; Okechukwu Uchendu; Jess Eric Solier.
Res., 280 Washington Ave., 10801. Tel: 914-632-0675; Fax: 914-633-4264.
Catechesis/Religious Programs—Students 135.

4—Holy Family, (1913), Rev. Msgr. John Mescall; Rev. Gary Mead.
Res., 83 Clove Rd., 10801. Tel: 914-632-0673; Fax: 914-576-8556.
Church—Mayflower Ave. & Mt. Joy Pl., 10801.
School—(1921), Mayflower Ave., 10801. Tel: 914-632-3810.
Lay Teachers 10; Students 204.
Catechesis/Religious Programs—Tel: 914-636-6758.
Students 365.
Chapels—Ursuline Sisters, 1352 N. Ave., 10804. Tel: 914-636-3456; Fax: 914-576-2620; Iona Grammar and Preparatory Schools, 173 Stratton Rd., 10804. Tel: 914-633-7744; 632-2727; Fax: 914-235-6338; Iona College, 715 N. Ave., 10801. Tel: 914-633-2000; Fax: 800-633-2329; New Rochelle, St. Patrick Prov., 30 Montgomery Circle, 10801. Tel: 914-633-6851; Fax: 914-633-5579; New Rochelle, St. Joseph Chapel, Tel: 914-632-6592; Fax: 914-533-4264; Edmond Rice Hall, 33 Pryer Ter., 10804. Tel: 914-636-6194; Fax: 914-636-0021; Crosier Fathers, 125 Paine Ave., 10804. Tel: 914-636-3614; Fax: 914-636-4261; Opus Dei, 99 Overlook Cir., 10804. Tel: 914-235-1201; Fax: 914-235-7805; Holy Cross Brothers Provincialate, 85 Overlook Cir., 10804. Tel: 914-632-1951; Fax: 914-632-2490.

5—Holy Name of Jesus, (1929), Revs. Martin J. Biglin; John P. DeLora; Deacons Carmine DeMarco; Robert Gontcharuk.
Res., 75 Lispenard Ave., 10801. Tel: 914-636-4856.
Church—Petersville Rd. and Halligan St., 10801.
School—(1954), 70 Petersville Rd., 10801. Tel: 914-576-6672; Fax: 914-576-6676. Mr. Albert D'Angelo, Prin.
Sisters 1; Lay Teachers 12; Students 268.
Catechesis/Religious Programs—Tel: 914-576-6038.
Students 192.
Chapel—Sisters of Charity Convent, 78 Petersville Rd., 10801. Tel: 914-636-4354.

New Windsor, Orange Co., St. Joseph (1962), Rev. Laurence H. Gibney; Deacons Joseph Lieby; Anthony Ferraiuolo.
Res., 4 St. Joseph Pl., 12553. Tel: 914-561-8467; Fax: 914-562-3269.
School—148 Windsor Hwy., 12553. Tel: 914-565-5110.
Sisters 1; Lay Teachers 12; Students 208.
Catechesis/Religious Programs—Tel: 914-561-8475.
Students 374.

North Tarrytown, Westchester Co., St. Teresa of Avila (1853) (Spanish-Portuguese), Rev. Francis P. Gorman.
Res., 130 Beekman Ave., 10591. Tel: 914-631-0720; Fax: 914-366-6459.

Catechesis/Religious Programs—Tel: 914-631-1831.
Students 244.
Holy Cross (1921) (Slovak-Polish), Rev. Francis P. Gorman; Rev. Msgr. Cyril J. Potocek.
Res., 118 Beekman Ave., 10591. Tel: 914-631-1493.
Immaculate Conception (1917) (Italian), Revs. Louis J. Mazza; Salvatore Fiore, S.J., (Italy) (Retired).
Res., 199 N. Broadway, 10591. Tel: 914-631-0446.

Nyack, Rockland Co., St. Ann (1869), Rev. Msgr. Edmund Netter, Pastor Emeritus; Revs. Robert P. Henry; Peter J. Kihm; Leo Fredrick Perera (Sri Lanka); Thomas Aidoo (Ghana).
Res., 16 Jefferson St., 10960. Tel: 914-358-4707; Fax: 914-358-3246.
School—(1892), Tel: 914-358-0125; Fax: 914-358-7911. Mrs. Evelyn Jensen Ortiz, Prin.
Lay Teachers 5; Students 75.
Catechesis/Religious Programs—19 Jefferson St., 10960. Tel: 914-358-3758. Ms. Julie LePore, D.R.E.
Students 195.
Convent—150 Third Ave., 10960. Tel: 914-358-2697.

Obernburg, Sullivan Co., St. Mary (1854) (German), Rev. John M. Richardson, O.F.M.; Deacon Lawrence Knack.
Res., 12767. Tel: 914-482-5541; Fax: 914-482-9340. [CEM]

Ossining, Westchester Co., St. Augustine (1853), Rev. Msgr. Hilary Franco; Rev. Msgr. Robert F. McCormick, Pastor Emeritus; Rev. Robert G. Hilfiker.
Res., Eagle Park Rte. 9, 10562. Tel: 914-941-0067. [CEM]
School—(1893), Tel: 914-941-3849. Sr. Mary Elizabeth Donoghue, Prin.
Priests 2; Sisters of St. Dominic (Columbus) 1; Lay Teachers 25; Students 46.
St. Ann (1927), Rev. Edward G. Byrne; Sr. Eileen Finnerty, Pastoral Assoc.; Deacon Jose DeJesus. In res., Rev. Matthias Noulaka (Nigeria).
Res., 25 Eastern Ave., 10562. Tel: 914-941-2556; Fax: 914-923-9239.
School—16 Elizabeth St., 10562. Tel: 914-941-0312. Mrs. Dorethea Muccigrosso, Prin.
Sisters 1; Lay Teachers 12; Students 387.
Catechesis/Religious Programs—Tel: 914-941-2420.
Students 360.
Convent—10 Elizabeth St., 10562.

Otisville, Orange Co., Holy Name (1969), Rev. Gerard J. Di Senso.
Res., P.O. Box 597, 10963. Tel: 914-386-1320. [CEM]
Catechesis/Religious Programs—Tel: 914-386-2327. Mrs. Nancy Doran, D.R.E.
Students 267.

Patterson, Putnam Co., Sacred Heart (1957), Revs. James P. Flynn, Pastor Emeritus; Ralph W. La Belle, Admin.
Res., 414 Haviland Dr., 12563. Tel: 914-279-4832; Fax: 914-278-0432.
Catechesis/Religious Programs—Mrs. Karin Frick, D.R.E.
Students 391.

Pawling, Dutchess Co., St. John the Evangelist (1848), Revs. John J. Duff; James J. Moriarty, Pastor Emeritus.
Res., 39 E. Main St., 12564. Tel: 914-855-5488; Fax: 914-855-1273. [CEM]
Catechesis/Religious Programs—Tel: 914-855-9408.
Students 355.

Pearl River, Rockland Co., St. Margaret (1923), Revs. Rudolph Eisler; George Stewart; Deacons William Donovan; William Tobin.
Res., 115 W. Central Ave., 10965. Tel: 914-735-4746; Fax: 914-735-3511.
School—(1953), N. Magnolia St., 10965. Tel: 914-735-2855; Fax: 914-735-0131. Mrs. Nancy Langehennig, Prin.
Lay Teachers 13; Students 285.
Catechesis/Religious Programs—Tel: 914-735-5489. Sr. Maryann Lawlor, O.P., D.R.E.
Students 640.
St. Aedan (1966), Rev. Msgr. Joseph P. Penna; Rev. Msgr. Edward J. Quirk, Pastor Emeritus; Rev. John M. Lagiovane.
Res., 23 Reld Dr., 10965. Tel: 914-735-7405; Fax: 914-735-4125.
Catechesis/Religious Programs—Tel: 914-735-2531.
Students 623.

Peekskill, Westchester Co., Assumption (1859) (Indian-Hispanic), Rev. Msgr. Francis J. Ansbro; Revs. Arthur R. Leo; Steven E. Clark; Deacon James F. Roberts.
Res., 131 Union Ave., 10566. Tel: 914-737-2071; Fax: 914-737-1633. [CEM]
School—(1907), S. Division & First St., 10566. Tel: 914-737-0680.
Sisters 3; Lay Teachers 9; Students 250.
Catechesis/Religious Programs—Students 175.
Chapel—St. Joseph Home, Tel: 914-737-3373; Fax: 914-73-9614.

Pelham, Westchester Co., St. Catharine (1896), Rev. Peter F. Bannan.
Res., 25 Second Ave., 10803. Tel: 914-738-1491.
Catechesis/Religious Programs—Tel: 914-738-1332.
Students 270.

Pelham Manor, Westchester Co., Our Lady of Perpetual Help (1954), Rev. Msgr. Hugh D. Curran; Deacon Guy Pellegrini.
Res., 559 Pelham Manor Rd., 10803. Tel: 914-738-1449; Fax: 914-738-9454.
School—(1957), 575 Fowler Ave., 10803. Tel: 914-738-5158. Sr. Marie Morris, S.C., Prin.
Sisters 2; Lay Teachers 11; Students 215.
Catechesis/Religious Programs—Tel: 914-738-0670.
Students 530.

Phoenicia, Ulster Co., St. Francis de Sales (1902), Revs. Aloysius M. McPartland, M.S.; Hector O. LaChapelle, M.S.
Res., Main St., P.O. Box 25, 12464. Tel: 914-688-5617. [CEM]
Missions—Allaben, Ulster Co., Our Lady of Lourdes, Rte. 28, Allaben, 12480.; Boiceville, Ulster Co., Our Lady of La Salette, Rte. 28, Boiceville, 12412.

Piermont, Rockland Co., St. John (1852), Rev. John T. Dwyer.
Res., 895 Piermont Ave., 10968. Tel: 914-359-0078.

Pine Bush, Orange Co., The Infant Saviour (1951), Rev. Msgr. James S. Conlan; Rev. Martin Suitan.
Res., Holland Ave., P.O. Box 81, 12566. Tel: 914-744-2391.
Catechesis/Religious Programs—Tel: 914-744-9944.
Students 470.
Mission—Walker Valley, Ulster Co., Our Lady of the Valley, Walker Valley, 12588.

Pine Island, Orange Co., St. Stanislaus (1912) (Polish), Rev. Joaquim J. Olendzki.
Res., Pulaski Hwy., 10969. Tel: 914-258-4426. [CEM]

Pine Plains, Dutchess Co., St. Anthony (1958), Rev. William A. White, Admin.; Deacon Salvatore P. Patricola.
Res., 68 Poplar Ave., 12567. Tel: 518-398-7115; Fax: 518-398-9146.
Catechesis/Religious Programs—Students 170.

Plattekill, Ulster Co., Our Lady of Fatima, Rev. John Jaume, C.R.
Res., P.O. Box 77, 12568. Tel: 914-564-4972.
Catechesis/Religious Programs—Students 175.

Pleasant Valley, Dutchess Co., St. Stanislaus Kostka (1903), Revs. Charles P. Quinn; Cyril Kuragama.
Res., Main St., P.O. Box 558, 12569. Tel: 914-635-1700; Fax: 914-635-8675.
Catechesis/Religious Programs—Tel: 914-635-8611.
Students 501.

Pleasantville, Westchester Co., Holy Innocents (1894), Revs. Raymond Daley, O.P.; James B. Sheridan, O.P.; John P. Sullivan, O.P.; Sean J. McConway, O.P.; Harry T. Donoghue, O.P. In res., Rev. Joseph Payne, O.P.
Res., 431 Bedford Rd., 10570. Tel: 914-769-0025; Fax: 914-747-2476. [CEM]
Catechesis/Religious Programs—Tel: 914-769-3297. Linda DeMarkey, D.R.E.
Students 600.
Mission—Pleasantville Park, Westchester Co., Our Lady of Pompeii.

Pocantico Hills, Westchester Co., The Magdalene (1894), Rev. Msgr. Donald J. Pryor; Rev. Msgr. Stephen J. Fitzgerald, Pastor Emeritus.
Res., 525 Bedford Rd., North Tarrytown, 10591. Tel: 914-631-0529.

Port Chester, Westchester Co.,

1—Our Lady of Mercy, (1854), Rev. Ralph V. Curcio; Rev. Msgr. Cornelius M. O'Brien, Pastor Emeritus; Rev. Msgr. James T. Gorman; Revs. Joe Braganza; Longinus Nazareth; Sr. Lorraine Dougherty, P.B.V.M., Pastoral Assoc.; Deacons Raymond H. Daur; Robert A. Fien. In res., Rev. Domingo Lopez.
Res., 260 Westchester Ave., 10573. Tel: 914-939-0612; Fax: 914-939-2807. [CEM]
Catechesis/Religious Programs—Tel: 914-937-5288. Mrs. Kathleen McCarthy, D.R.E.
Students 220.
Chapel—Sister of Charity, 18 Spring St., 10573. Tel: 914-937-2440.

2—Corpus Christi, (1925) (Italian), Revs. James A. McKenna, S.D.B.; Peter Granzotto, S.D.B.; John Blanco, S.D.B.; Gus W. Baek, S.D.B.; Armand Quinto, S.D.B.; Deacons John B. Munnick, Jr.; Dan Ciccone.
Res., 136 S. Regent St., 10573. Tel: 914-939-3169; Fax: 914-939-7249.
School—135 S. Regent St., 10573. Tel: 914-937-4407; Fax: 914-937-6904.
Sisters, Daughters of Mary Help of Christians 4; Lay Teachers 15; Students 400.
Catechesis/Religious Programs—Students 400.

3—Our Lady of the Rosary, (1904) (Italian), Revs. Joseph Chirruete, S.D.B.; Bill Burk, S.D.B.; Emiliano Chiriboga, S.D.B.
Church—22 Don Bosco Pl., 10573. Tel: 914-939-0547.
Res., 23 Nicola Pl., 10573. Tel: 914-937-5532.
School—(1945), Central Ave., 10573. Tel: 914-939-1021. Ms. Colleen Fitzgerald, Prin.
Lay Teachers 17; Students 210.
Chapel—Port Chester, Eucharistic Adoration.

4—Sacred Heart of Jesus, (1917), Rev. Henry G. d'Anjou.
Res., 229 Willett Ave., 10573. Tel: 914-939-1497.

Port Ewen, Ulster Co., Presentation of the Virgin Mary (1856), Rev. Paul A. Miller, C.SS.R.
Res., Fr. Kelley Dr., 12466. Tel: 914-331-0053.
Catechesis/Religious Programs—Students 200.
Mission—Esopus, Ulster Co., Sacred Heart, P.O. Box 219, Esopus, 12429. Tel: 914-384-6828. Rev. Eugene J. Grohe, C.SS.R.

Port Jervis, Orange Co., Immaculate Conception (1851), Rev. John J. Murray; Deacon Philip Bouwmans. Pastor Emeriti: Revs. John E. Rooney; Thomas J. Melican.
Res., 46 Ball St., Box 712, 12771. Tel: 914-856-8212; Fax: 914-858-8375. [CEM]
Catechesis/Religious Programs—Students 350.
Most Sacred Heart (1899), Rev. David A. De Simonc.
Res., 12 McAllister St., 12771. Tel: 914-856-1331; Fax: 914-858-0687.

Poughkeepsie, Dutchess Co.,

1—St. Peter, (1837), Rev. Leo R. Prince; Deacons James R. Hayes; George F. Cacchione; Albert J. Klein.
Res., 424 Violet Ave., 12601. Tel: 914-452-8580.
School—(1853), Tel: 914-471-6600.
Sisters of Charity of St. Vincent de Paul 3; Lay Teachers 15; Students 230.
Catechesis/Religious Programs—Students 250.
Chapels—Poughkeepsie, Convent of St. Peter.; Poughkeepsie, Hudson River Psychiatric Center, Our Lady of the Holy Rosary, Tel: 914-471-2537.
Catechesis/Religious Programs—Students 250.

2—St. Mary, (1873), Revs. John J. Brinn, M.A.; John J. Hunter, M.S.; Deacon Richard Dingee. In res., Rev. Anthony S. Marian, Ph.D (India) Chap. Vassar Brothers Hospital.
Res., 269 Church St., 12601-4201. Tel: 914-452-8250; Fax: 914-452-8266.
Catechesis/Religious Programs—Tel: 914-471-4747.
Students 152.

3—Holy Trinity, (1921), Revs. Joseph P. LaMorte; James L. Cerbone, S.D.B. In res., Rev. Gamini E. Fernando (Sri Lanka) Chap., Green Haven Correctional Facility.
Res., 775 Main St., 12603. Tel: 914-452-1863; Fax: 914-452-1867.
School—(1952), 20 Springside Ave., 12603. Tel: 914-471-0520. Mrs. Mary Ann McGivney, Prin.
Sister Servants of the Immaculate Heart of Mary 3; Lay Teachers 9; Students 289.
Catechesis/Religious Programs—Tel: 914-471-5838. Sr. Maureen Davey, S.U., D.R.E.
Students 465.
Chapel—Holy Trinity Convent, 769 Main St., 12603. Tel: 914-454-2160.

4—St. John the Baptist, (1923), Rev. Richard A. La Monte, Admin.
Res., 1 Grand St., 12601. Tel: 914-452-4943.

5—St. Joseph, (1901) (Polish), Rev. Jan Jacmierski.
Res., 9 Lafayette Pl., 12601. Tel: 914-452-2333.
Chapels—Poughkeepsie, Rectory.; Cemetery Chapel, Evergreen Ave., 12601.

6—St. Martin de Porres, (1962), Revs. Brian E. McWeeney, D.Min.; Philip Tran; Kenneth Horst. Pastoral Assoc.: Deacons Robert Jarmick; Victor Salamone; Patrick Hogan.
Res., 40 Cedar Valley Rd., 12603. Tel: 914-473-4222; Fax: 914-473-4223. [CEM]
School—38 Cedar Valley Rd., 12603. Tel: 914-452-4428. Mrs. Mary Jane Daley, Prin.
Lay Teachers 11; Students 296.
Catechesis/Religious Programs—Tel: 914-471-8728. Eileen Andros, D.R.E.
Students 779.

7—Our Lady of Mt. Carmel, (1910), Rev. Richard A. LaMorte.
Res., 11 Mt. Carmel Pl., 12601. Tel: 914-454-0340; Fax: 914-454-0393.

School—Tel: 914-471-2460. Mr. Gabriel F. Ponte, Prin.
Lay Teachers 15; Students 276.

Red Hook, Dutchess Co., St. Christopher (1875), Revs. Charles P. Coen; Peter Kulandai.
Res., 58 S. Broadway, 12571. Tel: 914-758-3732; Fax: 914-758-1214. [CEM]
Catechesis/Religious Programs—Tel: 914-758-5506.
Students 351.

Rhinebeck, Dutchess Co., The Good Shepherd (1901), Revs. George J. Kuhn; Lawrence Xavier.
Res., 3 Mulberry St., 12572. Tel: 914-876-4583; Fax: 914-876-3912. [CEM]
Catechesis/Religious Programs—Tel: 914-876-7298.
Students 340.
Mission—Rhinecliff, Dutchess Co., St. Joseph, Church St., Rhinecliff, 12574.
Chapels—Astor Home for Children, Tel: 914-876-4081; Fax: 914-876-2020; Rhinebeck, Ferncliff Nursing Home, Tel: 914-876-2011; Fax: 914-876-4810; Rhinecliff, Holy Cross Campus of Pius XII School, Tel: 914-876-4084; Fax: 914-876-4199; Rhinebeck, Sisters of St. Ursula, Linwood Retreat House, Tel: 914-876-4178; Fax: 914-876-6544.

Rosendale, Ulster Co., St. Peter (1855), Revs. Paul Dmoch; Raphael Nwachukwu (Nigeria); Deacons John J. Larkin; John J. Liggan.
Res., 12472. Tel: 914-658-3117; Fax: 914-658-3540. [CEM]
School—(Old: 1890; New: 1965), Tel: 914-658-9209; Fax: 914-658-9827. Gerianne O'Rourke, Prin.
School Sisters of St. Francis (Milwaukee, WI) 1; Lay Teachers 10; Students 120.
Catechesis/Religious Programs—Tel: 914-658-8911.
Students 345.
Mission—High Falls, Ulster Co., Our Lady Help of Christians, J.F.K. Ln., High Falls, 12440.

Rye, Westchester Co., Resurrection (1880), Most Rev. Anthony F. Mestice, D.D.; Rev. Msgr. Daniel A. Peake; Revs. Jack Arlotta; Zacharias Nadackal, C.M.I. (India); Rev. Msgr. Thomas McMahon, Pastor Emeritus.
Res., 910 Boston Post Rd., 10580. Tel: 914-967-0142; 967-0254; Fax: 914-967-6494.
School—(1906), 116 Milton Rd., 10580. Tel: 914-967-1218; Fax: 914-967-0295.
Sisters 1; Lay Teachers 15; Students 265.
Catechesis/Religious Programs—Tel: 914-967-1270.
Students 800.
Chapel—Seton Hall Convent of the Sisters of Charity, Tel: 914-967-7085.

Saugerties, Ulster Co., St. Mary of the Snow (1833), Revs. Hugh R. Grace; Christopher H. Berean; Deacons Perry Bunyar; Donald Trees; Karl Pietkiewicz; Arnie Hyland.
Res., 36 Cedar St., 12477. Tel: 914-246-4913; Fax: 914-246-4996. [CEM]
School—(1881), 25 Cedar St., 12477. Tel: 914-246-6381. Miss Christine M. Molinelli, Prin.
Lay Teachers 11; Students 176.
Chapel—Saugerties, Parish Center.
Catechesis/Religious Programs—Tel: 914-246-7534; Fax: 914-246-7354.
Students 167.

Scarsdale, Westchester Co., Immaculate Heart of Mary (1912), Rev. Msgr. John J. Scanlon; Revs. Thomas J. Tolentino; Joseph S. Dietz; Deacons Ernest F. Salomone; Robert di Targiani.
Res., 8 Carman Rd., 10583. Tel: 914-723-0276; Fax: 914-722-0628.
School—(1928), 201 Boulevard, 10583. Tel: 914-723-5608; Fax: 914-723-8004. Robert W. Billings, Prin.
Lay Teachers 19; Students 270.
Catechesis/Religious Programs—Tel: 914-723-7593; Fax: 914-723-7209.
Students 992.

Our Lady of Fatima (1948), Rev. Msgr. Hugh F. McManus; Rev. Thomas J. McCaffrey; Deacons Francis Griffin; Michael J. Fox. In res., Rev. Gerard F. Rafferty; Irene Ingham Kollar, Pastoral Assoc.
Res., 5 Strathmore Rd., 10583. Tel: 914-723-7421; Fax: 914-723-7229.
School—(1950), Tel: 914-723-0460. Mrs. Barbara Stofko, Prin.
Lay Teachers 10; Students 225.

St. Pius X (1954), Rev. Msgr. Francis J. Melican; Rev. Francis J. Fajella, M.Ss.A.; Deacons Theodore A. Gaskin; William J. Hill.
Res., 91 Secor Rd., 10583. Tel: 914-725-2755; Fax: 914-725-2782.
School—(1957), 85 Palmer Ave., 10583. Tel: 914-725-0541.
Sisters 1; Lay Teachers 9; Students 151.

Shrub Oak, Westchester Co., Saint Elizabeth Ann Seton (1963), Rev. Msgr. James F. McCarthy; Revs. Matthew Grier, M.H.M.; S. Kulandairajan. In res., Rev. Mark Connell.
Res., Main St., 10588. Tel: 914-528-3547; Fax: 914-528-4216.
School—Tel: 914-528-3563. Sr. Gabriel Miriam, S.C., Prin.
Sisters 2; Lay Teachers 23; Students 575.
Catechesis/Religious Programs—Tel: 914-528-8553. Sr. Maureen Fitzpatrick, F.S.P., Prin.
Students 945.

Sloatsburg, Rockland Co., St. Joan of Arc (1966), Rev. John P. Gallant.
Res., 32 Eagle Valley Rd., 10974. Tel: 914-753-5239.
Catechesis/Religious Programs—Tel: 914-753-5193.
Students 203.

Spring Valley, Rockland Co., St. Joseph (1894), Revs. Rudolph F. Gonzalez; Carl Sansaricq; Armand Iavarone, O.SS.T.
Res., 333 Sneden Pl. W., 10977. Tel: 914-356-0311; Fax: 914-352-8126.
School—(1927), 245 N. Main St., 10977. Tel: 914-356-0054. Mrs. Dorothy Kelly, Prin.
Lay Teachers 11; Students 215.
Catechesis/Religious Programs—Tel: 914-352-5686.
Students 400.

Stony Point, Rockland Co., Immaculate Conception (1889), Revs. Robert J. Staar; Michael Challinor; Abraham Lotha (India); Deacon Philip Marino.
Res., 26 John St., 10980. Tel: 914-786-2742; Fax: 914-942-2614.
School—(1902), Main St., 10980. Tel: 914-786-5245.
Lay Teachers 10; Students 257.
Catechesis/Religious Programs—Tel: 914-786-5298.
Students 523.

Suffern, Rockland Co., Sacred Heart (1868), Rev. Msgr. Joseph P. Meehan; Revs. Ronald M. Vierling, P.F.; Patrick O. Balogun (Ijebu-Ode, Nigeria); Deacons John Baterbury; Robert J. Johnson; Joseph R. Verboys; Joseph A. Witt.
Res., 125 Lafayette, 10901. Tel: 914-357-0035; Fax: 914-368-0393.
School—(1909), 60 Washington Ave., 10901. Tel: 914-357-1684; Fax: 914-357-0318. Sr. Rose Andrew, Prin.
Sisters 3; Lay Teachers 21; Students 446.
Catechesis/Religious Programs—Tel: 914-357-6044.
Students 615.
Chapels—Dominican Sisters Convent, Tel: 914-357-1544; Good Samaritan Hospital, Tel: 914-368-5000; Tagaste Monastery, Tel: 914-357-0067; Fax: 914-369-0625.

Tappan, Rockland Co., Our Lady of the Sacred Heart (1952), Rev. John F. Dwyer.
Res., 120 King's Hwy., 10983. Tel: 914-359-1230.
Catechesis/Religious Programs—Tel: 914-359-1410.
Students 225.

Tarrytown, Westchester Co., Transfiguration (1896), Rev. Alfred J. Isacsson, O.Carm. In res., Revs. Robert P. Tracy, O.Carm.; Matthias Des Lauriers.
Res., 268 S. Broadway, 10591. Tel: 914-631-1672; Fax: 914-524-9352.
School—(1949), Prospect Ave., 10591. Tel: 914-631-3737; Fax: 914-631-6640. Mary Margaret Henshaw, Prin.
Sisters 1; Lay Teachers 14; Students 235.
Catechesis/Religious Programs—Tel: 914-631-2380.
Students 228.

Tivoli, Dutchess Co., St. Sylvia (1890), Rev. H. Theriault, M.Div.
Res., 104 Broadway, P.O. Box 95, 12583-0095. Tel: 914-757-2442. [CEM]

Tuckahoe, Westchester Co., Immaculate Conception (1853), Rev. Msgr. Vincent T. Case; Revs. Patrick A. Walsh, S.M.A.; Robert F. Ashman.
Res., 53 Winterhill Rd., 10707. Tel: 914-961-3643; Fax: 914-961-0283. [CEM]
School—(1913), Tel: 914-961-3785; Fax: 914-961-6054. Dr. Elaine Farrell, Prin.; Dr. James Morgan, Asst. Prin.
Sisters 2; Lay Teachers 22; Students 499.
Catechesis/Religious Programs—Tel: 914-961-1076. Lynn Callahan, D.R.E.
Students 692.
Chapel—Sisters Convent, Tel: 914-961-3970.

Assumption (1911) (Italian), Rev. Msgr. Vincent T. Case.
Res., 53 Winterhill Rd., 10707. Tel: 914-961-3643; Fax: 914-961-0283.
Church—100 Pleasant Ave., 10707.

Tuxedo, Orange Co., Our Lady of Mt. Carmel (1895), Rev. John F.X. Smith.
Res., Rte. 17, P.O. Box 697, 10987. Tel: 914-351-5284.

Valhalla, Westchester Co., Holy Name of Jesus (1896), Revs. Salvatore Matarazzo, O.P.; Leo Pelkington, O.P.; Patrick P. Walsh, O.P.
Res., Two Broadway, 10595. Tel: 914-949-2323; Fax: 914-868-6325.
School—Tel: 914-948-1744. Judith Foster, Prin.
Lay Teachers 12; Students 150.
Catechesis/Religious Programs—Tel: 914-949-1422.
Students 552.

Verplanck, Westchester Co., St. Patrick (1843), Revs. Francis M. Newman, Pastor Emeritus; Andrew E. Kurzyna.
Res., 240 11th St., 10596. Tel: 914-737-0635. [CEM]
Catechesis/Religious Programs—Students 165.
Chapel—Convent, Seventh St., 10596. Tel: 914-737-1373.

Walden, Orange Co., Most Precious Blood (1894), Rev. Kenneth M. Loughman.
Res., 42 Walnut St., 12586. Tel: 914-778-5719.
School—Tel: 914-778-3028.
Sisters of St. Dominic (Sparkill) 2; Lay Teachers 8; Students 200; PreK 17.
Catechesis/Religious Programs—Tel: 914-778-7081.
Students 385.
Mission—Wallkill, Ulster Co., St. Benedict, Wallkill, 12589.

Wappingers Falls, Dutchess Co., St. Mary (1850), Rev. Msgr. Francis P. Bellew.
Res., 19 Clinton St., 12590. Tel: 914-297-6261; 6262; Fax: 914-297-3227. [CEM]
School—(1890 and 1955), Convent Ave., 12590. Tel: 914-297-7500. Sr. Miriam Gregory, Prin.
Sisters 2; Lay Teachers 12; Students 216.
Catechesis/Religious Programs—Tel: 914-297-7586. Patricia Manuli, D.R.E.
Students 670.
Chapel—Mt. Carmel, St. Mary Convent.

Warwick, Orange Co., St. Stephen (1865), Rev. Desmond O'Connor; Rev. Msgr. Bernard Corrigan, Pastor Emeritus; Rev. Peter J. Madori.
Res., 75 Sanfordville Rd., 10990. Tel: 914-986-4028; Fax: 914-986-4109. [CEM]
School—Tel: 914-986-3533.
Lay Teachers 13; Students 237.
Catechesis/Religious Programs—Tel: 914-986-2231.
Students 932.
Mission—Florida, Orange Co., St. Edward, (1881) Florida, 10921.

Washingtonville, Orange Co., St. Mary (1902), Rev. Msgr. James F. Cox.
Res., 2 Fr. Tierney Cir., 10992. Tel: 914-496-3730; Fax: 914-496-3159. [CEM]
Catechesis/Religious Programs—Tel: 914-496-4101.
Students 1,500.

Wesley Hills, Rockland Co., St. Boniface (1966), Rev. John Keaveney.
Res., 5 Willow Tree Rd., 10952. Tel: 914-354-7307.
Catechesis/Religious Programs—Students 437.

West Hurley-Woodstock, Ulster Co., St. John (Woodstock) (1860), Rev. George W. Hommel.
Res., 12 Holly Hills Dr., Woodstock, 12498. Tel: 914-679-7696; Fax: 914-679-8393.
Catechesis/Religious Programs—Tel: 914-679-2869.
Students 320.
Mission—West Shokan, Ulster Co., St. Augustine, Watson Hollow Rd., West Shokan, 12494. Tel: 914-657-2190.

West Nyack, Rockland Co., St. Francis of Assisi (1964), Rev. Edward J. Weber; Deacon Donald O'Brien. In res., Rev. John Breen.
Res., 128 Parrott Rd., 10994. Tel: 914-634-4957; Fax: 914-639-6629.
Catechesis/Religious Programs—Tel: 914-638-4215.
Students 511.

West Point, Orange Co., Catholic Chapel of the Most Holy Trinity (1899), Revs. Edson J. Wood, O.S.A.; Owen J. Mullen; John T. McLoughlin.
Res., United States Military Academy, 699 Washington Rd., 10996. Tel: 914-446-5575; Fax: 914-446-6851.
Catechesis/Religious Programs—Tel: 914-446-2656.
Students 254.

White Plains, Westchester Co.,

1—St. Anthony, (1952) (Italian), Revs. Lawrence C. Inzeo; Peter C. Scaramuzzo; Deacon Arthur Manzione.

Res., 85 Harrison St., West Harrison, 10604. Tel: 914-948-1480; Fax: 914-948-0488.
School—(1957), Gainsborg Ave., West Harrison, 10604. Tel: 914-949-6986.
Sisters of Divine Compassion 5; Students 177.
Catechesis/Religious Programs—Tel: 914-949-0212.
Students 375.

2—ST. JOHN THE EVANGELIST, (1868), Rev. Msgr. James M. McDermott; Rev. Msgr. William B. Delaney, Pastor Emeritus; Revs. Christopher H. Daly; Thomas J. Joyce; Donald V. O'Brien, S.J.; Thomas Kalarickal, C.M.I. (India).
Res., 148 Hamilton Ave., 10601. Tel: 914-949-0439; Fax: 914-949-0462. [CEM]
School—(1890), 146 Hamilton Ave., 10601. Tel: 914-949-4374.
Lay Teachers 9.
Catechesis/Religious Programs—Students 270.

3—ST. BERNARD, (1926), Revs. Edward M. Roos; Jose Vilaplana, S.J. (Spain); George Spiteri (Malta); Benedict J. Kuolt, Chap.; Deacon Robert Whiteman.
Res., 51 Prospect St., 10606. Tel: 914-949-2111; Fax: 914-949-6044.
Catechesis/Religious Programs—Students 511.

4—OUR LADY OF MT. CARMEL, (1902), Rev. Albert Azrak, C.S.S. In res., Revs. Leonard DellaBadia, C.S.S.; Donald Toner, C.S.S.
Res., 92 S. Lexington Ave., 10606. Tel: 914-948-5909.

5—OUR LADY OF SORROWS, (1929), Revs. Patrick J. Dunne; Ignatius Vu; Rev. Msgr. John K. Daly, Pastor Emeritus.
Res., 920 Mamaroneck Ave., 10605. Tel: 914-949-9819; Fax: 914-949-4148.
School—(1957), Tel: 914-761-0124; Fax: 914-761-0176. Sr. Marie Cecile, Prin.
Lay Teachers 13; Students 221.
Catechesis/Religious Programs—Tel: 914-761-5257.
Students 291.

Woodbourne, Sullivan Co., Immaculate Conception (1957), Rev. John J. Lynch.
Res., P.O. Box 66, 12788. Tel: 914-434-7643; Fax: 914-436-7370.
Catechesis/Religious Programs—Tel: 914-436-7370.
Students 215.

Wurtsboro, Sullivan Co., St. Joseph (1880), Rev. Hugh A. Dardis.
Res., Sullivan St., P.O. Box 277, 12790. Tel: 914-888-4522. [CEM]

Yonkers, Westchester Co.,

1—ST. ANTHONY, (Nepera Park) (1923), Rev. Msgr. Harold J. Robertson; Revs. Philip J. Gagliano; John F. Fraser.
Res., 10 Squire Ave., 10703. Tel: 914-965-2733; Fax: 914-963-2285.
Church—1405 Nepperhan Ave., 10703.
School—Tel: 914-476-8489. Sr. Constance Christie, Prin.
Sisters 1; Lay Teachers 10; Students 205.

2—ST. ANTHONY, (Willow St.). Closed. For inquiries for parish records contact Our Lady of Mt. Carmel, Yonkers.

3—ST. ANN, (1947), Revs. Anthony M. Napolitano; John Carson; Lazar Sundararaj (India).
Res., 854 Midland Ave., 10704. Tel: 914-965-1555; 965-5584; Fax: 914-965-0678.
School—40 Brewster Ave., 10704. Tel: 914-965-4333. Sr. Joanne Shortall, Prin.
Lay Teachers 11; Students 287.
Catechesis/Religious Programs—Students 156.

4—ST. BARTHOLOMEW, (1911), Rev. Brian P. McCarthy; Rev. Msgr. Charles J. McManus, Pastor Emeritus; Rev. John Coppinger, S.A., Pastoral Assoc.; Deacon Robert A. Clemens.
Res., 15 Palmer Rd., 10701. Tel: 914-965-0566.
School—(1958), 278 Saw Mill River Rd., 10701. Tel: 914-476-7949. Sr. Ann Marie McMahon, P.B.V.M., Prin.
Sisters 2; Lay Teachers 13; Students 320.

5—ST. CASIMIR, (1899) (Polish), Rev. John Michalak, O.S.P.; Deacon John Radzilowicz.
Res., 239 Nepperhan Ave., 10701. Tel: 914-963-1254.
School—(1906), 259 Nepperhan Ave., 10701-3461. Tel: 914-965-2730. Mr. Paul Henshaw, Prin.
Lay Teachers 8; Students 132.

6—CHRIST THE KING, (1927), Rev. Msgr. A. Francis Burns; Revs. George C. Lodi; Daniel Maichiki.
Res., 740 N. Broadway, 10701. Tel: 914-963-7474; 963-7564; Fax: 914-963-7548.
School—(1955), 750 N. Broadway, 10701. Tel: 914-476-1711. Mrs. Elizabeth Pollock, Prin.
Sisters 3; Lay Teachers 10; Students 324.

7—ST. DENIS, (1910), Rev. Edward O'Halloran; Rev. Msgr. David B. Welsh, Pastor Emeritus; Rev. Varghese Maliakal (India).
Res., 470 Van Cortlandt Park Ave., 10705. Tel: 914-963-8468.
School—(1928), McLean Ave. & Lawrence St., 10705. Tel: 914-963-3438. Sr. John Maria Reeves, Prin.
Sisters 1; Lay Teachers 9; Students 252.
Catechesis/Religious Programs—Tel: 914-476-8077. Deacon Joseph Mulryan, D.R.E.
Students 110.

8—ST. EUGENE, (1949), Rev. Msgr. James P. Sullivan, Admin.; Revs. James P. Griffin; Leonard F. Villa, Admin. In res., Rev. P.J. Thawale; Deacon Donald M. Quigley, Pastoral Assoc.
Res., 32 Massitoa Rd., 10710. Tel: 914-779-5460; Fax: 914-793-8913.
School—(1951), 707 Tuckahoe Rd., 10710. Tel: 914-779-2956; Fax: 914-779-7668.
Sisters 3; Lay Teachers 20; Students 500.
Catechesis/Religious Programs—Tel: 914-793-2158.
Students 165.
Chapel—Yonkers, Franciscan Sisters Convent.

9—IMMACULATE CONCEPTION, (1848) (Spanish-Arabic), Rev. Msgr. Hugh J. Corrigan; Revs. Sami Totah (Jordan); Virgilio Compentente (Philippines).
Res., 103 S. Broadway, 10701. Tel: 914-963-0156; Fax: 914-963-1803. [CEM]
School—(1860), 15 St. Mary's St., 10701. Tel: 914-965-7048; Fax: 914-423-2826. Bro. Robert Falcone, Prin.
Sisters 3; Lay Teachers 9; Students 240.
Chapel—Sisters of Charity, St. Mary Convent, 4 St. Mary's St., 10701. Tel: 914-963-1449.
Good Shepherd Arabic Community of St. Mary—Rev. Sami Totah (Jordan) Dir.

10—ST. JOSEPH, (1871), Revs. Patrick M. Carroll; Paul V. Sullivan; Canice Osuji (Nigeria); Deacon Abraham Santiago.
Res., 141 Ashburton Ave., 10701. Tel: 914-963-0730; 963-0780. [CEM]
Convent—Tel: 914-965-1351. Sisters of Charity Sisters 7.

11—ST. JOHN THE BAPTIST, (1903) (Italian-Irish), Revs. John W. Lennon; Peter A. Migueli; Peter McKeown; Deacon Martin J. Olivieri.
Res., 670 Yonkers Ave., 10704. Tel: 914-963-1486; Fax: 914-963-1503.
School—(1954), Tel: 914-965-2356.
Sisters 3; Lay Teachers 8; Students 360.
Catechesis/Religious Programs—Marian Caputo, D.R.E.
Students 175.
Chapel—Convent, 176 Sweetfield Circle, 10704. Tel: 914-965-1837.

12—ST. MARGARET OF HUNGARY, (1928), Rev. Gabriel Kiss, S.J., (Hungary) Admin.; Deacon Louis Ju-Hasz.
Res., 76 Locust Hill Ave., 10701. Tel: 914-423-2211.

13—OUR LADY OF MT. CARMEL, (1913) (Italian), Revs. Terzo Vinci, S.A.C.; Barry Bossa, S.A.C.; Deacons Alfred R. Impallomeni; Nick A. Mazzei, Jr.
Res., 70 Park Hill Ave., 10701. Tel: 914-963-4766; Fax: 914-375-1069.
School—Mt. Carmel-St. Anthony, 85 Linden St., 10701. Tel: 914-476-8888; Fax: 914-375-1069. Mrs. Kathleen Conley, Prin.
Lay Teachers 10; Students 230.
Catechesis/Religious Programs—Tel: 914-423-8848.
Students 305.

14—OUR LADY OF THE ROSARY, (1907) (Portuguese), Revs. Daniel O'Shea, S.A.; George Ribeiro, S.A.; Bros. De Porres Poncia, S.A.; John Baptist Hildreth, S.A. In res., Rev. Carmen Giuliano, S.A.
Res., 226 Warburton Ave., 10701. Tel: 914-963-0806; Fax: 914-963-3958.

15—ST. PAUL THE APOSTLE, (1923), Rev. Msgr. John A. Gallagher; Sr. Eileen Treanor, Parish Ministry; Deacon James Hamilton.
Res., 602 McLean Ave., 10705. Tel: 914-963-7330.
Church—Lincoln Pl., 10705.
School—(1949), 77 Lee Ave., 10705. Tel: 914-965-2165. Grace Mallardi, Prin.
Lay Teachers 10; Students 312.

16—ST. PETER, (1894), Rev. Edward J. Keehan; Rev. Msgr. John A. Carlin; Deacons Pedro Irizarry; Randy Velez. In res., Rev. Brendan McCabe.
Res., 91 Ludlow St., 10705. Tel: 914-963-0822; Fax: 914-968-9305.
School—(1894 and 1955), 204 Hawthorne Ave., 10705. Tel: 914-963-2314; Fax: 914-966-8822.
Sisters 2; Lay Teachers 10; Students 278.
Catechesis/Religious Programs—Tel: 914-476-7946.
Students 463.

17—SACRED HEART, (1891), Revs. Bernard M. Maloney, O.F.M.Cap., Guardian; Christopher Dietrich, O.F.M.Cap.; James Gavin, O.F.M.Cap.; Thomas Murphy, O.F.M.Cap.; Peter McCall, O.F.M.Cap.; John B. Riordan, O.F.M.Cap., Community Vicar; Bros. Roger Deguire, O.F.M.Cap.; Walter Puhal, O.F.M.Cap.; Richard Therrien, O.F.M.Cap.; Bernard Twomey, F.S.C.
Res., 110 Shonnard Pl., 10703. Tel: 914-963-4205; Fax: 914-476-4960.
School—(1893), 108 Shonnard Pl., 10703. Tel: 914-963-5318. Ms. Mary Teresa Singer, Prin.
Sisters 1; Lay Teachers 12; Students 257.
High School—34 Convent Ave., 10703. Tel: 914-965-3114; Fax: 914-965-4510. Mrs. Bernadette Dunne, Prin.
Sisters 2; Lay Teachers 19; Students 302.
Convent—27 Convent Ave., 10703.

18—MOST HOLY TRINITY, (1894) (Slovak), Rev. Anthony J. Pleho.
Res., 18 Trinity Pl., 10701. Tel: 914-963-0720.
Chapel—Franciscan Friars of the Renewal, 15 Trinity Pl., 10701. Tel: 914-476-7279. Rev. Andrew D. Apostoli, C.F.R.

19—OUR LADY OF FATIMA, (1977) (Portuguese), Revs. Francisco Jorge; Aderbal T. De Paula.
Res., Portuguese R.C. Center, 355 S. Broadway, P.O. Box 283, 10705. Tel: 914-423-9688; Fax: 914-476-9434.

Yorktown Heights, Westchester Co., St. Patrick (1898), Rev. Msgr. Dermot R. Brennan; Revs. Alan F. Travers; Louis Jerome; Deacon Paul V. Vorel.
Res., 137 Moseman Rd., 10598. Tel: 914-962-5050; 5051; Fax: 914-962-0595.
School—(1953), 117 Moseman Rd., 10598. Tel: 914-962-2211.
Sisters 2; Lay Teachers 22; Students 343.
Catechesis/Religious Programs—Tel: 914-962-5586; Fax: 914-962-3207.
Students 1,860.

Youngsville, Sullivan Co., St. Francis of Assisi, Rev. Edward Greene, O.F.M.
Res., 12791. Tel: 914-482-4640.

Yulan, Sullivan Co., St. Anthony of Padua (1907) (Irish), Rev. Evan J. Greco, O.F.M.
Res., 12792. Tel: 914-557-8512; Fax: 914-557-3527. [CEM]
Mission—Pond Eddy, Sullivan Co., Sacred Heart, Berme Church Rd., Pond Eddy, 12770.

Chaplains of Public Institutions

Military Installations

NEW YORK. *National Catholic Community Service*. (Cardinal Spellman Servicemen's Club) 487 Park Ave., 10022. Rev. Msgr. Richard Cahill, Dir.
New York City Veterans Administration Hospital 406 First Ave., 10022. Rev. Edmund McCaffrey, O.Carm.

BRONX. *Veterans Administration Hospital* 130 W. Kingsbridge Rd., 10460. Rev. Edward A. Kozlowski; Rev. Msgr. Charles P. Boccio.

MONTROSE. *Franklin D. Roosevelt Hospital*. Revs. Daniel F. Lynch, O.Carm.; Albert Daly, O.Carm.; William J. O'Donnell.

WEST POINT. *Stewart Field*. Rev. Nash P. Geany.
West Point. U.S. Military Academy, 10966.

Societies

NEW YORK. *Marine and Aviation Department*. Vacant.
New York Fire Department. Rev. Msgr. Marc Filacchione.
New York Police Department. Rev. Msgr. Joseph J. Zammit.
New York Postal Service. Rev. John Lennon.
New York Sanitation Department. Rev. John Lennon.

YONKERS. *Yonkers Fire Department*. Rev. John Lennon.
Yonkers Police Department. Rev. John Lennon.

Prisons

CITY. *Adolescent Remand & Detention Center*. Sr. Margaret McCabe; Rev. John Wilkinson, 11-11 Hazen St., East Elmhurst, 11370. Tel: 718-546-7223.
Anna M. Kross Center. Revs. George Dash, O.F.M.Cap.; Thomas Houle, O.F.M.Cap., 18-18 Hazen St., East Elmhurst, 11370. Tel: 718-546-3623.
Bronx House of Detention. Revs. Vincent P. McNamara; Reginaldo John, 653 River Ave., Bronx, 10451. Tel: 718-579-4371.
Correctional Institution for Men. Sr. Mary O'Connor; Rev. Frank Passenant, 10-10 Hazen St., East Elmhurst, 11370. Tel: 718-546-5796.
George M. Motchan Detention Center. Revs. Joseph P. Kane, S.J.; Thomas Mestriparampil, 15-15 Hazen St., East Elmhurst, 11370. Tel: 718-956-2611.
George Viero Center. Rev. Joseph P. Kane, S.J.; Sr. Marie Hermann, 09-09 Hazen St., East Elmhurst, 11370. Tel: 718-204-5079, Ext. 2254.

James A. Thomas Center. Sr. Simone Ponnet; Rev. Thomas Houle, O.F.M.Cap., 14-14 Hazen St., East Elmhurst, 11370. Tel: 718-546-5425.

Manhattan Detention Center. Deacon Kenneth Radcliff, 125 White St., New York, 10013. Tel: 212-618-9538.

North Infirmary Command. Rev. Lawrence E. Lucas; Sr. Amy Henry, 15-00 Hazen St., East Elmhurst, 11370. Tel: 718-546-1256.

Otis Bantum Correctional Center. Revs. Lawrence E. Lucas; Thomas Mestriparampil; Sr. Constance Kennedy, 16-00 Hazen St., East Elmhurst, 11370. Tel: 718-546-6617.

Rose M. Singer Center. Rev. Joseph P. Kane, S.J. Tel: 718-546-7498; Sr. Marion DeFeis, 19-19 Hazen St., East Elmhurst, 11370.

Spofford Juvenile Center. Vacant. 1221 Spofford Ave., Bronx, 10474. Tel: 718-579-0100.

West Facility. Rev. Frank Passenant, 16-06 Hazen St., East Elmhurst, 11370. Tel: 718-546-4495.

COUNTY. *Dutchess County Jail*. Rev. Ernest D'Onofrio, O.F.M., Tel: 914-297-5706.

Orange County Jail. Attended from St. John, Goshen. Tel: 914-294-5328.

Putnam County Jail. Attended by St. James, Carmel. Tel: 914-225-2079.

Rockland County Jail. Attended by St. Augustine, New City. Tel: 914-634-3641.

Sullivan County Jail. Attended by St. Peter, Monticello. Tel: 914-794-5577.

Ulster County Jail. Attended by Church of St. Joseph, Kingston. Tel: 914-338-1554.

Westchester County Jail. Rev. Brendan McCabe, Box 389, Valhalla, 10595. Tel: 914-347-6132.

FEDERAL. *Federal Correctional Institution*. Rev. Michael O'Hara, O.M.I., Otisville, 10963. Tel: 914-386-5855.

Metropolitan Correctional Center. Rev. Juan Soles, 150 Park Row, New York, 10007-1779. Tel: 212-791-9130.

STATE. *Arthur Kill Correctional Facility*. Rev. Frank Naccarato, 2911 Arthur Kill Rd., Staten Island, 10309-1197. Tel: 718-356-7333.

Bayview Correctional Facility. Rev. George J. Dash, O.F.M.Cap., 550 W. 20th St., New York, 10011-2878. Tel: 212-255-7590.

Beacon Correctional Facility. Rev. Michael O'Hara; Deacon John O'Reilly, Box 780, Beacon, 12508-0780. Tel: 914-831-4200.

Bedford Hills Correctional Facility. Rev. Michael O'Shea, 247 Harris Rd., Bedford Hills, 10507-2499. Tel: 914-241-3100.

Downstate Correction Facility. Rev. Donald B. Licata; Deacon Anthony Gruerio, Box 445, Fishkill, 12524-0445. Tel: 914-831-6600.

Eastern Correctional Facility. Rev. Jose Mappilamattel; Deacon Franklyn Russell, Napanoch, 12458-0338. Tel: 914-647-7400.

Edgecombe Correctional Facility. Deacon Nicholas Mazzei, 611 Edgecombe Ave., New York, 10032-4398. Tel: 212-923-2575.

Fishkill Correctional Facility. Rev. Donald B. Licata, Box 307, Beacon, 12508. Tel: 914-831-4800.

Fulton Correctional Facility. Deacon Nicholas Mazzei, 1511 Fulton Ave., Bronx, 10457-8398. Tel: 718-583-8000.

Green Haven Correctional Facility. Rev. Msgr. Edward J. Donovan; Rev. Gamini E. Fernando, Stormville, 12582. Tel: 914-221-2711.

Lincoln Correctional Facility. Deacon Nicholas Mazzei, 31-33 W. 110 St., New York, 10026-4398. Tel: 212-860-9400.

Mid-Orange Correctional Facility. Deacon Ricardo Rosado; Rev. Augustine Graap, O.Carm., Warwick, 10990-0990. Tel: 914-986-2291.

Otisville Correctional Facility. Rev. Augustine Graap, O.Carm.; Deacon Eugene Bormann, Box 8, Otisville, 10963-0008. Tel: 914-386-1490.

Parkside Correctional Facility. Deacon Nicholas Mazzei, 10 Mt. Morris Park W., New York, 10027-6395. Tel: 212-860-6835.

St. Clare's Secure Unit. Revs. Thomas McCall, S.J.; George Dash, O.F.M.Cap., 415 W. 51st St., New York, 10019. Tel: 212-459-8227.

Shawangunk Correctional Facility. Rev. Joseph Kenlon, O.F.M.Cap., Box 750, Wallkill, 12589-0750. Tel: 914-895-2081.

Sing Sing Correctional Facility. Rev. Ronald J. Lemmert; Sr. Antonia Maguire, 354 Hunter St., Ossining, 10562-5442. Tel: 914-941-0108.

Sullivan Correctional Facility. Rev. Stanislaus Ogbonna, P.O. Box AG, Fallsburg, 12733-0116. Tel: 914-434-2080.

Taconic Correctional Facility. Sr. Antonia Maguire; Rev. George Dash, O.F.M.Cap., 250 Harris Rd., Bedford Hills, 10507-2498. Tel: 914-241-3010.

Ulster Correctional Facility. Deacons Richard D. Dingee; Joseph Doherty, Berme Rd., P.O. Box 800, Napanoch, 12458. Tel: 914-647-1670.

Wallkill Correctional Facility. Rev. Joseph Kenlon, O.F.M.Cap., Box G, Wallkill, 12589-0286. Tel: 914-895-2021.

Woodbourne Correctional Facility. Rev. Marcelo Blazquez Rodrigo, Pouch 1, Woodbourne, 12788. Tel: 914-434-7730.

Hospitals

BEACON. *Craig House Hospital*. Serviced by St. Joachim, Beacon. Tel: 914-831-1200.

BRONX. *Bronx Municipal Hospital Center, Abraham Jacobi Hospital, Nathan B. VanEtten Hospital*. Revs. Sancho G. Garrote; Robert Holick, M.H.M. Tel: 212-430-8771.

Bronx Psychiatric Center Tel: 212-931-0600. Rev. James J. Cunningham.

Bronx-Lebanon Hospital Center Tel: 212-590-1800; 518-5059. Revs. Robert A. Jeffers; Ruben Cammayo; Sr. Catherine Mary Doran, L.S.A.; Deacon Alfonso Ramos.

Calvary Hospital Tel: 212-518-2114. Rev. Michael J. Alessandro, Chap.; Sr. Mary Teresa O'Neill, R.S.H.M., Asst. Admin. Pastoral Ministries.

Lincoln Medical and Mental Health Center Tel: 212-579-5000; 579-5059. Sr. Eileen Finnerty, O.S.U.; Rev. Abel Alvarez, O.S.U.

Montefiore Medical Center Tel: 212-920-4997. Rev. Brendan McCabe, Dir. Pastoral Care.

North Central Bronx Hospital. Rev. Varghese Chethipuzha, Tel: 212-519-5000.

Our Lady of Mercy Medical Center. Revs. Frederick J. Becker, Vice Pres. Pastoral Svcs.; Thomas P. D'Angelo; Bernard Iheoha; Sr. Cathanne McVicar, S.M.; Sr. Joan Marie O'Leary, O.P.; Bro. Henry Owens, F.S.C.,

Pelham Bay Division, Sr. Kathleen Doyle, F.S.P., Tel: 212-920-9086; 920-9000.

St. Barnabas Hospital Tel: 212-960-9000. Revs. Thomas McGarry; Godfrey Anyaka; Sr. Miriam Hanratty, O.P.; Deacon Victor Pino.

U.S.V.A. Medical Center. Revs. John F. Dwyer; Bernardine Saglimbeni; Gregory Little, Tel: 212-584-9000, Ext. 1878.

Union Hospital. Serviced by St. Barnabas Hospital. Tel: 212-200-2020.

Westchester Square Hospital. Serviced by Santa Maria Parish. Tel: 718-828-2380.

BRONXVILLE. *Lawrence Hospital* Tel: 914-337-7300. Rev. Paul Vezhaparambil, C.M.I.; Sr. Agnes Regina Hughes, S.C.

CALLICOON. *Community General Hospital* Tel: 914-887-5530. Rev. Edward Burke, O.F.M.

CARMEL. *Putnam Hospital Center*. Serviced by St. James the Apostle, Carmel. Tel: 914-279-5711.

CASTLE POINT. *Veterans Administration Medical Center* Tel: 914-831-2000, Ext. 5453. Revs. Raymond Pavlick; John W. Borzuchowski; Robert Brennan; Donald B. Licata; Richard De La Pena.

COLD SPRING. *Julia L. Butterfield Memorial Hospital*. Serviced by Our Lady of Loretto, Cold Spring. Tel: 914-265-3642.

CORNWALL. *The Cornwall Hospital*. Serviced by St. Thomas of Canterbury, Cornwall-on-Hudson. Tel: 914-534-2547.

DOBBS FERRY. *Community Hospital of Dobbs Ferry*. Serviced by Sacred Heart, Dobbs Ferry. Tel: 914-693-0700.

St. Cabrini Nursing Home Tel: 914-693-6800. Sr. Suzanne Poulin, C.N.D.; Rev. Patrick Boyle, O.F.M.

ELLENVILLE. *Ellenville Community Hospital*. Serviced by the Church of St. Mary & St. Andrew, Ellenville. Tel: 914-647-6080.

GOSHEN. *Arden Hill Hospital*. Serviced by St. John, Goshen. Tel: 914-294-5441.

HARRIS. *Community General Hospital of Sullivan County*. Serviced by St. Peter, Monticello. Tel: 914-292-4525.

HARRISON. *St. Vincent Hospital and Medical Center of New York*. Rev. Joseph F. Cavoto, S.A., Dir. Pastoral Care, Tel: 914-967-6500.

HAWTHORNE. *Rosary Hill Home* Tel: 914-769-0114. Rev. John Proppe, O.F.M.Cap.

KINGSTON. *Benedictine Hospital* Tel: 914-338-2500. Sr. Kathleen Sharkey, O.S.B., Dir. Pastoral Care.; Revs. Martin Svitan; Lionel G. Trudel, M.M.

Kingston City Hospital Tel: 914-331-3131. Rev. Cornelius C. Woulfe, C.S.Sp.

MANHATTAN. *Beekman Downtown - New York Infirmary* Tel: 212-312-5000; 233-5300. Revs. Thomas McKeon, S.S.S.; Peter Ma.

Bellevue Hospital. Revs. John Logan, O.Carm.; Robert Greco, O.Carm.; Philip Marani, O.Carm.; Sr. Mary Elizabeth Steffens, R.G.S.

Beth Israel Medical Center Tel: 212-420-2000. Rev. Edwin J. Conlin.

Bird S. Coler Memorial Hospital and Home Tel: 212-838-8155. Revs. Harold F.X. O'Donnell, S.J.; Joseph N. Pershe, S.J.

Cabrini Medical Center Tel: 212-995-6056. Rev. Andrew Sioleti, O.F.M., Coord. Patient/Chaplaincy Svcs., Chaplains: Revs. Raymond G. Pierini, M.M.; John Dias, C.S.C.; Sr. Jean Cook, I.C.M.; Sr. Sofia Unneta Wood, R.S.C.J.; Sr. Stephanie Kabacinksi, M.S.C.; Sr. Consolata Demma, M.S.C.

Columbia Presbyterian Medical Center. Revs. Ralph La Belle; Donald Johnson; Fred Carrigan,

Allen Pavilion, Rev. Linus Iwuanyanwu; Deacon Miguel Granda.

Doctor's Hospital. Serviced by St. Joseph. Tel: 212-870-9000.

Goldwater Memorial Hospital Tel: 212-750-6800; 750-6674. Chaplains: Rev. Timothy A. Healey, S.J.; Mrs. Margaret Karwoski; Mrs. Roselaine Simonis, Assoc. Chap.

Gouverneur Hospital Tel: 212-374-4000. Rev. Dennis J. Sullivan; Sr. Clare Roche, P.B.V.M.

Gracie Square. Serviced by St. Jean Baptiste. Tel: 212-988-4400.

Harlem Hospital. Serviced by St. Mark. Tel: 212-491-8061.

Hospital for Special Surgery Tel: 212-606-1000. Rev. John Alexander Gregory Maturi, O.P.

Lenox Hill Hospital Tel: 212-439-2547. Rev. Edmund Slattery, S.S.S.; Bro. Michael Perez, S.S.S.; Sr. Denise Lafferriere, C.N.D.

Manhattan Eye, Ear & Throat Hospital. Serviced by St. Vincent Ferrer. Tel: 212-838-9200.

Manhattan Psychiatric Center Tel: 212-369-0500, Ext. 2530. Rev. Andrew Cuu Nguyen.

Medical Arts Center Hospital. Serviced by St. Patrick Cathedral. Tel: 212-755-0200.

Memorial Sloan Kettering Cancer Center Tel: 212-639-5982. Revs. William Robert Gannon, O.P.; Jerome Conroy, O.P.

Metropolitan Hospital Tel: 212-230-6262. Rev. Michael J. Sala, S.J.

Mount Sinai Medical Center. Revs. George Baker; Owen Lafferty; Sr. Mary Damian Glenane, S.A.

New York Eye & Ear Infirmary Tel: 212-673-3480.

New York Hospital Tel: 212-746-4690. Revs. Vincent Ferrer McHenry, O.P.; Paul B. Fu, O.P.; Robert Philip Fitzsimmons, O.P.; Athanasius Sullivan, O.P.; Sr. Margaret T. Oettinger, O.P.

New York University Medical Center Tel: 212-263-7300. Revs. Francisco Abaya; Albert J. DeLuca; John Gibson,

Hospital for Joint Disease, Serviced by Mary Help of Christians, 212-254-0058. Rev. Dennis Kelleher.

North General Hospital. Serviced by All Saints. Rev. Lawrence E. Lucas, Tel: 212-650-4511.

Rockefeller University Tel: 212-570-8000. Rev. John T. Murphy, O.P.

St. Clare's Hospital & Health Center Tel: 212-586-1500. Rev. John J. Donahue, C.S.C.; Sr. Pascal Conforti, O.S.U.

St. Luke's-Roosevelt Hospital Center Tel: 212-523-2016.

Roosevelt Site, Rev. James F. McQuade, C.S.P.

St. Vincent Hospital Tel: 212-790-7000. Revs. John Bickle, O.F.M., Dir. Pastoral Care; Praxid DeSilva; Sr. Eileen Lambert, O.S.F.; Sr. Bernadette Baer, S.C.; Rev. Jefferson Hammer.

Terence Cardinal Cooke Health Care Center Tel: 212-360-1000. Rev. Ronald Green; Sr. Joan Gannon, R.S.C.J.

U.S.V.A. Medical Center Tel: 212-686-7500. Revs. Charles Lovato, S.F.; Edmund McCaffrey, O.Carm.; Francis C. Morgan, SS.CC.

MIDDLETOWN. *Horton Memorial Hospital*. Serviced by St. Joseph, Middletown. Tel: 914-343-2424.

Middletown Psychiatric Center. Vacant. Tel: 914-342-5511.

MONTROSE. *FDR DVA Hospital*. Revs. Daniel F. Lynch, O.Carm.; William J. O'Donnell.

MOUNT KISCO. *Northern Westchester Hospital*. Serviced by St. Francis, Mt. Kisco. Tel: 914-666-1200.

MOUNT VERNON. *Mount Vernon Hospital*. Rev. Isaac Agambi, Tel: 914-664-8000.

NEW HAMPTON. *MID Hudson Psychiatric Center*. Rev. John Eyrrick, Senior Chap., Tel: 914-374-3171, Ext. 3601.

NEW ROCHELLE. *South Shore Medical Center*. Rev. John Muscat, Tel: 914-632-5000.

NEWBURGH. *St. Luke Hospital*. Serviced by St. Patrick, Newburgh. Tel: 914-561-4400.

NORTH TARRYTOWN. *Phelps Memorial Hospital*. Serviced by St. Theresa's, Sleepy Hollow. Tel: 914-631-0720.

NYACK. *Nyack Hospital*. Serviced By St. Ann, Nyack. Shirley Blair, Dir. Pastoral Care, Tel: 914-358-6200.

ORANGEBURG. *Rockland Psychiatric Center*. Revs. Donald T. Driscoll; John Sullivan, O.P., Tel: 914-359-1000, Ext. 3589.

OSSINING. *Stony Lodge Hospital*. Serviced by St. Augustine, Ossining. Tel: 914-941-7400.

PEEKSKILL. *Hudson Valley Hospital Center*. Serviced by Holy Spirit, Cortlandt Manor. Tel: 914-737-9000.

POMONA. *Dr. Robert L. Yeager Health Center*. Susan Osborne, Pastoral Care, Tel: 914-354-0200, Ext. 2889.

PORT CHESTER. *United Hospital.* Serviced by Our Lady of Mercy, Portchester. Tel: 914-939-0612.

PORT JERVIS. *Mercy Community Hospital* Tel: 914-856-5351. Sr. Margaret Costa, R.S.M., Dir. Pastoral Care; Rev. Bernard McDonald; Sr. M. Audrey Hallahan, R.S.M.; Deacon John Nash.

POUGHKEEPSIE. *Hudson River Psychiatric Center* Tel: 914-452-8000, Ext. 378. Rev. James J. LeBar; Deacon George Cacchone, Assoc. Chap.

St. Francis Hospital Tel: 914-471-2000. Rev. Thomas A. McDonald, M.S., Dir. Pastoral Care, Pastoral Care Assocs.: Sr. Mary Ellen Smith, O.S.F.; Sr. Marie Colette, O.S.F.

Vassar Brothers Hospital Tel: 914-454-8500. Rev. Anthony S. Marian.

RHINEBECK. *Northern Dutchess Hospital.* Serviced by Good Shepherd, Rhinebeck. Tel: 914-876-4583.

RYE. *Rye Psychiatric Hospital Center.* Serviced by Church of the Resurrection, Rye. Tel: 914-967-4567.

STATEN ISLAND. *Bayley Seton Hospital* Tel: 718-390-6000. Rev. Edward J. Datty, S.A., Dir. Pastoral Care, Chaplains: Sr. Claire Marian Barton, S.C.; Bro. Kieran Cullen, S.A.

Doctor's Hospital of Staten Island. Serviced by St. Sylvester. Tel: 718-727-4639.

St. Vincent's Medical Center of Richmond Tel: 718-876-1234. Rev. Msgr. Charles McDonough, Dir. Pastoral Care, Chaplains: Rev. Ralph Dawis; Bro. Vincent Basile, C.P.; Sr. Jean Klimczak, O.S.F.

Seaview Hospital and Home Tel: 718-371-3000, Ext. 3284. Rev. Blase B. Kardos, O.F.M.Conv.

Staten Island University Hospital North. Rev. Simon Savarimuthu; Sr. Francesca Cloutier; Deacon Rosario J. Tirella.

Staten Island University Hospital South Tel: 718-260-2000. Rev. Pius Ejifor.

SUFFERN. *Good Samaritan Hospital* Tel: 914-357-3300. Sr. Sheila Mullins, O.P., Dir. Pastoral Care; Rev. Gerardo DeFillippes; Sr. Anne Tonne, S.C.; Revs. George Mattioni, O.A.R.; Frank Cregon, O.A.R.

TUXEDO PARK. *Tuxedo Memorial Health Care Center.* Vacant. Tel: 914-351-4751.

VALHALLA. *Blythdale Children's Hospital.* Serviced by Holy Name of Jesus, Valhalla. Tel: 914-592-7555.

Westchester County Medical Center Tel: 914-347-7000. Revs. Michael Connolly, O.F.M.Cap.; James Stewart, O.F.M.Cap.; Paul Tolve, O.F.M.Cap.

WARWICK. *St. Anthony Community Hospital* Tel: 914-986-2276. Rev. Edward Sullivan, O.F.M.

WASSAIC. *Wassaic Development Center.* Revs. Sylvan J. Conover, O.F.M.Cap.; John Longweld, O.F.M.Cap.

WEST HAVERSTRAW. *Helen Hayes Hospital.* Rev. Anthony Louis, S.D.B.

WHITE PLAINS. *Burke Rehabilitation Center* Tel: 914-948-0050. Revs. Patrick J. Dunne, Pastor; John Quinn; Sr. Laura Morgan, F.M.S.C.

New York Hospital - Cornell Medical Center. Rev. Richard Liew, Dir. Pastoral Care & Education.

St. Agnes Hospital Tel: 914-681-4500. Sr. Mary Virginia Brady, R.D.C., Dir. Pastoral Care; Sr. Mary Vogl, Pastoral Assoc.; Rev. James Larkin, M.SS.A., Chap.; Sr. Mary Lusk, P.B.V.M.

White Plains Hospital Tel: 914-681-0600. Rev. Benedict J. Kuolt.

WINGDALE. *Harlem Valley Psychiatric Center* Tel: 914-832-6611, Ext. 1152. Rev. Anthony Donahue, O.F.M.Cap.

YONKERS. *St. John Hospital.* (Night Call-Christ the King, Yonkers, 914-963-7474) Tel: 914-964-4444. Rev. Neal Kerrigan, O.F.M.Cap.

St. Joseph Hospital Tel: 914-378-7000. Sr. Carolyn Parker, R.S.M., Dir. Pastoral Care; Sr. Dolores Doyle, P.B.V.M., Pastoral Care Assoc.; Revs. Thomas Murphy, O.F.M.Cap.; Richardson Donaldson, O.F.M.Cap.

Yonkers General Hospital. See Archdiocesan Directory for Parishes that Service Nursing Homes and Homes for the Aged. Tel: 914-964-7399. Rev. Henry Pushporoj.

On Duty Outside the Archdiocese:

Most Rev.—

McCormack, William J., Society for the Propagation of the Faith

Reverend Monsignors—

Balvo, Charles D., Apostolic Nunciatura, Prague, Czech Republic
Meier, John P., Catholic University of America, Washington, DC
Murnion, Philip J., National Pastoral Life Conference
O'Brien, William B., Daytop Village, 54 W. 40th St., New York, NY 10018

Reverend Fathers—

Brown, Charles, Congregation Pro, Doctrina Fidei
Carson, David L., O.F.M., Dept. of Veterans Affairs, Bath, NY
Chiang, John B., Oblates of Hong Kong
Dillon, Richard J., Fordham University, Fordham Rd., Bronx, NY 10458
Haggerty, Donald, Mt. St. Mary's Seminary, Emmitsburg, MD
Hartmann, Edward, Archdiocese of Fairbanks
Imbelli, Robert, Boston College
Irwin, Kevin W., Catholic University of America, Washington, DC
Kang, Paul, St. Andrew Kim, Orange, NJ
Kennedy, Robert T., Catholic University of America, Washington, DC
Komonchak, Joseph A., Catholic University of America, Washington, DC
Lonek, Stephen C., Diocese of Wilmington
Malcolm, Dennis E.
Marino, Umberto J.
McDonald, Thomas M., Fordham University, Lincoln Center, NY
O'Donnell, William J., V.A. Hospital, Montrose, NY
Pavone, Frank A., Pontifical Council for the Family, Rome
Rafferty, Raymond M., Netherlands
Rutler, George W., Legatus Apostolate
Serra, Dominic, St. Pauls Seminary, St. Paul, MN
Smarsh, Charles F., University of Maryland
Tou, John, Holy Family, Singapore
White, William, St. Vincent de Paul Seminary, Boynton Beach, FL
Whitson, Robley E., United Institute, Bethelem, CT
Young, William E., Archdiocese of Santa Fe, St. Anthony's Church, P.O. Box 200, Questa, NM 87556

Military Chaplains:

Reverend Fathers—

Adams, Walter C., U.S.A.F., Peterson Air Force Base, Colorado Springs, CO 80914
Borkowski, Francis, U.S.A.
Deponai, Joseph J., U.S.A.
Gallagher, Michael F., U.S.N.
Hill, Philip, U.S.A.
Keeley, Patrick P., (Retired), U.S.N.
Kelly, John R., U.S.A.
Lindblad, Karl-Albert, U.S.N.
Mandato, Kieran, U.S.N.
McGeory, Peter, U.S.N.
Mullin, Thomas
O'Reilly, Edward M., U.S.A.
Panek, Robert M., U.S.N.
Pugliese, Francis A.
Sandi, Thomas P., U.S.A.F.
Zoshak, William H., U.S.A.F.

On Special or Other (Arch)Diocesan Assignment:

Reverend Monsignors—

Barrett, Harry C., New York Medical College, Valhalla, NY 10595
Vaughey, James K., Exec. Dir., Cemeteries, The Trustees of St. Patrick's Cathedral in the City of New York, Inc.

Reverend Fathers—

O'Malley, Francis P., M.S. in Education, St. Vincent Hospital and Medical Center of New York, NY 10014

Graduate Studies:

Reverend Fathers—

Dillon, Robert
Hull, Michael
Lauri, John
Lynch, Thomas
Mustaciuolo, Gregory
Oonnoonny, George

Absent on Sick leave:

Most Rev.—

Vaughan, Austin

Reverend Fathers—

Coleman, John
Conlan, James S.
Coyne, James F.
Gilhooley, James
Jordan, Patrick J.
McKay, Frank
Mulloy, Matthew F.
O'Connor, Maurice
Sandstrom, Philip J.
Slattery, Maurice C.

Absent on Leave:

Reverend Fathers—

Antony, Charles
Barjacoba, Peter
Brogan, William
Calabrese, Daniel
Calhoun, C. John
Carden, Robert J.
Cassiero, Daniel
Ciaravolo, Ronald
Clark, Andrew
Dalton, Howard
Doherty, John B.
Donahue, Joseph
Elmo, Francis E.
Eremito, Anthony
Geraghty, James
Gollinge, Donald
Hoehmann, George
Hoffay, Thomas
Holhmann, George
Horst, Kenneth
Kovach, Raymond J.
LeBlanc, Paul
Malone, Donald
McGill, Joseph F.
McLucas, James
Mulloy, William
Mulvanerty, Thomas
Pane, Andrew
Peluso, Michael J.
Pipala, Edward A.
Plo, John
Quigley, Patrick
Quinn, James
Surace, Robert J.

Retired:

Most Rev.—

Ahern, Patrick, St. Thomas More, 65 E. 89th St., New York, NY 10128
Mahoney, James P., Assumption, 131 Union Ave., Peekskill, NY 10566

Reverend Monsignors—

Arpie, Robert A., 5 Lyon Ct., Hampton Bays, NY 11946
Bardes, George F., Stephinac H.S., 950 Mamaroneck Ave., White Plains, NY 10605
Bourke, Myles M., Portsmouth Abbey School, Portsmouth, RI
Brady, Daniel J., St. Patrick's, 29 Cox Ave., Armonk, NY 10504
Brennan, Francis P., Terrence Cardinal Cooke Nursing Home, 1249 5th Ave., New York, NY 10029
Brennan, Francis M., 6 Beech Rd., Suffern, NY 10901
Brooks, John N., Box 26, Rifton, NY 12471
Byrne, Harry J., 222 E. 93rd St., Apt. 39E, New York, NY 10128
Carlin, John A., 5635 Netherland Ave., Bronx, NY 10471
Clyne, Vincent F., 376 Baden Pl., Staten Island, NY 10306
Cohalan, Florence, St. Agnes, 143 E. 43rd St., New York, NY 10017
Connors, Edward M., Stepinac High School, 950 Mamaroneck Ave., White Plains, NY 10605
Considine, John J., Cardinal Spellman High School, 1991 Needham Ave., Bronx, NY 10466
Corrigan, Bernard J., St. Stephen, 75 Sanfordville Rd., Warwick, NY 10990
Costello, Francis M., 30 Inlets Blvd., Nokomis, FL 34275
Curtin, Richard B., Lucas Ave., Cottekill, NY 12419
Daly, John, 14309 A Canalview Dr., Delray Beach, FL 33484
Delaney, William B., 43 W. Orland Rd., Milford, CT 06460
Devlin, Joseph M., 190 Hollywood Ave., Bronx, NY 10465
DiBlasi, Augustine J., Stepinac High School, 950 Mamaroneck, White Plains, NY 10605
Doherty, John T., Stepinac High School, 950 Mamaroneck Ave., White Plains, NY 10605
Duffy, Francis X., 1083 Washington Green, New Windsor, NY 12553
Dugan, Edward T., St. Mary's, Main St., Marlboro, NY 12542
Dunne, Joseph A., 10777 Sample Rd., Coral Springs, FL 33065
Dwyer, Michael F., 3121 Ninth Ave. N., St. Petersburg, FL 33713
Fitzgerald, Stephen J., Francis Schervier Home, 2975 Independence Ave., Box 10463, Bronx, NY 10463
Forrester, Henry W., 210 Sand Ln., Staten Island, NY 10306
Fowler, Eugene A., Hearts Content Rd., Roxbury, CT 12474
Gallagher, Thomas V., Our Lady of Consolation, 3103 Arlington Ave., Bronx, NY 10463
Geissler, Robert, 196 Azalea Cir., Jackson, NY 08527
Gillen, John J., St. John Newmann Residence, 5655 Arlington Ave., Bronx, NY 10471
Glynn, Francis J., Holy Family, 366 Watchogue Rd., Staten Island, NY 10314
Goodwine, Joseph G., 960 Palm View Rd., Naples, FL 33942
Gordon, John, St. Margaret Mary, 560 Lincoln Ave., Staten Island, NY 10306
Green, Gerard A., 66 Van Cortlandt Park, Bronx, NY 10463

Guido, William F., 121 Egbert Ave., Staten Island, NY
Hammer, Edmond, Bethel Nursing Home, Ossining, NY 10562
Hanlon, James J., 150 Riverside Dr., New York, NY 10024
Harrington, John M., St. Margaret, 115 W. Central Ave., Pearl River, NY 10965
Higgins, William, Our Lady of Consolation, 3103 Arlington Ave., Bronx, NY 10463
Jablonski, Stanislaus, St. Valentine, 810 E. 221 St., Bronx, NY
Jeffers, Vincent W., Stepinac High School, 950 Mamaroneck Ave., White Plains, NY 10605
Keating, James V., St. Joseph, 242 Wall St., Kingston, NY 12401
Kelleher, Stephen, Kateri Nursing Home, 150 Riverside Dr., New York, NY 10024
Kelly, George A., 107-10 Shore Front Pkwy., Rockaway Beach, NY 11694
Kelly, Robert J., 644 Clawson St., Staten Island, NY 10306
Keogh, Thomas J., 4 Dogwood Rd., Hampton Bays, NY 11946
Loftus, Robert, Kateri Nursing Home, 150 Riverside Dr., New York, NY 10024
Mahoney, Francis, 141 Port Royal Dr., Toms River, NJ 08757
Marbach, Joseph, 3410 Amalfi Dr., West Palm Beach, FL 33417
Marinacci, Nicholas, St. Patrick's Old Cathedral, 263 Mulberry St., New York, NY 10012
Mazziotta, Robert R., P.O. Box 705, Philmont, NY 12565
McCaffrey, Thomas F., Our Lady of Fatima, 5 Strathmore Rd., Scarsdale, NY 10580
McCormack, Robert, 910 Boston Post Rd., Rye, NY 10580
McDonnell, James T., New Horizens, 400 Hemenway St., Marlboro, MA 01752
McMahon, Thomas, Stepinac High School, 950 Mamaroneck Ave., White Plains, NY 10605
McMahon, William J., Holy Spirit, 1969 Crompond Rd., Cortland Manor, NY 10566
McManus, Charles J., St. Gabriel, 3250 Arlington Ave., Bronx, NY 10461
Montano, Edward J., 4 Fiero Rd., P.O. Box 152, Malden-on-Hudson, NY 12453
Narkun, Peter P., Cardinal Hayes High School, 650 Grand Concourse, Bronx, NY 10451
Netter, Edmund W., c/o Joseph Robertson, 275 Amberfield Dr., NJ 08054
O'Brien, Cornelius M., Stepinac High School, 950 Mamaroneck Ave., White Plains, NY 10605
O'Connor, James, St. Francis Gardens, 904 Las Lomas Rd., Albuquerque, NM 87102
Pavis, Victor C., Cardinal Hayes High School, 650 Grand Concourse, Bronx, NY 10451
Potocek, Cyril J., Holy Cross, 118 Beekman Ave., N., Tarrytown, NY 10591
Quinn, Andrew F., Sacred Heart, 981 Castleton Ave., Staten Island, NY 10310
Quinn, John J., St. Joseph's Seminary, Yonkers, NY 10704
Quinn, Joseph J., John Paul II Residence, 603 First Ave., New York, NY 10016
Raimondo, Joseph J., St. Gregory the Great, 215 Halstead Ave., Harrison, NY 10528
Reisig, William E., 1230 Lafayette Ave., Bronx, NY 10474
Reynolds, Edward J., John Paul II Residence, 603 First Ave., New York, NY 10016
Rigney, James, 40 Dick Finn Rd., P.O. Box 8192, New Fairfield, CT 06812
Rigney, Raymond P., Stepinac High School, 950 Mamaroneck Ave., White Plains, NY 10605
Rinschler, William J., 445 21st St., New York, NY 10011
Rooney, Hugh J., Our Lady of Consolation Residence, 3103 Arlington Ave., Bronx, NY 10463
Rossbach, George F., 45-315 Lilipuna Rd., B202, Kaneoke, HI 96744
Rosselli, Charles, 9765 B Tabebuia Tree Dr., Boynton Beach, FL 33436
Ryan, Gerald J., St. Luke's, Bronx, NY
Santulin, Joseph M., John Paul II Residence, 603 First Ave., New York, NY 10016
Schroeder, Walter L., 525 Bedford Rd., North Tarrytown, NY 10591
Shevlin, John G., Immaculate Conception, Bangal, NY
Snee, Joseph T.V., St. Bernard, 328 W. 14th St., New York, NY 10014
Sullivan, Daniel L., Blessed Sacrament, 30 Manor Rd., Staten Island, NY 10310
Vier, Henry J., Stepinac High School, 950 Mamaroneck Ave., White Plains, NY 10605
Walsh, James J., 950 Mamaroneck Ave., White Plains, NY 10605
Welsh, David B., 470 Van Cortlandt Park Ave., Yonkers, NY 10705
Wilders, James G., Mary Manning Walsh Home, 1339 York Ave., New York, NY 10021

Reverend Fathers—
Adamo, Joseph P., Our Lady of Consolation, 3103 Arlington Ave., Bronx, NY 10463
Alessandro, Michael J., 1496 Commonwealth Ave., Bronx, NY 10460
Basile, Nicholas F., Our Lady of Mt. Carmel, 627 E. 187 St., Bronx, NY 10458
Breen, John F., St. Francis of Assisi Rectory, 128 Parrott Ave., W. Nyack, NY 10994
Brennan, Robert J., 35 Cerone Pl., Apt. 507, Newburgh, NY 12550
Buttinelli, Anthony, Via Valle della Storta 75, Rome, Italy 00123
Cavanaugh, John L., Stepinac High School, 950 Mamaroneck Ave., White Plains, NY 10605
Cholette, John B., 6606 Fairpines Rd., Chesterfield, VA 23832
Conlin, Edward, Immaculate Conception, 414 E. 14th St., New York, NY 10009
Connolly, Martin J., John Paul II Residence, 603 First Ave., New York, NY 10016
Conroy, Edward, St. Raymond, 1759 Castle Hill Ave., Bronx, NY 10462
Conte, James W., 2555 Willow St., San Diego, CA 92106
Conti, John P., 537 Third St., Brooklyn, NY 11215
Crotty, John M., 660 Americana Dr., Annapolis, MD 21403
Cusma, Joseph S., 255 Bronx River Rd., Apt. 8N, Yonkers, NY 10704
d'Anjou, Henry G., Stepinac High School, 950 Mamaroneck Ave., White Plains, NY 10605
D'Antonio, Anthony, Our Lady of Mt. Carmel, 627 E. 187 St., Bronx, NY 10458
D'Auriol, Vincent, Sts. Peter & Paul Parish, 833 St. Ann Ave., Bronx, NY 10456
Darby, Thomas J., John Paul II Residence, 603 First Ave., New York, NY 10016
Derrenbacher, James W., St. John Evangelist, 915 Rte. 212, Woodstock Rd., Saugerties, NY 12477
Doersam, Carl G., Ferncliff Nursing Home
Donachie, Joseph J., 900 Intervale St., Bronx, NY 10459
Doyle, Philip R., Box 1088, Carmel, NY 10512
Duane, Robert J., 8000 Shore Front Pkwy., Rockaway Beach, NY 11693
Duffy, Edwin, c/o Corroon, 612 Purchase, Rye, NY 10580
Dumpson, Roland J., 15 W. 124th St., New York, NY 10027
Dunn, Robert T., 854 Hudis St., Rohnert Park, CA 94928
Fagnani, Anthony G., 357 Yankee Lake Rd., Wurtsboro, NY 12790
Fiorillo, Antimo, 2352 St. Raymond's Ave., Bronx, NY 10462
Flannery, Michael, 8200 Shore Front Pkwy., Rockaway Beach, NY 11693
Fleming, John F., 1083 Washington Green, New Windsor, NY 12553
Flynn, James P., 1310 Stoneybrook Ave., Mamaronek, NY 10543
Fogarty, Daniel, 6333 Rancho Mission Rd., San Diego, CA 92108
Gallagher, Eugene P., 40 W. Point Hwy., Highland Falls, NY 10928
Giammarino, George, 1789 Seminole Ave., Bronx, NY 10461
Gussoni, Lino, Via Rodini Tedeschi 19, Piacenza, 29100 Italy
Halpin, Leo F., 5 Tanglewylde Ave., Apt. 6H, Bronxville, NY 10708
Holihan, John W., c/o Alandy, 18 DeKarla Dr., Middletown, NJ 07748
Jacolino, Dominic, John Paul II Residence, 603 First Ave., New York, NY 10016
Jenko, Aloysius, New York, NY 10016
Kelly, William E., Our Lady of Consolation, 3103 Arlington Ave., Bronx, NY 10463
Kennedy, William J., John Paul II Residence, 603 First Ave., New York, NY 10016
Kuolt, Benedict, St. Bernard, 51 Prospect St., White Plains, NY 10606
Larkin, John P., John Paul II Residence, 603 First Ave., New York, NY 10016
Laurenzano, Roch M., 8753 Como Lake Dr., Jacksonville, FL 32216
Magee, Andrew T., John Paul II Residence, 603 First Ave., New York, NY 10016
Maher, John J., 43 Hearth Dr., New Windsor, NY 10704
McGann, Joseph F., P.O. Box 2593, Montauk, NY 11954
McHale, Charles P., 266 Near Rd., Red Hook, NY 12571
McKenna, John J., St. Joan of Arc, 32 Eagle Valley Rd., Sloatsburg, NY 10974
Meade, John F., 65 Wright Ave., Malverne, NY 11565
Miller, Frederick J., 56 Sprague Ave., Staten Island, NY 10307
Minielli, Anthony, Via Colombo 9, 70028 Sannicandro, Bari
Molony, Francis J., Our Lady of Consolation Residence, 3103 Arlington Ave., Bronx, NY 10463
Moran, Thomas J., Ferncliff Nursing Home, 52 River Rd., Rhinebeck, NY 12572
Moriarty, James J., St. John the Evangelist, Pawling, NY
Murphy, Jerome J., Ferncliff Nursing Home, 52 River Rd., Rhinebeck, NY 12572
Neilson, Richard J., Our Savior, Park Ave. at 38th St., New York, NY 10016
Newman, Francis M., 174 Westchester Ave., Buchanan, NY
O'Hara, Eugene R., Our Lady of Consolation Residence, 3103 Arlington Ave., Bronx, NY 10463
O'Keefe, Thomas E., Stepinac High School, 950 Mamaroneck Ave., White Plains, NY 10605
O'Shea, Joseph J., St. Helena, 1315 Olmstead Ave., Bronx, NY 10462
O'Toole, Kenneth E., 15 St. John's Pl., Chappaqua, NY 10514
Pacacha, Joseph E., 1820 Smith Dr., N., Titesville, FL 32780
Parsons, Harold J., 227 Sunset Ave., Island Park, NY 11558
Phillips, Thomas, Our Lady of Consolation, 3103 Arlington Ave., Bronx, NY 10463
Pisanelli, Humbert D., Our Lady of Consolation, 3103 Arlington Ave., Bronx, NY 10463
Quirk, Edward J., c/o Jeanne Quirk, 7 Normandy Village, Nanuet, NY 10954
Sheridan, Eugene, HC 1, Box 34, Greenfield Park, NY 12435
Smolinski, Joseph J., 11 Dale Ave., Apt. 21, Highland Falls, NY 10928
Smyth, James, 616 Warburton Ave., Hastings-on-Hudson, NY 10706
Sullivan, Paul V., St. Joseph, 141 Ashburton Ave., Yonkers, NY 10701
Thenen, James, St. Peter's, 53 St. Marks Pl., Staten Island, NY 10301
Tobin, James B., Stepinac High School, 950 Mamaroneck Ave., White Plains, NY 10605
Tubridy, James J., 1214 Springdale Rd., Croton-on-Hudson, NY 10520
Vala, John B., John Paul II Residence, 605 First Ave., New York, NY 10016

Permanent Deacons:
Abbamont, Thomas J., St. Ursula, Mount Vernon
Aglietti, Richard, St. Mary's, Mt. Vernon
Almanzar, Andres A., St. John Vianney, Bronx
Alvarado, William, St. Columba, Hopewell Junction
Anderson, John J., Plant City, FL
Armo, John, St. John Evangelist, Mahopac
Attridge, James C., St. James the Apostle, Carmel
Aviles, Stanley, St. Denis, Hopewell Junction
Baerga, Luis, St. John the Evangelist, Goshen
Banker, Howard A., Our Lady of Assumption, Bronx
Barbieri, Nicola A., Our Lady of Pompeii, Dobbs Ferry
Baterbury, John J., Sacred Heart of Jesus, Suffern
Battersby, William L., St. Mary, Mount Vernon
Bellacicco, John A., St. Augustine, Highland
Bello, Rafael J., Our Lady of Guadalupe, South Manhattan
Bernal, Enrique, Our Lady of Guadalupe, South Manhattan
Biasotti, John C.
Biskup, William E., Regina Coeli, Hyde Park
Blake, George W., Block Island, RI
Bonanno, Joseph M., Regina Coeli, Hyde Park
Bormann, Eugene, St. Anastasia, Harriman
Borsavage, Charles T., St. James the Apostle, Carmel
Bouwmans, Philip R., Immaculate Conception, Port Jervis
Brigande, Vincent G., St. Charles, Staten Island
Brockmann, Peter, Sacred Heart, Monroe
Brown, James A., SS. John & Paul, Larchmont
Bruno, Gaspare F., St. Elizabeth Ann Seton, Shrub Oak
Buckley, John J., St. Mary, Newburgh
Bunyar, Perry A., St. Mary of the Snow, Saugerties
Buonocore, Dominc A., St. Paul, Congers
Burke, Eugene F., St. Gabriel, Bronx
Burnett, Robert V., Antigua, West Indies
Burns, James T., Sacred Heart, Monroe
Cacchione, George F., St. Peter, Poughkeepsie
Calafiore, Michael R., St. Charles, Staten Island
Calimano, Ross J., Our Lady Queen of Peace, Staten Island
Camacho, Ismael, Joan of Arc, Bronx
Camacho, Vidal J., St. Elizabeth of Hungary, FL
Canals, Dhoel M., Holy Family, Bronx
Carlino, Frank R., St. Columba, Chester

Carroll, Harold N., St. Charles Borromeo, Gardiner
Casadone, Dominic G., Sacred Heart, Newburgh
Cassaneto, Anthony P., St. Theresa of the Child Jesus, Bronx
Castellanos, Luis, Miami Beach, FL
Charlesworth, Myles J., Our Lady of Lourdes Parish, Raleigh, NC
Check, Raymond P., Virginia Beach, VA
Ciccone, Daniel J., Corpus Christi, Port Chester
Clemens, Robert A., St. Bartholomew, Yonkers
Collins, George J., St. Thomas More, Boynton Beach, FL
Conner, Albert C., Annunciation, Crestwood
Coppola, John J., St. Columbanus, Peekskill
Cosme, Felix, Gainesville, GA
Cotto, Angel L., Caguas, Puerto Rico
D'Aiello, Joseph, Holy Rosary, Bronx
D'Arconte, Benjamin, Sacred Heart, Hartsdale
Darlestin, Leones J., Holy Name of Jesus, Manhattan
Dauerer, Walter P., St. Denis, Hopewell Junction
Daur, Raymond, Our Lady of Mercy, Port Chester
De Jesus, Jose L., St. Ann, Ossining
De Los Santos, German, Incarnation, North Manhattan
De Maio, Donald J., Naples, FL
De Marco, Carmine J., Holy Name of Jesus, New Rochelle
De Meis, John, Italo-Greek Albanian Community
Degenhardt, Carl, St. Ursula, Mount Vernon
Del Campo, Francis, Our Lady Rosary, Port Chester
Delgado, Luis, Our Lady of Angels, Bronx
Deschler, Bernard M., Breezy Point
di Targiani, Robert, Immaculate Heart of Mary, Scarsdale
Dingee, Richard D., Ulster Correctional Facility, Napanoch
Doherty, Joseph, St. Joseph, Kingston
Donovan, William, St. Margaret, Pearl River
Dringus, William L., East Greenbush
Droulette, Donald L., St. Joseph, Kingston
Eccleston, Arthur W., Our Lady of Good Counsel, Staten Island
Edgerton, John M., St. Patrick's Parish, Tarpon Springs, FL
Esposito, Robert A., St. John the Evangelist, Mahopac
Estela, Jorge, Our Lady of Mercy, Bronx
Fama, Arthur, St. Joseph-St. Thomas, Staten Island
Feliciano, Ulises, Tagaste Monastery, Suffern
Fernandez, Roberto, St. Raymond, Bronx
Ferraiuolo, Anthony P., St. Joseph, New Windsor
Ferreira, Emetrio
Fien, Robert A., Our Lady of Mercy, Port Chester
Fontanez, Luis, Holy Cross, Bronx
Fox, Michael J., Our Lady of Fatima, Scarsdale
Francis, James, Our Lady of Pity, Bronx
Frohbose, John M., Our Lady of Mt. Carmel, Middletown
Frohmiller, Richard J., St. Joseph, Kingston
Gallagher, Daniel J., Boynton Beach, FL
Garcia, Rene, Our Lady of Guadalupe, New York
Gaskin, Theodore A., St. Pius X, Scarsdale
Giglio, Pasquale, St. Ursula, Mount Vernon
Glover, William, St. Patrick, Newburgh
Gohl, Frank, Regina Coeli, Hyde Park
Gontcharuk, Robert, Holy Name of Jesus, New Rochelle
Gonzalez, Faustino, Santiago de Compostella, Spain
Gonzalez, Ismael, Caguas, Puerto Rico
Gorman, James, St. Paul, Congers
Gorzka, Stephen S.
Graf, Joseph J., St. Margaret Mary, Staten Island
Granda, Miguel E., St. Paul, Manhattan
Griffin, Francis J., Our Lady of Fatima, Scarsdale
Grosso, Edward, Assumption, Maybrook
Gruerio, Anthony G., St. James, Carmel
Hafemann, Joseph R., St. Joachim, Beacon
Haight, Peter R., Sacred Heart, Newburgh
Hamilton, Eugene R., St. Peter, Haverstraw
Hamilton, James J., St. Paul the Apostle, Yonkers
Hanson, Lee, Sun City West, AZ
Hayes, James R., St. Peter, Poughkeepsie
Hennessy, John L., St. Barnabas, Bronx
Hernandez, Narcisco, Our Lady Queen of Martyrs, Manhattan
Hill, William J., St. Pius X, Scarsdale
Hodges, Raymond, Our Savior, Pine Bush
Hogan, Patrick J., St. Martin de Porres, Poughkeepsie
Hooghuis, Joseph, St. Patrick, Staten Island
Hopkins, Farrell J., Key West, FL
Horvath, Robert J., St. Thomas More Parish, Sarasota, FL
Howley, Herbert, Greenwich
Hudson, Alan A.
Impallomeni, Alfred R., Our Lady of Mount Carmel, Yonkers
Ippolito, Steve J.
Irizarry, Pedro, St. Peter, Yonkers
Jarmick, Robert E., St. Martin de Porres, Poughkeepsie
Jean-Gilles, Gabriel
Johnson, Robert, Sacred Heart, Suffern
Johnson, Thomas R., St. Joseph, Greenwich Village
Juhasz, Lajos, St. Margaret of Hungary, Yonkers
Kawula, Lawrence, Sacred Heart, Newburgh
Kazimir, Martin, St. Mary, Fishkill
Kelleher, John C., St. Catharine, Blauvelt
Klein, Albert J., St. Peter, Poughkeepsie
Klein, John P., Ward, SC
Knack, Lawrence F.
Knight, Charles C., Marysville, OH
Koch, George J., Sun City West, AZ
Kollar, John J.
Lagotta, Anthony A., Our Lady of Mt. Carmel & St. Benedicta, Staten Island
Larkin, John J., St. Peter, Rosendale
Laurato, Vincent I., St. Barnabas, Bronx
Le Blanc, Vincent F.
Leasiolagi, Taulafoga, St. John Vianney, Bronx
Li Greci, Christopher, St. Michael Chapel, Manhattan
Lieby, Joseph, St. Joseph, New Windsor
Liggan, John J., St. Peter, Rosendale
Longo, Ralph D., Holy Rosary, Greenwood Lake
Lopez, Domingo, St. Joseph of the Holy Family, Harlem
Lopez, Francisco, St. Martin of Tours, Bronx
Lugo, Alejandro, St. Cecilia, Manhattan
Maher, James, St. Aedans, Pearl River
Maldonado, Eusebio
Maloney, John R., St. Anthony, Nanuet
Manning, Cornelius J., St. Barnabas, Bronx
Manzione, Arthur, St. Anthony of Padua, West Harrison
Marino, Philip A., Immaculate Conception, Stony Point
Maroon, Phillip J., St. Rita, Staten Island
Martinez, Luis A., Our Lady Queen of Angels, Manhattan
Martinez, Rafael, Caguas, Puerto Rico
Mazza, Albert, Holy Name of Mary, Croton-on-Hudson
Mazzei, Nicholas A., Our Lady of Mt. Carmel, Yonkers
McCabe, Michael G., St. Augustine, New City
McCarthy, Richard, Sacred Heart, Monroe
McCormick, Daniel F., Virginia Beach, VA
McGowan, George J., Visitation B.V.M., Bronx
McNeill, Lawrence C., Holy Cross, Manhattan
McSherry, John W., St. Paul, Congers
Meier, Anthony C., Willow Springs, NC
Mercado, Carlos V., Immaculate Conception, Bronx
Mirando, Wilfredo, St. Lucy, Bronx
Mitchell, Richard F., St. Clare, Staten Island
Monegro, Juan, Incarnation, Manhattan
Moran, Bernard, St. Clare's, Bronx
Morillo, Felix M., Holy Spirit, Bronx
Morrette, Thomas, SS. John & Mary, Chappaqua
Mueller, William J., St. Mary Star of the Sea, Bronx
Mulryan, W. Joseph, St. Denis, Yonkers
Munnick, John B., Corpus Christi, Port Chester
Munoz, Jose A., Prison Chap., Scranton, PA
Murphy, John G., St. Frances de Chantal, Bronx
Nash, John J., Mercy Hospital, Port Jervis
Nielsen, William, St. Thomas of Canterbury, Cornwall-on-Hudson
Nolasco, Ronald, Our Lady of Mercy, Bronx
Nunez, Acadio, Puerto Rico
O'Brien, Donald, St. Francis of Assisi, West Nyack
O'Brien, Henry F., Spanish Fort, AL
O'Connor, Gerard R., Center of Jesus the Lord, New Orleans, LA
O'Reilly, John F.
O'Toole, Lawrence, St. Augustine, New York
Ocasio, Roberto, Kissimmee, FL
Olivieri, Martin J., St. John the Baptist, Yonkers
Orlando, Francis B., Blessed Sacrament, New Rochelle
Ortiz, Louis, Ponce, Puerto Rico
Ortiz, Pablo, St. Thomas Aquinas, Bronx
Ottaviano, Frank S., St. Augustine, Highland
Pacheco, Angel, St. Isaac Jogues Parish, Orlando, FL
Padron, Jose R., St. Pius V, Bronx
Palladino, Joseph, St. Joseph, New Paltz
Pappalardo, Augustine A., St. Gregory Barbarigo, Garnerville
Parchen, Raymond, Holy Spirit, Peekskill
Patricola, Salvatore P., St. Anthony's, Pine Plains
Pelella, John V., St. Thomas of Canterbury, Cornwall-on-Hudson
Pellegrini, Guy A., Our Lady Perpetual Help, Pelham
Perez, Primitiro, St. Stephen/Our Lady of Scapular, New York
Peters, John, St. Joseph, Kingston
Pietkiewicz, Karl J., St. Mary of the Snow, Saugerties
Pino, Victor M., St. John Chrysostom, Bronx
Pipher, Jesse E., Sarasota, FL
Piro, Vincent T., Our Lady of Mt. Carmel, Mt. Vernon
Pollick, Donald F., Westchester Medical Center Hospital, Valhalla
Porcel, Carlos M.
Portalatin, Epimegnio, Blessed Sacrament, Bronx
Preti, Aldo, St. Raymond, Bronx
Price, Joseph E.
Quigley, Donald M., St. Eugene, Yonkers
Quinn, Thomas J., Holy Child, Staten Island
Radcliffe, Kenneth L., Resurrection, Central Harlem
Radzilowicz, John, St. Casimir, Yonkers
Ramos, Alfonso, Sacred Heart, Bronx
Ramos, Edmundo A.
Ramos, Epifanio, Altamonte Springs, FL
Ramos, Rafael, St. John Vianney, Bronx
Rausch, Paul A., St. Thomas Aquinas, Forestburg
Reilly, John P., St. Columba, Hopewell Junction
Rentkowski, Joseph, St. Adalbert, Staten Island
Repke, John W., St. Mary, Marlboro
Rescildo, Ralph J., Hartford, CT
Rettino, P. Robert, St. Joseph, Spring Valley
Reynolds, Peter E., Our Lady of Mt. Carmel, Elmsford
Riley, John M., St. Peter, Liberty
Rivera, Andrew A., St. John, Kingsbridge Ave., Bronx
Rivera, Jose A., Aquas Buenas, Puerto Rico
Rizzo, Charles A., Blessed Sacrament, New Rochelle
Roberts, James F., Our Lady of the Assumption, Peekskill
Rodriguez, Arnaldo, Nativity, Manhattan
Rodriguez, Cristobal, Immaculate Conception, Bronx
Rodriguez, Hector, St. Philip Neri, Bronx
Rodriguez, Jacinto, St. Anthony, Bronx
Rodriguez, Jesus, Guayanilla, Puerto Rico
Rodriguez, Juan J., Holy Cross, Bronx
Rodriguez, Porfirio, St. Jude, Manhattan
Romagosa, Guillermo P., Manhattan College, Bronx
Rosado, Alejandro, St. Athanasius, Bronx
Rosado, Odalis R., St. Elizabeth, New York
Rosado, Reynaldo, St. Martin of Tours, Bronx
Rosado, Ricardo, Mid-Orange Correctional Facility, Warwick
Rush, James J., Charleston, SC
Russell, Franklyn R., St. Patrick, Newburgh
Russo, Richard J., St. Jean Baptist, Manhattan
Salamone, Victor A., St. Martin de Porres, Poughkeepsie
Salomone, Ernest F., Immaculate Heart of Mary, Scarsdale
Sanchez, Oscar, Trujillo Alto, Puerto Rico
Santana, Richard, Holy Name of Mary, Croton-on-Hudson
Santana, Robert, SS. Philip & James, Bronx
Santiago, Abraham, St. Joseph, Yonkers
Schlitt, Ronald, St. Christopher, Buchanan
Sepulveda, Miguel A., Ponce, Puerto Rico
Serrano, Jose I.
Seymour, John L., St. Francis of Assisi, Newburgh
Sheeley, Robert B., Holy Name of Jesus, Kingston
Shepard, John, St. Mary, Washingtonville
Shiel, Thomas P., Incarnation, Tampa, FL
Shkreli, Marash, St. Lawrence O'Toole, Brewster
Simpson, John J., St. Benedict, Bronx
Sin-Garciga, Felipe, St. Angela Merici, Bronx
Singler, John A., Our Lady Help of Christians, Staten Island
Smith, John A., Lewes, DE
Solanto, Joseph P., Holy Rosary, Bronx
Soto, Constancio, Ascension, Manhattan
Stahlnecker, James J., St. Mary of the Assumption, Staten Island
Steup, Fredrick C., St. Patrick, Newburgh
Stewart, George, St. Columba, Hopewell Junction
Suarez, Israel, Guaynabo, Puerto Rico
Sullivan, John D., Holy Trinity, West Harwich, MA
Sullivan, John M., St. Mary, Kingston
Sweeney, Walter F., Our Lady of Good Counsel, Staten Island
Tayco, Renato
Testa, Warren, St. Columba, Hopewell Junction
Then, Rafael, Good Shepherd, Manhattan
Thompson, Albert, Our Lady of Good Counsel, Staten Island
Tirado, Alberto, St. Ann's, Bronx
Tirella, Rosario J., Holy Rosary, Staten Island
Tobin, William D., St. Margaret, Pearl River
Tola, Vincente, Sunrise, FL
Topple, Edwin R., St. John the Evangelist, Centerville
Torres, Gilberto, Deltona, FL
Torres, Luis, Mayaguez, Puerto Rico
Torres, Luis A., St. Pius V., Bronx
Trapani, Richard, St. Joseph, Middletown

Trees, Donald F., St. Mary of the Snow, Saugerties
Treiling, John F., St. Joseph Home & Hospital, Yonkers
Troy, Patrick D., Sacred Heart, Dobbs Ferry
Vaccaro, William N., Our Lady of the Rosary, Port Chester
Vargas, Thomas A., Holy Trinity, Mamaroneck
Vazquez, Juan F., St. Martin of Tours, Bronx
Velez, Randy, St. Peter, Yonkers
Venezia, Ignatius, St. Boniface, Wesley Hills
Verboys, Joseph, Sacred Heart, Suffern
Vorel, Vladislav P., St. Patrick, Yorktown Heights
Wallace, Benjamin S., St. Lawrence O'Toole, Brewster
Weinstein, David, Immaculate Conception, Amenia
Weir, John E., Bridgeport, CT
Weireter, Paul J., St. Patrick, Highland Mills
Weiss, Robert W., St. Augustine, Highland
Welhous, Albert V., SS. Philip & James, Bronx
Wendelken, Charles L., Blessed Sacrament, New Rochelle
Wetherall, Edward J., Our Lady Help of Christians, Staten Island
Winrow, Robert P., St. Joseph, Kingston
Witt, Joseph A., Sacred Heart, Suffern
Woods, Edward J., Our Lady of Mt. Carmel, Middletown
Wyka, Stanley A., St. Casimir, Yonkers
Zatarga, Michael, North Palm Beach, FL

INSTITUTIONS LOCATED IN THE ARCHDIOCESE

[A] SEMINARIES, ARCHDIOCESAN

NEW YORK. *Cathedral Preparatory Seminary*. Archdiocesan Preparatory Seminary, 946 Boston Post Rd., Rye, 10580. Tel: 914-921-3994. Revs. Arthur Mastrolia, Headmaster; Frank Dias, Dean of Students; Mr. Nicholas Cecere, Academic Dean. Priests 2; Lay Teachers 9; Students 52.

Bishop Ford Residence, St. Joseph's Seminary, Dunwoodie, Yonkers, 10704. Tel: 914-968-2916. In res. Revs. Arthur Mastrolia; Frank Dias. Students 32.

BRONX. *St. John Neumann Residence*, 5655 Arlington Ave., 10471. Tel: 718-549-4511; Fax: 718-796-5163. Rev. Msgr. James E. White, Rector; Revs. Richard D. Baker, Dir. Liturgy & Field Svcs.; Thomas F. Madden, M.S., Spiritual Dir.; John P. O'Brien, Procurator & Dean of Students; Edward L. Warnken, Academic Dean. In res. Rev. Msgr. John J. Gillen; Rev. Robert McKeon.

YONKERS. *St. Joseph's Seminary*, Archdiocesan Major Seminary, 201 Seminary Ave., 10704-1852. Tel: 914-968-6200; Fax: 914-968-7912. Rev. Msgr. Francis J. McAree, S.T.D., Rector; Rev. Msgr. William B. Smith, S.T.D.; Rev. Msgr. John J. Farley, M.Ed.; Rev. Msgr. Lorenzo Albacete, S.T.D.; Rev. Msgr. James Connolly, Ph.D.; Rev. Msgr. John J. Quinn, M.A.; Revs. John Coughlin, J.C.D., Spiritual Dir.; Joseph P. Tierney, M.Div., Dean of Students & Dir. Pastoral Formation; Peter John Cameron, O.P., M.F.A.; Edmund J. Whalen, S.T.D., Vice-Rector; Anthony D. Sorgie, Ed.D., Vice-Rector for Academics & Dir. of Music; Edward L. Warnken, M.Div., Dean of Spirituality Year-Northampton; Joseph R. Giandurco, J.C.D., Faculty Sec. & Dean of Admissions.
Non-Resident Faculty: Rev. Kevin McMorrow, S.A., S.T.D.; Dr. Mary Ellen Hubbard, Ph.D., Dean of Institute of Religious Studies; Revs. Thomas J. Shelly, Ph.D.; Andrew D. Apostoli, C.F.R., M.S.; Dr. Francisco M. Alvarez, Ph.D.; Mrs. Frances Broderick, M.A.; Dr. Philip Cristantiello, Ph.D.; Dr. Paul L. Moglia, Ph.D.; Sr. Janet Baxendale, S.C., M.A.; Sr. M. Timothea Elliott, R.S.M., S.S.D.; Sr. Marie Pappas, C.R., M.A.; Rev. Paul Zilonka, C.P., S.S.L.; Mr. Christopher M. Bellitto, Ph.D.; Revs. Donald J. Keefe, S.J., S.T.D.; Frederick L. Miller, S.T.D.; Rev. Msgr. George J. Cascelli, M.S.; Revs. Gerard F. Rafferty, S.S.L.; Richard J. Neuhaus, M.Div.; Robert G. Kelly, S.J., M.A.T.; James B. Lloyd, C.S.P., Ph.D.; Robert McKeon, Vocation Dir.; John Long, S.J., Scholar in Residence; Sr. Regina Anne Melican, O.P., M.S.L.S., Dir. of Library; Mrs. Isabel Cartolano, Registrar. Priests 26; Sisters 4; Lay Teachers 3; Students 73 (of Archdiocese 42); North American College 9.

Mark Seven - DePaul House of Studies, c/o St. Joseph's Seminary, 201 Seminary Ave., 10704-1852. Tel: 914-375-3466.

[B] SEMINARIES, RELIGIOUS OR SCHOLASTICATES

NEW YORK. *St. Francis Novitiate*, 500 Todt Hill Rd., 10304. Tel: 718-981-3131; 981-3212. Revs. Justin A. Biase, O.F.M.Conv., Guardian & Novice Dir.; Blase Kardos, O.F.M.Conv., Chap.; Shawn Nolan, O.F.M.Conv., Retreat Dir.; Bros. Joseph Freitag, O.F.M.Conv., Hospice Chap.; Thomas Purcell, O.F.M.Conv., Advanced Studies.

Friars Minor Conventual Immaculate Conception Province Charitable Trust.

Society of St. Paul, 2187 Victory Blvd., 10314. Tel: 718-761-0047; Fax: 718-761-0057. Rev. Ignatius Staniszewski, S.S.P., Supr. & Dir. Alba House Publications; Bro. Peter C. Lyne, S.S.P., Vocations Dir. Book Stores Coordinators: Bros. Kevin J. Cahill, S.S.P.; Augustine Condon, S.S.P.; Lawrence H. Schubert, S.S.P., Bursar; Revs. Edmund C. Lane, S.S.P.; Victor L. Viberti, S.S.P.; Clarence A. Warren, S.S.P. Priests 4; Brothers 15.

BEACON. *St. Lawrence of Brindisi Friary*, Province of the Stigmata of St. Francis, 182 Sargent Ave., 12508-3993. Tel: 914-831-0394; 831-0451; 838-0759 (Infirmary); Fax: 914-831-0918. (Friary and Infirmary). Bros. Hilary Rodgers, O.F.M.Cap., Guardian; Efrain Sosa, O.F.M.Cap., Vicar & Dir. of Infirmary; Revs. Innocent Amore, O.F.M.Cap.; Seraphin Tirone, O.F.M.Cap.; Bros. John Boehm, O.F.M.Cap.; Lawrence Emmert, O.F.M.Cap.; Revs. John Frega, O.F.M.Cap.; Gerard De Leonardis, O.F.M.Cap.; Henry D'Angelis, O.F.M.Cap.; Sylvester Catallo, O.F.M.Cap.; Stanley Kobel, O.F.M.Cap.; Anthony Guidice, O.F.M.Cap.; Bros. Douglas Soik, O.F.M.Cap.; George Tucker, O.F.M.Cap.; Rev. Justin Joos, O.F.M.Cap.; Bro. Norbert G. Barron, O.S.F.; Rev. Carmine Fazio, O.F.M.Cap. Priests 10; Brothers 7; Lay Staff 11.

BRONX. *Ciszek Hall*, 2502 Belmont Ave., 10458-6282. Tel: 718-365-8752; Fax: 718-365-3166. Residence for Jesuit Scholastics engaged in Philosophy and Theology Studies at Fordham University. Revs. Kenneth J. Caufield, S.J., Rector; Raymond M. Sweitzer, S.J., Min.; Edward F. Salmon, S.J., Spiritual Dir.; Thomas W. Florek, S.J., Prof. Theology. Scholastics 17.

MARYKNOLL. *Center for Mission Research and Study at Maryknoll*, P.O. Box 305, 10545-0305. Tel: 914-941-7590; Fax: 914-941-5753.
E-mail: cmrsm@maryknoll.org
Web site: http://www.maryknoll.org/society/cmrs
Rev. William D. McCarthy, M.M., Exec. Dir.; Anne Reissner, Dir. of Study; Jean Paul Weist, Dir. of Research; Thomas Bamat, Senior Researcher; Mary Ann Cejka, Assoc. Researcher; Catherine McDonald, Coord., Society History.
Purpose: To investigate the contexts, trends and challenges of Christian Mission among Christians and peoples of other living faiths, and to foster reflection on the practical implications of these investigations. Priests 1; Lay Persons 5.

SUFFERN. *Tagaste Monastery*, 220 Lafayette Ave., 10901. Tel: 914-357-0067. Major Seminary of the Province of St. Augustine of the Augustinian Recollect Fathers & Brothers. Revs. John A. Gruben, Prior; Roberto Rodriguez, Sub-Prior & Prefect of Students; George Mattioni, O.A.R.; Francis Moriones, O.A.R. (Spain); Francis A. Cregan, O.A.R.; Deacon Ulises Feliciano, O.A.R.; Bros. Paul Rodriguez, O.A.R.; Joseph Joly, O.A.R.; Gerardo DeFillippo, O.A.R. Priests 4; Brothers 3; Permanent Deacons 1; Simple Professed 5; Solemn Professed Clerics 3.

[C] COLLEGES AND UNIVERSITIES

NEW YORK. *College of Mount Saint Vincent*, 6301 Riverdale Ave., 10471-1093. Tel: 718-405-3200; Fax: 718-549-2603.
E-mail: cfinegan@cmsv.edu
Web site: http://www.cmsv.edu
For a complete listing, refer to the Colleges and Universities section.

Marymount Manhattan College, 221 E. 71st St., 10021. Tel: 212-517-0400
For a complete listing, refer to the Colleges and Universities section.

*BRONX. *Fordham University*, (1841) Fordham Rd., 10458 Fax: 718-817-4925
For a complete listing, refer to the Colleges and Universities section.

Manhattan College, Manhattan College Pkwy., 10471. Tel: 718-862-7200; 800-MC2-XCEL.
Web site: http://www.manhattan.edu
For a complete listing, refer to the Colleges and Universities section.

DOBBS FERRY. *Mercy College in Dobbs Ferry*, 541 Broadway, 10522. Tel: 914-693-4500
For a complete listing, refer to the Colleges and Universities section.

*NEW ROCHELLE. *College of New Rochelle*, 29 Castle Pl., 10805. Tel: 914-654-5000; Fax: 914-654-5290.
E-mail: info@cnr.edu
Web site: http://www.cnr.edu
For a complete listing, refer to the Colleges and Universities section.

Iona College, 715 North Ave., 10801. Tel: 914-633-2000.
E-mail: webmaster@iona.edu
Web site: http://www.iona.edu
For a complete listing, refer to the Colleges and Universities section.

NEWBURGH. *Mt. St. Mary College*, (1954), 12550. Tel: 914-561-0800.
E-mail: coyne@msmc.edu
Web site: http://www.msmc.edu
For a complete listing, refer to the Colleges and Universities section.

ORANGEBURG. *Dominican College of Blauvelt*, 10962. Tel: 914-359-7800.
Web site: http://www.dc.edu
For a complete listing, refer to the Colleges and Universities section.

POUGHKEEPSIE. *Marist College*, 12601-1328. Tel: 914-575-3000.
E-mail: hmaltmi@marista.marist.edu
Web site: http://www.marist.edu
For a complete listing, refer to the Colleges and Universities section.

SPARKILL. *St. Thomas Aquinas College*, 10976. Tel: 914-398-4000; Fax: 914-359-8136
For a complete listing, refer to the Colleges and Universities section.

STATEN ISLAND. *St. John's University Staten Island Campus*, 300 Howard Ave., 10301. Tel: 718-390-4545; Fax: 718-816-4520
For a complete listing, refer to the Colleges and Universities section.

TARRYTOWN. *Marymount College*, 10591. Tel: 914-631-3200.
E-mail: admiss@mmt.marymt.edu
Web site: http://www.marymt.edu
For a complete listing, refer to the Colleges and Universities section.

[D] DEPARTMENT OF EDUCATION

NEW YORK. *Department of Education*, 1011 First Ave., 10022. Tel: 212-371-1000. Rev. Msgr. Thomas J. Bergin, Vicar for Education; Sr. Eileen Clifford, O.P., Assoc. Vicar for Education; Rev. Michael C. Crimmins, Assoc. Vicar for Higher Education; Sr. Lois Darold, C.S.J.B., Consultant.

Office of Finance. Mr. John D. Poling, Dir.; Mr. Gerald Judge, Controller; Mr. John Coyne, Asst. Controller.

Office of Seminary Education. St. Joseph's Seminary, Seminary Ave., Yonkers, 10704. Tel: 914-968-6200. Most Rev. Patrick Sheridan, D.D., Chancellor of the Seminary System; Rev. Msgr. Francis McAree, S.T.D., Rector; Revs. Anthony D. Sorgie, Ed.D., Vice Rector, Academics; Edmund J. Whalen, S.T.D., Vice Rector, Development.

Neumann Residence. Rev. Msgr. James White, Rector, 5655 Arlington Ave., Bronx, 10471. Tel: 718-549-4511.

Cathedral Prep. Seminary. Rev. Arthur Mastrolia, Headmaster, 946 Boston Post Rd., Rye, 10580. Tel: 914-921-3994.

Permanent Diaconate. Deacon Anthony Cassaneto, M.A., M.S.Ed., St. Joseph's Seminary, Yonkers, 10704. Tel: 914-968-6200.

Institute for Religious Studies. Mary Ellen Hubbard, Ph.D., Dean, St. Joseph's Seminary. Tel: 914-476-1172; Fax: 914-476-1185.

Vocations Office. Rev. Robert McLeon, Special Asst. to the Archbishop for Vocations, St. Joseph's Seminary. Tel: 914-968-1340. Sr. Deanna Sabetta, C.N.D., Special Asst. to the Archbishop for Vocations to Religious Life, 1011 First Ave., 10022. Tel: 212-371-1000.

Division of Elementary and Secondary Education, 1011 First Ave., 10022. Tel: 212-371-1000. Dr. Catherine Hickey, Supt. of Schools; Mr. Paul Ward, Deputy Supt. Assoc. Supts.: Sr. Dorothy Flanagan, Religious Education; Dr. Mary Jane Krebbs, Curriculum; Mr. James Mahoney, Publicly Assisted Programs; Bro. Thomas Schady, Secondary Education; Mr. James Simone, Special Education; Sr. Kathleen Sullivan, S.C., Teacher Recruitment. Asst. Supts.: Jeanette Galvin, Admin.; Sr. Winifred Lyons, S.C., Pro-Life Coord., Parent Volunteer Program & Teachers Institute; Mrs. Nora Murphy, Communications Mktg. Directors: Sr. Breda Galavan, R.S.H.M., Writing to Read; Sr. Angela Palermo, R.C.D., Catechist Formation; Sr. Lucy Sabatini, O.S.F., Early Childhood, 215 W. 15th St., 10011. Tel: 212-243-1881. Ann Maschin, Admin. Asst. District Supts.: Sr. Patricia Anastasio, P.B.V.M., Bronx; Mrs. Donna Carolan, Dutchess & Ulster; Sr. Kathleen FitzSimons, C.N.D., Staten Island; Deacon Arthur Manzione, Westchester & Putnam; Sr. Marilyn O'Brien, P.B.V.M., Rockland, Orange & Sullivan; Sr. June Clare Tracy, O.P., Manhattan.

Archdiocesan Drug Abuse Prevention Program. Mrs. Frances Maturo, Dir., 2789 Schurz Ave., Bronx, 10465. Tel: 718-904-1333.

Child Nutrition and School Management Service. Mr. Edward Albano, 323 E. 91st St., 10128. Tel: 212-722-0111; Fax: 212-722-5252.

Head Start Program. Mrs. Nora Feury, 1720 Metropolitan Ave., Bronx, 10462. Tel: 718-409-1277; Fax: 718-409-3219.

Cooke Center for Learning and Development. Dr. Gay Culverhouse, Dir., 475 Riverside Dr., Ste. 730, 10115. Tel: 212-280-4473.

Seton Foundation for Learning. Ms. Diane D. Cunningham, Exec. Dir., 104 Gordon St., 10304. Tel: 718-447-1750.

Bronx Alternative Special Education. James A. Simone, Assoc. Supt.; Mrs. Mary Carman, Admin. Asst., 1725 Castle Hill Ave., Bronx, 10462. Tel: 718-792-9669.

St. Ursula Learning Center. Mrs. Barbara Stefaniki, Educ. Dir., 183 Rich Ave., Mt. Vernon, 10550. Tel: 914-664-6656.

Joan Ann Kennedy Memorial Preschool. Ms. Kathryn Meyer, Educ. Dir., 26 Sharpe Ave., Staten Island, 10302. Tel: 718-876-0939.

Family Life/Respect Life Office, 1011 First Ave., 10022. Tel: 212-371-1000. Rev. John S. Bonnici, S.T.D., Dir.; Mr. Patrick Del Zoppo, Ph.D., CAS., Asst. Dir. & Coord. of Bereavement Ministry & Project Rachel Ministry; Mr. Edward Mechmann, Asst. Dir. & Coord. of Marriage Preparation Programs; Dr. Charles Potter, Assoc. Dir., Natural Family Planning; Vera V. Galeas, Coord., Hispanic Activities; Dana Larson-Super, Coord., Wedding Anniversary Awards Ceremony; Mr. Kevin S.D. Connelly, Coord., Pro-Life Activities; Mrs. Nancy Rizzi, Coord., Pro-Life Activities & Marriage Enrichment; Mrs. Eileen Murphy, Assoc. Dir., Educ. for Parenting, Hudson River East, Box L, 103 Jackson St., Fishkill, 12524. Tel: 914-896-0728. Mrs. Virginia Brown, Assoc. Dir., Educ. for Parenting, Hudson River West, 149 Cottage St., Middletown, 10940. Tel: 914-342-0908. Jim & Joanne Martin, Coord. Couple, Engaged Encounter, Tel: 914-228-1002. Jim & Nancy Rizzi, Coord. Couple, Marriage Encounter, Tel: 718-966-0990; 317-5881.

Archdiocesan Catechetical Office, 1011 First Ave., 10022. Tel: 212-371-1000. Sr. Joan Curtin, C.N.D., Archdiocesan Dir.; Miss Anne Coghlan, Special Religious Education (Consultant); Sr. Mary Elizabeth Kelleher, O.P., Dir. Catechist Formation; Sr. Teresita Morse, R.J.M., Dir. Formation of Directors/Coordinators; Mrs. Frances De Frange, Chm., Catechetical Congress; Bro. Francis Zaglauer, F.M.S., Dir., Adult Catechesis.

Catechetical Regional Offices.

Bronx, 323 E. 198th St., Bronx, 10458. Tel: 718-367-0420; Fax: 718-367-0420. Sr. Katherine Naughton, O.S.U., Dir.

Manhattan, c/o Mother Cabrini High School, 701 Fort Washington Ave., 10040. Tel: 212-923-0950. Sr. Catherine Ryan, F.S.P., Dir.

East and South Manhattan. Sr. Maria Elena Dio, S.C.H., Regional Dir., c/o St. Stephen of Hungary, 414 E. 82nd St., 10028. Tel: 212-879-6498.

Staten Island, 203 Sand Ln., Staten Island, 10305. Tel: 718-273-3833; Fax: 718-273-3833. Mrs. Frances De Frange, Dir.

Dutchess & Ulster Counties, Dutchess Office: 26 S. Hamilton Ave., Poughkeepsie, 12601-2599. Tel: 914-471-5427.

Ulster Office, 157 Broadway, Kingston, 12401. Tel: 914-338-3222. Sr. Miriam Eugene Fenton, S.C., Dir.

Westchester & Putnam Counties, 50 Washington Ave., New Rochelle, 10801. Tel: 914-633-3631; Fax: 914-633-3631. Sr. Kathleen Harrington, P.V.B.M., Dir.

Orange & Rockland Counties, Orange Office: John S. Burke Catholic High School, Fletcher St., P.O. Box 114, Goshen, 10924. Tel: 914-294-6428. Rockland Office: 798 Rte. 304 & Germonds Rd., P.O. Box 9162, Bardonia, 10954-1694. Tel: 914-627-1236. Sr. Anne Connelly, O.P., Dir.

Sullivan County, Blessed Kateri Tekakwitha Center, P.O. Box 1011, Liberty, 12754. Tel: 914-292-9100. Sr. Kevin John Shields, O.P., Dir.

Commission on Church Music, 1011 First Ave., 10022. Tel: 212-371-1000. Mr. John Michael Caprio, Exec. Dir.

Center for Spiritual Development, 96 Milton Rd., Rye, 10580. Tel: 914-967-7328. Anne Marie Wallace, Ph.D., Dir.

Office of Spiritual Development, 1 Pryor Manor Rd., Larchmont, 10538. Tel: 914-235-6839. Rev. Benedict J. Groeschel, C.F.R., Dir.

Trinity Retreat House, 1 Pryor Manor Rd., Larchmont, 10538. Tel: 914-235-6839. Rev. Eugene Fulton, Dir.

Instructional Television, 215 Seminary Ave., Yonkers, 10704. Mr. Michael Lavery, Administrative Dir. Tel: 914-968-7800. Elementary School: Full-Time Sisters 306; Part-Time Sisters 60; Full-Time Brothers 29; Part-Time Brothers 7; Full-Time Order Priests 5; Part-Time Order Priests 4; Full-Time Lay Teachers 3,222; Part-Time Lay Teachers726; Total Parish Enrollment 74,599; Total Inter-Parish Enrollment 1,422; Total Private Enrollment 3,913. High School: Full-Time Sisters 196; Part-Time Sisters 29; Full-Time Brothers 65; Part-Time Brothers 9; Full-Time Order Priests 42; Part-Time Order Priests 9; Full-Time Diocesan Priests 36; Part-Time Diocesan Priests 6; Full-Time Lay Teachers 1,688; Part-Time Lay Teachers 181; Total Diocesan Enrollment 8,308; Total Parish Enrollment 5,516; Total Private Enrollment 14,597; Total Seminary Enrollment 51.

[E] HIGH SCHOOLS, ARCHDIOCESAN

NEW YORK. *Cardinal Hayes High School,* 650 Grand Concourse, 10451. Tel: 718-292-6100; Fax: 718-292-5607. (Boys). Rev. Msgr. John K. Graham, Prin.; Mr. James G. Clarkin, Dean of Studies; Revs. Harry Burke; James T. Byrnes; Alfred D'Incecco; Matthew Fernan; Jeffrey Galens; Robert Harrison; John N. Paddack; Rev. Msgr. Victor C. Pavis. In res. Rev. Msgr. Peter P. Narkun. Priests 9; Brothers 3; Sisters 2; Lay Teachers 52; Students 1,060.

Cardinal Spellman High School. One Cardinal Spellman Pl., Bronx, 10466. Tel: 718-881-8000; Fax: 718-515-6615. Rev. Msgr. Jeremiah P. Monahan, Prin.; Revs. Emil L. Bettley; James J. Corrigan; John R. Kraljic; John T. Monaghan; James J. O'Shaughnessy; Lawrence M. Paolicelli; Peter R. Pilsner; Francis J. Principe. In res. Rev. Msgr. John J. Considine; Revs. Francis J. Corry; Vincent T. Euk; Richard F. Gorman. Priests 9; Sisters 3; Lay Teachers 77; Students 1,532.

Cathedral High School, 350 E. 56th St., 10022. Tel: 212-688-1545; Fax: 212-754-2024.
E-mail: egraham477@aol.com
(Girls). Rev. Msgr. Thomas Bergin, Pres.; Sr. Mary Kilmartin, S.C., Prin.; Sr. Elizabeth Graham, O.P., Asst. Prin.; Rev. Robert Poveromo. Priests 1; Sisters 14; Lay Teachers 42; Students 782.

Monsignor Farrell High School, 2900 Amboy Rd., 10306. Tel: 718-987-2900; Fax: 718-987-4241. Revs. Emmet R. Nevin, Prin.; John P. Comiskey; Robert G. Macchietto. Priests 3; Brothers 4; Sisters 3; Lay Teachers 67; Students 1,180.

Moore Catholic High School, 100 Merrill Ave., 10314. Tel: 212-761-9200. Revs. Robert I. Gannon; Edmund P. Connors. Priests 2; Sisters of the Presentation 1; Lay Teachers 32; Students 772.

GOSHEN. *John S. Burke Catholic High School,* Fletcher St., 10924. Tel: 914-294-5481. Sr. Josephine Ortner, P.B.V.M., Prin.; Rev. Trevor Nicholls. Priests 1; Sisters 3; Lay Teachers 34; Students 538.

HARTSDALE. *Maria Regina High School,* 500 W. Hartsdale Ave., 10530. Tel: 914-761-3300.
E-mail: mariaregina@cloud9.net
Sisters of the Resurrection. Sr. Eustelle Kozakiewicz, C.R., Supr.; Sr. Danielle M. Baran, C.R., Prin. Sisters 10; Lay Teachers 25; Students 450.

HURLEY. *John A. Coleman Catholic High School,* 430 Hurley Ave., 12443. Tel: 914-338-2750; Fax: 914-388-0250. Bro. Thomas Lee, F.M.S., Prin. Brothers 3; Sisters 1; Lay Teachers 20; Students 260.

POUGHKEEPSIE. *Our Lady of Lourdes High School,* 131 Boardman Rd., 12603. Tel: 914-471-0400. Bros. Donnell Neary, F.M.S., Pres.; Larry Lavallee, F.M.S., Prin.; Larry Gordon, F.M.S., Dean of Studies; Larry Hanshumacher, F.M.S.; Vincent Moriarty, F.M.S.; George DiCarluccio, F.M.S.; Armand Lamagna, F.M.S.; Henry Sawicki, F.M.S.; Gregory DelaNoy, F.M.S.; James Stevens, F.M.S.; Mr. William Dahncke, Dean of Men; Mrs. Judith Maher, Dean of Women; Sr. Lois Dee, O.P., Admin. Asst. Priests 2; Brothers 10; Lay Teachers 32; Students 804.

SOMERS. *John F. Kennedy High School,* 54 Rte. 138, 10589. Tel: 914-232-5061; Fax: 914-232-3416. Sisters of Divine Compassion. Revs. Anthony D. Marchitelli, Prin.; Francis Corry, Academic Dean; Mark J. Connell; Brian McSweeney; Sr. Barbara Heil, Treas.; Mr. Thomas Dolan, Dean of Students; Sr. M. Christopher, R.D.C., Dir. of Alumni Affairs. Priests 4; Sisters 8; Lay Teachers 37; Students 620.

WHITE PLAINS. *Archbishop Stepinac High School,* 950 Mamaroneck Ave., 10605. Tel: 914-946-4800; Fax: 914-686-3615. Rev. Msgr. John J. O'Keefe, Pres.; Mr. Ronald Tedesco, Headmaster; Mr. Ralph Nicoletti, Admin. Asst. & Dean of Students; Rev. Eric P. Raaser, Assoc. Dean of Students. Staff of School: Revs. Patrick M. Carroll; Thomas E. Collins; Philip J. Quealy. In res. Rev. Msgr. George F. Bardes; Rev. John L. Cavanaugh; Rev. Msgr. Edward M. Connors; Rev. Henry G. d'Anjou; Rev. Msgr. Augustine J. DiBlasi; Rev. Msgr. John T. Doherty; Rev. Msgr. Robert A. Ford; Rev. Msgr. Vincent W. Jeffers; Rev. Msgr. Thomas V. McMahon; Rev. Msgr. Cornelius O'Brien; Rev. Thomas E. O'Keefe; Rev. Msgr. Raymond P. Rigney; Rev. James B. Tobin; Rev. Msgr. Henry J. Vier; Rev. Msgr. James J. Walsh. Priests 5; Sisters 3; Lay Teachers 38; Students 630.

[F] HIGH SCHOOLS, PRIVATE

NEW YORK. *Academy of Mount St. Ursula,* 330 Bedford Park Blvd., 10458. Tel: 718-364-5353; Fax: 718-584-1507.
E-mail: ursula@con2.com
(Girls). Ursuline Nuns. Sr. Mary Beth Read, O.S.U., Prin. Sisters 7; Lay Teachers 35; Students 500.

All Hallows Institute. (also known as All Hallows High School). 111 E. 164th St., 10452. Tel: 212-293-4545.
E-mail: alhallow@aol.com
(Boys). Mr. Sean J. Sullivan, Prin.; Bro. Thomas R. Leto, Pres.; Rev. Peter Lekwot. Priests 1; Congregation of Christian Brothers 6; Lay Teachers 34; Students 450.

Aquinas High School. 685 E. 182nd St., Bronx, 10457. Tel: 718-367-2113; Fax: 718-295-5864.
E-mail: aqhs@aol.com
Sisters 21; Lay Teachers 35; Students 804. (Girls). Sr. Margaret Ryan, O.P., Prin.

Convent of the Sacred Heart, One E. 91st St., 10128-0654. Tel: 212-722-4745. (Girls). Religious of the Sacred Heart. Sr. N. Salisbury, R.S.C.J., Headmistress. Sisters 8; Lay Teachers 63; Students 518.

Dominican Academy, 44 E. 68th St., 10021. Tel: 212-744-0195; Fax: 212-744-0375.
E-mail: danyc@mail.con2.com
(Girls). Sr. Martha Kunesh, O.P., Prin. Sisters 9; Lay Teachers 21; Students 229.

Fordham Preparatory School, E. Fordham Rd., 10458. Tel: 718-367-7500; Fax: 718-367-7598. (Boys). Mr. Kevin R. Hackett, Chm. Bd.; Rev. Joseph P. Parkes, S.J., Pres.; Mr. Robert J. Gomprecht, Headmaster; Rev. John J. Mattimore, S.J., Asst. Headmaster; Mr. Bruce G. Bott, Dean of Students; Rev. Mallick J. Fitzpatrick, S.J., Dir. Guidance; Bro. Sebastian A. Boccabella, S.J.; Revs. Pierce A. Brennan, S.J.; Matthew C. Flood, S.J.; John J. Leonard, S.J.; Stanley J. O'Konsky, S.J.; William J. O'Malley, S.J.; Joseph S. Rooney, S.J.; Charles D. Sullivan, S.J.; Raymond M. Sweitzer, S.J. Priests 11; Lay Teachers 73; Students 970.

La Salle Academy, 44-50 E. Second St., 10003. Tel: 212-475-8940; Fax: 212-529-3598. (Boys). Brothers of The Christian Schools. Bros. Carl Malacalza, F.S.C., Pres.; Michael Farrell, F.S.C., Prin. Brothers 6; Sisters 1; Lay Teachers 28; Students 543.

Loyola School, 980 Park Ave., 10028. Tel: 212-288-3522.
Web site: http://www.loyola-nyc.org
(Coed). Society of Jesus. Mr. Gregory McLaughlin, Chm. Bd.; Revs. Joseph J. Papaj, S.J., Pres. & Headmaster; James J. Curry, S.J.; Eugene J. Prior, S.J.; Thomas S. Prout, S.J.; Michael E. Sehler, S.J. Priests 5; Lay Teachers 18; Students 202.

Mother Cabrini High School. (Grades 9-12), 701 Ft. Washington Ave., 10040. Tel: 212-923-3540. (Girls). Brian Donahue, Prin. Sisters 3; Lay Teachers 30; Students 430.

Notre Dame Academy High School, 134 Howard Ave., 10301. Tel: 718-447-8878. Congregation of Notre Dame. Mrs. Angela T. Ferrando, Prin. Sisters 2; Lay Teachers 30; Girls 365.

Notre Dame School of Manhattan, 104 St. Mark Pl., 10009. Tel: 212-982-0740.
E-mail: adnyntdamehs@connectinc.com
(Girls). Mr. John Joven, Prin. Sisters 5; Lay Teachers 14; Students 205.

Preston High School, 2780 Schurz Ave., 10465. Tel: 718-863-9134. (Girls). Sr. Lucille Coldrick, R.D.C., Prin. Asst. Principals: Linda Youngren; Sr. Laura Donovan, R.D.C. Sisters of the Divine Compassion 7; Lay Teachers 31; Students 452.

Regis High School, 55 E. 84th St., 10028. Tel: 212-288-1100; Fax: 212-794-1221.
Web site: http://www.regis-nyc.org
(Boys). Society of Jesus. Revs. J. Thomas McClain, S.J., Pres.; Thomas H. Feely, S.J., Headmaster; Mr. Francis J. Walsh, Asst. Headmaster; Mr. Daniel T. Dougherty, Dean of Students; Revs. Arthur C. Bender, S.J.; Vincent L. Biagi, S.J.; James R. Carney, S.J.; James J. DiGiacomo, S.J.; Joseph A. Dorgan, S.J.; Stephen V. Duffy, S.J.; Charles F. Gilley, S.J. Priests 9; Scholastics 1; Lay Teachers 42; Students 516. Res., 53 E. 83rd St., 10028.

Rice High School, 74 W. 124th St., 10027. Tel: 212-369-4100.
E-mail: adnyricehs@connectinc.com
(Boys). Congregation of Christian Brothers. Bro. John M. Walderman, C.F.C., Pres. Brothers 5; Lay Teachers 23; Students 315.

St. Catharine Academy, 2250 Williamsbridge Rd., 10469. Tel: 718-882-2882; Fax: 718-231-9099. (Girls). Francine Scioli, Prin. Sisters 9; Lay Teachers 54; Students 980.

St. John Villa Academy High School, 26 Landis Ave., 10305. Sr. Anne Dolores VanWagenen, C.S.J.B., Prin. Brothers 1; Sisters 8; Lay Teachers 42; Girls 630.

St. Joseph by the Sea, High School, 5150 Hylan Blvd., 10312. Tel: 718-984-6500; Fax: 718-984-6503; 227-6816.
E-mail: j.f.bolger@msn.com
(Coed). Rev. Msgr. Joseph C. Ansaldi, Prin.; Rev. James Garisto; Rev. Msgr. James Bolger; Rev. Michael P. Reilly. Priests 4; Sisters 7; Lay Teachers 61; Students 1,300.

Xavier High School, 30 W. 16th St., 10011. Tel: 212-924-7900.
Web site: http://www.xavier.nyc.ny.us
(Boys). Society of Jesus. Revs. Daniel J. Gatti, S.J., Pres.; David S. Ciancimino, S.J., Headmaster; Mr. Franklin N. Caesar, Asst. Headmaster; Mr. Franklin D. Gregory, Dean of Students; Revs. Christopher C. Casey, S.J.; Vincent E. Butler, S.J.; John F. Garvey, S.J.; William J. McGowan, S.J.; Robert V. O'Hare, S.J.; Marc J. Roselli, S.J.; Russell J. Sloun, S.J.; Vincent A. Taylor, S.J.; Joseph J. Walter, S.J.; David F. White, S.J.
(See listing for Xavier Jesuit Community for additional names of priests and brothers.). Priests 11; Scholastics 1; Lay Teachers 58; Students 857.

BARDONIA. *Albertus Magnus*, 798 Rte. 304, 10954. Tel: 914-623-8842.
Web site: http://www.lanline.com/~armadm
Sisters of St. Dominic (Sparkill) 7; Lay Teachers 28; Students 385.

BRONX. *Mount St. Michael Academy*, 4300 Murdock Ave., 10466. Tel: 718-515-6400; Fax: 718-994-7729. (Boys). Bros. John P. Bantz, F.M.S., Pres.; James Kearney, F.M.S., Prin. Priests 1; Sisters 2; Brothers 14; Lay Teachers 56; Students 996.

Junior High School. Mrs. Lillian Dippolito, F.M.S., Prin. Lay Teachers 5; Students 115.

DOBBS FERRY. *Our Lady of Victory Academy High School*, 565 N. Broadway, 10522. Tel: 914-693-1633.
E-mail: olva@computer.net
(Girls). Sisters of Mercy. Sr. Patricia Vetrano, R.S.M., Prin. Sisters 10; Lay Teachers 22; Students 382.

NEW ROCHELLE. *Iona Preparatory School*, 255 Wilmot Rd., 10804. Tel: 914-632-0714; Fax: 914-632-9760.
E-mail: jjoc97@ionaprep.pvt.k12.ny.us
Web site: http://www.ionaprep.pvt.k12.ny.us
(Boys). Congregation of Christian Brothers. Bro. John J. O'Connor, C.F.C., Pres.; Mr. Edward O'Neill, Headmaster; Mr. John Fogler, Asst. Headmaster; Mr. Dan Poccia, Asst. Headmaster; Bros. Anthony K. Cavet, C.F.C., Supr.; Gerard M. Gaffney, C.F.C., Dean of Faculty; Mr. Brian Terhune, Business Mgr. Brothers 10; Lay Teachers 45; Students 780.

Salesian High School, 148 Main St., 10801. Tel: 914-632-0248; Fax: 914-632-1362.
E-mail: salhsnr@aol.com
Web site: http://members.aol.com/salhsnr
Rev. John J. Serio, S.D.B., Dir. & Pres.; Mr. John P. Flaherty, Prin.; Sr. Barbara Wright, O.P., Asst. Prin.; Mr. Joseph Meade, Dean of Students; Bro. Thomas Sweeney, S.D.B., Coord. of Youth Ministry; Mr. Kwame Boakye-Yiadom, Business Mgr.; Mr. Paul Krebbs, Vice Pres. Inst. Advancement; Rev. Richard Rosin, S.D.B., Guidance Dir. & Vicar; Bros. Kevin Connolly, S.D.B.; Michael Brinkman, S.D.B.; Joseph Lody, S.D.B. Priests 2; Brothers 3; Scholastics 1; Sisters 1; Lay Teachers 33; Students 445.

Ursuline School. (Grades 6-12), 1354 North Ave., 10804. Tel: 914-636-3950; Fax: 914-636-3949.
E-mail: adnyursuline@connectinc.com
(Girls). Sr. Jean Baptiste Nicholson, O.S.U., Prin. Priests 1; Sisters 8; Lay Teachers 55; Students 700.

RYE. *School of the Holy Child*. (Grades 5-12), Westchester Ave., 10580. Tel: 914-967-5622; Fax: 914-967-6476. (Girls). Sr. Jean Marie O'Meara, S.H.C.J., Head. Society of the Holy Child Jesus 2; Lay Teachers 26; Students 193.

STATEN ISLAND. *St. Joseph Hill Academy*, 850 Hylan Blvd., 10305-2095. Tel: 718-447-1374. (Girls). Daughters of Divine Charity. Sr. Marie Claire, F.D.C., Prin. Sisters 3; Lay Teachers 25; Students 372.

WHITE PLAINS. *Academy of Our Lady of Good Counsel*, 52 N. Broadway, 10603. Tel: 914-949-0178; Fax: 914-949-5169.
E-mail: adnyolgdcoun@connectinc.com
Web site: http://www.law.pace.edu/goodcounsel/
(Girls). Ms. Joan Close, Prin. Sisters of the Divine Compassion 4; Lay Teachers 26; Students 428.

[G] SPECIAL SCHOOLS

NEW YORK. *Grace Institute*, 1233 Second Ave., 10021. Tel: 212-832-7605. Sisters of Charity, Mt. St. Vincent. Sr. Mary Ellen O'Boyle, Admin. Sisters 6; Lay Teachers 6; Students 800.

Mount St. Ursula Speech Center. 200th St. and Marion Ave., Bronx, 10458. Tel: 718-584-7679. Ursuline Nuns. Sr. M. Winifred Danwitz, Ph.D., Admin. Sisters 1; Lay Clinicians 8; Support Staff 6; Total Enrollment 150.

Seton Foundation for Learning, Inc. 104 Gordon St., Staten Island, 10304. Tel: 718-447-1750. Rev. Msgr. Joseph C. Ansaldi, Chm.; Mr. John Haugen, Pres.; Diane Cunningham, Exec. Dir. Lay Teachers 4; Assistants 5; Enrollment 43.

BRONX. *St. Joseph's School for the Deaf*, 1000 Hutchinson River Pkwy., 10465. Tel: 718-828-9000; 828-1671 (TDD); Fax: 718-792-6631.
E-mail: SJSDpmar@aol.com
(Birth to 14 years). Directed by Daughters of the Heart of Mary. Ms. Patricia Martin, Exec. Dir. Capacity 200; Enrollment 140.

MILLBROOK. *Cardinal Hayes School for Special Children*, North Ave., P.O. Box CH, 12545-0140. Tel: 914-677-6363; Fax: 914-677-6691. Fred Apers, Exec. Dir. Educational programs for multi-handicapped children. Lay Teachers 5; Capacity 35; Enrollment 30.

[H] ELEMENTARY SCHOOLS, PRIVATE

NEW YORK. *Academy of St. Dorothy*, 1305 Hylan Blvd., 10305. Tel: 718-351-0939.
E-mail: smccar98@aol.com
Sr. Sharon A. McCarthy, S.S.D., Prin. Sisters of St. Dorothy 3; Lay Teachers 7; Students 320.

Convent of the Sacred Heart, 1 E. 91st St., 10128. Tel: 212-722-4745. (Girls). Sr. N. Salisbury, R.S.C.J., Headmistress. Sisters 7; Lay Teachers 65; Students 572.

Marymount School. (Grades Nursery-12), 1026 Fifth Ave., 10028. Tel: 212-744-4486; Fax: 212-744-0163. Religious of the Sacred Heart of Mary. Sr. Kathleen Fagan, R.S.H.M., Headmistress. Sisters 6; Lay Teachers 49; Students 360.

Notre Dame Academy-Elementary School, 78 Howard Ave., 10301. Tel: 718-273-9096. Congregation of Notre Dame. Sr. Rose Mary Galligan, C.N.D., Prin. Lay Teachers 13; Students 340.

Sacred Heart Private Elementary School, Inc., 1651 Zerega Ave., 10462. Tel: 718-863-5047. Apostles of the Sacred Heart of Jesus. Sr. Mary Grace Walsh, A.S.C.J., Prin. Sisters 6; Lay Teachers 7; Students 150.

St. John Villa Academy Elementary School, Mailing Address: 57 Cleveland Pl., 10305. Sr. Rita Marie Carey, C.S.J.B., Prin. Sisters 9; Lay Teachers 10; Students 418.

St. Joseph Hill Academy Elementary, 850 Hylan Blvd., 10305. Sr. M. Mercedes, F.D.C., Prin. Sisters 3; Lay Teachers 30; Students 568.

Villa Maria Academy, 3335 Country Club Rd., 10465. Tel: 718-824-3260. Congregation of Notre Dame. Sr. Teresa Barton, C.N.D., Prin. Sisters 3; Lay Teachers 26; Students 564.

NEW ROCHELLE. *Iona Grammar School*. (Grades PreK-8), 173 Stratton Rd., 10804; Fax: 914-235-6338. (Boys). Bro. John D. Dugan, C.F.C., Pres. & Headmaster. Brothers 4; Lay Teachers 18; Students 240.

NEWBURGH. *Bishop Dunn Memorial School*, 50 Gidney Ave., 12550. Sisters of St. Dominic. Mrs. Kathleen Mellon, Prin. Sisters 2; Lay Teachers 10; Students 212.

PORT JERVIS. *Trinity Catholic School*, 44 Ball St., 12771. Carol Doll, Prin. Sisters 1; Lay Teachers 6; Enrollment 120.

WHITE PLAINS. *Academy of Our Lady of Good Counsel*. (Elementary Dept.). 52 N. Broadway, 10603. Tel: 914-949-8186. Sr. Clare Arenholz, R.D.C. Sisters 2; Lay Teachers 12; Students 172.

[I] THE CATHOLIC CHARITIES OF THE ARCHDIOCESE OF NEW YORK

NEW YORK. *The Catholic Charities of the Archdiocese of New York*, 1011 First Ave., 10022. Tel: 212-371-1000. Rev. Msgr. James J. Murray, Exec. Dir.; Rev. Msgr. William J. Toohy, Assoc. Exec. Dir. & Dir. Social Research; Rev. Kevin L. Sullivan, Chief Oper. Officer; Mr. Kenneth Dempsey, Chief Financial Officer; Rev. Richard F. Gorman; Ms. Joanne Abruzzese, Dir. Personnel; Rev. Michael F. Gannon, Coord. Upstate Counties, 240 Church St., Poughkeepsie, 12601. Tel: 914-452-1400.
Departments: Sr. Una McCormack, O.P., Dir. Child Care; Mary Healy-Sedutto, Ph.D., Dir. Health & Hospitals; Sr. Alice Biegen, R.S.H.M., Dir. Housing; Mr. John J. Hughes, Dir. Mental Health Svcs.; Ms. Roseann Micallef, Dir. Migration Svcs.; Ms. Patricia Brennan, Dir. Parish & Community Outreach; Mr. George B. Horton, Dir. Social & Community Development; Mr. Joseph Panepinto, Exec. Dir. CYO/Youth Svcs.

The Ladies of Charity of the Catholic Charities of the Archdiocese of New York, 1011 First Ave., 10022. Tel: 212-371-1000, Ext. 2540; Fax: 212-319-8265. Ms. Christina Krupa, Pres.; Ms. Susan Grady, Exec. Dir. Spiritual Dirs.: Rev. Msgr. William J. Toohy; Rev. Msgr. Peter Finn.

Catholic Charities Counselling Service, Archdiocese of New York, 1011 First Ave., 10022. Tel: 212-371-1000; Fax: 212-826-8795. Rev. Kevin L. Sullivan.

Roman Catholic Fund for Children and Other Purposes, 1011 First Ave., 10022. Tel: 212-371-1000; Fax: 212-826-8795. Rev. Msgr. James J. Murray.

Holy Name Centre for Homeless Men, Inc., 18 Bleeker St., 10012. Tel: 212-226-5848. Rev. Msgr. John B. Ahern, Dir.

Providence Health Services, 1249 Fifth Ave., 10029. Mary Healey-Sedutto, Ph.D., Pres.

[J] HOUSING

NEW YORK. *Catholic Charities Department of Housing, Housing Development Institute, Inc.*, 1011 First Ave., 10022. Tel: 212-371-1000, Ext. 2587; Fax: 212-753-7827. Sr. Alice Biegen, R.S.H.M., Dir.

[K] MENTAL HEALTH SERVICES

NEW YORK. *Catholic Charities Department of Mental Health Services*, 1011 First Ave., 10022. Tel: 212-371-1000, Ext. 2000; Fax: 212-826-8377
For a complete listing, refer to the Special Care Facilities section.

[L] MIGRATION SERVICES

NEW YORK. *Catholic Charities Department of Migration Services*, 1011 First Ave., 10022. Tel: 212-371-1000, Ext. 2260; Fax: 212-826-6254. Ms. Roseann Micallef, Dir.

Immigrant Services, 1011 First Ave., 10022. Tel: 212-371-1000, Ext. 2260; Fax: 212-826-6254. Mrs. Gladys Romani, Assoc. Dir.

Refugee Resettlement, 1011 First Ave., 10022. Tel: 212-371-1000, Ext. 2485; Fax: 212-826-6254. Ms. Patricia O'Callaghan, Coord.

Project Irish Outreach, 1011 First Ave., 10022. Tel: 212-371-1000, Ext. 2485; Fax: 212-826-6254. Ms. Patricia O'Callaghan, Coord.

[M] PARISH AND COMMUNITY OUTREACH

NEW YORK. *Catholic Charities Department of Parish and Community Outreach*, 1011 First Ave., 10022. Tel: 212-371-1000, Ext. 2004. Ms. Patricia Brennan, Dir.
Catholic Charities Centers: Central Harlem, 202 W. 141st St., 10030. Tel: 212-694-3939; Fax: 212-694-4242. Sr. Ann Shea, D.C., Lower Manhattan, 530 Grand St., 10002. Tel: 212-777-3111; Fax: 212-677-9057. Sr. Mary Matthew Labunski, M.S.B.T., Central Manhattan, 1011 First Ave., 10022. Tel: 212-371-1000, Ext. 2031; Fax: 212-826-8377. Mr. John Stanolevich, South Bronx, 420 E. 145th St., Bronx, 10454. Tel: 718-401-8342; Fax: 718-401-8345. Sr. Ann Shea, D.C., Staten Island, 120 Anderson Ave., Staten Island, 10302. Tel: 718-447-6330; Fax: 718-447-6060. Mr. James Ryan, Dutchess County, 240 Church St., Poughkeepsie, 12601. Tel: 914-452-1400; Fax: 914-452-3336. Orange County, 185 Liberty Ave., P.O. Box 64, Newburgh, 10977. Tel: 914-561-3452; Fax: 914-561-2825. Mrs. Maria McTiernan, Rockland County, 333 Sneden Pl., W., Spring Valley, 10977. Tel: 914-426-3436; Fax: 914-426-0881. Sullivan County, North St. & Liberty St., P.O. Box 395, Monticello, 12701. Tel: 914-791-6023; Fax: 914-791-6104. Ulster County, 157 Broadway, Kingston, 12401. Tel: 914-340-9170; Fax: 914-340-9596. Ms. Pat LaRue.

Parish Social Ministry, 1011 First Ave., 10022. Tel: 212-371-1000, Ext. 2032; Fax: 212-826-8377. Mrs. Dorothy Meehan.

Ministry to Seniors, 1011 First Ave., 10022. Tel: 212-371-1000, Ext. 2003; Fax: 212-826-8377. Mrs. Eleanor Ramos.

Office for the Homeless and Hungry, 1011 First Ave., 10022. Tel: 212-371-1000, Ext. 2529; Fax: 212-319-0405. Ms. Victoria Wells.

[N] SOCIAL AND COMMUNITY DEVELOPMENT

NEW YORK. *Catholic Charities Department of Social and Community Development*, 1011 First Ave., 10022. Tel: 212-371-1000, Ext. 2480; Fax: 212-391-0405. Mr. George B. Horton, Dir.

Office for Justice and Peace, 1011 First Ave., 10022. Tel: 212-371-1000, Ext. 2480; Fax: 212-391-0405.

Office of Criminal Justice, 1011 First Ave., 10022. Tel: 212-371-1000, Ext. 3166; Fax: 212-391-0405. Mr. Kenneth Hoffarth, Dir.

New York Institute for Human Development, Inc., 1011 First Ave., 10022. Tel: 212-371-1000, Ext. 2495; Fax: 212-391-0405. Mr. Jean Vernet, Dir.

[O] SERVICES TO THE DISABLED

NEW YORK. *Catholic Guild for the Blind*, 1011 First Ave., 6th Floor, 10022. Tel: 212-371-1000, Ext. 2017; Fax: 212-826-8377
For a complete listing, refer to the Special Care Facilities section.

New York Catholic Deaf Center, 1011 First Ave., 6th Floor, 10022. Tel: 212-371-1000; Fax: 212-826-8377
For a complete listing, refer to the Special Care Facilities section.

Mental Health & Community Residences:

NEW YORK. *Beacon of Hope House*, Central Administrative Office, 116 E. 16th St., 5th Fl., 10003-2112. Tel:

212-982-3560; Fax: 212-982-2869. Alan H. Bernstein, Exec. Dir.; Joan Noguera, Assoc. Exec. Dir.; Joy Jasper, Dir. Personnel; Ravi Ramaswamy, C.P.A., Controller.

Supervised Units, 1400 Waters Pl., Bronx, 10461. Tel: 212-892-3494; Fax: 212-892-5507. Christine Lawry, Admin. Asst.; Robert Franco, Prog. Mgr., Beacon I: Vadim Moldovan, Prog. Supvr. Tel: 718-931-0600 Ext. 3376, Beacon II: Kimberly Jones, Prog. Supvr. Tel: 718-931-0600 Ext. 2637, Beacon III: Susana Vasquez, Prog. Supvr. Tel: 718-931-0600 Ext. 3289.

Terence Cardinal Cooke Residence, 2467 Bathgate Ave., Bronx, 10458. Tel: 718-367-6990; Fax: 718-365-2544. Hope Goshea, Prog. Supvr.

Supervised Units, 777 Seaview Ave., Bldg. D, 2nd Fl., Staten Island, 10305. Tel: 718-980-1072; Fax: 718-980-1077. Dennis Scimone, Regl Dir., Brooklyn & Staten Island Svcs.; Sharon Quattrachi, Admin. Sec., Beacon I: Barbara Ignatenko, Prog. Supvr., Beacon II: Marlene Rosenberg, Prog. Supvr.

Staten Island Apartment Programs. Laurence Baker, Prog. Mgr., 90-92 Hancock St., Staten Island, 10305. Tel: 718-979-6241; Fax: 718-979-6941.

Highbridge Neighborhood Supported Housing Program, 1435 Ogden Ave., Bronx, 10452. Tel: 718-293-1009; Fax: 718-293-0939. Rick Downes, Prog. Supv.

Kingsborough Intensive Supported Apartment Program, 647 Vanderbilt Ave., Brooklyn, 11238. Tel: 718-398-4556; Fax: 718-398-4807. Veronica Rose, Prog. Supv.

Services to the St. Anthony's Residence, 410 E. 156th St., Bronx, 10455. Tel: 718-993-5060; Fax: 718-993-4758. Margo Gill, Prog. Mgr.

East Bronx Supported Housing, 707 Brady Ave., Bronx, 10462. Tel: 718-829-7177; Fax: 718-829-7376. Nancy Santos, Prog. Mgr.

Barnes Avenue Program, 2758 Barnes Ave., Bronx, 10461. Tel: 718-654-4750; Fax: 718-654-4804. Hope Goshea, Prog. Supvr.

The Clubhouse, 512 Southern Blvd., Bronx, 10455. Tel: 718-993-1078; Fax: 718-993-0216. Juan Ramos, Prog. Mgr.

BARRYVILLE. *New Hope Manor*, 35 Hillside Rd., 12719; Fax: 914-557-6603.
E-mail: newhopemnr@aol.com
Nicholas A. Roes, Dir.
See Miscellaneous listing for further details. Board of Directors: Revs. Daniel Egan, S.A.; Arte Johnson, S.P.; Sr. Rita Shea, O.P.; Sr. Madeline Murphy, O.P.; Sr. Cecilia La Pietra, O.P. Staff: Rev. Aquinas Thomas, S.A., Dir., In-Service Training; Sr. Maureen Conway, O.P., Dir. of Educ., Housemother, Counselor & Teacher; Sr. Patricia Conway, O.P., Housemother, Counselor & Teacher; Sr. Rose Respol, O.P., Dir., Religious Ed.

SPRING VALLEY. *Good Counsel / The Cardinal Cooke Residence*, 22 Linden Ave., 10977. Tel: 914-356-0517; Fax: 914-356-4175. Christopher Bell, Exec. Dir.; Kathleen Ferdinandsen, House Mgr. A program of Good Counsel in Hoboken, NJ, helping pregnant and single mothers with children. For information and intake referral, call 800-723-8331.

Good Counsel / The Paraclete Foundation, 1157 Fulton Ave., Bronx, 10456. Tel: 718-328-8620. Christopher Bell, Exec. Dir.; Anna Anekwe, House Mgr.

Good Counsel, 38 N. Clinton St., Poughkeepsie, 12601. Tel: 914-452-2944. Christopher Bell, Exec. Dir.; Kathy Aldrich, House Mgr.

Good Counsel, 38 Wiman Pl., Staten Island, 10305. Tel: 718-727-8266. Christopher Bell, Exec. Dir.; Ann Jarosz, House Mgr. Total Assisted 336; Total Staff 32.

[P] YOUTH SERVICES

NEW YORK. *Catholic Youth Organization of the Archdiocese of New York Inc.*, Executive Office, 1011 First Ave., 10022-4187. Tel: 212-371-1000, Ext. 2064; Fax: 212-371-1000, Ext. 3465. Mr. Henry Humphreys, Acting Pres.; Mr. Joseph E. Panepinto, Exec. Dir.; Mrs. Anne Navarro-Sullivan, Dir. Fundraising & Pub. Rels.; Sr. Judy Frasinetti, S.M.R., Consultant to Young Adult Ministry; Mrs. Antoinette Kerins, Dir. Teenage Federation & Blair Lodge; Mr. David Dennis, Dir. Outdoor Ministry.

Archdiocesan Committee on Scouting: Rev. Anthony D. Marchitelli, Archdiocesan Boy Scout Chap.; Sr. Kathleen Finnerty, O.S.U., Archdiocesan Girl Scout Chap.; Rev. Lawrence J. Quinn, Sea Cadet Chap.; Deacon Larry Battersby, Dir. of Parish-Based Youth Ministry.

CYO Manhattan County: Mr. Anthony D'Angelo, 242 Bathgate Ave., Bronx, 10458. Tel: 718-367-7659.

Grace Youth Ministry Center: Mr. Jorge Gonzalez, Dir., 218 W. 108th St., 10025. Tel: 212-666-6598.

Cardinal Spellman Center: Mr. Thomas Rosati, Dir., 137 E. Second St., 10009. Tel: 212-677-6600.

Lt. Joseph P. Kennedy, Jr., Memorial Center: Mr. Les Edwards, Dir., 34 W. 134th St., 10037. Tel: 212-882-6401.

CYO Staten Island Office: Judith Trancucci. 120 Anderson Ave., Staten Island, 10302. Tel: 718-448-4950.

Staten Island Center. Fran Mitilieri, Dir.; Laurie Maneski, Asst. Dir., 120 Anderson Ave., Staten Island, 10302. Tel: 718-448-4949.

CYO Westchester / Putnam Offices: Frank Magaletta, 9 Brookview Blvd., Chestnut Ridge, 10977. Tel: 914-623-2785. Blair Lodge Youth Ministry Center, Peekskill Rd., Putnam Valley, 10579. Tel: 914-528-5005. Mrs. Antoinette Kerins.

CYO Orange Office: Ann Lawrence, Teen Federation Coord., 260 Carpenter, Newburgh, 12550. Tel: 914-561-6264. John Smith, Sports Coord., P.O. Box 234, Highland Mills, 10930. Tel: 914-534-7700.

CYO Rockland Office: Thomas F. Collins, 34 Granecy Ct., Pearl River, 10965. Tel: 914-620-1662.

CYO Dutchess Office: John Van Voorhis, 33 Meadow Dr., Wappinger Falls, 12590. Tel: 914-297-7721. Mary Marshall, Catholic Center, 240 Church St., Poughkeepsie, 12601. Tel: 914-452-1400.

CYO Ulster Office: Thomas Brinkmann, 157 Broadway, Kingston, 12401. Tel: 914-340-9170.

CYO Sullivan County: Sr. Kevin John Shields, Box 1011, Liberty, 12750. Tel: 914-292-9100.

[Q] SOCIETY OF ST. VINCENT DE PAUL

NEW YORK. *Society of St. Vincent De Paul, Archdiocesan Central Council of New York*, 1011 First Ave., 10022. Tel: 212-755-8615. Legal Title: *The Society of St. Vincent de Paul of the Archdiocese of New York, Inc.* Territory: Archdiocese of New York. Mr. Ramon Vidal, Pres.; Rev. Robert T. Ritchie, Spiritual Advisor.

District Council of Manhattan, 1011 First Ave., Ste. 607, 10022. Tel: 212-755-8615. Legal Title: *The Society of St. Vincent de Paul in the City of New York*. Territory: Manhattan. Mr. Edmund Keane, Pres.; Rev. Msgr. Wallace A. Harris, Spiritual Advisor; Mr. Vincent D. Reilly, Exec. Sec.

District Council of the Bronx, 402 E. 152nd St., Bronx, 10455. Tel: 718-292-9090. Virginia Mulligan, Pres.

District Council of Staten Island, 28 Bryson Ave., Staten Island, 10302. Carmen Malandro, Pres.

Council of Rockland County, 37 E. Mayer Dr., Suffern, 10901. Deacon Joseph Verboys, Pres.

BRONX. *District Council of the Bronx*, 402 E. 152nd St., 10455. Tel: 718-292-9090. Legal Title: *The Society of St. Vincent de Paul, District Council of the Bronx, Inc.* Territory: Borough of The Bronx & Lower Westchester. Rev. Walter A. Birkle, Spiritual Dir.; Virginia M. Mulligan, Pres.

STATEN ISLAND. *Particular Council of Staten Island*. Carmen Malandro, Pres.; Deacon Joseph Graf, Spiritual Dir.

[R] INSTITUTIONS FOR DEPENDENT CHILDREN

NEW YORK. *Covenant House Under 21*, 460 W. 41st St., 10036
For a complete listing, refer to the Special Care Facilities section.

Pius XII Youth and Family Services, Inc., Office of the Pres., 570 Lexington Ave., 33rd Fl., 10022. Tel: 212-319-0464
For a complete listing, refer to the Special Care Facilities section.

BLAUVELT. *St. Dominic Home*, 10913. Tel: 914-359-3400; Fax: 914-359-4253
For a complete listing, refer to the Special Care Facilities section.

BRONX. *Saint Dominic's Home - Prevention Program (ASTAAN)*, 2345 University Ave., 10468. Tel: 718-584-4407
For a complete listing, refer to the Special Care Facilities section.

NANUET. *St. Agatha Home of the New York Foundling Hospital*, 135 Convent Rd., 10954. Tel: 914-623-3461
For a complete listing, refer to the Special Care Facilities section.

WEST PARK. *St. Cabrini Home*, 12493. Tel: 914-384-6500; Fax: 914-384-6001
For a complete listing, refer to the Special Care Facilities section.

WHITE PLAINS. *Cardinal McCloskey Services*, Two Holland Ave., 10603. Tel: 914-997-8000
For a complete listing, refer to the Special Care Facilities section.

[S] SPECIALIZED CHILD CARING HOMES

NEW YORK. *Good Shepherd Services*, 305 7th Ave., 9th Floor, 10001. Tel: 212-243-7021.
E-mail: palomonaco@aol.com
Web site: http://www.goodshepherds.org
For a complete listing, refer to the Special Care Facilities section.

Kennedy Child Study Center, 151 E. 67th St., 10021. Tel: 212-988-9500
For a complete listing, refer to the Special Care Facilities section.

Lavelle School for the Blind, 221st St. and Paulding Ave., 10469. Tel: 718-882-1212
For a complete listing, refer to the Special Care Facilities section.

Mission of the Immaculate Virgin Mount Loretto Staten Island, 10309. Tel: 718-317-2600.
For a complete listing, refer to the Special Care Facilities section.

New York Foundling Charitable Corp., 590 Avenue of the Americas, 10011. Tel: 212-633-9300
For a complete listing, refer to the Special Care Facilities section.

New York Foundling Hospital for Pediatric, Medical and Rehabilitative Care, Inc., 590 Avenue of the Americas, 10011. Tel: 212-633-9300
For a complete listing, refer to the Special Care Facilities section.

New York Foundling Hospital, The, 590 Avenue of the Americas, 10011. Tel: 212-633-9300
For a complete listing, refer to the Special Care Facilities section.

MILLBROOK. *Cardinal Hayes Home for Children*, North Ave., P.O. Box CH, 12545. Tel: 914-677-6363; Fax: 914-677-6691
For a complete listing, refer to the Special Care Facilities section.

RHINEBECK. *Astor Home for Children, The*, 36 Mill St., P.O. Box 5005, 12572-5005. Tel: 914-876-4081; Fax: 914-876-2020
For a complete listing, refer to the Special Care Facilities section.

Astor Learning Center, The, 36 Mill St., P.O. Box 5005, 12572-5005. Tel: 914-876-4081; Fax: 914-876-2020
For a complete listing, refer to the Special Care Facilities section.

[T] CHILDREN'S AGENCIES & PROTECTIVE INSTITUTIONS

NEW YORK. *Catholic Guardian Society*, 1011 First Ave., 10022. Tel: 212-371-1000
For a complete listing, refer to the Special Care Facilities section.

Catholic Home Bureau, 1011 First Ave., 10022. Tel: 212-371-1000
For a complete listing, refer to the Special Care Facilities section.

Guild of the Infant Savior, 1011 First Ave., Room 1287, 10022. Tel: 212-371-1000, Ext. 2440
For a complete listing, refer to the Special Care Facilities section.

Pelletier School & Services, 147 W. 70th St., 10023
For a complete listing, refer to the Special Care Facilities section.

LINCOLNDALE. *Lincoln Hall*, P.O. Box 600, 10540. Tel: 914-248-7474; Fax: 914-248-5173.
E-mail: pt.lincolnhall@worldnet.att.net
For a complete listing, refer to the Special Care Facilities section.

[U] CATHOLIC CHARITIES - CHILD CARING AGENCIES

OSSINING. *The Cardinal McCloskey Emergency Residential School*, 155 N. Highland Ave., 10562
For a complete listing, refer to the Special Care Facilities section.

[V] DAY NURSERIES

NEW YORK. *Featherbed Lane Day Care Center*. 98108 Featherbed Ln., Bronx, 10452. Tel: 212-583-8970. Mrs. Joyce Thompson, Dir. Group Day Care Children 33; Family Day Care Children 76.

Nazareth Nursery, 214-216 W. 15th St., 10011-6501. Tel: 212-243-1881. Montessori Day Care. Sr. Lucy Sabatini, O.S.F., Dir. & Admin. Sisters of St. Francis of the Mission of the Immaculate Virgin 2; Capacity 55 Children; Total Staff 14.

Providence Rest Child Day Care Center, Inc., 3310 Campbell Dr., 10465. Tel: 718-823-3588. Total Assisted 20/Day; Total Staff 6.

St. Benedict's Day Nursery, Day Care Center, 34 W. 134th St., 10037. Tel: 212-283-3350. Sr. Miriam Cecilia, Dir., Day Nursery. Handmaids of the Most Pure Heart of Mary 4; Children 82.

St. Cecilia's Day Nursery, 118 E. 106th St., 10029. Tel: 212-534-8423. Sr. Frances Arduini, S.A., Dir. Franciscan Sisters of the Atonement 3; Capacity 30; Total Served 30.

San Jose Day Nursery, 432 W. 20th St., 10011. Tel: 212-929-0839. Sr. Guadalupe Sordo, Supr.; Josefina Jimenez, Dir. Mothers of the Helpless 9; Children 57.

Sr. Elizabeth Boyle Child Learning Center, Inc. Bay St. and Vanderbilt Ave., Staten Island, 10304. Tel: 718-390-5655. Total Assisted 73; Total Staff 12.

MILLBROOK. *Hayes Nursery School and Day Care Center*, North Ave., P.O. Box CH, 12545. Tel: 914-677-6363; Fax: 914-677-6691. Fred Apers, Exec. Dir. Capacity 75.

YONKERS. *Queen's Daughters Day Care Center, Inc.*, 73 Buena Vista Ave., 10701. Tel: 914-969-4491. Barbara Berrios, Dir. Children 175; Total Staff 20.

[W] GENERAL HOSPITALS

NEW YORK. *Bayley Seton Hospital* 75 Vanderbilt Ave. Staten Island, 10304. Tel: 718-390-6000.
For a complete listing, refer to the Hospitals section.

Cabrini Medical Center (Cabrini Development Council, Inc.), 227 E. 19th St., 10003. Tel: 212-995-6000
For a complete listing, refer to the Hospitals section.

Our Lady of Mercy Medical Center 233rd St. Division, 600 E. 233 St. Bronx, 10466. Tel: 718-920-9000.
For a complete listing, refer to the Hospitals section.

St. Clare's Hospital and Health Center, 415 W. 51st St., 10019. Tel: 212-586-1500
For a complete listing, refer to the Hospitals section.

St. Vincent's Hospital and Medical Center of New York, 153 W. 11th St., 10011. Tel: 212-604-7000
For a complete listing, refer to the Hospitals section.

Saint Vincent's Medical Center of Richmond 355 Bard Ave. Staten Island, 10310. Tel: 718-876-1234.
For a complete listing, refer to the Hospitals section.

BEACON. *St. Francis Hospital*, Delavan Ave., 12508. Tel: 914-831-3500
For a complete listing, refer to the Hospitals section.

KINGSTON. *Benedictine Hospital*, 105 Mary's Ave., 12401. Tel: 914-338-2500
For a complete listing, refer to the Hospitals section.

PORT JERVIS. *Mercy Community Hospital*, 160 E. Main St., 12771. Tel: 914-856-5351; Fax: 914-858-5402
For a complete listing, refer to the Hospitals section.

POUGHKEEPSIE. *St. Francis Hospital*, North Rd., 12601. Tel: 914-471-2000
For a complete listing, refer to the Hospitals section.

SUFFERN. *Good Samaritan Hospital of Suffern*, 10901. Tel: 914-368-5000
For a complete listing, refer to the Hospitals section.

WARWICK. *St. Anthony Community Hospital, Inc.*, 15-19 Maple Ave., 10990. Tel: 914-986-2276
For a complete listing, refer to the Hospitals section.

WHITE PLAINS. *St. Agnes Hospital and Children's Rehabilitation Center*, 305 North St., 10605. Tel: 914-681-4500; Fax: 914-681-4974
For a complete listing, refer to the Hospitals section.

YONKERS. *St. Joseph's Medical Center*, 127 S. Broadway, 10701. Tel: 914-378-7000; Fax: 914-965-4838.
E-mail: SJMCgen@interactive.net
Web site: http://saintjosephs.org
For a complete listing, refer to the Hospitals section.

[X] SPECIAL HOSPITALS AND SANATORIA FOR INVALIDS

NEW YORK. *Calvary Hospital* 1740 Eastchester Rd. Bronx, 10461. Tel: 718-863-6900.
For a complete listing, refer to the Special Care Facilities section.

St. Rose's Home, 71 Jackson St., 10002. Tel: 212-677-8132
For a complete listing, refer to the Special Care Facilities section.

Terence Cardinal Cooke Health Care Center, 1249 Fifth Ave., 10029. Tel: 212-360-1000.
E-mail: tccgen@chcn.org
Web site: http://www.chcn.org
For a complete listing, refer to the Special Care Facilities section.

HARRISON. *St. Vincent's Hospital and Medical Center of New York, Westchester Branch*, 275 North St., 10528. Tel: 914-967-6500; Fax: 914-925-5157
For a complete listing, refer to the Special Care Facilities section.

HAWTHORNE. *Rosary Hill Home*, 10532. Tel: 914-769-0114
For a complete listing, refer to the Special Care Facilities section.

YONKERS. *St. Eleanora's Home for Convalescents*, 127 S. Broadway, 10701. Tel: 914-378-7000.
E-mail: sclegras@erols.com
For a complete listing, refer to the Special Care Facilities section.

[Y] ORDERS OF NURSING SISTERS

NEW YORK. *Convent of the Little Sisters of the Assumption*, 2604 Davidson Ave., 10468. Sr. Jean McCormack, Prov. Coord.; Sr. Mary Joseph, Local Coord. Sisters 6.

Family Health Service, Inc.; Little Sisters of the Assumption, 426 E. 119th St., 10035. Tel: 212-987-4422; Fax: 212-987-4430. Sr. Judith Garson, Exec. Dir.

BRONX. *Convent of the Sisters Servants of Mary S.M.*, 3305 Country Club Rd., 10465-1296. Tel: 718-829-0428. Mother Angeles Aizpurua. Mission: Private nursing in the homes. Sisters 20.

OSSINING. *Dominican Sisters Family Health Services, Inc.*, 299 N. Highland Ave., 10562. Tel: 914-941-1710. Community-based, certified, voluntary Home Health Agency and Long Term Home Health Care and AIDS Programs serving all of Westchester, Suffolk and the South Bronx. Sr. Virginia Hanrahan, O.P., B.S.N., M.S., Ph.D., Pres. & CEO; Sr. Margaret Flood, O.P., B.S.N., M.A., M.P.A.

Bronx Office, 279 Alexander Ave., Bronx, 10454. Tel: 718-665-6557. Margaret Sweeney, B.S.N., M.A., Admin.

Westchester Offices, 299 N. Highland Ave., 10562. Tel: 914-941-1654. Evelyn Bobb, B.S.N., Admin.

Suffolk County Office, 103-6 W. Montauk Hwy., Box 209, Hampton Bays, 11946. Tel: 516-728-0181. Box 866, Amagansett, 11930. Tel: 516-267-1090. Joanna O'Connell, B.S.N., Admin. Total Assisted 6,500.

STATEN ISLAND. *Pax Christi Hospice*, 355 Bard Ave., 10310. Hospice and Home Care Services for the terminally ill. Sisters of Charity Health Care System.

[Z] NURSING HOMES

NEW YORK. *Kateri Residence*, 150 Riverside Dr., 10024-2201. Tel: 212-769-0744; Fax: 212-873-0658.
E-mail: 1bond@chcn.org
Web site: http://www.chcn.org/kateri
For a complete listing, refer to the Special Care Facilities section.

Mary Manning Walsh Home, 1339 York Ave., 10021. Tel: 212-628-2800
For a complete listing, refer to the Special Care Facilities section.

St. Vincent dePaul Residence, 900 Intervale Ave., 10459. Tel: 718-589-6965
For a complete listing, refer to the Special Care Facilities section.

Terence Cardinal Cooke Health Care Center, 1249 Fifth Ave., 10029. Tel: 212-360-1000; Fax: 212-289-2739
For a complete listing, refer to the Special Care Facilities section.

BRONX. *Franciscan Health System of New York, Inc.*, 2975 Independence Ave., 10463-4699. Tel: 718-548-1700; Fax: 718-601-3384
For a complete listing, refer to the Special Care Facilities section.

Jeanne Jugan Residence, 3200 Baychester Ave., 10475 Fax: 718-671-0305
For a complete listing, refer to the Special Care Facilities section.

Medical Missionaries of Mary, 563 Minneford Ave., 10464-1118. Tel: 718-885-0945; Fax: 718-885-0010.
E-mail: mmmci@aol.com
Web site: http://www.medical-missionaries.com
For a complete listing, refer to the Special Care Facilities section.

Providence Rest, 3304 Waterbury Ave., 10465. Tel: 718-931-3000
For a complete listing, refer to the Special Care Facilities section.

St. Patrick's Home for the Aged and Infirm, 66 Van Cortlandt Park S., 10463. Tel: 718-519-2800
For a complete listing, refer to the Special Care Facilities section.

DOBBS FERRY. *St. Cabrini Nursing Home*, 115 Broadway, 10522. Tel: 914-693-6800
For a complete listing, refer to the Special Care Facilities section.

MIDDLETOWN. *St. Teresa's Nursing Home*, 120 Highland Ave., 10940. Tel: 914-342-1033; Fax: 914-344-5631
For a complete listing, refer to the Special Care Facilities section.

RHINEBECK. *Ferncliff Nursing Home*, 52 River Rd., 12572. Tel: 914-876-2011; Fax: 914-876-2019
For a complete listing, refer to the Special Care Facilities section.

STATEN ISLAND. *Carmel Richmond Nursing Home, Inc.*, 88 Old Town Rd., 10304-4299. Tel: 718-979-5000
For a complete listing, refer to the Special Care Facilities section.

WARWICK. *Villa Frances at the Knolls*, 20 Grand St., 10990. Tel: 914-986-2267
For a complete listing, refer to the Special Care Facilities section.

[AA] ADULT RESIDENCES

NEW YORK. *Centro Maria, Inc.*, 539 W. 54th St., 10019.
E-mail: centroma@erols.com
For a complete listing, refer to the Special Care Facilities section.

Cor Mariae, c/o 1011 First Ave., Rm. 1130, 10022. Tel: 212-371-1000, Ext. 2435
For a complete listing, refer to the Special Care Facilities section.

The Dwelling Place, 409 W. 40th St., 10018. Tel: 212-564-7887
For a complete listing, refer to the Special Care Facilities section.

El Carmelo Residence, 249 W. 14th St., 10011. Tel: 212-242-8224
For a complete listing, refer to the Special Care Facilities section.

The Jeanne d'Arc Residence, 253 W. 24th St., 10011. Tel: 212-989-5952
For a complete listing, refer to the Special Care Facilities section.

Kolping Society of New York Men's Residence (Catholic Kolping Society New York, Inc.), 165 E. 88th St., 10128. Tel: 212-369-6647
For a complete listing, refer to the Special Care Facilities section.

Kolping-on-Concourse 2916 Grand Concourse Bronx, 10458. Tel: 212-733-6119.
For a complete listing, refer to the Special Care Facilities section.

Leo House, 332 W. 23rd St., 10011. Tel: 212-929-1010; Fax: 212-366-6801
For a complete listing, refer to the Special Care Facilities section.

Padre Pio Shelter for Homeless Men 419 E. 155th St. Bronx, 10455. Tel: 718-292-3713.
For a complete listing, refer to the Special Care Facilities section.

Sacred Heart Residence, 432 W. 20th St., 10011. Tel: 212-929-5790
For a complete listing, refer to the Special Care Facilities section.

St. Agnes' Residence, 237 W. 74th St., 10023. Tel: 212-874-1361
For a complete listing, refer to the Special Care Facilities section.

St. Joseph's Immigrant Home, 425 W. 44th St., 10036-4402. Tel: 212-246-5363
For a complete listing, refer to the Special Care Facilities section.

St. Mary's Residence, 225 E. 72nd St., 10021. Tel: 212-249-6850
For a complete listing, refer to the Special Care Facilities section.

St. Zita's Home for Adults, 143 W. 14th St., 10011. Tel: 212-243-7200
For a complete listing, refer to the Special Care Facilities section.

Thorpe Family Residence, Inc., 2252 Crotona Ave., 10457
For a complete listing, refer to the Special Care Facilities section.

GARRISON. *St. Christopher's Inn*, P.O. Box 150, 10524-0150. Tel: 914-424-3616
For a complete listing, refer to the Special Care Facilities section.

MONTROSE. *Kolping-on-Hudson*, 95 Montrose Point Rd., 10548. Tel: 914-737-9547
For a complete listing, refer to the Special Care Facilities section.

[BB] CATHOLIC CAMPS

NEW YORK. *The Catholic Camp Association Inc.*, 1011 First Ave., Room 1287, 10022. Tel: 212-371-1000.
John V. Mara CYO Camps, Putnam Valley.
Hill Camp. Capacity 120.
Valley Camp. Capacity 120. Total Assisted 147; Total in Residence 271; Total Staff 48.

[CC] COMMUNITY CENTERS

NEW YORK. *Cardinal Spellman Center, Inc.*, 137 E. Second St., 10009. Tel: 212-677-6600; Fax: 212-995-8537. Mr. Thomas Rosati, Dir. All Centers are engaged in full time recreational and educational activities. Serves Lower East Side parishes and includes Cardinal Spellman Headstart. Total Staff 35; Total Assisted 1,550.

Casita Maria Inc. 928 Simpson St., Bronx, 10459; Fax: 718-842-4622. Cristina Toosie, Exec. Dir.; Mrs. Jacqueline Weld, Chm. Serves the Bronx and East Harlem. Casita Maria serves over 5,500 individuals each year through after school recreation, social services, senior citizens centers, and homeless seniors.

Casita Maria-Carver Community Center, 55 E. 102nd St., 10029. Cristina Toosie, Exec. Dir.; Orlando Tomas Martinez, Dir. Serves Carver Houses and adjacent areas of East Harlem.

Drew-Hamilton CYO Center, 220 W. 143rd St., 10030. Serves Central Harlem.

Lieut. Joseph P. Kennedy, Jr. Memorial Community Center, 34 W. 134th St., 10037. Mr. Les Edwards, Exec. Dir. Serves Central Harlem. Serves 200 youth in afternoon and afterschool programs and 500 teenagers in evening programs.

Life Experience and Faith Sharing Association, 149 E. 117th St., 10035. Tel: 212-996-7303. LEFS Team: James Addison; Diane Baker; Sr. Dorothy Gallant, S.C.; Darryl Gillis; Jimmie Robinson; Sr. Teresa H. Skehan, R.S.M.; Kara Cain; Sr. Cecilia Palange, S.C.I.M.; Ralph Thomas; Godfrey Xaba. Total Assisted 2,500.

Staten Island CYO Center, 120 Anderson Ave., Port Richmond, Staten Island, 10302. Tel: 718-448-4949; Fax: 718-273-8361. Frances M. Mitilieri, Dir. Serves residents of Port Richmond and surrounding areas.

[DD] MONASTERIES AND RESIDENCES OF PRIESTS AND BROTHERS

NEW YORK. *"America;" Residence and publication office of the America Press*, 106 W. 56th St., 10019. Tel: 212-581-4640; Fax: 212-399-3596. Revs. George W. Hunt, S.J., Editor-in-Chief; Robert C. Collins, S.J.; James J. DiGiacomo, S.J.; John W. Donohue, S.J.; Vincent T. O'Keefe, S.J., Supr.; John J. Gallen, S.J.; Eugene J. O'Brien, S.J.; Patrick H. Samway, S.J.; Charles M. Whelan, S.J.; Walter J. Smith, S.J.; Edward J. Mattimoe, S.J.; Vincent J. Duminuco, S.J.; Frederick J. O'Brien, S.J.; Dennis Linehan, S.J.; Charles J. O'Byrne, S.J.; T. A. John, S.J.; John F. Long, S.J.; Michael E. Sehler, S.J.; James P. Stehr, S.J.; James S. Torrens, S.J. Priests 20.

Apostolic Society of the Crusade of the Holy Spirit. c/o St. John's Rectory, 35 Willow St., Beacon, 12508. Tel: 914-831-0422; Fax: 914-831-1009. Revs. Ignatius Peries, C.Sp. (Argentina), Dir. Gen., Argentina; Bernard Kelly, C.Sp. (U.K.), Vicar Gen., U.K.; Nimal Mendis, C.Sp. (U.S.A.), Asst. Gen., Sec. Gen. & Treas. Gen., U.S.A.

Atonement Friars, 138 Waverly Pl., 10014-3845. Tel: 212-243-4692. Rev. Elias D. Mallon, S.A., Dir. Graymoor Ecumenical & Interreligious Institute; Bro. William Martyn, S.A., Exec. Sec. Commission on Ecumenical & Interreligious Affairs, Archdiocese of NY; Rev. Joseph F. Cavoto, S.A., Vocation Dir., Tel: 212-675-6389. Rev. James J. Gardiner, S.A., Natl. Pastoral Life Center, Tel: 212-255-6731. Rev. Charles Sharon, S.A., Admin.

Augustinian Recollects Provincial Residence, Province of St. Nicholas of Tolentine, 2800 Schurz Ave., 10465. Tel: 718-823-0460. Legal Title: *The Province of St. Nicholas of Tolentine of the Augustinian Recollect Fathers*. Revs. Jose Luis Duenas Navarro, O.A.R.; Jesus Sobejano, O.A.R.

Brothers of the Christian Schools of Manhattan College, Inc. 4415 Post Rd., Bronx, 10471. Tel: 212-884-0613. Bros. Kenneth Fitzgerald, F.S.C., Dir.; Luke Salm, F.S.C., Sub-Dir.; Thomas Scanlan, F.S.C., Pres. In res. Rev. Anthony L. Rubsys, F.S.C.A. Total Staff 9; Total in Residence 38.

Calasanzian Fathers (Piarists), 88 Convent Ave., 10027. Tel: 212-234-1919. Revs. Felix Jimenez, Sch.P.; Jose M. Clavero, Sch.P.; Felix Ganuza, Sch.P.

Crosier (Canons Regular of the Order of the Holy Cross), Holy Cross Priory, 326 W. 14th St., 10014. E-mail: crosier2@aol.com
Very Rev. Francis Kelly Scheets, O.S.C., Prior; Revs. Roger Vaughn, O.S.C.; Theodore K. Parker, O.S.C.; Adrian C. Piotrowski, O.S.C.; Timothy C. Conlon, O.S.C.; Bros. Fernando Rivera, O.S.C.; Gregory Madigan, O.S.C.; Gabriel Guerrero, O.S.C.; Timothy Tomczak, O.S.C.

Franciscan Friars, Order of Friars Minor, Holy Name Province, Holy Name Province Provincialate, 126 W. 32nd St., 10001-3202. Tel: 212-967-6300.
E-mail: HNP@aol.com
Web site: http://www.nji.com/~rbiasiot/index.htm
Legal Title: *Franciscan Friars, Order of Friars Minor of the Province of the Most Holy Name*. Revs. John M. Felice, O.F.M., Prov. Minister; Charles J. Miller, O.F.M., Prov. Vicar.
Priests of the Province in Residences not listed elsewhere: Rev. Justin J. Bailey, O.F.M., St. Bonaventure Friary, 56 Spadina Rd., Toronto, Ontario, M5R 2T3, Canada. Rev. Raymond A. Beane, O.F.M., Mailing Address: Box 590, Big Pine Key, FL, 33043-0590. Rev. David M. Bossman, O.F.M., Seton Hall University, South Orange, NJ, 07079-2696. Rev. Patrick C. Callaghan, O.F.M., Rte. 1, Saint Regis Falls, 12980-9712. Rev. Russell Becker, O.F.M., East Asian Pastoral Institute, Ateneo de Manila University, P.O. Box 221, 1101 U.P. Campus Q.C., Philippines. Rev. Owen Colligan, O.F.M., Staff Chap., Fort Bayard Medical Center, P.O. Box 219, Fort Bayard, NM, 88036-0219. Rev. Joseph Ganssle, O.F.M., 4165 Eaton St., Denver, CO, 80212-7306. Rev. Depaul A. Genska, O.F.M., Catholic Theological Union, 5401 S. Cornell Ave., Chicago, IL, 60615-5608. Rev. John Coughlin, O.F.M., St. Joseph's Seminary, Dunwoodie, Yonkers, 10704-1852. Rev. J. Patrick Kelly, O.F.M., FrancisCare, Elmwood Park Plaza, 475 Market St., Elmwood Park, NJ, 07407-3104. Rev. Venant Lalonde, O.F.M., St. Agnes Rectory, 143 E. 43 St., 10017-4065. Rev. John Pierce, O.F.M., Holy Family Parish, P.O. Box 502218, St. Thomas, U.S. Virgin Islands, 00805. Rev. Andrew Nargaj, O.F.M., Our Lady of Shkodra Church, 361 W. Hartsdale Ave., Hartsdale, 10530-0704. Rev. Demetrius O'Friel, O.F.M., 1755 Riverside Dr., P.O. Box 2804, Ottawa, Canada, K1G 3TG. Rev. Rene F. Phillips, O.F.M., 850 Thomas Ln., Angola, 14006-9572. Rev. Lawrence Schulmeister, O.F.M., 612 Warner St., Baltimore, MD, 21230. Rev. Richard Mucowski, O.F.M., St. Mary College, 4100 S. 4th St., Leavenworth, KS, 66048-5082. Rev. Benedict M. Taylor, O.F.M., Create Inc., 73 Lenox Ave., 10026. Rev. Gerard Lee, O.F.M., 341 Manning Blvd., Albany, 12206-1815. Rev. Gerald M. Dolan, O.F.M., 609 S. Convent Rd., Aston, PA, 19014. Rev. Edward C. Metzger, O.F.M., St. John the Baptist Rectory, 1085 Englewood Ave., Buffalo, 14223. Rev. James Vacco, O.F.M., Fredonia Newman Center, 222 Temple St., Fredonia, 14063. Rev. Peter S. Chepaitis, Bethany Ministries, Box 420, Middleburgh, 12122-0420. Rev. Douglas R. Glassman, O.F.M., 221 Windward St., Venice, CA, 90291-3764. Rev. Alfonso D. Guzman, O.F.M., Centro Vocacional Franciscano, Apartado 173, Sabana Seca, PR, 00952.
Military Chaplains: Rev. Louis V. Iasiello, O.F.M., Commander Naval Surface Force, US Atlantic Fleet, 1430 Mitscher Ave., Norfolk, VA, 23551-2494. Rev. Alan Sullivan, O.F.M., 3310 First Ave., San Diego, CA, 92103. Rev. Conrad W. Loftus, O.F.M., Fitzsimons Medical Center, Dept. of Ministry & Pastoral Care, Aurora, CO, 80045-5000.
Priests Abroad: Rev. Edward J. Dillon, O.F.M., Gethsemane, P.O. Box 186, 91001 Jerusalem, Israel. Rev. Howard O'Shea, 27 rue du Grand Madier, La Ciotat, France, 13600. For Information Regarding Vocations to the Brotherhood & Priesthood, write Franciscan Vocation Office, St. Francis Friary, 134 W. 32nd St., New York, NY 10001. Solemnly Professed Priests (including 4 Bishops) 479; Brothers 99; Temporary Vows: Brothers 2; Clerics 13; Novices 6; Permanant Deacons 3; Affiliates 11.

Franciscan Province of the Immaculate Conception, 125 Thompson St., 10012. Tel: 212-674-4388; 674-5490. Franciscan Province of the Immaculate Conception of New York City. Legal Title: *Friars Minor of the Order of St. Francis, Incorporated, New York, 1871*. Revs. Robert M. Campagna, O.F.M., Minister Prov.; Steven M. Sysol, O.F.M., Vicar Prov.; Simeon Distefano, O.F.M., Prov. Sec.; Alban V. Montella, O.F.M., Prov. Promoter of Missions.
Franciscan Mission Associates, 274-280 W. Lincoln Ave., Mt. Vernon, 10550. Ms. Madeline Bonnici, Exec. Dir.; Rev. Claude Scrima, O.F.M., Dir. of Secular Franciscans, St. Christopher Friary, P.O. Box 230, Boston, MA, 02113. Pious League of Saint Anthony, 151 Thompson St., P.O. Box 489, 10013-0489.
Priests of the Province Abroad: Rev. Giles Barreda, O.F.M., Franciscan Chapel Center, 2-37 Roppong; 4-Chome; Minatu-Ku 106, Tokyo, Japan. Rev. Gilbert Silverio, O.F.M., Convento San Francesco, Via Nicolo V, 35, 00165 Rome, Italy.
Military Chaplains: Rev. Charles Soto, O.F.M., Command Chap., Comregsuppgru, P.O. Box 280057, Mayport, FL, 32228-0057. Rev. Michael Travaglione, O.F.M., HHC USASA, Unit 15716, Box 189, APO AP, 96271. Rev. Brennan Egan, O.F.M., Marine Corps Air Station, 1841 A. Dyer Ct., Tustin, CA, 92782.
Retired Military Chaplains: Rev. Edwin Bobrek, O.F.M., 1427 Ave. de las Adelsas, Encinatas, CA, 92024. Rev. Jack Hoak, O.F.M., Serra Friary, 200 Hershey St., McKeesport, PA, 15132.
Priests of the Province Residing Elsewhere: Rev. Sigmund Brambilla, O.F.M. 15A Park Ave., Northampton, MA, 01060. Rev. Felician Napoli, O.F.M., Incarnation Church, 5124 Gateway Dr., Tampa, FL, 33615. Rev. Bartholomew De Simone, O.F.M., St. Gregory Church, 200 N. University Dr., Plantation, FL, 33324. Rev. Thaddeus Palmieri, O.F.M., Mary Help of the Christians Church, 6281 N.W. 66th Way, Parkland, FL, 33067. Rev. Clement Procopio, O.F.M., St. Cecilia Church, P.O. Box 366, Clarksdale, AZ, 86324. Rev. Boniface Rezza, O.F.M., 8 Garden Pl., Bay Shore, 11706. Rev. Victor Cesario, O.F.M., 2467 Finlandia Ln. #73, Clearwater, FL, 34623. Rev. John Bucchino, O.F.M., 14 Stuyvesant Oval #5D, 10009. Rev. Louis De Tommaso, O.F.M., St. Ignatius Rectory, P.O. Box 1306, Tarpon Springs, FL, 34688-1306. Rev. Ralph Di Pasquale, O.F.M., 2008 Crowberry Dr., Port St. Lucie, FL, 34983. Rev. Francis Hanudel, O.F.M., 50 Luisser St., Clifton, NJ, 07012. Rev. Mark Leone, O.F.M., Elizabeth Seton Residence, 125 Oakland St., Wellesley Hills, MA, 02181. On Sick Leave: Rev. Xavier Carnicelli, O.F.M., St. Cabrini Nursing Home, 115 Broadway, Dobbs Ferry, 10552. Rev. Vincent Mele, O.F.M., Kateri Residence, 150 Riverside Dr., 10024. Rev. Cyril Morisco, O.F.M., St. Joseph Manor Nursing Care Facility, 1133 Washington Ave., Portland, ME, 04103.
Residing in Canada: Immaculate Conception Friary, 2 Richardson Ave., Toronto, Ont., M6M 3R4. Revs. Amadeo Nardone, O.F.M.; Marcellinus Borg, O.F.M.; Benedict Goveas, O.F.M., St. Charles Borromeo Friary, 811 Lawrence Ave., Toronto, Ont., M6A 1C3. Revs. Antonio Nardoianni, O.F.M.; Salvatore DeBenedictis, O.F.M.; Michael D'Cruz, O.F.M., St. Francis Friary, 72 Mansfield Ave., Toronto, Ont., M6J 2B2. Revs. Gregory Botte, O.F.M.; Isidoro di Miglio, O.F.M.; Frederick Mazzarella, O.F.M.; James Wells, O.F.M., St. Lawrence Friary, 2210 Lawrence Ave. E., Scarborough, Ont., M1P 2P9. Rev. Ralph Paonessa, O.F.M., St. Bonaventure, 56 Spadina Rd., Toronto, Ont., M5R 2T3. Revs. Celestine Pennisi, O.F.M.; Frank Jannetta, O.F.M., St. Jane Francis Friary, 2747 Jane St., Downsview, Ont., M3L 2E8. Revs. Claudio Moser, O.F.M.; Brennan Egan, O.F.M., (Awaiting Military Assignment); Augustin Donini, O.F.M., St. Jude Friary, 3265 Weston Rd., Weston, Ont., M9M 2T9. Revs. Celestino Canzio, O.F.M.; Frank Jannetta, O.F.M.; Blaise Tranchida, O.F.M.
St. Francis Center for Religious, 208501 Hwy. #9, R.R. #8 (Mono Mills), Orangeville, Canada, L9W 3T5. Bro. Philip Adamo, O.F.M., Temp. Admin. Priests 154; Brothers 28; Permanent Deacons 3; Bishops 3.

The Franciscan Vocation Ministry of Holy Name Province, 135 W. 31st St., 10001-3439. Tel: 212-629-5868; 800-677-7788.
E-mail: fribro@aol.com or NathanaelN@aol.com
Rev. Peter V. Brophy, O.F.M., Dir., HNP Vocation Ministry; Bro. Nathanael Necaster, O.F.M., Admin. Asst.

Immaculate Conception Friary, 754 E. Gun Hill Rd., 10467. Tel: 212-653-2200. Capuchin Friars of the Province of the Stigmata of St. Francis. Revs. Robert Grix, O.F.M.Cap.; Pius Caccavalle, O.F.M.Cap.; Robert Yurgel, O.F.M.Cap.; Eric Hall, O.F.M.Cap. Total Assisted 190; Total Staff 20; Priests 4; Brothers 2.

Jesuit Community at Fordham University, 441 E. Fordham Rd., 10458. Tel: 212-817-5322. Priests 89; Scholastics 2; Brothers 2; Total in Residence 93; Total Staff 37. Loyola Hall, Jesuit Community. Very Rev. Joseph A. Novak, S.J., Rector; Revs. Edward F. Maloney, Supr.; David J. Casey, S.J., Min.; Joseph V. Dolan, S.J., Sub Min.; John D. Alexander, S.J.; Albert P. Bartlett, S.J.; Thomas V. Bermingham, S.J.; John D. Boyd, S.J.; William E. Boyle, S.J.; Francis P. Canavan, S.J.; Edward F. Clark, S.J.; W. Norris Clarke, S.J.; T. Gerard Connolly, S.J.; Frederick J. Dillemuth, S.J.; G. Richard Dimler, S.J.; Robert R. Dobbins, S.J.; Edward T. Dowling, S.J.; Gerard F. Fagan, S.J.; Daniel J. Fitzpatrick, S.J.; Joseph R. Frese, S.J.; C. Homer Giblin, S.J.; L. Augustine Grady, S.J.; Thomas C. Hennessy, S.J.; George B. Hoch, S.J.; William T. Hogan, S.J.; Bro. Frank W. Jensen, S.J.; Revs. J. Raymond Johnson; Robert G. Kelly, S.J.; John J. King, S.J.; Albert J. Loomie, S.J.; George C. McCauley, S.J.; Gerald A. McCool, S.J.; Joseph Mitros, S.J. (Poland); Vincent M. Novak, S.J.; Ladislas Orsy, S.J.; John W. Ortner, S.J.; Jung-Woo Park, S.J. (Korea); Louis B. Pascoe, S.J.; Eugene J. Quigley, S.J.; James H. Reid, S.J.; Herbert W. Rogers, S.J.; Robert J. Roth, S.J.; James A. Sadowsky, S.J.; Deacon Stephen A. Schoenig, Jesuit Scholastic; Revs. Robert J. Sealy, S.J.; J. Francis Stroud, S.J.; Daniel J. Sullivan, S.J.; Patrick J. Sullivan, S.J.; Edward J. Sweeney, S.J.; Eamon G. Taylor, S.J., Jesuit Community, Kohlmann Hall. Tel: 718-584-1638. Revs. Joseph P. Parkes, S.J., Supr.; John J. Scully, S.J., Min.; John J. Leonard, S.J., Sub-Min.; Pierce A. Brennan, S.J.; Michael P. Corcoran, S.J.; Mallick J. Fitzpatrick, S.J.; Matthew C. Flood, S.J.; Philip G. Judge, S.J.; Stanley J. O'Konsky, S.J.; William J. O'Malley, S.J.; Joseph S. Rooney, S.J.; Charles D. Sullivan, S.J.; Heiner T. Wilmer, S.J. (Germany), Cardinal Spellman Hall, Jesuit Community. Tel: 718-817-5330. Very Revs. Joseph A. Novak, S.J., Rector; Joseph A. O'Hare, S.J., Pres.; Rev. Daniel J. O'Brien, S.J., Min.; Bro. Donald J. Kavanagh, S.J., Sub Min.; Revs. Jeffrey P. Baerwald, S.J.; Dean P. Bechard, S.J.; Robert D. Cloney, S.J.; John J. Conley, S.J.; Deacon James K. Coughlin, S.J., Jesuit Scholastic; Revs. Joseph A. Currie, S.J.; Brian Davies, O.P. (England); Avery Dulles, S.J.; John T. Dzieglewicz, S.J.; Rev. Msgr. Charles J. Fahey (SY); Revs. Garrett J. Fitzgerald, S.J.; Robert R. Grimes, S.J.; Martin A. Hegyi, S.J. (Hungary); Alfred T. Hennelly, S.J.; Joseph W. Koterski, S.J.; Miguel B. Lambino, S.J.; Joseph T. Lienhard, S.J.; Nicholas D. Lombardi, S.J.; Mark S. Massa, S.J.; Donald C. Matthews, S.J.; George J. McMahon, S.J.; Joseph M. McShane, S.J.; John A. Mullin, S.J.; Richard J. Regan, S.J.; Patrick J. Ryan, S.J.; Raymond A. Schroth, S.J.; Thomas J. Scirghi, S.J.

Jesuit Provincial's Office, 39 E. 83rd St., 10028. Tel: 212-774-5500; Fax: 212-774-5510.
E-mail: nyprovsj@compuserve.com
Very Rev. Kenneth J. Gavin, S.J., Prov.; Revs. Thomas E. Smith, S.J., Exec. Asst. to Prov.; Frederick J. O'Brien, S.J., Asst. for Secondary Education; James F. Joyce, S.J., Asst. Social & Pastoral Ministries; Bro. Gilbert J. Scott, S.J., Asst. to Prov.;

Revs. J. Raymond Johnson, S.J., Prov. Treas., Auditor & American Rep. of the Missions of the Society of Jesus, Vatican City; William T. Wood, S.J., Asst. to the Prov. for the Intl. Apostolate; Thomas P. Gaunt, S.J., Asst. for Formation for Maryland & New York Provinces; Joseph S. Costantino, S.J., Vocation Dir. for Maryland & New York Provinces.
Priests of the Province Abroad: Rev. Vincent F. Blehl, S.J., Rabenkopfstr. 2, Apt. 229, Freiburg, Germany, 79102. Revs. James J. Bowes, S.J.; Alfred L. Fiorino, S.J., C.P. 6139, 00195 Rome, Italy. Revs. John M. McDermott, S.J.; Michael P. Hilbert, S.J.; Paul W. McNellis, S.J., Pontificia Universita Gregoriana, Piazza della Pilotta 4, 00187 Rome, Italy. Rev. Henry J. Bertels, S.J., Pontifical Biblical Institute, via della Pilotta 25, 00187 Rome, Italy. Rev. Keith F. Pecklers, S.J., Coll Bellarmino, Via del Seminario 120, 00186 Rome, Italy. Rev. John J. Halligan, S.J., Apdo. 17-01-3112, Quito, Ecuador. Rev. Michael F. Suarez, S.J., Campion Hall, Oxford, England, 0X1 1QS. Rev. Dennis M. Leder, S.J., Parroquia La Merced, Apartado Postal 2436, 01901. Rev. Charles J. Beirne, S.J., Universidad Rafael Landivar, Apartado 39C, Zona 16, Guatemala, C.A., 01016. Rev. J. Dean Brackley, S.J., UCA-Centro Mons Romero, Apdo. 01-168, San Salvador, El Salvador. Rev. Charles H. Lohr, S.J., Raimundus-Lullus Institute der Universitat-Freiburg, Werthmann Platz, 3, D-79085 Freiburg i Br., Germany.
Priests of the Province in Residences Not Listed Elsewhere: Rev. Theodore V. Francois, S.J., 507 Macon St., Brooklyn, 11233. Rev. Gerard H. Ettlinger, S.J., 10-01 162nd St., Apt. 50, Whitestone, 11357. Rev. John F. Walters, S.J., IAM Counseling Center, Tesserville Farm, R.D. 1, Box 75, New Albany, PA, 18833. Rev. Edward J. Mally, S.J., 1S 150 Spring Rd., Apt. 2E, Oakbrook Terrace, IL, 60181. Rev. John J. Gerhard, S.J., 850 Hylan Blvd., Staten Island, 10305. Rev. Louis A. Padovano, S.J., 169 E. 78 St., Apt 7-C, 10021. Rev. Joseph P. Kane, S.J., 2674 Valentine Ave., Apt., 1A, Bronx, 10458. Rev. Gerard P. Bell, S.J., 8611 Cedar St., Silver Spring, MD, 20910. Rev. John H. Rainaldo, S.J., 3 Stephan Ave., New Hyde Park, 11040. Rev. George H. Belgarde, S.J., St. Regis Mission, P.O. Box 429, Hogansburg, 13655.
Awaiting Assignment: Revs. Robert W. Dahlke, S.J.; Richard P. Grogan, S.J.
Leave of Absence: Revs. Martin Doyle, S.J.; Michael E. Donahue, S.J.

Jesuit Community, 860 Manida St., Bronx, 10474. Tel: 718-542-2283. Connected with Nativity Rectory. 44 Second Ave., 10003. In res., Rev. Joseph C. Towle, S.J.

Marist Brothers Residence. Our Lady of Grace Residence, 850 E. 226th St., Bronx, 10466. Tel: 212-652-1848. Bros. Francis Kelly, F.M.S.; John Malich, F.M.S.; Michael E. Flanigan, F.M.S.

Marist Brothers Champagnat Hall Community, 4300 Murdock Ave., Bronx, 10466. Tel: 718-994-4227. Bros. John Bantz, Dir.; Joseph Cerin Balet; Valerian Doiron; Peter Leonard; Simeon Gerald; Dennis Buckley; Francis Hughes; Godfrey Robertson; John Colbert; Kenneth Marino; James Gaffney; Robert Leclerc; Denis Caverley; Vincent Xavier; George L. Mathews; Christopher Shannon; Thomas Simmons; Frederick Sambor; Eugene Birmingham.

Marist Residence, 156 E. 38th St., 10016. Tel: 212-889-1176. Bros. James Devine, Dir.; Matthew Snowden; Patrick Tyrrell; James Kearney.

Marist Residence, 143 W. 87th St., 10024. Tel: 212-362-4039. Bros. Donnell Neary, Dir.; Anthony Iazzetti; Gerald Doherty; Thomas Schady.

Marist Provincial House, 26 First Ave., Pelham, 10803. Tel: 914-738-1218. Bros. Patrick McNamara, Prov.; Dermot Healy, Asst. Prov.; Thomas Long; Vincent B. Moriarty.

Marist Brothers, 40 S. Hamilton St., Poughkeepsie, 12601. Tel: 914-471-4077. Bros. George DiCarluccio, Dir.; James Stevens; Lawrence Gordon; Lawrence Lavallee.

Marist Brothers, 2 Eden Ter., Poughkeepsie, 12601-4803. Tel: 914-471-8354. Bros. John Nash, Dir.; Michael Williams.

Maryknoll House, 121 E. 39th St., 10016. Tel: 212-697-4470. Catholic Foreign Mission Society. Bros. Donald Miriani, M.M.; Brendan Corkery, M.M.

Murray-Weigel Hall, 515 E. Fordham Rd., 10458-5004. Tel: 718-430-4900; Fax: 718-365-8650. Revs. Gerald J. McMahon, S.J., Supr.; Edward C. Lynch, S.J., Min.; Joseph C. McKenna, S.J., Sub Min.; Bro. Gerard W. Schade, S.J., Infirmary; Revs. Thomas E. Ambrose, S.J.; Edward J. Berbusse, S.J.; Andrew J. Brady, S.J.; John E. Browning, S.J.; James F. Coleman, S.J.; John F.X. Condon, S.J.; Eugene K. Culhane, S.J.; Theodore J. Cunnion, S.J.; Paul J. Curtin, S.J.; James A. Daly, S.J.; Roy A. Drake, S.J.; George F. Driscoll, S.J.; Richard P. English, S.J.; John K. Fahey, S.J.; John L. Farrand, S.J.; William J. Farrell, S.J.; William J. Farricker, S.J.; James J. Fedigan, S.J.; James J. Finley, S.J.; William J. Gleason, S.J.; Robert J. Haskins, S.J.; Edwin C. Haungs, S.J.; Lawrence B. Hill, S.J.; John F. Hoek, S.J.; Henry A. Hoffen, S.J.; Anton M. Knees, S.J.; Joseph V. Landy, S.J.; William G. Lawlor, S.J.; Howard A. McCaffrey, S.J.; John McConnell, S.J.; Thomas F. McGann, S.J.; James J. McGinley, S.J.; Stephen J. Meany, S.J.; John A. Morrison, S.J.; John A. Nicholson, S.J.; Robert Jerome O'Connell, S.J.; Robert John O'Connell, S.J.; Richard J. Pendergast, S.J.; Eugene J. Quigley, S.J.; William E. Rively, S.J.; Peter J. Roslovich, S.J.; Joseph D. Ryan, S.J.; Joseph B. Schuyler, S.J.; Gary W. Schwartzkopf, S.J.; David E. Sippel, S.J.; Louis E. Soloman, S.J.; Francis J. Tierney, S.J.; Richard F. Timone, S.J.; Adalbert Umwech, S.J. (CI); James J. Wheeler, S.J.; Bros. Stephen J. Andrews, S.J.; Sebastian Boccabella, S.J.; Gerald F. Boyle, S.J.; Ignatius J. Fitzroy, S.J.; Sidney C. Saucier, S.J.; Carl J. Seitz, S.J. Priests 53; Brothers 7.

Our Lady of Consolation Residence, 3103 Arlington Ave., Corner of W. 231st St., Bronx, 10463. Tel: 718-548-0889. Rev. Charles R. Klein, Dir.; Most Rev. Austin B. Vaughan; Rev. Msgr. Thomas V. Gallagher; Rev. Msgr. William Higgins; Rev. Msgr. Hugh J. Rooney; Revs. Joseph P. Adamo; William E. Kelly; Francis J. Molony; Eugene P. O'Hara; Maurice C. Slattery; Humbert D. Pisanelli. In res. Rev. Stanislaus K. Treu, O.S.A.

Padua Friary, 151 Thompson St., 10012. Tel: 212-254-9553. Revs. Francis X. D'Alessandro, O.F.M., Guardian, Prov. Treas.; John-Marie Cassese, O.F.M., Vicar, Prov. Archivist & Chronicler; Bro. Luke Storino, O.F.M., Prov. Bookkeeper; Revs. Marion Cascino, O.F.M., FMU Prom.; Emmanuel Faraone, O.F.M.; Sebastian Buccellato, O.F.M.; George Mazzocchia, O.F.M.; Peter Walsh, O.F.M.

Pallottine Fathers, Society of the Catholic Apostolate, 414 E. 116th St., 10029. Revs. Peter J. Rofrano, S.A.C.; Severino Dominicis, S.A.C., Mt. Carmel Society & Catholic Apostolate Assoc.; Girolamo D'Ambrosi, S.A.C.; Tony Kelly, S.A.C., Spanish Apostolate. Total Assisted 300; Total Staff 15.

Passionist Spiritual Center, 5801 Palisade Ave., Riverdale, 10471. Very Rev. John Powers, C.P., Rector; Revs. Benedict Berlo, C.P.; Richard Scheiner, C.P.; Donald Ware, C.P., Retreat Dir.; Bros. Damian Carroll, C.P.; James Johnson, C.P.; Terence Skorka, C.P.

Pope John Paul II Residence, 603 First Ave., 10016. Tel: 212-686-3483. Rev. James S. Pfeiffer, Dir.; Rev. Msgr. Joseph J. Quinn; Revs. Martin Connolly; Dominic Jacolino; John B. Vala; Thomas J. Darby; William J. Kennedy; Harry Tiercelin; Andrew T. Magee; Rev. Msgr. Edward J. Reynolds; Rev. Msgr. Joseph M. Santulin; Rev. John P. Larkin.

Pope Paul VI Residence.
Frances Schervier Long Term Home Health Care. 2975 Independence Ave., Bronx, 10463. Rev. Albert Pellicane, C.P.

St. Catherine of Siena Priory, 411 E. 68th St., 10021. Tel: 212-988-8300; Fax: 212-988-6918. Very Rev. Christopher Johnson, O.P., Prior; Revs. Vincent Ferrer McHenry, O.P., Subprior; John Jerome Conroy, O.P.; Patrick Francis Connolly, O.P.; John Thaddeus Murphy, O.P.; Robert Philip Fitzsimmons, O.P.; Bartholomew Paul Fu, O.P.; George Lawrence Concordia, O.P.; Frank Bede Shipps, O.P.

St. Clare Friary, 440 W. 36th St., 10018.
E-mail: allgoode@aol.com
Revs. James E. Goode, O.F.M., Ph.D., Dir. of Solid Ground, A Franciscan Ministry with American Families; Stephen Caforio, O.F.M.; Placid Stroike, O.F.M., Chap., Covenant House. Total in Residence 3; Total Staff 2.

St. Crispin Friary. Franciscan Friars of the Renewal, 420 E. 156th St., Bronx, 10455. Tel: 718-665-2441. Revs. Robert Lombardo, C.F.R., Local Servant; Terry Messer, C.F.R., Vicar; Benedict J. Groeschel, C.F.R.; Stanley Fortuna, C.F.R. Priests 4; Brothers 5.

St. Ignatius Loyola Residence, 53 E. 83rd St., 10028. Tel: 212-288-6200. Revs. Arthur C. Bender, S.J., Rector; James F. O'Brien, S.J., Minister; William J. Bergen, S.J.; Vincent L. Biagi, S.J.; Gerard E. Braun, S.J.; Edwin J. Brooks, S.J.; Bro. John J. Campbell, S.J.; Revs. James R. Carney, S.J.; Francis J. Cosgrove, S.J.; Joseph S. Costantino; James J. Curry, S.J.; Joseph A. Dorgan, S.J.; Francis K. Drolet, S.J.; Stephen V. Duffy, S.J.; Francis X. Elsinghorst, S.J.; Thomas H. Feely, S.J.; Kenneth J. Gavin, S.J.; Charles F. Gilley, S.J.; Mark Hallinan, S.J.; Timothy A. Healey, S.J.; Anthony F. LaBau, S.J.; Joseph A. Latella, S.J.; Thomas D. McCall, S.J.; J. Thomas McClain, S.J. (Detroit); Bro. Jerome P. Menkhaus, S.J.; Revs. Walter F. Modrys, S.J.; Daniel G. O'Hare, S.J.; Joseph J. Papaj, S.J.; Eugene J. Prior, S.J.; Thomas S. Prout, S.J.; William J. Scanlon, S.J.; Bro. Gilbert J. Scott, S.J.; Revs. Thomas E. Smith, S.J.; Paul J. Tabor, S.J. (BO); William T. Wood, S.J.

St. Joseph's Friary. (Franciscan Friars of the Renewal), 523 W. 142nd St., 10031. Tel: 212-234-9089. (Novitiate). Rev. Glenn Sudano, C.F.R., Local Servant & Novice Dir. Novices 17.

St. Vincent de Paul Residence, 900 Intervale Ave., 10459. Total Assisted 3,120; Total Staff 8.

St. Vincent Ferrer Priory, 869 Lexington Ave., 10021. Tel: 212-744-2080; Fax: 212-327-3011. Dominican Friars Provincial House (Province of St. Joseph). Very Revs. Norman Alfred Haddad, O.P., Prov.; James Boniface Ramsey, O.P., Prior; Kevin Dominic Robb, O.P., Vicar Prov. & Socius; Revs. Albert Augustine Caprio, O.P., Prov. Treas.; John Peter Gerhard, O.P., Subprior; John James Sullivan, O.P.; Joaquin Bernardo, O.P. (Spain); William Robert Gannon, O.P.; Raymond Ferrer Halligan, O.P.; Deacon Edward Thomas Aquinas Dolan, O.P.; Bros. Bernard Christopher McCabe, O.P.; John Damian McCarthy, O.P.
Priests assigned but serving elsewhere: Revs. John Aedan McKeon, O.P.; Alan Augustine Evans, O.P.; James Moneta Moyna, O.P.; Robert William Vaughn, O.P.; Ronald Henery, O.P.; Peter John Cameron, O.P.; Joseph Hugh Mulhern, O.P.; Robert Urban Sharkey, O.P.; John Aquinas Farren, O.P.; John Patrick Burchill, O.P.; Joseph Anthony Scordo, O.P.; John Patrick McGuire, O.P.

Vincentian Fathers, 1834 Third Ave., 10029. Tel: 212-289-5589; Fax: 212-289-8321. Legal Title: *Padres Paules Community (Vincentians) Inc.* Revs. Victor Elia, C.M., Supr.; Candido Arrizurieta, C.M.; Santiago Lluch, C.M.

West Side Jesuit Community, 220 West 98th St., 10025. Tel: 212-866-6156.
E-mail: moore@murray.fordham.edu
Revs. Daniel J. Berrigan, S.J.; W. Alan Briceland, S.J.; Robert E. Carter, S.J.; Owen W. Daley, S.J.; Theodore V. Francois, S.J.; Gerald T. Huyett, S.J.; Robert J. Keck, S.J.; Jose Magadia, S.J.; Bro. Edward L. McCarthy, S.J.; Revs. William McNichols, S.J.; John G. McSherry, S.J.; Donald J. Moore, S.J., Supr.; Edward J. Murphy, S.J.; Peter Murray, S.J.; Enrico Raulli, S.J.; Joseph Roccosalvo, S.J.; Gary G. Seibert, S.J.; Robert Springer, S.J.; David S. Toolan, S.J.; Edward G. Zogby, S.J.

Xavier Jesuit Community, 30 West 16th St., 10011. Tel: 212-924-7900; Fax: 212-337-7545. Revs. Donald C. Gannon, S.J., Rector; Alfred E. Caruana, S.J.; Bro. Daniel M. Hoey, S.J.; Revs. James P. Jurich, S.J.; Joseph G. Musselman, S.J.; Michael V. Tueth, S.J.; Harold F. O'Donnell, S.J.; Leo Peter Prengaman, S.J.; Joseph J. Walter, S.J.; James J. Yannarell, S.J.; David P. Marcotte, S.J.; Edward J. McMahon, S.J.; Louis P. Sogliuzzo, S.J.; Henry J. Zenorini, S.J.; James A. Catalano, S.J.

Jesuit Residence. 126 W. 17th St., 10011. Tel: 212-620-0537. Revs. William P. Cain, S.J.; Thomas E. Clarke, S.J.; John P. Bucki, S.J., Supr.; Bro. Michael E. Breault, S.J.
(For list of faculty see the high school listing for Xavier High School).

BRONX. *Idente Missionaries - Santa Maria Residence*, 2352 St. Raymond Ave., 10462. Tel: 718-828-2380. Revs. Fernando Real, M.ID., Prov. Supr.; Robert Badillo, M.ID., Formation Dir.; Eduardo Rodriguez, M.ID., Residence Rector.

Our Lady of the Angels Friary. (Franciscan Friars of the Renewal), 423 E. 155th St., 10455. Tel: 718-993-3405. (Postulant House). Rev. Conrad Osterhout, C.F.R., Local Servant & Postulant Dir. Postulants 12.

CORNWALL. *Jogues Retreat*, Mailing Address: P.O. Box F, 12518. Tel: 914-534-7570; Fax: 914-534-3276. Revs. Herbert T. Kane, S.J., Supr. & Guest Master; Edward H. McGlinchy, S.J., Treas.

ESOPUS. *Marist Brothers F.M.S. (Province of St. Joseph)*, Mailing Address: P.O. Box 197, 12429. Bros. Henry J. Sawicki, F.M.S., Dir.; Donald Nugent, F.M.S., Retreat Dir. Brothers 7.

Redemptorist Priests and Brothers C.Ss.R. (Province of Baltimore), Mount Saint Alphonsus, Rte. 9W, P.O. Box 219, 12429. Tel: 914-384-6550. Very Rev. John G. Kingsbury, C.Ss.R., Rector; Bro. Robert Skinner, C.Ss.R.; Revs. Francis J. Gargani, C.Ss.R.; Dennis Kelleher, C.Ss.R.; Raymond Weithman, C.Ss.R., Parish Missionary; Kevin Milton, C.Ss.R. In res., Revs. Eugene J. Grohe, C.Ss.R.; John Kennington, C.Ss.R.; Paul A. Miller, C.Ss.R.; W. Richard Bonner, C.Ss.R. Priests 9; Brothers 1.

GARRISON. *Franciscan Friars of the Atonement*, Graymoor, P.O. Box 300, 10524-0300. Tel: 914-424-3671; 3672; 3673; Fax: 914-424-3635. Revs. Fred Alvarez, S.A.; Norman Boyd, S.A.; Bros. Joseph Buettner, S.A.; John Joseph Bursis, S.A.; Rev. Xavier Butler, S.A.; Bros. Raphael Colaciello, S.A.; Jeremiah Dalton, S.A.; Revs. Daniel Egan, S.A.; Joseph Egan, S.A.; Walter Gagne, S.A.; Bros. Francis Gutman, S.A.; Stephen Hanley, S.A.; Revs. Simeon Heine, S.A.; Alphonsus Hoban, S.A.; Pius F. Keating, S.A.; Alexander Kelliher, S.A.; Bonaventure Koelzer, S.A.; Thomas Orians, S.A.; Bros. Chrysostom Lane, S.A.;

Pius MacIsaac, S.A.; Joseph O'Gara, S.A.; Gregory Lucrezia, S.A.; Dominic McDonnell, S.A.; James McHugh, S.A.; Revs. Kevin McMorrow, S.A.; Noel McSweeney, S.A.; Cuthbert Micali, S.A.; Charles Murphy, S.A.; Owen Murphy, S.A.; William Murphy, S.A., Guardian, Senior Community; Bro. Theodore Novak, S.A.; Rev. Mark O'Connor, S.A.; Bro. Rocco Pace, S.A.; Revs. Normand Prevost, S.A.; George Ribeiro, S.A.; Bosco Schmidt, S.A.; Bros. Denis Sennett, S.A.; Edmund Sheridan, S.A.; Richard Skolinski, S.A.; Rev. Timothy Sullivan, S.A.; Bro. Robert Taylor, S.A.; Revs. Peter Taran, S.A.; Patrick Walsh, S.A.; Bros. Liam Young, S.A.; Joseph Marie Zakia, S.A.

St. Francis of Assisi Novitiate, Graymoor, P.O. Box 300, 10524-0300. Rev. Henry Marchese, S.A., Novice Dir.; Bros. Raymond Saville, S.A.; William Weeks, S.A. Novices 3.

St. Christopher's Inn, Graymoor, P.O. Box 150, 10524-0150. Rev. Bernard Palka, S.A., Dir.; Bros. Thomas Banacki, S.A.; George Clay, S.A.; Donald Perry, S.A.; Benedict Terasawa, S.A.; Revs. Robert Warren, S.A.; Charles Angell, S.A.

Graymoor Ecumenical and Interreligious Institute, 475 Riverside Dr., Room 1960, New York, 10115-1999. Tel: 212-870-2342; 870-2330; Fax: 212-870-2001. Rev. Elias D. Mallon, S.A., Dir.

Generalate of the Franciscan Friars of the Atonement-St. James Friary, Mailing Address: P.O. Box 5, 10524-0005. Tel: 914-424-3539; Fax: 914-424-3978. Very Rev. Emil F. Tomaskovic, S.A., Minister Gen.; Rev. Thomas Gumprecht, S.A., Vicar General; Bros. Peter Gannon, S.A.; Raymond Saville, S.A., Sec. Gen.; Revs. Bernard Palka, S.A., Treas. Gen.; Elias D. Mallon, S.A., 2nd General Councillor; Henry Marchese, S.A., 3rd General Councillor; Dennis Polanco, S.A., 4th General Councillor; Bro. William Martyn, S.A., Procurator General to the Holy See.

Friar-Priests serving in Japan, Diocese of Yokohama: Revs. Pacificus Von Essen, S.A.; Peter Katsuno, S.A.; Fidelis Fujihara, S.A. (Japan); Cyril Colton, S.A.; Charles Brozat, S.A.; Joseph Hiramatsu, S.A. (Japan), Regl. Min.; Gabriel Shiraki, S.A. (Japan); Damian Sato, S.A.; Eric Tampe, S.A.

Friars on assignments or studies: Revs. Pius F. Keating, S.A.; William Linakis, S.A.; Joseph Scerbo, S.A.

Friars stationed in England: Revs. Robert Mercer, S.A. (England); Michael Seed, S.A. (England); Emmanuel Sullivan, S.A.; Bro. Gerard Hand, S.A.

Friars stationed in Canada, Archdiocese of Vancouver: Rev. Celestine Leahy, S.A.; Bros. Savio McNeice, S.A.; Daniel Houde, S.A.; Timothy MacDonald, S.A.

Diocese of London, Ontario, Canada: Revs. Damian MacPherson, S.A. (Canada); Walter Gagne, S.A.; Michael Graham, S.A.; Paschal Breau, S.A. (Canada).

Archdiocese of Toronto, Canada: Revs. John Kiesling, S.A., Holy Cross Parish, Toronto; Peter Tomaino, S.A.; Timothy MacDonald, S.A.; Bede MacEachen, S.A. (Canada); Bro. Guy Gartland, S.A.; Rev. Brian Terry, S.A.; Bros. Denis Burgelin, S.A.; Philip Buckley, S.A.; Daniel Sylvain, S.A.

Archdiocese of Halifax, N.S. Canada: Revs. Arthur Gouthro, S.A. (Canada); David Poirier, S.A.

Friars in Military Service: Rev. William Dillon, S.A.

Friars residing in Italy: Rev. James Puglisi, S.A.

St. Joseph's Rehabilitation Center, Inc., Saranac Lake.

Graymoor Ecumenical & Interreligious Institute. (G.E.I.I.), 475 Riverside Dr., Room 1960, New York, 10115-1999. Tel: 212-870-2330; Fax: 212-870-2001. Legal Titles: *Friars of the Atonement, Inc.; St. Christopher's Inn, Inc.; Union That Nothing Be Lost, Inc.; St. Joseph's Rehabilitation Center, Inc.; Paul Wattson Human Resources Fund, Inc.*

St. Christopher's Friary, Mailing Address: Box 150, 10524-0150. Tel: 914-424-3616. Revs. Charles Angell, S.A., Guardian; Robert Warren, S.A.; Bros. George Clay, S.A.; Donald Perry, S.A.; Benedict Terasawa, S.A.; Thomas Banacki, S.A.; Charles Kenny, S.A.

St. Francis Friary (Glenclyffe).

Capuchin Franciscan Province of St. Mary, New York, New England. Mailing Address: Box 191, Garrison (Glenclyffe), 10524. Tel: 914-424-3488. Web site: http://www.capuchins.org

Revs. David Couturier, O.F.M.Cap., Center of Structural Conversion; Anthony Vetrano, O.F.M.Cap., Youth & Family Ministries, Vicar; Robert Abbatiello, O.F.M.Cap., Guardian & Vocation Ministry; Bros. Francis Liermann, O.F.M.Cap.; Antonine Lizama, O.F.M.Cap.

HARTSDALE. *Mill Hill Fathers Residence*, 222 W. Hartsdale Ave., 10530-1667. Tel: 914-682-0645; Fax: 914-682-0862. Very Rev. Terence J. Lee, M.H.M., Regl. Rep.; Revs. Cornelius M. Snoeren, M.H.M.; Emile Frische, M.H.M.; Bro. Theodore Tolboom, M.H.M.

JAMAICA ESTATES. *Paulist Fathers Generalate*, 86-11 Midland Pkwy., 11432. Tel: 718-291-5995; Fax: 718-291-6646. Very Rev. Francis P. DeSiano, C.S.P., Pres.; Revs. Robert J. O'Donnell, C.S.P.; Thomas W. Jones, C.S.P.; Edward D. Whitley, C.S.P.

Paulist Priests at Paulist Foundations outside the U.S.: Via Venti Settembre 14, Rome, Italy, 00187. Revs. Paul G. Robichand, C.S.P.; Dennis W. Hickey, C.S.P.; Gregora Apparcel, C.S.P., 659 Markham St., Toronto, Ontario, Canada, M6G 2M1. Revs. Michael P. Kerrigan, C.S.P.; Ronald A. Franco, C.S.P.; Thomas R. Marshall, C.S.P.; Thomas P. Murphy, C.S.P.; Deacon Richard J. Boudreau, C.S.P.

Military Chaplains: Revs. Gregory G. Caiazzo, C.S.P.; Thomas P. Hall, C.S.P.

On Special Assignment in the U.S. and Abroad: Revs. Edward R. Donovan, C.S.P.; Justin J. McCormick, C.S.P.; Mark-David Janus, C.S.P.; Thomas A. Kane, C.S.P.; Joachim Lally, C.S.P.; Norman J. O'Connor, C.S.P.; Martin J. O'Looney, C.S.P.; Thomas F. Stransky, C.S.P.

Retired: Revs. Charles W. Albright, C.S.P.; Walter Anthony, C.S.P.; Robert W. Baer, C.S.P.; Wilfred Brimley, C.S.P.; William J. Cantwell, C.S.P.; Ralph T. Carpenter, C.S.P.; John A. Carr, C.S.P.; Thomas E. Comber, C.S.P.; Leo E. Conlin, C.S.P.; Phillip J. Cunningham, C.S.P.; Robert P. Curtis, C.S.P.; Wilfred Dewan, C.S.P.; Francis X. Diskin, C.S.P.; John P. Donahue, C.S.P.; Charles A. Donovan, C.S.P.; Harry J. Dooley, C.S.P.; J. Aloysius Farrell, C.S.P.; James F. Fisher, C.S.P.; Joseph P. Flynn, C.S.P.; Donal F. Forrester, C.S.P.; Harold J. Foye, C.S.P.; Joseph T. Griffin, C.S.P.; Joseph M. Hanly, C.S.P.; George F. Helmich, C.S.P.; Donald E. Howard, C.S.P.; William J. Kenney, C.S.P.; James B. Lloyd, C.S.P.; Edward J. Lyons, C.S.P.; Stanley F. MacNevin, C.S.P.; Edward A. Maher, C.S.P.; William F. Manning, C.S.P.; Thomas J. Marley, C.S.P.; Harold J. Masterson, C.S.P.; Edward J. McDonald, C.S.P.; Neil J. McEleney, C.S.P.; Kenneth H. McGuire, C.S.P.; Louis F. McKernan, C.S.P.; James F. McLean, C.S.P.; James D. McNulty, C.S.P.; Robert P. Michele, C.S.P.; John Dennis Mitchell, C.S.P.; Ernest C. Mort, C.S.P.; John W. Mulhall, C.S.P.; Thomas P. Murphy, C.S.P.; Robert A. O'Donnell, C.S.P.; Edward P. O'Hern, C.S.P.; Harold J. Powers, C.S.P.; Robert F. Quinn, C.S.P.; John C. Reynolds, C.S.P.; Vincent J. Sampietro, C.S.P.; Warren H. Seedorf, C.S.P.; Arthur J. Spear, C.S.P.; Robert J. Stulting, C.S.P.; Walter J. Sullivan, C.S.P.; Joseph F. Troy, C.S.P.; Rudolph T. Vorisek, C.S.P.; James G. Walsh, C.S.P.; Richard J. Walsh, C.S.P.; Charles S. White, C.S.P.; Clarence E. Wilson, C.S.P.; Edward D. Wroblewski, C.S.P.

On Leave: Revs. Gregory G. Caiazzo, C.S.P.; Philip W. Hart, C.S.P.; Albert K.H. Kim, C.S.P.; James Kolb, C.S.P.; Kevin F. Novack, C.S.P.; Gregory A. Romanski, C.S.P.; Leslie M. Sieg, C.S.P.; Robert A. Sirico, C.S.P.; Joseph F.X. Smith, C.S.P.; Timothy F. Sullivan, C.S.P.; Thomas M. Tureman, C.S.P.; James M. Utendorf, C.S.P.; Nathan Wilburn, C.S.P.; Christopher P. Witt, C.S.P.

MARYKNOLL. *M.M.A.F. Charitable Trust*, Treasury Office, P.O. Box 306, 10545-0306. Tel: 914-941-7590; Fax: 914-941-2411. Rev. Richard B. Callahan, M.M., Contact Person.

Maryknoll Fathers and Brothers, 10545-0305. Tel: 914-941-7590; Fax: 914-762-0316. General Council: Revs. Raymond J. Finch, M.M., Supr. Gen.; Jeremiah R. Burr, M.M., Vicar Gen.; Thomas P. Henehan, M.M., Asst. Gen.; Michael J. Snyder, M.M., Asst. Gen.; Bro. Wayne J. Fitzpatrick, M.M., Asst. Gen.; Revs. Richard B. Callahan, M.M., Treas. Gen.; Norbert J. Rans, M.M., Asst. Treas.; Joseph P. LaMar, M.M., Asst. Treas.; Edward J. Manning, M.M., Asst. Treas.; Jose A. Aramburu, M.M.; Joseph B. Arsenault, M.M.; Brian Barrons, M.M.; Richard A. Bell, M.M.; Joseph E. Brannigan, M.M.; John T. Brinkman, M.M.; Robert J. Carleton, M.M.; Peter L. Chabot, M.M.; John E. Conway, M.M.; William S. Donnelly, M.M.; Edward V. Davis, M.M.; Wayman P. Deasy, M.M.; Stephen T. DeMott, M.M.; Thomas F. Donnelly, M.M.; Edward M. Dougherty, M.M.; Michael A. Duggan, M.M.; Emile E. Dumas, M.M.; George A. Egan, M.M.; Joseph Fedora, M.M.; William B. Frazier, M.M.; William J. Galvin, M.M.; Charles F. Girnius, M.M.; Fidelis C. Goodman, M.M.; Ronald L. Green, M.M.; J. Gerard Greene, M.M.; John K. Halbert, M.M.; Scott T. Harris, M.M.; Edward A. Hayes, M.M.; Charles T. Huegelmeyer, M.M.; James H. Kroeger, M.M.; Daniel P. Jensen, M.M.; David J. Jones, M.M.; Stephen P. Judd, M.M.; John M. Kaserow, M.M.; Thomas H. Keefe, M.M.; Joseph P. LaMar, M.M.; Carmen G. La Mazza, M.M.; Peter M. Le Jacq, M.M.; Francis J. Leong, M.M.; Lawrence J. Lewis, M.M.; Robert J. Lloyd, M.M.; Martin J. Lowery, M.M.; John J. McAuley, M.M.; Leo F. McCarthy, M.M.; William D. McCarthy, M.M.; William T. Madden, M.M.; John P. Martin, M.M.; John J. Mihelko, M.M.; William F. Mullan, M.M.; Edward J. Manning, M.M.; George F. Painter, M.M.; John A. Rich, M.M.; Alan J. Ryan, M.M.; James M. Scanlon, M.M.; Steven Scherrer, M.M.; Leo B. Shea, M.M.; Michael A. Simone, M.M.; Leo J. Sommer, M.M.; John H. Spain, M.M.; Raymond F. Sullivan, M.M.; Joseph L. Thaler, M.M.; Eugene A. Thalman, M.M.; Kenneth F. Thesing, M.M.; Kevin T. Thomas, M.M.; William J. Tokus, M.M.; Joseph W. Towle, M.M.; John C. Tynan, M.M.; Joseph R. Veneroso, M.M.; Edward F. Walck, M.M.; David I. Walsh, M.M.; John J. Walsh, M.M.; Michael P. Walsh; Edward M. Wroblewski, M.M.

Maryknoll Fathers and Brothers. 728 Kitchawan Rd., Ossining, 10562. Rev. Brian Barrons, M.M., Mailing Address: 10545-0305. Tel: 914-923-3711.

Maryknoll St. Teresa's Residence, 10545-0321. Tel: 914-941-4240; 941-4247. Staff: Revs. Thomas B. Kirchmyer, M.M., Dir.; James P. Nieckarz, M.M., Asst. Dir.; John P. Hudert, M.M. In res., Revs. Donald W. Aubry, M.M.; Joseph E. Avery, M.M.; John E. Bergwall, M.M.; Donat W. Chatigny, M.M.; William J. Coleman, M.M.; William J. Eggleston, M.M.; Albert V. Fedders, M.M.; Gregory J. Gilmartin, M.M.; Thomas C. Higgins, M.M.; Gregory J. Keegan, M.M.; August R. Kircher, M.M.; Most Rev. William F. Kupfer, M.M.; Revs. Theodore M. Kuechmann, M.M.; J. Edmund McClear, M.M.; Thomas F. McDermott, M.M.; Edwin R. McDevitt, M.M.; Michael J. McKillop, M.M.; Robert J. Reiley, M.M.; Bernard F. Wieland, M.M.; Most Rev. John W. Comber, M.M.; Revs. Gervis J. Coxen, M.M.; Allan J. Dennis, M.M.; Christopher W. Gibbons, M.M.; Most Rev. Richard J. Ham, M.M.; Revs. Eugene F. Higgins, M.M.; Raymond C. Hohlfeld, M.M.; Robert E. Lee, M.M.; Arthur C. Kiernan, M.M.; Most Rev. William F. Kupfer, M.M.; Revs. John F. Fay, M.M.; Joseph P. Meaney, M.M.; Francis S. Meccia, M.M.; William R. McCarthy, M.M.; James E. McLaughlin, M.M.; George McPeak, M.M.; John J. O'Brien, M.M.; Thomas P. O'Rourke, M.M.; Dennis J. Slattery, M.M.; James F. Smith, M.M.; Paul J. Sommer, M.M.; Joseph E. VanDenBogaard, M.M.; John Kelly Walsh, M.M.; Bernard F. Wieland, M.M.; Robert H. Winkels, M.M.

Special Assignments: Revs. Edward R. Arnold, M.M.; Patrick A. Bergin, M.M.; Ronald J. Boccieri, M.M.; Stephen R. Booth, M.M.; Roy L. Bourgeois, M.M.; Joseph E. Brannigan, M.M.; John T. Brinkman, M.M.; Curtis R. Cadorette, M.M.; James A. Collignon, M.M.; George G. Cotter, M.M.; Joseph F. Croghan, M.M.; Donald J. Doherty, M.M.; Paul J. Duffy, M.M.; Joseph Fedora, M.M.; Francis J. Flynn, M.M.; Bartholomew J. Galvin, M.M.; Most Rev. Hugo M. Gerbermann, M.M.; Revs. David J. Jones, M.M.; Richard S. Kardian, M.M.; John E. Keegan, M.M.; Edward R. Killackey, M.M.; John R. King, M.M.; Joseph R. Lang, M.M.; Daniel A. Lanza, M.M.; Robert L. Mackesy, M.M.; Thomas J. Maney, M.M.; John L. Martin, M.M.; William E. McCarthy, M.M.; Thomas P. McDonnell, M.M.; John J. Meaney, M.M.; George M. Mikolajczyk, M.M.; William H. Moeschler, M.M.; Peter P. Mullen, M.M.; Laurence T. Murphy, M.M.; James B. Nagle, M.M.; Albert J. Nevins, M.M.; Raymond J. Nobiletti, M.M.; Richard E. Paulissen, M.M.; Raymond G. Pierini, M.M.; Joseph S. Pulaski, M.M.; Albert I. Reymann, M.M.; Patrick J. Ryan, M.M.; J. Daniel Schneider, M.M.; Edward R. Schoellmann, M.M.; Daniel J. Sherman, M.M.; Joseph S. Smith, M.M.; Donald R. Steed, M.M.; Lionel G. Trudel, M.M.; Wayne T. Weinlader, M.M.; Walter W. Winrich, M.M.; C. Thomas Wilcox, M.M.; John F. Wymes, M.M.

The Maryknoll Fathers & Brothers Charitable Trust, 10545. Trustees: Revs. Richard B. Callahan, M.M.; Edward V. Davis, M.M.; Wayman P. Deasy, M.M.; Thomas H. Keefe, M.M.; Thomas B. Kirchmyer, M.M.; William F. Mullan, M.M.; Bro. Adrian Mazuchowski, M.M.

Maryknoll Fathers and Brothers. 586 McLean Ave., 10705. Tel: 914-963-0270. Revs. Alan J. Ryan, M.M.; John C. Tynan, M.M.; Carmen G. La Mazza, M.M.

MIDDLETOWN. *Brandsma Priory*, Carmelite Interprovincial Novitiate, Carmelite Dr., P.O. Box 2127, 10940-0439. Tel: 914-343-2959. Carmelite Friars (North American Prov. of St. Elias and Most Pure Heart of Mary Province). Revs. David McEvoy, O.Carm., Novice Dir.; Paul Denault, O.Carm., Vicar & Novice Dir. Novices 3.

St. Albert's Priory, Mailing Address: P.O. Box 868, Carmelite Dr., 10940-0868. Tel: 914-344-2220. Rev. Richard Champigny, O.Carm., Dir., Natl. Shrine of Our Lady of Mt. Carmel & Prior, St. Albert's Community, Tel: 914-344-0876; Fax: 914-344-0093. Revs. Albert Daly, O.Carm.; Sean Reid, O.Carm.; Brendan Hourihan, O.Carm.; Very Rev. Richard Nagle, O.Carm.; Revs. Daniel F. Lynch, O.Carm.; Norbert P. Hansen, O.Carm.; Very Rev. Charles J. Haggerty, O.Carm.; Revs. Augustine Graap, O.Carm.; Patrick McGuigan, O.Carm.; Bro. James Andrews.

Provincial Offices: Carmelite Dr., P.O. Box 3079, 10940-3079. Carmelite Friars (North American

Prov. of St. Elias). Very Rev. Mario Esposito, O.Carm., Prior Prov. Tel: 914-344-2223; Revs. Paul Denault, O.Carm., Prov. Procurator. Tel: 914-344-2224; Michael Kissane, O.Carm., Vocation Dir. Tel: 914-344-2225; Very Rev. Matthias DesLauriers, O.Carm., Dir., Devel. Office. Tel: 914-344-0876.

MOUNT VERNON. *Kolbe Friary*, 274-280 W. Lincoln Ave., 10550. Franciscan Friars, Province of the Immaculate Conception. Bro. Angelo Monti, O.F.M., Guardian.

St. Bernardine of Siena Friary, 25 Laurel Ave., 10552-1018. Tel: 914-699-1221. Franciscan Friars, Province of Immaculate Conception. In res., Revs. Patrick D. Boyle, O.F.M., Guardian; Alban V. Montella, O.F.M., Vicar; Anthony P. Abate, O.F.M.; Benedict J. D'Alessandro, O.F.M.; John R. Scarangello, O.F.M. Priests 5.

NEW PALTZ. *St. Joseph Friary*, 34 S. Chestnut St., 12561. Tel: 914-255-5635; Fax: 914-255-5679. Capuchin Friars, Province of St. Mary. Revs. Michael Banks, O.F.M.Cap., Supr.; Barnabas Keck, O.F.M.Cap.; Knute Kenlon, O.F.M.Cap., Chap., Wallkill Correctional Facility; Bro. Timothy Jones, O.F.M.Cap., Chap., State University at New Paltz.

NEW ROCHELLE. *Brothers of Holy Cross of the Eastern Province of the United States of America, Inc.*, 85 Overlook Cir., 10804. Tel: 914-632-4468; 632-4469; Fax: 914-632-2490.
E-mail: gleasonjoh@aol.com
Bros. John Gleason, C.S.C., Prov.; Stephen LaMendola, C.S.C., Asst. Prov. & Councilor Schools; Peter Martin, C.S.C., Councilor for Fin. Svcs. Councilors: Bros. Mark Knightly, C.S.C.; John Thornton, C.S.C.; Paul Bednarczyk, C.S.C. In res., Bros. George Schmitz, C.S.C.; William Farrell, C.S.C.; John Nicpon, C.S.C.; Rev. Jack Replogle, S.J. Professed Brothers 6.

Holy Cross Brothers, Eastern Province, Charitable Trust, 85 Overlook Cir., 10804. Trustees: Bros. Peter Martin, C.S.C., Treas.; Renatus Foldenauer, C.S.C.; Richard Kiniry, C.S.C.; Stephen LaMendola, C.S.C.; George Schmitz, C.S.C.

Saint Joseph's Residence, Inc., 30 Montgomery Cir., 10804-4413. Tel: 914-633-6851; Fax: 914-633-5579. Congregation of Christian Brothers. Bros. James B. Moffett, C.F.C., Pres.; Robert J. Roepke, C.F.C., Vice Pres. Admin.; Thomas C. Higgins, Sec.; Thomas F. Feerick, Vice Pres. Finance. A facility of limited care for male religious. Total in Residence 18; Total Staff 4.

St. Patrick's Provincial House (Congregation of Christian Brothers), 21 Pryer Terr., 10804. Tel: 914-636-6194; Fax: 914-636-0021. Bros. James B. Moffett, C.F.C., Prov.; Brian M. Walsh, C.F.C., Deputy Prov. Consultors: Bros. Lawrence A. Killelea, C.F.C.; V. Gregory McNally, C.F.C.; J. Edward Roepke, C.F.C.; Vincent J. Dougherty, Prov. Treas.; James P. Hamilton, C.F.C., Dir. Vocations; H. Michael Delaney, C.F.C., Dir. Devel.; Charles F. Miller, C.F.C., Dir. Mission Education; A. Eugenio DeLorenzo, C.F.C., Dir. Archives; John J. McCarthy, C.F.C., Dir. Assoc.; S. Anthony Ferro, C.F.C., Dir. Communications; John W. Casey, C.F.C., Dir. Education; Kevin Griffith, C.F.C., Dir. Formation, St. Joseph Care Center, 30 Montgomery Cir., 10804. Tel: 914-633-6851. Limited facility for male religious. Brothers Living in Community 6; Limited Care Center Total in Residence 15; Total Staff 7.

Salesian Cooperators of St. John Bosco, 148 Main St., 10802. Tel: 914-636-4225. Denis Cahill, Prov. Coord.; Rev. Francis X. Aracil, S.D.B., Prov. Delegate.

Salesian Provincial House, 148 Main St., P.O. Box 639, 10802-0639. Tel: 914-636-4225; Fax: 914-636-0159.
E-mail: sdbsue@aol.com
Very Rev. Patrick Angelucci, S.D.B., Prov.; Revs. Javier Aracil, S.D.B.; Paul Aronica, S.D.B.; Edward Cappelletti, S.D.B.; James Chiosso, S.D.B.; Dennis Donovan, S.D.B., Vicar, Devel. Dir.; David Gonder, S.D.B., Prov. Treas.; Joseph Maffei, S.D.B.; Michael Mendl, S.D.B.; David Moreno, S.D.B., Supr.; Philip Pascucci, S.D.B.; Peter Pong, S.D.B.; Joseph Ros, S.D.B. (Antilles); Robert Savage, S.D.B.; Anthony Spano, S.D.B., Financial Admin.; Waclav Swierzbiolek, S.D.B.; Louis Vyoral, S.D.B.; Bros. Andrew Lacombe, S.D.B.; Charles Mayer, S.D.B.; Aldo Roman, S.D.B.; David Tierney, S.D.B. Priests 17; Brothers 4.

PELHAM MANOR. *St. Vincent's Residence*, 190 Mt. Tom Rd., 10803-3309. Tel: 914-738-6138. The Passionists. Revs. Leo J. Gorman, C.P., Supr.; Stephen Haslach, C.P.; Paschal Smith, C.P.; Vincent Youngberg, C.P.

RYE. *Legionaries of Christ*, 815 Boston Post Rd., 10580. Tel: 914-967-7403. Revs. Peter Hopkins, L.C., Supr.; William Slattery, L.C.; Bros. Thomas Rudkins, L.C.; Paul Clarke, L.C.

SCARBOROUGH. *Carmelite Fathers, NY Prov. of St. Elias*, Carmelite Priory, 3 Woodlea Ln., 10510. Tel: 914-762-3719. Revs. Timothy C. Donohue, O.Carm.; Joachim J. Snyder, O.Carm.

STATEN ISLAND. *Scalabrinian Missionaries*, 209 Flagg Pl., 10304. Tel: 718-351-0232. Scalabrinian Mission Center, The Center for Migration Studies; St. Charles Residence. Revs. Dominic Rodighiero, C.S., Supr. & Dir. Devel. Office; Lydio Tomasi, C.S., Dir. Center for Migration Studies. In res. Revs. James Viero, C.S.; Henry S. Gentile, C.S.; Bro. Louis Calisto, C.S.

SUFFERN. *Parish Mission Team Residence*, 38 Montebello Rd., 10901.
E-mail: pmteam@aol.com
Rev. Thomas P. Devery; Sr. Beth Ann Herrmann, O.S.F.; Jaime Rickert; Scott Krug; Barbara Dombroski. In res. Rev. Msgr. James S. Conlan; Jose Antonio Suarez; Katie Feeney.

TAPPAN. *St. Eliseus Priory*. (Carmelite Pre-novitiate), P.O. Box 27, 10983-0027. Tel: 914-359-5299; Fax: 914-359-0856.
E-mail: ocarmvoc@frontiernet.net
Web site: http://frontiernet.net/~ocarmvoc
Rev. Michael Kissane, O.Carm., Dir. Students 4.

Office of Lay Carmelites. (Carmelite Third Order). Tel: 914-359-0535. Rev. Brocard Connors, O.Carm., Dir.

WASSAIC. *Guardian Angel Chapel*, Mailing Address: Box 443, 12592. Tel: 914-877-6821, Ext. 3350. Rev. Brian Gallagher.

WEST PARK. *Congregation of Christian Brothers*, Santa Maria-on-Hudson, 12493. Tel: 914-384-6750. Bros. D. D. Crimmins, Supr.; W. S. Barry; J. L. Heathwood; P. C. Leavy; John F. Farrel, F.S.C. Total in Residence 5.

WHITE PLAINS. *St. Conrad Friary*, 30 Gedney Park Dr., 10605. Tel: 914-761-3008; Fax: 914-948-6429.
E-mail: NYNEPROV1@juno.com
Legal Titles: *The Province of St. Mary of the Capuchin Order.*; *Capuchin Friars International, Inc.* (For Finance). Provincial Headquarters of the Province of St. Mary of the Capuchin Order. Development Office: 210 W. 31st St., New York, 10001. Very Rev. Bernard Smith, O.F.M.Cap., Min. Prov.; Revs. Regis Armstrong, O.F.M.Cap., Vicar Prov.; Paul Steffan, O.F.M.Cap., Exec. Asst.; Jerome McHugh, O.F.M.Cap., Sec.-Treas.; Paul Tolve, O.F.M.Cap., Chap.; James Stewart, O.F.M.Cap., Chap.; Bro. Joseph Yakimovich, O.F.M.Cap., Asst. Sec.-Treas. Priests 6; Brothers 1. (Nature of Apostolate: Provincial Administration, Hospital, Prison, Preaching, Recruitment). Subject to the Provincial. Revs. Jose McCarthy, O.F.M.Cap., Puerto Rico; Gregory Reisert, O.F.M.Cap., Washington, DC; Brendan Buckley, O.F.M.Cap., Sabbatical; Michael Connolly, O.F.M.Cap., West Harrison, NY; Paul Engel, O.F.M.Cap., New York, NY; John Rathschmidt, O.F.M.Cap., Ossining, NY; Philip Fabiano, O.F.M.Cap., Sabbatical; Ephram Karwowski, O.F.M.Cap., Peoria, IL; George Dash, O.F.M.Cap., Queens, NY; Bro. Terence Taffe, O.F.M.Cap., Minneapolis, MN.
Serving in the Military: Rev. James Jones, O.F.M.Cap., Chap., U.S.A. Total in Residence 65; Total Staff 11.

YONKERS. *St. Clare Friary*, 110 Shonnard Pl., 10703. Tel: 914-423-2392. Capuchin Franciscan Friars, Province of St. Mary. Residence for senior friars. Revs. Senan Taylor, O.F.M.Cap., Vicar; Darius Devito, O.F.M.Cap., Guardian; Neal Kerrigan, O.F.M.Cap.; Donatus Goetz, O.F.M.Cap.; John Langweld, O.F.M.Cap.; Celsus Repole, O.F.M.Cap.; Sylvan J. Conover, O.F.M.Cap.; Charles Repole, O.F.M.Cap.; James McIntyre, O.F.M.Cap.; Bros. Bernard Frey, O.F.M.Cap.; Paul Murray, O.F.M.Cap.; Peter Reilley, O.F.M.Cap. Total in Residence 15; Total Staff 3.

St. Felix Friary. (Franciscan Friars of the Renewal), 15 Trinity Plaza, 10701. Tel: 914-476-7279. (House of Studies). Revs. Andrew D. Apostoli, C.F.R., Gen. Community Servant; Robert Stanion, C.F.R., Vicar; Bros. Richard Roemer, C.F.R.; Bernard Murphy, C.F.R.; Seraphin Mange, C.F.R.; Leo Fisher, C.F.R.

St. Leopold's Friary. (Franciscan Friars of the Renewal), 259 Nepperhan Ave., 10701-3461. Tel: 914-965-8143. (House of Studies). Bro. Michael Kmiotek, C.F.R., Local Servant; Rev. Herald Brock, C.F.R., Local Vicar; Bros. Fidelis Moscinski, C.F.R.; Angelus Marie Houle, C.F.R.; Thomas Cacciola, C.F.R.

[EE] CONVENTS AND RESIDENCES OF SISTERS

NEW YORK. *Academy of St. Dorothy*. 1305 Hylan Blvd., Staten Island, 10305. Tel: 718-987-0677. Sisters of St. Dorothy. Sr. Mary Ann Keegan, S.S.D., Coord. Sisters 9.

Blessed Trinity Missionary Cenacle, 414 E. 14th St., 10009. Tel: 212-475-1450. Missionary Social Work and Parish Ministry. Family Division of Catholic Charities of New York, Campus Ministry N.Y.U. Missionary Servants of the Most Blessed Trinity 10; Total Assisted 3,873; Total Staff 6. Catholic Charities Family and Children's Services, 530 Grand St., 10002.

Carmelite Sisters Teresas of St. Joseph, Inc., 249 W. 14th St., 10011. Sr. Angela Perez, Supr.

Convent of Our Lady of the Presentation, 419 Woodrow Rd., 10312. Tel: 718-356-2121. Motherhouse and Novitiate of the Sisters of the Presentation. Sr. Mary O'Keefe, P.B.V.M. Sisters 34.

Convent of Sisters of the Congregation de Notre Dame, 76 Howard Ave., 10301. Tel: 718-447-0291. Sisters 9.

Corpus Christi Monastery, 1230 Lafayette Ave., 10474. Tel: 718-328-6996. Sr. Lee, Prioress. Solemnly Professed 14; Perpetually Professed 2; Novices 7.

Dalton Center for Mission and Peace. Sisters of the Holy Child Jesus, 325 E. 33rd St., 10016. Tel: 212-689-3548; 889-3886; Fax: 212-545-7804.
E-mail: shcj-apdo@aol.com
Total in Residence 7; Total Staff 4.

Daughters of Mary Immaculate, 15 Stori Rd., 12550. Sr. Putorti, Admin. Total Assisted 240; Total Staff 3.

The Dwelling Place of New York, Inc., 409 W. 40th St., 10018. Tel: 212-564-7887. Sr. Nancy Chiarello, Admin. Sisters 4.

Franciscan Handmaids of Mary Convent, 15 W. 124th St., 10027. Generalate of the Franciscan Handmaids of Mary. Sr. Loretta Theresa Richards, F.H.M., Supr. Sisters 22; Total Assisted 300; Total Staff 20. Other Convents: Camp St. Edward, 445 Woodvale Ave., Staten Island, 10309. St. Benedict Convent, 34 W. 134th St., 10037.

Handmaids of Mary Novitiate, 444 Woodvale Ave., Staten Island, 10309. Tel: 718-984-1625. Novitiate of the Franciscan Handmaids of the Most Pure Heart of Mary. Sr. Maria Goretti, Dir., Formation. Sisters 2; Associates 2.

Franciscan Missionaries of Mary. Provincialate, 3305 Wallace Ave., Bronx, 10467-6599. Tel: 718-547-4604; Fax: 718-547-4607.
E-mail: fmmprov@aol.com
Web site: http://www.fmm.org or www.fmmusa.org
Holy Name Convent, 204 W. 97th St., 10025-5620. Tel: 212-678-6901; Fax: 212-678-6865. Cardinal Hayes Home Convent, Box K, Millbrook, 12545. Tel: 914-677-6739.

Franciscan Sisters of Little Falls, Minnesota, 20 Walden Ave., 10306. Sisters 2.

Franciscan Sisters of the Poor Foundation, Inc., 708 Third Ave., Ste. 200, 10017. Tel: 212-818-1987; Fax: 212-808-0096.

Franciscan Sisters of the Poor Health System, Inc., 708 Third Ave., Ste. 200, 10017. Tel: 212-818-1987; Fax: 212-808-0096.

Little Sisters of the Assumption, 214 E. 30 St., 10016. Tel: 212-889-4310; Fax: 212-889-7358.
E-mail: littlesrs@aol.com
Web site: http://www.littlesisters.org
Sr. Jean McCormack, Prov. Coord. Sisters 26; Sisters in Province 48; Total Assisted 3,000; Total Staff 35.
Other residences in New York: 218 E. 105th St., 10029. Tel: 212-534-4932. 475 E. 115th St., 10029. Tel: 212-369-2097. 310 E. 120th St., 10035. 410 Grand St., Apt. 26H, 10002. Tel: 212-533-6496. 2604 Davidson Ave., Bronx, 10468. Tel: 212-933-0377. 98 Gladstone Ave, Walden, 12586. Tel: 914-778-7252. 159-A Johnston St., Newburgh, 12550. Tel: 914-562-0700.

Missionaries of Charity, Inc., 335 E. 145th St., 10451. Tel: 718-292-0019. Sr. M. Sabita, M.C., Reg. Supr.; Sr. M. Dominga, M.C., Supr., 406 W. 127th St., 10027. Tel: 212-222-7229. Sr. M. Fredina, M.C., Supr., 657 Washington St., 10014. Tel: 212-645-0587. Sr. M. Rochelle, M.C., Supr. Total Assisted 1,200; Total Staff (shared apostolates) 24.

Missionary Sisters of the Immaculate Heart of Mary. District House, 238 E. 15th St., Apt. 5, 10003-3901. Sr. Alene Grothues, Supr. Sisters 3. St. Joseph Convent, 238 E. 15th St., 10003-3901. Sr. Jean Cook, Supr. Sisters 4.

Monastery of St. Clare, 142 Hollywood Ave., 10465. Tel: 718-822-7271. Sr. Mary Bernadette Quinn, O.S.C., Abbess. Sisters 14.

Oblate Sisters of the Most Holy Redeemer, 1027 Grand Concourse, 10452. Tel: 293-9180. Sr. Ligia M. Latorre, Supr.

Oblates of the Mother of Orphans, 20 E. 72nd St., 10021. Sr. Maria Isabel Reina, Supr.

Parish Visitors of Mary Immaculate. 2151 Watson Ave., Bronx, 10472. Tel: 718-823-0350. Sr. Rose Aimee Tremblay, P.V.M.I., Supr. Sisters 5.

Sacred Heart Catechetical Center, 248 E. 62nd St., 10021. Tel: 212-838-0033. Mission Helpers of the Sacred Heart. Sisters 7.

St. Benedict's Convent, 34 W. 134th St., 10037. Tel: 212-234-6870. Franciscan Handmaids of the Most Pure Heart of Mary. Mother Miram Cecilia, Supr. Sisters 3.

St. Joseph Provincialate, 205 Major Ave., 10305. Tel: 718-720-4377. Provincialate of the Daughters of Divine Charity. Sisters 2; In Province 71.

Schoenstatt Sisters of Mary, Secular Institute, 337 Cary Ave., 10310. Tel: 718-727-8005. Sisters 7; Total Staff 4.

Shalom Convent, 714 W. 231st St., 10463. Franciscan Sisters of the Poor 4.

Sisters of Charity Center, Mount Saint Vincent, 6301 Riverdale Ave., 10471-9930; Fax: 718-884-3013. Sr. Elizabeth A. Vermaelen, Pres. Legal Titles: *The Sisters of Charity of Saint Vincent de Paul of New York.; Sisters of Charity Center.; Mount Saint Vincent on Hudson.; The Sisters of Charity of Saint Vincent de Paul of New York Pension Trust.* Total in Congregation 573; In Archdiocese 533.

The Elizabeth Seton Federation, Inc., Sisters of Charity Center, 6301 Riverdale Ave., Bronx, 10471. Sr. Mary McCormick, S.C., Pres.

Sisters of the Good Shepherd, 337 E. 17th St., 10003-3804. Tel: 212-475-4245. Legal Title: *Sisters of the Good Shepherd-New York City.* Sr. M. Victoria Andreoli, R.G.S., Supr. Sisters 10.

Society of Helpers. 385 W. 263rd St., Bronx, 10471. Tel: 718-884-3100.
E-mail: nyhelper@claret.org
Web site: http://www.claret.org/~srmoore/goodc.html
Sr. Geraldine Finan, Supr. Sisters 7.

Society of the Sacred Heart, R.S.C.J., 363 W. 51st St., 10019. Tel: 212-581-4698; 581-5746.
Other Residences: 436 W. 49th St., 10019. Tel: 212-581-3894. 222 E. 93rd St., 10128. Tel: 212-876-2276. 406 E. 80st. St., 10021. Tel: 212-288-1986; 288-5116. 515 E. 118th St., 10035. Tel: 212-876-2895. 236 E. 15th St., 10003. Tel: 212-529-3447. 519 E. 118th St., 10035. Tel: 212-410-3465. 253 E. 110th St., #2, 10029. Tel: 212-410-4315.

Ursuline Bedford Park Convent, 2885 Marion Ave., 10458. Tel: 212-364-1289; 220-3387. Sr. Marie Jerome Murray, O.S.U., Supr. Sisters 41.

Ursuline Provincialate. 323 E. 198th St., Bronx, 10458. Tel: 718-365-7410.
E-mail: ursruepr@aol.com
Provincialate of the Ursulines of the Roman Union, Eastern Province. Sr. Marie-Celine Miranda, O.S.U., Prov. Sisters in Province 205.

Ursuline Sisters of Andrews Avenue, Inc., 323 E. 198th St., Bronx, 10458. Sr. Marie-Celine Miranda, O.S.U., Pres.

BEACON. *Carmelite Monastery*, 139 De Puyster Ave., 12508-3540.
E-mail: mafj55d@prodigy.com
Sr. Marjorie Robinson, Prioress. Professed Nuns 10.

BLAUVELT. *Congregation of St. Dominic General Motherhouse of the Sisters of St. Dominic of Blauvelt*, 496 Western Hwy., 10913. Tel: 914-359-5600; Fax: 914-359-5773. Sr. Barbara Werner, O.P., Pres.; Sr. Julia O'Brien, O.P., Asst. to the Pres.; Revs. John L. Sullivan, O.P., Chap.; John P. Farrell, O.P., Chap., Emeritus. Sisters 247. Legal Title: *Congregation of Saint Dominic General Motherhouse of the Sisters of St. Dominic of Blauvelt.*

BRONX. *Our Lady of Guadalupe Convent.* (Franciscan Sisters of the Renewal), 3537 Bainbridge Ave., 10467. Tel: 718-547-9840. (House of Formation). Sr. Lucille Cutrone, C.F.R., Community Servant. Sisters 7.

Sisters of Life, St. Francis Convent, 198 Hollywood Ave., 10465. Tel: 718-881-8008. Mother Agnes Mary Donovan, S.V.

Sisters of St. John the Baptist, 10465. Tel: 718-518-7820; Fax: 718-518-8930. Provincial Residence. Sr. Mary Cecile Swanton, C.S.J.B., Prov. Supr.

Mt. St. John Convent, Purchase, 10577. Sr. Frederick Mary DePew, C.S.J.B., Supr. Sisters 28; In Province 126; In Archdiocese 105; Total Assisted 45; Total Staff 9.

Immaculate Heart Novitiate, 150 Anderson Hill Rd., Purchase, 10577. Sr. Loretta Marie Florio, Dir. Formation.

Ursuline Communities, Inc., 323 E. 198 St., 10458. Sr. Marie-Celine Miranda, O.S.U., Pres.

ESOPUS. *Mother of Perpetual Help Monastery*, 12429.
E-mail: rednuns@juno.com
Redemptoristine Nuns. Sr. Paula Schmidt, O.SS.R., Prioress. Professed Sisters 12; Novices 1.

GRAYMOOR. *Mother Lurana House.* Old W. Point Rd., Rte. 1, Box 186, Garrison, 10524. Franciscan Sisters of the Atonement. Adult Social Day Care. Sr. Barbara Ohl, S.A., Directress.

Motherhouse and Novitiate of the Franciscan Sisters of the Atonement, St. Francis Convent, R1, Box 163B, 10524-9717. Legal Title: *Franciscan Sisters of the Atonement, Inc.* Sr. Diane Bernier, S.A., Congregation Minister. Local Coord.: Sr. Eilish Sweeney, S.A.; Sr. Theresa Meehan, S.A. Sisters 73.

Our Lady's Guest and Retreat House, Graymoor, R.I. Box 163B, 10524-9717. Tel: 914-424-3300. Franciscan Sisters of the Atonement. Sr. Ita Flynn, S.A., Directress. Sisters 4.

HARRIMAN. *St. Patrick's Villa*, 10926. Provincial Retirement Home and Provincialate of the Sisters of the Catholic Apostolate (Pallottine). Sr. M. Nataline, Supr.; Sr. M. Kathleen Thompson, Prov.; Rev. Lawrence X. McCaffrey, S.J., Chap. Sisters 36.

HARTSDALE. *Institute of the Sisters of Mercy of the Americas, Regional Community of New York*, 150 Ridge Rd., 10530-2205. Tel: 914-328-3200; Fax: 914-328-3761.
E-mail: SrPWolf@aol.com
Sisters of Mercy. Sr. Patricia Wolf, R.S.M., Reg. Pres. Sisters of Mercy of the Americas 202.

HASTINGS-ON-HUDSON. *Sisters of St. Francis*, 49 Jackson Ave., 10706-3217; Fax: 914-478-5470. Sisters of St. Francis, Hastings-on-Hudson. Motherhouse and Novitiate. Sr. M. Bernadette Wyman, O.S.F., Gen. Minister; Rev. Robert Cheesman, C.Ss.R., Chap. Sisters 84.

HAVERSTRAW. *Sisters of St. Francis of Peace*, Congregation Center, 20 Ridge St., 10927. Sr. Margaret Gaffikin, Congregation Min.

HAWTHORNE. *Motherhouse & Novitiate of the Sisters of St. Dominic, Congregation of St. Rose of Lima*, 10532. Mother Anne Marie, O.P., Mother Gen.; Rev. John Proppe, O.F.M.Cap., Chap. Legal Title: *Motherhouse and Novitiate of the Sisters of St. Dominic, Congregation of St. Rose of Lima.* Professed Sisters 28; Sisters in Community 80; In Archdiocese 40.

HIGHLAND MILLS. *Religious of Jesus and Mary*, 10930. Sr. Margaret M. Quinn, R.J.M., Supr.; Rev. Thomas E. Clarke, S.J. Sisters 13; Total Staff 4.

HOPEWELL JUNCTION. *St. Aloysius Novitiate*, Beekman Rd., P.O. Box 98, 12533. Oblates to the Blessed Trinity. Mother Gloria Castro, Supr. Gen. Sisters 11; Novices 2; Postulants 2; Total in Residence 41; Total Staff 31.

LIBERTY. *Blessed Kateri Tekakwitha Religious Education Center*, Mailing Address: Box 1011, 12754. Tel: 914-292-9100. Dominican Sisters.

LIVINGSTON MANOR. *Monastic Sisters of Bethlehem and of the Assumption of the Virgin*, Grooville Rd., 12758. Sr. Amena Figeat, M.S.B.A.V., Supr. Total in Residence 12.

MARYKNOLL. *Maryknoll Community, Inc.*, 77 Ryder Rd., P.O. Box 306, 10545-3060.

Maryknoll Residential Care, Maryknoll Sisters Center, 10545-0311. Tel: 914-941-9230; Fax: 914-941-0213.
E-mail: mconnell@mksisters.com
Skilled Nursing home for the Maryknoll sisters only. Sr. Mary T. Connell, M.M., Admin. Beds 58; Sisters 54.

Maryknoll Sisters Charitable Trust, Treasury Office, P.O. Box 306, 10545-0306. Rev. Richard B. Callahan, M.M., Contact Person.

Maryknoll Sisters Contemplative Community, Mailing Address: P.O. Box 311, 10545-0311. Contemplative Community of the Maryknoll Sisters of St. Dominic. Sr. Theresa Baldini, M.M., Coord. Sisters 13.

Maryknoll Sisters of St. Dominic Inc., P.O. Box 311, 10545-0311. Tel: 914-941-7575; Fax: 914-923-0733.
Web site: http://www.maryknoll.org
Sr. Rosemary Healy, Center Coord. Professed Sisters 223; Total in Residence 226.

MILLBROOK. *Franciscan Missionaries of Mary*, Mailing Address: Box K, 12545. Sr. Anne Turbini, F.M.M., Local Coord. Sisters 4.

MONROE. *Parish Visitors of Mary Immaculate*, Mailing Address: Box 658, 10950-0658. Tel: 914-783-2251; Fax: 914-783-2085. Sr. Carole Marie Troskowski, Gen. Supr. Professed Sisters 63; Novices 8.

St. Joseph's Convent-Day Care Center, Harriman Heights Rd., R.R. 3, Box 165, 10950; Fax: 914-782-5645. Sr. M. Olivia Reginella, Coord. Sisters of the Catholic Apostolate (Pallottine) 6; Total Assisted 45; Total Staff 4.

MONSEY. *St. Zita's Villa*, 10952. Motherhouse and Novitiate of Sisters of Reparation of the Congregation of Mary. Sr. Maureen Francis, Supr. Sisters 14.

MONTICELLO. *St. Thomas Villa*, 12701. Sr. Rita Epilone, C.S.J., Admin. Summer residence for Sisters of St. Joseph, Brentwood.

NANUET. *St. Patrick Villa*, 2 Duryea Ln., 10954. Tel: 914-623-3371. Sisters of Charity of St. Vincent de Paul. Sr. Eileen A. Grubert, Admin. Sisters 29.

NEW ROCHELLE. *Ursuline Convent of St. Teresa*, 39 Willow Dr., 10805. Tel: 914-632-1199; Fax: 914-633-5281. Legal Title: *Ursuline Convent of St. Teresa's, New York.* Sr. Phyllis Hinchcliffe, O.S.U., Supr. Sisters 53.

Ursuline Residence, Inc., 1338 North Ave., 10804. Tel: 914-636-3456; Fax: 914-576-2620. Sr. Kathleen M. Donohue, O.S.U., Supr. Sisters 30.

NEW WINDSOR. *Mt. St. Joseph*, 880 Jackson Ave., 12553. Tel: 914-564-6620. Motherhouse of the Sisters of the Presentation of the Blessed Virgin Mary of New Winsor. Sr. Carla Lorenz, Pres.; Sr. Laura Follmer, Community Archivist. Ministry in the field of academic education in parochial and high schools; pastoral services; health care; social services. Sisters 123.

NEWBURGH. *Center of Hope Sisters' Residence*, 320 Powell Ave., 12550. Dominican Sisters of Hope. Sr. Maura Schefter, O.P., Admin.

Daughters of Mary Immaculate, 15 Stori Rd., 12550. Tel: 914-565-5034. Italian Apostolate in Sacred Heart Church.

OSSINING. *Dominican Sisters of Hope*, 299 N. Highland Ave., 10562. Tel: 914-941-4420.
E-mail: hopeteam@aol.com
Sr. Catherine Walsh, O.P., Prioress.

PEEKSKILL. *Mt. St. Francis, Motherhouse & Infirm of Franciscan Missionary Sisters of Sacred Heart*, 250 South St., 10566. Tel: 914-737-5409. Sr. Rose Cecilia Bozzo, F.M.S.C., Prov. Supr.; Sr. Ann Charles Maye, F.M.S.C., Supr. Legal Title: *Missionary Sisters of the Third Order of St. Francis.* Sisters of the Good Shepherd 3.
Canonical Name: Franciscan Missionary Sisters of the Sacred Heart.

Mt. St. Francis Infirmary, 250 South St., 10566.

Novitiate. Sr. Petra Zanghi, F.M.S.C., Directress of Formation.

Sisters of the Good Shepherd, 250 South St., 10566. Tel: 914-737-0019. Sisters of the Good Shepherd 4.

PURCHASE. *Society of the Sacred Heart*, Manhattanville College, 10577. Tel: 914-694-2200.
Web site: sofie.org/rscj/

RHINEBECK. *Linwood Spiritual Center*, 139 S. Mill Rd., 12572.
E-mail: ijksu@aol.com
Sisters of St. Ursula. Sr. Mary Isaac Koenig, S.U., Reg. Supr.; Sr. Maureen Steeley, S.U., Dir. Spiritual Center.

RYE. *Convent of the Holy Child*, 25 Convent Ln., 10580. Tel: 914-967-5544. H.C. Carriage House, 9 Convent Ln. Tel: 914-967-9440. Sisters 27.

SLOATSBURG. *St. Mary's Villa, Spiritual & Educational Center*, 150 Sisters Servants Ln., P.O. Box 6, 10974-0006. Tel: 914-753-5100. Sisters Servants of Mary Immaculate.

SPARKILL. *Dominican Convent of Our Lady of the Rosary*, 175 Rte. 340, 10976-1047.
E-mail: margmurph@aol.com
Motherhouse and General Novitiate of Dominican Sisters of Congregation of Our Lady of the Rosary. Sr. Kathleen Kane, O.P., Pres. Sisters 117 in Residence in Dominican Convent; Sisters 468 in Congregation.

STATEN ISLAND. *Daughters of St. Paul, Pious Society*, 78 Fort Pl., 10301. Tel: 718-447-5071. Missionary Sisters of the Communications Media. Sr. Deborah James Timmis, F.S.P., Supr. Sisters 9.

Pious Disciples of the Divine Master, Regional and Formation House, 60 Sunset Ave., 10314. Tel: 718-761-2323; 494-8597; Fax: 718-494-8521. Sr. M. Lucille Van Hoogmoed, Regional Supr. Sisters 9.

SUFFERN. *Sisters of Our Lady of Christian Doctrine aka Institute of Christian Doctrine*, Marydell Center, 23 Haskell Ave., 10901. Tel: 914-357-0046. Sr. Virginia Johnson, R.C.D., Pres. Sisters 38; Total in Residence 2; Total Staff 4.

Marydell Faith & Life Center, 640 N. Midland Ave., Nyack, 10960.

TARRYTOWN. *Provincial Center, Religious Sacred Heart of Mary*, 50 Wilson Park Dr., 10591. Tel: 914-655-3440; 631-8872; Fax: 914-631-7803. Sr. Martina Crowley, Supr. Prov. Councillors: Sr. Letizia Pappalardo; Sr. Edna O'Connor; Sr. Frances Lane, Sec.; Sr. Marion Therese Shanahan, Treas.; Sr. Monica Walsh, Dir. Formation; Sr. Joanne Safian, Dir. Communications. Total in Residence 66; Total Staff 32.

WALDEN. *Convent of Most Precious Blood*, 100 Ulster Ave., 12586. Sisters 2.

Little Sisters of the Assumption, 98 Gladstone Ave., 12586. Sr. Jean McCormack, Provincial; Sr. Ann Mary Blute, Local Coord. Sisters 8.

WARWICK. *Blessed Sacrament Monastery*, 235 Bellvale Lakes Rd., 10990-3403. Tel: 914-988-5424. Sacramentine Nuns. Sr. Mary Veronica Kiley, Prioress. Sisters 14.

Franciscan Sisters of Poor, Mt. Alverno Center, Inc. Franciscan Health Systems of Warwick, Inc., 20 Grand St., 10990. Tel: 914-986-2267. Ms. Jeanne Lee, CEO; Miss Jean Wetstine, Admin.; Sr. Mary Veronica Donohue, S.F.P., Community Minister; Rev. Edward Sullivan, O.F.M., Chap. Legal Title: *Franciscan Sisters of the Poor Mt. Alverno Center, Inc. Franciscan Health System of Warwick, Inc.*

WHITE PLAINS. *Convent of Our Lady of Good Counsel*, 52 N. Broadway, 10603; Fax: 914-949-5169. Motherhouse of the Sisters of the Divine Compassion. Sr. Helen Coldrick, R.D.C., Pres.

RDC Center for Counseling and Human Development, Inc., 52 N. Broadway, 10603. Sr. Patricia Sheridan, R.D.C. To provide counseling services for laity, religious and clergy. Individual and group counseling are offered as well as marital and family therapy. Sisters 51.

[FF] RETREAT HOUSES

NEW YORK. *Cardinal Spellman Retreat House*, Passionist Spiritual Center, 5801 Palisade Ave., 10471. Tel: 718-549-6500. Rev. Donald Ware, C.P., Dir.; Mr. William J. Gilberg, Admin. Ministry Staff: Rev. Benedict Berlo, C.P.; Bro. Damian Carroll, C.P. Retreats for adults and youths and hosted nonprofit groups.

BEDFORD VILLAGE. *Cenacle Retreat House*, Rte. 22, P.O. Box 467, 10506. Tel: 914-234-3344. Sr. Thelma Hall, R.C., Dir. Directed retreats, Spiritual Direction, Days of prayer for individuals or small groups (religious or lay). Total in Residence 1; Total Staff 1.

BRONX. *St. Joseph's Center*. (Spanish Cursillo Center), 275 W. 230th St., 10463. Tel: 718-796-4340. Revs. Francis E. Peluso, O.A.R., Dir.; Gregario Arista, O.A.R. (Mexico); Domingos Machado, O.A.R. (Portugal); Bro. Mario Alvarez, O.A.R., Admin. Total in Residence 1; Total Staff 4.

ESOPUS. *Marist Brothers of Ulster County*, Mailing Address: P.O. Box 197, 12429. Tel: 914-384-6106; 384-6620. Mid Hudson Valley Camp - Summer camp for disadvantaged children. Bro. Donald Nugent, F.M.S., Dir. Total Staff 3.

Mount St. Alphonsus Redemptorist Retreat Center, 12429. Tel: 914-384-6550. Redemptorist Fathers and Brothers. Very Rev. John G. Kingsbury, C.Ss.R., Rector; Bro. Robert Skinnner, C.Ss.R.; Revs. Francis J. Gargani, C.Ss.R.; Kevin Milton, C.Ss.R. Groups and individual retreats, conferences, workshops, and days of prayer. Available for Religious Chapters. Capacity 106 Rooms; Beds 161.

HIGHLAND MILLS. *Bethany Retreat House*, County Rd. 105, P.O. Box 1003, 10930. Tel: 914-928-2213. Religious of Jesus and Mary. Sr. Catherine Kenny, R.J.M., Dir. In res., Rev. Thomas E. Clarke. Total in Residence 16; Total Staff 7.

LARCHMONT. *Trinity Retreat*, 1 Pryer Manor Rd., 10538. Tel: 914-235-6839. Revs. Eugene Fulton, Dir.; Benedict J. Groeschel, C.F.R., Assoc. Dir.

MIDDLETOWN. *National Shrine of Our Lady of Mount Carmel*, Carmelite Dr., P.O. Box 868, 10940-0868. Tel: 914-344-0876; Fax: 914-344-0093. Very Rev. Matthias DesLauriers, O.Carm., Dir. Total Staff 8.

NEWBURGH. *Our Lady of Hope Center*, 434 River Rd., 12550. Conducted by the Oblates of Mary Immaculate of the Eastern Province. Revs. Gordon Orsino, O.M.I., Supr.; Patrick Brady, O.M.I.; Gerard McCormick, O.M.I.; Richard Kulwiec, O.M.I.; George M. White, O.M.I.; Charles Beausoleil, O.M.I.; Bros. Charles E. Quinn, O.M.I.; Charles Timothy Fuqua, O.M.I.

SLOATSBURG. *St. Mary's Villa*, 150 Sisters Servants Ln., P.O. Box 6, 10974-0006. Tel: 914-753-5100. Spiritual and Educational Center. (Retreats). Sisters Servants of Mary Immaculate. Total in Residence 8; Total Staff 4.

STATEN ISLAND. *Mount Manresa Jesuit Retreat House*, 239 Fingerboard Rd., 10305. Tel: 718-727-3844.
E-mail: skellym@tribeca.ios.com
Web site: http://www.cptryon.org/manresa
Jesuits. Revs. John T. Ryan, S.J., Dir.; Joseph T. Browne, S.J., Supr.; Richard P. Grogan, S.J.; Robert E. Groenewold, S.J.; John J. King, S.J.; Joseph E. Moltesz, S.J.; Thomas J. Quinn, S.J. Total in Residence 7; Total Staff 7.

WALDEN. *St. Andrew's Retreat House*, 257 St. Andrew's Rd., 12586. Tel: 914-778-5941. Sr. Deana Kohlman, Supr. Gen.; Sr. Ellen Patrick Stapleton, Business Mgr. North American Union Sisters of Our Lady of Charity.

WAPPINGERS FALLS. *Mt. Alvernia Retreat House*, 12590. Revs. Thomas More Nicastro, O.F.M.; Ernest D'Onofrio, O.F.M.; Armand Padula, O.F.M.; Andre Cirino, O.F.M.; Roch Ciandella, O.F.M.; Bros. Joseph Messina, O.F.M.; Giles Kelly, O.F.M.

WARWICK. *Mount Alverno Center and Convent*, 20 Grand St., 10990. Tel: 914-986-2267. Franciscan Sisters of the Poor. Miss Jean Wetstine, Exec. Dir.; Sr. Mary Veronica Donohue, S.F.P., Local Community Min.; Rev. Edward Sullivan, O.F.M., Chap.

WEST HAVERSTRAW. *Don Bosco Retreat Center and Marian Shrine*, Filors Ln., Box 9000, 10993. Tel: 914-947-2200; Fax: 914-947-2203.
E-mail: rshelly@aol.com
Founded 1947. Bros. Mario Audero, S.D.B.; Jerry Meegan, S.D.B., Retreat Coord.; Richard Pasiak, S.D.B.; Jerome Cincotta, S.D.B.; Thomas J. Higgs, S.D.B.; Emil Dube, S.D.B., Vocations; Bernard Zdanowicz, S.D.B.; Alfred Flatoff, S.D.B.; Joseph Botto, S.D.B.; Mario Audero, S.D.B.; Carlos Thenier, S.D.B.; Revs. Peter Lappin, S.D.B.; Richard Crager, S.D.B., Finances; Gennaro Sesto, S.D.B., Shrine Coord.; Chester Szemborski, S.D.B.; Roy J. Shelly, S.D.B., Dir.; William Burke, S.D.B.; Anthony Luzzi, S.D.B.; John Divizia, S.D.B.; Paul Kselman, S.D.B.; Eugene Walter, S.D.B.; Domenic DiGuardo, S.D.B.; A. Joseph Louis, S.D.B.; Frank A. Wolfram, S.D.B. Salesian Lay Ministers: Ms. J. Ellen Harder; Mr. Eloy Mendez-Olvera. Total in Residence 26; Total Staff 30.

Marian Shrine, Filors Ln., P.O. Box 9000, 10993. Tel: 914-947-2200; Fax: 914-947-2203.
E-mail: rshelly@aol.com
Revs. Roy J. Shelly, S.D.B., Dir.; John Divizia, S.D.B.; Gennaro Sesto, S.D.B., Shrine Coord.; William Burke, S.D.B.; Peter Lappin, S.D.B.; Richard Crager, S.D.B., Finances; Paul Kselman, S.D.B.; Domenic DiGuardo, S.D.B.; A. Joseph Louis, S.D.B.; Frank R. Wolfram, S.D.B.; Chester Szemborski, S.D.B.; Anthony Luzzi, S.D.B.; Eugene Walter, S.D.B.; Bros. Mario Audero, S.D.B.; Jerry Meegan, S.D.B., Retreats Coord.; Jerome Cincotta, S.D.B.; Thomas Higgs, S.D.B.; Emile Dube, S.D.B., Vocations; Richard Pasaik, S.D.B.; Alfred Flatoff, S.D.B.; Joseph Botto, S.D.B.; Bernard Zdanowicz, S.D.B.; Carlos Thenier, S.D.B. Salesian Lay Ministers: Ms. J. Ellen Harder; Mr. Ron Killoran; Mr. Eloy Mendez-Olvera. Total in Residence 23; Total Staff 30.

YONKERS. *Sisters of Mary Reparatrix*, 287 Hayward St., 10704. Sr. Margaret Hoey, S.M.R., Prov. Supr. Sisters 4.

[GG] UNIVERSITY APOSTOLATES

NEW YORK. *University Apostolate*, 1011 First Ave., 10022. Tel: 212-371-1000, Ext. 2805. Rev. Michael C. Crimmins, Coord.

Bronx Community College, 2352 St. Raymond Ave., Bronx, 10462. Tel: 718-828-2380. Rev. Eduardo Rodriguez.

City College of New York, 469 W. 142nd St., 10031. Tel: 212-650-5866. Mr. Gregory Pope.

Columbia University, 110 Earl Hall, 10027. Tel: 212-854-5110; 866-1500 (Notre Dame Rectory). Rev. Msgr. Christopher Maloney; Rev. Thomas Valenti.

Fashion Institute of Technology (SUNY), 227 W. 27th St., 10022. Tel: 212-564-9070, Ext. 231. Rev. Ray Frias, O.F.M.Cap.

Dominican College, 470 Western Hwy., Orangeburg, 10962. Tel: 914-359-7800, Ext. 255. Sr. Barbara McEneany, O.P.

Fordham University at Lincoln Center, 113 W. 60th St., Room 217, 10023. Tel: 212-636-6267. Ms. Joan Cavanagh.

Fordham University at Rosehill, Bronx, 10458. Tel: 718-817-4500 (C.M. Office); 817-1000 (Info.); Fax: 718-817-4505. Rev. Joseph Currie, S.J.; Deacon James Coughlan; Mr. Frank Rizzo; Sr. Ann Walsh, R.S.H.M.; Rev. John A. Mullin, S.J.; Mr. Robert Minotti.

Herbert H. Lehman College, Student Life Bldg.(222E), Bedford Park Blvd. W., Bronx, 10468. Tel: 718-960-4979. Sr. Madeleine Smith, S.H.C.J.; Mrs. Kathryn Mastriaco.

Hostos Community College, 500 Grand Concourse, Room C371, Bronx, 10451. Tel: 718-518-6561. Ms. Lidia Fernandez.

Hunter/Baruch College, 695 Park Ave., Room 1206 E. Bldg., 10021. Tel: 212-772-4752 (Hunter); 802-6809 (Baruch). Sr. Barbara Ann Mueller, O.P.

Iona College, New Rochelle, 10801. Tel: 914-633-2340; 633-2632. Rev. Louis Phillips, F.A.C.; Mr. Michael Hovey; Mr. Carl Procario-Foley; Bro. Robert Fitzsimmons, C.F.C.; Ms. Barbara Hetzel.

Manhattan College, Bronx, 10471. Tel: 718-920-0972. Rev. Cesar Russo; Bros. Dennis Lee, F.S.C.; James Loxham, F.S.C.

Manhattanville College, 125 Purchase St., Purchase, 10577. Tel: 914-323-5150. Rev. J. Joseph Flynn, O.F.M.Cap.

Marist College, Poughkeepsie, 12601. Tel: 914-575-3000, Ext. 2130; Fax: 914-471-6213. Rev. Luke McCann, Ph.D., Chap. Tel: 914-452-7330; Bros. Frank Kelly, F.M.S.; Michael Williams, F.M.S.

Marymount College, Tarrytown, 10591. Tel: 914-332-8248. Sr. Victoria Busch, R.S.H.M.

Marymount Manhattan College, 221 E. 71st St., 10021. Tel: 212-517-0597. Sr. Rosaleen O'Haloran.

Mt. St. Mary College, Campus Ministry Office, Newburg, 12550. Tel: 914-569-3154. Rev. James Gilhooley.

College of Mt. St. Vincent, Riverdale, 10471. Tel: 718-405-3200; 405-3215; 3216. Rev. John A. Vigilanti; Mrs. Harriet Carew; Mr. Terence McCorry.

College of New Rochelle, 29 Castle Pl., New Rochelle, 10805. Tel: 914-654-5339. Sr. Joan Garvey, O.P.

New York Maritime College, Fort Schyler, Bronx, 10465. Tel: 718-409-7200. Rev. Michael Moynihan.

New York Medical College, Valhalla, 10595. Tel: 914-993-4000. Deacon Lawrence O'Toole.

New York University, Catholic Center at NYU, 58 Washington Square South, 10012. Tel: 212-674-7236. Revs. John McGuire, O.P.; John Gregory Maturi; Sr. Thomasmari Gore, M.S.B.T.

Pace University, 20 Cardinal Hayes Pl., 10007. Tel: 212-962-3972. Rev. Paul Bernier, S.S.S.

Pace University-Westchester, SUNY, Purchase, 72 Carman Rd., Scarsdale, 10583. Tel: 914-723-0972. Mrs. Dorothy Lambert.

Rockland Community College, 145 College Rd., Suffern, 10901. Tel: 914-574-4531; Fax: 914-574-4425. Mr. Michael Ver'Schneider.

St. John's University, 300 Howard Ave., Staten Island, 10301. Tel: 718-390-4973; Fax: 718-390-4497. Rev. John Concagh, C.M.; Bro. Joe Tauraso, C.M.; Ms. Ellen Rhatigan.

St. Thomas Aquinas, 175 Rte. 340, Sparkill, 10976. Tel: 914-398-4062; Fax: 914-398-4061. Sr. Catherine Patrice Morgan, O.P.; Rev. Bernard L. Keitz, O.P.

SUNY/New Paltz, St. Joseph's Church, 34 S. Chestnut, New Paltz, 12561. Tel: 914-257-3024. Bro. Tim Jones, O.F.M.Cap.

United States Military Academy, Most Holy Trinity, West Point, 10996. Tel: 914-445-5575. Rev. John T. McLoughlin.

Wagner College & the College of Staten Island, Kairos House, 631 Howard Ave., Staten Island, 10301. Tel: 718-390-3461; 526-3595. Sr. Elaine R. Schenk, M.ID.

Vassar College, University Apostolate, Vassar College Box 381, Poughkeepsie, 12601-6198. Tel: 914-437-5847. Rev. Marc Oliver; Mrs. Valerie Oliver. Tel: 914-437-5548.

[HH] MISCELLANEOUS

NEW YORK. *Alfred E. Smith Memorial Foundation, Inc., The*, 1011 First Ave., 10022-4134. Tel: 212-371-1000, Ext. 3315. Rev. Msgr. Charles M. Kavanagh, Exec. Vice Pres.

America Press, Inc., The, Business & Editorial Offices,106 W. 56th St., 10019. Tel: 212-581-4640. Revs. George W. Hunt, S.J., Pres.; Charles M. Whelan, S.J., Vice. Pres.; Robert C. Collins, S.J., Sec. & Treas.

American Committee on Italian Immigration, Inc., 352 W. 44th St., 10036-5419. Tel: 212-247-7373; Fax: 212-265-5793.
E-mail: ACIMNY@aol.com
Web site: http://www.cyberitaly.com/acim
Rev. Peter P. Polo, C.S., Natl. Exec. Sec. Total Staff 3. To insure fair immigration policy favoring reunion of families and cultural integration of Italian Americans.

Apostolate for Family Consecration, Inc., Canonical Global Center, 350 Fifth Ave., Ste. 3304, 10118-0069. Tel: 212-971-1370. Jerome Coniker, Pres.

Archdiocesan Council of Catholic Nurses. (Includes Manhattan), 1011 First Ave., 10022. Tel: 212-371-1000.

Brooklyn Prep Alumni Association, Loyola Hall, Fordham Univ., 10458. Tel: 718-817-5447; Fax: 718-733-4456.
E-mail: mborelli@interport.net
Web site: http://users.interport.net/~mborelli/bpaa.htm
Rev. John D. Alexander, S.J., Moderator. Membership 4,500.

Calvary Fund, Inc. 1740 Eastchester Rd., Bronx, 10461. Tel: 718-518-2077; Fax: 718-518-2477.
E-mail: webmaster@calvaryhospital.org
Web site: calvaryhospital.org
Frank A. Calamari, Pres.; Dennis E. Berberich, Chm.

Cardinal Cooke Guild, 1011 First Ave., 10022. Tel: 212-371-1000. Official organization for information on the cause of canonization of Cardinal Terence J. Cooke. Sr. M. Aloysius McBride, O.Carm., Coord.

Cardinal Cooke Memorial Foundation, 1011 First Ave., Room 1940, 10022.

Cardinal's Fund for Children, 1011 First Ave., Room 1130, 10022.

Carmel Housing Development Fund Co., Inc., 1011 First Ave., 10022. Tel: 212-371-1000. Rev. Kevin L. Sullivan, Pres.

Catholic Actors Guild of America, Inc., The, 1501 Broadway, Ste. 518, 10036; Fax: 212-398-1868. William O'Mally, Pres.; Rev. Thomas Donlan, Chap.

Catholic Alumni Club of the Archdiocese of New York, 83 Christopher St., 10014. Tel: 212-243-6513; 243-0901. Geraldine Voelkel, Pres.

Catholic Big Brothers of New York, Inc., 45 E. 20th St., 10003. Tel: 212-477-2250; Fax: 212-477-2739. Total Assisted 275; Total Staff 14.

The Catholic Big Sisters, Archdiocese of New York-Manhattan Family Court, 60 Lafayette St., 10013. Tel: 212-349-4400; Fax: 212-349-4403. Total Families Assisted 180; Total Staff 6.

Catholic Daughters of the Americas and Its Courts, 10 W. 71st St., 10023. Tel: 212-877-3041; Fax: 212-724-5923. Mrs. Grace M. Rinaldi, National Regent; Mrs. Margaret O'Brien, Contact Person.

Catholic Foundation for the Dominican Republic, 1011 First Ave., Room 1150, 10022. Rev. Msgr. James P. Cassidy, Ph.D., Pres.; Oscar de la Renta, Chm.; Gerald Cunningham, Treas.; Richard Concannon, Sec.

Catholic Health Care Network, 1011 First Ave., Ste. 1150, 10022. Tel: 212-371-1000.
E-mail: rweaving@chcn.org
Web site: http://www.chcn.org
Mary Healey-Sedutto, Ph.D., Exec. Dir.

Catholic High School Association of New York, 1011 First Ave., Room 1856, 10022. Tel: 212-371-1000.

Catholic High Schools' Athletic Association of the Archdiocese of New York, 650 Grand Concourse, 10451. Tel: 718-585-5556. 4300 Murdock Ave., Bronx, 10466. Tel: 718-325-6423. Mr. Richard Tricario, Pres.

Catholic Interracial Council of N.Y., The, 899 10th Ave., 10019. Tel: 212-237-8255. Herbert A. Johnson, Exec. Dir.

Catholic Medical Mission Board, Inc., National Headquarters, 10 W. 17th St., 10011. Tel: 212-242-7757; Fax: 212-807-9161; 242-0930.
E-mail: cmmb@compuserve.com
His Eminence John Cardinal O'Connor; Rev. Vincent M. Cooke, S.J.; Rev. Msgr. Ferdinando D. Berardi; Revs. Robert J. Fuhrman; William T. Wood, S.J.; Sr. Marilyn Fischer, S.F.P.; Theodore J. Dubuque, Jr., M.D.; Thomas F. Murphy, Jr.; Thomas P. Melady, Ambassador; Floyd J. Donahue, M.D.; Terry Kirch, Pres. & CEO; Thomas V. Whelan; John A. Donnelly; James A. Cunningham.

Catholic Near East Welfare Association, 1011 First Ave., 10022.
E-mail: cnewa@cnewa.org
His Eminence John Cardinal O'Connor, Pres. & Treas.; His Eminence William H. Keeler, Vice Pres.; Rev. Msgr. Robert L. Stern, Sec. Gen.; Rev. Denis Madden, Assoc. Sec. Gen.

Catholic Social Policy Coalition of the Archdiocese of New York, The, 1011 First Ave., Room 1287, 10022. Agnes Kearns, Pres.

Catholic Women's Union. c/o Eunice Vasile, 15-25 Utopia Pkwy., Queens, 11357. Eunice Vasile, Pres.; Anna K. Weisz, Vice Pres.; Hilda McGlew, Treas.; Mary Sophie Ruedi, Sec.

The Center for Spirituality and Justice. 323 E. 198th St., Bronx, 10458. Rev. Thomas F. Madden; Bro. Charles A. Reutemann, F.S.C., Vice Pres.; Sr. Miriam Cleary, O.S.U., Sec. Total Assisted 15; Total Staff 3.

Centro Carismatico Catolico Hispano De La Arquidiocesis De Nueva York. 826 E. 166th St., Bronx, 10459. Tel: 718-378-1734; Fax: 718-378-1819. Rev. Josu Iriondo, Dir.

Chinese Catholic Information Center, 86 Riverside Dr., 10024. Tel: 212-787-6969. Rev. Paul Chan (Taiwan), Dir. Total in Residence 3; Total Staff 3.

Chinese Clergy & Religious Association in North America, 29 Mott St., 10013. Tel: 212-962-5157; 732-8558. Rev. Joseph S. Chiang, Coord.

Christ House, Inc. 432 E. 142nd St., Bronx, 10454. Tel: 718-665-8740. Shared Residence for Religious and Young Men Lacking Family Support. Bros. Thomas P. Draney, C.F.C., Dir.; James V. Hanney, C.F.C., Asst. Dir.

The Christophers, 12 E. 48th St., 10017. Tel: 212-759-4050; Fax: 212-838-5073.
E-mail: tci@idt.net
Web site: http://www.christophers.org
Rev. Thomas J. McSweeney, Dir. A multi-media organization reaching millions with the Gospel message. Total Staff 39.

Committe for Mission Responsibility Society, Inc. The Propagation of the Faith, 1011 First Ave., 10022. Tel: 212-371-1000, Ext. 2700. Rev. Msgr. Ferdinando Berardi, Dir.

Community of St. Egidio, U.S.A., Inc., P.O. Box 250299, 10025-1534. Tel: 212-663-1483. Paola Piscitelli, Pres.

Cornelia Connelly Center for Education, Holy Child Middle School, 220 E. 4th St., 10009. Tel: 212-982-2287. Sr. Mary Claire Ryan, S.H.C.J., Dir.; Sr. Susan Slater, S.H.C.J., Contact Person.

Courage, St. Michael Rectory, 424 W. 34th St., 10001. Tel: 212-421-0426; Fax: 212-268-7150.
E-mail: courage@world.std.com
Web site: http://world.std.com/~courage
Rev. John F. Harvey, O.S.F.S., Dir. Total Staff 2.

**CUSA - An Apostolate of the Sick or Disabled, Inc.*, 63 Wall St., Ste. 1802, 10005.
E-mail: ams4@juno.com
Mrs. Joan Donnelly, Pres.

Dominican Friars' Guilds, 141 E. 65th St., 10021.

St. Jude Dominican Missions, 141 E. 65th St., 10021. Tel: 212-744-2410. Rev. Raymond F. Halligan, O.P., Dir.

Dominican Rosary Apostolate, 141 E. 65th St., 10021. Tel: 212-744-2410.

Deserving Poor Boys Priesthood Association, 141 E. 65th St., 10021. Tel: 212-744-2410; Fax: 212-737-3875.

St. Martin de Porres Guild, 141 E. 65th St., 10021. Tel: 212-744-2410.

Dominican Shrine of St. Jude, Inc., St. Catherine of Siena Priory, 411 E. 68th St., 10021. Tel: 212-249-6067; 988-8300.
E-mail: georgec@interactive.net
Very Rev. Christopher Johnson, O.P.; Rev. George Lawrence Concordia, O.P., Admin. Dir.

**Don Bosco Harlem Association, Inc.*, 147-159 St. Nicholas Ave., 10026. Tel: 212-662-2693. Rev. George Hanna, S.D.B., Contact Person.

Felix Varela Foundation, Inc., The, 1011 First Ave., 10022. Rev. Msgr. Octavio Cisneros, Pres.

Franciscan Missionary Union, Province of the Most Holy Name. Headquarters, St. Francis Friary, 135 W. 31st St., 10001-3439. Tel: 212-736-8500. Bro. Denis Clark, O.F.M., Prov. Promoter.
Three schools in Brazil.

Franciscans of the Holy Name Province Sick, Aged and Retired Trust, 126 W. 32nd St., 10001-3202.
E-mail: hnp@aol.com
Web site: http://www.ofm.org

Franciscans of the Holy Name Province Education and Formation Trust.

Friends of American Art in Religion, Inc., 143 E. 43rd St., 10017. Tel: 212-661-3290. His Eminence John Cardinal O'Connor, Pres.; Rev. Msgr. Eugene V. Clark, Sec. & Treas.

Friends of RADIO MARIA, Inc., 352 W. 44th St., 10036. Tel: 212-246-9620; Fax: 212-265-5793.
E-mail: mciscoacim@aol.com
Rev. Mariano Cisco, C.S., Sec.

Fundacion Guadalupe, Inc., 1011 First Ave., Ste. 1233, 10022. Mr. Mario Paredes, Contact Person.

Global Education Associates, 475 Riverside Dr., Ste. 1848, 10115-1022. Tel: 212-870-3290; Fax: 212-870-2729. Sr. Sharon Fritsch, C.S.J.

Gregorian University Foundation, The, 106 W. 56th St., 10019. Tel: 212-582-5433.
E-mail: gregorian@mindspring.com
Rev. Eugene J. O'Brien, S.J., Pres.

Guild of Catholic Lawyers, The. Mailing Address: 6 MacDonald Pl., Scarsdale, 10583. Tel: 914-723-3211. 1011 First Ave., 10022. Tel: 212-371-1000, Ext. 2950. Rev. George W. Rutler, Spiritual Dir.; Gregory de Sousa, Pres., Emeritus, Exec. Dir.

Healing Through God Word Ministries, Inc., P.O. Box 080525, 10308-0007. Sr. Jean Marie Timko, O.P., Pres. Legal Title: *Healing Through God Word Ministries, Inc./Apostolate of Intercession Healing & Teaching the Word of God*. An evangelistic ministry of teaching the scriptures, intercession, and healing. Involves missions, retreats, days of renewal, healing services, and Bible studies.

Hispanic Catholic Charismatic Center of the Archdiocese of New York. 826 E. 166th St., Bronx, 10459. Tel: 718-378-1734; Fax: 718-378-1819. Rev. Josu Iriondo, Dir.

House of Peace, Inc. 1291 Allerton Ave., P.O. Box 696, Bronx, 10469-0696. Tel: 718-547-3230. Rev. Peter McCall, O.F.M.Cap.; Maryanne Lacy. Healing Prayer Center for the Peace of Christ Prayer Ministry.

The Housing Fund of the Archdiocese of New York, 1011 First Ave., 10022. Rev. Msgr. James J. Murray, Pres.; Rev. Kevin L. Sullivan, Vice. Pres.; Rev. Msgr. Donald Sakano, Sec. & Treas.

Hungarian Catholic League of America, Inc., 30 E. 30th St., 10016. Tel: 212-684-3623. Rev. Dominic L. Csorba, O.F.M., Pres.; Rev. Msgr. William I. Varsany, P.A., Chm. Bd.; Mr. Adam Tarnoczy, Exec. Sec.

Incarnation Children's Center Fund, Inc., 1290 St. Nicholas Ave., 10033. Capacity 18.

Institute of the Helpers. 385 W. 263rd St., Bronx, 10471. Sr. Teresa Cole, Pres.

Intercommunity Center for Justice & Peace, 20 Washington Square N., 10011. Tel: 212-475-6677.
E-mail: icjpny@aol.com
Sr. Marie Danaher, O.P., Exec. Dir. Peace and Justice Center is Sponsored by 39 religious congregations. The congregation assists its members in implementing values of peace and justice according to social teachings of the church. Total Staff 6.

International Catholic Child Bureau/North America, Inc., 595 West End Ave., #10C, 10024. Tel: 212-595-9180; Fax: 212-595-3917. Mr. David J. Sauer, Vice Pres., Admin. Svcs., The Catholic Health Association. An international convening agency for child care professionals interested in developing pilot projects, training seminars, research and advocacy for the physical, psychological, social, spiritual and religious well being of all children worldwide.

Jesuit Seminary and Mission Bureau, Inc., 39 E. 83rd St., 10028. Tel: 212-734-1144; Fax: 212-794-1036.
E-mail: wscanlonsj@aol.com
Revs. William J. Scanlon, S.J., Dir.; Gerard E. Braun, S.J.; Anthony F. LaBau, S.J.; James F. O'Brien, S.J.; Bros. John J. Campbell, S.J.; Jerome P. Menkhaus, S.J.

John LaFarge Institute, The, c/o America Press, Inc., 106 W. 56th St., 10019. Tel: 212-581-4640. Rev. Vincent T. O'Keefe, S.J., Dir.

La Casa Sollievo Della Sofferenza Opera Di Padre Pio. (The Home for the Relief of Suffering), c/o St. John, 210 W. 31st. St., 10001-2876. Tel: 212-564-9070, Ext. 236; Fax: 212-564-3964. Official United States Office. Rev. Armand Dasseville, O.F.M.Cap., Natl. Dir. & Coord.

LAMP Ministries, Inc. 2704 Schurz Ave., Bronx, 10465. Tel: 718-409-5062; Fax: 718-904-0048.
Web site: http://www.catholicity.com/cathedral/lamp/default.html
Co-Directors: Tom Scheuring, Ph.D.; Lyn Scheuring, Ph.D. Assoc. Directors: Marybeth Greene; Ed Greene.

LaSalle New York City, Inc., 44 E. 2nd St., 10003; Fax: 212-529-3598. Bros. Michael Corry, F.S.C., Chm.; Carl Malacalza, F.S.C., Vice Chm. Total Assisted 500; Total Staff 46.

Legion of Mary, Office, 1011 First Ave., 10022. Tel: 212-752-7966. Rev. Lawrence M. Paolicelli, Spiritual Dir.

Lower East Side Catholic Area Conference-Pastoral Center, 23 Oliver St., 10038. Tel: 212-962-1850; Fax: 212-571-4126.

Lumen Dei, 340 W. 53rd St., 10019. Tel: 212-586-4447; Fax: 212-586-1640. Rev. Wilberto Reyes Garced, Reg. Supr. Priests of Lumen Dei 1; Sisters of Lumen Dei 8.

Manhattan North Community Services, Inc., 91 Arden St., 10040. Niki Montaluo, Pres.

Maria Droste Services, 386 Park Ave. S., Ste. 903, 10016-8804. Tel: 212-889-4042; Fax: 212-889-3936. Legal Title: *St. Germaine's Services*. Betsy Selman-Babinecz, Dir.

**Monsignor Robert Fox Memorial Shelter Housing Development, Inc.*, Fox House, 111 E. 117th St., 10035. Sr. Florence Speth, Exec. Dir. Total Assisted 151; Total Staff 17.

Narnia Catechetical & Cultural Centre, Inc., 20 Sutton Pl. S., 10022. Mrs. Charles Teetor, Pres.; Mr. George Sim Johnston, Sec.-Treas.

National Federation for Life, 1011 First Ave., 10022.

Nativity Mission Center, Inc., 204 Forsyth St., 10002. Rose Allocca, Acting Dir. Students 55; Total Staff 15.

**Nazareth Housing, Inc.*, 519 E. 11th St., 10009.
E-mail: nazareth@earthlink.net

New York Catholic Forum, c/o St. Thomas More Church, 65 E. 89th St., 10128. George Sim Johnston, Chm.

New York Foundling Charitable Corp., 590 Ave. of the Americas, 10011. Sr. Elizabeth Vermaelen, Pres.

Nocturnal Adoration Society of the United States, 184 E. 76th St., 10021. Tel: 212-288-5082. Congregation of the Blessed Sacrament. Rev. Bernard J. Camire, S.S.S., Natl. Dir.

North American College of Rome, Alumni Assoc. of. Mailing Address: St. Joseph's Seminary, 201 Seminary Ave., Yonkers, 10704. Rev. Warren Wall, P.O. Box 1966, Mobile, AL, 36633. Rev. Edmund J. Whalen, S.T.D., St. Joseph's Seminary, 201 Seminary Ave., Yonkers, 10704.

Northeast Hispanic Catholic Center, Inc., 1011 First Ave., 10022. Tel: 212-751-7045. His Eminence John Cardinal O'Connor, Pres.; Mr. Mario J. Paredes, Exec. Dir.

Partnership for Quality Education, Inc., 1011 First Ave., 10022. Rev. Msgr. Charles M. Kavanaugh, Vicar Devel. Partnership for quality educaton, assisting 16 inner-city schools.

Passionist Residence. 5801 Palisade Ave., Bronx, 10471. Tel: 718-548-1182; Fax: 718-548-2945. Revs. Paul Fagan, C.P., Contact Person; Edward Beck, C.P.; Paul Wierichs, C.P.; Bros. Andre Mathieu, C.P.; Michael Moran, C.P. Total in Residence 5.

Patrons of the Arts in the Vatican Museums, 143 E. 43rd St., 10017. His Eminence John Cardinal O'Connor, Chm. of the Board; Rev. Msgr. Eugene V. Clark, Pres. Total Staff 2.

Pauline Books & Media. 78 Fort Pl., Staten Island, 10301. Tel: 718-447-5071; 447-5086; Fax: 718-816-1332. Legal Title: *Pauline Books & Media*. Other location: 150 E. 52nd St., 10022. Tel: 212-754-1110; Fax: 212-754-2268. Total in Residence 9; Total Staff 15.

Pax Christi Metro New York, 135 W. Fourth St., 10012. Tel: 212-420-0250; Fax: 212-673-0826.
E-mail: nypaxchristi@igc.apc.org
Rachel Keeler, Dir. We are a regional chapter of Pax Christi USA, the national Catholic movement for peace.

Perpetual Help Center. Redemptorist Fathers of New York. 294 E. 150th St., Bronx, 10451. Tel: 718-585-3678. Bro. Stephen Lendvay, C.SS.R.

Pius XII Foundation, Inc., 570 Lexington Ave., 10022. Tel: 212-319-0464. Bro. Robert Fontaine, C.S.C., Pres.

Polish Knights of Malta, Inc., 15 E. 65th St., 10021. Mr. Witoli Sulimirski, Pres.

Regina Coeli Society, Mailing Address: P.O. Box 939, 10272-0604. Tel: 212-374-5060. First Friday Club for the Catholic Women of New York City Police Dept. Jacquelyn Fleming, Pres.

S.H.A.R.E. - New York, Inc 1601 Bronxdale Ave., Bronx, 10462. Tel: 718-518-1513.
E-mail: SHARNYFood@aol.com
Ms. Elisa Perry, Exec. Dir.

St. Ansgar Scandinavian Catholic League, 40 W. 13th St., 10011. Tel: 212-675-0400. Rev. Philip J. Sandstrom, Spiritual Dir.; Dr. Astrid M. O'Brien, Pres.; Revs. Thomas A. Nielson, Chap.; John E. Halborg, Dir. Programs, Editor of the Bulletin; Mr. Nicholas Falco, Vice Pres. Membership.

St. Anthony Welfare Center, c/o Chancery Office, Room #1940, 1011 First Ave., 10022. Rev. Msgr. William J. McMahon, Dir.

St. Benedict the Moor Center, 283 St. Ann's Ave., 10454. Tel: 212-665-9693. James Roundtree, Pres. Total Assisted 36,000; Total Staff 8.

St. Joseph's Union of Staten Island, New York Inc. 108 Bedell St., Staten Island, 10309. Tel: 718-984-9296. Sr. Una McCormack, O.P., Treas.

St. Paul's Guild, Inc., 1011 First Ave., Room 1940, 10022. Rev. Msgr. Francis X. Duffy, Exec. Sec.

St. Rose's Settlement, 1011 First Ave., Room 1940, 10022. Tel: 212-371-1000.

St. Thomas Aquinas Foundation. National Headquarters (Order of Preachers, St. Joseph Prov.), 141 E. 65th St., 10021. Tel: 212-737-5757. Very Rev. Norman A. Haddad, O.P., Pres. Legal Title: *St. Thomas Aquinas Foundation of the Dominican Fathers of the United States (STAF)*.

Scalabrini Pastoral Center, 352 W. 44th St., 10036-5419. Tel: 212-247-7373.
E-mail: PPPOLO@aol.com
Web site: http://www.scalabrini.org
Directed by The Pius Society of the Missionaries of St. Charles Borromeo, Inc. (NY Prov.). Rev. Peter P. Polo, C.S., Dir. Total Staff 2.

American Committee on Italian Migration (A.C.I.M.).
Radio Maria.
Scalabrini Promotion Office.
Scalabrinian Italian Apostolate.

Shrine of St. Jude, Inc., St. Stephen of Hungary Parish, 414 E. 82nd St., 10028. Tel: 800-688-JUDE. Revs. John M. Felice, O.F.M., Pres.; Neil J. O'Connell, O.F.M., Spiritual Dir.; Sr. Natalie M. Runfola, R.S.C.J., Exec. Sec.

Sisters of Charity Health Care System Corp. 75 Vanderbilt Ave., Staten Island, 10304. Tel: 718-390-5080.
Web site: http://www.schcs.com

Sisters of Charity of New York Charitable Trust. Sisters of Charity Center, 6301 Riverdale Ave., Bronx, 10471-9930; Fax: 718-884-3013. Trustees: Sr. Elizabeth A. Vermaelen; Sr. Mary Ellen Brosnan; Sr. Mary Ellen Butler; Sr. Kathleen Hanrahan; Sr. Helen Mary Marks.

Sisters of the Holy Child Jesus-African Province Office, 325 E. 33rd St., 10016-9401. Tel: 212-696-5503; Fax: 212-545-7804.
E-mail: shcjapdo@aol.com
Sr. Margaret Rogers, S.H.C.J., Interim Dir. Legal Title: *Sisters of the Holy Child Jesus - African Province Office for the African Apostolates.*

Society for the Renewal of Christian Art, The, 217 E. 66th St., 10021. Tel: 212-288-8186. Rt. Rev. Alban W. Boultwood, O.S.B., Chm. of the Bd.; Albert J. Bouchard, Pres. Purpose: To work for the renaissance of Christian Art in our time and to foster a Christian dimension in the New York art world.

Contemporary Christian Art, Inc., 217 E. 66th St., 10021. Tel: 212-288-8186.
(Affiliated with the Society for the Renewal of Christian Art.). Emily Bouchard, Dir. Purpose: To work with artists in designing and producing Christian Art, art used in worship, presented in a contemporary manner. To bring the creators of Christian art and their works into contact with those who seek good art.

Society of Helpers. 385 W. 263rd St., Bronx, 10471. Tel: 718-884-3100.
E-mail: nyhelper_nyhelper@claret.org
Web site: http://www.claret.org/~srmoore/goodc.html
Sr. Geraldine Finan, Supr. Sisters 7.

**St. Elizabeth Seton Women's Center, Inc.*, 133 W. 70th St., 10023. Tel: 718-549-9200. Sr. Elizabeth A. Vermaelen, S.C., Pres.

**The Catholic League for Religious and Civil Rights*, 1011 First Ave., 10022. Tel: 212-371-3191; Fax: 212-371-3394.
E-mail: cl@catholicleague.org
Web site: http://www.catholicleague.org
Dr. William A. Donohue, Pres. Total Staff 11.

**The Elizabeth Seton Housing Development Fund Corporation*, 1991 Lexington Ave., 10035. Sr. Elizabeth Vermaelon, Pres. Total Assisted 400; Total Staff 3.

Thorpe Family Residence, Inc. 2252 Crotona Ave., Bronx, 10457. Total Assisted 64; Total Staff 12.

Tri-State Coalition for Responsible Investment, 20 Washington Sq. N., 10011. Tel: 212-475-6677; Fax: 212-475-6969.
E-mail: tricri@cpatch.com
Sr. Patricia Daly, O.P., Exec. Dir.

United States Catholic Historical Society, The, 1011 First Ave., Ste. 1940, 10022. Tel: 800-225-7999. Dr. Brian Butler, Pres. & Chm. of the Bd.; Mr. Charles J. James, Exec. Dir.

Xavier Society for the Blind, 154 E. 23rd St., 10010. Tel: 212-473-7800; Fax: 212-473-7801. Revs. Alfred E. Caruana, S.J., Exec. Dir.; James P. Jurich, S.J.; Joseph A. Latella, S.J.

BARRYVILLE. *New Hope Manor*, 35 Hillside Rd., 12719. Tel: 914-557-8353. Nicholas A. Roes, Exec. Dir.; Barbara Skidmore, Program Dir.; Sr. Maureen Conway, Dir. Education; Rev. Aquinas Thomas, S.A., Dir. Inservice Training. Members of the Board: Revs. Daniel Egan, S.A.; Arte Johnson, S.A.; Sr. Cecelia LaPietra, O.P.; Sr. Rita Shea, O.P. Sparkill Dominican Sisters. A live-in therapeutic community for the substance abuse rehabilitation of women 13-40 years old.

BRONX. *Abraham House, Inc.*, 342 Willis Ave., 10452. Rev. Msgr. Howard W. Calkins, Pres. Total Assisted 600; Total Staff 2.

American St. Boniface Society, Incorporated, Mailing Address: P.O. Box D, 10466-0604. Tel: 718-994-0989; Fax: 718-994-6119. Rev. Joachim Von Kersenbrock, S.J., Prov.; Germainiae Septentrionalis, Exec. Dir.

Angela House, Inc. Ursuline Provincialate, 323 E. 198th St., 10458. Sr. M. Winifred Danwitz, Ph.D., Exec. Dir. A transitional residence for homeless women and their young children.

Foundation of Christ the Redeemer & Institute Id, Misioneros y Misioneras Identes, 2352 St. Raymond Ave., 10462.

Marian Residence Fund, 323 E. 198th St., 10458. Tel: 718-365-7410. Sr. Madeline Welch, O.S.U., Trustee.

O.S.U. Charitable Trust, 323 E. 198th St., 10458. Tel: 718-365-7410. Sr. Madeline Welch, O.S.U., Prov.

St. Joseph's Center, 275 W. 230th St., 10463. Rev. Francis E. Peluso, O.A.R., Contact Person. For the development of Lay Leaders, Cursillo Center, Marriage Encounter. (Spanish). Total in Residence 1; Total Staff 4; Capacity 45.

St. Joseph's School for the Deaf Childrens Fund, Inc., 1000 Hutchinson River Pkwy., 10465. St. Joseph's School for the Deaf assists the students and faculty in their study, work, living, and extracurricular activities.

Saint Jutta Foundation, Inc., c/o Rev. John Adam, S.J., Fordham University, Loyola Hall, 10458.
E-mail: hegyi@murray.fordham.edu
Rev. John Adam, S.J., Contact Person.

**The Resource Center for Community Development, Inc.*, 1900 Crotona Pkwy., 10460. Tel: 718-893-0778. Most Rev. Francisco Garmedia, Pres. Total Assisted 5,000; Total Staff 35.

**Tolentine-Zeiser Community Life Center, Inc.*, 2345 University Ave., 10468; Fax: 718-733-1653. Total Assisted 172; Total Staff 19.

Ursuline Social Outreach, Inc., 323 E. 198th St., 10458. Sr. Eileen Fane, O.S.U., Pres.

Yarumal Mission Society, Inc., Office of the Pres., 2317 Washington Ave., 10458. Tel: 718-295-9600. Rev. Tulio Ramirez, M.X.Y.

CHELSEA. *The Fellowship of the Beloved Disciple*, Mailing Address: Box 38, 12512. Tel: 914-831-7791. The Word of the Cross Community. Co-Directors: Rev. Owen Lally, C.P.; Yvonne Zeller.

ESOPUS. *Holy Shroud Guild.* Mailing Address: P.O. Box 993, Canandaigua, 14424. Tel: 716-394-2606. Material Distribution Center, 294 E. 150th St., Bronx, 10451. Tel: 212-585-3678. Executive Council: Rev. Adam J. Otterbein, C.SS.R., Pres.; Very Rev. Frederick C. Brinkmann, C.SS.R., Pres., Protem.; Revs. John V. McGuire, C.SS.R., Sec.-Treas.; Hilary Conti, O.S.B.; John Kennington, C.Ss.R.; Frederick C. Brinkmann, C.SS.R.

GARRISON. *House of Nazareth Life Institute Ltd. (Nazareth Life Center)*, Philipse Brook Rd., Box 242, 10524. Tel: 914-424-3116. Sr. Marita Paul, F.S.P., Dir. Total in Residence 8; Total Staff 2.

HIGHLAND FALLS. *Ladycliff College Alumnae Association, Inc.*, P.O. Box 104, 10928. Tel: 914-446-2973; 446-5921.

HIGHLAND MILLS. *Thevenet Montessori School*, 202 Country Rte. 105, Box 1003, 10930-1003. Religious of Jesus and Mary. PreK-1 Enrollment 140.

HYDE PARK. *Focolare Movement National Center.* (Women), 204 Cardinal Rd., 12538. Tel: 914-229-9712; Fax: 914-229-1770. Miss Sharry Silvi, Dir., (Men), 196 Cardinal Rd., 12538. Tel: 914-229-0307; Fax: 914-229-0269. Mr. Julian Ciabattini, Dir. Founded in Trent, Italy in 1943. International Headquarters are in Rome, Italy. Movement was approved in March 1962 with the aim of working toward the fulfillment of Christ's prayer for unity, that all may be one. More than four million people, in all walks of life, married and single, are committed in or connected with the Movement. Centers in over fifty countries. Call for additional information.

LIVINGSTON MANOR. *The Monastic Family of Bethlehem*, Grooville Rd., 12758.

MARYKNOLL. *Friends of St. Maria Goretti, U.S.A., Inc.*, P.O. Box 0043, 10545-0043. Tel: 914-941-6372; Fax: 914-945-0715.
E-mail: mariagoretti@igc.apc.org
Bro. Goretti Zilli, Pres.; Rev. William T. Madden, M.M., Treas.; Mrs. Marie Finn, Sec.

Maryknoll Mission Association of the Faithful, P.O. Box 307, 10545-0307. Tel: 914-762-6364; Fax: 914-762-7031.
E-mail: bethany@igc.apc.org
Web site: http://www.maryknoll.org
Center Coordinating Team: Sheila Matthews; Thomas J. Rowan; Victoria Armour-Hileman. Leadership Team: Revs. Charles Dittmeier; William Vos; Barbara Fraser; Mary Mallahan Hicken; Sheila Matthews; Kathryn Vargas. Purpose: promoting and further developing a Catholic global mission effort which is open to Catholic lay, clerical, and religious mission vocations. The Association recruits and trains Catholic lay women, lay men, Priests, Brothers, and Sisters to conduct mission work. The Association sponsors Catholic lay men, lay women, Priests, Brothers, and Sisters in the performance of mission work and provides them with financial and other necessary support in the performance of mission work. Active in Bolivia, Brazil, Cambodia, Chile, China, El Salvador, Japan, Kenya, Mexico, Peru, Sudan, Tanzania, Thailand, United States, Venezuela, and Vietnam.

Maryknoll Mission Association of the Faithful, Inc., Philadelphia, PA.

Maryknoll Mission Association of the Faithful, Inc., El Paso, TX.

Maryknoll Mission Association of the Faithful, Inc., Castro Valley, CA.

MIDDLE VILLAGE. *National Italian Apostolate Conference*, 66-05 79th Pl., 11379. Tel: 718-326-1911.
E-mail: wazo2@aol.com
Rev. Msgr. William A. Varvaro, S.T.L., J.C.D., Exec. Dir.

MOUNT VERNON. *Franciscan Mission Associates*, 274-280 W. Lincoln Ave., P.O. Box 598, 10550. Tel: 914-664-5604; Fax: 914-664-3017. Province of the Immaculate Conception. Very Rev. Robert M. Campagna, O.F.M., Prov.; Madeline Bonnici, Exec. Dir.

St. Dymphna Devotion, 274-280 W. Lincoln Ave., P.O. Box 598, 10550. Tel: 914-664-5604; Fax: 914-664-3017. Province of the Immaculate Conception. Very Rev. Robert M. Campagna, O.F.M., Prov.; Madeline Bonnici, Exec. Dir.

NEW ROCHELLE. *The Christian Brothers Foundation, Inc.*, 33 Pryor Ter., 10804. Bros. James B. Moffett, C.F.C., Pres.; Charles J. Gattone, C.F.C., Vice Pres.; J. Barry Lynch, C.F.C., Sec. Purpose: To further Christian education and prophetic action on behalf of the materially poor and providing support for the Christian Brothers involved in this vocation.

Songcatchers, Inc., 44 Liberty Ave., 10801. Tel: 914-576-6774. Sr. Beth Dowd, O.S.U., Dir.

Ursuline Companions in Mission, Inc., College of New Rochelle, College Center - Room 155, 10805. Tel: 914-654-5270; Fax: 914-654-5290.
Web site: http://pages.map.com/lil/

NEWBURGH.

**Newburgh Ministry*, 9 Johnston St., 12550. Tel: 914-561-0070. Sr. Jean McCormack, L.S.A., Chairperson, Bd. of Dir.

Our Lady of Comfort Women's Center, 91 Ann St., 12550. Tel: 914-561-6267; Fax: 914-565-0572. Nina Faulkner, Treas. Shelter for Women & Children.

NORTH TARRYTOWN. *RSHM Life Center, Inc.*, 32-34 Beekman Ave., N., 10591. Sacred Heart of Mary. Total Assisted 265; Adults 150; Children 115; Total Staff 3.

OSSINING. *Dominican Sisters of Hope Ministry Trust*, 299 N. Highland Ave., 10562.

PEEKSKILL. *My Father's House, Inc.*, 143 Lafayette Pl., 10566. Rev. Ronald J. Lemmert, Pres.

PELHAM. *Passionist Communications, Inc.*, Mailing Address: P.O. Box 440, 10803-0440.
E-mail: sundaymass@aol.com
Rev. Leo J. Gorman, C.P., Exec. Producer. Assoc. Producers: Revs. Paschal Smith, C.P.; Stephen Haslach, C.P.

Passionist Communications Center, 19 Second Ave., 10803-1417. Tel: 914-738-3344; Fax: 914-738-7652.

PORT CHESTER. *Priests for Life*, P.O. Box 307, 10573. Tel: 914-937-8243; Fax: 914-937-9207.
E-mail: pfl@ix.netcom.com
Web site: http://www.priestsforlife.org
Rev. Frank A. Pavone, International Dir.; Anthony DeStefano, Exec. Dir.

RIVERDALE. *Holy Innocents Foundation*, 5272 Post Rd., 10471. Kevin T. O'Reilly, Pres.

RYE. *Alpha Omega Family Center, Inc.*, 815 Boston Post Rd., 10580. Total Assisted (annually) 1,500; Total Staff 3.

Center for Family Life, Inc., 815 Boston Post Rd., 10580. Tel: 203-281-4798. Rev. Anthony Bannon, L.C., Contact Person.

Center for Spiritual Development, 96 Milton Rd., 10580. Tel: 914-967-7328; Fax: 914-967-7387. Ann Marie Wallace, Ph.D., Dir.; Sr. Mary Frances Mills, O.S.F., Assoc. Dir.

Legion of Christ, Incorporated, 815 Boston Post Rd., 10580. Bro. Juan Sabadell, L.C., Contact Person.

SCARSDALE. *Catholic Charismatic Renewal Office*, 194 Gaylor Rd., 10583. Tel: 914-725-1773; Fax: 914-725-5227.
E-mail: charismny@aol.com
Co-Liaisons: Sr. Pauline Cinquini, S.C.; Rev. William B. Cosgrove, Tel: 914-227-8382; Fax: 914-227-3951.

The United States Catholic Widows and Widowers Association, Inc., c/o William B. Oakes, Jr., P.O. Box 40 H, 10583. Tel: 914-769-4386. Total Staff 1.

SPARKILL. *Hallel Institute*, 175 Rte. 340, 10976-1047. Tel: 914-365-2277.
E-mail: hallel@worldnet.att.net
Rev. George J. Torok, Pres. Total in Residence 37; Total Staff 9.

SUFFERN. *Covenant Corporation of Suffern, NY*, c/o Good Samaritan Hospital, 255 Lafayette Ave., 10901. Sr. Barbara Conroy, Pres.

Good Samaritan Foundation for Better Health, Inc., 255 Lafayette Ave., 10901-4869. Sr. M. Angelica Doris, Pres.; Michael A. Divers, Exec. Dir. Fundraising arm of Good Samaritan Hospital, Suffern, NY.

TARRYTOWN. *Ladycliff College Alumnae Association*, 88 Wilson Park Dr.

Religious of the Sacred Heart of Mary Charitable Trust, 50 Wilson Park Dr., 10591. Tel: 914-631-2979. Sr. Bernadette Kenny, Contact Person. Total in Residence 5; Total Staff 5.

THORNWOOD. *Familia USA, Inc.*, 500 Columbus Ave., 10549. Tel: 203-281-4798.

Montessori Community, Inc., 118 Whittier Dr., 10594. Mary McElroy, Vice. Pres.

Summertime Activities, Inc., 500 Columbus Ave., 10549. Tel: 203-281-4798. Bro. Juan Sabadell, L.C.

WALDEN. *Contemplative Outreach, Ltd.*, 257 St. Andrews Rd., 12586. Rt. Rev. Thomas Keating, O.C.S.O., Pres.; Gail Fitzpatrick-Hopler, Exec. Dir. Total Staff 5.

WHITE PLAINS. *Company of St. Paul*, 52 Davis Ave., 10605. Rev. Stuart Sandberg, Pres.

Religious of Divine Compassion Charitable Trust, 52 N. Broadway, 10603.

YONKERS. *Leviticus 25:23 Alternative Fund, Inc.*, 928 McLean Ave., 10704-4103. Tel: 914-237-3306; Fax: 914-237-3916.
E-mail: levf@erols.com
Bro. George C. Schmitz, C.S.C., Exec. Dir.; Sr. Agnes O'Grady, Loan Servicing Officer; Sr. Patricia Walsh, S.C., Admin. Asst.

[II] PERSONAL PRELATURES

NEW ROCHELLE. *Opus Dei (Prelature of the Holy Cross and Opus Dei)*, 99 Overlook Cir., 10804. Tel: 914-235-0198.
E-mail: newyork@opusdei.org
Web site: http://www.opusdei.org
Rev. Msgr. James A. Kelly, Ph.D., Reg. Vicar; Revs. Robert A. Brisson; Edward Maristany.
Other priests residing in New York: Revs. Bradley K. Arturi, J.C.D.; Orestes Gonzales, 117 Overlook Cir., 10804. Tel: 914-235-6128. Revs. Martin J. Miller; Robert A. Connor, 330 Riverside Dr., New York, 10025. Tel: 212-222-3285.

RELIGIOUS INSTITUTES OF MEN REPRESENTED IN THE ARCHDIOCESE

For further details refer to the corresponding bracketed number in the Religious Institutes of Men or Women section.

[0130]—*Assumptionists.*—A.A.
[0140]—*The Augustinians.* (Prov. of St. Joseph).—O.S.A.
[0330]—*Brothers of the Christian Schools.* (New York Prov.).—F.S.C.
[0600]—*Brothers of the Congregation of Holy Cross.*—C.S.C.
[0400]—*Canons Regular of the Order of the Holy Cross.* (Prov. of St. Odilia, Minneapolis, MN).—O.S.C.
[0470]—*The Capuchin Friars.* (St. Mary Prov.).—O.F.M.Cap.
[0270]—*Carmelite Fathers & Brothers.* (St. Elias Prov.).—O.Carm.
[0310]—*Congregation of Christian Brothers.* (Eastern U.S.).—C.F.C.
[0220]—*Congregation of the Blessed Sacrament.*—S.S.S.
[1330]—*Congregation of the Mission.*—C.M.
[1210]—*Congregation of the Missionaries of St. Charles.*—C.S.
[1000]—*Congregation of the Passion.* (St. Paul Prov.).—C.P.
[0480]—*Conventual Franciscans.* (Immaculate Conception Prov.).—O.F.M.Conv.
[0520]—*Franciscan Friars.* (Provs. of Most Holy Name of Jesus, Immaculate Conception; Commissariats of Holy Cross, Holy Family).—O.F.M.
[0530]—*Franciscan Friars of the Atonement.*—S.A.
[0650]—*Holy Ghost Fathers.* (Eastern Prov.).—C.S.Sp.
[0690]—*Jesuit Fathers and Brothers.* (New York Prov.).—S.J.
[0730]—*Legionaries of Christ.*—L.C.
[]—*Little Brothers of the Gospel.*—.
[0770]—*The Marist Brothers.*—F.M.S.
[0780]—*Marist Fathers.* (Northeastern Prov.).—S.M.
[0800]—*Maryknoll.*—M.M.
[0830]—*Mill Hill Missionaries.*—M.H.M.
[0720]—*The Missionaries of Our Lady of La Salette.*—M.S.
[0910]—*Oblates of Mary Immaculate.* (Eastern Prov.).—O.M.I.
[0430]—*Order of Preachers-Dominicans.* (St. Joseph Prov.).—O.P.
[0150]—*Order of the Augustinian Recollects.*—O.A.R.
[1020]—*Pauline Fathers and Brother.*—S.S.P.
[1030]—*Paulist Fathers.*—C.S.P.
[1040]—*Piarist Fathers.*—Sch.P.
[1070]—*Redemptorist Fathers.* (Baltimore Prov.).—C.SS.R.
[1190]—*Salesians of Don Bosco.* (St. Philip Prov.).—S.D.B.
[0990]—*Society of the Catholic Apostolate.*—S.A.C.
[1280]—*Stigmatine Fathers and Brothers.*—C.S.S.
[1300]—*Theatine Fathers.*—C.R.
[0560]—*Third Order Regular of Saint Francis.*—T.O.R.

RELIGIOUS INSTITUTES OF WOMEN REPRESENTED IN THE ARCHDIOCESE

[0130]—*Apostles of the Sacred Heart of Jesus.*—A.S.C.J.
[0230]—*Benedictine Sisters of Pontifical Jurisdiction.*—O.S.B.
[0330]—*Carmelite Sisters for the Aged and Infirm.*—O.Carm.
[3110]—*Congregation of Our Lady of the Retreat in the Cenacle.*—R.C.
[2410]—*Congregation of the Marianites of Holy Cross.*—M.S.C.
[3710]—*Congregation of the Sisters of Saint Agnes.*—C.S.A.
[1920]—*Congregation of the Sisters of the Holy Cross.*—C.S.C.
[1710]—*Congregation of the Third Order of St. Francis of Mary Immaculate.*—O.S.F.
[0760]—*Daughters of Charity of St. Vincent de Paul.*—D.C.
[0790]—*Daughters of Divine Charity.* (St. Joseph Prov.).—F.D.C.
[0850]—*Daughters of Mary Help of Christians.*—F.M.A.
[0860]—*Daughters of Mary of the Immaculate Conception.*—D.M.
[0950]—*Daughters of St. Paul.*—F.S.P.
[0810]—*Daughters of the Heart of Mary.*—D.H.M.
[0420]—*Discalced Carmelite Nuns.*—O.C.D.
[1050]—*Dominican Contemplative Nuns.*—O.P.
[1070-02]—*Dominican Sisters.*—O.P.
[1070-03]—*Dominican Sisters.*—O.P.
[1070-05]—*Dominican Sisters.*—O.P.
[1070-06]—*Dominican Sisters.*—O.P.
[1070-11]—*Dominican Sisters.*—O.P.
[1070-13]—*Dominican Sisters.*—O.P.
[1070-15]—*Dominican Sisters.*—O.P.
[1070-16]—*Dominican Sisters.*—O.P.
[1070-23]—*Dominican Sisters.*—O.P.
[1120]—*Dominican Sisters of the Roman Congregation.*—O.P.
[1170]—*Felician Sisters.*—C.S.S.F.
[1260]—*Franciscan Handmaids of the Most Pure Heart of Mary.*—F.H.M.
[1370]—*Franciscan Missionaries of Mary.*—F.M.M.
[1400]—*Franciscan Missionary Sisters of the Sacred Heart.* (Peekskill, NY).—F.M.S.C.
[1180]—*Franciscan Sisters of Allegany, New York.*—O.S.F.
[1310]—*Franciscan Sisters of Little Falls, Minnesota.*—O.S.F.
[1425]—*Franciscan Sisters of Peace.*—F.S.P.
[1190]—*Franciscan Sisters of the Atonement.*—S.A.
[1440]—*Franciscan Sisters of the Poor.*—S.F.P.
[3790]—*Institute of the Sisters of St. Dorothy.*—S.S.D.
[2310]—*Little Sisters of the Assumption.*—L.S.A.
[2340]—*Little Sisters of the Poor.*—L.S.P.
[2470]—*Maryknoll Sisters of St. Dominic.*—M.M.
[2480]—*Medical Missionaries of Mary.*—M.M.M.
[2680]—*Misericordia Sisters.*—S.M.
[2720]—*Mission Helpers of the Sacred Heart.*—M.H.S.H.
[2710]—*Missionaries of Charity.*—M.C.
[1360]—*Missionary Franciscan Sisters of the Immaculate Conception.*—O.S.F.
[2790]—*Missionary Servants of the Most Blessed Trinity.*—M.S.B.T.
[2900]—*Missionary Sisters of St. Charles Borromeo.*—M.S.S.C.B.
[2750]—*Missionary Sisters of the Immaculate Heart of Mary.*—I.C.M.
[2860]—*Missionary Sisters of the Sacred Heart.*—M.S.C.
[2920]—*Mothers of the Helpless.*—M.D.
[3030]—*Oblates of the Most Holy Redeemer.*—O.SS.R.
[3035]—*Oblates of the Mother of Orphans.*—O.M.O.
[3760]—*Order of St. Clare.*—O.S.C.
[2010]—*Order of the Most Holy Redeemer.*—O.SS.R.
[3160]—*Parish Visitors of Mary Immaculate.*—P.V.M.I.
[3450]—*Religious of Jesus-Mary.*—R.J.M.
[3460]—*Religious of Mary Immaculate.*—R.M.I.
[2070]—*Religious of the Holy Union of the Sacred Hearts.*—S.U.S.C.
[3465]—*Religious of the Sacred Heart of Mary.* (Eastern North American Prov.).—R.S.H.M.
[2519]—*Religious Sisters of Mercy, Alma, MI.*—R.S.M.
[3490]—*Sacramentine Nuns.*—O.S.S.
[2970]—*School Sisters of Notre Dame.*—S.S.N.D.
[1680]—*School Sisters of St. Francis.*—O.S.F.
[0980]—*Sister Disciples of the Divine Master.*—P.D.D.M.
[1830]—*Sister of the Good Shepherd.*—R.G.S.
[3020]—*Sisters Oblates of the Blessed Trinity.*—O.B.T.
[0590]—*Sisters of Charity of Saint Elizabeth, Convent Station.*—S.C.
[0650]—*Sisters of Charity of St. Vincent de Paul, New York.*—S.C.
[0660]—*Sisters of Christian Charity.*—S.C.C.
[2360]—*Sisters of Loretto.*—S.L.
[2575]—*Sisters of Mercy of the Americas.*—R.S.M.
[3000]—*Sisters of Notre Dame de Namur.*—S.N.D.deN.
[3080]—*Sisters of Our Lady of Christian Doctrine.*—R.C.D.
[3740]—*Sisters of St. Casimir.*—S.S.C.
[1510]—*Sisters of St. Francis of the Mission of the Immaculate Virgin.*—O.S.F.
[3820]—*Sisters of St. John the Baptist.*—C.S.J.B.
[3830-05]—*Sisters of St. Joseph.*—C.S.J.
[3890]—*Sisters of St. Joseph of Peace.*—C.S.J.P.
[0260]—*Sisters of the Blessed Sacrament for Indians and Colored People.*—S.B.S.
[3140]—*Sisters of the Catholic Apostolate (Pallottine).*—C.S.A.C.
[2980]—*Sisters of the Congregation de Notre Dame.*—C.N.D.
[0970]—*Sisters of the Divine Compassion.*—R.D.C.
[1000]—*Sisters of the Divine Providence of Kentucky.*—C.D.P.
[1990]—*Sisters of the Holy Names of Jesus & Mary.*—S.N.J.M.
[3320]—*Sisters of the Presentation of the B.V.M.* (Newburgh; Staten Island).—P.B.V.M.
[3320]—*Sisters of the Presentation of the B.V.M.* (Aberdeen, SD).—P.B.V.M.
[3470]—*Sisters of the Reparation of the Congregation of Mary.*—S.R.C.M.
[3480]—*Sisters of the Resurrection.*—C.R.
[1490]—*Sisters of the Third Franciscan Order (Syracuse).*
[3600]—*Sisters, Servants of Mary.*—S.M.
[2160]—*Sisters, Servants of the Immaculate Heart Of Mary.*—I.H.M.
[1890]—*Society of Helpers.*—H.H.S.
[2460]—*Society of Mary Repartrix.*—S.M.R.
[4040]—*Society of St. Ursula.*—S.U.
[4060]—*Society of the Holy Child Jesus.*—S.H.C.J.
[4070]—*Society of the Sacred Heart.*—R.S.C.J.
[4110]—*Ursuline Nuns.*—O.S.U.
[4130]—*Ursuline Sisters (Tildonk).*—O.S.U.
[4230]—*Xaverian Missionary Sisters.*—X.M.M.

ARCHDIOCESAN CEMETERIES

HAWTHORNE. *Cemetery of the Gate of Heaven.*
LONG ISLAND CITY. *Calvary.*
MONSEY. *Cemetery of the Ascension.*
STATEN ISLAND. *Cemetery of the Resurrection.*

NECROLOGY

† Brogan, Edward P., (Retired). —Died July 24, 1997.
† Connolly, Rev. Msgr. James M., Bronxville, NY, St. Joseph. —Died Dec. 15, 1997.
† Dale, James E., (Retired). —Died April 10, 1997.
† DiRaffaele, William F., Yonkers, NY, Christ the King. —Died Jan. 28, 1997.
† Fagnani, Anthony G., (Retired). —Died Jan. 4, 1998.
† Finnerty, Edward G., (Retired). —Died Oct. 8, 1997.
† Finnerty, Rev. Msgr. Edward M., (Retired). —Died Oct. 8, 1997.
† Goodwine, Rev. Msgr. John, (Retired). —Died Dec. 2, 1997.
† Gordon, Rev. Msgr. John J., (Retired). —Died Jan. 20, 1998.
† Heide, Rev. Msgr. Herman L., (Retired). —Died May 17, 1997.
† Joyce, Richard C., Patterson, NY, Sacred Heart. —Died Feb. 22, 1997.
† Keogh, Rev. Msgr. John P., (Retired). —Died Nov. 21, 1997.
† Leonard, Rev. Msgr. Francis X., Pine Island, NY, St. Stanislaus. —Died March 22, 1997.
† Maltese, Rev. Msgr. Anthony L., Tuckahoe, NY, Immaculate Conception. —Died June 15, 1997.
† Mangan, Eugene, Staten Island, NY, St. Sylvester. —Died June 25, 1997.
† McEnaney, Owen, (Retired). —Died Sept. 3, 1997.
† McNamara, Thomas E., Bronx, NY, Sts. Philip & James. —Died Nov. 25, 1997.
† McPeak, William J., (Retired). —Died Aug. 9, 1997.
† McShane, Vincent J., Croton-on-Hudson, NY, Holy Name of Mary. —Died March 11, 1997.
† Moore, Rev. Msgr. Robert E., Gardiner, NY, St. Charles Borromeo. —Died March 22, 1997.
† O'Brien, Rev. Msgr. Edward M., New York, NY, Guardian Angel. —Died April 3, 1997.
† Pucci, Rev. Msgr. Anthony, Yonkers, NY, Most Holy Trinity. —Died May 27, 1997.
† Richard, Rev. Msgr. Eugene, New Rocelle, NY, Blessed Sacrament. —Died Oct. 6, 1997.
† Sweeney, Rev. Msgr. William J., New York, NY, Our Lady of the Rosary. —Died April 4, 1997.
† Szarama, Roman J., Yonkers, NY, St. Eugene. —Died July 8, 1997.

Diocese of Norwich

(Dioecesis Norvicensis)

Most Reverend

DANIEL A. HART, D.D.

Bishop of Norwich; ordained February 2, 1953; consecrated Auxiliary Bishop of Boston October 18, 1976; appointed September 12, 1995; installed as Bishop of Norwich November 1, 1995. *Res., 274 Broadway, Norwich, CT, 06360.*

ESTABLISHED AUGUST 6, 1953.

Square Miles 1,978.

CORPORATE TITLE: *The Norwich Roman Catholic Diocesan Corporation.*

Comprises the Counties of Middlesex, New London, Tolland and Windham in the State of Connecticut and Fishers Island, a portion of Suffolk County in the State of New York.

For legal titles of parishes and diocesan institutions, consult the Chancery Office.

Chancery: 201 Broadway, P.O. Box 587, Norwich, CT, 06360. Tel.: 860-887-9294; Fax: 860-886-1670.

STATISTICAL OVERVIEW

Personnel	
Bishop	1
Priests: Diocesan Active in Diocese	101
Priests: Active Outside Diocese	5
Priests: Retired, Sick or Absent	37
Number of Diocesan Priests	143
Religious Priests in Diocese	60
Extern Priests in Diocese	6
Ordinations:	
Diocesan Priests	2
Transitional Deacons	4
Permanent Deacons in Diocese	49
Total Brothers	27
Total Sisters	320
Parishes	
Parishes	78
With Resident Pastor:	
Resident Diocesan Priests	66
Resident Religious Priests	11
Without Resident Pastor:	
Administered by Priests	1
Missions	10
Pastoral Centers	23
Professional Ministry Personnel:	
Brothers	3
Sisters	26
Lay Ministers	12
Welfare	
Homes for the Aged	3
Total Assisted	250
Special Centers for Social Services	1
Total Assisted	126
Educational	
Diocesan Students in Other Seminaries	11
Seminaries, Religious	1
Total Seminarians	11
High Schools, Diocesan and Parish	3
Total Students	1,750
High Schools, Private	2
Total Students	321
Elementary Schools, Diocesan and Parish	23
Total Students	4,658
Catechesis/Religious Education:	
High School Students	2,728
Elementary Students	15,155
Total Students Under Catholic Instruction	24,623
Teachers in the Diocese:	
Priests	1
Brothers	1
Sisters	15
Lay Teachers	23
Vital Statistics	
Receptions into the Church:	
Infant Baptism Totals	3,165
Adult Baptism Totals	132
Received into Full Communion	203
First Communions	2,983
Confirmations	1,655
Marriages:	
Catholic	732
Interfaith	281
Total Marriages	1,013
Deaths	2,082
Total Catholic Population	223,511
Total Population	625,829

Former Bishops—Most Rev. BERNARD J. FLANAGAN, D.D., J.C.D., cons. Nov. 30, 1953; installed Dec. 9, 1953; transferred to See of Worcester, Aug. 12, 1959; died Jan. 28, 1997.—Most Rev. VINCENT J. HINES, D.D., J.C.D., cons. March 17, 1960; retired June 17, 1975; died April 23, 1990.—Most Rev. DANIEL P. REILLY, D.D., cons. Aug. 6, 1975; transferred to See of Worcester, Dec. 8, 1994.

Office of the Bishop

Seretary to the Bishop—Rev. MICHAEL PHILLIPPINO; Mrs. ALICE PUDVAH, Administrative Asst.; Mrs. REGINA WIEGERT, Sec.

The Chancery

Chancery—201 Broadway, P.O. Box 587, Norwich, 06360. Tel: 860-887-9294; Fax: 860-886-1670.

Vicar General—Rev. Msgr. THOMAS R. BRIDE, P.A., V.G.; Mrs. ANNA DEPTA, Sec.

Chancellor—Rev. Msgr. ROBERT L. BROWN; Mrs. SUSAN SULLIVAN, Sec.

Diocesan Advisor on Canonical Matters—Rev. Msgr. HENRY J. DZIADOSZ, J.C.D.

Diocesan Archivist Consultant and Historian—Rev. J. RALPH KELLEY, (Retired).

Diocesan Attorney—MICHAEL E. DRISCOLL, Esq., *22 Courthouse Sq., Norwich, 06360.* Tel: 860-889-3321.

Diocesan Attorney Emeritus—JAMES J. DUTTON, JR., Esq., K.S.G., *22 Courthouse Sq., Norwich, 06360.* Tel: 860-889-3321.

Diocesan Computer Center—Rev. ANTHONY P. GRUBER, Computer Consultant; Miss JEAN MARTIN, System Admin.

Diocesan Finance Office—Mr. WILLIAM J. CONNELL, Chief Financial Officer; Mr. KEVIN KEEGAN, Asst. Controller; Mr. VICTOR WELTIG, Internal Auditor; MARY ANN JACOBS, Bookkeeper, Lay Pension; Ms. ROBIN HOLTSCLAW, Risk Mgr. (CMRS); Miss JANET WEST, Accounts Receivable.

College of Consultors—Rev. Msgr. THOMAS R. BRIDE, P.A., V.G.; Rev. Msgr. HENRY N. ARCHAMBAULT, P.A.; Rev. Msgr. ROBERT L. BROWN; Rev. Msgr. ANTHONY ROSAFORTE; Revs. RUSSELL BOISVERT; LAURENCE LAPOINTE; MARK O'DONNELL; MICHAEL O'HARA; JOHN W. MCWEENEY, M.S.

Presbyteral Council—Most Rev. DANIEL A. HART, D.D., Pres.; Revs. ROBERT CRONIN, Chm. RUSSELL BOISVERT, Vice Chm. LAURENCE LAPOINTE, Sec. Members: Rev. Msgr. THOMAS R. BRIDE, P.A., V.G.; Rev. Msgr. HENRY ARCHAMBAULT, P.A.; Rev. Msgr. ROBERT L. BROWN; Rev. Msgr. HENRY DZIADOSZ; Rev. Msgr. RICHARD P. LAROCQUE; Rev. Msgr. ANTHONY S. ROSAFORTE; Revs. ROBERT BARNES; ANTHONY GRUBER; CHARLES MCGRAIL; JOHN MCWEENEY, M.S.; MARK O'DONNELL; MICHAEL O'HARA; MICHAEL SMITH; JOHN WHITE.

Deans—Rev. FRANCIS J. O'KEEFE, Putnam; Rev. Msgr. M. DAVITT FOX, Middletown; Revs. LAURENCE LAPOINTE, Willimantic; JOHN J. WHITE, Vernon; Rev. Msgr. HENRY N. ARCHAMBAULT, P.A., Norwich; Revs. R. THOMAS MCCONAGHY, New London; MICHAEL J. O'HARA, Old Saybrook.

Diocesan Pastoral Council—Rev. Msgr. HENRY ARCHAMBAULT, P.A.; Ms. DIANE BAKER; Rev. ROBERT BARNES; Ms. SARAH BECKER; Rev. Msgr. THOMAS BRIDE, P.A., V.G.; Rev. Msgr. ROBERT BROWN; Mrs. CAROL CONKLIN; Mr. AL FECTEAU; Rev. Msgr. M. DAVITT FOX; Mrs. NOREEN GRAVEL, R.N.; Bro. J. ROBERT HOULIHAN, C.F.X.; Mrs. AGNES KELLY; Sr. MARY ALICE KLINE, R.S.M.; Dr. ROBERT MILLER; Dr. PETER MOORE, Ph.D.; Mrs. JUDITH PAPPAGALLO; Mrs. SUSAN ROURKE; Mrs. NANCY RUDEK; Mr. ALEXANDER SAUNDERS; Mrs. FRANCES SCHOEN; Mr. JAMES SMART; Rev. Msgr. WILLIS WEST.

The Tribunal

Diocesan Tribunal—17 Otis St., P.O. Box 587, Norwich, 06360. Tel: 860-887-9294.

Judicial Vicar—Rev. Msgr. HENRY N. ARCHAMBAULT, P.A., J.C.D.

Associate Judicial Vicar—Rev. JOHN W. MCWEENEY, M.S.

Judges—Revs. J. CLIFFORD CURTIN; JOHN J. WHITE; FRANCIS J. O'KEEFE; JOSEPH CASTALDI, J.C.L.; WILLIAM FLYNN; LESZEK JANIK, J.C.L.; JOSEPH MORRISSETTE; J. LAWRENCE OUIMET; MICHAEL O'HARA; Sr. SALLY TOLLES, D.H.S., J.D., J.C.L.

Defender of the Bond—Rev. ROGER J. LAMOUREUX, O.M.I.

Advocates—Revs. RUSSELL L. BOISVERT; MICHAEL T. DONOHUE; WILLIAM T. FLYNN; PAUL J. GAUMOND; PAUL L. HEBERT; RUSSELL F. KENNEDY; FRANCIS A. LISZEWSKI; LEO S. SUTULA; STANLEY J. SZCZAPA; ROBERT WASHABAUGH; Sr. BEATRICE THEROUX, D.H.S.

Secretary of the Tribunal—Mrs. MARY J. SHEA.

Notaries—Rev. Msgr. THOMAS R. BRIDE, P.A., V.G.; Rev. Msgr. ROBERT L. BROWN; Mrs. MARY J. SHEA.

Vicar for Clergy—Rev. Msgr. RICHARD P. LAROCQUE; Mrs. SUSAN GARDINER, Sec.

Diocesan Offices, Ministries, Societies

Annual Bishop's Appeal (ABA)—See Development, Diocesan Office.

Bishop's Delegate to Hispanic Permanent Deacons—Mr. JESUS A.DIEZ CANSECO, *110 Pruett Pl., Oakdale, 06370.*

Diocesan Finance Council—Most Rev. DANIEL A. HART, D.D., Chm.; Rev. Msgr. THOMAS R. BRIDE, P.A., V.G.; Rev. Msgr. M. DAVITT FOX; Revs. RUSSELL BOISVERT; ANTHONY GRUBER; ANTHONY ROSAFORTE; THOMAS SMITH; WILLIAM SCHNEIDER; KENNETH FLINT; JOHN WHITE; Mr. JAMES CRONIN; Mr. FRED PERKINS, C.P.A.; Mr. PETER LAMALFA; Mrs. JOYCE PAGE; Mr. BERNARD PHANEUF; Mr. WILLIAM MCGURK; Mrs. DIANE KELLY; Mr. TERRENCE CAHILL; Mr. KENNETH PARZYCH; Mr. THOMAS GALLIVAN; Mr. VINCENT ROEMMELE.

Diocesan Panel of Pastors, Canon 1742—Rev. Msgr. M. DAVITT FOX; Rev. Msgr. ANTHONY ROSAFORTE; Revs. RUSSELL BOISVERT; ANTHONY GRUBER; WILLIAM SCHNEIDER; JOHN WHITE.

Diocesan Pastoral Council—See Chancery listing.

Bishop's Liaison with the Retired Clergy—Rev. Msgr. RICHARD P. LAROCQUE, *The Chancery, 201 Broadway, Norwich, 06360.* Tel: 860-887-9294.

Board of Education—See School Office.

Building Commission—Rev. Msgr. M. DAVITT FOX, Chm.; Rev. Msgr. WILLIS W. WEST; Revs. JOHN J. WHITE; MICHAEL DONOHUE.

Campaigns—

Campaign for Human Development—Rev. MICHAEL T. DONOHUE, *St. Matthias Rectory, Boston Post Rd., P.O. Box 25, East Lyme, 06333.* Tel: 860-691-2235.

Catholic Relief Services—Rev. Msgr. ROBERT L. BROWN, Dir.; Mrs. SUE SULLIVAN; Sec., *P.O. Box 587, Norwich, 06360.* Tel: 860-887-9294.

Campus Ministry—Rev. LAURENCE A.M. LAPOINTE, Diocesan Dir., *Newman Hall, 290 Prospect St., Willimantic, 06226.* Tel: 860-423-0856. (See separate category under Institutions for details).

Catechetical Ministry, Office of Director—See Faith Formation, Office for.

Catholic Charities-Catholic Family Services—Mr. JOHN SMEY, Diocesan Dir., *11 Bath St., Norwich, 06360.* Tel: 860-889-8346; Fax: 860-889-2658. Counsellors: Sr. SUZANNE GEBRIAN, M.H.S.H.; Mr. MICHAEL PETRIDES; Ms. SANDRA COULLARD, M.S.W.

District Offices—New London: *10 Pearl St., New London, 06320.* Tel: 860-443-5328. JULEIGH WILSON, Supvr. Comprehensive Emergency Svcs.; Windham: JENNIFER LAMOUREAUX, Supvr. Comprehensive Emergency Svcs., *61 Club Rd., Windham, 06280.* Tel: 860-423-7065.

Catholic Mental Health Clinic—11 Bath St., Norwich, 06360. Tel: 860-889-8346.

Catholic Mutual Relief Society—Diocesan Insurance, Ms. ROBIN HOLTSCLAW, Risk Mgr., *467 Bloomfield Ave., Bloomfield, 06002.* Tel: 1-800-331-2561. National Office, *4223 Center St., Omaha, NE, 68105.* Tel: 1-800-228-6108.

Catholic Youth Organization (CYO)—See Faith Formation, Office for.

CCD—See Faith Formation, Office for.

Cemetery Corporation and Subsidiaries, Diocesan Cemeteries—Rev. Msgr. WILLIS W. WEST, Dir., *St. Joseph Rectory, 99 Jackson St., Willimantic, 06226.* Tel: 860-423-8439. NICHOLAS W. MIGNONE, Mgr., Office: *815 Boswell Ave., Norwich, 06360.* Tel: 860-887-1019; Fax: 860-889-4804. (For details on individual cemeteries see separate listing.).

Commission on Women—Mrs. V. JANE LEGER, Diocesan Dir., *323 Main St., Norwich, 06360.* Tel: 860-889-7374 (Office); 449-9584 (Home).; Sr. THERESE MORNEAU, D.H.S.; Ms. JENNIFER BARRY; Ms. JEANNE BIAGIARELLI; Ms. IRENE BOULEY; Mrs. PAULINE CLOUTIER; Ms. CYNTHIA DELUCIA; Ms. JANE ENGELKE; Ms. KATHLEEN GRAVEL; Mrs. JANET GRIFFIN; Ms. RUTH KULMACZ; Ms. MARTHA KOWAC; Mrs. JANE LEGER; Ms. LINNEA LINDSTROM; Ms. BEATRICE MACKENZIE; Mrs. JUDY PAPPAGALLO; Mrs. JOHANNA REILLY; Miss JOSEPHINE RISICA.

Communications, Office of—Miss JACQUELINE M. KELLER, Dir. LOUISE DUMAINE, Sec., *The Bishop Flanagan Ministry Center, 1595 Norwich-New London Tpke., Uncasville, 06382.* Tel: 860-848-2237.

Community Ministries—Mrs. BARBARA BELLONE, *323 Main St., Norwich, 06360.* Tel: 860-889-7374 (Office). MARDIE FISHER, Asst. Admin., *323 Main St., Norwich, 06360.*

The Hope Shop—327 Main St., Norwich, 06360.

Saint Vincent de Paul Place—Norwich: *323 Main St., Norwich, 06360.* Tel: 860-889-7374. Middletown: *617 Main St., P.O. Box 398, Middletown, 06457.* Tel: 860-344-0097; Fax: 860-343-0023. Mr. PETER HARDING, Dir.; Sr. CAROL BEAUDOIN, R.S.M., Soup Kitchen Coord. Tel: 860-265-6999.

Connecticut Catholic Conference—Dr. MARIE HILLIARD, Exec. Dir., *134 Farmington Ave., Hartford, 06105.* Tel: 860-524-7882.

Continuing Education and Formation Commission—Rev. MARK O'DONNELL, Chm.; Rev. ROLAND C. CLOUTIER; DENNIS M. PERKINS; MICHAEL S. SMITH; Sr. MURIEL AUDETTE, S.S.A.; Sr. MARYANNE GUERTIN, S.S.J.

Council of Catholic Nurses—Rev. THOMAS SMITH, Diocesan Moderator, *St. Mary Rectory, 10 Huntington St., New London, 06320.* Tel: 860-437-1889.

Council of Catholic Women—Tel: 860-889-8346. Rev. EDWARD KONOPKA, Moderator, *St. Peter Rectory, 30 St. Peter Ln., P.O. Box 707, Higganum, 06441.* Tel: 860-345-8018. District Moderators: Revs. RICHARD T. BUONGIRNO, Middletown Deanery; MARTIN J. JONES, New London Deanery; EUGENE PILATOWSKI, Norwich Deanery; CHARLES LEBLANC, Putnam Deanery; Rev. Msgr. WILLIS W. WEST, Willimantic Deanery; Rev. PAUL MURDOCK, Rockville Deanery.

The Deaf, Ministry to—Sr. M. ESTHER COCKBURN, M.H.S.H., Dir., *God's Gift House, 325 Main St., P.O. Box 813, Norwich, 06360.* Tel: 860-886-1281 (Voice & TTY).

Development, Diocesan Office of (DOD)—Mr. RICHARD COSTELLO, Exec. Dir., *31 Perkins Ave., Norwich, 06360.* Tel: 860-886-1928.

Annual Bishop's Appeal—Mr. RICHARD COSTELLO, Dir., *31 Perkins Ave., Norwich, 06360.* Tel: 860-886-1928.

Planned Giving Office—Mr. RICHARD COSTELLO, Dir., *31 Perkins Ave., Norwich, 06360.* Tel: 860-886-1928.

Disabilities-People with—See His Able People, Ministry of.

Ecumenism—

Diocesan Commission for Ecumenical and Interreligious Affairs—Sr. MARYANNE GUERTIN, S.S.J., Dir., *Bishop Flanagan Ministry Center, 1595 Norwich-New London Tpke., Uncasville, 06382-1319.* Tel: 860-848-2237. Revs. GERALD COHEN, C.S.C.; RICHARD K. GROSS, S.J.; MARK D. O'DONNELL; Bro. THOMAS BERUBE, S.S.E.; Mrs. ROBERT CALABRO; Mrs. CAROL HANSEN; Mrs. DENISE NAULT; Mrs. ANITA POWERS; Mrs. GEORGIA TRACEY; Mr. MICHAEL TURCIO.

Evangelization & Catechumenate (RCIA), Office of—SUSAN MYSHRALL, Admin. Asst. R.C.I.A. Team: Rev. STANLEY J. SZCZAPA; ERNEST GOLNIK; Sr. KATHERINE MCKENNA, P.B.V.M.; GAYLE MADDEN; THOMAS MADDEN; MILDRED STEARNS; SUSAN MYSHRALL, *The Bishop Flanagan Ministry Center, 1595 Norwich-New London Tpke., Uncasville, 06382-1319.* Tel: 860-848-2237.

Faith Formation, Office for—Bishop Flanagan Ministry Center, 1595 Norwich-New London Tpke., Uncasville, 06382-1319. Tel: 860-848-2237. Sr. ELEANOR PERFETTO, Dir. Assoc. Dirs.: Sr. ELEANOR O'MALLEY; Mrs. DONNA GILLILAND; Sr. BETTY PAUL, S.P., Assoc. Dir., Diocesan Media Center; Mrs. EILEEN PASSERO.

Family Life, Office of—Sr. JOANNE CAMPANINI, I.H.M., Coord., *The Bishop Flanagan Ministry Center, 1595 Norwich-New London Tpke., Uncasville, 06382-1319.* Tel: 860-848-2237.

"Four County Catholic"—See Newspaper.

God's Gift House—See Community Ministries.

Haitian Ministries—EMILY SMACK, Acting Dir., *Bishop Flanagan Ministry Center, 1595 Norwich-New London Tpke., Uncasville, 06382-1319.* Tel: 860-848-2237. EMILY SMACK, Chm. Members: Mr. ANDREW HOFFMAN; Ms. LOUISE LABBE; Ms. SUSAN PETROSINO; Sr. MARILYN CANNING, R.S.M.; Mrs. EVELYN KIRBY; Rev. ANTHONY GRUBER; Ms. RUTH SANZO; Ms. JANET MINELLA-DIDIER; Mr. FRANCIS TRAINOR; Dr. THOMAS GORIN; BERNYCE RUIZ; Mr. WILLIAM MCGURK; Mr. GREG SECORD.

His Able People, Ministry of—Deacon EDUARDO DOGUE, Dir., *P.O. Box 242, Wauregan, 06387.* Tel: 860-779-0362.

Hispanic Ministry—Sr. MARY JUDE LAZARUS, S.C.M.C., Interim Dir., *61 Club Rd., Windham, 06280.* Tel: 860-423-8617.

New London—Rev. RUSSELL KENNEDY, Priest Dir., New London Area, *St. Mary Rectory, 70 Central Ave., Norwich, 06360.* Tel: 860-887-2565. Deacon MARIANO RAMOS; Sr. IRMA GARCIA, R.O.D.A.; Sr. MARIELOS BALLESTEROS, Pastoral Assoc.

Windham—Rev. PAUL MURDOCK, Dir.; Deacon FELIPE SILVA; Sr. MARY JUDE, S.C.M.C., Pastoral Assoc., *La Iglesia del Sagrado Corazon de Jesus Office, 61 Club Rd., 06280.* Tel: 860-423-8617.

Middletown—Revs. JOSEPH ASHE, Pastor; RUSSELL KENNEDY, Priest Dir., *St. John, 19 St. John Sq., Middletown, 06457.* Tel: 860-343-0466.

Norwich—Rev. RUSSELL KENNEDY, Priest Dir.; Sr. BERTA NAJERA, R.O.D.A., Pastoral Assoc., *St. Mary Church, 70 Central Ave., Norwich, 06360.* Tel: 860-887-2565.

Rockville—Rev. PAUL MURDOCK, Priest Dir.; Deacon MICHAEL BERSTENE, *St. Bernard Church, 25 St. Bernard's Terr., Rockville, 06066.*

Holy Childhood—See Pontifical Association of the Holy Childhood.

Holy Name Societies—Holy Name Societies, c/o Msgr. Thomas Bride, P.A., V.G., 201 Broadway, P.O. Box 587, Norwich, 06360. Tel: 860-887-9294.

Insurance—See Catholic Mutual Relief Society (C.M.R.S.).

Justice & Peace, Office of—Mr. RAY MASTRONUNZIO, Dir., *The Bishop Flanagan Ministry Center, 1595 Norwich-New London Tpke., Uncasville, 06382.* Tel: 860-848-2237.

Lawyers, Guild of Catholic—Mailing Address: *The Chancery, 201 Broadway, Norwich, 06360.* Tel: 860-887-9294. Atty. MICHAEL E. DRISCOLL, Pres.; Mrs. REGINA WIEGERT, Sec.; Rev. Msgr. HENRY ARCHAMBAULT, P.A., Chap.

Legion of Mary—Rev. ROBERT B. LYNCH, Diocesan Spiritual Dir., *St. Mary Rectory, 70 Central Ave., Norwich, 06360.* Tel: 860-887-2565.

Liturgy, Office of—Bishop Flanagan Ministry Center. Tel: 860-848-2237.

Marriage Encounter—The Bishop Flanagan Ministry Center, 1595 Norwich-New London Tpke., Uncasville, 06382. Tel: 860-848-2237.

Mercy Xavier Development Corporation—Mr. JAMES JOYCE, Pres., *181 Randolph Rd., Middletown, 06457.* Tel: 860-347-2343; 346-7735.

Ministry Formation and Permanent Diaconate, Office of—Deacon ROLAND J. LACASSE, Asst. Delegate, *The Bishop Flanagan Ministry Center, 1595 Norwich-New London Tpke., Uncasville, 06382.* Tel: 860-848-2237.

Newspaper—Official monthly newspaper of Diocese of Norwich—*"Four County Catholic"*; Mr. PETER L. GILL, Editor; Mr. BRUCE AVERY, Advertising Mgr., *Office of Communications, Bishop Flanagan Ministry Center, 1595 Norwich-New London Tpke., Uncasville, 06382.* Tel: 860-889-0202; Fax: 860-848-2816.

Nurses—See Council of Catholic Nurses.

Pastoral Planning, Office of—Sr. MARY ALICE KLINE, R.S.M., Coord., *Bishop Flanagan Ministry Center, 1595 Norwich-New London Tpke., Uncasville, 06382.* Tel: 860-848-2237.

People with Disability—See His Able People, Ministry of.

Permanent Deacon, Office of—Rev. Msgr. RICHARD P. LAROCQUE, Vicar for Clergy, *The Chancery, 201 Broadway, Norwich, 06360.* Tel: 860-887-9294.

Planned Giving Office—See Development, Diocesan Office of.

Pontifical Association of the Holy Childhood—Rev. Msgr. THOMAS R. BRIDE, P.A., V.G., Dir., *201 Broadway, P.O. Box 587, Norwich, 06360.* Tel: 860-887-9294.

Pontifical Society for the Propagation of the Faith—Rev. Msgr. THOMAS R. BRIDE, P.A., V.G., Dir.; Mrs. ANN DEPTA, Sec., *201 Broadway, P.O. Box 587, Norwich, 06360.* Tel: 860-887-9294.

Priests on Duty Outside Diocese—Revs. THOMAS M. ANGELO; JOHN GWUDZ; GERARD KIRBY; ADOLFO KLIMANSKIS; DEUS-DEDIT BYABATO.

Prison Ministry for Diocese of Norwich—Ms. MEG BRODHEAD, Dir.; Deacon DENNIS F. DOLAN, *Bishop Flanagan Ministry Center, 1595 Norwich-New London Tpke., Uncasville, 06382.* Tel: 860-848-2237.

Pro-Life Activities—Mr. JOSEPH P. COLLISON, Dir., *201 Broadway, P.O. Box 587, Norwich, 06360.* Tel: 860-887-9294.

Project Northeast—A program of Evangelization for the unchurched poor. Rev. RICHARD L. ARCHAMBAULT, Dir., *81 Church St., Putnam, 06260.* Tel: 860-928-4078. Sr. ELEANOR BALDONI, D.H.S., Assoc. Dir., *67 Railroad Ave., Putnam, 06260.* Tel: 860-928-5965.

RCIA—See Catechumenate, Office of.

Religious—See Vicar for Religious.

Retired Clergy—Rev. Msgr. BRONISLAW GADAROWSKI; Rev. Msgr. THADDEUS F. MALANOWSKI; Rev. Msgr. JAMES J. O'BRIEN; Rev. Msgr. PAUL ST. ONGE; Revs. LEO ALMENDRA; HENRY BIALOWSKI; ROBERT W. CRONIN; J. CLIFFORD CURTIN; EDWARD J. DAVIS; KENNETH FLINT; ALBERT GIAQUINTO; JOSEPH HORAN; J. RALPH KELLEY; JOHN KOZON; ANTHONY P. KUZDAL; ALFRED R. LANDRY; JOHN MARCINIAK; DANIEL F. MCGRATH; ROBERT E. MCNULTY; HUGH J. MURPHY; JOSEPH E. NICHOLS; EDWARD J. POULIN; ADAM PUPSYS; PAUL F. RAMEN; JOSEPH M. RICARD; JOHN J. SULLIVAN; EDWARD J. WISNESKI; ROBERT J. WOOD; THEODORE E. BERUBE; ESLYN J. DRUMMOND; GEORGE H. PARKER; EDWARD F. FRIGAULT.

Retirement—See Priests' Retirement Commission.

School Office, Diocesan—Dr. HOWARD BENNETT, Supt.; Sr. MARIE TREANOR, S.N.D., Assoc. Supt.; Sr. RACHEL ANDERSON, C.S.C., Sec., *43 Perkins Ave., Norwich, 06360.* Tel: 860-887-4086; 887-9371.

Board of Education—Mrs. GAY MULLEN; Sr. MARIE TREANOR, S.N.D., Chm.; Mrs. ANDREA BULLARD; Mrs. MARGARET LANGER, Chm.; Dr. HOWARD BENNETT; ELMO GIANANTONI; Rev. Msgr. ANTHONY S. ROSAFORTE, Pastor with a school. Ex Officios: Rev. Msgr. THOMAS R. BRIDE P.A., V.G.; Mrs. PATRICIA

AUSTIN; Mr. JOHN CIRILLO, Vice-Chm.; Rev. ROBERT W. BARNES; WILLIAM F. O'NEIL, JR., K.S.G.

Scouting—See Faith Formation, Office for.

Sick, Ministry to the—Sr. RITA JOHNSON, S.S.N.D., Dir., *W.W. Backus Hospital, 326 Washington St., Norwich, 06360.* Tel: 860-889-8331.

Soup Kitchen—See Community Ministries, Saint Vincent de Paul Place.

Spanish Speaking Apostolate—See Hispanic Ministry.

The Spiritual Renewal Services of the Diocese of Norwich—Rev. RAYMOND D. INTROVIGNE, Diocesan Dir.; Mrs. JUDITH HUGHES, Assoc. Dir., *God's Gift House, 325 Main St., P.O. Box 6, Norwich, 06360.* Tel: 860-887-0702. Dial-A-Prayer. Tel: 860-887-7767.

Vicar for Religious—Rev. JOHN W. MCWEENEY, M.S., J.C.L.; Sr. SALLY J. TOLLES, D.H.S., J.D., J.C.L., Assoc. Vicar, *The Tribunal, Otis St., P.O. Box 587, Norwich, 06360.* Tel: 860-887-9294.

Vocation Review Committee, Diocesan—Rev. Msgr. THOMAS R. BRIDE, P.A., V.G.; Rev. Msgr. RICHARD P. LAROCQUE; Rev. Msgr. WILLIS W. WEST; Revs. R. THOMAS MCCONAGHY; MARK O'DONNELL; MICHAEL PHILLIPPINO; Bro. WILLIAM CIGANEK, C.F.X.; Sr. JOYCE RIDICK, S.S.C.

Vocations—Rev. Msgr. THOMAS R. BRIDE, P.A., V.G., Diocesan Dir.; Revs. MICHAEL PHILLIPPINO, Asst. Dir. Vocations; MARK O'DONNELL, Diocesan Dir. for Promotion & Devel.; Mrs. ANN DEPTA, Sec.; Mrs. REBECCA CADY, Sec., *201 Broadway, P.O. Box 587, Norwich, 06360-0587.* Tel: 860-887-9294.

Youth Ministry—See Faith Formation, Office of.

Youth Retreat Centers—*Alpha House East,* Griswold, *Alpha House West,* Higganum. For details, contact; Sr. BETTY PAUL, S.P., *Bishop Flanagan Ministry Center, 1595 Norwich-New London Tpke., Uncasville, 06382.* Tel: 860-848-2237.

Women, Commission on—See Commission on Women.

CLERGY, PARISHES, MISSIONS AND PAROCHIAL SCHOOLS

CITY OF NORWICH
(New London County)

1—ST. PATRICK CATHEDRAL (1879), Rev. Msgr. Anthony S. Rosaforte; Revs. Gregory P. Galvin; Stephen S. Gulino; Deacon Al R. Fecteau.
Res., 213 Broadway, 06360. Tel: 860-889-8441; Fax: 860-889-2978.
School—211 Broadway, 06360. Tel: 860-889-4174. Sr. Mary Bernard Rivest, S.C.M.C., Prin.
Sisters of Charity of Our Lady Mother of the Church 2; Lay Teachers 9; Students 223.
Catechesis/Religious Programs—Tel: 860-886-1060.
Students 202.

2—SACRED HEART (Norwichtown) (1902), Rev. J. Lawrence Ouimet; Deacon Robert P. Hayes. In res., Rev. Michael L. Phillippino.
Res., 52 W. Town St., Norwichtown, 06360. Tel: 860-887-1030; Fax: 860-887-6550.
Catechesis/Religious Programs—Tel: 860-887-1715.
Students 104.
Mission—Fitchville, New London Co., St. John, 190 Fitchville Rd., Bozrah, 06334.

3—ST. JOSEPH, New London Co., (1904) (Polish), Rev. Eugene Pilatowski.
Res., 120 Cliff St., 06360. Tel: 860-887-1565.
Catechesis/Religious Programs—Tel: 860-887-4565.
Students 216.

4—ST. MARY (1845), Rev. Robert B. Lynch; Deacon Dennis Doyle. In res., Revs. Joseph G. Finnerty; Russell F. Kennedy.
Res., 70 Central Ave., 06360. Tel: 860-887-2565.
Catechesis/Religious Programs—Tel: 860-889-8347.
Students 80.

5—SS. PETER AND PAUL (1938), Rev. Barry C. Meehan, S.J.
Res., 181 Elizabeth St., 06360. Tel: 860-887-9857; Fax: 860-886-4728.

OUTSIDE THE CITY OF NORWICH

Ballouville, Windham Co., St. Anne (1882), Rev. Sylva P. LeCours.
Res., Box 125, 06233. Tel: 860-774-6164.
Catechesis/Religious Programs—Tel: 860-774-4023.
Students 79.

Baltic, New London Co., St. Mary of the Immaculate Conception (1886), Rev. Joseph Tito.
Res., 06330. Tel: 860-822-6378. [CEM]
School—St. Joseph, Tel: 860-822-6141; Fax: 860-822-6141.
Sisters of Charity of Our Lady Mother of the Church 5; Lay Teachers 5; Students 120.
Catechesis/Religious Programs—Students 140.

Bolton, Tolland Co., St. Maurice (1954), Rev. William J. Olesik.
Res., 32 Hebron Rd., 06043. Tel: 860-643-4466.
Catechesis/Religious Programs—Tel: 860-643-8374.
Students 251.

Brooklyn, Windham Co., Our Lady of La Salette (1968), Rev. Thomas G. Sickler, M.S. In res., Rev. John W. McWeeney, M.S.
Res., 06234. Tel: 860-774-6275; Fax: 860-774-0679.
Catechesis/Religious Programs—Students 320.
Mission—Hampton, Windham Co., Our Lady of Lourdes, 06234.

Canterbury, Windham Co., St. Augustine (1978), Rev. Gonzalo E. Regalado.
Res., 144 Westminister Rd., 06331. Tel: 860-546-6074.
Catechesis/Religious Programs—Students 205.

Chester, Middlesex Co., St. Joseph (1885), Rev. Thomas W. Ahern.
Res., 48 Middlesex Ave., 06412. Tel: 860-526-5495. [CEM]
Catechesis/Religious Programs—Students 210.

Clinton, Middlesex Co., St. Mary of the Visitation (1934), Rev. Michael Sequeira (India); Deacon Paul Weber.
Res., 54 Grove St., 06413-1999. Tel: 860-669-8512; Fax: 860-669-9052. [CEM]
Catechesis/Religious Programs—Tel: 860-669-7375.
Students 473.

Colchester, New London Co., St. Andrew (1860), Revs. Michael C. Giannitelli; Frank W. McKenna; Deacons Robert Barlow; Dennis Dolan.
Res., 128 Norwich Ave., 06415. Tel: 860-537-2355; Fax: 860-537-2356. [CEM 2][JC 2]
Catechesis/Religious Programs—Tel: 860-537-5415.
Students 684.

Columbia, Tolland Co., St. Columba (1960), Rev. Daniel C. Cronin.
Res., Rte. 66 at Rte. 87, P.O. Box 146, 06237. Tel: 203-228-3735.
Catechesis/Religious Programs—Tel: 860-228-3727.
Students 208.

Coventry, Tolland Co., St. Mary (1877), Rev. Paul Boudreau.
Res., 1600 Main St., P.O. Box 250, 06238. Tel: 860-742-0681. [CEM]
Catechesis/Religious Programs—Students 352.
Mission—Eagleville, Tolland Co., St. Joseph.

Cromwell, Middlesex Co., St. John (1882), Revs. Raymond Borkowski, O.F.M.Conv.; Hilary Brzostowski, O.F.M.Conv.
Res., 5 St. John Ct., 06416. Tel: 860-635-5590; Fax: 860-635-5591.
Catechesis/Religious Programs—Tel: 860-635-5156.
Students 629.

Danielson, Windham Co., St. James (1869), Revs. John J. O'Neill, M.S.; Brian D. Schloth, M.S.; Joseph F. Whalen, M.S.; John E. Welch, M.S.
Res., 12 Franklin St., 06239. Tel: 860-774-3900; Fax: 860-774-4205. [CEM]
School—Tel: 860-774-3281; Fax: 860-779-2137. Ms. Marguerite Ovellette, Prin.
Lay Teachers 11; Students 267.
Catechesis/Religious Programs—Tel: 860-774-8459.
Students 270.
Mission—East Killingly, Windham Co., Our Lady of Peace, 06239.

Dayville, Windham Co., St. Joseph (1874), Rev. William J. McNulty.
Res., 350 Hartford Pike, Box 487, 06241. Tel: 860-774-8656. [CEM]
Catechesis/Religious Programs—Tel: 860-774-2451. D.R.E.: Alyce Chartier; Norma Pokoski.
Students 104.
Convent—21 Williamsville Rd., Box 158, Rogers, 06263. Tel: 860-774-8154. Parish House Daughters of the Holy Spirit

Durham, Middlesex Co., Notre Dame (1953), Rev. Augustine Naduvilekoot.
Res., 272 Main St., 06422. Tel: 860-349-3058.
Catechesis/Religious Programs—Tel: 860-349-3059. Mr. Charles Colella, D.R.E.
Students 293.

East Hampton, Middlesex Co., St. Patrick (1879), Rev. Thomas G. Twomey; Deacon Warren J.F. Cyr.
Res., 47 W. High St., 06424-1077. Tel: 860-267-6644. [CEM]
Catechesis/Religious Programs—Students 311.

East Lyme, New London Co., St. Matthias (Flannders) (1939), Rev. Michael T. Donohue.
Res., 20 Church Lane, Unit 9, P.O. Box 25, 06333. Tel: 860-691-2235; Fax: 860-739-0524.
Catechesis/Religious Programs—Students 260.

Ellington, Tolland Co., St. Luke (1961), Rev. Louis M. Galluppi; Deacon Richard A. Boucher.
Res., 141 Maple St., P.O. Box 246, 06029. Tel: 860-875-8552; Fax: 860-872-6548.
Catechesis/Religious Programs—Tel: 860-875-4951.
Students 428.

Essex, Middlesex Co., Our Lady of Sorrows (1926), Revs. Francis W. Murphy; Bradley Pierce, M.Ss.A.
Res., 14 Prospect St., 06426. Tel: 203-767-1284.
Catechesis/Religious Programs—Tel: 203-767-2938.
Students 184.

Fishers Island, Suffolk Co., Our Lady of Grace (1902), Rev. Zenon A. Smilga Tel: 516-788-7353.
Res., Alpine Ave., Box 425, 06390. Tel: 516-788-7353.

Gales Ferry, New London Co., Our Lady of Lourdes (1960), Revs. William F. Schneider; Justinian B. Rweyemamu; Sr. Muriel Audette, S.S.A., Pastoral Assoc.; Deacon Steve Reed.
Res., 1650 Rte. 12, P.O. Box 278, 06335. Tel: 860-464-7251; Fax: 860-464-7252.
Catechesis/Religious Programs—Tel: 860-464-6676.
Students 534.

Groton, New London Co., Sacred Heart (1905), Revs. John J. Meagher, S.S.E.; Francis X. McMahon, S.S.E.
Res., 56 Sacred Heart Dr., 06340. Tel: 860-445-2905; 445-6648; Fax: 860-445-6648.
School—(Grades PreK-8). Tel: 460-445-0611. Sr. Linda Corona, A.S.C.J., Prin.
Lay Teachers 18; Aides 4; Students 383.
Catechesis/Religious Programs—Students 190.

St. Mary (1964), Rev. Theodore J. Klein; Sr. Jacquelyn Donohue, I.H.M., Pastoral Assoc.
Res., 69 Groton Long Point Rd., 06340. Tel: 860-445-1446; Fax: 860-448-0529.
Catechesis/Religious Programs—Students 260.

Hebron, Tolland Co., The Church of the Holy Family (1987), Rev. Roland C. Cloutier; Sr. Mary Ann DeFrancesco, R.S.M., Pastoral Assoc.
Mailing Address: P.O. Box 146, 06248. Tel: 860-228-0096; Fax: 860-228-1629.
Catechesis/Religious Programs—Mark L. McCann, D.R.E.
Students 450.

Higganum, Middlesex Co., St. Peter (1958), Rev. Edward M. Konopka.
Res., 30 St. Peter Ln., P.O. Box 707, 06441. Tel: 860-345-8018; Fax: 860-345-4067.
Catechesis/Religious Programs—Tel: 860-345-4726.
Students 206.

Jewett City, New London Co., St. Mary (1870), Revs. Gerald Boulanger, M.S., Co-Pastor; Rene L. Parent, M.S., Co-Pastor; Rev. Msgr. Henry N. Archambault, P.A., Dean; Rev. Msgr. Richard P., LaRocque, Vicar for Clergy; Rev. Msgr. Thomas R. Bride, Vicar General; Deacon Paul R. Baillargeon.
Res., 34 N. Main St., 06351. Tel: 860-376-2044. [CEM 2]
School—54 N. Main St., 06351. Tel: 860-376-0446; Fax: 860-376-4200. Fred Cale, Prin.
Lay Teachers 10; Students 170.
Catechesis/Religious Programs—Tel: 860-376-5150.
Students 274.

Killingworth, Middlesex Co., St. Lawrence (1978), Deacon Raymond Gosselin.
Res., 7 Hemlock Dr., 06419. Tel: 860-663-2576; Fax: 860-663-2576.
Catechesis/Religious Programs—Students 191.

Lebanon, New London Co., St. Francis of Assisi (1980), Rev. Peter B. Liszewski.
Res., W. Town St., P.O. Box 172, 06249. Tel: 860-642-6711.
Catechesis/Religious Programs—Students 188.

Middlefield, Middlesex Co., St. Colman (1890), Rev. Lester G. Morris; Sr. Pauline Semkow, R.S.M., Pastoral Assoc.
Res., 145 Hubbard St., P.O. Box 457, 06455. Tel: 860-349-3868.
Catechesis/Religious Programs—Tel: 860-349-8074.
Students 180.

Middletown, Middlesex Co.,

1—ST. FRANCIS, (1903), Rev. Msgr. Michael D. Fox; Revs. Richard T. Buongirno; Robert Washabaugh.
Res., 10 Elm St., 06457. Tel: 860-347-4684; Fax: 860-347-7669.

Catechesis/Religious Programs—Tel: 860-344-1098.
Students 131.

2—ST. JOHN, (1843), Rev. Joseph C. Ashe; Sr. Ann Mack, R.S.M., Pastoral Assoc.
Res., 19 John's Sq., 06457. Tel: 860-347-5626. [CEM]
School—Tel: 860-347-3202.
Lay Teachers 14; Students 245.
Catechesis/Religious Programs—Students 72.

3—ST. MARY OF CZESTOCHOWA, (1903) (Polish), Revs. Aloysius J. Kisluk; Clement Jarnot, O.F.M.Conv.; Marek Masnicki. In res., Rev. John J. Sullivan.
Res., 79 S. Main St., 06457. Tel: 860-347-2365; Fax: 860-347-2110. [CEM]
School—87 S. Main St., 06457. Tel: 860-347-2978. Mrs. Kathleen Dutil, Prin.
Lay Teachers 10; Students 270.
Catechesis/Religious Programs—Students 160.

4—ST. PIUS X, (1957), Revs. Frederick Nickle, O.F.M.Cap.; James Hammer, O.F.M.Cap. In res., Revs. Colman Boylan, O.F.M.Cap., (Retired); Cyprian Murray, O.F.M.Cap.; Richard Donaldson, O.F.M.Cap., (Retired); Bruce Quinn, O.F.M.Cap., Hospital Chap.; Gabriel Massaro, O.F.M.Cap.; Bro. Eugene Sheehan, O.F.M.Cap.
Res., 310 Westfield St., 06457-2047. Tel: 860-347-4441; 4442; Fax: 203-347-3001.
Catechesis/Religious Programs—Tel: 860-346-9100.
Students 550.

5—ST. SEBASTIAN, (1930) (Italian), Revs. Joseph D. Sibilano, O.S.J.; Daniel L. Schwebs, O.S.J.; Joseph L. Iannuzzi, O.S.J.; Deacons John P. Catalano; Nicholas J. Cannata.
Res., 155 Washington St., 06457. Tel: 860-347-2638; Fax: 860-347-6736. [CEM]
School—61 Durant Ter., 06457. Tel: 860-347-3438. Sr. Patricia Dora, C.S.J., Prin.
Lay Teachers 10; Students 153.
Catechesis/Religious Programs—Students 386.

Montville, New London Co., St. John (1881), Rev. Russel L. Boisvert Tel: 203-848-1257; Deacon Melvin Nygaard. In res., Rev. Msgr. Robert L. Brown, Chancellor, Tel: 860-848-3771; Rev. Mark D. O'Donnell, Chap. St. Bernard High School, Tel: 860-848-1271.
Res., 22 Maple Ave., Uncasville, 06382. Tel: 860-848-9335. [CEM]
Catechesis/Religious Programs—Tel: 203-848-1409. Jim Rood, D.R.E.
Students 270.

Moodus, Middlesex Co., St. Bridget (1914), Rev. Msgr. Henry J. Dziadosz.
Res., 75 Moodus-Leesville Rd., P.O. Box 422, 06469-0422. Tel: 860-873-8623. [CEM]
Catechesis/Religious Programs—Students 270.

Moosup, Windham Co., All-Hallows (1859), Revs. Anthony Gruber; Gregorz P. Brozonowicz, Parochial Vicar.
Res., 130 Prospect St., 06354. Tel: 860-564-2668; Fax: 860-564-3941. [CEM]
School—Plainfield Catholic, Tel: 860-564-3476.
Lay Teachers 12; Students 254.
Catechesis/Religious Programs—Tel: 860-230-0141.
Students 271.
Mission—Sterling, Windham Co., St. Joseph.

Mystic, New London Co., St. Patrick (1870), Rev. Charles A. McGrail.
Res., 32 E. Main St., P.O. Box 236, 06355. Tel: 860-536-1800; Fax: 860-536-9635. [CEM]
Catechesis/Religious Programs—Tel: 860-536-6808.
Students 209.

New London, New London Co., St. Joseph (1907) (Italian), Revs. Joseph Castaldi; Martin J. Jones; Rev. Msgr. Paul J. St. Onge, (Retired); Rev. Joseph DeCosta; Deacon Gerard Gaynor.
Res., 17 Squire St., 06320. Tel: 860-443-5393.
School—Tel: 860-442-1720.
Lay Teachers 10; Students 226.
Catechesis/Religious Programs—Students 240.

St. Mary, Star of the Sea (1870), Rev. Thomas J. Smith; Rev. Msgr. Thomas R. Bride, P.A.; Revs. Dennis M. Perkins; Pasquale Taliercio, M.S.A.; Russell P. Kennedy, Dir. of Hispanic Min.; Deacons Mariano Ramos; Jesus A. Diez-Canseco; Sr. Brta Najela, R.O.D.A., Hispanic Min. Pastoral Assocs.: Sr. Giuseppina Frontini, S.C.I.C.; Sr. Gemma Mancini, S.C.I.C.
Res., 10 Huntington St., 06320-6198. Tel: 860-447-1431; Fax: 860-437-1889.
School—Tel: 860-443-7758; Fax: 860-444-2465. Sr. Angese Quarta, S.C.I.C., Prin.
Priests 2; Sisters 4; Lay Teachers 14; Students 268.
Catechesis/Religious Programs—Tel: 860-443-5870; Fax: 860-443-8552. Sr. Immacolata DeCossio, S.C.I.C., D.R.E.
Students 425.
Convent—28 Huntington St., 06320. Sr. Giuseppina Frontini, S.C.I.C., Supr. The Sisters of Charity of the Immaculate Conception of Ivrea.
Convent—197 Broadway, Norwich, 06360. Tel: 860-886-6092. Sr. Brta Najela, R.O.D.A., Supr. The Oblate Sisters of Divine Love.
Hispanic Ministry—60 Jay St., 06320. Tel: 860-437-1285. Rev. Russell P. Kennedy, Dir.

Niantic, New London Co., St. Agnes (1922), Rev. Arthur A. Archer; Deacons Roland J. LaCasse; Maurice J. Walsh.
Res., 22 Haigh Ave., 06357. Tel: 860-739-9722.
Catechesis/Religious Programs—Tel: 860-739-9992.
Students 323.
Chapel—Crescent Beach, St. Francis Chapel (Summer).

North Grosvenordale, Windham Co., St. Joseph (1872), Rev. Brian J. Converse.
Res., 12 Main St., P.O. Box 897, 06255. Tel: 860-923-2361; Fax: 860-923-3396. [CEM]
School—Tel: 860-923-2090; Fax: 860-923-3609. Sr. M. Elaine Moorcraft, S.C.M.C., Prin.
Sisters of Charity of Our Lady Mother of the Church 4; Lay Teachers 9; Students 156.
Catechesis/Religious Programs—Students 279.
Mission—Mechanicsville, Windham Co., Sacred Heart, P.O. Box 897, 06255.

North Stonington, New London Co., St. Thomas More (1977), Rev. John C. Nash.
Res., 87 Mystic Rd., 06359. Tel: 860-535-1601.
Catechesis/Religious Programs—Tel: 860-535-3229.
Students 208.

Oakdale, New London Co., Our Lady of the Lakes (1966), Rev. Michael J. Gill.
Res., 752 Norwich, Salem Tpke., 06370. Tel: 860-859-1575.
Catechesis/Religious Programs—Students 264.

Occum, New London Co., St. Joseph (1887), Rev. Robert W. Barnes.
Res., Box 256, Versailles, 06383-0256. Tel: 860-822-8020.
Catechesis/Religious Programs—Tel: 860-822-6963. Mrs. Monica Bernier, D.R.E.
Students 173.
Saint Society Church—(Corporate Title: St. Joseph Church Society of Occum, CT, Inc.).

Old Lyme, New London Co., Christ the King (1934), Rev. Msgr. Richard P. LaRocque; Rev. Leszek T. Janik; Sr. Katherine M. McKenna, P.B.V.M., Pastoral Assoc.
Office: 20 Lyme St., P.O. Box 443, 06371. Tel: 860-434-1669; Fax: 860-434-7140.
Res., 30 Lyme St., P.O. Box 443, 06371. Tel: 860-434-1660.
Catechesis/Religious Programs—Tel: 860-434-9873. Louise Young, D.R.E.
Students 307.
Chapel—Our Lady of Good Counsel at Sound View. (Summer Chapel) Shore Rd., 06371.

Old Saybrook, Middlesex Co., St. John (1884), Revs. Joseph H. Hanks; Robert A. Murphy.
Res., 161 Main St., 06475. Tel: 860-388-3787; Fax: 860-388-6008. [CEM]
School—42 Maynard Rd., 06475. Tel: 860-388-0849; Fax: 860-388-6265. Sr. Maria Goretti, S.C.M.C., Prin.
Sisters 3; Lay Teachers 16; Students 231.
Catechesis/Religious Programs—06475. Tel: 203-388-6288.
Students 310.

Pawcatuck, New London Co., St. Michael (1860), Revs. R. Thomas McConaghy; Dariusz K. Dudzik.
Res., 60 Liberty St., 06379. Tel: 860-599-5580; Fax: 860-599-8079. [CEM]
School—Tel: 860-599-1084. Richard B. Woodworth, Prin.
Lay Teachers 9; Students 223.
Catechesis/Religious Programs—Tel: 860-599-0040. Mrs. Crystal F. Wilcox, D.R.E.
Students 213.

Plainfield, Windham Co., St. John the Apostle (1907), Rev. Charles R. LeBlanc.
Res., 10 Railroad Ave., 06374. Tel: 860-564-3313. [CEM]
Catechesis/Religious Programs—12 Railroad Ave., 06374. Tel: 860-564-8380.
Students 206.

Pomfret, Windham Co., Most Holy Trinity (1886), Rev. Paul L. Hebert.
Res., 568 Pomfret St., P.O. Box 235, 06258-0235. Tel: 860-928-5830.
Catechesis/Religious Programs—Students 268.

Portland, Middlesex Co., St. Mary (1872), Rev. John F. Ashe; Sr. Mary Ida Dolan, R.S.M., Pastoral Assoc., Tel: 860-342-4913. In res., Rev. Michael S. Smith.
Res., 51 Freestone Ave., P.O. Box 307, 06480. Tel: 860-342-2328; Fax: 860-342-1433. [CEM]
Catechesis/Religious Programs—Tel: 860-342-2308.
Students 400.

Preston, New London Co., St. Catherine of Siena (1975), Rev. V. Anthony J. Alaharasan; Sr. Laurie Doucette, C.S.C., Pastoral Assoc.
Res., 243 Rte. 164, 06365-8726. Tel: 860-887-9966; Fax: 860-889-7640.
Catechesis/Religious Programs—Students 125.

Putnam, Windham Co., St. Mary (1866), Revs. Francis J. O'Keefe; Thomas Plathottam; Marcel G. Lachance; Deacons Pierre M. Desilets; Bernard A. Phaneuf.
Res., 218 Providence St., 06260. Tel: 860-928-6535; Fax: 860-928-7246. [CEM]
School—23 Marshall St., 06260. Tel: 860-928-7046; 928-1104; Fax: 860-928-9379. Ms. Phyllis Hickey, Prin.
Catechesis/Religious Programs—15 Marshall St., 06260. Tel: 860-928-4507; Fax: 860-928-2032.
Students 150.

Quaker Hill, New London Co., Our Lady of Perpetual Help (1904) (Polish), Rev. Leo S. Sutula; Deacon Ronald S. Kitlinski.
Res., 63 Old Norwich Rd., P.O. Box 329, 06375. Tel: 860-443-1875.
Catechesis/Religious Programs—Students 96.
Convent—59 Old Norwich Rd., 06375. Tel: 860-447-3550. Sisters of St. Joseph of Third Order of St. Francis

Quinebaug, Windham Co., St. Stephen (1955), Rev. William J. O'Rourke.
Res., Junction Rtes. 131 & 197, 06262. Tel: 860-935-5205; Fax: 860-935-5205.
Catechesis/Religious Programs—Students 68.

Rockville, Tolland Co., St. Bernard (1854), Revs. John J. White; Joseph F. DeCosta. In res., Rev. Roger M. Comtois.
Res., 25 St. Bernard's Terr., 06066. Tel: 860-875-0753. [CEM]
School—20 School St., 06066. Tel: 860-875-0475; Fax: 860-872-2444. Sr. Mary Gerald, R.S.M., Prin.
Sisters 2; Lay Teachers 8; Students 145.
Catechesis/Religious Programs—22 School St., 06066. Tel: 860-872-3828.
Students 225.
Convent—32 School St., 06066. Tel: 860-875-4016. Sisters of Mercy
Cemetery Office:—Tel: 203-872-6601.

St. Joseph (1905) (Polish), Revs. Joseph M. Olczak, O.S.P.P.E.; Bartholomew P. Marciniak, O.S.P.
Res., 33 West St., 06066. Tel: 860-871-1970; Fax: 860-872-0333.
School—41 West St., 06066. Tel: 860-875-4943. Sr. Janice Marie Gaudette, Prin.
Felician Sisters 3; Lay Teachers 10; Students 165.
Catechesis/Religious Programs—Students 144.

Rogers, Windham Co., St. Ignatius (1939), Rev. William J. McNulty.
Res., 350 Hartford Pike, Box 487, Dayville, 06241. Tel: 860-774-8656.
Church—21 Williamsville Rd., Box 158, 06263.
Convent—17 Williamsville Rd., Box 158, 06263. Tel: 860-774-8154. St. Ignatius Parish House Daughters of the Holy Spirit

Somersville, Tolland Co., All Saints (1915), Rev. Timothy C. Valliere; Deacons James J. Burgess; Lawrence W. Deraleau; John J. Abdalla, D.R.E.
Res., 25 School St., P.O. Box M, 06072. Tel: 860-749-8625.
Catechesis/Religious Programs—Tel: 860-763-0348.
Students 405.

Stafford Springs, Tolland Co., St. Edward (1869), Revs. Richard-Jacob Forcier, O.F.M.Conv.; Mark-Thomas Booth, O.F.M.Conv.; Bro. Dennis Sokolowski, O.F.M.Conv.
Mailing Address: 6 Benton St., 06076. Tel: 860-684-2705; Fax: 860-684-0757.
Res., 55 High St., 06076. [CEM]

School—(Grades Pre K-8). Tel: 860-684-2600. Lay Teachers 10; Students 202.
Catechesis/Religious Programs—Students 240.
Mission—Staffordville, Tolland Co., St. Joseph, 6 Benton St., 06076.

Stonington, New London Co., St. Mary (1850), Rev. Philip J. Geogan; Deacon Henry E. O'Reilly.
Res., 95 Main St., 06378-1219. Tel: 860-535-1700. [CEM]
Catechesis/Religious Programs—Tel: 860-535-4252. Mrs. Mary Maranell, D.R.E.
Students 180.

Storrs, Tolland Co., St. Thomas Aquinas (1947), Revs. Paul D. Holland, S.J.; Richard K. Gross, S.J.; James J. Dressman, S.J.; Sr. Alberta Surowiec, F.S.S.J.
Res., 46 N. Eagleville Rd., 06268. Tel: 860-429-6436; Fax: 860-486-5591.
Catechesis/Religious Programs—Tel: 860-429-6436. Bro. Edward J. Hall, C.P., D.R.E.
Students 200.

Taftville, New London Co., Sacred Heart (1883), Rev. Msgr. Henry N. Archambault, P.A. In res., Rev. Raymond D. Introvigne, Diocesan Dir. Spiritual Renewal Svcs.
Res., 156 Providence St., P.O. Box 208, 06380. Tel: 860-887-3072; Fax: 203-887-3072.
School—15 Hunters Ave., 06380. Tel: 860-887-1757; Fax: 860-889-7276. Sr. Mary David, Prin.
Sisters of Charity of Our Lady Mother of the Church 4; Lay Teachers 6; Students 145.
Catechesis/Religious Programs—Students 100.

Tolland, Tolland Co., St. Matthew (1964), Rev. James P. Carini; Deacon Ronald Freedman.
Mailing Address: P.O. Box 100, 06084-0100. Tel: 860-872-0200; Fax: 860-875-4413.
Catechesis/Religious Programs—Tel: 860-875-8663. D.R.E.: Peter R. Chabot, (Grades 6-12); Mrs. Nancy Rudek, (Grades K-5).
Students 648.

Vernon, Tolland Co., Sacred Heart (1958), Rev. Stanley J. Szczapa; Deacon Charles B. White.
Church—550 Hartford Tpke., 06066-5000. Tel: 860-875-4563; Fax: 860-872-2535.
Catechesis/Religious Programs—Students 120.

Voluntown, New London Co., St. Thomas Apostle (1892), Rev. James Joseph Sucholet.
Res., 61 Preston City Rd., P.O. Box 99, 06384. Tel: 860-376-2293. [CEM]
Catechesis/Religious Programs—49 Preston City Rd., 06384. Tel: 860-376-8352.
Students 112.
Mission—Glasgo, New London Co., St. Ann, Rte. 201, 06384.

Warrenville, Windham Co., St. Philip (1937), Rev. Joseph P. Murphy.
Res., 64 Pompey Hollow Rd., Ashford, 06278-1540. Tel: 860-429-2860; Fax: 860-487-5730. [CEM 2]
Catechesis/Religious Programs—Tel: 860-429-1921; 450-1544.
Students 144.

Waterford, New London Co., St. Paul (1960), Rev. Richard F. Roughan; Deacon Richard K. Walker.
Res., 170 Rope Ferry Rd., 06385. Tel: 860-443-5587.
Catechesis/Religious Programs—Tel: 860-443-3375.
Students 277.

Wauregan, Windham Co., Sacred Heart (1889) (French), Revs. Paul J. Gaumond; Theodore E. Berube, Pastor Emeritus.
Res., 620 Wauregan Rd., P.O. Box 468, 06387. Tel: 860-774-6892. [CEM]

West Willington, Tolland Co., St. Jude (1981), Rev. Thomas W. Sennik.
Res., 25 Old Farms Rd., P.O. Box 240, Willington, 06279. Tel: 860-429-9655.
Catechesis/Religious Programs—Tel: 860-429-8604.
Students 100.

Westbrook, Middlesex Co., St. Mark (1961), Rev. Richard Albamonti.
Res., 222 McVeagh Rd., P.O. Box 551, 06498. Tel: 860-399-9207.
Catechesis/Religious Programs—Students 189.

Windham, Windham Co., Sagrado Corazon de Jesus (1991) (Hispanic), Rev. Paul J. Murdock; Sr. Mary Jude Lazarus, S.C.M.C., Pastoral Assoc.; Deacon Felipe Silva.
Mailing Address: 61 Club Rd., 06280. Tel: 860-423-8617.
Catechesis/Religious Programs—Students 130.

Willimantic, Windham Co., St. Joseph (1859), Rev. Msgr. Willis W. West; Revs. Luke A. Walaszek, O.P.; Ted F. Tumicki. In res., Rev. Edward F. Frigault.
Res., 99 Jackson St., 06226. Tel: 860-423-8439; Fax: 860-423-6825. [CEM]
School—St. Mary-St. Joseph, 35 Valley St., 06226. Tel: 860-423-8479. Sr. M. Regina, Prin.
Catechesis/Religious Programs—Tel: 860-423-1544.
Students 250.
Convent—88 Jackson St., 06226. Tel: 203-423-5122.
Mission—Scotland, Windham Co., St. Margaret, Rte. 14, Scotland, 06264. Tel: 203-423-1791.

St. Mary (1903) (French), Revs. Roger J. Lamoureux, O.M.I.; George J. Richards, Jr.
Res., 80 Maple Ave., 06226. Tel: 860-423-5835; Fax: 860-423-9933.
School—St. Mary-St. Joseph, 35 Valley St., 06226. Tel: 860-423-8479; Fax: 860-423-8365. Mother Marie Dominica, S.C.M.C., Prin.
Sisters 5; Lay Teachers 10; Students 304.
Catechesis/Religious Programs—Students 120.
Convent—88 Jackson St., 06226. Tel: 860-423-5122. Sisters of Charity of Our Lady
Faith Formulation—Tel: 203-423-9700. Mrs. Tina Popeleski, Dir.

Chaplains of Public Institutions

NORWICH. *William W. Backus Hospital* 06360. Tel: 860-889-8331. Sr. Rita Johnson, S.S.N.D., Chaplaincy Svcs.

MIDDLETOWN. *Connecticut Valley Hospital* Eastern Dr., P.O. Box 351, 06457. Tel: 860-344-2546; 344-2666. Rev. Jose Rizal Dimapilis, O.P., Prin. Chap.
Long Lane School. Mailing Address: P.O. Box 882, 06457. Tel: 860-344-2820. Rev. Noel G. Ahrems, O.Carm.
Middlesex Memorial Hospital 28 Crescent St., 06457-0822. Tel: 860-347-9471, Ext. 6725. Rev. Richard Dolandson, O.F.M.Cap.

NEW LONDON. *Lawrence and Memorial Hospitals* Montauk Ave., 06320. Tel: 860-442-0711, Ext. 2609. Bro. Robert Vozzo, C.S.C., Chap.; Deacons Ron Kitlinski; Roland J. LaCasse.

NIANTIC. *State Farm for Women*. Vacant.

On Special or Other (Arch)Diocesan Assignment:
Reverend Monsignors—
Bride, Thomas R., P.A., Vicar Gen., The Chancery
Brown, Robert L., Chancellor, The Chancery

On Duty Outside the Diocese:
Reverend Fathers—
Bissonnette, Bernard
Caiazzo, Nicholas
Cronin, Robert W., 11 Middleford Dr., West Hartford, CT 06107
Giaquinto, Albert C., Theological College, 401 Michigan Ave., N.E., Washington, DC 20002
Kirby, Gerald S., Diocesan Mission House, c/o Lynx Air, P.O. Box 407139, Ft. Lauderdale, FL 33340
Klimanskis, Adolfo, St. Casimir Rectory, 350 Smith St., Providence, RI 02908
Shea, Thomas W.

Military Chaplains:
Reverend Fathers—
Angelo, Thomas M., Ch., Capt., 23 Wg/MC, Pope AFB, NC 28308
Gwudz, John S., Office of Chap., U.S.S. Independence, CV 62, FPO, AP 96618-2760

Absent on Leave:
Reverend Fathers—
Bolieau, Henry G.
Dempsey, Edward M., 75 Bushnell St., Hartford, CT 06114
Gaulin, Roger M.
Jean, Raymond J., 6 Foster Leigh Rd., Niantic, CT 06357
Liszewski, Francis A.
Surprenant, John L., 943 High St., Akron, PA 17501

Retired:
Reverend Monsignors—
Gadarowski, Bronislaw A., Winter, 357 Pineview Dr., Venice, FL 34293
Malanowski, Thaddeus F., 908 S. Prospect Ave., Clearwater, FL 34616
O'Brien, James J., St. Mary Home, 2021 Albany Ave., West Hartford, CT 06117
St. Onge, Paul J., 45 Squire St., New London, CT 06320
Reverend Fathers—
Almendra, Leoncio T., Real St. Abuyog, Leyte, Philippines
Berube, Theodore E., Sacred Heart Rectory, W. Main St., P.O. Box 468, Wauregan, CT 06387. Tel: 860-774-6892
Bialkowski, Henry A., 162 Eddy Glover Blvd., New Britain, CT 06053. Tel: 203-223-4242
Curtin, Clifford J., 799 Prospect Ave. B-6, West Hartford, CT 06105. Tel: 860-236-2493
Davis, Edward J., 179 Train St., Dorchester, MA 02122. Tel: 617-282-0479
Flint, Kenneth, Box 4, Charlestown, RI 02813. Tel: 401-364-1071
Giaquinto, Albert C., Theological College, 401 Michigan Ave., N.E., Washington, D.C. 20064
Horan, Joseph, P.O. Box 1043, Cowpens, SC 29330
Kelley, J. Ralph, Heritage Commons, 38 Boston Rd., Middletown, CT 06457. Tel: 860-343-0164
Kozon, John A., 3780 Isherwood Cove, Memphis, TN 38125
Kuzdal, Anthony P., 1714 Beach Pkwy., A-2, Cape Coral, FL 33904. Tel: 813-542-9261
Landry, Alfred R., St. Joseph Living Center, 14 Club Rd., Windham, CT 06280. Tel: 860-456-1107
Liszewski, Francis A., 8 Hillcrest Dr., Tolland, CT 06084
Marciniak, John, 70 W. 18th Rd., Broad Channel, NY 11693
McGrath, Daniel F., 2433 Main St., Rocky Hill, CT 06067
McNulty, Robert E., 5 Holmes St., E-14, Mystic, CT 06355. Tel: 860-536-1758
Morrissette, Joseph H., 30 School Hill Rd., Baltic, CT 06330
Murphy, Hugh J., P.O. Box 261, Pomfret, CT 06258
Nichols, Joseph E., 810 Walnut St., Lebanon, PA 17042
Poulin, Edward C., 13 Blissville Rd., Lisbon, CT 06351. Tel: 860-887-3689
Pupsys, Adam, P.O. Box 2163, Westerly, RI 02891
Ramen, Paul F., 350 Pond Hill Rd., Moosup, CT 06354. Tel: 860-887-2565
Ricard, Joseph M., 233 Spanish Moss Rd., Davenport, FL 33837
Sullivan, John J., St. Mary Rectory, 79 S. Main St., Middletown, CT 06457
Wisneski, Edward, S.T.D., Ph.D., 78 E. Ridge Rd., Middletown, CT 06457
Wood, Robert J., P.O. Box 1896, Statesboro, GA 30458

Permanent Deacons:
Abdalla, John, All Saints, Somerville
Bachand, Francis J., St. Mary Church, Jewett City
Baillargeon, Paul R., St. Mary, Jewett City
Barlow, Robert C., St. Andrew, Colchester
Berstene, Michael C., St. Bernard, Rockville
Boucher, Richard A., St. Luke Church, Ellington
Burgess, James J., All Saints & Office of Evangelization, Somersville
Cannata, Nicholas J., St. Sebastian Church, Middletown
Cartier, L. Roger
Catalano, John P., St. Sebastian Church, Middletown
Cote, Albert J., St. Francis, Lebanon
Cyr, Warren, St. Patrick, East Hampton
Danesi, Peter H., III, St. Mary, Groton
Deraleau, Lawrence W., All Saints Church, Somersville
Desilets, Pierre M., Project Northeast & St. Mary, Putnam
Diez Conseco, Jesus A., St. Mary, Hispanic Apostolate New London & Bishop's Delegate to Hispanic Permanent Deacons
Dogue, Eduardo, Ministry to Handicapped, Wauregan
Dolan, Dennis F., Prison Ministry
Donahue, Donald J., St. Thomas More Church, N. Stonington
Doyle, Dennis A., III, St. Mary, Norwich
Fecteau, Al R., Cathedral of St. Patrick, Norwich
Freedman, Ronald, St. Matthew Church, Tolland
Gaynor, Gerard J., Saint Joseph Church, New London
Goodwin, Lawrence, St. Margaret Mission Church, Scotland
Gosselin, Raymond P., St. Lawrence, Killingworth
Grospitch, Harry J., St. Bernard, Rockville
Hayes, Robert P., St. John, Fitchville
Kitlinski, Ronald S., Our Lady Perpetual Help, Quaker Hill
LaCasse, Roland J., Chap. Asst., Lawrence & Memorial Hospitals, Asst., St. Agnes
LaPlante, Joseph A., Manset, ME
McMahon, James R., Sr., St. Michael Church, Pawcatuck
Melendez, Carlos
Nygaard, Melvin G., St. John Church, Uncasville
O'Reilly, Henry E., St. Mary, Stonington
O'Sullivan, W. Ridgely, Bishop's Delegate for Permanent Deacons, St. Joseph Church, Chester
Osuba, Jose, Columbia
Phaneuf, Bernard A., St. Mary, Putnam
Ramos, Mariano, Hispanic Ministry, St. Mary, New London

Reed, Steven W., Our Lady of Lourdes, Gales Ferry
Saunders, Alexander, St. Bernard Church, Rockville
Silva, Felipe, St. Joseph Church, Willimantic
Walker, Richard K., St. Paul Church, Waterford
Walsh, Maurice, St. Agnes, Niantic
Weber, F. Paul, St. Mary of the Visitation Church, Clinton
White, Charles B., St. Luke Church, Ellington

INSTITUTIONS LOCATED IN THE DIOCESE

[A] SEMINARIES, RELIGIOUS OR SCHOLASTICATES

CROMWELL. *Holy Apostles College and Seminary*, 33 Prospect Hill Rd., 06416. Tel: 860-632-3000; 632-3010 (Admissions); Fax: 860-632-0176.
E-mail: Holy_Apostles@msn.com
Web site: www.novavista.com/holyapostles
Revs. Douglas L. Mosey, C.S.B., Ph.D., Pres. & Rector; Maurice Sheehan, O.F.M.Cap.; James Pepitone, Business Mgr.; Revs. Raymond Halliwell, M.Ss.A., Dir. of Admissions & Vice Rector; Addison Hallock, M.Ss.A., Spiritual Dir.; Bradley Pierce, M.Ss.A., Dir. Field Education; Ronan P. Callahan, C.P.; Philip Kiley, S.J.; Benedict Klucinec, M.Ss.A., Priestly Formation; Matthew Malnar; David Q. Liptak; Marc Daniel Kirby, O.Cist.; Ronald H. Mikasauskas, M.Ss.A.; Brian T. Mullady, O.P.; Joseph Olczak; Robert Sickler, M.Ss.A. Priests 25; Brothers 6; Sisters 5; Lay Teachers 6; Seminarians 68; Seminary Division Lay Students 45; Total 160.

ENDERS ISLAND. *St. Edmund's Novitiate*, P.O. Box 399, 06355. Tel: 860-572-9538; Fax: 203-572-7655.
Web site: www.sse.org
Society of St. Edmund. Revs. Stanely M. Deresienski, S.S.E., Supr.; Thomas F.X. Hoar, S.S.E.; Paul Pinard, S.S.E.; Bros. Martin Slattery, S.S.E.; Thomas Berube, S.S.E.; Sr. Jeanette Serra, S.S.C. Priests 3; Brothers 2; Sisters 1.

MYSTIC. *Edmundite Seminary Guild.* Society of St. Edmund of Connecticut, Inc., 06355. Tel: 860-536-4949; Fax: 203-536-7540. Revs. Roger J. LaCharite, S.S.E., Exec. Dir.; Joseph L. Hart, S.S.E., Dir.; Thomas F.X. Hoar, S.S.E., Treas.

[B] HIGH SCHOOLS, DIOCESAN

MIDDLETOWN. *Mercy High School*, 1740 Randolph Rd., 06457. Tel: 860-346-6659; Fax: 860-344-9887. Sisters of Mercy. Sr. Mary A. McCarthy, R.S.M., Prin.; Sr. Jean Dwyer, C.N.D., Vice Prin.; Mr. Steven Brickey, Dean of Students; Sr. Margaret O'Neill, R.S.M., Admin. Asst.; Miss Ann Derbacher, Campus Min.; Rev. Michael S. Smith, Chap. Sisters 10; Lay Teachers 39; Students 570.
Xavier High School, 181 Randolph Rd., 06457. Tel: 860-346-7735; Fax: 860-346-6859. Brothers of St. Francis Xavier. Bro. William Ciganek, C.F.X., Prin.; Rev. Michael S. Smith, Chap. Brothers 7; Lay Teachers 47; Students 784.

UNCASVILLE. *St. Bernard High School*, 1593 Norwich-New London Tpke., 06382-1399. Tel: 860-848-1271; Fax: 860-848-1274.
E-mail: sbhs@snet.net
Rev. Joseph Nguyen, Chap.; Sr. Mary Patrick, S.C.M.C., Prin.; Mother Mary Luke, S.C.M.C., Headmistress. Priests 2; Lay Teachers 34; Students 400.
St. Bernard Academy. (Grades 7-8). (Middle School), 1593 Norwich-New London Tpke., 06382-1399. Tel: 860-848-1271; Fax: 860-848-1274. Mother Mary Luke, S.C.M.C., Prin. Lay Teachers 4; Students 60.

[C] HIGH SCHOOLS, PRIVATE

BALTIC. *Academy and Boarding-School of the Holy Family*, 54 W. Main St., 06330. Tel: 860-822-9272. Sisters of Charity of Our Lady Mother of the Church. Sr. Marie-Alberta, S.C.M.C., Prin.; Rev. M.R.P. Sevastian, C.S.C. Sisters 6; Lay Teachers 8; Students 81.

THOMPSON. *Marianapolis Preparatory School*, P.O. Box 368, 06277-0368. Tel: 860-923-9565.
E-mail: bromic1@aol.com
Marian Fathers. Revs. Timothy Roth, M.I.C., Supr. & Headmaster; Albin Gurkis, M.I.C.; Bros. Donald Schaefer, M.I.C., Treas., Registrar & Dir. Devel.; Brian Manian, M.I.C., Asst. Resident Dir.; Victor Incardona, M.I.C.; Joseph Keil, M.I.C.; Lonny Welte, Candidate. Brothers 4; Lay Teachers 22; Students 186.

[D] PROTECTIVE INSTITUTIONS

DEEP RIVER. *Mount St. John*, 135 Kirtland St., 06417. Tel: 203-526-5391; Fax: 203-526-3846
For a complete listing, refer to the Special Care Facilities section.

[E] HOMES FOR AGED

WILLIMANTIC. *Holy Family Home and Shelter, Inc.*, 88 Jackson St., P.O. Box 884, 06226. Tel: 860-423-7719; Fax: 860-423-7719
For a complete listing, refer to the Special Care Facilities section.

WINDHAM. *St. Joseph Living Center*, 14 Club Rd., 06280. Tel: 860-456-1107; Fax: 860-450-7114
For a complete listing, refer to the Special Care Facilities section.

[F] MONASTERIES AND RESIDENCES OF PRIESTS AND BROTHERS

BALTIC. *Marian Friary of Our Lady of Guadalupe*, 22 School Hill Rd., 06330. Tel: 860-822-8606.
E-mail: ffi@connix.com
Web site: http://www.connix.com/~ffi/
Rev. Angelo Mary Geiger, Guardian; Bro. Pio Mary Pante, Vicar; Revs. Thomas Mary Huff; Joseph Mary McShane. Priests 3; Brothers 1; Postulants 2.

CROMWELL. *Missionaries of the Holy Apostles*, 33 Prospect Hill Rd., 06416. Tel: 860-632-3039; 623-3000; Fax: 860-632-3035. Society of the Missionaries of the Holy Apostles. Revs. Benedict Klucinec, M.Ss.A., Provincial Animator; Martin D. Rooney, M.Ss.A., Dir. Vocations, Dir. Mission Office, & Sec. to the Provincial; Robert McQueeney, M.Ss.A.; Pasquale Taliercio, M.Ss.A.; John Marcoux, M.Ss.A.; Raymond Halliwell, M.Ss.A.; Ronald Mikasauskas, M.Ss.A.; Robert Murphy, M.Ss.A.; Bradley Pierce, M.Ss.A.; Richard Skarbek, M.Ss.A.; Addison Hallock, M.Ss.A.; Laurence Preston, M.Ss.A.
Working Outside the Diocese: Revs. David Zercie; George Realmuto; J. Patrick Boyhan.

HAMPTON. *Brothers of St. Francis Xavier*, P.O. Box 177, 06247. Tel: 860-774-3340.

MIDDLETOWN. *Congregation of the Brothers of St. Francis Xavier*, 181 Randolph Rd., 06457-5606. Tel: 860-346-8585; Fax: 860-346-6859. Bros. William Ciganek, C.F.X., Prin.; James Boyle, C.F.X., Dir.; D. Paschal Alford, C.F.C.; Eugene Behenna, C.F.X.; Labre Dillon; J. Robert Houlihan, C.F.X.; John J. McDonald, C.F.X.; K. Paul McGlade, C.F.C.; H. Lawrence Nyhan, C.F.X.; Harold Pray, C.F.X.; Thomas Ryan, C.F.X.; Andre Shine, C.F.X. Total in Residence 12.

MYSTIC. *Society of St. Edmund*, P.O. Box 399, 06355. Tel: 860-572-9538; Fax: 860-572-7655.
E-mail: endersisle@aol.com
Web site: www.sse.org
Revs. Stanley M. Deresienski, S.S.E., Supr.; Thomas F.X. Hoar, S.S.E.; Paul Pinard, S.S.E.; Bros. Martin Slattery, S.S.E.; Thomas Berube, S.S.E.; Sr. Jeanette Serra, S.S.C., Dir. of the Apostolate Ctr. Total in Residence 6.

THOMPSON. *Marian Fathers*, Marianapolis Prep School, 06277. Tel: 860-923-9798.
E-mail: timothy.roth@snet.net
Revs. Timothy Roth, M.I.C., Supr. & Headmaster; Donald Finney, M.I.C., Asst. Headmaster & Second Councillor; Peter Barauskas, M.I.C.; Albin Gurkis, M.I.C.; Albin Sheputa, M.I.C.; Bros. Donald Schaefer, M.I.C., Treas. & First Councillor; Brian Manian, M.I.C.; Victor Incardona, M.I.C.; Joseph Keil, M.I.C.; Lonny Welte, Candidate. Total in Residence 9.

WILLIMANTIC. *Oblates of Mary Immaculate*, 289 Windham Rd., P.O. Box 55, 06226-0055. Tel: 860-423-8484; Fax: 860-423-5285. Revs. Daniel Nassaney, O.M.I., Supr. & Dir.; Henri A. DeLisle, O.M.I.; Roger Couture, O.M.I.; Bro. Donat Daigle, O.M.I.; Rev. Olivier Renaud, O.M.I. Total in Residence 5; Total Staff 12.

[G] CONVENTS AND RESIDENCES FOR SISTERS

NORWICH. *School Sisters Notre Dame*, 7 Otis St., 06360. Tel: 860-886-6948.

BALTIC. *Holy Family Motherhouse*, 06330. Tel: 860-822-8241. Sisters of Charity of Our Lady, Mother of the Church. Mother M. Theresita, Supr. Gen.; Rev. M.R.P. Sevastian, Chap. Professed 78; Junior Professed 10; Novices 3; Postulants 2; Total Assisted 210; Total Staff 7.
Sisters of the Holy Cross, 133 Main St., Box 199, 06330. Tel: 203-822-6794.

HIGGANUM. *Apostles of the Sacred Heart of Jesus*, Sacred Heart on the Lake, 529 Brainard Hill Rd., 06441. Tel: 860-345-4653. Total in Residence 4.

MIDDLETOWN. *Mill Hill Sisters*, 6 Bluebird Rd., 06457. Total in Residence 3.
Sisters of Mercy, 251 Hunting Hill Ave., 06457. Tel: 860-343-1642.
Other Locations: 421 High St., 06457. Tel: 860-346-4906. 94 Warner Ave., 06457. Tel: 860-343-8533. 419 High St., 06457. Tel: 860-344-8569. 203 East St., Hebron, 06248. Tel: 860-228-0849. 56 Beaver Brook Rd., R.D. 3, Lyme, 06371-3201. Tel: 860-434-0724. 103 Golden St., #3, Norwich, 06360. Tel: 860-886-9196. 159 Otrobando Ave., Norwich, 06360. Tel: 860-887-5168. 32 School St., P.O. Box 177, Rockville, 06066. Tel: 860-875-4016. 28 Liberty St., Pawcatuck, 06379. Tel: 860-599-4816. 43 W. High St., East Hampton, 06424. Tel: 860-267-6112. 4 S. View Cir., Old Saybrook, 06475. Tel: 860-395-0913.
Sisters of Our Lady of the Garden, 67 Round Hill Rd., 06457. Tel: 203-346-5765. Convent and Nursery School. Sr. Mary Eugene Sanita, O.L.G., Supr. Total Assisted 82; Total Staff 9.
Sisters of St. Joseph, T.O.S.F., 9 Woodman St., 06457. Tel: 860-347-8936.

MOODUS. *Sisters of St. Joseph of Chambery*. Mailing Address: P.O. Box 22, 06469. Tel: 203-873-1581.

MYSTIC. *Society of the Sisters for the Church*. Sr. Jeanette Serra, S.S.C., Edmundite Apostolate Center, P.O. Box 399, 06355. Tel: 860-572-9787.

PUTNAM. *Holy Spirit Provincial House*, 72 Church St., 06260-1810. Tel: 860-928-0891. Daughters of the Holy Spirit. Sr. Bonnie Morrow, Prov.; Sr. Anita Paul, Coord.; Rev. Richard L. Archambault, Chap. Sisters 65.
Other Locations: Madonna Community, 207 Sabin St., Apt. 42, 06260. Tel: 860-928-2466. Ker Joa Community, 31 Ravine St., 06260. Tel: 860-928-6197. Notre Dame Community, 4 Ravine St., 06260. Tel: 860-928-6163; 928-9129. Our Lady of Peace Community, 26 Church St., 06260. Tel: 860-928-6869. 67 Railroad St., 06260. Tel: 860-928-5965. 357 Church St., 06260. Tel: 860-928-7806. 51 Meadowbrook Rd., Apt. 48, Ellington, 06029. Tel: 860-870-5138. St. Ignatius Parish House Community, 17 Williamsville Rd., Rogers, 06263. Tel: 860-774-8154. 185 Farm Hill Rd., Middletown, 06457. Tel: 860-347-4382. Provincialate Community, 124 Rte. 169, Woodstock, 06281. Tel: 860-928-7072; 928-3882. St. Mary Convent, 40 N. Main St., Jewett City, 06351. Tel: 860-376-4020. All Hallows Convent, 152 Prospect St., Moosup, 06354. Tel: 860-564-5409. 815B Boswell Ave., Norwich, 06360. Tel: 860-885-0419. 124 Rte. 169, Woodstock, 06281. Tel: 860-928-9649. 33 Pinecrest Ridge, Apt. E, Woodstock, 06281. Tel: 860-928-2099. DHS, 12 St. Regis Dr., Danielson, 06239. Tel: 860-779-0790. 14 Windsor Ave., E-20, Plainfield, 06374. Tel: 860-564-0617. 31 Lincoln Park Rd., B-4, Preston, 06365. Tel: 860-886-2993.
Immaculate Conception Convent, Spiritual Renewal Center and Novitiate, 600 Liberty Hwy., 06260-2503. Tel: 860-928-7955; Fax: 860-928-1930. Sr. M. Paul Savickas, Prov. Sisters of the Immaculate Conception of the Blessed Virgin Mary 12; Total in Residence 15; Total Staff 7.
Matulaitis Nursing Home Inc., 10 Thurber Rd., 06260. Tel: 860-928-7976; Fax: 860-963-1920. Sisters of the Immaculate Conception of the Blessed Virgin Mary. Jane Logan, Admin.; Rev. Rapolas Krasauskas, Chap. Sisters 10; Residents 119.

UNCASVILLE. *Emmaus Community*, 24 Maple Ave., 06382. Tel: 860-848-3379. Total in Residence 3; Total Staff 3.

WILLIMANTIC. *Sisters of Charity of Our Lady, Mother of the Church*, St. Joseph Convent, 88 Jackson St., 06226. Total in Residence 9; Total Staff 9.

WINDHAM. *Carmelite Sisters of the Eucharist*, 1 Stanley Rd., 06280. Tel: 203-423-0067. Other Location, 26 Deborah Ln., Colchester, 06415. Tel: 860-267-1149. Sr. Mary Grace.

WOODSTOCK. *Provincialate Community of the Daughters of the Holy Spirit*, 124 Rte. 169, 06281; Fax: 860-928-6496. Sr. Bonnie Morrow, D.H.S., Prov. Tel: 860-928-7072; Sr. Linda Babineau, D.H.S., Prov. Councillor. Tel: 860-928-3882.

[H] PRIVATE ASSOCIATIONS OF THE FAITHFUL

ASHFORD. *Benedictine Monastery*. Community of Our Lady of Mount Caritas Monastery, O.S.B.; Sisters of the Order of St. Benedict. Contemplative. Seckar Rd., 06278. Tel: 860-429-7457. Rev. Mother Mary Peter, O.S.B., Supr. Professed 2; Lay Oblates 6; Novices 1.

WINDHAM. *Carmelite Sisters of the Eucharist*, One Stanley Rd., 06280. Tel: 860-423-0067. 26 Deborah Ln., Colchester, 06415. Tel: 860-267-1149. Sr. Mary Grace.

[I] RETREAT HOUSES

ENDERS ISLAND. *St. Edmund's Retreat*, P.O. Box 399, 06355-0399. Tel: 860-536-0565; Fax: 860-572-7655.
E-mail: enderisle@aol.com
Web site: www.sse.org
Rev. Thomas F.X. Hoar, S.S.E., Dir. of Devel.; Sr. Jeanette Serra, S.S.C., Dir. Retreats; Rev. Stanley M. Deresienski, S.S.E., Coord. of Pastoral Counseling & Spiritual Direction; Mr. Mark Goroom, Dir. Operations; Mrs. Claire St. Clair, Dir. Svcs. Total in Residence 6; Total Staff 5.

HAMPTON. *Community of the Way*. Mailing Address: P.O. Box 177, 06247. Tel: 860-774-3340. Bro. John M. Collins, C.F.X., Dir. Total in Residence 2; Total Staff 2.

MOODUS. *My Father's House*, Box 22, 39 N. Moodus Rd., 06469. Co-Directors: Rev. William McCarthy, M.S.A.; Sr. Bernadette Sheldon, C.S.J. A Christian renewal and retreat center. Total in Residence 12; Total Staff 19.

WAUREGAN. *Ministry of His Able People*. Mailing Address: P.O. Box 242, 06387. Tel: 860-779-0362. Deacon Eduardo Dogue, Dir.

Ave Maria Place. Rev. Patrick Martin. Tel: 203-774-0278. Total in Residence 2; Total Staff 2.

WILLIMANTIC. *Immaculata Retreat House*, 06226-0055. Tel: 860-423-8484; Fax: 860-423-5285. Oblate of Mary Immaculate: Northern Province. Revs. Daniel Nassaney, O.M.I., Supr. & Dir.; Henri A. Delisle, O.M.I., Treas.; Roger Couture, O.M.I.; Olivier Renaud, O.M.I. Total in Residence 5; Total Statff 12.

[J] RENEWAL CENTERS

PORTLAND. *Affirmation Counseling Center*, 553 Portland Cobalt Rd., 06480. Tel: 860-342-0760; Fax: 860-342-4226. Sr. Arlene Vannie, R.S.M., M.A., Dir. Total Assisted 960; Total Staff 12.

UNCASVILLE. *Emmaus-Diocesan Spiritual Life Center*, 24 Maple Ave., 06382. Tel: 860-848-3427. Sr. Mary Barbara Hobbs, P.B.V.M., Dir. Associate Directors: Sr. Julia Grey, O.P.; Sr. Jane Higgins, R.S.M.; Rev. Joseph G. Finnerty, St. Mary Rectory, 70 Central Ave., 06360. Tel: 860-889-6657; 848-0555. Sisters 3; Total in Residence 3; Total Staff 4.

[K] CAMPUS MINISTRY

WILLIMANTIC. *Campus Ministry*. Eastern Connecticut State University, Newman Hall. 290 Prospect St., 06226. Tel: 860-423-0856.
E-mail: lapointel@ecsuc.ctstateu.edu
Rev. Laurence A.M. LaPointe, Diocesan Dir. Campus Ministry.
Wesleyan University-The University Ministry (Middletown), Office of the University Chaplains, 171 Church St., Middletown, 06457. Tel: 860-685-2277. Rev. Gerald P. Cohen, C.S.C., Chap.
Connecticut College (New London), Harknes Chapel, 270 Mohegan Ave., New London, 06320-4196. Tel: 860-439-2452. Rev. Laurence A.M. LaPointe, Catholic Chap.
University of Connecticut (Storrs), St. Thomas Aquinas Chapel, 46 N. Eagleville Rd., Storrs, 06268-1710. Tel: 860-429-6436. Chaplains: Revs. James J. Dressman, S.J.; Richard K. Gross, S.J.; Paul Holland, S.J.

[L] SECULAR INSTITUTES

CROMWELL. *Little Franciscan Family*. A secular institute for women. 319 Main St., 06416. Julie Curley, Contact Person. Tel: 860-635-6384.

[M] MISCELLANEOUS

CROMWELL. *Basilian Fathers of Connecticut, Inc.*, 33 Prospect Hill Rd., 06416. Tel: 860-632-3010. Rev. Douglas L. Mosey, C.S.B., Pres.-Rector.

MIDDLETOWN. *Assisted Living Services, Inc. - Diocese of Norwich*, 10 Elm St., 06457. Rev. Msgr. M. Davitt Fox, Contact Person.

Marian Housing Corporation, 10 Elm St., 06457. Rev. Msgr. M. Davitt Fox, Contact Person.

Mercy Development Office, 1740 Randolph Rd., 06457. Tel: 860-347-8957; Fax: 860-344-9887. Karen Wall, Dir.

Mercy-Xavier Fund Corporation, 181 Randolph Rd., 06457.

Xavier Alumni & Development Office, 181 Randolph Rd., 06457. Tel: 203-347-6079. Total in Residence 12; Total Staff 76.

PUTNAM. *The Daughters of the Holy Spirit Charitable Trust*, 72 Church St., 06260. Tel: 860-928-0891. Sr. Bonnie Morrow, D.H.S., Trustee & Contact Person.

The Holy Spirit Health Care Center, Inc., 72 Church St., 06260. Tel: 860-928-0891. Sr. Bonnie Morrow, D.H.S., Prov. & Contact Person; Mrs. Annemarie Shiroka, Admin.

WILLIMANTIC. *Saint Joseph's Home for the Aged, Inc.*, 88 Jackson St., 06226.

WINDHAM. *Sagrado Corazon de Jesus, Inc. of Windham*, 61 Club Rd., 06280.

RELIGIOUS INSTITUTES OF MEN REPRESENTED IN THE DIOCESE

For further details refer to the corresponding bracketed number in the Religious Institutes of Men or Women section.

[0200]—*Benedictine Monks*.—O.S.B.
[1350]—*Brothers of St. Francis Xavier*. (St. Joseph Prov.).—C.F.X.
[0610]—*Brothers of the Congregation of Holy Cross*.—C.S.C.
[0470]—*The Capuchin Friars*. (Prov. of St. Mary).—O.F.M. Cap.
[0270]—*Carmelite Fathers and Brothers*.—O.Carm.
[0480]—*Conventual Franciscans*.—O.F.M.Conv.
[0533]—*Franciscan Friars of the Immaculate*.—F.F.I.
[0690]—*Jesuit Fathers and Brothers*.—S.J.
[0740]—*Marian Fathers*.—M.I.C.
[0720]—*The Missionaries of Our Lady of La Salette*. (American Prov.).—M.S.
[0910]—*Oblates of Mary Immaculate*. (St. John the Baptist Prov.).—O.M.I.
[0930]—*Oblates of St. Joseph*. (Eastern Prov.).—O.S.J.
[0430]—*Order of Preachers (Dominicans)*.—O.P.
[0440]—*Society of St. Edmund*.—S.S.E.
[0590]—*Society of the Missionaries of the Holy Apostles*.—M.S.A.
[1280]—*Stigmatine Fathers and Brothers*.—C.S.S.

RELIGIOUS INSTITUTES OF WOMEN REPRESENTED IN THE DIOCESE

[0130]—*Apostoles of the Sacred Heart of Jesus*.—A.S.C.J.
[1920]—*Congregation of Sisters of Holy Cross*.—C.S.C.
[0820]—*Daughters of the Holy Spirit*.—D.H.S.
[1070]—*Dominican Sisters*.—O.P.
[1170]—*Felician Sisters*.—C.S.S.F.
[]—*Franciscan Apostolic Sisters*.—F.A.S.
[2575]—*Institute of the Sisters of Mercy of the Americas*.—R.S.M.
[1410]—*Mill Hill Sisters*.—F.M.S.J.
[2720]—*Mission Helpers of the Sacred Heart*.—M.H.S.H.
[3465]—*Religious of the Sacred Heart of Mary*.—R.S.H.M.
[3430]—*Religious Teachers Filippini*.—M.P.F.
[]—*Roncalli Sisters*.
[2970]—*School Sisters of Notre Dame*.—S.S.N.D.
[]—*Servants of Immaculate Heart of Mary*.—I.H.M.
[]—*Sisters Oblates to Divine Love*.—R.O.D.A.
[]—*Sisters of Charity of Immaculate Conception of Irea, Italy*.—S.C.I.C.
[0530]—*Sisters of Charity of Our Lady, Mother of the Church*.—S.C.M.C.
[]—*Sisters of Holy Cross*.—C.S.C.
[3000]—*Sisters of Notre Dame de Namur*. (Connecticut Prov.).—S.N.D.deN.
[]—*Sisters of Our Lady of the Garden*.—O.L.G.
[3360]—*Sisters of Providence of Saint Mary-of-the-Woods, Indiana*.—S.P.
[3720]—*Sisters of Saint Anne*.—S.S.A.
[3830]—*Sisters of St. Joseph*.—S.S.J.
[3930]—*Sisters of St. Joseph of the Third Order of St. Francis*.—S.S.J.-T.O.S.F.
[3180]—*Sisters of the Cross of Passion*.—C.P.
[1970]—*Sisters of the Holy Family of Nazareth*. (Immaculate Heart of Mary Prov.).—C.S.F.N.
[2140]—*Sisters of the Immaculate Conception of the Blessed Virgin Mary (Lithuanian)*.
[3320]—*Sisters of the Presentation of the B.V.M.*—P.B.V.M.
[]—*Society of the Sisters for the Church*.—S.S.C.

NECROLOGY

† McKenna, Rev. Msgr. Edward I., Middletown, CT, St. John. —Died June 26, 1997.
† Murphy, Thomas W., Somersville, CT, All Saints. —Died April 15, 1997.
† O'Hara, Michael J., Killingworth, CT, St. Lawrence. —Died Jan. 29, 1997.

Diocese of Oakland

(Dioecesis Quercopolitana)

Most Reverend

JOHN S. CUMMINS, D.D.

Bishop of Oakland; ordained January 24, 1953; appointed Titular Bishop of Lambesi and Auxiliary Bishop of Sacramento February 26, 1974; consecrated May 16, 1974; appointed Bishop of Oakland May 3, 1977; installed June 30, 1977. *Res., 634 21st St., Oakland, CA, 94612.*

ESTABLISHED JANUARY 13, 1962.

Square Miles 1,467.

Comprises two Counties in the State of California—viz., Alameda and Contra Costa.

Legal Title: The Roman Catholic Bishop of Oakland, a Corporation Sole.

For legal titles of parishes and diocesan institutions, consult the Chancery Office.

Chancery Office: 2900 Lakeshore Ave., Oakland, CA, 94610. Tel.: 510-893-4711; Fax: 510-893-0945.

E-mail address: chancellor@Oakdiocese.org

STATISTICAL OVERVIEW

Personnel

Bishop	1
Priests: Diocesan Active in Diocese	163
Priests: Retired, Sick or Absent	40
Number of Diocesan Priests	203
Religious Priests in Diocese	101
Extern Priests in Diocese	12
Ordinations:	
Diocesan Priests	3
Permanent Deacons in Diocese	80
Total Brothers	16
Total Sisters	320

Parishes

Parishes	89
With Resident Pastor:	
Resident Diocesan Priests	59
Resident Religious Priests	16
Without Resident Pastor:	
Administered by Priests	12
Administered by Lay People	1
Completely Vacant	1
Missions	3
Pastoral Centers	11
Professional Ministry Personnel:	
Brothers	1
Sisters	35
Lay Ministers	319

Welfare

Catholic Hospitals	1
Total Assisted	29,000
Homes for the Aged	2
Total Assisted	1,221
Day Care and Extended Day Care Centers	5
Total Assisted	1,400
Specialized Homes	6
Total Assisted	20,000
Special Centers for Social Services	3
Total Assisted	25,000
Residential Care of Disabled	1
Total Assisted	736
Other Institutions	4
Total Assisted	19,038

Educational

Diocesan Students in Other Seminaries	18
Students Religious	71
Total Seminarians	89
Colleges and Universities	3
Total Students	4,500
High Schools, Diocesan and Parish	3
Total Students	1,922
High Schools, Private	6
Total Students	4,090
Elementary Schools, Diocesan and Parish	51
Total Students	6,012
Catechesis/Religious Education:	
High School Students	1,750
Elementary Students	9,882
Total Students Under Catholic Instruction	28,245
Teachers in the Diocese:	
Brothers	16
Sisters	19
Lay Teachers	848

Vital Statistics

Receptions into the Church:	
Infant Baptism Totals	9,443
Adult Baptism Totals	543
Received into Full Communion	1,028
First Communions	6,992
Confirmations	2,584
Marriages:	
Catholic	1,219
Interfaith	426
Total Marriages	1,645
Deaths	2,799
Total Catholic Population	500,000
Total Population	2,209,629

Former Bishops—Most Rev. FLOYD L. BEGIN, S.T.D., cons. May 1, 1947; appt. Bishop of Oakland on Feb. 21, 1962; died April 26, 1977.

Chancery Office—2900 Lakeshore Ave., Oakland, 94610-3697. Tel: 510-893-4711; Fax: 510-893-0945. Office Hours: 8:30-4:45.

Vicar General / Director of Pastoral Life—Rev. PAUL ROSS VASSAR, V.G.

Chancellor / Office of the Bishop—Sr. BARBARA FLANNERY, C.S.J.

Vicar of Finance—Rev. ALBANO G. OLIVEIRA.

Director of Financial Services—Rev. DAVID STAAL.

Director of Services and Resources—KENNETH J. REGGIO.

Judicial Vicar / Director of Canonical Services—DONALD R. HUDSON, J.C.L.

Adjutant Judicial Vicars & Canonical Consultant to the Bishop—Revs. ROBERT J. MCCANN, J.C.L.; GARY M. LUIZ, C.PP.S., J.C.L.

Director of Planning & Communication Services—CHARLES SIEBENAND.

Director of School Services—Dr. ANN MEYERS MANCHESTER.

Director of Ethnic & Cultural Services—Sr. FELICIA SARATI, C.S.J.

Canon Law Department—

Judicial Vicar—Rev. DONALD R. HUDSON, J.C.L.

Adjutant Judicial Vicar and Canonical Consultants to the Bishop—Revs. ROBERT J. MCCANN, J.C.L.; GARY M. LUIZ, C.PP.S., J.C.L.

Defender of the Bond—Rev. ANTHONY PHAN LAM, J.C.D.

Pro Synodal Judges—Revs. ANTHONY PHAN LAM, J.C.D.; ROBERT J. MCCANN, J.C.L.; GARY M. LUIZ, C.PP.S., J.C.L.

Notaries of the Tribunal—ALICE VIZCAINO; MARY O'SULLIVAN; MELISSA MATSUOKA; CAROL GAISER.

Promoter of Justice—Rev. ROBERT J. MCCANN, J.C.L.

Auditors of the Tribunal—MERCEDES C. CORRAL; CAROL GAISER; ED KENT; THERESA KOBAK; JOANNE MORGRET.

Consultors—Revs. DANIEL CARDELLI; FERNANDO CORTEZ; VINCENT COTTER; DANIEL DANIELSON; QUANG DONG; JAYSON LANDEZA; JOHN MAXWELL; GERARD MORAN; FRED RICCIO; LARRY SILVA; PAUL VASSAR.

Presbyteral Council—Revs. FRED RICCIO, Pres. VINCENT COTTER, Vice Pres. JAYSON LANDEZA, Sec. DANIEL CARDELLI; FERNANDO CORTEZ; DANIEL DANIELSON; QUANG DONG; JOHN MAXWELL; GERARD MORAN; LARRY SILVA; PAUL VASSAR.

Deans—#1: Rev. DANIEL DANIELSON, #2: Rev. PATRICK GOODWIN, #3: Rev. JOHN MALLON, #4: Rev. ROGER LUCEY, S.J., #5: Rev. BRIAN JOYCE, #6: Rev. FRANCISCO VICENTE, O.P., #7: Rev. HELMUT RICHTER, #8: Rev. RICHARD MANGINI, #9: Rev. JEREMIAH HOLLAND, SS.CC., #10: Rev. SEAMUS GENOVESE, #11: Rev. JOSEPH SCOTT, #12: Rev. JAMES MATTHEWS, #13: Rev. LARRY SILVA, #14: Rev. Msgr. MANUEL C. SIMAS, #15: Rev. RAMON J. GOMEZ, #16: Rev. JEFFREY FINLEY, C.PP.S., #17: Rev. RAY ZIELEZIENSKI, #18: Rev. JOHN CRUMLISH, #19: Rev. ALEXANDER SNYDER, #20: Rev. GEORGE CRESPIN, O.P., #21: Rev. ANTONIO A. VALDIVIA, #22: Rev. JOHN F. MAXWELL, #23: Rev. MELVIN HARY.

Pastoral Leadership Placement Board (PBPB)—Most Rev. JOHN S. CUMMINS; Ms. CATHY BROWN; Sr. CYNTHIA CANNING, S.N.J.M.; Rev. VINCENT COTTER; Revs. MICHAEL JOYCE; WILLIAM MACCHI; Ms. JOANN MASS; Rev. MICHAEL NORKETT; Mr. MICHAEL RAMOS; Sr. FELICIA SARATI; Revs. TIMOTHY STIER; PAUL VASSAR; Mr. BERNIE SUTTLE; Rev. Msgr. MARTIN WALSH.

Ethnic Pastoral Centers—Sr. FELICIA SARATI, C.S.J., Dir. Ethnic and Cultural Svcs. Div., *3014 Lakeshore Ave., Oakland, 94610.* Tel: 510-763-0301.

African American Catholic—Dr. TOINETTE EUGENE, *3014 Lakeshore Ave., Oakland, 94610.* Tel: 510-763-0301.

Chinese Catholic—Rev. THOMAS NG, Dir., *176 Ridgeway Ave., Oakland, 94611.*

Ethnic Youth Director—ARIEL SAN PEDRO, *521 Boden Way, Oakland, 94610.* Tel: 510-763-0301.

Director of Spanish Youth—JOSE MORAN, *521 Boden Way, Oakland, 94610.* Tel: 510-763-0301.

Filipino Catholic—STANLEY LEE, Dir., *3014 Lakeshore Ave., Oakland, 94610.* Tel: 510-893-4711.

Ge'ez Community—Rev. TEKLE YOHANIS, Bay Area Reg. Dir., *600 Parker St., San Francisco, 94118.* Tel: 415-666-6420.

Hispanic Pastoral Center—MICHAEL RAMOS, Dir., *3014 Lakeshore Ave., Oakland, 94610.* Tel: 510-763-0301.

Khmmu/Laotian Catholic Community—Rev. DON MACKINNON, C.SS.R., *Holy Redeemer Center, 8945 Golf Links Rd., P.O. Box 5007, Oakland, 94605.* Tel: 510-653-6341.

Korean Catholic—Rev. JAMES SOONG, Dir., *St. Andrew Kim Catholic Pastoral Center, 6226 Camden St., Oakland, 94605.* Tel: 510-562-3843.

Polish Center—Rev. LESZEK BARTOSZEWSKI, Dir., *1631-A Monument, Concord, 94520.* Tel: 510-825-7646.

Portuguese Pastoral Center—Rev. ANTONIO DOS REIS, Dir., *997 Sueirro Dr., Hayward, 94541.* Tel: 510-887-2912.

St. Joseph's Center for Deaf and Hard of Hearing—ARDITH A. LYNCH, Dir., *3880 Smith St., Union City, 94587.* Tel: 510-489-9784 (Voice). Tel: 510-489-9786 (TTY).

Tongan Community—Sr. SOFIA LANGE, Bay Area Reg. Dir., *1515 Dolan Ave., San Mateo, 94401.* Tel: 415-342-2470.

Vietnamese Catholic—Vacant, *3014 Lakeshore Ave., Oakland, 94610.* Tel: 510-763-0311.

Bishop's Representative for Eastern Rite Catholics—Rev. DAVID LINK.

Bishop's Representative for Permanent Deacons—Deacon DAVID REZENDES.

Bishop's Representative for Catholic Charismatics—CHARLES PEISSNER.

Bishop's Representative for Italian Speaking Faithful—Rev. DANIEL E. CARDELLI.

The Roman Catholic Welfare Corporation of Oakland—*2900 Lakeshore Ave., Oakland, 94610.*

Diocesan Offices and Directors

Apostleship of the Sea—Deacon STANLEY LEE, Port Chaplain, *3014 Lakeshore Ave., Oakland, 94610.* Tel: 510-893-4711.

Archivist/Records Management—MARY C. BATIZA, *3014 Lakeshore Ave., Oakland, 94610.*

Design Review Board—Revs. GERARD MORAN, Chm. PATRICK GOODWIN; ROBERT LOUGHERY, C.S.C.; RON SCHMIDT; DAVID STAAL; LAWRENCE YOUNG; Ms. LAURA HELD; WILLIAM GILLIS, A.I.A.; DAVID MESSINGER, S.E.

Facilities & Planning Services—C. J. FINNEY, Dir. ALEX HERNANDEZ, Assoc. Dir. J. H. MCCANN, Property Mgr.

Campaign for Human Development—PAUL WOOLEY, Dir., *433 Jefferson St., Oakland, 94607.*

Catholic Charities—Mrs. BARBARA TERRAZAS, Dir., *433 Jefferson St., Oakland, 94607.* Legal Title: *Catholic Charities of the Diocese of Oakland.*

Catholic Relief Services—PAUL WOOLLEY, Dir., *433 Jefferson St., Oakland, 94607.*

Cemeteries—ANTHONY SILVA, Dir., *1965 Reliez Valley Rd., P.O. Box 488, Lafayette, 94549.*

Censor—Rev. ROBERT J. MCCANN.

Clergy Personnel, Office of—Rev. PAUL SCHMIDT, *3014 Lakeshore Ave., Oakland, 94610.* Tel: 510-763-0301.

Cursillo Movement—Rev. FERNANDO CORTEZ, Spiritual Dir., *5562 Clayton Rd., Concord, 94521.* Tel: 510-672-5800.

Diocesan Pastoral Council—Vacant, *2900 Lakeshore Ave., Oakland, 94610.*

Ecumenical Affairs, Office of—Vacant, *3014 Lakeshore Ave., Oakland, 94610.* Tel: 510-763-0301.

Special Religious Education Department (SPRED)—Sr. AURORA PEREZ, Dir., *4025 Martin Luther King, Jr. Way at 40th St., Oakland, 94609.* Tel: 510-654-2869.

Education—Mrs. ANN MEYERS MANCHESTER, Ed.D., Supt. of Schools; Ms. PENNY PENDOLA, Assoc. Supt. of Schools: Curriculum and Personnel Svcs.; Sr. BARBARA BRAY, S.N.J.M., Asst. Supt.

FACE (Family Aid Catholic Education)—A division of The Roman Catholic Welfare Corporation of Oakland, ANNE RYNDERS, Exec. Dir., *2900 Lakeshore Ave., Oakland, 94610.*

Family Life Center and Divorced & Separated Catholics—Mrs. RITA BILLECI, Dir. Family Life; JUAN AMBRIZ, Assoc. Dir. SUE MEDINA, Coord. Divorced & Separated Catholics; Respect Life, Women's Pregnancy Service and Bioethics; MONIKA RODMAN, *2350 Pacheco St., Concord, 94520.* Tel: 510-680-8510.

Hospital Ministries—Rev. JOHN RANALLO, Dir., *3014 Lakeshore Ave., Oakland, 94610.* Tel: 510-763-0301.

Legion of Mary—*2900 Lakeshore Ave., Oakland, 94610.*

Newspaper: "The Catholic Voice"—MONICA CLARK, Editor, *3014 Lakeshore Ave., Oakland, 94610.* Tel: 510-893-5339.

Department of Human Resources—Vacant, *3014 Lakeshore Ave., Oakland, 94610.* Tel: 510-763-0301.

Office for Episcopal Liturgies—Mrs. CARMEN VINELLA, Dir., *521 Boden Way, Oakland, 94610.* Tel: 510-834-7311.

Vicar for Religious—Sr. BARBARA FLANNERY, C.S.J.

Liturgical Commission—Rev. PAUL VASSAR, Contact, *2900 Lakeshore Ave., Oakland, 94610.*

Christian Initiation—Mr. MARK GONZALEZ.

Environment and Art—Revs. JOHN KASPER, Co-Chm. RON SCHMIT, Co-Chm.

Music—Vacant.

Department for Faith and Ministerial Formation (Diocesan Institute for Ministerial Leadership; Permanent Diaconate Formation Program)

Director—Rev. Msgr. THEODORE W. KRAUS, Ph.D., *521 Boden Way, Oakland, 94610.* Tel: 510-834-7311.

Associate Director for In-Service Programming—Sr. PAT CHOONG.

Associate Director for Spanish Programming—CARLOS RIVAS.

Administrative Associate for Faith Services—Mr. LUIS RIVILLA, M.Div.

Department for Youth and Young Adults

Director—Mr. WILLIAM FORD, *521 Boden Way, Oakland, 94610.* Tel: 510-893-7311.

Associate Director of CYO Athletics and Catholic Scouting—Mr. WILLIAM FORD.

Associate Director of Youth Ministry—Ms. EVELYN GONZALEZ.

Associate Director of Spanish Youth Ministry—Mr. JOSE MORAN.

Associate Director of Ethnic Youth Ministry—ARIEL SAN PEDRO.

Office of the Bishop's Representative to Deacons

Bishop's Representative—Deacon DAVID REZENDES, *521 Boden Way, Oaklands, 94610.* Tel: 510-834-7311.

Diocesan Division for Parish Life

Director—Rev. PAUL R. VASSAR, V.G., *2900 Lakeshore Ave., Oakland, 94610.* Tel: 510-983-4711.

Resource Specialists—Parish Catechetics: Mr. MARC GONZALEZ, Latino Catechetics; Ms. ALICIA RESTREPO. Renewal: Ms. NORA PETERSEN, (Parish); Mr. HECTOR MEDINA, (Latino); LINDA KREHMEIER, Liturgical Resource.

Pontifical Association of the Holy Childhood—Rev. GARY B. TOLLNER, Dir.; Sr. MARIE STAFFORD, S.H.F., Assoc. Dir., *3014 Lakeshore Ave., Oakland, 94610.*

Propagation of the Faith—Rev. GARY B. TOLLNER, Dir., *3014 Lakeshore Ave., Oakland, 94610.* Legal Title: Oakland Society for the Propagation of the Faith.

Development/Stewardship—Ms. KATHERINE KING, *2900 Lakeshore Ave., Oakland, 94610.*

St. Peter the Apostle Society—Rev. GARY B. TOLLNER, *3014 Lakeshore Ave., Oakland, 94610.*

St. Vincent de Paul Society—VAUGHN DONOHUE, Alameda County Dir., *9235 San Leandro St., Oakland, 94603.* Tel: 510-638-7600. CHAREE LORD, Contra Costa County Dir., *2210 Gladstone Dr., Pittsburg, 94565.* Tel: 510-439-5060.

Vocations, Priestly and Religious—Rev. FERNANDO CORTEZ, Dir. & Dir. for Seminarians.

Diocesan Admissions Committee for Seminarians—In process of reformation.

Women, Diocesan Council of Catholic—SHIRLEY MANNETTE.

CLERGY, PARISHES, MISSIONS AND PAROCHIAL SCHOOLS

CITY OF OAKLAND (Alameda County)

1—CATHEDRAL OF ST. FRANCIS DE SALES (1886). Merged with St. Mary, Immaculate Conception to form St. Mary, Immaculate Conception-St. Francis de Sales.

2—ST. ANDREW-ST. JOSEPH (1965) (Latino-African American), Revs. Larry Silva; Thomas Edwards; Deacons Morris Soublet; Leo Edgerly; Eugene Stelly. In res., Rev. Ernest Brainard.
Res., 925 Brockhurst St., 94608. Tel: 510-653-7411; Fax: 510-652-5839.
Schools—St. Martin De Porres School.; St. Patrick Campus, (Grades 6-8). Tel: 510-832-1757; Fax: 510-832-6481.; Sacred Heart Campus, (Grades K-5). Tel: 510-652-2220; Fax: 510-652-2294.; St. Columba Campus, (Grades PreK-K). (future site), Tel: 510-652-2956.

3—ST. ANTHONY'S (1871), Rev. Thuong Hoai Nguyen; Deacon Arcadio Torres. In res., Revs. Prisco Cajes; Jeff Acebo; Huynh Huu Khoai.
Res., 1535 16th Ave., 94606. Tel: 510-534-2117; Fax: 510-534-2119.
School—Tel: 510-534-3334; Fax: 510-534-3378.
Lay Teachers 9; Students 144.
Catechesis/Religious Programs—Tel: 510-534-4420.
Students 144.

4—ST. AUGUSTINE'S (1907), Rev. William Johnson; Margaret Roncalli, Pastoral Assoc.
Res., 400 Alcatraz Ave., 94609. Tel: 510-653-8631; Fax: 510-652-4219.
School—410 Alcatraz Ave., 94609. Tel: 510-652-6727.
Sisters 2; Lay Teachers 14; Students 265.
Catechesis/Religious Programs—Students 265.

5—ST. BENEDICT (1930), Rev. James Matthews; Deacon John Gilbert. In res., Rev. Cuthbert Aronyu (Uganda).
Res., 2245 82nd Ave., 94605. Tel: 510-632-1847; Fax: 510-633-2092.

6—ST. BERNARD'S (1912) (Hispanic-African American), Revs. Joseph Scott, S.V.D.; Roberto Flores, S.V.D., Pastoral Assoc.; Deacon Javier Fuentes. In res., Revs. Stephen Ernest, S.V.D.; Peter Sam Nguyen, S.V.D.
Res., 1620-62nd Ave., 94621. Tel: 510-632-3013; Fax: 510-633-1714.
School—1630-62nd Ave., 94621. Tel: 510-632-6323; Fax: 510-632-6110.
Lay Teachers 8; Students 200.
Catechesis/Religious Programs—Students 292.

7—ST. COLUMBA'S (1898), Rev. Mario L. Borges.
Res., 6401 San Pablo Ave., 94608. Tel: 510-654-7600; Fax: 510-654-7615.

8—ST. CYRIL (1926) (Korean-Vietnamese), Rev. John Fernandes, Parochial Admin. In res., Revs. Javier F. Kutsche; James Song (Korea) Korean Pastoral Center; Anthony Phan Lam; Robert Ponciroli.
Res., 6226 Camden St., 94605. Tel: 510-638-1447; Fax: 510-638-5244.
School—3200 Second Ave., 94605. Tel: 510-638-9445; Fax: 510-638-0744.
Lay Teachers 8; Students 151.

9—ST. ELIZABETH'S (1892), Revs. Marco Antonio Figueroa, O.F.M.; Tommy King, O.F.M.; Peter Krieg, O.F.M.; Deacons Arcadio Torres; Noe Gonzalez. In res., Revs. Kenny Scott, O.F.M.; Gordon Urbine, O.F.M.
Res., 1500 34th Ave., 94601. Tel: 510-536-1266; Fax: 510-536-8560.
School—Tel: 510-532-7392; Fax: 510-532-0321.
Sisters 2; Lay Teachers 17; Students 496.
Catechesis/Religious Programs—Tel: 510-532-3766.
Students 765.
Mission—Oakland, Alameda Co., Mary Help of Christians, 2611 E. 9th St., 94601. Tel: 510-534-3501; Fax: 510-436-5157.

10—ST. JARLATH'S (1910), Revs. Raymond G. Breton; Denis A. Des Rosiers. In res., Revs. Robert A. Mathews; Alberto de Mingo Kaminouchi, C.SS.R. (Spain).
Res., 2620 Pleasant St., 94602. Tel: 510-532-2068; Fax: 510-532-3745.
School—2634 Pleasant St., 94602. Tel: 510-532-4387.
Lay Teachers 9; Students 270.

11—ST. LAWRENCE O'TOOLE (1916), Rev. Robert W. Charm.
Res., 3725 High St., 94619. Tel: 510-530-0761; Fax: 510-530-0974.
School—Tel: 510-530-0266; Fax: 510-530-7568.
Lay Teachers 17; Students 277.

12—ST. LEO'S (1911), Rev. Timothy K. Johnson. In res., Rev. Thomas Ng.
Res., 176 Ridgeway Ave., 94611-5122. Tel: 510-654-6177; Fax: 510-654-4203.
School—Tel: 510-654-7828; Fax: 510-654-4057.
Lay Teachers 10; Students 265.

13—ST. LOUIS BERTRAND (1908) (Hispanic-African American), Rev. Edgar Haasl.
Res., 1410-100th Ave., 94603. Tel: 510-568-1080; Fax: 510-635-8618.
School—1445-101st Ave., 94603. Tel: 510-568-1067.
Lay Teachers 9; Students 275.
Catechesis/Religious Programs—Students 875.

14—ST. MARGARET MARY (1922), Revs. George D. Sullivan (STO) Admin.; Paul J. Schmidt.
Res., 1219 Excelsior Ave., 94610. Tel: 510-482-0596; Fax: 510-482-0596.

15—MARY HELP OF CHRISTIANS CHURCH (1915) (Spanish), Rev. Marco Antonio Alvarado; Jose Felipe Patino, Admin.
Res., 2611 E. Ninth St., 94601. Tel: 510-534-3501.
School—One Estates Dr., Piedmont.

16—ST. MARY, IMMACULATE CONCEPTION. Merged with St. Francis de Sales to form St. Mary, Immaculate Conception-St. Francis de Sales.

17—ST. MARY, IMMACULATE CONCEPTION-ST. FRANCIS DE SALES (1993), Rev. Peter McGrath, S.J. In res.,

Revs. Joseph Carroll, S.J.; Binh Quach, C.S.Sp.; Joseph Thuan Nguyen, O.P.
Res. & Office: St. Francis de Sales Rectory: 634 21st St., 94612. Tel: 510-832-5057; Fax: 510-832-0212.
Catechesis/Religious Programs—Students 150.

18—OUR LADY OF LOURDES (1921), Rev. Seamus D. Genovese; Sr. Mary Gallagher, S.H.J.M.
Res., 2808 Lakeshore Ave., 94610. Tel: 510-451-1790; Fax: 510-893-6443. [CEM]

19—ST. PASCHAL BAYLON (1955), Rev. Robert K. Rien.
Res., 3700 Dorisa Ave., 94605. Tel: 510-636-0335; Fax: 510-636-0287.
School—Tel: 510-635-7922; Fax: 510-635-4219.
Lay Teachers 9; Students 195.

20—ST. PATRICK'S (1879) (African American-Hispanic), Rev. Charles D. Burns, S.V.D.
Res., 1023 Peralta St., 94607. Tel: 510-444-1081; Fax: 510-444-1113.
School—1630 10th St., 94607. Tel: 510-832-1757; Fax: 510-832-6481.
Lay Teachers 3; Students 59.

21—SACRED HEART (1876), Revs. Jose R. Arong, O.M.I.; Tom J. Edwards.
Res., 4025 Martin Luther King Way, 94609. Tel: 510-655-9209; Fax: 510-652-1958.
School—St. Martin De Porres, 664 41st St., 94609. Tel: 510-652-2220; Fax: 510-652-2294.
Lay Teachers 10; Students 250. Co-Principals: Mr. Robert Ratto; Rhuepell Stroud.
Catechesis/Religious Programs—Special Religious Education Department. (SPRED). Tel: 510-654-2869; Fax: 510-654-3067. Sr. Aurora Perez, S.H.F., D.R.E.
Students 16.

22—ST. THERESA OF THE INFANT JESUS (THE LITTLE FLOWER) (1925), Rev. Msgr. Bernard J. Moran; Rev. Hy Khac Nguyen.
Res., 30 Mandalay Rd., 94618. Tel: 510-547-2777; Fax: 510-653-3575.
School—Tel: 510-547-3146; Fax: 510-547-3253.
Lay Teachers 13; Students 290.
Catechesis/Religious Programs—Students 108.

OUTSIDE THE CITY OF OAKLAND

Alameda, Alameda Co.,

1—ST. ALBERT, (1976). Unassigned.
Res., 1022 Holly St., 94502. Tel: 510-522-2185; Fax: 510-522-1055.

2—ST. BARNABAS, (1925), Revs. Jeffrey R. Keyes, C.PP.S.; Timothy Erwin, C.PP.S.
Res., 1427 Sixth St., 94501. Tel: 510-522-8933; Fax: 510-522-8380.
School—Tel: 510-521-0595; Fax: 510-521-3560.
Lay Teachers 9; Students 210.

3—ST. JOSEPH BASILICA, (1885), Revs. Jeremiah Holland, SS.CC.; Patrick J. Crowley, SS.CC.
Res., 1109 Chestnut St., 94501. Tel: 510-522-0181; Fax: 510-522-2864.
School—St. Joseph Elementary School, Tel: 510-522-4457; Fax: 510-522-2890.
Lay Teachers 15; Students 312.
High School—See separate category under High Schools, Parochial. Tel: 510-523-1526; Fax: 510-523-2181.
Catechesis/Religious Programs—Tel: 510-522-0445. D.R.E.: Charles Sevin; Steve Mullin.
Students 840.

4—ST. PHILIP NERI, (1925), Revs. Jerrold F. Kennedy; Michael Lacey, M.S.C.
Res., 3108 Van Buren St., 94501. Tel: 510-522-2299; Fax: 510-522-1625.
School—1335 High St., 94501. Tel: 510-521-0787; Fax: 510-521-2418.
Lay Teachers 16; Students 293.

Antioch, Contra Costa Co., Holy Rosary (1874), Revs. Francisco Vicente; Mark C. Padrez, O.P.; Joseph Sergott, O.P.; Mrs. Jackie Hooke, Pastoral Assoc.
Res., 1313 A St., 94509. Tel: 510-757-4020; Fax: 510-757-6828. [CEM][JC]
School—Tel: 510-757-1270; Fax: 510-757-9309.
Lay Teachers 24; Students 457.
Catechesis/Religious Programs—21 E. 15th St., 94059. Tel: 510-757-9515.
Students 700.

St. Ignatius (1979), Revs. Vince Cotter; Leo Edgerly, Jr.; Deacon Al Fleischer.
Res., 209 Tanganyika Ct., 94509. Tel: 510-778-0768; Fax: 510-778-0845. [CEM]
Catechesis/Religious Programs—3351 Contra Loma Blvd., 94509. Tel: 510-778-1314.
Students 460.

Berkeley, Alameda Co.,

1—ST. AMBROSE, (1909), Rev. Thomas J. Ryan.
Res., 1145 Gilman St., 94706. Tel: 510-525-2620; Fax: 510-525-5399.

2—HOLY SPIRIT PARISH, (1967). (U.C. Newman Hall). Revs. Michael B. McGarry, C.S.P.; Frank Sabatte, C.S.P.; Albert Moser, C.S.P.
Res., 2700 Dwight Way, 94704-3113. Tel: 510-848-7812; Fax: 510-848-0179. [CEM]
Catechesis/Religious Programs—Students 180.

3—ST. JOSEPH THE WORKER, (1879), Revs. George E. Crespin; William J. O'Donnell. In res., Revs. Thomas Martin (Australia); Thomas J. McElligott (SFR); Gerard E. Reid (Jamaica) (Montego Bay).
Res., 1640 Addison St., 94703. Tel: 510-843-2244; Fax: 510-843-2730.
School—2125 Jefferson St., 94703. Tel: 510-845-6266; Fax: 510-845-6185.
Sisters 1; Lay Teachers 9; Students 193.

4—ST. MARY MAGDALEN, (1923), Revs. George M. Matanic, O.P.; Bruno Gibson, O.P. In res., Revs. Gregory Tatum, O.P.; Hilary Martin, O.P.
Res., 2005 Berryman St., 94709. Tel: 510-526-4811; Fax: 510-525-3638.
School—School of the Madeleine, 1225 Milvia St., 94709. Tel: 510-526-4744; Fax: 510-526-5152.
Lay Teachers 22; Students 314.

Brentwood, Contra Costa Co., Immaculate Heart of Mary (1949) (English-Spanish), Revs. John G. Garcia; Daniel E. Crahen, O.M.I.; Deacon Frank Bustos.
Res., 813 First St., 94513. Tel: 510-634-4154; Fax: 510-516-9340.
School—One Estates Dr., Piedmont.
Catechesis/Religious Programs—Students 423.

Byron, Contra Costa Co., St. Anne (1916), Rev. Ronald G. Schmit.
Mailing Address: Camino Diablo Rd. at McCabe Dr., P.O. Box 476, 94514.
Res., 5604 Schooner Loop, Discovery Bay, 54514. Tel: 510-634-6625; Fax: 510-634-4194.
Catechesis/Religious Programs—Students 175.

Castro Valley, Alameda Co., Our Lady of Grace (1947), Revs. Robert W. Gavotto, O.S.A.; Thomas W. Behan, O.S.A.; Paul Quante, O.S.A.; Deacon Robert Dowling.
Res., 3433 Somerset Ave., 94546-3398. Tel: 510-537-0806; Fax: 510-537-6281.
School—19950 Anita Ave., 94546-3398. Tel: 510-581-3155; Fax: 510-581-1059.
Lay Teachers 14; Students 287.
Catechesis/Religious Programs—Tel: 510-538-3464; 582-9266; 889-7017.
Students 380.

Transfiguration (1961), Rev. John C. Crumlish; Deacons Timothy L. Moore; Burt Rigley. In res., Rev. John E. Ranallo.
Res., 4000 E. Castro Valley Blvd., 94552. Tel: 510-538-7941; Fax: 510-538-7983.
Catechesis/Religious Programs—Tel: 510-537-1502.
Students 330.

Concord, Contra Costa Co.,

1—ST. AGNES, (1964), Revs. George E. Mockel; Donald Crosby, S.J.
Res., 3966 Chestnut Ave., 94519. Tel: 510-689-0838; Fax: 510-689-7899.
School—3886 Chestnut Ave., 94519. Tel: 510-689-3990; Fax: 510-689-3455.
Lay Teachers 15; Students 343.
Catechesis/Religious Programs—Tel: 510-689-3757.
Students 383.

2—ST. BONAVENTURE, (1957), Revs. Richard A. Mangini; Walter Borkowski; Salvador Macias; David Lawrence, S.J.
Res., 5562 Clayton Rd., 94521. Tel: 510-672-5800; Fax: 510-672-4606.
Catechesis/Religious Programs—Tel: 510-672-5500.
Students 652.

3—ST. FRANCIS OF ASSISI, (1984). (Formerly Most Precious Blood, 1955). Revs. William V. Macchi; (Eugene) Thomas P. Bonacci; Deacons William E. Bothe; Charles Palomares. In res., Rev. Msgr. Edward Varni, Pastor Emeritus.
Res., 860 Oak Grove Rd., 94518. Tel: 510-682-5447; Fax: 510-682-5491.
School—866 Oak Grove Rd., 94518. Tel: 510-682-5414; Fax: 510-682-5480.
Sisters 2; Lay Teachers 17; Students 338.
Catechesis/Religious Programs—Tel: 510-682-5422.
Students 248.

4—QUEEN OF ALL SAINTS, (1923), Revs. Michael Cunningham; Joseph Welch; Stan Zak. Pastoral Assocs.: Ellen L. Midgley; Deacons George Peters; Robert Karp.
Res., 2390 Grant St., 94520. Tel: 510-825-0350; Fax: 510-825-6975. [CEM]
School—2391 Grant St., 94520. Tel: 510-685-8700; Fax: 510-685-2034.
Lay Teachers 13; Students 263.
Catechesis/Religious Programs—Tel: 510-685-8707.
Students 100.

Crockett, Contra Costa Co., St. Rose of Lima (1912), Rev. Ciarian Dillon, O.M.I.
Res., 555 Third Ave., 94525. Tel: 510-787-2052; Fax: 510-787-2163.
Mission—Crockett, Contra Costa Co., St. Patrick, c/o St. Rose, 94525.

Danville, Contra Costa Co., St. Isidore's (1910), Revs. Daniel E. Cardelli; Terry Tompkins. In res., Revs. James E. Driscoll, (Retired); Frank L. Colacicco (SAN).
Res., 445 LaGonda Way, 94526-2522. Tel: 510-837-2122; Fax: 510-837-3954.
School—Tel: 510-837-2977; Fax: 510-837-2407.
Lay Teachers 26; Students 585.
Catechesis/Religious Programs—Tel: 510-837-1306; Fax: 510-837-3348.
Students 600.

Dublin, Alameda Co., St. Raymond (1961), Revs. Patrick A. Goodwin; John Blaker.
Res., 11555 Shannon Ave., 94568. Tel: 510-828-2460; Fax: 510-828-8610.
School—Tel: 510-828-4064; Fax: 510-828-2454.
Lay Teachers 15; Students 301.
Catechesis/Religious Programs—Tel: 510-828-4033.
Students 521.

El Cerrito, Contra Costa Co., St. Jerome's (1941), Rev. E. Donald Osuna.
Res., 308 Carmel Ave., 94530. Tel: 510-525-0876; Fax: 510-526-2721.
School—310 San Carlos, 94530. Tel: 510-525-9484; Fax: 510-525-5227.
Sisters of the Sacred Hearts of Jesus and Mary 1; Lay Teachers 15; Students 311.

St. John the Baptist (1925), Revs. John Maxwell; Leo Asuncion; Raymond Ogbemure; Deacon Thomas McGowan.
Res., 11150 San Pablo Ave., 94530. Tel: 510-232-5659; Fax: 510-236-0960.
School—Tel: 510-234-2244.
Sisters of Mercy (Ireland) 2; Lay Teachers 9; Students 314.
Catechesis/Religious Programs—Students 144.

El Sobrante, Contra Costa Co., St. Callistus (1952), Rev. Dana Michaels. In res., Rev. Richard Gagliardi.
Res., 3580 San Pablo Dam Rd., 94803. Tel: 510-223-1153; Fax: 510-223-1137.
Catechesis/Religious Programs—Tel: 510-222-0432.
Students 130.

Fremont, Alameda Co.,

1—CORPUS CHRISTI, (1914), Rev. Timothy Stier; Deacon Luis Trucios.
Res., 37891 Second St., 94536. Tel: 510-790-3207; Fax: 510-790-3227.
Catechesis/Religious Programs—Tel: 510-790-3226.
Students 235.

2—HOLY SPIRIT, (1886), Revs. Gerard K. Moran; Larry Young; Patrick Bishop; Deacons Rudolph Brazil; William Drobick; Richard Yee.
Res., 37588 Fremont Blvd., 94536. Tel: 510-797-1660; Fax: 510-797-7080. [CEM]
School—Tel: 510-793-3553.
Lay Teachers 11; Students 325.
Catechesis/Religious Programs—Tel: 510-797-5395.
Students 800.

3—ST. JAMES THE APOSTLE, (1972), Rev. Paul E. Cleu.
Res., P.O. Box 7084, 94537. Tel: 510-792-1962.

4—ST. JOSEPH MISSION CHURCH, (1797), Rev. Msgr. Manuel C. Simas; Rev. Jayson J. Landeza.
Res., P.O. Box 3276, Mission San Jose, 94539. Tel: 510-656-2364; Fax: 510-656-2438. [CEM]
School—43222 Mission Blvd., 94539. Tel: 510-656-6525; Fax: 510-656-3608.
Dominican Sisters of San Jose 2; Lay Teachers 12; Students 283.
Catechesis/Religious Programs—Tel: 510-657-0905; Fax: 510-657-4165.
Students 485.

5—ST. LEONARD, (1959), Rev. Joseph Cantillon. In res., Rev. Gerard Beigel.
Res., 3600 St. Leonard's Way, 94538. Tel: 510-656-4921; Fax: 510-226-0714.
School—3635 St. Leonard's Way, 94538. Tel: 510-657-1674; Fax: 510-657-3659.
Sisters 2; Lay Teachers 8; Students 290.
Catechesis/Religious Programs—Tel: 510-651-4966.
Students 380.

6—SANTA PAULA, (1965), Rev. Pascual Ramirez; Deacons Ovide Guesnon; Bill Martinez.
Res., 4358 Bora Bora Ave., 94538. Tel: 510-657-4043; 657-4040; Fax: 510-657-4055.
Catechesis/Religious Programs—Tel: 510-657-3777.
Students 377.

Hayward, Alameda Co.,

1—ALL SAINTS, (1898), Revs. Robert J. McCann; Mark Wiesner; Emmanuel H. Gardon, C.P.; Deacon Nelson Gonsalves. In res., Rev. Matthew Hills.
Church—22824 Second St., 94541. Tel: 510-581-2570; Fax: 510-581-9538. [CEM]
School—Tel: 510-582-1910; Fax: 510-582-0866.
Lay Teachers 15; Students 310.
Catechesis/Religious Programs—Tel: 510-538-2711; Fax: 510-581-3642.
Students 354.

2—ST. BEDE, (1955), Revs. Seamus J. Farrell; Marciano Santiago, II (Philippines); Jose de Jesus Nieto-Ruiz; Rev. Msgr. George J. Francis, Pastor Emeritus; Deacons Denis Ryken; Gabriel Hernandez.
Res., 26950 Patrick Ave., 94544. Tel: 510-782-2171; Fax: 510-782-9712.
School—26910 Patrick Ave., 94544. Tel: 510-782-3444; Fax: 510-782-2243.
Lay Teachers 13; Students 305.
Catechesis/Religious Programs—Tel: 510-782-4292.
Students 650.

3—ST. CLEMENT, (1953), Revs. Thomas McNally, C.S.C.; William Phifer, C.S.C. In res., Rev. Robert J. Loughery, C.S.C.
Res., 738 Calhoun St., 94544. Tel: 510-582-7282; 582-7240; Fax: 510-582-1875.
School—790 Calhoun St., 94544. Tel: 510-538-5885. Mrs. Joan Burman, Prin.
Lay Teachers 12; Students 303.
Catechesis/Religious Programs—Students 506.

4—ST. JOACHIM, (1951), Revs. Ray Zielezienski; Sergio Mora.
Res., 21250 Hesperian Blvd., 94541. Tel: 510-783-2766; Fax: 510-783-2760.
School—Tel: 510-783-3177; Fax: 510-783-2161.
Lay Teachers 13; Students 304.
Catechesis/Religious Programs—Tel: 510-785-1818.
Students 304.

Lafayette, Contra Costa Co., St. Perpetua (1952), Rev. John Kasper, O.S.F.S. In res., Rev. Francis J. Houdek, S.J.
Res., 3454 Hamlin Rd., 94549. Tel: 510-283-0272; Fax: 510-283-6534.
School—Tel: 510-284-1640; Fax: 510-284-5676.
Lay Teachers 15; Students 268.
Catechesis/Religious Programs—Students 335.

Livermore, Alameda Co., St. Charles Borromeo (1964), Rev. Richard McCafferty, S.J.
Res., 1315 Lomitas Ave., 94550. Tel: 510-447-4549; Fax: 510-373-7088. [JC]
Catechesis/Religious Programs—Tel: 510-449-0133.
Students 175.

St. Michael's (1878), Revs. Michael Joyce; Scott Chavez; David E. Staal; Deacons David Rezendez; Bill Archer. In res., Revs. Augustine Koilparampil (India); Walter W. Mayer.
Res., 458 Maple St., 94550. Tel: 510-447-1585; Fax: 510-447-0520. [CEM]
School—Tel: 510-447-1888; Fax: 510-447-6720.
Sisters 2; Lay Teachers 14; Students 350.
Catechesis/Religious Programs—Tel: 510-447-8814.
Students 394.

Martinez, Contra Costa Co., St. Catherine of Siena (1873), Revs. Vincent R. Brylka; Carl H. Seewald, S.V.D.
Res., 1100 Estudillo St., 94553. Tel: 510-228-2230; Fax: 510-228-1318. [CEM]
School—Tel: 510-228-4140; Fax: 510-228-0697. Mr. Mark DeMarco, Prin.
Lay Teachers 10; Students 275.
Catechesis/Religious Programs—1125 Ferry St., 94553. Tel: 510-228-5087.
Students 244.

Moraga, Contra Costa Co., St. Monica (1965), Mrs. Cath McGhee, Pastoral Admin.; Rev. Declan Deane; Deacons Jack Jordan; Luis Rivilla. In res., Rev. Thomas M. Mulvanerty (NY).
Res., 1001 Camino Pablo, P.O. Box 128, 94556. Tel: 510-376-6900; Fax: 510-376-9796.
Catechesis/Religious Programs—Tel: 510-376-0500.
Students 453.

Newark, Alameda Co., St. Edward's (1920), Revs. Ronald P. Wiecek, C.PP.S.; Jeffrey Finley, C.PP.S.; Gene Wilson, C.PP.S.; Deacons Ernest Perez; Nick Bruckner; Roger Wedl; Antonio Barreto.
Res., 5788 Thornton Ave., 94560. Tel: 510-797-0241; Fax: 510-797-4557.
School—P.O. Box 245, 94560. Tel: 510-793-7242.
Sisters 2; Lay Teachers 10; Students 312.
Catechesis/Religious Programs—Tel: 510-797-5588.
Students 1,265.

Oakley, Contra Costa Co., St. Anthony (1925) (English-Spanish-Portuguese), Rev. Bernardino Andrade; Deacons Joseph Tovar; Alan Layden.
Res., 971 O'Hara Ave., 94561. Tel: 510-625-2048; Fax: 510-625-4433. [JC]
Catechesis/Religious Programs—Tel: 510-625-2077.
Students 210.

Orinda, Contra Costa Co., Santa Maria (1947), Rev. J. Roger Lucey, S.J. In res., Rev. Paul B. Steinmetz, S.J.
Res., 20 Santa Maria Way, 94563. Tel: 510-254-2426; Fax: 510-254-2468.
Catechesis/Religious Programs—Tel: 510-254-0554. D.R.E.: Dorothy Harrington, (Children); Dianna Rees, (Youth-CLW).
Students 284.

Piedmont, Alameda Co., Corpus Christi (1929), Revs. Albano Oliveira; Brian Timoney. In res., Rev. Basil DePinto.
Res., 322 St. James Dr., 94611. Tel: 510-530-4343; Fax: 510-530-6824.
School—One Estates Dr., 94611. Tel: 510-530-4056; Fax: 510-530-5926.
Lay Teachers 14; Students 285.
Catechesis/Religious Programs—Students 214.

Pinole, Contra Costa Co., St. Joseph's (1947), Revs. P. Michael Galvan; Quang Minh Dong; Ramiro Flores; Deacon Benjamin P. Agustin.
Parish Center, Office & Mailing Address: 2100 Pear St., 94564.
Church—837 Tennent Ave., 94564. Tel: 510-741-4900; Fax: 510-724-9185.
School—Tel: 510-724-0242.
Lay Teachers 20; Students 320.
Catechesis/Religious Programs—Tel: 510-741-4912; 4913.
Students 658.

Pittsburg, Contra Costa Co., Good Shepherd (1965), Revs. Helmut W. Richter; Louis Dabovich, Pastor Emeritus; James Pickett; Deacon Ferris J. Anthony.
Res., 3200 Harbor St., 94565. Tel: 510-432-6404; Fax: 510-432-6748.
Catechesis/Religious Programs—Tel: 510-439-1091.
Students 600.

Our Lady Queen of the World (1962), Revs. Theo Palis, Pastor Emeritus; Richard J. Culver, Admin.; Thomas Duong Binh Minh.
Res., 3155 Winterbrook Dr., 94565. Tel: 510-458-4718; Fax: 510-458-3161.
Catechesis/Religious Programs—Tel: 510-458-4574.
Students 310.

St. Peter Martyr of Verona (1914), Revs. Ricardo A. Chavez; Agerico Galang.
Res., 740 Black Diamond St., 94565. Tel: 510-432-4771; Fax: 510-432-3389.
School—Tel: 510-439-1014; Fax: 510-439-1506.
Lay Teachers 10; Students 302.
Catechesis/Religious Programs—Tel: 510-432-7200.
Students 308.

Pleasant Hill, Contra Costa Co., Christ the King (1951), Rev. Msgr. James J. Wade, Pastor Emeritus; Revs. Brian T. Joyce; Paul Nourie, O.M.I.; Jim McGee, S.S.; Margo Schorno, Pastoral Assoc.
Res., 199 Brandon Rd., 94523. Tel: 510-682-2486; Fax: 510-682-5021.
School—Tel: 510-685-1109; Fax: 510-685-1289. Sr. Carmel Garcia, C.S.J., Prin.
Sisters of St. Joseph of Carondelet 5; Lay Teachers 12; Students 328.
Catechesis/Religious Programs—Tel: 510-686-1017.
Students 730.

Pleasanton, Alameda Co., St. Augustine (1901), Revs. Daniel E. Danielson; Anthony W. Herrera; Geoffrey Baraan; Deacons Richard Martin; Thomas Perry; James Campbell; Ernest Freeman; Edward Quigley.
Res., 3999 Bernal Ave., P.O. Box 817, 94566. Tel: 510-846-4489; Fax: 510-426-0586. [CEM]
Catechesis/Religious Programs—Tel: 510-846-3531; Fax: 510-846-3543.
Students 1,439.
Mission—Pleasanton, Alameda Co., St. Elizabeth Seton, (1991) 4001 Stoneridge Dr., 94566. Tel: 510-484-5020.

Point Richmond, Contra Costa Co., Our Lady of Mercy (1902), Rev. James C. Clift.
Res., 301 W. Richmond Ave., 94801. Tel: 510-232-1843; Fax: 510-232-1805.

Richmond, Contra Costa Co., St. Cornelius (1952), Revs. Antonio A. Valdivia; Stephan Kappler; Deacon Juan Beltran.
Res., 225-28th St., 94804. Tel: 510-233-5215; Fax: 510-233-7342. [CEM]
School—201-28th St., 94805. Tel: 510-232-3326; Fax: 510-232-4071.
Lay Teachers 11; Students 216.
Catechesis/Religious Programs—Students 180.

St. David of Wales (1952), Rev. Ronald E. Atwood.
Res., 5641 Esmond Ave., 94805. Tel: 510-237-1531; Fax: 510-237-3801.
School—871 Sonoma St., 94805. Tel: 510-232-2283; Fax: 510-231-0484. Mrs. Barbara Kringle, Prin.
Lay Teachers 15; Students 336.
Catechesis/Religious Programs—5418 Esmond Ave., 94805. Tel: 510-236-6690.
Students 336.

St. Mark's (1912), Rev. Antonio A. Valdivia, Admin.
Res., 159 Harbour Way, 94801. Tel: 510-234-5886; Fax: 510-236-5711.

Rodeo, Contra Costa Co., St. Patrick's (1923), Revs. Melvin J. Hary; Augustine Joseph, S.D.B. (India).
Res., 825 Seventh St., 94572. Tel: 510-799-4406; Fax: 510-799-5681.
School—907 Seventh St., 94572. Tel: 510-799-2506; Fax: 510-799-6781.
Sisters of the Immaculate Heart of Mary 2; Lay Teachers 12; Students 285.

San Leandro, Alameda Co.,

1—ASSUMPTION OF THE BLESSED VIRGIN MARY, (1951), Rev. Msgr. Michael Lucid; Rev. Joseph Duong Phan. In res., Rev. Michael Norkett.
Res., 1100 Fulton Ave., 94577. Tel: 510-352-1537; Fax: 510-352-9155.
School—Tel: 510-357-8772; Fax: 510-357-7018.
Lay Teachers 20; Students 293.

2—ST. ALPHONSUS LIGUORI, (1955), Rev. Raymond Sacca.
Res., 2085 Miramar Ave., 94578. Tel: 510-276-3907.

3—ST. FELICITAS, (1952), Revs. Wayne Campbell; Patrick Hannon; Deacon Jose Prado, (Retired). In res., Rev. Tran Thuc Dinh (Vietnam) (Retired).
Res., 1662 Manor Blvd., 94579. Tel: 510-351-5244; Fax: 510-351-5730.
School—1650 Manor Blvd., 94579. Tel: 510-357-2530; Fax: 510-357-5358.
Sisters of St. Joseph of Wichita 2; Lay Teachers 7; Students 304.
Catechesis/Religious Programs—Tel: 510-483-4880.
Students 270.

4—ST. LEANDER, (1864), Revs. John Prochaska; Thomas Lester; Deacons Dennis Davis; Victor Silveira; Antonio Baptista; Frank Beville. In res., Revs. Matthew R.D. Regan; Antonio Reis.
Office: 474 W. Estudillo Ave., 94577. Tel: 510-895-5631; Fax: 510-352-3578.
School—Tel: 510-351-4144; Fax: 510-483-6060.
Lay Teachers 9; Students 308.
Catechesis/Religious Programs—Students 347.

5—OUR LADY OF GOOD COUNSEL, (1966), Rev. Alexander N. Snyder.
Res., 14112 Azores Pl., 94577. Tel: 510-483-6731; Fax: 510-483-7705.

San Lorenzo, Alameda Co., St. John the Baptist (1925), Revs. David Link; William J. Dunn; Deacon Leonard J. Bettencourt.
Res., 264 E. Lewelling Blvd., 94580. Tel: 510-351-5050; Fax: 510-276-0397.
School—Tel: 510-276-6632; Fax: 510-276-5645. Arlene Marseille, Prin.
Sisters 2; Lay Teachers 11; Students 309.
Catechesis/Religious Programs—Tel: 510-278-5080.
Students 220.

San Pablo, St. Paul (1864), Revs. Paul Fazio, O.F.M.Conv.; Ignatius Hinkle, O.F.M.Conv.; Bro. George Cherrie, O.F.M.Conv.; Deacons Ysidro Madrigal; Isidoro R. Flores; Donaciano Perez.
Res., 1845 Church Ln., 94806. Tel: 510-232-5931; Fax: 510-232-1846.
School—Tel: 510-233-3080; Fax: 510-231-8777.
Lay Teachers 12; Students 308.
Catechesis/Religious Programs—1825 Church Ln., 94806.
Students 457.

San Ramon, Contra Costa Co., St. Joan of Arc (1979), Revs. Fred A. Riccio; Herman M. Leong; Deacons Charles Marchese; Ruben Gomez.
Res., 2601 San Ramon Valley Blvd., 94583. Tel: 510-830-0600; Fax: 510-830-5059.
Catechesis/Religious Programs—Tel: 510-830-4710.
Students 1,330.

Union City, Alameda Co., Our Lady of the Rosary (1951), Rev. Jose M. Leon; Deacons Federico Ceja, (Retired); Richard L. Folger; Gustaaf Roemers; Luis Trucios. In res., Rev. Roy Eco (Philippines).
Res., 703 C St., 94587. Tel: 510-471-2609; Fax: 510-471-4601.
School—Tel: 510-471-3765.
Lay Teachers 8; Students 181.

Catechesis/Religious Programs—Tel: 510-471-7419.
Students 390.

St. Anne (1973), Revs. Ramon J. Gomez; Louis Shen, S.J.
Res., 32223 Cabello St., P.O. Box 292, 94587. Tel: 510-471-7766; Fax: 510-487-6540.
Catechesis/Religious Programs—Tel: 510-489-2080.
Students 665.

Walnut Creek, Contra Costa Co.,

1—St. Anne, (1965), Rev. Msgr. John T. McCracken; Revs. Anthony S. Hannick (YAK); William Kegel, S.J.; Sr. Ruth Anne Saunders, C.S.J., Pastoral Assoc.
Res., 1600 Rossmoor Pkwy., 94595-2507. Tel: 510-932-2324; Fax: 510-932-4628.

2—St. John Vianney, (1965), Revs. Vincent J. Scott; Christopher Berbena.
Res., 1650 Ygnacio Valley Rd., 94598. Tel: 510-939-7911; Fax: 510-939-0450.
Catechesis/Religious Programs—Tel: 510-939-9544.
Students 507.

3—St. Mary's, (1941), Revs. John J. Mallon; John R. Kenny; George Palamattathil. In res., Rev. Peter Charankat (India).
Res., 1201 Alpine Rd., 94596. Tel: 510-934-2544; Fax: 510-934-1358.
School—Tel: 510-935-5054; Fax: 510-935-5063. Mrs. Mary Lou Curtis, Prin.
Lay Teachers 16; Students 272.
Catechesis/Religious Programs—2039 Mt. Diablo Blvd., 94596. Tel: 510-937-2414; Fax: 510-937-6487. Marlene Preun, D.R.E.
Students 255.

4—St. Stephen, (1966), Rev. Harry B. Morrison.
Res., 525 Madonna Ln., 94596. Tel: 510-939-3826; Fax: 510-988-0417.

Chaplains of Public Institutions

Hospitals

Oakland. *Children's Hospital*. Sr. Bernice Gotelli, P.B.V.M. Tel: 510-428-3325; 428-3000.
Highland Hospital. Sr. Maura O'Connor, S.N.J.M. Tel: 510-437-4800.
Kaiser-Permanente Medical Center Tel: 510-428-5000. Rev. Basil DePinto; Mrs. Jodi Henrekin Tel: 510-596-1000.
Summit Medical Center, Pastoral Care. Attended by Sacred Heart Parish. Tel: 510-835-4500.

Antioch. *Delta Memorial Hospital*. Attended by Holy Rosary Parish.

Berkeley. *Alta Bates Hospital*. Sr. Kathleen Corbett, C.S.J. Tel: 510-204-4444.
Alta Bates-Herrick Hospital. Attended by St. Joseph the Worker Parish, Berkeley.

Castro Valley. *Eden Hospital*. Rev. John Ranallo, O.S.A. Tel: 510-537-1234.

Concord. *Mount Diablo Hospital, Pastoral Care*. Attended by Queen of All Saints Church. Tel: 510-682-8200.

Fremont. *Washington Hospital*. Rev. Richard Peiris Tel: 510-505-0599; 797-1111; Sr. Jeanne Sullivan, S.N.D. Tel: 510-797-1111; Rev. Jeffrey Finley, C.PP.S. Tel: 510-797-1111.

Hayward. *Kaiser-Permanente Medical Center*. Attended by St. Bede Parish.

Livermore. *Veterans Administration Hospital*. Rev. Augustine Koilparampil Tel: 510-447-2560; 447-1585.

Martinez. *Contra Costa Hospital*. Attended by St. Catherine of Siena Parish.
Kaiser-Permanente Medical Center. Sr. Moira MacPherson Tel: 510-372-1000.

Pinole. *Doctor's Hospital*. Attended by St. Joseph Parish, Pinole.

Pittsburg. *Los Medanos Hospital*. Attended by Good Shepherd Parish.

Richmond. *East Bay Hospital*. Attended by St. Cornelius Parish & St. Mark Parish.
Kaiser-Permanente. Attended by St. Mark Parish.

San Leandro. *Fairmont Hospital, Redemptorists* Tel: 510-667-3251. Bro. Rick Fischer.
Humana Hospital. Attended by St. Leander Parish.
Physicians Community Hospital. Attended by Assumption Parish.

San Pablo. *Brookside-Hospital*. Attended by St. Paul Parish. Tel: 510-235-7000.

San Ramon. *San Ramon Regional Medical Center*. Attended by St. Joan of Arc Parish. Tel: 510-275-9200 (Hospital).

Santa Cruz. *Dominican Santa Cruz Hospital* 1555 Soquel Dr., 95065. Rev. Scott F. Hill, O.M.I., 121 New St., 95060.

Walnut Creek. *John Muir Memorial Hospital, Pastoral Care*. Attended by St. John Vianney Parish. Tel: 510-939-3000 (Hospital).
Kaiser-Permanente Medical Center. Rev. Peter Charankat Tel: 510-372-1000.
Walnut Creek Hospital. Attended by St. John Vianney Parish.

Prisons and Jails

Oakland. *North County Jail*. Deacon Eugene Stelley Tel: 510-652-5453.
Victim Offender Reconciliation Program. (VORP). Rick Mockler, Dir., Tel: 510-834-5656.

Martinez. *Contra Costa County Jails*. Pat Conroy Tel: 510-672-7822.
Contra Costa County Juvenile Institution. Deacon Frank Beville Tel: 510-834-5656.

Pleasanton. *Alameda County Jail-Santa Rita Rehabilitation Center*. Deacon Frank Beville Tel: 510-834-5656; 828-5400, Ext. 261.
Federal Correctional Institution. Sr. Joan Campbell, P.B.V.M.; Rev. Efrin Casio Tel: 510-829-3522.

San Leandro. *Alameda County Juvenile Institutions*. Deacon Frank Beville, Coord., Tel: 510-834-5656.

On Special Assignment:
Reverend Fathers—
Vella, Francis, Chap., V.A. Medical Center, Alexandria, LA

Military Chaplains:
Reverend Monsignors—
Walsh, Martin E., Army Reserves
Reverend Fathers—
Brennan, Bernard F., Oakland Army Base, Oakland
Buenaventura, Cesar, Lt., C.H.C., U.S. Naval Reserves
Hannick, Anthony S., Veterans Admin. Hospital, Martinez
Koilparampil, Augustine, U.S. Veterans Hospital, Livermore
Lagasse, Ronald J., Lt. Col., U.S. Army Reserves, Schofield Army Base, Hawaii
Pokladowski, Gregory F., Cmdr., C.H.C., U.S. Navy, Oak Knoll Naval Hospital, Oakland
Starbuck, James
Wydeven, John

Graduate Studies:
Reverend Fathers—
Macias, Salvadore

Retired:
Reverend Monsignors—
Adams, Robert
Clogher, John J.
Francis, George J.
McGinty, Michael J.
Mullen, William J.
Varni, Edward
Wade, James J.
Walsh, Martin E.
Zitko, Aloysius
Reverend Fathers—
Brainard, Ernest B.
Broderson, Donald
Cabral, Kenneth J.
Daly, George
Dollard, John J.
Driscoll, James
Eggerling, Milton
Gallagher, Thomas B.
Hayburn, Edmund L.
Keane, James
Kozina, Vladimir
Lu, Matthias
Manning, John
Marshall, William
McLeod, Daniel
Mifsud, Carmelo
Morgan, John
Murray, Adrian
Ribero, Arthur
Ruffing, Norman
Russell, Kenneth
Schwab, Joseph

Permanent Deacons:
Agustin, Benjamin, St. Joseph, Pinole
Anthony, Ferris J., Good Shepherd, Pittsburg
Archer, William, St. Michael, Livermore
Baptista, Antonio, St. Leander, San Leandro
Barnes, Frank, Christ the King, Pleasant Hill
Barnes, James, St. Patrick, Oakland
Barreto, Antonio, St. Edward, Newark
Beltran, Juan, Unassigned
Bettencourt, Leonard, St. John the Baptist Church, San Lorenzo
Beville, Frank, St. Leander, San Leandro
Bothe, William, St. Francis of Assisi, Concord
Brazil, Rudolph, Holy Spirit, Fremont
Bruckner, Nick, St. Edward, Newark
Bustos, Frank, Immaculate Heart of Mary, Brentwood
Cain, Jerry, Leave of Absence
Calub, Benigno, St. Ann, Union City
Campbell, James, St. Augustine, Pleasanton
Ceja, Federico, Our Lady of the Rosary, Union City
Davis, Dennis, St. Leander, San Leandro
Dowling, Robert, Our Lady of Grace, Castro Valley
Drobick, William, Holy Spirit, Fremont
Duhe, Gaston J., St. Patrick, West Oakland
Edgerly, Leo, Sr., St. Andrew-St. Joseph, Oakland
Fihn, Norbert, St. Mary's College
Fleischer, Alfred, St. Ignatius, Antioch
Flores, Isidore, St. Paul, San Pablo
Flores, Jose, Most Holy Rosary, Antioch
Folger, Richard, Our Lady of the Rosary, Union City
Freeman, Ernest, St. Augustine, Pleasanton
Frumkin, Paul, St. Clement, Hayward
Fuentes, Javier, St. Bernard, Oakland
Gall, William, St. Bonaventure, Concord
Gilbert, John, St. Benedict, Oakland
Gomez, Ruben, St. Joan of Arc, San Ramon
Gonsalves, Nelson, All Saints, Hayward
Gonzalez, Noe, St. Elizabeth, Oakland
Grigg, Jerry, Most Holy Rosary, Antioch
Guesnon, Ovide, Santa Paula, Fremont
Hagenbach, Robert, On Duty Outside the Diocese
Hernandez, Gabriel, St. Bede, Hayward
Hoblitzell, Ross, St. Michael, Livermore
Horan, Ronald, Unassigned
Jordan, Jack, St. Monica, Moraga
Layden, Alan, St. Anthony, Oakley
Lee, Stanley, The Filipino Pastoral Center
Lewandowski, Daniel, On Duty Outside the Diocese
Madrigal, Ysidro, St. Paul, San Pablo
Marchese, Charles, Jr., Corpus Christi, Fremont
Martin, Richard, St. Augustine, Pleasanton
Martinez, Bill, (Retired)
McGowan, Thomas, St. John, El Cerrito
Moll, Herbert, On Duty Outside the Diocese
Moore, Timothy, Transfiguration, Castro Valley
Palomares, Charles, St. Francis of Assisi, Concord
Perez, Donaciano, St. Paul, San Pablo
Perez, Ernest, St. Edward, Newark
Perry, Thomas, St. Augustine, Pleasanton
Peters, George, Queen of All Saints, Concord
Prado, Jose, St. Felicitas, San Leandro
Quigley, Edward, St. Augustine, Pleasanton
Rabuy, Carlos, St. Ann, Union City
Rezendes, David, St. Michael, Livermore
Rigley, Burton, Transfiguration, Castro Valley
Rivilla, Luis, Faith and Ministerial Formation
Romers, Gustaaf, St. Ann, Union City
Ryken, Dennis, St. Bede, Hayward
Silva, Richard, On Duty Outside the Diocese
Silveira, Victor, St. Leander, San Leandro
Smith, Leo, (Retired)
Soublet, Morris, St. Andrew-St. Joseph, Oakland
Stelly, Eugene, St. Andrew-St. Joseph, Oakland
Torres, Arcadio, (Retired)
Tovar, Joseph, St. Anthony, Oakley
Turcios, Luis, Corpus Christi, Fremont
Victoria, Hector, St. Raymond, Dublin
Warren, William, Jr., On Duty Outside the Diocese
Wedl, Roger, St. Edward, Newark
Yee, Richard, Holy Spirit, Fremont

INSTITUTIONS LOCATED IN THE DIOCESE

[A] SEMINARIES, RELIGIOUS OR SCHOLASTICATES

Oakland. *Graduate School of Theology, School of Applied Theology*, 5890 Birch Ct., 94618. Tel: 510-652-1651.
E-mail: SATPRES@aol.com
Apostolate of the California Province of the Society of Jesus. Graduate School of Sabbaticals and Christian Leadership. An Affiliate of the Graduate Theological Union. Dr. Frank B. Nieman, Ph.D., Pres. & Dean; Sr. Therese McGroddy, R.S.H.M., Dir. Admissions.
Trustees: Mr. William J. Boyle, C.P.A.; Claude Welch, Ph.D.; Dr. Glenn Bucher; Sr. Rosemary Chinnici; Sr. Barbara Green, O.P.; Mr. James Jackson; Rev. Francis J. Houdek, S.J.; Ms. Jennie Magid; Mr. James Penna, J.D.; Revs. Eugene R. Zimmers, S.J.; Francis Buckley, S.J. Sisters 2; Lay Teachers 1; Students 50.

Berkeley. *Dominican School of Philosophy and Theology*, 2401 Ridge Rd., 94709. Tel: 510-849-2030.
E-mail: 104547.1164@compuserve.com
(Dominican House of Studies at the Graduate Theological Union). Revs. Gregory Rocca, O.P., Pres. &

Faculty (Regular); Edward Krasevac, O.P., Dean & Faculty; Ms. Cheryl A. Trainor, Registrar; Ms. Teresa O'Rourke, Dean Student Affairs & Admissions; Mrs. Eleanor Westbrooke, Sec.
Faculty (Regular): Rev. Luke D. Buckles, O.P.; Mr. Mark Delp; Revs. Stephen Ernest, S.V.D.; Michael Dodds, O.P.; Sr. Barbara Green, O.P.; Revs. Edward Krasevac, O.P.; Eugene M. Ludwig, O.F.M.Cap.; John Hilary Martin, O.P.; Michael T. Morris, O.P.; Gregory Rocca, O.P.; Richard Schenk, O.P.; Gregory Tatum, O.P.
Faculty (Adjunct): Revs. Joseph Boenzi, S.D.B.; Owen Carroll; Dr. Marilyn Anne Coffy; Revs. Arthur Lenti, S.D.B.; Michael Ribotta, S.D.B. Priests 15; Brothers 1; Sisters 1; Lay Teachers 5; Students 95.

Franciscan School of Theology, 1712 Euclid Ave., 94709. Tel: 510-848-5232; Fax: 510-549-9466. Rev. William M. Cieslak, O.F.M.Cap., Pres.; Bro. William J. Short, O.F.M., Academic Dean; Rev. Mario DiCicco, O.F.M., Dir. Devel.; Sr. Paschal Hocum, O.S.F., Registrar; Mr. Dale Gilson, Coord. of Student Svcs.
Faculty: Revs. Michael D. Guinan, O.F.M.; William M. Cieslak, O.F.M.Cap.; Rigoberto Caloca-Rivas, O.F.M.; Richard Gula, S.S.; Kenan B. Osborne, O.F.M.; Xavier J. Harris, O.F.M.; Joseph P. Chinnici, O.F.M.; Thomas West, O.F.M.; Sr. Mary McGann, R.S.C.J.; Sr. Eva Lumas, S.S.S.; Bro. William J. Short, O.F.M. Priests 9; Brothers 1; Sisters 3; Lay Teachers 1; Total Enrollment 100.

Franciscan School of Theology Student Residence, 1920-7th St., 94710. Tel: 510-841-4102.
E-mail: Sevenstr@aol.com
Revs. Tommy King, O.F.M., Dir.; Walter Gomez, O.F.M.; Bros. Jeremiah Grimaud, O.F.M.; John Kiesler, O.F.M.; Edgar Magana, O.F.M.; Dan Barica, O.F.M.; Charles Talley, O.F.M.; Tran Nguyen, O.F.M.; Garrett Galvin, O.F.M. Priests 1; Brothers 1.

The Jesuit School of Theology at Berkeley, 1735 LeRoy Ave., 94709. Tel: 510-841-8804.
E-mail: sargyris@jstb.edu
A Pontifical Faculty of Theology. One of two theological centers of the U.S. Jesuit Conference, Society of Jesus. A Member of the Graduate Theological Union (GTU), Berkeley. Revs. George E. Griener, S.J., Acting Academic Dean; William J. Rewak, S.J., Pres.; George R. Murphy, S.J., Vice Pres. & Dean of Students; Dr. Paul Jacobson, Acting Vice Pres. Devel. & Pub. Rels.; Mr. Robert Lassalle-Klein, Dir. of Field Education; Rev. Donald Arel, O.M.I., Dir., Institute for Spirituality & Worship; Ms. Lorna Wallace McKeown, Asst. Academic Dean & In-House Registrar; Mrs. Karen Ripsom, Asst. Treas.; Ms. Alice Ducey, Dir. of Admissions; Mr. Steven Argyris, Vice Pres. for Finance & Admin.
Faculty (Emeriti): Revs. Harry T. Corcoran, S.J.; John E. Huesman, S.J.; John H. Wright, S.J.; Richard A. Hill, S.J.; Joseph M. Powers, S.J.
Faculty: Rev. John F. Baldovin, S.J.; Sr. Anne Brotherton, S.F.C.C.; Revs. James T. Bretzke, S.J.; Thomas E. Buckley, S.J.; John Donahue, S.J.; Sr. Mary Ann Donovan, S.C.; Rev. John C. Endres, S.J.; Dr. Alejandro Garcia-Rivera; Revs. Donald L. Gelpi, S.J.; George E. Griener, S.J.; Dr. Gina Hens-Piazza; Rev. Francis J. Houdek, S.J.; Mr. Robert Lassalle-Klein; Revs. William R. O'Neill, S.J.; T. Howland Sanks, S.J.; Sr. Sandra M. Schneiders, I.H.M.; Rev. David J. Stagaman, S.J.; Dr. Seung Ai Yang. Sisters 1; Lay Teachers 4; Full-time faculty 18; Students 165. (See listing for The Jesuit Community at The Jesuit School of Theology at Berkeley).

MORAGA. *St. Mary's College, Assumption Hall Vocation Office*, Mailing Address: P.O. Box 4687, 94575. Tel: 510-631-4186.
E-mail: FSCinSF@earthlink.net
Bros. James Joost, F.S.C.; Norman Coole, F.S.C.; Camillus Chavez, F.S.C. Brothers 2.

[B] COLLEGES AND UNIVERSITIES

OAKLAND. *Holy Names College*, (1868) 3500 Mountain Blvd., 94619. Tel: 510-436-1000
For a complete listing, refer to the Colleges and Universities section.

FREMONT. *Queen of the Holy Rosary College* Mailing Address: P.O. Box 3908 Mission San Jose, 94539. Tel: 510-657-2468; Fax: 510-657-1734.
For a complete listing, refer to the Colleges and Universities section.

MORAGA. *St. Mary's College*, 94575. Tel: 510-631-4000
For a complete listing, refer to the Colleges and Universities section.

[C] HIGH SCHOOLS, DIOCESAN

OAKLAND. *Bishop O'Dowd High School*, 9500 Stearns Ave., 94605. Tel: 510-577-9100; Fax: 510-638-3259.
E-mail: odowd.pvt.K12.ca.us
Web site: odowd.pvt.K12.ca.us
Basilian Fathers (Congregation of St. Basil). Revs. John Huber, C.S.B.; Richard A. Ranalletti, C.S.B., Prin.; John B. Malo, C.S.B., Supr.; Robert H. Glass, C.S.B.; David Weise, C.S.B.; Benjamin Owens, C.SS.R.; Les F. Schaefer, C.S.B.; Iain DeJong, C.S.B. Priests 8; Lay Teachers 57; Students 1,095.

St. Elizabeth High School, 1530-34th Ave., 94601. Tel: 510-532-8947. Dr. Matilda Ignacio, Prin. Sisters 3; Lay Teachers 23; Students 330.

[D] HIGH SCHOOLS, PAROCHIAL

ALAMEDA. *Saint Joseph Notre Dame High School*, 1011 Chestnut St., 94501. Tel: 510-523-1526; Fax: 510-523-2181.
E-mail: SJNDPilots@Connectinc.com
Mr. Anthony V. Aiello, Prin. Priests 1; Lay Teachers 50; Students 540.

[E] HIGH SCHOOLS, PRIVATE

OAKLAND. *Holy Name High School*, 4660 Harbord Dr., 94618. Tel: 510-450-1110.
E-mail: ahancock@hnhs.pvt.k12.ca.us
Sisters of the Holy Names of Jesus and Mary. Laura M. Held, Pres.; Sr. Adele Hancock, P.B.V.M., Prin. Sisters 8; Lay Teachers 21; Students 270.

BERKELEY. *Saint Mary's College High School of Berkeley, Inc.*, 94706. Tel: 510-526-9242; Fax: 510-559-6298. Brothers of the Christian Schools. Bro. Albert Villagomez, F.S.C., Pres.; Dr. John T. Collins, Prin. Brothers 5; Lay Teachers 43; Students 620.

CONCORD. *Carondelet High School*, 1133 Winton Dr., 94518-3598. Tel: 510-686-5353; Fax: 510-671-9429. Sisters of St Joseph of Carondelet. Sr. Kathleen Lang, C.S.J., Prin. Sisters 6; Lay Teachers 50; Students 820.

De La Salle High School of Concord, Inc. dba De La Salle High School. (Boys), 1130 Winton Dr., 94518. Tel: 510-686-3310; Fax: 510-686-3474. Brothers of the Christian Schools (De La Salle Christian Brothers). Mr. James Tschann, Pres.; Bros. Robert J. Wickman, F.S.C., Prin.; Tom Westberg, F.S.C., Asst. Prin. & Brothers' Community Dir.; Mr. Robert Jordan, Dir. of Campus Min. Brothers 8; Lay Teachers 51; Students 900.

HAYWARD. *Moreau Catholic High School*, 27170 Mission Blvd., 94544. Tel: 510-881-4300; Fax: 510-582-8405. Brothers of Holy Cross. Patricia Geister, Prin.; Joseph Connell, Ph.D., Pres.; Margaret J. Walsh, Corp. Treas. Lay Teachers 64; Students 1,260.

RICHMOND. *Salesian High School*, 2851 Salesian Ave., 94804. Tel: 510-234-4433; Fax: 510-236-4636. Salesians of St. John Bosco. Rev. John Itzaina, S.D.B., Dir. & Prin.; Bro. Patrick Maloney, S.D.B., Business Mgr.; Revs. Arthur Brainard, S.D.B., (Retired); Laurence Byrne, S.D.B., (Retired); Mel Trindad, S.D.B., D.R.E.; Angel Baldonado, S.D.B.; Bro. Jerry Weirich, S.D.B., Dean of Discipline. Priests 5; Brothers 2; Lay Teachers 30; Students 460.

[F] EARLY CHILDHOOD EDUCATION CENTERS

MISSION SAN JOSE. *Dominican Kindergarten*, 43326 Mission Blvd., P.O. Box 3908, 94539; Fax: 510-657-1734.
E-mail: DominicanKin@connectinc.com
Web site: http://www.infolane.com/msjsisters/
Sr. Kathleen McAvoy, O.P., Dir. & Teacher. Sisters 1; Students 33.

[G] SUMMER SCHOOLS

OAKLAND. *Holy Names College*, 3500 Mountain Blvd., 94619. Tel: 510-436-1000. Sisters of the Holy Names of Jesus and Mary. Resident and Non-Resident Students.

MISSION SAN JOSE. *Queen of the Holy Rosary College*, 43326 Mission Blvd., P.O. Box 3908, 94539. Tel: 510-657-2468; Fax: 510-657-1734. Sisters of the Third Order of St. Dominic of the Congregation of the Queen of the Holy Rosary. Priests 1; Sisters 18; Lay Teachers 2; Students 252.

MORAGA. *St. Mary's College*, 94575. Brothers of the Christian Schools, District of San Francisco. Priests 1; Brothers 13; Lay Teachers 109.

[H] CATHOLIC CHARITIES OF THE DIOCESE OF OAKLAND

OAKLAND. *Catholic Charities of the Diocese of Oakland, Inc.*, 433 Jefferson St., 94607. Tel: 510-834-5656. Legal Title: *Catholic Charities of the Diocese of Oakland, Inc., A Non-Profit Corporation.* Barbara S. Terrazas, Exec. Dir.; Marilyn Kihara, Controller; Marilyn Lovelace, Human Resources Dir.; Esme Marconi, CFRE, Dir., Fund Dev./Public Affairs; Solomon Belette, Cluster Admin.
COMMUNITY AND PARISH SERVICES: Pat Spohn, Dir.
Counseling Services:
Alameda County Area Supervisor, 433 Jefferson St., 94607. Tel: 510-834-5656.
Chancery Annex, 3014 Lakeshore Ave., 94610. Tel: 510-763-0301. Regional Offices.
Alameda, 1109 Chestnut St., Alameda, 94501. Tel: 510-569-9307.
Antioch, 21 E. 15th St., Antioch, 94509. Tel: 510-778-7929.
Berkeley, 2700 Dwight Way, Berkeley. Tel: 510-834-5657, Ext. 4022.
East Oakland, 6226 Camden St., 94605. Tel: 510-569-9307.
Fremont Offices, 3767 Decoto Rd., Fremont, 94536. Tel: 510-792-2444. Fremont-Mission San Jose, 43148 Mission Blvd., Fremont, 94539. Tel: 510-490-5452.
Hayward, 22824 Second St., Hayward, 94541. Tel: 510-886-1331.
Hayward, 21250 Hesperian Blvd., Hayward, 94541. Tel: 510-886-1462.
Livermore, 458 Maple St., Livermore, 94550. Tel: 510-828-1462.
Concord, 2350 Pacheco St., Concord, 94521. Tel: 510-825-3099. Pat Spohn, Contra Costa County Area Supervisor.
Pinole, 2150 Pear Ave., Pinole, 94564. Tel: 510-724-6263.
Pittsburg, 455 W. Fourth St., Pittsburg, 94565. Tel: 510-432-7363.
Richmond, 225 Civic Center St., Richmond, 94804. Tel: 510-232-1377.
San Ramon, 2601 San Ramon Valley Blvd., San Ramon, 94583. Tel: 510-828-1462.
Services to Parish Schools, 433 Jefferson St., 94607. Tel: 510-834-5656.
Department of Aging, 433 Jefferson St., 94607. Tel: 510-834-5656.
HIV/AIDS Services, 433 Jefferson St., 94607. Tel: 510-834-5656. Randy Marcotte, Dir.
Services to Gays & Lesbians & Their Families, 433 Jefferson St., 94607. Tel: 510-834-5656. Rev. James Schexnayder, Dir.
Victim Offender Reconciliation Program, 433 Jefferson St., 94607. Tel: 510-834-5656. Lou Ann Aaberg, Dir.
Detention Ministry, 433 Jefferson St., 94607. Tel: 510-834-5656. Frank Beville, Coord.
Social Justice Resource Center, 1232-33rd Ave., 94601. Tel: 510-532-3518. Paul Woolley, Dir.
COMMUNITY SERVICES:
433 Jefferson St., 94607. Tel: 510-834-5656.
Emergency Services, 433 Jefferson St., 94607. Tel: 510-834-5656. Angelina Toscano, Dir.
English Action Center, 2369 Barrett Ave., Richmond, 94804. Tel: 510-234-5110. Barbara Racek, Dir.
English Action Center-Verde School, 2000 Giaramita, Room 17 & 18, Richmond, 94808. Tel: 510-234-5305.
English Action Center, 3200 Barrett Ave., Richmond, 94804. Tel: 510-234-2416.
HIV Prison Project, 433 Jefferson Ave., 94607. Tel: 510-834-5656. Judy Greenspan, Dir.
Housing Services, 433 Jefferson Ave., 94607. Tel: 510-834-5656. Kenneth Richardson, Dir.
Refugee and Immigrant Services, 1232-33rd Ave., 94601. Tel: 510-261-1538. Raquel Aguirre, Dir.
Refugee Employment Assistance Center, 100 Hacienda Ave., P.O. Box 247, San Lorenzo, 94580. Tel: 510-481-0131. Vu Pham, Dir.
Refugee Employment Assistance Center, 707 Jefferson St., 94607. Tel: 510-465-0642.
Refugee Employment Assistance Center, 4700 Calaveras Ave., Fremont, 94538. Tel: 510-745-8731.
SPECIAL PROGRAMS:
Campaign for Human Development (CHD), 433 Jefferson St., 94607. Tel: 510-834-5656. Paul Woolley, Diocesan Dir.
Catholic Relief Services (CRS), 433 Jefferson St., 94607. Tel: 510-834-5656. Paul Woolley, Dir.

[I] SOCIETY OF ST. VINCENT DE PAUL

OAKLAND. *Society of St. Vincent de Paul of Alameda County*, 9235 San Leandro St., 94603. Tel: 510-638-7600; Fax: 510-638-8354. Donald Gerigk, Pres.

Society of St. Vincent de Paul of Alameda County. Free Dinning Room, 675 23rd St., 94612. Tel: 510-451-7676. Total Assisted 12,000; Total Staff 12.

PITTSBURG. *Society of St. Vincent de Paul of Contra Costa County*, 2210 Gladstone Dr., 94565. Tel: 510-439-5060. Marianne Hawkins, Pres.

[J] DAY NURSERIES

OAKLAND. *Saint Vincent's Day Home, Inc.*, 1086 Eighth St., 94607-2697. Tel: 510-832-8324; Fax: 510-832-5021.
E-mail: vincent@dnai.com
Web site: www.otan.dni.us/hubiv/svdh
Legal Title: *Saint Vincent's Day Home, A Corporation.* Corinne M. Mohrmann, CEO. Religious 1; Lay Staff 35; Capacity 199; Total Assisted 300; Total Staff 36. Purpose: To provide quality child care services to those in greatest need while assisting parents in meeting their parental obligations.

[K] GENERAL HOSPITALS

HAYWARD. *St. Rose Hospital*, 27200 Calaroga Ave., 94545-4383. Tel: 510-264-4000.
For a complete listing, refer to the Hospitals section.

[L] ORGANIZATIONS FOR DEAF AND HARD OF HEARING

UNION CITY. *St. Joseph's Center for Deaf and Hard of Hearing*, 3880 Smith St., 94587. Tel: 510-489-9784 (Voice); 489-9786 (TDD). Legal Title: *St. Joseph's Center for the Deaf and Hard of Hearing, A Corporation*. Ardith A. Lynch, Diocesan Dir.

[M] RETIREMENT AND CARE FACILITIES

OAKLAND. *Bishop Begin Villa*, 3418 E. 18th St., 94601
For a complete listing, refer to the Special Care Facilities section.

Mercy Retirement and Care Center, 3431 Foothill Blvd., 94601. Tel: 510-534-8540; Fax: 510-261-7551
For a complete listing, refer to the Special Care Facilities section.

[N] MONASTERIES AND RESIDENCES OF PRIESTS AND BROTHERS

OAKLAND. *Dominican Order (Western Province), St. Albert's Priory*, Dominican House of Formation, 5890 Birch Ct., 94618. Tel: 510-596-1800. Very Rev. Jose Pimentel, O.P., Prior; Revs. Vincent A. Serpa, O.P., Novice Master; Michael Dodds, O.P., Master of Students; Finbarr Hayes, O.P.; Charles Hess, O.P.; Fabian Parmisano, O.P.; Sergius R. Propst, O.P.; Antoninus Wall, O.P.; Janko Zagar, O.P.; Luke D. Buckles, O.P.; Martin Walsh, O.P.; Bros. Robert Lavigne, O.P.; Jose Romero, O.P. In res. Revs. Donald Bramble, O.P.; Jude Eli, O.P.; Basil B. Cole, O.P.; Gerard Ehler, O.P.; Richard Schenk, O.P.; Bros. Roberto Bravo, O.P.; Alejandro Crosthwaite-Martinez, O.P.; Steven Maekawa, O.P.; Carl Schlicte, O.P.; Jordan Vajda, O.P.; Timothy Budde; Garry Cappleman; Paul Detweiler; Patrick Havel; David Orique; Robert Sheely; James Thompson; John Evans; Francis Le; Anselm Ramelow; Peter Rogers. Novices 11; Total in Residence 45.

Dominican Order, Siena House, 5730 Presley Way, 94618. Tel: 510-654-8735. Revs. Emmerich Vogt, O.P., Supr. Mission Band; David O'Rourke, O.P.; Leo Tubbs, O.P.; Gregory Rocca, O.P., Pres., Dominican School of Philosophy and Theology; Michael Carey, Dir., Santa Fe Institute; Michael Morris, O.P., Prof., Dominican School of Philosophy and Theology. Priests 6.

Franciscan Friars, St. Elizabeth Friary, 1500 34th Ave., 94601. Tel: 510-536-1287. Revs. Kenny Scott, O.F.M., Vicar; Peter Krieg, O.F.M.; Tom West, O.F.M.; Gordon Urbine, O.F.M.; Rigoberto Caloca-Rivas, O.F.M.; Marco Antonio Figueroa, O.F.M., Pastor; Melvin Stanley, O.F.M.; Bros. John Gutierrez, O.F.M., Guardian; Antonio Herrera, O.F.M.; Jose Alberto Barrera, O.F.M.; David Gaa, O.F.M.; Raul Alejos, O.F.M.; Balbino Rodriguez, O.F.M.; James Locksman, O.F.M.; Alberto Villafan, O.F.M.; Hoang Trinh, O.F.M.; Gustavo Castillanos, O.F.M.; Cesar Montelongo, O.F.M.; Ramiro Munoz, O.F.M.; John Gibbons, O.F.M.; Alvin Cachola, O.F.M.; Jose Luis Nerio, O.F.M.; Thomas More Ganmy, O.F.M.

Franciscan Friars Provincial Office, Province of St. Barbara, 1500-34th Ave., 94601. Tel: 510-536-3722; Fax: 510-536-3970.
E-mail: ofmcamain@aol.com
Web site: www.sbfranciscans.org
Revs. Finian McGinn, O.F.M., Prov.; Stephen Barnufsky, O.F.M., Vicar Prov.; Melvin A. Jurisich, O.F.M., Sec.; Ms. Guadalupe Aceves, Treas.; Rev. John S. Hardin, O.F.M., Assoc. Treas.; Bro. Angelo Cardinalli, O.F.M., Vocation; Rev. Miguel Obregon, O.F.M., Vocations. Priests 5; Total Staff 16.
On Duty Outside the Province: Revs. Angus Cooper, O.F.M., General Curia, Rome, Italy; Christopher F. Tomatis, O.F.M., The Antonanium Rome, Italy; Thomas Herbst, O.F.M., Oxford University, England; Oscar Mendez, O.F.M., The National University, El Salvador.

Franciscan Friars, 1508 Arch St., Berkeley, 94708. Tel: 510-845-1124. Revs. John Hardin, O.F.M., Guardian; Joseph P. Chinnici, O.F.M.; Melvin A. Jurisich, O.F.M.; Stephen Barnufsky, O.F.M.; William M. Cieslak, O.F.M.Cap.; Josef Prochnow, O.F.M.; Mario DiCicco, O.F.M.; Bro. William Short, O.F.M.

Murray Residence Community, 171 Santa Rosa Ave., 94610-1316. Tel: 510-655-8334. Revs. John A. Baumann, S.J., Supr.; Bernard M.C. Chu, S.J.; Thomas C. Weston, S.J.; David C. Schwartz, S.J.; Thomas J. Savage, S.J.

Oblate Provincial House & Procure, 290 Lenox Ave., 94610. Tel: 510-452-1550; Fax: 510-452-3421.
E-mail: omioak@aol.com
Provincial Headquarters of the Oblates of Mary Immaculate, Western Prov. Very Rev. David Ullrich, O.M.I., Prov.; Revs. Thomas Rush, O.M.I., 1st Asst. & Vicar Prov.; Paul Waldie, O.M.I., 2nd Asst.; William Antone, O.M.I., 3rd Asst.; Richard Haslam, O.M.I., 4th Asst./Sec.; Leo Dummer, O.M.I., Prov. Treas. In res. Revs. James P. McSorley, O.M.I.; Ruben Martinez, O.M.I.; John Kelly, O.M.I. Legal Title: *Oblate Fathers Western Province Inc.; Western Oblates Support Trust Fund*. Total in Residence 5; Total Staff 2.

Order of Preachers (Southern Province). De Porres House of Studies. 2215 Rose St., Berkeley, 94709. Tel: 510-644-8247; Fax: 510-644-8249. Revs. Jude Siciliano, O.P., Supr. & Prof., DSPT. Tel: 510-644-8247; John Markey, O.P., Assoc. Dir. Formation.

Redemptorists, 8945 Golf Links Rd., 94605. Tel: 510-562-9740; Fax: 510-562-1406. Very Rev. Stephen Meyer, C.Ss.R., Supr.; Revs. Fred Arpin, C.Ss.R.; Carlyle Blake, C.Ss.R.; Robert Kirkpatrick, C.Ss.R.; James Farrell; Patrick Leehan, C.Ss.R.; Francis McMahon, C.Ss.R.; John Shaughnessy, C.Ss.R.; Donald Mackinnon, C.Ss.R.; Bros. Denis Schroeder, C.Ss.R.; Martin Temple, C.Ss.R.; Richard Fischer, C.Ss.R.; Damian Bronson, C.Ss.R. Legal Title: *Redemptorist Society of California*.

Holy Redeemer Retreat and Conference Center, P.O. Box 5427, 94605. Tel: 510-635-6341.

Western Dominican Province, 5877 Birch Ct., 94618-1626. Tel: 510-658-8722; Fax: 510-658-1061. Province of the Holy Name of Jesus. Very Revs. Daniel Syverstad, O.P., Prior Prov.; Robert Christian, O.P., Vicar Prov. & Socius; Reginald Martin, O.P., Dir. Shrine of St. Jude, Asst. Province Treas. & Devel. Dir.; Revs. Donald J. Bramble, O.P., Dir. Dominican Mission Foundation; Jordan Bradshaw, O.P., Sec. Dominican Family; Luke Buckles, O.P., Regent Studies; G. Albert Buckley, O.P., Dir. Western Dominican Preaching; Anthony Cordeiro, O.P., Treas.; Thomas DeMan, O.P., Promoter Campus Ministry; Michael Dodds, O.P., Student Master; Paul Duffner, O.P., Promoter Rosary Confraternity; Raymond Finerty, O.P., Promoter Permanent Formation; Thomas Hayes, O.P., Promoter Holy Name Society; Patrick LaBelle, O.P., Dir. Planning & Ministry & Promoter Preaching & Media; Frederick Lucci, O.P., Promoter Social Justice; George Matanic, O.P., Promoter Dominican Laity; Vincent Serpa, O.P., Novice Master; Michael Sweeney, O.P., Promoter Parish Ministry.
Serving in Latin America: Revs. David Bello, O.P.; Vincent Foerstler, O.P.; Thomas Kraft, O.P.; Bro. Raymond Bertheaux, O.P.
Serving in Kenya: Rev. Kieran Healy, O.P.
Serving in Vatican City: Rev. Allen Duston, O.P., Dir., Office of the Patrons of the Arts in the Vatican Museums. Total in the Province 157.

BERKELEY. *Capuchin Franciscan Order, House of Studies*, 1534 Arch St., 94708. Tel: 510-841-2229. Saint Conrad Friary. Rev. Harold Snider, O.F.M.Cap., Student Dir.; Bros. Francis Driscoll, O.F.M.Cap., Formation Team, Dir. Assocs.; Peter Ciolino, O.F.M.Cap., Formation Team, Guardian. Friars in residence 11; Friars in formation 8; Total Staff 3.

Carmelite (Discalced) House of Studies, 2542 Hilgard Ave., 94709. Tel: 510-549-3918. Revs. David Centner, O.C.D.; John Melka, O.C.D. Total in Residence 6; Total Staff 2.

Holy Cross Fathers-Holy Cross Center, 2597 Virginia St., 94709. Tel: 510-548-8515; Fax: 510-548-7903. Revs. Donald G. Fetters, C.S.C., Religious Supr.; Daniel G. Groody, C.S.C.; William J. Dohar, C.S.C.; Terence H. Linton, C.S.C.; Bro. Ronald Whelan, C.S.C.

Jesuit Community at Jesuit School of Theology at Berkeley, 2621 Ridge Rd., 94709-1098. Tel: 510-841-2487; Fax: 510-549-1114. Rev. Charles L. Moutenot, S.J., Rector; Bro. Joseph M. Ritzman, S.J., Asst. Rector, Minister, & Treas.; Revs. Jose A. Aguilar, S.J. (Columbia); John F. Baldovin, S.J. (New York); Kevin M. Bradt, S.J. (New York); James T. Bretzke, S.J. (Wisconsin); Thomas J. Buckley, S.J. (California); Hartono Budi, S.J. (Indonesia); James J. Burshek, S.J. (Missouri); Andrew Cameron-Mowat, S.J. (Spain); Joseph P. Carroll, S.J. (California); John A. Coleman, S.J. (California); Harry T. Corcoran, S.J. (California); Donald F. Crosby, S.J. (California); Declan Deane, S.J. (Ireland); John R. Donahue, S.J. (Maryland); John C. Endres, S.J. (Oregon); Robert J. Fabing, S.J. (California); Donald L. Gelpi, S.J. (New Orleans); George E. Griener, S.J. (New Orleans); Simon J. Hendry, S.J. (New Orleans); Fred M. Henley, S.J. (Detroit); Francis J. Houdek, S.J. (Detroit); John E. Huesman, S.J. (California); William M. Kegel, S.J. (Wisconsin); Mathew Jayanth Kodekkanel, S.J. (India); Stephen T. Krupa, S.J. (Detroit); David L. Lawrence, S.J. (New Orleans); Lester E. Love, S.J. (Chicago); J. Roger Lucey, S.J. (Wisconsin); Francis X. McAloon, S.J. (Maryland); Peter R. McGrath, S.J. (New England); George R. Murphy, S.J. (New England); Robert J. Ochs, S.J. (Chicago); William R. O'Neill, S.J. (California); Joseph M. Palacios, S.J. (California); Joseph M. Powers, S.J. (California); Thierry-Jean Robouam, S.J. (Japan); T. Howland Sanks, S.J. (Maryland); David J. Stagaman, S.J. (Chicago); Osamu Takeuchi, S.J. (Japan); Aquilene Tarimo, S.J. (Africa); John H. Wright, S.J. (Oregon).
(See also listing for The Jesuit School of Theology at Berkeley).

Marist Fathers and Brothers, 2335 Warring St., 94704. Tel: 510-486-1232; 486-1276; Fax: 510-848-7204. Rev. Thomas M. Hamilton, S.M., Supr. & Formation Dir.; Bro. Peter DiFrancescantonio, S.M., Formation Staff. Legal Title: *Marist Society of California*.
Seminary Name: St. Peter Chanel Seminary - Marist Theologate.

Salesian Community, Don Bosco Hall, 1831 Arch St., 94709. Tel: 510-204-0800; Fax: 510-843-4335.
E-mail: BoscoLink@aol.com
Web site: http:/www.wenet.net/~jmrasor/
Revs. Arthur Lenti, S.D.B.; Ralph J. Murphy, S.D.B., Treas.; Michael Ribotta, S.D.B.; Joseph Boenzi, S.D.B., Dir.; Am Nguyen, S.D.B. (Vietnam); Joseph Nguyen Phuoc, S.D.B. (Vietnam); Denis Kong, S.D.B (Hong Kong); Henry Woo, S.D.B. (Korea); Avelino Lorenzo, S.D.B.; Ian Murdoch, S.D.B. (Australia); Yarat Chaiyara, S.D.B. (Thailand); Virendra Coutts, S.D.B. (India); Firmochito Dajao, S.D.B. (Philippines); Paul D'Souza, S.D.B. (India); Prasert Somngam, S.D.B. (Thailand). Total in Residence 24; Total Staff 3.

Servite Community, Sarpi Priory. (Western Province), 2414 Virginia St., 94709-1206. Tel: 510-848-4086. Rev. Bruce J. Klikunas, O.S.M. Total in Residence 1.

Society of the Precious Blood, 2800 Milvia St., 94703. Tel: 510-848-3076.
E-mail: rpw2644@aol.com
Revs. Ronald P. Wiecek, C.PP.S., Dir.; Gary M. Luiz, C.PP.S.; James Sloan, C.PP.S.
Candidates: Agustin Ramirez, C.PP.S.; Arturo Neri, C.PP.S.; Luis Motta; Gerardo Rivas; Javier Soto; Miguel Martinez. Total in Residence 8.

MORAGA. *Dominican Community*, Siena Hall, St. Mary's College, P.O. Box 5185, 94575-5185. Tel: 510-631-4315; Fax: 510-631-4315. Dominican Order. Revs. John McDonough, O.P., Supr.; Michael Carey, O.P.; Michael T. Morris, O.P. Priests 3.

SAN LEANDRO. *Society of the Precious Blood*, 2337 W. Ave. 134th, 94577-4132. Tel: 510-357-4982. Province of the Pacific, Provincial Headquarters, Provincial Center. Very Rev. James E. Franck, C.PP.S., Prov. Dir.; Rev. Joseph L. Brown, C.PP.S., Treas., St. Boniface Church, P.O. Box 86, Westphalia, IA, 51578. Rev. John R. Klopke, C.PP.S., Sec. Total in Residence 2; Total Staff 2.

SAN PABLO. *Franciscans, Conventual of California*, St. Francis of Assisi Friary, House of Studies, 1850 Church Ln., 94806-3706. Tel: 510-235-9119; Fax: 510-235-2045. Rev. Paul Fazio, O.F.M.Conv., Guardian and Dir. of Candidates. Total in Residence 10; Total Staff 1.

[O] CONVENTS AND RESIDENCES FOR SISTERS

OAKLAND. *Dominican Sisters of Mission San Jose*, St. Elizabeth Convent, 1555-34th Ave., 94601. Tel: 510-532-8344. Sisters 18.

Dominican Sisters of Oakford, Bethany House, 919 Aileen St., 94608. Tel: 510-652-0986. Sisters 2.

Dominican Sisters of San Rafael, House of Hope, 4264 Howe St., 94611. Tel: 510-654-8334. 1927 Haste, Berkeley, 94704. Tel: 510-631-4316.

Franciscan Missionaries of Mary, 570 Boden Way, Apt. 2, 94610. Tel: 510-444-8265. Sisters 3.

Franciscan Sisters of St. Francis of Penance and Christian Charity, 1815-33rd Ave., 94601. Tel: 510-534-4330; Fax: 510-436-5298. Sisters 5.
Novitiate House. Novices 1; Candidates 1; Professed 3. House of Hope, 2027 Nina Ct., Hayward, 94541. Tel: 510-537-1026; Fax: 510-655-3520.

Holy Names Sisters. Mailing Address: Provincial Administration, P.O. Box 907, Los Gatos, 95031. Tel: 408-395-5150; Fax: 408-354-8305.
E-mail: snjmcaadasst@connectinc.com
Holy Names College Convent, 3500 Mountain Blvd., 94619. Tel: 510-436-1635. Sr. Rose Eleanor Ehret. Tel: 510-436-1208; Sr. Dianne Fagan. Tel: 510-436-1502; Sr. Mary Christine Fleitz. Tel: 510-436-1636; Sr. Virginia Ghigliotti. Tel: 510-436-1637; Sr. Christine Patrinos. Tel: 510-436-1473; Sr. Grace Reeder. Tel: 510-436-1642; Sr. Ethel Mary Tinnemann. Tel: 510-436-1503; Sr. Alice Tobriner. Tel: 510-436-1645; Sr. Francesca Cabrini Weber. Tel: 510-436-1558. Sisters 9. Holy Names High School Convent, 4660 Harbord Dr., 94618. Tel: 510-547-1468; Fax: 510-547-3111. Sr. William Marie Ayres; Sr. Collette Carroll; Sr. Rita Caulfield; Sr. Doreen Crossett; Sr. Mary Elizabeth Doherty; Sr. Mary Louise Guenther; Sr. Paul Gerard Gustafson; Sr. Miriam Henry Hussey; Sr. Gerarda Joubert; Sr. Agnes Rita Judge; Sr. Virginia Rose Malone; Sr. Maura O'Connor; Sr. David Emmanuel Paula; Sr. Monica Perry; Sr. Mary Herbert Raphael; Sr. Mary Bernardina Wilson, Sisters 16. St. Theresa Convent, 4850 Clarewood Dr.,

94618. Tel: 510-547-1354. Sr. Rosemary Delaney; Sr. Marcia Frideger; Sr. Maureen Hester; Sr. Christine Wood, Sisters 4. St. Bede Convent, 26900 Patrick Ave., Hayward, 94544. Tel: 510-782-6700. Sr. Dolores Cazares; Sr. Nora Christian; Sr. Elizabeth Davis; Sr. Mary Anselm Grover; Sr. Marguerite Kirk; Sr. Molly Neville, Sisters 6. Coloma Residence, 2317 Coloma St., 94602. Tel: 510-531-4012. Sr. Deborah Church; Sr. Anne Dinneen; Sr. Patricia Kenny, Elbert Residence, 1011 Elbert St., 94602. Tel: 510-530-3267. Sr. Cynthia Canning; Sr. Donna Maynard; Sr. Maureen Webb, San Antonio Community, 1834 San Antonio Ave., Alameda, 94501. Tel: 510-522-6042. Sr. Noel Girard; Sr. Margaret Kennedy; Sr. Mary Rogers; Sr. Barbara Williams, West Oakland Community. Mailing Address: P.O. Box 20067, 94620. Sr. Rosario Asturias; Sr. Jean Elizabeth Griffin, 1490 34th St., #A, 94608. Tel: 510-601-9486. Sr. June Kearney; Sr. Marian Wright, 3232 Helen St., #B, 94608. Tel: 510-653-9705. Sr. Elizabeth Adams; Sr. Nancy Teskey, 4138 Whittle Ave., 94602. Tel: 510-530-3206. Sr. Mary Anderson, 412 Euclid Ave., #3, 94610. Tel: 510-836-5676. Sr. Sylvia Bartheld, 1245-B Broadway, Alameda, 94501. Tel: 510-523-2923. Sr. Barbara Bray; Sr. Jo Anne Quinlivan, 4349 Hyacinth Ave., 94619. Tel: 510-336-0919. Sr. Margaret Campbell, 2151 Central Ave., Alameda, 94501. Tel: 510-523-7296. Sr. Roberta Carson, 4081 Clayton Rd., #334, Concord, 94521. Tel: 510-827-2007. Sr. Victoria Dempf; Sr. Ruth Raftery, 621 18th St., 94612. Tel: 510-465-9996. Sr. Diane Enos, 3033 Wisconsin St., 94602. Tel: 510-530-0708. Sr. Theresa Fenzl, 2145 Santa Clara Ave., #F, Alameda, 94501. Tel: 510-864-8799. Sr. Maureen Patricia McCall, 456 Wayne Ave., #304, 94606. Tel: 510-268-8840. Sr. Kathleen Marie McCann, 2835 Bissell Ave., Richmond, 94804. Tel: 510-215-1504. Sr. Thomasine McMahon, 703 Atlantic Ave., #102, Alameda, 94501. Tel: 510-748-0544. Sr. Linda Orrick; Sr. Carol Sellman, 801 San Antonio Ave., Alameda, 94501. Tel: 510-523-3648. Sr. Delores Rashford, 2251 Buena Vista Ave., #9, San Leandro, 94577. Tel: 510-357-2270. Sr. Carol Selak, 410 Merritt Ave., #5, 94610. Tel: 510-893-9224. Sr. Shirley Sexton, 680 41st St., 94609. Tel: 510-652-3915. Sr. Maleada Mary Strange, 358 N. Murrieta Blvd., Livermore, 94550. Tel: 510-449-6335. Sr. Maureen Viani, 1045 Elbert St., 94602. Tel: 510-530-7425.

Presentation Sisters, 11 Warren St., No. 7, 94611. 1725 Oxford St., #308, Berkeley, 94709. 1725 Oxford St., #104, Berkeley, 94709. 1055 47th St., #C, Emeryville, 94608. 1515 Lincoln St., Berkeley, 94703.

Providence Sisters, Summit South, 3100 Summit St., P.O. Box 23020, 94623-9966. Tel: 510-835-4500. Sisters 4.

St. Lawrence O'Toole Convent, 3693 High St., 94619-2105. Tel: 510-530-2621. Adrian Dominican Sisters 4; Grand Rapids Dominicans 1.

Sisters of Charity of Cincinnati, 809-42nd St., 94608. Tel: 510-658-7990. 529-41st St., No. 9, 94609. Tel: 510-654-7328.

Sisters of Mercy, Burlingame, Mercy Retirement and Care Center, 3431 Foothill Blvd., 94601. Tel: 510-534-8540. Sisters 4.

Sisters of St. Joseph of Carondelet, 1520 E. 15th St., 94606-4422. 1133 Winton Dr., Concord, 94518. Tel: 510-686-9697. Sisters 4. St. Francis of Assisi Community, 866 Oak Grove Rd., Concord, 94518. Tel: 510-682-5418. Sisters 3. Bay Area Crisis Nursery, Inc., 1506 Mendocino Dr., Concord, 94521. Tel: 510-685-8052; 510-685-9740. Concord Residential Club, 2141 California St., Concord, 94520. Tel: 510-689-4939. Kwanza House Community, 529 Jean St., 94610. Tel: 510-655-2382. Sisters 2. Christ the King Community, Pleasant Hill, 94523. Tel: 510-691-4194. Sisters 3. St. Anthony Community, 1520 E. 15th St., 94606. Tel: 510-532-9455. Sisters 4. St. Catherine of Siena Community, 1125 Ferry St., Martinez, 94553. Tel: 510-228-9051. Sisters 5.

Social Service Sisters, 4000 Waterhouse, 94602. 851 Trestle Glen Rd., 94610. Sisters 6.

BERKELEY. *Dominican Sisters of Mission San Jose*, St. Mary Magdalen Community, 2004 Eunice St., 94709. Tel: 510-527-4817. Sisters 7.

Dominican Sisters of San Rafael, Benincase House of Formation, 2901 Channing Way, 94704. Tel: 510-540-6658.
E-mail: Purple115@juno.com
Sisters 6.

Franciscan Sisters of Little Falls, MN, 1418 A Fifth St., 94710.

Sisters of Charity, B.V.M., 1746 Addison St., 94703. Tel: 510-841-8791. 1708 Euclid Ave., No. 11, 94709. Tel: 510-843-0684. Sisters 2.

Sisters of Notre Dame de Namur, 1717 Oxford St., No. 101, 94709. Tel: 510-845-2113. 1717 Oxford St., No. 202, 94709. Tel: 510-540-6896. 1725 Oxford St., No. 210, 94709. Tel: 510-848-7439.

Sisters of St. Joseph of Carondelet, 2025 Durant Ave. #110, 94704. Tel: 510-540-0796; 486-8061. Sisters 3.

CASTRO VALLEY. *Sisters of St. Joseph in the Third Order of St. Francis*, 22120 Center St., No. 523, 94546. Tel: 510-886-1170. 2063 Boniface St., Concord, 94520. Tel: 510-680-7396. Sr. Madeline Antoskiewicz; Sr. Marie Myers, 5427 Valley View Rd., El Sobrante, 94803. Tel: 510-222-0492. Sr. Rosita Wisniewski, 141 Belleview Dr., Apt. 307, San Leandro, 94577.

Sisters of the Holy Family, Holy Family Convent, 19697 Redwood Rd., 94546. Tel: 510-582-7314. Sr. M. John Bosco Crivello, Local Coord. Total in community 12.

CONCORD. *Sisters of St. Joseph of the Third Order of St. Francis*, 2301 Mt. Diablo St., 94520. Tel: 510-680-7396; 825-2091.

EL CERRITO. *Franciscan Sisters of Perpetual Adoration (FSPA)*, 1317 Liberty St., No. 17, 94530. Tel: 510-233-9797. 2629 34th Ave., Oakland, 94601. Tel: 510-536-1266.

Mercy Sisters, Ireland, St. John the Baptist Convent, 11154 San Pablo Ave., 94530. Tel: 510-233-6769. Sisters 4.

Sisters of Sacred Hearts of Jesus and Mary, St. Jerome Convent, 310 San Carlos Ave., 94530. Tel: 510-525-6554.
E-mail: MaryGSHJM@JPS
Sisters 7.

EL SOBRANTE. *Sisters of St. Joseph of the Third Order of St. Francis, S.S.J.-T.O.S.F.*, 5427 Valley View Rd., 94803. Tel: 510-222-0492. 22120 Center St., #523, Castro Valley, 94546. Tel: 510-886-1170. 2063 Bonifacio St., Concord, 94520. Tel: 510-680-7396. Sisters 6.

FREMONT. *Sisters of the Holy Family*, Callison Day Home, Inc., 159 Washington Blvd., 94539. Tel: 510-624-4598. Legal Title: *Callison Day Home. Sisters of the Holy Family.*

HAYWARD. *Dominican Sisters of Adrian, MI*, 23910 Second St. #36, 94541. Tel: 510-582-2568.

Holy Names Sisters, St. Bede Convent, 26900 Patrick Ave., 94544. Tel: 510-782-6700.
E-mail: snjmcaadasst@connectinc.com
Sisters 6.

Sisters of St. Joseph of Wichita, KS, 1626 Ashbury Ln., 94545. Tel: 510-782-5960. Sisters 4.

KENSINGTON. *Discalced Carmelite Nuns*, 68 Rincon Rd., 94707. Tel: 510-526-5050. Solemn Professed 6.

Holy Names Sisters, 224 Lake Dr., 94708. Tel: 510-524-2231.

LIVERMORE. *Dominican Sisters of San Rafael*, St. Michael Convent, 375 Maple St., 94550. Tel: 510-443-1666; Fax: 510-447-6720.
E-mail: stmichaelliv@connectinc.com
Sisters 5.

MARTINEZ. *Sisters of St. Joseph of Carondelet*, St. Catherine of Siena Convent, 1125 Ferry St., 94553. Tel: 510-228-9051. Sisters 5.

MISSION SAN JOSE. *Dominican Sisters of Mission San Jose*, 43326 Mission Blvd., P.O. Box 3908, 94539. Tel: 510-657-2468; Fax: 510-657-1734.
E-mail: secgenmsj@connectinc.com
Web site: www.infolane.com/msjsisters/
Generalate Motherhouse and Novitiate of the Dominican Sisters of Mission San Jose, Congregation of The Queen of the Holy Rosary. Sr. Rose Marie Hennessy, Prioress Gen. Sisters 137.

Queen of Peace Community. Sr. Rebecca Shinas, O.P., Supr.

St. Joseph Priory. Sr. Mary LaSalette Fuselier, O.P., Prioress.

St. Martin Infirmary. Sr. Evelyn Casper, O.P., Supr.

San Domenico Community. Sr. Rose Marie Hennessy, O.P., Supr./Prioress Gen.

Siena House. Sr. Phyllis Marie Bridenbecker, O.P., Supr.

St. Edward Convent, 37088 Arden St., Newark, 94560-3702. Tel: 510-793-9447. Sr. Mary Paul Mehegan, O.P., Supr.

St. Elizabeth Convent, 1555-34th Ave., P.O. Box 7465, Oakland, 94601-0465. Tel: 510-532-8344. Sr. Kathleen Marie Ramirez, O.P., Supr.

St. Mary Magdelen Convent, 2004 Eunice St., Berkeley, 94709-1926. Tel: 510-527-4817. Sr. Ingrid Clemmensen, O.P., Supr.

Our Lady of Guadalupe Convent, 631 Aztec Ct., Fremont, 94539-7164. Tel: 510-490-6902. Sr. Andre Marie Fujier, O.P., Supr.

NEWARK. *Dominican Sisters of Mission San Jose*, St. Edward Convent, 37088 Arden St., 94560. Tel: 510-793-9447. Sisters 4.

PLEASANT HILL. *Holy Family Sisters*, Holy Family Center, 2059 Pleasant Hill Rd., 94523. Tel: 510-935-6151. Sisters 4; Total in Residence 4; Total Staff 2.

Sisters of St. Joseph of Carondelet, 368 Gladys Dr., 94523. Tel: 510-682-0533. Sisters 3; Total Assisted 65; Total Staff 4.

RODEO. *Sisters of Immaculate Heart of Mary*, St. Patrick Convent, 815 Seventh St., 94572. Tel: 510-799-6683. Sisters 3.

SAN LEANDRO. *Dominican Sisters of Oakford*, Our Lady of Guadalupe House of Formation, 327 Woodland Park, 94577. Tel: 510-569-9189. Total in Residence 4; Total Staff 1. Sisters 4.

Sisters of St. Joseph of Wichita, St. Felicitas Convent, 1662 Manor Blvd., 94579. Tel: 510-351-5244. Sisters 3.

SAN LORENZO. *Presentation Sisters, Kildare, Ireland*, St. John the Baptist Convent, 16642 Ashland Ave., 94580. Tel: 510-278-7128. Sisters 6.

[P] PASTORAL CENTERS

BERKELEY. *Jesuit Volunteer Corps Southwest*. Non-Profit Corporation. Mailing Address: P.O. Box 3266, 94703. Tel: 510-653-8564; Fax: 510-653-5145.
E-mail: jvcsw1@aol.com
Web site: http://gvweb.georgetown.edu/jvc
Mary Ashley, Exec. Dir. Volunteers 110.

DANVILLE. *San Damiano Retreat*, Franciscan Retreat House, Mailing Address: Box 767, 94526. Tel: 510-837-9141; Fax: 510-837-0522.
Web site: http://www.ctnba.org/CTN/catholic/retreat.htm#7
Retreat House for men, women and married couples. Revs. Raymond J. Bucher, O.F.M., Dir.; Larry Dunphy, O.F.M., Guardian. In res. Revs. Barry Brunsman, O.F.M., Retreat Master; Emmanuel Muessiggang, O.F.M.; Rufino Zaragoza, O.F.M. Total in Residence 6; Total Staff 29.

LAFAYETTE. *Diocesan Youth Retreat Center*, 1977 Reliez Valley Rd., 94549. Tel: 510-934-5802; 934-5800; Fax: 510-934-5802. Total in Residence 5; Total Staff 3.

PLEASANT HILL. *Holy Family Center*, 2059 Pleasant Hill Rd., 94523. Tel: 510-935-6151. Ministries: Personal Growth Programs, Counseling, Spiritual, Direction, Adult Faith Formation.

[Q] NEWMAN CENTERS

OAKLAND. *Holy Names College Campus Ministry*, 3500 Mountain Blvd., 94619.
Web site: http://www.hnc.edu
Sr. Sharon Casey, O.P., Dir. Campus Min.

Mills College Newman Center, 5000 MacArthur Blvd., 94605. Rev. Donald C. Pologruto, C.S.P., Chap.

HAYWARD. *California State University/Campus Ministry Center*, 25580 Campus Dr., 94542-1199. Tel: 510-581-1970; Fax: 510-581-1026.
E-mail: bobcsc@aol.com
Rev. Robert J. Loughery, C.S.C., Dir. Total Staff 1.

MORAGA. *St. Mary's College Campus Ministry*, Box 4777, 94575-4777. Tel: 510-631-4366; Fax: 510-631-4332. Rev. Salvatore Ragusa, S.D.S.; Sr. Ingrid Clemmensen, O.P.; Mr. Christopher Fuller; Ms. Martha Gonzalez; Mr. Scott Connolly.

[R] PERSONAL PRELATURES

BERKELEY. *Opus Dei (Prelature of the Holy Cross and Opus Dei)*, Garber House, 2710 College Ave., 94705. Tel: 510-548-2819. Rev. Paul A. Dolan.

[S] MISCELLANEOUS LISTINGS

OAKLAND. *Adventus*, 2900 Lakeshore Ave., 94610. Tel: 510-893-4711; Fax: 510-893-0945. Rev. David E. Staal. Purpose: To support the mission of the Roman Catholic Diocese of Oakland.

The Benilde Religious & Charitable Trust, c/o Plageman & Lund LLP, 1999 Harrison St., Ste. 2700, 94612. Mr. William Plageman, Jr., Contact Person. Charitable trust fund to benefit the educational activities of the Brothers of the Christian Schools of San Francisco.

Casa Vincentia, 3210 62nd Ave., 94605. Tel: 510-729-0316. Home for single pregnant women, 18-25 yrs. Barbara Jackson, Exec. Dir. Total in Residence 5; Total Staff 2.

Catholic Ladies' Aid Society, Grand Chaplain, 3014 Lake Shore Ave., 94610. Tel: 510-893-4711; Fax: 510-273-4946. Rev. Gary B. Tollner.

Catholic Parent Teacher Groups, 2900 Lake Shore Ave., 94610. Sr. Rose Marie Hennessy, O.P., Moderator.

Dominican Community Support Charitable Trust, 5877 Birch Ct., 94618. Tel: 510-658-8722. Anthony J. Cordeiro, O.P., Contact Person. Tel: 510-658-8722.

A Friendly Manor/A Friendly Place, 2298 San Pablo Ave., 94612. Tel: 510-451-8923. Sr. Maureen Lyons, C.S.J. Purpose: Daytime hospitality center for homeless women. Total Assisted 19,500; Total Staff 2.

Hesed Community, Benedictine Urban Community of Christian Meditation, 3745 Elston Ave., 94602. Tel: 510-482-5573.
E-mail: Hesedone@aol.com
Sr. Barbara Hazzard, O.S.B. Total in Residence 1; Total Staff 1.

Institute of Lay Theology, 5890 Birch Ct., 94618. Revs. Eugene R. Zimmers, S.J.; Michael J. Zimmers, S.J.; Frank B. Nieman, Ph.D., Sec.; Revs.

John A. Privett, S.J., Pres.; Robert L. St. Clair, S.J., Vice Pres. A Study Center and Promoter of Evangelization.

Italian Catholic Federation, 2900 Lake Shore Ave., 94610. Rev. Daniel E. Cardelli.

Missionaries of the Kingship of Christ, 1500-34th Ave., 94601. Tel: 510-536-1266. A Franciscan Secular Institute for Women, Men, Priests. Rev. Geoffrey Bridges, O.F.M., Contact Person. Tel: 510-647-2704.

**Oakland Elizabeth House*, 6423 Colby St., 94618. Tel: 510-601-1213. Martha McCarthy, Contact Person. Purpose: Transitional housing for low-income women and children.

Pacific Institute for Community Organization, 171 Santa Rosa Ave., 94610. Tel: 510-655-2801; Fax: 510-655-4816.
E-mail: BaumannPICO@compuserve.com
Rev. John A. Baumann, S.J., Exec. Dir.; Dr. Carlos Prietto, Chm.; Rev. Msgr. Norman Rotert, Vice Chm.

St. Mary's Center, 635-22nd St., 94612. Tel: 510-893-4723.
E-mail: ellie@stmc.org
Sr. Marilyn Medau, Dir. Food for all Ages Prog.; Carol Jackson, Dir. Senior Svcs.; Corinne Lund, Dir. Pre-School Prog.; Rev. Eleanor Shepardson, Exec. Dir. Total Assisted 1,750; Total Staff 17.

**The Gamelin-California Association*, Providence House, 540-23rd St., 94612-1718. Tel: 510-444-0839. Apartment building designed for disabled persons and persons with AIDS. Timothy Zaricznyj, Dir. Units 40.

Vietnamese Senior Care Center, 3014 Lakeshore Ave., 94610. Tel: 510-273-4986. Sr. Nicole Nguyen, D.C., Contact Person. Purpose: special outreach to the elder Vietnamese population.

BERKELEY. *Academy of American Franciscan History*, 1712 Euclid Ave., 94709. Tel: 510-848-5232; 548-1755 (Library).
E-mail: AcadaFH@aol.com
Total Staff 1.

Incarnation Monastery, Camaldolese Benedictines, 1369 La Loma Ave., 94708. Tel: 510-845-0601; Fax: 510-548-6439. Rev. Andrew Colnaghi, Prior. In res. Bros. Cassian Hardie, O.S.B.Cam.; Randy Sweringen, O.S.B.Cam. Total in Residence 3.

Inter-Friendship House Association, Friendship Center, 1646 Addison St., 94703. Tel: 510-843-7675. Rev. Bernard M.C. Chu, S.J. (China), Dir. Total Staff 1.

Multicultural Institute, 1712 Euclid Ave., 94709. Tel: 510-848-4075; Fax: 510-848-4095. Board of Directors: Revs. Rigoberto Caloca-Rivas, O.F.M., Exec. Dir.; Joseph Baur, O.F.M.; George E. Crespin; Bernie V. Elissagaray; Jose Joel Garcia, Ph.D., J.D.; Deborah Chu-Lan Lee, B.A.; Revs. Finian McGinn, O.F.M., Ph.D.; Kenan B. Osborne, O.F.M., Ph.D.; Alfredo Terrazas, J.D.; Barbara Terrazas, M.P.H.

CONCORD. *East Bay Services to the Developmentally Disabled*, 1485 Enea Cir., Ste. 1470, 94520. Tel: 510-825-2091; Fax: 510-825-2439. Nonresidence Serves 1,600; Residence 65; Staff 60.

EMERYVILLE. *Lasallain Educational Opportunities, Inc.*, 1266-61st St., 94608. Tel: 510-450-0555. Bro. Christopher Bassen, F.S.C., Prog. Dir. Total Assisted 210; Total Staff 6.

LAFAYETTE. *La Casa de la Luz / The Institute for Spiritual Direction*, 936 Dewing Ave., Ste. I, 94549. Tel: 510-284-5714. Spiritual Direction and Personal Growth of Men and Women. Pamela Prime Sullivan, Dir. Total Staff 4.

MISSION SAN JOSE. *Dominican Sisters of Mission San Jose Foundation (A Non-Profit Corp.)*, Mailing Address: P.O. Box 3908, 94539. Tel: 510-657-2468; Fax: 510-657-1734.
E-mail: secgenmsj@connectinc.com
Web site: www.infolane.com/msjsisters/
Sr. Charlotte Shea, O.P., Exec. Vice Pres.; Hugh Campbell, Pres.; Catherine Lyons, Sec. & Treas.

SAN LEANDRO. *Venerable Merlini Foundation*, 2337 W. Ave. 134th, 94577-4132. Tel: 510-357-4982. Jerome Stack, Pres.; Joseph L. Brown, Treas.

RELIGIOUS INSTITUTES OF MEN REPRESENTED IN THE DIOCESE

For further details refer to the corresponding bracketed number in the Religious Institutes of Men or Women section.

[0140]—*The Augustinians*.—O.S.A.
[0170]—*Basilian Fathers*.—C.S.B.
[0330]—*Brothers of the Christian Schools*. (Prov. of San Francisco).—F.S.C.
[0600]—*Brothers of the Congregation of Holy Cross*. (Southwest Prov.).—C.S.C.
[0200]—*Camaldolese Benedictines*.—O.S.B.Cam.
[0470]—*The Capuchin Friars*.—O.F.M.Cap.
[0480]—*Conventual Franciscans*.—O.F.M.Conv.
[0260]—*Discalced Carmelite Friars*.—O.C.D.
[1140]—*Fathers of the Sacred Hearts*.—SS.CC.
[0520]—*Franciscan Friars*. (Santa Barbara Prov.).—O.F.M.
[0530]—*Franciscan Friars of the Atonement*.—S.A.
[0690]—*Jesuit Fathers and Brothers*.—S.J.
[0770]—*The Marist Brothers*.—F.M.S.
[0910]—*Oblates of Mary Immaculate*. (Western Prov.).—O.M.I.
[0920]—*Oblates of St. Francis De Sales*.—O.S.F.S.
[0430]—*Order of Preachers-Dominicans*. (Prov. of Holy Name of Jesus).—O.P.
[1030]—*Paulist Fathers*.—C.S.P.
[0610]—*Priests of the Congregation of Holy Cross*.—C.S.C.
[1070]—*Redemptorist Fathers*. (Oakland Prov.).—C.SS.R.
[1190]—*Salesians of Don Bosco*. (Turin, Italy).—S.D.B.
[1240]—*Servites*. (Western Prov.).—O.S.M.
[0760]—*Society of Mary*.—S.M.
[0420]—*Society of the Divine Word*. (Techny, IL).—S.V.D.
[1060]—*Society of the Precious Blood*. (Prov. of the Pacific).—C.PP.S.

RELIGIOUS INSTITUTES OF WOMEN REPRESENTED IN THE DIOCESE

[0340]—*Carmelite Sisters of Charity*.—C.aCh.
[1780]—*Congregation of the Sisters of the Third Order of St. Francis of Perpetual Adoration*. (Spokane, WA).—F.S.P.A.
[0420]—*Discalced Carmelite Nuns*.—O.C.D.
[1070-03]—*Dominican Sisters*.—O.P.
[1070-04]—*Dominican Sisters*.—O.P.
[1070-12]—*Dominican Sisters*.—O.P.
[1070-13]—*Dominican Sisters*.—O.P.
[1070-30]—*Dominican Sisters*.—O.P.
[2470]—*Maryknoll Sisters of St. Dominic*.—M.M.
[]—*Sisters for Christian Community*.—S.F.C.C.
[0430]—*Sisters of Charity of the Blessed Virgin Mary*. (Mt. Carmel, Dubuque, IA).—B.V.M.
[2360]—*Sisters of Loretto At the Foot of the Cross*. (Nerink, KY).—S.L.
[2516]—*Sisters of Mercy*.—S.M.
[2570]—*Sisters of Mercy*. (Burlingame, CA).—S.M.
[3000]—*Sisters of Notre Dame de Namur*. (Prov. of California).—S.N.D.deN.
[3350]—*Sisters of Providence*. (Sacred Heart Prov.).—S.P.
[4080]—*Sisters of Social Service of Los Angeles, Inc*.—S.S.S.
[1630]—*Sisters of St. Francis of Penance and Christian Charity*.—O.S.F.
[1650]—*Sisters of St. Francis of Philadelphia*.—O.S.F.
[3840]—*Sisters of St. Joseph of Carondelet*. (Los Angeles Prov.).—C.S.J.
[3830-03]—*Sisters of St. Joseph of Orange*.—C.S.J.
[3930]—*Sisters of St. Joseph of the Third Order of St. Francis*. (Prov. of Our Lady of Czestochowa).—S.S.J.-T.O.S.F.
[3830-18]—*Sisters of St. Joseph of Wichita*.—C.S.J.
[1960]—*Sisters of the Holy Family*.—S.H.F.
[1990]—*Sisters of the Holy Names of Jesus and Mary*. (Prov. of Calif.).—S.N.J.M.
[3320]—*Sisters of the Presentation of the B.V.M*. (San Francisco, CA).—P.B.V.M.
[3680]—*Sisters of the Sacred Heart of Jesus and Mary*.—S.H.J.M.
[2150]—*Sisters, Servants of the Immaculate Heart of Mary*.—I.H.M.
[3330]—*Union of the Sisters of the Presentation of the Blessed Virgin Mary*.—P.B.V.M.

DIOCESAN CEMETERIES AND MAUSOLEUMS

OAKLAND. *The Roman Catholic Cemeteries of the Diocese of Oakland*, 2900 Lakeshore Ave., 94610. Tel: 510-893-4711; Fax: 510-893-0945. Directors: Most Rev. John S. Cummins; Revs. Albano Oliveira; David E. Staal; Sr. Barbara Flannery, C.S.J.
St. Mary's.

ANTIOCH. *Holy Cross*.

HAYWARD. *Holy Sepulchre Cemetery and Mausoleum*.

LAFAYETTE. *Queen of Heaven*.

PLEASANTON. *Christ the King*.

SAN PABLO. *St. Joseph's Cemetery and Mausoleum*.

NECROLOGY

† Autard, Joseph, (Retired). —Died March 7, 1997.
† Harcar, Anthony J., (Retired). —Died Dec. 17, 1997.
† Keeley, James T., Oakland, CA, St. Mary, Immaculate Conception-St. Francis De Sales. —Died Jan. 3, 1997.

Diocese of Ogdensburg

(Dioecesis Ogdensburgensis)

Most Reverend

PAUL S. LOVERDE, D.D., S.T.L., J.C.L.

Bishop of Ogdensburg; ordained December 18, 1965; appointed Titular Bishop of Ottabia and Auxiliary Bishop of Hartford February 3, 1988; consecrated April 12, 1988; transferred to Ogdensburg November 11, 1993; installed January 17, 1994. *Res., 624 Washington St., Ogdensburg, NY, 13669.*

ERECTED BY HIS HOLINESS PIUS IX, FEBRUARY 16, 1872.

Square Miles 12,036.

Incorporated by a special act of the Legislature of the State of New York, April 10, 1945, with the title: The Roman Catholic Diocese of Ogdensburg, New York.

Comprises that part of Herkimer and Hamilton Counties north of the northern line of the townships of Ohio and Russia as existing in 1872 with the entire Counties of Lewis, Jefferson, St. Lawrence, Franklin, Clinton and Essex in the State of New York.

For legal titles of parishes and diocesan institutions, consult the Chancery Office.

Chancery Office: 622 Washington St., P.O. Box 369, Ogdensburg, NY, 13669. Tel.: 315-393-2920; Fax: 315-394-7401.

STATISTICAL OVERVIEW

Personnel	
Bishop	1
Priests: Diocesan Active in Diocese	114
Priests: Active Outside Diocese	9
Priests: Diocesan in Foreign Missions	2
Priests: Retired, Sick or Absent	43
Number of Diocesan Priests	168
Religious Priests in Diocese	17
Extern Priests in Diocese	1
Ordinations:	
Diocesan Priests	2
Permanent Deacons in Diocese	58
Total Brothers	12
Total Sisters	194
Parishes	
Parishes	123
With Resident Pastor:	
Resident Diocesan Priests	87
Resident Religious Priests	6
Without Resident Pastor:	
Administered by Priests	28
Administered by Women Religious	2
Missions	28
Pastoral Centers	9
Professional Ministry Personnel:	
Brothers	2
Sisters	32
Lay Ministers	24
Welfare	
Health Care Centers	2
Total Assisted	48,100
Homes for the Aged	3
Total Assisted	880
Day Care and Extended Day Care Centers	1
Total Assisted	26
Special Centers for Social Services	8
Total Assisted	15,700
Other Institutions	15
Total Assisted	14,000
Educational	
Seminaries, Diocesan	1
Students from This Diocese	8
Students from Other Diocese	15
Diocesan Students in Other Seminaries	10
Total Seminarians	18
Colleges and Universities	1
Total Students	335
High Schools, Diocesan and Parish	2
Total Students	689
Elementary Schools, Diocesan and Parish	24
Total Students	4,427
Catechesis/Religious Education:	
High School Students	3,008
Elementary Students	9,885
Total Students Under Catholic Instruction	18,362
Teachers in the Diocese:	
Priests	2
Brothers	1
Sisters	30
Lay Teachers	371
Vital Statistics	
Receptions into the Church:	
Infant Baptism Totals	1,989
Adult Baptism Totals	163
Received into Full Communion	94
First Communions	2,090
Confirmations	1,701
Marriages:	
Catholic	492
Interfaith	272
Total Marriages	764
Deaths	1,667
Total Catholic Population	139,447
Total Population	495,263

Former Bishops—Rt. Rev. EDGAR P. WADHAMS, D.D., cons. May 5, 1872; died Dec. 5, 1891.—Rt. Rev. HENRY GABRIELS, D.D., cons. May 5, 1892; died April 23, 1921.—Most Rev. JOSEPH H. CONROY, D.D., LL.D., cons. May 1, 1912; succeeded to the See, Nov. 21, 1921; died March 20, 1939.—Most Rev. FRANCIS J. MONAGHAN, S.T.D., LL.D., cons. June 29, 1936; succeeded to the See, March 20, 1939; died Nov. 13, 1942.—Most Rev. BRYAN J. MCENTEGART, D.D., LL.D., cons. Aug. 3, 1943; transferred to Titular See of Aradi, Aug. 19, 1953; appt. June 26, 1953 to Rectorship of Catholic University of America, Washington, D.C., appt. Bishop of Brooklyn, April 16, 1957; installed June 13, 1957; appt. Archbishop, April 15, 1966; retired and appt. Titular Archbishop of Gabii, July 17, 1968; died Sept. 30, 1968.—Most Rev. WALTER P. KELLENBERG, D.D., cons. Oct. 5, 1953; appt. to Ogdensburg, Jan. 19, 1954; transferred to See of Rockville Centre, April 16, 1957; installed May 27, 1957; died Jan. 11, 1986.—Most Rev. JAMES J. NAVAGH, D.D., cons. Sept. 24, 1952; appt. to Ogdensburg, May 8, 1957; transferred to Paterson, Feb. 12, 1963; died in Rome, Oct. 2, 1965.—Most Rev. LEO R. SMITH, D.D., appt. Auxiliary Bishop of Buffalo, July 9, 1952; cons. Sept. 24, 1952; appt. Bishop of Ogdensburg, Feb. 12, 1963; died in Rome Oct. 9, 1963.—Most Rev. THOMAS A. DONNELLAN, D.D., appt. March 4, 1964; cons. April 9, 1964; appt. to Atlanta, May 29, 1968; transferred to Archdiocese of Atlanta, July 16, 1968; died in Atlanta, Oct. 15, 1987.—Most Rev. STANISLAUS J. BRZANA, S.T.D., LL.D, ord. June 7, 1941; appt. Titular Bishop of Cufruta and Auxiliary of Buffalo, May 24, 1964; cons. June 29, 1964; transferred to Ogdensburg, Oct. 22, 1968; retired Nov. 11, 1993; died March 1, 1997.

Chancery Office—622 Washington St., P.O. Box 369, Ogdensburg, 13669. Tel: 315-393-2920; Fax: 315-394-7401. Office Hours: Mon.-Fri. 8:15-4:30 (Sept.-June); Summer hours: 8:45-4.

Secretary to the Bishop—Bro. DAVID EDDY C.F.X., *P.O. Box 369, Ogdensburg, 13669.* Tel: 315-393-2920.

Vicar General—Rev. Msgr. ROBERT L. LAWLER, P.A., V.G., *St. Mary's Rectory, P.O. Box 187, Waddington, 13694.* Tel: 315-388-4466; Fax: 315-388-4722.

Moderator of the Curia and Episcopal Vicar for Pastoral Services—Rev. Msgr. JOHN R. MURPHY, S.T.L., M.A.

Chancellor and Episcopal Vicar for Diocesan Services—Rev. TERRY R. LAVALLEY, J.C.L.

Fiscal Officer—Mr. JOHN J. GRAY, JR., C.P.A., M.B.A.

Diocesan Archivist—Rev. LAWRENCE E. COTTER, S.T.L., *622 Washington St., P.O. Box 369, Ogdensburg, 13669.* Tel: 315-393-2920.

Judicial Vicar—Rev. Msgr. HARRY K. SNOW, M.A., J.C.L.

Secretary to the Tribunal—Sr. MARY PATRICK MURPHY, S.S.J., M.S.; Rev. DOUGLAS J. LUCIA, Assoc. Sec.

Adjutant Judicial Vicars—Revs. PHILIP T. ALLEN; TERRY R. LAVALLEY, J.C.L.

Promoter of Justice—Rev. Msgr. PETER R. RIANI, S.T.D., M.Ed.

Defenders of the Bond—Rev. Msgr. JOHN F. PENDERGAST; Rev. Msgr. PAUL E. WHITMORE; Revs. LAWRENCE E. COTTER; JAMES A. DELBEL; RAYMOND J. MOREAU; JOSEPH MORGAN; KEVIN O'BRIEN; ALAN D. SHNOB; J. LEE SNOW; JOHN R. YONKOVIG.

Pro-Synodal Judges—Rev. Msgr. ROBERT H. AUCOIN; Rev. Msgr. BERNARD E. CHRISTMAN; Rev. Msgr. CLARENCE M. DEVAN; Rev. Msgr. HERBERT J. HANNAN; Rev. Msgr. ANTHONY A. MILIA; Rev. Msgr. FRANCIS A. WHITE; Revs. FLOYD J. BLEAUX; ROBERT L. COTTER; JOSEPH W. ELLIOTT; DANIEL T. KEEFE; CLYDE A. LEWIS; GILBERT B. MENARD; EARL W. NICHOLS; F. JAMES SHURTLEFF.

Notary—Mrs. DIANNA SHAVER.

Advocates—Sr. MARY PATRICK MURPHY, S.S.J., M.S.; Rev. Msgr. DENNIS J. DUPREY; Rev. Msgr. JOHN R. MURPHY, S.T.L., M.A.; Revs. FAY W. AGER; DOUGLAS A. DECKER; GARVIN J. DEMARAIS; GARRY B. GIROUX; ALBERT J. HAUSER; ALAN J. LAMICA; WILLIAM G. REAMER; DERK M. SCHUDDE.

Diocesan Consultors—Rev. Msgr. ROBERT L. LAWLER, P.A., V.G.; Rev. Msgr. BERNARD E. CHRISTMAN; Rev. Msgr. CLARENCE M. DEVAN; Rev. Msgr. LEEWARD J. POISSANT; Revs. F. JAMES SHURTLEFF; DONALD J. MANFRED; KEVIN J. O'BRIEN.

Deans—Rev. TIMOTHY J. SOUCY, V.F., Adirondack; Rev. Msgr. C. JOHN MCAVOY, V.F., Clinton; Rev. Msgr. FRANCIS A. WHITE, V.F., Essex; Rev. Msgr. DENNIS J. DUPREY, V.F., Franklin; Rev. LAWRENCE E. MARULLO, V.F., Hamilton and Herkimer; Rev. Msgr. ANTHONY A. MILIA, V.F., Jefferson; Rev. LEO A. WILEY, V.F., Lewis; Rev. ANDREW J. AMYOT, V.F., St. Lawrence.

Council of Priests—Most Rev. PAUL S. LOVERDE, Chm.; Rev. Msgr. BERNARD E. CHRISTMAN, Vice Chm.; Rev. Msgr. ROBERT L. LAWLER, P.A., V.G.; Revs. KEVIN J. O'BRIEN; STEVEN M. MURRAY; RICHARD S. STURTZ;

Rev. Msgr. WILLIAM J. ARGY; Revs. JOHN R. YONKOVIG; THOMAS E. KORNMEYER; PETER MULLEN, M.M.; MARK MCDONALD, M.S.C.; LEO A. WILEY, V.F.; DONALD J. MANFRED; F. JAMES SHURTLEFF.

Co-Vicars for Religious—Rev. Msgr. DENNIS J. DUPREY; Sr. CATHERINE LIVERS, S.P., *Chancery Office, 622 Washington St., P.O. Box 369, Ogdensburg, 13669-0369.*

Diocesan Offices and Directors

Apostleship of Prayer—Rev. ALBERT J. HAUSER, Dir.

Building Commission—Most Rev. PAUL S. LOVERDE, Chm. Members: Rev. TERRY R. LAVALLEY, J.C.L.; Rev. Msgr. ROBERT J. GIROUX; Rev. Msgr. JOHN R. MURPHY, S.T.L., M.A.

Campus Ministry—Rev. HARRY E. GIROUX, Diocesan Dir.; Deacon WILLIAM S. RAVEN; Revs. TIMOTHY SOUCY; J. ROGER MCGUINNESS; FRANCIS J. FLYNN.

Catholic Charities of the Diocese of Ogdensburg—Ogdensburg Office—Sr. DONNA FRANKLIN, D.C., Diocesan Dir., *P.O. Box 296, Ogdensburg, 13669.* Tel: 315-393-2255; Fax: 315-393-2402. Mr. PATRICK LYONS, Dir., *P.O. Box 296, Ogdensburg, 13669.* Tel: 315-393-2660. Watertown Office—Mrs. ANNE BOULTER-DAVIS, Dir., *812 State St., Watertown, 13601.* Tel: 315-788-4330; Fax: 315-786-0539. Plattsburgh Office—PAMELA WILSON, M.S., Dir., *4914 S. Catherine St., Plattsburgh, 12901.* Tel: 518-561-0470; Fax: 518-561-0472. Malone Office— *63 E. Main St., P.O. Box 896, Malone, 12953.* Tel: 518-483-1460; Fax: 518-483-1460. Lowville Office— *7514 S. State St., Lowville, 13367.* Tel: 315-376-4141. Port Henry Office— *14 Park Pl., Port Henry, 12974.* Tel: 518-546-3565. Tupper Lake Office— *60 Park St., P.O. Box 701, Tupper Lake, 12986.* Tel: 518-359-7688.

Catholic Relief Services—Sr. DONNA FRANKLIN, D.C., *P.O. Box 296, Ogdensburg, 13669.* Tel: 315-393-2255.

Cemeteries—Rev. TERRY R. LAVALLEY, Acting Dir., *622 Washington St., P.O. Box 369, Ogdensburg, 13669.*

Censor Librorum—Rev. LAWRENCE E. COTTER, B.S., S.T.L., M.S.

Charismatic Renewal—Rev. FRANCIS CORYER, Liaison, *St. Henry's Church, 3 Josephine St., Dekalb Junction, 13630.*

Clergy and Pastoral Personnel—Rev. JOSEPH A. MORGAN, Dir., *P.O. Box 369, Ogdensburg, 13669.* Tel: 315-393-2920.

Department of Communications—

Bureau of Information—Rev. TERRY R. LAVALLEY, J.C.L., Chancellor, *P.O. Box 369, Ogdensburg, 13669.* Tel: 315-393-2920; Fax: 315-394-7401.

Newspaper—"North Country Catholic"; Mrs. MARY LOU KILIAN, Editor; Mr. SCOTT WILSON, Circulation/Advertising, *P.O. Box 326, Ogdensburg, 13669.* Tel: 315-393-2540.

Media Bureau—Mrs. LINDA KELLEY, Dir., *1900 State Hwy. 11B, Potsdam, 13676.* Tel: 315-265-0261; Fax: 315-268-7104.

Continuing Education of Clergy—Rev. J. ROGER MCGUINNESS, Chm.

Development Office—Bishop's Fund Appeal, Planned Giving, Bishop's Heritage Circle; Mrs. JANICE SHOEN, Dir.

Stewardship—Rev. Msgr. GERALD H. SERVICE, Dir., *622 Washington St., P.O. Box 369, Ogdensburg, 13669.* Tel: 315-393-2920.

Ecumenical Commission—Rev. Msgr. JOSEPH G. BAILEY, Chm.

Education—Sr. KATHLEEN MURPHY, O.S.F., Supt., Schools; Mrs. DOROTHY HOBBS, Asst. Supt., *622 Washington St., P.O. Box 369, Ogdensburg, 13669.* Tel: 315-393-2920.

Employee Benefits—Mrs. DEBRA L. MOUSAW, *P.O. Box 369, Ogdensburg, 13669.*

Office of Evangelization—Sr. MARY ELLEN BRETT, S.S.J., Dir., *Mater Dei College, 5428 State Hwy. 37, Ogdensburg, 13669.* Tel: 315-393-5930, Ext. 410.

Family Life and Pre-Cana—Deacon EDWARD MAZUCHOWSKI; Mrs. LOUISE MAZUCHOWSKI, *177 Gene LeFevre Rd., Cadyville, 12918.*

Formation for Ministry—Sr. JUDITH BAUMERT, S.S.J., Dir., *Mater Dei College, 5428 State Hwy. 37, Ogdensburg, 13669.* Tel: 315-393-5930, Ext. 401.

Legion of Mary—Rev. Msgr. EDMUND H. DUMAS, *St. Alphonsus Church, P.O. Box 166, Tupper Lake, 12986.*

Mission Aid Societies—Rev. GEORGE F. MAROUN, Dir., *604 Washington St., Ogdensburg, 13669.* Tel: 315-393-0368; Fax: 315-393-0981.

The Society for The Propagation of the Faith—Rev. GEORGE MAROUN, Dir., *604 Washington St., Ogdensburg, 13669.* Tel: 315-393-0368.

Holy Childhood Association—Rev. GEORGE MAROUN, Dir., *604 Washington St., Ogdensburg, 13669.*

Ogdensburg Peruvian Apostolate—Revs. JAY SEYMOUR; PATRICK MUNDY, *San Martin de Porres, Casilla 105, Mollendo, Peru, S.A.*

Natural Family Planning Services—Mr. ANGELO PIETROPAOLI, Pres.; Mrs. ANGELO PIETROPAOLI, Pres., *36 1st St., Malone, 12953.*

Pastoral Council—Most Rev. PAUL S. LOVERDE, Chm.; Sr. MARY PATRICK MURPHY, S.S.J., Sec., *Mater Dei College, Riverside Dr., Ogdensburg, 13669.*

Pastoral Planning—Rev. Msgr. JOHN R. MURPHY, Dir.; Rev. TERRY R. LAVALLEY, J.C.L.; Rev. Msgr. DENNIS J. DUPREY, *P.O. Box 369, Ogdensburg, 13669.* Tel: 315-393-2920.

Permanent Diaconate—Rev. HOWARD J. VENETTE, Formation Dir., *P.O. Box 315, Colton, 13625.* Deacon FREDERICK BROUSSEAU, Dir. Ordained Deacons, *32 Chestnut St., Potsdam, 13676.*

Personnel Board—Rev. JOSEPH A. MORGAN, Dir., Clergy Personnel; Rev. Msgr. JOHN F. PENDERGAST; Revs. J. MICHAEL GAFFNEY; L. WILLIAM GORDON; RAYMOND J. MOREAU; DONALD A. ROBINSON.

Priests' Eucharistic League—Rev. ALBERT J. HAUSER, Dir.

Department of Christian Formation—Mr. MICHAEL WAGNER, Diocesan Dir., *866 Arsenal St., Watertown, 13601.* Tel: 315-782-3620; Fax: 315-782-2009. Ogdensburg Regional Center, *604 Washington St., Ogdensburg, 13669.* Tel: 315-393-0368. Sr. MOLLY SMITH, D.C., Ogdensburg Reg. Dir. Plattsburgh Regional Center, *114A Cornelia St., Plattsburgh, 12901.* Tel: 518-563-2022; Fax: 518-563-2138. Sr. IMELDA KIRKEY, O.S.M, Plattsburgh Dir. Watertown Regional Center, *866 Arsenal St., Watertown, 13601.* Tel: 315-782-3620. Mr. MICHAEL WAGNER, Watertown Reg. Dir.

Youth Ministry—Mrs. GAYLE FRANK, Dir., *P.O. Box 369, Ogdensburg, 13669.* Tel: 315-393-0368.

St. Vincent de Paul Society—Vacant.

Scouts—Sr. MARY RITA KEMPNEY, S.S.J., Diocesan Liaison, *866 Arsenal St., Watertown, 13601.* Tel: 315-782-3620.

Council of Religious—Sr. RITA MARY MORRISSETTE, O.S.M., Pres.; Sr. JOAN CASEY, R.S.M., Vice Pres.; Sr. RUTH SEGUIN, R.S.M., Sec.; Sr. PATRICIA MURTAGH, R.S.M., Treas.

Vocations—Revs. DONALD A. ROBINSON, Dir. Vocations & Dir. Seminarians Assoc. Vocations Directors; Revs. TIMOTHY CANAAN; CHRISTOPHER CARRARA, *Wadhams Hall, 6866 State Hwy. 37, Ogdensburg, 13669.* Tel: 315-393-4231.

Worship—ALBERT J. HAUSER, Dir., *P.O. Box 369, Ogdensburg, 13669.* Tel: 315-393-0368.

CLERGY, PARISHES, MISSIONS AND PAROCHIAL SCHOOLS

CITY OF OGDENSBURG
(St. Lawrence County)

1—ST. MARY'S CATHEDRAL (1748), Rev. Msgr. Harry K. Snow, Rector; Rev. Kris C. Lauzon; Rev. Msgr. William J. Argy; Rev. Joseph P. Wheelock; Sr. Mary Theresa La Brake, G.N.S.H., Pastoral Assoc.; Deacons D. Thomas Sharrow; William M. Taylor; Richard E. Winter. In res., Rev. Thomas G. Votraw.
Res., 415 Hamilton St., 13669. Tel: 315-393-3930; Fax: 315-393-6680. [CEM]
Catechesis/Religious Programs—Tel: 315-393-1820. Mrs. Michele Rosteck, D.R.E.
Students 253.

2—NOTRE DAME (1859), Revs. John M. Hunt; John M. Demo; Sr. Mary Bernard Shanley, C.S.J., Pastoral Assoc.; Deacons Victor Demers; Thomas Kilian. In res., Rev. Joseph A. Morgan; Rev. Msgr. Robert J. Giroux.
Res., 125 Ford Ave., P.O. Box 149, 13669. Tel: 315-393-5050; Fax: 315-393-5962. [CEM]
School—Ogdensburg Catholic Central School, (Grades K-5) 315 Gates St., 13699. Tel: 315-393-0165. Ms. Nancy LaRue, Prin.
Lay Teachers 9; Students 125.
Catechesis/Religious Programs—Bishop Conroy Christian Formation Program, 214 Morris St., 13669. Tel: 315-393-1820.
Students 170.

OUTSIDE CITY OF OGDENSBURG

Adams, Jefferson Co., St. Cecilia (1870), Rev. Douglas Decker.
Res., 19 Grove St., 13605. Tel: 315-232-2392. [CEM]
Catechesis/Religious Programs—Students 230.

Alexandria Bay, Jefferson Co., St. Cyril of Alexandria (1000 Islands) (1885), Rev. Thomas F. Driscoll.
Res., Box 477, 13607. Tel: 315-482-2670. [CEM]
Catechesis/Religious Programs—Students 107.

Altona, Clinton Co., Holy Angels (1865) (Irish-French Canadian), Rev. Gilbert O. Boisvert.
Res., P.O. Box 113, 12910. Tel: 518-236-5848; Fax: 518-236-4942. [CEM]
Oratory—Jericho, St. Alexis.
Catechesis/Religious Programs—Mary Ellen Tomo, D.R.E.
Students 142.

Antwerp, Jefferson Co., St. Michael (1849), Rev. Liam O'Doherty.
Res., 30 Maple St., P.O. Box 70, 13608. Tel: 315-659-8372; Fax: 315-659-8372. [CEM]
Mission—Philadelphia, Jefferson Co., St. Joseph, 13608.

Au Sable Forks, Clinton Co., Holy Name (1848), Rev. Donald F. Kramberg; Deacon Joseph H. Gilbert, II.
Res., 10 Church St., P.O. Box 719, 12912. Tel: 518-647-8225. [CEM]
School—(Grades PreK-6) 5 Pleasant St., 12912. Tel: 518-647-8444. Mrs. Susan Pulitzer, Prin.
Lay Teachers 9; Students 114.
Catechesis/Religious Programs—Students 110.

Black Brook, Clinton Co., St. Matthew (1848), Rev. Donald F. Kramberg; Deacon Joseph H. Gilbert, II.
Res., 10 Church St., P.O. Box 719, Au Sable Forks, 12912. Tel: 518-647-8225. [CEM]

Black River, Jefferson Co., St. Paul (1901), Rev. Theodore M. Gillette.
Res., 208 LeRay St., 13612. Tel: 315-773-5672.
Church—210 LeRay St., 13612.
Catechesis/Religious Programs—Students 83.

Bloomingdale, Essex Co., St. Paul (1897), Rev. Joseph P. Trombley.
Res., 50 Saranac Ave., P.O. Box 356, 12913. Tel: 518-891-0144; Fax: 518-891-5259. [CEM 2]
Mission—Gabriels, Franklin Co., Assumption of the B.V.M., Rte. 86, Gabriels, 12939.
Catechesis/Religious Programs—Tel: 518-891-3576. D.R.E. Thelma Niederbuhl, (Grades 1-5); Kathy Gonyea, (Grades 6-12).
Students 103.

Bombay, Franklin Co., St. Joseph (1912), Rev. Martin Farrell, O.S.D.
Res., P.O. Box 499, Fort Covington, 12937. Tel: 518-358-4471; Fax: 518-358-2500.
Catechesis/Religious Programs—Tel: 518-358-2500.
Students 70.

Brasher Falls, St. Lawrence Co., St. Patrick (1830), Rev. Clark S. White; Deacons Floyd J. Barton; Francis Horan. In res., Rev. Msgr. Herbert J. Hannan.
Res., P.O. Box 208, 13613. Tel: 315-389-5401.
Parish Center: Tel: 315-389-5191. [CEM]
Catechesis/Religious Programs—Helen Brown, D.R.E.
Students 199.

Brownville, Jefferson Co., Immaculate Conception of the B.V.M. (1874)(Irish-Italian), Rev. Joseph W. Elliott; Sr. Norah Phelan C.S.C., Pastoral Assoc. & D.R.E.
Res., 119 W. Main St., P.O. Box 99, 13615. Tel: 315-782-1143.
Catechesis/Religious Programs—Tel: 315-788-7240.
Students 281.
Mission—Dexter, Jefferson Co., St. Elizabeth Seton, 13615. Tel: 315-639-3888.

Brushton, Franklin Co., St. Mary (1870), Rev. Alfred H. Fish.
Res., 12916. Tel: 518-529-7433; Fax: 518-529-6720. [CEM]
Catechesis/Religious Programs—Marian Roscoe, D.R.E.
Students 309.

Burke, Franklin Co., St. George (1874), Rev. Bill Edwards.
Res., P.O. Box 105, Main St., 12917. Tel: 518-483-5687; Fax: 518-483-5687, Ext. 51. [CEM]

Cadyville, Clinton Co., St. James Minor (1854), Rev. George W. Tobin.
Res., P.O. Box 117, 12918-0117. Tel: 518-293-7026. [CEM]
Catechesis/Religious Programs—Students 146.

Canton, St. Lawrence Co., St. Mary (1874), Rev. Msgr. Gerald H. Service.
Res., 66 Court St., P.O. Box 308, 13617. Tel: 315-386-2543. [CEM]
School—(Grades PreK-6) 2 Powers St., 13617. Tel: 315-386-3572. Mrs. Eleanor Beauvais, Prin.
Lay Teachers 9; Students 136.
Catechesis/Religious Programs—Mrs. Jeannine Ballard, D.R.E.
Students 186.

St. Thomas More (1959). (Campus Parish). Rev. Harry E. Giroux.
Res., 39 Court St., P.O. Box 424, 13617. Tel: 315-386-8425; Fax: 315-386-1200.

Cape Vincent, Jefferson Co., St. Vincent of Paul, Rev. E. Thomas Silver.
Res., Box 288, 13618. Tel: 315-654-2662; Fax: 315-654-4721. [CEM]

Carthage, Jefferson Co., St. James Minor (1818), Revs. Kevin J. O'Brien; Christopher C. Carrara; Sr. M. Victorine Brenon, S.S.J., Pastoral Assoc.; Deacon Richard J. Staab.
Res., 327 West St., 13619. Tel: 315-493-3224; Fax: 315-493-3280. [CEM]
School—Augustinian Academy, (Grades PreK-8) 317 West St., 13619. Tel: 315-493-1301. Sr. John Mary Brockway, S.S.J., Prin.; Sr. M. Victorine Brenon, S.S.J., Supr.
Sisters of St. Joseph 1; Lay Teachers 12; Students 231.
Catechesis/Religious Programs—Students 181.
Convent—Tel: 315-493-1672.
Mission—Natural Bridge, Jefferson Co., St. Henry.

Champlain, Clinton Co., St. Mary (1861), Rev. L. William Gordon; Deacon Leonard Patrie.
Res., 86 Church St., P.O. Box 368, 12919. Tel: 518-298-8244; Fax: 518-298-2879. [CEM 2]
School—(Grades PreK-6). Tel: 518-298-3372; Fax: 518-298-3372. Sr. Marie Cordata Kelly, S.S.J., Prin.
Daughters of Charity of the Sacred Heart of Jesus 2; Lay Teachers 8; Students 145.
Catechesis/Religious Programs—Students 170.

Chasm Falls, Franklin Co., St. Helen (1881), Rev. Msgr. Dennis J. Duprey; Sr. Sheila Moran, S.S.J., Admin.
Res., Rte. 1, Box 311, Malone, 12953. Tel: 518-483-1515. [CEM]
Church Office: Rte. 1, Box 311, Malone, 12953. Tel: 518-483-1515.
Catechesis/Religious Programs—Students 71.
Missions—Lake Titus, Franklin Co., St. Mary, 12953.; Owl's Head, Franklin Co., St. Joseph, 12953.

Chateaugay, Franklin Co., St. Patrick (1848), Rev. Fay W. Ager; Sr. Mary Hallahan, O.S.U., Pastoral Assoc.
Res., 11 W. Main St., P.O. Box 908, 12920. Tel: 518-497-6673. [CEM]
Catechesis/Religious Programs—Tel: 518-497-6165.
Students 295.
Mission—Brainardsville, Franklin Co., St. Jude, 12920.

Chaumont, Jefferson Co., All Saints (1922), Rev. John J. Cosmic.
Res., P.O. Box 100, 13622. Tel: 315-649-2717. [CEM]
Catechesis/Religious Programs—27396 Madison St., 13622
Students 75.

Chazy, Clinton Co., Sacred Heart, Rev. Louis C. Gardner; Deacon Robert J. LeClair.
Res., P.O. Box 459, 12921. Tel: 518-846-7650; Fax: 518-846-7655. [CEM]

Churubusco, Clinton Co., Immaculate Heart of Mary (1880), Rev. Howard McCasland, Admin.
Res., Rte. 189, 12923. Tel: 518-497-9956. [CEM]
Catechesis/Religious Programs—St. Edmund's Center, Ellenburg, Tel: 518-594-3907.
Students 62.

Clayton, Jefferson Co., St. Mary of Clayton (1838), Rev. Daniel L. Chapin; Deacon Gary A. Frank.
Res., 521 James St., 13624. Tel: 315-686-3398 (Rectory); 686-2638 (Parish Office). [CEM 2][JC]
Catechesis/Religious Programs—515 Mary St., 13624. Tel: 315-686-2638.
Students 110.

Colton, St. Lawrence Co., St. Patrick (1864), Revs. Howard J. Venette; Lawrence E. Cotter, Pastor Emeritus.
Res., P.O. Box 315, 13625. Tel: 315-262-2871; 262-2188 (Parish Center); Fax: 315-262-2871. [CEM]
Catechesis/Religious Programs—Students 70.
Missions—South Colton, St. Lawrence Co., St. Paul, 13625.; Parishville, St. Lawrence Co., St. Michael, 13625.

Constable, Franklin Co., St. Francis of Assisi (1872), Rev. Garry B. Giroux; Deacon Garry N. Burnell.
Res., Maple St., P.O. Box 86, 12926. Tel: 518-483-2775 (Rectory); 483-0486 (Parish Office). [CEM]
Catechesis/Religious Programs—Students 320.
Mission—Westville, Franklin Co., Our Lady of Fatima, 12926.

Constableville, Lewis Co., St. Mary (1820), Rev. Paschal Rys, O.F.M.Conv.
Res., P.O. Box 382, 13325. Tel: 315-397-2556. [CEM][JC 2]
Catechesis/Religious Programs—Students 117.

Cooperville, Clinton Co., St. Joseph (1790), Rev. Normand C. Cote.
Res., 74 Mason Rd., Champlain, 12919-9763. Tel: 518-298-8619. [CEM]
Catechesis/Religious Programs—Students 90.

Copenhagen, Lewis Co., St. Mary (1901) (Irish-French), Rev. Charles E. Chase.
Res., High St., P.O. Box 12, 13626. Tel: 315-688-2683. [CEM]
Catechesis/Religious Programs—Students 75.
Mission—New Boston, Lewis Co., SS. Peter and Paul. [CEM]

Croghan, Lewis Co., St. Stephen (1869), Rev. Leo A. Wiley.
Res., Main St., P.O. Box 38, 13327-0038. Tel: 315-346-6958; Fax: 315-346-1200. [CEM]
Catechesis/Religious Programs—Tel: 315-346-6963. Thomas Schneeberger, D.R.E.
Students 309.
Oratories—Belfort, St. Vincent de Paul; New Bremen, St. Peter. [CEM 3]

Crown Point, Essex Co., Sacred Heart Church (1874), Revs. William G. Muench; William G. Reamer; Sr. Leila Spaulding, S.A., Pastoral Assoc.; Deacon Elliott A. Shaw.
Church—12928. Tel: 518-597-3924. [CEM]

Dannemora, Clinton Co., St. Joseph (1853), Rev. John J. Looby; Deacon Edward Mazuchowski. In res., Rev. Peter M. Berg.
Res., 179 Smith St., Box 418, 12929-0418. Tel: 518-492-7118; Fax: 518-492-7742. [CEM 2]
Catechesis/Religious Programs—Tel: 518-492-2524. Lynn Lynch, D.R.E.
Students 222.

Deferiet, Jefferson Co., St. Rita (1900), Revs. Kevin J. O'Brien; Christopher C. Carrara.
Res., 327 West St., Carthage, 13619. Tel: 315-493-3224; Fax: 315-493-3280.

De Kalb Junction, St. Lawrence Co., St. Henry (1893), Rev. Francis J. Coryer.
Res., 3 Josephine St., 13630. Tel: 315-347-3540; Fax: 315-347-4925. [CEM]
Catechesis/Religious Programs—Students 8.
Mission—Russell, St. Lawrence Co., St. Rene Goupil, 24 Pestle St., Russell, 13684.

Edwards, St. Lawrence Co., Sacred Heart (1894), Rev. Francis J. Coryer; Deacon Peter J. Lawless.
Res., P.O. Box 301, De Kalb Junction, 13630. Tel: 315-347-3540; Fax: 315-347-4925.
Catechesis/Religious Programs—Students 10.

Elizabethtown, Essex Co., St. Elizabeth (1881), Rev. Msgr. Francis A. White, V.F.
Res., P.O. Box 368, 12932. Tel: 518-873-6760. [CEM]
Catechesis/Religious Programs—Students 108.

Ellenburg, Clinton Co., St. Edmund, Rev. Gilbert B. Menard; Deacon Larry Debiec.
Res., 12933. Tel: 518-594-3907. [CEM]
Catechesis/Religious Programs—D.R.E.: Marie Trombley; Betty Bulriss.
Students 281.

Essex, Essex Co., St. Joseph, Rev. Bruce T. Favreau.
Res., P.O. Box 607, Willsboro, 12996. Tel: 518-963-4524; Fax: 518-963-7719. [CEM][JC]

Evans Mills, Jefferson Co., St. Mary (1847), Rev. Pierre Aubin, M.S.C.
Res., 8408 S. Main St., P.O. Box 179, 13637. Tel: 315-629-4425; Fax: 315-629-4581. [CEM]
Mission—Theresa, Jefferson Co., St. Theresa of Avila, 318 Main St., Theresa, 13691. Tel: 315-628-4512; Fax: 315-629-4581.

Fort Covington, Franklin Co., St. Mary (1837), Rev. Martin Farrell, O.S.D.
Res., P.O. Box 499, 12937. Tel: 518-358-4471; Fax: 518-358-2500. [CEM 2]
Catechesis/Religious Programs—Tel: 518-358-2500.
Students 115.

Glenfield, Lewis Co., St. Mary (1919), Revs. David Wisniewski; Bernard Jacubco, M.S.C. In res., Rev. Robert L. Cotter.
Res., 5441 Shady Ave., Lowville, 13367. Tel: 315-376-6662; Fax: 315-376-6663. [CEM]
Catechesis/Religious Programs—Students 84.
Mission—Greig, Lewis Co., St. Thomas, (1876). [CEM]

Gouverneur, St. Lawrence Co., St. James (1875), Rev. Vicente Jazmines.
Res., 164 E. Main St., 13642. Tel: 315-287-0114; Fax: 315-287-0114. [CEM 2]
School—(Grades PreK-6) S. Gordon St., 13642. Tel: 315-287-0130. Sr. Ronald Marie Hax, S.S.J., Prin.
Sisters 2; Lay Teachers 7; Students 154.
Catechesis/Religious Programs—Elizabeth Bradford, D.R.E.
Students 181.

Hammond, St. Lawrence Co., St. Peter (1905), Rev. Msgr. Lawrence M. Deno.
Res., P.O. Box 218, 13646. Tel: 315-324-5718; Fax: 315-324-6338.
Catechesis/Religious Programs—Students 80.
Mission—Rossie, St. Lawrence Co., St. Patrick, 13646. [CEM]

Harrisville, Lewis Co., St. Francis Solanus (1879), Rev. Mark Traenkle, S.A.; Deacon Philip Looby.
Res., P.O. Box 208, 13648. Tel: 315-543-2421; Fax: 315-543-7637. [CEM]
Oratory—Lake Bonaparte, St. Rita.

Heuvelton, St. Lawrence Co., St. Raphael's (1880), Rev. Rolland A. Hart.
Res., 5 Clinton St., P.O. Box 377, 13654. Tel: 315-344-2383.
Catechesis/Religious Programs—Students 92.

Hogansburg, Franklin Co., St. Patrick (1834) (Irish), Rev. Msgr. Clarence M. Devan, Admin.
Res., Church St., P.O. Box 427, 13655. Tel: 518-358-2557. [CEM][JC]

Hopkinton, St. Lawrence Co., Church of the Holy Cross, Rev. James A. Delbel.
Res., P.O. Box 288, St. Regis Falls, 12980. Tel: 518-856-9456. [CEM]

Houseville, Lewis Co., St. Hedwig (1922) (Polish), Revs. David Wisniewski; Bernard Jakubco.
Res., St. Peter's Church, 5441 Shady Ave., Lowville, 13367-1615. Tel: 315-376-6662; Fax: 315-376-6663.

Indian Lake, Hamilton Co., St. Mary's (1958), Rev. William G. Reamer, Temp. Admin.
Res., Rte. No. 28, P.O. Box 332, 12842. Tel: 518-648-5422; Fax: 518-648-5422. [CEM]
Catechesis/Religious Programs—Students 52.
Mission—Blue Mountain Lake, Hamilton Co., St. Paul, 12842.

Inlet, Hamilton Co., St. Anthony of Padua (1897), Rev. Lawrence Marullo, V.F.; Deacon Ronald Ste.-Marie.
Mailing Address: P.O. Box 507, 13360. Tel: 315-369-3554.

Keene, Essex Co., St. Brendan (1868), Rev. Alan J. Lamica.
Res., P.O. Box 130, 12942-0130. Tel: 518-576-4434; Fax: 518-576-9318.
Mission—Wilmington, Essex Co., St. Margaret.

Keeseville, Clinton and Essex Cos., Church of the Immaculate Conception (1835) (Irish-French), Rev. Msgr. Joseph Aubin.
Res., 1804 Main St., 12944-3745. Tel: 518-834-7100. [CEM]
Oratory—Clintonville, St. Catherine of Sienna. (Closed).

St. John the Baptist (1853) (French-Irish), Rev. Msgr. Joseph Aubin.
Res., 1804 Main St., 12944-3745. Tel: 518-834-7100. [CEM]
Catechesis/Religious Programs—1806 Main St., 12944-3745. Tel: 518-834-6002.
Students 165.

Lafargeville, Jefferson Co., St. John the Evangelist (1898), Rev. Daniel L. Chapin.
Res., 521 James St., Clayton, 13624. Tel: 315-686-3398.
Church—35923 Rte.180, P.O. Box 157, 13656. Tel: 315-658-2295 (Parish Center). [CEM]

Lake Clear, Franklin Co., St. John in the Wilderness (1887), Revs. Timothy J. Soucy; Mark Raymond Reilly. Pastoral Assocs.: Sr. Cecilia Carey, O.P.; Sr. Ann Marie Conway, O.P.
Mailing Address: P.O. Box 260, 12945. Tel: 518-891-2286.
Res., 19 St. Bernard's St., Saranac Lake, 12983. Tel: 518-891-4616; Fax: 518-891-4619. [CEM][JC]
Catechesis/Religious Programs—Pius X Inter-Parish Religious Education Center, 23 River St., Saranac Lake, 12983. Tel: 518-891-3111.
Students 50.
Mission—Paul Smiths, Franklin Co., St. Gabriel, Pickett Hall #106, Paul Smiths, 12970. Tel: 518-327-6225.
Summer Station—Fish Creek, State Campsite.

Lake Placid, Essex, Co., St. Agnes (1896), Rev. J. Michael Gaffney.
Res., 6 Hillcrest Ave., 12946. Tel: 518-523-2200; Fax: 518-523-2203. [CEM]
School—(Grades PreK-6) 4 Hillcrest Ave., 12946. Tel: 518-523-3771. Gregory F. Camelo, Prin.
Lay Teachers 10; Students 160.
Catechesis/Religious Programs—Tel: 518-523-3998. Mrs. Margaret Malone, D.R.E.
Students 125.

Lake Pleasant, Hamilton Co., St. James, Major (1924), Rev. Paul J. Kelly.
Res., P.O. Box 214, Speculator, 12164. Tel: 518-548-6275.

Lisbon, St. Lawrence Co., SS. Philip and James (1870), Rev. Msgr. William J. Argy; Sr. Joan Marie Casey, R.S.M., Admin. Lay Ministers: Elaine Craig; David Sandburg.
Mailing Address: P.O. Box 175, 13658. Tel: 315-393-3796.
Catechesis/Religious Programs—Students 53.

Long Lake, Hamilton Co., St. Henry (1908), Rev. Robert L. Decker.
Mailing Address: P.O. Box 455, 12847.

Res., 5 Adams Ln., Newcomb, 12852. Tel: 518-624-2541. [JC]

Louisville, St. Lawrence Co., St. Lawrence (1930), Rev. Thomas A. Moody; Sr. Mary Stephen Durant, O.S.M., Pastoral Assoc.
Res., 30 Willard Rd., Massena, 13662. Tel: 315-769-3120. [CEM]
Catechesis/Religious Programs—Tel: 315-764-0488.
Students 220.

Lowville, Lewis Co., St. Peter (1870), Revs. David Wisniewski; Bernard Jakubco, M.S.C.
Res., 5441 Shady Ave., 13367. Tel: 315-376-6662; Fax: 315-376-6663.
School—(Grades PreK-6) 5445 Shady Ave., 13367. Tel: 315-376-2424; Fax: 315-376-2568.
Sisters of St. Joseph 1; Lay Teachers 8.
Catechesis/Religious Programs—Students 142.

Lyon Mountain, Clinton Co., St. Bernard (1875), Rev. Msgr. Bernard E. Christman; Deacons Reginald Merrill; Francis Siskavich.
Res., 10 Church Pond Rd., P.O. Box 23, 12952. Tel: 518-735-4357. [CEM]
Catechesis/Religious Programs—Students 125.
Mission—Standish, Clinton Co., St. Michael. [CEM]

Madrid, St. Lawrence Co., St. John the Baptist (1869), Rev. Thomas A. Moody. In res., Rev. Lawrence E. Cotter.
Church—3715 County Rte. 14, P.O. Box 68, 13660.
Res., 30 Willard Rd., Massena, 13662. Tel: 315-769-3120. [CEM]
Catechesis/Religious Programs—Tel: 315-322-5661.
Students 92.

Malone, Franklin Co., Notre Dame (1868), Rev. Msgr. Dennis J. Duprey; Rev. Thomas E. Kornmeyer; Sr. Maureen Welch, O.S.U., Pastoral Assoc.
Res., 11 Church Pl., P.O. Box 547, 12953. Tel: 518-483-4074; Fax: 518-483-4185. [CEM]
School—Holy Family, (Grades PreK-8). (Multi-Parish). Tel: 518-483-4443; Fax: 518-483-4446. Sr. Jeraldine Fritz, D.C., Prin.
Sisters 6; Lay Teachers 14; Students 278.
Catechesis/Religious Programs—Diane Grant, D.R.E. (Grades K-8 & Confirmation).
Students 200.

St. John Bosco (1935), Rev. Roland V. Menard.
Res., 57 Rennie St., 12953. Tel: 518-483-3642. [CEM]
Catechesis/Religious Programs—Students 181.

St. Joseph's (1837), Rev. F. James Shurtleff; Deacon Richard D. Hart, Pastoral Assoc.
Res., 132 W. Main St., 12953. Tel: 518-483-1300; Fax: 518-483-1300, Ext. 51. [CEM 2]
Catechesis/Religious Programs—Mrs. Tamra Murphy, D.R.E.
Students 219.

Massena, St. Lawrence Co., Sacred Heart (1874), Rev. Msgr. John F. Pendergast; Revs. James M. Larche; Sony George Pulickal, C.M.F. (India); Sr. Juliana Fitzpatrick, O.S.M., Pastoral Assoc.; Deacon James J. Hotte.
Res., 212 Main St., P.O. Box 329, 13662. Tel: 315-769-2469; Fax: 315-769-6973. [CEM]
Catechesis/Religious Programs—Students 356.

St. Joseph, Rev. John L. Downs.
Res., 72 Malby Ave., 13662. Tel: 315-769-3972 (Rectory); 769-9076 (Office); Fax: 315-764-5409. [JC]

St. Mary (1913), Rev. Alan D. Shnob.
Res., 105 Cornell Ave., P.O. Box 609, 13662. Tel: 315-764-0239; Fax: 315-769-5526. [JC]
School—Trinity Catholic School, (Grades PreK-6) 188 Main St., 13662. Tel: 315-769-5911. Sr. Mary Eamon Lyng, S.S.J., Prin.
Sisters of Saint Joseph and Servants of Mary 4; Lay Teachers 14; Students 352.
Catechesis/Religious Programs—D.R.E.: Anne Borsellino, (Grades K-6); Sr. Maureen Sweeney, S.S.J., (Grades 7-12).
Students 206.

Mineville, Essex Co., The Church of All Saints (1872), Rev. Michael A. Toth.
Mailing Address: P.O. Box C, 12956. Tel: 518-942-5953.
Res., 17 St. Patrick's Pl., Port Henry, 12974. Tel: 518-546-7254. [CEM]
Catechesis/Religious Programs—Students 90.

Mooers, Clinton Co., St. Joseph, Rev. Gerald A. Cerank. In res., Rev. Cyril W. Rapin.
Res., 83 Maple St., 12958. Tel: 518-236-7142. [CEM]
Mailing Address: P.O. Box 98, Mooers Forks, 12959. Tel: 518-236-5632.
Catechesis/Religious Programs—Students 110.

Mooers Forks, Clinton Co., St. Ann (1860), Rev. Gerald A. Cerank; Deacon Tyrone A. Rabideau.
Res., 3062 Rte. 11, P.O. Box 98, 12959. Tel: 518-236-5632. [CEM]
Catechesis/Religious Programs—Students 137.

Morrisonville, Clinton Co., St. Alexander (1897), Revs. Stephen H. Gratto; James P. Loughren.
Res., 5 Church St., P.O. Box 159, 12962. Tel: 518-561-5039. [CEM][JC]
School—(Grades PreK-8). Tel: 518-563-5615. Bro. Rolland Gaudette, F.I.C.
Daughters of Charity of the Sacred Heart of Jesus 2; Lay Teachers 10; Students 122.
Catechesis/Religious Programs—Tel: 518-563-7855. Pamela Ballantine, D.R.E.
Students 276.

Morristown, St. Lawrence Co., St. John the Evangelist (1941), Rev. Msgr. Leeward J. Poissant.
Res., P.O. Box 216, 13664. Tel: 315-375-6571.
Catechesis/Religious Programs—Students 115.
Mission—Brier Hill, St. Lawrence Co., Our Lady of Grace, 13664.

Newcomb, Essex Co., St. Therese (1902), Rev. Robert L. Decker.
Res., 5 Adams Ln., 12852. Tel: 518-582-3671. [CEM]

Norfolk, St. Lawrence Co., Visitation of the B.V.M. (1880), Rev. Andrew J. Amyot.
Res., 3 Morris St., P.O. Box 637, 13667. Tel: 315-384-4242. Rev. Msgr. Thomas J. Robillard.; Res., 11 Hepburn St., P.O. Box 505, 13667. Tel: 315-384-3847. [CEM]
Catechesis/Religious Programs—Students 106.

North Bangor, Franklin Co., St. Augustine (1887), Rev. Raymond J. Moreau; Deacon John C. Dwyer.
Res., P.O. Box 327, 12966. Tel: 518-483-6674; Fax: 518-481-6351. [CEM]
Catechesis/Religious Programs—Jean Jacques, D.R.E.
Students 200.
Mission—West Bangor, Franklin Co., St. Edward, 12966.

North Lawrence, St. Lawrence Co., St. Lawrence (1875), Rev. Clark S. White.
Res., P.O. Box 208, Brasher Falls, 13613. Tel: 315-389-5401. [CEM]

Norwood, St. Lawrence Co., St. Andrew (1876), Rev. Paul F. Worczak.
Res., 2 Park Ave., 13668. Tel: 315-353-7303. [CEM]
Catechesis/Religious Programs—Tel: 315-353-2824.
Students 121.

Old Forge, Herkimer Co., St. Bartholomew (1897), Rev. Lawrence Marullo, V.F.
Res., P.O. Box 236, 13420. Tel: 315-369-3554.

Olmstedville, Essex Co., St. Joseph (1871), Rev. Richard S. Sturtz.
Mailing Address: Box 368, Schroon Lake, 12870. Tel: 518-251-2565; 532-7100; Fax: 518-532-7461. [CEM]

Peru, Clinton Co., St. Augustine (1883), Rev. Peter R. Riani.
Res., 3035 Main St., P.O. Box 569, 12972. Tel: 518-643-2435; Fax: 518-643-0960.
School—Tel: 518-643-9505. Sr. Mary Helen Herman, S.S.J., Prin.
Sisters 2; Lay Teachers 7; Students 180.
Catechesis/Religious Programs—Tel: 518-643-0089.
Students 370.
Mission—West Peru, Clinton Co., St. Patrick, 12972. [CEM 2]

Plattsburgh, Clinton Co.,

1—Our Lady of Victory, (1907) (French), Rev. Floyd J. Bleaux, Jr.
Res., 4919 S. Catherine St., 12901. Tel: 518-561-1842; Fax: 518-561-2269. [CEM]
School—Our Lady of Victory Academy, 4917 S. Catherine St., 12901. Tel: 518-563-4262; Fax: 518-562-5403. Lorraine Laframboise, Prin.
Sisters 1; Lay Teachers 9; Students 143.
Catechesis/Religious Programs—Students 130.
Convent—4907 S. Catherine St., 12901. Tel: 518-563-7419. Our Lady of Victory Sr. Bernadette Ducharme, S.C.S.L., Regl. Supr.

2—St. John the Baptist, (1837) (Irish), Rev. Msgr. C. J. McAvoy; Rev. Timothy Canaan. Pastoral Assocs.: Sr. Mary Felicitas Wells, R.S.M.; Sr. Elizabeth Sayah, R.S.M. In res., Rev. John M. Crable.
Res., 7 Margaret St., 12901. Tel: 518-563-0730; Fax: 518-563-0754. [CEM]
School—(Grades PreK-8) 59 Broad St., 12901. Tel: 518-563-2260; Fax: 518-563-4553. John Fairchild, Prin.
Priests 1; Sisters 1; Lay Teachers 25; Students 286.
Catechesis/Religious Programs—Tel: 518-561-6694.
Students 286.

3—St. Joseph, (Treadwells Mill) (1935), Revs. Stephen H. Gratto; James P. Loughren.
Res. & Mailing Address—5 Church St., P.O. Box 159, Morrisonville, 12962. Tel: 518-563-6301.

4—St. Mary of the Lake, (Cumberland Head) (1965), Rev. Danel T. Keefe.
Res., 1202 Cumberland Head Road, P.O. Box 704, 12901. Tel: 518-561-2488; Fax: 518-561-3732. [CEM]
Catechesis/Religious Programs—Eunice Trombly, D.R.E.
Students 100.

5—St. Peter, (1853), Revs. John R. Yonkovig; Christopher J. Fusco; Deacons Robert King; Robert Diehl, Spiritual Life Dir. In res., Rev. Msgr. Morris L. Dwyer; Rev. Joseph A. Conti.
Res., 114 Cornelia St., 12901. Tel: 518-563-1692. [CEM]
School—(Grades PreK-8) St. Charles St., 12901. Tel: 518-561-7132. Mrs. Jean Mockry, Prin.
Sisters 2; Lay Teachers 19; Students 271.
Catechesis/Religious Programs—Tel: 518-563-3278. Sr. Ellen Donahue, S.A., D.R.E.
Students 198.

6—Newman Parish, John XXIII College Community, (1970), Rev. J. Roger McGuinness; Sr. Bernadette Ducharme, S.C.S.L., Pastoral Assoc.; Mrs. Eileen Ward, Admin. Asst.
Res., 90 Broad St., 12901. Tel: 518-563-6852; 561-7545 (Office); Fax: 518-561-1004.

Port Henry, Essex Co., St. Patrick (1854), Rev. Michael A. Toth.
Res., 17 St. Patrick's Pl., 12974. Tel: 518-546-7254; Fax: 518-546-3439. [CEM]
Catechesis/Religious Programs—Tel: 518-546-3374.
Students 195.

Port Leyden, Lewis Co., St. Martin (1879), Rev. Msgr. Paul E. Whitmore.
Res., P.O. Box 431, 13433. Tel: 315-348-6104; Fax: 315-348-6104. [CEM]
Catechesis/Religious Programs—Students 207.
Mission—Lyons Falls, Lewis Co., St. John.

Potsdam, St. Lawrence Co., St. Mary (1841), Revs. John P. Kennehan; Edward E. Papp; Deacon Frederick A. Brousseau. In res., Rev. Francis J. Flynn.
Res., 17 Lawrence Ave., 13676. Tel: 315-265-9680; Fax: 315-268-1443. [CEM]
School—(Grades PreK-6). Tel: 315-265-3511.
Lay Teachers 7; Students 119.
Catechesis/Religious Programs—Tel: 315-265-6220.
Students 230.

St. Francis of Assisi Campus Parish (Newman Center) (1969), Rev. Francis J. Flynn.
Office: 39-41 Main St., 13676-2004. Tel: 315-265-9520; Fax: 315-268-1946.
Catechesis/Religious Programs—Students 57.

Raquette Lake, Hamilton Co., St. William, Rev. Lawrence Marullo, V.F.
Mailing Address: P.O. Box 326, Old Forge, 13360. Tel: 315-369-3551.

Raymondville, St. Lawrence Co., St. Raymond (1920), Rev. J. Everett Denesha.
Res., P.O. Box 178, 13678-0178. Tel: 315-384-3191.

Redford, Clinton Co., Assumption of the B.V.M. (1869), Rev. Philip T. Allen.
Res., 78 Clinton St., 12978. Tel: 518-293-6259. [CEM]
School—(Grades K-6). Tel: 518-293-6231. Mrs. Beth Newell, Prin.
Lay Teachers 6; Students 57.

Redwood, Jefferson Co., St. Francis Xavier (1848), Rev. Thomas F. Driscoll. In res., Rev. James L. Meehan, (Retired).
Mailing Address: P.O. Box 477, Alexandria Bay, 13607. Tel: 315-482-2670.
Res., P.O. Box 903, 13679. Tel: 315-482-6359. [CEM]

Rosiere, Jefferson Co., St. Vincent de Paul (1871), Rev. E. John Silver. In res., Rev. Eugene A. Kelly.
Res., 31385 County Rte. 4, Cape Vincent, 13618. Tel: 315-654-2576. [CEM]

Rouses Point, Clinton Co., St. Patrick (1860), Rev. Wilfred L. DeRoche; Deacon Noel A. Hinerth.
Res., 138 Lake St., P.O. Box 217, 12979. Tel: 518-297-7361. [CEM][JC]
Catechesis/Religious Programs—Tel: 518-297-6945; 297-6387. Patricia Canning, D.R.E.
Students 130.

Sackets Harbor, Jefferson Co., St. Andrew (1886), Rev. Douglas G. Comstock; Deacon Norman Hunneyman.
Res., 110 E. Main St., Box 530, 13685. Tel: 315-646-3341; Fax: 315-646-3341.
Catechesis/Religious Programs—Students 60.
Mission—Henderson, Jefferson Co., Queen of Heaven, 13685.

Saint Regis Falls, Franklin Co., St. Ann, Rev. James A. Delbel.
Res., P.O. Box 288, 12980. Tel: 518-856-9456. [CEM]
Oratory—Santa Clara, St. Peter.

Saranac Lake, Franklin Co., St. Bernard (1888), Revs. Timothy J. Soucy; Mark Raymond Reilly; Sr. Rita Mary Morrissette, O.S.M., Pastoral Assoc.; Deacons Frederick R. Oberst; Joseph Szwed.
Res., 19 St. Bernard St., 12983. Tel: 518-891-4616; Fax: 518-891-4619. [CEM][JC]
School—Tel: 518-891-2830. Rebecca P. Marlowe, Prin.
Lay Teachers 7; Students 165.
Catechesis/Religious Programs—Pius X Center, 32 River St., 12983. Tel: 518-891-3111. Mrs. Kathy Gonyea, D.R.E.
Students 230.

Schroon Lake, Essex Co., Our Lady of Lourdes (1883), Rev. Richard S. Sturtz.
Res., P.O. Box 368, 12870. Tel: 518-532-7100; Fax: 518-532-7461. [CEM]

Sciota, Clinton Co., St. Louis (1899) (French Canadian), Rev. Gilbert O. Boisvert.
Res., P.O. Box 113, Altona, 12910. Tel: 518-236-5848. [CEM]

Star Lake, St. Lawrence Co., St. Hubert (1893), Rev. Eugene J. Beaudet.
Res., 1046 Oswegatchie Trail Rd., P.O. Box 9, 13690. Tel: 315-848-3612. [CEM]
Catechesis/Religious Programs—Students 60.
Missions—Newton Falls, St. Lawrence Co., St. Anthony of Padua, Newton Falls, 13666.; Fine, St. Lawrence Co., St. Michael, Fine, 13635-0008. [CEM]

Ticonderoga, Essex Co., St. Mary (1852), Revs. William G. Muench; William G. Reamer; Sr. Leila Spaulding, S.A., Pastoral Assoc.; Deacon Elliott A. Shaw.
Res., 12 Father Jogues Pl., 12883. Tel: 518-585-7144; Fax: 518-585-3632. [CEM]
School—(Grades K-8) 301 Amherst Ave., 12883. Tel: 518-585-7433; Fax: 518-585-3632. Sr. Sharon Anne Dalton, S.S.J., Prin.; Sr. M. Juliana Raymond, S.S.J., Supr.
Sisters 2; Lay Teachers 7; Students 213.
Catechesis/Religious Programs—Students 150.
Convent—307 Lake George Ave., 12883. Tel: 518-585-6547.

Trout River, Franklin Co., St. Bridget (1865), Rev. Garry B. Giroux; Deacon Garry Burnell.
Res., Maple St., P.O. Box 86, Constable, 12926. Tel: 518-483-2775 (Rectory); 483-0486 (Office). [CEM]

Tupper Lake, Franklin Co., Holy Name of Jesus (Faust) (1904), Rev. Robert M. Shurtleff.
Res., 114 Main St., 12986. Tel: 518-359-9194. [CEM]
Catechesis/Religious Programs—Tel: 518-359-8089. D.R.E.: Mrs. Claire Maroun; Sr. Elizabeth Menard, O.P.
Students 309.

St. Alphonsus, Rev. Donald J. Manfred; Rev. Msgr. Edmund H. Dumas, Pastor Emeritus; Sr. Barbara R. McCarthy, O.P., Pastoral Assoc.; Deacons James T. Ellis; James R. Keough; Gerald H. Savage.
Res., 48 Wawbeek Ave., P.O. Box 1166, 12986. Tel: 518-359-3405. [CEM]
School—Holy Ghost Academy, (Grades PreK-6). Tel: 518-359-2203.
Lay Teachers 7; Students 122.

Waddington, St. Lawrence Co., St. Mary (1826), Rev. Msgr. Robert L. Lawler, P.A., V.G.
Res., P.O. Box 187, 13694. Tel: 315-388-4466; Fax: 315-388-4722. [CEM 3]
Catechesis/Religious Programs—Msgr. Arquett Parish Center, Tel: 315-388-4423.
Students 85.

Watertown, Jefferson Co.,

1—Holy Family, (1895), Revs. Clyde A. Lewis; Albert R. Plante; Scott D. Fobare; Deacons Edward R. Miller; Douglas J. Marlow; Andrew Yarchuk; David F. Moltz; Richard Gaebel.
Res., 129 Winthrop St., 13601. Tel: 315-782-2468; Fax: 315-782-4684.
School—(Grades N-8). Tel: 315-788-7011. Sr. Ellen Rose Coughlin, S.S.J., Prin.
Sisters of St. Joseph 2; Lay Teachers 18; Students 371.
Catechesis/Religious Programs—Holy Family Religious Education Office, Sterling Pl., 13601. Tel: 315-782-6750.
Students 259.

2—Our Lady of the Sacred Heart, Missionaries of the Sacred Heart, (1922), Revs. Mark McDonald, M.S.C.; Benoit C. Dostie, M.S.C.; Richard Huber, M.S.C.; William Connor, M.S.C.; Paul E. Labrosse, M.S.C.; Mark A. Zacker, M.S.C.; Deacon David N. Henningan. In res., Rev. Timothy M. Ladden.
Parish Office: 664 Thompson St., 13601. Tel: 315-782-1474; Fax: 315-782-0473.
Res., 668 Thompson St., 13601. Tel: 315-782-3480; Fax: 315-782-0473. [JC]
School—(Grades K-8) 320 W. Lynde St., Tel: 315-782-3060. Sr. Bernadette Marie Collins, S.S.J., Prin.
Sisters 3; Lay Teachers 12; Students 195.
Preschool and Day Care—Tel: 315-782-3060.
Catechesis/Religious Programs—Beverly A. Hennigan, D.R.E.
Students 150.

3—St. Anthony, (1913) (Italian), Rev. Msgr. Anthony A. Milia, V.F.; Deacons Vincent J. Frattali; Richard C. Warner, Sr. In res., Rev. Steven M. Murray.
Res., 850 Arsenal St., 13601. Tel: 315-782-1190. [JC]
School—(Grades PreK-8). Tel: 315-788-1461; Fax: 315-788-1461. Mrs. Annette M. Connolly, Prin.
Lay Teachers 10; Students 188.
Catechesis/Religious Programs—Students 52.

4—St. Patrick, (1854), Rev. Arthur J. LaBaff; Deacon William G. Schmidt; Sr. Mary William Argy, S.S.J., Pastoral Assoc.
Res., 724 Ives St., 13601. Tel: 315-782-6086; Fax: 315-782-2909. [CEM]
School—(Grades K-8) 733 S. Massey St., 13601. Tel: 315-788-3935; Fax: 315-788-4447. Mrs. Gail Baker-Graham, Prin.
Lay Teachers 10; Students 168.
Catechesis/Religious Programs—Mrs. Dorothy Neamand, D.R.E.
Students 111.

Wells, Hamilton Co., St. Anne, Rev. Paul J. Kelly.
Mailing Address: P.O. Box 214, Speculator, 12164. Tel: 518-548-6275. [CEM]
Catechesis/Religious Programs—Students 8.

West Chazy, Clinton Co., St. Joseph (1884), Rev. Garvin J. Demarais; Deacons Gerald Defayette; Victor Fisher.
Res., P.O. Box 224, 12992. Tel: 518-493-4521. [CEM]
Catechesis/Religious Programs—12992. Tel: 518-493-5222.
Students 296.

West Leyden, Lewis Co., St. Mary's Nativity, Rev. Victor E. Lamore.
Res., P.O. Box 305, 13489. Tel: 315-942-2595. [CEM]
Mission—Fish Creek, SS. Peter & Paul. [CEM]

Westport, Essex Co., St. Philip Neri (1879), Rev. Euclid A. Marier.
Res., 66 Pleasant St., Box M, 12993. Tel: 518-962-8610. [CEM]

Willsboro, Essex Co., St. Philip of Jesus, Rev. Bruce T. Favreau.
Res., P.O. Box 607, 12996. Tel: 518-963-4524; Fax: 518-963-7719. [CEM]
Catechesis/Religious Programs—Students 65.

Witherbee, Essex Co., St. Michael (1911). Closed. For inquiries for parish records contact the Chancery.

Chaplains of Public Institutions

Military and Medical

Ogdensburg. *St. Lawrence Psychiatric Center* St. Vincent's Chapel, 13669. Tel: 315-393-3000. Sr. Kathryn Healey, G.N.S.H., Chap.

Plattsburgh. *Champlain Valley Physicians Hospital Medical Center* 75 Beekman St., 12901. Tel: 518-561-2000. Rev. John M. Crable, Chap.

Tupper Lake, (Sunmount). *Sunmount Developmental Center* 403 Park St., 12986. Deacon Joseph Szwed, Chap.

Watertown. *Samaritan Medical Center* 830 Washington St., 13601. Tel: 315-785-4000. Jean Clark, Chap. and Coord.
U.S. Army Headquarters Fort Drum. Revs. Aloysius M. Rodriguez; James J. Madden.

Prisons

Ogdensburg. *Ogdensburg Correctional Facility* One Correction Way, 13669. Tel: 315-393-0281. Deacon Larry Debiec; Rev. Stephen R. Rocker.
Riverview Correctional Facility Box 158, 13669. Tel: 315-393-8400. Deacon D. Thomas Sharrow; Rev. Joseph A. Morgan.

Altona. *Altona Correctional Facility* P.O. Box 125, 12910. Tel: 518-236-7841; Fax: 518-236-6235. Deacon Victor J. Fisher; Rev. Garvin Demarais.

Cape Vincent. *Cape Vincent Correctional Facility* 13618. Tel: 315-654-4100, Ext. 548. Deacon Thomas F. Kilian; Rev. William Connor, M.S.C.

Dannemora. *Clinton Correctional Facility* P.O. Box 798, 12929-0798. Tel: 518-492-2511, Ext. 301. Deacon Eliseo Melendez; Rev. Peter M. Berg Tel: 518-492-7118.

Gabriels. *Gabriel's Correctional Facility* P.O. Box 100, 12939. Tel: 518-327-3111, Ext. 258. Rev. Joseph P. Trombley, Chap.

Gouverneur. *Gouverneur Correctional Facility* Scotch Settlement Rd., P.O. Box 370, 13642. Tel: 315-287-7351; Fax: 315-287-2533. Deacon Vincent E. Irvin, Jr.; Rev. Rolland A. Hart.

Lyon Mountain. *Lyon Mountain Correctional Facility* P.O. Box 23, 12952. Tel: 518-735-4540. Rev. Msgr. Bernard E. Christman.

Malone. *Barehill Correctional Facility* Cady Rd., 12953. Tel: 518-483-8411, Ext. 409. Deacon John Trombly; Rev. Robert O. Lamitie.
Franklin Correctional Facility P.O. Box 10, 12953-9720. Tel: 518-483-6040, Ext. 2402. Deacon John Trombly; Rev. Bill Edwards.

Moriah. *Moriah Shock Incarceration Correctional Facility.* Fisher Hill Rd., P.O. Box 999, Mineville, 12956-0999. Tel: 518-942-7561. Rev. Euclid A. Marier.

Ray Brook. *Adirondack Correctional Facility* Box 110, 12977-0110. Tel: 518-891-1343. Rev. Peter P. Mullen, M.M., Res., Star Rte., Box 152, Saranac Lake, 12983. Tel: 518-891-6540, 891-1343.
Federal Correctional Institution P.O. Box 300, 12977. Tel: 518-891-5400. Deacon Fred Mader; Rev. Peter P. Mullen, M.M.

Watertown. *Watertown Correctional Facility* 13601. Tel: 315-782-7490, Ext. 445. Rev. William Connor, M.S.C., Chap., Res., Missionaries of the Sacred Heart, 666 Thompson St., 13601. Tel: 315-782-3480.

Special Assignment:
Reverend Fathers—
Wertman, Raymond, Credo Foundation, 138 Winthrop St., Watertown, NY 13601

On Duty Outside the Diocese:
Reverend Fathers—
Ledermann, Paul F., Veterans Home, P.O. Box 7, Yountville, CA 94599
Leehy, Stephen G., 9 San Camille Ct., St. Charles, MO 63303
Lucia, Douglas J., North American College, Casa Santa Maria dell' Umilta, Via dell' Umilta 30, 00187 Rome, Italy
Mundy, Patrick W., San Martin De Porres, Casilla 105, Mollendo, Peru S.A.
O'Neil, Maurice L., 505 N. La Canada Dr., Green Valley, AZ 85614
Sestito, Joseph N., 114 Stanwood Ln., Manlius, NY 13104
Seymour, James W., San Martin De Porres, Casilla 105, Mollendo, Peru, S.A.

Military Chaplains:
Reverend Fathers—
Demers, Richard D., U.S. Air Force, 31 Sharon Dr., Edwards AFB, CA 03523
Mulvaney, Andrew R., Chap., U.S. Army, CMR 430, Box 1301, 221 BSB, APO AE, 09096
Ratigan, Patrick A., Chap. U.S. Army, 7445 Van Noy Loop, Fort Meade, MD 20755
Sykes, Gregory, Chap., U.S. Army, 148 Cullum Rd., West Point, NY 10996

Absent on Leave:
Reverend Fathers—
Andrews, Lawrence W.
Donoghue, Kelly C.
Schudde, Derk M.

Absent on Sick Leave:
Reverend Fathers—
Fallon, John, The Towers, 401b, 5400 Montgomery, Albuquerque, NM 87109
Franklin, Edward L., Clearview Mobile Home, 12220 5th St., S.P. 105, Yucaipa, CA 92399
Gonyo, Roland G.
Votraw, Thomas G., St. Mary's Cathedral, 415 Hamilton St., Ogdensburg, NY 13669

Retired:
Reverend Monsignors—
Argy, William, St. Mary's Cathedral Rectory, Ogdensburg, NY 13669. Tel: 315-393-3930
Bailey, Joseph G., R.D. 169 Butler Rd., Hammond, NY 13646
Berube, Louis D., 613 Green St., Ogdensburg, NY 13669
Devan, Clarence M., St. Patrick's Church, P.O. Box 307, Hogansburg, NY 13655
Dumas, Edmund H., 48 Wawbeek Ave., Tupper Lake, NY 12986
Dwyer, Morris L., St. Peter's Rectory, Plattsburgh, NY
Gefell, Gerard J., 2332 Humphrey Rd., Cape Vincent, NY 13618. Tel: 315-654-3504
Gefell, Joseph G., 2332 Humphrey Rd., Cape Vincent, NY 13618. Tel: 315-654-3504

Giroux, Robert J., Notre Dame Rectory, 125 Ford Ave., P.O. Box 149, Ogdensburg, NY 13669. Tel: 315-393-5050
Hannan, Herbert J., St. Patrick's Church, Brasher Falls, NY 13613
McCarthy, Robert J., 324 Pratt St., Watertown, NY 13601
Phillips, George M., P.O. Box 10, Jemez Springs, NM 87026
Robillard, Thomas J., 11 Hepburn St., Norfolk, NY 13667
Stinebrickner, David W., St. Joseph's Home, 420 Lafayette St., Ogdensburg, NY 13669

Reverend Fathers—
Beyette, Paul V., HC Box 218, Loon Lake, N.Y. 12989
Branche, John S., Two Fordham Hill Oval, #10C, Bronx, NY 10468
Callaghan, Patrick, O.F.M., Spruce St., St. Regis Falls, NY 12980. Tel: 518-856-9729
Canning, John W., P.O. Box 712, Parishville, NY 13672
Coffey, William H., 109 Ten Eyck St., Watertown, NY 13601. Tel: 315-788-1394
Cotter, Charles B., Genesis Healthcare Center, Watertown, NY 13601
Cotter, Lawrence E., 3715 County Rte. 14, P.O. Box 68, Madrid, NY 13660
Cotter, Robert L., St. Mary Rectory, Glenfield, NY 13343
Igo, James P., 10 Daniels St., Arlington, MA 02174
Jarecki, Michael S., R.R. 1, Box 25B, Constable, NY 12926
Jollet, Robert, M.S.C., Wadhams Hall Seminary, 6866 State Hwy. 37, Ogdensburg, NY 13669
Kelly, Eugene A., St. Vincent De Paul Rosiere, 31385 County Route 4, Cape Vincent, NY 13618
Labrosse, Paul E., M.S.C., 668 Thompson St., Watertown, NY 13601
Ladden, Timothy M., 668 Thompson St., Watertown, NY 13601
LaLonde, Emile G., P.O. Box 1193, LeHigh Acres, FL 33970
Lamitie, James F., 4062 70th Ct., Riviera Beach, FL 53404
Lyddy, Daniel F., 31 Sydney St., Lowell, MA 01852. Tel: 508-459-9448
Marier, Euclid A., St. Philip Neri Church, 66 Pleasant St., Box M, Westport, NY 12993
Martin, Roger, 54 W. Main St., P.O. Box 25, Baltic, CT 06330
McCasland, Howard, Immaculate Heart of Mary, Rt. 189, Churubusco, NY 12923
Meehan, James L., St. Francis Xavier, Redwood
Menard, Francis A., 6862 E. Main St. Rd., Rte. #1, Box 35, Malone, NY 12953
Nichols, Earl W., 32 Church St., Apt. 15, Brasher Falls, NY 13613
Njeim, Elias, Colonial Manor, Apt. 9, Watertown, NY 13601
Patterson, Terrence R., Mailing Address: Box 288, Potsdam, NY 13676. Tel: 315-265-2986
Plante, Albert R., 129 Winthrop St., Watertown, NY 13601
Poupore, Norman E., P.O. Box 824, Pierrepont Manor, NY 13674
Rapin, Cyril W., St. Joseph's Church, P.O. Box 288, Mooers, NY 12958-0288
Richard, Charles J., Mater Dei College, 5428 State Hwy. 37, Ogdensburg, NY 13669
Snow, J. Lee, 1631 Palmland Dr., Boynton Beach, FL 33436

Permanent Deacons:
Barton, Floyd, St. Patrick, Brasher Falls
Brousseau, Frederick A., St. Mary, Potsdam
Burnell, Garry N., St. Francis of Assisi, Constable
Debiec, Larry, St. Edmund, Ellenburg
Defayette, Gerald R., St. Joseph, West Chazy
Demers, Victor, Notre Dame, Ogdensburg
Diehl, Robert, St. Peter, Plattsburgh
Dwyer, John C., St. Augustine, N. Bangor
Ellis, James T., St. Alphonsus, Tupper Lake
Fisher, Victor J., St. Joseph, West Chazy
Frank, Gary A., St. Mary, Clayton
Frattali, Vincent J., St. Anthony, Watertown
Gaebel, Richard M., Holy Family, Watertown
Gilbert, Joseph H., Holy Name, Ausable Forks
Gilner, Gerard, St. Mary, Indian Lake
Hart, Richard D., St. Joseph, Malone
Hennigan, David N., Our Lady of the Sacred Heart, Watertown
Hinerth, Noel A., St. Patrick, Rouses Point
Horan, Francis W., St. Patrick, Brasher Falls
Hotte, James J., Sacred Heart, Massena
Hunneyman, Norman L., St. Andrew, Sackets Harbor
Irvin, Vincent E., Jr., Correctional Facility, Gouverneur
Keough, James R., St. Alphonsus, Tupper Lake
Kilian, Thomas F., Cape Vincent Correctional Facility, Cape Vincent
King, Robert A., St. Peter, Plattsburgh
Lawless, Peter J., Sacred Heart, Edwards
LeClair, Robert J., Sacred Heart, Chazy
Looby, Phillip M., St. Francis, Solanus, Harrisville
Mader, Frederick J., St. Paul, Bloomingdale
Marlow, Douglas, Holy Family, Watertown
Mazuchowski, Edward, St. Joseph, Dannemora
Melendez, Eliseo, Clinton Correctional Facility
Merrill, Reginald F., St. Bernard, Lyon Mountain
Miller, Edward R., Holy Family, Watertown
Moltz, David, Holy Family, Watertown
Oberst, Frederick R., St. Bernard, Saranac Lake
Patrie, Leonard L., St. Mary, Champlain
Rabideau, Tyrone, St. Ann, Mooers Forks
Raven, William S., St. Paul, Black River
Savage, Gerald H., St. Alphonsus, Tupper Lake
Schmidt, William G., St. Patrick, Watertown
Sharrow, Thomas, St. Mary's Cathedral, Ogdensburg
Shaw, Elliott A., St. Mary's, Ticonderoga
Siskavich, Francis, St. Bernard, Lyon Mountain
Staab, Richard J., St. James, Carthage
Ste. - Marie, Ronald, St. Anthony, Inlet
Szwed, Joseph, St. Bernard, Saranac Lake
Taylor, William M., St. Mary's Cathedral, Ogdensburg
Trombly, John J., Franklin Correctional Facility, Malone
Warner, Richard C., Sr., St. Anthony, Watertown
Winter, Richard E., St. Mary's Cathedral, Ogdensburg
Yarchuk, Andrew, Holy Family, Watertown

INSTITUTIONS LOCATED IN THE DIOCESE

[A] SEMINARIES, DIOCESAN

OGDENSBURG. *Wadhams Hall*, 6866 State Hwy. 37, 13669-4420. Tel: 315-393-4231; 393-3596 (Student); Fax: 315-393-4249.
E-mail: whsc@gisco.net
Open to candidates for the Diocesan and religious priesthood (and Christian Leadership Program). Four-year College and two-year Pre-Theology Program. Rev. Msgr. Robert H. Aucoin, S.T.L., M.Ed., Rector-Pres., Chm. & Asst. Prof. Languages; Rev. Donald Robinson, M.A., Vice Pres., Chm. & Prof. Social Science, Dir. Health, Dir. of Admissions, Asst., Prof. of History; Rev. Msgr. Joseph G. Bailey, M.A., Prof. Religious Studies; Rev. Msgr. Leeward J. Poissant, Ph.D., Prof. Philosophy; Revs. Albert J. Hauser, S.T.L., M.A., Asst. Prof. Latin, Religious Studies; George F. Maroun, B.A., Dir. Spiritual Formation, Asst. Prof. Religious Studies & Spanish, Dir. Social J; Edward J. Sheedy, M.A., M.S., Asst. Prof. Religious Studies; Stephen R. Rocker, Ph.D., Chm. & Prof. Philosophy, Dean of Students; Bro. Guy Roddy, F.I.C., B.A., M.A., M.S., D.Min., Chm. of Religious Studies, Dir. Special Prog., Assoc. Prof. of Social Sciences; Rev. Robert Jollet, M.S.C., M.S.L.S., Dir Library; Sr. Mary Christine Taylor, Ph.D., Academic Dean & Prof. Social Sciences; Mr. Donald K. Fellows, M.M., Chair Fine Arts, Asst. Professor Music, Dir. Liturgical Music; Mrs. Diana C. Krisciunas, M.A., Chair. & Asst. Prof. English; Sr. Constance Sylver, M.M.Ed., Instructor, Developmental Studies; Mrs. Nancy C. Orologio, B.S., Dir. Finance; Mrs. Jeanne Becker, M.A., Instructor, French; Mrs. Beth O. Reynolds, M.S., Visiting Prof. Mathematics; Rev. Msgr. Lawrence M. Deno, Ph.D., Prof., Education. Priests 10; Brothers 1; Sisters 2; Lay Teachers 5; Total Staff 18. Students 24.

[B] COLLEGES AND UNIVERSITIES

OGDENSBURG. *Mater Dei College*, 5428 State Hwy. 37, 13669. Tel: 315-393-5930; Fax: 315-393-5056
For a complete listing, refer to the Colleges and Universities section.

[C] HIGH SCHOOLS, INTERPAROCHIAL

PLATTSBURGH. *Seton Catholic Central*, 5135 N. Catherine St., 12901. Tel: 518-561-4031; Fax: 518-563-1193. Dr. Philip R. Fusco, Ed.D., Prin.; Rev. Joseph A. Conti, Chap. Priests 1; Sisters 2; Brothers 3; Lay Teachers 23; Students 344.

WATERTOWN. *Immaculate Heart Central High School*, 1316 Ives St., 13601. Tel: 315-788-4670.
E-mail: ihc@gisco.net
Web site: www.gisco.net/ihc
Mr. Pat A. Fontana, Prin.; Rev. Steven Murray, Spiritual Dir. Priests 1; Sisters 5; Lay Teachers 15; Students 313.

[D] RELIGIOUS EDUCATION

OGDENSBURG. *Bishop Conroy School of Religion*, 214 Morris St., 13669-1714.

SARANAC LAKE. *Pius X Center*, 32 River St., 12983.

WATERTOWN. *Watertown Catechetical Office*, Sterling Pl., 13601. Tel: 315-782-0030. Special Religious Education. Sr. Mary Maurice Black, S.S.J., Coord.

[E] SPECIAL HOSPITALS AND HOMES FOR INVALIDS AND AGED

OGDENSBURG. *St. Joseph's Home*, 420 Lafayette St., 13669. Tel: 315-393-3780; Fax: 315-393-3847
For a complete listing, refer to the Special Care Facilities section.

LAKE PLACID. *St. Margaret Convent*, 420 Old Military Rd., 12946. Tel: 518-523-2929; Fax: 518-523-1401
For a complete listing, refer to the Special Care Facilities section.

Uihlein Mercy Center, 420 Old Military Rd., 12946. Tel: 518-523-2464; Fax: 518-523-1401
For a complete listing, refer to the Special Care Facilities section.

SARANAC LAKE. *St. Joseph's Rehabilitation Center, Inc.*, 99 Glenwood Estates, P.O. Box 470, 12983. Tel: 518-891-3950; 891-4135 (Admissions); Fax: 518-891-3986.
E-mail: stjoes@northnet.org
For a complete listing, refer to the Special Care Facilities section.

TUPPER LAKE. *Mercy Healthcare Center, Inc.*, 114 Wawbeek Ave., 12986. Tel: 518-359-3355; Fax: 518-359-9044
For a complete listing, refer to the Special Care Facilities section.

[F] MONASTERIES AND RESIDENCES OF PRIESTS AND BROTHERS

SARANAC LAKE. *Atonement Friars*, 69 Franklin Ave., 12983. Tel: 518-891-2395. Revs. Daniel P. Callahan, S.A.; Arthur M. Johnson, S.A. Total in Residence 2.

St. Joseph's Friary, P.O. Box 470, 12983. Tel: 518-891-3494. Bros. Alan Lemay, S.A.; Paschal Steen, T.S.A. Total in Residence 2.

[G] CONVENTS AND RESIDENCES FOR SISTERS

OGDENSBURG. *Mater Dei College, Sisters of St. Joseph*, 5428 State Hwy. 37, 13669. Tel: 315-393-5930. Sr. Mary Patrick Murphy, S.S.J., Supr.

St. Joseph's Convent, Grey Nuns of the Sacred Heart, 709 Franklin St., 13669. Tel: 315-393-1763. Sr. Joan McElwain, G.N.S.H., Supr.

CARTHAGE. *St. James Convent, Sisters of St. Joseph*, 317 West St., 13619. Tel: 315-493-1672. Sr. Victorine Brenon, S.S.J., Supr. Total Staff 3; Total in Residence 3.

CHAMPLAIN. *St. Mary's Convent*, 1060 Rte. 9, 12919. Tel: 518-298-3141.

CHASM FALLS. *St. Helen's, Sisters of St. Joseph*, R.D. 1, P.O. Box 311, 12953. Tel: 518-483-1515.

CLAYTON. *Sisters of Holy Cross*, 38289 Rte. 12 E., 13624. Tel: 315-686-3640. Sr. Margaret Fleming, C.S.C. Sisters 2.

ELLENBURG CENTER. *Our Lady of the Adirondack's Inc. House of Prayer, Franciscan Sisters of the Atonement*, 7270 Star Rd., Rte. 190, 12934-9708. Tel: 518-594-3253. Sr. Jean T. Beyette, S.A., Dir. Our Lady of Adirondacks Community. Rita S. Parrott, O.L.A.; Theresa M. Lindsey, O.L.A.; Rev. Joseph P. Trombley, Spiritual Dir.

GOUVERNEUR. *St. James' Convent, Sisters of St. Joseph*, 28 S. Gordon St., 13642. Tel: 315-287-0658. Sr. Jane Frances Cutting, S.S.J., Supr. Total Staff 2; Total in Residence 2.

KEESEVILLE. *St. Stanislaus Convent*, 1808 Main St., Rte. 22, 12944. Tel: 518-834-9312. Sisters of Mercy of the Americas, Regional Community of Vermont. Sr. Patricia Murtagh, R.S.M.

LOWVILLE. *St. Peter's Convent, Sisters of St. Joseph*, 5445 Shady Ave., 13367. Tel: 315-376-6362. Sr. Judy Adams, S.S.J.

MALONE. *Daughters of Charity*, 27 Webster St., 12953. Tel: 518-483-1203. Sr. Helen Kelley, D.C.; Sr. Jeraldine Fritz, D.C.

St. Joseph's Ursuline Convent, Ursuline Nuns, 90 Elm St., 12953. Tel: 518-483-2880; Fax: 518-483-7091. Sr. Ann Peterson, O.S.U., Supr. Sisters 13.

Ursuline Community, Ursuline Nuns, 104 Park St., 12953. Tel: 518-483-5356.
E-mail: mtwosu@juno.com
Sr. Maureen Welch, O.S.U., Coord.

MASSENA. *Sacred Heart Convent*, 188 Main St., P.O. Box 91, 13662. Tel: 315-769-6238. Total in Residence 3.

St. Joseph's Convent, Sisters of St. Joseph, 36 Alden St., 13662. Tel: 315-764-0379. Sr. Mary Eamon Lyng, S.S.J.; Sr. Mary Christine Taylor, S.S.J.; Sr. Maureen Sweeney, S.S.J. Total in Residence 3.

PERU. *St. Augustine's Convent, Sisters of St. Joseph (SSJ)*, 3012 N. Main St., Box 567, 12972. Tel: 518-643-6768. Total in Residence 2.

PLATTSBURGH. *Franciscan Sisters of the Atonement*, 5209 N. Catherine St., 12901. Tel: 518-563-8893. Sr. Rita LaPoint, S.A.

Regina Maria Retreat House, Daughters of the Heart of Mary, 77 Brinkerhoff St., 12901. Tel: 518-561-3421. Mary Curran, D.H.M.

St. John's Convent, 62 Court St., 12901. Tel: 518-561-9689; Fax: 518-563-0754. Sisters of Mercy 2.

St. Louis Community, Sisters of Charity of St. Louis, 4907 S. Catherine St., 12901. Tel: 518-563-7410; 563-0383 (Office); Fax: 518-563-0383.

St. Peter's Convent, Dominican Sisters of Hope, 5240 N. Catherine, 12901. Tel: 518-563-4451. Sr. Mary Stephanie Frenette, O.P., Contact Person. Total in Residence 2.

SARANAC LAKE. *St. Bernard's Convent, Servants of Mary-Omaha*, 30 River St., 12983. Tel: 518-891-4363. Sr. Rita Marie Morrissette, O.S.M.

St. Joseph's Carmelite Monastery, Discalced Carmelite Nuns, 68 Franklin Ave., 12983. Tel: 518-891-0655. Sr. Marie Gertrude Haughney, O.C.D., Prioress; Rev. Peter G. Helfrich, Chap.

Sisters of Mercy of the Americas, Rte. 1, Box 351, 12983. Tel: 518-891-3234. Sr. Carolyn Madden, R.S.M.

TICONDEROGA. *St. Mary's Convent, Sisters of St. Joseph*, 307 Lake George Ave., 12883. Tel: 518-585-6547. Sr. Sharon Anne Dalton, S.S.J., Co-Supr.; Sr. M. Juliana Raymond, S.S.J., Co-Supr. Total Staff 2; Total in Residence 2.

TUPPER LAKE. *Dominican Sisters of Hope, Ossining*, 37 Lake St., 12986. Tel: 518-359-9632. Sr. Barbara McCarthy, O.P.; Sr. Elizabeth Menard, O.P. Total in Residence 2.

Holy Spirit Convent, 48 High St., 12986. Tel: 518-359-3838. Sr. Gertrude DeMars, D.H.S.; Sr. Alice Carron, D.H.S. Daughters of the Holy Spirit 2.

WATERTOWN. *Grey Nuns of the Sacred Heart*, 502 Dimmick St., Rear Apt., 13601-3911. Tel: 315-788-2548. Sr. Kathleen E. Hannan, G.N.S.H., Psychotherapy.

Precious Blood Monastery, Sister Adorers of the Prescious Blood, 400 Pratt St., 13601. Tel: 315-788-1669. Sr. Martha Emery, A.P.B., Supr. Total Staff 8; Total in Residence 8.

Sisters of Mercy, Watertown, NY, 251 Stone St., 13601-3252. Tel: 315-788-2232. Sr. Rose Curtin, R.S.M., Coord., Additional Address: Villa Catherine, Chaumont, 13622. Tel: 315-649-2983. Sisters 4.

Sisters of St. Joseph Motherhouse, 1425 Washington St., 13601. Tel: 315-782-3460. Sr. M. Damien Quenville, S.S.J., Supr.; Sr. Annunciata, S.S.J., Major Supr. Total Staff 15; Total in Residence 39.

[H] RETREAT HOUSES

PLATTSBURGH. *Regina Maria Retreat House*, 77 Brinkerhoff St., 12901. Tel: 518-561-3421. Mary A.E. Curran, D.H.M. Daughters of the Heart of Mary 3.

[I] INCORPORATED CEMETERIES

BRASHER FALLS. *St. Patrick's Cemetery Association of Brasher Falls, N.Y.*, 13613.

CARTHAGE. *St. James Cemetery Corporation*, 13619.

CROGHAN. *St. Stephen's Cemetery Association, Inc.*, 13327.

MALONE. *Notre Dame Cemetery of Malone, N.Y., Inc.*, 12953.

St. Joseph's Cemetery of Malone, N.Y., Inc., 12953.

PLATTSBURGH. *Mount Carmel Cemetery*, St. John the Baptist Church, 7 Margaret St., 12901.

WATERTOWN. *Calvary Cemetery Association of Watertown, N.Y.*, Sacred Heart Church, 664 Thompson, 13601.

[J] MISCELLANEOUS LISTINGS

OGDENSBURG. *St. Joseph's Foundation, Inc.*, 420 Lafayette St., 13669.

HOGANSBURG. *St. Regis Mission* (Akwesasne), Box 429, 13655. Tel: 613-575-2066. Reservation and parish on both sides of U.S.-Canadian border. Rev. George H. Belgarde, Admin. Priests 1; Brothers 1.

Roman Catholic Community Center, Inc. (Kateri Tekakwitha Center). Miss Debra Wilcox, Religious Education Coord. Tel: 518-358-2931.

PLATTSBURGH. *Christ Child Day Nursery*, 5115 N. Catherine, 12901. Tel: 518-561-6451. Mrs. Nancy Fournier, Dir. Total Staff 5; Total Assisted 26.

SARANAC LAKE. *Guggenheim Center for Religious Programs*, P.O. Box 664, 12983. Tel: 518-891-0809; 891-3323 (Dorm). Mr. Ralph Bennett, Dir., Res., 15 Leona St., 12983. Tel: 518-891-2844.

WATERTOWN. *Mission Project Service*, 662 Thompson St., 13601. Tel: 315-782-2382.
E-mail: misprojser@aol.com
Beverly Hennigan, Exec. Dir.; Rev. Pierre Aubin, M.S.C., Dir.

Sacred Heart Foundation, 668 Thompson St., 13601. Tel: 315-782-3480. Rev. Pierre Aubin, M.S.C., Dir.

RELIGIOUS INSTITUTES OF MEN REPRESENTED IN THE DIOCESE

For further details refer to the corresponding bracketed number in the Religious Institutes of Men or Women section.

[0320]—*Brothers of Christian Instruction*. (Alfred, ME).—F.I.C.
[1350]—*Brothers of St. Francis Xavier*.—C.F.X.
[0360]—*Claretian Missionaries*.—C.M.F.
[0520]—*Franciscan Friars*.—O.F.M.
[0530]—*Franciscan Friars of the Atonement*.—S.A.
[0690]—*Jesuit Fathers and Brothers*. (French Canadian Prov. of Montreal).—S.J.
[1110]—*Missionaries of the Sacred Heart*.—M.S.C.

RELIGIOUS INSTITUTES OF WOMEN REPRESENTED IN THE DIOCESE

[0760]—*Daughters of Charity of St. Vincent de Paul*.—D.C.
[0750]—*Daughters of the Charity of the Sacred Heart of Jesus*.—F.C.S.C.J.
[0810]—*Daughters of the Heart of Mary*.—D.H.M.
[0820]—*Daughters of the Holy Spirit*.—D.H.S.
[0420]—*Discalced Carmelite Nuns*.—O.C.D.
[1070-03]—*Dominican Sisters*.—O.P.
[1070-22]—*Dominican Sisters*.—O.P.
[1105]—*Dominican Sisters of Hope*.—O.P.
[1190]—*Franciscan Sisters of the Atonement*.—S.A.
[1840]—*Grey Nuns of the Sacred Heart*.—G.N.S.H.
[2575]—*Institute of the Sisters of Mercy of the Americas*. (Burlington, VT; Providence, RI; New York, NY).—R.S.M.
[3590]—*Servants of Mary*. (Servite Sisters).—O.S.M.
[3340]—*Sister of Providence*.—S.P.
[0110]—*Sisters Adorers of the Precious Blood*.—A.P.B.
[0620]—*Sisters of Charity of St. Louis*.—S.C.S.L.
[1930]—*Sisters of Holy Cross*.—C.S.C.
[1800]—*Sisters of St. Francis of the Third Order Regular*.—O.S.F.
[3840]—*Sisters of St. Joseph of Carondelet*.—C.S.J.
[3830-12]—*Sisters of St. Joseph of Watertown*.—S.S.J.
[4110]—*Ursuline Nuns*.—O.S.U.

NECROLOGY

✠ Brzana, Most Rev. Stanislaus J., (Retired). —Died March 1, 1997.
† Boyea, Ivan G., Watertown, NY, St. Patrick. —Died Oct. 31, 1996.
† Coseo, Rev. Msgr. Francis G., (Retired). —Died Feb. 5, 1997.
† Flattery, James M., (Retired). —Died Aug. 9, 1997.
† Pease, Anthony F., Combermere, Ontario, Madonna House. —Died Jan. 8, 1997.
† Salmon, Albert G., Brushton, NY, St. Mary's. —Died Aug. 21, 1997.

Archdiocese of Oklahoma City

(Archidioecesis Oklahomapolitana)

Most Reverend

EUSEBIUS J. BELTRAN, D.D.

Archbishop of Oklahoma City; ordained May 14, 1960; appointed Bishop of Tulsa February 28, 1978; installed April 20, 1978; appointed Archbishop of Oklahoma City November 24, 1992; installed January 22, 1993. *Res., P.O. Box 32180, Oklahoma City, OK, 73123.*

Most Reverend

CHARLES A. SALATKA, D.D.

Retired Archbishop of Oklahoma City; ordained February 24, 1945; appointed Titular Bishop of Cariana and Auxiliary of Grand Rapids December 9, 1961; consecrated March 6, 1962; appointed Bishop of Marquette January 10, 1968; installed March 25, 1968; appointed Archbishop of Oklahoma City September 27, 1977; installed December 15, 1977; retired November 24, 1992. *Res., P.O. Box 32180, Oklahoma City, OK, 73123.*

Pastoral Office: 7501 Northwest Expy., P.O. Box 32180, Oklahoma City, OK, 73123. Tel.: 405-721-5651; Fax: 405-721-5210.

ESTABLISHED FEBRUARY 6, 1973.

ERECTED INTO A VICARIATE APOSTOLIC BY BRIEF OF MAY 29, 1891. ERECTED INTO THE DIOCESE OF OKLAHOMA WITH THE SEE IN OKLAHOMA CITY BY A BRIEF OF POPE PIUS X, AUGUST 17, 1905. NAME CHANGED TO DIOCESE OF OKLAHOMA CITY AND TULSA BY BULL OF POPE PIUS XI, NOVEMBER 14, 1930. ERECTED INTO ARCHDIOCESE OF OKLAHOMA CITY BY A BULL OF POPE PAUL VI, DECEMBER 13, 1972. THE PROVINCE INCLUDES THE DIOCESES OF TULSA AND LITTLE ROCK.

Comprises the following 46 Counties: Alfalfa, Beaver, Beckham, Blaine, Caddo, Canadian, Carter, Cimarron, Cleveland, Comanche, Cotton, Custer, Dewey, Ellis, Garfield, Garvin, Grady, Grant, Greer, Harmon, Harper, Jackson, Jefferson, Johnston, Kay, Kingfisher, Kiowa, Lincoln, Logan, Love, McClain, Major, Marshall, Murray, Noble, Oklahoma, Pontotoc, Pottawatomie, Roger Mills, Seminole, Stephens, Texas, Tillman, Washita, Woods and Woodward.

Square Miles 42,470.

For legal titles of parishes and archdiocesan institutions, consult the Pastoral Office.

STATISTICAL OVERVIEW

Personnel	
Archbishop	1
Retired Archbishops	1
Abbots	1
Retired Abbots	3
Priests: Diocesan Active in Diocese	70
Priests: Active Outside Diocese	5
Priests: Diocesan in Foreign Missions	1
Priests: Retired, Sick or Absent	17
Number of Diocesan Priests	93
Religious Priests in Diocese	24
Extern Priests in Diocese	7
Ordinations:	
Diocesan Priests	2
Permanent Deacons in Diocese	48
Total Brothers	10
Total Sisters	151
Parishes	
Parishes	75
With Resident Pastor:	
Resident Diocesan Priests	60
Resident Religious Priests	12
Without Resident Pastor:	
Administered by Priests	3
Missions	46
Pastoral Centers	1
Closed Parishes	1
Professional Ministry Personnel:	
Sisters	23
Lay Ministers	71
Welfare	
Catholic Hospitals	6
Total Assisted	617,440
Homes for the Aged	5
Total Assisted	333
Day Care and Extended Day Care Centers	2
Total Assisted	374
Special Centers for Social Services	1
Total Assisted	668
Residential Care of Disabled	1
Total Assisted	25
Educational	
Diocesan Students in Other Seminaries	9
Total Seminarians	9
Colleges and Universities	1
Total Students	600
High Schools, Diocesan and Parish	1
Total Students	706
High Schools, Private	1
Total Students	250
Elementary Schools, Diocesan and Parish	18
Total Students	3,540
Elementary Schools, Private	1
Total Students	285
Catechesis/Religious Education:	
High School Students	2,765
Elementary Students	8,762
Total Students Under Catholic Instruction	16,917
Teachers in the Diocese:	
Priests	2
Sisters	12
Lay Teachers	241
Vital Statistics	
Receptions into the Church:	
Infant Baptism Totals	2,174
Adult Baptism Totals	386
Received into Full Communion	572
First Communions	1,826
Confirmations	1,188
Marriages:	
Catholic	406
Interfaith	356
Total Marriages	762
Deaths	828
Total Catholic Population	93,262
Total Population	2,029,229

Former Bishops—Rt. Rev. THEOPHILE MEERSCHAERT, D.D., ord. Dec. 23, 1871; appt. first Vicar-Apostolic of Indian Territory and Titular Bishop of Sidyma by Bulls of June 2, 1891; cons. in Natchez, Sept. 8, 1891; appt. first Bishop of Oklahoma, Aug. 23, 1905 made assistant at the pontifical throne, Nov. 30, 1916; died Feb. 21, 1924.—Most Rev. FRANCIS C. KELLEY, D.D., LL.D., Ph.D., Litt.D., Bishop of Oklahoma City & Tulsa; ord. Aug. 24, 1893; appt. Bishop of Oklahoma, June 25, 1924; cons. Holy Name Cathedral, Chicago, IL, Oct. 2, 1924; died Feb. 1, 1948.—Most Rev. EUGENE J. MCGUINNESS, D.D., Bishop of Oklahoma City & Tulsa; ord. May 22, 1915; cons. Bishop of Raleigh, Dec. 21, 1937; appt. Coadjutor, Oklahoma City and Tulsa *"cum jure successionis,"* Nov. 11, 1944; installed Jan. 10, 1945; succeeded to the See, Feb. 1, 1948; died Dec. 27, 1957.—Most Rev. VICTOR J. REED, D.D., Bishop of Oklahoma City & Tulsa; ord. Dec. 21, 1929; cons. March 5, 1958; died Sept. 8, 1971.—Most Rev. JOHN R. QUINN, D.D., ord. July 19, 1953; appt. Auxiliary Bishop of San Diego and Titular Bishop of Thisiduo, Oct. 21, 1967 Episcopal ordination, Dec. 12, 1967; translated to Oklahoma City and Tulsa, Nov. 18, 1971; appt. as Archbishop of the Archdiocese of Oklahoma City, Dec. 13, 1972; installed as Archbishop of Oklahoma City, Feb. 6, 1973; transferred to Archbishop of San Francisco, April 26, 1977.

Vicars General—Revs. JAMES A. KASTNER, V.G.; EDWARD J. WEISENBURGER, V.G.

Regional Vicars Region I—Vacant, *3901 S.W. 29th. St., Oklahoma City, 73119. Region II,* Rev. LOWELL STIEFERMAN, *7336 W. Britton Rd., Oklahoma City, 73132. Region III,* Rev. JOHN VRANA, *125 E St. S.W., Ardmore, 73401. Region IV,* Rev. JAMES D.M. STAFFORD, *P.O. Box 2546, Lawton, 73502. Region V,* Rev. THOMAS O'TOOLE, *P.O. Box 864, Elk City, 73648. Region VI,* Rev. EDWARD MENASCO, *P.O. Box 708, Woodward, 73802. Region VII,* Rev. JAMES J. MICKUS, *P.O. Box 3527, Enid, 73702. Region VIII,* Rev. JOHN MICHALICKA, *P.O. Box 1330, Ponca City, 74602. Region IX,* Rev. PHILIP DONOHOE, *208 S. Evans, El Reno, 73036.*

Pastoral Office—7501 Northwest Expy., P.O. Box 32180, Oklahoma City, 73123. Tel: 405-721-5651; Fax: 405-721-5210. Office Hours: Mon.-Fri. 8:30-4:30.

Chancellor—Rev. JOHN A. STEICHEN.

Vicar for Ministries—Rev. ANTHONY B. TAYLOR.

Spiritual Direction for Priests—Rev. DAVID M. LAFFERTY, Coord.

Archdiocesan Tribunal—7501 Northwest Expy., P.O. Box 32180, Oklahoma City, 73123. Tel: 405-721-5651.

Judicial Vicar—Rev. CHARLES H. SCHETTLER, S.T.L., J.C.D.

Assistant Judicial Vicar—Rev. EDWARD WEISENBURGER, V.G., M.A., J.C.L.

Pro-Synodal Judge—Revs. JOHN A. PETUSKEY, M.A.; EDWARD WEISENBURGER, V.G., M.A., J.C.L.; Mr. GEORGE RIGAZZI, J.C.L.

Defenders of the Bond—Revs. LOWELL STIEFERMAN; ALAN J. LOTH; JOHN W. FEEHILY.

Advocates—Rev. EDWARD MENASCO; Mrs. MONA CROSS; Mrs. WANDA J. LANE; Mrs. SUSAN LINDLEY.

Notaries—Mrs. MONA CROSS; Mrs. HELEN L. SELLERS; Mrs. TONI NICHOLLS.

Interdiocesan Tribunal of Second Instance for the Province of Oklahoma City—P.O. Box 32180, Oklahoma City, 73123. Tel: 405-721-5651.

Judicial Vicar—Rev. ROBERTO QUANT, J.C.L.

Judges—Revs. JAMES A. KASTNER, V.G.; GERARD A. MACAULAY.

Defenders of the Bond—Revs. PHILIP M. DONOHOE; ELMER C. SCHWARZ.

Consultors Archdiocesan—Revs. THOMAS BOYER; JAMES A. KASTNER, V.G.; BRUCE NATSUHARA; JOSEPH R. ROSS; JOHN A. STEICHEN; EDWARD J. WEISENBURGER, V.G.

Council of Priests Archdiocesan—Rev. JOSEPH R. ROSS, Chm., *P.O. Box 20508, Oklahoma City, 73156.* Revs. THOMAS BOYER; MICHAEL CHAPMAN; JAMES A. KASTNER, V.G.; EDWARD MENASCO; DAVID F. MONAHAN; BRUCE NATSUHARA; WILLIAM B. ROSS; JOACHIM SPEXARTH, O.S.B.; JOHN A. STEICHEN; ANTHONY B. TAYLOR; EDWARD J. WEISENBURGER, V.G.

Health Panel, Archdiocesan—Rev. WILLIAM B. ROSS, Chm., *P.O. Box 1280, Purcell, 73080.* Tel: 405-527-3077.

Personnel Committee—Revs. RAY ACKERMAN; JAMES A. KASTNER, V.G.; WILLIAM B. ROSS; LOWELL STIEFERMAN.

Archdiocesan Offices and Directors

Office of Stewardship and Development—Mr. JAMES A. WEINMANN, Dir., *P.O. Box 32180, Oklahoma City, 73123.* Tel: 405-721-5651.

Archdiocesan Development Fund—formerly *Diocesan Development Fund;* also formerly known as *Diocesan Fund, Bishop's Fund for Diocesan Development;* Mr. JAMES A. WEINMANN, Dir., *7501 N.W. Expy., P.O. Box 32180, Oklahoma City, 73123.* Tel: 405-721-5651.

Planning Commission Archdiocesan—P.O. Box 32180, Oklahoma City, 73123.

Archdiocese of Oklahoma City Educational Trust Fund—Sr. CATHERINE POWERS, C.N.D., Dir., *7501 N.W. Expy., P.O. Box 32180, Oklahoma City, 73123.*

Associated Catholic Charities—Mr. TIMOTHY O'CONNOR, Dir., *1501 N. Classen Blvd., Oklahoma City, 73106.* Tel: 405-523-3000; Fax: 405-523-3030.

Archdiocesan Finance Council—Most Rev. EUSEBIUS J. BELTRAN, D.D.; Revs. JOHN A. STEICHEN; THOMAS O'TOOLE; ANTHONY B. TAYLOR; Deacon DALE NEIKIRK; WILLIAM BEAVERS; Mr. ANTHONY KNAPSTEIN; Mrs. SUSAN LOOSEN; Mr. MICHAEL MILLIGAN; Mrs. JENNIFER HOANG PHAM; Mr. HUGH D. RICE; Mr. MICHAEL R. STERKEL; Mr. DAVID JOHNSON, Business Mgr., *Business Office: P.O. Box 32180, Oklahoma City, 73123.* Tel: 405-721-5651.

Building Committee—Mr. DAVID JOHNSON, *P.O. Box 32180, Oklahoma City, 73123.* Tel: 405-721-5651.

Catholic Foundation of Oklahoma, Inc.—Mr. DAVID JOHNSON, Sec./Treas.; Mr. JAMES A. WEINMANN, Dir., Devel., *7501 Northwest Expy., P.O. Box 32180, Oklahoma City, 73123.* Tel: 405-721-5651.

Catholic Lawyers Guild—Rev. RAYMOND K. ACKERMAN, Spiritual Moderator, *2801 South Shartel, Oklahoma City, 73108.* Tel: 405-631-8865.

Catholic Social Services—1501 N. Classen Blvd., Oklahoma City, 73106. Tel: 405-523-3000; Fax: 405-523-3030.

Charismatic Renewal—Rev. MARVIN F. LEVEN, Episcopal Moderator, *P.O. Box 7948, Lawton, 73506.* Tel: 580-536-6351.

Communications, Archdiocesan Department of—Ms. JEANNE DEVLIN, Dir., *P.O. Box 32180, Oklahoma City, 73123.* Tel: 405-721-1810; 721-5651.

Correction Related Ministry—Rev. MARK MASON, *21 N. Cherokee, Hennessey, 73742.* Tel: 405-853-4425; Fax: 405-853-2166.

Council of Catholic Women, Archdiocesan—Rev. JOSEPH C. KOLB; Mrs. LEONARD KOOS, *1313 S. Midwest Blvd., Midwest City, 73110.*

Ecumenical and Interreligious Affairs, Office for Archdiocesan Dir.—Rev. JOHN A. PETUSKEY, *P.O. Box 510, Edmond, 73083.* Tel: 405-340-0691.

Education—Sr. CATHERINE POWERS, C.N.D., Archdiocesan Dir., *P.O. Box 32180, Oklahoma City, 73123.* Tel: 405-721-4202; 721-5651.

Catholic Schools, Office of—Sr. CATHERINE POWERS, C.N.D., Supt.; Sr. MARIA YECK, R.S.M., Assoc. Supt., *P.O. Box 32180, Oklahoma City, 73123.* Tel: 405-721-4202; 721-5651.

Religious Education, Office of—Mrs. D'ESTA VERDICCHIO, Dir. MARCO OCANA, Assoc. Dir., Hispanic Religious Education, *P.O. Box 32180, Oklahoma City, 73123.* Tel: 405-721-1415; 721-5651.

Pastoral Ministry Office—Mrs. SHEILA MUELLER, Dir., *P.O. Box 32180, Oklahoma City, 73123.* Tel: 405-721-1415; 721-5651. Affiliated with Kansas Newman College, Wichita, KS, and Aquinas Institute, St. Louis, MO.

Campus Ministry, Department of—Rev. C. JOSEPH MEINHART, *100 E. Stinson, Norman, 73072.* Tel: 405-321-0990.

Clergy Education, Department of—Rev. JAMES A. KASTNER, V.G., Dir., *P.O. Box 32180, Oklahoma City, 73123.* Tel: 405-721-5651.

Evangelization, Office of—Miss JOAN DARK, Dir., *P.O. Box 32180, Oklahoma City, 73123.* Tel: 405-728-3561; 721-5651, Ext. 150.

Family Life Department—Mr. NICK BAGILEO, *P.O. Box 32180, Oklahoma City, 73123.* Tel: 405-721-8943; 721-5651.

Indian Ministries, Inc.—(Oklahoma), Rev. MICHAEL WHEELAHAN, Liaison, *P.O. Box 628, Anadarko, 73005.* Tel: 405-247-5255.

Justice and Human Development, Commission for—Mrs. SHIRLEY COX, *1501 N. Classen Blvd., Oklahoma City, 73106.* Tel: 405-532-3000.

Legal Counsel—Mr. JACK R. LAWRENCE, *3030 Northwest Expy., Oklahoma City, 73112.* Tel: 405-948-6000.

Master of Ceremonies—Revs. ROBERT WOOD; TIMOTHY FULLER, Asst.

Millennium Committee—Rev. PAUL GALLATIN, *5024 North Grove, Oklahoma City, 73122.* Tel: 405-789-2595.

Ministry to Priests Program—Rev. ANTHONY B. TAYLOR, Dir., *P.O. Box 32180, Oklahoma City, 73123.* Tel: 405-721-5651.

Mission "Micatokla"—Archdiocesan Mission of Satiago Atitlan, Guatemala—Rev. JOHN A. STEICHEN, Archdiocesan Coord., *P.O. Box 32180, Oklahoma City, 73123.* Tel: 405-721-5651; Fax: 405-721-5210.

Newspaper—"The Sooner Catholic"; Ms. JEANNE DEVLIN, Editor, *P.O. Box 32180, Oklahoma City, 73123.* Tel: 405-721-1810; 721-5651.

Permanent Diaconate—Rev. C. JOSEPH MEINHART, Dir., *P.O. Box 32180, Oklahoma City, 73123.* Tel: 405-721-5651. Deacon JAMES YOUNG, Asst. to the Dir.

Priests' Medical Fund—formerly known as *Infirmed Priest Fund;* Rev. JOHN A. STEICHEN, *P.O. Box 32180, Oklahoma City, 73123.* Tel: 405-721-5651.

Priests' Retirement Board—Most Rev. EUSEBIUS J. BELTRAN, D.D.; Revs. JOHN A. PETUSKEY; JOHN A. STEICHEN; ANTHONY B. TAYLOR, Chm., *Pastoral Office, P.O. Box 32180, Oklahoma City, 73123.* Tel: 405-721-5651.

Propagation of the Faith, Holy Childhood Assoc., Missionary Cooperation Plan—Rev. JOHN A. STEICHEN, *P.O. Box 32180, Oklahoma City, 73123.* Tel: 405-721-5651.

Rural Life—Rev. JAMES GREINER, Dir., *1100 N. Sara Road, P.O. Box 246, Mustang, 73064.* Tel: 405-376-9435.

Scouting—Rev. MICHAEL WHEELAHAN, *P.O. Box 628, Anadarko, 73005.* Tel: 405-247-5255.

St. Ann's Retirement Village—Mrs. JOY ECKER, Dir. Admin., *9400 St. Ann Dr., Oklahoma City, 73162.* Tel: 405-728-7888.

St. Francis de Sales Seminary (Legal Title)—Most Rev. EUSEBIUS J. BELTRAN, D.D., Pres.; Rev. JOHN A. STEICHEN, Sec. Trustees: Rev. DAVID F. MONAHAN; Mr. DAVID JOHNSON, Treas., *P.O. Box 32180, Oklahoma City, 73123.*

St. Vincent dePaul, Society of Oklahoma City District Council—Rev. JOHN A. PETUSKEY, Spiritual Moderator, *P.O. Box 510, Edmond, 73083.* Tel: 405-340-0691.

Vocations and Seminarians—Rev. JOHN METZINGER, Dir., *Archdiocesan Pastoral Center, P.O. Box 32180, Oklahoma City, 73123.* Tel: 405-721-9351; 721-5651.

Worship and Spiritual Life, Office of—Rev. STEPHEN BIRD, Dir.; Sr. JOANNE YANKAUSKIS, O.S.B., Co-Dir., *P.O. Box 32180, Oklahoma City, 73123.* Tel: 405-721-5651.

Youth and Young Adult Ministry, Office of—Mrs. NANCY HOUSH, Dir.; Miss BECKY JANKA, Assoc. Dir., *P.O. Box 32180, Oklahoma City, 73123.* Tel: 405-721-9220; 721-5651.

CLERGY, PARISHES, MISSIONS AND PAROCHIAL SCHOOLS

OKLAHOMA CITY
(Oklahoma County)

1—CATHEDRAL OF OUR LADY OF PERPETUAL HELP, Revs. Thomas J. Boyer, Rector; Hoa Nguyen. In res., Revs. Ray Ackerman; Paul Mollan.
Res., 3214 N. Lake Ave., 73118. Tel: 405-525-2349; Fax: 405-525-3628. [JC]
School—Bishop John Carroll, 1100 N.W. 32, 73118. Tel: 405-525-0956; Fax: 405-523-3053.
Lay Teachers 13; Students 166.

2—ST. ANDREW DUNG-LAC (Vietnamese), Rev. Dominic Hung Hoang; Deacon San Nguyen.
Church—2337 N.W. 19th St., 73107. Tel: 405-528-2537; 528-4986; Fax: 405-524-0893.
Mailing Address: P.O. Box 75875, 73107.

3—ST. CHARLES BORROMEO, Revs. Paul H. Gallatin; William Novak; Deacons John Pitt; Marc LeWand; Walter Cullinan.
Res., 5024 N. Grove St., 73122. Tel: 405-789-2595; Fax: 405-789-4394. [JC]
School—5000 N. Grove St., 73122. Tel: 405-789-0224; Fax: 405-789-6292.
Lay Teachers 17; Students 259.

4—CHRIST THE KING, Revs. Joseph R. Ross; James A. Kastner, V.G.; Deacon David Best.
Res., 8005 Dorset Dr., P.O. Box 20508, 73156. Tel: 405-842-1481; Fax: 405-843-0539. [JC]
School—Tel: 405-843-3909; Fax: 504-843-6519. Leslie Bloomer, Prin.
Lay Teachers 17; Students 262.

5—CORPUS CHRISTI, Rev. Larok Obwano Martin (Uganda); Deacon James Barton.
Res., 1005 N.E. 15th St., 73117. Tel: 405-236-4301; Fax: 405-235-0032. [JC]
School—Tel: 405-232-4811.
Lay Teachers 9; Students 110.

6—CHURCH OF THE EPIPHANY OF THE LORD, Rev. Lowell L. Stieferman.
Res., 7336 W. Britton Rd., 73132. Tel: 405-722-2110; Fax: 405-722-6719.

7—ST. EUGENE'S, Rev. Bill Pruett; Deacon Patrick Reynolds.
Res., 2400 W. Hefner Rd., P.O. Box 20930, 73156. Tel: 405-751-7115; Fax: 405-751-8722. [JC]
School—Tel: 405-751-0067.
Lay Teachers 35; Students 320.

8—ST. FRANCIS OF ASSISI, Rev. Thomas R. Dowdell; Deacon Roland Benoit. In res., Rev. Charles H. Schettler.
Res., 1901 N.W. 18th St., P.O. Box 60569, 73146. Tel: 405-528-0485; Fax: 405-524-1260. [JC]
School—Rosary, 1910 N.W. 19th St., 73106. Tel: 405-525-9272. Mrs. Beverly Warden, Prin.
Sisters 1; Lay Teachers 14; Students 253.

9—ST. PAUL, APOSTLE, Rev. Kenneth E. Kulinski; Deacon Philip LePage; Rev. Mary Joseph Choo, (Korean Chap.).
Res., 3901 S. Sunnylane Rd., Del. City, 73115. Tel: 405-677-4873; Fax: 405-619-0596. [JC]
Mission—Del City, Korean Roman Catholic Community, 3405 S. Wofford, 73115.

10—HOLY ANGELS (1924), Rev. Roberto Quant; Deacon Lucio Nieto.
Res., 317 N. Blackwelder St., 73106. Tel: 405-232-6572; Fax: 405-235-8334. [JC]
Convent—1522 N.W. Third St., 73106. Tel: 405-236-3407. Carmelite Missionaries of St. Teresa

11—IMMACULATE CONCEPTION, Rev. A. Gerard MacAulay; Deacon Agustin Hernandez.
Res., 3901 S.W. 29th St., 73119. Tel: 405-685-4224; Fax: 405-685-4483. [CEM]

12—ST. JAMES, Revs. Larry B. Gatlin; James A. Goins; Deacons Otis Davis; Marti Gulikers.
Res., 4308 S. Blackwelder St., 73119. Tel: 405-636-6800; Fax: 405-636-6848.
School—1224 S.W. 41st St., 73109. Tel: 405-636-6810; Fax: 405-636-6818.
Sisters 2; Lay Teachers 17; Students 246.
Convent—4212 S. Blackwelder, 73119. Tel: 405-636-6830. Sisters of Charity of Leavenworth

13—ST. JOSEPH. (Old Cathedral). Rev. Louis J. Lamb.
Church—301 N.W. 4th St., 73102. Fax: 405-815-6644.
Res., 307 N.W. 4th St., 73102. Tel: 405-235-4565. [JC]

14—OUR LADY OF MOUNT CARMEL AND ST. THERESE LITTLE FLOWER, Revs. Jenaro De La Cruz, O.C.D.; Ruben Garcia.
Res., 1125 S. Walker Ave., Box 26127, 73126. Tel: 405-235-2037; Fax: 405-235-7023. [JC]
Mission—Packing Town, Oklahoma Co., Our Lady of Guadalupe, 2123 S.W. 11th St., Packing Town, 73108.

15—ST. PATRICK, Rev. Stephen J. Bird. In res., Rev. Donald C. Moore.
Res., 2121 N. Portland, P.O. Box 75835, 73147. Tel: 405-947-2275; 946-4441; Fax: 405-942-4894.

16—ST. PHILIP NERI (Midwest City), Rev. Robert T. Wood; Deacons Matthew Browne; James G. Young.
Res., 301 Wilson Dr., Midwest City, 73110. Tel: 405-739-0456; Fax: 405-732-7823. [JC]
School—1121 Felix Pl., 73110. Tel: 405-737-4496; Fax: 405-732-7823.
Lay Teachers 18; Students 286.

17—Sacred Heart, Revs. Timothy D. Luschen; Thomas W. Darnall; Deacons George Leal; Michael Rockey.
Res., 2706 S. Shartel Ave., 73109. Tel: 405-634-2458; Fax: 405-634-2459. [JC]
School—2700 S. Shartel Ave., 73109. Tel: 405-634-5673. Mrs. Rosemary Kerber, Prin.
Lay Teachers 11; Students 182.

OUTSIDE OKLAHOMA CITY

Ada, Pontotoc Co., St. Joseph, Rev. George J. Pupius; Deacon Michael Radosevich.
Res., 1300 E. Beverly St., P.O. Box 1585, 74821. Tel: 580-332-4811; Fax: 580-436-1226.

Altus, Jackson Co., Prince of Peace, Rev. Joseph A. Jacobi.
Res., 1500 Falcon Rd., P.O. Box 894, 73522. Tel: 405-482-3363; Fax: 580-482-3367.
Mission—Hollis, Harmon Co., Our Lady of Guadalupe, P.O. Box 107, Hollis, 73550. Tel: 580-688-2233.

Alva, Woods Co., Sacred Heart, Rev. David B. Imming.
Res., 627 12th St., 73717. Tel: 580-327-0339; Fax: 580-327-0710.
Mission—Waynoka, Woods Co., Our Mother of Mercy, 210 South Main St., Waynoka, 73860.

Anadarko, Caddo Co., St. Patrick's, Rev. Michael Wheelahan.
Res., 1115 W. Petree Rd., Box 628, 73005. Tel: 405-247-5255; Fax: 405-247-5410.
Missions—Binger, Binger Co., Our Lady of the Most Holy Rosary, Hwy. 152, Binger, 73009.; Carnegie, Caddo Co., St. Richard, Hwy. 9, Carnegie, 73015.

Ardmore, Carter Co., St. Mary, Revs. John P. Vrana; Juan Manuel Guerrero.
Res., 125 E St. S.W., 73401. Tel: 580-223-0231; Fax: 580-226-2129. [CEM]
Missions—Healdton, Carter Co., St. Cecilia, 300 E. Lincoln Ave., Healdton, 73438.; Marietta, Love Co., Good Shepherd, Broadway & N. 7th, Marietta, 73448.

Bison, Garfield Co., St. Joseph's, Rev. Alan J. Loth.
Res., Box 117, 73720. Tel: 580-758-3558; Fax: 580-758-1219. [CEM]
Mission—Fairview, Major Co., St. Ann, 6th & Locust, Fairview, 73737. Tel: 580-229-2270.

Blackwell, Kay Co., St. Joseph's, Rev. Joseph W. Burger.
Res., 315 W. Blackwell Ave., P.O. Box 578, 74631. Tel: 580-363-2096; Fax: 580-363-2096.

Calumet, Canadian Co., Immaculate Heart of Mary, Rev. Omar Tabing.
Mailing Address: P.O. Box 99, 73014.
Church—239 Freehoma, 73014. Tel: 405-893-2336; Fax: 405-893-2715.

Chandler, Lincoln Co., Our Lady of Sorrows, Rev. David M. Lafferty.
Res., 409 Price Ave., P.O. Box 543, 74834. Tel: 405-258-1239; Fax: 405-258-1259. [CEM]
Mission—Stroud, Lincoln Co., St. Louis, Hwy. 99 & Eighth Ave., Stroud, 74079.

Cherokee, Alfalfa Co., St. Cornelius, Rev. David B. Imming; Deacon Gary Means.
Res., 404 S. Massachusetts, P.O. Box 197, 73728. Tel: 580-596-3228. [CEM]

Chickasha, Grady Co., Holy Name, Rev. Elmer C. Schwarz.
Res., 210 S. Seventh St., Box 748, 73023. Tel: 405-224-7513; Fax: 405-224-4434. [CEM]

Clinton, Custer Co., St. Mary's, Rev. Michael R. Vaught.
Res., 714 S. 12th St., 73601. Tel: 580-323-0309; Fax: 580-323-0345.
Mission—Cordell, Washita Co., St. Anne, 522 E. Third, Cordell, 73632.

Duncan, Stephens Co., Assumption, Revs. James F. Rapp, O.S.F.S.; Marc J. Clifford, O.S.F.S.; Charles A. LaPenta, O.S.F.S.; Deacon Bernard T. O'Loughlin.
Res., 711 Hickory Ave., 73533. Tel: 580-255-0590; Fax: 580-255-0590. [CEM]
Missions—Marlow, Stephens Co., Immaculate Conception, Fourth & Comanche, Marlow, 73055.; Rush Springs, Grady Co., St. Francis of Assisi, Fifth & Choctaw, Rush Springs, 73082.; Ryan, Jefferson Co., San Jose, 1117 Lincoln Ave., Ryan, 73565. Tel: 580-757-2830.

Edmond, Oklahoma Co., St. John the Baptist, Revs. John A. Petuskey; Kevin J. Ratterman; Deacons Bill Bawden; Bill Coyle.
Res., 900 S. Littler St., P.O. Box 510, 73083. Tel: 405-340-0691; Fax: 405-340-5715.
School—St. Elizabeth Ann Seton School, 925 South Blvd., 73083. Tel: 405-348-5364; Fax: 405-340-9627.
Lay Teachers 23; Students 450.
St. Monica, Revs. Anthony B. Taylor; Carlos Castillo (Costa Rica).
Mailing Address: 2001 North Western, 73003. Tel: 405-359-2700; Fax: 405-341-0023.
Res., 1121 N.W. 199th St., 73003. Tel: 405-330-2699. [CEM]

Elgin, Comanche Co., St. Ann, Rev. Peter Ashurst.
Res., 910 Eighth Street, P.O. Box 10, 73538. Tel: 580-492-5914; Fax: 580-492-5908.
Missions—Sterling, Comanche Co., Our Lady of Perpetual Help, 220 N. A Street, Sterling, 73567.; Apache, Caddo Co., Mother of Sorrows, 521 E. Wallace, Elgin, 73006.

Elk City, Beckham Co., St. Matthew's, Rev. Thomas L. O'Toole.
Mailing Address: 3001 E. Hwy. 6, P.O. Box 864, 73648.
Res., 121 Merritt Rd., 73648. Tel: 580-225-0066;225-0000; Fax: 580-225-3522. [CEM]
Mission—Sayre, Beckham Co., Queen of All Saints, 914 N. 5th St., Sayre, 73662. Tel: 580-928-5124.

El Reno, Canadian Co., Sacred Heart, Rev. Philip M. Donohoe.
Res., 208 S. Evans St., 73036. Tel: 405-262-1405; Fax: 405-262-2251. [CEM]
School—Sacred Heart School, 210 S. Evans, 73036. Tel: 405-262-2284. Mrs. Lois Jeffrey, Prin.
Teachers 5; Students 64.

Enid, Garfield Co., St. Francis Xavier, Rev. James J. Mickus; Deacon Anthony Crispo.
Res., 110 N. Madison, Box 3527, 73702. Tel: 580-237-0812; Fax: 580-237-0909. [JC]
St. Gregory the Great, Rev. Lawrence T. Kowalski.
Church—1924 W. Willow, 73703. Tel: 580-233-4589; Fax: 580-233-4590.
Res., 2045 Lantern Ln., 73703. Tel: 580-233-1845.
Mission—Goltry, Alfalfa Co., St. Michael, Main St., Goltry, 73739. [CEM]

Frederick, Tillman Co., St. Helen, Rev. Carl W. Janocha.
Res., 507 E. Highview Ave., Rte. No. 2, 73542. Tel: 580-335-3298; Fax: 580-335-3953.
Mission—Tipton, Tillman Co., Sacred Heart, 300 Frederick St., Tipton, 73570.

Guthrie, Logan Co., St. Mary's, Rev. Denis G. Hanrahan; Deacons Roy Ellison; Richard Washko.
Res., 411 N. Elm St., 73044. Tel: 405-282-4239; Fax: 405-282-5610. [CEM]
School—Lay Teachers 6; Students 84.
Mission—Crescent, Logan Co., St. Margaret Mary, P.O. Box 632, Crescent, 73028. Tel: 405-969-2351.

Guymon, Texas Co., St. Peter's, Revs. Charles R. Murphy; Scott Adams; Deacons Joe Cruz; Simon Guerra.
Res., 1220 N. Quinn St., P.O. Box 731, 73942. Tel: 580-338-7212; Fax: 580-338-5584. [CEM]
Missions—Hooker, Texas Co., Sacred Heart, 106 N. Albright, Hooker, 73945.; Boise City, Cimarron Co., Good Shepherd, S. Ellis at Second, Boise City, 73933.

Harrah, Oklahoma Co., St. Teresa of Avila, Rev. James Murphy, O.S.B.
Res., 1576 Tim Holt Dr., Box 418, 73045. Tel: 405-454-2819; Fax: 405-454-0981. [CEM]

Hennessey, Kingfisher Co., St. Joseph's, Rev. Mark E. Mason.
Res., 211 N. Cherokee St., 73742. Tel: 405-853-4425; Fax: 405-853-2166. [CEM]
Mission—Marshall, Logan Co., St. Camillus, Main St., Marshall, 73056.

Hitchcock, Blaine Co., Sacred Heart Mission. Closed. For inquiries for parish records contact the Chancery.

Jones, Oklahoma Co., St. Robert Bellarmine, Rev. Gary W. Kayler, Admin.
Church—First at Atlanta, P.O. Box 280, 73049. Tel: 405-321-8495.
Mission—Luther, Oklahoma Co., Saint Theresa of the Infant Jesus, Ash & Third, P.O. Box 358, Luther, 73054.

Kingfisher, Kingfisher Co., SS. Peter and Paul, Rev. David H. True.
Res., 309 S. Main St., 73750. Tel: 405-375-4581; Fax: 405-375-3858. [CEM]
School—Tel: 405-375-4616.
Carmelite Sisters 1; Lay Teachers 6; Students 98.
Mission—Watonga, Blaine Co., St. Rose of Lima, 900 N. Clarence Nash, Watonga, 73772.

Konawa, Pottawatomie Co., Sacred Heart, Rev. Matthew J. Brown, O.S.B.
Res., Rte. 1, Box 101, 74849. Tel: 580-925-2145; Fax: 580-925-2145. [CEM]
Missions—Wanette, Pottawatomie Co., St. Mary; Wewoka, Seminole Co., St. Joseph.

Lawton, Comanche Co., Blessed Sacrament, Rev. James D.M. Stafford; Deacon Bill Adamson.
Res., 12 S.W. Seventh St., Box 2546, 73502. Tel: 580-355-2054; Fax: 580-355-2055.
School—St. Mary's, 611 A Ave., 73501. Tel: 405-355-5888.
Sisters of Divine Providence 5; Lay Teachers 13; Students 189.
Holy Family. (Formerly St. Barbara). Rev. Marvin F. Leven; Deacons Herman Lawrence; Leo Martinez, Jr.
Res., 1010 N.W. 82nd St., P.O. Box 7948, 73506. Tel: 580-536-6351; Fax: 580-536-6352.

Loyal, Kingfisher Co., St. Joseph Mission. Closed. For inquiries for parish records contact the Chancery.

Mangum, Greer Co., Sacred Heart, Rev. Joseph C. Kolb; Deacon Pedro Maldonado.
Res., 501 N. Byers, P.O. Box 310, 73554. Tel: 580-782-2657; Fax: 580-782-2457.
Mission—Hobart, Kiowa Co., Sts. Peter & Paul, 324 S. Randlett, P.O. Box 371, Hobart, 73651. Tel: 580-726-3925. [CEM]

McLoud, Pottowatomie Co., St. Vincent de Paul, Rev. Eugene C. Marshall, O.S.B.
Res., 122 S. 10th St., P.O. Box 585, 74851. Tel: 405-964-5606 (Res.); 878-5452; Fax: 405-878-5189.

Medford, Grant Co., St. Mary's, Rev. Michael Hughes.
Res., 214 W. Cherokee, Box 360, 73759. Tel: 580-395-2148. [CEM]
Missions—Wakita, Grant Co., St. Mary's Assumption, Main & Birch, Wakita, 73771.; Pond Creek, Grant Co., St. Joseph's, S. Hwy. 81, Pond Creek, 73766.

Moore, Cleveland Co., St. Andrew's, Rev. John W. Feehily; Deacons Angus Watford; James L. Keene.
Res., 800 N.W. Fifth, Box 6261, 73153. Tel: 405-799-3334; Fax: 405-799-4951.

Mustang, Canadian Co., Church of the Holy Spirit, Rev. James A. Greiner.
Church—1100 N. Sara Rd., P.O. Box 246, 73064. Tel: 405-376-9435; 376-5218; Fax: 405-376-4929.

Newkirk, Kay Co., St. Francis of Assisi, Rev. Richard J. Beckman.
Res., 610 W. Ninth St., P.O. Box 11, 74647. Tel: 580-362-3320; Fax: 580-362-3320.

Nicoma Park, Oklahoma Co., Our Lady of Fatima, Rev. Wilbur E. Moore.
Res., 2255 W. Meyer Cir., Box 368, 73066. Tel: 405-769-2490; Fax: 405-769-9113.

Norman, Cleveland Co., St. Joseph's, Revs. Ernest A. Flusche; Matthew Price Oswalt; Deacon Larry Sousa.
Res., 425 E. Tonhawa, 73071. Tel: 405-321-8080; Fax: 405-321-4360. [CEM]
Church of St. Mark the Evangelist, Rev. John Metzinger.
Mailing Address: P.O. Box 722217, 73070. Tel: 405-366-7676.
Res., 3701 Castlerock Rd., 73072. Tel: 405-447-3085; Fax: 405-447-0480.
Church—3939 W. Tecumseh Rd., 73070.
St. Thomas More University Parish, Rev. C. Joseph Meinhart; Deacons John Warren; James Knight.
Church—100 E. Stinson, 73072. Tel: 405-321-0990; Fax: 405-321-0964.
Res., 1501 Lincoln, 73072. Tel: 405-329-5319.

Okarche, Kingfisher Co., Holy Trinity, Rev. Edward J. Weisenburger.
Res., 211 W. Missouri, Box 185, 73762. Tel: 405-263-7930; Fax: 405-263-7721. [CEM]
School—Box 485, 73762. Tel: 405-263-4422; Fax: 405-263-7475. Sr. Marita Rother, A.S.C., Prin.
Lay Teachers 8; Students 128.

Okeene, Blaine Co., St. Anthony's, Rev. Bruce K. Natsuhara.
Res., 211 S. Fifth St., Box 767, 73763. Tel: 580-822-3511; 822-3544; Fax: 580-822-3542. [CEM]
Mission—Seiling, Dewey Co., St. Thomas, 105 W. McAlister, Seiling, 73663.

Pauls Valley, Garvin Co., St. Catherine of Siena, Rev. David F. Monahan.
Res., 205 W. Bert St., 73075. Tel: 405-238-3741; Fax: 405-238-5325.
Mission—Lindsay, Garvin Co., St. Peter's, E. Second & Quapah, Lindsay, 73052.

Perry, Noble Co., St. Rose of Lima, Rev. Kevin Devlin.
Res., 421 Ninth St., 73077. Tel: 580-336-9300; Fax: 580-336-9795. [CEM]
Mission—Billings, Noble Co., Sacred Heart, Broadway & Lowe, Billings, 74630.

Ponca City, Kay Co., Church of St. Mary, Revs. John J. Michalicka; J. Bosco Pudhota (India).
Res., 707 E. Ponca St., Box 1330, 74602. Tel: 580-765-6031; Fax: 580-765-1327. [CEM]
Schools—St. Mary, 415 S. 7th, 74601. Tel: 580-765-4387; Fax: 580-765-1352.; Sisters of St. Joseph of Wichita, 311 Fairview St., 74601. Tel: 580-765-0482; Fax: 580-765-0562. Sally Caughlin, Prin.
Sisters 1; Lay Teachers 19; Students 266.

Prague, Lincoln Co., St. Wenceslaus, National Shrine of the Infant Jesus of Prague, Rev. Adrian Vorderlandwehr, O.S.B.
Res., Fourth St. & Broadway St., Box 488, 74864. Tel: 405-567-3404; Fax: 405-567-3404. [CEM]
Mission—Meeker, Lincoln Co., St.Michael, Hwy. 62, Meeker, 74855.

Purcell, McClain Co., Our Lady of Victory, Rev. William B. Ross.
Res., 316 W. Jefferson St., Box 1280, 73080. Tel: 405-527-3077; Fax: 405-527-3077.
Mission—Lexington, Cleveland Co., St. John the Baptist, 309 S.E. 3rd St., Lexington, 73051. [CEM]

Seminole, Seminole Co., Immaculate Conception, Rev. Basil Keenan, O.S.B.
Res., Hwy. 9 W., Box 164, 74868. Tel: 405-382-3602; Fax: 405-382-3602.
Mission—Maud, Seminole Co., St. Cecelia, Main St., Maud, 74854.

Shawnee, Pottawatomie Co., St. Benedict, Rev. Charles Massoth, O.S.B.
Res., 632 N. Kickapoo, 74801. Tel: 405-275-0001; Fax: 405-214-9181. [CEM]

Sulphur, Murray Co., St. Francis Xavier, Rev. Timothy M. Fuller.
Res., 1313 E. Seventh, 73086. Tel: 580-622-3070; Fax: 580-622-2863.
Church—700 E. Oklahoma Ave., 73086. Tel: 580-622-3780.
Missions—Madill, Marshall Co., Holy Cross, 14 W. Francis, Madill, 73446. Tel: 580-795-3721; Tishomingo, Johnston Co., St. Anthony, 305 E. Wilson, Tishomingo, 73460.

Tonkawa, Kay Co., St. Joseph's, Rev. Joseph W. Burger.
Res., 320 W. North St., P.O. Box 525, 74653. Tel: 580-628-2416. [CEM]

Union City, Canadian Co., St. Joseph's, Rev. John A. Steichen.
Res., 404 N. Kate Boevers Ave., Box 100, 73090. Tel: 405-483-5329; Fax: 405-483-5329. [CEM]

Walters, Cotton Co., St. Patrick, Rev. Vincent dePaul Traynor, O.S.B.
Mailing Address: P.O. Box 305, 73572. Tel: 580-875-3855; Fax: 580-875-2369.
Res., 209 E. Iowa, 73572.
Missions—Grandfield, Tillman Co., Our Lady of Perpetual Help, S. Main St. & 8th St., Grandfield, 73546.; Waurika, Jefferson Co., St. Thomas Aquinas, 400 Block E, D St., Waurika, 73573.

Watonga, St. Joseph. Closed. For inquiries for parish records contact the Chancery.
Sacred Heart. Closed. For inquiries for parish records contact the Chancery.

Weatherford, Custer Co., St. Eugene's, Rev. Michael L. Chapman; Deacon Joseph Dubey.
Res., 704 N. Bryan, Box 407, 73096. Tel: 580-772-3209; Fax: 580-772-3541. [CEM 3]
Missions—Thomas, Custer Co., Blessed Sacrament, 520 N. Oklahoma, Thomas, 73669.; Hinton, Caddo Co., Sacred Heart, 204 N. Clark Ave., Hinton, 73047.

Woodward, Woodward Co., St. Peter's, Revs. Edward Menasco; Joseph Arledge.
Res., 2020 Oklahoma Ave., Box 708, 73802. Tel: 580-256-5305; Fax: 580-256-5840.
Missions—Mooreland, Woodward Co., Sacred Heart, 301 N. Main, Mooreland, 73852.; Shattuck, Ellis Co., Holy Name, 600 S. Main, Shattuck, 73858.; Beaver, Beaver Co., St. Frances Cabrini, 101 Ave. C, Beaver, 73932.; Buffalo, Harper Co., St. Joseph, 325 S.W. 2nd, Buffalo, 73834.

Yukon, Canadian Co., St. John Nepomuk, Rev. Ben Zoeller; Deacon Hi Joseph Roberts.
Mailing Address: P.O. Box 850249, 73085.
Church—600 S. Garth Brooks Blvd., 73099. Tel: 405-354-2743; Fax: 405-354-2770.
School—Tel: 405-354-2509. Sr. Laurentia Koehler, A.S.C., Prin.
Sisters 1; Lay Teachers 11; Students 125.

Special Assignment:
Reverend Fathers—
Ackerman, Raymond K., Pres., Mt. St. Mary High School, 2801 S. Shartel, Oklahoma City, OK 73109. Tel: 405-842-6639
Bash, Cletus, Chap. Mercy Health Center, 4300 W. Memorial Rd., Oklahoma City, OK 73120
Bird, Stephen J., Dir., Office of Worship & Spiritual Life, P.O. Box 32180, Oklahoma City, OK 73123. Tel: 405-721-5651
Lafferty, David, Spiritual Direction Coord., Priests' Prayer House, 700 N. E. 19th, Oklahoma City, OK 73105
Mason, Mark, Coord., Correction Related Ministry, 211 N. Cherokee, Hennessey, OK 73742
McSherry, Thomas, Micatokla, Santiago-Atitlan, Departmento Solola, Guatemala
Meinhart, Joseph C., Dir. Permanent Diaconate, P.O. Box 32180, Oklahoma City, OK 73123
Metzinger, John R., Dir., Seminarians & Vocations, P.O. Box 32180, Oklahoma City, OK 73123
Mollan, Paul F., Chap., Deaconess and Baptist Hospitals, 3214 N. Lake, Oklahoma City, OK 73118
Moore, Donald C., St. Ann's Home, 9400 St. Ann's Dr., Oklahoma City, OK 73162
Roberson, Henry, Chap., 2829 Williamsburg, Enid, OK 73702
Seeton, Philip, Chap., McGuinness High School, 901 N.W. 50th, Oklahoma City, OK 73118
Taylor, Anthony B., Vicar for Ministries, P.O. Box 32180, Oklahoma City, OK 73123. Tel: 405-721-5651
Vas, Joseph S., Chap. St. Anthony Hospital, 1000 N. Lee St., P.O. Box 205, Oklahoma City, OK 73101. Tel: 405-272-6263
Wolf, Don, Pres., NFPC, 1337 W. Ohio St., Chicago, IL 60622. Tel: 312-226-3334

On Duty Outside the Archdiocese:
Reverend Fathers—
Cowden, David, 432 E. Fireweed Ave., Palmer, AK 99645
Parker, Rick, 26245 Ocean View Ave., Carmel, CA 93923

Graduate Studies:
Reverend Fathers—
Stansberry, Richard, North American College, Casa Santa Maria, Via dell 'Umilta 30, Rome, 00187 Italy

---

Military Chaplains:
Reverend Fathers—
Creider, Philip B., Office of the Chaplain, 810 Avenger Ave., Lemore, CA 209-998-4618

Absent on Leave:
Reverend Fathers—
Aultz, Gary C.
Siebs, Robert L.

Absent on Sick Leave:
Reverend Fathers—
Grimes, Price D., Jr., P.O. Box 32180, Oklahoma City, OK 73123. Tel: 405-720-9871
Schiff, John S.

Prison Ministry:
Reverend Fathers—
Mason, Mark, Coord., Correction Related Ministry, 211 N. Cherokee, Hennessey, OK 73742. Tel: 405-853-4425; Fax: 405-853-2166
McMenamin, John, P.O. Box 32180, Oklahoma City, OK 73123. Tel: 405-720-7258

Retired:
Reverend Fathers—
Darnall, Thomas W., 2706 S. Shartel, Oklahoma City, OK 73109
Hardesty, Leo, 9400 St. Ann's Dr., Oklahoma City, OK 73162
McLaughlin, Joseph, 110 Rudy Dr., Apt. 15, Gallup, NM 87301. Tel: 505-973-2398
Ross, James H., P.O. Box 32180, Oklahoma City, OK 73123. Tel: 405-720-9874
Scheller, John, P.O. Box 32180, Oklahoma City, OK 73123. Tel: 405-722-1902
Schwarz, Bernard F., Rte. 3, Box 203, Marlow, OK 73055
Talloen, Jerome G., 9243 N. MacArthur, Apt. D., Oklahoma City, OK 73132
VandeWalle, Victor, P.O. Box 32180, Oklahoma City, OK 73123
Walch, John, P.O. Box 32180, Oklahoma City, OK 73123
White, Charles G., 2716 S. Cincinnati, Tulsa, OK 74114. Tel: 918-745-9317
Wrigley, Franklin, 700 N.E. 19th, Oklahoma City, OK 73105. Tel: 405-524-1118
Zagar, John T., 19000 N. County Line Rd, Piedmont, OK 73078. Tel: 405-341-1048

Permanent Deacons:
Adamson, Bill, Blessed Sacrament, Lawton
Amend, Carl, On Duty Outside the Archdiocese
Avila, Tomas, On Duty Outside the Archdiocese
Barton, James D., Corpus Christi, Oklahoma City
Bawden, Bill, St. John the Baptist Church, Edmond
Benoit, Roland, St. Francis of Assisi Church, Oklahoma City
Best, David, Christ the King Church
Browne, Matt, St. Philip Neri, Midwest City
Christophe, Norman, Retired
Collier, E. Charles, (Retired)
Coyle, Bill, Jr., St. John the Baptist, Edmond
Crispo, Anthony, St. Francis Xavier, Enid
Cruz, Joe M., St. Peter, Guymon
Cullinan, Walter, St. Charles Borromeo Church, Oklahoma City
Davis, Otis L., St. James, Oklahoma City
Descher, Duane, Oklahoma Medical Complex, Oklahoma City
Dollins, Belvin G., (Retired)
Dubey, Joe, St. Eugene, Weatherford
Ellison, Roy, St. Mary's, Guthrie
Forgue, Joseph, Chap., Federal Penitentiary, El Reno
Guerra, Simon, St. Peter, Guymon
Gulikers, Marti, St. James, Oklahoma City
Hernandez, Agustin, Immaculate Conception, Oklahoma City
Huff, Louis, St. Robert Bellarmine Church, Jones
Jones, Bro. Justin, O.S.B., St. Gregory Abbey, Shawnee
Keene, James, St. Andrew Church, Moore
Knight, James, Asst. to Dir. of Diaconate, St. Thomas More University Parish, Norman
Knipp, Stanley, Medical Leave
Lawrence, Herman, Holy Family, Lawton
Leal, George, Sacred Heart Church, Oklahoma City
LePage, Philip, St. Paul Apostle, Del City
LeWand, Marc, St. Charles, Oklahoma City
Maldonado, Pedro, St. Peter and Paul, Hobart
Marchessault, Arthur, On Leave
Martinez, Leopoldo, Holy Family Church, Lawton
McLauchlin, Robert, Medical Leave
Means, Gary, St. Cornelius, Cherokee
Neikirk, Dale, On Leave
Nguyen, San, St. Andrew Dung-Lac Church, Oklahoma City
Nieto, Lucio, Holy Angels, Oklahoma City
O'Loughlin, Bernard, Assumption Church, Duncan
Pitt, John, St. Charles Borromeo, Oklahoma City
Radosevich, Michael, St. Joseph, Ada
Reisinger, Conrad C., (Retired)
Reynolds, Patrick, St. Eugene, Oklahoma City
Roberts, Hi Joseph, St. Nepomuk, Yukon
Robinson, Richard, St. Mary, Ponca City
Rockey, Michael, Sacred Heart Church, Oklahoma City
Sousa, Larry, St. Joseph, Norman
Thelin, Carl, On Leave
Tindall, Bill, (Retired)
Warren, John, St. Thomas More, Norman
Washko, Richard, St. Mary Church, Guthrie
Watford, Angus, St. Andrew, Moore
Young, James G., St. Philip Neri, Midwest City

INSTITUTIONS LOCATED IN THE ARCHDIOCESE

[A] COLLEGES AND UNIVERSITIES

SHAWNEE. *St. Gregory's University*, 74801. Tel: 405-878-5100; Fax: 405-878-5170
For a complete listing, refer to the Colleges and Universities section.

[B] HIGH SCHOOLS, ARCHDIOCESAN

OKLAHOMA CITY. *Bishop McGuinness High School*. (Coed), 801 N.W. 50th St., 73118. Tel: 405-842-6638. Mr. Stephen Parsons, Pres.; Rev. Philip Seeton. Priests 1; Sisters 1; Lay Teachers 56; Students 706.

[C] HIGH SCHOOLS, PRIVATE

OKLAHOMA CITY. *Mount St. Mary High School*. (Coed), 2801 S. Shartel Ave., 73109. Tel: 405-631-8865; 8866. Sisters of Mercy of the Americas. Rev. Raymond K. Ackerman, Chap., Pres.; Mrs. Mary Jane Wittrock; Mrs. Joanne Forgue, Chm., Rel. Studies Dept. Priests 1; Sisters 1; Lay Teachers 19; Students 250.

[D] ELEMENTARY SCHOOLS, PRIVATE

OKLAHOMA CITY. *Villa Teresa*. (Grades N-4), 1216-1300 Classen Dr., 73103. Tel: 405-232-4286. Carmelite Sisters of St. Therese of the Infant Jesus. Mrs. Pamela Graham, Prin. Sisters 7; Lay Teachers 30; Students 285.

Villa Teresa Moore. (Grades N-K), 13501 S. Western Ave., 73170. Tel: 405-691-7737. Carmelite Sisters of St. Therese of the Infant Jesus. Mrs. Pamela Gra ham, Prin.; Sr. Sylvia Negrete, Dir. Sisters 1; Lay Teachers 10; Students 89.

NORMAN. *All Saints Catholic School*, 451 E. Tonhawa, 73071-5842. Tel: 405-447-4600. Ms. Glenda Peters, Prin. Lay Teachers 14; Grades: Pre-K 5; Students 234.

[E] GENERAL HOSPITALS

OKLAHOMA CITY. *Hillcrest Health Center, Inc.*, 2129 S.W. 59th St., 73119. Tel: 405-685-6671; Fax: 405-680-2817
For a complete listing, refer to the Hospitals section.

Mercy Memorial Health Center, 4300 W. Memorial Rd., 73120. Tel: 405-755-1515
For a complete listing, refer to the Hospitals section.

St. Anthony Hospital, 1000 N. Lee St., P.O. Box 205, 73101. Tel: 405-272-7000; Fax: 405-272-7075
For a complete listing, refer to the Hospitals section.

ARDMORE. *Mercy Memorial Health Center, Inc. (MMHC)*, 1011 14th Ave., N.W., 73401. Tel: 580-221-6611
For a complete listing, refer to the Hospitals section.

ENID. *St. Mary Mercy Hospital*, 305 S. 5th St., Box 232, 73701. Tel: 580-233-6100
For a complete listing, refer to the Hospitals section.

PONCA CITY. *St. Joseph Regional Medical Center*, 14th and Hartford, 74602. Tel: 580-765-3321; Fax: 580-765-0379
For a complete listing, refer to the Hospitals section.

[F] SPECIAL CARE FACILITIES

OKLAHOMA CITY. *St. Ann's Home Inc.*, 9400 St. Ann's Dr., 73162. Tel: 405-728-7888; Fax: 405-728-1302
For a complete listing, refer to the Special Care Facilities section.

[G] ECUMENICAL CENTERS

OKLAHOMA CITY. *Archdiocesan Pastoral Center*, 7501 Northwest Expwy., P.O. Box 32180, 73123. Tel: 405-721-5651; Fax: 405-721-5210. Mr. James Weinmann, Dir.; Mrs. Jeanine McFall, Events Coord. Used for Archdiocesan Chancery; ecumenical activities; retreat-meeting center for ecumenical and non-profit organizations; and retired priests' residence.

[H] HOMES FOR THE AGED

OKLAHOMA CITY. *Trinity Place Apartments*, Associated Catholic Charities, 3825 N.W. 19th St., 73107. Tel: 405-947-4143; Fax: 405-947-4199
For a complete listing, refer to the Special Care Facilities section.

Villa Isenbart, Inc., c/o Associated Catholic Charities, 1501 Classen Blvd., 73106
For a complete listing, refer to the Special Care Facilities section.

PONCA CITY. *St. Mary's Housing Foundation*, 408 S. 8th St., 74601
For a complete listing, refer to the Special Care Facilities section.

Westminster Village, Inc., 1601 Academy Rd., 74604. Tel: 405-762-0927
For a complete listing, refer to the Special Care Facilities section.

[I] MONASTERIES AND RESIDENCES OF PRIESTS AND BROTHERS

OKLAHOMA CITY. *House of Prayer for Priests*, 700 N.E. 19th, 73105. Tel: 405-525-0477. Rev. David Lafferty, Coord. Spiritual Direction.

Monastery of Our Lady of Mount Carmel and Little Flower, 1125 S. Walker Ave., Box 26127, 73126. Tel: 405-235-2037. Order of Discalced Carmelites (Oklahoma Province).

Little Flower Clinic: Free medical service for the Poor. Assisted annually 1,500.

SHAWNEE. *St. Gregory Abbey*, 1900 W. MacArthur Dr., 74801. Tel: 405-878-5490; Fax: 405-878-5198. Legal Title: *Benedictine Fathers of Sacred Heart Mission, Inc.* Order of St. Benedict, including University, Novitiate, and Mabee-Gerrer Museum of Art. Rt. Rev. Martin Lugo, O.S.B., Abbot; Revs. Patrick McCool, O.S.B., Prior; Joachim Spexarth, O.S.B., Subprior. Retired Abbots: Rt. Revs. Philip A. Berning, O.S.B.; Charles Massoth, O.S.B.; Adrian R. Vorderlandwehr, O.S.B.; Revs. Matthew J. Brown, O.S.B.; Charles Buckley, O.S.B., Dir.; Augustine S. Horn, O.S.B.; Maurus P. Jaeb, O.S.B.; Basil Keenan, O.S.B.; Eugene C. Marshall, O.S.B.; James D. Murphy, O.S.B.; Thomas R. Rabideau, O.S.B.; Victor W. Roberts, O.S.B.; Theodore T. Seneschal, O.S.B.; Lawrence R. Stasyszen, O.S.B.; Daniel M. Suellentrop, O.S.B.; Vincent dePaul Traynor, O.S.B.; Paul J. Zahler, O.S.B. Priests 24; Brothers 10; Deacons 1.

[J] CONVENTS AND RESIDENCES FOR SISTERS

OKLAHOMA CITY. *Alverno Community*, 3108 Northwest Expwy., #101, 73112. Tel: 405-942-2947. Franciscan Sisters of Mary. Sisters 2. Bethlehem Community, 600 N.W. 4th, #320, 73102. Tel: 405-235-4670. Sisters 2.

Carmelite Sisters of St. Therese of the Infant Jesus Motherhouse, Villa Teresa, 1300 Classen Dr., 73103. Tel: 405-232-7926. Sr. Immaculata Commet, C.S.T., Supr. Sisters in Community 28; Resident Sisters 22; Postulants 1; Novices 1.

Sisters of Mercy of the Americas, Mercy Health Center Convent, 4300 W. Memorial Rd., 73120. Tel: 405-755-1515. Retirement Center for Sisters of Mercy of Oklahoma. Sr. M. Rose Elizabeth Power, R.S.M., Coord. Sisters 17.

PIEDMONT. *Carmel of St. Joseph*, 20,000 N. County Line Rd., 73078. Tel: 405-348-3947. Discalced Carmelite Nuns (Cloistered). Sr. Therese Ranallo, O.C.D., Prioress. Professed Sisters 11; Novices 1; Postulants 1.

Sisters of Benedict Red Plains Monastery, 728 Richland Rd., SW, 73078-9324. Tel: 405-373-4565; 373-4569. Sr. Marie Ballmann, O.S.B., Prioress. Sisters in Community 13; Scholastics 2.

PONCA CITY. *Sisters of St. Joseph of Wichita*, 311 Fairview St., 74601. Tel: 580-765-0482. Sisters 4.

[K] CAMPUS MINISTRY & NEWMAN CENTERS

NORMAN. *Campus Ministry for the Archdiocese of Oklahoma City*, 100 East Stinson, 73072. Rev. C. Joseph Meinhart, Dir.

University of Oklahoma, 100 E. Stinson, 73072. Tel: 405-321-0990. Rev. C. Joseph Meinhart.

Oklahoma City University, P.O. Box 60569, Oklahoma City, 73146. Tel: 405-528-0485. Rev. Thomas Dowdell.

East Central State University, P.O. Box 1585, Ada, 74820. Tel: 580-332-4811. Rev. George Pupius.

Northwestern Oklahoma State College, 627 12th St., Alva, 73717. Tel: 580-327-0339. Rev. David B. Imming.

University of Science & Arts of Oklahoma, P.O. Box 748, Chickasha, 73023. Tel: 405-224-7513. Rev. Elmer C. Schwarz.

University of Central Oklahoma, 321 E. Clegern, Edmond, 73034. Tel: 405-340-6300. Rev. Kevin J. Ratterman.

Oklahoma Panhandle State University, P.O. Box 277, Goodwell, 73942. Tel: 580-338-7212. Revs. Charles R. Murphy; Scott Adams.

Cameron University, P.O. Box 7948, Lawton, 73506. Tel: 580-536-6351. Rev. Marvin F. Leven.

Northern Oklahoma College, P.O. Box 525, Tonkawa, 74653. Tel: 580-628-2416. Rev. Joseph W. Burger.

Southwestern Oklahoma State University, P.O. Box 407, Weatherford, 73096. Tel: 580-772-3209. Rev. Michael L. Chapman; Deacon Joe Dubey.

[L] MISCELLANEOUS

CANTON. *Las Casas Dominican Ministry Among the Cheyenne and Arapaho*, 524 W. Pine, 73724-9703. Tel: 405-886-3413. THE WHITE EARTH CENTER.

PIEDMONT. *Benedictine Spirituality Center*. Location at Red Plains Monastery, 728 Richland Rd., SW, 73078-9324. Tel: 405-373-4565.

SHAWNEE. *Oklahoma Benedictine Institute on Mental Retardation, Inc.*, 1900 W. MacArthur, 74801. Tel: 405-878-5288; Fax: 405-878-5114. Rev. Paul Zahler, O.S.B., Ph.D, Dir.

Oklahoma Benedictine Institute on Mental Retardation.

Harold C. and Connie Brand Early Child Development Center.

Home Start Program.

Lyle H. Boren Child Development Center.

Home Integration Program.

Community Integration Program.

Employment Integration Program.

St. Michael Foundation.

Ostrich Outreach Program.

Oklahoma Benedictine Institute TV Network for Success.

"The Greatest of These is Love" Fund.

International Institute on Mental Retardation.

RELIGIOUS INSTITUTES OF MEN REPRESENTED IN THE ARCHDIOCESE

For further details refer to the corresponding bracketed number in the Religious Institutes of Men or Women section.

[0200]—*Benedictine Monks.*—O.S.B.

[0260]—*Discalced Carmelite Friars.* (Oklahoma Prov.).—O.C.D.

[0920]—*Oblates of St. Francis De Sales.*—O.S.F.S.

RELIGIOUS INSTITUTES OF WOMEN REPRESENTED IN THE ARCHDIOCESE

[0100]—*Adorers of the Blood of Christ.*—A.S.C.

[0230]—*Benedictine Sisters of Pontifical Jurisdiction.*—O.S.B.

[0380]—*Carmelite Sisters of St. Therese of the Infant Jesus.*—C.S.T.

[0390]—*Congregation of Missionary Carmelites of St. Therese.* (Houston, TX).—C.M.S.T.

[0420]—*Discalced Carmelite Nuns.*—O.C.D.

[1070-13]—*Dominican Sisters.* (Adrian, MI).—O.P.

[1070-06]—*Dominican Sisters.* (Newburgh, NY).—O.P.

[1900]—*Eucharistic Missionaries of St. Theresa.* (Mexico).—M.E.S.T.

[1415]—*Franciscan Sisters of Mary.*—F.S.M.

[]—*Hermanas Catequistas Guadalupanas.*—H.C.G.

[1680]—*School Sisters of St. Francis.*—S.S.S.F.

[0480]—*Sisters of Charity of Leavenworth.*—S.C.L.

[2980]—*Sisters of Congregation de Notre Dame.*—C.N.D.

[1010]—*Sisters of Divine Providence of San Antonio, Texas.*—C.D.P.

[2575]—*Sisters of Mercy of the Americas.*—R.S.M.

[3840]—*Sisters of St. Joseph of Carondelet.*—C.S.J.

[2150]—*Sisters, Servants of the Immaculate Heart of Mary.*—I.H.M.

CEMETERIES

OKLAHOMA CITY. *Resurrection Memorial*, P.O. Box 32865, 73123. Tel: 405-721-4191.

NECROLOGY

† Dockers, Anthony R., (Retired). —Died Dec. 14, 1996.

† Eichhoff, William M., Oklahoma City, OK, St. Francis of Assisi. —Died April 8, 1997.

† Garvey, John, (Retired). —Died Oct. 3, 1996.

† Moras, Edward, Oklahoma City, OK, St. James. —Died July 3, 1997.

† Prather, Edward, (Retired). —Died Nov. 26, 1996.

† Wilkiemeyer, Philip, (Retired). —Died Dec. 31, 1996.

Archdiocese of Omaha

(Archidioecesis Omahensis)

Most Reverend

ELDEN FRANCIS CURTISS

Archbishop of Omaha; ordained May 24, 1958; appointed Bishop of Helena March 4, 1976; consecrated April 28, 1976; appointed Archbishop of Omaha May 4, 1993; installed June 25, 1993. *Chancery Office: 100 N. 62nd St., Omaha, NE, 68132-2795.*

Most Reverend

DANIEL E. SHEEHAN, D.D., J.C.D.

Retired Archbishop of Omaha; ordained May 23, 1942; appointed Titular Bishop of Capsu and Auxiliary January 4, 1964; consecrated March 19, 1964; succeeded to See June 11, 1969; retired. *Chancery Office: 100 N. 62nd St., Omaha, NE, 68132-2795.*

Chancery Office: 100 N. 62 St., Omaha, NE, 68132-2795. Tel.: 402-558-3100; Fax: 402-551-4212.

E-mail address: archbishopomaha@compuserve.com

ESTABLISHED AS A VICARIATE-APOSTOLIC JANUARY 6, 1857.

ERECTED A DIOCESE OCTOBER 2, 1885; ARCHDIOCESE AUGUST 7, 1945.

Square Miles 14,051.

Comprises the Counties of Boyd, Holt, Merrick, Nance, Boone, Antelope, Knox, Pierce, Madison, Platte, Colfax, Stanton, Wayne, Cedar, Dixon, Dakota, Thurston, Cuming, Dodge, Burt, Washington, Douglas and Sarpy in the State of Nebraska.

For legal titles of parishes and archdiocesan institutions, consult the Chancery Office.

STATISTICAL OVERVIEW

Personnel	
Archbishop	1
Retired Archbishops	1
Retired Bishops	2
Abbots	1
Retired Abbots	1
Priests: Diocesan Active in Diocese	161
Priests: Active Outside Diocese	10
Priests: Retired, Sick or Absent	60
Number of Diocesan Priests	231
Religious Priests in Diocese	132
Extern Priests in Diocese	11
Ordinations:	
Diocesan Priests	7
Transitional Deacons	3
Permanent Deacons in Diocese	131
Total Brothers	26
Total Sisters	343
Parishes	
Parishes	141
With Resident Pastor:	
Resident Diocesan Priests	121
Resident Religious Priests	4
Without Resident Pastor:	
Administered by Priests	15
Administered by Permanent Deacons	1
Missions	18
Closed Parishes	1
Professional Ministry Personnel:	
Sisters	18
Lay Ministers	267
Welfare	
Catholic Hospitals	4
Total Assisted	268,064
Health Care Centers	1
Total Assisted	220
Homes for the Aged	4
Total Assisted	361
Day Care and Extended Day Care Centers	5
Specialized Homes	1
Special Centers for Social Services	13
Total Assisted	121,703
Other Institutions	2
Total Assisted	29,802
Educational	
Diocesan Students in Other Seminaries	39
Seminaries, Religious	1
Students Religious	11
Total Seminarians	50
Colleges and Universities	2
Total Students	7,361
High Schools, Diocesan and Parish	12
Total Students	3,534
High Schools, Private	6
Total Students	2,704
Elementary Schools, Diocesan and Parish	60
Total Students	15,900
Elementary Schools, Private	3
Total Students	301
Non-residential Schools for the Disabled	1
Total Students	55
Catechesis/Religious Education:	
High School Students	3,905
Elementary Students	15,503
Total Students Under Catholic Instruction	49,315
Teachers in the Diocese:	
Priests	23
Brothers	4
Sisters	41
Lay Teachers	1,300
Vital Statistics	
Receptions into the Church:	
Infant Baptism Totals	4,447
Adult Baptism Totals	223
Received into Full Communion	545
First Communions	4,373
Confirmations	3,444
Marriages:	
Catholic	933
Interfaith	533
Total Marriages	1,466
Deaths	1,889
Total Catholic Population	214,523
Total Population	818,677

Former Bishops—Rt. Rev. JAMES O'GORMAN, O.C.S.O., D.D., Vicar-Apostolic and Titular Bishop of Raphanea; cons. May 8, 1859; died July 4, 1874.—Rt. Rev. JAMES O'CONNOR, D.D., Vicar-Apostolic and Titular Bishop of Dibona; cons. Aug. 20, 1876; appt. first Bishop of Omaha, Oct. 2, 1885; died May 27, 1890.—Rt. Rev. RICHARD SCANNELL, D.D., cons. Bishop of Concordia, Nov. 30, 1887; transferred to Omaha, Jan. 30, 1891; died Jan. 8, 1916.—Most Rev. JEREMIAH J. HARTY, D.D., ord. April 28, 1878; cons. Archbishop of Manila, P.I., Aug. 15, 1903; transferred to Omaha, May 16, 1916; died Oct. 29, 1927.—Most Rev. FRANCIS J. BECKMAN, D.D., Bishop of Lincoln and Apostolic Administrator of Omaha from June 1, 1926 to July 4, 1928.—Most Rev. JOSEPH FRANCIS RUMMEL, D.D., Bishop of Omaha; appt. March 30, 1928; cons. May 29, 1928; installed July 4, 1928; transferred to the Archdiocese of New Orleans, March 9, 1935.—Most Rev. JAMES H. RYAN, D.D., appt. Titular Bishop of Modra, Aug. 15, 1933; cons. Oct. 25, 1933; transferred to See of Omaha, Aug. 3, 1935; installed Nov. 21, 1935 elected to Archepiscopal dignity, Aug. 7, 1945; died Nov. 23, 1947.—Most Rev. GERALD T. BERGAN, D.D., ord. Oct. 28, 1915; appt. Bishop of Des Moines, March 24, 1934; cons. June 13, 1934; promoted to Omaha, Feb. 7, 1948; retired June 18, 1969 made Titular Archbishop of Tacarata; died July 12, 1972.—Most Rev. DANIEL E. SHEEHAN, D.D., J.C.D., ord. May 23, 1942; appt. Titular Bishop of Capsu and Auxiliary, Jan. 4, 1964; cons. March 19, 1964; succeeded to See, June 11, 1969; retired.

Vicar General—Most Rev. DANIEL E. SHEEHAN, D.D., J.C.D.

Vicar for Religious—Very Rev. JAMES R. CAIN, J.C.D.

Chancery Office—100 N. 62nd St., Omaha, 68132-2795. Tel: 402-558-3100; Fax: 402-551-4212. Office Hours: Mon.-Fri. 9-5.

Chancellor—Rev. MICHAEL F. GUTGSELL, J.C.L.

Moderator of the Curia—Rev. R. MICHAEL FITZPATRICK, J.C.L., S.T.L.

Finance Director (canonical)—Rev. R. MICHAEL FITZPATRICK, J.C.L., S.T.L.

Business and Finance Director—HERBERT L. KARRER.

Archdiocesan Tribunal—100 N. 62nd St., Omaha, 68132.

Judicial Vicar—Rev. R. MICHAEL FITZPATRICK, J.C.L., S.T.L.

Associate Judicial Vicar—Rev. MICHAEL F. GUTGSELL, J.C.L.

Judges—Rev. Msgr. ANTHONY B. MICKELLS, J.C.D.; Rev. GERALD P. MELCHIOR, J.C.L.

Promoter of Justice—Rev. JAMES R. CAIN, J.C.D.

Defenders of the Bond—Revs. JAMES R. CAIN, J.C.D.; Rev. VALENTINE J. PETER, S.T.D., J.C.D.

Advocates—Rev. PATRICK C. HARRISON; Deacon JERRY OVERKAMP.

Attorneys—Appointed for each matrimonial case.

Appeal Court—The Tribunal of the Diocese of Lincoln, NE is the Appeal Court for Omaha.

Consultors—Most Rev. DANIEL E. SHEEHAN, D.D., J.C.D.; Revs. NORMAN F. HUNKE; MICHAEL B. MALLOY; MELVIN J. MERWALD; FRANK A. PARTUSCH; ROLAND A. PESCHEL; MICHAEL G. PRINTY; RICHARD J. REISER; JAMES P. SCHOLZ; DANIEL F. SOLTYS; STEVEN J. STILLMUNKS.

Deans—U.S.C.: Rev. FRANK A. PARTUSCH, U.S.E.: Rev. JOHN O. MCCASLIN, U.N.E.: Rev. NORMAN F. HUNKE, U.N.W.: Rev. DANIEL KAMPSCHNEIDER, U.W.: Rev. STEVEN J. STILLMUNKS, R.S.W.: Rev. RICHARD WHITEING, R.N.C.: Rev. ALFRED SALANITRO, R.S.E.: Rev. WILLIAM L'HEUREUX, R.C.: Rev. OWEN W. KORTE, R.N.W.: Rev. RICHARD REISER, R.N.E.: DAVID W. LAPLANTE.

Finance Council—Most Rev. ELDEN FRANCIS CURTISS; Revs. R. MICHAEL FITZPATRICK, J.C.L., S.T.L.; GERALD E. GONDERINGER; FRANK LORDEMANN; Mr. HERBERT L. KARRER; Mr. ROMAN UHING; Mr. HERMAN D. WEIST.

Archdiocesan Offices and Directors

Boy Scouts—Rev. DANIEL L. WITTROCK, Chap.

Building Commission—Rev. R. MICHAEL FITZPATRICK, J.C.L., S.T.L.; Mr. LEE KARRER, Contact Person; Rev. JAMES R. CAIN, J.C.D.; Mr. THOMAS L. FINLEY; Rev. ROBERT J. SMITH; Mr. DANIEL WITT; Bro. WILLIAM WOEGER, F.S.C.

Catholic University, Friends of—Rev. R. MICHAEL FITZPATRICK, J.C.L., S.T.L., Dir.

Cemeteries—Rev. ROBERT J. GASS, Dir.

Censor Librorum—Rev. VAL J. PETER, J.C.D., S.T.D.

Charities—SCOT L. ADAMS, Dir., *3300 N. 60th St., Omaha, 68104.*

Omaha Priests Retirement Plan and Trust, The—Revs. FRANCIS E. KUBART; THOMAS R. FURLONG; Mr. JAMES KINEEN; Mr. DONALD E. RUTH; Mr. DAVID DUREN; Mr. HERBERT L. KARRER.

Commission for Ecumenical Affairs—Rev. GERALD P. MELCHIOR.

Commission on Divine Worship—Bro. WILLIAM WOEGER, F.S.C., Coord., Environment & Art; Rev. RONALD NOECKER, Coord., Music.

Council of Catholic Women, Archdiocesan—Rev. EDGAR J. WORTMANN, Archdiocesan Moderator, *3020 Curtis, Omaha, 68111.*

Deaf—Rev. JAMES VANCE, C.SS.R.

Diaconate Program—Revs. THOMAS J. ADAMS, Urban Dir. Tel: 402-455-4966. PAUL ORTMEIER, Rural Dir. Tel: 402-373-2233.

Catholic School Office—Sr. PATRICIA MULCAHEY, O.P., Supt., Schools, *3212 N. 60th St., Omaha, 68104.* Tel: 402-554-8493.

Religious Formation, Office of—*3212 N. 60th St., P.O. Box 4130, Omaha, 68104.* Mr. JAMES CORR, Dir.; Ms. LORI SPANBAUER, Asst. Dir., Young Adult; Ms. RITA RAMOS, Asst. Dir., Youth; Ms. MARY ALICE O'REILLY, Asst. Dir., Elementary Formation; Ms. NANCY KOLEY, Asst. Dir., Catechist Cert. & Media Resources. Tel: 402-554-8493; Fax: 402-554-8402.

Family Life—Sr. BARBARA MARKEY, N.D., Dir., *3214 N. 60th St., Omaha, 68104.* Tel: 402-551-9003.

Hispanic Ministry—Vacant, *3218 N. 60th St., Omaha, 68104.* Tel: 402-551-2255.

Holy Name Society—Rev. JOHN S. MICHALAK, Dir.

Hospitals—Rev. JAMES QUINN, S.J.

Legion of Mary—Rev. PETER F. DUNNE, Dir.

Natural Family Planning—Sr. BARBARA MARKEY, N.D., Dir., Family Life Office: *3214 N. 60th St., Omaha, 68104.* Tel: 402-551-9003.

Newspaper—Mr. CHARLIE WIESER, Editor, *"The Catholic Voice", 6060 N.W. Radial Hwy., Omaha, 68104.* Tel: 402-558-6611; Fax: 402-558-6614.

Nocturnal Adoration Society—Vacant.

Pastoral Planning Office—MARY JO HUSTEN, Dir. Tel: 402-551-2255.

Priests' Eucharistic League—Rev. WILLIAM WHELAN.

Propagation of the Faith, Pontifical Association of Holy Childhood and Catholic Students Mission Crusade—Rev. R. MICHAEL FITZPATRICK, J.C.L., S.T.L., Dir., *100 N. 62nd St., Omaha, 68132.*

Retreats, Laymen—Rev. ALBAN SUEPER, S.S.C., Dir.

Rural Life Conference—Rev. FRANK J. BAUMERT.

St. Vincent de Paul Society—Rev. JOHN L. PIETRAMALE, Spiritual Dir.; Mr. PATRICK MCCARTHY, Pres., *2101 Leavenworth St., Omaha, 68102.*

St. Vincent de Paul Store, Inc.—*2101 Leavenworth St., Omaha, 68102.*

Priests' Council—

Officers—Revs. OWEN KORTE, Pres. NORMAN HUNKE, Vice Pres. DANIEL KAMPSCHNEIDER, Sec. ROBERT PREISINGER, Treas.

Age Groups—Revs. FRANCIS KUBART; THOMAS FANGMAN; DAMIAN ZUERLEIN; KENNETH VAVRINA; ROBERT SMITH; MICHAEL GREWE; JOHN L. PIETRAMALE.

Religious Orders—Revs. ROBERT TILLMAN, S.J.; GERMAR NEUBERT, O.S.B.; ROBERT OELERICH, C.S.S.R.

Deans—Revs. FRANK A. PARTUSCH, (USC); JOHN O. MCCASLIN, (USE); MICHAEL GREWE, (US); NORMAN HUNKE, (UNE); DANIEL KAMPSCHNEIDER, (UNW); STEVEN STILLMUNKS, (UW); RICHARD WHITEING, (RSW); ALFRED SALANITRO, (RNC); RICHARD REISER, (RNW); WILLIAM L'HEUREUX, (RSE); DAVID W. LAPLANTE, (RNE); OWEN W. KORTE, (RC).

Archbishop's Appointees—Revs. R. MICHAEL FITZPATRICK, J.C.L., S.T.L.; MICHAEL F. GUTGSELL, J.C.L.

Ex Officio—Most Rev. DANIEL E. SHEEHAN, D.D., J.C.D.; Revs. MEL MERWALD, Consultor; MICHAEL MALLOY; MICHAEL PRINTY; DANIEL SOLTYS.

Social Ministry Commission—Sr. MARY HOGAN, O.S.M., Coord.

Sodalities—Rev. THOMAS A. HALLEY, S.J.

Catholic Charities, Inc.—SCOT L. ADAMS, Exec. Dir., *3300 N. 60th St., Omaha, 68104.* Tel: 402-554-0520.

Catholic Charities, Inc. Satellite Offices and Services—

The Shelter—Care for battered women, children, therapy for spouse abusers. KATHY SCHINKER, Contact Person, *P.O. Box 4346, Omaha, 68104.* Tel: 402-558-5700.

St. Martin de Porres Center—Social Justice education, counseling, food pantry, refugee program. A'JAMAL BYNDON, Emergency Svcs. JUNITA ELLIOTT, Vision of H.O.P.E., *2417 Burdette St., Omaha, 68111.* Tel: 402-341-4004.

St. Gabriel's Center—Detoxification, inpatient treatment and extended care for low-income and indigent alcoholics. JAN VAN DOREN, Contact Person, *3483 Larimore Ave., Omaha, 68111.* Tel: 401-451-4264.

UCSS Counseling Services—JACK WRIGHT, *Sheehan Center, 3300 N. 60th St., Omaha, 68104.* Tel: 402-554-0520. RAY WILSON, Substance Abuse, *3300 N. 60th St., Omaha, 68104.* Tel: 402-554-0520.

Catholic Family Services—GORDON GREEN, Contact Person, *1761 26th Ave., P.O. Box 573, Columbus, 68602-0573.* Tel: 402-563-3833.

Catholic Family Services—*1255 4th St., Ste. 220, Norfolk, 68701.* Tel: 402-371-3555.

Vocations—Rev. MARK D. FILIPS, Dir.

Youth-Young Adult Ministry—Ms. RITA RAMOS, *3216 N. 60th St., Omaha, 68104.* Tel: 402-551-5070.

CLERGY, PARISHES, MISSIONS AND PAROCHIAL SCHOOLS

CITY OF OMAHA
(Douglas County)

1—ST. CECILIA'S CATHEDRAL, Revs. Norman F. Hunke; Joseph M. Wray; Donald Stortz. In res., Rev. R. Michael Fitzpatrick.
Res., 701 N. 40 St., 68131. Tel: 402-551-2313; Fax: 402-551-2306.
School—Tel: 402-556-6655.
Congregation of the Most Holy Rosary, (Sinsinawa, WI) 2; Lay Teachers 26; Students 509.
Catechesis/Religious Programs—Bonnie Pryor, D.R.E.
Students 70.

2—ST. ADALBERT, Rev. Frank A. Partusch.
Res., 2617 S. 31 St., 68105. Tel: 402-345-1621.
Catechesis/Religious Programs—2124 S. 32 Ave., 68105. Tel: 402-341-5604.
Students 15.

3—ST. AGNES, Rev. Damian Z. Zuerlein.
Res., 2215 Q St., 68107. Tel: 402-731-0100.

4—ST. ANN, Rev. John C. Rizzo. In res., Rev. Nguyen Loi.
Res., 2247 Poppleton Ave., 68108. Tel: 402-341-6613.
School—All Saints Catholic School. See Elementary Schools, Interparochial Under Institutions Located in the Archdiocese.
Catechesis/Religious Programs—Students 14.

5—ST. ANTHONY, Rev. Carl F. Sodoro.
Res., 5401 S. 33 St., 68107. Tel: 402-733-2423.

6—ASSUMPTION, B.V.M., Rev. Rodney V. Kneifl.
Res., 5434 S. 22 St., 68107. Tel: 402-734-4500; Fax: 402-734-4502.
School—Tel: 402-734-4504.
Lay Teachers 12; Students 157.

7—ST. BENEDICT THE MOOR, Rev. Walter E. Boehme, S.J.
Res., 2423 Grant St., 68111. Tel: 402-348-0631.

8—ST. BERNADETTE, Revs. Robert F. Preisinger; Roland A. Peschel; Deacons Ron Casart; Pete Digilio; Duane Thome; Sebastian Enzolera. In res., Rev. Msgr. Albert L. Krejci.
Res., 7600 S. 42 St., Omaha, 68147. Tel: 402-731-4694; Fax: 402-731-8735.
School—Tel: 402-731-3033. Mrs. Lisa Nelson, Prin.
Lay Teachers 25; Students 459.
Catechesis/Religious Programs—Tel: 402-731-9421. Sr. Maureen Heegan, C.S.J., D.R.E.
Students 95.

9—ST. BERNARD, Rev. Jerome I. Spenner; Deacons Donald Kemp; Skip Baughman; Carl Miller; Edward Osterhaus. In res., Rev. Gerald P. Melchior.
Res., 3601 N. 65 St., 68104. Tel: 402-551-0269; Fax: 402-551-2311.
School—Tel: 402-553-4993. David Peters, Prin.
Lay Teachers 21; Students 340.
Catechesis/Religious Programs—Joanne Raleigh, D.R.E.
Students 144.

10—BLESSED SACRAMENT, Rev. Edgar J. Wortmann.
Res., 3020 Curtis Ave., 68111. Tel: 402-455-5200.
School—Tel: 402-455-4030.
Lay Teachers 12; Students 119.

11—ST. BRIDGET, Rev. James L. Weeke. In res., Rev. Paul Begley.
Res., 4112 S. 26 St., 68107. Tel: 402-733-8811.
Catechesis/Religious Programs—Students 24.

12—CHRIST THE KING, Revs. Robert J. Gass; John L. Pietramale; Deacon Glenn Tylutki.
Res., 654 S. 86 St., 68114. Tel: 402-391-3606; Fax: 402-391-1498.
School—Tel: 402-391-0977; Fax: 402-391-2418. Mrs. Mary Anderson, Prin.
Lay Teachers 27; Students 336.
Catechesis/Religious Programs—Tel: 402-391-3624. Colleen Leise, D.R.E.
Students 92.

13—ST. ELIZABETH ANN, Revs. Joseph G. Hanefeldt; William Safranek; Deacons Jack Finney; Richard Nelson; Ernie Gencarelli; Martin Crowley.
Res., 11212 Grande Ave., 68164. Tel: 402-493-2186; Fax: 402-493-0630.
School—St. James-Seton School. See Elementary Schools, Interparochial Under Institutions Located in the Archdiocese.
Catechesis/Religious Programs—Tel: 402-572-0369; Fax: 402-572-0368. Mrs. Doris Grillo, D.R.E.
Students 240.

14—ST. FRANCES CABRINI, Rev. Roger Kalscheuer, S.J., Admin.; Deacon Anthony Filipcic.
Res., 1334 S. Ninth St., 68108. Tel: 402-342-2464; Fax: 402-342-2470.
School—All Saints Catholic School. See Elementary Schools, Interparochial Under Institutions Located in the Archdiocese.

15—ST. FRANCIS ASSISI, Revs. John C. Starostka; John R. Buckson, Hispanic Ministry; Deacon Paul L. Matukewicz.
Res., 4513 S. 32nd St., 68107-1499. Tel: 402-731-2699.
School—Sisters 1; Lay Teachers 2; Students 43.

16—HOLY CROSS, Revs. Charles F. Swanson; Mark Bridgman. In res., Rev. Msgr. Edward C. O'Donnell, V.G.; Rev. Ralph Librea; Deacon George Elster.
Res., 4803 William St., 68106. Tel: 402-553-7500; Fax: 402-553-7735.
School—Tel: 402-551-3773.
Lay Teachers 23; Students 387.
Catechesis/Religious Programs—Students 73.

17—HOLY FAMILY, Deacon Ralph L. Hueser, Admin.
Res., 1715 Izard St., 68102. Tel: 402-345-1062; Fax: 402-344-8136.

18—HOLY GHOST, Revs. Ralph J. Steffensmeier; Timothy M. Podraza; Deacons Tom Schulte; Paul Eubanks.
Res., 5219 S. 53rd St., 68117. Tel: 402-731-3176; Fax: 402-738-1409.
School—Tel: 402-731-5161; Fax: 402-738-1409. Jane Barreuther, Prin.
Lay Teachers 11; Students 239.
Catechesis/Religious Programs—Tel: 402-731-4574. Mary Fenton, D.R.E.
Students 65.

19—HOLY NAME, Revs. Brian Johnson, C.SS.R.; Robert Oelerich, C.SS.R.; Stephen Benden, C.SS.R.; James Vance, C.SS.R.; Bro. William Cloughley, C.SS.R.
Res., 3014 N. 45th St., 68104. Tel: 402-451-6622; Fax: 402-457-6901.
School—(Grades K-8). Tel: 402-451-5403. Sofia Kock, Prin.
Lay Teachers 15; Students 274.
Catechesis/Religious Programs—Tel: 402-453-0873. Catherine Snyder, D.R.E.
Students 60.

20—IMMACULATE CONCEPTION, B.V.M., Rev. John O. McCaslin.
Res., 2708 S. 24th St., 68108. Tel: 402-342-1074; Fax: 402-342-1074.
School—All Saints Catholic School. See Elementary Schools, Interparochial Under Institutions Located in the Archdiocese.
Catechesis/Religious Programs—Students 6.

21—ST. JAMES, Rev. Michael W. Grewe; Rt. Rev. Raphael Walsh, O.S.B.; Deacons Jerry Gau; Larry Heck; Stan Kurtz; Pat Lenz; Wayne Young. In res., Rev. James V. Brown, O.A.R.
Res., 9025 Larimore Ave., 68134. Tel: 402-572-0499; Fax: 402-572-6864.
School—St. James-Seton School. See Elementary Schools, Interparochial Under Institutions Located in the Archdiocese.
Catechesis/Religious Programs—Tel: 402-572-0369; Fax: 402-572-0368. Mrs. Doris Grillo, D.R.E. Students 170.

22—ST. JOAN OF ARC, Revs. Emmett F. Meyer; Joseph Broudou.
Res., 3122 S. 74 St., 68124. Tel: 402-393-2005.
School—Tel: 402-393-2314.
Sisters of Mercy 2; Lay Teachers 21; Students 365.
Catechesis/Religious Programs—Tel: 402-391-1906. Marilyn Opitz, D.R.E.
Students 162.

23—ST. JOHN, Revs. Bert Thelen, S.J.; Thomas A. Halley, S.J.; Philip Amidon, S.J.; John Horn, S.J.; Deacon Ken Kalkowski.
Office: 2500 California Pl., 68178. Tel: 402-280-3030; Fax: 402-280-2465.

24—ST. JOHN VIANNEY, Revs. Paul J. Schwaab; Thomas D. Furlong; Deacons Pete DesRosiers; Frank Telich. In res., Rev. James M. Sullivan (HEL).
Res., 5801 Oak Hills Dr., 68137. Tel: 402-895-0808; Fax: 402-895-0896.
Catechesis/Religious Programs—Anne Waldron, D.R.E.
Students 537.

25—ST. JOSEPH, Rev. Walter Wancewicz.
Res., 1730 S. 16th St., 68108. Tel: 402-342-1618.
School—All Saints Catholic School. See Elementary Schools, Interparochial Under Institutions Located in the Archdiocese.
Catechesis/Religious Programs—Students 64.

26—ST. LEO, Revs. R. Patrick McCaslin; Jeffrey L. Zyla.
Res., 1920 N. 102nd St., 68114. Tel: 402-397-0407; Fax: 402-397-2887.
School—St. Pius X-St. Leo School. See Elementary Schools, Interparochial Under Institutions Located in the Archdiocese.
Catechesis/Religious Programs—Students 445.

27—ST. MARGARET MARY, Revs. Melvin Merwald; Randall Donner.
Res., 6116 Dodge St., 68132. Tel: 402-558-2255; Fax: 402-551-5631.
School—Tel: 402-551-6663.
Lay Teachers 20; Students 523.
Catechesis/Religious Programs—Students 180.

28—ST. MARY, Revs. Carl F. Sodoro; Daniel F. Brick.
Res., 3529 Q St., 68107. Tel: 402-731-0204.
School—Lay Teachers 13; Students 166.

29—ST. MARY MAGDALENE, Revs. William L. Kelligar; Fernando C. Benliro.
Res., P.O. Box 3285, 68103. Tel: 402-342-4807; Fax: 402-344-0941.
School—All Saints Catholic School. See Elementary Schools, Interparochial Under Institutions Located in the Archdiocese.

30—MARY OUR QUEEN, Revs. Carl A. Salanitro; Ralph B. O'Donnell; Deacon Paul Rooney.
Res., 3535 S. 119 St., 68144. Tel: 402-333-8662; Fax: 402-333-4504.
School—3405 S. 119 St., 68144. Tel: 402-333-8663; Fax: 402-334-3948.
Lay Teachers 28; Students 586.
Catechesis/Religious Programs—Tel: 402-333-8231. Barb Eastridge, D.R.E.
Students 502.

31—MOTHER OF PERPETUAL HELP. (Church of the Deaf). Rev. James Vance, C.SS.R.
Res., 5215 Seward St., 68104. Tel: 402-558-4214.

32—OUR LADY OF GUADALUPE, Revs. Damian J. Zuerlein; John R. Buckson; Gustavo Barrientos; Stanley L. Kasun; Deacons Joe Ramirez; Duane Bronk.
Res., 2310 O St., 68107. Tel: 402-731-2196; Fax: 402-731-2196.
Catechesis/Religious Programs—Sr. Marcianne Trujillo, D.R.E.
Students 462.

33—OUR LADY OF LOURDES, Revs. Frank A. Partusch; Paul M. Albenesius; Deacons Frank Hilt; Michael Reynolds.
Res., 2110 S. 32nd Ave., 68105. Tel: 402-346-0900; Fax: 402-346-0901.
School—2124 S. 32nd Ave., 68105. Tel: 402-341-5604. Mr. Kenneth Hajek, Prin.
Sisters 1; Lay Teachers 20; Students 360.
Catechesis/Religious Programs—Students 45.

34—ST. PATRICK, Revs. Lucian S. Astuto; Chad A. Ripperger, F.SS.P.
Res., 1404 Castelar St., 68108. Tel: 402-341-1305; Fax: 402-342-5510.
School—All Saints Catholic School. See Elementary Schools, Interparochial Under Institutions Located in the Archdiocese.
Catechesis/Religious Programs—Students 18.

35—ST. PETER, Rev. John C. Rizzo.
Res., 709 S. 28th St., 68105. Tel: 402-341-4560.

36—SS. PETER AND PAUL, Revs. Donald W. Shane; Norman B. Parr.
Res., 5912 S. 36th St., 68107. Tel: 402-731-4578.
School—Tel: 402-731-4713. Joan Miller, Prin.
Lay Teachers 18; Students 341.
Catechesis/Religious Programs—Tel: 402-733-3344. Julie Bizal, D.R.E.
Students 233.

37—ST. PHILIP NERI, Revs. Daniel J. Kampschneider; LuVerne W. Steffes; Deacons Dick Edgerton; Fred Hendrick.
Res., 8200 N. 30th St., 68112. Tel: 402-455-1289; Fax: 402-455-8398.
School—Tel: 402-455-8666; Fax: 402-453-3620. Barbara Marchese, Prin.
Lay Teachers 13; Students 229.
Catechesis/Religious Programs—Tel: 402-455-2190. Joanne Raleigh, D.R.E.
Students 106.

38—ST. PIUS X, Revs. Lloyd A. Gnirk; Daniel L. Wittrock. In res., Rev. Paul C. Zaccone.
Res., 6905 Blondo St., 68104. Tel: 402-558-8446; Fax: 402-558-4986.
School—St. Pius X-St. Leo School. See Elementary Schools, Interparochial Under Institutions Located in the Archdiocese.
Catechesis/Religious Programs—Tel: 402-558-1898. Susie Naatz, D.R.E.
Students 130.

39—ST. RICHARD, Rev. Daniel P. Herek. Co-Administrators: Rev. Msgr. Charles Brodersen; Rev. Edward Schad.
Res., 4320 Fort St., 68111. Tel: 402-455-2865.
School—Tel: 402-451-0692. Ms. Sue McCaslin, Prin.
Sisters 1; Lay Teachers 14; Students 192.

40—ST. ROBERT BELLARMINE, Rev. Msgr. Blase J. Cupich; Rev. John S. Andrews; Deacons Fred Alexander, (Retired); William Fell; John Kronschnabel. In res., Rev. Michael F. Gutgsell.
Res., 11802 Pacific St., 68154. Tel: 402-333-8989; Fax: 402-333-5489.
School—Tel: 402-334-1929; Fax: 402-333-7188. Craig V. Estee, Prin.
Lay Teachers 29; Students 570.
Catechesis/Religious Programs—Tel: 402-333-1959. Wilma D. Smith, D.R.E.
Students 200.

41—ST. ROSE, Rev. Mark D. Filips, Admin.
Res., 4102 S. 13th St., 68107. Tel: 402-733-9327; Fax: 402-731-9937.

42—SACRED HEART, Rev. James P. Scholz; Deacons Charles Weskirchen; James Chambers.
Res., 2218 Binney St., 68110. Tel: 402-451-5755; Fax: 402-451-1731.
School—Tel: 402-451-5858.
Lay Teachers 12; Students 150.

43—ST. STANISLAUS, Rev. Richard L. Swolek.
Res., 4002 J St., 68107. Tel: 402-731-4152; Fax: 402-731-4389.
School—Tel: 402-731-0484.
Poor Sisters of St. Francis Seraph of Perpetual Adoration 1; Lay Teachers 8; Students 160.
Catechesis/Religious Programs—Students 21.

44—ST. STEPHEN THE MARTYR, Revs. Gerald E. Gonderinger; Thomas S. Gall; Larry Toms.
Res., 17053 M St., 68135. Tel: 402-896-9682.
Church—16701 S St., 68135. Tel: 402-896-9675; Fax: 402-896-1990.
School—Tel: 402-896-0754. Mr. John Smith Prin.
Students 401.
Catechesis/Religious Programs—Students 1,441.

45—ST. THERESE OF THE CHILD JESUS, Rev. Thomas J. Adams.
Res., 5316 N. 14th Ave., 68110. Tel: 402-455-4966.

46—ST. THOMAS MORE, Revs. John E. Vernon; Craig J. Loecker. In res., Revs. Stanislaus Golik; Bernardine Hahn, O.F.M.
Res., 4804 Grover St., 68106. Tel: 402-556-1456.
School—Lay Teachers 22; Students 396.

47—ST. VINCENT DE PAUL, Sarpy Co., Revs. Dennis A. Hanneman; Thomas F. O'Brien; Francis A. Nigli; Deacon Donald K. Clausen.
Res., 14330 Eagle Run Dr., 68164. Tel: 402-496-7988 (Pastoral Center); 498-8425 (Rectory); Fax: 402-496-9933.
School—Tel: 402-492-2111. Dr. Vicky Grandy, Prin.
Students 660.
Catechesis/Religious Programs—Tel: 402-493-1642.
Students 605.

48—ST. WENCESLAUS, Revs. Franklin A. Dvorak; Mark J. McKercher; Deacons John Cerveny; Elvon Anderson; Donald Cowles; Joseph Friend. In res., Rev. James E. Gilg.
Res., 15353 Pacific St., Omaha, 68154. Tel: 402-330-0304; Fax: 402-330-1476.
School—(Grades K-8). Tel: 402-330-4356. Mary McGuire, Prin.
Students 700.
Catechesis/Religious Programs—Tel: 402-330-1889. Judy Thorne, D.R.E.
Students 1,034.

OUTSIDE THE CITY OF OMAHA

Albion, Boone Co., St. Michael, Rev. Wilfred J. Spenner.
Res., 524 W. Church St., 68620. Tel: 402-395-2393.
School—Tel: 402-395-2926.
Priests 1; Religious 1; Lay Teachers 8; Students 96.
Catechesis/Religious Programs—Students 235.

Aloys, Cuming Co., St. Aloysius, Rev. Stephen J. Gutgsell.
Res., 700 Hwy. 32, West Point, 68788. Tel: 402-372-2789. [CEM]

Atkinson, Holt Co., St. Joseph, Rev. Wayne W. Schlautman; Deacons Gerald Gonderinger, (Retired); Art Villemure.
Res., 317 W. State St., P.O. Box 220, 68713. Tel: 402-925-2122; Fax: 402-925-5320. [CEM]
School—Tel: 402-925-2104.
Lay Teachers 10; Students 80.
Catechesis/Religious Programs—Tel: 402-925-5854. D.R.E.: Dennis Ryan; Patti Skrdla.
Students 90.

Bancroft, Cuming Co., Holy Cross, Rev. David W. LaPlante.
Res., P.O. Box 524, Lyons, 68038. Tel: 412-846-5550.

Battle Creek, Madison Co., St. Patrick's, Rev. Michael P. Eckley.
Res., 107 N. Third St., P.O. Box 40, 68715. Tel: 402-675-2485.
Catechesis/Religious Programs—Christine Brandl, D.R.E.
Students 150.
Mission—Schoolcraft, Madison Co., St. Francis de Sales.

Beemer, Cuming Co., Holy Cross, Rev. Ronald J. Noecker.
Res., 517 Fraisier St. N., P.O. Box 212, 68716. Tel: 402-528-3475. [CEM]

Bellevue, Sarpy Co., St. Mary, Revs. Thomas R. Ward; Michael P. Keating; Deacons Ralph Hueser; Duane Iwanski; Chuck L'Archevesque; Andy Foray.
Res., 811 W. 23rd Ave., 68005. Tel: 402-291-1350; Fax: 402-291-1375.
School—(Grades PreK-8). Tel: 402-291-1666. Sr. Regina Wagner, Prin.
Lay Teachers 18; Students 310.
Catechesis/Religious Programs—Tel: 402-291-3964. Nina Tisinger, D.R.E.
Students 469.

Blair, Washington Co., St. Francis Borgia, Rev. Hugh F. Schwartz.
Res., P.O. Box 548, 68008. Tel: 402-426-3823. [CEM]
Catechesis/Religious Programs—402-426-5145 David Kaslon, D.R.E.
Students 418.

Bellevue, Sarpy Co., St. Matthew The Evangelist Church of Bellevue, Rev. Dennis R. Stolinksi.
Res., 3605 Looking Glass Dr., 68123. Tel: 402-292-7418.
School—(Grades K-8) 12210 S. 36th St., 68123. Tel: 402-291-2039. Patricia Buettell, Prin.
Lay Teachers 15; Students 212.

Bloomfield, Knox Co., St. Andrew, Rev. Paul Ortmeier.
Res., 304 S. McNamara St., P.O. Box 416, 68718. Tel: 402-373-2233. [CEM]
Catechesis/Religious Programs—Tel: 402-373-2696. Barb Jackson, D.R.E.
Students 134.

Bow Valley, Cedar Co., SS. Peter and Paul, Rev. Mark A. Tomasiewicz.
Res., 106 W. 889th Rd. (Bow Valley), Hartington, 68739. Tel: 402-254-3311. [CEM]
School—East Catholic Elementary School. See Elementary Schools, Interparochial Under Institutions Located in the Archdiocese.
Catechesis/Religious Programs—Students 128.

Boys Town, Douglas Co., Immaculate Conception B.V.M., Rev. Valentine J. Peter. In res., Rev. Msgr. Peter F. Dunne; Revs. Eugene McReynolds, O.S.B.; Aloysius J. McMahon.
Res., 68010. Tel: 402-498-1111.
Catechesis/Religious Programs—Students 570.

Butte, Boyd Co, SS. Peter and Paul, Rev. Lydell T Lape.
Res., P.O. Box 8, 68722. Tel: 402-775-2452. [CEM]
Mission—Naper, Boyd Co., Sacred Heart. [CEM]

Cedar Rapids, Boone Co., St. Anthony, Rev. Urban Schmitt, O.S.C., Admin.
Res., P.O. Box 56, 68627. Tel: 308-358-0773. [CEM]
Catechesis/Religious Programs—Students 123.
Mission—Primrose, Boone Co., St. Mary, 68627. [CEM]

Central City, Merrick Co., St. Michael, Rev. Nelson A. Newman; Deacon Robert Flesch.
Res., 2402 20th Ave., 68826. Tel: 308-946-2855; Fax: 308-946-2982.
Catechesis/Religious Programs—D.R.E.: Teresa Hartwig; Marie Nicholas.
Students 138.

Clarks, Merrick Co., St. Peter, Rev. Kenneth P. Vavrina.
Res., P.O. Box 185, 68628. Tel: 308-773-2282. [CEM]
Catechesis/Religious Programs—Tel: 308-548-2573. Linda Yrkoski, D.R.E.
Students 54.

Clarkson, Colfax Co., SS. Cyril and Methodius, Rev. Floyd A. Wessling.
Res., 120 Cherry St., P.O. Box 457, 68629. Tel: 402-892-3464.
School—St. John Neumann, Tel: 402-892-3474.
Lay Teachers 4; Students 74.
Catechesis/Religious Programs—Students 191.

Coleridge, Cedar Co., St. Michael, Rev. Dennis DeGuzman.
Res., 315 S. Madison, R.R. 1, 68727. Tel: 402-283-4614.
Catechesis/Religious Programs—Students 96.

Columbus, Platte Co., St. Anthony, Rev. Christopher J. Grimmond; Deacons Michael Placzek; Robert Obershaw; Michael McGuire.
Res., 562 17th Ave., 68601. Tel: 402-564-3313; Fax: 402-563-1005.
School—Tel: 402-564-4767; Fax: 402-563-1005. Mary Jane Noble, Prin.
Lay Teachers 8; Students 129.
Catechesis/Religious Programs—Lori Olson, D.R.E.
Students 187.

St. Bonaventure, Revs. Daniel E. Keller; Anthony Espinosa; Deacons Arthur Spenner; Lawrence Mielak. In res., Rev. Steven D. Emanuel.
Res., 1565 18th Ave., 68601. Tel: 402-564-7151; Fax: 402-562-6025. [CEM]
School—Tel: 402-564-7153. Mr. Don E. Day, Prin.
Sisters 2; Lay Teachers 13; Students 232.
Catechesis/Religious Programs—D.R.E.: Rose V. Arp; Mary Gabriel.
Students 320.

St. Isidore, Revs. Joseph A. Miksch; Michael D. Schmitz.
Res., 3921 20th St., 68601. Tel: 402-564-8993; Fax: 402-564-8955.
School—Tel: 402-564-2604.
Missionary Benedictine Sisters 4; Lay Teachers 12; Students 220.
Catechesis/Religious Programs—Students 264.

Constance, Knox Co., St. Joseph. (Mission of Crofton). Rev. Robert K. English.
Mailing Address: Box 335, Crofton, 68730. Tel: 402-388-4814. [CEM]
School—West Catholic Elementary. See Elementary Schools, Interparochial Under Institutions Located in the Archdiocese.

Creighton, Knox Co., St. Ludger, Rev. Keith D. Rezac.
Res., 908 Lake St., 68729-9509. Tel: 402-358-3596.
School—410 Bryant Ave., 68729. Tel: 402-358-3501; Fax: 402-358-3501.
Sisters 3; Lay Teachers 5; Students 59.
Catechesis/Religious Programs—Tel: 402-358-3501. D.R.E.: Sr. Margaret Sibbel, S.S.S.F.; Beate Wilmes; Sr. Mary Hettich, S.S.S.F.
Students 84.

Crofton, Knox Co., St. Rose of Lima, Rev. Robert K. English.
Res., 1316 W. Fifth St., P.O. Box 335, 68730. Tel: 402-388-4814. [CEM]
School—Tel: 402-388-4393.
Lay Teachers 8; Students 151.
Catechesis/Religious Programs—D.R.E.: Arlene Steffen, (Grades 1-8); Charlotte Arens, (Grades 9-12).
Students 143.

Dodge, Dodge Co., St. Wenceslaus, Rev. Melvern A. Wiese.
Res., 743 Second St., 68633. Tel: 402-693-2235. [CEM 2]
School—Tel: 402-693-2819. Sr. Rosalima Wilkinson, R.S.M., Prin.
Lay Teachers 5; Students 71.
Catechesis/Religious Programs—Tel: 402-693-2347. Joan Ruskamp, D.R.E.
Students 102.

Duncan, Platte Co., St. Stanislaus, Rev. James F. McCluskey.
Res., P.O. Box 192, 68634. Tel: 402-897-2625. [CEM]
Catechesis/Religious Programs—Students 113.

Elgin, Antelope Co., St. Boniface, Rev. Owen W. Korte; Deacon Dennis Wiehn.
Res., P.O. Box B, 68636-0433. Tel: 402-843-2345; Fax: 402-843-2253. [CEM]
School—Tel: 402-843-5460.
Sisters 2; Lay Teachers 8; Students 114.
Catechesis/Religious Programs—Students 230.

Elkhorn, Douglas Co., St. Patrick, Rev. Ronald S. Wasikowski.
Res., 20500 W. Maple Rd., 68022. Tel: 402-289-4289; Fax: 402-289-4288. [CEM]
Catechesis/Religious Programs—Tel: 402-289-4947.
Students 193.

Emerson, Dakota Co., Sacred Heart, Rev. James V. Kramper.
Res., Sixth St. & Main St., P.O. Box 250, 68733. Tel: 402-695-2342. [CEM]
School—Tel: 402-695-2513.
Lay Teachers 4; Students 45.

Ewing, Holt Co., St. Peter de Alcantara, Rev. Gerald A. Leise, Jr.
Res., P.O. Box 37, 68735. Tel: 402-626-7605.
Catechesis/Religious Programs—Helen Larson, D.R.E.
Students 103.

Fordyce, Cedar Co., St. John the Baptist, Rev. Gregory Benkowski, Admin.
Res., P.O. Box 170, 68736. Tel: 402-357-3506; Fax: 402-357-3708. [CEM]
School—West Catholic Elementary. See Elementary Schools, Interparochial Under Institutions Located in the Archdiocese.
Catechesis/Religious Programs—Kathy Magorian, D.R.E.
Students 67.

Fort Calhoun, Washington Co., St. John the Baptist, Rev. James F. Schwertley.
Res., 608 N. 13th St., Box 163, 68023. Tel: 402-468-5348.

Fremont, Dodge Co., St. Patrick, Revs. Francis W. Lordemann; David M. Korth; John Whalen; Deacons Robert Chapman; Edward Gentrup; Justin Lauer; Hugh Robinson; LeRoy Spieker.
Res., 422 E. Fourth St., 68025. Tel: 402-721-6611; Fax: 402-727-8167. [CEM]
High School—Archbishop Bergan, (Grades 7-12). Tel: 402-721-9683; Fax: 402-721-5366. Timothy George, Prin.
Lay Teachers 22; Students 288.
Catechesis/Religious Programs—Tel: 402-721-9710. Helen Kuiper, D.R.E.
Students 555.

Fullerton, Nance Co., St. Peter, Rev. Richard J. Whiteing.
Res., 315 N. Esther, P.O. Box 368, 68638. Tel: 308-536-2574. [CEM]
Catechesis/Religious Programs—Students 156.

Genoa, Nance Co., St. Rose of Lima, Rev. Robert H. Nienaber.
Res., 116 N. Elm St., P.O. Box 490, 68640-0490. Tel: 402-993-2323.
Catechesis/Religious Programs—Students 135.

Gretna, Sarpy Co., St. Patrick, Rev. Daniel F. Soltys.
Res., 508 Angus, 68028. Tel: 402-332-4444; Fax: 402-332-5107. [CEM]
Catechesis/Religious Programs—Tel: 402-332-3242. Elaine Sedlacek, D.R.E.
Students 365.

Hartington, Cedar Co., Holy Trinity, Revs. William E. Sanderson; Stanley T. Schmit.
Res., 404 S. Broadway Ave., P.O. Box 278, 68739. Tel: 402-254-6559. [CEM]
School—Tel: 402-254-6496.
Lay Teachers 10; Students 197.
Catechesis/Religious Programs—Students 177.

Heun, Colfax Co., Holy Trinity, Rev. Ray O. Bonham.
Res., P.O. Clarkson Rte. 1, Box 49, 68629. Tel: 402-986-1627. [CEM]
School—See Elementary Schools, Interparochial Under Institutions Located in the Archdiocese.
Catechesis/Religious Programs—Students 65.
Mission—Tabor, Colfax Co., St. Mary. [CEM]

Hooper, Dodge Co., St. Rose of Lima, Rev. William D. L'Heureux.
Res., 405 Elk St., P.O. Box 443, 68031. Tel: 402-654-3449. [CEM]
Catechesis/Religious Programs—Students 47.
Mission—Scribner, Dodge Co., St. Lawrence, 405 Elk St. Box 443, 68031. Tel: 402-654-3449. [CEM]
Catechesis/Religious Programs—Students 43.

Howells, Colfax Co., SS. Peter and Paul, Rev. Thomas J. Sellentin.
Res., 614 Center St., P.O. Box 40, 68641. Tel: 402-986-1653.
School—Howells Community Catholic School. See Elementary Schools, Interparochial Under Institutions Located in the Archdiocese.
Catechesis/Religious Programs—Students 60.

St. John Nepomucene, Rev. Thomas J. Sellentin.
Res., 614 Center St., P.O. Box 40, 68641. Tel: 402-986-1653. [CEM]
School—Howells Community Catholic School. See Elementary Schools, Interparochial Under Institutions Located in the Archdiocese.
Catechesis/Religious Programs—Students 55.

Humphrey, Platte Co., St. Francis, Rev. J. Brian Beilman. In res., Rev. Wayne S. Pavela.
Res., P.O. Box 116, 68642. Tel: 402-923-0913; Fax: 402-923-1590. [CEM]
School—(Grades K-6). Tel: 402-923-0611; Fax: 402-923-1590.
Lay Teachers 8; Students 182.
High School—Tel: 402-923-0818.
Lay Teachers 15; Students 153.
Catechesis/Religious Programs—Students 79.

Jackson, Dakota Co., St. Patrick, Rev. Michael G. Printy.
Res., 203 E. Elk St., P.O. Box 87, 68743. Tel: 402-632-4292.
Catechesis/Religious Programs—Claudette Albenesius, D.R.E.
Students 118.
Mission—Hubbard, Dakota Co., St. Mary, P.O. Box 126, Hubbard, 68741. Tel: 402-632-4283. [CEM 2]

Krakow, Nance Co., SS. Peter and Paul, Rev. Robert H. Nienaber, Admin.
Res., P.O. Genoa, R.R. 2, P.O. Box 18, 68640. Tel: 402-993-6600.

Laurel, Cedar Co., St. Mary, Rev. Alfred J. Salanitro; Deacon LeRoy Creamer.
Res., 406 Elm St., P.O. Box 828, 68745. Tel: 402-256-3303.
Catechesis/Religious Programs—Marietta Freeman, D.R.E.
Students 93.
Mission—Dixon, Dixon Co., St. Anne.

Leigh, Colfax Co., St. Mary, Rev. Francis E. Kubart.
Res., 220 W. Third St., P.O. Box 385, 68643. Tel: 402-487-2666. [CEM]
Catechesis/Religious Programs—Agnes Thalken, D.R.E.
Students 95.

Lindsay, Platte Co., Holy Family, Rev. James F. Novotny.
Res., P.O. Box 68, 68644. Tel: 402-428-2455. [CEM]
School—(Grades 1-6). Tel: 402-428-3455; Fax: 402-428-3231.
Lay Teachers 7; Students 102.
High School—(Grades 7-12). Tel: 402-428-3215; Fax: 402-428-3231.
Lay Teachers 13; Students 111.
Catechesis/Religious Programs—Students 72.

Lynch, Boyd Co., Assumption B.V.M., Rev. Donald M. Kros.
Res., P.O. Box 167, 68746. Tel: 402-569-2421. [CEM]

Lyons, Burt Co., St. Joseph, Rev. David W. LaPlante.
Res., 430 Lincoln St., P.O. Box 524, 68038. Tel: 402-687-2102.
Catechesis/Religious Programs—Students 87.

Madison, Madison Co., St. Leonard, Rev. William F. Weidner.
Res., 504 S. Nebr. St., P.O. Box 368, 68748. Tel: 402-454-3529. [CEM]
School—Tel: 402-454-3525.
Lay Teachers 4; Students 57.
Catechesis/Religious Programs—Students 171.

Menominee, Cedar Co., St. Boniface, Rev. Gregory Benkowski, Admin.; Deacon Clarence Jansen.
Res., P.O. Box 170, Fordyce, 68736. Tel: 402-357-3506; Fax: 402-357-3795. [CEM]
School—West Catholic Elementary. See Elementary Schools, Interparochial Under Institutions Located in the Archdiocese.

Monterey, Cuming Co., St. Boniface, Rev. Stephen J. Gutgsell.
Res., 450 12th Rd., West Point, 68788. Tel: 402-372-3681. [CEM]

Neligh, Antelope Co., St. Francis, Rev. Frank J. Baumert; Deacons Bernard Burbach; Leonard Obershaw.
Res., 702 W. 11th St., P.O. Box 259, 68756. Tel: 402-887-4521.
Catechesis/Religious Programs—Students 311.
Mission—Neligh, Antelope Co., St. Theresa, 702 West 11th, 68756.

Newcastle, Dixon Co., St. Peter, Rev. James J. Bartak. Mailing Address: P.O. Box 898, Ponca, 68770-0898. Res., P.O. Box 127, 405 Annie St., 68757. Tel: 402-355-2620 (rectory); 402-755-2773 (office).
Catechesis/Religious Programs—Tel: 402-692-3232. Barb Wieseler, D.R.E.
Students 81.

Norfolk, Madison Co., Sacred Heart, Revs. Harold J. Buse; Thomas M. Fangman; Joseph C. Taphorn; Deacons Jim Doolittle; Richard Mueting; Irving St. Arnold.
Res., 202 S. Fifth St., 68701. Tel: 402-371-2621; Fax: 402-371-0403.
School—(Grades K-12). Tel: 402-371-4584 (K-6); 371-2784 (7-12); Fax: 402-379-8129 (K-6); 379-2929 (7-12). Principals: Ron Brewer, (Grades K-6); Jeff Bellar, (Grades 7-12).
Priests 4; Lay Teachers 51; Students 776.
Catechesis/Religious Programs—Tel: 402-371-8658. Mary Throener, D.R.E. (Grades K-12).
Students 639.

North Bend, Dodge Co., St. Charles Borromeo, Rev. Daniel E. Galas.
Res., P.O. Box 457, 68649. Tel: 402-652-8484.
Catechesis/Religious Programs—Betty Marxsen, D.R.E.
Students 213.

Olean, Colfax Co., Sacred Heart. (mission of St. Wenceslaus, Dodge). Rev. Melvern Wiese.
Res., 743 Second St., Dodge, 68633. Tel: 402-693-2335. [CEM]
School—Howells Community Catholic School. See Elementary Schools, Interparochial Under Institutions Located in the Archdiocese.
Mission—Dodge, St. Wenceslaus.

O'Neill, Holt Co., St. Patrick, Revs. Richard J. Reiser; Mark K. Merkel; Deacon Robert Shoemaker; Lisa Lueninghoener, Liturgist.
Res., 301 E. Adams, 68763. Tel: 402-336-1602; Fax: 402-336-1613. [CEM]
School—Tel: 402-336-2664.
Sisters 1; Lay Teachers 11; Students 129.
High School—Tel: 402-336-4455.
Sisters 1; Lay Teachers 15; Students 121.
Catechesis/Religious Programs—Tel: 402-336-1602. Linda Lieswald, D.R.E.
Students 225.
Mission—Amelia, Holt Co., St. Joseph, Tel: 402-482-5283.

Osmond, Pierce Co., St. Mary of the Seven Dolors, Rev. Kenneth M. Potts.
Res., 509 Hill St., P.O. Box 397, 68765. Tel: 402-748-3340. [CEM]
School—Tel: 402-748-3433.
Lay Teachers 4; Students 59.
Catechesis/Religious Programs—Students 73.

Papillion, Sarpy Co., St. Columbkille, Revs. Steven J. Stillmunks; Leo Rigatuso; Joseph E. Weiss, S.J.; Deacons Ralph Tharp; Frank Mascarello; Jerry Overkamp; Eldon Lauber; Roland Kaiser.
Res., 200 E. Sixth St., 68046. Tel: 402-339-3285; Fax: 402-592-4753.
School—Tel: 402-339-8706; Fax: 402-592-4147.
Lay Teachers 22; Students 561.
Catechesis/Religious Programs—Tel: 402-339-0990; Fax: 402-339-3977. Marge Koenigsman, D.R.E.
Students 801.

Pender, Thurston Co., St. John, Rev. James V. Kramper.
Res., 108 N. Fifth St., P.O. Box 96, 68047. Tel: 402-385-3258.
Catechesis/Religious Programs—Students 95.

Petersburg, Boone Co., St. John the Baptist, Rev. Gerald A. Connealy.
Res., Fourth St. & Norman St., P.O. Box 8, 68652. Tel: 402-386-5580. [CEM]
School—Tel: 402-386-5472.
Sisters 1; Lay Teachers 3; Students 30.
Catechesis/Religious Programs—Students 74.
Mission—Raeville, Boone Co., St. Bonaventure, P.O.Box 8, 68652.

Pierce, Pierce Co., St. Joseph, Rev. Thomas DeBacker.
Res., 116 W. Willow St., 68767. Tel: 402-329-4200. [CEM]
Catechesis/Religious Programs—Tel: 402-329-6655.
Students 190.

Plainview, Pierce Co., St. Paul, Rev. James M. Buckley.
Res., P.O. Box 387, 68769. Tel: 402-582-4413. [CEM]
Mission—Brunswick, Antelope Co., St. Ignatius.

Platte Center, Platte Co., St. Joseph, Rev. James C. Ryberg.
Res., P.O. Box 155, 68653-0155. Tel: 402-246-2255. [CEM]
Catechesis/Religious Programs—Tel: 402-246-5700. Angela Dolezal, D.R.E.
Students 120.

Ponca, Dixon Co., St. Joseph, Rev. James J. Bartak; Deacon Paul Poulosky.
Res., P.O. Box 127, Newcastle, 68757. Tel: 402-355-2620; 755-2773 (office). [CEM]
Catechesis/Religious Programs—D.R.E.: Kari Richards; K.J. Knere.
Students 119.

Raeville, Boone Co., St. Bonaventure, Rev. Gerald A. Connealy.
Res., Petersburg, 68652. Tel: 402-386-5580. [CEM]

Ralston, Douglas Co., St. Gerald, Revs. Lawrence J. Dorsey; Thomas Weisbecker.
Res., 7859 Lakeview St., 68127. Tel: 402-331-1955; Fax: 402-331-1961.
School—Tel: 402-331-4223; Fax: 402-331-1961. David Garland, Prin.
Lay Teachers 17; Students 380.
Catechesis/Religious Programs—Tel: 402-331-4523.
Students 520.

Randolph, Cedar Co., St. Frances de Chantal, Rev. Ronald A. Battiato; Deacon Vincent Schmit.
Res., P.O. Box B, 68771. Tel: 402-337-0644. [CEM]
Catechesis/Religious Programs—Tel: 402-337-0341. La Donna Leiting, D.R.E.
Students 245.

St. Charles, Cuming Co., St. Anthony, Rev. Stephen J. Gutgsell.
Res., 445 15th Rd., West Point, 68788. Tel: 402-372-3681. [CEM]

St. Edward, Boone Co., St. Edward, Rev. Edward B. Gill.
Res., 805 Washington St., P.O. Box A, 68660-0136. Tel: 402-678-2642. [CEM]
Catechesis/Religious Programs—Sr. Agatha Marie Sadler, D.R.E.
Students 95.

St. Helena, Cedar Co., Immaculate Conception, Rev. Mark Tomasiewicz.
Res., Sts. Peter & Paul Church (Bow Valley), R.R. 3, 106 W. 889th Rd., Hartington, 68739. Tel: 402-357-2465. [CEM]
School—East Catholic Elementary. See Elementary Schools, Interparochial Under Institutions Located in the Archdiocese.
Catechesis/Religious Programs—Students 38.

St. James, Cedar Co., SS. Philip and James, Rev. Jay L. Kruse.
Res., P.O. Box 65, Wynot, 68792. Tel: 402-357-2146. [CEM]
School—East Catholic Elementary. See Elementary Schools, Interparochial Under Institutions Located in the Archdiocese.

St. John, Holt Co., St. John, Rev. Gerald A. Leise, Jr.
Res., R.R. 1, P.O. Box 150, Clearwater, 68726. Tel: 402-485-2430.
Catechesis/Religious Programs—Beth Schueth, D.R.E.
Students 48.

Schuyler, Colfax Co., St. Augustine, Rev. William S. Whelan; Deacons Marvin Capoun; James DeBlauw.
Res., 619 Banner St., 68661. Tel: 402-352-3521. [CEM]
Catechesis/Religious Programs—320 W. 10 St., 68661. Tel: 402-352-2149.
Students 167.

St. Mary, Rev. Ralph A. Lammers; Deacon Evan Drozda.
Res., 308 W. 10 St., 68661. Tel: 402-352-3540; Fax: 402-352-2149.
Catechesis/Religious Programs—Tel: 402-352-2149. Leona Kracl, D.R.E.
Students 199.

Silver Creek, Merrick Co., St. Lawrence, Rev. Kenneth Vavrina.
Res., P.O. Box 332, 68663. Tel: 308-773-2282. [CEM]
Catechesis/Religious Programs—Tel: 402-897-2510. Linda Yrkoski, D.R.E.
Students 54.

Snyder, Dodge Co., St. Leo, Rev. Daniel E Galas.
Res., P.O. Box 188, 68664. Tel: 402-568-2520. [CEM]
Catechesis/Religious Programs—Tel: 402-568-2586. Joyce Kreikemeier, D.R.E.
Students 49.

South Sioux City, Dakota Co., St. Michael, Revs. David F. Liewer; Ross Burkhalter.
Res., 1405 First Ave., 68776. Tel: 402-494-5423; Fax: 402-494-6342.
School—Tel: 402-494-1526.
Lay Teachers 14; Students 190.
Catechesis/Religious Programs—1414 Third Ave., 68776. Tel: 402-494-2827; Fax: 402-494-2344.
Students 300.
Mission—Homer, Dakota Co., St. Cornelius.

Spencer, Boyd Co., St. Mary, Rev. Frank E. Jindra, Admin.
Res., South St. & Harmon St., P.O. Box 149, 68777. Tel: 402-589-0067; Fax: 402-589-1068.
Catechesis/Religious Programs—D.R.E.: Mary Kirpatrick, (Grades 1-6), Tel: 402-589-1266; Bill Engelhaupt, (Grades 7-12), Tel: 402-589-9016.
Students 86.

Springfield, Sarpy Co., St. Joseph, Rev. James R. Cain.
Res., 102 S. Ninth St., P.O. Box 345, 68059. Tel: 402-253-2889.
Catechesis/Religious Programs—Tel: 402-253-2949. Linda Keller, D.R.E.
Students 150.

Stanton, Stanton Co., St. Peter, Rev. Timothy J. Lange.
Res., P.O. Box 557, 68779. Tel: 402-439-2147.
Catechesis/Religious Programs—D.R.E.: Valerie Morfeld Tel: 402-396-3207; Karen Petersen Tel: 402-439-2331.
Students 140.

Stuart, Holt Co., St. Boniface, Rev. Douglas P. Scheinost.
Res., 106 E. Fourth, P.O. Box 190, 68780. Tel: 402-924-3262; Fax: 402-924-3494. [CEM]
School—Tel: 402-924-3803.
Lay Teachers 4; Students 56.
Catechesis/Religious Programs—Students 124.

Tarnov, Platte Co., St. Michael, Rev. Leonard C. Ficenec, Admin.
Res., R.R. 1, P.O. Box 202, Humphrey, 68642. Tel: 402-246-4821. [CEM]

Tekamah, Burt Co., St. Patrick, Rev. Martin P. Conley.
Res., 1323 R St., 68061-1542. Tel: 402-374-1692.
Catechesis/Religious Programs—Tom Olson, D.R.E.
Students 77.
Mission—Decatur, Burt Co., Holy Family.

Tilden, Madison Co., Our Lady of Mt. Carmel, Rev. Robert A. Schmitz.
Res., P.O. Box 458, 68781. Tel: 402-368-7710.
Catechesis/Religious Programs—Tel: 402-368-5919. Corine Frey, D.R.E.
Students 105.

Valley, Douglas Co., St. John, Rev. Robert J. Smith; Deacon Gary Hennessey.
Res., 209 E. Sunset, 68064. Tel: 402-359-5783.
Catechesis/Religious Programs—Tel: 402-289-4067. Vonnie Abbott, D.R.E.
Students 240.

Verdigre, Knox Co., St. Wenceslaus, Rev. Michael B. Malloy.
Res., 409 S. Third St., P.O. Box 9, 68783-009. Tel: 402-668-2331. [CEM]
Catechesis/Religious Programs—Students 151.
Mission—Verdigre, Knox Co., St. William, P.O. Box 9, 68783-0009.

Walthill, Thurston Co., St. Joseph, Revs. Thomas E. Bauwens; Steven Boes.
Res., P.O. Box GG, Winnebago, 68071. Tel: 402-846-5550; Fax: 402-878-2760.

Wayne, Wayne Co., St. Mary, Rev. Donald M. Cleary.
Res., 412 E. 8th St., 68787. Tel: 402-375-2000. [CEM]
School—Tel: 402-375-2337.
Lay Teachers 8; Students 61.
Catechesis/Religious Programs—Students 218.

West Point, Cumming Co., Assumption B.V.M., Revs. Gary L. Ostrander; Charles R. Uhlik; Deacons Vincent Maly; Kenneth Batenhorst.
Res., 343 N. Monitor St., 68788. Tel: 402-372-2188. [CEM]
School—Guardian Angel, Tel: 402-372-5328. Sr. Carol Seidl, Prin.
Priests 2; Sisters 3; Lay Teachers 20; Students 356.
Catechesis/Religious Programs—Carol Praest, D.R.E.
Students 138.

Winnebago, Thurston Co., St. Augustine's. (Indian Mission). Revs. Thomas E. Bauwens; Steven Boes.
Res., P.O. Box GG, 68071. Tel: 402-878-2402; Fax: 402-878-2760.
School—Tel: 402-878-2291.
Missionary Benedictine Sisters 4; Lay Teachers 6; Students 83.
Mission—Macy, Thurston Co., Our Lady of Fatima.

Wisner, Cuming Co., St. Joseph, Rev. David D. Belt.
Res., 1318 G Ave., W., P.O. Box 623, 68791. Tel: 402-529-3242. [CEM]
Catechesis/Religious Programs—Tel: 402-529-3891. Anne McManigal, D.R.E.
Students 122.

Wynot, Cedar Co., Sacred Heart, Rev. Jay L. Kruse.
Res., P.O. Box 65, 68792. Tel: 402-357-2400. [CEM]
Catechesis/Religious Programs—Deanna Klug, D.R.E.
Students 89.

On Duty Outside the Archdiocese:
Reverend Fathers—
Baxter, Gregory P., Theological Studies, Rome, Italy

Greisen, Thomas A., Conception Seminary, Conception, MO
Harrison, Patrick, Canon Law Studies, Rome, Italy

Military Chaplains:
Reverend Fathers—
Dendinger, William J., Chap., U.S.A.F.
Dillon, Jerome V., Chap., U.S.N.R.
Hall, Douglas C., U.S.A.F.
Harbour, Linn S., U.S.A.F.
Reeson, David G., U.S.A.F.

Absent on Leave:
Reverend Fathers—
Fiala, John M.
Gaughan, James M.
Herek, Daniel P.
Mainelli, Vincent P., C.O.
Matt, Thomas S.
McKamy, Eldon J.
McNeil, Joel
Rowe, Douglas L.
Rush, Gerald V.

Absent on Sick Leave:
Reverend Fathers—
Finch, Joseph E.

Retired:
Reverend Monsignors—
Ariano, Joseph W.
Hupp, Robert P., 7508 Walnut St., Omaha, NE 68124
Krejci, Albert L., 7600 S. 42 St., Omaha, NE 68147
Michaels, Anthony B., 2405 S. 48th Ave., Omaha, NE 68106
O'Donnell, Edward C., 4803 William St., Omaha, NE 68106
Werner, Cyril J., P.O. Box 562, Hartington, NE 68739
Reverend Fathers—
Bartek, James F., 900 N. 90th St., Omaha, NE 68114
Bartek, William C., 7323 Shirley Ct., Omaha, NE 68124
Beacom, John F., 757 E. Decatur, West Point, NE 68788
Begley, Paul, 4112 S. 26th St., Omaha, NE 68107
Brodersen, Charles F., 9230 Burt St. #223, Omaha, NE 68114
Carroll, Patrick A., 4752 N. 14th Ave., Omaha, NE 68110
Ciurej, Richard S., 4107 S. 38 St., Omaha, NE 68107
Dickes, Jerome H., 500 E. 8th St., Yankton, SD 57078
Duffy, Robert P., 7323 Shirley Ct., Omaha, NE 68124
Dunne, Peter F., Boys Town Center, Boys Town, NE 68010
Fangman, Paul J., Rte. 1, Box 139, Humphrey, NE 68642
Ficenec, Leonard C., R.R. 1, Box 202, Tarnov, NE 68642
Fitzgerald, William F.
Flisiak, Stefan, R.R. 2, Box 18, Genoa, NE 68640
Golik, Stanislaus, 4804 Grover St., Omaha, NE 68106
Hebert, John M., 2325 Fifth Ave., Marshalltown, IA 50158
Hunkeler, Edward J., 5605 N. 105th Plaza-3, Omaha, NE 68134
Kelly, Michael J., 900 N. 90th St., Omaha, NE 68114
Kenny, James E., 7232 Shirley Ct., Omaha, NE 68124
Koros, John J., 120 Citrus Rd. N.E., Lake Placid, FL 33852
Kovar, Vaclav, General Delivery, Dodge, NE 68633
Krajicek, Robert P.
Kreikemeier, Leo A., Rte. 1, P.O. Box 25E, Cedar Bluffs, NE 68015
LaRocque, Benedict J., O.S.B., Saint Benedict Abbey, Atchison, KS 66002
Meiergerd, Godfrey A., Rte. 1, Box 250, Cedar Bluffs, NE 68124
Meister, Andrew H., P.O. Box 25D, Cedar Bluffs, NE 68015
Micek, Joseph S., 1655 E. Sahara, Apt. 1056, Las Vegas, NV 89104
Mitera, Stanislaus C., 1938 S. 38 Ave., Apt. 116, Omaha, NE 68105
Moreci, Francis A., 2642 N. Newland Ave., Chicago, IL 60635
Musteikis, Leonard, 420 Preston Circle, Sunny Hills, FL 32428
Peter, Paul F., 7323 Shirley Ct., Omaha, NE 68107
Petrasic, Martin J., 2603 S. 50 St., Omaha, NE 68106
Petrusic, Anthony A., 322 Virginia St., Hollywood, FL 33019
Price, Francis R., 401 N. 18th St., Norfolk, NE 68701
Stevens, Clifford J.
Tuma, Anthony F., 1870 S. 75th St., Omaha, NE 68124
Wilwerding, Anthony P., #8 Madonna Dr., Hardy, AR 72542
Wolbach, Richard A., 4001 S. 36th St., Omaha, NE 68107

Permanent Deacons:
Alexander, Fred
Anderson, Andy
Archibald, Joseph
Barbour, Frank
Bartman, Frank
Batenhorst, Kenneth F.
Baughman, Charles
Brich, James
Brisson, Ralph
Bronk, Duane
Capoun, Marvin
Casart, Ronald
Cerveny, John
Chambers, James
Chapman, Robert
Clausen, Donald
Creamer, LeRoy
Crowley, Martin
Cuva, Fred
Davis, Dennis
DeBlawn, James L.
DesRosiers, Peter
Dethlefs, Dennis
Digilio, Peter
Dineen, Lonnie
Doolittle, James
Dreifuerst, Lester
Drozda, Evan
Dunn, Donald
Edgerton, Richard
Elster, George
Enzolera, Sebastian
Eubanks, Paul
Fell, William
Filipcic, Anthony
Finney, Jack
Fitzgerald, Thomas
Flesch, Robert
French, Gary
Friend, Joseph
Gau, Jerome
Gencarelli, Ernest
Gentrup, Edward
Gonderinger, Gerald
Gurney, David
Heck, Lawrence
Hendricks, Fred
Hennessey, Gary
Hills, Lyle
Hilt, Frank
Horner, Ron
Huck, John
Hueser, Ralph
Iwanski, Duane
Jansen, Clarence
Janssen, Daniel
Johnson, Donald
Kaiser, Roland G.
Kalkowski, Kenneth
Kedrowski, Kirk
Kemp, Donald
Kessler, Joseph
Knockenhauer, George F.
Kronschnabel, John
Kube, Norman
Kurtz, Stanley
L'Archevesque, Charles
Lauber, Eldon
Lauer, Justin
Lenz, Patrick
Livingston, Tom
Maly, Vince
Mascarello, Frank
Mascarello, John
Matukewicz, Paul
McGuire, Michael
Mendick, Daniel
Mielak, Lawrence
Miles, Patrick
Miller, Carl
Moore, Fred
Mueting, Richard
Murphy, Thomas
Narducci, Warren
Nelson, Richard
Obershaw, Leonard
Obershaw, Robert
Overkamp, Jerry
Placzek, Michael
Poulosky, Paul
Purnell, Thomas
Ramirez, Joseph
Reynolds, Michael
Ridder, Frederick
Robinson, Hugh
Rooney, Paul
Sanders, Thomas
Schimonitz, Eugene
Schmmidt, Vincent
Schulte, Thomas
Schumacher, Allan
Shoemaker, Robert
Sommer, Fred
Spenner, Arthur
Spicer, Ernest
Spieker, LeRoy
St. Arnold, Irving
Staroski, Jim
Steenson, Gerald
Steffen, Andrew
Telich, Frank
Tharp, Bud
Thoene, Sylvan
Thome, Duane
Tylutki, Glenn
Villemure, Arthur
Werthmann, Ralph
Weskirchen, Charles
Wiehn, Dennis
Young, Wayne

INSTITUTIONS LOCATED IN THE ARCHDIOCESE

[A] COLLEGES AND UNIVERSITIES

OMAHA. *College of St. Mary*, 1901 S. 72 St., 68124. Tel: 402-399-2400.
E-mail: enroll@csm.edu
Web site: www.csm.edu
For a complete listing, refer to the Colleges and Universities section.

**Creighton University*, 2500 California Plaza, 68178. Tel: 402-280-2700.
E-mail: fmm@creighton.edu
Web site: http:www.creighton.edu
For a complete listing, refer to the Colleges and Universities section.

[B] HIGH SCHOOLS, DIOCESAN

OMAHA. *Daniel J. Gross Catholic High School of Omaha*, 7700 S. 43rd St., 68147. Tel: 402-734-2000; Fax: 402-734-4270.
Web site: http://www.gross.creighton.edu
William Ford, Pres. & Contact. Assistant Principals: Dorothy Ostrowski; Rebecca Cleveland; Michelle Pohlman, Campus Ministry; Rev. Walter G. Wancewicz. Lay Teachers 45; Students 680.

Roncalli Catholic High School of Omaha, 6401 Sorensen Pkwy., 68152. Tel: 402-571-7670. Dr. Duane Gross, Pres. & Contact; Dr. Duane Gross, Prin. Sisters 1; Lay Teachers 25; Students 345.

V.J. & Angela Skutt Catholic High School of Omaha, 3131 S. 156 St., 68130. Tel: 402-333-0818. Rev. James E. Gilg, Pres. & Contact; Dr. W. Patrick Durow, Prin.; John Stanten, Activities Dir.; Joan Koneck-Wilcox, Campus Minister. Priests 1; Lay Teachers 38; Students 514.

COLUMBUS. *Scotus Central Catholic High School*. (Grades 7-12), 1554 18th Ave., 68601. Tel: 402-564-7165.
E-mail: wgannon@gilligan.esu7.K12.ne.us
Web site: gillligan.esu.ne.us/~scoweb/scotus.html
Mr. William Gannon, Supt.; Mr. Thomas Walding, Prin. & Contact; Rev. Steven Emanuel, Campus Min. Priests 1; Lay Teachers 32; Students 486.

ELGIN. *Pope John XXIII Central Catholic High School at Elgin*, P.O. Box 179, 68636. Tel: 402-843-5325.
E-mail: dcannon@esu8.esu8.K12.ne.us.
Dennis Cannon, Prin. Priests 4; School Sisters of St. Francis 1; Lay Teachers 12; Students 110.

HARTINGTON. *Cedar Catholic High School*, 401 S. Broadway, 68739. Tel: 402-254-3906.
E-mail: gary@cchs.esu1.K12.ne.us.
Web site: http://www.cchs.cedar.esu1.K12.ne.us
Gary Dunn, Admin. & Contact; Rev. Dennis De Guzman, Spiritual Dir. Lay Teachers 20; Students 263.

NORFOLK. *Norfolk Catholic High School*, 2300 Madison Ave., 68701. Tel: 402-371-2784.
Web site: http://www.ncknights.org
Mr. Richard Bancke, Prin.; Mr. Jeff Beller, Prin. & Contact. Priests 3; Lay Teachers 32; Students 315.

WEST POINT. *Central Catholic High School*, 68788. Tel: 402-372-5326.
E-mail: jj92705@navix.net

Web site: http://pathfinder.esu2.K12.ne.us/ccatholic Mr. John James, Prin. & Contact. Franciscan Sisters of Christian Charity 2; Lay Teachers 13; Students 155.

[C] HIGH SCHOOLS, PRIVATE

OMAHA. *Creighton Preparatory School*, 7400 Western Ave., 68114. Tel: 402-393-1190.
E-mail: rtillman@creighton.edu
Web site: http://dante.creighton.edu
Revs. Robert V. Hotz, S.J., Pres.; Robert J. Tillman, S.J., Supr. & Contact; Mr. John Naatz, Prin.; Revs. Burnell B. Bisbee, S.J.; Robert E. Brodzeller, S.J.; Thomas C. Donohoe, S.J.; William J. Doran, S.J.; Willard J. Dressel, S.J.; Harry Eglsaer, S.J.; Todd W. Harrison, S.J.; Michael J. Marco, S.J.; Mark E. Niemann, S.J.; William F. O'Leary, S.J.; James A. Sinnerud, S.J.; Bros. James E. Garvey, S.J.; Paul J. Kemper, S.J.; Gerald E. Peltz, S.J. Priests 13; Brothers 3; Scholastics 2; Lay Teachers 59; Students 965.

Duchesne Academy of the Sacred Heart, 36th & Burt Sts., 68131. Tel: 402-558-3800. Mrs. Sheila K. Haggas, Head of School & Contact. Society of the Sacred Heart 4; Lay Teachers 24; Girls 217.

Marian High School, 74th and Military Ave., 68134. Tel: 402-571-2618.
E-mail: ekmarian@marian.creighton.edu
Web site: http://marian.creighton.edu
Servants of Mary. Elizabeth Kish, Head of School & Contact. Sisters 4; Lay Teachers 44; Girls 627.

Mercy High School, 1501 S. 48th St., 68106. Tel: 402-553-9424.
E-mail: burnellj@mercy.creighton.edu
Web site: http://www.mercyhigh.org
Sr. Johanna Burnell, R.S.M., Pres. & Contact; Carolyn Jaworski, Prin. Sisters of Mercy of the Americas 5; Lay Teachers 27; Girls 310.

BOYS TOWN. *Father Flanagan's Boys' Home*, 68010. Rev. Valentine J. Peter, Contact.
See Protective Institutions.

ELKHORN. *Mount Michael High School*, 22520 Mt. Michael Rd., 68022-3400. Tel: 402-289-2544; Fax: 442-289-4539.
E-mail: bosborne@knightnet.creighton.edu
Web site: http://mtmike.creighton.edu
Rt. Rev. Theodore Wolff, O.S.B., Abbot; Brian Osborne, Prin. & Contact; Revs. Robert Halter, O.S.B.; Charles Zach, O.S.B., Pres.; Richard Thell, O.S.B.; John Hagemann, O.S.B.; Michael Liebl, O.S.B.; Daniel Lenz, O.S.B.; Louis Sojka, O.S.B.; Stephen J. Plank, O.S.B. Priests 4; Sisters 1; Professed Brothers 2; Lay Teachers 12; Students 141.

[D] ELEMENTARY SCHOOLS, INTER-PAROCHIAL

OMAHA. *All Saints Catholic School*, 1335 S. 10th St., 68108. Tel: 402-346-5757. Diane Cronin, Prin. & Contact. Serving parishes of St. Ann, St. Frances Cabrini, St. Joseph, St. Mary Magdalene Immaculate Conception, St. Patrick. Lay Teachers 15; Students 259.

St. Agnes School of Omaha, Inc., 2211 Q St., 68107. Tel: 402-731-1601. Therese Palandino, Prin.

St. James-Seton School, 9212 Tomahawk Blvd., 68134. Tel: 402-572-0339.
E-mail: tcrum@marian.creighton.edu
Web site: http://mentor.creighton.edu/sjs/
Terry Crum, Prin. & Contact. Servants of Mary 2; Lay Teachers 34; Students 758.

St. Pius X-St. Leo School, 6905 Blondo St., 68104. Tel: 402-551-6667. Mrs. Joyce Gubbels, Prin. & Contact. Servants of Mary 2; Lay Teachers 44; Students 827.

FORDYCE. *West Catholic Elementary*, 303 Omaha St., Box 167, 68736-0167. Tel: 402-357-3507. Serving parishes in Constance, Fordyce & Menominee. Mrs. Marilyn Wiebelhaus, Prin. & Contact. Lay Teachers 5; Students 65.

HARTINGTON. *East Catholic Elementary*, 108 W. 889 Rd., 68739-6079. Tel: 402-357-2146. Marilyn Wiebelhaus, Prin. Serving parishes in Bow Valley, St. Helena & St. James. Lay Teachers 3; Students 45.

HOWELLS. *Howells Community Catholic School*, Box 70, 68641. Tel: 402-986-1689. Serving parishes in Howells, Olean, Heun, Aloys & Tabor. Mrs. Mary Ann Spicka, Prin. (Grades 1-6) & Contact. Lay Teachers 7; Students 116.

[E] ELEMENTARY SCHOOLS, PRIVATE

BOYS TOWN. *Father Flanagan's Boys' Home*. Rev. Valentine J. Peter, Contact. See Protective Institutions below.

[F] SPECIAL EDUCATION

OMAHA. *Christian Urban Education Service Foundation*, 2218 Binney, 68110. Rev. James P. Scholz, Contact. Sisters 1; Lay Teachers 10; Students 150.

The Jesuit Middle School of Omaha, 2311 N. 22nd St., 68110. Tel: 402-346-4464. Rev. James L. Michalski, S.J., Pres. & Contact Person. Lay Teachers 2; Students 30.

Madonna School for Exceptional Children, 2537 N. 62nd, 68104. Tel: 402-556-1883. John Palladino, Prin. Lay Teachers 8; Students 55.

Madonna Shop, 2014 N. 66, 68104. Tel: 402-551-5441. Robin Moses, Mgr.

St. Matthew the Evangelist School. (Grades PreK-8), 12210 S. 36th St., 68123. Patricia A. Buttell, Prin. & Contact. Lay Teachers 15; Students 212.

[G] GENERAL HOSPITALS

OMAHA. *Alegent Health - Bergen Mercy Health System*, 1010 N. 96th St., Ste. 200, 68114. Tel: 402-343-4430; Fax: 402-343-4337
For a complete listing, refer to the Hospitals section.

**Archbishop Bergan Mercy Medical Center*, 7500 Mercy Rd., 68124. Tel: 402-398-6060; Fax: 402-398-6920
For a complete listing, refer to the Hospitals section.

Boys Town National Research Hospital, 555 N. 30 St., 68131. Tel: 402-498-6511; Fax: 402-498-6357
For a complete listing, refer to the Hospitals section.

Catholic Health Corp., 920 S. 107 Ave., 68114. Tel: 402-393-7661
For a complete listing, refer to the Hospitals section.

NORFOLK. *Faith Regional Health Services*, 1500 Koenigstein Ave., 68701. Tel: 402-371-3402; Fax: 402-644-7468
For a complete listing, refer to the Hospitals section.

O'NEILL. *St. Anthony's Hospital*, 68763. Tel: 402-336-2611; Fax: 402-336-2815.
E-mail: sahml@inetnebr.com
For a complete listing, refer to the Hospitals section.

WAYNE. *Providence Medical Center*, 1200 Providence Rd., 68787
For a complete listing, refer to the Hospitals section.

WEST POINT. *Franciscan Care Services, Inc., dba St. Francis Memorial Hospital*, 430 N. Monitor St., 68788-1595. Tel: 402-372-2404; Fax: 402-372-2360.
E-mail: fc70656@navix.net
For a complete listing, refer to the Hospitals section.

[H] NURSING AND CONVALESCENT HOMES

*OMAHA. *Bergan Mercy Care Center*, 1870 S.75th St., 68124. Tel: 402-398-6800
For a complete listing, refer to the Special Care Facilities section.

Mercy Villa, 1845 S. 72 St., 68124
For a complete listing, refer to the Special Care Facilities section.

New Cassel Retirement Center, 900 N. 90th St., 68114. Tel: 402-393-2277
For a complete listing, refer to the Special Care Facilities section.

NORFOLK. *St. Joseph Nursing Home*, 401 N. 18th St., 68701. Tel: 402-371-9404.
E-mail: stjoeadm@ncfcomm.com
For a complete listing, refer to the Special Care Facilities section.

WEST POINT. *Franciscan Care Services, Inc., (d.b.a. St. Joseph Retirement Community)*, 320 E. Decatur, 68788. Tel: 402-372-3477
For a complete listing, refer to the Special Care Facilities section.

[I] PROTECTIVE INSTITUTIONS

*BOYS TOWN. *Father Flanagan's Boys' Home*, 68010. Tel: 402-498-1111
For a complete listing, refer to the Special Care Facilities section.

[J] FAMILY SERVICE CENTERS

OMAHA. *Catholic Charities*, Daniel E. Sheehan Center, 3300 N. 60th St., 68104. Tel: 402-554-0520; Fax: 402-554-0365.
E-mail: ccomaha@aol.com
Web site: http://tcvomaha.org/ccomaha/cathc-l.htm
Scot L. Adams, Contact.

COLUMBUS. *Catholic Charities*, 1761 26th Ave., P.O. Box 573, 68602-0573. Tel: 402-563-3833. Gordon Green, Dir. & Contact.

NORFOLK. *Catholic Charities Counselling Services*, 1109 S. 13th St., Ste. 302, 68701. Tel: 402-371-3555. Gordon Green, Dir. & Contact.

[K] MONASTERIES AND RESIDENCES OF PRIESTS AND BROTHERS

OMAHA. *Campion House*, 518 N. 19th St., 68102. Tel: 402-341-2408. Revs. David G. Schultenover, S.J.; Lawrence E. Gillick, S.J.; Thomas N. Schloemer, S.J.; John P. Fitzgibbons, S.J. Scholastics 9.

Jesuit Community At Creighton University, 2500 California St., 68178. Tel: 402-280-2700.
E-mail: jesuits@creighton.edu
Web site: http://www.creighton.edu
Revs. Thomas J. Shanahan, S.J., Rector; James J. Gladstone, S.J., Min. & Contact; Philip R. Amidon, S.J., Min. & Contact; Andrew Alexander, S.J.; Thomas E. Bannantine, S.J.; Walter E. Boehme; Gail G. Bohr, S.J.; Robert O. Burns, S.J.; Neil Cahill, S.J.; Gregory I. Carlson, S.J.; James F. Clifton; Donald A. Doll, S.J.; Donald D. Driscoll, S.J.; James A. Egan, S.J.; Lawrence W. Flanagan, S.J.; Michael J. Flecky, S.J.; James J. Gladstone, S.J.; Thomas A. Halley, S.J.; M. Dennis Hamm, S.J.; Thomas J. Hansen, S.J.; Robert P. Hart, S.J.; Richard J. Hauser, S.J.; Bro. James Heidrick, S.J.; Revs. Lawrence C. Helmueller, S.J.; Michael L. Hindelang, S.J.; Robert E. Hoene, S.J.; Thomas A. Hoffman, S.J.; John G. Holbrook, S.J.; John P. Horn, S.J.; Eugene J. Jakubek, S.J.; John P. Jelinek, S.J.; Howard E. Kalb, S.J.; William F. Kelley, S.J.; Charles T. Kestermeier, S.J.; William T. Kolarec, S.J.; James P. Kramper, S.J.; G. Thomas Krettek, S.J.; Edward A. Larkin, S.J.; Norbert J. Lemke, S.J.; Leland E. Lubbers, S.J.; John J. Lynch, S.J.; Paul A. Mahowald, S.J.; Thomas Manahan, S.J.; David G. Matzko, S.J.; Robert F. McEniry, S.J.; Richard D. McGloin, S.J.; Dennis P. McNeilly, S.J.; Thomas S. McShane, S.J.; James L. Michalski, S.J.; Michael G. Morrison, S.J.; Charles F. Mullen, S.J.; James J. O'Leary, S.J.; Bernard J. Portz, S.J.; Francis A. Prokes, S.J.; Michael Proterra, S.J. (Baltimore); James J. Quinn, S.J.; Virgil J. Roach, S.J.; Perry L. Robinson, S.J.; John M. Scott, S.J.; Robert J. Shanahan, S.J.; Thomas J. Shanahan, S.J.; Edward A. Sharp, S.J.; Most Rev. John R. Sheets, S.J., D.D.; Bros. Robert E. Smith, S.J.; Edmund W. Stetzen, S.J.; Revs. Gerard L. Stockhausen, S.J.; Albert R. Thelen, S.J.; Ernesto Travieso, S.J.; Martin O. Vaske, S.J.; George E. Von Kaenel, S.J.; Clarence M. Wagener, S.J.; Joseph E. Weiss, S.J.; Bro. Michael R. Wilmot, S.J.; Revs. M. John Wymelenberg, S.J.; John D. Zuercher, S.J. Priests 69; Brothers 6. Legal Title: *Jesuit Community at Creighton University.*

ELKHORN. *Mount Michael Abbey*, 22520 Mount Michael Rd., 68022-3400. Tel: 402-289-2541; Fax: 402-289-4539.
E-mail: abbottheodore@knightnet.creighton.edu
Web site: http://mountmike.creighton.edu
Benedictine Fathers. Rt. Rev. Theodore J. Wolff, O.S.B., Abbot & Contact; Very Rev. Robert Halter, O.S.B., Prior; Bro. Jerome Kmiecik, O.S.B., Sub-Prior; Rt. Rev. Raphael Walsh, O.S.B.; Revs. Frederic Schindler, O.S.B.; Benedict Dohle, O.S.B.; Albert Massmann, O.S.B.; Adrian Liable, O.S.B.; Nathanael Foshage, O.S.B.; Eugene McReynolds, O.S.B.; Bernard Sheehan, O.S.B.; Charles Zach, O.S.B.; Richard Thell, O.S.B.; John Hagemann, O.S.B.; Michael Liebl, O.S.B.; Daniel Lenz, O.S.B.; Louis L. Sojka, O.S.B.; Stephen J. Plank, O.S.B. Priests 17; Professed Brothers 9.

ST. COLUMBANS. *St. Columban's Foreign Mission Society*. (Corporate Title: St. Columban's Foreign Mission Society), 68056. Tel: 402-291-1920.
E-mail: stcolne.us@aol.com
Web site: http://stcolumban.org
Regional Headquarters and Administration Offices of the Columban Fathers in the United States. Very Rev. Brendan O'Sullivan, S.S.C., Dir. & Contact; Revs. James J. Hastings, S.S.C., Vice Dir.; Richard Steinhilber, S.S.C., Editor "Columban Mission"; Paul E. Casey, S.S.C.; J. Donald Devine, S.S.C.; Edward Dolan, S.S.C.; P. Gerard Dunne, S.S.C.; Oliver Kennedy, S.S.C.; Donal O'Farrell, S.S.C.; Robert O'Rourke, S.S.C.; Colm Stanley, S.S.C.; Alban Sueper, S.S.C.; William Sweeney, S.S.C. Priests 14. Other Assignments: Revs. W. Aedan McGrath, S.S.C., Legion of Mary; Thomas Normanly, S.S.C., Buffalo, NY; Robert Clark, S.S.C., U.S. Navy; Otto Imholte, S.S.C., Studies; Arturo Aguilar, S.S.C., El Paso; George Da Roza, S.S.C., Studies; Thomas Vaughan, S.S.C., Pending; Gerard Markey, S.S.C., Pending; Michael Donnelly, S.S.C., El Paso; George V. Herrgott, S.S.C., Studies; Sean McGrath, S.S.C., Los Angeles; William Schmitt, S.S.C., Las Cruces; John Wanaurny, El Paso.

SCHUYLER. *Benedictine Mission House*, Christ the King Priory, 68661. Tel: 402-352-2177; Fax: 402-352-2176.
E-mail: benedict.center@navix.net
Revs. Germar Neubert, Prior & Contact; Herman Kornbrust, O.S.B.; Adam Patras, O.S.B.; Volker Futter, O.S.B., Sub-prior; Thomas Aquinas Leitner, O.S.B. Brothers 7.

[L] CONVENTS AND RESIDENCES FOR SISTERS

OMAHA. *Contemplative Sisters of the Good Shepherd*, 3321 Fontenelle Blvd., 68104-3633. Sr. Clare Filipowicz, Supr. & Contact. Sisters 14. Attended by Jesuit Fathers.

Monastery of St. Clare, 3626 N. 65th Ave., 68104. Tel: 402-558-4916. Poor Clares (Second Order of St. Francis). Sr. Veronia Luebbert, Contact. Sisters 9. Attended by Jesuit Fathers.

Motherhouse of the Servants of Mary, Convent of Our Lady of Sorrows, 7400 Military Ave., 68134. Tel: 402-571-2547; Fax: 402-573-6055. Sr. Terese Lux,

O.S.M., Prov. & Contact; Sr. Zita Marie Sharrow, O.S.M., Asst. Prov. Professed 122; Sisters in Motherhouse 45.

Provincial Motherhouse and Novitiate of the Notre Dame Sisters, 3501 State St., 68112. Tel: 402-455-2994.
E-mail: maz@creighton.edu
Sr. Mary Ann Zimmer, N.D., Prov. Pres. & Contact. Professed 70; Sisters living at Motherhouse 38.

Regional Office of the Sisters of Mercy of the Americas (Regional Community of Omaha), 7262 Mercy Rd., 68124. Tel: 402-393-8225.
E-mail: smomaha@aol.com
Sr. Patricia McDermott, R.S.M., Pres.; Sandy Elsasser, Contact. Perpetually Professed 267.

School Sisters of St. Francis, Regional Office, 2117 S. 33rd St., 68105-3117. Tel: 402-342-5570; Fax: 402-342-5680.
E-mail: sssf@infobridge.com
Sr. Nedine Ferris, Contact.

Sisters of the Annunciation of the Archdiocese of Omaha, P.O. Box 24970, 68124-0970. Tel: 402-391-3606. Revs. Robert J. Gass; Matthew J. Gutowski; Carl F. Sodoro.

Sisters of the Good Shepherd (R.G.S.), 1106 N. 36th St., 68131. Tel: 402-551-2966. Sr. Eileen Schiltz. Sisters 5.

NORFOLK. *Immaculata Convent*, 300 N. 18th St., 68701-3687. Tel: 402-371-3438; Fax: 402-379-2877.
E-mail: maryagnes@conpoint.com
Sr. Agnes Salber, O.S.B., Prioress & Contact. Legal Title: *Immaculata Convent, Priory Motherhouse and Novitiate of the Missionary Benedictine Sisters*. Sisters 41; Postulants 1; Novices 2.

O'NEILL. *St. Anthony's Convent*, 210 E. Adams St., 68763. Tel: 402-336-3576. Sr. Agnesmarie Slaight, Contact. Sisters of St. Francis of Penance and Christian Charity 4.

[M] SECULAR INSTITUTES

OMAHA. *Apostolic Oblates*, 11002 N. 204th St., 68002. Tel: 402-289-2670.
E-mail: psm@mitec.net
Web site: www.mitec.net/~psm/index.html
Teresa Monaghen, Local Moderator. Secular Institute for women dedicated to promoting spiritual growth among the laity. 6762 Western Ave., 68002. Tel: 402-553-4418. Franco Salvo, National Moderator; Palmira Tafani, Contact.

Institute of the Apostolic Oblates, 6762 Western Ave., 68132. Tel: 402-553-4418.
E-mail: aoomaha@mitec.net
Franca Salvo, National Moderator. A secular institute for women with the aim of promoting the universal call to holiness, through working apostolate of the Pro Sanctity Movement.

Apostolic Sodales - Secular Institute for Priests, Boys Town Center, 68010. Tel: 402-498-1469. Rev. Peter Dunne; Palmira Tafani, Contact.

ELKHORN. *Pro Sanctity Movement*, 11002 N. 204th St., 68022. Tel: 402-289-2670; Fax: 402-289-1938. Teresa Monaghen, National Dir. Tel: 402-289-2670; Leonard Gabriel, Dir. Tel: 402-496-6210; Teresa Monaghen, Contact. Ecclesial organization: Promotes apostolates of holiness; teaches, supports and guides people seeking to deepen their spiritual life.

[N] EDUCATIONAL FOUNDATIONS AND TRUST FUNDS

OMAHA. *The Omaha Archdiocesan Educational Foundation, Inc.*, Department of Education, 3212 N. 60th St., 68104. Tel: 402-554-8493; Fax: 402-554-8402.

St. Michael Church of Albion, NE, Educational Endowment Trust, Albion.
St. Michael Church of Albion, NE, Parish Endowment Trust, Albion.
St. Joseph Church Educational Endowment Trust, Atkinson.
St. Mary Church Educational Endowment Trust, Bellevue.
SS. Peter and Paul Parish Endowments, Bow Valley.
East Catholic Elementary School Endowment, Bow Valley/St. Helena.
St. Anthony Church Endowment Trust, Cedar Rapids.
Parish Endowment Trust Fund of St. Michael Catholic Church, Central City.
St. Peter Parish Endowment Trust, Clarks.
Church of St. Theresa of Avila Educational Endowment, Clearwater.
Church of St. Theresa of Avila Parish Endowment, Clearwater.
St. Bonaventure Church Endowment Trust, Columbus.
St. Isidore Church Endowment Trust, Columbus.
St. Isidore Elementary School Endowment Trust, Columbus.
Scotus Central Catholic High School Endowment, Columbus.
St. Ludger Parish Endowment Trust, Creighton.
St. Rose of Lima Parish Endowment, Crofton.
St. Wenceslaus Educational Endowment, Dodge.
St. Stanislaus Church Educational Endowment Trust, Duncan.
St. Boniface School Endowment Trust, Elgin.
St. Boniface Parish Endowment Trust, Elgin.
Mt. Michael Foundation, Inc., Elkhorn.
St. Patrick School Tuition Assistance Endowment Trust, Elkhorn.
St. Patrick School Endowment Trust, Elkhorn.
St. Patrick Parish Endowment Trust, Elkhorn.
Sacred Heart Parish Educational Endowment Trust, Emerson.
West Catholic Educational Endowment, Fordyce/Menominee.
St. John the Baptist Church Educational Endowment Trust, Fort Calhoun.
St. Patrick Catholic Church Endowment Trust, Fremont.
St. Patrick Parish Educational Endowment (Lauer), Fremont.
St. Peter Catholic Church Endowment Trust, Fullerton.
Holy Trinity Parish Endowment, Hartington.
SS. Peter and Paul Catholic Church Endowment Trust for Howells Community Catholic School, Howells.
St. Patrick Parish Endowment Trust, Jackson.
St. Leonard Parish Endowment Trust, Madison.
Church of St. Boniface of Menominee, Menominee.
St. Boniface Parish Endowment, Menominee.
Church of St. Francis of Assisi Parish Educational Endowment, Neligh.
Church of St. Francis of Assisi Parish Endowment Fund, Neligh.
Sacred Heart Parish Endowment Fund, Norfolk.
Archbishop Sheehan Adult Education Fund.
All Saints Catholic School Endowment.
Black Students Educational Endowment.
Blessed Sacrament Parish Educational Endowment.
Christ the King Educational Endowment Trust.
Church of the Assumption Scholarship Educational Endowment.
Robert G. Cunningham Endowment Trusts.
John Flynn Family Endowment Trust.
Fr. James E. Fitzgerald Educational Memorial.
Holy Cross School/Clete and Claire Haney Memorial.
Holy Ghost Educational Endowment.
Marian High School, Inc. Scholarship Endowment Trust.
Marian High School, Inc. Endowment Trust.
Mary Our Queen Educational Endowment Trust.
McAuley Fund.
Music in Catholic Schools.
OAEF, Inc.- C.J. Miller Trust.
Our Lady of Lourdes Educational Endowment Trust.
Religious Education Department-St. Andrew Evangelization Fund.
Roncalli High School Endowment Funds.
St. Adalbert Church Educational Endowment Fund.
St. Bernard Memorial Endowment Fund.
St. Bernard Religious Educational Endowment Fund.
St. Cecilia Cathedral Endowment Trust.
St. Francis of Assisi Church of South Omaha Educational Endowment Fund.
St. James/Seton School Endowment Fund.
St. Joan of Arc Parish Educational Endowment Fund.
St. Joan of Arc Parish Endowment.
St. John Vianney Church of Millard Parish Endowment Trust.
St. Joseph High School Endowment Trust.
St. Margaret Mary Church Educational Endowment Trust.
St. Patrick Church Educational Endowment Trust.
St. Philip Neri Church of Omaha Endowment Trust.
St. Robert Bellarmine Church Educational Endowment Trust.
St. Robert Bellarmine Parish Endowment Trust.
St. Rose Parish Endowment.
St. Stanislaus Parish Endowment Trust.
St. Stanislaus School and Educational Endowment Trust.
St. Thomas More School Endowment Trust.
St. Wenceslaus Church of Omaha Educational Endowment Trust.
Skutt Catholic High School Endowment Trust.
St. Vincent dePaul School Educational Endowment.
St. Vincent dePaul Parish Endowment Trust.
Dolores Vipond Memorial Endowment.
St. Patrick Parish/St. Mary School Endowment, O'Neill.
St. Patrick Foundation, O'Neill.
St. Columbkille Educational Endowment Trust, Papillion.
Immaculate Conception School Endowment-Heine Memorial, St. Helena.
Cedar Catholic High School Endowment (Halemba), St. Helena.
SS. Philip & James Parish Educational Endowment, St. James.
St. Michael Educational Endowment, South Sioux City.
St. Mary Catholic Church Endowment, Spencer.
St. Boniface Elementary School Endowment Fund, Stuart.
St. Wenceslaus Church Parish Endowment Trust, Verdigre.
St. Mary Educational Endowment Fund, Wayne.
Church of the Assumption of the B.V.M. Parish Endowment Trust, West Point.
Guardian Angels Grade School Educational Endowment Trust, West Point.
West Point Central Catholic High School Educational Endowment Trust, West Point.
St. Augustine Indian Mission Endowment, Winnebago.

ST. COLUMBANS. *Columban Fathers Regional Administration*, P.O. Box 10, 68056-0010. Tel: 402-291-1920; Fax: 402-291-8693.
E-mail: stcolneus@aol.com
Web site: http://st.columban.org.
St. Columban's Central Administration.
St. Columban's D-M-P Trust.
St. Columban's Gift Annuity Trust.
St. Columban's Education Trust.
St. Columban's Priests Health Program Trust.
St. Columban's Retirement Fund Trust.
St. Columban's Seminary Reserve Trust.
St. Columban's Masses in Trust.
St. Columban's Donors/Personal Trust.
St. Columban's Regional Trust.
St. Columban's Burse Estate Trust.

[O] MISCELLANEOUS

OMAHA. *Archdiocesan Consultation Service*, 3300 N. 60th St., 68104. Tel: 402-551-1135; Fax: 402-554-0365. Sr. Marie Micheletto, R.S.M., Dir. & Contact.

Archdiocesan Hispanic Ministry Office, 3216 N. 60th St., 68104. Tel: 402-558-3134. Mary Ann Sharp, Sec.

Beginning Experience, 3214 N. 60th St., 68104. Tel: 402-551-9003; Fax: 402-551-3050. Sr. Barbara Markey, Contact.

**Bergan Mercy Foundation, Inc.* (Provides support to the mission of Bergen Mercy Health System dba Alegent Health), 7500 Mercy Rd., 68124. Tel: 402-343-4430. Sr. Norita Cooney, R.S.M., Contact Person.

Cardinal Spellman Catholic Education, 12210 S. 36th St., 68123. Tel: 402-291-2030. Mrs. Patty Buttell, Prin. & Contact.

Cathedral Arts Project, Inc., 100 N. 62nd St., 68132. Tel: 402-558-3100. Bro. William J. Woeger, F.S.C., Exec. Dir. & Contact.

**Catholic Charities Foundation*, 3300 N. 60th St., 68104. Tel: 402-554-0520; Fax: 402-551-8797.
E-mail: ccomaha@aol.com
Web site: http://www.tcvomaha.org/ccomaha/cathc_1.htm
Scot L. Adams, Ph.D., Pres. & Contact.

Catholic County Jail Ministry, 701 S. 28th St., 68105-1511. Tel: 402-342-7142. Sr. Carol Kowalski, O.S.M., Dir. & Contact.

Christ Child Society of Omaha, 1248 S. 10th St., 68108. Tel: 402-342-4566. C. Timothy Connor, Exec. Dir. & Contact.
Day care centers. Total Assisted 200.
Special care centers. Total Assisted 4,500.

Christian Family Movement (CFM), 3514 N. 63rd St., 68104. Tel: 402-558-1710. Contacts: Edwin & Sheila Osterhaus.

Christian Urban Education Service, 2218 Binney St., 68110. Rev. James P. Scholz.

Christians Encounter Christ, 1938 S. 149th Cir., 68144. Tel: 402-334-2497. Jan Ekstrom, Contact Person. Purpose: To promote the transferring of environments through Christian leaders who are willing to live and share their principles of being Christian. Through the ongoing development of their Christian Personality, strengthened by their 4th Day, these leaders strive to instill the spirit and sense of gospel to all environments in which they are actively involved.

Francis House. (Men's Sheltering.), 1702 Nicholas St., P.O. Box 217, 68102. Tel: 402-341-1821. Paul A. Koch, Dir. & Contact.

Harrington Homes Program, 7262 Mercy Rd., Ste. 102, 68124-2348. Tel: 402-398-6614; Fax: 402-398-6370. Sr. Carolyn Coffey, R.S.M., Contact Person.

Health System of Mercy, 7262 Mercy Rd., 68124. Tel: 402-393-8225.
E-mail: smomaha@ad.com
Sr. Joan Martin, R.S.M., Contact Person.

Heart of Mary Publishing Company, Incorporated dba Heart of Mary Ministry, 1613 Vinton St., #4, 68108-1430. Tel: 402-342-9265.
E-mail: srmaryluch@aol.com
Web site: http://www.heartofmaryministry.com
Sr. Mary Lucy Astuto, Contact.

Holy Name Housing Corp., 3014 N. 45th St., 68104. Tel: 402-453-6100; Fax: 402-451-7187. Sr. Marilyn Ross, R.S.M., Exec. Dir. & Contact.

The Institute for Priestly Formation, 320 North 20th St., #1208, 68178. Tel: 402-546-6384.
E-mail: rgabuzda@creighton.edu
Web site: http://www.creighton.edu/summersessions/institute.htm
Richard J. Gabuzda, Contact Person. Purpose: To offer program and support for the integration of theological study, spiritual growth and direction, and retreat experiences for diocesan seminarians and priests.

Marriage Encounter, 3912 Burt St., 68131. Joe & Joan Wilcox, Exec. Team.

McAuley Bergan Center, 3552 Farnam St., 68131. Tel: 402-342-1688. 3534 S. 108th St., 68144. Tel: 402-393-2696. Paul Maginn, Dir. & Contact. Adult Day Care Centers.

McDermott Place, 7262 Mercy Rd., Ste. 102, 68124. Tel: 402-398-6614; Fax: 402-398-6370. Sr. Carolyn Coffey, R.S.M., Contact.

Mercy Housing dba Mercy House, 7262 Mercy Rd., 68124. Tel: 402-398-6614; Fax: 402-398-6032. Sr. Carolyn Coffey, R.S.M., Contact Person.

**Mercy Housing Midwest*.
Mercy Northglen.
Mercy Western Manor.
Mercy Crestview Village.
Mercy Twin Cities - Mercy Oakwood Gardens, 7262 Mercy Rd., Ste. 102, 68124. Tel: 402-398-6614; Fax: 402-398-6370. Sr. Carolyn Coffey, R.S.M., Contact Person. Purpose: To provide affordable housing to the economically poor.

New Covenant Center: Education for Justice and Peace, 2712 S. 24th St., 68108-1342. Tel: 402-345-5111. Sr. Maureen Connolly, S.S.S.F., Prog. Coord.

Notre Dame Housing, Inc., 3501 State St., 68112-1709. Tel: 402-455-2994; Fax: 402-455-3974.
E-mail: maz@creighton.edu
Sr. Mary Ann Zimmer, N.D., Contact Person.
Purpose: To provide housing for elderly and persons of low-income or otherwise unable to afford market rate housing.

Notre Dame Living Center, Inc., 3501 State St., 68112-1709. Tel: 402-455-2994.
E-mail: maz@creighton.edu
Sr. Mary Ann Zimmer, N.D., Contact Person & Pres. Purpose: Provides affordable housing to the elderly, particularly those of low-income status.

The Omaha Archdiocesan Community Foundation and Donor Directed Depository, P.O. Box 4130, 68104-0130. Tel: 402-554-8493. This foundation receives asset gifts and distributes earnings at the direction of the donor participants for the support of Catholic ministries in the archdiocese.

Omaha Archdiocesan Educational Foundation, Inc., P.O. Box 4130, 68104. Mrs. Rosemary Daly, Pres.

Omaha Catholic Jail Ministry, 2500 California St., 68178. Tel: 402-280-2700.

Douglas County Correction Center, 710 S. 17th St., 68102. Tel: 402-444-7400.

Pope Paul VI Institute for the Study of Human Reproduction, 6901 Mercy Rd., 68106. Tel: 402-390-6600; Fax: 402-390-9851. Thomas W. Hilgers, M.D., Dir.

St. James Manor, Inc., 3118 N. 60th St., 68104. Tel: 402-551-4243. Joseph V. Rysavy, Pres. & Contact.

Siena - Francis House, Inc., P.O. Box 217, D.T.S., 68101. Tel: 402-341-1821; Fax: 402-341-5270. Paul A. Koch, Dir. & Contact.

Siena House. (Women's Sheltering), 1702 Nicholas St., P.O. Box 217, 68102. Tel: 402-341-1821; Fax: 402-341-5270. Paul A. Koch, Dir. & Contact.

TEC, Box 4130, 68104. Tel: 402-554-8493. Rita Ramos, Asst. Dir. Youth Ministry.

Widowed and Divorced Catholics of Omaha, 3214 N. 60th St., 68104. Tel: 402-551-9003. Nancy Davis, Contact.

The Young Adult Beginning Experience, 3214 N. 60th St., 68104. Tel: 402-551-9003. Sr. Barbara Markey, Contact.

LYNCH. *Niobrara Valley House of Renewal*, P.O. Box 117, 68746. Rev. Donald M. Kros, Contact.

PETERSBURG. *John Paul II Religious Education Center*, Box 9, 4th & Norman St., 68652-0009. Tel: 402-386-5747. Sr. Lee Agnes Hodapp, O.S.F., Dir. & Consultant.

WINNEBAGO. *St. Augustine's Indian Mission*, P.O. Box GG, 68071. Revs. Thomas E. Bauwens, Dir.; Steven Boes, Contact.

RELIGIOUS INSTITUTES OF MEN REPRESENTED IN THE ARCHDIOCESE

For further details refer to the corresponding bracketed number in the Religious Institutes of Men or Women section.

[0200]—*Benedictine Monks*.—O.S.B.
[0330]—*Brothers of the Christian Schools*. (St. Louis, MO).—F.S.C.
[0690]—*Jesuit Fathers and Brother*. (Wisconsin Prov.).—S.J.
[0150]—*Order of the Augustinian Recollects*. (St. Augustine Prov.).—O.A.R.
[1070]—*Redemptorist Fathers*. (St. Louis Prov.).—C.SS.R.
[0370]—*Society of St. Columban*.—S.S.C.

RELIGIOUS INSTITUTES OF WOMEN REPRESENTED IN THE ARCHDIOCESE

[0230]—*Benedictine Sisters of Pontifical Jurisdiction*.—O.S.B.
[1070-03]—*Dominican Sisters*.—O.P.
[1230]—*Franciscan Sisters of Christian Charity*.—O.S.F.
[1430]—*Franciscan Sisters of Our Lady of Perpetual Help*.—O.S.F.
[2575]—*Institute of the Sisters of Mercy of the Americas*.—R.S.M.
[0210]—*Missionary Benedictine Sisters*.—O.S.B.
[2960]—*Notre Dame Sisters*.—N.D.
[3760]—*Order of St. Clare*.—O.S.C.
[1680]—*School Sisters of St. Francis*. (Our Lady of Angels Prov.).—O.S.F.
[3580]—*Servants of Mary*.—O.S.M.
[1630]—*Sisters of St. Francis of Peace and Christian Charity*. (Denver Prov.).—O.S.F.
[1640]—*Sisters of St. Francis of Perpetual Adoration*. (Colorado Springs, CO).—O.S.F.
[1830]—*Sisters of the Good Shepherd*.—R.G.S.
[3270]—*Sisters of the Most Precious Blood* . (O'Fallon, MO).—C.PP.S.
[3320]—*Sisters of the Presentation of the B.V.M.*.—P.B.V.M.
[4070]—*Society of the Sacred Heart*.—R.S.C.J.
[4120]—*Ursuline Nuns, of the Congregation of Paris*.—O.S.U.

ARCHDIOCESAN CEMETERIES

OMAHA. *Calvary*.
Holy Sepulchre.
Resurrection.
St. Mary.
St. Mary Magdalene.

NECROLOGY

† Flynn, Rev. Msgr. John A., Omaha, NE, Archdiocesan Community Foundation. —Died Sept. 15, 1997.
† Foster, William A., (Retired). —Died May 14, 1997.
† Hulsman, Rev. Msgr. Francis J., (Retired). —Died Sept. 14, 1997.
† Kleffman, William C., Omaha, NE, St. Agnes. —Died Aug. 21, 1997.
† Tresnak, Anthony J., (Retired). —Died May 11, 1997.

Diocese of Orange in California

(Arausicanae in California)

Most Reverend

NORMAN F. MCFARLAND, D.D., J.C.D.

Bishop of Orange; ordained June 15, 1946; appointed Titular Bishop of Bida and Auxiliary of San Francisco June 5, 1970; consecrated September 8, 1970; appointed Apostolic Administrator December 6, 1974; appointed Bishop of Reno-Las Vegas February 10, 1976; installed March 31, 1976; appointed Bishop of Orange December 29, 1986; installed February 24, 1987. *Res., 200 W. La Veta Ave., Orange, CA, 92866. Office: Marywood Center, 2811 E. Villa Real Dr., Orange, CA, 92867.*

Most Reverend

MICHAEL P. DRISCOLL, M.S.W., D.D.

Auxiliary Bishop and Vicar General; ordained May 1, 1965; appointed Titular Bishop of Massita and Auxiliary December 19, 1989; consecrated March 6, 1990. *Res., 200 W. La Veta Ave., Orange, CA, 92866.*

Chancellor's Office: 2811 E. Villa Real Dr., P.O. Box 14195, Orange, CA, 92863-1595. Tel.: 714-282-3000; Fax: 714-282-3029.

ESTABLISHED JUNE 18, 1976.

Square Miles 782.

Comprises the County of Orange in the State of California.

DIOCESAN PATRON: Our Lady of Guadalupe.

Legal Titles: *(Prot. No. CD 528-76)*

The Roman Catholic Bishop of Orange, a Corporation Sole.

Diocese of Orange Education and Welfare Corporation.

Catholic Charities of Orange.

For legal titles of parishes and diocesan institutions, consult the Diocesan Pastoral Service Office.

STATISTICAL OVERVIEW

Personnel	
Bishop	1
Auxiliary Bishops	1
Abbots	1
Retired Abbots	1
Priests: Diocesan Active in Diocese	117
Priests: Active Outside Diocese	8
Priests: Diocesan in Foreign Missions	1
Priests: Retired, Sick or Absent	52
Number of Diocesan Priests	178
Religious Priests in Diocese	94
Extern Priests in Diocese	16
Ordinations:	
Diocesan Priests	2
Religious Priests	1
Transitional Deacons	2
Permanent Deacons in Diocese	49
Total Brothers	7
Total Sisters	360
Parishes	
Parishes	54
With Resident Pastor:	
Resident Diocesan Priests	46
Resident Religious Priests	8
Without Resident Pastor:	
Missions	5
Pastoral Centers	4
Professional Ministry Personnel:	
Brothers	4
Sisters	49
Lay Ministers	165
Welfare	
Catholic Hospitals	1
Total Assisted	34,488
Health Care Centers	2
Total Assisted	170,986
Homes for the Aged	1
Total Assisted	55
Day Care and Extended Day Care Centers	1
Total Assisted	100
Specialized Homes	5
Total Assisted	15,801
Special Centers for Social Services	3
Total Assisted	375,479
Residential Care of Disabled	2
Total Assisted	51
Other Institutions	1
Total Assisted	100
Educational	
Diocesan Students in Other Seminaries	50
Seminaries, Religious	1
Students Religious	11
Total Seminarians	61
High Schools, Diocesan and Parish	3
Total Students	4,633
High Schools, Private	3
Total Students	1,076
Elementary Schools, Diocesan and Parish	35
Total Students	13,257
Elementary Schools, Private	2
Total Students	718
Catechesis/Religious Education:	
High School Students	7,645
Elementary Students	30,660
Total Students Under Catholic Instruction	58,050
Teachers in the Diocese:	
Priests	11
Brothers	1
Sisters	51
Lay Teachers	933
Vital Statistics	
Receptions into the Church:	
Infant Baptism Totals	17,767
Adult Baptism Totals	811
Received into Full Communion	652
First Communions	11,211
Confirmations	4,406
Marriages:	
Catholic	2,938
Interfaith	776
Total Marriages	3,714
Deaths	2,748
Total Catholic Population	606,484
Total Population	2,636,888

Former Bishops—Most Rev. WILLIAM R. JOHNSON, appt. Titular Bishop of Biera and Auxiliary Bishop of Los Angeles, Feb. 9, 1971; cons. March 25, 1971; installed as first Bishop of Orange, June 18, 1976; died July 28, 1986.

Vicar General—Most Rev. MICHAEL P. DRISCOLL, D.D., Office: *Marywood Center, 2811 E. Villa Real Dr., Orange, 92867.* Tel: 714-282-3000.

Chancellor/Moderator of the Curia—Rev. Msgr. JOHN URELL, Office: *2811 E. Villa Real Dr., Orange, 92867.* Tel: 714-282-3000.

Vice Chancellor—Rev. J. MICHAEL MCKIERNAN, *P.O. Box 14195, Orange, 92863-1595.* Tel: 714-282-3000.

Secretary to the Bishop—Rev. Msgr. JOHN URELL.

Master of Ceremonies—Rev. J. MICHAEL MCKIERNAN, *P.O. Box 14195, Orange, 92863-1595.*

Vicar for Religious Communities—Most Rev. MICHAEL P. DRISCOLL, D.D., *2811 E. Villa Real Dr., Orange, 92867.* Tel: 714-282-3000.

Vicar for Hispanic Communities—Rev. Msgr. JAIME SOTO, Office: *2811 E. Villa Real Dr., Orange, 92867.* Tel: 714-282-3000.

Vicar for Priests—Rev. EAMON O'GORMAN. Tel: 714-282-3000.

Vicar for Religious Education—Rev. CHRISTOPHER SMITH, Office: *2811 E. Villa Real Dr., Orange, 92867.* Tel: 714-282-3000.

Vicar for Pastoral and Community Affairs—Rev. Msgr. JOHN F. SAMMON, P.A., *Res., 200 W. La Veta Ave., Orange, 92866.* Office: *2811 E. Villa Real Dr., Orange, 92867.* Tel: 714-282-3000.

Diocesan Pastoral Service Office—2811 E. Villa Real Dr., Orange, 92867. Tel: 714-282-3000. Office Hours: Mon-Fri. 9-5, *P.O. Box 14195, Orange, 92863-1484;* Fax: 714-282-3029.

Diocesan Tribunal—2811 E. Villa Real Dr., Orange, 92867. Tel: 714-282-3080.

Judicial Vicar—Rev. WILLIAM J. VOHSING, J.C.L.

Adjutant Judicial Vicars—Rev. Msgr. DANIEL J. MURRAY, J.C.L.; Rev. Msgr. DANIEL H. BRENNAN; Rev. JACK K. SEWELL, J.C.L.

Secretary to the Tribunal—Rev. B. JEFFREY BLANGIARDI, S.J., J.C.D.

Promotor of Justice—Rev. Msgr. HUGH O'CONNOR.

Judges—Rev. Msgr. DANIEL H. BRENNAN; Rev. Msgr. JOHN G. CAMPBELL; Rev. Msgr. PAUL MARTIN; Rev. Msgr. JOHN URELL, M.S.W.; Rev. Msgr. DANIEL J.

MURRAY, J.C.L.; Very Rev. ARTHUR A. HOLQUIN, S.T.L.; Revs. B. JEFFREY BLANGIARDI, S.J., J.C.D.; JAMES HARTNETT; THOMAS HA; DANIEL R. HOPCUS; JOHN R. KELLER; JOSEPH NETTEKOVEN; TED OLSON; KENNETH SCHMIT; JACK K. SEWELL, J.C.L.; WILLIAM J. VOHSING, J.C.L.; JOHN CARONAN, O.Praem., J.C.L.

Defenders of the Bond—Revs. TIMOTHY RAMAEKERS; JOHN A. BRADLEY; TUAN JOSEPH PHAM, J.C.L.; DOUGLAS COOK, J.C.L.

Ecclesiastical Notaries—SANDRA K. DALTON; LINDA BRAUN; LAURIE MARMOLEJO.

National Organization for Decent Literature—Rev. Msgr. JOHN F. SAMMON, Dir., *2811 E. Villa Real Dr., Orange, 92867.* Tel: 714-282-3000.

Newman Apostolate—Rev. PATRICK PHILBIN, S.M., Dir., *P.O. Box 6030, Irvine, 92616.* Tel: 714-856-0211.

Parish Councils and Parish Development—Rev. Msgr. JOHN F. SAMMON, Dir., *2811 E. Villa Real Dr., Orange, 92867.* Tel: 714-282-3000.

Diaconate—Sr. JOANN TABOR, C.S.J., Dir. JACK BRENNAN, Asst. Dir., *2811 E. Villa Real Dr., Orange, 92867.* Tel: 714-282-3000.

Clergy Personnel Board—Rev. Msgr. WILLIAM MCLAUGHLIN, Chm.; Rev. Msgr. DANIEL MURRAY; Rev. Msgr. JOHN URELL, Auditor; Revs. CIRILO FLORES; RUDOLPH PRECIADO; JEROME KARCHER, *2811 E. Villa Real Dr., Orange, 92867.* Tel: 714-282-3000.

Communications Office—Rev. Msgr. LAWRENCE J. BAIRD, Dir., *2811 E. Villa Real Dr., Orange, 92867.* Tel: 714-282-3000.

Conciliation & Arbitration Office—Ms. DOLORES CHURCHILL, L.C.S.W., *2811 E. Villa Real Dr., Orange, 92867.* Tel: 714-282-3000.

Diocesan Council of Catholic Women—Rev. DOUGLAS COOK, Moderator; DORIS CANTLAY, Pres., *2811 E. Villa Real Dr., Orange, 92867.* Tel: 714-282-3000.

Priests' Relief—Rev. EAMON O'GORMAN, *2811 E. Villa Real Dr., Orange, 92867.* Tel: 714-282-3000.

Council of Priests—Most Rev. MICHAEL DRISCOLL; Most Rev. NORMAN F. MCFARLAND; Rev. Msgr. JOHN SAMMON; Rev. Msgr. PAUL MARTIN; Rev. WILLIAM VOHSING; Rev. Msgr. JAIME SOTO; Rev. Msgr. JOHN URELL; Rev. Msgr. PETER TIEN; Rev. Msgr. ANTONIO SUDARIO; Revs. RICHARD DELAHUNTY; TIMOTHY FREYER; BRUCE PATTERSON; AL BACA; RUDOLPH PRECIADO; PATRICK RUDOLPH; KENNETH KRAUSE; J. MICHAEL MCKIERNAN; STEVE SALLOT; JOE JUSTICE; MICHAEL HEHER; BRENDAN SMITH, S.T.; VINCE GILMORE, O.Praem.; JOHN LENIHAN; JUSTIN MACCARTHY, *2811 E. Villa Real Dr., Orange, 92867.* Tel: 714-282-3000.

Consultors—Most Rev. MICHAEL DRISCOLL, D.D.; Rev. WILLIAM VOHSING; Rev. Msgr. JOHN SAMMON; Rev. Msgr. JAIME SOTO; Rev. Msgr. PETER TIEN; Rev. Msgr. JOHN URELL; Revs. JOHN LENIHAN; JUSTIN MACCARTHY.

Propagation of the Faith—Rev. Msgr. JOHN F. SAMMON, Dir., *2811 E. Villa Real Dr., Orange, 92867.* Tel: 714-282-3000.

Religious Institute of Orange Executive Board—Sr. JEAN SCHULTE, S.P.; Sr. CLARE BRIODY, D.M.J.; Sr. EYMARD FLOOD, O.S.C.; Sr. VICKY BRADY, R.S.M.; Sr. MAURA FITZSIMMON, P.B.V.M.; Sr. HELEN LOUISE LACEY, C.S.J.

Society of St. Vincent de Paul of Orange County—Mr. JAMES D. KAY; Rev. PEREGRINE GRAFFIUS, O.S.M., Spiritual Dir., *180 S. Cypress, Orange, 92866.* Tel: 714-633-9194.

Schools Office—Bro. WILLIAM CARRIERE, F.S.C., Supt.; Sr. MARY CATHERINE EVANS, O.P., Assoc. Supt., *2811 E. Villa Real Dr., Orange, 92867.* Tel: 714-282-3000.

Schools Advisory Board of Education—*2811 E. Villa Real Dr., Orange, 92867.* Tel: 714-282-3000.

Vocations Office—Rev. Msgr. DANIEL J. MURRAY, Dir., *2811 E. Villa Real Dr., Orange, 92867.* Tel: 714-282-3000.

Campaign for Human Development—Rev. Msgr. JOHN URELL, Dir.

Board of Directors—DOLORES CHURCHILL; Deacon FRANK CHAVEZ; WALTER DALY; DIETER MYERS GONZALES; EDWARD EGAN; WILLIAM ERICKSON; VIRGINIA FAULKNER; Sr. REBECCA RODRIGUEZ, C.S.J.; FRED VEGA, *2811 E. Villa Real Dr., Orange, 92867.* Tel: 714-282-3000.

Diocesan Offices and Directors

Apostleship of Prayer—Rev. Msgr. HUGH O'CONNOR, *2050 W. Ball Rd., Anaheim, 92804.* Tel: 714-774-2595.

Archivist—Rev. WILLIAM KREKELBERG, Office: *Mission San Juan Capistrano, 31522 Camino Capistrano, San Juan Capistrano, 92675-0691.*

Boy Scouts—Rev. Msgr. JOHN F. SAMMON, *2811 E. Villa Real Dr., Orange, 92867.* Tel: 714-282-3000.

Liturgical Environment-Art Committee—Rev. ROD STEPHENS, Chm.; Very Rev. ARTHUR HOLQUIN; Revs. KERRY BEAULIEU; PAUL LEVESQUE, *2811 E. Villa Real Dr., Orange, 92867.* Tel: 714-282-3000.

Land Advisory Board—Most Rev. NORMAN F. MCFARLAND, Pres.; Most Rev. MICHAEL P. DRISCOLL, D.D., Admin.; Mr. ARTHUR BIRTCHER; Mr. TERENCE K. BARRY; Mr. JOSEPH HENNESSEY; Mr. DANIEL HOLDEN; Mr. R. RAND SPERRY; Rev. Msgr. JOHN URELL; KENNETH TAIT. Staff: Mr. PHIL REIS; Mr. DON CROUGH.

Diocesan Construction Board—Most Rev. NORMAN F. MCFARLAND; Mr. TERRANCE BARRY, Chm.; Mr. RON GAGNON; Mr. FRANK REYNOLDS; Mr. MARKO E. BOTICH; Mr. EDWARD REYNOLD; Mr. HARRY G. KREIDER; Mr. ARTHUR BIRTCHER; Mr. RICHARD HUNSAKER; Most Rev. MICHAEL P. DRISCOLL. Staff: Mr. PHIL RIES; Mr. DON CROUGH, Construction Mgr.

Diocesan Finance Council—Most Rev. MICHAEL DRISCOLL; Most Rev. NORMAN F. MCFARLAND; Mr. JACK DERLOSHON, Chm.; Mr. TOM KLEINBAUER; Mr. GORDON LEE; Rev. Msgr. JOHN URELL; Mr. LEE MEYER; Mr. WILLIAM CRAWFORD; GUY WILSON; PAUL SCHLOEMER. Staff: Mr. PHIL RIES, Dir.; Mr. CARLOS VASQUEZ.

Director of Finance—Mr. PHIL RIES, Dir.; Mr. CARLOS VASQUEZ, Controller, *P.O. Box 14195, Orange, 92867.* Tel: 714-282-3000.

Catholic Charities of Orange—Most Rev. MICHAEL P. DRISCOLL, D.D., Vicar, Charities; KRISTAN SCHLICHTE, Exec. Dir., Office: *1506 Brookhollow, Ste. 112, Santa Ana, 92705.* Tel: 714-662-7500.

Cemeteries—Mr. THOMAS FLYNN, Dir., *2811 E. Villa Real Dr., Orange, 92867.* Tel: 714-282-3000.

Cemeteries Board—Rev. Msgr. JOHN F. SAMMON, Chm.; Most Rev. MICHAEL P. DRISCOLL, D.D.; Rev. Msgr. SINON F. FALVEY.

Ministry to Priests—Rev. EAMON O'GORMAN, Vicar, Priests; Rev. Msgr. BILL MCLAUGHLIN; Rev. Msgr. DANIEL BRENNAN; Rev. Msgr. HUGH O'CONNOR; Most Rev. MICHAEL P. DRISCOLL, D.D.; Revs. MICHAEL HOAN; RUDOLPH PRECIADO; LAURENCE DOLAN; AL BACA; RICHARD DELAHUNTY; KEN SCHMIT; JOHN MCANDREW; GORDON MORELAND, S.J.; JOSEPH JUSTICE; MICHEL PECHARICH; STEVE SALLOT, *2811 E. Villa Real Dr., Orange, 92867.* Tel: 714-282-3000.

Cursillo Movement—Revs. RAYMOND SKONEZNY, Exec. Spiritual Dir. DAVID VUELVAS-ARIAS, Spiritual Dir., Hispanic Cursillo; PETER VU DINH TRAC, Spiritual Dir., Vietnamese Cursillo, *2811 E. Villa Real Dr., Orange, 92867.* Tel: 714-538-2096.

Office for Deaf Ministry—CONNIE WILD, Dir.

Office for Religious Education—Rev. CHRISTOPHER H. SMITH, Vicar; RUTH BRADLEY, Dir. NURIA CHEKOURAS, Coord./Consultant, Hispanic Adult, Family and Child Religious Education; MARY BROSSEAU, Consultant, Special Religious Education. Assoc. Dirs., Youth & Young Adult Ministries: NANCY HORMUTH, Dir. JAVIER CASTILLO, Assoc. Dir.

Library/Media Center—DIANE MURRAY, Dir.

Catechetical Institute—JOAN KULIK, Dir., *2811 E. Villa Real Dr., Orange, 92867.* Tel: 714-282-3000.

Religious Education Board—VIRGINIA CURLEY; RUTH BRADLEY; Bro. WILLIAM CARRIERE, F.S.C.; Sr. JENNIFER NGUYEN, L.H.C.; SHERRIE OLDHAM; STEVE ELLAIR; SUE LINKHORN; EUGENE O'TOOLE; MITZI PONGINETTI; Rev. CHRISTOPHER H. SMITH, *2811 E. Villa Real Dr., Orange, 92867.* Tel: 714-282-3000.

Ecumenical and Interreligious Affairs—Rev. Msgr. LAWRENCE J. BAIRD, Chm.; Sr. MARYANNE HUEPPER, C.S.J.; Rev. JOHN MONESTERO; Dr. CHARLES FRAZEE; Mrs. CECIL PIANTADOSI; Mrs. SUE MONTANO FENWICK; Dr. GEORGE E. SAINT-LAURENT; Rev. PAUL LEVESQUE; Mrs. JOSEPHINE BALL, *2811 E. Villa Real Dr., Orange, 92867.* Tel: 714-282-3000.

Family Life—CARMELA TREANOR, Dir., *2811 E. Villa Real Dr., Orange, 92867.* Tel: 714-282-3045. Commission Members: RICE BERKSHIRE; LINDA BERKSHIRE; Deacon TIM CARVER; DONNA CARVER; Deacon TOM KLOSS; MANNY COLOSO; DORIS COLOSO; BOB DAUSCH; MARY DAUSCH; IRMA FORTIN; RUDY GOMEZ; LALI GOMEZ; Rev. JOHN JANZE; RICH JENISON; MARY JENISON; CAROL KOPPENHEFFER; Rev. BRUCE LAVERY; Sr. DOROTHY MORRIS; EUGENE O'TOOLE; BILL PERRY; MARSHA PERRY; EILEEN PFAFF; ALMA REGAN; JULIA RAMIREZ; HUMBERTO RAMIREZ; DENNIS STOICA; SANDY STOICA; Rev. ROBERT VIDAL; STEVE WHITE; EARL WILLIAM.

Office of Hispanic Ministry—Rev. Msgr. JAIME SOTO, Dir.; Mrs. JUANA MARIA AMEZQUITA, Admin., *2811 E. Villa Real Dr., Orange, 92867.* Tel: 714-282-3000.

Holy Childhood—Rev. Msgr. JOHN F. SAMMON, Dir., *2811 E. Villa Real Dr., Orange, 92867.* Tel: 714-282-3000.

Holy Name Society—Rev. Msgr. JOHN F. SAMMON, Dir., *2811 E. Villa Real Dr., Orange, 92867.* Tel: 714-282-3000.

Insurance—Mr. THOMAS FLYNN, Dir., *2811 E. Villa Real Dr., Orange, 92867.* Tel: 714-282-3000.

Legion of Mary—Rev. Msgr. PEDRO YRIGAN, Dir., *Res., 922 N. Newhope St., Santa Ana, 92703.* Tel: 714-554-3437. Rev. Msgr. HUGH O'CONNOR, *Res., 2050 W. Ball Rd., Anaheim, 92804.* Tel: 714-774-2595.

Liturgy, Music, Evangelization & Adult Education—Rev. ROD STEPHENS, Dir., *2811 E. Villa Real Dr., Orange, 92867.* Tel: 714-282-3000.

Marriage Encounter—JOE CRUZ; TERI CRUZ, *2811 E. Villa Real Dr., Orange, 92867.* Tel: 714-282-3000.

Respect Life Program NCCB—Rev. Msgr. JOHN F. SAMMON, Dir., *2811 E. Villa Real Dr., Orange, 92867.* Tel: 714-282-3000.

Catecumenate—Rev. ROD STEPHENS, Dir., *2811 E. Villa Real Dr., Orange, 92867.* Tel: 714-282-3000.

Stewardship Office—BARBARA NELSON, Dir., *2811 E. Villa Real Dr., Orange, 92867.* Tel: 714-282-3000.

Planned Giving Office—Rev. Msgr. LAWRENCE BAIRD, *2811 E. Villa Real Dr., Orange, 92867.* Tel: 714-282-3000.

Perpetual Adoration Programs—Rev. Msgr. JOHN SAMMON, Dir., *2811 E. Villa Real Dr., Orange, 92867.* Tel: 714-282-3000.

CLERGY, PARISHES, MISSIONS AND PAROCHIAL SCHOOLS

CITY OF ORANGE

1—CATHEDRAL OF THE HOLY FAMILY (1921), Very Rev. Arthur Holquin, Rector; Revs. Patrick Rudolph; Gregory Gilroy, O.F.M.Conv.; J. Michael McKiernan. In res., Rev. Malcolm Smith, M.Afr.

Res., 566 S. Glassell St., 92866. Tel: 714-639-2900; Fax: 714-639-8022.

School—530 S. Glassell St., 92866. Tel: 714-538-6012; Fax: 714-633-5892.

Lay Teachers 28; Students 594.

Catechesis/Religious Programs—Tel: 714-538-2800.

Students 706.

2—LA PURISIMA (1964), Revs. Valentin Ramon, C.M.F.; Richard Wozniak, C.M.F.; William Paiz, C.M.F.; Peter Vu Dinh Trac; Deacon Dr. Anthony Bube.

Res., 11712 N. Hewes, 92869. Tel: 714-633-5800; Fax: 714-633-8364.

School—Tel: 714-633-5411; Fax: 714-633-1588. Sr. Cecilia Duran, O.D.N., Prin.

Sisters of the Company of Mary 1; Lay Teachers 15; Students 320.

Catechesis/Religious Programs—Tel: 714-633-5344; Fax: 714-633-1588.

Students 1,077.

3—ST. NORBERT (1963), Revs. John M. Joyce; John-Paul Hopping. In res., Rev. Msgr. Peter Esterka; Rev. Jude Lucier, O.Praem; Deacons Timothy Carver; Jay Milam.

Res., 300 E. Taft Ave., 92865. Tel: 714-637-4360; Fax: 714-637-0201.

School—Tel: 714-637-6822; Fax: 714-637-3682.

Union of the Sisters of the Presentation of the Blessed Virgin Mary 2; Lay Teachers 11; Students 319.

Catechesis/Religious Programs—Tel: 714-998-1070. D.R.E.: Sr. Marie Clare Fox, P.B.V.M.; Sydney Costello.

Students 780.

ORANGE COUNTY OUTSIDE THE CITY

Anaheim

1—ST. ANTHONY CLARET (1955) (English-Spanish), Rev. Marito F. Rebamontan; Rev. Msgr. James F. Nash, Pastor Emeritus; Revs. Paul Levesque; Carlos Martinez.

Res., 1450 E. La Palma Ave., 92805. Tel: 714-776-0270; Fax: 714-776-6022.

School—Tel: 714-535-3284; Fax: 714-535-8558.

Lay Teachers 10; Students 268.

Catechesis/Religious Programs—Tel: 714-778-0580. D.R.E.: Maria Holper; Leonard Beckman.

Students 786.

2—ST. BONIFACE (1860), Rev. Msgr. Wilbur Davis; Revs. David Vuelvas-Arias; Louis Abdoo, I.M.C.; Quang Vinh Chu.

Res., 120 N. Janss St., 92805. Tel: 714-956-3110; Fax: 714-956-3034.

School—500 W. Chartres St., 92805. Tel: 714-772-3060.

Dominican Sisters (Mission San Jose) O.P. 1; Lay Teachers 19; Students 309.

Catechesis/Religious Programs—Tel: 714-776-6473.

Students 1,123.

3—ST. JUSTIN MARTYR (1958), Rev. Joseph Nettekoven; Rev. Msgr. Hugh O'Connor, Pastor Emeritus; Revs. J. Douglas Dale; Antonio Zapata. In res., Rev. John Monestero.

Res., 2050 W. Ball Rd., 92804. Tel: 714-774-2595; Fax: 714-774-9849.
Church—Ball Rd. and Empire, 92804.
School—2030 W. Ball Rd., 92804. Tel: 714-772-4902; Fax: 714-772-2092.
Lay Teachers 13; Students 290.
Catechesis/Religious Programs—Tel: 714-535-6111.
Students 380.
Mission—Anaheim, Sacred Heart, 10852 Harcourt, 92804. Tel: 714-821-3133.

4—SAN ANTONIO (1977), Rev. Seamus A. Glynn. In res., Rev. William J. Vohsing; Deacons Doug Cook; Thomas Klos.
Res., 5800 E. Santa Ana Canyon Rd., 92807. Tel: 714-974-1416; Fax: 714-974-9630.
Catechesis/Religious Programs—Tel: 714-974-2053. Carolyn Buehler, D.R.E.
Students 931.

Brea, St. Angela Merici (1962), Rev. Theodore Olson; Rev. Msgr. Emmett McCarthy, Pastor Emeritus; Revs. John McAndrew; Fabian Richards; Deacons Fred von Voigt; Carlos Navarro.
Res., 585 Walnut St., 92821. Tel: 714-529-1821; Fax: 714-529-0569.
Church—Walnut and Fir, 92821.
School—575 S. Walnut Ave., 92821. Tel: 714-529-6372; Fax: 714-529-7755.
Lay Teachers 13; Religious 1; Students 295.
Catechesis/Religious Programs—Tel: 714-529-2311.
Students 761.

Buena Park, St. Pius V (1948), Revs. Thomas McManus, O.S.A.; Patrick Crilly, O.S.A.; Thomas Tevington, O.S.A.; Patrick A. Brennan, O.S.A.; Declan (Finbarr) Fogarty, O.S.A.
Res., 7691 Orangethorpe Ave., 90621. Tel: 714-522-2193; Fax: 714-522-1730.
School—Tel: 714-522-5313; Fax: 714-522-1767.
Lay Teachers 19; Students 590.
Catechesis/Religious Programs—Tel: 714-522-3971.
Students 600.

Capistrano Beach, San Felipe de Jesus (1950) (Spanish), Rev. John A. Bradley; Rev. Msgr. John V. Coffield, Pastor Emeritus; Deacon Victor Samano.
Res., 27045-B Camino de Estrella, 92624. Tel: 714-661-7500; Fax: 714-661-7500.
Church—Domingo St. & Sepulveda, 92624.
Catechesis/Religious Programs—27045-B Camino de Estrella, 92624.
Students 135.

Costa Mesa, St. Joachim (1947), Revs. Joseph R. Robillard; Douglas Cook; Michael Galinada, S.M.
Res., 1964 Orange Ave., 92627. Tel: 714-574-7400; Fax: 714-574-7407.
School—Tel: 714-574-7411.
Sisters of the Company of Mary 2; Lay Teachers 17; Students 335.
Catechesis/Religious Programs—Tel: 714-574-7416.
Students 965.

St. John the Baptist (1960), Revs. Jerome M. Henson; Tran Phuc Long; Bruce A. Patterson. In res., Rev. Msgr. Daniel H. Brennan.
Res., 1015 Baker St., 92626. Tel: 714-540-2214; Fax: 714-540-5902.
School—Tel: 714-557-5060; Fax: 714-557-9263.
Sisters of Mercy 2; Lay Teachers 20; Students 605.
Catechesis/Religious Programs—Tel: 714-546-4102.
Students 630.

Cypress, St. Irenaeus (1961), Rev. Michael Heher; Rev. Msgr. Antonio Sudario; Revs. Roy Kim; Huy P. Pham; Deacon James Thompson.
Res., 5201 Evergreen Ave., 90630. Tel: 714-826-0760; Fax: 714-826-1608.
School—9201 Grindlay St., 90630. Tel: 714-827-4500; Fax: 714-827-2930.
Sisters 2; Lay Teachers 18; Students 589.
Catechesis/Religious Programs—9211 Grindlay St., 90630. Tel: 714-826-1140.
Students 851.

Dana Point, St. Edward (1969), Revs. John P. Lenihan; John W. Procter; Denis Lyons; Deacons John McQuade; Jesse Michel.
Res., 33926 Calle La Primavera, 92629. Tel: 714-496-1307; Fax: 714-496-1557.
School—33866 Calle La Primavera, 92629. Tel: 714-496-1241; Fax: 714-496-1819.
Lay Teachers 11; Students 346.
Catechesis/Religious Programs—Tel: 714-496-6011.
Students 700.

El Toro, Santiago de Compostela (1979), Revs. Kenneth A. Schmit; George P. Blais.
Res., 21682 Lake Forest Dr., Lake Forest, 92630. Tel: 714-951-8599; Fax: 714-951-2687.
Catechesis/Religious Programs—Tel: 714-951-0792.
Students 905.

Fountain Valley, Holy Spirit (1972), Revs. Joseph Knerr; Philip Hart, C.S.P.; Tuan Pham. In res., Rev. Philip T. Smith, O.Praem., S.T.M.
Res., 17270 Ward St., 92708. Tel: 714-963-1811; Fax: 714-968-1775.
Catechesis/Religious Programs—Tel: 714-963-7871. Sr. Regina Stewart, D.R.E.
Students 519.

Fullerton, St. Juliana Falconieri (1965), Revs. Jude M. Herlihy, O.S.M.; Donald M. Duplessis, O.S.M.; Joseph P. Cheah, O.S.M., Chap. (California State Univ. - Newman Club); Deacons William Schlater; Jay L. Milam. In res., Rev. David M. Kondik, O.S.M.
Office: 1319 N. Acacia Ave., 92831. Tel: 714-879-1965; Fax: 714-526-6673.
Res., 1316 N. Acacia Ave., 92831. Tel: 714-879-1965.
School—1320 N. Acacia Ave., 92831. Tel: 714-871-2829.
Lay Teachers 8; Students 323; Part-Time Teachers 5.
Catechesis/Religious Programs—Students 265.

St. Mary's (1912), Revs. Gerard Cosgayon, O.A.R.; Frank T. Wilder, O.A.R.; Deacons Carlos Gonzalez; Manuel Chavira.
Res., 400 W. Commonwealth Ave., 92832. Tel: 714-525-2500; Fax: 714-525-3837.
School—Tel: 714-525-9689.
Sisters of St. Joseph of Orange 1; Lay Teachers 13; Students 223.
Catechesis/Religious Programs—Tel: 714-992-5070.
Students 416.

St. Philip Benizi (1958), Revs. Paul E. Gins, O.S.M.; Ignatius M. Kissel, O.S.M.; Manuel Maya, O.S.M.; Patrick Donovan, O.S.M.; Deacons Jack Brennan; Richard Glaudini.
Res., 235 S. Pine Dr., 92833-3294. Tel: 714-871-3610; Fax: 714-871-5827.
School—215 S. Pine Dr., 92833-3293. Tel: 714-871-6121; Fax: 714-992-4167. Neil Donat, Prin.
Lay Teachers 12; Students 281.
Catechesis/Religious Programs—Tel: 714-870-0561. Carol Meglio, D.R.E.
Students 495.

Garden Grove, St. Callistus (1961) (English-Spanish-Vietnamese), Revs. Rudolph J. Preciado; Joseph Tuan Pham; Gerardo J. Tanilong. In res., Rev. Msgr. Daniel J. Murray; Rev. Paul Chu Van Chi (Australia) (Sydney).
Res., 12921 Lewis St., 92840. Tel: 714-971-2141; Fax: 714-971-9112.
Church—Garden Grove Blvd. and Lewis St., 92840.
School—12901 Lewis St., 92840. Tel: 714-971-2023; Fax: 714-971-2031.
Dominican Sisters 2; Lay Teachers 10; Students 288.
Catechesis/Religious Programs—Tel: 714-971-2091. Maureen Ross, D.R.E.
Students 1,120.

St. Columban (1953), Revs. Donald Romito; Michael P. Hanifin; Raphael Ho Xuan Nguyen; Dominic Hoa Nguyen; Deacon Robert Kelleher.
Res., 10801 Stanford Ave., 92640. Tel: 714-534-1174; Fax: 714-534-1937.
School—10855 Stanford Ave., 92640. Tel: 714-534-3947.
Religious Sisters of Charity 2; Lay Teachers 12; Students 331.
Catechesis/Religious Programs—Students 1,311.

Huntington Beach

1—ST. BONAVENTURE (1965), Revs. Kerry Beaulieu; John R. Keller; Martin Benzoni, O.Praem.; Joseph Luan Nguyen.
Res., 16400 Springdale St., 92649. Tel: 714-846-3350; 846-3359; Fax: 714-840-0480.
School—Tel: 714-846-2472; Fax: 714-840-0498.
Union of the Sisters of the Presentation of the Blessed Virgin Mary 3; Lay Teachers 23; Students 630.
Catechesis/Religious Programs—16377 Bradbury Lane, 92647. Tel: 714-846-2472. Virginia Curley, D.R.E.
Students 900.

2—ST. MARY'S BY THE SEA (1977), Revs. Daniel Johnson; Eamon Mackin, C.H.S.
Res., 321 10th St., 92648. Tel: 714-536-6913; Fax: 714-536-2464.
Catechesis/Religious Programs—Students 165.

3—SS. SIMON AND JUDE (1912), Revs. Laurence P. Dolan, O.F.M.; Christian Mondor, O.F.M.; Gustave R. Krumm, O.F.M. In res., Revs. Felipe Baldonado, O.F.M.; Emery Tang, O.F.M.
Res., 20444 Magnolia St., 92646. Tel: 714-962-3333; Fax: 714-965-6456.
School—Tel: 714-962-4451; Fax: 714-968-1329.
Lay Teachers 30; Students 629.
Catechesis/Religious Programs—Tel: 714-963-0014. Sherrie Oldham, D.R.E.
Students 500.

4—ST. VINCENT DE PAUL (1977), Revs. Jerome T. Karcher; Sy Uy Nguyen.
Res., 8345 Talbert Ave., 92646. Tel: 714-842-3000; Fax: 714-842-6780.
Catechesis/Religious Programs—Students 529.

Irvine, St. Elizabeth Ann Seton (1976), Revs. Thomas Pado; Alex H. Ha.
Res., 9 Hillgate, 92612-3265. Tel: 714-854-1000; Fax: 714-854-0079.
Catechesis/Religious Programs—Students 370.

St. John Neumann (1978), Revs. Colm Conlon; John E. Shetler; Ray Skonezny.
Res., 5101 Alton Pkwy., 92604-5499. Tel: 714-559-4006; Fax: 714-857-4788.
Catechesis/Religious Programs—Tel: 714-786-6105; Fax: 714-786-6102. Edith Marik, D.R.E.
Students 1,060.

St. Thomas More (1996), Rev. John E. Janze. In res., Rev. William Krekelberg.
Res., 4112 Escudero Dr., 92620-3212. Tel: 714-551-8601; Fax: 714-551-5879.
Catechesis/Religious Programs—Students 380.

Laguna Beach, St. Catherine of Siena (1923), Rev. Msgr. John Urell; Rev. Stephen Duffin.
Res., 990 Temple Ter., 92651. Tel: 714-494-9701; Fax: 714-497-2610.
School—3090 S. Coast Hwy., 92651. Tel: 714-494-7339; Fax: 714-376-5752.
Lay Teachers 9; Students 280.
Catechesis/Religious Programs—Tel: 714-499-5876.
Students 165.

Laguna Hills, St. Nicholas (1965), Revs. Juan Caboboy; Joseph Son Nguyen; Deacon Ray Havert. In res., Rev. Jeffrey Blangiardi, S.J.
Res., 24252 El Toro Rd., 92653. Tel: 714-837-1090; Fax: 714-837-9510.
Catechesis/Religious Programs—Tel: 714-837-7676.
Students 438.

Laguna Niguel, St. Timothy (1980), Revs. Bruce Lavery; Fred K. Bailey; Donald Kolda, S.J.; Deacon Ed Salgado.
Res., 29102 Crown Valley Pkwy., 92677. Tel: 714-249-4091; Fax: 714-249-4094.
Catechesis/Religious Programs—Tel: 714-495-4126.
Students 535.

La Habra, Our Lady of Guadalupe (1947), Revs. Justin H. MacCarthy; Cirilo Flores. In res., Rev. Eamon O'Gorman.
Res., 900 W. La Habra Blvd., 90631. Tel: 562-691-0533; Fax: 562-694-8328.
School—Tel: 562-697-9726; Fax: 562-905-0095.
Sisters of St. Joseph of Orange 2; Lay Teachers 21; Students 495.
Catechesis/Religious Programs—Tel: 562-691-2104; Fax: 562-697-6391.
Students 605.

Los Alamitos, St. Hedwig (1960), Revs. Daniel R. Hopcus; Thomas J. Keller, M.S.C.; Rafael Luevano.
Res., 11482 Los Alamitos Blvd., 90720. Tel: 562-430-0509; Fax: 562-431-9989.
School—Tel: 562-431-5001; Fax: 562-799-1791.
Irish Sisters of Charity 1; Lay Teachers 21; Students 603.
Catechesis/Religious Programs—Tel: 562-493-2521.
Students 550.

Mission Viejo, St. Kilian (1970), Rev. James P. Dunning. In res., Rev. Craig Butters.
Res., 26872 Estanciero Dr., 92691. Tel: 714-586-4440; Fax: 714-454-1043.
Catechesis/Religious Programs—Tel: 714-586-4550. Marcia Burns, D.R.E.
Students 950.

Newport Beach, Our Lady of Mount Carmel (1923), Revs. Kenneth J. Krause; Patrick A. Doherty; Deacon Glenn Erwin.
Res., 1441 W. Balboa Blvd., 92661-1010. Tel: 714-673-3775; Fax: 714-673-3137.
Catechesis/Religious Programs—Tel: 714-673-2719.
Students 168.

Our Lady Queen of Angels (1953), Rev. Msgr. William McLaughlin; Rev. Msgr. William R. Harvey, Pastor Emeritus; Revs. Benjamin Benedicto; Robert W.P. Puhlman.
Res., 2046 Mar Vista Dr., 92660. Tel: 714-644-0200; Fax: 714-644-1349.
School—750 Domingo Dr., 92660. Tel: 714-644-1166; Fax: 714-644-6213.
Lay Teachers 24; Students 347.
Catechesis/Religious Programs—Tel: 714-640-1272.
Students 490.

Convent—2108 Aralia St., 92660. Tel: 714-644-0660.
Chapel—St. John Vianney, Tel: 714-675-2221. Rev. Msgr. Lawrence J. Baird.

Placentia, St. Joseph (1953), Revs. Timothy Ramaekers; James C. Ries; Deacons Chuck Gagnon; Ed Faulk. In res., Rev. Rod Stephens.
Res., 717 N. Bradford Ave., 92870-4599. Tel: 714-528-1487; Fax: 714-528-1569.
School—801 N. Bradford Ave., 92870-4599. Tel: 714-528-1794; Fax: 714-528-0668.
Lay Teachers 16; Students 300.
Catechesis/Religious Programs—Tel: 714-993-0830. D.R.E.: Pat Hobbs; Eloisa Ramirez, (Spanish).
Students 680.
Mission—Atwood, Orange Co., St. Theresa Chapel, 636 Van Buren Ave., Atwood, 92811.

Rancho Santa Margarita, San Francisco Solano Church (1989), Revs. Michael Pecharich; Alex K. Kim; Sr. Barbara Reder, S.P., Pastoral Assoc.
Res., 22082 Antonio Pkwy., 92688. Tel: 714-589-7767; Fax: 714-589-7768.
Catechesis/Religious Programs—Tel: 714-589-1709.
Students 1,588.

San Clemente, Our Lady of Fatima (1947), Revs. Frank Moran; Timothy Freyer; Rev. Msgr. Anthony McGowan, Pastor Emeritus.
Res., 105 La Esperanza, 92672. Tel: 714-492-4101; Fax: 714-492-4856.
School—Tel: 714-492-7320; Fax: 714-492-3793.
Lay Teachers 13; Students 313.
Catechesis/Religious Programs—Tel: 714-492-1663.
Students 400.

San Juan Capistrano, (Old Mission) (1776) (Spanish), Rev. Msgr. Paul M. Martin; Rev. Msgr. John Campbell; Rev. Joseph Droessler; Deacons Joseph Halka; David Sire; Viviano Mireles. In res., Rev. Harold Fumo.
Res., P.O. Box 697, 92693. Tel: 714-248-2000; Fax: 714-248-2008 (parish office). [CEM]
School—Tel: 714-248-2050; Fax: 714-240-8091.
Lay Teachers 18; Students 439.
Catechesis/Religious Programs—Tel: 714-248-2010; Fax: 714-248-2056. Linda Berkshire, D.R.E.
Students 655.

Santa Ana

1—Immaculate Heart of Mary (1960), Revs. Enrique Sera; Ignatius Lau; Ismael Silva; Deacon Gerardo de Santos.
Res., 1100 S. Center St., 92704. Tel: 714-751-5335.
School—Tel: 714-545-8185.
Sisters 3; Lay Teachers 9; Students 230.
Catechesis/Religious Programs—Tel: 714-546-5186.
Students 868.

2—Our Lady of Guadalupe (1927), Rev. Alonso Caceres. In res., Rev. Msgr. Jaime Soto.
Res., 541 E. Central Ave., 92707. Tel: 714-540-0902; Fax: 714-540-3053.
Catechesis/Religious Programs—Tel: 714-540-9231. Rosa Castro, D.R.E.
Students 1,127.

3—Our Lady of Guadalupe (1938) (Spanish), Revs. Anthony Palos, O.A.R.; Etelvino Iglesias, O.A.R.
Res., 1322 E. Third St., 92701. Tel: 714-836-4142; Fax: 714-836-7417.
Catechesis/Religious Programs—Tel: 714-835-8933. Margarita Garza, D.R.E.
Students 470.

4—Our Lady of Lourdes (1985) (Mexican), Rev. William Barman.
Res., 5021 W. 16th St., 92703. Tel: 714-636-3260; Fax: 714-539-0783.
Catechesis/Religious Programs—Students 254.

5—Our Lady of the Pillar (1965) (Hispanic), Revs. Alfredo de Dios, O.A.R.; Galo Espinoza, O.A.R.; Robert Huse, O.A.R.; Joachim Goni, O.A.R.; Euben Capacillo, O.A.R.
Res., 1622 W. 6th St., 92703. Tel: 714-543-1700; Fax: 714-543-9640.
School—601 N. Western Ave., 92703. Tel: 714-542-5177.
Catechesis/Religious Programs—Tel: 714-542-4684.
Students 1,405.

6—St. Anne's (1923) (Hispanic), Revs. Joseph C. Justice; Cesar M. Salazar; Leonicio Segura; Deacon Carlos Evyoque.
Res., 109 Borchard Ave., P.O. Box 2425, 92707. Tel: 714-835-7434; Fax: 714-835-4506.
School—Tel: 714-542-9328; Fax: 714-542-3431.
Sisters 5; Lay Teachers 11; Students 277.
Catechesis/Religious Programs—Tel: 714-542-1213.
Students 735.

7—St. Barbara's (1962), Revs. Richard C. Kennedy; Salvador Landa; Kiem Van Tran; Nguyen Van Thanh.
Res., 730 S. Euclid St., 92704. Tel: 714-775-7733; Fax: 714-775-9467.
School—Tel: 714-775-9477; Fax: 714-775-9468.
Lay Teachers 24; Students 456.
Catechesis/Religious Programs—Tel: 714-775-9475.
Students 1,436.

8—St. Joseph's (1887), Revs. Christopher H. Smith; Alfred S. Baca. In res., Rev. Steven Sallot.
Res., 727 Minter St., 92701. Tel: 714-542-4411; Fax: 714-542-9770.
School—Tel: 714-542-2704.
Sisters 2; Lay Teachers 7; Students 210.
Catechesis/Religious Programs—Tel: 714-550-8096.
Students 450.

Seal Beach, St. Anne's (1921), Rev. Robert S. Vidal; Rev. Msgr. Michael Collins, Pastor Emeritus.
Res., 340 Tenth St., 90740. Tel: 562-431-0721; Fax: 562-431-3050.
Catechesis/Religious Programs—Students 86.
Holy Family (1969), Rev. Msgr. Brian Coghlan; Rev. Msgr. James J. Pierse, Pastor Emeritus.
Res., 13900 Church Pl., 90740. Tel: 562-430-8170; Fax: 562-493-4643.

Stanton, St. Polycarp (1961) (English-Spanish-Vietnamese), Revs. Edward Poettgen; Vincent Hung Pham; John P. Graven; Thomas Ha.
Res., 8100 Chapman Ave., 90680. Tel: 714-893-2766; Fax: 714-898-6675.
School—8182 Chapman Ave., 90680. Tel: 714-893-8882.
Lay Teachers 9; Students 237.
Catechesis/Religious Programs—Tel: 714-892-3158.
Students 820.

Tustin, St. Cecilia (1957) (Vietnamese-Spanish), Revs. Timothy MacCarthy; Christopher Heath; Tuyen Nguyen; Deacons Lee Meyer; Jerry Miller; Rafael Romero; Jon Schlemmer.
Res., 1301 S.E. Sycamore, 92680. Tel: 714-544-3250; Fax: 714-838-1996.
School—Tel: 714-544-1533; Fax: 714-544-0643.
Lay Teachers 15; Students 355.
Catechesis/Religious Programs—Tel: 714-838-4466.
Students 1,050.

Westminster, Blessed Sacrament (1947), Revs. James Hartnett; Agustin Escobar; Michael Hoan; Tuan Nguyen. In res., Rev. Jack Sewell.
Res., 14072 S. Olive St., 92683. Tel: 714-892-4489; Fax: 714-892-5560.
School—14146 S. Olive St., 92683. Tel: 714-893-7701. Roisin McAree, Prin.
Lay Teachers 12; Students 327.
Catechesis/Religious Programs—14144 S. Olive St., 92683. Tel: 714-897-2142. Ann Przygocki, D.R.E.
Students 852.

Yorba Linda, St. Martin (1970), Revs. Richard A. Delahunty; John T. Hiltz, (Retired); David Gruver.
Res., 19767 Yorba Linda Blvd., 92886. Tel: 714-970-2771; Fax: 714-970-5654.
Catechesis/Religious Programs—Tel: 714-970-2521. D.R.E.: Pam Bender; Jackie Schultz, (Adult); Pasquale Talarico, (Youth).
Students 1,105.

Chaplains Of Public Institutions

Orange. *Juvenile Hall* 331 The City Dr., 92868. Tel: 714-634-7611. Rev. Brendan Smith, S.T., 422 Almond, 92866. Tel: 714-633-6527.
Orange County Medical Center 101 The City Dr. S., 92868. Tel: 714-634-5678. Served by St. Callistus Parish. 12921 Lewis St., Garden Grove, 92840. Tel: 714-971-2141.
Theo Lacy Minimum Security Facility. (Branch Jail), 501 The City Dr., 92862. Tel: 714-834-3090. Rev. Brendan Smith, S.T., Chap., 422 Almond, 92866. Tel: 714-633-6527.

Costa Mesa. *Fairview Developmental Center* 2501 Harbor, 92626. Tel: 714-545-9331. Rev. Charles Willingham, O.Praem.

El Toro. *El Toro Marine Base.* Revs. Marc Boisvert; Chin Van Dang; Thomas P. Hall, C.S.P., Station Chapel: U.S.M.C.A.S., 92709. Tel: 714-726-3824.

Garden Grove. *Palm Harbor General Hospital* 12601 Garden Grove Blvd., 92804. Tel: 714-537-5160. Served by St. Callistus Parish. 12921 Lewis St., 92804. Tel: 714-971- 2141.

Tustin. *Marine Corps Air Station.* (H). Rev. Timothy J. Janning, M.C.A.S. (H), 92701. Tel: 714-726-7311.

Special Assignment:
Reverend Monsignors—
Duc Tien, Peter, Dir., Vietnamese Center, 1538 N. Century Blvd., Santa Ana, CA 92703. Tel: 714-554-4211
Sammon, John F., P.A., Vicar for Pastoral and Community Affairs
Reverend Fathers—
Brazil, Sean, S.S.C., Dir., Korean Center, 7655 Trask Ave., Westminster, CA 92683
Cho, Laurentius, St. Thomas Korean Catholic Center, Anaheim, CA 92801-6710
Karp, Joseph A., Dir., Polish Center, Yorba Linda
Kim, Benedict, St. Thomas Korean Catholic Center, Anaheim, CA 92801-6710
Moreland, J. Gordon, S.J., Dir., House of Prayer for Priests, 7734 Santiago Canyon Rd., Orange, CA 92869

On Duty Outside the Diocese:
Reverend Fathers—
Buckman, Franklin J., Our Lady of Mt. Carmel Church, 503 W. Chocktoot, P.O. Box 396, Chiloquin, OR 79624
Daley, Wallace
Fama, Benjamin Joseph, Society of Our Lady of the Most Holy Trinity, P.O. Box 152, Robstown, TX 78380
Hung, Joseph K., Gethsemane Abbey, KY

Military Chaplains:
Reverend Fathers—
Fry, James Q.
Shimotsu, John
Sweeney, Kevin

Absent on Sick Leave:
Reverend Fathers—
Croal, Thomas
DiStefano, Joseph
Fee, Pat
Fumo, Harold
Gonzales, George
Kinzer, Gary
Kolberg, Lawrence R.
Luongo, John
Monestero, John
Tu, Joachim Vu

Inactive Leave:
Reverend Monsignors—
Harris, Michael
Reverend Fathers—
Colleran, Desmond
Coughlin, Richard
Coulombe, Dale
Croal, James Joseph
Farris, James M.
Frost, Stephen
Geraughty, Michael
German, Timothy J.
Gibbons, Francis X.
Harvey, James
Jagosz, Mitchell
Melito, Joseph
Nguyen, Joseph Chuan
O'Callaghan, John
Perez, Henry
Ramos, Eleuterio
Ruhl, John
Ryder, Matthais
Schmidt, Nicholas
Theis, Jeffrey
Tressler, Robert
Widera, Siegfried

Retired:
Reverend Monsignors—
Coffield, John V.
Collins, Michael
Doyle, Timothy
Falvey, Sinon
Harvey, William R.
Hughes, Michael
Keenan, John C.
McCarthy, Emmett
McGowan, Anthony
Nash, James F.
O'Brien, Terrence
O'Connor, Hugh
Pierse, James J.
Scannell, Peter
Yrigan, Pedro
Reverend Fathers—
Chinh, Peter
Ho, Mathias
Morales, Jose
Powers, Joseph
Sheahan, John A.

Permanent Deacons:
Antunez, Jay, St. Polycarp, Stanton
Barth, John, On Duty Outside the Diocese
Brenes-Rios, Anthony, Our Lady of Guadalupe, La Habra

Brennan, John, St. Philip Benizi, Fullerton
Bube, Anthony, La Purisima, Orange
Carver, Timothy, St. Norbert, Orange
Chavez, Frank, St. Martin de Porres, Yorba Linda
Chavira, Manuel, St. Mary, Fullerton
Cook, Douglas, San Antonio de Padua, Anaheim Hills
Coughlin, Charles, Blessed Sacrament, Westminster
Dennis, Irving, On Duty Outside the Diocese
DeSantos, Gerardo, Immaculate Heart of Mary, Santa Ana
Duthoy, Raymond, St. Justin Martyr, Anaheim
Erwin, Glenn, Our Lady of Mt. Carmel, Newport Beach
Euyoque, Carlos, St. Anne, Santa Ana
Faulk, Edward, St. Joseph, Placentia
Garza, Domingo, Our Lady of Guadalupe, Santa Ana
Glaudini, Richard, St. Philip Benizi, Fullerton
Gonzales, Carlos, St. Mary, Fullerton
Halka, Joseph, Mission San Juan Capistrano, San Juan Capistrano
Havert, Raymond, St. Nicholas, Laguna Hills
Jones, Wesley, St. Boniface, Anaheim
Kelleher, Robert, St. Columban, Garden Grove
Klos, Thomas, San Antonio de Padua, Anaheim Hills
Larkin, James, St. Polycarp, Stanton
Luna, Frank, Catholic Deaf Center, Orange
McQuade, John, St. Edward, Dana Point
Melton, Harold, On Duty Outside the Diocese
Merandi, Louis, Holy Cross Greek Melkite
Meyer, Leon, St. Cecilia, Tustin
Michel, Jesse, St. Edwards, Dana Point
Milam, Jay, St. Juliana Falconieri, Fullerton
Miller, Gerald, St. Cecilia, Tustin
Mireles, Viviano, Mission San Juan Capistrano, San Juan Capistrano
Myers, Paul, On Duty Outside the Diocese
Nalbach, George, Our Lady of Fatima, San Clemente
Navarro, Carlos, St. Angela Merici, Brea
Porcella, Roger, On Duty Outside the Diocese
Pyne, Gerald, Our Lady of Guadalupe, La Habra
Reynoso, Jose Luis, St. Boniface, Anaheim
Richeson, James, Our Lady Queen of Angels, Newport Beach
Rivera, Manuel, St. Anne, Santa Ana
Romero, Rafael, St Cecilia, Tustin
Salgado, Fernando, St. Timothy, Laguna Niguel
Samano, Victor, San Felipe de Jesus, Capistrano Beach
Schlater, William, St. Juliana Falconieri, Fullerton
Schlemmer, Jon, St. Cecilia, Tustin
Sire, David, Mission San Juan Capistrano, San Juan Capistrano
Stripling, Joseph, Blessed Sacrament, Westminster
Sullivan, Neill, Our Lady Queen of Angels, Newport Beach
Swift, Bernard, (Retired)
Thompson, James, St. Irenaeus, Cypress
vonVoigt, Fred, St. Angela Merici, Brea
Zambrano, Jose, On Duty Outside the Diocese

INSTITUTIONS LOCATED IN THE DIOCESE

[A] SEMINARIES AND SCHOLASTICATES FOR RELIGIOUS

MIDWAY CITY. *St. Patrick's Novitiate and Scholasticate*, 7820 Bolsa Ave., 92655. Tel: 714-897-8181; Fax: 714-898-9020. Conducted by the Brothers of St. Patrick. Brothers 4.

SILVERADO. *St. Michael's Norbertine Postulancy, Novitiate and Juniorate*, 19292 El Toro Rd., 92676. Tel: 714-858-0222. Conducted by the Norbertine Fathers. Rt. Rev. Eugene J. Hayes, O.Praem., Abbot; Revs. Thomas W. Nelson, O.Praem., Dir. Formation & Novice Master; Augustine R. Puchner, O.Praem., Asst. Dir. Formation; Very Rev. Hugh C. Barbour, O.Praem, Ph.D., Prof. Philosophy; Revs. John E. Caronan, O.Praem., Prof. Latin; Gregory M. Dick, O.Praem, Prof. Scripture; Hubert S. Szanto, O.Praem., Prof. Latin. For listing of other Norbertine priests working in the Diocese, refer to St. Michael College Prep High School.

[B] COLLEGES AND UNIVERSITIES

ORANGE. *St. Joseph College, Orange*, 480 S. Batavia St., 92868. Tel: 714-633-8121; Fax: 714-744-3165
For a complete listing, refer to the Colleges and Universities section.

[C] HIGH SCHOOLS, DIOCESAN

FULLERTON. *Rosary High School*. (Girls), 1340 N. Acacia Ave., 92831. Tel: 714-879-6302; Fax: 714-879-0853.
E-mail: rosary@ix.netcom.com
Web site: http://www.rc.net/orange/rosary
Mrs. Trudy Mazzarella, Prin. Sisters 1; Lay Teachers 42; Students 686.

RANCHO SANTA MARGARITA. *Santa Margarita Catholic High School*, 22062 Antonio Pkwy., 92688. Tel: 714-858-3350; Fax: 714-858-4399. Merritt V. Hemenway, Prin. Priests 2; Sisters 2; Lay Teachers 105; Students 1,820.

SANTA ANA. *Mater Dei High School*. (Coed), 1202 W. Edinger, 92707-2191. Tel: 714-754-7711; Fax: 714-754-1880. Norbertine Fathers; Franciscan Fathers; Brothers of St. Patrick; Sisters of St. Joseph of Orange; Religious Sisters of Charity; Sisters de l'Union Chretienne de St. Chaumond; Sisters of St. Louis; Sisters of the Company of Mary. Mr. Patrick Murphy, Prin.; Revs. Steven Sallot, Rector/Chaplain; Eugene David Burnett, O.F.M.; Robert S. Hodges, O.Praem.; Joseph K. Horn, O.Praem.; Luke Laslavich, O.Praem. Priests 5; Brothers 1; Sisters 8; Lay Teachers 126; Students 2,135.

[D] HIGH SCHOOLS, PRIVATE

ANAHEIM. *Cornelia Connelly School of the Holy Child*. (Girls), 2323 W. Broadway, 92804. Tel: 714-776-1717; Fax: 714-776-2534.
E-mail: cornelia@exo.com
Sisters of the Holy Child Jesus. Sr. Francine Gunther, S.H.C.J., Head of School.
Cornelia Connelly School Development Fund.
Cornelia Connelly School Scholarship Fund. Lay Teachers 20; Students 208.
Servite High School; Servite High School Development Fund, 1952 W. La Palma, 92801. Tel: 714-774-7575; Fax: 714-774-1404. Servite Friars. Rev. Gerald M. Horan, O.S.M., Pres.; Mr. Raymond Dunne, Prin.; Revs. Edward M. Penonzek, O.S.M.; Michael P. Pontarelli, O.S.M.; Eugene M. Smith, O.S.M.; Bros. Philip M. Eikmeyer, O.S.M.; Joel A. Lechner. Priests 4; Brothers 2; Sisters 1; Lay Teachers 47; Students 815.

SIVERADO. *St. Michael's College Preparatory High School*. (Grades 9-12). (Boarding school for boys), 19292 El Toro Rd., 92676-9710. Tel: 714-858-0222; Fax: 714-858-7365. Revs. Gabriel D. Stack, O.Praem., Prin.; Stephen M. Boyle, O.Praem.; Vincent M. Gilmore, O.Praem., Dean Students; Jerome M. Molokie, O.Praem.; Charles W. Willingham, O.Praem.; Adrian J. Connor, O.Praem.; Justin S. Ramos, O.Praem.; Nicholas M. Tacito, O.Praem, Spiritual Dir.; Jordan S. Anderson, O.Praem; James G. Smith, O.Praem.; Eugene J. Hayes, O.Praem. Priests 11; Brothers 1; Lay Teachers 9; Students 60.

[E] ELEMENTARY SCHOOLS AND DAY NURSERIES, PRIVATE

ANAHEIM. *St. Catherine's Military School*, 215 N. Harbor Blvd., 92805. Tel: 714-772-1363. Legal Title: *St. Catherine's Military School, a Corp.* Sr. Carolyn Marie Monahan, Admin. & Prin. Dominican Sisters of Mission San Jose 19; Sisters 9; Lay Teachers 14; Students 190.

RANCHO SANTA MARGARITA. *Serra Catholic School*, 23652 Antonio Pkwy., 92688-1993. Tel: 714-888-1990.
E-mail: serra@serraschool.org
Web site: www.serraschool.org
Mrs. Audrey Tellers, Prin. Lay Teachers 27; Students 650.

SANTA ANA. *Santa Clara Day Nursery and Kindergarten*, 1021 N. Newhope, 92703. Tel: 714-554-8850; Fax: 714-554-58-86. Poor Clare Missionary Sisters (M.C.). Sisters 12; Children 100.

TUSTIN. *Saint Jeanne de Lestonnac School*, 16791 E. Main, 92870. Tel: 714-542-4271.
E-mail: jeanne@OCweb.com
Web site: www.ocweb.com/sj
Sr. Mary of Jesus Rodriguez, O.D.N., Prin. Sisters of the Company of Mary 7; Lay Teachers 27; Students 535.

[F] GENERAL HOSPITALS

ORANGE. *St. Joseph Health System*, 440 S. Batavia St., 92868. Tel: 714-997-7690
For a complete listing, refer to the Hospitals section.

FULLERTON. *St. Jude Medical Center*, 101 E. Valencia Mesa Dr., 92834. Tel: 714-871-3280
For a complete listing, refer to the Hospitals section.
St. Jude Memorial Foundation, P.O. Box 4138, 92834. Tel: 714-992-3033; Fax: 714-738-0691
For a complete listing, refer to the Hospitals section.

MISSION VIEJO. *Mission Hospital Regional Medical Center*, 27700 Medical Center Rd., 92691. Tel: 714-364-1400.
E-mail: srma@0103.stjoe.org
For a complete listing, refer to the Hospitals section.

[G] SPECIAL SERVICES

ORANGE. *St. Vincent de Paul Society*, 180 S. Cypress, 92866. Tel: 714-633-9195; Fax: 714-771-2748. Mr. Dan Harney, Pres.; Mr. Joseph D. Kay, Exec. Dir.; Rev. Peregrine Graffius, O.S.M., Spiritual Dir. Total Staff 97; Total Assisted 305,000.
Special Works of the St. Vincent de Paul Society:
Second Harvest Food Bank of Orange County, 426-A W. Almond, 92866. Tel: 714-771-1343. Mr. Thomas M. Seeberg.
Mary's Home, Transitional Housing, La Habra, 180 S. Cypress, 92866. Tel: 714-547-5566.
St. Vincent de Paul Center for Community Reconciliation, 777 S. Main St., Ste. 200, 92868. Tel: 714-836-8100. Programs include: Catholic Detention Ministry, Friends Outside and Institute for Conflict Management.
Stores and Workshops, 180 Cypress, 92866. Tel: 714-633-9194.
Search of Orange County, Inc., P.O. Box 4191, 92867. Tel: 714-753-3533.

ANAHEIM. *St. Thomas Korean Catholic Center*, 412 N. Crescent Way, 92801. Tel: 714-772-3993; Fax: 714-772-3636. Revs. Benedict Kim, Dir.; Laurentius Cho.

SANTA ANA. *Holy Family Services, Adoption and Foster Care*, 1403 S. Main St., 92707. Tel: 714-835-5551; Fax: 714-973-4971. Debra Richardson, Exec. Dir.
St. Francis Home, 1718 W. 6th St., 92703. Tel: 714-542-0381. Franciscan Sisters of the Immaculate Conception, Inc. Sr. Leticia Rodriguez, O.S.F., Admin. Sisters 22.
Vietnamese Catholic Center, 1538 N. Century Blvd., 92703. Tel: 714-554-4211; 554-5565; Fax: 714-265-1161. Rev. Msgr. Peter Nguyen Duc Tien, Dir. In res. Rev. Joachim Vu Tu. Total in Residence 2; Total Staff 5.

SILVERADO. *St. Michael's Summer Camp*, St. Michael's Abbey, 19292 El Toro Rd., 92676-9801. Tel: 714-858-0444. Boys aged 6-12 years. Capacity 120.

WESTMINSTER. *Korean Catholic Ministry*, 7655 Trask Ave., 92683. Tel: 714-897-6510. Revs. Sean Brazil, S.S.C., Dir. Korean Martyrs Center; Michael Morrissey. Tel: 714-891-6961.

YORBA LINDA. *Polish Center*, 3999 Rose Dr., 92886. Tel: 714-996-8161. Rev. Joseph A. Karp, Dir.

[H] MONASTERIES AND RESIDENCES OF PRIESTS AND BROTHERS

ORANGE. *Brothers of the Christian Schools*, Marywood Center, P.O. Box 14195, 92863-1595. Tel: 714-282-3000. Bro. William Carriere, F.S.C., Ph.D.
Claretian Missionaries, La Purisima, 11712 N. Hewes, 92869. Tel: 714-633-5800.
E-mail: lps@ocweb.com
Web site: www.ocweb.com/.lps.
Total in Residence 3; Total Staff 12.
Jesuits, House of Prayer, 7734 Santiago Canyon Rd., 92869. Tel: 714-639-9740. Rev. J. Gordon Moreland, S.J. Total in Residence 2; Total Staff 1.
Marianists, House of Prayer, 7734 Santiago Canyon Rd., 92869. Tel: 714-633-2698. Rev. Patrick Philbin, S.M.
Missionaries of Africa, 566 S. Glassell St., 92866-3017. Tel: 714-639-2900.
Servite Fathers and Brothers, Sisters of St. Joseph of Orange, Regina Residence, 430 S. Batavia, 92868. Tel: 714-744-3153. Rev. Gerard M. Calkins, O.S.M.
Theatine Fathers, St. Joseph Hospital, 1100 W. Stewart Dr., 92692. Tel: 714-771-8137. Rev. David Maes, C.R.

ANAHEIM. *Servite Fathers and Brothers*. Servite Friars, Servite Priory, 1922 W. La Palma Ave., 92801-3595. Tel: 714-774-7575. Revs. Eugene M. Smith, O.S.M., Prior; Mel M. Corcoran, O.S.M.; Peregrine M. Graffius, O.S.M.; Gerald M. Horan, O.S.M.; Michael M. Pontarelli, O.S.M.; Bros. Philip M. Eikmeyer, O.S.M.; Joel M. Lechner, O.S.M.
De familia members of the community living outside the priory: Revs. Gerard M. Calkins, O.S.M.; Edward M. Penonzek, O.S.M., Servite High School, 1952 W. La Palma Ave., 92801-3595. Tel: 714-774-7575.

BUENA PARK. *Augustinian Fathers*, St. Pius V, 7691 Orangethorpe Ave., 90621. Tel: 714-522-2193.
E-mail: cherbers@packbell.net
Total in Residence 5; Total Staff 3.
Servite Fathers And Brothers, Servite Provincial Center, 5210 Somerset St., 90621-1498. Tel: 714-523-5810.
E-mail: osmwest@aol.com
Revs. Peregrine M. Graffius, O.S.M., Prov.; Ignatius M. Kissel, O.S.M., Asst. Prov. Councillors: Revs. Eugene M. Smith, O.S.M.; Joseph M. Cheah, O.S.M.; John M. Topper, O.S.M.; Ignatius M. Kissel, O.S.M., Treas.; Donald M. Siple, O.S.M., Vocation Dir.
Personnel assigned outside the Province and Country: Rev. Robert M. Anderson, O.S.M., Monte Berico Novitiate, P.O. Box 1457, Nigel, Republic of South Africa, 1490. Revs. Christopher M. Ross, O.S.M.,

Vicar Provincial of Western Australia; Robert M. Zivkovic, O.S.M.; Frank Christi, O.S.M.; Carlo M. Marchetti, O.S.M.; Patrick Boyle, O.S.M.; Leo M. Spicer, O.S.M.; Liam Mackle, O.S.M.; Myles Lynch, O.S.M.; Bros. Stephen Barker, O.S.M.; Oscar Aguilara, O.S.M.

The Grotto, 8840 N.E. Skidmore St., Portland, OR, 97220. Residents 7; Religious 4; Lay Teachers 50.

COSTA MESA. *Fairview Developmental Center*, 2501 Harbor Blvd., 92626. Tel: 714-957-5242. Rev. Joseph McEneany, SS.CC.

FULLERTON. *Augustinian Recollects*, St. Mary, 400 W. Commonwealth Ave., 92832-1713. Tel: 714-525-2500.

Servite Fathers and Brothers, St. Juliana Falconieri, 1316 N. Acacia, 92831. Tel: 714-879-1971. St. Philip Benizi, 235 S. Pine Dr., 92833-3294. Tel: 714-871-3613. Total in Residence 4; Total Staff 3.

HUNTINGTON BEACH. *Franciscan Fathers*, SS. Simon and Jude, 20444 Magnolis St., 92646. Tel: 715-962-3333.

LAGUNA NIGUEL. *Jesuits*, St. Timothy, 29102 Crown Valley Pkwy., 92677. Tel: 714-249-4091. Rev. Donald Kolda, S.J.

MIDWAY CITY. *Brothers of St. Patrick, St. Patrick's Novitiate and Scholasticate*, 7820 Bolsa Ave., 92655. Tel: 714-897-8181. Bros. Livinus Bellew, F.S.P.; Aquinas Cassin, F.S.P.; Edwin Guidera, F.S.P.; Matthew Regan, F.S.P.

SANTA ANA. *Augustinian Recollects*, Our Lady of Guadalupe, 1322 E. 3rd St., 92701-5104. Tel: 714-836-4142. Our Lady of the Pillar, 1622 6th St., 92703. Tel: 714-543-1700.

Franciscan Fathers, Mater Dei High School, 1202 W. Edinger St., 92707. Tel: 714-754-7711. Rev. Eugene David Burnett, O.F.M.

Trinitarian Missionaries/Missionary Servants of the Most Holy Trinity, Trinitarian House, P.O. Box 1933, 92702. Tel: 714-541-4840. Revs. Brendan Smith, S.T.; Edward J. Molumby, S.T.; John T. Seymour, S.T.

SILVERADO. *Norbertine Fathers of Orange Inc.*, St. Michael's Abbey (O.Praem.), 19292 El Toro Rd., 92676-9710. Tel: 714-858-0222; Fax: 714-858-4583. Rt. Revs. Eugene J. Hayes, O.Praem., Abbot; Ladislas K. Parker, O.Praem., (Retired) Abbot Emeritus; Very Rev. Hugh C. Barbour, O.Praem., Prior; Rev. Jordan S. Anderson, O.Praem., St. Michael's Prep. Parish Apostolates: Revs. Martin R. Benzoni, O.Praem.; Michael U. Perea, O.Praem.; Hermann-Joseph K. Rettig, O.Praem.; Stephen M. Boyle, O.Praem., St. Michael's Prep; John E. Caronan, O.Praem., Abbey Treas.; Leo J. Celano, O.Praem., Prison Chap.; Adrian J. Connor, O.Praem., St. Michael's Prep; Gregory M. Dick, O.Praem., Formation Asst.; Patrick D. Foutts, O.Praem., Mary Star of the Sea; Paul L. Gelencser, O.Praem., (Retired); Vincent M. Gilmore, O.Praem., Subprior, St. Michael's Prep; Francis M. Gloudeman, O.Praem., Home Schooling; Robert S. Hodges, O.Praem., Mater Dei; Joseph K. Horn, O.Praem., Mater Dei; Benedict A. Horvath, O.Praem., (Retired); Gerlac A. Horvath, O.Praem., (Retired); Bernard M. Johnson, O.Praem., Mary Star of the Sea; Lawrence C. Johnson, O.Praem., Mary Star of the Sea; Anthony Mary J. Kopp, O.Praem., Mary Star of the Sea; Luke S. Laslavich, O.Praem., Mater Dei; Jerome M. Molokie, O.Praem., St. Michael's Prep; Maximilian A. Moreno, O.Praem., (On Leave); Peter D. Muller, O.Praem., Santa Margarita; Thomas W. Nelson, O.Praem., Dir. Formation; Pascal B. Nguyen, O.Praem., Mary Star of the Sea; Gilbert L. O'Brien, O.Praem., Military Chap.; Raymond L. Perez, O.Praem., Educ. Leave & Parish Apostolate; Augustine R. Puchner, O.Praem., Asst. Dir. Formation; Justin S. Ramos, O.Praem., St. Michael's Prep; Clement A. Rudnay, O.Praem., (Retired); James G. Smith, O.Praem., High School Treas.; Philip T. Smith, O.Praem., Mary Star of the Sea; Theodore R. Smith, O.Praem., Teaching in Hungary; Gabriel D. Stack, O.Praem., Prin., St. Michael's Prep; Hubert S. Szanto, O.Praem., (Retired); Nicholas M. Tacito, O.Praem., St. Michael's Prep; Werenfried P. van Straaten, O.Praem., Aid to the Church in Need; Charles W. Willingham, O.Praem., St. Michael's Prep; Norbert G. Wood, O.Praem., Prin., Mary Star of the Sea. Priests 43; Clerics 11; Novices 2; Postulants 3.

WESTMINSTER. *Columban Fathers*, Korean Martyrs Catholic Center, 7655 Trask Ave., 92683. Tel: 714-897-6510. Revs. Sean Brazil, S.S.C.; Michael Morrissey. Tel: 714-891-6961.

[I] CONVENTS AND RESIDENCES FOR SISTERS

ORANGE. *Adrian Dominicans*, Marywood Center, 2811 E. Villa Real Dr., 92867. Tel: 714-282-3000.

Daughters of Mary and Joseph, 1129 W. Palmyra Ave., #c, 92868. Tel: 714-744-3726.

Servants of Mary, St. Joseph Motherhouse, 480 S. Batavia St., 92668. Tel: 714-633-8121.

Sisters of Charity of Leavenworth, 2427 Northumberland, 92865. Tel: 714-974-8518.

Sisters of Providence, Marywood Center, 2811 E. Villa Real Dr., 92867. Tel: 714-282-3000.

Sisters of St. Joseph of Carondelet, Sisters of St. Joseph of Cluny, Center for Spiritual Development, 434 S. Batavia, 92868. Tel: 714-744-3175.

Sisters of St. Joseph of Orange Motherhouse Community, 480 S. Batavia, 92868. Tel: 714-633-8121, Ext. 735. Sr. Michelle Tochtrop, C.S.J., Gen. Sec. & Contact. Sisters 34. Regina Residence Community, 430 S. Batavia St., 92868. Tel: 714-744-3109. Sisters 67. Palmyra Community, 940 W. Palmyra, 92868. Tel: 714-744-3150. Sisters 6. Casa Magnolia Community, 954 W. Palmyra, 92868. Tel: 714-639-1030. Sisters 3. St. Joseph Hospital Community, P.O. Box 5600, 92868. Tel: 714-771-8040. Sisters 9. Greengrove Community, 2075 Greengrove St., 92665. Tel: 714-974-9079. Sisters 4.

Sisters of the Company of Mary, La Purisima Convent, 11712 N. Hewes, 92869. Tel: 714-538-0811.
E-mail: lps@ocweb.com
Web site: ocweb.com/lps
Sisters 6.

Sisters of the Holy Cross, 92868. Tel: 714-771-1738 (Work).

Sisters of the Presentation of the Blessed Virgin Mary, St. Norbert Convent, 343 E. Chestnut, 92867. Tel: 714-637-7390. Sisters 3.

ANAHEIM. *Cornelia Connelly Convent*, 2323 W. Broadway, 92804. Tel: 714-538-6228. Sisters of the Holy Child. Sisters 3. 9351 Greenwich, 92804. Tel: 714-776-9444. Sisters 2. Corporate Title: Society of the Holy Child Jesus, Inc.

Dominicans, Mission San Jose, St. Catherine Military School, 215 N. Harbor Blvd., 92805-2596. Tel: 714-772-1363.
E-mail: OrStCathMil@connectinc.com
Sisters 16.

Religious Sisters of Mercy of the Americas, St. Boniface Parish, 120 N. Janss St., 92805. Tel: 714-956-3110. St. Justin Martyr, 2050 W. Ball Rd., 92804. Tel: 714-774-2407.

BREA. *Sisters of St. Clare*, St. Clare's Garden, 449 S. Pine Ave., 92821-6644. Tel: 714-257-1113. Sisters 1. 446 S. Poplar Ave., 92821-6644. Sisters 4.

BUENA PARK. *Sisters of Our Lady of Perpetual Help*, 6751 Western Ave., 90621. Tel: 714-521-1345. Sisters 4.

COSTA MESA. *Sisters of Mercy of Ireland*, St. John the Baptist Convent, 2960 Mendoza Dr., 92626. Tel: 714-545-2116. Sisters 4.

Sisters of the Company of Mary, St. Joachim Convent, 1943 Orange Ave., 92727. Tel: 714-574-7408.
E-mail: stjoachim@ioc.net
Sisters 4.

CYPRESS. *Sisters of the Blessed Virgin Mary*, St. Irenaeus Convent, 5201 Evergreen Ave., 90630. Tel: 714-527-4844.

DANA POINT. *Sisters of Social Service*, St. Edward, 33926 Calle La Primavera, 92629-2018. Tel: 714-496-1307.

Sisters of St. Joseph of Orange, Mission Hospital Community, 33392 Via Lenita, 92629. Tel: 714-488-0433.
E-mail: srma@0103.stjoe.org
Sr. Michelle Tochtrop, C.S.J., Gen. Sec. & Contact. Tel: 714-633-8121 Ext. 735; Sr. Martha Ann Fitzpatrick, C.S.J.; Sr. Maura Judge, C.S.J.; Sr. Marian Schubert, C.S.J.; Sr. Beth McPherson, C.S.C.

FOUNTAIN VALLEY. *Sisters of Social Service*, 9076 La Colonia, 92708. Tel: 714-847-8981.

FULLERTON. *Sisters of St. Joseph of Orange*, Rosary Community, 1601 E. Alto Ln., 92831. Tel: 714-526-3141. Sr. Michelle Tochtrop, C.S.J., Gen. Sec. & Contact. Tel: 714-633-8121 Ext. 735. Sisters 7. St. Jude Hospital Community, P.O. Box 4138, 92634. Tel: 714-992-3000. Sisters 8. St. Mary Convent, 920 N. Grandview, 92832. Tel: 714-526-7349. Sisters 4.

GARDEN GROVE. *Eucharistic Missionaries of the Most Holy Trinity*, 11892 E. Lampson Ave., 92840. Tel: 714-530-5727. Sisters 4.

Religious Sisters of Charity, St. Columban Convent, 12555 Westlake St., 92650. Tel: 714-534-1003. Sisters 4.

Sisters of the Presentation of the Blessed Virgin Mary, St. Columban Residence, 10871 Stanford Ave., #18, 92840-5118. Tel: 714-537-2015.

HUNTINGTON BEACH. *Sisters of Charity of the Blessed Virgin Mary*, SS. Simon & Jude Convent, 20512 Tobermory Cir., 92646-5837. Tel: 714-968-2237.
E-mail: vsmurlo@pacbell.net

Sisters of the Presentation of the Blessed Virgin Mary, St. Bonaventure Convent, 16441 Bradbury Ln., 92647. Tel: 714-846-6212. Sisters 5.

LA HABRA. *Sisters of St. Joseph of Carondelet*, Villa Maria House of Prayer, 1252 N. Citrus Dr., 90631. Tel: 310-691-5838. Sisters 4.

Sisters of St. Joseph of Orange, Our Lady of Guadalupe Community, 920 W. La Habra Blvd., 90631. Tel: 310-691-9612. Sr. Michelle Tochtrop, C.S.J., Gen. Sec. & Contact. Sisters 2.

LAGUNA BEACH. *Benedictines*, St. Catherine of Siena Convent, 3090 S. Coast Hwy., 92651. Tel: 714-494-7339.

LAGUNA HILLS. *Sisters of Little Company of Mary*, St. Nicholas Convent, 24652 La Cienega, 92653. Tel: 714-643-8688. Sisters 2.

LAKE FOREST. *School Sisters of St. Francis*, 24001 Muirlands Blvd. #146, 92630. Tel: 714-951-8681.
E-mail: sssf@earth.execpc.com
Web site: www.homeboyz.com/sssf

NEWPORT BEACH. *Community of the Holy Spirit*, Our Lady Queen of Angels Convent, 2108 Aralia St., 92660. Tel: 714-644-0660.

RANCHO SANTA MARGARITA. *Sisters of Providence*, 243 Via Serena, 92688. Tel: 714-589-3322.

Sisters of the Holy Cross, 7 Via Amistosa, Apt. B, 92688.

SANTA ANA. *Dominicans, Mission San Jose*, St. Callistus Convent, 2541 N. Forest Ave., 92706. Tel: 714-953-4322.
E-mail: msjcallistus@connectinc.com
Sisters 4.

Franciscan Missionary Sisters of the Immaculate Conception, St. Francis Home for the Aged, 1718 W. 6th St., 92703. Tel: 714-542-0381. Sisters 22.

Franciscans, Rochester, Immaculate Heart of Mary Convent, 2202 McFadden, 92704. Tel: 714-545-7916. Sisters 5.

Lovers of the Holy Cross, 1401 S. Sycamore St., 92707. Tel: 714-973-1951. Sisters 9.

Poor Clare Missionary Sisters of the Blessed Sacrament, 1019 N. Newhope St., 92703. Tel: 714-554-8850; Fax: 714-554-5886. Sisters 15.

Sisters of Mercy of the Americas, 16350 Harbor Blvd., #2602, 92704-3836. Tel: 714-839-7893.

Sisters of St. Joseph of Carondelet, Hogar de San Jose, 507 N. Linwood Ave., 92701. Tel: 714-541-6480. St. Joseph, 727 Minter St., 92701. Tel: 714-550-8096.

Sisters of St. Joseph of Orange, Casa Guadalupe Community, 414 S. Broadway, 92701. Tel: 714-834-9381. Sr. Michelle Tochtrop, C.S.J., Gen. Sec. & Contact. Tel: 714-633-8121 Ext. 735. Sisters 5. Fifth Street Community, 519 E. 5th St., 92701. Tel: 714-543-6661. Sisters 3.

Sisters of the Company of Mary, St. Anne's Convent, 1339 S. Broadway, 92707. Tel: 714-558-1340. Sisters 3.

Society Devoted to the Sacred Heart, Heart of Jesus Retreat Center, 2927 S. Greenville St., 92704. Tel: 714-557-4538. Sisters 7. Sacred Heart Convent, 2911 S. Greenville St., 92704. Tel: 714-751-6335. Sisters 6.

SEAL BEACH. *Franciscans, Syracuse*, St. Anne Convent, 328 1/2 10th St., 90740. Tel: 310-493-4630.

SILVERADO. *Rosarian Dominicans*, St. Michael's Convent, 19292 El Toro Rd., 92676. Tel: 714-858-0487. Sisters 7.

TUSTIN. *Adrian Dominicans*, St. Jeanne de Lestonnac Convent, 16791 E. Main St., 92780. Tel: 714-541-3125.

Sisters de L'Union-Chretienne de Saint Chaumond, 14391 Clarissa Ln., 92780. Tel: 714-730-1475. Sisters 3.

Sisters of Providence, 14692 Charloma Dr., 92780. Tel: 714-544-9021. Sisters 3.

Sisters of St. Louis, 131 Hall Cir., #59, 92780.

Sisters of the Company of Mary, Provincial House, 16791 E. Main St., 92780. Tel: 714-541-3125; Fax: 714-835-0648.
E-mail: odn@ocweb.com
Web site: www.ocweb.com/sj
Sisters 16.

WESTMINSTER. *Korean Sisters of our Lady of Perpetual Help*, 7655 Trask Ave., 92683. Tel: 714-373-2556. Sisters 2.

YORBA LINDA. *Sisters of Providence Residence*, Providence House, 4580 Casa Oro Dr., 92886. Tel: 714-996-5027.
E-mail: dpaula996@juno.com
Sr. Jan Craven, S.P.; Sr. Paula Damiano, S.P. Sisters 2.

[J] CATHOLIC CHARITIES

SANTA ANA. *Catholic Charities of Orange County, Inc.*, 1506 Brookhollow Dr., Ste. 112, 92705. Tel: 714-662-7500; Fax: 714-662-1861. Kristan Schlichte, M.S., Exec. Dir.; Most Rev. Michael P. Driscoll, M.S.W., Vicar for Charities.

Counseling Services. Patricia Burgoyne, M.S.W., L.C.S.W., Program Dir.

Family Resource Center. Tara Brennon, Admin.

Columbian House, Anaheim Hills. Frank Bartosik, Facility Mgr.

Columbian House, Garden Grove. Ann, Wohlgenant, Faculty Mgr. Residential care for children with developmental disabilities.

Family Support Center. Gilbert Rivera, Admin.

Employment Services. Mr. Xang Yang, Prog. Dir.
Family Service Center. Raoul Aroz, Admin.
Resettlement, Immigration & Citizenship Services. Thu Tran, Program Dir.

[K] RETREAT HOUSES

ORANGE. *Center for Spiritual Development*, 434 S. Batavia St., 92868-3907. Tel: 714-744-3175, Ext. 404. Sr. Jane Delisle, C.S.J., Exec. Dir. Total Staff 12.
House of Prayer for Priests, 7734 Santiago Canyon Rd., 92869. Tel: 714-639-9740. Rev. J. Gordon Moreland, S.J., Dir. In res. Rev. Patrick B. Philbin, S.M. Total in Residence 2; Total Staff 1.
Marywood Retreat Center, 2811 E. Villa Real Dr., 92867. Tel: 714-282-3099 (Evenings & Weekends). Mrs. Eileen Pfaff, Facilities Coord., Tel: 714-282-3098 (Days Mon.-Fri.). Sr. Joseph Patrice Shea, S.P., Res. Dir. Retreats for youth, men, women & married couple groups. Capacity 120.

LA HABRA. *Villa Maria House of Prayer*, 1252 N. Citrus Dr., 90631. Tel: 562-691-5838. Sisters of St. Joseph of Carondelet.

SANTA ANA. *Heart of Jesus Retreat Center*, 2927 S. Greenville St., 92704. Tel: 714-557-4538; Fax: 714-668-9780. Society Devoted to the Sacred Heart. Sisters 9; Total Staff 6.

[L] NEWMAN CENTERS

FULLERTON. *California State University Fullerton, Newman Center*, St. Juliana Falconieri, 1316 N. Acacia Ave., 92831. Tel: 714-526-7189.
E-mail: csufnewman@newman.org
Rev. Joseph P. Cheah, O.S.M.

IRVINE. *Campus Ministry-Diocese of Orange*, U.C.I. Interfaith Center, P.O. Box 6030, 92616-6030. Tel: 714-856-0211; 753-3373, Ext. 3. Rev. Patrick Philbin, S.M., Diocesan Dir. Campus Ministry.
University of California, Irvine, U.C.I. Interfaith Center, P.O. Box 6030, 92616-6030. Tel: 714-856-0211; 753-3373, Ext. 3. Rev. Patrick Philbin, S.M., Diocesan Dir. Campus Ministry.

[M] SECULAR INSTITUTES

FULLERTON. *Pro Sanctity Spirituality Center, Retreat House*, 205 S. Pine Dr., 92833. Tel: 714-956-1020.
E-mail: ApostolicO@aol.com
Agnes Rus, Dir. Capacity: 27-40 for day use.
Pro Sanctity Movement. Barbara Wagner, Dir.

[N] MISCELLANEOUS LISTINGS

ORANGE. *Sisters of St. Joseph Healthcare Foundation*, 480 S. Batavia St., 92868. Tel: 714-633-8121; Fax: 714-744-3165. Sr. Diane Hejna, C.S.J., Exec. Dir.

ANAHEIM. *Orange County Catholic Alumni Club*, P.O. Box 4541, 92803. Tel: 714-502-8086.

EL TORO. *Aid to the Church In Need, Inc.*, P.O. Box 1000, 92630. Tel: 714-858-0222; 800-628-6333.
Web site: www.churchinneed.org
Mr. David Budinger, Jr., Pres.; Revs. Hubert S. Szanto, O.Praem., Board Member; Gabriel D. Stack, O.Praem.; Mr. Robert W. Lulley, Natl. Dir.

FULLERTON. *Apostolic Oblates*, 2125 W. Walnut Ave., 92833. Tel: 714-871-5768.
E-mail: ApostolicO@aol.com
House of Formation for Professed Apostolic Oblates. Secular Institute of the Apostolic Oblates, Inc. Agnes Rus, Local Moderator.

SILVERADO. *Norbertine Association of St. Joseph, Inc.*, St. Michael's Abbey, 19292 El Toro Rd., 92676-9710. Tel: 714-858-0222, Ext. 216; Fax: 714-858-4583. Officers: Rt. Rev. Eugene J. Hayes, O.Praem., Pres.; Rev. Thomas M. Nelson, O.Praem., Vice Pres. & Chap.; Monique Petit, Moderator. A public association of the faithful for unmarried lay women wishing to live a more intense Norbertine spirituality in common.

RELIGIOUS INSTITUTES OF MEN REPRESENTED IN THE DIOCESE

For further details refer to the corresponding bracketed number in the Religious Institutes of Men or Women section.

[0140]—*Augustinian Fathers.*—O.S.A.
[0150]—*Augustinian Recollects.*—O.A.R.
[1160]—*Brothers of St. Patrick.*—F.S.P.
[0330]—*Brothers of the Christian Schools.*—F.S.C.
[0360]—*Claretian Missionaries.*—C.M.F.
[0370]—*Columban Fathers.*—S.S.C.
[0520]—*Franciscan Fathers.*—O.F.M.
[0690]—*Jesuit Fathers and Brothers.*—S.J.
[0780]—*Marist Fathers.*—S.M.
[0850]—*Missionaries of Africa.*—M.Afr.
[0900]—*Norbertine Fathers.*—O.Praem.
[1140]—*Sacred Heart Fathers.*—SS.CC.
[1240]—*Servite Fathers and Brothers.*—O.S.M.
[0420]—*Society of the Divine Word.*—S.V.D.
[1300]—*Theatine Fathers.*—C.R.
[0840]—*Trinity Missionaries.*—S.T.

RELIGIOUS INSTITUTES OF WOMEN REPRESENTED IN THE DIOCESE

[]—*Benedictine Sisters.* (Grand Terrace).—O.S.B.
[]—*Benedictine Sisters.* (Rapid City, SD).—O.S.B.
[2020]—*Community of the Holy Spirit.*—C.H.S.
[1920]—*Congregation of Sisters of the Holy Cross* .—C.S.C.
[0880]—*Daughters of Mary and Joseph.*—D.M.J.
[1070-13]—*Dominican Sisters.* (Adrian, MI).—O.P.
[]—*Dominican Sisters.* (Mission San Jose).—O.P.
[]—*Eucharistic Missionaries of the Most Holy Trinity.*—M.E.S.S.T.
[1350]—*Franciscan Missionary Sisters of the Immaculate Conception.*—O.S.F.
[]—*Franciscan Sisters.* (Rochester, MN).—O.S.F.
[]—*Franciscan Sisters.* (Syracuse, NY).—O.S.F.
[1650]—*Franciscan Sisters, Philadelphia Foundation.*—O.S.F.
[2390]—*Lovers of the Holy Cross Sisters.*—L.H.C.
[2840]—*Poor Clare Missionaries of Blessed Sacrament.*—M.C.
[3280]—*Presentation Sisters of Blessed Virgin Mary.*—P.B.V.M.
[3400]—*Religious Sisters of Charity.*—R.S.C.
[]—*Rosarian Dominican Sisters.*—O.P.
[1680]—*School Sisters of St. Francis.*—S.S.S.F.
[3580]—*Servants of Mary.*—O.S.M.
[]—*Sisters of Charity of Leavenworth.* (KS).—S.C.L.
[]—*Sisters of Charity of Poitiers.*—S.C.P.
[0430]—*Sisters of Charity of the Blessed Virgin Mary.*—B.V.M.
[1940]—*Sisters of Holy Faith.*—C.H.F.
[]—*Sisters of Mercy of Ireland.*—S.M.
[2575]—*Sisters of Mercy of the Americas.*—R.S.M.
[]—*Sisters of Our Lady of Perpetual Help.*—S.O.L.P.H.
[]—*Sisters of Providence.*—S.P.
[4090]—*Sisters of Social Service.*—S.S.S.
[3770]—*Sisters of St. Clare.*—O.S.C.
[3830-03]—*Sisters of St. Joseph.* (Orange).—C.S.J.
[3840]—*Sisters of St. Joseph of Carondelet.*—C.S.J.
[3840]—*Sisters of St. Joseph of Carondelet.* (Albany Prov.).—C.S.J.
[3860]—*Sisters of St. Joseph of Cluny.*—S.J.C.
[3935]—*Sisters of St. Louis.*—S.S.L.
[0700]—*Sisters of the Company of Mary.*—O.D.N.
[1990]—*Sisters of the Holy Names of Jesus and Mary.*—S.N.J.M.
[2270]—*Sisters of the Little Company of Mary.*—L.C.M.
[4050]—*Sisters of the Society Devoted to the Sacred Heart.*—S.D.S.H.
[4060]—*Society of the Holy Child Jesus.*—S.H.C.J.

DIOCESAN CEMETERIES

ORANGE. *Holy Sepulcher*, 7845 Santiago Canyon Rd., 92869. Steve Haupert, Supt.

ANAHEIM. *Holy Cross.*

HUNTINGTON BEACH. *Good Shepherd Cemetery and Mausoleum*, 8301 Talbert Ave., 92646. Joe Hernandez, Supt.

LAKE FOREST. *Ascension*, 24754 Trabuco Rd., 92630. John D. Callaghan, Jr., Supt.

NECROLOGY

(No Deaths)

Diocese of Orlando

(Dioecesis Orlandensis)

Most Reverend

NORBERT M. DORSEY, C.P., D.D., S.T.D.

Bishop of Orlando; ordained April 28, 1956; appointed Auxiliary Bishop of Miami January 10, 1986; ordained Titular Bishop of Mactaris and Auxiliary Bishop of the Archdiocese of Miami March 19, 1986; appointed Bishop of Orlando March 20, 1990; installed as Third Bishop of Orlando May 25, 1990. *Office: 421 E. Robinson, P.O. Box 1800, Orlando, FL, 32802.*

Most Reverend

THOMAS J. GRADY, D.D.

Retired Bishop of Orlando; ordained April 23, 1938; appointed Auxiliary Bishop of Chicago June 21, 1967; ordained Titular Bishop of Vamalla August 24, 1967; appointed Bishop of Orlando November 9, 1974; installed as Second Bishop of Orlando December 16, 1974; retired May 25, 1990. *Mailing Address: 421 E. Robinson, P.O. Box 1800, Orlando, FL, 32802.*

ESTABLISHED JUNE 18, 1968.

Square Miles 10,776.

Comprises the Counties of Brevard, Lake, Marion, Orange, Osceola, Polk, Seminole, Sumter and Volusia in the State of Florida.

For legal titles of parishes and diocesan institutions, consult the Chancery.

Chancery: 421 E. Robinson, P.O. Box 1800, Orlando, FL, 32802-1800. Tel.: 407-246-4800; Fax: 407-246-4942.

STATISTICAL OVERVIEW

Personnel	
Bishop	1
Retired Bishops	1
Priests: Diocesan Active in Diocese	101
Priests: Active Outside Diocese	7
Priests: Retired, Sick or Absent	26
Number of Diocesan Priests	134
Religious Priests in Diocese	65
Extern Priests in Diocese	45
Ordinations:	
Transitional Deacons	3
Permanent Deacons	5
Permanent Deacons in Diocese	123
Total Brothers	13
Total Sisters	142
Parishes	
Parishes	70
With Resident Pastor:	
Resident Diocesan Priests	60
Resident Religious Priests	10
Without Resident Pastor:	
Missions	10
Professional Ministry Personnel:	
Brothers	2
Sisters	49
Lay Ministers	179
Welfare	
Day Care and Extended Day Care Centers	9
Total Assisted	900
Specialized Homes	2
Total Assisted	105
Special Centers for Social Services	6
Total Assisted	25,000
Other Institutions	9
Total Assisted	900
Educational	
Diocesan Students in Other Seminaries	19
Total Seminarians	19
High Schools, Diocesan and Parish	4
Total Students	2,370
Elementary Schools, Diocesan and Parish	32
Total Students	12,809
Non-residential Schools for the Disabled	1
Total Students	61
Catechesis/Religious Education:	
High School Students	3,877
Elementary Students	21,757
Total Students Under Catholic Instruction	40,893
Teachers in the Diocese:	
Priests	1
Sisters	36
Lay Teachers	826
Vital Statistics	
Receptions into the Church:	
Infant Baptism Totals	5,926
Adult Baptism Totals	670
Received into Full Communion	917
First Communions	5,683
Confirmations	3,690
Marriages:	
Catholic	907
Interfaith	692
Total Marriages	1,599
Deaths	3,296
Total Catholic Population	312,609
Total Population	2,992,581

Former Bishops—Most Rev. WILLIAM D. BORDERS, D.D., ord. May 18, 1940; appt. Bishop of Orlando, May 2, 1968; cons. June 14, 1968; transferred to Baltimore, March 25, 1974 as Archbishop.—Most Rev. THOMAS J. GRADY, D.D., ord. April 23, 1938; appt. Second Bishop of Orlando, Nov. 9, 1974; installed Dec. 16, 1974; retired May 25, 1990.

Chancery—421 E. Robinson, P.O. Box 1800, Orlando, 32802-1800. Tel: 407-246-4800; Fax: 407-246-4942.

Vicar General—Rev. PATRICK J. CAVERLY, V.G., *P.O. Box 1800, Orlando, 32802.* Tel: 407-246-4800.

Archivist—JANE QUINN.

Chancellor—Sr. LUCY VAZQUEZ, O.P., J.C.D., *P.O. Box 1800, Orlando, 32802.* Tel: 407-246-4800.

Tribunal—421 E. Robinson, P.O. Box 1800, Orlando, 32802. Tel: 407-246-4850.

Officialis—Rev. MATTHEW J. CONNOLLY.

Adjutant Judicial Vicar—Rev. PAIGE BLAKELY, J.C.L.

Director of Tribunal—Sr. LUCY VAZQUEZ, O.P., J.C.D.

Promoter of Justice—Sr. LUCY VAZQUEZ, O.P., J.C.D.

Defenders of the Bond—Revs. PAIGE BLAKELY, J.C.L.; MATTHEW J. CONNOLLY; J. FERNANDO GIL, J.C.L.; Sr. LUCY VAZQUEZ, O.P., J.C.D.

Judges—Revs. PAIGE BLAKELY, J.C.L.; NED PRENDIVILLE, J.C.L.; Sr. LUCY VAZQUEZ, O.P., J.C.D.; Revs. MATTHEW CONNOLLY; JOHN GIEL, J.C.L.

Comptroller—JOHN T. WETTACH.

Deans—Rev. ROBERT FUCHECK, Northern Deanery; Rev. SEAN HESLIN, Central Deanery South; Rev. CHARLES I. MITCHELL, Central Deanery North; Rev. PAUL KAMIDE, Eastern Deanery; Rev. ANTHONY BLUETT, Western Deanery; Rev. DAVID P. PAGE, Southern Deanery.

Priests' Council—Executive Committee: Most Rev. NORBERT M. DORSEY, C.P., Pres.; Revs. THOMAS MCMACKIN, Chm. JOHN GIEL, Sec. PATRICK J. CAVERLY, V.G., Ex Officio; EMILE GENTILE, T.O.R., Ex Officio. Members: Revs. FELIX BANOS; WILLIAM HANLEY; ANTHONY BLUETT; WILLIAM ENNIS; MANUEL FERNANDEZ; ROBERT FUCHECK; SEAN HESLIN; PAUL KAMIDE; CHARLES MITCHELL; PAUL HENRY; DAVID P. PAGE; MICHAEL GIGLIO; PETER UNIOWSKI; RICHARD WALSH.

Consultors—Revs. PATRICK J. CAVERLY, V.G.; SEAN HESLIN; ANTHONY BLUETT; PAUL KAMIDE; CHARLES I. MITCHELL; DAVID P. PAGE; ROBERT FUCHECK.

Bishop's Executive Staff—Most Rev. NORBERT M. DORSEY; Revs. PATRICK J. CAVERLY, V.G.; JOHN FLYNN, O.S.A.; EMILE GENTILE, T.O.R.; ROBERT WEBSTER; Sr. LUCY VAZQUEZ, O.P., J.C.D.; THOMAS AGLIO; JOHN WETTACH.

Vicar for Religious—Sr. LUCY VAZQUEZ, O.P., J.C.D., *P.O. Box 1800, Orlando, 32802.*

Vicar for Clergy—Rev. EMILE GENTILE, T.O.R.

Diocesan Offices and Organizations

B.A.S.E.—VITO NAPOLETANO, Dir.; Rev. PATRICK J. CAVERLY, V.G., *P.O. Box 1800, Orlando, 32802.* Tel: 407-246-4842.

Black & Haitian Ministry—Vacant, *P.O. Box 1800, Orlando, 32802.* Tel: 407-246-4925.

Building Commission—WILLIAM G. KRAMER, A.I.A., Co-ord., *P.O. Box 1800, Orlando, 32802.* Tel: 407-246-4870.

Campus Ministry—Rev. EMILE GENTILE, T.O.R., Dir., *P.O. Box 1800, Orlando, 32802.* Tel: 407-246-4875.

Catholic Social Services—THOMAS AGLIO, Dir., *1771 N. Semoran Blvd., Orlando, 32807.* Tel: 407-658-1818; Fax: 407-282-2891.

Cemeteries—Rev. THOMAS BARRETT, Dir., *P.O. Box 1800, Orlando, 32802.* Tel: 407-246-4870.

Censor of Books—Sr. LUCY VAZQUEZ, O.P., J.C.D., *Chancery Office, P.O. Box 1800, Orlando, 32802.*

Cursillos de Cristiandad—Rev. CARL VACEK, T.O.R., Dir., *Immaculate Heart of Mary, P.O. Box 310, Candler, 32111.* Tel: 352-687-4031.

Prison & Jail Ministry—THOMAS GILLAN, *1771 N. Semoran Blvd., Orlando, 32807.* Tel: 407-658-1818.

Diocesan Pastoral Council—VITO NAPOLETANO, Bishop's Rep., *P.O. Box 1800, Orlando, 32802.* Tel: 407-246-4840.

Ecumenical Office—Rev. LARRY LOSSING, *P.O. Box 1800, Orlando, 32802.*

Education, Board of—JERRY ALLENDER, Chm.

Education, Department of—MAUREEN HUNTINGTON, Ed.S., Supt., *P.O. Box 1800, Orlando, 32802.* Tel: 407-246-4900; Fax: 407-246-4940.

Family Life—ELAINE HENRIS, Dir., *P.O. Box 1800, Orlando, 32802.* Tel: 407-246-4865.

Catholic Gay & Lesbian Ministry—Rev. JOHN R. FLYNN, O.S.A., Dir., *P.O. Box 1800, Orlando, 32802-1800.* Tel: 407-695-3262; Fax: 407-246-4942.

Farmworker Ministry, Office for—Rev. ROBERT MARKUNAS, Dir., *P.O. Box 1800, Orlando, 32802.* Tel: 407-246-4930; Fax: 407-246-4932.

Finance Committee—GERALD F. HILBRICH, *KPMG Peat Marwick, LTD., P.O. Box 3031, Orlando, 32802.*

Fiscal Management—JOHN WETTACH.

Hispanic Ministry Office—Rev. ROBERT MARKUNAS, Dir., *P.O. Box 1800, Orlando, 32802.* Tel: 407-246-4930; Fax: 407-246-4942.

Immigration Services—RICHARD LOGUE, Dir., *1771 N. Semoran Blvd., Orlando, 32807.* Tel: 407-658-0113; Fax: 407-249-5699.

Insurance Committee—VITO NAPOLETANO, Acting Chm.

Lay Ministry Development—Dr. LINDA PERRONE ROONEY, Dir., *P.O. Box 1800, Orlando, 32802.* Tel: 407-246-4880; Fax: 407-246-4884.

Liturgical Commission—Rev. ROBERT WEBSTER, Dir., *P.O. Box 1800, Orlando, 32802.* Tel: 407-246-4860.

Newspaper—*"The Florida Catholic"*, HENRY LIBERSAT, Editor-Mgr., *P.O. Box 609512, Orlando, 32860-9512.* Tel: 407-660-9141.

Permanent Diaconate—Rev. EMILE GENTILE, T.O.R., Dir.; Deacon BOB KINSEY, Co-Dir., *P.O. Box 1800, Orlando, 32802.* Tel: 407-246-4875; Fax: 407-246-4942.

Priests' Continuing Education—Rev. RICHARD WALSH.

Priests Personnel—Rev. EMILE GENTILE, T.O.R., *P.O. Box 1800, Orlando, 32802.* Tel: 407-246-4875.

Propagation of the Faith—Rev. JOHN MCCORMICK, Dir., *Holy Redeemer, 1603 N. Thacker Ave., Kissimmee, 34741.* Tel: 407-846-3700.

Real Estate Committee—Rev. NICHOLAS KING, Chm., *P.O. Box 1800, Orlando, 32802.* Tel: 407-246-4800.

Refugee Resettlement—RICHARD LOGUE, Dir., *1771 N. Semoran Blvd., Orlando, 32807.* Tel: 407-658-0110; Fax: 407-249-5699.

Religious Education—Sr. LINDA L. GAUPIN, C.D.P., Ph.D., Dir., *P.O. Box 1800, Orlando, 32802.* Tel: 407-246-4910; Fax: 407-246-4940.

Media Center—ROZAN JORDAN, Dir., *329 Broadway, Orlando, 32803.* Tel: 407-246-4895; Fax: 407-246-4942.

Respect Life Office—DEBORAH SHEARER, Dir., *1771 N. Semoran Blvd., Orlando, 32807.* Tel: 407-277-7266; Fax: 407-282-2891.

Scouting—*Office of Youth Ministry, P.O. Box 1800, Orlando, 32802.* Tel: 407-246-4910.

Sister Diocese-Mission Office—Sr. BERNADETTE MACKAY, O.S.U., Dir., *P.O. Box 1800, Orlando, 32802.* Tel: 407-246-4890; Fax: 407-246-4942.

Sister's Council—Sr. ELIZABETH MARIE STOUP, S.S.J.

Society of St. Vincent de Paul—*P.O. Box 1800, Orlando, 32802.*

Spiritual Development—Rev. CARL VACEK, T.O.R., *2400 Dike Rd., Winter Park.* Tel: 407-671-6322.

Vietnamese Ministry—Rev. DUNG VAN "JOSEPH" BUI, *4001 Edgewater Dr., Orlando, 32804.* Tel: 407-293-9556.

Vocations—Rev. THOMAS BARRETT, Dir., *P.O. Box 1800, Orlando, 32802.* Tel: 407-246-4875; Fax: 407-246-4942.

Youth Ministry—JULIE BUTSON MICKLER, M.A., *P.O. Box 1800, Orlando, 32802.* Tel: 407-246-4911; Fax: 407-246-4940.

CLERGY, PARISHES, MISSIONS AND PAROCHIAL SCHOOLS

CITY OF ORLANDO
(Orange County)

1—ST. JAMES CATHEDRAL (1881), Revs. Sean Heslin; J.P. Morgan; Rafael Villegas; Deacons Sam Ryan; Bruce Simpson.
Church—215 N. Orange Ave., 32801. Tel: 407-422-2005; Fax: 407-422-2009.
School—Tel: 407-841-4432; Fax: 407-648-4603.
Lay Teachers 32; Students 468.
Catechesis/Religious Programs—Tel: 407-422-8624; Fax: 407-422-4009.
Students 371.
Mission—Orlando, Orange Co., St. Ignatius Kim Korean Mission, 1504 Muriel St., 32806. Tel: 407-897-6587; Fax: 407-897-6587. Rev. John Park.

2—BLESSED TRINITY (1965), Revs. Joe Aquino, M.S.; Camillo Avitabile, M.S.; Ron Gagne, M.S. In res., Rev. Matthew J. Connolly.
Res., 4545 E. Anderson Rd., 32812. Tel: 407-277-1702; Fax: 407-277-1973.
Catechesis/Religious Programs—Students 465.

3—GOOD SHEPHERD (1956), Revs. Brian Sheridan, M.S.; Joseph Kettner, M.S., Vicar; Daniel P. Bradley, M.S.; Stephen J. Krisanda, M.S.; Deacon Jose Garcia.
Mailing Address: 5900 Oleander Dr., 32807. Tel: 407-277-3938; Fax: 407-273-5148.
Res., 567 Hewitt Dr., 32807. Tel: 407-277-3938; Fax: 407-273-5148.
School—Tel: 407-277-3973; Fax: 407-277-2605.
Sisters 2; Lay Teachers 26; Students 588.
Pre-School—Tel: 407-277-1857.
Sisters 1; Lay Teachers 11; Students 102.
Catechesis/Religious Programs—Tel: 407-277-4200. Martha Solar, D.R.E.
Students 412.

4—HOLY CROSS (1992), Rev. Robert Kurber.
Res., 12600 Marsfield Rd., 32837. Tel: 407-438-0990; Fax: 407-438-4090.
Catechesis/Religious Programs—Students 708.

5—HOLY FAMILY (1975), Revs. William Ennis; John O'Holohan, S.J.; Michael E. Giglio.
Res., 5125 S. Apopka-Vineland Rd., 32819. Tel: 407-876-2211; Fax: 407-876-1167. [JC]
School—5129 S. Apopka-Vineland Rd., 32819. Tel: 407-876-9344; Fax: 407-876-8775. Sr. Dorothy Sayers, M.P.F., Prin.; Sr. Angela Bulla, M.P.F., Asst. Prin.
Sisters 3; Lay Teachers 22; Students 670.
Catechesis/Religious Programs—Tel: 407-876-6331; Fax: 407-876-8775.
Students 1,000.

6—ST. ANDREW (1957), Revs. Ben Berinti, C.PP.S.; Rick Friebel, C.PP.S.; Tito Rojas; Deacons James M. Flynn; Jose Cruz; Rafael Hernandez.
Res., 801 Hastings, 32808. Tel: 407-293-0730; Fax: 407-293-0739.
School—Tel: 407-295-4230; Fax: 407-290-0959.
Lay Teachers 24; Students 656.
Catechesis/Religious Programs—Students 220.

7—ST. CHARLES BORROMEO (1954), Revs. Donald G. Mainardi; Frank Cerio; Joseph Dung Van Bui; Deacon Richard Rupp. In res., Rev. Thomas Barrett.
Res., 4001 Edgewater Dr., 32804. Tel: 407-293-9556; Fax: 407-293-9213.
School—Tel: 407-293-7691; Fax: 407-293-9213.
Sisters of St. Joseph of St. Augustine 4; Lay Teachers 28; Students 660.
Preschool—Tel: 407-295-7041.
Lay Teachers 6; Students 54.
Catechesis/Religious Programs—Tel: 407-297-0284.
Students 114.

8—ST. ISAAC JOGUES (1987), Revs. Robert Hoeffner; Hernan Afanador; Deacons Robert Kloznick; Orlando Lendoiro; Lee Cochoran; Angel Pacheco.
Mailing Address: P.O. Box 720009, 32872. Tel: 407-249-0906; Fax: 407-273-3236.
Catechesis/Religious Programs—Students 622.

9—ST. JOHN VIANNEY (1959), Revs. Paul J. Henry; Timothy Daly; Vidal Arboleda, (Retired); Carlos Bedoya; Deacons Miguel Beltran; Kevin Mills; Terri Tagye, Pastoral Asst.
Res., 6200 S. Orange Blossom Tr., 32809. Tel: 407-855-5391; Fax: 407-859-3631.
School—Tel: 407-855-4660; Fax: 407-857-2760. Sr. Elizabeth Murphy, Prin.
Sisters of St. Francis of Philadelphia 4; Lay Teachers 26; Students 690.
Catechesis/Religious Programs—Tel: 407-859-1158. Deacon Tom Tagye, D.R.E.
Students 550.

10—ST. JOSEPH (1962) (Polish-Philippino), Revs. Robert W. Brown; Larry Lossing; Joseph Piatek.
Res., 1501 N. Alafaya Tr., 32828. Tel: 407-275-0841.
Catechesis/Religious Programs—Tel: 407-282-7784.
Students 350.

OUTSIDE THE CITY OF ORLANDO

Altamonte Springs, Seminole Co., St. Mary Magdalen (1959), Revs. Charles I. Mitchell; Edward J. Thompson; Jose F. Munoz; Thomas Smith; Deacons Henry Libersat; Norm Kazyk; Jerry Kelly.
Res., 861 Maitland Ave., 32701. Tel: 407-831-1212; Fax: 407-831-1560.
School—Tel: 407-339-7301; Fax: 407-339-9556.
Sisters 3; Lay Teachers 28; Students 532.
Catechesis/Religious Programs—Tel: 407-834-2211.
Students 475.

Annunciation (1982), Revs. Patrick J. Caverly; Michael J. Cannon (Ireland); Christopher P. Caracci; Charles J. Deeney, O.M.I.
Mailing Address: P.O. Box 3846, Longwood, 32779. Tel: 407-869-9472; Fax: 407-869-4661.
Res., 1020 Montgomery Rd., 32714.
School—Annunciation Catholic Academy, (Grades K-8). Tel: 407-774-2801; Fax: 407-774-2826.
Lay Teachers 25; Students 500.
Catechesis/Religious Programs—Tel: 407-869-0934.
Students 2,000.

Apopka, Orange Co., St. Francis of Assisi (1966), Revs. Clyde A. Bonar; Tito Rojas; Deacons Heriberto Santana; Laurence Herbert.
Res., 834 S. Orange Blossom Trail, 32703. Tel: 407-886-4602; Fax: 407-886-9758.
Catechesis/Religious Programs—Students 459.

Barefoot Bay, Brevard Co., St. Luke (1986), Rev. Patrick J. Carroll.
Res., P.O. Box 779-114, 32976. Tel: 561-664-9310; Fax: 561-664-3374. [JC]

Bartow, Polk Co., St. Thomas Aquinas (1956), Rev. Domingo Gonzalez.
Res., 1305 E. Mann Rd., 33830. Tel: 941-533-4514.
Missions—Fort Meade, Polk Co., St. Elizabeth Ann Seton, 101 Edgewood, Fort Meade, 33841. Tel: 941-285-7390; Wahneta, Polk Co., Our Lady of Guadalupe, 2150 State Rd. 559, Wahneta, 33880. Tel: 941-299-3854; Fax: 941-299-8247. Rev. Norman Farland.
Catechesis/Religious Programs—Tel: 941-533-4514.
Students 79.

Belleview, Marion Co., St. Theresa (1951), Rev. James MacLoughlin.
Res., 11526 S.E. U.S. Hwy. 301, 34420. Tel: 352-245-2458; Fax: 352-245-1521.
Catechesis/Religious Programs—Tel: 352-245-5300; Fax: 352-245-1521.
Students 185.

Bushnell, Sumter Co., St. Lawrence (1959), Rev. Fabian Sheganoski.
Res., 223 E. Vermont Ave., 33513. Tel: 352-793-4636.
Church—320 E. Dade Ave., 33513. Tel: 352-793-7788.
Catechesis/Religious Programs—Fax: 352-793-4787.
Students 85.
Mission—Wildwood, Sumter Co., St. Vincent de Paul Mission, 5195 E. CR 462, Wildwood, 34785. Tel: 904-330-0220.

Casselberry, Seminole Co., St. Augustine (1969), Revs. Joseph A. Genito, O.S.A.; John R. Flynn, O.S.A.; Kevin C. Mullins, O.S.A.
Res., 375 Sunset Dr., 32707. Tel: 407-695-3262; Fax: 407-699-8998.
Catechesis/Religious Programs—Students 370.

Clermont, Lake Co., Blessed Sacrament (1961), Rev. Andrew Wawrzycki; Deacon Paul Schneider.
Res., 720 12th St., 34711. Tel: 352-394-3562; Fax: 352-394-3562.
Catechesis/Religious Programs—Tel: 352-394-1097.
Students 307.

Cocoa, Brevard Co., Blessed Sacrament (1967), Rev. Edmund S. Czarnecki; Deacon Richard J. Basso.
Mailing Address: P.O. Box 40, Sharpes, 32959.
Office: 5135 U.S. No. 1 N., 32927. Tel: 407-632-6333; Fax: 407-631-2560.
Catechesis/Religious Programs—Students 262.

Cocoa Beach, Brevard Co., Church of Our Saviour (1956), Rev. Eamon Tobin.
Res., 5301 N. Atlantic Ave., 32931. Tel: 407-783-4554; Fax: 407-868-6743.
School—Tel: 407-783-2330; Fax: 407-784-6330.
Lay Teachers 16; Students 233.
Catechesis/Religious Programs—Students 202.

Daytona Beach, Volusia Co., St. Paul's (1881), Revs. Robert E. Webster; Diego Londono; Peter A. Sagorski; Deacon Robert Landers.
Res., 317 Mullally St., P.O. Box 646, 32115. Tel: 904-252-5422; Fax: 904-252-1936.

School—Tel: 904-252-7915; Fax: 904-238-7903.
Lay Teachers 18; Students 325.
Catechesis/Religious Programs—Students 130.

Our Lady of Lourdes (1953), Rev. Philip J. Egitto. In res., Rev. Thomas J. Connery.
Res., 304 Cornell Dr., 32118. Tel: 904-675-7975.
School—Tel: 904-252-0391; Fax: 904-238-1175.
Lay Teachers 15; Students 243.
Catechesis/Religious Programs—Tel: 904-255-0433.
Students 76.

DeBary, Volusia Co., St. Ann's (1959), Rev. Paige A. Blakely; Deacon William Cavins.
Res., 26 Dogwood Tr., P.O. Box 218, 32713-0218. Tel: 407-668-8270; Fax: 407-668-8471.
Catechesis/Religious Programs—Students 212.

De Land, Volusia Co., St. Peter's (1883), Rev. Msgr. Thomas Cannon, S.J.; Rev. William Gohring; Deacons Chester DeMarsh; Michael Alverez; Robert LaPlante; Joseph Costa; Robert Kinsey; Edward Rinderle; Jack Lahart; Wilfred Steinmetz; Ronald Keehner.
Mailing Address: P.O. Box 3700, 32723. Tel: 904-822-6000; Fax: 904-822-6034.
Res., 359 W. New York Ave., 32720.
School—Tel: 904-822-6010; Fax: 904-822-6013. Mrs. Joan Kinsey, Prin.
Lay Teachers 18; Students 313.
Catechesis/Religious Programs—Ms. Colette Martineau, D.R.E.
Students 303.
Mission—Barberville, Volusia Co., San Jose Mission, 165 Emporia Rd., Barberville, 32005. Tel: 904-749-9372.

Deltona, Volusia Co., Our Lady of the Lakes (1970), Revs. Michael Hanrahan; Harry C. Wallace (SY); Esau N. Garcia, C.P.; Deacons Hervey Mondor; Ray Doyle; Bruno Wiencek; Dan Feinbaum; Gilberto Perez; Ricardo Gonzalez.
Res., 1310 Maximilian St., 32725. Tel: 407-574-2131; Fax: 407-860-0074.
Catechesis/Religious Programs—Tel: 407-574-4620.
Students 860.

St. Clare (1989), Rev. Christopher A. Hoffmann; Deacons Joseph Robert; Gilberto Torres; Charles Bernard.
Res., 2961 Day Rd., 32738. Tel: 904-789-9990; Fax: 904-789-2430.
Catechesis/Religious Programs—Students 235.

Dunnellon, Marion Co., St. John the Baptist (1976), Rev. Emilio G. Garcia; Deacon Fred Crawford, Jr.
Res., U.S. 41 N., P.O. Box 310, 34430. Tel: 352-489-3166; Fax: 352-489-3166.
Catechesis/Religious Programs—Students 113.

Eustis, Lake Co., St. Mary of the Lakes (1912), Revs. Manuel A. Fernandez; Richard E. Oser, S.J.; Deacons Louis Klein; Francis McDonald.
Res., 234 E. Badger Ave., 32726. Tel: 352-483-3500; Fax: 352-483-1370.
Catechesis/Religious Programs—Tel: 352-483-3458.
Students 292.

Haines City, Polk Co., St. Ann (1969). (Formerly Transfiguration). Revs. Antonio Pons; Joseph T. Gomolski.
Res., 1311 E. Robinson Dr., P.O. Box 1285, 33845. Tel: 941-422-4370; Fax: 941-421-2522.
Catechesis/Religious Programs—Students 385.

Indialantic, Brevard Co., Holy Name of Jesus (1959), Revs. David Page; Robert McDonnell, C.S.C.; David Scotchie; Deacons Charles Foy; Joseph Richiuso; James Seidel.
Res., 3050 Hwy. A1A, 32903. Tel: 407-773-2783; Fax: 407-777-0929.
School—Tel: 407-773-1630; Fax: 407-773-7148.
Sisters 1; Lay Teachers 28; Students 499.
Catechesis/Religious Programs—Tel: 407-773-3905.
Students 557.

Kissimmee, Osceola Co., Holy Redeemer (1917) (Spanish), Revs. John McCormick; Luiz Bastos; Sante Reale, C.PP.S.
Res., 1603 N. Thacker Ave., 34741. Tel: 407-847-2500; 846-3700; Fax: 407-847-9687.
School—(1993) (Grades PreK-8) 1800 W. Columbia Ave., 34741. Tel: 407-870-9055; Fax: 407-870-2214. Maureen Kane, Prin.
Sisters of St. Joseph 1; Lay Teachers 18; Students 342.
Catechesis/Religious Programs—Bro. James Needham, D.R.E.
Students 890.
Mission—Kissimmee, Osceola Co., St. Catherine of Siena, 430 Otter Creek Dr., P.O. Box 450698, 34745-0698. Tel: 407-344-9607; Fax: 407-344-9160. Rev. Vidal Martinez, O.S.M.

Lady Lake, Lake Co., St. Timothy (1985), Revs. Robert Fucheck; Louis J. Gonter; Deacons Richard K. Del Papa; Nicholas Deutsch.
1351 Paige Pl., 32159. Tel: 352-753-0989; Fax: 352-753-9602.

Lakeland, Polk Co.,

1—Church of the Resurrection, (1963), Revs. Val J. Sheedy; Andrew Mallick; Deacon Joseph Wortman.
Res., 3720 Old Hwy. 37, 33813. Tel: 941-646-3556; Fax: 941-644-8697.
Catechesis/Religious Programs—Tel: 941-644-0585.
Students 324.

2—St. Anthony's, (1982), Revs. Vianney Cunningham, T.O.R.; Roderick Soha, T.O.R.; Joseph M. Hayden; Deacon Frank F. Oettinger; Rev. Richard Tucker (SY).
Res., 820 Marcum Rd., P.O. Box 90164, 33804-0164. Tel: 941-858-8047; Fax: 941-859-1036.
School—(Grades PreK-4) 820 Marcum Rd., 33809. Tel: 941-858-0671. Sr. Michael Patrick Koegel, O.S.F.
Lay Teachers 5; Students 124.
Catechesis/Religious Programs—Tel: 941-858-8611.
Students 262.

3—St. John Neumann, (1988), Rev. Peter Uniowski.
Res., P.O. Box 1064, Mulberry, 33860-1064. Tel: 941-644-7201; Fax: 941-647-3691.
Church—501 E. Carter Rd., 33813. Tel: 941-647-3400.
Catechesis/Religious Programs—Tel: 941-647-3404.
Students 210.

4—St. Joseph's, (1898), Revs. John Caulfield; Franklin G. Buck; Reynord Araya-Morales; Deacons Joseph McCabe; James Coughlin; Antonio Martinez.
Res., 210 W. Lemon St., P.O. Box 30, 33802. Tel: 941-682-0555; Fax: 941-686-9546.
School—Tel: 941-686-6415.
Sisters of Notre Dame 2; Lay Teachers 17; Students 299.
Catechesis/Religious Programs—Tel: 941-687-8873.
Students 195.

Lake Wales, Polk Co., Holy Spirit (1927), Revs. Felix Banos; Leo Dobo, (Retired); Joseph R. Gurdak, O.F.M.Cap; Deacon Donald E. Raymond.
Res., 644 S. 9th St., P.O. Box 232, 33853. Tel: 941-676-1556; Fax: 941-676-2962.
Catechesis/Religious Programs—Tel: 813-678-1083.
Students 262.
Station—Nalcrest, Tel: 941-692-1057.

Leesburg, Lake Co., St. Paul's (1954), Revs. John C. Giel; Nicholas J. O'Brien; Deacon Lawrence Holder.
Res., 1330 Sunshine Ave., 34748. Tel: 352-787-6354; Fax: 352-787-5971.
School—Tel: 352-787-4657.
Lay Teachers 13; Students 177.
Catechesis/Religious Programs—Tel: 352-365-4252.
Students 190.

Longwood, Seminole Co., Church of the Nativity (1960), Revs. Kenneth R. Schnipke, C.PP.S.; Henry L. Frantz, C.PP.S.; Deacon Constantino Ferriola. In res., Rev. Norbert Adelman.
Res., 3255 N. County Rd. 427, 32750. Tel: 407-322-3961; Fax: 407-322-3981.
Catechesis/Religious Programs—Students 922.

Melbourne, Brevard Co., Our Lady of Lourdes (1931) (Spanish), Revs. William Nanley; Jose Bautista. In res., Rev. Matthew Mello; Deacons Dennis Jones; Sergio Colon.
Res., 1626 Oak St., 32902. Tel: 407-723-3636; Fax: 407-951-8029.
School—420 E. Fee Ave., 32901. Tel: 407-723-3631.
Lay Teachers 20; Students 272.
Catechesis/Religious Programs—Students 253.

Ascension (1959), Revs. Francis X.J. Smith; Anthony Quinlivan, C.SS.R.; Deacons Richard Storum; Michael McElwee.
Mailing Address: 2950 N. Harbor City Blvd., 32935-6259. Tel: 407-254-1595; Fax: 407-255-3490.
School—Tel: 407-254-5495; Fax: 407-259-0993.
Sisters of Mercy (Ardee, Ireland) 2; Lay Teachers 24; Students 583.
Catechesis/Religious Programs—Tel: 407-259-6693.
Students 589.

Melbourne Beach, Brevard Co., Immaculate Conception (1978), Rev. Joseph A. Nolan; Deacon Howard Pettengill, Jr.
Res., 3780 S. Hwy. A1A, 32951. Tel: 407-725-0552; Fax: 407-727-8218.
Catechesis/Religious Programs—Students 115.

Merritt Island, Brevard Co., Divine Mercy (1964), Revs. Edward McCarthy; Colin Kidd, O.F.M., (Retired); Kent A. Walker.
Res., 1940 N. Courtenay Pkwy., 32953. Tel: 407-452-5955; Fax: 407-455-2268.
School—Tel: 407-452-0263; Fax: 407-453-7573.
Sisters of Mercy (Galway) 2; Lay Teachers 16; Students 290.
Catechesis/Religious Programs—Tel: 407-459-2819.
Students 347.
Convent—1930 N. Courtenay Pkwy., 32953. Tel: 407-452-1279.
Sisters 2.

Mims, Brevard Co., Holy Spirit (1967), Rev. Bill Zamborsky.
Office: 2399 Holder Rd., 32754-2103. Tel: 407-269-2282; Fax: 407-269-2252.
Res., 2309 Holder Rd., 32754-2103. [JC]
Catechesis/Religious Programs—Tel: 407-269-7785.
Students 212.

Mount Dora, Orange Co., St. Patrick's (1973) (Hispanic), Revs. Emile A. Gentile, T.O.R.; Blase Romano, T.O.R.; Alfredo Ortiz; Deacons William Fisher; Julio Morales.
Res., 6801 Old Hwy. 441 S., P.O. Box 211, 32756. Tel: 904-383-8556; Fax: 904-383-8443. [CEM]
Catechesis/Religious Programs—Students 135.

New Smyrna Beach, Volusia Co., Sacred Heart (1926), Revs. Eugene Daigle, C.ss.R.; William Biffar, C.ss.R.; John Cavanaugh, C.ss.R.; John Barry, C.ss.R.; Deacons George McMahon; Thomas Murray.
Res., 998 Father Donlan Dr., Box 729, 32170. Tel: 904-428-6426; Fax: 904-423-4088.
School—Tel: 904-428-4732; Fax: 904-428-4087.
Lay Teachers 18; Students 262.
Catechesis/Religious Programs—Blake Buruazos, D.R.E.
Students 200.
Mission—Edgewater, Volusia Co., St. Gerard, 114 West Ocean Ave., Edgewater, 32141. [CEM]

Our Lady Star of the Sea (1973), Rev. Thomas J. Bergin; Rev. Msgr. Francis Campagnone (BGP) (Retired); Deacon Paul Rock.
Res., 3837 Sandstone Ct., 32169. Tel: 904-427-4530; Fax: 904-423-6245.
Catechesis/Religious Programs—Tel: 904-423-6245.
Students 113.

Ocala, Marion Co.,

1—Blessed Trinity, (1922), Revs. Patrick J. Sheedy; Luis A. Barerra; Steven Phillips; Deacons James Boerstler; Harold Timmis.
Res., 5 S.E. 17th St., 34471. Tel: 352-629-8092; Fax: 352-351-8872.
School—Tel: 352-622-5808; Fax: 352-622-1660.
Lay Teachers 46; Students 603.
Catechesis/Religious Programs—Students 447.
Mission—Citra, Marion Co., Christ the King, 14047 N. U.S. Hwy. 301, Citra, 32112. Tel: 352-595-5605; Fax: 352-595-5605.

2—Our Lady of the Springs, (1982), Rev. William J. Neumann; Deacon John G. Collier, III.
Office—4047 N.E. 21st St., 34470. Tel: 352-236-2230; Fax: 352-236-1475.
Catechesis/Religious Programs—Fran Lopez, D.R.E. (Grades K-8).
Students 145.
Missions—Ocala National Forest, Marion Co., St. Joseph of the Forest, 17301 E. Hwy. 40, Silver Springs, 34488. Tel: 352-625-4222; Astor, Lake Co., St. Hubert of the Forest, P.O. Box 715, Astor, 32102. Tel: 352-236-2230.

3—Queen of Peace, (1987), Rev. Patrick J. O'Doherty; Deacon Richard Lacina.
Res., 6455 S.W. State Rd. 200, 34476. Tel: 904-854-2181; Fax: 904-854-7840. [JC]
Catechesis/Religious Programs—Students 110.

4—St. Jude's, (1983), Rev. Anthony Palmese; Deacon Santos Santiago.
Res., 453 Marion Oaks Dr., 34473. Tel: 352-347-0154; Fax: 352-347-5211.
Church—443 Marion Oaks Dr., 34473.
Catechesis/Religious Programs—Students 60.

Ormond Beach, Volusia Co., St. Brendan (1960), Revs. John J. Ryan; Steve Baumann.
Res., 136 Banyan Dr., 32176. Tel: 904-441-1505; Fax: 904-441-0774.
School—Tel: 904-441-1331.
Lay Teachers 22; Students 304.
Catechesis/Religious Programs—Students 180.

Prince of Peace (1966), Revs. Thomas P. McMackin; Leo Hodges.
Res., 600 S. Nova Rd., 32174. Tel: 904-672-5272; Fax: 904-677-3224.
Catechesis/Religious Programs—Students 475.

Palm Bay, Brevard Co., Our Lady of Grace (1989), Revs. James Dore, O.S.M.; John Martin, O.S.M.; Deacons Richard C. Shaw; Francis Falatico. In res., Rev. Damian Charboneau, O.S.M.
Res., 115 Battersea S.E., 32909. Tel: 407-786-8742.
Church—300 Malabar Rd. S.E., 32907. Tel: 407-725-3066; Fax: 407-725-9534.
Catechesis/Religious Programs—Students 487.

St. Joseph (1914), Revs. Michael A. Farrell; Chau Nguyen; Deacon Alfred P. Somma.
Res., 5330 Babcock St. N.E., P.O. Box 060507, 32906. Tel: 407-727-1565; Fax: 407-676-2579. [CEM]
School—Tel: 407-723-8866; Fax: 407-727-1181.
Lay Teachers 20; Students 414.
Catechesis/Religious Programs—Students 322.

Poinciana, Kissemmee Co., St. Rose of Lima (1994), Rev. Fernando Gil.
Res., 140 Pompei Dr., 34758. Tel: 407-932-5004; Fax: 407-932-0407.
Catechesis/Religious Programs—Students 148.

Port Orange, Volusia Co., Epiphany (1962), Rev. Paul T. Kamide. In res., Rev. Peter Mitchell.
Res., 201 Lafayette St., 32127. Tel: 904-767-6111; Fax: 904-767-0017.
Catechesis/Religious Programs—Students 310.

Our Lady of Hope (1981), Rev. Raymond J. O'Leary.
Res., P.O. Box 290216, 32129. Tel: 904-788-6144; Fax: 904-761-8840.
Catechesis/Religious Programs—Tel: 904-788-6747.
Students 380.

Rockledge, Brevard Co., St. Mary's (1917), Rev. Nicholas King; Rev. Msgr. Terence J. Farrelly, Pastor Emeritus; Rev. Robert Mitchell.
Mailing Address: 75 Barton Ave., 32955. Tel: 407-636-6834; Fax: 407-632-4301. [JC]
School—Tel: 407-636-4208; Fax: 407-636-0591.
Sisters of Mercy (Limerick) 4; Lay Teachers 25; Students 594.
Catechesis/Religious Programs—Tel: 407-633-9985.
Students 224.

St. Cloud, Osceola Co., St. Thomas Aquinas (1968), Revs. Fabian G. Gimeno; Felicito S. Baybay.
Res., 701 Brown Chapel Rd., P.O. Box 700368, 34770-0368. Tel: 407-957-4495.
Church—900 Brown Chapel Rd., 34769.
School—800 Brown Chapel Rd., 34769. Tel: 407-957-1772; Fax: 407-957-0131.
Lay Teachers 26; Students 494.
Catechesis/Religious Programs—Tel: 407-957-4057.
Students 310.

Sanford, Seminole Co., All Souls (1911), Revs. Richard W. Trout; David Vivero.
Res., 800 S. Oak Ave., 32771. Tel: 407-322-3795; Fax: 407-322-1131. [CEM]
School—Tel: 407-322-7090; Fax: 407-321-7255.
Lay Teachers 16; Students 300.
Catechesis/Religious Programs—Students 305.

Silver Springs Shores, Marion Co., Immaculate Heart of Mary (1983), Revs. Sean Shine; Con Shine; Deacon Lou Bonneau.
Mailing Address: P.O. Box 310, Candler, 32111. Tel: 904-687-4031; Fax: 904-687-1811.
Catechesis/Religious Programs—Tel: 904-687-8818.
Students 48.

Titusville, Brevard Co., St. Teresa (1958), Revs. John S. Murray; Charles Viviano; Deacons Donald Boland; Charles I. Robichaud.
Res., 203 Ojibway St., P.O. Box 1598, 32781. Tel: 407-268-3441; Fax: 407-268-3270.
School—Tel: 407-267-1643; Fax: 407-268-5124.
Sisters of Mercy (Gort, Ireland) 3; Lay Teachers 13; Students 305.
Catechesis/Religious Programs—Tel: 407-268-0440; Fax: 407-268-3720.
Students 289.
Convent—3380 Muirfield Dr., 32780. Tel: 407-267-1610.
Sisters 2.

Winter Garden, Orange Co., Resurrection (1967), Rev. Andrew O'Reilly, C.PP.S.
Church and Res.: P.O. Box 771257, 34777. Tel: 407-656-3113; Fax: 407-654-4935.
Catechesis/Religious Programs—Tel: 407-654-4935.
Students 350.

Winter Haven, Polk Co., St. Joseph's (1923), Revs. Anthony Bluett; Joseph Pinchock; Deacon Nuoc Van Dang.
Res., 532 Ave. M N.W., 33881. Tel: 941-294-3144; Fax: 941-299-9709.
School—Tel: 941-293-3311.
Sisters of Notre Dame, Chardon, Ohio Province 1; Lay Teachers 21; Students 438.
Catechesis/Religious Programs—Tel: 941-299-9709.
Students 275.

St. Matthew (1973), Rev. Fred R. Ruse.
Res., 365 Pasco Ct., 33884. Tel: 941-324-0357; Fax: 941-324-9181.
Church—651 Carl Floyd Rd., 33884.
Catechesis/Religious Programs—Tel: 941-324-3559.
Students 215.

Winter Park, Orange Co., St. Margaret Mary (1947), Revs. Richard Walsh; Robert Wiseman, C.S.C.; Kurt Ewen; Deacons Jack Timmes; Nemsy Gubatan.
Res., 526 N. Park Ave., 32789. Tel: 407-647-3392; Fax: 407-647-4492.
School—Tel: 407-644-7537; Fax: 407-644-7357.
Lay Teachers 30; Students 535.
Catechesis/Religious Programs—Tel: 407-647-5171; Fax: 407-647-4492.
Students 430.

Saints Peter and Paul (1967), Revs. Sean K. Cooney; Pedro C. Puntal (Philippines); Deacons Al Castellana; James Campbell.
Res., 5300 Old Howell Branch Rd., 32792. Tel: 407-657-6114; Fax: 407-657-9375.
Catechesis/Religious Programs—Fax: 407-657-9530.
Students 800.

Winter Springs, Seminole Co., St. Stephen (1985), Rev. John J. Bluett.
Res., 575 Tuskawilla Rd., 32708. Tel: 407-699-5683; Fax: 407-699-8408.
Catechesis/Religious Programs—Students 1,600.

Shrines

1—Mary Queen of the Universe Shrine (1986), Revs. F. Joseph Harte; Barry Dowd; Fortune Frenoy, S.M.; William M. Boyle; Sr. Ita Hickey, O.S.C.
Res., 8300 Vineland Ave., 32821. Tel: 407-239-6600; Fax: 407-239-1362.

Special Assignment:
Reverend Fathers—
Barrett, Thomas, Office of Cemeteries & Office of Vocations
Connolly, Matthew J., Officialis
Gentile, Emile A., T.O.R., Vicar for Clergy
Lossing, Larry, Office of Ecumenism
Markunas, Robert, Hispanic & Farmworker Ministry
Prendiville, Ned, Tribunal
Walsh, Richard, Priests' Continuing Education
Webster, Robert, Office of Liturgy

On Duty Outside the Diocese:
Reverend Fathers—
Henry, Peter, Switzerland
Ingram, James A., U.S. Military
Kandel, Timothy, Miami
Mueller, Michael, U.S. Military
Stahl, Allen, U.S. Military
Traupman, Robert, Maryland

Sabbatical:
Reverend Fathers—
Bendixen, Arthur, Inactive
Cleare, Rudi, On Leave
Collins, Michael, Inactive
Coyle, James, Inactive
Danen, Lyle, Inactive
Finley, William, Inactive
Granahan, Gerard, Inactive
Olds, Steve, Advanced Studies
Uhran, Vernon, Inactive

Retired:
Mitred Archpriest—
Berko, Matthew, St. Mary Ukrainian, 20 E. Nightingale St., Apopka, FL 32712. Tel: 407-880-1640
Reverend Monsignors—
Bartok, Charles, 3753 Grove Circle, Zellwood, FL 32798
Campagnone, Francis, 215 Cherry Wood Ln., Edgewater, FL 32132. Tel: 904-423-7360
Denehy, John, 460 Grant Ave., Satellite Beach, FL 32937
Farrelly, Terence J., 56 Barton Ave., Rockledge, FL 32955. Tel: 407-636-9099
Farris, Semaan, 604 Tupelo Dr., Melbourne, FL 32935. Tel: 407-255-2505
Reverend Fathers—
Angles, Sebastian, 2601 Muscatello St., Orlando, FL 32837. Tel: 407-851-1934
Arboleda, Vidal, St. John Vianney, 6200 S. Orange Blossom Tr., Orlando, FL 32809. Tel: 407-855-5391
Benitez, Eduardo, P.O. Box 1524, Davenport, FL 33837
Buzek, Joseph J., 1858 Maywood Rd., Winter Park, FL 32792. Tel: 407-671-1264
Cosgrove, J. Kelly, 4182 Mount Vernon Ave., Titusville, FL 32780. Tel: 407-267-8601
Dobo, Leo, P.O. Box 7245, Indian Lake Estates, FL 33855. Tel: 941-692-1057
Donnelly, Brendan, P.O. Box 686, Southbury, CT 06488-0686. Tel: 203-264-5071
Donohue, Peter, C.S.C., Christopher Lodge, 323 Arthur Ave., Cocoa Beach, FL 32931. Tel: 407-799-8383
Edwards, James F., P.O. Box 2188, Ormond Beach, FL 32175. Tel: 904-258-5293
Fanning, Leo M., 14 Polar Bear Pk., Ormond Beach, FL 32174. Tel: 904-672-1725
Foley, William A., S.M., 31 Fillmore Ct., Satellite Beach, FL 32937. Tel: 407-773-7631
Franczek, Walter, 5062 S.E. 115th St., Belleview, FL 32620. Tel: 352-347-7289
Garvy, John, Blue Ridge Apartments, 108 N. Blue Ridge Rd., Black Mountain, NC 28711
Gonter, Louis J., 9980 S.E. 161st. Pl., Summerfield, FL 32691. Tel: 352-347-7289
Goodman, Frank, 900 Mosley Rd., Lake Alfred, FL 33850
Grasso, Richard E., 88 Marvin Rd., Ormond Beach, FL 32176. Tel: 904-677-0188
Hamilton, Edward A., 1540 Waldorf Circle, N.E., Palm Bay, FL 32905. Tel: 407-768-6299
Hannon, Michael, 5216 Karlsburg Pl., Palm Harbor, FL 34685. Tel: 813-934-2469
Hayden, Joseph Mark, 4747 Road 33 N., #354, Lakeland, FL 33805. Tel: 941-686-8046
Hennes, Paul R., 102 Wild Cherry Ave., Leesburg, FL 34748. Tel: 904-728-4716
Holland, Cajetan, C.S.C., 325 Arthur Ave., Cocoa Beach, FL 32931-4065
Jennings, Francis, C.SS.R., St. Alphonsus Villa, P.O. Box 548, New Smyrna Beach, FL 32170
Jordan, Patrick, 880 Lancaster Rd., Deland, FL 32720. Tel: 904-740-1123
Karwacki, Marion T., 236 Lake Ira Dr. W., Winter Haven, FL 33884. Tel: 941-324-1385
Kidd, Colin, O.F.M., Divine Mercy, 1940 N. Courtenay Pkwy., Merritt Island, FL 32953. Tel: 407-452-5955
Knoll, Mark, C.SS.R., P.O. Box 1529, New Smyrna Beach, FL 32170-1529. Tel: 904-427-3094
Lambour, Stephen, C.S.C., 325 Arthur Ave., Cocoa Beach, FL 32931-4065
Letourneau, F. E., The Veranda Nursing & Rehabilitation Center, 830 W. 29th St., Orlando, FL 32805
Lloyd, Vincent A., 713 Egret Ct., Edgewater, FL 32141. Tel: 904-423-8432
Lochner, Robert J., C.S.C., Christopher Lodge, 323 Arthur Ave., Cocoa Beach, FL 32931. Tel: 407-799-8383
McNeil, John, 26608 Bella Vista Blvd., Howey-in-the-Hills, FL 34737. Tel: 904-324-2664
McNicholas, Stephen, 220-8 Moree Loop, Winter Springs, FL 32708
Mena, Jose, 501 N. Ocean St., Apt. 1703, Jacksonville, FL 32202
Moreau, George, (Jan.-May), P.O. Box 07267, Fort Myers, FL 33919
Moser, Charles J., S.M.A., 165 Bonita St., Titusville, FL 32780. Tel: 407-267-6863
Murphy, James, 1742 Colleen, Orlando, FL 32809. Tel: 407-851-1742
Nacca, John J., St. John the Baptist, P.O. Box 310, Dunnellon, FL 32630. Tel: 352-489-3166
Nolin, Joseph A., 219 Essex Dr., Ormond Beach, FL 32176. Tel: 904-441-2055
O'Farrell, William J., 320 Fleming Ave., Port Orange, FL 32019. Tel: 904-767-6114
O'Reilly, P. J., 2891 Nokomis Ave., Palm Bay, FL 32905. Tel: 407-724-6702
Pawlak, Edwin F., 2465 S. Washington Ave., Unit A106, Titusville, FL 32780. Tel: 407-269-6089
Power, Virgil, Sandy Oaks Park, 6760 N. Lecanto Hwy., Beverly Hills, FL 32665
Quinn, Peter, P.O. Box 7022, Daytona Beach, FL 32116
Redmond, Lawrence, P.O. Box 4159, St. Augustine, FL 32085
Rimshaw, Joseph J., S.S.J., 411 E. Lincoln Ave., Melbourne, FL 32901-4536. Tel: 407-723-1708
Ross, Kenneth, 604 White Plains Rd., Eastchester, NY 10709. Tel: 914-337-2488
Serraino, Frederick, C.S.C., Christopher Lodge, 325 Arthur Ave., Cocoa Beach, FL 32931. Tel: 407-783-6312
Slafkosky, Andrew L., 610 Pine Rd., Silver Springs Shores, FL 34472. Tel: 352-687-8677
Tucker, Richard, 375 Brannen Rd., #229, Lakeland, FL 33813. Tel: 941-646-8744
VanNufflen, Albert, C.I.C.M., Aliki Condominium, 2828 N. Atlantic Ave., #202, Daytona Beach, FL 32118. Tel: 904-672-9098
Whipple, Donald W., C.S.C., Christopher Lodge, 323 Arthur Ave., Cocoa Beach, FL 32931. Tel: 407-799-8383
Zammit, Francis X., P.O. Box 291242, Port Orange, FL 32129. Tel: 904-761-1388

Permanent Deacons:
Agers, Allen, (Retired), Holy Spirit, Mims
Almodovar, Ismael, Resurrection, Winter Garden
Alvarez, Jose M., St. Peter, DeLand
Barbieri, Robert, Inactive
Basso, Richard, Blessed Sacrament, Sharpes

Beltran, Miguel, St. John Vianney, Orlando
Bernard, Charles, St. Clare, Deltona
Boerstler, James, Blessed Trinity, Ocala
Boland, Donald, St. Teresa, Titusville
Bonneau, Louis, Immaculate Heart of Mary, Silver Springs Shores
Bradley, Francis, Holy Spirit, Mims
Busing, Marvin, St. Joseph, Lakeland
Campbell, James, Sts. Peter & Paul, Goldenrod
Casares, Gabriel, St. Rose of Lima, Poinciana
Castellana, Al, Sts. Peter & Paul, Goldenrod
Cavins, William, St. Ann, DeBary
Collier, John, Our Lady of the Springs, Ocala
Colon, Hector, Unassigned
Colon, Sergio, Our Lady of Lourdes, Melbourne
Costa, Joseph, St. Peter, DeLand
Coughlin, James, St. Joseph, Lakeland
Crawford, Fred J., Jr., St. John the Baptist, Dunnellon
Crotty, John, St. Joseph, Orlando
Cruz, Jose F., St. Andrew, Orlando
Dang, Nuoc Van, St. Joseph, Winter Haven
Decatrel, Leon, St. Joseph, Orlando
Del Papa, Richard, St. Timothy, Lady Lake
DeMarsh, Chester, Prince of Peace, Ormond Beach
Desjardins, Roland, On Duty Outside the Diocese
Deutsch, Nicholas, St. Timothy, Lady Lake
Diaz, Celso, Holy Cross, Orlando
Doyle, Raymond, (Retired), Our Lady of the Lakes, Deltona
Dwyer, Bruce, St. Mary, Rockledge
Falatico, Francis E., Our Lady of Grace, Palm Bay
Feinbaum, Daniel, Our Lady of the Lakes, Deltona
Ferriola, Constantino, Jr., Nativity, Longwood
Fisher, William, Jr., St. Patrick, Mount Dora
Flynn, James, St. Andrew, Orlando
Foy, Les, Holy Name of Jesus, Indialantic
Garcia, Jose M., Good Shepherd, Orlando
Gonzalez, Julio, Resurrection, Winter Garden
Gonzalez, Raphael, Resurrection, Winter Garden
Gonzalez, Ricardo, Our Lady of the Lakes, Deltona
Green, Howard, Our Lady of Lourdes, Melbourne
Gubatan, Nemsy, St. Margaret Mary, Winter Park
Henry, Vernon, Our Saviour, Cocoa Beach
Herbert, Larry, St. Francis of Assisi, Apopka
Hernandez, Rafael, St. Andrew, Orlando
Hindes, John T., St. Joseph of the Forest Mission, Silver Springs
Holder, Lawrence, St. Paul, Leesburg
Jones, Dennis, Our Lady of Lourdes, Melbourne
Kazyk, Norm, St. Mary Magdalen, Altamonte Springs
Keehner, Ron, St. Peter, DeLand
Kelly, Gerard, St. Mary Magdalen, Altamonte Springs
Kinsey, Robert, St. Peter, DeLand
Klein, Louis, (Retired), St. Mary of the Lakes, Eustis
Kloznick, Robert, St. Isaac Jogues, Orlando
Krajeski, Vernon, On Duty Outside the Diocese
Lacina, Richard, Queen of Peace, Ocala
Lahart, John, St. Peter, DeLand
Lammers, Jack, St. Joseph of the Forest Mission, Silver Springs
Landers, Robert, St. Paul, Daytona Beach
LaPlante, Robert, St. Peter, DeLand
Lendoiro, Orlando, St. Issac Jogues, Orlando
Libersat, Henry, St. Mary Magdalen, Altamonte Springs
Maddex, Edwin, Unassigned
Martin, Jack, Holy Cross, Orlando
Martin, Leonard, Holy Name of Jesus, Indialantic
Martinez, Antonio, St. Joseph, Lakeland
McCabe, Joseph, St. Joseph, Lakeland
McDonald, Francis L., St. Mary of the Lakes, Eustis
McElwee, Michael, Ascension, Melbourne
McMahon, George, Sacred Heart, New Smyrna Beach
Messinger, George, Unassigned
Mills, Kevin, St. John Vianney, Orlando
Monat, Noe, St. Ann, Haines City
Mondor, Hervey, Our Lady of the Lakes, Deltona
Morales, Julio, St. Francis of Assisi, Apopka
Morales, Ramon, Holy Cross, Orlando
Murello, Andy, St. Mary, Rockledge
Murray, Thomas, Sacred Heart, New Smyrna Beach
Neris, Susano, St. Rose of Lima, Poinciana
Ocasio, Roberto, St. Catherine of Siena Mission, Kissimmee
Oetinger, Frank, St. John Neumann, Mulberry
Olivo, Agapito, Centro Guadalupano Mission, Wahneta
Otradovec, Byron, St. Lawrence, Bushnell
Pacheco, Angel, St. Isaac Jogues, Orlando
Pellosie, John, Sts. Peter & Paul, Goldenrod
Perez, Gilberto, Our Lady of the Lakes, Deltona
Pettengill, Howard, Jr., Immaculate Conception, Melbourne Beach
Ramos, Epifanio, Inactive
Raymond, Donald, Holy Spirit, Lake Wales
Richiuso, Joseph, Holy Name of Jesus, Indialantic
Rinderle, Edward, St. Peter, DeLand
Rivera, Jose, St. Rose of Lima, Poinciana
Robert, Joseph, St. Clare, Deltona
Robichaud, Charles, St. Teresa, Titusville
Rock, Paul J., Our Lady Star of the Sea, New Smyrna Beach
Roy, Reginald, On Duty Outside the Diocese
Rupp, Richard T., St. Charles Borromeo, Orlando
Ryan, Sam, St. James, Orlando
Sanborn, Philip, St. Theresa, Belleview
Santana, Heriberto, St. Andrew, Orlando
Santiago, Santos, St. Jude, Ocala
Schneider, Paul A., Blessed Sacrament, Clermont
Seidel, James B., Holy Name of Jesus, Indialantic
Shaw, Richard, Our Lady of Grace, Palm Bay
Simpson, Bruce, St. James, Orlando
Somma, Alfred P., St. Joseph, Palm Bay
Sowinski, James, On Duty Outside the Diocese
Steinmetz, Wilfred, St. Peter, DeLand
Storum, Richard, Ascension, Melbourne
Swart, Homer, Epiphany, Port Orange
Tagye, Thomas, St. John Vianney, Orlando
Timmes, John, St. Margaret Mary, Winter Park
Timmis, Harold, Christ the King Mission, Ocala
Torres, Gilberto, St. Clare, Deltona
Trapani, Richard J., St. Thomas Aquinas, St. Cloud
Warner, Donald, St. Isaac Jogues, Orlando
Wendel, David, St. John Neumann, Lakeland
White, Gerard, On Duty Outside the Diocese
Wiencek, Bruno, Our Lady of the Lakes, Deltona
Wortman, Joseph, Resurrection, Lakeland
Wuenschel, Cyril, Unassigned

INSTITUTIONS LOCATED IN THE DIOCESE

[A] HIGH SCHOOLS, DIOCESAN AND PAROCHIAL

ORLANDO. *Bishop Moore High School*, 3901 Edgewater Dr., 32804. Tel: 407-293-7561. Rev. Tom Barrett. Priests 1; Lay Teachers 58; Students 1,075.

DAYTONA BEACH. *Father Lopez High School*, 960 Madison Ave., 32114. Tel: 904-253-5213. Mr. David Gonsalves, Prin.; Rev. Thomas Connery, Chap. Priests 1; Lay Teachers 27; Students 315.

LAKELAND. *Santa Fe Catholic High School*. (Grades 8-12), 3110 Highway 92 E., 33801. Tel: 941-665-4188; Fax: 941-665-4151. Ms. Mary Ellen Smith, Prin. Sisters 1; Lay Teachers 25; Students 320.

MELBOURNE. *Central Catholic High School*, 100 E. Florida Ave., 32901. Tel: 407-727-0793; Fax: 407-727-1134.
E-mail: dioorl48@mcc
Mr. Joe Mancini, Prin.; Rev. Matthew Mello, School Pastor. Lay Teachers 52; Students 660.

[B] SPECIAL SCHOOLS

ORLANDO. *Morning Star School*, 954 Leigh Ave., 32804-2299. Tel: 407-295-3077. Sr. Elizabeth Marie Stoup, S.S.J., Prin. School for Exceptional Children. Sisters of St. Joseph of St. Augustine 2; Lay Teachers 7; Students 65.

[C] HOUSING ACCOMMODATIONS FOR THE ELDERLY

ORLANDO. *Monsignor Bishop Manor Apts., Inc.*, 824 Borders Cir., 32808. Tel: 407-293-3339; Fax: 407-293-0085.
E-mail: Bishopmanor@juno.com
For a complete listing, refer to the Special Care Facilities section.

DAYTONA BEACH. *Casa San Pablo*, 401 N. Ridgewood Ave., 32114. Tel: 904-253-2828; Fax: 904-253-0842
For a complete listing, refer to the Special Care Facilities section.

MELBOURNE. *Ascension Manor*, 2960 Pineapple Ave., 32935. Tel: 407-757-9828
For a complete listing, refer to the Special Care Facilities section.

OCALA. *Trinity Villas I, Inc.*, 3728 N.E. 8th Pl., 34470-1093. Tel: 904-694-5507; Fax: 904-694-7434
For a complete listing, refer to the Special Care Facilities section.

Trinity Villas II, Inc., 3728 N.E. 8th Pl., 34470-1093. Tel: 904-694-5507; Fax: 904-694-7434
For a complete listing, refer to the Special Care Facilities section.

ORMOND BEACH. *Prince of Peace Villas, Inc.*, 664 S. Nova Rd., 32174. Tel: 904-673-5080; Fax: 904-673-2008
For a complete listing, refer to the Special Care Facilities section.

PORT ORANGE. *Epiphany Manor*, 4792 S. Ridgewood Ave., 32127
For a complete listing, refer to the Special Care Facilities section.

WINTER HAVEN. *Episcopal Catholic Apartments*, 500 Ave. L N.W., 33881. Tel: 941-299-4481
For a complete listing, refer to the Special Care Facilities section.

[D] RETREAT CENTERS

WINTER PARK. *San Pedro Spiritual Development Center*, 2400 Dike Rd., 32792. Tel: 407-671-6322; Fax: 407-671-3992.
E-mail: spcdove@aol.com
Web site: www.theguide.com
Revs. Carl Vacek, T.O.R., Dir.; Seraphin Conley, T.O.R.; Bros. Terence Thielen, T.O.R., Admin.; David Liedl, T.O.R. In res. Rev. Robert J. D'Aversa, T.O.R. Total Staff 4; Total in Residence 5.

[E] NEWMAN CENTERS OF CENTRAL FLORIDA

ORLANDO. *University of Central Florida Newman Center*, P.O. Box 26000, 32816. Tel: 407-823-5337. Rev. John R. Flynn, O.S.A.

DAYTONA BEACH. *Embry-Riddle Aeronautical University*, Office of the Chaplain, 600 S. Clyde Morris Blvd., 32114-3900. Tel: 904-226-6580. Rev. Leo Hodges, University Chap. & Dir. Campus Ministry.

DE LAND. *Stetson University Catholic Campus Ministry*, Newman House, 523 N. Amelia Ave., 32724. Tel: 904-822-8156.
E-mail: choffmann@stetson.edu
Rev. Chris Hoffmann; Deacon Edward Rinderle, Co-Dir. Total Staff 1.

LAKELAND. *Florida Southern College Newman Center*, c/o St. Anthony, P.O. Box 90164, 33804-0164. Tel: 941-858-8047. Rev. Vianney Cunningham, T.O.R. Total Staff 2; Total in Residence 2.

MELBOURNE. *Florida Institute of Technology Campus Ministry*, 150 W. University Blvd., 32901-6988. Tel: 407-768-8000, Ext. 8045.
E-mail: dbailey@fit.edu
Rev. Douglas Bailey, S.D.S. Total Staff 2.

WINTER PARK. *Rollins College Campus Ministry*, c/o St. Margaret Mary, 526 Park Ave., N., 32789. Tel: 407-647-3392. Rev. Robert A. Wiseman, C.S.C.

[F] MONASTERIES AND RESIDENCES OF PRIESTS AND BROTHERS

ORLANDO. *Bethany House of Beutel*, 1600 Lakeside Dr., 32803-1508. Tel: 407-894-8175; Fax: 407-897-1133. Rev. Jordan K. Grimes, C.P., Supr.; Bro. Philip Frank, C.P. Prayer Center for Passionist Priests and Brothers.

COCOA BEACH. *Holy Cross Fathers, Eastern Priests Province*, 325 Arthur Ave., 32931-4065. Tel: 407-799-8383; Fax: 407-783-6312. Revs. Robert J. Brennan, C.S.C., Supr.; Stephen Lambous, C.S.C.; Robert J. Lochner, C.S.C.; Peter Donohue, C.S.C.; Cajetan Holland, C.S.C.; Philip C.M. Kelly, C.S.C.; Donald W. Whipple, C.S.C.; Bros. John Dolan, C.S.C.; Jerome Healey, C.S.C.; Herman Zaccarelli, C.S.C. Total Staff 2; Total in Residence 10.

NEW SMYRNA BEACH. *Redemptorist Fathers of the Vice Province of Richmond*, 313 Hillman St., P.O. Box 1529, 32170. Tel: 904-427-3094; Fax: 904-423-1270. Very Rev. Edward J. Gray, C.SS.R.; Bro. Thomas Kuhn, C.SS.R., Vice Prov. Procurator; Revs. Jack J. Fiske, C.SS.R., Leave of Absence; Karl Krauser, C.SS.R., Leave of Absence; Robert M. Pagliari, C.SS.R.; George Kelly, C.SS.R. Total Staff 6; Total in Residence 57.

St. Alphonsus Villa-Redemptorist Fathers and Brothers, 318 N. Riverside Dr., P.O. Box 548, 32170-0548. Tel: 904-428-6481. Revs. George Dorn, C.SS.R., Supr.; Walter Bueche, C.SS.R.; Mark Knoll, C.SS.R.; Lawrence Dolan, C.SS.R.; Paul T. Gillen, C.SS.R.; John Salamon, C.SS.R.; Leonard Cordier, C.SS.R.; Joseph Ellison, C.SS.R.; Donald Bolton, C.SS.R.; Francis Donlan, C.SS.R.; Henry O'Toole, C.SS.R.; Leo Lanigan, C.SS.R.; James O'Malley, C.SS.R.; Daniel Bowen, C.SS.R.; Bros. Thomas Kuhn, C.SS.R.; Louis Hoerner, C.SS.R. Total Staff 8; Total in Residence 16.

WINTER PARK. *Franciscan Friars, T.O.R., Provincial Residence, San Pedro Friary*, 2400 Dike Rd., 32792-8118. Tel: 407-671-6322; Fax: 407-671-3992.
Friars in Residence: Revs. Robert J. D'Aversa, T.O.R.; Seraphin Conley, T.O.R.; Carl Vacek, T.O.R.; Bros. Terence Thielen, T.O.R.; David Liedl, T.O.R. Total Staff 4; Total in Residence 5.

San Pedro Center, Third Order Regular of St. Francis, 2400 Dike Rd., 32792. Tel: 407-671-6322; Fax: 407-671-3992. Revs. Carl Vacek, T.O.R., Dir.; Seraphin Conley, T.O.R.; Robert J. D'Aversa, T.O.R.; Bros. Terence Thielen, T.O.R., Admin.; David Liedl, T.O.R. Total Staff 4; Total in Residence 5.

[G] MISCELLANEOUS

ORLANDO. *Good Shepherd Corporation of Orlando, Inc.*, 597-9 Bablonica Dr., 32807. Tel: 407-658-2909; Fax: 407-658-0005. Sr. Mary Brigid Lawlor, Pres. Total Assisted 30; Total Staff 2.

GOLDENROD.

**Catholic Volunteers in Florida, Inc.*, P.O. Box 702, 32733-0702. Tel: 407-331-6444; Fax: 407-331-6446. E-mail: cvif@mindspring.com
National recruitment for statewide (FL) placement of full-time volunteers in one-year service assignments. Co-sponsored by Florida's bishops, the Episcopal Advisor, is Most Reverend John J. Snyder. Ella Kalenberg, S.L.W., Volunteer Coord.; Mr. John R. Geiger, Dir. Staff 2; Lay Volunteers 8.

WINTER GARDEN. *Sisters of St. Joseph's Architectural Stained Glass*, 930 Carter Rd., Ste. 212, 34787. Tel: 407-877-3220.

RELIGIOUS INSTITUTES OF MEN REPRESENTED IN THE DIOCESE

For further details refer to the corresponding bracketed number in the Religious Institutes of Men or Women section.

[0140]—*Augustinians.*—O.S.A.
[0610]—*Congregation of the Holy Cross (Southern Province).*—C.S.C.
[1000]—*Congregation of the Passion.*—C.P.
[0520]—*Franciscan Fathers.*—O.F.M.
[0690]—*Jesuit Fathers & Brothers.*—S.J.
[0760]—*Marist Fathers Society of Mary.*—S.M.
[0720]—*Missionaries of Our Lady of LaSalette.*—M.S.
[0910]—*Oblates of Mary Immaculate.*—O.M.I.
[1070]—*Redemptorist Fathers (Baltimore Province).*—C.SS.R.
[1190]—*Salesians of Don Bosco.*—S.D.B.
[1240]—*Servants of Mary (Servites).*—O.S.M.
[0110]—*Society of African Missions.*—S.M.A.
[1200]—*Society of the Divine Savior.*—S.D.S.
[1060]—*Society of the Precious Blood (Cincinnati Province).*—C.PP.S.
[0560]—*Third Order Regular of Saint Francis (Province of the Immaculate Conception).*—T.O.R.

RELIGIOUS INSTITUTES OF WOMEN REPRESENTED IN THE DIOCESE

[0230]—*Benedictine Sisters of Pontifical Jurisdiction.* (St. Petersburg).—O.S.B.
[3710]—*Congregation of the Sisters of St. Agnes.*—C.S.A.
[1070]—*Dominican Sisters.*—O.P.
[1180]—*Franciscan Sisters of Allegany, New York.*—O.S.F.
[2720]—*Mission Helpers of the Sacred Heart.*—M.H.S.H.
[2750]—*Missionary Sisters of the Immaculate Heart of Mary.*—I.C.M.
[3770]—*Order of St. Clare.*—O.S.C.
[3130]—*Our Lady of Victory Missionary Sisters.*—O.L.V.M.
[3320]—*Presentation Sisters of the Blessed Virgin Mary.*—P.B.V.M.
[2070]—*Religious of the Holy Union of the Sacred Hearts.*—S.U.S.C.
[3430]—*Religious Teachers Filippini.*—M.P.F.
[2970]—*School Sisters of Notre Dame.*—S.S.N.D.
[3590]—*Servants of Mary (Servite Sisters).*—O.S.M.
[]—*Sisters for Christian Community.*—S.F.C.C.
[0440]—*Sisters of Charity of Cincinnati, Ohio.*—S.C.
[0430]—*Sisters of Charity of the Blessed Virgin Mary.*—B.V.M.
[0990]—*Sisters of Divine Providence.*—C.D.P.
[2360]—*Sisters of Loretto at the Foot of the Cross.*—S.L.
[2640]—*Sisters of Mercy from Ireland.* (Meath Community).—R.S.M.
[2535]—*Sisters of Mercy from Ireland.* (Galway).—R.S.M.
[2523]—*Sisters of Mercy from Ireland.* (Longford).—R.S.M.
[2530]—*Sisters of Mercy from Ireland.* (Ardee-Dundalk).—R.S.M.
[2560]—*Sisters of Mercy from Ireland.* (Ennis).—R.S.M.
[2550]—*Sisters of Mercy from Ireland.* (Limerick).—R.S.M.
[2575]—*Sisters of Mercy of the Americas.*—R.S.M.
[2990]—*Sisters of Notre Dame.* (Chardon, OH).—S.N.D.
[3000]—*Sisters of Notre Dame de Namur.*—S.N.D.deN.
[1630]—*Sisters of St. Francis of Penance & Christian Charity.*—O.S.F.
[1650]—*Sisters of St. Francis of Philadelphia.*—O.S.F.
[1570]—*Sisters of St. Francis of the Holy Family.*—O.S.F.
[3840]—*Sisters of St. Joseph of Carondelet.* (St. Louis, MO).—C.S.J.
[3850]—*Sisters of St. Joseph of Chambery.*—C.S.J.
[3900]—*Sisters of St. Joseph of St. Augustine, Florida.*—S.S.J.
[1830]—*Sisters of the Good Shepherd.*—R.G.S.
[1990]—*Sisters of the Holy Names of Jesus and Mary.*—S.N.J.M.
[2350]—*Sisters of the Living Word.*—S.L.W.
[2160]—*Sisters, Servants of the Immaculate Heart of Mary.* (Scranton, PA).—I.H.M.
[4110]—*Ursuline Nuns.*—O.S.U.

NECROLOGY

† Grimillion, Rev. Msgr. John E., (Retired). —Died Feb. 21, 1997.
† Grogan, Patrick, Rockledge, FL, St. Mary. —Died Aug. 12, 1997.
† Thomas, Fred J., (Retired). —Died Feb. 23, 1997.

Diocese of Owensboro

(Dioecesis Owensburgensis)

Most Reverend

JOHN J. MCRAITH, D.D.

Bishop of Owensboro; ordained February 21, 1960; appointed October 23, 1982; consecrated December 15, 1982. *Res., 501 W. Fifth St., Owensboro, KY, 42301. Address correspondence to: 600 Locust St., Owensboro, KY, 42301; Fax: 502-683-6883.*

Catholic Pastoral Center: 600 Locust St., Owensboro, KY, 42301. Tel.: 502-683-1545; Fax: 502-683-6883.

Web site address: http://www.catholic-church.org/owensboro

E-mail address: boonej@brescia.edu

CREATED DECEMBER 9, 1937.

ERECTED FEBRUARY 23, 1938.

Square Miles 12,502.

Comprises the following thirty-two Counties in the western part of the State of Kentucky: Allen, Ballard, Breckinridge, Butler, Caldwell, Calloway, Carlisle, Christian, Crittenden, Daviess, Edmonson, Fulton, Graves, Grayson, Hancock, Henderson, Hickman, Hopkins, Livingston, Logan, Lyon, McCracken, McLean, Marshall, Muhlenberg, Ohio, Simpson, Todd, Trigg, Union, Warren and Webster.

For legal titles of parishes and diocesan institutions, consult the Catholic Pastoral Center.

STATISTICAL OVERVIEW

Personnel	
Bishop	1
Priests: Diocesan Active in Diocese	63
Priests: Active Outside Diocese	5
Priests: Retired, Sick or Absent	16
Number of Diocesan Priests	84
Religious Priests in Diocese	13
Extern Priests in Diocese	1
Ordinations:	
Diocesan Priests	4
Religious Priests	2
Total Brothers	4
Total Sisters	239
Parishes	
Parishes	79
With Resident Pastor:	
Resident Diocesan Priests	48
Resident Religious Priests	3
Without Resident Pastor:	
Administered by Priests	26
Administered by Women Religious	2
Pastoral Centers	2
New Parishes Created	1
Professional Ministry Personnel:	
Brothers	3
Sisters	31
Lay Ministers	34
Welfare	
Catholic Hospitals	1
Total Assisted	85,000
Health Care Centers	2
Total Assisted	8,000
Homes for the Aged	2
Total Assisted	176
Day Care and Extended Day Care Centers	3
Total Assisted	136
Special Centers for Social Services	2
Total Assisted	16,000
Educational	
Diocesan Students in Other Seminaries	12
Total Seminarians	12
Colleges and Universities	1
Total Students	750
High Schools, Diocesan and Parish	3
Total Students	1,064
Elementary Schools, Diocesan and Parish	19
Total Students	4,434
Catechesis/Religious Education:	
High School Students	1,354
Elementary Students	3,774
Total Students Under Catholic Instruction	11,388
Teachers in the Diocese:	
Priests	1
Brothers	1
Sisters	14
Lay Teachers	353
Vital Statistics	
Receptions into the Church:	
Infant Baptism Totals	1,074
Adult Baptism Totals	155
Received into Full Communion	265
First Communions	1,020
Confirmations	1,250
Marriages:	
Catholic	246
Interfaith	246
Total Marriages	492
Deaths	567
Total Catholic Population	51,932
Total Population	778,235

Former Bishops—Most Rev. FRANCIS R. COTTON, D.D., First Bishop of Owensboro; ord. June 17, 1920; appt. Dec. 16, 1937; cons. Feb. 24, 1938; died Sept. 25, 1960.—Most Rev. HENRY J. SOENNEKER, D.D., Second Bishop of Owensboro; ord. May 26, 1934; appt. March 10, 1961; cons. April 26, 1961; installed May 9, 1961; retired June 17, 1982; died Sept. 24, 1987.

Catholic Pastoral Center—600 Locust St., Owensboro, 42301. Tel: 502-683-1545; Fax: 502-683-6883. Refer all official business to this address.

Vicar General—Rev. JOSEPH M. MILLS, J.C.L., *Res., 5856 Ky. 81, Owensboro, 42301.* Tel: 502-685-0339.

Chancellor—Sr. JOSEPH ANGELA BOONE, O.S.U.

Archivist—Sr. EMMA CECILIA BUSAM, O.S.U.

Diocesan Tribunal—

Judicial Vicar—Rev. J. PATRICK REYNOLDS, J.C.L.

Adjutant Judicial Vicar—Vacant.

Defenders of the Bond—Revs. KEVIN KARL; JOSEPH M. MILLS; GREGORY G. TRAWICK.

Judges—Revs. LEONARD ALVEY; J. PATRICK REYNOLDS, J.C.L.; JOHN VAUGHAN, J.C.D.; RICHARD MEREDITH.

Advocates—Priests and pastoral ministers of the diocese.

Case Promoters—Sr. VIVIAN MARIE BOWLES, O.S.U.

Administrative Assistants—Mrs. MARY ANN KURZ; Mrs. KAY M. RHODES.

Clinical Psychologist— PATRICIA G. CAMPBELL.

Diocesan Boards and Councils

Diocesan Pastoral Council—Mr. MIKE THOMPSON; Mr. CHARLES RUCKS; Mr. JIM SHANAHAN; Sr. MAGGIE COOPER, S.C.N.; Mr. DAN RALPH; Ms. DEBBIE RALPH; Sr. EVA BOONE, O.S.U.; Mr. TOM HAYDEN; Sr. EULA JOHNSON, S.C.N.; Mr. PERRY ELDER; Ms. SHARON EBELHAR; Rev. HENRY WIEDER; Ms. SUE GRAY; Rev. RAY CLARK; Ms. JUDY MCCELLAN; Ms. HELEN WILLETT; Ms. BARBARA PENNER; Mr. LARRY HIGDON; Ms. JANE HOBBS; Mr. RAY GIARDINELLA; Mr. JIM SCOTT; Mr. PAUL BACHI; Mr. ZACK HODGES.

Consultors—Revs. KEVIN KARL; RAY CLARK; MARTIN HAYES; LEONARD ALVEY; Rev. Msgr. GEORGE HANCOCK.

Deans—Rev. RICHARD MEREDITH, Bowling Green; Rev. J. EDWARD BRADLEY, Central; Rev. ANTHONY BICKETT, Eastern; Rev. DELMA CLEMONS, Fancy Farm; Rev. JERRY BAKER, Hopkinsville; Rev. MAURICE TIELL, The Lakes; Rev. JOHN VAUGHAN, Owensboro; Rev. HENRY WIEDER, Paducah.

Priests' Council—Revs. JOSEPH M. MILLS; MAURICE TIELL; RICHARD MEREDITH; LEONARD ALVEY; KEVIN KARL; RAY CLARK; ANTHONY BICKETT; MARTIN HAYES; Rev. Msgr. GEORGE HANCOCK; Revs. HENRY WIEDER; DELMA CLEMONS; JERRY BAKER; JOHN VAUGHAN; J. EDWARD BRADLEY.

Council of Religious—Sr. EVA BOONE, O.S.U.; Sr. MARY LOUISE ALVEY, O.S.U.; Sr. ALICIA COOMES, O.S.U.; Sr. CHARLES MARY BURNS, S.C.N.; Sr. EULA JOHNSON, S.C.N.; Sr. JOLINDA NAAS, O.S.B.; Sr. JOANN MARK, A.S.C.; Sr. MARY MATTHIAS WARD, O.S.U.; Sr. NANCY MURPHY, O.S.U.; Sr. ROSEMARY ESTERKAMP, G.H.M.S.

Pastoral Office for Administration—Sr. JOSEPH ANGELA BOONE, O.S.U., Dir.

Pastoral Office for Stewardship—Mr. TOM LILLY, Dir.

Committee for Administration—Mr. HOMER BARTON; Ms. JANET BERRY; Ms. BECKY MILLAY; Sr. JOANN MARK, A.S.C.; Mr. CHARLES KAMUF; Mr. JOSEPH HANCOCK; Mr. LOUIS HAAS; Revs. BRAD WHISTLE; JOE MILLS; MARTY HAYES; Mr. MIKE THOMPSON.

Pastoral Office for Education—

Superintendent of Schools—Mr. JOSEPH O'BRYAN.

Director of Office for Religious Education—Sr. KATHY GALLO, O.S.U.; Sr. JULIA MARIE HEAD, Faith Devel.

Committee for Education—Mr. DEL HAYDEN; Rev. LEONARD ALVEY; Ms. JUDY MCCLELLAN; Sr. JOLINDA NAAS, O.S.B.; Rev. BRIAN JOHNSON; Dr. DAN STUMPF; Ms. VICKIE CASH; Mr. PHIL HAIRE; Mr. STEVE SHOULTA; Ms. BARBARA KOONCE; Sr. ROSEANNE SPALDING, O.S.U.; Ms. BONNIE MARKS; Ms. JANET MURPHY; Ms. ANGEL PAYNE; Ms. CAROL HIGDON; Mr. KEVIN LAURENT.

Director of Ecumenism—Rev. JOSEPH O'DONNELL, Glmy., *9515 Ky. 144, Knottsville, 42366.* Tel: 502-281-4802; Fax: 502-281-9556.

Youth Ministry—Rev. HENRY WIEDER, Dir.; Ms. MELINDA PRUNTY, Assoc. Dir.

Director of Communications and Editor of the Diocesan Newspaper "Western Kentucky Catholic"—Mr. MEL HOWARD.

Communications Committee—Rev. JOHN LITTLE; JIM TIDWELL; ZACK HODGES; JACK ALLARD; LANE RHODES; CHIP PRIDE; H. J. RUMAGE.

Pastoral Office for Worship—Rev. LARRY MCBRIDE, Dir. MARTHA HAGAN, Assoc. Dir.; Ms. PATTY BROWN, Dir. Diocesan Office for Music.

Diocesan Liturgical Committee—Revs. THOMAS CLARK; LARRY MCBRIDE, Chm.; Sr. LARRAINE LAUTER, O.S.U., Chm.; Ms. MARTHA HAGAN; Ms. PATTY BROWN; Mr. MICHAEL BOGDAN; Ms. SUE ECKMANS; Sr. ANNALITA LANCASTER, O.S.U.; Rev. JOHN THOMAS; Ms. CLEO HIGDON; Sr. ALICIA COOMES, O.S.U.

Pastoral Office for Spiritual Life—Sr. AMELIA STENGER, O.S.U., Dir., *Mount St. Joseph, Maple Mount, 42356*. Tel: 502-229-4103.

Cursillo—Rev. TERRY DEVINE, Dir., *1317 Main St., Sturgis, 42459*. Tel: 502-333-4645.

Pastoral Office for Outreach and Lay Ministry—Sr. PATRICIA FRONING, O.S.F., Dir.

Pastoral Office for Social Concerns—Sr. LEETA SHUECRAFT, O.S.U., Dir. RITA BROTHERS, Assoc. Dir.

Diocesan Social Concerns Committee—LIZ FRANCIS; Sr. MAGGIE COOPER, S.C.N.; Sr. ROSE JEAN POWERS; Mr. JACK ALLARD; Ms. GLORIA ADAMS.

Catholic Relief Service Director—Sr. LEETA SHUECRAFT, O.S.U.

Campaign for Human Development—Sr. LEETA SHUECRAFT, O.S.U.

Respect Life Office—Sr. LEETA SHUECRAFT, O.S.U.

Rural Life Office—Sr. LEETA SHUECRAFT, O.S.U.

Mission Office—Rev. JOSEPH M. MILLS.

Pastoral Office for Family Life—EDWINA HYLAND, Dir.

Diocesan Family Life Committee—JUDY KAPELSOHN; TOM HEILERS; KAREN HEILERS; MARTHA CRABTREE; TOM HAYDEN; JOYCE HAYDEN; Rev. ED BRADLEY; GERALD GILLIAM; CASSIE GILLIAM; GAIL CRITCHELOW; CAROL YANIK.

Natural Family Planning—EDWINA HYLAND.

Pastoral Office for Personnel—

Priest Personnel Committee—Revs. GERALD CALHOUN; BRUCE FOGLE; PAUL POWELL; JERRY RINEY; BRIAN ROBY; DARRELL VENTERS.

Vocations Office—Rev. BRAD WHISTLE, *St. Romuald Parish, Hardinsburg, 40143*. Tel: 502-756-2356.

Continuing Education for Priests—Rev. RICHARD MEREDITH, *St. Joseph Parish, 434 Church St., Bowling Green, 42101*. Tel: 502-842-2525.

[*]Roman Catholic Diocese of Owensboro Charitable Trust Fund, Inc.—Most Rev. JOHN J. MCRAITH; Revs. JOE MILLS; KEVIN KARL.

Hispanic Ministries—Rev. STAN PURYEAR, Dir., *St. Joseph Parish, 434 Church St., Bowling Green, 42101*. Tel: 502-842-2525.

Organizations

St. Vincent de Paul Society—DAVID OSBORNE, *3507 Dove Loop N., Owensboro, 42301*.

Scouting Activities—Rev. HENRY WIEDER; Rev. STEVE ULRICH, Chap., *600 Locust St., Owensboro, 42301*. Tel: 502-683-1545.

Holy Childhood Association—Rev. JOSEPH M. MILLS.

Teens Encounter Christ—Rev. HENRY WIEDER, *600 Locust St., Owensboro, 42301*. Tel: 502-683-1545.

Legion of Mary—

CLERGY, PARISHES, MISSIONS AND PAROCHIAL SCHOOLS

CITY OF OWENSBORO
(Daviess County)

1—ST. STEPHEN CATHEDRAL, Revs. John R. Vaughan; David William Kennedy; Michael E. Williams. Pastoral Assocs.: Sr. Ann McGrew; Mr. Michael Conley; Mr. Ron Greenwell; Mr. Larry Lyon.
Res., 614 Locust St., 42301. Tel: 502-683-6525; Fax: 502-683-3621.
Chapel—Blessed Sacrament, 602 Sycamore St., 42301. Tel: 502-926-4741. [CEM] Rev. William Allard; Gloria Adams, Admin.

2—BLESSED MOTHER, Revs. C. Phil Riney; Isaac Daniel Kreutzer; Jan Storm, Admin. Asst.; Patricia Blair, Pastoral Assoc.
Office: 515 E. 22nd St., 42303.
Res., 601 E. 23rd St., 42303. Tel: 502-683-8444.

3—THE IMMACULATE, Rev. Timothy Sweeney, O.S.B.; Sr. Geneva Stumler, O.S.B., Pastoral Assoc.
Parish Office: 2516 Christie Pl., 42301. Tel: 502-683-0689; Fax: 502-926-9016.
Res., 2601 Christie Pl., 42301.

4—OUR LADY OF LOURDES, Rev. John Meredith.
Res., 4029 Frederica St., 42301. Tel: 502-684-5369; Fax: 502-683-8008.

5—PRECIOUS BLOOD, Rev. Darrell Venters. Pastoral Assocs.: Sr. Larraine Lauter, O.S.U.; Sr. Elaine Byrne.
Res., 3306 Fenmore St., 42301. Tel: 502-684-6888; Fax: 502-684-1304.

6—ST. PIUS TENTH, Rev. Larry McBride.
Res., 3512 E. Sixth St., 42303. Tel: 502-684-5517; Fax: 502-684-2709.

7—SS. JOSEPH AND PAUL, Rev. Freddie Byrd; Martha McCarty, Pastoral Min.; Lisa Mattingly, Admin.
Res., 609 E. 4th St., 42303. Tel: 502-683-5641; Fax: 502-685-4766.

OUTSIDE THE CITY OF OWENSBORO

Aurora, Marshall Co., St. Henry, Rev. Richard L. Cash.
Res., 16097 U.S. Hwy. 68 E., Hardin, 42048. Tel: 502-474-8058. [CEM]

Axtel, Breckinridge Co., St. Anthony, Rev. Bruce Fogle.
Res., R.R. 3, Hardinsburg, 40143. Tel: 502-257-2132. [CEM]

Bardwell, Carlisle Co., St. Charles, Rev. Anthony Stevenson.
Res., R.R. 2, Box 317, 42023. Tel: 502-642-2586; Fax: 502-642-2586. [CEM]

Beaver Dam, Ohio Co., Holy Redeemer, Rev. Fidelis Levri, Glmy.; Sr. Luisa Bickett, O.S.U., Pastoral Assoc.
Office: P.O. Box 106, 42320. Tel: 502-274-3414.; 768 Horse Branch Loop, Horse Branch, 42349. Tel: 502-274-4285.

Big Clifty, Grayson Co., St. Mary. Closed. Records kept at St. Paul's Church, 1821 St. Paul Rd., Leitchfield, KY 42754. Tel: 502-242-7436.

Bowling Green, Warren Co., St. Joseph's, Rev. Richard Meredith.
Res., 434 Church St., 42101. Tel: 502-842-2525; Fax: 502-746-9696. [CEM]
Holy Spirit, Revs. W. Jerry Riney; Carl McCarthy; Ms. Anita Willoughby, Pastoral Assoc.
Res., 2232 Smallhouse Rd., 42104-4141. Tel: 502-842-7777; Fax: 502-842-6174. [CEM]

Brown's Valley, Daviess Co., St. Anthony, Rev. Tony Jones.
Church—261 St. Anthony Rd., Utica, 42376. Tel: 502-733-4341. [CEM]

Cadiz, Trigg Co., St. Stephen, Rev. Leonard Arcilesi.
Res., 1698 Canton Rd., 42211. Tel: 502-522-3801; Fax: 502-522-3801.

Calhoun, McLean Co., St. Sebastian, Rev. Steve Ulrich.
Res., 180 State Rte. 136 W., 42327-9521. Tel: 502-273-3185.

Calvert City, Marshall Co., St. Pius Tenth, Rev. Aloysius Powers, Admin. Pastoral Assocs.: Sr. Lisa Marie Cecil, O.S.U.; Sr. Mary Angela Matthews, O.S.U.
Res., P.O. Box 495, 42029. Tel: 502-395-4727.

Central City, Mulenberg Co., St. Joseph, Rev. Francis Mastrovito, T.O.R.; Sr. Rose Karen Johnson, O.S.U., Pastoral Assoc.
Res., 113 S. Third St., 42330. Tel: 502-754-1164.

Clarkson, Grayson Co., St. Elizabeth of Hungary, Rev. Charles G. Fischer.
Res., 1821 St. Paul Rd., Leitchfield, 42754. Tel: 502-242-7436. [CEM]
Catechesis/Religious Programs—306 Clifty Ave., 42726. Tel: 502-242-4414.

Clinton, Hickman Co., St. Jude, Rev. Mike Clark; Sr. Diane M. Payne, O.S.U., Pastoral Assoc.
Res., 42031. Tel: 502-653-6869.

Cloverport, Breckinridge Co., St. Rose, Rev. Tom Clark.
Res., 118 Chestnut St., 40111. Tel: 502-788-6422. [CEM]

Curdsville, Daviess Co., St. Elizabeth, Rev. Robert Drury.
Mailing Address: P.O. Box 9-A, 42334. Tel: 502-229-4134.

Dawson Springs, Hopkins Co., Resurrection, Rev. Martin Mattingly.
Res., 530 Industrial Park Rd., 42408. Tel: 502-383-4743; Fax: 502-383-5819.
Church—Tel: 502-797-8665.

Earlington, Hopkins Co., Immaculate Conception, Rev. Martin Mattingly.
Res., 125 S. Day St., 42410. Tel: 502-383-4743; Fax: 502-383-5819.

Eddyville, Lyon Co., St. Mark Church, Rev. Maurice J. Tiell.
Res., 302 Peachtree Ln., 42038. Tel: 502-388-2133.
Stations—Kentucky State Penitentiary, Tel: 502-388-2133; Western Kentucky Correctional Complex, Tel: 502-388-2133.

Elkton, Todd Co., St. Susan, Rev. Thomas S. Charters. Pastoral Assocs.: Sr. Bernadette Hengstebek, G.H.M.S.; Sr. Catherine Schoenborn, G.H.M.S.
Res., P.O. Box 788, 42220. Tel: 502-265-5263.

Fancy Farm, Hickman Co., St. Denis, Rev. Anthony Stevenson.
Res., St. Charles Church, R.R. 2, Box 317, Bardwell, 42023. Tel: 502-642-2586; Fax: 502-642-2586. [CEM]
St. Jerome, Graves Co., Rev. Delma Clemons.
Res., P.O. Box 38, 42039. Tel: 502-623-8181; Fax: 502-623-6341. [CEM]
Catechesis/Religious Programs—Sr. Anastasia Lamb, D.R.E.
Students 250.

Fordsville, Ohio Co., St. John the Baptist, Revs. Joseph O'Donnell, Glmy.; Fidelis Levri, Glmy.; Sr. Eva Marie Boone, O.S.U., Pastoral Assoc.
Res., P.O. Box 127, 42343. Tel: 502-276-3619.

Franklin, Simpson Co., St. Mary of the Woods, Rev. Frank Ruff, Glmy., Sacramental Min.; Sr. Lene Rubly, O.S.F., Pastoral Coord.; Sr. Davida Loosbrock, O.S.F., Pastoral Assoc.
Res., Box 388, 42135. Tel: 502-586-4515. [CEM]

Fulton, Fulton Co., St. Edward, Rev. J. Michael Clark.
Res., 504 Eddings St., 42041. Tel: 502-472-2742; Fax: 502-472-2742.

Grand Rivers, Livingston Co., St. Anthony of Padua. (Grand Rivers Catholic Church). Rev. Msgr. George H. Hancock; Sr. Rosemary Esterkamp, G.H.M.S.
Res., 1518 J.H. O'Bryan Ave., P.O. Box 447, 42045. Tel: 502-362-0408.

Grayson Springs, Grayson Co., St. Augustine, Rev. Gary Hayes.
Res. & Mailing Address: c/o St. Anthony Church, 1256 St. Anthony Church Rd., Clarkson, 42726. Tel: 502-242-4791; Fax: 502-242-2601. [CEM]

Guthrie, Todd Co., Sts. Mary & James, Rev. Thomas S. Charters, G.H.M.S. Pastoral Ministers: Sr. Bernadette Hengstebeck, G.H.M.S.; Sr. Catherine Schoenborn, G.H.M.S.
Res., P.O. Box 325, 42234. Tel: 502-483-2571.

Hardinsburg, Breckinridge Co., St. Romuald, Revs. J. Brad Whistle; Pete Hughes; Sr. Martha Keller, O.S.U., Pastoral Assoc.
Res., 40143. Tel: 502-756-2356; Fax: 502-756-2099. [CEM]

Hawesville, Hancock Co., Immaculate Conception, Rev. Tony Bickett. Pastoral Assocs.: Sr. Karla Marie Kaelin, O.S.U.; Sr. Rita Lechner, S.P.
Res., 42348. Tel: 502-927-8419. [CEM]

Henderson, Henderson Co., Holy Name of Jesus, Revs. J. Edward Bradley; Andrew Ausenbaugh; Deacon Ken Mikulcik; Sr. Pauletta Kane, S.C.N., Pastoral Assoc.
Res., 511 Second St., 42420. Tel: 502-826-2096; Fax: 502-827-1494. [CEM]
School—618 Second St., 42420. Tel: 502-827-3425; Fax: 502-827-3432.
Sisters of Charity of Nazareth 1; Lay Teachers 31; Students 588.

Henshaw, Union Co., St. Ambrose, Rev. Terry Devine; Sr. Markan Freking, O.S.U., Pastoral Assoc.
Res., c/o St. Francis Borgia, 1308 N. Adams St., Sturgis, 42459. Tel: 502-333-4645. [CEM]

Hickman, Fulton Co., Sacred Heart, Rev. J. Michael Clark; Sr. Mary Agnes VonderHaar, O.S.U., Pastoral Assoc.
Res., 411 Moulton St., 42050-1327. Tel: 502-236-2071.

Hopkinsville, Christian Co., SS. Peter and Paul, Rev. Gerald H. Baker. In res., Rev. Ben Cameron, C.P.M.
Res., 902 E. Ninth St., 42240. Tel: 502-885-8522; Fax: 502-885-5296.
School—Tel: 502-886-0172; Fax: 502-887-9924.
Lay Teachers 10; Students 219.

Irvington, Breckinridge Co., Holy Guardian Angels, Rev. J. Brad Whistle; Pete Hughes, Pastoral Assoc.
Mailing Address: P.O. Box 86, 40146. Tel: 502-547-7314.
301 W. High St., 40146. Tel: 502-257-2132.
Rectory:—215 Caroline St., 40146. Tel: 502-547-7314.

Knottsville, Daviess Co., St. William, Rev. Martin Hayes.
Res., 9515 Kentucky 144, Philpot, 42366. Tel: 502-281-4802; Fax: 502-281-9556. [CEM]
School—Mary Carrico Memorial School, Tel: 502-281-5546.
Ursuline Sisters 2; Lay Teachers 7; Students 138.

LaCenter, Ballard Co., St. Mary, Revs. Henry Wieder; Brian Roby; Sr. Alicia Coomes, Pastoral Assoc.
Church—P.O. Box 514, 42056. Tel: 502-665-5551 (Office); 665-5654 (Res.); Fax: 502-665-9033. [CEM]

Leitchfield, Grayson Co., St. Joseph's, Rev. Dave Johnson; Sr. Ruth Mattingly, O.S.U., Pastoral Min.
Res., 109 W. Walnut St., 42754. Tel: 502-259-3028. [CEM]

Lewisport, Hancock Co., St. Columba, Rev. Tony Bickett. Pastoral Assocs.: Sr. Rita Lechner, S.P.; Sr. Karla Marie Kaelin, O.S.U.
Res., 815 Pell St., P.O. Box 358, 42351. Tel: 502-927-8419. [CEM]

Livermore, McLean Co., St. Charles, Rev. Steve Ulrich.
Res., St. Sebastian Church, 180 State Rte. 136 W., Calhoun, 42327-9521. Tel: 502-685-2559.
Church—506 Hill Ave., 42352.

McQuady, Breckinridge Co., St. Mary-of-the-Woods, Rev. Bruce Fogle.
Res., R.R. 3, Hardinsburg, 40143. Tel: 502-756-2093. [CEM]

Madisonville, Hopkins Co., Christ the King, Rev. Francis Roof.
Res., 1600 Kingsway Dr., 42431. Tel: 502-821-5494; Fax: 502-825-8612.
School—Tel: 502-821-8271; Fax: 502-825-9394.
Lay Teachers 11; Students 139.
Preschool—Tel: 502-821-3954.
Students 58.

Marion, Crittenden Co., St. William, Rev. Terry Devine; Sr. Mary Louise Alvey, O.S.U., Pastoral Assoc.
Res., 860 S. Main St., 42064. Tel: 502-965-2477. [CEM]

Mayfield, Graves Co., St. Joseph, Rev. Ray Clark.
Res., 702 W. Broadway St., 42066. Tel: 502-247-2843; Fax: 502-247-6835. [CEM]
School—Tel: 502-247-4420; Fax: 502-247-6835.
Lay Teachers 11; Students 149.

Morganfield, Union Co., St. Ann's, Rev. Patrick M. Bittel; Ms. Patricia Claussen, Pastoral Min.
Res., 304 Church St., 42437. Tel: 502-389-2287; Fax: 502-389-0219. [CEM]

Morgantown, Butler Co., Holy Trinity, Rev. Fidelis Levri, Glmy.
Res., 766 Logansport Rd., P.O. Box 222, 42261. Tel: 502-526-3723.

Murray, Calloway Co., St. Leo, Rev. Ray Goetz; Sr. Mary Matthias Ward, O.S.U., Pastoral Assoc.
Res., 401 N. 12th St., 42071. Tel: 502-753-3876; 759-1621 (Office); Fax: 502-759-2073.

Oak Grove, Christian Co., St. Michael the Archangel, Rev. Leonard Arcilesi.
Res., 440 State Line Rd., P.O. Box 1285, 42262. Tel: 502-640-9580; 502-522-3801 (Rectory).

Paducah, McCracken Co.,

1—St. Francis de Sales, Revs. Gerald Calhoun; Brian Anthony Johnson; Adam Rewa, Pastoral Assoc.
Res., 116 S. Sixth St., 42001. Tel: 502-442-1923; Fax: 502-443-4616.

2—Rosary Chapel, Revs. Gerald Calhoun; Brian Anthony Johnson.
Res., 711 Ohio St., 42001. Tel: 502-444-6383.

3—St. John the Evangelist, Rev. Benjamin F. Luther. In res., Rev. Louis Caporiccio, C.P.M.
Res., 6705 Old U.S. Hwy. 45, 42003. Tel: 502-554-3810; Fax: 502-554-3810.
School—7450 St. John Church Dr., 42003. Tel: 502-554-8826; Fax: 502-554-8826.
Lay Teachers 7; Students 107.

4—St. Thomas More, Revs. Henry Wieder; Brian Roby; Sr. Marie Goretti Browning, O.S.U., Pastoral Assoc.
Office: 209 Wallace La., 42001. Tel: 502-444-7404; Fax: 502-444-9064.
Res., 5645 Blandville Rd., 42001.

Peonia, Grayson Co., St. Anthony's, Rev. Gary Hayes.
Res., 1256 St. Anthony Church Rd., Clarkson, 42726. Tel: 502-242-4791. [CEM]

Philpot, Daviess Co., St. Lawrence, Rev. Martin E. Hayes.
Res., 9515 Kentucky 144, Knottsville, 42366. Tel: 502-281-4802; Fax: 502-281-9556. [CEM]

Princeton, Caldwell Co., St. Paul, Rev. Richard T. Danhauer.
Res., 813 S. Jefferson, 42445. Tel: 502-365-6786.

Providence, Webster Co., Holy Cross, Rev. Kevin Karl. Pastoral Assocs: Bros. Ken Grondin, C.F.C.; Tim Smyth, C.F.C.
Church—730 North Highway 41A, 42450.

Reed, Henderson Co., St. Augustine, Rev. Msgr. Bernard Powers.
Res., 16777 Hwy. 60 E., 42451. Tel: 502-764-5599. [CEM]

Rome, Daviess Co., St. Martin, Rev. Joseph M. Mills; Rose Ann Payne, Pastoral Assoc.
Res., 5856 Kentucky 81, Owensboro, 42301. Tel: 502-685-0339.

Russellville, Logan Co., Sacred Heart, Rev. Lucian P. Hayden.
Res., 296 W. 6th St., 42276. Tel: 502-726-6963.

Scottsville, Allen Co., Christ the King, Rev. Frank Ruff, Glmy., Sacramental Min.; Sr. Lene Rubly, O.S.F., Pastoral Coord.; Sr. Davida Loosbrock, O.S.F., Pastoral Assoc.
Res., P.O. Box 463, 42164. Tel: 502-586-4515; 237-4404.

Sebree, Webster Co., St. Michael, Rev. Kevin Karl.
Res., P.O. Box 705, Church St., 42455. Tel: 502-835-2584.

St. Joseph, Daviess Co., St. Alphonsus, Rev. Robert Drury.
Res., 7950 Cummings Rd., Owensboro, 42301. Tel: 502-229-4566. [CEM]

St. Paul, Grayson Co., St. Paul, Rev. Charles G. Fischer.
Res., 1821 St. Paul Rd., Leitchfield, 42754. Tel: 502-242-7483. [CEM]
School—Tel: 502-242-7483.
Lay Teachers 5; Students 46.

Sorgho, Daviess Co., St. Mary Magdalene, Rev. J. Patrick Reynolds.
Res., 7232 Kentucky 56, Owensboro, 42301. Tel: 502-771-4436. [JC]

Stanley, Daviess Co., St. Peter of Alcantara, Rev. Paul P. Powell.
Res., 81 Church St., Owensboro, 42301. Tel: 502-764-1983. [CEM]

Sturgis, Union Co., St. Francis Borgia, Rev. Terry Devine; Sr. Marcan Freking, O.S.F., Pastoral Assoc.
Res., 1308 N. Adams St., 42459. Tel: 502-333-4645.

Sunfish, Edmondson Co., St. John the Evangelist, Rev. Dave Johnson. Pastoral Assocs.: Sr. Dolorita Robinson, O.S.U.; Sr. Rosaria Ray, O.S.U.
Church—430 St. John Church Rd., 42284. Tel: 502-286-4366. [CEM]

Uniontown, Union Co., St. Agnes, Sr. Jolinda Naas, O.S.B., Pastoral Assoc.
Res., P.O. Box 607, 42461. Tel: 502-822-4416; Fax: 502-822-4416. [CEM]

Waverly, Union Co., Sacred Heart, Rev. Anthony Ziegler.
Res., 201 E. Market St., 42462. Tel: 502-389-4224; Fax: 502-389-4224. [CEM]
St. Peter, Rev. Anthony Ziegler.
Res., 201 E. Market St., 42462. Tel: 502-389-4224; Fax: 502-389-4224. [CEM]

Wax, Grayson Co., St. Benedict, Rev. Gary Hayes.
Res., St. Anthony Church, 1256 St. Anthony Church Rd., Clarkson, 42726. Tel: 502-242-4791. [CEM]

Whitesville, Daviess Co., St. Mary of the Woods, Revs. Richard M. Powers; Maury Riney; Sr. Clarita Browning, O.S.U., Pastoral Assoc.
Res., 10534 Main Cross, P.O. Box 1, 42378. Tel: 502-233-4196; Fax: 502-233-5557. [CEM]
School—St. Mary's Grade School, Tel: 502-233-5253; Fax: 502-233-9360.
Lay Teachers 12; Students 260.

Non-Parochial Assignments:
Reverend Fathers—
Alvey, Leonard J., Brescia College, 717 Frederica St., Owensboro, KY 42301
Piskula, Louis, Chap., 2501 Old Hartford Rd., Owensboro, KY 42303
Reisz, Leonard, 617 E. 23rd St., Owensboro, KY 42301
Shonis, Anthony J., Chap., Mount St. Joseph, Maple Mount, KY 42356

On Duty Outside the Diocese:
Reverend Fathers—
Thomas, John, St. Meinrad, IN, St. Meinrad Seminary

Studying Outside the Diocese:
Reverend Fathers—
Hostetter, Laurence, Casa Santa Maria, Via dell' Umilta 30, 00187, Rome, Italy. Tel: 001-39-6-69001; (Fax)001-39-6-679-1448
Trawick, Gregory G., Divine Word College. Tel: 202-529-5206

On Sabbatical:
Reverend Fathers—
Willett, Robert

Absent on Leave:
Reverend Fathers—
Dunn, Stephen
McCarty, Bruce
Odom-Green, William
Payne, Gary

Military Chaplains:
Reverend Fathers—
Wheatley, Carroll, NAVSCUPPACT Memphis, 512 Elrod Loop, Millington, TN 38503
Willett, William D., CMR 438, Box 286, APO, AE 09111

Retired:
Reverend Fathers—
Clements, Richard
DeNardi, Charles A., Ambassador Shores, 1705 St. Paul Rd., Leitchfield, KY 42754
Glahn, Carl, Bishop Cotton Apts., 2501 Old Hartford Rd., Owensboro, KY 42303
Hagman, William J., Bishop Cotton Apts., 2501 Old Hartford Rd., Owensboro, KY 42303
Hancock, Walter, 102 Houston St., Cloverport, KY 40111
Hite, James C., Bishop Cotton Apts., 2501 Old Hartford Rd., Owensboro, KY 42303
Miller, Joseph C., Box 319, Nevis, MN 56467
O'Bryan, Henry, P.O. Box 114, Owensboro, KY 42302-0114
Rhodes, Joseph, Bishop Cotton Apts., 2501 Old Hartford Rd., Owensboro, KY 42303
Willett, Henry L., 6143 St. Lawrence Rd., Philpot, KY 42366. Tel: 502-281-9691
Wolford, Charles, Nazareth Village, I Apt. 318, P.O. Box 210, Nazareth, KY 40048

INSTITUTIONS LOCATED IN THE DIOCESE

[A] COLLEGES AND UNIVERSITIES

Owensboro. *Brescia College*, 717 Frederica St., 42301. Tel: 502-685-3131.
Web site: http://brescia.edu
For a complete listing, refer to the Colleges and Universities section.

[B] HIGH SCHOOLS, INTER-PAROCHIAL

Owensboro. *Owensboro Catholic High School*, 1524 W. Parrish Ave., 42301. Tel: 502-684-3215; Fax: 502-684-7050. Mr. Harold Staples, Prin.; Rev. Tony Jones, Chm. Religion Dept.; Ms. Kelly Wathen, Devel. Dir. Priests 1; Lay Teachers 45; Students 685.

Paducah. *St. Mary High School*, 1243 Elmdale Rd., 42003. Tel: 502-442-1681; Fax: 502-442-7920. Rosann Whiting, Prin. Sisters 1; Lay Teachers 18; Students 202.

Whitesville. *Trinity High School*, 42378. Tel: 502-233-5533. Mr. Steve Winkler, Prin. Priests 1; Lay Teachers 11; Students 177.

[C] ELEMENTARY SCHOOLS, INTER-PAROCHIAL

Owensboro. *Catherine Spalding School*. (Grades K-6), 4017 Frederica St., 42301. Tel: 502-684-7583. Mrs. Sandy Fleming, Prin. Lay Teachers 17; Students 317.

Francis R. Cotton School. (Grades K-6), 3418 U.S. Hwy. 60 E., 42303. Tel: 502-683-2268. Mrs. Joyce Hoffman, Prin. Ursuline Sisters 1; Lay Teachers 13; Students 233.

Henry J. Soenneker School. (Grades K-6), 3400 Fenmore St., 42301. Tel: 502-684-6487. Mr. P. J. Hayden, Prin. Lay Teachers 6; Students 116.

Holy Angels Elementary, 5712 Kentucky Hwy. 56, 42301. Tel: 502-771-4773. Sr. Betsy Moyer, Prin. Lay Teachers 10; Students 191.

Holy Family (Middle) School. (Grades 7-8). (Owensboro Catholic Middle School), 2540 Christie Pl., 42301. Tel: 502-683-0480; Fax: 502-683-0495. Mr. James T. Duffy, Prin. Lay Teachers 23; Students 352.

St. Angela Merici School. (Grades K-6), 525 E. 23rd St., 42303. Tel: 502-683-6989. P. J. Hayden, Prin. Ursuline Sisters 1; Lay Teachers 19; Students 385.

Bowling Green. *St. Joseph School*, 416 Church Ave., 42101-1887. Tel: 502-842-1235. Ms. Joanne Powell, Prin. Lay Teachers 17; Students 274.

Hardinsburg. *St. Romuald School*, N. Main St., 40143. Tel: 502-756-5504. Ms. Doris Waldeck, Prin. Lay Teachers 10; Students 192.

Morganfield. *St. Ann Interparochial School*, 320 Church St., 42437. Tel: 502-389-1898. Mrs. Janet Gill, Prin. Lay Teachers 11; Students 211.

Paducah. *St. Mary Elementary*, 377 Highland Blvd., 42003. Mrs. Marina Burchett, Prin. Lay Teachers 19; Students 371.

St. Mary Middle School. (Grades 6-8), 1243 Elmdale Rd., 42003. Ms. Rosann M. Whiting, Prin. Sisters 1; Lay Teachers 8; Students 167.

[D] GENERAL HOSPITALS

PADUCAH. *Lourdes Hospital*, 1530 Lone Oak Rd., P.O. Box 7100, 42002-7100. Tel: 502-444-2444
For a complete listing, refer to the Hospitals section.

[E] HOMES FOR AGED

OWENSBORO. *Carmel Home*, 2501 Old Hartford Rd., 42303. Tel: 502-683-0227
For a complete listing, refer to the Special Care Facilities section.

KNOTTSVILLE. *Bishop Soenneker Home* 9545 Kentucky 144 Philpot, 42366. Tel: 502-281-4881.
For a complete listing, refer to the Special Care Facilities section.

[F] MONASTERIES AND RESIDENCES OF PRIESTS AND BROTHERS

HARTFORD. *Glenmary House*, 300 Peach Alley, 42347. Tel: 502-298-9886. The Home Missioners of America. Directors: Bros. Dennis Craig; Larry Johnson.

SOUTH UNION. *Fathers of Mercy*, 42283. Tel: 502-542-4146. Very Rev. William P. Casey, C.P.M., Supr. Gen.; Revs. David M. Wilton, C.P.M., Vicar Gen., Mission Dir.; Joseph H. Burgdorf, C.P.M., Novice Master; John R. O'Brien, C.P.M.; John J. Molloy, C.P.M.; Daniel Sheehan, C.P.M.; Francis T. Sherry, C.P.M.; Denis Blais, C.P.M.

[G] CONVENTS AND RESIDENCES FOR SISTERS

OWENSBORO. *The Glenmary Center*, P.O. Box 22264, 42304-2264. Tel: 502-686-8401. Glenmary Home Mission Sisters of America. Sr. Christine Beckett, Pres.
Special Centers for Social Services & Assistance. Total Assisted 4,000; Total Staff 7. Professed Sisters in Community 12.

LIVERMORE. *The Glenmary Center for Mission Training*. Formation Program. 220 E. 7th St., P.O. Box 520, 42352-0520. Tel: 502-278-5239. Sr. Mae Koenig, Dir.; Sr. Martha Schuler, Assoc. Dir.; Sr. Patricia Leighton.

MAPLE MOUNT. *Mount St. Joseph*, 42356. Tel: 502-229-4103. Motherhouse and Convent of the Ursuline Nuns of the Congregation of Paris. Sr. Rose Marita O'Bryan, O.S.U., Supr.; Rev. Anthony J. Shonis, Chap.; Sr. Emma Cecilia Busam, O.S.U., Archivist. Professed Sisters in Community 223.

WHITESVILLE. *St. Joseph's Monastery*, 8564 Crisp Rd., 42378. Tel: 502-233-4571; Fax: 502-233-4356.
E-mail: SMAHiggs@mindspring.com
Religious of the Passion of Jesus Christ, (Passionist Nuns, Cloistered Contemplative). Sr. Mary Agnes Higgs, C.P., Supr.; Rev. Louis Piskula, Chap. Professed Sisters 18.

[H] RETREAT CENTERS

MAPLE MOUNT. *Mt. St. Joseph Retreat Center*, 42356. Tel: 502-229-4103. Sr. Amelia Stenger, O.S.U., Dir. Assoc. Directors: Rev. Msgr. Bernard Powers; Sr. Elaine Burke, O.S.U.

[I] NEWMAN CENTERS

BOWLING GREEN. *Western Kentucky University Newman Center*, St. Thomas Aquinas Chapel, 1403 College St., P.O. Box 10170, 42102-4770. Tel: 502-843-3638.
E-mail: LittlJT@PREMIERNET.NET
Web site: www.PREMIERNET.NET/~WKUCNC
Rev. John Little, Dir.; Damian Oliver, Pastoral Min. Students 1,100.

MURRAY. *Murray State University Newman House*, 220 N. 13th St., 42071. Tel: 502-753-1391.
E-mail: sisterMary@mursuky.campus.mci.net
Sr. Mary Matthias Ward, O.S.U.; Rev. J. Raymond Goetz. Students 800.

[J] MISCELLANEOUS LISTINGS

OWENSBORO. *Cathedral Preschool*, 600 Locust St., 42301. Tel: 502-926-1652. Students 206.
The Catholic Foundation of Western Kentucky, 600 Locust St., 42301.
**Daniel Pitino Shelter, Inc.*, 501 Walnut St., 42301. Tel: 502-688-9000. Provides soup kitchen seven days a week, shelter for 36 homeless, education facilities, food bank, legal aid and medical services for those unable to pay. Total Assisted 30,000; Employees 3; Volunteers 150.
**Glenmary Sisters Charitable Trust*, 1500 Avon Pl., 42301. Mr. Frank Harris, Chm.; Sr. Patricia Leighton, Sec.; Mr. Charles Reid.
Interparish Deposit Loan Fund Corp., 600 Locust St., 42301-2130. Sr. Joseph Angela Boone, Contact Person.
Owensboro Catholic Consolidated School System, 1524 W. Parrish Ave., 42301. Sr. Susan Mary Mudd, O.S.U., Dir.
**The Roman Catholic Diocese of Owensboro Kentucky Charitable Trust Fund, Inc.*, 600 Locust St., 42301. Tel: 502-683-1545; Fax: 502-683-6883. Sr. Joseph Angela Boone, O.S.U.

BOWLING GREEN. *Diocesan Shrine of Mary Mother of the Church and Model of all Christians*, St. Joseph, 434 Church St., 42101. Tel: 502-842-2525.

PADUCAH. *Our Lady of the Pines Prayer House, Inc.*, 717 S. 6th St., 42001. Tel: 502-443-3650.
St. Mary High School Benefit Fund, 1243 Elmdale Rd., 42003.

RELIGIOUS INSTITUTES OF MEN REPRESENTED IN THE DIOCESE

For further details refer to the corresponding bracketed number in the Religious Institutes of Men or Women section.

[0200]—*Benedictine Monks.*—O.S.B.
[0820]—*Congregation of the Fathers of Mercy.*—C.P.M.
[0570]—*Glenmary Home Missioners.* (Glendale OH).—Glmy.
[0560]—*Third Order Regular of Saint Francis.*—T.O.R.

RELIGIOUS INSTITUTES OF WOMEN REPRESENTED IN THE DIOCESE

[0100]—*Adorers of the Blood of Christ.*—A.S.C.
[0230]—*Benedictine Sisters of the Pontifical Jurisdiction.* (Ferdinand, IN).—O.S.B.
[0360]—*Carmelite Sisters of the Divine Heart of Jesus.*—Carmel D.C.J.
[2080]—*Home Mission Sisters of America.*—G.H.M.S.
[2575]—*Institute of the Sisters of Mercy of the Americas.* (Cincinnati, OH; Detroit, MI).—R.S.M.
[3170]—*Religious of the Passion of Jesus Christ.*—C.P.
[0500]—*Sisters of Charity of Nazareth.*—S.C.N.
[3360]—*Sisters of Providence of Saint Mary-of-the-Woods, Indiana.*—S.P.
[2260]—*Sisters of the Lamb of God.*—A.D.
[1760]—*Sisters of the Third Order of St. Francis of Penance and Charity.* Tiffin, OH.—O.S.F.
[1720]—*Sisters of the Third Order Regular of St. Francis of the Congregation of Our Lady of Lourdes.* Rochester, MN.—O.S.F.
[4120]—*Ursuline Nuns, of the Congregation of Paris.*—O.S.U.
[1570]—*Sisters of St.Francis of the Holy Family.* Dubuque, IA.—O.S.F.

INTERPAROCHIAL CEMETERIES

OWENSBORO. *Mater Dolorosa*, 1860 W. 9th St., 42301.
Resurrection, 5404 Leitchfield Rd., 42303. Mr. Art Hodde, Dir.

NECROLOGY

† Boehmicke, George, (Retired). —Died Nov. 6, 1996.

Diocese of Palm Beach

Most Reverend

J. KEITH SYMONS, D.D.

Bishop of Palm Beach; ordained May 18, 1958; appointed Titular Bishop of Siguritanus and Auxiliary of St. Petersburg January 16, 1981; consecrated March 19, 1981; appointed Second Bishop of Pensacola-Tallahassee September 29, 1983; installed November 8, 1983; appointed Second Bishop of Palm Beach June 2, 1990; installed July 31, 1990; Fax: 561-775-7035.

ESTABLISHED OCTOBER 24, 1984.

Square Miles 5,115.

Comprises the Counties of Palm Beach, Martin, Indian River, Okeechobee and St. Lucie in the State of Florida.

Legal Corporate Title: *The Diocese of Palm Beach.*

For legal titles of parishes and diocesan institutions, consult the Chancery.

The Pastoral Center:. Mailing Address: P.O. Box 109650, Palm Beach Gardens, FL, 33410-9650. Location: 9995 N. Military Tr., Palm Beach Gardens, FL, 33410. Tel.: 561-775-9500; Fax: 561-775-9556.

Web site address: http://diocese.maco.net

E-mail address: diocese@maco.net

STATISTICAL OVERVIEW

Personnel	
Bishop	1
Priests: Diocesan Active in Diocese	72
Priests: Active Outside Diocese	5
Priests: Retired, Sick or Absent	19
Number of Diocesan Priests	96
Religious Priests in Diocese	42
Extern Priests in Diocese	14
Ordinations:	
Diocesan Priests	1
Religious Priests	1
Transitional Deacons	3
Permanent Deacons in Diocese	37
Total Brothers	3
Total Sisters	183
Parishes	
Parishes	46
With Resident Pastor:	
Resident Diocesan Priests	40
Resident Religious Priests	6
Without Resident Pastor:	
Missions	5
Professional Ministry Personnel:	
Brothers	1
Sisters	28
Lay Ministers	45
Welfare	
Catholic Hospitals	1
Total Assisted	15,862
Homes for the Aged	1
Total Assisted	120
Day Care and Extended Day Care Centers	2
Total Assisted	120
Specialized Homes	1
Total Assisted	16
Special Centers for Social Services	21
Total Assisted	19,251
Residential Care of Disabled	2
Total Assisted	12
Educational	
Seminaries, Diocesan	1
Students from This Diocese	13
Students from Other Diocese	60
Diocesan Students in Other Seminaries	11
Total Seminarians	24
High Schools, Diocesan and Parish	3
Total Students	2,067
Elementary Schools, Diocesan and Parish	14
Total Students	5,357
Elementary Schools, Private	2
Total Students	562
Catechesis/Religious Education:	
High School Students	2,377
Elementary Students	13,530
Total Students Under Catholic Instruction	23,917
Teachers in the Diocese:	
Priests	19
Sisters	22
Lay Teachers	420
Vital Statistics	
Receptions into the Church:	
Infant Baptism Totals	4,397
Adult Baptism Totals	280
Received into Full Communion	349
First Communions	3,675
Confirmations	1,960
Marriages:	
Catholic	789
Interfaith	368
Total Marriages	1,157
Deaths	2,347
Total Catholic Population	219,470
Total Population	1,438,844

Former Bishop—Most Rev. THOMAS V. DAILY, D.D., ord. Jan. 10, 1952; appt. Titular Bishop of Bladia and Auxiliary Bishop of Boston, Dec. 31, 1974; cons. Feb. 11, 1975; appt. first Bishop of Palm Beach, July 17, 1984; installed Oct. 24, 1984; transferred to Bishop of Brooklyn, Feb. 20, 1990.

The Pastoral Center—Mailing Address: P.O. Box 109650, Palm Beach Gardens, 33410-9650. Tel: 561-775-9500; Fax: 561-775-9556. *9995 N. Military Trail, Palm Beach Gardens, 33410.*

Vicars General—Rev. Msgr. IRVINE J. NUGENT; Very Rev. CHARLES E. HAWKINS.

Episcopal Vicars—Rev. Msgr. JOHN R. MCMAHON; Revs. FRANCIS J. LECHIARA; TIMOTHY J. LYNCH; RICHARD MURPHY; ARTHUR J. VENEZIA.

Moderator of Curia—Rev. Msgr. IRVINE J. NUGENT, V.G.

Administrative Assistant to Bishop—Sr. MARIE CONSILIA MANTELLO, A.S.C.J.

Executive Secretary to Bishop—Miss ANNE LAPORTE.

Master of Ceremonies—Revs. MICHAEL EDWARDS.

Matrimonial Tribunal—

Judicial Vicar—Rev. Msgr. THOMAS J. KLINZING, J.C.L.

Judges—Rev. Msgr. RAYMOND BLAIR, J.C.D.; Rev. Msgr. THOMAS KLINZING, J.C.L.; Revs. ARTHUR ESPELAGE, O.F.M., J.C.D.; GERALD HUGHES, J.C.D.; DAMIAN TOWEY, C.P., J.C.D.

Defender of the Bond—Rev. Msgr. JOSEPH MARBACH, J.C.D.; Revs. TIMOTHY J. LYNCH, J.C.L.; WILLIAM MARTIN, O.M.I., J.U.D.

Assessors—Rev. Msgr. JAMES BURKE; Revs. MICHAEL W. EDWARDS; GLEN POTHIER; Mrs. LORRAINE SABATELLA.

Promotor of Justice—Rev. DAMIAN TOWEY, C.P., J.C.D.

Director of the Tribunal—Mrs. LORRAINE SABATELLA, B.A.

Notaries—Rev. MICHAEL W. EDWARDS; Ms. MARY LOU HUGHES; Mrs. LORRAINE SABATELLA.

Secretaries—Mrs. GEMA FERNANDEZ; Mrs. SANDRA DUBEAU.

Advocates—Rev. GLEN J. POTHIER; Rev. Msgr. JAMES BURKE; Sr. MARIE JAMES MCCALLEN, R.S.M.; Mrs. JOANN AUGUSTYN; Mr. BERNARD CONKO; Mrs. KATHLEEN CONTE; Mrs. ELAINE WOLLING; Mr. JOHN MCGREEVY; Ms. SYLVIA RAFTERY.

Chancellor—Rev. MICHAEL W. EDWARDS. Tel: 561-627-2411.

Administrative Assistant to Vicar General/Chancellor—Ms. MARY LOU HUGHES.

Archives—Ms. MARY LOU HUGHES.

Archives Committee—Rev. MICHAEL W. EDWARDS, Chm.

Vicariate for Christ's Faithful

Episcopal Vicar—Rev. ARTHUR J. VENEZIA.

Diocesan Office of Evangelization—Rev. FRANCIS REARDON, Dir.

Office for Seminarians—Rev. ARTHUR J. VENEZIA, Dir.

Office for Vocations—Rev. LOUIS GUERIN, Dir.

Diocesan Vocations Admissions Committee—Rev. CHARLES E. HAWKINS, Chm.

Vicar for Permanent Deacons—Deacon JACK PIERCE, Vicar.

Vicar for Religious—Rev. MARK A. SZANYI, O.F.M.Conv.; Sr. JOHN KEVIN MCNULTY, O.S.F., Assoc. Vicar for Religious.

Dir. for Religious Vocations—Sr. JOHN KEVIN MCNULTY, O.S.F., Assoc. Vicar.

Diocesan Commission of Religious—Sr. JEANNE DREA, O.P., Chm.

Laity—

Office for Black Catholic Ministry—Mrs. LORRAINE LYLES, Dir.

Office for Haitian Ministry—Deacon EMILE AMBROISE, Dir.

Office for Hispanic Ministry—Sr. REGINA TUTZO, R.M.I.

Office for Hispanic Ministry in Indian River and St. Lucie Counties—Rev. DON REDDEN.

Rural Life Migrant Ministry—P.O. Box 1203, Stuart, 34995. Mrs. MARIA CHRISTINA MARQUEZ, Coord.

Holy Childhood Association—Rev. MICHAEL W. EDWARDS, Dir., *P.O. Box 109650, Palm Beach Gardens, 33410-9650.*

Legion of Mary—Rev. KEVIN MACGABHANN, Spiritual Moderator; Deacon ROBERT JACOBI, Assoc. Spiritual Moderator.

Vicariate for Catholic Charities

Vicar—Rev. Msgr. JOHN R. MCMAHON.

Catholic Charities—Mr. MARCEL O. CHARPENTIER, A.C.S.W., Exec. Dir.; Ms. MADELEINE SCHUTZ, L.C.S.W., Assoc. Dir.

Belle Glade Office—Sr. AMADEE MAXWELL, S.B.S.

Birthline Crisis Pregnancy Center—Mrs. ARLENE CONKLIN.

Campaign for Human Development & Catholic Relief Services—Mrs. BARBARA ROTH.

Elder Affairs Case Management & Guardianship—Sr. MARYROSE CROWLEY, S.S.N.D.

Emmaus Residence for Persons Living with AIDS—Rev. JOHN EDWARDS, S.J.

Lifeline Crisis Pregnancy Center—Mrs. ARLENE CONKLIN.

Martin County Offices (Hope Sound, Indiantown, East Stuart, Stuart)—Ms. PAMELA BLACK.

Maurawood Community Outreach for Pregnancy/Parenting—Ms. PAIGE STUHR.

Nazareth Homes-Adult Group Homes for People with Developmental Disabilties—Alhambra House: Sr. RITA BAUM, S.S.J. Bethlehem House: Sr. RITA BAUM, S.S.J.

Office of Housing Management & Development—Ms. ROBIN LUNN.

Okeechobee Outreach Center/After School Program—Ms. BARBARA ISAMAN.

Family First Family Program—Ms. MADELEINE SCHUTZ.

Refugee Resettlement & Immigration Services—Mr. DEXTER ORANGE.

Saint Lucie County Office—Ms. CARMEN SIBRUN.

Samaritan Center for Homeless Families—Ms. KRIS ALTMAN; Mrs. JOYCE WILD.

Villa Assumpta Housing for the Elderly—Ms. LINDA MATZ.

Villa Franciscan Housing for the Elderly—Mr. WILLIAM KERR, Mgr.

Villa Madonna Housing for the Elderly—Ms. ROSEMARY MCMAHON, Mgr.

Vicariate for Education

Vicar—Rev. FRANCIS J. LECHIARA.

Office of Catechesis and Leadership Development—Deacon JAMES CAMPBELL, Dir.

Missionary Cooperative Plan—Rev. MICHAEL W. EDWARDS, *P.O. Box 109650, Palm Beach Gardens, 33410-9650.*

Propagation of the Faith—Rev. MICHAEL W. EDWARDS, *P.O. Box 109650, Palm Beach Gardens, 33410-9650.*

Office of Communications—Rev. MICHAEL EDWARDS, Dir.

Office of "The Florida Catholic"—Mr. THOMAS TRACY, Editor.

Office of the Catholic Schools—Sr. JOAN DAWSON, O.S.F., Supt.; Mrs. PATRICIA CANTIERI, Asst. Supt.

Office of Special Education - C.O.M.E.—Mrs. PATRICIA CANTIERI, Dir.

Vicariate for Marriage and the Family

Vicar—Rev. TIMOTHY J. LYNCH.

Family Life—

Office of Family Life Ministry—Directors: WALTER ATWELL; GERALDINE ATWELL.

Office of Youth Ministry and Young Adult Ministry—Rev. AIDAN LACY, Spiritual Moderator; Sr. JUDE RUGGERI, A.S.C.J., Dir.

Cursillo Movement—10970 State Rd. 703, N. Palm Beach, 33408. Rev. MICHAEL TSCHUDI, Spiritual Dir.

Cursillo Movement for Hispanics—9600 W. Atlantic Ave., Delray Beach, 33446. Rev. MATTHEW DIDONE, C.S., Spiritual Dir.

Office of Ministry with People with Disabilities—Sr. RITA BAUM, S.S.J., Dir.

Office of Prison Ministry—Sr. BETTY FRASCINO, O.S.F., Dir.

Office of Ecumenical and Inter-Faith Activities—Revs. EDMUND SZPIEG, Dir. MICHAEL TSCHUDI, Assoc. Dir.

Office for Liturgy—Rev. MICHAEL DRISCOLL, O.Carm., Dir.

Office for Campus Ministry—Rev. MARTIN DEVEREAUX, Dir., Lynn University; Rev. FRANCIS DIXON, O.Carm, Dir., Florida Atlantic University.

Chaplain for Catholic Scouting—Rev. THOMAS EUTENEUER, Chap.

Liaison to Charismatic Movement—Rev. WALTER DOCKERILL.

World Wide Marriage Encounter—Rev. FRANK B. GUINAN, Spiritual Moderator. Exec. Couple: LARRY BALIK; HERMIE BALIK, *220 Colony Way W., Jupiter, 33458.*

Office for Respect Life—Mr. DONALD KAZIMIR, Dir.

Vicariate for Pastoral Services

Vicar—Rev. RICHARD MURPHY.

Diocesan Financial Administrator—Mr. BASIL ZALOOM.

Financial Advisory Board—Rev. RICHARD MURPHY, Chm.

Office for Building and Renovations—Mr. PATRICK MOLAMPHY, Dir.

Commission for Building—Rev. RICHARD MURPHY, Chm.

Office of Cemeteries—Rev. THOMAS VENGAYIL, Dir.

Office of Data Processing—Rev. RICHARD MURPHY.

Office of Resource Development—Mrs. DORIS HANLON, Admin. Asst.

Pastoral Center Personnel—Mr. BASIL ZALOOM.

Committee for Parish Boundaries—Revs. JOHN G. BLOCK, Chm.

Legal Affairs—Mr. J. PATRICK FITZGERALD, ESQ., *110 Merrick Way, Ste. 3-B, Coral Gables, 33134.* Tel: 561-659-6438; Fax: 305-443-6613.

Consultative Bodies

College of Consultors—Rev. Msgr. THOMAS KLINZING, J.C.L.; Rev. Msgr. IRVINE J. NUGENT, V.G.; Very Rev. CHARLES E. HAWKINS, V.G.; Rev. Msgr. JOHN R. MCMAHON; Revs. JOHN G. BLOCK; MICHAEL EDWARDS; FRANCIS J. LECHIARA; TIMOTHY J. LYNCH; RICHARD MURPHY; JAMES MURTAGH; ARTHUR J. VENEZIA.

Presbyteral Council—Rev. Msgr. IRVINE J. NUGENT, V.G.; Rev. Msgr. JOHN R. MCMAHON; Rev. Msgr. THOMAS KLINZING, J.C.L.; Very Rev. CHARLES E. HAWKINS, V.G.; Revs. CHRISTOPHER ALLEN; EDWARD MALONEY; JAMES MURTAGH; LOUIS GUERIN; MICHAEL W. EDWARDS; FRANCIS X. FENECH; THOMAS OTTO; CHARLES E. NOTABARTOLO; FRANCIS J. LECHIARA; TIMOTHY J. LYNCH; RICHARD MURPHY; JOHN EDWARDS, S.J.; FRANCIS REARDON; ARTHUR J. VENEZIA; THOMAS VENGAYIL.

Miscellaneous

Society of St. Vincent de Paul, District Council of the Treasure Coast—Mrs. FRANCES ASKLAND, *1063 S.W. McCoy Ave., Port St. Lucie, 34953.* Tel: 561-336-9054.

CLERGY, PARISHES, MISSIONS AND PAROCHIAL SCHOOLS

CITY OF PALM BEACH GARDENS
(Palm Beach County)

1—CATHEDRAL OF ST. IGNATIUS LOYOLA (1984), Rev. Msgr. Thomas Klinzing, Rector; Revs. Glen K. Pothier; Donald Finney, M.I.C.
Res., 9999 N. Military Tr., Palm Beach Gardens, 33410. Tel: 561-622-2565; Fax: 561-624-9489.
Catechesis/Religious Programs—Students 625.

OUTSIDE THE CITY OF PALM BEACH GARDENS

Belle Glade, Palm Beach Co., St. Philip Benizi, Revs. Luis Aineto, S.D.B.; James Horan, O.S.B.; Jeremiah Reen, S.D.B.; Attilio Klinger, S.D.B; Bros. Michael Brinkman; Lino Seneci, S.D.B.
Res., 710 S. Main St., 33430. Tel: 561-996-3870; Fax: 561-996-3899.
Catechesis/Religious Programs—Students 324.

Boca Raton, Palm Beach Co.,

1—ASCENSION, Revs. Matthew A. Morgan; Donald R. Munro.
Res., 7250 N. Federal Hwy., 33487. Tel: 561-997-5486; Fax: 561-997-5862.

2—OUR LADY OF LOURDES, Rev. Martin B. Mulqueen; Rev. Msgr. Joseph H. O'Shea, Pastor Emeritus; Revs. Andrew Riley; Joseph M. Kuczborski (PEO).
Res., 20094 S.W. 57th Ave., 33428. Tel: 561-483-2440; Fax: 561-482-0626.
Catechesis/Religious Programs—Students 1,200.

3—ST. JOAN OF ARC, Rev. Msgr. John McMahon; Revs. Thomas J. Skindeleski (PH); John Sutton (PAT).
Res., 370 S.W. 3rd St., 33432. Tel: 561-392-0007; Fax: 561-392-0074.
School—Sisters of Mercy, Skibbereen. Sr. Ellen Murphy R.S.M., Prin.
Sisters 3; Lay Teachers 27; Students 639.
Catechesis/Religious Programs—Students 861.

4—ST. JOHN THE EVANGELIST, Rev. Michael O'Flaherty.
Res., 19785 Hampton Dr., Ste. #4, 33434. Tel: 561-488-1373.

5—ST. JUDE, Revs. Michael Driscoll, O.Carm.; Timothy Johnson, O.Carm.; Aquinas E. Stack, O.Carm. In res., Rev. Eugene Foley, O.Carm.
Res., 21693 Club Villa Terrace, 33433.
Church—21689 Toledo Rd., 33433. Tel: 561-392-8172; Fax: 561-362-0845.
School—Tel: 561-392-9160. Sr. Debbie Armstrong, R.S.M., Prin.
Sisters 1; Lay Teachers 16; Students 360.
Catechesis/Religious Programs—Students 604.

Boynton Beach, Palm Beach Co., St. Mark, Revs. Mark Szanyi, O.F.M.Conv.; Joseph Lotz, O.F.M.Conv.
Res., 643 N.E. 4th Ave., 33435. Tel: 561-734-9330; Fax: 561-735-3463.
School—Sisters of Charity of St. Elizabeth. Miss Phyllis Pacilli, Prin.
Sisters 2; Lay Teachers 18; Students 315.

St. Thomas More, Rev. Frank O'Loughlin.
Res., 10935 S. Military Tr., 33436. Tel: 561-737-3095; Fax: 561-737-8697.

Delray Beach, Palm Beach Co.,

1—EMMANUEL, Rev. Raymond Hubert.
Res., 15700 S. Military Tr., 33484. Tel: 561-496-2480.

2—OUR LADY OF PERPETUAL HELP MISSION, Rev. Roland Desormeaux, C.S.; Rev. Msgr. Jean Gerard Yves Lapierre (Haiti).
Residence and Church—510 S.W. Eighth Ave., 33444. Tel: 561-276-4880; Fax: 561-276-7036.

3—OUR LADY QUEEN OF PEACE, Rev. Matthew DiDone, C.S., Admin.
Res., 9600 W. Atlantic Ave., 33446. Tel: 561-499-6234; Fax: 561-499-5513.
Claritian Missionaries 4.

4—ST. VINCENT FERRER, Revs. John A. Skehan; John Barrow; Aidan Lacy.
Res., 840 George Bush Blvd., 33483. Tel: 561-276-6892; Fax: 561-276-8068.
School—715 N.E. 8th Ave., 33483.
Sisters of Mercy (Kinsale, Ireland) 4; Lay Teachers 15; Students 322.

Fellsmere, Indian River Co., Our Lady of Guadalupe Mission, Rev. Don Redden.
Mailing Address: P.O. Box 9, 32948.
Res., 2410 Florida Ave., Fort Pierce, 34950. Tel: 561-464-2285.
Mission—Fellsmere, Indian River Co., Rte. 512, P.O. Box 9, 32948. Tel: 561-571-9875; Fax: 561-571-8321.

Fort Pierce, St. Lucie Co., Notre Dame Mission, Rev. Antoine Richert, S.M.M.
Res., 217 N. U.S. Hwy. #1, 34950. Tel: 561-466-9617.

St. Anastasia, Rev. Mark Christopher.
Res., 407 S. 33rd St., P.O. Box 430, 34954-0430. Tel: 561-461-2233.
School—Tel: 561-461-2232; Fax: 561-468-2037. Mrs. Vickie Guettler, Prin.
Sisters 1; Lay Teachers 24; Students 601.

St. Mark, Revs. Richard Murphy; Sean de Leis, C.S.Sp.
Mailing Address: P.O. Box 2020, 34954.
Res., 1924 Zephyr Ave., 34982. Tel: 561-461-8150.

Highland Beach, Palm Beach Co., St. Lucy, Revs. Gerald Grace; Anthony J. Chepanis, Pastor Emeritus; Louis T. Guerin.
Res., 3510 S. Ocean Blvd., 33487. Tel: 561-278-1280; Fax: 561-278-8509.

Hobe Sound, Martin Co., St. Christopher, Revs. Leslie Cann; Richard Vilie (MIA); Aidan Hynes.
Mailing Address: P.O. Box 607, 33475.
Res., 12001 S.E. Federal Hwy., 33455. Tel: 561-546-5150; Fax: 561-546-8820.

Indiantown, Martin Co., Holy Cross, Revs. Thomas Euteneur, Admin.; Juan de la Calle, Pastor Emeritus.
Mailing Address: P.O. Box 999, 34956.
Res., 15927 S.W. 150 St., 34956. Tel: 561-597-2798; Fax: 561-597-2741.

Jensen Beach, Martin Co., St. Martin de Porres, Revs. Robert L. Magee; Thomas J. Rynne, Pastor Emeritus.
Mailing Address: P.O. Box 1087, 34958.
Res., 2555 N.E. Savanna Rd., 34958. Tel: 561-334-4214; Fax: 561-334-8627.

Juno Beach, Palm Beach Co., St. Patrick, Rev. Frank Guinan.
Res., 2549 Hope Ln., W., Palm Beach Gardens, 33410. Tel: 561-626-8626; Fax: 561-622-6471.

Jupiter, Palm Beach Co., St. Peter, Rev. Charles Notabartolo. In res., Rev. Michael W. Edwards.
Res., 1701 Indian Creek Pkwy., 33458. Tel: 561-575-0837; Fax: 561-575-6784.
Catechesis/Religious Programs—Students 950.

Lake Worth, Palm Beach Co., Sacred Heart, Revs. Peter Van Nguyen; Francis X. Fenech, Pastor Emeritus; Irvine M. Nugent.
Mailing Address: P.O. Box 551, 33460.
Res., 425 N. M St., 33460. Tel: 561-582-4736; Fax: 561-588-5238.
School—410 N. M St., 33460. Sr. Breeden Connolly, S.S.J., Prin.
Sisters 4; Lay Teachers 13; Students 283.

St. Luke, Revs. Daniel V. Cronin; Larkin Connolly, Pastor Emeritus; George L. Batista (NEW); Francis E. Maloney.
Res., 2892 S. Congress Ave., 33461. Tel: 561-965-8980; Fax: 561-965-1384.

School—Tel: 561-965-8190; Fax: 561-965-2404. Sr. Janet Finely, O.S.F., Prin.

Lay Teachers 11; Students 284.

St. Matthew, Rev. Clemens Hammerschmitt.

Res., 5417 Fearnley Rd., 33467-5654. Tel: 561-966-8878; Fax: 561-968-1238.

Lantana, Palm Beach Co., Holy Spirit, Revs. Kevin MacGabhann; William O'Dea, Pastor Emeritus; James Fiore; Jacob Aymanamkuzhy.

Res. and Mailing—1000 Lantana Rd., P.O. Box 2978, 33465. Tel: 561-585-5970; Fax: 561-575-8482.

North Palm Beach, Palm Beach Co., St. Clare, Revs. William D. O'Shea; Thomas P. O'Flanagan.

Res., 821 Prosperity Farms Rd., 33408. Tel: 561-622-7477; Fax: 561-624-0022.

School—Tel: 561-622-7171; Fax: 561-627-4426. Mr. Andrew J. Houvouras, Prin.

Lay Teachers 25; Students 547.

St. Paul of the Cross, Revs. Arthur Venezia; Michael Tschudi. In res., Rev. Peter Duvelsdorf, S.D.B (RVC).

Res., 10970 State Rd. 703, 33408. Tel: 561-626-1873; Fax: 561-622-7307.

Okeechobee, Okeechobee Co., Sacred Heart, Rev. Hugh Duffy.

Mailing Address: P.O. Box 716, 34973.

Res., 701 S.W. Sixth St., 34973. Tel: 941-763-3727; Fax: 941-763-9334.

Pahokee, Palm Beach Co., St. Mary, Rev. John J. Mericantante.

Res., 1200 E. Main St., 33476. Tel: 561-924-7305; Fax: 561-924-9394.

Palm Beach, Palm Beach Co., St. Edward, Rev. Francis J. Lechiara; Rev. Msgr. James Burke. In res., Rev. Danis Ridore (Canada).

Res., 144 N. County Rd., 33480. Tel: 561-832-0400; Fax: 561-833-3359.

Palm City, Martin Co., Holy Redeemer, Rev. Bernard F. Powell.

Mailing Address: P.O. Box 916, 34991.

Res., 1964 Capri St., 34990. Tel: 561-286-4590.

Port St. Lucie, St. Lucie Co., St. Lucie, Revs. Matthew Fitzgerald; Peter C. Dolan, Pastor Emeritus; Rodney Q. Titus; Richard Allen Schaefer.

Res., 446 S.W. Irving St., 34983. Tel: 561-878-1215; Fax: 561-878-1299.

Catechesis/Religious Programs—Students 550.

St. Elizabeth Ann Seton, Rev. Clarence Podgorski.

Church—930 S.W. Tunis Ave., 34953. Tel: 561-336-0282; Fax: 561-336-1494.

Holy Family, Revs. Thomas F. Cauley; Thomas Otto. Mailing Address: P.O. Box 8447, 34985. Tel: 561-335-2385; Fax: 561-335-2517.

Res., 2330 Mariposa Ave., 34953.

Riviera Beach, Palm Beach Co., St. Francis of Assisi, Revs. William P. McSweeney, O.M.I.; Rolland Bennett, O.M.I. In res., Rev. Robert Colfer, O.M.I.

Res., 200 W. 20th St., 33404. Tel: 561-842-2482; Fax: 561-863-2985.

School—Mrs. Judith Edelman, Prin. Lay Teachers 10; Students 160.

Royal Palm Beach, Palm Beach Co., Our Lady Queen of the Apostles, Revs. Michael Woodcock; Edmund L. Szpieg.

Res., 172 Kings Way, 33411. Tel: 561-798-5661; Fax: 561-798-5663.

Mailing Address: 100 Crestwood Blvd., S., 33411.

Sebastian, Indian River Co., St. Sebastian, Revs. Timothy Sockol; Tomasz Makowski.

Mailing Address: P.O. Box 78-1212, 32978-1212.

Res., 13075 U.S. Hwy. 1, 32958. Tel: 561-589-5790; Fax: 561-388-0084.

Stuart, Martin Co., St. Joseph, Revs. A. Christopher Allen; John Morrissey; John Kasparek.

Res., 1200 E. 10th St., 34996. Tel: 561-287-2727; Fax: 561-278-4998.

School—Tel: 561-287-6975; Fax: 561-287-4733. Mrs. Marie Privuznak, Prin.

Lay Teachers 21; Students 423.

Mission—Stuart, Martin Co., St. Andrew.

Tequesta, Palm Beach Co., St. Jude, Revs. Thomas Vengayil; John J. McAtavey, Pastor Emeritus; Edward Campbell, O.S.B.

Mailing Address: P.O. Box 3726, 33469.

Res., 204 U.S. Hwy. 1, 33469. Tel: 561-746-7974; Fax: 561-743-6127.

Vero Beach, Indian River Co., St. Helen, Rev. Msgr. Irvine Nugent, V.G.; Revs. John F. Flynn, S.M.A.; Ramon J. Echeverria.

Res., 2085 Tallahassee Ave., P.O. Box 2927, 32961. Tel: 561-567-5129; Fax: 561-567-4823.

School—2050 Vero Beach Ave., 32960.

Lay Teachers 9; Students 265.

Holy Cross, Revs. Richard Murphy; John B. O'Hare, Pastor Emeritus; Francis Reardon.

Res., 500 Iris Ln., 32964. Tel: 561-231-0671; Fax: 561-234-5653.

St. John of the Cross, Rev. John A. Crowley. In res., Rev. Donal O'Hare (WCH).

Res., 950 82nd Ave., 32966. Tel: 561-563-0057; Fax: 561-563-0057.

Wellington, Palm Beach Co., St. Rita, Revs. Walter J. Dockerill; Julian Harris; Maciej Piotrowicz.

Res., 13645 Paddock Dr., 33414. Tel: 561-793-8544; Fax: 561-793-4082.

West Palm Beach, Palm Beach Co.,

1—HOLY NAME OF JESUS, Revs. James Murtagh; John Cunningham; Alberto Rodrigues, O.S.S.T.

Res., 345 S. Military Tr., 33415. Tel: 407-683-3555; Fax: 407-683-1051.

School—Sr. Kathleen Curtin, R.S.M., Prin. Sisters 1; Lay Teachers 13; Students 300.

2—MARY IMMACULATE, Rev. Timothy J. Lynch. In res., Rev. Arthur Espelage, O.F.M.

Res., 390 Sequoia Dr., 33409. Tel: 561-686-8128; Fax: 561-686-8406.

3—ST. ANN, Revs. William J. Mayer, S.J.; Wayne Herpin, S.J. In res., Revs. John Edwards, S.J.; Eugene Bannin, S.J.

Res., 310 N. Olive Ave., 33410. Tel: 561-832-3757; Fax: 561-659-1465.

School—Sisters 6; Lay Teachers 12; Students 200.

4—ST. JOHN FISHER, Revs. William Martin, O.M.I., Pastor; John Vereb, Pastor Emeritus; Joseph Pallard, O.M.I. In res., Revs. Joseph Milford, O.M.I.; Joseph Pucci, O.M.I.

Res., 4001 North Shore Dr., 33407. Tel: 561-842-1224.

5—ST. JULIANA, Revs. Charles E. Hawkins; Nestor Rodriguez; Adrian Torres (Columbia).

Res., 4500 S. Dixie Hwy., 33405. Tel: 561-833-9745.

School—Mrs. Mary Beth Quick, Prin. Sisters of St. Joseph 4; Lay Teachers 15; Students 261.

Special Assignment:

Reverend Fathers—

Armbrust, Leo F., 11380 Prosperity Farms Rd., Palm Beach Gardens, FL 33410

Devereaux, Martin C., Chap., Lynn University, 3601 N. Military Trail, Boca Raton, FL 33431. Tel: 561-994-0770

Dixon, Francis, O.Carm., Campus Ministry at Florida Altantic University, 777 Glades Rd., Boca Raton, FL 33431. Tel: 561-367-3000

On Duty Outside the Diocese:

Reverend Fathers—

Allison, Michael, St. Paul, 1617 Walnut St., Erie, PA 16502

Block, John G., St. Bonaventure, 16400 Springdale St., Huntington Beach, CA 92649-2786

McNally, Michael

Ryan, Patrick

Schulz, Ronald, Catholic Theological Union, 5401 S. Cornell Ave., Chicago, IL 60615-5698

Retired:

Reverend Monsignors—

O'Shea, Joseph H.

Reverend Fathers—

Calle, Juan de la
Chepanis, Anthony J.
Connolly, Larkin
Dolan, Peter C.
Fenech, Francis
Flynn, Francis
Hare, John B.
LeSage, Joseph
Malvey, James
McAtavey, John J.
O'Dea, William
O'Donnell, Richard
Profeta, Salvatore
Rynne, Thomas
Sheehan, James
Stack, Christopher
Vereb, John
Victor, Al

Permanent Deacons:

Allgaier, John (NEW)
Ambroise, Emile
Arnold, Daniel
Campbell, James
Castellanos, Luis, (Retired)
Clifford, Frank
Collins, George (NY)
DiLeonardo, Ignatius (MIA)
DiMauro, Joseph
Galard, John (MIA)
Gallagher, Daniel (NY)
Gluhosky, Frank (HRT)
Jacobi, Robert
Johnson, Louis
Kucera, John
Lopez, Jesus
Melendez, Carlos
Mieses, Luis J. (Santo Domingo)
Pagliara, Daniel
Pfeiffer, Robert
Pierce, Jack
Raisch, Jack
Ramos, Geraldo (BGP)
Sawney, Ira (Grenada)
Seppanen, Henry (CAM)
Shellheimer, Bill (NEW)
Toussaint, Henk
Venezia, Richard
Wesley, Albert (FTW)

INSTITUTIONS LOCATED IN THE DIOCESE

[A] SEMINARIES, RELIGIOUS OR SCHOLASTICATES

BOYNTON BEACH. *St. Vincent de Paul Regional Seminary*, 10701 S. Military Tr., 33436. Tel: 561-732-4424; Fax: 561-737-2205.
E-mail: po31869b@pbseflin.org
Rev. Msgr. Pablo A. Navarro, S.T.L. (MIA), Rector / Pres.; Revs. Stephen Bosso, S.S.L. (PEN), Academic Dean & Vice Rector; Mark Heuberger, M.A. (VEN), Treas.; Alfredo Hernandez, S.T.L.; Stephen Tzecieski, C.M., B.A., M.A., Spiritual Dir.; Sr. Janet Sullivan, O.S.F., Continuing Education Dir.; Dr. Sixto Garcia, Ph.D.; Dr. Antonio Lopez, Ph.D.; Mr. Art Quinn, L.S., Librarian; Rev. Msgr. William White, M.A. (NY); Revs. Steven O'Hala, S.T.D. (MIA); Peter Plourde, S.S.L. (SP); Juan Quijano, S.T.L. (MIA); Sr. Margarita Gomez, R.M.IK, S.T.L.

[B] HIGH SCHOOLS, DIOCESAN AND PAROCHIAL

BOCA RATON. *Pope John Paul II High School*, 4001 N. Military Tr., 33431. Tel: 561-994-8998. Revs. Raymond V. Maher, O.Carm., Pres.; Guy Fiano, O.Carm.; Thomas Zalewski, O.Carm.; James Hess, O.Carm.; Kenneth Murphy, O.Carm.; Bro. Roberto Perez, O.Carm.; Sr. Eileen Sullivan, O.P., Prin. Sisters 2; Lay Teachers 49; Students 741.

FORT PIERCE. *John Carroll High School*, 3402 Delaware Ave., 34947-6116. Tel: 561-464-5200; Fax: 561-464-5233.
E-mail: jchs@gate.net
Web site: www.vero.com/vol/jchs
Rev. Michael Sajda, O.F.M.Conv., Pres.; Mr. Clyde L. Russell, Prin.; Rev. Joseph Dorniak, O.F.M.Conv. Sisters 3; Lay Teachers 27; Students 445.

WEST PALM BEACH. *Cardinal Newman High School*, 512 Spencer Dr., 33409. Tel: 561-683-6266; Fax: 561-683-7307.
E-mail: cnhs@flinet.com
Web site: http://www.flinet.com/~cnhs
Revs. David Carr, Pres.; Richard George, Chap.; Thomas Barrett. Lay Teachers 57; Students 861.

[C] SCHOOLS, PRIVATE

INDIANTOWN. *Hope Rural School*. (Grades K-6), 15929 S.W. 150th St., 34956. Tel: 561-597-2203.
E-mail: hopesch@gate.net
Web site: http://www.gate.net/~hopesch
Sr. Marie Celeste Gatti, O.P., Dir.; Sr. Marion Hangsterfer, O.P., Prin. Sisters 3; Lay Teachers 7; Students 190.

WEST PALM BEACH.

**Rosarian Academy*. (Grades PreK-8), 807 N. Flagler Dr., 33401. Tel: 561-832-5131. Sisters of St. Dominic (Adrian, MI). Rev. William Martin, O.M.I., Chap.; Sr. Jean Aufderheide, O.P., Prin. Sisters 6; Lay Teachers 26; Students 317.

[D] GENERAL HOSPITALS

WEST PALM BEACH. *St. Mary's Hospital, Inc.*, 901 45th St., 33407-2495. Tel: 561-881-2865; Fax: 561-881-2864

For a complete listing, refer to the Hospitals section.

[E] HOMES FOR AGED

WEST PALM BEACH. *Noreen McKeen Residence for Geriatric Care*, 315 Flagler Dr., S., 33401. Tel: 561-655-8544

For a complete listing, refer to the Special Care Facilities section.

[F] PERSONAL PRELATURES

DELRAY BEACH. *Opus Dei.* (Prelature of the Holy Cross and Opus Dei), 4409 Frances Dr., 33445. Tel: 561-498-1249. Legal Title: *The Work of God, Inc.* Revs. Jay Alvarez; Christopher Schmitt.

[G] MONASTERIES AND RESIDENCES OF PRIESTS AND BROTHERS

BOCA RATON. *St. Elias Priory-Order of Carmelites, NY*, 4944 Rabbit Hollow, 33487. Tel: 561-995-6762; 997-2089. Revs. Thomas Zalewski, O.Carm.; Guy Fiano, O.Carm., Prior; Raymond V. Maher, O.Carm.; James Hess, O.Carm.; Kenneth Murphy, O.Carm.; Francis Dixon, O.Carm.

NORTH PALM BEACH. *Our Lady of Florida Spiritual Center*, 1300 U.S. Hwy. No. 1, 33408. Tel: 561-626-1300; Fax: 561-627-3956. Revs. Francis Finnigan, C.P., Dir. Retreats; Damian Towey, C.P.; Isaias Powers, C.P.; Raphael Amrhein, C.P.; Roger Gannon, C.P.; Sr. Breda Eustace, C.P. Priests 4.

TEQUESTA. *P.I.M.E. Missionaries*, 1550 Beach Rd., 33469. Tel: 561-746-7767.
E-mail: nichom@aol.com
Web site: http://www.pime.org
Revs. Nicholas Maestrini, P.I.M.E., Rector; Pasquale Persico, P.I.M.E.

VERO BEACH. *Paulist Fathers Retirement Home*, 1225 20th Ave., 32960. Tel: 561-562-0500. Revs. Thomas J. Marley, C.S.P.; Edward J. Lyons, C.S.P.; William J. Cantwell, C.S.P.; George F. Helmich, C.S.P.; Thomas J. Connellan, C.S.P.

[H] CONVENTS AND RESIDENCES FOR SISTERS

DELRAY BEACH. *Christ the King Monastery of St. Clare.* (Solemn Vows, Papal Enclosure), 3900 Sherwood Blvd., 33445-5699. Tel: 561-498-3294. Sr. Mary Veronica Butler, O.S.C., Abbess. Cloistered Sisters 9; Extern Sisters 3; Novices 1.

Claretian Missionary, Sisters of Florida, Inc., 9600 W. Atlantic Ave., 33446. Tel: 561-498-9239.
E-mail: claretian.sr.delray@worldnet.att.net

WEST PALM BEACH. *Adrian Dominican Sisters, Florida Mission Chapter*, 810 N. Olive Ave., 33401. Tel: 561-832-6521; Fax: 561-820-8750.
E-mail: flmich@aol.com
Web site: http://www.op.org/adrian/
Sr. Marie Carleen Maly, O.P., Chapter Prioress.

[I] RETREAT HOUSES

LANTANA. *The Cenacle Spiritual Life Center*, 1400 S. Dixie Hwy., 33462-5492. Tel: 561-582-2534; Fax: 561-582-8070. Spiritual Life Center for laity and religious. Sisters 7.

NORTH PALM BEACH. *Our Lady of Florida Spiritual Center*, 1300 U.S. Hwy. No. 1, 33408. Tel: 561-626-1300; Fax: 561-627-3956.
E-mail: finnigan@gate.net
Web site: http://www.webhighway.com/ourlady

[J] MISCELLANEOUS LISTINGS

PALM BEACH GARDENS. *Catholic Charities of the Diocese of Palm Beach, Inc.*, 34410-9650. Mailing Address: P.O. Box 109650, 34410-9650. 9995 N. Military Tr., West Palm Beach, 34410.

Con El, Inc., 33410-9650. Mailing Address: P.O. Box 109650, 33410-9650.

Diocesan Council of Catholic Women, 33410-9650. Mailing Address: 17574 Lake Park Rd., Boca Raton, 33487. Rev. Clemens Hammerschmitt, Diocesan Moderator; Mrs. Cindy Nau, Pres.

Diocesan Health Plan Trust, 33410. Mailing Address: P.O. Box 109650, 33410-9650. Most Rev. J. Keith Symons; Rev. Francis J. Lechiara, Chm.

Diocesan Pension Plan Trust, 33410. Mailing Address: P.O. Box 109650, 33410.
Members: Most Rev. J. Keith Symons; Rev. Francis J. Lechiara, Chm.

Diocesan Property & Liability Insurance Committee, 34410-9650. Mailing Address: P.O. Box 109650, 33410-9650. Rev. Richard Murphy, Chm.

Diocese of Palm Beach Endowment Trust, 33410-9650. Mailing Address: P.O. Box 109650, 33410-9650.

The Florida Catholic of Palm Beach, Inc., 33410-9650. Mailing Address: P.O. Box 109650, 33410-9650.

BOCA RATON. *Christ Child Society of Boca Raton*, P.O. Box 811025, 33481-1025.

BOYNTON BEACH. *St. Vincent de Paul Regional Seminary Endowment Trust*, 10701 S. Military Tr., 33436.

JENSEN BEACH. *Villa Assumpta, Inc.*, 2539 N.E. Mission Dr., 9-8, 34957. Tel: 561-334-0009; Fax: 561-334-2168. Ms. Linda Matz, Res. Mgr.

LAKE WORTH. *Villa Madonna*, 4809 Lake Worth Rd., 33463-3455.

NORTH PALM BEACH. *Christ Child Society of Palm Beach*, P.O. Box 14441, 33408.

PALM CITY. *St. Raphael Family Life Center*, 9440 S.W. 48th Ave., 34991. Tel: 561-781-0350.

PORT ST. LUCIE. *District Council of the Treasure Coast, Society of St. Vincent de Paul*, 1063 S.E. McCoy Ave., 34953. Tel: 561-336-9054.

RIVIERA BEACH. *Society of St. Vincent de Paul, District Council*, 2567 Old Dixie Hwy., 33404. Tel: 561-845-0562. Mr. Joseph Kaht, Contact Person.

Villa Franciscan, Inc., 2101 Avenue F, 33404. Tel: 561-840-0444; Fax: 561-840-9444. Mr. William Kerr, Mgr.

VERO BEACH. *Society of St. Vincent de Paul, St. Sebastian Conference*, 5480 85th St., 32967. Tel: 561-589-3338. Mr. Paul Ouellette, Contact Person.

WEST PALM BEACH. *Emmaus Residence*, P.O. Box 247, 33402-8999. Tel: 561-863-9227; Fax: 561-863-1680. Rev. John J. Edwards, S.J., Dir.

RELIGIOUS INSTITUTES OF MEN REPRESENTED IN THE DIOCESE

For further details refer to the corresponding bracketed number in the Religious Institutes of Men or Women section.

[0200]—*Benedictine Monks.*—O.S.B.
[1330]—*Congregation of Mission.*—C.M.
[1030]—*Congregation of St. Paul.*—C.S.P.
[1000]—*Congregation of the Passionists.*—C.P.
[0480]—*Conventual Franciscans.*—O.F.M.Conv.
[0520]—*Franciscan Friars.* (Holy Name Prov.).—O.F.M.
[0520]—*Franciscan Friars.* (Immaculate Conception Prov.).—O.F.M.
[0740]—*Marians of the Immaculate Conception.*—M.I.C.
[1210]—*Missionaries of St. Charles-Scalabrinians.*—C.S.
[0870]—*Monfort Missionaries.*—S.M.M.
[0270]—*Order of Carmelites.*—O.Carm.
[0910]—*Order of Mary Immaculate.*—O.M.I.
[1310]—*Order of the Most Holy Trinity.*—O.S.S.T.
[1050]—*Pontifical Institute for Foreign Missions.*—P.I.M.E.
[1190]—*Salesians of Don Bosco.*—S.D.B.
[0110]—*Society of African Missions.*—S.M.A.
[0690]—*Society of Jesus.*—S.J.
[0370]—*Society of St. Columban.*—S.S.C.

RELIGIOUS INSTITUTES OF WOMEN REPRESENTED IN THE DIOCESE

[0130]—*Apostles of the Sacred Heart of Jesus.*—A.S.C.J.
[0330]—*Carmelite Sisters for the Aged and Infirm.*—O.Carm.
[0685]—*Claretian Missionary Sisters.*—R.M.I.
[]—*Congregation of Sisters of the Passion.*—C.P.
[1070-03]—*Dominican Sisters.* (Sinsinawa, WI).—O.P.
[1070-13]—*Dominican Sisters.*—O.P.
[1070-06]—*Dominican Sisters.* (Newburgh, NY).—O.P.
[1070-16]—*Dominican Sisters.* (Ossining, NY).—O.P.
[1070-22]—*Dominican Sisters.* (Fall River, MA).—O.P.
[]—*Dominican Sisters of St. Catherine de Ricci.*—O.P.
[1140]—*Eucharistic Missionaries of St. Dominic.*—O.P.
[]—*Franciscan Sisters.* (Milwaukee, WI).—O.S.F.
[1180]—*Franciscan Sisters of Allegany, NY.*—O.S.F.
[1310]—*Franciscan Sisters of Little Falls.*—O.S.F.
[1845]—*Guadalupana Missionaries of the Holy Spirit.*—M.G.Sp.S.
[]—*Hermitage of Diocese of Palm Beach.*
[2575]—*Institute of Sisters of Mercy of the Americas.*—R.S.M.
[]—*Marians of the Immaculate Conception.*—M.I.C.
[3760]—*Order of St. Clare.*—O.S.C.
[3460]—*Religious of Mary Immaculate.*—R.M.I.
[3110]—*Religious of Our Lady of the Cenacle.*—R.C.
[3465]—*Religious of the Sacred Heart of Mary.*—R.S.H.M.
[2970]—*School Sisters of Notre Dame.*—S.S.N.D.
[1680]—*School Sisters of St. Francis.*—S.S.S.F.
[0440]—*Sisters of Charity of Cincinnati, OH.*—S.C.
[0500]—*Sisters of Charity of Nazareth.*—S.C.N.
[0430]—*Sisters of Charity of the Blessed Virgin Mary.*—B.V.M.
[2110]—*Sisters of Humility of Mary.*—H.M.
[2560]—*Sisters of Mary Reparatrix.*—S.M.R.
[3000]—*Sisters of Notre Dame de Namur.*—S.N.D.deN.
[3340]—*Sisters of Providence.*—S.P.
[0590]—*Sisters of St. Elizabeth, Convent Station.*—S.C.
[1800]—*Sisters of St. Francis of the Third Order Regular.* (Williamsville, NY).—O.S.F.
[3840]—*Sisters of St. Joseph of Carondelet.*—C.S.J.
[]—*Sisters of St. Joseph of St. Augustine.*—S.S.J.
[0260]—*Sisters of the Blessed Sacrament.*—S.B.S.
[1990]—*Sisters of the Holy Names of Jesus and Mary.*—S.N.J.M.
[]—*Sisters of the Most Holy Soul of Jesus.*
[2150]—*Sisters, Servants of the Immaculate Heart of Mary.*—I.H.M.
[2490]—*Society of Catholic Medical Missionaries.*—S.C.M.M.

DIOCESAN CEMETERIES

WEST PALM BEACH. *Our Lady Queen of Peace Catholic Cemetery, Inc.*, 10941 Southern Blvd., 33406. Tel: 561-793-0711. Mrs. Marian Harris, Admin.

NECROLOGY

† LeSage, Joseph Vincent, Sebastian, FL, St. Sebastian. —Died Nov. 29, 1997.

† McGrenehan, Rev. Msgr. Bernard Joseph, Pastor Emeritus, Palm Beach, FL, St. Edward. —Died Aug. 31, 1997.

Diocese of Paterson

(Dioecesis Patersonensis)

Most Reverend

FRANK J. RODIMER, D.D., J.C.D.

Bishop of Paterson; ordained May 19, 1951; appointed Bishop of Paterson December 13, 1977; ordained and installed February 28, 1978. *Res., 178 Derrom Ave., Paterson, NJ, 07504.*

ESTABLISHED DECEMBER 9, 1937.

Square Miles 1,214.

Comprises the Counties of Passaic, Morris and Sussex in the State of New Jersey.

For legal titles of parishes and diocesan institutions, consult the Chancery Office.

Diocesan Center: 777 Valley Rd., Clifton, NJ, 07013. Tel.: 973-777-8818; Fax: 973-777-8976.

STATISTICAL OVERVIEW

Personnel	
Bishop	1
Abbots	2
Retired Abbots	5
Priests: Diocesan Active in Diocese	176
Priests: Active Outside Diocese	24
Priests: Retired, Sick or Absent	63
Number of Diocesan Priests	263
Religious Priests in Diocese	194
Extern Priests in Diocese	18
Permanent Deacons in Diocese	138
Total Brothers	42
Total Sisters	944
Parishes	
Parishes	111
With Resident Pastor:	
Resident Diocesan Priests	98
Resident Religious Priests	12
Without Resident Pastor:	
Administered by Priests	1
Pastoral Centers	5
Professional Ministry Personnel:	
Brothers	2
Sisters	53
Lay Ministers	117
Welfare	
Catholic Hospitals	3
Total Assisted	701,290
Homes for the Aged	9
Total Assisted	470
Residential Care of Children	2
Total Assisted	56
Day Care and Extended Day Care Centers	20
Total Assisted	900
Specialized Homes	2
Total Assisted	16,000
Special Centers for Social Services	13
Total Assisted	37,500
Residential Care of Disabled	8
Total Assisted	60
Educational	
Diocesan Students in Other Seminaries	9
Seminaries, Religious	4
Students Religious	8
Total Seminarians	17
Colleges and Universities	2
Total Students	1,793
High Schools, Diocesan and Parish	5
Total Students	2,424
High Schools, Private	5
Total Students	1,547
Elementary Schools, Diocesan and Parish	58
Total Students	15,946
Elementary Schools, Private	3
Total Students	578
Catechesis/Religious Education:	
High School Students	9,281
Elementary Students	33,290
Total Students Under Catholic Instruction	64,876
Teachers in the Diocese:	
Priests	37
Brothers	19
Sisters	206
Lay Teachers	1,171
Vital Statistics	
Receptions into the Church:	
Infant Baptism Totals	8,815
Adult Baptism Totals	166
Received into Full Communion	319
First Communions	7,500
Confirmations	4,163
Marriages:	
Catholic	1,616
Interfaith	557
Total Marriages	2,173
Deaths	3,716
Total Catholic Population	380,293
Total Population	1,055,369

Former Bishops—Most Rev. THOMAS H. MCLAUGHLIN, S.T.D., LL.D., cons. July 25, 1935; transferred to Paterson, Dec. 16, 1937; died March 17, 1947.—Most Rev. THOMAS A. BOLAND, S.T.D., cons. July 25, 1940; transferred to Paterson, June 21, 1947; transferred to Newark as Archbishop, Nov. 15, 1952; died March 16, 1979.—Most Rev. JAMES A. MCNULTY, D.D., appt. Auxiliary Bishop of Newark, Aug. 2, 1947; cons. Oct. 7, 1947; appt. Bishop of Paterson, April 9, 1953; transferred to Diocese of Buffalo, Feb. 12, 1963; died Sept. 4, 1972.—Most Rev. JAMES J. NAVAGH, D.D., cons. Sept. 24, 1952; appt. Bishop of Ogdensburg, May 8, 1957; transferred to Bishop of Paterson, Feb. 12, 1963; died Oct. 2, 1965.—Most Rev. LAWRENCE B. CASEY, D.D., appt. Auxiliary Bishop of Rochester, Feb. 10, 1953; cons. May 5, 1953; appt. Bishop of Paterson, March 9, 1966; died June 15, 1977.

Vicar General—Rev. Msgr. JOSEPH R. BRESTEL.

Vicar for Administration, Moderator of the Curia—Rev. Msgr. HERBERT K. TILLYER.

Vicar for Planning and Priorities—Rev. Msgr. JAMES T. MAHONEY.

Vicar for Retired Priests—Rev. RAYMOND LOPATESKY.

Vicar for Religious—Sr. JOAN KERWIN LAWLER, C.S.J.P.

Vicar for Deacons—Rev. ROBERT DIACHEK.

Deans—Rev. Msgr. THOMAS J. COLETTA, Paterson; Rev. VICTOR J. MAZZA, Clifton; Rev. Msgr. JOHN PODGORNY, Passaic; Rev. Msgr. EUGENE BOLAND, Mid Passaic County; Rev. FRANK MCHUGH, O.F.M., Northern Passaic County; Rev. WILLIAM NAUGHTON, Southwestern Morris County; Rev. Msgr. RONALD AMANDOLARE, Southeastern Morris County; Rev. MARTIN MCDONNELL, Eastern Morris County; Rev. Msgr. JOHN J. CARROLL, Northeastern Morris County; Rev. JOSEPH J. GOODE, Northern Morris County; Rev. Msgr. JOHN FITZPATRICK, Western Morris County; Rev. WILLIAM P. STOBER, Sussex County.

Diocesan Center—777 Valley Rd., Clifton, 07013. Tel: 973-777-8818; Fax: 973-777-8976. Office Hours: Mon.-Fri. 9-4:30. All mail should be addressed to this office.

Chancellor—Rev. Msgr. HERBERT K. TILLYER.

Vice Chancellors—Rev. T. MARK CONDON; Sr. JOAN KERWIN LAWLER, C.S.J.P.

Archivist—Rev. RAYMOND J. KUPKE.

Secretary to the Bishop—Rev. T. MARK CONDON.

Admin. Asst. to the Bishop—Mrs. KIT SPRINGER.

Admin. Asst. to the Chancellor—Mrs. GRACE MAZZA.

Secretary to the Vice Chancellor—Mrs. MARY PORTELLI.

Diocesan Counsel—Mr. JAMES EVERS.

Diocesan Tribunal—

Judicial Vicar—Rev. EDWARD J. KURTYKA, J.C.D.

Adjutant Judicial Vicars—Revs. JOSEPH T. ANGINOLI, J.C.L.; JOHN E. HART, J.C.L.

Advocates—Revs. JOHN T. CONNOLLY, M.Div.; MARK A. MANCINI, M.Div.; MICHAEL BURKE, S.T.M., J.D.

Auditors—Rev. PAUL IOVINO; Miss ANN SMITH HUGHES.

Defenders of the Bond—Rev. Msgr. KENNETH E. LASCH, J.C.D.; Revs. T. MARK CONDON, J.C.L.; EDWARD J. HINDS, J.C.L.; GEORGE F. HUNDT, J.C.L.; Sr. JOAN KERWIN LAWLER, C.S.J.P.

Pro-Synodal Judges—Rev. Msgr. JOHN J. CARROLL, Ed.D.; Rev. JOHN T. CATOIR, J.C.D.; Rev. Msgr. JOHN J. DEMKOVICH; Rev. Msgr. JOHN H. DERICKS; Rev. Msgr. HERBERT K. TILLYER, M.Ch.A.; Rev. Msgr. THOMAS J. TRAPASSO, S.T.L.; Rev. REGIS P. WALLACE, O.S.B.

Administrative Assistants and Notaries—Mrs. JULIE BARAM; Mrs. PATRICIA CZERNIEWSKI; Mrs. ROSE LUCIGNANI.

Consulting Psychologist—EDMUND J. RUBIN, Ph.D.; JAMES A. SAVAGE, Psy.D.

Presbyteral Council—Rev. Msgr. JOSEPH R. BRESTEL; Rev. Msgr. JOHN J. CARROLL; Rev. Msgr. PAUL KNAUER; Rev. Msgr. HERBERT K. TILLYER; Revs. HERNAN ARIAS; MICHAEL J. DRURY; Rev. Msgr. JAMES L. FALLON; Revs. GEORGE F. HUNDT; PAUL S. MANNING; PAUL DALY; MARTIN G. GLYNN; RICHARD RENTO; JOSEPH SANTA-BIBIANA, S.D.B.; ROBERT WISNIEFSKI.

College of Consultors—Rev. Msgr. JOSEPH R. BRESTEL; Rev. Msgr. PAUL F. KNAUER; Rev. Msgr. HERBERT K. TILLYER; Revs. HERNAN ARIAS; MICHAEL J. DRURY; Rev. Msgr. JAMES L. FALLON; Revs. PAUL S. MANNING; GEORGE F. HUNDT; PAUL DALY; MARTIN G. GLYNN; RICHARD RENTO; ROBERT WISNIEFSKI.

Diocesan Secretariats

Communications Secretariat—Mr. VICTOR F. WINKLER, *869 Broadway, Paterson, 07514.* Tel: 973-278-3491; Fax: 973-278-3202.

"The Beacon"—Diocesan Newspaper, Mr. VICTOR F. WINKLER, Editor-in-Chief; Mr. RICHARD A. SOKERKA, Gen. Mgr.; Mr. JOSEPH TINTLE, News Editor, *597 Valley Rd., P.O. Box 1887, Clifton, 07015.* Tel: 973-279-8845.

Office of Evangelization / Communications—Rev. JOHN T. CATOIR, Dir., *63 Monroe St., Passaic, 07055.* Tel: 973-777-0303; Fax: 973-742-5033.

Communications Office—MARIANNA THOMPSON, Dir., *597 Valley Rd., P.O. Box 1887, Clifton, 07015.* Tel: 973-278-3202; Fax: 973-279-2265.

Secretariat For Parish Life—Mr. PHILIP A. RUSSO, Exec. Sec., *777 Valley Rd., Clifton, 07013.* Tel: 973-777-8818.

Office of Family / Respect Life—Mrs. MARY LYNN TOWNSLEY, Consultant.

Project Rachael Post-Abortion Helpline—Tel: 800-886-6449; 973-777-6449.

Engaged Encounter—Rev. ROBERT J. MITCHELL, Spiritual Dir. Tel: 973-347-3190. Coordinators: TODD SCHMIDT; DEBBIE SCHMIDT. Tel: 973-726-7016. Registration Couple: DAVID DE MARTINO; LINDA DE MARTINO. Tel: 973-764-5711.

Natural Family Planning—Rev. PAUL DUGGAN, Spiritual Dir. Chair Couple: FRANK TRACEY; DIANA TRACEY. Tel: 973-398-6246. Registration Couple: ANTHONY HOFFMAN; SHARON HOFFMAN. Tel: 973-785-4372.

Office of Parish Catechetics—Mr. THOMAS BROWN, Consultant.

Catechetical Leaders Association—Ms. LIZ TOMLINSON. Tel: 973-548-6028.

Office of Ministry Among Hispanics—Vacant; Ms. IVANNIA VEGA, Consultant for Hispanic Youth & Family Ministry.

Commission for Hispanic Catholic Ministry—Rev. HERNAN ARIAS, Chm. Tel: 973-345-4070.

Office of Worship and Spirituality—Dr. PATRICIA BARTLE.

Liturgical Commission—Rev. ELIAS LORENZO, O.S.B., Chm. Tel: 973-538-3231.

Office of Youth Ministry—Mr. PHILIP RUSSO, Consultant.

Catholic Scouting—Rev. WAYNE VARGA. Tel: 973-334-2090.

Office for Campus Ministry—Rev. LOUIS J. SCURTI, Coord., Catholic Campus Ministers. Tel: 973-595-6184.

Ecumenical Officer—Rev. CHARLES J. PARR, *737 Valley Rd., Clifton, 07013.*

Media Resourcing—Mrs. GINGER MOLL.

Related Organizations—

Catholic Deaf Society—Rev. JOSEPH J. GOODE, Moderator. Tel: 973-627-0422. Rev. Msgr. THOMAS J. TRAPASSO, Asst. Moderator.

Charismatic Renewal—Rev. BRENDAN J. MURRAY, Liaison. Tel: 973-627-0313.

English Cursillos—Ms. MARY ANN ROGERS, Lay Dir. Spiritual Advisors: Rev. JOHN A. CONNELL; Deacon JOSEPH PARLAPIANO. Tel: 908-637-6174. Sr. MARIANNE JOYCE, S.L.

Spanish Cursillos—Mr. MANUEL SANTANA, Lay Dir. Tel: 973-595-9327. Revs. PETER NAPOLI, O.F.M.Cap. Tel: 973-742-2142. JOSEPH SANTA-BIBIANA, S.D.B. Tel: 973-742-9695.

World Wide Marriage Encounter—Exec. Couple: KATHY FRIEL; TOM FRIEL. Tel: 800-499-6552. Registration Couple: EILEEN PEREZ; RALPH PEREZ. Tel: 800-499-6552.

Pastoral Administration

Division of Clergy and Personnel—

Clergy Personnel Office—Rev. Msgr. THOMAS ZAZZELLA, Dir.; Mrs. ROSEMARY J. DONNELLY, Admin. Asst., *737 Valley Rd., Clifton, 07013.* Tel: 973-777-2955.

Deacon Internship Program—Rev. FRANCIS J. DUFFY, Dir., *6 Sussex Ave., Morristown, 07960.* Tel: 973-538-4851.

Ministry for Priestly Formation and Education—Rev. CHARLES J. PARR, Dir., *737 Valley Rd., Clifton, 07013.* Tel: 973-777-5651.

Mission Office—Rev. Msgr. JOHN J. DEMKOVICH, Dir.; Mrs. ELEANOR MATAS, Office Mgr., *24 DeGrasse St., Paterson, 07505.* Tel: 973-278-3491.

Office of Health Care Ministry—Rev. ROBERT M. DIACHEK, Dir., *74 Kahdena Rd., Morristown, 07960.* Tel: 973-538-3500.

Office of the Permanent Diaconate—Rev. ROBERT M. DIACHEK, Vicar, *74 Kahdena Rd., Morristown, 07960.* Tel: 973-538-6849.

Vicar for Religious Communities—Sr. JOAN KERWIN LAWLER, C.S.J.P., Vicar. Tel: 973-777-8818.

Vocations Office—Rev. PAUL S. MANNING, Dir., *737 Valley Rd., Clifton, 07013.* Tel: 973-472-2812.

Division of Finance and Budget—

Business Office—Mr. WILLIAM H. HINKES, Finance Officer; Mr. WAYNE G. LONG, Business Mgr.; Mr. JOSEPH LIPARI, Controller; Miss. DEBORAH MINNICH, Bookkeeper; Mrs. JOYCE LARSEN, Sec.; Mr. TIMOTHY POTTER, Dir., Devel., *777 Valley Rd., Clifton, 07013.*

Diocesan Facilities Manager—Mr. JAMES FIERRO.

Insurance Office—Mrs. JAYNE CICCARELLI, Employee Benefits; Mrs. DIVINA RAMOS, Property-Liability-Auto Claims; Mrs. DENISE GLICKMAN, Claims Adjuster, *777 Valley Rd., Clifton, 07013.* Tel: 973-777-8818.

Buildings and Sites Commission—Rev. Msgr. GEORGE DUDAK, Chm., *Rte. 24, Schooleys Mountain, 07870.* Tel: 908-876-4395.

Diocesan Cemetery Office—Rev. Msgr. HERBERT K. TILLYER, Dir.; Mr. JOHN M. CAVANAUGH, Asst. Dir., *58 McLean Blvd., Paterson, 07513.* Tel: 973-279-2900.

School Division—Mr. FRANK PETRUCELLI, Supt.; Sr. MARY LOU LAFFERTY, O.S.F., Asst. Supt., Elementary Education; Sr. DOROTHY BANASHAK, S.S.C., Asst. Supt., Secondary Education and Governmental Programs; Sr. URSULA BUTLER, O.S.B., Asst. Supt., Elementary Education; Sr. NANCY GRASSIA, O.S.F., Asst. Supt., Planning and Research; Sr. MAUREEN SULLIVAN, S.C., Asst. Supt., Elementary Education; Mr. PATRICK PEACE, Dir., School Finance; Mr. EDWIN PETERSON, Education Council Pres.; Ms. KAREN FASANELLA, Elementary Principals' Assoc. Pres., *777 Valley Rd., Clifton, 07013.* Tel: 201-777-8818.

Social Ministries—Mr. JOSEPH F. DUFFY, Exec. Sec., *476 17th Ave., Paterson, 07504.* Tel: 973-523-7361.

Catholic Family and Community Services—Mr. JOSEPH F. DUFFY, Exec. Dir.; Ms. PATRICIA DERDERIAN, Admin. Asst.; Ms. VIRGINIA GROSSI, Staff Attorney; Mr. ROBERT JACOBS, Controller, *24 De Grasse St., Paterson, 07501.* Tel: 973-279-7100.

Aging Services—Ms. PATRICIA REIDY, Dir., *24 DeGrasse St., Paterson, 07501.* Tel: 973-279-7100.

Family Services—Rev. THOMAS MCGRATH, Dir., *476 17th Ave., Paterson, 07504.* Tel: 973-523-9595.

Friendship Corner—Ms. JANET TERRY, Dir., *Alabama Ave., Paterson, 07509.* Tel: 973-684-3742.

Parish Social Ministries—Mr. THOMAS MCCANN, Dir., *476 17th Ave., Paterson, 07504.* Tel: 973-527-7361.

Hispanic Information Center—Mr. LORENZO HERNANDEZ, Dir., *270 Passaic St., Passaic, 07055.* Tel: 973-779-7022.

Immigration and Refugee Services—Ms. MAI LIEU, Dir., *24 DeGrasse St., Paterson, 07501.* Tel: 973-279-7100.

Italian Catholic Center—Miss PHILOMENA DESOPO, Dir., *24 DeGrasse St., Paterson, 07501.* Tel: 973-278-4955.

Mt. St. Joseph's Children Center—Sr. DOROTHY SHEAHAN, S.C., *124 Shepherd Ln., Totowa, 07512.* Tel: 973-595-5720.

Multi-Lingual Center—Ms. ROSE KARDASHIAN, Dir., *24 DeGrasse St., Paterson, 07501.* Tel: 973-279-7100.

The Palloti Center—Miss KATHERINE CIRSTOV, Dir., *44 Ward St., Paterson, 07051.* Tel: 973-523-5144.

Partnership for Social Services—Sr. THOMASINA GEBHARD, S.S.M., Dir., *48 Wyker Rd., Franklin, 07416.* Tel: 973-827-4702.

Father English Multi-Purpose Community Center—Deacon ROBERT VESOTA, Exec. Dir., *435 Main St., Paterson, 07501.* Tel: 973-881-0280.

Pre School Day Care Center Programs—A Child's World-El Mundo del Nino; EUNICE RAMIREZ, Dir. A Child's Time-El Tiempo del Nino; LILA BANKS, Dir., *433 Main St., Paterson, 07501.* Tel: 973-278-3110. El Mundo de Colores; LAURA ZARIFE, Dir., *44 Ward St., Paterson, 07505.* Tel: 973-523-0919.

Youth Haven—Shelter-Crisis Intervention, Ms. DENISE MEZA, Dir., *212 Slater St., Paterson, 07501.* Tel: 973-881-1611.

Catholic Social Services of Morris County, Inc. (Hope House)—Mrs. DIANNE KWIATKOWSKI, Exec. Dir.; Ms. REBECCA JACOB, Asst. to Exec. Dir.; Mrs. CAROL STOLZ, Coord., Fix-It Program; Mr. NELSON ROBINSON, Coord., Alcoholism Programs; Mr. MICHAEL DAVID-WILSON, Dir., Aids Center; Mr. KARL MANGER, Asst. Dir., Aids Center; Mrs. MARY MURDTER, Coord., Home Sharing Program; GAIL CASSESE, Dir., Substance Abuse Program; Ms. JEANINE DAKIN, Dir., Finance and Admin.; Ms. FRANCES CHIODO, Coord., Chore Program; MARTHA OSTER, Dir., Gen. Counseling; Mrs. DULCE B. HALEY, Clinical Supvr.; Ms. SHARON MATUSA, Coord., AIDS Pastoral Care, *19-21 Belmont Ave., Dover, 07801.* Tel: 973-361-5555.

Department for Persons with Disabilities—Mr. THOMAS A. BARRETT, Exec. Dir.; Ms. JULIE TATTI, Assoc. Dir. Quality Improvement Specialists: Ms. JENNIFER MURPHY; Ms. BARBARA OCKER; Mr. SCOTT MILLIKEN, Staff Trainer; Sr. JOAN KATHLEEN GERCKE, S.S.J., Dir., Human Resources; Mr. ROCCO ZAPPILE, Comptroller, *1049 Weldon Rd., Oak Ridge, 07438.* Tel: 973-697-4394.

Group Homes—

Murray House—Ms. DEBBIE LICHTER, Dir., *86 Allwood Pl., Clifton, 07015.* Tel: 973-470-5694.

Wayne Marathon House—Mrs. JOANN VALLES, Dir., *648 Black Oak Ridge Rd., Wayne, 07470.* Tel: 973-628-9074.

Finnegan House—Ms. BETTY PORMAN, Dir., *1049 Weldon Rd., Oak Ridge, 07438.* Tel: 973-697-1246.

Alexander House—Ms. ARLENE GROSENBECK, Dir., *1049 Weldon Rd., Oak Ridge, 07438.* Tel: 973-697-1812.

Columbus House—Ms. CHERYL SLATE, Dir., *1049 Weldon Rd., Oak Ridge, 07438.* Tel: 973-697-1644.

Wehrlen House—Ms. MARGARET DOYLE, Dir., *18 Bisset Dr., West Milford, 07480.* Tel: 973-208-1883.

Gruenert Adult Training Center—Mrs. KATHY DE YOUNG, Dir., *Belmont Ave., Dover, 07801.* Tel: 973-328-7479.

Basile Apartment—Mrs. GRISELDA MANJARRES, Dir., *Kings Arms Apts., Byrne Ct., Wayne, 07470.* Tel: 973-633-1809.

Keleher Apartments—Ms. PAMELA VAN ACK, Dir., *67B Pike Dr., Wayne, 07470.* Tel: 973-697-4394.

Straight and Narrow, Inc.—Rev. NORMAN O'CONNOR, C.S.P., Exec. Dir. LORNA TONGARA, Exec. Asst.; Dr. RICHARD GUILD, Dir., Adult Residential Treatment; Mrs. KAREN BAILEY, Dir., Alpha Program; REBECCA GRANEY, Dir., Meadowview Program; Secaucus, NJ: Ms. PHYLLIS ANDERSON, R.N., Supt., Nurses; Dr. RICHARD GUILD, Dir., Cedar Out-Patient Clinic; Bro. KENNETH HARDING, O.F.M., Dir., Juvenile Treatment Unit; Revs. MICHAEL MOORE, (YAK) Dir. Pastoral Care Unit; GREG DROGON, Counselor; THOMAS G. RAINFORTH, Admissions, *296 Straight St., Paterson, 07501.* Tel: 973-345-6000.

McNulty Half-Way House—Mr. ANGELO ZECCA, Dir., *101 Cedar St., Paterson, 07501.* Tel: 973-279-7003.

Medical Day Care Center—HENRIETTA LEMON, R.N., Dir., *180 E. 19th St., Paterson.*

Methadone Maintenance Centers—JAMES GUINN, Dir., *Bergen Pines Hospital, E. Ridgewood Ave., Paramus, Bergen Pines Hospital, 75 E. Broadway, Hackensack.*

Affiliated Organizations—

Apostleship of Prayer—Rev. CHRISTOPHER DILELLA, Dir., *26 Green Village Rd., Madison, 07040.* Tel: 973-377-4000.

Diocesan Council of Catholic Women—Rev. Msgr. JOSEPH A. CIAMPAGLIO, Dir., *152 Mt. Pleasant Ave., Dover, 07801.* Tel: 973-366-7095. Mrs. KATHLEEN LEVENDUSKY, *126 Day St., Clifton, 07011.* Tel: 973-772-5918.

Justice and Peace Commission—Rev. PATRICK RICE.

Diocesan Holy Name Federation—Mr. FRANK STEINER, Pres.

Legion of Mary—Rev. Msgr. JOHN J. DEMKOVICH, Spiritual Dir. GEORGE A. PATINO, Pres., *63 Monroe St., Passaic, 07055.* Tel: 973-779-0427.

Priests Eucharistic League—Rev. CHRISTOPHER DILELLA, Dir., *26 Green Village Rd., Madison, 07040.* Tel: 973-377-4000.

Commission for Black Catholic Ministries—Mr. BRUCE B. LAWSON, Pres. Tel: 973-898-9260.

Commission for Hispanic Catholic Ministries—Rev. HERNAN ARIAS, Chm.

CLERGY, PARISHES, MISSIONS AND PAROCHIAL SCHOOLS

CITY OF PATERSON

(Passaic County)

1—CATHEDRAL OF ST. JOHN THE BAPTIST (1820), Rev. Msgr. Mark J. Giordani; Revs. Gilberto Gutierrez (Colombia); Luis A. Rendon (Colombia). In res., Deacon Manuel Santiago.

Res., 381 Grand St., 07505. Tel: 973-345-4070; Fax: 973-345-7831. [CEM]

School—Pope John Paul II School. See Elementary Schools, Diocesan under Institutions Located in the Diocese for details.

2—ST. AGNES (1883), Rev. Luciano Cruz; Deacons Percy Silva; Pedro Acevedo.

Res., 681 Main St., 07503. Tel: 973-279-0250; Fax: 973-357-1218.

3—ST. ANTHONY'S (1909) (Italian), Revs. Joseph Santa-Bibiana, S.D.B.; Kenneth Shaw, S.D.B.; Vincent Duffy, S.D.B.

Res., 138 Beech St., 07501. Tel: 973-742-9695; Fax: 973-881-0522.
School—(1921), 144 Beech St., 07501. Tel: 973-279-3510; Fax: 973-523-1757.
Salesian Sisters, Daughters of Mary Help of Christians 5; Lay Teachers 10; Students 290.

4—BLESSED SACRAMENT (1911) (Italian), Rev. Richard A. Rusconi. In res., Rev. John F. Heusser.
Res., 224 E. 18th St., 07524. Tel: 973-523-5002; Fax: 973-523-3766.
School—(1953), 2896-Sixth Ave., 07524. Tel: 973-278-8787; Fax: 973-278-6436.
Maestre Pie Filippini (Religious Teachers Filippini) 3; Lay Teachers 12; Students 264.

5—ST. BONAVENTURE (1877), Revs. Alvin V. Faddish, O.F.M.; John T. Piccione, O.F.M.; Deacon Joseph Balough. In res., Rev. Angelus P. Gambatese, O.F.M.
Res., 174 Ramsey St., 07501. Tel: 973-279-1016; Fax: 973-279-2507.

6—ST. CASIMIR'S (1911) (Lithuanian), Rev. Msgr. Anthony Bertasius, Admin.
Res., 147 Montgomery St., 07501. Tel: 973-279-1922.

7—ST. GEORGE (1897), Revs. Nicholas G. Bozza; Jose Javier Nieves; Deacon William Hussey. In res., Rev. Thomas G. Rainforth.
Res., 408 Getty Ave., 07503. Tel: 973-742-0350; Fax: 973-754-0657.
School—(1897), 30 Michigan Ave., 07503. Tel: 973-684-6754; Fax: 973-684-1988.
Lay Teachers 12; Students 380.

8—ST. GERARD MAJELLA (1962), Revs. George F. Hundt; John P. Hanley; Deacon Joseph Sisco.
Res., 501 W. Broadway, 07522. Tel: 973-595-8446; Fax: 973-790-0778.
School—(1965).
Salesian Sisters of St. John Bosco 4; Lay Teachers 8; Students 252.

9—ST. JOSEPH'S (1867), Revs. Robert W. Wisniefski; Gregory Colucci.
Res., 399 Market St., 07501. Tel: 973-278-0030.
School—Pope John Paul II School. See Elementary Schools, Diocesan under Institutions Located in the Diocese for details.

10—ST. MARY'S (1873). (Auxilium Christianorum). Revs. Joseph G. Buffardi; Jorge Rodriguez, O.F.M.Conv.
Res., 410 Union Ave., 07502. Tel: 973-790-8651.
School—(1874), 196 Wayne Ave., 07502.
Salesian Sisters of St. John Bosco 5; Lay Teachers 11; Students 370.

11—ST. MICHAEL THE ARCHANGEL (1903) (Italian), Rev. Joseph J. Orlandi. In res., Rev. Greg Drogon.
Res., 70 Cianci St., 07501. Tel: 973-523-8413; Fax: 973-253-4279.

12—OUR LADY OF LOURDES (1882), Rev. Peter Napoli, O.F.M.Cap.
Res., 440 River St., 07524. Tel: 973-742-2142; Fax: 973-345-9136.
School—(1883), Tel: 973-278-0164; Fax: 973-278-3030.
Lay Teachers 9; Students 268.

13—OUR LADY OF POMPEI (1916) (Italian), Rev. Sal J. Panagia; Deacon Henry Gallo.
Res., 70 Murray Ave., 07501. Tel: 973-742-1969; Fax: 973-742-1335.

14—OUR LADY OF VICTORIES (1882), Rev. Msgr. Thomas J. Coletta; Deacon Leo Gardner.
Res., 100 Fair St., 07501. Tel: 973-279-0487.

15—ST. STEPHEN'S (1903) (Polish), Rev. John T. Connolly. In res., Rev. Francis Maliszewski.
Res., 86 Martin St., 07501. Tel: 973-742-2822.

16—ST. THERESE (1926), Revs. Charles J. Waller; Juan Carlos Ruiz.
Res., 80-13th Ave., 07504. Tel: 973-881-0400.
School—(1953), 765 14th Ave., 07504. Tel: 973-278-4135. Deacon Nicholas Varsalona, Prin.
Lay Teachers 11; Students 395.

OUTSIDE THE CITY OF PATERSON

Andover, Sussex Co., Good Shepherd (1976), Rev. Richard A. Steiger; Deacons John S. Larkin; Joseph Hilber; Thomas Sullivan.
Office: Rte. 517 (Tranquility Rd.), P.O. Box 464, 07821. Tel: 973-786-6631; 786-5520 (Res.).

Boonton, Morris Co., Our Lady of Mount Carmel (1847), Rev. Edward J. Hinds; Deacon Barry Costello.
Res., 910 Birch St., 07005. Tel: 973-334-1017; Fax: 973-335-1833. [CEM]
School—(1868), 205 Oak St., 07005. Tel: 973-334-2777.
Franciscan Sisters of Sacred Heart 1; Lay Teachers 8; Students 110.

SS. Cyril and Methodius (1907) (Slovak), Revs. James J. Termyna; Zdzislaw Nawrocki, S.Ch.; Sr. Ursala Carr, S.C., Pastoral Assoc.
Res., 215 Hill St., 07005. Tel: 973-334-0139; Fax: 973-402-9512. [CEM]

Branchville, Sussex Co., Our Lady Queen of Peace (1951), Rev. William P. Stober.
Res., 209 Rte. 206, 07826. Tel: 973-948-3185; Fax: 973-948-4799.

Budd Lake, Morris Co., St. Jude (1946), Revs. Robert J. Mitchell, Admin.; George Kuzhippallil; Deacon Anthony C. Siino.
Res., Mt. Olive Rd., 07828. Tel: 973-691-1561.

Butler, Morris Co., St. Anthony (1878), Revs. Frank McHugh, O.F.M.; John J. Doyle, O.F.M.; Sr. Cecilia Burns, S.C., Pastoral Assoc.
Res., 65 Bartholdi Ave., 07405. Tel: 973-838-0031; Fax: 973-838-0649. [CEM]
School—(1882), Tel: 973-838-0854; Fax: 973-838-1460.
Brothers 1; Lay Teachers 9; Students 201.
Parish House—71 Bartholdi Ave., 07405. Tel: 973-838-8585.

Cedar Knolls, Morris Co., Notre Dame of Mt. Carmel (1917), Revs. Jude S. Salus, O.S.B.; Donal R. Fox, O.S.B.; Bro. James Konchalski, O.S.B.
Res., 13 Halko Dr., 07927. Tel: 973-538-1358; Fax: 973-538-7403.

Chatham, Morris Co., St. Patrick's (1874), Rev. Msgr. Ronald A. Amandolare; Rev. Owen Moran; Deacons Joseph A. Wisneski; Francis P. McQuade.
Res., 85 Washington Ave., 07928. Tel: 973-635-0625; Fax: 973-635-0119.
School—(1872), 45 Chatham St., 07928. Tel: 973-635-4623; Fax: 973-635-2311.
Lay Teachers 24; Students 336.

Chatham Township, Morris Co., Corpus Christi (1966), Rev. Msgr. James Mahoney.
Res., 234 Southern Blvd., Chatham, 07928. Tel: 973-635-0070; Fax: 973-675-5518.

Chester, Morris Co., St. Lawrence the Martyr (1950), Rev. Msgr. P. Kevin Flanagan; Rev. Lancelot Reis; Deacon Frank Owens.
Res., Main St., P.O. Box 730, 07930. Tel: 908-879-5371.

Clifton, Passaic Co.,

1—SACRED HEART, (1897) (Italian), Rev. Msgr. Julian B. Varettoni; Revs. Andrew T. Perretta; Michael D. Joly.
Res., 145 Randolph Ave., 07011. Tel: 973-546-6012; Fax: 973-546-1814.
School—(1953), 43 Clifton Ave., 07011. Tel: 973-546-4695; Fax: 973-546-8774.
Lay Teachers 15; Students 282.

2—ST. ANDREW THE APOSTLE, (Allwood) (1938), Rev. Msgr. Peter J. McHugh; Rev. Philip Le Beau; Deacon Robert J. Ayers.
Res., 400 Mt. Prospect Ave., 07012. Tel: 973-779-6873; Fax: 973-779-0573.
School—(1953), 410 Mt. Prospect Ave., 07012. Tel: 973-473-3711; Fax: 973-473-6611.
Sisters of the Presentation 2; Lay Teachers 10; Students 241.

3—ST. BRENDAN, (1945), Revs. Richard G. Rento; Frank W. Weber. In res., Revs. Alan F. Savitt; Francis Matarazzo.
Res., 154 E. First St., 07011. Tel: 973-772-1115; Fax: 973-772-0497.
School—(1946), 155 E. First St., 07011. Tel: 973-772-1149; Fax: 973-773-1163.
Lay Teachers 12; Students 283.

4—ST. CLARE'S, (1913), Rev. Msgr. Brendan P. Madden; Rev. Thomas J. Fitzgerald.
Res., 69 Allwood Rd., 07014. Tel: 973-777-7588.
School—(1959), Tel: 973-777-7582; Fax: 973-473-0127.
Lay Teachers 17; Students 255.

5—SS. CYRIL AND METHODIUS, (1913) (Slovak), Rev. Msgr. Thomas J. Zazella; Deacon John Teresinski. In res., Revs. T. Mark Condon; Patrick O. Erwin.
Res., 218 Ackerman Ave., 07011. Tel: 973-546-4390; Fax: 973-546-3269.

6—ST. JOHN KANTY, (1930) (Polish), Revs. Alex B. Cymerman, O.F.M.Conv.; Waclaw Sokolowski, O.F.M.Conv.; Michael Zielke, O.F.M.Conv.; Deacon Robert Atilio.
Res., 49 Speer Ave., 07013. Tel: 973-779-4102; Fax: 973-779-2104.
School—(1958), 61 Wesley St., 07013. Tel: 973-471-9407; Fax: 973-773-0421.
Felician Sisters 1; Lay Teachers 13; Students 230.

7—ST. PAUL, (1914), Revs. Victor J. Mazza; Brian Flanagan; Deacon Joseph Puskas. In res., Rev. Robert K. Hooper.
Res., 124 Union Ave., 07011. Tel: 973-546-2746; Fax: 973-340-2083.
School—(1916), Tel: 973-546-2161; Fax: 973-546-0057.
Sisters of Charity 3; Lay Teachers 10; Students 200.

8—ST. PHILIP THE APOSTLE, (1943), Revs. Peter J. Doody; Robert J. Gordon; Deacon Gregory DeLorenzo.
Res., 797 Valley Rd., 07013. Tel: 973-779-6200; Fax: 973-779-2959.
School—(1954), Tel: 973-779-4700.
Franciscan Sisters of Peace 3; Lay Teachers 28; Students 604.

Convent Station, Morris Co., St. Thomas More (1966), Rev. Msgr. J. Francis Feenan. In res., Rev. Zbigniew Kluba.
Res., Madison Ave., Box 286-C, 07961. Tel: 973-267-5330.

Denville, Morris Co., St. Mary's (1926), Rev. Msgr. James H. Murray; Rev. Richard V. Tartaglia; Deacons David McCaffrey; Al Klose; Charles Burrows.
Res., 15 Myers Ave., 07834. Tel: 973-627-0269.
School—(1954), Tel: 973-627-2606; Fax: 973-627-9316.
Sisters of St. Joseph 1; Lay Teachers 10; Students 256.

Dover, Morris Co., St. Mary's (1845), Revs. Richard H. Oliveri; John J. Klein.
Res., 425 W. Blackwell St., 07801. Tel: 973-366-0184; Fax: 973-366-5377. [CEM]
School—(1878), S. Main St., 07801. Tel: 973-366-0309; Fax: 973-366-6252.
Sisters of Christian Charity Wharton, NJ 1; Lay Teachers 15; Students 192.

Our Lady Queen of the Most Holy Rosary (1959) (Hispanic), Rev. Elias Tamayo.
Res., 77 Richards Ave., 07801. Tel: 973-361-2725; Fax: 973-266-0814.

Sacred Heart (1904), Rev. Ronald J. Tully; Deacons Eugene P. Dolan; Brian Drury; Henry Hyle; Edward Whelan; Richard Zeich. In res., Rev. Msgr. Charles F. Powers.
Res., 4 Richards Ave., 07801. Tel: 973-366-0060.
School—(1923), 30 N. Essex St., 07801. Tel: 973-366-2068; Fax: 973-366-9428.
Sisters of Sorrowful Mother 1; Lay Teachers 11; Students 245.

East Hanover, Morris Co., St. Rose of Lima (1957), Rev. Msgr. William McCarthy; Deacons Robert A. Lang; Alfredo Fanelli; Frank Puglia. Pastoral Assocs.: Sr. Dolores Alfone, F.S.R.; Sr. Concepta D'Amato, F.S.R.
Res., 312 Ridgedale Ave., 07936. Tel: 973-887-5572; Fax: 973-884-0476.
School—(1961), Tel: 973-887-6990.
Lay Teachers 12; Students 206.

Flanders, Morris Co., St. Elizabeth Ann Seton (1985), Rev. Msgr. John B. Wehrlen; Deacons James McGrory; Stephen P. Natafalusy.
Res., 61 Main St., 07836. Tel: 973-927-1629; Fax: 973-927-1629.

Florham Park, Morris Co., Holy Family (1950), Revs. Raymond J. Kupke; William J. Mooney. Pastoral Assocs.: Mrs. Barbara Froetscher; Mrs. Patricia Danishek; Mrs. Virginia Akhoury; Deacons William F. Ward; Mark McCabe.
Res., Lloyd Ave., 07932. Tel: 973-377-1817; Fax: 973-377-6350.
School—(1954), Tel: 973-377-4181; Fax: 973-377-0273.
Sisters of Christian Charity 2; Lay Teachers 18; Students 262.

Franklin, Sussex Co., Immaculate Conception (1867), Rev. Martin G. Glynn.
Res., 75 Church St., 07416. Tel: 973-827-9575; Fax: 973-827-7375. [CEM]

Green Pond, Morris Co., St. Simon the Apostle (Rockaway Twp.) (1942), Rev. Joseph T. Anginoli.
Res., 1010 Green Pond Rd., 07435. Tel: 973-697-4699.

Hainesville, Sussex Co., St. Thomas the Apostle (1941), Rev. Gerald F. Lewis, Admin.
Mailing Address: P.O. Box 187, Layton, 07851. Tel: 973-948-2296; Fax: 973-293-8933.

Hamburg, Sussex Co., St. Jude the Apostle (1966), Rev. William B. Collins.
Res., Beaver Run Rd., P.O. Box 1, 07419. Tel: 973-827-8030.

Haskell, Passaic Co., St. Francis of Assisi (1905), Rev. Msgr. Remigio G. Rocco; Rev. Vincent M. Klim.
Res., 868 Ringwood Ave., 07420. Tel: 973-835-0480; Fax: 973-835-3277.
School—(1912), Tel: 973-835-3268; Fax: 973-616-7644.
Lay Teachers 11; Students 188.

Hawthorne, Passaic Co., St. Anthony's (1908), Rev. Msgr. Elso C. Introini; Rev. Eugene R. Sylva; Deacons Richard J. Brudzynski; Anthony E. Bernardine; George W. Forshay. In res., Rev. Msgr. Joseph R. Brestel, P.A., V.G.
Res., 276 Diamond Bridge Ave., 07506. Tel: 973-427-1478; Fax: 973-427-4826.
School—(1912), 268 Diamond Bridge Ave., 07506. Tel: 973-423-1818; Fax: 973-423-6065.
Sisters 1; Lay Teachers 12; Students 273.

Hewitt, Passaic Co., Our Lady Queen of Peace (1921),

Rev. William Scully, O.F.M.; Deacons Charles Roche; Jack Ehrlich.
Res., Friary, 1911 Union Valley Rd., 07421. Tel: 973-728-8162; Fax: 973-728-0258.
School—(1960), Tel: 973-728-9339.
Franciscan Sisters 1; Lay Teachers 9; Students 165.

Highland Lakes, Sussex Co., Our Lady of Fatima (1954), Rev. Msgr. Aloysius J. Busch.
Mailing Address: P.O. Box 242, 07422. Tel: 973-764-4457.

Hopatcong, Sussex Co., St. Jude's (1931), Revs. George J. Gothie; John J. McGuigan; Deacon Vincent F. Hanwacker.
Res., 40 Maxim Dr., 07843. Tel: 973-398-6377.

Kinnelon, Morris Co., Our Lady of the Magnificat (1961), Rev. Msgr. John J. Carroll; Rev. Timothy Dowling; Deacon Joseph Richardson. In res., Rev. David L. Coppola.
Res., 2 Miller Rd., 07405. Tel: 973-838-6838; Fax: 973-838-0710. [CEM]
School—(1964), Tel: 973-838-6222; Fax: 973-838-0409. Ms. Karen Fasanella, Prin.
Lay Teachers 11; Students 250.

Lake Hopatcong, Morris Co., Our Lady Star of the Sea (Jefferson Twp.) (1910), Rev. P. Christopher Muldoon.
Res., Espanong Rd., P.O. Box 337, 07849. Tel: 973-663-0211; Fax: 973-663-4302.

Lincoln Park, Morris Co., St. Joseph's (1922), Rev. Dennis J. Hogan; Sr. Eileen Halloran, F.S.P., Pastoral Assoc.; Deacon Stephen Marabeti.
Res., 216 Comly Rd., 07035. Tel: 973-696-4411.

Little Falls, Passaic Co., Our Lady of the Holy Angels (1883), Revs. Thomas M. Gallagher, O.F.M.; Flavian Walsh, O.F.M.; John Leonard, O.F.M.; Deacon Frank Muoio. Pastoral Assocs.: Sr. Margaret Lucille Peterson, O.P.; Sr. Joanna Glover, O.P.
Res., 07424. Tel: 973-256-5200; Fax: 973-256-0185.
School—(1903), 465 Main St., 07424. Tel: 973-256-1132. Sr. Mary Byrnes, P.B.V.M., Prin.
Franciscan Missionary Sisters of the Sacred Heart 1; Lay Teachers 9; Students 197.

Long Valley, Morris Co., St. Luke (1982), Rev. Michael J. Drury.
Res., 3 Carl Ln., P.O. Box 416, 07853. Tel: 908-876-3515.
Church—265 W. Mill Rd., 07853.
St. Mark the Evangelist (1986), Rev. Allen F. Stepien.
Res., 59 Lane Rd., 07853. Tel: 908-850-0652.

Madison, Morris Co., St. Vincent Martyr (1805), Revs. Christopher C. DiLella; Peter V.B. Wells; Deacon Henry De Mena. In res., Rev. James O'Kielty.
Res., 26 Green Village Rd., 07940. Tel: 973-377-4000; Fax: 973-377-8242. [CEM]
School—(1848), Tel: 973-377-1104.
Lay Teachers 15; Students 345.

McAfee, Sussex Co., St. Francis de Sales (1963), Rev. Msgr. John V. Boland; Rev. Frederick Walters.
Mailing Address: P.O. Box 785, 07428. Tel: 973-827-3248.

Mendham, Morris Co., St. Joseph's (1853), Rev. Msgr. Kenneth E. Lasch; Deacon Robert F. Santos.
6 New St., 07945. Tel: 973-543-5950; Fax: 973-543-2562. [CEM]
School—(1963), Tel: 973-543-7474.
Sisters of Christian Charity 1; Lay Teachers 11; Students 260.

Montague, Sussex Co., St. James the Greater (1943), Rev. Gerald F. Lewis, Admin.
Res., 75 River Rd., 07827. Tel: 973-293-3379; Fax: 973-293-8933.

Montville, Morris Co., St. Pius X (1959), Revs. Joseph J. Garbarino; John A. Tarantino; Deacon Andrew L. Cavaliere.
Res., 18 Changebridge Rd., 07045. Tel: 973-334-4506; 334-4510; Fax: 973-331-1706.
School—(1963), Tel: 973-335-1253; Fax: 973-335-2392. Sr. June Morrissey, S.C., Prin.
Lay Teachers 10; Students 180.

Morris Plains, Morris Co., St. Virgilius (1881), Revs. John Andrew Connell; Ronald Sordillo; Sr. Mary Larkin, Pastoral Assoc.; Deacons Sylvester Mazzoccoli; Daniel Scrone; Merle Sisler. In res., Rev. Msgr. James L. Fallon, Pastor Emeritus.
Res., 18 W. Hanover Ave., 07950. Tel: 973-538-1418; Fax: 973-538-2992.
School—(1910), 11 W. Hanover Ave., 07950. Tel: 973-539-7267.
Sisters of St. Dominic 2; Lay Teachers 15; Students 250.

Morristown, Morris Co., Assumption of the Blessed Virgin Mary (1848), Rev. Msgr. Martin F. Rauscher; Rev. William L. Winston; Deacons P. Michael Hanly; Gabriel Lasch; William Harty; Tony DiLorenzo; Frank Para; Tom Spruiell. In res., Revs. William P. Glennon; Joseph M. Casey.
Res., 91 Maple Ave., 07960. Tel: 973-539-2141; Fax: 973-984-0632. [CEM]
School—(1850), 63 MacCulloch Ave., 07960. Tel: 973-538-0590; Fax: 973-984-3632.
Sisters of Charity 4; Lay Teachers 34; Students 570.
St. Margaret's (1930), Revs. Francis J. Duffy; Andrew Velez. In res., Rev. Msgr. Christian D. Haag, P.A.; Bro. Hugh McGrath, O.S.F.
Res., 6 Sussex Ave., 07960. Tel: 973-538-0874; Fax: 973-538-4581.

Mountain Lakes, Morris Co., St. Catherine of Siena (1956), Revs. Patrick Rice; A. Richard Carton; Deacon Joseph Parlapiano.
Res., 10 N. Pocono Rd., 07046. Tel: 973-334-7131; Fax: 973-334-3202.

Mount Arlington, Morris Co., Our Lady of the Lake (1888), Revs. Joseph Ryan; Desmond O'Connor, S.P.S.
Res., One Park Ave., 07856. Tel: 973-398-0240; Fax: 973-398-3667.

Mount Hope, Morris Co., St. Bernard's (1855), Rev. Joseph G. Farias.
Res., 446 Mt. Hope Rd., Wharton, 07885-2814. Tel: 973-627-0066; Fax: 973-627-3631.

Netcong, Morris Co., St. Michael's (1873), Rev. Msgr. Thomas J. Trapasso; Deacons Alex Buckholtz; Philip Pawlows; Joseph Keenan; Stuart Murphy. In res., Rev. Msgr. James J. Doyle, Pastor Emeritus; Rev. Robert G. Hoffmann.
Res., 4 Church St., 07857. Tel: 973-347-0032; Fax: 973-347-1560. [CEM]
School—(1922), Tel: 973-347-0039; Fax: 973-347-0054.
Sisters of Christian Charity 2; Lay Teachers 16; Students 460.

Newton, Sussex Co., St. Joseph's (1854), Revs. Edward M. Davey; Zbigniew Tyburski; Deacons Arthur Van Vleet; John Grimes; Raymond Biersbach. In res., Rev. Angelus Croce.
Res., 17 Elm St., 07860. Tel: 973-383-1985; Fax: 973-383-8164. [CEM]

New Vernon, Morris Co., Christ the King (1956), Revs. Patrick G. O'Donovan; Paul Duggan.
Res., Blue Mill Rd., 07976. Tel: 973-539-4955; Fax: 973-267-7070.

Oak Ridge, Morris Co., St. Thomas, the Apostle (1949), Rev. Msgr. John E. Fitzpatrick.
Res., 5635 Berkshire Valley Rd., 07438. Tel: 973-208-0090; Fax: 973-208-0092. [CEM]

Ogdensburg, Sussex Co., St. Thomas of Aquin (1881), Rev. Stanley C. Barron.
Res., 53 Kennedy Ave., 07439. Tel: 973-827-3190; Fax: 973-827-9738. [CEM]

Parsippany, Morris Co., St. Christopher (1944), Rev. Msgr. Frank B. Ferraioli; Rev. Sean McDonnell (Ireland); Deacons John J. Kelly; Michael Pirylis; John Bernero; Edward Lally; Henry Rohrman.
Res., 1050 Littleton Rd., 07054. Tel: 973-539-7050; Fax: 973-539-3601.
School—(1962), Tel: 973-539-7053.
Sisters of St. Dominic 4; Lay Teachers 15; Students 413.
St. Ann (1982), Rev. Martin McDonnell; Sr. Frances Sanzo, S.S.C., Pastoral Assoc.; Deacons Donald O'Leary; Alfred Frank.
Res., 781 Smith Rd., 07054. Tel: 973-884-1986; Fax: 973-884-0940.
St. Peter the Apostle (1938), Rev. Msgr. Herbert K. Tillyer; Revs. Peter Filipkowski; Wayne M. Varga; Sr. Sylvia Berzinski, S.S.C., Pastoral Assoc.; Sr. Regina McTiernan, C.S.J.B.; Deacons David Collins; Daniel Ferry.
Res., 179 Baldwin Rd., 07054. Tel: 973-334-2090; Fax: 973-334-5397.
School—(1958), Tel: 973-334-4704; Fax: 973-334-0622.
Sisters 2; Lay Teachers 12; Students 250.
Catechesis/Religious Programs—189 Baldwin Rd., 07054. Tel: 973-335-9713.
Students 652.

Passaic, Passaic Co.,

1—St. Nicholas, (1868), Rev. Msgr. Robert B. Carroll; Rev. Daniel A. Kelly; Deacon Edward Ramirez. In res., Rev. Michael Burke.
Res., 153 Washington Pl., 07055. Tel: 973-779-7867; Fax: 973-815-1893.
School—(1874), 123 Jefferson St., 07055. Tel: 973-779-1987.
Sisters of Charity 2; Lay Teachers 11; Students 264.

2—St. Anthony of Padua, (1917) (Italian), Rev. Herman Arias.
Res., 95 Myrtle Ave., 07055. Tel: 973-777-4793; Fax: 973-779-6864.
School—(1960), 40 Tulip St., 07055. Tel: 973-773-0970.
Sisters 5; Lay Teachers 9; Students 255.

3—Assumption of the Blessed Virgin Mary, (1891) (Slovak), Rev. Msgr. John J. Demkovich. In res., Rev. John T. Catoir.
Res., 63 Monroe St., 07055. Tel: 973-779-0427; Fax: 973-472-5033.

4—Holy Rosary, (1918) (Polish), Rev. Msgr. John Podgorny; Revs. Stanley Lesniowski; Stefan Las.
Res., 6 Wall St., 07055. Tel: 973-473-1578.

5—Holy Trinity, (1900) (German), Revs. Mark Olenowski; Antonio Rodriguez.
Res., 226 Harrison St., 07055. Tel: 973-778-9763.
School—(1906), 228 Hope Ave., 07055. Tel: 973-473-1043.
Sisters of St. Dominic 4; Lay Teachers 7; Students 145.

6—St. Joseph's, (1892) (Polish), Revs. Joseph Czerkies; Stanislaw Drzal, S.Ch.
Res., 7 Parker Ave., 07055. Tel: 973-473-0921.

7—Mt. Carmel, (1902) (Italian), Rev. Sam Frapaul, O.F.M.Cap.
Res., 10 St. Francis Way, 07055. Tel: 973-473-0246.
School—(1954).
Franciscan Sisters 3; Lay Teachers 12; Students 280.

8—Our Lady of Fatima, (1954) (Hispanic), Rev. Msgr. Raul Guzman; Revs. Hector Melendez; Nelson Betancur; Deacons Jesus Cortes; Juan Ortiz.
Res., 32 Exchange Pl., 07055. Tel: 973-472-0815; Fax: 973-472-0250.

9—St. Stephen's, (1902) (Magyar), Rev. Stephen N. Mustos, Sch.P.
Res., 223 Third St., 07055. Tel: 973-779-0332; Fax: 973-778-4263.

Pequannock, Morris Co., Holy Spirit (1949), Revs. Alfred J. Lampron; Edward A. Collins; Deacons Gil Leifer; Thomas Kimak.
Res., 318 Tpke., 07440. Tel: 973-696-1234; Fax: 973-305-9390.
School—(1956), Tel: 973-835-5680; Fax: 973-835-1757.
Maestre Pie Filippini (Religious Teachers Filippini) 2; Lay Teachers 15; Students 350.
Convent—Tel: 973-694-2111.
Our Lady of Fatima Chapel (Tridentine) (1994), Rev. Joseph P. Terra, F.S.S.P. In res., Revs. Kenneth Baker, S.J.; Nicolas Zolnerovicz.
Res., 32 West Franklin Ave., 07440. Tel: 973-694-6727; Fax: 973-694-7629.
School—St. Maximilian Kolbe School, 18 First St., 07440. Tel: 973-694-1034. Mrs. Mary Lou Bednar, Prin.
Lay Teachers 4; Students 40.

Pompton Lakes, Passaic Co., Our Lady of the Assumption (1906), Revs. John Carnevale, O.F.M.; Kevin Downey, O.F.M.; Sr. Arlene Kollar, S.S.C., Pastoral Assoc.; Bro. Richard McFeeley, O.F.M.; Deacons Paul A. Liotard; Edward Higgins; Steven Madreperla. In res., Rev. Thomas Hartle, O.F.M.
Res., St. Mary's Friary, 52 Lenox Ave., 07442. Tel: 973-839-1975; Fax: 973-835-8432.
School—(1951), Tel: 973-835-2010; Fax: 973-835-7529. Ms. Kathleen Berlino, Prin.
Lay Teachers 16; Students 253.

Pompton Plains, Morris Co., Our Lady of Good Counsel (1962), Rev. Patrick J. Scott; Deacons Don X. Bancroft; Ronald Ochner; Edward Jaroszewski; Charles Mallory. In res., Rev. Michael J. Lombardo.
Res., 155 W. Pkwy., P.O. Box 218, 07444. Tel: 973-839-2447; Fax: 973-839-9492.

Prospect Park, Passaic Co., St. Paul's (1924), Revs. Edward J. Kurtyka; Steven G. Shadwell.
Res., 286 Haledon Ave., Paterson, 07508. Tel: 973-790-8169.
School—(1955), 13 Wagaraw Blvd., 07508. Tel: 973-942-9428.
Lay Teachers 10; Students 180.

Randolph, Morris Co., Resurrection (1978), Revs. William M. Naughton; Brendan McLoughlin; Ashiono Anthony Mabango; Deacons Keith S. Farber; Robert M. Flavin; Gerard Hand; Roger La Couture; Kenneth Weaver.
Res., 651 Millbrook Ave., 07869. Tel: 973-895-4224; Fax: 973-895-3224.
St. Matthew the Apostle (1988), Rev. David McDonnell; Deacon William Peters.
Res., 267 Dover-Chester Rd., 07869. Tel: 973-584-1101.

Ringwood, Passaic Co., St. Catherine of Bologna (1917), Rev. Msgr. Patrick G. Panos; Rev. Gerald B. Kanzic; Deacons James Elliott; Richard Michalski.
Res., 112 Erskine Rd., 07456. Tel: 973-962-7032.
School—(1948), Tel: 973-962-7131; Fax: 973-962-0585.
Franciscan Sisters of Ringwood 1; Lay Teachers 17; Students 310.

Rockaway, Morris Co., St. Cecilia's (1869), Revs. John E. Hart; Brendan J. Murray; J. Patrick Ryan (ALB). In res., Rev. Paul S. Manning.
Res., 70 Church St., 07866. Tel: 973-627-0313; 627-0316; Fax: 973-627-4811. [CEM]
School—(1958), Halsey Ave., 07866. Tel: 973-252-0760; Fax: 973-627-5217.

Sisters of Christian Charity 2; Lay Teachers 11; Students 310.

Sacred Heart (1923) (Slovak), Rev. Joseph J. Goode. In res., Rev. Marc Mancini.
Res., 63 E. Main St., 07866. Tel: 973-627-0422; Fax: 973-627-6249.
School—(1965). Sisters of the Sorrowful Mother. Tel: 973-627-7689.
Lay Teachers 9; Students 271.

Rockaway Township, Morris Co., St. Clement, Pope and Martyr (1964), Rev. Msgr. Joseph A. Ciampaglio; Deacon Harry Dachisen.
Res., 154 Mt. Pleasant Ave., Dover, 07801. Tel: 973-366-7095; Fax: 973-366-7095.

Schooley's Mountain, Morris Co., Our Lady of the Mountain (1954), Rev. Msgr. George A. Dudak.
Res., Rte. 24, 07870. Tel: 908-876-4395. [CEM]

Sparta, Sussex Co., Our Lady of the Lake (1935), Rev. Msgr. Paul F. Knauer. In res., Rev. Chukwudi Obiajunwa (Nigeria).
Res., 294 Sparta Ave., 07871. Tel: 973-729-6107; Fax: 973-729-7203.
School—(1954), Tel: 973-729-9174; Fax: 973-729-0318. Ms. Barbara Campione, Prin.
Lay Teachers 25; Students 490.

Blessed Kateri Tekakwitha (1988), Revs. Daniel W. Murphy; Gregory A. White; Sr. Barbara Moore, O.P., Pastoral Assoc.; Deacons Frank Padden; Andrew Calandriello; Paul Puleo; Edward Reading; Charles Mathias.
Res., 427 Stanhope Rd., 07871. Tel: 973-729-1682; Fax: 973-729-0702.

Stirling, Morris Co., St. Vincent de Paul (1886), Revs. Patrick E. Brown; Arthur J. Colaiacovo; Albert Nix.
Res., Bebout Ave., 07980. Tel: 908-647-0118; Fax: 908-647-5992. [CEM]
School—(1955), Tel: 908-647-0421.
Lay Teachers 25; Students 272.

Stockholm, Sussex Co., St. John Vianney (1958), Rev. Matthew J. Twiggs; Deacons Edmund Galinski; Thomas Kronyak; Stanley Sisson.
Res., 07460. Tel: 973-697-6550; Fax: 973-697-6882.

Succasunna, Morris Co., St. Therese (1957), Revs. Joseph P. Davis; James A.D. Smith; Deacon Anthony Signorelli.
Res., 7 Hunter St., 07876. Tel: 973-584-8271; Fax: 973-584-0684.
School—(1963), Tel: 973-584-0812; Fax: 973-584-2029.
Sisters 2; Lay Teachers 8; Students 198.

Sussex, Sussex Co., St. Monica (1881), Rev. Charles A. Perricone; Deacon Jerome Schenker.
Res., 33 Unionville Ave., 07461. Tel: 973-875-4521; Fax: 973-875-7538.

Swartswood, Sussex Co., Our Lady of Mt. Carmel (1951), Rev. John J. Quinlan; Deacons Ellis F. Schweitzer; Robert T. Davis; Edward J. Muller.
Mailing Address: P.O. Box 124, 07877. Tel: 973-383-3566; Fax: 973-383-3831.

Totowa Borough, Passaic Co., St. James of the Marches (1926), Rev. Msgr. Eugene M. Boland; Revs. Paul Iovino; Joseph Murphy.
Res., 32 St. James Pl., Totowa, 07512. Tel: 973-790-0288; Fax: 973-790-7064.
School—(1956), Tel: 973-956-8824. Sr. Mary Ann Grimes, Prin.
Sisters 1; Lay Teachers 11; Students 180.

Wayne, Passaic Co.,

1—ANNUNCIATION, (1963), Rev. Msgr. Stanislaus E. Schinski; Rev. Absalom Coutinho; Deacons Charles Tenga; Andrew Kostic.
Res., 45 Urban Club Rd., 07470. Tel: 973-694-5700; Fax: 973-694-5706.

2—HOLY CROSS, (1925), Rev. John M. Heekin.
Res., 17 Van Duyne Ave., 07470. Tel: 973-696-1065.

3—IMMACULATE HEART OF MARY, (1956), Rev. Msgr. Louis J. Bihr; Rev. George T. Shema; Deacons John Gaffney; Jaime Llanso; Philip Healy. In res., Rev. Roger Hebert.
Res., 580 Ratzer Rd., 07470. Tel: 973-694-3400; Fax: 973-694-3459.
School—(1958), Tel: 973-694-1225; Fax: 973-872-9043.
Lay Teachers 13; Students 220.

4—OUR LADY OF CONSOLATION, (1963), Rev. James R. Hertel, J.C.D.; Deacon Robert Pringle.
Res., 1799 Hamburg Tpke., 07470. Tel: 973-839-3444; Fax: 973-839-9695.
School—(1967), Tel: 973-839-2323; Fax: 973-839-2428.
Sisters 3; Lay Teachers 12; Students 210.

5—OUR LADY OF THE VALLEY, (1960), Rev. Msgr. James H. O'Rorke; Deacon Michael Wallace.
Res., 614 Valley Rd., 07470. Tel: 973-694-4585.
School—(1962), Tel: 973-696-2212.
Sisters of St. Joseph 1; Lay Teachers 20; Students 358.

West Milford Township, Passaic Co., St. Joseph (1765), Revs. Boniface F. Hanley, O.F.M.; Bernard J. Splawski, O.F.M.; Deacon Milton Smilek.
Res., 454 Germantown Rd., West Milford, 07480. Tel: 973-697-6100; Fax: 973-697-3716.
School—(1956), Tel: 973-697-6896.
Lay Teachers 11; Students 220.

Whippany, Morris Co., Our Lady of Mercy (1854), Revs. John DeMattia; John P. Pilipie; Sr. Eileen Side, S.S.J., Pastoral Assoc.; Sr. Ann McKeon, G.N.S.H., Youth Min.
Res., 9 Parsippany Rd., 07981. Tel: 973-887-0050; Fax: 973-887-0991. [CEM]
School—Tel: 973-887-2611. Sr. Catherine Duignan, C.S.J.P., Prin.
Lay Teachers 8; Students 196.

Chaplains of Public Institutions

Hospitals

PATERSON. *Preakness Hospital* P.O. Box V, 07509. Tel: 973-278-6800. Rev. John F. Heusser.
St. Joseph Hospital 703 Main St., 07503. Tel: 973-754-2000; 754-2060 (Office). Sr. Jane Frances Brady, Pres. & CEO; Revs. William N. Cramer, Dir. Pastoral Care; Francis Hanudel, O.F.M.; Sr. Bernice Romanick, F.S.P.; Sr. Marie Josetta Wethington, S.C.

DENVILLE. *St. Clare Hospital* Pocono Rd., 07834. Tel: 973-627-3000. Chaplains: Revs. Thomas A. Heffernan; Charles Lovato, S.A.; Stuart Baer; Noel Clarke.

DOVER. *Dover General Hospital* Jardine St., 07801. Tel: 973-939-3000. Rev. Jeremiah O'Riordan.

MORRIS PLAINS. *Greystone Park Psychiatric Hospital*. Vacant. 07950. Tel: 973-538-1800.

MORRISTOWN. *Morristown Memorial Hospital* 100 Madison Ave., 07960. Tel: 973-540-5307. Revs. Zbigniew Kluba; Joseph M. Casey.

NEWTON. *Newton Memorial Hospital* 175 High St., 07860. Tel: 973-383-2121. Rev. John J. Quinlan.

PASSAIC. *Passaic General Hospital* 350 Blvd., 07055. Tel: 973-345-4300. Rev. Francis Matarazzo.
St. Mary Hospital 211 Pennington Ave., 07055. Tel: 973-473-1000. Revs. Luke Guastella, O.F.M.Cap.; Vincent Liuzzo, O.F.M.Cap.

POMPTON PLAINS. *Chilton Memorial Hospital* 07444. Tel: 973-831-5000. Rev. Michael J. Lombardo.

TOTOWA. *North Jersey Developmental Center*. Rev. Louis J. Scurti.

WAYNE. *Wayne General Hospital* Hamburg Tpke., 07470. Tel: 973-942-6900. Rev. Michael J. Lombardo.

Correctional Facilities

PATERSON. *Passaic County Jail*. Rev. Msgr. Mark J. Giordani; Rev. Hernan Arias.

MORRIS PLAINS. *Morris County Youth Center*. Rev. Robert G. Hoffmann.

MORRISTOWN. *Morris County Jail*. Rev. Patrick E. Brown.

NEWTON. *Sussex County Jail*. Rev. Robert G. Hoffmann.

Special Assignment:
Reverend Fathers—
McGrath, Thomas M., 476 17th Ave., Paterson, NJ 07504. Tel: 201-523-9595

On Duty Outside the Diocese:
Reverend Monsignors—
Conway, Michael, Orlando, FL
Reverend Fathers—
Belanich, Giordano, Fairview, NJ
Brown, Patrick, Larchmont, NY
DiCristina, Frank A., Redlands, CA
Grasso, Richard, Daytona Beach, FL
Holterhoff, Edward G., Monterey, CA
Mancini, Marc A., Washington, D.C.
Mastroeni, Anthony, Gaming, Austria
McLeod, David, Manahawkin, NJ
Pavlick, Raymond A., Walden, NY
Reading, Edward, Trenton, NJ
Stephenson, Alphonse J., Point Pleasant, NJ
Valerio, Thomas A., Berryville, VA
Vitillo, Robert J., Washington, DC
Weis, John H., Midland, MI

Military Chaplains:
Reverend Fathers—
Briganti, Philip J., USA
Cusack, John J., USAF
O'Grady, Frank, USA
Parisi, Michael, USN
Sodano, Ralph H., USN
Walsh, Michael A., USN

Sabbatical:
Reverend Monsignors—
Carvajal, Felipe
Longua, Paul
Reverend Fathers—
Daly, M. Paul

Absent on Leave:
Reverend Monsignors—
Alonso, Jose A.
Reverend Fathers—
Gorrell, Paul
Holliday, David D.
Moss, James T.
O'Connor, John H.
Pisarcik, John G.

Unassigned:
Reverend Monsignors—
McBride, Peter A.
Reverend Fathers—
Erwin, Patrick O.
Lambro, Edward
Peretta, Andrew J.
Scolamiero, Dominic A.
Scott, James C.

Retired:
Reverend Monsignors—
Biesiada, Louis W., 2001 N.E. 38th St., Lighthouse Point, FL 33064
Bischoff, Francis J., 140 Shepherd Ln., Totowa, NJ 07512
Carey, Leo P., Nazareth Village, Main St., Box 635, Chester, NJ 07930
Cassidy, Charles C., 516 Oak Hill Ct., Lanoka Harbor, NJ 08734
Corr, John F., 83 Primose Tr., Morristown, NJ 07960
Dericks, John H., 288 Lackawanna Dr., Andover, NJ 07821
Doyle, James J., 4 Church St., Netcong, NJ 07857
Fallon, James L., 10 W. Hanover Ave., Morris Plains, NJ 07950
Ferrito, Joseph L., 516 Oak Hill Ct., Lanoka Harbor, NJ 08734
Flek, Ladis Laus J., 140 Shepherd Ln., Totowa, NJ 07512
Gallo, Joseph J., 55 Quartz Ln., Paterson, NJ 07510
Gallo, Louis J., Nazareth Village, Main St., Box 635, Chester, NJ 07930
Haag, Christian D., 6 Sussex Ave., Morristown, NJ 07960
Hayes, Denis A., 140 Shepherd Ln., Totowa, NJ 07512
Lee, Thaddeus, P.O. Box 2044, Beach Haven, NJ 08008
McQuaid, Eugene, P.O. Box 628, Dingmans Ferry, PA 18328
Meyer, Joseph J., 140 Shepherd Ln., Totowa, NJ 07512
Morris, John E., 18 William St., Lincoln Park, NJ 07035
Powers, Charles, 4 Richards St., Dover, NJ 07801
Puma, Vincent E., 970 Black Oak Ridge Rd., Wayne, NJ 07470
Rugel, James J., 12 Grove Rd., Oak Ridge, NJ 07438
Russo, Charles J., 27 Livingston Rd., Morristown, NJ 07960
Ryan, John R., Nazareth Village, Main St. Box 635, Chester, NJ 07930
Ryan, Leo P., Nazareth Village, Main St. Box 635, Chester, NJ 07930
Wolsin, Carl J., Nazareth Village, Main St., Box 635, Chester, NJ 07930
Reverend Fathers—
Connolly, Martin C., Nazareth Village, Main St., Box 635, Chester, NJ 07930
Costigan, George, St. Francis Convent, Windemere Ave., Mt. Arlington, NJ 07856
Fanning, Leo M., 14 Polar Bear Path, Ormond Beach, FL 32174
Feeney, Bernard, R.R. 6, Box 399, Branchville, NJ 07826
Grieco, Charles, Nazareth Village, Main St., Box 635, Chester, NJ 07930
Hanley, James T.
Hebert, Roger, 580 Ratzer Rd., Wayne, NJ 07470
Hewitt, Kenneth R., 490 Windemere Ave., Mount Arlington, NJ 07856
Jacobs, Richard A., 7 Middlesex Rd., E. Greenbush, NY 12061
Jasaitis, Raymond J., 61 Main St., Flanders, NJ 07836
Krajewski, Paul A., 10 Prime Rose Ln., Mount Arlington, NJ 07856
LoGatto, Joseph J., 424 Third St., Carlstadt, NJ 07072
Lugo, Joseph W., 78 Chestnut St., Bridgewater, NJ 08807
Maliszewski, Francis, 86 Martin St., Paterson, NJ 07501
McHugh, Dennis, Our Lady's Shrine, Knock, County Mayo, Ireland
Morris, Robert J., Nazareth Village, Main St., Box

635, Chester, NJ 07930
Mullan, Patrick, Nazareth Village, Main St., Box 635, Chester, NJ 07930
Mushinsky, John E., 22 Boston Rd., Neptune, NJ 07753
Ruddy, Edward J., St. Attracta's Nursing Home, Knock Rd., Charlestown, County Mayo, Ireland
Sullivan, John A., 730 Linnwood Ave., Brick, NJ 08723

Permanent Deacons:
Acevedo, Pedro, St. Agnes, Paterson
Altilio, Robert M., St. John Kanty, Clifton
Ayers, Robert, St. Andrew the Apostle, Clifton
Balough, Joseph, St. Bonaventure, Paterson
Bancroft, Don X., Our Lady of Good Counsel, Pompton Plains
Bernardine, Anthony E., St. Anthony, Hawthorne
Bernero, John, St. Christopher, Parsippany
Bianchi, Roland, Archdiocese of Newark, NJ
Biersbach, Raymond, St. Joseph, Newton
Bitecola, Daniel
Brudzynski, Richard, St. Anthony, Hawthorne
Buckholtz, Alexander E., St. Michael Church, Netcong
Burrows, Charles, St. Mary, Denville
Calandriello, Andrew, Blessed Kateri Tekakwitha, Sparta
Cassidy, Joseph, Retired
Cavaliere, Andrew L., St. Pius X, Montville
Ciampa, Alfred
Collins, David, St. Peter the Apostle, Parsippany
Cortes, Jesus, Our Lady of Fatima, Passaic
Costello, Barry, Mt. Carmel Church, Boonton
Costello, John, St. Luke, Long Valley
Dachisen, Harry, St. Clement Pope and Martyr, Rockaway Township
Damato, Larry, Archdiocese of St. Louis, MO
Davis, Robert T., Our Lady of Mount Carmel, Swartswood
de Mena, Henry, St. Vincent Martyr, Madison
DeLorenzo, Gregory, St. Philip Church, Clifton
DiLorenzo, Anthony, Assumption, Morristown
Dolan, Eugene P., Sacred Heart, Dover
Drury, Brian, Sacred Heart, Dover
Ehrlich, Jacob B., Our Lady Queen of Peace, Hewitt
Elliott, James, St. Catherine of Bologna, Ringwood
Fanelli, Alfredo, St. Rose of Lima, East Hanover
Farber, Keith, Resurrection, Randolph
Ferry, Daniel F., St. Peter the Apostle, Parsippany
Flavin, Robert
Fohn, Kurt, Diocese of Charlotte, NC
Forshay, George W., St. Anthony, Hawthorne
Frank, Alfred E., St. Ann, Parsippany
Gaffney, John F., Immaculate Heart of Mary Church, Wayne
Galinski, Edmund V., St. John Vianney, Stockholm
Gallo, Henry, Our Lady of Pompei, Paterson
Gardner, Leo, Our Lady of Victories, Paterson
Grimes, John, St. Joseph, Newton
Grish, Kevin, Immaculate Conception, Franklin
Hand, Gerard, Resurrection, Randolph
Hanly, P. Michael, Assumption, Morristown
Hanwacker, Vincent F., St. Jude Church, Hopatcong
Harty, William, Assumption, Morristown
Healy, Philip, Immaculate Heart of Mary, Wayne
Healy, Thomas F., Jr., St. Luke, Long Valley
Higgins, Edward J., St. Mary, Pompton Lakes
Hilber, Joseph, Good Shepherd, Andover
Hussey, William E., St. George Church, Paterson
Hyle, Henry, Sacred Heart, Dover
Jaroszewski, Edward, Our Lady of Good Counsel Church, Pompton Plains
Jones, Frederick B., Jr., APO Germany
Keegan, Edward, St. Matthew, Randolph
Keenan, Joseph, St. Michael, Netcong
Kelly, John, St. Christopher, Parsippany
Kimak, Thomas J., Holy Spirit, Pequannock
Klose, Albert P., St. Mary, Denville
Kostic, Andrew, Annunciation, Wayne
Kronyak, Robert, Diocese of Charleston, SC
Kronyak, Thomas, St. John Vianney, Stockholm
Kruk, Leonard, Diocese of Trenton, NJ
Lacouture, Roger, Resurrection, Randolph
Lally, Edward J., St. Christopher, Parsippany
Lang, Robert A., St. Rose of Lima, East Hanover
Larkin, John S., Good Shepherd, Andover
Lasch, Gabriel L., Assumption BVM Church, Morristown
Lebron, Florencio G., St. Mary, Paterson
Leifer, Gil, Holy Spirit, Pequannock
Liotard, Paul A., St. Mary, Pompton Lakes
Llanso, Jamie, Father English Center, Paterson
Llibre, John, Unassigned
Madreperla, Steven A., St. Mary Church, Pompton Lakes
Mallory, Charles, Our Lady of Good Counsel Church, Pompton Plains
Manning, Tim, St. Peter the Apostle, Parsippany
Marabeti, Stephen J., St. Joseph Church, Lincoln Park
Mathias, Charles T., Bl. Kateri Tekakwitha, Sparta
Mazzaccoli, Sylvester A., St. Virgil Church, Morris Plains
McCabe, Mark, Holy Family, Florham Park
McCaffrey, David, St. Mary, Denville
McGrory, James G., St. Elizabeth Ann Seton, Flanders
McMullin, Robert
McNally, Peter J.
McQuaid, Francis P., St. Patrick, Chatam
Meyer, John, Diocese of Charleston, SC
Michalski, Richard, St. Catherine of Bologna, Ringwood
Minicozzi, John
Morris, James
Muller, Edward J., Our Lady of Mount Carmel, Swartswood
Munoz, Mario, Our Lady of Victories, Paterson
Muoio, Frank, Holy Angels Church, Little Falls
Murphy, Stuart, St. Michael, Netcong
Natafalusy, Stephen P., St. Elizabeth Ann Seton, Flanders
O'Leary, Donald, St. Ann, Parsippany
Ochner, Ronald, Our Lady of Good Counsel Church, Pompton Plains
Ortiz, Juan, Our Lady of Fatima Church, Passaic
Owens, Frank, St. Lawrence the Martyr, Chester
Padden, Frank J., Blessed Kateri Tekawitha, Sparta
Para, Frank, Assumption, Morristown
Parlapiano, Joseph J., St. Catherine of Siena, Mountain Lakes
Pawlows, Philip T., St. Michael, Netcong
Peters, William L., St. Matthew, Randolph
Pirylis, Michael, St. Christopher, Parsippany
Pomales, Jose, St. John Cathedral, Paterson
Pringle, Robert H., Our Lady of Good Counsel, Pompton Plains
Puglia, Frank, St. Rose of Lima, East Hanover
Puleo, Paul A., Blessed Kateri Tekakwitha, Sparta
Puskas, Joseph, St. Paul, Clifton
Quinn, Joseph, Notre Dame of Mt. Carmel, Cedar Knolls
Ramirez, Edward, St. Nicholas, Passaic
Raymond, Thomas, Archdiocese of Boston, MA
Reading, Edward J., Blessed Kateri Tekakwitha, Sparta
Reed, Daniel, St. Brendan, Clifton
Richardson, Joseph, Our Lady of Magnificat, Kinnelon
Roche, Charles, St. Francis of Assisi, Haskell
Rodriguez, Angel, Our Lady of Lourdes Church, Paterson
Rohrman, Harry, St. Christopher, Parsippany
Santana, Heriberto, Diocese of Orlando, FL
Santiago, Manuel, St. John the Baptist Cathedral, Paterson
Santos, Robert F., St. Joseph, Mendham
Schenker, Jerome, St. Monica, Sussex
Schwietzer, Ellis F., Our Lady of Mount Carmel, Swartswood
Scrone, Daniel, St. Virgil, Morris Plains
Sheehan, Patrick, St. Matthew, Randolph
Shoemaker, William, Diocese of Austin, TX
Signorelli, Anthony, St. Therese, Succasunna
Siino, Anthony C., St. Jude, Budd Lake
Silva, Percy, St. Agnes, Paterson
Simeone, Enio, Passaic General Hospital
Sisco, Joseph, St. Gerard Majella, Paterson
Sisler, Merle F., St. Virgil, Morris Plains
Sisson, Stanley, St. John Vianney, Stockholm
Smilek, Milton, St. Joseph, West Milford
Spruiell, Thomas, Assumption, Morristown
Sullivan, Thomas, Good Shepherd, Andover
Tenga, Charles, Annunciation, Wayne
Teresinski, John S., SS. Cyril & Methodius Church, Clifton
Turner, John
Van Ormen, Patrick, Our Lady of the Mountain, Schooleys Mountain
Van Vleet, Arthur H., St. Joseph, Newton
Varsalona, Nicholas, St. Therese Church, Paterson
Vesota, Robert, Father English Center, Paterson
Walker, John
Wallace, Michael J., Our Lady of the Valley, Wayne
Walsh, Frank, Diocese of Phoenix, AZ
Ward, William, Holy Family, Florham Park
Weaver, Kenneth, Resurrection, Randolph
Whaley, Bruce, Archdiocese of Philadelphia, PA
Whelan, Edward, Sacred Heart, Dover
Wisneski, Joseph A., St. Patrick, Chatham
Zeich, Richard, Sacred Heart, Dover

INSTITUTIONS LOCATED IN THE DIOCESE

[A] SEMINARIES, RELIGIOUS OR SCHOLASTICATES

OAK RIDGE. *Paulist Novitiate*, 243 Mt. Paul Rd., 07438. Tel: 973-697-6341. Missionary Society of St. Paul the Apostle (Paulist Fathers). Elaine Morin, Admin.

[B] COLLEGES AND UNIVERSITIES

HALEDON. *Salesian College*, 655 Belmont Ave., 07508
For a complete listing, refer to the Colleges and Universities section.

MENDHAM. *Assumption College for Sisters*, 07945 Fax: 973-543-9459.
E-mail: socc@tsa.net
For a complete listing, refer to the Colleges and Universities section.

MORRISTOWN. *College of Saint Elizabeth*, 2 Convent Rd., 07961. Tel: 973-290-4000.
Web site: http://www.st-elizabeth.edu
For a complete listing, refer to the Colleges and Universities section.

[C] HIGH SCHOOLS, DIOCESAN

PATERSON. *Paterson Catholic Regional High School*, 764-11th Ave., 07514. Tel: 973-278-1024. Sr. Gloria Perez, P.B.V.M., Prin.; Albert Hernandez, Asst. Prin.; Michele R. Fierro, Asst. Prin. Priests 1; Sisters 3; Brothers 3; Lay Teachers 24; Students 460.

DENVILLE. *Morris Catholic High School*, 07834. Tel: 973-627-6674. Bro. Hugh McGrath, O.S.F., Prin.; Sr. Jonathan Moyles, S.C.C., Asst. Prin.; Rev. Paul S. Manning, Chap. Priests 2; Sisters 11; Lay Teachers 25; Students 440.

MADISON. *Bayley-Ellard High School*, 07940. Tel: 973-377-2486.
E-mail: bayley@nac.net
Web site: hhtp:/www.nac.net/bayley
Mr. Frank O. Mattiace, Exec. Dir. & Prin.; Rev. Msgr. John F. Corr; Rev. Msgr. James Fallon; Rev. Edward J. Dillon. Priests 3; Sisters 5; Lay Teachers 19; Students 201.

SPARTA. *Pope John XXIII High School*, 07871. Tel: 973-729-6125.
E-mail: dipathspj@connectinc.com.
Rev. Kieran A. McHugh, Prin. Lay Teachers 46; Students 668.

WAYNE. *De Paul High School*, 1512 Alps Rd., 07470. Tel: 973-694-3702; Fax: 973-633-5381. Sr. Patricia Flarity, Prin.; Rev. David L. Coppola. Sisters 1; Brothers 1; Lay Teachers 46; Students 625.

[D] HIGH SCHOOLS, PRIVATE

PATERSON. *Don Bosco Technical High School*, 202 Union Ave., 07502. Tel: 973-595-8800. Revs. Patrick Angelucci, S.D.B., Dir.; A. J. Louis, S.D.B.; Paul P. Avallone, S.D.B.; Patrick Diver, S.D.B.; Thomas McGahee, S.D.B.; Stephen Ryan, S.D.B.; Bros. Bruno Busatta, S.D.B.; John Andres, S.D.B.; Thomas Dion, S.D.B.; Louis Konopeski, S.D.B.; Henry VanDer-Velden, S.D.B.; Andrew Bertello, S.D.B. Priests 6; Brothers 6; Sisters 2; Lay Teachers 20; Students 325.

Don Bosco Volunteers, Inc. Rev. Paul P. Avallone, S.D.B., Contact Person.

CONVENT STATION. *Academy of St. Elizabeth*, 07961. Tel: 973-292-6414. Sisters of Charity. Sr. Patricia Mary McMullen, S.C., Prin. Sisters 6; Lay Teachers 26; Students 205.

MORRISTOWN. *Delbarton School*, 230 Mendham Rd., 07960. Tel: 973-538-3231. Day School for Boys. (Grades 7-12). Rev. Giles P. Hayes, O.S.B., Headmaster. Asst. Headmasters: Mr. John Kowalik; Mr. Edward Kim; Revs. Luke Travers, O.S.B., Dir. of Admissions; Edward Seton Fittin, O.S.B., Dir. Campus Min. Monks 20; Laymen 70; Students 515.

Villa Walsh Academy, 07960. Tel: 973-538-3680. College Preparatory for girls (Grades 7-12). Conducted by Religious Teachers Filippini. Sr. Patricia Pompa, M.P.F., Prin. Sisters 12; Lay Teachers 20; Students 222.

NORTH HALEDON. *Mary Help of Christians Academy*, 659-723 Belmont Ave., 07508. Tel: 973-790-6200.
E-mail: fma24@cyberney.net
Daughters of Mary Help of Christians (Salesian Sisters). Sr. Carmen Pena, F.M.A., Supr.; Sr. Karen Dunn, F.M.A., Prin.; Rev. Kenneth Shaw, S.D.B., Chap. Sisters 24; Lay Teachers 12; Students 255.

[E] ELEMENTARY SCHOOLS, DIOCESAN

CLIFTON. *Pope John Paul II School*. Serving St. John the Baptist Cathedral and St. Joseph, Paterson, 775 Valley Rd., 07013. Tel: 973-458-9282. Sr. Judith Suprys, F.M.A., Prin. Asst. Principals: Ms. Kathleen Fields; Sr. Theresa Samson, F.M.A. Sisters 6; Lay Teachers 27; Students 760.

[F] REGIONAL ELEMENTARY SCHOOLS

FRANKLIN. *Immaculate Conception Regional School*, 65 Church St., 07416. Mrs. Sheila O'Leary, Prin. Serves Immaculate Conception, Franklin; Our Lady of Fatima, Highland Lakes; St. John Vianney, Stockholm; St. Monica, Sussex; St. Thomas of Aquin, Ogdensburg; St. Francis De Sales, McAfee; St. Jude, Hamburg. Sisters 3; Lay Teachers 10; Students 287.

NEWTON. *St. Joseph Regional School*, Jefferson St., 07860. Tel: 973-383-2909; Fax: 973-383-6353.
E-mail: sba@nac.net
Sr. Betty Ann Martinez, F.M.A., Prin. Serves St. Joseph, Newton; Our Lady Queen of Peace, Branchville; Our Lady of Mount Carmel, Swartswood. Sisters 1; Lay Teachers 9; Students 207.

PASSAIC. *Passaic Catholic Regional School*, 212 Market St., 07055. Sr. Joselle Ratka, C.S.S.F., Prin. Serves Holy Rosary, St. Joseph, St. Stephen, St. Mary, Our Lady of Fatima, in Passaic. Sisters 1; Lay Teachers 10; Students 216.

[G] PRIVATE PRESCHOOL

FLORHAM PARK. *Magic Kingdom Day Care Nursery School*, 88 Brookline Rd., 07932. Tel: 973-966-9762. Vocationist Sisters. Sr. Romilda A. Borges, S.D.V., Prin. Sisters 9; Lay Teachers 3; Students 85.

NEWTON. *Camp Auxilium Center*, 14 Old Swartswood Rd., 07860. Tel: 973-383-2621.
E-mail: fmaca@juno.com
Salesian Sisters. Sr. Lou Ann Fantauzza, F.M.A., Prin. Sisters 4; Lay Teachers 12; Students 275.

PARSIPPANY. *St. Elizabeth's Nursery and Montessori School, Inc.*, 499 Park Rd., 07054. Tel: 973-540-0721. Sr. Rosa Maria Miranda, F.S.S.E., Contact Person. Students 180.

[H] CHILDREN'S CENTERS

DENVILLE. *St. Peter's Village*, 170 Diamond Spring Rd., 07834. Tel: 973-627-0212; Fax: 973-627-3338. Staffed by School Sisters of Notre Dame. Sr. Katherine M. Kinnally, S.S.N.D., Dir. Sisters 1; Residents 16.

TOTOWA. *Mt. St. Joseph Children's Center*, 124 Shepherds Ln., 07512. Tel: 973-595-5720. Residential Treatment Center for Emotionally Disturbed Boys. Under the direction of Catholic Family and Community Services. Sr. Dorothy Sheahan, S.C., Dir. Residents 32; Day Students 8.

[I] RETREAT HOUSES & HOUSES OF PRAYER

BRANCHVILLE. *Sanctuary of Mary-Our Lady of the Holy Spirit*, 252 Wantage Ave., 07826. Tel: 973-875-7625. Rev. Silvester J. Livolsi (NEW).

CHESTER. *Hermits of Bethlehem of the Heart of Jesus*, Pleasant Hill Rd., 07930. Rev. Eugene L. Romano, Desert Father. Priests 1; Brother Candidates 1; Sisters 4.

CONVENT STATION. *Xavier Center*, 07961. Tel: 973-290-5100; Fax: 973-290-5121.
E-mail: cahxavier@aol.com
A retreat & conference center. Sr. Carol Heller, S.C., Admin.

FLORHAM PARK. *Vocationist Fathers Retreat Center*, 90 Brooklake Rd., 07932. Tel: 973-966-6262. Rev. Edgar Da Cunha, S.D.V., Dir.

MENDHAM. *Villa Pauline*, 07945. Retreat House for Men & Women. Sisters of Christian Charity 5.

MORRISTOWN. *Good Shepherd Retreat Center*, 74 Kahdena Rd., 07960. Tel: 973-538-4233. Legal Title: *Sisters of the Good Shepherd of New Jersey*. Sr. Marie Barbara, R.G.S., Supr. Sisters 2.

Loyola House of Retreats, 161 James St., 07960. Tel: 973-539-0740. Society of Jesus. Revs. William P. Walsh, S.J., Supr. & Dir.; Richard J. Anable, S.J.; Donald G. Devine, S.J.; John J. McDonald, S.J.; Edmund W. Nagle, S.J.; Robert E. O'Donnell, S.J.; Emmet J. Norton, S.J.; William R. O'Leary, S.J., Admin.; Thomas F. Walsh, S.J.; Sr. Barbara Connell, S.C.; Sr. Irene M. Garvey, O.P. Priests 9; Sisters 2.

St. Mary's Abbey Retreat Center, 230 Mendham Rd., 07960. Tel: 973-538-5231, Ext. 2100. Rev. Beatus T. Lucey, O.S.B., Dir.

MOUNT ARLINGTON. *Felician Retreat House*, 35 Windemere Ave., 07856. Tel: 973-398-9806. Sr. Mary Gilbert Szaroleta, C.S.S.F., Dir.

NEWTON. *Queen of Peace Retreat House*, St. Paul's Abbey, P.O. Box 7, 07860. Tel: 973-383-2470; 393-0660. Rt. Rev. Joel Macul, O.S.B.; Deacon Edward J. Reading.

Sacred Heart Retreat Center, 20 Old Swartswood Rd., 07860. Tel: 973-383-2620.
E-mail: shcenter@juno.com
Daughters of Mary Help of Christians. Sr. Catherine Hurley, F.M.A., Supr. Sisters 6.

OAK RIDGE. *Mount Paul Retreat Center*, 243 Mt. Paul Rd., 07438. Tel: 973-697-6341. Annette Morin, Admin.

RINGWOOD. *Mt. St. Francis Retreat Center*, 474 Sloatsburg Rd., 07456. Tel: 973-962-9778. Sr. Theresa Regina, F.S.R., Admin.

[J] GENERAL HOSPITALS

PATERSON. *St. Joseph's Hospital and Medical Center*, 703 Main St., 07503. Tel: 973-754-2000
For a complete listing, refer to the Hospitals section.

DENVILLE. *Northwest Covenant Medial Center*, 25 Pocono Rd., 07834
For a complete listing, refer to the Hospitals section.

Sisters of the Sorrowful Mother Ambulatory Care Corp., c/o 25 Pocono Rd., 07834
For a complete listing, refer to the Hospitals section.

PASSAIC. *St. Mary's Hospital*, 211 Pennington Ave., 07055. Tel: 973-470-3000
For a complete listing, refer to the Hospitals section.

[K] HOMES FOR AGED

PATERSON. *St. Joseph Rest Home for Aged Women*, 46 Preakness Ave., 07522
For a complete listing, refer to the Special Care Facilities section.

DENVILLE. *Franciscan Oaks Independent Living Units & Health Center*, 21 Pocono Rd., 07834
For a complete listing, refer to the Special Care Facilities section.

St. Francis Health Resort, 07834 Fax: 973-625-9245.
E-mail: billmili@aol.com
For a complete listing, refer to the Special Care Facilities section.

TOTOWA. *St. Joseph's Home for the Elderly*, 140 Shepherd Ln., 07512. Tel: 973-942-0300
For a complete listing, refer to the Special Care Facilities section.

[L] RESIDENCES FOR WOMEN

PATERSON. *St. Frances Residence*, 25 Jackson St., 07501. Sr. Joyce Vincent, S.C., Admin. Sisters of Charity of St. Elizabeth, NJ 3; Residents 35.

MORRISTOWN. *Dericks Residence*, 70 MacCulloch Ave., 07960. Tel: 973-292-9517. Mr. James Stauner, Dir. Residents 25.

POMPTON LAKES. *Eugene Kennedy Residence*, 31 Pompton Ave., 07442. Tel: 973-835-1476. Sr. M. Beatrice Kereszi, F.S.P., Admin. Residents 13.

WAYNE. *Bethany Residence*, 738 Rte. 23, 07470. Tel: 973-628-8109. Sr. Joseph Loretto, M.S.B.T., Admin. Residents 12.

Kilroy Residence, 584 Ratzer Rd., 07470. Tel: 973-694-3594. Sr. Roseanna Seifert, F.S.P., Dir.; Sr. Maria Francis Shebellock, F.S.P., Asst. Dir. Residents 12.

WEST PATERSON. *Holy Family Residence*, 44 Rifle Camp Rd., P.O. Box 536, 07424. Conducted by the Missionary Sisters of the Immaculate Conception of the Mother of God. M. Catherine Dulio, Admin. Residents 44.

[M] MONASTERIES AND RESIDENCES OF PRIESTS AND BROTHERS

PATERSON. *St. Benedict the Moor Friary*, 146 Danforth Ave., 07501. Tel: 973-523-0808; Fax: 973-523-5904. Rev. Claude Lenehan, O.F.M.; Bros. Vincent Casamento, O.F.M.; Robert Frazzetta, O.F.M.; Edward Higgins, O.F.M.; Paul Santoro, O.F.M., Guardian.

BUTLER. *St. Anthony Friary*, 63 Bartholdi Ave., 07405. Tel: 973-838-4080. Order of Friars Minor. Revs. Richard P. Biasiotto, O.F.M., Guardian; John S. Ahearn, O.F.M.; Emmett A. Barrett, O.F.M.; Giulio F. Basetti-Sani, O.F.M.; Maurice J. Brick, O.F.M.; Patrick M. Brown, O.F.M.; Kieran A. Cassion, O.F.M.; Bernard R. Creighton, O.F.M.; Emmanuel Duffy, O.F.M.; Cary Kean, O.F.M.; Matthew L. Gaskin, O.F.M.; Charles V. Hayes, O.F.M.; Cordius P. Kazanchy, O.F.M.; Leonard A. Kelly, O.F.M.; Basil F. Lobby, O.F.M.; Gerald R. McDonald, O.F.M.; Anthony McGuire, O.F.M.; Edward A. McGuire, O.F.M.; Frederick McKeever, O.F.M.; Theodore A. McNally, O.F.M.; Alexus J. Mulrenan, O.F.M.; LaSalle O'Friel, O.F.M.; Michael V. Perry, O.F.M.; J. Felton Robertson, O.F.M.; Jude Smith, O.F.M.; Bros. Peter R. Butler, O.F.M.; Fintan Duffy, O.F.M.; Rosario Vieira, O.F.M.; Daniel F. Murray, O.F.M., Vicar. Priests 25; Brothers 4.

CLIFTON. *Holy Face of Jesus Monastery*, 1697 State Hwy. 3, P.O. Box 691, 07012. Sylvestrine Benedictine Monks. Revs. Hilary Conti, O.S.B.; Bruno Daniel, O.S.B.; Thomas Toomey, O.S.B.; Joseph Kulathinal, O.S.B. Priests 4.

FLORHAM PARK. *Father Justin Vocationary*, 90 Brooklake Rd., 07932. Tel: 973-966-6262. Revs. Mario Muccitelli, S.D.V., Delegate; Edgar da Cunha, S.D.V., Supr.; Ugo Fraraccio, S.D.V.; Robert Vass, S.D.V.

LAFAYETTE. *St. Francis Center*, 07848. Tel: 973-383-6465. Capuchin Friars. Bro. Julius Tkaczyk, O.F.M.Cap., Vicar; Rev. Brian Tomlinson, O.F.M.Cap., Local Minister. Priests 1; Brothers 1.

MORRISTOWN. *St. Mary's Abbey*, Delbarton, 230 Mendham Rd., 07960. Tel: 973-538-3231. Rt. Revs. Gerald P. Lair, O.S.B., Abbot; Brian H. Clark, O.S.B., Abbot Emeritus; Leonard G. Cassell, O.S.B., Abbot Emeritus; Martin J. Burne, O.S.B., Abbot Emeritus; Very Rev. Elias R. Lorenzo, O.S.B., Prior; Revs. Jerome Borski, O.S.B.; Kevin M. Bray, O.S.B.; Thomas J. Confroy, O.S.B.; Benet W. Caffrey, O.S.B.; Christian J. Casper, O.S.B.; Gabriel M. Coless, O.S.B.; Michael J. Collins, O.S.B.; Mark W. Confroy, O.S.B.; Conall R. Coughlin, O.S.B.; Richard J. Cronin, O.S.B.; Edward Seton J. Fittin, O.S.B.; Jerome B. Fitzpatrick, O.S.B.; Germain L. Fritz, O.S.B.; Simon P. Gallagher, O.S.B.; Giles P. Hayes, O.S.B.; John E. Hesketh, O.S.B.; Joel J. Leikhim, O.S.B.; Beatus T. Lucey, O.S.B.; Adrian T. McLaughlin, O.S.B.; Kenneth H. Mayer, O.S.B.; Peter J. Meaney, O.S.B.; James O'Donnell, O.S.B.; Hilary O'Leary, O.S.B.; Rembert F. Reilly, O.S.B.; Joachim B. Schweitzer, O.S.B.; Andrew T. Smith, O.S.B.; Luke L. Travers, O.S.B.; Regis P. Wallace, O.S.B. Total Priests 42; Serving Out of Diocese 10; Brothers 9. Bros. John Babicz, O.S.B.; Damian B. Breen, O.S.B.; Paul J. Diviney, O.S.B.; Tarcisius Hoang-Hoa, O.S.B.; Jonathan M. Hunt, O.S.B.; Ambrose J. Kelly, O.S.B.; Christopher K. Rosa, O.S.B.; Anthony s. Sargent, O.S.B.; Kiernan M. Shiek, O.S.B.; Brendan A. Tumalty, O.S.B.
Resident Outside the Abbey: Revs. Timothy J. Brennan, O.S.B.; Donal R. Fox, O.S.B.; Patrick M. Hurley, O.S.B.; Karl J. Roesch, O.S.B.; Jude S. Salus, O.S.B.; Wilfred G. Schulz, O.S.B.; Bruno A. Ugliano, O.S.B.; Benedict Michael Worry, O.S.B.; Justino Capato, O.S.B.; Bro. James Konchalski, O.S.B. Total Priests 42; Serving Out of Diocese 9; Brothers 11.

NEWTON. *St. Paul's Abbey*, 07860. Tel: 973-383-2470; Fax: 973-383-5782. (Formerly the Little Flower Monastery). Order of St. Benedict, Congregation of St. Ottilien. Rt. Revs. Joel P. Macul, O.S.B., Abbot; Justin E. Dzikowicz, O.S.B., Resigned; Augustine J. Hinches, O.S.B., (Resigned); Charles V. Coriston, O.S.B., (Resigned); Revs. Boniface D. Cronin, O.S.B.; Andrew C. O'Sullivan, O.S.B.; Jude C. Bradley, O.S.B.; Patrick J. Bonner, O.S.B.; Bede E. Classick, O.S.B.; Basil J. Wallace, O.S.B.
Priests Residing Outside the Monastery: Mailing Address: P.O. Box 213, Lushoto, Tanzania. Rev. Damian J. Milliken, O.S.B., Inkamana Abbey, P/Bag X9333, Vayheid 3100, South Africa. Rev. Peter W. Blue, O.S.B. Priests 12; Lay Monks 2.

OAK RIDGE-MILTON. *St. Stanislaus B. M. Friary*, Manor Dr., 07438. Tel: 973-697-7757. Capuchin Fathers. Revs. Hyacinth M. Dabrowski, O.F.M.Cap.; Henry T. Krajewski, O.F.M.Cap., Superior; Francis Mucharski, O.F.M.Cap.; Francis J. Salwowski, O.F.M.Cap.; Sigmund M. Klimowicz, O.F.M.Cap.; Peter Gacki, O.F.M.Cap.; Francis Majewski, O.F.M.Cap., Vicar; George J. Korytkowski, O.F.M.Cap.; Joseph M. Kubiak, O.F.M.Cap.; Stephen Laliberte, O.F.M.Cap.; Ivot Miszkel, O.F.M.Cap. Priests 9.

RINGWOOD. *Holy Name Friary, Inc.*, 2 Morris Rd., 07456. Tel: 973-962-7200. Revs. A. Francis Soucy, O.F.M., Supr. & Contact Person; Arthur Butler, O.F.M.; Francis Carroll, O.F.M.; Flavian Colligan, O.F.M.; Justin Eeles, O.F.M.; Robert Gabel, O.F.M.; Cosmas Girard, O.F.M.; Hugh King, O.F.M.; Roch Knopke, O.F.M.; Gerard Lewis, O.F.M.; Valentine Long, O.F.M.; Cyprian Lynch, O.F.M.; Raphael McDonald, O.F.M.; Kieran F. McMahon, O.F.M.; Lucian Mulhern, O.F.M.; Owen J. Ormsby, O.F.M.; Lawrence F. Pafchik, O.F.M.; Vincent Shea, O.F.M.; Eric Shoppe, O.F.M.; Hilary Scott, O.F.M.; Gregory Toomey, O.F.M.; Bros. Hormisdas Marcotte, O.F.M.; Gilbert McEvoy, O.F.M.; Joseph P. Trunk, O.F.M.; Agapitus Rothmann, O.F.M.; Paul Slaby, O.F.M.

STIRLING. *Holy Spirit Missionary Cenacle*, 1050 Long Hill Rd., 07980. Tel: 908-647-0208. Missionary Servants of the Most Holy Trinity. Revs. Peter Krebs, S.T., Custodian; Vincent Fitzpatrick, S.T.; Cajetan McDyre, S.T.; Ralph Frisch, S.T.; Campion Murphy, S.T.; Stephen Quinn, S.T.; Bro. Martin Pacholek, S.T. Priests 6; Brothers 1.

Serenity Retreat League, 1292 Long Hill Rd., Box 10, 07980. Tel: 908-647-1539. Sr. Mary T. Lynch, S.F.C.C., Dir.

Shrine of St. Joseph, 1050 Long Hill Rd., 07980. Tel: 908-647-0208. Rev. Peter Krebs, S.T., Custodian. Priests 6; Brothers 1; Sisters 6.

WAYNE. *P.I.M.E. Missionaries Residence*, 34 Grandview Dr., 07470. Tel: 973-694-1790; Fax: 973-694-0444.
E-mail: pimeusanj@aol
Web site: www.rc.net/pime
Revs. Luigi Acerbi, P.I.M.E.; Claudio Corti, P.I.M.E.; Luciano Ghezzi, P.I.M.E.

Xaverian Missionary Fathers, Provincial House, 12 Helene Court, 07470. Tel: 973-942-2975.
E-mail: xavmissionsnj@msn.com
Revs. Francis Signorelli, S.X., Prov.; Dario Maso, S.X.; Frank Grappoli, S.X.; Herondi Fernandes, S.X.
Mission Assignments: Makeni, Sierra Leone: Revs.

Gerard Furlan, S.X.; Victor Mosele, S.X.; Luciano Peterlini, S.X.
Belem, Brazil: Revs. Francis Gugliotta, S.X.; Danilo Lago, S.X.; Mario Pezzotti, S.X.
Cameroon: Rev. Rene Lovat, S.X.
Uvira, Dem. Rep. of the Congo: Rev. Noel Tomasi, S.X.
Sao Paulo, Brazil: Rev. Gino Nasini, S.X.
Padang, Indonesia: Revs. Bruno Orru, S.X.; Frank Qualizza, S.X.
Buenaventura, Columbia: Rev. Mark Marangone, S.X.
Torreon, Mexico: Revs. Danilo Boschetto, S.X.; Adolph Menendez, S.X.
Bujumbura, Burundi: Rev. Joseph Tavera, S.X.
Taiwan: Revs. Julian Perozzi, S.X.; Martino Roia, S.X.; Joseph Matteucig, S.X.

[N] CONVENTS AND RESIDENCES FOR SISTERS

PATERSON. *Daughters of Charity of the Most Precious Blood*, 46 Preakness Ave., 07522. Sr. Maria Goretti Chaloux, D.C.P.B., Supr. Sisters 11.
Daughters of Mary Help of Christians. Sr. Carmen Pena, F.M.A., Supr.
Missionary Sisters of the Immaculate Conception of the Mother of God, 779 Broadway, 07509. Mailing Address: P.O. Box 3026, 07509-3026. Sr. Margaret Reid, S.M.I.C., Prov. Coord.
Missionary Sisters of the Immaculate Conception of the Mother of God, 396 E. 38th St., 07504. Sisters 2.
Missionary Sisters of the Immaculate of the Mother of God, 374-18th Ave., 07504. Sisters 6.

CHESTER. *Carmel of the Immaculate Heart of Mary.* Hermits of Our Lady of Mt. Carmel (Diocesan Community), 80 Pleasant Hill Rd., 07930-2135. Tel: 908-879-4990. Sr. Mary of Jesus and St. Joseph, H.O.Carm., Desert Mother. Sisters 5.

CONVENT STATION. *Motherhouse of the Sisters of Charity.* Mailing Address: P.O. Box 476, 07961. Tel: 973-290-5424.
E-mail: escharity@aol.com
Sr. Barbara Conroy, S.C., General Supr. Professed Sisters 105.
St. Anne Villa. Mailing Address: P.O. Box 476, 07961. Tel: 973-292-6555.
E-mail: srcsc@aol.com
Sisters of Charity of St. Elizabeth. Home for retired and infirm Sisters. Sr. Rosanne Caiazzo, S.C., Admin.; Rev. Mark W. Confroy, O.S.B., Chap. Bed Capacity 115.

DENVILLE. *Our Lady of Sorrows Convent, Sisters of Sorrowful Mother*, 9 Pocono Rd., 07834.
Residences: 4 Pocono Rd., 07834. 45 N. Shore Dr., 07834. 21 Cooper Rd., Boonton, 07005. 40 E. Main St., Rockaway, 07866. R.R. 1, Box 390, Hamburg, 07419. Sisters 39.

FLORHAM PARK. *Sister Joanna House of Formation*, 88 Brooklake Rd., 07932. Tel: 973-966-9762. Sr. Anna Maria Mancino, S.D.V., Delegate & Superior; Sr. Romilda A. Borges, S.D.V., Prin. Sisters 9.

GLADSTONE. *Mt. St. John Convent*, 07934. Tel: 908-234-1074; 234-0640. Sisters of St. John the Baptist. Sr. Angelita Vazzano, C.S.J.B., Admin. Sisters 8.

HALEDON. *Institute of the Daughters of Mary Help of Christians*, 655 Belmont Ave., 07508. Tel: 973-790-7964. Provincialate of Daughters of Mary Help of Christians. Mother Theresa Kelly, F.M.A., Prov.; Sr. Grace Ruiz, F.M.A., Supr.; Rev. Innocent Clementi, S.D.B., Chap. Daughters of Mary Help of Christians (Salesian Sisters) 46.

HEWITT. *St. Joseph's Convent*, Long House Dr., 07421. Sisters of Mercy, Daughters of Charity of St. Vincent de Paul of Hungary. Sisters 6.

MENDHAM. *Mallinckrodt Convent-Motherhouse and Novitiate of the Sisters of Christian Charity*, 07945. Tel: 973-543-6528.
E-mail: socc@tsa.net
Daughters of the Blessed Virgin Mary of the Immaculate Conception. Sr. Mary Edward Spohrer, S.C.C., Prov. Supr. Sisters 54; Novices 4; Postulants 3.

MORRISTOWN. *Monastery Discalced Carmelite Nuns of the Most Blessed Virgin Mary of Mt. Carmel*, 189 Madison Ave., 07960. Mother Mary Michael, O.C.D., Prioress. Professed Nuns 7; Extern Sisters 1; Postulants 2.
St. Lucy Provincialate of the Religious Teachers Filippini, Novitiate, Villa Walsh Academy, 455 Western Ave., 07960-4928. Tel: 973-538-2886.
E-mail: mpfprovoffice@msn.com
Legal Title: *Pontifical Institute of the Religious Teachers Fillippini.* Sr. Frances Lauretti, M.P.F., Prov.; Sr. Ascenza Tizzano, M.P.F., Supr.; Sr. Dolores Potkay, M.P.F., Dir. Formation. Sisters 86; Junior Professed 3.

MOUNT ARLINGTON. *Felician Sisters of St. Francis of Assisi Convent*, 37 Windemere Ave., 07856. Sr. Mary Josita, C.S.S.F., Local Supr. Professed Sisters 7.

OAK RIDGE. *Society of the Sisters of the Church*, 15 Heritage Ct., 07438. Tel: 973-208-1456. Sr. Sylvia Berzinski, S.S.C., Coord. Sisters 11.

PARSIPPANY. *St. Francis of Assisi Novitiate-Franciscan Sisters of St. Elizabeth*, 499 Park Rd., 07054. Tel: 973-539-3797.
E-mail: ludovico@garden.net
Mother Gina Maria Amico, F.S.S.E., Delegate General; Rev. Philip W. Nielsen, O.F.M., Chap., Tel: 973-605-8729; Fax: 973-539-3347. Perpetually Professed Sisters 17; Temp. Professed Sisters 15; Novices 7; Postulants 1.

PASSAIC. *Missionary Sisters of Divine Providence*, 302 Madison Ave., 07542. Tel: 973-278-1030. Sr. Faustina Paulino, M.S.D.P., Supr. Sisters 3; Associates 3.
Our Lady of Mt. Carmel Convent, Franciscan Sisters of Ringwood, 47 Reid Ave., 07055. Tel: 973-471-6352. Sr. M. Berard, F.S.R., Supr. Sisters 5.
St. Joseph Convent, 9 Quincy St., 07055. Sr. Krystyna Kwasniak, D.P.H.M., Supr.

RINGWOOD. *Mt. St. Francis*, 07456. Tel: 973-962-7411. General Motherhouse and Novitiate of the Franciscan Sisters. Sr. Annette Lucchese, F.S.R., Gen. Coord.; Rev. Lawrence Burke, O.F.M. Professed Sisters 32.

STIRLING. *Blessed Trinity Missionary Cenacle*, 1190 Long Hill Rd., 07980. Tel: 908-647-1165. Missionary Servants of the Most Blessed Trinity 3.
Holy Trinity Convent, 1026 Long Hill Rd., 07980. Tel: 908-647-6584. Sr. Anna Karusat, Supr. Servants of Jesus 6.

WEST PATERSON. *Missionary Sisters of the Immaculate Conception of the Mother of God*, Generalate, 48 Garden Ave., 07424. Sr. Luci Fontenele, S.M.I.C., Coord. Gen. Sisters 4.
Missionary Sisters of the Immaculate Conception, Convent of the Immaculate Conception, 44 Rifle Camp Rd., 07424. Tel: 973-279-2621; Fax: 973-754-1577. Sr. Margaret Mary Newkirk, S.M.I.C., Coord.; Rev. Donald Sella, Chap.
The Society of Sisters for the Church, 396 Rifle Camp Rd., 07424. Sr. Dorothy Wilkinson, S.S.C., Pres. Sisters 22; Companions 3; Observers 3.

[O] NEWMAN CENTERS

CONVENT STATION. *College of St. Elizabeth Newman Center*, 07960. Tel: 973-290-4300; Fax: 973-290-4312.
E-mail: @liza.st.elizabeth.edu
Web site: http://www.st.elizabeth.edu
Rev. Anthony J. Ciorra.

HALEDON. *William Paterson University of New Jersey Catholic Campus Ministry Center*, 219 Pompton Rd., 07508.
E-mail: scurti@frontier.wilpaterson.edu
Web site: www.wilpaterson.edu/clubs/ccmc-mast.htm
Rev. Louis J. Scurti.

MADISON. *Drew University Catholic Campus Ministry.* Chaplain's Office, President's House Annex, 07940. Tel: 973-408-3027. Rev. Joseph G. Farias. Tel: 973-627-0066.
Fairleigh Dickinson University and Drew University. Catholic Campus Ministry, Fairleigh Dickinson University, 285 Madison Ave., 07940. Tel: 973-593-8651. Rev. Joseph G. Farias, Res: 446 Mt. Hope Rd., Wharton, 07885-2814. Tel: 973-627-0066.

[P] MISCELLANEOUS LISTINGS

PATERSON. *Martin de Porres Village Corporation*, Green St., 07501. Tel: 973-881-8022. Rev. Msgr. Herbert K. Tillyer, Pres. Sponsoring Martin De Porres, Vill.
Riese Corporation, Twentieth Ave., 07501. Tel: 973-279-2262. Rev. Msgr. Joseph R. Brestel, Pres. Sponsoring Governor Paterson Towers, Maurice Brick Residence, Brestel Residence, William F. Hinchcliffe Manor.
St. Anthony's Guild, 07509. Tel: 973-777-3737.
E-mail: anthonian@aol.com
Membership organization supports the work of The Franciscan Friars of Holy Name Province. Revs. Joseph M. Hertel, O.F.M., Dir.; Cassian A. Miles, O.F.M.; Allan Von Kobs, O.F.M.; Felician A. Foy, O.F.M.; Rayner F. Williams, O.F.M.

CHESTER. *Nazareth Village*, Main St., Box 635, 07930. Retirement residence for diocesan priests. Rev. Raymond M. Lopatesky, Dir. In res. Revs. Martin Connolly; Charles Grieco; Robert J. Morris; Patrick Mullan; Raymond J. Jasaitis; Rev. Msgr. Carl J. Wolsin; Rev. Msgr. Joseph J. Gallo; Rev. Msgr. Louis J. Gallo; Rev. Msgr. John R. Ryan; Rev. Msgr. Leo P. Ryan; Rev. Msgr. Walter Pruschowitz; Rev. Msgr. Leo P. Carey.

CONVENT STATION. *Seton Health Care, Inc.*, Convent of Saint Elizabeth, P.O. Box 476, 07961. Tel: 973-292-6545. Sr. Barbara Conroy, S.C., Pres.

MORRISTOWN. *Priests Residence*, 74 Kahdena Rd., 07960. Revs. Robert M. Diachek; Hugh P. Murphy.

PASSAIC. *St. Jude Media Ministries*, 63 Monroe St., 07055. Tel: 973-777-0303; Fax: 973-472-5033. Rev. John T. Catoir, Dir.

STIRLING. *Father Judge Apostolic Center*, 1292 Long Hill Rd., 07980. Tel: 908-647-7112; 647-2422 (Res.); Fax: 908-647-6045.
E-mail: fjac3@aol.com
Rev. Dennis Berry, S.T., Dir.; Bonnie Hackett, Admin.; Melissa Enzmann, Communications Dir.
Trinity Mission Center, 1292 Long Hill Rd., 07980. Tel: 908-647-7003.
Sponsored by: Missionary Servants of the Most Holy Trinity. Rev. Dennis Berry, S.T. Service opportunities through the Missionary Cenacle Family.

WAYNE. *Siena Village*, 1000 Siena Village, 07470. Tel: 973-226-0730. Sr. Alice Matthews, O.P., Dir.
Via Caritas Health System, Inc., 57 Willowbrook Blvd., Ste. 205, 07470. Tel: 973-625-6681. Sr. Jane Frances Brady, S.C., Chm.; Joseph Trunfio, Ph.D., Pres. & CEO.

RELIGIOUS INSTITUTES OF MEN REPRESENTED IN THE DIOCESE

For further details refer to the corresponding bracketed number in the Religious Institutes of Men or Women section.

[0200]—*Benedictine Monks.* (St. Mary, St. Paul Abbeys; Holy Face of Jesus Residence).—O.S.B.
[0470]—*The Capuchin Friars* .(Italian, Polish). —O.F.M.Cap.
[0480]—*Conventual Franciscans.*(Polish).—O.F.M.Conv.
[0520]—*Franciscan Friars.* (Holy Name Prov.).—O.F.M.
[0690]—*Jesuit Fathers and Brothers.* (New York Prov.).—S.J.
[0840]—*Missionary Servants of the Most Holy Trinity.* (Silver Spring, MD).—S.T.
[1030]—*Paulist Fathers.* (New York).—C.S.P.
[1190]—*Salesians of Don Bosco.* (Turin, Italy).—S.D.B.
[1340]—*Vocationist Fathers.*—S.D.V.
[1360]—*Xaverian Missionary Fathers.* (Wayne).—S.X.

RELIGIOUS INSTITUTES OF WOMEN REPRESENTED IN THE DIOCESE

[0230]—*Benedictine Sisters of Pontifical Jurisdiction.*—O.S.B.
[0740]—*Daughters of Charity of the Most Precious Blood.*—D.C.P.B.
[0850]—*Daughters of Mary Help of Christians.*—F.M.A.
[]—*Daughters of the Most Pure Heart of the Most Holy Virgin Mary.* (Passaic).
[0420]—*Discalced Carmelite Nuns.*—O.C.D.
[1070-06]—*Dominican Sisters.*—O.P.
[1070-18]—*Dominican Sisters.*—O.P.
[1170]—*Felician Sisters.*—C.S.S.F.
[1400]—*Franciscan Missionary Sisters of the Sacred Heart.* (Peekskill).—F.M.S.C.
[1420]—*Franciscan Sisters of Ringwood.*—F.S.R.
[1460]—*Franciscan Sisters of St. Elizabeth.*—F.S.S.E.
[]—*Hermits of Our Lady of Mt. Carmel.*—H.O.Carm.
[2340]—*Little Sisters of the Poor.*—L.S.P.
[2790]—*Missionary Servants of the Most Blessed Trinity.*—M.S.B.T.
[2760]—*Missionary Sisters of the Immaculate Conception of the Mother of God.*—S.M.I.C.
[3430]—*Religious Teachers Filippini.*—M.P.F.
[2970]—*School Sisters of Notre Dame.*—S.S.N.D.
[1700]—*School Sisters of the Third Order of St. Francis.*—O.S.F.
[3560]—*Servants of Jesus.* (Starling).—S.J.
[3580]—*Servants of Mary.*—O.S.M.
[0590]—*Sisters of Charity of Saint Elizabeth, Convent Station.*—S.C.
[0660]—*Sisters of Christian Charity.*—S.C.C.
[3820]—*Sisters of St. John the Baptist.*—C.S.J.B.
[3830]—*Sisters of St. Joseph.* (Chestnut Hill, PA).—C.S.J.
[3890]—*Sisters of St. Joseph of Peace.*—C.S.J.P.
[1830]—*Sisters of the Good Shepherd.*—R.G.S.
[3320]—*Sisters of the Presentation of the B.V.M.*.—P.B.V.M.
[4100]—*Sisters of the Sorrowful Mother (Third Order of St. Francis).*—S.S.M.
[]—*The Society of the Sisters of the Church.* (Passaic).
[4210]—*Vocationist Sisters.*—S.D.V.

NECROLOGY

† Cassidy, Joseph A., Budd Lake, NJ St. Jude. —Died Oct. 21, 1997.
† Conlin, Raymond E., Clifton, NJ, St. Philip the Apostle. —Died Sept. 19, 1997.
† Donnelly, James, Paterson, NJ St. Stephen. —Died Sept. 24, 1997.
† Mahon, Rev. Msgr. David, Mountain Lakes, NJ, St. Catherine of Siena. —Died July 15, 1997.
† McCluskey, Vincent S., Denville, NJ, Morris Catholic High School. —Died April 7, 1997.

Diocese of Pensacola-Tallahassee

(Dioecesis Pensacolensis-Tallaseiensis)

Most Reverend

JOHN H. RICARD, S.S.J., D.D., PH.D., V.G.

Bishop of Pensacola-Tallahassee; ordained May 25, 1968; ordained Auxiliary Bishop of Baltimore July 2, 1984; appointed Bishop of Pensacola-Tallahassee January 21, 1997.

ESTABLISHED NOVEMBER 6, 1975.

Square Miles 14,044.

Comprises the following Counties: Bay, Calhoun, Escambia, Franklin, Gadsden, Gulf, Holmes, Jackson, Jefferson, Leon, Liberty, Madison, Okaloosa, Santa Rosa, Taylor, Wakulla, Walton and Washington Counties.

For legal titles of parishes and diocesan institutions, consult the Pastoral Center.

Pastoral Center: P.O. Drawer 17329, Pensacola, FL, 32522. Tel.: 904-432-1515; Fax: 904-436-6424.

E-mail address: CHANOF12529@aol.com

STATISTICAL OVERVIEW

Personnel	
Bishop	1
Priests: Diocesan Active in Diocese	52
Priests: Active Outside Diocese	8
Priests: Retired, Sick or Absent	14
Number of Diocesan Priests	74
Religious Priests in Diocese	9
Extern Priests in Diocese	28
Ordinations:	
Diocesan Priests	1
Permanent Deacons in Diocese	45
Total Brothers	5
Total Sisters	61
Parishes	
Parishes	49
With Resident Pastor:	
Resident Diocesan Priests	41
Resident Religious Priests	6
Without Resident Pastor:	
Administered by Priests	2
Missions	9
Professional Ministry Personnel:	
Brothers	5
Sisters	6
Lay Ministers	6
Welfare	
Catholic Hospitals	1
Total Assisted	20,269
Homes for the Aged	3
Total Assisted	186
Day Care and Extended Day Care Centers	3
Total Assisted	366
Special Centers for Social Services	7
Total Assisted	50,362
Educational	
Diocesan Students in Other Seminaries	9
Total Seminarians	9
High Schools, Diocesan and Parish	1
Total Students	600
Elementary Schools, Diocesan and Parish	8
Total Students	1,737
Non-residential Schools for the Disabled	1
Total Students	16
Catechesis/Religious Education:	
High School Students	1,582
Elementary Students	5,332
Total Students Under Catholic Instruction	9,276
Teachers in the Diocese:	
Sisters	8
Lay Teachers	139
Vital Statistics	
Receptions into the Church:	
Infant Baptism Totals	1,139
Adult Baptism Totals	155
Received into Full Communion	254
First Communions	1,217
Confirmations	906
Marriages:	
Catholic	208
Interfaith	199
Total Marriages	407
Deaths	541
Total Catholic Population	63,985
Total Population	1,256,474

Former Bishops—Most Rev. RENE H. GRACIDA, D.D., ord. May 23, 1959; appt. Titular Bishop of Masuccaba and Auxiliary of Miami, Dec. 6, 1971; cons. Jan. 25, 1972; appt. first Bishop of Pensacola-Tallahassee, Oct. 1, 1975; installed Nov. 6, 1975; transferred to Bishop of Corpus Christi, May 19, 1983.—Most Rev. J. KEITH SYMONS, D.D., Bishop of Pensacola-Tallahassee; ord. May 18, 1958; Titular Bishop of Siguritanus and Auxiliary of St. Petersburg; appt. Jan. 16, 1981; cons. March 19, 1981; Bishop of Pensacola-Tallahassee; appt. Sept. 29, 1983; installed Nov. 8, 1983; transferred to Bishop of Palm Beach, June 2, 1990.—Most Rev. JOHN M. SMITH, J.C.D., D.D., Bishop of Pensacola-Tallahassee; ord. May 27, 1961; Titular Bishop of Tre Taverne and Auxiliary of Newark; appt. Dec. 1, 1987; cons. Jan. 25, 1988; Bishop of Pensacola-Tallahassee; appt. June 25, 1991; installed July 31, 1991; transferred to Coadjutor of Trenton, Nov. 21, 1995.

Pastoral Center—11 N. "B" St., Pensacola, 32501. Tel: 850-432-1515; Fax: 850-436-6424., *Mailing Address: P.O. Drawer 17329, Pensacola, 32522.*

Chancellor—Rev. Msgr. JAMES AMOS, J.C.L.

Vicars for Priests—Revs. JOHN CASSIDY; MICHAEL FOLEY.

Vicar for Permanent Deacons—Deacon JOHN MORGAN.

Vicar for Religious—Rev. Msgr. JAMES AMOS, J.C.L.

Vice Chancellor & Notary—Rev. MICHAEL REED.

Vicars Forane—Very Rev. RICHARD J. BOWLES, V.F., Cathedral Vicariate Forane; Very Rev. MICHAEL MOONEY, V.F., Northwest Vicariate Forane; Very Rev. STEVEN O'CONNOR, V.F., Southwest Vicariate Forane; Very Rev. FRANCIS SZCZYKUTOWICZ, V.F., North Central Vicariate Forane; Rev. Msgr. RAYMOND MULLINS, West Central Vicariate Forane; Rev. Msgr. WILLIAM A. CROWE, V.F., East Central Vicariate Forane; Very Rev. JOHN V. O'SULLIVAN, V.F., Eastern Vicariate Forane.

Diocesan Tribunal—1000 W. Garden St., Pensacola, 32501. Mailing Address: P.O. Drawer 17329, Pensacola, 32522. Tel: 850-436-6454.

Judicial Vicar—Very Rev. JAMES J. FLAHERTY, J.C.L.

Associate Judicial Vicar—Rev. Msgr. JAMES AMOS, J.C.L.

Judges—Very Rev. JAMES J. FLAHERTY, J.C.L.; Revs. WILLIAM P. BROWN, J.C.L.; TODD O. HEVIA, J.C.D.

Promoter of Justice—Rev. TODD O. HEVIA, J.C.D.

Auditors—Revs. THOMAS BONANTI; JOSEPH CALLIPARE; EUGENE D. CASSERLY; MICHAEL REED.

Defender of the Bond—Rev. Msgr. JAMES AMOS, J.C.L.

Notaries—Revs. JOSEPH CALLIPARE; MICHAEL REED; Deacons GERARD WILLIAMSON; RAMON BONANNO.

College of Consultors—Rev. Msgr. JAMES AMOS, J.C.L.; Rev. Msgr. RAYMOND MULLINS, V.F.; Very Rev. JAMES J. FLAHERTY; Revs. MICHAEL MOONEY; DANIEL BUTLER.

Administrative Council—Rev. Msgr. JAMES AMOS, J.C.L.; Very Revs. MICHAEL CHERUP; JAMES J. FLAHERTY; MICHAEL MOONEY; Rev. MICHAEL REED, Sec.; Sr. ELLEN KIERAN, M.S.B.T.; Mr. J. PATRICK REMICH.

Council of Permanent Deacons—Rev. Msgr. JAMES AMOS; Rev. Msgr. LUKE HUNT; Revs. JIM FLAHERTY; MARTIN HOLLEY; CRAIG WILLIAMS; Sr. CHRIS WILTRAKIS; Deacons JOHN MORGAN, Vicar for Deacons; HENRY BURRELL; THOMAS FRAITES; DALE JOHNSON; Dr. RAY BANANNO; Mr. PAT REMICH; Mrs. MINNIE SEABROOK.

Council of Sisters—Sr. MARGARET KUNTZ, A.S.C.J., Chm.; Sr. MARILYN DOUCETTE, C.N.D., Vice Chm.; Sr. MARGUERITE GIBBS, I.H.M., Sec. & Treas.; Sr. BARBARA MURRAY, R.S.M., Recording Sec.

Diocesan Commissions, Departments, And Offices

Apostleship of the Sea, Office of the—Very Rev. RICHARD J. BOWLES, V.F., Chap., *P.O. Drawer 17329, Pensacola, 32522.* Tel: 850-432-1515.

Archivist—FELECIA C. SONNIER, *P.O. Drawer 17329, Pensacola, 32522.* Tel: 850-432-1515.

Black Catholics, Office of—Deacon BRADLEY SEABROOK, Dir., *P.O. Drawer 17329, Pensacola, 32522.* Tel: 850-432-1515.

Building & Renovation, Diocesan Commission for—Rev. Msgr. GEORGE E. SINDIK, Chm.; Rev. Msgr. JAMES AMOS, J.C.L.; Rev. Msgr. LUKE HUNT; Mr. B. J. NICKELSEN; Mr. THEODORE J. RUCKSTUHL; Mr. J. PATRICK REMICH; FELECIA C. SONNIER, *P.O. Drawer 17329, Pensacola, 32522.* Tel: 850-432-1515.

Building & Renovation, Office of—Mr. B. J. NICKELSEN, Dir., *P.O. Drawer 17329, Pensacola, 32522.* Tel: 850-432-1515.

Campaign for Human Development, Office of—Rev. MICHAEL REED, Dir., *P.O. Drawer 17329, Pensacola, 32522.* Tel: 850-432-1515.

Campus Ministry—P.O. Drawer 17329, Pensacola, 32522. Tel: 850-432-1515. Pensacola-University of West Florida: Rev. MICHAEL FLYNN, Dir., *9945 Hillview Dr., Pensacola, 32514.* Tel: 850-477-3221. Tallahassee-Florida Agricultural & Mechanical University, St. Eugene Chapel: Rev. JOHN BOATENG-MENSAH, Dir., *701 Gamble St., Tallahassee, 32310.* Tel: 850-222-6482. Florida State University: Rev. TOM COLLINS, Dir., *P.O. Box 2395, Tallahassee, 32316.* Tel: 850-222-9630.

Catholic Daughters of the Americas—Rev. ROBERT F. MORRIS, Court Chap.; Mrs. JOYCE PFEIFFER, Regent, *304 N. Sunset Blvd., Gulf Breeze, 32507.*

Catholic Women, Diocesan Council of—Very Rev. RICHARD J. BOWLES, V.F., Spiritual Dir.; Mrs. JEANNETTE SCHAAL, Pres., *P.O. Drawer 17329, Pensacola, 32522.* Tel: 850-432-1515.

Catholic Social Services, Department of—Sr. ELLEN KIERAN, M.S.B.T., Dir. Offices—Pensacola: *222 E. Government St., Pensacola, 32501.* Tel: 850-436-6410. Fort Walton Beach:: Mrs. MARTI DEADRICK, Supvr., *40 Beal Pkwy. S.W., Fort Walton Beach, 32548.* Tel: 850-244-2825. Panama City:: Mrs. MILLIE DICKENS, Supvr., *3218 E. 11th St., Panama City, 32401.* Tel: 850-763-0475. Tallahassee:: Ms. WENDY J. BLAIR, Supvr., *P.O. Box 20165, Tallahassee, 32316.* Tel: 850-222-2180.

Cemetery Office—Deacon JEAN WHITE, Dir., *P.O. Drawer 17329, Pensacola, 32522.* Tel: 850-432-1515. *Holy Cross Cemetery, 1300 E. Hayes St., Pensacola, 32503.* Tel: 850-432-0878. Deacon JEAN WHITE, Dir., *Calvary Cemetery, 834 Sunny Hills Blvd., Sunny Hills, 32428.* Tel: 850-773-2165. Mr. FRED MCEVOY, Dir.

Charismatic Renewal, Diocesan Commission for—Rev. EUGENE PATHE, Moderator; Dr. YOLANDA RAMOS, Chm., *P.O. Drawer 17329, Pensacola, 32522.* Tel: 850-432-1515.

Christian Formation, Office of—Sr. CHRISTINE WILTRAKIS, M.S.B.T., Dir.; Sr. REBECCA BETZ, M.S.B.T., Assoc. Dir.; Mrs. RITA TOLBERT, Resource Center Coord., *P.O. Drawer 17329, Pensacola, 32522.* Tel: 850-436-6455.

Communications, Office of—Rev. MICHAEL MOONEY, Dir., *P.O. Drawer 17329, Pensacola, 32522.* Tel: 850-432-1515.

"The Florida Catholic"—Ms. BRENDA LAWRENCE, Reporter for the Diocese of Pensacola-Tallahassee Edition of *"The Florida Catholic", P.O. Drawer 17329, Pensacola, 32522.* Tel: 850-432-5215.

Cursillo Movement—Rev. MICHAEL FOLEY, Spiritual Dir.; Mr. WILLIAM E. SCHAAL, Diocesan Lay Dir., *P.O. Drawer 17329, Pensacola, 32522.* Tel: 850-432-1515.

Ecumenical & Interreligious Affairs, Office of—Very Rev. RICHARD J. BOWLES, V.F., Dir., *P.O. Box 12423, Pensacola, 32582.* Tel: 850-438-4985.

Education, Department of—*P.O. Drawer 17329, Pensacola, 32522.* Tel: 850-432-1515.

Schools, Diocesan Commission for—Mrs. CAROLYN KETCHEL, Chm.; Rev. MARTIN HOLLEY; Mr. JOHN DOHERTY; Mr. ROBIN DICKSON; Mrs. CYNTHIA LACOUR; Sr. MARY CAPLICE, C.N.D., Admin. Officer; Mrs. ROSLYN GUYETTE; Mrs. ANGELA HEARD; Mr. RICHARD LURTON; Mrs. FRANCINE NEAL; Mr. ROBIN DICKSON; Dr. CATHERINE O'MALLEY; Dr. NANCY ROBERTS; Dr. MARION WILLIAMS, *P.O. Drawer 17329, Pensacola, 32522.* Tel: 850-432-1515.

Superintendent of Schools, Office of the—Sr. MARY CAPLICE, C.N.D., Supt., *P.O. Drawer 17329, Pensacola, 32522.* Tel: 850-432-1515.

Marriage & Family Life Ministries, Department of—Mrs. LOUISE RITZ, Dir., *P.O. Drawer 17329, Pensacola, 32522.* Tel: 850-432-1515. Ministries: Engaged Encounter, Leadership Development for Family, Marriage Encounter and Natural Family Planning (NFP).

Respect Life, Office of—Very Rev. JAMES J. FLAHERTY, Dir.

Finance, Diocesan Commission for—Mr. ROBERT EMMANUEL, Chm.; Rev. Msgr. LUKE HUNT, Sec.; Rev. Msgr. JAMES AMOS, J.C.L.; Mr. ROBERT HAMEL; Mr. ERIC NICKELSEN; Mr. VINCE WHIBBS, JR.; Mr. ALBERT WILLIAMS, JR., *P.O. Drawer 17329, Pensacola, 32522.* Tel: 850-432-1515.

Finance, Department of—Mr. J. PATRICK REMICH, Dir., *P.O. Drawer 17329, Pensacola, 32522.* Tel: 850-432-1515.

Hispanic Ministry, Office of—Vacant, *P.O. Drawer 17329, Pensacola, 32522.* Tel: 850-432-1515.

Holy Childhood Association—Sr. MARY CAPLICE, C.N.D., Dir., *P.O. Drawer 17329, Pensacola, 32522.* Tel: 850-432-1515.

Holy Name Society—*P.O. Drawer 17329, Pensacola, 32522.* Tel: 850-432-1515.

Justice and Peace, Office of—Vacant, *P.O. Drawer 17329, Pensacola, 32522.* Tel: 850-432-1515.

Knights of Columbus—Rev. Msgr. LUKE HUNT, Diocesan Chap., *P.O. Drawer 17329, Pensacola, 32522.* Tel: 850-432-1515.

Legion of Mary—Rev. SLADE CRAWFORD, Diocesan Spiritual Dir., *P.O. Drawer 17329, Pensacola, 32522.* Tel: 850-432-1515.

Liturgy, Office of—Rev. J. CRAIG WILLIAMS, Dir., *P.O. Drawer 17329, Pensacola, 32522.* Tel: 850-436-6455.

Permanent Diaconate Formation Board—Rev. Msgr. JAMES AMOS, J.C.L.; Rev. C. SLADE CRAWFORD; Very Rev. JAMES J. FLAHERTY; Deacons HENRY BURRELL; THOMAS KENNELL; MACK SHOOK; Mrs. LOUISE RITZ; Mrs. JUANITA SANKS, *P.O. Drawer 17329, Pensacola, 32522.* Tel: 850-432-1515.

Permanent Diaconate, Office of—Deacon JOHN MORGAN, Vicar for Deacons, *P.O. Drawer 17329, Pensacola, 32522.* Tel: 850-432-1515.

Priestly Life and Ministry, Office of—Very Rev. ROBERT MORRIS, Dir., *P.O. Drawer 17329, Pensacola, 32522.* Tel: 850-432-1515.

Priests' Pension Plan, Board for—Rev. Msgr. WILLIAM A. CROWE, V.F.; Rev. Msgr. LUKE HUNT; Rev. Msgr. RAYMOND MULLINS, V.E.; Revs. EUGENE CASSERLY; JOHN CASSIDY; MICHAEL FOLEY. Consultants:: Mr. JOHN A. PANYKO, ESQ.; Mr. J. PATRICK REMICH.

Priests' Personnel Board—Rev. Msgr. GEORGE E. SINDIK; Rev. Msgr. JAMES AMOS, J.C.L.; Very Rev. JOHN V. O'SULLIVAN; Revs. MICHAEL FOLEY; KEVIN T. JOHNSON, *P.O. Drawer 17329, Pensacola, 32522.* Tel: 850-432-1515.

Propagation of the Faith, Office of—Rev. FRANCIS SZCZYKUTOWICZ, Dir., *P.O. Drawer 17329, Pensacola, 32522.* Tel: 850-432-1515.

Real Estate, Diocesan Commission for—Rev. Msgr. LUKE HUNT, Chm.; Rev. Msgr. WILLIAM A. CROWE, V.F.; Very Revs. RICHARD J. BOWLES, V.F.; JOHN V. O'SULLIVAN, V.F.; Rev. FRANCIS SZCZYKUTOWICZ, V.F.; Mr. ROBERT EMMANUEL; Mr. J. PATRICK REMICH; Mr. JOHN DONOVAN; Mr. JOHN MORGAN, Sec., *P.O. Drawer 17329, Pensacola, 32522.* Tel: 850-432-1515.

Real Estate, Office of—Mr. JOHN MORGAN, Dir., *P.O. Drawer 17329, Pensacola, 32522.* Tel: 850-432-1515.

St. Vincent de Paul Society—Pensacola Particular Council, Rev. OLIVER BARRETT, C.S.Sp., Spiritual Dir.; Mr. AL GODWIN, Pres., *2200 W. Desoto St., Pensacola, 32505.* Tel: 850-434-6615. Tallahassee Chapter, Very Rev. MICHAEL W. TUGWELL, Spiritual Dir.; Mr. ALBERT A. RELATION, Pres., *P.O. Box 2395, Tallahassee, 32316.* Tel: 850-576-6099.

Seminarian Candidate Review Board—Very Rev. MICHAEL W. TUGWELL, Chm.; Rev. Msgr. JAMES AMOS, J.C.L.; Rev. JOSEPH CALLIPARE; Mr. WILLIAM NADICKSBERND; Sr. ELLEN KIERAN, M.S.B.T.; Mrs. ROSEMARY MASON, *P.O. Drawer 17329, Pensacola, 32522.* Tel: 850-432-1515.

Seminarians, Office of—Rev. SLADE CRAWFORD, Dir., *P.O. Drawer 17329, Pensacola, 32522.* Tel: 850-432-1515.

Vocations, Office of—Rev. SLADE CRAWFORD, Dir., *Drawer 17329, Pensacola, 32522.* Tel: 850-432-1515.

Serra Club—Pensacola: Rev. MICHAEL B. SHAW, Spiritual Dir.; Mr. JOSEPH PASTUCHA, Pres.; Tallahassee: Mr. STANLEY KUPISZEWSKI, Pres.; Fort Walton Beach-Niceville: Rev. EDMOND PERJAK, Spiritual Dir.; Mr. RICHARD HICKENBOTHAM, Pres., *P.O. Drawer 17329, Pensacola, 32522.* Tel: 850-432-1515.

Youth Ministry, Office of—Rev. MICHAEL A. CHERUP, Dir.; Miss JENNIFER MIHALCIK, Sec., *P.O. Drawer 17329, Pensacola, 32522.* Tel: 850-432-1515.

CLERGY, PARISHES, MISSIONS AND PAROCHIAL SCHOOLS

GREATER PENSACOLA
(Escambia County)

1—CATHEDRAL OF THE SACRED HEART (1905), Revs. Michael A. Cherup, Rector; Michael B. Shaw; Deacons Henry Burrell; Jean White.
Res., 1101 E. Mallory St., P.O. Box 2248, 32503. Tel: 850-438-3131; Fax: 850-436-6428.
School—Sacred Heart Cathedral School, 1603 N. 12th Ave., 32503. Tel: 850-436-6440; Fax: 850-436-6444. Apostles of the Sacred Heart. Sr. Elizabeth Knight, A.S.C.J., Prin.
Catechesis/Religious Programs—Students 87.
Convent—1700 Conway Dr., 32503. Tel: 904-438-0560.

2—LITTLE FLOWER (Myrtle Grove) (1945), Revs. C. Slade Crawford; Viet Huynh. In res., Rev. Ernest Patrick.
Res., 6495 Lillian Hwy., P.O. Box 3009, Myrtle Grove, 32516. Tel: 850-455-5641.
School—Congregation of Notre Dame Sisters, Tel: 850-455-4851. Sr. Rose Mary Sullivan, C.N.D., Prin.
Sisters 1; Lay Teachers 10; Students 262.
Catechesis/Religious Programs—Students 167.

3—HOLY SPIRIT (Warrington) (1968), Rev. Msgr. James Amos, V.G.; Rev. Msgr. James Gallagher, Pastor Emeritus; Deacons Eugene Geri; Clayton L. Overton.
Res., 10650 Gulf Beach Hwy., 32507. Tel: 850-492-0837 (Office).
Catechesis/Religious Programs—Students 76.

4—NATIVITY OF OUR LORD (1969), Revs. Michael P. Mooney; Michael J. Flynn; Deacons Randall Comeau; Dennis Dobransky.
Res., 9945 Hillview Rd., 32514. Tel: 850-477-3221; Fax: 850-494-1503.
Catechesis/Religious Programs—.
Students 300.

5—OUR LADY QUEEN OF MARTYRS, MISSION (1977), Rev. Augustine Nguyen Thanh Hue (Vietnamese).
Res., 3295 S. Barrancas Ave., 32507. Tel: 850-455-2712.

6—ST. ANNE (Bellview) (1964), Rev. John F. Gray, Admin.; Deacon John C. McLellan. In res., Rev. Thomas O'Flaherty.
Res., 5200 Saufley Field Rd., 32526-1626. Tel: 850-456-5966; Fax: 850-453-3138.
Preschool—Tel: 850-453-2119. Mrs. Anne M. Clapsadl, Dir.
Students 40.

7—ST. ANNE (Brownsville) (1953), Rev. D. Oliver Barrett, C.S.Sp.
Res., 2910 W. Gadsden St., 32505. Tel: 850-433-5467; Fax: 850-453-3138.

8—ST. ANTHONY OF PADUA (1941) (African American), Rev. Thomas A. Bonanti.
Res., 1804 N. Davis St., 32503. Tel: 850-436-6422; Fax: 850-436-6422.

9—ST. JOHN THE EVANGELIST (1859), Revs. Richard L. Altenbaugh; Joseph G. Going, O.P.; Deacons Gerard Williamson; Stanley Barrows.
Res., 303 S. Navy Blvd., 32507. Tel: 850-455-0356; Fax: 850-455-5109.
School—Sisters of Mercy, Tel: 850-456-5218; Fax: 850-456-5956. Sr. Patricia Ann Pepitone, R.S.M., Prin.
Sisters 3; Lay Teachers 15; Students 209.
Convent—325 S. Navy Blvd., 32507. Tel: 850-455-0355.

10—ST. JOSEPH (1891) (African American), Rev. Thomas A. Bonanti; Sr. Maureen Joseph Kirwan, S.C., Pastoral Assoc.
Mailing Address: P.O. Box 13566, 32591. Tel: 850-436-6461; Fax: 850-436-6462.
Res., 141 W. Intendencia St., 32501.
Catechesis/Religious Programs—Students 89.

11—ST. MARY (1941), Revs. Eugene D. Casserly; Eugene W. Pathe (England); Sr. Marilyn Doucette, C.N.D., Pastoral Outreach.
Mailing Address: P.O. Box 6117, 32503.
Res., 401 Van Pelt Ln., 32505. Tel: 850-478-2797.
Catechesis/Religious Programs—Tel: 850-478-1635.
Students 185.

12—ST. MICHAEL (1559), Very Rev. Richard J. Bowles, V.F.
Res., 19 N. Palafox St., P.O. Box 12423, 32582. Tel: 850-438-4985.

13—ST. PAUL (1963), Rev. Msgr. George E. Sindik, V.E.; Revs. Joseph Callipare; Martin Holley; Deacons John P. Morgan; Russell C. Packard.
Res., 3131 Hyde Park Rd., 32503. Tel: 850-434-2551; Fax: 850-436-6449.
School—Apostles of the Sacred Heart (Hamden, CT), Tel: 850-436-6435; Fax: 850-436-6437. Sr. M. Lizabeth Doty, A.S.C.J., Prin.
Sisters 2; Lay Teachers 18; Students 309.
Catechesis/Religious Programs—Tel: 850-436-6446.
Students 367.
Convent—1700 Conway Dr., 32503. Tel: 850-438-0560.
Mission—Pensacola, Escambia Co., Church of Our Savior, 6700 Old Spanish Tr., 32504.

14—ST. STEPHEN (1922), Rev. Hector R.G. Perez, S.T.D.
Res., 900 W. Garden St., 32501. Tel: 850-432-9362.

15—ST. THOMAS MORE (1954), Rev. John T. Cassidy.
Mailing Address: 510 Bayshore Dr., 32507. Tel: 850-456-2543; Fax: 850-456-8537.

CITY OF TALLAHASSEE
(Leon County)

1—CO-CATHEDRAL OF ST. THOMAS MORE (1968), Revs. Michael W. Tugwell, Rector; Thomas S. Collins.
Res., 832 W. Tennessee St., P.O. Box 2395, 32316. Tel: 850-222-7371; 222-9630 (Office); Fax: 850-222-6430.
Catechesis/Religious Programs—Students 125.
Chapel—St. Eugene, Florida A&M University, 701 W. Gamble St., 32310. Tel: 850-222-6482. [JC]
Rev. John Boateng-Mensah, Chap.

2—BLESSED SACRAMENT, Very Rev. John V. O'Sullivan, V.F.; Revs. Kevin Johnson; James F. Cregan.
Res., 624 Miccosukee Rd., 32308. Tel: 850-222-1321; Fax: 850-222-9772.
School—Trinity Catholic, Tel: 850-222-0444; Fax:

850-224-5067. Sr. Aileen McClain, O.P., Prin.
Sisters 2; Lay Teachers 34; Students 565.

3—GOOD SHEPHERD (1973), Revs. Michael Foley; Thomas Guido; Deacons Andrew Radigan; Robert Vossler.
Office: 4665 Thomasville Rd., 32308. Tel: 850-893-1837; 893-2381.
Catechesis/Religious Programs—Bette Scaringe, D.R.E.
Students 695.

4—ST. LOUIS (1979), Rev. David McCreanor, Ph.D.; Deacons Nelson Madera, Ph.D.; Mack Shook.
Res., 4151 Miraflores Ln., 32303. Tel: 850-562-5140.
Catechesis/Religious Programs—Students 99.

OUTSIDE THE CITIES OF PENSACOLA AND TALLAHASSEE

Apalachicola, Franklin Co., St. Patrick (1851), Rev. Roger Latosynski.
Res., 27 Sixth St., P.O. Box 550, 32320. Tel: 904-653-9453. [JC]

Bayou George, Bay Co., Our Lady of the Rosary, Rev. W. P. Brown.
Res., 5622 Julie Dr., Panama City, 32404. Tel: 850-769-5067.
Catechesis/Religious Programs—Students 25.
Mission—Fountain, Bay Co., Our Lady Queen of Peace.

Blountstown, Calhoun Co., St. Francis of Assisi, Rev. John P. Selleck, Admin.
Res., 334 Gaskin St., 32424. Tel: 850-674-4482.
Mission—Wewahitchka, Gulf Co., St. Lawrence, Box 651, Wewahitchka, 32465. Tel: 850-639-5787.

Bonifay, Holmes Co., Blessed Trinity (1979), Rev. John F. Kelly.
Res., Rte. 4, Box 643, 32425. Tel: 850-547-3735.

Cantonment, Escambia Co., St. Jude Thaddeus (1966), Rev. Richard E. Dawson; Deacons John Bartoszewicz; Bradley Seabrook; Tom Simard.
Res., 303 Rocky Ave., 32533. Tel: 850-968-6189; Fax: 850-968-1578. [CEM]
Mission—Barrineau Park, Escambia Co., St. Elizabeth of Hungary, 303 Rocky Ave., 32533. Tel: 850-587-2550.
Catechesis/Religious Programs—Students 68.

Chattahoochee, Gadsden Co., Holy Cross Parish (1972), Rev. Jacob M. Pallivathukkall (India) Admin.
Res., R.R. 1, Box 1562, 32324. Tel: 850-663-4610.

Chipley, Washington Co., St. Joseph the Worker (1968), Rev. John F. Kelly.
Res., P.O. Box 266, 32428. Tel: 850-638-7654.
Catechesis/Religious Programs—Students 43.

Crestview, Okaloosa Co., Our Lady of Victory (1954), Rev. Michael V. Reed, Admin.
Res., 143 Jeff Dr., 32536. Tel: 904-682-4622; Fax: 904-689-0335.
Catechesis/Religious Programs—Students 380.

De Funiak Springs, Walton Co., St. Margaret, Very Rev. James J. Flaherty.
Res., Hwy. 331 N., Box 590, 32433. Tel: 904-892-9247.
Catechesis/Religious Programs—Students 51.
Mission—Freeport, Walton Co., Christ the King, Hwy. 331 S., 32439.

Destin, Okaloosa Co., Corpus Christi (1977), Rev. Robert F. Morris; Deacons Joseph Rose; Anthony Restivo.
Res., 307 Beach Dr., P.O. Box 635, 32540. Tel: 904-654-5422.
Catechesis/Religious Programs—Students 68.
Church of the Resurrection, Walton Co., (1981), Rev. Roy C. Marien.
Res., 259 Miramar Beach Dr., 32541. Tel: 850-837-0357; Fax: 850-837-2062.

Fort Walton Beach, Okaloosa Co., St. Mary (1914), Rev. Msgr. Raymond Mullins, V.F.; Revs. Peter Zalewski; Sean Garrett (SAT); Deacons Robert J. Saxer; Charles Wolf; Charles Shettle; John Howell.
Res., 110 St. Mary Ave., S.W., 32548-6645. Tel: 850-243-3742; Fax: 850-243-1271.
School—Tel: 850-243-8913; Fax: 850-243-7895. Mrs. Joy Webb, Prin.
Lay Teachers 20; Students 405.
Catechesis/Religious Programs—Tel: 850-244-1833. Sr. Evelyn Rogers, S.U.S.C., D.R.E.
Students 394.

Fountain, Bay Co., Our Lady Queen of Peace Mission, Rev. William P. Brown.
Mailing Address: P.O. Box 213, 32438. Tel: 850-769-5067.
Church—18005 Lazy Ln., 32438.

Freeport, Walton Co., Christ the King Mission (1984), Very Rev. James J. Flaherty.
Hwy. 331 N., P.O. Box 590, De Funiak Springs, 32422. Tel: 904-892-9247. See St. Margaret Parish, De Funiak Springs.

Gulf Breeze, Santa Rosa Co., St. Ann (1948), Rev. Msgr. Luke Hunt; Rev. William Condren; Deacons Robert Kostic; Patrick O'Connell.
Res., 100 Daniel Dr., P.O. Drawer 1057, 32562. Tel: 850-932-2859; Fax: 850-934-2804.
St. Ann Discovery School—(Extended Care & Preschool). Tel: 850-932-9330. Mrs. Carol Lyvers, Dir. Teachers 25; Students 235.
Catechesis/Religious Programs—Students 450.
Mission—Gulf Breeze, Santa Rosa Co., Our Lady of the Assumption, 920 Via de Luna, P.O. Box 1057, Pensacola Beach, 32561. Tel: 850-934-0222.

Lanark Village, Franklin Co., Sacred Heart of Jesus (1960), Rev. James F. Cregan.
Res., 109 Newman Dr., P.O. Box 729, 32323. Tel: 850-697-3445.

Madison, Madison Co., St. Vincent de Paul (1907), Rev. Joseph C. Schwab, O.M.I.
Res., 402 N.W. Sumter St., P.O. Box 730, 32341. Tel: 850-973-2428.

Marianna, Jackson Co., St. Anne (1947), Rev. Hugh Dolan.
Res., 3009 Fifth St., P.O. Box 1547, 32447. Tel: 850-482-3734. [JC]

Mary Esther, Okaloosa Co., St. Peter (1975), Rev. Edward A. Kirby; Deacon David P. Robinson.
Res., 100 Francis St., 32569. Tel: 850-581-2556.
Catechesis/Religious Programs—Students 80.

Medart, Wakulla Co., St. Elizabeth Ann Seton (1975), Rev. James B. MacGee, O.M.I.
Mailing Address: 3609 Coastal Hwy., Crawfordville, 32327. Tel: 850-926-1797. [CEM]
Catechesis/Religious Programs—Students 38.
Mission—Woodville, Leon Co., St. Stephen the Protomartyr, Natural Bridge Rd., P.O.Box 1142, Woodville, 32362. Tel: 850-421-9094.

Mexico Beach, Bay Co., Our Lady of Guadalupe Mission. See St. Dominic, Panama City.

Milton, Santa Rosa Co., St. Rose of Lima (1957), Rev. Todd O. Hevia; Deacons David Davey; Thomas Kennell.
Res., 515 Park Ave., S.W., 32570. Tel: 850-623-3600. [JC]
Catechesis/Religious Programs—Students 230.

Monticello, Jefferson Co., St. Margaret (1917), Rev. Joseph C. Schwab, O.M.I.
Res., P.O. Box 730, Madison, 32341. Tel: 850-973-2428.
Church—U.S. Hwy. 90 E., 32334. Tel: 850-997-3622.

Niceville, Okaloosa Co., Christ Our Redeemer (1989), Rev. J. Craig Williams; Deacons Michael Carucci; Joaquin Trevino; Grant Boughton.
Res., 1028 White Point Rd., 32578. Tel: 850-897-7797; Fax: 850-897-2422.
Catechesis/Religious Programs—Tel: 850-897-2974.
Students 300.
Holy Name of Jesus (1964), Revs. Daniel J. Butler; Dominic Phan Sa; Deacons David Casey; Thomas Fraites; Louis Marini; Willie O'Neal.
Res., 1200 Valparaiso Blvd., P.O. Box 576, 32588. Tel: 850-678-7813; Fax: 850-678-5775.
Catechesis/Religious Programs—Students 227.

Panama City, Bay Co., St. Dominic (1917), Rev. Msgr. William A. Crowe, V.F.; Revs. Joseph P. Caffrey; James J. Lambert; John B. Cayer; Deacon James Gardner.
Res., 3308 E. 15th St., 32405-7414. Tel: 850-785-4574; Fax: 850-872-0800.
Catechesis/Religious Programs—Tel: 904-763-7393.
Students 296.
Mission—Mexico Beach, Bay Co., Our Lady of Guadalupe, 1500 N. 15th St., Mexico Beach, 32410. Tel: 850-648-3006.
St. John the Evangelist (1945), Revs. Donald Suberlak, C.R.; Martin Bratek, C.R., Vicar; Deacons Dale Johnson; Earl C. Mirus; John Kreppein.
Res., 1008 Fortune Ave., P.O. Box 978, 32401. Tel: 850-763-1821.
School—Tel: 850-763-1775. Miss Sally Lorei, Prin. Sisters of the Resurrection 3; Lay Teachers 17; Students 289.
Catechesis/Religious Programs—Students 132.
SS. Peter & Paul Mission (1981) (Vietnam), Rev. Andrew Nguyen Minh Tu (Vietnam) Admin.
Res., 3129 Fifth St., P.O. Box 3087, 32401. Tel: 850-785-6191. [JC]
Catechesis/Religious Programs—Students 34.

Panama City Beach, Bay Co., St. Bernadette (1956), Rev. David T. O Shea.
Res., 1214 Moylan Rd., 32407. Tel: 850-234-3490; Fax: 850-234-3266.
Catechesis/Religious Programs—Students 180.

Pensacola Beach, Escambia Co., Our Lady of the Assumption Mission (1979),
Mailing Address: P.O. Box 1057, Gulf Breeze, 32561.
920 Via de Luna, 32561. Tel: 850-934-0222. See St. Ann, Gulf Breeze.

Perry, Taylor Co., Immaculate Conception (1918), Rev. Edward Hauf, O.M.I. In res., Rev. Francis Bagan, O.M.I.
Res., 2750 S. Byron Butler Pkwy., 32347. Tel: 850-584-3169; Fax: 850-584-5736.
Center—Tel: 850-584-8853.

Port St. Joe, Gulf Co., St. Joseph (1925), Rev. Thom A. Crandall.
Res., 2006 Monument Ave., P.O. Box 820, 32457-0820. Tel: 850-227-1417.
Church—20th & Monument Sts., 32457-0820. Tel: 850-229-8637.
Mission—Port St. Joe, Gulf Co., San Blas Catholic Mission.

Quincy, Gadsden Co., St. Thomas the Apostle (1957), Sr. Maria Lauren Donohue, M.S.B.T., Pastoral Assoc. & Hispanic Ministry Contact; Deacons William Strange; Luis Benavides.
Res., Hwy. 90, Box 451, 32353. Tel: 850-627-2350.
Catechesis/Religious Programs—Tel: 850-627-8807. Sr. Maria Rincon, M.S.B.T., D.R.E.
Students 180.
Hispanic Ministry Office of St. Thomas—Religious Education Office.
Mission Juan Diego—Outreach Center for the Hispanic Migrants/Farmworkers, Greensboro, Tel: 850-442-9023. Mrs. Mary Matthews, Contact.
Mission—Greensboro, Gadsden Co., Casa Guadalupana, Catholic Center for Evangelization, P.O. Box 59, Greensboro, 32330. Tel: 850-442-4337.

Santa Rosa Beach, Walton Co., St. Rita (1982), Rev. Dennis O'Brien, Admin.
Mailing Address: 20 St. Rita Ln., P.O. Box 1223, 32459. Tel: 850-267-2761; Fax: 850-267-3711.

Sunny Hills, Washington Co., St. Theresa, Rev. Francis S. Szczykutowicz; Deacon Joseph Dealy.
Res., 2056 Sunny Hills Blvd., 32428. Tel: 850-773-3406; Fax: 850-773-7008.

Tiger Point, Santa Rosa Co., St. Sylvester (1979), Very Rev. Steven J. O'Connor; Deacon Frank Wines.
Res., 3507 Gulf Breeze Pkwy., Gulf Breeze, 32561. Tel: 850-932-6807; Fax: 850-932-6338.
Catechesis/Religious Programs—Students 182.

Wewahitchka, Gulf Co., St. Lawrence Mission, c/o 334 Gaskin St., Blountstown, 32424. See St. Francis of Assisi, Blountstown.

Woodville, Leon Co., St. Stephen the Protomartyr (1979),
Mailing Address: P.O. Box 1142, 32362. Tel: 850-421-9094. See St. Elizabeth Ann Seton, Medart.

Chaplains of Public Institutions

PENSACOLA. *Escambia County Jail*. Deacon Stanley Barrows.
TALLAHASSEE. *Federal Correctional Institution*. Vacant.
CHATTAHOOCHEE. *Florida State Hospital*. Vacant.
River Junction Correctional Institution. Vacant.
EGLIN. *Eglin Federal Prison Camp Eglin Air Force Base*. Deacon Joaquin Trevino, Chap.
MARIANNA. *Dozier School for Boys Sunland Training Center, Jackson Vocation Center*. Vacant.
Florida Correctional Institutions. Sr. Ann Marie Raftery, O.S.F.
SNEADS. *Apalachee Correctional Institution*. Deacon Robert Moore.

On Duty Outside the Diocese:
Reverend Monsignors—
Kerr, William A., La Roche College, 9000 Babcock Blvd., Pittsburgh, PA 15237
Reverend Fathers—
Bosso, Stephen C., St. Vincent de Paul Regional Seminary, 10701 E. Military Tr., Boynton Beach, FL 33436
Roland, Charles, St. Joseph Church, 2011 Darling Ave., Waycross, GA 31501
Sarmiento, Oscar, St. Isidro Parish, 2310 Martin Luther King Blvd., Pompano Beach, FL 33609-1591

Military Chaplains:
Reverend Fathers—
Bluett, James K.
Krzywicki, Lance P., Chap., PSC 810, Box 14, FPO, AE 09169
McClanahan, Robert P., NAS, Patuxent River, MD 20670
Voyt, Stephen A., Maj., Wright Patterson AFB, OH 45424

On Leave of Absence:
Rev.—
Wood, Peter N.

Retired:
Reverend Monsignors—
Cunningham, Patrick

Gallagher, James
Reverend Fathers—
Dzienkiewicz, Edwin
Halstead, Philip
Hogarty, Paul
Jordan, James J.
Joseph, William
Kiem, Anthony
Patrick, Ernest E.
Watters, Joseph

Permanent Deacons:
Barrows, Stanley, St. John the Evangelist, Warrington
Bartoszewicz, John M., St. Jude Thaddeus, Cantonment
Bodish, William, St. Mary, Fort Walton Beach
Bonanno, Frederick R., St. Mary, Fort Walton Beach
Boughton, Grant, Christ our Redeemer, Niceville
Burrell, Henry N., Cathedral of the Sacred Heart, Pensacola
Carucci, Michael J., Christ Our Redeemer, Niceville
Casey, David R., Holy Name of Jesus, Niceville
Cloud, Millard F., Inactive
Comeau, Randall O., Nativity of Our Lord, Pensacola
Davey, David, St. Rose of Lima, Milton
Dealy, Michael J., (Retired)
Dobransky, Dennis, Nativity, Pensacola
Fraites, Thomas J., Holy Name of Jesus, Niceville
Gaines, William G., Leave of Absence
Gardner, James L., St. Dominic, Panama City
Geri, Eugene A., Holy Spirit, Pensacola
Greskovich, Frank J., Leave of Absence
Howell, John, St. Mary, Fort Walton Beach
Hromadka, Joseph J., St. Rita, Mexico Beach
Johnson, Dale R., St. John the Evangelist, Panama City
Kennell, Thomas H., St. Rose of Lima, Milton
Kostic, Robert B., St. Ann, Gulf Breeze
Kreppein, John, St. John the Evangelist, Panama City
Madera, Nelson I., St. Louis, Tallahassee
Marini, Louis, Holy Name of Jesus, Niceville
McLellan, John, St. Anne, Bellview
Mirus, Earl C., St. John the Evangelist, Panama City
Morgan, John P., St. Paul, Pensacola
O'Connell, Patrick F., (Retired)
O'Neal, Willie, Holy Name of Jesus, Niceville
Overton, Clayton, (Retired)
Packard, Russell C., St. Paul, Pensacola
Radigan, Terence A., Good Shepherd, Tallahassee
Restivo, Anthony, Corpus Christi, Destin
Richardson, Walter H., St. Mary, Fort Walton
Robinson, David P., St. Peter, Mary Esther
Rose, Joseph, Corpus Christi, Destin
Saxer, Robert J., St. Mary, Fort Walton Beach
Seabrook, Bradley M., St. Jude, Cantonment
Shettle, Charles G., (Retired)
Shook, Mack D., St. Louis, Tallahassee
Simard, Thomas, St. Jude, Cantonment
Trevino, Joaquin D., Christ Our Redeemer, Niceville
Vossler, Robert J., Good Shepherd, Tallahassee
Vota, Joseph L., (Retired)
White, Jean F., Cathedral of the Sacred Heart, Pensacola
Williamson, Gerard, St. John the Evangelist, Warrington
Wines, Frank, St. Sylvester (Diocese of Lansing, MI)
Wolf, Charles R., St. Mary, Fort Walton Beach

INSTITUTIONS LOCATED IN THE DIOCESE

[A] HIGH SCHOOLS, DIOCESAN

PENSACOLA. *Pensacola Catholic High School*, 3043 W. Scott St., 32505. Tel: 850-436-6400; Fax: 850-436-6405.
E-mail: martinK@amaranth.com
Sr. Kierstin Martin, A.S.C.J., Prin. Sisters 2; Lay Teachers 56; Students 600.

[B] ELEMENTARY SCHOOLS, DIOCESAN

PENSACOLA. *St. Michael*, 601 N. Palafox St., 32501. Tel: 850-438-4059.
E-mail: StMichael@pen.net
Web site: http://wwwpensacolastmichael.org
Sisters of St. Joseph (Buffalo). Sr. Robert Anne, S.S.J., Prin. Sisters 2; Lay Teachers 13; Students 284.

[C] GENERAL HOSPITALS

PENSACOLA. *The Mother Seton Guild of Sacred Heart Hospital, Inc.*, 32504
For a complete listing, refer to the Hospitals section.
Sacred Heart Foundation, Inc., 4475 Bayou Blvd., 32503
For a complete listing, refer to the Hospitals section.
Sacred Heart Hospital of Pensacola, 5151 N. Ninth Ave., 32504. Tel: 850-416-7000
For a complete listing, refer to the Hospitals section.

[D] HOMES FOR AGED

PENSACOLA. *Haven of Our Lady of Peace*, 5203 N. Ninth Ave., 32504. Tel: 850-477-0531; Fax: 850-477-6782
For a complete listing, refer to the Special Care Facilities section.

[E] APARTMENTS FOR THE ELDERLY AND HANDICAPPED

TALLAHASSEE. *Casa Calderon, Inc.*, 800 W. Virginia St., 32304. Tel: 850-222-4026.
E-mail: karkoel@aol.com.
For a complete listing, refer to the Special Care Facilities section.

[F] CONVENT AND RESIDENCES FOR SISTERS

PENSACOLA. *Blessed Trinity Missionary Cenacle*, 412 Bayshore Dr., 32507. Tel: 850-456-4141. Sisters 5.
Notre Dame Convent, Sisters of the Congregation of Notre Dame, 1001 Deason St., 32505. Tel: 850-438-5906. Sisters 5.
Sacred Heart Hospital Convent, 5151 N. Ninth Ave., 32504. Tel: 850-474-7920.
St. Michael Convent, 18 W. Jackson St., 32501-3956. Tel: 850-436-6460. Sisters of Mercy of the Americas; Sisters of St. Joseph (Buffalo); Sisters of Charity of St. Elizabeth of New Jersey. Sisters 3.

APALACHICOLA. *Martin House*, 149 10th St., 32320. Tel: 850-653-8774. Sinsinawa Dominicans Congregation of the Most Holy Rosary 2. Total Assisted 1,460.

MARIANNA. *Mission Helpers of the Sacred Heart Convent*, 3007 Fifth St., 32446. Tel: 850-526-3290. Sisters 2.

SUNNY HILLS. *Vestiarki Sisters of Jesus (Poland)*, 3919 Vistula Dr., 32428. Tel: 850-773-3302. Sisters 5; Total Assisted 4.

[G] HOMELESS SHELTERS

TALLAHASSEE. *Holy Family Home*. Catholic Social Services-Tallahassee. Rte. #7, Box 725, 32308. Tel: 850-877-6736.

PANAMA CITY. *Naomi House*, 2941 11th St., 32401. Tel: 850-769-5756.
St. Barnabas House, 2943 11th St., 32401. Tel: 850-769-0314. Coordinators: Dan Coleman, M.C.V.; Sheila Coleman, M.C.V. Total in Residence 77; Total Staff 5.

[H] RETREAT HOUSES

TALLAHASSEE. *The Saint John Neumann Spiritual Renewal Center*, 685 Miccosukee Rd., 32308. Tel: 850-224-2971. Sr. Christine Kelly, S.S.J., Dir. Sisters 3.

NAVARRE. *Casa Stella Maris*, 7650 Clark St., 32566. Tel: 850-932-6807. Very Rev. Steven J. O'Connor, Dir. Total Staff 1.

[I] MISCELLANEOUS

PENSACOLA. *Diocese of Pensacola-Tallahassee Education Foundation, Inc.*, P.O. Drawer 17329, 32522. Tel: 850-432-1515.
E-mail: DIOPCTAL75@aol.com
St. Michael Cemetery Foundation, Inc., P.O. Drawer 17329, 32522. Tel: 850-432-1515.

RELIGIOUS INSTITUTES OF MEN REPRESENTED IN THE DIOCESE

For further details refer to the corresponding bracketed number in the Religious Institutes of Men or Women section.

[0340]—*Cistercian Fathers.*—O.Cist.
[1080]—*Congregation of the Resurrection.* (Chicago Prov.).—C.R.
[0650]—*Holy Ghost Fathers.*—C.S.Sp.
[0590]—*Missionaries of the Holy Apostles.*—M.Ss.A.
[0910]—*Oblates of Mary Immaculate.* (Eastern American Prov.).—O.M.I.
[0430]—*Order of Preachers-Dominicans.* (Southern Prov.).—O.P.

RELIGIOUS INSTITUTES OF WOMEN REPRESENTED IN THE DIOCESE

[0130]—*Apostles of the Sacred Heart of Jesus.*—A.S.C.J.
[0760]—*Daughters of Charity of St. Vincent de Paul.* (Eastern Prov.).—D.C.
[1070-03]—*Dominican Sisters.*—O.P.
[1070-13]—*Dominican Sisters.*—O.P.
[1070-14]—*Dominican Sisters.*—O.P.
[2720]—*Mission Helpers of the Sacred Heart.*—M.H.S.H.
[2790]—*Missionary Servants of the Most Blessed Trinity.*—M.S.B.T.
[0430]—*Sisters of Charity of Blessed Virgin Mary.*—B.V.M.
[0590]—*Sisters of Charity of Saint Elizabeth, Convent Station.*—S.C.
[0990]—*Sisters of Divine Providence.*—C.D.P.
[2575]—*Sisters of Mercy of the Americas.* (Baltimore, MD).—R.S.M.
[1660]—*Sisters of Saint Francis of the Providence of God.*—O.S.F.
[3900]—*Sisters of St. Joseph of St. Augustine, Florida.*—S.S.J.
[2980]—*Sisters of the Congregation de Notre Dame.* (Blessed Sacrament Prov.).—C.N.D.
[3480]—*Sisters of the Resurrection.*—C.R.
[2150]—*Sisters, Servants of the Immaculate Heart of Mary.*—I.H.M.
[]—*Vestiarski Sisters of Jesus.* (Poland).—V.S.

NECROLOGY

† Lorigan, Thomas, Milton, FL, St. Rose of Lima. —Died Sept. 8, 1997.
† Ryan, Brian G., Crestview, FL, Our Lady of Victory. —Died Nov. 12, 1996.

Diocese of Peoria

(Dioecesis Peoriensis)

Most Reverend

JOHN J. MYERS, D.D., J.C.D.

Bishop of Peoria; ordained December 17, 1966; appointed July 14, 1987; consecrated September 3, 1987; acceded to See of Peoria January 23, 1990. *Res., 607 N.E. Madison Ave., Peoria, IL, 61603.* Tel.: 309-671-1550; Fax: 309-671-5079.

Most Reverend

EDWARD W. O'ROURKE, D.D.

Retired Bishop of Peoria; ordained May 28, 1944; appointed May 24, 1971; consecrated July 15, 1971; installed July 15, 1971; retired January 23, 1990. *Res., St. Augustine Manor, 1301 N.E. Glendale, Peoria, IL, 61603.* Tel.: 309-673-0446.

Chancery: 607 N.E. Madison Ave., P.O. Box 1406, Peoria, IL, 61655. Tel.: 309-671-1550; Fax: 309-671-5079.

ESTABLISHED 1877.

Square Miles 16,933.

A cross-section of Illinois, bounded on the north by the Counties of Whiteside, Lee, De Kalb, Grundy and Iroquois, and on the east by Kendall, Grundy, Kankakee and Ford, and on the south by Adams, Brown, Cass, Menard, Sangamon, Macon, Moultrie, Douglas and Edgar; comprising the Counties of Bureau, Champaign, Dewitt, Fulton, Hancock, Henderson, Henry, Knox, La Salle, Livingston, Logan, Marshall, Mason, McDonough, McLean, Mercer, Peoria, Piatt, Putnam, Rock Island, Schuyler, Stark, Tazewell, Vermilion, Warren and Woodford.

For legal titles of parishes and diocesan institutions, consult the Chancery.

STATISTICAL OVERVIEW

Personnel	
Bishop	1
Retired Bishops	1
Abbots	1
Retired Abbots	1
Priests: Diocesan Active in Diocese	182
Priests: Active Outside Diocese	14
Priests: Retired, Sick or Absent	60
Number of Diocesan Priests	256
Religious Priests in Diocese	57
Extern Priests in Diocese	1
Ordinations:	
Diocesan Priests	10
Transitional Deacons	4
Permanent Deacons	17
Permanent Deacons in Diocese	96
Total Brothers	9
Total Sisters	336
Parishes	
Parishes	165
With Resident Pastor:	
Resident Diocesan Priests	142
Resident Religious Priests	21
Without Resident Pastor:	
Administered by Priests	2
Missions	39
Pastoral Centers	5
Professional Ministry Personnel:	
Brothers	3

Sisters	36
Lay Ministers	29
Welfare	
Catholic Hospitals	8
Total Assisted	923,194
Homes for the Aged	2
Total Assisted	203
Residential Care of Children	1
Total Assisted	58
Day Care and Extended Day Care Centers	3
Total Assisted	363
Specialized Homes	2
Total Assisted	90
Special Centers for Social Services	1
Total Assisted	17,426
Residential Care of Disabled	1
Total Assisted	4
Other Institutions	5
Total Assisted	1,624
Educational	
Diocesan Students in Other Seminaries	26
Total Seminarians	26
Colleges and Universities	1
Total Students	152
High Schools, Diocesan and Parish	6
Total Students	2,590

Elementary Schools, Diocesan and Parish	48
Total Students	12,478
Catechesis/Religious Education:	
High School Students	3,409
Elementary Students	13,589
Total Students Under Catholic Instruction	32,244
Teachers in the Diocese:	
Priests	5
Sisters	45
Lay Teachers	726
Vital Statistics	
Receptions into the Church:	
Infant Baptism Totals	3,216
Adult Baptism Totals	513
Received into Full Communion	578
First Communions	3,211
Confirmations	3,114
Marriages:	
Catholic	664
Interfaith	606
Total Marriages	1,270
Deaths	2,298
Total Catholic Population	230,481
Total Population	1,436,473

Former Bishops—Most Rev. JOHN LANCASTER SPALDING, D.D., cons. May 1, 1877; resigned Sept. 11, 1908; Titular Archbishop of Scitopolis; appt. Oct. 14, 1908; died Aug. 25, 1916.—Most Rev. EDMUND M. DUNNE, D.D., ord. June 24, 1887; cons. Sept. 1, 1909; died Oct. 17, 1929.—Most Rev. JOSEPH H. SCHLARMAN, D.D., Ph.D., J.C.D., ord. June 29, 1904; cons. June 17, 1930; named Assistant at Papal Throne, Nov. 16, 1950; Archbishop *ad personam; appt. June 27, 1951; died Nov. 10, 1951.—Most Rev.* WILLIAM E. COUSINS, D.D., ord. April 23, 1927; Titular Bishop of Forma and Auxiliary Bishop of Chicago; appt. Dec. 17, 1948; cons. March 7, 1949; Bishop of Peoria; appt. May 19, 1952; Archbishop of Milwaukee; appt. Dec. 17, 1958.—Most Rev. JOHN B. FRANZ, D.D., ord. June 13, 1920; Bishop of Dodge City; appt. May 29, 1951; cons. Aug. 29, 1951; transferred Peoria, Aug. 8, 1959; retired June 1, 1971; died July 3, 1992.—Most Rev. EDWARD W. O'ROURKE, D.D., ord. May 28, 1944; Bishop of Peoria; appt. May 24, 1971; cons. July 15, 1971; retired Jan. 23, 1990.

Chancery—607 N.E. Madison Ave., P.O. Box 1406, Peoria, 61655. Tel: 309-671-1550. Please direct all calls for all departments to this number; Fax: 309-671-5079. Office Hours: Mon.-Fri. 8:30-4:30.

Vicar General—Rev. Msgr. JAMES F. CAMPBELL, Vicar General/Chancellor, *Sheen Pastoral Center, 412 N.E. Madison Ave., Peoria, 61603.* Tel: 309-671-1550; Fax: 309-671-1558.

Chancellor—Rev. Msgr. JAMES F. CAMPBELL, Vicar General/Chancellor, *Sheen Pastoral Center, 412 N.E. Madison Ave., Peoria, 61603.* Tel: 309-671-1550; Fax: 309-671-1558.

Moderator of the Curia—Rev. Msgr. JAMES F. CAMPBELL, *Sheen Pastoral Center, 412 N.E. Madison Ave., Peoria, 61603.* Tel: 309-671-1550; Fax: 309-671-1558.

Vice Chancellors—Rev. Msgr. STEVEN P. ROHLFS, *St. Philomena Rectory, 3300 Tweleve Oaks Dr., Peoria, 61604.* Tel: 309-682-8642; Fax: 309-682-8955. Revs. JOSEPH P. DONTON; MARK MERDIAN, *607 N.E. Madison Ave., Peoria, 61603.* Tel: 309-671-1550; Fax: 309-671-5079.

Director of Development—Mr. EDWARD N. LAUGHLIN, *Sheen Pastoral Center, 412 N.E. Madison Ave., Peoria, 61603.* Tel: 309-671-1550; Fax: 309-671-1595.

Director of Finance—Mr. ALLYN G. SCHMID, *Sheen Pastoral Center, 412 N.E. Madison Ave., Peoria, 61603.* Tel: 309-671-1550; Fax: 309-671-1595.

Diocesan Tribunal—Sheen Pastoral Center, 412 N.E. Madison Ave., Peoria, 61603. Tel: 309-671-1550; Fax: 309-677-6798.

Judicial Vicar—Very Rev. RICHARD SOSEMAN, M.A., J.C.L.

Defender of the Bond—Rev. J. BRIAN REJSEK, J.C.L.

Adjutant Judicial Vicars—Rev. J. BRIAN REJSEK, J.C.L.; Rev. Msgr. JOSEPH A. ZUBE, J.C.L.; Rev. Msgr. RICK OBERCH, J.C.L.

Auditor—Sr. MARIANNE BURKHARD, O.S.B., J.C.L.

Judges—Rev. Msgr. Richard G. Fitzsimmons; Revs. Jerome Jung, J.C.D.; Dale R. Maloy; Rev. Msgr. Clarence J. Hettinger, J.C.L.; Sr. Marianne Burkhard, O.S.B., J.C.L.

Advocates—Mrs. Cheryl Criss; Mr. David Reising.

Notaries—Mrs. Debra Williams; Mrs. Janice Vicary; Mrs. Nancy Paul.

Diocesan College of Consultors—Most Rev. John J. Myers, D.D., J.C.D.; Rev. Msgr. James F. Campbell, V.G.; Rev. Msgr. Richard Fitzsimmons; Rev. Msgr. Albert Hallin; Rev. Msgr. Steven P. Rohlfs; Rev. Msgr. Dale Wellman; Revs. Thomas E. Mack; Terrance O'Brien; George F. Remm; Paul E. Showalter; Gerald J. Verdun; John Mark Williams, *Sheen Pastoral Center, 412 N.E. Madison Ave., Peoria, 61603.* Tel: 309-671-1550; Fax: 309-671-1558.

Vicariates and Vicars—Rev. Thomas W. Maloney, Bloomington; Rev. Terrance P. O'Brien, Champaign; Rev. Thaddeus Pracz, Danville; Rev. Patrick K. O'Neal, Henry; Rev. Duane C. Jack, Kewanee; Rev. Msgr. Richard Fitzsimmons, La Salle; Rev. Msgr. Norman D. Goodman, Lincoln; Rev. Richard Pricco, Macomb; Ernest Pizzamiglio, Monmouth; Rev. Rev. Msgr. Raymond Boyle, Ottawa; Rev. James J. Swaner, Pekin; Rev. Msgr. S. P. Rohlfs, Peoria, N.W.; Rev. J. Mark Williams, Peoria, S.E.; Rev. E. E. Higgins, Pontiac; Rev. Paul E. Showalter, Rock Island.

Diocesan Offices and Directors

Finance Council (Canon 492)—Most Rev. John J. Myers, D.D., J.C.D., Pres.; Rev. Msgr. James F. Campbell, V.G.; Sr. Diane Marie McGrew, O.S.F.; Rev. Robert E. Lee; Rev. William Watson; Mr. Gerald T. Wombacher; Mr. David DeJaegher; Mrs. Doris Bermingham; Mr. Daniel Reynolds; Mr. Toby Gualandri; Mr. Allyn G. Schmid, *Sheen Pastoral Center, 412 N.E. Madison Ave., Peoria, 61603.* Tel: 309-671-1550; Fax: 309-671-1595.

Art and Architecture Commission—Rev. Terrance P. O'Brien, *1303 Lincolnshire Dr., Champaign, 61821.* Tel: 217-359-4224; Fax: 217-359-9846.

Catholic Cemeteries—Rev. John Anderson, *Sheen Pastoral Center, 412 N.E. Madison Ave., Peoria, 61603.* Tel: 309-671-1550; Fax: 309-671-1595.

Catholic Education Office—Dr. Melvin Kuhbander, Ph.D., Supt., Catholic Schools; Mrs. Patricia Kawczynski, Assoc. Supt.; Mr. William A. Janicki, Dir., Religious Education Dept.; Ms. Barbara McAtee, Assoc. Dir., *Sheen Pastoral Center, 412 N.E. Madison Ave., Peoria, 61603.* Tel: 309-671-1550; Fax: 309-671-1595.

Catholic Men, Council of—Rev. Donald R. Schladen, Moderator, *Box 26, Marseilles, 61341.* Tel: 815-795-2240.

Catholic Relief Services—Rev. John C. Anderson, *412 N.E. Madison Ave., Peoria, 61603.* Tel: 309-671-1550; Fax: 309-671-1595.

Catholic Women, Council of—Rev. Msgr. Dale Wellman, Moderator, *312 W. 1st St., Milan, 61264.* Tel: 309-787-4593.

Censor Librorum—Rev. Msgr. Steven P. Rohlfs, *3300 N. Twelve Oaks Dr., Peoria, 61604.* Tel: 309-682-8642; Fax: 309-682-8955.

Clergymen's Aid Society—Most Rev. John J. Myers, D.D., J.C.D., Chm./Ex-officio; Rev. Msgr. James F. Campbell, Exec. Sec./Treas. & Ex-Officio; Rev. Thomas E. Mack, Vice Pres.; Rev. Msgr. Albert W. Hallin, Sec.; Revs. Thomas Maloney; David C. Heinz; Rev. Msgr. Norman D. Goodman; Rev. Mark J. Merdian, *412 N.E. Madison Ave., Peoria, 61603.* Tel: 309-671-1550; Fax: 309-671-1558.

Commission for Ecumenism—Rev. Msgr. Albert W. Hallin, *405 W. Clark St., Champaign, 61820.* Tel: 217-352-8748.

Communications, Office of—Mrs. Kate Kenny, Dir., *Sheen Pastoral Center, 412 N.E. Madison Ave., Peoria, 61603.* Tel: 309-671-1550; Fax: 309-671-1595.

Council of Conciliation and Arbitration—Rev. Msgr. James F. Campbell, Chm., *Sheen Pastoral Center, 412 N.E. Madison Ave., Peoria, 61603-2720.* Tel: 309-671-1550; Fax: 309-671-1558.

Cursillo Program—Rev. Timothy Nolan, Spiritual Dir., *Spalding Renewal Center, 401 N.E. Madison Ave., Peoria, 61603.* Tel: 309-676-4001.

Diocesan Office of Development—Mr. Edward N. Laughlin, Dir.; Mr. John Howard, Planned Giving Dir., *Sheen Pastoral Center, 412 N.E. Madison Ave., Peoria, 61603.* Tel: 309-671-1550; Fax: 309-671-1595.

Diocesan Education Commission—*Sheen Pastoral Center, 412 N.E. Madison Ave., Peoria, 61603.* Tel: 309-671-1550; Fax: 309-671-1595.

Diocesan Office of Finance—Mr. Allyn G. Schmid, Dir.; Mr. Toby Gualandri, Auditor, Finance Office: *Sheen Pastoral Center, 412 N.E. Madison Ave., Peoria, 61603.* Tel: 309-671-1550; Fax: 309-671-1595.

Diocesan Pastoral Council—Rev. Msgr. James Campbell, V.G., *Sheen Pastoral Center, 412 N.E Madison Ave., Peoria, 61603.* Tel: 309-671-1550; Fax: 309-671-1558.

Diocesan Personnel Board—Rev. Msgr. James F. Campbell, V.G., Dir., *Sheen Pastoral Center, 412 N.E. Madison Ave., Peoria, 61603.* Tel: 309-671-1550; Fax: 309-671-1558.

Divine Worship, Office of—Mrs. Barbara A. Logan, Dir., *Sheen Pastoral Center, 412 N.E. Madison Ave., Peoria, 61603.* Tel: 309-671-1550; Fax: 309-671-1595.

Evangelization—Rev. John Mark Williams, Dir., *Sheen Pastoral Center, 412 N.E. Madison Ave., Peoria, 61603.* Tel: 309-671-1550; Fax: 309-671-1595.

Family Life, Office of—Ms. Maureen McNamara, Dir. Assoc. Dirs.: Ms. Jeanne Whalen; Mr. Patrick DiVetri, *Sheen Pastoral Center, 412 N.E. Madison Ave., Peoria, 61603.* Tel: 309-671-1550; Fax: 309-671-1595.

Natural Family Planning Dept.—417 N.E. Madison Ave., Peoria, 61603. Tel: 309-671-1570; Fax: 309-671-1576.

Holy Childhood Association—Rev. John C. Anderson, Dir., *412 N.E. Madison Ave., Peoria, 61603.* Tel: 309-671-1550; Fax: 309-671-1595.

Newspaper—"The Catholic Post"—Most Rev. John J. Myers, Publisher; Mr. Thomas Dermody, Editor-in-Chief, *409 N.E. Monroe Ave., Peoria, 61603.* Tel: 309-673-3603; Fax: 309-673-0334.

Nurses, Council of—Vacant.

Permanent Diaconate, Office of—Rev. Msgr. Charles J. Beebe, Episcopal Vicar/Dir., *1508 W. Wilhelm Rd., Dunlap, 61525.* Tel: 309-243-7811; Fax: 309-243-7810.

Priests' Eucharistic League—Rev. Msgr. Joseph A. Zube, J.C.L., *Sheen Pastoral Center, 412 N.E. Madison Ave., Peoria, 61603.* Tel: 309-671-1550; Fax: 309-671-1595.

Propagation of the Faith—Rev. John C. Anderson, Dir., *412 N.E. Madison Ave., Peoria, 61603.* Tel: 309-671-1550; Fax: 309-671-1595.

Priests' Purgatorial Society—Rev. Msgr. James F. Campbell, Dir., *Sheen Pastoral Center, 412 N.E. Madison Ave., Peoria, 61603.* Tel: 309-671-1550; Fax: 309-671-1558.

Rural Life Conference—Rev. Gregory K. Ketcham, Dir., *Church of the Immaculate Conception, 218 W. Broadway, Monmouth, 61462.* Tel: 309-634-7533.

Presbyteral Council—Rev. Thomas E. Mack, Pres.; Rev. Philip D. Halfacre, Sec./Treas.; Rev. Msgr. Norman D. Goodman, Vice Pres., *Sheen Pastoral Center, 412 N.E. Madison, Peoria, 61603.* Tel: 309-671-1550; Fax: 309-671-1558.

Social Service—Miss Peggy A. Arizzi, Diocesan Dir.; Mr. Jeff Turnbull, Assoc. Dir., *2900 W. Heading Ave., P.O. Box 817, Peoria, 61652.* Tel: 309-671-5700., Rock Island Office: *816 20th St., Rock Island, 61201.* Tel: 309-788-9581., Bloomington Office: *106 W. Chestnut, Bloomington, 61701.* Tel: 309-788-9581., Champaign Office: *610 1-2 E. Park St., Champaign, 61820.* Tel: 217-352-5279., LaSalle Office: *535 3rd St., LaSalle, 61301.* Tel: 815-223-4007., Galesburg Office: *2401 N. Broad St., Galesburg, 61401.*, Macomb Office: *105 S. Johnson St., Macomb, 61455.* Tel: 309-833-1791.

TEC—Rev. Timothy Nolan, Dir., *Spalding Renewal Center, 401 N.E. Madison Ave., Peoria, 61603.* Tel: 309-676-4001.

Vocations—Rev. Joseph Donton, Dir., *607 N.E. Madison Ave., P.O. Box 1406, Peoria, 61655.* Tel: 309-671-1568; Fax: 309-671-5079.

CLERGY, PARISHES, MISSIONS AND PAROCHIAL SCHOOLS

CITY OF PEORIA
(Peoria County)

1—St. Mary's Cathedral (1846), Most Rev. John J. Myers, S.T.L., J.C.D., Bishop of Peoria; Rev. Joseph P. Donton.
Res., 607-A N.E. Madison Ave., 61603. Tel: 309-671-1568; Fax: 309-671-1577.

2—Holy Family (1956), Revs. Steve McKinley, O.F.M.Conv.; Patrick Stoffer, O.F.M.Conv.; Bro. Martin Schmitz, O.F.M.Conv.; Deacon James Maubach.
Res., 3720 N. Sterling, 61615. Tel: 309-688-3427; Fax: 309-688-2174.
School—2329 W. Reservoir, 61615. Tel: 309-688-2931; Fax: 309-681-5687. Gary Parmelee, Prin.
Lay Teachers 21; Students 420.

3—Sacred Heart (1879) (German), Revs. Marne Breckensiek, O.F.M.; Casimir Kolesar, O.F.M.; Deacon Michael Reid.
Res., 504 Fulton St., 61602. Tel: 309-673-6316; 6317.

4—St. Ann (1994), Rev. Richard E. Horvath; Deacons Richard Jones; Joseph Koeppel.
Mailing Address: 1010 S. Louisa St., 61605. Tel: 309-674-5072; Fax: 309-655-1566.

5—St. Bernard's, Rev. David C. Heinz.
Res., 509 E. Kansas Ave., 61603. Tel: 309-682-1221; Fax: 309-6823462.
School—Tel: 309-682-5823.
Sisters 2; Lay Teachers 12; Students 155.

6—St. Boniface's (1881) (German). Merged with St. John's Parish July 1, 1994, to form St. Ann's Parish at 1010 S. Louisa St., 61605.
School—Consolidated with St. John and St. Martin de Porres, Tel: 309-674-0531.
Convent—1009 S. Louisa St., 61605. Tel: 309-674-0225. Sisters of St. Benedict

7—St. Cecilia's. Closed. For Sacramental records write St. Philomena, 3300 N. Twelve Oaks Dr., Peoria, IL 61604.

8—St. John's (1890) (Irish). Merged with St. Boniface July 1, 1994, to form St. Ann's Parish at 1010 S. Louisa St., 61605.
School—Consolidated with St. Ann and St. Martin de Porres, 1406 W. Antoinette St., 61605.

9—St. Jude's (1975), Rev. Msgr. Charles J. Beebe; Deacon Thomas Rapach.
Res., 1406 Wilhelm Rd., Dunlap, 61525. Tel: 309-243-7811; Fax: 309-243-7810. [CEM]
Catechesis/Religious Programs—Tel: 309-243-7324.
Students 283.

10—St. Mark's (1891), Revs. Robert G. Schladen; Jeffrey I. Windy; Deacons Bernard Filzen; Charles Tuerk; John Skender.
Res., 1113 W. Bradley Ave., 61606. Tel: 309-673-1263.
School—Lay Teachers 16; Students 310.
Catechesis/Religious Programs—Tel: 309-673-2212.
Students 85.

11—St. Martin de Porres (1976), Rev. Glenn Fontana.
Res., 103 S. Sheridan, 61605. Tel: 309-676-0726.
Southside Catholic Child Care Center—1010 W. Johnson, 61605. Tel: 309-674-7340.

12—St. Peter's (1897), Rev. John Mark Williams; Deacon Richard Zimmerman. In res., Rev. Mark Merdian.
Res., 2719 N.E. Madison Ave., 61603. Tel: 309-685-3861; Fax: 309-688-1502.

13—St. Philomena's (1945), Rev. Msgr. Steven P. Rohlfs; Revs. Christopher G. Haake; Donald Roszkowski; Deacons Robert England; Richard Hammel; Harry Ohl; David Reising. In res., Rev. Timothy Nolan.
Res., 3300 N. Twelve Oaks Dr., 61604-1464. Tel: 309-682-8642; Fax: 309-682-8955. [JC]
School—Sisters of St. Francis, Tel: 309-685-1208.
Sr. Mary Joseph Bickett, O.S.F., Prin.
Sisters 4; Lay Teachers 19; Students 465.
St. Philomena Endowment Trust—.

14—St. Thomas (1937), Revs. William A. Watson; D. Giles Brom; Bowan Schmitt; Sr. Rachel Bergschneider, O.S.B., Pastoral Assoc. & D.R.E.; Deacons Donald Efinger; Robert Waldschmidt; Francis S. Eaton; Earl Hietter; William Kelly, Sr.
Res., 904 E. Lake Ave., Peoria Heights, 61614. Tel: 309-688-3446; Fax: 309-688-3467.
School—4229 N. Monroe, Peoria Heights, 61614. Tel: 309-685-2533.
Lay Teachers 26; Students 480.
Catechesis/Religious Programs—Students 140.

15—St. Vincent De Paul (1962), Revs. Thomas R. Miller; John M. Verrier; Deacon Robert W. Myers, Sr. In res., Rev. Msgr. Clarence J. Hettinger.
Res., 6001 N. University St., 61614. Tel: 309-691-3602; Fax: 309-691-3687.
School—6003 N. University St., 61614. Tel: 309-691-5012.
Lay Teachers 22; Students 400.
Catechesis/Religious Programs—Tel: 309-691-6513.
Students 78.

OUTSIDE THE CITY OF PEORIA

Abingdon, Knox Co., Sacred Heart (1924), Rev. Francis M. Oman, I.C.
Res., 506 N. Main St., 61410. Tel: 309-462-3421.

Aledo, Mercer Co., St. Catherine's Church (1914), Rev. Gregory J. Plunkett.
Res., 106 N.E. Fourth, 61231. Tel: 309-582-7500; Fax: 309-582-2033. [CEM]
Catechesis/Religious Programs—Students 137.
Missions—Keithsburg, Mercer Co., St. Mary's, 602 S. 10th St., Keithsburg, 61442. Tel: 309-374-2420;

New Boston, Mercer Co., St. Theresa of the Little Flower, 109 Washington, New Boston, 61272.

Alexis, Warren Co., St. Theresa's (1877) (Swedish), Rev. William C. Keebler, Jr.
Res., 131 Main St., 61412. Tel: 309-482-3935. [CEM]
Mission—Wataga, Knoxville Co., St. Aloysius, N. Depot St., Wataga, 61488. Tel: 309-375-6835.

Andalusia, Rock Island Co., St. Patrick's (1974), Rev. James G. Pallardy.
Mailing Address: Box 211, 61232.
Res., 9616 140th St. W., Taylor Ridge, 61284. Tel: 309-798-2098.
Catechesis/Religious Programs—Tel: 309-798-2630.
Students 150.

Annawan, Henry Co., Sacred Heart (1893), Rev. Timothy J. Sauppe.
Res., 305 W. South Ave., 61234. Tel: 309-935-6911. [CEM]

Arlington, Bureau Co., St. Patrick's (1864), Rev. Kevin Gorman, O.S.B.
Res., 61312. Tel: 815-638-2323. [CEM]

Atkinson, Henry Co., St. Anthony's (1870) (Belgian), Rev. Donnelly J. Fitzpatrick.
Res., 204 W. Main St., P.O. Box 210, 61235-0210. Tel: 309-936-7900; Fax: 309-936-7900. [CEM]

Bartonville, Peoria Co., St. Anthony (1969), Rev. Thomas F. Kelly; Sr. Eleanor Hoffmann, O.P., Pastoral Assoc. & D.R.E.; Deacons Richard Hammond; Louis Tomlianovich.
Res., 2525 Skyway Rd., P.O. Box 4152, 61607. Tel: 309-697-0645; Fax: 309-697-2188.
Catechesis/Religious Programs—Students 230.

Bement, Piatt Co., St. Michael, Rev. Vien Van Do; Deacon Edward Nichols.
Res., 332 S. Macon, 61813. Tel: 217-762-2566.

Benson, Woodford Co., St. John (1873), Rev. Neri Greskoviak, O.F.M.
Res., 506 W. Randolph, Roanoke, 61561. Tel: 309-394-2615; Fax: 309-923-3031. [CEM]

Blackstone, Livingston Co., St. Bernard. Closed. For sacramental records contact, Immaculate Conception, Streater.

Bloomington, McLean Co.,

1—Holy Trinity, (1853), Revs. John J. Dietzen; Gregory Nelson; Deacons Brendan Carolan; Lewis Roesch.
Res., 704 N. Main St., 61701. Tel: 309-829-2197; Fax: 309-829-2243. [CEM]
School—705 N. Roosevelt, 61701. Tel: 309-828-7151; Fax: 309-827-8131.
1909 E. Lincoln St., 61701. Tel: 309-662-3712; Fax: 309-663-9115.
Sisters 2; Lay Teachers 26; Students 615.
Catechesis/Religious Programs—Tel: 309-828-8242. Mrs. Sharon Priester, D.R.E.
Students 245.

2—St. Mary's, (1867) (German), Revs. Ric Schneider, O.F.M.; Damian Cesanek, O.F.M.; Deacon Darrel Petri.
Res., 527 W. Jackson St., 61701. Tel: 309-827-8526; Fax: 309-829-3061. [CEM]
School—603 W. Jackson St., 61701. Tel: 309-828-5954.
Lay Teachers 10; Students 96.
Catechesis/Religious Programs—Students 173.

3—St. Patrick's, (1892), Revs. Glenn H. Harris, Admin.; Vincent E. Dietzen, Pastor Emeritus.
Res., 1209 W. Locust St., 61701. Tel: 309-829-1355. [JC]

4—St. Patrick Church of Merna, (1890), Revs. Gerald T. Ward; Lawrence A. Morlan.
Church—R.R. 1, Box 38, 61704. Tel: 309-662-7361; Fax: 309-664-6167. [CEM]
Catechesis/Religious Programs—Sr. Rita Ann Bregenhorn, O.S.U., D.R.E.
Students 226.

Bradford, Stark Co., St. John the Baptist (1876), Rev. John Thieryoung.
Res., 218 First St., Box 310, 61421. Tel: 309-897-4081; Fax: 309-897-8007. [CEM]

Brimfield, Peoria Co., St. Joseph's (1852) (Irish), Rev. Joseph J. Kelly.
Res., 314 W. Clay St., 61517. Tel: 309-446-3275. [CEM]
Mission—Williamsfield, Knox Co., St. James, Williamsfield, 61489. Tel: 309-446-3275.

Budd, Livingston Co., St. Bernard's. Closed. For parish records contact Church of the Immaculate Conception, Streator.

Bushnell, McDonough Co., St. Bernard (1877), Rev. David L. Kurt.
Res., 376 W. Hail St., 61422. Tel: 309-772-2333.

Camp Grove, Marshall Co., St. Patrick (1866) (Irish). Rev. Michael J. Driscoll.
Res., 115 W. Camp St., 61424. Tel: 309-493-5261. [CEM]

Campus, Livingston Co., Sacred Heart (Irish), Rev. James E. Rickey, Admin.
Res., P.O. Box 68, 60920. Tel: 815-584-3522; Fax: 815-584-1148. [CEM]

Canton, Fulton Co., St. Mary's (1862), Rev. Arthur D. Meyer; Deacon Victor Kovachevich.
Res., 229 N. 3rd Ave., 61520. Tel: 309-647-1473. [CEM 2]
Catechesis/Religious Programs—Tel: 309-647-0261.
Students 174.

Carthage, Hancock Co., Immaculate Conception (1860), Rev. Glenn J. Fontana.
Res., 125 N. Fayette, 62321. Tel: 217-357-3087. [CEM]
Mission—West Point, Hancock Co., St. Mary.

Champaign, Champaign Co.,

1—Holy Cross, (1912), Rev. Msgr. Albert W. Hallin; Rev. Robert D. Spilman; Deacons Henry Hart; John Lalande.
Res., 405 W. Clark St., 61820. Tel: 217-352-8748; Fax: 217-366-2929.
School—410 W. White St., 61820. Tel: 217-356-9521; Fax: 217-356-1745.
Lay Teachers 17; Students 417.
Catechesis/Religious Programs—Sr. Joan Kaucher, C.S.J., D.R.E.
Students 147.

2—St. John's Catholic Chapel, (1918). (For Catholic Students at the University of Illinois). Revs. Stuart W. Swetland, Chap.; Thomas Gibson; Robert Barry, O.P.
Res., Newman Hall, 604 E. Armory Ave., 61820. Tel: 217-344-1184; Fax: 217-344-4957.

3—St. Mary's, (1857), Rev. Thomas J. Royer.
Res., 612 E. Park Ave., 61820. Tel: 217-352-8364; Fax: 217-352-6859. [CEM]

4—St. Matthew, Revs. Terrance P. O'Brien; John-Peter Pham; David J. Erickson.
Res., 1303 Lincolnshire Dr., 61821. Tel: 217-359-4224; Fax: 217-359-9846.
School—1307 Linconshire Dr., 61821. Tel: 217-359-4114; Fax: 217-359-7507.
Lay Teachers 19; Students 474.
Catechesis/Religious Programs—Tel: 217-359-8761.
Students 299.

Chatsworth, Livingston Co., SS. Peter and Paul (1877) (French), Rev. Richard W. Brunskill.
Res., 406 N. Fifth St., P.O. Box 546, 60921. Tel: 815-635-3127. [CEM]

Chenoa, McLean Co., St. Joseph's (1859), Rev. Terry Cassidy.
Res., 225 W. Owsley, 61726. Tel: 815-945-2561; Fax: 815-945-7634. [CEM]
Catechesis/Religious Programs—Students 186.
Mission—Lexington, McLean Co., St. Mary, Tel: 815-945-7987.

Cherry, Bureau Co., Holy Trinity (1904), Rev. Kevin Gorman, O.S.B.
Res., P.O. Box 159, 212 S. Main, 61317. Tel: 815-894-2006; Fax: 815-894-2090. [CEM]

Chillicothe, Peoria Co., St. Edward's (1900), Rev. Anthony M. Ego; Deacons Gregory Serangeli; Bob Pomazel.
Res., 1216 N. 6th St., 61523. Tel: 309-274-3809. [CEM]
School—Tel: 309-274-2994; Fax: 309-274-4150.
Lay Teachers 13; Students 230.

Clinton, De Witt Co., St. John the Baptist's (1879), Rev. Robert H. Hoffmann.
Res., 502 N. Monroe St., 61727. Tel: 217-935-3727.
Catechesis/Religious Programs—Tel: 217-935-3727.
Students 114.

Coal Valley, Rock Island Co., St. Maria Goretti (1972), Rev. Richard F. Bresnahan; Deacons Charles Breeden; Robert Zimmerman.
Res., P.O. Box 159, 210 E. 22nd Ave., 61240. Tel: 309-799-3414.
Catechesis/Religious Programs—Tel: 309-799-7283.
Students 112.

Colfax, McLean Co., St. Joseph's (1850), Rev. Edward S. Kopec.
Res., P.O. Box 169, 107 W. North, 61728. Tel: 309-723-6229; Fax: 309-723-6527.
Mission—Strawn, Livingston Co., St. Rose.

Colona, Henry Co., St. Patrick's (1941), Rev. Edward E. Bush.
Res., 201 First St., P.O. Box 197, 61241. Tel: 309-792-3854. [JC]
Catechesis/Religious Programs—Tel: 309-949-2200. Jean Sottos, D.R.E.
Students 346.

Creve Coeur, Tazewell Co., Sacre Coeur (1954), Rev. James E. King.
Res., 301 Roosevelt St., 61610. Tel: 309-699-8223.
Church:—601 Rusche Ln., 61610. Tel: 309-699-8511.

Cullom, Livingston Co., St. John's (1881), Rev. Richard W. Brunskill.
Res., 113 Van Alstyne, P.O. Box 376, 60929. Tel: 815-689-2367.

Dalzell, Bureau Co., St. Thomas More (1934) (Italian), Rev. Placid W. Hatfield, O.S.B.; Deacon Robert Beltramini.
Res., 302 Chestnut, 61320. Tel: 815-663-6201.

Danville, Vermilion Co., Holy Family (1978), Rev. Ted Pracz; Deacons Herman Bott; Richard Smith.
Church—444 E. Main St., 61832. Tel: 217-431-5100; Fax: 217-431-5103. [CEM]
School—Tel: 217-431-5108.
Lay Teachers 14; Students 255.

St. Paul's (1915), Revs. Douglas J. Hennessy; R. Anthony Lee; Jeffrey Lawrence; Sr. Charles Allen, Pastoral Assoc.
Res., 1303 N. Walnut St., 61832. Tel: 217-442-5313; Fax: 217-442-5356. [JC]
School—1307 N. Walnut St., 61832. Tel: 217-442-3880; Fax: 217-442-5852.
Lay Teachers 26; Students 393.
Catechesis/Religious Programs—Students 150.

Delavan, Tazewell Co., St. Mary's (1859), Rev. Gregory J. Jozefiak.
Res., Box 769, 61734. Tel: 309-244-8516. [CEM]
Mission—Hopedale, Tazewell Co., St. Joseph's.

Depue, Bureau Co., St. Mary's (1908), Rev. Mubarak A. Amar.
Res., 312 Park St., Box 19, 61322. Tel: 815-447-2552. [CEM]

Downs, McLean Co., St. Mary's (1910), Rev. Stephen A. Willlard.
Church—101 N. Lincoln, P.O. Box 66, 61736. Tel: 309-378-4679; Fax: 309-378-4080.
Catechesis/Religious Programs—Students 153.

Dunlap, Peoria Co., St. Clement's. Closed. For inquiries for parish records contact the Chancery.

Dwight, Livingston Co., St. Patrick's (1862) (Irish), Rev. James E. Rickey.
Res., 126 W. Mazon Ave., P.O. Box 70, 60420. Tel: 815-584-3522; Fax: 815-584-3400. [CEM]
Catechesis/Religious Programs—Tel: 815-584-3110. Ginger Connor, D.R.E.
Students 292.

Eagle Township, La Salle Co., Annunciation of Blessed Virgin Mary (1869) (Irish), Rev. Charles A. McCarthy, C.S.Sp.
Church—Rte. 3, Eagle Township, Streator, 61364. Tel: 815-672-6500.
Res., Rte 1, 957 N. 17th Rd., Tonica, 61370. Tel: 815-856-2502. [CEM]

Earlville, La Salle Co., St. Theresa's (1904), Rev. William D. Virtue.
Res., 221 Union St., Box 90, 60518. Tel: 815-246-4321; Fax: 815-246-9581. [CEM 2]

East Moline, Rock Island Co., St. Anne (1919), Rev. Robert D. O'Connor; Sr. Mary O'Connor, B.V.M, Pastoral Assoc.
Res., 555 18th Ave., 61244. Tel: 309-755-5071.
School—Tel: 309-755-9771; Fax: 309-755-7407.
Sisters of Charity of the B.V.M. 4; Lay Teachers 11; Students 236.

St. Mary's (1907) (Belgian-Spanish), Rev. Donald L. Levitt; Deacon Jerry Buyck.
Res., 1908 13th St., 61244. Tel: 309-755-4111. [JC]
School—Tel: 309-755-4352.
Lay Teachers 16; Students 160.
Catechesis/Religious Programs—1925 13th St., 61244.
Students 150.

East Peoria, Tazewell Co., St. Monica's (1898), Rev. Kenneth L. Marchulones; Sr. Marjorie Meismer, O.S.F., Pastoral Assoc.; Deacons Ronald Rager; William Sloman.
Res., 303 Campanile Dr., 61611. Tel: 309-694-2061.
Catechesis/Religious Programs—Tel: 309-699-8458. Mrs. Jana Densberger, D.R.E.
Students 139.

Elkhart, Logan Co., St. Patrick (1856), Rev. Patrick DeMeulemeester.
Res., 213 S. Bogardus, P.O. Box 19, 62634. Tel: 217-947-2714.
Missions—Mount Pulaski, Logan Co., St. Thomas Aquinas, St. Patrick's, 62634.; Middletown, Logan Co., St. John the Baptist, St. Patrick's, 62634.

Elmwood, Peoria Co., St. Patrick's (1870) (Irish), Rev. Thomas E. Seibert, I.C.; Deacon Deane Keefer.
Res., P.O. Box 440, 61529. Tel: 309-742-4921. [CEM]

El Paso, Woodford Co., St. Mary's (1863), Rev. Lawrence P. Morrissey.
Res., 79 W. Third, P.O. Box 197, 61738. Tel: 309-527-4555. [CEM 2]

Catechesis/Religious Programs—Tel: 309-744-2490. Mrs. Judy Hinshaw, D.R.E.
Students 128.

Eureka, Woodford Co., St. Luke's (1982), Rev. Dominic J. Vitaliano.
Res., 301 E. Pearson St., 61530. Tel: 309-467-4855. [JC]
Church—904 E. Regan Dr., P.O. Box 226, 61530.

Fairbury, Livingston Co., St. John the Baptist (1857), Rev. Scott Archer.
Res., 110 E. Ash, 61739. Tel: 815-692-2555. [CEM]
Catechesis/Religious Programs—Students 123.
Mission—Forrest, Livingston Co., St. James, 322 S. William, Forrest, 61741.

Farmer City, De Witt Co., Sacred Heart (1899), Rev. Gerald J. Benbenek.
Res., 612 N. Plum St., 61842. Tel: 309-928-3855. [CEM]
Mission—Bellflower, Mclean Co., St. John.

Farmington, Fulton Co., St. Matthew's (1904) (Italian), Rev. Thomas E. Seibert, I.C.; Deacon John Burton.
Res., 156 E. Vernon St., 61531. Tel: 309-245-4351.

Galesburg, Knox Co., Corpus Christi (1885), Rev. James P. McAteer, I.C.
Res., 273 S. Prairie St., 61401. Tel: 309-343-8256; Fax: 309-343-4793. [CEM]
School—Costa Catholic School. Operates with Immaculate Heart and St. Patrick. 2726 Costa Dr., 61401. Tel: 309-344-3151.
Sisters 1; Lay Teachers 22; Students 311.
Catechesis/Religious Programs—Students 140.

Immaculate Heart of Mary (1956), Rev. Ernest E. Pizzamiglio.
Mailing Address: P.O. Box 550, 61402. Tel: 309-344-3108; Fax: 309-344-1205.
Res., 2401 N. Broad St., 61401.
School—See Corpus Christi Parish.
Catechesis/Religious Programs—Students 130.

St. Patrick's (1863), Rev. Frederick Bruce King, I.C.; Deacons Jesse M. Ramirez; James D. Haneghan.
Mailing Address: P.O. Box 589, 61402-0589. Tel: 309-343-9874; Fax: 309-343-9944.
Res., 858 S. Academy St., 61401. [JC]
School—See Corpus Christi Parish.

Galva, Henry Co., St. John's (1882) (Swedish), Rev. Bruce D. Lopez.
Res., 212 N.E. 1st St., 61434. Tel: 309-932-2409; Fax: 309-932-8238. [CEM]

Geneseo, Henry Co., St. Malachy's (1866), Revs. Michael G. Pakula; John A. Mahoney, Pastor Emeritus; Deacons Harley Chaffee; Walter Verbeck; Harley Harris; Thomas Wachtel; Larry Honzel.
Res., 595 E. Ogden Ave., 61254. Tel: 309-944-5393; Fax: 309-944-5319.
School—Tel: 309-944-3230.
Lay Teachers 8; Students 170.
Catechesis/Religious Programs—Tel: 309-944-3518. Liz Fristensky, D.R.E.
Students 341.

Georgetown, Vermilion Co., St. Isaac Jogues (1942), Rev. John Paninski, M.S.
Res., 109 W. Seventh St., 61846. Tel: 217-662-6708.

Granville, Putnam Co., Sacred Heart Of Jesus (1908) (Italian), Rev. Patrick K. O'Neal.
Res., P.O. Box 217, 61323. Tel: 815-339-2138. [CEM]
Catechesis/Religious Programs—Students 132.
Mission—Bureau, Bureau Co., St. Francis Xavier, P.O. Box 217, 61323.

Havana, Mason Co., St. Patrick's, Rev. Eugene A. Radosevich.
Res., P.O. Box 345, 423 S. Orange, 62644. Tel: 309-543-6373; Fax: 309-543-3241. [CEM]
Mission—Manito, Mason Co., Immaculate Conception, 505 S. Adams, P.O. Box 242, Manito, 61546. Deacon William Meyer.

Hennepin, Putnam Co., St. Patrick's (1865), Rev. John A. Kwak.
Res., 10 St., P.O. Box 200, 61327. Tel: 815-925-7066; 925-7500. [CEM]
Mission—Mount Palatine, Putnam Co., Immaculate Conception, P.O. Lostant, Lostant, 61335. Tel: 815-882-2337. [CEM]

Henry, Marshall Co., St. Joseph's (1878) (Irish), Rev. Walter A. Breuning.
Res., 401 South St., Box 75, 61537. Tel: 309-364-2224. [CEM 2]

St. Mary's (1851) (German), Rev. Walter A. Breuning.
Res., Box 75, 61537. Tel: 309-364-2224. [CEM 2]
Catechesis/Religious Programs—Tel: 309-364-2011. Sr. Anita D.R.E.
Students 201.

Hoopeston, Vermilion Co., St. Anthony's (1877), Rev. Jerome R. Pilon; Deacon William C. Ringler.
Church—423 S. Third St., P.O. Box 414, 60942. Tel: 217-283-6211; Fax: 217-283-6252.

Hooppole, Henry Co., St. Mary's. Attended by Annawan.

Ivesdale, Champaign Co., St. Joseph's (1863) (Irish), Rev. Thomas J. Royer.
Res., 612 E. Park, Champaign, 61820. Tel: 217-352-8364; Fax: 217-352-6859. [CEM]

Kewanee, Henry Co., St. Francis of Assisi (1906) (Polish), Rev. John Burns.
Res., 1009 N. Burr, 61443. Tel: 309-852-2761.
Mission—Cambridge, Henry Co., St. John Vianney, 313 S. West St., Cambridge, 61238. Tel: 309-937-3304.

St. Mary's Catholic Church, Rev. Duane C. Jack; Deacons Martin Van Meltebeck; John T. Mock; Raymond Van Wassenhove.
Res., Parish Center, 406 W. Central Blvd., 61443-2010. Tel: 309-852-4549; Fax: 309-853-4106. [CEM]
School—Visitation, 107 S. Lexington, 61443. Tel: 309-856-7451.
Lay Teachers 13; Students 186.
Catechesis/Religious Programs—Tel: 309-856-5451. Mrs. Phyllis Elliott, D.R.E.
Students 152.

Kickapoo, (Edwards) Peoria Co., St. Mary's of Kickapoo (1837), Rev. Harry A. Pierjok. In res., Rev. Msgr. Robert C. Livingston.
Res., 9910 W. Knox St., Kickapoo (Edwards), 61528. Tel: 309-691-2030 (Church); Fax: 309-691-2898. [CEM]
School—Tel: 309-691-3015.
Lay Teachers 6; Students 67.

Lacon, Marshall Co., Immaculate Conception (1853), Rev. Ronald E. Enderlin; Deacon J. Robert Murphy.
Res., 418 N. Center St., 61540. Tel: 309-246-5145. [CEM]

Ladd, Bureau Co., St. Benedict's (1893), Rev. Harold L. Datzman, O.S.B.
Res., 314 Bureau St., 61329. Tel: 815-894-2319; Fax: 815-894-2265.
Mission—Seatonville, Bureau Co., St. Gertrude, 711 Railroad Ave., Seatonville, 61359.

La Salle, La Salle Co.,

1—Queen of the Holy Rosary, (1925) (Italian), Rev. Dale R. Maloy.
Res., 529 Fourth St., 61301. Tel: 815-223-7129. [JC]

2—St. Hyacinth's, (1875), Rev. Joseph W. Anderson; Deacon Charles Burgess.
Res., 927 10th St., 61301. Tel: 815-223-0934. [CEM]
School—LaSalle Catholic, Tel: 815-223-5088. Mr. John Ranger, Prin.
Sisters 1; Lay Teachers 16; Students 165.

3—Resurrection, (1979), Rev. John M. Onderko.
Res., 913 Fifth St., 61301. Tel: 815-223-1459.
School—LaSalle Catholic School, Tel: 815-223-5088.
Sisters 1; Lay Teachers 9; Students 165.
Mission—Dimmick Township, Sacred Heart.

4—St. Patrick's, (1838) (Irish), Rev. M. Duane Leclercq.
Res., 725-Fourth St., 61301. Tel: 815-223-0641; Fax: 815-223-0523. [CEM]
School—Daughters of Charity of St. Vincent de Paul, Tel: 815-223-1166.
Sisters 4; Lay Teachers 12; Students 207.

Leonore, La Salle Co., SS. Peter and Paul's (1860) (German), Rev. Charles A. McCarthy, C.S.Sp.
Res., Rte. 1, Tonica, 61370. Tel: 815-856-2502; Fax: 815-856-2502. [CEM]

Lewistown, Fulton Co., St. Mary's (1865), Rev. Robert W. O'Connor.
Res., 705 N. Broadway St., P.O. Box 106, 61542. Tel: 309-547-3226; Fax: 309-547-3226. [CEM]
Mission—St. David, Fulton Co., St. Michael.

Lincoln, Logan Co., Holy Family (1857), Revs. Thomas Mack; Daniel Wilder.
Res., 316 S. Logan St., 62656. Tel: 217-732-4019; Fax: 217-732-8842. [CEM 2]
School—Carroll Catholic School, Tel: 217-732-7518; Fax: 217-732-7518.
Lay Teachers 13; Students 235.
Catechesis/Religious Programs—Holy Family Religious Education Center, 103 Fourth St., 62656. Tel: 217-735-3520.
Students 511.
Missions—Atlanta, Logan Co., St. Mary, Atlanta, 61723.; Mason City, Mason Co., St. Columba, Mason City, 62664.

Loretto, Livingston Co., St. Mary's (1873) (German). Closed. For inquiries contact St. Patrick, Dwight.

Lostant, La Salle Co., St. John the Baptist's (1862), Rev. William M. Gardner.
Res., P.O. Box 486, Wenona, 61377. Tel: 815-853-4558.
Church—301 S. Sheridan, 61334. Tel: 815-368-3339. [CEM]

Macomb, McDonough Co., St. Paul's (1854), Rev. Richard A. Pricco.
Res., 309 W. Jackson, 61455. Tel: 309-833-2496; Fax: 309-833-1560. [CEM]
School—Tel: 309-833-2470.
Lay Teachers 8; Students 138.
Catechesis/Religious Programs—Tel: 309-837-1024.
Students 211.
Mission—Tennessee, McDonough Co., Sacred Heart.

Mahomet, Champaign Co., Our Lady of the Lake (1981), Rev. John C. Horton; Deacon Robert Baxley.
Res., 501 W. State St., P.O. Box 109, 61853. Tel: 217-586-5153; Fax: 217-586-5924.
Catechesis/Religious Programs—Tel: 217-586-5141. Sr. Constance Heidewald, R.S.M., D.R.E.
Students 412.

Marseilles, La Salle Co., St. Joseph's (1902), Rev. Donald R. Schladen.
Res., 200 Broadway St., P.O. Box 26, 61341. Tel: 815-795-2240.
Catechesis/Religious Programs—Students 78.

Matherville, Mercer Co., St. Anthony's Church (1916), Rev. Richard Slavish.
Office: P.O. Box 208, 61263. Tel: 309-754-8711. [CEM 2]
Mission—Viola, Mercer Co., St. John, Viola, 61486. Tel: 309-596-2950.

Mendota, La Salle Co., Holy Cross (1863), Rev. Msgr. Richard G. Fitzsimmons; Rev. Joseph Dondanville; Deacon Vincent Slomian.
Res., 1010 Jefferson St., 61342. Tel: 815-538-6151; Fax: 815-539-5014. [CEM]
School—1000 Jefferson St., 61342. Tel: 815-538-6016.
Sisters of the Third Order of St. Dominic (Springfield) 1; Lay Teachers 12; Students 267.
Catechesis/Religious Programs—Tel: 815-539-6050. Karen Zolper, D.R.E.
Students 175.

Metamora, Woodford Co., St. Mary's (1864) (German), Revs. Dacian Batt, O.F.M.; Benno Heidlage, O.F.M.; Charles B. Miller, O.F.M., (Retired); Alan Heet, O.F.M., (Retired); Deacon Marvin Smith.
Res., 415 W. Chatham St., P.O.Box 319, 61548. Tel: 309-367-4407; Fax: 309-367-4437. [CEM]
School—Tel: 309-367-2528; Fax: 309-367-4437.
Sisters of St. Francis of the Immaculate Conception 1; Lay Teachers 11; Students 163.
Catechesis/Religious Programs—Tel: 309-367-2507. Sr. Anita Pauwels, O.S.F., D.R.E.
Students 114.

St. Mary of Lourdes, Rev. Robert Weakley, O.F.M.; Deacon Jack Gaetz.
Res., Rte. 2, 61548. Tel: 309-383-4460; Fax: 309-383-4467.

Milan, Rock Island Co., St. Ambrose (1924), Rev. Msgr. Dale L. Wellman; Sr. Charlotte Sonneville, O.S.B., Pastoral Assoc.; Deacon Frank Randazzo.
Res., 312 W. First St., 61264. Tel: 309-787-4593; Fax: 309-787-6403.
School—Operates as part of Jordan Catholic School of Rock Island, Tel: 309-793-7363.
Students 68.
Catechesis/Religious Programs—Tel: 309-787-6240. Diane Hansen, D.R.E.
Students 127.

Minonk, Woodford Co., St. Patrick's (1878), Rev. Robert F. Gilles.
Res., 420 E. Sixth St., Box 107, 61760-0107. Tel: 309-432-2700; Fax: 309-432-2700. [CEM]
Mission—Flanagan, Livingston Co., St. Joseph.
Catechesis/Religious Programs—Students 160.

Moline, Rock Island Co., Christ the King (1967), Rev. Richard Barclift.
Parish Center: 3205 60th St., 61265. Tel: 309-762-4634; Fax: 309-762-7848.
Catechesis/Religious Programs—Tel: 309-797-5202. D.R.E.: Janet Myers, (PreK-6); Paula Anderson, (Jr. High School).
Students 170.

Sacred Heart (1906) (Belgian), Revs. Robert E. Lee; Brian K. Brownsey; Stanley L. Deptula; Sr. Kathleen Mullin, Pastoral Assoc.; Deacons John Landry; Dennis De Vooght.
Lee Parish Center—1608 13th St., 61265. Tel: 309-762-2362; Fax: 309-757-5502.
School—Seton Catholic School, (Grades PreK-8). Tel: 309-757-5500.
Sisters 1; Lay Teachers 30; Students 605.
Catechesis/Religious Programs—Rita Luebbers, D.R.E.
Students 231.

St. Mary's (1876) (Hispanic), Rev. Deo Gratias R. Mutefunya; Deacon Russell W. Smith.
Res., 412 10th St., 61265. Tel: 309-764-1562; Fax: 309-764-0317. [CEM]
School—Seton Catholic School, (Grades 6-8). Tel: 309-764-5418.
Sisters 1; Lay Teachers 13; Students 195.
Catechesis/Religious Programs—Tel: 309-762-6575. Mrs. Claire Sally Van Oteghem, D.R.E.
Students 115.

Monmouth, Warren Co., Immaculate Conception, Revs. Carl LoPresti; Gregory K. Ketcham; Sr. Paula Helenthal, O.S.B., Pastoral Care Min.; Deacon William Clark.
Church—218 W. Broadway, 61462. Tel: 309-734-7533; Fax: 309-734-6082. [CEM]
School—Tel: 309-734-6037.
Lay Teachers 10; Students 157.
Convent—116 North A, 61462. Tel: 309-734-6327.
Mission—Oquawka, Henderson Co., St. Andrew.

Monticello, Piatt Co., St. Philomena, Rev. Vien Van Do; Deacon Edward S. Nichols.
Res., 1301 N. Market St., 61856. Tel: 217-762-2566. [CEM]

Morton, Tazewell Co., Blessed Sacrament (1957), Rev. Eugene L. Finnell; Deacon Thomas Moran.
Res., 261 E. Greenwood St., 61550. Tel: 309-266-9721; Fax: 309-266-9201.
School—Tel: 309-263-8442; Fax: 309-263-8443.
Lay Teachers 12; Students 214.
Catechesis/Religious Programs—Tel: 309-266-6791. Judy Krumholz, D.R.E.
Students 351.

Nauvoo, Hancock Co., SS. Peter and Paul's (1848) (German), Rev. Gregory K. Ketcham.
Res., 150 N. Wells St., 62354. Tel: 217-453-2428. [CEM]
School—Tel: 217-453-2511.
Lay Teachers 4; Students 41.
Catechesis/Religious Programs—Students 87.
Mission—Dallas City, Hancock Co., Sacred Heart, Dallas City, 62330.

Normal, McLean Co., Epiphany (1966), Rev. Tom Maloney; Deacon Richard Grimler.
Res., 1006 E. College Ave., 61761. Tel: 309-452-2585; 452-3223; Fax: 309-452-4851.
School—Tel: 309-452-3268.
Lay Teachers 14; Students 330.
Catechesis/Religious Programs—Mary Jean Kraft, D.R.E.
Students 430.

Odell, Livingston Co., St. Paul's (1901) (Irish), Rev. Francis J. Ryan.
Res., 313 W. Hamilton, 60460. Tel: 815-998-2197. [CEM]
School—Tel: 815-998-2194.
Lay Teachers 5; Students 138.

Oglesby, La Salle Co., Holy Family (1953), Revs. Anthony J. Trosley; David Whiteside.
Res., 311 Woodland Ave., 61348. Tel: 815-883-8233.
School—Tel: 815-883-8916; Fax: 815-883-8943.
Lay Teachers 12; Students 193.

Ohio, Bureau Co., Immaculate Conception Church (1875) (Irish), Rev. Binh K. Tran.
Res., c/o St. John's, 204 N. Main St., Walnut, 61376-0370. Tel: 815-379-2602. [CEM]

Orion, Henry Co., Mary, Our Lady of Peace (1962), Rev. R. Michael Schaab.
Res., 1402 10th St., P.O.Box 175, 61273-0175. Tel: 309-526-8106.
Catechesis/Religious Programs—Students 200.

Ottawa, La Salle Co.,

1—St. Columba, (1844) (Irish), Revs. David Kipfer; Gerald J. Meyer; Deacon Estal C. Daron.
Res., 122 W. Washington St., 61350. Tel: 815-433-0700; Fax: 815-433-0305. [CEM]
School—1110 LaSalle St., 61350. Tel: 815-433-1199.
Lay Teachers 13; Students 230.
Catechesis/Religious Programs—Students 125.

2—St. Francis of Assisi, (1858), Rev. Leo H. Gildner.
Res., 820 Sanger St., P.O. Box 2333, 61350-2333. Tel: 815-434-0969; Fax: 815-434-1073. [CEM]

3—St. Mary's, (1927), Rev. Harold F. Schmitt.
Res., 2005 Center St., Ottawa (Naplate), 61350. Tel: 815-433-2404; Fax: 815-433-9458.

4—St. Patrick's, (1893) (Irish), Rev. Robert J. Creager.
Res., 726 W. Jefferson St., 61350. Tel: 815-434-0768; Fax: 815-434-0768.
School—801 W. Jefferson St., 61350. Tel: 815-433-2889.
Dominican Sisters (Sinsinawa, WI) 3; Lay Teachers 10; Students 159.
Catechesis/Religious Programs—Tel: 815-433-3752. Mrs. Mary Jean Weihman, D.R.E.
Students 170.
Convent—727 W. Jefferson, 61350. Tel: 815-433-2637.

Pekin, Tazewell Co., St. Joseph's (1863), Revs. Gerald J. Verdun; James Kruse; Vandennis Nguyen; Deacons Charles Murray; Martin Pogioli; Ernie Whited.
Res., 303 S. Seventh St., 61554. Tel: 309-347-6108; Fax: 309-347-6959. [CEM 2]
School—Tel: 309-347-7194. Joan Moore, Prin.
Lay Teachers 16; Students 330 (including Preschool).
Catechesis/Religious Programs—Martha Novak, D.R.E.
Students 355.

Penfield, Champaign Co., St. Lawrence's (1898), Rev. Howard C. Barch.
Res., P.O. Box 49, 61862. Tel: 217-595-5560; Fax: 217-595-5439. [CEM]
Mission—Rankin, Vermilion Co., Holy Trinity, 200 S. Main, Rankin, 60960. Tel: 217-397-2967.

Peru, La Salle Co., St. Joseph's (1854), Revs. Henry H. Fritz, O.S.B.; Joseph J. Heyd, O.S.B.
Res., P.O. Box 608, 61354. Tel: 815-223-0718; Fax: 815-223-5690. [CEM]
School—Peru Catholic School System, (Grades PreK-8). Operated jointly by the Peru parishes. 2003 Fifth St., 61354. Tel: 815-224-1914.
Sisters 4; Lay Teachers 14; Students 286.
Catechesis/Religious Programs—Sandra Weger, D.R.E.
Students 140.

St. Mary's (1867) (Irish), Rev. Richard Kolczaski; Deacon Fred Sims.
Res., 1319 Sixth St., 61354. Tel: 815-223-2672.
School—Peru Catholic School System. See St. Joseph's for details. Tel: 815-224-1914.

St. Valentine's (1891) (Polish), Rev. Thomas Badovsky.
Res., 1109 Pulaski St., 61354. Tel: 815-223-0315. [CEM]
School—Peru Catholic School System. See St. Joseph's for details. Tel: 815-224-1914.
Catechesis/Religious Programs—Tel: 815-223-8471. Lynda Martin, D.R.E.
Students 110.

Pesotum, Champaign Co., St. Mary (1875) (German), Rev. Joseph M. Mai Chi Thanh.
Res., P.O. Box 169, 61863. Tel: 217-867-2434. [CEM]

St. Joseph (1904) (German), Rev. Joseph M. Mai Chi Thanh.
Res., P.O. Box 619, 61863. Tel: 217-867-2434. [CEM]

Peterstown, La Salle Co., SS. Peter and Paul (1872), Rev. Richard Fitzsimmons.
Res., 1010 Jefferson St., Mendota, 61342. Tel: 815-538-6151; Fax: 815-539-5014. [CEM]

Philo, Champaign Co., St. Thomas (1869), Rev. Dominic Vitaliano.
Res., 310 E. Madison, P.O. Box 266, 61864. Tel: 217-684-2571; Fax: 217-684-2571. [CEM]
School—Tel: 217-684-2309.
Sisters of the Third Order of St. Dominic (Springfield) 2; Lay Teachers 9; Students 153.
Mission—Bongard, Champaign Co., Immaculate Conception, 61864. [CEM]

Pontiac, Livingston Co., St. Mary's (1877), Revs. E. E. Higgins; Edward J. Roberts.
Res., 119 E. Howard St., P.O. Box 374, 61764. Tel: 815-844-7683; Fax: 815-842-4345. [CEM]
School—414 N. Main St., 61764. Tel: 815-844-6585; Fax: 815-844-6987.
Lay Teachers 10; Students 251.
Catechesis/Religious Programs—Students 127.

Princeton, Bureau Co., St. Louis (1865), Rev. Edward O. Harkrader.
Res., 616 S. Gosse Blvd., 61356. Tel: 815-879-0181; Fax: 815-879-8010.
School—Tel: 815-872-8521.
Sisters 2; Lay Teachers 11; Students 142.
Catechesis/Religious Programs—Tel: 815-872-1033.
Students 217.

Princeville, Peoria Co., St. Mary of the Woods (1867), Rev. J. Brian Rejsek.
Res., 407 S. Walnut, 61559. Tel: 309-385-4370. [CEM]

Ransom, La Salle Co., St. Patrick's (1883), Rev. William Arthur Ryan.
Res., 110 Wallace, P.O. Box 127, 60470. Tel: 815-586-4266. [CEM]
Mission—Grand Ridge, LaSalle Co., St. Mary, R.R. 1, Grand Ridge, 61325. Tel: 815-249-6871.

Rantoul, Champaign Co., St. Malachy's (1888), Revs. Jeffrey G. Laible; Stanley J. Malinowski, Pastor Emeritus; Deacon William Shipp Tel: 217-893-0741.
Office: Tel: 217-892-2023; Fax: 217-892-2378.
Res., 311 E. Grove Ave., 61866. Tel: 217-892-2044. [CEM]
School—340 E. Belle Ave., 61866. Tel: 217-892-2011.
Sisters 3; Lay Teachers 12; Students 186.
Convent—304 E. Belle Ave., 61866. Tel: 217-892-2870. Sisters of the Third Order of St. Dominic (Springfield)

Rapids City, Rock Island Co., St. John the Baptist (1857), Rev. James P. DeBisschop.
Res., 1416 Third Ave., P.O. Box 258, 61278. Tel: 309-496-2414; Fax: 309-755-1650. [CEM]
Catechesis/Religious Programs—Students 164.
Mission—Hampton, Rock Island Co., St. Mary, 708 State Ave., Rte. 84, Hampton, 61256. Tel: 309-755-5033. Deacon James Quinn.

Raritan, Henderson Co., Church of St. Patrick (1876) (Irish), Rev. Carl LoPresti; Deacon William Clark.
Res., P.O. Box 24, 61471. Tel: 309-734-7533.

Roanoke, Woodford Co., St. Joseph (1874), Rev. Neri Greskoviak, O.F.M.
Res., 506 W. Randolph, 61561. Tel: 309-923-3031; Fax: 309-926-3031.

Raritan, Henderson Co., St. Patrick's,
Res., P.O. Box 24, NJ 61471. Tel: 309-746-6223.

Rock Island, Rock Island Co.,

1—St. Mary, (1851) (German). (Formerly Immaculate Conception). Revs. James K. Ramer; George J. Schroeder, Pastor Emeritus (Retired).
16 Waverly Dr., 61201. Tel: 309-793-1897.
Rectory—2208 Fourth Ave., 61201-8904. Tel: 309-788-3322.

2—Sacred Heart, (1900), Rev. Ambrose Cunningham; Sr. Mary Veronica Grennan, Pastoral Assoc.; Deacon Jack Kettering.
Res., 2810 Fifth Ave., 61201. Tel: 309-794-0660.
School—Jordan Catholic School of Rock Island, Tel: 309-793-7350.
Sisters 2; Lay Teachers 30; Students 584.

3—St. Joseph's, (1876), Rev. J. M. Logan, Admin.; Sr. Germaine Cupp, O.S.B., Pastoral Assoc.
Res., 1316 Second Ave., 61201. Tel: 309-794-9793.
School—Operates as part of Jordan Catholic School of Rock Island.

4—St. Pius X, (1955), Revs. Paul E. Showalter; Francis M. Gallagher; Deacons Timothy Granet; Paul Martin; Philip Sailer. In res., Rev. Jeffrey Stirniman.
Res., 2502 29th Ave., 61201. Tel: 309-793-7373; Fax: 309-793-7361.
School—Operates as part of Jordan Catholic School of Rock Island. Tel: 309-793-7350.
Sisters 2; Lay Teachers 35; Students 248.
Catechesis/Religious Programs—Students 106.

Rushville, Schuyler Co., St. Rose (1870), Rev. Robert E. Reynolds.
Res., 319 N. Franklin St., P.O. Box 194, 62681-0292. Tel: 217-322-3424. [JC]

Rutland, La Salle Co., Sacred Heart (1895) (Irish), Rev. James C. Kretz.
Res., c/o 311 W. Santa Fe Ave., P.O. Box 165, Toluca, 61369. Tel: 815-452-2043. [CEM]

St. Augustine, Knox Co., St. Augustine (1863), Rev. Francis M. Oman, I.C.
Mailing Address: 506 N. Main St., Abingdon, 61410. Tel: 301-462-3421. [CEM]

Seneca, La Salle Co., St. Patrick's (1853), Rev. Msgr. Raymond J. Boyle.
Parish Center: 183 W. Union, 61360. Tel: 815-357-8509; Fax: 815-357-6239. [CEM]
Res., 176 W. Union St., 61360. Tel: 815-357-6239; Fax: 414-785-9567.
Catechesis/Religious Programs—Tel: 815-357-8509; Fax: 815-357-8509.
Students 190.

Seymour, Champaign Co., St. Boniface (1878), Rev. George E. Wuellner, Pastor Emeritus.
Res., 416 County Rd., 1100 N., 61875. Tel: 217-863-2190. [CEM]

Sheffield, Bureau Co., St. Patrick's (1885), Rev. Paul J. Meismer.
Res., 231 W. Atkinson St., 61361. Tel: 815-454-2251. [CEM]
Mission—Wyanet, Bureau Co., St. Margaret Mary.

Silvis, Rock Island Co., Our Lady of Guadalupe (1927) (Hispanic), Rev. Patrick M. Riordan; Deacon Henry Sandoval.
Res., 800 17th St., 61282. Tel: 309-792-3867.
Catechesis/Religious Programs—Students 115.

Spring Valley, Bureau Co.,

1—Immaculate Conception, (1884), Rev. Charles H. Kelly.
Res., 202 N. Greenwood St., 61362. Tel: 815-663-5351. [CEM]

2—St. Anne's. Closed. For sacramental records contact SS. Peter and Paul's, Spring Valley.

3—St. Anthony's, (1904) (Italian), Rev. Donald R. Henderson.
Res., P.O. Box 150, 510 Richard A. Mautino Dr., 61362-0150. Tel: 815-663-3731.
Catechesis/Religious Programs—Charles Palia, D.R.E.
Students 160.

4—SS. Peter and Paul's, (1891) (Polish), Rev. Donald R. Henderson. In res., Rev. Valentine Liss.
Res., 220 N. Terry St., P.O. Box 209, 61362. Tel: 815-663-3041. [CEM]

Streator, La Salle Co.,

1—Immaculate Conception, (1868) (Irish), Rev. Msgr. James L. Morrissey.
Res., 404 N. Park St., 61364. Tel: 815-672-2034.

[CEM]
School—St. Mary's, Tel: 815-672-3811. Mrs. Janice M. Corrigan, Prin.
Lay Teachers 10; Students 109.

2—ST. ANTHONY OF PADUA, (1881), Revs. Jerome Ham; Jerome Smith.
Res., 407 S. Park St., 61364. Tel: 815-672-4523; Fax: 815-672-0378. [CEM]
School—410 S. Park St., 61364. Tel: 815-672-3847.
Sisters 1; Lay Teachers 14; Students 216.
Catechesis/Religious Programs—Students 123.

3—ST. CASIMIR, (1916) (Polish), Rev. Gregory Mikula.
Res., 405 Illinois St., 61364. Tel: 815-672-2206. [CEM]
Catechesis/Religious Programs—Students 12.

4—ST. STEPHEN'S, (1884) (Slovak), Rev. Msgr. Peter E. Bolerasky; Revs. Jeffery Small; Edward U. Ohm; Michael Monclova.
Res., 711 Lundy St., 61364. Tel: 815-672-2474. [CEM 2]
School—807 E. Lundy St., 61364. Tel: 815-672-3265.
Sisters 3; Lay Teachers 7; Students 232.

Thomasboro, Champaign Co., St. Elizabeth's (1893), Rev. Charles P. Robards.
Res., 100 Church St., Box 367, 61878. Tel: 217-643-3395; Fax: 217-643-3395. [CEM]
Mission—Ludlow, Champaign Co., Sacred Heart, Ludlow, 60949.

Tiskilwa, Bureau Co., St. Mary's (1881), Rev. Michael Driscoll; Deacon John P. Murphy.
Res., P.O. Box 179, 61368. Tel: 815-646-4451; Fax: 815-646-4376. [CEM]
Mission—Bureau, Bureau Co., St. Francis Xavier. St. Xavier Mission merged with Sacred Heart of Jesus Parish, Granville.

Tolono, Champaign Co., St. Patrick's (1859), Rev. Dennis H. O'Riley.
Res., 212 E. Washington St., P.O. Box K, 61880. Tel: 217-485-5194. [CEM]
Mission—Homer, Champaign Co., St. Charles Borromeo, 110 S. East, Homer, 61849.

Toluca, Marshall Co., St. Ann's (1895) (Italian), Rev. James C. Kretz.
Res., 311 W. Santa Fe Ave., Box 165, 61369. Tel: 815-452-2043. [CEM]

Urbana, Champaign Co., St. Patrick's (1901), Revs. George F. Remm; Eugene Kane, (Retired); Sr. Charlene Cesario, S.S.C.M., Pastoral Assoc.; Deacon Dan Murphy.
Res., 708 W. Main St., 61801. Tel: 217-367-2665; Fax: 217-383-1002.
Catechesis/Religious Programs—Carolyn McElrath, D.R.E.
Students 465.

Utica, La Salle Co., St. Mary Church (1858), Rev. Philip D. Halfacre.
Res., 303 Division St., 61373. Tel: 815-667-4677; Fax: 815-667-4097. [CEM]

Walnut, Bureau Co., St. John's (1912), Rev. Binh K. Tran.
Res., P.O. Box 370, 204 N. Main St., 61376-0370. Tel: 815-379-2602.

Wapella, De Witt Co., St. Patrick's (1858), Rev. Robert H. Hoffmann.
Res., 308 S. Locust St., 61777. Tel: 217-935-9242. [CEM]

Warsaw, Hancock Co., Sacred Heart (1874) (German), Rev. Raymond M. Lukoskie.
Res., 245 S. 9th St., 62379. Tel: 217-256-3284. [CEM]
Catechesis/Religious Programs—Students 134.
Mission—Hamilton, Hancock Co., St. Mary. Deacons William Gray; Eugene Heintz.

Washburn, Woodford Co., St. Elizabeth, Revs. Dacian Batt, O.F.M.; Benno Heidlage, O.F.M.
Mailing Address: P.O. Box 219, Metamora, 61548. Tel: 309-367-4407 (St. Mary's Metamora). [CEM]

Washington, Tazewell Co., St. Patrick's (1941), Rev. James J. Swaner; Deacon Paul Neakrase.
Res., 705 E. Jefferson, 61571. Tel: 309-444-3524; Fax: 309-444-4070.
School—Tel: 309-444-4345; Fax: 309-444-7100.
Sisters of St. Mary of the Presentation 2; Lay Teachers 13; Students 205.
Catechesis/Religious Programs—Tel: 309-444-4139. Michelle Cooper, D.R.E.
Students 157.

Wedron, La Salle Co., St. Joseph's (1947), Rev. John G. Waugh.
Res., Box 60, 60557. Tel: 815-433-2962.

Wenona, Marshall Co., St. Mary's (1867), Rev. William M. Gardner. In res., Rev. Jerome V. Morrissey, (Retired).
Res., P.O. Box 486, 61377. Tel: 815-853-4558. [CEM]

Westville, Vermilion Co., St. Mary's (1903), Rev. Dean M. Huguet.
Res., 231 N. State St., 61883. Tel: 217-267-3334; Fax: 217-267-3335. [CEM]
School—225 N. State St., 61883. Tel: 217-267-7730; Fax: 217-267-3327.
Lay Teachers 14; Students 156.
SS. Peter and Paul. Closed. For inquiries for parish records contact St. Mary's, Westville.

Woodhull, Henry Co., St. John's (1889) (Swedish), Rev. Bruce D. Lopez.
Res., 390 E. Highway Ave., P.O. Box 248, 61490. Tel: 309-334-2180; Fax: 309-334-3317. [CEM 2]

Wyoming, Stark Co., St. Dominic's (1881), Rev. Thomas R. Brajkovich.
Res., 303 Galena Ave., 61491. Tel: 309-695-4031. [CEM]
Mission—Toulon, Stark Co., St. John, Toulon, 61483.

Chaplains of Public Institutions

DANVILLE. *Veterans' Administration Hospital* Tel: 217-442-8000. Rev. John Schultz, Military Chap.

DWIGHT. *Dwight Correctional Center.* Attended from St. Patrick's, Dwight. Tel: 815-584-3522. Rev. James E. Rickey.

LINCOLN. *Lincoln State School* Tel: 217-735-2361. Rev. Eugene Prendeville, O.M.I., Chap.
Logan Correctional Center. Vacant. Tel: 217-947-2714; 309-244-8516.

PONTIAC. *Illinois State Penitentiary.* Rev. Jonas Callanan, I.C., Chap., Res., 811 Hill St., 61704. Tel: 815-842-1150.

SHERIDAN. *Illinois Industrial School for Boys.* Rev. John G. Waugh, Chap.

Special Residence:
Reverend Fathers—
Carney, Edward
Zube, Joseph

Special Assignment:
Reverend Monsignors—
Hettinger, Clarence J., Diocesan Tribunal
Reverend Fathers—
Anderson, John C., Propagation of the Faith, Holy Childhood Assn., Catholic Relief Society

---

On Duty Outside the Diocese:
Reverend Fathers—
Baer, M. Stuart, 25 Pocono Rd., Denville, NJ 07834-2995
Collins, Patrick W., Archdiocese of Chicago
Guthrie, Raymond P., Diocese of Joliet
Henseler, J. Thomas, Diocese of Springfield, IL
Kuczborski, Joseph M., St. Joan of Arc, 370 W. Third St., Boca Raton, FL 33432
Myers, James E., 32 Middlefield Rd., Menlo Park, CA 94025
Pillon, Gordon, Diocese of Charolette
Powell, Eric S., Congregation for Oriental Churches, Rome
Prendergast, John J., Chap., U.S. Air Force
Przybyla, Kenneth, Diocese of Colorado Springs
Reese, Benjamin B., Diocese of Rapid City
Sepich, Lawrence, Archdiocese of Milwaukee
Sierra, Angel, Diocese of Springfield

Graduate Studies:
Reverend Fathers—
Dittmer, Antonio, North American College, Rome
Gray, Jason, North American College, Rome

Absent on Leave:
Reverend Fathers—
Engels, Francis C., P.O. Box 272, Kewanee, IL 61443-0272
Harbert, William S., 550 E. Carl Sandberg, Apt. 142, Galesburg, IL 61401
Hochstatter, Theodore, 3747 E. 4th Rd., Mendota, IL 61342
McDermott, Paul B., 1500 Wadsworth, Wadsworth, IL 60083
Ryan, John J., 5500 South Shore Dr., Chicago, IL 60637
Shea, Thomas, Rte. 1, Secor, IL 61771
Taylor, Thomas, 997 E. Fifth St., St. Paul, MN 55106

Retired:
Ciesielski, Heinc, 1553 Sobieski, LaSalle, IL 61301
Culleton, James P., 320 George St., Apt. W.2, Morris, IL 60450
Divan, Anthony L.
Hiland, George, 374 Benchopst, Sebastian, FL 32958
Reverend Monsignors—
Carton, George A., 2223 W. Heading Ave., Peoria, IL 61604
Haas, Murray V., 48 Riverview Dr., East Peoria, IL 61611
Hettinger, Clarence J., 6001 N. University, Peoria, IA 61614
Livingston, Robert C., St. Mary's Rectory, 8819 W. Knox St., Kickapoo, IL 61525
Motsett, C. Bourke, 1806 Washington, Danville, IL 61832
O'Dea, Joseph J., R.R. 3, Box 102AA, Pontiac, IL 61764
Render, Bernard A., 1301 N.E. Glendale Ave., Peoria, IL 61603
Reverend Fathers—
Aldrich, Ralph, 1817 Dale St., San Diego, CA 92102
Bawiec, Edward J., 424 W. First St., Oglesby, IL 61348
Blough, E. C., St. Augustine Manor, 1301 N.E. Glendale, Peoria, IL 61603
Colgan, Marvin, St. Joseph's, 401 9th St., Lacon, IL 61540
Condon, Louis M., P.O. Box 10319, 3538 70th St., Moline, IL 61265
Crawford, Richard E., 1414 S. Monroe, Streator, IL 61364
Dietzen, Vincent E., 436 South St., Danville, IL 61832
Gaughran, John, 312 N. State St., Westville, IL 61883
Gould, Eugene, 2551 19th Ave., Rock Island, IL 61201. Tel: 309-788-8510
Graves, Joseph A., 5335 Red Sky Dr., Colorado Springs, CO 80915
Hettinger, Paul W., R.R. 2, 3888 E. 1st Rd., Mendota, IL 61342
Hughes, Robert T., 1103 Peppertree Ln., Eureka, IL 61530
Jesiolowski, Sylvester E., 315 E. Second Ave., Box 21, Oglesby, IL 61348
Kane, Eugene, 1831 County Rd. 2500 N., Thomasboro, IL 61878
Karl, Charles, 3633 Richwoods Blvd., Peoria, IL 61604
King, John, P.O. Box 79, Starrucla, PA 18462
Krewer, Edward M., 1177 N. Gooding St., La Salle, IL 61301-1581
Lassuy, Raymond J., 7036 E. Orange Blossom Ln., Scottsdale, AZ 85253
Liss, Valentine, 220 Terry, Spring Valley, IL 61362
Mahoney, John A., 620 E. Ogden, Geneseo, IL 61254-1145
Malinowski, Stanley, 17 Golf Dr., Loda, IL 60948
Mooney, Harold T., 712 W. Green, Champaign, IL 61820
Morrissey, Jerome V., St. Augustine Manor, 1301 N.E. Glendale Ave., Peoria, IL 61603
Morrissey, Lawrence M., St. Augustine Manor, 1301 N.E. Glendale, Peoria, IL 61603
Mullen, Richard, 2414 Heritage Dr., Champaign, IL 61821
Niemeyer, John, 132 Mobile-Land Ct., Bloomington, IL 61701
O'Connor, John F., 407 N. Franklin, River Forest, IL 60305
O'Toole, John J., R.R. 2, P.O. Box 85-A, Lexington, IL 61753
Prendergast, Robert E., P.O. Box 548, Kewanee, IL 61443
Purcell, James, 19 Pinewood Park, Chillcothe, IL 61523
Raney, Richard E., 685 Mantanzas Ct., Fort Myers Beach, FL 33931
Reynolds, Robert E., 319 N. Franklin, Rushville, IL 62681-0292
Russo, Nicodemus A., 613 Fenwick, San Antonio, TX 78239
Schroeder, George J., 16 Waverly Dr., Rock Island, IL 61201
Shaughnessy, James D., St. Margaret's Living Center, 610 E. First, Spring Valley, IL 61362
Skirkus, Joseph K., Stark Co. Nursing Home, R.R. 1, Box 14, Toulon, IL 61483
Sors, Vladimir, 308 S. Monroe St., Streator, IL 61364
Sprague, George Raymond, St. Augustine Manor, 1301 N.E. Glendale, Peoria, IL 61603
Thompson, George M., 3026 55th St., Moline, IL 61265
Verhoye, Gerard A., 202 N. State, Box 603, Atkinson, IL 61235
Weishar, John A., St. Francis Continuing Care, 210 S. Fifth St., Burlington, IA 52601
Wuellner, George E., St. Boniface Church, 416 County Rd. 1110 N., Seymour, IL 61875
Very Rev. Canon—
Flattery, John J., Canon in Perpetuum, 20967 Walnut Hill, Danville, IL 61834. Tel: 217-442-2603

Permanent Deacons:
Adams, J. Rodger, Leave of Absence
Barr, Earl, Diocese of Phoenix
Baxley, Robert, Our Lady of the Lake, Mahomet
Beltramini, Robert, St. Thomas More, Dalzell

Bott, Herman J., Holy Family, Danville
Breeden, Charles, St. Maria Goretti, Coal Valley
Brinker, Kenneth, Leave of Absence
Burgess, Charles E., St. Hyacinth's, LaSalle
Burton, John, St. Matthew, Farmington
Carolan, Brendan, Holy Trinity, Bloomington
Chaffee, Harley, St. Malachy, Genesco
Clark, William H., Immaculate Conception, Monmouth
Daron, Estal, St. Columba, Ottawa
DeVooght, Dennis, Sacred Heart, Moline
Eaton, Francis, St. Thomas, Peoria Heights
Efinger, Donald, St. Thomas, Peoria
England, Robert, (Retired)
Fahey, Dennis, St. Martin de Porres, Peoria
Filzen, Bernard R., St. Mark's Church, Peoria
Gaetz, Dale, Co.Admin. of Permanent Deacons, St. Mary, Lourdes
Granet, Timothy, St. Pius X, Rock Island
Gratkowski, Daniel, Leave of Absence
Gray, William, St. Mary Mission, Hamilton
Grimler, Richard, Epiphany, Normal
Hammel, Richard F., Proctor Community Hospital, Peoria
Hammond, Richard G., St. Anthony's Church, Bartonville
Haneghan, James, St. Patrick, Galesburg
Harris, Harley, St. Malachy, Geneseo
Hart, Henry, Holy Cross, Champaign
Heintz, Eugene, St. Mary Mission, Hamilton
Hietter, Earl E., St. Thomas, Peoria Heights
Honzel, Larry, St. Malachy, Genesco
Hunter, Roger, St. Jude, Dunlop
Jones, Richard W., St. Ann's, Peoria
Kauth, Richard, Leave of Absence
Keefer, Wesley, St. Patrick, Elmwood
Kelly, William, St. Thomas, Peoria Heights
Kettering, Jack M., Sacred Heart, Rock Island
Koeppel, Joseph, St. Ann's, Peoria
Kovachevich, Victor, St. Mary, Canton
La Hood, Joseph, St. Martin de Porres, Peoria & Prison Ministry
Lalande, John, Holy Cross, Champaign
Landry, John, Sacred Heart, Moline
Mancuso, Terry, Leave of Absence
Martin, Paul, St. Pius X, Rock Island
Maubach, James, Holy Family, Peoria
McClellan, William, Leave of Absence
Meyer, William, Immaculate Conception, Manito
Moch, John, St. Mary, Kewanee
Moran, Thomas, Blessed Sacrament, Morton
Murphy, John P., St. Mary, Tiskilwa
Murphy, John R., Immaculate Conception, Lacon
Murphy, R. Daniel, Leave of Absence, St. Patrick, Urbana
Murray, Charles, St. Joseph, Pekin
Myers, Robert, St. Vincent de Paul, Peoria
Neakrase, Paul, St. Patrick, Washington
Nevinger, Ronald, Leave of Absence
Nichols, Ed, St. Philomena, Monticello
Oenning, Frank W., Leave of Absence
Ohl, Harry, St. Philomena, Peoria
Petri, Darrel, St. Mary, Bloomington
Pogioli, Martin, St. Joseph, Pekin
Pomazal, Robert, St. Edward, Chillicothe
Quinn, James, St. Mary Mission, Hampton
Rager, Ronald L., St. Monica's Church, East Peoria
Ramirez, Jesse, St. Patrick's, Galesburg
Randazzo, Frank G., St. Ambrose, Milan
Rapach, Thomas, St. Jude's, Dunlap
Reid, Michael, Sacred Heart, Peoria
Reising, David, St. Philomena, Peoria
Ringler, William, St. Anthony's, Hoopeston
Roesch, Lewis, Holy Trinity, Bloomington
Sailer, Philip, St. Pius X, Rock Island
Sandoval, Henry, Our Lady of Guadalupe, Silvis
Scanlan, Richard, St. Matthew, Champaign
Serangeli, Gregory, St. Edward's, Chillicothe, Co-Admin. of Permanent Deacons
Shipp, William, St. Malachy's, Rantoul
Simon, Nicholas, St. Anthony, Atkinson
Sims, Fred, St. Mary, Peru
Skender, John, St. Mark, Peoria
Sloman, William, St. Francis Medical Center, Peoria
Slomian, Vincent, Holy Cross, Mendota
Smith, Frank, (Retired)
Smith, Marvin, St. Mary, Metamora
Smith, Richard, Holy Family, Danville
Swim, Russ, St. Mary, Moline
Tomlianovich, Louis A., St. Anthony's, Bartonville
Tuerk, Charles W., St. Mark's Church, Peoria
Van Meltebeck, Martin, St. Mary, Kewanee
Van Wassenhove, Raymond, St. Mary, Kewanee
Verbeck, Walter, St. Malachy, Geneseo
Wachtel, Thomas, St. Malachy, Geneseo
Waldschmidt, Robert, St. Thomas, Peoria
Whited, Ernie, St. Joseph, Pekin
Zimmerman, Richard, St. Peter, Peoria
Zimmerman, Robert, St. Maria Goretti, Coal Valley

INSTITUTIONS LOCATED IN THE DIOCESE

[A] SEMINARIES, RELIGIOUS OR SCHOLASTICATES

PEORIA. *Rosminian Novitiate*, 2327 W. Heading Ave., 61604. Tel: 309-676-6341.
E-mail: wtmic@juno.com
Revs. James Nugent, I.C., Asst./Vocation Dir.; William T. Miller, I.C., Novice Master. In res. Priests 2; Laymen 3; Total Staff 5.

PERU. *St. Bede Abbey and Academy*, 61354. Tel: 815-223-3140; Fax: 815-223-3140, Ext. 292.
Permanent Staff: Priests 11; Brothers 4; Sisters 1; Lay Staff 49. The Benedictine Society of St. Bede. Rt. Revs. Roger F. Corpus, O.S.B., Abbot; Marion E. Balsavich, O.S.B., (Resigned); Very Rev. John F. Fitzgerald, O.S.B., Subprior; Bro. Nathaniel Grossman, O.S.B., Prior, Novice Master, Junior Master; Revs. Raymond A. Matulenas, O.S.B.; Stephen J. Souse, O.S.B.; Eugene A. Lauer, O.S.B.; William J. Kirk, O.S.B.; Sebastian C. Lewis, O.S.B.; Kevin D. Gorman, O.S.B.; Alfred J. Scheidler, O.S.B.; Henry H. Fritz, O.S.B.; Bernard A. Horzen, O.S.B.; Claude J. Peifer, O.S.B.; Dunstan R. Morrissey, O.S.B.; Joseph J. Heyd, O.S.B.; Arthur G. Schmit, O.S.B.; Allen J. Mattingly, O.S.B.; Ambrose B. Hessling, O.S.B.; Placid W. Hatfield, O.S.B.; Matthew C. Mazzuchelli, O.S.B.; Benedict B. McKean, O.S.B.; Gabriel G. Bullock, O.S.B.; Harold L. Datzman, O.S.B.; Philip D. Davey, O.S.B.; Ronald L. Margherio, O.S.B.; Samuel D. Pusateri, O.S.B.; Patrick A. Fennell, O.S.B.; Dominic M. Garramone, O.S.B.; James M. Murray, O.S.B.; Bros. George J. Matsouka, O.S.B.; Bede D. Schuda, O.S.B.; Mark F. Strassburger, O.S.B.; Luke E. McLachlan, O.S.B.; Michael M. Calhoun, O.S.B. Priests 29; Brothers 6.

[B] HIGH SCHOOLS, DIOCESAN AND INTER-PAROCHIAL

PEORIA. *Notre Dame High School*, 5105 N. Sheridan, 61614. Tel: 309-691-8741; Fax: 309-691-0875.
E-mail: Peorianotredame@ocslink.com
Mrs. Jane Hense, Dir. Devel.; Revs. Thomas E. Seibert, I.C., Asst. Chap.; Gary Caster, Asst. Chap.; Jeff Windy.
Peoria Notre Dame Scholarship Trust, 5105 N. Sheridan Rd., 61614. Rev. James J. Swaner, Pres.; Dr. James Maher, Vice Pres.; Carl Anderson, Sec.; John Wagner, Treas. Priests 3; Sisters 4; Lay Teachers 52; Students 1,004.

BLOOMINGTON. *Central Catholic High School*, 712 N. Center St., 61701. Tel: 309-827-5373; Fax: 309-827-0173.
E-mail: CCHS@ice.net
Web site: http://www/ice.net/~cchs
Mrs. Joy Allen, Prin.; Rev. Stephen Willard. Priests 1; Lay Teachers 25; Students 302.

DANVILLE. *Schlarman High School*, 61832. Tel: 217-442-2725; Fax: 217-442-0293.
E-mail: stittp@SHS.com
Web site: www.schlarman.com
Vernon O. Carr, Admin.; Rev. R. Anthony Lee. Lay Teachers 14; Students 154.

OTTAWA. *Marquette High School*, 61350. Tel: 815-433-0125; Fax: 815-433-2632.
E-mail: XAVMHS@THERAMP.NET
Web site: www.1th2.K12.IL.US/Marquette
James Messaglia, Prin.; Rev. Philip Halfacre, Chap. Priests 2; Lay Teachers 20; Students 251.

ROCK ISLAND. *Alleman High School*, 1103 40th St., 61201. Tel: 309-786-7793; Fax: 309-786-7834. Colin Letendre, Prin.; Revs. Daniel J. Mirabelli, C.S.V., Dir. of Devel.; Jeffrey Stimiman, Chap. Priests 2; Sisters 4; Lay Teachers 29; Students 570.

[C] HIGH SCHOOLS, PRIVATE

NAUVOO. *St. Mary's Academy*, 62354. Tel: 217-453-6619; Fax: 217-453-2316. Sr. Phyllis McMurray, O.S.B., Head of School.

PERU. *St. Bede Academy*, 61354. Tel: 815-223-3140. Full-time Teachers: Priests 4; Brothers 1; Sisters 5; Lay Teachers 16. Benedictine Fathers and Brothers. Rev. Philip Davey, O.S.B., Supt.; Mr. Joseph R. Benning, Prin.; Revs. Stephen J. Souse, O.S.B., Registrar; Dominic M. Garramone, O.S.B., Chap.; Bro. Bede Schuda, O.S.B., CFO; Mr. Bernie Moore, Dean of Students; Mr. Robert Leclercq, Dir. Guidance; Mr. Thomas McGunnigal, Business Mgr. Benedictine Priests 7; Brothers 2; Lay Teachers 18; Students 311.

[D] ELEMENTARY SCHOOLS, PRIVATE

PEORIA. *Father Sweeney School*, 403 N.E. Madison Ave., 61603. Tel: 309-637-6305; Fax: 309-637-6347. (Grades 4-8). The Father John Sweeney Memorial Program for the Academically Gifted. Mrs. Anne Carignan, Prin. Lay Teachers 10; Students 119.

[E] ELEMENTARY SCHOOLS INTER-PAROCHIAL

PEORIA. *Immaculate Conception Pre-Kindergarten*, 2408 W. Heading Ave., 61604. Tel: 309-674-6168. Sr. M. Elaine Haertjens, O.S.F., Dir. Sponsored by the Sisters of St. Francis of the Immaculate Conception. Students 20.

LA SALLE. *La Salle Catholic School*, 1055 Sixth St., 61301. Tel: 815-223-5088.
Web site: www.ASD.com
John D. Ranger, Prin. Lay Teachers 10; Students 165.

MOLINE. *Seton Catholic School*, 1320-16th Ave., 61265. Tel: 309-757-5500. Sr. Paula Vasquez, O.S.F., Admin. Sisters 2; Lay Teachers 30; Students 635.

ROCK ISLAND. *Jordan Catholic School of Rock Island, Inc.* Facilities at St. Ambrose, St. Pius, and Sacred Heart. 2901-24th St., P.O. Box 3490, 61204-3490. Tel: 309-793-7350.
E-mail: JCSoffice@Revealed.net
Web site: http://home.revealed.netJCSoffice/index.html
Daniel Lievens, Admin.
Directs the Elementary School System for the Rock Island-Milan area, operating facilities at Sacred Heart, St. Pius X. Parishes in Rock Island and St. Ambrose in Milan. Sisters 2; Lay Teachers 30; Students 584.
Commission on Education for Jordan Catholic School, P.O. Box 3490, 61204-3490. Tel: 309-793-7350. Sisters 2; Lay Teachers 30; Students 584.

[F] RELIGIOUS EDUCATION CENTERS, PRIVATE

PERU. *Sisters of St. Benedict*, 26 W. U.S. Hwy. 6, 61354. Tel: 815-223-6741. Sr. Margaret Suerth, O.S.B., IVCC College; Sr. Catherine Maloney, O.S.B., Hospice Care, Illinois Valley Community Hospital, Peru, IL.

[G] CATHOLIC SOCIAL SERVICE OF PEORIA

WEST PEORIA. *Catholic Social Service of Peoria*, 2900 W. Heading Ave., 61604. Tel: 309-671-5730; Fax: 309-674-1664. Ms. Peggy A. Arizzi, Exec Dir.; Mr. Jeff Turnbull, Assoc. Dir.
Catholic Social Service West, 2900 W. Heading Ave., 61604. Tel: 309-671-5700. Foster Home Programs. Tel: 309-671-5750.
Catholic Social Service Institutions, 2900 W. Heading Ave., 61604. Guardian Angel Home. Tel: 309-671-5760. St. Anne Hall. Tel: 309-671-5755. Cabrini Hall Maternity Home. Tel: 309-671-5743. Jesu Children's Enrichment Center. Tel: 309-671-5660.
Peoria Community Area Project/LaCasa Center, 100 Walnut, Suite 404, Peoria, 61602. Tel: 309-637-6327. Family Counseling, Adoption Services, Senior Citizens In-Home Counseling, Women's Counseling & Support Services.
Catholic Social Service Counseling, 413 N.E. Monroe, Peoria, 61603. Tel: 309-672-2707.
Catholic Social Service Branch Offices: 603 N. Center St., Bloomington, 61701. Tel: 309-829-6307. 2714 McGraw Dr., Bloomington, 61704. Tel: 309-662-3840. 416 W. Locust St., Canton, 61520. Tel: 309-647-5014. 1315A Curt Dr., Champaign, 61820. Tel: 217-352-5179. 600 Sager Ave., Danville, 61832. Tel: 217-443-1772; 443-9111. 292 N. Chambers, Galesburg, 61401. Tel: 309-342-1136. 542 Crosat, LaSalle, 61301. Tel: 815-223-4007. 310 S. Logan, Lincoln, 62656. Tel: 217-732-3771. 103 S. 5th St., Lincoln, 62656. Tel: 217-732-9714. 527 Grant St., P.O. Box 355, Macomb, 61455-0355. Tel: 309-833-1791. 15 S. Capital, Ste. 215, Pekin, 61554. Tel: 309-353-9500. 816 20th St., Rock Island, 61201. Tel: 309-794-2200. 823 20th St., Rock Island, 61201. Tel: 309-786-0770. Fort Armstrong, 1900 3rd Ave., Rock Island, 61201. Tel: 309-788-9581.
Catholic Social Service Outreach Offices: Dwight Outreach Office, 126 Mazon Ave., Dwight, 60420. Tel: 815-584-3110. Geneseo Outreach Office, 217 N. Russell, Geneseo, 61254. Tel: 309-944-3518. Kewanee Outreach Office, 223 W. Central Blvd., Kewanee, 61443. Tel: 309-852-2564. Pontiac Outreach Office, 501 N. Chicago, Pontiac, 61764. Tel: 815-844-3629. Streator Outreach Office, 111 E. Spring St., Streator, 61364. Tel: 815-673-2311. Total Institutional Staff 133; Other Staff 520.

[H] CHILDREN'S HOMES

WEST PEORIA. *Catholic Social Service Foster Care Program*, 2900 W. Heading Ave., 61604. Tel: 309-671-5750; Fax: 309-671-1046
For a complete listing, refer to the Special Care Facilities section.
Guardian Angel Home, 2900 W. Heading Ave., 309-671-5760

For a complete listing, refer to the Special Care Facilities section.

St. Anne Residential Treatment Center, 2900 W. Heading Ave., 61604. Tel: 309-671-5755

For a complete listing, refer to the Special Care Facilities section.

[I] DAY CARE CENTERS

PEORIA. *South Side Catholic Child Care Center*, 1010 W. Johnson St., 61605. Tel: 309-674-7340; Fax: 309-682-2065. Ollie Bracket, Dir. Children 103; Total Staff 15.

WEST PEORIA. *Jesu Children's Enrichment Centers*, 2900 W. Heading Ave., 61604. Tel: 309-671-5660. Staff 45; Capacity 185; Served 225.

[J] GENERAL HOSPITALS

PEORIA. *OSF Healthcare System*, 800 N.E. Glen Oak Ave., 61603-3200.
Web site: OSFHEALTHCARE.org
For a complete listing, refer to the Hospitals section.

St. Francis' Medical Center, 530 N.E. Glen Oak Ave., 61637. Tel: 309-655-2000; Fax: 309-655-2347
For a complete listing, refer to the Hospitals section.

BLOOMINGTON. *OSF St. Joseph Medical Center*, 2200 E. Washington, 61701. Tel: 309-662-3311; Fax: 309-662-7143
For a complete listing, refer to the Hospitals section.

DANVILLE. *United Samaritans Medical Center*, 812 N. Logan, 61832. Tel: 217-443-5000; Fax: 217-443-1965
For a complete listing, refer to the Hospitals section.

GALESBURG. *St. Mary Medical Center*, 3333 N. Seminary St., 61401-1299. Tel: 309-344-3161; Fax: 309-344-9494
For a complete listing, refer to the Hospitals section.

PONTIAC. *Saint James Hospital*, 610 E. Water, 61764. Tel: 815-842-2828; Fax: 815-842-4912
For a complete listing, refer to the Hospitals section.

SPRING VALLEY. *St. Margaret's Hospital*, 600 E. First St., 61362. Tel: 815-664-5311; Fax: 815-664-1335.
Web site: http://www.St.Margarets.com
For a complete listing, refer to the Hospitals section.

STREATOR. *St. Mary's Hospital*, 111 E. Spring St., 61364. Tel: 815-673-2311; Fax: 815-673-4541
For a complete listing, refer to the Hospitals section.

URBANA. *Covenant Medical Center of Champaign/ Urbana*, 1400 W. Park St., 61801. Tel: 217-337-2000; Fax: 217-337-4541
For a complete listing, refer to the Hospitals section.

[K] SPECIAL HOSPITALS AND SANATORIA

PEORIA. *Cabrini Hall Maternity Home*, 2900 W. Heading Ave., 61604. Tel: 309-671-5743
For a complete listing, refer to the Special Care Facilities section.

LACON. *St. Joseph's Nursing Home*, 801 Ninth St., 61540. Tel: 309-246-2175
For a complete listing, refer to the Special Care Facilities section.

ROCK ISLAND. *St. Anthony's Continuing Care Center*, 767 30th St., 61201. Tel: 309-788-7631
For a complete listing, refer to the Special Care Facilities section.

[L] HOMES FOR AGED

PEORIA. *St. Augustine Manor*, 1301 N.E. Glendale Ave., 61603. Tel: 309-674-7069
For a complete listing, refer to the Special Care Facilities section.

St. Joseph's Home of Peoria, 2223 W. Heading Ave., 61604. Tel: 309-673-7425
For a complete listing, refer to the Special Care Facilities section.

[M] RETREAT HOUSES

GEORGETOWN. *LaSalette Missionaries*, 5065 Olivet Rd. (Olivet), 61846. Tel: 217-662-6671. Revs. John Paninski, c/o St. Issac Jognes Parish, Georgetown; Thaddeus Plawny, M.S.; Bro. Anthony Sepanik, M.S. Priests 2; Brothers 1; Total Staff 2.

HENRY. *King's House of Retreats - Diocese of Peoria*, 61537. Tel: 309-364-3084. Rev. John C. Anderson, Admin.; Deacon Frederick J. Kruse, Dir. Priests 1; Total in Residence 2; Total Staff 3.

[N] CONVENTS AND RESIDENCES FOR SISTERS

PEORIA. *Immaculate Conception Convent*. 2408 W. Heading Ave., West Peoria, 61604-5096. Tel: 309-674-6168. Motherhouse of the Sisters of St. Francis of the Immaculate Conception. Sr. M. Barbara Buckley, O.S.F., Pres.; Rev. James F. Campbell, Chap. Sisters 18; Professed Sisters 59.

Missionaries of Charity Convent, 506 Hancock St., 61603. Tel: 309-674-7160. Sr. M. Davis, M.C., Supr. Sisters 4; Total Assisted 138; Total Staff 2.

The Poor Clares. Our Lady of the Angels Convent, 3432 W. Baskin Ridge, 61604. Tel: 309-682-3182. Sisters 4.

St. Francis Medical Center Hospital - Convent, 740 N. Glen Oak Ave., 61603. Tel: 309-655-4014. Sr. M. Ildefonsa Richter, O.S.F., Supr., Tel: 309-655-2083; 655-2044. The Sisters of the Third Order of St. Francis 11.

St. Martin de Porres Convent, 709 W. Hurlburt, 61605. Tel: 309-673-4103. Franciscan Apostolic Sisters. Sisters 2; Total Assisted 92; Total Staff 10.

BRIMFIELD. *Sisters of the Community of St. John*, 16225 W. Hwy. 150, 61517; Fax: 309-446-9813. Sisters 2.

EAST PEORIA. *Motherhouse, The Sisters of the Third Order of St. Francis*, 1175 Saint Francis Ln., 61611-1299. Tel: 309-699-7215. Sr. Mary Ellen Flannery, O.S.F., Major Supr. Sisters in Residence 34; Total Sisters in Community 71.

Mt. Alverno Novitiate, 1175 Saint Francis Ln., 61611-1299. Tel: 309-699-9313. Rev. Msgr. Rick J. Oberch, Chap. Novitiate of The Sisters of the Third Order of St. Francis. Sisters 2; Novices 1; Postulants 1.

LACON. *St. Joseph Motherhouse and Novitiate*, 61540. Tel: 309-246-2175. Daughters of St. Francis of Assisi. Sr. M. Vaclava Ballon, Prov. Supr. Sisters 16; Sisters in Community (Professed) 30.

NAUVOO. *St. Mary Monastery, Motherhouse and Novitiate*, 62354. Tel: 217-453-2227. Sr. Ruth Ksycki, O.S.B., Prioress. Benedictine Sisters of Pontifical Jurisdiction. Sisters in Community 71.

OTTAWA. *Sisters of Mercy of the Americas*, 906 Canal St., Apt. 516, 61350. Tel: 815-433-1357. Sisters 1; Total Asssisted 1,000; Total Staff 6.

ROCK ISLAND. *St. Mary of the Angels Convent*, 1000-30th St., 61201. Tel: 309-786-3733. Sr. Mary Dolores, O.S.F., Supr.; Rev. Raphael Fabish, Chap. Sisters in Residence 7.

STREATOR. *Franciscan Sisters*, 1509 E. Hickory St., 61364. Tel: 815-673-1259. Sr. Jean-Marie Schwarz, O.S.F., Coord.; Sr. Eleanora Marie Maurer, O.S.F.; Sr. Catherine Wiseen. Sisters in Residence 2.

WEST PEORIA. *Mother of Peace Home*, 2223 W. Heading Ave., 61604. Total Residents 12; Total Staff 15.

[O] NEWMAN CENTERS

PEORIA. *Newman Foundation at Bradley University & Illinois Central College*, 1116 W. College Ave., 61606-1728. Tel: 309-497-3759; 674-0208 (Office); Fax: 309-497-3759.
E-mail: StJohn@camelot.bradley.edu
Gina McKenna, Office Mgr. Congregation of St. John. Revs. Joseph Mary; Bernard Mary.

CHAMPAIGN. *St. John's Catholic Student Chapel and Newman Foundation, University of Illinois*, 604 E. Armory Ave., 61820. Tel: 217-344-1184; Fax: 217-344-4957. Revs. Stuart W. Swetland; Thomas Gibson; Robert Barry, O.P. Total in Residence 3; Total Staff 4.

MACOMB. *St. Francis of Assisi Newman Center*, 1401 University Dr., 61455. Tel: 309-837-3988. Rev. Mark DeSutter, Chap.

NORMAL. *St. Robert Bellarmine Newman Center, Illinois State University*, 501 S. Main St., 61761-2996. Tel: 309-452-5046; 452-3983.
E-mail: RLPALME@ILSTU.edu
Web site: www.ITS.ILSTU.edu/newman
Rev. Ronald L. Palmer, Chap. Total Staff 3.

ROCK ISLAND. *Augustana College Catholic Campus Ministry*, 61201. Tel: 309-794-7272.
E-mail: AMNMR@Augustana.edu
Sr. Marilyn Ring, O.S.B.

[P] PERSONAL PRELATURES

URBANA. *Opus Dei*. (Prelature of the Holy Cross and Opus Dei), Lincoln Green Center, 715 W. Michigan, 61801. Tel: 217-367-6650; Fax: 217-344-2987.
Web site: www.opusdei.org
In res. Rev. Jerome Jung.

[Q] MISCELLANEOUS

PEORIA. *Northside Office of Christian Response*, 1825 N.E. Adams St., 61603. Tel: 309-637-0322. Mr. John Truitt, Dir. Total Assisted 161; Total Staff 1.

St. Augustine Community, 1301 N.E. Glendale, 61603. Tel: 309-674-7069. Rev. Mario Shaw, Chap.

Highwood Learning Center, 1301 N.E. Glendale Ave., 61603. Dick Langjahr, Admin. Total Assisted 80; Total Staff 16.

St. Vincent De Paul Society, 3612 N.E. Monroe St., 61603. Diocesan Council and Particular Council of Peoria. John and Mary Truitt, Co-Presidents. Total Assisted; over 800 Families.

SHARE Food Program of Central Illinois, Inc., 1825 N.E. Adams St., 61603. Tel: 309-637-0282. Total Staff 5.

Society for Religious Vocations, P.O. Box 0911, 61653-0911. Tel: 708-424-4550; Fax: 708-424-4550.
E-mail: William.fairman@trincomm.org
Web site: http://www.ewtn.com/religiouslife
Mr. William D. Fairman, Coord. Total in Residence 2; Total Staff 1.

BLOOMINGTON. *Homes of Hope, Inc.* Homes of Hope, 1570 Hunt Dr., Normal, 61761.

MOLINE. *The Order of the Legion of Little Souls of the Merciful Heart of Jesus*, 428 39th St., 61265-1641. Tel: 309-797-8491. Teresa I. Huyten, Moderator; Rev. Michael L. Menner, Diocesen Chap.

RELIGIOUS INSTITUTES OF MEN REPRESENTED IN THE DIOCESE

For further details refer to the corresponding bracketed number in the Religious Institutes of Men or Women section.

[0200]—*Benedictine Monks*. (St. Bede Abbey).—O.S.B.
[]—Congregation of St. John.—F.J.
[1320]—*Clerics of St. Viator*.—C.S.V.
[0480]—*Conventual Franciscans*.—O.F.M.Conv.
[0520]—*Franciscan Friars*. (Prov. of St. John the Baptist).—O.F.M.
[0300]—*Institute of Charity*. (Rome, Italy).—I.C.
[0720]—*The Missionaries of Our Lady of La Salette*.—M.S.
[0910]—*Oblates of Mary Immaculate*. (Central Prov.).—O.M.I.
[0430]—*Order of Preachers (Dominicans)*. (Prov. of St. Albert the Great).—O.P.

RELIGIOUS INSTITUTES OF WOMEN REPRESENTED IN THE DIOCESE

[0230]—*Benedictine Sisters of Pontifical Jurisdiction*.—O.S.B.
[2100]—*Congregation of the Humility of Mary*.—C.H.M.
[1920]—*Congregation of the Sisters of the Holy Cross*.—C.S.C.
[1730]—*Congregation of the Sisters of the Third Order of St. Francis, Oldenburg, IN*.—O.S.F.
[1710]—*Congregation of the Third Order of St. Francis of Mary Immaculate, Joliet, IL*.—O.S.F.
[0760]—*Daughters of Charity of St. Vincent de Paul*.—D.C.
[0920]—*Daughters of St. Francis of Assisi*.—D.S.F.
[1070-03]—*Dominican Sisters*.—O.P.
[1070-10]—*Dominican Sisters*.—O.P.
[1450]—*Franciscan Sisters of the Sacred Heart*.—O.S.F.
[1820]—*Hospital Sisters of the Third Order of St. Francis*.—O.S.F.
[2575]—*Institute of the Sisters of Mercy of the Americas*.—R.S.M.
[2710]—*Missionaries of Charity*.—M.C.
[3230]—*Poor Handmaids of Jesus Christ*.—P.H.J.C.
[2970]—*School Sisters of Notre Dame*.—S.S.N.D.
[1680]—*School Sisters of St. Francis*.—O.S.F.
[3520]—*Servants of the Holy Heart of Mary*.—S.S.C.M.
[0430]—*Sisters of Charity of the Blessed Virgin Mary*.—B.V.M.
[0660]—*Sisters of Christian Charity*.—S.C.C.
[2450]—*Sisters of Mary of the Presentation*.—S.M.P.
[3360]—*Sisters of Providence of Saint Mary-of-the-Woods, Indiana*.—S.P.
[1540]—*Sisters of Saint Francis, Clinton, Iowa*.—O.S.F.
[1705]—*The Sisters of St. Francis of Assisi*.—O.S.F.
[1580]—*Sisters of St. Francis of the Immaculate Conception*.—O.S.F.
[3840]—*Sisters of St. Joseph of Corondelet*.—C.S.J.
[]—*Sisters of the Community of St. John*.
[1820]—*Sisters of the Third Order of St. Francis (East Peoria, Illinois)*.—O.S.F.

DIOCESAN CEMETERIES

PEORIA. *Catholic Cemetery Association of Peoria, IL*. Tel: 309-674-2760. Operates St. Mary's Cemetery, St. Joseph's Cemetery and Resurrection Cemetery in Peoria.

BLOOMINGTON. *Holy Cross Cemetery Association of Bloomington, IL*. Tel: 309-829-2197.

DANVILLE. *Resurrection Catholic Cemetery Association of Danville, IL*. Tel: 217-431-5100.

FARMER CITY. *St. Joseph Cemetery Association of Farmer City, IL*. Tel: 309-928-3855.

GALESBURG. *St. Joseph's Cemetery Association of Galesburg, IL*. Tel: 309-342-1913.

PEKIN. *Catholic Cemetery Association of Pekin, IL*. Tel: 309-347-6109.

ROCK ISLAND. *Calvary Cemetery Association of Rock Island, IL*. Tel: 309-788-6197; 764-1928.

NECROLOGY

† Isermann, William D., (Retired). —Died Dec. 9, 1996.
† Jacobowski, Raymond G., On Duty Outside the Diocese. —Died Feb. 23, 1997.
† Van Raes, Michael T., (Retired). —Died June 25, 1997.

Archdiocese of Philadelphia

(Archidioecesis Philadelphiensis)

Most Reverend

JOHN J. GRAHAM, D.D.

Retired Auxiliary Bishop of Philadelphia and Titular Bishop of Sabrata; ordained February 26, 1938; appointed Auxiliary Bishop of Philadelphia and Titular Bishop of Sabrata November 25, 1963; consecrated January 7, 1964; retired November 8, 1988. *Res., St. Joseph the Worker Church, 9172 New Falls Rd., Fallsington, PA, 19054.*

Most Reverend

MARTIN N. LOHMULLER, D.D.

Retired Auxiliary Bishop of Philadelphia and Titular Bishop of Ramsbury; ordained June 3, 1944; appointed Auxiliary Bishop of Philadelphia and Titular Bishop of Ramsbury February 11, 1970; consecrated April 2, 1970; retired October 11, 1994. *Res., Villa Maria House of Studies, King Rd., Immaculata, PA, 19345.*

Most Reverend

LOUIS A. DE SIMONE, D.D.

Retired Auxiliary Bishop of Philadelphia and Titular Bishop of Cillio; ordained May 10, 1952; appointed Auxiliary Bishop of Philadelphia and Titular Bishop of Cillio June 27, 1981; consecrated August 12, 1981; retired April 2, 1997. *Res., St. Monica Church, 2422 S. 17th St., Philadelphia, PA, 19145.*

His Eminence

ANTHONY CARDINAL BEVILACQUA, D.D., M.A., J.C.D., J.D.

Archbishop of Philadelphia; ordained June 11, 1949; appointed Titular Bishop of Aquaealba and Auxiliary Bishop of Brooklyn October 7, 1980; consecrated November 24, 1980; appointed Bishop of Pittsburgh October 7, 1983; installed December 12, 1983; installed Archbishop of Philadelphia February 11, 1988; Created Cardinal Priest June 28, 1991. *Office: 222 N. 17th St., Philadelphia, PA, 19103-1299.; All official correspondence should be sent to this office.*

The Chancery: 222 N. 17th St., Philadelphia, PA, 19103-1299. Tel.: 215-587-4538; Fax: 215-587-3907.

Web site address: http://www.archdiocese-phl.org

Most Reverend

ROBERT P. MAGINNIS, D.D., V.G.

Auxiliary Bishop of Philadelphia and Titular Bishop of Siminina; ordained May 13, 1961; consecrated March 11, 1996. *Res., St. Coleman Rectory, 11 Simpson Rd., Ardmore, PA, 19003-2812.* Tel.: 610-642-0545.

Most Reverend

JOSEPH F. MARTINO, D.D., V.G.

Auxiliary Bishop of Philadelphia and Titular Bishop of Cellae in Mauritania; ordained December 18, 1970; consecrated March 11, 1996. *Res., St. Charles Borromeo Seminary, Overbrook, 100 E. Wynnewood Rd., Wynnewood, PA, 19096.* Tel.: 610-667-3394.

DIOCESE ESTABLISHED APRIL 8, 1808.

ERECTED AN ARCHDIOCESE FEBRUARY 12, 1875.

Square Miles 2183.28.

Comprises all the City and County of Philadelphia, and the Counties of Bucks, Chester, Delaware and Montgomery in the State of Pennsylvania.

PATRONS OF THE DIOCESE: I. Immaculate Conception B.V.M., December 8; II. Saints Peter and Paul, Apostles, June 29. This Archdiocese was solemnly consecrated to the Sacred Heart of Jesus on the Feast of Saint Teresa of Avila, October 15, 1873. On May 23, 1952, the Archdiocese of Philadelphia was solemnly consecrated to the Immaculate Heart of Mary at the Shrine of Our Lady of Fatima, Portugal.

For legal titles of parishes and archdiocesan institutions, consult The Chancery.

STATISTICAL OVERVIEW

Personnel	
Cardinal	1
Auxiliary Bishops	3
Retired Bishops	3
Retired Abbots	1
Priests: Diocesan Active in Diocese	597
Priests: Active Outside Diocese	27
Priests: Diocesan in Foreign Missions	4
Priests: Retired, Sick or Absent	182
Number of Diocesan Priests	810
Religious Priests in Diocese	439
Extern Priests in Diocese	24
Ordinations:	
Diocesan Priests	6
Religious Priests	4
Transitional Deacons	11
Permanent Deacons	12
Permanent Deacons in Diocese	150
Total Brothers	137
Total Sisters	3,977
Parishes	
Parishes	287
With Resident Pastor:	
Resident Diocesan Priests	261
Resident Religious Priests	20
Without Resident Pastor:	
Administered by Priests	6
Missions	9
Pastoral Centers	18
Welfare	
Catholic Hospitals	8
Total Assisted	682,720
Health Care Centers	9
Homes for the Aged	19
Total Assisted	6,973
Residential Care of Children	5
Total Assisted	931
Day Care and Extended Day Care Centers	12
Total Assisted	521
Specialized Homes	3
Total Assisted	1,466
Special Centers for Social Services	13
Total Assisted	79,396
Residential Care of Disabled	4
Total Assisted	314
Other Institutions	7
Total Assisted	3,987
Educational	
Seminaries, Diocesan	1
Students from This Diocese	84
Students from Other Diocese	112
Seminaries, Religious	1
Students Religious	12
Total Seminarians	96
Colleges and Universities	11
Total Students	32,400
High Schools, Diocesan and Parish	25
Total Students	23,020
High Schools, Private	15
Total Students	6,640
Elementary Schools, Diocesan and Parish	221
Total Students	86,186
Elementary Schools, Private	21
Total Students	5,363
Non-residential Schools for the Disabled	5
Total Students	405
Catechesis/Religious Education:	
High School Students	6,240
Elementary Students	46,325
Total Students Under Catholic Instruction	206,675
Teachers in the Diocese:	
Priests	181
Brothers	64
Sisters	894
Lay Teachers	8,669
Vital Statistics	
Receptions into the Church:	
Infant Baptism Totals	20,260
Adult Baptism Totals	1,151
Received into Full Communion	744
First Communions	14,011
Confirmations	12,502
Marriages:	
Catholic	5,098
Interfaith	2,127
Total Marriages	7,225
Deaths	13,200
Total Catholic Population	1,421,570
Total Population	3,723,835

Former Bishops—Most Rev. MICHAEL FRANCIS EGAN, O.F.M., D.D., cons. Oct. 28, 1810; died July 22, 1814.—Most Rev. HENRY CONWELL, D.D., cons. Sept. 24, 1820; died April 22, 1842.—Most Rev. FRANCIS PATRICK KENRICK, D.D., cons. June 6, 1830; transferred to Baltimore in 1851; died July 8, 1863.—Saint JOHN NEPOMUCENE NEUMANN, C.SS.R., D.D., cons. March 28, 1852; died Jan. 5, 1860 Canonized June 19, 1977.—Most Rev. JAMES FREDERIC WOOD, D.D., cons. coadjutor, cum iure successionis, April 26, 1857; Bishop of Philadelphia, Jan. 5, 1860; appt. Archbishop Feb. 12, 1875; Sacred Pallium, June 17, 1875; died June 20, 1883.—Most Rev. PATRICK JOHN RYAN, D.D., cons. April 14, 1872 Bishop of Tricomia and Coadjutor with right of succession to the Archbishop of St. Louis; appt. Titular Archbishop of Salamis, Jan. 6, 1884 Archbishop of Philadelphia, June 8, 1884; died Feb. 11, 1911.—Most Rev. EDMOND FRANCIS PRENDERGAST, D.D., cons. Feb. 24, 1897, Titular Bishop of Scillio; Auxiliary Bishop of Philadelphia; Archbishop of Philadelphia, May 27, 1911; died Feb. 26, 1918.—His Eminence DENNIS CARDINAL DOUGHERTY, appt. Bishop of Nueva Segovia, P.I., April 7, 1903; cons. June 14, 1903; transferred to Jaro, P.I., April 19, 1908; transferred to Buffalo Nov. 30, 1915; transferred to Philadelphia April 30, 1918; installed as Archbishop of Philadelphia July 10, 1918 Pallium conferred May 6, 1919; created Cardinal Priest, March 7, 1921; died May 31, 1951.—His Eminence JOHN CARDINAL O'HARA, C.S.C., appt. Military Delegate of Armed Forces and Titular Bishop of Mylasa Dec. 11, 1939; cons. Jan. 15, 1940; transferred to Buffalo Mar. 10, 1945; transferred to Philadelphia Nov. 28, 1951; installed as Archbishop of Philadelphia Jan. 9, 1952 Pallium conferred Jan. 12, 1953; created Cardinal Priest Dec. 15, 1958; died Aug. 28, 1960.—His Eminence JOHN CARDINAL KROL, D.D., J.C.D., ord. Feb. 20, 1937; appt. Titular Bishop of Cadi and Auxiliary Bishop of Cleveland July 11, 1953; cons. Sept. 2, 1953; appt. Archbishop of Philadelphia Feb. 11, 1961; created Cardinal Priest June 26, 1967; retired Feb. 11, 1988; died March 3, 1996.

Vicars General—Rev. JOSEPH R. CISTONE,V.G. Tel: 215-587-4507. Most Rev. ROBERT P. MAGINNIS, D.D., V.G. Tel: 610-642-0545. Most Rev. JOSEPH F. MARTINO, D.D., V.G. Tel: 215-587-4649.

Office of the Cardinal Archbishop—His Eminence ANTHONY CARDINAL BEVILACQUA, D.D., M.A., J.C.D., J.D., Archbishop of Philadelphia; Rev. MICHAEL F. BURBIDGE, Admin. Sec. to the Cardinal Archbishop, *222 N. 17th St., Philadelphia, 19103-1299*. Tel: 215-587-3800.

Office of the Vicar for Administration—Rev. Joseph R. CistoneV.G., Vicar General. Tel: 215-587-4507; 587-4549; Fax: 215-587-4545. Assocs. to the Vicar Admin.: Rev. JOSEPH P. DUNCAN; Bro. JOSEPH WILLARD, F.S.C.; Mr. JAMES J. BOCK, JR.; Sr. LINDA M. SARIEGO, O.S.F., *222 N. 17th St., Philadelphia, 19103-1299*.

Regional Vicars—Rev. Msgr. JOHN V. BARTOS, Vicar for Bucks County, *685 York Rd., Warminster, 18974*. Tel: 215-957-1525. Rev. Msgr. JAMES T. McDONOUGH, A.C.S.W., Vicar for Chester County, *2 Forrest Lane, Strafford, 19087-2504*. Tel: 610-995-9450. Rev. MICHAEL T. McCULKEN, Vicar for Delaware County, *14th St. & Lansdowne Ave., Darby, 19023*. Tel: 610-461-0220. Rev. JOHN C. MARINE, Vicar for Montgomery County, *354 Conshohocken State Rd., Gladwyne, 19035*. Tel: 610-896-0567. Rev. FRANCIS W. BEACH, Vicar for Philadelphia-North, *632 W. Erie Ave., Philadelphia, 19140*. Tel: 215-228-1960. Rev. JOHN T. CONWAY, Vicar for Philadelphia-South, *525 Cobbs Pkwy., Philadelphia, 19143*. Tel: 215-476-7484. The Vicar for Philadelphia-South Supervises The St. Peter Claver Evangelization Center. *502 S. 12th St., Philadelphia, 19147*. Tel: 215-735-3164. The Vicar for Philadelphia-North Supervises The Catholic Institute for Evangelization. *4404 N. 5th St., Philadelphia, 19104*. Tel: 215-324-8291.

Office of the Vicar for Religious—

Vicar for Religious—Rev. ALEXANDER J. PALMIERI, J.C.L.

Coordinator for Vocations to Religious Life—Sr. KATHLEEN LEARY, S.S.J., Office: *222 N. 17th St., Philadelphia, 19103-1299*. Tel: 215-587-3795; Fax: 215-587-3790.

The Chancery—Rev. ALEXANDER J. PALMIERI, J.C.L., Chancellor, *222 North 17th St., Philadelphia, 19103-1299*. Tel: 215-587-4538; Fax: 215-587-3907.

Archivist—JOSEPH J. CASINO, M.A., M.S.L.S., Office: *St. Charles Borromeo Seminary, 100 E. Wynnewood Rd., Wynnewood, 19096-3001*. Tel: 610-667-2125.

Metropolitan Tribunal—*222 N. 17th St., Philadelphia, 19103-1299*. Tel: 215-587-3750; Fax: 215-587-0508. Communications should be sent to the above address.

Judicial Vicar—Rev. Msgr. JAMES J. GRAHAM, J.C.D.

Assistant Judicial Vicars—Revs. JOSEPH C. DIECKHAUS, J.C.L.; PAUL A. DIGIROLAMO, J.C.D.; EDUARDO G. MONTERO, J.C.L.

Archdiocesan Judges—Revs. MICHAEL J. FITZGERALD, J.D., J.C.D.; STEVEN J. HARRIS, J.C.D.; ALEXANDER J. PALMIERI, J.C.L.; Rev. Msgr. SAMUEL E. SHOEMAKER, J.C.D.; Rev. Msgr. VINCENT M. WALSH, J.C.D.; Sr. CARLOTTA BARTONE, S.H.C.J., J.C.

Promoter of Justice—Rev. THOMAS A. KANE, J.C.D.

Defenders of the Bond—Revs. JAMES D. BEISEL, M.Div.; JOHN P. BOLAND, M.A.; MICHAEL C. DIIORIO, M.Div.; THOMAS A. KANE, J.C.D.; GERARD C. MESURE, J.C.D.; JAMES M. OLIVER, J.C.L.; ROBERT J. POWELL, D.M.A.; JOHN D. REARDON, M.Div.; VINCENT F. WELSH, J.C.L.

Approved Advocates—Revs. EDWARD H. BELL, M.Div.; JOSEPH W. BONGARD, M.A.; MARK J. HUNT, S.T.L.; W. FRED KINDON, M.A.; KENNETH P. McATEER, M.Div.; JOSEPH J. NICOLO, M.Div.; Rev. Msgr. RICHARD T. POWERS; Revs. DANIEL J. SULLIVAN, M.A.; THOMAS J. WISNIEWSKI, M.Div.; KARL A. ZEUNER, S.T.L.

Secretary—Rev. W. FRED KINDON, M.A.

Notaries—JOAN McDOWELL; WINIFRED CANNON; MARY KAY DEVLIN.

Office of the Vicar for Renewal and Evangelization—Rev. Msgr. CHARLES V. DEVLIN, Vicar, *222 N. 17th St., Philadelphia, 19103-1299*. Tel: 215-587-0500.

Office for Ecumenical and Interreligious Affairs—Most Rev. JOSEPH F. MARTINO, D.D., H.E.D., *222 N. 17th St., Philadelphia, 19103-1299*. Tel: 215-587-3624.

Management Information Services—Mr. BRUCE JENSEN, Dir. Tel: 215-587-3687; Fax: 215-587-3808.

Office for Audit Services—Mr. PHILIP H. GALLAGHER, JR., C.P.A., Dir. Tel: 215-587-2474; Fax: 215-587-0512.

Office for General Services—Rev. Msgr. LOUIS A. D'ADDEZIO, Dir. Tel: 215-587-3633; Fax: 215-587-2481.

Office for Renewal of Pastoral Life—Most Rev. JOSEPH F. MARTINO, D.D., S.T.L., H.E.D., Dir. Tel: 215-587-0500.

Office for Research and Planning—ROBERT J. MILLER, Ed.D., Dir. Tel: 215-587-3545; Fax: 215-587-3817.

Secretariat for Catholic Education

All addresses are: *222 N. 17th St., Philadelphia, 19103*, unless otherwise indicated.

Secretary for Catholic Education—Rev. Msgr. PHILIP J. CRIBBEN, M.A. Tel: 215-587-3700; Fax: 215-587-5644.

Office of Catholic Education—Rev. Msgr. PHILIP J. CRIBBEN, M.A., Sec. for Catholic Education; RICHARD V. McCARRON, JR., Supt. of Schools; Rev. DANIEL J. KUTYS, Archdiocesan Dir. of Religious Education. Asst. Supts.: THOMAS ROONEY, Secondary Schools; Sr. MARGARET GRADL, I.H.M., Elementary Schools; Mrs. ELIZABETH O'DONNELL, Special Education.

Office for Youth and Young Adults—Rev. THOMAS M. HIGGINS, Dir.; Mr. LEONARD J. DIPAUL, Asst. Dir., *105 Argyle Rd., Ardmore, 19003*. Tel: 610-649-9476.

Parish Youth Ministry—Mr. LEONARD J. DIPAUL, Dir. Tel: 610-649-9410.

Archdiocesan Boy Scout—Rev. JOHN B. WENDRYCHOWICZ, Chap. Tel: 610-649-9476.

Camp Neumann Conference Center—STEPHEN TAYLOR, Dir. Tel: 215-343-6552.

Community Service Corps—DAVID McKENZIE, Dir. Tel: 215-567-4280.

Secretariat For Catholic Human Services

All addresses are: *222 N. 17th St., Philadelphia, 19103*. Tel: 215-587-3900, unless otherwise indicated.

Secretary for Catholic Human Services—Rev. TIMOTHY C. SENIOR, L.S.W., M.B.A. Tel: 215-587-3903.

Deputy Secretary—Rev. TIMOTHY C. SENIOR, L.S.W., M.B.A. Tel: 215-587-3908.

Chief Financial Officer—Mr. EDWARD T. CAHILL. Tel: 215-587-3889.

Catholic Social Services (300)—

Catholic Charities of the Archdiocese of Philadelphia—Rev. TIMOTHY C. SENIOR, L.S.W., M.B.A., Exec. Dir. Tel: 215-587-3903. Mr. EDWARD T. CAHILL, Chief Financial Officer. Tel: 215-587-3889. Mr. JAMES AMATO, L.S.W., Asst. Dir. Tel: 215-587-0529. Ms. ANNE MARIE BUCK, M.S., Asst. Dir. Tel: 215-587-3590. Ms. LORRAINE KNIGHT, Asst. Dir. Tel: 215-587-3906. Mr. JOHN C. SMITH, L.S.W., Dir. Children's & Residential Services. Tel: 215-587-3754.

Family Service Centers—

Philadelphia Family Services Department—MARTIN FRICK, Admin., *227 N. 18th St., Philadelphia, 19103*. Tel: 215-854-7030.

Senior Adult Services—Ms. KAREN BECKER, L.S.W., Admin. Tel: 215-854-7070.

Immigration Services—*227 N. 18th St., Philadelphia, 19103*. MARTIN FRICK, Admin. Tel: 215-854-7030.

North Philadelphia Service Center—*Casa del Carmen, Reese & Blavis Sts., Philadelphia, 19140*. Tel: 215-329-5660. W. GIOVANNI MORANTE, M.A., Admin.

Northeast Philadelphia Service Center—*7340 Jackson St., Philadelphia, 19136*. Tel: 215-624-5920. Ms. AMY STONER, L.S.W., Admin.

Bucks County Service Center—*100 Levittown Pkwy., Levittown, 19054*. Tel: 215-945-2550. MARGUERITE POWERS, L.S.W., Admin.

Chester County Service Center—*37 S. Pennsylvania Ave. - P.O. Box 119, Avondale, 19311*. Tel: 610-268-3510. Mr. WILLIAM KEFER, L.S.W., Site Supvr.

Delaware County Service Center—*130 E. 7th St., Chester City, 19013*. Tel: 610-876-9183. Mr. JAMES McMASTER, Admin.

Montgomery County Service Center—*353 E. Johnson Hwy., Norristown, 19401*. Tel: 610-279-7372. Sr. PATRICIA KELLY, M.S.B.T., M.S.W., Site Supvr.

Specialized Services—

Adoption Services Department—*227 N. 18th St., Philadelphia, 19103*. Tel: 215-854-7050. MARY MERMAN, L.S.W., Admin.

Child Care Department—*222 N. 17th St., Philadelphia, 19103*. Tel: 215-587-3575. TERESA THOMPSON, L.S.W., Admin.

Housing/Homeless Services—*227 N. 18th St., Philadelphia, 19103*. Tel: 215-854-7060. JOHN M. WAGNER, Admin.

Office for Human Relations—Sr. MARION DILLON, M.S.B.T., Dir. Tel: 215-587-5655.

Research & Managememt Information Systems—*227 N. 18th St., Philadelphia, 19103*. Tel: 215-854-7065. LOUISE MAIA, Mgr.

Volunteer Program—*227 N. 18th St., Philadelphia, 19103*. Tel: 215-854-7058. WILLIAM TANGRADI, L.S.W., Coord.

Nutritional Development Services—PATRICK F.E. TEMPLE-WEST, Dir., *111 S. 38th St., Philadelphia, 19104*. Tel: 215-895-3470.

Secretariat For Catholic Life and Formation

All addresses are: *222 N. 17th St., Philadelphia, 19103*; Fax: 215-587-5631. unless otherwise indicated

Secretary for Catholic Life and Formation—BERNADETTE A. O'CONNELL, M.S., L.S.W. Tel: 215-587-5629.

Deputy Secretary for Catholic Life and Formation—THOMAS WAVRO. Tel: 215-587-5667.

Office for Black Catholics—Mrs. LINDA B. LOVE, Dir. Tel: 215-587-3634.

Family Life Office—Deacon FRANCIS T. CLARK, M.A., Dir., *St. Charles Borromeo Seminary, 1000 E. Wynnewood Rd., Wynnewood, 19096-3069*. Tel: 610-660-9002.

Office for Hispanic Catholics—ANNA C. VEGA, Dir. Tel: 215-587-3786.

Office for Formation of the Laity—Tel: 215-587-5630; 3552.

Parish Pastoral Councils—MARY GINDHART, Program Coord. Tel: 215-587-3694.

Office for Pastoral Care of Migrants and Refugees—Rev. THOMAS BETZ, O.F.M.Cap., Dir. Tel: 215-587-3540.

Apostleship of the Sea—Bro. HUGH MAGUIRE, F.S.C., Coord., *Seamen's Church Institute, 249 Arch St., Philadelphia, 19106*. Tel: 215-922-2562.

Cambodian Apostolate—Sr. MARY THERESA NGUYEN, A.C.J., Contact, *St. Thomas Aquinas Rectory, 1719 Morris St., Philadelphia, 19145*. Tel: 215-334-2312.

Chinese Apostolates—During regular school hours call 215-922-0999; other times call St. John the Evangelist Rectory. Tel: 215-563-4145.

Filipino Apostolate—Sr. LORETTO MAPA, R.A., Coord. Tel: 215-334-2312.

Haitian Apostolate—Rev. JAMES J. McGINNIS, Coord., *Office: St. Martin de Porres Rectory, 2340 W. Lehigh Ave., Philadelphia, 19132*. Tel: 215-228-8330.

Hungarian Apostolate—Contact: Office for Pastoral Care for Migrants & Refugees. Tel: 215-587-3540.

Indian Apostolate, Syro Malabar Rite—Rev. JOHN THARAYIL, C.M.I., Coord., *St. Thomas Aquinas Rectory, 601 Bristol Pike, Croydon, 19021*. Tel: 215-788-2989.

Indian Apostolate, Syro Malankara Rite—Rev. ALEXANDER PANAMKUNNIL, Coord. Tel: 215-329-2320.

Irish Apostolate—Revs. MICHAEL J. KELLY, Contact, *St. Charles Borromeo Seminary, 100 E. Wynnewood Rd., Wynnewood, 19096-3099*. Tel: 610-667-3394, Ext. 268. JOSEPH C. McLOONE, Contact, *Cathedral Basilica of SS. Peter and Paul, 1723 Race St., Philadelphia, 19103*. Tel: 215-561-1313. MICHAEL J. McCLEANE, Contact, *Ascension of Our Lord Rectory, 725 E. Westmoreland St., Philadelphia, 19134*. Tel: 215-739-1670.

Korean Apostolate—Vacant. Tel: 215-548-5535.

Laotian Apostolate—Contact: Office for Pastoral Care for Migrants & Refugees. Tel: 215-587-3540.

Portuguese Apostolate—Rev. JOSE NUNES, Coord., *Office: Incarnation of Our Lord Rectory, 5105 N. 5th St., Philadelphia, 19120*. Tel: 215-329-2320.

Vietnamese Apostolate—Rev. PETER N. QUINN, Coord. Tel: 215-727-0205.

Respect Life Office—Mrs. HELEN P. KELLEHER, Dir. Tel: 215-587-3530.

Department for AIDS Ministry—Rev. JOHN T. MAHER, C.M., Admin. Tel: 215-587-3839.

Department for Pastoral Care for Persons with Disabilities—Mrs. HELEN P. KELLEHER, Admin. Tel: 215-587-3530 (Voice); 0510 (TDD).

Apostolate to Deaf Persons—Rev. ANTHONY RUSSO, C.SS.R., Coord., *St. Boniface Church, 174 Diamond St., Philadelphia, 19122*. Tel: 215-423-9547 (Voice/TDD).

Department for Pro-Life Activities—Mrs. PATRICIA BARCLIFF, Admin. Tel: 215-587-3703. Rev. PAUL S. QUINTER, S.T.D., M.S., Delegate of the Cardinal to Pro-Life Organizations. Tel: 215-587-3703.

Pontifical Society for the Propagation of the Faith—Rev. JAMES FITZPATRICK, Dir. Tel: 215-587-3944.

Pontifical Society of St. Peter Apostle—Rev. JAMES FITZPATRICK, Dir. Tel: 215-587-3944.

Pontifical Missionary Society of the Holy Childhood (Holy Childhood Assn.)—Rev. JAMES FITZPATRICK, Dir. Tel: 215-587-3944.

Pontifical Missionary Union—Rev. JAMES FITZPATRICK, Dir. Tel: 215-587-3944.

Office for Worship—Rev. DANIEL E. MACKLE, Dir. Tel: 215-587-3537.

Secretariat For Clergy

All addresses are: *222 N. 17th St., Philadelphia, 19103*, unless otherwise indicated.

Secretary for Clergy—Rev. WILLIAM J. LYNN. Tel: 215-587-4532.

Office for Clergy—
*Department Priest Personnel—*Revs. WILLIAM J. LYNN, Dir. GERARD C. MESURE, Asst. Dir. Tel: 215-587-4532.
*Priests' Personnel Board—*Most Rev. EDWARD P. CULLEN; Most Rev. ROBERT P. MAGINNIS; Most Rev. JOSEPH F. MARTINO; Rev. Msgr. JOHN V. BARTOS; Rev. Msgr. JAMES T. MCDONOUGH; Revs. FRANCIS W. BEACH; MICHAEL F. BURBIDGE; JOHN T. CONWAY; THOMAS J. DEMPSEY; J. MICHAEL FLOOD; MATTHEW J. KORNACKI; WILLIAM J. LYNN; JOHN C. MARINE; MICHAEL T. MCCULKEN; JOSEPH C. MCLOONE; BARTHOLOMEW J. O'BRIEN.
*Department of Chaplaincies—*Rev. Msgr. FRANCIS A. MENNA, Admin.
*Department of Continuing Formation for Diocesan Priests—*Rev. THOMAS M. MULLIN, Dir.
*Department Retired Clergy—*Vacant.
*Department Permanent Deacons—*Rev. ANDREW J. GOLIAS, S.T.D., Admin.; Sr. VERONICA GROSS, R.S.M., Asst. Admin., *St. Charles Borromeo Seminary, 100 E. Wynnewood Rd., Wynnewood, 19096.* Tel: 610-664-2213.
*St. Charles Borromeo Seminary—*Rev. Msgr. JAMES E. MOLLOY, M.Div., M.A., Rector, *100 E. Wynnewood Rd., Wynnewood, 19096.* Tel: 610-667-3394.
*Vocations Office for Diocesan Priesthood—*Rev. JOSEPH P. DEVLIN, Dir., *St. Charles Borromeo Seminary, 100 E. Wynnewood Rd., Wynnewood, 19096.* Tel: 610-667-5778.

Secretariat For Temporal Services and Chief Financial Officer
All addresses are: *222 N. 17th St., Philadelphia, 19103,* unless otherwise indicated.
*Secretary for Temporal Services and Chief Financial Officer—*Mr. GLENN J. MASAKOWSKI, M.MGT. Tel: 215-587-3959; Fax: 215-598-0599.
*Secretariat Coordinator—*Ms. MAUREEN VAN THUYNE. Tel: 215-587-3958; Fax: 215-587-0599.
*Secretariat Coordinator/Dir.-Parish Financial Services—*Mr. EDWARD M. MERENDA, M.B.A., C.P.A. Tel: 215-587-2435; Fax: 215-587-3939.
*Secretariat Coordinator/Training & Development—*Mr. FRANCIS P. COUGHLIN, M.A., M.S. Tel: 215-587-5654; Fax: 215-587-0599.
*Office for Capital Projects—*DONALD RAUB, M.MGT., Dir. Tel: 215-587-3560; Fax: 215-587-0599.
*Catholic Cemeteries Office—*Mr. ROBERT WHOMSLEY, Dir., *111 S. 38th St., Philadelphia, 19104.* Tel: 215-895-3450; Fax: 215-587-3458.
*Human Resources Office—*Ms. MARLENE LOGLISCI, Dir. Tel: 215-587-3910; Fax: 215-587-3572.
*Office for Insurance Services—*CHARLES J. DEBEVEC, C.P.C.U., Dir. Tel: 215-587-3644; Fax: 215-587-2498.
*Office for Legal Services—*Rev. MICHAEL J. FITZGERALD, J.D., J.C.D., Dir. Tel: 215-587-0511; Fax: 215-587-0512.
*Real Estate Office—*EUGENE F. BRAZIL, ESQ., Dir. Tel: 215-587-2453; Fax: 215-598-0512.
*Office for Accounting Services—*Mrs. LAURA J. MONTGOMERY, Dir. Tel: 215-587-3943; Fax: 215-587-3939.
*Educational Financial Services—*Mr. DAVID J. MAGEE, M.B.A., Dir. Tel: 215-587-3755; Fax: 215-587-3525.

Secretariat for External Affairs All addresses are: *222 N. 17th St., Philadelphia, 19103.* unless otherwise indicated
*Secretary for External Affairs—*Mr. STAN H. RETIF. Tel: 215-587-3507; Fax: 215-587-3649.
*Office for Public Affairs—*Mr. GUY L. CIARROCCHI, Dir. Tel: 215-587-3509; Fax: 215-587-0515.
*Office for Communications—*Vacant. Tel: 215-587-3747; Fax: 215-587-3871.
*Newspaper - "Catholic Standard and Times"—*Rev. PAUL S. QUINTER, S.T.D., M.S., Editor. Tel: 215-587-3660; Fax: 215-587-3979.
*Office for Development—*STAN H. RETIF, Dir. Tel: 215-587-5650; Fax: 215-587-3647.

Archdiocesan Offices, Boards, Commissions and Committees
All addresses are: *222 N. 17th St., Philadelphia, 19103-1299* unless otherwise indicated.
*Blind, Guild for all the—*Rev. JOHN J. SHELLEM, Moderator. Tel: 215-587-3592.
*Board of Trustees of Lay Employees Retirement Plan—*His Eminence ANTHONY CARDINAL BEVILACQUA, D.D., M.A., J.C.D., J.D., Chm.; Mr. GLENN J. MASAKOWSKI, Vice Chm.
*Diocesan Priests' Compensation and Benefits Committee—*Rev. WILLIAM J. LYNN, Chm.; Rev. Msgr. JOHN E. BRESLIN; Rev. Msgr. FRANCIS A. MENNA; Rev. Msgr. LEON J. PECK; Revs. GREGORY J. FAIRBANKS; CHARLES E. GORMLEY; FRANCIS P. GROARKE; KENNETH W. SHARP; Mr. GLENN MASAKOWSKI; Mr. ROBERT SIMS; Revs. DANIEL J. SULLIVAN; SAMUEL A. VERRUNI; ROBERT C. VOGAN.
*Building Committee—*Rev. Msgr. RICHARD J. SKELLY, Chm. (Drawings of building plans are reviewed by this committee).
*Cardinal's Committee for Christian Home and Family—*Rev. JOSEPH T. MARINO, M.A., Dir., *St. Charles Borromeo Seminary, 100 E. Wynnewood Rd., Wynnewood, 19096.* Tel: 610-660-9002.
*Catholic Health Association of the United States, The—*Rev. TIMOTHY C. SENIOR, M.S.W., M.B.A., Moderator.
*Catholic Relief Services—*Rev. Msgr. WILLIAM J. PAUL, Dir., *St. John the Evangelist Church, 752 Big Oak Rd., Morrisville, 19067.* Tel: 215-295-4102.
*Censores Librorum—*Rev. Msgr. JAMES MCGRATH, J.C.D.; Revs. JOSEPH J. ANDERLONIS, S.T.D.; FRANCIS A. BARSZCZEWSKI, S.T.L., M.S.L.S.; ANDREW J. GOLIAS, S.T.D.
*Charismatic Prayer Groups—*Contact Office for Formation of the Laity: Tel: 215-587-5642.
*Charismatic Publication Office - Key of David Publications—*Rev. Msgr. VINCENT M. WALSH, J.C.D., *Presentation B.V.M. Church, 204 Haverford Rd., Wynnewood, 19096.* Tel: 610-642-8341.
*Church Ministry Training Program—*Rev. ANDREW J. GOLIAS, S.T.D., Coord.; Sr. VERONICA GROSS, R.S.M., Asst. Coord., *St. Charles Borromeo Seminary, 100 E. Wynnewood Rd., Wynnewood, 19096.* Tel: 610-664-2213.
*College of Consultors—*Most Rev. EDWARD P. CULLEN, D.D., V.G.; Most Rev. ROBERT P. MAGINNIS, D.D., V.G.; Most Rev. JOSEPH F. MARTINO, D.D., V.G.; Rev. Msgr. WALTER J. CONWAY; Rev. Msgr. ROBERT T. MCMANUS; Rev. Msgr. ALBERT V. NORRELL; Rev. Msgr. BERNARD J. TRINITY; Revs. EDWARD H. BELL; MATTHEW J. KORNACKI; WILLIAM J. LYNN; ALEXANDER J. PALMIERI, J.C.L.
*Council of Managers for Development—*Most Rev. EDWARD P. CULLEN, D.D., V.G., Chm.; Most Rev. ROBERT P. MAGINNIS, D.D., V.G., Vice Chm. Tel: 215-587-4507.
*Council of Priests—*Most Rev. EDWARD P. CULLEN, D.D., V.G.; Most Rev. ROBERT P. MAGINNIS, D.D., V.G.; Most Rev. JOSEPH F. MARTINO, D.D., V.G.; Rev. Msgr. WALTER J. CONWAY; Rev. Msgr. PAUL F. CURRAN; Rev. Msgr. JAMES E. MALLOY; Rev. Msgr. ROBERT T. MCMANUS; Rev. Msgr. ALBERT V. NORRELL; Rev. Msgr. BERNARD J. TRINITY; Revs. EDWARD H. BELL; MICHAEL J. BURKE; ROBERT J. CARROLL; MICHAEL A. CHAPMAN; JAMES E. DALTON, O.S.F.S.; JAMES J. FOLEY; EDWARD J. HALLINAN; JOHN M. HALLORAN; MATTHEW J. KORNACKI; MICHAEL J. LONERGAN; WILLIAM J. LYNN; GEORGE A. MAJOROS; JOSEPH P. MCGEOWN; JOHN J. MCINTYRE; ALEXANDER J. PALMIERI, J.C.L.
*Educational Fund—*Office for Financial Services. Tel: 215-587-3959.
*Holy Name Society—*Rev. JOSEPH D. DOUGHERTY, Spiritual Dir., *St. John Bosco Rectory, 235 E. County Line Rd., Hatboro, 19040.* Tel: 215-672-7280.
*Information Line, Archdiocesan—*Tel: 215-587-3600.
*Interparochial Cooperation, Commission for—*Rev. ARTHUR E. RODGERS, *St. Matthias Rectory, 128 Bryn Mawr Ave., Bala Cynwyd, 19004.* Tel: 610-664-0207.
*Legion of Mary—*Rev. Msgr. THOMAS B. FALLS, D.D., *5109 N. Broad St., Philadelphia, 19141.* Tel: 215-457-6343.
*Moderator of Priests Conferences—*Rev. WILLIAM J. LYNN, Sec. for Clergy. Tel: 215-587-4532.
*Parish Sites and Boundaries, Commission for—*Rev. Msgr. JAMES E. MORTIMER, Chm.
*Pastors Review Board—*Rev. Msgr. ROBERT T. MCMANUS; Rev. Msgr. ALBERT V. NORRELL; Rev. Msgr. BERNARD TRINITY; Revs. MICHAEL J. BURKE; JOSEPH P. MCGEOWN.
Pennsylvania Catholic Conference—(Harrisburg). Board of Governors: His Eminence ANTHONY CARDINAL BEVILACQUA, D.D., M.A., J.C.D., J.D. Administrative Board: Rev. JOSEPH R. CISTONE; Mr. HERBERT G. KEENE, JR., Esq.; Rev. Msgr. PHILIP J. CRIBBEN, M.A.; Mr. RICHARD V. MCCARRON, JR., Education Dept.; Ms. MARGUERITE POWERS; Rev. TIMOTHY C. SENIOR, M.A., M.S.W., M.B.A., Social Welfare Dept.; Sr. MARION DILLON, M.S.B.T.; Mr. STAN H. RETIF, Justice and Rights Dept.
*Priests Eucharistic League—*Rev. Msgr. JOHN E. GILLESPIE, Dir., *Our Lady of Calvary Church, 11024 Knights Rd., Philadelphia, 19154.* Tel: 215-637-7515.
*The Papal Foundation—*Rev. Msgr. THOMAS J. BENESTAD, Exec. Dir. Tel: 215-587-4501., *222 N. 17th St., Philadelphia, 19103-1299.*

CLERGY, PARISHES, MISSIONS AND PAROCHIAL SCHOOLS

CITY OF PHILADELPHIA
(Philadelphia County)

1—CATHEDRAL BASILICA OF SS. PETER AND PAUL (1846), Rev. Msgr. James J. Howard; Revs. Joseph C. McLoone; William S. Murphy. In res., Rev. Msgr. John J. Caulfield; Rev. Daniel E. Mackle; Deacon Epifano DeJesus.
Res., 1723 Race St., 19103. Tel: 215-561-1313; 1314.
*Catechesis/Religious Programs—*Students 67.
*Chapel—*Our Lady of the Miraculous Medal, Tel: 215-972-8116.

2—ST. ADALBERT (1904) (Polish), Rev. Francis S. Feret; Rev. Msgr. Anthony E. Jaworowski, Pastor Emeritus; Revs. Jerome H. Pohl; Joseph Piesiur.
Res., 2645 E. Allegheny Ave., 19134. Tel: 215-739-3500; Fax: 215-739-5706.
*School—*3236 Edgemont St., 19134. Tel: 215-739-1920; Fax: 215-739-0519.
Sisters of the Holy Family of Nazareth 3; Lay Teachers 14; Students 328.

3—ST. AGATHA-ST. JAMES. Consolidated 1976. Rev. Karl A. Zeuner. Pastoral Assocs.: Revs. Charles J. Brinkman; George Strausser; Charles J. Pfeffer; Rayford E. Emmons.
Res., 3728 Chestnut St., 19104. Tel: 215-386-9732; 9733; Fax: 215-386-9734.

4—ST. AGNES-ST. JOHN NEPOMUCENE (1907) (Slovak). Consolidated January 1, 1980. Rev. Francis G. Lendacky.
Res., 319 Brown St., 19123. Tel: 215-627-0340.

5—ALL SAINTS (Bridesburg) (1860), Rev. Edward P. Burke.
Res., 2651 Buckius St., 19137. Tel: 215-535-4411; Fax: 215-744-6533. [CEM]
*School—*4623 E. Thompson St., 19137. Tel: 215-743-0715; 535-3699.
Sisters of St. Francis of Philadelphia 2; Lay Teachers 7; Students 149.

6—ALL SAINTS CHAPEL. Located at Philadelphia General Hospital. Spiritual records transferred to St. Agatha-St. James Church.

7—ST. ALOYSIUS (1894), Rev. John J. Bradley.
Res., 2600 Tasker St., 19145. Tel: 215-468-1088.
*School—*1624 S. 26th St., 19145. Tel: 215-334-0339. Bro. Aloysius Hammond, F.C., Prin.
Lay Teachers 9; Students 150.

8—ST. ALPHONSUS. Closed. Located at 1400 S. Fourth St. from 1852 to 1972. Spiritual records are kept at Sacred Heart of Jesus Church.

9—ST. AMBROSE (1923), Revs. James N. Catagnus; Herbert J. Sperger; Raphael Kannanaickal, C.M.I.
Res., 363 E. Roosevelt Blvd., 19120. Tel: 215-329-7900; 7901; Fax: 215-328-9206.
*Church—*C St. & Roosevelt Blvd., 19120.
*School—*405 E. Roosevelt Blvd., 19120. Tel: 215-457-3083.
Sisters of St. Joseph 2; Lay Teachers 13; Students 396.

10—ST. ANDREW (1924) (Lithuanian), Revs. Peter M. Burkauskas, Admin.; George D. Degutis, Pastor Emeritus.
Res., 1913 Wallace St., 19130. Tel: 215-765-2322; Fax: 215-765-0124.

11—ST. ANNE, Revs. Thomas J. Kelley; Lawrence F. Crehan. In res., Rev. Joseph R. Cistone.
Res., 2328 E. Lehigh Ave., 19125. Tel: 215-739-4590; Fax: 215-739-0983.
*School—*2343 E. Tucker St., 19125. Tel: 215-634-4231.
Sisters of St. Joseph 2; Lay Teachers 19; Students 641.

12—ANNUNCIATION B.V.M., Revs. Pasquale R. Catullo, Admin.; William S. Lange.
Res., 1511 S. 10th St., 19147. Tel: 215-334-0159.
*School—*12th & Wharton Sts., 19147.
Sisters, Servants of the Immaculate Heart of Mary 3; Lay Teachers 7; Students 250.

13—ST. ANSELM (1962), Revs. James J. Shields; George B. Cadwallader; James A. Lyons. In res., Rev. Msgr. William A. Doolin; Deacon Gerald J. Whartenby.
Res., 12669 Dunks Ferry Rd., 19154. Tel: 215-637-3525; Fax: 215-637-4915.
*School—*12670 Dunks Ferry Rd., 19154. Tel: 215-632-1133. Sr. Seraphine I.H.M., Prin.
Sisters of the Immaculate Heart of Mary 9; Lay Teachers 30; Students 1,010.

14—ST. ANTHONY OF PADUA (1886), Rev. David C. Sicoli.
Res., 2321 Fitzwater St., 19146. Tel: 215-545-6232; Fax: 215-546-3635.

15—ASCENSION OF OUR LORD (1899), Revs. Michael J. McCleane; Michael S. Olivere; Deacon Leo Gladnick.

Res., 725 E. Westmoreland St., 19134. Tel: 215-739-1670; Fax: 215-739-1455.
School—735 E. Westmoreland St., 19134. Tel: 215-739-6226.
Sisters of St. Joseph 2; Lay Teachers 9; Students 210.

16—ASSUMPTION B.V.M. (1848). Closed. For inquiries for parish records contact St. John the Evangelist.

17—ST. ATHANASIUS (1928), Rev. Herbert A. Bevard; Deacon Sidney M. Harper.
Res., 2050 Walnut Ln., 19138. Tel: 215-548-2700; Fax: 215-927-6615.
School—St. Athanasius-Immaculate Conception School. See Consolidated Parish Schools under Institutions Located in the Archdiocese.
Sisters 3; Lay Teachers 8; Students 280.
Catechesis/Religious Programs—Students 302.

18—ST. AUGUSTINE (1796). First foundation of Augustinian Order in U.S.A. Revs. Walter J. Quinn, O.S.A.; Pascal A. DeCicco, O.S.A., Pastoral Assoc. In res., Revs. William J. Krupa, O.S.A.; W. Howard McGraw, O.S.A.
Res., 243 N. Lawrence S., 19106-1195. Tel: 215-627-1838; Fax: 215-627-3911.
School—St. Mary Interparochial School. See Consolidated Parish Schools under Institutions Located in the Archdiocese.

19—ST. BARBARA (1921), Revs. John T. Lyons; Thomas F. Loughrey, Pastor Emeritus. In res., Rev. Joseph F. Gleason.
Res., 5359 Lebanon Ave., 19131. Tel: 215-473-1044; Fax: 215-473-5252.
School—5343 Lebanon Ave., 19131. Tel: 215-477-3456.
Catechesis/Religious Programs—Students 163.
Convent—5336 Diamond St., 19131. Tel: 215-477-3839.

20—ST. BARNABAS (1919), Revs. Bernard J. Herron; John F. Babowitch; James J. McLaughlin; Deacon Leonard J. Wolkowicz.
Res., 6300 Buist Ave., 19142. Tel: 215-726-1119; 1120; Fax: 215-726-1180.
School—64th St. & Buist Ave., 19142-3097. Tel: 215-729-3603.
Sisters of Immaculate Heart of Mary 6; Lay Teachers 19; Students 580.
Catechesis/Religious Programs—Students 181.
Convent—6328 Buist Ave., 19142. Tel: 215-729-1572.

21—ST. BARTHOLOMEW (1919), Revs. Joseph P. Denny; Carl F. Janicki; James J. Anziano. In res., Revs. Ildebrando E. Schifalacqua; John C. Dougherty; Deacon John J. Bean.
Res., 5600 Jackson St., 19124. Tel: 215-831-1224; 1225; Fax: 215-831-0467.
School—Jackson & Sanger St., 19124. Tel: 215-744-6393.
Lay Teachers 26; Students 666.
Catechesis/Religious Programs—Students 175.

22—ST. BENEDICT (1922), Rev. George B. Moore; Deacons Stephen Hopkins; James T. Walker; Calvin C. Smith.
Res., 1940 E. Chelten Ave., 19138. Tel: 215-924-4401; Fax: 215-924-4390.
School—1935 Medary Ave., 19138. Tel: 215-424-8073.
Lay Teachers 9; Students 185.
Convent—1942 E. Chelten Ave., 19138. Tel: 215-924-2876.

23—ST. BERNARD (1927), Revs. Charles J. Sullivan; Thomas J. Dunleavy; David Machain; Rev. Msgr. John B. Fee, Pastor Emeritus.
Res., 7341 Cottage St., 19136. Tel: 215-333-0446; Fax: 215-333-3215.
School—7340 Jackson St., 19136. Tel: 215-624-5204; Fax: 215-624-8806.
Lay Teachers 29; Students 805.

24—ST. BONAVENTURE (1889-1993). Closed. Spiritual records are kept at St. Veronica Church.

25—ST. BONIFACE (1865), Revs. Sean J. McGillicuddy, C.Ss.R.; Wenceslaus J. Smutny, C.SS.R.; Richard S. Bennett, C.Ss.R.; Bro. Manuel Martinez, C.SS.R.; Deacon Mario Lozada. In res., Revs. Anthony T. Russo, C.SS.R., Deaf Apostolate; Norman J. Simmons, C.SS.R.; Gerard J. Brinkmann, C.SS.R.; James W. Gilmour, C.SS.R.; Alexander F. Ortiz, C.S.s.R.; Kevin R. Murray, C.SS.R.; Bro. Edgardo Lugo, C.Ss.R.
Res., 174 W. Diamond St., 19122. Tel: 215-739-6376; Fax: 215-739-5102.
School—142 W. Diamond St., 19122. Tel: 215-634-6588.
Religious 1; Lay Teachers 10.
Catechesis/Religious Programs—Students 230.

26—ST. BRENDAN (1925-1934). Closed. Spiritual records are kept at St. Francis of Assisi Church.

27—ST. BRIDGET (1853), Rev. Richard R. York.
Res., 3667 Midvale Ave., 19129. Tel: 215-844-4126; Fax: 215-842-2536.
School—3636 Stanton St., 19129. Tel: 215-843-2828. Sr. Christine Konopelski, S.S.J., Prin.
Sisters of St. Joseph 3; Lay Teachers 11; Students 223.
Catechesis/Religious Programs—Students 267.
Convent—3665 Midvale Ave., 19129. Tel: 215-844-5663.

28—ST. CALLISTUS (1921), Revs. John F. Hummell; Carmen F. Taraborelli.
Res., 700 N. 67th St., 19151-3614. Tel: 215-473-4417; Fax: 215-473-6728.

29—ST. CARTHAGE (1915), Rev. Msgr. Albert V. Norrell. In res., Rev. John T. Conway.
Res., 525 Cobbs Creek Pkwy., 19143. Tel: 215-747-3250; Fax: 215-476-9974.
School—6225 Cedar Ave., 19143. Tel: 215-748-4450. Lawrence C. Schoppet, IV, Prin.
Sisters of St. Joseph 1; Lay Teachers 9; Students 240.

30—ST. CASIMIR (1803) (Lithuanian), Revs. Peter Burkauskas, Admin.; Eugene A. Wassel, Pastor Emeritus.
Res., 324 Wharton St., 19147. Tel: 215-468-2052; Fax: 215-468-0354.
School—Tel: 215-334-8407. Mrs. Ann O'Connor, Prin.
Lay Teachers 8; Students 149.
Catechesis/Religious Programs—Students 161.

31—ST. CATHERINE OF SIENA (1910-1972). Closed. For inquiries for parish records contact the Chancery.

32—ST. CECILIA (1911), Rev. Msgr. Francis X. Dreger; Revs. Thomas C. Hagan; George J. Monahan; Scott D. Brockson; Deacon Louis Malfara.
Res., 535 Rhawn St., 19111. Tel: 215-725-1240; Fax: 215-725-2130.
School—525 Rhawn St., 19111. Tel: 215-725-8588.
Sisters of the Immaculate Heart of Mary 9; Lay Teachers 32; Students 1,025.
Catechesis/Religious Programs—Tel: 215-725-2580.
Students 188.

33—ST. CHARLES BORROMEO (1868), Rev. George A. Majoros.
Res., 902 S. 20th St., 19146. Tel: 215-735-0600.
Church—20th & Christian Sts., 19146.
School—2019 Montrose St., 19146. Tel: 215-735-6879; 735-1475; Fax: 215-735-5523. Sr. Denise Ware, S.F.C.C., Prin.
Lay Teachers 10; Students 300.
St. Charles Preschool—1941 Christian St., 19146.
Lay Teachers 3; Students 78.
Catechesis/Religious Programs—Tel: 215-735-6898.
Students 55.

34—CHRIST THE KING (1963), Revs. Henry G. Birkhead; Gregory J. Fairbanks; James T. Henry; Deacon Walter C. Fulmer.
Res., 3252 Chesterfield Rd., 19114. Tel: 215-632-1144; Fax: 215-632-4933.
School—3205 Chesterfield Rd., 19114. Tel: 215-632-1375; 637-3838.
Sisters of St. Joseph 5; Lay Teachers 20; Students 502.

35—ST. CHRISTOPHER (1950), Rev. Msgr. Joseph P. Garvin; Revs. Vincent F. Welsh; Robert Marczewski; Joseph F. Smith, Pastor Emeritus.
Res., 13301 Proctor Rd., 19116. Tel: 215-673-5177; Fax: 215-698-0585.
School—13307 Proctor Rd., 19116. Tel: 215-673-5787; Fax: 215-673-8511.
Sisters of Mercy 2; Lay Teachers 34; Students 912.
Catechesis/Religious Programs—Students 203.

36—ST. CLEMENT (1865), Revs. John J. Cox; James P. Gorman; Deacon Walter Lance. In res., Rev. Joseph W. McCloskey.
Res., 2210 S. 71st St., 19142-1108. Tel: 215-729-0500.
School—SS. Clement-Irenaeus Consolidated School. See Consolidated Parish Schools under Institutions Located in the Archdiocese. Tel: 215-729-8368.
Sisters, Servants of the Immaculate Heart of Mary 8; Lay Teachers 18; Students 453.

37—ST. COLUMBA (1895-1993). Closed. Spiritual records are kept at St. Martin De Porres Church.

38—CORPUS CHRISTI (1921-1987). Closed. Spiritual records are kept at St. Martin De Porres Church.

39—ST. DOMINIC (1849), Revs. James J. Mulligan; Joseph A. McCloskey, Pastor Emeritus; Bernard J. Benischeck; John F. Meyers; James F. Sullivan.
Res., 8504 Frankford Ave., 19136. Tel: 215-624-5502; 5503; Fax: 215-333-1750. [CEM]
School—8512 Frankford Ave., 19136. Tel: 215-333-6703; Fax: 215-333-6727.
Sisters, Servants of the Immaculate Heart of Mary 14; Lay Teachers 26; Students 690.
Convent—8510 Frankford Ave., 19136. Tel: 215-333-0144.

40—ST. DONATO (1910) (Italian), Rev. Ferdinand Buccafurni.
Res., 403 N. 65th St., 19151. Tel: 215-747-4131.
School—405 N. 65th St., 19151. Tel: 215-748-2994; Fax: 215-748-0288.
Sisters 1; Lay Teachers 10; Students 238.

41—ST. EDMOND (1912), Rev. Francis P. Groarke. In res., Rev. Joseph J. Kelley.
Res., 2130 S. 21st St., 19145. Tel: 215-334-3755; Fax: 215-334-2081.
School—23rd and Mifflin Sts., 19145. Tel: 215-334-0398; Fax: 215-334-2848.
Sisters, Servants of the Immaculate Heart of Mary 2; Lay Teachers 10; Students 214.

42—ST. EDWARD THE CONFESSOR (1865-1993). Closed. Spiritual records are kept at Visitation Church.

43—ST. ELIZABETH (1872-1993). Closed. Spiritual records are kept at St. Martin De Porres Church.

44—EPIPHANY OF OUR LORD (1889), Revs. Dominic M. Chiaravalle; John E. Calabro; Peter C. Funk; Paul F. Maurer, Pastor Emeritus.
Res., 1121 Jackson St., 19148. Tel: 215-334-1035; Fax: 215-334-7885.
School—13th & Jackson Sts., 19148. Tel: 215-467-5385.
Lay Teachers 18; Students 500.

45—ST. FRANCIS OF ASSISI (1899), Rev. William S. Harrison; Deacon Allen Stevens.
Res., 4821 Greene St., 19144. Tel: 215-842-1287; Fax: 215-842-3338.
School—St. Martin De Porres School (Germantown). See Consolidated Parish Schools under Institutions Located in the Archdiocese. Tel: 215-842-1266. Miss Denise Winterberger, Prin.
Lay Teachers 8; Students 225.

46—ST. FRANCIS DE SALES (1890), Rev. Anthony W. Janton. In res., Rev. Paul A. DiGirolamo, J.C.D.
Res., 4625 Springfield Ave., 19143. Tel: 215-222-5819; Fax: 215-222-5821.
School—917 S. 47th St., 19143. Tel: 215-387-1749; 727-3929.
Sisters, Servants of the Immaculate Heart of Mary 5; Lay Teachers 17; Students 518.
Catechesis/Religious Programs—Students 18.

47—ST. FRANCIS XAVIER, Revs. Paul C. Convery; Aloysius H. Vath, Pastor Emeritus. In res., Rev. George G. Thiers.
Res., 2319 Green St., 19130. Tel: 215-765-4568.
Oratory—2321 Green St., 19130. Tel: 215-765-4049.
School—24th & Wallace Sts., 19130. Tel: 215-763-6564.
Sisters, Servants of the Immaculate Heart of Mary 5; Lay Teachers 7; Students 269.
Convent—2324 Green St., 19130. Tel: 215-665-1340.

48—ST. GABRIEL (1895), Rev. Francis X. Cortese, O.Praem.; Sr. Rene Wentzel, I.H.M., Pastoral Min.; Rev. Edward J. Kimpel, O.Praem., (Retired).
Res., 2917 Dickinson St., 19146. Tel: 215-463-4060; Fax: 215-755-2680.
School—30th & Dickinson Sts., 19146. Tel: 215-468-7230.
Sisters, Servants of the Immaculate Heart of Mary 3; Lay Teachers 13; Students 302.

49—ST. GEORGE (1902) (Lithuanian), Rev. Joseph J. Anderlonis.
Res., 3580 Salmon St., 19134. Tel: 215-739-3102; Fax: 215-739-7217.
School—2700 E. Venango St., 19134. Tel: 215-634-8803.
Lay Teachers 9; Students 183.
Convent—3570 Salmon St., 19134. Tel: 215-739-0472.
Sisters 2.

50—GESU (1868-1993). Closed. Spiritual records are kept at St. Malachy Church.

51—GOOD SHEPHERD (1925), Revs. Thomas J. Smith; Peter N. Quinn; Joseph P. Gausch, Pastor Emeritus. In res., Rev. William J. Chiriaco.
Res., 6667 Chester Ave., 19142. Tel: 215-727-8300; Fax: 215-727-5932.
School—66th St. & Chester Ave., 19142. Tel: 215-729-8766.
Sisters, Servants of the Immaculate Heart of Mary 2; Lay Teachers 10; Students 273.
Convent—Tel: 215-729-4043.

52—ST. GREGORY. Closed. Located at 52nd and Warren Sts. from 1895 to 1981. Spiritual records kept at St. Rose of Lima Church.

53—ST. HEDWIG (1907) (Polish), Rev. Joseph C. Stec. In res., Rev. Edward J. Kennedy.
Res., 802 N. 24th St., 19130. Tel: 215-765-8550.

54—ST. HELENA (1924), Rev. Craig F. Brugger; Most Rev. John J. Graham, Pastor Emeritus; Revs. Albert C. DiGiacobbe; John M. Donohie.
Res., 6161 N. Fifth St., 19120-1497. Tel: 215-424-1300; Fax: 215-424-9152.
School—6101 N. Fifth St., 19120. Tel: 215-549-2947.
Sisters of St. Joseph 4; Lay Teachers 14; Students 418.

55—ST. HENRY (1916-1993) (German). Closed. Spiritual records are kept at Incarnation Church.

56—HOLY ANGELS (1906), Rev. Edward J. Chwieroth. In res., Rev. Chang Yu.
Res., 70th Ave. & Old York Rd., 19126. Tel: 215-548-5535; Fax: 215-224-6615.
Catechesis/Religious Programs—Students 200.

57—HOLY CHILD (1909-1993). Closed. Spiritual records are kept at Our Lady of Hope Church.

58—HOLY CROSS (1890), Rev. H. James Hutchins; Deacon Richard Coyne. In res., Rev. Ronald M. Jakows.
Res., 154 E. Mt. Airy Ave., 19119. Tel: 215-247-0661.
School—144 E. Mt. Airy Ave., 19119. Tel: 215-242-0414.
Sisters of St. Joseph 3; Lay Teachers 10; Students 254.
Convent—148 E. Mt. Airy Ave., 19119. Tel: 215-247-0262.
Catechesis/Religious Programs—Tel: 215-247-3405. Mr. James Nelson, D.R.E.
Students 25.

59—HOLY FAMILY (1885), Revs. Francis X. McKee; James J. Martin; John W. Gsell, Pastor Emeritus. In res., Rev. Thomas F. Gibbons, M.M.; Deacon Eugene R. Leahy.
Res., 234 Hermitage St., 19127. Tel: 215-482-0450; 482-8608; Fax: 215-482-7531.
School—242 Hermitage St., 19127. Tel: 215-487-2796; 483-0903; Fax: 215-487-9134.
Sisters of the Immaculate Heart of Mary 4; Lay Teachers 14; Students 300.
Catechesis/Religious Programs—Interparochial C.C.D. Program - St. Josaphat's, Tel: 215-483-4470; Fax: 215-483-4471.
Students 37.

60—HOLY INNOCENTS (1927), Revs. Daniel J. Sullivan; Stephen C. White; Paul A. Castellani.
Res., 1337 E. Hunting Park Ave., 19124. Tel: 215-743-2600; Fax: 215-743-8041.
School—1312 E. Bristol St., 19124. Tel: 215-743-5909.
Sisters, Servants of the Immaculate Heart of Mary 7; Lay Teachers 23; Students 774.

61—HOLY NAME OF JESUS (Kensington) (1904), Very Rev. Stephen F. Carmody, O.P.; Rev. Ralph V. Townsend, O.P., Pastoral Assoc.
Res., 701 E. Gaul St., 19125-2896. Tel: 215-739-3960; Fax: 215-739-7597.
School—E. Berks & Gaul Streets, 19125. Tel: 215-423-3334; Fax: 215-425-9353.
Sisters, Servants of the Immaculate Heart of Mary 5; Lay Teachers 12; Students 230.
Preschool:—Kensington, Tel: 215-423-3041. Sr. Christine Lamb, I.H.M., Prin.

62—HOLY REDEEMER (1941) (Chinese). Unassigned. (Mission Chapel of the Church of St. John the Evangelist).
School—915 Vine St., 19107. Tel: 215-922-0999; Fax: 215-922-6674.
Lay Teachers 9; Students 238.
Parish House:—916 Wood St., 19107. Tel: 215-627-5293; Fax: 215-563-9980.

63—HOLY SPIRIT (1964), Revs. John E. Mulgrew; Davis T. Vadakkumpadan, C.M.I.
Res., 1900 Geary St., 19145. Tel: 215-334-4242.
School—1845 Hartranft St., 19145. Tel: 215-389-0715; Fax: 215-336-7719.
Poor Servants of the Mother of God 2; Lay Teachers 8; Students 182.
Catechesis/Religious Programs—Students 220.

64—HOLY TRINITY (1789) (German). Attended by Old St. Mary's Church, Sixth and Spruce Streets.
252 South Fourth St., 19106. Tel: 215-923-7930. [CEM]
School—St. Mary Interparochial School. See Consolidated Parish Schools under Institutions Located in the Archdiocese.

65—ST. HUBERT (1924). Closed. Formally located at Torresdale and Cottman Aves. from 1924-1940. Spiritual records transferred to St. Bernard Church. Tel: 215-333-0446.

66—ST. HUGH OF CLUNY (1922), Rev. Dennis M. Mooney; Deacon Jose L. Lozada-Figueroa. In res., Rev. Nelson J. Perez.
Res., 145 W. Tioga St., 19140. Tel: 215-634-1800.
School—3533 N. Mascher St., 19140. Tel: 215-634-3060; 634-3183.
Sisters of St. Joseph 2; Lay Teachers 9; Students 273.
Catechesis/Religious Programs—Students 169.

67—ST. IGNATIUS OF LOYOLA (1893), Rev. Federico A. Britto.
Res., 636 N. 43rd St., 19104. Tel: 215-386-5065; 386-1058; Fax: 215-386-2832.
School—617 N. 43rd St., 19104. Tel: 215-222-3626. Sr. Christine Smith, S.B.S., Prin.
Sisters of the Blessed Sacrament 5; Lay Teachers 7; Students 267.
Convent—644 N. 43rd St., 19104. Tel: 215-386-0302.
Chaplaincy—St. Ignatius Nursing Home, Tel: 215-349-8800; Fax: 215-222-3078.

68—IMMACULATE CONCEPTION (1869), Revs. William A. Dombrow; Edmund C. Wesolowski.
Res., 1020 N. Front St., 19123. Tel: 215-627-2702; Fax: 215-627-7344.

69—IMMACULATE CONCEPTION (1902), Revs. Stephen F. Cantwell, C.M.; Richard J. Rock, C.M. In res., Revs. William J. O'Brien, C.M.; Charles T. Plock, C.M.; John W. Gouldrick, C.M.; Michael Mazurchuk, C.M.
Res., 1020 E. Price St., 19138. Tel: 215-843-9468; Fax: 215-843-6570.
School—St. Athanasius-Immaculate Conception School. See Consolidated Parish Schools under Institutions located in the Archdiocese.

70—IMMACULATE HEART OF MARY (1952), Revs. Bartholomew J. O'Brien; Edward C. Kelly; Frank A. Giuffre. In res., Rev. Francis W. Beach.
Res., 819 Cathedral Rd., 19128. Tel: 215-483-1000; Fax: 215-483-1732.
School—815 Cathedral Rd., 19128. Tel: 215-482-2029.
Lay Teachers 35; Students 515.

71—INCARNATION OF OUR LORD (1900), Revs. John M. Halloran; John Kallor. In res., Revs. John Didgeon; Jose Nunes, (Portuguese Apostolate).
Res., 5105 N. Fifth St., 19120. Tel: 215-329-2320; Fax: 215-329-6149.
School—Tel: 215-457-2779. Sr. Patricia A. Walsh, I.H.M., Prin.
Sisters, Servants of the Immaculate Heart of Mary 4; Lay Teachers 15; Students 585.
Convent—401 W. Lindley Ave., 19120. Tel: 215-329-0672.

72—SAINT IRENAEUS (1966), Revs. Gavin W. Muir; A. James Chapman, Pastor Emeritus; Deacon Michael Arno.
Res., 2728 South 73rd St., 19153. Tel: 215-727-2888; Fax: 215-329-6149.
School—SS. Clement-Irenaeus Consolidated School. See Consolidated Parish Schools under Institutions Located in the Archdiocese. Tel: 215-729-8368.

73—ST. JAMES (1850-1976). Consolidated with St. Agatha to form St. Agatha-St. James. See separate listing for details.

74—ST. JEROME (1955), Revs. Joseph B. Graham; William J. Bispels; Martin F. O'Hara, Pastor Emeritus; James J. Brennan, M.A.; Deacon Charles Pavonarius. In res., Rev. Edward V. Avery.
Res., 8100 Colfax St., 19136. Tel: 215-333-4461; Fax: 215-333-6791.
School—3031 Stamford St., 19136. Tel: 215-624-0637; Fax: 215-624-5711. William McDowell, Prin.
Sisters of St. Joseph 3; Lay Teachers 30; Students 914.

75—ST. JOACHIM (1845), Revs. Robert Bazzoli, O.S.F.S.; Mark Plaushin, O.S.F.S.; Deacon Steven P. Wetzel.
Res., 1527 Church St., 19124. Tel: 215-535-0580; Fax: 215-831-1788. [CEM]
School—Penn & Church Sts., 19124. Tel: 215-288-9501.
Sisters, Servants of the Immaculate Heart of Mary 5; Lay Teachers 11; Students 315.
Catechesis/Religious Programs—Students 110.
Convent—1509 Church St., Tel: 215-535-6177.
Servants of the Immaculate Heart of Mary 10.

76—ST. JOAN OF ARC (1919), Revs. James P. Matteo; Michael J. Heim. In res., Rev. Msgr. Philip J. Cribben.
Res., 2025 E. Atlantic St., 19134. Tel: 215-535-4641; 535-5138; Fax: 215-535-7477.
School—3556 Frankford Ave., 19134. Tel: 215-533-3210.
Sisters, Servants of the Immaculate Heart of Mary 6; Lay Teachers 9; Students 272.
Convent—3550 Frankford Ave., 19134. Tel: 215-533-0959.

77—ST. JOHN THE BAPTIST (1831), Revs. Frederick J. Riegler; John A. Freeman. In res., Rev. Thomas J. Grumm.
Res., 146 Rector St., 19127. Tel: 215-482-4600; Fax: 215-482-2976. [CEM]
School—4211 Cresson St., 19127. Tel: 215-483-0903; Fax: 215-482-2451.
Sisters, Servants of the Immaculate Heart of Mary 7; Lay Teachers 11; Students 520.

78—ST. JOHN CANTIUS (1892) (Polish), Rev. Msgr. Bernard E. Witkowski; Rev. Msgr. Adam J. Bydlon, Pastor Emeritus; Revs. Stanislaw Kolano; Andrew D. McCormick; Dennis J. Witalec.
Res., 4415 Almond St., 19137. Tel: 215-535-6667; Fax: 215-535-7107.
School—4435 Almond St., 19137. Tel: 215-535-3446.
Sisters of the Holy Family of Nazareth 4; Lay Teachers 16; Students 340; Kindergarten 21.

79—ST. JOHN THE EVANGELIST (1830), Revs. James Menkhus, O.F.M.Cap.; Dennis Klemash, O.F.M.Cap.; Roman M. Kozacheson, O.F.M.Cap.; Benjamin Regotti, O.F.M.Cap.; Bro. James Gavin, O.F.M.Cap. In res., Revs. Thomas Betz, O.F.M.Cap.; Anselm Martin, O.F.M.Cap.
Res., 21 S. 13th St., 19107. Tel: 215-563-4145; Fax: 215-563-1770. [CEM]
School—St. Mary Interparochial School. See Consolidated Parish Schools under Institutions Located in the Archdiocese.
Mission—Philadelphia, Philadelphia Co., Holy Redeemer Chinese Church, 915 Vine St., 19107. Tel: 215-922-0999; Fax: 215-922-6674.

80—ST. JOHN NEPOMUCENE (Slovak). Consolidated with St. John Nepomucene and St. Agnes January 1, 1980. Spiritual records transferred to St. Agnes.

81—ST. JOSAPHAT (1898) (Polish), Rev. Leonard A. Furmanski.
Res., 124 Cotton St., 19127. Tel: 215-483-4470; Fax: 215-483-4037.
School—137 Grape St., 19127. Tel: 215-482-0285; Fax: 215-483-4053.
Bernardine Sisters of St. Francis 2; Lay Teachers 9; Students 250.

82—OLD ST. JOSEPH'S (1733), Revs. William C. Rickle, S.J.; Leo A. Murray, S.J.; Robert Yankevitch, S.J. In res., Revs. James M. English, S.J.; Edward A. Jarvis, S.J.
Res., 321 Willings Alley, 19106. Tel: 215-923-1733; 1734; Fax: 215-574-8529.
School—St. Mary Interparochial School. See Consolidated Parish Schools under Institutions Located in the Archdiocese.

83—ST. KATHERINE OF SIENA (1922), Rev. Msgr. James P. McBride; Revs. Marshall J. Kloda; John P. O'Connor; William F. Drobel, Pastor Emeritus; Joseph L. Coffey.
Res., 9700 Frankford Ave., 19114. Tel: 215-637-7548; Fax: 215-637-0146.
School—9720 Frankford Ave., 19114. Tel: 215-637-2181. Sr. M. John, C.S.F.N., Prin.
Sisters of the Holy Family of Nazareth 3; Lay Teachers 29; Students 750.
Catechesis/Religious Programs—Tel: 215-637-1464. Donna Heeney, D.R.E.
Students 60.

84—KING OF PEACE (1926) (Italian), Rev. Ralph J. Chieffo.
Res., 2530 Wharton St., 19146. Tel: 215-468-4107; Fax: 215-468-2882.
School—26th & Reed Sts., 19146. Tel: 215-468-7400. Sr. Janet Roddy, M.F.I.C., Prin.
Missionary Franciscan Sisters of the Immaculate Conception 7; Lay Teachers 9; Students 207.
Convent—1309 S. 26th St., 19146. Tel: 215-389-5414.

85—ST. LADISLAUS (1906) (Polish), Rev. George Ostaszewski.
Res., 1650 W. Hunting Park Ave., 19140. Tel: 215-225-8148.

86—ST. LAURENTIUS (1882) (Polish), Revs. Francis A. Gwiazda; Anthony F. Ziemba, Pastor Emeritus.
Res., 1608 E. Berks St., 19125. Tel: 215-739-1776.
School—1612 E. Berks St., 19125. Tel: 215-423-8834.
Felician Sisters of St. Francis 7; Lay Teachers 9; Students 265.
Catechesis/Religious Programs—Students 359.
Convent—1648 E. Berks St., 19125. Tel: 215-739-4447.

87—ST. LEO (1884), Revs. John J. Farry; Joseph E. O'Brien; James J. Coonan.
Res., 6658 Keystone St., 19135. Tel: 215-333-0340; Fax: 215-333-7590.
School—6649 Tulip St., 19135. Tel: 215-624-8669.
Sisters of St. Joseph 4; Lay Teachers 18; Students 409.
Catechesis/Religious Programs—Students 604.
Convent—4900 Unruh St., 19135. Tel: 215-624-1253.

88—ST. LUCY (Italian), Rev. Francis J. Sabatini. Pastor Emeriti: Revs. Albert J. Burruano; Francis J. Rauseo.
Res., 4503 Smick St., 19127. Tel: 215-483-0554.
School—146 Green Ln., 19127. Tel: 215-482-6578.
Lay Teachers 10; Students 225.

89—ST. LUDWIG (1891-1975) (German). Closed. Spiritual records transferred to St. Francis Xavier Church.

90—ST. MADELEINE SOPHIE (1925), Rev. Donald G. Birch. In res., Rev. John S. Heim.
Res., 6440 Greene St., 19119. Tel: 215-438-9464; Fax: 215-848-7953.
School—St. Martin De Porres School (Germantown). See Consolidated Parish Schools under Institutions Located in the Archdiocese.

91—St. Malachy (1850), Rev. John P. McNamee. In res., Rev. Robert A. McLaughlin.
Res., 1429 N. 11th St., 19122. Tel: 215-763-1305; Fax: 215-763-2023.
School—1419 N. 11th St., 19122. Tel: 215-232-0696.
Lay Teachers 11; Students 230.
Convent—1415 N. 11th St., 19122. Tel: 215-763-5366.

92—Saint Martha (1966), Revs. James G. Gannon, O.F.M.; Gerard H. Scherf, Pastor Emeritus; Marcel Kolakowski, O.F.M.
Res., 11301 Academy Rd., 19154. Tel: 215-632-3720; Fax: 215-632-7737.
School—11321 Academy Rd., 19154. Tel: 215-632-0320.
Lay Teachers 28; Students 660.

93—St. Martin De Porres (1993), Revs. Edward J. Hallinan; James McGinnis; Deacons William Stewart; Edward J. Andrews; Thomas A. Shields.
Res., 2340 W. Lehigh Ave., 19132. Tel: 215-228-8330; Fax: 215-221-6516.
School—23rd St. & Lehigh Ave., 19132. Tel: 215-223-6872.
Sisters of St. Joseph 5; Lay Teachers 18; Students 480.

94—St. Martin of Tours (1923), Revs. Thomas A. Murray; Matthew J. Kornacki; Charles D. Smith; Peter J. Talocci; Charles J. Zlock; Rev. Msgr. Michael F. Marley, Pastor Emeritus.
Res., 5450 Roosevelt Blvd., 19124. Tel: 215-535-2962; Fax: 215-535-3091.
School—Loretto Ave. & Sanger St., 19124. Tel: 215-533-3050.
Sisters of the Immaculate Heart of Mary 20; Lay Teachers 45; Students 1,455.
Catechesis/Religious Programs—Tel: 215-535-3090. Sr. Phyllis Direnzo, I.H.M., D.R.E.
Students 279.

95—Old St. Mary's (1763), Rev. Msgr. John A. Sharkey.
Res., 252 S. Fourth St., 19106. Tel: 215-923-7930. [CEM]
School—St. Mary Interparochial School. See Consolidated Parish Schools under Institutions Located in the Archdiocese.
Lay Teachers 9; Students 242.

96—St. Mary of the Assumption (1849) (German), Revs. John J. Sibel; Emil C. Oestreich, Pastor Emeritus; Deacon Joseph Sexton.
Res., 176 Conarroe St., 19127. Tel: 215-482-4264; Fax: 215-508-1731. [CEM]
School—167 Conarroe St., 19127. Tel: 215-482-1611; Fax: 215-508-1536.
Sisters 2; Lay Teachers 10; Students 323.

97—St. Mary of Czestochowa (1927) (Polish), Revs. Bernard J. Herron, Admin.; John S. Klapp, Pastor Emeritus.
Res., 59th St. & Elmwood Ave., 19143-6098. Tel: 215-729-2292.

98—St. Mary of the Eternal (Italian). Closed. Spiritual records are kept at St. Martin De Porres Church.

99—St. Mary Magdalen de Pazzi (1852) (Italian), Revs. Donato P. Silveri; Alfred M. Natali, O.S.A., (Retired).
Res., 712 Montrose St., 19147. Tel: 215-922-3695.

100—Mater Dolorosa (1911) (Italian), Revs. Joseph L. Logrip; Albert B. Palombo, Pastor Emeritus.
Res., 1676 Ruan St., 19124. Tel: 215-535-4036; 743-4718; Fax: 215-535-1267.
School—Paul & Ruan Sts., 19124. Tel: 215-743-4753. Miss Grace McGuirl, Prin.
Lay Teachers 12; Students 197.
Catechesis/Religious Programs—Students 273.

101—Maternity B.V.M. (1870), Rev. Msgr. Anthony W. McGuire; Revs. Ross J. Macartney; Francis E. Fox; Thomas M. Sodano; Deacons Victor Bonilla; Phillip Heaney; John C. Hynes.
Res., 9220 Bustleton Ave., 19115. Tel: 215-673-8127; 676-5144; Fax: 215-673-6597.
School—9322 Bustleton Ave., 19115. Tel: 215-673-0235. Sr. Bonita Smith, R.S.M., Prin.
Sisters of Mercy 2; Lay Teachers 30; Students 899.
Convent—Tel: 215-673-8118.

102—St. Matthew (1927), Rev. Msgr. Charles E. McGroarty; Revs. Gregory J. Hamill; Eugene M. Tully; Thomas D. Graham; Richard E. Rudy. In res., Rev. James F. Gough.
Res., 3000 Cottman Ave., 19149. Tel: 215-333-0585; Fax: 215-333-0757.
School—3040 Cottman Ave., 19149. Tel: 215-333-3142.
Sisters, Servants of the Immaculate Heart of Mary 7; Lay Teachers 36; Students 1,409.

103—St. Michael (1831), Rev. John M. Harkins; Deacon Zoilo Martes. In res., Rev. Francis Piro.
Res., 1445 N. Second St., 19122. Tel: 215-739-2358. [CEM]
School—1429 N. Second St., 19122. Tel: 215-426-5424.
Sisters of St. Joseph 4; Lay Teachers 6; Students 142.
Convent—1434 N. Second St., 19122. Tel: 215-739-3677.

104—St. Michael Mission. (Formerly located in Torresdale.) Spiritual records transferred to Our Lady of Calvary Church.

105—St. Michael of the Saints. Closed. Located at 4811 Germantown Ave. from 1924 to 1982. Spiritual records kept at St. Francis of Assisi Church.

106—St. Monica (1895), Most Rev. Louis A. De Simone; Revs. Charles L. Sangermano; Christopher J. Papa. In res., Rev. Clement Kurowski, O.F.M.; Deacons John C. Orlando; Leonard D. DeMasi.
Res., 2422 S. 17th St., 19145. Tel: 215-334-4170.
School—1714 Ritner St., 19145. Tel: 215-467-5338; 334-3777.
Sisters, Servants of the Immaculate Heart of Mary 5; Lay Teachers 25; Students 776.
Catechesis/Religious Programs—Students 129.

107—Most Blessed Sacrament (1901), Rev. Roland D. Slobogin. In res., Rev. Joseph M. Corley.
Res., 5628 Chester Ave., 19143. Tel: 215-729-0694; Fax: 215-729-0712.
School—5601 Kingsessing Ave., 19143. Tel: 215-727-1863.
Sisters, Servants of Immaculate Heart of Mary 3; Lay Teachers 7; Students 220.

108—Most Precious Blood (1907-1993). Closed. Spiritual records are kept at St. Martin De Porres Church.

109—Mother of Divine Grace (1926) (Italian), Rev. Angelo R. Citino; Deacon Joseph A. Micucci. In res., Rev. John B. Wendrychowicz.
Res., 2918 E. Thompson St., 19134. Tel: 215-739-0353; Fax: 215-739-9910.
School—2612 E. Monmouth St., 19134. Tel: 215-426-7325.
Lay Teachers 10; Students 212.
Catechesis/Religious Programs—Students 255.
Mission—Philadelphia, Philadelphia Co., St. Roch Chapel, E. Ontario, 19134.

110—Nativity of the Blessed Virgin Mary (1882), Revs. Richard J. McAndrews; Joseph F. Okonski. In res., Rev. Michael J. Blaine.
Res., 2535 E. Allegheny Ave., 19134. Tel: 215-739-2735; Fax: 215-739-2748.
School—3255 Belgrade St., 19134. Tel: 215-739-8761; Fax: 215-739-8781.
School Sisters of Notre Dame 3; Lay Teachers 20; Students 434.
Catechesis/Religious Programs—Tel: 215-739-4667. Mrs. Susan Campbell, D.R.E.
Students 86.
Convent—3224 Belgrade St., 19134. Tel: 215-427-3261; Fax: 215-427-3263. Novitiate-Sisters of Our Lady of Mercy

111—St. Nicholas of Tolentine (1912) (Italian), Revs. Nicholas Martorano, O.S.A.; Peter J. Toscani, O.S.A.; Eugene DelConti, O.S.A.; Edward Doran, O.S.A. In res., Rev. Anthony Gasparro, O.S.A., (Retired); Bro. John Holt, O.S.A.; Deacon Raymond Jacobucci.
Res., 910 Watkins St., 19148. Tel: 215-463-1326; Fax: 215-463-0888.
Church—Ninth St. below Morris St., 19148.
School—913 Pierce St., 19148. Tel: 215-468-0353; Fax: 215-334-9661.
Religious Sisters Filippini 4; Religious 2; Lay Teachers 20; Students 516.

112—Our Lady of Angels (1907) (Italian), Rev. Ferdinand Buccafurni, Admin.
Res., St. Donato Church, 403 N. 65th St., 19151. Tel: 215-747-4131.
Church—4970 Master St., 19131.

113—Our Lady of the Blessed Sacrament (1910-1972). Closed. Spiritual records transferred to Cathedral Basilica of SS. Peter and Paul.

114—Our Lady of Calvary (1958), Rev. Msgr. John E. Gillespie; Revs. John P. Hutter; Sylwester Wiejata.
Res., 11024 Knights Rd., 19154. Tel: 215-637-7515; Fax: 215-637-7517.
School—11027 Kipling Ln., 19154. Tel: 215-637-1648; Fax: 215-632-3810.
Sisters of the Holy Family of Nazareth 3; Lay Teachers 31; Students 1,055.
Catechesis/Religious Programs—Tel: 215-632-1342.
Students 156.

115—Our Lady of Consolation (1917) (Italian), Rev. Michael C. DiIorio.
Res., 7056 Tulip St., 19135. Tel: 215-333-0442; 333-5774.
School—Princeton & Edmund Sts., 19135. Tel: 215-624-0505. Miss Patricia Quinter, Prin.
Sisters of St. Francis of Philadelphia 1; Lay Teachers 9; Students 338.
Convent—7052 Tulip St., 19135. Tel: 215-332-4426.

116—Our Lady of Good Counsel (1898-1932). Closed. Spiritual records are kept at St. Paul Church.

117—Our Lady Help of Christians (1885) (German), Rev. Leo J. McGee. In res., Rev. Gregory J. Hickey.
Res., 3160 Gaul St., 19134. Tel: 215-739-2211.
School—2424 E. Allegheny Ave., 19134. Tel: 215-427-3499.
Sisters of Christian Charity 4; Lay Teachers 9; Students 285.
Catechesis/Religious Programs—Students 342.
Convent—Tel: 215-739-7890.

118—Our Lady of the Holy Souls (1909-1993). Closed. Spiritual records are kept at Our Lady of Hope Church.

119—Our Lady of Hope (1993), Revs. Kenneth P. McAteer; James R. Bajorek; Thomas P. Kletzel; Deacons Israel Rosario; William Champagne.
Res., 5200 N. Broad St., 19141-1628. Tel: 215-329-8100; 329-8164; Fax: 215-324-4660.
School—5218 N. Broad St., 19141-1626. Tel: 215-324-4211.
Lay Teachers 12; Students 280.

120—Our Lady of Loreto (1932) (Italian), Rev. Vito J. Carbone.
Res., 6214 Grays Ave., 19142-2903. Tel: 215-726-5221; Fax: 215-726-8602.
School—2412 S. 62nd St., 19142. Tel: 215-727-1551; Fax: 215-727-2828.
Lay Teachers 10; Students 230.

121—Our Lady of Lourdes (1894), Revs. James C. Sherlock; Patrick E. Sweeney; George W. Crowe.
Res., 6315 Lancaster Ave., 19151. Tel: 215-473-1669; 1670.
School—1940 N. 63rd St., 19151. Tel: 215-877-2727.
Sisters of Mercy 2; Lay Teachers 12; Students 225.

122—Our Lady of Mercy (1889-1984). Closed. Records transferred to St. Malachy.

123—Chapel of Our Lady of the Miraculous Medal (1912) (Spanish). Attended by Cathedral Basilica of SS. Peter and Paul, 1723 Race St., Philadelphia, PA 19103. Tel: 215-561-1313; 1314. Rev. William S. Murphy.
Church—1903 Spring Garden St., 19130. Tel: 215-972-8116.

124—Our Lady of Mt. Carmel, Revs. Joseph M. Derrig; Robert T. Feeney; Leonard A. Lewandowski; Mrs. Lucille Hillerman, Parish Svcs. Dir.
Res., 2319 S. Third St., 19148. Tel: 215-334-7766; Fax: 215-334-3269.
School—2339 S. Third St., 19148. Tel: 215-334-0584.
Sisters of Mercy 3; Lay Teachers 17; Students 450.
Convent—251 Ritner St., 19148. Tel: 215-334-6800.

125—Our Lady of Pompeii (1914-1993) (Italian). Closed. Spiritual records are kept at St. Veronica Church.

126—Our Lady of Ransom (1955), Revs. William F. McGeown; Laurence J. Gleason. In res., Rev. Msgr. Joseph J. McGlinn.
Res., 6701 Calvert St., 19149. Tel: 215-332-6166; Fax: 215-332-6811.
School—6740 Roosevelt Blvd., 19149. Tel: 215-332-4352.
Sisters, Servants of the Immaculate Heart of Mary 4; Lay Teachers 14; Students 526.
Convent—Tel: 215-624-1954.

127—Our Lady of the Rosary (1886), Rev. Joseph J. Nicolo.
Res., 345 N. 63rd St., 19139. Tel: 215-476-6511; 476-2050.
School—344 N. Felton St., 19139. Tel: 215-474-4011; Fax: 215-474-7807. Mrs. Margeuritte Henry, Prin.
Lay Teachers 10; Students 207.

128—Our Lady of the Rosary (Germantown) (1928-1977) (Italian). Closed. Spiritual records transferred to Immaculate Conception Church, Germantown.

129—Our Lady of Victory (1899), Rev. Henry J. McKee; Deacon Richard G. Nightingale. In res., Rev. Thomas M. Higgins.
Res., 5412 Vine St., 19139. Tel: 215-747-7567; 747-6731; Fax: 215-748-6269.
School—54th & Summer Sts., 19139. Tel: 215-747-8004. Sr. Catherine Lengle, S.S.J., Prin.
Sisters of St. Joseph 6; Lay Teachers 9; Students 239.
Convent—5330 Vine St., 19139. Tel: 215-747-7040.

130—Our Mother of Consolation (1855), Revs. Francis A. Sirolli, O.S.A.; Thomas J. Dillon, O.S.A., Hospital Chap.; Anthony J. Tomasulo, O.S.A.; Bro. William C. Harkin, O.S.A.; Deacons Clifford W. Brown; James M. Tormey.
Res., 9 E. Chestnut Hill Ave., 19118. Tel: 215-247-0430; Fax: 215-247-2506.

School—17 E. Chestnut Hill Ave., 19118. Tel: 215-247-1060. Mary P. Boyle, Prin.
Sisters of St. Joseph 7; Lay Teachers 6; Students 248.
Convent—23 E. Chestnut Hill Ave., 19118. Tel: 215-247-0552.

131—OUR MOTHER OF MERCY PRISON CHAPLAINCY, Rev. John M. Bonavitacola, Chap.
Res., 1350 Vernon Rd., 19150. Tel: 215-549-3760; Fax: 215-549-1271. Ministry to Philadelphia County Prisons; House of Correction; Detention Center; Curran-Fromhold Correctional Facility; Philadelphia Industrial Correctional Center, Special Detention Facilities, Tel: 215-685-8385. Fax: 215-685-8938.

132—OUR MOTHER OF SORROWS (1852), Revs. Alexander Masluk; James P. Daly, Pastor Emeritus.
Res., 1030 N. 48th St., 19131. Tel: 215-878-0875; Fax: 215-878-7420.
School—1020 N. 48th St., 19131. Tel: 215-473-5828; Fax: 215-477-3096.
Sisters of St. Joseph 1; Sisters of Mercy 1; Lay Teachers 9; Students 265.
Convent—St. Carthage, Tel: 215-747-0122.

133—ST. PATRICK (1839), Rev. Msgr. Philip J. Dowling; Rev. Peter A. Fitzpatrick, Pastor Emeritus.
Res., 242 S. 20th St., 19103. Tel: 215-735-9900; Fax: 215-732-0998.
School—St. Mary Interparochial School, Tel: 215-923-7522.

134—ST. PAUL (1843), Rev. Michael J. Gambone. In res., Rev. Thomas J. Rossi, O.Praem.
Res., 808 S. Hutchinson St., 19147. Tel: 215-923-0355.
School—910 Christian St., 19147. Tel: 215-922-3049.
Lay Teachers 8; Students 175.

135—ST. PETER THE APOSTLE (1842), Rev. Joseph C. Tizio, C.SS.R.; Deacon Miguel Betancourt. In res., Rev. Msgr. George Tomichek; Rev. Charles G. Fehrenbach, C.SS.R.
Tel: 215-627-2386; Fax: 215-627-2366.
St. John Neumann Apostolate—Tel: 215-627-3080; Fax: 215-627-2366. Revs. Michael Barrett; Seamus M. Quinn, C.SS.R.; Paul Bryan, C.SS.R.
Mission Band—Revs. William C. Maggs, C.SS.R.; Donald C. Miniscalco, C.SS.R.; Francis Sullivan, C.SS.R.
Res., 1019 N. Fifth St., 19123. Tel: 215-627-2386; Fax: 215-627-2366. [CEM]
School—1005 N. Fifth St., 19123. Tel: 215-627-3954; 922-5958.
School Sisters of Notre Dame 8; Lay Teachers 9; Students 294.

136—ST. PETER CLAVER (1889-1985). Closed. Spiritual records transferred to St. John the Evangelist Church.

137—ST. PHILIP NERI (1840), Rev. W. Fred Kindon. In res., Rev. Msgr. Louis A. D'Addezio.
Res., 218 Queen St., 19147. Tel: 215-468-1922; Fax: 215-465-3147.

138—ST. RAPHAEL (1904-1989). Closed. Spiritual records are kept at St. Irenaeus.

139—ST. RAYMOND OF PENAFORT (1941), Rev. John F. O'Brien. In res., Revs. Emil C. Oestreich; John M. Bonavitacola.
Res., 1350 Vernon Rd., 19150. Tel: 215-549-3760; Fax: 215-549-1271.
School—7940 Williams Ave., 19150. Tel: 215-548-1919.
Sisters of Mercy 1; Lay Teachers 10; Students 245.

140—RESURRECTION OF OUR LORD (1928), Revs. William C. Kaufman; Robert L. Brennan; Mardean E. Miller; Thomas J. Rooney.
Res., 2000 Shelmire Ave., 19152. Tel: 215-745-3211; Fax: 215-745-0587.
School—2020 Shelmire Ave., 19152. Tel: 215-742-1127; Fax: 215-742-0947. Ms. Elizabeth M. Keating, Prin.
Sisters of Notre Dame de Namur 1; Lay Teachers 31; Students 919.
Catechesis/Religious Programs—Students 300.

141—ST. RICHARD (1924), Revs. Joseph J. Gallagher; John J. Morley, Pastor Emeritus.
Res., 3010 S. 18th St., 19145. Tel: 215-468-4777; Fax: 215-468-3161.
School—19th & Pollock Sts., 19145. Tel: 215-467-5430.
Servants of the Immaculate Heart of Mary 5; Lay Teachers 10; Students 228.
Convent—1827 Pollock St., 19145. Tel: 215-467-1878.

142—ST. RITA OF CASCIA (1907), Revs. Michael F. Di Gregorio, O.S.A.; James L. Galligan, O.S.A.; John F. O'Rourke, O.S.A.; Deacon Leroy F. O'Kedas. In res., Rev. Edward J. Griffin, O.S.A.
Res., 1166 S. Broad St., 19146. Tel: 215-546-8333; Fax: 215-732-3510.

143—ST. ROSE OF LIMA (1921), Rev. Msgr. Wilfred J. Pashley.
Res., 1535 N. 59th St., 19151. Tel: 215-877-2991; Fax: 215-877-8255.
School—1522 N. Wanamaker St., 19131. Tel: 215-473-6030; Fax: 215-473-2338.
Sisters, Servants of the Immaculate Heart of Mary 3; Lay Teachers 7; Students 294.

144—SACRED HEART OF JESUS (1871), Revs. Michael J. Sheehan; William E. Dean. In res., Rev. Kevin C. Lawrence.
Res., 1404 S. Third St., 19147-6099. Tel: 215-465-4050; 4051.
School—1329 Moyamensing Ave., 19147. Tel: 215-462-4129; Fax: 215-462-9429. Sr. Janet Walters, I.H.M., Prin.
Sisters of the Immaculate Heart of Mary 4; Lay Teachers 8; Students 215.
Convent—1420 S. Third St., 19147. Tel: 215-463-8719.

145—SACRED HEART (1913-1977) (Hungarian). Closed. For inquiries for parish records contact St. Michael Church.

146—ST. STANISLAUS (Polish), Rev. Joseph B. Jarosz.
Res., 242 Fitzwater St., 19147. Tel: 215-925-2631.
School—St. Mary Interparochial School. See Consolidated Parish Schools under Institutions Located in the Archdiocese.

147—STELLA MARIS (1954), Rev. Msgr. James F. Connelly, S.T.L., H.E.D.; Revs. Patrick J. Brady; Edmund J. Maher.
Res., 2901 S. 10th St., 19148. Tel: 215-465-2336; 2337.
School—814 Bigler St., 19148. Tel: 215-467-6262.
Sisters of St. Joseph 3; Lay Teachers 11; Students 300.
Convent—2929 S. 10th St., 19148. Tel: 215-462-1111.

148—ST. STEPHEN (1843-1993). Closed. Spiritual records are kept at Our Lady of Hope Church. Tel: 215-329-8100.

149—ST. TERESA OF AVILA (1853-1972). Closed. Spiritual records are kept at St. Rita Church. Tel: 215-546-8333.

150—ST. THERESE OF THE CHILD JESUS (1925), Rev. Steven J. Harris, J.C.D.; Deacon Edward M. Purnell.
Res., 6611 Ardleigh St., 19119. Tel: 215-438-5279; Fax: 215-438-8031.
School—Anderson & Upsal Sts., 19119. Tel: 215-844-5654; Fax: 215-844-8461. Mrs. Camille Brown, Prin.
Lay Teachers 13; Students 273.

151—ST. THOMAS AQUINAS (1885), Revs. Arthur I. Taraborelli; Joseph Dinh C. Huynh; John P. Gutekunst.
Res., 1719 Morris St., 19145. Tel: 215-334-2312; Fax: 215-755-9369.
School—18th & Morris Sts., 19145. Tel: 215-334-0878.
Lay Teachers 18; Students 650.

152—ST. TIMOTHY (1928), Revs. Anthony W. Dieckhaus; Francis X. Morrison; John J. LaRosa; Francis P. Rogers; Joseph W. Callahan.
Res., 3001 Levick St., 19149. Tel: 215-624-6188; Fax: 215-624-1316.
School—Hawthorne & Levick Sts., 19149. Tel: 215-338-9797; Fax: 215-331-6457. Sr. Marie Notwick, S.S.J., Prin.
Sisters of St. Joseph 5; Lay Teachers 44; Students 1,181.
Catechesis/Religious Programs—Students 1,567.
Convent—3033 Levick St., 19149. Tel: 215-624-8333.

153—TRANSFIGURATION OF OUR LORD (1905), Rev. James A. Callahan.
Res., 5533 Cedar Ave., 19143. Tel: 215-476-1207; Fax: 215-476-4324.
School—5501 Cedar Ave., 19143. Tel: 215-474-7611.
Sisters, Servants of the Immaculate Heart of Mary 5; Lay Teachers 15; Students 410; Daycare 45.
Convent—Tel: 215-472-2936.

154—ST. VERONICA (1872), Revs. Michael A. Chapman; Angelo J. Hernandez, Parochial Vicar; Deacons Rafael Maldonado; Alfonzo Fernandez. In res., Rev. Edward A. Pelezar.
Res., 533 W. Tioga St., 19140. Tel: 215-228-4878; 225-5677.
School—Sixth & Tioga St., 19140. Tel: 215-225-1575; Fax: 215-225-2595. Sr. Virginia Paschall, I.H.M., Prin.
Sisters, Servants of the Immaculate Heart of Mary 3; Lay Teachers 7; Students 226.
Catechesis/Religious Programs—Tel: 215-228-4878. Sr. Kathleen Brown, I.H.M., D.R.E.
Students 190.
Convent—3521 N. Sixth St., 19140. Tel: 215-223-9107.
Casila Outreach Program—606 W. Eric Ave., 19140. Tel: 215-226-3507. Sr. Angelica Perez, O.P., Supr. Dominican Sisters of Our Lady of the Rosary of Fatima.

155—ST. VINCENT DE PAUL (1851), Revs. Gregory P. Cozzubbo, C.M.; Aidan R. Rooney, C.M.; John Maher, C.M.; Bro. Alfred J. Smith, C.M.
Res., 109 E. Price St., 19144. Tel: 215-438-2925; Fax: 215-438-4856.
School—St. Martin De Porres School (Germantown). See Consolidated Parish Schools under Institutions Located in the Archdiocese.

156—VISITATION B.V.M. (1874), Rev. Msgr. Edward M. Deliman; Revs. Augusto Concha, O.P.; Joseph T. Trinh.
Res., 2625 B St., 19125. Tel: 215-634-1133; Fax: 215-634-6622.
School—Lehigh Ave. & B St., 19125. Tel: 215-634-7280.
Sisters of St. Joseph 4; Lay Teachers 15; Students 397.
Catechesis/Religious Programs—Students 140.

157—ST. WILLIAM (1920), Rev. Msgr. James E. Mortimer; Revs. Thomas J. McManus, S.T.L.; Winson Parekkat, C.M.I.; Michael J. Saban. In res., Rev. Msgr. Walter J. Conway, J.C.D., (Retired).
Res., 6200 Rising Sun Ave., 19111. Tel: 215-745-1389; Fax: 215-745-2650.
Primary School—6200 Palmetto St., 19111. Tel: 215-342-3369.
Intermediate School—Rising Sun and Robbins Aves., 19111. Tel: 215-342-4488.
Middle School—Rising Sun and Devereaux Aves., 19111. Tel: 215-725-2574.
Sisters, Servants of the Immaculate Heart of Mary 12; Lay Teachers 42; Students 1,182.
Day Care Center—514 Devereaux Ave., 19111. Tel: 215-745-7708.
Convent—6226 Rising Sun Ave., 19111. Tel: 215-745-3513.
Pastoral Care Ministry: Tel: 215-742-9992.

OUTSIDE THE CITY OF PHILADELPHIA

Abington, Montgomery Co., Our Lady Help of Christians (1953), Revs. Joseph D. Bowen; Thomas A. Nasta; Rev. Msgr. J. Clement Bennington, Pastor Emeritus; Deacon Joseph T. Rooney. In res., Rev. Albert J. Santorsola.
Res., 1500 Marian Rd., 19001. Tel: 215-886-3456; Fax: 215-886-7312.
Preschool—.
Lay Teachers 3; Students 51.
School—Elkins & Crater Rds., 19001. Tel: 215-887-3067.
Lay Teachers 10; Students 204.
Catechesis/Religious Programs—Tel: 215-887-3466.
Students 200.

Ambler, Montgomery Co., St. Anthony of Padua (1886), Revs. Stephen P. McHenry; Thomas B. Troy; Deacon David E. Jones.
Res., 259 Forest Ave., 19002-5999. Tel: 215-646-4742; Fax: 215-646-4864. [CEM]
School—Ambler Catholic Elementary School. See Consolidated Parish Schools under Institutions Located in the Archdiocese.
Sisters of St. Joseph 5; Lay Teachers 14; Students 286.
Catechesis/Religious Programs—Tel: 215-646-0586.
Students 328.
Convent—251 Forrest Ave., 19002. Tel: 215-646-0426.

St. Joseph (1920), Rev. Daniel J. Cavanaugh.
Res., 16 S. Spring Garden St., 19002-4797. Tel: 215-646-0494; Fax: 215-643-6389.
School—Ambler Catholic Elementary School. See Consolidated Parish Schools under Institutions Located in the Archdiocese.
Catechesis/Religious Programs—Tel: 215-646-0586.
Students 328.

Ardmore, Montgomery Co., St. Colman (1907), Most Rev. Robert P. Maginnis; Rev. Joseph M. Arnholt. Pastor Emeriti: Rev. Msgr. Francis J. Statkus; Rev. Joseph A. St. Clair. In res., Rev. Richard J. Wright.
Res., 11 Simpson Rd., 19003. Tel: 610-642-0545; Fax: 610-642-6853.
School—SS. Colman-John Neumann School. See Consolidated Parish Schools under Institutions Located in the Archdiocese. Tel: 610-642-0545.

Ardsley, Montgomery Co., Queen of Peace (1954), Rev. Msgr. Thomas J. Hilferty; Rev. John C. Moloney; Rev. Msgr. Joseph E. Lynaugh, Pastor Emeritus. In res., Rev. William J. Lynn.
Res., 820 North Hills Ave., 19038. Tel: 215-887-1838; Fax: 215-887-8328.
School—835 North Hills Ave., Tel: 215-886-4782; Fax: 215-886-2142.
Sisters of the Holy Family of Nazareth 1; Lay Teachers 11; Students 262.

Catechesis/Religious Programs—Sr. Jean Marie, C.S.F.N., D.R.E.
Students 298.
Convent—825 North Hills Ave., Tel: 215-887-4785.

Aston, Delaware Co., St. Joseph (1947), Revs. Robert C. Vogan; James M. Iannarella.
Res., 256 Concord Rd., 19014. Tel: 610-497-3340; Fax: 610-497-3383.
School—Tel: 610-494-0147. Ms. Anne Cook, Prin.
Lay Teachers 19; Students 459.
Catechesis/Religious Programs—Tel: 610-494-4358. Ms. Patricia McGeever, D.R.E.
Students 315.

Bala Cynwyd, Montgomery Co., St. Matthias (1906), Rev. Arthur E. Rodgers; Rev. Msgr. James J. Vizzard; Revs. Charles E. Gormley; Thomas A. Kane, Pastor Emeritus, (Retired); Deacon Gerald Kelly.
Res., 128 Bryn Mawr Ave., 19004-3099. Tel: 610-664-0207; Fax: 610-664-3559.
School—122 Bryn Mawr Ave., 19004. Tel: 610-664-1942.
Sisters of Mercy 4; Lay Teachers 15; Students 206.
Convent—108 Highland Ave., 19004. Tel: 610-667-1399.

Bensalem, Bucks Co.,

1—St. Charles Borromeo, (1903), Revs. Francis A. Carbine; Michael F. Hennelly. In res., Rev. Thomas M. Kohler.
Res., 1731 Hulmeville Rd., 19020. Tel: 215-638-3625; Fax: 215-245-8578.
School—(Grades PreK-8) 1704 Bristol Pike, Tel: 215-639-3456.
Sisters, Servants of the Immaculate Heart of Mary 8; Lay Teachers 12; Students 550.
Catechesis/Religious Programs—Students 150.
Convent—1080 Kings Ave., Tel: 215-639-0113.

2—St. Elizabeth Ann Seton, (1976), Revs. William T. Joseph; John J. Duffy, Pastor Emeritus; Deacons Francis C. Klauder; Joseph W. Niland. In res., Rev. Joseph P. Kerrigan.
Res., 1200 Park Ave. East, 19020. Tel: 215-245-6122; Fax: 215-245-4211.
Catechesis/Religious Programs—Tel: 215-245-9756.
Students 42.

3—Saint Ephrem, (1966), Rev. James E. McGuire; Rev. Msgr. Edward S. Musial, Pastor Emeritus; Revs. Joseph E. Howarth; Anthony F. Orth.
Res., 5400 Hulmeville Rd., 19020. Tel: 215-245-1698; Fax: 215-245-4787. [CEM]
School—5340 Hulmeville Rd., 19020. Tel: 215-639-9488; Fax: 215-639-0206.
Sisters, Servants of the Immaculate Heart of Mary 7; Lay Teachers 24; Students 755.
Catechesis/Religious Programs—Students 380.
Convent—5300 Hulmeville Rd., 19020. Tel: 215-638-1024.

4—Our Lady of Fatima, (1954), Revs. Thomas D. Homa; John A. Griffin, Pastor Emeritus. In res., Rev. Richard J. Griffin.
Res., Fatima Acres, 19020. Tel: 215-639-4254.
School—Tel: 215-638-3256; Fax: 215-638-3256.
Sisters, Servants of the Immaculate Heart of Mary 6; Lay Teachers 6; Students 284.
Convent—2915 Street Rd., 19020. Tel: 215-639-1916. Fatima Acres

Berwyn, Chester Co., St. Monica (1897), Rev. George G. Hagenbach.
Res., 635 First Ave., 19312. Tel: 610-644-0110; Fax: 610-695-0850. [CEM]
School—First and Woodside Aves., Tel: 610-644-8848. Mrs. Mary Dunwoody, Prin.
Lay Teachers 16; Students 241.
Catechesis/Religious Programs—Tel: 610-647-4757.
Students 274.

Boothwyn, Delaware Co., St. John Fisher (1971), Rev. Sidney C. Burgoyne.
Res., 4225 Chichester Ave., 19061. Tel: 610-485-0441; Fax: 610-859-2109.
School—Holy Saviour-St. John Fisher School. See Consolidated Parish Schools under Institutions Located in the Archdiocese.
Catechesis/Religious Programs—Tel: 610-485-0581.
Students 267.

Bridgeport, Montgomery Co., St. Augustine (1892), Rev. Msgr. Francis X. Schmidt; Rev. Francis H. Gallen, Pastor Emeritus. In res., Rev. Charles J. Kennedy.
Res., 464 Ford St., 19405. Tel: 610-272-4088; Fax: 610-272-6396. [CEM]
School—St. Augustine-Our Lady of Mount Carmel School. See Consolidated Parish Schools under Institutions Located in the Archdiocese. Tel: 610-275-8676.
Sisters, Servants of the Immaculate Heart of Mary 4; Lay Teachers 9; Students 202.
Convent—512 Bush St., 19405. Tel: 610-275-3348.
Catechesis/Religious Programs—Students 55.

Our Lady of Mt. Carmel (1924) (Italian), Rev. Salvatore J. Pronesti.
Res., 502 Ford St., 19405. Tel: 610-272-3479; Fax: 610-272-5449.
School—St. Augustine-Our Lady of Mount Carmel. See Consolidated Parish Schools under Institutions Located in the Archdiocese.

Our Mother of Sorrows (1926) (Slovak), Revs. Gregory Parlante; John M. Matsko, Pastor Emeritus.
Res., 504 Holstein St., 19405. Tel: 610-275-3170; Fax: 610-275-0728.
School—St. Augustine-Our Lady of Mount Carmel School. See Consolidated Parish Schools under Institutions Located in the Archdiocese.

Bristol, Bucks Co., St. Ann (1906) (Italian), Revs. James R. Day, O.SS.T.; John DiMatteo, O.SS.T., Pastor Emeritus; Daniel Houde, O.SS.T.
Res., 357 Dorrance St., P.O. Box 1175, 19007. Tel: 215-788-2128; Fax: 215-781-9782.
School—418 Jefferson Ave., 19007. Tel: 215-788-2030.
Sisters of the Most Holy Trinity 3; Lay Teachers 7; Students 215.
Convent—430 Jefferson Ave., 19907. Tel: 215-788-2531.
Mission—Tullytown, Bucks Co., Sacred Heart of Jesus, Main St., 19007.

St. Mark (1845), Revs. Michael J. Ryan; John J. McIntyre; Deacon Jose Antonio Morales.
Res., 1025 Radcliffe St., 19007. Tel: 215-788-2319. [CEM]
School—1024 Radcliffe St., 19007. Tel: 215-785-0973.
Lay Teachers 12; Students 250.
Catechesis/Religious Programs—Students 151.
Convent—921 Radcliffe St., 19007.

Brookhaven, Delaware Co., Our Lady of Charity (1952), Revs. Andrew J. Hanlon; James J. Kelly; John D. Schiele; Edmond J. Speitel.
Res., 231 Upland Rd., 19015. Tel: 610-872-6192; Fax: 610-872-1120.
School—249 Upland Rd., 19015. Tel: 610-874-0410.
Sisters, Servants of the Immaculate Heart of Mary 9; Lay Teachers 17; Students 420.
Catechesis/Religious Programs—Students 208.
Convent—245 Upland Rd., 19015. Tel: 610-874-8101.

Brookline, Delaware Co., Annunciation B.V.M. (1927), Revs. Ignatius L. Murray; Timothy J. Buckley. In res., Rev. Michael T. McCulken.
Res., 410 Sagamore Rd., Havertown, 19083. Tel: 610-449-1613; Fax: 610-449-7041.
School—411 Brookline Blvd., Havertown, 19083. Tel: 610-446-8430.
Sisters of Mercy 1; Lay Teachers 18; Students 298.
Catechesis/Religious Programs—Students 246.
Convent—421 Brookline Blvd., Havertown, 19083.

Broomall, Delaware Co., St. Pius X (1955), Revs. James J. Kelly; James T. McCabe; William T. Small. In res., Deacon Joseph E. Iannucci.
Res., 220 Lawrence Rd., 19008. Tel: 610-353-4880; Fax: 610-356-1084.
School—204 Lawrence Rd., 19008. Tel: 610-356-7222.
Sisters, Servants of the Immaculate Heart of Mary 5; Lay Teachers 25; Students 500.
Catechesis/Religious Programs—Tel: 610-353-6950.
Students 444.

Bryn Mawr, Delaware Co., St. John Neumann (1964), Rev. Msgr. James H. Meehan; Sr. Carol Kelly, S.S.J., Pastoral Min. In res., Rev. Msgr. David E. Walls; Rev. Michael J. Matz.
Res., 380 Highland Ln., 19010. Tel: 610-525-3100; Fax: 610-525-6363.
School—SS. Colman-St. John Neumann School. See Consolidated Parish Schools under Institutions Located in the Archdiocese. Tel: 610-525-3266; Fax: 610-525-6103. Mrs. Mary Ann DeAngelo, Prin.
Sisters 1; Lay Teachers 17; Students 246.
Catechesis/Religious Programs—Students 167.
Convent—340 Highland Ln., 19010. Tel: 610-527-1220; 527-3115.

Our Mother of Good Counsel, Montgomery Co., (1885), Revs. James E. Martinez, O.S.A.; Adrian Gilligan, O.S.A., Prior. In res., Revs. Anthony P. Burrascano, O.S.A.; Harry A. Cassel, O.S.A., (Retired).
Res., 31 Pennswood Rd., 19010. Tel: 610-525-0147; Fax: 610-525-0157.
School—St. Thomas-Good Counsel School. See Consolidated Parish Schools under Institutions Located in the Archdiocese.
Lay Teachers 10; Students 195.
Catechesis/Religious Programs—Fax: 610-525-0157.
Students 131.

Center Square, Montgomery Co., St. Helena (1919), Revs. Joseph A. Vadino; John T. Coates, Pastor Emeritus. In res., Rev. David E. Diamond.
Res., P.O. Box 5085, 19422-0809. Tel: 610-275-7711; Fax: 610-275-7610.
School—Tel: 610-279-3345.
Sisters of Mercy 1; Lay Teachers 16; Students 358.
Catechesis/Religious Programs—Students 241.
Convent—Tel: 610-272-1383.

Chadds Ford, Delaware Co., St. Cornelius (1963), Rev. James E. Locke.
Res., 110 Ridge Rd., 19317. Tel: 610-459-2502.
Catechesis/Religious Programs—Students 292.

Chalfont, Bucks Co., St. Jude (1962), Rev. Msgr. James P. McCoy; Rev. Michael J. Gerlach; Deacons Vincent G. Ceneviva; John T. Riordan.
Res., 321 W. Butler Ave., 18914-2329. Tel: 215-822-0179; Fax: 215-822-0638.
School—323 W. Butler Ave., 18914. Tel: 215-822-9225. Sr. Marie Melanie, R.S.M., Prin.
Sisters 2; Lay Teachers 18; Students 406.
Catechesis/Religious Programs—Tel: 215-822-7553. Ms. Margaret F. McMenamin, Prin.
Students 461.

Cheltenham, Montgomery Co., St. Joseph (1953), Rev. Joseph J. Qunidlen. In res., Rev. Edward J. Chwieroth.
Res., 120 Hilldale Rd., 19012. Tel: 215-635-5533; Fax: 215-635-4578.
School—Boncouer & Water Rds., Tel: 215-635-0102; Fax: 215-635-4881.
Daughters of Our Lady of the Sacred Heart 2; Lay Teachers 8; Students 217.
Convent—7633 Waters Rd., Tel: 215-224-2159.

Presentation of Blessed Virgin Mary (1890), Revs. John J. Shelley; John R. McFadden; Sr. Joan Anne Melley, S.S.J., Parish Service Dir. In res., Rev. Joseph A. Tracy.
Res., 100 Old Soldiers Rd., 19012. Tel: 215-379-1364; 379-1599; Fax: 215-379-1456.
School—Hasbrook Ave. & Old Soldiers Rd., 19012. Tel: 215-379-3798; Fax: 215-379-4430.
Lay Teachers 20; Students 516.
Catechesis/Religious Programs—Students 160.
Convent—107 Old Soldiers Rd., 19012. Tel: 215-379-8343.

Chester, Delaware Co.,

1—St. Anthony of Padua, (1908-1993) (Italian). Closed. Spiritual records are kept at Blessed Katharine Drexel Church. Tel: 610-872-3731.

2—Blessed Katharine Drexel, (1993), Revs. Kevin P. Murray; Clemens J. Gerdelman; Ignatius Marneni. 1920 Providence Ave., 19013. Tel: 610-872-3731; Fax: 610-872-0545.
School—Tel: 610-872-7358; Fax: 610-872-7833.
Convent—1902 Providence Ave., 19013. Tel: 610-876-4916.
Mission—Chester, Delaware Co., Blessed Katharine Drexel Center for Evangelization, 2nd & Norris St., 19013. Tel: 610-872-3731; Fax: 610-872-0545.

3—St. Hedwig, (1902-1993) (Polish). Closed. Spiritual records are kept at Blessed Katharine Drexel Church. Tel: 610-872-3731.

4—Immaculate Heart of Mary, (1873-1993). Closed. Spiritual records are kept at Blessed Katharine Drexel Church. Tel: 610-872-3731.

5—St. Michael, (1842-1993). Closed. Spiritual records are kept at Blessed Katharine Drexel Church. Tel: 610-872-3731.

6—Our Lady of Vilna, (1924-1972) (Lithuanian). Closed. Sacramental records are kept at Blessed Katharine Drexel Church. Tel: 215-872-3731.

7—Resurrection of Our Lord, (1911-1993). Closed. Spiritual records are kept at Blessed Katharine Drexel Church. Tel: 610-872-3731.

8—St. Robert, (1922-1993). Closed. Spiritual records are kept at Blessed Katharine Drexel Church. Tel: 610-872-3731.

Chester Heights, Delaware Co., St. Thomas the Apostle (1729), Revs. Richard C. Williams; Anthony G. Flynn; Deacon Charles Devine.
Res., 430 Valley Brook Rd., Glen Mills, 19342. Tel: 610-459-2224; Fax: 610-459-2677. [CEM]
School—Tel: 610-459-8134; Fax: 610-459-8120.
Lay Teachers 14; Students 295.
Catechesis/Religious Programs—Tel: 610-459-3477. Joseph Doyle, D.R.E.
Students 381.
Chaplaincies—Glen Mills Schools; Delaware County Prison; Brinton Manor; Rosehill.

Clifton Heights, Delaware Co., Sacred Heart (1910) (Polish), Rev. Francis A. Barszczewski, S.T.L.; Rev. Msgr. Francis J. Urbanowicz, Pastor Emeritus; Rev. Jan Palkowski; Deacon Boleslaw S. Wojewodka.
Res., 316 E. Broadway, 19018. Tel: 610-623-0409; Fax: 610-623-2926.
Kindergarten & Preschool—301 E. Berkley Ave., 19018. Tel: 610-623-4861.
Convent—300 E. Berkley Ave., 19018. Tel: 610-623-8804.

Mission—Chester, Delaware Co., St. Hedwig Chapel, 4th & Hayes Sts., Chester, 19013.

Coatesville, Chester Co.,

1—ST. CECILIA, (1870), Revs. Francis J. Schlett; Francis C. Lewis.
Res., 99 N. 6th Ave., 19320. Tel: 610-384-0422; Fax: 610-384-4415. [CEM]
School—Coatesville Area Catholic Elementary School. See Consolidated Parish Schools under Institutions Located in the Archdiocese.
Sisters, Servants of the Immaculate Heart of Mary 4; Lay Teachers 16; Students 533.
Catechesis/Religious Programs—Students 150.
Convent—603 E. Lincoln Hwy., Tel: 610-384-0733; Fax: 610-384-5730.

2—OUR LADY OF THE ROSARY, (1917) (Italian), Rev. Harry A. Romano; Deacon Richard Stoughton.
Res., 80 S. 17th Ave., 19320. Tel: 610-384-1415.
School—Coatesville Area Catholic Elementary School. See Consolidated Parish Schools under Institutions Located in the Archdiocese.
Catechesis/Religious Programs—Tel: 610-384-1415.
Students 383.

3—ST. JOSEPH, (1924) (Slovak), Rev. John V. Oulds, Admin.
Res., 404 Charles St., 19320. Tel: 610-384-0360.
School—Coatesville Area Catholic Elementary School. See Consolidated Parish Schools under Institutions Located in the Archdiocese.

4—ST. STANISLAUS KOSTKA, (1907) (Polish), Rev. John V. Oulds.
Res., 209 W. Lincoln Hwy., 19320. Tel: 610-384-1172. [CEM]
School—Coatesville Area Catholic Elementary School. See Consolidated Parish Schools in the Institutions Located in the Archdiocese.

Collegeville, Montgomery Co., St. Eleanor (1911), Revs. John A. Franey; James P. McKelvey; Deacons Gerald McGrath; James Burns; Michael Woodal. In res., Revs. Philip J. Lowe; Francis P. Lennon, Pastor Emeritus.
Res., 647 Locust St., 19426. Tel: 610-489-1647; Fax: 610-489-7469.
School—Tel: 610-489-9434.
Lay Teachers 27; Students 520.
Catechesis/Religious Programs—Tel: 610-489-4677.
Students 590.
Convent—111 Sixth Ave., 19426. Tel: 610-489-1573.

Collingdale, Delaware Co., St. Joseph (1916), Revs. Donald E. Leighton; Michael J. Lonergan; William G. Donovan; David A. Fernandes.
Res., 500 Woodlawn Ave., 19023. Tel: 610-583-4530; Fax: 610-583-7730.
School—Bartram & Woodlawn Aves., Tel: 610-586-0356. Sr. Rosemary Dougherty, I.H.M., Prin.
Sisters, Servants of the Immaculate Heart of Mary 13; Lay Teachers 26; Students 755.

Conshohocken, Montgomery Co., SS. Cosmas and Damian (1912) (Italian), Revs. Gasper A. Genuardi; Nicholas A. Lazzaro, Pastor Emeritus. In res., Rev. Alexander J. Palmieri, M.A., J.C.L.; Deacon Armand J. Maresca.
Res., 209 W. Fifth Ave., 19428. Tel: 610-828-0101; Fax: 610-828-5294.
School—See Consolidated Parish Schools under Institutions Located in the Archdiocese. Conshohocken Catholic School, Tel: 610-828-2007; Fax: 610-825-8796.

St. Mary (1905) (Polish), Rev. Msgr. Robert J. Grudowski.
Res., 140 W. Hector St., 19428. Tel: 610-828-0260; Fax: 610-828-9665. [CEM]

St. Matthew (1851), Rev. James W. Donlon. In res., Rev. John J. Ames.
Res., 219 Fayette St., 19428. Tel: 610-828-0424; Fax: 610-825-5168. [CEM]
School—Conshohocken Catholic School. See Consolidated Parish Schools under Institutions Located in the Archdiocese. Tel: 610-828-2007.
Catechesis/Religious Programs—Students 133.
Convent—Third Ave. & Harry St., Tel: 610-828-0174.

Croydon, Bucks Co., St. Thomas Aquinas (1922), Revs. Francis M. Gallagher, M.A.; John Tharayil, C.M.I.; Deacon Lawrence J. Gibson.
Res., 601 Bristol Pike, 19021-5496. Tel: 215-788-2989; 788-5813; Fax: 215-788-7626.
School—Walnut Ave. & Bristol Pike, Tel: 215-785-1130.
Lay Teachers 17; Students 330.

Darby, Delaware Co., Blessed Virgin Mary (1913), Rev. Peter J. Foley.
Res., 1101 Main St., 19023. Tel: 610-583-2128; Fax: 610-583-9829.
School—47 MacDade Blvd., 19023. Tel: 610-586-0638.
Sisters, Servants of the Immaculate Heart of Mary 3; Lay Teachers 13; Students 280.
Catechesis/Religious Programs—Tel: 610-586-2490.
Students 163.

Delphi, Montgomery Co., St. Mary (1926), Revs. Charles J. McElroy; Donald J. Mills.
Res., 40 Spring Mount Rd., Schwenksville, 19473. Tel: 610-287-8156; Fax: 610-287-4226.
School—Tel: 610-287-7757.
Lay Teachers 13; Students 230.
Catechesis/Religious Programs—Tel: 610-287-0102.
Students 428.

Downingtown, Chester Co., St. Joseph (1851), Rev. Msgr. Robert T. McManus; Revs. William J. Smith, Pastor Emeritus; Walter J. Benn; Raymond J. Overstreet; Joseph A. Toth; Deacon Edward R. Schiappa.
Res., 338 Manor Ave., 19335. Tel: 610-269-8294; Fax: 610-269-2487. [CEM]
School—340 Manor Ave., 19335. Tel: 610-269-8999.
Sisters, Servants of the Immaculate Heart of Mary 3; Lay Teachers 20; Students 640.
Catechesis/Religious Programs—Tel: 610-873-8798.
Students 1,384.
Convent—336 Manor Ave., 19335. Tel: 610-363-6559.

Doylestown, Bucks Co., Our Lady of Mount Carmel (1850), Rev. Msgr. John E. Breslin; Revs. John J. Davids; Gerard C. Chapman, M.Div.; Daniel J. Gallagher; Rev. Msgr. Martin J. McDonough, Pastor Emeritus; Bro. Richard C. Ekmann, O.S.A.; Deacons George Corwell; Joseph Gousie, Sr.; Walter Kelly.
Res., 235 E. State St., 18901. Tel: 215-348-4190; Fax: 215-348-3104. [CEM]
School—E. Ashland St., 18901. Tel: 215-348-5907; Fax: 215-348-5671.
Sisters of St. Francis of Philadelphia 4; Lay Teachers 23; Students 607.
Catechesis/Religious Programs—Tel: 215-345-7089. Sr. Christa DeBacher, D.R.E.
Students 1,400.
Convent—209 E. State St., 18901. Tel: 215-348-4663.

Drexel Hill, Delaware Co.,

1—ST. ANDREW, (1916), Rev. Msgr. D. James McGettigan; Revs. James E. McVeigh; Girard J. Cusatis; Deacon Daniel N. DeLucca.
Res., 3500 School Ln., 19026. Tel: 610-259-1169; Fax: 610-259-0556.
School—529 Mason Ave., 19026. Tel: 610-259-5145. Mrs. Eileen Wilson, Prin.
Sisters of St. Joseph 3; Lay Teachers 22; Students 562.
Catechesis/Religious Programs—Students 405.
Convent—535 Mason Ave., 19026. Tel: 610-259-6130.

2—ST. BERNADETTE, (1947), Revs. William A. Wright; John H. Roebuck. In res., Rev. Daniel J. Kutys.
Res., 1035 Turner Ave., 19026. Tel: 610-789-7676; Fax: 610-789-9539.
School—1015 Turner Ave., 19026. Tel: 610-449-6126; Fax: 610-789-0890.
Oblate Sisters of St. Francis de Sales 3; Lay Teachers 22; Students 470.
Catechesis/Religious Programs—Tel: 610-853-1740. John Blisard, D.R.E.
Students 310.
Convent—Tel: 610-789-2325.

3—ST. CHARLES BORROMEO, (1849), Rev. Msgr. Daniel A. Murray, S.T.L., S.S.L.; Rev. Francis J. Cauterucci; Deacons Francis Fabrizio; Peter Calabrese.
Res., 3422 Dennison Ave., 19026. Tel: 610-623-3800; Fax: 610-284-9583. [CEM]
School—3400 Dennison Ave., 19026. Tel: 610-626-4687.
Sisters, Servants of the Immaculate Heart of Mary 2; Lay Teachers 19; Students 447.
Catechesis/Religious Programs—Tel: 610-256-4389.
Students 270.
Convent—3407 Dennison Ave., 19026. Tel: 610-623-0965.

4—ST. DOROTHY, (1947), Rev. Msgr. Frederick J. Helduser; Rev. Michael D. Murphy; Deacon John J. Davaro.
Res., 4910 Township Line, 19026. Tel: 610-789-7788; 789-7338; Fax: 610-789-6936.
School—Tel: 610-789-4100.
Sisters of Mercy of the Americas 1; Lay Teachers 21; Students 472.
Catechesis/Religious Programs—Tel: 610-853-1499.
Students 350.
Convent—1201 Burmont Rd., 19026. Tel: 610-789-4112.

East Goshen, Chester Co., SS. Peter and Paul (1967), Revs. James J. Foley; Louis D. Kovacs, Pastor Emeritus; Joseph W. Dragon; Deacons Arthur G. Harrison; Thomas J. Horan; Robert J. Kefer.
Res., 1325 Boot Rd., West Chester, 19380. Tel: 610-692-2216; Fax: 610-692-7103.
Catechesis/Religious Programs—Tel: 610-692-5886.
Students 740.

East Greenville, Montgomery Co., St. Philip Neri (1919), Revs. John J. Scarcia; Edmond J. Speitel, Pastor Emeritus.
Res., 1325 Klinerd Rd., Pennsburg, 18073. Tel: 215-679-9275; 679-9330; Fax: 215-679-0386. [CEM]
School—Sixth & Washington Sts., 18041. Tel: 215-679-7481; Fax: 215-679-8370.
Students 144.
Catechesis/Religious Programs—Students 262.

East Lansdowne, Delaware Co., St. Cyril of Alexandria (1928), Revs. Peter D. Burke; Donald J. Farrell, Pastor Emeritus.
Res., 153 Penn Blvd., 19050-2698. Tel: 610-623-5160; Fax: 610-622-2479.
School—716 Emerson Ave., 19050. Tel: 610-623-1113.
Sisters, Servants of the Immaculate Heart of Mary 3; Lay Teachers 12; Students 344.
Catechesis/Religious Programs—19050. Tel: 610-623-1406.
Students 225.
Convent—171 Penn Blvd., 19050. Tel: 610-623-6590.

Eddystone, Delaware Co., St. Rose of Lima (1890), Revs. Gerald D. Canavan; Charles P. McMullen, Pastor Emeritus.
Res., 1901 Chester Pike, 19013. Tel: 610-876-6170; Fax: 610-876-6128.
School—St. Madeline-St. Rose School. See Consolidated Parish Schools under Institutions Located in the Archdiocese.
Catechesis/Religious Programs—Students 216.

Elkins Park, Montgomery Co., St. James (1923), Rev. Raymond J. Himsworth.
Res., 8320 Brookside Rd., 19027. Tel: 215-635-6210.
School—8304 Brookside Rd., 19027. Tel: 215-635-4673; Fax: 215-635-3521.
Lay Teachers 11; Students 225.

Essington, Delaware Co., St. Margaret Mary Alacoque (1921), Revs. John J. Nevins; Francis J. Cornely, Pastor Emeritus.
Res., 500 Wanamaker Ave., 19029. Tel: 610-521-9177.

Exton, Chester Co., SS. Philip and James (1959), Rev. Michael J. Burke; Rev. Msgr. John J. Caulfield, Pastor Emeritus; Revs. John D. Silcox, Jr.; Quan Tran; Deacons Frank M. Bizal; Charles W. Polley, Jr. In res., Rev. Samuel A. Verruni, Chap.
Res., 107 N. Ship Rd., 19341. Tel: 610-363-6536; Fax: 610-524-7359.
School—721 N. Ship Rd., 19341. Tel: 610-363-6530. Sr. Marita Shaun, I.H.M., Prin.
Sisters, Servants of the Immaculate Heart of Mary 4; Lay Teachers 20; Students 663.
Catechesis/Religious Programs—Tel: 610-363-1307. Sr. Eunice Marie, I.H.M., D.R.E.
Students 527.
Convent—105 N. Ship Rd., 19341. Tel: 610-363-7068.

Fairless Hills, Bucks Co., St. Frances Cabrini (1952), Rev. Msgr. John J. Miller; Rev. Leo P. Oswald.
Res., 325 S. Oxford Valley Rd., 19030. Tel: 215-946-4040; 943-1116.
School—10 Goble Ct., 19030. Tel: 215-946-6334.
Lay Teachers 21; Students 420.
Catechesis/Religious Programs—Tel: 215-946-1115.
Students 320.

Fallsington, Bucks Co., St. Joseph the Worker (1956), Rev. John J. Foster. In res., Most Rev. John J. Graham, (Retired).
Res., 9172 New Falls Rd., 19054. Tel: 215-945-4486; Fax: 215-945-3292.
School—9160 New Falls Rd., 19054. Tel: 215-945-4312; Fax: 215-945-8733.
Lay Teachers 14; Students 232.
Catechesis/Religious Programs—Tel: 215-945-4680.
Students 212.

Feasterville, Bucks Co., Assumption B.V.M. (1950), Revs. Daniel P. Devine; Albert T. Kostelnick; Charles J. Noone. Pastoral Assocs.: Sr. Diane Wolf, S.S.J.; Sr. Madeline Dolores, I.H.M. In res., Rev. Robert H. Roedel.
Res., 1900 Meadowbrook Rd., 19053. Tel: 215-357-1221; Fax: 215-357-2283.
School—Tel: 215-357-5499.
Sisters, Servants of the Immaculate Heart of Mary 4; Lay Teachers 19; Students 476.
Catechesis/Religious Programs—Tel: 215-357-3445. Sr. Kathryn Benham, I.H.M., D.R.E.
Students 340.

Convent—55 Bristol Rd., 19053. Tel: 215-355-3898.

Flourtown, Montgomery Co., St. Genevieve (1953), Revs. Joseph A. Duffey, O.S.A.; William A. Recchuti, O.S.A. In res., Rev. John P. Hennessy, O.S.A.; Deacon Joseph Manson.
Res., 1225 Bethlehem Pike, 19031. Tel: 215-836-2828; Fax: 215-836-7218.
School—1237 Bethlehem Pike, 19031. Tel: 215-836-5644; Fax: 215-836-0159.
Sisters of St. Joseph 4; Lay Teachers 16; Students 240.
Catechesis/Religious Programs—Students 167.
Convent—1301 Bethlehem Pk., 19031. Tel: 215-233-4392.

Gladwyne, Montgomery Co., St. John Baptist Vianney (1927), Rev. John P. Gallagher. Pastor Emeriti: Revs. Ignatius C. Reynolds; Martin J. O'Halloran; Deacon Paul Kern.
Res., 1110 Vaughans Ln., 19035. Tel: 610-642-0938.

Glenolden, Delaware Co., St. George (1923), Rev. Michael P. McCormac.
Res., 22 E. Cooke Ave., 19036-1497. Tel: 610-237-1633; Fax: 610-237-9626.
School—Glen & Lamont Aves., 19036-1497. Tel: 610-583-0419.
Sisters 1; Lay Teachers 8; Students 208.
Catechesis/Religious Programs—Tel: 610-583-2460.
Students 287.
Convent—11 E. Lamont Ave., 19036-1497. Tel: 610-583-5160.

Glenside, Montgomery Co., St. Luke the Evangelist (1905), Revs. J. Michael Flood; Joseph T. Murphy; Dennis G. Van Thuyne. In res., Rev. Daniel J. Kearns.
Res., 2316 Fairhill Ave., 19038. Tel: 215-572-0128; Fax: 215-572-0482.
School—2336 Fairhill Ave., 19038. Tel: 215-884-0843; Fax: 215-884-4607. Sr. Helen Frederick, S.S.J., Prin.
Sisters of St. Joseph 4; Lay Teachers 23; Students 457.
Catechesis/Religious Programs—Tel: 215-884-2080. Mary Jane Dean, D.R.E.
Students 230.
Convent—2324 Fairhill Ave., 19038. Tel: 215-884-0225.

Hatboro, Montgomery Co., St. John Bosco (1953), Revs. Joseph D. Dougherty; Louis J. Kolenkiewicz.
Res., 235 E. County Line Rd., 19040. Tel: 215-672-7280.
School—215 E. County Line Rd., 19040-1298. Tel: 215-675-1484.
Sisters, Servants of the Immaculate Heart of Mary 3; Lay Teachers 8; Students 227.
Catechesis/Religious Programs—Students 315.
Convent—189 E. County Line Rd., 19040. Tel: 215-675-2301.

Hatfield, Montgomery Co., St. Maria Goretti (1953), Revs. Leonard N. Peterson; Vincent Pham The Tung; Edward A. Windhaus.
Res., 1601 Derstine Rd., 19440. Tel: 215-721-0199; Fax: 215-721-4320.
School—Hatfield Valley Rd., 19440. Tel: 215-721-9098.
Sisters, Servants of the Immaculate Heart of Mary 4; Lay Teachers 10; Students 305.
Catechesis/Religious Programs—Tel: 215-368-0669.
Students 608.
Convent—Cowpath Rd., 19440. Tel: 215-368-1190.

Havertown, Delaware Co., St. Denis (1825), Revs. Joseph T. Marino; Kenneth W. Sharp; Deacons John F. Schlegel; David B. Schaffer.
Res., 2401 St. Denis Ln., 19083. Tel: 610-446-0200; Fax: 610-446-4638. [CEM]
School—300 E. Eagle Rd., 19083. Tel: 610-446-4608.
Sisters of Mercy 2; Lay Teachers 30; Students 550.
Catechesis/Religious Programs—Tel: 610-449-7892.
Students 253.
Convent—Tel: 610-446-1263.

Highland Park, Delaware Co., St. Laurence (1917), Rev. Msgr. Thomas J. Herron; Revs. A. Jason Kulczynski; William S. Lange.
Res., 30 St. Laurence Rd., Upper Darby, 19082. Tel: 610-449-0600; 0601; Fax: 610-449-4299.
School—8245 W. Chester Pike, 19082. Tel: 610-789-2670.
Sisters, Servants of the Immaculate Heart of Mary 3; Lay Teachers 21; Students 554.
Catechesis/Religious Programs—Students 303.
Convent—Tel: 610-449-7042.

Hilltown, Bucks Co., Our Lady of the Sacred Heart (1919), Rev. John F. McBride. In res., Rev. James P. Olson, M.A.
Res., Rte. 152 & Broad St., 18927. Tel: 215-822-9224; Fax: 215-822-9102. [CEM]
School—St. Agnes-Sacred Heart School. See Consolidated Parish Schools under Institutions Located in the Archdiocese.
Catechesis/Religious Programs—Tel: 215-822-9020.
Students 385.

Holland, Bucks Co., St. Bede the Venerable (1966), Revs. Eugene G. Cusick; Gary Pacitti; Thomas J. Furey.
Res., 1054 Holland Rd., 18966. Tel: 215-357-5720; Fax: 215-396-0704.
School—1053 Holland Rd., 18966. Tel: 215-357-4720.
Sisters of St. Casimir 2; Lay Teachers 20; Students 471.
Catechesis/Religious Programs—Tel: 215-357-2130.
Students 752.
Convent—1071 Holland Rd., 18966. Tel: 215-355-2132.

Honey Brook, Chester Co., St. Peter (1963), Rev. William J. Cox.
Res., 1080 N. Manor Rd., 19344-9608. Tel: 610-942-2112.
Catechesis/Religious Programs—Tel: 610-942-4518.
Students 466.

Horsham, Montgomery Co., St. Catherine of Siena (1963), Revs. Henry J. Smyth; James E. Goerner; Deacons Timothy Urbanski; Richard Haddon.
Res., 321 Witmer Rd., 19044. Tel: 215-672-2881; 674-1025.
School—317 Witmer Rd., 19044. Tel: 215-674-1904; Fax: 215-674-1466.
Sisters of Mercy 1; Lay Teachers 21; Students 376.
Catechesis/Religious Programs—Tel: 215-674-8549.
Students 650.
Convent—319 Witmer Rd., 19044. Tel: 215-672-7221.

Huntingdon Valley, Montgomery Co., St. Albert the Great (1962), Rev. Msgr. Paul F. Curran; Rev. John J. Kelly; Sr. Maria Rachfalski, O.S.F., Parish Services Dir.
Res., 212 Welsh Rd., 19006. Tel: 215-947-3500; Fax: 215-938-9071.
School—216 Welsh Rd., 19006. Tel: 215-947-2332. Mary Randles, Prin.
Lay Teachers 21; Students 540.
Catechesis/Religious Programs—Students 215.

Jamison, Bucks Co., St. Cyril of Jerusalem (1965), Rev. Robert J. Powell, D.M.A., M.A., M.Div.; Deacon Joseph Windish. In res., Rev. Robert W. Povish, M.A.
Res., 1410 Almshouse Rd., 18929. Tel: 215-343-1288; Fax: 215-343-3924.
Catechesis/Religious Programs—Tel: 215-343-3139.
Students 490.

Jenkintown, Montgomery Co., Immaculate Conception (1866), Revs. John J. Conahan; Francis J. Gallagher; Deacon Paul Hagerty.
Res., 604 West Ave., 19046. Tel: 215-884-4022; 887-0181; Fax: 215-887-4163.
School—606 West Ave., 19046. Tel: 215-887-1312.
Lay Teachers 15; Students 218.
Catechesis/Religious Programs—Tel: 215-885-5586.
Students 285.

Kennett Square, Chester Co., St. Patrick (1869), Revs. Victor F. Sharrett; Daniel J. Dougherty; Deacon James K. Madonna.
Res., 218 S. Meredith St., 19348. Tel: 610-444-2128; Fax: 610-444-4941. [CEM]
Parish Office: 212 Meredith St., 19348. Tel: 610-444-4364; Fax: 610-444-2129.
School—210 Meredith St., 19348. Tel: 610-444-3104; Fax: 610-444-3166.
Lay Teachers 10; Students 193.
Catechesis/Religious Programs—Tel: 610-444-2214. Mrs. Patricia Lohr, D.R.E.
Students 305.

Kimberton, Chester Co., St. Basil the Great (1965), Rev. Msgr. Joseph A. Shields. In res., Rev. William E. Grogan.
Res., Kimberton Rd. off Rte. 113, Box 637, 19442-0637. Tel: 610-933-2110; 933-4730; Fax: 610-933-0627.
School—Tel: 610-933-2453.
Lay Teachers 12; Students 300.
Catechesis/Religious Programs—Tel: 610-935-1261.
Students 236.
Convent—Tel: 610-933-2345. Sisters of St. Francis Residence

King of Prussia, Montgomery Co., Mother of Divine Providence (1954), Revs. Thomas P. Gaynard; William J. Dougherty; Francis G. Marszalek.
Res., 333 Allendale Rd., 19406. Tel: 610-265-4178; Fax: 610-265-1653.
School—405 Allendale Rd., 19406. Tel: 610-265-2323.
Grey Nuns of the Sacred Heart 2; Lay Teachers 15; Students 319.
Catechesis/Religious Programs—Tel: 610-337-2173.
Students 347.
Convent—Tel: 610-278-9439.

Lafayette Hill, Montgomery Co., St. Philip Neri (1945), Rev. Msgr. Richard T. LaHart; Rev. Edward J. Kelly.
Res., 437 Ridge Pike, 19444. Tel: 610-828-5717; 834-1975; Fax: 610-834-0392.
School—3015 Chestnut St., 19444. Tel: 610-828-3082; Fax: 610-828-2943.
Sisters of St. Joseph 8; Lay Teachers 19; Students 448.
Catechesis/Religious Programs—Students 131.
Convent—Tel: 610-828-2866.

Lansdale, Montgomery Co., St. Stanislaus (1876), Rev. Msgr. Joseph W. Murray; Revs. Francis J. Bartos; John B. Flanagan; Stephen A. Moerman; Rev. Msgr. Paul J. Cahill, Pastor Emeritus; Deacons Mathieu Tielemans; C. Stephens Vondercrone.
Res., 51 Lansdale Ave., 19446. Tel: 215-855-3133; Fax: 215-855-5478. [CEM]
School—493 E. Main St., 19446. Tel: 215-368-0995; Fax: 215-393-4869. Diane McCaughan, Prin.; Mrs. Barbara Kelly, Asst. Prin.
Lay Teachers 35; Students 791.
Catechesis/Religious Programs—Tel: 215-855-9893.
Students 403.

Lansdowne, Delaware Co., St. Philomena (1898), Revs. Robert J. Chapman; Thomas J. Dempsey, Pastor Emeritus.
Res., 41 E. Baltimore Ave., 19050. Tel: 610-622-2420; Fax: 610-622-1215.
School—21 N. Highland Ave., 19050. Tel: 610-259-6817. Mrs. Mary Calderone, Prin.
Lay Teachers 9; Students 242.

Lenni, Delaware Co., St. Francis de Sales, Revs. Charles P. Vance; Joseph E. Walsh, Pastor Emeritus.
Res., 35 New Rd., P.O. Box 97, 19052. Tel: 610-459-2203. [CEM]
School—Tel: 610-459-0799.
Sisters of St. Francis of Philadelphia 2; Lay Teachers 9; Students 188.
Convent—28 New Rd., Aston, 19014. Tel: 610-459-2501.
Stations—Delaware County Home.; Fair Acres Farm.; Sleighton School.

Levittown, Bucks Co., Immaculate Conception B.V.M. (1954), Revs. James J. Bones; John Mulholland.
Res., 5201 Emilie Rd., 19057-2505. Tel: 215-946-1638; 1639; Fax: 215-946-2149.
School—3810 Oxford Valley Rd., 19057. Tel: 215-949-2848.
Sisters, Servants of the Immaculate Heart of Mary 2; Lay Teachers 15; Students 396.
Catechesis/Religious Programs—Tel: 215-945-0826.
Students 225.
Convent—Tel: 215-945-4664.

St. Michael the Archangel (1953), Rev. Msgr. Richard T. Powers; Revs. Luke L. Chow; Francis X. Trauger; Joseph N. Accardi.
Res., 66 Levittown Pkwy., 19054. Tel: 215-945-1166; Fax: 215-945-6988.
School—130 Levittown Pkwy., 19054. Tel: 215-943-0222; Fax: 215-943-9068.
Lay Teachers 33; Students 820.
Catechesis/Religious Programs—Tel: 215-547-2518.
Students 409.
Convent—88 Levittown Pkwy., 19054. Tel: 215-943-8232.

Queen of the Universe (1955), Revs. Paul A. Wiedmann; Thomas A. McCann; Rev. Msgr. James A. Coyle, Pastor Emeritus; Deacon Joseph Upcavage. In res., Rev. Henry E. Dougherty.
Res., 2443 Trenton Rd., 19056. Tel: 215-945-8750; Fax: 215-945-0413.
School—Tel: 215-945-1866.
Sisters of St. Joseph 3; Lay Teachers 11; Students 309.
Catechesis/Religious Programs—Tel: 215-945-2704.
Students 509.
Convent—Tel: 215-945-6116.

Linfield, Montgomery Co., St. Clare (1963), Rev. Thomas J. Duffy.
Res., 228 Main St., 19468-1020. Tel: 610-495-7263.

Linwood, Delaware Co., Holy Saviour (1915), Rev. Thomas P. McKelvey.
Res., 108 E. Ridge Rd., 19061. Tel: 610-485-2520; 2521.

School—Holy Saviour-St. John Fisher School. See Consolidated Parish Schools under Institutions Located in the Achdiocese. Judith Ann Devine, B.A., M.A., Prin.
Catechesis/Religious Programs—Students 136.
Convent—122 E. Ridge Rd., 19061. Tel: 610-485-7320.

Lower Makefield, Bucks Co., St. John the Evangelist (1964), Rev. Msgr. William J. Paul; Rev. Edward H. Bell; Deacon James E. Hartman.
Res., 752 Big Oak Rd., Morrisville, 19067. Tel: 215-295-4102; Fax: 215-295-3128.
School—728 Big Oak Rd., Morrisville, 19067. Tel: 215-295-0629; Fax: 215-295-6258.
Bernardine Sisters of St. Francis 1; Lay Teachers 12; Students 258.
Catechesis/Religious Programs—Tel: 215-295-9239.
Students 637.
Convent—Tel: 215-295-8201.

Malvern, Chester Co., St. Patrick (1915), Revs. James J. Ambrogi; Joseph G. Watson; Francis N. McDevitt, Pastor Emeritus; Deacon Lawrence P. Froio.
Res., 104 Channing Ave., 19355. Tel: 610-647-2345; Fax: 610-647-4997.
School—115 Channing Ave., 19355. Tel: 610-644-5797.
Catechesis/Religious Programs—Tel: 610-296-8899.
Students 520.

Manoa, Delaware Co., Sacred Heart (1927), Revs. George J. Boyle; James J. Whelan; Deacons John J. Suplee; Thomas J. Woods. Pastor Emeriti: Rev. Msgr. James McGrath; Rev. Msgr. Thomas B. Falls. In res., Rev. Joseph Duncan.
Res., 105 Wilson Ave., Havertown, 19083. Tel: 610-449-3000; Fax: 610-449-2364.
School—Tel: 610-446-9198.
Sisters, Servants of the Immaculate Heart of Mary 2; Lay Teachers 13; Students 298.
Catechesis/Religious Programs—Tel: 610-446-7597. Eileen V. Lynch, D.R.E.
Students 315.
Convent—108 Shelbourne Rd., 19083. Tel: 610-446-3694.

Maple Glen, Montgomery Co., St. Alphonsus (1963), Revs. Wilfred F. Maloney; J. Jerome Wild; Thomas J. Kelly, Pastor Emeritus.
Res., 33 Conwell Dr., 19002. Tel: 215-646-4600; Fax: 215-646-0180.
School—29 Conwell Dr., 19002. Tel: 215-646-0150.
Lay Teachers 24; Students 407.
Catechesis/Religious Programs—Tel: 215-643-7938.
Students 271.
Convent—1563 Temple Dr., 19002. Tel: 215-646-6644.

Marcus Hook, Delaware Co., Immaculate Conception (1917) (Italian), Rev. Joseph A. Amalfitano.
Res., 21 W. Eighth St., P.O. Box 355, 19061. Tel: 610-485-1026.

Media, Delaware Co., St. Mary Magdalen (1963), Revs. James F. Hughes; Jonathan U. Mbah, C.S.Sp.; Deacon E. Peter Zurbach.
Res., 2400 N. Providence Rd., 19063. Tel: 610-566-8821; Fax: 610-566-1005.
School—2430 N. Providence Rd., 19063. Tel: 610-565-1822; Fax: 610-627-9670.
Lay Teachers 20; Students 395.
Catechesis/Religious Programs—Tel: 610-565-5782.
Students 170.

Nativity of the Blessed Virgin Mary (1868), Revs. Francis A. Giliberti; Peter J. DiMaria; James F. Bradley, Pastor Emeritus. In res., Rev. Joseph J. Kennedy, Pastor Emeritus.
Res., 30 E. Franklin St., 19063. Tel: 610-566-0185. [CEM]
School—Gayley St., 19063. Tel: 610-566-6881.
Servants of the Most Sacred Heart of Jesus 5; Lay Teachers 7; Students 210.
Catechesis/Religious Programs—Students 330.
Convent—Tel: 610-565-8399.

Milmont Park, Delaware Co., Our Lady of Peace (1922), Revs. Charles M. O'Rourke; David W. Givey.
Res., 501 Belmont Ave., 19033. Tel: 610-532-8081; 8082.
School—200 Milmont Ave., 19033. Tel: 610-534-0689. Sr. Denise Clifford, S.S.J., Prin.
Sisters of St. Joseph 4; Lay Teachers 11; Students 272.
Catechesis/Religious Programs—Students 302.
Convent—Tel: 610-532-4699.

Morrisville, Bucks Co., Holy Trinity, Rev. John C. Eckert.
Res., 201 N. Pennsylvania Ave., 19067. Tel: 215-295-3045. [CEM]
School—Osborne Ave. & Stockham Ave., 19067. Tel: 215-295-6900. Mrs. Barbara Nuzzolo, Prin.
Lay Teachers 11; Students 288.

Morton, Delaware Co., Our Lady of Perpetual Help (1907), Rev. Msgr. Richard J. Skelly; Rev. Timothy F. O'Sullivan. In res., Rev. Msgr. Joseph P. McFadden.
Res., O.L.P.H. Ct., 2130 Franklin Ave., 19070. Tel: 610-543-1046; Fax: 610-543-6150.
School—#5 O.L.P.H. Ct., 2130 Franklin Ave., 19070. Tel: 610-543-8350.
Sisters of St. Francis of Philadelphia 2; Lay Teachers 19; Students 402.
Catechesis/Religious Programs—Tel: 610-543-5448.
Students 390.
Convent—#3 O.L.P.H. Ct., 2130 Franklin Ave., 19070. Tel: 610-543-0186.

Narberth, Montgomery Co., St. Margaret (1900), Rev. Msgr. James J. Flood; Rev. John E. Fitzgerald. In res., Rev. Stephen J. Dougherty.
Res., 208 N. Narberth Ave., 19072. Tel: 610-664-3770.
School—227 N. Narberth Ave., 19072. Tel: 610-664-2640; Fax: 610-664-4677.
Sisters of Mercy 1; Lay Teachers 14; Students 250.
Catechesis/Religious Programs—Tel: 610-664-5715. Ms. Mary Katherine Roach, D.R.E.
Students 146.
Convent—301 Windsor Ave., 19072. Tel: 610-664-2748.

New Garden Township, Chester Co., St. Gabriel of the Sorrowful Mother (1988), Rev. Richard J. Maisano. Mailing Address: P.O. Box 709, Avondale, 19311. Tel: 610-268-0296; Fax: 610-268-5022.
Catechesis/Religious Programs—Students 170.

New Hope, Bucks Co., St. Martin of Tours (1885), Revs. John P. Schmeer; Paul J. Carey, Pastor Emeritus.
Res., 111 New St., 18938. Tel: 215-862-5472; Fax: 215-862-1829. [CEM]
Catechesis/Religious Programs—Students 159.

Newtown, Bucks Co., St. Andrew (1880), Revs. Michael C. Picard; J. Brian Bransfield; Edward T. Kearns. In res., Rev. John P. Paul.
Res., 81 Swamp Rd., 18940. Tel: 215-968-2262; Fax: 215-579-9344. [CEM]
School—51 Wrights Rd., 18940. Tel: 215-968-2685; Fax: 215-968-4795.
Preschool—138 S. Sycamore St., 18940. Tel: 215-968-3464; Fax: 215-968-8606.
Sisters, Servants of the Immaculate Heart of Mary 6; Lay Teachers 40; Students 900.
Catechesis/Religious Programs—Tel: 215-968-6929.
Students 975.
Convent—Tel: 215-968-6568.

Newtown Square, Delaware Co., St. Anastasia (1912), Revs. John J. Shellem; Michael A. Colagreco; Dennis L. Sullivan, T.O.R.; Rev. Msgr. Richard J. Simons, Pastor Emeritus. In res., Rev. Joseph F. Rymdeika.
Res., 3301 W. Chester Pike, 19073. Tel: 610-356-1613; Fax: 610-356-8332.
School—Tel: 610-356-6225.
Sisters of St. Joseph 4; Lay Teachers 30; Students 648.
Catechesis/Religious Programs—Tel: 610-356-5069.
Students 420.
Convent—3305 W. Chester Pike, 19073. Tel: 610-356-0273.

Norristown, Montgomery Co.,

1—Epiphany of Our Lord, (1957), Revs. James F. Baldrick; Patrick G. McCormick; Deacons William R. Radetzky; Kenneth P. Clancy; Joel M. Ziff. In res., Rev. Joseph P. Gentili.
Res., 3050 Walton Rd., 19401. Tel: 610-828-8634; Fax: 610-828-1802.
School—3040 Walton Rd., 19401. Tel: 610-825-0160.
Lay Teachers 12; Students 221.
Catechesis/Religious Programs—Tel: 610-825-6790. Mrs. Julia Noble, D.R.E.
Students 325.

2—St. Francis of Assisi, (1923), Rev. Msgr. Jerry Duraczynski; Revs. George P. Ettorre; Kevin C. Trautner; Lee J. Makowski, O.S.A.; Sr. Mary Jane Dunleavy, S.S.J., Pastoral Assoc. In res., Rev. Dominick F. Finn, O.S.F.S.
Res., 600 Hamilton St., 19401. Tel: 610-272-0402; Fax: 610-272-1794.
School—Oak & Buttonwood Sts., 19401. Tel: 610-272-0501; Fax: 610-272-8011.
Sisters of St. Joseph 2; Lay Teachers 14; Students 352.
Catechesis/Religious Programs—Students 165.
Convent—Tel: 610-272-3686.

3—Holy Saviour, (1903) (Italian), Rev. Msgr. Arthur J. Centrella; Revs. Louis P. Bellopede; Anthony J. Cossavella; Rev. Msgr. John J. Busco, Pastor Emeritus; Deacons John Parker; Donald Kretsch.
Res., 407 E. Main St., 19401. Tel: 610-275-0958; Fax: 610-275-8464.
School—Airy & Walnut Sts., 19401. Tel: 610-272-8864.
Lay Teachers 12; Students 240.
Catechesis/Religious Programs—Students 292.
Mission—Black Horse, Montgomery Co., Our Lady of Mount Carmel, 460 Fairfield Rd., 19401. Tel: 610-277-7739. [CEM]

4—St. Patrick, (1835), Rev. Louis C. Bier; Deacon Ismael Fuentes Cintron. In res., Rev. James T. McGuinn.
Res., 714 DeKalb St., 19401. Tel: 610-272-1408; Fax: 610-275-0238. [CEM]
Religious Education Building: Chestnut & Green Sts., 19401. Tel: 610-272-4500.
Convent—630 DeKalb St., 19401. Tel: 610-277-5962. Missionaries of Charity

5—St. Paul, (1963), Rev. Harry E. McCreedy; Deacon Michael Dayoc. In res., Revs. Henry B. Degnan; Walter Duraczynski (SFS).
Res., 2007 New Hope St., 19401. Tel: 610-279-6725; Fax: 610-275-6771.
School—351 E. Johnson Hwy., 19401. Tel: 610-275-2990; Fax: 610-275-0470.
Lay Teachers 12; Students 224.

6—St. Titus, (1962), Rev. Robert E. Brennan. In res., Rev. Joseph W. Bongard; Rev. Msgr. Thomas J. Scanlon.
Res., 3006 Keenwood Rd., 19403. Tel: 610-279-4990; Fax: 610-279-8640.
School—Keenwood Rd. & Norriton Dr., 19403. Tel: 610-279-6043.
Bernardine Sisters of St. Francis of Philadelphia 1; Lay Teachers 16; Students 370.
Convent—Tel: 610-279-3111.

North Wales, Montgomery Co., Mary, Mother of the Redeemer (1987), Revs. Philip C. Ricci; Harry G. Richards.
Res., 1325 Upper State Rd., 19454. Tel: 215-362-7400; 362-8966; Fax: 215-362-4127.
Catechesis/Religious Programs—Students 705.

St. Rose of Lima (1919), Rev. John P. Boland. In res., Rev. Msgr. James J. Graham; Rev. Gerald S. Smith; Deacon Edward A. Konarski.
Res., 428 S. Main St., 19454-3224. Tel: 215-699-4617; Fax: 215-699-4452.
School—425 W. Pennsylvania Ave., 19454-3498. Tel: 215-699-8831; Fax: 215-661-1691.
Lay Teachers 20; Students 235.
Catechesis/Religious Programs—Students 369.

Norwood, Delaware Co., St. Gabriel (1891), Revs. Daniel M. Dooley; John J. Large; Gerardo M. Caruso; Joseph J. Blanchfield, Pastor Emeritus.
Res., 233 Mohawk Ave., 19074. Tel: 610-586-1225.
School—Cleveland Ave., Tel: 610-532-3234.
Lay Teachers 18; Students 440.
Catechesis/Religious Programs—Tel: 610-534-7709.
Students 580.

Oreland, Montgomery Co., Holy Martyrs (1949), Rev. David A. Doyne. In res., Revs. Raymond F. Tribuiani; Ignatius J. Szal, Pastor Emeritus.
Res., 120 Allison Rd., 19075. Tel: 215-884-8575; Fax: 215-884-5924.
School—121 Allison Rd., 19075. Tel: 215-887-2044. Catherine C. McGough, Prin.
Lay Teachers 12; Students 173.
Preschool—207 Ulmer Ave., 19075. Tel: 215-572-8605.
Catechesis/Religious Programs—Students 192.

Ottsville, Bucks Co., St. John the Baptist (1743), Rev. Joseph Tobias, M.S.C.; Deacons Ernest D'Angelo; John O'Brien.
Res., 4050 Durham Rd., 18942. Tel: 610-847-5521. [CEM]
School—Tel: 610-847-5523; Fax: 610-847-5523.
Lay Teachers 13; Students 219.
Catechesis/Religious Programs—Tel: 610-847-5522.
Students 181.
Mission—Upper Black Eddy, Bucks Co., St. Joseph, Marienstein Rd., Upper Black Eddy, 18972.

Oxford, Chester Co., Sacred Heart (1914), Rev. William B. Dooner; Deacon Francis Murphy.
Res., 203 Church Rd., 19363. Tel: 610-932-5040.
Catechesis/Religious Programs—Students 417.

Paoli, Chester Co., St. Norbert (1956), Revs. Domenic A. Rossi, O.Praem.; Nicholas R. Terico, O.Praem.; Walter J. Burke, O.Praem, Pastor Emeritus.
Res., 78 Leopard Rd., 19301. Tel: 610-644-1655; Fax: 610-644-1928.
School—Greenlawn & Leopard Rds., 19301. Tel: 610-644-1670; Fax: 610-644-0201.
Grey Nuns of the Sacred Heart 2; Lay Teachers 14; Students 278.
Catechesis/Religious Programs—Tel: 610-664-1342.
Students 247.
Convent—Tel: 610-644-1576.

Parkesburg, Chester Co., Our Lady of Consolation (1853), Revs. Victor J. Eschbach; George P. Schneider, Pastor Emeritus. In res., Rev. John Van De Paer, C.I.C.M.
Res., 603 Second Ave., 19365. Tel: 610-857-3510; Fax: 610-857-2353. [CEM]
School—Coatesville Area Catholic Elementary School. See Consolidated Parish Schools under Institutions Located in the Archdiocese.
Catechesis/Religious Programs—10 Cemetery Rd., 19365. Tel: 610-857-1003.
Students 450.
Mission—Doe Run, Chester Co., St. Malachy. [CEM]

Penndel, Bucks Co., Our Lady of Grace (1908), Revs. Robert J. Conner; Robert A. Roncase; William J. Teverzczuk.
Res., 225 Bellevue Ave., 19047. Tel: 215-757-7700; 757-7786; Fax: 215-757-5377. [CEM]
School—300 Hulmeville Ave., 19047. Tel: 215-757-5287.
Sisters, Servants of the Immaculate Heart of Mary 3; Lay Teachers 21; Students 572.
Catechesis/Religious Programs—Tel: 215-757-5530.
Students 571.
Convent—338 Hulmeville Ave., 19047. Tel: 215-757-2272.

Penn Valley, Montgomery Co., St. Justin Martyr (1964), Rev. John B. De Mayo. In res., Rev. Thomas J. Wisniewski.
Res., 1222 Hagysford Rd., Narberth, 19072. Tel: 610-664-0165; Fax: 610-664-5612.

Phoenixville, Chester Co.,

1—St. Ann, (1907), Revs. John J. Newns; Michael G. Murtha.
Res., 502 Main St., 19460. Tel: 610-933-3732; Fax: 610-935-7958. [CEM]
School—Holy Family School. See Consolidated Parish Schools under Institutions Located in the Archdiocese.
Lay Teachers 15; Students 340.
Catechesis/Religious Programs—Tel: 610-933-9350; Fax: 610-935-7958.
Students 212.
Parish Center—602 S. Main St., 19460.

2—Holy Trinity, (Polish), Rev. Joseph A. Daniel.
Res., 219 Dayton St., 19460. Tel: 610-933-3023. [CEM]
School—Holy Family School. See Consolidated Parish Schools under Institutions Located in the Archdiocese.
Convent—221 Dayton St., 19460. Tel: 610-983-9446. Bernardine Sisters of the Third Order of St. Francis

3—St. Mary of the Assumption, (1840), Rev. John C. Wilz.
Res., 212 Dayton St., 19460. Tel: 610-933-2526; Fax: 610-935-1706. [CEM 2]
School—Holy Family School. See Consolidated Parish Schools under Institutions Located in the Archdiocese.

4—Sacred Heart, (1900) (Slovak), Rev. Msgr. John M. Galyo.
Res., 148 Church St., 19460. Tel: 610-933-3830. [CEM]
School—Holy Family School. See Consolidated Parish Schools under Institutions Located in the Archdiocese.

Pottstown, Montgomery Co., St. Aloysius (1856), Revs. John F. McCole; Dominic Tran Minh Duc; Edward J. Jablonski.
Res., 214 N. Hanover St., 19464. Tel: 610-326-5877; Fax: 610-326-0901. [CEM 2]
School—Third & Hanover Sts., 19464. Tel: 610-326-6167.
Sisters of St. Francis of Philadelphia 2; Lay Teachers 20; Students 480.
Catechesis/Religious Programs—Tel: 610-970-0675.
Students 366.
Convent—223 Beech St., 19464. Tel: 610-326-1498.

Holy Trinity (1899) (Slovak), Rev. Msgr. John M. Galyo, Admin.; Rev. Andrew L. Slafkosky, Pastor Emeritus.
Res., 370 South St., 19464. Tel: 610-326-2432. [CEM]

St. Peter (1924) (Polish), Rev. Edward P. Kuczynski.
Res., 1128 South St., 19464. Tel: 610-326-5023.
School—1126 South St., 19464. Tel: 215-323-6730; Fax: 215-323-6730.
Bernardine Sisters of St. Francis 1; Lay Teachers 9; Students 200.
Convent—1124 South St., 19464. Tel: 610-323-9378.

Primos, Delaware Co., St. Eugene (1955), Rev. Joseph J. Meehan. In res., Rev. Joseph C. Bordonaro.
Res., 200 Oak Ave., 19018. Tel: 610-626-2866; Fax: 610-626-1904.
School—110 Oak Ave., 19018. Tel: 610-622-2909.
Lay Teachers 9; Students 241.
Catechesis/Religious Programs—Students 185.

Quakertown, Bucks Co., St. Isidore (1886), Revs. Henry C. Graf; Thomas J. Brennan.
Res., 531 W. Broad St., 18951. Tel: 215-536-4389. [CEM]
School—603 W. Broad St., Tel: 215-536-6052; Fax: 215-536-8647.
Lay Teachers 13; Students 265.
Catechesis/Religious Programs—Students 450.

Richboro, Bucks Co., St. Vincent de Paul (1968), Revs. Joseph J. McLaughlin; John D. Gabin; William T. McBride, Pastor Emeritus.
Res., 654 Hatboro Rd., 18954-1039. Tel: 215-357-5905; Fax: 215-953-8190.
Catechesis/Religious Programs—Tel: 215-322-1932.
Students 595.

Ridley Park, Delaware Co., St. Madeline, Revs. Daniel J. Cavanaugh; Gavin W. Muir; Anthony C. Rodo.
Res., 110 Park St., 19078. Tel: 610-532-6880; Fax: 610-532-6653.
School—St. Madeline-St. Rose School. See Consolidated Parish Schools under Institutions Located in the Archdiocese.
Lay Teachers 16; Students 370.
Catechesis/Religious Programs—Students 256.

Riegelsville, Bucks Co., St. Lawrence (1974), Revs. Robert H. Breen; Joseph A. Henry, J.C.D., Pastor Emeritus.
Res., 345 Elmwood Ln., P.O. Box 126, 18077. Tel: 610-749-2684. [JC]

Roslyn, Montgomery Co., St. John of the Cross (1953), Revs. Thomas J. Duane; John J. Kilgallon; Paul C. Brandt.
Res., 2741 Woodland Rd., 19001. Tel: 215-659-4460; Fax: 215-659-2551.
School—2805 Woodland Rd., Tel: 215-659-1365. Sr. Patricia Maureen Mount, I.H.M., Prin.
Sisters, Servants of the Immaculate Heart of Mary 5; Lay Teachers 13; Students 300.
Catechesis/Religious Programs—Tel: 215-659-1451.
Students 212.
Convent—2803 Woodland Rd., Tel: 215-659-4483.

Royersford, Montgomery Co., Sacred Heart (1973), Rev. Thomas F. Doyle; Deacon Michael J. Conroy. In res., Rev. Vincent R. Morabito.
Res., 838 Walnut St., P.O. Box 64, 19468. Tel: 610-948-5915; 948-4087.
School—Area Catholic Elementary School of the Sacred Heart, Lewis Rd. & Washington St., 19468. Tel: 610-948-7206.
Lay Teachers 14; Students 240.
Catechesis/Religious Programs—Tel: 610-792-2997.
Students 400.

Rydal, Montgomery Co., St. Hilary of Poitiers (1962), Rev. Msgr. Michael J. Carroll. In res., Rev. Paul M. Kennedy, M.A.
Res., 820 Susquehanna Rd., 19046. Tel: 215-884-3252.
School—920 Susquehanna Rd., 19046. Tel: 215-887-4520; Fax: 215-887-6337.
Students 248.

Secane, Delaware Co., Our Lady of Fatima (1952), Revs. Engelbert G. Michel; William S. Kirk. In res., Rev. Thomas R. Urian.
Res., 1 Fatima Dr., 19018. Tel: 610-532-5800.
School—10 Fatima Dr., 19018. Tel: 610-586-7539.
Sisters, Servants of the Immaculate Heart of Mary 3; Lay Teachers 14; Students 474.
Catechesis/Religious Programs—Tel: 610-532-7430.
Students 216.
Convent—5 Fatima Dr., 19018. Tel: 610-532-1190.

Sellersville, Bucks Co., St. Agnes (1919), Rev. Msgr. Michael J. Long; Rev. John F. Bowe; Deacon Harry Tucker.
Res., 445 N. Main St., 18960. Tel: 215-257-2128. [CEM]
School—St. Agnes-Sacred Heart School. See Consolidated Parish Schools under Institutions Located in the Archdiocese. Tel: 215-257-3571.
Lay Teachers 22; Students 515.
Catechesis/Religious Programs—Tel: 215-257-1811.
Students 400.

Sharon Hill, Delaware Co., Holy Spirit (1892), Revs. Martin E. Woodeshick; John A. Fitzgibbons; Daniel J. Kehoe, Pastor Emeritus; Deacons Albert Rayner; Thomas Butcavage.
Res., 1028 School St., 19079. Tel: 610-583-2220; Fax: 610-583-5130.
School—1036 School St., 19079. Tel: 610-532-7557; Fax: 610-532-3614.
Lay Teachers 9; Students 238.
Catechesis/Religious Programs—Tel: 610-532-1154.
Students 109.

Southampton, Bucks Co., Our Lady of Good Counsel (1923), Rev. Msgr. Bernard J. Trinity; Revs. Charles H. Hagan; Mark J. Haynes.
Res., 611 Knowles Ave., 18966. Tel: 215-357-1300, Ext. 100; Fax: 215-357-4452.
School—Second St. Pike, 18966. Tel: 215-357-1300, Ext. 101. Mr. Frank Mokriski, Prin.
Lay Teachers 25; Students 645.
Catechesis/Religious Programs—Tel: 215-357-1300, Ext. 126.
Students 533.

South Coventry, Chester Co., St. Thomas More (1968), Rev. Hugh J. Dougherty; Deacon George W. Leonhardt, Jr. In res., Rev. Robert H. Mulligan.
Res., 2101 Pottstown Pike, Pottstown, 19465. Tel: 610-469-9304; Fax: 610-469-9315.
Catechesis/Religious Programs—Tel: 610-469-9302.
Students 318.

Spring City, Chester Co., St. Joseph, Rev. John J. Dinda. In res., Revs. Michael W. Rzonca; Robert I. Riedy, Pastor Emeritus.
Res., 3640 Schuylkill Rd., 19475. Tel: 610-948-7760.

Springfield, Delaware Co., St. Francis of Assisi (1923), Revs. Salvatore M. Riccio; James C. Otto; Deacons James D. Kane, Sr.; Arthur M. McGuire.
Res., 136 Saxer Ave., 19064. Tel: 610-543-0848; Fax: 610-604-0283.
School—112 Saxer Ave., Tel: 610-543-0546.
Lay Teachers 18; Students 375.
Catechesis/Religious Programs—Students 405.

Holy Cross (1948), Revs. Edward B. Cahill; Mark G. Swope; Sr. Antoinette Marie, R.S.M., Pastoral Min. In res., Deacon Robert Frankenberger.
Res., 651 E. Springfield Rd., 19064. Tel: 610-626-3321; Fax: 610-622-2920.
School—Bishop & Springfield Rds., 19064. Tel: 610-626-1709.
Sisters of Mercy 1; Lay Teachers 16; Students 335.
Catechesis/Religious Programs—Tel: 610-543-4892.
Students 245.
Convent—Tel: 610-626-2492.

St. Kevin (1955), Revs. John J. Kane; Philip A. Scully, Pastor Emeritus. In res., Rev. Michael J. Fitzpatrick.
Res., Tel: 610-544-8777; 8778; Fax: 610-544-7832.
School—Tel: 610-544-4455; Fax: 610-544-7092.
Sisters of St. Joseph 10; Lay Teachers 14; Students 353.
Convent—Tel: 610-544-4535.

Stowe, Montgomery Co., St. Gabriel (1929), Revs. James W. Gormley; Patrick A. Duddy, Pastor Emeritus. In res., Rev. James A. Murphy, (Retired). Parish Center: 127 E. Howard St., 19464. Tel: 610-326-5127.
Res., 421 Jefferson St., 19464. Tel: 610-327-2248.

Strafford, Chester Co., Our Lady of the Assumption (1908) (Italian), Revs. Eugene J. Carbo; Daniel J. Hoy. In res., Rev. Msgr. James T. McDonough.
Res., 35 Old Eagle School Rd., 19087. Tel: 610-688-1178; 688-6147; Fax: 610-293-9680. [CEM]
Preschool—135 Fairfield Ln., 19087. Tel: 610-688-5277.
Catechesis/Religious Programs—Tel: 610-688-6590.
Students 170.

Swarthmore, Delaware Co., Notre Dame de Lourdes (1959), Rev. William J. Benonis; Deacons Michael McAndrews; James Basilio. In res., Rev. Joseph L. Maloney.
Res., 950 Michigan Ave., 19081. Tel: 610-544-1270; Fax: 610-544-1271.
School—990 Fairview Rd., 19081. Tel: 610-328-9330.
Lay Teachers 13; Students 325.

Swedesburg, Montgomery Co., Sacred Heart (1907) (Polish), Rev. Joseph J. Zingaro; Rev. Msgr. Anthony E. Jaworowski, (Retired); Deacon T. Eric Makoid.
Res., 120 Jefferson St., 19405. Tel: 610-275-1750; Fax: 610-275-0480.
School—631 E. Fourth St., 19405. Tel: 610-277-4133; Fax: 610-277-4725.
Lay Teachers 12; Students 190.
Parish Center—635 E. Fourth St., 19405.

Trooper, Montgomery Co., Visitation B.V.M. (1954), Rev. Msgr. Francis J. Clemins; Revs. Francis X. Herron; Francis J. Mulranen; Zachary W. Navit. In res., Rev. Henry C. Schuyler.
Res., 196 N. Trooper Rd., Norristown, 19403. Tel: 610-539-5572; Fax: 610-539-3240.
School—N. Trooper Rd., R.D. 1, Norristown, 19403. Tel: 610-539-6080; Fax: 610-630-7946.
Sisters of the Holy Family of Nazareth 4; Lay Teachers 28; Students 777.

Catechesis/Religious Programs—Tel: 610-539-6211. Roseanne Terranova, D.R.E.
Students 776.
Convent—Tel: 610-539-5558.

Upper Darby, Delaware Co., St. Alice (Stonehurst) (1922), Revs. William P. Donnelly; Joseph Tran Kim Thien, Pastoral Assoc.; Rev. Msgr. William A. Doolin, Pastor Emeritus. In res., Revs. John P. Collins; David F. Brackenridge; Matthew Michael (ALX); Deacon Joseph F. Coyle.
Res., 150 Hampden Rd., 19082. Tel: 610-352-1431.
School—135 Copley Rd., 19082. Tel: 610-352-0725.
Sisters, Servants of the Immaculate Heart of Mary 4; Lay Teachers 9; Students 250.
Catechesis/Religious Programs—Students 195.

Upper Gwynedd, Montgomery Co., Corpus Christi (1964), Revs. Thomas P. Flanigan, Ed.D.; Joseph L. Farrell; Francis J. Loughran, Pastor Emeritus. In res., Rev. Martin T. Cioppi.
Res., 900 Sumneytown Pike, Lansdale, 19446. Tel: 215-855-1311; Fax: 215-855-3631.
School—920 Sumneytown Pike, Lansdale, 19466. Tel: 215-368-0582; Fax: 215-361-5927.
Sisters of St. Joseph 7; Lay Teachers 18; Students 575.
Catechesis/Religious Programs—Tel: 215-362-2292. Theresa McHale, D.R.E.
Students 835.
Convent—1622 Supplee Rd., Lansdale, 19446. Tel: 215-368-0737.

Valley Forge, Montgomery Co., St. Teresa of Avila (1918), Revs. Francis E. Kelly; Thomas F. Walsh, Pastor Emeritus. In res., Rev. Michael P. O'Malley, M.A.
Mailing Address: Box 248, 19481. Tel: 610-666-5820; Fax: 610-666-7511.
Res., 1260 S. Trooper Rd., Norristown, 19403.
School—2550 S. Parkview Dr., Norristown, 19403. Tel: 610-666-6069.
Lay Teachers 8; Students 232.
Catechesis/Religious Programs—Tel: 610-666-0644.
Students 183.

Villanova, Delaware Co., St. Thomas of Villanova Parish Community (1848), Revs. Dennis J. Harten, O.S.A.; Michael Bielecki, O.S.A.; Deacon Albert T. Derivan. In res., Rev. Anthony M. Genovese, O.S.A.
Res., 1229 W. Lancaster Ave., Rosemont, 19010. Tel: 610-525-4801; Fax: 610-525-6041.
School—St. Thomas-Good Counsel School. See Consolidated Parish Schools under Institutions Located in the Archdiocese.
St. Thomas of Villanova Preschool—1236 Montrose Ave., Rosemont, 19010. Tel: 610-525-7554.

Wallingford, Delaware Co., St. John Chrysostom (1952, Revs. Joseph P. McGeown; Efren V. Esmilla; Rev. Msgr. Frederick J. Stevenson, Pastor Emeritus; Deacon Raymond Vadino.
Res., 617 S. Providence Rd., 19086. Tel: 610-874-3418; Fax: 610-872-1741.
School—607 Providence Rd., 19086. Tel: 610-876-7110.
Sisters of St. Joseph 5; Lay Teachers 21; Students 267.
Catechesis/Religious Programs—605 S. Providence Rd., 19086. Tel: 610-872-4673.
Students 615.
Convent—Tel: 610-872-7194.

Warminster, Bucks Co., Nativity of Our Lord (1956), Revs. William J. O'Donnell; Stephen F. Katziner; Kenneth G. Putz. In res., Rev. Msgr. John V. Bartos; Rev. James F. Endres.
Res., 625 W. Street Rd., 18974. Tel: 215-675-1925; Fax: 215-674-3787.
School—585 W. Street Rd., 18974. Tel: 215-675-2820.
Sisters of St. Joseph 1; Lay Teachers 25; Students 660.
Catechesis/Religious Programs—Tel: 212-672-5316.
Students 340.
Convent—615 W. Street Rd., 18974. Tel: 215-672-0147.

Warrington, Bucks Co., St. Joseph (1922), Revs. James A. Grant; Robert G. Suskey; Rev. Msgr. Leon J. Peck, Pastor Emeritus; Deacons Karl Hartmann; Frank Cavaliere. In res., Rev. Richard P. Connors.
Res., 1795 Columbia Ave., 18976. Tel: 215-672-3020; Fax: 215-672-3114.
School—St. Joseph & St. Robert Bellarmine School. See Consolidated Parish Schools under Institutions Located in the Archdiocese.
Sisters, Servants of the Immaculate Heart of Mary 3; Lay Teachers 18; Students 504.
Catechesis/Religious Programs—Tel: 215-672-9990. Sr. Anna Marie McDermott, I.H.M., D.R.E.
Students 255.
Station—Willow Grove Naval Air Station, Tel: 215-443-6002.

St. Robert Bellarmine (1968), Revs. Joseph T. Kane; Joseph M. McDermott.
Res., 856 Euclid Ave., 18976. Tel: 215-343-0315; Fax: 215-343-8592.
School—St. Joseph & St. Robert Bellarmine School. See Consolidated Parish Schools under Institutions Located in the Archdiocese.
Catechesis/Religious Programs—Euclid Ave. & Carriage Way, 18976. Tel: 215-343-9433.
Students 510.
Convent—189 E. County Line Rd., Hatboro, 19040. Tel: 215-675-2301.

Wayne, Chester Co., St. Isaac Jogues (1970), Rev. Msgr. Joseph C. Cunningham. In res., Rev. Boniface A.A. Osuji, Ph.D.
Res., 50 W. Walker Rd., 19087. Tel: 610-687-3366; Fax: 610-293-9529.
Catechesis/Religious Programs—Tel: 610-687-2481. Kathy Aaronson, D.R.E.
Students 225.

St. Katharine of Siena, Delaware Co., (1893), Rev. Msgr. John J. Jagodzinski; Rev. Msgr. Joseph P. Cooney, Pastor Emeritus; Sr. Elizabeth O'Hara, S.S.J., Parish Svcs. Dir.; Deacon George Bolter. In res., Rev. Pascal A. Monteleone.
Res., 104 S. Aberdeen Ave., 19087. Tel: 610-688-4584; Fax: 610-688-7951.
School—229 Windemere Ave., 19087. Tel: 610-688-5451. Sr. William Therese, I.H.M., Prin.
Sisters, Servants of the Immaculate Heart of Mary 4; Lay Teachers 15; Students 308.
Catechesis/Religious Programs—Tel: 610-688-7890. Mr. James Orega, D.R.E.
Students 244.

West Chester, Chester Co., St. Agnes (1793), Rev. Msgr. Thomas P. Craven; Revs. Robert B. McDermott; Joseph B. Jung; Rafael Mendez; Deacon Victor Gonzalez. In res., Rev. Joseph D. Brandt; Rev. Msgr. Laurence F. Kelly, Pastor Emeritus.
Res., 233 W. Gay St., 19380. Tel: 610-692-2990; Fax: 610-692-9623. [CEM]
School—211 W. Gay St., 19380. Tel: 610-696-1260.
Sisters, Servants of the Immaculate Heart of Mary 4; Lay Teachers 23; Students 508.
Catechesis/Religious Programs—209 W. Gay St., 19380. Tel: 610-436-4640.
Students 591.
Convent—205 W. Gay St., 19380.

SS. Simon and Jude (1961), Revs. Francis X. Meehan; Michael Davis; Deacons James Lyon; Ben Stam. In res., Rev. James J. Melle.
Res., 8 Cavanaugh Ct., 19382. Tel: 610-696-3624; Fax: 610-696-3971.
School—6 Cavanaugh Ct., Tel: 610-692-5249; Fax: 610-696-4682.
Sisters, Servants of the Immaculate Heart of Mary 5; Lay Teachers 18; Students 622.
Catechesis/Religious Programs—Tel: 610-692-3118.
Students 519.
Convent—Tel: 610-692-4394.

West Conshohocken, Montgomery Co., St. Gertrude (1888), Rev. James J. McKeaney. In res., Rev. T. Christopher Reday.
Res., 209 Merion Ave., 19428. Tel: 610-828-0268.
PreK-Kindergarten—150 Cedar Ave., 19428. Tel: 610-828-2161.

West Grove, Chester Co., Assumption B.V.M. (1873), Rev. John W. Graf. In res., Rev. Francis J. Depman.
Res., 107 Evergreen St., 19390. Tel: 610-869-2722; Fax: 610-869-3252. [CEM]
School—290 State Rd., 19390. Tel: 610-869-9576. Sr. Francis Eileen Tiernan, I.H.M., Prin.
Sisters, Servants of the Immaculate Heart 3; Lay Teachers 13; Students 284.
Catechesis/Religious Programs—Tel: 610-869-8575.
Students 465.
Convent—105 Evergreen St., 19390. Tel: 610-869-9832.
Mission—Avondale, Chester Co., Santa Maria, Madra de Dios, P.O. Box 1019, Avondale, 19311. Tel: 610-268-3365; Fax: 610-869-9395.

Westtown, St. Maximilian Kolbe (1986), Revs. Hugh P. Campbell; William A. Trader; Deacon Lawrence Brandon.
Res., 15 E. Pleasant Grove Rd., West Chester, 19382. Tel: 610-399-6936; 399-9642; Fax: 610-399-4828.
Catechesis/Religious Programs—Students 600.

Willow Grove, Montgomery Co., St. David (1919), Revs. Richard T. Bolger; Francis V. Bielski. In res., Rev. William G. Donovan.
Res., 316 N. Easton Rd., 19090. Tel: 215-657-0252; Fax: 215-659-6516.
School—401 N. Easton Rd., 19090. Tel: 215-659-6393.
Sisters, Servants of the Immaculate Heart of Mary 7; Lay Teachers 14; Students 310.
Catechesis/Religious Programs—Tel: 215-659-4059.
Students 392.
Convent—400 N. Easton Rd., 19090. Tel: 215-659-0445.

Wyndmoor, Montgomery Co., Seven Dolors (1916), Revs. William J. Stanton, M.A., M.Div.; John F. Cullen, M.A., Pastor Emeritus. In res., Rev. John D. Reardon, M.Div.
Res., 1200 E. Willow Grove Ave., 19038-7614. Tel: 215-233-2552; Fax: 215-233-2553.

Wynnewood, Montgomery Co., Presentation B.V.M. (1954), Rev. Msgr. Vincent M. Walsh, J.C.D.; Rev. Msgr. John C. Kavanagh, Pastor Emeritus; Sr. Alice Price, R.S.M., Pastoral Assoc.
Res., 204 Haverford Rd., 19096. Tel: 610-642-8341; Fax: 610-896-1970.
School—230 Haverford Rd., 19096. Tel: 610-642-8040. Kay Kelly, Prin.
Lay Teachers 13; Students 198.
Convent—240 Haverford Rd., 19096. Tel: 610-642-3803.
Sisters 3.

Yardley, Bucks Co., St. Ignatius of Antioch (1920), Rev. Msgr. Samuel E. Shoemaker, J.C.D.; Rev. James D. Tortorici, M.A. In res., Rev. Mark J. Hunt, S.T.L.
Res., 999 Reading Ave., 19067. Tel: 215-493-3377; Fax: 215-493-0450. [CEM][JC]
School—Tel: 215-493-3867.
Lay Staff 20; Students 305.
Catechesis/Religious Programs—Tel: 215-493-5204.
Students 684.

Yeadon, Delaware Co., St. Louis (1928), Rev. Charles E. Bonner.
Res., 821 W. Cobbs Creek Pkwy., 19050. Tel: 610-623-0553.

Chaplains of Public Institutions

PHILADELPHIA. *Philadelphia Prison System* 8001 State Rd., 19136. Tel: 215-276-2288. Rev. John M. Bonavitacola, Chap.
Veterans Administration Medical Center University & Woodland Aves., 19104. Tel: 215-823-5800, Ext. 2776. Rev. James E. King, Chap.

COATESVILLE. *Veterans Administration Medical Center*. Vacant. 19320. Tel: 215-384-7711, Ext. 190.

GRATERFORD. *Graterford State Correctional Institution* 19426. Tel: 215-489-4151. Rev. Michael W. Rzonca, Chap.

NORRISTOWN. *Norristown State Hospital* 19401. Tel: 215-270-1104. Rev. Dominick Finn, O.S.F.S., Chap.

On Duty Outside the Archdiocese:
Reverend Monsignors—
Bransfield, Michael J., National Shrine of the Immaculate Conception, Fourth St. & Michigan Ave., N.E., Washington, DC 20017
Green, James P., Apostolic Nunciature, Carnegielaan, 5, 2517 KH Den Haag, Netherlands
Pepe, Joseph A., Tribunal, Archdiocese of Santa Fe, 4000 Saint Joseph Pl., N.W., Albuquerque, NM 87120
Thomas, Daniel E., Official, Congregation for Bishops, Pontifical North American College, Vatican City State, 00120 Europe. Tel: 011-39-6849-3846
Reverend Fathers—
Donofrio, Michael J., Parroquia San Pedro, Apartado 13, Andanuaylas, Apurimac, Peru
Garzarelli, Santo R., Bishop's House, P.O. Box 205, Vanimo, Papua New Guinea
Grous, Albin J., SS. Cyril and Methodius Seminary, 3535 Indian Tr., Orchard Lake, MI 48324-1623
McNamara, Donald P., Misioneros De Maryknoll, Apartado Postal 20.273, San Martin, Caracas 1020-A Venezuela, S.A.
Menei, Francis T., Trinity Spiritual Center, 3609 Simpson Ferry Rd., Shiremanstown, PA 17011
Ragan, Gerald P., Immaculate Conception Church, 204 N. Church St., Dublin, GA 31021
Shields, Hugh J., Sociedad de Santiago Apostol, Apartado 18-1025 Miraflores, Lima 18 Peru
Skindeleski, Thomas J., Saint Joan of Arc Church, 370 S.W. Third St., Boca Raton, FL 33432
Walsh, Edward J., St. Catherine of Sienna, 33 New Hyde Park Rd., Franklin Square, NY 11010

Military Chaplains:
Reverend Fathers—
Benz, David H.
Boyle, Dennis P.
Burns, Vincent P.
Concha, Alfonso J.
DiGregorio, Joseph L.
Foley, Francis P.
Glatts, Joseph M.
McManus, Gerald D.

Graduate Studies:
Reverend Fathers—
Costa, Anthony J., Casa Santa Maria, Via dell'Umilta 30, Rome 00187 Italy
Gentili, Joseph P., Casa Santa Maria, Via dell'Umilta 30, Rome, 00187 Italy
Gill, G. Dennis, Casa Santa Maria, Via dell'Umilta 30, Rome 00187 Italy
Hunt, Mark J., St. Ignatius Rectory, 999 Reading Ave., Yardley, PA 19067
Magee, Michael K., Casa Santa Maria, Via dell'Umilta 30, Rome, 00187 Italy
Mahoney, Shaun L., Casa Santa Maria, Via dell'Umilta, Rome, 00187 Italy
O'Driscoll, John C., Casa Santa Maria, Via dell'Umilta 30, Rome, 00187 Italy
Oliver, James M., Casa Santa Maria, Via dell'Umilta 30, Rome, 00187 Italy
Pesarchick, Robert A., Casa Santa Maria, Via dell'Umilta 30, Rome, 00187 Italy
Prior, Joseph G., Casa Santa Maria, Via dell'Umilta 30, Rome, 00187 Italy
Tracy, Joseph A., Casa Santa Maria, Via dell'Umilta 30, Rome, 00187 Italy

Absent on Sick Leave:
Reverend Monsignors—
Nace, Arthur J.
Reverend Fathers—
Bloh, Stephen R.
Connors, Richard P.
Dougherty, William J.
Durney, Charles W.
Fala, John G.
Farley, Bernard C.
Kohler, Thomas M.
McCarthy, Michael J.
Moriarity, Daniel J.
Roedel, Robert H.
Satchell, Martin J.
Smart, Raymond W.
Wesolowski, Edmund C.

Absent on Leave:
Reverend Monsignors—
Walls, David E.
Reverend Fathers—
DePaoli, Edward M.
DiPaul, Lawrence M.
Donnelly, Russell J.
Fisher, Craig B.
Galanaugh, Joseph T.
Gillin, Thomas P.
Grailey, Joseph P.
Heron, J. Thomas
Knotek, Marcel
McLoughlin, Richard J.
O'Brien, Mark J.
Swierzy, Michael W.

Retired:
Reverend Monsignors—
Bennington, J. Clement, 3508 Bay Ave., Ocean City, NJ 08226
Busco, John J., Holy Savior Rectory, 407 E. Main St., Norristown, PA 19041-5119
Bydlon, Adam J., Villa Saint Joseph, 1436 Lansdowne Ave., Darby, PA 19023-1298
Cahill, Paul J., Villa Saint Joseph, 1436 Lansdowne Ave., Darby, PA 19023-1298
Caufield, John J., Cathedral Basilica SS. Peter and Paul, 1723 Race St., Philadelphia, PA 19103
Conway, Walter J., Saint William Rectory, 6200 Rising Sun Ave., Philadelphia, PA 19111
Cooney, Joseph P., Villa Saint Joseph, 1436 Lansdowne Ave., Darby, PA 19023-1298
Doolin, William A., Saint Anselm Rectory, 12669 Dunks Ferry Rd., Philadelphia, PA 19154
Falls, Thomas B., Villa Saint Joseph, 1436 Lansdowne Ave., Darby, PA 19023-1298
Fee, John B., Villa Saint Joseph, 1436 Lansdowne Ave., Darby, PA 19023-1298
Fitzmaurice, Francis J., Villa Saint Joseph, 1436 Lansdowne Ave., Darby, PA 19023
Jaworowski, Anthony E., Sacred Heart Rectory, 120 Jefferson St., Swedesburg, PA 19405
Kavanaugh, John C., Presentation B.V.M. Rectory, 204 Haverford Rd., Wynnewood, PA 19096
Kelly, Laurence F., Saint Agnes Rectory, 233 W. Gay St., West Chester, PA 19380
Keul, Francis X., Regina Coeli Residence for Priests, 685 York Rd., Warminster, PA 18974
Lynaugh, Joseph E., Villa Saint Joseph, 1436 Lansdowne Ave., Darby, PA 19023-1298
Marley, Michael F., Villa Saint Joseph, 1436 Lansdowne Ave., Darby, PA 19023-1298
McDonough, Martin J., Villa Saint Joseph, 1436 Lansdowne Ave., Darby, PA 19023-1298
McGlinn, Joseph J., Our Lady of Ransom Rectory, 6701 Calvert St., Philadelphia, PA 19149
McGrath, James, 6101 34th St. W., 10 E, Bradenton, FL 34210-3701
Monaghan, Charles J., Villa Saint Joseph, 1436 Lansdowne Ave., Darby, PA 19023-1298
Musial, Edward S., Saint Mary Rectory, 140 W. Hector St., Conshohocken, PA 19428
Mynaugh, Charles B., Regina Coeli Residence for Priests, 685 York Rd., Warminster, PA 18974
Nugent, Arthur W., 1341 Osbourne Ave., Roslyn, PA 19001
Peck, Leon J., Regina Coeli Residence for Priests, 685 York Rd., Warminster, PA 18974
Pryor, Thomas P., Villa Saint Joseph, 1436 Lansdowne Ave., Darby, PA 19023
Schaeflein, Charles J., Mount Nazareth, 2775 Holme Ave., Philadelphia, PA 19152
Sikora, Joseph G., Saint Francis Country House, 1412 Lansdowne Ave., Darby, PA 19023-1298
Simons, Richard J., Villa Saint Joseph, 1436 Lansdowne Ave., Darby, PA 19023-1298
Statkus, Francis J., 208 E. Trenton Ave., Wildwood Crest, NJ 08260
Stevenson, Frederick J., Saint John Chrysostom Rectory, 605 S. Providence Rd., Wallingford, PA 19086-6998
Urbanowicz, Francis J., Sacred Heart Rectory, 316 E. Broadway Ave., Clifton Heights, PA 19018-1723
Vizzard, James J., Saint Matthias Rectory, 128 Bryn Mawr Ave., Bala Cynwyd, PA 19004
Reverend Fathers—
Barnes, Gerard J., Villa Saint Joseph, 1436 Lansdowne Ave., Darby, PA 19023-1298
Barr, Philip R., 1511 Grant Rd., West Chester, PA 19382
Benonis, Richard R., 7207 Southern Ridge Dr., Converse, TX 78109
Blanchfield, Joseph J., St. Gabriel Rectory, 233 Mohawk Ave., Norwood, PA 19074-4019
Boland, Edward G., Villa Saint Joseph, 1436 Lansdowne Ave., Darby, PA 19023-1298
Bradley, James F., Villa Saint Joseph, 1436 Lansdowne Ave., Darby, PA 19023-1298
Calpin, Thomas J., Villa Saint Joseph, 1436 Lansdowne Ave., Darby, PA 19023-1298
Carey, Paul J., 1165 Beverly Rd., Rydal, PA 19046
Catullo, Pasquale R., Villa Saint Joseph, 1436 Lansdowne Ave., Darby, PA 19023-1298
Cellucci, Carl D., 902 Surf Ave., North Wildwood, NJ 08260
Chapman, A. James, Villa Saint Joseph, 1436 Lansdowne Ave., Darby, PA 19023-1298
Coates, John T., Regina Coeli Residence for Priests, 685 York Rd., Warminster, PA 18974
Cornely, Francis J., 1140-B Hidden Cove Dr., Mount Pleasant, SC 29464
Cudemo, Nicholas V., 1310 Grovania Ave., Abington, PA 19001
Cullen, John F., Seven Dolors Church, 1200 E. Willow Grove Rd., Wyndmoor, PA 19038
Czarnota, Reynold A., Villa Saint Joseph, 1436 Lansdowne Ave., Darby, PA 19023
Daly, James P., Villa Saint Joseph, 1436 Lansdowne Ave., Darby, PA 19023-1298
Daly, John J., Villa Saint Joseph, 1436 Lansdowne Ave., Darby, PA 19023-1298
Degnan, Henry B., St. Paul Rectory, 2007 New Hope St., Norristown, PA 19401
Degutis, George D., 8815 Calvert St., Philadelphia, PA 19152-1305
Dempsey, Thomas J., Villa Saint Joseph, 1436 Lansdowne Ave., Darby, PA 19023-1298
Devlin, Joseph F., Villa St. Joseph, 1436 Lansdowne Ave., Darby, PA 19023-1298
Dougherty, Henry E., Queen of the Universe Rectory, 2443 Trenton Rd., Levittown, PA 19056
Dougherty, John C., Saint Bartholomew Rectory, 5600 Jackson St., Philadelphia, PA 19124
Drobel, William F., Villa Saint Joseph, 1436 Lansdowne Ave., Darby, PA 19023-1298
Duddy, Patrick A., Villa Saint Joseph, 1436 Lansdowne Ave., Darby, PA 19023-1298
Duffy, John J., Five Whalerman Cove, Brigantine, NJ 08203
Dunne, Peter J., 815 Haycock Run Rd., Kintnersville, PA 18930
Durney, Charles W., P.O. Box 138, Tuscarora, PA 17982
Dux, James M., Villa Saint Joseph, 1436 Lansdowne Ave., Darby, PA 19023-1298
Dziadosz, Edward T., 438 W. Mahanoy Ave., Mahanoy City, PA 17948-0095
Egan, Francis M., 625 Turkey Point Rd., Port Norris, NJ 08349
Fala, John G., Saint Bernard Rectory, 7341 Cottage St., Philadelphia, PA 19136
Farrell, Donald J., Saint Cyril of Alexandria Rectory, 153 Penn Blvd., East Lansdowne, PA 19050
Feeney, Thomas M., 1341 Osbourne Ave., Roslyn, PA 19001
Fitzpatrick, Peter A., St. Patrick Rectory, 242 S. 20th St., Philadelphia, PA 19103
Gallen, Francis H., Hershey Mill, 118 Chandler Dr., West Chester, PA 19380
Gausch, Joseph P., 1240 Ohio Ave., Cape May, NJ 08240
Gibas, John J., 8018 Large St., Philadelphia, PA 19152
Glynn, John P., 137 105th St., Stone Harbor, NJ 08247
Gough, James F., St. Matthew Rectory, 3000 Cottman Ave., Philadelphia, PA 19149
Griffin, John A., Our Lady of Fatima Rectory, 2933 Street Rd., Fatima Acres, Bensalem, PA 19020
Griffin, Richard J., Our Lady of Fatima Rectory, 2933 Street Rd., Fatima Acres, Bensalem, PA 19020
Gsell, John W., Villa Saint Joseph, 1436 Lansdowne Ave., Darby, PA 19023-1298
Hartnett, Walter J., Villa Saint Joseph, 1436 Lansdowne Ave., Darby, PA 19023-1298
Henry, Joseph A., 1815 Carwithen St., Philadelphia, PA 19152
Jaworowski, Leon E., Villa Saint Joseph, 1436 Lansdowne Ave., Darby, PA 19023-1298
Kane, Aloysius T., Villa Saint Joseph, 1436 Lansdowne Ave., Darby, PA 19023-1298
Kane, Thomas A., St. Matthias Rectory, 128 Bryn Mawr Ave., Bala Cynwyd, PA 19004
Kehoe, Daniel J., Holy Spirit Rectory, 1028 School St., Sharon Hill, PA 19079
Kelly, James J., Villa Saint Joseph, 1436 Lansdowne Ave., Darby, PA 19023-1298
Kelly, Thomas J., Saint Francis Country House, 1412 Lansdowne Ave., Darby, PA 19023-1298
Kennedy, Joseph J., Nativity B.V.M. Rectory, 30 E. Franklin St., Media, PA 19096
Kerrigan, Joseph P., Saint Elizabeth Ann Seton Rectory, 1200 Park Ave. E., Bensalem, PA 19020
Kerwick, Robert J., Villa Saint Joseph, 1436 Lansdowne Ave., Darby, PA 19023-1298
Klapp, John S., 5630 N. Arbor St., Philadelphia, PA 19120
Klitsch, Anthony L., Villa Saint Joseph, 1436 Lansdowne Ave., Darby, PA 19023-1298
Koob, Edward H., 6612 Pleasure Ave., Sea Isle City, NJ 08243-1450
Kovacs, Louis D., Villa Saint Joseph, 1436 Lansdowne Ave., Darby, PA 19023-1298
Krick, Howard K., 2420 McCullough, Apt. 222, San Antonio, TX 78212-3565
Lazzaro, Nicholas A., Villa Saint Joseph, 1436 Lansdowne Ave., Darby, PA 19023
Leary, James V., Sacred Heart Rectory, 148 Church St., Phoenixville, PA 19460
Lennon, Francis P., St. Eleanor Rectory, 647 Locust St., Collegeville, PA 19426-2541
Lepleiter, Robert P., Regina Coeli Residence for Priests, 685 York Rd., Warminster, PA 18974
Loughran, Francis J., Villa Saint Joseph, 1436 Lansdowne Ave., Darby, PA 19023-1298
Loughrey, Thomas F., 651 W. Pine Ave., West Wildwood, NJ 08260
Maguire, Connell J., 2800 N. Ocean Dr., Apt. B15a, Riviera Beach, FL 33404
Mangan, John J., Villa Saint Joseph, 1436 Lansdowne Ave., Darby, PA 19023-1298
Matsko, John M., St. Francis Country House, 1412 Lansdowne Ave., Darby, PA 19023-1218
Maurer, Paul F., Epiphany of Our Lord Church, 1121 Jackson St., Philadelphia, PA 19148
McBride, William T., Regina Coeli Residence for Priests, 685 York Rd., Warminster, PA 18974
McCaffrey, Gerard D., Regina Coeli Residence for Priests, 685 York Rd., Warminster, PA 18974
McCloskey, Joseph A., St. Francis Country House, 1412 Lansdowne Ave., Darby, PA 19023-1218
McDermott, Francis A., St. Patrick Rectory, 242 S. 20th St., Philadelphia, PA 19103
McDevitt, Francis N., Villa Saint Joseph, 1436 Lansdowne Ave., Darby, PA 19023-1298
McMullen, Charles P., Saint Francis Country House, 1412 Lansdowne Ave., Darby, PA 19023-1218
Morley, John J., Villa Saint Joseph, 1436 Lansdowne Ave., Darby, PA 19023-1298
Morrison, Robert A., c/o Secretary for Clergy, 222 N. 17th St., Philadelphia, PA 19103
Murphy, James A., St. Gabriel Rectory, 127 E. Howard St., Stowe, PA 19464
Murphy, James J., 227 Brazilian Ave., Palm Beach, FL 33480
Murphy, James F., Saint Francis Country House, 1412 Lansdowne Ave., Darby, PA 19023-1218
Murphy, Joseph T., 812 Rowland Ave., Cheltenham, PA 19012
Murphy, Lawrence J., Villa Saint Joseph, 1436 Lansdowne Ave., Darby, PA 19023-1298
Murray, John J., Villa Saint Joseph, 1436 Lansdowne Ave., Darby, PA 19023-1298
O'Connor, John P., Saint Katherine of Siena Rectory, 9700 Frankford Ave., Philadelphia, PA 19114-2896

O'Halloran, Martin J., Regina Coeli Residence for Priests, 685 York Rd., Warminster, PA 18974
O'Hara, Martin F., St. Jerome Rectory, 8100 Colfax St., Philadelphia, PA 19136-1801
Oestreich, Emil C., St. Raymond of Penafort Rectory, 1350 Vernon Rd., Philadelphia, PA 19150-2123
Palombo, Albert B., 14211 Alto Cedro Dr., Del Ray Beach, FL 33484-2550
Reino, Joseph C., 910 Wynnewood Rd., Philadelphia, PA 19151-4501
Reynolds, Ignatius C., Villa Saint Joseph, 1436 Lansdowne Ave., Darby, PA 19023-1298
Riedy, Robert I., Saint Francis Country House, 1412 Lansdowne Ave., Darby, PA 19023-1218
Rilley, John F., Villa St. Joseph, 1436 Lansdowne Ave., Darby, PA 19023
Rogers, Francis P., St. Timothy Rectory, 3001 Levick St., Philadelphia, PA 19149
Rossi, Anthony M., Villa Saint Joseph, 1436 Lansdowne Ave., Darby, PA 19023-1298
Ryan, Robert F., St. Gabriel's Hall, P.O. Box 7280, Audubon, PA 19407
Sabadish, Joseph F., 60 Stone Rd., Branch Dale, PA 17923
Scherf, Gerard H., Saint Martha Rectory, 11301 Academy Rd., Philadelphia, PA 19154
Schifalacqua, Ildebrando E., St. Bartholomew Rectory, 5600 Jackson St., Philadephia, PA 19124
Schneider, George P., 109 Chestnut St., Parkesburg, PA 19365
Schuyler, Henry C., Visitation B.V.M. Rectory, 196 N. Trooper Rd., Norristown, PA 19403-2665
Scully, Philip A., Villa Saint Joseph, 1436 Lansdowne Ave., Darby, PA 19023-1298
Senske, Joseph A., Gillet Convent, Immaculata College, P.O. Box 731, Immaculata, PA 19345
Shea, Thomas F., Villa Saint Joseph, 1436 Lansdowne Ave., Darby, PA 19023-1298
Sheridan, James B., Villa Saint Joseph, 1436 Lansdowne Ave., Darby, PA 19023-1298
Slafkosky, Andrew L., 610 Pine Rd., Silver Spring Shores, Ocala, FL 34472-6167
Smith, Joseph F., Viilla Saint Joseph, 1436 Lansdowne Ave., Darby, PA 19023-1298
Smith, Martin G., 111 Walnut Ave., Villas, NJ 08251
Smith, William J., 4051 Asbury Ave., Ocean City, NJ 08226
Soreth, James F., Saint Francis Country House, 1412 Lansdowne Ave., Darby, PA 19023-1218
Spaits, George S., Villa Saint Joseph, 1436 Lansdowne Ave., Darby, PA 19023-1298
Spicijaric, Anthony, Villa Saint Joseph, 1436 Lansdowne Ave., Darby, PA 19023-1298
St. Clair, Joseph A., Villa Saint Joseph, 1436 Lansdowne Ave., Darby, PA 19023-1298
Szal, Ignatius J., 460 Sunbury St., Minersville, PA 17954
Van Stone, John J., Villa Saint Joseph, 1436 Lansdowne Ave., Darby, PA 19023-1298
Walker, Norbert J., 401 W. Brigantine Ave., Brigantine, NJ 08203
Walsh, George J., Villa Saint Joseph, 1436 Lansdowne Ave., Darby, PA 19023
Walsh, John M., Villa Saint Joseph, 1436 Lansdowne Ave., Darby, PA 19023-1298
Walsh, Joseph E., Saint Francis de Sales Rectory, 35 New Rd., P.O. Box 97, Lenni, PA 19052
Walsh, Michael L., Camilla Hall, Immaculata, PA 19345
Walsh, Thomas F., 730 Salem Ct., Yardley, PA 19067
Wassel, Eugene A., Saint Francis Country House, 1412 Lansdowne Ave., Darby, PA 19023-1298
Wright, Richard J., Saint Colman Rectory, 11 Simpson Rd., Ardmore, PA 19003
Ziemba, Anthony F., Saint Laurentius Rectory, 1608 E. Berks St., Philadelphia, PA 19125

Permanent Deacons:
All locations are Philadelphia unless otherwise indicated.
Andrews, Edward J., St. Martin De Porres Church
Arno, Michael R., St. Irenaeus Church
Basilio, James A., Notre Dame De Lourdes Church, Swarthmore
Bean, John J., St. Bartholomew Church
Belanger, A. Kenneth, St. Helena Church, Center Square
Bentancourt, Miguel, St. Peter the Apostle Church
Bizal, Francis M., SS. Philip and James Church, Exton
Bolter, George A., St. Monica Church, Berwyn
Bonilla, Victor M., Maternity B.V.M. Church
Brandon, Lawrence G., St. Maximilian Kolbe Church, West Chester
Brown, Clifford W., Our Mother of Consolidation Church
Burns, James H., St. Eleanor Church, Collegeville
Butcavage, Thomas E., Holy Spirit Church, Sharon Hill
Calabrese, Peter J., St. Charles Borromeo Church, Drexel Hill
Cavaliere, Francis M., St. Joseph Church, Warrington
Ceneviva, Vincent G., St. Jude Church, Chalfont
Champagne, William E., Our Lady of Hope Church
Clancy, Kenneth P., Epiphany of Our Lord Church, Norristown
Clark, Francis T., St. Joseph Church, Ambler
Collazo, Apolonio, Visitation B.V.M. Church
Conroy, Michael F., Sacred Heart Church, Royersford
Corwell, George V., Our Lady of Mt. Carmel Church, Doylestown
Coyle, Joseph P., St. Alice Church, Upper Darby
Coyne, Richard C., Holy Cross Church
Cruz, Felipe, Incarnation of Our Lord Church
D'Angelo, Ernest, St. John the Baptist Church, Ottsville
Davaro, John J., St. Dorothy Church, Drexel Hill
Dayoc, Michael J., St. Paul Church, Norristown
DeJesus, Epifanio, Cathedral Basilica of SS. Peter & Paul
Del Valle, Maximino, Incarnation of Our Lord Church
DeLucca, Daniel N., St. Andrew Church, Drexel Hill
DeMasi, Leonard, St. Monica Church
Derivan, Albert T., St. Thomas of Villanova Church, Rosemont
Devine, Charles F., St. Thomas the Apostle Church, Chester Heights
Diana, Leonard J., St. Kevin Church, Springfield
Dymek, Edward J., St. Ephrem Church, Bensalem
Eichman, Thomas E., St. Kevin Church, Springfield
Eliason, William F., St. David Church, Willow Grove
Fabrizio, Francis S., St. Charles Borromeo Church, Drexel Hill
Favinger, M. Eugene, Our Lady of Consolation Church, Parkesburg
Fernandez, Alfonzo, St. Veronica Church
Finn, Michael J., Blessed Katharine Drexel Church, Chester
Fontanez, Jose, Incarnation of Our Lord Church
Frankenberger, Robert J., Holy Cross Church, Springfield
Froio, Lawrence P., St. Patrick Church, Malvern
Fuentes, Ismael, St. Patrick Church, Norristown
Fulmer, Walter C., Christ the King Church
Gibson, Lawrence J., St. Thomas Aquinas Church, Croyden
Gladnick, Leo T., Ascension of Our Lord Church
Gonzalez, Victor M., St. Agnes Church, West Chester
Gousie, Joseph N., Our Lady of Mount Carmel Church, Doylestown
Gravlin, John J., St. Matthew Church
Guinane, William J., St. Madeline Church, Ridley Park
Haddon, Richard S., St. Catherine of Siena Church, Horsham
Hagerty, Paul B., Immaculate Conception Church, Jenkintown
Hannum, Stephen W., Unassigned
Harkin, William C., Our Mother of Consolation Church
Harper, Sidney M., St. Athanasius Church
Harrison, A. Gerald, SS. Peter and Paul Church, West Chester
Hartmann, James E., St. John the Evangelist Church, Morrisville
Hartmann, Karl J., St. Joseph Church, Warrington
Heaney, Philip E., Maternity B.V.M. Church
Hernandez, Jose, Incarnation of Our Lord Church
Hopkins, Stephen, St. Benedict Church
Horan, Thomas J., SS. Peter & Paul Church, West Chester
Hynes, John, Maternity B.V.M. Church
Iannucci, Joseph E., St. Pius X Church, Broomall
Jacobucci, Raymond, St. Nicholas of Tolentine Church
Jones, David E., St. Anthony of Padua Church, Ambler
Kane, James D., Sr., St. Francis of Assisi Church, Springfield
Kefer, Robert J., SS. Peter & Paul Church, West Chester
Kelly, Gerald F., St. Matthias Church, Bala Cynwyd
Kelly, Walter E., Our Lady of Mount Carmel Church, Doylestown
Kern, Paul R., St. John Baptist Vianney Church, Gladwyne
Klauder, Francis, St. Elizabeth Ann Seton Church, Bensalem
Konarski, Edward A., St. Rose of Lima Church, North Wales
Kretsch, Donald J., Holy Savior Church, Norristown
Lance, Walter C., St. Clement Church
Leahy, Eugene R., Holy Family Church
Leonhardt, George W., St. Thomas More Church, South Coventry
Lozada, Jose Luis, St. Hugh of Cluny Church
Lozada, Mario, St. Boniface Church
Lyon, James E., SS. Simon & Jude Church, West Chester
Madonna, James K., St. Patrick Church, Kennett Square
Makoid, T. Eric, Sacred Heart Church, Swedesburg
Maldonado, Rafael, St. Veronica Church
Malfara, Louis S., St. Cecilia Church
Manson, Joseph J., St. Genevieve Church, Flourtown
Manzano, Edwin R., Visitation B.V.M. Church
Maresca, Armand J., SS. Cosmas & Damian Church, Conshohocken
Martes, Zoilo, St. Michael Church
McAndrews, Michael J., Notre Dame DeLourdes Church, Swarthmore
McGovern, Clement J., St. Cornelius Church, Chadds Ford
McGrath, Gerard P., St. Eleanor Church, Collegeville
McGuire, Arthur M., St. Francis of Assisi Church, Springfield
Mendez, Jose M., St. Ambrose Church
Micucci, Joseph A., Mother of Divine Grace Church
Morales, Jose A., St. Mark Church, Bristol
Morris, George E., St. Robert Bellarmine Church, Warrington
Murphy, Francis X., Sacred Heart Church, Oxford
Nightingale, Richard G., Our Lady of Victory Church
Niland, Joseph W., St. Elizabeth Ann Seton Church, Bensalem
O'Brien, Gregory R., St. Madeline Church, Ridley Park
O'Kedas, Leroy F., St. Rita of Cascia Church
Oliver, Joseph M., Our Lady of Perpetual Help, Morton
Orlando, John C., St. Monica Church
Parker, John, Holy Saviour Church, Norristown
Pavonarius, Charles A., St. Jerome Church
Polley, Charles W., Jr., Ss. Philip and James Church, Exton
Purnell, Edward M., St. Theresa of the Child Jesus Church
Radetsky, William R., Epiphany of Our Lord Church, Norristown
Rayner, Albert E., Holy Spirit Church, Sharon Hill
Rebuck, Charles H., St. Gabriel Church, Stowe
Riordan, John T., St. Jude Church, Chalfont
Rooney, Joseph T., Our Lady Help of Christians Church, Abington
Rosario, Israel, Our Lady of Hope Church
Rouse, Daniel J., St. John Bosco Church, Hatboro
Ruiz, Luis, St. Ambrose Church
Schaffer, David B., St. Denis Rectory, Havertown
Schiappa, Edward R., St. Joseph Church, Downingtown
Schlegel, John F., St. Denis Rectory, Havertown
Seda, Victor, St. Helena Church
Sexton, Joseph F., St. Mary of the Assumption Church
Shields, Thomas A., St. Martin De Porres Church
Skawinski, Robert J., St. Ignatius Church, Yardley
Smith, Calvin C., St. Benedict Church
Stam, Bernardus C., SS. Simon & Jude Church, West Chester
Stevens, Allen T., St. Francis of Assisi Church
Stewart, Robert J., St. Ignatius Church, Yardley
Stewart, William H., St. Martin De Porres Church
Stoughton, Richard L., Our Lady of the Rosary Church, Coatesville
Suplee, John J., Sacred Heart Church, Havertown
Thompson, Vincent J., St. Francis Xavier Church
Tielemans, Mathieu M., St. Stanislaus Church, Lansdale
Tormey, James M., Our Mother of Consolation Church
Tucker, Henry E., St. Agnes Church, Sellersville
Upcavage, Joseph R., Queen of the Universe Church, Levittown
Urbanski, Timothy E., St. Catherine of Siena Church, Horsham
Vadino, Raymond M., St. John Chrysostom Church, Wallingford
Verna, Louis, Blessed Virgin Mary Church, Darby
Vondercrone, C. Stephens, St. Stanislaus Church, Lansdale
Walker, James T., St. Benedict Church
Wetzel, Steven P., St. Joachim Church
Whartenby, Gerald J., St. Anselm Church
Windish, Joseph F., St. Cyril of Jerusalem Church, Jamison

Wirth, Richard D., St. Cornelius Church, Chadds Ford

Wojewodka, Boleslaw S., Sacred Heart Church, Clifton Heights

Wolkowicz, Leonard J., St. Barnabas Church

Woodall, Michael V., St. Eleanor Church, Collegeville

Woods, Thomas J., Sacred Heart Church, Havertown

Ziff, Joel M., Epiphany of Our Lord Church, Norristown

Zurbach, E. Peter, St. Mary Magdalen Church, Media

INSTITUTIONS LOCATED IN THE ARCHDIOCESE

[A] SEMINARIES, ARCHDIOCESAN

WYNNEWOOD. *Theological Seminary of St. Charles Borromeo, Overbrook*, Administration: 100 E. Wynnewood Rd., 19096. Tel: 610-667-3394; Fax: 610-664-7913. Rev. Msgr. James E. Molloy, M.Div., M.A., Rector; Revs. Christopher J. Schreck, S.S.L., Ph.D., S.T.D. (SAV), Vice Rector, Educational Admin.; John A. Close, M.Div., M.S., M.A., Vice Rector Institutional Advancement; Elaine K. Rice, M.B.A., Vice Pres., Finance; Ruth Suder, B.S., Vice Pres., Operations; Revs. Kevin T. McMahon, S.T.B., S.T.L., S.T.D. (WIL), Academic Dean, Theology Division; John J. DelliCarpini, M.Div., M.A., Ph.D., Academic Dean, College Division; Frederick L. Miller, M.A., S.T.L., S.T.D. (NEW), Academic Dean, Religious Studies Division; Thomas J. Owens, M.Div., Dean Formation Theology Division; Michael J. Kelly, M.Div., M.A., Dean of Formation, College Division; Robert J. Carroll, M.Div., M.A., Dir. Spiritual Formation, Theology Division; Paul V. Dougherty, M.Div., M.A., Dir. Spiritual Formation, College Division; Steven J. Marinucci, M.Div., Dir., Pastoral and Apostolic Formation; Lorena F. Boylan, M.S.L.S., M.A., Dir. of Library Svcs.; Lawrence A. Heyman, Ed.M., Registrar; Revs. John M. Savinski, M.Div., M.A., Dir., Spirituality Year Prog.; Peter J. Welsh, M.Div., M.A., Ph.D., Coord. Spiritual Formation & Spirituality Year Prog.

Full Time Institutional Faculty: Mark E. Bradford, M.Mus.; Revs. Stephen J. Brett, S.S.J., Ph.D, J.D. (WDC); Augustine M. Esposito, O.S.A., M.Div., Ph.D., M.A.; Janet Haggerty, M.A., Ph.D.; Atherton C. Lowry, M.A., Ph.D.; Rev. Msgr. Richard Malone, M.A., J.C.L., S.T.D.; Gerald H. Malsbary, M.A., Ph.D.; Rev. Michael J. McNally, M.Div., M.Th., M.A., Ph.D (PMB); Elizabeth M. Nagel, M.A., S.S.D.; John Saward, M.A., M.Litt.; John D. Thornbrugh, M.A., Ph.D.

Adjunct Faculty: Rev. George A. Aschenbrenner, S.J., S.T.D.; J. Brian Benestad, M.A., Ph.D.; Rev. Msgr. Michael J. Chaback, S.T.D. (ALN); Rev. Stephen J. Dougherty, M.Div., M.A.; Mary Ellen Fattori, M.A.; Rev. Msgr. Ronald W. Gainer, M.A., J.C.L. (ALN); Rev. Andrew J. Golias, S.T.D.; Rev. Msgr. James J. Graham, M.Div., J.C.D.; Barbara Guiliano, M.S., M.A.; Paul T. Klucsarits, M.A.; Sr. Mary Elizabeth Kratzinger, S.S.J., M.A.; Revs. Joseph L. Logrip, M.A., M.Div.; Daniel E. Mackle, M.Div., M.A.; Elizabeth Mintzer, M.A.; Revs. Stephen P. McHenry, M.A., Ph.D.; Thomas M. Mullin, M.Div., M.A., S.S.L.; Alexander J. Palmieri, M.Div., M.A., J.C.L.; Paul S. Quinter, M.Div., M.A., M.S., S.T.D; Joseph F. Rymdeika, M.Div., M.A.; Joseph C. Stec, M.A.; David A. Wortman, M.A., M.Phil., Rabbi; Shawn Weldon, M.A.

Additional Formation Personnel: Revs. Dennis J. Carbonaro, M.Div., M.A.; Curtis L. Clark, M.Div., M.A., S.T.L. (ARL); James J. Fitzpatrick, M.Div.; Joseph T. Szolack, M.Div. (CAM). In res. Most Rev. Joseph F. Martino, D.D., S.T.L., H.E.D.; Rev. Msgr. Thomas J. Benestad, M.Div. (ALN). Priests 35; Sisters 1; Lay Staff 19; College and Theology Division Students 196; Religious Studies Division Students 263; Seminarians from Archdiocese 84; Seminarians from other Dioceses 112.

[B] SEMINARIES, RELIGIOUS OR SCHOLASTICATES

PHILADELPHIA. *Brothers of the Christian Schools Scholasticate*, Jeremy House, 6633 Ardleigh St., 19119-3898. Tel: 215-843-1884.
E-mail: jeremyhouse@juno.com
Bro. Dennis Malloy, F.S.C., Dir. Professed Brothers 4; Scholastics 2.

DePaul Novitiate, 5710 Magnolia St., 19144. Tel: 215-843-1581. Revs. Thomas J. Butler, C.M., Asst. Dir.; Charles M. Shanley, C.M., Asst. Dir. In res. Revs. Joseph L. Levesque, C.M.; Thomas F. McKenna, C.M.; Peter A. Campbell, C.M. National Novitiate for the Congregation of the Mission (Vincentians).

St. Vincent's Seminary, 500 E. Chelten Ave., 19144-1296. Tel: 215-848-1985. Very Rev. Joseph L. Levesque, C.M., Prov.; Revs. Thomas F. McKenna, C.M., Asst. Prov.; William W. Sheldon, C.M., Supr.; Richard J. Kehoe, C.M., Dir. Missions; John W. Gouldrick, C.M., Treasurer; William J. O'Brien, C.M., Dir. Miraculous Medal Association; John W. Carven, C.M., Provincial Archivist. Central House of the Eastern Province of the Congregation of the Mission, (Vincentians).

PAOLI. *Daylesford Abbey*, 220 S. Valley Rd., 19301-1900. Tel: 610-647-2530; Fax: 610-651-0219. Legal Title: *Norbertine Fathers, Inc.* Rt. Rev. Ronald J. Rossi, O.Praem., Prior; Rev. John J. Novielli, O.Praem., SubPrior; Rt. Rev. John E. Neitzel, O.Praem., Abbot Emeritus; Revs. Theodore J. Antry, O.Praem., Vocation Dir.; Joseph A. Serano, O.Praem., Treas. Priests 10; Brothers 1.

SPRINGFIELD. *Don Guanella House of Formation*, 1795 S. Sproul Rd., 19064. Tel: 610-328-3406. Congregation of the Servants of Charity. Rev. Silvio De Nard, S.C. Priests 1.

VILLANOVA. *St. Augustine Friary*, 214 Ashwood Rd., 19085. Tel: 610-527-0325, Ext. 243. Bro. John J. DelCasale, O.S.A., Prior. In res. Bros. John Konwerski, O.S.A.; Joseph T. Spindler, O.S.A.; Revs. Daniel E. Doyle, O.S.A.; John F. McAtee, O.S.A.; James D. McBurney, O.S.A.; Francis J. Caponi, O.S.A.; Edward J. Enright, O.S.A.; Thomas F. Martin, O.S.A.; Alfred E. Murphy, O.S.A.; Stanley C. Smith, O.S.A.; Robert A. Turnbull, O.S.A.

[C] COLLEGES AND UNIVERSITIES

PHILADELPHIA. *Chestnut Hill College*, 19118. Tel: 215-248-7000; Fax: 215-248-7155.
Web site: www.chc.edu
For a complete listing, refer to the Colleges and Universities section.

Holy Family College, (1954) Grant and Frankford Aves., 19114. Tel: 215-637-7700; Fax: 215-637-3787.
E-mail: fonley@hslc.org
For a complete listing, refer to the Colleges and Universities section.

LaSalle University, 1900 W. Olney Ave., 19141. Tel: 215-951-1000; Fax: 215-951-1783
For a complete listing, refer to the Colleges and Universities section.

St. Joseph's University, 5600 City Ave., 19131. Tel: 610-660-1000; Fax: 610-660-1201
For a complete listing, refer to the Colleges and Universities section.

ASTON. *Neumann College*, One Neumann Dr., 19014-1298. Tel: 610-459-0905.
E-mail: neumann@smtpgate.neumann.edu
Web site: http://www.neumann.edu
For a complete listing, refer to the Colleges and Universities section.

GWYNEDD VALLEY. *Gwynedd-Mercy College*, 19437. Tel: 215-646-7300; Fax: 215-641-5509
For a complete listing, refer to the Colleges and Universities section.

IMMACULATA. *Immaculata College*, 19345. Tel: 610-647-4400.
Web site: http://www.immaculata.edu
For a complete listing, refer to the Colleges and Universities section.

RADNOR. *Cabrini College*, (1957) 610 King of Prussia Rd., 19087. Tel: 610-902-8100
For a complete listing, refer to the Colleges and Universities section.

ROSEMONT. *Rosemont College of the Holy Child Jesus*, 19010-1699. Tel: 610-526-2984; Fax: 610-527-0341.
E-mail: jfrogers@rosemont.edu
Web site: www.rosemont.edu
For a complete listing, refer to the Colleges and Universities section.

VILLANOVA. *Villanova University*, 19085. Tel: 610-519-4500; Fax: 610-519-4514
For a complete listing, refer to the Colleges and Universities section.

[D] HIGH SCHOOLS, ARCHDIOCESAN

PHILADELPHIA. *Archbishop Ryan High School*, 11201 Academy Rd., 19154-3397. Tel: 215-637-1800. Opened September 7, 1966. Franciscan Friars, Order of Friars Minor. Revs. Charles Newman, O.F.M., Prin.; Rene Barczak, O.F.M.; Carl Graczyk, O.F.M.; Francis Kelly, O.F.M.; Gabriel A. Rosetti, O.F.M.; Louis Stislow, O.F.M., Chap.; Michael Surufka, O.F.M. Priests 7; Brothers 9; Sisters 21; Lay Teachers 105; Students 2,461.

Cardinal Dougherty High School, 6301 N. 2nd St., 19120. Tel: 215-276-2300; Fax: 215-276-2306.
E-mail: cdhs@libertynet.org
Web site: http://www.libertynet.org/~cdhs
(Coed) Opened September 1956. Rev. Paul M. Kennedy, M.A., M.Div., Pres.; Mrs. Joanne H. Walls, M.S., Prin.; Rev. John B. Wendrychowicz, School Minister. Priests 6; Sisters 18; Lay Teachers 39; Students 1,076.

Father Judge High School for Boys, 3301 Solly Ave., 19136. Tel: 215-338-9494; Fax: 215-338-0250. Opened September 1954. Oblates of St. Francis de Sales. Revs. Thomas J. Erbrick, O.S.F.S., Supr.; Joseph A. DiMauro, O.S.F.S., Prin.; Charles F. Engelhardt, O.S.F.S.; Joseph A. Dougherty, O.S.F.S.; Thomas P. Gallagher, O.S.F.S.; Charles C. Garst, O.S.F.S.; Eugene L. Kelly, O.S.F.S.; Dennis W. Killion, O.S.F.S.; Gerard J. Mahoney, O.S.F.S.; David M. Merchant, O.S.F.S.; Edward L. Rauch, O.S.F.S., Pres.; Edward J. Roszko, O.S.F.S.; William O. Seelaus, O.S.F.S.; Al Smith; John Nees; Frank Greene; John J. Dennis, O.S.F.S.; Stanley Dobkiewicz; Gerald M. Dunne, O.S.F.S.; Bro. Thomas Brophy. Priests 19; Brothers 1; Lay Teachers 57; Students 1,400.

John W. Hallahan Catholic Girls High School, 311 N. 19th St., 19103-1198. Tel: 215-563-8930; Fax: 215-563-3809. Opened September 18, 1901. Mrs. Lorraine S. Rice, Pres.; Sr. Marita Carmel, I.H.M., Prin.; Rev. Joseph M. Corley, School Min. Priests 1; Sisters 14; Lay Teachers 25; Students 700.

Little Flower Catholic High School for Girls, 10th and Lycoming Sts., 19140. Tel: 215-455-6900. Opened September 1, 1939. Sr. Kathleen Klarich, R.S.M., Prin.; Sr. Joan Rychalsky, I.H.M., Pres.; Rev. Joseph J. Kelley, School Minister. Sisters 21; Lay Teachers 34; Students 832.

Northeast Catholic High School for Boys, 1842 E. Torresdale Ave., 19124-4418. Tel: 215-831-1234.
E-mail: mspmurray@aol.com
Opened September 7, 1926. Oblates of St. Francis de Sales. Res., 1840 E. Torresdale Ave., 19124-4418. Revs. Michael S. Murray, O.S.F.S, Pres.; Nicholas R. Waseline, O.S.F.S., Prin.; Very Rev. William E. Davis, O.S.F.S., Supr.; Rev. William T. McCandless, O.S.F.S., School Min. Priests 13; Brothers 3; Lay Faculty 47; Students 950.

Roman Catholic High School for Boys, 301 N. Broad St., 19107. Tel: 215-627-1270; 627-1570.
Web site: http://philanet.com/~roman/
Opened September 8, 1890. Revs. Francis W. Beach, M.A., Pres. & Rector; Gerard J. Hoffman, Prin.; Joseph F. Gleason, School Minister; Ronald M. Jakows, Teacher. Priests 4; Sisters 2; Lay Teachers 38; Students 846.

St. Hubert's Catholic High School for Girls, 7320 Torresdale Ave., 19136. Tel: 215-624-6840.
E-mail: sthubert@nni.com
Web site: www.asd.com
Opened September 1941. Sr. Alma Rose Schlosser, S.S.J., Pres.; Rev. John J. Pidgeon, Dir. School Ministry; Sr. Marie Esther Hart, I.H.M., Prin. Priests 1; Sisters 16; Lay Teachers 61; Students 1,455.

St. John Neumann High School. (Formerly Southeast Catholic High School), 2600 Moore St., 19145-1798. Tel: 215-389-4900; Fax: 215-462-3577. (Boys) Opened September 1, 1934. Canons Regular of Premontre Diocesan Priests forming Faculty. Revs. Michael J. Lee, O.Praem., Pres.; Ronald J. Rossi, O.Praem., Prin.; Steven J. Albero, O.Praem.; Hubert N. Beaudoin, O.Praem., School Ministry; John Zagarella, O.Praem; John M. Cagney, O.Praem., (Retired); James C. Rodia, O.Praem.; Bros. Joseph W. Mulholland, O.Praem.; John Michael Zychowski, O.deM.; Blase G. Corso, O.Praem.; John B. Ginder, O.Praem. Priests 7; Sisters 1; Brothers 4; Lay Teachers 37; Students 753.

St. Maria Goretti High School, 1736 S. 10th St., 19148. Tel: 215-465-8437. (Girls) Opened September 1955. Sr. M. Sheila Foy, I.H.M., Pres.; Candida Antonelli, Prin.; Rev. Michael Blaine, School Min. Sisters 23; Lay Teachers 36; Students 790.

West Philadelphia Catholic High School, 4501 Chestnut St., 19139. Tel: 215-386-2244. Opened September 6, 1989. Bro. John McDonnell, F.S.C.; Rev. William J. Chiriaco, Dir. School Ministry. Priests 1; Religious 23; Lay Teachers 29; Students 820.

DREXEL HILL. *Archbishop Prendergast High School*, 401 N. Lansdowne Ave., 19026. Tel: 610-259-0265.
E-mail: prendie@nni.com
Open September 1956. Sr. Catherine Robinson, S.S.J., Pres.; Mrs. Carol Ann Blair, Prin.; Rev. Michael J. Fitzpatrick, Dir. School Ministry. Priests 1; Sisters 18; Lay Teachers 40; Girls 905.

Monsignor Bonner High School, 403 N. Lansdowne Ave., 19026-1196. Tel: 610-259-0280; Fax: 610-259-1630. (Boys) Opened September 1953 as Archbishop Prendergast High School for Boys. New name adopted September 1956. Revs. John T. Denny, O.S.A., Prin.; William E. Atkinson, O.S.A.; Francis X. Devlin, O.S.A.; Augustine M. Esposito, O.S.A., Prior; John J. Ferrence, O.S.A.; George P. Magee, O.S.A.; Daniel McLaughlin, O.S.A.; Thomas M. Mahoney, O.S.A. Priests 8; Sisters 3; Lay Teachers 45; Students 995.

FAIRLESS HILLS. *Conwell-Egan Catholic High School*, 611 Wistar Rd., 19030. Tel: 215-945-6200. Formerly Bishop Egan High School, Fairless Hills, and Bishop Conwell High School, Levittown. Mr. William L. Galante, Pres.; Miss Helen T. Chaykowsky, Prin.; Revs. Gabriel Zeis, T.O.R., School Min.; Fidelis F. Weber, T.O.R., Guidance Dir. Sisters 10; Brothers 5; Deacons 1; Lay Teachers 60; Students 1,394.

NORRISTOWN. *Kennedy-Kenrick Catholic High School*, 250 E. Johnson Hwy., 19401. Tel: 610-275-2846. Formerly Bishop Kenrick High School, Norristown, and Archbishop Kennedy High School, Conshohocken. Rev. Gregory J. Hickey, Prin.; Harry R. Neenhold, Pres.; Revs. Joseph W. Bongard; James McQuinn; John P. Paul. Sisters 16; Lay Teachers 27; Students 641.

POTTSTOWN. *St. Pius X High School*, 844 N. Keim St., 19464. Tel: 610-326-8990. Opened 1954. Rev. Philip J. Lowe, Ed.D., Prin.; Mr. Salvatore DiNenna, Pres. Priests 4; Sisters 1; Lay Teachers 30; Students 578.

RADNOR. *Archbishop John Carroll High School*, 211 Matson Ford Rd., 19087. Tel: 610-688-7610; Fax: 610-688-8326.
Web site: achs.library.net
Opened September 1967. Rev. T. Christopher Redcay, Dir. of School Ministry. Priests 3; Sisters 6; Lay Teachers 43; Students 1,017.

SPRINGFIELD. *Cardinal O'Hara High School*, 1701 S. Sproul Rd., 19064. Tel: 610-544-3800; Fax: 610-544-1189. (Coed) Opened September, 1963. Rev. Msgr. Joseph P. McFadden, Pres.; Revs. John J. Ames; John P. Collins; Joseph Maloney; Joseph C. Bordonaro; Pascal A. Monteleone; Thomas R. Urian. Priests 7; Sisters 9; Lay Teachers 62; Students 1,717.

WARMINSTER. *Archbishop Wood Catholic High School*, 655 York Rd., 18974. Tel: 215-672-5050.
E-mail: jbeisel@archwood.org
Web site: www.archwood.org
Opened September 1964. Revs. James D. Beisel, Pres.; Robert W. Povish, Chap.; James F. Endres; John P. Paul; William G. Donovan. Priests 5; Sisters 13; Brothers 1; Lay Teachers 54; Students 1,180.

WEST CHESTER. *Bishop Shanahan High School*, 103 N. Everhart Sts., 19380. Tel: 610-696-7604.
E-mail: shanahan@voicenet.com
Web site: http://voicenet.com/shanahan/
(Coed) Formerly St. Agnes High School opened in 1909; became diocesan high school September 1957. Sr. Helen Rapine, I.H.M., Pres.; Sr. Nancy McFadden, I.H.M., Prin.; Revs. Joseph Rymdeika; James J. Melle; Joseph D. Brandt. Sisters, Servants of the Immaculate Heart of Mary 9; Priests 3; Lay Teachers 35; Students 825.

WYNCOTE. *Bishop McDevitt High School*, 125 Royal Ave., 19095-1198. Tel: 215-887-5575.
E-mail: APMcDev30@nni.com
Web site: users.nni.com/apmcdev30/mcdevitt.html
Opened September 1958. Frederick J. Ciao, Ph.D., Pres.; Revs. Paul C. Brandt; James R. Jugenheimer; Albert J. Santorsola. Priests 3; Sisters 8; Lay Teachers 41; Students 860.

[E] VOCATIONAL HIGH SCHOOLS

PHILADELPHIA. *Mercy Vocational High School*, 2900 W. Hunting Park Ave., 19129-1803. Tel: 215-226-1225.
E-mail: apmervoc@nni.com
Sr. Rosemary Herron, R.S.M., Prin.; Mr. William J. Donahue, Vice Prin. Sisters of Mercy 8; Lay Teachers 24; Students 377.

[F] HIGH SCHOOLS, PAROCHIAL

LANSDALE. *Lansdale Catholic High School*, 700 Lansdale Ave., 19446-2995. Tel: 215-362-6160; 242-6160 (Philadelphia). Opened 1949 as a school of St. Stanislaus Parish. Mr. Stephen P. Gary, Prin.; Rev. Martin T. Cioppi, Pres. Religious Sisters of Mercy 1; Sisters of Notre Dame 1; Priests 3; Lay Teachers 43; Students 920.

[G] HIGH SCHOOLS, PRIVATE

PHILADELPHIA. *Nazareth Academy High School*, 4001 Grant Ave., 19114-2999. Tel: 215-637-7676; Fax: 215-637-8523. Sr. Rosemarie Griffin, C.S.F.N., Prin. Sisters 17; Lay Teachers 43; Girls 431.

St. Joseph's Preparatory School, Office of the President, 1733 W. Girard Ave., 19130. Tel: 215-978-1950; Fax: 215-765-1710. Rev. David A. Sauter, S.J., Pres.; Dr. Michael J. Coury, Prin.; Mr. Bernard E. Kueny, Jr., Admin. Vice Pres.; Mr. Charles J. Johnson, Treas.; Ms. Sara M. Adkins, Registrar; Mr. Kevin J. Kelly, Dean of Students; Revs. Peter P. D'Alessandro, S.J.; Stephen A. Garber, S.J.; F. Joseph Michini, S.J.; Francis E. Skechus, S.J.; Ryan J. Maher, S.J. Priests 5; Sisters 1; Lay Teachers 55; Students 917.

BENSALEM. *Holy Ghost Preparatory School*, 2429 Bristol Pike, 19020. Tel: 215-639-2102; Fax: 215-639-4225.
Web site: www.holyghostprep.bensalem.pa.us
Rev. James P. McCloskey, C.S.Sp., Headmaster. Holy Ghost Fathers 5; Lay Teachers 38; Boys 455.

BRYN MAWR. *Country Day School of the Sacred Heart*, 480 Bryn Mawr Ave., 19010. Tel: 610-527-3915; Fax: 610-527-0942. Sr. Matthew Anita MacDonald, S.S.J., Head of School; Rev. Thomas P. Gillin. Sisters 2; Lay Teachers 36; Students 233.

DEVON. *Devon Preparatory School*, 19333. Tel: 610-688-7337; Fax: 610-688-2409.
E-mail: sjcalasanctius@juno.com
Piarist Fathers. Revs. James P. Shea, Sch.P., Rector & Headmaster; Richard S. Wyzykiewicz, Sch.P., Chap.; Ferdinand Negrillos, Sch.P.; Louis G. Mesko, Sch.P.; Geza Pazmany, Sch.P. Priests 3; Lay Teachers 21; Students 187.

FLOURTOWN. *Mt. St. Joseph Academy*, 120 W. Wissahickon Ave., 19031. Tel: 215-233-3177. Sr. Mary Dacey, S.S.J., Pres.; Sr. Karen Dietrich, S.S.J., Prin. Sisters of St. Joseph 19; Lay Teachers 32; Students 526.

GWYNEDD VALLEY. *Gwynedd-Mercy Academy*, 1345 Sumneytown Pike, 19437-0902. Tel: 215-646-8815. Sr. Mary Alice, R.S.M., Prin. Sisters 15; Lay Teachers 28; Girls 388.

HOLLAND. *Villa Joseph Marie High School for Girls*, 18966. Tel: 215-357-8810. Sr. M. Elaine, S.S.C., Prin.; Rev. John A. Cannon, Chap. Priests 1; Sisters of St. Casimir 5; Lay Teachers 20; Students 300.

MALVERN. *Malvern Preparatory School for Boys*, 19355. Tel: 610-644-5454. Revs. David J. Duffy, O.S.A., Pres.; Harry J. Erdlen, O.S.A., Prior; Richard J. Cochrane, O.S.A.; James R. Flynn, O.S.A.; Ronald A. Hamaday, O.S.A.; John H. Melton, O.S.A.; John R. Liggio, O.S.A. Priests 7; Lay Teachers 51; Students 527.

Villa Maria Academy High School, 370 Old Lincoln Hwy., 19355. Tel: 610-644-2551.
E-mail: apvmah30@nni.com
Web site: http://users.nni.com/vma
Sr. Mary Kelly, I.H.M., Prin. Sisters, Servants of the Immaculate Heart of Mary 15; Lay Teachers 32; Girls 416.

MERION. *Merion Mercy Academy*, 19066. Tel: 610-664-6655; Fax: 610-664-6322. Day School for Girls. Sr. Teresa Mary, Prin. Sisters of Mercy 16; Lay Teachers 32; Students 399.

VILLANOVA. *Academy of Notre Dame de Namur*, 560 Sproul Rd., 19085. Tel: 610-687-0650; Fax: 610-687-1912. Sr. Regina Finnegan, Pres.; Mrs. Margaret Farrell, Prin. Sisters 10; Lay Teachers 55; Girls 460.

WYNDMOOR. *LaSalle College High School*, 8605 Cheltenham Ave., 19038. Tel: 215-233-2911; Fax: 215-233-1418. Bro. Rene Sterner, F.S.C., Pres.; Mr. David T. Diehl, Prin.; Bro. Timothy Ahern, F.S.C., Religious Supr. Priests 1; Brothers of the Christian Schools 13; Lay Teachers 65; Students 947.

[H] CONSOLIDATED PARISH SCHOOLS

PHILADELPHIA. *St. Athanasius-Immaculate Conception School*, 7101 Limekiln Pike, 19138. Tel: 215-424-5045; Fax: 215-927-6615. Consolidated school for St. Anthanasius Parish and Immaculate Conception Parish. Sisters 3; Lay Teachers 8; Students 280.

St. Martin de Porres School (Germantown), 44 W. Logan St., 19144. Tel: 215-842-1266. Consolidated school for St. Francis of Assisi Parish, St. Madeleine Sophie Parish and Saint Vincent de Paul Parish. Lay Teachers 8; Students 225.

St. Mary Interparochial School, 5th & Locusts Sts., 19106. Tel: 215-923-7522. Consolidated school for St. Stanislaus Parish, Old St. Joseph Parish, Old St. Mary Parish, St. John the Evangelist Parish, St. Augustine Parish and Holy Trinity Parish. Lay Teachers 9; Students 242.

SS. Clement-Irenaeus School, 72nd St. & Paschall Ave., 19142-1108. Tel: 215-729-8368. Consolidated school for St. Clement Parish and St. Irenaeus Parish. Servants of the Immaculate Heart of Mary 8; Lay Teachers 18; Students 453.

AMBLER. *Ambler Catholic Elementary School*, 260 Forest Ave., 19002. Tel: 215-646-6150; Fax: 215-646-7435. Consolidated school for St. Anthony of Padua Parish and St. Joseph Parish. Sisters of St. Joseph 5; Lay Teachers 14; Students 286.

BRIDGEPORT. *St. Augustine-Our Lady of Mount Carmel School*. (Grades K-4), 418 Jefferson Ave., 19007. Tel: 610-275-8676; Fax: 610-272-6396. Consolidated schools for St. Augustine Parish, Our Lady of Mount Carmel Parish and Our Mother of Sorrows Parish. Servants of the Immaculate Heat of Mary 4; Lay Teachers 9; Students 202.

BYRN MAWR. *SS. Colman-John Neumann School*, 372 Highland Ln., 19010. Tel: 610-525-3266. Mrs. Mary Ann DeAngelo, Prin. Consolidated school for St. Colman Parish and St. John Neumann Parish. Sisters 1; Lay Teachers 17; Students 246.

COATESVILLE. *Coatesville Area Catholic Elementary School*, 605 E. Lincoln Hwy., 19320. Tel: 610-384-5961; Fax: 610-384-5730. Consolidated for St. Cecilia Parish, St. Joseph Parish, Our Lady of Consolation, Parksburg. Servants of the Immaculate Heart of Mary 4; Lay Teachers 16; Students 533.

CONSHOHOCKEN. *Conshohocken Catholic School*, 205 Fayette St., 19428. Tel: 610-828-0755. Mrs. Jacqueline Kerrigan, Prin., SS. Cosmas & Damian Primary Campus. (Grades PreK-K). Tel: 610-828-0755. St. Matthew Elementary Campus. (Grades 1-8). Tel: 610-828-2007; Fax: 610-825-8796. Consolidated school for SS. Cosmas & Damian Parish and St. Matthew Parish.

LINWOOD. *Holy Saviour-St. John Fisher School*, 116 E. Ridge Rd., 19061. Tel: 610-485-0363. Judith Ann Devine, B.A., M.A., Prin. Consolidated school for Holy Saviour Parish and St. John Fisher Parish. Lay Teachers 17; Students 384.

PHOENIXVILLE. *Holy Family School*, Third & Buttonwood Sts., 19460. Tel: 610-933-7562..Consolidated school for St. Ann Parish, Holy Trinity Parish, St. Mary of the Assumption Parish and Sacred Heart Parish..Lay Teachers 15; Students 340.

RIDLEY PARK. *St. Madeline-St. Rose School*, Tome & Rogers Sts., 19078. Tel: 610-583-3662. Consolidated School for St. Madeline Parish and St. Rose of Lima Parish. Lay Teachers 16; Students 370.

SELLERSVILE. *St. Agnes-Sacred Heart School*, 393 N. Main St., 18960. Tel: 215-257-3571. Consolidated school for St. Agnes Parish and St. Robert Bellarmine Parish. Lay Teachers 22; Students 515.

VILLANOVA. *St. Thomas-Good Counsel School*. Pennswood Rd., Bryn Mawr, 19010. Tel: 610-525-1407; Fax: 610-525-0157. Lay Teachers 10; Students 195. Consolidated school for St. Thomas of Villanova Parish and Our Mother of Good Counsel Parish.

WARRINGTON. *SS. Joseph-St. Robert School*, 1701 Columbia Ave., 18976. Tel: 215-672-0724. Consolidated school for St. Joseph Parish and St. Robert Bellarmine Parish. Servants of the Immaculate Heart of Mary 3; Lay Teachers 18; Students 504.

[I] ELEMENTARY SCHOOLS, PRIVATE

PHILADELPHIA. *Cecilian Academy*, 100-144 W. Carpenter Ln., 19119. Tel: 215-849-3252. (PreK-8 and Learning Disabilities Program). Sr. Elizabeth Joseph, Prin. Convent, 6818 Chesheim Rd., 19119. Sisters of St. Joseph 9; Lay Teachers 12; Students 192.

The Gesu School, 18th & Thompson Sts., 19121. Tel: 215-763-3660; 763-9077(Development); Fax: 215-763-9844. Rev. George Bur, S.J., Pres.; Sr. Ellen Convey, I.H.M., Prin.; Rev. Neil Ver-Schneider, S.J.; Sr. Patricia McGrenra, I.H.M.; Sr. Carmela Anne Dauerbach, I.H.M. Priests, Society of Jesus 2; Sisters, Servants of the Immaculate Heart of Mary 3; Lay Teachers 19; Students 420.

Nazareth Academy Grade School, 4701 Grant Ave., 19114. Tel: 215-637-7777.
E-mail: www.duffy@nni.com
Sr. M. Martin, C.S.F.N., Prin. Sisters of the Holy Family of Nazareth 5; Lay Teachers 14; Students 234.

Norwood-Fontbonne Academy for Boys and Girls, 8891 Germantown Ave., 19118. Tel: 215-247-3811. Sr. Monica Osaben, S.S.J., Dir. Sisters of St. Joseph 4; Lay Teachers 32; Students 476.

BRYN MAWR. *St. Aloysius Academy*. (Grades PreK-8), 401 S. Bryn Mawr Ave., 19010. Tel: 610-527-0506; 525-1670. Sr. Carolyn M. Dimick, I.H.M., Prin. Sisters, Servants of the Immaculate Heart of Mary 11; Lay Teachers 24; Students 293.

DREXEL HILL. *School of the Holy Child Jesus*. (Grades PreK-8), 450 Penn Ave., 19026. Tel: 610-259-2712. Sr. Barbara Foy, S.H.C.J., Prin. Sisters of the Holy Child Jesus 2; Lay Teachers 35; Students 234.

IMMACULATA. *Villa Maria Academy*, 19345. Tel: 610-644-4864. Sr. Mary A. Burke, I.H.M., Prin. Sisters, Servants of the Immaculate Heart of Mary 8; Lay Teachers 24; Girls 368.

MERION. *Waldron Mercy Academy*, 513 Montgomery Ave., 19066. Tel: 610-664-9847.
E-mail: wmaweb@mciunix.mciu.k12.pa.us
Sr. Patricia Smith, R.S.M., Prin.; Mr. Stephen Stritch, Vice Prin. Sisters of Mercy 7; Lay Teachers 36; Students 559.

RADNOR. *Armenian Sisters Academy*, 440 Upper Gulph Rd., 19087. Tel: 610-687-4100. Montessori for ages 3-6. Ungraded Elementary for ages 7-14. Sr. Louisa Kassarjian, Prin. Sisters 3; Lay Teachers 24; Students 212.

ROSEMONT. *Rosemont School of the Holy Child,* 1344 Montgomery Ave., 19010. Tel: 610-525-1876; Fax: 610-525-7128.
E-mail: rosemontslt@aol.com
Sr. Mary Broderick, S.H.C.J., Prin. Sisters of the Holy Child Jesus 2; Lay Teachers 34; Students 270.

SPRING HOUSE. *Gwynedd-Mercy Academy.* (Grades K-8), Elementary Division, Norristown Rd., P.O. Box 241, 19477. Tel: 215-646-4916; 646-2406 (Business Office); Fax: 215-628-8441. Sr. Anne Crampsie, R.S.M., Prin. Sisters of Mercy 3; Lay Teachers 39; Students 450.

WYNCOTE. *Ancillae-Assumpta Academy.* (Grades PreK-8). (Coed), 2025 Church Rd., 19095. Tel: 215-885-1636.
E-mail: emccoy@erols.com
Sr. Elizabeth McCoy, A.C.J., Dir.; Sr. Maureen Gillespie, A.C.J., Prin. Handmaids of the Sacred Heart of Jesus 8; Lay Teachers 52; Students 557.

YARDLEY. *Grey Nun Academy,* 1750 Quarry Rd., 19067. Tel: 215-968-4151. (Coed Day School). Sr. Dolores Beatty, G.N.S.H., Prin. Grey Nuns of the Sacred Heart 4; Lay Teachers 25; Students 248.

[J] SPECIAL EDUCATION

PHILADELPHIA. *Our Lady of Confidence Day School,* 10th and Lycoming Sts., 19140. Tel: 215-329-2697; Fax: 215-324-7440. Mentally Handicapped. Sr. Francis Christi, S.S.J., Prin. Sisters of St. Joseph 1; Lay Teachers 10; Students 135.

LEVITTOWN. *Queen of the Universe Day Center,* 2443 Trenton Rd., 19056. Tel: 215-945-6090. Mrs. Sallie LaMorgia, Prin. Mentally Retarded and Developmental Delay Students. Lay Teachers 4; Students 45.

NORWOOD. *Archbishop Ryan School for Children with Hearing Impairment,* 233 Mohawk Ave., 19074.
Web site: http://www.ces/msaorg
Mrs. Judith Sexton, M.A., C.E.D., Prin. Convent. Tel: 610-583-5160. Sisters of St. Joseph 4; Lay Teachers 8; Students 46.

UPPER DARBY. *St. Lucy Day School for Children with Visual Impairments,* 130 Hampden Rd., 19082. Tel: 610-352-4550; 352-4555.
E-mail: stlucydayschool@compuserve.com
Web site: http://www.homepagecreations.com/stlucy/index.html
Sr. M. Margaret Fleming, I.H.M., Prin. Sisters, Servants of the Immaculate Heart of Mary 4; Lay Teachers 4; Students 30.

WYNNEWOOD. *St. Katherine Day School,* 930 Bowman Ave., 19096. Tel: 610-667-3958; Fax: 610-667-3625. Children with Developmental Delay/Mental Retardation. Miss Lisa M. Cetroni, Prin. Lay Teachers 12; Students 131.

[K] THE CATHOLIC SOCIAL SERVICES OF THE ARCHDIOCESE OF PHILADELPHIA

PHILADELPHIA. *The Catholic Social Services of the Archdiocese of Philadelphia,* 222 N. 17th St., 19103. Tel: 215-587-3900; Fax: 215-587-2479. All addresses unless otherwise indicated. Rev. Timothy C. Senior, L.S.W., M.B.A., Exec. Dir.; Edward T. Cahill, Chief Financial Officer; John C. Smith, L.S.W., Dir. Children's & Residential Svcs.; John Amato, L.S.W., Asst. Dir.; Anne Marie Buck, M.S., Asst. Dir.; Lorraine Knight, Asst. Dir.; Teresa Thompson, L.S.W., Admin. Child Care Dept.; Lorraine Knight, Admin.; David Moore, Mgr.
Office for Human Relations. Tel: 215-587-5655. Sr. Marion Dillon, M.S.B.T., L.S.W., Dir.
Service Centers:
Philadelphia:
Northeast Philadelphia, 7340 Jackson St., 19136. Tel: 215-624-5920. Amy Stoner, L.S.W., Admin.
North Philadelphia, Casa del Carmen, Reese St. & Blavis St., 19140. Tel: 215-329-5660. W. Giovanni Morante, M.A., Admin.
Bucks County:
Levittown, 100 Levittown Pkwy., Levittown, 19054. Tel: 215-945-2550. Marguerite Powers, L.S.W., Admin.
Middle Bucks County:
Southampton, 611 Knowles Ave., Southampton, 18966. Tel: 215-355-1960. Marguerite Powers, L.S.W., Admin.
Chester County:
Avondale, 37 S. Pennsylvania Ave., P.O. Box 119, Avondale, 19311. Tel: 610-268-3510. William Kefer, L.S.W., Site Supvr.
Downingtown:
Downingtown, 141 E. Lancaster Ave., Downingtown, 19335. Tel: 610-269-4060. William Kefer, L.S.W., Site Supvr.
Delaware County:
Chester, 130 E. 7th St., Chester, 19013. Tel: 610-876-9183. James McMaster, M.B.A., Admin.
Springfield, 1797 S. Sproul Rd., Springfield, 19064. Tel: 610-328-7090. James McMaster, M.B.A., Admin.
Montgomery County:
Norristown, 353 E. Johnson Hwy., Norristown, 19401. Tel: 215-279-7372. Sr. Patricia Kelly, M.S.B.T., L.S.W., Site Supvr.
Holy Family Center, 227 N. 18th St., 19103.
Volunteer Program, 227 N. 18th St., 19103.
Immigration Services, 227 N. 18th St., 19103. Martin Frick, Admin. Family Svcs. Dept.; M. Louise Maia, Mgr. Research & Mgmt. Information Systems; Mary Merman, L.S.W., Admin. Adoption Svcs. Dept.; Karen Becker, L.S.W., Admin.; John M. Wagner, Admin. & Housing/Homeless Svcs.; William Tangradi, L.S.W., Volunteer Coord. Total Assisted 79,396; Total Staff 226.

[L] INSTITUTIONS FOR DEPENDENT CHILDREN

PHILADELPHIA. *Catholic Home for Girls,* 5238 N. Broad St., 19141. Tel: 215-324-2610
For a complete listing, refer to the Special Care Facilities section.
St. Joseph's House for Boys, 4010-4012 Ashburner St., 19136-2801. Tel: 215-332-3490
For a complete listing, refer to the Special Care Facilities section.
St. Vincent's Orphanage Tacony, 7201 Milnor St., 19135. Tel: 215-624-5601
For a complete listing, refer to the Special Care Facilities section.

AMBLER. *St. Mary's Villa for Children,* 701 Bethlehem Pike, P.O. Box 388, 19002-0388. Tel: 215-242-0376; 643-7676.
E-mail: csfn@juno.com
For a complete listing, refer to the Special Care Facilities section.

BENSALEM. *St. Francis Homes for Boys,* 857 Langstroth Ln., 19020-5735. Tel: 215-638-9310
For a complete listing, refer to the Special Care Facilities section.

[M] RESIDENTIAL SCHOOLS FOR MENTALLY HANDICAPPED CHILDREN AND ADULTS

SPRINGFIELD. *Cardinal Krol Center,* 1799 S. Sproul Rd., 19064. Tel: 610-543-3380. Rev. Romano DiRuscio, S.C., M.A., Admin. A residential facility for 131 mentally retarded male adults which provides an environment, both day and residential, that contributes to the individuals own growth and development by fulfilling their potential in the physical, mental, emotional, social, psychological, and spiritual areas of their lives. Priests 4; Residential Capacity 131; Day Program 20; Total Assisted 170; Total Staff 250.
Divine Providence Village, 686 Old Marple Rd., 19064. Tel: 610-328-7730. Sr. Gertrude LaBarbera, D.S.M.P., Admin.; Revs. James J. Brennan, Chap.; Timothy Senior, Chap. Care & specialized training for developmentally disabled females. Sisters 6; Capacity 96.
Don Guanella School for Retarded Boys, 1797 S. Sproul Rd., 19064-1195. Tel: 610-543-1418. Rev. Romano DiRuscio, S.C., M.A., Admin. Provides specialized care and treatment program for mentally retarded boys ages 6-21. Capacity: Residents 40; Day Students 30.

[N] RESIDENTIAL HOMES FOR PHYSICALLY HANDICAPPED CHILDREN

ROSEMONT. *St. Edmond's Home for Children,* 320 S. Roberts Rd., 19010. Tel: 610-525-8800
For a complete listing, refer to the Special Care Facilities section.

[O] PROTECTIVE INSTITUTIONS

PHILADELPHIA. *St. Gabriel's System,* Administrative Offices, 117 S. 17th St., Ste. 1701, 19103. Tel: 215-665-8777; Fax: 215-665-8821
For a complete listing, refer to the Special Care Facilities section.

AUDUBON. *St. Gabriel's Hall,* Box 7280, 19407-7280. Tel: 215-247-2776 (Philadelphia); 610-666-7970 (Audubon)
For a complete listing, refer to the Special Care Facilities section.

[P] DAY TREATMENT CENTERS

PHILADELPHIA. *De La Salle-In-Towne Day Treatment Center,* 25 S. Van Pelt St., 19103. Tel: 215-567-5500; Fax: 215-567-6922. Bro. Robert J. Kinzler, F.S.C., M.S.W., Exec. Dir.; Charles E. Gaus, Dir. A community based day treatment program for court-committed delinquent boys, ages 14-17. Capacity 110; Total Staff 35; Total Assisted 275.

BENSALEM. *De La Salle Vocational Day Treatment Center,* Box 344, 19020. Tel: 215-464-0344. Bros. Robert Kinzler, F.S.C., M.S.W., Exec. Dir.; Dennis Malloy, F.S.C., A.C.S.W., M.A., Dir. A community based day treatment program for court-committed delinquent boys, ages 15-18. Capacity 125; Total Staff 40.

[Q] RESIDENCES FOR UNMARRIED MOTHERS

HAVERTOWN. *St. Vincent's Maternity Residence,* 104 E. Township Line Rd., 19083. Tel: 610-446-0105. Sr. Louise Kane, S.S.J., L.S.W., Admin. Capacity 12. Information and Referrals. Tel: 215-324-2610. Total Assisted 100; Total Staff 12.

[R] SENIOR CITIZEN CENTERS

PHILADELPHIA. *Norris Square Senior Citizens Center,* 2121 N. Howard St., 19133. Tel: 215-423-7241. Carmen Constable, Coord. Total Assisted 100; Total Staff 9.
St. Anne's Center, 2607 E. Cumberland St., 19125. Tel: 215-423-2772. Barbara Jo Gibson, Center Coord. Total Staff 6; Total Assisted 11,288.
St. Bernard's Senior Adult Program, 7340 Jackson St., 19136. Tel: 215-624-5920. Ms. Claire Mansfield, Prog. Dir.
St. Rita's Senior Citizen Center, 1150-1154 S. Broad St., 19146. Tel: 215-735-4300; Fax: 215-735-0935. Daryl Kezell, L.S.W., Coord. Total Staff 11; Total Assisted 400.
Star Harbor Center, 4700 Springfield Ave., 19143. Tel: 215-726-7468; Fax: 215-726-7496. Maryrose Smith, Coord.

[S] OUTREACH CENTERS

PHILADELPHIA. *Casa del Carmen,* 4400 N. Reese St., 19140. Tel: 215-329-5660. W. Giovanni Morante, M.A. Offers emergency crisis social services to the Spanish speaking community in Philadelphia and surrounding areas.
Catholic Center for the Deaf and Hard of Hearing, St. Boniface Rectory, 174 W. Diamond St., 19122. Tel: 215-423-9547. Rev. Anthony T. Russo, C.SS.R., Dir.
Mass and Homily in Sign Language: Resurrection Church, Castor Ave. & Vista St., 19152. St. Mary's Manor, 701 Lansdale Ave., Lansdale, 19446. Tel: 215-368-0900. St. Stanislaus Church, Main St. and Lansdale Ave., Lansdale, 19446. Tel: 215-855-3133. St. Charles Borromeo Church, Burmont Rd and Dennison Ave., Drexel Hill, 19026. Tel: 215-623-3800. Rev. Paul V. Dougherty, M.A.
Mass with Sign Language Interpreter: St. Francis of Assisi Church, Marshall and Buttonwood Sts., Norristown, 19401. Tel: 215-272-0402. S.S. Peter and Paul, Boot Rd. & Rte. 202, West Chester, 19380. Tel: 610-692-2216. St. Francis of Assisi, Marshall St. & Buttonwood St., Norristown, 19401. Tel: 610-272-0402. St. Joseph's Church, Bartram and Woodlawn Ave., Collingdale, 19023. Tel: 610-583-4530. St. Thomas Aquinas Church, Bristol Pike and Walnut Ave., Croydon, 19021.
Drueding Center, 413 W. Master St., 19122. Tel: 215-769-1830; 769-1931; Fax: 215-787-0999.
Subsidiary of Holy Redeemer Health System, Inc. Sponsor: Sisters of the Holy Redeemer, C.S.R. Communications Department, c/o 1648 Huntingdon Pike, Meadowbrook, 19046. Provides transitional housing and support services for homeless women with children; daycare is provided for the children.
Mercy Hospice, 334 S. 13th St., 19107. Tel: 215-545-5153. Suzanne O'Grady, Dir. Provides temporary and extended shelter care, hot meals, clothing, casework and referral services to homeless and transient women and women with children. Total Staff 33; Total Assisted 2,700.
St. John Hospice for Men, 1221 Race St., 19107. Tel: 215-563-7763; Fax: 215-563-7763. Staffed by Catholic Social Services Archdiocese of Philadelphia. Rev. Kevin C. Lawrence, Program Dir.
Women of Hope, 1210 Lombard St., 19147. Tel: 215-732-1341. Una Edwards, Dir. Residential Facility for chronically mentally ill homeless women. Capacity 24.
Women of Hope, 251 N. Lawrence St., 19106. Tel: 215-592-9116. Sr. Maureen Crissy, R.S.M., Prog. Dir. Residential facility for chronically mentally ill homeless women. Capacity 22; Total Staff 18; Total Assisted 22.

CHESTER. *Bernardine Center,* 2625 Ninth St., 19013. Tel: 215-497-3225. Sr. Rose MacDermott, O.S.F., Dir. Emergency food cupboard, motivation, education toward self-sufficiency, advocacy and social spirituality education. Sisters 4.

[T] DAY CARE CENTERS

PHILADELPHIA. *Bambino Gesu Child Development Center,* 5210 N. Broad St., 19141. Tel: 215-457-4330; Fax: 215-457-4216. Sr. Mary Julia Apolonio, O.S.P., Admin. Oblate Sisters of Providence 4; Total Staff 11.
St. Monica Day Care Center, 1441 Porter St., 19145. Tel: 215-334-6001. Sister, Servants of the Immaculate Heart of Mary. Sr. Maria Clemens, I.H.M., Admin. Total Staff 12; Total Assisted 115.

St. Vincent's Day Care Center, 7201 Milnor St., 19135. Tel: 215-624-5600; Fax: 215-624-8355. Rev. Msgr. William A. Koenig, Pres., Bd. of Mgrs.; Agnes Healey, Dir. Day Care.

[U] GENERAL HOSPITALS

PHILADELPHIA. *Mercy Hospital of Philadelphia*, 501 S. 54th St., 19143. Tel: 215-748-9000
For a complete listing, refer to the Hospitals section.
Nazareth Hospital, 2601 Holme Ave., 19152. Tel: 215-335-6000
For a complete listing, refer to the Hospitals section.
St. Agnes Medical Center, 1900 S. Broad St., 19145. Tel: 215-339-4100
For a complete listing, refer to the Hospitals section.

DARBY. *Mercy Catholic Medical Center*, Fitzgerald Mercy Hospital, Lansdowne Ave. and Baily Rd., 19023. Tel: 215-237-4000
For a complete listing, refer to the Hospitals section.

HAVERFORD. *Mercy Haverford Hospital*, 2000 Old West Chester Pike, 19083. Tel: 215-645-3600
For a complete listing, refer to the Hospitals section.

HUNTINGDON VALLEY. *Holy Redeemer Foundation*, 521 Moredon Rd., 19006. Tel: 215-938-0505; Fax: 215-938-8717.
E-mail: foundtn@phillynet.com
Web site: www.holyredeemer.com
For a complete listing, refer to the Hospitals section.
HRH Management Corporation, 727 Welsh Rd., 19006. Tel: 215-938-0180; Fax: 215-938-1237
For a complete listing, refer to the Hospitals section.

LANGHORNE. *St. Mary Medical Center* Langhorne-Newton Rd., 19047. Tel: 215-750-2000.
For a complete listing, refer to the Hospitals section.

MEADOWBROOK. *Holy Redeemer Hospital and Medical Center*, 1648 Huntingdon Pike, 19046. Tel: 215-947-3000
For a complete listing, refer to the Hospitals section.

NORRISTOWN. *Sacred Heart Hospital and Rehabilitation Center*, 1430 DeKalb St., 19401. Tel: 215-278-8200
For a complete listing, refer to the Hospitals section.

[V] SPECIAL HOSPITALS AND SANATORIA

PHILADELPHIA. *Mount Nazareth*, 2755 Holme Ave., 19152. Tel: 215-338-8992
For a complete listing, refer to the Special Care Facilities section.

ASTON. *Assisi House*, 600 Red Hill Rd., 19014. Tel: 215-459-8990
For a complete listing, refer to the Special Care Facilities section.

DARBY. *Villa Saint Joseph*, 1436 Lansdowne Ave., 19023-1298. Tel: 610-586-8535
For a complete listing, refer to the Special Care Facilities section.

DOWNINGTOWN. *St. John Vianney Hospital*, 151 Woodbine Rd., 19335. Tel: 610-269-2600
For a complete listing, refer to the Special Care Facilities section.

FLOURTOWN. *St. Joseph Villa*, 110 W. Wissahickon Ave., 19031-1898. Tel: 215-836-4179
For a complete listing, refer to the Special Care Facilities section.

IMMACULATA. *Camilla Hall Nursing Home*, P.O. Box 100, 19345-0100. Tel: 610-644-1152
For a complete listing, refer to the Special Care Facilities section.

MERION STATION. *McAuley Convent*, 517 Montgomery Ave., 19066. Tel: 610-667-2775
For a complete listing, refer to the Special Care Facilities section.

VENTNOR. *Villa St. Joseph by the Sea*, 114 S. Princeton Ave., 08406. Tel: 609-822-7184
For a complete listing, refer to the Special Care Facilities section.

WARMINSTER. *Regina Coeli Residence for Priests*, 685 York Rd., 18974. Tel: 215-441-4642
For a complete listing, refer to the Special Care Facilities section.

[W] AFFILIATED SERVICES

PHILADELPHIA. *Holy Name Province.*
Franciscan Volunteer Ministry, Inc., P.O. Box 29276, 19125. Tel: 215-427-3070; Fax: 215-427-3059.
Jean Donovan House Volunteer Residence, 1809 E. Hagert St., 19125. Franciscan Volunteer, Inc. staff residence.
St. Francis Inn, 2441 Kensington Ave., 19125. Tel: 215-423-5825. Rev. Michael A. Duffy, O.F.M., Contact Person. Brothers 4. A hot meal and shelter service for the poor.
Thea Bowman's Women's Center, 2858 Kensington Ave., 19134. Sr. Xavier Kozubal, C.S.F.N., Contact Person. Total Staff 4; Total Assisted 35. Women's day activity center.
St. Joseph's Mens Shelter, 2436 N. Front St., 19133. Men's homeless shelter.
Mary House, 1805 E. Hagert St., 19125. Overnight volunteer housing.
Canticle House, 1811 E. Hagert St., 19125. Lay staff residence.
Franciscan Volunteer Ministry, Inc., Franciscan Friars, 2443 Kensington Ave., 19125.
Franciscan Volunteer Ministry, Inc., Staff Residence, 1811 E. Hagert St., 19125.
Franciscan Volunteer Ministry, Inc., Volunteer Residence, 1809 E. Hagert St., 19125.
**Holy Redeemer, Nazareth & St. Mary Home Health Services.* *Holy Redeemer Support Services, 12265 Townsend Rd., Ste. 400, 19154. Tel: 215-671-9200; Fax: 215-671-1950. Subsidiary of Holy Redeemer Health System, Inc. Sponsor: Sisters of the Holy Redeemer. Denise Collins, Pres., Communications Department, c/o 1648 Huntingdon Pike, Meadowbrook, 19046. Medicare certified home health agency serving patients in their own homes; Medicare certified hospice program serving terminally ill patients and their families.
St. Benedict Thrift Shop, 437 W. Girard Ave., 19122. Tel: 215-235-1848. Karen Pushaw, Contact Person. A clothing and furniture thrift store operated by Franciscans.

LANGHORNE. *St. Mary's Child Development Center*, c/o St. Mary's Hospital, Langhorne-Newton Rd., 19047. Tel: 215-750-5720. Ms. Judy McGovern.

PHOENIXVILLE. *St. Mary's Franciscan Shelter*, 209 Emmett St., 19460. Tel: 610-933-3097; Fax: 610-917-9845. Sr. Emma Mary Steckel, O.S.F., Dir.; Sr. Mary Teresa Coll, O.S.F., Housekeeping; Sr. Regina Carmel McMonagle, O.S.F., Coord. Volunteer and Food Prog.; Sr. Christine Kranichfeld, Maintenance Coord.; Rose Dougherty, Case Mgr. Total Staff 6; Families Assisted 26.

[X] NURSING AND CONVALESCENT HOMES

PHILADELPHIA. *Sacred Heart Free Home for Incurable Cancer*, 1315 W. Hunting Park Ave., 19140. Tel: 215-329-3222
For a complete listing, refer to the Special Care Facilities section.
St. Ignatius Nursing Home, 4401 Haverford Ave., 19104. Tel: 215-349-8800; Fax: 215-222-3078
For a complete listing, refer to the Special Care Facilities section.
St. John Neumann Nursing Home, 10400 Roosevelt Blvd., 19116. Tel: 215-698-5600
For a complete listing, refer to the Special Care Facilities section.

DARBY. *St. Francis Country House*, 1412 Lansdowne Ave., 19023-1218. Tel: 610-461-6510; Fax: 610-461-3558
For a complete listing, refer to the Special Care Facilities section.

DOWNINGTOWN. *St. Martha Manor*, 470 Manor Ave., 19335. Tel: 610-873-8490
For a complete listing, refer to the Special Care Facilities section.

FLOURTOWN. *Sisters of St. Joseph of Philadelphia, St. Joseph Villa Staff*, 110 W. Wissahickon Ave., 19031-1898
For a complete listing, refer to the Special Care Facilities section.

[Y] BOARDING HOMES FOR THE AGED

PHILADELPHIA. *Holy Family Home*, 5300 Chester Ave., 19143-4993. Tel: 215-729-5153
For a complete listing, refer to the Special Care Facilities section.
Immaculate Mary Home, 2990 Holme Ave., 19136-1829. Tel: 215-335-2100; Fax: 215-331-1016
For a complete listing, refer to the Special Care Facilities section.
Sacred Heart Manor, 6445 Germantown Ave., 19119. Tel: 215-438-5268
For a complete listing, refer to the Special Care Facilities section.
St. Joseph Housing Corporation
For a complete listing, refer to the Special Care Facilities section.

DARBY. *Little Flower Manor*, 1201 Springfield Rd., 19023. Tel: 610-534-6000; Fax: 610-534-6039
For a complete listing, refer to the Special Care Facilities section.
Villa St. Teresa, 1215 Springfield Rd., 19023. Tel: 610-583-0700
For a complete listing, refer to the Special Care Facilities section.

ELVERSON. *St. Mary of Providence Center*, 227 Isabella Rd., 19520. Tel: 610-942-4166
For a complete listing, refer to the Special Care Facilities section.

FLOURTOWN. *Bethlehem Retirement Village*, 100 W. Wissahickon Ave., 19031. Tel: 215-233-0998.
E-mail: j.grelisejuno.com
For a complete listing, refer to the Special Care Facilities section.

HOLLAND. *St. Joseph Home for the Aged*, 1182 Holland Rd., 18966. Tel: 215-357-5511; Fax: 215-357-1701
For a complete listing, refer to the Special Care Facilities section.

HUNTINGDON VALLEY. *Redeemer Long Term Care & Elder Services*, 727 Welsh Rd., 19006. Tel: 215-938-0180; Fax: 215-938-1237
For a complete listing, refer to the Special Care Facilities section.
Redeemer Village, 1551 Huntingdon Pike, 19006. Tel: 215-947-8168
For a complete listing, refer to the Special Care Facilities section.

LANSDALE. *St. Mary Manor*, 701 Lansdale Ave., 19446. Tel: 215-368-0900; Fax: 215-362-2891
For a complete listing, refer to the Special Care Facilities section.

YARDLEY. *D'Youville Manor*, 1750 Quarry Rd., 19067. Tel: 215-579-1750
For a complete listing, refer to the Special Care Facilities section.

[Z] RESIDENCES FOR WOMEN

PHILADELPHIA. *Blessed Katharine Drexel Residence*, 7919 Forrest Ave., 19150. Tel: 215-549-5765. Carolyn Harrington, Dir.
Lucy Eaton Smith, The, 1929 Sansom St., 19103. Tel: 215-564-0561. Dominican Sisters of the Congregation of St. Catherine de Ricci. Total Staff 7; Residents 150.
St. Mary's Convent: Residence for Women, 5th and Locust Sts., 19106. Tel: 215-627-8655. Religious Sisters of Mercy. Sr. Catherine Rawley, R.S.M., Admin. Residents 33; Total Staff 6.

[AA] MONASTERIES AND RESIDENCES OF PRIESTS AND BROTHERS

PHILADELPHIA. *Archdiocesan Oratory of St. Philip Neri (C.O.)*, 2321 Green St., 19130-3196. Tel: 215-765-4568. Revs. George G. Thiers, Provost; Paul C. Convery; Bro. Brian Gaffney.
Augustinian Community (O.S.A.), 910 Watkins St., 19148. Tel: 215-463-1326; Fax: 215-463-0888. Rev. Eugene Del Conte, O.S.A., Contact Person.
Brothers of Charity, St. Aloysius Residence, 2026 S. 28th St., 19145. Tel: 215-468-0251. Bro. Jerome Benway, F.C. Total in Residence 2.
Brothers of Charity (F.C.), 6522 Belmar St., 19142. Tel: 215-729-4417. Bro. William Riley, F.C.
Brothers of the Christian Schools, West Catholic Community, 1919 S. 23rd St., 19145. Tel: 215-551-4191. Bro. Richard Buccina, F.S.C.
Brothers of the Christian Schools, St. Mary's Hall, 7018 Boyer St., 19119-1801. Tel: 215-248-2434; Fax: 215-248-4327. Bro. Edward Davis, F.S.C., Dir. Total in Residence 5.
Congregation of the Mission, St. Vincent's Seminary, 500 E. Chelten Ave., 19144-1203. Tel: 215-848-1985; Fax: 215-844-2085. Central House of the Congregation of the Mission (Vincentian Community), Eastern Province. Novitiate, Central Shrine of the Miraculous Medal in the United States, The Central Association of the Miraculous Medal and St. Catherine's Infirmary, The Brother Bertrand Ducournau Archives of the Eastern Province of the Congregation of the Mission.
Provincial Administration: Very Rev. Joseph L. Levesque, C.M., Prov.; Revs. Thomas F. McKenna, C.M., Asst. Prov.; John W. Gouldrick, C.M., Prov. Treas.; Joseph L. Boegel, C.M., Assoc. Prov. Treas.; Bro. Peter A. Campbell, C.M., Prov. Planner.
House Administration: Revs. William W. Sheldon, C.M., Supr.; William J. Bamber, C.M., Asst. Supr.; Gerald E. Deitzer, C.M., Treas. In res. Revs. William J. Bamber, C.M.; Robert J. Brandenberger, C.M.; Joseph L. Boegel, C.M.; George E. Browne, C.M.; John W. Carven, C.M., Prov. Archivist; William J. Casey, C.M.; Gerard D. Conroy; John J. Cusack, C.M.; Gerald E. Deitzer, C.M.; Walter F. Dirig, C.M.; Thomas M. Finley, C.M.; William P. Finn; Patrick J. Fleming, C.M.; Frederick J. Gaulin, C.M.; Fredric P. Gehring, C.M.; Aloysius P. Grass, C.M.; John J. Hodnett, C.M.; John D. Hummel, C.M.; John V. Kennedy, C.M.; Thomas R. Kennedy, C.M.; John F. King, C.M.; Daniel J. Kramer, C.M.; Richard A. Loeffler, C.M.; Edward C. Mannion, C.M.; William E. McKeon, C.M.; Terence J. Mooney, C.M.; Paul M. Murphy, C.M.; Bartholomew J. O'Malley, C.M.; Charles J. O'Connor, C.M.; John S. Pearce, C.M.; James E. Power, C.M.; William W. Sheldon, C.M.; David L. Symes, C.M.; Joseph J. Symes, C.M.
St. Catherine Infirmary. Revs. Joseph P. McCaffrey, C.M.; John A. Murray, C.M.; Vincent J. Nugent, C.M.; Vincent E. Trunk, C.M.
Vincentian Fathers of the Eastern Province of the Congregation of the Mission serving on special assignments other than the Motherhouse:
Ethiopia: Revs. John J. Buckley, C.M.; Francis X. Maguire, C.M.

Rome, Italy: Very Rev. Robert P. Maloney, C.M.; Rev. Patrick J. Griffin, C.M.
Philippines: Rev. Robert P. Crawford, C.M.
Solomon Islands: Rev. Thomas J. Hynes, C.M.
Taiwan: Rev. Thomas A. Sendlein, C.M.
District of Columbia: Rev. Brian J. O'Connell, C.M.
Florida: Revs. Lester T. DeMott, C.M.; Robert P. Galchus, C.M.; Edward F. McQuillan, C.M.; Jose Sanchez, C.M.; Stephen P. Trzecieski, C.M.
Michigan: Revs. Alfred R. Pehrsson, C.M.; Michael M. Shea, C.M.
New York: Rev. William J. Gormley, C.M.
Pennsylvania: Revs. James E. Claffey, C.M.; Bruce J. Krause, C.M.; John P. Murray, C.M.; Edward J. Smith, C.M.; Joseph J. Snoha, C.M.
South Carolina: Rev. John J. Lawlor, C.M.
West Virginia: Rev. Carl L. Pieber, C.M. Total in Residence 38.

Father Judge Faculty House, 3301 Solly Ave., 19136. Tel: 215-624-1604. Revs. Joseph G. Campellone, O.S.F.S.; James E. Dalton, O.S.F.S.; John J. Dennis, O.S.F.S.; Joseph A. Dougherty, O.S.F.S.; Gerald M. Dunne, O.S.F.S.; Charles F. Engelhardt, O.S.F.S.; Thomas P. Gallagher, O.S.F.S.; Francis J. Green, O.S.F.S.; Eugene L. Kelly, O.S.F.S.; James D. Keenan, O.S.F.S.; Dennis W. Killion, O.S.F.S.; Gerard J. Mahoney, O.S.F.S.; David M. Merchant, O.S.F.S.; Robert G. Mulligan, O.S.F.S.; Edward L. Rauch, O.S.F.S.; William O. Seelaus, O.S.F.S.; Bro. Thomas Brophy, O.S.F.S. Total Staff 7; Total in Residence 17.

Gesu School Jesuit Community and Outreach Center(S.J.), 1236 N. 18th St., 19121. Tel: 215-235-1662. Rev. George Bur, S.J., Contact Person. Total Assisted 500; Total Staff 2.

Holy Ghost Fathers, 8101 Cresco Ave., 19136. Tel: 215-331-1039. Rev. Francis R. Duffy, C.S.Sp., Ph.D. Total in Residence 1.

Holy Name Priory, Dominican Friars. Province of St. Joseph. 701 E. Gaul St., 19125-2896. Tel: 215-739-3960; Fax: 215-739-7597. Revs. Stephen F. Carmody, O.P., Prior; Ralph V. Townsend, O.P., Councillor.

Holy Spirit Missonary Cenacle, 1301 Oak Ln., 19126. Tel: 215-924-2257; Fax: 215-224-6808. Missionary Servants of the Most Holy Trinity. Bro. Paul Michalenko, S.T.

Inner City House, 1904 N. 22nd St., 19121. Tel: 215-765-1904. Rev. David I. Hagan, O.S.F.S., Dir. Total in Residence 1; Total Assisted 750.

Jesuit Community at St. Joseph's University, 5600 City Ave., 19131. Tel: 610-660-1400.
E-mail: jgodfrey@sju.edu
Web site: http://www.sju.edu/JESUIT_COMMUNITY
Loyola Center: Revs. Joseph J. Godfrey, S.J., Rector; Francis H. McGauley, S.J., Dir. Infirmary; Nicholas J. Rashford, S.J., Pres.; H. Cornell Bradley, S.J., Father Min.; Joseph A. Arroyo, S.J. (Spain); Michael L. Barber, S.J.; John E. Bennett, S.J.; Bruce M. Bidinger, S.J.; Michael J. Blee, S.J.; Edward C. Bradley, S.J.; Francis F. Burch, S.J.; Joseph A. Cawley, S.J.; Peter A. Clark, S.J.; Donald G. Clifford, S.J.; Richard J. Colgan, S.J.; Jerome B. Coll, S.J.; John M. Comey, S.J.; Mark J. Connelly, S.J.; Thomas J. Doyle, S.J.; Joseph A. Duke, S.J.; Edward J. Farren, S.J.; Gerald F. Finnegan, S.J.; Christopher S. Fronk, S.J.; Stephen A. Garber, S.J.; Edward A. Geary, S.J.; Vincent J. Genovesi, S.J.; Paul J. Gilvary, S.J.; James J. Gormley, S.J.; Howard J. Heim, S.J.; Frederick A. Homann, S.J.; Albert H. Jenemann, S.J.; Joseph L. Lombardi, S.J.; Bernard J. McConnell; John W. McDaniel, S.J.; Eric McDermott, S.J.; Michael A. McElwee, S.J.; Dennis E. McNally, S.J.; James W. Moore, S.J.; Patrick F. Murray, S.J.; William I. Nuttall, S.J.; Anthony P. Roberts, S.J.; William J. Ruppenthal, S.J.; William A. Ryan, S.J.; Patrick R. Shaules, S.J.; Eugene F. Shaw, S.J.; Francis E. Skechus, S.J.; Herbert F. Smith, S.J.; Robert A. Thoman; Martin R. Tripole, S.J.; Eric A. Zimmer, S.J.; Bros. Robert J. Fitzgerald, S.J.; Francis J. Boyle, S.J.; Bartholomew Sheehan, S.J. Priests 50; Brothers 3.

St. Alphonsus House. Tel: 215-477-9220. Revs. Anthony J. Berret, S.J.; Joseph J. Feeney, S.J.; Joseph M. Kakalec, S.J.; Bro. John J. McLane, S.J. Priests 3; Brothers 1; Scholastics 1.

Maryknoll House, 6367 Overbrook Ave., 19151. Tel: 215-477-5892.
E-mail: mklphil@igc.apc.org
Web site: http://www.maryknoll.org
Maryknoll Fathers and Brothers (Catholic Foreign Mission Society of America, Inc.). Rev. Frank Higdon, M.M.

Monastery of Our Lady of Mercy, 6398 Drexel Rd., 19151-2596. Tel: 215-877-4858; Fax: 215-877-7208. Order of the B.V.M. of Mercy (Mercedarian Friars). Post Novitiate formation house for the Order. Revs. Arcangelo Manzi, O.de.M., M.A., Local Supr.; Antonio Fortunato, O.de.M., Master of Students, Philosophy & Theology. Total in Residence 9; Total Staff 3.

Oblates of St. Francis De Sales, Northeast Catholic High School Faculty House, 1840 E. Torresdale Ave., 19124-4418. Tel: 215-535-9080. Oblates of St. Francis De Sales. Very Rev. W. E. Davis, O.S.F.S., Supr.; Revs. Robert D. Ashenbrenner, O.S.F.S.; Leon V. Bonikowski, O.S.F.S.; Joseph A. DiMauro, O.S.F.S.; John V. DiFilippo, O.S.F.S.; Thomas M. Gillespie, O.S.F.S.; Joseph J. Griffin, O.S.F.S.; Robert P. Hanlon, O.S.F.S.; William T. McCandless, O.S.F.S.; Michael S. Murray, O.S.F.S.; Francis J. Pileggi, O.S.F.S.; William G. Scholl, O.S.F.S.; Edward J. Simons, O.S.F.S.; John J. Sullivan, O.S.F.S.; Cornelius F. Kilty, O.S.F.S.; Nicholas R. Waseline, O.S.F.S.; Bros. Harry G. Schneider, O.S.F.S.; Gerald M. Sweeney, O.S.F.S.; James F. Williams, O.S.F.S.; Daniel Wisniewski, O.S.F.S.; Mr. Serge Vasilevsky, Scholastics. Total in Residence 21.

Order of Friars Minor of the Province of the Most Holy Name aka Holy Name Province, St. Francis Inn, 1802 E. Hagert St., 19125. Tel: 215-423-2859. Revs. Michael A. Duffy, O.F.M.; Charles V. Finnegan, O.F.M.; Francis Pompei, O.F.M.; Bros. Xavier de la Huerta, O.F.M.; Thomas Ennis, O.F.M.

St. Alphonsus House, 5800 Overbrook Ave., 19131. Tel: 215-477-9220. Jesuit Fathers. Revs. Anthony J. Berret, S.J.; Joseph J. Feeney, S.J.; Joseph M. Kakalec, S.J.; Bro. John J. McLane, S.J. Priests 3; Brothers 1.

St. Joseph's Preparatory School Jesuit Community, Arrupe House, 1226 N. 18th St., 19121. Tel: 215-765-1875. Residence of Jesuit Fathers. Revs. Herbert B. Keller, S.J., Rector; Peter P. D'Alessandro, S.J.; F. Joseph Michini, S.J.; David A. Sauter, S.J.; J. Vincent Taggart, S.J.

St. Michael's Passionist Residence, 6300 N. Seventh St., 19126. Tel: 215-549-1761. Revs. Alexis Paul, C.P., Dir.; Columkille Regan, C.P.; Fidelis Connolly, C.P. Total Staff 3; Total in Residence 4; Students 1.

St. Norbert Priory, 1815 S. 27th St., 19145. Tel: 215-389-5575.
E-mail: snpriory@netaxs.com
Canons Regular of Premontre Faculty residence for Norbertine Fathers who teach at St. John Neumann High School. Revs. Steven J. Albero, O.Praem.; Richard J. Antonucci, O.Praem., Supr.; Hubert N. Beaudoin, O.Praem.; John M. Cagney, O.Praem.; Michael J. Lee, O.Praem.; James C. Rodia, O.Praem.; John C. Zagarella, O.Praem.; Bros. Joseph Mulholland, O.Praem.; William Kelly, O.Praem.; John B. Ginder, O.Praem.

St. Pius X Friary, 11051 Academy Rd., 19154. Tel: 215-632-1300. Order of Friars Minor, Assumption B.V.M. Province. Faculty Residence for Archbishop Ryan High School. Revs. Louis Stislow, O.F.M., Guardian; Rene Barczak, O.F.M.; Roderick Drag, O.F.M.; Carl Graczyk, O.F.M.; Francis X. Kelly, O.F.M.; Linus E. Kopczewski, O.F.M.; Charles Newman, O.F.M.; Warren Rector, O.F.M.; Gabriel A. Rosetti, O.F.M.; Michael Surufka, O.F.M.; Joel Szydlowski, O.F.M.; Rudolph Wieszczek, O.F.M.

Society of the Brothers of the Holy Spirit (B.H.S.), Providence House, 3531 N. 19th St., 19140. Tel: 215-225-7231. Bro. Darryl-Joseph Branch, B.H.S., Contact Person. Total in Residence 3.

AUDUBON. *Christian Brothers (F.S.C.)*, St. Gabriel Hall Community, Pawlings Rd., P.O. Box 7280, 19407-7280. Tel: 215-247-2776: 610-666-7970.

BENSALEM. *Congregation of the Holy Ghost*, Spiritan Hall, 2401 Bristol Pike, 19020. Tel: 215-638-0232; 0233.
E-mail: rnroach@aol.com
Faculty Residence for Priests & Brothers Teaching at Holy Ghost Preparatory School; Also Residence for Retired Priests and Brothers.
School Community: Revs. James P. McCloskey, C.S.Sp., Supr.; Robert N. Roach, C.S.Sp.; John A. Sawicki, C.S.Sp.; Christopher H. McDermott, C.S.Sp., Bursar; Denis P. Robinson, C.S.Sp.; Norman E. Bevan, C.S.Sp.
Retirement Community: Revs. Robert N. Roach, C.S.Sp., Supr.; Jeremiah A. Falvey, C.S.Sp., Bursar; Anthony S. Kliche, C.S.Sp.; John R. Muka, C.S.Sp.; Vincent J. Niederberger, C.S.Sp.; Albert M. Seichepine, C.S.Sp.; Stephen A. Zamborsky, C.S.Sp.; Bro. Dominic Reardon, C.S.Sp.

BRYN MAWR. *Augustinians Brothers (O.S.A.)*, Our Mother of Good Counsel Community, 31 Pennswood Rd., 19010-3475. Tel: 610-525-0147. Rev. Adrian Gilligan, O.S.A., Contact Person.

DEVON. *Piarist Fathers (Order of the Pious Schools)*, 363 Valley Forge Rd., 19333. Tel: 610-688-6807.
E-mail: sjcalasanctius@juno.com
Priests who teach at Devon Preparatory School: Revs. James J. Shea, Sch.P., Headmaster; Richard S. Wyzykiewicz, Sch.P., Prov.; Ladislaus Magyar, Sch.P.; Louis G. Mesko, Sch.P.; Ferdinand Negrillos, Sch.P.; Geza Pazmany, Sch.P.

Piarist Fathers Latin Mission. Revs. Richard Wyzykiewicz, Sch.P.; Mario B. Vizcaino, Sch.P. Total Staff 3; Total in Residence 18.

DOYLESTOWN. *Pauline Fathers Monastery, Shrine of Our Lady of Czestochowa*, 654 Ferry Rd., P.O. Box 2049, 18901. Tel: 215-345-0607; Fax: 214-348-2148. Office. Tel: 215-345-0600; 0601. Revs. Lucius Tyrasinski, O.S.P.P.E., Prov.; George J. Maj, O.S.P.P.E., Prior; Jan Kolmaga, O.S.P.P.E., Sub-Prior; Stephen Z. Wozniczka, O.S.P.P.E., Shrine Dir.; Zdzislaw Kikowski, O.S.P.P.E.; Angelus P. Ferrara, O.S-.P.P.E.; Albert P. Ostatek, O.S.P.P.E.; Marian Zalecki, O.S.P.P.E.; Michael Zembrzuski, O.S.P.P.E.; Bros. Casimir Pasnik; Didak Turi; Luke Mitura; Peter Lisiecki.

FAIRLESS HILLS. *St. Anthony Friary*, 607 Wistar Rd., 19030. Tel: 215-943-4810. Franciscan Friars T.O.R. Bro. James Boyle, T.O.R., Local Min.; Revs. Fidelis F. Weber, T.O.R., Guidance Dir.; Neil Saller, T.O.R.; M. Gerald Gordon, T.O.R.; John Grinnen, T.O.R.; Donald F. Vuketich, T.O.R.; Gabriel Zeis, T.O.R.; Bros. James A. Boyle, T.O.R.; John T. Carosella, T.O.R.; John Patrick Calvey, T.O.R.; Francis M. Haworth, T.O.R.; Lawrence Hilferty, T.O.R. Faculty residence for priests and brothers who teach at Conwell-Egan Catholic High School. Total in Residence 11.

FLOURTOWN. *Augustinians (O.S.A.)*, St. Genevieve Friary, 1225 Bethlehem Pike, 19031-1902. Tel: 215-836-2830. Revs. Joseph A. Duffey, O.S.A., Contact Person; John P. Hennessy, O.S.A.; William A. Recchuti, O.S.A. Total in Residence 13.

LANGHORNE. *Society of Mary, Marist Fathers*, St. Mary's Hospital, 19047. Tel: 215-750-2558. Rev. George Wallace, S.M., Contact.

LAVEROCK. *Brothers of Charity (F.C.)*, Triest Hall, 7720 Doe Ln., 19038. Tel: 215-887-6361; 887-6372. Total in Residence 3.

MALVERN. *Augustinians (O.S.A.)*, Malvern Prep School Community, 19355. Tel: 610-644-5454; 647-8281. Rev. Harry J. Erdlen, O.S.A., Prior.

PAOLI. *Daylesford Abbey*, 220 S. Valley Rd., 19301-1900. Tel: 610-647-2530; Fax: 610-651-0219. Legal Title: *Norbertine Fathers, Inc.* Rt. Rev. Ronald J. Rossi, O.Praem., Prior; Revs. John J. Novielli, O.Praem., SubPrior; Theodore J. Antry, O.Praem., Vocation Dir.; Joseph A. Serano, O.Praem., Treas.; Maurice C. Avicolli, O.Praem.; Andrew D. Ciferni, O.Praem., House Supr. & Institute Dir.; William J. Fischer, O.Praem.; Edward J. Kimpel, O.Praem.; Joseph C. Laenen, O.Praem.; David T. Lawlor, O.Praem.; Joseph P. McLaughlin; Rt. Rev. John E. Neitzel, O.Praem., Abbot Emeritus; Revs. Thomas J. Rossi, O.Praem.; Charles T. Urban, O.Praem.; Bros. Blase G. Corso, O.Praem.; John B. Ginder, O.Praem.; William J. Kelly, O.Praem. Priests 24; Brothers 3.

SPRINGFIELD. *Servants of Charity (S.C.)*, Don Guanella Village, 1795 S. Sproul Rd., 19064. Tel: 610-328-3406. Rev. Romano DiRuscio, S.C., Contact Person. Total in Residence 7.

VILLANOVA. *Fray de Leon Community*, Villanova University, 19085. Tel: 610-519-5020. Augustinians. Rev. Edward T. Hastings, O.S.A., Contact. Total in Residence 4.

Order of St. Augustine, St. Thomas of Villanova, 109 Willowburn Rd., 19085-1313. Tel: 610-527-0856. Rev. Donald F. Reilly, O.S.A.

Provincial Offices of the Order of St. Augustine, Province of St. Thomas of Villanova, P.O. Box 338, 19085-0338. Tel: 610-527-3330; Fax: 610-520-0618. Very Rev. John E. Deegan, O.S.A., Prior Prov.; Revs. Anthony P. Burrascano, O.S.A., Treas. & Mission Procurator; Alfred E. Murphy, O.S.A., Prov. Archivist; John E. Rotelle, O.S.A., Contact Person, Prov. Sec., Dir. Communications, Augustinian Press; Joseph A. Jordan, O.S.A., Augustinian Seminary Guild; Richard D. Appicci, O.S.A., Mission Office; Francis J. Caponi, O.S.A., Coord. Vocation Activities. Tel: 610-525-7890, St. Augustine Friary, 214 Ashwood Rd., P.O. Box 338, 19085. Tel: 610-527-0325. Bro. John J. Del Casale, O.S.A. Total in Residence 12.

St. John Stone Friary, 37 Aldwyn Ln., 19085; Fax: 610-527-2315; 527-7925. Revs. John E. Deegan, O.S.A., Prior Prov.; Kail C. Ellis, O.S.A.; John E. Rotelle, O.S.A.; Michael J. Scanlan, O.S.A.; T. Shawn Tracy, O.S.A., Prior; Francis E. Chambers, O.S.A.; William J. Donnelly, O.S.A.

St. Thomas Monastery, 19085. Tel: 610-645-7500. Revs. Richard D. Appicci, O.S.A.; John P. Betoni, O.S.A.; Andrew J. Boyle, O.S.A.; John E. Bresnahan, O.S.A.; George F. Burnell, O.S.A.; Edward J. Burns, O.S.A.; Donald X. Burt, O.S.A.; Jan H. Busch, O.S.A.; George J. Callaghan, O.S.A.; Angus N. Carney, O.S.A.; John F. Casey, O.S.A.; Laurence J. Conneen, O.S.A.; Russell J. DeSimone, O.S.A.;

Edward J. Dixey, O.S.A., Prior; Edmund J. Dobbin, O.S.A., Pres., Villanova University; John M. Driscoll, O.S.A.; Gerard M. Duff, O.S.A.; Henry J. Eagan, O.S.A.; Francis A. Eigo, O.S.A.; John J. Farrell, O.S.A.; Francis A. Farsaci, O.S.A.; John J. Fitzgerald, O.S.A.; Charles R. Flynn, O.S.A.; Dennis J. Gallagher, O.S.A.; John J. Gallagher, O.S.A.; Karl A. Gersbach, O.S.A.; Joseph J. Gildea, O.S.A.; Dante L. Girolami, O.S.A.; Edwin T. Grimes, O.S.A.; John J. Hagen, O.S.A.; Joseph A. Jordan, O.S.A., Treas.; Patrick J. Kenny, O.S.A.; Charles P. Laferty, O.S.A.; Joseph F. Laverty, O.S.A.; Bernard A. Lazor, O.S.A.; John F. Lipp, O.S.A.; Neil J. McGettigan, O.S.A.; Francis X. McGuire, O.S.A.; John J. McKenzie, O.S.A.; Thomas J. Mahony, O.S.A.; Lee J. Makowski, O.S.A.; Francis L. Melcher, O.S.A.; Thomas M. Murnane, O.S.A.; Robert J. Murray, O.S.A.; William J. Murray, O.S.A.; James L. Nolan, O.S.A.; Bernard J. O'Dowd, O.S.A.; Bernard J. Murray, O.S.A.; John M. Quinn, O.S.A.; Patrick J. Rice, O.S.A.; George F. Riley, O.S.A.; Joseph C. Schnaubelt, O.S.A.; Albert C. Shannon, O.S.A.; Joseph L. Shannon, O.S.A.; Thomas J. Shea, O.S.A.; Ralph V. Shuhler, O.S.A.; Ralph C. Shurer, O.S.A.; Arthur F. Smith, O.S.A.; John P. Stack, O.S.A.; Robert E. Steinman, O.S.A.; Michael P. Sullivan, O.S.A.; Henry B. Syvinski, O.S.A.; William C. Van Breda, O.S.A.; Dennis G. Wilde, O.S.A.; Eugene M. Zega, O.S.A.; Bros. Nicholas Osuna, O.S.A.; James E. Farrell, O.S.A.; George J. Phillips, O.S.A. Total Staff 16; Total in Residence 67.

WILLOWBURN. *Order of St. Augustine*, St. Thomas of Villanova Prov. Friary, 109 Willowburn Rd., 19085. Tel: 610-527-0856. Rev. Edward L. Hamel, O.S.A.

WYNDMOOR. *Christian Brothers (F.S.C.)*, LaSalle High School Community, 8605 Cheltenham Ave., 19038. Tel: 215-233-3030. Bro. Timothy Ahern, F.S.C., Contact Person. Total in Residence 16.

Oblates of St. Francis de Sales (O.S.F.S.), Villa De Sales Oblate Residence, 8501 Flourtown Ave., 19038. Tel: 215-836-1472. Very Rev. Joseph F. Chorpenning, O.S.F.S., S.T.L., Ph.D., Religious Supr. & Contact Person. Total in Residence 7.

Villa de Sales Oblate Residence, 8501 Flourtown Ave., 19038. Tel: 215-836-1472. Very Rev. Joseph F. Chorpenning, O.S.F.S., S.T.L., Ph.D. Total in Residence 7.

[BB] CONVENTS AND RESIDENCES OF SISTERS

PHILADELPHIA. *Assumption Hall*, Sisters of St. Joseph, 8900 Norwood Ave., 19118. Tel: 215-247-3665; 248-2564. Sr. Ann Sweeney, S.S.J., Contact. Residence for Norwood-Fontbonne Academy Faculty.

Blessed Trinity Missionary Cenacle, 804 N. 24th St., 19130. Tel: 215-765-2237. Missionary Servants of the Most Blessed Trinity, Ministry in Catholic Social Services and various parish ministries.

Blessed Trinity Mother Missionary Cenacle, 3501 Solly Ave., 19136. Tel: 215-335-7550; Fax: 215-335-7559.
E-mail: msbtphl@aol.com
Generalate, Novitiate and Candidacy of the Missionary Servants of the Most Blessed Trinity. Mother Boniface Center. Sr. Siena Marie Wahl, M.S.B.T., Gen. Custodian; Sr. Joan Marie Keller, M.S.B.T., Gen. Sec. Total Staff 25; Total in Residence 105.

Carmelite Monastery, 66th Ave. and Old York Rd., 19126. Tel: 215-424-6143; Fax: 215-424-6143; 424-6145. Mother Pia of Jesus Crucified, Prioress.

Carmelite Sisters for the Aged and Infirm (O.Carm.), Sacred Heart Manor, 6445 Germantown Ave., 19119. Tel: 215-236-5268.

Congregation of the Sisters of St. Felix, St. Ignatius Convent, 4401 Haverford Ave., 19104. Tel: 215-222-2296; Fax: 215-222-3078. Sr. Mary Joanne Ustaszewska, Local Min.

Convent of the Daughters of Charity, 449 E. Locust Ave., 19144-1323. Tel: 215-438-3536. Sr. Anne Marie Graham, D.C., Supr. Total in Residence 5.

Convent of the Little Sisters of the Assumption, 6300 Drexel Rd., 19151. Tel: 215-877-8655. Total in Residence 6.

Convent of the Missionary Sisters of the Immaculate Heart of Mary, I.C.M., 1242 S. Broad St., 19146. Tel: 215-468-6368. Sr. Anna Verlinden, Supr.

Convent of the Sisters of the Good Shepherd, 733 Susquehanna Rd., 19111-1399. Tel: 215-742-4774. Total in Residence 2.

Daughters of St. Paul, 9171 A Roosevelt Blvd., 19114. Tel: 215-676-9494. Sr. Marjorina Zanatta, F.S.P., Supr.

Daughters of St. Paul Convent, 9610 Evans St., 19115. Tel: 215-969-5068.
E-mail: fspphila@aol.com
Web site: www.pauline.org
Sr. Marjorina Zanatta, F.S.P., Supr.

Dominican Sisters of Our Lady of the Rosary, O.P., 606 W. Erie Ave., 19140-4431. Tel: 215-226-3507.
E-mail: fatima@juno.com
Dominican Sisters of Our Lady of the Rosary of Fatima. Sr. M. Angelica Perez, O.P., Local Supr.

Emmaus Convent, 5358 Cedar Ave., 19143. Tel: 215-471-7260. Sisters of Mercy (R.S.M.). Total in Residence 4.

Franciscan Sisters of Allegany (O.S.F.), 2622 Potter St., 19125. Tel: 215-739-6441. Sr. Mary Augustini, O.S.F., Local Min.

Franciscan Sisters of Peace, Cecilian Academy, 6818 Cresheim Rd., 19119. Tel: 215-438-7515.

Grey Nuns of the Sacred Heart. St. Joseph the Worker Convent, 9168 New Falls Rd., Fallsington, 19054. Tel: 215-269-9783; Fax: 215-269-9789. Total Staff 1; Total in Residence 4.

Handmaids of the Sacred Heart of Jesus, 4001 N. 17th St., 19140. Tel: 215-225-2468.
E-mail: acjphilly@juno.com
Sr. Gloria Petrone, A.C.J., Supr. Total in Residence 7.

Hannah House, Sisters of St. Joseph, 2458 N. 16th St., 19132. Tel: 215-221-0211. Sr. Virginia Jenkins, S.S.J., Contact Person.

Immaculate Heart Convent, 7310 Torresdale Ave., 19136. Tel: 215-332-8299. Sr. Marie de Lourdes, I.H.M., Contact Person. Faculty Residence for Sisters, Servants of the Immaculate Heart of Mary, teaching at St. Hubert High School. Total in Residence 12.

Immaculate Heart Convent, 4904 Chestnut St., 19139. Tel: 215-474-8971. Sr. Regina Havens, I.H.M., Supr. Faculty Residence for Sisters, Servants of the Immaculate Heart of Mary, who teach at West Philadelphia Catholic High School. Total Staff 9; Total in Residence 9.

Little Servants of the Holy Family of Seoul, 70th & Old York Rd., 19126. Tel: 215-548-5535. Sr. Andrew Kim, L.S.H.F., Local Supr.

Little Sisters of the Assumption, 832 Ritner St., 19148. Tel: 215-334-8902. Sr. Marie Gervasi, L.S.A., Contact. Total in Residence 3.

Little Sisters of the Poor, Holy Family Home, 5300 Chester Ave., 19143. Tel: 215-729-5753; Fax: 215-729-5158.

Little Workers of the Sacred Hearts, Sacred Hearts Convent, 160 Carpenter Ln., 19119. Tel: 215-843-2266.

Mary Immaculate Convent, 1731 S. 11th St., 19148. Tel: 215-468-9133. Sr. Maureen Catherine, I.H.M., Supr. Faculty Residence for Sisters, Servants of the Immaculate Heart of Mary, who teach at St. Maria Goretti High School and John W. Hallahan High School. Total Staff 32; Total in Residence 32.

Medical Mission Sisters (M.M.S.), 217 E. Price St., 19144. Tel: 215-844-3672. Sr. Barbara Ann Brigham, M.M.S., Contact Person. Total in Residence 6.

Medical Mission Sisters, North American Sector, 8400 Pine Rd., 19111. Tel: 215-742-6100; Fax: 215-342-3948.
E-mail: mms@mms-sna.org
Web site: www.libertynet.org/~mmsl
Sr. Maria Hornung, M.M.S., Sector Coord.; Sr. Jane Gates, M.M.S., District Coord. Sisters in Sector 149; Total in Residence 55.

Missionary Servant of the Most Blessed Trinity, Holy Spirit Missionary Cenacle, 1835 Johnson St., Apt. 11, 19145. Tel: 215-467-4871. Sr. Marion Dillon, M.S.B.T., Contact Person.

Missionary Sisters of the Most Sacred Heart, Trinity House, 518 Devereaux Ave., 19111. Tel: 215-342-3498. Total in Residence 4.

Missionary Sisters of the Sacred Heart (Cabrini Sisters), 67th and Callowhill Sts., 19151. Tel: 215-472-7911. Sr. Patricia Dunleavy, M.S.C., Supr.

Monastery of the Visitation Nuns, 5820 City Ave., 19131-1295. Tel: 215-473-5888. Mother Frances de Sales Paganelli, V.H.M., Supr.; Rev. Joseph A. Duke, S.J., Chap. Total Staff 13; Total in Residence 13.

Mother of Peace House, 2622 Potter St., 19125. Tel: 215-739-6441. Franciscan Sisters of Allegany.

Mt. St. Joseph Convent, 9701 Germantown Ave., 19118-2694. Tel: 215-248-7200.
E-mail: MSJC19118@aol.com
Web site: http://home.earthlink.net/~roredassj/homepage/
Motherhouse of the Sisters of St. Joseph of Chestnut Hill, Philadelphia. Sr. Margaret Fleming, S.S.J., Supr.

Nazareth Convent, Religious Sisters of Mercy, 6369 Woodbine Ave., 19151. Tel: 215-477-3022. Sr. Patricia Smith, R.S.M., Contact Person.

Peace Hermitage, Society of Catholic Medical Missionaries, 8400 Pine Rd., 19111. Tel: 215-342-0961. Sr. Jane Burns, S.C.M.M., Contact Person.

Poor Servants of the Mother of God, 832 N. Judson St., 19130. Tel: 215-763-4526.

Portiuncula Convent, 4565 Cottman Ave., 19135. Tel: 215-332-0125; 0126. Residence for Sisters of St. Francis of Philadelphia. Total in Residence 5.

Provincial House of the Sisters of the Holy Family of Nazareth. Immaculate Conception Province, 4001 Grant Ave., 19114. Tel: 215-637-6464; Fax: 215-637-8475.
Web site: http://www.integra-net.com/csfn.phila
Sr. M. Michaelann Delaney, Prov. Supr.; Rev. Ronald J. Ferrier, Chap. Total in Residence 180.

Religious Sisters of the Assumption, Assumption Convent, 914 S. 49th St., 19143. Tel: 215-727-9430. Sr. Ann Palmer, Supr.

St. Clare Convent, 7375 Ditman St., 19136. Tel: 215-332-4750.
Faculty Residence for Sisters of St. Francis of Philadelphia serving St. Hubert, Cardinal Dougherty and Hallahan High Schools.

St. Francis Convent, 1727 S. 11th St., 19148. Tel: 215-463-7343. Residence of Sisters of St. Francis of Philadelphia employed at St. Maria Goretti and Hallahan High Schools, St. Agnes Hospital, Sacred Heart School, (Child/Family Treatment), and Archdiocesan Office.

St. Isaac House, Society of the Daughters of the Heart of Mary. 226 N. Essex Ave., #106, Narberth, 19072. Tel: 610-664-9546. Sr. Kathleen F. Devine, D.H.M., Supr.

St. Joseph Convent, 7300 Torresdale Ave., 19136. Tel: 215-338-4884. Faculty Residence for Sisters of St. Joseph, who teach at St. Hubert and Father Judge High School, St. Vincent's Orphanage and Nazareth Academy.

St. Joseph the Worker Convent, 2846 W. Allegheny Ave., 19132. Tel: 215-228-4030. Sisters of Mercy (R.S.M.). Sr. Mary Urban, Coord.

St. Michael Hall, 9001 Germantown Ave., 19118. Tel: 215-247-3698. Sr. Jean Faustman, S.S.J., Contact Person. Faculty Residence for Sisters of St. Joseph who staff Chestnut Hill College. Total in Residence 11.

School Sisters of Notre Dame, Nativity Community, 6346 Hegerman St., 19135. Tel: 215-333-5742. Sr. Mary Loraditch, S.S.N.D.

School Sisters of Notre Dame, St. Vincent Community, 7201 Milnor St., 19135. Tel: 215-624-5600; 624-5635. Total in Residence 6.

School Sisters of Notre Dame, 2141 N. Howard St., 19122. Tel: 215-634-2227.

School Sisters of Notre Dame, 158 E. Huntingdon St., 19125. Tel: 215-425-1350.

School Sisters of Notre Dame, Vistation Community, 3978 Constance Rd., 19114. Tel: 215-824-0754. Sr. Bernadette Marie Ravenstahl, S.S.N.D., Contact.

Shalom Convent, 5342-44 Cedar Ave., 19143. Tel: 215-474-5538. Residence of Religious Sisters of Mercy.

Sister Servants of the Holy Spirit of Perpetual Adoration (S.Sp.S.A.P.), Convent of Divine Love, 2212 Green St., 19130. Tel: 215-567-0123. Sr. Mary Catherine, S.Sp.S.A.P., Supr.; Rev. Joseph C. Dieckhaus, Chap.

Sisters of Charity of Nazareth, 1905 Brown St., 19130. Tel: 215-236-0993.

Sisters of Notre Dame de Namur, Resurrection Convent, 2037 Vista St., 19152. Tel: 215-745-3872. Total Staff 11; Total in Residence 11.

Sisters of Our Lady of Mercy, S.O.L.M., 3224 Belgrade St., 19134-5299. Tel: 215-427-3261; Fax: 215-427-3263. Sisters of the Christian Charity. Total in Residence 5.

Sisters of St. Francis of Philadelphia. Franciscan Formation House. 338 Warton St., 19147. Tel: 215-336-8915. Total in Residence 7.

Sisters of St. Francis of Philadelphia, Santa Chiara, 2238 S. 12th St., 19148. Tel: 215-465-2227. Sisters Residence for those who work at St. Agnes Medical Center and Epiphany Church.

Sisters of St. Francis of Philadelphia, St. Agnes Convent, 1900 S. Broad St., 19145. Tel: 215-465-1597. Total in Residence 10.

Sisters of St. Francis of Philadelphia (O.S.F.), 1342 Castle Ave., 19148. Tel: 215-755-2352.

Sisters of St. Francis of Philadelphia, Canticle House. Congregational Minister's Office, 609 S. Convent Rd., Aston, 19014. Tel: 610-558-7701.
Convent, 1626 Mifflin St., 19145. Tel: 215-551-2586.

Sisters of St. Joseph, Neumann Hall, 58 E. Northwestern Ave., 19118. Tel: 215-248-7282.

Sisters of St. Joseph of Philadelphia. Divine Shepherd Convent, 927 Bethlehem Pike, Erdenheim, 19038. Tel: 215-836-2082. Total in Residence 6.

Sisters of St. Joseph of Philadelphia, Immaculate Heart of Mary Convent, 823 Cathedral Rd., 19128. Tel: 215-482-8540. Sisters in Residence 7.

Sisters of St. Joseph of Philadelphia, Cecilian Academy, 6818 Cresheim Rd., 19119. Tel: 215-438-7515. Total in Residence 11.

Sisters of St. Joseph of Philadelphia, Fournier Community, Administration, 9701 Germantown Ave., 19118-2694. Tel: 215-248-7200.
E-mail: MSJC19118@aol.com
Web site: http://home.earthlink.net/~roredassj/homepage/
Sr. Margaret Fleming, S.S.J., Supr. Gen.

Sisters of St. Joseph of Philadelphia, Nazareth House. 931 Bethlehem Pike, Erdenheim, 19038. Tel: 215-836-2613. Total in Residence 5.

Sisters of the Blessed Sacrament, Acacia Community, 3533 N. 19th St., 19140. Total in Residence 4.
Sisters of the Good Shepherd, 5356 Chew Ave., 19138. Tel: 215-843-9411. Neighborhood ministry, mediation program. Total in Residence 4.
Sisters of the Good Shepherd (Contemplative), 715 Susquehanna Rd., 19111. Tel: 215-722-3970. Sr. Jude Ellen Golumbieski, C.G.S., Supr. Total in Residence 16.
Sisters of the Good Shepherd (R.G.S.), 8550 Verree Rd., 19111-1353. Tel: 215-342-5820. Sr. Maria Virginia Gordon, R.G.S.
Sisters of the Good Shepherd (R.G.S.), P.O. Box 44258, 19144. Tel: 215-849-2070. Sr. M. Loretta Clancy, R.G.S., Contact Person. Total in Residence 5.
Sisters of the Holy Child, 2362 E. York St., 19125. Tel: 215-423-9514.
Response-Ability Residence, 4724 Cedar Ave., 19143. Tel: 215-726-3947. Residence for volunteers for Teacher Service Project sponsored by the Society of Holy Child.
Sisters of the Holy Family of Nazareth, Holy Family College Convent, Grant and Frankford Aves., 19114. Tel: 215-637-6262.
Sisters of the Holy Family of Nazareth, Infant Jesus Convent, 2755 Holme Ave., 19152. Tel: 215-338-8992.
Sisters of the Holy Family of Nazareth, Nazareth Hospital Convent, 2723 Holme Ave., 19152-2015. Tel: 215-335-6380. Total in Residence 25.
Sisters of the Holy Redeemer, Emmaus Convent, 1117 Wakeling St., 19124. Tel: 215-288-5564.
E-mail: emmauscsr@aol.com
Total in Residence 3.
Sisters of the Holy Redeemer, Angelus-Formation Community, 705 Medary Ave., 19126. Tel: 215-276-0262. Total in Residence 4.

AMBLER. *Sisters of the Holy Family of Nazareth (C.S.F.N.)*, St. Mary's Villa for Children, 701 Bethlehem Pike, Box 388, 19002. Tel: 215-643-7676. Residential Treatment Center for Children.

ARDMORE. *Missionary Sisters of the Holy Rosary (M.S.H.R.)*, 205 Cricket Ave., 19003. Tel: 610-896-1786. Sr. Paula Molloy, M.S.H.R., Reg. Supr. Total in Residence 10.

ASTON. *Convent of Our Lady of Angels*. (Formerly Glen Riddle), 609 S. Convent Rd., 19014. Tel: 215-459-4125. Motherhouse of the Sisters of St. Francis of Philadelphia. Sr. Marie Lucey, O.S.F., Congregational Min.
Mt. Alvernia Convent, 602A S. Convent Rd., 19014. Tel: 215-459-5989. Sisters of St. Francis of Philadelphia. Sr. Helen St. Paul, O.S.F., Contact Person. Total in Residence 3.
Sisters of St. Francis of Philadelphia, Our Lady of the Valley Convent, 10 Red Hill Rd., 19014. Sr. Margarita Guggy, O.S.F., Contact. Total in Residence 140; Total Staff 110.
Sisters of St. Francis of Philadelphia, Portiuncula Convent, 610 Red Hill Rd., 19014. Tel: 610-459-8992. Sisters 12.
Sisters of St. Francis of Philadelphia, Assisi House, 600 Red Hill Rd., 19014. Tel: 610-459-8990. Total Staff 110; Total in Residence 140.
Sisters of St. Francis of Philadelphia, TAU Convent, 886 Concord Rd., 19014. Sr. Kathleen Donovan, O.S.F., Contact. Total in Residence 6.

BENSALEM. *Grey Nuns of the Sacred Heart*, Cornwell Station Apartments, 717 Station Ave., No. 0-120, 19020. Tel: 215-639-1613. Sr. Eileen White, G.N.S.H., Contact Person. Total in Residence 2.
St. Elizabeth Convent, 1663 Bristol Pike, 19020-8502. Tel: 215-244-9900.
Web site: SBS@libertynet.org
Motherhouse of the Sisters of the Blessed Sacrament for Indians and Colored People. Sr. Monica Loughlin, S.B.S., Pres.; Sr. Barbara Specker, S.B.S., Local Dir. Total in Residence 45; Total Staff 13.
St. Michael Hall, 1663 Bristol Pike, 19020-8502. Tel: 215-244-9900; 638-0865.
E-mail: SBS@libertynet.org
Web site: www.liberty.org/SBS
The Infirmary of the Sisters of the Blessed Sacrament.
Sisters of the Blessed Sacrament Novitiate, 1663 Bristol Pike, 19020. Mailing Address: P.O. Box 8502, 19020. Sr. Jacinta Franz, S.B.S., Contact Person; Sr. Amedee Maxwell, S.B.S. Professed Sisters 3; Novices 2; Total in Residence 5.

BRANDAMORE. *Medical Mission Sisters*, P.O. Box 216, 19316. Tel: 215-742-6100. Sr. Kathryn Gates, M.M.S., Personnel Asst.

BRYN MAWR. *Missionary Sisters of the Holy Rosary*, 741 Polo Rd., 19010. Tel: 610-520-1974. Total in Residence 8.
Sisters of the Holy Child, 621 Pembroke Rd. Residence for Sisters of the Holy Child Jesus in varied apostolates.
American Province Archives, 1355 Montgomery Ave., Rosemont, 19010-1698. Tel: 610-527-3486, Ext. 221.
Sisters of the Holy Child Jesus, 105 County Line Rd., 19010. Tel: 610-525-9955. Sr. Eileen Algeo, S.H.C.J., Contact Person. Retirement Residence for Sisters of the Holy Child Jesus.
Society of the Holy Child Jesus, 700 Old Lancaster Rd., 19010. Tel: 610-527-5076.
E-mail: countyl@juno.com
Residence of Sisters of the Holy Child Jesus. Total in Residence 7.

CHELTENHAM. *Daughters of Our Lady of the Sacred Heart*, St. Joseph Convent, 7633 Waters Rd., 19012. Tel: 215-224-2159. Total in Residence 2.

CHESTER. *Bernardine Sisters of St. Francis*, Sacred Heart Convent, 2601 W. Tenth St., 19013. Total in Residence 25.
Bernardine Sisters of St. Francis, Bernardine Center, 2625 W. Ninth St., 19013. Tel: 610-497-3225.
Bernardine Sisters of St. Francis, Blessed Katharine Drexel Convent, 2061 W. 10th St., 19013. Tel: 610-497-2368.
Missionaries of Charity, Gift of Mary, 2714 W. 9th St., 19013. Tel: 610-494-4724. Sr. M. Roberta, M.C., Contact. Total Assisted 273; Total Staff 4.

COATESVILLE. *Comboni Missionary Sisters*, 58 S. 6th Ave., 19320. Tel: 610-380-9229. Sr. Joan Ramus, C.M.S., Supr.

DARBY. *Religious Sisters of Mercy*, 3 Golf Rd., 19023. Tel: 610-461-7634. Sr. Mary Elizabeth Burke, R.S.M., Coord. Residence of Sisters, majority of whom minister at Mercy Health Corporation.
Sisters of the Divine Redeemer, Divine Redeemer Convent, 1209 Springfield Rd., 19023. Tel: 610-534-1688.

DEVON. *Congregation of the Benedictines of Jesus Crucified, O.S.B.*, Regina Mundi Priory, Inc., 550 S. Waterloo and Fairfield Rds., 19333-1798. Tel: 610-688-5130; Fax: 610-995-0477. Sr. Zita Wenker, O.S.B., Prioress. Total in Residence 17.

DREXEL HILL. *Holy Child Convent*, 453 Shadeland Ave., 19026. Tel: 610-259-1732.
E-mail: SHCJ@juno.com
Residence of Sisters of the Holy Child Jesus (S.H.C.J.).
St. Joseph Convent, 435 N. Lansdowne Ave., 19026-1190. Tel: 610-622-0440. Sr. Gertrude Friel, S.S.J., Local Coord. Faculty Residence for Sisters of St. Joseph who teach at Archbishop Prendergast High School, Msgr. Bonner High School, and Bishop Neuman and Villanova University.
Sisters of Notre Dame de Namur, 435 N. Lansdowne Ave. 19026-1190. Tel: 610-237-4760.
Sisters of the Holy Child Jesus (S.H.C.J.), 620 Edmonds Ave., 19026. Tel: 610-626-8223.
Society of the Holy Child Jesus, Provincial Office, 460 Shadeland Ave., 19026. Tel: 610-626-1400; Fax: 610-626-1454. Sr. Susan Slater, S.H.C.J., Prov. Legal Title: *Society of the Holy Child Jesus American Province, Inc.*
Xavier House, 454 Shadeland Ave., 19026. Tel: 610-623-8568. Sisters of the Holy Child Jesus.

ELKINS PARK. *Dominican Motherhouse, Congregation of St. Catherine de Ricci*, 750 Ashbourne Rd., 19027-2596. Tel: 215-635-6027; Fax: 215-635-2071. Sr. Rita McManus, O.P., Pres.
Dominican Retreat House, Convent of Our Lady of Prouille, 750 Ashborne Rd., 19027-2596. Tel: 215-782-8520; 224-0945. Total Staff 38; Total in Residence 20.
St. Catherine Hall, 750 Ashbourne Rd., 19027-2596. Tel: 215-635-4540. Retirement Residence for Dominican Sisters of St. Catherine de Ricci. Total Staff 5; Total in Residence 25.

ELVERSON. *Daughters of St. Mary of Providence (D.S.M.P.)*, St. Mary of Providence Center, 227 Isabella Rd., 19520. Tel: 942-4166. Sr. Bernardine Ugolini, D.S.M.P., Contact Person. Total in Residence 3; Total Staff 15.

ESSINGTON. *Bernardine Sisters of St. Francis*, St. Margaret Mary Convent, 546 Wanamaker Ave., 19029. Tel: 610-521-3286.

FEASTERVILLE. *Grey Nuns of the Sacred Heart*, 1825 Bridgetown Pike, 19053.

FLOURTOWN. *St. Rita Convent*, 1410 Bethlehem Pike, 19031. Tel: 215-836-1615. Sisters of Mercy of the Americas. Sr. Maureen McCann, R.S.M.
Sisters of St. Joseph of Philadelphia, Mt. St. Joseph Academy, 120 W. Wissahickon Ave., 19031-1922. Tel: 215-233-4368; Fax: 215-233-4734. Sr. Constance Gardner, S.S.J., Contact.

FOX CHASE MANOR. *Sisters of St. Basil (O.S.B.M.)*. Motherhouse of the Sisters of St. Basil. 710 Fox Chase Rd., 19046-4198. Tel: 215-663-9153.
E-mail: basilians@aol.com
Sr. Dorothy Ann Busowski, O.S.B.M., Prov.

GLENSIDE. *Medical Mission Sisters*. (Society of Catholic Medical Missionaries, Inc.), 15 E. Glenside Ave., 19038. Tel: 215-886-4036. Total in Residence 4.
Sisters of St. Francis of Assisi (Milwaukee), 229 Edge Hill Rd., 19038. Tel: 215-866-7388.

GWYNEDD VALLEY. *Sisters of Mercy of the Americas, Annunciation Convent*, Gwynedd Mercy College, Evans Rd., 19437. Tel: 215-646-8894.
Religious Sisters of Mercy, St. Joseph Convent, Evans Rd. & Sumneytown Pike, 19437. Tel: 215-646-5259.
Religious Sisters of Mercy, Treweryn Convent, Gwynedd Mercy College, Sumneytown Pike, 19437.
Tabor Convent-Gwynedd Mercy College, Sumneytown Pike, 19437. Tel: 215-641-5516.
Transfiguration Convent, Gwynedd Mercy Convent, 19437. Tel: 215-641-5512.
Visitation Convent, Gwynedd Mercy College, 19437. Tel: 215-641-5537.

HAVERFORD. *Provincial Residence of the Handmaids of the Sacred Heart of Jesus*, St. Raphaela Center, 616 Coopertown Rd., 19041. Tel: 610-642-5715; Fax: 610-642-3879. Sr. Gloria Petrone, A.C.J., Prov.; Sr. Asunta Thanh, A.C.J., Local Supr. Total in Residence 10.

HOLLAND. *Villa Joseph Marie*, 1180 Holland Rd., 18966. Tel: 215-357-8810. Sr. Ann Therese, S.S.C., Supr.; Rev. John A. Cannon, Chap.

HUNTINGDON VALLEY. *Sisters of the Holy Redeemer Provincialate*, 521 Moredon Rd., 19006. Tel: 215-938-0540; Fax: 215-938-7759. Sr. M. Regina Heilman, C.S.R., Prov. Supr.; Revs. Michael C. Bolesta, Chap.; Timothy M. Judge, Chap. Total in Residence 17.

IMMACULATA. *Sisters, Servants of the Immaculate Heart of Mary (I.H.M.)*, Pacis Hall, 19345. Tel: 610-889-1668. Sr. Eliz Seton, I.H.M., Contact. Total in Residence 42.
Sisters, Servants of the Immaculate Heart of Mary, (I.H.M.), Camilla Hall, Box 100, 19345. Tel: 610-644-1152.
Sisters, Servants of the Immaculate Heart of Mary (I.H.M.), Gillet Hall, Box 900, 19345-0901. Tel: 610-647-4400. Total in Residence 67.
Villa Maria House of Studies, 19345. Tel: 610-647-2160; Fax: 610-889-4874. Legal Title: *Villa Maria House of Studies, Motherhouse of the Sisters, Servants of the Immaculate Heart of Mary*. Ministry in the field of Academic Education at all levels, Early Childhood Center, Congregation Retirement and Health Care Center, Pastoral Ministry, Diocesan and Parish Administration, Literacy Center, Spirituality Center, Directors of Religious Education, Drug and Alcohol Counseling, Ministry to Hispanics. Total in Residence 1,317.

JENKINTOWN. *Grey Nuns of the Sacred Heart*, Immaculate Conception Convent, 600 West Ave., 19046. Tel: 215-884-9145. Sr. Kathleen M. Woody, G.N.S.H., Coord.
Sisters of the Holy Redeemer, St. Elizabeth Convent, 615 Fox Chase Rd., 19046. Tel: 215-379-0112.

KENNETT SQUARE. *Sisters of Notre Dame de Namur (S.N.D.deN.)*, 501 W. Cypress St., 19348. Tel: 610-444-1792.
E-mail: edna-snd@juno.com
Sr. Edna Maier, S.N.D.deN., Contact Person.

KING OF PRUSSIA. *Bernardine Franciscan Sisters*, Generalate, 403 Allendale Rd., 19406. Tel: 610-337-3864; Fax: 610-337-4359.
E-mail: bfgen@aol.com
Sr. Mary Margaret Jackson, O.S.F., Gen. Min.; Sr. Christine Marie Jasinowski, Gen. Sec. General Councilors: Sr. Madonna Marie Harvath; Sr. Maria Korick; Sr. Marilisa Helena da Silva.

LANGHORNE. *Monastery of St. Clare, Poor Clares*. Altar Bread Ministry. 1271 Langhorne-Newton Rd., 19047-1297. Tel: 215-968-5775; Fax: 215-968-6254.
E-mail: stclare@voicenet.com
Web site: http://www.voicenet.com/~stclare
Cloistered Contemplative Nuns.
San Damiano Convent, 104 Alberts Way, 19047. Tel: 215-860-7185. Total in Residence 3.
Sisters of St. Francis of Philadelphia, St. Mary Convent, 19047. Tel: 215-757-9494. Total in Residence 10.
Sisters of St. Francis of Philadelphia, Franciscan Residence, 113 Alberts Way, 19047. Tel: 215-860-1059. Sisters serving at St. Mary Medical Center.

LANSDALE. *Religious of the Assumption*, Assumption Convent, 500 E. Main St., 19446. Tel: 215-368-4427.

LANSDOWNE. *Sisters of Bon Secours*, 44 S. Lansdowne Ave., 19050. Tel: 610-626-8637. Sisters of Bon Secours caring for elderly women in their home.

MALVERN. *Villa Maria Convent*, 370 Old Lincoln Hwy., 19355. Tel: 215-647-4878. Sisters, Servants of the Immaculate Heart of Mary (I.H.M.). Total in Residence 14.

MEADOWBROOK. *Sisters of the Holy Redeemer*, Emmanuel Convent, 1600 Huntingdon Pike, 19046. Tel: 215-947-2735. Total in Residence 9.

MERION. *Sisters of Mercy of the Americas, Merion Regional Community, Convent*, 19066. Tel: 610-664-6650; Fax: 610-664-3429. Sr. Christine McCann, R.S.M., Reg. Pres.; Sr. Juliet Ferrari, R.S.M., Local

Coord.; Rev. Michael F. Burbidge, Chap. Motherhouse of the Sisters of Mercy of Merion, PA. Sisters 94; Total Staff 16.

Sisters of Mercy of the Americas, Merion Regional Community, Agape, 515 Montgomery Ave., 19066. E-mail: ryann38318@aol.com Sisters 2.

MERION STATION. *Religious of the Assumption*. Assumption Convent and Spiritual Center. 227 N. Bowman Ave., 19066. Tel: 610-664-3074; 664-1736. Sr. Anne Francoise, R.A., Supr.; Sr. Francis Joseph, R.A., Center Dir. Total in Residence 8; Total Staff 3.

Religious Sisters of Mercy, St. Anne Convent, 276 Meeting House Ln., 19066.

Religious Sisters of Mercy, Bethany House of Prayer, 272 Meeting House Ln., 19066. Tel: 610-667-3066.

Religious Sisters of Mercy, McAuley Convent (Infirmary), 517 Montgomery Ave., 19066. Tel: 610-660-7841. Rev. Thomas F.X. Wheeler, S.J., Chap.

Agape Convent, 515 Montgomery Ave., Merion, 19066.

MORTON. *Sisters of St. Francis of Philadelphia (O.S.F.)*, 2130 Franklin Ave., Ct. No. 3, 19070-1217. Tel: 610-543-0186. Total In Residence 5; Total Staff 5.

NEWTOWN. *Grey Nuns of the Sacred Heart*, 135 S. Sycamore St., 18940. Tel: 215-968-0735. Sr. Patricia Geary, G.N.S.H.; Sr. Jean Liston, G.N.S.H.; Sr. Dolores Beatty, G.N.S.H. Total in Residence 3.

NORRISTOWN. *Immaculate Heart Convent*, 1834 Arch St., 19401. Tel: 610-279-2616. Sr. Judith Trumbore, I.H.M., Supr. Faculty Residence for Sisters, Servants of the Immaculate Heart of Mary, who teach at Kennedy-Kenrick Catholic High School.

Missionaries of Charity, 630 DeKalb St., 19401-3944. Tel: 610-277-5962. Sr. M. Carmelina, M.C., Supr. Services include Food Distribution and Emergency Night Shelter. Sisters 4.

OVERBROOK. *Little Sisters of the Assumption (L.S.A.)*, 6300 Drexel Rd., 19151. Tel: 215-877-8655; Fax: 215-877-0958. Total in Residence 5.

PROSPECT PARK. *Sisters of St. Francis of Philadelphia*, Claddagh House, 518 13th Ave., 19076. Tel: 610-583-1113.

RADNOR. *Armenian Sisters of the Immaculate Conception*, 440 Upper Gulph Rd., 19087. Tel: 610-688-9360. Sr. Cecile Kehyayan, Supr. Total in Residence 4.

Missionary Sisters of the Sacred Heart of Jesus (Cabrini Sisters), Cabrini College Convent, 610 King of Prussia Rd., 19807-3698. Tel: 610-687-1823; 902-8233 (vocation office). Total in Residence 6.

ROSEMONT. *Daughters of St. Mary of Providence (D.S.M.P.)*, 320 Roberts Rd., 19010. Tel: 610-525-8800. Sr. Martha Scheessele, D.S.M.P., Contact Person. Sisters who work at St. Edmond's Home for Children.

Holy Child Infirmary, 1341 Montgomery Ave., 19010. Tel: 610-525-1329. Total Staff 20; Total in Residence 37.

Sisters of the Holy Child Jesus (S.H.C.J.), Henze House, 40 Rosemont Ave., 19010. Tel: 610-525-5843. Total in Residence 6.

Sisters of the Holy Child Jesus (S.H.C.J.), New Sharon Community, 1341 Montgomery Ave., 19010. Tel: 610-525-9900. Sr. Dorothy Cunnion, S.H.C.J., Coord. Total in Residence 24.

Infirmary - Community. Tel: 610-525-9000. Total in Residence 32.

Sisters of the Holy Child Jesus (S.H.C.J.), Carroll House Convent, 1301 Wendover Ave., 19010. Tel: 610-527-1025. E-mail: sullivan@rosemont.edu Total in Residence 4.

Sisters of the Holy Child Jesus (S.H.C.J.), Gracemere Convent, 1316 Wendover Ave., 19010. Tel: 610-525-5601. E-mail: gracemere@juno.com Total in Residence 5.

Sisters of the Holy Child Jesus (S.H.C.J.), Midhill Convent, 1355 Montgomery Ave., 19010. Tel: 610-527-3486. Total in Residence 12.

Sisters of the Holy Child Jesus (S.H.C.J.), Rosemont College Convent, 19010. Tel: 610-526-2970. Total in Residence 6.

SELLERSVILLE. *Bernardine Sisters of St. Francis*. House of Contemplation/Prayer. St. Agnes Convent, 427 N. Main St., 18960. Tel: 215-257-0845. Open to lay and religious for days of prayer, hermitage retreats, private retreats, and prayer week-ends. Call to inquire. Total in Residence 21.

SPRINGFIELD. *Daughters of St. Mary of Providence*, Divine Providence Village, 686 Old Marple Rd., 19064. Tel: 610-328-7730.

Immaculate Heart of Mary Convent, 1725 S. Sproul Rd., 19064. Tel: 610-544-0275. Sr. Mariann T. Guiniven, I.H.M., Supr. Faculty Residence for Sisters, Servants of the Immaculate Heart of Mary, who teach in Cardinal O'Hara High School and Archbishop Prendergast High School.

Our Lady of Mercy Convent, 1735 S. Sproul Rd., 19064. Tel: 610-544-0238. Faculty Residence for Sisters of Mercy who teach in Cardinal O'Hara and Archbishop Prendergast High Schools.

St. Anthony Convent, 1715 S. Sproul Rd., 19064. Tel: 610-544-4066. Residence for Sisters of St. Francis of Philadelphia who teach in Cardinal O'Hara High School and other Ministries. Total Staff 6; Total in Residence 6.

St. Joseph Convent, 1705 S. Sproul Rd., 19064. Tel: 610-544-4230. Sr. Joyce Ballerino, S.S.J. Sisters of St. Joseph Faculty House, Cardinal O'Hara High School. Total in Residence 10.

STRAFFORD. *Our Lady of the Assumption Convent*, 139 Fairfield Ln., 19087. Tel: 610-688-7889. Sisters, Servants of the Immaculate Heart of Mary. Sr. Patricia Hughes, I.H.M., Supr. Total in Residence 6.

VILLANOVA. *Sisters of Notre Dame de Namur*, Notre Dame Convent, 560 Sproul Rd., 19085. Tel: 610-688-8810. Residence for Sisters of Notre Dame de Namur who teach at Academy of Notre Dame.

WARMINSTER. *Immaculate Heart of Mary Convent*, 657 York Rd., 18974-2001. Tel: 215-674-0717; 674-0665. Sr. Loretta Therese, I.H.M., Supr. Faculty Residence for Sisters, Servants of the Immaculate Heart of Mary, who teach at Archbishop Wood High School. Total in Residence 9.

Sisters of St. Joseph of Philadelphia, Nativity of Our Lord Convent, 605 W. Street Rd., 18974. Tel: 215-672-0147. Residence of Sisters St. Joseph who teach at Archbishop Wood High School and Nativity Parish.

WYNCOTE. *Handmaids of the Sacred Heart of Jesus*, 2025 Church Rd., 19095. Tel: 215-576-6250. E-mail: acjwyncote@earthlink.net Sr. Rosa Maria Molina, A.C.J., Supr. Total in Residence 16; Total Staff 5.

YARDLEY. *Grey Nuns of the Sacred Heart (G.N.S.H.)*, St. Joseph Community, 1750 Quarry Rd., 19067. Tel: 215-968-4237. Sr. Marie Cecil Egan, G.N.S.H., Supr. Total in Residence 23; Total Staff 68.

Motherhouse of the Grey Nuns of the Sacred Heart, 1750 Quarry Rd., 19067. Tel: 215-968-4236. Sr. Jean Liston, G.N.S.H., Supr. Gen. Total In Residence 57; Total Staff 68.

YEADON. *St. Michael Convent*, 14 Baily Rd., 19050. Tel: 610-623-3631. Sr. Barbara McGeever, R.S.M., Supr. Residence of Religious Sisters of Mercy who staff Mercy Health Corporation of Southeastern PA.

[CC] RETREAT HOUSES

PHILADELPHIA. *Mother Boniface Center*, 3501 Solly Ave., 19136. Tel: 215-335-7541. Sr. Jennie Catanese, M.S.B.T. Sponsored by Missionary Servants of the Most Blessed Trinity. Mid-week and weekend programs; retreats, days of recollection, scripture study, meetings, workshops and hosting programs. Capacity 80; Total Staff 1.

Urban House of Prayer, 1919 Cambridge St., 19130. Tel: 215-236-8328. Sisters of Notre Dame de Namur. Sr. Marie Bodell, S.N.D.deN., Dir.; Rev. George W. Bur, S.J. Total in Residence 1.

ASTON. *Clare House*, 608 B. Legion Rd., 19014. Tel: 610-459-4077. Sr. Celeste Crine, O.S.F., Dir. Directed and Private Retreats. Staffed by Sisters of St. Francis of Philadelphia. Capacity 4; Total Staff 2; Total Guests 180.

ELKINS PARK. *Dominican Retreat House*, Convent of Our Lady of Prouille, 750 Ashbourne Rd., 19027-2596. Tel: 215-782-8520; 224-0945. Retreat house for laity and religious. Total Staff 38; Total in Residence 20.

FOLSOM. *The Marianist Center*, 901 Morton Ave., Ste. 11, 19033. Tel: 610-532-3116. A Center for Educational and Spiritual Growth. Programs include: retreats, days of reflection, scripture study, service/outreach to the poor and marginalized, workshops in small Christian communities and Marianist studies. Bro. Jack Ventura, S.M. Total Staff 7; Total Assisted 700.

HAVERFORD. *Saint Raphaela Center*, 616 Coopertown Rd., 19041. Tel: 610-642-5715; Fax: 610-642-3879; 642-6788. Handmaids of the Sacred Heart of Jesus. Sr. Mercedes Rojo, A.C.J., Dir.

MALVERN. *St. Joseph's-in-the-Hills*. (The Malvern Retreat House), 313 Warren Ave., 19355-0315. Tel: 610-644-0400. E-mail: malvernlrl@aol.com Owned and Operated by the Laymen's Retreat League. Rev. Dennis J.W. O'Donnell, Ph.D., Rector. Tel: 610-647-8581; Paul I. Ackerman, Pres.; Sr. Mary Catherine Walton, S.S.J., Midweek Dir. Offers weekend and midweek, overnight, twilight programs for men, women, students, seniors and clergy. Daily Capacity 323; Annual Retreatants over 22,000.

YARDLEY. *Providence Center*, 1750 Quarry Rd., 19067. Tel: 215-968-4236. Lawrence McElroy, Dir.

[DD] CAMPS

JAMISON. *Camp Neumann Conference Center*. Mailing Address: P.O. Box 297, 18929. Tel: 215-343-6552. Summer resident camp for boys and girls.

[EE] NEWMAN APOSTOLATE

PHILADELPHIA. *Newman Apostolate*, Newman Center, 2129 N. Broad St., 19122-1193. Tel: 215-232-3779; 235-1596; Fax: 215-235-7302. E-mail: 71107.373@compuserve.com Web site: http://www.libertynet.org/~tunewman Rev. Robert A. McLaughlin, Archdiocesan Dir. Full Time Chaplaincies:

University of Pennsylvania, Newman Hall, 3720 Chestnut St., 19104-6189. Tel: 215-898-7575; Fax: 215-386-5899. Rev. Charles J. Pfeffer, Newman Chap.; Robert Cardie, M.A., Asst. to the Chap.

Drexel University, Newman Center, 30 S. 33rd St., 19104-2509. Tel: 215-590-8760; Fax: 215-590-8634. Rev. Charles J. Brinkman, Chap.

Temple University, Newman Center, 2129 N. Broad St., 19122-1193. Tel: 215-232-3779; Fax: 215-235-7302. Rev. Robert A. McLaughlin, Chap.; Sr. Dorothy Giloley, S.S.J., Asst. to the Chap.

West Chester University, Newman Center, 409 Trinity Dr., West Chester, 19382-5362. Tel: 610-436-0891; Fax: 610-436-6247. Rev. Samuel A. Verruni, Chap.; Christine M. Silsby, M.A., Assoc. to Chap.

Tri-College Newman Cluster-Bryn Mawr, Haverford and Swarthmore Colleges, St. Pius X Rectory, 220 Lawrence Rd., Broomall, 19008. Tel: 610-353-4880; Fax: 610-356-1084. Rev. John A. Freeman, Chap.; Ms. Susan Harte, Asst. to Chap.

Part-time Chaplaincies:

Allegheny University of the Health Sciences, Hahnemann.

Center City.

Allegheny University of the Health Sciences, East Falls, St. Bridget's Church, 3667 Midvale Ave., 19129-1712. Tel: 215-844-4126. Rev. Richard R. York, Chap.

Allegheny University Hospitals, Bucks County, St. John Bosco Church, 235 East County Line Rd., Hatboro, 19040-1298. Tel: 215-672-7280. Rev. Joseph D. Dougherty, Chap.

Allegheny University Hopitals, Elkins Park, St. James Church, 8320 Brookside Dr., Elkins Park, 19027. Tel: 215-635-6210. Rev. Raymond J. Himsworth, Chap.

Beaver College, Glenside, St. Luke the Evangelist Church, 2316 Fairhill Ave., Glenside, 19038-4107. Tel: 215-572-0128. Rev. J. Michael Flood, Chap.

Bucks County Community College, St. Andrew Church, 81 Swamp Rd., Newtown, 18940. Tel: 215-968-2262.

Cheney University. Dr. Susan Arisman, Dean School of Education. Tel: 610-399-2353.

Community College of Philadelphia.

Delaware County Community College, Media. Frank Mulvaney, Contact, Math/Science Dept., Delaware County Community College, Math Science Dept., Media, 19063. Tel: 610-359-5206. Rev. Leonard N. Peterson, Chap.

St. Anastasia Church, 3301 West Chester Pike, Newtown Square, 19073. Tel: 610-356-1613; 356-3303; Fax: 610-356-8332.

Delaware Valley College of Science and Agriculture, St. Jude Church, 321 W. Butler Ave., Chalfont, 18914-2329. Tel: 215-822-0179; Fax: 215-822-0638. Rev. Michael J. Gerlach.

Harcum Junior College, Our Mother of Good Counsel, 31 Pennswood Rd., Bryn Mawr, 19010. Tel: 610-525-0147.

Haverford College.

Thomas Jefferson University.

Lincoln University, Sacred Heart Church, 101 Church Rd., Oxford, 19363. Tel: 610-932-5040. Rev. William B. Dooner, Chap.

Montgomery County Community College, St. Helena Church, P.O. Box 5085, Center Square, 19422. Tel: 610-275-7711.

Pennsylvania State University - Ogontz Campus, Our Lady Help of Christians, 1500 Marian Rd., Abington, 19001. Tel: 215-886-3456.

Pennsylvania State University - Delaware County Campus, St. Francis de Sales Church, New Rd., Box 97, Lenni, 19062. Tel: 610-459-2203.

Pennsylvania State University-Great Valley Campus.

Philadelphia College of Pharmacy and Science, St. Francis de Sales Church, 4625 Springfield Ave., 19143. Tel: 215-222-5819.

Philadelphia College of Textiles and Science, St. Bridget Church, 3667 Midvale Ave., 19129-1712. Tel: 215-844-4126. Rev. Richard R. York.

Roxborough Memorial School of Nursing, St. John the Baptist, 146 Rector St., 19127. Tel: 215-482-4600.

Swarthmore College.

Temple University, Ambler Division, St. Alphonsus Church, 33 Conwell Dr., Maple Glen, 19002. Tel: 215-646-4600; Fax: 215-646-0180.

University of the Arts, Assoc. Dean's Office, Broad and Pine Sts., 19102. Tel: 215-875-2236.

St. John the Evangelist Church, 21 S. 13th St., 19107. Tel: 215-563-4145. Dr. Annelte DiMedio, Ph.D., Contact.

Ursinus College, St. Eleanor Church, 647 Locust St., Collegeville, 19426-2541. Tel: 610-489-1647; Fax: 610-489-7469. Rev. John A. Franey, Chap.

Widener University, Blessed Katherine Drexel Church, 20th and Providence Ave., Chester, 19013. Tel: 610-872-3731; Fax: 610-872-0545. Rev. Clemens J. Gendelmann, Chap.

[FF] MISCELLANEOUS LISTINGS

PHILADELPHIA. *Alpha House Kindergarten*, Grant and Franklin Aves., 19114. Tel: 215-632-3366. Mrs. Sara LaSalle-Tarantin, Prin. Total in Residence 144; Total Staff 6.

Apostleship of Prayer, St. Joseph's University, 5600 City Ave., 19131. Tel: 610-660-1436; 660-1400. Rev. Herbert F. Smith, S.J., Dir.

Catholic Kolping Society, 5400 Rising Sun Ave., 19120. Tel: 215-324-9332. Rev. Engelbert G. Michel, Praeses; Mrs. Catherine Pinkerton, Pres.; Mr. Alphonse Ellerkamp, Vice-Praeses; Mr. Earl Asimos, Treas.; Mr. Alex Eli, Vice Pres.

Catholic League For Persons With Disabilities, 4110 Glenview St., 19135. Tel: 215-331-2617. Board of Directors 15; Total Membership 85.

Catholics United for the Faith. (St. John Neumann Philadelphia Area Chapter), 183 Hillcrest Ave., 19118. Tel: 215-247-2585. Mrs. Anne M. Wilson, Chm.

The Central Association of the Miraculous Medal, 475 E. Chelten Ave., 19144-5785. Tel: 215-848-1010; Fax: 215-848-1014; 1-800-523-3674. Rev. William J. O'Brien, C.M., Dir.; Mr. Charles P. Kelly, Gen. Mgr. & Contact Person Miraculous Medal Magazine.

CORA Services, 733 Susquehanna Rd., 19111. Tel: 215-342-7660; 535-2957 (Neumann Center); Fax: 215-745-9857.
E-mail: mck71@erols.com
Anthony F. Chunn, Ph.D., CEO; Sr. Mary Charity Kohl, Founding Admin. Legal Title: *CORA Services, Inc., Philadelphia, Pennsylvania*. Services provided for children, families and teen pregnancy. Programs available: counseling, speech and language, remediation and GED. Total Assisted 30,000; Total Staff 264.

Euphrasia House, Inc., P.O. Box 44258, 19144-3016. Tel: 215-849-3371. Sr. Mary Loretta Clancy, Dir. & Contact Person. Women-in-Transition. Sponsored by: Sisters of the Good Shepherd. Total Staff 6; Total in Residence 5.

Franciscan Volunteer Ministry, Inc., P.O. Box 29276, 19125. Tel: 215-427-3070; Fax: 215-427-3059.
E-mail: fvmpd@aol.com
Ms. Stephanie A. DeBenedetti, Prog. Dir. Purpose: To create and run a faith-based lay volunteer program in the United States.

Good Shepherd Neighborhood House. Mediation Program. 5356 Chew Ave., 19138. Tel: 215-843-5413.
E-mail: shepherd@libertynet.org
Web site: www.libertynet/~shepherd/
Cheryl Cutrona, Exec. Dir. Legal Title: *Good Shepherd Corporation, Philadelphia, Pennsylvania*.

**Holy Redeemer Physician Services*. c/o Gregory J. Nowak, Esq., Stradley, Ronon, Stevens & Young. 2600 One Commerce Square, 19103-7098.

IHM Center for Literacy and GED Programs, 425 W. Lindley Ave., 19120. Tel: 215-457-2232; Fax: 215-457-2232. Sr. M. Anne Smith, I.H.M., M.A., Dir., 929 S. Farragut St., 19143. Tel: 215-382-0292. Full-time program with courses in Adult Basic Education (ABE); English for Speakers of Other Languages (ESOL) and General Educational Development (GED).

Katherine Kiernan Chateau, Inc., c/o Catholic Social Services, 222 N. 17th St., Ste. 300, 19103. Tel: 215-587-3903; Fax: 215-587-2479.

Ladies of Charity, 222 N. 17th St., 19103. Tel: 215-587-3816. His Eminence Anthony J. Bevilacqua, O.P., M.A., O.C.L., J.D; Rev. Msgr. James T. McDonough, A.C.S.W., Moderator; Mrs. Dominick Lazanski, Pres.

St. Agnes Foundation, 1900 S. Broad St., 19145. Tel: 215-339-4225. James M. Wilson, Pres.

St. Matthew Elementary Campus. Tel: 610-828-2007; Fax: 610-825-8796.
St. Cosmas & Damian Primary Campus. (Grades PreK-K). Tel: 610-828-0755. Mrs. Jacqueline Kerrigan, Prin.

St. Vincent's Orphan Asylum-St. Vincent's Comprehensive Emergency Shelter Program, 7201 Milnor St., 19135. Tel: 215-MA4-5600; Fax: 215-624-8355. Rev. Eduardo G. Montero, J.C.L. Total Assisted 48; Total Staff 8.

Shrine of Our Lady of Victories at St. Peter Claver, 12th & Lombard Sts., 19147. Tel: 215-735-0799. Rev. William J. Maguire, C.S.Sp., S.T.L., Dir. Shrine & Archconfraternity of Our Lady of Victories.

Society of Catholic Medical Missionaries Generalate, Inc. (Effective 1991), 8400 Pine Rd., 19111. Tel: 215-742-6100; Fax: 215-342-3948. Sr. Clarita Hackman, M.M.S., Contact Person; Sr. Rita Syron, M.M.S., Pres. Corporation collects funds for charitable and missionary work, for Medical Mission Sisters; Assists in operation of hospitals, clinics and primary health care programs; Assists in care of poor, sick and infirm, in U.S. and overseas; Assists in training and educating men and women in medicine and nursing, and other health professions; Trains candidates for the Community; Provides assisted living care to sick and elder Medical Mission Sisters.

The Warner Perpetual Trust for the Benefit of Catholic Charities, Provident National Bank, P.O. Box 7648, 19101. Tel: 610-585-5698; Fax: 610-358-4275. Legal Title: *The Warner Perpetual Trust for the Benefit of Catholic Charities of the Archdiocese of Philadelphia*.
(The "Perpetual" Trust). Mr. Edward Nemanic, Trust Officer.

ASTON. *Franciscan Ministries Foundation, Inc.*, 609 S. Convent Rd., 19014. Tel: 610-558-7713; Fax: 610-558-1421. Sr. Eileen Valerie, Contact. Tel: 610-558-7701; Robert C. Wallis, Exec. Dir. Purpose: Raises funds to fulfill the needs of the Ministries and Retired Sisters of the Sisters of St. Francis of Philadelphia.

Sisters of St. Francis of Philadelphia, Charitable Trust I and Charitable Trust II, Our Lady of Angels Convent, 19014. Tel: 610-459-2112. Sr. Marie Lucey, O.S.F., Congregational Minister.

BALA CYNWYD. *Mercy Health Corp. of Southeastern PA*, One Bala Plaza, Ste. 402 E., 19004. Tel: 610-660-7440. Sr. Mary Christine McCann, R.S.M., Chm. Bd.; Plato A Marinakos, Pres. & CEO. Holding Company for diversified health care subsidiaries. Total Assisted 42; Total Staff 8.

CONSHOHOCKEN. *St. Vincent de Paul Society*, 210 Harry St., 19428. Tel: 610-825-8125.
E-mail: STVIN@libertynet.org
Most Rev. Robert P. Maginnis, D.D., Spiritual Advisor; Anthony R. George, Pres.; Elizabeth Dart, Exec. Sec.; Robert Lanzilotta, Stores Dir. Tel: 215-763-5668. Catholic Lay Organization serving those in need with spiritual, moral, material and financial support regardless of race, creed, etc.

FLOURTOWN. *Saint Joseph Guild*, Stenton and Wissahickon Aves., P.O. Box 36, 19031-0036. Tel: 215-248-7838; Fax: 215-248-7802. Sr. Ann Marguerite, S.S.J., Dir.

FORT WASHINGTON. *John Paul II Foundation for Peace, Justice & Human Rights*, The Copernicus House, P.O. Box 267, 19034. Tel: 215-646-4101.

HUNTINGDON VALLEY.
**Holy Redeemer Health System, Inc.*, 727 Welsh Rd., 19006. Tel: 215-938-0180; Fax: 215-938-1237. Mailing Address: Communications Department, c/o 1648 Huntingdon Pike, Meadowbrook, 19046. Sponsor: Sisters of the Holy Redeemer, C.S.R. Michael B. Laign, Pres. & CEO. Parent organization which maintains, manages, and operates the health care system composed of the various corporations sponsored and established by the Sisters of the Holy Redeemer, C.S.R. as follows: Drueding Center; Holy Redeemer, Nazareth & St. Mary Home Health Services; Holy Redeemer Support Services; Holy Redeemer Foundation; HRH Management Corp.; Holy Redeemer Visiting Nurse Agency (NJ); Holy Redeemer Managed Care Org.; HR Physician Services; Redeemer Long Term Care and Elder Serv.; Holy Redeemer Hosp. & Med. Ctr.; Redeemer-Nazareth Med. Supply Co.
Holy Redeemer Hospital and Medical Center.
Redeemer Center.
St. Joseph's Manor.
The Lafayette - Redeemer.
Holy Redeemer Foundation.
Holy Redeemer Home Health and Hospice Services.
Holy Redeemer Transitional Care Unit.
Holy Redeemer Support Services.
Holy Redeemer Multicare.
Holy Redeemer Visiting Nurse Agency.
Holy Redeemer Hospice.
Redeemer Village II.
Drueding Center.
HRH Management Corporation.

**HR Physician Services (aka Holy Redeemer Physician and Ambulatory Services).*

**Holy Redeemer Managed Care Organization.*

**Holy Redeemer Physician Services*, 727 Welsh Rd., Ste. 108, 19006. Tel: 215-938-4600; Fax: 215-938-7309. Mailing Address: Communications Department, c/o 1648 Huntingdon Pike, Meadowbrook, 19046.
Subsidiary of Holy Redeemer Health System, Inc. Sponsor: Sisters of the Holy Redeemer C.S.R. Michelle Urofsky, Pres. Nonprofit corporation formed to establish, operate and maintain family health clinics and practices, laboratories, dispensaries, buildings, and facilities relating to these purposes, and provide the services of physicians and other health care professionals in connection with the provision of health care services at Holy Redeemer Hospital and Medical Center, and other hospitals, clinics and health care facilities.

IMMACULATA. *Enserv Inc.*, King Rd., 19345. Tel: 610-647-4400, Ext. 3147.

KING OF PRUSSIA. *Bernardine Franciscans, Delaware County*, 403 Allendale Rd., 19406.
E-mail: bfgen@aol.com
Sr. Christine Jasinowski, Contact Person.

RADNOR. *Catholic Health East*, 100 Matsonford Rd., Bldg.3, Ste. 220, 19087. Tel: 610-971-9770; Fax: 610-688-5443. Mr. Daniel F. Russell, Pres. & CEO.

**Eastern Mercy Health System*, 3 Radnor Corporate Center, Ste. 220, 19087-4592. Tel: 610-971-9770; Fax: 610-688-5443.
E-mail: emhs@pond.com
Daniel F. Russell, Pres. & CEO. Eastern Mercy Health System is a multi-institutional Catholic health system sponsored by nine Regional Communities of the Sisters of Mercy of the Americas and the Franciscan Sisters of St. Joseph(Hamburg, NY). Founded in 1986 for the purpose of preserving and strengthening the Catholic health ministry, Eastern Mercy provides programs, services, and expertise which enhance the sponsorship, stewardship, and strategic positioning of participating health care organizations. Eastern Mercy includes regional health care systems and freestanding health care organizations and services throughout seven states. Eastern Mercy facilities and services include large tertiary hospitals, community acute care hospitals, skilled nursing facilities, residential living facilities, and expansive primary care, home care, and outreach services in diverse rural, urban, and suburban communities throughout the eastern United States.

YEADON. *Mercy Court*, 550 S. Lansdowne Ave., 19050. Tel: 610-623-3083. Sisters of Mercy. Sr. Mary Carmela, R.S.M., Prog. Mgr. Low income apartments for independent living for older adults. Total Assisted 102; Total Staff 6.

RELIGIOUS INSTITUTES OF MEN REPRESENTED IN THE ARCHDIOCESE

For further details refer to the corresponding bracketed number in the Religious Institutes of Men or Women section.

[0140]—*The Augustinians*(Provs. of St. Thomas Villanova & Our Mother of Good Counsel).—O.S.A.

[0290]—*Brothers of Charity.*—F.C.

[0330]—*Brothers of the Christian Schools.* (Baltimore Prov.).—F.S.C.

[]—*Brothers of the Holy Spirit.*—B.H.S.

[0900]—*Canons Regular of Premontre.*—O.Praem.

[0470]—*Capuchin Friars.*—O.F.M.Cap.

[0275]—*Carmelites of Mary Immaculate.*—C.M.I.

[0860]—*Congregation of the Immaculate Heart of Mary (Missionhurst).*—C.I.C.M.

[1330]—*Congregation of the Mission.* (Eastern Prov.).—C.M.

[0950]—*Congregation of the Oratory.*—C.O.

[1000]—*Congregation of the Passion.*—C.P.

[0650]—*Holy Ghost Fathers.* (Eastern Prov.).—C.S.Sp.

[0800]—*Maryknoll Fathers and Brothers.*—M.M.

[0825]—*Missionaries of the Blessed Sacrament.*—M.S.S.

[1110]—*Missionaries of the Sacred Heart.* (American Prov.).—M.S.C.

[0840]—*Missionary Servants of the Most Holy Trinity.*—S.T.

[0920]—*Oblates of St. Francis de Sales.*—O.S.F.S.

[0520]—*Order of Friars Minor.* (Assumption B.V.M. & Most Holy Name Provs.).—O.F.M.

[0480]—*Order of Friars Minor, Conventual.*—O.F.M.Conv.

[0970]—*Order of Our Lady of Mercy.*—O.deM.

[0430]—*Order of Preachers (Dominicans).* (Eastern Prov.).—O.P.

[1310]—*Order of the Holy Trinity.*—O.SS.T.

[1010]—*Pauline Fathers.*—O.S.P.P.E.

[1040]—*Piarist Fathers.*—Sch.P.

[1070]—*Redemptorist Fathers.* (Baltimore Prov.).—C.SS.R.

[1220]—*Servants of Charity.*—S.C.

[0690]—*Society of Jesus (Jesuits).* (Maryland Prov.).—S.J.

[0760]—*Society of Mary (Marianists).*—S.M.

[0780]—*Society of Mary (Marists).*—S.M.

[0560]—*Third Order Regular of Saint Francis.* (Prov. of the Most Sacred Heart).—T.O.R.

RELIGIOUS INSTITUTES OF WOMEN REPRESENTED IN THE ARCHDIOCESE

[1070-13]—*Adrian Dominican Sisters.*
[]—*Armenian Sisters of the Immaculate Conception.*—C.I.C.
[1810]—*Bernardine Sisters of the Third Order of St. Francis.*—O.S.F.
[0330]—*Carmelite Sisters for the Aged and Infirm.*—O.Carm.
[0690]—*Comboni Missionary Sisters.*—C.M.S.
[0270]—*Congregation of Bon Secours.*—C.B.S.
[2250]—*Congregation of the Benedictines of Jesus Crucified.*—O.S.B.
[]—*Contemplative Sister of the Good Shepherd.*—C.G.S.
[0760]—*Daughters of Charity of St. Vincent de Paul.*—D.C.
[]—*Daughters of Mary, Mother of Mercy.*—D.M.M.M.
[0900]—*Daughters of Our Lady of the Sacred Heart.*—F.D.N.S.C.
[0940]—*Daughters of St. Mary of Providence.*—D.S.M.P.
[0810]—*Daughters of the Heart of Mary.*—D.H.M.
[0420]—*Discalced Carmelite Nuns.*—O.C.D.
[1070-17]—*Dominican Sisters.*—O.P.
[1070-23]—*Dominican Sisters.*—O.P.
[1105]—*Dominican Sisters of Hope.*—O.P.
[]—*Dominican Sisters of Our Lady of the Rosary.*—O.P.
[1170]—*Felician Sisters.*—C.S.S.F.
[1180]—*Franciscan Sisters of Alleghany, New York.*—O.S.F.
[1425]—*Franciscan Sisters of Peace.*—F.S.P.
[1840]—*Grey Nuns of the Sacred Heart.*—G.N.S.H.
[1870]—*Handmaids of the Sacred Heart of Jesus.*—A.C.J.
[]—*Little Servants of the Holy Family of Seoul.*—L.S.H.F.
[2300]—*Little Servants Sisters of the Immaculate Conception.*—L.S.I.C.
[2310]—*Little Sisters of the Assumption.*—L.S.A.
[2340]—*Little Sisters of the Poor.*—L.S.P.
[2345]—*Little Workers of the Sacred Hearts.*—P.O.S.C.
[2490]—*Medical Mission Sisters.*—M.M.S.
[2710]—*Missionaries of Charity.*—M.C.
[1360]—*Missionary Franciscan Sisters of the Immaculate Conception.*—M.F.I.C.
[2790]—*Missionary Servants of the Most Blessed Trinity.*—M.S.B.T.
[2730]—*Missionary Sisters of the Holy Rosary.*—M.S.H.R.
[2750]—*Missionary Sisters of the Immaculate Heart of Mary.*—I.C.M.
[2800]—*Missionary Sisters of the Most Sacred Heart of Jesus of Hiltrup.*—M.S.C.
[2860]—*Missionary Sisters of the Sacred Heart.*(Eastern Prov.).—M.S.C.
[3060]—*Oblates Sisters of St. Francis de Sales.*—O.S.F.S.
[3730]—*Order of St. Basil the Great.*—O.S.B.M.
[3760]—*Order of St. Clare.*—O.S.C.
[1705]—*Order of St. Francis of Assisi.*—O.S.F.
[0950]—*Pious Society Daughters of St. Paul.*—F.S.P.
[3640]—*Poor Servants of the Mother of God.*—S.M.G.
[3390]—*Religious of the Assumption.*—R.A.
[3430]—*Religious Teachers Filippini.*—M.P.F.
[2970]—*School Sisters of Notre Dame.*—S.S.N.D.
[1700]—*School Sisters of St. Francis.*—O.S.F.
[]—*Servants of the Lord and of the Virgin of MATARA.*—V.E.
[3540]—*Sister Servants of the Holy Spirit of Perpetual Adoration.*—S.Sp.S.deA.P.
[2160]—*Sister Servants of the Immaculate Heart of Mary.* (Scanton).—I.H.M.
[3630]—*Sister Servants of the Most Sacred Heart of Jesus.*—S.S.C.J.
[0500]—*Sisters of Charity of Nazareth.*—S.C.N.
[0660]—*Sisters of Christian Charity.*—S.C.C.
[2575]—*Sisters of Mercy of the Americas, Merion, PA.*—R.S.M.
[0820]—*Daughters of the Holy Spirit.*—D.H.S.
[3000]—*Sisters of Notre Dame de Namur.*—S.N.D.deN.
[2670]—*Sisters of Our Lady of Mercy.*—S.O.L.M.
[3893]—*Sisters of Saint Joseph of Chestnut Hill, Philadelphia.*—S.S.J.
[3740]—*Sisters of St. Casimir.*—S.S.C.
[1650]—*Sisters of St. Francis of Philadelphia.*—O.S.F.
[0260]—*Sisters of the Blessed Sacrament for Indians and Colored People.*—S.B.S.
[1020]—*Sisters of the Divine Redeemer.*—S.D.R.
[1830]—*Sisters of the Good Shepherd.*—R.G.S.
[1970]—*Sisters of the Holy Family of Nazareth.*—C.S.F.N.
[2000]—*Sisters of the Holy Redeemer.*—C.S.R.
[2060]—*Sisters of the Most Holy Trinity.*—O.SS.T.
[1490]—*Sisters of the Third Franciscan Order of Syracuse.*—O.S.F.
[2170]—*Sisters, Servants of the Immaculate Heart of Mary (Immaculta).*—I.H.M.
[4060]—*Society of the Holy Child Jesus.*—S.H.C.J.
[4120]—*Ursuline Sisters of the Immaculate Conception.*—O.S.U.
[4190]—*Visitation Nuns.*—V.H.M.

ARCHDIOCESAN CEMETERIES

PHILADELPHIA. *Cathedral*, 48th St. and Lancaster Ave., 19131. Tel: 215-477-8918.
Holy Sepulchre, Cheltham Ave. & Ivy Hill Rd., 19150. Tel: 215-247-0691.
New Cathedral, 2nd & Butler Sts., 19140. Tel: 215-634-3212.
BENSALEM. *Resurrection*, 5201 Hulmeville Rd., 19020. Tel: 215-639-0965.
CHALFONT. *St. John Neumann*, 3797 County Line Rd., 18914. Tel: 215-822-0680.
GLENMOORE. *All Souls*, R.R. 322, 19343.
NEWTOWN. *All Saints*, R.R. 413, Twining Bridge Rd., 18940.
SPRINGFIELD. *SS. Peter and Paul*, Sproul Rd., 19064. Tel: 610-544-4933.
WEST CONSHOHOCKEN. *Calvary*, Gulph & Matsonford Rd., 19428. Tel: 610-525-2214.
WEST GROVE. *Holy Saviour* Penn Township.
YEADON. *Holy Cross*, Baily Rd., 19050. Tel: 610-626-2206; 215-476-3656.

NECROLOGY

† Bradley, John J., Philadelphia, PA, St. Aloysius. —Died March 5, 1997.
† Burns, Rev. Msgr. Vincent L., Drexel Hill, PA, St. Andrew. —Died March 6, 1997.
† Coyle, Rev. Msgr. James A., (Retired). —Died Sept. 20, 1997.
† Curran, Joseph B., Springfield, PA, Holy Cross. —Died Jan. 4, 1997.
† Fahey, William M., Eddystone, PA, St. Rose of Lima. —Died Oct. 4, 1997.
† Gaughan, Rev. Msgr. Francis J., Philadelphia, PA, St. Matthew. —Died Nov. 19, 1996.
† Kilgarriff, John J., Morton, PA, Our Lady of Perpetual Help. —Died March 11, 1997.
† Koenig, Rev. Msgr. William A., (Retired). —Died Nov. 5, 1996.
† Martusevich, Rev. Msgr. Vito J., Philadelphia, PA, St. George. —Died Aug. 23, 1997.
† Ponisciak, Cyril S., Coatesville, PA, St. Joseph. —Died May 17, 1997.
† Ruhl, George J., Milmont Park, PA, Our Lady of Peace. —Died Feb. 24, 1997.
† Shimkus, Bernard A., (Retired). —Died Nov. 10, 1996.
† Sikora, Rev. Msgr. Joseph G., Philadelphia, PA, St. Dominic. —Died Jan. 11, 1997.
† Teller, Rev. Msgr. Raymond J., Doylestown, PA, Our Lady of Mount Carmel. —Died March 2, 1997.
† Thomas, Joseph W., (Retired). —Died Dec. 8, 1996.
† York, James E., (Retired). —Died April 29, 1997.

Diocese of Phoenix

(Dioecesis Phoenicensis)

Most Reverend

THOMAS J. O'BRIEN, D.D.

Bishop of Phoenix; ordained May 7, 1961; consecrated January 6, 1982; installed January 18, 1982. *Res., 48 E. Wagon Wheel Dr., Phoenix, AZ, 85020. All correspondence to be sent to: 400 E. Monroe, Phoenix, AZ, 85004.*

ESTABLISHED DECEMBER 2, 1969.

Square Miles 43,967.

Comprises the Counties of Maricopa; Mohave; Yavapai & Coconino not to include the territorial boundaries of the Navajo Indian Reservation; Pinal—that portion of land known as the Gila River Indian Reservation in the State of Arizona.

Patroness of Diocese: Our Lady of Guadalupe.

For legal titles of parishes and diocesan institutions, consult the Chancery Office.

Diocesan Office: 400 E. Monroe, Phoenix, AZ, 85004. Tel.: 602-257-0030; Fax: 602-258-3425.

Web site address: http://www.catholicsun.org

E-mail address: tbow@cathdioc.org

STATISTICAL OVERVIEW

Personnel	
Bishop	1
Retired Bishops	1
Priests: Diocesan Active in Diocese	97
Priests: Active Outside Diocese	3
Priests: Retired, Sick or Absent	45
Number of Diocesan Priests	145
Religious Priests in Diocese	113
Extern Priests in Diocese	22
Ordinations:	
Diocesan Priests	2
Transitional Deacons	2
Permanent Deacons	12
Permanent Deacons in Diocese	175
Total Brothers	5
Total Sisters	230
Parishes	
Parishes	88
With Resident Pastor:	
Resident Diocesan Priests	63
Resident Religious Priests	19
Without Resident Pastor:	
Administered by Permanent Deacons	4
Administered by Women Religious	1
Completely Vacant	1
Missions	28
New Parishes Created	2
Closed Parishes	3
Professional Ministry Personnel:	
Brothers	2

Sisters	206
Lay Ministers	344
Welfare	
Catholic Hospitals	1
Total Assisted	311,481
Health Care Centers	2
Total Assisted	99,340
Homes for the Aged	9
Total Assisted	405
Day Care and Extended Day Care Centers	26
Total Assisted	983
Specialized Homes	8
Total Assisted	587
Special Centers for Social Services	11
Total Assisted	2,096,541
Residential Care of Disabled	1
Total Assisted	26
Educational	
Diocesan Students in Other Seminaries	25
Total Seminarians	25
High Schools, Diocesan and Parish	4
Total Students	2,526
High Schools, Private	1
Total Students	1,170

Elementary Schools, Diocesan and Parish	23
Total Students	7,816
Catechesis/Religious Education:	
High School Students	5,444
Elementary Students	30,437
Total Students Under Catholic Instruction	47,418
Teachers in the Diocese:	
Priests	17
Scholastics	4
Brothers	2
Sisters	43
Lay Teachers	577
Vital Statistics	
Receptions into the Church:	
Infant Baptism Totals	11,557
Adult Baptism Totals	463
Received into Full Communion	724
First Communions	6,032
Confirmations	3,049
Marriages:	
Catholic	1,210
Interfaith	493
Total Marriages	1,703
Deaths	3,392
Total Catholic Population	388,839
Total Population	3,109,820

Former Bishops—Most Rev. EDWARD A. MCCARTHY, D.D., installed Bishop of the Diocese of Phoenix, Dec. 2, 1969; transferred Coadjutor Archbishop of Miami, July 7, 1976; installed Sept. 17, 1976.—Most Rev. JAMES S. RAUSCH, D.D., Ph.D., installed March 22, 1977; died May 18, 1981.

Vicar General—Rev. Msgr. RICHARD MOYER, V.G., *Diocesan Center, 400 E. Monroe, Phoenix, 85004.* Tel: 602-257-0030.

Diocesan Office—400 E. Monroe, Phoenix, 85004. Tel: 602-257-0030; Fax: 602-258-3425.

Chancellor—Sr. MARY ANN WINTERS, S.C., *400 E. Monroe, Phoenix, 85004.* Tel: 602-257-0030.

Assistant Chancellor—Rev. MICHAEL L. DISKIN, *400 E. Monroe, Phoenix, 85004.* Tel: 602-257-0030.

College of Consultors—Rev. Msgr. RICHARD W. MOYER, V.G.; Revs. ALAN MALONE, J.V.; TIMOTHY DAVERN, V.F., J.C.L.; PETER DOBROWSKI, V.F.; CHARLES KIEFFER; ROBERT VOSS, V.F.; FRANK BARTEL, V.F.; JOHN COLEMAN, V.F.

Finance and Administration—Rev. MICHAEL STRALEY, Vicar, *400 E. Monroe, Phoenix, 85004.* Tel: 602-257-0030.

Vicars Forane—Revs. FRANK FERNANDEZ, V.F.; SCOTT BRUBAKER, V.F.; PETER DOBROWSKI, V.F.; CHARLES GORAIEB, V.F.; ROBERT VOSS, V.F.; EDWARD CALLANAN, S.J., V.F.; GERALD YAEGER, V.F.; FRANK BARTEL, V.F.; EARL D'EON, V.F.; TIMOTHY DAVERN, V.F.; J. C. ORTIZ, V.F.; JOHN COLEMAN, V.F.

Diocesan Tribunal—Office: *400 E. Monroe, Phoenix, 85004.* Tel: 602-257-5585; Fax: 602-257-5646.

Judicial Vicar—Rev. ALAN MALONE.

Adjutant Judicial Vicars—Revs. PHILIP ACQUARO, C.S.B., J.C.L.; TIMOTHY R. DAVERN, J.C.L.; MICHAEL F. DIEDERICHS, J.C.D.; PAUL OREL, J.C.L.

Diocesan Judges—Revs. PHILIP ACQUARO, C.S.B., J.C.L.; TIMOTHY R. DAVERN, J.C.L.; MICHAEL F. DIEDERICHS, J.C.D.; GREGORY M. KOTNIS, J.C.L.; ALAN MALONE; PAUL OREL, J.C.L.

Defenders of the Bond—Revs. VALENTINE L. BOYLE, O.Carm.; ROBERT J. CARUSO; CHARLES G. KIEFFER; FRANK P. SIMLIK; Sr. FRANCES WETZEL, O.P.

Advocates—Sr. ELEANOR GIBBONS, S.C.; Sr. RUTH KARNITZ, S.S.N.D.; SANDRA CONSIGLIO.

Auditors—Revs. PHILIP ACQUARO, C.S.B., J.C.L.; VALENTINE L. BOYLE, O.Carm.; TIMOTHY R. DAVERN, J.C.L.; MICHAEL DIEDERICHS, J.C.D.; ALAN MALONE; PAUL OREL, J.C.L.; Sr. ELEANOR GIBBONS, S.C.; Sr. RUTH KARNITZ, S.S.N.D.; Sr. FRANCES WETZEL, O.P.

Notaries—Rev. MICHAEL L. DISKIN; Sr. ELEANOR GIBBONS, S.C.; Sr. RUTH KARNITZ, S.S.N.D.; Sr. M. ANTHONY POERIO, I.B.V.M.; DOROTHY DALTON; MAUREEN HAMILTON; M. ANGELA JIMENEZ; WALDA SWEENEY.

Appellate Court Administrator-Diocese of Phoenix—MAUREEN HAMILTON.

Presbyteral Council—Most Rev. THOMAS J. O'BRIEN, D.D.; Rev. Msgr. RICHARD W. MOYER, V.G.; Revs. FRANK BARTEL, V.F.; SCOTT BRUBAKER, V.F.; EDWARD CALLANAN, S.J., V.F.; NATHAN CASTLE, O.P.; JOHN COLEMAN, V.F., Chm. EARL D'EON, V.F.; TIMOTHY DAVERN, J.C.L., V.F.; MARK DIPPRE; MICHAEL DISKIN, Asst. Chancellor; FRANK FERNANDEZ, V.F.; PETER DOBROWSKI, V.F.; EVAN HOWARD, O.F.M.; CHARLES GORAIEB, V.F.; CHARLES KIEFFER; ALAN MALONE, J.V.; J. C. ORTIZ, V.F.; PRUDENCIO RODRIQUEZ, C.M.; ROBERT VOSS, V.F.; GERALD YAEGER, V.F.; Sr. MARY ANN WINTERS, Chancellor.

Diocesan Pastoral Council—Most Rev. THOMAS J. O'BRIEN, D.D.; Rev. Msgr. RICHARD W. MOYER, V.G.; Revs. MICHAEL L. DISKIN, Exec. Sec. MICHAEL MINOGUE; Bro. RICHARD SUTTLE, C.M.F.; Sr. PATRICIA OLIVER, R.S.M.; Sr. MARY ANN WINTERS, S.C., Chancellor; Deacon BOB ANDERSON; MONICA DOMINGO; TIMOTHY HENLEY; RAQUEL HIDALGO; JO HINELINE; MICHAEL JOHNSEN, Chm. ALMA LANDA; HARVEY LESAN; JORGE LOPEZ; VERONICA LUCAS; KEVIN MCCARTHY; JEANNINE MOYLE; NANCY PERLICK, R.S.M., Vice Chm. JACQUELIN RIDEAU; MICHAEL SILLS-TRAUSCH;

ART STINE; CARLOS TEJEDA; NAN TROTTA; MARVIN VENS.

Arizona Catholic Conference—Rev. Msgr. EDWARD RYLE, M.S.W., Exec. Dir., *400 E. Monroe, Phoenix, 85004.* Tel: 602-257-0030.

Buildings & Property—JOSEPH GALANO, Dir., *Diocesan Center, 400 E. Monroe, Phoenix, 85004.* Tel: 602-257-0030. Rev. Msgr. JOHN J. MCMAHON, Vicar, *4633 N. 54th St., Phoenix, 85018.* Tel: 602-840-5066.

Catholic Community Foundation—Most Rev. THOMAS J. O'BRIEN, D.D., Pres. CARL S. MILLER, Exec. Dir., *400 E. Monroe, Phoenix, 85004.* Tel: 602-257-0030.

Cemeteries—Rev. WILLIAM MCKAY, Admin. GARY L. BROWN, Exec. Dir. St. Francis, Holy Cross, and Queen of Heaven. Office: *1438 W. Broadway, #B-245, Tempe, 85282.* Tel: 602-829-0221., Calvary Cemetery: *201 W. University, Flagstaff, 86001.* Tel: 520-774-9125.

"The Catholic Sun"—(Diocesan Newspaper); Mr. CHRISTOPHER GUNTY, Assoc. Publisher, *400 E. Monroe, Phoenix, 85004.* Tel: 602-257-0030; 257-5565; Fax: 602-258-6404.

Communications—MARGE INJASOULIAN, Dir., *400 E. Monroe, Phoenix, 85004.* Tel: 602-257-0030.

Information Services (Data Processing)—KIM BRISWALTER, Dir., *400 E. Monroe, Phoenix, 85004.* Tel: 602-257-0030.

Stewardship Office—(Charity & Development Appeal); BILL SCHWANEKAMP, Dir., *400 E. Monroe St., Phoenix, 85004.* Tel: 602-257-0030. (Annuities and Trusts); CARL S. MILLER, Exec Dir., *400 E. Monroe St., Phoenix, 85004.* Tel: 602-257-0030. JIM CRUTHOFF, Dir. of Planned Giving. Tel: 602-257-5641.

Ecumenical and Interreligious Affairs—Rev. MICHAEL L. DISKIN, Dir., *400 E. Monroe, Phoenix, 85004.* Tel: 602-257-0030.

Ministry of Christian Formation—Sr. DOLORETTE FARIAS, S.S.N.D., Dir., *400 E. Monroe, Phoenix, 85004.* Tel: 602-257-0030.

Diaconate Ministry—Deacon DANIEL PETERSON, Dir., *400 E. Monroe, Phoenix, 85004.* Tel: 602-257-0030. THOMAS KAYSER, Assoc. Continuing Education. Tel: 520-445-3141. Deacon RAY ROGER, Assoc. Ministry. Tel: 602-257-0030.

Vocations—Rev. ROBERT CLEMENTS, Dir., *400 E. Monroe, Phoenix, 85004.* Tel: 602-257-0030.

Office of Worship—Rev. SCOTT BRUBAKER, Vicar; Sr. MARY ANTHONY POERIO, I.B.V.M., Dir. TREVOR THOMPSON, Asst. Dir., *400 E. Monroe, Phoenix, 85004.* Tel: 602-257-0030.

Schools—MARYBETH MUELLER, Supt. Schools; MARY CATHERINE KEATING, Asst. Supt., *400 E. Monroe, Phoenix, 85004.* Tel: 602-257-0030.

Catechetical Ministry—Deacon JOHN MEYER, Dir. CAROL GASTELUM, Assoc. Dir., *400 E. Monroe, Phoenix, 85004.* Tel: 602-257-0030.

Youth-Young Adult Campus Ministry—LARRY FRAHER, Dir. MODESTO GARCIA, Asst. Dir. KEVIN STARRS, At-Risk Youth Resources, *400 E. Monroe, Phoenix, 85004.* Tel: 602-257-0030.

The Catholic Scouting Program—Rev. DENNIS O'ROURKE, Liaison, *7923 E. Latham, Scottsdale, 85257.* Tel: 602-945-8437; Fax: 602-945-4335.

Family Life Activities—RICHARD BERGKESSEL, Dir., *400 E. Monroe, Phoenix, 85004.* Tel: 602-257-0030.

Life Issues—JUDY GIFFORD, Coord., *400 E. Monroe, Phoenix, 85004.* Tel: 602-257-0030.

Mount Claret Retreat Center—Directors: Rev. Msgr. JOHN J. MCMAHON; Rev. EUGENE MAGUIRE; Ms. JO SWIGER, Asst. Dir.; Sr. REGINA MARIE BOSLET, S.C., Asst. Dir. Cursillo Movement: Revs. LEO DELGADO, Dir. THEO FUENTES, C.M.F., Assoc. Dir., *4633 N. 54th St., Phoenix, 85018.* Tel: 602-840-5066; Fax: 602-840-5732.

Special Services for Persons with Disabilities—ISABELLA RICE, Dir., *400 E. Monroe, Phoenix, 85004.* Tel: 602-257-0030.

Native American Ministry Office—Rev. JOHN HALL, Vicar, *400 E. Monroe, Phoenix, 85004.* Tel: 602-257-0030.

Diocesan Office of Social Ministry—Mr. GUY MIKKELSEN, *77 E. Thomas Rd., Ste. 100, Phoenix, 85012.* Tel: 602-285-1800; Fax: 602-285-1838.

Diocesan Attorney—GREGORY J. LEISSE, *400 E. Monroe, Phoenix, 85004.* Tel: 602-257-0030.

Priests' Assurance Association—Rev. MICHAEL L. DISKIN, Sec., *400 E. Monroe, Phoenix, 85004.* Tel: 602-257-0030.

Polish Apostolate—Rev. KLEMENS DABROWSKI, S.Ch., Admin., *Our Lady of Czestochowa, 6530 N. 7th St., Phoenix, 85014.* Tel: 602-212-1172; Fax: 602-212-1178.

Priest Personnel—Rev. THOMAS ZURCHER, C.S.C., Vicar, *400 E. Monroe, Phoenix, 85004.* Tel: 602-257-0030.

Advisory Board for the Continuing Formation of Priests—Rev. THOMAS ZURCHER, C.S.C., *400 E. Monroe, Phoenix, 85004.* Tel: 602-257-0030.

Priestly Life and Ministry Board—Rev. THOMAS ZURCHER, C.S.C., *400 E. Monroe, Phoenix, 85004.* Tel: 602-257-0030.

Priests' Placement Board—Rev. THOMAS ZURCHER, *400 E. Monroe, Phoenix, 85004.* Tel: 602-257-0030.

Prisons, Catholic Ministries To—Rev. KLEMENS PEPEL, Dir., *Estrella Jail, 2939 W. Durango, Phoenix, 85009.* Tel: 602-256-5574.

Prison Facilities—State and County Jails; Deacon PETER MURPHY. Tel: 602-591-3243 (Pager). Rev. KLEMENS PEPEL. Tel: 602-256-5574.

Arizona Center for Women—Deacon TOM SWISHER, *342 N. 32nd St., Phoenix, 85008.* Tel: 602-994-0952.

Arizona Correctional Training Center—Rev. EMIL COTE, *179th Ave. and McDowell Rd., Perryville, 85323.* Tel: 602-853-0304, Ext. 2198.

Alhambra Correctional Center—(Diagnostic Center); Deacon TOM SWISHER, Chap., *26th St. and Van Buren, Phoenix, 85008.* Tel: 602-994-0952.

Aspen Correctional Center—Deacon TOM SWISHER, Chap., *24th St. and Fillmore, Phoenix, 85008.* Tel: 602-994-0952.

Federal Correctional Institute—Rev. CHARLES BORMANN, Chap., *47900 N. 45th Ave., Phoenix, 85027.* Tel: 602-465-9757.

Arizona State Institutions—(Juveniles).

Adobe Mountain Juvenile Institute—(Boys & Girls); Diocesan Prison Ministry Staff *Black Canyon Hwy., 280 W. Pinnacle Peak Rd., Phoenix, 85027.* Tel: 602-869-9050, Ext. 270.

County Juvenile Detention Center—3125 W. Durango, Phoenix, 85009. Diocesan Prison Ministry Staff.

Propagation of the Faith—Sr. JEAN STEFFES, C.S.A., *400 E. Monroe, Phoenix, 85004.* Tel: 602-257-0030.

Holy Childhood Association—Sr. JEAN STEFFES, C.S.A, *400 E. Monroe, Phoenix, 85004.* Tel: 602-257-0300.

Hispanic Ministry—

Office of Hispanic Ministry—Rev. PRUDENCIO RODRIGUEZ DE YURRE, C.M., Ph.D., Vicar; MICHAEL HERNANDEZ NOWAKOWSKI, Dir., *400 E. Monroe, Phoenix, 85004.* Tel: 602-257-0030.

Office of Human Resources (Personnel)—JOHN UNGVARY, Dir., *400 E. Monroe, Phoenix, 85004.* Tel: 602-257-0030.

Religious, Office of—Sr. JEAN STEFFES, C.S.A., Dir., *400 E. Monroe, Phoenix, 85004.* Tel: 602-257-0030.

CLERGY, PARISHES, MISSIONS AND PAROCHIAL SCHOOLS

CITY OF PHOENIX
(Maricopa County)

1—SS. SIMON AND JUDE CATHEDRAL, Revs. Michael O'Grady, Rector; Patrick Mowrer. In res., Rev. Francis Peacock.
Res., 6351 N. 27th Ave., 85017. Tel: 602-242-1300; Fax: 602-249-3768.
School—Tel: 602-242-1299. Sr. M. Raphael Quinn, I.B.V.M., Prin.
Lorreto Sisters 5; Lay Teachers 17; Students 581.
Convent—Tel: 602-242-2544.
Mission—Phoenix, Maricopa Co., Santa Rosa Chapel, 1901 W. Ocotillo, 85017. Tel: 602-433-0658; Fax: 602-433-9465.

2—CORPUS CHRISTI, Revs. Louis A. Sigman; Albert F.H. Hoorman; Sr. Frances Ellsperman, O.P., Pastoral Assoc.; Deacons Alexander Gaudio; Patrick Flynn; Philip Simeone.
Res., 3550 E. Knox, 85044. Tel: 602-893-8770; Fax: 602-893-3291.

3—HOLY FAMILY, Rev. Jorge Canez.
Res., 6802 S. 24th St., 85040. Tel: 602-268-2632.

4—IMMACULATE HEART OF MARY, Revs. Antonio Sotelo; Lawrence Baumann; Graciela Albillar, Parish Admin. In res., Rev. Klemens Pepel.
Res., 909 E. Washington St., 85034. Tel: 602-253-6129; Fax: 602-253-4210.

5—MOST HOLY TRINITY, Revs. Michael Rolland, O.P.; Dominic Briese, O.P.; Bruno Mauricci, O.P.; Paul Tran, O.P.; Bro. Pasquale Manalio, O.P.; Deacon Guy Goubeaux.
Res., 8620 N. Seventh St., 85020. Tel: 602-944-3375; Fax: 602-943-2323.
School—535 E. Alice Ave., 85020. Tel: 602-943-9058. Ms. Christine Steele, Prin.
Lay Teachers 16; Students 368.
McHugh Hall/Small Hall—8820 N. Seventh St., 85020. Tel: 602-997-6726.
Vietnamese Catholic Community: Rev. Paul Tran.

6—ST. AGNES, Revs. Tiernan O'Callaghan, O.Carm.; John Larkin, O.Carm.; Patrick Gavin, O.Carm. In res., Revs. Ernest Larkin, O.Carm.; Michael Kwiecien, O.Carm.
Res., 1954 N. 24th St., 85008. Tel: 602-244-0349; Fax: 602-244-0054.
School—2311 E. Palm Ln., 85006. Tel: 602-244-1451. Catherine Downey, Prin.
Lay Teachers 11; Students 262.
Convent—1818 N. 23rd St., 85006. Tel: 602-244-1174.

7—SS. ANTHONY AND PIUS X, Rev. J. Saul Madrid.
Church & Res.—909 S. First Ave., 85003. Tel: 602-252-1771; Fax: 602-252-1669.
Missions—Phoenix, Maricopa Co., St. Pius X, 809 S. Seventh Ave., 85007. Rev. John Auther, S.J.; Phoenix, Maricopa Co., Our Lady of Fatima, 1414 S. 17th Ave., 85007. Tel: 602-254-4944. Rev. Francis A. Peacock, Admin.

8—ST. AUGUSTINE, Revs. David Sanfilippo; John Ebbesmier; Deacon Joe Hauser.
Res., 3630 N. 71st Ave., 85033. Tel: 602-849-3131; Fax: 602-849-5689.

9—ST. CATHERINE OF SIENA, Revs. Charles Goraieb; David Kelash; Deacons George Lazok; Joe Lessard.
Res., 6401 S. Central Ave., 85040. Tel: 602-276-5581; Fax: 602-276-2119.
School—6413 S. Central Ave., 85040. Tel: 602-276-5581, Ext. 251; Fax: 602-276-2241. Cynthia Bernacki, Prin.
Lay Teachers 10; Students 183.
Convent—313 W. Alta Vista, 85041. Tel: 602-268-5620; 276-5581 Ext. 240 (Voice Mail).

10—ST. EDWARD CONFESSOR, Rev. Jorge Canez; Deacon Peter Fejes.
Res., 4410 E. Southern Ave., 85040. Tel: 602-438-0043; Fax: 602-438-9305.

11—ST. FRANCIS XAVIER, Revs. Edward E. Callanan, S.J.; Patrick J. Reuse, S.J.; Arthur J. Wehr, S.J.; Gilbert Chacon, S.J.
Res., 4715 N. Central Ave., 85012-1796. Tel: 602-279-9547; Fax: 602-248-8968.
School—Tel: 602-266-5364. Mrs. Kristen Spucces, Prin.
Lay Teachers 27; Students 532.

12—ST. GREGORY, Revs. Michael Straley; Alonso Saenz.
Res., 3424 N. 18th Ave., 85015. Tel: 602-264-4488; Fax: 602-264-4489.
School—3440 N. 18th Ave., 85015. Tel: 602-266-9527. Ms. Eileen Marie Ripsen, Prin.
Lay Teachers 17; Students 302.
Convent—3437 N. 18th Ave., 85015. Tel: 602-265-2396. Sisters of the Institute of B.V.M.

13—ST. JEROME, Revs. L. Pierre Hissey; John Shetler; Deacons Robert Dedecker; Michael Phelan; Theodore Micek; Richard Rein.
Church—10815 N. 35th Ave., 85029. Tel: 602-942-5555; Fax: 602-504-9115.
School—Tel: 602-942-5644. Carl Hodus, Prin.
Lay Teachers 15; Students 307.

14—ST. JOAN OF ARC, Revs. Larry W. Weidner; John Cullinan; Gena McGowan, Pastoral Assoc.; Deacon Phil Locascio. In res., Rev. Gil Rutz.
Parish Center: 3801 E. Greenway Rd., 85032-4698. Tel: 602-867-9171; Fax: 602-482-7930.

15—ST. JOSEPH, Rev. Frank Fernandez; Deacons Harry Schwan; Charles Kelly.
Res., 11001 N. 40th St., 85028. Tel: 602-996-5120; Fax: 602-996-4011 (Call first).

16—ST. LUKE, Rev. Richard A. Milligan.
Res., 19644 N. Seventh Ave., 85027. Tel: 602-582-0561.
Mission—New River, Maricopa Co., Good Shepherd Mission, 45033 N. 12th St., 85027. Tel: 602-465-9740; 274-0442. Rev. Valentine L. Boyle, O.Carm., Admin.

17—ST. MARK, Rev. David Cooney, S.D.S.; Deacons Lou A. Burgess; Jose Hernandez. In res., Revs. Tulio Maya, S.D.S.; Roman Mueller, S.D.S.
Res., 400 N. 30th St., 85008. Tel: 602-267-0503.
Mission—Phoenix, Maricopa Co., St. Philip the Deacon Catholic Center, 615 N. 20th St., 85006. Tel: 602-253-1076. Deacon Louis Pardini, Admin.

18—ST. MARTIN DE PORRES, Deacon Jose Olivarez, Admin. Sacramental Ministers: Revs. Raymond Ritari; Frank Sevola, O.F.M.
Res., 3851 W. Wier Ave., 85041. Tel: 602-276-2466 (Church); Fax: 602-232-2147.

19—ST. MARY'S BASILICA, Rev. Evan Howard, O.F.M. In res., Revs. Lester Mitchell, O.F.M.; Blaise Cronin, O.F.M.; Lucius Grosso, O.F.M.; Luis Baldonado, O.F.M.
Res., 231 N. Third St., 85004. Tel: 602-252-7651; Fax: 602-256-2773.

20—ST. MATTHEW, Revs. Raymond Ritari; Frank Sevola, O.F.M.; Deacons Tony Beltran; Albert Gonzales.
Res., 320 N. 20th Dr., 85009. Tel: 602-258-1789; Fax: 602-258-6507.
School—2038 W. Van Buren, 85009. Tel: 602-254-0611. Dr. Robert Sherman, Prin.
Sisters 2; Lay Teachers 7; Students 224.
Convent—2106 W. Van Buren, 85009. Tel: 602-253-9124.

21—St. Paul, Revs. Eugene O'Carroll; L. Brendon Dorian; Deacons Robert England; Kenneth Marion. Res., 330 W. Coral Gables Dr., 85023. Tel: 602-942-2608; Fax: 602-993-0228.

22—Our Lady of the Valley, Revs. Scott Brubaker; Scott Ritchey.
Church—3220 W. Greenway Rd., 85023. Tel: 602-993-1213; Fax: 602-993-1223.

23—Sacred Heart, Rev. Luis Baldonado, O.F.M.
Church—1421 S. 12th St., 85034. Tel: 602-258-2089.

24—St. Theresa, Revs. Charles G. Kieffer; Fred Adamson. In res., Rev. Michael L. Diskin.
Res., 5045 E. Thomas Rd., 85018. Tel: 602-840-0850; Fax: 602-840-0871.
School—5001 E. Thomas Rd., 85018. Tel: 602-840-0010. Judy Setzkorn, Prin.
Sisters 1; Lay Teachers 25; Students 564.

25—St. Thomas the Apostle, Revs. John Spaulding; Mark Hebert; Joseph Fichtner, O.S.C.; Deacons Americo Gouveia; Donald Kuban; Kenneth Miller.
Res., 2312 E. Campbell Ave., 85016-5597. Tel: 602-954-9089; Fax: 602-956-3454.
School—4510 N. 24th St., 85016. Tel: 602-954-9089. Mr. Fredric Stephen, Prin.
Sisters 1; Lay Teachers 34; Students 591.
Convent—4550 N. 24th St., 85016-5299. Tel: 602-954-8489.

26—St. Vincent de Paul, Revs. John V. Shine, C.M.; John O'M. Sharpe, C.M.; J. Antonio Ruiz, C.M.; Gregory Schlarb, C.M.; Deacon Arnold Hernandez, C.M. In res., Rev. Michael J. Boyle, C.M.
Res., 3140 N. 51st Ave., 85031. Tel: 602-247-6871; Fax: 602-247-4457.
School—3130 N. 51st Ave., 85031. Tel: 602-247-8595. Sr. Theresa Marie McDermott, D.C., Prin.
Daughters of Charity 2; Lay Teachers 11; Students 249.
Convent—3130 N. 51st Ave., 85031. Tel: 602-247-8916. Daughters of Charity

OUTSIDE THE CITY OF PHOENIX

Bagdad, Yavapai Co., St. Francis of Assisi, Rev. Peter Taylor, Admin.
Mailing Address: P.O. Box 768, 86321. Tel: 520-633-4325.
Church & Rectory: 220 Cook St., 86321. Tel: 520-633-2389.

Bapchule, Pinal Co., St. Peter's, Sr. Anne Fischer, S.S.N.D., Admin.; Deacon Joseph Swisher, Admin.
Mailing Address: P.O. Box 545, Sacaton, 85247. Tel: 520-562-3716; Fax: 520-315-3963.
School—P.O. Box 840, 85221. Tel: 520-315-3835; Fax: 520-315-3963. Sr. Martha Mary Carpenter, O.S.F., Prin.
Franciscan Sisters of Christian Charity (Manitowoc, WI) 2; Lay Teachers 3; Students 171.
Missions of Gila River Catholic Community Team—.
Missions—Ak Chin, St. Francis; Blackwater, Holy Family; Sacaton Flats, Our Lady of Victory; Santan, St. Anne; Sacaton, St. Anthony.

Buckeye, Maricopa Co., Saint Henry, Rev. Richard Driscoll, S.D.S.; Deacon John R. Bilinski.
Res., 128 S. Third St., 85326. Tel: 602-386-6407; Fax: 602-386-4328.
Mission—Harquahala Valley, San Isidoro Labrador.

Bullhead City, Mohave Co., St. Margaret Mary, Rev. Peter P. Dobrowski; Deacon Richard Eckert.
Res., 1691 N. Oatman Rd., 86442. Tel: 520-758-7117; Fax: 520-758-2345.

Camp Verde, Yavapai Co., St. Frances Cabrini, Rev. James Kelly.
Res., P.O. Box 1677, 86322. Tel: 520-567-3543.
Church—608 W. General Crook Trail, 86322. Tel: 520-567-3543.
Mission—Black Canyon City, Yavapai Co., St. Philip Benizi, P.O. Box 138, Black Canyon City, 85324. Tel: 620-374-5392. Rev. Kevin Hunt Diaz.

Carefree, Maricopa Co., Our Lady of Joy, Rev. Msgr. Richard Moyer, V.G.
Res., P.O. Box 1359, 85377. Tel: 602-488-2229 (Church); 488-3090 (Rectory); Fax: 602-488-1085.

Cashion, Maricopa Co., St. William, Rev. Thomas G. Bielawa, S.D.S., Admin.
Mailing Address: P.O. Box 329, 85329.
Res., 11003 W. Third St., 85329. Tel: 602-936-6115.
Mission—Santa Maria, Our Lady of Guadalupe, 6807 Lower Buckeye Rd., Phoenix, 85043.

Chandler, Maricopa Co., St. Andrew the Apostle, Revs. Joseph I. Hennessy; Camille Prat, S.J.; Deacon Gary Jacobs.
Res., 3450 W. Ray Rd., 85226. Tel: 602-899-1990; Fax: 601-917-8475.
St. Mary's, Revs. George E. Highberger; Joseph McGaffin. In res., Rev. Robert Clements.
Res., 230 W. Galveston, 85224. Tel: 602-963-3207; Fax: 602-814-9417.
School—200 W. Galveston, 85224. Tel: 602-963-4951. Sr. Mary Norbert Long, Prin.
Sisters of Charity, Seton Hill 3; Lay Teachers 20; Students 512.
St. Benedict, Rev. Patrick Robinson; Deacon Stephen Beard.
Res., 660 N. Beck, 85226.
Church—6400 W. Del Rio St., 85226. Tel: 602-961-1610; Fax: 602-961-1794.

Cottonwood, Yavapai Co., Immaculate Conception, Rev. Emile "Bud" Pelletier; Deacons James Anderson; Onofre Duran; Ron Pelton.
Mailing Address: P.O. Box 995, 86326.
Res., 421 N. Willard St., 86326. Tel: 520-634-2933.
Mission—Clarkdale, Yavapai Co., St. Cecilia, P.O. Box 366, Clarkdale, 86324-0366. Tel: 520-634-2142. Rev. Michael F. Hurley, Admin.

El Mirage, Maricopa Co., Santa Teresita, Rev. George Wuest, S.J.; Deacon Jose Garza.
Church—14016 N. Verbena St., 85335.
Res., P.O. Box 67, 85335. Tel: 602-583-8183; Fax: 602-583-2963.

Flagstaff, San Francisco de Asis, Revs. Douglas Nohava; Kieran Kleczewski; Daniel McBride.
Mailing Address: P.O. Box 1946, 86002-1946. Tel: 520-779-1341; Fax: 520-779-2903.
Rectory: 520 W. Riordan Rd., 86002.
School—St. Mary's Regional School, 320 N. Humphrey, 86001. Tel: 520-779-1337. Dr. Marie Axman, Prin.
Institute of the Blessed Virgin Mary 1; Lay Teachers 14; Students 256.
Chapels—Nativity of B.V.M., 16 W. Cherry Ave., 86001.; Our Lady of Guadalupe, 225 S. Kendrick, 86001.; St. Pius X, 2257 E. Cedar Ave., 86004.

Fountain Hills, Maricopa Co., Ascension, Rev. Thomas O'Dea; Sr. Kathleen Storan, Pastoral Assoc.; Leann Gratz, Parish Mgr.
Church—12615 Fountain Hills Blvd., 85268. Tel: 602-837-1066; Fax: 602-837-9093.
Mission—Rio Verde, St. Dominic.

Gila Bend, Maricopa Co., St. Michael, Rev. Howard Kuhns, C.S.C.
Res., 515 W. Norma St., P.O. Drawer F, 85337. Tel: 520-683-6463.
Church—314 Dodson St., 85337.
Mission—Tohono O'Odham, St. Lucy, Paloma Ranch. (Native American Village). Sr. Barbara Anne Webster, O.S.F., Ministries Asst.

Gilbert, Maricopa Co., St. Anne, Revs. Douglas E. Lorig; Julio Higuera; Deacons Ken Kulinowski; Gerald O'Toole; James Salamone; Tom Phelan; Bobbi Friedrich, Pastoral Assoc.
Mailing Address: P.O. Box 228, 85299-0228. Tel: 602-892-4970; Fax: 601-892-6736.
Church—440 E. Elliot Rd., 85299-0228.
Mission—Queen Creek, Maricopa Co., Our Lady of Guadalupe, P.O. Box 856, Queen Creek, 85242. Tel: 602-963-3207.

Glendale, Maricopa Co.,

1—Our Lady of Perpetual Help, Revs. Fausto Penafiel; John Ebbesmier; Deacons James Marth; Tony Lopez; Robert Myers; Eddie Molina; Charles Hecter.
Res., 5614 W. Orangewood Ave., 85301. Tel: 602-939-9785; Fax: 602-934-8854.
School—7521 N. 57th Ave., 85301. Tel: 602-931-7288. Sr. Lucia Daluz, O.S.F., Prin.
Sisters 1; Lay Teachers 9; Students 241.
Chapel—Our Lady of Guadalupe, 55th Ave. & Lamar.

2—St. Helen, Revs. Robert Skagen; Louis R. Mraz, O.S.C.; Sr. Patricia Oliver, R.S.M., Pastoral Assoc.; Deacons Joseph Shinske; Robert Rudolph Campas; Paul Csuy.
Res., 5510 W. Cholla, 85304. Tel: 602-979-4202; Fax: 602-412-1226.

3—St. James, Rev. Kenneth A. Van De Ven; Deacon John O'Connor.
Church—19640 N. 35th Ave., 85308. Tel: 602-581-0707; Fax: 602-581-0110.
Res., 18225 N. 35th Dr., 85308. Tel: 602-843-0421.

4—St. Louis The King, Revs. John Slobig; Robert Bliven, O.S.C.; Deacon Gene Messer.
Mailing Address: 4331 W. Maryland Ave., 85301. Tel: 602-930-1127; Fax: 602-930-1129.
School—Tel: 602-939-4260. Sr. Jean Perry, C.S.A., Prin.
Sisters 1; Lay Teachers 10; Students 223.

5—St. Raphael, Revs. Cyprian Hibner, O.Carm.; James Mueller, O.Carm.; Deacons Forrest Briesch; Stewart Wood; Joseph Liotta.
Res., 5504 W. Acoma, 85306.
Church—5525 W. Acoma, 85306. Tel: 602-938-4227; Fax: 601-978-0305.

6—St. Thomas More, Rev. James Turner.
P.O. Box 11887, 85318-1887. Tel: 602-566-6215.

Goodyear, Maricopa Co., Saint John Vianney, Revs. Joseph V. Corpora, C.S.C.; John A. Herman, C.S.C.; Stephen Wilbright, C.S.C.
Office: 539 La Pasada Blvd., 85338. Tel: 602-932-3313; Fax: 602-932-1896.
Res., 11 Loma Linda, Avondale, 85323. Tel: 602-925-0418.

Grand Canyon, Coconino Co., El Cristo Rey, Rev. Francis D. Zagorc, C.S.C., Admin.
Res., Rectory Chapel, Boulder at Albright, P.O. Box 505, 86023. Tel: 520-638-2390.

Guadalupe, Maricopa Co., Our Lady of Guadalupe, Rev. Joseph A. Baur, O.F.M., Admin.; Deacon Santo Bernasconi.
Office: 5445 San Angelo, St. Guadelupe, 85283. Tel: 602-839-2860.
Res., 9004 Calle Maravilla, 85283. Tel: 602-839-2376.

Jerome, Yavapai Co., Holy Family. Unassigned.
St. Cecilia Mission: (Sacramental Records) P.O. Box 366, Clarkdale, 86324. Tel: 520-634-2142.

Kingman, Mohave Co., St. Mary's, Rev. James Alling; Deacons Bill Del Monaco; Jose Rodriguez.
Res., 302 E. Spring St., 86401. Tel: 520-753-3359; Fax: 520-753-2581.
Mission—Dolan Springs, Mohave Co., Our Lady of the Desert, P.O. Box 491, Dolan Springs, 86441. Tel: 520-767-3154.

Lake Havasu City, Mohave Co., Our Lady of the Lake, Rev. Michael Deptula; Deacons Robert B. Treichel; Thomas C. Coe; Robert W. Davey; Eamon Parsons.
Res., 1975 Daytona Dr., 86403. Tel: 520-855-2685; Fax: 520-855-7172.

Laveen, Maricopa Co., St. John The Baptist, Sr. Anne Fischer, S.S.N.D., Admin.; Deacon Tom Swisher, Admin.
Res., P.O. Box 693, 85339-0693. Tel: 520-550-2034.
Mission—Santa Cruz, St. Catherine.
Station—Lone Butte, St. Francis Xavier.

Litchfield Park, Maricopa Co., St. Thomas Aquinas, Revs. Franklin L. Bartel; Ray Greco, O.S.B.; Deacons Daniel O'Leary Peterson; Chuck Shaw.
Res., 447 S. Litchfield Rd., 85340. Tel: 602-935-2151; 935-3625; Fax: 602-935-5044.

Mesa, Maricopa Co.,

1—All Saints, Rev. Robert Caruso; Deacons Donnan Lukaszewski; T. Vincent Neeley; Ray Semmler; Reed Santa.
Church—1534 N. Recker Rd., 85205. Tel: 602-985-7655; Fax: 602-396-0837.

2—Christ the King, Revs. John Coleman; Christopher Carpenter; Deacons Joseph August; Philip Van Der Heyden; Stanley Humpal.
Res., 1505 E. Dana Ave., 85204.
Church—1551 E. Dana Ave., 85204. Tel: 602-964-1719; Fax: 602-844-4498.
School—Tel: 602-844-4480. Ms. Janice Merfeld, Prin.
Lay Teachers 12; Students 304.

3—Holy Cross, Rev. Dennis Riccitelli; Sr. Mary Eunice McGreevey, S.C., Pastoral Ministry; Deacons Tony Smerke; James Battista.
Res., 1244 S. Power Rd., 85206. Tel: 602-981-2021; Fax: 602-981-6844.

4—Queen of Peace, Revs. Karl LeClaire, S.D.S.; Lloyd P. Kramlich, S.D.S.; Paul Portland, S.D.S.; Thomas Tureman; Deacons Buddy Clapham; John Reidel.
Res., 141 N. Macdonald St., 85201. Tel: 602-969-9166; Fax: 602-969-8102.
School—109 N. Macdonald St., 85201. Tel: 602-969-0226. Ms. Shelley Conner, Prin.
Lay Teachers 11; Students 245.

5—St. Bridget, Rev. John F. Cunningham; Rev. Msgr. Bernard Collins, (Retired); Rev. Msgr. Michael Nestor, (Retired); Deacons Joe Scaccia; William Shea; Len Liszewski.
Res., 2850 E. Lockwood St., 85213. Tel: 602-924-9138.
Church—2213 N. Lindsay Rd., 85213. Tel: 602-924-9111; Fax: 602-924-3103.

6—St. Timothy, Revs. Dale J. Fushek; Mark Dippre; Deacons Ollie Babbitts; Thomas Bolduc; Barry Smith; Dutch Hurrish. In res., Rev. Paul Orel.
Res., 1730 W. Guadalupe, 85202. Tel: 602-838-8844; Fax: 602-820-7984.
Convent—2754 S. Pennington, 85202.
Sisters 4.
Catholic Life Productions, Inc. dba LIFE TEEN Program—Tel: 602-820-7001. Lin Tropio, Prog. Dir.

Peoria, Maricopa Co., St. Charles Borromeo, Rev. Hugo Gonzalez; Deacons Armando Mesquita; Bill Phares.
Mailing Address: P.O. Box 819, 85380-0819.
Res., 8617 W. Peoria Ave., 85345. Tel: 602-979-3418.
Church—8615 W. Peoria Ave., 85345. Fax: 602-412-2397.

Prescott, Yavapai Co., Sacred Heart, Revs. Fred LeClaire, C.M.F.; Francis Pyka, C.M.F.; James Griffin; Richard Farrell; Deacons William Davis; Thomas Kayser; John Lamon.

Res., 150 Fleury Ave., 86301. Tel: 520-445-3141; Fax: 520-717-1074.
School—131 N. Summit Ave., 86301. Tel: 520-445-2621. Ms. Donna Walsh, Prin.
Institute of the Blessed Virgin Mary Sisters 1; Lay Teachers 8; Students 190.
Convent—229 N. Summit St., 86301. Tel: 520-445-7861.
Missions—Congress Junction, Yavapai Co., Good Shepherd of the Desert; Yarnell, Yavapai Co., St. Mary's, P.O. Box 706, Yarnell, 85362. Tel: 520-427-3715. Rev. John Faustina.; Chino Valley, Yavapai Co., St. Catherine Laboure, P.O. Box 152, Chino Valley, 86323. Tel: 520-636-4071. Rev. John Salvador.

Prescott Valley, Yavapai Co., St. Germaine, Revs. Gerald Yaeger; Kevin Hunt Diaz.
Res., 7997 E. Dana Dr., 86314. Tel: 520-772-6350; Fax: 520-772-4413.
Missions—Mayer, St. Joseph; Humboldt, St. Lawrence.

Sacaton, Native American Catholic Community, Mailing Address: c/o Sr. Anne Fischer, S.S.N.D., P.O. Box 545, 85247. Tel: 520-562-3716.

Scottsdale, Maricopa Co.,

1—Blessed Sacrament, Revs. Eugene Young; Mathew Plathottam; Deacons Clem Czapinski; Pat Hughes; Harry Hude. In res., Rev. Thomas Walsh, (Retired).
Res., 11300 N. 64th St., 85254. Tel: 602-948-8370; Fax: 602-951-3844.

2—Our Lady of Perpetual Help, Revs. William P. Healy; John Bernbrock, S.J.; Deacons Irving Fleming; James Hoyt. In res., Rev. Alan Malone.
Res., 7655 E. Main St., 85251. Tel: 602-947-4331; Fax: 602-874-3798.
School—3801 N. Miller Rd., 85251. Tel: 602-874-3720. Sr. Marian Grace Brandt, S.C., Prin.
Sisters of Charity 3; Lay Teachers 25; Students 580.
Convent—7634 E. Second St., 85251. Tel: 602-945-3867.

3—St. Bernadette, Rev. Richard Felt; Deacons Alan Bowslaugh; John Meyer; Roy Rooker.
Office: 14415 N. 73rd St., #107, 85260-3130. Tel: 602-905-0221; Fax: 602-905-0249.

4—St. Bernard of Clairvaux, Rev. Robert Voss; Deacons Fred Giesner; George Reinert.
Res., 10755 N. 124th St., 85259. Tel: 602-661-9843; Fax: 602-614-8092.

5—St. Daniel the Prophet, Revs. Francis R. Zappitelli; Dennis J. O'Rourke; Simon Jeon; Deacons Roy Anderson; Ranald Guldan; Charles Raymond; Richard Regan. In res., Rev. Patrick Smith.
Res., 7923 E. Latham St., 85257. Tel: 602-945-8437; Fax: 602-945-4335.
School—Tel: 602-949-8034. Sr. Mary Lucilla Wertz, S.C., Prin.
Lay Teachers 11; Students 224.
Convent—7830 E. Roosevelt, 85257. Tel: 602-423-5240.
Korean Catholic Community: Rev. Simon Jeon.

6—St. Maria Goretti, Revs. Blase Myer; Rudolph Kundert; John Picardi; Deacons Herve Lemire; Len Zbiegien; Tom Bills; Anthony Dudzic.
Res., 8344 E. Edward Ave., 85250.
Church—6261 N. Granite Reef Rd., 85250. Tel: 602-948-8380; Fax: 602-948-8815.

7—St. Patrick, Rev. Eric Tellez; Deacon Jim Buchanan.
Office: 10815 N. 84th St., 85260. Tel: 602-998-3843; Fax: 602-998-5218.

Sedona, Yavapai Co., St. John Vianney, Rev. J.C. Ortiz; Deacon Bob Anderson.
Res., 180 Soldier Pass Rd., P.O. Box 3909, W. Sedona, 86340. Tel: 520-282-7545; Fax: 520-282-1798.
Chapel—Holy Cross, 780 Chapel Rd., P.O. Box 1043, 86339. Tel: 520-282-4069.

Seligman, Yavapai Co., St. Francis, Rev. Isidore Garcia, C.M.F., Admin.
Res., P.O. Box 308, 86337. Tel: 520-422-3354.
Church—104 Schoney, 86337.
Mission—Ashfork, St. Anne.

Sun City, Maricopa Co., St. Clement of Rome, Revs. Earl D'Eon; Ed Coleman, O.M.I.; Mathew Mampara; Deacons Edward Owen; Irving Dennis; Stanley Giza.
Res., 15800 Del Webb Blvd., 85351. Tel: 602-974-5867; Fax: 602-974-0562.

St. Elizabeth Seton, Revs. Joseph Gillespie; William Waldron; Richard P. Ciesniewski; William Harnischfeger; Deacon William Tone.
Res., 9728 Palmeras Ln., 85373. Tel: 602-972-2129; Fax: 602-974-0654.

Church of St. Joachim & St. Anne, Revs. Frank P. Simlik; Richard Ryan.
Mailing Address: P.O. Box 748, 85372.
Res., 11625 111th Ave., 85351-3746. Tel: 602-972-1179; Fax: 602-972-1170.

Sun City West, Maricopa Co., Our Lady of Lourdes, Revs. Michael Minogue; Harold Graf; Deacons Lee Hanson; Maurice Arnold; Jack Cummings; George Koch.
Res., 19002 N. 128th Ave., 85375. Tel: 602-546-2767; Fax: 602-214-1246.

Sun Lakes, Maricopa Co., St. Steven, Rev. Emmett J. FitzPatrick.
Mailing Address: 24827 S. Dobson Rd., 85248. Tel: 602-895-9266.
Res., 10324 E. Michigan Ave., 85248. Tel: 602-895-9304.

Tempe, Maricopa Co.,

1—Holy Spirit, Rev. John Hanley; Deacon Frank Danna.
Office: 1815 E. Gemini Dr., 85283. Tel: 602-838-7474; Fax: 602-838-6720.

2—Our Lady of Mt. Carmel, Revs. Timothy R. Davern, J.C.L.; Donald Kline.
Res., 2121 S. Rural Rd., 85282. Tel: 602-967-8791; Fax: 602-967-4919.
School—2117 S. Rural Rd., 85282. Tel: 602-967-5567. Dr. Vincent Sheridan, Prin.
Lay Teachers 31; Students 480.
Tongan Catholic Community: Rev. Timothy Davern, Liaison.

3—Resurrection, Revs. Thomas F. Hever; Bruce Downs. In res., Rev. Joseph G. Krijnen.
Res., 3201 S. Evergreen Rd., 85282. Tel: 602-838-0207; Fax: 602-756-1501.

4—St. Margaret, Deacon Frank G. Galarza, Admin.
Res., 2435 E. McArthur Dr., 85281. Tel: 602-967-0379; Fax: 602-967-3825.
Missions—Salt River Indian, St. Francis; Lehi, St. Paschal Baylon, P.O. Box 3334, Scottsdale, 85257. Tel: 602-994-0952.

Tolleson, Maricopa Co., Blessed Sacrament, Revs. Bruce Cecil, C.S.C.; Brent Kruger; Deacon Antonio M. Chavez, Sr.
Res., 312 N. 93rd Ave., P.O. Box 248, 85353. Tel: 602-936-7107; Fax: 602-936-9536.

Wickenburg, Maricopa Co., St. Anthony of Padua, Rev. John Vogt.
Res., 232 N. Tegner St., 85390. Tel: 520-684-2096; Fax: 520-684-3539.
Mission—Aguila, Our Lady of Guadalupe.

Williams, Coconino Co., St. Joseph's, Rev. J.F. Michael Bain.
Res., 900 W. Grant, 86046. Tel: 520-635-2430; Fax: 520-635-2430, Ext. 51.

Chaplains of Public Institutions

Phoenix. *Arizona State Hospital* 2500 E. Van Buren St., 85008. Tel: 602-220-6190. Chaplains: Sr. Patricia Pieper, D.deN.; Deacons George Valverde; Joseph Shinske.
Good Samaritan Medical Center 1111 E. McDowell Rd., 85006. Tel: 602-239-4324. Rev. Patrick J. Adkins, O.S.C.
Maricopa Medical Center 2601 E. Roosevelt St., 85008. Tel: 602-267-5011. Rev. Tulio Maya, S.D.S., Chap.
Phoenix Indian Medical Center. (For Sacramental Records Contact St. Francis Xavier at 602-279-9547) 4212 N. 16th St., 850. Tel: 602-263-1017. Deacon Alex Roy, Chap., Tel: 602-946-0859.
St. Joseph's Hospital P.O. Box 2071, 85001. Tel: 602-406-3275. Ms. Theresa M. Ehrsam, Dir., Chaplaincy Svcs.
St. Luke's Medical Center. Vacant. 1800 E. Van Buren St., 85006. Tel: 602-251-8100.
United States Veterans Affairs Medical Center 650 E. Indian School Rd., 85012. Tel: 602-222-6422. Revs. Bernard L. Young, Chap.; Peter Morello, Chief of Chap. Svcs.; Kenneth Klieber, Chap.

Chandler. *Chandler Regional Hospital* 475 S. Dobson Rd., 85224. Tel: 602-821-7639. Sr. Anna Oven, O.P., Chap.

Luke Air Force Base. *Luke Air Force Base* 58 FW/HC, 13968 Shooting Star St., 85309-1932. Tel: 602-856-6211. Rev. Redmond Raux, Chap.

Prescott. *United States Veterans Hospital (Prescott)* Veterans Administration Medical Center, 86313. Tel: 520-776-6029, Ext. 6478. Rev. Gerald Caffrey, C.M.F., Chap.

Scottsdale. *Scottsdale Memorial Hospital* 7400 E. Osborn Rd., 85251. Tel: 602-481-4000; 945-8437. Rev. Patrick Smith, Chap.

Special Assignment:
Reverend Monsignors—
McMahon, John J., Dir. Mount Claret Retreat Center, 4633 N. 54th St., Phoenix, AZ 85018. Tel: 602-840-5066
Reverend Fathers—
Acquaro, Philip, C.S.B., Diocesan Ctr., Tribunal Office, 400 E. Monroe, Phoenix, AZ 85004. Tel: 602-257-0030
Benjamin, Don, O.Carm., Exec. Dir. Kino Institute, 1224 E. Northern Ave., Phoenix, AZ 85020
Clements, Robert, Vocation Dir., 400 E. Monroe St., Phoenix, AZ 85004. Tel: 602-257-0030
Diskin, Michael L., Asst. Chancellor & Ecumenical Officer, Diocesan Center, 400 E. Monroe, Phoenix, AZ
Goulet, Wayne F., 8540 N. Central Ave., #13, Phoenix, AZ 85020
Hall, John, Vicar, Native American Ministry, 400 E. Monroe, Phoenix, AZ 85004
Malone, Alan, Judicial Vicar, 400 E. Monroe, Phoenix, AZ 85004
Orel, Paul, Diocesan Center Tribunal Office, 400 E. Monroe, Phoenix, AZ
Pepel, Klemens, Dir., Prison Ministry, 400 E. Monroe St., Phoenix, AZ 85004
Prudencio, Rodriguez, C.M., Vicar, Hispanic Ministry, Diocesan Center, 400 E. Monroe, Phoenix, AZ 85004
Ryle, Edward J., Exec. Dir., Arizona Catholic Conference, 400 E. Monroe St., Phoenix, AZ 85004
Sharp, David L., C.S.B., Campus Min., Glendale Community College
Straley, Michael, Vicar & Vicar Admin. Svcs., 400 E. Monroe, Phoenix, AZ

On Duty Outside the Diocese:
Reverend Fathers—
Brogan, Leo T.
Draves-Arpaia, Neil
Lessard, Joseph

On Leave:
Reverend Fathers—
Gauthier, John
Parker, Charles

Unassigned:
Reverend Fathers—
Boulanger, Andre
Bredemann, George
Briceno, Joseph
Lehman, Mark A.
Sherwood, Lan S.

Retired:
Reverend Monsignors—
Donohoe, Robert J., 2345 W. Orangewood Ave., Phoenix, AZ 85021
Reverend Fathers—
Bourbon, Arthur, 11121 Desert Butte, Sun City, AZ 85351
Boyle, Thomas, 325 W. Holly St., Phoenix, AZ 85003
Colton, Bernard, 122A Clanabogan Rd., Omagh, Co. Tyrone, BT 7815 N Northern Ireland
Cullinan, John F., St. Joan of Arc, 3801 E. Greenway Rd., Phoenix, AZ 85032-4698
Diederichs, Michael F., 2002 W. Sunnyside Dr., #3315, Phoenix, AZ 85029-3552
Faustina, John M., St. Mary, P.O. Box 706, Yarnell, AZ 85362
Feit, Matthias, 12036 103rd Ave., Sun City, AZ 85351
Florez, Laurence A., P.O. Box 74, Youngtown, AZ 85363
Glass, Gerald J., 8141 N. 16th St., #7, Phoenix, AZ 85020
Groves, Edmund, St. Paul's Convent, Bushmount, Clonakilty, Co. Cork, Ireland
Hodges, Henry D., 4730 W. Northern Ave., #2083, Glendale, AZ 85302
Kelly, Martin C., 10637 Saratoga Cir., Sun City, AZ 85351
Kotnis, Gregory M., P.O. Box 3081, Lake Havasu City, AZ 86405-3081
Krijnen, Joseph G., Resurrection Parish, 3201 S. Evergreen Rd., Tempe, AZ 85282
Long, Francis C., HC63 Box 5589, Snowflake, AZ 85937
Maguire, Eugene, 4701 N. 68th St., #103, Scottsdale, AZ 85251
McCready, Daniel A., 918 E. Broadmor, Tempe, AZ 85282
McGovern, Michael A., 10206 Snead Cir., Sun City, AZ 85351
McKay, William E., 6457 E. Dodge St., Mesa, AZ 85205
Mitchell, William J., 1675 Leisure World, Mesa, AZ 85206
Morales, Raul, P.O. Box 1143, Gilbert, AZ 85299
Moynihan, Cornelius A., 18626 Spanish Garden Dr., Sun City West, AZ 85375
O'Hern, Charles A., Sun Terrace, 1825 W. Emelita, #339, Mesa, AZ 85202
O'Reilly, Francis J., Churchfield Lawns, Knock, Co. Mayo, Ireland
Pirrung, George, P.O. Box 995, Cottonwood, AZ 86326

Portmann, Frederick, 1255 W. Osborn Rd., Phoenix, AZ 85013
Schwartz, Anthony, Villa Guadalupe Home, 1900 Mark Ave., Gallup, NM 87301
Smith, Paul P., 6301 N. 34th Ln., Phoenix, AZ 85017
Sullivan, John T., Nazareth House, 6333 Rancho Mission Rd., San Diego, CA 92108
Wajda, Edward J., 214 S. Laveen Dr., Chandler, AZ 85226
Walsh, Thomas A., Blessed Sacrament, 11300 N. 64th St., Scottsdale, AZ 85254
Wasielewski, Henry R., P.O. Box 939, Tempe, AZ 85280-0939

Permanent Deacons:
Aird, Gordon, Unassigned
Anderson, Bob, Jr., St. John Vianney, Sedona
Anderson, James, Immaculate Conception, Cottonwood
Anderson, Roy, St. Daniel the Prophet, Scottsdale
Arnold, Maurice, (Retired), Our Lady of Lourdes, Sun City West
August, Joe, Christ the King, Mesa
Babbits, Oliver, St. Timothy, Mesa
Barelli, John, St. Thomas the Apostle, Phoenix
Barr, Earl, SS. Simon & Jude Cathedral, Phoenix
Battista, James, Holy Cross, Mesa
Beard, Stephen, St. Benedict, Chandler
Beltran, Anthony N., St. Matthew's, Phoenix
Bernasconi, Santo R., Our Lady of Guadalupe, Guadalupe
Bilinski, John, St. Henry, Buckeye
Bills, Tom, St. Maria Goretti, Scottsdale
Boehle, Jack, San Francisco de Asis, Flagstaff
Bolduc, Thomas, St. Timothy, Mesa
Bolton, Edward L., St. Gregory, Phoenix
Bowslaugh, Alan P., St. Bernadette, Scottsdale
Boyer, Terry, On Leave
Brett, James, St. Theresa, Phoenix
Briesch, Forrest, St. Raphael, Glendale
Buchanan, James, St. Patrick, Scottsdale
Burgin, Edward, Indian Ministry
Burke, Edward, St. Joseph Hospital, Phoenix
Campas, Rudolph, St. Helen, Glendale
Chavez, Antonio, Blessed Sacrament, Tolleson
Clapham, Buddy, Queen of Peace, Mesa
Coe, Tom, Our Lady of the Lake, Lake Havasu City
Conn, Richard A., Our Lady of Mount Carmel, Tempe
Csuy, Paul E., St. Helen, Glendale
Cummings, Jack, Our Lady of Lourdes, Sun City West
Curran, Richard, Diocesan Ministry, St. Maria Goretti, Scottsdale
Czapinski, Clemens, Blessed Sacrament Scottsdale
D'Agnolo, Louis A.
Danna, Frank, Holy Spirit, Tempe
Davey, Bob, Our Lady of the Lake, Lake Havasu City
Davis, William, Sacred Heart, Prescott
DeDecker, Robert, St. Jerome Church, Phoenix
Del Monaco, William, St. Mary, Kingman
Dennis, Irving, St. Clement of Rome, Sun City
Dudzic, Anthony, St. Maria Goretti, Scottsdale
Duran, Onofre, Immaculate Conception, Cottonwood
Eckert, Dick, St. Margaret Mary, Bullhead City
England, Robert E., St. Paul, Phoenix
Fejes, Peter, St. Edward, Phoenix
Ferski, Andy, Unassigned
Fleming, Irving, Our Lady of Perpetual Help Church, Scottsdale
Flynn, Patrick F., Corpus Christi, Phoenix
Fronske, Robert, (Retired)
Galarza, Frank, St. Margaret, Tempe
Garza, Jose, Santa Teresita, El Mirage
Gaudio, Alexander L., Corpus Christi, Phoenix
Gehringer, William D., (Retired)
Giesner, Fred, St. Bernard, Scottsdale
Giza, Stanley, St. Clement of Rome, Sun City
Gonzales, Albert, St. Augustine, Phoenix
Goubeaux, Guy, Most Holy Trinity, Phoenix
Gouveia, Americo, St. Thomas the Apostle, Phoenix
Gregory, Tom, Sacred Heart, Prescott
Guldan, Ranald, St. Daniel the Prophet, Scottsdale
Guzman, Juan, St. Augustine, Phoenix
Hamilton, James, On Leave
Heeter, Charles, Our Lady of Perpetual Help, Glendale
Henn, Thomas, Luke Air Force Base, Litchfield
Hernandez, Arnold, St. Vincent de Paul, Phoenix
Hernandez, Jose, St. Mark, Phoenix
Herrmann, Richard E., St. Agnes, Phoenix
Hickcox, Edward M., San Francisco de Asisi, Flagstaff
Hintze, Craig, St. Mary, Chandler
Holgin, Alex, Our Lady of Mount Carmel, Tempe
Houser, Joseph, St. Augustine, Phoenix
Hoyt, James, Our Lady of Perpetual Help, Scottsdale
Hude, Harry, Blessed Sacrament, Scottsdale
Hughes, Patrick, Blessed Sacrament, Scottsdale
Humpal, Stanley, Christ the King, Mesa
Humphrey, Charles A., Sacred Heart, Prescott
Hurley, Dan A., St. Joachim & St. Anne, Sun City
Hurrish, Dutch, St. Timothy, Mesa
Jacobs, Gary, St. Andrew the Apostle, Chandler
Jimenez, Ramon H., Our Lady of Guadalupe, Guadalupe
Kayser, Thomas E., Assoc. Dir. of the Permanent Diaconate, Sacred Heart, Prescott
Kelly, Charles, St. Joseph, Phoenix
Kloft, Lee, St. Gregory Parish, Phoenix
Koch, George, Our Lady of Lourdes, Sun City West
Kuban, Donald, St. Thomas the Apostle, Phoenix
Kulinowski, Kenneth, St. Anne, Gilbert
Lamon, John, Sacred Heart Parish, Prescott
Lazok, George, St. Catherine of Siena, Phoenix
LeClair, Douglas, Unassigned
Lemire, Herve, St. Maria Goretti, Scottsdale
Leone, Robert, All Saints Newman Center, Tempe
Lessard, Joseph M., Mount Claret Retreat Center, Phoenix
Liotta, Joe, St. Raphael, Glendale
Liszewski, Leonard, St. Briget, Mesa
LoCascio, Phil, St. Joan of Arc, Phoenix
Lopez, Tony, Our Lady of Perpetual Help, Glendale
Lukaszewski, Don, All Saints, Mesa
Mader, Charles J., St. Charles Borromeo, Peoria
Marion, Kenneth, St. Paul, Phoenix
Marth, Jim, Our Lady of Perpetual Help, Glendale
Martin, Stephen J., SS. Simon and Jude Cathedral, Phoenix
Meli, John, Our Lady of the Valley, Glendale
Mesquita, Armando, St. Charles Borromeo, Peoria
Messer, Gene, St. Louis the King, Glendale
Meyer, John A., Diocesan Dir. of Catechetical Ministry, St. Bernadette, Scottsdale
Micek, Theodore, St. Jerome, Phoenix
Miller, John, St. Thomas the Apostle Byzantine, Gilbert
Miller, Kenneth, Chap., Kolping Society, St. Thomas the Apostle, Phoenix
Molina, Eddie, Our Lady of Perpetual Help, Glendale
Mosley, William, San Francisco de Asis, Flagstaff
Murphy, Peter, Prison Ministry, St. Gregory Parish, Phoenix
Myers, Robert P., Our Lady of Perpetual Help, Glendale
Neely, Vincent, All Saints, Mesa
O'Connor, John, St. James, Glendale
O'Toole, Gerald, St. Anne Parish, Gilbert
Olivarez, Jose D., St. Martin de Porres, Phoenix
Ortega, Elisandro G., St. Mark, Phoenix
Owen, Edward, St. Clement of Rome, Sun City
Pardini, Louis, Ph.D., St. Philip the Deacon, Phoenix
Parsons, Eamon, Our Lady of the Lake, Lake Havasu City
Pelton, Ron, Immaculate Conception, Cottonwood
Peterson, Daniel, Dir. Diaconate, St. Thomas Aquinas, Litchfield Park
Pfleger, James, Luke Air Force Base, Litchfield
Phares, William, St. Charles Borromeo, Peoria
Phelan, Mike, St. Jerome, Phoenix
Phelan, Thomas J., St. Anne, Gilbert
Rade, Douglas, San Francisco de Asis, Flagstaff
Raymond, Charles J., St. Daniel the Prophet, Scottsdale
Raymond, Robert, Unassigned
Regan, W. Richard, St. Daniel the Prophet, Scottsdale
Rein, Richard, St. Jerome, Phoenix
Reinert, George, (Retired)
Riedel, John, Queen of Peace, Mesa
Rocha, Felix, Unassigned
Rodriguez, Jose, St. Mary, Kingman
Roger, Ray, St. Vincent de Paul, Phoenix
Rooker, Roy, St. Bernadette, Scottsdale
Roy, Alex, St. Francis Indian Mission, Mesa Chaplain, Indian Hospital
Salamone, James, St. Anne Parish, Gilbert
Sanchez, Harry E., St. Agnes, Phoenix
Santa, Reed, All Saints, Mesa
Scaccia, Joe, St. Bridget, Mesa
Scarabino, Anthony G., Diocese of Gallup
Schwan, Harry, St. Joseph, Phoenix
Sejba, Jim, Our Lady of Joy, Carefree
Semmler, Raymond, All Saints, Mesa
Shaw, Chuck, St. Thomas Aquinas, Litchfield Park
Shea, William, St. Bridget, Mesa
Shinske, Joseph, Chap., Arizona State Hospital, St. Helen's, Glendale
Simeone, Philip, Corpus Christi, Phoenix
Smerke, Tony, Holy Cross, Mesa
Smith, Barry, St. Timothy, Mesa
Starrs, William, Sacred Heart, Prescott
Stevenson, William, Dayton, OH
Swisher, Thomas, Prison Ministry, St. John the Baptist & St. Peter
Tone, William, (Retired), St. Elizabeth Seton, Sun City
Treichel, Robert, Our Lady of the Lake, Lake Havasu City
Valverde, W. George, Chap., Arizona State Hospital & St. Philip the Deacon, Phoenix
Van Der Hayden, Philip, Christ the King, Mesa
Vera, Emidio B., Holy Family, Phoenix
Vivio, William, St. Paul, Phoenix
Walsh, Franklyn, Unassigned
Walsh, Thomas, Blessed Sacrament, Scottsdale
Whelan, Laurence, San Francisco de Asis, Flagstaff
Wood, Stewart, St. Raphael, Glendale
Zanon, Thomas, Unassigned
Zbiegien, Leonard J., St. Maria Goretti, Scottsdale

INSTITUTIONS LOCATED IN THE DIOCESE

[A] HIGH SCHOOLS, DIOCESAN

PHOENIX. *Bourgade Catholic High School*, 4602 N. 31st Ave., 85017. Tel: 602-973-4000.
E-mail: diophxbourga@connectinc.com
Sr. Mary McGreevy, S.S.N.D., Prin.; Sr. Kathleen Janiak, R.S.M., Dir. Studies; Mr. Thomas Kurry, Dir. Students; Rev. John Ebbesmier, Chap. Sisters 3; Brothers 1; Lay Teachers 23; Students 312.

St. Mary's High School, 2525 N. Third St., 85004. Tel: 602-254-6371.
E-mail: diophxstmhs@connect.com
Mr. Bill Lehman, Prin.; Mrs. Suzanne Fessler, Asst. Prin.; Tom Miller, Counselor; Rev. Blaise Cronin, O.F.M., Spiritual Dir. Academic Advisors: Sr. Jeanette Shean, I.B.V.M.; Bro. Joseph Schwab, O.F.M.; Daniel Johansen. Priests 2; Sisters 2; Brothers 1; Lay Teachers 44; Students 756.

Seton Catholic High School, 1150 N. Dobson Rd., 85224. Tel: 602-963-1900; Fax: 602-963-1974.
E-mail: diophxseton@connectinc.com
Mr. George Majoue, Prin. Asst. Principals: Ms. Judy Krick; Dr. Frank Klajda. Sisters of Charity of Seton Hill 3; Lay Teachers 29; Students 470.

Xavier College Preparatory, 4710 N. Fifth St., 85012. Tel: 602-277-3772; Fax: 602-279-1346.
E-mail: diophxxavier@connectinc.com
Sr. M. Joan Fitzgerald, B.V.M., Prin.; Sr. Lynn Winsor, B.V.M., Vice Prin. Sisters 10; Lay Teachers 64; Students 988.

[B] HIGH SCHOOLS, PRIVATE

PHOENIX. *Brophy College Preparatory*, Faculty Res., 4701 N. Central Ave., 85012. Tel: 602-264-5291; Fax: 602-266-3642. Jesuit Fathers. Boys day school. Rev. Edward Reese, S.J., Pres.; Mr. Edwin J. Hearn, Prin.; Ms. Kimberly Cavnar, Asst. Prin.; Mrs. Dorothy Dunnion, Asst. Prin.; Mr. A. Joseph Helm, Jr., Treas.; Revs. E. Louis Bishop, S.J.; Francis A. Moore, S.J., Devel.; William Kopas, Dean of Students; Revs. Peter J. Pabst, S.J., Rector; Kevin Dilworth, S.J.; J. Cameron Ayers, S.J.; James E. Flynn, S.J.; John J. Perlite, S.J., Sub-Min.; Joseph J. Fice, S.J.; James R. Menard, S.J.; Anton J. Renna, S.J.; John R. Becker, S.J.; Harry T. Oliver, S.J.; Richard T. Coz, S.J. Scholastics: Revs. Doanh Nguyen, S.J.; Stephen Hurley, S.J. Priests 14; Scholastics 4; Lay Teachers 65; Students 1,170.

[C] GENERAL HOSPITALS

PHOENIX. *Mercy Services Corporation*, 350 W. Thomas Rd., 85013
For a complete listing, refer to the Hospitals section.

St. Joseph's Hospital and Medical Center, 350 W. Thomas Rd., P.O. Box 2071, 85001. Tel: 602-285-3000
For a complete listing, refer to the Hospitals section.

[D] HOMES FOR THE AGED & HANDICAPPED

PHOENIX. *Desert Crest Apartments*, 2101 E. Maryland Ave., 85016. Tel: 602-264-6427
For a complete listing, refer to the Special Care Facilities section.

Senior Village, 3541 W. Vogel, 85051. Tel: 602-843-3008
For a complete listing, refer to the Special Care Facilities section.

Sweetwater Gardens Apartments, 2035 E. Sweetwater, 85022. Tel: 602-867-4549
For a complete listing, refer to the Special Care Facilities section.

AVONDALE. *Vianney Villas Apartments*, 750 S. Fourth St., 85323. Tel: 602-932-2036
For a complete listing, refer to the Special Care Facilities section.

KINGMAN. *Kingman Heights Apartments*, 1020 Detroit Ave., 86401. Tel: 602-753-2425
For a complete listing, refer to the Special Care Facilities section.

LAKE HAVASU CITY. *Becket House Apartments*, 865 Cashmere Dr., 86403. Tel: 602-855-7178
For a complete listing, refer to the Special Care Facilities section.

WICKENBURG. *Padua Hills Apartments*, 460 S. West Rd., 85390. Tel: 602-684-7034
For a complete listing, refer to the Special Care Facilities section.

WILLIAMS. *St. Agnes Apartments*, 200 S. Ninth, 86046. Tel: 602-635-2913
For a complete listing, refer to the Special Care Facilities section.

[E] CONVENTS AND RESIDENCES OF SISTERS

PHOENIX. *Dominican Sisters*, 3901 E. Pinnacle Rd., #183, 85024-8115.
Institute of Blessed Virgin Mary (I.B.V.M.). (Regional House), 2521 W. Maryland Ave., 85017. Tel: 602-433-0658; Fax: 602-864-8620. Sisters 4.
Missionaries of Charity, 1414 S. 17th Ave., 85007. Tel: 602-258-5504. Sisters 4.
Sisters of Charity of the Blessed Virgin Mary. (Xavier Convent), 4712 N. Third St., 85012. Tel: 602-264-0445. Sisters 8.
Sisters of Divine Savior, 323 E. Elm St., 85012. Tel: 602-274-0228. Sisters 3.
Sisters of St. Benedict of Phoenix, 6407 W. Indian School Rd., 85033. Tel: 602-848-9608.
Day Care Center. Capacity 8; Children 5.
Union of Sisters of the Presentation of the Blessed Virgin Mary. (Provincial House), 729 W. Wilshire Dr., 85007. Tel: 602-271-9687; 258-9476; Fax: 602-253-9166. Sr. Catherine Burke, P.B.V.M., Prov. Sisters 4.

MESA. *Sisters of Notre Dame de Namur.* (Casa Guadalupe), 548 W. Third St., 85201. Tel: 602-964-3685.

TEMPE. *Sisters of Charity.* (Seton House), 1014 S. George Dr., 85281. Tel: 602-967-5538. Sisters 2.

[F] MONASTERIES AND RESIDENCES OF PRIEST AND BROTHERS

PHOENIX. *Carmelite Community*, 1717 W. Flower, 85015. Revs. Valentine L. Boyle, O.Carm., (Retired); Don Benjamin, O.Carm.; Bro. Anton Hagan, O.Carm., (Retired). Priests 2; Brothers 1.
Crosier Community of Phoenix (Canons Regular of the Order of the Holy Cross), 2617 E. Campbell Ave., 85016. Tel: 602-224-0434; Fax: 602-224-0722. E-mail: crosiercwk@aol.com
Revs. Joseph P. Cain, O.S.C.; Joseph J. Bruemmer, O.S.C.; Richard N. Ohlemacher, O.S.C.; Louis R. Mraz, O.S.C.; Fridolin P. Mischke, O.S.C.; Robert J. Bliven, O.S.C.; Leo W. Kapphahn, O.S.C.; Patrick J. Adkins, O.S.C.; Joseph A. Fichtner, O.S.C.; Charles Kunkel, O.S.C., Prior; Robert V. Zylla, O.S.C. Priests 11.
Holy Cross Congregation of Casa Santa Cruz, 7126 N. Seventh Ave., 85021. Tel: 602-944-6000. Bro. Remigius Bullinger, C.S.C.; Revs. Eugene A. Burke, C.S.C.; Milton N. Adamson, C.S.C.; Joseph F. O'Donnell, C.S.C., Dir.; Ambrose J. Wheeler, C.S.C.; Robert L. Kramer, C.S.C., Asst. Supr.; Thomas K. Zurcher, C.S.C., Vicar; Louis Rink, C.S.C.; John B. Wababa, C.S.C. Priests 7; Brothers 1.

TEMPE. *Dominicans (Dominican Community-Jordan House)*, 1042 E. Campus, 85282. Tel: 602-829-1804. Revs. Nathan G. Castle, O.P., Supr.; Joseph O'Brien, O.P.; Daniel Rolland, O.P. Priests 3.

[G] RETREAT HOUSES

PHOENIX. *Mt. Claret Retreat Center*, 4633 N. 54th St., 85018. Tel: 602-840-5066. Rev. Msgr. John J. McMahon, Dir. Asst. Directors: Rev. Eugene Maguire; Sr. Regina Marie Boslet, S.C.; Jo Swiger.
Cursillo Movement: Revs. Leo Delgado, C.M.F., Dir.; Theo Fuentes, C.M.F., Asst. Dir. Priests 2.

BLACK CANYON CITY. *Contemplative House of Prayer.* (Our Lady of Solitude), P.O. Box 1140, 85324. Tel: 602-374-9204. Sr. Mary Therese Sedlock, O.S.F., Dir.

SCOTTSDALE. *Franciscan Renewal Center, Inc. (Casa de Paz Y Bien)*, 5802 E. Lincoln Dr., P.O. Box 220, 85252. Tel: 602-948-7460; Fax: 602-948-2325. Donna Gordon, Admin.; Revs. Alexander Manville, O.F.M., Retreat Master; Alonso de Blas, O.F.M.; William Shaughnessy, O.F.M., Bro. Mario Vasquez, O.F.M. Priests 3; Brothers 1.

[H] NEWMAN CENTERS

PHOENIX. *Office of Youth and Young Adult Ministries*, 400 E. Monroe, 85004. Larry Fraher, Dir.; Modesto Garcia, Assoc. Dir.; Kevin Starr, Youth At Risk Coord. Mesa Community College, Chandler; Gilbert Community College; Glendale Community College; Scottsdale Community College; Paradise Valley Community College; ASU West.
American Graduate School of International Management. (Glendale), Thunderbird Campus, 15249 N. 59th Ave., Glendale, 85306. Tel: 602-978-7011. Joaquin Duarte. Tel: 602-978-7184.
Glendale Community College, P.O. Box 1562, Wickenburg, 85358. Tel: 520-684-7779. Rev. David L. Sharp, C.S.B.
Yavapai College, Emery Riddle Aeronautical University. (Prescott), Sacred Heart Parish, 150 Fleury Ave., Prescott, 86301. Tel: 502-445-3141. Mrs. Gail Schimberg.
Arizona State University. (Tempe), All Saints Catholic Newman Center, 230 E. University Dr., P.O. Box 1987, Tempe, 85281. Tel: 602-967-7823. Revs. Nathan Castle, O.P., Dir.; Daniel Rolland, O.P.; Deacon Robert Leone, Chap.
Mesa Community College, P.O. Box 1175, Cashion, 85329. Tel: 602-936-4221.
Catholic Committee on Scouting. Tel: 602-945-8437. Rev. Dennis J. O'Rourke, Chap.

[I] ACADEMIES OF RELIGIOUS TEACHING

PHOENIX. *Kino Institute*, 1224 E. Northern Ave., 85020-4295. Tel: 602-997-7397; Fax: 602-870-8871.
E-mail: kino@cathdioc.org
Kino Institute Bookstore. Tel: 602-906-9798.
Kino Institute Library. Tel: 602-906-9798.
Kino Institute Media Center. Tel: 602-906-9798. Mary Ajamie, Sec.; Teofilo Argueta-Ramirez, Dir. La Programa de Formacion Pastoral. Tel: 602-216-9682; Rev. Don C. Benjamin, O.Carm., Exec. Dir. Kino Institute. Tel: 602-212-1745; Sr. Joyce Braun, C.S.A., Bookstore & Library Asst.; Kathy Brown, Dean School of Ministry; Pat Julian, Dir. Spirituality Program & Spiritual Direction Training Program; Revs. Michael Kwiecien, O.Carm., Emeritus Faculty; Vernon Meyer, Dean School of Biblical Studies; Tom Missey, Media Ctr. Asst.; Margaret Newman, Business Mgr.; Lisa Padula, Admin. Asst.; Sr. Bibiane Roy, O.P., Librarian, Dir. Bookstore & Media Ctr. Tel: 602-906-9798; Rev. Gilbert J. Rutz, Editor Kino Forum & Dir. Kino Ambassadors; Diana Stickney, Dir. University San Francisco Graduate Program. Tel: 602-678-5675 (fax); Joe Velazquez, Dir. Survival School Church Mgmt.; Bob Vyslouzil, Plant Mgr.; Zdenka Vyslouzil, Custodian. Total Staff 18.

[J] MISCELLANEOUS LISTINGS

PHOENIX. *Andre House of Arizona*, 213 S. 11th Ave., 85007-3132. Hospitality House, Indiana Province of the Congregation of Holy Cross. Mailing Address: P.O. Box 2014, 85001-2014. Tel: 602-255-0580. Revs. John J. Dougherty, C.S.C., Dir.; Brent Kruger, C.S.C.; John Wababa, C.S.C.; Bro. Richard Armstrong, C.S.C.
Casa De Merced, 222 W. Thomas Rd., #214, 85013. Tel: 602-406-6218. Gloria Munoz, Pres.
Catholic Social Services of Central and Northern Arizona, Inc., 1610 W. Camelback Rd., 85015. Tel: 602-285-1999; Fax: 602-285-0311. Christopher Bavasi, Pres.; Paul Martodam, M.P.A., CEO; Kristen Schmidt, M.S.W., Ph.D., Deputy Dir.
Regional Agencies:
Catholic Social Service of Phoenix, 1610 W. Camelback Rd., 85015-3525. Tel: 602-997-6105; Fax: 602-870-3891.
West Valley Office, 14010 N. El Mirage Rd., El Mirage, 85323. Tel: 602-972-1576.
Head Start Office, 8438 N. 39th Ave., 85051. Tel: 602-937-5230. Maureen Webster, A.C.S.W., C.I.S.W., Agency Dir.
East Valley Catholic Social Service, 18 E. University Dr., Ste. 101, Mesa, 85201. Tel: 602-964-8771; Fax: 602-964-8865. 24 hour Domestic Violence Hotline Tel: 602-821-1024. Ellie Gersten, A.C.S.W., Agency Dir.
Catholic Social Service Flagstaff, 201 West University Ave., Flagstaff, 86001. Tel: 520-774-9125; Fax: 520-774-0697. John Allen, Agency Dir.
Catholic Social Service of Yavapai, 116 N. Summit, Prescott, 86301. Tel: 520-778-2531; Fax: 520-771-9531.
Verde Valley Office, 736 North Main St., Cottonwood, 86326. Tel: 520-634-4254; Fax: 520-639-4368. John Allen, C.M.C., Agency Dir.
Catholic Social Service of Mohave, 1370 Ramar Rd., Ste. D, Bullhead City, 86442. Tel: 520-758-4176; Fax: 520-758-5141.
1849 Airfield, Kingman, 86401. Tel: 520-718-1117; Fax: 520-718-1124.
Lake Havasu Office, 1975 Daytona Blvd., Lake Havasu City, 86403. Tel: 520-855-4960; Fax: 520-453-9629. Marty Adams, M.S.W., A.C.S.W., Agency Dir.
Westside Head Start, 7400 W. Olive Ave., Ste. 10, Peoria, 85345. Tel: 602-486-9868; Fax: 602-486-9988. 27 Head Start Centers. Mary Ann Perez, Agency Dir.
Pregnancy Parenting & Adoption Services, 1825 W. Northern Ave., 85021. Tel: 602-997-6105; Fax: 602-331-4071. Connie Mitchell, A.S.C.W., C.I.S.W., Dir.
Office of Peace & Justice, 1610 W. Camelback Rd., 85015. Tel: 602-285-1999; Fax: 602-285-0311.
Residential Facilities:
Casa Linda Lodge. Tel: 602-943-6461. Pregnant and parenting teens. Morgan Taylor Kane, M.A., Res. Sup.
Sundance Lodge. Tel: 602-870-0376. Group Transitional living for homeless mothers and their children. Sheila Lucas, Program Coord.
My Sister's Place. Tel: 602-964-8771. Domestic Violence Shelter. Teresa Grates, M.C., Supvr.
Crossroads Shelter. Tel: 602-997-6105. Abused and neglected adolescent girls. Morgan Taylor Kane, M.A., Res. Sup.
Spring Haven Group Home. Tel: 602-997-6105. Abused and neglected adolescent girls. Morgan Taylor Kane, M.A., Res. Sup.
Stepping Stones Group Home. Tel: 602-997-6105. Abused and neglected girls. Morgan Taylor Kane, M.A., Res. Sup.
Aspen House, 304 O'Leary, Flagstaff, 86001. Tel: 520-779-5017. Pregnancy shelter.
Child Care Centers.
Carefree Child Development Center, 621 W. Clay St., Flagstaff, 86001. Tel: 520-774-1722. Shanna Gencarelle, Dir.
Residential Facilities.
Christ Child Society, P.O. Box 15945, 85060-5945. Tel: 602-893-2711. Ann Schwanekamp, Pres.
El Mirage Senior Village, 222 W. Thomas Rd, #214, 85013. Tel: 602-406-6218. Gloria Munoz, Pres.
Foundation for Senior Living, 77 E. Thomas Rd., Ste. 100, 85012. Tel: 602-285-1800; Fax: 602-285-1838. Murray Gibson, Chm.; Guy Mikkelsen, Pres.
Foundation for Senior Adult Living, Inc. Sweetwater Gardens (Apartments for the Handicapped), Phoenix; Kingman Heights Apartments, Kingman.
FSAL Desert Crest. (Desert Crest Apartments).
FSAL Development Corp. (Sun Terrace Apartments, Mesa).
FSAL Management.
FSAL Nursing Care Centers.
FSAL Programs. Adult Day Health Care Centers; In-Home Care Services; Home Safety & Repair Program; Community Action Programs/Senior Centers; Adult Foster Care; Oasis (Older Adult Service & Information System); Pathways Program (Resources and Referral-Care Management).
FSAL Rural Development. Becket House Apartments, Lake Havasu City; Vianney Villas Apartments, Avondale; Padua Hills Apartments, Wickenburg; St. Agnes Apartments, Williams.
Payson Senior Living, Inc. (Pineview Manor Apartments, Payson).
FSL Pathways. Assisted Group Living Program (Nine Houses), Phoenix.
The Malta Center, 3033 N.7th Ave., 85013. Tel: 602-212-0222; Fax: 602-212-1360. Rev. Joseph O'Brien, O.P., Exec. Dir.; John O'Brien, Pres. Pastoral and spiritual resources for persons with AIDS, their family members and caregivers.
Mercy Housing Arizona, 222 W. Thomas, #214, 85013. Tel: 602-406-6218. Gloria Munoz, Pres.
Mercy Properties Arizona, 222 W. Thomas Rd., #214, 85013. Tel: 602-406-6218. Gloria Munoz, Pres.
**Natural Family Planning*, 4945 E. Thomas Rd., 85018. Tel: 602-381-1884; Fax: 602-852-9582. Mrs. Janet Kistler, Dir. & Diocesan Coord. for N.F.P. Svcs. Center provides Natural Family Planning Services, Instructional Series, Introductions for Marriage Preparation, and Chastity Education for Adolescents and Parents and offers classes in Spanish and Mother/Daughter, Father/Son Workshops in Fertility Appreciation. Program is endorsed by the Diocesan Development Plan for N.F.P., National Council of Catholic Bishops.
Plazas de Merced, 222 W. Thomas Rd., #214, 85013. Tel: 602-402-6218; Fax: 602-650-7141. Gloria Munoz, Pres.
St. Joseph the Worker. (Job Service), 213 S. 11th Ave., 85007-3503. Tel: 602-257-4390; Fax: 602-254-3834. E-mail: stjoe@internetmcl.com
Mailing Address: P.O. Box 13503, 85002. Matthew Feeney, Chm. Bd. of Dir.; Janet M. Gray, Exec. Dir.; Richard Hoyet, Vice Pres.; Bro. Richard Armstrong, C.S.C., Treas. To assisst homeless and those on the verge of homelessness, in their efforts to secure and keep full-time, meaningful employment.
St. Mary's Scholarship & Benefit Fund, 2525 N. Third St., 85004. David Cantelme, Pres.

St. Vincent De Paul Society, P.O. Box 13600, 85002. Tel: 602-495-3004; 254-3338; Fax: 602-495-3029. Stephen J. Zabilski, Exec. Dir.; Nancy Spencer, Pres.; Rev. Msgr. John J. McMahon, Spiritual Advisor.

**Southwest Catholic Health Network Corp.*, 2800 N. Central Ave., Ste. 400, 85004. Tel: 602-263-3066; Fax: 602-263-2098. Katherine J. Byrne, Pres.

CHANDLER. *The Catholic Retreat for Young Singles, Inc.*, 637 S. Danyell Dr., 85225. Tel: 602-848-5184. David Gannon, Liaison.

GOODYEAR. *St. John Vianney School Development Fund*, 539 La Pasada Blvd., 85338. Tel: 602-932-3313; Fax: 602-932-1896. Rev. Joseph V. Corpora, C.S.C., Pres.

TEMPE. *City of the Lord*, 711 W. University Dr., 85281. Tel: 602-968-5895; Fax: 602-921-9175.
E-mail: cotljudith@juno.com
James R. Jones, Overall Coord.

**Friends of the Orphans*, 19 W. Alameda Dr, Ste. 108, 85285-5507. Tel: 602-967-9449. Dee Campbell, Exec. Dir.

RELIGIOUS INSTITUTES OF MEN REPRESENTED IN THE DIOCESE

For further details refer to the corresponding bracketed number in the Religious Institutes of Men or Women section.

[0170]—*Basilian Fathers.* (Western Prov.).—C.S.B.
[0200]—*Benedictine Monks.* (St. Meinrad Archabbey).—O.S.B.
[0600]—*Brothers of the Congregation of Holy Cross.*—C.S.C.
[0400]—*Canons Regular of the Order of the Holy Cross.*—O.S.C.
[0270]—*Carmelite Fathers and Brothers.* (Prov. of St. Elias).—O.Carm.
[0350]—*Cistercian Order of the Strict Observance (Trappists).*—O.C.S.O.
[0360]—*Claretian Missionaries.* (Western Prov.).—C.M.F.
[1330]—*Congregation of the Mission.* (Prov. of the West).—C.M.
[0520]—*Franciscan Friars.* (Prov. of Santa Barbara).—O.F.M.
[0650]—*Holy Ghost Fathers.* (Western Prov.).—C.S.Sp.
[0690]—*Jesuit Fathers and Brothers.* (California, Oregon, & Chicago Provs.).—S.J.
[0910]—*Oblates of Mary Immaculate.* (Our Lady of Hope).—O.M.I.
[0430]—*Order of Preachers (Dominicans).* (Western Prov.).—O.P.
[0610]—*Priests of the Congregation of Holy Cross.*—C.S.C.
[1200]—*Society of the Divine Savior.* (North American Prov.).—S.D.S.

RELIGIOUS INSTITUTES OF WOMEN REPRESENTED IN THE DIOCESE

[0230]—*Benedictine Sisters of Pontifical Jurisdiction.* (Duluth, St. Paul, MN).—O.S.B.
[0990]—*Congregation of Divine Providence.* (Pittsburgh, PA).—C.D.P.
[1780]—*Congregation of Sisters of the Third Order of St. Francis of Perpetual Adoration.* (La Crosse, WI).—F.S.P.A.
[3710]—*Congregation of the Sisters of St. Agnes.* (Fond du Lac, WI).—C.S.A.
[1710]—*Congregation of the Third Order of St. Francis of Mary Immaculate.* (Joliet, IL).—O.S.F.
[0760]—*Daughters of Charity.* (Los Altos Hills, CA).—D.C.
[0850]—*Daughters of Mary Help of Christians.* (San Antonio, TX).—F.M.A.
[0810]—*Daughters of the Heart of Mary.* (Holyoke, MA).—D.H.M.
[1070-03]—*Dominican Sisters.* (Sinsinawa, WI).—O.P.
[1070-11]—*Dominican Sisters.* (Sparkill, NY).—O.P.
[1070-13]—*Dominican Sisters.* (Adrian, MI).—O.P.
[1070-24]—*Dominican Sisters.* (Great Bend, KS).—O.P.
[1070-28]—*Dominican Sisters.* (Akron, OH).—O.P.
[1070-30]—*Dominican Sisters.* (Mountain View, CA).—O.P.
[1120]—*Dominican Sisters of Roman Congregation.* (Iowa City, IA).—O.P.
[1140]—*Eucharistic Missionaries of St. Dominic.* (New Orleans, LA).—O.P.
[1230]—*Franciscan Sisters of Christian Charity.* (Manitowoc, WI).—O.S.F.
[1430]—*Franciscan Sisters of Our Lady of Perpetual Help.* (St. Louis, MO).—O.S.F.
[1440]—*Franciscan Sisters of the Poor.* (Brooklyn, NY).—F.S.P.
[2370]—*Institute of the Blessed Virgin Mary (Loretto Sisters).* (Toronto, Ont., Canada).—I.B.V.M.
[2380]—*Institute of the Blessed Virgin Mary (Loretto Sisters).* (Rathfarnham, Dublin, Ireland).—I.B.V.M.
[2740]—*Maryknoll Sisters of St. Dominic.* (Maryknoll, NY).—M.M.
[2710]—*Missionaries of Charity.* (Calcutta, India).—M.C.
[2790]—*Missionary Servants of Most Blessed Trinity.*—M.S.B.T.
[3130]—*Our Lady of Victory Missionary Sisters.* (Huntington, IN).—O.L.V.M.
[2970]—*School Sisters of Notre Dame.* (Milwaukee, WI; Irving, TX).—S.S.N.D.
[1680]—*School Sisters of St. Francis.* (Milwaukee, WI).—S.S.S.F.
[1690]—*School Sisters of the Third Order of St Francis.* (Pittsburgh, PA).—O.S.F.
[0440]—*Sisters of Charity of Cincinnati, Ohio.*—S.C.
[0570]—*Sisters of Charity of Seton Hill, Greensburg, Pennsylvania.*—S.C.
[0430]—*Sisters of Charity of the B.V.M..* (Dubuque, IA).—B.V.M.
[2575]—*Sisters of Mercy of the Americas.* (Pittsburgh, PA; Rochester, NY; Burlingame, CA; Chicago, IL; Omaha, NE; Providence, RI).—R.S.M.
[3000]—*Sisters of Notre Dame de Namur.* (Cincinnati, OH).—S.N.D.deN.
[1540]—*Sisters of St. Francis.* (Clinton, IA).—O.S.F.
[1705]—*The Sisters of St. Francis of Assisi.* (Milwaukee, WI).—O.S.F.
[1630]—*Sisters of St. Francis of Penance and Charity.* (Redwood City, CA).—O.S.F.
[1630]—*Sisters of St. Francis of Penance and Charity.* (Redwood City, CA).—O.S.F.
[1570]—*Sisters of St. Francis of the Holy Family.* (Dubuque, IA).—O.S.F.
[3830-05]—*Sisters of St. Joseph.* (Brentwood, NY).—C.S.J.
[3830-11]—*Sisters of St. Joseph.* (Nazareth, MI).—S.S.J.
[3830-15]—*Sisters of St. Joseph.* (Concordia, KS).—C.S.J.
[3935]—*Congregation of the Sisters of St. Louis.* (Woodland Hills, CA).—S.S.L.
[3840]—*Sisters of St. Joseph of Carondelet.*—C.S.J.
[3930]—*Sisters of St. Joseph of the Third Order of St. Francis.* (South Bend, IN).—S.S.J.-T.O.S.F.
[1030]—*Sisters of the Divine Savior.* (Milwaukee, WI).—S.D.S.
[3730]—*Sisters of the Order of St. Basil the Great.* (Uniontown, PA).—O.S.B.M.
[3260]—*Sisters of the Precious Blood.* (Dayton, OH).—C.PP.S.
[2090]—*Sisters, Home Visitors of Mary.* (Detroit, MI).—H.V.M.
[2150]—*Sisters, Servants of the Immaculate Heart of Mary.*—I.H.M.
[3330]—*Union of the Sisters of the Presentation of the B.V.M..* (Phoenix, AZ).—P.B.V.M.

NECROLOGY

† Bechtel, Francis, (Retired). —Died Nov. 10, 1997.
† Crossan, Seamus S., Williams, AZ, St. Joseph. —Died April 15, 1997.
† Doran, John, (Retired). —Died April 20, 1997.

Diocese of Pittsburgh

(Dioecesis Pittsburgensis)

Most Reverend

DONALD W. WUERL, S.T.D.

Bishop of Pittsburgh; ordained December 17, 1966; appointed Titular Bishop of Rosemarkie and Auxiliary Bishop of Seattle December 3, 1985; consecrated January 6, 1986; appointed and canonically installed Bishop of Pittsburgh February 12, 1988; liturgically installed March 25, 1988. *Office: 111 Blvd. of the Allies, Pittsburgh, PA, 15222-1618. All official correspondence should be sent to this office.*

Most Reverend

JOHN B. MCDOWELL, PH.D.

Retired Auxiliary Bishop of Pittsburgh; Titular Bishop of Tamazuca; ordained November 4, 1945; appointed July 18, 1966; consecrated September 8, 1966; resigned September 30, 1996. *Mailing Address: c/o Diocese of Pittsburgh, 111 Blvd. of the Allies, Pittsburgh, PA, 15222-1618.*

Most Reverend

WILLIAM J. WINTER, V.G., S.T.D.

Auxiliary Bishop of Pittsburgh and Titular Bishop of Uthina; ordained December 17, 1955; appointed December 27, 1988; consecrated February 13, 1989. *Res., Sacred Heart Church, 310 Shady Ave., Pittsburgh, PA, 15206-4389.*

Most Reverend

DAVID A. ZUBIK, V.G., D.D.

Auxiliary Bishop of Pittsburgh; ordained May 3, 1975; appointed February 18, 1997; installed April 6, 1997. *Mailing Address: c/o 111 Blvd. of the Allies, Pittsburgh, PA, 15222-1618.*

ESTABLISHED AUGUST 8, 1843.

Square Miles 4,092.

Comprises the Counties of Allegheny, Beaver, Lawrence, Washington, Greene, and Butler in the State of Pennsylvania.

For legal titles of parishes and diocesan institutions, consult the Legal Office.

Pastoral Center: 111 Blvd. of the Allies, Pittsburgh, PA, 15222-1618. Tel.: 412-456-3000.

Web site address: http://www.diopitt.org

STATISTICAL OVERVIEW

Personnel	
Bishop	1
Auxiliary Bishops	2
Retired Bishops	1
Priests: Diocesan Active in Diocese	371
Priests: Active Outside Diocese	25
Priests: Diocesan in Foreign Missions	1
Priests: Retired, Sick or Absent	116
Number of Diocesan Priests	513
Religious Priests in Diocese	124
Extern Priests in Diocese	59
Ordinations:	
Diocesan Priests	2
Religious Priests	1
Permanent Deacons in Diocese	22
Total Brothers	46
Total Sisters	1,837
Parishes	
Parishes	218
With Resident Pastor:	
Resident Diocesan Priests	198
Resident Religious Priests	14
Without Resident Pastor:	
Administered by Priests	6
Professional Ministry Personnel:	
Brothers	1
Sisters	72
Lay Ministers	205
Welfare	
Catholic Hospitals	5
Total Assisted	666,923
Health Care Centers	1
Total Assisted	35
Homes for the Aged	12
Total Assisted	3,085
Residential Care of Children	4
Total Assisted	484
Day Care and Extended Day Care Centers	98
Total Assisted	610
Specialized Homes	5
Total Assisted	519
Special Centers for Social Services	4
Total Assisted	64,355
Residential Care of Disabled	1
Total Assisted	88
Other Institutions	4
Total Assisted	180
Educational	
Seminaries, Diocesan	1
Students from This Diocese	11
Diocesan Students in Other Seminaries	15
Total Seminarians	26
Colleges and Universities	3
Total Students	13,436
High Schools, Diocesan and Parish	8
Total Students	3,700
High Schools, Private	3
Total Students	639
Elementary Schools, Diocesan and Parish	105
Total Students	28,435
Elementary Schools, Private	4
Total Students	792
Non-residential Schools for the Disabled	2
Total Students	158
Catechesis/Religious Education:	
High School Students	6,988
Elementary Students	49,083
Total Students Under Catholic Instruction	103,257
Teachers in the Diocese:	
Priests	7
Brothers	16
Sisters	155
Lay Teachers	2,027
Vital Statistics	
Receptions into the Church:	
Infant Baptism Totals	8,951
Adult Baptism Totals	484
Received into Full Communion	1,089
First Communions	9,295
Confirmations	8,643
Marriages:	
Catholic	2,559
Interfaith	1,141
Total Marriages	3,700
Deaths	9,465
Total Catholic Population	754,149
Total Population	2,009,092

Former Bishops—Rt. Rev. MICHAEL J. O'CONNOR, D.D., ord. June 1, 1833; cons. Aug. 15, 1843; transferred to Erie and then to Pittsburgh Dec. 20, 1853; resigned May 23, 1860; entered the Society of Jesus Dec. 22, 1860; died at Woodstock College, MD, Oct. 18, 1872.—Rt. Rev. MICHAEL DOMENEC, C.M., D.D., ord. June 30, 1839; cons. Dec. 9, 1860; transferred to Allegheny, Jan. 11, 1876; resigned July 29, 1877; died at Tarragona, Spain, Jan. 5, 1878.—Rt. Rev. JOHN TUIGG, D.D., ord. May 14, 1850; cons. March 19, 1876; transferred as Apostolic Administrator of Allegheny 1877; died at Altoona Dec. 7, 1889.—Rt. Rev. RICHARD PHELAN, D.D., ord. May 4, 1854; cons. Aug. 2, 1885; Titular Bishop of Cibyra and Coadjutor to the Rt. Rev. John Tuigg; succeeded to Bishop Tuigg, Dec. 7, 1889; died Dec. 20, 1904.—Most Rev. J. F. REGIS CANEVIN, D.D., ord. June 4, 1879; cons. Titular Bishop of Sabrata and Coadjutor, Feb. 24, 1903; succeeded to the See of Pittsburgh, Dec. 20, 1904; resigned Nov. 26, 1920; Titular Archbishop of Pelusium; appt. Jan. 9, 1921; died March 22, 1927.—Most Rev. HUGH C. BOYLE, D.D., ord. July 2, 1898; succeeded to the See of Pittsburgh, June 16, 1921; cons. June 29, 1921; died Dec. 22, 1950.—His Eminence JOHN CARDINAL DEARDEN, S.T.D., ord. Dec. 8, 1932; Titular Bishop of Sarepta and Coadjutor Bishop of Pittsburgh; appt. March 13, 1948; cons. May 18, 1948; succeeded to the See, Dec. 22, 1950; assistant at the Pontifical Throne, Oct. 15, 1957; installed at the Archdiocese of Detroit, Dec. 18, 1958; created Cardinal, April 28, 1969; died Aug. 2, 1988.—His Eminence JOHN CARDINAL WRIGHT, S.T.D., ord. Dec. 8, 1935; Titular Bishop of Aegeae and Auxiliary of Boston; appt. May 10, 1947; cons. June 30, 1947; transferred to Bishop of Worcester, Jan. 28, 1950; transferred to Pittsburgh, Jan. 23, 1959; to the Roman Curia as Prefect of the Sacred Congregation for the Clergy; appt. April 23, 1969; created Cardinal, April 28, 1969; died at Cambridge, MA, Aug. 10, 1979.—Most Rev. VINCENT M. LEONARD, D.D., ord. June 16, 1935; appt. Titular Bishop of Arsacal and Auxiliary, Feb. 28, 1964; cons. April 21, 1964; succeeded to the See, June 1, 1969; resigned June 30, 1983; died Aug. 28, 1994.—His Eminence ANTHONY CARDINAL BEVILACQUA, D.D.,

J.C.D., J.D., ord. June 11, 1949; Titular Bishop of Aquae Albae and Auxiliary Bishop of Brooklyn; appt. Oct. 4, 1980; cons. Nov. 24, 1980; Bishop of Pittsburgh; appt. Oct. 10, 1983; installed Dec. 12, 1983; appt. Archbishop of Philadelphia, Feb. 11, 1988; created Cardinal, June 29, 1991.

Pastoral Center—111 Blvd. of the Allies, Pittsburgh, 15222. Tel: 412-456-3000. All official correspondence should be directed to this office.

Chancellor—Sr. MARGARET HANNAN, R.S.M. Tel: 412-456-3129.

Vicars General—Most Rev. WILLIAM J. WINTER, V.G., S.T.D.; Most Rev. DAVID A. ZUBIK, V.G., D.D.

Bishop's Office—Most Rev. DONALD W. WUERL, S.T.D.; Rev. PAUL J. ZYWAN, Admin. Sec.; Rev. JAMES A. WEHNER, Master of Ceremonies, Direct all official correspondence to the Bishop at this address: *111 Blvd. of the Allies, Pittsburgh, 15222.* Tel: 412-456-3010.

General Secretary—Most Rev. DAVID A. ZUBIK, V.G., D.D. Tel: 412-456-3131; Fax: 412-456-3197.

Associate General Secretary—Sr. MARGARET HANNAN, R.S.M. Tel: 412-456-3129.

Vicar for Canonical Services—Very Rev. LAWRENCE A. DINARDO, V.E., J.C.L.,address all correspondence to: *111 Blvd. of the Allies, Pittsburgh, 15222-1698.* Tel: 412-456-3135; Fax: 412-456-3173.

Matrimonial Concerns, Office for—Canonical Consultants: Revs. RICHARD M. LELONIS, J.C.L.; JAMES P. MCDONOUGH, S.T.L., J.C.L.

Tribunal Office—Address all correspondence to: *111 Blvd. of the Allies, Pittsburgh, 15222-1698.* Tel: 412-456-3033; Fax: 412-456-3173.

Judicial Vicar—Very Rev. ROBERT J. AHLIN, J.C.L.

Adjutant Judicial Vicar—Very Rev. JAMES R. BEDILLION, J.C.L.

Judges—Revs. JAMES L. AARON, M.S.Ed.; PAUL J. BRADLEY, M.S.W.; Very Rev. LAWRENCE A. DINARDO, V.E., J.C.L.; Rev. TIMOTHY G. EVANS, S.T.L.; Very Rev. WILLIAM P. FEENEY, V.F., M.Div.; Very Rev. LEO V. VANYO, V.F., J.C.D.; Revs. ROBERT F. GUAY, M.Div.; JAMES E. KUNKEL, S.T.M.; RICHARD M. LELONIS, J.C.L.; JOSEPH R. LEMP, S.T.L.; THOMAS M. O'DONNELL, M.Div.; THEODORE A. RUTKOWSKI, S.T.L.; JOSEPH C. SCHEIB; CHARLES W. SPEICHER, Ph.D., S.T.M.; ROBERT R. WERTHMAN, M.Div.; Mrs. RITA FERKO JOYCE, J.D., J.C.L.

Promoter of Justice—Rev. JEROME A. DIXON, J.C.L.

Defenders of the Bond—Revs. MARTIN F. BARKIN, M.Div.; J. LAWRENCE BRUNEY, M.Div.; ROBERT J. CLARKE, M.Div.; DENNIS J. COLAMARINO, M.Div.; LOUIS L. DENINNO, M.Div.; JEROME A. DIXON, J.C.L.; ROBERT M. FRANCO, M.Ch.A.; JAMES P. MCDONOUGH, S.T.L., J.C.L.; JOHN R. RUSHOFSKY, M.S.Ed.; BENEDETTO P. VAGHETTO, J.C.L.

Director of Cases—Mrs. RITA FERKO JOYCE, J.D., J.C.L.

Auditors-Assessors—Revs. FRANK D. ALMADE, Ph.D.; CHARLES S. BOBER, S.T.D.; ROBERT J. CEDOLIA; DAVID D. DEWITT, M.Div.; KEVIN J. DOMINIK, M.Div.; MARK A. ECKMAN, M.Div.; ANDREW C. FISCHER, M.Div.; JOSEPH F. KEENAN, M.Div.; EDWARD L. KRYSTON, M.Div.; WILLIAM P. O'MALLEY, M.Div.

Advocates—Revs. CARMEN A. D'AMICO, M.Div.; MICHAEL W. DECEWICZ, M.Div.; ANDREW C. FISCHER, M.Div.; JOSEPH F. KEENAN, M.Div.; PAUL J. ZYWAN, M.Div.

Notaries—DARLENE C. PETERSON; ANNETTE W. SEMAN; DARLENE WILCE.

Secretary for Clergy and Religious—Very Rev. JAMES S. RUGGIERO, V.E., *111 Blvd. of the Allies, Pittsburgh, 15222.* Tel: 412-456-3060; Fax: 412-456-3188.

Secretary for Education—Rev. KRIS D. STUBNA, S.T.D., *111 Blvd. of the Allies, Pittsburgh, 15222.* Tel: 412-456-3100; Fax: 412-456-3101.

Secretary for Pastoral Life—Rev. RONALD P. LENGWIN, *111 Blvd. of the Allies, Pittsburgh, 15222.* Tel: 412-456-3021; Fax: 412-456-3168.

Secretary for Social Concerns—Rev. FRANK D. ALMADE, Ph.D., *111 Blvd. of the Allies, Pittsburgh, 15222.* Tel: 412-456-3156; Fax: 412-456-3180.

Deans and Deaneries—Most Rev. WILLIAM J. WINTER, V.G., S.T.D., Chm., College of Deans; Very Rev. LEO V. VANYO, V.F., J.C.D., Central (Allegheny County); Very Rev. THOMAS B. FERRIS, V.F., Northside (Allegheny County); Very Rev. ROBERT G. DUCH, V.F., Allegheny Valley (Allegheny County); Very Rev. GEORGE C. NEWMEYER, V.F., Northwest (Allegheny County); Very Rev. JOSEPH M. MELE, V.F., East Suburban (Allegheny County); Very Rev. BERNARD M. HARCARIK, V.F., South Pittsburgh (Allegheny County); Very Rev. HUGH J. LANG, V.F., Steel Valley (Allegheny County); Very Rev. WALTER A. SOBON, V.F., Southwest (Allegheny County); Very Rev. ROBERT J. REARDON, V.F., South Hills (Allegheny County); Very Rev. STEPHEN M. CHERVENAK, V.F., Mon Yough (Allegheny County); Very Rev. ROBERT F. GUAY, V.F., Beaver County; Very Rev. JAMES F. MURPHY, V.F., Butler County; Very Rev. MAURO J. CAUTELA, V.F., Lawrence County; Very Rev. ALBIN C. MCGINNIS, V.F., Greene County; Very Rev. WILLIAM P. FEENEY, V.F., Washington County East; Very Rev. PHILIP J. DONATELLI, V.F., Washington County West.

Office for the Delegate for Religious—Sr. ANNE WINSCHEL, C.D.P., Delegate, *2900 Noblestown Rd., Pittsburgh, 15205-4227.* Tel: 412-928-5844.

Priest Council—Most Rev. DONALD W. WUERL, S.T.D., Pres.; Most Rev. WILLIAM J. WINTER, V.G., S.T.D.; Most Rev. DAVID A. ZUBIK, V.G., D.D.; Revs. HARRY R. BIELEWICZ; CHARLES S. BOBER, S.T.D., S.T.L.; PAUL J. BRADLEY, M.S.W.; J. LAWRENCE BRUNEY; MICHAEL W. DECEWICZ; Very Rev. LAWRENCE A. DINARDO, V.E., M.Ch.A., J.C.L.; Very Rev. JAMES S. RUGGIERO, V.E.; Revs. JOHN P. GALLAGHER, S.T.L.; RICHARD A. INFANTE; PAUL M. KUPPE, O.F.M.Cap.; JOHN P. MALONEY; G. MALCOLM MCDONALD; THOMAS D. O'NEIL; MICHAEL SALVAGNA, C.P.; MICHAEL S. SUSLOWICZ; JOHN P. SWEENEY; DAVID H. TAYLOR; BENEDETTO P. VAGHETTO, J.C.L.; LOUIS F. VALLONE; JAMES G. YOUNG.

College of Consultors—Most Rev. DONALD W. WUERL, S.T.D.; Most Rev. WILLIAM J. WINTER, V.G., S.T.D.; Most Rev. DAVID A. ZUBIK, V.G., D.D.; Revs. CHARLES S. BOBER, S.T.D.; PAUL J. BRADLEY, M.S.W.; MICHAEL W. DECEWICZ; JOHN P. GALLAGHER, S.T.L.; JOHN P. MALONEY; MALCOLM MCDONALD; MICHAEL SALVAGNA, C.P.; JOHN P. SWEENEY; DAVID H. TAYLOR; BENEDETTO P. VAGHETTO, J.C.L.; JAMES G. YOUNG.

Diocesan Development Board—Revs. RONALD P. LENGWIN, Chm. FRANK D. ALMADE, Ph.D.; Mrs. NANCY F. BECK; Sr. PATRICIA CAIRNS, C.S.J.; Mr. GREGORY R. DUFOUR; Sr. MARGARET HANNAN, R.S.M.; Mr. CHARLES A. KOEMPEL, C.P.A.; Mr. JOSEPH G. LUTTRINGER; Mr. AMBROSE MURRAY; Revs. JOHN M. O'TOOLE; KRIS D. STUBNA, S.T.D.; GEORGE A. WILT.

Diocesan Finance Council—Most Rev. DONALD W. WUERL, S.T.D., Pres.; Most Rev. DAVID A. ZUBIK, V.G., D.D., Chm.; Sr. MARGARET HANNAN, R.S.M.; Mr. MICHAEL J. HANNON; Mr. MARTIN G. MCGUINN; Mr. HARRY F. MURRAY; Mr. FRED O'BRIEN; Very Rev. ROBERT J. REARDON, V.F.; Mr. FRANK J. SCHNEIDER; Mr. LEO W. YOCHUM.

Diocesan Pastoral Council—Most Rev. DONALD W. WUERL, S.T.D., Chm.; Most Rev. WILLIAM J. WINTER, V.G., S.T.D.; Most Rev. DAVID A. ZUBIK, V.G., D.D.; Ms. BARBARA ANTROM; Dr. JOHN A. BAMONTE; Mr. EDWARD BERNOT; Ms. MARY ANN BOBER; Mr. BRAD CATON; Very Rev. STEPHEN M. CHERVENAK, V.F.; Bro. JOHN DEMPSEY, S.M.; Rev. PHILIP N. FARRELL; Mrs. LILLIAN GERMAINE; Mr. RICHARD P. JACOB; Mrs. KATHY KRISFALUSY; Mrs. CHARLES KUDZMA; Mrs. ANNE LAYCHAK; Mr. JOHN LAYTON; Sr. DELIA MARIE MCNEIRNEY, I.H.M.; Rev. STEVEN M. PALSA; Mr. JAMES PARHAM; Sr. MARY PRICE, S.C.; Sr. MARY CABRINI PROCOPIO, C.S.S.F.; Mrs. MONA RUSH; Mr. DONALD SHAW; Ms. JEANNE SMALL; Mr. JAMES WEILAND.

Priest Personnel Board—Most Rev. DONALD W. WUERL, S.T.D.; Most Rev. WILLIAM J. WINTER, V.G., S.T.D.; Most Rev. DAVID A. ZUBIK, V.G., D.D.; Very Rev. JAMES S. RUGGIERO, V.E., Chm.; Revs. CHARLES S. BOBER, S.T.D.; DAVID J. BONNAR; EDWARD J. BURNS; CARMEN A. D'AMICO; JOHN R. HANEY; RICHARD A. INFANTE; RONALD P. LENGWIN; KENNETH E. OLDENSKI; JOHN M. O'TOOLE.

Diocesan Administration

Administrative Procedures, Office for—Very Rev. LAWRENCE A. DINARDO, V.E., J.C.L., Admin. Tel: 412-456-3135.

Adult and Family Catechesis, Office for—Rev. RONALD D. LAWLER, O.F.M.Cap., Ph.D., Dir. Tel: 412-456-3117.

Archives and Records Center—Mr. KENNETH A. WHITE, Dir.; Mr. BURRIS E. ESPLEN, Archivist, *125 N. Craig St., Pittsburgh, 15213-1555.* Tel: 412-621-6217.

Bishop, Office of the Diocesan—Revs. PAUL J. ZYWAN, Admin. Sec. JAMES A. WEHNER, Master of Ceremonies. Tel: 412-456-3010.

Bishop Boyle Center—Vacant, *120 E. 9th Ave., Homestead, 15120-1600.* Tel: 412-462-8516.

Black Catholic Ministries, Office for—Mrs. MARGARETTA STOKES TUCKER, Dir. Tel: 412-456-3170.

Budget and Planning - Secretariat for Education, Office for—Mr. ROY CARTIER, Dir. Tel: 412-456-3108.

Building Commission—Mr. GENE T. ODATO, Exec. Sec., *4721 5th Ave., Pittsburgh, 15213.* Tel: 412-621-6206.

Building Services, Office for—Mrs. DARLENE M. HOLZER, Mgr. Tel: 412-456-3016.

Campus Ministry, Office for—Rev. ROBERT L. SEEMAN, Dir., *Newman Center, 342 Normal Ave., Slippery Rock, 16057.* Tel: 412-794-6620.

Canonical Services, Office for—Very Rev. LAWRENCE A. DINARDO, V.E., J.C.L. Tel: 412-456-3135.

Cardinal Wright Center—Rev. DAVID J. BONNAR, Dir.; Ms. DIANE GASBARRO, Mgr., *10745 Babcock Blvd., Gibsonia, 15044.* Tel: 412-961-6884.

Catechesis, Office for—Mr. KENNETH M. OGOREK, Dir. Tel: 412-456-3114.

Catechetical Ministries, Office for—Ms. SHARON T. TYBOROWSKI, Dir. Tel: 412-456-3110.

Catholic Charities—Sr. PATRICIA CAIRNS, C.S.J., Exec. Dir., *212 9th St., Pittsburgh, 15222.* Tel: 412-456-6999., Allegheny County: *212 9th St., Pittsburgh, 15222.* Tel: 412-456-6999., Beaver County: *1260 N. Brodhead Rd., Monaca, 15601.* Tel: 412-775-0758., Butler County: *407 A W. Jefferson St., Butler, 16001.* Tel: 412-287-4011., Greene County: *32 Church St., Ste. 3, Waynesburg, 15370.* Tel: 412-627-6410., Lawrence County: *15 W. Washington St., New Castle, 16101.* Tel: 412-658-5526., Washington County: *331 S. Main St., Washington, 15301.* Tel: 412-228-7722., Roselia Center: *624 Clyde St., Pittsburgh, 15213.* Tel: 412-682-4410; 4411. Services for single pregnant women. Maryhouse Residence for Women: *1113 Creedmoor Ave., Pittsburgh, 15226.* Tel: 412-563-3312., St. Joseph's House of Hospitality, Inc.: *1635 Bedford Ave., Pittsburgh, 15219.* Tel: 412-471-0666., Ozanam Cultural Center: *1833 Wylie Ave., Pittsburgh, 15219.* Tel: 412-281-4046.

Catholic Cemeteries Assoc.—Ms. ANNABELLE MCGANNON, Exec. Dir., *718 Hazelwood Ave., Pittsburgh, 15217-2807.* Tel: 412-521-9133.

Catholic Schools, Department for—Mr. ROBERT L. PASERBA, Ed.D., Supt.-Schools; Sr. MARY JO MUTSCHLER, S.C., Asst. Supt.-Elementary Schools; Mrs. ANNA MARIE CATANZARO, Asst. Supt.-Secondary Schools; Mr. RONALD T. BOWES, D.A., Asst. Supt.-Public Policy & Devel. Tel: 412-456-3090.

Educational Consultants—Sr. BENITA DEMATTEIS, O.S.B.; Sr. URSULA KELLY, S.S.N.D.; Sr. CATHERINE ANN KOLLER, C.D.P.; Sr. LORETTA KRALL, C.S.J.; Mr. WILLIAM C. LLOYD; Sr. M. DENISE MAHER, C.S.J.; Sr. IRENE MARY WILBURN, S.C., *135 1st Ave., Pittsburgh, 15222.* Tel: 412-456-3070.

Chaplaincies, Office for—Rev. JOHN J. KEANE, Dir., *4721 5th Ave., Pittsburgh, 15213.* Tel: 412-621-6209.

Charismatic Prayer Groups—Rev. JOHN P. SWEENEY, Moderator, *St. Titus Parish, 952 Franklin St., Aliquippa, 15001.* Tel: 412-378-8561.

Chief Financial Officer—Mr. CHARLES A, KOEMPEL, C.P.A. Tel: 412-456-3137.

Clergy and Ministerial Formation, Department for—Rev. DAVID J. BONNAR, Dir., *St. Paul Seminary, 2900 Noblestown Rd., Pittsburgh, 15205-4227.* Tel: 412-928-5840.

Clergy Personnel, Dept. for—Rev. EDWARD J. BURNS. Tel: 412-456-3060.

Communications, Office for—Mr. JOHN F. MCMAHON, Dir.; Mr. RAYMOND G. FLECKENSTEIN, Dir. of Communication Services. Tel: 412-456-3020.

Cultural Diversity, Commission on—Rev. RONALD P. LENGWIN, Chm. Tel: 412-456-3021.

Data Automation, Office for—Mr. JOHN F. ZDILLA, Dir. Tel: 412-456-3152.

Deaf Persons, Office for—Mrs. KAREN M. MCGANN, Dir.; Rev. WALTER G. RYDZON, Chap., *135 1st Ave., Pittsburgh, 15222.* Tel: 412-456-3119 (Voice); 456-3122 (TTY).

Development Office—Mr. GREGORY R. DUFOUR, Acting Dir. Tel: 412-456-3085.

Diaconate, Office for the—Rev. DAVID J. BONNAR, Dir., *St. Paul Seminary, 2900 Noblestown Rd., Pittsburgh, 15205-4227.* Tel: 412-928-5840.

Diocesan National Black Catholic Congress Leadership Team—Ms. BARBARA ANTROM, Team Leader, *324 Baker Ave., Clairton, 15025.* Tel: 412-233-3492.

Diocesan Purchasing Commission—Mr. JAMES W. PEARCE, Exec. Dir., *2900 Noblestown Rd., Pittsburgh, 15205.* Tel: 412-922-6400.

Disabilities, Department for Persons with—Ms. GRACE T. HARDING, Dir., *135 1st Ave., Pittsburgh, 15222.* Tel: 412-456-3119 (Voice); 456-3122 (TTY).

Ecumenical and Interfaith Commission—Rev. RONALD P. LENGWIN, Chm. Tel: 412-456-3021.

Educational Media, Department for—Mr. CHARLES A. BEAUDRY, Dir., *St. Paul Seminary, 2900 Noblestown Rd., Pittsburgh, 15205-4227.* Tel: 412-928-5817.

Educational Special Events, Office for—Sr. M. IGNATIUS ROONEY, R.S.M., Dir. Tel: 412-456-3075; or 928-5830.

Electronic Media, Office for—Mrs. NANCY K. LIPPERT, Dir., *St. Paul Seminary, 2900 Noblestown Rd., Pittsburgh, 15205-4227.* Tel: 412-928-5923.

Employment Development and Community Concerns, Office for—Mr. JOSEPH A. CARR, Dir. Tel: 412-456-3164.

Evangelization and Christian Initiation, Office for—Rev. M. ERIC DISKIN, M.Div., Dir. Tel: 412-456-3083.

Family Life and Family Concerns, Office for—Mrs. MAUREEN H. WOOD, Dir. Tel: 412-456-3160.

Financial Services, Office for—Mr. JOSEPH G. LUTTRINGER, Dir. Tel: 412-456-3025. Central Accounting Dept.: Tel: 412-456-3032. Parish Accounting Dept.: Tel: 412-456-3025. Auditing Dept.: Tel: 412-456-3028.

Foundation, Catholic Diocese of Pittsburgh—Mr. GREGORY R. DUFOUR, Acting Dir. Tel: 412-456-3085.

Gilmary Diocesan Center—Mr. RONALD W. RAGAN, Dir., *601 Flaugherty Run Rd., Coraopolis, 15108-3899.* Tel: 412-264-8400.

Insurance/Employee Benefits, Office for—Mr. DAVID S. STEWART, Mgr. Tel: 412-456-3045.

Justice and Peace Commission—Ms. VERONICA MORGAN-LEE, Ph.D., Chm. Tel: 412-456-3162.

Learning Media Center—Mr. CHARLES A. BEAUDRY, Dir., *St. Paul Seminary, 2900 Noblestown Rd., Pittsburgh, 15205-4227.* Tel: 412-928-5817.

Legal Office—Mr. WILLIAM A. STEIDLE, JR., ESQ., Gen. Counsel. Tel: 412-456-3126.

Mental Retardation and Special Religious Education, Office for Persons with—Mrs. ELEANOR G. MARSHALL, Dir., *135 1st Ave., Pittsburgh, 15222.* Tel: 412-456-3119.

Millennium Celebration, Office for the—Rev. JOHN E. KOZAR, M.Div., Exec. Dir. Tel: 412-456-3065.

Ministries, Institute for—Sr. PATRICIA ROGAN, O.S.F., Dir., *St. Paul Seminary, 2900 Noblestown Rd., Pittsburgh, 15205-4227.* Tel: 412-928-5827.

Missions, Office for—Rev. JOHN E. KOZAR, M.Div., Dir. Tel: 412-456-3065.

Music Ministry, Office for—Rev. JAMES J. CHEPPONIS, Dir. Tel: 412-456-3042.

Natural Family Planning Advisory Committee—Mr. ROBERT GANNON, M.D., Chm. Tel: 412-456-3160.

Parish Services, Office for—Sr. MARILYN HOEING, O.S.F., Dir. Tel: 412-456-3057.

Payroll, Office for—Mr. JOHN G. CVETIC, Mgr. Tel: 412-456-3006.

Personnel, Office for—Mrs. DARLENE M. HOLZER, Mgr. Tel: 412-456-3016.

Physical Disabilities, Office for Persons with—Rev. PATRICK F. RAGER, Chap. Tel: 412-461-6393.

Pilgrimage Office—Rev. JOHN E. KOZAR, Dir. Tel: 412-456-3065.

Pornography, Commission to Counter—Mrs. NORMA NORRIS, Chm. Tel: 412-456-3160.

Pre-Ordination Formation, Department for—Rev. DAVID J. BONNAR, Dir., *St. Paul Seminary, 2900 Noblestown Rd., Pittsburgh, 15205-4227.* Tel: 412-928-5840.

Property Planning and Development, Office for—Mr. GENE T. ODATO, Dir., *4721 5th Ave., Pittsburgh, 15213.* Tel: 412-621-6206.

Public Affairs, Department for—Rev. RONALD P. LENGWIN, Dir. Tel: 412-456-3021.

Religious Education/CCD, Department for—Mr. BRIAN M. KEANE, Dir. Tel: 412-456-3112.

Research and Planning, Office for—Mr. JOHN P. FLAHERTY, Dir. Tel: 412-456-3146.

Retired Priests, Office for—Very Rev. THOMAS J. KRAM, V.E., Vicar. Tel: 412-881-3675.

Retired Priests, Residences for—Sr. GABRIELLA SECHI, O.S.H.J., Admin., *St. John Vianney Manor, 2600 Morange Rd., Pittsburgh, 15205.* Tel: 412-928-0825. Rev. H. MICHAEL KERNAN, Dir., *Cardinal Dearden Center, 4721 5th Ave., Pittsburgh, 15213.* Tel: 412-687-8022.

St. Paul Seminary—Revs. DAVID P. BONNAR, Rector; ROBERT P. CONNOLLY, Vice Rector; Sr. JUDITH WORDEN, R.S.M., Coord. of Apostolic Works; Sr. M. IGNATIUS ROONEY, R.S.M., Admin. Asst. to Rector, *St. Paul Seminary, 2900 Noblestown Rd., Pittsburgh, 15205.* Tel: 412-921-5800.

Social Awareness, Department for—Mr. MICHAEL ANDREOLA, Dir. Tel: 412-456-3161.

Social Programs and Community Development, Department for—Mr. W. JOHN HANNIGAN, M.S.W., Dir. Tel: 412-456-3162.

Society for the Propagation of the Faith—Rev. JOHN E. KOZAR, M.Div., Dir. Tel: 412-456-3065.

Synodal Commission—Most Rev. DAVID A. ZUBIK, V.G., D.D., Chm. Tel: 412-456-3131.

Television and Radio Production—Refer to Electronic Media, Office for.

Theological Commission—Rev. JOSEPH J. KLEPPNER, S.T.L., Ph.D., Chm. Tel: 412-775-6363.

Vision Impairments, Office for Persons with—Rev. Msgr. PAUL M. LACKNER, Chap., *135 1st Ave., Pittsburgh, 15222.* Tel: 412-456-3119.

Vocations, Office for—Rev. DAVID J. BONNAR, Dir., *St. Paul Seminary, 2900 Noblestown Rd., Pittsburgh, 15205-4227.* Tel: 412-928-5836.

Worship, Office for—Rev. M. ERIC DISKIN, Dir. Tel: 412-546-3041.

Worship Commission—Rev. M. ERIC DISKIN, Chm. Tel: 412-456-3041.

Youth and Young Adult Ministry, Office for—Mrs. JOYCE A. GILLOOLY, Dir.; Rev. EDWARD M. CZEMERDA, Coord.-Spiritual Formation; Mr. GARY M. SLIFKEY, Coord.-Outreach and Athletic Ministry, *Gilmary Diocesan Center, 601 Flaugherty Run Rd., Coraopolis, 15108-3899.* Tel: 412-264-9530.

CLERGY, PARISHES, MISSIONS AND PAROCHIAL SCHOOLS

CITY OF PITTSBURGH, PROPER
(Allegheny County)

1—ST. PAUL CATHEDRAL (1834), Very Rev. Leo V. Vanyo, V.F., Rector; Revs. G. Malcolm McDonald; Joseph Sioli, C.O. In res., Rev. Paul J. Zywan.
Res., 108 N. Dithridge St., 15213. Tel: 412-621-4951; Fax: 412-621-4951.

2—ST. AGNES. Closed. For sacramental records contact St. Paul Cathedral.

3—ST. ANN (Hungarian). Closed. See St. Stephen.

4—ST. AUGUSTINE (German). Closed. See Our Lady of the Angels.

5—ST. BEDE (1922), Rev. Edward M. Bryce. In res., Revs. Joseph C. Beck; Felix Owino, A.J.
Res., 509 S. Dallas Ave., 15208. Tel: 412-661-7222; Fax: 412-661-9337.
School—6920 Edgerton Ave., 15208. Tel: 412-661-9425.
Lay Teachers 18; Students 293.

6—ST. BENEDICT THE MOOR (1889) (African American), Rev. Carmen A. D'Amico.
Res., 91 Crawford St., 15219. Tel: 412-281-3141; Fax: 412-391-7151.
School—2900 Webster Ave., 15219. Tel: 412-682-3755; Fax: 412-682-4058.
Sisters of St. Joseph 5; Lay Teachers 7; Students 224.
Convent—Tel: 412-621-0519.

7—ST. CATHERINE OF SIENA (Beechview) (1902), Revs. Aloysius Berk; Louis DeNinno. In res., Rev. Aloysius Joseph, S.N.B. (India).
Res., 1901 Broadway Ave., 15216. Tel: 412-531-2135; Fax: 412-531-8543.
School—(Grades K-8) 1915 Broadway Ave., 15216. Tel: 412-561-0399; Fax: 412-561-6160.
Sisters of St. Joseph 1; Lay Teachers 10; Students 139.
Catechesis/Religious Programs—Tel: 412-561-8242.
Students 247.

8—ST. CHARLES LWANGA PARISH (1992). Consolidated from the following churches: Corpus Christi, Holy Rosary, Mother of Good Counsel, Our Lady Help of Christians, Our Lady of the Most Blessed Sacrament and SS. Peter & Paul. Rev. David H. Taylor. In res., Revs. Gregory Ugah (Nigeria); Cornelius Okochi (Nigeria).
Res., 7114 Kelly St., 15208. Tel: 412-731-3020; Fax: 412-731-1615.
School—Holy Rosary, 7120 Kelly St., 15208. Tel: 412-731-2567; Fax: 412-731-3476.
Lay Teachers 15; Students 283.

9—CORPUS CHRISTI. Closed. See St. Charles Lwanga.

10—ST. ELIZABETH OF HUNGARY (Slovak). Closed. See St. Patrick-St. Stanislaus Kostka.

11—EPIPHANY (1903) (Irish), Revs. Robert E. Spangenberg, C.S.Sp.; John F. Walsh, Hospital Chap.
Res., 1018 Centre Ave., 15219. Tel: 412-471-0257; Fax: 412-471-1345.

12—OUR LADY HELP OF CHRISTIANS (Italian). Closed. See St. Charles Lwanga.

13—HOLY FAMILY (Polish). Closed. See Our Lady of the Angels.

14—HOLY ROSARY. Closed. See St. Charles Lwanga.

15—ST. HYACINTH (Polish). Closed. See St. Regis.

16—IMMACULATE CONCEPTION (1834) (Italian), Revs. Dale E. DeNinno, Admin.; William R. Siple; Edward J. Kunco. In res., Rev. Paul A. Holzer, (Retired).
Res., 4712 Liberty Ave., 15224. Tel: 412-682-5353; Fax: 412-682-6766.
School—Tel: 412-621-5199.
Sisters of the Holy Spirit, Pittsburgh 4; Lay Teachers 15; Students 415.

17—IMMACULATE HEART OF MARY (1897) (Polish), Rev. Joseph E. Swierczynski.
Res., 3058 Brereton Ave., 15219. Tel: 412-621-5170; Fax: 412-621-7445.

18—ST. JOACHIM. Closed. See St. Rosalia.

19—ST. JOHN THE BAPTIST. Closed. See Our Lady of the Angels.

20—ST. JOSEPH (1872) (German), Revs. Dale E. DeNinno, Admin.; William R. Siple; Edward J. Kunco. In res., Rev. Paul A. Holzer, (Retired).
Res., 4712 Liberty Ave., 15224. Tel: 412-682-2354; Fax: 412-682-6766.

21—ST. KIERAN. Closed. See St. Matthew.

22—ST. LAWRENCE O'TOOLE (East End) (1897), Rev. James G. Graham. In res., Rev. Arthur R. Merrell.
Res., 5323 Penn Ave., 15224. Tel: 412-363-1771.

23—ST. MARTIN (West End). Closed. See Guardian Angels.

24—ST. MARY'S (Lawrenceville). Closed. See Our Lady of the Angels.

25—ST. MARY ASSUMPTION (Lawrenceville). Closed. See St. Matthew.

26—ST. MARY OF MERCY (1870), Revs. John M. O'Toole; Francis A. Siler. In res., Rev. Msgr. Francis A. Glenn, (Retired); Revs. Ronald P. Lengwin; William M. Miller.
Res., 202 Stanwix St., 15222. Tel: 412-261-0110; Fax: 412-261-0113.

27—ST. MATTHEW (1993). Consolidated from St. Kieran and St. Mary Assumption. Rev. Robert K. Yetsko, T.O.R.
Res., 5322 Carnegie St., 15201. Tel: 412-781-6701; Fax: 412-781-1331.
Catechesis/Religious Programs—Tel: 412-781-5192.
Students 95.

28—MOTHER OF GOOD COUNSEL (Italian). Closed. See St. Charles Lwanga.

29—OUR LADY OF THE ANGELS (1993). Consolidated from St. Augustine, Holy Family, St. John the Baptist and St. Mary. Revs. Paul M. Kuppe, O.F.M.Cap.; Gervase Degenhardt, O.F.M.Cap.; John Getsy, O.F.M.Cap. In res., Revs. Ralph Zehe, O.F.M.Cap.; Kenan Crowley, O.F.M.Cap.; Michael Joyce, O.F.M.Cap.
Res., 225 37th St., 15201. Tel: 412-682-6888; 682-0929 (Office); Fax: 412-682-6889. [CEM]
School—St. John Neumann Regional Catholic Elementary School. See Consolidated Schools under Institutions Located in the Diocese. Tel: 412-682-5096; Fax: 412-682-0811.

30—OUR LADY OF THE MOST BLESSED SACRAMENT. Closed. See St. Charles Lwanga.

31—ST. LOUISE DE MARILLAC (1961), Revs. Thomas E. Kredel; John M. Bachkay; Francis M. Kurimsky.
Res., 312 McMurray Rd., 15241. Tel: 412-833-1010; Fax: 412-833-6624.
School—310 McMurray Rd., 15241. Tel: 412-835-0600.
Felician Sisters 3; Lay Teachers 25; Students 563.
Catechesis/Religious Programs—Tel: 412-835-1155.
Students 1,091.

32—ST. PATRICK (Strip District). Closed. See St. Patrick-St. Stanislaus Kostka.

33—SS. PETER AND PAUL (East Liberty). Closed. See St. Charles Lwanga.

34—ST. PHILOMENA Squirrel Hill. Closed. See St. Bede.

35—ST. RAPHAEL (1911), Revs. Joseph V. Kurutz; Domenic Mancini. In res., Rev. John J. Charnoki.
Res., 1118 Chislett St., E., 15206. Tel: 412-661-3100; Fax: 412-661-4105.
School—1154 Chislett St., 15206. Tel: 412-661-0288.
Sisters of St. Joseph 2; Lay Teachers 16; Students 272.
Convent—1101 Jancey St., 15206. Tel: 412-661-6569.

36—ST. REGIS (1993). Merged with St. Hyacinth. Rev. William J. Cheetham.
Res., 3235 Parkview Ave., 15213. Tel: 412-681-9365; Fax: 412-681-1175.

37—ST. ROSALIA. Merged with St. Joachim. Revs. Joseph W. Reschick; Gary W. Oehmler.
Res., 411 Greenfield Ave., 15207. Tel: 412-421-5766; Fax: 412-421-4529.
School—Tel: 412-521-3005.
Sisters of the Immaculate Heart of Mary 7; Lay Teachers 21; Students 360.

38—SACRED HEART (1872), Most Rev. William J. Winter, V.G.; Revs. Francis J. Murhammer; John A. Reifsnyder; Miles Eric Diskin.
Res., 310 Shady Ave., 15206. Tel: 412-661-0187; Fax: 412-661-7932.
School—325 Emerson St., 15206. Tel: 412-441-1582.
Sisters of Charity 3; Lay Teachers 21; Students 475.

39—ST. STANISLAUS (Strip District) (Polish). Closed. See St. Patrick-St. Stanislaus Kostka.

40—ST. PATRICK-ST. STANISLAUS KOSTKA (1993). Consolidated of St. Stanislaus, St. Patrick and St. Elizabeth of Hungary. Rev. Thomas G. Schaefer, C.S.Sp. In res., Revs. Ben Adzogba, C.S.Sp.; Jean Claude Mbemba, C.S.Sp.

Parish Office: 1711 Liberty Ave., 15222. Tel: 412-471-4767; Fax: 412-471-1209.
Res., 57 21st St., 15222. Tel: 412-471-0434.

41—ST. STEPHEN (1993). Merged with St. Ann. Rev. Cornelius W. McCaulley, S.T.L.
Mailing Address: 5115 Second Ave., 15207.
Res., 131 E. Elizabeth St., 15207. Tel: 412-421-9210.
School—134 E. Elizabeth St., 15207. Tel: 412-421-9447.
Sisters of Charity 1; Lay Teachers 10; Students 155.

SOUTH SIDE

42—ST. ADALBERT (Polish). Closed. See Prince of Peace.

43—ST. BASIL (1907) (German), Revs. Robert J. Meyer; Robert J. Miller. In res., Rev. Joseph C. Scheib.
Res., 1735 Brownsville Rd., 15210. Tel: 412-882-9763; Fax: 412-882-2476.
School—1803 Concordia St., 15210. Tel: 412-884-4434.
Sisters of Divine Providence 1; Lay Teachers 12; Students 289.
Catechesis/Religious Programs—Tel: 412-881-4440.
Students 491.
Convent—30 W. Willock Rd., 15227. Tel: 412-881-0638.

44—ST. CANICE (Knoxville). Closed. See St. John Vianney.

45—ST. CASIMIR (Lithuanian). Closed. See Prince of Peace.

46—ST. GEORGE (Allentown). Closed. See St. John Vianney.

47—GUARDIAN ANGELS (West End) (1994). Merged with St. James and St. Martin. Revs. Robert J. Clarke; Mark A. Thomas.
Res., 1030 Logue St., 15220. Tel: 412-921-4077; Fax: 412-922-4945. [CEM]
School—Elizabeth Seton Elementary. See Holy Innocents (West End). Tel: 412-331-4529.

48—ST. HENRY. Closed. See St. John Vianney.

49—HOLY ANGELS (1903), Rev. J. David Crowley, M.A.
Res., 408 Baldwin Rd., 15207. Tel: 412-461-6906; Fax: 412-461-0961.
Catechesis/Religious Programs—Tel: 412-461-8500.
Students 500.

50—HOLY INNOCENTS (1900), Revs. Donald N. Buchleitner; John B. Corbett.
Res., 3011 Landis St., 15204. Tel: 412-331-0268.
School—Elizabeth Seton Elementary, 3021 Landis St., 15204. Tel: 412-331-4529.
Sisters 1; Lay Teachers 20; Students 387.

51—ST. JAMES (West End). Closed. See Guardian Angels.

52—ST. JOHN THE EVANGELIST. Closed. See Prince of Peace.

53—ST. JOSAPHAT (Polish). Closed. See Prince of Peace.

54—ST. JOHN VIANNEY (Hilltop) (1994). Consolidation of the the following churches: St. Canice, St. George, St. Henry, and St. Joseph. Revs. Charles S. Bober; Douglas A. Boyd; John E. Hissrich; Mark A. Eckman.
823 Climax St., 15210. Tel: 412-381-8300; Fax: 412-431-3790. [JC]
School—Bishop Leonard Catholic School, 430 Cathedral Ave., 15210. Tel: 412-381-3541; Fax: 412-381-8611.
Students 395.
Catechesis/Religious Programs—Tel: 412-381-5581.
Students 326.

55—ST. JUSTIN (Mt. Washington) (1917), Rev. Walter C. Rydzon.
Res., 539 Boggs Ave., 15211. Tel: 412-381-9878.

56—ST. MARY OF THE MOUNT (Mt. Washington) (1873), Rev. Louis F. Vallone; Deacon Robert Barth. In res., Revs. Canice Crawford; Joachim Msaki; Rev. Antony Kalapura.
Res., 403 Grandview Ave., 15211. Tel: 412-381-0212; Fax: 412-381-9921.
School—Bigham St. & Grandview Ave., 15211. Tel: 412-431-4645.
Sisters of the Immaculate Heart of Mary 4; Sisters of Divine Providence 1; Lay Teachers 10; Students 237.

57—ST. MATTHEW (Slovak). Closed. See Prince of Peace.

58—ST. MICHAEL (German). Closed. See Prince of Peace.

59—OUR LADY OF LORETO (1959), Rev. James W. Dolan.
Res., 1905 Pioneer Ave., 15226. Tel: 412-341-6161.

60—ST. PAMPHILUS (1960), Rev. James T. Merlino, O.F.M. In res., Rev. R. Stephen Almango, O.F.M.
Res., 948 Tropical Ave., 15216. Tel: 412-341-1000; Fax: 412-341-6956.
Church—1000 Tropical Ave., 15216. Tel: 412-531-8449.

61—ST. PETER. Closed. See Prince of Peace.

62—ST. PIUS X (1954), Rev. Thomas M. Marpes. In res., Rev. Michael Mukasa (Uganda).
Res., 3040 Pioneer Ave., 15226. Tel: 412-563-5423.
School—Brookline Regional Catholic School, (Grades PreK-8) 2690 Waddington Ave., 15226. Tel: 412-563-0858; 341-6163.
Lay Teachers 25; Students 503.
Catechesis/Religious Programs—Tel: 412-563-1588.
Students 150.

63—PRINCE OF PEACE (1992). Consolidated from the following churches: St. Adalbert, St. Casimir, St. John the Evangelist, St. Josaphat, St. Matthew, St. Michael and St. Peter. Revs. Bernard M. Harcarik, V.F.; John B. Lendvai.
Res., 81 S. 13th St., 15203-1897. Tel: 412-481-8380; Fax: 412-431-0209. [CEM 6]

64—RESURRECTION (Brookline) (1909), Revs. Joseph P. Grosko; Victor J. Rocha; Deacon Richard Very. In res., Rev. Paul Mwangi.
Res., 1100 Creedmoor Ave., 15226. Tel: 412-563-4400; Fax: 412-563-4403.
Catechesis/Religious Programs—Tel: 412-343-7111.
Students 225.

65—ST. VINCENT (Esplen). Closed. See St. John of God, McKees Rocks.

66—ST. WENDELIN (Carrick) (1873), Revs. Thomas M. O'Donnell; Joseph G. Luisi.
Res., 2728 Custer Ave., 15227. Tel: 412-882-1480. [CEM]
School—Bishop John B. McDowell Regional School, 3198 Schieck St., 15227. Tel: 412-884-5676.
Catechesis/Religious Programs—Tel: 412-882-3414.
Students 175.

NORTH SIDE

67—ST. AMBROSE. Merged with St. Boniface to form Holy Wisdom.

68—ANNUNCIATION. Closed. See Incarnation of the Lord.

69—ST. BONIFACE. Merged with St. Ambrose to form Holy Wisdom.

70—ST. CYRIL OF ALEXANDRIA (1924), Very Rev. Thomas B. Ferris, V.F. In res., Rev. Charles L. Christen.
Res., 3854 Brighton Rd., 15212. Tel: 412-761-1552; Fax: 412-761-1059.
School—Tel: 412-761-5043; Fax: 412-761-0840.
Sisters of Mercy of the Diocese of Pittsburgh 2; Lay Teachers 12; Students 253.
Catechesis/Religious Programs—Tel: 412-734-0505. Jean M. DiDonato, D.R.E.
Students 172.
Convent—3830 Parviss St., 15212. Tel: 412-766-8338.

71—ST. FRANCIS XAVIER. Closed. See Risen Lord.

72—ST. GABRIEL ARCHANGEL (Slovak). Closed. See Risen Lord.

73—HOLY WISDOM (1994), Very Rev. Lawrence A. DiNardo, M.Ch.A., J.C.L., V.E.; Rev. Msgr. Donald W. Kraus; Rev. Eugene J. Dougherty.
Res., 1025 Haslage Ave., 15212-3429. Tel: 412-231-1116; Fax: 412-231-1072. [CEM]

74—INCARNATION OF THE LORD (1993). Consolidated from Annunciation and Nativity of Our Lord. Rev. Joseph F. Keenan; Sr. Catherine Fedewa, C.F.S.N., Pastoral Assoc. In res., Rev. Matthew Ekwuribe (Nigeria).
Res., 4071 Franklin Ave., 15214. Tel: 412-931-2911; Fax: 412-931-2832.
School—4072 Franklin Rd., 15214. Tel: 412-931-2330.
Sisters 1; Lay Teachers 9; Students 194.

75—ST. JOSEPH. Closed. See St. Peter.

76—ST. LEO. Closed. See Risen Lord.

77—OUR LADY QUEEN OF PEACE. Closed. See St. Peter.

78—MOST HOLY NAME OF JESUS (Troy Hill) (1868) (German), Rev. W. David Schorr. In res., Revs. Dominic Dery; James L. Aaron, (Retired); Anthony Anomah, C.S.Sp.; Anthony Naaeke.
Res., 1700 Harpster St., 15212-4393. Tel: 412-231-2994; Fax: 412-231-7180. [CEM]
School—1515 Tinsbury St., 15212. Tel: 412-322-6226.
Lay Teachers 9; Students 149.
Catechesis/Religious Programs—Tel: 412-231-3002.
Students 129.
Chapel—St. Anthony's, (1880). Sr. Margaret Liam Glenane, S.A., Asst. Dir.

79—NATIVITY OF OUR LORD. Closed. See Incarnation of the Lord.

80—ST. NICHOLAS (Croatian). Closed. See St. Nicholas.

81—ST. PETER (1993). Consolidated from St. Cyprian, St. Mary's, Mary Immaculate & Our Lady, Queen of Peace, St. Joseph, St. Peter and St. Wenceslaus. Revs. Benjamin Walker, O.S.B.; Eric Vogt, O.S.B.
Res., 720 Arch St., 15212. Tel: 412-321-0711; Fax: 412-321-7807. [CEM]
School—711 W. Commons St., 15212. Tel: 412-231-8248; Fax: 412-231-0835.
Lay Teachers 10; Students 167.

82—REGINA COELI (Italian). Closed. For sacramental records contact St. Cyril of Alexandria.

83—RISEN LORD (1993). Consolidated from the following churches: St. Francis Xavier, St. Gabriel Archangel, St. Leo and Our Lady of Perpetual Help. Rev. Thomas J. Galvin. In res., Rev. Robert Schweitzer.
Res., 3250 California Ave., 15212. Tel: 412-761-1507; Fax: 412-761-1508.

84—ST. WENCESLAUS. Closed. See St. Peter.

OUTSIDE THE CITY OF PITTSBURGH

Aleppo Township, Allegheny Co., St. Mary (1852), Rev. John E. Kozar.
Res., 444 Glenfield Rd., Sewickley, 15143. Tel: 412-741-6460. [CEM]

Aliquippa, Beaver Co., St. Titus (1994). Merged with St. Joseph, West Aliquippa. Revs. John P. Sweeney; Robert J. Grecco.
Res., 952 Franklin Ave., 15001. Tel: 412-378-8561; Fax: 412-378-2392. [JC 2]
School—107 Sycamore St., 15001. Tel: 412-378-7940; Fax: 412-375-8893.
Sisters of St. Joseph 1; Lay Teachers 12; Students 152.
Catechesis/Religious Programs—Tel: 412-378-8665.
Students 200.

Allison Park, Allegheny Co., St. Ursula (1908), Revs. Garret D. Dorsey; Ernest Strelinski, P.A.
Res., 3937 Kirk Ave., 15101. Tel: 412-486-6700.
School—Tel: 412-486-5511.
Sisters 1; Lay Teachers 15; Students 224.
Catechesis/Religious Programs—Tel: 412-486-3374.
Students 445.

Ambridge, Beaver Co.,

1—ST. VERONICA. Closed. See Good Samaritan.

2—DIVINE REDEEMER. Closed. See Good Samaritan.

3—ST. STANISLAUS. Closed. See Good Samaritan.

4—CHURCH OF CHRIST THE KING. Closed. See Good Samaritan.

5—HOLY TRINITY, (Croatian). Closed. See Good Samaritan.

6—GOOD SAMARITAN, (1994). Consolidated from the following churches: St. Veronica, Divine Redeemer, St. Stanislaus, Christ the King and Holy Trinity. Revs. John Bauer; John Skirtich; Mark Thomas, S.T.L.
Res., 725 Glenwood Ave., 15003. Tel: 412-266-6565; Fax: 412-266-5570. [CEM][JC]
School—Tel: 412-266-1670.
Catechesis/Religious Programs—Tel: 412-266-2194.
Students 187.

Aspinwall, Allegheny Co., St. Scholastica, Rev. Robert G. Duch, Ph.D.
Res., 309 Brilliant Ave., 15215. Tel: 412-781-0186.
School—205 Brilliant Ave., 15215.
Sisters of the Third Order of St. Francis 1; Lay Teachers 13; Students 211.
Catechesis/Religious Programs—Third & Maple Sts., Pittsburgh, 15215. Fax: 412-781-4316.
Students 383.

Avella, Washington Co., St. Michael (1917), Rev. Pierre G. Sodini, S.T.L.
Res., 95 Highland Ave., P.O. Box 145, 15312. Tel: 412-587-3570. [CEM]

Baden, Beaver Co., St. John the Baptist (1866), Rev. Joseph J. Dascenzo.
Res., Linmore Ave., P.O. Box 171, 15005. Tel: 412-869-2280; Fax: 412-869-0305. [CEM]

Bairdford, Allegheny Co., St. Victor (1919), Revs. C. William Hausen; Roland Ripoli, O.S.B.
Res., Box 149, 15006. Tel: 412-265-2070; Fax: 412-265-6316.
Catechesis/Religious Programs—Tel: 412-265-4040.
Students 500.

Baldwin Boro, Allegheny Co., St. Albert the Great (1956), Revs. Charles W. Speicher, Ph.D.; Edward Kryston; Deacon Robert J. Becker. In res., Rev. Msgr. Daniel A. Gearing.
Res., 3171 Churchview Ave., 15227. Tel: 412-884-7744; Fax: 412-884-2300.
School—Bishop John B. McDowell Regional School,

(Grades PreK-8) 3198 Schieck St., 15227. Tel: 412-884-5676; Fax: 412-884-8610.
Lay Teachers 17; Students 257.
Catechesis/Religious Programs—Tel: 412-884-8282. Anita Bridge, D.R.E.
Students 390.

Beaver, Beaver Co., SS. Peter and Paul (1830), Rev. Msgr. Raymond T. Schultz, V.F.; Rev. Daniel B. Dixon. In res., Rev. Regis R. Alberth.
Res., 200 Third St., 15009. Tel: 412-775-4111. [CEM]
School—370 E. End Ave., 15009. Tel: 412-774-4450.
Sisters of Divine Providence 1; Lay Teachers 11; Students 169.
Catechesis/Religious Programs—Students 321.

Beaver Falls, Beaver Co., Divine Mercy (1994). Consolidated from St. Mary and Holy Trinity. Rev. Donald R. Bischof. In res., Rev. Paul J. Savage, S.T.L.
Res., 605 Tenth St., 15010. Tel: 412-846-4585; Fax: 412-846-6868. [CEM]
School—609 Tenth St., 15010. Tel: 412-846-5955.
Lay Teachers 10; Students 144.
Catechesis/Religious Programs—Tel: 412-846-8133.
Students 190.

Holy Trinity (Polish). Closed. See Divine Mercy.

St. Philomena (1948), Rev. J. Francis Frazer.
Res., 3908 Sixth Ave., 15010. Tel: 412-843-7375.
School—Tel: 412-846-2272.
Lay Teachers 8; Students 163.

Bellevue, Allegheny Co., Assumption of the Blessed Virgin Mary on the Beautiful River (1903), Revs. Robert J. Boyle; John P. Hickey; Paul W. Merkovsky.
Res., 45 N. Sprague Ave., 15202. Tel: 412-766-6660; Fax: 412-766-4836.
School—35 N. Jackson Ave., 15202. Tel: 412-761-7887.
Lay Teachers 20; Students 285.
Catechesis/Religious Programs—Pittsburgh, Tel: 412-766-4046.
Students 425.

Bentleyville, Washington Co., St. Luke. Closed. See Ave Maria, Ellsworth.

Bessemer, Lawrence Co., St. Anthony (1909), Rev. James A. Downs.
Res., W. Poland Ave., P.O. Box 3, 16112. Tel: 412-667-7737. [CEM]

Bethel Park, Allegheny Co., St. Germaine (1957), Rev. Nicholas A. Pesanka; Sr. Mary Faith Balawejder, C.S.S.F., Pastoral Assoc.
Res., 7003 Baptist Rd., 15102. Tel: 412-833-0661; Fax: 412-833-4036.
School—7001 Baptist Rd., 15102. Tel: 412-833-0223.
Felician Sisters 2; Lay Teachers 13; Students 175.
Catechesis/Religious Programs—Tel: 412-833-6662.
Students 256.

St. Thomas More (1953), Revs. Kenneth R. White; David J. Bonnar; J. Edward Suhoza.
Res., 126 Fort Couch Rd., Pittsburgh, 15241. Tel: 412-833-0031; Fax: 412-833-5995.
School—134 Fort Couch Rd., Pittsburgh, 15241. Tel: 412-833-1412.
Lay Teachers 15; Students 265.
Catechesis/Religious Programs—Tel: 412-835-6996; Fax: 412-833-5995.
Students 545.

St. Valentine (1931), Revs. John A. Harvey; F. Raymond Trance; Kevin J. Dominik.
Res., 2710 Ohio St., 15102. Tel: 412-835-4415; Fax: 412-835-4417.
School—(Grades PreK-8) 2709 Mesta St., 15102. Tel: 412-835-3780.
Lay Teachers 15; Students 257.
Catechesis/Religious Programs—Tel: 412-831-6466.
Students 760.

Blawnox, Allegheny Co., St. Edward (1938), Rev. Russell J. Maurer. In res., Rev. Thomas M. Kirby.
Res., 450 Walnut St., Pittsburgh, 15238. Tel: 412-828-4066.
Catechesis/Religious Programs—Tel: 412-828-7310.
Students 135.

Bobtown, Greene Co., St. Ignatius of Antioch (1924), Rev. Alvin Gutierrez.
Res., Box 63, 15315. Tel: 412-839-7122.
Catechesis/Religious Programs—Tel: 412-839-7208; 943-3844.
Students 117.
Mission—Bobtown, Greene Co., Holy Family.

Boyers, Butler Co., St. Alphonsus (1841). Merged with Epiphany, St. Paschal and St. Louis, W. Sunbury. Rev. Albert C. Koser.
Mailing Address: P.O. Box 46, 16020.
Res., 2709 W. Sunbury Rd., 16020. Tel: 412-791-2393. [CEM][JC 3]
Catechesis/Religious Programs—Students 200.

Braddock, Allegheny Co., Good Shepherd (1985), Revs. Albert L. Zapf; Robert J. Zajdel. In res., Rev. Joseph D. Karabin.
Res., 416 Verona St., 15104. Tel: 412-271-1515; Fax: 412-271-6634.
School—1025 Braddock Ave., 15104. Tel: 412-271-2492. Russell Firestone, Prin.
Sisters 3; Lay Teachers 8; Students 132.
Convent—Tel: 412-271-1736.

Braddock Hills, Allegheny Co., Sacred Heart (1897) (Polish), Rev. Albert L. Zapf, Admin.
Res., 1600 Brinton Rd., 15221-4902. Tel: 412-829-2161.

Brentwood, Allegheny Co., St. Sylvester (1927), Revs. Robert R. Werthman; Leroy A. DiPietro; Very Rev. Robert J. Ahlin; Deacon Joseph R. Mueller.
Res., 3754 Brownsville Rd., 15227. Tel: 412-882-8593; Fax: 412-882-0153.
School—30 W. Willock Rd., 15227. Tel: 412-882-9900.
Sisters of Divine Providence 1; Lay Teachers 12; Students 240.
Catechesis/Religious Programs—Tel: 412-881-4142.
Students 364.

Bridgeville, Allegheny Co.,

1—St. Agatha, (1894). Closed. See Holy Child.

2—Holy Child, (1994). Consolidated from St. Agatha and St. Anthony. Revs. Frederick L. Cain; Pierce M. Falkenhan; George T. DeVille, Senior Priest.
Res., 212 Station St., 15017. Tel: 412-221-5213. [CEM]
School—Tel: 412-221-4720.
Sisters 2; Lay Teachers 14; Students 276.
Catechesis/Religious Programs—Tel: 412-221-6514. Mrs. Marilyn Spitzig.
Students 459.
Convent—509 Coulter St., 15017. Tel: 412-221-8930.

3—St. Anthony, (1915) (Lithuanian). Closed. See Holy Child.

4—St. Barbara, (1894), Rev. William F. Kohler.
Res., 45 Prestley Rd., 15017-1971. Tel: 412-221-5152. [CEM]

Bulger, Washington Co., St. Ann (1917), Rev. Rudolph M. Silvers.
Res., 967 Grant St., Box 488, 15019-0488. Tel: 412-796-3791.

Burgettstown, Washington Co., Our Lady of Lourdes (1916), Rev. Richard J. Tusky.
Res., 621 S. Main St., 15021. Tel: 412-947-3363; Fax: 412-947-9348. [CEM]
School—620 Main St., 15021. Tel: 412-947-5076; Fax: 412-947-5065.
Lay Teachers 10; Students 171.
Catechesis/Religious Programs—Students 155.

Butler, Butler Co.,

1—St. Fidelis of Sigmaringen, (1995), Revs. James F. Murphy; George Palick.
Res., 125 Buttercup Rd., 16001. Tel: 412-482-2690; Fax: 412-482-2315.
Catechesis/Religious Programs—Tel: 412-482-2362. Mrs. Edythe M. Schirra.
Students 482.

2—St. Michael the Archangel, (1909) (Italian-French), Rev. Matthew R. Cirilli.
Res., 432 Center Ave., 16001. Tel: 412-282-4107; Fax: 412-282-9365. [CEM]
School—Butler Consolidated Schools. See separate listing. Tel: 412-285-4276; Fax: 412-285-4896.
Catechesis/Religious Programs—Tel: 412-282-3156.
Students 298.

3—St. Paul, (1867) (Territorial), Revs. Hugh M. Gloninger; James L. Armstrong; Harry R. Bielewicz; Deacons Raymond C. Rice; Gerald C. Stein, (Retired). In res., Rev. Henry S. Preneta (GBG) Hospital Chap.
Res., 128 N. McKean St., 16001. Tel: 412-287-1759.
School—Butler Consolidated Schools. See separate listing. Tel: 412-285-4276; Fax: 412-285-4896.
Catechesis/Religious Programs—Students 360.

4—St. Peter, (1821) (German), Rev. Jack Nanz.
Res., 127 Franklin St., 16001. Tel: 412-287-2743; Fax: 412-287-8447. [CEM]
School—Butler Consolidated Schools. See separate listing. Tel: 412-285-4276.
Catechesis/Religious Programs—201 Franklin St., 16001. Tel: 412-285-3249.
Students 299.

5—St. Wendelin, (1863), Rev. Michael Greb, O.F.M.Cap.
Res., 210 St. Wendelin Rd., 16002. Tel: 412-287-0820. [CEM]
Preschool—.
Students 46.
School—(Grades PreK-6) 211 St. Wendelin Rd., 16001. Tel: 412-285-4986.
Lay Teachers 7; Students 73.
Catechesis/Religious Programs—Students 112.

Cabot, Butler Co., St. Joseph (1904), Rev. Louis J. Petruha, O.F.M.Cap.; Bro. John McCloskey O.F.M.Cap.; Sr. Natalie Lann, C.S.J., Pastoral Assoc.
Res., 315 Stoney Hollow Rd., 16023. Tel: 412-352-2149; Fax: 412-352-7174.
Catechesis/Religious Programs—Tel: 412-352-3030.
Students 351.

California, Washington Co., St. Thomas Aquinas (1888), Rev. Timothy F. Whalen, M.A.
Res., 213 Fourth St., 15419. Tel: 412-938-3204; Fax: 412-938-0434. [CEM]

Canonsburg, Washington Co., St. Patrick (1993). Merged with St. Genevieve. Revs. Philip J. Przybyla; James E. Seeger; Patrick Hynes; Deacon Joseph C. Meyer, Jr.
Res., 317 W. Pike St., 15317. Tel: 412-745-6560; Fax: 412-746-1112. [CEM]
School—Hutchinson & Murdock Sts., 15317. Tel: 412-745-7977.
Priests 3; Sisters of St. Francis 1; Lay Teachers 11; Students 187.
Catechesis/Religious Programs—Tel: 412-745-3787.
Students 591.

St. Genevieve (Polish). Closed. See St. Patrick.

Carmichaels, Greene Co., St. Hugh (1951), Rev. Francis A. Nazimek.
Res., 408 Rte. 88, 15320. Tel: 724-966-7270.
Catechesis/Religious Programs—Students 157.

Carnegie, Allegheny Co.,

1—St. Elizabeth Ann Seton, (1992) (Italian-German). Consolidated from the following churches: Holy Souls, St. Ignatius de Loyola, Immaculate Conception, St. Joseph, St. Luke and St. Vincent de Paul, Walkers Mill. Revs. Rudolph F. Smoley; Robert M. Staszewski.
Res., 206 Mary St., 15106-2489. Tel: 412-276-1011; Fax: 412-276-0816. [CEM]
Catechesis/Religious Programs—127 Finley Ave., 15106. Tel: 412-279-8118.
Students 387.

2—Holy Souls. Closed. See St. Elizabeth Ann Seton.

3—St. Ignatius de Loyola, (Polish). Closed. See St. Elizabeth Ann Seton.

4—Immaculate Conception, (Polish). Closed. See St. Elizabeth Ann Seton.

5—St. Joseph, (German). Closed. See St. Elizabeth Ann Seton.

6—St. Luke. Closed. See St. Elizabeth Ann Seton.

Castle Shannon, Allegheny Co., St. Anne (1889), Revs. Donald P. Breier; Michael L. Yaksick; Dam Nguyen. In res., Rev. Msgr. Charles O. Rice, Pastor Emeritus.
Res., 400 Hoodridge Dr., Pittsburgh, 15234. Tel: 412-531-5964; Fax: 412-531-6136. [CEM]
School—4040 Willow Ave., Pittsburgh, 15234. Tel: 412-561-7720; Fax: 412-561-7927.
Lay Teachers 14; Students 277.
Catechesis/Religious Programs—Tel: 412-561-0101.
Students 580.

Cecil, Washington Co., St. Mary (1909), Rev. Msgr. Robert P. Garland.
Res., 10 St. Mary's Ln., Box 285, 15321. Tel: 412-221-1560; Fax: 412-221-1561. [CEM]
Catechesis/Religious Programs—Tel: 412-221-0595.
Students 239.

Center Township, Beaver Co., St. Frances Cabrini (1961), Revs. Joseph J. Kleppner, S.T.L., Ph.D.; Chuck Baptiste.
Res., 115 Trinity Dr., Aliquippa, 15001. Tel: 412-775-6363; Fax: 412-775-3848.
Catechesis/Religious Programs—Tel: 412-774-4888.
Students 621.

St. Andrew, Butler Co., (1964), Rev. James G. Salberg.
Res., 1660 N. Main St., Ext., Butler, 16001. Tel: 412-287-7781; Fax: 412-287-7346.

Charleroi, Washington Co.,

1—St. Jerome. Closed. See Mary Mother of the Church.

2—SS. Cyril and Methodius, (Slovak). Closed. See Mary Mother of the Church.

3—Mary Mother of the Church, (1892). Consolidated from SS. Cyril & Methodius, St. Jerome and Mother of Sorrows. Team Ministry: Revs. John A. Marcucci, Moderator; David F. Dzermejko Tel: 412-483-4572.
Res., 624 Washington Ave., 15022-1989. Tel: 412-483-5533; Fax: 412-483-0122. [CEM]
Catechesis/Religious Programs—Students 480.

4—Mother of Sorrows, (Italian). Closed. See Mary Mother of the Church.

Chicora, Butler Co., Mater Dolorosa (1910), Rev. Bartley A. Sorensen.
Res., P.O. Box 243, 16025. Tel: 412-445-2275.
Catechesis/Religious Programs—Students 220.

Chippewa Township, Beaver Co., Christ the Divine Teacher (1969), Rev. Harry R. Sangl.
Res., 116 Thorndale Dr., Beaver Falls, 15010. Tel: 412-846-7540.
Catechesis/Religious Programs—Tel: 412-847-4750.
Students 265.

Churchill Borough, Allegheny Co., St. John Fisher (1960), Rev. Carl J. Gentile.
Res., 33 Lewin Ln., Pittsburgh, 15235. Tel: 412-241-4722; Fax: 412-241-4653.
Catechesis/Religious Programs—Tel: 412-241-4653.
Students 151.

Clairton, Allegheny Co., St. Clare of Assisi (1994). Consolidated from the following churches: St. Joseph, St. Paulinus and St. Clare. Revs. Peter P. Murphy; Emil W. Fischer, O.F.M.Cap.
Office: 314 Wilson Ave., 15025. Tel: 412-233-7870; Fax: 412-233-0742. [CEM]
School—336 Wilson Ave., 15025. Tel: 412-233-7598.
Catechesis/Religious Programs—Students 182.
St. Joseph. Closed. See St. Clare of Assisi.
St. Paulinus. Closed. See St. Clare of Assisi.

Clarksville, Washington Co., St. Thomas (1992) (Polish-Italian), Rev. Thomas R. Miller.
Res., R.D. No. 1, 15322. Tel: 412-377-2588. [CEM]

Conway, Beaver Co., Our Lady of Peace (1941), Revs. Robert Guay; Patrick Hynes; David C. Menegay.
Res., 1000 Third Ave., 15027. Tel: 412-869-3024; Fax: 412-869-3025.
Catechesis/Religious Programs—Tel: 412-869-4723.
Students 345.

Coraopolis, Allegheny Co., St. Joseph (1891), Revs. Lawrence V. Holpp; Timothy Dawes.
Res., 1304 Fourth Ave., 15108. Tel: 412-264-6162. [CEM]
School—Tel: 412-264-6141.
Felician Sisters 3; Lay Teachers 8; Students 170.
Catechesis/Religious Programs—1313 Fifth Ave., 15108. Tel: 412-262-2828.
Students 120.

Coylesville, Butler Co., St. John, Rev. Raymond C. Boccardi, Admin.
Res., 455 Clearfield Rd., Fenelton, 16034. Tel: 412-287-7590. [CEM]
Catechesis/Religious Programs—Students 220.

Crafton, Allegheny Co., St. Philip (1839) (Irish), Revs. James J. Schmitt; Kenneth R. Keene, Parochial Vicar.
Res., 50 W. Crafton Ave., Pittsburgh, 15205. Tel: 412-922-6300; Fax: 412-920-7310. [CEM]
School—52 W. Crafton Ave., Pittsburgh, 15205. Tel: 412-928-2742.
Sisters of Charity 3; Lay Teachers 23; Students 329.
Catechesis/Religious Programs—Tel: 412-928-2744.
Students 255.

Cranberry Township, Butler Co., St. Ferdinand (1961), Revs. John P. Gallagher; Joseph P. Newell; Deacon John J. Walsh; Barbara McCarthy, Pastoral Assoc.
Res., 2535 Rochester Rd., 16066-6496. Tel: 412-776-2888; Fax: 412-776-2378.
Catechesis/Religious Programs—Tel: 412-776-9177. Clara Kana, D.R.E.
Students 1,778.

Creighton, Allegheny Co., Holy Family (East Deer Twp.) (1949) (Territorial), Rev. Robert F. Rishel.
Res., 787 Freeport Rd., 15030. Tel: 412-224-1626.

Darlington, Beaver Co., St. Rose of Lima (1871), Rev. James B. Krah.
Res., 3357 Constitution Blvd., 16115. Tel: 412-843-0152.
Catechesis/Religious Programs—Students 184.
Mission—New Galilee, Beaver Co., St. Ann, New Galilee, 16141.

Donora, Washington Co.,

1—St. Charles. Closed. See Our Lady of the Valley.

2—St. Dominic, (Slovak). Closed. See Our Lady of the Valley.

3—Holy Name of the Blessed Virgin Mary. Closed. See Our Lady of the Valley.

4—Our Lady of the Valley, (1992). Consolidated from the following churches: St. Charles Borromeo, St. Dominic, Holy Name of the Blessed Virgin Mary and St. Philip Neri. Revs. David J. Kriss; Kenneth Agede (Nigeria); Joseph Nietlong (Nigeria).
Res., 571 Thompson Ave., 15033. Tel: 412-379-4777; 379-7777; Fax: 412-379-6242. [CEM]
Catechesis/Religious Programs—Second St. Ext. & Park Manor Rd., 15033. Tel: 412-379-5977.
Students 215.

5—St. Philip Neri, (Italian). Closed. See Our Lady of the Valley.

Duquesne, Allegheny Co., Holy Name. Closed. See Christ the Light of the World.
St. Joseph (1897) (German), Rev. L. James Susany. In res., Rev. Emmanuel C. Agbakwuru (Nigeria).
Res., 817 W. Grant Ave., 15110. Tel: 412-466-1304. [CEM]
School—Duquesne Catholic School. See separate listing. Tel: 412-466-3895.
Christ the Light of the World (1994). Consolidated from St. Hedwig and Holy Name. Rev. Dennis Colamarino.
Res., 32 S. First St., 15110. Tel: 412-469-0196. [CEM]
Catechesis/Religious Programs—Students 154.

East McKeesport, Allegheny Co., St. Robert Bellarmine (1952), Revs. John G. Oesterle; David Scharf.
Res., 1313 Fifth Ave., 15035. Tel: 412-824-2644; 824-2635; Fax: 412-824-2635.
Catechesis/Religious Programs—Tel: 412-824-3688. Robert Koslosky, D.R.E.
Students 250.

East Pittsburgh, Allegheny Co., St. William. Closed. See Holy Cross.
St. Helen (Slovak). Closed. See Holy Cross.
Holy Cross (1994). Consolidated from St. William and St. Helen. Rev. Miroslaus A. Wojcicki.
Res., 905 Main St., 15112. Tel: 412-829-1146.
Convent—(Allison Park) 515 Howard St., 15112. Tel: 412-829-0815. Sisters of Divine Providence Sisters 4.

Elizabeth, Allegheny Co., St. Michael (1849), Revs. Timothy G. Evans; R. Donald Jones.
Res., 101 McLay Dr., 15037. Tel: 412-751-0663; Fax: 412-751-2161. [CEM]
School—Sixth & Bayard St., 15037. Tel: 412-384-9400.
Lay Teachers 7; Students 134.
Catechesis/Religious Programs—Students 425.

Ellsworth, Washington Co., Ave Maria (1994). Consolidated from St. Luke, St. Clement, and St. Joseph. Rev. Mark J. Skertich.
Mailing Address: P.O. Box 650, 15331.
Res., 126 Church St., Bentleyville, 15314. Tel: 412-239-3591. [CEM 2]
School—Ave Maria School, Tel: 412-239-2226; Fax: 412-239-2272.
Catechesis/Religious Programs—Students 136.

Ellwood City, Lawrence Co., St. Agatha (1895) (Territorial), Rev. Vincent Velas, Admin.
Res., 124 Fifth St., 16117. Tel: 412-758-7587. [CEM]
Catechesis/Religious Programs—Tel: 412-752-1271.
Students 281.
Purification of the Blessed Virgin Mary (1914) (Italian), Revs. Mauro Cautela; Nicholas A. Spirko.
Res., 415 Fourth St., 16117. Tel: 412-758-4411; Fax: 412-752-1466. [JC]
School—(Grades K-6). Tel: 412-758-5591.
Sisters 3; Lay Teachers 11; Students 220.
Catechesis/Religious Programs—Tel: 412-758-5562.
Students 392.

Elrama, Allegheny Co., St. Isaac Jogues (1950), Rev. Robert Andrew Kohuch.
Res., Box 600, 15038. Tel: 412-384-4406.

Emsworth, Allegheny Co., Sacred Heart (1891), Revs. John P. Skaj, C.S.Sp.; Francis P. Meenan, C.S.Sp.
Res., 154 Orchard Ave., Pittsburgh, 15202. Tel: 412-761-6651; Fax: 412-766-8298.
Catechesis/Religious Programs—Tel: 412-761-3806. Linda McKenzie, D.R.E.
Students 207.

Etna, Allegheny Co., All Saints (1902), Rev. John Vojtek.
Res., 19 Wilson St., Pittsburgh, 15223-1798. Tel: 412-781-0530; Fax: 412-784-8769.
Preschool—20 Wilson St., Pittsburgh, 15223. Tel: 412-781-4692.
School—19 Dewey St., Pittsburgh, 15223. Tel: 412-782-0939. Bernadine Srocki, M.Ed, Ed.D, Prin.
Lay Teachers 11; Students 172.
Catechesis/Religious Programs—19 1/2 Dewey St., Pittsburgh, 15223. Tel: 412-782-3307. Sr. Mary Catherine Blooming, H.M., D.R.E.
Students 283.
Social Service—Tel: 412-781-2044.

Evans City, Butler Co., St. Matthias (1939), Rev. William J. Ritzert.
Res., 417 E. Main St., 16033. Tel: 412-538-5331.
Catechesis/Religious Programs—Students 168.

Finleyville, Washington Co., St. Francis of Assisi (1893), Rev. John Gudewicz.
Res., 3609 Washington Ave., 15332. Tel: 412-348-7145; Fax: 412-348-7522. [CEM]
Catechesis/Religious Programs—Tel: 412-348-6190.
Students 225.

Forest Hills, Allegheny Co., St. Maurice (1949), Revs. Robert M. Franco, M.Ch.A.; Martin R. Conley.
Res., 2001 Ardmore Blvd., Pittsburgh, 15221. Tel: 412-271-0809; Fax: 412-271-2415.
School—Tel: 412-351-5403.
Sisters of Mercy (Pittsburgh) 5; Lay Teachers 19; Students 390.
Catechesis/Religious Programs—Tel: 412-352-5404; Fax: 412-271-2415.
Students 270.

Franklin Park Borough, Allegheny Co., Saints John and Paul (1994), Rev. Albert J. Semler.
Res., 2586 Wexford-Bayne Rd., Sewickley, 15143. Tel: 412-935-2104; Fax: 412-935-8320.
Catechesis/Religious Programs—Tel: 412-935-7153. Phyllis Haney, D.R.E.
Students 790.
St. John Neumann (1979), Revs. William R. Bovard; Robert R. Coyne.
Res., 1543 Old Orchard Rd., Pittsburgh, 15237. Tel: 412-366-2020; Fax: 412-366-2866.
Catechesis/Religious Programs—2230 Rochester Rd., Pittsburgh, 15237. Tel: 412-366-5885.
Students 757.

Fredericktown, Washington Co., St. Michael the Archangel. Closed. See St. Oliver Plunkett, Marianna.

Freedom, Beaver Co., St. Felix (1906) (Italian), Rev. Leon Leitem, O.F.M.Cap.
Res., 450 13th St., 15042. Tel: 412-775-1476; Fax: 412-775-5684. [CEM]
Catechesis/Religious Programs—Tel: 412-728-4421.
Students 125.

Glade Mills, Butler Co., Holy Sepulcher (1944), Rev. John P. Maloney. In res., Rev. Gregory Mallya (Tanzania).
Res., 1304 E. Cruikshank Rd., Butler, 16001. Tel: 412-586-7610; Fax: 412-586-7247.
School—Tel: 412-586-5022.
Lay Teachers 11; Students 173.
Catechesis/Religious Programs—Tel: 412-586-7276.
Students 508.

Glassport, Allegheny Co., St. Cecilia. Closed. See Queen of the Rosary.
Queen of the Rosary (1994). Consolidated from Holy Cross and St. Cecilia. Rev. Casimir Kedzierski.
Res., 530 Michigan Ave., 15045. Tel: 412-672-7209; Fax: 412-672-6390.
School—St. Joseph Regional School. See separate listing. 15133. Tel: 412-678-0659.
Catechesis/Religious Programs—Tel: 412-672-7910.
Students 175.

Glenshaw, Allegheny Co., St. Bonaventure (1957), Revs. George C. Newmeyer; James R. Gretz; James R. Torquato.
Res., 2001 Mount Royal Blvd., 15116. Tel: 412-486-2606; Fax: 412-492-9329.
School—Tel: 412-486-2608; Fax: 412-487-8657.
Sisters of Divine Providence 1; Lay Teachers 27; Students 565.
Catechesis/Religious Programs—Tel: 412-486-0800.
Students 480.
St. Mary (1834), Revs. Walter J. Benz; Paul Grunebach; John McKenna.
Res., 2510 Middle Rd., 15116. Tel: 412-486-4100; Fax: 412-486-4150. [CEM]
School—Tel: 412-486-7611; Fax: 412-487-9509.
Sisters of Divine Providence 1; Lay Teachers 24; Students 429.
Catechesis/Religious Programs—Tel: 412-486-5521; 492-9344. Rose Stegman, D.R.E., (Elementary).
Students 672.

Green Tree, Allegheny Co., St. Margaret (1938), Revs. Harry E. Nichols; Philip N. Farrell.
Res., 310 Mansfield Ave., Pittsburgh, 15220. Tel: 412-921-0745; Fax: 412-921-0707.
School—915 Alice St., Pittsburgh, 15220. Tel: 412-922-4765; Fax: 412-922-4647.
Lay Teachers 20; Students 340.
Catechesis/Religious Programs—Tel: 412-921-7999.
Students 400.

Harmarville, Allegheny Co., St. Francis of Assisi, Rev. Hugh J. McCormley.
Res., 2599 Freeport Rd., Pittsburgh, 15238. Tel: 412-828-3123.

Harwick, Allegheny Co., Our Lady of Victory (1944), Rev. Alfred C. Cicola.
Res., 1319 Low Grade Rd., Box 198, 15049. Tel: 412-274-8575; Fax: 412-274-0529.

Catechesis/Religious Programs—Tel: 412-274-6445.
Students 210.

Herman, Butler Co., St. Mary of the Assumption (1842), Rev. James Kurtz, O.F.M.Cap.
Res., 16039. Tel: 412-285-3285; Fax: 412-285-3285. [CEM]
School—Tel: 412-283-2129.
Sisters of Divine Providence 1; Lay Teachers 9; Students 146.
Catechesis/Religious Programs—Students 158.

Hillsville, Lawrence Co., St. Lawrence (1904) (Italian), Rev. James A. Downs.
Res., Martin Kelly Speer Rd., Box 23, 16132. Tel: 412-667-7721. [CEM]

Holiday Park, Allegheny Co., Our Lady of Joy (1968), Revs. Robert J. Cedolia; Nicholas Mastrangelo.
Res., 2000 O'Block Rd., Pittsburgh, 15239. Tel: 412-795-3388; Fax: 412-793-5308.
Catechesis/Religious Programs—Tel: 412-795-4389.
Students 834.

Homestead, Allegheny Co.,

1—St. Anne. Closed. See St. Maximilian Kolbe, Munhall.

2—St. Anthony. Closed. See St. Maximilian Kolbe, Munhall.

3—St. Mary Magdalene. Closed. See St. Maximilian Kolbe, Munhall.

4—SS. Peter and Paul, (Lithuanian). Closed. See St. Maximilian Kolbe, Munhall.

Hopewell Township, Beaver Co., Our Lady of Fatima, Revs. Thomas J. McKenna; Micah Muhlen, O.F.M.
Res., 4001 Broadhead Rd., Aliquippa, 15001. Tel: 412-375-7626; Fax: 412-375-0219.
School—Lay Teachers 7; Students 102.
Catechesis/Religious Programs—Tel: 412-378-8020; Fax: 412-378-1931.
Students 589.

Imperial, Allegheny Co., St. Columbkille (1908), Revs. Dennis M. Buranosky; Richard J. Wesoloski.
Res., 103 Church Rd., 15126. Tel: 412-695-7325. [CEM]
Catechesis/Religious Programs—Tel: 412-695-2146.
Students 455.

Industry, Beaver Co., St. Christine. Closed. See St. Blaise, Midland.

Ingram, Allegheny Co., Ascension (1967), Rev. Walter A. Sobon.
Res., 114 Berry St., Pittsburgh, 15205. Tel: 412-921-1230; Fax: 412-922-1279.
Catechesis/Religious Programs—Brian M. Keane, D.R.E.
Students 260.

Jefferson Boro, Allegheny Co., St. Thomas A'Becket (1957), Rev. Gerard D. Kelly.
Res., 509 Gill Hall Rd., Jefferson Boro, Clairton, 15025. Tel: 412-655-2885; Fax: 412-655-0615.
Catechesis/Religious Programs—139 Gill Hall Rd., 15025. Tel: 412-653-4322.
Students 410.

Kennedy Township, Allegheny Co., St. Malachy (1953), Revs. John D. Brennan; Paul R. Staud; James Chepponis.
Res., 343 Forest Grove Rd., Coraopolis, 15108. Tel: 412-771-5483.
School—Tel: 412-771-4545.
Lay Teachers 17; Students 287.
Catechesis/Religious Programs—Tel: 412-771-7480.
Students 529.

Koppel, Beaver Co., Queen of Heaven (1992). Consolidated from St. Monica, Wampum and St. Theresa, Koppel. Rev. Joseph R. Lemp, S.T.L.
Res., 6421 Sixth Ave., P.O. Box A, 16136-0601. Tel: 412-846-5702; Fax: 412-846-2219. [CEM]
Catechesis/Religious Programs—Tel: 412-846-9559.
Students 185.

St. Teresa. Closed. See Queen of Heaven.

Lawrence, Washington Co., St. Elizabeth. Closed. See St. Mary, Cecil.

Liberty Boro, Allegheny Co., St. Eugene. Closed. See St. Mark, Port Vue.

Library, Allegheny Co., St. Joan of Arc (1923), Rev. Phillip Pribonic.
Res., 6414 Montour St., 15129. Tel: 412-833-2400; Fax: 412-835-1764.
School—6470 Library Rd., 15129. Tel: 412-833-2433.
Lay Teachers 13; Students 189.
Catechesis/Religious Programs—Tel: 412-835-3724.
Students 580.

Lyndora, Butler Co., St. John (1904) (Slovak). Closed. See St. Fidelis of Sigmaringen, Butler.

St. Stanislaus Kostka (1919) (Polish). Merged with St. Conrad, Meridian, and St. John, Lyndora, to form St. Fidelis, Butler.

McDonald, Washington Co., St. Alphonsus (1892), Rev. Edward J. Trzeciakowski.
Res., 219 W. Lincoln Ave., 15057. Tel: 412-926-2984; Fax: 412-926-5120.
Catechesis/Religious Programs—Students 264.

McKeesport, Allegheny Co.,

1—St. Martin de Porres, (1993). Consolidated from St. Mary, Holy Trinity, Sacred Heart and St. Peter. Revs. John R. Rushofsky; James E. Kunkel; Deacon Ken Gleason.
Res., 704 Market St., 15132. Tel: 412-672-9763; Fax: 412-672-2817. [CEM 3]
School—St. Joseph Regional School, Tel: 412-678-0659.
Catechesis/Religious Programs—Tel: 412-672-7440.
Students 118.

2—St. Peter. Closed. See St. Martin de Porres.

3—St. Mary, (German). Closed. See St. Martin de Porres.

4—St. Mary Czestochowa, (1893) (Polish), Rev. Francis B. Lachowicz.
Res., 2515 Versailles Ave., 15132. Tel: 412-672-0765. [CEM]
School—McKeesport Central Catholic School. See separate listing.
Catechesis/Religious Programs—2412 Versailles Ave., 15132. Tel: 412-751-2873.
Students 112.

5—Holy Trinity. Closed. See St. Martin de Porres.

6—St. Pius V, (1903). Merged with St. Stephen. Rev. John J. Keane, Admin.
Res., 2911 Versailles Ave., 15132. Tel: 412-673-8878. [CEM]
School—McKeesport Central Catholic School. See separate listing. Tel: 412-672-4612.

7—St. Stephen, (1899) (Hungarian). Closed. See St. Pius V.

8—Sacred Heart, (Croatian). Closed. See St. Martin de Porres.

9—St. Perpetua. Closed. See St. Patrick, Versailles.

McKees Rocks, Allegheny Co.,

1—St. Mary Help of Christians, (German). Closed. See St. John of God.

2—St. Francis de Sales. Closed. See St. John of God.

3—St. John of God, (1993). Consolidated from the following churches: St. Francis de Sales, SS. Cyril & Methodius, St. Maria Goretti Chapel, St. Mark, St. Mary Help of Christians, Mother of Sorrows and St. Vincent, Pittsburgh. Team Ministers: Revs. Paul C. Householder; Lawrence R. Smith; William R. Terza, Team Moderator. In res., Revs. Richard M. Lelonis, J.C.L.; Regis J. Ryan; Christopher Mbogu (Nigeria).
Office—810 Chartiers Ave., 15136. Tel: 412-771-5646; Fax: 412-331-0678.
School—See Consolidated Schools under Institutions Located in the Diocese. Tel: 412-331-0220.
Catechesis/Religious Programs—Tel: 412-331-8627. Mr. John Fatula, D.R.E.
Students 348.

4—St. Maria Goretti Chapel. Closed. See St. John of God.

5—Mother of Sorrows, (Italian). Closed. See St. John of God.

6—St. Mark, (Slovak). Closed. See St. John of God.

7—SS. Cyril and Methodius, (Polish). Closed. See St. John of God.

Fredericktown, Washington Co., St. Oliver Plunkett (1994). Consolidated from Saints Mary & Ann, Marianna, and St. Michael Archangel, Fredericktown. Rev. Edward S. Litavec.
Res., Box 638, 15333. Tel: 724-377-0128. [CEM]
Catechesis/Religious Programs—Students 170.

Mars, Butler Co., St. Kilian (1920), Rev. John W. Rebel.
Res., Clarke & Cherry Sts., P.O. Box 394, 16046. Tel: 412-625-1665.
Catechesis/Religious Programs—Hook St., 16046. Tel: 412-625-1288.
Students 250.

Meadowlands, Washington Co., Our Lady of the Miraculous Medal (1949), Rev. Ferdinand F. Lech.
Res., Box 366, 15347. Tel: 412-222-1911. [JC]

Meridian, Butler Co., St. Conrad. Merged with St. John and St. Stanislaus Kostka, Lyndora to form St. Fidelis, Butler.

Midland, Beaver Co., St. Blaise (1994), Rev. Dennis J. Bradley.
Res., 772 Ohio Ave., 15059. Tel: 412-643-4050; Fax: 412-643-6533.
Catechesis/Religious Programs—757 Penn Ave., 15059. Tel: 412-643-4663.
Students 265.

Millvale, Allegheny Co.,

1—St. Ann. Closed. See Holy Spirit.

2—St. Anthony, (German). Closed. See Holy Spirit.

3—Holy Spirit, (1994). Consolidated from St. Anthony and St. Ann. Revs. John R. Weber, C.S.Sp.; John L. Marini, C.S.Sp. In res., Rev. Joseph F. Rengers, C.S.Sp.
Res., 608 Farragut St., Pittsburgh, 15209. Tel: 412-821-4424.
School—100 Howard St., Pittsburgh, 15209. Tel: 412-821-4805; Fax: 412-821-4714.
Lay Teachers 13; Students 253.
Catechesis/Religious Programs—Tel: 412-821-2099; Fax: 412-821-9305.
Students 315.

4—St. Nicholas, (Croatian). Closed. See the new St. Nicholas.

5—St. Nicholas, (1994) (Croatian). Merged. Very Rev. Romildo Hrboka, T.O.R.; Rev. Grgo Sikiric, T.O.R.
Administrative Center: 24 Maryland Ave., Pittsburgh, 15209. Tel: 412-821-3438; Fax: 412-821-8726. [CEM][JC 2]

Monaca, Beaver Co., St. John the Baptist (1888), Revs. Philip J. De Carlo; Robin S. Evanish.
Res., 1409 Pennsylvania Ave., 15061. Tel: 412-775-3940; Fax: 412-775-6886. [CEM]
School—Virginia Ave. & 15th St., 15061. Tel: 412-775-5774.
Lay Teachers 12; Students 271.
Catechesis/Religious Programs—Students 373.

Monongahela, Washington Co., Transfiguration (1865), Rev. William P. Feeney.
Res., 722 W. Main St., 15063. Tel: 412-258-7742; Fax: 412-258-8733. [CEM 2]
School—731 Chess St., 15063. Tel: 412-258-3199.
Lay Teachers 7; Students 155.
Madonna Catholic Middle School—.
Lay Teachers 5; Students 89.
Catechesis/Religious Programs—Students 200.

St. Anthony (1905) (Italian-Slavic), Rev. Joseph E. Feltz, Admin.
Res., 225 Park Ave., 15063. Tel: 412-258-9710.
Catechesis/Religious Programs—St. Anthony School, Chass St., 15063. Tel: 412-258-9233. Sr. Mary Laurentia Varga, D.R.E.
Students 130.

Monroeville, Allegheny Co., St. Bernadette (1955), Revs. Michael W. Decewicz; Michael A. Caridi; Richard A. Infante.
Res., 245 Azalea Dr., 15146. Tel: 412-373-0050; Fax: 412-374-8113.
School—(Grades PreK-8). Tel: 412-372-7255.
Sisters 2; Lay Teachers 13; Students 343.
Catechesis/Religious Programs—Tel: 412-373-1797.
Students 745.

North American Martyrs (1960), Revs. Anthony G. DeLuca; Bernard B. Costello; Deacon Regis C. Cunningham.
Res., 2526 Haymaker Rd., 15146. Tel: 412-373-0330.
School—(Grades K-6). Tel: 412-373-0889.
Lay Teachers 8; Students 145.
Catechesis/Religious Programs—Tel: 412-372-8149.
Students 392.

Moon Township, Allegheny Co., St. Margaret Mary (1956), Rev. John Ayoob.
Res., One Parish Pl., 15108-2697. Tel: 412-264-2573; Fax: 412-264-4327.
Catechesis/Religious Programs—Tel: 412-264-9368.
Students 717.

Mt. Lebanon, Allegheny Co., St. Bernard (1919), Revs. George A. Wilt; Thomas V. Manning; Thomas R. Wilson.
Res., 311 Washington Rd., Pittsburgh, 15216. Tel: 412-561-3301; Fax: 412-563-0211.
School—(Grades PreK-8) 315 Washington Rd., Pittsburgh, 15216. Tel: 412-341-5444; Fax: 412-341-2044.
Lay Teachers 20; Students 495.
Catechesis/Religious Programs—Tel: 412-561-0199.
Students 540.

St. Winifred (Pittsburgh) (1960), Rev. Jeremiah T. O'Shea. In res., Rev. John K. Takyi (Ghana).
Res., 550 Sleepy Hollow Rd., Pittsburgh, 15228. Tel: 412-344-5010; Fax: 412-563-7279.
Catechesis/Religious Programs—Tel: 412-563-1414.
Students 426.

Munhall, Allegheny Co.,
1—St. Margaret. Closed. See St. Maximilian Kolbe.
2—St. Maximilian Kolbe, (1992). Consolidated from the following churches: St. Margaret, Munhall; St. Michael, Munhall; St. Anne, Homestead; St. Anthony, Homestead; St. Mary Magdalene, Homestead; SS. Peter & Paul, Homestead. Rev. Henry R. Krawczyk. In res., Revs. Mark W. Glasgow Tel: 412-462-1807; James McDonough Tel: 412-462-1718.
Office—605 Ninth Ave., 15120-1996. Tel: 412-461-1054; Fax: 412-462-1718.
3—St. Michael, (Slovak). Closed. See St. Maximilian Kolbe.
4—St. Rita, (1936), Rev. Alvin J. Adams.
Res., 218 W. Schwab Ave., 15120. Tel: 412-461-4204.
5—St. Theresa of Lisieux, (1925), Very Rev. Hugh J. Lang; Rev. Howard W. Campbell. In res., Rev. Joseph C. Girdis, (Retired).
Res., One St. Theresa Ct., 15120. Tel: 412-462-8161; Fax: 412-462-4817.
School—Three St. Theresa Ct., 15120. Tel: 412-462-8163.
Sisters of Charity 2; Lay Teachers 21; Students 397.
Catechesis/Religious Programs—Tel: 412-461-7680. Ms. Lori Ellis, D.R.E.
Students 260.

Muse, Washington Co., Holy Rosary (1963), Rev. Edward R. Schleicher.
Res., Orchard St., Box 447, 15350-0447. Tel: 412-745-3531.
Catechesis/Religious Programs—Students 166.

Natrona, Allegheny Co., St. Joseph (1992). Merged with St. Ladislaus and St. Mathias. Rev. Donald J. Sotak.
Res., 96 Pond St., 15065-2630. Tel: 412-224-1336. [CEM]
High School—St. Joseph Catholic High School, 800 Montana Ave., Natrona Heights, 15065. Tel: 412-224-5552.
Catechesis/Religious Programs—Students 125.
St. Ladislaus (Polish). Closed. See St. Joseph.
St. Mathias. Closed. See St. Joseph.

Natrona Heights, Allegheny Co., Blessed Sacrament. Closed. See Our Lady of the Most Blessed Sacrament.
Our Lady of the Most Blessed Sacrament (1992) (Polish-Slovak). Consolidated from Most Blessed Sacrament and Our Lady of Perpetual Help. Revs. Stan M. Gregorek; Aaron J. Kriss; John J. Batykefer.
Res., 1526 Union Ave., 15065-2008. Tel: 412-226-4900; Fax: 412-224-3559.
Catechesis/Religious Programs—Tel: 412-224-3339.
Students 565.
Our Lady of Perpetual Help. Closed. See Our Lady of the Most Blessed Sacrament.

Nemacolin, Greene Co., Our Lady of Consolation (1923), Rev. Michael S. Suslowicz.
Res., P.O. Box 206, 15351. Tel: 412-966-7909. [CEM]

Neshannock, Lawrence Co., St. Camillus (1959), Rev. David A. Driesch. In res., Rev. Francis C. Graff.
Res., 314 W. Englewood Ave., New Castle, 16105. Tel: 412-652-9471.
Catechesis/Religious Programs—Tel: 412-652-9497.
Students 490.

New Bedford, Lawrence Co., St. James (1844), Rev. Joseph R. McCaffrey.
Res., P.O. Box 207, 16140. Tel: 412-964-8276; Fax: 412-964-1108. [CEM]
Catechesis/Religious Programs—Students 185.

New Brighton, Beaver Co., Holy Family (1994). Consolidated from St. Joseph and SS. Cyril and Methodius. Rev. Harry E. Parsons.
Catechesis/Religious Programs—Tel: 412-846-9622; Fax: 412-847-3585.
Students 222.
SS. Cyril and Methodius (Slovak). Closed. See Holy Family.

New Castle, Lawrence Co.,
1—Mary, Mother of Hope, (1993). Consolidated from St. Mary and Madonna of Czestochowa. Revs. Victor J. Molka, Jr.; Robert M. Miller.
Res., 124 N. Beaver St., 16101. Tel: 412-658-2564; Fax: 412-658-9024. [CEM][JC]
Catechesis/Religious Programs—Tel: 412-656-1017.
Students 306.
2—St. Mary. Closed. See Mary, Mother of Hope.
3—St. Joseph the Worker, (1888), Very Rev. Norbert J. Campbell.
Res., 1111 S. Cascade St., 16101. Tel: 412-658-1683. [JC]
Catechesis/Religious Programs—Tel: 412-654-9739.
Students 450.
4—St. Vitus, (1901) (Italian), Revs. John D. Petrarulo; J. Lawrence Bruney; John J. Baver.
Res., 910 S. Mercer St., 16101. Tel: 412-652-3422. [JC]
School—915 S. Jefferson St., 16101. Tel: 412-654-9297; Fax: 412-654-9364.
Apostles of the Sacred Heart of Jesus 5; Lay Teachers 14; Students 300.
Catechesis/Religious Programs—Tel: 412-654-9371.
Students 520.
5—Madonna of Czestochowa. Closed. See Mary, Mother of Hope.
6—St. Michael, (Slovak). Closed. See St. Vincent de Paul.
7—SS. Philip and James, (Polish). Closed. See St. Vincent de Paul.
8—St. Lucy, (Italian). Closed. See St. Vincent de Paul.
9—St. Margaret. Closed. See St. Vincent de Paul.
10—St. Vincent de Paul, (1993). Consolidated from the following churches: St. Lucy, St. Michael, SS. Philip & James, St. Margaret and Holy Cross, West Pittsburgh. Revs. Benedetto P. Vaghetto, J.C.L.; Daniel Vallecorsa, M.A., S.T.L.; Frank Erdeljac, M.Div.
Res., One Lucymont Dr., 16102. Tel: 412-652-5829; Fax: 412-656-0413. [CEM 2]
Catechesis/Religious Programs—Clayton St., 16102. Tel: 412-654-2822.
Students 250.

North Oakland, Butler Co., St. Joseph (1872), Rev. Bartley A. Sorensen, Admin.
Res., Main St., P.O. Box 243, Chicora, 16025. Tel: 412-445-2275. [CEM]
Catechesis/Religious Programs—Students 99.

North Rochester, Beaver Co., St. Pudentiana. Closed. See St. Cecilia, Rochester.

Oakdale, Allegheny Co., St. Patrick (1866), Rev. William J. Schwartz.
Res., 7322 Noblestown Rd., 15071. Tel: 412-693-9260; Fax: 412-693-9247. [CEM]

Oakmont, Allegheny Co., St. Irenaeus (1908), Rev. William P. O'Malley.
Res., 387 Maryland Ave., 15139. Tel: 412-828-3065.
School—Tel: 412-828-8444. Ms. Mary Frances Panian, Prin.
Lay Teachers 9; Students 211.
Catechesis/Religious Programs—634 Fourth St., 15139. Tel: 412-828-9450.
Students 264.

O'Hara Township, Allegheny County, St. Joseph (1845), Rev. Walter W. Dworak.
Res., 330 Dorseyville Rd., Pittsburgh, 15215. Tel: 412-963-8885. [CEM]
Catechesis/Religious Programs—342 Dorseyville Rd., Pittsburgh, 15215. Tel: 412-963-9252.
Students 464.

Overbrook, Allegheny Co., St. Norbert (1914) (German), Revs. Michael C. MacVeigh; Joseph P. Pudichery.
Res., 2413 Off Saw Mill Run Blvd., Pittsburgh, 15234. Tel: 412-881-1316; 881-2474; Fax: 412-881-6728.
Catechesis/Religious Programs—Tel: 412-882-2040.
Students 67.

Penn Hills, Allegheny Co., St. Bartholomew (1950), Revs. James W. Garvey; Vincent F. Kolo. In res., Rev. Diego Cadri.
Res., 111 Erhardt Dr., Pittsburgh, 15235. Tel: 412-242-3374; Fax: 412-242-1488.
School—Tel: 412-242-2511; Fax: 412-242-0114.
Sisters 4; Lay Teachers 19; Students 405.
Catechesis/Religious Programs—Tel: 412-242-7207. Judy Kirk, D.R.E.
Lay Teachers 33; Students 275.
St. Gerard Majella (1964), Rev. Richard J. Czapinski.
Res., 121 Dawn Dr., Verona, 15147. Tel: 412-793-3333; Fax: 412-793-4726.
Catechesis/Religious Programs—Tel: 412-793-3959.
Students 298.
St. Susanna (1960), Rev. Raymond Michael Utz.
Res., 200 Stotler Rd., Pittsburgh, 15235-3598. Tel: 412-731-7465; Fax: 412-798-0479.
Catechesis/Religious Programs—Tel: 412-793-9448.
Students 185.

Perrysville, Allegheny Co., St. Teresa of Avila (1867), Revs. Thaddeus S. Maida; David J. Jastrab; David G. Poecking.
Res., 1000 Avila Ct., Pittsburgh, 15237. Tel: 412-367-9001; Fax: 412-366-8415. [CEM]
School—800 Avila Ct., Pittsburgh, 15237. Tel: 412-367-9001, Ext. 530; Fax: 412-364-1172.
Religious 3; Lay Teachers 22; Students 425.
Catechesis/Religious Programs—Tel: 412-367-9001, Ext. 549.
Students 875.

Peters Township, Washington Co., St. Benedict the Abbot (1962), Revs. Philip J. Donatelli; John E. Forbidussi; Deacon John Layton.
Res., 120 Abington Dr., McMurray, 15317. Tel: 412-941-9406; Fax: 412-941-9517.
Catechesis/Religious Programs—Tel: 412-941-9587.
Students 1,340.

Pitcairn, Allegheny Co., St. Michael (1895), Rev. James E. Somma.
Church—750 Wall Ave., 15140. Tel: 412-373-3400.
Res., 740 Wall Ave., 15140. Tel: 412-373-2610.

Pleasant Hills, Allegheny Co., St. Elizabeth (1942), Revs. Roy H. Conley; David Cillo; Thomas A. Wagner.
Res., Grove Pl., Pittsburgh, 15236. Tel: 412-881-7728; Fax: 412-882-8320.
School—Tel: 412-881-2958.
Lay Teachers 33; Students 684.
Catechesis/Religious Programs—Tel: 412-882-5023. D.R.E.: Kathleen Probo; Tisha Bridges.
Students 717.
Chapel of Convenience—St. David, Baldwin Boro., Pittsburgh.

Port Vue, Allegheny Co., St. Joseph. Closed. See St. Mark.
St. Mark (1993), Rev. Gerald S. Mikonis.
Administration Center: 1101 Romine Ave., 15133. Tel: 412-678-6275.; St. Joseph Worship Site: 1125 Romine Ave., 15133.
Res. & St. Eugene Worship Site—3210 Liberty Way, Liberty Borough, 15133. Tel: 412-678-6275.
School—St. Joseph Regional School. See Consolidated Schools under Institutions Located in the Diocese. Tel: 412-678-0659.
Catechesis/Religious Programs—Michelle Smith, D.R.E.
Students 243.

Prospect, Butler Co., St. Christopher (1974), Rev. Matthew Tosello.
Res., 229-232 N. Franklin St., 16052. Tel: 412-865-2430; Fax: 412-865-2430.
Catechesis/Religious Programs—Tel: 412-865-9840.
Students 135.

Rankin, Allegheny Co., Visitation of the Blessed Virgin Mary (Croatian). Closed. See Word of God, Swissvale.

Renton, Allegheny Co., St. Januarius (1950), Rev. Richard R. Ragni.
Res., 1450 Renton Rd., 15239. Tel: 412-793-4439.

Reserve Township, Allegheny Co., St. Aloysius (1892), Rev. William G. Rutledge.
Res., 3616 Mt. Troy Rd., Pittsburgh, 15212. Tel: 412-821-2351.
School—3614 Mt. Troy Rd., Pittsburgh, 15212. Tel: 412-821-5444.
Lay Teachers 10; Students 170.
Catechesis/Religious Programs—Tel: 412-821-2792.
Students 130.

Richeyville, Washington Co., St. Agnes (1994), Rev. Francis Z. Jurewicz.
Res., Box 406, 15358. Tel: 412-632-5858.

Richland Township, Allegheny Co., Saint Richard (1992), Rev. Kenneth E. Oldenski.
Res., 3841 Dickey Rd., Gibsonia, 15044. Tel: 412-444-1971; Fax: 412-444-6001.
Catechesis/Religious Programs—Students 423.

Robinson Township, Allegheny Co., Holy Trinity (Moon Run) (1944), Revs. Robert W. Herrmann; William J. Scholz. In res., Rev. John Fitzgerald.
Res., 5718 Steubenville Pike, P.O. Box 15567, Pittsburgh, 15244. Tel: 412-787-2140; 787-2143; Fax: 412-787-3799.
School—(Grades PreK-8). Tel: 412-787-2656; Fax: 412-787-9487.
Sisters of St. Francis. (Mt. Prov., Pittsburgh) 2; Lay Teachers 23; Students 429.
Catechesis/Religious Programs—Tel: 412-859-3467.
Students 420.

Rochester, Beaver Co., St. Cecilia (1856). Merged with St. Pudentiana. Revs. Ward Stakem, O.F.M.Cap.; William Gillum, O.F.M.Cap.; Marvin Justi, O.F.M.Cap.
Res., 303 Jackson St., 15074. Tel: 412-775-0801; Fax: 412-774-3056. [CEM]
Catechesis/Religious Programs—Tel: 412-775-2761.
Students 273.

Roscoe, Washington Co., St. Joseph (1904), In res., Rev. George J. Moneck, Admin.
Res., Box 486, 15477. Tel: 412-938-2324.

Ross Township, Allegheny Co., St. Sebastian (North Hills) (1952), Revs. Paul J. Bradley; Kenneth A. Sparks; Patrick C. Barkey.
Res., 311 Siebert Rd., Pittsburgh, 15237. Tel: 412-364-8999; Fax: 412-364-6330.
School—307 Siebert Rd., Pittsburgh, 15237. Tel: 412-364-7171.
Sisters 7; Lay Teachers 25; Students 503.
Catechesis/Religious Programs—Tel: 412-366-4000.
Students 460.

Russellton, Allegheny Co., Transfiguration (1916), Rev. Robert W. Habe.
Res., 15 Poma St., 15076. Tel: 412-265-1030. [CEM]
School—(Grades K-7) McKrell Rd., 15076. Tel: 412-265-3350.
Lay Teachers 8; Students 99.
Catechesis/Religious Programs—Tel: 412-265-4860.
Students 242.

Scott Township, Allegheny Co., SS. Simon and Jude (1955), Revs. Richard E. Ward; John Dinello. In res., Rev. Kris D. Stubna.
Res., 1607 Greentree Rd., Pittsburgh, 15220. Tel: 412-563-3189; Fax: 412-563-8524.
School—1625 Greentree Rd., Pittsburgh, 15220. Tel: 412-563-1353; Fax: 412-563-8617.
Lay Teachers 19; Students 344.
Catechesis/Religious Programs—Tel: 412-563-1199.
Students 285.

Our Lady of Grace (1947), Revs. Theodore A. Rutkowski; Ray A. Gualtieri; Michael Maranowski. In res., Rev. Cletus Mbarikatta, C.S.Sp.
Res., 310 Kane Blvd., Pittsburgh, 15243. Tel: 412-279-7070.
School—1734 Bower Hill Rd., Pittsburgh, 15243. Tel: 412-279-6611; Fax: 412-279-6755.
Lay Teachers 23; Students 333.
Catechesis/Religious Programs—1730 Bower Hill Rd., Pittsburgh, 15243. Tel: 412-276-0277.
Students 569.

Sewickley, Allegheny Co., St. James (1863), Revs. Raymond Rhoden; Louis F. Pascazi. In res., Rev. Harold E. Baily.
Res., 200 Walnut St., 15143. Tel: 412-741-6650; Fax: 412-741-4782. [CEM]
School—201 Broad St., 15143. Tel: 412-741-5540.
Sisters of St. Joseph 3; Lay Teachers 12; Students 220.
Catechesis/Religious Programs—Tel: 412-741-6766.
Students 220.

Sharpsburg, Allegheny Co., St. John Cantius (1906) (Polish), Rev. Andrew C. Fischer.
Res., 220 9th St., 15215. Tel: 412-781-6119; Fax: 412-781-4461.

St. Mary (1994), Rev. Thomas F. Manion.
Res., 210 Penn St., Pittsburgh, 15215. Tel: 412-781-2857; Fax: 412-781-9589. [CEM]
Catechesis/Religious Programs—Tel: 412-781-5150.
Students 136.

Madonna of Jerusalem (1904) (Italian), Rev. Andrew C. Fischer.
Res., 220 Ninth St., 15215. Tel: 412-781-6119; Fax: 412-781-4461.

Slippery Rock, Butler Co., St. Peter (1938), Rev. Donald C. Fisher.
Res., 670 S. Main St., 16057. Tel: 412-794-2880; Fax: 412-794-1255. [CEM]
Catechesis/Religious Programs—Tel: 412-794-5101.
Students 205.
Mission—Forestville, Butler Co., St. Anthony, (1908) P.O. Box 6, Forestville, 16035. Tel: 412-735-2638.

South Park Township, Allegheny Co., Nativity (1905), Rev. F. Terrence Fedigan. In res., Revs. Innocent Jooji (Nigeria); Paschal Kabura (Uganda).
Res., 5802 Curry Rd., Pittsburgh, 15236. Tel: 412-655-3000; Fax: 412-650-4658.
School—(Grades PreK-8) 5811 Curry Rd., Pittsburgh, 15236. Tel: 412-653-1500; Fax: 412-653-2619.
Lay Teachers 12; Students 154.
Catechesis/Religious Programs—Tel: 412-655-1565.
Students 354.

Springdale, Allegheny Co., St. Alphonsus (1901), Rev. George E. Saladna, S.T.L., S.S.L.
Res., 249 James St., 15144-1699. Tel: 412-274-5084; Fax: 412-274-7035.
Catechesis/Religious Programs—Tel: 412-274-2547.
Students 160.

Swissvale, Allegheny Co.,

1—St. Anselm. Closed. See Word of God.

2—Word of God, (1994) (Irish-Croatian). Consolidated from the following churches: St. Anselm, St. Barnabus and Visitation of the Blessed Virgin Mary, Rankin. Revs. Frank J. Drabiska; Paul Cwynar; Paul Henne. In res., Rev. Peter Debo (Uganda).
Res., 7446 McClure Ave., Pittsburgh, 15218. Tel: 412-241-1372; Fax: 412-241-0168.
School—7438 McClure Ave., Pittsburgh, 15218. Tel: 412-371-8587.
Sisters of Charity 3; Lay Teachers 19; Students 425.
Catechesis/Religious Programs—Tel: 412-351-0670.
Students 425.

3—Saint Barnabas, (Slovak). Closed. See Word of God.

4—Madonna del Castello, (1920) (Italian), Rev. John J. Cassella, M.Div.
Res., 2021 S. Braddock Ave., Pittsburgh, 15218. Tel: 412-271-5666; Fax: 412-271-5667.

Tarentum, Allegheny Co., Holy Martyrs (1992) (Slovak). Consolidated from St. Clement and Sacred Heart, St. Peter. Rev. Donald Chortos.
Res., 353 W. Ninth Ave., 15084. Tel: 412-224-0770; Fax: 412-224-7070. [CEM][JC 2]
Catechesis/Religious Programs—216 W. 9th Ave., 15084. Tel: 412-224-1234.
Students 275.

Sacred Heart - St. Peter. Closed. See Holy Martyrs.
St. Clement. Closed. See Holy Martyrs.

Turtle Creek, Allegheny Co., St. Colman (1882), Revs. John A. Geinzer; John W. Markell.
Res., 100 Tri-Boro Ave., 15145. Tel: 412-823-2564.
School—(Grades PreK-8) 547 Hunter St., 15145. Tel: 412-823-4871; Fax: 412-823-6326.
Sisters of Mercy of the Americas 2; Lay Teachers 14; Students 321.
Catechesis/Religious Programs—Tel: 412-823-9114.
Students 275.

Unity, Allegheny Co., St. John the Baptist (1915), Revs. Joseph M. Mele; Edward L. Yuhas; Martin F. Barkin.
Res., 444 St. John St., Pittsburgh, 15239. Tel: 412-793-4511; 793-4580; Fax: 412-793-4311. [CEM]
School—418 Unity Center Rd., Pittsburgh, 15239. Tel: 412-793-0555; Fax: 412-793-4001.
Lay Teachers 21; Students 368.
Catechesis/Religious Programs—Tel: 412-795-6376.
Students 627.

Upper St. Clair, Allegheny Co., St. John Capistran (1968), Very Rev. Robert J. Reardon.
Res., 1610 McMillan Rd., Pittsburgh, 15241. Tel: 412-221-6275; Fax: 412-257-3789.
Catechesis/Religious Programs—Tel: 412-221-5445.
Students 282.

Verona, Allegheny Co., St. Joseph (1866), Revs. Edwin J. Wichman; Trieu Ngoc Le. In res., Rev. John Ugobueze (Nigeria).
Res., 825 Second Ave., 15147-1498. Tel: 412-795-5114. [CEM]
School—Tel: 412-828-7213.
Lay Teachers 13; Students 219.
Catechesis/Religious Programs—Tel: 412-828-7715.
Students 205.

Versailles, Allegheny Co., St. Denis. Closed. See St. Patrick.

McKeesport, Allegheny Co., St. Patrick (1993). Merged with St. Denis and St. Perpetua, McKeesport. Rev. Gerald Lutz.
Res., 310 32nd St., 15132. Tel: 412-673-4110; Fax: 412-678-7259. [CEM]

Wampum, Lawrence Co., St. Monica. Closed. See Queen of Heaven, Koppel.

Washington, Washington Co., Immaculate Conception (1854), Revs. James G. Young; Frank M. Kurimsky; Kevin F. McKnight; Theodore P. Zabowski; Deacon Leon Abraham.
Res., 119 W. Chestnut St., 15301. Tel: 412-225-1425. [CEM 3]
School—111 W. Spruce St., 15301. Tel: 412-225-1680.
Lay Teachers 30; Students 500.
Catechesis/Religious Programs—135 W. Chestnut St., 15301. Tel: 412-225-0382.
Students 845.

St. Hilary (1919), Rev. Thomas D. O'Neil.
Res., 320 Henderson Ave., 15301. Tel: 412-222-4087.
Catechesis/Religious Programs—Tel: 412-222-1381.
Students 159.

Waynesburg, Greene Co., St. Ann (1839), Rev. Albin C. McGinnis.
Res., 232 E. High St., 15370. Tel: 412-627-7568. [CEM]
Catechesis/Religious Programs—Students 235.

West Aliquippa, Beaver Co., St. Joseph. Closed. See St. Titus, Aliquippa.

West Mifflin, Allegheny Co.,

1—St. Agnes, (1867), Rev. Michael J. Polak.
Res., 622 St. Agnes Ln., 15122. Tel: 412-466-2655. [CEM]
School—653 St. Agnes Ln., 15122. Tel: 412-466-6238.
Sisters of the Holy Spirit 5; Lay Teachers 8; Students 185.
Catechesis/Religious Programs—Students 286.
Convent—635 St. Agnes Ln., 15122.

2—Holy Spirit, (1963), Rev. Daniel A. Valentine.
Res., 2603 Old Elizabeth Rd., 15122-2598. Tel: 412-466-5048; Fax: 412-466-4983.
Catechesis/Religious Programs—Tel: 412-466-1264.
Students 387.

3—Holy Trinity, (1901) (Slovak), Rev. Edward P. Bunchek.
Res., 529 Grant Ave. Ext., 15122. Tel: 412-466-6545. [CEM]
School—Duquesne Consolidated Schools. See separate listing.

4—Resurrection, (1936), Rev. Robert G. Turner.
Res., 3909 Donna Ave., 15122. Tel: 412-461-8087.
School—James LaVelle, One Majka Dr., 15122. Tel: 412-462-4344; Fax: 412-461-1230.
Lay Teachers 11; Students 225.
Catechesis/Religious Programs—Tel: 412-461-4049.
Students 190.

West Pittsburg, Lawrence Co., Holy Cross. Closed. See St. Vincent de Paul, New Castle.

West Sunbury, Butler Co., St. Louis. Closed. See St. Alphonsus, Boyers.

West View, Allegheny Co., St. Athanasius (1905), Revs. Robert A. Norton; James M. Bachner. In res., Rev. Edward F. McSweeney.
Res., 7 Chalfonte Ave., Pittsburgh, 15229. Tel: 412-931-4624; Fax: 412-939-3516.
School—2 Wentworth Ave., Pittsburgh, 15229. Tel: 412-931-6633. Ms. Gabrielle Yingling, Prin.
Lay Teachers 13; Students 164.
Catechesis/Religious Programs—Tel: 412-931-3670. Mary Mercer, D.R.E.
Students 439.

Wexford, Allegheny Co., St. Alexis (1961), Rev. Steven Palsa. In res., Rev. Harry F. Petrie.
Res., 10090 Old Perry Hwy., 15090. Tel: 412-935-4343; Fax: 412-935-1270.
School—(Grades PreK-5). Tel: 412-935-3190.
Lay Teachers 15; Students 310.
Catechesis/Religious Programs—Tel: 412-935-0877.
Students 450.

St. Alphonsus (1840) (German), Revs. William H. Schroeder; Richard J. Thompson.
Res., 201 Church Rd., 15090. Tel: 412-935-1151; Fax: 412-934-3877. [CEM][JC]
School—Tel: 412-935-1152.
Sisters of the Holy Spirit 1; Lay Teachers 19; Students 530.
Catechesis/Religious Programs—Fax: 412-934-3788.
Students 360.

Whitehall, Allegheny Co., St. Gabriel of the Sorrowful Virgin (1944), Revs. John R. Haney; Alan E. Morris. In res., Rev. Thomas F. Carey.
Res., 5200 Greenridge Dr., Pittsburgh, 15236. Tel: 412-881-8115; 881-8117.
School—Tel: 412-882-3353.
Sisters 1; Lay Teachers 23; Students 578.
Catechesis/Religious Programs—Tel: 412-881-7950.
Students 476.

White Oak Boro, Allegheny Co., St. Angela (1958), Rev. Stephen M. Chervenak; Sr. Patricia Marie Buranosky, O.S.F., Pastoral Assoc.
Res., 1732 Fawcett Ave., White Oak, 15131. Tel: 412-672-2365.
School—1640R Fawcett Ave., White Oak, 15131. Tel: 412-672-2360; Fax: 412-672-0880.
Lay Teachers 14; Students 290.
Catechesis/Religious Programs—Tel: 412-672-0913.
Students 270.

Wildwood, Allegheny Co., St. Catherine of Sweden (1953), Revs. Regis M. Farmer; Miroslaw; Margaret A. Kirchner, M.S., Parish Mgr. In res., Rev. Gregory Swiderski.
Res., 2308 W. Hardies Rd., 15091. Tel: 412-443-2087; 961-0399; 443-5876; Fax: 412-443-3633.
Catechesis/Religious Programs—Students 836.

Wilkinsburg, Allegheny Co., St. James (1869), Rev. Warren W. Metzler.
Res., 718 Franklin Ave., Pittsburgh, 15221. Tel: 412-241-1392; Fax: 412-241-6625.
School—721 Rebecca Ave., Pittsburgh, 15221. Tel: 412-242-3515.
Lay Teachers 19; Students 247.

Wilmerding, Allegheny Co., St. Jude the Apostle (1994). Consolidated from St. Aloysius and St. Leocadia. Rev. John J. O'Malley.
Res., 405 Westinghouse Ave., 15148. Tel: 412-823-8390; 823-1117. [CEM]
St. Leocadia (Polish). Closed. See St. Jude the Apostle.

Wireton, Allegheny Co., St. Catherine of Siena (1911), Rev. John R. Huber.
Res., 20 McGovern Blvd., 15001. Tel: 412-457-7026.
Catechesis/Religious Programs—Tel: 412-457-0106.
Students 251.

Zelienople, Butler Co., St. Gregory (1906), Rev. Charles B. Bergman.
Res., 2 W. Beaver St., 16063. Tel: 412-452-7245; Fax: 412-452-4064. [CEM]
School—115 Pine St., 16063. Tel: 412-452-9731.
Lay Teachers 8; Students 150.
Catechesis/Religious Programs—Students 280.

Chaplains of Public Institutions

ALLEGHENY COUNTY. *Auberle Home* Tel: 412-462-6866.
Depaul Institution Tel: 412-561-4848. Rev. Richard L. Conboy Tel: 412-299-7846.
East Liberty Family Health Care Center Tel: 412-661-2802.
Gateway Rehab Tel: 412-766-8700.
Holy Family Institute Tel: 412-734-2887.
Robinson Development Center Tel: 412-771-0232.
St. Anthony Home for Exceptional Children Tel: 412-882-1333.
St. Joseph House of Hospitality Tel: 412-471-0666.
Seneca Hills Village. Attended by St. Bartholomew Parish, Tel: 412-242-3343. Tel: 412-793-1700.
South Hills Family Hospice Tel: 412-561-4900.

BEAVER COUNTY. *McGuire Memorial Home* Tel: 412-843-3400. Rev. Regis Alberth Tel: 412-775-4111.

BUTLER COUNTY. *The United Presbyterian Home for Children* Tel: 412-625-3141. Rev. Arthur Merrell Tel: 412-363-4143.

WASHINGTON COUNTY. *Western Center* Tel: 412-873-3274. Rev. Ladis J. Cizik Tel: 412-941-4360.

Hospitals

ALLEGHENY COUNTY. *AUMC Forbes Metro*. Attended by St. James, Wilkinsburg. Tel:412-241-1392.
AUMC Forbes Regional. Sr. Monique Dietz, L.B. Tel: 412-781-4022; Rev. James E. Somma Tel: 412-373-2610.
AUMC/University Medical Centers - Allegheny Valley Hospital. Attended by Our Lady of the Most Blessed Sacrament, Natrona Heights. Tel:412-226-4900.
Children's Hospital Tel: 412-647-5326. Sr. Nora Egan Tel: 412-372-6758.
Jefferson Hospital Tel: 412-469-5000. Rev. Robert Kohuch Tel: 412-384-4406.
Magee-Women's Hospital Tel: 412-647-1000. Sr. Nora Egan, C.S.J. Tel: 412-372-6758.
McKeesport Hospital Tel: 412-664-2000. Rev. John M. Elanjileth (ROM) Tel: 412-673-5552.
Mercy Health System of Pittsburgh Tel: 412-232-8111. Revs. Alan S. Evans Tel: 412-232-7512; Richard S. Jones Tel: 412-232-8047.
Mercy Providence Hospital Tel: 412-323-5600. Rev. Robert Mellott Tel: 412-931-0173.
Ohio Valley General Hospital Tel: 412-777-6161. Rev. Regis J. Ryan Tel: 412-771-5646.
St. Clair Memorial Hospital. Attended by Our Lady of Grace, Pittsburgh. Tel:412-279-7070; 412-561-4900.
St. Francis Central Hospital Tel: 412-562-3000. Rev. John Walsh Tel: 412-471-0654.
St. Francis Medical Center Tel: 412-622-4343. Revs. Robert Craig, O.F.M.Cap. Tel: 412-682-6103; Bonaventure Stefun, O.F.M.Cap. Tel: 412-471-4390; Sr. Mary Joseph Trimbur, O.S.F. Tel: 412-622-4741.
Sewickley Valley Hospital Tel: 412-741-6000. Rev. Harold E. Baily Tel: 412-741-8836.
Suburban General Hospital. Attended by Assumption of the Blessed Virgin Mary on the Beautiful River, Bellevue. Tel:412-766-6660 Tel: 412-734-6000.
University of the Health Science - Allegheny General Campus. Revs. Frank A. Mitolo Tel: 412-359-4269; Charles L. Christen, Asst. Chap., Tel: 412-359-3131.
UPMC Braddock Tel: 412-636-5000. Rev. Joseph D. Karabin Tel: 412-271-1515.
UPMC Passavant Hospital Tel: 412-367-6700. Rev. W. Peter Horton Tel: 412-366-9256; Sr. Caritas Marshall, C.S.J. Tel: 412-364-5938.
UPMC Shadyside Hospital Tel: 412-623-2121. Revs. Edward L. Hoffman Tel: 412-621-5679; Gilbert Puznakoski Tel: 412-621-5679.
UPMC Southside Hospital Tel: 412-488-5550. Rev. John Walsh Tel: 412-471-0654.
UPMC St. Margaret Hospital Tel: 412-784-4000. Rev. Thomas M. Kirby Tel: 412-826-9048.
UPMC University of Pittsburgh Medical Center Tel: 412-647-2020. Revs. Samuel J. Esposito Tel: 412-621-5679; Patrick George, T.O.R.; Michael McDermott Tel: 412-621-0364; Carlo Napoli, T.O.R. Tel: 412-782-4755; Richard Terdine Tel: 412-621-5679; Sr. Mary Kay Hamond, C.S.J. Tel: 412-882-7593.
West Penn Hospital Tel: 412-578-5000. Revs. Edward L. Hoffman Tel: 412-621-5679; John M. Jordan Tel: 412-621-5679.

BEAVER COUNTY. *The Medical Center Beaver* Tel: 412-728-7000. Revs. Marvin Justi, O.F.M.Cap. Tel: 412-774-6046; Kenneth Myers Tel: 412-843-7375.
UPMC Beaver. Attended by St. Titus, Aliquippa. Tel:412-378-8561 Tel: 412-875-1212.

BUTLER COUNTY. *Butler Memorial Hospital* Tel: 412-283-6666. Sr. Mary Sheehan, I.H.M. Tel: 412-283-2640.

GREENE COUNTY. *Greene County Memorial*. Attended by St. Ann, Waynesburg. Tel:412-627-7568 Tel: 412-627-3101.

LAWRENCE COUNTY. *Ellwood City Hospital*. Attended by St. Agatha, Ellwood City. Tel:412-758-7587 Tel: 412-752-0081.
Jameson Memorial Hospital Tel: 412-658-9001. Rev. Frank G. Erdeljac Tel: 412-535-4786.
St. Francis Hospital Tel: 412-658-3511. Rev. Frank Erdeljac Tel: 412-535-4786.

WASHINGTON COUNTY. *Canonsburg Hospital* Tel: 412-745-6100. Rev. Ladis J. Cizik Tel: 412-941-4360.
Mon Valley Hospital. Attended by Transfiguration, Monongahela. Tel:412-258-7742 Tel: 412-258-2000.
Washington Hospital. Attended by Immaculate Conception, Washington. Tel:412-225-1425 Tel: 412-225-7000.

Veterans Administration Hospitals

ALLEGHENY COUNTY. *Department of Veterans Affairs Medical Center Aspinwall* Tel: 412-688-6000, Ext. 6729. Revs. Ralph Zehe, O.F.M.Cap. Tel: 412-682-0929; Emitt Schuler, O.F.M.Cap. Tel: 412-531-4545.
Department of Veterans Affairs Medical Center Oakland Tel: 412-683-3000. Revs. Ralph Zehe, O.F.M.Cap. Tel: 412-682-6430; Mark W. Glasgow Tel: 412-461-1054; Emitt Schuler, O.F.M.Cap. Tel: 412-531-4545.

BUTLER COUNTY. *Department of Veterans Affairs- Deshon Hospital* Tel: 412-287-4781. Rev. William J. Ritzert Tel: 412-538-5331.

Rehabilitation, Nursing and Geriatric Care Facilities

ALLEGHENY COUNTY. *Asbury Heights*. Attended by St. Bernards. Tel:412-561-3300 Tel: 412-341-1030.
Atrium I Nursing Research and Rehabilitation Center Tel: 412-787-2483. Rev. George Leech.
Baldwin Health Care. Attended by St. Elizabeth of Hungary, Pittsburgh. Tel:412-882-8744 Tel: 412-885-8400.
Beverly Manor of Monroeville. Attended by North American Martyrs, Monroeville. Tel: 412-373-0330; 856-7570.
Collins Nursing Center Tel: 412-661-1740. Rev. George T. Leech Tel: 412-922-6300.
DT Watson Rehab Hospital. Attended by St. James, Sewickley. Tel:412-741-6650 Tel: 412-741-9000.
Forbes Nursing Center Tel: 412-665-3232. Rev. Joseph C. Beck Tel: 412-661-7222.
Greater Pittsburgh Rehab Hospital Tel: 412-856-2400. Rev. Joseph Beck Tel: 412-661-7222.
Healthsound Harmarville Rehabilitation Hospital Tel: 412-781-5700. Rev. Thomas Kirby Tel: 412-826-9048.
Heartland Health Care Center Tel: 412-665-2400. Rev. George T. Leech Tel: 412-922-6300.
Heritage Shadyside. Attended by Sacred Heart, Pittsburgh. Tel:412-661-0187 Tel: 412-422-5100.
Independence Court of Mt. Lebanon. Attended by St. Ann, Castle Shannon, Tel:412-531-5964 and St. Thomas More, Bethel Park, Tel:412-883-0031; 341-4400.
Independent Court of Monroeville Tel: 412-373-3030. Rev. Joseph Beck Tel: 412-661-7222.
James P. Wall Home for the Aged Tel: 412-761-5373. Rev. Jerome Dixon Tel: 412-3033.
Kane Regional Center - Glen Hazel Tel: 412-422-6800. Rev. Joseph C. Beck Tel: 412-661-7222; Sr. Donna Marie Mulligan, S.C. Tel: 412-461-0968.
Kane Regional Center - McKeesport Tel: 412-675-8600. Rev. Kenan Crowley, O.F.M.Cap. Tel: 412-682-6888.
Kane Regional Center - Ross Tel: 412-369-2000. Rev. Ernest Strzelinski Tel: 412-486-6700.
Kane Regional Center - Scott Tel: 412-429-3000. Rev. Richard L. Conboy, S.T.L. Tel: 412-429-3040.
Manorcare Health Services Greentree Rd., Tel: 412-344-7744. Rev. Thomas F. Carey Tel: 412-881-8115.
Manorcare Health Services McMurray Rd., Tel: 412-941-3080. Margaret Reismeyer.
Manorcare Health Services Highland Dr., Tel: 412-831-6050. Rev. Thomas F. Carey Tel: 412-881-8115.
Manorcare Health Services Perry Hwy., Tel: 412-369-9955. Rev. Joseph Beck Tel: 412-661-7222.
Manorcare Health Services. Attended by North American Martyrs, Monroeville. Tel: 412-373-0330; 856-7071.
Marian Manor, Inc Tel: 412-563-6866. Rev. Henry Szarnicki Tel: 412-563-2011.
Mt. Lebanon Manor Convalescent Center Tel: 412-257-4444. Rev. Thomas F. Carey Tel: 412-881-8115.
Oakmont Nursing Center. Attended by St. Irenaeus, Oakmont. Tel: 412-828-3085; 828-7300.
Presbyterian Seniorcare Westminister Place. Attended by St. Irenaeus, Oakmont. Tel:412-828-3065; 826-6088.
Regency Hall Nursing Home Tel: 412-366-8540. Revs. Gregory Swiderski Tel: 412-449-2536; David Dixon, Asst., Tel: 412-928-0825.
Rehabilitation Institute of Pittsburgh. Attended by St. Bede, Pittsburgh. Tel:412-661-7222; 521-9000.
Ridgepoint. Attended by Nativity, South Park Twp. Tel:412-655-3000; 653-6870.
Riverview Center for Jewish Seniors. Attended by St. Rosalia, Pittsburgh. Tel:412-421-5766; 521-5900.
St. Joseph Nursing and Health Care Center Tel: 412-665-5100. Rev. George Leech Tel: 412-922-6300.
St. Margaret Senca Place. Attended by St. Bartholomew, Penn Hills. Tel:412-242-3374; 798-8000.
Shadyside Nursing and Rehabilitation Center Tel: 412-362-3500. Rev. George Leech Tel: 412-922-6300.
Southwestern Nursing and Rehabilitation Center Tel: 412-466-0600, Ext. 5989. Rev. Thomas F. Carey Tel: 412-881-8115.
UPMC Canterbury Place. Attended by Our Lady of the Angels, Pittsburgh. Tel: 412-682-0929; 622-9000.
Vincentian Home for the Chronically Ill Tel: 412-366-5600. Revs. Gregory Swiderski Tel: 412-449-2536; David Dixon, Asst., Tel: 412-928-0825.
Woodhaven Convalescent Center Tel: 412-856-4770. Rev. Joseph C. Beck Tel: 412-661-7222.

BEAVER COUNTY. *Beaver Valley Geriatric Center* Tel: 412-775-7100. Revs. Paul J. Savage Tel: 412-846-4585; Kenneth E. Myers Tel: 412-843-7375.

BUTLER COUNTY. *Sunnyview Home* Tel: 412-282-1800. Sr. Mary Sheehan, I.H.M. Tel: 412-283-2640.

GREENE COUNTY. *Curry Memorial Home*. Attended by St. Ann, Waynesburg. Tel:412-627-7568; 627-3153.
Franklin Care Center. Attended by St. Ann, Waynesburg. Tel:412-627-7568; 852-2020.

LAWRENCE COUNTY. *Almira Home* Tel: 412-652-4131. Rev. Francis C. Graff Tel: 412-652-9471.
Belvedere Residence, Inc Tel: 412-924-2191. Rev. Francis C. Graff Tel: 412-652-9471.
Castle Manor Tel: 412-654-4377. Rev. Francis C. Graff Tel: 412-652-9471.
Cedar Manor Tel: 412-654-8050. Rev. Francis C. Graff Tel: 412-652-9471.
Golden Hill Nursing, Inc Tel: 412-654-7791. Rev. Francis C. Graff Tel: 412-652-9471.
Haven Convalescent Home Tel: 412-654-8833. Rev. Francis C. Graff Tel: 412-652-9471.
Highland Hall Care Center Tel: 412-658-4781. Rev. Francis C. Graff Tel: 412-652-9471.
Hill View Manor Tel: 412-658-1521. Rev. Francis C. Graff Tel: 412-652-9471.
Indian Creek Nursing Center Tel: 412-653-6340. Rev. Francis C. Graff Tel: 412-652-9471.
Jack Rees Nursing and Rehabilitation Services Tel: 412-652-3863. Rev. Francis C. Graff Tel: 412-652-9472.
Majors Manor Tel: 412-924-9568. Rev. Francis C. Graff Tel: 412-652-9471.
Overlook Nursing Home Tel: 412-946-3511. Rev. Francis C. Graff Tel: 412-652-9471.
Shenango United Presbyterian Home Tel: 412-946-3516. Rev. Francis C. Graff Tel: 412-652-9471.
Silver Oak Nursing Tel: 412-652-3863. Rev. Francis C. Graff Tel: 412-652-9471.

WASHINGTON COUNTY. *Canon House* Tel: 412-745-7771. Rev. Ladis Cizik Tel: 412-941-4360.
Charles House Home for the Aged Tel: 412-745-6355. Rev. Ladis Cizik Tel: 412-941-4360.
Greenery Nursing Home Tel: 412-745-8000. Rev. Ladis Cizik Tel: 412-941-4360.
Horizon Senior Care Tel: 412-746-5040. Rev. Ladis Cizik Tel: 412-941-4360.
Pine Lawn Home Tel: 412-746-1460. Rev. Ladis Cizik Tel: 412-941-4360.
Rest Haven Personal Care Home I Tel: 412-745-3333. Rev. Ladis Cizik Tel: 412-941-4360.
Rest Haven Personal Care Home II Tel: 412-746-3233. Rev. Ladis Cizik Tel: 412-941-4360.
Rest Haven Personal Care Home V Tel: 412-746-4666. Rev. Ladis Cizik Tel: 412-941-4360.

South Hills Convalescent Center Tel: 412-746-1300. Rev. Ladis Cizik Tel: 412-941-4360.

Mental Health Facilities

ALLEGHENY COUNTY. *Mayview State Hospital* Tel: 412-257-6500. Rev. George T. DeVille Tel: 412-221-5213.
Western Psychiatric Hospital. UPMC Chaplains. Tel:412-647-9071; 624-2100.

WASHINGTON COUNTY. *New Life Treatment Center* Tel: 412-746-2400. Rev. Ladis Cizik Tel: 412-941-4360.

Correctional Institutions

ALLEGHENY COUNTY. *Allegheny County Jail* Tel: 412-350-2000. Revs. Robert Schweitzer Tel: 412-761-1507; Arthur R. Merrell Tel: 412-363-4143.
Shuman Center Tel: 412-661-6806. Rev. Arthur R. Merrell Tel: 412-363-4143.

BEAVER COUNTY. *Beaver County Jail*. Rev. Msgr. Raymond T. Schultz Tel: 412-775-4111.

BUTLER COUNTY. *Butler County Jail*. Rev. Hugh M. Gloninger Tel: 412-287-1759.

GREEN COUNTY. *State Correctional Institute at Green* Tel: 412-852-2902. Rev. George Moneck Tel: 412-938-2324.
State Correctional Institution at Waynesburg (Women's Facility) Tel: 412-627-6185. Rev. Albin C. McGinnis Tel: 412-627-7568; Sr. Yvonne Dursh, O.S.F. Tel: 412-882-3470.
Waynesburg County Jail Tel: 412-627-7780. Rev. Albin C. McGinnis Tel: 412-627-7568.

LAWRENCE COUNTY. *Lawrence County Jail* Tel: 412-654-5384. Rev. James A. Downs Tel: 412-667-7737.
Youth Development Center Tel: 412-656-7300. Rev. Joseph McCaffrey Tel: 412-964-8276; Sr. Noreen Sterns, H.M.

WASHINGTON COUNTY. *Washington County Jail*. Attended by Immaculate Conception, Washington. Tel:412-225-1425; 561-7557.

On Duty Outside the Diocese:
Reverend Fathers—
Arnott, John J., P.O. Box 129, Cambridge, VT 05444
Bleichner, Howard P., Theological College of Catholic Univ., 401 Michigan Ave. N.E., Washington, DC 20017
Cellini, Ronald R., St. Peter Parish, 70 Lady's Island Dr., Beauford, SC 29901
Connolly, Brian W., 2444 Matson Rd., Apt. 911, Cincinnati, OH 45208
Fay, William J., St. Vincent Seminary, Frasier Purchase Rd., Latrobe, PA 15650
Friday, Robert M., Catholic Univ., 620 Michigan Ave., N.E., Washington, DC 20064-0001
Hebda, Bernard A., Palazzo Delle Congregazioni, Piazza pio XII, 00120 Citta' del Vaticano
Johnson, David R., Immaculate Conception, P.O. 1609, Denham Springs, LA 70726
Lauer, Eugene F., Univ. of Notre Dame, 1201 Hesburgh Library, Notre Dame, IN 46556
Mazurek, James K., SS. Cyril & Methodius Seminary, Orchard Lake, MI 48324
Mueller, Richard J., Epiphany Cathedral, 310 Sarasota St., Venice, FL 34285
Ogrodowski, William M., North American College, 00120 Vatican City State, Rome, Italy
Paone, Ernest C., 1556 Glacier Rd., Oceanside, CA 92054
Roos, H. Jules, Centro de Obras Sociales, Apartado 473, Chimbote, Peru
Taylor, Augustus R., Jr., 1812 W. 48th St., Los Angeles, CA 90062

Graduate Studies:
Reverend Fathers—
Maurer, Daniel J., North American College, 00120 Vatian City State, Europe
Welding, Brian J., North American College, 00120 Vatican City State, Europe

---

Military Chaplains:
Reverend Fathers—
Brzek, Jon J., P.O. Box 8026, Camp Lejeune, NC 28547-8026
Dansak, Thomas E., MCAS, Chaplain's Office, PSC. Box 8033, Cherry Point, NC 28533
Fix, Donald P., USS Tarawa, LHA-1, FPO-AP, 96622-1600
Hennessy, Joseph P., 7WG/HC, 158 Ave. B, Dyess AFB, TX 79607-1458
Laboon, Joseph D., VA Medical Center, 1601 Perdido St., New Orleans, LA 70146
Lamonde, Joseph R., Commarforpac, Box 64105, Camp Smith, HI 96861
Malinsky, Gregory J., 24 Wing-HC (ACC), Howard AFB, APOAE, 34001-5000 (Panama)
Sagala, James F., Veterans Administration Medical Center, Tremont Ave., East Orange, NJ 07019
Valko, Robert A., CHC USNR, LCDR, Office of the Wing Chap., 2nd MAW, Cherry Point, NC 28533
Yagesh, Richard C., DPTNAVSCI USMERMARCAD, Kings Point, NY 11024-1699

Absent on Sick Leave:
Reverend Fathers—
Patriquin, Garry D.
Rager, Patrick F.

Retired:
Reverend Monsignors—
Darkowski, Leon S., 235 The Boulevard, Pittsburgh, PA 15210
Dravecky, Michael A., 1471 Guffey Rd., North Huntingdon, PA 15642
Findlan, Joseph G., St. John Vianney Manor, 2600 Morange Rd., Pittsburgh, PA 15205
Gearing, Daniel A., St. Albert the Great, 3171 Church Ave., Pittsburgh, PA 15227
Glenn, Francis A., St. Mary of Mercy, 202 Stanwix St., Pittsburgh, PA 15222
Keefer, Oliver D., Cardinal Dearden Ctr., 4721 5th Ave., Pittsburgh, PA 15213-2915
Lackner, Paul M., Cardinal Dearden Center, 4721 Fifth Ave., Pittsburgh, PA 15213-2915
McCarren, John C., St. Ursula, 3937 Kirk Ave., Allison Park, PA 15101-3691
Meenan, Joseph S., Cloverleaf Estates W, 494 Canterbury Cir., Carnegie, PA 15106
Rice, Charles O., St. Anne Church, 400 Hoodridge Dr., Pittsburgh, PA 15234-1794
Rooney, Francis J., Marian Manor Nursing Home, 2695 Winchester Dr., Pittsburgh, PA 15220-4099
Seli, John J., Cape Hacienda #202, 6655 Ridgewood Ave., Cocoa Beach, FL 32931
Sojka, Ferdinand M., St. John Vianney Manor, 2600 Morange Rd., Pittsburgh, PA 15205
Reverend Fathers—
Beck, Leo J., St. John Vianney Manor, 2600 Morange Rd., Pittsburgh, PA 15205
Biondi, Nicholas A., St. John Vianney Manor, 2600 Morange Rd., Pittsburgh, PA 15205
Blough, William G., 421 Washington Ave., Oakmont, PA 15139
Bolvary, Paul L., Pe'cs Berfseuy'u.16, F632, Hungary
Burchianti, Leo R., St. John Vianney Manor, 2600 Morange Rd., Pittsburgh, PA 15205
Carey, Thomas F., St. Gabriel Sorrowful Virgin, 5200 Greenridge Dr., Pittsburgh, PA 15236
Cercone, Raymond A., c/o R.D. 3, Box 46, Eighty Four, PA 15330-9712
Charnoki, John J., St. Raphael, 1118 Chislett St., Pittsburgh, PA 15206-1304
Conner, Glenn T., St. John Vianney Manor, 2600 Morange Rd., Pittsburgh, PA 15205
Cvelbar, Joseph, St John Vianney Manor, 2600 Morange Rd., Pittsburgh, PA 15205
Deblasio, Dominck A., 605 Market St., Freeport, PA 16229
Dismachek, Francis M., St. John Vianney Manor, 2600 Morange Rd., Pittsburgh, PA 15205
Dompka, John A., 1150 Tranter, Green Tree, PA 15220
Filip, Francis B., Vincentian Home, Perrymont Rd., Pittsburgh, PA 15237
Fording, John D., St. John Vianney Manor, 2600 Morange Rd., Pittsburgh, PA 15205
Gelati, Dario, Via Vela, 46030 Sustinente (MN), Italy
Getty, Roy G., Cardinal Dearden Center, 4721 Fifth Ave., Pittsburgh, PA 15213-2915
Gibson, John W., 12 Lawrence St., P.O. Box 252, Lawrence, PA 15055
Girdis, Joseph C., St. Therese, 1 St. Therese Ct., Munhall, PA 15120
Goralka, Albert A., 301 W. Ninth Ave., Tarentum, PA 15084
Griffith, John O., R.D. No. 2, Box S-27, McDonald, PA 15057
Gubanich, Michael T., 106 S. Pine St., Ellsworth, PA 15331
Henry, Leo G., St. John Vianney Manor, 2600 Morange Rd., Pittsburg, PA 15205
Holzer, Paul A., Immaculate Conception & St. Joseph, c/o 4712 Liberty Ave., Pittsburgh, PA 15224-1794
Horner, Thomas J., St. John Vianney Manor, 2600 Morange Rd., Pittsburgh, PA 15205
Hutnik, William J., Cardinal Dearden Center, 4721 Fifth Ave., Pittsburgh, PA 15213-2915
Jackovic, George V., 124 Bennington Dr., Canonsburg, PA 15317
Jones, Patrick F., St. Jude the Apostle, 405 Westinghouse Ave., Wilmerding, PA 15148-1123
Jozwiak, Stanislaus J., 2103 Fawcett Ave., White Oak, PA 15131-1819
Kato, Stephen M., St. Stephen Rectory, 2125 Beacon St., McKeesport, PA 15132
Kernan, Michael H., Cardinal Dearden Center, 4721 Fifth Ave., Pittsburg, PA 15213-2915
Kilarecki, George W., Vincentian Home, Perrymont Rd., Pittsburgh, PA 15237
Klein, John P., Vincentian Home, Perrymont Rd., Pittsburgh, PA 15237
Kopecky, Joseph A., 1503 Sylvan Ave., Natrona Heights, PA 15065-1642
Kuczynski, Francis I., Vincentian Home, Perrymont Rd., Pittsburgh, PA 15237
Kuenzig, Aloysius A., 2715 Custer Ave., Pittsburgh, PA 15227
Kuenzig, Peter A., 2715 Custer Ave., Pittsburgh, PA 15227
Lackner, Francis J.X., St. Bernard, 311 Washington Rd., Pittsburgh, PA 15216
Luteri, Evaristo, St. John Vianney Manor, 2600 Morange Rd., Pittsburgh, PA 15205
Majda, Francis A., 1809 Hanna St., New Castle, PA 16101
Maliszewski, Edward C., P.O. Box 1075, Monroeville, PA 15146-1075
Marconyak, Albert J., Little Sisters of the Poor, 1028 Benton Ave., Pittsburgh, PA 15212
Massung, Francis G., St. John Vianney Manor, 2600 Morange Rd., Pittsburgh, PA 15205
Mastrangelo, Joseph A., 1111 S. Mercer St., New Castle, PA 16101
McColligan, Raymond A., 98 S.W. 15th Ct., Boynton Beach, FL 33426
McIlvane, Donald W., 5700 Bunkerhill St., Apt. 1005, Pittsburgh, PA 15206-1166
McSweeney, Edward F., St. Athanasius, 7 Chalfonte Ave., Pittsburgh, PA 15229-1824
Michaels, John L., St. John Vianney Manor, 2600 Morange Rd., Pittsburgh, PA 15205
Miller, Joseph W., Vincentian Home, Perrymont Rd., Pittsburgh, PA 15237
Molnar, Richard L., 237 E. Eugene St., Munhall, PA 15120
Murphy, Thomas R., 6346 Walnut St., Pittsburgh, PA 15206
Nee, Thomas M., St. John Vianney Manor, 2600 Morange Rd., Pittsburgh, PA 15205
O'Brien, Bernard P., 2217 Los Angeles Ave., Pittsburgh, PA 15216
O'Brien, John, Cardinal Dearden Center, 4721 Fifth Ave., Pittsburgh, PA 15213-2915
O'Connell, Thomas C., Vincentian Home, Perrymont Rd., Pittsburgh, PA 15237
Palko, John A., St. Martin de Porres, c/o 705 Shaw Ave., McKeesport, PA 15132-2334
Paluse, Richard V., 37 Forsythe Rd., Pittsburgh, PA 15220
Parme, George J., Villa St. Joseph, 1030 State St., Baden, PA 15005
Petrie, Harry F., St. Alexis, 10090 Old Perry Hwy., Wexford, PA 15090-9320
Pietrzynski, Boleslaus J., Vincentian Home, Perrymont Rd., Pittsburgh, PA 15237
Plantes, Francis P., St. John Vianney Manor, 2600Morange Rd., Pittsburgh, PA 15205
Pucci, Francis L., Sisters of Divine Redeemer, 999 Rock Run Rd., Elizabeth, PA 15037
Roach, Charles B., 8990 E. Washington St., Chagrin Falls, OH 44023
Rodgers, Francis M., St. John Vianney Manor, 2600 Morange Rd., Pittsburgh, PA 15205
Rodgers, Thomas M., Cardinal Dearden Center, 4721 Fifth Ave., Pittsburgh, PA 15213-2915
Scanlon, John J., 1337 Fifth Ave., North Versailles, PA 15137
Schirra, Peter M., 421 Marsh Hill Rd., McHenry, MD 21541
Sedlak, Valentine G., Cardinal Dearden Center, 4721 Fifth Ave., Pittsburgh, PA 15213-2915
Smith, Thomas E., 621 Swallow Dr., Casselberry, FL 32707
Soisson, Clifford F., St. John Vianney Manor, 2600 Morange Rd., Pittsburgh, PA 15205
Stuparitz, George P., St. John Vianney Manor, 2600 Morange Rd., Pittsburgh, PA 15205
Szarnicki, Zygmunt V., St. John Vianney Manor, 2600 Morange Rd., Pittsburgh, PA 15205
Turlik, Andrew J., St. John Vianney Manor, 2600 Morange Rd., Pittsburgh, PA 15205
Unger, John M., St. John Vianney Manor, 2600 Morange Rd., Pittsburgh, PA 15205
Vecchio, Michael J., 502 Sewickley Heights Dr., Sewickley, PA 15143
Vollmer, Raymond A., 148 Monastery Ave., Pittsburgh, PA 15203-1432
Weirauch, William P., 181 44th St., Pittsburgh, PA 15201
Wichmanowski, Walter F., St. John Vianney Manor, 2600 Morange Rd., Pittsburgh, PA 15205
Zolnierzak, Stanislaus J., St. John Vianney Manor, 2600 Morange Rd., Pittsburgh, PA 15205

Permanent Deacons:
Abraham, Leon B., Immaculate Conception, Washington
Bane, John J., St. Bernard, Mount Lebanon
Barth, Robert V., Catholic Cemeteries

Becker, Robert J., St. Albert the Great, Baldwin Boro
Brabender, Herbert C., Allegheny General Hospital
Cunningham, Regis C., North American Martyrs, Monroeville
Giconi, Mario W.
Gleason, Kenneth V., The Intersection, McKeesport
Hathaway, Ralph B., St. Bernard, Mount Lebanon
Layton, John, St. Benedict the Abbot, Peters Township
McKelvey, Albert T.
Meyer, Joseph C., St. Patrick, Canonsburg
Mueller, Joseph R., St. Sylvester, Brentwood
O'Keefe, Charles L., Little Sisters of the Poor
Rice, Raymond C., St. Paul, Butler
Rubio-Roman, Silverio, St. Victor, Bairdford
Schaefer, Jerome R., St. Fidelis, Meridian/Lyndora
Schaffner, Thomas A., St. Fidelis, Meridian/Lyndora
Stein, Gerald C., St. Paul, Butler
Very, Richard, Resurrection, Brookline
Walsh, John, St. Ferdinand, Cranberry Twp.

INSTITUTIONS LOCATED IN THE DIOCESE

[A] SEMINARIES, RELIGIOUS OR SCHOLASTICATES

PITTSBURGH. *Saint Paul Seminary*, College & Pre-Theology, 2900 Noblestown Rd., 15205. Tel: 412-921-5800. Revs. Edward J. Burns, Rector; Robert P. Connolly, Vice Rector & Dir. Spiritual Formation; Sr. Judith Worden, R.S.M., Coord. Apostolic Works; Sr. Ignatius Rooney, R.S.M., Admin. Asst. to the Rector. Priests 2; Sisters 2; Students (attending Duquesne University) 11.

[B] COLLEGES AND UNIVERSITIES

PITTSBURGH. *Carlow College*, 3333 5th Ave., 15213. Tel: 412-578-6000
For a complete listing, refer to the Colleges and Universities section.

Duquesne University of the Holy Ghost, 600 Forbes Ave., 15282. Tel: 412-396-6000; Fax: 412-396-5785
For a complete listing, refer to the Colleges and Universities section.

La Roche College, 9000 Babcock Blvd., 15237. Tel: 412-367-9300
For a complete listing, refer to the Colleges and Universities section.

[C] HIGH SCHOOLS, DIOCESAN

PITTSBURGH. *Canevin Catholic High School*, 2700 Morange Rd., 15205. Tel: 412-922-7400.
E-mail: canevinhs@canevin.k12.pa.us
Mr. John Maurer, Headmaster; Rev. Alvin J. Adams, Chap. Priests 2; Sisters 1; Lay Teachers 35; Students 537.

Central District Catholic High School. (Boys), 4720 Fifth Ave., 15213. Tel: 412-621-8189; Fax: 412-631-0758. The school is a Diocesan institution under the care of the Christian Brothers. Bro. Lawrence Monroe, F.S.C., Prin. Priests 1; Brothers 11; Lay Teachers 48; Students 857.

North Catholic High School. (Coed), 1400 Troy Hill Rd., 15212. Tel: 412-321-4823; Fax: 412-321-0599.
E-mail: nctrojanatnauticom.net
Priests 1; Brothers 4; Sisters 5; Lay Teachers 32; Students 501.

Oakland Catholic High School, 144 N. Craig St., 15213. Priests 1; Sisters 1; Lay Teachers 40; Students 519.

BADEN. *Quigley Catholic High School*, 200 Quigley Dr., 15005. Tel: 412-869-2188; 343-6722.
E-mail: diopghquighs@connecting.com
Rev. David C. Menegay, Prin. Priests 1; Sisters 1; Lay Teachers 17; Students 201.

MCKEESPORT. *Serra Catholic High School*, 200 Hershey Dr., 15132. Tel: 412-751-2020.
E-mail: serrahs@aol.com; diopghserra@connectinc.com
Under the direction of the Franciscan Friars (Province of the Immaculate Conception). Rev. Michael Dominic Ledoux, O.F.M., Headmaster. Priests 4; Brothers 2; Sisters 3; Lay Teachers 19; Students 355.

MT. LEBANON. *Seton-LaSalle Catholic High School*, 1000 McNeilly Rd., 15226. Tel: 412-561-3583; Fax: 412-561-9097.
Under care of Christian Brothers and Sisters of Charity. Rev. Mark A. Eckman, Chap.

[D] HIGH SCHOOLS, PRIVATE

PITTSBURGH. *Mt. Alvernia High School*, 146 Hawthorne Rd., 15209. Tel: 412-821-3858. Sisters of St. Francis. Dorothy K. McGinley, Prin. Sisters 5; Lay Teachers 13; Students 153.

Vincentian High School, Peebles Rd. & McKnight Rd., 15237. Tel: 412-364-1616. Vincentian Sisters of Charity 2; Lay Teachers 13; Students 188.

CORAOPOLIS. *Our Lady of the Sacred Heart High School*, 1504 Woodcrest Ave., 15108. Tel: 412-264-5140. Felician Sisters, C.S.S.F. State approved day high school. Sr. Mary Francine Horos, C.S.S.F., Prin. Priests 1; Sisters 3; Lay Teachers 20; Students 300.

[E] ELEMENTARY SCHOOLS, DIOCESAN

PITTSBURGH. *St. Agnes Diocesan School*, 120 Robinson St., 15213. Sr. Elizabeth Ann Herbert, R.S.M., Prin. Sisters 2; Lay Teachers 10; Students 225.

[F] CONSOLIDATED SCHOOLS

PITTSBURGH. *Prince of Peace Catholic School*, 85 S. 14th St., 15203. Sisters 3; Lay Teachers 9; Students 151.

St. John Neumann Regional, Catholic Elementary, 250 44th St., 15201. Sisters 3; Lay Teachers 18; Students 348.

AMBRIDGE. *Glenwood*, 8th Ave., 15003. Serving Good Samaritan Parish. Sisters 2; Lay Teachers 10; Students 214.

BUTLER. *Butler Catholic School*. St. Michael. (Grades 1-3), 130 Glenn Ave., 16001. St. Paul. (Grades K, 4-8), 515 E. Locust St., 16001. Sisters 2; Lay Teachers 25; Students 465. Serving the parishes of St. Paul, St. Michael, St. Fidelis, St. Andrew, and St. Peter's, Butler. Butler Montessori School, St. Paul Bldg., 515 E. Locust St., 16001.

DUQUESNE. *Duquesne Catholic School*. (Grades PreK-8), 12 Norman St., 15110. Serving the Parishes of Christ the Light of the World and St. Joseph, Duquesne. Lay Teachers 6; Students 123.

ELLSWORTH. *Ave Maria School*, Box 590, 15331. Serving the parishes of Ave Maria: St. Luke, Bentleyville; St. Clement, Ellsworth; and St. Joseph, Cokeburg. Lay Teachers 7; Students 115.

MCKEES ROCKS. *St. John of God School*. (Grades PreK-8), 115 Margaret St., 15136. Lay Teachers 6; Students 123.

MCKEESPORT. *McKeesport Central Catholic*, 2412 Versailles Ave., 15132. Tel: 412-672-4612. Serving the parishes of St. Stephen, St. Pius V, St. Mary Czestochowa. Felician Sisters, C.S.S.F. 2; Lay Teachers 7; Students 145.

PORT VUE. *St. Joseph Regional School*. (Grades PreK-8), 1125 Romine Ave., 15133. Mrs. Elizabeth M. Kinol, Prin. Serving the parishes of Queen of Rosary, St. Martin de Porres, St. Mark, St. Patrick. Lay Teachers 18; Students 400.

[G] ELEMENTARY SCHOOLS, PRIVATE

PITTSBURGH. *Carlow College Campus School*. (Grades PreK-8), 3333 5th Ave., 15213. Sisters of Mercy. Sisters 2; Lay Teachers 25; Students 271.

ALLISON PARK. *Providence Heights Alpha School*, 9000 Babcock Blvd., 15101. Tel: 412-366-4455. Sisters of Divine Providence. Ms. Karen Lehman, Prin.; Sisters 6; Lay Teachers 12; Students 184.

BADEN. *Mount Gallitzin Academy*, 1016 State St., 15005-1399. Tel: 412-869-2505; 869-2151.
Web site: www.classroom.net/schools/BMountGallitzinAcaemyB.html
Sisters of St. Joseph. Sr. Norma Zanieski, C.S.J., Prin. Sisters 9; Lay Teachers 10; Students 283.

Mount Gallitzin Academy Corp., 1020 State St., 15005-1399. Tel: 412-562-3745. Rosemary L. Corsetti, Esquire. Purpose: to engage in educational activities and the operation of educational program of the Sisters of St. Joseph. Funds, distributions, gifts, bequests, endowments, grants, and contributions from other charitable organizations and student tuitions will be used to support applicant organization's programs and ministry outreach.

[H] DEPARTMENT OF SPECIAL EDUCATION

PITTSBURGH. *The De Paul Institute*, Castlegate Ave., 15226. Tel: 412-561-4848. Day school for children with hearing losses and speech and language disabilities. James R. Farwell, Exec. Dir.; Sr. Virginia Pascaretta, S.C., Educational Dir. Sisters 5; Lay Teachers 16; Students 73.

St. Anthony School Programs, 2718 Custer Ave., 15227. Tel: 412-882-1333; Fax: 412-882-1668. Resource rooms for students with special needs in 6 elementary schools and 2 high schools. Kim Scanlon Lieb, Exec. Dir. Lay Teachers 12; Students 84.

NEW BRIGHTON. *McGuire Memorial*, 2119 Mercer Rd., 15066. Tel: 412-843-3400; 734-0134.
Web site: www.trfn.clpgh.org/mmhf
Residential Facility- Intermediate Care for Developmentally Challenged. Sisters 10; Lay Staff 250; Residents 88.

[I] CHILD CARE INSTITUTIONS

PITTSBURGH. *Franciscan Child Day Care Center*, 1401 Hamilton Rd., 15234-2399. Tel: 412-882-5085.
E-mail: srsosfprov@aol.com
For a complete listing, refer to the Special Care Facilities section.

Mt. Alvernia Day Care & Learning Center, 146 Hawthorne Rd., 15209
For a complete listing, refer to the Special Care Facilities section.

Providence Child Care Center, 400 Hoodridge Dr., 15234. Tel: 412-562-3745
For a complete listing, refer to the Special Care Facilities section.

Vincentian Child Care, Inc., 8200 McKnight Rd., 15237. Tel: 412-366-8588
For a complete listing, refer to the Special Care Facilities section.

ALLISON PARK. *Providence Connections, Inc.*, Corporate Office, 9000 Babcock Blvd., 15101. Tel: 412-931-5241; Fax: 412-635-5416
For a complete listing, refer to the Special Care Facilities section.

EMSWORTH. *Holy Family Institute*, 8235 Ohio River Blvd., 15202. Tel: 412-766-4030
For a complete listing, refer to the Special Care Facilities section.

[J] GENERAL HOSPITALS

PITTSBURGH. *Mercy Hospital of Pittsburgh*, 1400 Locust St., 15219. Tel: 412-232-8111.
Web site: www.mercylink.org
For a complete listing, refer to the Hospitals section.

Mercy Providence Hospital, 1004 Arch St., 15212. Tel: 412-323-5600; Fax: 412-323-5685
For a complete listing, refer to the Hospitals section.

Pittsburgh Mercy Foundation, Forbes-Stevenson Bldg., 1401 Locust St., Ste. 2, 3rd Fl., 15219-5125.
Web site: www.mercylink.org
For a complete listing, refer to the Hospitals section.

Pittsburgh Mercy Health System, Inc., 1400 Locust St., 15219. Tel: 412-232-7510.
E-mail: jmastal@mercy.PMHS.org
Web site: www.mercylink.org
For a complete listing, refer to the Hospitals section.

St. Francis Central Hospital, 1200 Centre Ave., 15219. Tel: 412-562-3301
For a complete listing, refer to the Hospitals section.

St. Francis Medical Center, 400 45th St., 15201. Tel: 412-622-4343
For a complete listing, refer to the Hospitals section.

St. Francis Nursing Center-East, 745 N. Highland Ave., 15206. Tel: 412-362-6622
For a complete listing, refer to the Hospitals section.

**St. Francis Health System*, 4401 Penn Ave., 15224-1380. Tel: 412-622-4343.
Web site: www.sfhs.edu
For a complete listing, refer to the Hospitals section.

CRANBERRY TOWNSHIP. *St. Francis Nursing Center-North*, One St. Francis Way, 16066. Tel: 412-772-5350
For a complete listing, refer to the Hospitals section.

NEW CASTLE. *St. Francis Hospital of New Castle*, 1000 S. Mercer St., 16101. Tel: 412-658-3511
For a complete listing, refer to the Hospitals section.

[K] SPECIAL HOSPITALS AND SANATORIA FOR INVALIDS

PITTSBURGH. *Villa De Marillac Nursing Home*, 5300 Stanton Ave., 15206. Tel: 412-361-2833
For a complete listing, refer to the Special Care Facilities section.

Vincentian Home Inc., 111 Perrymont Rd., 15237. Tel: 412-366-5600
For a complete listing, refer to the Special Care Facilities section.

[L] HOMES FOR THE AGED

PITTSBURGH. *Home for the Aged of the Little Sisters of the Poor*, 1028 Benton Ave., 15212. Tel: 412-761-5373
For a complete listing, refer to the Special Care Facilities section.

Marian Hall Home, Inc., 934 Forest Ave., 15202. Tel: 412-761-1999; 761-2556; Fax: 412-761-2556
For a complete listing, refer to the Special Care Facilities section.

Marian Manor Corp., 2695 Winchester Dr., 15220-4099. Tel: 412-563-6866 (Admin.); 563-1244 (Nursing Service)
For a complete listing, refer to the Special Care Facilities section.

St. Joseph Nursing and Health Care Center, Inc., 5324 Penn Ave., 15224-1798. Tel: 412-665-5100
For a complete listing, refer to the Special Care Facilities section.

St. Paul Manor, 148 Monastery Ave., 15203. Tel: 412-381-4744
For a complete listing, refer to the Special Care Facilities section.

St. Pius X Residence, Inc., 2681 Waddington Ave., 15226. Tel: 412-563-5040; Fax: 412-563-3776
For a complete listing, refer to the Special Care Facilities section.

**St. Francis Plaza, Inc.*, 451 44th St., 15201-1122. Tel: 412-683-6252; Fax: 412-683-4269
For a complete listing, refer to the Special Care Facilities section.

ALLISON PARK. *Regency Hall Nursing Home, Inc.*, 9399 Babcock Blvd., 15101. Tel: 412-366-8540; Fax: 412-369-9789
For a complete listing, refer to the Special Care Facilities section.

*BADEN. *Villa St. Joseph of Baden, Inc.*, 1030 State St., 15005. Tel: 412-869-6300
For a complete listing, refer to the Special Care Facilities section.

[M] REHABILITATION, NURSING AND GENERIC CARE FACILITIES

PITTSBURGH. *Marian Hall Home, Inc.*, 934 Forest Ave., 15202-1118. Tel: 412-761-1999; Fax: 412-761-2556
For a complete listing, refer to the Special Care Facilities section.

[N] PERSONAL PRELATURES

PITTSBURGH. *Opus Dei.* (Prelature of the Holy Cross and Opus Dei.), 5090 Warwick Terr., 15213. Tel: 412-683-8448.
Web site: www.opusdei.org
Legal Title: *The Work of God, Inc.* Revs. Francis J. Hoffman, J.C.D.; Joseph Landauer.

[O] MONASTERIES AND RESIDENCES OF PRIESTS AND BROTHERS

PITTSBURGH. *Congregation of the Oratory of St. Philip Neri*, The Pittsburgh Oratory, 4450 Bayard St., 15213. Tel: 412-681-3181. Very Rev. Bryan F. Summers, C.O., Provost; Revs. Drew P. Morgan, C.O.; David S. Abernethy, C.O.; Joseph C. Linck, C.O.; Joseph E. Sioli, C.O. Total Staff 6.

Consolata Fathers, 7110 Thomas Blvd., 15208. Tel: 412-241-3995; Fax: 412-247-5173. Revs. Alex Moreschi, I.M.C., Supr.; Alphonsus Mwariri, I.M.C., Admin. Priests 3.

Croatian Commissariate, T.O.R., 24 Maryland Ave., 152090. Tel: 412-821-3438; Fax: 412-821-8276. Very Rev. Romildo Hrboka, Commissary Prov. Councillors: Revs. Gabriel Badurina, T.O.R.; Grgo Sikiric, T.O.R.

Franciscan Friars, T.O.R., Queen of Peace Friary, 5324 Carnegie St., 15201. Tel: 412-782-4755. Very Rev. Edmund F. Carroll, T.O.R., Min. Prov. in res. Tel: 412-781-1232 (Office); Rev. Patrick Donahoe, T.O.R.; Bro. Albert Gentile, T.O.R., Local Min. Hospital Ministry: Revs. Carlo Napoli, T.O.R.; Patrick George, T.O.R.; Bernard Tickerhoof, T.O.R., Retreat Ministry. In res. Revs. Canice Crawford, T.O.R.; Patrick Donahoe, T.O.R.

Marianist Community, 1400 Troy Hill Rd., 15212. Tel: 412-321-7234. Bro. William Grundish, Dir.; Rev. James R. McKay, S.M., Chap.; Bros. Al Gillis, S.M.; Daniel Stupka, S.M.; John Dempsey, S.M.; C. Philip Alesandro, C.S.C. Priests 1; Brothers 5.

St. Augustine Friary, 221 36th St., 15201. Tel: 412-682-6430; Fax: 412-682-6148. Revs. Gregory Chervenak, O.F.M.Cap., Guardian; Robert Craig, O.F.M.Cap., Vicar; Jerome Dunn, O.F.M.Cap.; Paul Farkas, O.F.M.Cap.; Francis Fugini, O.F.M.Cap., Sec. Archives & Annals, Coord. for Missions and Provincial Fund Raising; Brendan Malloy, O.F.M.Cap., Communications Dir., Prov. Spiritual Asst. S.F.O.; Roland Raible, O.F.M.Cap.; Bertin Roll, O.F.M.Cap., Dir. Archconfraternity of Christian Mothers; Pascal Schaller, O.F.M.Cap.; Scott Seethaler, O.F.M.Cap.; DeSales Young, O.F.M.Cap.; Armand Yeaglin, O.F.M.Cap; Bros. David Cira, O.F.M.Cap.; Richard Lubomski, O.F.M.Cap.; Charles O'Connor, O.F.M.Cap.; Thomas Tomasunas, O.F.M.Cap.

St. Conrad Friary. 9448 Babcock Blvd., Allison Park, 15101. Tel: 412-364-8240; Fax: 412-366-8331. Revs. Blaise J. Fusco, O.F.M.Cap., Chaplain, Jubilarian; W. David Nestler, O.F.M.Cap., Guardian & Dir. Novices; Mark Carter, O.F.M.Cap., Vicar, Postulant Dir., Vocation Dir.; Vincent Fortunato, O.F.M.Cap., Asst. Dir. Novices. Novices 8; Total in Residence 12; Total Staff 1.

St. Francis Friary, 2905 Castlegate Ave., 15226. Tel: 412-531-4545. Revs. Thomas A. Dutkiewicz, Vicar, Confessor, St. Mary of Mercy Church, Pittsburgh; Ronald Lawler, Dir. Office for Adult & Family Catechesis; Emil William Fischer, Preaching Ministry, Guardian; Emett Schuler, VA Chap.; Maurice Sheehan, Dean, Holy Apostles Seminary; Charles Knoll, Replacement Ministry. Residents 6.

St. John Vianney Manor, 2600 Morange Rd., 15205. Tel: 412-928-0825; 928-0908. Retired priests' residence. In res. Revs. Leo J. Beck; Nicholas A. Biondi; Leo R. Burchianti; Glenn T. Conner; Joseph Cvelbar; Francis M. Dismachek; David C. Dixon; Rev. Msgr. Joseph G. Findlan; Revs. John D. Fording; Leo G. Henry; Evaristo Luteri; Francis G. Massung; John L. Michaels; Thomas M. Nee; Francis P. Plantes; Francis M. Rodgers; F. Clifford Soisson; Rev. Msgr. Ferdinand M. Sojka; Revs. George P. Stuparitz; Zygmunt V. Szarnicki; Andrew J. Turlik; John M. Unger; Walter F. Wichmanowski; Stanislaus J. Zolnierzak. Total in Residence 24; Total Staff 8.

St. Patrick Friary, 1711 Liberty Ave., 15222. Tel: 412-471-4310.
E-mail: friars@capuchin.com
Web site: www.capuchin.com
Revs. William Graham, O.F.M.Cap., Vicar, Prov. Exec. Sec.-Treas.; Bonaventure Stefan, O.F.M.Cap., Chap., St. Francis Medical Center, Pittsburgh; Edward Laurent, O.F.M.Cap., Supr., Dir. of St. Fidelis Devel. Office; Philip Fink, O.F.M.Cap., Prov.

St. Paul of the Cross Monastery. Retreat Center, Passionist Overseas Missions. 148 Monastery Ave., S.S., 15203. Tel: 412-381-1188. Very Rev. Xavier Vitacolonna, C.P., Local Supr.; Bro. Matthew Krawchyk, C.P., Asst. Local Supr.; Revs. Timothy Fitzgerald, C.P.; Gerald Laba, C.P.; John F. McMillan, C.P., Dir. Confraternity of the Passion; Edwin Moran, C.P.; Anthony Neary, C.P.; Clement Pavlick, C.P.; Jerome Vereb, C.P.; Mark Ward, C.P., Assoc. Retreat Dir.; Michael Salvagna, C.P., Retreat Dir.; Dan Sullivan, C.P.; Bros. Leo Di Fiore, C.P., Passionist Overseas Missions Dir.; Joseph Holzer, C.P.; Benedict Palese, C.P.
Mission Band: Revs. Vincent Segotta, C.P.; Timothy Fitzgerald, C.P.; Edwin Moran, C.P.; Dan Sullivan, C.P.
Retreat Center: Revs. Michael Salvagna, C.P., Dir. Tel: 412-381-7676; Mark Ward, C.P.
Passionist Overseas Missions: Bro. Leo Di Fiore, C.P., Rel. Admin. Coord. Tel: 412-381-1189 Ext. 21. Total Assisted 5,000; Residents 19; Total Staff 15.

Society of The Divine Word, 207 Lytton, 15213. Tel: 412-683-4030. Rev. Walter Ostrowski, S.V.D., Mission Dir. Tel: 412-683-0640. Total in Residence 3.

Third Order Regular of Saint Francis - Province of the Most Sacred Heart of Jesus, 215 57th St., 15201-2338. Tel: 412-781-8333; Fax: 412-781-1219. Very Rev. Edmund F. Carroll, T.O.R., Prov. Min., Queen of Peace Friary, 5324 Carnegie St., Pittsburg, 15201. Tel: 412-782-4755. Residents 6; Total Staff 2.

AVALON. *Holy Family Friary.* (Friars Minor), The Franciscans. Vice-Province of the Most Holy Savior.
E-mail: jrya45a@prodigy.com
232 S. Home Ave., Pittsburgh, 15202. Tel: 412-761-2550; 761-8470; Fax: 412-761-2959. Friars David Kohut, O.F.M., Prov.; Lawrence Pollack, O.F.M.; Jerome Pavlik, O.F.M.; David A. Moczulski, O.F.M.; Gilbert Maga, O.F.M.; John Joseph Gonchar, O.F.M.; Micah Muhlen, O.F.M. Friars 10.

Franciscan House of Evangelization, 2428 Arlington Ave., Pittsburgh, 15210. Tel: 412-431-4476; Fax: 412-431-4478. Friars Daniel Barrett, O.F.M.; Thomas Gerchak, O.F.M.; Mark Hudak, O.F.M.; David Moczulski, O.F.M. Friars 4.

BEAVER FALLS. *Our Lady of Peace Monastery*, 71 Darlington Rd., 15010. Tel: 412-843-6110. Rev. Bruno Raspudic, O.F.M., Supr.

BEN AVON. *St. Anthony Friary and Mission House.* 226 Rostrevor Pl., Pittsburgh, 15202-1919. Tel: 412-761-4831. Franciscan Fathers of the Assumption of the Blessed Virgin Mary Province (Order of Friars Minor). Revs. Jerome B. Staniszewski, O.F.M., Guardian & Dir. Missions; Sylvester E. Makarewicz, O.F.M., Vicar, (On Medical Leave); Marcel M. Pasiecznik, O.F.M.; Michael Lacienski, O.F.M.; Felix Reczek, O.F.M. Fathers 5.

BETHEL PARK. *Holy Ghost Fathers and Brothers Provincialate*, 6230 Brush Run Rd., 15102. Tel: 412-831-0302.
E-mail: cppromise@aol.com
Very Rev. Christopher P. Promis, C.S.Sp., Prov.; Revs. Girard J. Kohler, Mission Procurator; Henry J. Koren, C.S.Sp., Archivist. Residents 3; Total Staff 4.

HERMAN. *St. Mary's Friary*, 16039. Tel: 412-285-3285. Capuchin Friars. Revs. Louis J. Petruha, O.F.M.Cap., Guardian; DePaul Ripko, O.F.M.Cap.; Michael Greb, O.F.M.Cap.; James Kurtz, O.F.M.Cap., Vicar; Lester Knoll, O.F.M.Cap.; Melvin Averman, O.F.M.Cap.; Bros. James Townsend, O.F.M.Cap.; Robert Herrick, O.F.M.Cap.

MCKEESPORT. *Franciscan Friars.* Faculty Res. Serra Catholic High School, 200 Hershey Dr., 15132. Tel: 412-751-1250. Friars John-Michael Pinto, O.F.M., Guardian; Alexis Anania, O.F.M.; Michael Dominic W. Ledoux, O.F.M., Vicar; Sean Mary Fitzwater, T.O.R.; Jack W. Hoak, O.F.M.

ROCHESTER. *St. Cecilia Friary*, 303 Jackson St., 15074. Tel: 412-775-0801; 774-6046.
E-mail: rochester@juno.com
Capuchin Friars. Revs. Ward Stakem, O.F.M.Cap.; William Gillum, O.F.M.Cap.; Leon Leitem, O.F.M.Cap., St. Felix Friary, Freedom, 15042. Rev. Bernard Finerty, O.F.M.Cap., St. Felix Friary, Freedom, 15042. Bro. Joseph Day, O.F.M.Cap. In res. Rev. Marvin Justi, O.F.M.Cap., Vicar.

[P] CONVENTS AND RESIDENCES FOR SISTERS

PITTSBURGH. *Convent of Mercy*, 3333 Fifth Ave., 15213. Tel: 412-578-6225.
E-mail: gscarpino@carlow.edu
Motherhouse of Sisters of Mercy of the County of Allegheny. Established in 1843. Sr. Georgine Scarpino, R.S.M.; Rev. Robert J. George, Chap. Sisters 218; Total Professed Sisters 219.

Holy Family Manor, 301 Bellevue Rd., 15229-2194. Tel: 412-931-6996. Residence for Retired Sisters. Sisters 52.

Jesus Redeemer Convent, 285 Bellevue Rd., 15229-2195. Tel: 412-931-5388.

Ladies of Bethany, 1004 Oglethorpe Ave., 15201-2151. Tel: 412-781-4022.
Other Convents: 276 Bruin Rd., Petrolia, 16050. Tel: 412-753-2294.

Motherhouse and Novitiate of the Vincentian Sisters of Charity, 8200 McKnight Rd., 15237. Tel: 412-364-3000; Fax: 412-364-9055. Sr. Rita Gesue, V.S.C., Supr. Gen.; Rev. Blaise J. Fusco, O.F.M.Cap., Chap.

Our Lady of Sorrows Convent of the Passionist Nuns, 2715 Churchview Ave., 15227. Tel: 412-881-1155.
Motherhouse and Novitiate of the Religious of the Passion. (Passionist Nuns). Mother Mary Ann, C.P., Supr. Professed Sisters 9; Novices 1.

St. Benedict Monastery, Benedictine Sisters of Pontifical Jurisdiction, 4530 Perrysville Ave., 15229-2296. Tel: 412-931-2844; Fax: 412-931-8970. Motherhouse and Novitiate of the Benedictine Sisters in the Diocese. Sr. Roberta Campbell, O.S.B., Prioress. Sisters 89.

Benedictine Center, Inc. Sr. Roberta Campbell, O.S.B., Pres.

St. Benedict Academy, Inc.

Pittsburgh Benedictine Ministries, Inc.

Sisters of Our Lady of Charity, N.A.U., 4100 Vinceton St., 15214. Tel: 412-931-2299. North American Union of the Sisters of Our Lady of Charity, Inc. Sr. Thomas Aul, Local Supr. Sisters 14.

Sisters of St. Francis of the Providence of God, St. Francis Convent Motherhouse, 3603 McRoberts Rd., 15234-2398. Tel: 412-882-9911.
E-mail: srsosfprov@aol.com
Sr. Joanne Brazinski, O.S.F., Gen. Supr.; Rev. Thomas Kram, Chap. Sisters 116.

Sisters of the Holy Family of Nazareth of Western Pennsylvania, 285 Bellevue Rd., 15229-2195. Tel: 412-931-4775. Sr. Maria Kruszewski, C.S.F.N., Prov. Supr. Tel: 412-931-4778; Fax: 412-931-9746. Legal Title: *Sisters of the Holy Family of Nazareth of Western Pennsylvania.* Professed Sisters in Provincialate 39; Total Professed Sisters 151.

ALLISON PARK. *The Sisters of Divine Providence*, Providence Heights Motherhouse, 9000 Babcock Blvd., 15101-2793. Tel: 412-931-5241. Motherhouse and Novitiate of the Sisters of Divine Providence in the Diocese (Pittsburgh Province). Sr. Mary Ellen Rufft, C.D.P., Prov. Dir. & Pres.; Rev. Frank D. Almade. In Motherhouse 113; In Province (including Puerto Rico) 281.

BADEN. *St. Joseph Convent*, 15005. Tel: 412-869-2151; 761-3700; Fax: 412-869-3336.
E-mail: secofcsj@usaor.net
Web site: www.nd.edu/~csjus/Baden/home.html
Motherhouse of Sisters of St. Joseph. Rev. Kenneth E. Kezmarsky, M.Div., Chap. In Community 321 (Final Professed); Temporary 3; Novices 1.

BELLEVUE. *Mount Assisi Convent.* Motherhouse of the School Sisters of the Third Order of St. Francis, 934 Forest Ave., Pittsburgh, 15202. Tel: 412-761-6004. In res. Rev. James R. Bedillion. Sisters 89; Residents 37; Total Staff 17.

CORAOPOLIS. *Our Lady of the Sacred Heart Convent.* 1500 Woodcrest Ave., Pittsburgh, 15108. Tel: 412-264-2890; 269-2881; Fax: 412-264-7047.
Provincial House and Novitiate of the Felician Sisters of Pennsylvania C.S.S.F. Sr. Mary Cabrini Procopio, C.S.S.F., Prov. Min.; Rev. Arthur L. Garbin, Chap. Professed 143; Total in Residence 89; Total Staff 31.

Infirmary of St. Joseph Hall, 1500 Woodcrest Ave., 15108. Tel: 412-264-2890; 269-2881. Rev. Richard L. Conboy, S.T.L., Chap.

ELIZABETH. *Divine Redeemer Motherhouse*, 999 Rock Run Rd., 15037. Tel: 412-751-8600; Fax: 412-751-0355. Motherhouse and Novitiate of the Sisters of the Divine Redeemer. Sr. M. Monica Kosztolnyik, S.D.R., Prov. In res. Rev. Francis L. Pucci, Chap. In the Community 59.

EMSWORTH. *Mother Frances Convent.* 140 Allegheny Ave., Pittsburgh, 15202-1402. Tel: 412-766-6702.

MILLVALE. *St. Francis Convent.* Mt. Alvernia, 146 Hawthorne Rd., Pittsburgh, 15209. Tel: 412-821-2200; Fax: 412-821-3318.
E-mail: information@millvalefranciscans.org
Web site: www.millvalefranciscans.com
Sisters of St. Francis of Millvale, PA. Motherhouse and Novitiate of the Order in the Diocese. In the Community: Professed Sisters 225; Juniors 1; Associates 31; In the Motherhouse: Professed Sisters 97. Attended by Capuchin Fathers from St. Augustine, Pittsburgh.

ROSS TOWNSHIP. *Motherhouse, Sisters of the Holy Spirit (S.H.S.).* 5246 Clarwin Ave., Pittsburgh, 15229. Tel: 412-931-1917. Sr. Marita Juras, S.H.S., Gen. Supr.; Most Rev. David A. Zubik, Chap. Professed Sisters 67; Total in Community 67.

VILLA MARIA. *Sisters of the Humility of Mary,* Villa Maria Community Center, P.O. Box 914, 16155. Tel: 412-964-8861; Fax: 412-964-8082.
E-mail: vmcc@hmis.org
Sr. Ruthmary Powers, H.M., Major Supr.; Rev. Frank Erdeljac. Tel: 412-535-4786. Professed Sisters 252; Candidates 1; Novices 3; Residents 73; Total Staff 139.

[Q] RETREAT HOUSES

PITTSBURGH. *Franciscan Spirit and Life Center,* 3605 McRoberts Rd., 15234-2340. Tel: 412-881-9207; Fax: 412-885-7210. Sisters of St. Francis of the Providence of God. Sr. Barbara Ann Zilch, O.S.F., Dir.; Sr. J. Lora Dambroski, O.S.F., Retreat & Program Dir.
Purpose: To provide a facility to individuals for retreats and spiritual programs. Overnight accomodations for 23. Conference room and dining facility. Three hermitages available on daily, overnight or weekly basis. Total Staff 6.

Martina Spiritual Renewal Center, Inc., 5244 Clarwin Ave., 15229. Tel: 412-931-9766.
Conducted by Sisters of the Holy Spirit.
Purpose: To provide a facility to individuals and groups for retreats and spiritual programs. Sr. Marita Juras, S.H.S., Pres.; Sr. Mary Richard Mehelich, S.H.S., Dir.; Sr. Madalyn Chlebowski, S.H.S., Staff; Sr. Christina Marie Janusek, S.H.S., Staff.

St. Paul of the Cross Retreat Center, 148 Monastery Ave., 15203. Tel: 412-381-7676; 381-7677; Fax: 412-431-3044. Revs. Michael Salvagna, C.P., Dir.; Mark Ward, C.P., Asst. Dir.; Jean Simok, Business Mgr. Assocs.: Dr. Susan Stangl; Dr. Salvatore Mascari.

**The Burning Bush: Franciscan House of Prayer,* 32-40 Pius St., 15203-1617. Tel: 412-381-3819; Fax: 412-381-1585.
E-mail: burnbush@nb.net
Purposes: A Franciscan-oriented House of Prayer and retreat facility for contemplation, rest, prayer and spiritual nourishment; motherhouse for formation and prayer of Lay Franciscans of Adoration. Contact Persons: Fred Koerner, L.F.A., Mod.; Sr. Damian Tosi, O.L.C., L.F.A., Asst. Mod. Total in Residence 3.

ALLISON PARK. *Kearns Spirituality Center,* 9000 Babcock Blvd., 15101-2713. Tel: 412-366-1124; Fax: 412-635-5416. Sisters of Divine Providence. Directors: Sr. Agnes Raible, C.D.P.; Sr. Marilyn Seidel, C.D.P.
Conference room for 250; overnight accommodations for 60; dining facilities for 200. Total Staff 7.

BETHEL PARK. *Holy Ghost Animation Center,* 6230 Bush Run Rd., 15102. Tel: 412-835-3510. Revs. Constantine J. Conan, C.S.Sp.; Francis X. Hanley, C.S.Sp., Dir.; Girard J. Kohler, C.S.Sp.; Henry J. Koren, C.S.Sp.; James F. Pergl, C.S.Sp.; John S. Rondeau, C.S.Sp.; John P. McAndrew, C.S.Sp.; John M. Jendzura. Total in Residence 8; Total Staff 20.

CORAOPOLIS. *Gilmary Diocesan Center,* 601 Flaugherty Run Rd., 15108-3899. Tel: 412-264-8400; Fax: 412-264-8415.
Web site: www.diopitt.org
Ronald W. Ragan, Dir.
Overnight facilities for 219; meeting rooms for one-day programs; separate adult and youth facilities; 150 seat dining room, 150 seat chapel, indoor heated swimming pool, gymnasium, outdoor volleyball and basketball courts and ballfield.

Office for Adolescent Formation & Youth Ministry. Joyce Gillooly, Dir. Tel: 412-264-9530: Fax: 412-264-9539. Total Staff 11.

GIBSONIA. *John Cardinal Wright Vocation and Prayer Center,* 10745 Babcock Blvd., 15044. Mrs. Diane Gasbarro, Mgr. Total Staff 10.

[R] OFFICES FOR CAMPUS MINISTRY

PITTSBURGH. *Office of Chaplaincies,* 4721 Fifth Ave., 15213. Tel: 412-621-6209. Rev. John J. Keane, Dir.

SLIPPERY ROCK. *Office for Campus Ministry,* 342 Normal Ave., 16057. Tel: 412-794-6620. Rev. Robert L. Seeman, Dir., Art Institute of Pittsburgh. (Pittsburgh), Downtown Campus Ministry, 135 1st Ave. #118, Lawrence Hall Rm. 709, Pittsburgh, 15222. Tel: 412-392-4732. Rev. Joseph C. Linck, C.O., Carlow College, 3333 5th Ave., Pittsburgh, 15213. Tel: 412-578-6069. Nellene Groetsch, Carnegie-Mellon University, Ryan Catholic Newman Center, 4450 Bayard St., Pittsburgh, 15213. Tel: 412-681-3181. Very Rev. Bryan F. Summers, C.O.; Sr. Bernadette Young, C.D.P.; Revs. David S. Abernethy, C.O.; Malcolm McDonald; Drew P. Morgan, C.O.; Joseph Scioli, C.O., Chatham College, Ryan Catholic Newman Center, 4450 Bayard St., Pittsburgh, 15213. Tel: 412-681-3181. Very Rev. Bryan F. Summers, C.O.; Sr. Bernadette Young, C.D.P.; Revs. David S. Abernethy, C.O.; Malcolm McDonald; Drew P. Morgan, C.O.; Joseph Scioli, C.O., Community College of Allegheny College - Boyce Campus, 5245 Azalea Dr., Monroeville, 15146. Tel: 412-373-0050. Rev. Richard Infante, Community College of Allegheny College - North Campus, 720 Arch St., Pittsburgh, 15212-5296. Tel: 412-321-0711. Rev. Eric T. Vogt, O.S.B., Community College of Allegheny College - South Campus, 2603 Old Elizabeth Rd., West Mifflin, 15122. Tel: 412-466-5048. Rev. Daniel Valentine, Duquesne University, Campus Ministry, Pittsburgh, 15282. Tel: 412-396-6020. Revs. Donald McEachin, C.S.Sp.; Raymond D. French, C.S.Sp.; Jocelyn Gregoire, C.S.Sp.; William Headley, C.S.Sp.; Sr. Bernadette Campbell, O.P.; Ms. Kate Fletcher, Geneva College, Rte. 18 College Hill, Beaver Falls, 15010. Tel: 412-773-3839. Patrick Corcoran, Dir.; Rev. Francis Frazer, La Roche College, Campus Ministry, 9000 Babcock Blvd., Pittsburgh, 15237. Tel: 412-367-9300, Ext. 141. Rev. W. Peter Horton, Pennsylvania State University, Beaver Campus, Broadhead Rd., Monaca, 15061. Tel: 412-773-3839. Mr. Patrick W. Corcoran, Dir., Point Park College, Downtown Campus Ministry, 135 1st Ave., Lawrence Hall Rm. 709, Pittsburgh, 15222. Tel: 412-392-4732. Rev. Joseph C. Linck, C.O., Robert Morris College, Moon Township Campus, St. James, 200 Walnut St., Sewickly, 15143. Tel: 412-741-0836; 262-8313. Rev. Harold E. Baily, Robert Morris College, Pittsburgh Campus, Downtown Campus Ministry, Lawrence Hall Rm. 709, Pittsburgh, 15222. Tel: 412-392-4732. Rev. Joseph C. Linck, C.O., University of Pittsburgh, Ryan Catholic Newman Center, 4450 Bayard St., Pittsburgh, 15213. Tel: 412-681-3181. Very Rev. Bryan F. Summers, C.O., Dir.; Revs. David S. Abernethy, C.O.; Malcolm McDonald; Drew P. Morgan, C.O.; Joseph Scioli, C.O.; Sr. Bernadette Young, C.D.P., California University (California), 213 4th St., California, 15419. Tel: 412-938-4573. Faye E. Abbondanza, Campus Min.; Rev. Timothy F. Whalen, Dir., Westminster College, 313 W. Englewood Ave., New Castle, 16105. Tel: 412-652-9471. Rev. David A. Driesch, Slippery Rock University, Newman Center (Slippery Rock), 342 Normal Ave., 16057. Tel: 412-794-8459. Rev. Robert L. Seeman, Dir.; Ms. Diane Magliocca, Campus Min., Washington and Jefferson College (Washington), Newman Center, 1 S. College St., Washington, 15301. Tel: 412-228-7044. Rev. Kevin F. McKnight, Chap., Waynesburg College (Waynesburg), St. Ann Church, 32 S. Cumberland St., Waynesburg, 15370. Tel: 412-627-8191. Rev. Albin C. McGinnis.

[S] MISCELLANEOUS LISTINGS

PITTSBURGH. *The Capuchin Franciscan Volunteer Corps, Inc.,* 220 37th St., 15201. Tel: 412-682-6011.
E-mail: volunteers@capuchin.com
Web site: www.capuchin.com
Province of St. Augustine of the Capuchin Order. Rev. William Talentino, O.F.M.Cap., Dir.
Purpose: To promote, train, supervise and support Catholic lay missions and missionaries throughout the world, especially in conjunction with the ministries and fraternities of the Capuchin Order.

Cardinal Tardini Charitable Trust, 111 Blvd. of the Allies, 15222. Tel: 412-456-3000.

Catholic Business Alliance, 107 Shannon Dr., 15238. Tel: 412-967-0613; Fax: 412-255-9868. Mr. Frederick P. O'Brien, Contact Person.
Purpose: To devote talents and resources to assist Catholic Charities, special Diocesan projects approved by the Bishop, and enrich spiritual life of membership.

Catholic Diocese of Pittsburgh Foundation, 111 Blvd. of the Allies, 15222. Tel: 412-456-3085.
E-mail: development@diopitt.org

The Catholic Historical Society of Western Pennsylvania, Synod Hall, 125 N. Craig St., 15213. Tel: 412-531-5725. Mr. Anthony P. Joseph, Jr., Pres.
Purpose: To promote the teaching of the Catholic Church in the United States, especially the Church in Western Pennsylvania; to recognize the growth, development and contribution of the Catholic Church by the preservation of artifacts, records and documents related to that history; to make available the results of research and study.

Chimbote Foundation, 111 Blvd. of the Allies, 15222-1618.

Christ Child Society of Pittsburgh, P.O. Box 11324, 15238-1324. Tel: 412-682-4102. Mrs. Jean Katarincic, Contact; Rev. Frank D. Almade, Chap.
Purpose: To foster a personal love of Christ expressed in service for needy children and youths. Total Assisted 700; Volunteers 50.

Congregations of Religious Women Charitable Trust, 285 Bellevue Rd., 15229. Sr. Michele Collins, C.S.F.N., Chm.

Elizabeth Seton Center Inc., 1900 Pioneer Ave., 15226. Tel: 412-561-8400. Sr. Barbara Ann Boss, S.C., Exec. Dir. Day Care Programs for Children and Adults; Senior Citizens Center; Suzuki School of Music. Sisters of Charity 16; Total Assisted 1,030; Total Staff 54.

The Epiphany Association, 947 Tropical Ave., 15216-3031. Tel: 412-341-7494; Fax: 412-341-7495.
E-mail: epiphany@steelcity.net
Web site: www.geocities.com/Eureka/Park/1773
Total Staff 4.

Holy Family Foundation, 8325 Ohio River Blvd., Ste. 200, 15202-1594. The Holy Family Foundation was formed in 1992 to promote & support the public charitable works & educational purposes of Holy Family Institute.

Jesuit Community of Pittsburgh. Corpus Christi Pastoral Center. 1550 Lincoln Ave., 15206. Tel: 412-361-2167. Rev. Robert B. Cullen, S.J. Total Assisted 5.

Mercy Hospital School of Nursing Alumni Association, 1400 Locust St., 15219. Tel: 412-232-7941. Sr. Carolyn Schallenberger, R.S.M., Dir. School of Nursing.

Mount Nazareth Center, Inc., 285 Bellevue Rd., 15229-2195. Tel: 412-931-9761; Fax: 412-931-7255. Mr. Fred D. Just, Exec. Dir. Tel: 412-931-1039. Total Assisted 725; Total Staff 46.

Mt. Nazareth Learning Center. Child Care: Infants; Toddlers; Pre-School; Kindergarten. Tel: 412-931-9761; 931-9241.

Nazareth Housing Services. Housing Counseling; Low Income Home Ownership. Tel: 412-931-3510.

Nazareth Family Services. Family Counseling; Family Life Education. Tel: 412-931-1026. Total Assisted 1,390; Total Staff 64.

Nazareth Family Foundation, 285 Bellevue Rd., 15229. Tel: 412-931-4778.
E-mail: csfnsjpsmc@juno.com
Sr. Michele Collins, Pres. Purpose: To promote family life through financial support of facilities, programs, and services which enhance individual and family well-being. Total Assisted 3; Total Staff 3.

North Catholic Endowment Fund, 111 Blvd. of the Allies, 15222.

Pension Plan for the Diocese of Pittsburgh. (Lay Pension Plan), 111 Blvd. of the Allies, 15222. Tel: 412-456-3137; Fax: 412-456-3130. Mr. Charles A. Koempel, Dir.

Pittsburgh Catholic Publishing Associates. Purpose: To promote for Catholics and other readers an understanding of the mission and teachings of the Church and its role in the community. 135 First Ave., Ste. 200, 15222-1506. Tel: 412-471-1252.
E-mail: pghcatholic@pittsburgh.net
Mr. Greg Brown, Editor; Ms. Carmella A. Weismantle, Comptroller.
Purpose: To promote for Catholics and other readers an understanding of the mission and teachings of the Church and its role in the community.

Pittsburgh Diocese Knights of Columbus Bishop Wright Project, (Incorporated), 2718 Custer Ave., 15227. Tel: 412-882-1333. Project for benefit of St. Anthony School for Programs and McGuire Memorial.

Priests' Benefit Plan of the Diocese of Pittsburgh, 111 Blvd. of the Allies, 15222. Tel: 412-456-3137; Fax: 412-456-3139.
E-mail: finserv@diopitt.orf
Rev. Thomas Kram, Chm.
Purpose: To provide certain retirement and health-related benefits to eligible priests.

St. Francis Academy Corporation, 1401 Hamilton Rd., 15234. Tel: 412-882-9911.
E-mail: srsosfprov@aol.com
Sr. Elise Mora, O.S.F., Pres.

St. Joseph's House of Hospitality, Inc., 1635 Bedford Ave., 15219. Tel: 412-471-0666. A subsidiary of Catholic Charities. Ms. Phyllis A. Malchano, Exec. Dir. Seton Hill Sisters of Charity 6; Residents 60; Total Assisted 140; Total Staff 18.

Maryhouse Residence for Women, 1113 Creedmoor Ave., 15226. Tel: 412-563-3312. Residents 30; Sisters of St. Francis 1.

St. Regis Residence for Ladies. (Non-Sectarian), 50 Congress St., 15219. Tel: 412-281-9888. Accommodations for 73 boarders, and is under the direction of a Board of Lay Managers. Donna Tomosky, Mgr. Permanent Residents 35; Staff 6.

Saint Thomas More Society, 300 Four PPG Pl., 15222-5404. Tel: 412-338-4750. Mr. Brian O'Connor, Pres.

St. Vincent de Paul Society, 1917 Brownsville Rd., 15210.

Sisters of Mercy Continuing Support Trust Fund, 3333 Fifth Ave., 15213.
E-mail: gscarpino@carlow.edu
Sr. Georgine Scarpino, Pres.

Sisters of St. Francis of the Providence of God Ministries Corporation, 3603 McRoberts Rd., 15234-2398. Tel: 412-882-9911. Sr. Marian Blodis, O.S.F., Pres. Program: Franciscan Spirit and Life Center.

Society of Saint Vincent de Paul, Council of Pittsburgh, 1243 N. Franklin St., 15233. Tel: 412-321-1071; Fax: 412-321-9131. Pete Jeffrey, Pres.; Rev. Thomas M. Rodgers, Spiritual Advisor. Total Assisted 28,000.

**The Burning Bush*, 32 Pius St., 15203-1617. Tel: 412-381-3819; Fax: 412-381-1585.
E-mail: burnbush@nb.net
Franciscan House of Prayer. Total in Residence 3; Total Staff 2.

Toner Trust, Catholic Institute of Pittsburgh, 111 Blvd. of the Allies, 15222.

Trust for Theological Studies, 111 Blvd. of Allies, 15222. Most Rev. John B. McDowell, Ph.D., D.D., V.G.

Vincentian Sisters of Charity Collaborative Services, 8200 McKnight Rd., 15237. Tel: 412-364-3000. Sr. Rita Gesue, Pres.
Purpose: To provide coordination and supervision of facilities and services operating under the auspices of the Vincentian Sisters of Charity.

ALLISON PARK. *Divine Providence Foundation*, 9000 Babcock Blvd., 15101. Tel: 412-931-5241; Fax: 412-635-5416. Sr. Mary Ellen Rufft, C.D.P., Pres.
Purpose: To perform, foster, and support acts of Christian charity among the sick and ailing.

Sisters of Divine Providence Charitable Trust, 9000 Babcock Blvd., 15101-2793. Tel: 412-931-5241; Fax: 412-635-5416. Sr. Mary Ellen Rufft, C.D.P., Pres.

BADEN.
**Girls Hope of Pittsburgh, Inc.*, 1020 Baden St., 15005. Tel: 412-869-2868. Sr. Donna Marie Tahaney, Contact Person.
Purpose: To provide a supportive home environment and a quality education through college for girls who have potential for leadership but who because of poverty, abuse, neglect or abandonment cannot remain in their own homes. Total Assisted 15; Total Staff 6.

CLAIRTON. *Sisters Place, Inc.*, 460 Reed St., 15025. Tel: 412-233-3903; Fax: 412-233-3904.
Purpose: To provide hospitality, housing and advocacy to women and children who are homeless or of low income. Sr. Cynthia Serjak, R.S.M., Pres.; Kathi Boyle, Exec. Dir.

ELIZABETH. *Divine Redeemer Health Care Ministeries Corp.*, 999 Rock Run Rd., 15037; Fax: 412-751-0355.

Sisters of Divine Redeemer Charitable Trust, 999 Rock Run Rd., 15037. Tel: 412-751-8600; Fax: 412-751-0355.

MCKEESPORT. *Auberle*, 1101 Hartman St., 15132. Tel: 412-673-5800. Mr. Lynn M. Knezevich, Exec. Dir.
Purpose: To provide services to at risk children and their families. Total in Residence 150; Total Staff 200.

Pauline Auberle Foundation, 1101 Hartman St., 15132. Tel: 412-673-5800. Raymond M. Niedenberger, Exec. Dir. Continues mission of Pauline Auberle Foundation while providing support to Auberle through fundraising, rental agreements, and overall management and leadership services. Total Staff 13.

VILLA MARIA. *The Center for Learning*, Evergreen Rd., Box 910, 16155. Tel: 800-767-9090; 412-964-8083; Fax: 888-767-8080.
E-mail: cfl@stratos.net
Web site: www.centerforlearning.org
Educational Development Center and Publisher of values-based instructional materials: Religion for Catholic schools and parishes; English/Language Arts, Social Studies, Novel/Drama and Elementary Curriculum Units for all schools. Sr. Rose Schaffer, H.M., M.A., Pres. & CEO; Sr. Bernadette Vetter, H.M., M.A., Vice Pres. Owned and operated by the Sisters of the Humility of Mary. Directed by an Ecumenical Lay Board. Shipping-business office in Villa Maria. Administrative-Editorial Office, 21590 Center Ridge Rd., Rocky River, OH, 44116. Tel: 440-331-1404; Fax: 440-331-5414.

Sisters of the Humility of Mary Charitable Trust, Villa Maria Community Center, P.O. Box 313, 16155. Tel: 412-964-8861.
E-mail: vmcc@hmis.org
Sr. Mildred Ely, H.M., Contact.

Villa Maria Education Center, 16155. Sr. Rose Marie Kramer, H.M., Dir. A center for adolescents and pre-adolescents which provides programs to foster the development of strong spiritual and personal values, self-worth, respect for others, and social awareness. Total Assisted 2,360; Total Staff 10.

Villa Maria Residential Services. (Villa Maria Apartments), P.O. Box 230, 16155. Tel: 412-964-8099; Fax: 412-964-8082. Housing for low & moderate income for senior citizens 62 & over. Sr. Mary Ida Schaffer, H.M., Pres. & CEO. Apartments 37.

RELIGIOUS INSTITUTES OF MEN REPRESENTED IN THE DIOCESE

For further details refer to the corresponding bracketed number in the Religious Institutes of Men or Women section.

[0200]—*Benedictine Monks.* (St. Vincent Archabbey).—O.S.B.
[0330]—*Brothers of the Christian Schools.* (Prov. of Baltimore).—F.S.C.
[0470]—*The Capuchin Friars.* (Prov. of St. Augustine).—O.F.M.Cap.
[1000]—*Congregation of the Passion.* (Eastern Prov.).—C.P.
[]—*Croatian Franciscans.* Croatian Commissariate.—T.O.R.
[0520]—*Franciscan Friars.* (Provs. of Assumption B.V.M. & Immaculate Conception; Custodies of Most Holy Savior).—O.F.M.
[0650]—*Holy Ghost Fathers.* (Eastern Prov.).—C.S.Sp.
[0950]—*Oratorians.*—C.O.
[0430]—*Order of Preachers (Dominicans).* (Province of St. Joseph).—O.P.
[0760]—*Society of Mary (Marianists).* (Cincinnati Prov.).—S.M.
[0420]—*Society of the Divine Word.*—S.V.D.
[0560]—*Third Order Regular of Saint Francis.* (Prov. of Sacred Heart of Jesus).—T.O.R.

RELIGIOUS INSTITUTES OF WOMEN REPRESENTED IN THE DIOCESE

[0130]—*Apostles of the Sacred Heart of Jesus.*—A.S.C.J.
[0230]—*Benedictine Sisters of Pontifical Jursidiction.*—O.S.B.
[]—*Daughters of Mary, Mother of the Church.*—D.M.
[1070-24]—*Dominican Sisters.*—O.P.
[]—*Dominican Sisters, Congregation of the Most Holy Rosary.*
[1170]—*Felician Sisters.*—C.S.S.F.
[1190]—*Franciscan Sisters of Atonement.*—S.A.
[2575]—*Institute of the Sisters of Mercy of the Americas.* (Pittsburgh, PA; Erie, PA; Scranton, PA).—R.S.M.
[]—*Ladies of Bethany.*—L.B.
[2340]—*Little Sisters of the Poor.*—L.S.P.
[2720]—*Mission Helpers of the Sacred Heart.*—M.H.S.H.
[3071]—*North American Union Sisters of Our Lady of Charity.*—O.L.C.
[3050]—*Oblate Sisters of the Sacred Heart of Jesus.*—O.S.H.J.
[]—*Our Lady of the Way (Secular Institute).*
[3170]—*Religious of the Passion of Jesus Christ.*—C.P.
[3430]—*Religious Teachers Filippini* (St. Lucy Filippini Prov.).—M.P.F.
[2970]—*School Sisters of Notre Dame.*—S.S.N.D.
[1690]—*School Sisters of St. Francis.*—O.S.F.
[0570]—*Sisters of Charity of Seton Hill, Greensburg, Pennsylvania.*—S.C.
[0990]—*Sisters of Divine Providence.*—C.D.P.
[1660]—*Sisters of Saint Francis of the Providence of God.*—O.S.F.
[3830-13]—*Sisters of Saint Joseph.*—C.S.J.
[1620]—*Sisters of St. Francis of Millvale, Pennsylvania.*—O.S.F.
[3840]—*Sisters of St. Joseph of Carondelet.* (St. Paul, MN & Albany, NY Prov.).—C.S.J.
[1020]—*Sisters of the Divine Redeemer.*—S.D.R.
[1970]—*Sisters of the Holy Family of Nazareth.*—C.S.F.N.
[2040]—*Sisters of the Holy Spirit.*—S.H.S.
[2110]—*Sisters of the Humility of Mary.*—H.M.
[2160]—*Sisters, Servants of the Immaculate Heart of Mary.*—I.H.M.
[4120-03]—*Ursuline Nuns of the Congregation of Paris.*—O.S.U.
[]—*Ursuline Sisters of the Immaculate Conception.* (Cleveland).—O.S.V.
[4160]—*Vincentian Sisters of Charity.*—V.S.C.

DIOCESAN CEMETERIES

PITTSBURGH. *Catholic Cemeteries Association, Inc.*, Central Office, 718 Hazelwood Ave., 15217-2807. Tel: 412-521-9133; Fax: 412-521-7019.

All Saints Cemetery (Braddock), 1560 Brinton Rd., 15221-4899. Tel: 412-271-5950; Fax: 412-271-8219.

Calvary Cemetery & Mausoleum, 718 Hazelwood Ave., 15217-2807. Tel: 412-421-9959; Fax: 412-521-7019.

Christ Our Redeemer Cemetery & Mausoleum (North Side), 204 Cemetery Ln., 15237-2722. Tel: 412-931-2206; Fax: 412-931-2229.

St. Mary, c/o Calvery Cemetery, 718 Hazelwood Ave., 15217-2807. Tel: 412-421-9959; Fax: 412-621-6439.

St. Stanislaus & St. Anthony, 700 Soose Rd., 15209-1544. Tel: 412-821-4324; Fax: 412-821-4718.

Queen of Heaven Cemetery & Mausoleum, 2900 Washington Rd., Bridgeville, 15017-1793. Tel: 412-831-3360; 941-7601; Fax: 412-942-2550.

Resurrection Cemetery & Mausoleum, R.D. #4, Box 398, Corapolis, 15108-9804. Tel: 412-695-2999; Fax: 412-695-3032.

Sacred Heart Cemetery and Mausoleum, 97 Sacred Heart Rd., Monongahela, 15063-9605. Tel: 412-258-2885; Fax: 412-258-2275.

Good Shepherd Cemetery & Mausoleum, 733 Patton St., Monroeville, 15146-4530. Tel: 412-824-0355; Fax: 412-823-9083.

Saint Joseph Cemetery & Mausoleum, 1443 Lincoln Hwy., North Versailles, 15137-2448. Tel: 412-823-9111; Fax: 412-823-6655.

Holy Souls, c/o Resurrection Cemetery, R.D. #4, Box 398, Coraopolis, 15108-9804. Tel: 412-695-3063; Fax: 412-695-3032.

Our Lady of Hope Cemetery & Mausoleum, 1898 Bakerstown Rd., Tarentum, 15084. Tel: 412-224-2785; Fax: 412-224-0211.

Holy Savior Cemetery, 4629 Bakerstown Rd., Gibsonia, 15044. Tel: 412-625-3822; Fax: 412-625-3880.

Mount Carmel Cemetery & Mausoleum, 7601 Mt. Carmel Rd., Verona, 15147. Tel: 412-241-1260; Fax: 412-241-5041.

NECROLOGY

† Biller, James C., Cranberry Twp., PA, St. Ferdinand. —Died Aug. 28, 1996.
† DeNapoli, Ettore J., Butler, PA, St. Michael. —Died May 15, 1997.
† Erkens, William J., Churchill, PA, St. John Fisher. —Died Feb. 6, 1997.
† Farina, Edward R., (Retired). —Died March 19, 1997.
† Froehlich, Raymond P., Sewickley, PA, St. James. —Died May 8, 1997.
† Knorr, Rev. Msgr. Joseph H., Bloomfield, PA, Immaculate Conception/St. Joseph. —Died Sept. 28, 1996.
† Malinak, Joseph G., Tarentum, PA, St. Clement. —Died May 14, 1997.
† Romero, Oswald E., (Retired). —Died Feb. 7, 1997.
† Stebler, Lawrence F., Perrysville, PA, St. Teresa of Avila. —Died June 9, 1997.

Diocese of Portland (In Maine)

(Dioecesis Portlandensis)

Most Reverend

JOSEPH JOHN GERRY, O.S.B.

Bishop of Portland; ordained June 12, 1954; ordained Titular Bishop of Praecausa and Auxiliary Bishop of Manchester April 21, 1986; appointed Bishop of Portland December 21, 1988; installed February 21, 1989. *Res., 199 Western Promenade, Portland, ME, 04102. Mailing Address: P.O. Box 11559, Portland, ME, 04104-7559.*

Most Reverend

EDWARD CORNELIUS O'LEARY, D.D.

Bishop Emeritus; ordained June 15, 1946; appointed Titular Bishop of Moglaena and Auxiliary November 17, 1970; consecrated January 25, 1971; succeeded to See December 4, 1974; installed December 18, 1974; resigned September 27, 1988. *Res., Cathedral Residence, 307 Congress St., Portland, ME, 04101.*

Most Reverend

MICHAEL RICHARD COTE, D.D.

Auxiliary Bishop of Portland; ordained June 29, 1975; ordained Titular Bishop of Cebarades and Auxiliary Bishop of Portland July 27, 1995. *Mailing Address: P.O. Box 11559, Portland, ME, 04104-7559.*

ESTABLISHED JULY 29, 1853.

Square Miles 33,040.

Comprises the State of Maine.

Corporate Title: *Roman Catholic Bishop of Portland, a Corporation Sole.*

For the legal titles of other diocesan-related institutions, please consult Chancery.

Chancery: 510 Ocean Ave., P.O. Box 11559, Portland, ME, 04104-7559. Tel.: 207-773-6471; Fax: 207-773-0182.

STATISTICAL OVERVIEW

Personnel	
Bishop	1
Auxiliary Bishops	1
Retired Bishops	1
Priests: Diocesan Active in Diocese	120
Priests: Active Outside Diocese	7
Priests: Retired, Sick or Absent	62
Number of Diocesan Priests	189
Religious Priests in Diocese	53
Extern Priests in Diocese	14
Ordinations:	
Diocesan Priests	4
Transitional Deacons	1
Permanent Deacons in Diocese	11
Total Brothers	28
Total Sisters	483
Parishes	
Parishes	138
With Resident Pastor:	
Resident Diocesan Priests	103
Resident Religious Priests	13
Without Resident Pastor:	
Administered by Priests	21
Administered by Lay People	1
Missions	54
New Parishes Created	1
Closed Parishes	1
Professional Ministry Personnel:	
Sisters	15
Lay Ministers	78
Welfare	
Catholic Hospitals	3
Total Assisted	220,987
Health Care Centers	1
Total Assisted	73
Homes for the Aged	8
Total Assisted	930
Day Care and Extended Day Care Centers	4
Total Assisted	530
Specialized Homes	4
Total Assisted	79
Special Centers for Social Services	7
Total Assisted	2,685
Educational	
Diocesan Students in Other Seminaries	13
Total Seminarians	13
Colleges and Universities	1
Total Students	4,685
High Schools, Diocesan and Parish	1
Total Students	241
High Schools, Private	2
Total Students	631
Elementary Schools, Diocesan and Parish	18
Total Students	4,079
Elementary Schools, Private	1
Total Students	174
Catechesis/Religious Education:	
High School Students	4,448
Elementary Students	16,669
Total Students Under Catholic Instruction	30,940
Teachers in the Diocese:	
Priests	4
Sisters	30
Lay Teachers	289
Vital Statistics	
Receptions into the Church:	
Infant Baptism Totals	3,134
Adult Baptism Totals	240
Received into Full Communion	364
First Communions	3,238
Confirmations	6,309
Marriages:	
Catholic	895
Interfaith	464
Total Marriages	1,359
Deaths	2,751
Total Catholic Population	233,927
Total Population	1,227,927

Former Bishops—The first Bishop-Elect, Very Rev. J. COSKERY V.G.,of Baltimore, declined the nomination.—Rt. Rev. DAVID W. BACON, D.D., cons. April 22, 1855; died Nov. 5, 1874.—Rt. Rev. JAMES AUGUSTINE HEALY, D.D., cons. June 2, 1875; died Aug. 5, 1900.—His Eminence WILLIAM CARDINAL O'CONNELL, cons. Bishop of Portland, May 19, 1901; named Coadjutor Archbishop of Boston, Feb. 8, 1906; succeeded to the See of Boston, Aug. 30, 1907; created Cardinal, Nov. 27, 1911; died April 22, 1944.—Rt. Rev. LOUIS S. WALSH, D.D., cons. Oct. 18, 1906; died May 12, 1924.—Rt. Rev. JOHN GREGORY MURRAY, D.D., ord. April 14, 1900; cons. April 28, 1920; transferred to the Archdiocese of St. Paul, Oct. 29, 1931; died Oct. 11, 1956.—Most Rev. JOSEPH EDWARD MCCARTHY, D.D., ord. July 4, 1903; cons. Aug. 24, 1932; died Sept. 8, 1955.—Most Rev. DANIEL JOSEPH FEENEY, D.D., LL.D., Bishop of Portland; ord. May 21, 1921; appt. Titular Bishop of Sita and Auxiliary of Portland, June 22, 1946; cons. Sept. 12, 1946; Apostolic Administrator of the Diocese; appt. July 27, 1948; Coadjutor "cum jure successionis"; appt. March 4, 1952; succeeded to See, Sept. 8, 1955; died Sept. 15, 1969.—Most Rev. PETER LEO GERETY, D.D., ord. June 29, 1939; appt. March 4, 1966; cons. June 1, 1966; appt. Apostolic Administrator, Feb. 18, 1967; succeeded to See, Sept. 15, 1969; transferred Archdiocese of Newark, NJ, April 2, 1974.—Most Rev. EDWARD C. O'LEARY, D.D., ord. June 15, 1946; Titular Bishop of Moglaena and Auxiliary Bishop of Portland; appt. Nov. 17, 1970; cons. Jan. 25, 1971; Apostolic Administrator; appt. June 29, 1974 ninth Bishop of Portland, Dec. 4, 1974; installed Dec. 18, 1974; resigned Sept. 27, 1988.

Vicar General—Most Rev. MICHAEL R. COTE.

Chancery—510 Ocean Ave., P.O. Box 11559, Portland, 04104-7559. Tel: 207-773-6471; Fax: 207-773-0182. Office Hours: Mon.-Fri. 9-4:30. Closed Holidays.

Co-Chancellors—Rev. MARC B. CARON, S.T.L.; Sr. RITA-MAE BISSONNETTE, R.S.R., J.C.L.

Bishop's Delegate for Clergy—Rev. PAUL F. STEFANKO, J.C.L.

Public Affairs—Mr. MARC R. MUTTY.

Diocesan Tribunal—510 Ocean Ave., P.O. Box 11559, Portland, 04104-7559. Tel: 207-773-6471.

Officialis—Rev. PAUL F. STEFANKO, J.C.L.

Promoter of Justice—Rev. MARK P. NOLETTE, J.C.L.

Defenders of the Bond—Sr. RITA-MAE BISSONNETTE, R.S.R., J.C.L.; Sr. CLAUDIA BARBRE, R.S.M., J.C.L.; Rev. PAUL F. STEFANKO, J.C.L.; Sr. ANN KEEVAN, C.S.J., J.C.D.; Rev. MARK P. NOLETTE, J.C.L.; Most Rev. MICHAEL R. COTE, J.C.L., D.D.; Mr. GEORGE G. PAVLOFF, J.C.D.

Advocates—Sr. CLAUDIA BARBRE, R.S.M., J.C.L.; Sr. ANN KEEVAN, C.S.J., J.C.D.; Revs. MARK P. NOLETTE, J.C.L.; PAUL F. STEFANKO, J.C.L.; Mr. GEORGE G. PAVLOFF, J.C.D.; Sr. RITA-MAE BISSONNETTE, R.S.R.

Office Coordinator—Rev. PAUL F. STEFANKO, J.C.L.

Notaries—Mrs. NAJLIA KERRIGAN; Mrs. FRANCESCA M. FORTIN.

Associate Judges—Rev. Msgr. RAYMOND F. BEGIN, S.T.L., J.C.D.; Rev. JOSEPH J. KOURY, J.C.D.; Sr. RITA-MAE BISSONNETTE, R.S.R., J.C.L.; Revs. MARK P. NOLETTE, J.C.L.; Most Rev. MICHAEL R. COTE, J.C.L., D.D.; Mr. GEORGE G. PAVLOFF, J.C.D.

Guardian—Rev. MARC B. CARON, S.T.L.

Deans—Rev. Msgr. ROBERT G. LAVOIE, V.F.; Rev. Msgr. CHARLES M. MURPHY; Very Revs. JOHN F. O'HARA, V.F.; RENE T. MATHIEU, V.F.; NORMAND P. RICHARD, V.F.; ROYAL J. PARENT; NORMAND CARPENTIER, V.F.; ANTONIO AMATO, V.F.; PAUL A. PLANTE, V.F.; GEORGES J. PLANTE, V.F.; LEOPOLD G. NICKNAIR, V.F.; JEAN PAUL LABRIE, V.F.; BRIAN D. BLANCHETTE, V.F.; PAUL E. COTE, V.F.; LAURENT R. LAPLANTE, V.F.; CLEMENT D. THIBODEAU, V.F.; FRANK J. MURRAY, V.F.; JOSEPH J. KOURY, V.F.

Diocesan Consultors—Rev. Msgr. VINCENT A. TATARCZUK; Revs. THOMAS M. MURPHY; GEORGES J. PLANTE, V.F.; CLEMENT D. THIBODEAU; RENE T. MATHIEU; Most Rev. MICHAEL R. COTE, J.C.L., D.D.; Revs. FRANCIS P. MORIN; JAMES J. MORRISON.

Diocesan Offices and Directors

Campaign for Human Development—Ms. GLORIA A. DUGAN, L.C.S.W., *P.O. Box 10660, Portland, 04104.* Tel: 207-781-8550; Fax: 207-781-8560.

Catholic Stewardship Appeal—Mr. DAVID P. TWOMEY, C.P.A., Dir.; Mrs. ANNETTE DIMILLO, Coord., *510 Ocean Ave., P.O. Box 11559, Portland, 04104-7559.* Tel: 207-773-6471.

Catholic Relief Services—Ms. ANN P. FOLEY, *510 Ocean Ave., P.O. Box 11559, Portland, 04104-7559.* Tel: 207-773-6471.

Catholic Schools Office—Sr. ROSEMARY T. DONOHUE, S.N.D., Supt., Schools, *510 Ocean Ave., P.O. Box 11559, Portland, 04104-7559.* Tel: 207-773-6471.

Catholic Scouting—CHARLES MATTHEW, Co-Chm., *6 Cottage St., Fairfield, 04937.* CARL PARADIS, Co-Chm., *7 Valee Ave, Waterville, 04901.* JOYCE ROSSIGNOL, Girl Scout Liaison, *P.O. Box 812, Waterville, 04901.*

Catholic Charismatic Renewal Diocesan Liaison—Rev. RICHARD P. RICE, *66 North Ave., Sanford, 04073.*

Catholic Charities Maine—Central Services: GLORIA A. DUGAN, L.C.S.W., A.C.S.W., Exec. Dir.; Mr. PAUL L. MORGAN, Contracting Dir.; Ms. BONNIE J. BAGLEY, Services Dir.; Ms. SANDRA L. BOYD, Operations Dir.; Mr. PAUL J. LUISE, Pub. Rels. Dir., *P.O. Box 10660, Portland, 04104.* Tel: 207-781-8550; Fax: 207-781-8560. PETER J. TURNER, M.B.A., Finance Dir. CONNIE JONES, Human Resources Dir.; Mr. NORMAND D. HOULE, Information Technology Dir., *P.O. Box 10660, Portland, 04104.* Tel: 207-781-8550; Fax: 207-781-8560.

Clergy Benefit Plan-Clergy Pension Plan—Prudential Committee: Rev. Msgr. VINCENT A. TATARCZUK, Chm., *P.O. Box 218, Raymond, 04071.* Most Rev. JOSEPH J. GERRY, O.S.B., Pres.; Revs. J. JOSEPH FORD, Chm. Bd. CLAUDE J. ALBERT, Treas. NORMAND E. CARPENTIER, Sec. Members: Rev. Msgr. PAUL D. GLEASON; Revs. RICHARD R. OUELLETTE; LIONEL G. CHOUINARD; GEORGES J. PLANTE, V.F.; MARCEL G. CHOUINARD; JOHN L. DOUGHER; TIMOTHY NADEAU; JOHN E. HARRIS; MARC B. CARON; Mrs. SALLY I. NELSON, Plan Admin.; Mr. JOHN R. ROSSIGNOL, Plan Accountant.

Diocesan Archivist—Sr. THERESE PELLETIER, S.C.I.M.

Diocesan Board of Education—Mrs. DORIS OUELLETTE, Chm.; Sr. ROSEMARY T. DONOHUE, S.N.D., Exec Sec. ANNE E. PELLETIER, Recording Sec. Members: Sr. ANNE-MARIE BOURQUE, R.S.M.; Rev. STEPHEN CONCANNON; PRISCILLA DENTON; Mr. CHARLES KENNEDY; Mr. MICHAEL WELCH; Mr. JAMES A. WARD; Rev. RICHARD ST. CYR; Rev. JAMES KEEGAN, S.J.; Sr. EDWARD MARY KELLEHER, R.S.M.; Rev. RICHARD MCLAUGHLIN; NOREEN MINKLER.

Diocesan Bureau of Housing—Most Rev. JOSEPH J. GERRY, O.S.B., Bishop of Portland/Pres.; Mr. DAVID P. TWOMEY, Treas. ROBERT C. ROBINSON, ESQ., Clerk, *P.O. Box 11559, Portland, 04104-7559.*

Diocesan Council of Priests—Rev. Msgr. VINCENT A. TATARCZUK; Revs. NORMAND E. CARPENTIER; ALFRED JACQUES; RENALD D. LABARRE; GEORGES J. PLANTE; PAUL PLANTE; RENE T. MATHIEU, Chm. CLEMENT D. THIBODEAU; PAUL R. MARQUIS; FRANCIS P. MORIN; JAMES L. NADEAU; MARK NOLETTE; PAUL R. KERNS; ROBERT C. VALLAINCOURT; JOHN KEEGAN, S.J.; JAMES J. MORRISON, V.F.; CLAUDE GENDREAU; MICHAEL MCGARRIGLE. Ex Officio: Most Rev. MICHAEL R. COTE, J.C.L., D.D.; Rev. Msgr. CHARLES MURPHY; Rev. MARC B. CARON.

Diocesan Director of Pastoral and Educational Services—Sr. PATRICIA C. FLYNN, R.S.M., *Chancery Office, 510 Ocean Ave., P.O. Box 11559, Portland, 04104-7559.*

Diocesan Finance Council—Most Rev. JOSEPH J. GERRY, O.S.B.; Most Rev. MICHAEL R. COTE; Rev. CLAUDE ALBERT; Mr. WILLIAM STOLOSKI; Mr. MICHAEL MCNAMARA; JOHN DECKRO, Vice-Chm. MARTIN F. MORGAN, JR.; Rev. JAMES J. MORRISON; KEVIN O'NEIL; CHARLES PRINN; MARY ANN NEWCOMB; GREGG H. GINN; JOHN SCHIAVI; RICHARD RODERICK, Chm. GREGORY ST. ANGELO; Sr. MARY DENIS SCHWARTZ, R.S.M. Ex Officio Members: Rev. MARC B. CARON. Staff: DAVID P. TWOMEY, C.P.A.; Mr. ANTHONY SILVIA; Mr. JOHN R. ROSSIGNOL; WILLIAM RICHARDS.

Diocesan Office of Catechetics and Initiation—BARBARA A. SMITH, Diocesan Dir.; Mrs. KATHY DYER, Region I Resource Person, *25 Coolidge Ave., Caribou, 04736.* Tel: 207-496-0520. Sr. CATHERINE GREEN, R.S.M., Region II Resource Person, *492 Main Rd., Hampden, 04444.* Tel: 207-947-5381. Region III Resource Persons: AGNES DINN; JAMES DINN, *24 Hayford St., Farmingdale, 04344.* Tel: 207-622-2874. BARBARA A. SMITH, Region IV Resource Person, *Chancery Office, 510 Ocean Ave., P.O. Box 11559, Portland, 04104-7559.* Tel: 207-773-6471.

Diocesan Office of Public Affairs—Mr. MARC R. MUTTY, Dir., *510 Ocean Ave., P.O. Box 11559, Portland, 04104-7559.*

Diocesan Office of Family Life & Natural Family Planning Program and Respect Life Office—Mr. STEPHEN J. BEIRNE, Dir., *P.O. Box 11559, Portland, 04104-7559.* Tel: 207-773-6471.

Diocesan Office of Ministry to Persons with Disabilities—Sr. CLAIRE BLAIS, C.S.J., *P.O. Box 11559, Portland, 04104-7559.*

Bishop's Delegate for Priests—Rev. PAUL F. STEFANKO, J.C.L., Dir., *510 Ocean Ave., P.O. Box 11559, Portland, 04104-7559.* Tel: 207-773-6471.

Diocesan Office of Small Christian Communities—Sr. PATRICIA C. FLYNN, R.S.M., Coord., *P.O. Box 11559, Portland, 04104-7559.* Tel: 207-773-6471.

Diocesan Office for Worship—Mrs. SUZANNE PROULX POWELL, Dir., *510 Ocean Ave., P.O. Box 11559, Portland, 04104-7559.* Tel: 207-773-6471.

Diocesan Office of Youth Ministry—Mrs. JEANNE S. BIGELOW, Dir. Youth Ministry Regional Coordinators: Region I, KAREN OUELLETTE. Tel: 207-834-8355; Fax: 207-834-6835. Region II, WILLIAM ROMANO, *P.O. Box 623, Waterville, 04901.* Tel: 207-862-6149; Fax: 207-862-4041. Region III, MICHAEL THURLOW, . Fax: 207-588-0305.

Financial Management—Mr. DAVID P. TWOMEY, Finance Officer; Mr. ANTHONY SILVA, Controller; Mr. JOHN ROSSIGNOL, Asst. Controller, *510 Ocean Ave., P.O. Box 11559, Portland, 04104-7559.* Tel: 207-773-6471.

General Counsel—Mr. ROBERT C. ROBINSON, *12 Portland Pier, P.O. Box 568, Portland, 04112.*

Liturgical Commission—Members: Revs. RENALD LABARRE; RIGINALD BRISSETTE; MARC B. CARON; Mr. KEVIN BIRCH; Rev. MICHAEL J. HENCHAL, J.C.L.; SUZANNE PROULX POWELL, Exec. Sec.

Maine Diocesan Council of Catholic Women—Most Rev. JOSEPH J. GERRY, Episcopal Chm.; Rev. LAWRENCE CONLEY, V.F., Diocesan Moderator, *St. Catherine Parish, 29 Paris St., Norway, 04268-1132.* Mrs. DOROTHY TURMELLE, Diocesan Pres.

Newman Apostolate—Rev. JOSEPH J. KOURY, J.C.D., Coord. Assoc. Pastors: Revs. ALBIN A. ANDRUS; PHILIP A. TRACY; LARCH FIDLER, IV; CLAUDE GENDREAU; ERNEST L'HEUREUX; GERALD A. LEVESQUE; JOHN MARQUIS, S.M.; JOSEPH J. CARTER; JOHN F. O'HARA. Pastoral Assocs.: Rev. JOHN J. TOPAZ, O.F.M.Cap.; Sr. MARY SWEENEY; Sr. SYLVIA COMER.

Vicar for Religious—Most Rev. MICHAEL R. COTE, F.I.C.

Personnel Board—Revs. JOHN SKEHAN; REGINALD R. BRISSETTE; STEPHEN CONCANNON; MICHAEL J. HENCHAL, J.C.L.; REAL J. NADEAU; MARCEL DUMOULIN; FRANK MURRAY; PAUL F. STEFANKO, J.C.L.; MARC B. CARON; RICHARD OUELLETTE; CHRISTOPHER LAROCHE. Officio Members: Most Revs. JOSEPH J. GERRY, Pres. MICHAEL R. COTE, Vice Pres.; Rev. Msgr. CHARLES M. MURPHY, Dir., Seminarians.

Pontifical Association of Holy Childhood—Ms. ANN P. FOLEY, Dir., *510 Ocean Ave., P.O. Box 11559, Portland, 04104-7559.* Tel: 207-773-6471.

Pontifical Society for the Propagation of the Faith—Ms. ANN P. FOLEY.

Seminarians, Director of—Rev. Msgr. CHARLES M. MURPHY, *510 Ocean Ave., P.O. Box 11559, Portland, 04104-7559.* Tel: 207-773-6471.

Vocations—Revs. DANIEL P. GREENLEAF, Diocesan Dir., *510 Ocean Ave., P.O. Box 11559, Portland, 04104-7559.* Tel: 207-773-6471 (office); 877-0953 (residence).

CLERGY, PARISHES, MISSIONS AND PAROCHIAL SCHOOLS

CITY OF PORTLAND
(Cumberland County)

1—CATHEDRAL OF THE IMMACULATE CONCEPTION, Rev. James A. Nadeau, Rector. In res., Most Revs. Edward C. O'Leary, (Retired); Michael R. Cote; Revs. Robert E. Lee, O.Carm.; Harold Nicknair; John J. Scahill; Albin Andrus; Patrick J. Barrett.
Res., 307 Congress St., 04101. Tel: 207-773-7746 (Rectory); 774-5101 (Res.); Fax: 207-879-5547.
School—14 Locust St., 04101. Tel: 207-775-1491. Sr. Theresa Rand, R.S.M., Prin.
Sisters of Mercy 1; Sisters of the Holy Rosary 1; Lay Teachers 6; Students 150.
Catechesis/Religious Programs—Tel: 207-772-0276. Donna Lebel, D.R.E.
Students 125.

2—ST. DOMINIC'S. Merged to form Sacred Heart/St. Dominic's, Portland.

3—ST. JOSEPH'S, Revs. Patrick Glavin, O.F.M.Cap.; Don Bosco Duquette, O.F.M.Cap.; Theodosius Corley, O.F.M.Cap.; John Tokaz, O.F.M.Cap.
Res., 673 Stevens Ave., 04103. Tel: 207-797-7026; Fax: 207-797-2679.
School—697 Stevens Ave., 04103. Tel: 207-797-7073. Ms. Lori Ann Lee, Prin.
Sisters of Mercy 1; Lay Teachers 16; Students 218.
Catechesis/Religious Programs—Tel: 207-797-9509. D.R.E.: Eleanor Bernabei; Sylvia Harlow.
Students 363.

4—ST. LOUIS (Polish), Rev. Msgr. Vincent A. Tatarczuk, Admin.
Res., 279 Danforth St., 04102. Tel: 207-773-4176.

5—ST. PATRICK'S, Revs. Coleman P. O'Toole; John D. Civiello.
Res., 1342 Congress St., 04102. Tel: 207-772-6325.
School—1251 Congress St., 04102. Tel: 207-772-2521. Mrs. Barbara Ann Arnoldo, Prin.
Sisters of Mercy 2; Lay Teachers 9; Students 259.
Catechesis/Religious Programs—Tel: 207-772-3521. Cynthia McGarry, D.R.E.
Students 65.

6—ST. PETER'S (Italian), Rev. Kieran Monahan, O.F.M.; Bro. Mark Brown, O.F.M.
Res., 72 Federal St., 04101. Tel: 207-773-0748; Fax: 207-879-0557.
Catechesis/Religious Programs—Bro. Mark Brown, D.R.E.
Students 140.

7—SACRED HEART/ST. DOMINIC. Merged with St. Dominic, Portland. Rev. Frank P. Morin.
Res., 80 Sherman St., 04101-2216. Tel: 207-772-6182; 772-7877.
Catechesis/Religious Programs—Students 56.

8—ST. CHRISTOPHER'S (Peaks Island), Rev. Robert Bouchard.
Res., 107 Island Ave., 04108-1125. Tel: 207-766-2585.
Mission—Long Island, Great Diamond Island.

9—ST. PIUS X, Revs. Arthur H. Pare, S.J., Pastor; Robert F. Regan, S.J., Pastoral Assoc. In res., Rev. John W. Keegan, S.J.
Res., 492 Ocean Ave., 04103. Tel: 207-775-3032; Fax: 207-874-7514.
Catechesis/Religious Programs—Tel: 207-775-2185. Donna Beattie, D.R.E.
Students 297.

OUTSIDE THE CITY OF PORTLAND

Ashland, Aroostook Co., St. Mark's, Rev. Mark P. Nolette.
Res., School St., P.O. Box E, 04732-0545. Tel: 207-435-3591. [CEM]
Catechesis/Religious Programs—Tel: 207-435-6440. Carol H. Bushey, D.R.E.
Students 90.
Mission—Portage, Our Lady of the Lakes.

Auburn, Androscoggin Co., St. Louis, Rev. Richard D. Bertrand, S.J.; Sr. Irene Platt, C.O.C., Pastoral Assoc. & D.R.E.
Res., 24 Dunn St., 04210. Tel: 207-784-4146. [JC]
Catechesis/Religious Programs—Tel: 207-784-0012.
Students 110.
Parish Center—101 Second St., 04210.

St. Philip's, Rev. Roger P. Chabot.
Res., 365 Turner Rd., 04212-8410. Tel: 207-784-6486; Fax: 207-784-6487.
Catechesis/Religious Programs—Students 116.

Sacred Heart, Rev. Maurice T. Lebel; Sr. Elizabeth Platt, C.O.C., Pastoral Assoc. & RCIA Coord.
Res., 267 Minot Ave., 04210. Tel: 207-782-8096.
Catechesis/Religious Programs—Sandra Tardiff, D.R.E., Tel: 207-782-4005.
Students 181.

Augusta, Kennebec Co., St. Mary's, Rev. Paul R. Kerns. In res., Revs. D. Joseph Manship; William F. Modlin; John I. Audibert.
Res., 41 Western Ave., P.O. Box 547, 04332. Tel: 207-623-8823; Fax: 207-623-7574. [CEM 2]
School—56 Sewall St., 04332. Tel: 207-623-3491; Fax: 207-626-5818. Sr. Barbara Brennan, R.S.M., Prin.
Sisters of Mercy 2; Lay Teachers 11; Students 251.
Catechesis/Religious Programs—D.R.E.: Gretchen Franz, (Grades K-5) Tel: 207-622-3450; Michael Thurlow, (Grades 6-12) Tel: 207-626-5940.
Students 150.
St. Andrew's. Unassigned.
Res., St. Andrew St., R.F.D. 10, Box 1350, 04330. Tel: 207-623-8543; Fax: 207-626-0287.
Catechesis/Religious Programs—Tel: 207-623-3159. Suzanne Allarie-Dowling, D.R.E.
Students 146.
St. Augustine's, Rev. Lionel G. Chouinard.
Res., One Kendall St., 04330. Tel: 207-622-2184; Fax: 207-621-4064. [CEM 2]
School—24 Washington St., 04330. Tel: 207-622-1771. Sr. Rachel Boucher, Prin.
Sisters of the Presentation of Mary 2; Lay Teachers 10; Students 188.
Catechesis/Religious Programs—Lisa Couture, D.R.E.
Students 89.

Bangor, Penobscot Co., St. John's, Revs. Gerard G. Gosselin; Richard O'Brien; Robert J. Sullivan, S.J. Pastoral Assocs.: Sr. Patricia Mooney, R.S.M.; Sr. Celestine Theriault, R.S.M.
Res., 207 York St., 04401. Tel: 207-942-6941; Fax: 207-947-5984.
School—166 State St., 04401. Tel: 207-945-0023. Mrs. Susan Inman, Prin.
Lay Teachers 14; Students 143.
Catechesis/Religious Programs—Tel: 207-945-0023. Joan Winstead, D.R.E.
Students 443.
St. Mary's, Revs. Frank J. Murray; Richard O'Brien.
Res., 768 Ohio St., 04401-3106. Tel: 207-945-5018.
School—Tel: 207-947-7063. Sr. Margaret Walsh, R.S.M., Prin.
Lay Teachers 8; Students 140.
Catechesis/Religious Programs—Tel: 207-942-1643.
Students 570.

Bar Harbor, Hancock Co., Holy Redeemer, Rev. Joseph F. Daniels.
Res., 21 Ledgelawn Ave., 04609. Tel: 207-288-3535.
Catechesis/Religious Programs—Tel: 207-288-3421.
Students 54.

Bath, Sagadahoc Co., Immaculate Conception, Rev. Joseph R. Mckenna.
Res., 144 Lincoln St., 04530. Tel: 207-443-3423.
Catechesis/Religious Programs—Tel: 207-443-4987. Nancy Lewis, D.R.E.
Students 169.

Belfast, Waldo Co., St. Francis of Assisi, Rev. Constanzo J. Piscilli, Admin.
Res. & Mailing Address—81 Court St., 04915-6134. Tel: 207-338-4433.
Catechesis/Religious Programs—Tel: 207-338-6688. Sr. Aline Roy, D.R.E.
Students 124.
Mission—Isleboro, St. Mary of the Isles.

Benedicta, Aroostook Co., St. Benedict's, Rev. Joseph H. Blattner.
Res., 04733. Tel: 207-365-4128. [CEM]
Catechesis/Religious Programs—Tel: 207-365-4269. Anna Robinson, D.R.E.
Students 59.
Mission—Sherman Station, Penobscot Co., St. Joseph's Church, P.O. Box 27, Sherman Station, 04733.

Berwick, York Co., Our Lady of Peace, Rev. Hilary J. Cameron.
Res., 25 Berwick St., 03901-2109. Tel: 207-698-1072.
Catechesis/Religious Programs—Students 160.

Biddeford, York Co., St. Andre's, Rev. Reginald R. Brissette.
Mailing Address: 6 St. Mary St., 04005.
Res., 73 Bacon St., 04005. Tel: 207-282-3333. [JC]
School—St. James School. See St. Joseph's for details.
Catechesis/Religious Programs—Tel: 207-282-4812.
Students 191.
St. Joseph's, Revs. Renald D. LeBarre; Joseph F. Carter; Sr. June Rita Fortier, S.C.I.M.
Office—6 St. Mary St., P.O. Box 408, 04005. Tel: 207-282-9352; Fax: 207-286-8679.
Res., 43 Center St., 04005.
School—New Consolidated School - St. James, (Grades K-8) P.O. Box 5039, 25 Graham St., 04007. Tel: 207-282-4084. Ms. Marie Klement, Prin.
Sisters 1; Lay Teachers 28; Students 416.
Catechesis/Religious Programs—Tel: 207-282-4812. Nancy P. Labbe, D.R.E. & Pastoral Assoc.
Students 191.
St. Mary's, Rev. John Andrew Allen, Pastor.
Res., P.O.Box 515, 04005. Tel: 207-284-5363; Fax: 207-286-8679. [CEM]
School—St. James School. See St. Joseph's for details. Tel: 207-282-4084.
Catechesis/Religious Programs—Tel: 207-282-4812.
Students 191.
Mission—Biddeford Pool, York Co., St. Brendan.

Bingham, Somerset Co., St. Peter's, Rev. Robert V. Paskey, S.J.
Res., Owens St., Box No. 667, 04920. Tel: 207-672-3912.
Catechesis/Religious Programs—Students 71.
Mission—West Forks, SS. Philip & James.

Boothbay Harbor, Lincoln Co., Our Lady, Queen of Peace, Rev. Royal J. Parent.
Res., 82 Atlantic Ave., 04538. Tel: 207-633-2680; Fax: 207-633-1164.
Catechesis/Religious Programs—Students 47.

Bradley, Penobscot Co., St. Ann, Rev. Timothy J. Nadeau.
Res., Box 137, 04411. Tel: 207-827-2087. [JC]
Catechesis/Religious Programs—Tel: 207-827-7643. Mary Shorette, D.R.E.
Students 65.

Brewer, Penobscot Co., St. Joseph's, Revs. Joel R. Cyr, Admin.; Brendan Harnett.
Res., 531 N. Main St., 04412. Tel: 207-989-5388. [JC]
Catechesis/Religious Programs—Tel: 207-989-5343.
Students 184.
St. Teresa's, Revs. Joel R. Cyr, Admin.; Brendan Harnett.
Res., 440 S. Main St., 04412. Tel: 207-989-7049; Fax: 207-989-4992.
Catechesis/Religious Programs—Tel: 207-989-6129.
Students 88.

Bridgton, Cumberland Co., St. Joseph, Rev. Joseph E. Whitlock.
Mailing Address: P.O. Box 310, 04009-0310. Tel: 207-647-2334.
Catechesis/Religious Programs—Tel: 207-647-8154.
Students 101.
Mission—Fryeburg, Oxford Co., St. Elizabeth Ann Seton, P.O. Box 332, Fryeburg, 04037. Tel: 207-935-4245.

Brownville Junction, Piscataquis Co., St. Francis Xavier, Rev. Myles Cyr, O.M.I., Admin.
Res., Front St., Box 385, 04415. Tel: 207-965-2341.
Catechesis/Religious Programs—Tel: 207-943-5160. Deborah Moulton, D.R.E.
Students 31.
Mission—Milo, St. Paul.

Brunswick, Cumberland Co., St. John the Baptist, Revs. Walter Gaudreau, S.M.; Edward Sheehan, S.M.; Kenneth Ridgeway, S.M. In res., Rev. Robert McDonald, S.M.
Res., 39 Pleasant St., 04011. Tel: 207-725-8756; Fax: 207-798-4792. [CEM]
School—St. John's School, 37 Pleasant St., 04011. Tel: 207-725-5507. Sr. Angela Krippendorff, Prin.
Lay Teachers 21; Students 237.
Catechesis/Religious Programs—Tel: 207-729-5966. Carolyn Ruggles, D.R.E.
Students 210.
Mission—Pejepscot, Topsham Co., St. Andrew, Rte. 196, Pejepscot, 04086.
St. Charles, Rev. Stephen F. Concannon.
Office: 132 McKeen St., 04011. Tel: 207-725-2624.
Catechesis/Religious Programs—Students 173.
Missions—Bailey Island, Precious Blood; South Harpswell, St. Mary-by-the-Sea.

Bucksport, Hancock Co., St. Vincent de Paul, Rev. John F. O'Hara, V.F.
Res., 158 Franklin St., P.O. Box S, 04416. Tel: 207-469-3322. [CEM]
Catechesis/Religious Programs—Mary O'Shea, D.R.E.
Students 136.

Calais, Washington Co., Immaculate Conception, Rev. Brian D. Blanchette.
Res., 17 Calais Ave., 04619. Tel: 207-454-3413.
Catechesis/Religious Programs—Leah McLean, D.R.E.
Students 120.

Camden, Knox Co., Our Lady of Good Hope, Rev. Eugene F. Gaffey.
Res., 7 Union St., 04843. Tel: 207-236-4785; Fax: 207-236-9422.
Catechesis/Religious Programs—Students 178.
Mission—North Haven, Our Lady of Peace.
Station—Vinalhaven, Our Lady of Peace.

Cape Elizabeth, Cumberland Co., St. Bartholomew, Rev. Michael J. Henchal; Sr. Ruth Hayden, Pastoral Assoc.
Res., 8 Two Lights Rd., 04107. Tel: 207-799-5528; Fax: 207-799-1532.
Catechesis/Religious Programs—Tel: 207-767-3436.
Students 211.

Caribou, Aroostook Co., Holy Rosary, Revs. Leopold G. Nicknair; Christopher J. LaRoche. In res., Rev. Msgr. Gilman Chaloult.
Res., 31 Thomas Ave., P.O. Box 625, 04736. Tel: 207-498-2536.
Catechesis/Religious Programs—Tel: 207-498-8655. D.R.E.: Michael McCormack; Ronald Willey; Jacqueline Lambert.
Students 292.
Mission—Washburn, St. Catherine.
Sacred Heart, Rev. Joachim Thanh Nguyen.
Res., 1143 Van Buren Rd., 04736. Tel: 207-498-2763.
Catechesis/Religious Programs—Betty Thompson, D.R.E., Tel: 207-498-8741.
Students 105.

Daigle, Aroostook Co., Holy Family, Rev. Jean Paul Labrie.
Res., 11 E. Main St., Fort Kent, 04743. Tel: 207-834-5656. [CEM]
Catechesis/Religious Programs—Students 15.

Dexter, Penobscot Co., St. Ann's, Very Rev. Antonio Amato, V.F.
Res., 59 Free St., 04930. Tel: 207-924-7104.
Catechesis/Religious Programs—Tel: 207-924-7993.
Students 90.

Dover-Foxcroft, Piscataquis Co., St. Thomas, Rev. Paul R. Marquis.
Res., 45 High St., 04426. Tel: 207-564-2842.
Catechesis/Religious Programs—Tel: 207-564-0867. Louise DuLac, D.R.E.
Students 60.
Mission—Sangerville, Holy Family.

Eagle Lake, Aroostook Co., St. Mary's, Rev. James R. Albert.
Res., Church St., 04739. Tel: 207-444-5119.
Catechesis/Religious Programs—Mildred Pelletier, D.R.E.
Students 30.

East Millinocket, Penobscot Co., St. Peter's, Rev. George W. Beaudet.
Res., 56 Cedar St., P.O. Box 400, 04430. Tel: 207-746-3861.
Catechesis/Religious Programs—Tel: 207-746-3333. Julie Fiske, D.R.E.
Students 140.

Eastport, Washington Co., St. Joseph, Rev. Paul M. Sullivan, S.J.
Res., 51 Washington St., 04631. Tel: 207-853-2825. [JC]
Catechesis/Religious Programs—Students 28.
Mission—Pembroke, St. John the Evangelist.

Ellsworth, Hancock Co., St. Joseph's, Rev. Leo James Michand.
Res., 231 Main St., 04605. Tel: 207-667-2342. [CEM]
Catechesis/Religious Programs—Mimi Colawell, D.R.E.
Students 175.
Missions—Green Lake, Our Lady of the Lake; Winter Harbor, St. Margaret.

Fairfield, Somerset Co., Immaculate Heart of Mary, Rev. Marcel L. Dumoulin; Kimberly Suttie, Pastoral Assoc.
Res., 21 High St., 04937. Tel: 207-453-6131; Fax: 207-453-8334.
Catechesis/Religious Programs—Tel: 207-453-7940.
Students 153.

Falmouth, Cumberland Co., Holy Martyrs, Rev. Msgr. Charles M. Murphy, S.T.D.; Mrs. Judith Dominick, Pastoral Assoc.
Catechesis/Religious Programs—266 Foreside Rd., 04105. Tel: 207-781-4573; Fax: 207-781-3961.
Students 386.

Farmington, Franklin Co., St. Joseph's, Rev. Gerald A. Levesque.
Mailing Address: c/o The Pastoral Center, 13 Middle St., 04938-1598. Tel: 207-778-2778; Fax: 207-778-0268.
Catechesis/Religious Programs—David Levensalor, D.R.E.
Students 153.

Fort Fairfield, Aroostook Co., St. Denis, Rev. William J. Carrigg, Admin.
Res., 43 Main St., 04742-1223. Tel: 207-473-7329. [CEM 2]

Catechesis/Religious Programs—Students 73.

Fort Kent, Aroostook Co., St. Louis, Rev. Jean Paul Labrie.
Res., 11 E. Main St., 04743. Tel: 207-834-5656. [CEM]
Catechesis/Religious Programs—Tel: 207-834-3984. D.R.E.: Ziona Straub, (Grades K-6/SPRED); Irene Harvey, (Grades 7-8).
Students 594.

Frenchville, Aroostook Co., St. Luce's (Upper), Rev. Angelo LeVasseur.
Mailing Address: P.O. Box 98, Upper Frenchville, 04745-0098. Tel: 207-543-7313; Fax: 207-543-6193. [CEM]
Catechesis/Religious Programs—Tel: 207-543-5150. Marie Textor, D.R.E.
Students 203.

Gardiner, Kennebec Co., St. Joseph's, Rev. Clement D. Thibodeau. In res., Rev. L. David Mani.
Res., One Lincoln Ave., 04345-2188. Tel: 207-582-2385. [CEM]
Catechesis/Religious Programs—Tel: 207-582-1149.
Students 328.

Gorham, Cumberland Co., St. Anne, Rev. Ernest L. L'Heureux.
Res., 299 Main St., 04038. Tel: 207-839-4857; 839-3082; Fax: 207-839-3082.
Catechesis/Religious Programs—Tel: 207-839-3082. Claire Sirois, D.R.E.
Students 486.
Mission—East Sebago, Our Lady of Sebago.

Grand Isle, Aroostook Co., St. Gerard-Mt. Carmel, Rev. Richard R. Ouellette.
Res., 04746. Tel: 207-895-3436. [CEM]
Catechesis/Religious Programs—Verna Beaulieu, D.R.E.
Students 96.

Gray, Cumberland Co., St. Gregory, Rev. Msgr. Robert G. Lavoie.
Res., 24 N. Raymond Rd., P.O. Box 345, 04039-0345. Tel: 207-657-4241.
Catechesis/Religious Programs—Tel: 207-627-4693.
Students 75.

Greenville, Piscataquis Co., Holy Family, Rev. Anthony Rotunno.
Res., Pritham Rd., P.O. Box 478, 04441. Tel: 207-695-2262.
Catechesis/Religious Programs—Tel: 207-695-2009. Lucy Fay, D.R.E.
Students 25.
Mission—Rockwood, Somerset Co., St. Joseph's. [CEM]

Hallowell, Kennebec Co., Sacred Heart, Rev. Richard G. Lonsdale.
Res., 12 Summer St., 04347. Tel: 207-623-3424.
Catechesis/Religious Programs—Tel: 207-623-3807. Mary Bourque, D.R.E.
Students 76.

Hamlin, Aroostook Co., St. Joseph, Rev. Joseph S. Chasse, S.M.
Res., 336 Main St., Van Buren, 04785. Tel: 207-868-2718. [CEM]
Catechesis/Religious Programs—Tel: 207-868-2835.
Students 361.

Hampden, Penobscot Co., St. Matthew, Rev. George W. Hickey.
Res., 70 Western Ave., P.O. Box 280, 04444. Tel: 207-862-3517.
Catechesis/Religious Programs—Tel: 207-862-5404. Mrs. Pam Smith, D.R.E.
Students 189.

Houlton, Aroostook Co., St. Mary's, Rev. Philip Cyr; Sr. Carol Martin, P.F.M., Pastoral Assoc.
Res., 110 Military St., 04730. Tel: 207-532-2871.
Catechesis/Religious Programs—Students 291.

Howland, Penobscot Co., St. Leo, Rev. Andre L. Houle, O.M.I.
P.O. Box 329, 04448. Tel: 207-732-3495.
Catechesis/Religious Programs—Tel: 207-732-4559.
Students 65.

Indian Township, Washington Co., St. Ann (1929), Rev. Michael Sheridan.
Church—P.O. Box 358, 04668. Tel: 207-796-5013.
Mission—Indian Township, St. Theresa's Chapel.

Island Falls, Aroostook Co., St. Agnes, Rev. Joseph H. Blattner.
Mailing Address: P.O. Box 27, Benedicta, 04733. Tel: 207-365-4128. [CEM]
Catechesis/Religious Programs—Students 20.
Mission—Patten, St. Paul.

Jackman, Somerset Co., St. Anthony, Rev. Richard C. Malo.
Res., 04945. Tel: 207-668-2881. [CEM]
Catechesis/Religious Programs—Students 48.

Jay, Franklin Co., St. Rose of Lima, Rev. George C. Pelletier.
Res., One Church St., 04239. Tel: 207-897-2173; Fax: 207-897-2478.
Catechesis/Religious Programs—Students 184.

Kennebunk, York Co., St. Martha's, Rev. Laurant R. Laplante.
Res., 34 Portland Rd., P.O. Box 510, 04043. Tel: 207-985-6252; Fax: 207-985-7740.
Catechesis/Religious Programs—Mrs. Rosanne Smith, D.R.E.
Students 286.
Mission—Kennebunk, St. Monica's.

Kittery, York Co., St. Raphael's, Rev. Robert D. Lariviere.
Res., 8 Whipple Rd., 03904-1758. Tel: 207-439-0442; Fax: 207-439-0442.
Catechesis/Religious Programs—Faith Formation Center, 6 Whipple Rd., 03904-1739. Tel: 207-439-2642.
Students 132.

Lewiston, Androscoggin Co.,

1—ST. JOSEPH'S, Rev. Richard McLaughlin.
Res., 253 Main St., 04240. Tel: 207-784-5328; Fax: 207-795-5078. [JC]
School—393 Main St., 04240. Tel: 207-784-8811; Fax: 207-783-9522. Mrs. Andree Tostevin, Prin.
Religious 1; Lay Teachers 9; Students 234.
Catechesis/Religious Programs—Tel: 207-782-2286. Connie Ayotte, D.R.E.
Students 158.

2—HOLY CROSS, Revs. Rene T. Mathieu; Mark S. Reinhardt.
Res., 16 Ste. Croix St., P.O. Box 1540, 04241-1540. Tel: 207-782-9463; Fax: 207-782-5968. [JC]
School—17 Baird St., 04241. Tel: 207-783-9323. Mrs. Patricia Berthiaume, Prin.
Sisters of Presentation of Mary 2; Lay Teachers 29; Students 586.
Catechesis/Religious Programs—Tel: 207-783-7241. Ms. Ruth Oakley, D.R.E.
Students 409.

3—HOLY FAMILY, Revs. Claude J. Albert, Jr.; John J. Austin; Germaine Marquis, Pastoral Assoc. In res., Rev. Rene G. Lavoie.
Res., 607 Sabattus St., 04240. Tel: 207-782-8928; Fax: 207-782-3179.
Catechesis/Religious Programs—Tel: 207-783-7330. Linda Grandmaison, D.R.E.
Students 325.

4—ST. MARY'S, Rev. Richard D. Bertrand, S.J.
Mailing Address: 24 Dunn St., Auburn, 04210-6896.
Res., 88 Oxford St., 04243-3061. Tel: 207-784-4146.
Catechesis/Religious Programs—Tel: 207-784-0012. Sr. Irene Platt, C.O.C., D.R.E.
Students 93.

5—ST. PATRICK'S, Revs. Real J. Nadeau; Andrew Dubois. In res., Rev. Bertrand R. Poussard.
Pastoral Center: 135 Ash St., 04240. Tel: 207-777-1200; Fax: 207-782-0110.
Res., 220 Bates St., 04240. Tel: 207-782-1997. [CEM]
Catechesis/Religious Programs—Fax: 207-786-9223. Hugh Keene, D.R.E.
Students 62.

6—SS. PETER AND PAUL, Revs. Real J. Nadeau; Andrew Dubois.
Res., 135 Ash St., 04240. Tel: 207-777-1200; Fax: 207-786-9223.
School—250 Bates St., 04240. Tel: 207-782-0721; Fax: 207-782-0110. Mrs. Donna Sawyer, Prin.
Lay Teachers 10; Students 175.
Catechesis/Religious Programs—Mrs. Marie Badeau, D.R.E.
Students 64.

Limerick, York Co., St. Matthew, Rev. Richard A. Nadeau.
Res., R.R. 1, Box 155, 04048. Tel: 207-793-2244.
Catechesis/Religious Programs—Tel: 207-642-3231. Marc Hildreth, D.R.E.
Students 330.

Limestone, Aroostook Co., St. Louis, Rev. William J. Carrigg, Admin.; Janet Beckwith, Pastoral Assoc. In res., Rev. L. Chanel Cyr.
Res., 302 Main St., 04750-1116. Tel: 207-325-4843.
Catechesis/Religious Programs—Tel: 207-325-4656. Diane Edgecomb, D.R.E.
Students 115.

Lincoln, Penobscot Co., St. Mary, Revs. George Sirois, O.M.I.; Roger Cyr; Deacon Thomas Krapf.
Res., 168 Main St., 04457. Tel: 207-794-6333.
Catechesis/Religious Programs—Dawn Sinclair, D.R.E.
Students 142.
Missions—Kingman, St. James; Winn, Sacred Heart; Danforth, St. Ann; Vanceboro, Guardian Angel.

Lisbon, Androscoggin Co., St. Anne's. Merged with Holy Family and SS. Cyril and Methodius to form Holy Trinity, Lisbon Falls.

Lisbon Falls, Androscoggin Co., Holy Trinity (1995), Revs. Anthony F. Kuzia, C.M., Pastor; Julian Szumilo, C.M.
Res., 51 Main St., 04252-1597. Tel: 207-353-6725; 353-2792 (Office); Fax: 207-353-6192. [CEM 3]
Catechesis/Religious Programs—Tel: 207-353-6306.
Students 180.

SS. Cyril and Methodius (Slovak). Merged with St. Anne's and Holy Family to form Holy Trinity, Lisbon Falls.

Lubec, Washington Co., Sacred Heart, Rev. Richard A. Lembo.
Res., 19 Church St., 04652. Tel: 207-733-2214.
Catechesis/Religious Programs—Tel: 207-853-2494.
Students 30.
Mission—Campobello, St. Timothy's, New Brunswick, Canada E09 3H0.

Lyman, York Co., St. Philip, Rev. Thomas M. Lee.
Res., 404 Goodwins Mills Rd., 04002. Tel: 207-499-2940. [JC]
Catechesis/Religious Programs—Lucille Prescott, D.R.E.
Students 147.

Machias, Washington Co., Holy Name of Jesus, Rev. W. Larch Fidler, IV, Admin.
Res., 11 Free St., P.O. Box 248, 04654. Tel: 207-255-3731.
Catechesis/Religious Programs—Carlene Holmes, D.R.E.
Students 46.
Mission—Cherryfield, St. Michael's.

Madawaska, Aroostook Co., St. David's, Rev. Richard R. Ouellette.
Res., Rte. 2, Box 85, 04756. Tel: 207-728-3366. [CEM]
Catechesis/Religious Programs—Tel: 207-728-4012. Sharon M. Oullettte, D.R.E.
Students 98.

St. Thomas Aquinas, Rev. Michael L. Doucette.
Mailing Address: P.O. Box 128, 04756. Tel: 207-728-7531; Fax: 207-728-4217. [CEM]
Catechesis/Religious Programs—Tel: 207-728-7135. Ann Marie Clavette, D.R.E.
Students 374.

Madison, Somerset Co., St. Sebastian, Rev. Georges J. Plante.
Res., 149 Main St., 04950-1599. Tel: 207-696-3203. [CEM]
Catechesis/Religious Programs—Elisabeth Crowley, D.R.E.
Students 80.

Mars Hill, Aroostook Co., St. Joseph, Rev. Thomas Lequin.
Mailing Address: St. Mary's Rectory, P.O. Box 813, Presque Isle, 04769. Tel: 207-768-3671; 429-9805 (Church).
Catechesis/Religious Programs—P.O. Box 197-A, 04758. Tel: 207-429-9074. Julie Tweedie, D.R.E.
Students 40.

Mechanic Falls, Androscoggin Co., Our Lady of Ransom, Rev. Harold D. Moreshead.
Res., 117 Elm St., P.O. Box 206, 04256. Tel: 207-345-2691.
Catechesis/Religious Programs—D.R.E.: Sandy Ferland; Sheila Priola; Ellen Morrison.
Students 120.
Mission—Mechanic Falls, Oxford Co., St. Mary, P.O. Box 206, 04256.

Mexico, Oxford Co., St. Theresa, Rev. Joseph Lange.
Res., 3 Brown St., 04257. Tel: 207-364-2593. [JC]
Catechesis/Religious Programs—Katherine Bisson, D.R.E.
Students 45.
Mission—Dixfield, St. Joseph.

Millinocket, Penobscot Co., St. Martin of Tours, Rev. Normand P. Richard.
Res., 18 Colby St., 04462. Tel: 207-723-5902 (Office); 723-8533 (Rectory); Fax: 207-723-9533.
Catechesis/Religious Programs—Tel: 207-723-9904. Paula Miller, D.R.E.
Students 280.

Newcastle, Lincoln Co., St. Patrick, Rev. Raymond Picard.
Mailing Address: P.O. Box 598, 04553. Tel: 207-563-3240.
Catechesis/Religious Programs—St. Patrick's Parish Ctr., Academy Hill Rd., 04553. Tel: 207-563-6038.
Students 97.

Northeast Harbor, Hancock Co., St. Ignatius, Rev. Joseph E. Daniels; Deacon Joseph LaPlante.
Res., 21 Ledgelawn Ave., Bar Harbor, 04609. Tel: 207-288-3535.
Catechesis/Religious Programs—436 Seawall Rd, 04679. Tel: 207-244-0445.
Students 35.
Missions—Islesford, Our Lady Star of the Sea; Manset, St. Peter's.

North Vassalboro, Kennebec Co., St. Bridget's, Rev. Donald R. Daigle.
Mailing Address: P.O. Box 159, 04962. Tel: 207-873-3204.
Catechesis/Religious Programs—Tel: 207-445-4802. Mrs. Ann Morgan, D.R.E.
Students 104.
Mission—China Lake, St. Peter.

Norway, Oxford Co., St. Catherine of Sienna, Rev. Lawrence J. Conley.
Res., 32 Paris St., 04268-1132. Tel: 207-743-2606.
Catechesis/Religious Programs—Armand Bonneau, D.R.E.
Students 225.
Mission—Bethel, Oxford Co., Our Lady of the Snows, Rte. 26, Bethel, 04217. Tel: 207-824-2933.

Oakland, Kennebec Co., St. Theresa, Rev. Joseph W. Cahill.
Res., 25 Church St., 04963. Tel: 207-465-3856.
Catechesis/Religious Programs—Tel: 207-465-7951. Sr. Cecile Grenier, D.R.E.
Students 90.
Mission—Belgrade Lakes, St. Helena.

Old Orchard Beach, York Co., St. Margaret's, Rev. Normand E. Carpentier.
Res., 6 Saco Ave., P.O. Box 289, 04064. Tel: 207-934-2322; Fax: 207-934-2322.
Catechesis/Religious Programs—Tel: 207-934-4232.
Students 206.
Chapel—Old Orchard, St. Luke's.

Old Town, Penobscot Co.,

1—HOLY FAMILY, Rev. Robert C. Vaillancourt.
Res., 262 S. Main St., 04468. Tel: 207-827-4000. [JC]
Catechesis/Religious Programs—Tel: 207-827-2377.
Students 233.

2—ST. JOSEPH'S. Closed. See Holy Family.

3—ST. MARY'S. Closed. See Holy Family.

4—ST. ANN CHURCH, INDIAN ISLAND, Rev. Timothy J. Nadeau.
Mailing Address: P.O. Box 560, 04468. Tel: 207-827-2172. [CEM]
Catechesis/Religious Programs—Mrs. Terry Paul, D.R.E.
Students 36.

Oquossoc, Franklin Co., Our Lady of the Lakes, Very Rev. Paul E. Cote, V.F.
Res., Box 333, 04964. Tel: 207-864-3795.
Catechesis/Religious Programs—Students 50.
Missions—Rangeley, St. Luke; Stratton, St. John, Tel: 207-246-3277; Sugarloaf U.S.A., Richard H. Bell Memorial Chapel, Tel: 207-246-3277.

Orono, Penobscot Co., St. Mary's, Rev. Joseph J. Koury, Pastor.
Res., 89 Main St., 04473. Tel: 207-866-3372. [JC]
Catechesis/Religious Programs—Students 40.

Our Lady of Wisdom Personal Campus Parish, Rev. Joseph J. Koury; Sr. Mary Sweeney, S.C.
Res., University of Maine, Newman Center, 83 College Ave., 04473. Tel: 207-866-2155; Fax: 207-866-4543.
Catechesis/Religious Programs—Margaret Hallee, D.R.E.
Students 118.
Newman Campus Ministry Center—Tel: 207-866-2155; Fax: 207-866-4543.

Perry, Washington Co., St. Ann (Pleasant Point), Rev. Paul M. Sullivan, S.J., Temp. Admin.
Res., 04667. Tel: 207-853-4718. [CEM]
Catechesis/Religious Programs—Students 30.

Pittsfield, Somerset Co., St. Agnes, Rev. C. James Martel; Deacon David Scammon.
Res., 5 High St., P.O. Box 369, 04967. Tel: 207-487-2777.
School—6 Pine St., 04967. Tel: 207-487-3899. Sr. Elizabeth Cobb, R.S.M., Prin.
Diocesan Sisters of Mercy 2; Lay Teachers 4; Students 51.
Catechesis/Religious Programs—Students 120.

Presque Isle, Aroostook Co., Nativity of B.V.M., Rev. Thomas Lequin.
Res., 6 Roberts St., P.O. Box 813, 04769-0813. Tel: 207-768-3671. [CEM 2]
Catechesis/Religious Programs—Tel: 207-764-0161. Ann Albert, D.R.E.
Students 321.

Richmond, Sagadahoc Co., St. Ambrose, Rev. Paul M. Pare.
Res., 27 Kimball St., P.O. Box 38, 04357. Tel: 207-737-4713.
Catechesis/Religious Programs—Students 102.
Mission—Litchfield, Kennebec Co., St. Leo, Litchfield, 04350. Tel: 207-268-4727.

Rockland, Knox Co., St. Bernard's, Rev. Valmont R. Gilbert.
Res., 150 Broadway, 04841. Tel: 207-594-4322; Fax: 207-594-4322. [CEM]
Catechesis/Religious Programs—Tel: 207-594-5204. Sr. Lucille Menard, S.A., D.R.E.
Students 85.
Mission—Thomaston, Knox Co., St. James.

Rumford, Oxford Co., St. Athanasius-St. John, Rev. Alfred Jacques.
Res., 126 Maine Ave., 04276. Tel: 207-364-4555. [JC]
School—115 Maine Ave., 04276. Tel: 207-364-2528. Walter Buotte, Prin.
Lay Teachers 13; Students 185.
Catechesis/Religious Programs—Mary Theriault, D.R.E.
Students 171.
Mission—Roxbury Pond, St. Mary's Chapel.

Sabattus, Androscoggin Co., Our Lady of the Rosary, Rev. John F. Harris; Sr. Lucille Fournier, O.P., Pastoral Assoc.
Res., 65 High St., 04280. Tel: 207-375-6951.
Catechesis/Religious Programs—Tel: 207-375-6581.
Students 41.
Mission—Greene, St. Francis, Tel: 207-946-5758.

Saco, York Co., Most Holy Trinity, Revs. George B. Mulligan, C.S.C.; Patrick Walsh, C.S.C.; Sr. Rita Bujold, C.S.J., Pastoral Assoc. In res., Rev. James F. Murphy, C.S.C.
Res., 271 Main St., Box 310, 04072. Tel: 207-282-3321; Fax: 207-284-2274.
Catechesis/Religious Programs—Tel: 207-282-6392.
Students 404.

Notre Dame de Lourdes, Rev. Richard E. St. Cyr.
Res., 16 Cutts Ave., 04072. Tel: 207-282-1392; Fax: 207-282-1392. [JC]
School—50 Beach St., 04072. Tel: 207-283-3111. Sr. Linda Mae Plourde, P.M., Prin.
Sisters of the Presentation of Mary 3; Lay Teachers 9; Students 200.
Catechesis/Religious Programs—Tel: 207-282-0911. Marcel Bertrand, D.R.E.
Students 70.

St. Agatha, Aroostook Co., St. Agatha's, Rev. Michael P. Gendreau.
Res., 04772. Tel: 207-543-7447; Fax: 207-543-9392.
Catechesis/Religious Programs—Tel: 207-543-6119. Judy Michaud, D.R.E.
Students 134.
Mission—Madawaska, Aroostook Co., St. Michael's Chapel, Birch Point Rd., Madawaska, 04756. Tel: 207-728-7845. [CEM 2]

St. Francis, Aroostook Co., St. Charles, Rev. Claude R. Gendreau.
Res., 04774. Tel: 207-398-3530. [CEM]
Catechesis/Religious Programs—Students 120.
Mission—Allagash Plantation, St. Paul.

St. John, Aroostook Co., St. John, Rev. Claude R. Gendreau.
Mailing Address: P.O. Box 68, St. Francis, 04774. Tel: 207-398-3530. [CEM]

Sanford, York Co., Holy Family, Rev. Richard P. Rice; Joyce M. St. Pierre, Pastoral Assoc.
Res., 66 North Ave., 04073. Tel: 207-324-2420; Fax: 207-324-5318. [JC]
School—St. Thomas Consolidated School. For Holy Family, St. Ignatius and Notre Dame, Springvale. Tel: 207-324-2549; Fax: 207-324-2549. Norman Provost, Prin.
Sisters 1; Lay Teachers 11; Students 242.
Catechesis/Religious Programs—Students 79.

St. Ignatius Martyr, Rev. Raymond D. Auger; Gerald Coutu, Pastoral Assoc. & D.R.E.
Res., 10 St. Ignatius St., 04073. Tel: 207-324-6040; Fax: 207-324-6041. [CEM]
Catechesis/Religious Programs—Tel: 207-324-6231. Gerald Coutu, D.R.E.
Students 209.

Scarborough, Cumberland Co., St. Maximilian Kolbe, Rev. Thomas M. Murphy.
Mailing Address: P.O. Box 57, 04074. Tel: 207-883-2597; Fax: 207-883-4246.
Catechesis/Religious Programs—Tel: 207-883-1742. Kathy Sparda, D.R.E.
Students 698.
Mission—Pine Point, Scarborough Co., St. Jude, Rte. 9, 04074.

Sinclair, Aroostook Co., St. Joseph, Rev. Michael P. Gendreau.
Res., St. Agatha, 04772. Tel: 207-543-7447; Fax: 207-543-6119. [CEM]
In res., P.O. Box 69, 04779. Tel: 207-243-7563
Catechesis/Religious Programs—P.O. Box 69, Sinclaire, 04779. Tel: 207-243-7563.
Students 23.

Skowhegan, Somerset Co., Notre Dame De Lourdes, Rev. Marcel G. Chouinard; Sr. Claudette Darisse, S.A.S.V., Pastoral Assoc.
Res., 222 Water St., P.O. Box 369, 04976. Tel: 207-474-2039; Fax: 207-474-2039. [CEM]
Catechesis/Religious Programs—Tel: 207-474-9844. Beth Crowe, D.R.E.
Students 250.

South Berwick, York Co., St. Michael, Rev. Philip Michael Tracy; Sr. Jacqueline Moreau, R.S.M., Pastoral Assoc. & D.R.E.
Res., 29 Young St., 03908. Tel: 207-384-4241; Fax: 207-384-4289. [CEM]
Catechesis/Religious Programs—Students 158.

South Portland, Cumberland Co., Church of the Holy Cross, Revs. Paul E. Coughlin, Pastor; Frederick H. Morse, Pastoral Assoc.
Mailing Address: 30 Emery St.; P.O. Box 2708, 04116-2708.
Res., 11 Aspen Ave., 04106. Tel: 207-799-4611; 772-7489.
School—436 Broadway, 04106. Sr. Maura Murphy, R.S.M., Prin.
Sisters of Mercy 2; Lay Teachers 13; Students 251.
Catechesis/Religious Programs—Tel: 207-799-8345. D.R.E.: Carol Kilroy; Constance Libby.
Students 218.

St. John the Evangelist, Rev. Paul E. Coughlin. In res., Rev. Frederick H. Morse.
Res., 11 Aspen Ave., 04106. Tel: 207-772-7489.
Catechesis/Religious Programs—Sr. Marie Roy, D.R.E.
Students 175.

Springvale, York Co., Notre Dame, Rev. Armand R. Neault.
Res., 10 Payne St., Box 278, 04083. Tel: 207-324-6630. [CEM]
Catechesis/Religious Programs—Rebecca Carlson, D.R.E.
Students 346.

Stockholm, Aroostook Co., St. Therese, Rev. Joachim Thamh Nguyen.
Mailing Address: 1143 Van Buren Rd., Caribou, 04736.
Church—04783. Tel: 207-498-2763.
Catechesis/Religious Programs—Diane Dickinson, D.R.E.
Students 79.

Stonington, Hancock Co., St. Mary Star of the Sea, Revs. John F. O'Hara; George McCormick (CAM).
Res., Thurlow Hill, Box 25, 04681. Tel: 207-367-2343.
Mission—Castine, Hancock Co, Our Lady of Holy Hope, Pleasant St., Box 413, Castine, 04421. Tel: 207-326-8228.

Van Buren, Aroostook Co., St. Bruno - St. Remi, Revs. Joseph S. Chasse, S.M.; David Lajoie, S.M.; Marcel Lajoie, S.M.
Res., 336 Main St., 04785. Tel: 207-868-2718. [CEM]
Catechesis/Religious Programs—Tel: 207-868-2835. Rebecca Devost, D.R.E.
Students 345.
Mission—Van Buren, Aroostock Co., St. Rose Chapel.

St. Remi. Merged with St. Bruno. For further details see separate listing under St. Bruno.

Wallagrass, Aroostook Co., St. Joseph's, Rev. James R. Albert.
Church—R.R. 1, P.O. Box 1205, Soldier Pond, 04781. Tel: 207-444-5135. [CEM 3]
Res., Church St., P.O. Box 249, Eagle Lake, 04739. Tel: 207-444-5119. [CEM]
Catechesis/Religious Programs—Students 40.

Waterville, Kennebec Co., Holy Spirit. Merging St. Francis de Sales, Sacred Heart and Notre Dame Parishes. Revs. James S. Plourde; Scott Mower; Sr. Line Rioux, C.S.J., Pastoral Assoc.
Res., 72 Pleasant St., 04901-5405. Tel: 207-872-2281; Fax: 207-877-0675. [JC]
Catechesis/Religious Programs—Tel: 207-872-2264; Fax: 207-877-0675. D.R.E.: Rachel Matthews; Monica Bolduc.
Students 352.

Sacred Heart. Merged with Notre Dame and St. Francis de Sales to form Holy Spirit, Waterville.

Notre Dame. Merged with Sacred Heart and St. Francis de Sales to form Holy Spirit, Waterville.

Wells, York Co., St. Mary, Rev. J. Joseph Ford.
Res., Eldredge Rd., P.O. Box 368, 04090. Tel: 207-646-5605; Fax: 207-646-9437.
Catechesis/Religious Programs—Students 212.

Mission—Ogunquit, All Saints.

Westbrook, Cumberland Co., St. Edmund (Prides Corner), Rev. Albert B. Colpitts.
Res., 355 Bridgton Rd., 04092. Tel: 207-797-8233.
Catechesis/Religious Programs—Tel: 207-797-4539. Mrs. Sandra Bois, D.R.E.
Students 130.

St. Hyacinth, Rev. James P. Brewer; Sr. Christine Plouffe, O.P., Pastoral Assoc.
Res., 295 Brown St., 04092. Tel: 207-854-2003. [CEM]
Catechesis/Religious Programs—Tel: 207-854-8214; 854-8019. D.R.E.: Frances Gray; Rosalie Aube.
Students 130.

St. Mary's, Rev. John L. Dougher.
Res., 625 Main St., 04092. Tel: 207-854-2753; Fax: 207-856-7318. [JC]
Catechesis/Religious Programs—Tel: 207-854-8669. Larry Guertin, D.R.E.
Students 184.

Whitefield, Lincoln Co., St. Denis, Rev. John L. Audibert; Deacon Joseph Reid.
Res., 298 Grand Army Rd, 04353-3419. Tel: 207-549-7425. [CEM]
Catechesis/Religious Programs—Students 75.

Wilton, Franklin Co., St. Mary. Closed. For further details see separate listing for St. Joseph, Farmington.

Windham, Cumberland Co., Our Lady of Perpetual Help, Rev. Donald R. Proulx.
Res., Rte. 302, 919 Roosevelt Tr., P.O. Box 1030, 04062-1030. Tel: 207-892-8288.
Catechesis/Religious Programs—Tel: 207-892-8922.
Students 237.
Mission—East Raymond, St. Raymond, Rte. 85 at Crescent Lake, East Raymond, 04071.

Winslow, Kennebec Co., St. John the Baptist, Rev. Paul A. Plante; Mrs. Elaine Gordon, Pastoral Assoc. In res., Rev. Daniel P. Greenleaf Tel: 207-877-0953.
Res., 47 Monument St., 04901. Tel: 207-872-2373. [JC]
School—36 1/2 Garand St., 04901. Tel: 207-872-7115. Mr. Kevin Scully, Prin.
Lay Teachers 7; Students 125.
Catechesis/Religious Programs—Students 300.

Winterport, Waldo Co., St. Gabriel, Rev. George W. Hickey.
Res., St. Matthew's, 70 Western Ave., P.O. Box 280, Hampden, 04444. Tel: 207-862-3517.
Catechesis/Religious Programs—Tel: 207-233-4341. Darlene Duffy, D.R.E.
Students 70.

Winthrop, Kennebec Co., St. Francis Xavier, Rev. Sylvio J. Levesque.
Res., 10 Lake St., 04364. Tel: 207-377-2922. [JC]
Catechesis/Religious Programs—Tel: 207-377-6844. Nancy Lynn Yocono, D.R.E.
Students 212.
Mission—Monmouth, Kennebec Co., St. Stanislaus.

Woodland, Washington Co., St. James the Greater, Rev. Michael Sheridan, Sacramental Min.; Ms. Patricia Phillips, Parish Coord.
Res., 24 Summit St., P.O. Box 369, 04694. Tel: 207-427-6908.
Catechesis/Religious Programs—Tel: 207-427-3236. Mrs. Mary White, D.R.E.
Students 88.

Yarmouth, Cumberland Co., Sacred Heart, Rev. Richard A. O'Donnell. Pastoral Assocs.: John Munroe; Cherie Piper.
Res., 33 Main St., 04096. Tel: 207-846-5584. [CEM]
Catechesis/Religious Programs—Tel: 207-846-6003. D.R.E.: Ann Peacock; Cherie Piper; John Munroe.
Students 305.
Mission—Freeport, St. Jude's.

York Harbor, York Co., St. Christopher-by-the-Sea, Rev. James J. Morrison.
Res., One Lilac Ln., P.O. Box 1225, 03911. Tel: 207-363-2111; Fax: 207-363-1586.
Catechesis/Religious Programs—Tel: 207-363-4177; Fax: 207-363-1586. Rose Cronin, D.R.E.
Students 395.
Mission—York Beach, St. Mary, Star of the Sea.

Chaplains of Public Institutions

PORTLAND. *Maine Medical Center* Tel: 207-871-0111. Chaplains: Revs. Patrick Glavin, O.F.M.Cap.; Donald McAllister; Albin Andrus; Mrs. Anne Monaghan.
Mercy Hospital Tel: 207-879-3358. Rev. Donald McAllister; Mrs. Agnes LaStoria; Sr. M. Michael Connelly, R.S.M.
St. Joseph's Manor Tel: 207-797-0600. Rev. Robert E. Lee.

AUGUSTA. *Augusta Mental Health Institute*. Vacant. Tel: 207-289-7334.
Kennebec Valley Medical Center Tel: 207-626-1000. Mr. Stephen Vinette, Pastoral Assoc.

BANGOR. *Eastern Maine Medical Center*. Taylor Hospital, Bangor Convalescent Center, Tel: 207-942-6941. Rev. Robert J. Sullivan, S.J.
St. Joseph's Hospital Tel: 207-947-8311. Rev. Richard V. Rokos; Sr. Mary Edmund, C.S.S.F., Pastoral Assoc.

BIDDEFORD. *Southern Maine Medical Center* Tel: 207-283-3663. Sr. Jacqueline Vezina, R.H.S.J.

LEWISTON. *Central Maine Medical Center* Tel: 207-795-0111. Mrs. Kathleen O'Wril.
St. Mary's Regional Medical Center. Rev. Bertrand R. Poussard, Campus Ave., P.O. Box 291, 04243-0291. Tel: 207-777-8520. Sr. Madeline Normand, P.M.; Sr. Huguette Allard, S.G.M.; Mr. Kenneth Rancort.

SOUTH PORTLAND. *Maine Youth Center* Tel: 207-828-4921. Rev. William F. Modlin.
Men's Correctional Center Tel: 207-828-4921. Rev. William F. Modlin.

THOMASTON. *Maine State Prison* Tel: 207-828-4921. Rev. William F. Modlin.

TOGUS. *Dept. of Veteran Affairs* Tel: 207-622-1134, Ext. 5176. Rev. L. David Mani.

WARREN. *Super Maximum Facility & Minimum Facility* Tel: 207-828-4921. Rev. William F. Modlin.

WATERVILLE. *Mid-Maine Medical Center* Tel: 207-872-1000. Mrs. Angeline Hubert.

Special or Other Diocesan Assignment:
Reverend Fathers—
Caron, Marc B., P.O. Box 11559, Portland, ME 04104-7559
Roux, G. Albert
Skehan, John R., P.O. Box 11559, Portland, ME 04104-7559
Stefanko, Paul F., P.O. Box 11559, Portland, ME 04104-7559

On Duty Outside the Diocese:
Reverend Fathers—
Carrigan, Fredrick, 342 Willis Ave., P.O. Box 172, Bronx, NY 10454

Military Chaplains:
Reverend Fathers—
Cote, David P., USAF Academy, 2330 Faculty Dr., Bolder, CO 80840
Goudreau, Joseph L., 24AU Lee Ave., Ft. Myers, VA 22211. Tel: 703-696-3532
Morency, Raymond P., 3509 Lake Ave., Apt. 1052, Columbus, SC 29206. Tel: 803-782-2141
Welch, Bernard J., USCG Tracen, 1 Munro Ave., Cape May, NJ 08204-5001. Tel: 609-523-8542/898-6974; Fax: 609-898-6848

Sabbatical:
Reverend Fathers—
Caron, Antonin R.
Girouard, Robert J.
Robitaille, Marcell L.
Seavey, Michael J., 4141 Guilford Dr., College Park, MD 20740
Thomson, Edward A., P.O. Box 11559, Portland, ME 04104-7559

Retired:
Reverend Monsignors—
Begin, Raymond F., P.O. Box 434, Raymond, ME 04071
Chaloult, Gilman, 31 Thomas Ave., Caribou, ME 04736
Gleason, Paul D., P.O. Box 1938, Hampton, NH 03842. Tel: 613-926-5442
Tatarczuk, Vincent A., P.O. Box 218, Raymond, ME 04071. Tel: 207-655-3672
Reverend Fathers—
Auger, Gaston E., Box 476, West Kennebunk, ME 04094. Tel: 207-985-7059
Barrett, Patrick J., Cathedral Residence, 307 Congress St., Portland, ME 04101. Tel: 207-874-2830
Berube, Louis, P.O. Box 8054, Lewiston, ME 04243. Tel: 207-777-1692
Bill, J. Armand, 402A Sandpiper Dr., Fort Pierce, FL 34948. Tel: 407-467-1011
Bureau, Germain H., Mount St. Joseph Home, 7 Highwood St., Waterville, ME 04901
Burns, T. Lee, 3103 Vesper Ave., Sarasota, FL 34232. Tel: 813-377-4961
Carrier, Herve G., P.O. Box 3061, Lewiston, ME 04243-3061
Carrier, Joseph S., 133 S. Main St., Auburn, ME 04210. Tel: 207-786-2231
Cormier, Norman R., Pleasant Hill Rd., R.R. 1, Box 441, Limerick, ME 04048-9735. Tel: 207-793-2377
Cournoyer, Napoleon, c/o Pat Menongian, 151 Virginia Ave., Portland, ME 04103
Cyr, L. Chanel, 302 Main St., Limestone, ME 04750-1116. Tel: 207-325-4843
Davis, John P., 68 Webster Ave., Lewiston, ME 04240
Feeney, John J., 51 Tamarlan, Portland, ME 04103
Franck, Marc E., Mount St. Joseph Home, 7 Highwood St., Rm 5, Waterville, ME 04901
Frechette, Leonard A., 350 Elm St., #302, Biddeford, ME 04005. Tel: 207-284-7573
Gorham, Peter P., P.O. Box 515, Ellsworth, ME 04605-0515
Goudreau, George W., P.O. Box 28, Rumford, ME 04276
Gower, James M., 23 High Brook Rd., Bar Harbor, ME 04609. Tel: 207-288-9780
Harvey, Richard R., 12 Bayberry Rd., Brewer, ME 04412-1202. Tel: 207-989-8007
Huot, Leopold J., 19 Lambert St., Biddeford, ME 04005. Tel: 207-282-4325
Jacques, Donald W., 17 Larisa Ln., Milford, NH 03055
Kane, Francis J., 677 Cherry Valley Rd., #47, Guilford, NH 03246
Knox, James, 31 Clearview Dr., Scarborough, ME 04074-8319. Tel: 207-883-9652
Lauzon, Raymond J., Pranceskona Vienuolynus, Vilniaus 2, Kretinga, 5700 Lithuania
Lavoie, Rene G., Holy Family Rectory, 607 Sabattus St., Lewiston, ME 04240
Lavoie, Robert R., Mt. St. Joseph Home, Highwood St., Waterville, ME 04901
Lee, Robert E., Cathedral Residence, 307 Congress St., Portland, ME 04101. Tel: 207-773-6980
Letourneau, Francis E., P.O. Box 5577, Orlando, FL 32855-5577
Leveille, Rudolph J., 69 Juniper St., Bangor, ME 04401
Marquis, J. Alphee, Northern Maine Medical Center, 143 E. Main St., Fort Kent, ME 04743. Tel: 207-834-3155
Martel, Robert T., Mount St. Joseph Home, Highwood St., Waterville, ME 04901. Tel: 207-873-0006
McCarthy, Richard C., 58 Pitt St., Portland, ME 04103. Tel: 207-772-1211
McGarrigle, Michael, 76 Ward Cir., Brunswick, ME 04011-9343. Tel: 207-725-5764
McInnis, Richard W., 16 Lochness Rd., Rumford, ME 04276. Tel: 207-364-8717
Mulkern, Stephen M., P.O. Box 474, New Harbor, ME 04554. Tel: 207-677-2881
Nicknair, Bernard L., 135 Willard Rd., Auburn, ME 04210
Nicknair, Harold, Cathedral Residence, 307 Congress St., Portland, ME 04101. Tel: 207-828-8835
O'Brien, Edward J., Seaside Nursing Home, 850 Baxter Blvd., Portland, ME 04103
Ouellette, Roger J., Mount St. Joseph Home, Highwood St., Waterville, ME 04901. Tel: 207-873-0432
Paquet, Hubert J., 46 Wentworth St., Biddeford, ME 04405
Pare, Paul U., 27 Marion St., Biddeford, ME 04005. Tel: 207-282-4155
Patenaude, Gilbert A., 47 River St., Augusta, ME 04330. Tel: 207-622-3832
Patenaude, Laurent O., Mount St. Joseph Home, Highwood St., Waterville, ME 04901. Tel: 207-873-4873
Pollard, Daniel E., 5 Ocean Way Condo, P.O. Box 118, York Beach, ME 03910
Proulx, Roger F., Mount St. Joseph Home, Highwood St., Waterville, ME 04901. Tel: 207-872-4903
Romani, Joseph, 264 Eastern Promenade, Portland, ME 04101. Tel: 207-773-2449
Scahill, John J., Cathedral Residence, 307 Congress St., Portland, ME 04101
Sims, Henry F.H., Park Danforth, Apt. 415, Stevens Ave., Portland, ME 04103. Tel: 207-878-2843
Soucy, D. Wilfrid, Robin Dr., New Port Richey, FL 33552. Tel: 813-842-1497
St. Pierre, Romeo A., 15 Garden Cir. N., Caribou, ME 04736. Tel: 207-498-6049
Sullivan, John L., Mount St. Joseph, Highwood St., Waterville, ME 04901
Tracy, George E., 1229 Broadway, Ste. 400, Bangor, ME 04401-2596. Tel: 207-941-2400; Fax: 207-941-2401
Vallely, James P., Proctor Ave., Goose Rocks Beach, ME 04046. Tel: 207-967-2718

INSTITUTIONS LOCATED IN THE DIOCESE

[A] COLLEGES AND UNIVERSITIES

STANDISH. *Saint Joseph's College*, 278 Whites Bridge Rd., 04084-5263. Tel: 207-893-7711; Fax: 207-893-7867

For a complete listing, refer to the Colleges and Universities section.

[B] HIGH SCHOOLS, REGIONAL

LEWISTON. *St. Dominic Regional High School*, 179 Blake St., 04240. Tel: 207-782-6911. Mr. G. Michael Welch, Prin. Sisters 1; Lay Teachers 20; Students 241.

[C] HIGH SCHOOLS, PRIVATE

PORTLAND. *Catherine McAuley High School*, 631 Stevens Ave., 04103. Tel: 207-797-3802. Sr. Edward Mary Kelleher, R.S.M., Prin. Sisters of Mercy 9; Lay Teachers 21; Girls 249.

Cheverus High School, 267 Ocean Ave., 04103. Tel: 207-774-6238.
E-mail: info@cheverus.org
Web site: http://www.cheverus.org
Faculty resides at St. Ignatius Residence. See separate listing for details. Rev. John W. Keegan, S.J., Pres.; Mr. John H.R. Mullen, Prin.; Revs. Calvin M. Goodwin, S.J.; John W. Michalowski, S.J., Supr.; James F. Talbot, S.J.; John W. Keegan, S.J.; Bro. Bill Quegan, S.J. Lay Teachers 26; Students 382.

[D] ELEMENTARY SCHOOLS, PRIVATE

WATERVILLE. *Mount Merici Elementary School*, 142 Western Ave., 04901. Tel: 207-873-3773.
E-mail: MMPVT-HM@MOUNT-MERCI.PVT.K12.ME.US
Web site: http://www.mount-merci.pvt.K12.ME.US
Susan Cote, Prin. Lay Teachers 11; Students 175.

[E] DIOCESAN HUMAN RELATIONS SERVICES

FALMOUTH. *Catholic Charities Maine*. Mailing Address: P.O. Box 10660, Portland, 04104. 356 U.S. Rte. 1, 04105. Tel: 207-781-8550. Most Revs. Joseph J. Gerry, O.S.B., Pres.; Michael R. Cote, Vice Pres.; Mr. Gregory W. Boulos, Chm.; Mr. Gregory M. Smith, C.P.A., Treas.; Ms. Gloria A. Dugan, Exec. Dir.; Peter J. Turner, Finance Dir.; Ms. Connie Jones, Human Resources Dir. Tel: 207-781-8550.

Office of Social Justice and Peace, 562 Congress St., Portland, 04101. Tel: 207-879-1130 Ext. 279. Mr. Paul Christian, Dir.

Parish Social Ministry, P.O. Box 748, Caribou, 04736. Tel: 207-498-2575. Mr. Leo Paquin, Coord.

Arnie Hanson Center, 65 India St., Portland, 04101. Tel: 207-871-7452. Bonnie Bagley, Interim Dir.

Evodia House, 79 Allen Ave., Portland, 04103. Tel: 207-878-5251. Lawrence Hames, Dir.

St. Francis House, 88 Third St., Auburn, 04210. Tel: 207-784-2011. Bonnie Bagley, Interim Dir.

The Fellowship House, 95 Blake St., Lewiston, 04240. Tel: 207-784-2901. Bonnie Bagley, Interim Dir.

St. Elizabeth's Child Development Center, 87 High St., Portland, 04101. Tel: 207-871-7444. Daniel Murphy, Dir.

St. Louis Child Care Center, 116 Hill St., P.O. Box 645, Biddeford, 04005. Tel: 207-282-3790. Jeffrey Burges, Dir.

Catholic Charities Maine Family Child Care, 15 Westminster St., Lewiston, 04240. Tel: 207-786-0925. Carolyn Davis, Dir.

Child Development Center - Peaks Island, Central Ave., P.O. Box 07, Peaks Island, 04108. Tel: 207-766-2854. Janine Blatt, Dir.

St. Louis Child Care Center, 116 Hill St., P.O. Box 645, Biddeford, 04005. Tel: 207-282-3790. Jeffrey Burgess, Dir.

Catholic Charities Maine Counseling Services, 562 Congress St., Portland, 04101. Tel: 207-775-5671. Cecile Gagne, Dir.

Catholic Charities Maine Support & Recovery Services, 66 State St., P.O. Box 797, Portland, 04104. Tel: 207-871-7431. Mr. Donald Harden, Dir.

Catholic Charities Maine Mental Health Services, 66 Western Ave., P.O. Box 378, Fairfield, 04937-5231. Tel: 207-453-4365; 800-660-5231. Mr. William Bois, Dir.

Refugee Resettlement Services, 562 Congress St., Portland, 04101. Tel: 207-871-7437. Doris Hohman, Dir.

Birthline Pregnancy Support Services, 562 Congress St., Portland, 04101. Tel: 207-871-7464. Annette Rioux, Dir.

SEARCH (Seek Elderly Alone, Renew Courage, and Hope), 15 Westminster St., Lewiston, 04240. Tel: 207-784-0157. Ann Corbin, Dir.

Catholic Charities Maine Adult and Family Services, 1066 Kenduskeag Ave., Bangor, 04401. Tel: 207-941-2855. Mary Menair, Dir.

Jessie Albert Memorial Dental Center, 15 Commercial St., Bath, 04530. Tel: 207-443-9721. Deanna Grosso-Keith, D.M.D.

Chester Dental Center, R.R. 1, Box 341 A, Lincoln, 04458. Tel: 207-794-8185. Gary Steinberg, D.M.D.

Volunteer Services, 562 Congress St., Portland, 04101. Tel: 207-879-1130, Ext. 238. Ann Corbin, Dir.

St. Michael's Center Emergency Foster Care, 1066 Kenduskeag Ave., Bangor, 04401. Tel: 207-941-2855. Mr. Paul Vestal, Jr., Dir. Legal Title: *St. Michael's Center Emergency Foster Care, Juvenile Jail Diversion Program and Home Based Family Services and Tracker Services.*

Educational Services for Blind and Visually Impaired Children, 1066 Kenduskeag Ave., Bangor, 04401. Tel: 207-941-2855. Jean Small, Dir.

Downeast Big Brothers - Big Sisters, 1066 Kenduskeag Ave., Bangor, 04401. Tel: 207-941-2855. Thomas Godfrey, Dir.

Educational Services for Blind and Visually Impaired Children-Instructional Materials Center, 562 Congress St., Portland, 04101. Tel: 207-871-7440. Ms. Youngok Raymond, Mgr. Legal Title: *Educational Services for Blind and Visually Impaired Children, Instructional Materials Center.*

Therapeutic Foster Care, 15 Westminster St., Lewiston, 04240. Tel: 207-784-0157. Stephen Letourneau, Dir.

The Christopher Home, P.O. Box 748, Caribou, 04736. Tel: 207-498-2575. Dixie Dumond, Dir.

Juvenile Jail Diversion Program, P.O. Box 748, Caribou, 04736. Tel: 207-498-2575.

Group Home After Care, P.O. Box 748, Caribou, 04736. Tel: 207-498-2575.

Educational Services for Blind and Visually Impaired Children-Satellite Office, P.O. Box 748, Caribou, 04736. Tel: 207-498-2575.

Emergency Foster Care, Caribou, 04736. Tel: 207-498-2575.

Educational Services for Blind and Visually Impaired Children-Satellite Office, 15 Westminster St., Lewiston, 04240. Tel: 207-786-0925.

Educational Services for Blind and Visually Impaired Children-Satellite Office, 66 Western Ave., P.O. Box 378, Fairfield, 04937-0378. Tel: 207-453-4365.

[F] SPECIAL RESIDENTIAL SERVICES

PORTLAND. *McAuley Residence, Inc.*, 91 State St., 04101. Tel: 207-773-5289. Transitional Housing and support services for women with or without children. Sr. Carol Lachance, R.S.M., Dir.

AUBURN. *St. Joseph Child Care Center*, 270 Minot Ave., 04210. Tel: 207-782-2711. Ms. Constance R. Ouellette, Dir.

BANGOR. *St. Andre's Group Home for Single Mothers with Infants.* Mailing Address: 283 Elm St., Biddeford, 04005. 87 Ohio St., 04401. Tel: 207-945-5021. Group Home Parenting Services for single mothers with infants. Eileen Ward, Program Dir.

BIDDEFORD. *St. Andre Home, Inc.*, Admin. Office, 283 Elm St., 04005-3093. Tel: 207-282-3351.
E-mail: SaintAndre@aol.com
Dr. Gregory C. Foltz, Exec. Dir. Pregnant and Parenting Young Women, Adoption Services, Service to Troubled Teens, Infant Foster Care Homes, Emergency Placement; Public Information-Education; Community Outreach Services.

St. Andre's Group Home for Pregnant and Parenting Young Women. Mailing Address: 283 Elm Street, 04005. 168 Prospect St., 04005. Tel: 207-284-7436. Sr. Simonne Janelle, S.C.I.M., Supr.

LEWISTON. *St. Andre's Group Home for Troubled Girls.* Mailing Address: 283 Elm St., Biddeford, 04005. 188 Sabattus St., 04240. Suzanne Dionne, Supvr.

[G] HOMES FOR THE AGED

PORTLAND. *Deering Pavilion Apartment House for Senior Citizens*, 880 Forest Ave., 04103. Tel: 207-797-8777

For a complete listing, refer to the Special Care Facilities section.

St. Joseph's Manor, 1133 Washington Ave., 04103. Tel: 207-797-0600; Fax: 207-797-4168

For a complete listing, refer to the Special Care Facilities section.

BANGOR. *St. Xavier's Home*, 119 Somerset St., 04401. Tel: 207-942-4815

For a complete listing, refer to the Special Care Facilities section.

BIDDEFORD. *St. Andre Health Care Facility*, 407 Pool St., 04005-9716. Tel: 207-282-5171

For a complete listing, refer to the Special Care Facilities section.

LEWISTON. *Maison Marcotte*, 100 Campus Ave., 04240. Tel: 207-786-0062

For a complete listing, refer to the Special Care Facilities section.

**St. Marguerite d'Youville Pavilion*, 102 Campus Ave., 04240. Tel: 207-777-4200

For a complete listing, refer to the Special Care Facilities section.

WATERVILLE. *Mt. St. Joseph Holistic Care Community*, Highwood St., 04901. Tel: 207-873-0705

For a complete listing, refer to the Special Care Facilities section.

Seton Village Inc., 1 Carver St., 04901. Tel: 207-873-0178

For a complete listing, refer to the Special Care Facilities section.

[H] GENERAL HOSPITALS

*PORTLAND. *Mercy Hospital*, 144 State St., 04101. Tel: 207-879-3000

For a complete listing, refer to the Hospitals section.

BANGOR. *St. Joseph Hospital*, 360 Broadway, 04401. Tel: 207-262-1000

For a complete listing, refer to the Hospitals section.

BUCKSPORT. *Bridgewell, Inc.*, Box 836, 04416

For a complete listing, refer to the Hospitals section.

LEWISTON. *Community Clinical Services, Inc.*, 100 Campus Ave, Ste. #1, 04240. Tel: 207-777-8841

For a complete listing, refer to the Hospitals section.

Sisters of Charity Health System, Inc., 97 Campus Ave., 04240. Tel: 207-777-8802

For a complete listing, refer to the Hospitals section.

**St. Mary's Regional Medical Center*, Campus Ave., P.O. Box 291, 04243-0291. Tel: 207-777-8100

For a complete listing, refer to the Hospitals section.

[I] MONASTERIES AND RESIDENCES OF PRIESTS AND BROTHERS

PORTLAND. Retreat Masters. Revs. Raymond Lebrun, O.M.I.; Michael Lauze, O.M.I., Supr.; Marcel Bolduc, O.M.I., Dir.; Bros. Robert Dutil, O.M.I.; Paul Ricard, O.M.I.; Donat Daigle, O.M.I. Priests 3; Brothers 3.

St. Ignatius Residence, 271 Ocean Ave., 04103-5795. Tel: 207-774-7226. Jesuit Fathers (New England Prov.). Revs. John W. Michalowski, S.J., Supr.; Calvin M. Goodwin, S.J.; James F. Talbot, S.J.; Bro. Bill Quegan, S.J. Priests 3; Brothers 1.

ALFRED. *Notre Dame Institute*, Shaker Hill Rd., P.O. Box 159, 04002. Tel: 207-324-6612; Fax: 207-490-2370. Provincial House of Brothers of Christian Instruction. Bros. Francis Blouin, F.I.C., Prov. Tel: 207-324-0067; James Lacasse, F.I.C., Supr. Tel: 207-324-6612; Rev. Theodore Letendre, F.I.C., Dir., Notre Dame Spiritual Center. Tel: 207-324-6160. Rev. Theodore Letendre, F.I.C., Chap. Tel: 207-324-1017. Brothers 19.

KENNEBUNKPORT. *St. Anthony's Friary*. Franciscan Vice-Province of St. Casimir in Lithuania,Canada and United States, Office of the Magazine "The Bell of St. Francis" (in Lithuanian language). St. Anthony's Friary, Guest House and St. Anthony's Shrine. P.O. Box 980, 04046. Tel: 207-967-2011. Revs. Placid Barius, O.F.M., Prov. Lithuanian Vice-Province; Leonard Andriekus, O.F.M., Supr., Guardian; George S. Gailiusis, O.F.M., Dir., Gift Shop; Gabriel Baltrusaitis, O.F.M., Vicar of the Friary, Procurator and Dir.- Guest House; Raphael J. Sakalys, O.F.M., Procurator and Mgr. of Magazine Varpelis; John J. Bacevicius, O.F.M., Counsellor; Robert Des Roches, O.F.M., Provincial Spiritual Asst. to Sec. Franciscan Order; Robert Barber, O.F.M., Liturgist; Andrew R. Bisson, Parish Ministry. Priests 9.

LEWISTON. *SS. Peter and Paul Priory*, 27 Bartlett St., 04240. Tel: 207-784-7309; Fax: 207-777-0056. Residence for Dominican Fathers or Friar Preachers. Very Revs. Robert Comtois, O.P., Prior; Martin Dionne, O.P., Sub-Prior; Revs. Jean Marie Lapointe, O.P. (Canada); James Donovan, O.P. (Canada); Raymond Corriveau, O.P.; Rosaire Pelletier, O.P.; Bros. Irenee Richard, O.P.; Robert Beaulieu, O.P. Priests 6; Brothers 2.

American Dominican Friars Serving in Canada. Revs. Thomas Demers, O.P.; Thomas R. Potvin, O.P.; Bernard M. Remillard, O.P.; Claude Richard, O.P.

WATERVILLE. *Mt. St. Joseph Priest Retirement Home*, Highwood St., 04901. Tel: 207-873-0705. Revs. Germain Bureau; Robert R. Lavoie; Robert T. Martel; Roger J. Ouellette; John L. Sullivan; Laurent Patenaude; Marcel Robitaille; Roger F. Proulx; Mark Franck.

[J] CONVENTS AND RESIDENCES OF SISTERS

PORTLAND. *House of Formation*, 605 Stevens Ave., 04103. Tel: 207-797-6957. Sr. Jean Little, R.S.M., Contact Person. Sisters of Mercy of the Americas 3.

Mercy Convent, 144 State St., 04101. Tel: 207-773-5560. Sr. Mary Michael Connelly, R.S.M., Supr. Sisters of Mercy of the Americas 5.

Monastery of the Precious Blood, 166 State St., 04101-3794. Tel: 207-774-0861. Sr. Mary Jo Divney, Supr. Adorers of the Precious Blood 4.

Motherhouse of the Sisters of Mercy of the Americas, 605 Stevens Ave., 04103-0146. Tel: 207-797-7861; Fax: 207-797-7861. Sr. Mary Laboure Morin, R.S.M., Pres.; Sr. Margaret Anne Burke, R.S.M., Local Coord. Motherhouse; Rev. Theodosius Corley, O.F.M.Cap., St. Joseph Rectory, Stevens Ave. Sisters in Residence at Motherhouse 82.

St. Catherine's Residence, 242 Walton St., Apt. 207, 04103. Tel: 207-878-8476. Sr. Anne-Marie Bourque, R.S.M., Coord. Sisters of Mercy of the Americas 2.

St. Patrick, 17 Frances St., 04102. Tel: 207-772-0723. Sisters of Mercy of the Americas 4.

Sisters of Charity, 1137 Washington Ave., 04103. Tel: 207-797-8607. Sr. Diane Beaudoin, Contact Person. Sisters 5.

Sisters of Mercy of the Americas, 289 Congress St., 04101. Tel: 207-773-8039. Sr. Theresa Rand, R.S.M., Contact Person. Sisters of Mercy of the Americas 4.

Sisters of Our Lady of the Holy Rosary, 20 Thomas St., 04102. Tel: 207-774-3756. Sr. Carole Jean Lappa, R.S.R., Reg. Supr. Tel: 207-772-3130. Sisters of Our Lady of the Holy Rosary 3.

Sisters of St. Joseph, 38 Malilly Rd., 04103. Tel: 207-775-2466; Fax: 207-773-0182. Sr. Ann Keevan, C.S.J., Contact Person.

ALFRED. *Sisters of Our Lady of the Holy Rosary*. Notre Dame Institute, 04002-0159. Tel: 207-324-0647. Sr. Regina Drody, R.S.R., Coord.; Rev. Theodore Letendre, F.I.C. Sisters 2.

AUBURN. *Companions of Christ*, 133 Western Ave., 04210. Tel: 207-784-5960. Sr. Elizabeth Platt, C.O.C., Contact Person. Sisters 2.

Sisters of Saint Joseph, 270 Minot Ave., 04210. Tel: 207-782-1548. Sr. Madeleine Grandmaison, Contact Person. Sisters of St. Joseph 2.

AUGUSTA. *St. Augustine*, 5 Kendall St., 04330. Tel: 207-622-2494. Sisters of the Presentation of Mary. Sr. Joan Desmarais, P.M., Supr. Sisters 2.

St. Mary, 8 Lincoln St., 04330. Tel: 207-623-4033. Sisters of Mercy of the Americas 3.

BANGOR. *St. Joseph Convent*, 360 Broadway, 04401-3900. Tel: 207-262-1000; Fax: 207-262-1939. Sr. Barbara Theresa Martis, C.S.S.F., Contact Person. Felician Sisters 11.

BIDDEFORD. *Marie Fitzbach Convent*, 290 Elm St., 04005. Tel: 207-282-2714. Sr. Jacqueline Bilodeau, S.C.I.M., Supr. Servants of the Immaculate Heart of Mary (Good Shepherd) 9.

Marie Joseph Spiritual Center, R.F.D. 2, Lester Orcutt Blvd., 04005. Tel: 207-284-5671. Sr. Cecile Plasse, P.M., Supr.; Rev. James Murphy, C.S.C., Chap. Sisters of the Presentation of Mary 15.

St. Joseph's Convent, 409 Pool St., 04005. Tel: 207-284-8381. Sr. Claire Ouellette, S.C.I.M., Supr. Section A & B; Sr. Bertha Duperry, Supr. Section C. Sisters of the Immaculate Heart of Mary (Good Shepherd) 44.

BRUNSWICK. *St. John the Baptist Convent*, 37 Pleasant St., 04011. Tel: 207-725-5484. Sr. Angela Krippendorf, O.S.U., Supr. Ursuline Sisters 8.

CASCO. *Community of the Resurrection*, P.O. Box 284, 04015-0284. Tel: 207-627-7184. Sr. Renata Camenzind, Supr. Total in Residence 5.

FORT KENT. *St. Louis*, 12 E. Main St., 04743. Tel: 207-834-5023. Sr. Gloria Ouellette, P.F.M., Supr. Little Franciscans of Mary 3.

HAMPDEN. *Sisters of Mercy of the Americas*, 692 Main Rd., 04444. Tel: 207-947-5381. Sr. Catherine Green, R.S.M.

HOULTON. *Marie Claire Residence*, 7 Cleveland St., 04730. Tel: 207-532-2324. Sr. Carol Martin, P.F.M., Contact Person. Little Franciscans of Mary 3.

INDIAN ISLAND. *St. Ann's Convent*. Penobscot Reservation, P.O. Box 566, Old Town, 04468. Tel: 207-827-4862. Sr. Janet Campbell, R.S.M., Prin. & Supr., Indian Island School. Tel: 207-827-4285. Sisters of Mercy of the Americas 2.

KENNEBUNK. *Sisters of St. Joseph*, 215 Sea Rd., 04043. Tel: 207-967-5986. Sr. Claire Blais, C.S.J. Sisters 3.

KITTERY. *St. Raphael Convent*, 6 Whipple Rd., 03904-1739. Tel: 207-439-2322. Sr. Maureen Hurley, D.W., Coord. Sisters 3.

LEWISTON. *Daughters of Wisdom*, 169 College St., Apt. #1, 04240. Tel: 207-777-1912. Sr. Jeanne Nicknair, D.W., Contact Person.

Dominican Sisters of the Roman Congregation, 18 Tampa St., 04240. Tel: 207-782-7480; Fax: 207-753-1945. Sr. Monique Belanger, O.P., Prioress. Sisters 6.

Grey Nuns of Montreal Residence, 18 Golden St., Apt. A, 04240. Tel: 207-782-6849. The Society of the Grey Nuns of Montreal. Sr. Huguette Allard, S.G.M. Sisters 2.

Holy Cross, 15 Baird Ave., 04240. Tel: 207-782-0263. Sr. Nora Dumais, Supr. Sisters of the Presentation of Mary 6.

Holy Family, 2 Rideout Ave., 04240. Tel: 207-783-0693. Sr. Jeanne Page, P.M., Supr. Sisters of Presentation 2.

House of Discernment, 67 Webster St., 04240. Tel: 207-786-3723. Sr. Margaret Camire, Supr. Sisters of Presentation 4.

Sisters of Charity, Sisters' Residence, 98 Campus Ave., P.O. Box 701, 04243-0701. Tel: 207-782-0798. Sr. Louise Morrissette, Supr. Sisters 2.

Sisters of St. Joseph, 121 Webber Ave., 04240. Tel: 207-783-9069. Sr. Laurette Levasseur, C.S.J., Contact Person. Sisters 2.

OAKLAND. *St. Theresa Community*, 30 Church St., 04963. Tel: 207-465-7605. Sr. Anne Xavier Loubert, C.S.J., Contact Person. Sisters of St. Joseph 2.

OLD ORCHARD BEACH. *Sisters of Our Lady of the Holy Rosary*. Regional House, 25 Portland Ave., 04064. Tel: 207-934-0592. Sr. Olla Laplante, Superior. Sisters 4.

ORLAND. *Missionary Sisters of the Immaculate Conception*. P.O. Box 836, 04416. Tel: 207-469-7616. Sr. Miriam Devlin, S.M.I.C., Contact Person. Sisters 2.

PITTSFIELD. *St. Agnes*, 9 High St., 04967-1213. Tel: 207-487-5040. Sr. Elizabeth Cobb, Contact Person. Diocesan Sisters of Mercy 2.

PLEASANT POINT. *St. Ann's Convent*, P.O. Box 126, 04667. Tel: 207-853-2944. Sr. Maureen Wallace, R.S.M., Supr. Sisters of Mercy of the Americas 2.

PRESQUE ISLE. *St. Mary's Convent*, 331 Main St., 04769. Tel: 207-762-7711. Sr. Mary O'Donnell, R.S.M., Contact Person. Diocesan Sisters of Mercy 2.

ROCKLAND. *St. Bernard's Convent*, 152 Broadway, 04841. Tel: 207-594-7271. Sr. Jeanne Miller, S.A., Contact Person. Franciscan Sisters of the Atonement (Graymoor, NY) 2.

SABATTUS. *Dominican Sisters*, Lisbon Rd., R.F.D. No. 1, Box 3125, 04280-9761. Tel: 207-375-6583.
E-mail: Lucille@ime.net
Sr. Lucille Fournier, O.P., Prioress. Dominican Sisters of the Roman Congregation 8.

SACO. *Bay View Community*, 187 Bay View Rd., 04072. Tel: 207-283-3636. Sr. Cecile Labrecque, S.C.I.M., Supr.; Rev. James E. Connor, Chap., Tel: 207-284-8863. Servants of the Immaculate Heart of Mary (Good Shepherd Sisters) 34.

Notre Dame de Lourdes, 27 Thornton Ave., 04072. Tel: 207-284-8943. Sr. Sylvia Lariviere, Supr. Sisters of the Presentation of Mary 3.

Provincial Residence, 313 Seaside Ave., 04072-3410. Tel: 207-284-6429; Fax: 207-282-7376. Servants of the Immaculate Heart of Mary. Sr. Theresa Rounds, S.C.I.M., Prov. Supr. Sisters 4.

Religious Hospitallers of St. Joseph, 44 High St., 04072. Tel: 207-282-3585. Sr. Mary Annunciata, R.H.S.J., Coord. Sisters 3.

ST. AGATHA. *Our Lady of Wisdom Convent*, 380 Main St., P.O. Box 108, 04772-0108. Tel: 207-543-7523. Sr. Yvette Raymond, D.W., Coord. Daughters of Wisdom 7.

SANFORD. *Daughters of the Charity of the Sacred Heart of Jesus*, 20 Lenox St., 04073-3221. Tel: 207-324-4931. Sr. Bonita A. Cote, F.C.S.C.J., Contact Person. Sisters 2.

St. Ignatius, 14 St. Ignatius St., 04073. Tel: 207-324-2034. Sr. St. Benoit Plante, O.S.U., Supr. Sisters 4.

SCARBOROUGH. *Sisters of Notre Dame*, 9 Coach Lantern Ln., 04074. Tel: 207-885-0791. Sr. Rosemary Donohue, S.N.D., Contact Person.

SOUTH PORTLAND. *Holy Cross Convent*, 30 Emery St., 04106. Tel: 207-799-1175. Sr. Annemarie Kiah, Contact Person & Supr. Sisters of Mercy of the Americas 3.

Our Lady of Mercy Convent, 265 Cottage Rd., 04106. Tel: 207-767-5804. Sr. M. Eunice Boyd, R.S.M., Supr. Gen. Diocesan Sisters of Mercy of Portland 9.

STANDISH. *Honoratus Residence*. St. Joseph College, 278 Whites Bridge Rd., 04084-5263. Tel: 207-892-9611. Sr. Michele T. Aronica, R.S.M. Sisters of Mercy of the Americas 2.

Marian Hall, 04084. Tel: 207-892-5542. St. Joseph's College, 278 Whites Bridge Rd., 04084-5263. Tel: 207-892-6766. Sr. Joyce Mahany, R.S.M., Contact Person. Sisters of the Americas 5.

VAN BUREN. *St. Bruno Convent*, 300 Main St., 04785. Tel: 207-868-5266. Sr. Dorina Chasse, S.C.I.M., Supr. Servants of the Immaculate Heart of Mary 8.

WATERVILLE. *Blessed Sacrament Convent*, 101 Silver St., 04901. Tel: 207-872-7072. Servants of the Blessed Sacrament. Sr. Patricia Ann Keane, S.S.S., Supr. Sisters 10.

Mt. Merici Convent, 142 Western Ave., 04901-4617. Tel: 207-873-3515. Sr. Agnes Marie Proulx, O.S.U., Prioress. Ursuline Sisters 15.

Mt. St. Joseph Fontbonne Community, Highwood St., 04901. Tel: 207-873-5377. Sr. Cecile Roux, C.S.J., Coord. Sisters of St. Joseph 12.

Mt. St. Joseph Sisters' Residence, Highwood St., 04901. Tel: 207-873-4804. Sr. Yvette Poulin, C.S.J., Coord. Sisters of St. Joseph 3.

Sisters of St. Joseph, 24 Glen Ave., 04901. Tel: 207-873-5247. Sr. Dorine Moreau, C.S.J., Coord. Sisters of St. Joseph 4.

Ursuline Sisters Infirmary, 142 Western Ave., 04901. Tel: 207-873-1931. Sr. Aimee Bouffard, O.S.U., Supr. Ursuline Sisters 15.

Ursuline Sisters' Residence, 140 1/2 Western Ave., 04901. Tel: 207-872-9375. Sr. Theresa Pelletier, O.S.U., Contact Person. Sisters 3.

WINSLOW. *Inter-Community*. Sisters of St. Joseph/Mercy. 17 Boston Ave. #2, 04901. Tel: 207-877-7896. Sisters 2.

Provincialate of the Sisters of St. Joseph, 93 Halifax St., 04901. Tel: 207-872-2878. Sr. Dorothy Bujold, Coord. Sisters 4.

[K] HERMITAGES

ORLAND. *John of the Cross Monastery Hermitage*, 166 Upper Falls Rd., 04472. Tel: 207-469-3456. Sr. Margaret Dorgan, D.C.M. Carmelite Sisters 2.

ST. ALBANS. *Divine Mercy Hermitage*, 57 Bryant Rd., 04971. Tel: 207-938-5586; Fax: 207-938-5586. Sr. B. Emmanuel Bryant.

Sky-Arch Hermitage, 47 Byrant Rd., 04971. Tel: 207-938-5586.
E-mail: srhermit@somtel.com
Web site: http://www.somtel.com/~srhermit
Sr. Margaret Mary Cuddeback.

THORNDIKE. *Transfiguration Hermitage*, R.R. 1, Box 398, 04986-9709. Tel: 207-568-3731. Sr. Elizabeth Wagner, Contact Person.

[L] RETREAT HOUSES

ALFRED. *Notre Dame Retreat & Spiritual Center*, P.O. Box 159, 04002-0159. Tel: 207-324-6160; Fax: 207-324-5044. Bro. Theodore Letendre, F.I.C., Dir.

AUGUSTA. *St. Paul Retreat House and Cursillo Center*. (Men and Women). Mailing Address: c/o Chancellor, P.O. Box 11559, Portland, 04104-7559.

BIDDEFORD. *Marie Joseph Spiritual Center*, R.F.D. #2, Lester Orcutt Blvd., 04005. Tel: 207-284-5671. Sr. Claire Vanasse, P.M., Dir.; Rev. James F. Murphy, C.S.C., Chap. Sisters of the Presentation of Mary.

LITCHFIELD. *Dominican Sisters*, Buker Pond, 04350. Mailing Address: 18 Tampa St., Lewiston, 04240. Sr. Monica Dubois, O.P., Dir.

PEAKS ISLAND. *Mother of the Good Shepherd Monastery by the Sea*, 235 Pleasant Ave., 04108. Tel: 207-766-2717. The Servants of God of St. Augustine. Rt. Rev. A.M. Seamus Kuebler, O.A.S., Abbot; Bro. Nicholas Druin. Purpose is to especially pray and minister to priests and brothers.

SACO. *Bay View Villa, Guest and Retreat House*, 187 Bay View Rd., 04072. Tel: 207-286-8762. Servants of the Immaculate Heart of Mary. Sr. Anita Therrien, S.C.I.M., Dir. Guests 30.

UPPER FRENCHVILLE. *Christian Life Center*. P.O. Box 530, 04745. Tel: 207-543-6193; Fax: 207-543-6193. Rev. Angelo LeVasseur, Dir.

[M] NEWMAN CENTERS

PORTLAND. *University of Southern Maine*. Portland Campus c/o Sacred Heart Rectory, 80 Sherman St., 04101-2216.
Gorham Campus: Rev. Ernest L. L'Heureux, Chap.

Westbrook College. Res. St. Joseph Church, 673 Stevens Ave., 04103. Revs. Theodosius Corley, O.F.M.Cap.; Patrick Glavin, O.F.M.Cap.; Don Bosco Duquette, O.F.M.Cap.

BIDDEFORD. *University of New England*. Res. St. Joseph Rectory, P.O. Box 408, 04005. Rev. Joseph F. Carter, Chap.

BRUNSWICK. *Bowdoin College*. Newman Center, 04011. Tel: 207-725-8541. Rev. Philip A. Tracey.

CASTINE. *Maine Maritime Academy*, 158 Franklin St., P.O. Box S, 04416. Tel: 207-469-3322. Rev. John F. O'Hara, V.F., Chap.

FARMINGTON. *University of Maine at Farmington*. c/o The Pastoral Center, 13 Middle St., 04938. Rev. Gerald A. Levesque, Chap.; Susan Anzivino, Moderator.

FORT KENT. *University of Maine at Fort Kent*. St. Louis Rectory, 11 E. Main St., 04743.

LEWISTON. *Bates College*, 163 Wood St., 04240. Tel: 207-786-8272.
E-mail: kallen2@bates.edu
Rev. Philip A. Tracey.

MACHIAS. *University of Maine at Machias*, 9 O'Brien Ave., 04654. Rev. W. Larch Fidler, IV.

ORONO. *University of Maine*. Our Lady of Wisdom Parish/Newman Center, 83 College Ave., 04473-1596. Tel: 207-866-2155; Fax: 207-866-4543.
E-mail: koury@saturn.caps.maine.edu
Rev. Joseph J. Koury; Sr. Mary Sweeney, S.C., Campus Min.

PRESQUE ISLE. *University of Maine at Presque Isle*. St. Mary's Rectory, 6 Roberts St., P.O. Box 813, 04769. Tel: 207-768-3671.

SOUTH PORTLAND. *Southern Maine Technical College*. Holy Cross Rectory, 11 Aspen St., 04106. Tel: 207-799-4611. Rev. Paul F. Coughlin.

STANDISH. *Saint Joseph's College*. Campus Ministry Office., 04084-5263. Tel: 207-893-7791. Rev. John Tokaz, O.F.M.Cap.; Sr. Sylvia Comer, R.S.M., Chap.

WATERVILLE. *Colby College*, Mid Maine Campus Ministry, 04901. Tel: 207-872-3559. Dean of Students Office, Colby College. Rev. John E. Marquis, S.M., Chap.

Thomas College, Mid Maine Campus Ministry, 04901. Tel: 207-872-3559. Dean of Students Office, Colby College. Rev. John E. Marquis, S.M., Chap.

[N] MISCELLANEOUS LISTINGS

PORTLAND. *St. Elizabeth's Child Development Center*, 87 High St., 04101. Tel: 207-871-7444. Daniel Murphy.

BANGOR. *St. Michael's Center*, 1066 Kenduskeag Ave., 04401. Tel: 207-941-2855. Paul Vestal, Jr., Dir. Emergency Foster Care Juvenile Jail Diversion Program, Home Based Family Services, and Case Management Services.

BIDDEFORD. *St. Andre Housing, Inc.*, 39 Sullivan St., 04005. Tel: 207-773-6471. Chris Rose, Contact Person. Sponsored by: Roman Catholic Diocese of Portland. Purpose: to provide low income housing for the elderly in a deprived area of the state.

RELIGIOUS INSTITUTES OF MEN REPRESENTED IN THE DIOCESE

For further details refer to the corresponding bracketed number in the Religious Institutes of Men or Women section.

[0320]—*Brothers of Christian Instruction.*—F.I.C.
[0470]—*The Capuchin Friars.* (Prov. of St. Mary).—O.F.M.Cap.
[1330]—*Congregation of the Mission.*—C.M.
[0480]—*Conventual Franciscans.*—O.F.M.Conv.
[0520]—*Franciscan Friars.* (Custody of St. Casimer).—O.F.M.
[0690]—*Jesuit Fathers and Brothers.* (New England Prov.).—S.J.
[0780]—*Marist Fathers.* (Boston Prov.).—S.M.
[0910]—*Oblates of Mary Immaculate.* (Prov. of St. John the Baptist).—O.M.I.
[0430]—*Order of Preachers (Dominicans).* (Canadian Prov.).—O.P.
[0610]—*Priests of the Congregation of the Holy Cross.* (Eastern Prov.).—C.S.C.

RELIGIOUS INSTITUTES OF WOMEN REPRESENTED IN THE DIOCESE

[]—*Community of the Resurrection.*
[]—*Companions of Christ.*—C.O.C.
[3100]—*Congregation of Our Lady of the Holy Rosary.*—R.S.R.
[2230]—*Congregation of the Infant Jesus.*—C.I.J.
[0750]—*Daughters of Charity of the Sacred Heart of Jesus.*—F.C.S.C.J.
[0960]—*Daughters of Wisdom.*—D.W.
[]—*Diocesan Carmelites of Maine.*—D.C.M.
[]—*Diocesan Sisters of Mercy.*—R.S.M.
[1120]—*Dominican Sisters of the Roman Congregation.*—O.P.
[1170]—*Felician Sisters.*—C.S.S.F.
[1190]—*Franciscan Sisters of the Atonement.*—S.A.
[2575]—*Institute of the Sisters of Mercy of the Americas.*—R.S.M.
[2280]—*Little Franciscan of Mary.*—P.F.M.
[2760]—*Missionary Sisters of the Immaculate Conception of the Mother of God.*—S.M.I.C.
[3440]—*Religious Hospitallers of Saint Joseph.*—R.H.S.J.
[3500]—*Servants of the Blessed Sacrament.*—S.S.S.
[3550]—*Servants of the Immaculate Heart of Mary.*—S.C.I.M.
[0490]—*Sisters of Charity of Montreal (Grey Nuns).*—S.G.M.
[0610]—*Sisters of Charity of St. Hyacinthe (Grey Nuns).*—S.C.S.H.
[3000]—*Sisters of Notre Dame de Namur.*—S.N.D.deN.
[3750]—*Sisters of St. Chretienne.*—S.S.Ch.
[3870]—*Sisters of St. Joseph (Lyons, France).*—C.S.J.
[0150]—*Sisters of the Assumptions.*—S.A.S.V.
[0110]—*The Sisters of the Precious Blood.*—A.P.B.
[3310]—*Sisters of the Presentation of Mary.*—P.M.
[4110]—*Ursuline Nuns (Roman Union).* (Northeastern Prov.).—O.S.U.
[0640]—*Sisters of Charity of St. Vincent de Paul.* (Halifax).—S.C.

DIOCESAN CEMETERIES

BANGOR. *Mount Pleasant*, 449 Ohio St., 04401. Tel: 207-947-4322. Mr. William Foley.

BIDDEFORD. *St. Joseph*, West St., P.O. Box 391, 04005. Tel: 207-282-0747. Mr. Paul Garriepy.

LEWISTON. *St. Peter*, Switzerland Rd., 04240. Tel: 207-782-8721.

SOUTH PORTLAND. *Calvary*, 1461 Broadway, 04106. Tel: 207-773-5796. Mr. David Nee.

WATERVILLE. *St. Francis*, 78 Grove St., 04901. Tel: 207-872-2770. Mr. Clarence Hebert.

NECROLOGY

† McDonald, Michael J., Portland, ME, Cathedral of the Immaculate Conception. —Died June 20, 1997.

† Schmit, Ronald N., Brewer, ME, St. Joseph. —Died June 13, 1997.

† Ward, Rev. Msgr. Edward F., (Retired). —Died Feb. 18, 1997.

Archdiocese of Portland in Oregon

(Archidioecesis Portlandensis in Oregon)

Most Reverend

JOHN G. VLAZNY, D.D.

Archbishop of Portland in Oregon; ordained December 20, 1961; appointed Auxiliary Bishop of Chicago and Titular Bishop of Stagno October 31, 1983; consecrated December 13, 1983; appointed Bishop of Winona May 19, 1987; installed July 29, 1987; appointed Archbishop of Portland in Oregon October 28, 1997; installed December 19, 1997

Most Reverend

KENNETH D. STEINER, D.D.

Archdiocesan Administrator; ordained May 19, 1962; appointed Titular Bishop of Avensa and Auxiliary December 6, 1977; ordained March 2, 1978. *Office: 2838 E. Burnside St., Portland, OR, 97214.*

ERECTED AS A VICARIATE-APOSTOLIC DECEMBER 1, 1843.

CREATED ARCHDIOCESE OF OREGON CITY, JULY 24, 1846; NAME CHANGED BY PAPAL DECREE TO "ARCHDIOCESE OF PORTLAND IN OREGON," SEPTEMBER 26, 1928.

Square Miles 29,717.

Comprises that part of the State of Oregon lying between the summit of the Cascades and the Pacific Ocean.

For legal titles of parishes and archdiocesan institutions, consult the Archdiocesan Pastoral Center.

Archdiocesan Pastoral Center: 2838 E. Burnside St., Portland, OR, 97214-1895. Tel.: 503-234-5334; Fax: 503-234-2545.

Web site address: http://www.archdpdx.org/

E-mail address: @archdpdx.org

STATISTICAL OVERVIEW

Personnel	
Archbishop	1
Auxiliary Bishops	1
Abbots	2
Retired Abbots	1
Priests: Diocesan Active in Diocese	102
Priests: Active Outside Diocese	4
Priests: Diocesan in Foreign Missions	2
Priests: Retired, Sick or Absent	42
Number of Diocesan Priests	150
Religious Priests in Diocese	193
Extern Priests in Diocese	24
Ordinations:	
Diocesan Priests	3
Transitional Deacons	2
Permanent Deacons in Diocese	16
Total Brothers	84
Total Sisters	577
Parishes	
Parishes	125
With Resident Pastor:	
Resident Diocesan Priests	78
Resident Religious Priests	38
Without Resident Pastor:	
Administered by Priests	5
Administered by Lay People	4
Missions	26
Pastoral Centers	1
Professional Ministry Personnel:	
Sisters	24
Lay Ministers	156
Welfare	
Catholic Hospitals	9
Total Assisted	1,525,424
Health Care Centers	5
Total Assisted	1,692
Homes for the Aged	5
Total Assisted	1,496
Day Care and Extended Day Care Centers	4
Total Assisted	1,585
Specialized Homes	6
Total Assisted	2,779
Special Centers for Social Services	14
Total Assisted	937,267
Residential Care of Disabled	3
Total Assisted	35
Educational	
Seminaries, Diocesan	1
Students from This Diocese	13
Students from Other Diocese	112
Diocesan Students in Other Seminaries	2
Students Religious	29
Total Seminarians	44
Colleges and Universities	2
Total Students	5,584
High Schools, Diocesan and Parish	3
Total Students	1,591
High Schools, Private	6
Total Students	3,171
Elementary Schools, Diocesan and Parish	41
Total Students	8,990
Elementary Schools, Private	1
Total Students	383
Catechesis/Religious Education:	
High School Students	2,404
Elementary Students	12,125
Total Students Under Catholic Instruction	34,292
Teachers in the Diocese:	
Priests	51
Scholastics	2
Brothers	8
Sisters	73
Lay Teachers	1,268
Vital Statistics	
Receptions into the Church:	
Infant Baptism Totals	5,092
Adult Baptism Totals	732
Received into Full Communion	637
First Communions	3,802
Confirmations	1,960
Marriages:	
Catholic	738
Interfaith	563
Total Marriages	1,301
Deaths	1,974
Total Catholic Population	286,741
Total Population	2,767,100

Former Bishops—Most Rev. FRANCIS NORBERT BLANCHET, D.D., First Vicar Apostolic of Oregon Territory; cons. July 25, 1845, Titular Bishop of Drasa; appt. Archbishop of Oregon City, July 24, 1846 when the Vicariate was erected into an ecclesiastical province; resigned 1880; died June 18, 1883.—Most Rev. CHARLES JOHN SEGHERS, D.D., cons. June 29, 1873; Bishop of Vancouver Island, British Columbia; coadjutor to the Archbishop of Oregon City, Dec. 10, 1878; Archbishop, Dec. 20, 1880; resigned 1884 and; transferred to Vancouver Island, British Columbia; died Nov. 28, 1886.—Most Rev. WILLIAM H. GROSS, C.SS.R., D.D., Archbishop of Oregon City; cons. Bishop of Savannah, GA April 27, 1873 promoted by His Holiness Leo XIII Feb. 1, 1885 from Savannah to the Archiepiscopal See of Oregon City; died Nov. 14, 1898.—Most Rev. ALEXANDER CHRISTIE, D.D., Archbishop of Oregon City; cons. June 29, 1898, Bishop of Vancouver Island, B. C. promoted by His Holiness Leo XIII February 12, 1899 from Vancouver Island to the Archiepiscopal See of Oregon City; died April 6, 1925.—Most Rev. EDWARD D. HOWARD, D.D., LL.D., Titular Archbishop of Albule; ord. June 12, 1906; cons. Titular Bishop of Isauria and Auxiliary Bishop of Davenport, April 6, 1924; appt. to the See of Oregon City, April 30, 1926 asst. at the Pontifical Throne, May 2, 1939; transferred to the Titular See of Albule and as Archbishop of Portland in Oregon, Dec. 9, 1966; died Jan. 2, 1983.—Most Rev. ROBERT JOSEPH DWYER, D.D., Ph.D., ord. June 11, 1932; cons. Bishop of Reno, August 5, 1952; appt. Archbishop of Portland in Oregon, Dec. 9, 1966; resigned Jan. 22, 1974; died March 24, 1976.—Most Rev. CORNELIUS MICHAEL POWER, D.D., J.C.D., ord. June 3, 1939; appt. Bishop of Yakima, Feb. 5, 1969; cons. May 1, 1969; appt. Archbishop of Portland in Oregon, Jan. 22, 1974; retired July 3, 1986; died May 22, 1997.—Most Rev. WILLIAM J. LEVADA, S.T.D., ord. Dec. 20, 1961; appt. Titular Bishop of Capri and Auxiliary Bishop of Los Angeles, March 29, 1983; appt. Archbishop of Portland in Oregan,

July 1, 1986; installed Sept. 21, 1986; appt. Coadjutor Archbishop of San Francisco, Aug. 17, 1995; transferred Oct. 24, 1995.—Most Rev. FRANCIS E. GEORGE, O.M.I., Ph.D., S.T.D., ord. Dec. 21, 1963; appt. Bishop of Yakima July 10, 1990; installed Sept. 21, 1990; appt. Archbishop of Portland in Oregon, April 29, 1996; installed May 27, 1996; appt. Archbishop of Chicago April 8, 1997; installed May 7, 1997.

Office of the Archbishop

Archdiocesan Pastoral Center—2838 E. Burnside St., Portland, 97214-1895. Tel: 503-234-5334; Fax: 503-234-2545.

Vicars and Directors

Vicar General—Rev. PAUL PERI.

Vicar for Clergy—Rev. CHARLES LIENERT.

Vicar for Finance—Rev. PAUL PERI.

Department Directors—
Business Affairs—PAULETTE FURNESS.
Clergy—Rev. CHARLES LIENERT.
Education—ROBERT MIZIA.
Chancellor / Public Services—MARY JO TULLY.
Pastoral Services—Rev. MICHAEL MASLOWSKY.

Vicariate For Southeast Asians—Rev. VINCENT MINH, C.SS.R., Episcopal Vicar, *5404 N.E. Alameda Dr., Portland, 97213.* Tel: 503-249-5892.

Chancellor—MARY JO TULLY.

College of Consultors—Most Rev. KENNETH D. STEINER; Rev. Msgr. FRANK CAMPBELL; Very Rev. PATRICK BRENNAN; Revs. JOSEPH BROWNE, C.S.; DONALD BUXMAN; ARTHUR DERNBACH; JOSEPH JACOBBERGER; CHARLES LIENERT; GREGORY MOYS; PAUL PERI.

Area Vicars—Rev. JOSEPH JACOBBERGER, Downtown Portland; Rev. CATHAL BRENNAN, North Portland; Rev. ROBERT KRUEGER, Northeast Portland; Rev. PETER KIRWIN, O.F.M., Southeast Portland; Rev. JOSEPH S. MCMAHON, East Portland Suburban; Rev. D. BRUCE BROWN, South Portland Suburban; Rev. RICHARD ROSSMAN, West Portland Suburban; Rev. WAYNE FORBES, Beaverton Suburban; Rev. THOMAS FARLEY, Yamhill County; Rev. CARL FLACH, Tualatin Valley; Rev. ELWIN SCHWAB, Columbia County; Rev. MARK BACHMEIER, North Coast; Vacant; Marion County; Rev. MICHAEL HEMMING, Metropolitan Salem; Vacant; Santiam; Most Rev. KENNETH D. STEINER, Albany-Corvallis; Rev. TIMOTHY MOCKAITIS, Metropolitan Eugene; Rev. JACK WELLS, Middle Coast; Rev. JOHN MCGUIRE, South Coast; Rev. WILLIAM RYAN, O.S.A., Douglas County; Rev. JAMES CLIFFORD, Southern Oregon.

Personnel Board—Revs. PAUL F. PERI, Chm. JOHN KERNS; ROBERT KRUEGER; WAYNE FORBES; JOSEPH JACOBBERGER; CHARLES LIENERT, (Ex Officio); JACK MOSBRUCKER.

Tribunal

Judicial Vicar—Rev. THOMAS YURCHAK, J.C.L.; LINDA WEIGEL, J.C.L., Dir. Tel: 503-233-8381.
Adjutant Judicial Vicar—Revs. CARL FLACH; BERTRAM GRIFFIN, J.C.D.
Judges—Revs. CARL J. FLACH; CARL GIMPL; GARY JACOBSON; THOMAS YURCHAK, J.C.L.; PATRICK BRENNAN, J.C.L.; THOMAS BROCKHAUS, O.S.B., J.C.D.; BERTRAM GRIFFIN, J.C.D.; JOSEPH JACOBBERGER; HENRY LACERTE, J.C.D.; Rev. Msgr. EDMUND VAN DER ZANDEN.

Defenders of the Bond—Revs. JAMES MAYO; GREGORY MOYS; LINDA WEIGEL, J.C.L.; KELLY VANDEHEY.

Auditors—ALEXANDRIA GUERRA-SUNDBERG; PEG WILLS.

Notary—MARGARET PALMER.

Advocates—All priests with Archdiocesan assignments and pastoral ministers by appointment.

Archdiocesan Offices and Agencies

Archives—MARY A. GRANT, Archivist. Tel: 503-233-8334., *2838 E. Burnside St., Portland, 97214-1895.*

Building Commission—Most Rev. JOHN G. VLAZNY; Revs. THEODORE WEBER, Chm. PAUL PERI; JOSEPH HEUBERGER; ALEXANDER PLASKER, O.S.B.; A. P. DIBENEDETTO, F.A.I.A.; JOHN BROCKAMP; ROBERT STOCHOSKY; DELIA WILSON; DONALD BENZ; JOSEPH PELLICANO; EDWARD CURTIN; PAULETTE FURNESS, Ex Officio; KEN SCOTT, Sec. Tel: 503-234-5334.

Business Affairs—PAULETTE FURNESS, Dir., *2838 E. Burnside St., Portland, 97214-1895.* Tel: 503-234-5334.

Campus Ministry—Rev. MICHAEL MASLOWSKY, Dir., *2838 E. Burnside St., Portland, 97214-1895.* Tel: 503-234-5334.

Catholic Charities, Inc.—DENNIS KEENAN, Exec. Dir., *231 S.E. 12th Ave., Portland, 97214-9813.* Tel: 503-231-4866.

Catholic Deaf Ministry—Sr. LINDA ROBY, B.V.M., Dir., *2838 E. Burnside St., Portland, 97214-1895.* Tel: 503-233-8398 (V-TDD).

"Catholic Sentinel"—(Official Newspaper of the Archdiocese), Most Rev. JOHN G. VLAZNY, Publisher-in-Chief; JOHN J. LIMB, Publisher; ROBERT PFOHMAN, Editor, *5536 N.E. Hassalo, Portland, 97213-3638.* Tel: 503-281-1191.

Catholic Youth Organization—KRISTA VON BORSTELL, Exec. Dir., *Oregon Plaza, 825 N.E. 20th St., Ste. 320, Portland, 97232.* Tel: 503-231-9484.

Cemeteries—Rev. PAUL PERI, V.G., Dir. TIM CORBETT, Supt., *Mt. Calvary Cemetery, 333 S.W. Skyline Blvd., Portland, 97221.* Tel: 503-292-6621.

Clergy Personnel—Rev. CHARLES LIENERT, Vicar for Clergy, *2838 E. Burnside St., Portland, 97214-1895.* Tel: 503-233-8366.

Communications, Office of—BUD BUNCE, Dir., *2838 E. Burnside St., Portland, 97214-1895.* Tel: 503-233-8373.

Continuing Education for Clergy—Rev. PAUL PERI, Dir. Board Members: Revs. EDMOND BLIVEN; DONALD BUXMAN; J. PATRICK MOORE; TIMOTHY MURPHY; SCOTT VANDEHEY, *2838 E. Burnside St., Portland, 97214-1895.* Tel: 503-234-5334.

Development Office—JONATHAN WEAVER, Dir., Devel. & Annual Catholic Appeal; ROBERT BELDING, Dir. Planned Giving & CEEF, *2838 E. Burnside St., Portland, 97214-1895.* Tel: 503-233-8333.

Ecumenical and Interreligious Affairs—Rev. RICHARD SIRIANNI, Dir. MARY JO TULLY, Assoc. Dir., *3123 N.E. 24th Ave., Portland, 97212.* Tel: 503-281-5777.

Education, Religious—Bro. ROBERT RODRIGUES, O.F.M., Dir. CATHY SHANNON, Assoc. Dir., *2838 E. Burnside St., Portland, 97214-1895.* Tel: 503-234-5334.

Family Life Office—Vacant, *2838 E. Burnside St., Portland, 97214-1895.* Tel: 503-233-8341.

Finance Council—Most Rev. JOHN G. VLAZNY, Chair; Rev. PAUL PERI; Rev. PATRICK WALSH; ARTHUR SCHULTE, JR., Ph.D.; LEO C. SHERRY, JR.; MYRON FLECK; ROGER CONKLING; HENRIETTA SAALFELD; PATRICK REILLY; LEONARD VUYLSTEKE; DENNIS FERGUSON; EDWARD HERINCKX, *2838 E. Burnside St., Portland, 97214-1895.* Tel: 503-233-8350.

Financial Services—LEONARD VUYLSTEKE, Dir., *2838 E. Burnside St., Portland, 97214-1895.* Tel: 503-233-8359.

Hispanic Ministeries—RAUL VELAZQUEZ, Dir., *2838 E. Burnside St., Portland, 97214.* Tel: 503-233-8324.

Historical Commission—JOSEPH SCHIWEK, JR., *2838 E. Burnside St., Portland, 97214-1895.*

Holy Childhood, Pontifical Association of—MARY JO TULLY, Dir., *2838 E. Burnside St., Portland, 97214-1895.* Tel: 503-233-8323.

Immigration Counseling Services—SUSAN ROSSITER, Dir., *434 N.W. 6th Ave., Ste. 202, Portland, 97209.* Tel: 503-221-1689.

Justice and Peace—FRANK FROMHERZ, Dir., *2838 E. Burnside St., Portland, 97214-1895.* Tel: 503-233-8361.

Ministry Formation—Rev. MICHAEL MASLOWSKY, Dir., *2838 E. Burnside St., Portland, 97214-1895.* Tel: 503-233-8391.

Mission Office—MARY JO TULLY, Dir., *2838 E. Burnside St., Portland, 97214-1895.* Tel: 503-233-8323.

Office for People with Disabilities—DOROTHY DESMARTEAU-COUGHLIN, Dir. RUTH HAYES-BARBA, Assoc. Dir., *2838 E. Burnside St., Portland, 97214-1895.* Tel: 503-233-8396 (V/TTY).

Oregon Catholic Conference—Most Rev. JOHN G. VLAZNY, Pres.; Most Rev. THOMAS J. CONNOLLY (BAK), Vice Pres.; Most Rev. KENNETH STEINER; ROBERT CASTAGNA, Exec. Dir., *2838 E. Burnside St., Portland, 97214-1895.* Tel: 503-233-8387.

Oregon Catholic Press—Most Rev. JOHN G. VLAZNY, Publisher-in-Chief; JOHN J. LIMB, Publisher; DAN HUMPHRIES, Gen. Mgr., *5536 N.E. Hassalo, Portland, 97213.* Tel: 503-281-1191.

Pastoral Services, Evangelization, Pastoral Councils, Charismatic Renewal—Rev. MICHAEL MASLOWSKY, Dir., *2838 E. Burnside St., Portland, 97214-1895.* Tel: 503-233-8385.

Permanent Diaconate—Rev. RICHARD HUNEGER, Dir.; Deacon JOHN RIES, Assoc. Dir., *2838 E. Burnside St., Portland, 97214-1895.* Tel: 503-234-5334.

Pro-Life Activities—ROBERT CASTAGNA, Exec. Dir., Oregon Catholic Conference, *2838 E. Burnside St., Portland, 97214-1895.* Tel: 503-233-8387.

Project Rachel—*231 S.E. 12th Ave., Portland, 97214-9813.* Tel: 1-800-249-8074.

Propagation of the Faith, Pontifical Society for the—MARY JO TULLY, Dir., *2838 E. Burnside St., Portland, 97214-1895.* Tel: 503-233-8322.

St. Mary's Home for Boys—EMMA DENNIS, Exec. Dir., *16535 S.W. Tualatin Valley Hwy., Beaverton, 97006.* Tel: 503-649-5651.

School Office—ROBERT MIZIA, Supt. Tel: 503-233-8300. Bro. WILLIAM CAMPBELL, S.M., Asst. Supt., School Personnel/Technology; Sr. RITA RAE SCHNEIDER, R.S.M., Asst. Supt., Faith Formation/Curriculum, *2838 E. Burnside St., Portland, 97214-1895.*

Vocations—Rev. LIAM CARY, Dir., *2838 E. Burnside St., Portland, 97214-1895.* Tel: 503-233-8368.

Worship—*2838 E. Burnside St., Portland, 97214-1895.* Tel: 503-234-5334.

Youth Ministry—DONALD CIFFONE, Dir., *2838 E. Burnside St., Portland, 97214-1895.* Tel: 503-233-8395.

CLERGY, PARISHES, MISSIONS AND PAROCHIAL SCHOOLS

CITY OF PORTLAND
(Multnomah County)

1—CATHEDRAL OF THE IMMACULATE CONCEPTION (1851), Revs. Joseph Jacobberger; Luan Tran; Deacon John Ries.
Res., 1716 N.W. Davis St., 97209. Tel: 503-228-4397; Fax: 503-242-2568.
School—110 N.W. 17th Ave., 97209. Tel: 503-227-4297; Fax: 503-243-3819.
Order of Servants of Mary 2; Lay Teachers 10; Students 225.

2—ST. AGATHA (1911), Rev. Cosmas White, O.S.B. In res., Rev. Matthias Burger, O.S.B.
Res., 1403 S.E. Nehalem St., 97202. Tel: 503-236-4747; Fax: 503-236-4747.
School—(Grades K-8). Tel: 503-234-5500.
Sisters 1; Lay Teachers 11; Students 155.

3—ALL SAINTS (1917), Rev. John Kerns.
Res., 3847 N.E. Glisan, 97232. Tel: 503-232-4305; Fax: 503-234-9685.
School—601 N.E. 39th Ave., 97232. Tel: 503-236-6205; Fax: 503-236-0781.
Lay Teachers 21; Students 358.
Catechesis / Religious Programs—Students 42.

4—ST. ANDREW (1907), Rev. Robert W. Krueger.
Res., 806 N.E. Alberta St., 97211. Tel: 503-281-4429; Fax: 503-281-4411.

5—ST. ANTHONY (1917), Rev. Michael Maslowsky.
Res., 3725 S.E. 80th Ave., 97206. Tel: 503-771-6039; Fax: 503-775-6119.

6—ASCENSION (1892), Rev. Peter Kirwin, O.F.M. In res., Rev. Loren Kerkof O.F.M.; Bros. Mark Schroeder, O.F.M.; Robert Rodrigues, O.F.M.
Church: 7507 S.E. Yamhill, 97215. Tel: 503-256-3897; Fax: 503-257-4681.
Res., 404 S.E. 68th, 97215. Tel: 503-253-8305.
Catechesis / Religious Programs—Tel: 503-256-3897; Fax: 503-257-4681.
Students 138.

7—ASSUMPTION (1909), Rev. Joseph Baccellieri.
Res., 7406 N. Smith St., 97203. Tel: 503-286-0203.

8—ST. BIRGITTA (1954), Rev. Joseph P. Browne, C.S.C.
Res., 11820 N.W. St. Helens Rd., 97231-2319. Tel: 503-286-3929.
Chapel—Portland, Chapel of Our Lady of Sinj.

9—BLESSED SACRAMENT (1913), Rev. Cathal Brennan; Sr. Raphael Balduc, O.S.F., Pastoral Assoc.
Office: 4610 N. Maryland Ave., 97217. Tel: 503-284-4689; Fax: 503-284-0376. [CEM]
Res., 4620 N. Maryland Ave., 97217. Tel: 503-281-6758.

10—ST. CHARLES (1914), Rev. Jacob Mosbrucker. Pastoral Assocs.: Barbara Hays; Martha Stephenson.
Parish Center: 5310 N.E. 42nd, 97218. Tel: 503-281-6461; Fax: 503-281-6828.
School—Archbishop Howard School, (Grades PreK-8) 5309 N.E. Alameda Dr., 97213. Tel: 503-281-1912.
Lay Teachers 11; Students 272.

11—CHURCH OF KOREAN MARTYRS (1990) (Korean), Rev. Andrew Sung Han Kim.
Res., 10840 S.E. Powell Blvd., 97266. Tel: 503-762-6880; Fax: 503-760-6601.

12—ST. CLARE (1913), Rev. Donald A. Durand.
Res., 8535 S.W. 19th Ave., 97219. Tel: 503-244-1037; Fax: 503-246-2665.
School—Tel: 503-244-7600.
Sisters of Charity 1; Lay Teachers 14; Students 227.

13—ST. ELIZABETH OF HUNGARY (1953), Revs. John B. Wironen, C.S.C.; William E. Wickham, C.S.C., Chap. VA Hospital.
Res., 4112 S.W. Sixth Ave. Dr., 97201. Tel: 503-222-2168.

14—ST. FRANCIS OF ASSISI, Rev. Charles Lieneri, Mod.; Valerie Chapman, Pastoral Admin.; Silivelio Alaalatoa, Pastoral Assoc.; Joe Rastatter, Soc. Min.
Res., 330 S.E. 11th Ave., 97214. Tel: 503-232-5880.

15—HOLY CROSS (1901), Rev. Cathal Brennan.
Res., 5227 N. Bowdoin St., 97203. Tel: 503-289-2834; Fax: 503-283-7056.
School—Tel: 503-289-3010; Fax: 503-286-5006.
Sisters 4; Lay Teachers 8; Students 200.

Chapel—Christ The Teacher, University of Portland, 5000 N. Willamette Blvd., 97203. Tel: 503-283-7311; Fax: 503-283-7399.

16—HOLY FAMILY (1931), Rev. Robert Barricks. 3732 S.E. Knapp, 97202. Tel: 503-774-1428; Fax: 503-774-1854.
Res., 3708 S.E. Flavel St., 97202. Tel: 503-788-2051; Fax: 503-774-1854.
School—Tel: 503-774-8871. Sandy Stanton, Prin.
Lay Teachers 14; Students 214.

17—HOLY REDEEMER (1906), Revs. Richard Schiblin, C.S.S.R.; Vincent Minh, C.S.S.R.; Anthony Phuc Nguyen, C.S.S.R.; Joseph K. Nuttman, C.S.S.R.; M. Durkin Fitzgerald, C.SS.R.
Res., 25 N. Portland Blvd., 97217. Tel: 503-285-4539; Fax: 503-285-8216.
School—Tel: 503-283-5197.
Sisters of the Holy Names of Jesus and Mary 7; Lay Teachers 20; Students 391.

18—HOLY ROSARY PARISH & DOMINICAN PRIORY (1894), Rev. Anthony Cordeiro, O.P.; Very Rev. Paul Ratory O.P., Prior; Rev. Thomas J. McGreevy, O.P. In res., Revs. Paul A. Duffner, O.P.; Dominic Hoffman, O.P.; Christopher H. Moschini, O.P.; Christopher Terry, O.P.
Res., 375 N.E. Clackamas St., 97232. Tel: 503-235-3163; Fax: 503-235-3164.
Confraternity of the Most Holy Rosary—P.O. Box 3617, 97208. Tel: 503-236-8393; Fax: 503-236-8394.
Catechesis/Religious Programs—Students 134.

19—ST. IGNATIUS (1907), Revs. Roy Antunez, S.J.; Stephen M. Hess, S.J.
Res., 3400 S.E. 43rd Ave., 97206. Tel: 503-777-1491; Fax: 503-777-3142. [JC]
School—3330 1/2 S.E. 43rd St., 97206. Tel: 503-774-5533; Fax: 503-788-1134.
Sisters of the Holy Names of Jesus and Mary 4; Lay Teachers 14; Students 252.
Convent—4130 S.E. Brooklyn, 97206. Tel: 503-231-6538. Sisters of the Holy Names of Jesus and Mary

20—IMMACULATE HEART OF MARY (1888), Rev. Nicolaus Marandu.
Res., 2926 N. Williams Ave., 97227-1628. Tel: 503-287-3724; Fax: 503-287-5011.

21—ST. JOHN FISHER (1959), Rev. Wayne A. Forbes.
Res., 7007 S.W. 46th Ave., 97219. Tel: 503-246-4686; Fax: 503-452-8570.
School—Tel: 503-246-3234; Fax: 503-246-4117.
Lay Teachers 17; Aides 7; Students 267.
Catechesis/Religious Programs—Tel: 503-244-5784.
Students 80.

22—CHURCH OF ST. JOSEPH THE WORKER (1885), Rev. Jack Krall.
Res., 2310 S.E. 148th, 97233. Tel: 503-761-8710; Fax: 503-761-8545.

23—ST. MARY MAGDALENE (1911). (The Madeleine). Rev. Richard D. Sirianni.
Res., 3123 N.E. 24th Ave., 97212. Tel: 503-281-5777; Fax: 503-281-5787.
School—3240 N.E. 23rd Ave., 97212. Tel: 503-288-9197. Bernadette Kunnen, Prin.
; Lay Teachers 12; Students 265.

24—CHURCH OF ST. MICHAEL, THE ARCHANGEL (1894), Rev. Bertram F. Griffin; Celeste Granato, Pastoral Min.
Res., 424 S.W. Mill St., 97201. Tel: 501-228-8629; Fax: 501-827-7689.

25—OUR LADY OF SORROWS (1917), Rev. Robert Beltrami, O.F.M.
Res., 5221 S.E. Knight St., 97206. Tel: 503-775-6731; Fax: 503-775-6732.
School—Tel: 503-771-3592; Fax: 503-774-5390.
Sisters 4; Lay Teachers 13; Students 172.

26—ST. PATRICK (1885), Rev. Frank Knusel, Admin.
Res., 1623 N.W. 19th Ave., 97209. Tel: 503-222-4086.

27—ST. PETER (1911), Rev. Dale T. Waddill.
Office: 8648 S.E. Foster Rd., 97266. Tel: 503-777-3321; Fax: 503-777-3321.
Res., 5736 S.E. 86th St., 97266. Tel: 503-777-1026.

28—ST. PHILIP NERI (1912), Revs. Stephen E.M. Bossi, C.S.P.; Richard W. Chilson, C.S.P.; Vincent Sampietro, C.S.P.; Joseph J. Scott, C.S.P. Pastoral Assocs.: Kim Armbruster; Claire Meyer; Charlene Scales; Liz Anctil-Frane.
Res., 2408 S.E. 16th Ave., 97214. Tel: 503-231-4955; Fax: 503-736-1383.

29—ST. PIUS X (Cedar Mill) (1953), Revs. Neil J. Moore; Heiko T. Junge; Deacon Robert Little.
Office: 1280 N.W. Saltzman Rd., 97229. Tel: 503-644-5264; Fax: 503-626-6540.
School—1260 N.W. Saltzman Rd., 97229. Tel: 503-644-3244; Fax: 503-646-6568.
Lay Teachers 13; Students 266.
Catechesis/Religious Programs—Tel: 503-626-3154.
Students 665.

30—QUEEN OF PEACE (1924), Rev. Amancio Rodrigues.
Res., 2434 N. Farragut St., 97217. Tel: 503-283-1100; Fax: 503-289-2144.

31—ST. RITA (1924), Rev. Richard Boyle, O.S.M.
Mailing Address: 10029 N.E. Prescott St., 97220. Tel: 503-252-3403; Fax: 503-256-9682.

32—ST. ROSE OF LIMA (1911), Rev. Richard J. Huneger.
Res., 2727 N.E. 54th Ave., 97213. Tel: 503-281-5318; Fax: 503-284-8350.
School—Archbishop Howard School, Tel: 503-281-1912; Fax: 503-281-0554.
Lay Teachers 12; Students 269.

33—SACRED HEART (1893), Rev. Benedict Suing, O.S.B.
Res., 3910 S.E. 11th Ave., 97202. Tel: 503-231-9636.

34—ST. STANISLAUS (1907) (Polish), Rev. Richard G. Philiposki, S.Ch.
Res., 3916 N. Interstate Ave., 97227-1063. Tel: 503-281-7532; Fax: 503-281-7532.

35—ST. STEPHEN (1907), Rev. Morton Park.
Res., 1112 S.E. 41st Ave., 97214. Tel: 503-234-5019; Fax: 503-239-5985.
School—4235 S.E. Salmon, 97214. Tel: 503-235-7040; Fax: 503-239-5985.
Lay Teachers 6; Students 130.

36—ST. THERESE OF THE CHILD JESUS (1955), Revs. Louis J. Urbanski; Cletus C. Osuji (Nigeria); Mr. Vernon Korchinski, Pastoral Assoc.
Res., 1260 N.E. 132nd Ave., 97230. Tel: 503-256-5850; Fax: 503-253-3560.
School—Tel: 503-253-9400; Fax: 503-253-9571.
Dominican Sisters of Mission San Jose 2; Lay Teachers 14; Students 260.

37—ST. THOMAS MORE (1936), Rev. Galdino Monteiro; Deacon Edward Morin.
Res., 3525 S.W. Patton Rd., 97221. Tel: 503-222-2055; Fax: 503-227-5661.
School—Tel: 503-222-6105.
Sisters of St. Francis 1; Lay Teachers 17; Students 225.

38—ST. VINCENT DE PAUL (1919). (Downtown Chapel). Revs. Richard F. Berg, C.S.C.; Stephen J. Sedlock, C.S.C. In res., Rev. Gary N. Smith, S.J.
Res., 601 W. Burnside St., 97209. Tel: 503-228-0746; Fax: 503-402-1607.

OUTSIDE THE CITY OF PORTLAND

Albany, Linn Co., Our Lady of Perpetual Help (1885), Rev. John C. Betts. Pastoral Assocs.: Ellen Ketsdever; Kathleen Gyovai; Sharon Tebb.
Res., 728 Ellsworth St., 97321. Tel: 541-926-1449; Fax: 541-926-2191.
School—815 S. Broadalbin, Tel: 541-928-7474.
Sisters 2; Lay Teachers 4; Students 148.
Catechesis/Religious Programs—Tel: 541-926-9327.
Students 274.

Aloha, Washington Co., St. Elizabeth Ann Seton (1982), Rev. J. Pat Moore.
Res., 3145 S.W. 192nd Ave., 97006. Tel: 503-649-9044; 649-6211; Fax: 503-848-2915.
Catechesis/Religious Programs—Students 94.

Ashland, Jackson Co., Our Lady of the Mountain (1959), Revs. Anthony Rosevear, O.P.; Raymond Finerty, O.P., Newman Center; Brendan McAnerney, O.P. In res., Rev. Paschal (Donald) Salisbury, O.P.
Res., 987 Hillview Dr., 97520. Tel: 541-482-1146; Fax: 541-488-5174.
Catechesis/Religious Programs—Students 166.

Astoria, Clatsop Co., St. Mary, Star of the Sea (1874), Rev. Mark V. Bachmeier.
Res., 1465 Grand Ave., 97103. Tel: 503-325-3671; Fax: 503-325-7983. [JC]
School—Tel: 503-325-3771.
Lay Teachers 9; Students 101.
Mission—Hammond, Clatsop Co., St. Francis de Sales.

Bandon, Coos Co., Holy Trinity (1883), Rev. William E. Karath.
Res., 355 Oregon Ave., Box 1037, 97411. Tel: 541-347-2309; Fax: 541-347-9256. [CEM]
Mission—Port Orford, Curry Co., St. John the Baptist, P.O. Box 884, Port Orford, 97465.

Beaverton, Washington Co., St. Cecilia (1876), Revs. Dennis J. O'Donovan; Richard Thompson; Luke O'Donnell, O.S.B.
Res., 5105 S.W. Franklin Ave., 97005. Tel: 503-644-2619; Fax: 503-626-7204.
School—Tel: 503-644-7647.
Sisters 1; Lay Teachers 15; Students 270.
Catechesis/Religious Programs—Tel: 503-644-0203; Fax: 503-626-7205.
Students 667.

Holy Trinity (1962), Rev. John Waldron.
Res., 13715 S.W. Walker Rd., 97005. Tel: 503-643-9528; Fax: 503-644-8426.
School—Tel: 503-644-5748; Fax: 503-644-8486.
Lay Teachers 18; Students 265.

Catechesis/Religious Programs—Tel: 503-646-0331.
Students 124.

Brookings, Curry Co., Star of the Sea (1923), Rev. Edmund K. Ryan, O.P.
Mailing Address: Box 1066, 97415.
Res., 820 Old County Rd., 97415. Tel: 541-469-2313; Fax: 541-469-2683.
Mission—Gold Beach, Curry Co., St. Charles Borromeo, 94323 Gauntlet, P.O. Box 33, Gold Beach, 97444. Tel: 541-247-2453. Rev. Thomas F. Mannion.

Canby, Clackamas Co., St. Patrick (1882), Rev. Thomas D. Yurchak.
Res., 498 N.W. Ninth, P.O. Box 730, 97013. Tel: 503-266-9411; Fax: 503-263-2293. [CEM]
Preschool:—Tel: 503-263-8584. Theresa Jensen, Dir.
Lay Teachers 1; Children 4.
Catechesis/Religious Programs—488 N.W. 9th, 97013. Tel: 503-266-2401.
Students 231.

Central Point, Jackson Co., Shepherd of the Valley (1978), Rev. James Clifford, O.S.A.
Office: 600 Beebe Rd., 97502. Tel: 541-664-1050; Fax: 541-664-9312.

Coos Bay, Coos Co., St. Monica (1888), Rev. Terry J. O'Connell.
Mailing Address: 696 Donnelly Ave., 97420-1553.
Church—Sixth St. between Donnelly & Bennett, 97420. Tel: 541-267-7421; Fax: 541-269-0339.

Coquille, Coos Co., Holy Name (1915), Rev. John F. McGuire.
Res., 12 N. Dean St., 97423. Tel: 541-396-3849; Fax: 541-396-4620.
Missions—Myrtle Point, Coos Co., Sts. Ann and Michael, 209 Second St., Myrtle Point, 97458. Tel: 541-396-3849; Powers, Coos Co., St. Bridget, 580 Third & Spruce, Powers, 97466.

Cornelius, Washington Co., St. Alexander (1881), Revs. Martin R. Senko, Admin.; Evaristo Santa Aria (Mexico) Co-Admin.
Mailing Address: P.O. Box 644, 97113.
Res., 183 N. 11th, 97113. Tel: 503-359-0304; 357-8167 (Hispanic). [CEM]
Catechesis/Religious Programs—Students 126.

Corvallis, Benton Co., St. Mary (1861), Most Rev. Kenneth D. Steiner, D.D.; Rev. Martin L. King; Deacon Francis Potts; Gloria J. Holt, Contact Person.
Res., 501 N.W. 25th St., 97330. Tel: 541-757-1988; Fax: 541-757-2788. [CEM]
Catechesis/Religious Programs—Tel: 541-757-1675.
Students 644.

Cottage Grove, Lane Co., Our Lady of Perpetual Help (1897), Rev. James Dowd; Sr. Elizabeth Hecker, S.N.J.M., Pastoral Assoc.
Res., 1025 N. 19th St., 97424. Tel: 541-942-3420.
Mission—Creswell, Lane Co., St. Philip Benizi, Cresswell.

Dallas, Polk Co., St. Philip (1920), Rev. Gerald Quintal.
Office: 825 S.W. Mill St., 97338. Tel: 503-623-2440. [JC]

Estacada, Clackamas Co., St. Aloysius (1924), Rev. Robert J. Palladino.
Res., P.O. Box 1199, 97023. Tel: 503-630-2416. [JC]

Eugene, Lane Co.,

1—ST. JUDE, (1969), Rev. Peter A. Roerig.
Office: 4330 Willamette, 97405. Tel: 541-344-1191; Fax: 541-345-6001.

2—ST. MARK, (1962), Rev. Daniel Reynolds.
Res., 1760 Echo Hollow Rd., 97402. Tel: 541-689-0725; Fax: 541-689-0569.

3—ST. MARY, (1887), Revs. Scott Vandehey; James Stange.
Res., 1062 Charnelton St., 97401. Tel: 541-342-1139; Fax: 541-334-6996. [CEM]
Catechesis/Religious Programs—Students 118.

4—ST. PAUL, (1955), Rev. Timothy Mockaitis.
Res., 1201 Satre St., 97401. Tel: 541-686-2345; Fax: 541-686-0037.
School—Tel: 541-344-1401; Fax: 541-344-2572.
Sisters 1; Lay Teachers 18; Students 268.
Catechesis/Religious Programs—Students 117.

5—ST. PETER, (1955), Rev. David Ronald Cullings.
Res., 1150 Maxwell Rd., 97404. Tel: 541-688-1051; Fax: 541-689-0782. [JC]

6—ST. THOMAS MORE, (1915). (University Parish). Revs. Michael Fones, O.P., Admin.; Christopher Renz, O.P.; Sr. Janet Ryan, S.N.J.M., Pastoral Assoc. In res., Revs. Augustine Thompson, O.P.; Vincent Lopez, O.P.; Vincent Benoit, O.P.; Bede Wilks, O.P.
Res., 1850 Emerald St., 97403. Tel: 541-343-7021; 346-4468; Fax: 541-686-8028.

Florence, Lane Co., St. Mary, Our Lady of the Dunes (1951), Rev. Donald K. Gutmann.
Res., 85060 U.S. Hwy. 101 S., Box 2640, 97439. Tel: 541-997-2312.

Forest Grove, Washington Co., St. Anthony (1908), Rev. David Gutmann; Sandra S. Zajdel, Pastoral Assoc., Tel: 503-357-8147; Lois Boogaard, Bus. Mgr.
Res., 1660 Elm St., 97116. Tel: 503-357-2989; Fax: 503-357-2217.
Catechesis/Religious Programs—Tel: 503-357-8147.
Students 180.

Gervais, Marion Co., Sacred Heart-St. Louis (1847), Rev. Kenneth Jacques, O.S.B.
Res., 680 Elm Ave., P.O. Box 236, 97026. Tel: 503-792-4231; Fax: 503-792-3749. [CEM]
School—Tel: 503-792-4541; Fax: 503-792-3826. Judy Howard, Prin.
Sisters 1; Lay Teachers 4; Students 108.

Grand Ronde, Yamhill Co., St. Michael (1860), Rev. James Crunican.
Res., 48520 S.W. Hebo Rd., 97347. Tel: 503-843-2206.

Grants Pass, Josephine Co., St. Anne (1896), Revs. Gregory Moys; Todd Molinari.
Res., 1131 N.E. 10th St., 97526. Tel: 541-476-2240; Fax: 541-476-2194.
Parish Center—1133 N.E. 10th St., 97526. Tel: 541-479-4848.
School—(Grades K-6). Tel: 541-479-1582. Mr. Frankie Bytheway, Prin.
Lay Teachers 8; Students 145.
Kelly Youth Center—1129 N.E. 10th St., 97526. Tel: 541-476-5802.
Catechesis/Religious Programs—Tel: 541-479-4848.
Students 203.
Missions—Cave Junction, Josephine Co., St. Patrick, 407 W. River St., Cave Junction, 97523. Tel: 541-592-3658. Rev. Harry Holwell.; Rogue River, Jackson Co., Rogue River Catholic Community, P.O. Box 1596, Rogue River, 97537. Tel: 541-582-1373. Deacon Robert Chapin.

Gresham, Multnomah Co., St. Anne (1957), Rev. J. Michael Morrissey.
Res., 1015 S.E. 182nd Ave., 97233-5099. Tel: 503-665-4935; Fax: 503-661-2116.
Catechesis/Religious Programs—Students 246.

St. Henry (1913), Revs. Joseph S. McMahon; E. Slider Steuernol. In res., Rev. Charles J. Lienert.
Office: 346 N.W. First St., 97030. Tel: 503-665-9129; Fax: 503-665-8238.
Catechesis/Religious Programs—Students 253.

Hillsboro, Washington Co., St. Matthew (1902), Revs. Carl J. Flach; Gary Zerr.
Res., 447 S.E. 3rd Ave., 97123-4499. Tel: 503-648-1998; Fax: 503-648-4489. [CEM]
School—Tel: 503-648-2512.
Lay Teachers 11; Students 250.
Catechesis/Religious Programs—Tel: 503-648-6213.
Students 235.

Independence, Polk Co., St. Patrick (1908), Rev. Victoriano Perez.
Office: 1275 E St., 97351. Tel: 503-838-1242; Fax: 503-838-6873.
Res., 1258 E St., 97351. Tel: 503-838-5137.

Jordan, Linn Co., Our Lady of Lourdes (1885), Rev. W. Thomas Jones, S.M.
Res., 39043 Jordan Rd., 97374. Tel: 503-394-2437. [CEM]
Mission—Lyons, Linn Co., St. Patrick, 7th St., Lyons 97358.

Junction City, Lane Co., St. Helen (1916), Rev. Joseph Black.
Res., 1350 W. Sixth Ave., 97448. Tel: 541-998-8053; Fax: 541-998-9474. [CEM]

Keizer, Marion Co., St. Edward (1967), Rev. Philip M. Hemming.
Office: 5303 River Rd., N., 97303. Tel: 503-393-5323; Fax: 503-393-5323. [CEM]
Catechesis/Religious Programs—Tel: 503-463-5439.
Students 171.

Lake Oswego, Clackamas Co., Our Lady of the Lake (1890), Revs. Rock Sassano; Xavier Panneer Selvam.
Mailing Address: 650 A Avenue, 97034-2943. Tel: 503-636-7687; Fax: 503-636-9415. [CEM]
School—715 A Ave., 97034-2943. Tel: 503-636-2121; Fax: 503-635-7760. Joan M. Codd, Prin.
Sisters 2; Lay Teachers 18; Students 249.
Catechesis/Religious Programs—Students 600.

Lebanon, Linn Co., St. Edward (1903), Rev. Paul P. Maher, O.M.I.; Deacon Richard E. Triska.
Office (Mailing Address): 100 Main St., 97355. Tel: 541-258-5333.
Res., 251 Second St., 97355.
Catechesis/Religious Programs—Tel: 541-258-5333.
Students 200.

Lincoln City, Lincoln Co., St. Augustine (1925), Rev. Mell Stead.
Res., 1139 N.W. Hwy. 101, 97367. Tel: 541-994-2216.

McMinnville, Yamhill Co., St. James (1876), Rev. Thomas B. Farley.
Res., 1145 E. First St., 97128. Tel: 503-472-5232; Fax: 503-472-4414. [CEM]
School—Tel: 503-472-2661.
Lay Teachers 10; Students 134.
Catechesis/Religious Programs—Students 79.
Mission—Dayton, Yamhill Co., St. Martin de Porres, 407 Ferry St., Dayton, 97114. Tel: 503-864-2378; Fax: 503-864-3211.

Medford, Jackson Co., Sacred Heart of Jesus (1928), Revs. Mark Cach; Kelly Vandehey.
Res., 449 S. Ivy St., 97501. Tel: 541-779-4661; Fax: 541-732-0633. [JC]
School—Tel: 541-772-4105. Perry Martin, Prin.
Lay Teachers 12; Students 190.
Mission—Jacksonville, Jackson Co., St. Joseph, 280 N. 4th, Jacksonville, 97530.
Catechesis/Religious Programs—Students 427.

Milwaukie, Clackamas Co., Christ the King (1960), Revs. Augustine Kulbis, O.S.M.; Joseph Cheah, O.S.M.
Res., 7414 S.E. Michael Dr., 97222. Tel: 503-659-1475; Fax: 503-659-6138.
School—Tel: 503-654-0601; Fax: 503-654-0168. Ruth Gill, Prin.
Lay Teachers 14; Students 245.
Catechesis/Religious Programs—Tel: 503-786-0102.
Students 170.

St. John the Baptist (1912), Revs. Bruce Brown; John Amsberry; Sr. Rae Skinner, S.N.J.M., R.C.I.A. Dir. In res., Rev. Joseph J. Neuville.
Res., 10955 S.E. 25th, 97222. Tel: 503-654-5449; Fax: 503-653-9567.
School—10956 S.E. 25th, 97222. Tel: 503-654-0200; Fax: 503-654-8419.
Lay Teachers 17; Students 203.
Catechesis/Religious Programs—Tel: 503-659-2760; Fax: 503-653-9567.
Students 197.

Molalla, Clackamas Co., St. James (1962), Rev. Edward Altstock.
Res., 301 Frances St., 97038. Tel: 503-829-2080; Fax: 503-829-2806.
Catechesis/Religious Programs—Students 144.

Monroe, Benton Co., St. Rose (1883), Rev. Joseph Black; William J. Richardson, Jr., Admin.
Mailing Address: P.O. Box 516, 97456.
Res., 00470 S. Fifth, 97456. Tel: 541-847-5454. [CEM]

Mt. Angel, Marion Co., St. Mary (1880), Revs. Edmund Smith, O.S.B.; Emmanuel W. Clark, O.S.B.
Res., Box 465, 97362. Tel: 503-845-2296; Fax: 503-845-2297. [CEM 2]
Catechesis/Religious Programs—Tel: 503-845-9248.
Students 294.
Mission—Scotts Mills, Marion Co., Holy Rosary. [CEM]

Myrtle Creek, Douglas Co., All Souls (1952), Rev. William A. Ryan, O.S.A.
Res., 1242 N.E. Spruce St., P.O. Box 810, 97457. Tel: 541-863-3271. [JC]
Mission—Glendale, Douglas Co., Holy Family, 243 Marshall Ave., Glendale, 97442.

Newberg, Yamhill Co., St. Peter (1909), Rev. Gregory A. Gage; Lee Allard, Pastoral Assoc.
Res., 608 S. Columbia St., 97132. Tel: 503-538-4312.

Newport, Lincoln Co., Sacred Heart Parish (1889), Rev. Jack M. Wells.
Res., 927 N. Coast Hwy., P.O. Box 843, 97365. Tel: 541-265-5101; Fax: 541-265-7582. [JC]
Mission—Siletz, Lincoln Co., St. Mary, 231 E. Logsden Rd, Siletz, 97380.

North Bend, Coos Co., Holy Redeemer (1906), Rev. Karl Schray.
Res., 2250 16th St., 97459. Tel: 541-756-6901; Fax: 541-756-3234. [JC]
Catechesis/Religious Programs—Tel: 541-756-0161.
Students 240.

North Plains, Washington Co., St. Edward (1913), Rev. Msgr. Frank Campbell.
Res., P.O. Box 507, 97133. Tel: 503-644-1932; 647-2131 (Parish). [CEM]

Oakridge, Lane Co., St. Michael (1941), Rev. William M. O'Malley, S.J.
Res., 76387 Crestview St., P.O. Box 422, 97463. Tel: 541-782-3262.
Mission—Dexter, Lane Co., St. Henry, 38925 Dexter Rd., P.O. Box 65, Dexter, 97431. Tel: 541-937-3033. [JC]

Oregon City, Clackamas Co., St. John the Apostle (1842), Rev. Donald R. Buxman.
Res., 417 Washington St., 97045. Tel: 503-656-3474; Fax: 503-656-0486. [CEM]
School—Tel: 503-656-5123. Alan Loboy, Prin.
Lay Teachers 10; Students 196.
Catechesis/Religious Programs—Tel: 503-656-7755.
Students 245.

Rainier, Columbia Co., Nativity B.V.M. (1909), Rev. Emmett B. Painter, S.J.
Res., 204 E. C St., P.O. Box 340, 97048. Tel: 503-556-5641.
Mission—Clatskanie, Columbia Co., St. John the Baptist.

Redland, Clackamas Co., St. Philip Benizi (1969), Rev. Theodore R. Weber.
Res., 18211 S. Henrici Rd., Oregon City, 97045. Tel: 503-631-2882; Fax: 503-631-7443.
Catechesis/Religious Programs—Tel: 503-631-7124.
Students 159.

Reedsport, Douglas Co., St. John the Apostle (1924), Rev. Don Gutmann.
Res., 12 St. Johns Way, 97467. Tel: 541-271-5621.

Rockaway, Tillamook Co., St. Mary by the Sea (1927), Rev. William A. Maat, O.S.B.
Res., P.O. Box 390, 97136. Tel: 503-355-2345. [JC]
Church—275 S. Pacific St., Tel: 503-355-2661 (Office).

Roseburg, Douglas Co., St. Joseph (1867), Rev. Ray Elam, O.S.A.
Res., 800 W. Stanton St., 97470. Tel: 541-673-5157; Fax: 541-672-5022. [CEM]
School—Tel: 541-672-1751.
Lay Teachers 7; Students 123.
Catechesis/Religious Programs—Tel: 541-672-7239.
Students 270.
Station—Glide, Tel: 541-496-3999.

Roy, Washington Co., St. Francis of Assisi (1908), Rev. Stephen Breitenstein.
Res., 39135 N.W. Harrington Rd., Banks, 97106. Tel: 503-324-2231. [CEM]
School—39085 N.W. Harrington Rd., Banks, 97106. Tel: 503-324-2182.
Sisters of St Mary of Oregon 2; Lay Teachers 9; Students 138.

St. Helens, Columbia Co., St. Frederic (1910), Rev. Elwin C. Schwab.
Res., 175 S. 13th St., 97051. Tel: 503-397-0148.

St. Louis, Marion Co., St. Louis. Closed. For sacramental records contact Sacred Heart-St. Louis, Gervias.

St. Paul, Marion Co., St. Paul (1839), Rev. Charles D. Borho, Admin.
Res., 20217 Christie St. N.E., P.O. Box 454, 97137. Tel: 503-633-4611. [CEM]
School—20327 Christie St., N.E., P.O. Box 188, 97137. Tel: 503-633-4622. Ms. Christina Meadows, B.S., M.A., Prin.
Sisters 1; Lay Teachers 7; Students 108.

Salem, Marion Co., St. Joseph (1864), Revs. Carl Gimpl; Petrus Binh Hoang.
Res., 721 Chemeketa St. N.E., 97301. Tel: 503-581-1623; Fax: 503-581-7271. [JC]
School—Tel: 503-581-2147.
Sisters of the Holy Names of Jesus and Mary 2; Sisters of St. Mary 1; Lay Teachers 28; Students 279.
Catechesis/Religious Programs—Tel: 503-585-5095.
Students 275.
Mission—Salem, Marion Co., San Jose.

Queen of Peace (1963), Rev. George Wolf. Pastoral Assocs.: Sr. Joan Jett, S.N.J.M.; Darlene Joynt.
Office: P.O. Box 3016, 97302. Tel: 503-364-7202; Fax: 503-364-5882.
School—4227 Lone Oak Rd., S.E., Tel: 503-362-3443; Fax: 503-589-9411.
Lay Teachers 10; Students 168.
Catechesis/Religious Programs—Tel: 503-364-7202; Fax: 503-364-5882. D.R.E.: Tricia Boyle, Preschool-Elem.; Sheila Mousel, Youth Min., Young Adult (Grades 9-12).
Students 327.

St. Vincent de Paul (1925), Rev. Patrick McNamee; Sr. Joyce Barsotti, S.S.M.O.; Raoul Van Landuyt, Pastoral Assoc.; Kimberly Allain, Pastoral Asst.
Res., 1025 Columbia St., 97303. Tel: 503-363-4589; Fax: 503-363-9493. [JC]
School—Tel: 503-363-8457; Fax: 503-363-1516.
Sisters 1; Lay Teachers 12; Students 145.
Catechesis/Religious Programs—1015 Columbia St. N.E., 97303. Tel: 503-363-2166.
Students 150.

Sandy, Clackamas Co., St. Michael the Archangel (1898), Rev. J. Aidan Mayo.
Res., 18090 S.E. Langensand Rd., 97055. Tel: 503-668-4446; Fax: 503-668-5018.
Mission—Welches, Clackamas Co., St. John the Evangelist, Tel: 503-622-6338.

Scappoose, Columbia Co., St. Wenceslaus (1911), Rev. Stephen M. Clovis.
Parish Office: Tel: 503-543-2110; Fax: 503-543-5159.
Res., 51555 Old Portland Rd., 97056. [CEM]
Catechesis/Religious Programs—Tel: 503-534-7425.
Students 120.

Scio, Linn Co., St. Bernard (1912), Rev. Kevin O'Conner, O.M.I.
Res., P.O. Box 45, 97374. Tel: 503-394-2625.
Mission—Jefferson, Marion Co., St. Thomas, 647 Third St., Jefferson, 97352. Tel: 541-327-2343.

Seaside, Clatsop Co., Our Lady of Victory (1913), Rev. Nicholas Nilema, A.L.C.P.
Res., 120 Ocean Way, 97138.
Parish Office—Tel: 503-738-6161.
Mission—Seaside, Clatsop Co., St. Peter the Fisherman, Tel: 503-436-2876.
Mailing Address: 120 Ocean Way, 97138.

Shady Cove, Jackson Co., Our Lady of Fatima (1955), Rev. William McHugh, O.M.I.
Res., 37 Church Ln., P.O. Box 116, 97539. Tel: 541-878-2479.

Shaw, Marion Co., St. Mary (1906), Rev. G. James Brady, C.S.C.
Mailing Address: P.O. Box 338, Aumsville, 97325-0338. Tel: 503-362-6159.
Res., 9168 Silver Falls Hwy., S.E., Aumsville, 97325. [CEM]

Sheridan, Yamhill Co., Good Shepherd (1908), Rev. James Crunican.
Res., 127 N.E. Hill St., 97378. Tel: 503-843-2206.

Sherwood, Washington Co., St. Francis (1921), Rev. Thomas McCarthy, S.J.
Mailing Address: P.O. Box 279, 97140. Tel: 503-625-6185; Fax: 503-625-6187.
Res., 400 S. Pine St., 97140. Tel: 503-625-6186.
Church—400 N.E. Oregon St., 97140. Tel: 503-625-5914.
Catechesis/Religious Programs—Tel: 503-625-6187; Fax: 503-625-6187.
Students 377.

Silverton, Marion Co., St. Paul (1914), Rev. Ed Coleman; Deacon Loris A. Buccola.
Res., 1410 Pine St., 97381. Tel: 503-873-2044. [CEM]

Springfield, Lane Co., St. Alice (1947), Rev. Patrick Walsh.
Res., 1520 F St., 97477. Tel: 541-747-7041; Fax: 541-744-2272.

Stayton, Marion Co., Immaculate Conception (1903), Rev. Richard Wallace.
Res., 525 E. Santiam, Box 535, 97383. Tel: 503-769-2656; Fax: 503-769-5621. [CEM]
School—Tel: 503-769-2718.
Sisters of St. Mary of Oregon 1; Lay Teachers 16; Students 267.
Catechesis/Religious Programs—1077 N. Sixth St., 97383. Tel: 503-769-2557.
Students 120.

Sublimity, Marion Co., St. Boniface (1879), Rev. Arthur P. Dernbach.
Res., 375 E. Church St., 97385. Tel: 503-769-5664. [CEM]
Missions—Mill City, Marion Co., St. Catherine of Siena, First & Ivy, Mill City, 97360.; Detroit, Marion Co., St. Christopher, Santian Ave., Detroit, 97342.

Sutherlin, Douglas Co., St. Francis Xavier (1957), Rev. J. Brendan Fleming.
Res., P.O. Box 1048, 97479-1048. Tel: 541-459-4042 (Office); 459-7599 (Rectory).
Mission—Drain, Douglas Co., St. John the Apostle, P.O. Box 457, Drain, 97435-0457. Tel: 541-836-2891.

Sweet Home, Linn Co., St. Helen (1953), Rev. Andrew Harris, O.M.I.
Res., 815 Fifth Ave., 97386. Tel: 541-367-2530.
Mission—Brownsville, Linn Co., Holy Trinity, 104 Blakely Ave., Brownsville, 97327.

Tigard, Washington Co., St. Anthony (1910), Revs. Leslie M. Sieg, C.S.P., Parish Admin.; Peter Makalla, A.L.C.P.
Res., 9905 S.W. McKenzie St., 97223. Tel: 503-639-4179; Fax: 503-624-2364. [CEM]
School—Tel: 503-639-4979; Fax: 503-620-5117. Jeanne Bloudek, Prin.
Lay Teachers 20; Students 337.
Catechesis/Religious Programs—Students 414.

Tillamook, Tillamook Co., Sacred Heart (1890), Rev. John Henderson, O.F.M.Conv.
2411 Fifth St., 97141. Tel: 503-842-6647; Fax: 503-842-3897. [CEM]
Mission—Cloverdale, Tillamook Co., St. Joseph, P.O. Box 9, Cloverdale, 97112. Tel: 503-392-3685. Rev. Bill C. Hausmann, S.J., Admin.

Tualatin, Clackamas Co., Church of the Resurrection (1981), Rev. Richard Rossman.
Mailing Address: 21060 S.W. Stafford Rd., 97062. Tel: 503-638-1579; Fax: 503-638-8754.
Catechesis/Religious Programs—Students 305.

Veneta, Lane Co., St. Catherine of Siena (1954), Rev. Joseph Black, Moderator; Gene Modrich, Parish Admin.
Res., 25181 E. Broadway, P.O. Box 277, 97487. Tel: 503-541-3933.

Verboort, Washington Co., Visitation B.V.M. (1875), Rev. Joseph Heuberger.
Res., 4285 N.W. Visitation Rd., Forest Grove, 97116. Tel: 503-357-3860. [CEM]
School—Tel: 503-357-6990; Fax: 503-359-0819.
Sisters of St. Mary of Oregon (S.S.M.O.) 1; Sisters of the Holy Names (S.N.J.M.) 1; Lay Teachers 8; Students 151.

Vernonia, Columbia Co., St. Mary (1923), Rev. Ronald C. Millican; Lelana L. Vandehey, Pastoral Admin.
Church—960 Missouri Ave., 97064. Tel: 503-429-8841; Fax: 503-429-8841.

Waldport, Lincoln Co., St. Anthony (1949), Rev. Gerard Steckler, S.J., Admin.
Res., P.O. Box 770, 97394. Tel: 503-563-3246; Fax: 503-563-3246.

Wilsonville, Clackamas Co., St. Cyril (1926), Rev. Paul Peri; Deacon Jim Myers.
Res., 9210 S.W. Fifth St., 97070. Tel: 503-682-2332; Fax: 503-682-0898.
Catechesis/Religious Programs—Students 154.

Woodburn, Marion Co., St. Luke (1899), Revs. David Zegar; Michael P. Johnston; Deacon Jerry McKenzie.
Office: 417 Harrison St., 97071. Tel: 503-981-5011; Fax: 503-981-5012.
Res., 521 W. Lincoln St., 97071. Tel: 503-981-1531. [CEM]
School—529 Harrison St., 97071. Tel: 503-981-7441.
Sisters 4; Lay Teachers 7; Students 191.
Mission—Hubbard, Marion Co., St. Agnes, 3052 D St., Hubbard, 97032.
Catechesis/Religious Programs—Students 148.

Yamhill, Yamhill Co., St. John (1910), Revs. David Gutmann, Admin.; John J. Kindall, S.J.; Beth Heesacker, Pastoral Assoc.
Mailing Address: P.O. Box 580, 97148. Tel: 503-662-4291.

SOUTHEAST ASIAN VICARIATE

1—Southeast Asian Vicariate, Multnomah Co., (1982), 5404 N.E. Alameda Dr., 97213. Tel: 503-249-5892; Fax: 503-249-1776. Revs. Vincent Minh, C.S.S.R., Episcopal Vicar; John B. Hong-Phuc, C.S.S.R.; James Pham-Van-Ninh, S.E.; Joseph Nguyen Duc Hau, S.E.
Catechesis/Religious Programs—Students 800.

Chaplains of Public Institutions

Portland. *Department of Veterans' Affairs Medical Center* 3710 S.W. U.S. Veterans' Hospital Rd., Box 1034, 97207. Tel: 503-220-8262, Ext. 7027, 7021. Rev. William E. Wickham, C.S.C.
Oregon Health Sciences University St. Elizabeth, 4112 Sixth Ave. Drive, 97201. Tel: 503-222-2168. Rev. John B. Wironen, C.S.C.

Roseburg. *U.S. Veterans' Administration Hospital* 913 N.W. Garden Valley Blvd., 97470-6513. Tel: 541-440-1000, Ext. 4720. Rev. Leroy Calkins, O.S.M., V.A.M.C.

Salem. *Mill Creek Correctional Facility* 5485 Turner Rd., 97310-9400. Tel: 503-378-2333. Rev. James Jacobson, S.J.
Oregon State Correctional Institution 3405 Deer Park Dr. S.E., 97310. Tel: 503-373-0147. Rev. Michael Sprauer.
Oregon State Penitentiary 2605 State St., 97310. Tel: 503-378-2333; Fax: 503-378-3897. Rev. James Jacobson, S.J.
Oregon Women's Correction Center 2809 State St., 97310. Tel: 503-378-2441. Rev. Michael Sprauer.
Santiam Correctional Institution 4005 Aumsville Hwy. S.E., 97310-9112. Tel: 503-378-2333. Rev. James Jacobson, S.J.
Youth Correctional Facility 2450 Strong Rd., 97310. Tel: 503-986-0421; Fax: 503-378-2175. Rev. Ted Frison.

Sheridan. *Federal Correctional Institution* 27072 Ballston Rd., 97378-9601. Tel: 503-843-4442, Ext. 254. Rev. Phong Bui.

White City. *U.S. Veternan's Affiars Domiciliary* 97503. Tel: 541-826-2111, Ext. 3321. Revs. Joseph E. Shirey, S.J.; Paschal Donald Salisbury, O.P.

Woodburn. *MacLaren Youth Correctional Facility* 2630 N. Pacific Hwy., 97071. Tel: 503-981-9531, Ext. 316. Rev. Ted Frison.

Special Assignment:
Reverend Fathers—
Brennan, Patrick, Mount Angel Seminary
Carey, Raymond, Mount Angel Seminary, St. Benedict, OR 97373

On Duty Outside the Archdiocese:
Reverend Fathers—
Adams, Daniel, St. Benedict, 1801 Octavia St., San Francisco, CA 94109
Clark, David, St. Vincent de Paul Church, 36 Altenburg Gardens, Clapham Common, London, SWII IJJ England
Coleman, James, Padres de Santiago Apostol, Castilla 919, Santa Cruz, Bolivia
Dare, Glenn, Diocese of Sacramento
Killingsworth, Bradley, Parroquia Fatima, Castilla 919, Santa Cruz
Olsen, Kenneth, #302-2250 Manor Pl., Comox, BC V9M 1C4 Canada

---

Absent on Leave:
Reverend Fathers—
Chun, Francis, P.O. Box 66277, Portland, OR 97266
Galluzzo, James, c/o 4545 S.E. Tibbetts, Portland, OR 97206
Law, Michael, 19885 S.W. Oak St., Aloha, OR 97007
McHugh, Donald, 1623 S.E. Miller St., Portland, OR 97202

Retired:
Reverend Fathers—
Alvares, Augustine, 12075 Mount Hamilton Rd., San Jose, CA 95140
Beno, Joseph, 484 S. 17th St., P.O. Box 1012, St. Helens, OR 97051
Bliven, Edmond, 3311 S.W. First Ave., Portland, OR 97201
Brouillard, John, 17704 N.W. Shadyfir Loop, Space 39, Beaverton, OR 97006
Chao, Joseph, 4595-A St. John Vianney Way, Beaverton, OR 97007
Cieslinski, Robert, St. John Vianney Residence, 4630-D S.W. St. John Vianney Way, Beavertown, OR 97007
Cohan, Francis J., Mailing Address: P.O. Box 26, Sheridan, OR 97378
Cunniff, Vincent, 4655-D S.W.,St. John Vianney Way, Beaverton, OR 97007
Denman, Donald, St. John Vianney Residence, 4630-B S.W. St. John Vianney Way, Beaverton, OR 97007
DePra, Italo, 1148 Third Ave. #62, Chula Vista, CA 91911
Dieringer, James J., P.O. Box 683, Pacific City, OR 97135
Domin, John M., 14645 S.W. Farmington, Beaverton, OR 97007
Engel, John, 17704 N.W. Shadyfir Loop, Space 39, Beaverton, OR 97006
Fritz, Norbert, St. John Vianney Residence, 4595-A S.W. St. John Vianney Way, Beaverton, OR 97007
Gothe, Marcus, 4655-B S.W. St. John Vianney Way, Beaverton, OR 97007
Grammond, Maurice, Mailing Address: P.O. Box 8475, Portland, OR 97207
Harris, James M., 14295 S.W. Jenkins Rd., Space 23, Beaverton, OR 97005
Hume, Kenneth, 19453 Stillmeadow Dr., Oregon City, OR 97045
Hwang, Bernard, O.S.B., 19526 Lazy Creek Ln., Oregon City, OR 97045
Jacobson, Gary, St. John Vianney Residence, 4595 S.W. St. John Vianney Way, Beaverton, OR 97007
Kennedy, Alan, St. John Vianney Residence, 4655-A S.W. St. John Vianney Way, Beaverton, OR 97007
Kies, Emil, Mailing Address: P.O. Box 5869, Charleston, OR 97420
Kolasinski, Daniel, P.O. Box 526, Reedsport, OR 97467
Linehan, Cornelius, 8736 N.E. Russell Pl., Portland, OR 97220
Linehan, Jeremiah, 6908 N.E. Tillamook St., Portland, OR 97210
McKean, Louis, P.O. Box 1121, Chula Vista, CA 91912
McMahon, Joseph M., 4525-B St. John Vianney Way, Beaverton, OR 97007
Neuville, Joseph, P.O. Box 586, Aurora, OR 97002
Reedy, John J., St. John Vianney Residence, 4630-A S.W. St. John Vianney Way, Beaverton, OR 97007
Ridi, Pio, 6806 N. Sedro, Portland, OR 97203

Rodakowski, Louis, P.O. Box 177, Vida, OR 97488
Saalfeld, Lawrence, 14506 S.E. Carol Ave., Milwaukie, OR 97267
Stipe, Jack H., St. John Vianney Residence, 4525-D S.W. St. John Vianney Way, Beaverton, OR 97007
Taaffe, Charles Q, 1085 Columbia St. N.E., Salem, OR 97303
Thielen, Martin, 4655-C S.W. St. John Vianney Way, Beaverton, OR 97007
Van Der Zanden, Edmund, 4525-C S.W. St. John Vianney Way, Beaverton, OR 97007
Vandehey, Ervin S., St. John Vianney Residence, 4630-C S.W. St. John Vianney Way, Beaverton, OR 97007
Williams, Alfred, 85 S.W. Lexington Way, Beaverton, OR 97006
Wiseman, Thomas, c/o Raymond Heuberger, P.O. Box 243, Sublimity, OR 97385
Wraszczak, Chester, 850 S.E. 169th Dr., Portland, OR 97233

Permanent Deacons:
Buccola, Loris, St. Paul, Silverton
Chapin, Robert L., Jr., St. Anne, Grants Pass
Conley, Roger, St. Vincent de Paul, Salem
Filardi, Ronald, Sacred Heart, Medford
Little, Robert, St. Pius X, Portland
McKenzie, Gerald, St. Luke, Woodburn
Mendez, Jose R., St. Luke, Woodburn; St. Joseph, Salem
Morin, Edward, St. Thomas More, Portland
Myers, James, St. Cyril, Wilsonville
Potts, Francis, St. Mary, Corvallis
Ries, John D., The Cathedral, Portland
Soper, Leonard, St. Benedict Lodge, McKensie Bridge
Stenbeck, John H., St. Joseph, Roseburg
Stromberg, Alton, Our Lady of Victory, Seaside
Triggs, Donald J., St. Mary, Corvallis
Triska, Richard, St. Edward, Lebanon

INSTITUTIONS LOCATED IN THE ARCHDIOCESE

[A] SEMINARIES, RELIGIOUS, ARCHDIOCESAN OR SCHOLASTICATES

PORTLAND. *Franciscan Formation Community*, 827 N.E. Alberta, 97211. Tel: 503-287-9223.
E-mail: postulancy.worldnet.att.net
Web site: www.sbfranciscans.org
Bro. Thomas M. Nichols, O.F.M., Dir. Priests 1; Brothers 1; Postulants 8.
Jesuit Novitiate of St. Francis Xavier, 3301 S.E. 45th Ave., 97206. Tel: 503-774-5699.
E-mail: orenev@teleport.com
Rev. Patrick J. Lee, S.J., Dir. Novices; Bro. Wayne M. Gsell, S.J., Socius/Minister. In res. Rev. John J. Kindall, S.J. Priests 1; Brothers 1; Novices 8.

ST. BENEDICT. *Mount Angel Seminary*, 97373. Tel: 503-845-3951; Fax: 503-845-3126.
E-mail: registrar@mtangel.edu
Rt. Rev. Joseph Wood, O.S.B., Abbot & Chancellor; Very Rev. Patrick Brennan, Pres. & Rector; Marina Keys, Admin. Asst. & Contact Person; Dr. Ernest Skublics, S.T.B., S.T.L, Ph.D., Academic Dean; Revs. Gregory Duerr, O.S.B., Spiritual Dir.; Dave Rogerson, O.S.B. (SEA), Theology I-II Dir. Personal Formation; William Hammelman, O.S.B., Formation Dir. Pre-Theology; Liem Nguyen, O.S.B., Formation Dir. ESL I-II & Theology I; Philip Waibel, O.S.B., Dir. Pastoral Education; Mr. John Degnin, Dir. Devel.; Revs. Odo Recker, O.S.B., Admissions Dir. & Registrar; Thomas Carawan, Coordinator Liturgy; Richard Paperini, Formation Dir. Theology I, III-IV; Leif Kehrwald, Asst. Dir. Pastoral Educ.; Rev. William Miller, S.J., Formation Dir. PreTheology I-II; Mr. Thomas Bolton, Alumni Dir.; Rev. Vitaliano Ola'aiga, Formation Dir., College I-II, Theology I. Priests 19; Sisters 5; Brothers 5; Lay Teachers 18.

[B] COLLEGES AND UNIVERSITIES

*PORTLAND. *University of Portland*, 5000 N. Willamette Blvd., 97203. Tel: 503-283-7911.
E-mail: webmaster@uofport.edu
Web site: www.uofport.edu
For a complete listing, refer to the Colleges and Universities section.

MARYLHURST. *Marylhurst College*, 97036. Tel: 503-636-8141.
E-mail: president@marylhurst.edu
Web site: http://www.marylhurst.edu
For a complete listing, refer to the Colleges and Universities section.

[C] HIGH SCHOOLS, DIOCESAN

PORTLAND. *Central Catholic High School*. (Coed), 2401 S.E. Stark St., 97214. Tel: 503-235-3138; Fax: 503-233-0073. Rev. Timothy Murphy, Pres.; Ron Edwards, Prin.; Rev. Ron Millican. Priests 2; Sisters 3; Lay Teachers 61; Students 811.

MEDFORD. *St. Mary's School*. (Coed), 816 Black Oak Dr., 97504.
Web site: www.stmarys.medford.or.us
Barbara W. Callaway, Prin.; Rev. Thomas J. Whelan, O.S.A. Priests 1; Sisters 1; Lay Teachers 29; Lay Staff 13; Students 347.

STAYTON. *Regis High School*. (Coed), P.O. Box 65, 97383. Tel: 503-769-2159. Mr. Douglas J. Wasko, Prin. Lay Teachers 16; Students 235.
Regis High School Foundation, P.O. Box 65, 97383.

[D] HIGH SCHOOLS, PRIVATE

PORTLAND. *Jesuit High School*. (Coed), 9000 S.W. Beaverton-Hillsdale Hwy., 97225-2491. Tel: 503-292-2663.
E-mail: anton@teleport.com
Web site: http://www.teleport.com/jesuit
The Society of Jesus. Revs. William E. Hayes, S.J., Pres.; Anton T. Harris, S.J., Rector, Admin. & Contact Person; Mrs. Sandra Satterberg, Prin.; Mr. Paul Hogan, Academic Vice Prin.; Mr. Steve Beaird, Vice Pres. Development; Mr. Kevin G. Connell, S.J., Vice Prin. Student Life; Mr. Richard Gedrose, Exec. Vice Pres.; Mrs. Shirley Poppe, Admissions Dir.; Mr. Donald Clarke, Campus Min. Faculty: Revs. Richard H. Ganz, S.J.; Frank D. Masterson, S.J.; David S. Olivier, S.J.; Lawrence F. Robinson, S.J.; Bruce J. Schmidlkofer, S.J., Sabbatical. In res. Revs. Joseph R. DeJardin, S.J.; Gordon L. Keys, S.J.; Edward P. McTighe, S.J. Scholastics: Revs. Edward Lopez, S.J.; Jeffrey N. McDougall, S.J. School: Priests 8; Lay Staff 95; Students 1,014. Community: Priests 10.
St. Mary's Academy. (Girls), 1615 S.W. Fifth Ave., 97201. Tel: 503-228-8306. Patricia A. Thompson, Prin. Sisters 6; Lay Teachers 45; Students 564.

BEAVERTON. *Valley Catholic Middle & High Schools*. (Coed), 4275 S.W. 148th Ave., 97007. Tel: 503-644-3745. Sisters of St. Mary of Oregon. Sr. Wanda Marie Jordan, S.N.J.M., Prin. Sisters 5; Lay Teachers 31; Students 450.

EUGENE. *Marist High School*. (Coed), 1900 Kingsley Rd., 97401. Tel: 541-686-2234; Fax: 541-342-6451. Revs. Vincent Benoit, O.P.; Vincent Lopez, O.P., Prin. Priests 2; Lay Teachers 50; Students 570.

MILWAUKIE. *LaSalle High School*. (Coed), 11999 S.E. Fuller Rd., 97222.
E-mail: lasalle@northwest.com (MAC)
William S. George, Prin.; Gregory R. VanderZanden, Pres. Sisters 1; Lay Teachers 37; Students 604.

SALEM. *Salem Catholic Schools Foundation*, P.O. Box 13207, 97309. Tel: 503-371-9068.

[E] ELEMENTARY SCHOOLS, AREA

EUGENE. *O'Hara Area Elementary Catholic School*, 715 W. 18th, 97402. Elizabeth Moore, Prin. Comprised of students from the following parishes in Eugene: St. Jude, St. Mark, St. Mary, St. Paul, St. Peter, St. Alice and the Newman Center. Lay Teachers 16; Students 365.

[F] ELEMENTARY SCHOOLS, PRIVATE

PORTLAND. *Franciscan Montessori Earth School*, 14750 S.E. Clinton St., 97236. Staffed by Franciscan Sisters of the Eucharist. Mother Francine Cardew, F.S.E., Dir. Franciscan Sisters of the Eucharist 5; Lay Teachers 23; Students 400.

BEAVERTON. *St. Mary of the Valley School*, 4440 S.W. 148th, 97007. Tel: 503-626-7781. Sisters of St. Mary of Oregon. Jean Bomber, Prin. Sisters 2; Lay Teachers 24; Students 379.
Valley Catholic Middle School. (Grades 7-8), 4440 S.W. 148th, 97007. Sr. Adele Marie, S.S.M.O., Vice Prin. Sisters 1; Lay Teachers 5; Students 104.

[G] SOCIAL AND MINISTERIAL SERVICES

PORTLAND. *Catholic Charities of the Archdiocese of Portland in Oregon*, 231 SE 12th Ave., 97214. Tel: 503-231-4866. Dennis B. Keenan, M.S.W., Exec. Dir.; Richard Deml, C.P.A., Controller; Heather Kmetz, Pub. Rels. Mgr.; Cheryl Shepperd, Devel. Dir.
Catholic Charities Social Service Division of Portland, 231 S.E. 12th Ave., 97214. Tel: 503-231-4866. Douglas Alles, Social Svc. Dir.; Rev. Bruce Cwiekowski, AIDS Ministry Coordinator. Programs include: maternity and aftercare home, adoption, refugee resettlement, Hispanic health outreach, AIDS ministry, ministry to the elderly, Asian social services, and Project Rachel, and Immigration Legal Services.
Catholic Youth Organization/Camp Howard, 825 N.E. 20th, Ste. 320, 97232-2295. Tel: 503-231-9484. Krista Von Borstel, Exec. Dir. Programs include: Youth recreation & camping.
Immigration Counseling Services, 434 N.W. Sixth Ave. #202, 97209. Tel: 503-221-1689. Susan Rossiter, Exec. Dir. Programs include: Immigration legalization advocacy, court hearing representation.
Catholic Community Services of Lane County, 945 W. Seventh Ave., Eugene, 97402. Tel: 503-345-3642. Jeanne Benson, Exec. Dir. Programs include: Emergency shelter, utilities, and food, single mothers shelter, drug dependent mothers shelter, family shelter, young parents program, family self-sufficiency program.
Catholic Community Services of Mid-Willamette Valley and the Central Coast, 142 Glenbrook N., Keizer, 97307. Tel: 503-390-2600. Jim Seymour, Exec. Dir. Programs include: Center for delinquent youth, developmentally & physically disabled group homes, shelter for displaced youth, counseling center, Hispanic mental health outreach, child abuse prevention program.
Catholic Community Services of Southern Oregon, 440 S. Ivy St., Medford, 97501. Tel: 503-779-0803. Sean Crowley, Dir. Programs include: Emergency services, health clinics, community education, Alzheimer Respite Center.

[H] CHILD DEVELOPMENT CENTERS

PORTLAND.
**Providence Child Center*, 830 N.E. 47th Ave., 97213. Tel: 503-215-2400. Legal Title: *Sisters of Providence in Oregon*. Ethelyn G. Pankratz, Admin. Sisters 2. Children's Nursing Center providing skilled nursing care and habilitation/rehabilitation services for children who have physical and mental disabilities and multiple care needs. Long-term chronic care, short-term care for respite, transition, or pediatric hospice provided.
Providence Montessori School. Preschool education for children ages 2 1/2 to 6 with a broad array of developmental needs and abilities.
Wee Care. Day-care center for children of employees of Providence Medical Center, ages 6 weeks to 6 years.

[I] RESIDENTIAL SCHOOLS FOR YOUTHS WITH EMOTIONAL-SOCIAL PROBLEMS

BEAVERTON. *St. Mary's Home for Boys, Inc.*, 16535 S.W. Tualatin Valley Hwy., 97006. Tel: 503-649-5651. Residential & day treatment center for behaviorally & emotionally disturbed children. Emma Dennis, Exec. Dir. & Contact Person. Students 100.

[J] GENERAL HOSPITALS

PORTLAND. *Providence Portland Medical Center*, 4805 N.E. Glisan St., 97213. Tel: 503-215-1111
For a complete listing, refer to the Hospitals section.
Providence St. Vincent Medical Center, 9205 S.W. Barnes Rd., 97225. Tel: 503-297-4411; Fax: 503-291-2468
For a complete listing, refer to the Hospitals section.

*EUGENE. *Sacred Heart Medical Center*, 1255 Hilyard St., P.O. Box 10905, 97440. Tel: 541-686-7300
For a complete listing, refer to the Hospitals section.

FLORENCE. *Peace Harbor Hospital*, 400 Ninth St., 97439. Tel: 503-997-8412
For a complete listing, refer to the Hospitals section.

MEDFORD. *Providence Medford Medical Center*, 1111 Crater Lake Ave., 97504-6225. Tel: 541-732-5000
For a complete listing, refer to the Hospitals section.

*MILWAUKIE. *Providence Milwaukie Hospital*, 10150 S.E. 32nd Ave., 97222. Tel: 503-652-8300
For a complete listing, refer to the Hospitals section.

NEWBERG. *Providence Newberg Hospital*, 501 Villa Rd., 97132. Tel: 503-537-1701
For a complete listing, refer to the Hospitals section.

ROSEBURG. *Mercy Medical Center, Inc.*, 2700 Stewart Pkwy., 97470. Tel: 541-673-0611; Fax: 541-677-4830
For a complete listing, refer to the Hospitals section.

SEASIDE. *Providence Seaside Hospital*, 725 S. Wahanna Rd., 97138-7735. Tel: 503-717-7000; Fax: 503-717-7505
For a complete listing, refer to the Hospitals section.

[K] HOMES FOR AGED

PORTLAND. *Mt. St. Joseph Residence and Extended Care Center*, 3060 S.E. Stark St., 97214-3099. Tel: 503-232-6193; Fax: 503-235-2772
For a complete listing, refer to the Special Care Facilities section.

BEAVERTON. *Maryville Nursing Home*, 14645 S.W. Farmington Rd., 97007. Tel: 503-643-8626
For a complete listing, refer to the Special Care Facilities section.

MT. ANGEL. *Benedictine Nursing Center*, 540 S. Main St., 97362-9523. Tel: 503-845-6841
For a complete listing, refer to the Special Care Facilities section.

NORTH BEND. *Evergreen Court for Retirement Living, Inc.*, 451 O'Connell St., 97459. Tel: 541-756-2545
For a complete listing, refer to the Special Care Facilities section.
St. Catherine's Residence and Nursing Center, 9359 Sheridan Ave., 97459. Tel: 541-756-4151; Fax: 541-756-1049
For a complete listing, refer to the Special Care Facilities section.

[L] MONASTERIES AND RESIDENCES OF PRIESTS

PORTLAND. *Colombiere Community*, 2222 NW Hoyt St., 97210. Tel: 503-221-2332. Revs. James R. Laudwein, S.J., Supr.; Brian L. Ulrickson, S.J., Min.; Arnold R. Beezer, S.J.; Robert B. Grimm, S.J.; J. Patrick Hurley, S.J.; David G. King, S.J.; Henry H. Kohls, S.J.; John V. Murphy, S.J.; Brad R. Reynolds, S.J.; Wilfred P. Schoenberg, S.J.; Bro. James B. Wood, S.J.; Revs. James R. Conyard, S.J.; John J. Dunn, S.J.; Thomas R. Garvin, S.J.; James E. Jacobsen, S.J.; Robert J. Jones, S.J.; John McBride, S.J.; William T. Miller, S.J.; L. Michael Pope, S.J.; Charles A. Wollesen, S.J.
The Grotto, The National Sanctuary of Our Sorrowful Mother, 85th and N.E. Sandy Blvd., P.O. Box 20008, 97294-0008. Tel: 503-254-7371; 7372 (Monastery). Revs. John M. Topper, O.S.M., Prior & Exec. Dir.; Patrick M. McNamara, O.S.M.; Richard M. Boyle, O.S.M. In res. Revs. Philip M. Brennan, O.S.M.; Louis Breton, O.S.M. Brothers 3; Sisters 4.
Holy Cross Fathers & Brothers, C.S.C. - University of Portland, 5000 N. Willamette Blvd., 97203. Tel: 503-978-8024. Revs. James Connelly, C.S.C., Supr.; Richard F. Berg, C.S.C.; George C. Bernard, C.S.C.; Frederick Barr, C.S.C.; Thomas Bill, C.S.C.; G. James Brady, C.S.C.; Harry Bride, C.S.C.; Joseph Browne, C.S.C.; Michael M. DeLaney, C.S.C.; Paul Fryberger, C.S.C.; Barry J. Hagan, C.S.C.; Thomas Hosinski, C.S.C.; William Hund, C.S.C.; John Kurtzke, C.S.C.; Edwin Obermiller, C.S.C.; Dennis P. O'Hare, C.S.C.; Claude Pomerlau, C.S.C.; Chester Prusynski, C.S.C.; Richard Rutherford, C.S.C.; Jeffrey Schneibel, C.S.C.; Charles D. Sherrer, C.S.C.; Jeffrey Sobosan, C.S.C.; Philip Sopke, C.S.C.; Arthur Schoenfeldt, C.S.C.; Stephen Sedlock, C.S.C.; Adrien Ste. Marie, C.S.C.; David T. Tyson, C.S.C.; Arthur F. Wheeler, C.S.C.; Bros. Ken Allen, C.S.C.; Flugence Dougherty, C.S.C.; Daniel Mallon, C.S.C.; Frederick Williams, C.S.C.; Donald Stabrowski, C.S.C.; Daniel Mallon, C.S.C.
Holy Rosary Priory, 375 N.E. Clackamas St., 97232. Tel: 503-235-3163.
Jesuit Provincial Office (Society of Jesus, Oregon Prov.), 2222 N.W. Hoyt, 97210. Tel: 503-226-6977.
E-mail: 74513.2642@compuserve.com
Web site: www.europa.com/~rover/index.htm
Very Rev. Robert B. Grimm, S.J., Prov.; Revs. Brad R. Reynolds, S.J., Asst. for Formation, Exec. Asst. Socius; Brian Ulrickson, S.J., Dir. of Vocations; Michael A. Tyrrell, S.J., Prov. Treasurer; L. Paul Fitterer, S.J., Asst. for Secondary Schools; Mr. Matthew Senecal, Dir. of Devel.; Ms. Deb. Shannon, Communications Dir.; Mr. William Lockyear, Chief Fin. Officer; Mrs. Joyceann Hagen, Asst. for Ministries.
Oregon Province priests not listed elsewhere: Rev. David A. Myers, S.J., 5441 San Angelo St., Guadalupe, AZ, 85283. Rev. Thomas J. Bunnell, S.J., 1510 N. Edison St., Kennewick, WA, 99336. Rev. James K. Voiss, S.J., 2628 Trader Ct., South Bend, IN, 46628.
Oregon Province priests serving outside the US: Revs. Francis E. Case, S.J.; Joseph B. Danel, S.J.; Leo Donald Davis, S.J.; John V. Hennessy, S.J.; William J. Loyens, S.J.; John J. Morris, S.J.; Howard L. Morrison, S.J.; Bartholomew J. Murphy, S.J.; John J. Navone, S.J.; Dominic H. Nguyen, S.J.; Michael J. Schultheis, S.J.; Joseph H. Small, S.J.; Thomas E. Zeyen, S.J.

AMITY. *Brigittine Priory of Our Lady of Consolation - The Order of the Most Holy Savior*, 23300 Walker Ln., 97101. Tel: 503-835-8080. Bro. Benedict Kirby, O.Ss.S., Prior. Professed 12; Novices 1.

GOLD HILL. *Augustinian Community*, P.O. Box 310, 97525. Tel: 541-855-1333. Revs. James Clifford, O.S.A., Prior; Thomas J. Whelan, O.S.A.

LAFAYETTE. *The Cistercian (Trappist) Abbey of Our Lady of Guadalupe*, 97127. Tel: 503-852-7174; Fax: 503-852-7748. Order of Cistercians of the Strict Observance. Rt. Rev. Peter McCarthy, O.C.S.O.; Revs. John-Baptist Hasbrouck, O.C.S.O., Prior; Dismas Gannon, O.C.S.O.; Romain Payant, O.C.S.O.; Jerome Ebacher, O.C.S.O.; Mark Weidner, O.C.S.O.; Peter Plakut, O.C.S.O.; Howard Curtis, O.C.S.O.; Martin Cawley, O.C.S.O.; Francis King, O.C.S.O.; Timothy Michell, O.C.S.O.; Joseph-Benedict Donnelly, O.C.S.O.; Arnold Weller, O.C.S.O.; Richard Layton, O.C.S.O.; Timothy Clark, O.C.S.O.; Casey Bailey, O.C.S.O. Solemnly Professed 34; Priests 16; Total in Community 35.

ST. BENEDICT. *Mt. Angel Abbey*, 97373. Tel: 503-845-3030; Fax: 503-845-3594. Rt. Revs. Joseph Wood, O.S.B., Abbot; Peter Eberle, O.S.B., (Retired); Very Revs. Paul Thomas, O.S.B., Prior; Paschal Cheline, O.S.B., Subprior; Revs. Bruno Becker, O.S.B.; Thomas Aq. Brockhaus, O.S.B.; Isaac Jogues Brown, O.S.B.; Dominic Broxmeyer, O.S.B.; Athanasius Buchholz, O.S.B.; Matthias Burger, O.S.B.; Matthew Butsch, O.S.B.; Emmanuel W. Clark, O.S.B.; Thien Dang, O.S.B.; Augustine De Noble, O.S.B.; Daniel Hasenoehrl, O.S.B.; Jeremy Driscoll, O.S.B.; Gregory Duerr, O.S.B.; Hugh Feiss, O.S.B.; Richard Galvin, O.S.B.; William Hammelman, O.S.B.; Pius X Harding, O.S.B.; Stephen Hofmann, O.S.B.; Kenneth Jacques, O.S.B.; Joachim McCann, O.S.B.; Patrick Meagher, O.S.B.; Norbert Novak, O.S.B.; Lawrence Minder, O.S.B.; Liem Nguyen, O.S.B.; David Nicholson, O.S.B.; Bede Partridge, O.S.B.; Alexander Plasker, O.S.B.; Odo Recker, O.S.B.; Leo Rimmele, O.S.B.; Bernard Sander, O.S.B.; Timothy Sander, O.S.B.; Edmund Smith, O.S.B.; Vincent Trujillo, O.S.B.; Philip Waibel, O.S.B.; Jerome Young, O.S.B.; Cosmas White, O.S.B.; Placidus Zach, O.S.B.; Nathan Zodrow, O.S.B. Monks in perpetual vows 64 (divided as follows:); Priests 44; Brothers 22; Monks in triennial vows 3.

[M] CONVENTS AND RESIDENCES FOR SISTERS

PORTLAND. *"Rose Hall" Reparation and Prayer Center*, 2120 S.E. 24th Ave., 97214-5504. Tel: 503-236-4207. Mother Regina Rose, S.R., Dir.
Convent of Our Lady of Angels, 0858 S.W. Palatine Hill Rd., 97219. Tel: 503-635-4534.
Convent of Sisters of Reparation of the Sacred Wounds of Jesus. Novitiate, 2120 S.E. 24th Ave., 97214-5504. Tel: 503-236-4207. Mother Regina Rose, S.R., Supr. Gen.; Sr. Mary of the Angels, S.R., Asst. Sisters 4; Donne Members 80.
Convent of Sisters of Social Service, 21 S.E. Floral Pl., 97214. Tel: 503-232-5806. Sisters 7.
Other Addresses: 14405 S.W. Sexton Mt. Dr., Apt. A, 97005-7493. Tel: 503-641-6509. 1776 Madras St. S.E., Salem, 97306. Tel: 503-391-7498.
Convent of the Good Shepherd, 562 N. Portland Blvd., 97217. Tel: 503-283-4931.
Convent of the Society of the Holy Child Jesus, 5431 N. Strong St., 97203. Tel: 503-289-9975.
Franciscan Renewal Center, 0858 S.W. Palatine Hill Rd., 97219. Tel: 503-636-1590. Sr. Mary Jo Chaves, O.S.F.; Sr. Mary Smith, O.S.F.; Sr. Kathy Dauses, O.S.F.; Douglas Spears.
Holy Cross Convent (1670), 7408 S.E. Alder, 97215. Tel: 503-254-3284. Legal Title: *Vietnamese Adorers of the Holy Cross.* Sr. M. Kim Phuong T. Nguyen, M.T.G., Supr. Sisters 16; Novices 6; Candidates 10. First foundation in the United States in 1976, founded by Bishop Pierre Lambert de la Motte. Represented in the Archdiocese of Portland in Oregon and the Diocese of Arlington, VA.
Sisters of Mercy Convent, 3080 S.E. Stark St., 97214. Tel: 503-236-1972.

BEAVERTON. *Convent, Franciscan Missionary Sisters of Our Lady of Sorrows*, 3600 S.W. 170th Ave., 97006-5099. Tel: 503-649-1634; Fax: 503-649-8382. Sr. Anne Marie, O.S.F., Supr. Gen.; Sr. Carol Ann, O.S.F., Local Supr. Sisters 15.
St. Mary of the Valley Convent, 4440 S.W. 148th Ave., 97007. Tel: 503-644-9181. Motherhouse of the Sisters of St. Mary of Oregon. Sr. Delores Adelman, S.S.M.O., Supr. Gen.; Sr. Sharon Kirk, Local Supr.; Most Rev. Basil Meeking, Chap. Professed Sisters 96.

BRIDAL VEIL. *Convent, Franciscan Sisters of the Eucharist.* Administrative Center, 48100 E. Crownpoint Hwy., 97010. Tel: 503-695-2375. Sr. Mary Michael Costello, F.S.E., Supr. Sisters 7.

EUGENE. *Carmel of Maria Regina.* (Contemplative Order), 87609 Green Hill Rd., 97402. Tel: 541-345-8649. Mother Elizabeth Mary, O.C.D., Prioress. Professed Sisters 11.

MARYLHURST. *Convent of the Holy Names*, 97036. Tel: 503-636-8105. Provincial House of the Sisters of the Holy Names of Jesus & Mary, S.N.J.M. Sr. Eileen Brown, S.N.J.M., Prov. Dir.; Sr. Kathleen Hecht, S.N.J.M., House Admin. Professed Sisters 236; Temporarily professed 3; Candidates 1.

MT. ANGEL. *Queen of Angels Monastery*, 840 S. Main St., 97362. Tel: 503-845-6141; Fax: 503-845-6585.
E-mail: qam@open.org
Monastery of the Benedictine Sisters of Mt. Angel. Sr. Jeanette von Herrmann, O.S.B., Prioress & Contact Person. Sisters 59.

[N] RETREAT HOUSES

PORTLAND. *The Jesuit Spirituality Center*, 3220 S.E. 43rd Ave., 97206. Tel: 503-777-2225; Fax: 503-774-7382. Legal Title: *Loyola Retreat Association, S.J., Inc. dba The Jesuit Spirituality Center.* Rev. Peter D. Byrne, S.J., Dir.; Marilyn Kirvin-Quamme, Assoc. Dir.; Bro. Michael Bennett, S.J., Property Mgr.

BEAVERTON. *Our Lady of Peace Retreat*, 3600 S.W. 170th Ave., 97006-5099. Tel: 503-649-7127; Fax: 503-649-8382. Sr. Carol Ann, O.S.F., Supr.; Sr. M. Joseph, O.S.F., Asst. Supr. Franciscan Missionary Sisters of Our Lady of Sorrows 15.

GOLD HILL. *St. Rita's Retreat Center*, P.O. Box 310, 97525. Tel: 541-855-1333. Rev. Thomas J. Whelan, O.S.A., Dir. & Contact Person.

MCKENZIE BRIDGE. *St. Benedict Lodge-Dominican Retreat & Conference Center*, 56630 North Bank Rd., 97413-9614. Tel: 541-822-3572; Fax: 541-822-3631.
E-mail: bdtop@efn.org
Dominican Retreat & Conference Center. Lodge-retreat guests: 541-822-6151. Bro. Daniel Thomas, O.P., Dir. & Contact Person; Rev. Paul E. Scanlon, O.P., Chap., 46052 McKenzie Hwy., Vida, 97488. Tel: 541-896-0284. Deacon Leonard Soper; Sr. John Maureen Backenstos, S.N.J.M., Spiritual & Temporal Ministry, 55408 W. Delta Dr., 97413. Tel: 541-822-3937.

MT. ANGEL. *Benedictine Sisters Shalom Prayer Center*, 97362. Tel: 503-845-6773. Sr. Antoinette Traeger, O.S.B., Dir. Sisters 4.

PACIFIC CITY. *Nestucca Sanctuary*, P.O. Box 670, 97135-0670. Rev. Andrew J. Dufner, S.J., Retreat Dir. & Contact Person.

ST. BENEDICT. *Mount Angel Abbey Retreat House*, 97373. Tel: 503-845-3025. Rev. Isaac Jogues Brown, O.S.B., Dir.

[O] SOCIETY OF ST. VINCENT DE PAUL

PORTLAND. *Macdonald Center*, 601 W. Burnside, 97209. Tel: 503-222-5720. Mary Sue Richen, Program Dir.
St. Vincent de Paul Rehabilitation Service, Inc., 4867 N.E. Martin Luther King Jr. Blvd., 97211. Tel: 503-281-1289.
E-mail: janetblack@compuserve.com
Training & placement for adults with disabilities. Roy Soards, Exec. Dir.; Bennett Johnson, Dep. Dir. Employees/Trainees 800.
Society of St. Vincent de Paul. Portland Council, 3601 S.E. 27th Ave., 97202. Tel: 503-235-7837.

EUGENE. *Society of St. Vincent de Paul.* Archdiocesan Council. 705 S. Seneca St., 97402.
E-mail: sudpeug@efn.org
Dennis Maricle, Pres.
Society of St. Vincent de Paul. Eugene Council. 705 S. Seneca St., 97402. Tel: 541-687-5820; Fax: 541-683-9423. Donald Lamb, Pres.; Terrence R. McDonald, Exec. Dir.; Rebecca Larson, Contact Person.

MEDFORD. *Society of St. Vincent de Paul.* Rogue Valley Council, P.O. Box 1663, 97501. Tel: 541-772-3828. Lorie Harmon, Pres.; William J. Howe, Treas. & Contact Person.

SALEM.
**Society of St. Vincent de Paul.* Council of Mid-Willamette Valley, 730 Front St. N.E., 97301. Tel: 503-364-1062; Fax: 503-364-2708. Joseph Glandorf, Pres.; Nancy Cooney, Exec. Dir. & Contact Person.

[P] NEWMAN CENTERS

PORTLAND. *University of Portland*, Campus Ministry, 5000 N. Willamette Blvd., 97203. Tel: 503-283-7131. Revs. Philip Sopke, C.S.C., Dir.; Edwin Obermiller, C.S.C., Assoc.; Elizabeth McCabe, Assoc.; Daniel Sanone, Assoc.
Southern Oregon State College (Ashland), Walsh Memorial Newman Center, 1150 Ashland St., Ashland, 97520. Tel: 541-482-0825. Rev. Raymond Finerty, O.P., Dir. & Chap.
Oregon State University (Corvallis), Newman Center, 2111 N.W. Monroe St., Corvallis, 97330. Tel: 541-752-6818. Sue Gifford, Pastoral Dir.
University of Oregon (Eugene), Newman Center, 1850 Emerald St., Eugene, 97403. Tel: 541-343-7021; Fax: 541-686-8028. Rev. Jose Pimentel, O.P.; Sr. Janet Ryan, S.N.J.M., Pastoral Assoc.
Lane Community College, 4000 E. 30th Ave., Eugene, 97405. Tel: 541-747-4501, Ext. 2850.
Pacific University (Forest Grove). Rev. David Gutmann, Chap.; Kathy Yee, Campus Min., Res. St. Anthony Church, 1660 Elm St., Forest Grove, 97116. Tel: 503-357-8075; Fax: 503-357-2217.
Lewis & Clark (Lake Oswego). Rev. Xavier Panneer Selvam, Chap., Our Lady of the Lake Church, 650 A Avenue, Lake Oswego, 97034. Tel: 503-636-7687; Fax: 503-636-9415.
Linfield College (McMinnville). Rev. Thomas Farley, Campus Min., St. James Church, 1110 E. First St., McMinnville, 97128. Tel: 503-472-5232.
Marylhurst College (Marylhurst), Durocher Center for Campus Ministry. Rev. Henri LaCerte, O.S.B., Chap.; Sr. Elaine Kraft, S.N.J.M., Dir., Marylhurst, 97036. Tel: 503-636-3941, Ext. 351.
Western Oregon State College (Monmouth). Rev. Victor Perez, Chap., Res., 245 W. Main, Monmouth, 97361. Tel: 503-838-1242.
Willamette University (Salem). Rev. Carl Gimpl, Chap.; Chrissy Weston, Campus Min., St. Joseph Church, 721 Chemeketa St., N.E., Salem, 97301. Tel: 501-581-1623.

[Q] MISCELLANEOUS

PORTLAND. *Blanchet House of Hospitality*, 340 N.W. Glisan St., 97209. Tel: 503-226-3911. Al Riley, Dir.

**Franciscan Enterprise of Oregon, Inc.*, P.O. Box 11268, 97211. Tel: 503-284-8642; Fax: 503-284-4092. Karen Voiss, Exec. Dir. & Contact Person.

**Franciscan Ministry Network*, 4725 N.E. 9th Ave., 97211.
E-mail: tumultym@aol.com
Rev. Matt Tumulty, Exec. Dir. & Contact Person.

Jesuit Development & Communications Office, P.O. Box 4408, 97208. Tel: 503-227-1174.
E-mail: msenecal@compuserve.com
Web site: www.europa.com/~rover/index.htm
Mr. P. Matthew Senecal, Dir. Devel.; Ms. Deb Shannon, Communications Dir.; Ms. Shari Thompson, Asst. Dir. Devel.; Revs. John V. Murphy, S.J., Assoc. Dir. Devel.; Daniel C. Weber, S.J., Assoc. Dir. Devel.; Charles E. Schmitz, S.J., Liaison for Jesuit Intl. Min.

**Jesuit Volunteer Corps: Northwest*, P.O. Box 3928, 97208-3928. Tel: 503-335-8202. Martin Winch, Exec. Dir.

Metro Catholic Broadcasting, KBVM-FM, 88.3, P.O. Box 5888, 97228-5888. Tel: 503-283-7455. Caron Fox, Gen. Mgr.

Northeast Catholic Counseling Center, 8383 N.E. Sandy Blvd., Suite 205, 97220. Tel: 503-253-0964. Sr. Barbara Kennedy, O.S.M., Dir. & Contact Person. Sisters 2; Lay Counselors 4.

Oregon Catholic Conference, 2838 E. Burnside St., 97214. Tel: 503-233-8387; Fax: 503-235-2630. Most Revs. Thomas J. Connolly, O.M.I., Acting Pres.; Kenneth Steiner, Acting Vice Pres.; Rev. Gregory Moys, Sec.-Treasurer; Mr. Robert Castagna, Gen. Counsel & Exec. Dir.

Paulist Fathers Catholic Center for Evangelization, 2408 S.E. 16th Ave., 97214. Tel: 503-231-4955.
E-mail: phlneri@aol.com
Web site: www.paulist.org/portland/paulists.html
Revs. Stephen E. Bossi, C.S.P.; Richard W. Chilson, C.S.P.; Joseph J. Scott, C.S.P.; Joseph L. Schmidt, C.S.P., Student Intern.

St. Andrew Legal Clinic, 807 N.E. Alberta, 97211. Tel: 503-281-1500. Joel K. Overlund, Dir. & Contact Person.

**The Gamelin-Oregon Association-Emilie House*, 5520 N.E. Glisan, 97213-3169. Tel: 503-236-9779; Fax: 503-239-1867. Sisters of Providence. Sr. Alexis Melancon, S.P., Dir. & Contact Person. 41 apartments for the elderly and subsidized by the Department of Housing and Urban Development.

BEAVERTON. *Our Lady of Peace Institute in Catholic Teaching*, 3600 S.W. 170th Ave., 97006. Tel: 503-649-7127; Fax: 503-649-8382. Rev. Leo Slatterie, Dir.; Sr. Carol Ann, O.S.F., Coord. & Contact Person; Sr. Anne Marie, O.S.F., Asst. Coord. Staff 7; Students 60.

CORBETT. *Catholic Engaged Encounter of Oregon, Inc.*, 34926 E. Historical Columbia River Hwy., 97019; Fax: 503-695-5428. Marriage Preparation Program providing weekend retreats to engaged couples. Tim & Renee Jimenez. Couples served 475; Volunteers 56.

HILLSBORO. *St. Matthew Legal Clinic*, 232 S.E. Lincoln, Ste. H, 97123. Tel: 503-648-1600. Mr. Keith R. Raines, Contact Person.

MARYLHURST.
**Cornelia Connelly Pastoral Counseling Center*, Marylhurst College, Aquinas Hall, P.O. Box 251, 97036.
E-mail: jspearing@juno.com
Web site: www.cptryon.org/cornelia
Sr. Joan Spearing, S.H.C.J., Dir. & Contact Person.

MT. ANGEL. *Benedictine Foundation of Oregon*, Box 912, 97362. Tel: 503-845-2556.
E-mail: bfo@teleport.com
Steven Ritchie, Exec. Dir. & Contact Person.

Benedictine Housing, Inc., 540 S. Main St., 97362. Tel: 503-845-6841. Ms. Deanna Bettesworth, Housing Project Coord.

Benedictine Services Corporation, 540 S. Main St., 97362. Tel: 503-845-6841. Ms. Deanna Bettesworth, Housing Project Coord.

St. Joseph's Shelter, 925 S. Main, P.O. Box 1005, 97362. Tel: 503-845-6147. Sr. Adele Mansfield, O.S.B., Admin.

MYRTLE CREEK. *Council of Douglas County of the Society of St. Vincent dePaul*, 126 N. Main, P.O. Box 1258, 97457. Mr. Joe G. Heilman, Contact Person.

RELIGIOUS INSTITUTES OF MEN REPRESENTED IN THE ARCHDIOCESE

For further details refer to the corresponding bracketed number in the Religious Institutes of Men or Women section.

[]—*Apostolic Life Community Of Priests (Holy Spirit Fathers)*.—A.L.C.P.
[0140]—*The Augustinians*.—O.S.A.
[0200]—*Benedictine Monks*. (Mt. Angel, OR).—O.S.B.
[0895]—*Brigittine Monastery of Our Lady of Consolidation*.—O.Ss.S.
[0350]—*Cistercians Order of the Strict Observance (Trappists)*.—O.C.S.O.
[]—*Conventual Franciscans*.—O.F.M.Conv.
[0520]—*Franciscan Friars*. (Prov. of Santa Barbara).—O.F.M.
[0690]—*Jesuit Fathers and Brothers*. (Oregon Prov.).—S.J.
[]—*Missionaries Of The Holy Spirit*.—M.Sp.S.
[0910]—*Oblates of Mary Immaculate*.—O.M.I.
[0430]—*Order of Preachers (Dominicans)*. (Western Prov.).—O.P.
[1030]—*Paulist Fathers*.—C.S.P.
[0610]—*Priests of the Congregation of Holy Cross*.—C.S.C.
[1070]—*Redemptorist Fathers*. (Oakland Prov.).—C.SS.R.
[1240]—*Servites*. (Western Prov.).—O.S.M.
[1260]—*Society of Christ*.—S.Ch.
[]—*Society Of Mary*.—S.M.

RELIGIOUS INSTITUTES OF WOMEN REPRESENTED IN THE ARCHDIOCESE

[0230]—*Benedictine Sisters of Pontifical Jurisdiction*. (Mount Angel, OR).—O.S.B.
[0350]—*Carmelite Sisters (Corpus Christi)*.—O.Carm.
[1920]—*Congregation of the Sisters of Holy Cross*.—C.S.C.
[1780]—*Congregation of the Sisters of the Third Order of St. Francis of Perpetual Adoration*.—F.S.P.A.
[0420]—*Discalced Carmelite Nuns*.—O.C.D.
[1070-12]—*Dominican Sisters*.—O.P.
[]—*Dominican Sisters Of Caldwell, NJ*.—O.P.
[1390]—*Franciscan Missionary Sisters of Our Lady of Sorrows*.—O.S.F.
[]—*Holy Spirit Sisters*.
[1250]—*The Institute of the Franciscan Sisters of the Eucharist*.—F.S.E.
[2575]—*Institute of the Sisters of Mercy of the Americas*. (Omaha, NE).—R.S.M.
[]—*Oblates of Saint Martha*.—O.S.M.
[2519]—*Religious Sisters of Mercy of Alma, MI*.—R.S.M.
[3590]—*Servants of Mary (Servite Sisters)*.—O.S.M.
[]—*Sisters For Christian Community*.—S.F.C.C.
[0430]—*Sisters of Charity of the Blessed Virgin Mary*.—B.V.M.
[3350]—*Sisters of Providence*. (Prov. of the Sacred Heart).—S.P.
[]—*Sisters of Reparation of the Sacred Wounds of Jesus*.—S.R.
[4080]—*Sisters of Social Service of Los Angeles, Inc.*.—S.S.S.
[1630]—*Sisters of St. Francis of Penance and Christian Charity*.—O.S.F.
[1650]—*The Sisters of St. Francis of Philadelphia*.—O.S.F.
[1530]—*Sisters of St. Francis of the Congregation of Our Lady of Lourdes, Sylvania, Ohio*.—O.S.F.
[1570]—*Sisters of St. Francis of the Holy Family*. (Dubuque, IA).—O.S.F.
[3840]—*Sisters of St. Joseph of Carondelet*.—C.S.J.
[3890]—*Sisters of St. Joseph of Peace*. (Western Prov.).—C.S.J.P.
[3960]—*Sisters of St. Mary of Oregon*.—S.S.M.O.
[1830]—*The Sisters of the Good Shepherd*.—R.G.S.
[1990]—*Sisters of the Holy Names of Jesus and Mary*.—S.N.J.M.
[3320]—*Sisters of the Presentation of the B.V.M.*—P.V.B.M.
[4060]—*Society of the Holy Child Jesus*. (American Prov.).—S.H.C.J.
[4155]—*Vietnamese Adorers of the Holy Cross*.—M.T.G.

ARCHDIOCESAN CEMETERIES

PORTLAND. *Gethsemani*.
Mount Calvary.
EUGENE. *Mount Calvary*.
SALEM. *St. Barbara*.

NECROLOGY

✠ Power, Most Rev. Cornelius, (Retired). —Died May 22, 1997.
† Bianco, Hamilcar, (Retired). —Died April 6, 1997.
† Cormier, Joseph, (Retired). —Died June 28, 1997.
† Harrington, Emmet, (Retired). —Died July 14, 1997.
† Johnson, William G., Portland, OR, Mt. St. Joseph. —Died Jan. 18, 1997.
† Kiernan, Patrick Joseph, North Bend, OR, Holy Redeemer Parish. —Died Sept. 3, 1997.
† Schaefers, Rev. Msgr. Francis, (Retired). —Died Nov. 25, 1996.
† Schlatter, Glen F., (Retired). —Died June 26, 1997.

Diocese of Providence

(Dioecesis Providentiensis)

Most Reverend

ROBERT E. MULVEE, D.D., J.C.D.

Bishop of Providence; ordained June 30, 1957; appointed Auxiliary Bishop of Manchester and Titular Bishop of Summa February 15, 1977; consecrated April 14, 1977; installed Bishop of Wilmington February 19, 1985; installed April 11, 1985; appointed Coadjutor Bishop of Providence February 9, 1995; succeeded to the see June 11, 1997. *Res., 30 Fenner St., Providence, RI, 02903-3603. Mailing Address: One Cathedral Sq., Providence, RI, 02903-3695.* Tel.: 401-278-4545; Fax: 401-278-4548.

Most Reverend

LOUIS E. GELINEAU, D.D., S.T.L., J.C.L.

Former Bishop of Providence; ordained June 5, 1954; appointed December 6, 1971; consecrated January 26, 1972; retired June 11, 1997. *Res., 30 Fenner St., Providence, RI, 02903-3603. Mailing Address: One Cathedral Sq., Providence, RI, 02903-3695.* Tel.: 401-278-4545; Fax: 401-278-4548.

Most Reverend

GEORGE H. PEARCE, S.M., D.D.

Former Archbishop of Suva; ordained February 3, 1947; appointed Titular Bishop of Attalea in Pamphilia February 29, 1956; consecrated June 29, 1956; transferred to Apia June 21, 1966; promoted to Suva June 22, 1967; resigned April 10, 1976; Personal assistant to the Bishop of Providence. *Res. & Mailing Address: 30 Fenner St., Providence, RI, 02903-3603.* Tel.: 401-331-2434; Fax: 401-278-4530.

Corporate Title: *Roman Catholic Bishop of Providence.*

ESTABLISHED 1872.

Square Miles 1,085.

Comprises the State of Rhode Island.

Bishop's Office & Chancery Office: One Cathedral Square, Providence, RI, 02903-3695. Tel.: 401-278-4500; Fax: 401-278-4548.

Web site address: http://www.providence.com

E-mail address: jlplante@intap.net

STATISTICAL OVERVIEW

Personnel	
Retired Archbishops	1
Bishop	1
Retired Bishops	2
Abbots	1
Retired Abbots	1
Priests: Diocesan Active in Diocese	207
Priests: Active Outside Diocese	13
Priests: Diocesan in Foreign Missions	2
Priests: Retired, Sick or Absent	94
Number of Diocesan Priests	316
Religious Priests in Diocese	132
Extern Priests in Diocese	18
Ordinations:	
Diocesan Priests	3
Religious Priests	1
Transitional Deacons	1
Permanent Deacons in Diocese	83
Total Brothers	124
Total Sisters	769
Parishes	
Parishes	158
With Resident Pastor:	
Resident Diocesan Priests	142
Resident Religious Priests	9
Without Resident Pastor:	
Administered by Priests	7
Missions	8
Pastoral Centers	18
Professional Ministry Personnel:	
Brothers	5
Sisters	63
Lay Ministers	141
Welfare	
Catholic Hospitals	1
Total Assisted	201,000
Health Care Centers	1
Total Assisted	45
Homes for the Aged	13
Total Assisted	918
Day Care and Extended Day Care Centers	9
Total Assisted	672
Specialized Homes	2
Total Assisted	130
Special Centers for Social Services	11
Total Assisted	57,522
Other Institutions	13
Total Assisted	156,903
Educational	
Seminaries, Diocesan	1
Students from This Diocese	2
Diocesan Students in Other Seminaries	14
Total Seminarians	16
Colleges and Universities	2
Total Students	7,781
High Schools, Diocesan and Parish	4
Total Students	1,923
High Schools, Private	8
Total Students	3,383
Elementary Schools, Diocesan and Parish	46
Total Students	11,735
Elementary Schools, Private	4
Total Students	1,419
Catechesis/Religious Education:	
High School Students	11,117
Elementary Students	31,383
Total Students Under Catholic Instruction	68,757
Teachers in the Diocese:	
Priests	37
Brothers	43
Sisters	110
Lay Teachers	1,356
Vital Statistics	
Receptions into the Church:	
Infant Baptism Totals	7,066
Adult Baptism Totals	223
Received into Full Communion	360
First Communions	6,624
Confirmations	4,809
Marriages:	
Catholic	1,923
Interfaith	385
Total Marriages	2,308
Deaths	5,672
Total Catholic Population	632,978
Total Population	996,325

Former Bishops—Rt. Rev. THOMAS F. HENDRICKEN, D.D., cons. first Bishop of Providence, April 28, 1872; died June 11, 1886.—Rt. Rev. MATTHEW HARKINS, D.D., cons. second Bishop of Providence, April 14, 1887; died May 25, 1921.—Most Rev. WILLIAM A. HICKEY, D.D., ord. Dec. 22, 1893; appt. Coadjutor Bishop of Providence, *Cum jure successionis,* March 10, 1919; cons. Titular Bishop of Claudiopolis, April 10, 1919; succeeded to the See of Providence, May 25, 1921; died Oct. 4, 1933.—Most Rev. FRANCIS P. KEOUGH, D.D., cons. fourth Bishop of Providence, May 22, 1934; appt. Archbishop of Baltimore, Nov. 29, 1947; died Dec. 8, 1961.—Most Rev. RUSSELL J. MCVINNEY, D.D., appt. May 29, 1948; cons. July 14, 1948 fifth Bishop of Providence; died Aug. 10, 1971.—Most Rev. LOUIS E. GELINEAU, D.D., appt. Dec. 6, 1971; cons. sixth Bishop of Providence, Jan. 26, 1972; retired June 11, 1997.

Vicar General—Rev. Msgr. WILLIAM I. VARSANYI, J.C.D.

Episcopal Vicars—

Vicar for Canonical Affairs—Rev. Msgr. WILLIAM I. VARSANYI, J.C.D.

Vicar for Education—Rev. Msgr. ROBERT J. MCMANUS, M.A., S.T.D.

Vicar for Judicial Matters—Very Rev. JOEL A. LECUIVRE, J.C.L.

Vicar for Planning & Finance—Rev. Msgr. WILLIAM J. MCCAFFREY, S.T.B., M.A.

Vicar for Social Ministry—Rev. Msgr. GEORGE L. FRAPPIER, S.T.B., M.A.

Vicar for Spirituality and Evangelization—Rev. Msgr. JOHN C. ALLARD.

Vicars for Deaneries—Rev. JOHN A. KILEY, Deanery No. I; Rev. BERTRAND L. THEROUX, Deanery No. II; Rev. JOHN J. LAVIN, Deanery No. III; Rev. RAYMOND C. THEROUX, Deanery No. IV; Rev. JOSEPH P. HENRY, Deanery No. V; Rev. EDWARD J. MCGOVERN, Deanery No. VI; Rev. RAYMOND B. MALM, Deanery No. VII; Rev. WILFRID G. GREGOIRE, Deanery No. VIII; Rev. JOHN W. LOLIO, Deanery No. IX.

Bishop's Office & Chancery Office—One Cathedral Sq., Providence, 02903-3695. Office Hours: Mon.-Fri. 9-5. Tel: 401-278-4500; Fax: 401-278-4548.

Vicar General and Vicar for Canonical Affairs—Rev. Msgr. WILLIAM I. VARSANYI, J.C.D. Tel: 401-278-4520.

Moderator of the Curia—Rev. Msgr. PAUL D. THEROUX, S.T.B., J.C.L. Tel: 401-278-4535.

Chancellors—Rev. Msgr. JACQUES L. PLANTE, M.A. Tel: 401-278-4515. Rev. Msgr. ROBERT C. EVANS, J.C.L. Tel: 401-278-4517.

Secretary to the Bishop—Rev. PETER J. ANDREWS. Tel: 401-278-4547.

Diocesan Tribunal—One Cathedral Sq., Providence, 02903-3695. Tel: 401-278-4666.

Judicial Vicar—Very Rev. JOEL A. LECUIVRE, J.C.L.

Judges—Rev. Msgr. PAUL D. THEROUX, S.T.B., J.C.L.; Revs. JOHN J. DARCY, M.A., J.C.L.; JOSEPH A. HOWARTH, J.C.L., S.T.B.; FRANCIS P. KAYATTA, M.A., M.C.L., J.C.L.; RONALD P. SIMEONE, M.Div., J.C.L.

Assessors and Auditors—Rev. Msgr. ARTHUR A. SULLIVAN, Ph.D.; Rev. EDWARD J. MCGOVERN, S.T.L, M.S.W.

Promoter of Justice—Rev. Msgr. WILLIAM I. VARSANYI, J.C.D.

Defenders of the Bond—Very Rev. JOEL A. LECUIVRE, J.C.L.; Rev. JOHN J. LAVIN, J.C.D.

Assessors and Counselors—Sr. MADONNA CRAWFORD, R.S.M., M.A.; Mrs. DIANE DIFIORE, B.S.

Notary—Mrs. LINDA L. NASTARI.

Secretary—Very Rev. JOEL A. LECUIVRE, J.C.L.

Council of Priests—One Cathedral Sq., Providence, 02903-3695. Tel: 401-278-4517.

Officers—Most Rev. ROBERT E. MULVEE, Pres.; Very Rev. JOEL A. LECUIVRE, J.C.L., Moderator; Rev. Msgr. ROBERT C. EVANS, J.C.L., Sec. & Treas.

Council Members—Rev. Msgr. GEORGE L. FRAPPIER, S.T.B., M.A.; Rev. Msgr. WILLIAM J. MCCAFFREY, S.T.B., M.A.; Rev. Msgr. ROBERT C. NEWBOLD, Ph.D., J.D.; Rev. Msgr. WILLIAM I. VARSANYI, J.C.D.; Revs. STEPHEN P. AMARAL; RANDOLPH G. CHEW; W. DOUGLAS GRANT; DONALD J. KING; WILLIAM J. LEDOUX; EDWARD J. MCGOVERN; RAYMOND C. THEROUX; ARMAND V. VENTRE; HENRY P. ZINNO, JR.

College of Consultors—Rev. Msgr. ROBERT C. EVANS, J.C.L.; Rev. Msgr. GEORGE L. FRAPPIER, S.T.B., M.A.; Rev. Msgr. SALVATORE R. MATANO, S.T.L., J.C.D.; Rev. Msgr. WILLIAM J. MCCAFFREY, S.T.B., M.A.; Rev. Msgr. ROBERT C. NEWBOLD, Ph.D., J.D.; Rev. Msgr. WILLIAM I. VARSANYI, J.C.D.; Revs. HENRY J. BODAH; ANTHONY D. IWUC; DONALD J. KING; JOEL A. LECUIVRE, J.C.L.; EDWARD J. MCGOVERN; RAYMOND C. THEROUX.

Diocesan Finance Council—Most Rev. ROBERT E. MULVEE, Pres.; Rev. Msgr. WILLIAM I. VARSANYI, J.C.D.; Rev. Msgr. ROBERT C. EVANS, J.C.L.; Rev. Msgr. WILLIAM J. MCCAFFREY, S.T.B., M.A., Sec.; Rev. Msgr. JACQUES L. PLANTE, M.A.; Rev. Msgr. PAUL D. THEROUX, J.C.L.; Revs. GEORGE B. MCCARTHY; BERTRAND L. THEROUX; Sr. M. THERESE ANTONE, R.S.M.; Mr. JOSE ALEX ARIZA; Mr. JOHN W. FLYNN; Mr. JAMES C. FORTE; Hon. ANTHONY A. GIANNINI; Mr. ANTHONY T. GWIAZDOWSKI; Ms. MARIE J. LANGLOIS; Mr. THOMAS J. SKALA; Mr. PAUL J. TAVARES.

Finance Officer—Mr. JAMES P. SULLIVAN, C.P.A.

Diocesan Offices and Directors

AIDS Ministry—Rev. STEPHEN P. AMARAL, Coord., *Office of Community Services & Advocacy, 83 Stewart St., Providence, 02903.* Tel: 401-278-4585; 421-7833.

Apostolate for Deaf and Hearing Impaired—Rev. JOHN BOSCO VALENTE, O.F.M., Chap. for the Deaf, *58 Weybosset St., Providence, 02903.* Tel: 401-331-6510. Sr. GABRIEL M. CLUNE, O.P., Dir., *One Cathedral Sq., Providence, 02903-3695.* Tel: 401-278-4630; 331-3283 (voice & TTD).

Apostolate for Persons with Handicaps—(Legal Title: The Mercy Home and School). Rev. GERARD O. SABOURIN, Dir.; Sr. GABRIEL M. CLUNE, O.P., Dir., *One Cathedral Sq., Providence, 02903-3695.* Tel: 401-278-4630.

SPRED (Special Religious Education)—Ms. COLLEEN TOUCHETTE, *One Cathedral Sq., Providence, 02903-3695.* Tel: 401-658-1174.

Archives—Rev. Msgr. JACQUES L. PLANTE, M.A., Archivist, *One Cathedral Sq., Providence, 02903-3695.* Tel: 401-278-4522.

Black Catholic Ministry—Mrs. LOIS TABELA, Coord., *One Cathedral Sq., Providence, 02903-3695.* Tel: 401-278-4552.

Building Commission—Revs. RAYMOND P. LUFT, Chm. PETER J. ANDREWS; ROGER C. GAGNE; JOEL A. LECUIVRE; STEPHAN A. SILIPIGNI; Sr. MARYPATRICIA MURPHY, R.S.M.; Mr. DONALD J. SULLIVAN, P.E.; Mr. ROBERT W. CAMPAGNONE; Mr. JOSEPH CONNOLLY; Ms. VIRGINIA HESSE; Mr. FRANK R. SPIRITO.

Building Commission, Office of—Mr. DONALD J. SULLIVAN, P.E., Dir., Facilities; Mr. FRANK R. SPIRITO, Facilities Engineer; Ms. CAROL ANN NELSON, Facilities Mgr.; Mr. MAXIME E. GIROUARD, JR., Environmental Engineer, *One Cathedral Sq., Providence, 02903-3695.* Tel: 401-278-4636.

Catholic Campus Ministry—Sr. FRANCIS V. MURPHY, S.N.D., Interim, *Johnson & Wales University, 38 Laurel Ave., Providence, 02906.* Tel: 410-351-9035.

Catholic Charity Fund—Mr. ANTHONY T. GWIAZDOWSKI, Exec. Dir.; Rev. Msgr. WILLIAM J. MCCAFFREY, S.T.B., M.A., Moderator, *Diocesan Development Center, 80 St. Mary Dr., Cranston, 02920.* Tel: 401-943-6550.

Catholic Foundation of Rhode Island—Vacant Dir., *Diocesan Development Center, 80 St. Mary's Dr., Cranston, 02920.* Tel: 401-278-4528.

Catholic Inner City Center (cf. Community Services and Advocacy)—(Legal Title: *Catholic Inner City Apostolate, Inc.);* Mr. JOHN J. BARRY, III, *83 Stewart St., Providence, 02903.* Tel: 201-941-5600.

Catholic-Jewish Relations—Rev. EDWARD H. FLANNERY, Dir., *80 Farnum Pike, Georgiaville, 02917.* Tel: 401-231-8561.

Catholic Mutual Group—Mr. GREG CARLSON, Claims & Risk Mgr., *One Cathedral Sq., Providence, 02903-3695.* Tel: 401-278-4638; 278-4639.

Catholic Relief Services—Rev. Msgr. WILLIAM I. VARSANYI, J.C.D., Dir., *One Cathedral Sq., Providence, 02903-3695.* Tel: 401-278-4519.

Catholic School Office—Bro. WILLIAM DYGERT, C.S.C., Supt., *One Cathedral Sq., Providence, 02903-3695.* Tel: 401-278-4550.

Catholic Scouting-Boy Scouts, Girl Scouts, Camp Fire—One Cathedral Sq., Providence, 02903-3695. Tel: 401-278-4626.

Catholic Sexuality Education (cf. Respect Life Office)—

Catholic Youth Organization—(Legal title: *Catholic Youth Organization of the Diocese of Providence);* Miss LOUISE M. DUSSAULT, Dir., Youth Ministry, *One Cathedral Sq., Providence, 02903-3695.* Tel: 401-278-4626.

Cemeteries—(Legal title: *Catholic Cemeteries);* Rev. Msgr. GALLIANO J. CAVALLARO, Dir., *One Cathedral Sq., Providence, 02903-3695.* Tel: 401-278-4575.

Censors of Books—Rev. Msgr. JOHN F. COX, Ph.D.; Rev. Msgr. ROBERT C. NEWBOLD, Ph.D., J.D.

Charismatic Renewal—Rev. RAYMOND M. KELLY, *152 Holden St., Providence, 02908.* Tel: 401-421-7070.

Charisnewal RI—Co-Dirs.: Mr. BOB LAFAZIA; Mr. TED CARLSON, *244 Smith St., Providence, 02908.* Tel: 401-751-3345.

Child Care, Office of—Mrs. ALEXANDRA F. MOSER, Exec. Dir., *485 Mt. Pleasant Ave., Providence, 02908.* Tel: 401-274-3094.

Clergy Benefit Fund: Medical and Pension—(Legal Title: *Our Lady, Queen of the Clergy).*

Medical Advisory Board—Rev. Msgr. ROBERT C. EVANS; Rev. Msgr. WILLIAM I. VARSANYI; Rev. Msgr. GEORGE L. FRAPPIER, Sec.; Revs. DONAT A. BARRETTE; PAUL R. GRENON; JOSEPH P. HEANEY; ALFRED C. LONARDO; CHARLES B. MCDERMOTT; JAMES J. VERDELOTTI.

Pension Advisory Board—Rev. Msgr. ROBERT C. EVANS; Rev. Msgr. WILLIAM J. MCCAFFREY; Rev. Msgr. WILLIAM I.VARSANYI; Rev. Msgr. GEORGE L. FRAPPIER, Sec.; Rev. DONALD J. KING; Mr. JAMES P. SULLIVAN.

Communications—(Legal title: *Diocesan Catholic Telecommunications Network of Rhode Island);* (News Media, Radio, TV, Public Relations); Mr. WILLIAM G. HALPIN, Dir., *One Cathedral Sq., Providence, 02903-3695.* Tel: 401-278-4600; Fax: 401-278-4649.

Media Services Department—(Media Production, Audio-Visual, Photography, Creative Media Programming and Consultation); Mrs. ANN FORTE, *One Cathedral Sq., Providence, 02903-3695.* Tel: 401-278-4678.

Telecommunications Department—(Produces "Called to Serve" and other Catholic programming, Liaison with State Interconnect and CATV Companies, EWTN Liaison); Miss SUSAN MCCARTHY, Program Coord.; Mr. ANTHONY RIZZINI, Asst. to Dir., Radio & TV Prod., *One Cathedral Sq., Providence, 02903-3695.* Tel: 401-278-4608.

Community Services and Advocacy—(Legal Title: *Catholic Inner City Apostolate, Inc.);* Mr. JOHN J. BARRY, III, Dir., *83 Stewart St., Providence, 02903.* Tel: 401-278-4585; 421-7833.

Council of Religious—Sr. JACQUELINE DICKEY, S.S.C.H., Coord. Steering Committee: Bro. ALAN AUBIN, S.C.; Sr. COLETTE AUGER, P.M.; Bro. EDMOND PRECOURT, F.S.C.; Sr. MARTA INES TORO, O.P., *One Cathedral Sq., Providence, 02903-3695.* Tel: 401-278-4633.

Cursillo Movement—Rev. FRANK S. SALMANI, Spiritual Dir., *2 Russo St., Providence, 02904.* Tel: 401-861-5111. Mrs. KATHRYN ROBBIO, Lay Coord., *100 Empress Dr., E. Greenwich, 02818.* Tel: 401-884-2424.

Diaconate (Transitory)—Rev. EUGENE R. LESSARD, *1030 Dexter St., Central Falls, 02863.* Tel: 401-726-2600.

Ecumenical Commission—Rev. LIONEL A. BLAIN, Chm., *1200 Mendon Rd., Woonsocket, 02895.* Tel: 401-766-0626. Revs. JOSEPH D. SCHENICK; EDWARD G. ST. GODARD.

Education and Compliance—Lt. ROBERT N. MCCARTHY, Dir., *433 Elmwood Ave., Providence, 02907.* Tel: 401-941-0760.

Education, Department of—Rev. Msgr. ROBERT J. MCMANUS, M.A., S.T.D., Vicar for Education, *One Cathedral Sq., Providence, 02903.* Tel: 401-278-4587. Bro. WILLIAM DYGERT, C.S.C., Supt., Schools. Tel: 401-278-4550. Sr. SHEILA DURANTE, R.S.M., Asst. Supt.; Sr. FRANCIS V. MURPHY, S.N.D., Interim Dir., Campus Min., *Johnson & Wales Univ.* Tel: 401-351-9035. Mr. JOSEPH P. SINWELL, Dir., Office of Religious Education, C.C.D. Tel: 401-278-4646. Rev. GERARD O. SABOURIN, Dir., Diocesan Apostolate Persons with Handicapped. Tel: 401-278-4630. Ms. COLLEEN TOUCHETTE, SPRED (Special Religious Education). Tel: 401-658-1174.

Evangelization—Sr. MARTA INES TORO, O.P., Dir., *One Cathedral Sq., Providence, 02903-3695.* Tel: 401-278-4624.

Finance Office—(Cf. Planning and Finance Office).

Fiscal Office—Mr. J. TIMOTHY KOCAB, Diocesan Controller, *One Cathedral Sq., Providence, 02903-3695.* Tel: 401-278-4616.

Government Liaison—Rev. Msgr. ROBERT C. NEWBOLD, Ph.D., J.D., Diocesan Dir.

Grievance Committee—Revs. ROBERT P. PERRON, Chm. GERALD E. BEIRNE, Sec. THOMAS J. FERLAND; ROGER C. GAGNE; JOSEPH P. HEANEY; NICHOLAS I. IACOVACCI; FARRELL E. MCLAUGHLIN; JAMES T. TRAINOR.

Health Care Ministries, Office of—Rev. JOHN E. WATTERSON, Dir., *103 Pine Street, P.O. Box 518, Pawtucket, 02862.* Tel: 401-725-0160; Fax: 401-729-0341.

Hispanic Ministry—Mrs. AIDA HIDALGO, Dir., *One Cathedral Sq., Providence, 02903-3695.* Tel: 401-278-4526.

Holy Childhood Association—Rev. Msgr. WILLIAM I. VARSANYI, J.C.D., Dir., *One Cathedral Sq., Providence, 02903-3695.* Tel: 401-278-4519.

Holy Name Society—Rev. ANTHONY D. IWUC, Dir., *391 High St., Central Falls, 02863.* Tel: 401-723-5427.

Immigration and Refugee Services—(Legal Title: *Diocesan Bureau of Social Services);* Mr. GERARD A. NOEL, JR., Dir., *One Carter St., Providence, 02907.* Tel: 401-467-7200; Fax: 401-467-6310.

Insurance Commission—Rev. Msgr. WILLIAM J. MCCAFFREY, S.T.B., M.A., Chm.; Rev. Msgr. WILLIAM J. CAREY; Revs. JOHN T. CARTY; VICTOR M. VIEIRA; ROGER G. CHAMPIGNY; Mr. GREG CARLSON; Mr. PETER F. GOLDBECKER; Mr. J. TIMOTHY KOCAB; Mr. MICHAEL MCINTYRE; Ms. SANDRA G. PARRILLO; Mr. DONALD J. SULLIVAN, P.E.; Mr. ANTHONY J. ROURKE; Mr. JAMES P. SULLIVAN, C.P.A., *One Cathedral Sq., Providence, 02903-3695.* Tel: 401-278-4616.

Marriage and Family—(Legal Title: *Retreat House of the Immaculate Heart of Mary);* Mr. STEPHEN A. BURKE, M.S.W., Dir., *80 St. Mary's Dr., Cranston, 02920.* Tel: 401-943-7900.

Marriage Enrichment—DON SCHIAVONE; BONNY SCHIAVONE.

Marriage Preparation—Mrs. RITA DONAHUE.

Parish Outreach—ROLANDO MONTUTOR, S.D.R.W.

Separated, Divorced, Remarried & Widowed—Mrs. DOROTHY J. LEVESQUE.

Management Information Services—Ms. PEG RYAN, Dir., *One Cathedral Sq., Providence, 02903-3695.* Tel: 401-278-4611.

Media Services Department—(Cf. Communications).

Ministerial Formation—(Continuing Education of Priests, Permanent Deacons, Lay Ministers). Rev. Msgr. ROBERT J. MCMANUS, M.A., S.T.D., Dir., *One Cathedral Sq., Providence, 02903-3695.* Tel: 401-278-4587.

Ministry with Separated, Divorced, Remarried and Widowed Persons—(Cf. Marriage & Family Life Office).

Natural Family Planning—(Cf. Respect Life Office).

Occult Awareness Ministry—Rev. PAUL E. DESMARAIS, *c/o One Cathedral Sq., Providence, 02903-3695.* Tel: 401-273-1702.

Parish Evangelization and Renewal—Sr. MARTA INES TORO, O.P., Dir., *One Cathedral Sq., Providence, 02903-3695.* Tel: 401-278-4624.

Pastoral Planning—Ms. CONNIE THORNTON, Dir., *One Cathedral Sq., Providence, 02903-3695.* Tel: 401-278-4610.

Planning and Finance—Rev. Msgr. WILLIAM J. MCCAFFREY, S.T.B., M.A., Vicar; Mr. JAMES P. SULLIVAN, C.P.A., Finance Officer, *One Cathedral Sq., Providence, 02903*. Tel: 401-278-4540; Fax: 401-831-1947.

Priests, Minister for—Rev. NORMAND J. GODIN, *1045 Douglas Pike, Mohegan, Harrisville, 02830*. Tel: 401-568-7101.

Priests' Eucharistic League—Rev. JOSEPH P. HYNES, Dir., *358 Newport Ave., Pawtucket, 02861*. Tel: 401-722-4470.

Priests' Personnel Board—Rev. Msgr. ROBERT C. EVANS, J.C.L., Dir., *One Cathedral Sq., Providence, 02903-3695*. Tel: 401-278-4527. Rev. DONAT A. BARRETTE, Vice Chm.; Rev. JOHN E. UNSWORTH,Group I: Rev. ANTHONY D. IWUC,Group II: Rev. FRANCIS W. O'HARA,Group III: Rev. ROGER A. HOULE.

Project Hope / Projecto Esperanza—(Legal Title: *Project Hope / Projecto Esperanza*); Mr. JOHN J. BARRY, III, *400 Dexter St., Center Falls, 02863*. Tel: 401-728-0515.

Propagation of the Faith—(Legal title: *Society for the Propagation of the Faith, Diocese of Providence*); Rev. Msgr. WILLIAM I. VARSANYI, J.C.D., Dir., *One Cathedral Sq., Providence, 02903-3695*. Tel: 401-278-4519.

Radio & T.V. Producer—(Cf. Communications).

Religious, Office of—Sr. JACQUELINE DICKEY, S.S.C.H., Dir., *One Cathedral Sq., Providence, 02903-3695*. Tel: 401-278-4633.

Religious Education—Mr. JOSEPH P. SINWELL, *34 Fenner St., Providence, 02903*. Tel: 401-278-4646.

Renewal in the Spirit—Rev. JOHN F. RANDALL, *Res., 178 Dexter St., Providence, 02907*. Tel: 401-421-6441.

Resource Development Department—(Annual Appeal, Planned Giving, Bishop's Partnership in Charity); Mr. ANTHONY T. GWIAZDOWSKI, Stewardship & Devel. Dir.; Rev. Msgr. WILLIAM J. MCCAFFREY, Moderator, *Diocesan Development Center, 80 St. Mary's Dr., Cranston, 02920*. Tel: 401-943-6550.

Respect Life Office—(Legal Title: *House of the Good Shepherd of Providence*); Mr. LEE GROSSI, Dir., *433 Elmwood Ave., Providence, 02907-1793*. Tel: 401-467-7203; Fax: 401-467-7205.

Natural Family Planning—Mrs. SHEILA BURKE.

Social Justice and Peace Concerns—Ms. PAT JAEHNIG; Ms. CATHY MCELROY.

Catholic Sexuality Program—Ms. KATHY MORRISON.

Public Policy—Ms. MARIA PARKER.

Retreat House Program—Sr. JEAN MARIE MCGEE, R.S.M., Admin., *Our Lady of Peace Spiritual Life Center, Narragansett, 02882*. Tel: 401-884-7676; 783-2871.

Seminarians, Major, Advisory Board for—Revs. MARCEL E. PINCINCE; PETER J. ANDREWS; EUGENE R. LESSARD; RICHARD D. SHEAHAN; JOHN E. UNSWORTH; CLYDE J. WALSH, *485 Mt. Pleasant Ave., Providence, 02908-3301*. Tel: 401-331-1316.

Senior Care, Office of—Miss MARY ANN ALTRUI, Exec. Dir., *400 Mendon Rd., North Smithfield, 02896-6999*. Tel: 401-767-3500.

St. Vincent de Paul Society—(Emergency Assistance Network), *83 Stewart St., Providence, 02903*. Tel: 401-421-7833.

Social Ministry Vicariate—Rev. Msgr. GEORGE L. FRAPPIER, S.T.B., M.A., Vicar, *128 Green St., Woonsocket, 02895*. Tel: 401-769-7487.

Spirituality and Evangelization—Rev. Msgr. JOHN C. ALLARD, Vicar; Sr. MARTA INES TORO, O.P., Dir., Evangelization, *One Cathedral Sq., Providence, 02903-3695*. Tel: 401-278-4625.

SPRED (Cf. Special Religious Education)—Apostolate for Persons with Handicaps.

Stewardship and Development—Mr. ANTHONY T. GWIAZDOWSKI, Dir., *80 St. Mary's Dr., Cranston, 02920*. Tel: 401-943-6550.

Telecommunications—(Cf. Communications).

Vocations—Revs. MARCEL E. PINCINCE, Dir. PAUL E. DEMARAIS, Spiritual Dir., *485 Mt. Pleasant Ave., Providence, 02908*. Tel: 401-831-8011. Sr. JACQUELINE DICKEY, S.S.C.H., Assoc. Dir., Religious, *One Cathedral Sq., Providence, 02903-3695*. Tel: 401-278-4633.

Worship, Office for—Rev. PETER J. ANDREWS, Dir., *One Cathedral Sq., Providence, 02903-3695*. Tel: 401-278-4640.

Diocesan Liturgical Commission—Rev. PETER J. ANDREWS, Chm. Members: Revs. RONALD E. BRASSARD; JOSEPH A. HOWARTH, J.C.L., S.T.B.; STEVEN A. SILIPIGNI; JOSE OMAR ZULUAGA; Mrs. JOANNE MERCIER.

Hispanic Liturgy Committee—Rev. JOSE OMAR ZULUAGA, Chm. Members: Mr. SILVIO CUELLAR; Mrs. CECILIA MARIN; Mrs. MARY MENDEZ; Mrs. SONIA PFLIEGER.

Liturgical Education Committee—Mrs. JOANNE MERCIER, Chm. Members: Revs. JOHN J. DARCY; TIMOTHY J. GORTON; FARRELL E. MCLAUGHLIN; Mr. JOHN SILVIA; Mrs. PEGGY SIMMS; Mr. PAUL T. SULLIVAN.

Liturgy Policy & Guide Committee—Rev. JOSEPH A. HOWARTH, J.C.L., S.T.B., Chm. Members: Revs. RANDOLPH G. CHEW; DAVID W. MASELLO; RICHARD A. VALENTINE.

Music Committee—Rev. RONALD E. BRASSARD, Chm. Members: Revs. PAUL J. DAPONTE; ANTHONY MANCINI; THOMAS J. TREPANIER; Mr. MARK GIRARDIN; Sr. GAIL HIMROD, O.P.; Ms. SHERRY HUMES; Deacon PAUL LAMBERT; Mr. DAVID MARTINEZ; Mrs. LINDA REID; Mr. RONALD TURNQUIST.

Worship Environment Committee—Rev. STEPHAN A. SILIPIGNI, Chm. Members: Very Rev. JOEL A. LECUIVRE, J.C.L.; Rev. FRANCIS W. BROCATO, O.P.; Miss ADE BETHUNE; Mr. ALFRED OAKES.

Young Adult Ministry—Mr. CHRISTOPHER MAHAR, Coord., *One Cathedral Sq., Providence, 02903-3695*. Tel: 401-278-4525.

Youth Ministry—Miss LOUISE DUSSAULT, Dir., *One Cathedral Sq., Providence, 02903-3695*. Tel: 401-278-4636.

CLERGY, PARISHES, MISSIONS AND PAROCHIAL SCHOOLS

CITY OF PROVIDENCE
(Providence County)

1—CATHEDRAL OF SS. PETER AND PAUL (1837). (Legal title: SS. Peter and Paul's Church, Providence, Rhode Island). Rev. Francis J. Giudice, Rector. In res., Revs. Normand W. Valois; Peter J. Andrews.
Res., 30 Fenner St., 02903. Tel: 401-331-2434 (Office); 278-4510 (Cathedral Residence); Fax: 401-331-2435.
Convent—Tel: 401-272-4502.
Sisters of St. Joseph 5.

2—ST. ADALBERT (1902) (Polish). (Legal Title: Saint Adalbert's Church). Rev. Frederick V. Slota.
Res., 866 Atwells Ave., 02909-2596. Tel: 401-351-9306.
Convent—Tel: 401-831-3336. Sr. Mary Alexander, Supr.
Felician Sisters of St. Francis 3.
Catechesis / Religious Programs—864 Atwells Ave., 02909-2596.
Students 84.

3—ST. AGNES (1904). (Legal title: St. Agnes Church). Rev. Norman J. Godin, Admin.
Res., 351 Branch Ave., 02904. Tel: 401-861-7265; Fax: 401-454-6839.
Catechesis / Religious Programs—Students 69.

4—ST. ANN (1895) (Italian). (Legal title: Saint Ann's Catholic Church of Providence, Rhode Island). Revs. Raymond B. Bastia; Frank S. Salmani.
Res., 2 Russo St., 02904. Tel: 401-861-5111; Fax: 401-861-5112.
School—525 Branch Ave., 02904. Tel: 401-331-0891; Fax: 401-854-0870.
Lay Teachers 17; Students 194.
Catechesis / Religious Programs—Tel: 401-521-5220.
Students 105.

5—ST. ANTHONY (Olneyville) (1900). (Legal title: Saint Anthony's Church Corporation, Rhode Island). Rev. Joseph Protano, Jr.
Res., 549 Plainfield St., 02909. Tel: 401-943-2300.
Catechesis / Religious Programs—Tel: 401-943-4450.
Students 57.

6—ASSUMPTION OF THE BLESSED VIRGIN MARY (1871). (Legal title: The Church of the Assumption, Providence, Rhode Island). Revs. Daniel M. Trainor; Guillermo L. Corrales Bedoya (Columbia).
Res., 791 Potters Ave., 02907. Tel: 401-941-1248; Fax: 401-781-4887.
Catechesis / Religious Programs—Tel: 401-941-3768.
Students 230.

7—ST. AUGUSTINE (1929). (Legal title: Saint Augustine's Church, Providence, Rhode Island). Revs. Barry R.L. Connerton; Bernard A. Healey. In res., Rev. Joseph A. Howarth.
Res., 20 Old Rd., 02908. Tel: 401-831-3503; Fax: 401-421-9060.
School—635 Mt. Pleasant Ave., 02908. Tel: 401-831-1213. Mrs. Paul F. Morry, Prin.
Sisters 3; Lay Teachers 25; Students 361.
Catechesis / Religious Programs—Students 333.

8—ST. BARTHOLOMEW (1907) (Italian). Silver Lake District (Legal title: Saint Bartholomew's Church Corporation). Revs. Joseph F. Pranzo, C.S.; Francis Fiorentin, C.S. In res., Rev. Francis Minchiatti, C.S.
Res., 297 Laurel Hill Ave., 02909. Tel: 401-944-4466; Fax: 401-946-5866.
School—311 Laurel Hill Ave., 02909. Tel: 401-944-5662. Ms. Gertrude Blais, Prin.
Sisters 1; Lay Teachers 9; Students 160.
Catechesis / Religious Programs—Students 150.

9—BLESSED SACRAMENT (1888). (Legal title: The Church of the Blessed Sacrament in Providence, Rhode Island). Revs. Charles E. Maher; Robert W. Hayman; Deacon Thomas F. Boutier.
Res., 239 Regent Ave., 02908. Tel: 401-751-7575; Fax: 401-751-7567.
School—240 Regent Ave., 02908. Tel: 401-831-3993. Mrs. Susan Round, Prin.
Sisters Faithful Companions of Jesus 1; Lay Teachers 23; Students 368.
Catechesis / Religious Programs—Students 138.
Convent—350 Mount Pleasant Ave., 02908. Tel: 401-274-6578.
Sisters Faithful Companions of Jesus 4.

10—ST. CASIMIR (1919) (Lithuanian). (Legal title: Saint Casimir's Church, Providence, Rhode Island). Rev. Adolph Klimanskis (NOR) Admin.
Res., 350 Smith St., 02908. Tel: 401-331-1051.

11—ST. CHARLES BORROMEO (1874) (French). (Legal title: Saint Charles Borromeo Roman Catholic Church, Providence, Rhode Island). Revs. John F. Randall; John W. Gray.
Res., 178 Dexter St., 02907. Tel: 401-421-6441.
Catechesis / Religious Programs—Students 194.

12—ST. EDWARD (1874). (Legal title: The Church of St. Joseph Geneva Rhode Island). Rev. Richard J. Bushee.
Res., 10 Caxton St., 02904. Tel: 401-331-4035.
Church—997 Branch Ave., 02904.
Catechesis / Religious Programs—Students 70.

13—GENESIS COMMUNITY. Closed. For inquiries for parish records contact Cathedral of SS. Peter & Paul, Providence.

14—ST. HEDWIG. Closed. For inquiries for sacramental records contact St. Adalbert Parish, Providence.

15—HOLY CROSS (1949) (Italian). (Legal Title: Corporation of the Church of the Holy Cross). Rev. Anthony Mancini, Admin.
Res., 18 King Philip St., 02909. Tel: 401-274-5225; Fax: 401-274-6635.
Catechesis / Religious Programs—636 Hartford Ave., 02909. Tel: 401-751-1144. Mrs. June Carnevale, D.R.E.
Students 212.

16—HOLY GHOST (1889) (Italian). (Legal title: Corporation of the Church of the Holy Ghost, Rhode Island). Revs. Ignatius Battaglia, C.S.; Angelo J. Susin, C.S.
Res., 472 Atwells Ave., 02909. Tel: 401-421-3551; Fax: 401-421-3557.
School—35 Swiss St., 02909. Tel: 401-421-4455. Mrs. Carol Wood, Prin.
Sisters of Mercy of the Americas 1; Lay Teachers 8; Students 163.
Day Care Center—Tel: 401-521-9510. Sr. Dorothy I. Porcaro, R.S.M., Dir.
Lay Teachers 8; Children 75.
Catechesis / Religious Programs—Mr. Alfred Casinelli, D.R.E.
Students 73.

17—HOLY NAME OF JESUS (1882). (Legal title: Church of the Holy Name of Jesus at Providence, Rhode Island). Revs. Kevin R. Fisette; Marc-Arthur Jerome (Haiti); Deacon Frederick A. Young.
Res., 99 Camp St., 02906-1799. Tel: 401-272-4515; Fax: 401-272-4616.
School—Tel: 401-351-0533.
Lay Teachers 13; Students 167.
Catechesis / Religious Programs—Students 80.

18—IMMACULATE CONCEPTION. Closed. For inquiries for sacramental records contact St. Patrick Parish, Providence.

19—ST. JOHN. Closed. (Legal title: St. John Church of Providence Rhode Island). Sacramental records are located at St. Mary Church, Providence.

20—ST. JOSEPH (Foxpoint) (1851). (Legal title: St. Joseph's Church Providence Rhode Island). Rev. Msgr. William J. McCaffrey. In res., Revs. Henry J. Bodah; John J. Rainone; William F. Sears.
Res., 92 Hope St., 02906. Tel: 401-421-9137; Fax: 401-621-5349.

21—ST. MARON. (Legal title: Church of St. Maron in Providence). Rev. Msgr. Jacques L. Plante.
Res., One Cathedral Square, 02903-3695.

22—ST. MARY (Broadway) (1853). (Legal title: St. Mary's Church Providence Rhode Island). Rev. Roger C. Gagne. In res., Rev. Nicholas J. Iacovacci.
Res., 538 Broadway, 02909-3329. Tel: 401-274-3434.
School—30 Barton St., 02909. Tel: 401-274-5250. Mr. Robert Waldraff, Prin.
Sisters of the Congregation de Notre Dame 1; Lay Teachers 11; Students 209.

23—St. Michael the Archangel (South Providence) (1859). (Legal title: St. Michael's Providence, Rhode Island). Revs. Raymond B. Malm; Dennis A. Reardon.
Res., 239 Oxford St., 02905. Tel: 401-781-7210; Fax: 401-461-6164.
Catechesis/Religious Programs—Students 301.

24—Our Lady of Charity. (Legal title: Church of Our Lady of Charity of Providence). Rev. Msgr. William I. Varsanyi.
Res., One Cathedral Sq., 02903-3695.

25—Our Lady of Lourdes (1904) (French). (Legal title: Church of Our Lady of Lourdes). Rev. Msgr. Robert C. Newbold; Deacon Anthony Wendolowski.
Res., 901 Atwells Ave., 02909. Tel: 401-272-8127.

26—Our Lady of Mt. Carmel (1921) (Italian). (Legal title: Church of Our Lady of Mount Carmel, Providence). Revs. Raymond P. Luft; Hugo Carmona (Columbia).
Res., 12 Spruce St., 02903. Tel: 401-274-2113.

27—Our Lady of the Rosary (Portuguese). (Legal title: Church of Our Lady of the Rosary). Rev. Antonio M. Paiva.
Res., 463 Benefit St., 02903. Tel: 401-421-5621.
Convent—17 Traverse St., 02903. Tel: 401-751-9342, 401-751-6432.
Sisters of St. Dorothy 3.
Catechesis/Religious Programs—Sr. Fatima Simas, S.S.D., D.R.E.
Students 281.

28—St. Patrick's (1841). (Legal title: St. Patrick's Church, Providence, Rhode Island). Rev. Raymond M. Kelly.
Res., 152 Holden St., 02908. Tel: 401-421-7070.
Church—244 Smith St., 02908.
School—Tel: 401-421-9300. Mr. Stephen M. Raymond, Prin.
Lay Teachers 10; Students 161.
Catechesis/Religious Programs—Students 80.

29—St. Pius V (1918). (Legal title: Saint Pius Church, Providence, Rhode Island). Very Rev. Kenneth R. Letoile, O.P., Prior; Revs. Michael P. Trainor, O.P.; Michael DeTemple, O.P. In res., Bro. Denis Swann, O.P.
Res., 55 Elmhurst Ave., 02908. Tel: 401-751-4871; Fax: 401-273-1089.
School—49 Elmhurst Ave., 02908. Tel: 401-421-9750; Fax: 401-455-3928. Sr. Shirley Jeffcott, O.P., Prin.
Dominican Sisters 1; Lay Teachers 15; Students 276.
Catechesis/Religious Programs—Tel: 401-421-2263. Mrs. Louise Toomey, D.R.E.
Students 270.
Convent—30 Elmhurst Ave., 02908. Tel: 401-751-0362.

30—St. Raymond (1911). (Legal title: Saint Raymond's Church Corporation). In res., Rev. Peter J. Gower, Admin.
Res., 2 Matilda St., 02904-1812. Tel: 401-861-8169.
Church—1240 N. Main St., 02906. Tel: 401-351-4224; Fax: 401-274-3350.
Catechesis/Religious Programs—Students 60.

31—St. Sebastian (1915). (Legal title: Church of Saint Sebastian). Rev. Msgr. Salvatore R. Matano.
Res., 67 Cole Ave., 02906. Tel: 401-751-0196; Fax: 401-273-7406.
Catechesis/Religious Programs—Tel: 401-272-6062.
Students 128.

32—St. Teresa of Avila (Olneyville) (1883). (Legal title: Saint Teresa's Church Providence Rhode Island). Rev. Raymond L. Tetrault.
Res., 18 Pope St., 02909. Tel: 401-831-7714.

33—St. Thomas (Fruit Hill) (1886). (Legal title: St. Thomas' Church of Manton Rhode Island). Rev. Joseph R. Paquette; Deacon Albert DePetrillo.
Res., 65 Fruit Hill Ave., 02909. Tel: 401-272-7118.
School—See St. Thomas Regional School. Tel: 401-351-0403.
Catechesis/Religious Programs—Tel: 401-272-1443.
Students 334.
Convent—41 Edendale Ave., 02911. Tel: 401-272-1722.

OUTSIDE THE CITY OF PROVIDENCE

Barrington, Bristol Co., Holy Angels (1913) (Italian). (Legal title: Holy Angel's Church Corporation). Rev. David W. Masello.
Res., 341 Maple Ave., 02806. Tel: 401-245-7743; Fax: 401-245-9698.
Catechesis/Religious Programs—359 Maple Ave., 02806. Tel: 401-245-4332.
Students 114.

St. Luke (West Barrington) (1942). (Legal title: Saint Luke's Church Corporation, Barrington). Revs. William R. Jenkinson; David C. Procaccini. In res., Rev. Robert J. McManus.
Res., 108 Washington Rd., 02806-1133. Tel: 401-246-1212.
School—Waldron Ave., 02806. Tel: 401-246-0990; Fax: 401-246-2120. Mrs. Margaret C. Halpin, Prin.
Lay Teachers 19; Students 301.
Catechesis/Religious Programs—Tel: 401-246-1363. D.R.E.: Patricia Grattan, (Grades 1-5); Diane Comerford, (Grades 6-10).
Students 590.

Bristol, Bristol Co., St. Elizabeth (1913) (Portuguese). (Legal title: Saint Elizabeth's Church of Bristol). Revs. John C. Baker; Thomas J. Ferland; Deacon John Sardinha.
Res., 577 Wood St., 02809. Tel: 401-253-8366.
School—10 Monroe Ave., 02809. Tel: 401-253-7622. Sr. Cynthia Mello, S.S.D., Prin.
Sisters of St. Dorothy 1; Lay Teachers 11; Students 212.
Catechesis/Religious Programs—Tel: 401-253-3501. Lisa Correira, D.R.E.
Students 449.

St. Mary (1869). (Legal title: Saint Mary's Church, Bristol, Rhode Island). Rev. Barry J. Gamache; Deacons Benjamin Barboza; Bernard G. Theroux.
Res., 330 Wood St., 02809. Tel: 401-253-3300; Fax: 401-253-3300. [CEM]
Catechesis/Religious Programs—Tel: 401-253-2270.
Students 180.
Mission—Prudence Island, Newport, Our Lady of Prudence, 02872.

Our Lady of Mount Carmel (1917) (Italian). (Legal title: Church of Our Lady of Mount Carmel, Bristol). Revs. James J. Verdelotti; James D. Capoverdi, Jr.; Deacon Paul Bisbano.
Res., 141 State St., 02809. Tel: 401-253-9449; Fax: 401-253-5687. [JC]
School—Maestre Pie Filippini. (Religious Teachers Filippini) 117 State St., 02809. Tel: 401-253-8455; Fax: 401-253-5687. Sr. Concetta Millemaggi, M.P.F., Prin.
Sisters 2; Lay Teachers 12; Students 230.
Catechesis/Religious Programs—131 State St., 02809. Tel: 401-253-3984.
Students 250.

Burrilleville, Providence Co., St. Joseph (Pascoag) (1884). (Legal title: Saint Joseph's Roman Catholic Church of Pascoag). Rev. Clifford J. Cabral.
Res., 183 Sayles Ave., P.O. Box 188, Pascoag, 02859. Tel: 401-568-2411; Fax: 401-568-2586.
Catechesis/Religious Programs—Students 231.

Burrillville, Providence Co., Our Lady of Good Help (Mapleville) (1905). (Legal title: Eglise de Notre Dame de Bonsecours). Rev. Timothy J. Lemlin; Deacon Richard J. Lapierre.
Res., 1063 Victory Hwy., Box 158, Mapleville, 02839. Tel: 401-568-5272; Fax: 401-568-5351.
Catechesis/Religious Programs—Mrs. Patricia Ducharme, D.R.E.
Students 272.

St. Patrick (Harrisville) (1854). (Legal title: St. Patrick's Church, Burrillville, Rhode Island). Rev. Bernard M. O'Reilly, M.A., Ph.D., D.Min.
Res., 45 Main St., Harrisville, 02830. Tel: 401-568-5600. [CEM][JC 2]
Catechesis/Religious Programs—Tel: 401-568-5580.
Students 180.
Mission—Glendale, St. Louis Chapel, Old Victory Hwy., Glendale, 02826.

St. Theresa of the Child Jesus (Nasonville) (1923). (Legal title: Church of Saint Teresa of the Child Jesus, Nasonville). Rev. Paul T. Hurley.
Res., 35 Dion Dr., Harrisville, 02830. Tel: 401-568-8280. [CEM]
Catechesis/Religious Programs—Tel: 401-567-0705.
Students 198.

Central Falls, Providence Co.,

1—The Holy Spirit Catholic Community, (1997). Consolidation of the following three parishes: Holy Trinity, (Legal Title: Church of the Holy Trinity, Central Falls); Notre Dame, (Legal Title: Notre Dame Church); and St. Matthew, (Legal Title: Saint Matthew's Church of Central Falls). Revs. Robert P. Perron, Admin.; Robert M. Beirne; Eugene R. Lessard.
Res., 1060 Dexter St., 02863-1717. Tel: 401-726-6200; 725-1748; 723-5326.
Catechesis/Religious Programs—Tel: 401-722-3717.
Students 312.

2—Holy Trinity, (1989). Merged with Notre Dame, Central Falls and St. Matthew, Central Falls to form The Holy Spirit Catholic Communtity, Central Falls. (Legal title: Church of the Holy Trinity, Central Falls).

3—St. Joseph, (1906) (Polish). (Legal title: St. Joseph's Church of Central Falls). Rev. Anthony D. Iwuc.
Res., 391 High St., 02863-3109. Tel: 401-723-5427.

4—St. Matthew's, (1906) (French). Merged with Holy Trinity, Central Falls and Notre Dame, Central Falls to form The Holy Spirit Catholic Community, Central Falls. (Legal title: Saint Matthew's Church of Central Falls).

5—Notre Dame, (1873) (French). Merged with Holy Trinity, Central Falls and St. Matthew, Central Falls to form The Holy Spirit Catholic Community, Central Falls. (Legal title: Notre Dame Church).

Charlestown, Washington Co., St. Mary (Carolina) (1946). (Legal title: Saint Mary's Church Corporation, Carolina). Rev. John F. Heaney.
Res., P.O. Box 475, Carolina, 02812. Tel: 401-364-7214.
Catechesis/Religious Programs—Tel: 401-783-1849.
Students 362.
Mission—Charlestown, Washington Co., St. James, 2079 Mat. School House Rd., Charlestown, 02813. Tel: 401-364-7214.

Coventry, Kent Co., SS. John and Paul (1955). (Legal title: SS. John and Paul Parish Corporation, Coventry). Revs. Joseph P. Henry; Dariusz G. Jonczyk; William J. Ledoux; Deacon Robert A. Turbitt, II.
Res., 341 S. Main St., 02816. Tel: 401-821-5764; Fax: 401-828-5351.
School—Father John V. Doyle School, Tel: 401-821-3756. Mr. J. Robert McDermott, Prin.; Mrs. Vivian Ryan, Vice Prin.
Lay Teachers 19; Students 401.
Catechesis/Religious Programs—Tel: 401-821-5785.
Students 1,250.

Our Lady of Czenstochowa (Quidnick) (1909) (Polish). (Legal title: Church of Our Lady of Czenstochowa). Rev. John D. Dreher.
Res., 445 Washington St., 02816. Tel: 401-821-7991.
Catechesis/Religious Programs—Students 226.

St. Vincent de Paul (Anthony) (1937) (French). (Legal title: Church of Saint Vincent de Paul, Anthony, Rhode Island). Rev. Paul J. Laporte, Admin.; Deacon Edward Sadowski, Jr.
Res., 6 St. Vincent de Paul St., 02816. Tel: 401-821-8719.
Convent—8 St. Vincent de Paul St., 02816. Tel: 401-828-6506. Sr. Lorette Goucy, P.M., Supr.
Sisters of the Presentation of Mary 3.
Catechesis/Religious Programs—2 St. Vincent de Paul St., 02816. Tel: 401-828-3090.
Students 200.

Cranston, Providence Co.,

1—St. Ann, (1858). (Legal title: St. Anne's Church, Cranston, Rhode Island). Rev. John G. Greaves. In res., Rev. Msgr. Leo J. Hines (MAN).
Res., 1493 Cranston St., 02920. Tel: 401-942-2767.
Catechesis/Religious Programs—Tel: 401-942-0655.
Students 350.

2—Holy Apostles, (1991). (Legal title: Holy Apostles Church, Cranston, Rhode Island). Rev. Richard D. Sheahan.
Res., 800 Pippin Orchard Rd., 02921. Tel: 401-946-5586; Fax: 401-946-5066.
Catechesis/Religious Programs—Students 844.

3—Immaculate Conception, (Oaklawn) (1958). (Legal title: Immaculate Conception Church Corporation, Cranston). Rev. Ronald E. Brassard; Deacons Carmine Forlingieri; Raymond J. LaFrance; Thomas J. Lennon; Thomas R. Raspallo.
Res., 237 Garden Hills Dr., 02920. Tel: 401-942-1854; Fax: 401-942-2897.
Catechesis/Religious Programs—Tel: 401-942-1958. D.R.E.: Claudia Bertrand; Richard Raspallo.
Students 566.

4—St. Mark, (Garden City) (1950). (Legal title: Saint Mark's Church Corporation of Cranston). Revs. Richard A. Donnelly; M. Kevin Lynch.
Res., 9 Garden Ct., 02920. Tel: 401-942-1616.
Catechesis/Religious Programs—Tel: 401-942-3231.
Students 403.

5—St. Mary, (Knightsville) (1925) (Italian). (Santa Maria della Civita) (Legal title: Saint Mary's Church, Cranston). Revs. Alfred C. Lonardo; Daniel M. Azzarone; Joseph A. Pescatello; Deacon Peter A. Ceprano.
Res., 1525 Cranston St., 02920-5297. Tel: 401-942-1492; Fax: 401-946-2531.
School—Tel: 401-944-4107. Mrs. Elizabeth Mizzoni, Prin.
Lay Teachers 19; Students 316.
Catechesis/Religious Programs—Tel: 401-944-1323; Fax: 401-946-5231. Phyllis Ann Persson, D.R.E.
Students 500.

6—St. Matthew, (Auburn) (1909). (Legal title: St. Matthew's Church Corporation). Revs. Richard A. Walsh; Raymond J. Ferrick; James T. Ruggieri.
Res., 15 Frances Ave., 02910. Tel: 401-461-7172; Fax: 401-461-7173.
Church—Elmwood & Park Ave., 02910.
School—1301 Elmwood Ave., 02910. Tel: 401-941-8954. Ms. Elaine P. Dykstra, Prin.
Lay Teachers 14; Students 298.
Catechesis/Religious Programs—Tel: 401-781-4568; Fax: 401-461-7173. Sr. Rita E. McCoy, R.S.M., D.R.E.
Students 395.

7—St. Paul, (Edgewood) (1907). (Legal title: Saint Paul's Church of Edgewood). Revs. Randolf G. Chew; Paul J. DaPonte. In res., Rev. Robert J. Maynard.
Res., One St. Paul Pl., 02905. Tel: 401-461-5734; Fax: 401-786-3616.
School—1789 Broad St., 02905. Tel: 401-941-2030. Mrs. Jean Patterson, Prin.
Lay Teachers 11; Students 185.
Catechesis/Religious Programs—Tel: 401-941-5576.
Students 305.

Cumberland, Providence Co.,

1—St. Aidan, (1962). (Legal title: St. Aidan Church Corporation, Cumberland). Rev. Donald L. Depatie.
Res., 1060 Diamond Hill Rd., 02864. Tel: 401-333-5897; Fax: 401-333-5078.
Catechesis/Religious Programs—Tel: 401-333-9030.
Students 285.

2—St. Joan of Arc, (Cumberland Hill) (1929). (Legal title: Saint Joan's Church, Cumberland, Rhode Island). Rev. Norman W. Bourdon. In res., Rev. Msgr. Robert C. Evans.
Res., 3357 Mendon Rd., 02864-2195. Tel: 401-658-2084; Fax: 401-658-2086.
Catechesis/Religious Programs—Tel: 401-658-0734.
Students 582.

3—St. John Baptist Mary Vianney, (Diamond Hill) (1953). (Legal title: Saint John Baptist Mary Vianney Church Corporation, Diamond Hill). Rev. J. Raymond Theroux; Deacon Paul H. Lambert.
Res., 3609 Diamond Hill Rd., 02864. Tel: 401-333-6060; Fax: 401-333-0766.
Catechesis/Religious Programs—3587 Diamond Hill Rd., 02864. Tel: 401-333-2347.
Students 534.

4—St. Joseph, (Ashton) (1872). (Legal title: St. Joseph's Church, Ashton, Rhode Island). Rev. John W. Hunt.
Res., Mendon Rd., P.O Box 7005, 02864. Tel: 401-333-4013; Fax: 401-333-4013. [CEM]
Catechesis/Religious Programs—Tel: 401-333-4014.
Students 286.

5—Our Lady of Fatima, (Valley Falls) (1953) (Portuguese). (Legal title: Church of Our Lady of Fatima, Valley Falls). Revs. Dennis J. Kieton; Domingos M. da Cunha.
Res., Fatima Dr., 02864. Tel: 401-723-6719; Fax: 401-723-1698.
Catechesis/Religious Programs—Tel: 401-724-3454.
Students 426.

6—St. Patrick, (Valley Falls) (1861). (Legal title: St. Patrick's Church Corporation, Valley Falls, Rhode Island). Revs. David T. Perry; Joseph E. Davis.
Res., 301 Broad St., 02864. Tel: 401-725-0344; 725-7802. [CEM]
Catechesis/Religious Programs—Tel: 401-725-0344.
Students 250.

East Greenwich, Kent Co., Our Lady of Mercy (1853). (Legal title: Our Lady of Mercy, Greenwich, Rhode Island). Revs. John W. Lolio; Anthony W. Verdelotti. In res., Rev. John J. Darcy.
Res., 65 Third St., 02818. Tel: 401-884-4968; Fax: 401-884-1415. [CEM]
Catechesis/Religious Programs—Tel: 401-884-1061.
Students 908.
Convent—36 Fourth Ave., 02818. Tel: 401-884-9292.

East Providence, Providence Co.,

1—St. Brendan, (Riverside) (1909). (Legal title: St. Brendan's Church). Revs. John E. Unsworth; Robert L. Bailey; Marcel L. Taillon.
Res., 60 Turner Ave., Riverside, 02915. Tel: 401-433-2600; Fax: 401-433-1962.
School—55 Turner Ave., Riverside, 02915. Tel: 401-433-1290.
Lay Teachers 14; Students 232.
Catechesis/Religious Programs—Tel: 401-433-2680. John D. Sousa, D.R.E.
Students 780.

2—St. Francis Xavier, (Portuguese). (Legal title: Saint Francis Xavier's Church). Revs. Victor M. Vieira; Michael A. Sisco; Jay A. Finelli.
Res., 81 N. Carpenter St., 02914. Tel: 401-434-1878; Fax: 401-408-1950.
Catechesis/Religious Programs—Tel: 401-434-3153; 434-9421.
Students 975.

3—St. Margaret, (Rumford) (1888). (Legal title: Saint Margaret's Church Corporation, East Providence Rhode Island). Rev. Thomas L. Keenan.
Res., 1098 Pawtucket Ave., Rumford, 02916. Tel: 401-438-3230; Fax: 401-438-4221.
School—42 Bishop Ave., Rumford, 02916. Tel: 401-434-2338; Fax: 401-431-0266. Mr. Felipe M. Felipe, Prin.
Lay Teachers 25; Students 360.
Catechesis/Religious Programs—Tel: 401-435-4755.
Students 425.

4—St. Martha, (1956). (Legal title: St. Martha's Church Corporation, East Providence). Revs. Jude P. McGeough; Normand J. Demers.
Res., 2595 Pawtucket Ave., 02914. Tel: 401-434-4060.
Catechesis/Religious Programs—Tel: 401-434-7030.
Students 380.

5—Our Lady of Loreto, (1920) (Italian). (Legal title: Church of Our Lady of Loreto, East Providence). Rev. Stanley T. Nakowicz.
Res., 346 Waterman Ave., 02914. Tel: 401-434-3535.
Catechesis/Religious Programs—Students 112.

6—Sacred Heart, (1876). (Legal title: Church of the Sacred Heart). Rev. Peter S. DiTullio, S.C.
Res., 118 Taunton Ave., 02914. Tel: 401-434-0326; Fax: 401-434-7285.
School—56 Purchase St., 02914. Tel: 401-434-1080. Sisters 3; Lay Teachers 11; Students 180.
Nursery-Day Care—101 Taunton Ave., 02914. Tel: 401-434-2462.
Staff 7; Children 80.
Catechesis/Religious Programs—Students 116.

Foster, Providence Co., St. Paul the Apostle (1972). (Legal title: St. Paul's Church Corporation, Foster). Rev. Paul A. Charland.
Res., 116A Danielson Pike, 02825-1421. Tel: 401-647-3664; Fax: 401-647-3680.
Catechesis/Religious Programs—Students 360.

Glocester, Providence Co., St. Eugene (Chepachet) (1956). (Legal title: St. Eugene's Church Corporation, Chepachet). Rev. Charles P. Quinn.
Res., 1251 Putnam Pike, P.O. Box A, Chepachet, 02814. Tel: 401-568-5102.
Catechesis/Religious Programs—Students 180.

Hopkinton, Washington Co., St. Joseph (Hope Valley) (1939). (Legal title: Saint Joseph's Church, Hope Valley). Rev. Michael J. Leckie.
Res., P.O. Box 388, 1105 Main St., Hope Valley, 02832. Tel: 401-539-8311.
Catechesis/Religious Programs—Tel: 401-539-8312.
Students 311.

Our Lady of Victory (Ashaway) (1946). (Legal title: Church of Our Lady of Victory, Ashaway). Rev. James V. Farley.
Res., 169B Main St., Ashaway, 02804. Tel: 401-377-8830.
Catechesis/Religious Programs—Tel: 401-377-8435; Fax: 401-377-8830.
Students 90.

Jamestown, Newport Co., St. Mark (Jamestown) (1909). (Legal title: Saint Mark Church of Jamestown). Rev. William J. O'Neill.
Res., 60 Narragansett Ave., 02835. Tel: 401-423-1421. [CEM]
Catechesis/Religious Programs—Tel: 401-423-1518.
Students 314.

Johnston, Providence Co.,

1—St. Brigid, (Thornton) (1915). (Legal title: Saint Brigid's Church of Johnston). Rev. James L. Kelleher.
Res., 1231 Plainfield, 02919. Tel: 401-944-2232.
Catechesis/Religious Programs—Students 145.

2—Our Lady of Grace, (1913) (Italian). (Legal title: Church of Our Lady of Grace). Rev. Douglas J. Spina; Deacon Robert P. Troia. In res., Rev. Ronald P. Simeone.
Res., 4 Lafayette St., 02919. Tel: 401-231-2220; Fax: 401-231-3905.
Catechesis/Religious Programs—Tel: 401-231-8959; Fax: 401-231-8959.
Students 235.

3—St. Robert Bellarmine, (1963). (Legal title: St. Robert Bellarmine Church Corporation, Johnston). Rev. John G. LaPointe.
Res., 1804 Atwood Ave., 02919-3215. Tel: 401-232-5600.
Catechesis/Religious Programs—Students 500.

4—St. Rocco, (1903) (Italian). (Legal title: Saint Rocco Church of Johnston). Revs. Alfred P. Almonte, C.S.; Hector Sartori, C.S.; John A. Corrao, C.S.; Sr. Patricia Cigrand, A.S.C.J., Pastoral Assoc.; Deacon Robert P. Troia. In res., Rev. Settimo Basso, C.S.
Res., 927 Atwood Ave., 02919. Tel: 401-942-5203; Fax: 401-464-6422.
School—931 Atwood Ave., 02919. Tel: 401-944-2993; Fax: 401-944-3019. Sr. Mary Carol Gentile, A.S.C.J., Prin.
Apostles of the Sacred Heart of Jesus 5; Lay Teachers 20; Students 480.
Catechesis/Religious Programs—Tel: 401-944-6040. Sr. Rose Alfieri, C.P., D.R.E.
Students 350.

Lincoln, Providence Co., St. Ambrose (Albion) (1905). (Legal title: St. Ambrose Church, Albion, Rhode Island). Rev. Thomas J. Trepanier.
Res., 191 School St., Albion, 02802. Tel: 401-333-1568; Fax: 401-333-8941. [CEM]
Catechesis/Religious Programs—Tel: 401-334-3735.
Students 132.

St. James (Manville) (1874). (Legal title: Saint James Church of Manville, Rhode Island). Rev. Richard P. Desaulniers; Deacon Gregory Horton.
Res., 33 Division St., Box 60, Manville, 02838. Tel: 401-766-1558; Fax: 401-766-1561. [CEM]
Catechesis/Religious Programs—57 Division St., Manville, 02838. Tel: 401-769-2676; Fax: 401-766-1516.
Students 260.

St. Jude (Lincoln) (1946). (Legal title: St. Jude's Church, Lincoln). Rev. Bernard C. Lavin. In res., Rev. Msgr. Paul D. Theroux.
Res., 301 Front St., 02865. Tel: 401-725-8140.
Catechesis/Religious Programs—Tel: 401-725-8120. Sr. Mary Higgins, R.S.M., D.R.E.
Students 689.

Little Compton, Newport Co., St. Catherine of Siena (1930). (Legal title: St. Catherine's Church Corporation, Little Compton). Rev. Gerald W. Hussey.
Res., 74 Simmons Rd., P.O. Box 208, 02837-0208. Tel: 401-635-4420; Fax: 401-635-2214. [CEM]
Catechesis/Religious Programs—Students 120.

Middletown, Newport Co., St. Lucy (Middletown) (1952). (Legal title: Saint Lucy's Church Corp.). Rev. Eugene J. McKenna.
Res., 909 W. Main Rd., 02842-6351. Tel: 401-847-6153; Fax: 401-847-1545.
Catechesis/Religious Programs—Tel: 401-847-6154. D.R.E. Sr. Mary T. Burns, C.P.; Sr. Rosemary Burnham, R.S.M.; Sr. Assunta Riley, R.S.M.
Students 398.

Narragansett, Washington Co., St. Mary, Star of the Sea (Point Judith) (1960). (Legal title: St. Mary, Star of the Sea Church Corporation, Point Judith). Rev. Donald J. Bouressa.
Res., 864 Pt. Judith Rd., P.O. Box 3329, 02882. Tel: 401-783-4449; Fax: 401-783-0986.
Catechesis/Religious Programs—Tel: 401-789-7308; Fax: 401-783-0986.
Students 265.

St. Thomas More (1917). (Legal title: St. Thomas More Church, Narragansett Pier, Rhode Island). Rev. John C. Halloran; Deacon Paul J. Sullivan.
Res., 53 Rockland St., 02882. Tel: 401-789-7682.
Catechesis/Religious Programs—Tel: 401-783-2113.
Students 305.
Chapel—Bonnet Shores, St. Veronica Summer Chapel.

New Shoreham, Washington Co., St. Andrew (Block Island) (1917). (Legal title: Saint Andrew's Church Corporation, Block Island). Rev. Donal R. Kehew, Admin.
Res., Spring St., Block Island, 02807. Tel: 401-466-5519.

Newport, Newport Co.,

1—St. Augustin, (1911). (Legal title: Saint Augustin's Church of Newport). Rev. John McNulty; Sr. Josephine St. Leger, S.J.C., Pastoral Assoc.
Res., 2 Eastnor Rd., 02840. Tel: 401-847-0518; Fax: 401-848-2411.
Catechesis/Religious Programs—Students 108.

2—Jesus Saviour, (1926) (Portuguese). (Legal title: Church of Jesus-Saviour, Newport). Rev. Msgr. William J. Carey, Admin.
Res., One Vernon Ave., 02840. Tel: 401-847-1267; Fax: 401-846-3375.
Catechesis/Religious Programs—Tel: 401-846-4095.
Students 68.

3—St. Joseph, (1885). (Legal title: Saint Joseph's Church of Newport, Rhode Island). Rev. John J. Lavin. In res., Rev. Francis A. O'Loughlin.
Res., 5 Mann Ave., 02840. Tel: 401-847-0065; Fax: 401-849-2195.

Catechesis/Religious Programs—Tel: 401-847-9248; Fax: 401-849-2195.
Students 337.

4—ST. MARY, (1826). (Legal title: St. Mary's, Newport, Rhode Island). Rev. George B. McCarthy.
Res., 12 William St., P.O. Box 547, 02840. Tel: 401-847-0475; Fax: 401-845-9497. [CEM]
Catechesis/Religious Programs—Tel: 401-846-6057.
Students 215.

North Kingstown, Washington Co., St. Bernard (Wickford) (1874). (Legal title: St. Bernard's Roman Catholic Church of Wickford, Rhode Island). Rev. Gerard O. Sabourin; Deacon Ronald DePietro.
Office: 415 Tower Hill Rd., Wickford, 02852. Tel: 401-295-0387.
Catechesis/Religious Programs—Tel: 401-295-5235. D.R.E.: Sr. Roberta Giampaoli; Mrs. Michelle Jacomb.
Students 479.
Mission—Exeter, Washington Co., Blessed Kateri Tekakwitha, 84 Exeter Rd., Exeter, 02822. Tel: 401-295-0234.

St. Francis De Sales (Davisville) (1960). (Legal title: St. Francis de Sales Church Corporation, North Kingstown). Revs. Farrell E. McLaughlin; Douglas Grant.
Res., 381 School St., 02852. Tel: 401-884-2105; Fax: 401-885-4315.
Catechesis/Religious Programs—Tel: 401-885-3639. D.R.E.: Cathleen Dowd; Sara Kirtlink.
Students 1,085.

North Providence, Providence Co.,

1—ST. ANTHONY, (1944) (Italian). (Legal title: Saint Anthony's Church Corporation, North Providence). Revs. Edward S. Cardente; C. Brian Lagasse.
Res., 5 Gibbs St., 02904. Tel: 401-353-3120; Fax: 401-353-5126.
Catechesis/Religious Programs—Tel: 401-353-5125. D.R.E. Maryann Pallotta; Peg Ormond.
Students 540.

2—ST. LAWRENCE, (Centredale) (1907). (Legal title: Saint Lawrence Church of Centredale). Rev. David Piacentini. In res., Rev. Peter G. Young.
Res., 624 Woonasquatucket Ave., 02911-1652. Tel: 401-231-9126; Fax: 401-231-7425.
Catechesis/Religious Programs—Tel: 401-231-5255.
Students 261.

3—MARY, MOTHER OF MANKIND, (1967). (Legal title: Mary, Mother of Mankind Church Corporation, North Providence). Rev. Stephan A. Silipigni.
Res., 25 Fourth St., 02911. Tel: 401-231-3542; Fax: 401-232-0965.
Catechesis/Religious Programs—Students 252.

4—PRESENTATION OF THE BLESSED VIRGIN MARY, (Marieville) (1912) (French). (Legal title: Church of the Presentation of the Blessed Virgin Mary). Rev. Louis T. Natalizia. In res., Rev. John W. O'Brien; Deacon Louis A. Vani.
Res., 1081 Mineral Spring Ave., 02904. Tel: 401-722-7140; Fax: 401-722-6617.
Catechesis/Religious Programs—Tel: 401-722-8824.
Students 238.

North Smithfield, Providence Co., St. John the Evangelist (Slatersville) (1872). (Legal title: St. John's Church Society, Rhode Island). Revs. Raymond A. Tetreault; Chinnaiah Yerrnini, O.S.S. (India).
Res., 63 Church St., Slatersville, 02876. Tel: 401-762-0946; Fax: 401-762-0944. [CEM]
Catechesis/Religious Programs—Tel: 401-762-0966. Mrs. Sara D. Hickey, D.R.E.
Students 566.

Pawtucket, Providence Co.,

1—ST. ANTHONY, (1926) (Portuguese). (Legal title: Saint Anthony's Church Corporation, Pawtucket). Rev. Joseph A. Escobar, O.P., Admin.; Deacon Manuel Martins.
Res., 32 Lawn Ave., 02860. Tel: 401-723-9138; Fax: 401-725-5616.
Catechesis/Religious Programs—Students 259.

2—ST. CECILIA, (1910) (French). (Legal title: Saint Cecilia's Church Corporation). Rev. Francis C. Santilli.
Res., 1253 Newport Ave., 02861. Tel: 401-722-1101; Fax: 401-727-3844.
School—755 Central Ave., 02861. Tel: 401-723-9463; Fax: 401-722-1444.
Sisters 6; Lay Teachers 11; Students 332.
Catechesis/Religious Programs—Students 299.

3—ST. EDWARD, (1904). (Legal title: St. Edward's Church of Pawtucket). Rev. James R. Collins; Deacon Raymond E. Batalon.
Res., 58 Hancock St., 02860. Tel: 401-725-7036; Fax: 401-722-4090.
Catechesis/Religious Programs—61 Hope St., 02860. Tel: 401-725-7831.
Students 190.

4—IMMACULATE HEART OF MARY, (1979) (Cape Verdean). (An operation of Church of St. Maron in Providence). Rev. Arlindo A. Amarco, C.S.Sp., Admin.
Res., 35 Clay St., Central Falls, 02863. Tel: 401-725-1126.
Church—291 High St., 02860.
Catechesis/Religious Programs—Students 75.

5—ST. JOHN THE BAPTIST, (1884) (French). (Legal title: The Church of St. John the Baptist of Pawtucket Rhode Island). Revs. Joel A. Lecuivre, J.C.L.; Jose Omar Zuluaga (Colombia); Deacon Raymond M. Lagesse.
Res., 69 Quincy Ave., 02860. Tel: 401-722-9054; Fax: 401-724-3514.
Catechesis/Religious Programs—Students 173.

6—ST. JOSEPH, (1873). (Legal title: St. Joseph's Church). Rev. Charles B. McDermott. In res., Revs. Timothy L. Gillen; Richard C. Maynard; John J. McElroy, Pastor Emeritus.
Res., 193 Walcott St., 02860. Tel: 401-724-9190.
Catechesis/Religious Programs—Students 248.

7—ST. LEO THE GREAT, (1916). (Legal title: Church of Saint Leo the Great in Pawtucket). Revs. John A. Kiley; Christopher M. Davenport.
Res., 697 Central Ave., 02861. Tel: 401-722-1220; Fax: 401-722-1220.
School—723 Central Ave., 02861. Tel: 401-725-3620. Sr. Marie Lorraine Halpin, R.S.M., Prin.
Sisters 4; Lay Teachers 15; Students 305.
Catechesis/Religious Programs—Tel: 401-722-0744. Mrs. Linda Prew, D.R.E.
Students 275.

8—ST. MARIA GORETTI, (1953). (Legal title: St. Maria Goretti Church Corporation, Pawtucket). Rev. Kenneth J. Suibielski; Deacon Lucien Ouellette.
Res., 165 Power Rd., 02860. Tel: 401-725-4355; Fax: 401-729-5711.
Catechesis/Religious Programs—Tel: 401-729-5713.
Students 275.

9—ST. MARY OF THE IMMACULATE CONCEPTION, (1829). (Legal title: The Church of the Immaculate Conception of Pawtucket, Rhode Island). Revs. John E. Watterson; Albert A. Kenney; Deacon C. Patrick Sheehy.
Res., 103 Pine St., P.O. Box 518, 02862. Tel: 401-722-5425; Fax: 401-729-0341. [CEM]
School—(Grades PreK-8) 167 George St., 02862. Tel: 401-723-6695. Mrs. Patricia Baumgartel, Prin.
Sisters 1; Lay Teachers 10; Students 215.
Catechesis/Religious Programs—Students 109.

10—OUR LADY OF CONSOLATION, (1895) (French). (Legal title: Church of Our Lady of Consolation Rhode Island). Rev. Normand L. Courtemanche.
Res., 10 Webster St., 02860. Tel: 401-722-2804; Fax: 401-722-2804.
Catechesis/Religious Programs—Tel: 401-725-2409.
Students 101.

11—SACRED HEART OF JESUS, (1872). (Legal title: The Church of the Sacred Heart of Jesus of Pawtucket, Rhode Island). Rev. Paul E. Desmarais. In res., Rev. William H. Tanguay, Dir., Hmong Apostolate, Tel: 401-723-5480.
Res., 38 Park St., 02860. Tel: 401-722-3226.
Catechesis/Religious Programs—Tel: 401-722-9861.
Students 140.

12—ST. TERESA OF THE CHILD JESUS, (1929). (Legal title: Church of Saint Teresa of the Child Jesus, Pawtucket, Rhode Island). Revs. Joseph P. Hynes; Charles H. Galligan; Hugh O'Rourke, S.S.C.
Res., 358 Newport Ave., 02861. Tel: 401-722-4470; Fax: 401-722-2958.
School—150 Wood Haven Rd., 02861. Tel: 401-726-1414. Sr. Barbara Foley, R.S.M., Coord.; Sr. Maureen Sadlier, R.S.M., Prin.
Sisters of Mercy of the Americas 4; Lay Teachers 17; Students 290.
Catechesis/Religious Programs—Tel: 401-723-2266.
Students 313.

Portsmouth, Newport Co., St. Anthony (1901). (Legal title: Saint Anthony's Church of Portsmouth). Rev. Daniel J. Gray.
Res., P.O. Box 570, 2836 E. Main Rd., 02871. Tel: 401-683-0089.
Catechesis/Religious Programs—Tel: 401-683-3636.
Students 210.

St. Barnabas (1963). (Legal title: St. Barnabas Church Corporation, Portsmouth). Rev. Kevin J. Brassil.
Res., 1697 E. Main Rd., 02871. Tel: 401-683-1343; Fax: 401-683-5056.
Catechesis/Religious Programs—Tel: 401-683-3147.
Students 410.

Scituate, Providence Co., St. Joseph (North Scituate) (1940). (Legal title: Saint Joseph's Church Corporation, North Scituate). Rev. Francis J. Keefe.
Res., Danielson Pk., P.O. Box 236, North Scituate, 02857. Tel: 401-647-2255; Fax: 401-647-2968.
Catechesis/Religious Programs—Tel: 401-647-2650.
Students 487.

Smithfield, Providence Co., St. Michael (Georgiaville) (1875). (Legal title: St. Michael's Church, Georgiaville, Rhode Island). Rev. Richard A. Valentine; Deacon William Small, Ph.D. In res., Rev. Edward H. Flannery.
Res., 80 Farnum Pike, Georgiaville, 02917. Tel: 401-231-5119; Fax: 401-231-0523.
Catechesis/Religious Programs—Tel: 401-231-1340.
Students 530.

St. Philip (Greenville) (1852). (Legal title: St. Philip's Church Greenville Rhode Island). Revs. Gerald E. Beirne; Ronald L. Simoneau; Robert E. Lacombe; Deacons Harris J. Gederman; Carlo J. Sabetti.
Res., 622 Putnam Ave., Greenville, 02828-1403. Tel: 401-949-1500; Fax: 401-949-3504.
School—618 Putnam Ave., Greenville, 02828. Tel: 401-949-1130.
Sisters of Mercy of the Americas 1; Lay Teachers 15; Students 245.
Catechesis/Religious Programs—Tel: 401-949-0330. Jean Cedor, D.R.E.
Students 1,037.

South Kingstown, Washington Co., Christ the King (Kingston) (1950). (Legal title: Christ the King Church Corporation, Kingston). Rev. Joseph D. Creedon.
Res., 180 Old North Rd., Kingston, 02881. Tel: 401-783-7459; Fax: 401-789-3671.
Catechesis/Religious Programs—Tel: 401-789-0417.
Students 805.

St. Francis of Assisi (Wakefield) (1879). (Legal title: Saint Francis Church). Rev. Nicholas P. Smith. In res., Rev. Stephen P. Amaral.
Mailing Address: c/o St. Francis Church, 114 High St., Wakefield, 02879-3141. Tel: 401-783-4411; Fax: 401-783-9667.
Catechesis/Religious Programs—Tel: 401-792-8684.
Students 498.
Mission—Matunuck, Washington, St. Romuald, 61 Atlantic Ave., Wakefield, 02879.

Tiverton, Newport Co.,

1—ST. CHRISTOPHER, (1925). (Legal title: Saint Christopher's Church of Tiverton). Rev. Francis P. Kanda, C.S.Sp.
Res., 1660 Main Rd., 02878. Tel: 401-624-6644.
Catechesis/Religious Programs—Students 150.

2—HOLY GHOST, (North Tiverton) (1913). (Legal title: Church of the Holy Ghost, North Tiverton). Rev. Henry P. Zinno, Jr.; Deacon Raymond E. Levesque.
Res., 311 Hooper St., North Tiverton, 02878. Tel: 401-624-8131; Fax: 401-625-5156.
Catechesis/Religious Programs—Tel: 401-624-3664.
Students 380.

3—ST. MADELEINE SOPHIE, (1948). (Legal title: Saint Madeleine's Church Corporation of Tiverton). Rev. Joseph F. McDonough, C.S.Sp. In res., Rev. Joseph F. McNamara, C.S.Sp.
Res., 35 Lake Rd., 02878. Tel: 401-624-4226.
Catechesis/Religious Programs—Students 148.

4—ST. THERESA, (1960). (Legal title: St. Theresa's Parish Corporation, Tiverton). Rev. Bertrand N. Richman, Ph.D., Admin.; Deacon Jesse L. Martins.
Res., 265 Stafford Rd., 02878. Tel: 401-624-8746; Fax: 401-625-5384.
Catechesis/Religious Programs—Tel: 401-625-5576.
Students 175.

Warren, Bristol Co.,

1—ST. ALEXANDER, (1915) (Italian). (Legal title: Saint Alexander's Church Corporation, Warren). Rev. David W. Masello, Admin.
Res., 221 Main St., 02885. Tel: 401-245-6369. [CEM]
Catechesis/Religious Programs—Tel: 401-245-4332.
Students 45.

2—ST. CASIMIR, (1908) (Polish). (Legal title: Saint Casimir's Church of Warren). Rev. Matthew J. Strumski.
Res., 228 Child St., 02885-9998. Tel: 401-245-4422.

3—ST. JEAN BAPTISTE, (1877) (French). (Legal title: The Church of Saint Jean Baptiste of Warren Rhode Island). Rev. Emile A. Robert.
Res., 328 Main St., 02885. Tel: 401-245-8392. [CEM]
Catechesis/Religious Programs—Students 121.

4—ST. MARY OF THE BAY, (1851). (Legal title: Church of Saint Mary of the Bay). Revs. Bertrand L. Theroux; Paul J. O'Rourke, S.S.C.
Res., 645 Main St., 02885. Tel: 401-245-7000; Fax: 401-245-7093. [CEM]
Catechesis/Religious Programs—Tel: 401-245-2644.
Students 413.
Convent—430R Water St., 02885. Tel: 401-245-8629. Sisters of Mercy of the Americas

5—ST. THOMAS THE APOSTLE, (1952) (Portuguese). (Legal title: Saint Thomas the Apostle Church Corporation). Rev. Joel D. Oliveira (BO) Admin.
Res., 500 Metacom Ave., 02885. Tel: 401-245-4469.
Catechesis/Religious Programs—Tel: 401-245-4488.
Students 140.

Warwick, Kent Co.,

1—ST. BENEDICT, (Conimicut) (1914). (Legal title: St. Benedict's Church, Conimicut). Rev. Pierre J. Plante.
Res., 135 Beach Ave., P.O. Box 9485, 02889. Tel: 401-737-9492; Fax: 401-739-0974.
Catechesis/Religious Programs—70 Transit St., 02889. Tel: 401-738-2545.
Students 257.

2—ST. CATHERINE, (Apponaug) (1916). (Legal title: Saint Catherine's Roman Catholic Church of Warwick, Rhode Island). Rev. Roger G. Champigny; Deacon John F. Baker.
Res., 3252 Post Rd., 02886. Tel: 401-737-4455; Fax: 401-732-7739.
Catechesis/Religious Programs—Tel: 401-737-6234. D.R.E.: Margaret Boylan; Martha Capaldi.
Students 273.

3—ST. CLEMENT'S, (1961). Merged with St. Rose of Lima to form St. Rose of Lima/St. Clement, Warwick. (Legal title: St. Clement Church Corporation, Warwick).

4—ST. FRANCIS OF ASSISI, (Hillsgrove) (1943). (Legal title: Saint Francis Church Corporation, Hillsgrove). Rev. Timothy J. Gorton; Deacon Kevin P. Masse.
Res., 596 Jefferson Blvd., 02886. Tel: 401-737-5191; Fax: 401-737-1159.
School—610 Jefferson Blvd., 02886. Tel: 401-737-2721. Mrs. Judith A. Costa, Prin.
Sisters of St. Joseph 1; Lay Teachers 11; Students 166.
Catechesis/Religious Programs—Students 116.
Convent—639 Jefferson Blvd., 02886. Tel: 401-737-6014.

5—ST. GREGORY THE GREAT, (Cowesett) (1961). (Legal title: St. Gregory the Great Church Corporation, Warwick). Revs. Alfred V. Ricci; Roger M. Fortin; Deacon Robert V. Stone.
Res., 41 Sandro Dr., 02886. Tel: 401-884-1666; Fax: 401-884-2448.
Catechesis/Religious Programs—Tel: 401-884-0797.
Students 500.

6—ST. KEVIN, (1956). (Legal title: St. Kevin's Church Corporation, Warwick). Revs. Robert F. Hawkins; Francis W. O'Hara.
Res., 333 Sandy Ln., 02889. Tel: 401-737-2638; Fax: 401-732-2832.
School—39 Cathedral Rd., 02889. Tel: 401-737-7172; Fax: 401-738-2832.
Sisters of Notre Dame de Namur 1; Lay Teachers 24; Students 397.
Catechesis/Religious Programs—Tel: 401-739-6309. Carole Maddock, D.R.E.
Students 464.

7—ST. PETER, (Pawtuxet) (1933). (Legal title: St. Peter's Church, Warwick, Rhode Island). Revs. Peter M. Cavanaugh; John N. Dondapati (India). In res., Rev. Msgr. John F. Cox, Pastor Emeritus.
Res., 350 Fair St., 02888. Tel: 401-467-4895; Fax: 401-785-9282.
School—Tel: 401-781-9242; Fax: 401-467-5673.
Sisters of Mercy of the Americas 2; Lay Teachers 18; Students 270. Co-Principals: Sr. Mary Angelus, R.S.M.; Sr. Kathleen Farley, R.S.M.
Catechesis/Religious Programs—120 Mayfair Rd., 02888. Tel: 401-781-9243.
Students 309.

8—ST. RITA, (Oakland Beach) (1935). (Legal title: Saint Rita's Church Corporation, Oakland Beach). Rev. Bertil J. Anderson.
Res., 722 Oakland Beach Ave., 02886. Tel: 401-738-1800.
Catechesis/Religious Programs—Tel: 401-738-1806.
Students 259.

9—ST. ROSE OF LIMA, (Greenwood) (1950). Merged with St. Clement to form St. Rose of Lima/St. Clement, Warwick. (Legal title: Saint Rose's Church Corporation, Warwick).

10—ST. ROSE OF LIMA/ST. CLEMENT. Consolidation of St. Rose of Lima and St. Clement. (Legal title: St. Clement's Church Corporation, Warwick) (Legal title: St. Rose's Church Corporation, Warwick). Rev. Robert L. Marciano, Admin.
Res., 171 Inman Ave., 02886-1700. Tel: 401-739-0212; Fax: 401-732-4144.
School—St. Rose of Lima, 200 Brentwood Ave., 02886. Tel: 401-739-6937; Fax: 401-737-4632. Mrs. Linda E. LeBeau, Prin.
Lay Teachers 10; Students 240.

11—ST. TIMOTHY, (Hoxie) (1950). (Legal title: Saint Timothy's Church Corporation, Warwick). Revs. James J. Hamilton; David E. Green.
Res., 1799 Warwick Ave., 02889. Tel: 401-739-9552; Fax: 401-738-2466.
Catechesis/Religious Programs—101 Lake Shore Dr., 02889. Tel: 401-738-9079.
Students 355.

12—ST. WILLIAM, (Norwood) (1933). (Legal title: Saint William's Church Corporation, Norwood). Rev. George P. Behan; Deacon Thomas P. O'Hara.
Res., 200 Pettaconsett Ave., 02888. Tel: 401-781-7226; Fax: 401-781-4177.
Catechesis/Religious Programs—Tel: 401-781-0343.
Students 272.

Westerly, Washington Co.,

1—ST. CLARE, (Misquamicut) (1946). (Legal title: Saint Clare's Church Corporation, Misquamicut). Rev. Edmund H. Fitzgerald.
Res., 4 Saint Clare Way, Misquamicut, 02891. Tel: 401-348-8765.
Catechesis/Religious Programs—Tel: 401-596-1838.
Students 206.

2—IMMACULATE CONCEPTION, (1885). (Legal title: Church of the Immaculate Conception of Westerly, Rhode Island). Revs. Wilfrid G. Gregoire; Douglas S. Sweet; Deacon Robert Alessio.
Res., 111 High St., 02891. Tel: 401-596-2130.
Catechesis/Religious Programs—Tel: 401-596-0900; Fax: 401-348-2351. D.R.E.: Mrs. Rosemary Buonocore; Mrs. Lorraine Morrone.
Students 451.

3—ST. PIUS X, (1955). (Legal title: St. Pius X Parish Corporation, Westerly). Revs. Lawrence E. Toole; Raymond N. Suriani.
Res., 44 Elm St., 02891. Tel: 401-596-2535.
School—32 Elm St., 02891. Tel: 401-596-5735.
Lay Teachers 10; Students 200.
Catechesis/Religious Programs—Tel: 401-596-8530.
Students 214.

4—ST. VINCENT DE PAUL, (Bradford) (1946). (Legal title: Saint Vincent's Church Corporation, Bradford). Rev. James V. Farley.
Res., P.O. Box 277, 5 Church St., Bradford, 02808. Tel: 401-377-2289; Fax: 401-377-8830.
Catechesis/Religious Programs—Tel: 401-377-8435.
Students 199.

West Warwick, Kent Co.,

1—ST. ANTHONY, (Riverpoint) (1925) (Portuguese). (Legal title: Saint Anthony's Church Corporation, River Point). Rev. Reinaldo M. Cardoso.
Res., 10 Sunset Ave., 02893. Tel: 401-821-8342.
Catechesis/Religious Programs—Students 189.

2—CHRIST THE KING, (Centreville) (1931) (French). (Legal title: Church of Christ the King, West Warwick). Rev. George L. Allard. In res., Rev. David F. Ricard, Chap., Kent County Memorial Hospital, Warwick.
Res., 120 Legris Ave., 02893. Tel: 401-821-9228. [JC]
Catechesis/Religious Programs—130 Legris Ave., 02893. Tel: 401-823-3443. D.R.E.: Mrs. Janice Rousselle; Mrs. Laurie Masse.
Students 242.

3—ST. JAMES, (Arctic) (1908). (Legal title: Saint James Church of Arctic). Revs. James P. Hynes; Kevin R. Fisette.
Res., 1270 Main St., P.O. Box 1346, 02893. Tel: 401-821-7323; Fax: 401-821-7323.
Catechesis/Religious Programs—Tel: 401-828-5059.
Students 160.

4—ST. JOHN'S, (Arctic) (1874) (French). (Legal title: St. John the Baptist Church of Centreville, Rhode Island). Revs. Barry M. Meehan; Alphonse O. Lethiez (Haiti).
Res., 20 Washington St., 02893. Tel: 401-821-7661; Fax: 401-826-7274. [CEM]
School—St. John the Baptist School, 17 St. John St., 02893. Tel: 401-821-5285; Fax: 401-826-2950. Sr. Claudette Brunelle, P.M., Prin.; Sr. Claire Marie, P.M., Supr.
Sisters of the Presentation of Mary 5; Lay Teachers 12; Students 207.
Catechesis/Religious Programs—Students 143.

5—ST. JOSEPH, (Natick) (1873). (Legal title: St. Joseph's Church, Natick RI). Rev. Charles H. Downing; Deacons Laurence O. Gagnon; Robert L. Gallo, Hispanic Ministry.
Res., 854 Providence St., 02893-1140. Tel: 401-821-4072.
School—(Grades PreK-8) Wakefield St., 02893. Tel: 401-821-3450.
Religious 1; Deacons 1; Lay Teachers 20; Students 252.
Catechesis/Religious Programs—Students 204.

6—ST. MARY, (Crompton) (1844). (Legal title: St. Mary's Church, Crompton Rhode Island). Rev. Paul F. Reynolds.
Res., 70 Church St., 02893. Tel: 401-821-5555; 822-1006. [CEM][JC]
Catechesis/Religious Programs—Tel: 401-828-8756.
Students 229.

7—OUR LADY OF GOOD COUNSEL, (Phenix) (1897) (French). (Legal title: Church of Our Lady of Good Counsel, Warwick RI). Rev. Paul R. Lemoi.
Res., 60 Pleasant St., 02893. Tel: 401-821-6428. [CEM]
Catechesis/Religious Programs—Tel: 401-822-1869.
Students 147.

8—SS. PETER AND PAUL, (Phenix) (1853). (Legal title: SS. Peter and Paul's Church, Phoenixville, Rhode Island). Rev. Richard A. Bucci, Admin.
Res., 48 Highland St., 02893-5699. Tel: 401-821-2198. [CEM]
Catechesis/Religious Programs—Students 102.

9—SACRED HEART CHURCH, (Natick) (1929) (Italian). (Legal title: Church of the Sacred Heart, Natick RI). Rev. Robert J. Giardina.
Res., 820 Providence St., 02893. Tel: 401-821-4184; Fax: 401-828-8883.
Catechesis/Religious Programs—Tel: 401-828-5202.
Students 145.

Woonsocket, Providence Co.,

1—ST. AGATHA, (1953). (Legal title: Saint Agatha's Church Corporation, Woonsocket). Rev. Msgr. John C. Allard; Rev. Gerard J. Caron; Deacon Eugene Garceau. In res., Rev. Joseph P. Heaney.
Res., 34 Joffre Ave., 02895. Tel: 401-767-2950.
Catechesis/Religious Programs—Students 122.

2—ST. ALOYSIUS, (1902) (French). (Legal title: Saint Aloysius Church of Woonsocket). Rev. Frederic D. Dean.
Res., 323 Rathbun St., 02895. Tel: 401-762-1100.
Catechesis/Religious Programs—Students 52.

3—ST. ANN, (1890) (French). (Legal title: St. Ann's Church Corporation of Woonsocket RI). Revs. Roger A. Houle; Edward L. Pieroni.
Res., 82 Cumberland St., 02895. Tel: 401-766-0370; Fax: 401-765-6321. [JC]
Catechesis/Religious Programs—Tel: 401-766-5771.
Students 205.
Convent—120 Gaulin Ave., 02895. Tel: 401-766-2485. Sr. Louise Francoise, P.M., Supr.
Sisters of the Presentation of Mary 2.

4—ST. ANTHONY'S, (1924) (Italian). (Legal title: Saint Anthony's Church, Woonsocket RI). Rev. Francis P. Kayatta. In res., Rev. Msgr. George L. Frappier.
Res., 128 Greene St., 02895. Tel: 401-766-2640.
Catechesis/Religious Programs—Fax: 401-765-3646.
Students 60.

5—ST. CHARLES, (1846). (Legal title: St. Charles Borromeo's Church, Woonsocket RI). Rev. D. Bryan Finerty.
Res., 190 N. Main St., 02895. Tel: 401-766-0176; Fax: 401-766-0185. [CEM]
Catechesis/Religious Programs—Tel: 401-766-3088.
Students 78.

6—HOLY FAMILY, (1902) (French). (Legal title: Church of the Holy Family). Rev. Edward G. St. Godard.
Res., 414 S. Main St., 02895. Tel: 401-762-0830.
Catechesis/Religious Programs—Tel: 401-762-3441.
Students 260.

7—ST. JOSEPH, (East Woonsocket) (1929). (Legal title: Saint Joseph's Church, Woonsocket). Revs. Lionel A. Blain; Maurice L. Brindamour.
Res., 1200 Mendon Rd., 02895-3999. Tel: 401-766-0626; Fax: 401-766-0627.
Catechesis/Religious Programs—1210 Mendon Rd., 02895. Tel: 401-766-8233. Jeannine Allard, D.R.E.
Students 450.
Station—Woonsocket Health Center, Tel: 401-765-2100.

8—OUR LADY OF VICTORIES, (1909) (French). (Legal title: Church of Notre Dame des Victoires). Revs. Roger A. Houle, Admin.; Edward L. Pieroni.
Res., 170 Spring St., 02895. Tel: 401-762-0333.
Catechesis/Religious Programs—Students 73.

9—OUR LADY, QUEEN OF MARTYRS, (1953). (Legal title: Our Lady, Queen of Martyrs Church Corporation, Woonsocket). Revs. Paul R. Grenon; John E. Abreu.
Res., 1409 Park Ave., 02895-6597. Tel: 401-762-5117; Fax: 401-765-8875.
Catechesis/Religious Programs—Tel: 401-767-2576; Fax: 401-765-8875.
Students 381.

10—PRECIOUS BLOOD, (1843) (French). (Legal title: The Church of the Precious Blood of Woonsocket, Rhode Island). Rev. Msgr. John C. Allard, Admin.; Rev. Gerard J. Caron. In res., Revs. Henri D. Morin; Albert H. Brindamour.
Res., 94 Carrington Ave., 02895. Tel: 401-762-0326; 883-6600. [CEM]

11—SACRED HEART, (1895). (Legal title: Church of the Sacred Heart Woonsocket RI). Rev. Dennis J. Kieton, Admin.; Deacon Armand R. Brissette, Jr.
Res., 415 Olo St., 02895. Tel: 401-766-3150; Fax: 401-766-6864.
Catechesis/Religious Programs—Tel: 401-766-3151.
Students 152.

12—ST. STANISLAUS, (1905) (Polish). (Legal title: Saint Stanislaus Kostka Church of Woonsocket). Rev. Boguslaw T. Gibowski, Admin.
Res., 174 Harris Ave., 02895. Tel: 401-762-0021.

Chaplains of Public Institutions

PROVIDENCE. *Miriam Hospital* 164 Summit Ave., 02906. Tel: 401-274-3700. Rev. Peter J. Gower, Res., 124 Hillside Ave., Pawtucket, 02860.
Rhode Island Hospital 593 Eddy St., 02902. Tel: 401-277-4000. Rev. John J. Rainone, Res., 92 Hope St., 02906. Rev. John W. O'Brien, Res., 1081 Mineral Spring Ave. N., 02904. Rev. Jose Q. Dos Reis, Res., 2615 Warwick Ave., Warwick, 02889. Rev. Gerald G. Harbour; Sr. Perpetua Lester, R.S.M., Res., 367 Kenyon Ave., Pawtucket, 02861. Ms. Janice Hart, Chap.
Roger Williams Hospital. Pastoral care provided by local parishes. 825 Chalkstone Ave., 02908. Tel: 401-456-2000.
Veterans Administration Hospital Davis Park, 02908. Tel: 401-273-7100. Rev. Francis J. Crowley (BO).

BURRILLVILLE. *Rhode Island-Zambarano State Hospital*. Vacant. Pastoral care provided by Office of Health Ministries. Wallum Lake, 02859.

CRANSTON. *Department of Corrections*. Sr. Theresa Foley, S.S.J., 9 Alma Ave., East Providence, 02916. Archdeacon George Yany, 111 Cross St., Central Falls, 02863. Sr. Agnes Bonville, R.S.M., 716 Brayton Ave., Somerset, MA 02726.
Rhode Island State Institutions Eleanor Slater Hospital, 02893. Rev. Gerard Bernard, M.S.C., Res., 33 Andrews Ave., Apt. B, West Warwick, 02893. Tel: 401-826-0446. Rev. John E. Watterson, Res., 103 Pine St., P.O. Box 518, Pawtucket, 02862. Tel: 401-722-5425.

JOHNSTON. *Port of Providence Catholic Chaplain* 927 Atwood Ave., 02919-6291. Tel: 401-942-5203. Rev. Hector Sartori, C.S.

NEWPORT. *Newport Hospital*. Rev. Francis A. O'Loughlin, Res., 5 Mann Ave., 02840. Tel: 401-847-0065.

NORTH SMITHFIELD. *Landmark Medical Center, Fogarty Unit*. Pastoral care provided by local parishes.

PAWTUCKET. *Memorial Hospital of Rhode Island*. Pastoral care provided by local parishes.

SOUTH KINGSTOWN. *South County Hospital*. Rev. Nicholas P. Smith, Res., 114 High St., Wakefield, 02879-3141. Tel: 401-782-8000.

WARWICK. *Kent County Memorial Hospital*. Rev. David F. Ricard, Res., 120 Legris Ave., West Warwick, 02893.

WESTERLY. *The Westerly Hospital*. Pastoral care provided by local parishes. 25 Wells St., 02891. Tel: 401-596-6000.

WOONSOCKET. *Landmark Medical Center, Woonsocket Unit*. Pastoral care provided by local parishes.

On Duty Outside the Diocese:
Reverend Fathers—
Berthelette, Ernest H., Chap., U.S. Air Force
Bolton, Paul J., Chap., U.S. Army
Brodeur, Dennis A., 477 N. Lindbergh Blvd., St. Louis, MO 63141
Collins, Raymond F., Catholic University of America, Washington, DC
Gallagher, William M., One Cathedral Sq., Providence, RI 02903-3695
Haberek, Jerome A., Chap., U.S. Army
Kelley, Edward J., Chap., U.S. Army
LaMontagne, Bernard L., St. Mary of Woods, IN 47876
Lynch, Cornelius B., Society of St. James
Montecalvo, Carlo F., Chap., U.S. Air Force
O'Neill, Thomas D., Diocese of Victoria
Pincince, Gerald P., 191 Hadley Rd., Sugar Hill, NH 03585
Prendiville, Edmond P., St. Helen Church, 3033 NW 33rd Ave., Fort Lauderdale, FL 33310-1123
Rochon, Robert A., St. Ann's Hospital, Fall River, MA
Tanguay, William H., Dir. Hmong Ministry, c/o Sacred Heart Rectory, 38 Park St., Pawtucket, RI 02860

Absent on Leave:
Reverend Fathers—
Abruzzese, Joseph A.
Allaire, Robert A.
Archambault, Paul A.
Blais, Robert L.
Carpentier, Robert A.
LaMountain, Michael V.
Lepire, Roland M.
Scagnelli, Peter J.

Retired:
Reverend Monsignors—
Brock, Edmund J., St. Antoine Residence, 400 Mendon Rd., North Smithfield, RI 02895
Carey, William J., P.O. Box 16, Jamestown, RI 02835
Cavallaro, Galliano J., 50 Park Row West #712, Providence, RI 02903
Cerrito, Albert J., 402 Elm Ave., Port Charlotte, FL 33952
Cox, John F., 350 Fair St., Warwick, RI 02888
Dunn, Louis W., c/o One Cathedral Sq., Providence, RI 02903-3695
Dziob, Michael W., St. John Vianney Residence, 493 Mt. Pleasant Ave., Providence, RI 02908
Egan, Edward F., St. John Vianney Residence, 493 Mt. Pleasant Ave., Providence, RI 02908
Fagnant, Donat J., 2 Abbot St., Cumberland, RI 02864-8202
Ferland, Oscar R., 190 Usquepaugh Rd., West Kingston, RI 02892
Geoghegan, Arthur T., 1900 S. Ocean Ave., Ft. Lauderdale, FL 33316
Guilbault, Oscar A., 860 N. Quidnessett Rd., North Kingstown, RI 02852
Lloyd, Paul A., Jeanne Jugen Residence, 964 Main St., Pawtucket, RI 02860
Metsy, Norman G., 6467 Oak Shore Dr., Panama City, FL 32404
Murray, William F., P.O. Box 1366, Mashpee, MA 02649
Struck, John W., 7 Seawind Ter., Westerly, RI 02891
Sullivan, Arthur A., 35 Sweetfern Rd., Warwick, RI 02888
Tavares, John E., P.O. Box 1193, Eastham, MA 02642
Reverend Fathers—
Beaulieu, Raymond, P.O. Box 433, Jamestown, RI 02835
Belhumeur, Roger E., 1650 Douglas Ave., North Providence, RI 02904
Besse, Joseph A., 70 Landmark Ave., Warwick, RI 02886
Boland, Edward F., St. John Vianney Residence, 493 Mt. Pleasant Ave., Providence, RI 02908
Borkowski, John A., 19 Helen Ave., Freehold, NJ 07728
Brindamour, Albert H., Precious Blood Rectory, 94 Carrington Ave., Woonsocket, RI 02895-4594
Carmone, Anthony F., P.O. Box 9177, Port Charlotte, FL 33949-9177
Carnevale, Thomas J., 2543 W. Main Rd., Portsmouth, RI 02871
Carty, John T., 43 Phillips Rd., East Greenwich, RI 02818-0472
Dailey, Ronald G., 182 Eldridge St., Cranston, RI 02910
de Serpa, Roberto, Rua Recreio dos Artistas 46-10.D, 9700 Angra do Heroismo, Terceira, Azores
DeLellis, Francis V., 190 S. Weeden Rd., Wakefield, RI 02880
Deneault, Normand J., St. John Vianney Residence, 493 Mt. Pleasant Ave., Providence, RI 02908
Desrosiers, Alfred R., c/o One Cathedral Sq., Providence, RI 02903-3695
Diogo, Louis M., 26 Meadow Rd., Swansea, MA 02777
Doucet, Ovila T., Jeanne Jugan Residence, 964 Main St., Pawtucket, RI 02860
Doyle, John V., 49 Sherwood Valley Ln., Coventry, RI 02816
Dyer, Raymond E., Mt. St. Rita Health Center, 15 Sumner Brown Rd., Cumberland, RI 02864
Ethier, Robert D., 10 Webster St., Pawtucket, RI 02860
Farrell, John F., Box 689, West Kingstown, RI 02892
Fioretti, Jerome, Scalabrini Villa, 860 No. Quidnessett Rd., North Kingstown, RI 02852
Freitas, Fernando P., 29 Bullocks Pt. Ave., Apt. 3A, Riverside, RI 02915-5341
Gagne, Rene E., St. John Vianney Residence, 493 Mt. Pleasant Ave., Providence, RI 02908
Gallagher, Joseph T., P.O. Box 80066, South Dartmouth, MA 02748
Gillen, Timothy L., St. Joseph Rectory, 193 Walcott St., Pawtucket, RI 02860-3266
Gorman, George F., St. John Vianney Residence, 493 Mt. Pleasant Ave., Providence, RI 02908
Hart, Thomas B., P.O. Box 921, Portsmouth, RI 02871
Hazebrouck, Maurice L., 41 Hazebrouck St., Cumberland, RI 02864
Heaney, Joseph P., St. Agatha Rectory, 34 Joffre Ave., Woonsucket, RI 02895
Horgan, Joseph E., 25 Leading St., Johnston, RI 02919
Hunt, Patrick J., 23 Willis Dr., Cumberland, RI 02964
Iacovacci, Nicholas J., St. Mary Rectory, 538 Broadway, Providence, RI 02909
Johnson, Edward A., 719 Deer Run Villa, St. Simons Is., GA 31522
King, Donald J., St. John Vianney Residence, 493 Mt. Pleasant Ave., Providence, RI 02908
Lacasse, Roger, St. Ann Rectory, 82 Cumberland St., Woonsocket, RI 02895
Lambert, Joseph J., St. John Vianney Residence, 493 Mt. Pleasant Ave., Providence, RI 02908
Marot, Roger L., Father Marot CYO Center, 53-77 Federal St., Woonsocket, RI 02895
Maynard, Leon C., St. John Vianney Residence, 493 Mt. Pleasant Ave., Providence, RI 02908
Maynard, Richard C., St. Joseph Rectory, 193 Walcott St., Pawtucket, RI 02860-3266
Maynard, Robert J., 1 St. Paul Pl., Cranston, RI 02905
McElroy, John J., 193 Walcott St., Pawtucket, RI 02860
McGovern, Edward J., St. John Vianney Residence, 493 Mt. Pleasant Ave., Providence, RI 02908
Mendonsa, August F., 106 Allerton Ave., East Providence, RI 02914
Micarelli, Edmond C., c/o One Cathedral Sq., Providence, RI 02903-3695
Moniz, Hyacinth, 825 Wakefield St., Box 84, West Warwick, RI 02893
Morin, Henri D., 94 Carrington Ave., Woonsocket, RI 02895
Murphy, Joseph F.
Murphy, William F., St. John Vianney Residence, 493 Mount Pleasant Ave., Providence, RI 02908
Narewski, Peter J., St. John Vianney Residence, 493 Mt. Pleasant Ave., Providence, RI 02908
Rafferty, Raymond J., St. James Well, Greenore, County Louth, Ireland
Randall, Robert J., 2322 Oliver Hazzard Perry Hwy., Wakefield, RI 02880
Raspallo, Domenic, 38 Oaklawn Ave., Cranston, RI 02920
Robitaille, Henry J., 5 Costilla Lane, Spanish Lakes River Front, Port St. Lucie, FL 34952
Santurri, Joseph, Residenza Maria Marcella, Via della Vignaccia, 197 (Aurelio), 00163 Rome, Italy
Schenick, Joseph D., 70 Homer St., Providence, RI 02905
Shanley, Joseph D., 167 Blackstone St., Woonsocket, RI 02895
Silva, James M., c/o One Cathedral Sq., Providence, RI 02903
Sullivan, Timothy J., 309 Spring St., Newport, RI 02840
Szymanski, Bronislaus, Pl. Jana Pawla II, 1, Lomza, 18-400 Poland
Thadeu, Joseph S., 62 Griffith Dr., East Providence, RI 02915
Thomson, Paul van K., P.O. Box 814, Wakefield, RI 02880
Trainor, James T., St. John Vianney Residence, 493 Mt. Pleasant Ave., Providence, RI 02908
Turillo, B. Samuel, 215 Old Succotash Rd., South Kingstown, RI 02880
Valois, Normand W., 30 Fenner St., Providence, RI 02903
Walsh, Clyde J., St. John Vianney Residence, 493 Mt. Pleasant Ave., Providence, RI 02908
Young, Peter G., 624 Woonasquatucket Ave., North Providence, RI 02911

Permanent Deacons:
Alessio, Robert G., St. Clare, Misquamicut
Andrade, Charles, St. Patrick, Providence
Archambault, Bernard L., St. Joseph's, Woonsocket
Bacon, Normand J., St. Eugene, Chepachet
Baker, John F., St. Catherine, Warwick
Barboza, Benjamin, St. Mary, Bristol
Batalon, Raymond E., St. Edward, Pawtucket
Bisbano, Paul, Our Lady of Mount Carmel, Bristol
Bouchard, Thomas, St. Joseph, Woonsocket
Boutier, Thomas F., Blessed Sacrament, Providence
Braga, Joseph F., St. Charles, Providence

Brissette, Armand, Jr., Sacred Heart, Woonsocket
Callahan, Raymond F., St. Mary's, West Warwick
Carpenter, Robert A., Raleigh, NC
Ceprano, Peter A., St. Mary, Cranston
Conley, James E., St. Mary of the Bay, Warren
Cordeiro, Manuel, St. Patrick, Providence
Corey, John A., St. Kevin, Warwick
Dadlez, Mark A., St. Alexander, Warren
Daidone, Salvatore A., Christ the King, Jacksonville, FL
DePetrillo, Albert, St. Thomas, Providence
DePietro, Ronald H., St. Francis de Sales, North Kingstown
DiOrio, Dominic P., Holy Angels, Barrington
Dufour, John, St. Joan, Cumberland
Edsall, Noel, St. Francis de Sales, North Kingstown
Forlingieri, Carmine, Immaculate Conception, Cranston
Gagnon, Laurence O., Sr., St. Joseph, West Warwick
Gallo, Robert L., Sacred Heart, West Warwick
Garceau, Eugene, St. Agatha, Woonsocket
Garcia, Luis, Assumption, Providence
Gauthier, Clovis, Our Lady of Consolation, Pawtucket
Gederman, Harris J., St. Philip, Greenville
Gomez, Oscar, St. Teresa, Providence
Goulart, Joseph, Sr., St. Catherine's, Little Compton
Holder, Lawrence C., Diocese of Orlando, FL
Horton, Gregory, St. James, Manville
Johnson, Loring F., Assumption, Providence
Keogh, Richard B., Christ the King, Kingston
LaFleur, Norman R., St. John the Evangelist, Slatersville
LaFrance, Raymond J., St. Francis de Sales, North Kingstown
Lagesse, Raymond M., St. John's, Pawtucket
Lambert, Paul H., St. John Vianney, Cumberland
Lapierre, Richard J., Our Lady of Good Help, Mapleville
Lennon, Thomas J., Immaculate Conception, Cranston
Levesque, Raymond E., Holy Ghost, Tiverton
Lucian, Robert C., Diocese of St. Augustine, FL
MacLure, Robert, St. Patrick, Providence
Martins, Jesse L., St. Theresa, Tiverton
Martins, Manuel, St. Anthony, Pawtucket
Masse, Kevin P., St. Francis, Warwick
Masse, Paul, St. John the Evangelist, Slatersville
Maynard, Jacques, St. Mary's, West Warwick (Crompton)
McAdam, Robert, St. Augustine's, Providence
Millard, Charles E., M.D., St. Mary of the Bay, Warren
Morisseau, Robert M., St. Benedict, Warwick
Mulcahy, Robert, St. Joseph's, Woonsocket
Napolitano, Michael D., Our Lady of Good Counsel, West Warwick
Nicholson, Robert E., St. Teresa, Pawtucket
Nova, Leocadio, St. Aloysius, Woonsocket
O'Hara, Thomas P., St. William, Warwick
Ouellette, Lucien, St. Maria Goretti, Pawtucket
Ragosta, Armand, St, Mary, Cranston
Raspallo, Thomas R., Immaculate Conception, Cranston
Riccio, Raymond L., St. Rocco, Johnston
Rico, Jose, St. Charles Borromeo, Providence
Sabetti, Carlo J., St. Philip, Greenville
Sadowski, Edward J., Jr., St. Vincent de Paul, Coventry
Sardinha, John, St. Elizabeth's, Bristol
Sheehy, C. Patrick, St. Mary, Pawtucket
Sinesi, Rugiero A., Christ the King, West Warwick
Small, William A., St. Michael, Esmond
Stone, Francis J., St. Peter, Warwick
Stone, Robert V., St. Peter, Warwick
Sullivan, Paul J., St. Thomas More, Narragansett
Tanguay, Paul A., Sacred Heart, East Providence
Theroux, Bernard G., St. Mary, Bristol
Theroux, Paul A., St. Francis of Assisi, Wakefield
Tribelli, Anthony A., St. Ann's, Cranston
Troia, Robert, St. Rocco's, Thornton
Tumminelli, Joseph P., St. Robert Bellamine, Johnston
Turbitt, Robert A., II, SS. John and Paul, Coventry
Turcotte, Joseph G., St. Francis of Assisi, Wakefield
Urrico, Francis X., St. Bernard, North Kingstown
Vani, Louis A., Presentation of the Blessed Virgin Mary, North Providence
Wendoloski, Anthony, Jr., Our Lady of Lourdes, Providence
West, Harry A., Jr., St. Teresa, Providence
Young, Frederick A., Holy Name, Providence

INSTITUTIONS LOCATED IN THE DIOCESE

[A] SEMINARIES, DIOCESAN

PROVIDENCE. *Seminary of Our Lady of Providence*, (House of Formation for College Students), 485 Mt. Pleasant Ave., 02908. Tel: 401-331-1316.
E-mail: vocatione@aol.com
Revs. Marcel E. Pincince, Vocation Dir. - Rector; Paul E. Desmarais, Spiritual Dir. Legal Title: *Seminary of Our Lady of Providence*. Students 3.

[B] COLLEGES AND UNIVERSITIES

PROVIDENCE. *Providence College*, River Ave. & Eaton St., 02918. Tel: 401-865-1000; Fax: 401-865-2057.
E-mail: pcadmiss@providence.edu
Web site: http://www.providence.edu
For a complete listing, refer to the Colleges and Universities section.

NEWPORT. *Salve Regina University*, 02840-4192. Tel: 401-847-6650; Fax: 401-847-0372.
E-mail: sruadmis@salve.edu
Web site: www.salve.edu
For a complete listing, refer to the Colleges and Universities section.

[C] HIGH SCHOOLS, DIOCESAN

PAWTUCKET. *St. Raphael Academy*, 123 Walcott St., 02860. Tel: 401-723-8100; 723-8740. Rev. Francis C. Santilli, Chap.; Bro. Thomas Casey, F.S.C., Prin. Conducted by the Brothers of the Christian Schools with the Religious of the Holy Union of the Sacred Hearts, Sisters of Mercy of the Americas, and Sisters of St. Chretienne. Legal Title: *Saint Raphael's Academy*. Brothers 5; Sisters 4; Lay Teachers 34; Students-Boys 268; Girls 252.

SOUTH KINGSTOWN. *The Prout School*. 4640 Tower Hill Rd., Wakefield, 02879. Tel: 401-884-0264; 789-9262; Fax: 401-782-2262. Bro. Edmond Precourt, F.S.C., Prin. Brothers 1; Sisters 1; Lay Teachers 31; Students-Boys 171; Girls 213. Legal Title: *The Prout School*.

WARWICK. *Bishop Hendricken High School*, 2615 Warwick Ave., 02889. Tel: 401-739-3450; Fax: 401-732-8261. Revs. Marcel L. Taillon, Chap.; Jose Q. dos Reis, Chap. of the Brothers; Bro. Kevin Cawley, C.F.C., Pres. & Prin. Congregation of Christian Brothers. Legal Title: *Bishop Hendricken High School*. Priests 1; Brothers 8; Sisters 2; Lay Teachers 48; Boys 832.

[D] HIGH SCHOOLS, REGIONAL

PAWTUCKET. *Bishop Francis P. Keough Regional High School*, 145 Power Rd., 02860. Tel: 401-726-0335; Fax: 401-726-0336. Jeanne H. Leclerc, Prin. Sisters 2; Lay Teachers 10; Girls 75.

[E] HIGH SCHOOLS, PRIVATE

PROVIDENCE. *La Salle Academy*. (Grades 7-12), 612 Academy Ave., 02908. Tel: 401-351-7750; Fax: 401-453-6315.
E-mail: diaroche@loa.com
Web site: http://www.loa.com/lasalle
Bro. A. Jerome Corrigan, F.S.C., Pres.; Mr. Michael Scanlan, Prin.; Rev. Albert A. Kenney, Chap. Conducted by the Brothers of the Christian Schools. Legal Title: *St. John De La Salle Institute*. Priests 1; Brothers 8; Sisters 1; Lay Teachers 75; Students 1,155; Total Staff 107.

COVENTRY. *St. Xavier Academy*, 2 Saint Vincent de Paul St., 02816. Tel: 401-826-2130.
E-mail: cosxa001@llwsbe.wsbe.org
Friends of St. Xavier. Mrs. Kathleen Siok, Prin. Lay Teachers 10; Girls 60.

EAST PROVIDENCE. *St. Mary Academy*. (Grades 7-12). Bayview, 3070 Pawtucket Ave., Riverside, 02915. Tel: 401-434-0113; Fax: 401-483-5936. Sisters of Mercy of the Americas and Sisters of St. Joseph. Sr. Elizabeth McAuliffe, R.S.M., Pres.; Ms. Colleen Gribbon, Prin. Sisters 15; Lay Teachers 51; Girls 668.

PORTSMOUTH. *Portsmouth Abbey School*, Cory's Ln., 02871. Tel: 401-683-2000. Rt. Rev. F. Mark Serna, O.S.B., Headmaster. Legal Title: *Order of St. Benedict in Portsmouth, Rhode Island*. Priests 9; Brothers 3; Lay Teachers 38; Students 290.

SMITHFIELD. *Immaculate Conception Academy*. 60 Austin Ave., Greenville, 02828. Tel: 401-949-2820. Ms. Maria Bracket, Prin.; Rev. David Chaves, L.C., Chap. Boarding School Students 46.

WARREN. *Our Lady of Fatima High School*. (Grades 7-12), 360 Market St., Rte. 136, 02885. Tel: 401-245-4449. Sr. Mary Margaret Souza, S.S.D., Prin. Sisters of St. Dorothy. Sisters 4; Lay Teachers 14; Students 150.

WOONSOCKET. *Mt. St. Charles Academy*. (Grades 7-12), 02895-5599. Tel: 401-769-0310; Fax: 401-762-2327.
E-mail: mtstcharlesadmin@edgenet
Bros. Robert R. Croteau, S.C., Pres.; Clifford M. King, S.C., Prin. Brothers of the Sacred Heart. Legal Title: *Mount Saint Charles Academy, Inc.* Brothers 15; Sisters 1; Lay Teachers 44; Students 860.

[F] ELEMENTARY SCHOOLS, PRIVATE

PROVIDENCE. *San Miguel School*, 12 Carter St., 02907. Tel: 401-467-9777. Bro. Lawrence Goyette, F.S.C. Students 59; Brothers 2; Sisters 1; Lay Teachers 5.

CUMBERLAND. *Mercymount Country Day School*, Wrentham Rd., 02864. Tel: 401-333-5919.
E-mail: cmmda001@llwsbe.wsbe.org
Sr. Martha Mulligan, R.S.M., Prin. Sisters of Mercy of the Americas. Sisters 5; Lay Teachers 24; Students 387.

EAST PROVIDENCE. *St. Mary Academy*. Day Pupils. Bayview, 3070 Pawtucket Ave., Riverside, 02915. Tel: 401-438-4635. Sisters of Mercy of the Americas. Sr. Norma Fleming, R.S.M., Prin. Sisters 4; Lay Teachers 12; Students 288.

NEWPORT. *St. Joseph of Cluny Sisters' School, Inc.* (Grades K-8). Day School, Brenton Rd., 02840. Tel: 401-847-6043; Fax: 401-846-0281. Sr. Yvonne Kelly, S.J.C., Prin. Sisters 4; Lay Teachers 16; Students 247.

PORTSMOUTH. *St. Philomena School*, Cory's Lane, 02871. Tel: 401-683-0268. Sisters Faithful Companions of Jesus. Sr. Ann Marie Walsh, F.C.J., Prin. Teaching Sisters 2; Lay Teachers 32; Students 449.

[G] REGIONAL ELEMENTARY SCHOOLS

PROVIDENCE. *Bishop McVinney Regional School*, 155 Gordon Ave., 02905. Tel: 401-781-2370. (Grades PreK-3). Elementary Division: Sr. Lillian Dempsey, C.P., Prin. Sisters 2; Lay Teachers 8; Students 195.

Middle Division. (Grades 4-8), 155 Harrison St., 02907. Tel: 401-331-5714. Sr. Theresina Scully, C.P., Prin. & Exec. Dir. Sisters 1; Lay Staff 8; Students 159. Legal Title: *Catholic Association for Regional Education*.

St. Thomas Regional School, 15 Edendale Ave., 02911. Tel: 401-351-0403. Patricia A. Wolfert, Prin. Sisters 3; Lay Teachers 12; Students 270.

CENTRAL FALLS. *St. Elizabeth Ann Seton Academy*, 909 Lonsdale Ave., 02863. Tel: 401-728-6230. Sr. Ann McKenna, R.S.M., Prin. Sisters 5; Lay Teachers 19; Students 278.

CRANSTON. *Cranston-Johnston Catholic Regional School*, 43 Poplar Dr., 02920. Tel: 401-942-7245.
E-mail: crcrt027@wsbe.wsbe.org
Deacon Thomas R. Raspallo, Prin. Sisters 1; Deacons 1; Lay Teachers 22; Students 420.

EAST GREENWICH. *Our Lady of Mercy Regional School*. (Grades PreK-6), Fourth Ave., 02818. Tel: 401-884-1618. Miss Barbara C. Dwyer, Prin. Sisters 4; Lay Teachers 22; Students 341.

PAWTUCKET. *Woodlawn Catholic Regional School*. (Grades K-8), 61 Hope St., 02860. Tel: 401-723-3759.
E-mail: pawcaool@llushe.wsbe.org
Sr. Martha M. Serbst, R.S.M., Prin. Sisters 5; Lay Teachers 5; Students 262.

PORTSMOUTH. *All Saints Academy, The Newport County Catholic Regional School*. (Grades K-8), 2836 E. Main Rd., 02871. Tel: 401-683-1377. Sr. Marie Baldi, S.U.S.C., Prin. Sisters 3; Lay Teachers 8; Students 130.

WAKEFIELD. *Monsignor Matthew F. Clarke Regional School*. (Grades PreK-6), Tower Hill Rd., 02879. Tel: 401-789-0860. Sr. Aideen Langan, C.P., Prin. Sisters 1; Lay Teachers 16; Students 360.

WARWICK. *Overbrook Academy at Our Lady of Providence Center*. (Boarding School), 836 Warwick Neck Ave., 02889. Tel: 401-737-2850.
E-mail: overbrook@ids.net
Miss Bertha Del Toro, Prin./Dir.; Rev. David Chaves, L.C., Chap. Students 89.

WEST WARWICK. *Notre Dame Regional School*. (Grades K-8), 59 Pleasant St., 02893. Tel: 401-821-6334. Sr. Patricia Langton, O.P., Prin. Sisters 2; Lay Teachers 10; Students 191.

[H] THE GREATER WOONSOCKET CATHOLIC REGIONAL SCHOOL SYSTEM

Member Schools

BURRILLVILLE. *Father Holland Catholic Regional Elementary School*. (Grades PreK-6). 180 Sayles Ave., Pascoag, 02859. Tel: 401-568-4589. Students 185. Mailing Address: Regional Administration, P.O. Box 487, 1 Social St., Woonsocket, 02895. Tel: 401-762-1095. Shawn A. Carpon, Prin.

WOONSOCKET. *Good Shepherd Catholic Regional Middle School*. (Grades 6-8), 1210 Mendon Rd., 02895. Tel: 401-767-5906. Mrs. Marianne Alger, Admin.; Mrs. Louise P. Kane, Prin. Lay Teachers 9; Students 199.

Monsignor Gadoury Regional Primary School. (Grades PreK-3), 1371 Park Ave., 02895. Tel: 401-767-5902. Constance McClure, Prin. Lay Teachers 6; Students 156.

Our Lady of Victories Regional Primary School. (Grades K-3), 148 Spring St., 02895. Tel: 401-767-5904. Mr. Armand B. Houle, Prin. Lay Teachers 9; Students 202.

St. Joseph Intermediate Regional School. (Grades 4-5), 1210 Mendon Rd., 02895. Tel: 401-767-5907. Mrs. Louise Kane, Prin. Lay Teachers 6; Students 121.

[I] CHILD CARING FACILITIES

PROVIDENCE. *Group Home for Adolescent Boys,* (Whitemarsh House), 20 Eighth St., 02906. Tel: 401-351-7230. Bro. John McHale, O.L.P., Dir. Boys 60.

NARRAGANSETT. *Ocean Tides,* 635 Ocean Rd., 02882-1314. Tel: 401-789-1016. Bros. Brendan Gerrity, F.S.C., Pres.; Timothy Balfe, F.S.C., Dir. Social Svcs.; John Norton, F.S.C., Court Liaison. Legal Title: *Ocean Tides, Inc.* Brothers 6; Lay Teachers 14; Lay Staff 27; Students 70.

[J] DAY NURSERIES

PROVIDENCE. *Carter Day Nursery,* 239 Public St., 02905. Tel: 401-751-9752. Nicole F. Curran, B.S., Dir.; Mrs. Alexandra Moser, B.A., Exec. Dir. Day care provided for 126 children. Legal Title: *The Nazareth Home.* Total Asisted 100; Total Staff 17.

St. Vincent Day Care Center, 485 Mt. Pleasant Ave., 02908. Tel: 401-274-3094. Mrs. Alexandra F. Moser, B.A., Exec. Dir./Program Dir. Day care provided for 71 children. Legal Title: *Saint Vincent de Paul Infant Asylum.* Total Assisted 71; Total Staff 21.

LINCOLN. *Mount St. Francis Day Care Center,*. 57 Division St., Manville, 02838. Tel: 401-767-2829. Mrs. Alexandra Moser, B.A., Exec. Dir. & Program Dir. Day care provided for 121 children three years old through Kindergarten full day. Legal Title: *Mount St. Francois of Woonsocket, RI.* Total Assisted 121; Total Staff 19.

NEWPORT. *Garrettson Memorial Day Care Nursery,* 299 Spring St., 02840. Tel: 401-846-6470. Mary Ann Altrui, M.S.W., Dir. Day care & licensed kindergarten provided for 90 children between the ages of 2-6 years old. Legal Title: *The Saint Clare Home.* Lay Teachers 12.

[K] GENERAL HOSPITALS

PROVIDENCE. *St. Joseph Health Services of Rhode Island - St. Joseph Hospital for Specialty Care,* 21 Peace St., 02907. Tel: 401-456-3000.
Web site: www.saintjosephri.com
For a complete listing, refer to the Hospitals section.

NORTH PROVIDENCE. *St. Joseph Health Services of Rhode Island - Our Lady of Fatima Hospital,* 200 High Service Ave., 02904. Tel: 401-456-3000.
Web site: www.saintjosephri.com
For a complete listing, refer to the Hospitals section.

[L] VISITING AND NURSING OF THE SICK

PROVIDENCE. *Holy Spirit Convent,* 43 Westerly Ave., 02909. Tel: 401-946-5639. Daughters of the Holy Spirit. Sr. Louis Ernest Brodeur, D.H.S., Contact Person. Sisters 2; Visiting Sisters 2; Visits 187; Number of patients 45.

[M] HOMES FOR AGED

PROVIDENCE. *St. Joseph Living Center,* 153 Dean St., 02903. Tel: 401-272-3335
For a complete listing, refer to the Special Care Facilities section.

CUMBERLAND. *Mount St. Rita Health Centre,* 15 Sumner Brown Rd., 02864. Tel: 401-333-6352
For a complete listing, refer to the Special Care Facilities section.

NEWPORT. *St. Clare Home,* 309 Spring St., 02840. Tel: 401-849-3204; Fax: 401-849-5780
For a complete listing, refer to the Special Care Facilities section.

NORTH KINGSTOWN. *Scalabrini Villa,* 860 N. Quidnessett Rd., 02852. Tel: 401-884-1802.
E-mail: ejm@bdol.com
For a complete listing, refer to the Special Care Facilities section.

NORTH SMITHFIELD. *St. Antoine Residence,* 400 Mendon Rd., 02896. Tel: 401-767-3500
For a complete listing, refer to the Special Care Facilities section.

PAWTUCKET. *Jeanne Jugan Apartments,* 310 Sayles Ave., 02860
For a complete listing, refer to the Special Care Facilities section.

Jeanne Jugan Residence, 964 Main St., 02860. Tel: 401-723-4314; Fax: 401-727-2885
For a complete listing, refer to the Special Care Facilities section.

WOONSOCKET. *Saint Francis House,* 167 Blackstone St., 02895. Tel: 401-762-5255
For a complete listing, refer to the Special Care Facilities section.

[N] CAMPS AND COMMUNITY CENTERS

PROVIDENCE. *McAuley House,* 163 Niagara St., 02907. Tel: 401-941-9013. Legal Title: *The McAuley Corporation.* Sr. Ann L. Welch, R.S.M., Dir. Total under care annually 25,000.

McAuley Village, 325 Niagara St., 02907-2000. Tel: 401-467-3630. Legal Title: *The McAuley Corporation.* Sr. Dolores Crowley, R.S.M., Exec. Dir. Sisters of Mercy 2; Families assisted 22; Children in day care center 46; Total Staff 11.

St. Francis Chapel & City Ministry Center, 58 Weybosset St., 02903. Tel: 401-331-6510.
Web site: www.ids.net/st_francis_chapel
Rev. David I. Covertino, O.F.M., Guardian & Dir.

St. Martin de Porres Multi-Purpose Center, 160 Cranston St., 02907. Tel: 401-274-6783. Legal Title: *St. Martin de Porres Center.* Wayne B. Houle, Dir. Total under care 2,100; Total Assisted 2,300; Total Staff 12.

BURRILLVILLE. *Mater Spei Day Camp.* Box W, Chepachet, 02814. Tel: 401-568-2473. Maria Piccirilli, Dir.

CRANSTON. *Rejoice in Hope Youth Center,* 804 Dyer Ave., 02920. Tel: 401-942-6571. Patricia Kane, Dir.

EAST PROVIDENCE. *Emmaus Youth Center - Region 4.* 25 Metropolitan Park Dr., Riverside, 02915. Tel: 401-433-4327.
E-mail: emmauscyo@juno.com
Marie Piccirilli, Dir.

PAWTUCKET. *Father Barry CYO Center,* 38 Denver St., 02860. Tel: 401-723-5111; 723-5119; Fax: 401-723-1757.
E-mail: frbarrycyo@juno.com
Legal Title: *Father Barry CYO Center.* Ms. Colette M. Savaria, Dir.

SOUTH KINGSTOWN. *St. Dominic Savio Youth Center.* Broad Rock Rd., P.O. Box 67, Peace Dale, 02883. Tel: 401-783-4055; 783-9123; Fax: 401-789-4630. Legal Title: *St. Dominic Savio Boys' Center.* Ms. Marie L. Lachapelle, Dir.

Tower Hill Camp. Broad Rock Rd., P.O. Box 67, Peace Dale, 02883. Tel: 401-783-9123; Fax: 401-789-4630. Legal Title: *Rhode Island Home for Working Boys.* Ms. Marie L. Lachapelle, Dir.

WARWICK. *Our Lady of Providence Center,* 836 Warwick Neck Ave., 02889. Tel: 401-739-6850. Legal Title: *OLP Center, Inc.* Mrs. Paulette M. Turcotte, Dir.

WOONSOCKET. *Fr. Marot CYO Center,* 53 Federal St., 02895. Legal Title: *CYO of Northern Rhode Island.* Co-Directors: Miss Fern Dery; Mr. Roland Berard; Rev. Roger L. Marot, Spiritual Dir.

[O] PERSONAL PRELATURES

PROVIDENCE. *Opus Dei, Mathewson House,* 224 Bowen St., 02906. Tel: 401-272-7834. Rev. Michael J. Manz.

[P] MONASTERIES AND RESIDENCES OF PRIESTS AND BROTHERS

PROVIDENCE. *Brothers of Our Lady of Providence,* 164 Massachusetts Ave., 02907. Tel: 401-461-6638. Office, 20 Eighth St., 02906. Tel: 401-351-7230. Bro. John McHale, O.L.P., Supr. Brothers 2.

St. Francis Friary, 58 Weybosset St., 02903. Tel: 401-331-6510; Fax: 401-453-0034.
Web site: www.ids.net/st_francis_chapel
Legal Title: *St. Francis Weybosset Street Chapel, Inc.* Franciscan Friars. Revs. David I. Convertino, O.F.M., Guardian; William Beaudin, O.F.M., Vicar; John J. Marino, O.F.M.; Severin Brady, O.F.M.; Gerald H. Brennan, O.F.M.; Hugh Eller, O.F.M.; Stephen Lynch, O.F.M.; Ambrose Donehue, O.F.M.; Jude R. Murphy, O.F.M.; John B. Valente, O.F.M.; Michael Purich, O.F.M. Priests 10; Novices 7.

St. John Vianney Residence, 493 Mt. Pleasant Ave., 02908. Tel: 401-331-9870. Residence for Senior Priests. Rev. Edward J. McGovern, Coord. Residents: Rev. Msgr. Louis W. Dunn; Rev. Msgr. Michael W. Dziob; Rev. Msgr. Edward F. Egan; Revs. Edward F. Boland; Normand J. Deneault; Rene E. Gagne; George F. Gorman; Donald J. King; Joseph J. Lambert; Leon C. Maynard; Joseph F. Murphy; William F. Murphy; Peter J. Narewski; James T. Trainor; Clyde J. Walsh. Priests 16.

St. Pius Priory, 55 Elmhurst Ave., 02908. Tel: 401-751-4871; Fax: 401-273-1089. Legal Title: *Dominican Fathers.* Very Rev. Kenneth R. Letoile, O.P., Prior; Revs. Michael DeTemple, O.P.; Michael P. Trainor, O.P.; Bro. Denis Swann, O.P. Priests 4; Brothers 1.

St. Thomas Aquinas Priory at Providence College, 333 Eaton St., 02918-0001. Tel: 401-865-2101 (office). Legal Title: *Priory of St. Thomas Aquinas.* Dominican Friars.
Assigned & Residing in the Priory: Very Rev. Robert J. Hennessey, O.P., Prior; Most Rev. Ernest B. Boland, O.P., Retired Bishop of Multan; Revs. J. Iriarte Andujar, O.P.; Richard Joseph Barranger, O.P.; Albino F. Barrera, O.P.; Robert E. Bond, O.P.; Francis W. Brocato, O.P. (Chicago Prov.); Daniel J. Cassidy, O.P.; Edward L. Cleary, O.P. (Chicago Prov.); George L. Cochran, O.P.; Paul M. Conner, O.P. (Oakland Prov.); Thomas M. Coskren, O.P.; John F. Cunningham, O.P.; G. Adrian Dabash, O.P.; James J. Davis, O.P.; Vincent De Lucia, O.P.; John Martin Diggins, O.P.; James A. Driscoll, O.P.; William David Folsey, O.P.; Joseph J. Guido, O.P.; Kenneth R. Gumbert, O.P. (Oakland Prov.); Ralph T. Hall, O.P.; Leonard P. Hindsley, O.P.; G. Nicholas Ingham, O.P.; P. Augustine Judd, O.P.; Anthony A. Jurgelaitis, O.P.; Terence S. Keegan, O.P.; Bernard F. Langton, O.P.; Joseph L. Lennon, O.P.; Richard A. McAlister, O.P.; James R. McAvey, O.P.; Thomas D. McGonigle, O.P. (Chicago Prov.); J. Stuart McPhail, O.P.; Robert A. Morris, O.P.; Matthew F. Morry, O.P.; Edward T. Myers, O.P.; William P. Marquis, O.P.; Robert D. Myett, O.P.; Francis D. Nealy, O.P.; Mark D. Nowel, O.P.; Fortunate M. Ojiako, O.P. (Nigeria Prov.); John S. Peterson, O.P.; Matthew D. Powell, O.P. (Chicago Prov.); John J. Reid, O.P.; John C. Rubba, O.P.; Paul E. Seaver, O.P.; Kenneth Sicard, O.P.; John Dominic Skalko, O.P.; A. Philip Smith, O.P.; James T. Sullivan, O.P.; Walter Urban Voll, O.P.; Bros. M. Francis Liebold, O.P.; F. Kevin O'Connell, O.P.
Assigned but Living Outside the Priory: Revs. Brian Chrzastek, O.P., (Franciscan House, Chicago); Curtis E. Henritzy, O.P., (The Angelicum, Rome); James Ferrer Quigley, O.P., (The Angelicum, Rome, Italy); John A. Langlois, O.P., (Fribourg, Switzerland); William J. O'Shaughnessy, O.P., (Heritage Hills Nursing Center). Bishops in Residence 1; Priests in Residence 52; Brothers in Residence 2; Priests residing outside Priory 5.

BRISTOL. *St. Columban's Retirement House,* Box 65, Ferry Rd., 02809. Tel: 401-253-6909. Legal Title: *St. Columban's Foreign Mission Society.* Revs. William F. Sullivan, S.S.C., Supr.; Thomas L. Convery, S.S.C.; Norbert F. Feld, S.S.C.; Brian Gallagher, S.S.C.; Michael Harrison, S.S.C.; John C. Healey, S.S.C.; Rudolph Hoza, S.S.C.; Fintan Keegan, S.S.C.; Thomas A. McCormack, S.S.C.; Joseph McSweeney, S.S.C.; Joseph Murrin, S.S.C.; John O'Doherty, S.S.C.; David E. Richers, S.S.C.; James Roddy, S.S.C. Priests 14.

BURRILLVILLE. *Sacred Heart Brothers Provincial House.* Brothers of the Sacred Heart, New England Prov. Legal Title: *The Order of the Brothers of the Sacred Heart of New England, Inc.* Mailing Address: 685 Steere Farm Rd., Pascoag, 02859-4601. Tel: 401-568-8686; 568-3361; Fax: 401-568-9810. Bros. Robert F. Breault, S.C., Prov. Supr. of New England Prov.; Louis J. Laperle, S.C., Exec. Asst. for Finances; Fred U. Bouchard, S.C., Local Supr.; Edward Breault, S.C., Prov. Sec.; Paul F. Hebert, S.C., Exec. Asst. for Missions; Rev. Albert J. Morel, S.C., Chap. Brothers 28.

MANVILLE. *St. James Residence,* 57 Division St., 02838. Tel: 401-762-0769. Bro. Alan Aubin, S.C., Dir. Brothers of the Sacred Heart 10.

NARRAGANSETT. *Christian Brothers' Center,* 635 Ocean Rd., 02882. Tel: 401-789-0244; Fax: 401-783-5303.
E-mail: cbcjdl@aol.com
Legal Title: *Brothers of the Christian Schools, Long Island-New England Province.* Brothers of the Christian Schools. Bros. William Mann, F.S.C., Prov., Visitor; Daniel Casey, F.S.C., Auxiliary Prov., Education/Continuing-Initial Formation; Robert Hazard, F.S.C., Vocation Counselor; Peter Clifford, F.S.C., Dir. Finance/Development; Peter Corlano, Formation Counselor; Rev. Owen F. Goodwin, SS.CC., Chap. Brothers 27; Brothers in the Province 105.

PAWTUCKET. *Brothers of the Christian Schools,* 58 Hancock St., 02860-2629. Tel: 401-725-7815. Bro. Frederick C. Mueller, F.S.C., Dir. Brothers 4.

PORTSMOUTH. *Abbey of St. Gregory the Great,* 285 Cory's Lane, 02871. Tel: 401-683-2000; Fax: 401-683-5888. Legal Title: *Order of St. Benedict in Portsmouth, Rhode Island.* Benedictines of the English Congregation. Rt. Rev. F. Mark Serna, O.S.B., Abbot; Very Rev. R. Ambrose Wolverton, O.S.B., Prior; Rt. Rev. Matthew Stark, O.S.B., Retired Abbot; Revs. Peter Sidler, O.S.B.; H. David Hurst, O.S.B.; Julian Stead, O.S.B.; B. Benedict Lang, O.S.B.; F. Philip Wilson, O.S.B.; R. Maurus Fleming, O.S.B.; A. Damian Kearney, O.S.B.; Michael Stafford, O.S.B.; P. Geoffrey Chase, O.S.B.; Christopher Davis, O.S.B.; Paul McDonald, O.S.B.; T. Edmund Adams, O.S.B.; Caedmon Holmes; P. Paschal Scotti, O.S.B. Abbots 2; Priests 15; Brothers 2.

WOONSOCKET. *Brothers of the Sacred Heart,* 800 Logee St., 02895. Tel: 401-769-0313. Bro. Willie A. Morin, S.C., Local Supr.; Rev. Ronald Dupuis, S.C., Chap. Brothers 9.

St. John's Residence, 159 Earle St., 02895. Tel: 401-766-9677. Bro. John L. Collignon, S.C., Supr. Brothers 8.

[Q] CONVENTS AND RESIDENCES FOR SISTERS

BARRINGTON. *Monastery of Discalced Carmelites*, Nayatt Ave., 02806. Tel: 401-245-3421. Legal Title: *Monastery of Discalced Carmelites at Nayatt, Barrington, RI.* Sr. Genevieve Lawler, O.C.D., Prioress. Professed Sisters 14.

BRISTOL. *Mt. St. Joseph Provincialate*, 13 Monkeywrench Ln., 02809. Tel: 401-253-7835. Sisters of St. Dorothy. Sr. Eileen Egan, S.S.D., Prov. Coord.; Sr. Catherine Rebello, S.S.D., Local Coord. Sisters 5.

CUMBERLAND. *Sisters of Mercy of the Americas, Regional Community of Providence*, Highland View Rd., 02864. Tel: 401-333-6333.
E-mail: mercyri@aol.com
Legal Title: *Sisters of Mercy of Providence, Inc.* Sr. Barbara Riley, R.S.M., Pres. Councilors: Sr. Carol Mary Morrison, R.S.M.; Sr. Sheila Harrington, R.S.M.; Sr. Patricia Combies, R.S.M.; Sr. Maureen McElroy, R.S.M. Sisters 410; Temporary Vows 5; Candidates 3. Sisters of Mercy, Highland View Rd., 02864. Tel: 401-333-2439. Sisters of Mercy 2. Mercycrest Convent, 255 Wrentham Rd., 02864. Tel: 401-333-5283. Sisters of Mercy 2. Mercyknoll Convent, Highland View Rd., 02864. Tel: 401-333-6804. Sisters of Mercy 2. Mercymount Convent, Wrentham Rd., 02864. Tel: 401-333-0158. Sisters of Mercy 4.

EAST POVIDENCE. *St. Mary Convent*. Bay View, 3070 Pawtucket Ave., Ste. 2, Riverside, 02915-5197. Sr. Carmen Demeule, R.S.M., Co-Dir.; Sr. Rita Bartley, R.S.M., Co-Dir. Sisters of Mercy of the Americas 54.

NARRAGANSETT. *Sisters of the Cross & Passion Convent*, 24 Castle Rd., 02882. Tel: 401-783-6668. Sisters 3.

NEWPORT. *Benedictines of Jesus Crucified*, St. Paul's Priory, 61 Narragansett Ave., 02840-4099. Tel: 401-847-2423. Legal Title: *Benedictines of Jesus Crucified Inc.* Benedictine Sisters of Pontifical Jurisdiction. Convent of the Congregation of the Benedictines of Jesus Crucified, O.S.B. Sr. Marie Agathe Karunaratne, O.S.B., Prioress. Sisters 11.

Cluny Provincial House, 90 Brenton Rd., 02840-4256. Tel: 401-846-4757; Fax: 401-846-2276.
E-mail: clunyusa@wsii.com
Sisters of St. Joseph of Cluny.
Provincial House. Sr. Marie Cooper, S.J.C., Prov. Supr.; Sr. Josephine St. Leger, S.J.C., Prov. Councilor, St. Joseph of Cluny Convent. Tel: 401-847-3637; Fax: 401-847-4072. Sr. Eugenia Brady, S.J.C., Local Supr. Sisters 14; Sisters in Diocese 19; Sisters in Cluny Prov. of U.S.A. & Canada 43.

Corpus Christi Carmel, 516 Broadway, 02840. Tel: 401-847-6165. Corpus Christi Carmelite Sisters. Sr. Teresa Winefride, O.Carm., Supr.; Sr. Emerentiana, O.Carm., Regl. Supr., U.S.A. Sisters 3.

St. Clare Convent, Cutting Memorial, 301 Spring St., 02840. Tel: 401-846-1025. Legal Title: *The Saint Clare Home*. Sr. Simone Leblond, D.H.S., Coord. Daughters of the Holy Spirit 7.

NORTH KINGSTOWN. *Holy Family Convent*, 1 Wright Ln., 02852. Tel: 401-294-3554. Legal Title: *Sisters of the Holy Cross and Passion*. Provincial Office of the Sisters of the Cross and Passion. Sr. Ellen Downes, C.P., Prov. Sisters 2.

NORTH PROVIDENCE. *Franciscan Missionaries of Mary*, 399 Fruit Hill Ave., 02911. Tel: 401-353-5800. Legal Title: *Franciscan Missionaries of Mary*.

Holy Family Community, 399 Fruit Hill Ave., 02911. Tel: 401-353-5800. Sr. Virginia Daly, F.M.M., Supr. Sisters 12.

Our Lady, Queen of Peace, Assisted Living Community, 399 Fruit Hill Ave., 02911. Tel: 401-353-5800. Sr. Philomena Agudo, F.M.M., Supr.; Sr. Lois Ann Pereira, F.M.M., Admin. Sisters 22.

Trinity Community, Assisted Living Community, 399 Fruit Hill Ave., 02911. Tel: 401-353-5800. Sr. Joyce Gardella, F.M.M., Supr. Sisters 20.

Our Lady of the Lourdes Convent, 385 Fruit Hill Ave., 02911. Tel: 401-353-6381. Sr. Rosemarie Higgins, F.M.M., Supr. Sisters 4.

Bethany, (House of On-Going Formation), 397 Fruit Hill Ave., 02911. Tel: 401-353-5860. Sr. Josephine J. Iozzo, F.M.M., Dir.

De Chappotin Community, 399 Fruit Hill Ave., 02911. Tel: 401-353-9412. Sr. Rosalie McNaughton, F.M.M., Supr. Sisters 6.

NORTH SMITHFIELD. *Franciscan Missionaries of Mary*, Ein Karim Community, 318 Mendon Rd., 02895. Tel: 401-766-8242. Sr. Agnes Begley, F.M.M., Coord. Sisters 4.

PAWTUCKET. *St. John the Baptist Convent*, 85 Slater St., 02860-2863. Tel: 401-722-1850. Sr. Mary E. Ward, F.M.M., Coord.; Sr. Helen Kalogaras, F.M.M.; Sr. Mary Nancy Cabral, F.M.M.; Sr. Barbara Dopierla, F.M.M.; Sr. Aline Giroux, F.M.M.; Sr. Ann Tarnauskas, F.M.M. Franciscan Missionaries of Mary 6.

SOUTH KINGSTOWN. *Sisters of the Cross and Passion*. 364 Oakwoods Dr., Peace Dale, 02879. Tel: 401-783-5457. Sr. Margaret Mary Hanley, C.P., Coord. Sisters 4.

WOONSOCKET. *Emmanuel House*, 67 Highland St., 02895.

Franciscan Apostolic Sisters, 89 Morris St., 02895. Tel: 401-769-9395. Sr. Wilma J. Lopez, F.A.S., Supr. Sisters 4.

[R] RETREAT HOUSES

CUMBERLAND. *Mercy Lodge*, Summer Brown Rd., P.O. Box 7651, 02864. Tel: 401-333-2801.

NARRAGANSETT. *Our Lady of Peace Spiritual Life Center*, Ocean Rd., Box 507, 02882. Tel: 401-884-7676. Legal Title: *Our Lady of Peace Retreat House*. Sr. Jean Marie McGee, R.S.M., Dir. Team Members: Revs. Robert F. Caul; Richard M. Friedrichs; Ms. Veneta Rainville.

NEWPORT. *Nazareth Spiritual Enrichment Center*, 12 Cliff Terr., 02840. Tel: 401-847-1654. Sisters of St. Chretienne. Sr. Estelle Plante, S.S.Ch., Dir. Sisters 2.

St. Paul Priory Guest House, 61 Narragansett Ave., 02840-4099. Tel: 401-847-2423. Benedictines of Jesus Crucified, O.S.B. Sr. Marie Agathe Karunaratne, O.S.B., Prioress.

NORTH PROVIDENCE. *Bethany Renewal Center*, 397 Fruit Hill Ave., 02911. Tel: 401-353-5860. Conducted by the Franciscan Missionaries of Mary. Sr. Josephine J. Iozzo, F.M.M., Dir.

[S] NEWMAN CENTERS

PROVIDENCE. *Brown University*, Catholic Chaplain's Office, Box 1931, 02912. Tel: 401-863-2344.
E-mail: Henry-Bodah@brown.edu
Rev. Henry J. Bodah, Chap.

Johnson & Wales University, Friendship Bldg., 2 Richmond St., 02903. Tel: 401-598-1830. Sr. Francis V. Murphy, S.N.D., Campus Min.

Rhode Island College, Catholic Campus Ministry, Student Union 300, 600 Mt. Pleasant Ave., 02908. Tel: 401-456-8168. Mr. James Montavon, Campus Min.

BRISTOL. *Roger Williams University*, Catholic Chaplain's Office, 1 Old Ferry Rd., 02809. Tel: 401-254-3433. Rev. Barry J. Gmache.

SMITHFIELD. *Bryant College*, Chaplain's Office, 1150 Douglas Pike, Box 33, 02917-1284. Tel: 401-232-6045. Rev. Pierre J. Plante, Chap.

SOUTH KINGSTOWN. *University of Rhode Island Catholic Center*. Kingston, 02881. Tel: 401-874-2324.
E-mail: JSoar@Uriacc.ur.edu
Web site: http://www.uri.edu/student_life/chaps/catholic.html
Chaplains: Revs. John P. Soares; Joseph D. Creedon; Mrs. Carol Maddock, Campus Min.

WARWICK. *Community College of R.I.*, Knight Campus, Campus Ministry Office, 400 East Ave., 02886. Tel: 401-825-2226.
E-mail: ananderson@ccri.cc.ri.us
Ms. Angela M. Anderson, Campus Min., Flanagan Campus, Campus Ministry Office, Louisquisset Pike, Lincoln, 02865. Tel: 401-333-7013.

[T] SECULAR INSTITUTES

PROVIDENCE. *Opus Spiritus Sancti-East Coast USA Region*, 485 Mt. Pleasant Ave., 02908-3301. Tel: 401-278-4515; Fax: 401-278-4548. Rev. Msgr. Jacques L. Plante, Regl. Coord.

LINCOLN. *Oblate Missionaries of Mary Immaculate*. P.O. Box 303, Manville, 02838. Miss Ruth A. Valois.

SOUTH KINGSTOWN. *Regnum Christi*. 4780 Tower Hill Rd., Wakefield, 02879. Tel: 401-482-6200. Ms. Gabriella Garza, Dir.

[U] MISCELLANEOUS LISTINGS

PROVIDENCE. *Miscellaneous Listings for the Diocese of Providence*. Mailing address for all Providence listings, Chancery Office: 1 Cathedral Sq., 02903. Tel: 401-278-4500. For Further information contact. Rev. Msgr. Jacques L. Plante, Chancellor.
Catholic Charity Fund.
Catholic Information Center of Newport.
Catholic Investment Trust, Inc.
Catholic Teachers' College of Providence.
The Church of the Immaculate Conception, North Providence.
De LaSalle Academy Corporation.
Diocesan Service Corporation.
Homes for Hope Foundation.
Inter-Parish Loan Fund, Inc.
LaSalle Academy.
Little Sisters of the Assumption of Woonsocket.
Marian Association of Northern Rhode Island.
Mary, Mother of Youth Center.
The Mercy Home and School.
Mother of Hope Novitiate.
New England Conference of Diocesan Directors of Religious Education.
Our Lady of Providence Preparatory Seminary.
Our Lady, Queen of the Clergy.
Pius X Salvage Bureau.
Providence Catholic Schools Collaborative.
The Rhode Island Catholic Orphan Asylum (St. Aloysius Home).
Roman Catholic Bishop of Providence. A Corporation Sole.
St. Benedict's Hearth Corporation, East Providence.
Saint Hedwig's Church Corporation, Providence.
St. John's Church of Providence.
Saint Margaret's Home.
Saint Maria Society.
St. Mary Academy of the Visitation.
Saint Raphael's Industrial Home and School.
St. Vincent de Paul Home, Woonsocket.
Stella Maris Home for Convalescents.
Vision of Hope, Inc.

BURRILLVILLE. *Conference of Regional Treasurers*. 685 Steere Farm Rd., Pascoag, 02859-4601. Tel: 401-568-3361; Fax: 401-568-9810. Bro. Louis J. Laperle, S.C., Rep. of CORT I.

Father Andre Coindre Charitable Trust,. 685 Steere Farm Rd., Pascoag, 02859-9810. Bro. Louis J. Laperle, S.C., Corp. Sec.

NARRAGANSETT. *Saint Benilde Community Support Charitable Trust*, 635 Ocean Rd., 02882-1314. Tel: 401-789-0244; Fax: 401-783-5303.
E-mail: joes46@aol.com

NORTH PROVIDENCE. *Franciscan Missionaries of Mary*, 399 Fruit Hill Ave., 02911.
E-mail: mmotte@aol.com

Mission Resource Center. Tel: 401-353-4470; Fax: 401-353-8779. Sr. Mary Motte, F.M.M., Dir.; Sr. Alma Dufault, F.M.M., Assoc. Dir.

SOUTH KINGSTON. *Hombre Nueva (RI), Inc.*, 47 Crest Ave., 02879. Tel: 203-281-4798. Rev. Juan Sabadell, L.C., Contact Person.

SOUTH KINGSTOWN. *"Mater Ecclesiae" International Formation Center*. 4780 Tower Hill Rd., Wakefield, 02879. Tel: 401-782-6205; 782-6200. Members 72. (Regnum Christi Movement). Ms. Gabriela Garza, Dir.; Revs. Jose A. Alonso, L.C., Chap.; Jude Furlong, L.C., Prof.

The Legion of Christ (RI) Incorporated. 4780 Tower Hill Rd., Wakefield, 02879. Tel: 203-281-4798. Rev. Juan Sabadell, L.C., Contact Person.

Mater Ecclesiae, Inc. 4780 Tower Hill Rd., Wakefield, 02879. Tel: 203-281-4798. Rev. Juan Sabadell, L.C., Contact Person.

Overbrook, Incorporated, 02879. Tel: 203-281-4798. Rev. Juan Sabadell, L.C., Contact Person.

WEST WARWICK. *Tides Family Services*, Family Counseling, 1599 Main St., 02893. Tel: 401-822-1360. Bro. Michael Reis, F.S.C., Pres./Treas.
Branch Offices: Tides Outreach Project, 260 Highland Ave., Providence, 02906. Tides' Hispanic Outreach Project, 400 Dexter Ave., Central Falls, 02863. Staff 29; Assisted 1,500.

RELIGIOUS INSTITUTES OF MEN REPRESENTED IN THE DIOCESE

For further details refer to the corresponding bracketed number in the Religious Institutes of Men or Women section.

[]—*Apostolic Life Community of Priests in the Opus Spiritus Sancti.*—O.S.S.
[0200]—*Benedictine Monks.*—O.S.B.
[]—*Brothers of Our Lady of Providence.*—O.L.P.
[0330]—*Brothers of the Christian Schools.* (New England-Long Island Prov.).—F.S.C.
[1100]—*Brothers of the Sacred Heart.*—S.C.
[0310]—*Congregation of Christian Brothers.*—C.F.C.
[0520]—*Franciscan Friars.* (Prov. of the Most Holy Name).—O.F.M.
[0600]—*Holy Cross Brothers.*—C.S.C.
[0650]—*Holy Ghost Fathers.* (Eastern Prov.).—C.S.Sp.
[0730]—*Legionaires of Christ.*—L.C.
[0720]—*Missionaries of Our Lady of LaSalette.*—M.S.
[1210]—*Missionaries of St. Charles (Scalabrinians).*—C.S.
[1110]—*Missionaries of the Sacred Heart.*—M.S.C.
[0430]—*Order of Preachers (Dominicans).* (Prov. of St. Joseph).—O.P.
[1220]—*Servants of Charity.*—S.C.
[0370]—*Society of St. Columban.*—S.S.C.

RELIGIOUS INSTITUTES OF WOMEN REPRESENTED IN THE DIOCESE

[0130]—*Apostles of the Sacred Heart of Jesus.*—A.S.C.J.
[2250]—*Benedictines of Jesus Crucified.*—O.S.B.
[0350]—*Carmelite Sisters (Corpus Christi).*—O.Carm.
[0940]—*Daughters of St. Mary of Providence.*—D.S.M.P.
[0820]—*Daughters of the Holy Spirit.*—D.H.S.
[0420]—*Discalced Carmelite Nuns.*—O.C.D.
[1070-15]—*Dominican Sisters.*—O.P.
[1170]—*Felician Sisters.*—C.S.S.F.
[]—*Franciscan Apostolic Sisters.*—F.A.S.
[1370]—*The Franciscan Missionaries of Mary.*—F.M.M.

[]—*Franciscan Sisters.*—O.S.F.

[3790]—*Institute of the Sisters of St. Dorothy.*—S.S.D.

[2340]—*Little Sisters of the Poor.*—L.S.P.

[3450]—*Religious of Jesus and Mary.*—R.J.M.

[3110]—*Religious of the Cenacle.*—R.C.

[2070]—*Religious of the Holy Union of the Sacred Hearts.*—S.U.S.C.

[4070]—*Religious of the Sacred Heart.*—R.S.C.J.

[3430]—*Religious Teachers Filippini.*—M.P.F.

[2970]—*School Sisters of Notre Dame.*—S.S.N.D.

[3650]—*Servants of Our Lady, Queen of the Clergy.*—S.R.C.

[2575]—*Sisters of Mercy of the Americas.*—R.S.M.

[3000]—*Sisters of Notre Dame de Namur.*—S.N.D.deN.

[3720]—*Sisters of Saint Anne.*—S.S.A.

[3750]—*Sisters of St. Chretienne.*—S.S.CH.

[3815]—*Sisters of St. Jeanne d'Arc.*—S.J.A.

[3860]—*Sisters of St. Joseph of Cluny.*—S.J.C.

[3830]—*Sisters of St. Joseph of Springfield.*—S.S.J.

[2980]—*Sisters of the Congregation of Notre Dame.*—C.N.D.

[3180]—*Sisters of the Cross and Passion.*—C.P.

[1010]—*Sisters of the Divine Providence of Kentucky.*—C.D.P.

[3310]—*Sisters of the Presentation of Mary.*—P.M.

[3320]—*Sisters of the Presentation of the B.V.M.*—P.B.V.M.

[4040]—*Society of St. Ursula.*—S.U.

[4048]—*Society of the Sisters, Faithful Companions of Jesus.*—F.C.J.

DIOCESAN CEMETERIES

PROVIDENCE. *St. Patrick's.*
BARRINGTON. *Maria Del Campo.*
CRANSTON. *St. Ann's.*
CUMBERLAND. *Resurrection.*
EAST PROVIDENCE. *Gate of Heaven.*
MIDDLETOWN. *St. Columba.*
PAWTUCKET. *Mount St. Mary's.*
St. Francis.
WEST GREENWICH. *St. Joseph.*

NECROLOGY

† Broderick, John D., Newport, RI, Jesus Saviour. —Died Sept. 5, 1997.

† Davey, John J., Providence, RI, St. Ann. —Died July 18, 1997.

† Dery, Jean-Pierre, Nasonville, RI, St. Theresa of the Child Jesus. —Died Dec. 4, 1996.

† Pyne, William F., North Smithfield, RI, St. Antoine Residence. —Died March 14, 1997.

Diocese of Pueblo

(Dioecesis Pueblensis)

Most Reverend

ARTHUR N. TAFOYA, D.D.

Bishop of Pueblo; ordained May 12, 1962; appointed July 1, 1980; consecrated September 10, 1980; installed September 10, 1980. *Mailing Address: 1001 Grand Ave., Pueblo, CO, 81003.* Tel.: 719-544-9861; Fax: 719-544-1220.

Most Reverend

CHARLES A. BUSWELL, D.D.

Retired Bishop of Pueblo; ordained July 9, 1939; appointed August 8, 1959; consecrated September 30, 1959; installed October 6, 1959; retired September 18, 1979. *Res., 13 Tartan Ln., Pueblo, CO, 81001.*

DIOCESAN PATRON: St. Therese of the Child Jesus. Secondary Patroness: Our Lady of Guadalupe.

ERECTED A DIOCESE NOVEMBER 15, 1941.

Square Miles 48,155.

Comprises the 29 Counties of Alamosa, Archuleta, Baca, Bent, Conejos, Costilla, Crowley, Custer, Delta, Dolores, Fremont, Gunnison, Hinsdale, Huerfano, Kiowa, La Plata, Las Animas, Mesa, Mineral, Montezuma, Montrose, Otero, Ouray, Prowers, Pueblo, Rio Grande, Saguache, San Juan and San Miguel in the southern part of the State of Colorado.

For legal titles of parishes and diocesan institutions, consult the Business Office.

Catholic Pastoral Center: 1001 N. Grand Ave., Pueblo, CO, 81003. Tel.: 719-544-9861; Fax: 719-544-5202.

STATISTICAL OVERVIEW

Personnel	
Bishop	1
Retired Bishops	1
Retired Abbots	1
Priests: Diocesan Active in Diocese	39
Priests: Active Outside Diocese	4
Priests: Diocesan in Foreign Missions	1
Priests: Retired, Sick or Absent	33
Number of Diocesan Priests	77
Religious Priests in Diocese	39
Extern Priests in Diocese	1
Permanent Deacons in Diocese	10
Total Brothers	13
Total Sisters	102
Parishes	
Parishes	55
With Resident Pastor:	
Resident Diocesan Priests	33
Resident Religious Priests	17
Without Resident Pastor:	
Administered by Priests	4
Administered by Women Religious	1
Missions	61
Professional Ministry Personnel:	
Sisters	10
Lay Ministers	40
Welfare	
Catholic Hospitals	5
Total Assisted	1,462,029
Homes for the Aged	4
Special Centers for Social Services	1
Total Assisted	2,894
Educational	
Diocesan Students in Other Seminaries	6
Total Seminarians	6
High Schools, Private	1
Total Students	92
Elementary Schools, Diocesan and Parish	3
Total Students	886
Elementary Schools, Private	1
Total Students	234
Catechesis/Religious Education:	
High School Students	2,269
Elementary Students	4,429
Total Students Under Catholic Instruction	7,916
Teachers in the Diocese:	
Brothers	1
Sisters	8
Lay Teachers	102
Vital Statistics	
Receptions into the Church:	
Infant Baptism Totals	1,979
Adult Baptism Totals	137
Received into Full Communion	377
First Communions	1,611
Confirmations	925
Marriages:	
Catholic	306
Interfaith	127
Total Marriages	433
Deaths	1,269
Total Catholic Population	106,482
Total Population	547,287

Former Bishops—Most Rev. JOSEPH CLEMENT WILLGING, D.D., First Bishop of Pueblo; ord. June 20, 1908; appt. Dec. 6, 1941; cons. Feb. 24, 1942; Assistant at Pontifical Throne, Feb. 20, 1958; died March 3, 1959.

Catholic Pastoral Center—1001 N. Grand Ave., Pueblo, 81003. Tel: 719-544-9861; 1-800-354-2729; Fax: 719-544-5202. Office Hours: Mon.-Fri. 8-12 & 1-5.

Vicar General—Rev. EDWARD H. NUNEZ, V.G.

Director of the Curia—Mr. THOMAS M. DOERK, Dir.; Rev. MARK A. PLEWKA, J.C.L., Chancellor; Mrs. LORRAINE GUERIN, Vice Chancellor.

Diocesan Tribunal—

Judicial Vicar—Rev. MARK A. PLEWKA, J.C.L.

Adjutant Judicial Vicar—Rev. DAVID L. RICKEN, J.C.L.

Promotor Justitiae—Revs. JOSEPH P. MCGUINNESS; DAVID L. RICKEN, J.C.L.

Defensores Vinculi—Revs. RICHARD F. BECKER; ROGER P. DORCY; GEORGE T. HOLLAND; DANIEL R. HUBER; MICHAEL A. KURZ, J.C.L.; JOSEPH P. MCGUINNESS; EDWARD H. NUNEZ, V.G.; DAVID L. RICKEN, J.C.L.; RONALD ROCHE; JEROME A. RYKOWSKI; ERVIN J. SCHMITT; Ms. DONI R. NEEDHAM.

Judicial Experts—Rev. MARVIN J. KAPUSHION, M.S.W., J.C.L., L.C.S.W.; Dr. MICHAEL MILLARD, Ph.D.

Secretarial to the Tribunal—Ms. DONI NEEDHAM.

Judges—Revs. RICHARD F. BECKER; ROGER P. DORCY; EDWARD H. NUNEZ, V.G.

Ecclesiastical Notaries—Mrs. LORRAINE GUERIN; Ms. DONI NEEDHAM; Rev. MARK T. BETTINGER.

Presbyteral Council-College of Consultors—Ex-Officio: Most Rev. ARTHUR N. TAFOYA, D.D.; Revs. MARK A. PLEWKA, J.C.L.; EDWARD H. NUNEZ, V.G.; CHARLES A. SENA, Vice Chm. & Treas. JESSE PEREZ, Chm. THOMAS M. ADRIANS; ERVIN J. SCHMITT; JAMES F. KOENIGSFELD, V.F.

Deans—Rev. ROGER P. DORCY, V.F., Pueblo Deanery; Rev. CARLOS TRUJILLO, V.F., Alamosa Deanery; Rev. MICHAEL MCCLEARY, V.F., Durango Deanery; Rev. JAMES F. KOENIGSFELD, V.F., Grand Junction Deanery; Rev. THOMAS R. HINNI, C.M., V.F., La Junta Deanery; Rev. FRANK L. DAVIED, O.F.M., V.F., Walsenburg Deanery.

Archivist—Mrs. LORRAINE GUERIN.

Diocesan Offices and Specialists

Diocesan Offices—

Pastoral Services—

Shared Ministry Formation—Mr. JAMES SCIEGEL.

Stewardship—Mr. THOMAS J. WEAVER.

Social Justice—Mr. LARRY HOWE-KERR.

Worship—Mrs. PAULA GIORDANO, Contact.

Evangelization—Vacant.

Parish Social Ministry—Sr. SUE KENNEDY, S.C.L.

Administrative Services—

Business and Finance—Mrs. VIRGINIA JIMENEZ.

Human Resources—Mrs. THERESA FARLEY.

Clergy Services—Rev. J. WILLIAM HUBER.

Tribunal—Rev. MARK PLEWKA.

Bishop's Office—Mr. THOMAS M. DOERK.

The Bishop of Pueblo, a Corporation Sole—1001 N. Grand Ave., Pueblo, 81003. Tel: 719-544-9861.

Diocesan Director of Business & Finance—Mrs. VIRGINIA JIMENEZ, *1001 N. Grand Ave., Pueblo, 81003.*

Diocesan Office for Development—Mr. THOMAS J. WEAVER, C.F.R.E.

Finance Advisory Council—Mr. JAMES MURRAY, *40 Regency Blvd., #G, Pueblo, 81005.* Tel: 719-566-1413.

Diocesan Newspaper—"The Chronicle of Catholic Life"; Most Rev. ARTHUR N. TAFOYA, D.D., Publisher, *1001 Grand Ave., Pueblo, 81003.* Tel: 719-544-9861. Managing Editor: *109 Pawnee Ave., Manitou Springs, 80829.* Tel: 719-685-5202.

Coordinator for Schools—Sr. ANDREA VASQUEZ, O.S.B.

Liaison for Organizations—Mrs. LORRAINE GUERIN, Contact Person.
Missions—Mr. THOMAS M. DOERK, Dir. Curia, *1001 N. Grand Ave., Pueblo, 81003.* Tel: 719-544-9861.
Holy Childhood, Association—Mr. THOMAS M. DOERK, Dir. Curia, *1001 N. Grand Ave., Pueblo, 81003.* Tel: 719-544-9861.
Propagation of the Faith—Mr. THOMAS M. DOERK, Dir. Curia, *1001 N. Grand Ave., Pueblo, 81003.* Tel: 719-544-9861.
Family Life Ministries—Mr. LUCIO FLORES, *302 Jefferson St., Pueblo, 81004.* Tel: 719-544-4233.
Migrant Ministry—Sr. ANDREA VASQUEZ, O.S.B., Specialist.
Religious Education / Youth and Young Adult Ministry—Mr. JAMES SCIEGEL, Specialist, Resource Library; Mrs. FRANCES INGO. Tel: 719-544-9861.
Worship—Mrs. PAULA GIORDANO, Contact.
R.C.I.A.—Mr. JIM SCIEGEL, Coord.
Diocesan Liturgical Council—Most Rev. ARTHUR N. TAFOYA, D.D., Contact Person.
Campus Ministry—Mrs. JANET JOHNSON, *600 E. Georgia, Gunnison, 81230.* Tel: 970-641-0325.
Vocations—Rev. RAYMOND VANDORPE, C.M., Specialist.
Catholic Social Service, Inc.—Mr. LUCIO FLORES, Dir., *302 Jefferson St., Pueblo, 81004.* Tel: 719-544-4215.
Branch Offices—Catholic Relief Services, Family Counseling Center, 302 Jefferson St., Pueblo, 81004. Tel: 719-544-4215., *Grand Junction Office.* Tel: 970-241-8475., *La Junta Office.* Tel: 719-384-9244.
The Bishop Charles A. Buswell Trust—13 Tartan Ln., Pueblo, 81001. Tel: 719-543-2804.
Boy Scouts of America—Rev. Msgr. GEORGE T. HOLLAND, Diocesan Chap., *2204 Wyoming Ave., Pueblo, 81004.* Tel: 719-561-8697.
Cemetery Committee—Vacant.
Catholic Charismatic Renewal Center—519 W. 11th St., Pueblo, 81003. Tel: 719-543-7313.
Clergy Benefit Society of the Diocese of Pueblo, Inc.—Rev. EDWARD G. PETTIT, *919 E. Evans Ave., Pueblo, 81004.* Tel: 719-542-4702.
Clergy Formation Council—Rev. RAYMOND VANDORPE, C.M., *1001 N. Grand Ave., Pueblo, 81003.* Tel: 719-544-9861.
Cursillos in Christianity—Contact: *Chancery, 1001 N. Grand Ave., Pueblo, 81003.* Tel: 719-544-9861.
Diocesan Catechetical Council—Most Rev. ARTHUR N. TAFOYA, D.D., Contact Person, *1001 N. Grand Ave., Pueblo, 81003.* Tel: 719-544-9861.
Diocesan Council of Catholic Women—Rev. RICHARD F. BECKER, Moderator, *1145 S. Aspen Rd., Pueblo, 81006.* Tel: 719-544-1886.
Diocesan Liturgical Council—Most Rev. ARTHUR N. TAFOYA, D.D., Contact, *1001 N. Grand Ave., Pueblo, 81003.* Tel: 719-544-9861.
Diocesan Pastoral Council—Ms. NAOMI SALAZAR, Chm., *331 Riverwood Dr., Alamosa, 81101.* Tel: 719-259-6981.
Father John Powers Memorial Basketball League, Inc.—Mr. ROBERT J. DOUGLASS, Contact Person, *144 Harvard Ave., Pueblo, 81004.* Tel: 719-544-7192.
John Neumann Catholic School Foundation—330 Lake Ave., Pueblo, 81004. Tel: 719-543-8864.
Due Process Board—Mr. BERNARDINO ALVAREZ, Chm., *2010 E. 13th St., Pueblo, 81001.* Tel: 719-544-4671.
Human Development Commission of the Diocese of Pueblo—Mr. ANDY CARRILLO, Chm., *1638 Laguna St., Pueblo, 81006.* Tel: 719-545-6505.
Campaign for Human Development—Mr. LARRY HOWE-KERR, Chm., *140 Elm Ave., Grand Junction, 81501.*
Nocturnal Adoration Society—Sr. ELIZABETH MADDEN, S.S.S., *311 E. Mesa Ave., Pueblo, 81006.* Tel: 719-545-PRAY.
Presbyteral Council—Most Rev. ARTHUR N. TAFOYA, D.D., Pres.; Revs. JESSE PEREZ, Chm. CHARLIE SENA, Vice Chm. & Treas. TOM ADRIANS; ERVIN J. SCHMITT; EDWARD H. NUNEZ, V.G., Ex-Officio; MARK A. PLEWKA, J.C.L., Ex-Offico.
Standing Committees—
Clergy Assemblies—Revs. JESSE PEREZ, Chm. WILLIAM DOLL, Sec. LEONARD RACKI.
Continuing Education—Revs. J. WILLIAM HUBER, Ph.D., Chm. BOB CARDEN; DANIEL HUBER; JAMES KOENIGSFELD, V.F.
Sabbatical—Revs. J. WILLIAM HUBER, Ph.D., Chm. BEN BACINO; DANIEL R. HUBER.
Personnel—Revs. TOM ADRIANS, Chm. JESSE PEREZ; CHARLES SENA; WILLIAM GLEESON; JOHN COSTANZO; WILLIAM NELSON.
[*]Posada Shelter—Ms. ANNE STATTELMAN, Dir., *1008 N. Grand Ave., Pueblo, 81003.* Tel: 719-545-8776.
Clergy Conference of the Diocese of Pueblo—Rev. THOMAS ADRIANS, *1708 Horseshoe Dr., Pueblo, 81001.* Tel: 719-542-9248.
Las Hermanas de Pueblo—Mrs. ROSEANNA PADILLA, Pres., *P.O. Box 4116, Pueblo, 81001.* Tel: 719-544-2014.
SEARCH—Ms. SANDY HANSEN, *917 E. Evans, Pueblo, 81004.* Tel: 719-546-1015; 544-8246.
Sisters' Council—Sr. ANDREA VASQUEZ, O.S.B., *1001 N. Grand Ave., Pueblo, 81003-2948.* Tel: 719-544-9861.
Legion of Mary—Ms. JANE L. ALCON, Pres., *Pueblo Curia, 1414 E. Ash St., Pueblo, 81001.* Tel: 719-543-2610.

CLERGY, PARISHES, MISSIONS AND PAROCHIAL SCHOOLS

CITY OF PUEBLO
(Pueblo County)

1—SACRED HEART CATHEDRAL (1872), Rev. Anthony A. Wojcinski. In res., Rev. Frank Tinajero, S.V.D.
Parish Office: 414 W. 11th St., 81003. Tel: 719-544-5175; Fax: 719-584-9922.

2—CHRIST THE KING (1957), Rev. Thomas M. Adrians.
1708 Horseshoe Dr., 81001. Tel: 719-542-9248; Fax: 719-545-9826.
Convent—11 MacNaughton Rd., 81001. Tel: 719-543-2466; Fax: 719-545-9826.

3—HOLY FAMILY (1954), Revs. Jesse L. Perez; Benjamin J. Bacino, O.F.M.
2827 Lakeview Ave., 81005. Tel: 719-564-2696; Fax: 719-564-4396.
Catechesis / Religious Programs—Joseph DeFrier, D.R.E.
Students 350.
Mission—Rye, Pueblo Co., St. Aloysius, (1936). Rev. Marvin J. Kapushion.
Res., P.O. Box 186, Rye, 81069.

4—HOLY ROSARY (1954), Rev. Mark A. Plewka, J.C.L.
Office: 2400 W. 22nd St., 81003. Tel: 719-545-7219.
Res., 2207 W. 22nd St., 81003. Tel: 719-543-0917.

5—OUR LADY OF THE ASSUMPTION (1949), Revs. Ervin J. Schmitt; Edward G. Pettit.
Parish Office: 919 E. Evans, 81004. Tel: 719-543-2168.
Res., 217 E. Mesa Ave., 81006. Tel: 719-543-7576; Fax: 719-562-1195.

6—OUR LADY OF GUADALUPE (1968), Rev. Edward H. Nunez, V.G.
914 E. Second St., 81001. Tel: 719-542-1447.

7—OUR LADY OF THE MEADOWS (1979), Rev. Roger P. Dorcy, V.F.; Deacon Robert J. Myscofski, Pastoral Assoc.
23 Starling Dr., 81005. Tel: 719-561-3580; Fax: 719-561-1271.

8—OUR LADY OF MT. CARMEL (1902), Revs. John Waters, S.J.; Eugene D. Kelly, S.J.; Harry L. Sanford, S.J.
421 Clark St., 81003. Tel: 719-542-5952; Fax: 719-542-2310.

9—ST. ANNE (1956), Rev. James E. Friel.
Res., 2701 E. 12th St., 81001. Tel: 719-545-2644.

10—ST. ANTHONY OF PADUA. Closed. For inquiries for parish records contact the Chancery.

11—ST. FRANCIS XAVIER (1903), Rev. Ronald Roche.
611 Logan Ave., 81004. Tel: 719-564-1125.
Mission—Beulah, Pueblo Co., Our Lady of Lourdes.

12—ST. JOSEPH (1960), Revs. Richard F. Becker; Robert J. Carden.
Office: 1145 S. Aspen Rd., 81006. Tel: 719-544-1886.
Res., 1165 S. Aspen Rd., 81006. Tel: 719-543-0835.

13—ST. LEANDER (1921), Rev. Edward H. Nunez, V.G.
Office: 1402 E. Seventh St., 81001. Tel: 719-544-8411; Fax: 719-544-8202.

14—ST. MARY (1895), Revs. Ervin J. Schmitt; Edward G. Pettit.
Office & Mailing Address: 919 E. Evans, 81004. Fax: 719-562-1195.; 217 E. Mesa Ave., 81006. Tel: 719-543-3601.

15—ST. PATRICK (1882), Revs. Ervin J. Schmitt; Edward G. Pettit.
Office & Mailing Address: 919 E. Evans, 81004. Fax: 719-562-1195.
Res., 304 E. Routt Ave., 81004. Tel: 719-542-4702.

16—ST. PIUS X (1955), Rev. J. William Huber, Ph.D.
Parish Center: 3130 Morris Ave., 81008. Tel: 719-542-4264; Fax: 719-583-8103.
Mission—Pueblo West, Pueblo Co., St. Paul the Apostle, 3130 Morris Ave., 81008. Tel: 719-547-3725.

17—SHRINE OF ST. THERESE (1948), Rev. Vicente Paz en La Casa; Linda Davis, Pastoral Assoc.
300 Goodnight Ave., 81004. Tel: 719-542-1788; Fax: 719-542-2130.

OUTSIDE THE CITY OF PUEBLO

Aguilar, Las Animas Co., St. Anthony (1875), Rev. Frank L. Davied, O.F.M.
P.O. Box 577, 81020. Tel: 719-941-4124. [CEM]
Res., P.O. Box 86, Walsenburg, 81089.
Missions—Trujillo Creek, Mount Carmel; Gulnare, Las Animas Co., San Jose.

Alamosa, Alamosa Co., Sacred Heart (1887), Rev. Gary L. Kennedy.
P.O. Box 547, 81101. Tel: 719-589-3211; 589-5829 (Parish Center); Fax: 719-589-5829.
Station—Mosca, Adams State College, (Alamosa).

Avondale, Pueblo Co., Sacred Heart (1960), Rev. Maurice O. Gallagher.
P.O. Box 278, 81022. Tel: 719-947-3092.
Mission—Boone, Pueblo Co., St. William, Mailing Address: 52950 Bascal Rd., Boone, 81025. Tel: 719-947-3548.

Canon City, Fremont Co., St. Michael (1880), Rev. James E. King.
611 N. 11th St., 81212. Tel: 719-275-7549; Fax: 719-275-7540.

Capulin, Conejos Co., St. Joseph (1912), Rev. William T. Gleeson.
Mailing Address: P.O. Box 40, 81124. Tel: 719-274-5304; Fax: 719-274-9865. [CEM]
Missions—La Jara, Conejos Co., Our Lady of the Valley, 19617 S. Hwy. 285, La Jara, 81140. Tel: 719-274-5647; Manassa, Conejos Co., St. Therese of the Child Jesus, 115 Main St., Manassa, 81141.; Los Sauces, St. Anthony, 18900 County Rd. 28, Los Sauces, 81151.; Romeo, Conejos Co., Our Lady of the Immaculate Conception, 211 Blanca St., Romeo, 81148.

Center, Saguache Co., St. Francis Jerome (1951), Revs. Carlos B. Trujillo, V.F.; William R. Nelson.
P.O. Box 845, 81125. Tel: 719-754-3969.
Mission—Saguache, St. Agnes, 505 Gunnison, 81129. Tel: 719-655-2530.
Station—Crestone, Tel: 719-256-4778; Fax: 719-256-4719.

Conejos, Conejos Co., Our Lady of Guadalupe (1857), Rev. Doug Hunt, C.R.
Mailing Address: P.O. Box 305, Antonito, 81120. Tel: 719-376-5985; Fax: 719-376-2530. [CEM]
Missions—Antonito, Conejos Co., St. Augustine; Lobatos, Sagrada Familia; Ortiz, San Juan Nepomuceno y San Cayetano; San Antonio, San Antonio de Padua; San Rafael, San Pedro y San Rafael; San Miguel, San Miguel.

Cortez, Montezuma Co., St. Margaret Mary (1945), Revs. William K. Connor; Joseph P. McGuinness.
28 E. Montezuma Ave., 81321. Tel: 970-565-3308.
Mission—Dove Creek, Dolores Co., St. Jude.

Crested Butte, Gunnison Co., Queen of All Saints (1883). Attended by St. Peter Parish, Gunnison. Rev. James F. Koenigsfeld, V.F.
Church—P.O. Box 271, 81224. Tel: 970-641-0808; Fax: 970-641-4592.

Del Norte, Rio Grande Co., Holy Name of Mary (1879), Revs. Carlos B. Trujillo, V.F.; William R. Nelson.
645 Pine Ave., P.O. Box 97, 81132. Tel: 719-657-3147; Fax: 719-657-2613. [CEM]
Missions—Los Valdeses, St. Francis of Assisi; South Fork, Rio Grande Co., Holy Family; Creede, Mineral Co., Immaculate Conception.

Delta, Delta Co., St. Michael (1911), Rev. Charles A. Sena.
Parish Office: 628 Meeker St., 81416. Tel: 970-874-3300.
Res., 560 Meeker St., 81416. Tel: 970-874-5116.
Mission—Cedaredge, Delta Co., St. Philip Benizi, P.O. Box 713, Cedaredge, 81413. Tel: 970-856-6495.

Durango, La Plata Co., St. Columba (1881), Rev. Michael L. McCleary, V.F.
1830 E. Second Ave., 81301. Tel: 970-247-0044; Fax: 970-385-5737.
School—Tel: 970-247-5527.
Sisters of St. Dominic 2; Lay Teachers 14; Students 310.
Sacred Heart (1906), Rev. Joseph Gallegos, C.R.
254 Fifth Ave., 81301. Tel: 970-247-3997.

Florence, Fremont Co., St. Benedict (1895), Rev. Michael Murray, O.S.B.; Ms. Irene Goergen, Pastoral Assoc.
622 W. Second St., P.O. Box 189, 81226. Tel: 719-784-4879.
Mission—Rockvale, Fremont Co., St. Patrick.

Fruita, Mesa Co., Sacred Heart (1890), Rev. John J. Costanzo, Supvr.; Sr. Barbara Piotrowski S.C., Parish Dir.
Mailing Address: 513 E. Aspen Ave., 81521. Tel: 970-858-9605.

Gardner, Huerfano Co., Sacred Heart (1912), Rev. Frank L. Davied, O.F.M., V.F.
Mailing Address: P.O. Box 86, Walsenburg, 81089. Tel: 719-738-1204; Fax: 719-738-1206.

Grand Junction, Mesa Co., Immaculate Heart of Mary (1955), Revs. James H. Plough; John B. Farley.
776 Bookcliff Ave., 81501. Tel: 970-242-6121; Fax: 970-242-6778.
Mission—Palisade, Mesa Co., St. Ann, 535 W, 1st

St., Palisade, 81526. Tel: 970-464-5157. Sr. Ann Marie Dunn, O.S.F., Pastoral Assoc.
Stations—Debeque.; Collbran.

St. Joseph (1884), Revs. John J. Costanzo; Mark T. Bettinger.
Mailing Address: P.O. Box 246, 81502.
253 White Ave., 81501. Tel: 970-243-0209; Fax: 970-243-7493.
School—Holy Family School.
North: 800 Bookcliff, 81501. Tel: 970-242-6168; Fax: 970-242-4244.; South: 303 Grand Ave., 81501. Tel: 970-241-1489.
Lay Teachers 20; Students 395.

Gunnison, Gunnison Co., St. Peter (1881), Rev. James F. Koenigsfeld, V.F.
303 N. Wisconsin St., 81230. Tel: 970-641-0808; Fax: 970-641-4592.
Mission—Lake City, Hinsdale Co., St. Rose of Lima.

Holly, Prowers Co., St. Frances of Rome (1910), Rev. William P. Doll.
130 S. Fifth St., 81047. Tel: 719-537-6688.
Mailing Address: P.O. Box 130.
Mission—Bristol, Prowers Co., St. Mary.

Ignacio, La Plata Co., St. Ignatius Parish (1881), Rev. Edward J. Andary.
P.O. Box 352, 81137. Tel: 970-563-4241.
Missions—Bayfield, La Plata Co., St. Bartholemew, P.O. Box 214, Bayfield, 81122.; Arboles, Archuleta Co., SS. Peter & Rose, R.R. 2, 81137.
Station—Tiffany.

La Junta, Otero Co., La Junta Catholic Parish (1889). (Formerly St. Patrick-Our Lady of Guadalupe). Rev. Thomas R. Hinni, C.M., V.F.
222 Lincoln St., Box 1181, 81050. Tel: 719-384-4342; 384-4372; Fax: 719-384-7894.

Lamar, Prowers Co., St. Francis De Sales-Our Lady of Guadalupe (1930), Rev. Raymond P. Grimes.
600 E. Parmenter St., 81052. Tel: 719-336-7759.

Las Animas, Bent Co., St. Mary (1910), Rev. Philip J. Coury, C.M.
714 Elm St., 81054. Tel: 719-456-0357.

Mancos, Montezuma Co., St. Rita (1914), Revs. William K. Connor; Joseph P. McGuinness.
P.O. Box 150, 81328. Tel: 970-533-7388.
Missions—Dolores, Montezuma Co., Our Lady of Victory Church; Rico, Dolores Co., Immaculate Heart of Mary Chapel.
Station—Mesa Verde, National Park.

Monte Vista, Rio Grande Co., St. Joseph (1920), Revs. Carlos B. Trujillo, V.F. Tel: 719-852-2673; William R. Nelson; Sr. Johnette Sawyer, O.S.B., Pastoral Assoc.
425 Batterson, P.O. Box 587, 81144. Tel: 719-852-2523; Fax: 719-852-0623.
Stations—Morada.; Mountain Meadows, Tel: 719-852-5138; Homelake, Tel: 719-852-5118; High Valley, Tel: 719-852-5711.

Montrose, Montrose Co., St. Mary (1906), Rev. Daniel R. Huber; Deacons Dennis Putnam, Parish Dir.; Michael Rovella.
645 S. Fifth St., 81401. Tel: 970-249-3319; Fax: 970-249-9088.
Mission—Olathe, Montrose Co., Our Lady of Fatima, Tel: 970-323-6217.

Ouray, Ouray Co., St. Daniel the Prophet (1883), Rev. Nathanael Foshage, O.S.B.
P.O. Box 565, 81427. Tel: 970-325-4373.
Mission—Silverton, San Juan Co., St. Patrick, 1005 Reece, Silverton, 81433.

Pagosa Springs, Archuleta Co., Immaculate Heart of Mary (1923), Rev. John C. Bowe, C.R.
P.O. Box 451, 81147. Tel: 970-264-5702; Fax: 970-264-4876. [CEM]
Missions—Frances, St. Francis; Pagosa Junction, Archuleta Co., St. John Baptist; Trujillo, St. James.
Station—Chromo.

Paonia, Delta Co., Sacred Heart (1923), Rev. Michael N. Smith, S.J., Admin.
235 N. Fork Ave., P.O. Box 988, 81428. Tel: 970-527-3214; Fax: 970-527-5468.
Mission—Hotchkiss, Delta Co., St. Margaret Mary, 331 Bridge St., Hotchkiss, 81419. Tel: 970-872-2117.

Rocky Ford, Otero Co., St. Peter (1910), Rev. Richard L. Wehrmeyer, C.M.
1209 Swink Ave., 81067. Tel: 719-254-3565.
Missions—Manzanola, Otero Co., St. Joseph the Worker, P.O. Box 265, Manzanola, 81058.; Ordway, Crowley Co., St. Peter Church, P.O. Box 218, Ordway, 81063. Tel: 719-267-4645; Fowler, Otero Co., Mary Queen of Heaven, P.O. Box 214, Fowler, 81039. Tel: 719-263-4455.

San Luis, Costilla Co., Sangre de Cristo (1881) (Hispanic), Rev. Patrick M. Valdez, C.R.
Res., P.O. Box 326, 81152. Tel: 719-672-3685; Fax: 719-672-0300. [CEM]
Missions—Blanca, Costilla Co., St. James, Blanca, 81123. Tel: 719-672-3685; Fort Garland, Costilla Co., Holy Family, Fort Garland, 81133.; Chama, Costilla Co., Immaculate Conception, Chama, 81153.; San Acacio, Costilla Co., San Acacio, San Acacio, 81150.; San Pedro, Costilla Co., SS. Peter and Paul, San Pedro, 81153.; San Isidro, Costilla Co., St. Isidro; San Francisco, Costilla Co., St. Francis of Assisi, San Francisco, 81153.; Garcia, Costilla Co., Sacred Heart of Jesus, Garcia, 81134.
Catechesis/Religious Programs—Students 143.

Silverton, San Juan Co., St. Patrick (1883), Rev. Nathanael Foshage, O.S.B.
Mailing Address: P.O. Box 565, Ouray, 81427. Tel: 970-325-4373.

Springfield, Baca Co., Annunciation (1932), Rev. J. Patrick Walsh, S.J.
140 Kansas St., 81073. Tel: 719-523-6645.
Station—Walsh.

Telluride, San Miguel Co., St. Patrick (1896), Rev. Kevin F. Novack.
P.O. Box 398, 81435. Tel: 970-728-3387; Fax: 970-728-8029.
Mission—Nucla, Montrose Co., Our Lady of Sorrows, P.O. Box 451, Nucla, 81424. Tel: 970-864-7788.

Trinidad, Las Animas Co., Most Holy Trinity, Trinidad Area Catholic Community (Trinidad Cluster) (1885), Revs. Mark D. McKenzie, S.J., Supr.; Eugene C. Renard, S.J.; Harry H. Hoormann, S.J.; Robert A. Hagan, S.J.
235 N. Convent St., 81082. Tel: 719-846-3369; Fax: 719-846-4856. [CEM]
School—237 Church St., 81082. Tel: 719-846-7541. Sisters 3; Lay Teachers 21; Students 231.
Missions—Weston, Las Animas Co., Our Lord of Esquipula; Vigil, St. Isidore; Branson, Las Animas Co., Blessed Sacrament; Trinchera, Las Animas Co., Sacred Heart; Hoehne, Las Animas Co., St. John Baptist; Segundo, Las Animas Co., St. Ignatius.

Our Lady of Mt. Carmel, Trinidad Area Catholic Community (Trinidad Cluster) (1907), Revs. Mark D. McKenzie, S.J., Supr.; Harry H. Hoormann, S.J.; Eugene C. Renard, S.J., V.F.; Robert A. Hagan, S.J.
Mailing Address: 235 N. Convent St., 81082. Tel: 719-846-3369; Fax: 719-846-4856.
Mission—Cokedale, Las Animas Co., Sacred Hearts of Jesus and Mary.

St. Joseph, Trinidad Area Catholic Community (Trinidad Cluster) (1950), Revs. Mark D. McKenzie, S.J., Supr.; Eugene C. Renard, S.J.; Harry H. Hoormann, S.J.; Robert A. Hagan, S.J.
Mailing Address: 235 N Convent St., 81082. Tel: 719-846-3369; Fax: 719-846-4856.

Vineland, Pueblo Co., St. Therese (1928), Revs. Richard F. Becker; Robert F. Carden.
1133 Lane 36, Pueblo, 81006. Tel: 719-948-2410.

Walsenburg, Huerfano Co., St. Mary (1896), Rev. Frank L. Davied, O.F.M., V.F.; Sr. Carol Tlack, N.D., Senior Outreach Dir.
P.O. Box 86, 81089. Tel: 719-738-1204; Fax: 719-738-1206. [CEM]
Missions—La Veta, Huerfano Co., Christ the King, P.O. Box 752, La Veta, 81055.; Gardner, Huerfano Co., Sacred Heart, P.O. Box 228, Gardner, 81040.; Chama, Huerfano Co., Our Lady of Guadalupe.

Westcliffe, Custer Co., Our Lady of the Assumption (!870), Rev. Louis M. Kirby, O.S.B.
P.O. Box 359, 81252. Tel: 719-783-2340.

Chaplains of Public Institutions

PUEBLO. *Colorado State Hospital*. Vacant. Tel: 719-546-4434.

CANON CITY. *Fremont Correctional Facility*. Vacant. St. Dismas Chapel.

CROWLEY. *Arkansas Valley Correctional Facility*. Vacant.

FLORENCE. *Federal Correctional Institute at Florence*. Revs. John O'Flynn; Frank Tinajero, S.V.D.

FORT LYON. *Veterans Administration Hospital*. Vacant. Mailing Address:Mailing Address: P.O. Box 147, 81038. Tel: 719-456-1260, Ext. 3939.

TRINIDAD. *State Home for the Aged*. Administered by priests from Trinity area Catholic community.

On Duty Outside the Diocese:
Reverend Fathers—
Gini, John E., Jolon, CA
Haberman, C. Robert, San Rafael, CA
Kurz, Michael A., Rockford, IL
Norman, Clifford A., Mexico
Ricken, David L., J.C.L., Rome, Italy

Absent on Leave:
Reverend Fathers—
Bonfadini, Leo
Bouchard, Norman
Groves, William
Thill, Richard
Vandenberg, James

Military Chaplains:
Reverend Fathers—
Cerwonka, Clarence G., U.S. Army

Sabbatical:
Reverend Fathers—
Quinn, Thomas J.

Retired:
Reverend Monsignors—
Delaney, Howard L., 7-C Bonnymede, Pueblo, CO 81001
Holland, George T., 2204 Wyoming Ave., Pueblo, CO 81004
Kane, Joseph F., 4214 Minnequa, Apt. C, St. Louis, MO 63118
Reverend Fathers—
Beno, John R., 315 W. 15th St., Pueblo, CO 81003
Blong, Delbert F., 3336 S. Ammons, Unit 12-103, Lakewood, CO 80227
Cavanagh, Michael J., 56 Wentworth, Westwood, MA 02090
Corbett, Michael E., 2102 D. Chautard Dr., Pueblo, CO 81005
Danowski, Alexander J., 653 Country Court, Grand Junction, CO 81506
Kiernan, John G., 2185 Linda Ln., Grand Junction, CO 81501
Kukucka, Joseph G., 417 Indiana St., Sugar City, CO 81076
Marcantonio, Clement, 2nd General Hospital, APO AG, 09180
McDevitt, James J., St. Vincent's Church, 840 George Bush Blvd., Delray Beach, FL 33483
Mendrick, Paul P., 1312 Lakeview Ave., Apt. 204, Pueblo, CO 81004
Montoya, Jose J., Forrest Park Care Center, 7045 Stuart St., Westminister, CO 80030
Munson, Thomas N., Res., 16098 County Rd. 28.3, Dolores, CO 81323
O'Sullivan, John C., Livingston Baker Apts. #608, 1925 First Ave., Seattle, WA 98101
Powers, William V., 1414 E. 8th St., Pueblo, CO 81001
Racki, Leonard E., 31 Terrace Dr., Pueblo, CO 81001
Rykowski, Jerome A., 2675 Springside Ct. #3B, Grand Junction, CO 81506. Tel: 970-243-6234
Schoening, Sylvester H., Hermitage, 1250 Mountain View Ln., P.O. Box 553, Norwood, CO 81423
Smigiel, Walter J., 3517 Atlantic Dr., Colorado Springs, CO 80910
Sutton, John H., 310 3rd Ave., Cando, ND 58324
Sweeney, Eugene J., 120 Ashley Dr., Fairhope, AL 36532
Tomalonis, John, Tremont Nursing Home, 44 Donaldson Rd., Tremont, PA 17981
Wichmann, Edward W., 1225 Central Blvd., Apt. 903, Brownsville, TX 78520

Permanent Deacons:
Boies, James A., Sr.
Booth, William R.
Hawes, Lloyd
Myscofski, Robert, Our Lady of the Meadows, Pueblo
Pewters, William, St. Joseph, Grand Junction
Putnam, Dennis, Montrose
Reynolds, Philip
Rovella, Mike
Stoop, John
Swindells, George A., Pueblo

INSTITUTIONS LOCATED IN THE DIOCESE

[A] HIGH SCHOOLS, DIOCESAN

TRINIDAD. *Trinidad Catholic Schools*, 201 Church St, 81082. Tel: 719-846-7541; Fax: 719-846-4856. Mr. Joseph A. Reorda, Prin.(Grades K-12). Sisters 3; Lay Teachers 21; Students 231.

[B] HIGH SCHOOLS, PRIVATE

CANON CITY. *St. Scholastica Academy*, 615 Pike Ave., 81212. Tel: 719-275-7461; Fax: 719-269-9531. Girls boarding and day school. (Grades 6-12). Ms. Virginia T. Wilkinson, Prin. Benedictine Sisters of Chicago 8; Lay Teachers 13; Students 92.

[C] ELEMENTARY SCHOOLS, PRIVATE

PUEBLO. *John Neumann Catholic Schools*, 330 Lake Ave., 81004. Tel: 719-543-8407. Mrs. Diana Croasdell, Admin.

Elementary School, 2415 E. Orman Ave., 81004. Tel: 719-561-9419; 566-9636. Lay Teachers 18; Students 234.
Middle School, 330 Lake Ave., 81004. Tel: 719-543-8864. Lay Teachers 7; Students 96.
Preschool, 2415 E. Orman Ave., 81004. Tel: 719-561-9419. Mrs. Rose Mary Runyan, Dir. Lay Teachers 3; Students 82.

[D] GENERAL HOSPITALS

PUEBLO. *Centura Health-St. Mary-Corwin Hospital*, 1008 Minnequa Ave., 81004. Tel: 719-560-4000; Fax: 719-560-5823
For a complete listing, refer to the Hospitals section.
CANON CITY. *Centura Health-St. Thomas More Hospital*, 1338 Phay Ave., 81212. Tel: 719-269-2000; Fax: 719-269-2016
For a complete listing, refer to the Hospitals section.
DURANGO. *Centura Health-Mercy Medical Center*, 375 E. Park Ave., 81301. Tel: 970-247-4311; Fax: 970-382-1082
For a complete listing, refer to the Hospitals section.
GRAND JUNCTION. *Marillac Clinic, Inc.*, 600 Center Ave., Bldg. 3A, 81501
For a complete listing, refer to the Hospitals section.
St. Mary Hospital and Medical Center, P.O. Box 1628, 81502. Tel: 970-244-2273; Fax: 970-244-7510
For a complete listing, refer to the Hospitals section.

[E] SPECIAL CARE FACILITIES

PUEBLO. *Villa Pueblo*, 1111 Bonforte Blvd., 81001. Tel: 719-646-5911; Fax: 719-544-1354
For a complete listing, refer to the Special Care Facilities section.
CANON CITY. *Centura Health-Progressive Care Center*, 1338 Phay Ave., 81212. Tel: 719-269-2000; Fax: 719-269-2016
For a complete listing, refer to the Special Care Facilities section.
FLORENCE. *Centura Health-St. Joseph Manor*, 600 W. 3rd St., 81226-1117. Tel: 719-784-4893; Fax: 719-784-4308
For a complete listing, refer to the Special Care Facilities section.

[F] MONASTERIES AND RESIDENCES OF PRIESTS AND BROTHERS

CANON CITY. *Holy Cross Abbey*, P.O. Box 1510, 81215-1510. Tel: 719-275-8631; Fax: 719-275-7125. Kenneth C. Hein, O.S.B., Abbot; Rt. Revs. Edward J. Vollmer, O.S.B., Retired Abbot; Warren J. Heidgen, O.S.B., Retired Abbot; Revs. Ignatius J. Smith, O.S.B., Prior & Procurator; Stephen J. Sustrick, O.S.B.; Harold M. Glentzer, O.S.B.; Lambert W. Morrow, O.S.B., Subprior; William L. Thompson, O.S.B.; Bernard P. Gervais, O.S.B.; Bede J. Butler, O.S.B.; Louis M. Kirby, O.S.B.; Henry W. Lacerte, O.S.B.; Paul J. Montez, O.S.B.; Michael D. Murray, O.S.B.; Martin de Porres J. Muheim, O.S.B.; John Robinson, O.S.B.; Barnabas W. Stelzner, O.S.B.; Andrew J. Kemberling, O.S.B.; Bros. Bernard A.F. Best, O.S.B.; Matthew Bach, O.S.B.; Kevin J. Bachmann, O.S.B.; Aelred Wetli, O.S.B., Latin American Missions; Patrick J. Braskey, O.S.B.; David J. Downey, O.S.B.; Aloysius A.L. Shaima, O.S.B.; Gregory Legge, O.S.B. Priests of Monastery 18; Professed Brothers 6; Oblates 2.
TRINIDAD. *Trinidad Area Catholic Community*, 615 E. Goddard Ave., 81082. Tel: 719-846-3360. Business Address: 235 N. Convent St., 81082. Tel: 719-846-3369; Fax: 719-846-4856. Revs. Mark D. McKenzie, S.J., Supr.; Robert A. Hagan, S.J.; Harry H. Hoormann, S.J.; Eugene C. Renard, S.J., V.F.

[G] CONVENTS AND RESIDENCES FOR SISTERS

PUEBLO. *Servants of the Blessed Sacrament*, 311 E. Mesa Ave., 81006. Tel: 719-545-7729. Sr. Josephine Roney, S.S.S., Supr. Sisters 6.
GRAND JUNCTION. *Adrian Dominican Sisters, Southwest Mission Chapter*, 1983 S. Broadway, 81503-9592. Tel: 970-241-6152; Fax: 970-257-0812. Sr. Barbara Stanek, O.P., Chapter Prioress.
MONTROSE. *St. Mary Youth Minister Residence*, 529 S. Fifth St., 81401. Tel: 970-252-0418.

[H] NEWMAN CENTERS

GUNNISON. *Campus Ministry - Diocese of Pueblo*, 600 E. Georgia, 81230. Tel: 970-641-0325. Ms. Janet Johnson, Dir.
University of Southern Colorado, Campus Ministry. Tel: 719-542-9248. Ms. Sheilagh McGlynn.
Adams State College (Alamosa), United Campus Ministry College Center, Rm. 329, Alamosa, 81102. Tel: 719-589-7516; 274-5304. Mr. Daniel Borg.
Fort Lewis College. Fort Lewis College Center for Campus Ministry, North Complex #7, 1000 Rim Dr., Box 7211, Durango, 81301. Tel: 970-247-7460. Ms. Lisa Sauer, Campus Min.
Mesa State College (Grand Junction), Newman Center, 1135 College Pl., Grand Junction, 81501. Tel: 970-241-3670. Sr. Kathy Lentsch, O.S.F., Campus Min.
Western State College (Gunnison), Campus Ministry Center, 600 E. Georgia, 81230. Tel: 970-641-0325. Ms. Janet Johnson, Campus Min.
Otero Junior College (La Junta), P.O. Box 1181, La Junta, 81050. Tel: 719-384-4342. Mr. F. Anthony Gallegos, Contact Person.
Lamar Junior College (Lamar). (Contact Parish, St. Francis de Sales), 600 E. Parmenter, Lamar, 81052. Tel: 719-336-7759.
Trinidad State Junior College Campus Ministry (Trinidad), 600 Prospect, Trinidad, 81082. Tel: 719-846-5624. Mr. Allen Bachoroski, Contact Person.

[I] RETREAT WORK

CRESTONE. *Spiritual Life Institute of America, Inc.*, P.O. Box 219, 81131. Tel: 719-256-4778; Fax: 719-256-4719. Revs. William McNamara, O.C.D.; David Denny, Prior. Priests 2; Brothers 2; Sisters 3.
MONTROSE. *Spes in Deo Franciscan Family Retreat Center, Inc.*, 21661 Hwy. 550, 81401. Tel: 970-249-3526. M. Joyce Martin, Pres., Bd. of Directors.
WHITEWATER. *Whitewater Community, Inc.*, 8250 Kannah Creek Rd., 81527. Tel: 970-241-3847. Sisters 2.

[J] MISCELLANEOUS

PUEBLO.
**Catholic Diocese of Pueblo Foundation*, 1001 N. Grand Ave., 81003.
Deacon Candidate Formation Council, 1001 N. Grand Ave., 81003.
John Neumann Catholic School (Administration & Middle School), 330 Lake Ave., 81004. (John Neumann Catholic Schools housed at Seton Education Center).
Pueblo Community Soup Kitchen, Inc., 422 W. Seventh, 81003. Tel: 719-545-6540. Mrs. Myrtle Huff, Coord.
S.E.T. of Pueblo, Inc. A division of Catholic Health Initiatives Mountain Region. 1902 E. Orman Ave., 81004. Tel: 719-560-5886; Fax: 719-560-4655. Sr. Jacqueline Riggio, S.C., Exec. Dir. Purpose: A ministry to low-income, disadvantaged, and underserved persons, providing educational and health maintenance for empowerment and transformation.
St. Anthony Community, 18 Dartmouth, 81005. Tel: 719-566-1620.
SEARCH of Pueblo, 917 E. Evans, 81004. Tel: 719-544-8246.
Serra Club of Pueblo, 3216 Baltimore Ave., 81008. Tel: 719-542-8133. Mrs. Sophie Ruskin, Pres.
Sisters for Christian Community, 1081 S. Lynx Dr., 81007. Tel: 719-547-2416. Sallie Watkins, Sec.
CENTER. *Artes Del Valle (Hispanic Craft Cooperative)*, P.O. Box 627, 81125. Tel: 719-589-4769; 754-3191. Artes del Valle is under the auspices of St. Francis Jerome Church, Center.
DURANGO. *Mercy Health Foundation*, 375 E. Park Ave., 81301. Tel: 970-382-1273. Affiliate of Catholic Health Initiatives.
GRAND JUNCTION. *Grand Valley Catholic Outreach*, 240 White Ave., 81501. Tel: 970-241-3658. P.O. Box 246, 81502.
Grand Valley Peace and Justice, 253 White Ave., P.O. Box 246, 81501. Tel: 970-243-4378. Mrs. Bev Goodrich, Dir.
St. Mary's Hospital Foundation, 2635 N. 7th St., P.O. Box 1628, 81502-1628.
St. Mary's Rehabilitation Center, Inc., P.O. Box 1628, 81502.
PAGOSA SPRINGS. *Archuleta Housing Corporation*, 713 San Juan Ave. P.O. Box 355, 81147-0355. Tel: 970-264-2195.

RELIGIOUS INSTITUTES OF MEN REPRESENTED IN THE DIOCESE

For further details refer to the corresponding bracketed number in the Religious Institutes of Men or Women section.
[0200]—*Benedictine Monks.*—O.S.B.
[1330]—*Congregation of the Mission.* (Missouri Prov.).—C.M.
[0260]—*Discalced Carmelite Monks.*—O.C.D.
[0690]—*Jesuit Fathers and Brothers.* (Missouri Prov.).—S.J.
[]—*Missionaries of the Divine Word.*—S.V.D.
[]—*Order Franciscan Minor.*—O.F.M.
[1300]—*Theatine Fathers.* (Rome, Italy).—C.R.

RELIGIOUS INSTITUTES OF WOMEN REPRESENTED IN THE DIOCESE

[0230]—*Benedictine Sisters of Pontifical Jurisdiction.* (Chicago, IL; Covington, KY; Colorado Springs, CO; Yankton, SD).—O.S.B.
[1710]—*Congregation of the Third Order of St. Francis of Mary Immaculate, Joliet, IL.*—O.S.F.
[0420]—*Discalced Carmelite Nuns.*—O.C.D.
[1070-13]—*Dominican Sisters.*—O.P.
[1070-24]—*Dominican Sisters.*—O.P.
[]—*Guadalupanas Missionaries of the Holy Spirit.*
[2575]—*Institute of the Sisters of Mercy of the Americas.*—R.S.M.
[2960]—*Notre Dame Sisters.*—N.D.
[3130]—*Our Lady of Victory.*—O.L.V.M.
[3580]—*Servants of Mary.*—O.S.M.
[3500]—*Servants of the Blessed Sacrament.*—S.S.S.
[]—*Sisters for Christian Community.*—S.F.C.C.
[0440]—*Sisters of Charity of Cincinnati, Ohio.*—S.C.
[0480]—*Sisters of Charity of Leavenworth, Kansas.*—S.C.L.
[2360]—*Sisters of Loretto At the Foot of the Cross.*—S.L.
[1570]—*Sisters of St. Francis of the Holy Family.*—O.S.F.
[3830-15]—*Sisters of St. Joseph.*—C.S.J.
[3830-18]—*Sisters of St. Joseph.*—C.S.J.
[1720]—*Sisters of the Third Order Regular of St. Francis of the Congregation of Our Lady of Lourdes.*—O.S.F.
[]—*Sisters of Whitewater Community.*
[4060]—*Society of the Holy Child Jesus.*—S.H.C.J.

CEMETERIES, DIOCESAN AND PAROCHIAL

PUEBLO. *Gate of Heaven.* Legal Title: *Gate of Heaven Section, Roselawn Cemetery Assoc.*
AGUILAR. *St. Anthony.* (St. Anthony Parish).
CAPULIN. *St. Anthony; St. Francis; St. Joseph; and Capulin.* (St. Joseph Parish).
CONEJOS. *Conejos; Las Mesitas; San Antonio; Ortiz; and Labatos.* (Our Lady of Guadalupe Parish).
DEL NORTE. *St. Francis of Assisi.* (Holy Name of Mary Parish).
FRUITA. *Fruita Catholic.* (Sacred Heart Parish).
PAGOSA SPRINGS. *St. John the Baptist; St. Andrew Avelino; St. Francis; and St. James.* (Immaculate Heart of Mary Parish).
RYE. *Mount Olivet.* (St. Daniel Mission Parish). Legal Title: *The Rye Mount Olivet Cemetery.*
SAN LUIS. *San Luis; San Pedro; San Acacio; San Francisco; and Chama.* (Sangre de Cristo Parish).
TRINIDAD. *Trinidad Catholic.* Legal Title: Trinidad Catholic Cemetery Assoc. (Holy Trinity Parish).
WALSENBURG. *St. Mary.* Legal Title: St. Mary Cemetery Association, Inc. (St. Mary Parish).
WESTCLIFFE. *Silver Cliff Assumption Catholic.* (Our Lady of the Assumption Parish).

NECROLOGY

† Stauter, Rev. Msgr. Patrick C., (Retired). —Died Jan. 24, 1997.

Diocese of Raleigh

(Dioecesis Raleighiensis)

Most Reverend

F. JOSEPH GOSSMAN, D.D., J.C.D.

Bishop of Raleigh; ordained December 17, 1955; appointed Titular Bishop of Aguntum and Auxiliary Bishop of Baltimore July 15, 1968; ordained Bishop, September 11, 1968; appointed Fourth Bishop of Raleigh April 8, 1975; installed May 19, 1975. *Res., 1601 Westbridge Ct., Raleigh, NC, 27606. Office: 300 Cardinal Gibbons Dr., Raleigh, NC, 27606.* Tel.: 919-821-9702.

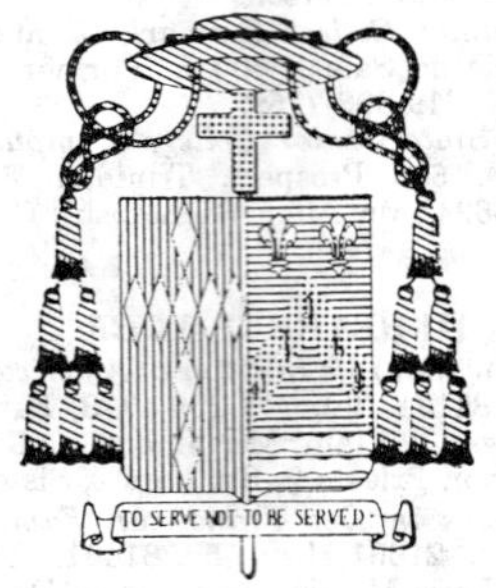

Most Reverend

GEORGE E. LYNCH, D.D.

Retired Auxiliary Bishop of Raleigh; Titular Bishop of Satafi; ordained May 29, 1943; appointed October 20, 1969; consecrated January 6, 1970; retired July 10, 1985. *Res., P.O. Box 3, Woodlawn Station, Bronx, NY, 10470.*

ESTABLISHED AS VICARIATE-APOSTOLIC OF NORTH CAROLINA BY POPE PIUS IX, MARCH 3, 1868

ESTABLISHED AS DIOCESE OF RALEIGH BY POPE PIUS XI, DECEMBER 12, 1924.

Square Miles 31,875.

Comprises the following Counties in the State of North Carolina: Alamance, Beaufort, Bertie, Bladen, Brunswick, Camden, Carteret, Caswell, Chatham, Chowan, Columbus, Craven, Cumberland, Currituck, Dare, Duplin, Durham, Edgecombe, Franklin, Gates, Granville, Greene, Halifax, Harnett, Hertford, Hoke, Hyde, Johnston, Jones, Lee, Lenoir, Martin, Moore, Nash, New Hanover, Northampton, Onslow, Orange, Pamlico, Pasquotank, Pender, Perquimans, Person, Pitt, Robeson, Sampson, Scotland, Tyrrell, Vance, Wake, Warren. Washington, Wayne and Wilson

For legal titles of parishes and diocesan institutions, consult the Chancery.

Catholic Center: 300 Cardinal Gibbons Dr., Raleigh, NC, 27606. Tel.: 919-821-9700; Fax: 919-821-9705.

Web site address: http://www.raldioc.org

E-mail address: chancery@raldioc.org

STATISTICAL OVERVIEW

Personnel	
Bishop	1
Retired Bishops	1
Priests: Diocesan Active in Diocese	54
Priests: Active Outside Diocese	4
Priests: Retired, Sick or Absent	19
Number of Diocesan Priests	77
Religious Priests in Diocese	52
Extern Priests in Diocese	7
Permanent Deacons in Diocese	22
Total Brothers	7
Total Sisters	83
Parishes	
Parishes	70
With Resident Pastor:	
Resident Diocesan Priests	39
Resident Religious Priests	25
Without Resident Pastor:	
Administered by Women Religious	6
Missions	14
Pastoral Centers	10
Professional Ministry Personnel:	
Sisters	23
Lay Ministers	67
Welfare	
Catholic Hospitals	1
Total Assisted	6,000
Day Care and Extended Day Care Centers	6
Total Assisted	705
Special Centers for Social Services	10
Total Assisted	47,452
Educational	
Diocesan Students in Other Seminaries	22
Total Seminarians	22
High Schools, Diocesan and Parish	1
Total Students	575
Elementary Schools, Diocesan and Parish	17
Total Students	4,969
Catechesis/Religious Education:	
High School Students	3,143
Elementary Students	13,015
Total Students Under Catholic Instruction	21,724
Teachers in the Diocese:	
Brothers	2
Sisters	16
Lay Teachers	243
Vital Statistics	
Receptions into the Church:	
Infant Baptism Totals	3,211
Adult Baptism Totals	246
Received into Full Communion	350
First Communions	2,890
Confirmations	1,347
Marriages:	
Catholic	360
Interfaith	404
Total Marriages	764
Deaths	674
Total Catholic Population	133,442
Total Population	3,590,238

Former Bishops of Diocese—Most Rev. WILLIAM J. HAFEY, D.D., cons. June 24, 1925; transferred to the See of Scranton, PA, Oct. 2, 1937; installed Nov. 15, 1937; died May 12, 1954.—Most Rev. EUGENE J. MCGUINNESS, D.D., cons. Dec. 21, 1937; transferred to the See of Oklahoma City and Tulsa, OK, Dec. 8, 1944; installed Jan. 10, 1945; died Dec. 27, 1957.—Most Rev. VINCENT S. WATERS, D.D., cons. May 15, 1945; installed June 6, 1945; died Dec. 3, 1974.

Former Bishops of Vicariate-Apostolic—His Eminence JAMES CARDINAL GIBBONS, cons. Aug. 16, 1868, Titular Bishop of Adramyttum, first Vicar-Apostolic; transferred to Richmond, VA, July 30, 1872; promoted to the See of Baltimore, Oct. 3, 1877; created Cardinal-Priest of S. Maria in Trastevere, June 7, 1886; died March 24, 1921.—Most Rev. JOHN J. KEANE, cons. Bishop of Richmond and Vicar-Apostolic of North Carolina, Aug. 25, 1878; transferred to the Titular See of Jasso, Aug. 12, 1888; elevated to the Archepiscopal Dignity with the title of Archbishop of Damascus, Jan. 9, 1897; transferred to the See of Dubuque, July 24, 1900; resigned April 3, 1911; appt. Titular Archbishop of Cios, April 28, 1911; died June 23, 1918.—Rt. Rev. H. P. NORTHROP, cons. Titular Bishop of Rosalia and Vicar-Apostolic of North Carolina, Jan. 8, 1882; transferred to Charleston, Jan. 27, 1883; died June 7, 1916.—Rt. Rev. LEO HAID, O.S.B., Vicar Apostolic of North Carolina and Abbot-Ordinary of Belmont Abbey; cons. Titular Bishop of Messene, July 1, 1888; died July 24, 1924.

Office of the Bishop—715 Nazareth St., Raleigh, 27606. Tel: 919-821-9702; Fax: 919-821-9755.

Vicar General—Rev. Msgr. JAMES E. MCSWEENEY, *715 Nazareth St., Raleigh, 27606.*

Vicar General & Moderator of the Curia—Very Rev. GERALD L. LEWIS, *715 Nazareth St., Raleigh, 27606.* Tel: 919-821-9702.

Chancellor—JOHN P. RIEDY, *715 Nazareth St., Raleigh, 27606.* Tel: 919-821-9704.

Vice Chancellor for Canonical Affairs—Rev. GIRARD M. SHERBA, J.C.L., *715 Nazareth St., Raleigh, 27606.* Tel: 919-821-9756.

Chancery—715 Nazareth St., Raleigh, 27606. Tel: 919-821-9703; Fax: 919-821-9705.

Deans—Rev. TERRENCE COLLINS, Albermarle; Rev. THOMAS P. HADDEN, Cape Fear; Rev. THOMAS J. GAUL, Fayetteville; Rev. FRANCIS MOESLEIN, New Bern; Rev. JOHN MCGEE, O.S.F.S, Piedmont; Rev. JOHN F. O'CONNOR, Raleigh; Rev. JAMES M. LABOSKY, Tar River.

Diocesan Attorney—CHARLES F. POWERS, III, *P.O. Box 1471, Raleigh, 27602.* Tel: 919-828-0684.

Diocesan Consultors—Revs. THOMAS P. HADDEN; JOSEPH G. VETTER; JOHN F. O'CONNOR; FRANCIS R. MOESLEIN; MICHAEL P. SHUGRUE; GERALD L. LEWIS.

Diocesan Tribunal—715 Nazareth St., Raleigh, 27606. Tel: 919-821-9700. All rogatorial commissions should be directed to the Tribunal.

Advocates—SR. BARBARA MARIE CADY, S.U.; DORIS S. ALBERNAZ; DONALD J. BALFE; ROBERT W. BARTOLDUS; BRUCE G. BEEZER, Ed.D.; BARBARA A. BLAIR; JOAN M. DOWD; ROSEMARY DUDASH; TEA DUDLEY;

NOELIE H. DUHE, M.P.A.; JOHN R. HALADA; BARBARA HAROLD; JOY M. HARSEN, M.P.H.; MARGARET E. HAST; Deacon JOHN L. HUBISZ, Ph.D.; SHIRLEY M. HUX; DOLORES MACK; EDWARD W. MACK; MARCELENE A. MCLURE; NANCY T. MILLER; ANN M. SAUNDERS; MARY L. WILSON.

Defenders of the Bond—Revs. JOSEPH MULRONEY J.C.L.; ALBAN HARMON, C.P., J.C.L.

Diocesan Judges—Rev. Msgr. JAMES E. MCSWEENEY; Revs. JAMES F. BUTLER; THOMAS P. HADDEN; JEFFREY A. INGHAM; WILLIAM L. PITTS.

Director of the Tribunal—Sr. PATRICIA M. WILSON, S.C.

Notaries—VIKKI NEWELL; ANNE SPEICHER.

Officialis—Rev. GIRARD M. SHERBA, J.C.L.

Promotor of Justice—Vacant.

Priests' Council—Revs. DAVID BROCKMAN; MICHAEL CLAY; TERRENCE COLLINS; JOHN J. FORBES; THOMAS J. GAUL; THOMAS P. HADDEN; DANIEL KENNA, O.M.F.; JAMES M. LABOSKY; DAVID MCBRIAR, O.F.M.; FRANCIS R. MOESLEIN; JOHN O'CONNOR; GIRARD M. SHERBA; MICHAEL SHUGRUE; DONALD STAIB; JOSEPH G. VETTER. Ex-Officio: GERALD LEWIS, V.G.; D. ROBERTO KEENAN.

Sisters' Council—Sr. MARGARET HARIG, S.N.D.

Vicar for Priests—Rev. MICHAEL P. SHUGRUE, *Duke University, Box 99057, Durham, 27708.*

Vicars for Religious—Sr. DAMIAN MARIE JACKSON, O.S.F., *711 Mason Rd., Durham, 27712.* Sr. MARGARET GALLAGHER, I.H.M., *P.O. Box 822, Plymouth, 27962.*

Diocesan Divisions and Departments

Business Services Division—RUSSELL ELMAYAN, Dir., *Catholic Center, 715 Nazareth St., Raleigh, 27606.* Tel: 919-821-9722.

Computer Services—JOHN ALLAN TALLANT. Tel: 919-821-9719.

Fiscal Services—KIM WARD. Tel: 919-821-9727.

Development Office—DEBORAH ROSSI. Tel: 919-821-9721.

Property / Construction—ARTHUR WESCHE. Tel: 919-821-9726.

Communications Division—FRANK MOROCK, Dir., *Catholic Center, 715 Nazareth St., Raleigh, 27606.* Tel: 919-821-9732.

Evangelization Office—TERRENCE JACKSON, Dir. Tel: 919-821-9746.

Freeman Media Resource Center—TERRI RING. Tel: 919-821-9743.

Graphic Services—TAMMY S. STANLEY. Tel: 919-821-9735.

NC Catholic Newspaper—JOHN STRANGE, Editor. Tel: 919-821-9736.

Campus Ministry—Rev. PHILLIP LEACH, Dir., *Newman Catholic Student Center, 218 Pittsboro St., Chapel Hill, 27516-2738.* Tel: 919-929-3730.

Catholic Schools—MICHAEL J. FEDEWA, Supt. Tel: 919-821-9748.

Faith Development—MARY DOWLING. Tel: 919-821-9771.

Marriage Preparation—Mrs. LINDA BEDO. Tel: 919-821-9753.

Youth Ministry—ELA MILEWSKA. Tel: 919-821-9770.

Young Adult Ministry—Tel: 919-821-9771.

Adult Faith Development—ROBERT JONES. Tel: 919-821-9740.

African-American Ministry—Sr. MAXINE TOWNS, S.A., *St. Alphonsus Center, 810 N. Reid St., Wilson, 27893.* Tel: 919-821-9762.

Hispanic Ministry—TERESA ALDAHONDO, *Catholic Center, 715 Nazareth St., Raleigh, 27606.* Tel: 919-821-9764.

Vicar for Hispanics—Rev. D. ROBERTO KEENAN, *c/o Diocese of Raleigh, Hispanic Ministry, 715 Nazareth St., Raleigh, 27606.* Tel: 919-821-9738.

Office of Liturgy—Rev. JOHN F. O'CONNOR, *Sacred Heart Cathedral, 226 Hillsborough St., Raleigh, 27603-1724.* Tel: 919-832-6030.

Vicar for Black Catholics—Rev. THOMAS P. HADDEN, *St. Mary Church, 412 Ann St., Wilmington, 28401-4596.* Tel: 910-762-5491.

Vocations—Rev. JOHN RANALLI, Dir., *Catholic Center, 715 Nazareth St., Raleigh, 27606.* Tel: 919-821-9713.

Catholic Social Ministries—KATHLEEN WALSH, A.C.S.W., Dir., *Catholic Center, 715 Nazareth St., Raleigh, 27606.* Tel: 919-821-9752.

Peace and Justice—Sr. JOAN JURSKI, O.S.F., *Catholic Center, 715 Nazareth St., Raleigh, 27606.* Tel: 919-821-9751.

Senior Housing—LINDA BEDO, *Catholic Center, 715 Nazareth St., Raleigh, 27606.* Tel: 919-821-9753.

Regional Offices—

Albemarle Deanery Office—JILLIAN MILLER, Dir., *123 Market St., Hertford, 27944.* Tel: 919-426-7717.

Cape Fear Deanery Office—DIANE PISCZEK, M.Ed., Dir., *2805 Market St., Wilmington, 28403.* Tel: 910-251-8130.

Fayetteville Deanery Office—DOROTHY ANN PYLE, Dir., *111 Boone Trail, Fayetteville, 28306.* Tel: 910-424-2020.

New Bern Deanery Office—MICHAEL MILES, C.C.S.W., Dir., *P.O. Box 1251, New Bern, 28560.* Tel: 919-638-2188.

Piedmont Deanery—SUSAN GILBERTSON, M.S.W., *P.O. Box 647, Durham, 27702.* Tel: 919-286-1964.

Raleigh Deanery—RODERICK B. O'CONNOR, C.C.S.W., *400 Oberlin Rd., Ste. 350, Raleigh, 27605.* Tel: 919-832-0225.

Tar River Deanery—ELAINE FRANZETTI, M.S.W., *P.O. Box 8241, Greenville, 27835-8241.* Tel: 919-355-5111.

Miscellaneous Offices—

Apostleship of Prayer—Rev. MICHAEL H. JORDAN, S.J., *P.O. Box 461, Erwin, 28339.* Tel: 910-897-2277.

Apostleship of the Sea—Rev. FRANCIS R. MOESLEIN, *St. Egbert Church, 1706 Evans St., Morehead City, 28557.* Tel: 919-726-3559.

Boy Scouts—HALL MOORE, JR., Scout Chap., *329 Meredith St., Raleigh, 27606.*

Censor Librorum—Rev. Msgr. JAMES E. MCSWEENEY.

Engaged Encounter—Marriage Preparation and Enrichment Office, *Catholic Center, 715 Nazareth St., Raleigh, 27606.* Tel: 919-821-9753.

Holy Childhood Pontifical Association—Rev. WILLIAM L. PITTS; Sr. THERESE CHURCH, *209 S. Lumina Ave., Wrightsville Beach, 28480.* Tel: 910-256-2471.

Marriage Encounter—ROGER BOLSER; TERESA BOLSER, *1604 Laughridge Dr., Cary, 27511.* Tel: 919-319-9100.

Personnel Director—LEO TAPLER, *Catholic Center, 715 Nazareth St., Raleigh, 27606.* Tel: 919-821-9711.

Propagation of the Faith—Rev. WILLIAM L. PITTS, *St. Therese Church, 209 S. Lumina Ave., Wrightsville Beach, 28480.* Tel: 910-256-2471.

CLERGY, PARISHES, MISSIONS AND PAROCHIAL SCHOOLS

CITY OF RALEIGH
(Wake County)

1—CATHEDRAL OF THE SACRED HEART (1924), Very Rev. John F. O'Connor, Rector.
Office: 226 Hillsborough St., 27603-1724. Tel: 919-832-6030; Fax: 919-833-4667.
Res., 15 N. McDowell St., 27603. Tel: 919-836-1790; Fax: 919-833-4667.
School—Tel: 919-832-4711. Sr. Marilyn Muldoon, O.S.U., Prin.
Ursuline Sisters 1; Lay Teachers 15; Students 265.
Catechesis / Religious Programs—Branch Ellison, D.R.E.
Students 178.
Convent—219 W. Edenton St., 27603. Tel: 919-832-1109.

2—CATHOLIC STUDENT CENTER, NORTH CAROLINA STATE UNIVERSITY (1974), Rev. Alan J. Dash.
Res., Aquinas House, 600 Bilyeu St., 27606. Tel: 919-833-9668; Fax: 919-833-1194.

3—OUR LADY OF LOURDES (1954), Revs. Jeffrey A. Ingham; Douglas P. Reed; Deacon Myles J. Charlesworth.
Office: 2718 Overbrook Dr., 27608. Tel: 919-782-1973; Fax: 919-571-9957.
Res., 2912 Anderson Dr., 27608. Tel: 919-781-9784.
School—2710 Overbrook Dr., 27608. Tel: 919-782-1670. Sr. M. Therese Grady, S.N.D., Prin.
Sisters of Notre Dame 3; Lay Teachers 20; Students 576.
Catechesis / Religious Programs—D.R.E.: Alexandra Stocking, (Adult); Donna Ashcraft, (PreK-8).
Students 370.

4—ST. FRANCIS OF ASSISI (1982), Revs. Daniel Kenna, O.F.M.; Mark Reamer, O.F.M.; Robert Sandoz, O.F.M.
Res., 11401 Leesville Rd., 27613. Tel: 919-870-8205; Fax: 919-870-1790.
Catechesis / Religious Programs—Tel: 919-847-8205. D.R.E.: Loretta Jean Schorr, (Adult); Peggy Dunbeck, (Grades PreK-8); Colleen McCarthy, (High School); Ann Murray, (Family).
Students 1,255.

5—ST. JOSEPH (1968), Rev. Thanh N. Nguyen.
Res., 630 Peartree Ln., 27610. Tel: 919-231-6364; Fax: 919-231-9884.
Catechesis / Religious Programs—Mary Jo Clark, D.R.E.
Students 100.

6—ST. LUKE THE EVANGELIST (1985), Rev. David D. Brockman.
Res., 12317 Bayleaf Church Rd., 27614-9165. Tel: 919-870-1490.
Church—12333 Bayleaf Church Rd., 27614-9165. Tel: 919-848-1533; Fax: 919-848-0662.
Catechesis / Religious Programs—Tel: 919-847-4973.
Students 238.

7—ST. RAPHAEL (1966), Revs. Robert S. Curry, S.J.; J. Michael Flynn, S.J.; William J. Kelley, S.J. Pastoral Assocs.: Sr. Patricia Cornell, C.S.C.; Sr. Dolores Glick, M.H.S.H.; Deacons Robert T. Madey; Frank Barnes.
Res., 5801 Falls of Neuse Rd., 27609. Tel: 919-876-1581; Fax: 919-872-3723.
St. Raphael Catholic School & Early Childhood Center—Tel: 919-876-3526. Rosalie Innacelli, Prin.
Students 260.
Catechesis / Religious Programs—Tel: 919-876-1668; Fax: 919-872-3723. Mary Lynn Whittaker, D.R.E.
Students 944.

OUTSIDE THE CITY OF RALEIGH

Ahoskie, Hertford Co., St. Charles Borromeo (1944), Rev. Stephen C. Worsley.
Res., P.O. Box 605, 27910. Tel: 919-332-2939.
Catechesis / Religious Programs—Students 15.
Mission—Scotland Neck, Halifax Co., St. Anne.

Apex, Wake Co., St. Andrew the Apostle (1984), Revs. William F. Schmidt, S.A.; Alban Carroll, S.A.; Kenneth Cienik, S.A.
Res., 1520 Cone Ave., 27502. Tel: 919-362-0414; Fax: 919-362-5778.
Catechesis / Religious Programs—Tel: 919-362-1673. Noelle Marino-Ruiz, D.R.E.
Students 1,435.

Burgaw, Pender Co., St. Joseph (1908), Rev. Christopher Balas, O.F.M.Conv.
Res., 220 Inlet Dr., Scotts Hill, Wilmington, 28405. Tel: 910-686-7724; Fax: 910-686-8270. [CEM]
Church—Rte. 1, Box 1714, 28425. Tel: 910-259-2601; Fax: 910-259-7695.
Catechesis / Religious Programs—Tel: 910-392-4778. D.R.E.: Despina Horvath, (St. Joseph); Beth Rich, (Transfiguration).
Students 20.
Mission—Wallace, Transfiguration.

Burlington, Alamance Co., Blessed Sacrament (1928), Revs. Alvin Somerville, O.F.M.Conv.; Terence Pascatore, O.F.M.Conv. In res., Revs. Daniel M. Quackenbush, O.F.M.Conv.; Michael Lorentsen, O.F.M.Conv.; Bro. Raymond Sobocinski, O.F.M.Conv.
Mailing Address: P.O. Box 619, 27216. Tel: 910-226-8796; Fax: 910-227-2896.
Res., 408 W. Davis St., 27215.
School—Tel: 910-570-0019. Mr. Thomas A. Kraft, Prin.
Lay Teachers 30; Students 360.
Catechesis / Religious Programs—Miss Sheila Murphy, D.R.E.
Students 284.

Buxton, Dare Co., Our Lady of the Seas, Rev. Andre C. Izac.
Mailing Address: P.O. Box 399, 27920. Tel: 919-995-6370.

Carolina Beach, New Hanover Co., Immaculate Conception (1925), Rev. Jim Behan, O.S.F.S.
Church—6650 Carolina Beach Rd., Wilmington, 28412. Tel: 910-791-1003; Fax: 910-791-0081.

Cary, Wake Co., St. Michael the Archangel (1962), Revs. John A. Wall; Robert T. Schriber.
Res., 804 High House Rd., 27513. Tel: 919-468-6100; Fax: 919-468-6130.
Catechesis / Religious Programs—Tel: 919-468-6120. Stephen O. Edwards, D.R.E.
Students 1,380.

Castle Hayne, New Hanover Co., St. Stanislaus Kostka (1914) (Polish), Rev. Briant Cullinane, O.F.M.Conv.
Res., 220 Inlet Dr.,Scotts Hill, Wilmington, 28405-6824. Tel: 910-686-7724; Fax: 910-675-2336. [CEM]
Church—4849 Castle Hayne Rd., 28429-4849. Tel: 910-675-3116 (Office & Hall).

Chapel Hill, Orange Co., St. Thomas More (1940), Revs. Michael G. Clay, D.Min.; Frank J. Stangl, S.T.D.; Harry B. Zerner, S.J. Pastoral Assocs.: Ms. Theresa Keller; Sr. Marie St. Paul Alspaugh, S.S.J.
Parish Offices: 940 Carmichael St., 27514. Tel: 919-942-1040; Fax: 919-942-6193.
Res., 740 Gimghoul Rd., 27514-3844. Tel: 919-967-8485.
School—(Grades K-8) 920 Carmichael St., 27514. Tel: 919-929-1546; Fax: 919-929-1783. Sr. Marie St. Leger, S.S.J., Prin.
Sisters 1; Lay Teachers 34; Students 444.
Catechesis / Religious Programs—Tel: 919-933-1041. Mrs. Jan Vallero, D.R.E.
Students 610.

Newman Catholic Student Center, University of North Carolina (1968), Revs. Phillip M. Leach; Edward P. Mahoney; Sr. Margaret Harig, S.N.D., Pastoral Assoc.
Res., 218 Pittsboro St., 27516-2738. Tel: 919-929-3730; Fax: 919-929-3778.
Catechesis/Religious Programs—Tel: 919-933-1041.
Students 114.

Clinton, Sampson Co., Immaculate Conception (1910), Revs. John Williams; Steven Carlson.
Mailing Address: P.O. Box 859, 28329. Tel: 910-592-1384; Fax: 910-592-8725.
Missions—Mount Olive, Wayne Co., St. Mary, (1916) 311 W. Main St., Mount Olive 28365. Tel: 919-658-4023; Mount Olive, Duplin Co., Posada Guadalupana, (1993).
Station—San Juan, Old Hwy. 701, Ingold, Tel: 910-592-1384.

Dunn, Harnett Co., Sacred Heart (1916), Rev. Trent L. Watts.
Mailing Address: P.O. Box 535, 28335. Tel: 910-891-1972; Fax: 910-891-5767.
Res., 209 S. Ellis Ave., 28334. Tel: 910-892-3414.
Catechesis/Religious Programs—Mrs. Jan Rebman, D.R.E.
Students 93.

Durham, Durham Co.,

1—Holy Cross, (1938) (African American), Rev. David E. Barry, S.J.
Res., 1400 S. Alston Ave., 27707. Tel: 919-682-4852; Fax: 919-688-6160.
Catechesis/Religious Programs—Tel: 919-688-6160. Helen Hudson, D.R.E.
Students 100.

2—Holy Infant, (1970), Revs. John E. McGee, O.S.F.S.; Richard E. Cleary, O.S.F.S.
Res., 5000 South Park Dr., 27713-9470. Tel: 919-544-7135; Fax: 919-544-1799. [CEM]
Catechesis/Religious Programs—Diane Quintal, D.R.E.
Students 256.

3—Immaculate Conception, (1906), Revs. David J. McBriar, O.F.M.; John J. Heffernan, O.F.M.; Patrick E. Tuttle, O.F.M.; Deacon Laurence DeCarolis.
Res., 725 Burch Ave., 27701. Tel: 919-682-3449; Fax: 919-682-7999.
School—Immaculata, 721 Burch Ave., 27701. Tel: 919-682-5847. Mr. William Abel, Prin.
Lay Teachers 29; Students 363.
Catechesis/Religious Programs—Barbara Pegg, D.R.E.
Students 323.

4—St. Matthew, (1990), Rev. J. Paul Byron.
Res., 1001 Mason Rd., 27712. Tel: 919-479-1001; Fax: 919-479-4848. [CEM]
Catechesis/Religious Programs—Lynn Sale, D.R.E.
Students 217.

Edenton, Chowan Co., St. Anne (1858), Rev. Eugene M. Grabowski.
Mailing Address: P.O. Box 422, 27932. [CEM]
Church—207 N. Broad St., 27932. Tel: 919-482-2617.
Catechesis/Religious Programs—Students 75.
Mission—Columbia, All Souls.

Elizabeth City, Pasquotank Co., Holy Family (1915), Rev. John L. Gillespie.
Mailing Address: 1453 N. Road St., 27906-1525. Tel: 919-338-2521; Fax: 919-338-4183.
Res., 1453 N. Road St., 27909. Tel: 919-335-4419.
Catechesis/Religious Programs—Mrs. Doreen Warren, D.R.E.
Students 177.
Station—Currituck, Currituck Senior Citizens Center, Tel: 919-232-3505.

Farmville, Pitt Co., St. Elizabeth (1931) (Lebanese), Sr. Grace Campbell, I.H.M., Pastoral Admin.
Mailing Address: P.O. Box 189, 27828. Tel: 919-753-4367; Fax: 919-753-4367.
Catechesis/Religious Programs—Students 8.

Fayetteville, Cumberland Co., St. Ann (1940) (African American), Rev. Thomas R. Davis.
Office:—365 N. Cool Spring St., 28301. Tel: 910-483-3216; Fax: 910-483-4185.
Res., 1100 Clarendon St., Apt. 301, 28305. Tel: 910-483-5871.
School—Tel: 910-483-3902. Sr. JoAnne Goecke, D.C., Prin.
Daughters of Charity 3; Lay Teachers 11; Students 204.
Catechesis/Religious Programs—Michael Patterson, D.R.E.
Students 121.
Convent—1933 Martindale Dr., 28304. Tel: 910-484-1675.

St. Elizabeth Ann Seton (1981), Rev. Willard Rucinski, O.S.F.S.
Res., 700 Carnegie St., 28311. Tel: 910-488-8274; Fax: 910-488-7116.
Catechesis/Religious Programs—Brenda Bissonnette, D.R.E.
Students 232.

St. Patrick (1824), Revs. John G. Durbin, S.T.L.; Ryszand Kolodziej; Deacon Louis Hanemann.
Mailing Address: 2840 Village Dr., 28304. Tel: 910-323-2410; Fax: 910-323-3006.
Res., 433 Holly Ln., 28305. Tel: 910-484-8253.
School—1620 Marlborough Rd., 28304. Tel: 910-323-1865; Fax: 910-484-1573. Mr. Tom Manion, Prin.
Lay Teachers 11; Students 262.
Catechesis/Religious Programs—Tel: 910-323-2410, Ext. 107; Fax: 910-323-3006. Tim McHale, D.R.E.
Students 471.

Fuquay-Varina, Wake Co., St. Bernadette (1987), Rev. Francis G. Maloney; Sr. Claudia Bronsing, Pastoral Admin.; Deacon Anthony Meier.
Mailing Address: 1005 Wilbon Rd., 27526-9702. Tel: 919-552-8758; Fax: 919-552-1846.
Catechesis/Religious Programs—Tel: 919-552-8758. Mrs. Michele Dexter, D.R.E.
Students 227.
Hispanic Office—Tel: 919-552-2922.

Garner, Wake Co., St. Mary, Mother of the Church (1966), Rev. Francis G. Maloney; Deacon Leo Tapler.
Res., 1008 Vandora Springs Rd., 27529. Tel: 919-772-5777; Fax: 919-772-5534.
Catechesis/Religious Programs—Tel: 919-779-4017. Mary Rider, D.R.E.
Students 310.

Goldsboro, Wayne Co., St. Mary (1889), Revs. William J. Ruhl, O.S.F.S.; Thomas P. Norris, O.S.F.S.
Res., 1000 N. Jefferson Ave., 27530-3141. Tel: 919-734-5033; Fax: 919-580-0730.
School—Tel: 919-735-1931; Fax: 919-735-1917. Lynn P. Magoon, Prin.
Sisters, Servants of the Immaculate Heart of Mary 3; Lay Teachers 13; Students 315.
Catechesis/Religious Programs—Mrs. Carole M. Sears, D.R.E.
Students 252.

Greenville, Pitt Co., St. Gabriel (1936), Rev. Thomas McCann, C.P.; Lucille Gorham, Pastoral Assoc.
Res., 1120 W. Fifth St., 27834. Tel: 919-758-1504; Fax: 919-758-1479.
Catechesis/Religious Programs—Students 58.

St. Peter's, Revs. Joseph R. Jones, C.P.; Alban Harmon, C.P.
Res., 2700 E. Fourth St., 27858. Tel: 919-757-3259; Fax: 919-752-1499.
School—Tel: 919-752-3529; Fax: 919-752-7604. Bro. Simon Jaworski, O.S.F., Prin.
Franciscan Brothers (Brooklyn) 2; Lay Teachers 27; Students 530.
Catechesis/Religious Programs—Sarah McPherson, D.R.E.
Students 25.

Hampstead, Pender Co., St. Jude the Apostle, Rev. Casimir Sabol, O.F.M.Conv.; Bro. Paul Hardison, O.F.M.Conv., Pastoral Assoc.
Mailing Address: P.O. Box 1790, 28443.
Res., 220 Inlet Dr., Scotts Hill, Wilmington, 28405. Tel: 910-686-7724.

Havelock, Craven Co., Annunciation (1953), Rev. Frederick R. Flaherty, M.S.
Mailing Address: Drawer B, 28532-0177. Tel: 919-447-2112; Fax: 919-447-2595.
School—Tel: 919-447-3137; Fax: 919-447-3138. Mrs. June Pietras, Prin.
Lay Teachers 20; Students 265.
Catechesis/Religious Programs—246 E. Main St., 28532. Tel: 919-447-2436; Fax: 919-447-2436. Mrs. Maureen McInerney, D.R.E.
Students 228.

Henderson, Vance Co., St. James the Greater (1925). Consolidated St. Paul and St. Catherine of Siena, Oxford merged to form St. James the Greater. Rev. J. William Long.
Res., 3275 Hwy. 158 Bypass, 27536. Tel: 919-438-3124; Fax: 919-438-3214. [JC]
Catechesis/Religious Programs—Donna Gaul, D.R.E.
Students 140.
Mission—Warrenton, Warren Co., St. Joseph, Norlina Rd., Warrenton, 27589. Tel: 919-438-3124.

Hillsborough, Orange Co., Holy Family (1989), Sr. Marie Therese Bugge, O.S.U., Pastoral Admin.
Mailing Address: P.O. Box 1061, 27278. Tel: 919-732-1030; Fax: 919-732-1030.
Catechesis/Religious Programs—Students 109.

Hope Mills, Cumberland Co., Good Shepherd (1981), Very Rev. Thomas J. Gaul, V.F.; Rev. John R. Kelly.
Res., 116 Oak St., 28348. Tel: 910-425-1590; Fax: 910-423-9973.
Catechesis/Religious Programs—Tel: 910-425-5617. Janice Carnahan, D.R.E.
Students 435.

Jacksonville, Onslow Co., Shrine of the Infant of Prague, Church of the Holy Spirit (1941), Revs. Denis Hackett, O.F.M.Conv., Admin.; John Ruffo, O.F.M. Conv.
Mailing Address: P.O. Drawer 556, 28541. Tel: 910-347-4196; Fax: 910-347-9338.
Res., 330 Mildred Ave., 28540. Tel: 910-347-4171.
School—St. Francis of Assisi, Tel: 910-353-1300; 455-0838; Fax: 910-353-1305. Michele Estep, Prin.
Lay Teachers 20; Students 288.
Catechesis/Religious Programs—Tel: 910-455-1296. Sr. Cecilia McClain, S.C., D.R.E.
Students 416.

Kill Devil Hills, Dare Co., Holy Redeemer (1935), Rev. Terrence Collins.
Mailing Address: P.O. Box 327, 27948-0327.
Office: 1206 N. Virginia Dare Tr., 27948. Tel: 919-441-8115; Fax: 919-441-8183.
Res., 109 Sunrise View, Kitty Hawk, 27949. Fax: 919-441-8115.
Missions—Nags Head, Dare Co., Holy Trinity; Buxton, Our Lady of the Seas, P.O. Box 399, Buxton, 27920-0399. Tel: 919-995-6370.
Stations—Ocracoke, Annunciation, Tel: 919-995-6370; Corolla, Corolla Chapel, Tel: 919-441-7220.

Kinston, Lenoir Co., Holy Trinity-Our Lady of the Atonement (1921) (African American-Hispanic), Revs. Girard M. Sherba, J.C.L.; Paul W. Brant, S.J.; Sr. Maria DiBello, R.S.M., Pastoral Assoc.
Mailing Address: P.O. Box 1455, 28503-1455. Tel: 919-523-8898; Fax: 919-527-9495.
Res., 28501. Tel: 919-523-4377.
Church—512 W. Vernon Ave., 28501.
Catechesis/Religious Programs—P.O. Box 1455, 28503. Sandra Murphy, D.R.E.
Students 91.

Laurinburg, Scotland Co., St. Mary (1946), Rev. Kevin Fahey.
Mailing Address: P.O. Box 1148, 28353-1148. Tel: 910-276-1478. [JC]
Catechesis/Religious Programs—Students 95.

Lumberton, Robeson Co., St. Francis De Sales (1938), Revs. Thomas Watkins; E. Fernando Torres (Columbia).
Mailing Address: P.O. Box 2249, 28359-2249. Tel: 910-739-4723; Fax: 910-739-5443.
Res., 2000 Elizabethtown Rd., 28358.
Mission—Red Springs, Robeson Co., St. Andrew, 506 E. 4th Ave., Red Springs, 28377. Tel: 910-843-3440.

Morehead City, Carteret Co., St. Egbert (1929), Very Rev. Francis R. Moeslein; Rev. Michael Butler; Deacon Albert Feneis.
Parish Hall—1706 Evans St., 28557. Tel: 919-726-3559; Fax: 919-726-2232.
Res., 1612 Evans St., 28557. Tel: 919-726-2535.
School—Tel: 919-726-3418. Mrs. Lesley Ferguson, Prin.
Lay Teachers 7; Students 152.
Catechesis/Religious Programs—Tel: 919-726-9696.
Students 92.

New Bern, Craven Co., St. Paul (1821), Revs. Ernest Ruede; Mark J. Betti; Deacon William Hunt.
Rectory: 3108 Farrior Cir., 28562. Tel: 919-638-4436.
Church—3005 Country Club Rd., 28562. Tel: 919-638-1984; Fax: 919-638-2144. [CEM]
School—3007 Country Club Rd., 28562. Tel: 919-633-0100; Fax: 919-633-4457. Sr. Susan Therese Armbruster, I.H.M., Prin.
Sisters, Servants of the Immaculate Heart of Mary 3; Lay Teachers 11; Students 310.
Catechesis/Religious Programs—Tel: 919-633-3030. Sr. Mildred McClain, S.C., D.R.E.
Students 222.

Newton Grove, Sampson Co., Our Lady of Guadalupe (1871), Rev. Joseph J. Yaeger.
Office: P.O. Box 100, 28366. Tel: 910-594-0287; Fax: 910-594-1749.
Res., 211 Irwin Dr., 28366. Tel: 910-594-0152. [CEM]
Catechesis/Religious Programs—Students 130.

Pinehurst, Moore Co., Sacred Heart (1919), Revs. Robert T. Lawson; Roch T. Drozdzik.
Mailing Address: P.O. Box 1768, 28370. Tel: 910-295-6550; Fax: 910-295-6450.
Catechesis/Religious Programs—Tel: 910-295-6878. Mrs. Barbara Kemple, D.R.E.
Students 165.
Mission—Robbins, Moore Co., Blessed Juan Diego, Woodmen of the World Bldg., Salisbury & Fourcher St., Robbins, 27325.

Plymouth, Washington Co., St. Joan of Arc (1959), Sr. Margaret Gallagher, I.H.M., Pastoral Admin.
Mailing Address: P.O. Box 822, 27962. Tel: 919-793-4052.

Raeford, Hoke Co., St. Elizabeth of Hungary (1959), Sr. M. Carol Loughney, I.H.M., Pastoral Admin.
Res., 124 Palmer St., 28376-9322. Tel: 910-875-8803; Fax: 910-875-8803.
Catechesis/Religious Programs—Students 50.

Riegelwood, Columbus Co., Christ the King (1964), Rev. J. Douglas Lawson, Admin.
Mailing Address: P.O. Box 155, 28456. Tel: 910-655-3313.

Roanoke Rapids, Halifax Co., St. John the Baptist (1931), Rev. Robert F. Shea.
Res., 115 E. Ninth St., 27870. Tel: 919-537-4667; Fax: 919-535-2076.
Catechesis/Religious Programs—Charles Boykin, D.R.E.
Students 138.

Rocky Mount, Nash & Edgecombe Cos., Our Lady of Perpetual Help (1912), Revs. JaVan J. Saxon; Richard W. Turner.
Mailing Address: 331 Hammond St., 27804. Tel: 919-972-0452.
Res., 501 Hammond St., 27804. Tel: 919-972-1949; Fax: 919-972-4780.
School—Tel: 919-972-1971. Sr. Mary Paula Hughes, C.S.J., Prin.
Sisters, Servants of the Immaculate Heart of Mary 2; Lay Teachers 6; Students 131.
Catechesis/Religious Programs—Tel: 919-972-0498. Dianne Young, D.R.E.
Students 185.

Roxboro, Person Co., SS. Mary and Edward (1935), Rev. Robert P. Staley.
Res., 611 N. Main St., 27573-5040. Tel: 910-599-4122.
Mission—Butner, St. Bernadette.

Sanford, Lee Co., St. Stephen (1932), Rev. John J. Forbes.
Res., 2402 Wicker St. Ext., P.O. Box 4659, 27331-4659. Tel: 919-776-1532; Fax: 919-775-1399.
Catechesis/Religious Programs—Tel: 919-776-3843.
Students 247.

Shallotte, Brunswick Co., St. Brendan the Navigator (1983), Rev. Francis P. Simeone, O.S.F.S.
Mailing Address: Box 2984, 28459-9999. Tel: 910-754-8544; Fax: 910-755-6046.
Church & Office: 5105 Ocean Hwy. W., 28459.
Catechesis/Religious Programs—Students 83.

Siler City, Chatham Co., St. Julia (1961), Rev. Daniel M. Quackenbush, O.F.M.Conv.
Mailing Address: 1002 W. Third St., 27344. Tel: 919-742-5584.

Smithfield, Johnston Co., St. Ann (1935), Rev. Joseph G. Mulroney, J.C.L.
Res., 113 N. Seventh St., 27577. Tel: 919-934-2084; Fax: 919-934-4639.
Catechesis/Religious Programs—Students 183.

Southern Pines, Moore Co., St. Anthony of Padua (1895), Rev. James F. Butler; Sr. Mary Anne Pierson, M.S.B.T., Pastoral Assoc.
Mailing Address: P.O. Box 29, 28388-0029. Tel: 910-692-6613; Fax: 910-692-4964.
Res., 23 Village in the Woods, 28387. Tel: 910-693-7789.
Catechesis/Religious Programs—Tel: 910-692-6241. Jamie Kovarik, D.R.E.
Students 196.

Southport, Brunswick Co., Sacred Heart (1941), Rev. J. Douglas Lawson; Deacon Eugene Gillis (CHL); Patricia Ciemnicki, Dir. Pastoral Svcs.
Mailing Address: 5269 Dosher Cutoff, S.E., 28461. Tel: 910-457-6173.
Res., 213 Yaupon Dr., 28461. Tel: 910-457-0223.
Catechesis/Religious Programs—Tel: 910-457-6173. D.R.E.: Patricia Novotny; Ruthann Horan.
Students 92.
Mission—Riegelwood, Christ the King.

Swansboro, Onslow Co., St. Mildred (1947), Rev. Emile Dusseault, M.S.
Mailing Address: P.O. Box 338, 28584-0338. Tel: 910-326-4370; Fax: 910-326-2642.
Res., 616 Sabiston Dr., 28584. Tel: 910-326-4370. [CEM]
Catechesis/Religious Programs—Tel: 910-326-5589. Laura Leblanc, D.R.E.
Students 175.

Tarboro, Edgecombe Co., St. Catherine (1934), Rev. William Murphy, C.P.
Res., 1004 St. David St., 27886. Tel: 919-823-3866; Fax: 919-824-0412.
Catechesis/Religious Programs—Students 50.

Wake Forest, Wake Co., St. Catherine of Siena (1940), Rev. Thomas S. Tully.
Church—520 W. Holding Ave., 27587. Tel: 919-556-4104; Fax: 919-554-8796.
Catechesis/Religious Programs—Elizabeth Edens, D.R.E.
Students 205.
Station—Louisburg, Louisburg College Chapel.

Washington, Beaufort Co., Mother of Mercy (1963), Rev. Donald G. Baribeau, M.S.
Res., 112 W. Ninth St., 27889. Tel: 919-946-2941; Fax: 919-946-1399.
Church—111 W. Ninth St., 27889.
Catechesis/Religious Programs—Tel: 919-946-8808. Ms. Blossom von Struve, D.R.E.
Students 68.

Wendell, Wake Co., St. Eugene (1948), Rev. Robert Diegelman.
Mailing Address: P.O. Box 188, 27591. Tel: 919-365-7114; Fax: 919-365-9431.
Catechesis/Religious Programs—Gail Hernandez, D.R.E.
Students 218.

Whiteville, Columbus Co., Sacred Heart (1938), Rev. Albert Gondek, O.S.F.S.
Res., 402 N. Lee St., 28472. Tel: 910-642-3895; Fax: 910-640-1948.
Catechesis/Religious Programs—Students 58.

Williamston, Martin Co., Holy Trinity, Sr. Elizabeth Bullen, I.H.M., Pastoral Admin.
Mailing Address: P.O. Box 894, 27892-0894. Tel: 919-792-4091.
Church—Hwy. 17-13 Bypass, 27892.

Wilmington, New Hanover Co., St. Mark (1978), Revs. Matthew D. Hendrick; Gregory D. Spencer.
Church—1011 Eastwood Rd., 28403.
Res., 145 Tanbridge Rd., 28405. Tel: 910-392-0720; Fax: 910-392-6777.
Catechesis/Religious Programs—Ms. Anne Doyle, D.R.E.
Students 609.

St. Mary (1821), Revs. Thomas P. Hadden; Bernard E. Shlesinger, III.
Res., 405 Ann St., 28401-4592. Tel: 910-762-5491; Fax: 910-762-9664. [JC]
School—Tel: 910-762-6517. Barbara Bourne, Prin.
Lay Teachers 24; Students 353.
St. Thomas Preschool—Tel: 910-762-7764. Lydia Braye, Dir.
Lay Teachers 8; Students 76.
Catechesis/Religious Programs—Tel: 910-251-9992. Sr. Barbara Marie Cady, S.U., D.R.E.
Students 237.

Wilson, Wilson Co., St. Alphonsus De Liguori. Closed. For sacramental records contact St. Therese, Wilson.

Church of St. Therese (1923), Very Rev. James M. Labosky, V.F.
Church and Office: 700 Nash St., N.E., 27893-3047. Tel: 919-237-3019; Fax: 919-237-2042.
Res., 200 Gray St., N.E., 27893-3710. Tel: 919-237-0143.
School—(Grades PreK-5). Tel: 919-237-5342; Fax: 919-237-2042.
Sisters 2; Lay Teachers 13; Students 137.
Catechesis/Religious Programs—Tel: 919-237-3019.
Students 207.

Wrightsville Beach, New Hanover Co., St. Therese (1939), Rev. William L. Pitts.
Res., 209 S. Lumina Ave., 28480. Tel: 910-256-2471; Fax: 910-256-2459.
Catechesis/Religious Programs—Tel: 910-395-2259. Mrs. Joan Walters, D.R.E.
Students 150.

Special Assignment:
Reverend Fathers—
Lewis, Gerald, Vicar Gen., 715 Nazareth St., Raleigh, NC 27606
Mahoney, Edward P., Duke University, Durham, NC 27706
Ranalli, John, 715 Nazareth St., Raleigh, NC 27606

On Duty Outside the Diocese:
Reverend Fathers—
Fitzgerald, R. Martin, 72 ABW/HC, 6170 Arnold St., Ste. 6, Tinker, AFB 73145-8100

Graduate Studies:
Reverend Fathers—
Garneau, James F., 300 Taylor St. N.E., Apt. L-22, Washington, DC 20017-1530
Rhodes, Ronald E., 66 Clifford St., Boston, MA 02119-2121. Tel: 617-445-9786

Absent on Leave:
Reverend Fathers—
Dorsel, John F.
Klaus, Joseph J.

Awaiting Assignment:
Reverend Fathers—
Watkins, Thomas

Retired:
Reverend Monsignors—
Jones, James, 2228 Fox Horn Rd., New Bern, NC 28562. Tel: 919-635-5318
Koch, Frederick A., St. Joseph of the Pines Villa, 592 Central Ave., Apt. D-7, Southern Pines, NC 28387
McSweeney, James E., 233 Hanover Pl., Cary, NC 27511-6624
Murphy, Francis, St. Joseph of the Pines Villa, Apt. C-13, Southern Pines, NC 28387. Tel: 919-692-8289
Reverend Fathers—
Bryon, Paul J., 5305 Quail Meadow Dr., Raleigh, NC 27609. Tel: 919-876-7232
Carcich, G. John, 592 Central Dr., Villa F1, Southern Pines, NC 28387
Creel, Jesse, St. Albans, 120-32 193rd St., Jamaica, NY 11412-3637. Tel: 708-525-0880
Ghisalberti, Giacomo G., P.O. Box 155, Riegelwood, NC 28456-0155
Giacomini, Antonio, O.F.M.Cap., Stratford Arms, Apt. 9-B, Greenville, NC 27858
Harper, John, St. Joseph of the Pines, 590 Central Dr., Room 540, Southern Pines, NC 28387
Jacobs, Allen A., St. Joseph of the Pines, Knollwood Campus, 590 Central Dr., Southern Pines, NC 28387-2899. Tel: 910-693-3704
Keaney, James P., 1316 E. Ninth St., Roanoke Rapids, NC 27870. Tel: 919-535-4093
Ketchersid, Corbin W., 117 H Feldspar Ln., Fayetteville, NC 28314. Tel: 910-488-1797
Mulholland, Charles H., 5305 Quail Meadow Dr., Raleigh, NC 27609. Tel: 919-876-7232
Parker, Kenneth, 704 McIntosh Rd., Carthage, NC 28327. Tel: 910-245-4640
Richardson, John L., 1889 Norwood St. S.W., Schooner's Pointe, Ocean Isle Beach, NC 28469

Permanent Deacons:
Barnes, Frank, St. Rafael, Raleigh
Broering, Harry, Mother of Mercy, Washington
Charlesworth, Myles, Our Lady of Lourdes, Raleigh
DeCarolis, Lawrence, Immaculate Conception, Durham
Evans, Forest, Immaculate Conception, Durham
Feneis, Al, St. Egbert, Morehead City
Foggie, Willie, St. Eugene, Wendell
Gillis, Eugene, Sacred Heart, Southport
Goodrow, Joseph, Infant of Prague, Jacksonville
Hanemann, Louis, St. Patrick, Fayetteville
Hubisz, John, N.C.S.U. Aquinas House, Raleigh
Hunt, William, St. Paul, New Bern
Kuntz, Edward
Lewandowski, Stephen, St. Joseph, Raleigh
Madey, Robert, St. Raphael, Raleigh
McGahran, Robert, St. Brendan, Shallotte
Meier, Anthony, St. Bernadette, Fuquay-Varina
Newton, Philip, St. Luke, Raleigh
Schoebel, James, St. Anthony, Southern Pines
Tapler, Leopold, Catholic Center, Raleigh
Wobser, Don, Holy Redeemer, Kill Devil Hills
Woodhall, Johnathan, St. Anthony, Southern Pines

INSTITUTIONS LOCATED IN THE DIOCESE

[A] HIGH SCHOOLS

RALEIGH. *Cardinal Gibbons Memorial High School*, 2401 Crusader Dr., 27606. Tel: 919-834-1625. Bro. Michel Bettigole, O.S.F., Prin. Brothers 4; Sisters 2; Lay Teachers 41; Students 575.

[B] CHILD CARE CENTERS

RALEIGH. *St. Joseph Pre-School*, 624 Peartree Ln., 27610.
St. Raphael Catholic School and Early Childhood Center, 5801 Falls of the Neuse Rd., 27609. Mrs. Rosalie P. Innacelli, Dir. Lay Teachers 16; Students 260.

APEX. *Saint Andrew Early Childhood Center*, 3008 Old Raleigh Rd., 27502. Tel: 919-387-8656. Eileen Vaughan, Dir. Total Staff 20; Students 121.

CARY. *St. Michael Early Childhood Center*, 804 High House Rd., 27513. Ms. Elana O'Connell, Dir. Total Staff 19; Students 139.

GARNER. *St. Mary Child Development Center*, 1008 Vandora Springs Rd., 27529. Tel: 919-772-0009. Ms. Karen Williams, Dir. Lay Teachers 7; Total Staff 16; Students 120.

WILMINGTON. *St. Thomas Child Development Center*, 109 S. Second St., 28401. Lydia Davis Braye, Dir. Total Staff 11; Lay Teachers 9; Students 65.

[C] GENERAL HOSPITALS

SOUTHERN PINES. *St. Joseph of the Pines*, 590 Central

Dr., 28387. Tel: 910-692-2212.
Web site: www.sjp.org
For a complete listing, refer to the Hospitals section.

[D] CATHOLIC SOCIAL SERVICES

RALEIGH. *Catholic Social Ministries of the Diocese of Raleigh, Inc.*, 715 Nazareth St., 27606-2187. Tel: 919-821-9750. Kathleen Walsh, A.C.S.W, Diocesan Dir. Total Staff 29; Total Assisted 47,452.
Regional Office, 400 Oberlin Rd. #350, 27605. Tel: 919-832-0225. Roderick B. O'Connor, C.C.S.W.
Regional Office, 2805 Market St., Wilmington, 28403. Tel: 910-251-8130. Diane Pisczek, M.Ed.
Regional Office, 1424 Broad St., P.O. Box 647, Durham, 27702. Tel: 919-286-1964. Susan Gilbertson, C.C.S.W.
Regional Office, 111 Boone Trail, Fayetteville, 28306. Tel: 910-424-2020. Dorothy Ann Pyle, C.C.S.W.
Regional Office, 502 Middle St., P.O. Box 1251, New Bern, 28560. Tel: 919-638-2188. Michael Miles, C.C.S.W.
Regional Office, 3219 Landmark St. 7A, P.O. Box 8241, Greenville, 27835-8241. Tel: 919-355-5111. Elaine Franzetti, C.C.S.W.
Regional Office, 123 Market St., Hertford, 27944. Tel: 919-426-7717. Julian Miller, M.S.W.
Peace and Justice Office, 300 Cardinal Gibbons Dr., 27606-2198. Tel: 919-821-9751. Sr. Joan Jurski, O.S.F.
Senior Housing Office, 715 Nazareth St., 27606-2187.

[E] MONASTERIES AND RESIDENCE OF PRIESTS AND BROTHERS

RALEIGH. *De Porres House*, 304 E. Park Dr., P.O. Box 12927, 27605-2927. Tel: 919-833-1893; Fax: 919-833-1449. Revs. James Burke, O.P.; James D. Campbell, O.P.; Arthur R. Kirwin, O.P.; Michael M. Burke, O.P.; Martin J. Iott, O.P.; Jude Siciliano, O.P.
Dominican Friars of Raleigh, Inc., De Porres House, 304 E. Park Dr., 27605. Rev. Jude Siciliano, Pres.
Dominican Community, De Porres House, 304 E. Park Dr., 27605-2927. Tel: 919-571-8123. Revs. James Burke, O.P.; Michael M. Burke, O.P.; James D. Campbell, O.P.; Martin J. Iott, O.P.; Arthur R. Kirwin, O.P.; Jude Siciliano, O.P.
Jesuit Community, 5801 Falls of the Neuse Rd., 27609. Tel: 919-876-1667.
Jesuits in Eastern North Carolina: Revs. Paul W. Brant, S.J.; Michael H. Jordan, S.J.; Harry B. Zerner, S.J.; Robert Curry, S.J.; William J. Kelley, S.J.; Michael J. Flynn, S.J.; David E. Barry, S.J.

BURLINGTON. *Conventual Franciscans*, Blessed Sacrament Church, 408 W. Davis St., P.O. Box 619, 27216. Tel: 910-226-8796; Fax: 910-227-2896. Revs. Alvin Somerville, O.F.M.Conv.; Terence Pescatore, O.F.M.Conv.; Daniel Quackenbush, O.F.M.Conv.; Michael Lorentsen, O.F.M.Conv.; Bro. Raymond Sobocinski. Total in Residence 5.

CHAPEL HILL. *Jesuit Residence, Robert Southwell House*, 211 McCauley St., 27516-2721. Revs. Mark B. Thesing, C.S.C.; Harry B. Zerner, S.J. Total in Residence 2.

GREENVILLE. *St. Peter Friary*, 2606 E. Fifth St., 27858.
E-mail: peterville@sprintmail.com
Franciscan Brothers of Brooklyn. Bros. Simon Jaworski, O.S.F.; Cletus Burke, O.S.F. Brothers 2.

WILMINGTON. *Conventual Franciscans O.F.M.Conv.*, Duns Scotus Friary, 220 Inlet Dr., Scots Hill, 28405. Tel: 910-686-7724. Bro. Paul Hardison, O.F.M.Conv. In res. Revs. Casimir Sabol, O.F.M.Conv.; Christopher Balas, O.F.M.Conv.; Douglas Reed, O.F.M.Conv.

[F] CONVENTS AND RESIDENCES FOR SISTERS

RALEIGH. *Cathedral Convent-Ursuline Sisters*, 219 W. Edenton St., 27603. Tel: 919-832-9035. Sisters 2.
Sisters of Charity of Seton Hill, 2433 Milburnie Rd., 27610.
Sisters of Divine Providence, 109 Autumn Chase Dr., 27613. Tel: 919-571-0325.
E-mail: ljschorr@juno.com
Sisters of Notre Dame, 3905 Yew Circle, 27612. Tel: 919-781-3739. Sisters 3.
Sisters of the Holy Cross, 1213-E Manassas Ct., 27609. Tel: 919-872-3418. Sisters 2.

AHOSKIE. *Sisters of St. Louis—California Region*, 409 W. Church St., 27910. Tel: 919-332-2220.

CARY. *Sisters of Mercy of the Americas*, 450 Pebble Creek Dr., 27511. Tel: 919-481-4402.
E-mail: aheath8573@aol.com
Web site: www.saintandrew.org
Sisters of St. Francis of Sylvania, Ohio, 1204-C Village Greenway, 27511. Tel: 919-460-6218.
E-mail: jurski@raldioc.org
Sisters 2.

CHAPEL HILL. *St. Thomas More Sisters' Residence*, 301 Colony Woods Dr., 27514. Tel: 919-929-1547. Sisters 2.
Sisters, Servants of the Immaculate Heart of Mary, 6 St. James Pl., 27514-3426.

DURHAM. *Dominican Congregation of St. Catherine De-Ricci*, 711 Mason Rd., 27712. Tel: 919-477-1285; Fax: 919-477-9485.
E-mail: djack@IX.netcom.com
Sisters of St. Francis of Philadelphia, 711 Mason Rd., 27712. Tel: 919-477-1285; Fax: 919-477-9485.
E-mail: djack@IX.netcom.com

FARMVILLE. *Sisters, Servants of the Immaculate Heart of Mary*, P.O. Box 189, 27828-0189. Tel: 919-753-4367.
E-mail: elizabet@greenvillenc.com

FAYETTEVILLE. *Daughters of Charity*, Marguerite Naseau House, 1933 Martindale Dr., 28304. Tel: 910-484-1675. Daughters of Charity of St. Vincent de Paul. Sisters 5.

FUQUAY-VARINA. *Sisters of Saint Francis*, 125 Church St., 27526. Tel: 919-557-5372.

GARNER. *Adrian Dominican Sisters of the Most Holy Rosary*, House of Preachers, 1411 Kenbrook Dr., 27529. Tel: 919-661-9324; Fax: 919-661-0817.

GOLDSBORO. *St. Mary's Convent*, 1603 Edgerton St., 27530. Tel: 919-735-0838. Sisters, Servants of the Immaculate Heart of Mary.

GREENVILLE. *Daughters of Wisdom*, 303 Oak St., 27858. Sisters 2.

JACKSONVILLE. *Holy Spirit Convent*, 3 East Dr., 28546. Tel: 910-353-1200. Total in Residence 4.

KINSTON. *Sisters of Mercy*, 716 West Rd., 28501. Tel: 919-523-9490.

KITTY HAWK. *Sisters of Charity*, 5110 Lindbergh Ave., 27949. Tel: 919-261-3335. Sr. Mary Kay Bush, S.C.; Sr. Francis Agnes Anthony, S.C.

NEW BERN. *St. Paul Convent*, 3003 Country Club Rd., 28562. Tel: 919-637-3726. Total in Residence 3.
Sisters of Charity of Seton Hill, 1307 B Stallings Pkwy., 28562.

PLYMOUTH. *Sisters, Servants of the Immaculate Heart of Mary*, P.O. Box 822, 27962. Tel: 919-793-4052.

RAEFORD. *St. Elizabeth of Hungary Parish House*, 124 Palmer St., 28376. Tel: 910-875-8803.
E-mail: StElizabet@aol.com

ROCKY MOUNT. *Our Lady of Perpetual Help Convent*, 120 Chesapeake Ct., 27804. Tel: 919-446-4515.
E-mail: mac4hbm
Sisters, Servants of the Immaculate Heart of Mary. Total in Residence 2.

ROLESVILLE. *Sisters For Christian Community*, P.O. Box 517, 27571.

SANFORD. *St. Mark's Convent*, 807 Valley Rd., 27330. Tel: 919-776-5350. Sisters of St. Joseph of St. Mark 2.

SOUTHERN PINES. *Missionary Servants of the Most Blessed Trinity*, 565 N. May St., 28387-5611. Tel: 910-692-4032.
St. Joseph of the Pines, 590 Central Dr., 28387. Tel: 910-692-6848. Sisters of Providence 3.

TARBORO. *Congregation of St. Agnes*, 701 Cedar Ln., 27886. Tel: 919-823-8801.

WILLIAMSTON. *Sisters, Servants of the Immaculate Heart of Mary*, 503 E. Simmons Ave., 27892. Tel: 919-792-4091.

WILMINGTON. *Sisters of St. Francis of Philadelphia*, 5009 Lord Tennyson Rd., 28405. Tel: 910-392-4778.
Sisters of St. Ursula, 216 S. Fifth Ave., 28401. Tel: 910-763-6770. Sisters 4.

WILSON. *Franciscan Sisters of the Atonement*, 810 Reid St. E., 27893.
Sisters of Notre Dame, 911 Branch St. N.W., 27893-2925. Total in Residence 3.

[G] RETREAT HOUSES

RALEIGH. *Madonna House*, 424 Rose Ln., 27610. Tel: 919-231-4049.
E-mail: madonnah@mv.igs.net
Web site: http://www.mv.igs.net/~madonnah
Carolyn Desch; Elsie Whitty; Carol Gordon; Miss Theresa Davis, Dir.

DURHAM. *Avila Retreat Center*, 711 Mason Rd., 27712. Tel: 919-477-1285; Fax: 919-477-9485.
E-mail: jacksond@raldioc.org
Web site: http://www.raldioc.org/avila.html
Sr. Damian Marie Jackson, O.S.F., Dir. Total Staff 8; Total in Residence 2.

[H] COLLEGE CAMPUS MINISTRY CENTERS

RALEIGH. *Catholic Student Center*, North Carolina State University, Aquinas House, 600 Bilyeu St., 27606. Tel: 919-833-9668.
E-mail: ajdash@unity.ncsu.edu
Web site: www2.ncsu.edu/ncsu/stud_orgs/aquinas_house/
Rev. Alan J. Dash.

CHAPEL HILL. *Newman Catholic Student Center*, University of North Carolina, 218 Pittsboro St., 27516. Revs. Phillip M. Leach; Edward P. Mahoney.

DURHAM. *Catholic Student Center for Students at Duke University*, Box 99057, 27708-9057. Tel: 919-684-8959. Rev. Michael P. Shugrue.
North Carolina Central University, 1400 S. Alston Ave., 27707. Tel: 919-682-4852. Rev. David E. Barry, S.J.

ELON COLLEGE. *Elon College*. Mailing Address: Catholic Campus Ministry, Campus Box 2960, 27244-2010. Tel: 910-538-2741. Rev. Michael Lorentsen, O.F.M.Conv., Campus Min.

GREENVILLE. *Catholic Student Center for Students at East Carolina University*, P.O. Box 2605, 27836-2605. Center, 953 E. 10th St., 27858. Tel: 919-757-3760. Office, 955 E. 10th St., 27858. Tel: 919-757-1991. Rev. Paul Vaeth, C.P. Total in Residence 1; Total Staff 1.

WILMINGTON. *Catholic Student Center*, University of North Carolina at Wilmington, 4802 College Acres Dr., 28403. Tel: 910-791-7167. Rev. William L. Pitts.

[I] MISCELLANEOUS

RALEIGH. *Catholic Housing Corporation*, 300 Cardinal Gibbons Dr., 27606.
Catholic Parish Outreach, 408 Capital Blvd., 27603. Tel: 919-834-9680. Total Staff 81; Total Assisted 16,306.
The Clergy Retirement Plan of Diocese of Raleigh, 715 Nazareth St., 27606.
Vocations Office, 715 Nazareth St., 27606-2187. Tel: 919-821-9713; Fax: 919-821-9705.
E-mail: ranalli@raldioc.org
Rev. John A. Ranalli, Dir.

NORTH TOPSAIL BEACH. *Marianist Family Ministry, Inc.*, Christian Family Living Center, 2006 Wicker St., 28460. Tel: 910-328-1584.
E-mail: cf12@juno.com
Joseph Dicostanzo. Total Staff 250; Total in Residence 1,400.

PINEHURST. *St. Joseph Home Care, Inc.*, 95 Aviemore Dr., 28374. Mr. George Kecatos, Pres.
St. Joseph of the Pines Home Health Agency, 95 Aviemore Dr., 28374. Tel: 910-295-3920. Legal Title: *St. Joseph of the Pines, Inc.* Lorena Moree, Exec. Dir. & Chief Oper. Officer.
Serving Moore, Lee, Hoke, Anson, Harnett, Davidson, Randolph, Montgomery, Robeson, Scotland, Chatham, Richmond, Mecklenburg and Cumberland Counties. Home Health Agencies 14; Long Term Care Facilities 2; Adult Day Care Center 1; Acute Care Beds 4; Retirement Villas, Low-income Housing for elderly.

SMITHFIELD. *Short Journey Center*, 2323 Cleveland Rd., 27577. Tel: 919-934-7463; Fax: 919-934-7464.
E-mail: karch@Raldioc.org

SOUTHERN PINES. *St. Joseph of the Pines Retirement Villa*, 592 Central Dr., 28387. Tel: 910-692-6455. Mrs. Denise Davidson, Dir. Total Staff 7; Total in Residence 75.

RELIGIOUS INSTITUTES OF MEN REPRESENTED IN THE DIOCESE

For further details refer to the corresponding bracketed number in the Religious Institutes of Men or Women section.

[0470]—*The Capuchin Friars.*—O.F.M.Cap.
[1000]—*Congregation of the Passion.*—C.P.
[0480]—*Conventual Franciscans.*—O.F.M.Conv.
[0520]—*Franciscan Friars.*—O.F.M.
[0530]—*Franciscan Friars of the Atonement.*—S.A.
[0690]—*Jesuit Fathers and Brothers.* (Maryland & New York Provs.).—S.J.
[0720]—*The Missionaries of Our Lady of La Salette.*—M.S.
[0920]—*Oblates of St. Francis De Sales.* (American Prov.).—O.S.F.S.
[0430]—*Order of Preachers (Dominicans).*—O.P.
[0610]—*Priests of the Congregation of Holy Cross.*—C.S.C.

RELIGIOUS INSTITUTES OF WOMEN REPRESENTED IN THE DIOCESE

[3710]—*Congregation of the Sisters of Saint Agnes.*—C.S.A.
[]—*Adrian Dominican Sisters of the Most Holy Rosary.* (Adrian, MI).—O.P.
[3935]—*Congregation of the Sisters of St. Louis.*—S.S.L.
[1920]—*Congregation of the Sisters of the Holy Cross.*—C.S.C.
[0760]—*Daughters of Charity of St. Vincent de Paul.*—D.C.
[0960]—*Daughters of Wisdom.*—D.W.
[1070-13]—*Dominican Sisters.*—O.P.
[1070-17]—*Dominican Sisters.*—O.P.
[1190]—*Franciscan Sisters of the Atonement.*—S.A.
[2575]—*Institute of the Sisters of Mercy of the Americas.* (Belmont, NC; Merion, PA; Hartford, CT).—R.S.M.
[]—*Mission Helpers of the Sacred Heart.*—M.H.S.H.

[2790]—*Missionary Servants of the Most Blessed Trinity.*—M.S.B.T.
[]—*Sisters for Christian Community.*—S.F.C.C.
[0570]—*Sisters of Charity of Seton Hill, Greensburg, Pennsylvania.*—S.C.
[0990]—*Sisters of Divine Providence.*—C.D.P.
[2990]—*Sisters of Notre Dame.* (Chardon, OH).—S.N.D.
[3340]—*Sisters of Providence.*—S.P.
[1650]—*Sisters of St. Francis of Philadelphia.*—O.S.F.
[3830]—*Sisters of St. Joseph.*—S.S.J.
[3910]—*Sisters of St. Joseph of St. Mark.*—S.J.S.M.
[1830]—*Sisters of the Good Shepherd.* (Silver Spring, MD).—R.G.S.
[1990]—*Sisters of the Holy Names of Jesus and Mary.*—S.N.J.M.
[2150]—*Sisters, Servants of the Immaculate Heart of Mary.*—I.H.M.
[2160]—*Sisters, Servants of the Immaculate Heart of Mary.*—I.H.M.
[2170]—*Sisters, Servants of the Immaculate Heart of Mary.*—I.H.M.
[4048]—*Society of Sisters Faithful Companions of Jesus.*—F.C.J.
[4040]—*Society of St. Ursula.*—S.U.
[]—*Ursuline Sisters.*—O.S.U.

NECROLOGY

† Chase, Chan H., (Retired). —Died April 1, 1997.
† Donohue, Raymond J., (Retired). —Died Oct. 10, 1997.
† O'Brien, John G., (Retired). —Died Feb. 2, 1997.

Diocese of Rapid City

(Dioecesis Rapidopolitana)

(Vacant See)

Chancery Office: 606 Cathedral Dr., P.O. Box 678, Rapid City, SD, 57709. Tel.: 605-343-3541; Fax: 605-348-7985.

FORMERLY THE DIOCESE OF LEAD.

ERECTED AUGUST 4, 1902; SEE TRANSFERRED TO RAPID CITY, AUGUST 1, 1930.

Square Miles 43,000.

Comprises the Counties of Bennett, Butte, Corson, Custer, Dewey, Fall River, Gregory, Haakon, Harding, Jackson, Jones, Lawrence, Lyman, Meade, Mellette, Pennington, Perkins, Stanley, Shannon, Todd, Tripp and Ziebach in the State of South Dakota.

For legal titles of parishes and diocesan institutions, consult the Chancery Office.

STATISTICAL OVERVIEW

Personnel	
Priests: Diocesan Active in Diocese	27
Priests: Active Outside Diocese	2
Priests: Retired, Sick or Absent	12
Number of Diocesan Priests	41
Religious Priests in Diocese	27
Extern Priests in Diocese	1
Ordinations:	
Diocesan Priests	2
Transitional Deacons	1
Permanent Deacons in Diocese	26
Total Brothers	9
Total Sisters	72
Parishes	
Parishes	63
With Resident Pastor:	
Resident Diocesan Priests	25
Resident Religious Priests	10
Without Resident Pastor:	
Administered by Priests	24
Administered by Permanent Deacons	1
Administered by Women Religious	1
Completely Vacant	2
Missions	17
Pastoral Centers	4
Professional Ministry Personnel:	
Brothers	3
Sisters	26
Lay Ministers	77
Welfare	
Residential Care of Children	1
Total Assisted	6
Day Care and Extended Day Care Centers	1
Total Assisted	20
Specialized Homes	1
Total Assisted	1,309
Special Centers for Social Services	2
Total Assisted	3,170
Educational	
Diocesan Students in Other Seminaries	14
Total Seminarians	14
High Schools, Diocesan and Parish	1
Total Students	265
High Schools, Private	1
Total Students	160
Elementary Schools, Diocesan and Parish	1
Total Students	555
Elementary Schools, Private	1
Total Students	378
Catechesis/Religious Education:	
High School Students	2,106
Elementary Students	4,451
Total Students Under Catholic Instruction	7,929
Teachers in the Diocese:	
Sisters	10
Lay Teachers	121
Vital Statistics	
Receptions into the Church:	
Infant Baptism Totals	1,202
Adult Baptism Totals	47
Received into Full Communion	141
First Communions	906
Confirmations	482
Marriages:	
Catholic	94
Interfaith	111
Total Marriages	205
Deaths	416
Total Catholic Population	37,702
Total Population	211,591

Former Bishops—Most Rev. JOHN STARIHA, D.D., cons. October 28, 1902; retired March 29, 1909 and named Titular Bishop of Antipatride; died in Laibach, Austria, Nov. 28, 1915.—Most Rev. JOSEPH F. BUSCH, D.D., cons. May 19, 1910; transferred to Saint Cloud, MN, Feb. 21, 1915; died May 31, 1953.—Most Rev. JOHN J. LAWLER, S.T.D., cons. Titular Bishop of Greater Hermopolis and Auxiliary Bishop of St. Paul, Minnesota, May 19, 1910; transferred to the See of Lead, Jan. 29, 1916; died March 11, 1948.—Most Rev. LEO F. DWORSCHAK, D.D., cons. Titular Bishop of Tium and Coadjutor Bishop of Rapid City "cum jure successionis," Aug. 22, 1946; transferred to Fargo, ND, April 10, 1947.—Most Rev. WILLIAM T. MCCARTY, C.SS.R., D.D., appt. Titular Bishop of Anaea and Delegate to the Military Vicar, Jan. 2, 1943; appt. Coadjutor Bishop of Rapid City "cum jure successionis," April 10, 1947; succeeded to March 11, 1948; retired Sept. 17, 1969; appt. Titular Bishop of Rotdon; died Sept. 14, 1972.—Most Rev. HAROLD J. DIMMERLING, D.D., appt. Bishop of Rapid City, Sept. 17, 1969; ord. May 2, 1940; cons. Oct. 30, 1969; died Dec. 13, 1987.—Most Rev. CHARLES J. CHAPUT, D.D., appt. Bishop of Rapid City, April 11, 1988; appt. Archbishop of Denver, Feb. 18, 1997.

Vicar General—Rev. Msgr. MICHAEL B. WOSTER, J.C.L.

Chancery Office—606 Cathedral Dr., P.O. Box 678, Rapid City, 57709. Tel: 605-343-3541; Fax: 605-348-7985. Office Hours: Mon.-Fri. 8-5 Address all official business to this office.

Chancellor—Sr. M. CELINE ERK, O.S.B.

Diocesan Tribunal—918 5th St., Rapid City, 57701. Tel: 605-343-8685; Fax: 605-348-1050.

Officialis—Rev. Msgr. MICHAEL B. WOSTER.

Diocesan Consultors—Revs. WILLIAM PAULY, S.J.; MICHEL MULLOY; PETER WILKE; ARNOLD KARI; BRIAN LANE; KERRY PRENDIVILLE.

Deaneries—Rev. PETER KOVARIK, Piedmont: Rev. GARY ORESHOSKI, Belle Fourche: Rev. MARK MCCORMICK, Hot Springs: Rev. DALE KUTIL, Ft. Pierre: Rev. JOE ZELLER, Timber Lake: Rev. MICHAEL HIGHT, Presho:

Presbyteral Council—Rev. BRIAN LANE, Pres.

Vicar for Retired Priests—Rev. D. CRAIG COWER.

Permanent Diaconate Program, Sioux Spiritual Center—Rev. JOHN HATCHER, S.J., *HCR 77, Box 271, Howes, 57748.* Tel: 605-985-5906.

Development and Stewardship Program—GRANT TROTTER, Dir.

Continuing Education of Clergy—Rev. Msgr. MICHAEL B. WOSTER.

Vocation Program—Rev. ARNOLD KARI, Dir., *P.O. Box 309, Philip, 57567-0309.* Tel: 605-859-2664.

Diocesan Finance Manager—SUSAN LAMBERT.

Diocesan Finance Council—Rev. Msgr. MICHAEL B. WOSTER, Pres.; Sr. CELINE ERK, O.S.B.; Rev. RAY DEISCH; CHRIS SCHMID; SHIRLEY STEC; JEFFREY VIKEN; ARTHUR KROETCH; RAY HILLENBRAND; PETE LIEN, JR.; JOHN BELL, Sec.; Mrs. SUSAN WILLIAMS; FRANK SHORT; JERRY GERDES; Mrs. CAROL VARLAND; Mrs. AGNES MOUSEL.

Holy Childhood Pontifical Association—Rev. PAUL DAHMS.

Propagation of the Faith—Rev. PAUL DAHMS.

Beginning Experience—918 5th St., Rapid City, 57701. Tel: 605-343-8685.

Birthright—918 5th St., Rapid City, 57701. Tel: 605-343-8685.

Blue Army—918 5th St., Rapid City, 57701. Tel: 605-343-8685.

Couple to Couple—918 5th St., Rapid City, 57701.

Cursillo—918 5th St., Rapid City, 57701.

Engaged Encounter—918 5th St., Rapid City, 57701.

Health Panel—Box 678, Rapid City, 57709.

Marriage Encounter—918 5th St., Rapid City, 57701.

Catholic Relief Service—Rev. PAUL DAHMS, Dir., *606 Cathedral Dr., Rapid City, 57701-5498.*

Native Concerns Office—PHYLLIS DECORY, Dir., *606 Cathedral Dr., Rapid City, 57701.* Tel: 605-343-3541.

Pro-Life Commission—SUE JIMMERSON, Chm., *606 Cathedral Dr., Rapid City, 57701.*

Right to Life—2109 5th St., Rapid City, 57701. Tel: 605-342-3101.

Director of Ongoing Formation—Rev. Msgr. WILLIAM J. O'CONNELL, *P.O. Box 539, McLaughlin, 57642-0539.* Tel: 605-823-4401.

Vicar of Education—THOMAS LANE.

Supt. of Schools—DICK THOMPSON, *300 Fairmont Blvd., Rapid City, 57701.* Tel: 605-343-8484.

Director of Rural Life—Rev. Msgr. MICHAEL B. WOSTER.

Office of Family Life—HARRIET YOUNG, Dir., *918 5th St., Rapid City, 57701.* Tel: 605-343-8685.

Diocesan Office of Religious Education—SEAN INNERST, Dir., *606 Cathedral Dr., Rapid City, 57701.* Tel: 605-343-3541.

Campaign for Human Development—Rev. PAUL DAHMS, Dir., *606 Cathedral Dr., Rapid City, 57701-5498.* Tel: 605-343-3541.

West River Catholic Newspaper—EILEEN SULLIVAN ROTERT, Editor, *606 Cathedral Dr., Rapid City, 57701.*

West River Catholic Youth Office—GLEN GAUER, Dir., *606 Cathedral Dr., Rapid City, 57701.*

Archives—Sr. CELINE ERK, O.S.B.

CLERGY, PARISHES, MISSIONS AND PAROCHIAL SCHOOLS

CITY OF RAPID CITY (Pennington County)

1—CATHEDRAL OF OUR LADY OF PERPETUAL HELP (1890), Revs. Peter B. Wilke, Rector; Janusz Korban; Michael F. Irwin, F.S.S.P.; Timothy Hoag; Deacons Tom Lane; George Gladfelter. Pastoral Ministers (Hospital/Hospice): Sr. Kathleen Clancy, O.S.F.; Patricia Petit.
Church—520 Cathedral Dr., 57701-5499. Tel: 605-342-0507.
School—St. Elizabeth Seton Central School. See separate listing under Institutions Located in the Diocese.
Catechesis / Religious Programs—Bro. Ward O'Connell, C.F.X., D.R.E.
Students 344.
Chapel—Immaculate Conception.
Missions—Keystone, Our Lady of Mount Carmel; Hermosa, St. Michael's.

2—BLESSED SACRAMENT (1947), Revs. Michel Mulloy; Brian C. Fawcett.
Res., 4500 Jackson Blvd., 57702-4999. Tel: 605-342-3336; Fax: 605-341-5668.
Catechesis / Religious Programs—Tel: 605-342-8730.
Students 566.

3—ST. THERESE THE LITTLE FLOWER (1941). Formerly known as The Church of St. John the Evangelist. Revs. Daniel Juelfs; Benjamin Reese (PEO); Deacon Claude Sauer.
Res., 532 Adams St., 57701. Tel: 605-342-1556. [JC]
Catechesis / Religious Programs—Tel: 605-348-6272.
Students 243.

4—ST. ISAAC JOGUES (1949) (Native American), Revs. Patrick M. McCorkell, S.J.; Bernard D. Fagan, S.J.; Deacons James Garnett; Leroy Decory.
Res., 220 Wright St., P.O. Box 1304, 57709-1304. Tel: 605-343-3257.
Catechesis / Religious Programs—Tel: 605-343-2165.
Students 180.
Mother Butler Center—Catechetical and Social Center for Indians. Tel: 605-343-2165.
Mission—Rapid City, Pennington Co., Indian Health Service, Sioux San Hospital and Pennington County Jail.

OUTSIDE THE CITY OF RAPID CITY

Belle Fourche, Butte Co., St. Paul (1905), Rev. David Orians.
Res., 855 Fifth St., 57717-1701. Tel: 605-892-3226. [JC]
Also attends St. Mary, Newell and St. Joseph's, Mud Butte.
Catechesis / Religious Programs—Tel: 605-892-3226.
Students 136.
Missions—Newell, St. Mary, Star of the Sea; Mud Butte, St. Joseph.

Bison, Perkins Co., Blessed Sacrament (1918), Rev. Leo Hausmann.
Res., P.O. Box 297, 57620. Tel: 605-244-5546. [JC]
Mission—Drew, Perkins Co., St. James, Tel: 605-244-5546.

Bonesteel, Gregory Co., Immaculate Conception (1906), Rev. James D. Becht.
Res., P.O. Box 376, 57317-0376. Tel: 605-654-2204. [CEM]
Also attends Church of St. Anthony, Fairfax and St. Francis Xavier, Ponca Creek.
Catechesis / Religious Programs—Students 78.

Buffalo, Harding Co., St. Anthony (1917). Attended by Blessed Sacrament, Bison. Revs. Leo Hausmann; Andrew Morvay, (Retired).
Res., P.O. Box 297, Bison, 57620-0297. Tel: 605-244-5546. [CEM][JC]
Catechesis / Religious Programs—Students 55.
Missions—Cox, Harding Co., St. Agnes; Ralph, Harding Co., St. Isidore; Reva, Harding Co., Our Lady of the Prairie.

Burke, Gregory Co., Sacred Heart (1905). Attended by St. Joseph, Gregory.
Res., P.O. Box 354, 57523-0354. Tel: 605-775-2532. [CEM 2]
Catechesis / Religious Programs—Students 69.

Clearfield, Tripp Co., St. Boniface. Closed. For sacramental records contact Immaculate Conception, Winner.

Colome, Tripp Co., St. Isidore (1909). Attended by Immaculate Conception, Winner. Deacon Michael Curtin, Pastoral Asst.
Res., P.O. Box 405, 57528-0405. Tel: 605-842-1437.
Catechesis / Religious Programs—Students 59.

Custer, Custer Co., St. John the Baptist (1911), Rev. Bryan Sorensen.
Res., P.O. Box 632, 57730-0632. Tel: 605-673-4426. [JC]
Also attends St. Rose of Lima, Hill City.
Catechesis / Religious Programs—Tel: 605-673-4426.
Students 124.

Deadwood, Lawrence Co., St. Ambrose (1877), Rev. Paul G. Dahms.
Res., 760 W. Main St., 57732-1003. Tel: 605-578-1519. [CEM]
Catechesis / Religious Programs—732 Main St., 57732-0320. Tel: 605-578-1921.
Students 86.

Eagle Butte, Dewey Co., All Saints (1911) (Native American), Revs. John Klingler, S.C.J.; Thomas Westhoven, S.C.J.; Bro. Frank Presto, S.C.J.; Deacon Theodore Knife.
Res., P.O. Box 110, 57625-0110. Tel: 605-964-3391; Fax: 605-964-3300. [CEM 8][JC]
Catechesis / Religious Programs—Students 64.
Missions—Bridger, Ziebach Co., Immaculate Conception; Cherry Creek, Ziebach Co., St. Joseph; Dupree, Ziebach Co., Sacred Heart; Promise, Dewey Co., St. Catherine; Red Scaffold, Ziebach Co., Sacred Heart; Ridgeview, Dewey Co., St. Joseph; Thunder Butte, Ziebach Co., St. Luke; White Horse, Dewey Co., St. Therese.

Edgemont, Fall River Co., St. James (1893). Attended by St. Anthony, Hot Springs. Deacon Earl Witte, (Retired).
Mailing Address: P.O. Box 969, Hot Springs, 57747-0969. Tel: 605-745-3393.
Mission—Ardmore, St. Aloysius, Tel: 605-662-7706.

Fairfax, Gregory Co., St. Anthony's (1904). Attended by Immaculate Conception, Bonesteel. Rev. James D. Becht.
Mailing Address: c/o P.O. Box 376, Bonesteel, 57317-0376. Tel: 605-654-2204. [CEM]
Catechesis / Religious Programs—Students attend religious education at Immaculate Conception, Bonesteel.

Faith, Meade Co., St. Joseph (1917), Rev. Dennis Riss.
Res., P.O. Box 307, 57626-0307. Tel: 605-967-2201; Fax: 605-967-2201. [CEM]
Catechesis / Religious Programs—Students 41.
Missions—Red Owl, Meade Co., St. Anthony; Plainview, Meade Co., Our Lady of Victory.

Fort Pierre, Stanley Co., St. John (1905), Rev. Dale Kutil.
Res., 206 W. Main, P.O. Box 670, 57532-0670. Tel: 605-223-2176. [JC]
Catechesis / Religious Programs—Tel: 605-223-2492.
Students 120.

Gregory, Gregory Co., St. Joseph (1905), Rev. Raymond J. Deisch.
Res., 414 Church St., 57533. Tel: 605-835-9290. [CEM 3]
Catechesis / Religious Programs—Mary Vale Hall, 411 Church St., Tel: 605-835-9396.
Students 122.

Hermosa, Custer Co., St. Michael's. Attended by Our Lady of Perpetual Help Cathedral, Rapid City.

Hill City, Pennington Co., St. Rose of Lima (1898). Attended by St. John the Baptist, Custer. Rev. Bryan Sorensen.
Res., P.O. Box 632, Custer, 57730. Tel: 605-673-4426. [JC]
Catechesis / Religious Programs—Tel: 605-574-2479.
Students 76.

Hot Springs, Fall River Co., St. Anthony's (1890), Rev. Mark McCormick.
Res., P.O. Box 969, 57747-0969. Tel: 605-745-3393. [JC]
Catechesis / Religious Programs—Students 195.
Missions—Oelrichs, Fall River Co., St. Martin, 7th & Main Sts., Oelrichs, 57763.; Edgemont, Fall River Co., St. James, 310 3rd St., Edgemont, 57735. Tel: 605-662-7706. Deacon Earl F. Witte.; Ardmore, Fall River Co., St. Aloysius, Ardmore, 57735.

Kadoka, Jackson Co., Our Lady of Victory (1908), Rev. Robert D. Baden; Deacon Eugene A. Heckathorne.
Res., P.O. Box 159, 57543-0159. Tel: 605-837-2219. [JC]

Kennebec, Lyman Co., St. Michael's (1906). Attended by St. Mary, Lower Brule.
Mailing Address: P.O. Box 185, Lower Brule, 57548-0185. Tel: 605-473-5335; Fax: 605-473-5453. [CEM]

Kenel, Corson Co., Assumption of the Blessed Virgin Mary (1879) (Native American). Attended by St. Bernard, McLaughlin.
Res., P.O. Box 539, McLaughlin, 57642-0539. Tel: 605-823-4401.

Kyle, Shannon Co., Our Lady of Sorrows (1910) (Native American), Rev. Joseph Damhorst, S.J.; Deacon Lawrence Whiting, (Retired). In res., Rev. James Ryan, S.J.
Res., P.O. Box 398, 57752-0398. Tel: 605-455-2888. [CEM 2]
Missions—Allen, Bennett Co., St. John of the Cross; Medicine Root, Shannon, St. Stephens.

Lead, Lawrence Co., St. Patrick's (1878), Rev. William A. Zandri.
Res., 141 S. Siever St., 57754. Tel: 605-584-2002. [CEM][JC]
Catechesis / Religious Programs—Students 115.

Lemmon, Perkins Co., St. Mary's (1909), Rev. Ronald B. Garry; Deacons Carl Orthman; Bill Dustman.
Res., P.O. Box 210, 57638. Tel: 605-374-3767. [JC]
Catechesis / Religious Programs—Peggy Falvey, D.R.E.
Students 109.
Missions—Morristown, Corson Co., Sacred Heart; Watauga, Corson Co., St. Michael.

Lower Brule, Lyman Co., St. Mary's (1923) (Native American), Revs. Yvon Sheehy, S.C.J.; James L. Walters, S.C.J.
Office: P.O. Box 185, 57568. Tel: 605-473-5335; Fax: 605-473-5453. [CEM]

Manderson, Shannon Co., St. Agnes (1901) (Native American). Attended by Our Lady of Sorrows, Kyle. Rev. James Ryan, S.J.
Res., P.O. Box 88, 57756. Tel: 605-867-5776. [CEM]
Missions—Wounded Knee, Shannon Co., Sacred Heart; Rockyford, Shannon Co., St. Peter's.

Martin, Bennett Co., Our Lady of the Sacred Heart (1918), Rev. John J. Hennessy, S.J.; Deacon Calvin Clifford.
Mailing Address: P.O. Box 567, 57551. Tel: 605-685-6232. [CEM][JC]
Catechesis / Religious Programs—Tel: 605-685-6274.
Students 107.

McIntosh, Corson Co., St. Bonaventure's (1913), Rev. Msgr. William O'Connell; Rev. Steven Biegler.
Res., P.O. Box 320, 57641. Tel: 605-273-4334; Fax: 605-823-2325. [CEM]
Catechesis / Religious Programs—Students 61.

McLaughlin, Corson Co., St. Bernard (1918), Rev. Msgr. William O'Connell; Rev. Steven Biegler; Deacons Vern Rath; Michael Kills Pretty Enemy; Paul Keller.
Res., P.O. Box 539, 57642. Tel: 605-823-4401; Fax: 605-823-2325. [CEM]
Catechesis / Religious Programs—Tel: 605-823-4210.
Sisters of St. Francis of the Immaculate Conception 2; Lay Teachers 16; Students 114.
Missions—Bullhead, Corson Co., St. Aloysius; Wakpala, Corson Co., St. Bede; Kenel, Corson Co., Our Lady of the Assumption Parish; McIntosh, Corson Co., St. Bonaventure, P.O. Box 320, McIntosh, 57641. Tel: 605-273-4334.

Midland, Haakon Co., St. William (1911). Attended by Sacred Heart, Philip.
Mailing Address: P.O. Box 309, Philip, 57567. Tel: 605-859-2664.

Mission, Todd Co., St. Thomas the Apostle (1933) (Native American). Attended by St. Francis, Mission. Rev. Ron Seminara, S.J.; Deacon Marlon J. Leneaugh.
Church—P.O. Box 151, 57555. Tel: 605-856-4618. [CEM]
Catechesis / Religious Programs—Tel: 605-856-2273. Gladys Bordeaux, D.R.E.
Students 61.
Mission—Okreek, Todd Co., St. Peter's, P.O. Box 499, St. Francis, 57572. Tel: 605-747-2362.

Morristown, Corson Co., Sacred Heart (1912). Attended by St. Mary's, Lemmon.
Mailing Address: P.O. Box 210, Lemmon, 57638. Tel: 605-374-3767. [JC]

Murdo, Jones Co., St. Martin (1906). Attended by Christ the King, Presho.
Mailing Address: P.O. Box 399, Presho, 57568. Tel:

605-669-2436. [CEM]
Catechesis/Religious Programs—Tel: 605-895-2534.
Students 36.

Newell, Butte Co., St. Mary Star of the Sea (1910). Attended by St. Paul, Belle Fourche.
Mailing Address: P.O. Box 72, 57760. Tel: 605-456-2221.
Catechesis/Religious Programs—Students 64.
Mission—Mud Butte, Meade Co., St. Joseph's Catholic Church, (1921) Mud Butte, 57758.

New Underwood, Pennington Co., St. John the Evangelist (1921), Rev. Reuben Valades.
Res., P.O. Box 305, 57761. Tel: 605-754-6446. [JC]
Mission—Lakeside, Meade Co., St. Margaret.

Norris, Melette Co., Sacred Heart (1955). Attended by St. Agnes, Parmelee. Rev. Joseph C. Gill, S.J.
Res., 14CR 76, Box 11A, Belvidere, 57521-9701. Tel: 605-747-2118. [JC]

Oglala, Shannon Co., Our Lady of the Sioux (1916) (Native American). Attended by Holy Rosary Mission, Pine Ridge. Sr. Julianne Brockamp, P.B.V.M., Pastoral Coord.
Res., P.O. Box 140, 57764. Tel: 605-867-5673. [CEM]

Parmelee, Todd Co., St. Agnes, Rev. Joseph C. Gill, S.J.
Res., P.O. Box 115, 57566. Tel: 605-747-2118.
Catechesis/Religious Programs—Students 90.
Missions—Upper Cutmeat, Sacred Heart; He Dog, St. Patrick Hall; Black Pipe-Corn Creek, St. Joseph Hall.

Philip, Haakon Co., Sacred Heart (1907), Rev. Arnold A. Kari.
Res., 307 W. Elm, P.O. Box 309, 57567. Tel: 605-859-2664. [JC]
Catechesis/Religious Programs—Students 116.
Missions—Milesville, Haakon Co., St. Mary; Midland, Haakon Co., St. William.

Piedmont-Black Hawk, Meade Co., Our Lady of the Black Hills (1916), Rev. Peter Kovarik; Deacon Walt Wilson.
Res., HCR 80, Box 481, 57769. Tel: 605-787-5168. [JC]
Catechesis/Religious Programs—Students 174.

Pine Ridge, Shannon Co., Sacred Heart (1890) (Lakota). Attended from Pine Ridge Reservation.
Res., P.O. Box 359, 57770. Tel: 605-867-5551; Fax: 605-867-1291. [JC]
Catechesis/Religious Programs—Students 37.

Porcupine, Shannon Co., Church of Christ the King (1901) (Native American). Attended by Our Lady of Sorrows, Kyle. Rev. James H. Ryan, S.J.
Res., P.O. Box 398, Kyle, 57752-0398. Tel: 605-867-1614; 455-2888. [CEM]
School—Our Lady of Lourdes Mission School, Tel: 605-867-5568; Fax: 605-867-5874. Cynthia Hillman, Prin.
Sisters 1; Lay Teachers 12; Students 168.
Missions—On the Creek, Shannon Co., St. Paul, P.O. Box 7, 57772. Tel: 605-867-1614. [CEM]
Manderson, Shannon Co., St. Agnes, P.O. Box 88, Manderson, 57756. Tel: 605-867-5776. [CEM]
Manderson, Shannon Co., St. Peter's, P.O. Box 88, Manderson, 57756. [CEM]
Wounded Knee, Sacred Heart.

Presho, Lyman Co., Christ the King (1906), Rev. Michael Hight.
Res., P.O. Box 399, 57568-0399. Tel: 605-895-2534. [CEM]
Catechesis/Religious Programs—Students 36.
Missions—Murdo, Jones Co., St. Martin of Tours; Draper, Jones Co., St. Anthony of Padua.

Reliance, Lyman Co., St. Mary's (1911). Attended by St. Mary's, Lower Brule.
Mailing Address: P.O. Box 185, Lower Brule, 57548-0185. Tel: 605-473-5335; Fax: 605-473-5453. [CEM]

Rosebud, Todd Co., St. Bridget, Rev. David Gau, S.J.
Res., P.O. Box 340, 57570-0340. Tel: 605-747-2496.
Catechesis/Religious Programs—Students 148.
Mission—Soldier Creek, St. Rose.

St. Francis, Todd Co., St. Charles (1886) (Native American), Rev. David Gau, S.J.; Deacon Ben Black Bear, Jr.
Res., Box 499, 57572. Tel: 605-747-2533; Fax: 605-747-5057. [CEM]
Catechesis/Religious Programs—Tel: 605-747-2567.
Students 321.
Missions—See listing under Indian Missions for Rosebud Reservation, St. Francis regarding details on personnel and missions.; Soldier Creek, Todd Co., St. Rose; Spring Creek, Todd Co., St. Patrick.

Spearfish, Lawrence Co., St. Joseph (1907), Rev. Kerry Prendiville.
Res., 844 5th St., 57783-2005. Tel: 605-642-2306; Fax: 605-642-1024. [JC]
Catechesis/Religious Programs—Students 404.

Sturgis, Meade Co., St. Francis of Assisi (1840), Rev. Gary Oreshoski; Deacon Roger Heidt.
Res., 1049 Howard St., 57785-1999. Tel: 605-347-3579. [CEM]
Catechesis/Religious Programs—Tel: 605-347-3996. Debi Dauer, D.R.E.
Students 238.

Timber Lake, Dewey Co., Holy Cross (1910), Rev. Joseph E. Zeller.
Res., P.O. Box 70, 57656-0070. Tel: 605-865-3653. [CEM][JC 3]
Catechesis/Religious Programs—Students 197.
Missions—Isabel, Dewey Co., St. Mary; Trail City, Corson Co., Holy Rosary.

Wall, Pennington Co., St. Patrick's (1917), Rev. Robert D. Baden.
Res., P.O. Box 405, 57790-0405. Tel: 605-279-2542. [JC]
Catechesis/Religious Programs—Students 79.
Mission—Interior, Jackson Co., Holy Rosary.

Wanblee, Jackson Co., Ignatius Loyola (1920) (Native American), Rev. Joseph Damhorst, S.J.
Res., P.O. Box 229, 57577. Tel: 605-462-6170. [CEM 3]
Catechesis/Religious Programs—Students 65.
Mission—Potatoe Creek, Jackson Co., St. Henry.

Watauga, Corson Co., St. Michael (1912). Attended by St. Mary's, Lemmon.
Mailing Address: P.O. Box 210, Lemmon, 57638-0210. Tel: 605-473-3767. [CEM]

White River, Mellette Co., St. Ignatius (1899) (Native American), Rev. Ron Seminara, S.J.
Res., P.O. Box 245, 57579-0245. Tel: 605-259-3381. [JC]
Catechesis/Religious Programs—Tel: 605-259-3313.
Students 31.
Mission—Wood, Melette Co., Our Lady of Good Counsel, Wood, 57585.
Sacred Heart, Melette Co., (1919), Rev. Ronald Seminara, S.J.
P.O. Box 245, 57579-0245. Tel: 605-259-3213. [JC]

Winner, Tripp Co., Immaculate Conception (1910), Rev. Brian Lane; Deacon Michael Curtin.
Res., 302 W. Fourth, P.O. Box 765, 57580. Tel: 605-842-3520.
Catechesis/Religious Programs—Students 207.
Mission—Keyapaha, Tripp Co., St. Ann.

INDIAN MISSIONS

Eagle Butte, Dewey Co., Cheyenne River Reservation (1911) (Native American), Revs. John Klingler, S.C.J.; Thomas Westhoven, S.C.J.; Bro. Frank Presto.
Mailing Address: All Saints, P.O. Box 110, 57625. Tel: 605-964-3391; Fax: 605-964-3300. [CEM]
Catechesis/Religious Programs—Students 64.
Missions—Bridger, Ziebach Co., Immaculate Conception; Dupree, Ziebach Co., Sacred Heart; Promise, Dewey Co., St. Catherine; Ridgeview, Dewey Co., St. Joseph; Cherry Creek, Ziebach Co., St. Joseph; Thunder Butte, Ziebach Co., St. Luke; Red Scaffold, Ziebach Co., Sacred Heart; White Horse, Ziebach Co., St. Therese.

Lower Brule, Lyman Co., Lower Brule Reservation (1895) (Native American), Revs. Yvon Sheehy, S.C.J.; James L. Walters, S.C.J.
Mailing Address: P.O. Box 185, 57548. Tel: 605-473-5335; 473-5215; Fax: 605-473-5453. [CEM]
Sisters 3.

Pine Ridge, Shannon Co., Holy Rosary (Pine Ridge Reservation) (1888) (Native American), Revs. David L. Smith, S.J.; Earl J. Kurth, S.J.; Joseph Damhorst, S.J., (Kyle, Wamblee); William Pauly, S.J., Supr., (Pine Ridge); Paul Manhart, S.J., (Kyle, Wamblee); James Ryan, S.J., (Manderson, Wounded Knee, Porcupine); William G. McKenney, S.J.; Kevin C. Schneider, S.J.; Peter J. Klink, S.J., Dir. Devel.; Thomas Merkel, S.J., Supt. of Red Cloud School.
Mailing Address: Pine Ridge P.O., 57770. Tel: 605-867-5491; Fax: 605-967-1291.
Priests 12; Lay Teachers 42; Brothers 3.
School—Red Cloud Indian School, Tel: 605-867-5491; Fax: 605-867-1291. Sr. Monica O.S.F., Coord.
Priests 12; Sisters of St. Francis of Penance and Christian Charity 3; Sisters of Charity of Cincinnati 1; School Sisters of Notre Dame of St. Louis 1; Congregation of Notre Dame 4; Lay Teachers 42; Students: Elementary 128; Middle School 82; High School 160.
Missions—Cuny Table, Shannon Co., St. Joseph; Oglala, Shannon Co., Our Lady of Sioux, P.O. Box 140, Oglala, 57764. Tel: 605-867-5673; No Water, Shannon Co., Our Lady of Good Counsel; Slim Butte, Shannon Co., Our Lady of Lourdes; Red Shirt Table, Shannon Co., St. Bernard.

St. Francis, Todd Co., Rosebud Reservation (1886) (Native American). St. Francis Mission and Rosebud Educational Society. Revs. Ronald S. Seminara, S.J., Supr., Mission; Joseph Gill, S.J.; John A. Hennessy, S.J., Our Lady of the Sacred Heart, Martin; Richard T. Jones, S.J.; Robert G. Gilroy, S.J.; Glendon R. Welshons, S.J.; David Gau, S.J., St. Bridget, Rosebud & St. Charles, St. Francis; Bro. Edward C. Gill, S.J.; Deacons Ben Black Bear, Jr.; Harold Condon; Marlon Leneaugh.
Mailing Address: P.O. Box 499, 57572-0499. Tel: 605-747-2361; Fax: 605-747-5057. [CEM]
Priests 7; Permanent Deacons 2; Brothers 3; Sisters 3.
Catechesis/Religious Programs—Tel: 605-747-2142.
Students 740.
Missions—St. Francis, Todd Co., St. Charles, Tel: 605-747-2533; Okreek, Todd Co., St. Peter, Tel: 605-747-2362; Soldier Creek, Todd Co., St. Rose, Tel: 605-747-2362; Spring Creek, Todd Co., St. Patrick, Tel: 605-747-2845; Parmelee, Todd Co., St. Agnes, Box 115, Parmelee, 57566. Tel: 605-747-2118; Upper Cutmeat, Todd Co., Sacred Heart, Box 115, Parmelee, 57566. Tel: 605-747-2118; Rosebud, Todd Co., St. Bridget, P.O. Box 340, Rosebud, 57570. Tel: 605-747-2436; White River, Mellette Co., St. Ignatius; Wood, Mellette Co., Our Lady of Good Counsel, Tel: 605-747-2362; Norris, Mellette Co., Sacred Heart, Box 115, Parmelee, 57566; Mission, Todd Co., St. Thomas, Box 151, Mission, 57555. Tel: 605-856-2273. Rev. Ron Seminara, S.J.

Standing Rock, Corson Co., Standing Rock Reservation (1918), Rev. Msgr. William J. O'Connell; Rev. Steven Biegler.
St. Bernard's Church: P.O. Box 539, McLaughlin, 57642. Tel: 605-823-4401; Fax: 605-823-2325.
Catechesis/Religious Programs—Tel: 605-823-4210.
Students 114.
Missions—Wakpala, Corson Co., St. Bede; Bullhead, Corson Co., St. Aloysius; Kenel, Corson Co., Assumption of the Blessed Virgin Mary Church.

Chaplains of Public Institutions

ELLSWORTH. *Ellsworth AFB*. Rev. Joseph Motsay, 28th BW/HC, Ellsworth AFB, 57706.

On Duty Outside the Diocese:
Reverend Fathers—
Novotny, Richard

Retired:
Reverend Fathers—
Birdsall, John M., 2110-C St. Martin Dr., Rapid City, SD 57702
Corry, John J., 2110-C St. Martin Dr., Apt. 107, Rapid City, SD 57702
Cower, D. Craig, 824 Columbus, #204, Rapid City, SD 57701-3578
Jordan, Collins P., c/o Lionel Bordeaux, Mission, SD 57555
Lambert, William, 163 Vondera St., Robertsville, MO 63072
Morvay, Andrew, P.O. Box 85, Buffalo, SD 57720-0085
Philbin, William, 1102 City Springs Rd. #104, Rapid City, SD 57702-0223
Plante, Richard A., W. Hills S., Rm. 202, 201 Anamaria Dr., Rapid City, SD 57701-7376
Scadron, Christopher, 5612 S. Forrest Ave., Tuscon, AZ 85746
Scherer, Gerald N., P.O. Box 268, Hermoso, SD 57744-0268
Staricek, Andrew, P.O. Box 7, Bison, SD 57620-0007

Permanent Deacons:
Black Bear, Ben, Jr., St. Francis Mission, St. Francis
Clifford, Calvin, Martin
Condon, Harold, Parmelee
Coy, Patrick, Hill City
Curtin, Michael, St. Isidore, Colome
DeCory, Leroy, Rapid City
Dustman, Bill, Lemmon
Garnet, James W., Rapid City
Gladfelter, George, Rapid City
Grant, Albert, Hot Springs
Heckathorne, Eugene A., Kadoka
Heidt, Roger, Sturgis
Hill, Ken, Albuquerque, New Mexico
Jetson, David, Rapid City
Keller, Paul, McLaughlin
Kills Pretty Enemy, Michael, McLaughlin
Knife, Theodore, Faith
Lane, Thomas, Silver City
Leneaugh, Marlon, Mission
McGeeney, Joe, (Retired)
Murray, Chet, (Retired), Rapid City
Orthman, Carl, Lemmon

Rath, Vern, McLaughlin
Richards, Reno, Allen Mission District
Sauer, Claude, (Retired), St. Therese, Rapid City
Usera, Luis, Colorado
Whiting, Lawrence, Kyle
Wilson, Walt, Piedmont
Witte, Earl Joseph, St. James, Edgemont

INSTITUTIONS LOCATED IN THE DIOCESE

[A] DIOCESAN CATHOLIC SCHOOL SYSTEM

RAPID CITY. *St. Thomas More High School*, 300 Fairmont Blvd., 57701. Tel: 605-343-8484; Fax: 605-348-1315.
E-mail: stmoore@sd.cybernex.net
Richard Thompson, Supt. Lay Teachers 27; Students 265; Total Staff 52.
St. Elizabeth Elementary and Middle School, 431 Oakland, 57701. Tel: 605-348-1477. Lay Teachers 40; Students 555; Staff 66.

[B] MONASTERIES AND RESIDENCES OF PRIESTS & BROTHERS

BETHLEHEM. *Holy Nativity Monastery*, 57708. Tel: 605-787-4606. Revs. Louis Marie, Supr.; Maron Morgan; Anthony Kramer; Elias Havel; Martin Ferland. Priests 5.

EAGLE BUTTE. *Sacred Heart Community House*, P.O. Box 110, 57625-0110. Tel: 605-964-3391; Fax: 605-964-3300. Revs. John Klinger, S.C.J., Coord.; Thomas Westhoven, S.C.J.; Bro. Frank Presto, S.C.J. Priests 2; Brothers 1.

HOWES. *Kino Jesuit Community*, HCR 77 Box 271, 57748-9505. Tel: 605-985-5906; Fax: 605-985-5908.
E-mail: smitten@sioux.sodak.net
In res. Revs. Bernard D. Fagan, S.J.; Thomas J. Tierney, S.J.; Stephen F. Mitten, S.J.; John A. Schwantes, S.J.; Patrick M. McCorkell, S.J.; John E. Hatcher, S.J. Priests 6.

LOWER BRULE. *SCJ Community House*, P.O. Box 185, 57548-0185. Tel: 605-473-5335; 473-5487. Revs. Yvon Sheehy, S.C.J.; James L. Walters, S.C.J. Priests 2; Total in Residence 2; Total Staff 2.

PINE RIDGE. *Jesuit Community of Holy Rosary Mission*, 57770-0001. Tel: 605-867-5491. Revs. William Pauly, S.J., Supr.; William G. McKenney, S.J., Pastor; Peter J. Klink, S.J., Dir. Devel.; Kevin C. Schneider, S.J.; Earl J. Kurth, S.J.; Joseph Damhorst, S.J.; Paul Manhart, S.J.; David Smith, S.J.; Tom Merkel, S.J., Supt., Red Cloud School; James S. Ryan, S.J. Priests 10; Brothers 3; Total in Residence 15; Total Staff 2.

[C] CONVENTS AND RESIDENCES FOR SISTERS

RAPID CITY.
**Benedictine Convent of St. Martin*, 2110 C St. Martin Dr., 57702-9392. Tel: 605-343-8011; Fax: 605-399-2723. Motherhouse and Novitiate of the Sisters of St. Benedict. Sr. Florence McManamen, O.S.B., Prioress. Sisters 43; Novices 1.
Benedictine Convent of St. Martin Retirement Trust, 2110-C St. Martin Dr., 57702-9392. Tel: 605-343-8011. Sr. Mary Wegher, Trustee & Contact Person.
St. Martin's Community Center, 2110-C St. Martin Dr., 57702-9392. Tel: 605-343-8011; Fax: 605-399-2723. Total Assisted 20; Total Staff 2.
Kateri Convent, 624 Adams, 57701-0809. Tel: 605-343-6261. Parish Office and Home Visitations, particularly Native Americans. Oblate Sisters of the Blessed Sacrament 2.

PORCUPINE. *Our Lady of Lourdes School Convent*, P.O. Box 7, 57772-0007. Notre Dame Sisters.

[D] MISCELLANEOUS

RAPID CITY. *The Catholic Education Fund, Inc.*, P.O. Box 678, 57709-0678.
Catholic Parish Association Contingency Fund, Inc., P.O. Box 678, 57709-0678.
Catholic Social Service of the Diocese of Rapid City, 918 5th St., 57701. Tel: 605-348-6086; Fax: 605-348-1050. James Kinyon, Dir.
Priest Retirement and Aid Association, 824 Columbus St., #204, 57701-3578. Revs. Raymond Deisch, Pres.; D. Craig Cower, Exec. Sec.; Rev. Msgr. Michael Woster, Vice Pres.; Revs. Dale Kutil; James Becht; Leo Hausmann.
St. Martin's Community Center, 2110 C St. Martin Dr., 57702-9392. Tel: 605-343-8011; Fax: 605-399-2723. Sr. Jane Frances Mullaney, O.S.B., Dir.
St. Martin's Learning Center, 2110-C St. Martin Dr., 57702-9392. Tel: 605-343-2243. Sr. Carol Kovarik, O.S.B., Dir. Sisters 2; Students 20.
Western South Dakota Catholic Foundation, Inc., P.O. Box 678, 57709-0678.

EAGLE BUTTE. *Sacred Heart Center*, 121 Landmark St., P.O. Box 2000, 57625-2000. Tel: 605-964-6062; Fax: 605-964-6060. Bro. Francis J. Presto, S.C.J., Dir. Total Assisted 495; Total Staff 28.

HOWES. *The Diocese of Rapid City Mahpiya na Maka Okoigna*. Sioux Spiritual Center, HCR 77, P.O. Box 271, 57748-9505. Tel: 605-985-5906; Fax: 605-985-5908. Revs. John E. Hatcher, S.J.; Stephen F. Mitten, S.J.; John A. Schwantes, S.J. Total in Residence 3; Total Staff 6.

MANDERSON. *St. Francis Home*, P.O. Box 122, 57756-0122. Tel: 605-455-2781. Sr. Geraldine Clifford, O.S.F., Minister; Sr. Colleen Mahoney, O.S.F. Sisters of St. Francis Marycrest. Home for abandoned and abused children (Licensed) 2-12 years of age.

RELIGIOUS INSTITUTES OF MEN REPRESENTED IN THE DIOCESE

For further details refer to the corresponding bracketed number in the Religious Institutes of Men or Women section.

[1350]—*Brothers of St. Francis Xavier.*—C.F.X.
[1130]—*Congregation of the Priests and Brothers of the Sacred Heart.*—S.C.J.
[0690]—*Jesuit Fathers and Brothers.*—S.J.

RELIGIOUS INSTITUTES OF WOMEN REPRESENTED IN THE DIOCESE

[0230]—*Benedictine Sisters of Pontifical Jurisdiction.* (Rapid City, SD).—O.S.B.
[1070-13]—*Dominican Sisters.* (Adrian, Michigan).—O.P.
[]—*Franciscan Sisters of Little Falls, MN.*
[2960]—*Notre Dame Sisters.* (Omaha, NE).—N.D.
[3010]—*Oblate Sisters of the Blessed Sacrament.* (Marty, SD).—O.S.B.S.
[2970]—*School Sisters of Notre Dame.* (St. Louis, MO; Dubuque, IA).—S.S.N.D.
[1680]—*School Sisters of St. Francis.* (Milwaukee, WI).—S.S.S.F.
[3580]—*Servants of Mary.* (Omaha, NE).—O.S.M.
[0660]—*Sister of Christian Charity.* (Wilmette, IL).—S.C.C.
[]—*Sisters of Charity of Cincinnati (Ohio).*—S.C.
[1630]—*Sisters of St. Francis of Penance and Christian Charity.* (Denver, CO).—O.S.F.
[]—*Sisters of St. Francis of Perpetual Adoration.* (Colorado Springs, CO).—O.S.F.
[1580]—*Sisters of St. Francis of the Immaculate Conception.* (Peoria, IL).—O.S.F.
[2980]—*Sisters of the Congregation of Notre Dame.* (Ridgefield, CT).—C.N.D.
[1030]—*Sisters of the Divine Savior.* (Milwaukee, WI).—S.D.S.
[3320]—*Sisters of the Presentation of the B.V.M.* (Aberdeen, SD; Dubuque, IA; Fargo, ND).—P.B.V.M.

DIOCESAN CEMETERIES

RAPID CITY. Catholic Cemeteries (all Diocesan) are located in the following parishes: Bear Butte, Belle Fourche, Bonesteel, Buffalo, Burke, Cherry Creek, Cheyenne Agency, Clearfield, Colome, Custer, Dallas, Deadwood, Dupree, Eagle Butte, Fairfax, Faith, Gregory, Glencross, Kadoka, Kenel, Kennebec, Lemmon, McIntosh, Martin Mission, Murdo, Pine Ridge, Porcupine, Presho, Reliance, St. Francis, Sturgis, Timber Lake, Trail City, Wakpala, Watauga, Winner, and Witten.

NECROLOGY

(No Deaths)

Diocese of Reno

(Dioecesis Renensis)

Most Reverend

PHILLIP F. STRALING, D.D.

Bishop of Reno; ordained March 19, 1959; appointed Bishop of San Bernardino July 18, 1978; installed November 6, 1978; appointed Bishop of Reno March 21, 1995; installed June 29, 1995. *515 Court St., Reno, NV, 89501.*

Pastoral Center: 515 Court St., Reno, NV, 89501. Mailing Address: P.O. Box 1211, Reno, NV, 89504. Tel.: 702-329-9274; Fax: 702-348-8619.

ERECTED AS THE DIOCESE OF RENO BY HIS HOLINESS POPE PIUS XI MARCH 27, 1931. CANONICAL ERECTION OF THE DIOCESE AUGUST 19, 1931; REDESIGNATED DIOCESE OF RENO-LAS VEGAS BY POPE PAUL VI, OCTOBER 13, 1976; REDESIGNATED DIOCESE OF RENO BY HIS HOLINESS POPE JOHN PAUL II MARCH 21, 1995.

Square Miles 70,852.

Legal Title: "The Roman Catholic Bishop of Reno and His Successors, a Corporation Sole".

Comprises the Counties of: Carson City, Churchill, Douglas, Elko, Eureka, Humboldt, Lander, Lyon, Mineral, Pershing, Storey, and Washoe.

PATRONS OF THE DIOCESE: *Our Lady of the Snows (August 5); The Holy Family (Sunday in the Octave of Christmas); Established through an Apostolic brief dated August 24, 1933.*

For legal titles of parishes and diocesan institutions, consult the Pastoral Center.

STATISTICAL OVERVIEW

Personnel	
Bishop	1
Priests: Diocesan Active in Diocese	15
Priests: Active Outside Diocese	2
Priests: Retired, Sick or Absent	5
Number of Diocesan Priests	22
Religious Priests in Diocese	13
Extern Priests in Diocese	7
Ordinations:	
Transitional Deacons	1
Permanent Deacons in Diocese	8
Total Brothers	4
Total Sisters	33
Parishes	
Parishes	28
With Resident Pastor:	
Resident Diocesan Priests	16
Resident Religious Priests	10
Without Resident Pastor:	
Administered by Women Religious	1
Completely Vacant	1
Missions	8
Professional Ministry Personnel:	
Brothers	1
Sisters	6
Lay Ministers	3
Welfare	
Catholic Hospitals	1
Total Assisted	142,566
Health Care Centers	3
Total Assisted	9,539
Day Care and Extended Day Care Centers	1
Total Assisted	187
Special Centers for Social Services	7
Total Assisted	182,000
Educational	
Diocesan Students in Other Seminaries	4
Total Seminarians	4
High Schools, Diocesan and Parish	1
Total Students	531
Elementary Schools, Diocesan and Parish	4
Total Students	1,143
Catechesis/Religious Education:	
High School Students	1,141
Elementary Students	4,135
Total Students Under Catholic Instruction	6,954
Teachers in the Diocese:	
Brothers	1
Sisters	4
Lay Teachers	66
Vital Statistics	
Receptions into the Church:	
Infant Baptism Totals	1,782
Adult Baptism Totals	162
Received into Full Communion	132
First Communions	1,166
Confirmations	573
Marriages:	
Catholic	175
Interfaith	85
Total Marriages	260
Deaths	322
Total Catholic Population	55,536
Total Population	513,019

Former Bishops—Most Rev. THOMAS K. GORMAN, D.D., D.Sc.Hist., ord. Bishop, July 22, 1931; appt. Coadjutor Bishop of Dallas "cum jure successionis," Feb. 8, 1952; succeeded to the See, Aug. 19, 1954; resigned Aug. 27, 1969; died Aug. 16, 1980.—Most Rev. ROBERT J. DWYER, D.D., Ph.D., ord. June 11, 1932; appt. May 20, 1952; cons. Aug. 5, 1952; elevated to Archiepiscopal Dignity and promoted to Portland in Oregon, Dec. 14, 1966; resigned Jan. 22, 1974; died March 24, 1976.—Most Rev. JOSEPH GREEN, D.D., ord. July 14, 1946; appt. Titular Bishop of Trisipa and Auxiliary of Lansing, June 22, 1962; cons. Aug. 28, 1962; appt. Bishop of Reno, March 10, 1967; installed May 5, 1967; resigned Dec. 6, 1974; died Aug. 31, 1982.—Most Rev. NORMAN F. MCFARLAND, D.D., J.C.D., ord. June 15, 1946; appt. Titular Bishop of Bida and Auxiliary of San Francisco, June 5, 1970; ord. Bishop, Sept. 8, 1970; appt. Apostolic Admin., Dec. 6, 1974; appt. Bishop of Reno, Feb. 10, 1976; transferred to Orange, Dec. 29, 1986; appt. Bishop of Orange, Feb. 24, 1987.—Most Rev. DANIEL F. WALSH, D.D., ord. March 30, 1963; appt. Titular Bishop of Tigia and Auxiliary of San Francisco; ord. Bishop, Sept. 24, 1981; appt. Bishop of Reno-Las Vegas, June 9, 1987; installed Aug. 6, 1987; appt. first Bishop of the newly established Diocese of Las Vegas, March 21, 1995; installed June 28, 1995.

Bishop's Office—

Bishop—Most Rev. PHILLIP F. STRALING.

Secretary—HELEN SCHMITT, Ext. 28.

Vicar-General—Rev. Msgr. THOMAS A. MEGER.

Chancellor—Bro. MATTHEW CUNNINGHAM, F.S.R., Ext. 29.

Secretary—JOAN TOPOIAN, Ext. 10.

Tribunal—

Judicial Vicar/Officialis—Rev. THOMAS FRANSISCUS, C.SS.R., J.C.L.

Secretary/Notary—CARMEN GODOY, Ext. 19.

Promoter of Justice—Rev. GEORGE WOLF.

Defenders of the Bond—Revs. ROBERT A. BOWLING; ALBERT M. FOSSELMAN.

Advocates—Bro. MATTHEW CUNNINGHAM, F.S.R.; Revs. JAMES SETELIK; CHARLES DURANTE; Sr. MARIE MCGLOIN, S.A.

Education, Department of—

Superintendent of Schools—Bro. MATTHEW CUNNINGHAM, F.S.R., Ext. 29.

Department of Catechetical and Youth Ministry—Rev. FRANCIS MURPHY, Dir., Ext. 34. PAT COLEMAN, Sec., Ext. 13.

Department of Religious Education-Audio/Visual—MARCIE ROSS, Ext. 13.

Curia—Most Rev. PHILLIP F. STRALING; Rev. Msgr. THOMAS A. MEGGER, V.G., Moderator; Revs. FRANCIS MURPHY; TOM FRANSISCUS, C.SS.R.; Bro. MATTHEW CUNNINGHAM, F.S.R.; Lt. Gen. MARTIN BRANDTNER, USMC (RET); Mr. KEVIN DAY; Mr. JOSE OJEDA; Mr. TIM WANNER.

Department of Development—Lt. Gen. MARTIN BRANDTNER, USMC (RET), Dir., Ext. 18.

Diaconate—Rev. GERALD HANLEY.

Diocesan Communications Committee—Most Rev. PHILLIP F. STRALING; Rev. ROBERT BOWLING; Bro. MATTHEW CUNNINGHAM, F.S.R.; Rev. Msgr. LEO MCFADDEN; Rev. GEORGE WOLF; Ms. DIANA SEIXAS.

Diocesan Board of Consultors—Rev. Msgr. THOMAS MEGER; Revs. ARIEL ARIAS; JAMES SETELIK; JOHN BAIN; JOHN CORONA; CHARLES DURANTE; ROBERT BOWLING; GEORGE WOLF.

Diocesan Development Committee—Most Rev. PHILLIP F. STRALING; Mr. LEROY ARRASCADA; Rev. ROBERT BOWLING; Mr. BOB CAPURRO; Bro. MATTHEW CUNNINGHAM, F.S.R.; Mr. KEVIN DAY; Rev. Msgr. LEO MCFADDEN; Mr. PETER PARKER; Rev. ROBERT SIMPSON; Mr. TIM WANNER; Lt. Gen. MARTIN BRANDTNER, USMC (RET).

Finance Office—

Finance Committee—Most Rev. PHILLIP F. STRALING; Rev. Msgr. THOMAS MEGER; Ms. VIRGINIA ZORIO; Mr. ED HOUSTON; Mr. BOB ARMSTRONG; Bro. MATTHEW CUNNINGHAM, F.S.R.; Mr. TIM WANNER.

Business Manager—TIM WANNER, Ext. 20.

Personnel Administrator—CINDI MITCHELL, Ext. 24.

Administrative Assistants—JUDY LUBICH, Ext. 23. JACKIE BURRIS, Ext. 22.

Frontier of the Faith—Tel: 702-348-6628. *310 W. 2nd St., Reno, NV, 89503., Mail: P.O. Box 10930, Reno, NV, 89510.*

Director—BETTIE ENGEBRETSON.

Secretary—ANNETTE EISELE.

Office of Hispanic Ministry—JOSE OJEDA, Dir., Ext. 26. MARIA DODSON, Sec., Ext. 31. MARIPAZ RAMOS, Diocesan Coord. Hispanic Youth, Ext. 31.

Institute of Ministry & Leadership Formation—Ms. FRAN MCMILLEN, Dir., Ext. 14.

Missionary Co-Op 1997—Bro. MATTHEW CUNNINGHAM, F.S.R., Ext. 29.

Natural Family Planning—JULIANNA JERVIS, O.P., Dir., *St. Mary's Hospital.* Tel: 702-323-2041.

"Northern Nevada Catholic" Newspaper—DIANA SEIXAS, Editor-in-Chief, *1725 S. McCarran, Reno, NV, 89502.* Tel: 702-359-5858; Fax: 702-359-6565.

Our Mother of Sorrows Cemetery—*310 W. 2nd St., Reno, NV, 89503.* Tel: 702-323-0133., *Mail: P.O. Box*

8505, Reno, NV, 89507; Fax: 702-323-1229. Sophie Mitchell, Oper. Mgr.; Sr. Ofelia Roibas, Staff.

Presbyteral Council—Revs. John Bain; Robert Bowling; John Corona; Charles Durante; Jim Setelik; George Wolf; Ariel Arias; Rev. Msgr. Thomas A. Meger.

Priests' Personnel Board—Most Rev. Phillip F. Straling; Rev. Msgr. Thomas Meger; Revs. Charles Durante; Jerry Hanley; George Wolf, Ex Officio Member; Bro. Matthew Cunningham, F.S.R.

Prison Ministry—Carson City Area: Margaret Sanborn; Russ Sanborn. Tel: 702-885-0480.

Property Management—Tim Wanner.

Respect Life Core Committee—Most Rev. Phillip F. Straling; Revs. Thomas Cronin, Dir. Charles Durante; Sr. Patricia Kelly, O.C.D.; Mr. Ross Barker; Ms. Brandi DuPont; Mrs. Margaret Graham; Ms. Julianna Jervis; Mrs. Marilee Railton.

Seminary Board—Most Rev. Phillip F. Straling; Rev. Charles Durante; Rev. Msgr. Thomas A. Meger, V.G.; Rev. Robert Simpson.

Vocations Board—Rev. Arthur Herkowski, Chm.; Revs. Omar Botia; Charles Shelton, O.F.M.Conv.; Mr. Bob Pascoe; Mr. Dick Penndorf; Ms. Connie West.

CLERGY, PARISHES, MISSIONS AND PAROCHIAL SCHOOLS

CITY OF RENO
(Washoe County)

1—St. Thomas Aquinas Cathedral (1907), Revs. Ronald Olson, O.F.M.Conv., Rector; Charles Shelton, O.F.M.Conv.; Viktor Perez, O.F.M.Conv. In res., Rev. Arthur Young, O.F.M.Conv.
Res., 310 W. Second St., 89503-5398. Tel: 702-329-2571; Fax: 702-329-2456.
Catechesis/Religious Programs—Jose Ramiro Cortez, D.R.E.(English & Spanish).
Students 140.

2—Our Lady of the Snows (1939), Rev. Msgr. Thomas Meger, V.G.; Rev. Robert E. Buchanan. In res., Rev. Francis J. Murphy.
Office: 1138 Wright St., 89509. Tel: 702-323-6894; Fax: 702-323-6749.
School—1125 Lander St., 89509. Tel: 702-322-2773. Mary E. Clark, Prin.
Lay Teachers 12; Students 276.
Catechesis/Religious Programs—Sr. M. Carmen Baca, D.R.E.
Students 550.

3—Our Lady of Wisdom (1965), Rev. Frank Hoffmann; Patrick Winans, Office Mgr.
Office: 1101 N. Virginia St., 89503. Tel: 702-322-4336; Fax: 702-322-3616.

4—St. Albert the Great (1948), Rev. Robert A. Simpson.
Mailing Address: 1259 St. Albert Dr., 89503.
Res., 1250 Wyoming Ave., 89503. Tel: 702-747-0722; Fax: 702-746-3976.
Catechesis/Religious Programs—Tel: 702-746-3976. D.R.E.: Marcy Welch, (Grades K-6); Judith Hall, (Grades K-6); Margaret Tharldson, (Grades 7-12).
Students 349.

5—St. Rose of Lima (1996), Rev. Thomas Donnelly.
Mailing Address: P.O. Box 18790, 89511-0790. Tel: 702-851-1874; Fax: 702-851-1727.

6—St. Therese Church of the Little Flower (1947). (St. Jude Shrine). Revs. Robert A. Bowling, V.F.; Francis Murphy; Omar Botia; Cyril Apassa; Deacon Robert Ruggiero. In res., Rev. Tom Cronin, Chap., Washoe Medical Center.
Office: 875 E. Plumb Ln., 89502. Tel: 702-322-2255; Fax: 702-322-0196.
Res., 339 Urban Rd., 89509.
School—1300 Casazza Dr., 89502. Tel: 702-323-2931. Sr. Margaret Oates, R.S.M., Prin.
Sisters of Mercy 2; Lay Teachers 8; Students 291.
Catechesis/Religious Programs—Tel: 702-322-3415. Sr. Carol Bettencourt, S.H.F., D.R.E.
Students 291.

OUTSIDE THE CITY OF RENO

Battle Mountain, Lander Co., St. John Bosco (1940), Rev. John Keefe, C.S.C., Admin.
Mailing Address: P.O. Box 428, 89820.
Office & Res.—384 S. Reese St., 89820. Tel: 702-635-2576; Fax: 702-635-5729.
Catechesis/Religious Programs—Bertha Dorthy, D.R.E.
Students 131.
Mission—Austin, St. Augustine.

Carlin, Elko Co., Sacred Heart (1910), Rev. Joseph Nuttman, C.Ss.R., Pastoral Admin.
Mailing Address: P.O. Box 235, 89822.
Office: 562 Fourth St., 89822. Tel: 702-754-6425; Fax: 702-754-2942.
Res., 315 Peters, 89822.

Carson City, Corpus Christi (1949), Rev. Ariel Arias; Deacon Roger Porcella.
Res., 5335 Snyder Ave., 89701. Tel: 702-882-1967; Fax: 702-882-2435.

St. Teresa's of Avila (1858), Revs. Gerald T. Hanley; Charles Durante; Sr. Marie McGloin, S.A., Pastoral Assoc.; Deacons Bob Evans; Craig LaGier; Wendell Schumacher; Dennis Schreiner.
Res., 108 N. Minnesota St., 89703. Tel: 702-882-1968; Fax: 702-883-7063.
School—567 S. Richmond Ave., 89703. Tel: 702-882-2079; Fax: 702-882-6135. Mrs. Judith Elges, Prin.
Lay Teachers 9; Students 236.
Catechesis/Religious Programs—400 W. King St., Ste. 104, 89703. Tel: 702-882-2130. Mary Ann Randall D.R.E.
Students 639.

Dayton, Lyon Co., St. Ann, Rev. Michael Dallmeier, O.F.M.
Mailing Address: P.O. Box 309, 89403. Tel: 702-246-7578; Fax: 702-246-3789.

Elko, Elko Co., St. Joseph's (1917), Rev. Norman King; Sr. Rosemary Boessen, R.S.M., Pastoral Assoc.
Office: 1035 C St., 89801. Tel: 702-738-6432; Fax: 702-738-0898 (Office Hrs. Only).
Res., 986 Highland Dr., 89801.
Catechesis/Religious Programs—Janie Bauer, D.R.E.
Students 550.
Missions—Wells, St. Thomas Aquinas, 619 Sixth St., P.O. Box 369, Wells, 89835. Tel: 702-752-3400; Jackpot, Elko Co., Blessed Miguel Pro, Box 462, Jackpot, 89825.

Eureka, Eureka Co., St. Brendan's (1872), Rev. Joseph Nuttman, C.Ss.R, Pastoral Admin.
Mailing Address: P.O. Box 305, 89316.
Res., 1022 O'Neill Ave., 89316. Tel: 702-237-5278.

Fallon, Churchill Co., St. Patrick (1920), Rev. Stanley T. Wisniewski, S.J.
Church & Mailing Address—850 W. Fourth St., 89406. Tel: 704-423-2846.
Res., 375 Tedford Ln., 89406.
Catechesis/Religious Programs—Tel: 702-423-5210. D.R.E.: Candy Cramer; Patty Fleming.
Students 200.

Fallon Naval Air Station Base Chapel (1977), Rev. James Connoly.
Office: Naval Air Station, 4755 Pasture Rd., Bldg. 351, 89496-5000. Tel: 702-426-2813; Fax: 702-426-2959.

Fernley, Lyon Co., St. Robert Bellarmine (1957), Sr. M. Christopher Schmidt, S.H.F., Parish Life Coord.
Mailing Address: P.O. Box 473, 89408.
Office: 190 S. West St., 89408. Tel: 702-575-4011; Fax: 702-575-7601.
Missions—Empire, St. Joseph the Worker; Silver Springs, Our Lady of the Blessed Sacrament.

Gardnerville, Douglas Co., St. Gall (1917), Rev. John J. Corona; Sr. Dorothy Sanchez, F.S.P.A., Pastoral Assoc.
Mailing Address: P.O. Box 788, 89410.
Office: 1343 Centerville Rd., 89410. Tel: 702-782-2852; Fax: 702-782-2622.
Res., 1740 Lavender Ct., Minden, 89423.
Catechesis/Religious Programs—Tel: 702-782-3784. Debbie Posnien, D.R.E., Tel: 702-782-3784.
Students 282.

Hawthorne, Mineral Co., Our Lady of Perpetual Help (1938), Rev. Jose Issac, Admin.
Mailing Address: P.O. Box 850, 89415. Office 804 A St., 89415. Tel: 702-945-2020; Fax: 702-945-1772.
Res., 794 A St., 89415.
Mission—Gabbs, St. Michael, Gabbs, 89409.

Incline Village, Washoe Co., St. Francis of Assisi (1965), Rev. Michael Q. Mahone.
Mailing Address: P.O. Box 4226, 89450. Tel: 702-831-0490; Fax: 702-831-2045.
Church—Mt. Rose Hwy. at Kelly Dr., 89450.

Lovelock, Pershing Co., St. John the Baptist (1875), Rev. Lorenzo Torrente.
Res. & Mailing Address—1045 Franklin Ave., 89419-0177. Tel: 702-273-2189.
Church—1085 Franklin Ave., 89419-0177.

Sparks, Washoe Co., Holy Cross Catholic Community (1967), Rev. George C. Wolf; Deacon Ron Schmitt.
Res., 3175 Goldy Way, 89434. Tel: 702-358-2544; Fax: 702-358-8239.
Catechesis/Religious Programs—Tel: 702-358-8239. D.R.E.: Laura Balmut, (Liturgy of the Word & Grades 1-7); Jill McAboy, (Grades 8-10 & Confirmation).
Students 350.

Immaculate Conception (1932), Revs. John J. O'Brien, S.A.C.; Timothy Twomey, S.A.C. In res., Rev. John Coen, S.A.C.
Res., 590 Pyramid Way, 89431. Tel: 702-358-5977; Fax: 702-359-3951.
Catechesis/Religious Programs—D.R.E.: Marilyn Heywood, (Elementary), Tel: 702-324-0555; Pat Giannotti, (High School), Tel: 702-358-3107.
Students 251.

Stead, Washoe Co., St. Michael's (1967), Rev. Thomas J. Fransiscus, C.Ss.R.
Res., 14075 Mt. Vida St., Reno, 89506. Tel: 702-972-7462; Fax: 702-972-9373.

Sun Valley, Washoe Co., St. Peter Canisius (1976), Rev. Larry Morrison, Pastoral Admin.
Res., 225 E. Fifth Ave., 89433. Tel: 702-673-2029; Fax: 702-673-2028.

Virginia City, Storey Co., St. Mary in the Mountains (1862), Rev. Bernard Michalik, O.F.M.Conv.
Mailing Address: P.O. Box 510, 89440.
Res., Taylor St. & E St., 89440. Tel: 702-847-9099; Fax: 702-847-0466.

Winnemucca, Humboldt Co., St. Paul (1883), Rev. Joseph E. Richard.
Mailing Address: 350 Melarkey St., 89445.
Res., Fourth St. & Melarkey St., 89445. Tel: 702-623-2928; Fax: 702-623-6816.
Catechesis/Religious Programs—Bonnie Hilbish, D.R.E.
Students 354.
Missions—Paradise Valley, Humboldt Co., St. Alphonsus; McDermitt, Humboldt Co., Sacred Heart.

Yerington, Lyon Co., Holy Family (1901), Rev. Thomas E. Wright.
Mailing Address: P.O. Box 839, 89447.
Res., 37 N. West St., 89447. Tel: 702-463-2882; Fax: 702-463-2162.
Church—43 N. West St., 89447.
Mission—Smith Valley, Lyon Co., St. John the Baptist, Hwy. 208, P.O. Box 36, Wellington, 89444. Tel: 702-465-2222.

Zephyr Cove, Douglas Co., Our Lady of Tahoe (1966), Rev. John K. Bain.
Mailing Address: P.O. Box 115, 89448.
Res., 630 Don Dr., 89448. Tel: 702-588-2080; Fax: 702-588-0211.
Catechesis/Religious Programs—Mary Beth Crosby, D.R.E., Tel: 916-542-2620.
Students 70.

On Duty Outside the Diocese:
Reverend Fathers—
Aitcheson, William M., 11 Irving Ave., Colonial Beach, VA 22443
Quilici, Lawrence, 7954 N. Jacqueline Pl., Tucson, AZ 85741. Tel: 520-579-3635

Leave of Absence:
Reverend Fathers—
Perrier, Martin
Vieages, Harold

Retired:
Reverend Monsignors—
McFadden, Leo E., 3363 Spring Creek Cir., Reno, NV 89509
Reverend Fathers—
Avella, William, 40 Penrose Ln., Yerington, NV 89447. Tel: 702-463-3958
Fanning, Gerard F., Ballymakenny (East Rand), County Louth, Drogheda Ireland
Fosselman, Albert, P.O. Box 5617, Incline Village, NV 89450. Tel: 702-831-5590
Herkowski, Arthur M., 1299 Flora Glen Dr., Sparks, NV 89434

Permanent Deacons:
Batson, Randol G., St. Mary's Regl. Medical Ctr., 235 W. Sixth St., Reno, NV 89520. Tel: 702-323-2041
Evans, Robert, 700 W. Adeline, Carson City, NV 89701. Tel: 702-883-2341
Lagier, Craig, 1217 Calaveras, Carson City, NV 89703. Tel: 702-883-9740
Porcella, Roger, 986 Ridgeview Dr., Carson City, NV 89705. Tel: 702-267-5110
Ruggiero, Robert L., 4697 W. Leonisio Dr., Sun Valley, NV 89433. Tel: 702-674-3086
Schmitt, Ron, 1095 E. York Way, Sparks, NV 89434. Tel: 702-358-1625
Schreiner, Dennis, 1809 Pyrenees, Carson City, NV 89703. Tel: 702-882-6864
Schumacher, Wendell, 52 Loire St., Carson City, NV 89703. Tel: 702-882-1883

INSTITUTIONS LOCATED IN THE DIOCESE

[A] HIGH SCHOOLS, DIOCESAN

RENO. *Bishop Manogue High School*, 400 Bartlett St., 89512. Tel: 702-329-0011. Dr. Carl Shaff, Pres.; Robert D. Sullivan, Prin.; Susan Smith, Business Mgr. Brothers 1; Sisters 1; Lay Teachers 28; Students 531.

[B] GENERAL HOSPITALS

RENO. *St. Mary's Regional Medical Center*, 235 W. Sixth St., 89520-0108. Tel: 702-323-2041; Fax: 702-789-3963

For a complete listing, refer to the Hospitals section.

[C] DAY NURSERIES

RENO. *Holy Child Day Home*, 440 Reno Ave., 89509. Tel: 702-329-2979; Fax: 702-329-8531. Mrs. Karen L. Barreras, Dir. Lay Teachers 38; Boys 103; Girls 84.

[D] MONASTERIES AND RESIDENCES FOR PRIESTS AND BROTHERS

RENO. *Brothers of Our Lady of the Holy Rosary Monastery*, 232 Sunnyside Dr., 89503-3510. Tel: 702-747-4441. Bros. Philip Napolitano, F.S.R., Supr.; Matthew Cunningham, F.S.R., Asst. Supr.; Edward Zuber, F.S.R. Brothers 3.

[E] CONVENTS AND RESIDENCES FOR SISTERS

RENO. Sacred Heart Sisters.

Discalced Carmelite Nuns.

Carmelite Monastery (O.C.D.), 1950 La Fond Dr., 89509-3099. Tel: 702-323-3236; Fax: 702-322-1532. Sr. Ann Weber, Prioress. Discalced Carmelite Nuns 14.

Little Flower Convent (S.M.), 1280 Casazza St., 89502. Tel: 702-322-5966. Sisters of Mercy. Sr. Sandra DiCianno, S.M., Contact Person. Sisters 2.

St. Mary's Convent (O.P.), 411 W. Sixth St., 89503. Tel: 702-323-5196. Sr. Patricia Simpson, O.P., Supr. Sisters of St. Dominic. Sisters 7.

Sisters of the Holy Family Convent, S.H.F., 6730 S. McCarran Blvd., 89509. Tel: 702-827-5370. Sr. Carmen Baca, S.H.F.; Sr. Carol Bettencourt, S.H.F.; Sr. Christopher Schmidt, S.H.F. Holy Family Sisters. Sisters 3.

GARDNERVILLE. *Franciscan Sisters of Perpetual Adoration*, 1450 Douglas, P.O. Box 788, 89410. Tel: 702-782-8405. Sr. Dorothy Sanchez, F.S.P.A.

SPARKS. *Sisters of St. Philip Neri*, 135 Pascus Pl., 89431. Tel: 702-331-0708. Sisters 3.

[F] CAMPUS MINISTRY

RENO. *University of Nevada, Newman Club*. Served by Our Lady of Wisdom, 1101 N. Virginia St., 89503. Tel: 702-322-4336. Rev. Frank Hoffmann, Chap.

[G] CATHOLIC COMMUNITY SERVICES OF NORTHERN NEVADA

RENO. *Catholic Community Services of Northern Nevada*. Mailing Address: P.O. Box 5099, 89513-5099. 275 E. Fourth St., 89501. Tel: 702-322-7073; Fax: 702-322-8197.

Adoption. Linda Maisel, Dir.

Emergency Assistance. Ida Yoas, Dir.

St. Vincent's Food Pantry. Mary Weeks, Dir.

St. Vincent's Thrift Shop. Mary Weeks, Dir.

Holy Child Day Home, 440 Reno Ave., 89509. Tel: 702-329-2979; Fax: 702-329-8537. Karen Barreras, Dir.

St. Vincent's Dining Room. Mailing Address: P.O. Box 5099, 89513-5099. 505 W. Third St., 89503. Tel: 702-329-5363. Ray Trevino, Dir.

St. Vincent's Haven. Mailing Address: P.O. Box 5099, 89513-5099. 1865 Montello Ave., 89506. Tel: 702-322-7073. James Millington, Dir.

St. Vincent's Residence, 395 Gould St., 89502. James Millington, Dir.

RELIGIOUS INSTITUTES OF MEN REPRESENTED IN THE DIOCESE

For further details refer to the corresponding bracketed number in the Religious Institutes of Men or Women section.

[0960]—*Brothers of the Congregation of Our Lady of the Holy Rosary*.—F.S.R.

[1140]—*Congregation of the Sacred Heart of Jesus*.

[0480]—*Conventual Franciscans*.—O.F.M.Conv.

[0520]—*Franciscan Friars*.

[0690]—*Jesuit Fathers and Brothers*.—S.J.

[0610]—*Priests of the Congregation of the Holy Cross*.

[1070]—*Redemptorist Fathers*.—C.Ss.R.

[0990]—*Society of the Catholic Apostolate*. (Irish Prov.).—S.A.C.

RELIGIOUS INSTITUTES OF WOMEN REPRESENTED IN THE DIOCESE

[1780]—*Congregation of the Sisters of the Third Order of St. Francis of Perpetual Adoration*.—F.S.P.A.

[0420]—*Discalced Carmelite Nuns*.—O.C.D.

[1070-04]—*Dominican Sisters*.—O.P.

[1190]—*Franciscan Sisters of the Atonement*.—S.A.

[2575]—*Sisters of Mercy*.—R.S.M. (Ireland).

[2523]—*Sisters of Mercy of Ardagh and Clonmacnois*.—R.S.M.

[]—*Sisters of St. Philip Neri*. (Madrid, Spain).

[1960]—*Sisters of the Holy Family*.—S.H.F.

DIOCESAN CEMETERIES

RENO. *Our Mother of Sorrows Cemetery & Mausoleum*, 2700 N. Virginia St., 89503. Mailing Address: P.O. Box 8505, 89507. Tel: 702-323-0133; Fax: 702-323-1229. Sophia Mitchell, Operations Mgr.

NECROLOGY

(No Deaths)

Diocese of Richmond

(Dioecesis Richmondiensis)

Most Reverend

WALTER F. SULLIVAN, D.D.

Bishop of Richmond; ordained May 9, 1953; appointed Titular Bishop of Selsey and Auxiliary Bishop of Richmond October 20, 1970; consecrated December 1, 1970; appointed Apostolic Administrator of Richmond April 30, 1973; succeeded to the See, June 6, 1974. *Res., 800 Cathedral Pl., Richmond, VA, 23220. Office: 811 Cathedral Pl., Suite B, Richmond, VA, 23220-4801.*

ESTABLISHED IN 1820.

Square Miles 36,711.

Comprises the State of Virginia, with the exception of the Counties of Arlington, Clarke, Culpeper, Fairfax, Fauquier, Frederick, King George, Lancaster, Loudoun, Madison, Northumberland, Orange, Page, Prince William, Rappahannock, Richmond, Shenandoah, Spottsylvania, Stafford, Warren and Westmoreland.

For legal titles of parishes and diocesan institutions, consult the Chancery Office.

The Chancery: 811 Cathedral Pl., Richmond, VA, 23220-4801. Tel.: 804-359-5661; Fax: 804-358-9159.

Web site address: http://www.diocric.org

STATISTICAL OVERVIEW

Personnel	
Bishop	1
Priests: Diocesan Active in Diocese	125
Priests: Active Outside Diocese	13
Priests: Retired, Sick or Absent	30
Number of Diocesan Priests	168
Religious Priests in Diocese	33
Extern Priests in Diocese	50
Ordinations:	
Diocesan Priests	1
Permanent Deacons	1
Permanent Deacons in Diocese	24
Total Brothers	9
Total Sisters	269
Parishes	
Parishes	139
With Resident Pastor:	
Resident Diocesan Priests	105
Resident Religious Priests	5
Without Resident Pastor:	
Administered by Priests	15
Administered by Permanent Deacons	2
Administered by Women Religious	6
Administered by Lay People	4
Administered by Pastoral Teams, etc.	2
Missions	11
Pastoral Centers	5
New Parishes Created	2
Professional Ministry Personnel:	
Brothers	9
Sisters	269
Welfare	
Catholic Hospitals	9
Total Assisted	449,572
Health Care Centers	1
Total Assisted	32,359
Homes for the Aged	15
Total Assisted	1,590
Residential Care of Children	1
Total Assisted	90
Day Care and Extended Day Care Centers	5
Total Assisted	615
Specialized Homes	1
Special Centers for Social Services	4
Total Assisted	10,180
Residential Care of Disabled	5
Total Assisted	203
Educational	
Diocesan Students in Other Seminaries	8
Total Seminarians	8
High Schools, Diocesan and Parish	5
Total Students	1,819
High Schools, Private	4
Total Students	901
Elementary Schools, Diocesan and Parish	22
Total Students	5,020
Catechesis/Religious Education:	
High School Students	5,631
Elementary Students	18,862
Total Students Under Catholic Instruction	32,241
Teachers in the Diocese:	
Priests	4
Brothers	2
Sisters	13
Lay Teachers	470
Vital Statistics	
Receptions into the Church:	
Infant Baptism Totals	3,377
Adult Baptism Totals	600
Received into Full Communion	1,028
First Communions	3,439
Confirmations	1,645
Marriages:	
Catholic	558
Interfaith	654
Total Marriages	1,212
Deaths	1,476
Total Catholic Population	187,263
Total Population	4,706,300

Former Bishops—Rt. Rev. PATRICK KELLY, D.D., first Bishop; cons. Aug. 24, 1820; translated Waterford and Lismore in 1822; died Oct. 8, 1829.—Rt. Rev. RICHARD V. WHELAN, D.D., second Bishop; cons. March 21, 1841; translated Wheeling, July 23, 1850; died July 7, 1874.—Rt. Rev. JOHN MCGILL, D.D., cons. Nov. 10, 1850; died Jan. 14, 1872.—His Eminence JAMES CARDINAL GIBBONS, D.D., cons. August 16, 1868 Bishop of Adramyttum, and Vicar-Apostolic of North Carolina; translated the See of Richmond, July 30, 1872; translated the See of Baltimore, Oct. 3, 1877; created Cardinal Priest of S. Maria in Trastevere, June 7, 1886; died March 24, 1921.—Rt. Rev. JOHN J. KEANE, D.D., cons. Aug. 25, 1878; resigned August, 1888 rector of the Catholic University, Washington, DC; transferred to Archbishopric of Dubuque, July 24, 1900; died June 27, 1918.—Rt. Rev. AUGUSTINE VAN DE VYVER, D.D., cons. Oct. 20, 1889; died Oct. 16, 1911.—Rt. Rev. DENIS JOSEPH O'CONNELL, D.D., cons. May 3, 1908 Titular Bishop of Sebaste and Auxiliary Bishop of San Francisco; appt. Bishop of Richmond, Jan. 19, 1912; resigned Jan. 15, 1926 and appointed Titular Archbishop of Marianne; died Jan. 1, 1927.—Most Rev. ANDREW J. BRENNAN, D.D., ord. December 17, 1904; cons. Titular Bishop of Thapsus and Auxiliary Bishop of Scranton, April 25, 1923; appt. Bishop of Richmond, May 28, 1926; resigned April 14, 1945; appt. Titular Bishop of Telmissus; died May 23, 1956.—Most Rev. PETER L. IRETON, D.D., ord. June 20, 1906; appt. Titular Bishop of Cime Coadjutor Bishop and Apostolic Administrator of Richmond, August 3, 1935; cons. October 23, 1935; named Bishop of Richmond, April 14, 1945; named Assistant at the Pontifical Throne, May 21, 1956; died April 27, 1958.—Most Rev. JOHN J. RUSSELL, D.D., ord. July 8, 1923; appt. Bishop of Charleston, Jan. 28, 1950; cons. March 14, 1950; appt. Bishop of Richmond, July 3, 1958; retired April 3, 1973; died March 17, 1993.

Central Administrative Offices

All Diocesan Offices are located at: 811 Cathedral Place, Richmond, VA 23220-4801. Tel: 804-359-5661; Fax: 804-358-9159, unless otherwise indicated

Vicars General—Rev. Msgr. THOMAS F. SHREVE, V.G., J.C.L.; Rev. Msgr. CHARLES A. KELLY, V.G.

Episcopal Vicars—Rev. Msgr. THOMAS J. CAROLUZZA, Eastern Vicariate; Rev. Msgr. CHARLES A. KELLY, Central Vicariate; Rev. Msgr. ROBERT M. PERKINS, Southside Vicariate; Rev. JAMES GREALISH, Western Vicariate.

Vicar for the Hispanic Apostolate—Rev. Msgr. MICHAEL S. SCHMIED; ELISA MONTALVO, Dir.

Ethinic and Special Ministries, Office of—ELISA MONTALVO, Dir. Tel: 804-359-5661, Ext. 204.

Ethnic and Special Liturgies—Filipino, Hispanic, Korean, Vietnamese; Tridentine Latin Mass, Deaf/Hearing Impaired—Please contact this office for locations and schedules.

Vicar for Ecumenism—Rev. Msgr. RAYMOND A. BARTON.

Chancellor—Mrs. ANNE C. EDWARDS.

Secretary to the Bishop—Rev. PASQUALE J. APUZZO.

Department Moderators—Mr. JOHN F. BARRETT; Ms. DIANE BIALKOWSKI; Dr. STEPHEN M. COLECCHI.

Diocesan Tribunal Central Offices—

Judicial Vicar—Rev. WILLIAM V. SULLIVAN, J.C.L., M.Ch.A.

Judges—Revs. MARTIN E. LAVIN, J.C.L.; J. SCOTT DUARTE, J.C.L.; J. KENNETH RUSH, D.Min.; JAMES GREALISH, B.A.; R. FRANCIS MUENCH, J.C.L.; RUSSELL E. SMITH.

Defenders of the Bond—Revs. MICHAEL M. DUFFY, J.C.L.; KEVIN J. O'BRIEN, S.T.B.; Deacon JOHN H. THOMAS; H. ROBERTA SMALL, J.C.L.

Field Offices—

Roanoke—P.O. Box 21784, Roanoke, 24018-0180.

Tidewater—145 Dupre Ave., Norfolk, 23503-3423. Tel: 804-588-2941.

Ecclesiastical Notaries—Mrs. BARBARA A. LEE; Mrs. L'TANYA LESANE; ANTHONY K. SPRATLEY; Ms. BARBARA WATTS.

Auditors—Ms. VALERIE MCAVOY.

Vicar for Priests—Vacant.

Vicar for Priestly Formation—Rev. MICHAEL A. RENNINGER.
Vocation Director for Promotion and Recruitment—Rev. MICHAEL MCCARRON.
Department of Pastoral Services—Ms. DIANE BIALKOWSKI, Moderator.
Office of Christian Formation—Mr. DENNIS BEEMAN, Dir. Assoc. Directors: Mrs. EMILY FILIPPI; Ms. PATRICIA NOVAK.
Office of Catholic Schools—Ms. DIANE BIALKOWSKI, Supt.; Ms. MAUREEN MCCABE; MICHAEL J. MARUCA, Asst. Supt. Schools.
Office of Campus and Young Adult Ministry—Bro. COSMAS RUBENCAMP, C.F.X., Dir.; Sr. DIANE GUY, S.N.D., Assoc. Dir.
Department of Social Action—Dr. STEPHEN M. COLECCHI, Moderator.
Office of Justice and Peace—Dr. STEPHEN M. COLECCHI, Dir. Assoc. Directors: Mr. MICHAEL E. STONE; Dr. KATHLEEN T. KENNEY.
Appalachian Office—Sr. GWEN HENNESSEY, Dir., *P.O. Box 660, St. Paul, 24283*. Tel: 540-762-5050.
Migrant Ministry—JAMES ALBRIGHT, Dir., *P.O. Box 584, Accomac, 23301*. Tel: 804-787-7862.
Office of Refugee Resettlement—Mrs. MARILYN BRESLOW, Exec. Dir.
Richmond Regional Dir.—KATHLEEN JACKSON.
Norfolk Regional Dir.—JANE COOK, Interim Dir., *1801 Ashland Ave., Norfolk, 23509*. Tel: 804-623-9131.
Roanoke Regional Dir.—Mrs. BARBARA SMITH, *1106 9th St. S.E., Roanoke, 24013*. Tel: 540-342-7561.
Ministry with Older Adults—Ms. MARY ELLEN COX, Coord. Tel: 804-227-3116.
Office of Black Catholics—Sr. CORA BILLINGS, R.S.M., Dir.
Office of Communications—Rev. PASQUALE J. APUZZO, Dir.
Department of Administrative Services—Mr. JOHN F. BARRETT, Moderator.
Office of Finance—Mr. JOHN F. BARRETT, Dir.; Mr. EDWARD L. SHRINER, C.P.A., Controller.
Office of Personnel—Mr. MICHAEL BECHELLI, Dir.; Ms. ETTA SHEPPERD, Assoc. Dir.
Management Information Services—Mrs. JOAN PARDUE, Dir.; Mrs. KAREN BISHOP, Programmer/Analyst.
Office of Development—Ms. CAROLE KAHWAJY.
Office of General Services—Mrs. SUSAN R. TEAL.
Office of Risk Management—Mr. WILLIAM J. WHELAN, Dir.
Theological Consultant—Bro. PHILIP DOUGHERTY, C.F.X.

Diocesan Councils

Apostleship of the Sea—Rev. SANTIAGO C. FRIAS, *155 W. Government Ave., Norfolk, 23503*. Tel: 804-480-3433.
Board of Conciliation and Arbitration—Vacant.
Campaign for Human Development—Mr. MICHAEL STONE, Diocesan Dir.
Catholic Relief Services—Dr. KATHLEEN KENNEY.
Catholic Historical Society of the Roanoke Valley—Mrs. MARY C. MAIER, *2609 Hillcrest Ave. N.W., Roanoke, 24012*.
Catholic Daughters of America—Ms. MARIAN E. NOWLAND, State Regent, *4617 Seminary Rd., Apt. 207, Alexandria, 22304*.
Catholic Golden Age—Ms. JEAN CAHEN, *2821 Hilliard Rd., Richmond, 23228*.
"Catholic Virginian" (Diocesan Newspaper)—Mr. CHARLES MAHON, Editor, *P.O. Box 26843, Richmond, 23261*. Tel: 804-359-5654; Fax: 804-359-5689. Mr. STEPHEN S. NEILL, Assoc. Editor; Mrs. JUDITH LINDFORS, Business Mgr./Circulation Dir.
Council of Catholic Women—Mrs. MARGARET DISNEY, *3801 Cedar Grove Rd., Richmond, 23235*.
Catholic Women's Club—Mrs. JOE F. CLARA, Pres., *4536 Phomcroft Dr., Glen Allen, 23060*.
Cemeteries—Rev. FREDERICK J. FEUSAHRENS, Dir. Tel: 804-329-0473.
Charismatic Communities—Mr. ROBERT BROWN, *HC02, Box 205, Buckingham, 23921*. Tel: 804-969-1755.
Councilium Board for Education—MAUREEN MCCABE, *811 Cathedral Pl., Richmond, 23220*. Tel: 804-359-5661.
Council of Priests—See Presbyteral Council.
Cursillio—Rev. JAMES KAUFFMANN, Spiritual Dir., *P.O. Box 396, Ladysmith, 22501*. Tel: 804-448-9064. Lay Co-Directors: JAMES MCGROGAN; ALBERTA MCGROGAN, *Rte. 1, Box 65-A, Fairfield, 24435*. Tel: 540-348-5939.
Commonwealth Catholic Charities—*1512 Willow Lawn Dr., Richmond, 23230-0565*. Tel: 804-285-5900. Rev. DAVID J. BERGNER, S.D.S., Exec. Dir.; Dr. STEPHEN M. COLECCHI, Diocesan Dir.
Catholic Charities of Hampton Roads, Inc.—*4855 Princess Anne Rd., Virginia Beach, 23462*. Tel: 757-467-7707. Mrs. MARGARET ROBERTSON, Exec. Dir.
Ecumenical Officer—Rev. RAYMOND A. BARTON, *208 E. Jefferson St., Charlottesville, 22901*.
Finance Council—Mr. H. GREGORY KILDUFF, *8936 River Crescent, Suffolk, 23433-1110*.
Haitian Ministry Commission—Bro. COSMOS RUBENCAMP, Exec. Sec., *811 Cathedral Pl., Richmond, 23220*. Tel: 804-359-5661.
Holy Childhood Association—Rev. Msgr. THOMAS F. SHREVE, J.C.L., V.G.
Knights of Columbus—THOMAS J. HOGAN, State Deputy, *3126 Barkley Dr., Fairfax, 22031*.
Nocturnal Adoration Society—Rev. DONALD F. SCALES, *300 N. Sheppard St., Richmond, 23220*.
Diocesan Pastoral Council—Mrs. ELLEN HEWITT, *2908 Scarsborough Dr., Richmond, 23235*.
Pax Christi Richmond—Mr. JOHN GALLINI, *2425 Triton Dr., Richmond, 23235*.
Pax Christi Virginia—Vacant.
Presbyteral Council—Rev. P. FRANCIS MUENCH, *St. Rose of Lima, 2114 Bay Ave., Hampton, 23661-2810*.
Promoter of Justice—Vacant.
Propagation of the Faith—Rev. Msgr. THOMAS F. SHREVE, J.C.L., V.G.
Respect Life—MICHAEL E. STONE, Coord.
Diocesan AIDS Task Force—Dr. STEPHEN LENTON, Chm., *P.O. Box 7087, Richmond, 23221-0087*.
Richmond Catholic Heritage Foundation—Rev. WILLIAM H. CARR, *St. Bede Church, 10 Harrison Ave., Williamsburg, 23185*.
Secular Carmelite Communities—
Community of the Holy Spirit—SUNNI COWLING, O.C.D.S., Pres., *1211 Mt. Erin Dr., Richmond, 23231*.
Community of Our Lady of the Annunication—TIRA KNIPSEL, O.C.D.S., Pres., *1288 Alanton Dr., Virginia Beach, 23454*.
Serra Club of Richmond—Mr. JAMES POLLOCK, Pres., *10800 Dominion Fairways Dr., Glen Allen, 23060*.
Scouting—Rev. ADRIAN HARMENING, Chap. Tel: 804-342-1319. Mr. JOHN CONRON, Diocesan Lay Chm. Tel: 804-272-5075.

CLERGY, PARISHES, MISSIONS AND PAROCHIAL SCHOOLS

CITY OF RICHMOND

1—CATHEDRAL OF THE SACRED HEART, Most Rev. Walter F. Sullivan, D.D.; Rev. Msgr. Charles A. Kelly, Rector; Rev. Michael A. Renninger, Vice-Rector.
Bishop's Office: 811 Cathedral Pl., 23220-4801. Tel: 804-359-5661.; Cathedral Office: 823 Park Ave., 23220. Tel: 804-359-5651; Fax: 804-359-8043. [JC]
Church—18 N. Laurel, 23220.

2—CHURCH OF THE EPIPHANY (Chesterfield Co), Rev. Msgr. Thomas F. Shreve; Deacon Peter Menting, Admin.
Mailing Address: 11000 Smoketree Dr., 23236-3144. Tel: 804-794-0222; 0223; Fax: 804-378-2013.
Mission—Amelia, Good Samaritan, P.O. Box 759, Amelia, 23002.

3—HOLY ROSARY, Rev. Arthur Dennis Conrad. In res., Rev. Kenneth Stofft.
Mailing Address: P.O. Box 23116, 23223.
Parish Office: 1209 N. 33rd St., 23223. Tel: 804-222-1105; Fax: 804-226-2204.
Res., 917 Old Denny St., 23221. Tel: 804-222-6568.
Church—N. 33rd & S St., 23223.
Child Care Center—1218 N. 34th St., 23223. Tel: 804-222-2590. Ms. Deborah Longs, Dir.
Students 120.

4—OUR LADY OF LOURDES (Henrico Co.), Revs. Thomas McDonnell, S.J.; Frank Wiggins.
Res., 8200 Woodman Rd., 23228-3237. Tel: 804-264-4990; 262-7315; 7314; Fax: 804-262-7337. [JC]
School—Tel: 804-262-1770. Lucy R. Reilley, Prin.
Lay Teachers 19; Students 302.

5—SACRED HEART, Rev. David Stokes, S.J.
Mailing Address: 1415 Perry St., 23224-2057.
Res., 1409 Perry St., 23224. Tel: 804-230-6430; 232-8964 (Office); Fax: 804-231-9931. [JC]
Church—1401 Perry St., 23224.

6—ST. AUGUSTINE (Chesterfield Co.), Rev. Msgr. Michael S. Schmied. In res., Rev. Ricardo Seidel.
Mailing Address: 4400 Beulah Rd., 23237-1850.
Res., 9608 Verlinda Ct., 23237. Tel: 804-778-4842.
Church—Corner of Hopkins & Beulah Rd., 23237. Tel: 804-275-7962; Fax: 804-271-4604.

7—ST. BENEDICT, Revs. Donald Scales, O.S.B. Tel: 804-254-8841; Augustine W. Ludwig, O.S.B.
Res., 3007 Hanover Ave., 23221. Tel: 804-254-8839. [JC]
Church—300 N. Sheppard St., 23221-2407. Tel: 804-254-8810; Fax: 804-355-5112.
School—3100 Grove Ave., 23221. Tel: 804-254-8850. Mary Claire Robinson, Prin.
Lay Teachers 15; Students 254.
Mission—Richmond, St. Joseph Tridentine Community, Tel: 804-342-1319. Rev. Adrian W. Harmening, O.S.B.

8—ST. BRIDGET (Henrico Co.), Rev. Msgr. Thomas G. Miller; Rev. Remi Sojka.
Church—6006 Three Chopt Rd., 23226-2797. Tel: 804-282-9511; Fax: 804-285-7227.
School—6011 York Rd., 23226. Tel: 804-288-1994. Mrs. Bettijo Loving, Prin.
Sisters 1; Lay Teachers 30; Students 472.

9—ST. EDWARD THE CONFESSOR, Revs. Ronald A. Ruth; Rene Castillo.
Mailing Address: 2700 Dolfield Rd., 23235-2618. Tel: 804-272-2948; Fax: 804-560-3565.
Res., 10908 Ashburn Rd., 23235-2618. Tel: 804-330-0772.
Church—Hugeunot Rd. & Dolfield Dr., 23235.
School—Regional School St. Edward-Epiphany, 10701 Huguenot Rd., 23235. Tel: 804-272-2881. Ms. Georgette Richards, Prin.

10—ST. ELIZABETH, Sr. Cora Marie Billings, R.S.M., Pastoral Coord.
Mailing Address: 1301 Victor St., 23222-3935. Tel: 804-329-4599; Fax: 804-321-0741. [JC]
Church—2712 Second Ave., 23222.
School—All Saints, 3418 Noble Ave., 23222. Tel: 804-329-7524. Mr. Kenneth Soistman, Prin.

11—ST. GABRIEL (Chesterfield Co.), Rev. John M. DeGiorgio.
Mailing Address: P.O. Box 129, Moseley, 23120. Tel: 804-639-6712; Fax: 804-639-6591.

12—ST. KIM TAEGON, Rev. Dominic Hwain Hwang.
Mailing Address: 3103 Maury St., 23224-3542. Tel: 804-232-0993; Fax: 804-232-0995.
Church—3100 Logandale Ave., 23224.

13—ST. MARY, Rev. Walter G. Lewis.
Mailing Address: 9505 Gayton Rd., 23229-5319. Tel: 804-740-4044; Fax: 804-740-2197.
School—Tel: 804-740-1048. Hazel Lewane, Prin.
Lay Teachers 21; Students 274.

14—ST. PATRICK, Rev. James K. Disney.
Mailing Address: 213 N. 25th St., 23223-7115. Tel: 804-648-0504; Fax: 804-648-5216.
School—2600 E. Grace St., 23223. Tel: 804-648-3621. Sr. Patricia Endres, D.C., Prin.

15—ST. PAUL, Rev. Frederick J. Feusahrens. In res., Rev. George E. Zahn.
Mailing Address: 909 Rennie Ave., 23227. Tel: 804-329-0473; 329-5512; Fax: 804-321-6454.
School—All Saints, 3418 Noble Ave., 23227. Tel: 804-329-7524. Mr. Kenneth Soistman, Prin.

16—ST. PETER, Rev. Robert A. Brownell.
Mailing Address: P.O. Box 933, 23218-0933. Tel: 804-643-4315; Fax: 804-783-6120.
Res., 4030 Forest Hill Ave., Apt. 27, 23225. Tel: 804-231-3941. [JC]
Church—800 E. Grace St., 23219.

17—CHURCH OF THE VIETNAMESE MARTYRS, Revs. Joseph Than Xuan Pham; Anthony Ngo.
Mailing Address: 67 Clopton St., 23225-3957. Tel: 804-231-4835; Fax: 804-231-4685.

OUTSIDE THE CITY OF RICHMOND

Abingdon, Christ the King, Rev. Robert L. Krenik.
Mailing Address: P.O. Box 1201, 24212-1201.
Res., 124 Park Blvd., Marion, 24354. Tel: 540-783-7282; 628-2941; Fax: 540-783-7282.
Church—820 E. Main St., 24212.

Appomattox, Our Lady of Peace, Rev. Robert Dillon; Deacon William K. Hayes.
Mailing Address: P.O. Box 668, 24522-0668. Tel: 804-352-0104.
Res., Rte. 3, Box 7260, Dillwyn, 23936. Fax: 804-969-2168.
Church—Intersection of Rte. 631 & Rte. 627, 24522.

Ashland, Hanover Co., St. Ann, Rev. Msgr. William V. Sullivan.
Church & Mailing Address—105 S. Snead St., 23005-1811. Tel: 804-798-5039; Fax: 804-798-5072.
Res., 202 Thompson St., 23005-1514. Tel: 804-752-5902.

Bedford, Holy Name of Mary, Rev. Timothy Huffman.
Mailing Address: 1307 Oakwood St., 24523-1613. Tel: 540-586-8988; Fax: 540-587-9080.
Res., 1531 Newton Cir., 24523. Tel: 540-586-9271.
Church—1301 Oakwood St., 24523.

Big Stone Gap, Wise Co., Sacred Heart, Rev. Anthony Rodrigues. In res., Rev. Leslie Schmidt, Glmy.
Mailing Address: 1821 Holton Ave., 24219-2611. Tel: 540-523-1588; Fax: 540-523-1602.

Blacksburg, Montgomery Co., St. Mary & Newman Community, Revs. Donald H. Lemay; James M. Cowles, Campus Min.; Deacon Mike Ellerbrock.
Mailing Address: 706 Harding Ave., 24060-3618.

Tel: 540-552-1091; Fax: 540-953-2962.
Res., 213 Price St., 24060. Tel: 540-951-2136.
Newman Community: 203 Otey St., 24060. Tel: 540-951-0032.

Blackstone, Nottoway Co., Immaculate Heart of Mary, Mrs. Therese Mansfield, Pastoral Coord.
Mailing Address: P.O. Box 266, 23824-0266. Tel: 804-292-5535; Fax: 804-292-5535.
Church—819 S. Main St., 23824.

Bristol, St. Anne, Rev. Thomas A. Ianucci; Deacon Harry Hall.
Mailing Address: 350 Euclid Ave., 24201-4014. Tel: 540-669-8200; Fax: 540-669-3523. [CEM]
Res., 922 Chester St., 24201. Tel: 540-466-4776.
School—300 Euclid Ave., 24201. Tel: 540-669-0048. Mrs. Jean Green, Prin.
Lay Teachers 21; Students 199.

Brookneal, Campbell Co., St. Elizabeth of Hungary, Rev. Matthias Newell.
Mailing Address: 800 John Randolph Blvd., South Boston, 24592-2943. Tel: 804-572-2285; Fax: 804-572-1725.
Res., 3302 W. Main St., South Boston, 24592. Tel: 804-572-3313.
Church—374 Juniper Cliff Rd., 24528. Tel: 804-572-2285.

Buckingham, Church of the Nativity, Rev. Robert Dillon.
Mailing Address: P.O. Box 241, 23921-0241. Tel: 804-969-2168 (Rectory).
Church—Rte. 60 E., 23921.

Buckner, Immaculate Conception, Rev. Rodney Rodis.
Mailing Address: P.O. Box 40, Mineral, 23117-0040. Tel: 540-894-4266; Fax: 540-894-4993.
Res., 106 Loving St., Louisa, 23093. Tel: 540-967-2465.
Church—1107 Frederick Hall Rd., 23024.

Cape Charles, Northampton Co., St. Charles, Rev. J. Michael Breslin.
Mailing Address: 545 Randolph Ave., 23310-3305. Tel: 804-331-1724.

Caroline County, St. Mary of the Annunciation, Rev. James F. Kauffmann.
Mailing Address: P.O. Box 396, Ladysmith, 22501.
Office & Church—(intersection Rt. 609 & Rt. 629) 10306 Ladysmith Rd., Ladysmith, 22501. Tel: 804-448-9064; 358-2427 (Rectory); Fax: 804-358-7025.

Charlottesville, Albemarle Co., Church of the Holy Comforter, Rev. Msgr. Raymond A. Barton; Rev. Joseph Torretto.
Mailing Address: 208 E. Jefferson St., 22902-5105. Tel: 804-295-7185; Fax: 804-295-7001.
Res., 660 Evergreen Ave., 22902. Tel: 804-977-5859.

Church of the Incarnation, Rev. William E. La Fratta.
Office: 635 Hillsdale Dr., 22901-1716. Tel: 804-973-4381; Fax: 804-973-1757.
Res., 2414 Commonwealth Dr., 22901. Tel: 804-978-4384.

St. Thomas Aquinas, Revs. Gregory Salomone, O.P.; Michael McCormack, O.P.; Aaron Laushway, O.P.; Jordan Lenaghan, O.P.
Mailing Address: 331 Kent Rd., 22903.
Office: Tel: 804-293-6472; 293-8081; Fax: 804-296-1941.
Res., 308 Alderman Rd., 22903. Tel: 804-977-5658.
Church—401 Alderman Rd., 22903.

Chesapeake

1—Prince of Peace, Rev. Christian Haydinger.
Mailing Address: 621 Cedar Rd., 23320-8300. Tel: 757-547-0356; 547-3903; Fax: 757-436-6477.
Res., 303 Elberon Ct., 23320. Tel: 757-547-2951.

2—St. Mary, Sr. Bernice McCourt, S.N.D., Pastoral Coord.
Mailing Address: P.O. Box 174-B, 23321-0174. Tel: 757-488-2663; 548-8426 (Rectory); Fax: 757-485-3699.
Church—536 Homestead Rd., 23321.

3—St. Stephen Martyr, Rev. James E. Gordon.
Mailing Address: 1544 S. Battlefield Blvd., 23322. Tel: 757-421-7416; 757-421-7416 (Rectory); Fax: 757-421-7488.

4—St. Therese of Lisieux, Rev. James C. Griffin.
Mailing Address: 4137 Portsmouth Blvd., 23321-2127. Tel: 757-488-2553; 2554; Fax: 757-465-4086.
Res., 3908 Parkway Rd., 23321. Tel: 757-488-5413.

Chincoteague, Accomack Co., St. Andrew, Rev. John A. Prinelli.
Mailing Address: P.O. Box 229, 23336-0229. Tel: 757-336-5432; Fax: 757-336-3515.
Res., 6319 Mumford St., 23336.
Church—6288 Church St., 23336.

Christiansburg, Holy Spirit Catholic Church, Rev. Louis R. Benoit.
Mailing Address: P.O. Box 98, 24073.
Church—Our Savior Lutheran Church, Cambria Rd., Pearisburg, 24073. Tel: 540-381-0299; 921-3547.

Clarksville, Mecklenburg Co., St. Catherine of Siena, Rev. James Fosnot.
Mailing Address: P.O. Box 1537, 23927.
Res., 810 Market St., 23927. Tel: 804-374-5040.
Church—805 Virginia Ave., 23927. Tel: 804-374-8408; Fax: 804-374-8408.

Clifton Forge, Alleghany Co., St. Joseph, Rev. Lawrence Mullaney.
Mailing Address: 620 Jefferson Ave., 24422-1715. Tel: 540-863-5371; Fax: 540-863-8963. [CEM]

Clintwood, Dickenson Co., St. Joseph, Rev. Robert B. Rademacher, Glmy.
Mailing Address: Box 1250, 24228-1250. Tel: 540-926-4123; Fax: 540-926-6304.
Church—Main St., 24228.

Colonial Heights, St. Ann, Rev. Msgr. Robert M. Perkins. In res., Rev. John P. Blankenship.
Mailing Address: 17111 Jefferson Davis Hwy., 23834-5396. Tel: 804-526-2548; Fax: 804-526-1922.
Res., 12861 Percival St., Chester, 23831. Tel: 804-796-9342.

Columbia, Fluvanna Co., St. Joseph, Rev. Gerald A. Przywara; Deacon Albert J. Carini.
Mailing Address: P.O. Box 808, 23038-0808. Tel: 804-589-5201; Fax: 804-589-5201.
Res., 15 Dogleg Rd., Palmyra, 22963. Tel: 804-589-5200.

Covington, Alleghany Co., Church of the Sacred Heart, Rev. David L. Nott.
Office: 214 W. Locust St., 24426-1537. Tel: 540-962-6541; Fax: 540-962-2147.
Res., 222 W. Locust St., 24426-1537. Tel: 540-965-5821.

Crewe, Nottoway Co., St. John the Baptist, Ms. Therese Mansfield, Pastoral Coord.
Mailing Address: 102 Oliver Ave., 23930-1410. Tel: 804-645-7509; Fax: 804-292-5535.
Mission—Meherrin, Sacred Heart, P.O. Box 62, Meherrin, 23954.

Danville, Pittsylvania Co., Sacred Heart, Rev. David V. McGuire.
Mailing Address: 288 W. Main St., 24541-2848. Tel: 804-792-9456; Fax: 804-792-9463.
Res., 154 College Ave., 24541. Tel: 804-792-0081.
School—540 Central Blvd., 24541. Tel: 804-793-2656; Fax: 804-793-2658. Marguerite S. Hancock, Prin.
Lay Teachers 23; Students 281.

Dinwiddie County, St. John, Rev. John J. Martinez, S.J.
Mailing Address: 7215 Squirrel Level Rd., Petersburg, 23805-7035. Tel: 804-861-0123; Fax: 804-861-0123.
Church—Squirrel Level Rd. & Flank Rd., Petersburg, 23805.

Elkton, Rockingham Co., Holy Infant, Rev. Daniel Bain.
Mailing Address: 101 W. Marshall Ave., 22827-1221. Tel: 540-298-1341.
Church—Rte. 33 & Rte. 340, 22827.

Emporia, Greensville Co., St. Richard, Rev. Leo Cervantes.
Mailing Address: 117 Laurel St., 23847-2506. Tel: 804-634-3524.
Mission—Lawrenceville, St. Bernard.

St. Peter the Apostle, Rev. Leo Cervantes.
Mailing Address: 117 Laurel St., 23847-2506. Tel: 804-634-3524.
Church—Rte. 46 & Rte. 626, Valentines, 23887.

Farmville, Prince Edward Co., St. Theresa, Rev. Joseph H. Metzger, III.
Mailing Address: 709 Buffalo St., 23901-1109. Tel: 804-392-3934; Fax: 804-392-1611.
Res., 400 Putney St., 23901. Tel: 804-392-8900.
Church—709 Buffalo St., 23901.

Fincastle, Botetourt Co., Church of the Transfiguration, Sr. Eveline Murray, Pastoral Coord.
Mailing Address: P.O. Box 416, 24090-0416. Tel: 540-473-2656; Fax: 540-473-2193.
Church—3650 Roanoke Rd., 24090.

Fort Monroe, St. Mary Star of the Sea, Rev. Joseph L. Clark.
Mailing Address: 7 Frank Ln., 23651-1010. Tel: 757-722-9855; 722-3138; Fax: 757-726-0083.
School—St. Mary Star of the Sea, 14 N. Willard Ave., Hampton, 23663. Tel: 757-723-6358. Sr. Mary Rose Bingham, O.P., Prin.
Sisters 2; Lay Teachers 15; Students 265.

Franklin, Southampton Co., St. Jude, Rev. Carl De Souza.
Mailing Address: 1014 Clay St., 23851-1309. Tel: 757-569-9600; Fax: 757-562-6974.
Mission—Wakefield, Infant of Prague.

Gate City, Scott Co., St. Bernard, Parish Coordinators: Lou Jane Gilmer; Leona Martin.
Mailing Address: 105 Linda St., 24251. Tel: 540-386-9665; Fax: 423-246-2279.
Mission—Dungannon, St. Patrick, Rte. 1, Box 135, Dungannon, 24245. Tel: 540-995-2305.

Glen Allen, Henrico Co., St. Michael, Rev. John E. Leonard.
Mailing Address: 4491 Springfield Rd., 23060. Tel: 804-527-1037; Fax: 804-527-1039.

Gloucester, St. Therese, the Little Flower, Rev. John E. Ridgell.
Mailing Address: P.O. Box 669, 23061.
Office: Tel: 804-693-5939; 693-9043 (Hall); Fax: 804-693-4766.
Res., 8051 Belroi Rd., 23061. Tel: 804-693-3380.
Church—6262 Main St., 23061.

Greene County, Shepherd of the Hills, Rev. Daniel Bain.
Mailing Address: P.O. Box 83, Quinque, 22965-0083. Tel: 804-985-3929.
Res., 101 W. Marshall Ave., Elkton, 22827. Tel: 540-298-1341.
Church—Rte. 633, Quinque.

Hampton

1—Immaculate Conception, Rev. Robert E. French.
Mailing Address: P.O. Box 7382, 23666-0382.
Res., 123 Tanglewood Dr., 23666. Tel: 757-826-0050.
Church—2150 Cunningham Dr., 23666. Tel: 757-826-0393; 826-0455; Fax: 757-825-0855.

2—St. Joseph, Revs. Joseph J. Majewski, C.SS.R.; Donald Winter, C.SS.R.; Anthony Morris, C.SS.R.
Mailing Address: P.O. Box 4126, 23664-0126.
Res., 410 Buckroe Ave., 23664-0126. Tel: 757-851-1711.
Church—414 Buckroe Ave., 23664-0126. Tel: 757-851-8800; Fax: 757-851-1875.

3—St. Rose of Lima, Rev. R. Francis Muench.
Mailing Address: 2114 Bay Ave., 23661. Tel: 757-245-5513; Fax: 757-245-1277.
Res., 2108 Bay Ave., 23661. Tel: 757-245-6313.

4—Our Lady of Viet Nam Chapel, Revs. Stephen Tan Nguyen; Thai Trinh.
Mailing Address: P.O. Box 1937, 23699. Tel: 757-722-2657; Fax: 757-622-4248.
Chapel—1307 LaSalle Ave., 23661.

Harrisonburg, Rockingham Co., Blessed Sacrament, Revs. Kenneth E. Wood; John A. Grace.
Mailing Address: P.O. Box 226, 22801-0226.
Res., 843 Meadowlark Dr., 22801. Tel: 540-433-5666.
Church—154 N. Main St., 22801. Tel: 540-434-4341; 434-8601; Fax: 540-434-0849.

Highland Springs, Henrico Co., St. John, Rev. James R. Guttendorf.
Mailing Address: P.O. Box 190, 23075-0190. Tel: 804-737-8028; Fax: 804-328-4683.
Res., 903 W. Nine Mile Rd., 23075. Tel: 804-737-4077.
Church—813 W. Nine Mile Rd., 23075.

Hopewell, St. James Church, Rev. Daniel Bond.
Mailing Address: 510 W. Poythress St., 23860-2508.
Res., 105 N. Fifth Ave., 23860. Tel: 804-458-9286.
Church—500 W. Poythress St., 23860. Tel: 804-458-9223; 458-9286 (evening); Fax: 804-458-1216.
Mission—Claremont, St. Anne.

Hot Springs, Bath Co., The Shrine of the Sacred Heart, Rev. David L. Nott.
Mailing Address: Drawer B, 24445-0047. Tel: 540-839-2603; Fax: 540-962-2147.

Hurt, Pittsylvania Co., St. Victoria, Rev. Robert J. McEleney.
Mailing Address: P.O. Box 640, 24563-0640. Tel: 804-324-4824; Fax: 804-324-4759.
Res., 305 Victoria Dr., 24563.

Lake Easton, Mecklenberg Co., St. Peter The Apostle. (Mission of St. Richard's, Emporia). Rev. Leo T. Cervantes.

Lebanon, Russell Co., Good Shepherd, Rev. Paul Maier.
Mailing Address: P.O. Box 730, 24266-0730. Tel: 540-889-1690; 889-0127.

Lexington, Rockbridge Co., St. Patrick, Rev. N. Alan Lipscomb.
Mailing Address: P.O. Box 725, 24450-0725. Tel: 540-463-3533; Fax: 540-463-6384.
Office: 221 W. Nelson St., 24450.
Res., 225 Denny Lane, 24450. Tel: 540-463-6819.
Church—219 W. Nelson St., 24450.

Lynchburg, Campbell Co., Holy Cross, Rev. Msgr. J. Kenneth Rush; Mrs. Judith Pasicznyk, Pastoral Assoc.
Office: 710 Clay St., 24504-2530. Tel: 804-846-5245; Fax: 804-846-7022. [CEM]
Res., 3766 Fort Ave., 24501. Tel: 804-846-5966.
Church—700 Clay St., 24504.
School—Regional School, (Grades PreK-12) 2125 Langhorne Rd., 24501. Tel: 804-847-5436. Mr. John P. Jones, Prin.
Lay Teachers 45; Students 317.

St. Thomas More, Rev. Kevin O'Brien.
3015 Roundelay Rd., 24502-2036. Tel: 804-237-5911; 237-8855 (Rectory); Fax: 804-237-8854.

Marion, Smyth Co., St. John the Evangelist Church, Rev. Robert L. Krenik.
124 Park Blvd., 24354. Tel: 540-783-7282.
Church—120 Park Blvd., 24354.

Martinsville, Henry Co., St. Joseph, Rev. Martin Lavin.
Mailing Address: 704 E. Church St., 24112-3107. Tel: 540-638-4779; 638-1192; Fax: 540-638-2218.
Res., 9 Booker Rd., 24112. Tel: 540-632-3710.

Mathews, Mathews Co., Church of Francis de Sales, Rev. John D. Boddie.
Mailing Address: P.O. Box 158, 23109-0158. Tel: 804-725-2776; Fax: 804-725-5463.
Church—Rte. 647 & Lover's Ln., 23109.

Mechanicsville, Hanover Co., Church of the Redeemer, Rev. James J. Begley.
Mailing Address: 8275 Meadowbridge Rd., 23111. Tel: 804-746-4911; Fax: 804-746-8804-746-8657.
Res., 7438 Shire Pkwy., 23111. Tel: 804-730-1844.
Church—Tel: 804-746-0633 (Hall).

Middlesex County, Church of the Visitation, Rev. John D. Boddie.
Mailing Address: P.O. Box 38, Topping, 23169-0038. Tel: 804-758-5160.
Res., Box 34, Cobbs Creek, 23035. Tel: 804-725-5463; Fax: 804-725-5463.
Church—Rte. 33, Harmony Grove, 23035.

Mineral, St. Jude, Rev. Rodney Rodis.
Mailing Address: P.O. Box 40, 23117-0040. Tel: 540-894-4266; Fax: 540-894-4993.
Res., 106 Loving St., Louisa, 23093. Tel: 540-967-2465.
Church—1937 Jefferson Davis Hwy., 23117.

Moneta, Bedford Co., Resurrection, Sr. Elizabeth Bagen, G.N.S.H., Pastoral Coord.
Mailing Address: 15353 Moneta Rd., 24121-9804. Tel: 540-297-5530; Fax: 540-297-6316.

Newport News, Newport Co.,

1—CATHOLIC COMMUNITY OF THE KOREAN MARTYRS, Rev. Andrew Lee.
Mailing Address: 8 Evelyn Dr., 23602-3318. Tel: 804-875-1202.

2—OUR LADY OF MOUNT CARMEL, Rev. Msgr. Michael D. McCarron; Revs. Peter Tran; Timothy Keeney; Deacon Paul Larkin.
100 Harpersville Rd., 23601-2324. Tel: 757-595-0385; 0386; 0387; Fax: 757-599-9285.
School—Tel: 757-596-2754. Sr. Mary Camille Poole, O.P., Prin.
Sisters of St. Dominic 4; Lay Teachers 16; Students 392.

3—ST. JEROME, Rev. Joseph B. Majewski; Deacon Peter Kwan.
Mailing Address: 116 Denbigh Blvd., 23608-3333. Tel: 757-877-5021; 874-3268; Fax: 757-898-1437.

4—ST. VINCENT DE PAUL, Rev. Lloyd Stephenson.
Mailing Address: P.O. Box 258, 23607-0258. Tel: 757-245-4234; Fax: 757-245-0039.
Church—230 33rd St., 23607.

Norfolk, Norfolk City Co.,

1—BLESSED SACRAMENT, Rev. Julian B. Goodman.
Mailing Address: 170 Painter St., 23505-4557. Tel: 757-423-8305; Fax: 757-451-3335. [JC]
Res., 110 W. Severn Rd., 23505. Tel: 757-423-2176.
Church—Newport Ave. & Painter St., 23505.

2—CHRIST THE KING, Rev. Brian Rafferty.
Office & Mailing Address—1803 Columbia Ave., 23509-1200. Tel: 757-622-1120; 622-9196; Fax: 757-627-8808.
Res., 1804 Ashland Ave., 23509. Tel: 757-627-1723.
School—3401 Tidewater Dr., 23509. Tel: 757-625-4951. Mrs. Patricia Suraci, Prin.
Lay Teachers 19; Students 301.

3—HOLY TRINITY, Rev. Lou Ruoff; Rev. Msgr. Santiago C. Frias.
Mailing Address: 155 W. Government Ave., 23503-2905. Tel: 757-480-3433; Fax: 757-480-8749. [JC]
Res., 175 W. Government Ave., 23503. Tel: 804-480-2430.
School—154 W. Government Ave., 23503. Tel: 757-583-1873. Ms. Deneane Nofplot, Prin.
Lay Teachers 17; Students 230.

4—SACRED HEART, Rev. John J. Dorgan.
Office: 520 Graydon Ave., 23507-1711. Tel: 757-625-6763; Fax: 757-627-1965.

5—BASILICA OF ST. MARY, Rev. Msgr. Walter C. Barrett, Rector.
Office: 1000 Holt St., 23504-4241. Tel: 757-622-4487; Fax: 757-625-7969. [JC]
Church—232 Chapel St., 23504.
School—St. Mary's Academy, 921 Holt St., 23504. Tel: 757-622-7246. Sr. Barbara Boyle, S.N.D., Prin.
Sisters 1; Lay Teachers 18; Students 211.
Convent—1000 Holt St., 23504. Tel: 757-627-5213.

6—OUR LADY OF LAVANG, Revs. Stephen Tan Nguyen, O.F.M.; Thai Trinh.
1806 Ashland Ave., 23509-1236.
Church—409 Compostella Rd., 23518. Tel: 757-622-5345; 545-5606; Fax: 757-622-4248.

7—ST. PIUS X, Rev. Williams J. Dale.
Mailing Address: 7800 Halprin Dr., 23518-4408. Tel: 757-583-0291; Fax: 757-583-0293.
Res., 1615 Longdale Dr., 23518. Tel: 757-855-3297.
School—7813 Halprin Dr., 23518. Tel: 757-588-6171; Fax: 757-587-8657. Sr. Anne Carroll, I.H.M., Prin.
Sisters Servants of the Immaculate Heart of Mary 2; Lay Teachers 26; Students 525.

Norge, James City Co., St. Olaf, Patron of Norway, Donna Young Whitley, Pastoral Coord.
Mailing Address: 104 Norge Ln., 23188-7229. Tel: 757-564-3819; Fax: 757-565-1099.

Norton, Wise Co., St. Anthony, Rev. Joseph C. Facura.
Mailing Address: 1009 Virginia Ave., 24273-1805. Tel: 540-679-2336; Fax: 540-679-4501.
Mission—Coeburn, St. Mary.
Station—Wise, Clinch Valley College of the University of Virginia.

Onley, Accomac Co., St. Peter's the Apostle, Rev. Daniel L. Kelly.
Mailing Address: P.O. Box 860, 23418-0860. Tel: 757-787-4592; Fax: 757-787-2899.

Palmyra, Fluvanna Co., Ss. Peter & Paul, Rev. Gerald A. Przywara; Deacon Albert J. Carini.
Mailing Address: Rte. 2, Box 142, 22963-9506. Tel: 804-589-5201; Fax: 804-589-5201.

Pearisburg, Giles Co., Holy Family, Rev. Louis R. Benoit.
Mailing Address: 516 Mason Court Dr., 24134-1832. Tel: 540-921-3547; Fax: 540-726-3907.

Pennington Gap, Lee Co., Church of the Holy Spirit, Rev. Anthony Rodrigues.
Mailing Address: P.O. Box 923, Jonesville, 24263.
Res., 1821 Holton Ave., Big Stone Gap, 24219. Tel: 540-523-6546; Fax: 540-523-1602.
Church—1010 Morgan Ave., 24277.

Petersburg, Prince George Co., St. Joseph, Rev. Robert M. Spener.
Mailing Address: P.O. Box 2006, 23804-1306.
Office: 11 N. Market St., PA 23804. Tel: 804-733-3115; Fax: 804-862-9931.
Res., 19 Centre Hill Ct., 23804. Tel: 804-732-5127. [CEM]
School—Tel: 804-732-3931. Ms. Miriam Cotton, Prin.
Lay Teachers 10; Students 192.

Pocahontas, Tazewell Co., St. Elizabeth (1896), Rev. Daniel O. Brady.
Mailing Address: P.O. Box 608, 24635-0608. Tel: 540-988-4626; Fax: 540-988-4626.

Portsmouth, Holy Angels, Rev. John J. Wagner, III.
Office: 34 Afton Pkwy., 23702-2739. Tel: 757-485-2142; 2143; Fax: 757-485-3699.
Church of the Resurrection, Rev. James V. Carr.
Mailing Address: 3501 Cedar Ln., 23703. Tel: 757-484-7335; 484-7408; Fax: 757-484-5857.
Res., 3420 Wilshire Rd., 23703. Tel: 757-484-7336.
School—Portsmouth Catholic Elementary School, 2301 Oregon Ave., 23701. Tel: 757-488-6744. Ms. Thea Haubrich, Prin.
St. Paul, Revs. Joseph S. Slowik; Robert J. Walsh.
Res., 518 High St., 23704-3516. Tel: 757-397-7066; Fax: 757-393-4334. [CEM]
Church—522 High St., 23704.

Powhatan, St. John Neumann, Rev. J. Morton Biber; Deacon John H. Thomas Tel: 804-379-9811.
Church—2480 Batterson Rd., 23139-7513. Tel: 804-598-3754; 794-9098; Fax: 804-598-1467.
Mission—Cartersville, St. Catherine.

Prince George County, Church of the Sacred Heart, Rev. James E. Gallagher.
Mailing Address: 4415 County Dr., Petersburg, 23805-7567. Tel: 804-732-6385; Fax: 804-732-6385. [CEM]

Quinton, New Kent Co., St. Elizabeth Ann Seton, Sr. Agnes Seebach, O.S.U., Pastoral Coord.
Mailing Address: P.O. Box 245, 23141-0245. Tel: 804-932-4125; Fax: 804-932-8126.
Church—2631 Pocahontas Trail, 23141.

Radford, St. Jude, Rev. Msgr. James Grealish.
Mailing Address: 1740 Tyler Rd., Christiansburg, 24073-6154. Tel: 540-639-5341; Fax: 540-639-4738.
Res., 900 Berkley St., 24141. Tel: 540-731-9541.

Richlands, Tazewell Co., St. Mary, Rev. Thomas R. Collins.
Mailing Address: 1118 E. Second St., 24641. Tel: 540-935-2815.
Mission—Grundy, St. Joseph.

Roanoke, Our Lady of Nazareth, Rev. Joseph P. Lehman.
Mailing Address: 2505 Electric Rd., S.W., 24018-3599. Tel: 540-774-0066 (Office); 774-0857 (Residence); Fax: 540-774-2148.
St. Andrew, Roanoke Co., Rev. Steven R. Rule.
Mailing Address: 631 N. Jefferson St., 24016-1401. Tel: 540-344-9814; Fax: 540-344-7879. [JC]
Res., 3025 Bancroft Dr., 24014. Tel: 540-345-7018.
St. Gerard, Roanoke Co., Rev. Wayne L. Ball.
809 Orange Ave., N.W., 24016-1117. Tel: 540-343-7744; Fax: 540-776-0903.
School—Roanoke Catholic Regional Elementary and High School, 621 N. Jefferson St., P.O. Box 11926, 24022. Tel: 540-982-3756. Ms. Karen Mabry, Prin.

Rocky Mount, Franklin Co., Francis of Assisi, Sr. Fidelis Rubbo, O.S.F., Pastoral Coord.
Mailing Address: 15 Glennwood Dr., 24151-2111. Tel: 540-483-9591; 483-8981; Fax: 540-483-5232.

St. Paul, Wise Co., St. Therese, Rev. Paul Maier.
Mailing Address: P.O. Box 56, 24283-0056. Tel: 540-762-5932; Fax: 540-762-5932.
Res., 3107 Sixth Ave., 24283.

Salem, Our Lady of Perpetual Help, Rev. Gregory Kandt.
Mailing Address: 314 Turner Rd., 24153-2308. Tel: 540-387-0491; Fax: 540-389-8237.
Res., 1408 Kathryn Ln., 24153. Tel: 540-387-1020.

Scottsville, Albemarle Co., St. George, Rev. Ralph Hamlet.
Mailing Address: P.O. Box 9, 24590-0009. Tel: 804-286-3724; Fax: 804-263-8509.
Missions—Lovingston, St. Mary, P.O. Box 375, Lovingston, 22949-0735. Tel: 804-263-4008; Amherst, Amherst Co., Catholic Community of Amherst, Amherst, 24521. Tel: 804-263-8509.

Smithfield, Good Shepherd, Rev. Thomas B. Nee.
Mailing Address: P.O.Box 840, 23431-0840.
Res., 600 Smith St., Suffolk, 23434. Tel: 757-925-0731; Fax: 757-538-0103.
Church—300 Smithfield Blvd., 23430.

South Boston, Halifax Co., St. Paschal Baylon, Rev. Matthias Newell.
Mailing Address: 800 John Randolph Blvd., 24592-2943.
Res., 3302 N. Main St., 24592. Tel: 804-572-3313; 572-2285 (Office); Fax: 804-572-1725.

South Hill, Mecklenburg Co., Good Shepherd, Rev. James Fosnot.
Mailing Address: P.O. Box 621, 23970-0621. Tel: 804-447-3622; Fax: 804-447-4729.
Church—1664 N. Mecklenburg Ave., 23970.

Staunton, Augusta Co., St. Francis of Assisi, Rev. John Adam Abe.
Church & Mailing Address—121 N. Augusta, 24401-3636. Tel: 540-886-2262; Fax: 540-885-5743.
Res., 126 N. New St., 24401. Tel: 540-886-9121.

Suffolk, St. Mary of the Presentation, Rev. Thomas B. Nee.
Office: 202 S. Broad St., 23434-5715. Tel: 757-539-5732; Fax: 757-538-0103.
Church—200 S. Broad St., 23434.

Tabb, York Co., Blessed Kateri Tekawitha, Rev. Thomas J. Quinlan.
Church & Office: 3800 Big Bethel Rd., 23693-3814. Tel: 757-766-3800; Fax: 757-766-1125.

Tappahannock, Essex Co., St. Timothy, Rev. Richard D. Dollard.
Mailing Address: P.O. Box 129, 22560-0129.
Church—Rte. 17 & Airport Rd., 22560. Tel: 804-443-2760; Fax: 804-443-2022.

Tazewell, St. Theresa, Rev. Daniel O. Brady.
Mailing Address: P.O. Box 345, 24651-0345. Tel: 540-988-4626; Fax: 540-988-4626.
Church—304 Tazewell Ave., 24651.

Virginia Beach

1—CHURCH OF THE ASCENSION, Revs. James E. Parke; Robert Cummins. In res., Revs. Robert Gloisten; Charles Faul.
Office: 4853 Princess Anne Rd., 23462-4446. Tel: 757-495-1886; 495-3833 (Rectory); Fax: 757-495-1516.
Catechesis/Religious Programs—Students 482.

2—CHURCH OF THE HOLY APOSTLES, Virginia Co. Anglican-Roman Catholic Congregation of Hampton Roads. Rev. Charles Faul.
Church—1598 Lynnhaven Pkwy., 23456-2008. Tel: 757-427-0963; Fax: 757-427-9434.

3—CRISTO REY HISPANIC APOSTOLATE, Virginia Co., Sr. Barbara Gerwe, D.C., Pastoral Coord.
Mailing Address: 269 Clearfield Ave., 23462-1815. Tel: 757-490-7896; Fax: 757-518-9638.

4—HOLY FAMILY, Virginia Co., Rev. Richard T. Mooney.
Parish Center: 1279 N. Great Neck Rd., 23454-2117. Tel: 757-481-5702; 340-5161; Fax: 757-481-3989.

5—HOLY SPIRIT, Virginia Co., Rev. Msgr. Thomas J. Caroluzza; Revs. Thomas E. Mattingly; Rolo Castillo; Deacon John T. Glynn.
Office: 1396 Lynnhaven Pkwy., 23456-2710. Tel: 757-468-3600; 3601; 3602; Fax: 757-468-3602.
Res., 3345 Clubhouse Rd., 23452. Tel: 804-340-3933.

6—ST. GREGORY THE GREAT, Virginia Co., Revs. Paschal Kneip, O.S.B.; Damian Abbaticchio, O.S.B.; John Peck; Luke Policicchio, O.S.B.; Anselm Ober, O.S.B.; Philip Ghys, O.S.B.; Deacon Raymond Check.
Office: 5347 Virginia Beach Blvd., Box 7, 23462. Tel: 757-497-8330; 497-7235; Fax: 757-490-1492.
School—5343 Virginia Beach Blvd., 23462-1896. Tel: 757-497-1811. Sr. Rose Marie Adams, I.H.M., Prin.
Sisters 3; Lay Teachers 28; Students 694.

7—ST. JOHN THE APOSTLE CHURCH, Virginia Co., Rev. Dwight E. Shrader. In res., Rev. Paul Gaughan, (Retired).
Church—800 Los Conaes Way, 23456-6421. Tel: 757-426-2180; Fax: 757-426-6857.

8—ST. LUKE, Virginia Co., Rev. Eugene J. Teslovic.
Mailing Address: 2304 Salem Rd., 23456-1215. Tel: 757-427-5776; Fax: 757-427-2260.

9—ST. MARK, Virginia Co., Rev. Daniel N. Klem.
Mailing Address: 1505 Kempsville Rd., 23464-7210. Tel: 757-479-1010; 479-0414.
Res., 4901 Whitewood Ln., 23464. Tel: 757-467-4932; Fax: 757-479-9453.

10—ST. MATTHEW, Virginia Co., Rev. Timothy A. Drake.
Office: 3314 Sandra Ln., 23464-1736. Tel: 757-420-6310; Fax: 757-420-6311.
Res., 806 Bridgeport Place, 23464. Tel: 757-523-1723.
School—3316 Sandra Ln., 23464. Tel: 757-420-2455. Ms. Barbara White, Prin.
Lay Teachers 28; Students 526.

11—ST. NICHOLAS, Virginia Co., Rev. James M. Noto.
Office & Church—712 Little Neck Rd., 23452. Tel: 757-340-7231; Fax: 757-340-2727.
Res., 3340 Old Kirkwood Dr., 23452-5807. Tel: 757-498-7834.

12—STAR OF THE SEA, Virginia Co., Rev. James E. Dorson.
Office: 1404 Pacific Ave., 23451-3439. Tel: 757-428-8547; 425-6583; Fax: 757-428-0788.
Res., 322 Arctic Ave., 23451. Tel: 757-425-9026.
School—1404 Pacific Ave., 23451. Tel: 757-428-8400. Mrs. Susan Fentress, Prin.
Sisters 2; Lay Teachers 15; Students 265.

Waynesboro, Augusta Co., St. John the Evangelist, Rev. William S. O'Brien.
Mailing Address: 344 Maple Ave., 22980-4706.
Office: Tel: 540-949-6145; 6146; Fax: 540-932-8512.
Res., 320 Maple Ave., 22980. Tel: 540-943-4051.
Church—300 Maple Ave., 22980.
Station—Fishersville, Woodrow Wilson Rehabilitation Center.

West Point, King William Co., Our Lady of the Blessed Sacrament, Rev. James M. Arsenault.
Mailing Address: 3510 King William Ave., 23181-9501.
Church—3570 King William Ave., 23181. Tel: 804-843-3125; Fax: 804-843-9158. [CEM]

Williamsburg, York Co., St. Bede's, Revs. William H. Carr; Antonio R. Malabad; Patrick Golden. In res., Rev. Charles Fisher.
Mailing Address: 10 Harrison Ave., 23185-3530. Tel: 757-229-3631; Fax: 757-229-5361.
Res., 601 College Ter., 23185. Tel: 757-229-4233.
Church—500 Richmond Rd., 23185.

Woodlawn, Carroll Co., St. Joseph's, Rev. Charles W. Brickner.
Mailing Address: 99 Joy Ranch Rd., 24381-1213. Tel: 540-236-7814; Fax: 540-238-8711.
Missions—Patrick Springs, Church of the Risen Lord; Floyd, Floyd Co., Church of All Saints.

Wytheville, St. Mary's, Rev. J. Ven Ilano.
Mailing Address: P.O. Box 7, 24382-0007. Tel: 540-228-3104; Fax: 540-228-3322. [CEM]
Church—370 E. Main St., 24382.
Mission—Pulaski, St. Edward, Tel: 540-980-6511.

Yorktown, York Co., St. Joan of Arc, Rev. Don Michael Hanna.
Office: 315 Harris Grove Ln., 23692-4014. Tel: 757-898-5570; Fax: 757-898-0737.

Chaplains of Public Institutions

RICHMOND. *McGuire VA Medical Center*. Rev. James K. Disney.
MCV Hospital. Rev. Blaise Perrello.

HAMPTON. *VA Medical Center* Chaplain Service, Bldg. 69, 23667. Tel: 804-722-9961, Ext. 3600. Revs. Lloyd F. Stephenson; Donald J. Cavey.

NORFOLK. *Depaul Medical Center*. The following are attended by Sacred Heart Church: Children's Hospital of the King's Daughters; Norfolk General Hospital. 150 Kingsley Ln., 23505. Tel: 804-889-5000. Rev. Jerome Turner.

PETERSBURG. *Federal Correctional Institution*. Rev. John P. Blankenship.

SALEM. *Salem VA Medical Center* Tel: 540-982-2463. Rev. Wayne L. Ball, Chap.

Special Assignment:
Reverend Fathers—
Guarnieri, Lee
Lane, Mark
Stofft, Kenneth

On Duty Outside the Diocese:
Reverend Fathers—
Funk, Virgil C., Washington, DC
McNally, Stephen, Bonn, Germany
Murphy, Dennis, Providence, RI
Natale, Samuel, New York
Slattery, Joseph A., Pretoria, South Africa
Thuy, Pham Quang
Williams, McKinley

Military Chaplains:
Reverend Fathers—
D'Aurora, Joseph
Dang, Chin Van
Hickman, J. Stephen
Huan, Joseph Van Tran
Kanicki, Philip A.
Moran, Edward C.

Absent On Leave:
Reverend Fathers—
Bonamo, James
Magri, Thomas

Unassigned:
Reverend Fathers—
Bostwick, John
Kruc, James
Lenning, Terry

Retired:
Reverend Monsignors—
Michael, Chester P., Route 2, Box 225, Afton, VA 22920
Reverend Fathers—
Beardsley, Frederick, 5910 Kensington Ave., Richmond, VA 23226
Bowers, Vernon J., Mailing Address: U.S. Post Office, Ware Neck, VA 23178
Cassidy, Patrick, 628 Toll Gate Ln., Petersburg, VA 23865
Chmura, Stanislaus, 717 Cooper Ave., Inverness, FL 34450
Condon, William F., P.O. Box 1742, Clarksville, VA 23927
Connelly, William P., 4605 Truman Ln., Virginia Beach, VA 23445
Dinga, William, 1324 Debree Ave., Norfolk, VA 23517
Dinges, Anthony, 102 Oliver Ave., Crewe, VA 23920
Ditty, James, 1316 Mill Lake Quarter, Chesapeake, VA 23320
Farley, Laurence F., 127 W. Birch St., Hazelton, PA 18201
Gallagher, Paul V., 34 Oakland Dr., Pulaski, VA 24301
Gaughan, Paul, St. John's Rectory, 800 Los Conaes Way, Virginia Beach, VA 23456
Gormley, George J., Our Lady of the Valley, Roanoke, VA 24016
Henry, Thomas, Our Lady of Peace, Charlottesville, VA 22901
Kloepfer, John S., P.O. Box 1472, Clarksville, VA 23927
McIntyre, Raymond T., 62 Manhattan Dr., Ashley, PA 18706
Naro, Carl J., Rte. 1, Box 151, Wingina, VA 24599
Naylor, Ronald J., 1060 Birnam Woods Dr., Virginia Beach, VA 23466
Pereira, Albert F., 4713 Clintwood Dr., Portsmouth, VA 23703
Rodriguez, D. Andres G., San Martin de Tabara, Zamora, Spain
Ruth, Robert F.
Stickle, William, 144 Bay Cliff Trail, Kill Devil Hills, NC 27948
Stockert, Donfred H., 183 Hitchcock Ave., Highland Springs, VA 23075
Walsh, Robert J., 518 High St., Portsmouth, VA 23704
Warren, Robert, P.O. Box 6194, Charlottesville, VA 22906
Welch, Thomas David, 305 Victoria Dr., Hurt, VA 24563

Permanent Deacons:
Birx, Charles R., St. Jude, Radford
Carini, Albert J., St. Joseph, Columbia
Cartwright, Gordon, Lynchburg, VA
Check, Raymond P., St. Gregory the Great, Virginia Beach
Cortezano, Alfredo, NAS, Norfolk
Dwyer, Bruce K., St. Joseph, Woodlawn
Ellerbrock, Michael, St. Mary, Blacksburg
Fournier, Keith, Virginia Beach, VA
Glynn, John, Holy Spirit, Virginia Beach
Hall, Harry, St. Anne, Bristol
Hanzlik, Edward, Sacred Heart, New Bohemia
Hayes, William, Our Lady of Peace, Appomattox
Horbowy, Thaddeus, FCI, Petersburg
Kwon, Peter H., Dr., St. Jerome, Newport News Korean Community
Larkin, Paul V., Langley AFB
McCormick, Daniel F., St. Mark, Virginia Beach
Menting, Peter J., Good Samaritan, Amelia
Pinto, Richard, Langley AFB
Ports, Francis J., Holy Name of Mary, Bedford
Roderique, Raymond, Forest, VA
Thomas, John H., Diocesan Tribunal
Torres, Patricio-Lisboa, Bishop's Office
Weir, Robert, Virginia Beach, VA

INSTITUTIONS LOCATED IN THE DIOCESE

[A] HIGH SCHOOLS, DIOCESAN

LYNCHBURG. *Holy Cross Regional School*, 2125 Langhorne Rd., 24501. Tel: 804-847-5436. John P. Jones, Prin. Lay Teachers 45; Students 377.

NEWPORT NEWS. *Peninsula Catholic High School*, 600 Harpersville Rd., 23601. Tel: 757-596-7247; Fax: 757-591-9718. Mrs. Francine Conway, Prin. Lay Teachers 28; Students 330.

PETERSBURG. *St. Vincent de Paul High School*, 240 Wagner Rd., 23803-9232. Tel: 804-733-4305; Fax: 804-862-3634. Daughters of Charity of Saint Vincent de Paul. Dr. Patricia A. Crisci, Prin. Sisters 1; Lay Teachers 17; Students 170.

ROANOKE. *Roanoke Catholic School*. (Grades PreK-12), 621 N. Jefferson St., 24016. Tel: 540-982-3532.
E-mail: res1@rbnet.com
Ms. Karen Mabry, Prin. Lay Teachers 40; Students 490.

VIRGINIA BEACH. *Catholic High School*, 4552 Princess Anne Rd., 23462. Tel: 804-467-2881; Fax: 804-467-0284. Rev. Msgr. William L. Pitt, Prin. Priests 3; Lay Teachers 34; Students 452.

[B] HIGH SCHOOLS, PRIVATE

RICHMOND. *Benedictine High School*, 304 N. Sheppard St., 23221. Tel: 804-342-1300.
E-mail: info@benedictinehighschool.org
Web site: www.benedictinehighschool.org
A Military High School in the Charge of the Benedictine Monks. Rt. Rev. Benedict R. McDermott, O.S.B., Pres.; Dr. David A. Bouton, Headmaster; Rev. Adrian W. Harmening, O.S.B. Priests 2; Lay Teachers 28; Students 287.
Saint Gertrude High School, 3215 Stuart Ave., 23221. Tel: 804-358-9114; Fax: 804-355-5682.
E-mail: sgregori@pen.K12.va.us
Sr. Charlotte Lange, O.S.B., Prin. Benedictine Sisters 1; Lay Teachers 28; Students 250.

POWHATAN. *Blessed Sacrament High School at Belmead*, P.O. Box 519, 23139. Tel: 804-598-4729. Dr. Lou Ross Hopewell, Prin. Religious 2; Lay Teachers 10; Students 90.

WILLIAMSBURG. *Walsingham Academy Upper School*, P.O. Box 8702, 23187-8702. Tel: 757-229-6026.
Web site: http://www.widomaker.com/~walsnhm
(Grades 8-12). Private Day School for Boys and Girls. Sr. Virginia Marie Kauffmann, R.S.M., Prin. Sisters of Mercy 5; Lay Teachers 26; Students 274.

[C] ELEMENTARY SCHOOLS, DIOCESAN

CHARLOTTESVILLE. *Charlottesville Catholic Elementary School*. (Grades K-2), 301-B Jefferson St., 22902. Tel: 804-977-7761.
E-mail: ccs@avenue.org
Edward E. Rossmoore, Prin. Lay Teachers 5; Students 66.

[D] ELEMENTARY SCHOOLS, PRIVATE

WILLIAMSBURG. *Walsingham Academy Lower School*, P.O. Box 8702, 23187-8702.
E-mail: walsingham@aol.com
(Grades PreK-7). Day School for Boys and Girls. Sr. Mary Jeanne Oesterle, R.S.M., Prin. Sisters 2; Lay Teachers 34; Students 423.

[E] GENERAL HOSPITALS

RICHMOND. *St. Mary's Hospital*, 5801 Bremo Rd., 23226. Tel: 804-285-2011
For a complete listing, refer to the Hospitals section.

NEWPORT NEWS. *Mary Immaculate Hospital*, 2 Bernardine Dr., 23602-4499. Tel: 757-886-6600
For a complete listing, refer to the Hospitals section.

NORFOLK. *Bon Secours - DePaul Health Foundation*, 150 Kingsley Ln., 23505
For a complete listing, refer to the Hospitals section.

Bon Secours De Paul Medical Center, Inc., 150 Kingsley Ln., 23505. Tel: 757-889-5000
For a complete listing, refer to the Hospitals section.

NORTON. *St. Mary's Hospital, Inc.*, P.O. Box 620, 24273. Tel: 540-679-9100
For a complete listing, refer to the Hospitals section.

PORTSMOUTH. *Maryview Medical Center*, 3636 High St., 23707. Tel: 757-398-2200
For a complete listing, refer to the Hospitals section.

[F] ORPHANAGES AND INFANT HOMES

RICHMOND. *St. Joseph's Villa*, 8000 Brook Rd., 23227-1338. Tel: 804-553-3200; Fax: 804-553-3259
For a complete listing, refer to the Special Care Facilities section.

NORFOLK. *St. Mary's Home for Disabled Children*, 317 Chapel St., 23504. Tel: 757-622-2208
For a complete listing, refer to the Special Care Facilities section.

ROANOKE. *The Achievement Center-St. Vincent's Home, Inc.* Mailing Address: P.O. Box 12368, 24025. Tel: 540-982-0128.
For a complete listing, refer to the Special Care Facilities section.

De Paul Family Services, Inc., 4502 Starkey Rd., S.W., 24014. Tel: 540-989-7355
For a complete listing, refer to the Special Care Facilities section.

[G] CHILD LEARNING CENTERS

RICHMOND. *Holy Angels*, 1307 Lakeside Ave., 23228. Tel: 804-266-7200. Sr. Juliana Paladini, Dir. Comboni Missionary Sisters 4; Lay Teachers 2; Children 44.

Holy Rosary Child Care Center, 1218 N. 34th St., Box 8046, 23223. Tel: 804-222-2590. Mrs. Deborah Longs, Dir. Children 120.

NORFOLK. *Christ the King Extended Care*, 3401 Tidewater Dr., 23509. Tel: 804-627-0119. Mrs. Uli Williford, Admin. Children 80.

[H] HOMES FOR THE AGED

RICHMOND. *Marywood Apartments*, 1261 Marywood Ln., 23229. Tel: 804-740-5567
For a complete listing, refer to the Special Care Facilities section.

Our Lady of Hope Health Center, Inc., 13700 N. Gayton Rd., 23233. Tel: 804-360-1960
For a complete listing, refer to the Special Care Facilities section.

St. Francis Home, Inc., 2511 Wise St., 23225-3952. Tel: 804-231-1043; Fax: 804-231-1065
For a complete listing, refer to the Special Care Facilities section.

St. Joseph's Home for the Aged, 1503 Michael Rd., 23229. Tel: 804-288-6245
For a complete listing, refer to the Special Care Facilities section.

St. Mary Wood's, 1257 Marywood Ln., 23229. Tel: 804-741-8624
For a complete listing, refer to the Special Care Facilities section.

CHARLOTTESVILLE. *Our Lady of Peace*, 751 Hillsdale Dr., 22901. Tel: 804-973-1155
For a complete listing, refer to the Special Care Facilities section.

HAMPTON. *Seton Manor*, 215 Marcella Rd., 23666. Tel: 757-827-6512
For a complete listing, refer to the Special Care Facilities section.

LYNCHBURG. *McGurk House Apartments*, 2425 Tate Springs Rd., 24501
For a complete listing, refer to the Special Care Facilities section.

Nott Homes, Inc., 3009-3011 Roundelay Rd., 24502
For a complete listing, refer to the Special Care Facilities section.

NEWPORT NEWS. *St. Francis Nursing Center*, 4 Ridgewood Pkwy., 23602
For a complete listing, refer to the Special Care Facilities section.

NORFOLK. *Madonna Home*, 814 W. 37th St., 23508. Tel: 757-623-6662
For a complete listing, refer to the Special Care Facilities section.

ROANOKE. *Our Lady of the Valley Retirement Community*, 650 N. Jefferson St., 24016. Tel: 540-345-5111
For a complete listing, refer to the Special Care Facilities section.

SUFFOLK. *Bon Secours-Maryview Nursing Care*, 4775 Bridge Rd., 23435. Tel: 757-686-0488
For a complete listing, refer to the Special Care Facilities section.

VIRGINIA BEACH. *Marian Manor*, 5345 Marian Ln., 23462. Tel: 804-456-5018
For a complete listing, refer to the Special Care Facilities section.

Our Lady of Perpetual Help Health Center, Inc., 4560 Princess Anne Rd., 23462-7905
For a complete listing, refer to the Special Care Facilities section.

Russell House, 900 First Colonial Rd., 23454. Tel: 804-481-0770
For a complete listing, refer to the Special Care Facilities section.

[I] HOME FOR HANDICAPPED ADULTS

RICHMOND. *St. Joseph's Villa Housing Corp.*, 8000 Brook Rd., 23227-1399. Tel: 804-553-3283; Fax: 804-553-3259
For a complete listing, refer to the Special Care Facilities section.

[J] SERVICES FOR THE DISABLED

RICHMOND. *Hollybrook I & II*. St. Joseph Villa, 7700 Brook Rd., 23229. Tel: 804-553-3283. Ms. Margaret Hill, Housing Mgr. Residents 80.

Outreach in Love. c/o Epiphany Church, 11000 Smoketree Dr., 23236. Tel: 804-794-0222. Lynda D. Heithaus, Coord. Religious education for people with disabilities.

Sean's Place, 713 N. First St., 23219. Tel: 804-344-8164. Mr. Pete Jones, Prog. Coord.

[K] SPECIALIZED SERVICES

RICHMOND. *Commonwealth Catholic Charities*, 1512 Willow Lawn Dr., 23230-0565. Tel: 804-285-5900.
E-mail: comcathric@aol.com
Web site: http://members.aol.com/COMCATHRIC/index.html
Rev. David J. Bergner, S.D.S., Exec. Dir. Satellite Offices: 820 Campbell Ave., S.W., Roanoke, 24016. Tel: 540-344-5107. Woodbrook Shopping Center, 1859-C3 Seminole Trail, Charlottesville, 22901. Tel: 804-974-6880. Connections, One Skyline Pl., Suite 1106, 5205 Leesburg Pike, Falls Church, 22041-3802. Tel: 703-820-1151. Family & Child Center, 3321 S. Crater Rd., Suite C, Petersburg, 23805. Tel: 804-862-3733. Elizabeth Ann Seton Center, 1512 Willow Lawn Dr., 23230-0565. Tel: 804-285-5987. Managed Home Care for the Elderly, 1512 Willow Lawn Dr., 23230-0565. Tel: 804-285-5900. Connections, 302 McClanahan St., S.W., Roanoke, 24014. Tel: 540-342-0411. Total Assisted 9,772.

Elizabeth Ann Seton Center, 1512 Willow Lawn Dr., 23230. Tel: 804-285-5900. Legal Title: *Catholic Charities of Richmond, Inc.* Mrs. Nikki Jones, Dir. Total Assisted 378.

CHARLOTTESVILLE. *Elizabeth Ann Seton Center*. Office, P.O. Box 6565, Richmond, 23230. Tel: 804-974-6880. Ms. Jane Hotchkiss, Dir.

VIRGINIA BEACH. *Catholic Charities of Hampton Roads, Inc.*, 4855 Princess Anne Rd., 23462. Tel: 757-467-7707; Fax: 757-495-3206. Margaret M. Robertson, Exec. Dir.
Branch Offices: 12829 Jefferson Ave., Suite 101, Newport News, 23608. Tel: 757-875-0060. 1301 Colonial Ave., Norfolk, 23517. Tel: 757-625-2568. 3804 Poplar Hill Rd., Suite A, Chesapeake, 23321. Tel: 757-484-0703. 1300 Jamestown Rd., Williamsburg, 23185. Tel: 757-253-2847. Total Assisted 4,500.

[L] MONASTERIES AND RESIDENCES OF PRIESTS AND BROTHERS

RICHMOND. *Mary Mother of the Church Abbey*, 12617 River Rd., 23233. Tel: 804-784-3508.
E-mail: bmcd@erols.com
Web site: www.benedictinehighschool.org
Benedictine Monks. Rt. Rev. Benedict R. McDermott, O.S.B.; Revs. Theophile W. Brown, O.S.B., Prior, Novice Master; Thomas C. Byrne, O.S.B.; Thomas W. Stumpf, O.S.B.; Adrian W. Harmening, O.S.B., Procurator; Donald F. Scales, O.S.B.; Augustine W. Ludwig, O.S.B.; Augustine W. Cunningham, O.S.B.; Bros. Paul Bateman, O.S.B.; Clement Carney, O.S.B.; Matthew Miller, O.S.B.; James Casey, O.S.B.; David Owen, O.S.B. Priests 8; Brothers 5.

WEST POINT. *Missionaries of the Holy Family, General Mission Office—M.S.F., Inc.*, P.O. Box 918, 23181. Tel: 804-843-2622. Rev. John Brieffies, M.S.F., Pres. & Dir.

[M] CONVENTS AND RESIDENCES FOR SISTERS

RICHMOND. *Benedictine Sisters of Virginia, St. Gertrude Convent*, 3215 Stuart Ave., 23221. Tel: 804-355-7227. Sr. Ernestine Johann. Sisters 3.

Comboni Missionary Sisters, Provincial House, 1307 Lakeside Ave., 23228. Tel: 804-266-2975; 262-8827. Sr. Ruth Bryden, C.M.S., Provincial. Sisters 22.

Daughters of Charity. St. Patrick School Community, 207 N. 26th St., 23223. Tel: 804-649-7437. Sr. Clara Pedo, Supr.

CROZET. *Cistercian Nuns of the Strict Observance (Virginia)*, 3365 Monastery Dr., 22932. Tel: 804-823-1452; Fax: 804-823-6379.
E-mail: angels@esinet.net
Web site: http://www.esinet.net/angels.html
Mother Marion Rissetto, Prioress. Legal Title: *Cistercian Nuns of the Strict Observance in Virginia, Inc. Our Lady of the Angels Monastery*. Professed 8.

NEWPORT NEWS. *Bernardine Sisters of the Third Order of St. Francis*, 8E Ridgewood Pkwy., 23602. Tel: 757-886-6398; 886-6765; Fax: 757-886-6751. Sr. Barbara Ann, Local Min. Sisters 13.

Bethlehem Monastery of the Poor Clare Nuns, 28 Harpersville Rd., 23601. Tel: 757-596-5942. Observing the Primitive Rule of St. Clare, Constitutions of the Poor Clare Federation of Mary Immaculate (strictly cloistered, solemn vows). Mother Mary Colette, Abbess. Solemnly Professed 12; Novices 1; Postulants 1. Attended by Our Lady of Mt. Carmel Church, Newport News.

NORFOLK. *Sisters Servants of the Immaculate Heart of Mary*. St. Pius X Convent, 7813 Halprin Dr., 23518. Tel: 804-587-8657. Sr. Anne Carroll, I.H.M., Supr. Sisters 4.

NORTON. *Poor Servants of the Mother of God*, P.O. Box 620, 24273. Tel: 540-679-0477; Fax: 540-679-7549. Sr. Mary Coughlan, S.M.G., Sister in charge. Sisters 6.

PETERSBURG. *Daughters of Charity*. St. Joseph Convent, 127 Franklin St., 23803-3308. Tel: 804-732-8501. Sr. Patricia Nee. Sisters 3.

PORTSMOUTH. *Sisters of Bon Secours*, 412 West Rd., 23707. Tel: 804-397-3869. Sr. Rita Thomas, Pres. Sisters 3.

ROCKVILLE. *Monastery of the Visitation Monte Maria*, 12221 Bienvenue Rd., 23146. Tel: 804-749-4885. Mother Margaret Mary McGuire, Supr. Visitation Sisters 17; Novices 3.

VIRGINIA BEACH. *Sisters Servants of I.H.M.* St. Gregory the Great Convent, 5349 Virginia Beach Blvd., 23462. Tel: 804-497-7517. Sr. Brenda Anne Query, Supr.

WILLIAMSBURG. *Sisters of Mercy*. Walsingham Academy, P.O. Box 8702, 1100 Jamestown Rd., 23187-8702. Tel: 757-229-2642. Sr. Rose Morris, R.S.M. Sisters 8.

[N] RETREAT HOUSES

RICHMOND. *The Dwelling Place*, 601 Holly Grove Ln., 23235. Tel: 804-323-3360.
Conducted by: Patricia Carreras; Audrey Stech.

Richmond Hill. Ecumenical Center, 2209 E. Grace St., 23235. Tel: 804-783-7903. Rev. Benjamin Campbell, Pastoral Dir.

HAMPTON. *Holy Family Retreat*, 1414 N. Mallory St., P.O. 3151, 23663. Tel: 757-722-3997.
E-mail: gerry15@juno.com
Rev. Gerard H. Schreiber, C.Ss.R., Supr. & Dir. Asst. Retreat Directors: Revs. Bernard J. Power, C.Ss.R.; Charles J. Brinkmann, C.Ss.R.

LYNCHBURG. *Tabor Retreat Center*, 2125 Langhorne Rd., 24501. Tel: 804-846-6475. Chris Barrett, Dir.

MONTPELIER. *Shalom House*. Retreat Center, P.O. Box 196, 23192. Tel: 804-883-6149. Ms. Catherine Cawley, Dir.

ROANOKE. *Madonna House*, 828 Campbell Ave., S.W., 24016. Tel: 540-343-8464. Ms. Linda Owen, Dir.

SMITHFIELD. *The Well*, 18047 Quiet Way, 23430. Tel: 757-255-2366. Co-Directors: Sr. Nancy Healy, S.F.C.C.; Diane Weymouth.

[O] MISCELLANEOUS

RICHMOND. *Sacred Heart Center, Inc.*, 1400 Perry St., 23224. Tel: 804-230-4399. Ms. Jeanine Harper, Exec. Dir. Neighbouring Communities Day Care, After School Care, Adult Education and Social Services.

St. Francis Home of Richmond Foundation, Ltd., 2511 Wise St., 23224. Provides grants to subsidize cost of care for aged, infirm and disabled residents of limited means.

Transitional Housing. Flagler Home-St. Joseph's Villa, 8000 Brook Rd., 23227-1399. Rebecca Lee, Dir. Women & Children in residence 70.

NEWPORT NEWS. *Family Focus*. (Community Churches sites for day and evening programs.), c/o Bernardine Sisters, 8E Ridgewood Pkwy., 23602.

NORFOLK. *Catholic Worker Hospitality House*, 1321 W. 38th St., 23508. Tel: 804-423-5420. Coordinators: Steve Baggerly; Kim Williams.

PORTSMOUTH. *Catholic Elementary Education Foundation of Hampton Roads*, 2301 Oregon Ave., 23701. Sr. Carol Durkin, Chm.

Maryview Psychiatric Hospital, 3636 High St., 23707. Allan D. Erbe, Admin. Beds 54.

ROANOKE. *Catholic Historical Society of the Roanoke Valley*. (Museum & religious goods), 402 W. Campbell Ave., 24016. Tel: 504-982-0152. Mary C. Maier, Contact.

St. Francis House, Inc., P.O. Box 2215, 24009. Tel: 540-345-9090. Eileen Stone, Dir. Food Distribution and Social Services.

RELIGIOUS INSTITUTES OF MEN REPRESENTED IN THE DIOCESE

For further details refer to the corresponding bracketed number in the Religious Institutes of Men or Women section.

[0200]—*Benedictine Monks*. (Latrobe, PA).—O.S.B.
[1350]—*Brothers of St. Francis Xavier*.—C.F.X.
[0630]—*Congregation of the Missionaries of the Holy Family*.—M.S.F.
[0570]—*The Glenmary Home Missioners*.—Glmy.
[0650]—*Holy Ghost Fathers*.—C.S.Sp.
[0690]—*Jesuits Fathers and Brothers*.—S.J.
[0430]—*Order of Preachers (Dominicans)*. (Province of St. Joseph).—O.P.
[1070]—*Redemptorist Fathers*. (Baltimore Prov.).—C.SS.R.

RELIGIOUS INSTITUTES OF WOMEN REPRESENTED IN THE DIOCESE

[0230]—*Benedictine Sisters of Pontifical Jurisdiction*.—O.S.B.
[1810]—*Bernardine Sisters of the Third Order of St. Francis*.—O.S.F.
[0670]—*Cistercian Nuns of the Strict Observance*.—O.C.S.O.
[0690]—*Comboni Missionary Sisters*.—C.M.S.
[0270]—*Congregation of Bon Secours*.—C.B.S.
[1070-09]—*Congregation of St. Catherine of Siena, Racine*.—O.P.
[1070-07]—*Congregation of St. Cecelia, Nashville*.—O.P.
[1070-02]—*Congregation of St. Mary of the Springs, Columbus*.—O.P.
[1070-13]—*Congregation of the Most Holy Rosary, Adrian*.—O.P.
[1070-06]—*Congregation of the Most Holy Rosary, Newburg*.—O.P.
[3830-05]—*Congregation of the Sisters of St. Joseph of Brentwood, NY*.—C.S.J.
[1920]—*Congregation of the Sisters of the Holy Cross*.—C.S.C.
[0760]—*Daughters of Charity of St. Vincent de Paul*.—D.C.
[0820]—*Daughters of the Holy Spirit*.—D.H.S.
[0960]—*Daughters of Wisdom*.—D.W.
[1180]—*The Franciscan Sisters*.—O.S.F.
[1840]—*Grey Nuns of the Sacred Heart*.—G.N.S.H.
[2575]—*Institute of the Sisters of Mercy of the Americas*.—R.S.M.
[2340]—*Little Sisters of the Poor*.—L.S.P.
[2490]—*Medical Mission Sisters*.—S.C.M.M.
[2480]—*Medical Missionaries of Mary*.—M.M.M.
[2720]—*Mission Helpers of the Sacred Heart*.—M.H.S.H.
[2790]—*Missionary Servants of the Most Blessed Trinity*.—M.S.B.T.
[3760]—*Order of St. Clare*.—P.C.C.
[3640]—*Poor Servants of the Mother of God*.—S.M.G.
[3465]—*Religious of the Sacred Heart of Mary*. (Eastern American Prov.).—R.S.H.M.
[2970]—*School Sisters of Notre Dame*.—S.S.N.D.
[1070-03]—*Sinsinawa Dominican Congregation of the Most Holy Rosary*.—O.P.
[]—*Sisters for Christian Community*.—S.F.C.C.
[0500]—*Sisters of Charity of Nazareth*.—S.C.N.
[0590]—*Sisters of Charity of St. Elizabeth, Convent Station*.—S.C.
[0990]—*Sisters of Divine Providence*. (Our Lady of Divine Providence Prov.).—C.D.P.
[2990]—*Sisters of Notre Dame*.—S.N.D.
[3000]—*Sisters of Notre Dame de Namur*.—S.N.D.deN.
[3950]—*Sisters of Saint Mary of Namur*.—S.S.M.N.
[1530]—*Sisters of St. Francis of the Congregation of Our Lady of Lourdes, Sylvania, Ohio*.—O.S.F.
[3840]—*Sisters of St. Joseph of Carondelet*.—C.S.J.
[2980]—*Sisters of the Congregation of Notre Dame*.—C.N.D.
[1990]—*Sisters of the Holy Names of Jesus and Mary*.—S.N.J.M.
[3260]—*Sisters of the Precious Blood*.—C.P.P.S.
[2170]—*Sisters, Servants of the Immaculate Heart of Mary*. (Immaculata, PA).—I.H.M.
[4110]—*Ursuline Nuns (Roman Union)*. (Eastern Prov.).—O.S.U.
[4130]—*Ursuline Sisters of the Congregation of Tildonk, Belgium*.—O.S.U.
[4190]—*Visitation Nuns*.—V.H.M.

DIOCESAN CEMETERIES

RICHMOND. *Holy Cross*, First Ave. & Daniels St., 23222. Tel: 804-321-5936.

Mount Calvary, 1400 S. Randolph St., 23220. Tel: 804-355-5271.

LYNCHBURG. *Holy Cross*, Bedford Ave. Mailing Address: 710 Clay St., 24504. Tel: 804-846-5245.

NORFOLK. *St. Mary's*, 722 E. 30th St., 23504. Tel: 804-627-2874.

PORTSMOUTH. *Portsmouth Catholic*, Elm Ave. & Portsmouth Blvd. Mailing Address: P.O. Box 155, 23705. Tel: 804-488-1723.

ROANOKE. *St. Andrew*, 3601 Salem Tpke., N.W., 24017. Tel: 703-342-9180.

NECROLOGY

† Jenkins, Paul D., Hopewell, VA, St. James. —Died Jan. 8, 1997.

† Warner, J. Anthony, Richmond, VA, Our Lady of Lourdes. —Died May 8, 1997.

Diocese of Rochester

(Dioecesis Roffensis)

Most Reverend

MATTHEW H. CLARK, D.D.

Bishop of Rochester; ordained December 19, 1962; appointed Bishop of Rochester April 23, 1979; consecrated May 27, 1979; installed June 26, 1979. *Res., 1150 Buffalo Rd., Rochester, NY, 14624.*

Most Reverend

DENNIS W. HICKEY, D.D., V.G.

Retired Auxiliary Bishop of Rochester; ordained June 7, 1941; appointed Titular Bishop of Rusuccuru and Auxiliary January 5, 1968; consecrated March 14, 1968; retired December 11, 1989. *Res., 415 Ames St., Rochester, NY, 14611.*

Most Reverend

JOSEPH L. HOGAN, S.T.D., D.D.

Retired Bishop of Rochester; ordained June 6, 1942; appointed Bishop of Rochester October 6, 1969; consecrated November 28, 1969; installed November 28, 1969; retired November 28, 1978. *Res., 123 Maple Ave., Victor, NY, 14564.*

ESTABLISHED MARCH 3, 1868.

Square Miles 7,107.

Comprises the Counties of Monroe, Livingston, Wayne, Ontario, Seneca, Cayuga, Yates, Steuben, Chemung, Tioga, Schuyler and Tompkins in the State of New York.

For legal titles of parishes and diocesan institutions, consult the Pastoral Center.

Legal Title of Diocese: The Diocese of Rochester.

Pastoral Center: 1150 Buffalo Rd., Rochester, NY, 14624-1890. Tel.: 716-328-3210; 800-388-7177; Fax: 716-328-3149.

E-mail address: dor@mail-frontiernet.net

STATISTICAL OVERVIEW

Personnel	
Bishop	1
Retired Bishops	2
Abbots	1
Priests: Diocesan Active in Diocese	169
Priests: Active Outside Diocese	6
Priests: Diocesan in Foreign Missions	1
Priests: Retired, Sick or Absent	94
Number of Diocesan Priests	270
Religious Priests in Diocese	62
Extern Priests in Diocese	12
Ordinations:	
Diocesan Priests	1
Transitional Deacons	2
Permanent Deacons	5
Permanent Deacons in Diocese	108
Total Brothers	32
Total Sisters	650
Parishes	
Parishes	161
With Resident Pastor:	
Resident Diocesan Priests	143
Resident Religious Priests	5
Without Resident Pastor:	
Administered by Priests	8
Administered by Permanent Deacons	2
Administered by Women Religious	2
Administered by Lay People	1
Missions	19
Closed Parishes	1
Professional Ministry Personnel:	
Sisters	73
Lay Ministers	318
Welfare	
Catholic Hospitals	3
Total Assisted	720,000
Health Care Centers	4
Total Assisted	1,500
Homes for the Aged	4
Total Assisted	1,500
Residential Care of Children	1
Total Assisted	400
Specialized Homes	7
Total Assisted	500
Special Centers for Social Services	35
Total Assisted	80,000
Residential Care of Disabled	10
Total Assisted	100
Educational	
Seminaries, Diocesan	1
Students from This Diocese	8
Diocesan Students in Other Seminaries	8
Total Seminarians	16
High Schools, Private	8
Total Students	3,509
Elementary Schools, Diocesan and Parish	50
Total Students	13,360
Elementary Schools, Private	5
Total Students	821
Non-residential Schools for the Disabled	1
Total Students	104
Catechesis/Religious Education:	
High School Students	3,651
Elementary Students	31,464
Total Students Under Catholic Instruction	52,925
Teachers in the Diocese:	
Priests	18
Brothers	14
Sisters	17
Lay Teachers	1,256
Vital Statistics	
Receptions into the Church:	
Infant Baptism Totals	5,624
Adult Baptism Totals	289
Received into Full Communion	645
First Communions	5,321
Confirmations	4,494
Marriages:	
Catholic	1,298
Interfaith	664
Total Marriages	1,962
Deaths	4,258
Total Catholic Population	370,162
Total Population	1,481,007

Former Bishops—Rt. Rev. BERNARD J. MCQUAID, D.D., cons. July 12, 1868; died Jan. 18, 1909.—Most Rev. THOMAS F. HICKEY, D.D., ord. March 25, 1884; cons. May 24, 1905; succeeded to the See, Jan. 18, 1909; appt. assistant at the Pontifical Throne, May 4, 1925 made Archbishop of the Titular See of Viminacium, Oct. 30, 1928; died Dec. 10, 1940.—Most Rev. JOHN FRANCIS O'HERN, D.D., ord. Feb. 17, 1901; appt. Bishop of Rochester, Jan. 8, 1929; cons. March 19, 1929; died May 22, 1933.—His Eminence EDWARD CARDINAL MOONEY, appt. Aug. 28, 1922; transferred to Detroit, May 26, 1937; installed Archbishop of Detroit, Aug. 3, 1937; created Cardinal, Feb. 18, 1946; died Oct. 25, 1958.—Most Rev. JAMES E. KEARNEY, D.D., ord. Sept. 19, 1908; appt. Bishop of Salt Lake, Utah, July 1, 1932; cons. Oct. 28, 1932; transferred to Rochester, July 31, 1937; installed Nov. 11, 1937; retired Oct. 26, 1966; died Jan. 12, 1977.—Most Rev. FULTON J. SHEEN, D.D., ord. Sept. 30, 1919; appt. Titular Bishop of Cesariana and Auxiliary of New York, May 28, 1951; cons. June 11, 1951; appt. to Rochester, Oct. 26, 1966; installed Dec. 15, 1966; resigned Oct. 15, 1969; appt. Titular Archbishop of Newport; died Dec. 9, 1979.

Pastoral Office Administration

Pastoral Center—1150 Buffalo Rd., Rochester, 14624-1890. Tel: 716-328-3210; 800-388-7177 (Toll Free within Diocese); Fax: 716-328-3149.

Vicar General and Pastoral Office Moderator—Rev. JOHN M. MULLIGAN.

Chancellor—Rev. KEVIN E. MCKENNA, J.C.D.

Judicial Vicar—Rev. LOUIS A. SIRIANNI, J.C.L.

Secretaries to the Bishop—Rev. TIMOTHY T. BROWN; Ms. JANIS CAMERON.

Diocesan Consultors—Most Rev. DENNIS W. HICKEY, D.D., V.G.; Revs. JOHN M. MULLIGAN, V.G.; BRIAN COOL; JACK PHILIPPS; ROBERT RING; GERRY APPELBY; KEVIN E. MCKENNA, J.C.D.; DANIEL HOLLAND.

Synod Office—Ms. KATHLEEN M. CANNON, Dir.

Consultative Bodies—

Bishop's Stewardship Council—Presidents: Most Rev. MATTHEW H. CLARK; Mr. JOSEPH BELL; Dr. KATHERINE KEOUGH; Mr. JAMES RYAN; Sr. SHEILA STEVENSON; Rev. JOHN MULLIGAN, V.G.; Mr. MATTHEW AUGUSTINE; Mr. R. CARLOS CARBALLADA; Mr. WILLIAM CARPENTER; Mr. JOSE CORONAS; Rev. PETER DECKMAN; Mr. PATRICK FOX; Mr. CUTBERTO GARZA; Mr. JOHN GOUGH; Ms. BARBARA KELLEY; Mr. LAURENCE KIRWIN; Ms. GERMAINE KNAPP; Mr. LOUIS LANGIE, JR.; Mr. THOMAS MCDERMOTT; Ms. CONSTANCE MITCHELL; Ms. JANE NAPIER; Mr. DAVID PEARTREE, ESQ.; Rev. JOHN PHILIPPS; Sr.

ROSEMARY ST. PETER, S.S.J.; Sr. PATRICIA SCHOELLES, S.S.J.; Ms. JOYCE SINICROPI; JUDY TOYER, ESQ.; SALLY TRUE, ESQ.; Rev. ROBERT WERTH; Ms. KATHLEEN WHELEHAN.

Priests' Council—Rev. JACK PHILIPPS, Chm.

Regional Coordinator—Rev. TIMOTHY BROWN, Liaison.

Commission of Women—GLORIA ULTERINO, Liaison.

Clergy Relief Society—Most Rev. MATTHEW H. CLARK, D.D., Pres.; Revs. ROBERT KRECKEL, Vice Pres. THOMAS H. WHEELAND, Treas. JOHN FIRPO, Sec. RICHARD R. BRICKLER; JOHN H. HAYES; CHARLIE MANNING; WILLIAM B. LEONE; GENE SWEENEY; RAY BOOTH.

"Catholic Courier"—Tel: 716-328-4340. KAREN FRANZ, Gen. Mgr. & Editor Board of Directors: Most Rev. MATTHEW H. CLARK, Pres.; Rev. JOHN MULLIGAN, Vicar General & V.P.; Rev. KEVIN E. MCKENNA, J.C.D., Sec.; Mr. WILLIAM KEDLEY, Treas.; Most Rev. DENNIS W. HICKEY; Revs. JOHN FORNI; WILLIAM SPILLY; Mr. MARTIN MOLL; Mrs. DELORES LOFTUS; Mrs. BARBARA KILEY; Mr. THOMAS FLYNN; Sr. ROBERTA TIERNEY, S.S.N.D.; Mr. RICHARD HARE; Ms. ELLEN DEBUONO; Mr. LEON SAWYKO.

Diocesan Missions Office (Propagation Of The Faith)—Rev. ROBERT C. BRADLER. Tel: 716-436-9200. World and Diocesan Missions.

Internal Support Ministries

Office of Development—

Director of Development—Mr. MARK S. SEEBERG.

Director of Major Gifts—Mrs. MARY L. CONSLER.

Director of Annual Giving—Mr. THOMAS C. D'AGOSTINO.

Administrative Assistant—Mrs. NANCY A. NASH.

Donor Relations Coordinator—Mrs. MICHELE GAMET.

Office of Communications—

Director of Communications—Ms. ELIZABETH BROWN.

Communications Assistant—CATHY RAUSCH.

Department of Financial Services—

Chief Financial Officer—Mr. JAMES M. RINEFIERD.

Controller—Mr. PAUL VISCA.

Manager of Buildings and Properties—Mr. ERIC PATCHKE.

Diocesan Building Commission—ERIC PATCHKE, Sec. DAVID ANDREWS; JOSEPH KIZINSKI; WILLARD STEANE; Sr. ESTELLE MARTIN, R.S.M.; WILLIAM MATTHEWS; Rev. WILLIAM J. AMANN; Ms. SANDY MCGREEVY; Rev. JOHN V. ROSSE.

Holy Sepulchre Cemetery—Most Rev. MATTHEW H. CLARK, D.D., Pres.; Rev. PETER T. BAYER, Vice Pres., Treas. & Sec.; Mr. E. ROBERT VOGT, Dir. & Asst. Treas.; Mr. MARTIN BIRMINGHAM; Mr. ALFRED M. HALLENBECK; Mr. WILLIAM MCGINN; Sr. MARIE MICHELLE PEARTREE, S.S.J.; Mr. JAMES M. RINEFIERD; Mr. LARRY O. STID; Mrs. MICHAEL TOMAINO; Rev. THOMAS WHEELAND.

Information Systems And Research—

Diocean Director—Ms. JOAN A. ZAIA.

AS/400 Coordinator—Mrs. LYNNE SUORSA.

Parish Computer Coordinator—Mr. TOM VEEDER; MAUREEN EASTERLY.

Department of Legal Services—

Director—Rev. KEVIN E. MCKENNA, J.C.D., Chancellor.

Secretary—Mrs. BEVERLY KELLY.

Due Process—

Conciliation Board—Mr. RICHARD PELINO, *18 Nettlecreek Rd., Fairport, 14450.* Tel: 716-223-2857.

Diocesan Archives—Rev. WILLIAM GRAF, Dir. Archival Services, *219 Stenson St., Rochester, 14606.* Tel: 716-458-6079. Rev. ROBERT F. MCNAMARA, Archivist, *4536 St. Paul Blvd., Rochester, 14617.* Tel: 716-338-1602. Sr. CONNIE DERBY, R.S.M., Exec. Asst., *1150 Buffalo Rd., Rochester, 14624.* Tel: 716-328-3210.

External Ministries

Faith Development Ministry—Sr. MARY ANN BINSACK, R.S.M., Dir.

Catholic Schools Office—Mr. TIMOTHY W. DWYER, Supt., Schools.

Assistant Superintendent of Business and Finance—Mr. DAVID MEISENZAHL.

Assistant Superintendents—Sr. PATRICIA CARROLL, S.S.J., Asst. Supt., Government Svcs & Admin.; Sr. VIRGINIA STEINWACHS, S.S.J., Asst. Supt., Human Resources; Sr. MARGARET MANCUSO, S.S.J., Asst. Supt., Curriculum & Instruction; Ms. MARY CAFFREY, Asst. Supt., Assessment & Staff Devel.; Sr. ANNE GUERIN, S.S.J., Asst. Supt., School Advancement; Sr. ELAINE ENGERT, S.S.J., Asst. Supt., WIN Programs.

Department of Evangelization and Catechesis—Ms. MARIBETH MANCINI, Dir.

Coordinator for Sacramental Catechesis—Mrs. BARBARA CARROLL.

Catechetical Consultant—Mrs. MARY BRITTON.

AV Resource Librarian—Mrs. MARY ELLEN FITZGIBBONS.

Coordinator of Youth Ministry—MICHAEL THEISEN.

Coordinator of Young Adult, Adult & Family Faith Formation—KAREN RINEFIERD.

Parish Support Ministries—

Director—Ms. KATHLEEN M. CANNON. Tel: 716-328-3228, Ext. 387 TDD (English). Tel: 716-328-3210 (Spanish).

Office Of Black Ministries—Ms. JACQUELYN DOBSON, Dir.

Office of Spanish Apostolate—Bro. LUIS RUBERTE, H.Ch., Dir., Field Office: *873 N. Clinton Ave., Rochester, 14605.* Tel: 716-232-4844.

Hispanic Pastoral Institute—Bro. LUIS RUBERTE, Dir.

Urban Subsidy Program—Ms. JACQUELYN DOBSON.

Office of Asian Pacific Ministry—Ms. HA NGUYEN.

Office of Pastoral Council Formation—Deacon CLAUDE LESTER.

Tribunal—Revs. LOUIS A. SIRIANNI, M.Div., J.C.L., Judicial Vicar; KEVIN E. MCKENNA, J.C.D., Promoter of Justice; Mr. JOHN SKVORAK, J.C.L., Judge; Sr. DOROTHY SCHLUETER, R.S.M., Certified Clinical Psychologist; Ms. LINDA SARACENI, Sec.

Case Instructors—Ms. PATRICIA A. KEOUGH; Deacon GEORGE W. BURNETT.

Pro-Synodal Judges—Revs. R. RICHARD BRICKLER; ROBERT COLLINS; DONALD J. CURTISS, J.C.L.; RONALD GAESSER; WILLIAM GRAF, D.Min.; JOHN S. HAYES; JOHN LYNCH; ROBERT F. O'NEILL, M.Ch.A., M.Div.

Defenders of the Bond—Revs. WILLIAM J. GORDINIER; M. GERARD HAFNER; WILLIAM LUM.

Office Of Ecumenical And Interreligious Affairs—Deacon BRIAN MCNULTY.

Commission for Ecumenical and Interreligious Affairs—Deacon BRIAN MCNULTY.

Commission on Christian/Jewish Relations—Rev. JOSEPH P. BRENNAN; Deacon BRIAN MCNULTY.

Director Office of Liturgy—Ms. JOAN WORKMASTER; Ms. VIRGINIA MILLER, Assoc. Dir.

Liturgical Commission—Sr. CHRIS J. TREICHEL, O.S.F., Chm. CHARLES DISPENZA, Vice Chm.; Ms. JOAN WORKMASTER, Exec. Sec.; Sr. ESTELLE MARTIN, R.S.M., Environment & Art Rep.; Rev. DANIEL MCMULLIN, Music Rep.

Catholic Charities of the Diocese of Rochester—JACK BALINSKY, Exec. Dir. PATRICK FOX, Chm., Board of Directors, *1150 Buffalo Rd., Rochester, 14624.* Tel: 716-328-3210.

Campaign for Human Development—JACK BALINSKY.

Catholic Relief Services—JUDY TAYLOR.

Communications Manager—JUDY TAYLOR.

Consistent Life Ethic Coordinator—SUZANNE SCHNITTMAN.

Catholic Charities Regional Offices—

Catholic Charities Community and Residential Services—PAUL T. PICKERING, Exec. Dir., *1945 E. Ridge Rd., Ste. 24, Rochester, 14622.* Tel: 716-339-9800.

Administrative Services—BARBARA POLING, Dir.

Community Services—Vacant.

Finances—JAMES CROWLEY, Dir.

Residential Services—KATHLEEN TERMINE, Dir.

AIDS Community Follow-up Program—JANE HALLINEN, Dir.

Community Awareness Program—LYN ZYLA.

Catholic Family Center—Ms. CAROLYN A. PORTANOVA, Pres. & CEO; Ms. JUDITH AZOFF, VP, Admin. Svcs. RITA AUGUSTINE, VP, Prog. Svcs. BEVERLY LUDKE, VP, Human Resources; BARBARA MURPHY, VP, Finance; ANTHONY LAPAGLIE, Chm., Regl. Board of Directors, All offices at: *25 Franklin St., Rochester, 14604.* Tel: 716-546-7220. unless otherwise indicated.

Departments of Catholic Family Center—

Catholic Youth Organization (CYO)—DWAYNE MAHONEY, Dir. Tel: 716-262-7008.

Children and Family Services—KAREN EMERTON, Dir. Tel: 716-262-7100.

Elder Services—IRENE COVENY, Dir. Tel: 716-262-7058.

Employee Assistance & Counseling—WENDY STRAUSS, Dir. Tel: 716-262-7034.

Homeless & Housing Services—MAUREEN SCHNORR, Dir. Tel: 716-463-5452. NORMAN ROBERTS. Tel: 716-423-9590.

Office of Social Policy & Research—JOE KENNEY, Dir. Tel: 716-262-7021.

Refugee and Immigration Services—EDWARD A. PATANE, Dir. Tel: 716-262-7082.

Restart Substance Abuse Services—CARL A. HATCH, Dir. Tel: 716-546-3046.

Wayne County—M. JOSH MCCROSSEN, Dir. Tel: 315-331-4867.

Finger Lakes Social Ministries—Serving Yates, Ontario, Wayne, Seneca and Cayuga Counties. GIOVINA CAROSCIO, Exec. Dir. SCARLETT EMERSON, Parish and Community Devel. Coord. JANE SORENSON, Prog. Devel. Dir. ALMA KUNES, Prog. Coord. BARRY ROACH, Chm., Regl. Board of Directors, Main office: *One Franklin Sq., Geneva, 14456.* Tel: 315-789-2686., Satellite offices at: *29 William St., Auburn, 13021.* Tel: 315-252-0018., *4440 E. Ridge Rd., Williamson, 14589.* Tel: 315-589-2600.

Catholic Charities of the Southern Tier—Serving Chemung, Schuyler, Steuben, Tompkins and Tioga Counties. ANTHONY BARBARO, Exec. Dir. JOE CAPARULO, Chm., Board of Directors, All offices at: *1700 College Ave., Elmira, 14901.* Tel: 607-734-9784.

Departments of Catholic Charities of the Southern Tier—

Emergency Services—CINDY SMITH, Dir. Tel: 607-734-4898.

Food Bank of the Southern Tier—JOHN P. FARRER, Dir. Tel: 607-796-6061.

Gateways Community Living Program—JEFF EATON, Dir. Tel: 607-733-8387.

Justice and Peace—KATHLEEN DUBEL, Dir. Tel: 607-734-5893.

Tioga Teens & Family Outreach—JOE FEDEROWICZ, Dir. Tel: 607-687-8607.

Transitions Counseling—AMY DENENBERG, Dir. Tel: 607-936-4695.

Catholic Charities of Livingston County—TIM MCMAHON, M.S.W., Exec. Dir. WILLIAM DERBY, Ph.D, Pres., Regl. Board of Directors, *10 Clinton St., Mt. Morris, 14510.* Tel: 716-658-4466.

Departments of Catholic Charities of Livingston County—

Livingston County Rural Outreach—Sr. NANCY O'BRIEN, Dir.

Community of Caring—Vacant.

Bishop Sheen Ecumenical Housing Foundation—ALLYNN SMITH, Exec. Dir. SHARON CONHEADY, Pres., Board of Directors, *835 East Ave., Rochester, 14607.* Tel: 716-461-4263.

Camp Stella Maris—MATTHEW FLANIGAN, Exec. Dir. JAY TRAVERS, Pres., Board of Directors, *3052 E. Lake Rd., Livonia, 14487.* Tel: 716-346-2243; 346-2251.

DePaul Mental Health Services, Inc.—MARK H. FULLER, Exec. Dir. ELLEN KREMER, Pres., Board of Directors, *1931 Buffalo Rd., Rochester, 14624.* Tel: 716-426-8000.

Kinship Family and Youth Services, Inc.—JOSEPH WEIDER, Exec. Dir. SARAH HEINEMAN, Pres., Board of Directors, *204 Main St., Hornell, 14843.* Tel: 607-324-0909.

Mercy Center with the Aging—Sr. ANNE MALOY, R.S.M., M.S.W., Dir.; Sr. GRATIA L'ESPERANCE, R.S.M., M.Div., Asst. Dir., *327 Warrington Dr., Rochester, 14618-1536.* Tel: 716-244-5190.

Providence Housing Development Corporation—MAGGIE BRINGEWATT, Exec. Dir. JACK BALINSKY, Pres., Board of Directors, *1150 Buffalo Rd., Rochester, 14624.* Tel: 716-328-3210.

St. Ann's Home and The Heritage—Ms. BETTY MULLIN, Pres. ANTHONY J. MALONE, P.E., Pres., Board of Directors, *1500 Portland Ave., Rochester, 14621.* Tel: 716-342-1700.

St. Joseph's Villa—M. JUDITH MCKAY, Exec. Dir. JOHN HORVATH, Pres., Board of Directors, *3300 Dewey Ave., Rochester, 14616.* Tel: 716-865-1550.

Human Resources—Mr. WILLIAM OLSEN, Dir.

Department of Recruitment Services—Mrs. BARBARA PEDEVILLE.

Department of Priest Personnel—Rev. ROBERT P. RING, Dir.

Coordinator of Clergy Services—Mrs. SANDRA GROCKI.

Priests' Personnel Board—Revs. ROBERT P. RING, Chm. PETER T. BAYER; MICHAEL F. CONBOY; DAVID J. FARAONE; R. WILLIAM E. GRAF; THOMAS P. MULL; JOHN V. ROSSE.

Intern Process—Rev. EDWARD L. PALUMBOS, Dir., *3003 Dewey Ave., Rochester, 14616.* Tel: 716-663-3230.

Ministry To Priests—Rev. R. RICHARD BRICKLER, *330 Gregory St., Rochester, 14620.* Tel: 473-4271.

Priests' Retirement Committee—Revs. ROBERT P. RING; ELMER W. HEINDL; Most Rev. DENNIS W. HICKEY; Revs. EUGENE MCFARLAND; FRANCIS H. VOGT; Mrs. SANDRA GROCKI.

Priests' Sabbatical Committee—Mrs. JUDITH ANN KOLLAR, Chm.; Revs. R. RICHARD BRICKLER; PETER A. DECKMAN; KEVIN E. MCKENNA, J.C.D.; ROBERT P. RING; GEORGE WIANT.

Office Of Vocations—Rev. JOHN A. DESOCIO, Dir., Becket Hall: *314 Gregory St., Rochester, 14620.* Tel: 716-461-2890.

Office Of Seminarians—Rev. JOHN A. DESOCIO, Dir., Becket Hall: *314 Gregory St., Rochester, 14620.* Tel: 716-461-2890.

Vicar for Religious—Vacant.

Deacon Personnel—Deacon THOMAS CASS, Dir.

CLERGY, PARISHES, MISSIONS AND PAROCHIAL SCHOOLS

METROPOLITAN ROCHESTER
(Monroe County)

1—SACRED HEART CATHEDRAL (1910), Most Rev. Matthew H. Clark, D.D.; Revs. Thomas P. Mull; Timothy T. Brown.
Res., 296 Flower City Pk., 14615. Tel: 716-254-3221; Fax: 716-254-8970.
School—Tel: 716-458-8088; Fax: 716-458-7155. Sr. M. Stephanine Riley, S.S.J., Prin.
Lay Teachers 21; Students 421; Preschool 83.
Catechesis/Religious Programs—Mrs. Patricia DiFabio, D.R.E.
Students 200.
Convent—287 Flower City Pk., 14615. Tel: 716-254-5048.

2—ST. AMBROSE (1921), Rev. Michael J. Schramel; Nancy Giordano, Pastoral Assoc.
Res., 25 Empire Blvd., 14609. Tel: 716-288-5000; Fax: 716-654-7658.
School—Tel: 716-288-0580. Rebecca Maloney, Prin.
Lay Teachers 25; Students 424.
Catechesis/Religious Programs—Tel: 716-288-1620. Mary Kay Oberst, D.R.E.
Students 334.
Convent—61 Waldo Ave., 14609. Tel: 716-288-9149.

3—ST. ANDREW (1914), Rev. Timothy E. Horan; Deacon William Schmitz; Sr. Anne Marie Lennon, R.S.M., Pastoral Assoc. In res., Rev. Robert Donovan.
Res., 923 Portland Ave., 14621. Tel: 716-342-8686.
School—Tel: 716-467-9201; Fax: 716-467-4191. Norman Fagnan, Prin.
Lay Teachers 10; Students 254.
Catechesis/Religious Programs—Tel: 718-342-6665. Sr. Lucille Nalbone, M.P.F., D.R.E.
Students 34.

4—ST. ANNE (1930), Rev. Frank E. Lioi. In res., Revs. Joseph M. Sasso; Thomas J. Hoctor; Gary L. Tyman; James R. Cosgrove.
Res., 1600 Mt. Hope Ave., 14620-4598. Tel: 716-271-3260; Fax: 716-271-7160.
Catechesis/Religious Programs—Students 59.

5—CHURCH OF THE ANNUNCIATION (1917) (Italian), Rev. Robert F. O'Neill; Deacon Victor Yanaitis.
Res., 1754 Norton St., 14609. Tel: 716-544-1050.
Catechesis/Religious Programs—Students 50.

6—ST. ANTHONY OF PADUA (1906) (Italian-Vietnamese), Revs. Paul J. Tomasso; Daniel McMullin; Louis Nhien, Vietnamese Ministry.
Res., 60 Lorimer St., 14608. Tel: 716-458-1180.

7—ST. AUGUSTINE (1898). Merged with Our Lady of Good Counsel and St. Monica to form Roman Catholic Community of the 19th Ward.
Res., 410 Chili Ave., 14611. Tel: 716-328-2442.

8—BLESSED SACRAMENT (1902), Rev. Bruce F. Ammering. In res., Rev. George Norton.
Res., 259 Rutgers St., 14607. Tel: 716-271-7240; Fax: 716-442-7517 (call first).
Catechesis/Religious Programs—Deacon David Paluskiewicz, D.R.E.
Students 58.

9—ST. BONIFACE (1860) (German), Rev. R. Richard Brickler.
Res., 330 Gregory St., 14620. Tel: 716-473-4271.
School—(Grades PreK-6). Tel: 716-271-6370. Sr. Mary Smith, S.S.N.D., Prin.
School Sisters of Notre Dame 2; Lay Teachers 12; Students 181.
Catechesis/Religious Programs—Students 55.

10—ST. BRIDGET (1854), Rev. Anthony P. Mugavero; Deacon Charles R. Dispenza.
Res., 8 Mark St., 14605.
Church—14 Mark St., 14605. Tel: 716-454-4236; Fax: 716-454-0835.
Catechesis/Religious Programs—Students 38.

11—ST. CECILIA (1949), Rev. Walter F. Cushing; Sr. Marie Therese S.S.N.D., Pastoral Assoc.
Res., 2732 Culver Rd., 14622. Tel: 716-467-4286; Fax: 716-544-8889. [CEM]
Catechesis/Religious Programs—Tel: 716-338-1051.
Students 180.

12—ST. CHARLES BORROMEO (1925), Revs. Edward L. Palumbos; Douglas Della Pietra; Francis E. Blighton. In res., Rev. Elmer W. Heindl.
Res., 3003 Dewey Ave., 14616. Tel: 716-663-3230; Fax: 716-663-8055.
School—64 Maiden Ln., 14616. Tel: 716-663-1220.
Students 305.
Catechesis/Religious Programs—Tel: 716-663-8000. Margaret A. Gray, D.R.E.
Students 231.

13—CHRIST THE KING (1955), Revs. Robert B. Hale, C.S.B.; Joseph A. Trovato, C.S.B.; Timothy J. Fitzgerald, C.S.B.
Res., 445 Kings Hwy., 14617. Tel: 716-266-1288; Fax: 716-266-1074.
School—Tel: 716-467-8730. Colleen D'Hondt, Prin.
Sisters of St. Joseph 1; Lay Teachers 19; Students 260; Preschool 55.
Catechesis/Religious Programs—Tel: 716-338-1146. Mrs. Mary Ann Obark, D.R.E.
Lay Teachers 25; Students 405.

14—CORPUS CHRISTI (1888), Revs. James B. Callan, Admin.; Enrique Cadena (Mexico); Mary Ramerman, Pastoral Assoc.
Res., 80 Prince St., 14605. Tel: 716-325-2424; Fax: 716-262-3576.
Church—864 Main St. E., 14605.
Catechesis/Religious Programs—Tel: 716-232-3032; Fax: 716-262-3576. Mimi Youngman, D.R.E.
Students 510.

15—ST. FRANCIS ASSISI (1929) (Spanish-Italian), Revs. Paul J. Tomasso; Daniel McMullin; Deacons Carlos Vargas; Thomas Phillips.
Res., 77 Whitney St., 14611. Tel: 716-436-6693.
Catechesis/Religious Programs—Students 68.

16—ST. FRANCIS XAVIER. (Canonically merged in 1985 and now known as Holy Redeemer-St. Francis Xavier). All inquiries should be directed to the listed address: 34 Teresa St., 14605-1696.

17—ST. GEORGE (1907) (Lithuanian), Rev. Charles L. Mockevicius.
Res., 545 Hudson Ave., 14605. Tel: 716-232-4111.

18—GUARDIAN ANGELS (1960), Mr. Dean Condon, Pastoral Admin.; Deacon Anthony Mercadel; Ms. Charlene Gabriel, Pastoral Assoc.
Res., 2061 E. Henrietta Rd., 14623. Tel: 716-334-1412; Fax: 716-334-7145.
Diocesan Child Care and Preschool—Tel: 716-334-7550.
Lay Teachers 3; Students 91.
Catechesis/Religious Programs—Tel: 716-334-6412. Ms. Gerry McLaughlin, D.R.E.
Students 200.

19—ST. HELEN (1940), Rev. John A. Firpo; Deacons Christopher Fisher; Richard Schuler, Pastoral Assoc. In res., Rev. Kevin E. McKenna, Chancellor.
Res., 310 Hinchey Rd., 14624. Tel: 716-235-1210; Fax: 716-235-2417.
School—Quadrant School, 150 Lettington Dr., 14624. Tel: 716-235-2391. Carol Robinson, Prin.
Lay Teachers 17; Students 285.
Catechesis/Religious Programs—Tel: 716-235-2407. Patricia Flass, S.S.J., D.R.E.
Students 149.

20—HOLY APOSTLES (1884), Revs. Paul J. Tomasso; Daniel McMullin.
Res., 7 Austin St., 14606. Tel: 716-254-7170.

21—HOLY CROSS (1873), Revs. Thomas H. Wheeland; Frederick F. Eisemann; Peter Enyan-Boadu; Sr. Kathleen Mary O'Connell, Pastoral Assoc.; Sr. Rita Biel, Parish Visitor.
Res., 4492 Lake Ave., 14612. Tel: 716-663-2244; Fax: 716-865-5379.
School—4488 Lake Ave., 14612. Tel: 716-663-6533; Fax: 716-663-7948. Sr. Marilyn Reeves, Prin.
Sisters 3; Lay Teachers 25; Students 515.
Catechesis/Religious Programs—Tel: 716-621-8133. Karen Henrichs, D.R.E.
Students 285.
Convent—4490 Lake Ave., 14612. Tel: 716-663-5351.

22—HOLY FAMILY (1864) (German), Deacons Patrick M. Shanley, Admin.; Angelo Coccia. In res., Most Rev. Dennis W. Hickey, D.D.; Rev. Louis A. Sirianni.
Res., 415 Ames St., 14611. Tel: 716-328-3110.
School—899 Jay St., 14611. Tel: 716-328-4800. Sr. Lorraine Burns, S.S.N.D., Prin.
Lay Teachers 12; Students 193.
Catechesis/Religious Programs—D.R.E.: Bernard Grizard; Debbie Difilippo.
Students 95.

23—HOLY GHOST (1875), Rev. Alexander H. Bradshaw; Sr. Janice Nadeau, S.S.N.D., Pastoral Assoc.
Res., 220 Coldwater Rd., 14624. Tel: 716-247-3535; Fax: 716-247-4223. [CEM]
Catechesis/Religious Programs—Tel: 716-426-1289. Sr. Karen Dietz, S.S.J., D.R.E.
Students 182.

24—HOLY NAME OF JESUS (1964), Rev. John V. Rosse; Deacon Richard Lombard.
Res., 15 St. Martin's Way, 14616. Tel: 716-621-4040; Fax: 716-621-6343.
Catechesis/Religious Programs—Tel: 716-621-6343.
Students 271.

25—HOLY REDEEMER-ST. FRANCIS XAVIER (1867-1888). Merged in 1985. Revs. Dennis Shaw; Laurence Tracy; Deacon Agenol Rodriguez.
Res., 34 Teresa St., 14605. Tel: 716-482-3211; Fax: 716-325-5771.
Church—300 Bay St., 14605.

26—HOLY ROSARY (1889), Rev. Lawrence V. Murphy; Deacon James Fitch; Rose Culligan Davis, Pastoral Assoc.
Res., 414 Lexington Ave., 14613. Tel: 716-458-4422; Fax: 716-458-8209.
School—420 Lexington Ave., 14613. Tel: 716-254-8180. Miss Mary Beth Fuehrer, Prin.
Lay Teachers 8; Students 120.
Catechesis/Religious Programs—Students 78.

27—IMMACULATE CONCEPTION (1849), Rev. Michael G. Upson.
Office: 445 Frederick Douglass St., 14608. Tel: 716-325-3893; Fax: 716-325-2082.

28—ST. JAMES (1949), Rev. John A. Lynch.
Res., 109 Brockley Rd., 14609. Tel: 716-482-9796.
School—Northeastern Quadrant Catholic School.

29—ST. JOHN THE EVANGELIST (1914), Rev. William V. Spilly. Pastoral Assocs: Sr. Chris Treichel, O.S.F.; Patricia Curtis. In res., Rev. Edward A. Zimmer.
Mailing Address: 150 Floverton St., 14610.
Res., 549 Humboldt St., 14610. Tel: 716-482-6211; 482-4280; Fax: 716-482-8213.
School—Tel: 716-654-9437; Fax: 716-654-8787.
Lay Teachers 15; Students 192; Pre-School 50.
Catechesis/Religious Programs—Students 92.

30—ST. JOHN EVANGELIST (1865) (Greece), Revs. Joseph F. D'Aurizio; Dennis Bonsignore.
Res., 2400 Ridge Rd., W., 14626. Tel: 716-225-8980; Fax: 716-723-9825.
School—2375 Ridge Rd., W., 14626. Tel: 716-225-3450. Mr. Robert Edelman, Prin.
Lay Teachers 20; Students 320.
Catechesis/Religious Programs—Tel: 716-225-4200.
Students 721.

31—ST. JOSEPH (1836). Closed. For inquiries for parish records contact Our Lady of Victory.

32—ST. JUDE THE APOSTLE (1968), Rev. John J. Steger.
Res., 4100 Lyell Rd., 14606. Tel: 716-247-5262; Fax: 716-429-5111.
Catechesis/Religious Programs—Tel: 716-247-5275.
Students 190.

33—OUR LADY OF GOOD COUNSEL (1928). Merged with St. Augustine and St. Monica to form Roman Catholic Community of the 19th Ward.
Res., 75 Ernestine St., 14619. Tel: 716-235-1130.

34—OUR LADY OF LOURDES (1928), Revs. John L. O'Connor; Otto J. Vogt.
Res., 150 Varinna Dr., 14618. Tel: 716-473-9656.
School—Seton Catholic School, (Grades PreK-6). See St. Thomas More for Grades 7 & 8. 165 Rhinecliff Dr., 14618. Tel: 716-473-6604; Fax: 716-473-3347.
Sisters 2; Lay Teachers 32; Students 380.
Catechesis/Religious Programs—Tel: 716-244-2361. Sr. Lucille Lenhard, D.R.E.
Students 128.

35—OUR LADY OF MERCY (1957), Rev. Stanley G. Kacprzak. Pastoral Assocs.: Roni Antenucci; Patricia Boyce.
Res., 36 Armstrong Rd., 14616. Tel: 716-865-0775; Fax: 716-865-9403.
Catechesis/Religious Programs—Tel: 716-865-2917. Sr. Kathryn Wahl, D.R.E.
Students 150.

36—OUR LADY OF MOUNT CARMEL (1909), Revs. Dennis Shaw; Laurence Tracy; Sr. Julia Norton, R.S.M.; Deacons Nemesio Martinez; Felix Medero.
Res., 53 Ontario St., 14605. Tel: 716-232-1133; Fax: 716-325-5771.
Catechesis/Religious Programs—Tel: 716-224-01777. Yolanda Ortiz-Vargas, D.R.E.
Students 77.
Convent—59 Ontario St., 14605. Tel: 716-454-6766.
St. Martin's Soup Kitchen—Tel: 716-325-6500.

37—OUR LADY OF PERPETUAL HELP (1905), Rev. Neil Miller; Sr. Livia Ann Ruocco, R.S.M., Pastoral Assoc.; Sr. Francisca Aguillon, O.L.C., Hispanic Pastoral Assoc. In res., Rev. Anthony P. Mugavero.
Res., 1089 Joseph Ave., 14621. Tel: 716-467-2725.
Catechesis/Religious Programs—Students 55.

38—OUR LADY QUEEN OF PEACE (1960), Rev. Joseph A. Hart; Deacon Albert Bergeron. Pastoral Assocs.: Sr. Jacqulyn Reichart, R.S.M.; Margaret Ostromecki.
Res., 95 Warren Ave., 14618-4311. Tel: 716-244-3010; Fax: 716-242-7733.
601 Edgewood Ave., 14618-4329.
Catechesis/Religious Programs—Students 165.

39—OUR LADY OF VICTORY-ST. JOSEPH (1848), Revs. Winfried M. Kellner, Admin.; Gerard J. McMahon.
Res., 210 Pleasant St., 14604. Tel: 716-454-2244; Fax: 716-454-2246.

40—OUR MOTHER OF SORROWS (1829) (Irish), Revs. Thomas R. Statt; Richard J. Shatzel; Sr. Mary Doran, S.S.J., Pastoral Assoc.
Res., 5000 Mt. Read Blvd., 14612. Tel: 716-663-5432; Fax: 716-663-5435. [CEM]

School—1701 Latta Rd., 14612. Tel: 716-621-3495. Sr. Sheila Luber, S.S.J., Prin.
Lay Teachers 27; Students 365.
Catechesis/Religious Programs—Tel: 716-621-3495. Mrs. Claudia Adams, D.R.E.
Students 528.

41—St. Lawrence (1959), Revs. Frank J. Falletta; Michael J. Volino; Donald J. Haycock, C.S.C.
Res., 1000 N. Greece Rd., 14626. Tel: 716-723-1350; Fax: 716-723-1361.
School—Tel: 716-225-3870; Fax: 716-225-1336. Sr. Diane Dennie, Prin.
Lay Teachers 23; Students 481.
Catechesis/Religious Programs—Tel: 716-225-7320. Rosanne Young, D.R.E.
Students 750.

42—St. Lucy (1912). Closed. For inquiries for parish records contact Immaculate Conception Church.

43—St. Margaret Mary (1929), Rev. Peter T. Bayer. In res., Rev. John T. Walsh.
Res., 401 Rogers Pkwy., 14617. Tel: 716-342-2100; Fax: 716-467-7694.
School—School at St. Margaret Mary's: Monroe County Catholic Schools, (Grades PreK-6) 400 Rogers Pkwy., 14617. Tel: 716-266-0413. Sr. Mary Alice O'Brien, R.S.M., Prin.
Lay Teachers 15; Students 265.
Catechesis/Religious Programs—Tel: 716-342-7114.
Students 430.

44—St. Mark (1964), Rev. Thomas M. Erdle; Deacons James L. Chatterton; Thomas Kluchko.
Res., 54 Kuhn Rd., 14612. Tel: 716-225-3710; Fax: 716-227-6824.
Catechesis/Religious Programs—Mary Margaret Chatterton, D.R.E.
Students 550.

45—St. Mary (1834), Rev. William Donnelly; Deacon William Coffey.
Res., 15 St. Mary's Place, 14607. Tel: 716-232-7140; Fax: 716-232-6289.
Catechesis/Religious Programs—Students 105.

46—Emmanuel Church of the Deaf of the Diocese of Rochester (1981), Rev. Raymond H. Fleming.
Res., 75 Ernestine St., 14619. Tel: 716-235-1812 (Voice); 235-3849 (TTY).

47—St. Michael (1872) (German-Hispanic), Revs. Dennis J. Shaw; Laurence Tracy.
Res., 869 Clinton Ave., N., 14605. Tel: 716-325-4040; Fax: 716-325-5771.
Catechesis/Religious Programs—Students 129.

48—St. Monica (1898) (Irish). Merged with Our Lady of Good Counsel and St. Augustine to form Roman Catholic Community of the 19th Ward. In res., Revs. Raymond H. Fleming; Richard C. O'Connell.
Res., 34 Monica St., 14619. Tel: 716-235-3322.
School—841 Genesee St., 14611. Tel: 716-235-4140. Sr. Mary Marvin, R.S.M., Prin.
Lay Teachers 13; Students 235.

49—Roman Catholic Community of the 19th Ward (1994). Consolidation of Our Lady of Good Counsel, St. Augustine, and St. Monica. Rev. Robert Werth; Lourdes Perez-Albuerne, Business Mgr.
Res., 34 Monica St., 14619. Tel: 716-235-3322.

50—St. Patrick (1832). Closed. (Old Cathedral). Records from 1832 thru May 1978 can be obtained from St. Anthony of Padua Church. Any information after that time contact St. Francis of Assisi.
1150 Buffalo Rd., 14624.

51—SS. Peter and Paul (1843), Revs. Paul J. Tomasso; Daniel McMullin.
Res., 720 Main St., W., 14611. Tel: 716-436-3110; Fax: 716-436-0373.

52—St. Pius Tenth (1954), Revs. Gerald T. Connor; Lance M. Gonyo; Deacon John E. Zierle.
Res., 3032 Chili Ave., 14624. Tel: 716-247-2566; Fax: 716-247-2511. [CEM]
School—(Grades PreK-6). Tel: 716-247-5650; Fax: 716-247-7409. Mr. Stephen Oberst, Prin.
Sisters of St. Joseph 2; Lay Teachers 20; Students 436.
Catechesis/Religious Programs—3000 Chili Ave., 14624. Tel: 716-247-5269; Fax: 716-247-7409. Ms. Ann Hastee, D.R.E.
Students 525.

53—St. Philip Neri (1929) (Italian), Rev. Timothy Horan, Temporary Admin.
Res., 1782 Clifford Ave., 14609. Tel: 716-482-2400.

54—Most Precious Blood (1930) (Italian), Rev. William E. Graf.
Res., 219 Stenson St., 14606. Tel: 716-458-6079.

55—St. Salome (1925), Rev. William G. Darling.
Res., 4282 Culver Rd., 14622. Tel: 716-323-1160; Fax: 716-544-4810.
Catechesis/Religious Programs—Students 96.

56—St. Stanislaus (1890) (Polish), Revs. Mitchell Zygadlo; Valentine A. Jankowiak; Adam Ogorzaly; Deacon Raymond Mielcarek.
Res., 34 St. Stanislaus St., 14621. Tel: 716-467-3068; Fax: 716-467-3072.
Catechesis/Religious Programs—Tel: 716-544-2614.
Students 60.

57—St. Theodore (1924), Revs. Daniel F. Holland; Frederick Helfrich; Jack Quinn. Pastoral Assocs: Sr. Catherine Pfleger, R.S.M.; Sr. Barbara Bartkowiak, O.S.F.; Sr. Mary Jean Smith, S.S.J.; Deacon Anthony Caruso. In res., Rev. Desmond O'Neill.
Res., 168 Spencerport Rd., 14606. Tel: 716-429-6811; Fax: 716-429-7726.
Catechesis/Religious Programs—Tel: 716-429-5650.
Students 444.

58—St. Theresa (1927) (Polish). Closed. For inquiries for parish records contact St. Stanislaus, Rochester.

59—St. Thomas the Apostle (1922), Revs. Robert C. Bradler; Ralph J. Fraats; Deacon Thomas H. Beck. In res., Rev. Robert F. McNamara.
Res., 4536 St. Paul Blvd., 14617. Tel: 716-342-2323.
Catechesis/Religious Programs—Tel: 716-342-1704. Mr. David Higbee, D.R.E.
Students 200.

60—St. Thomas More (1953), Rev. Andrew Grzela; Deacon Stephen Carroll; Sr. Ellen Galvin, S.S.J., Pastoral Assoc. In res., Revs. John S. Whalen; Richard J. Orlando; William I. Onuh (Nigeria).
Res., 2617 East Ave., 14610. Tel: 716-381-4200; Fax: 716-381-6327.
School—Siena Catholic Academy, (Grades 7-8). See Our Lady of Lourdes for Grades PreK-6. Tel: 716-381-1220.
Lay Teachers 27; Students 360.
Catechesis/Religious Programs—Tel: 716-381-0470.
Students 150.

OUTSIDE METROPOLITAN ROCHESTER

Addison, Steuben Co., St. Catherine of Siena (1854), Rev. Gerald T. O'Connor.
Res., 49 Maple St., 14801. Tel: 607-359-2115. [CEM]
Catechesis/Religious Programs—Students 65.

Apalachin, Tioga Co., St. Margaret Mary (1955), Rev. David P. Simon; Patricia Federowicz, Pastoral Assoc.; Deacon Joseph F. Federowicz.
Res., 1110 Pennsylvania Ave., 13732. Tel: 607-625-3191; Fax: 607-625-5717.
Catechesis/Religious Programs—Tel: 607-625-3192.
Students 142.

Auburn, Cayuga Co.,

1—Holy Family, (1834), Rev. Conrad J. Sundholm. In res., Rev. Robert M. Egan.
Res., 85 North St., 13021. Tel: 315-252-9576; Fax: 315-255-1506.
School—Cayuga County Catholic School, Tel: 315-253-8327; Fax: 315-253-2401.
Catechesis/Religious Programs—Tel: 315-252-9578; Fax: 315-255-1506.
Students 80.

2—Sacred Heart, (1955), Rev. Paul Brennan.
Res., 90 Melrose Rd., 13021. Tel: 315-252-7271; Fax: 315-255-0716. [JC]
School—St. Joseph School. A consolidation of the following parishes: Holy Family; Sacred Heart; and St. Alphonsus. Tel: 315-253-8327; Fax: 315-253-2401.
Catechesis/Religious Programs—Tel: 315-253-2712.
Students 350.
Mission—Owasco, Cayuga Co., St. Ann, (1912) 90 Melrose Rd., 13021. Tel: 315-252-7271.

3—St. Mary, (1868) (Irish), Rev. Robert J. Schrader. In res., Rev. James C. Enright.
Res., 15 Clark St., 13021. Tel: 315-252-9545.
Catechesis/Religious Programs—17 Clymer St., 13021. Tel: 315-252-3439.
Students 378.

4—St. Alphonsus, (1853), Rev. Foster P. Rogers. In res., Revs. Clarence W. Gardner, Pastor Emeritus; Joseph T. Gaynor; Paul J. Freemesser; Edward J. Foy.
Res., 10 Lewis St., 13021-2708. Tel: 315-252-7261; Fax: 315-252-7262. [JC]
School—St. Joseph's Elementary & Primary School. A consolidation of the parishes of Cayuga County. Tel: 315-253-8327.
Catechesis/Religious Programs—Tel: 315-253-6147. Marie Venaglia, D.R.E.
Students 152.

5—St. Aloysius. Closed. For inquiries for parish records contact the Chancery.

6—St. Hyacinth, (1905) (Polish), Revs. Robert M. Grzybowski, O.F.M.Conv.; Callistus Juras, O.F.M.Conv., Pastoral Assoc.; Xavier Nawrocki, O.F.M.; Deacon Gary DiLallo. In res., Rev. Matthew Swizdor, O.F.M.Conv.
Res., 61 Pulaski St., 13021. Tel: 315-252-7297; Fax: 315-255-3781. [JC]
School—St. Joseph School. A consolidation of the following parishes: Holy Family; Sacred Heart; St. Alphonsus; and St. Hyacinth. Tel: 315-253-8327.
Catechesis/Religious Programs—Tel: 315-252-5132.
Students 158.

7—St. Francis of Assisi, (1907) (Italian), Rev. Robert L. Beligotti. In res., Rev. C. Richard Nangle.
Res., 185 Clark St., 13021. Tel: 315-252-7593; Fax: 315-252-7593. [JC]
Catechesis/Religious Programs—Tel: 315-253-7921; Fax: 315-252-7593.
Students 87.

Aurora, Cayuga Co., St. Patrick (1858), Rev. Paul J. Ryan; Deacon John Prave.
Res., Main St., Box 296, 13026-0296. Tel: 315-364-7197; Fax: 615-364-7825. [CEM]
Catechesis/Religious Programs—Students 50.

Avon, Livingston Co., St. Agnes (1866), Rev. James C. Burke. In res., Rev. James T. Wolfe.
Res., 108 Prospect St., 14414. Tel: 716-226-2100; Fax: 716-226-6436. [CEM]
School—Tel: 716-226-8500. Gerald E. Benjamin, Ph.D., Prin.
Lay Teachers 8; Students 94.
Catechesis/Religious Programs—Tel: 716-226-3232.
Students 117.

Bath, Steuben Co., St. Mary (1860), Rev. Robert W. Hammond.
Res., 32 E. Morris St., 14810. Tel: 607-776-3327; Fax: 607-776-3409. [CEM]
Catechesis/Religious Programs—36 E. Morris St., 14810.
Students 120.

Bradford, Steuben Co., St. Stanislaus (1922) (Polish), Revs. Gerald T. O'Connor; Andrew J. Kalafsky.
Res., Main St., P.O. Box 153, 14815-0153. Tel: 607-583-4920.
Mission—Campbell, Steuben Co., St. Joseph, (1870) P.O. Box 153, 14815-0153.
Catechesis/Religious Programs—Students 57.

Brockport, Monroe Co., Nativity of the Blessed Virgin Mary (1848), Rev. Roy J. Kiggins.
Res., 152 Main St., 14420-1972. Tel: 716-637-4500; Fax: 716-637-4232. [CEM]
School—Holley & Utica St., 14420. Tel: 716-637-2100; Fax: 716-637-7420.
Lay Teachers 8; Students 123.
Catechesis/Religious Programs—Tel: 716-637-8490.
Students 305.

Caledonia, Livingston Co., St. Columba (1885), Rev. Walter J. Plominski, Admin.
Res., 198 North St., 14423. Tel: 716-538-2126. [CEM]
Catechesis/Religious Programs—Students 98.
Mission—Mumford, Monroe Co., St. Patrick, (1854) Church St., 14511. Mumford,

Canandaigua, Ontario Co., St. Mary (1844), Revs. Walter L. Wainwright; Brian C. Cool.
Res., 95 N. Main St., Canadaigua, 14424. Tel: 716-394-1220; Fax: 716-396-3230. [CEM]
School—16 Gibson St., 14424. Tel: 716-394-4300. Mrs. Eileen O'Neill, Prin.
Lay Teachers 14; Students 230.
Catechesis/Religious Programs—16 Gibson St., 14424. Tel: 716-394-4590.
Students 655.

Canisteo, Steuben Co., St. Joachim (1880), Rev. Daniel W. Heintz.
Res., 32 W. Main St., 14823. Tel: 607-698-4034.
Catechesis/Religious Programs—Students 87.

Cato, Cayuga Co., St. Patrick (1875), Rev. William B. Leone; Deacon John Tomandl; Sr. Virginia Taylor, R.S.M., Pastoral Assoc.
Res., 2667 Hamilton St., P.O. Box 266, Weedsport, 13166. Tel: 315-834-6266; Fax: 615-689-7090.
Catechesis/Religious Programs—Tel: 315-834-9203. Walter Sheehan, D.R.E.
Students 157.

Cayuga, Cayuga Co., St. Joseph (1870), Rev. Paul J. Ryan; Deacon John Prave.
Springport Cove, P.O. Box 139, Union Springs, 13160.
Res., Main St., Box 296, Aurora, 13026. Tel: 315-364-7197; Fax: 315-364-7825.
Catechesis/Religious Programs—Students 50.

Churchville, Monroe Co., St. Vincent De Paul (1869), Rev. William F. Laird, Admin.
Res., 11 N. Main St., Drawer I, 14428. Tel: 716-293-1400. [CEM]
Catechesis/Religious Programs—Tel: 315-293-1180.
Students 184.

Clifton Springs, Ontario Co., St. Felix (1856). Merged with St. Francis to form St. Felix / St. Francis Parish Cluster, Clifton Springs.
St. Felix / St. Francis Parish Cluster (1992), Rev. Edward J. Dillon.
Office: 12 Hibbard Ave., 14432. Tel: 315-462-2961; Fax: 315-462-3608. [CEM 2]
Catechesis/Religious Programs—Students 83.

Clyde, Wayne Co., St. John the Evangelist (1852), Rev. Leo J. Reinhardt; Deacon Gregory J. Kiley.
Res., 114 Sodus St., 14433. Tel: 315-923-3941. [CEM]
Catechesis/Religious Programs—Tel: 315-923-7315; Fax: 315-923-3941. Mary DeLisio, D.R.E.
Students 130.
Mission—Savannah, Wayne Co., St. Patrick, (1875) Grand Ave., Savannah, 13146. Tel: 315-365-3244.

Cohocton, Steuben Co., St. Pius V (1861) (German), Rev. Charles T. Manning.
Res., 35 Maple Ave., P.O. Box 387, 14826. Tel: 716-384-5500; Fax: 716-384-5500. [CEM 2][JC]
Catechesis/Religious Programs—Students 80.
Mission—Perkinsville, Steuben Co., Sacred Heart of Jesus, (1838) Chapel St., P.O. Box 389, Perkinsville, 14529. Tel: 716-728-5665.

Corning, Steuben Co., St. Mary (1848), Revs. Michael F. Conboy; Michael R. Brown; Deacon Raymond Defendorf; Sr. Joan Cawley, S.S.J., Pastoral Assoc. In res., Rev. Francis R. Davis.
Mailing Address: c/o 222 Dodge Ave., 14830. Tel: 607-936-4689; Fax: 607-936-0222. [CEM]
Catechesis/Religious Programs—Mary Ann Hinkley, D.R.E.
Students 60.
St. Patrick (1903), Revs. Michael F. Conboy; Michael R. Brown; Deacon Raymond Defendorf.
Office & Mailing Address: c/o 222 Dodge Ave., 14830. Tel: 607-936-4689; Fax: 607-936-0222.
Res., 155 State St., 14830. Tel: 607-962-0422. [JC]
Catechesis/Religious Programs—Mary Ann Hinkley, D.R.E.
Students 125.
St. Vincent de Paul (1913), Revs. Michael F. Conboy; Michael R. Brown; Deacon Ray Defendorf; Barbara Hesenius, Pastoral Assoc.
Res., c/o 222 Dodge Ave., 14830. Tel: 607-936-4688; Fax: 607-936-0222. [JC]
Catechesis/Religious Programs—Alene Goodman, D.R.E.
Students 125.

Dansville, Livingston Co., St. Mary (1845), Rev. Stephen Kraus.
Res., 40 Elizabeth St., 14437. Tel: 716-335-2700; Fax: 716-335-2713. [CEM]
School—Tel: 716-335-6800.
Lay Teachers 8; Students 155.
Catechesis/Religious Programs—Tel: 716-335-8700.
Students 174.

Dryden, Tompkins Co., Holy Cross (1962), Rev. John H. Hayes.
Res., 375 S. George Rd., Freeville, 13068. Tel: 607-844-8314; Fax: 607-844-9414. [CEM]
Catechesis/Religious Programs—Tel: 607-844-8358.
Students 230.

East Bay, Wayne Co., St. John Fisher (1935). Closed. All inquiries for mission records can be made at St. Mary Magdalen, Wolcott.

East Bloomfield, Ontario Co., St. Bridget (1850), Rev. John J. Philipps; Deacon Claude Lester.
Res., 15 Church St., 14443. Tel: 716-657-7626; Fax: 716-657-5349. [CEM]
Catechesis/Religious Programs—Students 157.

East Rochester, Monroe Co., St. Jerome (1905), Rev. Albert L. Delmonte; Sr. Clare Brown, S.S.J., Pastoral Assoc.
Res., 207 S. Garfield St., 14445. Tel: 716-586-3231; Fax: 716-586-0537.
Catechesis/Religious Programs—206 West Ave., 14445. Tel: 716-586-1625.
Students 294.

Elmira, Chemung Co.,

1—Sts. Peter and Paul of Eastside Catholic Parish, (1848), Rev. Patrick L. Connor; Sr. Kathleen Bayer, R.S.M., Pastoral Assoc.; Deacons Michael Capanelli; George Welch.
Office: 161 High St., 14901. Tel: 607-732-1994.
Res., 950 Lake St., 14901. Tel: 607-732-2455.
School—Holy Family Catholic Schools. Serving the parishes in Elmira. See St. Mary, St. Casimir, and Our Lady of Lourdes for details.
Catechesis/Religious Programs—Students 57.

2—St. Patrick, (1871), Rev. Joseph P. McCaffrey; Sr. Maureen Mylott, S.C., Pastoral Assoc.
Res., 604 Park Pl., 14901. Tel: 607-733-0300; Fax: 607-733-3606.
School—Holy Family Catholic Schools. Serving the parishes in Elmira. See St. Mary, St. Casimir, and Our Lady of Lourdes for details. Tel: 607-734-4414.
Catechesis/Religious Programs—Tel: 607-737-0536; Fax: 607-733-3606.
Students 76.

3—St. Mary, (1871), Rev. Richard T. Farrell; Deacon Robert Stowell.
Res., 224 Franklin St., 14904. Tel: 607-734-6254; Fax: 607-733-8890.
School—Holy Family Primary, (Grades PreK-3). See St. Casimir and Our Lady of Lourdes for Intermediate and Jr. High. 421 Fulton St., 14904. Tel: 607-732-3588; Fax: 607-732-1850. Constance Dunn, Prin.
Lay Teachers 13; Students 301.
Catechesis/Religious Programs—Donna Bennett, D.R.E.
Students 275.

4—St. John the Baptist of Eastside Catholic Parish, (1866) (German), Rev. Patrick L. Connor; Sr. Kathleen Bayer, R.S.M., Pastoral Assoc.; Deacons Michael Capanelli; George Welch.
Office: 161 High St., 14901. Tel: 607-732-1994.
Res., 950 Lake St., 14901. Tel: 607-732-2455.
Church—325 Lake St., 14901.
School—Holy Family Catholic Schools. Serving the parishes in Elmira. See St. Mary, St. Casimir, and Our Lady of Lourdes for details.

5—St. Casimir, (1890) (Polish), Rev. Christopher E. Linsler.
Res., 1004 Davis St., 14901. Tel: 607-734-1622.
School—Holy Family Jr. High. See St. Mary and Our Lady of Lourdes for Primary and Intermediate. 1008 Davis St., 14901. Tel: 607-734-0336. Mrs. Elizabeth Berliner, Prin.
Lay Teachers 9; Students 147.

6—St. Cecilia of Eastside Catholic Parish, (1904), Rev. Patrick L. Connor; Sr. Kathleen Bayer, R.S.M., Pastoral Assoc.; Deacons Michael Capanelli; George Welch.
Office: 161 High St., 14901. Tel: 607-732-1994.
Res., 950 Lake St., 14901. Tel: 607-732-2455.
School—Holy Family Catholic Schools. Serving the parishes in Elmira. See St. Mary, St. Casimir, and Our Lady of Lourdes for details.

7—St. Anthony, (1908) (Italian). Clustered with St. Patrick's Church. Rev. Joseph J. McCaffrey.
Res., 604 Park Pl., 14901. Tel: 607-733-0300; Fax: 607-733-3606.
School—Holy Family Catholic Schools. Serving the parishes in Elmira. See St. Mary, St. Casimir, and Our Lady of Lourdes for details. Tel: 607-734-4414.
Catechesis/Religious Programs—Tel: 607-737-0536; Fax: 607-733-3606.
Students 84.

8—Our Lady of Lourdes, (1940), Rev. Paul J. McCabe.
Res., 120 Fairmont Rd., 14905. Tel: 607-732-6261; Fax: 607-732-7256.
School—Holy Family Intermediate. See St. Mary and St. Casimir for Primary and Junior High. 301 Demarest Pkwy., 14905. Tel: 607-734-0841; Fax: 607-732-5432. Miss Brenda Lisi, Prin.
Lay Teachers 10; Sisters 1; Students 171.
Catechesis/Religious Programs—Tel: 607-734-0727. Eileen Sokolowski, D.R.E.
Students 255.

Elmira Heights, Chemung Co., St. Charles Borromeo (1904), Rev. Christopher E. Linsler; Deacon William P. Dougherty.
Res., 130 Oakwood Ave., 14903. Tel: 607-734-7619.
Catechesis/Religious Programs—Tel: 607-734-1622.
Students 85.

Fairport, Monroe Co., Assumption of the Blessed Virgin Mary (1866), Revs. Edward Golden; Paul Walsh, C.S.B.; Deacon Ronald J. Tocci; Sheryl Zabel, Pastoral Assoc.
Catechesis/Religious Programs—Assumption School of Religion, 10 Baumer Place, 14450. Tel: 716-223-0525. Cathy Tocci, D.R.E.
Students 940.
Church of the Resurrection (1973), Rev. Louis A. Vasile.
Res., 52 Mason Rd., 14450. Tel: 716-223-6686.
Church—63 Mason Rd., 14450. Tel: 716-223-5500; Fax: 716-223-6958.
Catechesis/Religious Programs—Students 245.
St. John of Rochester (1962), Revs. James E. Boyle; Michael C. Hogan; Sr. Kathleen A. Wayne, R.S.M.; Deacons Thomas J. Cleary; Daniel M. Kinsky.
Ministry Bldg.: 8 Wickford Way, 14450.
Res., 18 Wickford Way, 14450. Tel: 716-248-5993.
School—10 Wickford Way, 14450. Tel: 716-248-8836; Fax: 716-248-8839. Mrs. Marilyn Tripp, Prin.
Lay Teachers 13; Students 216.
Catechesis/Religious Programs—Tel: 716-248-8850. Judith Swagler, D.R.E.
Students 769.

Fleming, Cayuga Co., St. Isaac Jogues (1946), Rev. Albert J. Shamon, Admin.
Res., 5 S. Marvine Ave., Auburn, 13021. Tel: 315-255-2912; Fax: 315-255-2912.

Geneseo, Livingston Co., St. Mary (1854), Revs. William Gordinier; J. Walter Carron, Pastor Emeritus. In res., Rev. Eugene H. McFarland Tel: 716-243-2551.
Office: 13 North St., 14454. Tel: 716-243-1100; Fax: 716-243-0240.
Res., 4 Avon Rd., 14454. Tel: 716-243-2422. [CEM]
Catechesis/Religious Programs—Students 212.

Geneva, Ontario Co., St. Francis de Sales (1835), Rev. Ronald P. Harley. In res., Rev. Vincent P. Panepinto.
Res., 130 Exchange St., 14456. Tel: 315-789-0930; Fax: 315-781-1985. [CEM][JC 2]
School—Consolidated School. See St. Stephen and St. Francis de Sales.
Catechesis/Religious Programs—Students 110.
St. Stephen (1904). Consolidated with the following parishes: St. Francis de Sales and St. Stephen. Rev. Msgr. Gerard C. Krieg; Rev. Brian E. Jeffers; Mrs. Ruth Page, Pastoral Assoc.
Res., 48 Pulteney St., 14456. Tel: 315-789-1124; Fax: 315-789-1271. [JC]
School—(Grades PreK-8) 17 Elmwood Ave., 14456. Tel: 315-789-1828. Mrs. Elaine Morrow, Prin.
Sisters of St. Joseph 1; Lay Teachers 17; Students 304.
Catechesis/Religious Programs—21 High St., 14456. Tel: 315-781-2624. Walter Savaria, D.R.E.
Students 55.

Groton, Tompkins Co., St. Anthony (1873), Rev. Bernard L. Carges.
Res., 312 Locke Rd., R.D. 2, 13073. Tel: 607-898-5135. [CEM]
Catechesis/Religious Programs—Students 140.

Hamlin, Monroe Co., St. Elizabeth Ann Seton (1982), Rev. William Amann; Deacons Ramon Datz; John Holmes.
Res., 3747 Brick Schoolhouse Rd., 14464. Tel: 716-964-8627; Fax: 716-964-8200.
Catechesis/Religious Programs—Tel: 716-964-8200.
Students 240.

Hammondsport, Steuben Co., St. Gabriel (1845), Sr. Anne Michelle McGill, Pastoral Admin.
Res., 78 Shethar St., 14840. Tel: 607-569-3501; Fax: 607-569-3226. [CEM]

Henrietta, Monroe Co., Church of the Good Shepherd (1911), Rev. Michael J. Bausch; Sr. Barbara Stinard, R.S.M., Pastoral Assoc.; Deacon Eugene Edwards. In res., Rev. John M. Mulligan, V.G.
Res., 3318 E. Henrietta Rd., 14467. Tel: 716-334-3518; Fax: 716-334-6015.
School—3288 E. Henrietta Rd., 14467. Tel: 716-334-5100. Marie Arcuri, Prin.
Lay Teachers 12; Students 200.
Catechesis/Religious Programs—Tel: 716-334-3023.
Students 700.

Hilton, Monroe Co., St. Leo (1884), Rev. John J. Glogowski; Deacon James P. Steiger.
Res., 167 Lake Ave., 14468. Tel: 716-392-2710; Fax: 716-392-9254.
Catechesis/Religious Programs—Tel: 716-392-9694.
Students 435.

Honeoye, Ontario Co., St. Mary, Our Lady of the Hills (1868), Rev. Edward B. Zenkel.
Res., Rte. 20A, Box 725, 14471. Tel: 716-229-5007. [CEM]
Catechesis/Religious Programs—Students 78.

Honeoye Falls, Monroe Co., St. Paul of the Cross (1870), Lawrence A. Gross; Deacon Albro C. Wilson, Jr.
Res., 29 Monroe St., 14472. Tel: 716-624-1443; Fax: 716-624-5169. [CEM]
Catechesis/Religious Programs—Students 133.

Hornell, Steuben Co., St. Ann (1866), Revs. James P. Jaeger; Robert Kanka, (Retired); Deacon Robert W. McCormick.
Res., 31 Erie Ave., P.O. Box 605, 14843. Tel: 607-324-0410. [CEM][JC 2]
School—27 Erie Ave., 14843. Tel: 607-324-0733. Sr. Dolores Ann Stein, Prin.
Lay Teachers 13; Students 175.
Catechesis/Religious Programs—Tel: 607-324-7121. Marianne Logan, D.R.E.
Students 203.
St. Ignatius Loyola (1931), Rev. Jeremiah P. Moynihan.
Res., 343 Canisteo St., 14843. Tel: 607-324-5811.

Horseheads, Chemung Co., St. Mary Our Mother (1866), Revs. Thomas W. Burr; Scott M. Kubinski. In res., Rev. Robert C. MacNamara, (Retired).
Res., 816 W. Broad St., 14845. Tel: 607-739-3817;

Fax: 607-739-5628. [CEM]
School—811 Westlake St., 14845. Tel: 607-739-9157; Fax: 607-739-2532. Deacon Daniel R. Hurley, Prin.
Lay Teachers 14; Students 283.
Catechesis/Religious Programs—Tel: 607-739-8214.
Students 430.

Interlaken, Seneca Co., St. Francis Solanus (1875), Rev. Nelson J. Ruppert, O.F.M.Cap.
Mailing Address: c/o Holy Cross Rectory, P.O. Box 337, Ovid, 14521-0337. Tel: 607-532-8337; Fax: 607-869-9825.
Res., St. Fidelis Friary, 7790 County Rd. 153, 14847. Tel: 607-532-4423; Fax: 607-532-9271.
Church—Orchard St., 14847. Tel: 607-532-8337; Fax: 607-869-9825.

Ithaca, Tompkins Co., St. Catherine of Siena (1960), Rev. Ronald E. Gaesser. Pastoral Assocs.: Sr. Nancy Schmidt; Dora Hankey.
Res., 320 St. Catherine Cir., 14850. Tel: 607-257-2493; Fax: 607-257-5901.
Catechesis/Religious Programs—Tel: 607-257-2493; Fax: 607-257-5901.
Students 131.

Immaculate Conception (1848), Revs. George P. Heuman; Paul Bonnaci; Paul D'Sousa; Deacon James D. Hankey.
Res., 113 N. Geneva St., 14850. Tel: 607-273-6121; Fax: 607-273-0185. [CEM 2]
School—320 W. Buffalo St., 14850. Tel: 607-273-2707. Diana Baker, Prin.
Sisters of St. Joseph 1; Lay Teachers 12; Students 205.
Catechesis/Religious Programs—Tel: 607-273-0303.
Students 190.

King Ferry, Cayuga Co., Our Lady of the Lake, King Ferry (1868), Rev. Paul J. Ryan; Deacon John Prave.
Spring Port Cove, P.O. Box 139, Union Springs, 13160.
Res., Main St., P.O. Box 296, Aurora, 13026. Tel: 315-364-7197; Fax: 315-364-7825. [CEM]
Catechesis/Religious Programs—Students 50.

Lansing, All Saints (1913), Rev. Ronald E. Gaesser; Mary E. Wintish, R.S.M., Pastoral Assoc.
Res., 347 Ridge Rd., 14882. Tel: 607-533-7344.
Catechesis/Religious Programs—Students 68.

Leicester, Livingston Co., St. Thomas Aquinas (1897), Rev. Richard J. Beligotti.
Res., 175 Main St. Box 195, 14481. Tel: 716-382-3400.
Catechesis/Religious Programs—Students 120.
Mission—Retsof, Livingston Co., St. Lucy, (1912).

Lima, Livingston Co., St. Rose (1848), Rev. James F. Doyle.
Res., 1985 Lake Ave., 14485. Tel: 716-624-1005. [CEM]
Catechesis/Religious Programs—Tel: 716-624-1005.
Students 70.

Livonia, Livingston Co., St. Joseph (1911), Rev. Robert L. Collins.
Res., 14 Washington St., P.O. Box 77, 14487. Tel: 716-346-3815; Fax: 716-346-3815. [CEM]
Catechesis/Religious Programs—41 Spring St., 14487. Tel: 716-346-2500; Fax: 716-346-9445.
Students 218.
Mission—Conesus, Livingston Co., St. William, P.O. Box 77, 14487. Tel: 716-346-3757.

Livonia Center, Livingston Co., St. Michael (1848). Closed. For inquiries for parish records contact St. Mary's, Honeoye.

Lyons, Wayne, St. Michael (1852) (Italian), Rev. William M. Barrett.
Res., 3 Holley St., 14489-1505. Tel: 315-946-4182; Fax: 315-946-4736.
Catechesis/Religious Programs—Students 74.

Macedon, Wayne Co., St. Patrick (1883), Rev. Robert Scott Bourcy; Deacon Dominick N. Abballe.
Res., 52 Main St., 14502. Tel: 315-986-5671. [CEM]

Marion, Wayne, St. Gregory (1914), Rev. Robert Gaudio; Dr. Denise Mack, P.A.
Res., 136 Church St., Palmyra, 14522. Tel: 315-597-4571.
Office: 3806 Union St., 14522. Tel: 315-926-4323.
Catechesis/Religious Programs—Students 142.

Mendon, Monroe Co., St. Catherine of Siena (1902), Revs. Charles J. Latus; John P. Norris; Sr. Ruth Maier, S.S.J., Pastoral Assoc.; Deacon Fernando V. Ona, M.D.
Res., 26 Mendon-Ionia Rd., 14506. Tel: 716-624-4990; Fax: 716-624-4996.
Catechesis/Religious Programs—Mrs. Gail Brooks, D.R.E.
Students 380.
Convent—15 Mendon-Ionia Rd., 14506. Tel: 716-624-1538.

Montezuma, Cayuga Co., St. Michael (1865). Closed. For inquiries for parish records contact St. Joseph, Weedsport.

Moravia, Cayuga Co., St. Patrick (1872), Rev. John F. Gagnier.
Res., 51 Grove St., P.O. Box 111, 13118. Tel: 315-497-0626. [CEM]

Mount Morris, Livingston Co., St. Patrick (1869), Rev. Daniel J. Condon.
Res., 46 Stanley St., 14510. Tel: 716-658-2110. [CEM]
Parish Center, 33 Murray St., Mt. Morris, 14510.

Naples, Ontario, St. Januarius (1876), Rev. Philip J. Billotte.
Res., 180 N. Main St., P.O. Box 459, 14512. Tel: 716-374-2414; Fax: 716-374-2415.
Catechesis/Religious Programs—Students 83.

Newark, Wayne Co., St. Michael (1863), Revs. Peter C. Clifford; Peter M. DeBellis; Deacon Thomas Cass. In res., Rev. Joseph M. McDonnell, Pastor Emeritus.
Res., 401 Main St., 14513. Tel: 315-331-6753; Fax: 315-331-2925.
School—320 S. Main St., 14513. Tel: 315-331-2297. Mrs. Kathleen Peters, Prin.
Lay Teachers 20; Students 335.
Catechesis/Religious Programs—Tel: 315-331-3408. Rose Leisenring, D.R.E.
Students 265.

Newark Valley, Tioga County, St. John the Evangelist (1880), Rev. William A. Moorby; Deacon Warren M. Rutan.
Res., 24 Rock St., P.O. Box 458, 13811. Tel: 607-642-3328.
Catechesis/Religious Programs—Tel: 607-642-3258; Fax: 607-642-3258.
Students 100.
Mission—Catatonk, Tioga Co., St. Francis of Assisi, (1930) P.O. Box 458, 13811. Tel: 607-659-5959.

North Chili, Monroe Co., St. Christopher (1968), Rev. Bernard F. Dollen.
Res., 3350 Union St., 14514. Tel: 716-594-1400; Fax: 716-594-1403 (call first).
Catechesis/Religious Programs—Tel: 716-594-1441.
Students 691.

Nunda, Livingston Co., Holy Angels (1854), Rev. Daniel J. Condon.
Res., 46 Stanley St., Mount Morris, 14510. Tel: 716-468-3450; 658-2110.

Odessa, Schuyler Co., St. Benedict (1965), Rev. David L. Bonin.
Res., 905 N. Decatur St., Watkins Glen, 14891. Tel: 607-535-2786.
Church—Speedway, 14869. Tel: 607-594-2226.

Ontario, Wayne Co., St. Mary of the Lake (1869), Rev. Robert G. Kreckel; Deacons Gerald J. Skerrett; Lee Skerrett.
Res., 5823 Walworth Rd., P.O. Box 499, 14519. Tel: 315-524-2611; Fax: 315-524-7421. [CEM]
Catechesis/Religious Programs—5823 Walworth Rd., 14519. Tel: 315-524-7421.
Students 505.

Ovid, Seneca Co., Holy Cross (1849), Rev. Nelson J. Ruppert, O.F.M.Cap.
Res., 7227 S. Main St., P.O. Box 337, 14521-0337. Tel: 607-869-2261; Fax: 607-869-9825. [CEM]
Catechesis/Religious Programs—Students 64.

Owego, Tioga Co., St. Patrick (1842), Rev. William A. Moorby, Admin.; Deacon George Burnett.
Res., 300 Main St., 13827. Tel: 607-687-1068; Fax: 607-687-2676. [CEM]
School—Tel: 607-687-1770. Mrs. Loretta Hayton, Prin.
Lay Teachers 6; Students 139.
Catechesis/Religious Programs—Tel: 607-687-1331.
Students 275.

Painted Post, Steuben Co., Immaculate Heart of Mary (1952), Revs. Michael F. Conboy; Michael R. Brown; Deacon Raymond Defendorf; Sr. Mary Kay Ryan, S.S.J., Pastoral Assoc.
Mailing Address: c/o 222 Dodge Ave., Corning, 14830. Tel: 607-936-4688; 962-0422 (Res.); Fax: 607-936-0222. [CEM][JC]

Palmyra, Wayne Co., St. Anne (1850), Revs. Robert Gaudio; Francis H. Vogt, Pastor Emeritus.
Res., 136 Church St., 14522. Tel: 315-597-4571. [CEM]
Catechesis/Religious Programs—Tel: 315-597-4571. Ms. Marilyn Smith, D.R.E.
Students 101.

Penfield, Monroe Co., Holy Spirit (1965), Revs. Frederick W. Bush; Ronald A. Antinarelli. In res., Rev. Francis M. Feeney.
Res., 1355 Hatch Rd., Webster, 14580. Tel: 716-671-5520.
Catechesis/Religious Programs—Tel: 716-671-5680.
Students 304.

St. Joseph (1860), Revs. Kevin P. Murphy; Lee P. Chase; Deacon Thomas Ecker; Sr. Patricia M. Switzer, R.S.M., Pastoral Assoc. In res., Revs. L. John Hedges; Edward E. Steinkirchner.
Res., 43 Gebhardt Rd., 14526. Tel: 716-586-8089. [CEM]
School—39 Gebhardt Rd., 14526. Tel: 716-586-6968; Fax: 716-586-4619.
Sisters 1; Lay Teachers 24; Students 394.
Catechesis/Religious Programs—Andrew Desmarias, D.R.E.
Students 1,032.

Penn Yan, Yates Co., St. Michael (1850), Co-Pastors: Revs. Charles Mulligan; Peter Deckman; Deacon Claude Curtin.
Res., 312 Liberty St., 14527. Tel: 315-536-7459; Fax: 315-536-7450. [CEM 2]
School—210 Keuka St., 14527. Tel: 315-536-6112. Sr. Ann Lafferty, S.S.J., Prin.
Lay Teachers 7; Students 138.
Catechesis/Religious Programs—210 Keuka St., Tel: 315-536-3794. Sr. Mary Kay McNelis, S.S.J., D.R.E.
Students 122.
Mission—Dundee, Yates Co., St. Andrew, (1877) 312 Liberty St., P.O. Box 12, Dundee, 14837.

Phelps, Ontario Co., St. Francis (1869). Merged with St. Felix to form St. Felix / St. Francis Parish Cluster, Clifton Springs.

Pittsford, Monroe Co., St. Louis (1911), Revs. James A. Schwartz; Kip Correveau; Deacon Thomas J. Driscoll. In res., Revs. Protus Hamisi; John A. Reddington; James F. Slattery.
Res., 64 S. Main St., 14534. Tel: 716-586-5675; Fax: 716-387-9888.
School—11 Rand Pl., 14534. Tel: 716-586-5200. Kathleen Carroll, Prin.
Lay Teachers 19; Students 419.
Catechesis/Religious Programs—64 S. Main St., 14534. Tel: 716-381-4455.
Students 305.

Church of the Transfiguration (1983), Rev. Gerald J. Appelby; Deacon Michael Piehler; Barbara Swiecki, Pastoral Min.
Res., 50 W. Bloomfield Rd., 14534. Tel: 716-248-2427; Fax: 716-385-9870.
Catechesis/Religious Programs—Tel: 716-248-2465. Mary Presutti, D.R.E.
Students 825.

Rexville, Steuben Co., St. Mary (1845) (Irish), Rev. Daniel W. Heintz.
Res., 32 W. Main St., Canisteo, 14823. Tel: 607-698-4034. [CEM]

Rush, Monroe Co., St. Joseph (1863), Rev. John M. Mulligan, V.G., Sacramental Min.; Sr. Alice Cooney, S.S.J., Pastoral Admin.
Res., 1209 Rush West Rush Rd., 14543-0320. Tel: 716-533-1719.
Catechesis/Religious Programs—Tel: 716-533-1760.
Students 202.

Scipio Center, Cayuga Co., St. Bernard (1867), Rev. John F. Gagnier, Admin.
Mailing Address: 2814 Center Rd., P.O. Box 157, 13147. Tel: 315-364-8172.
Res., 51 Grove St., P.O. Box 111, Moravia, 13118. Tel: 315-497-0626. [CEM]

Scottsville, Monroe Co., St. Mary of the Assumption (1853), Rev. Kevin McKenna; Deacon Michael Mahoney, Admin.
Res., 99 Main St., P.O. Box 23, 14546. Tel: 716-889-3100; Fax: 716-889-7806. [CEM]
Catechesis/Religious Programs—Tel: 716-889-8440; Fax: 716-889-7806.
Students 198.

Seneca Falls, Seneca Co., St. Patrick (1831), Rev. David Gramkee.
Res., 97 W. Bayard St., 13148. Tel: 315-568-5203; Fax: 315-568-5203. [CEM]
School—Tel: 315-568-6295.
Lay Teachers 16; Students 176.
Catechesis/Religious Programs—81 W. Bayard St., 13148. Tel: 315-568-2573.
Students 202.

Shortsville, Ontario Co., St. Dominic (1885), Rev. William J. Cosgrove; Deacon Edward A. Smith.
Res., 6 Canandaigua St., 14548. Tel: 716-289-4164. [CEM]
Catechesis/Religious Programs—Students 205.

Sodus, Wayne Co., Epiphany (1922), Rev. David J. Faraone.
Res., 105 W. Main St., 14551. Tel: 315-483-6111; Fax: 315-483-0327.
Catechesis/Religious Programs—Ann Wilkins, D.R.E.
Students 158.

Mission—Sodus Point, Wayne Co., St. Rose, (1886).

Spencerport, Monroe Co., St. John the Evangelist (1867), Rev. William C. Michatek; Deacon Larry Van Etten. In res., Revs. Paul G. Wohlrab; M. Gerard Hafner.
Res., 60 Martha St., 14559. Tel: 716-352-5481. [CEM]
School—55 Martha St., 14559. Tel: 716-352-4550; Fax: 716-352-3759. Mr. Christopher Meagher, Prin. Lay Teachers 16; Students (K-8) 213; Students (PreK) 26.
Catechesis/Religious Programs—Tel: 716-352-0225. Shirley Curatolo, D.R.E.
Students 423.

Stanley, Ontario Co., St. Theresa (1875), Rev. Mark A. Miller.
Res., 2050 Main St., P.O. Box 416, 14561. Tel: 716-526-5566. [CEM]
Catechesis/Religious Programs—Students 130.
Mission—Rushville, Ontario Co., St. Mary, (1869) Gilbert St., 14561.

Trumansburg, Tompkins Co., St. James the Apostle (1857), Rev. Eugene O'Hara, O.F.M. Cap.
Res., 17 Whig St., P.O. Box 1, 14886. Tel: 607-387-6781; Fax: 607-387-3763. [CEM]
Catechesis/Religious Programs—Students 79.

Union Springs, Cayuga Co., St. Michael's (1851), Rev. Paul J. Ryan; Deacon John Prave.
Springport Cove, P.O. Box 135, 13160.
Res., Main St., Box 296, Aurora, 13026. Tel: 315-364-7197; Fax: 315-364-7825. [CEM]
Catechesis/Religious Programs—Students 50.

Van Etten, Chemung Co., St. Pius the Tenth (1954), Rev. Thomas H. Watts.
Mailing Address: c/o 132 Main St., 14889. Tel: 607-589-4494; Fax: 607-565-2014.
Res., 503 Clark St., Waverly, 14892. Tel: 607-565-2014; Fax: 607-565-2014.

Victor, Ontario Co., St. Patrick (1856), Rev. George Wiant.
Res., 115 Maple Ave., 14564. Tel: 716-924-7111; Fax: 716-742-3296. [CEM]
Catechesis/Religious Programs—115 Maple Ave., 14564. Tel: 716-924-2800.
Students 327.

Waterloo, Seneca Co., St. Mary (1868), Rev. Dennis R. Sewar; Patricia Albrecht, Pastoral Assoc.
Res., 25 Center St., 13165. Tel: 315-539-2944; Fax: 315-539-8841. [CEM]
School—Tel: 315-539-3772. Arlene F. McDermott, Prin.
Lay Teachers 13; Students 188.
Catechesis/Religious Programs—Tel: 315-539-8146.
Students 205.

Watkins Glen, Schuyler Co., St. Mary of the Lake (1846) (Irish-Italian), Rev. David L. Bonin.
Res., 905 N. Decatur St., 14891. Tel: 607-535-2786. [CEM 2]
Parish Center—10th St., 14891.
Catechesis/Religious Programs—Tel: 607-535-4507.
Students 176.

Waverly, Tioga Co., St. James (1881), Rev. Thomas H. Watts. In res., Rev. William A. Burns.
Res., 503 Clark St., 14892. Tel: 607-565-2014; Fax: 607-565-2014. [CEM]
Catechesis/Religious Programs—Students 115.

Wayland, Steuben Co., St. Joseph's (1881) (German), Rev. Paul R. Schnacky; Deacon Daniel Slattery.
Res., 206 Fremont St., 14572-1298. Tel: 716-728-2228. [CEM]
School—209 Fremont St., 14572. Tel: 716-728-5700.
Lay Teachers 8; Students 166.
Catechesis/Religious Programs—Tel: 716-728-2228.
Students 168.

Webster, Monroe Co., Holy Trinity (1861), Revs. Thomas F. Nellis; William M. Hart, (Retired); Deacon Leo Kester.
Res., 1460 Ridge Rd., 14580. Tel: 716-265-1616; Fax: 716-265-1616. [CEM]
School—1456 Ridge Rd., 14580. Tel: 716-265-2002; Fax: 716-265-3405. Mrs. Mary Lou Kime, Prin.
Lay Teachers 14; Students 190.
Catechesis/Religious Programs—Tel: 716-265-4750.
Students 376.

St. Paul (1967), Rev. Raymond Booth.
Res., 783 Hard Rd., 14580. Tel: 716-671-2100; Fax: 716-787-8907.
Catechesis/Religious Programs—Tel: 716-671-2110. Scott Rutan, D.R.E.
Students 822.

Weedsport, Cayuga Co., St. John (1865), Rev. William B. Leone; Sr. Virginia Taylor, R.S.M., Pastoral Assoc.; Deacon John Tomandl.
Res., 2667 Hamilton St., P.O. Box 266, 13166. Tel: 315-834-6266; Fax: 315-689-7090.
Catechesis/Religious Programs—Tel: 315-834-9203; Fax: 315-689-7090. Walter B. Sheehan, D.R.E.
Students 125.

St. Joseph (1854), Rev. William B. Leone; Sr. Virginia Taylor, R.S.M., Pastoral Assoc.; Deacon John Tomandl.
Res., 2667 Hamilton St., P.O. Box 266, 13166. Tel: 315-834-6266; Fax: 315-689-7090. [CEM]
Catechesis/Religious Programs—Tel: 315-834-9203; Fax: 315-689-7090. Walter Sheehan, D.R.E.
Students 182.

Webster, Monroe Co., St. Rita (1950), Revs. John T. Reif; Donald E. McCarthy, C.S.B.; Deacons Richard Mahany; Stan Douglas.
Res., 1008 Maple Dr., 14580. Tel: 716-671-1100; Fax: 716-671-1105 (call first).
School—Tel: 716-371-3132. Sr. Katherine Ann Rappl, R.S.M., Prin.
Sisters of Mercy 1; Lay Teachers 17; Students 360.
Catechesis/Religious Programs—Tel: 716-671-2079.
Students 706.

Wolcott, Wayne Co., St. Mary Magdalene (1940), Rev. John V. Forni.
Res., 11956 Washington St., 14590-1133. Tel: 315-594-9430.

St. Thomas the Apostle (1882), Rev. John V. Forni.
Mailing Address: 11956 Washington St., 14590-1133. Tel: 315-594-9430. [CEM]
Mission—Fair Haven, Cayuga Co., St. Jude Chapel, (1962). All inquiries for sacramental records for St. Thomas and St. Jude prior to July 1, 1985 can be made at St. Joseph, P.O. Box 266, Weedsport, NY 13166..

Chaplains of Public Institutions

Health Care Facilities

ROCHESTER. *Genesee Hospital*. Rev. George Norton, 224 Alexander St., 14607.
Highland Hospital. Vacant. 1000 South Ave., 14620.
Monroe Community Hospital. Rev. Desmond O'Neill, 435 E. Henrietta Rd., 14620. Tel: 716-473-4080.
Park Ridge Hospital 1555 Long Pond Rd., 14626. Rosemarie Zlotnick, Pastoral Care Assoc.
Rochester General Hospital. Rev. William Endres, 1425 Portland Ave., 14621.
St. Ann's Home/Heritage. Vacant. 1500 Portland Ave., 14621.
St. Mary's Hospital. Rev. James Cosgrove; Sr. Elaine Hollis, S.S.J., Dir. Spiritual Care, 89 Genesee St., 14611.
Strong Memorial Hospital. Revs. Donald J. Curtiss; Matthew A. Kawiak, 601 Elmwood Ave., 14642.

AUBURN, CAYUGA CO. *Mercy Health and Rehabilitation Center*. Cayuga Co. Sr. Mary Gertrude Dumas, O.S.F., 3 St. Anthony St., 13021.

BATH, STEUBEN CO. *Soliders' Home and Veterans' Hospital* Tel: 607-776-2111, Ext. 1382. Revs. Ronald Marecki; David Carson.

CANANDAIGUA, ONTARIO CO. *Veteran's Hospital* Tel: 716-394-2000, Ext. 3052. Revs. Miecislaus I. Curzydio; Francis Vogt.

ELMIRA, CHEMUNG CO. *St. Joseph Hospital*. Chemung Co. Rev. Joseph Brodnick; Sr. Margot Mann, S.S.J., 555 E. Market St., 14902. Tel: 607-733-6541.

HORNELL, STEUBEN CO. *St. James Mercy Hospital*. Steuben Co. Revs. Jeremiah P. Moynihan; Brian Diffenbacher, 411 Canisteo St., 14843.

State Facilities

ROCHESTER. *Finger Lakes DDSO - Rochester Site*. Vacant. 620 Westfall Rd., 14620. Tel: 716-461-8676.
Rochester Psychiatric Center 1111 Elmwood Ave., 14620. Rev. Thomas D. Hoctor.

AUBURN. *Auburn Correctional Facility* 135 State St., 13021. Revs. John D. Dillon; James C. Enright.

ELMIRA. *Elmira Correctional Facility, Center and Camp Monterey* P.O. Box 500, 14902. Tel: 607-734-3901. Rev. Joseph Brodnick; Mr. Peter G. Ladley; Mr. Michael Stanley.
Elmira Psychiatric Center 100 Washington St., 14901. Deacon Joseph Federowicz.

GENESEO, LIVINGSTON CO. *Finger Lakes DDSO - Geneseo Site* 3 Park St., 14454-1217. Tel: 716-243-6405. Deacon Edward Sergent.

INDUSTRY. *State Agricultural & Industrial School, Div. of Youth*. Vacant. 14474. Tel: 716-533-1700.

MORAVIA, CAYUGA CO. *Cayuga Correctional* P.O. Box 1150, 13118. Tel: 315-497-1110. Deacon Gregory Kiley.

NEWARK, WAYNE CO. *Finger Lakes DDSO - Newark Site* 703 E. Maple Ave., 14513. Tel: 315-331-1700. Deacon Edward Sergeant.

PINE CITY. *Southport Correctional Facility* P.O. Box 2000, 14871-2000. Tel: 607-737-0850. Chaplains: Rev. Richard Farrell; Mrs. Theresa Stanley.

RED CREEK. *Butler Correctional Facility* P.O. Box 388, 13143. Tel: 315-754-6216, Ext. 288. Rev. Robert G. Smith.

SONYEA, LIVINGSTON CO. *Groveland Correctional Facility* Rt. 36, P.O. Box 50, 14556. Tel: 716-658-2871, Ext. 362. Rev. William I. Onuh; Deacon Paul Clement.
Livingston Correctional Facility and Seneca Correctional Facility Rt. 36, P.O. Box 49, 14556. Rev. William Dnuh; Deacon Nemesio Martinez.

WILLARD, SENECA CO. *Drug Treatment Center* 7116 County Rd. 132, P.O. Box 303, 14588-0303. Tel: 607-869-5500, Ext. 2393. Rev. Vincent Panepinto.

County Jail Chaplains

ROCHESTER. *Livingston County Jail*. Vacant. 4 Church St., Geneseo, 14454. Tel: 716-243-1100.
Monroe County Jail. Vacant. Deacons William Baker; Brian Mahoney.
Tompkins County Jail. Vacant.
Yates County Jail. Vacant.

On Duty Outside the Diocese:
Reverend Fathers—
Bartollotta, Victor W., Jr., Bishop Lynch High School, 9750 Ferguson Rd., Dallas, TX 75228-3891
Celso, Thomas B., 163 Patterson, Newark, NY 14513-9119
Curran, Charles E., Southern Methodist University, 4125 Woodcreek Dr., Dallas, TX 75220
Fleming, Terence K., 1200 Seventh Ave. N., St. Petersburg, FL 33733
Metzger, Edwin B., St. Jude, P.O. Box 65, Athi River, Kenya

Military Chaplains:
Reverend Fathers—
Brown, Lewis E., CHC, USNR, Regional Support Group, 9170 2nd St., Ste. 120, Norfolk, VA 23511-2393

Absent on Leave:
Reverend Fathers—
DiSano, Frank E.
Lum, William
Schwab, Donald F.
Stacy, Ronald W.
Walczak, Melvin

Unassigned:
Reverend Fathers—
Emo, Eugene
Frederick, Ronald P.

Retired:
Reverend Monsignors—
Boyle, Charles V., 1500 Portland Ave., Rm. 813, Rochester, NY 14621
Cirrincione, Joseph A., Mailing Address: 81 Whitney St., Rochester, NY 14611
Cocuzzi, George A., St. Raymond Rectory, 1759 Castle Hill Ave., Bronx, NY 10462-4297
Duffy, John F., St. Pius X Home, 714 E. Brighton Ave, Apt. 208, Syracuse, NY 13205-2299
Gefell, Gerard J., 2332 Humphrey Rd., Cape Vincent, NY 13618
Gefell, Joseph G., 2332 Humphrey Rd., Cape Vincent, NY 13618
McMahon, Gerard J., 2523 Jackson St., Scranton, PA 18504
Murphy, J. Emmett, S.S.J. Convent Infirmary, 4199 East Ave., Rochester, NY 14618-3733
Quinn, Richard M., Sisters of Mercy Infirmary, 1437 Blossom Rd., Rochester, NY 14610
Roche, William M., Our Lady of Mt. Carmel Rectory, 300 Fulton St., Redwood City, CA 94062
Shannon, William H., Sisters of St. Joseph Motherhouse, 4095 East Ave., Rochester, NY 14618
Sullivan, Joseph J., S.S.J. Convent Infirmary, 4199 East Ave., Rochester, NY 14618-3733
Whalen, Leslie G., St. Ann's Home, 1500 Portland Ave., Rm. 834, Rochester, NY 14621
Reverend Fathers—
Alletto, Nicholas P., Lakeshore Nursing Home, 425 Beach Ave., Rochester, NY 14612
Brennan, Joseph P., 251 Bay Village Dr., Rochester, NY 14609
Burns, William A., St. James Rectory, 503 Clark St., Waverly, NY 14892
Calimeri, Anthony F., P.O. Box 24, Phelps, NY 14532
Callan, L. James, 500 Cook Rd., Hamlin, NY 14464
Carron, J. Walter, 1437 Blossom Rd., Rochester, NY 14610
Cloonan, Joseph F., 4383 Cascade Way, Paso Robles, CA 93446
Dailey, Joseph W., 1471 Long Pond Rd., Apt. 420, Rochester, NY 14626
Davis, Francis R., St. Mary's Rectory, 155 State St., Corning, NY 14830

Davis, Robert, Southfield Apartments, Quill Ave. & Clymer St., #D-13, Auburn, NY 13021
Donovan, Joseph D., S.S.J. Convent Infirmary, 4199 East Ave., Rochester, NY 14618-3733
Donovan, Robert, St. Andrews Rectory, 923 Portland Ave., Rochester, NY 14621. Tel: 716-342-8686
Downs, Robert, Southfield Apartments, Quill Ave. & Clymer St., Apt. D-13, Auburn, NY 13021
Egan, Joseph M., 3195 S. Main St., Horseheads, NY 14845
Egan, Robert, Holy Family, 85 North St., Auburn, NY 14580
Ehmann, Benedict A., S.S.J. Convent Infirmary, 4199 East Ave., Rochester, NY 14618-3733
Elsemann, Frederick F., 151 Sheppler St., Rochester, NY 14612
Erb, Francis J., P.O. Box 665, Savona, NY 14879
Feeney, Francis M., Holy Spirit Rectory, 1355 Hatch Rd., Webster, NY 14580
Foy, Edward J., St. Alphonsus Rectory, 10 Lewis St., Auburn, NY 13021
Gardner, Clarence W., St. Alphonsus Rectory, 10 Lewis St., Auburn, NY 13021
Gaynor, Joseph T., St. Alphonsus Rectory, 10 Lewis St., Auburn, NY 13021
Grace, Patrick J., 3742 Wildwood Rd., San Diego, CA 92107
Halloran, Emmet, St. Mary's Rectory, 95 N. Main St., Cannondaigna, NY 14424
Hanna, Austin B., Sisters of Mercy Infirmary, 1437 Blossom Rd., Rochester, NY 14610
Hart, William M., 1450 Ridge Rd., Webster, NY 14580
Hedges, L. John, St. Joseph's Rectory, 43 Gebhardt Rd., Penfield, NY 14526
Heindl, Elmer W., St. Charles Borromeo Rectory, 3003 Dewey Ave., Rochester, NY 14616
Hempel, John L., 109 Edgewood Ct., Forest Lakes, Oldsmar, FL 34677
Hogan, Michael C., St. John of Rochester Rectory, 18 Wickford Way, Fairport, NY 14450
Holberton, William B., 555 Spring St., Apt. 806, Bethlehem, PA 18018
Jankowiak, Valentine A., St. Stanislaus, 34 St. Stanislaus St., Rochester, NY 14621
Kalafsky, Andrew J., St. Anthony of Padua Friary, P.O. Box 414, Watkins Glen, NY 14891
Kanka, Robert, St. Ann's Rectory, 31 Erie Ave., P.O. Box 605, Hornell, NY 14843
Kelly, Gerald G., 434 Pine Glen Ln., Apt. B1, Lake Worth, FL 33463
MacNamara, Robert C., St. Mary Our Mother Rectory, 816 W. Broad St., Horseheads, NY 14845
Marvin, James J., 294 E. Lake Rd., P.O. Box 463, Honcoye, NY 14471
McCarthy, Charles L., 100 Antoinetta Dr., Rochester, NY 14623
McDonald, Elmer J., 6145 Sun Blvd., #505B, St. Petersburg, FL 33715
McDonnell, Joseph M., St. Michael's Rectory, 401 S. Main St., Newark, NY 14513
McFarland, Eugene H., St. Mary Rectory, 13 North St., Geneseo, NY 14454
McNamara, Elmer A., Mailing Address: St. Mark, P.O. Box 371, Kendall, NY 14476
McNamara, Joseph M., St. Pius X Home, 714 E. Brighton St., Syracuse, NY 13205
McNamara, Robert F., St. Thomas the Apostle Rectory, 4536 St. Paul Blvd., Rochester, NY 14617
Meng, Robert A., 7 Harwood Ln., East Rochester, NY 14445
Mockevicius, Charles L., 1156 Plank Rd., Webster, NY 14580
Mockevicius, Dominic, 1156 Plank Rd., Webster, NY 14580
Morgan, John A., 1986 Edgemont Dr., Camarillo, CA 93010
Murphy, David M., 51 Hall St., Waltham, MA 02154
Nacca, John J., Holy Family Cathedral, 122 W. 8th St., P.O. Box 3208, Tulsa, OK 74101
Nangle, C. Richard, St. Francis Rectory, 185 Clark St., Auburn, NY 13021
Nolan, Norbert L., 120 Holyoke St., Bldg. 4, Apt. 2, Rochester, NY 14615
Norris, John P., St. Catherine of Siena Rectory, 26 Mendon-Ionia Rd., Mendon, NY 14506
Nowak, Bernard, 601 Seneca Manor Dr., Apt. 14L, Rochester, NY 14621
O'Brien, Bartholomew J., 4199 East Ave., Rochester, NY 14618
O'Connell, James F., St. Ann's Home, Rochester, NY 14621
O'Connell, Richard C., St. Monica Rectory, 34 Monica St., Rochester, NY 14619
Orlando, Richard J., St. Thomas More Rectory, 2617 East Ave., Rochester, NY 14610
Reddington, John A., St. Louis Rectory, 46 S. Main St., Pittsford, NY 14534
Roach, John E., 9005 State Rd. 53, Naples, NY 14512
Sansom, Lawrence W., 571 Elmwood Terrace, Apt. B, Rochester, NY 14620
Sasso, Joseph M., 8112 Oatka Trail, LeRoy, NY 14482
Schifferli, Jerome F., 7 Washington St., Box 311, Livonia, NY 14487
Schmidt, Elmer J., St. Ann Rectory, 31 Erie Avenue, Hornell, NY 14843
Shamon, Albert J., 5 S. Marvine Ave., Auburn, NY 13021
Slattery, James F., St. Louis Rectory, 60 S. Main St., Pittsford, NY 14534
Steinkirchner, Edward E., St. Joseph's Rectory, 43 Gebhardt Rd., Penfield, NY 14526
Tormey, Daniel, American Catholic University, Louvain College, Naamestraat 100, 3000 Leuven Belgium
Ventura, Gennaro J., 8247 Dutch Hollow Rd., Wayland, NY 14572
Vogt, Francis H., 115 Throop St., Palmyra, NY 14522
Vogt, Otto J., Our Lady of Lourdes Rectory, 150 Varinna Dr., Rochester, NY 14618-3733
Wahl, Raymond J., S.S.J. Convent Infirmary, 4199 East Ave., Rochester, NY 14618-3733
Walsh, John T., St. Margaret Mary Rectory, 401 Rogers Pkwy., Rochester, NY 14617
Whalen, John S., St. Thomas More Rectory, 2617 East Ave., Rochester, NY 14610
Wohlrab, Paul G., St. John the Evangelist Rectory, 60 Martha St., Spencerport, NY 14559
Zimmer, Edward A., St. John the Evangelist Rectory, 549 Humboldt St., Rochester, NY 14610

Permanent Deacons:
Abballe, Dan, (Retired)
Almeter, Robert C., Diocese of Syracuse
Aman, Leo, St. Charles Borromeo, Rochester
Antenucci, John, Holy Apostles/St. Anthony Cluster, Rochester
Baker, William, Monroe County Jail Min.
Beck, Thomas, St. Thomas the Apostle, Rochester
Bergeron, Albert, Our Lady Queen of Peace, Rochester
Birx, Charles, Diocese of Richmond
Bowers, Owen F., St. James, Rochester
Burnett, George, Diocesan Tribunal
Cadregari, David, St. Ambrose, Rochester
Campanelli, Michael, (Retired)
Carrol, Stephen, St. Thomas More, Rochester
Caruso, Anthony, St. Theodore, Rochester
Casey, Lawrence B., On Duty Outside the Diocese
Cass, K. Thomas, St. Michael's, Newark
Chatterton, James, St. Mark's
Cleary, Thomas J., St. John of Rochester, Fairport
Clement, Paul F., Groveland Correctional Facility, Sonyea
Coccia, Angelo, Holy Family, Rochester
Coffey, William, St. Mary's, Rochester
Curtin, Claude, St. Michael's, Penn Yan
Datz, Ramon, St. Elizabeth Ann Seton, Hamlin
Defendorf, Raymond, St. Mary & St. Patrick, Corning
DiLallo, Gary R., St. Hyacinth, Auburn
Dispenza, Charles, St. Bridget's, Rochester
Dizer, Robert, Inactive
Doughtery, William P., St. Charles Borromeo, Elmira Heights
Douglas, Stanley, St. Rita's, Webster
Doyle, Gregory J., Matt Talbot Ministry, Rochester
Driscoll, Thomas J., St. Louis, Pittsford
Dwyer, Joseph, St. Charles Borromeo, Rochester
Ecker, Thomas R., St. Joseph, Penfield
Edwards, Eugene L., Jr., Good Shepherd, Henrietta
Erb, John, St. Felix, Clifton Springs
Federowicz, Joseph F., Elmira Psychiatric Center, Elmira
Fisher, Christopher, St. Helen's, Gates
Fitch, James E., Holy Rosary, Rochester
Fuerst, Eugene C., On Medical Leave of Absence
Giugno, John M, Most Precious Blood, Rochester
Glasgow, Joseph H., Fitz, Roman Catholic Community of the 19th Ward, Rochester
Graff, Stephen J., S.B.I., Rochester
Graybill, Patrick A., Unassigned
Grenn, Stanley J., St. Augustine, FL
Haber, Francis, St. Mary's of the Lake, Watkins Glen
Hankey, James D., Immaculate Conception, Ithaca
Hoerner, Gerard A., St. Mary's, Dansville
Holmes, John, Jr., On Duty Outside the Diocese
Hunt, William R., New Bern, NC
Hurley, Daniel R., St. Mary Our Mother, Horseheads
Kester, Leo A., (Retired)
Kiley, Gregory, Cayuga Correctional Facility
Kinsky, Daniel M., Church of the Resurrection, Fairport
Kluchko, Thomas J., St. Mark, Rochester
Kohlmeier, Charles P., Mercy Prayer Center
Krupiarz, Michael J., Sacred Heart Cathedral, Rochester
Lawson, Gregg K., Naperville, IL
Lebron, Juan, On Duty Outside the Diocese
Lester, Claude E., St. Bridget/St. Joseph, Bloomfield
Lombard, Richard J., Holy Name of Jesus, Rochester
Mahany, Richard E., St. Rita's, Webster
Mahoney, Brian, Monroe County Jail
Mahoney, Michael, St. Mary of the Assumption, Scottsville
Mangione, Michael, St. Anthony / St. Patrick, Elmira
Marini, Anthony, On Duty Outside the Diocese
Martinez, Nemesio, Livingston Correctional Facility, Sonyea
Maune, William D., Park Forest, IL
McCormick, Robert W., St. Ann's, Hornell
McGuire, Michael R., St. Januarius, Naples
McNulty, Brian J., 19th Ward RCC
Medero, Felix, Community of Hope, Rochester
Melendez, Eliseo, Clinton Correctional Facility
Mercadel, Anthony J., Guardian Angels, Rochester
Mercado, Conrado, On Duty Outside the Diocese
Mielcarek, Raymond, St. Stanislaus, Rochester
Morin, Kenneth, Unassigned
Nguyen, Hoc, St. Anthony of Padua, Rochester
Ona, Fernando V., St. Catherine's, Mendon
Palma, David, RIT Campus, Rochester
Paluskiewicz, David L., Blessed Sacrament, Rochester
Piehler, Michael J., Transfiguration, Pittsford
Prave, John J., Cayuga Team Ministry, Union Springs
Rodriguez, Agenol, Holy Redeemer, Rochester
Rutan, Warren, St. John the Evangelist, Newark Valley
Sampson, Gregory R., St. Anne, Rochester
Scarciotta, Kenneth A., (Retired)
Schmitz, William F., St. Andrew's, Rochester
Schraeder, Robert, Rochester Psychiatric Center
Schrage, Thomas, Campus Ministry, Brockport
Schuler, Richard, St. Helen, Rochester
Schultz, Klaus D., Borromeo Prayer Center
Sergeant, Edward R., Newark Development Center, Newark
Shanley, Patrick M., Holy Family, Rochester
Skerrett, Jerry, St. Mary's of the Lake, Ontario
Slattery, Daniel P., Groveland Correction Facility
Smith, Edward A., St. Dominic's, Shortsville
Srode, Walter E., Diocese of Albany
Steiger, James P., St. Leo, Hilton
Stowell, Robert, St. Mary's, Elmira
Swift, John G., Medical Leave of Absence
Tocci, Ronald, Church of the Assumption
Tomandl, John D., Northern Cayuga Cluster
Van Etten, Laurence A., On Leave of Absence
Vargas, Carlos H., St. Francis of Assisi, Rochester
Verkon, Ronald, On Duty Outside the Diocese
Welch, George J., Eastside Catholic Parish
Whitford, James, On Duty Outside the Diocese
Wilson, Albro C., Jr., St. Paul of the Cross, Honeoye Falls
Yanaitis, Victor M., Church of the Annunciation, Rochester
Zierle, John E., St. Pius Tenth, Rochester

INSTITUTIONS LOCATED IN THE DIOCESE

[A] GRADUATE SCHOOL OF THEOLOGY

ROCHESTER. *St. Bernard's Institute*, 1100 S. Goodman St., 14620. Tel: 716-271-3657
For a complete listing, refer to the Colleges and Universities section.

[B] HIGH SCHOOLS

ROCHESTER. *The Aquinas Institute*, 1127 Dewey Ave., 14613. Tel: 716-254-2020. Revs. Albert R. Gaelens, C.S.B., Dir. Alumni Rels.; Richard A. Wahl, C.S.B.; Dennis J. Kauffman, C.S.B. Under the direction of the Basilian Fathers. Priests 3; Lay Teachers 56; Students 880.

Bishop Kearney High School. (Coed), 125 Kings Hwy., 14617-5596. Tel: 716-342-4000; Fax: 716-342-4694. E-mail: kearney@frontiernet.net
Conducted by the Congregation of Christian Brothers in association with the School Sisters of Notre Dame, Wilton Province. Bro. Raymond J. Vercruysse, C.F.C., Pres.; Louis D'Angelo, Prin.; Mrs. Donna Gmelin, Asst. Prin. Brothers 6; Sisters 3; Lay Teachers 34; Students 530.

McQuaid Jesuit High School, 1800 S. Clinton Ave., 14618. Tel: 716-473-1130; Fax: 716-256-6171.
E-mail: jesuitres@mcquaid.org
Jesuit Fathers. Revs. William J. McCurdy, S.J., Supr.; James J. Fischer, S.J., Pres.; Mr. Franklin L. Kamp, Prin.; Revs. Thomas F. McManus, S.J., Asst. Treas.; Frederick G. Betti, S.J.; John P. Carriero, S.J.; John M. Costello, S.J.; James R. Dolan, S.J.; Joseph DeMaio, O.Carm.; Jack Healy, O.Carm.; Leon J. Hogenkamp, S.J.; William C. McCusker, S.J.; Francis J. McNamara, S.J., Alumni Dir.; James P. Malone, S.J.; Brian Murphy, O.Carm.; Lawrence J. Wroblewski, S.J. Priests 13; Sisters 1; Lay Teachers 40; Students 769.

Nazareth Schools: The Hall; The Academy, 1001 Lake Ave., 14613. Tel: 716-458-8583; Fax: 716-647-8717. Sisters of St. Joseph 16; Lay Teachers 60; Students 740.

Our Lady of Mercy High School. (Grades 7-12), 1437 Blossom Rd., 14610. Tel: 716-288-7120.
E-mail: mercy@netacc.net
Mrs. Evelyn J. Kirst, Prin. Sisters of Mercy 13; Lay Teachers 59; Students 595.

ELMIRA. *Notre Dame High School*, 1400 Maple Ave., 14904. Tel: 607-734-2267; Fax: 607-737-8903. Sr. Mary Walter Hickey, R.S.M., Prin.; Rev. Vincent McDonough, S.J., Chap. Priests 1; Sisters of Mercy 10; Lay Teachers 22; Students 350.

GENEVA. *De Sales High School*. (Incorporated under the laws of the State of New York), 14456. Tel: 315-789-5111.
E-mail: desales@epix.net
Web site: dhsoffice@lynnet.com
Edward J. Tracey, Prin. Lay Teachers 14; Students 150.

[C] JUNIOR HIGH SCHOOLS

ROCHESTER. *All Saints Catholic Jr. High*, 170 Spencerport Rd., 14606. Total Staff 16; Students 151.

Monroe County Catholic Schools, 1150 Buffalo Rd., 14624.

Northeastern Catholic Jr. High, 125 Kings Hwy. S., 14617. Total Staff 25; Students 260.

[D] ELEMENTARY SCHOOLS, PRIVATE

ROCHESTER. *Corpus Christi School*, 546 Oxford St., 14607. Tel: 716-473-3937. Sr. Eileen Daly, S.S.J., Prin. Sisters 4; Lay Teachers 8; Students 185.

Holy Family Catholic School System-Diocese of Rochester, 421 Fulton St., 14904.

Nazareth Hall Elementary School. (Coed), 180 Raines Park, 14613. Tel: 716-458-3786. Sr. Mary Anne Laurer, Dir. Sisters of St. Joseph 6; Lay Teachers 15; Students 230.

Nazareth Hall Middle School. (Coed), 1001 Lake Ave., 14613. Tel: 716-647-8716. Sr. Elizabeth Snyder, Dir. Sisters of St. Joseph 3; Lay Teachers 8; Students 120.

School of the Holy Childhood, 100 Groton Pkwy., 14623. Tel: 716-359-3710.
E-mail: admin@holychildhood.org
Web site: www.holychildhood.org
Day Programs and School for Mentally Retarded Children and Adults. Sr. M. Seraphine, S.S.J., Dir. Sisters of St. Joseph 5; Lay Teachers 21; Children 104; Adults 76.

EAST ROCHESTER. *Trinity Montessori School*, 501 S. Garfield St., 14445. Tel: 716-586-1044. Sr. Clare Francis Mogenhan, S.S.J., Admin. Sisters 2; Lay Teachers 16; Students 117.

[E] HOMES FOR AGED

ROCHESTER. *St. Ann's Home for the Aged*, 1500 Portland Ave., 14621. Tel: 716-342-1700.
Web site: www.stannsrochester.org
For a complete listing, refer to the Special Care Facilities section.

St. Ann's Nursing Home Co., Inc., 1450 Portland Ave., 14621.
Web site: www.stannsrochester.org
For a complete listing, refer to the Special Care Facilities section.

[F] CHILD CARE INSTITUTIONS

ROCHESTER. *St. Joseph's Villa of Rochester*, 3300 Dewey Ave., 14616. Tel: 716-865-1550
For a complete listing, refer to the Special Care Facilities section.

[G] CAMPS

LIVONIA. *Camp Stella Maris*, Conesus Lake, 4395 E.Lake Rd., 14487. Tel: 716-346-2243; Fax: 716-346-6921. Conesus Lake, 4395 E. Lake Rd., 14487. Tel: 716-346-2243; Fax: 716-346-6921. Matthew J. Flanigan, Exec. Dir.; Jay Travers, Board Pres.; Fiona Willis, Summer Camp Dir.
Purpose: Residential camping under Catholic auspices, for boys and girls (ages 7-14) of all faiths. Encampment period: Eight weeks during summer (July/August). Rental of facility available September-June for family/youth development retreats. ACA accredited. Day Camp Center for boys and girls (ages 5-10). Encampment period: Eight weeks during July/August in conjuction with resident camp. Adventure-Based Learning Experience (ABLE) high and low challenge ropes courses ideal for building trust, confidence, cooperation, teamwork, self-esteem, communication, and leadership skills.

[H] GENERAL HOSPITALS

ROCHESTER. *Unity Health System*, 89 Genesee St., 14611. Tel: 716-464-3000; Fax: 716-464-0044
For a complete listing, refer to the Hospitals section.

AUBURN. *Mercy Health & Rehabilitation Center Nursing Home Co., Inc.*, (1972) St. Anthony St., 13021. Tel: 315-253-0351; Fax: 315-258-3904.
E-mail: dfdonnelly@attmail
For a complete listing, refer to the Hospitals section.

ELMIRA. *St. Joseph's Health System, Inc. (Formerly St. Joseph's Hospital)*, 55 E. Market St., 14902. Tel: 607-733-6541.
Web site: www.stjosephs.org
For a complete listing, refer to the Hospitals section.

St. Joseph's Hospital Foundation, Inc., 555 E. Market St., 14902. Tel: 607-737-7004; Fax: 607-737-7837
For a complete listing, refer to the Hospitals section.

HORNELL. *St. James Mercy Hospital*, 411 Canisteo St., 14843. Tel: 607-324-8000
For a complete listing, refer to the Hospitals section.

[I] MONASTERIES AND RESIDENCES OF PRIESTS AND BROTHERS

ROCHESTER. *Basilian Residence*, 3497 East Ave., 14618. Tel: 716-586-4600. Revs. T. Paul Broadhurst, C.S.B.; Albert W. Cylwicki, C.S.B., Supr.; John L. Dugan, C.S.B.; Leo A. Hetzler, C.S.B., Councilor; Leo J. Klem, C.S.B.; John R. Lee, C.S.B.; William C. Marceau, C.S.B.; John C. Murray, C.S.B.; John A. Poluikis, C.S.B., Councilor. In res. Revs. Nathaniel Karisa (Kenya); Michael Murimi.
Priests of the Region Serving Elsewhere: Rev. William J. Sheehan, C.S.B., Collegio San Clemente, Via Labicana, 95, 00184, Rome, Italy. Rev. George Kosicki, C.S.B., Divine Mercy International, Eden Hill, Stockbridge, MA, 01263. Rev. J. Gareth Poupore, C.S.B., 16 Village Trail, Honeoye Falls, 14472. Rev. Donald E. McCarthy, C.S.B., St. Rita's Church, 1008 Maple Dr., Webster, 14580. Basilian Fathers of Fisher House, 224 Fairport Rd., East Rochester, 14445. Tel: 716-381-9283. Revs. Paul F. English, Rector. Tel: 716-264-9185; John R. Cavanaugh. Tel: 716-385-1353; Paul F. Walsh, C.S.B.; John Robbins.

Becket Hall, 314 Gregory St., 14620. Tel: 716-461-2890; Fax: 716-328-3149. Residence for Pre-Theologate candidates. Rev. John A. DeSocio, Dir. Students 6.

Residence of Basilian Fathers-The Aquinas Institute, 402 Augustine St., 14613. Tel: 716-254-1190. Revs. Dennis J. Kauffman, C.S.B., Supr.; Peter J. Etlinger, C.S.B.; Albert R. Gaelens, C.S.B.; Thomas M. Miller, C.S.B.; Richard A. Wahl, C.S.B. Priests 5.

St. George's Rectory, 545 Hudson Ave., 14605. Tel: 716-232-4111. Revs. Dominic Mockevicius, Admin.; Charles Mockevicius, Co-Admin.

Whitefriars Priory, 625 Colebrook Dr., 14617. Tel: 716-266-2560. Revs. Brian Murphy, O.Carm.; Joseph DeMaio, O.Carm.; Jack Healy, O.Carm., Prior; Matthew Temple, O.Carm. Total in Residence 4.

INTERLAKEN. *St. Fidelis Friary*, 7790 County Rd. 153, 14847. Tel: 607-532-4423; Fax: 607-532-9271. Capuchin Friars-Province of St. Mary (Order of Friars Minor Capuchin). Revs. Eugene O'Hara, O.F.M.Cap., Supr.; Nelson J. Ruppert, O.F.M.Cap., Vicar; Oliver J. O'Connor, O.F.M.Cap., Preaching Ministry; Julian Phelan, O.F.M.Cap., Preaching Ministry. Priests 4.

PIFFARD. *Abbey of the Genesee*, 14533. Tel: 716-243-0660; 243-2220 (Retreat House).
E-mail: abbeygen@frontiernet.net
Web site: http://web.lemoyne.edu/~bucko/genesee.htm
The Order of Cistercians of the Strict Observance (Trappists). Rt. Rev. John Eudes Bamberger, O.C.S.O., Abbot; Revs. Francis R. Steger, O.C.S.O., Prior; Thomas Aquinas Bond, O.C.S.O.; John J. Denburger, O.C.S.O.; Marcellus R. Earl, O.C.S.O.; Raymond J. Fournier, O.C.S.O.; Jerome J. Machar, O.C.S.O.; Robert J. Moore, O.C.S.O.; Regis C. Tompkins, O.C.S.O.; Justin R. Sheehan, O.C.S.O.; Joseph F. Stanton, O.C.S.O.; Aelred W. Wentz.
Absent on Leave: Rev. Michael M. Hayden, O.C.S.O. Professed Monks 27; Priests 13; Oblates 1; Total in Community (Piffard) 41.

PINE CITY. *Mount Saviour Monastery*, 231 Monastery Rd., 14871-9770. Tel: 607-734-1688; Fax: 607-734-1689.
E-mail: msavior@servtech.com
Web site: http://www.servtech.com/public/msaviour
Very Rev. Martin Boler, O.S.B., Prior; Revs. James Cronin, O.S.B.; James Kelly, O.S.B.; Timothy Courcy, O.S.B. Professed Monks 12; Professed Priests 4; Total in Community 16.

WATKINS GLEN. *St. Anthony of Padua Friary*, Lakeview Ave., P.O. Box 41, 14891. Tel: 607-535-2686. Franciscan Friars. Rev. Austin J. Budnick, O.F.M. Affiliated with the Assumption of the B.V.M. Province, with headquarters in Pulaski, Wisconsin. Priests 1.

[J] CONVENTS AND RESIDENCES FOR SISTERS

ROCHESTER. *Nazareth Convent*, 16 Lake View Park, 14613-1798. Tel: 716-458-3443; Fax: 716-254-6446. Sr. Anne Urquhart, Local Coord. Sisters 40.

North American Union-Sisters of Our Lady of Charity, OLC Holy Angels Convent, 1280 N. Winton Rd., 14609-5897. Tel: 716-654-8600. Sr. Frances Aguillon, Local Supr. Professed Sisters 5.

St. Joseph Convent Infirmary, 4199 East Ave., 14618-3733. Tel: 716-381-4064. Infirmary and home for retired Sisters of Saint Joseph of Rochester, Inc. Sr. Catherine Judge, S.S.J., Local Coord.; Sr. Jeannine Scheg, S.S.J., Admin.; Rev. Donald J. Curtiss, Chap. Sisters 76; Priests 6.

Sisters of Mercy of the Americas Regional Community of Rochester, 1437 Blossom Rd., 14610. Tel: 716-288-2710. Sr. Sheila Stevenson, Pres. In res. Rev. Matthew Kawlak. Tel: 716-288-6272. Professed Sisters 208; Temporary Professed 1; Perpetual Vows 207.

Sisters St. Joseph Motherhouse, 4095 East Ave., 14618-3798. Tel: 716-586-1000; Fax: 716-586-1193.
E-mail: ssjroch@aol.com
Motherhouse of the Sisters of St. Joseph of the Diocese of Rochester. Sr. Rosemary St. Peter, Congregational Pres.; Rev. Msgr. William H. Shannon, Chap. Professed Sisters in Community 431.

Spirit House, Inc., 72 Dorvid Rd., 14617. Tel: 716-544-5698.
E-mail: spirithouse1@juno.com
Sr. Mary Ann Ayers, R.S.M., Dir.

ELMIRA. *Monastery of Mary the Queen, Dominican Nuns*, 1310 W. Church St., 14905. Tel: 607-734-9506; Fax: 607-734-1452. Sr. Mary of the Sacred Heart, O.P., Prioress. Solemn Vows 12; Perpetual Vows 1.

PITTSFORD. *Monastery of Our Lady and St. Joseph Carmelite Monastery*, 1931 W. Jefferson Rd., 14534. Tel: 716-427-7094. Discalced Carmelite Nuns. Mother Miriam of the Angels, O.C.D., Prioress. Professed Nuns with Solemn Vows 8; Externs with Simple Vows 1; Novices 1.

[K] RETREAT HOUSES

ROCHESTER. *Mercy Prayer Center*, 65 Highland Ave., 14620. Conducted and subsidized by Sisters of Mercy. Total in residence 4; Total Staff 6.

S.S.J. Spirituality Center, 402 Rogers Pkwy., 14617. Tel: 716-336-4370.
E-mail: MLHSSJ@juno.com
Mary Louise Heffernan, S.S.J., Dir.; Total in residence 3; Total Staff 6.

CANANDAIGUA. *Notre Dame Retreat House*, Box 342, 5151 Foster Rd., 14424. Tel: 716-394-5700. Revs. Frederick C. Brinkman, C.SS.R., Dir.; Timothy F. Keating, C.Ss.R.; Leo F. Dunn, C.Ss.R.

CORNING. *Anawim Community Center*, 122 E. First St., 14830. Tel: 607-936-4965. Rev. Richard Rusk (MET), Admin.

[L] MISCELLANEOUS LISTINGS

ROCHESTER. *Apostleship of Prayer*, Diocesan Pastoral Center, 1150 Buffalo Rd., 14624. Tel: 716-328-3210. Rev. Thomas P. Mull; Mary Kessler, Diocesan Dir. Tel: 716-328-3210.

Archivist, 219 Stenson St., 14606. Tel: 716-458-6079. Rev. William E. Graf, Dir. of Archives and Records, 4536 St. Paul Blvd., 14617. Tel: 716-338-1602. Rev. Robert F. McNamara, Archivist.

Catherine McAuley Housing, 1694 St. Paul St., 14621. Tel: 716-338-7070. Sr. Janet Korn, R.S.M., Pres. Transitional Housing for Single Mothers and their Children. Total Staff 2; Families assisted 4.

Catholic Charismatic Renewal, 127 W. Meadows Dr., 14616. Tel: 716-321-1265. Diocesan Liaison Team: Don Germano; Louise Dale; David Valone; Robert Cirre; Rev. William A. Moorby, Spiritual Advisor.

Catholic Committee on Scouting, 1150 Buffalo Rd., 14624. Tel: 716-328-3210. Michael Theisen.

Catholic Gay & Lesbian Family Ministry, 1150 Buffalo Rd., 14624. Karen Rinefierd, Diocesan Liaison.

Censores Librorum, 1150 Buffalo Rd., 14624. Revs. Joseph A. Hart; Benedict A. Ehmann; Rev. Msgr. William H. Shannon; Rev. William E. Graf.

Dunn Tower Apartments, Inc., 100 Dunn Tower Dr., 14606. Ann R. Huber, Mgr.

Family Rosary For Peace, Inc., P.O. Box 11007, 14611. Tel: 716-436-6693. Rev. Paul J. Tomasso, Dir.; Dolores Mary Brien, Sec.

Holy Childhood Association, 1150 Buffalo Rd., 14624. Tel: 716-436-9200. Rev. Robert Bradler, Dir.

Marriage Encounter Apostolate. (Worldwide).
E-mail: johnandbel@aol.com
Web site: www.wwme.org
214 E. William St., Bath, 14810. Tel: 607-776-4870. John and Belinda Brasley; Rev. John Murray, C.S.B.

Melita House for Pregnant Women, 124 Evergreen St., 14605. Tel: 716-232-3656. Sisters of Mercy of Rochester. Contact Persons: Sr. Janet Korn, R.S.M.; Peggy Wyand-Block. Total Staff 6; Total assisted in residence 42; Total assisted in aftercare 100.

Providence Housing Development Corporation, 1150 Buffalo Rd., 14624.

Rochester Catholic Worker Bethany House, 169 St. Bridget's Dr., 14605. Tel: 716-454-4197. Donna Ecker, Contact Person. Total staff 4.

St. Francis de Sales Deaf Assn., 75 Ernestine St., 14619. Tel: 716-235-1812 (Voice); 235-3849 (TTY). Rev. Raymond H. Fleming, Dir.

St. Joseph's House of Hospitality (1941), 402 South Ave., 14603. Tel: 716-232-3262. Mailing Address: P.O. Box 1062, 14603. Tel: 716-232-3262. Sr. Marilyn Pray, S.S.J., Contact Person. Services provide soup kitchen, personal assistance to the needy, community garden and social justice advocacy. Total Staff 20; Total Assisted 100.

St. Joseph's Villa Foundation, 3300 Dewey Ave., 14616. Tel: 716-865-1550. Judith Van Bramer, Dir. of Development.

St. Theodore's Apartment Housing Development Fund Co., Inc. (Dunn Tower II Apts.), 200 Dunn Tower Dr., 14606.

Union Meadows Housing Development Fund Corp., 1150 Buffalo Rd., 14624. Maggie Bringewatt, Exec. Dir.; Jack Balinsky, Pres. & Board of Directors.

OWEGO. *Tioga County Rural Ministry, Inc.*, 60 North Ave., 13827. Tel: 607-687-3021. Sr. Lisette O'Brien, R.S.M., Pres. Total Staff 3; Total Assisted 7,005.

SENECA FALLS. *Patrician Fund Trust*, St. Patrick's Church, 97 W. Bayard St., 13148. Rev. David Gramkee.

SPENCERPORT. *Legion of Mary*, 60 Martha St., 14559. Tel: 716-352-9052. Rev. Paul G. Wohlrab, Spiritual Dir. - Rochester Comitium, Rochester Comitium, 191 Furlong St., Rochester, 14621-3959. Tel: 716-266-8087. Mrs. Vera Calnan, Pres.

[M] CAMPUS MINISTRY

ROCHESTER. *Diocesan Office of Campus Ministry*, Pastoral Center, 1150 Buffalo Rd., 14624. Tel: 716-275-4322.
E-mail: olsen@dor.org
Rev. Gary L. Tyman. Tel: 716-442-1402; Joelle LaPorte.

Catholic Students Organization Eastman School of Music, Nazareth College, 4245 East Ave., 14618. Tel: 716-389-2726.

Nazareth College of Rochester, 4245 East Ave., 14618. Tel: 716-389-2305; Fax: 716-389-2300. Sr. Kathleen Weider, S.S.J., Dir., Campus Min. Tel: 716-389-2305 Ext. 331; Deacon Leo Aman, Chap. Tel: 716-389-2306.

Catholic Campus Parish, Rochester Institute of Technology, Interfaith Center, 40 Lomb Memorial Dr., 14623. Tel: 716-475-2136. Rev. Joseph Catarise. Tel: 716-475-2135; Deacon David Palma. Tel: 716-475-2135.

Monroe Community College - Office of the Catholic Chaplain, 1000 E. Henrietta Rd., 14623. Tel: 716-292-2558, Ext. 292. Joan Ann Kirkeby-Prosser.

St. John Fisher College, 3690 East Ave., 14618. Tel: 716-385-8368. Revs. Paul F. English, C.S.B., Dir., Campus Ministry; John F. Robbins, C.S.B.; Deirdre McKiernan Hetzler.

State University College at Brockport, the Newman Oratory of Brockport, NY, Inc., 101 Kenyon St., 14420. Tel: 716-637-5036. Nancy J. Deryke; Rev. Theodore J. Auble; Sandra Shields; Deacon Thomas Schrage.

State University College at Geneseo (Geneseo), Newman Catholic Community at the Interfaith Center, 11 Franklin St., Box 265, Geneseo, 14454. Tel: 716-243-1460. Rev. James E. Hewes; David Desmond.

The Cornell Catholic Community, Inc. (Ithaca), Cornell University, G-22 Anabel Taylor Hall, Ithaca, 14853. Tel: 607-255-4228; Fax: 607-255-7793. Revs. Michael Mahler, Dir., Campus Ministry. Tel: 607-255-6013; Edward J. Ondrako, Ph.D., Assoc. Dir. Planning. Tel: 607-255-9380; Sr. Donna M. Fannon, M.H.S.H.; Sr. Margaret Brogden, M.H.S.H.; Dawn Redlin, Assoc. Dir. Admin. & Devel. Tel: 607-255-6012; Mr. Edward Kornuszko; Deborah Schoch.

The Catholic Community of Ithaca College, Muller Chapel, Ithaca College, 453 Danby Rd., Ithaca, 14850. Tel: 607-274-3103. Ms. Mary Humenay. Tel: 607-274-1117; Rev. Paul Bonacci. Tel: 607-274-3184.

Elmira College, 1 Park Place, Elmira, 14901. Tel: 607-735-1824, Ext. 1824. Rev. Severine Msemwa.

Finger Lakes Community College c/o St. Mary's Church, 95 N. Main St., Canandaigua, 14424. Rev. Brian C. Cool.

Corning Community College, 211 Academic Dr., Corning, 14830. Mary Skinner. Tel: 607-732-4552; 962-9413 (office).

Hobart and William Smith College, c/o St. Stephen's Church, 48 Pulteney St., Geneva, 14456. Rev. Msgr. Gerard C. Krieg. Tel: 315-789-1124.

Keuka College c/o St. Michael's Church, 312 Liberty St., Penn Yan, 14527. Revs. Charles Mulligan; Peter Deckman. Tel: 315-536-7459.

Roberts Wesleyan College c/o St. Christopher's Church, 3350 Union St., North Chili, 14514. Rev. Bernard Dollen. Tel: 716-594-1400; Sr. Carol Fox. Tel: 716-594-9125.

Wells College, c/o St. Patrick Church, Main St., P.O. Box 116, Aurora, 13026-0296. Rev. Paul J. Ryan. Tel: 315-364-7197.

Cayuga Community College, P.O. Box 1000, Auburn, 13021. Sr. Chris Lloyd, S.S.J., Chap. Tel: 315-255-1743.

New York Chiropractic College, c/o St. Patrick's Church, 97 W. Bayard St., Seneca Falls, 13148. Tel: 315-568-5203 (rectory); 568-3142 (college). Rev. Richard Murphy.

PENN YAN. *St. Michael's Church*, Keuka College, 312 Liberty St., 14527. Tel: 315-536-7459; Fax: 315-536-7450. Revs. Charles Mulligan; Peter Deckman.

RELIGIOUS INSTITUTES OF MEN REPRESENTED IN THE DIOCESE

For further details refer to the corresponding bracketed number in the Religious Institutes of Men or Women section.

[0170]—*Basilian Fathers*.—C.S.B.
[0200]—*Benedictine Monks*.—O.S.B.
[0470]—*The Capuchin Friars*. (Province of St. Mary).—O.F.M.Cap.
[0270]—*Carmelite Fathers and Brothers*.—O.Carm.
[0350]—*Cistercians Order of the Strict Observance (Trappists)*.—O.C.S.O.
[0310]—*Congregation of Christian Brothers*. (Eastern Prov.).—C.F.C.
[1140]—*Congregation of the Sacred Hearts of Jesus and Mary*.—SS.CC.
[0480]—*Conventual Franciscans*. (Buffalo & Immaculate Conception Provinces).—O.F.M.Conv.
[0520]—*Franciscan Friars*. (Assumption B.V.M. Prov.).—O.F.M.
[0690]—*Jesuit Fathers and Brothers*. (New York Province).—S.J.
[0610]—*Priests of the Congregation of Holy Cross*.—C.S.C.
[1070]—*Redemptorist Fathers*. (Baltimore Province).—C.SS.R.
[0760]—*Society of Mary (Marianists)*.—S.M.
[1060]—*Society of the Precious Blood*.—C.PP.S.
[0560]—*Third Order Regular of Saint Francis*.—T.O.R.

RELIGIOUS INSTITUTES OF WOMEN REPRESENTED IN THE DIOCESE

[3110]—*Congregation of Our Lady of the Retreat in the Cenacle*.—R.C.
[0760]—*Daughters of Charity of St. Vincent de Paul*.—D.C.
[0420]—*Discalced Carmelite Nuns*.—O.C.D.
[1050]—*Dominican Contemplative Nuns*.—O.P.
[1070-13]—*Dominican Sisters (Adrian, MI)*.—O.P.
[1070-05]—*Dominican Sisters (Amityville, NY)*.—O.P.
[2575]—*Institute of the Sisters of Mercy of the Americas*. (Rochester, NY).—R.S.M.
[2470]—*Maryknoll Sisters of St. Dominic*.—M.M.
[]—*Misioneras Guadalupanas del Espiritu Santo*.
[3070]—*North American Union Sisters of Our Lady of Charity*.—N.A.U.-O.L.C.
[3430]—*Religious Teachers Filippini*.—M.P.F.
[2970]—*School Sisters of Notre Dame*.—S.S.N.D.
[3950]—*Sisters of Saint Mary of Namur*.—S.S.M.N.
[1800]—*Sisters of St. Francis of the Third Order Regular (Williamsville, New York)*.—O.S.F.
[3830-14]—*Sisters of St. Joseph (Rochester)*.—S.S.J.
[3840]—*Sisters of St. Joseph of Carondolet*.—C.S.J.
[3730]—*Sisters of the Order of St. Basil the Great*.—O.S.B.M.
[1490]—*Sisters of the Third Franciscan Order*.—O.S.F.
[3620]—*Sisters, Servants of Mary Immaculate*.—S.S.M.I.
[2160]—*Sisters, Servants of the Immaculate Heart of Mary*.—I.H.M.

DIOCESAN CEMETERIES

ROCHESTER. *Holy Sepulchre*.

REGIONAL CEMETERIES

AUBURN. *St. Joseph's*.
CORNING. *St. Mary*.
ELMIRA. *SS. Peter and Paul's*.
GENEVA. *St. Mary's and St. Patrick's*.

NECROLOGY

† Gaynor, William, Auburn, NY, St. Alphonsus. —Died Sept. 12, 1997.
† Hayes, John S., (Retired). —Died May 20, 1997.
† Heisel, Raymond, Rochester, NY, Our Mother of Sorrows. —Died July 22, 1997.
† Hurley, John D., (Retired). —Died March 8, 1997.
† Reddington, Rev. John A., Pittsford, NY, St. Louis. —Died Dec. 30, 1997.
† Sweeney, Eugene P., Ithaca, NY, Immaculate Conception. —Died April 4, 1997.

Diocese of Rockford

(Dioecesis Rockfordiensis)

Most Reverend

THOMAS G. DORAN, D.D., J.C.D.

Bishop of Rockford; ordained December 20, 1961; appointed Bishop of Rockford April 19, 1994; consecrated June 24, 1994; installed June 24, 1994. *Res., 1243 N. Court St., Rockford, IL, 61103.*

Most Reverend

ARTHUR J. O'NEILL, D.D., V.G.

Retired Bishop of Rockford; ordained March 27, 1943; appointed Bishop of Rockford August 19, 1968; consecrated October 11, 1968; installed October 11, 1968; retired April 19, 1994. *Res., 14 Country Club Beach, Rockford, IL, 61103.* Tel.: 815-877-5078.

Diocesan Chancery: 1245 N. Court St., P.O. Box 7044, Rockford, IL, 61126-7044. Tel.: 815-962-3709; Fax: 815-968-2824.

ESTABLISHED SEPTEMBER 23, 1908.

Square Miles 6,457.

Comprises Jo Daviess, Stephenson, Winnebago, Boone, McHenry, Carroll, Ogle, DeKalb, Kane, Whiteside and Lee Counties in the State of Illinois.

For legal titles of parishes and diocesan institutions, consult the Chancery Office.

STATISTICAL OVERVIEW

Personnel	
Bishop	1
Retired Bishops	1
Abbots	1
Retired Abbots	2
Priests: Diocesan Active in Diocese	123
Priests: Active Outside Diocese	2
Priests: Retired, Sick or Absent	31
Number of Diocesan Priests	156
Religious Priests in Diocese	61
Extern Priests in Diocese	7
Ordinations:	
Diocesan Priests	6
Transitional Deacons	5
Permanent Deacons	1
Permanent Deacons in Diocese	108
Total Brothers	15
Total Sisters	450
Parishes	
Parishes	110
With Resident Pastor:	
Resident Diocesan Priests	93
Resident Religious Priests	8
Without Resident Pastor:	
Administered by Priests	8
Administered by Pastoral Teams, etc.	1
Missions	6
Professional Ministry Personnel:	
Sisters	34
Lay Ministers	72
Welfare	
Catholic Hospitals	4
Total Assisted	471,652
Health Care Centers	1
Total Assisted	375
Homes for the Aged	4
Total Assisted	557
Day Care and Extended Day Care Centers	1
Total Assisted	8,403
Specialized Homes	1
Total Assisted	431
Special Centers for Social Services	10
Total Assisted	312,797
Residential Care of Disabled	2
Total Assisted	76
Educational	
Diocesan Students in Other Seminaries	25
Total Seminarians	25
High Schools, Diocesan and Parish	6
Total Students	3,458
High Schools, Private	2
Total Students	894
Elementary Schools, Diocesan and Parish	41
Total Students	12,309
Catechesis/Religious Education:	
High School Students	4,900
Elementary Students	22,006
Total Students Under Catholic Instruction	43,592
Teachers in the Diocese:	
Priests	48
Sisters	34
Lay Teachers	905
Vital Statistics	
Receptions into the Church:	
Infant Baptism Totals	5,975
Adult Baptism Totals	254
Received into Full Communion	476
First Communions	5,506
Confirmations	3,780
Marriages:	
Catholic	945
Interfaith	465
Total Marriages	1,410
Deaths	1,926
Total Catholic Population	280,652
Total Population	1,079,500

Former Bishops—Most Rev. PETER J. MULDOON, D.D., ord. Dec. 18, 1886; cons. Titular Bishop of Tamassus and Auxiliary Bishop of Chicago, July 25, 1901; appt. Bishop of Rockford, Sept. 28, 1908; made Assistant to the Pontifical Throne, June 8, 1921; died Oct. 8, 1927.—Most Rev. EDWARD F. HOBAN, S.T.D., ord. July 11, 1903; cons. Titular Bishop of Colonia and Auxiliary Bishop of Chicago, Dec. 21, 1921; appt. Bishop of Rockford, Feb. 10, 1928; appt. Assistant at the Pontifical Throne, Nov. 25, 1937; appt. Titular Bishop of Listra and Coadjutor Bishop of Cleveland, Nov. 16, 1942; succeeded to the See of Cleveland, Nov. 2, 1945; died Sept. 22, 1966.—Most Rev. JOHN J. BOYLAN, D.D., Ph.D., ord. July 28, 1915; appt. Nov. 21, 1942; cons. Feb. 17, 1943; died July 19, 1953.—Most Rev. RAYMOND P. HILLINGER, D.D., ord. April 2, 1932; appt. Nov. 3, 1953; cons. Dec. 29, 1953; appt. Titular Bishop of Derbe and Auxiliary Bishop of Chicago, June 27, 1956; died Nov. 13, 1971.—Rt. Rev. DONALD M. CARROLL, D.D., appt. June 27, 1956; resigned Sept. 25, 1956.—Most Rev. LORAS T. LANE, D.D., ord. March 19, 1937; appt. Titular Bishop of Bencenna and Auxiliary of Dubuque, May 29, 1951; cons. Aug. 20, 1951; appt. to Rockford, Oct. 11, 1956; died July 22, 1968.

Diocesan Chancery—1245 N. Court St., P.O. Box 7044, Rockford, 61126-7044. Tel: 815-962-3709; Fax: 815-968-2824. Address all official business to this office. Office Hours: Mon.-Fri. 9-12, 1-3.

Vicars General—Most Rev. ARTHUR J. O'NEILL, D.D., V.G.; Rev. Msgr. DAVID D. KAGAN, V.G., J.C.L.; Rev. Msgr. THOMAS C. BRADY, P.A., V.G., Ph.D., *1245 N. Court St., P.O. Box 7044, Rockford, 61126.* Tel: 815-962-3709.

Moderator of the Curia—Rev. Msgr. DAVID D. KAGAN, V.G., J.C.L.

Episcopal Vicars and Secretaries—

Vicar for Clergy and Religious—Rev. Msgr. MICHAEL A. BINSFELD.

Vicar for Ministry to Hispanics—Very Rev. WILLIAM R. SCHUESSLER.

Vicar for Parish Consultations Process—Very Rev. F. JAMES LARSON.

Vicar for Social Ministries—Very Rev. LEO J. BARTEL.

Vicar for Spiritual Formation—Very Rev. KARL P. GANSS.

Secretary for Catholic Education—Sr. PATRICIA DOWNEY, O.P.

Secretary for Finance and Administration—Mr. WAYNE LENELL, C.P.A., Ph.D.

Chancellor—Rev. Msgr. CHARLES W. MCNAMEE, J.C.L.

Vice Chancellor—Rev. Msgr. MICHAEL A. BINSFELD.

Bishop's Secretary for Retired Priests—Rev. Msgr. CHARLES W. MCNAMEE, J.C.L.

Secretary to the Bishop—Rev. GLENN L. NELSON.

Diocesan Tribunal—850 N. Church St., Rockford, 61103. Tel: 815-963-8960; Fax: 815-963-9962. Address all official business to this office.

Judicial Vicar—Rev. Msgr. DAVID D. KAGAN, J.C.L.

Adjutant Judicial Vicar—Rev. MICHAEL KURZ, J.C.L.

Secretary and Director of the Tribunal—Sr. AUDREY STRAUB, S.S.N.D., J.C.L.

Secretary for Administrative Processes—Rev. ROBERT J. SWEENEY.

Promoter of Justice—Rev. Msgr. JOHN J. MITCHELL.

Defender of the Bond—Sr. AUDREY STRAUB, S.S.N.D., J.C.L.; Sr. ELAINE KERSCHER, O.S.F., J.C.L.

Pro Synodal Judges—Rev. Msgr. RAYMOND J. WAHL, P.A., J.C.D.; Rev. Msgr. CHARLES W. MCNAMEE, J.C.L.; Revs. GERALD P. KOBBEMAN; WILLIAM A. KRIEGSMANN; FRANCIS E. MCDONNELL.

Advocates—Rev. THOMAS J. MONAHAN, Ph.D.; Sr. BEVERLY JEANNE HOWE, O.P.; Sr. CARLEEN PETERS, S.S.N.D.

Experts—Rev. LAWRENCE M. URBANIAK, Ph.D.; Mr. MICHAEL M. KAGAN, M.A.

Notaries—Mrs. ORA CARTER-KEFALE; Mrs. DENISE GEORGE; Mrs. DONNA HAYES.

Diocesan Consultors—Rev. Msgr. THOMAS C. BRADY; Rev. Msgr. DAVID D. KAGAN; Rev. Msgr. THOMAS L. DZIELAK; Rev. Msgr. DANIEL J. HERMES; Rev. Msgr. JOHN J. MITCHELL; Rev. Msgr. WILLIAM H. SCHWARTZ; Rev. Msgr. RAYMOND J. WAHL; Very Rev. F. JAMES LARSON; Revs. WILLIAM J. CLAUSEN; GERALD P. KOBBEMAN; ANDREW J. PLESA; RICHARD M. RUSSO.

Deans—Rev. Msgr. EDWARD S. WRIGHT, Aurora Deanery; Very Rev. FRANCIS P. KENNEDY, DeKalb Deanery; Very Rev. ROBERT B. HOFFMAN, Elgin Deanery; Very Rev. P. WILLIAM MCDONNELL, Freeport Deanery; Rev. Msgr. PHILIP E. O'NEIL, McHenry County Deanery; Rev. Msgr. JOHN J. MITCHELL, Rockford Deanery; Very Rev. THOMAS E. BALES, Sterling Deanery.

Vicaress for Religious Women—Sr. JAMES MARIE O'CONNOR, S.S.N.D., *1245 N. Court St., P.O. Box 7044, Rockford, 61126.* Tel: 815-962-3709; Fax: 815-968-2824.

Diocesan Offices and Directors

Black Catholic Ministry—Vacant, *1526 S. Main St., Rockford, 61102.* Tel: 815-965-6993; Fax: 815-964-7101.

Campaign for Human Development—Mr. THOMAS MCKENNA, Dir., *921 W. State St., Rockford, 61102.* Tel: 815-965-0895; Fax: 815-965-6141.

Catholic Charismatic Renewal Services—Mr. RON BERGMAN, Diocesan Liaison, *1910 Bracknel Blvd., Rockford, 61103.* Tel: 815-654-4111.

Catholic Office of the Deaf—Rev. GLENN L. NELSON, Dir., *1245 N. Court St., P.O. Box 7044, Rockford, 61126.* Tel: 815-962-3709; 962-2994 (TTY).

Catholic Relief Services—Mr. THOMAS MCKENNA, *921 W. State St., Rockford, 61102.* Tel: 815-965-0895; Fax: 815-965-6141.

Cemeteries—Rev. Msgr. THOMAS C. BRADY, P.A., Dir., *8616 W. State St., Winnebago, 61088.* Tel: 815-965-1637; Fax: 815-965-9632.

Censores Librorum—Rev. Msgr. CHARLES W. MCNAMEE, J.C.L.; Rev. FRANCIS E. MCDONNELL.

Charities—Mr. BRISTON FERNANDES, Dir. Offices: *921 W. State St., Rockford, 61102.* Tel: 815-965-0895; Fax: 815-965-6141., *1700 N. Farnsworth Ave., Aurora, 60505, 1315 Pleasant St., DeKalb, 60115, 566 Dundee Ave., Elgin, 60120., 813 S. State Ave., Freeport, 61032, 202 Summit St., Galena, 61036, 5215 W. Bull Valley Rd., McHenry, 60050., 801 W. 11th St., Sterling, 61081.*

Satellite Offices—*860 Biester Dr., 206 C, Belvidere, 61008., 105 1/2 W. 1st St., Dixon, 61021.*

Clergy Relief Society, Priests' Retirement Committee—Rev. Msgr. CHARLES W. MCNAMEE, J.C.L., Exec. Sec., *1245 N. Court St., P.O. Box 7044, Rockford, 61126.* Tel: 815-962-3709; Fax: 815-968-2824.

Communications—Mr. OWEN PHELPS, JR., Dir., *921 W. State St., Rockford, 61102.* Tel: 815-963-3471; Fax: 815-968-2808.

Conciliation and Arbitration Office—Mr. HENRY J. CLOSE, Chm., *124 N. Water St., Ste. 300, P.O. Box 4749, Rockford, 61110.* Tel: 815-968-7591; Fax: 815-968-7507.

Council of Catholic Women, Diocesan—Rev. Msgr. THOMAS L. DZIELAK, Moderator, *708 10th Ave., Rock Falls, 61071.* Tel: 815-625-4508. Miss DORIS WITKOWSKI, Pres., *10478 Geneva St., Roscoe, 61073.* Tel: 815-623-2289.

Cursillo Movement—Rev. HAROLD L. NILGES, Dir., *340 Stott St., Genoa, 60135.* Tel: 815-784-2355.

Development Office—Mr. DAVID HOUGAN, Dir., *921 W. State St., Rockford, 61102.* Tel: 815-964-6711; Fax: 815-968-2808.

Divine Worship, Office for—(and RCIA Resources)—Rev. JOHN A. SLAMPAK, Dir., *921 W. State St., Rockford, 61102.* Tel: 815-963-0344; Fax: 815-963-9747.

Ecumenism, Office of—Rev. ROBERT JACKSON, Dir., *1005 Julien St., Belvidere, 61008.* Tel: 815-544-7788.

Education—Sr. PATRICIA DOWNEY, O.P., Sec. for Catholic Education/Supt., Schools; Sr. JEANETTE LANDUYT, O.P., Assoc. Supt.; Mr. JOHN MCGRATH, Dir., Rel. Educ. & Formation, *1260 N. Church St., Rockford, 61103.* Tel: 815-962-7791; Fax: 815-962-1767.

Ethicist for Health Care Issues, Diocesan—Rev. TIMOTHY L. DOHERTY, *921 W. State St., Rockford, 61102.* Tel: 815-963-4007; Fax: 815-962-2966.

Evangelization—Very Rev. KARL P. GANSS, Dir., *302 Fisk Ave., Dekalb, 60115.* Tel: 815-758-5432; Fax: 815-758-2487.

Family Life & Youth Ministry—Dirs.: Mr. DON GRAMER; Mrs. DON GRAMER, *7708 E. McGregor Rd., Rockford, 61102.* Tel: 815-965-5011; Fax: 815-965-5811.

Finance and Administration—Mr. WAYNE LENELL, C.P.A., Ph.D., Sec., Fin. & Admin., *921 W. State St., Rockford, 61102.* Tel: 815-964-5231; Fax: 815-964-5501.

Hispanic Ministry Offices—Very Rev. WILLIAM R. SCHUESSLER, Vicar, *921 W. State St., Rockford, 61102.* Tel: 815-962-8042. Offices in Diocese: Aurora Deanery: *Centro Cristo Rey, 315 N. Root St., Aurora, 60505.* DeKalb Deanery: *Centro Cuerpo de Cristo, 308 Fisk Ave., DeKalb, 60115.* Elgin Deanery: *Centro Jesus Resucitado, 90 N. Kennedy Dr., Carpentersville, 60110.* McHenry Deanery: *Centro San Jose, 207 E. Brainard St., Harvard, 60033.* Rockford Deanery: *Centro Sembrador, 921 W. State St., Rockford, 61102.* Sterling Deanery: *Tu C.A.S.A., 202 W. 6th St., Sterling, 61081.*

Holy Childhood Association—Sr. PATRICIA DOWNEY, O.P., Dir., *1260 N. Church St., Rockford, 61103.* Tel: 815-962-7791; Fax: 815-962-1767.

Investment and Loan—Mr. WAYNE LENELL, Sec., Fin. & Admin., *921 W. State St., Rockford, 61102.* Tel: 815-964-5231; Fax: 815-964-5501.

Lay Volunteer Ministry—Very Rev. KARL P. GANSS, Contact Person, *302 Fisk Ave., DeKalb, 60115.* Tel: 815-758-5432; Fax: 815-758-2487.

Legion of Mary—Rev. WILLIAM P. COLLINS, Dir., *2505 School St., Rockford, 61101.* Tel: 815-965-9539.

Liturgical Commission, Diocesan—Rev. JOHN A. SLAMPAK, Dir., *921 W. State St., Rockford, 61102.* Tel: 815-963-0344; Fax: 815-963-9747.

Ministry Formation, Office of—Mr. JOHN MCGRATH, Dir., *921 W. State St., Rockford, 61102.* Tel: 815-962-8873; Fax: 815-962-2966.

Ministry to Priests Program—Rev. Msgr. MICHAEL A. BINSFELD, Vicar, Clergy Sabbaticals and Diocesan Priests' Retreats, *1226 N. Church St., Rockford, 61103.* Tel: 815-965-5767; Fax: 815-965-5768.

Newman-Campus Ministry—Rev. STEPHEN J. KNOX, Dir., *512 Normal Rd., DeKalb, 60115.* Tel: 815-758-6667.

Newspaper—*"The Observer"*; Mr. OWEN PHELPS, JR., Mng. Editor, *921 W. State St., Rockford, 61102.* Tel: 815-963-3471; Fax: 815-968-2808.

Permanent Diaconate Program—Mr. THOMAS WELCH, Dir., *1266 N. Church St., Rockford, 61103.* Tel: 815-965-5837; Fax: 815-965-5768.

Priests' Eucharistic League—Rev. LAWRENCE M. URBANIAK, Dir., *15012 St. Patrick's Rd., Woodstock, 60098.* Tel: 815-338-7883.

Priest Personnel—Rev. Msgr. MICHAEL A. BINSFELD, Vicar, Clergy and Religious, *1226 N. Church St., Rockford, 61103.* Tel: 815-965-5767; Fax: 815-965-5768.

Pro-Life Activities, Office of—Rev. MICHAEL J. BOLGER, Dir., *229 W. Washington Pl., Freeport, 61032.* Tel: 815-232-7622.

Propagation of the Faith—Rev. ROBERT J. SWEENEY, Dir., *921 W. State St., Rockford, 61102.* Tel: 815-962-2934; Fax: 815-962-2966.

Research and Planning—Mr. MICHAEL CIESLAK, Dir., *921 W. State St., Rockford, 61102.* Tel: 815-963-7799; Fax: 815-962-2966.

Rural Life Conference—Mr. THOMAS MCKENNA, Dir., *921 W. State St., Rockford, 61102.* Tel: 815-965-0895.

Scouts—Rev. Msgr. WILLIAM H. SCHWARTZ, Dir., *1243 N. Church St., Rockford, 61103.* Tel: 815-965-2765; Fax: 815-965-0743.

Seton Center—Mr. RONALD DI TOMASSI, Building Dir., *921 W. State St., Rockford, 61102.* Tel: 815-965-2778.

Social Ministries, Office of—Very Rev. LEO J. BARTEL, Vicar, *921 W. State St., Rockford, 61102.* Tel: 815-965-5116; Fax: 815-965-0628.

Vocations—Rev. MARTIN G. HEINZ, Dir., *850 N. Church St., Rockford, 61103.* Tel: 815-963-1009; Fax: 815-963-9962.

CLERGY, PARISHES, MISSIONS AND PAROCHIAL SCHOOLS

CITY OF ROCKFORD
(Winnebago County)

1—ST. PETER CATHEDRAL (1922), Rev. Msgr. William H. Schwartz, Rector; Rev. Joseph P. Naill; Deacons Charles Cooper; Martin Czerniewski. In res., Revs. Timothy Doherty; Martin G. Heinz.
Res., 1243 N. Church St., 61103. Tel: 815-965-2765; 658-6060 (Rectory); Fax: 815-965-0743.
School—1231 N. Court St., Tel: 815-963-3620. Mr. Kevin Hart, Prin.
Lay Teachers 14; Students 310.
Catechesis/Religious Programs—Mr. Chris Weickert, D.R.E.
Students 112.

2—ST. ANTHONY OF PADUA (1909) (Italian), Revs. Luke Poczworowski, O.F.M.Conv.; Robert D. Melnick, O.F.M.Conv. In res., Rev. Dominic Wisz, O.F.M.Conv.; Deacons Sam Cassaro; Frank Barone.
Res., 1010 Ferguson St., 61102. Tel: 815-965-2761; Fax: 815-965-3244.
Catechesis/Religious Programs—Students 110.

3—ST. BERNADETTE (1957), Rev. Matthew T. Rudden; Deacon Richard Gerdeman; Rev. Casimir Muszynski.
Res., 2400 Bell Ave., 61103. Tel: 815-968-0904.
Church—Rockton Ave. & Bell Ave., 61103. Fax: 815-968-0904.
School—2300 Bell Ave., Tel: 815-968-2288. Mrs. Elizabeth Adams-Young, Prin.
Lay Teachers 15; Students 302.
Catechesis/Religious Programs—2300 Bell Ave., 61103. Tel: 815-968-2289. Mrs. Alice Kaczmarek, D.R.E.
Students 121.

4—ST. EDWARD (1929), Rev. Msgr. Raymond J. Wahl; Revs. James J. Murphy, Pastor Emeritus; Vincent J. Shindelar; Stanislaw Kos; Deacons Lambert Verstynen; Eugene Reilly.
Parish Office: 3004 11th St., 61109. Tel: 815-229-0282; Fax: 815-229-8912.
Res., 3026 11th St., 61109. Tel: 815-398-1249.
School—3020 S. 11th St., Tel: 815-396-2631; Fax: 815-398-2639. Mr. John Fitzsimmons, Prin.
Lay Teachers 11; Students 274.
Catechesis/Religious Programs—Tel: 815-229-0282. Lynette M. Ditzler, D.R.E.
Students 176.

5—HOLY FAMILY (1963), Rev. Msgr. Daniel J. Hermes; Revs. John A. Hanrahan, S.J.; Max J. Striedl, Jr.; Deacon Bob Bracken.
Office: 4401 Highcrest Rd., 61107. Tel: 815-398-4280; Fax: 815-398-4287.
School—4407 Highcrest Rd., Tel: 815-398-5331; Fax: 815-398-5902. Mr. Anthony Smerko, Prin.
Lay Teachers 30; Students 594.
Catechesis/Religious Programs—Tel: 815-397-9395. Joellen Lansing, D.R.E.
Students 729.

6—ST. JAMES (1853), Rev. David E. Beauvais. In res., Rev. Edgar Smigiel, O.F.M.
Res., 428 N. Second St., 61107. Tel: 815-962-1214. [JC]
School—409 N. First St., Tel: 815-962-8515; Fax: 815-962-8526. Ms. Margo Shifo, Prin.
Lay Teachers 15; Students 287.
Catechesis/Religious Programs—Tel: 815-962-5588. Sandra Lundy, D.R.E.
Students 128.

7—ST. MARY SHRINE, INSTITUTE OF CHRIST THE KING SOVEREIGN KING. For parish records, contact St. Anthony, Rockford. Rev. Brian Bovee.
Res., 517 Elm St., 61102. Tel: 815-968-0865.

8—ST. PATRICK (1919), Rev. William P. Collins. Pastoral Assocs.: Sr. Alyce Kelly, O.P.; Deacon Ron Graw.
Res., 2505 School St., 61101. Tel: 815-965-9539. [JC]
Catechesis/Religious Programs—Tel: 815-964-6591.
Students 65.

9—SS. PETER AND PAUL (1911) (Hispanic Hogar), Rev. Timothy Piasecki.
Res., 617 Lincoln Ave., 61102. Tel: 815-962-7171; Fax: 815-962-7171.
Catechesis/Religious Programs—Students 204.

10—ST. RITA (1914), Rev. Eric R. Barr; Deacons Alex Hainchek; Robert Martin; Michael Burch, Pastoral Assoc., Tel: 815-398-6483. In res., Rev. Michael Kurz.
Res., 6254 Valley Knoll Dr., 61109-1898. Tel: 815-398-0853; Fax: 815-397-7499.
School—6284 Valley Knoll Dr., 61109-1898. Tel: 815-398-3466. Ms. Joan Leonard, Prin.
Lay Teachers 13; Students 302.
Catechesis/Religious Programs—Tel: 815-398-6483. Ms. Barbara Malueg, D.R.E.
Students 340.

11—ST. STANISLAUS KOSTKA (1912) (Polish), Rev. John J. Mikula, O.F.M.Conv. In res., Rev. Hippolite Kuras, O.F.M.Conv.
Res., 201 Buckbee, 61104. Tel: 815-965-3913.

OUTSIDE THE CITY OF ROCKFORD

Algonquin, McHenry Co., St. Margaret Mary (1954), Revs. Michael J. Tierney; Wieslaw Grzela; Deacons Simon Grossmayer; Patrick Maher; Mrs. Kathleen Fuller, Pastoral Assoc. In res., Rev. Ephrem Karwowski, O.F.M.Cap.
Parish Office: 111 S. Hubbard St., 60102. Tel: 847-658-7625; Fax: 847-658-7882.
School—(Grades (PreK-8)) 113 Hubbard St., Tel: 847-658-5313; Fax: 847-854-0501. Mrs. Kathleen McMahon, Prin.
Lay Teachers 13; Students 293.
Catechesis/Religious Programs—Tel: 847-658-9339. Mrs. Sharon Prykop, D.R.E.
Students 1,110.

Amboy, Lee Co., St. Patrick (1857), Rev. Francis Daleiden, O.S.B.
Res., 32 N. Jones Ave., 61310. Tel: 815-857-2315; Fax: 815-857-2315. [CEM]
Catechesis/Religious Programs—Fax: 815-857-2314.
Students 272.

Apple River, Jo Daviess Co., St. Joseph, Rev. Everett J. Hiller.
Res., 107 Webster St., P.O. Box 3867, 61001. Tel: 815-594-2312. [CEM]

Aurora, Kane Co.,

1—Annunciation of the Blessed Virgin Mary, (1875), Rev. Mario Pedi, O.S.B.; Deacons Raymond Johnson; Harold Poss.
Res., 1820 Church Rd., 60504. Tel: 630-851-1436; Fax: 630-851-2435. [CEM]
School—1840 Church Rd., Tel: 630-851-4300; Fax: 630-851-4316. Mr. Norbert Rozanski, Prin.
Lay Teachers 10; Students 296.
Catechesis/Religious Programs—Students 105.

2—Holy Angels, (1892), Revs. Gerald P. Kobbeman; Daniel J. Deutsch; Deacons Tim White; Tom Hawksworth; Luke Cordes, (Retired).
Res., 720 Hardin Ave., 60506-4997. Tel: 630-897-1194; Fax: 630-897-1370.
School—720 Kensington Pl., 60506. Tel: 630-897-3613; Fax: 630-897-8233. Springfield Dominicans, Tel: 217-787-0491; Fax: 217-787-8169. Sr. Paul Mary Janssens, O.P., Prin.; Sr. Kathleen Gallagher, O.P., Asst. Prin.
Sisters 5; Lay Teachers 29; Students 737.
Catechesis/Religious Programs—Students 400.

3—St. Joseph, (1899), Rev. Jerome I. Leake; Deacon Norbert Szudarski, Pastoral Assoc., Tel: 630-897-0484. In res., Rev. Robert J. McClellan.
Mailing Address: P.O. Box 4395, 60507.
Res., 405 St. Joseph Ave., 60505. Tel: 630-844-3780; Fax: 630-844-1338. [CEM]
School—706 High St., 60507. Tel: 630-844-3781. Miss Marie Bockhaus, Prin.
Lay Teachers 30; Students 395.
Catechesis/Religious Programs—Tel: 630-844-3782.
Students 87.

4—St. Mary, (1872) (Irish), Rev. William F. Morrissey; Sr. Dorothy Hofer, O.S.F., Pastoral Assoc.; Deacons Richard Groom; William Rees; Mrs. Christine Rees. In res., Rev. Joseph M. Lessard.
Res., 430 E. Downer Pl., 60505-3475. Tel: 630-892-0480; Fax: 630-892-8664.
Catechesis/Religious Programs—432 E. Downer Pl., Tel: 630-859-3922.
Students 57.

5—St. Nicholas, (1862) (Hispanic), Rev. David R. Engbarth.
Res. & Mailing Address: 308 High St., 60505. Tel: 630-898-8707. [CEM]
School—Archbishop Romero School, 312 N. High St., Tel: 630-898-8690; Fax: 630-898-8866. Mrs. Jean Scanlan, Prin.
Lay Teachers 9; Students 218.
Catechesis/Religious Programs—Sr. Rita Mary Phalen, O.S.F., D.R.E.
Students 280.

6—Our Lady of Good Counsel, (1909), Rev. Edward F. Gillespie; Deacon James J. Valesano.
Res., 620 S. Fifth St., 60505. Tel: 630-851-1100; Fax: 630-851-4069.
School—601 Talma St., Tel: 630-851-4400; Fax: 630-851-8220. Sr. Nancy Ulrich, O.S.F., Prin.; Lucille Plachetka, Vice Prin.
Students 480.
Catechesis/Religious Programs—Students 81.

7—St. Peter, (1929), Rev. Edwin F. Millen.
Res., 925 Sard Ave., 60506. Tel: 630-896-6816.
School—915 Sard Ave., Tel: 630-892-1283. Sr. Margaret Fabrizius, O.P., Prin.
Sisters 2; Lay Teachers 5; Students 114.

8—St. Rita of Cascia, (1927), Rev. Robert J. Willhite.
Res., 750 W. Old Indian Trail Rd., 60506. Tel: 630-892-5918.
School—770 W. Old Indian Trail Rd., Tel: 630-892-0020; Fax: 630-892-4236. Ms. Elizabeth Baney, Prin.
Lay Teachers 14; Students 318.
Catechesis/Religious Programs—Tel: 630-892-9507. Judith Feiden, D.R.E.
Students 348.

9—Sacred Heart, (1861) (French), Revs. Gerald Paul, M.S.C.; Leo Petit, M.S.C.; Deacon Richard Groom.
Res., 771 Fulton St., 60505. Tel: 630-898-4165; Fax: 630-898-4165. [CEM]
School—Archbishop Romero School, Tel: 630-898-8690; Fax: 630-898-8866.
Catechesis/Religious Programs—Tel: 630-898-4165. Conchita Hurtado, D.R.E.
Students 225.

10—St. Therese of Jesus, (1925), Rev. Joseph T. Muller, M.S.C.
Res., 271 N. Farnsworth Ave., 60505. Tel: 630-898-5422; Fax: 630-898-5327.
School—255 N. Farnsworth Ave., Tel: 630-898-0620. Ms. Michelle Sunnen, Prin.
Sisters 1; Lay Teachers 7; Students 130.
Catechesis/Religious Programs—Students 255.

Batavia, Kane Co., Holy Cross (1854), Rev. Stephen St. Jules; Mrs. Nancy Brenski, Pastoral Assoc.
Res., 2300 Main St., 60510. Tel: 630-879-4750; Fax: 630-879-9502. [JC]
Catechesis/Religious Programs—Tel: 630-879-4751. D.R.E.: Mrs. Diane Downey; Mr. Bill Crow.
Students 930.

Belvidere, Boone Co., St. James (1886), Rev. Bernard J. Mullane.
Office: 535 Caswell St., 61008. Tel: 815-547-6397.
Res., 514 Caswell St., 61008. Tel: 815-547-6397. [CEM]
School—320 Logan Ave., 61008. Tel: 815-547-7633; Fax: 815-544-2294. Mrs. Barbara Majernik, Prin.
Lay Teachers 13; Students 222.
Catechesis/Religious Programs—Tel: 815-544-3698. Frank Zimmerman, D.R.E.
Students 470.

Byron, Ogle Co., St. Mary (1895), Rev. John A. Slampak; Deacon Bob Smits, Jr.
Res., P.O. Box 910, 232 E. Second St., 61010. Tel: 815-234-7431; Fax: 815-234-2133. [CEM]
Catechesis/Religious Programs—Tel: 815-234-5349. Marilyn Herrmann, D.R.E.
Students 329.

Carpentersville, Kane Co., St. Monica (1957), Revs. L. Thomas Risley; Robert Camacho; Deacons John Bach; J. Michael Frazier; Dennis Garber.
Res., 90 N. Kennedy Dr., 60110-1695. Tel: 847-428-2646; Fax: 847-428-0039. [JC]
Catechesis/Religious Programs—Tel: 847-428-7562. Marilyn Ernst, D.R.E.
Students 346.

Cary, McHenry Co., SS. Peter & Paul (1904), Revs. Donald M. Ahles; Miroslaw Reikowski; Deacon Thomas Welch.
Res., 410 N. First St., 60013. Tel: 847-516-2636; Fax: 847-639-3474.
School—416 N. First St., 60013. Tel: 847-639-3041; Fax: 847-639-5329. Sr. Katrina Lamkin, O.P., Prin.
Dominican Sisters 1; Lay Teachers 15; Students 279.
Catechesis/Religious Programs—Tel: 847-639-0414; Fax: 847-639-3474. Rosellyn Gilfether, D.R.E.
Students 1,282.

Crystal Lake, McHenry Co., St. Elizabeth Ann Seton (1978), Rev. Stephen K. Potter.
Office: 800 McHenry Ave., 60014. Tel: 815-459-3033; Fax: 815-459-3040.
Res., 445 Dartmoor Dr., 60014. Tel: 815-459-6223.
Catechesis/Religious Programs—Tel: 815-459-3096; Fax: 815-459-3040. Juliette Marsh, D.R.E.
Students 1,033.

St. Thomas the Apostle, Revs. Geoffrey Wirth; David Huber; Deacons Robert Nebel; Stephen Schaffer.
Res., 200 Washington St., 60014. Tel: 815-455-5407.
Pastoral Center: 272 King St., 60014. Tel: 815-455-5400; Fax: 815-455-2733.
School—265 King St., Tel: 815-459-0496; Fax: 815-459-0591. Mr. Warren Smith, Prin.
Lay Teachers 26; Students 465.
Catechesis/Religious Programs—Tel: 815-455-9787. Janet Kayser, D.R.E.
Students 1,851.

DeKalb, DeKalb Co., Christ the Teacher, University Parish of Northern Illinois University (1963), Rev. Stephen J. Knox; Deacon James Dombek. Pastoral Assocs.: Andrea Rusin; Terrence Beer.
Office: 512 Normal Rd., 60115. Tel: 815-758-6667; Fax: 815-758-2053.
Catechesis/Religious Programs—Dr. Laura Bird, D.R.E.
Students 126.

St. Mary (1861), Very Rev. Karl P. Ganss. In res., Rev. Anthony Vu Khac Long, C.M.C.
Office: 302 Fisk Ave., 60115.
Res., 321 Pine St., 60115. Tel: 815-748-5654. [CEM]
School—210 Gurler Rd., Tel: 815-756-7905; Fax: 815-758-1459. Sr. Dorothy Bertsch, S.M.P., Prin.
Sisters 1; Lay Teachers 20; Students 389.
Catechesis/Religious Programs—Tel: 815-758-8405; Fax: 815-758-2487.
Students 361.

Dixon, Lee Co., St. Anne (1928), Rev. Richard A. Rosinski; Sr. Lorraine Pratt, S.S.N.D., Pastoral Min.; Deacon James P. Ferolo.
Res., 1104 N. Brinton Ave., 61021. Tel: 815-288-3131; Fax: 815-288-3139.
School—1112 N. Brinton Ave., Tel: 815-288-5619; Fax: 815-288-3139. Sr. Marcianne Bzdon, S.S.N.D., Prin.
Lay Teachers 10; Students 165.
Catechesis/Religious Programs—Students 120.

St. Patrick (1856), Rev. John L. Stringini; Deacons Sam Berard; Bob Brandenburg.
Office: 612 S. Highland, 61021. Tel: 815-284-7719; Fax: 815-284-4758. [JC]
School—St. Mary Elementary & Junior High, (Grades PreK-8) 704 Peoria Ave., Tel: 815-284-6986; Fax: 815-288-2940. Mrs. Jean Spohn, Prin.
Lay Teachers 17; Students 256.
Catechesis/Religious Programs—Tel: 815-284-2867. Mrs. Sue Nielsen, D.R.E.
Students 275.

Dundee, Kane Co., St. Catherine of Siena (1914), Rev. William M. McKinstra.
Office: 845 W. Main St., 60118. Tel: 847-426-2217; Fax: 847-426-1130.
Res., 833 Royal Ln., 60118. Tel: 847-426-6253.
School—Tel: 847-426-4808. Mrs. Deborah Dedeo, Prin.
Lay Teachers 14; Students 287.
Catechesis/Religious Programs—Tel: 847-426-4712.
Students 452.
Mission—Gilbert, Kane Co., St. Mary, c/o 845 W. Main St., West Dundee, 60118. Tel: 847-836-8315. [CEM]

Durand, Winnebago Co., St. Mary (1862) (Irish), Rev. Thomas J. Monahan.
Mailing Address: St. Mary's Church. St. Mary's & St. Patrick's Cemeteries are jointly administered by St. Mary's Church, Durand. 606 W. Main St., 61024. Tel: 815-248-2490; Fax: 815-248-9100.
Catechesis/Religious Programs—Students 140.
Mission—Irish Grove Rd., Stephenson Co., St. Patrick. [CEM]

East Dubuque, Jo Daviess Co., St. Mary (1868), Rev. Raymond O. Holmgren.
Res., 170 Montgomery Ave., 61025. Tel: 815-747-3221. [JC]
School—701 Rte. 35 N., 61025. Tel: 815-747-3010. Mr. Michael Powers, Prin.
Lay Teachers 8; Students 120.
Catechesis/Religious Programs—Students 90.

Elburn, Kane Co., St. Gall (1870) (Irish), Rev. Richard W. Paddock; Sr. Valerie Sepenski, O.S.F., Pastoral Assoc. & D.R.E.
Res., 120 W. Shannon, P.O. Box 8020, 60119. Tel: 630-365-6030; Fax: 630-365-5483. [CEM]
Catechesis/Religious Programs—Tel: 630-365-9166.
Students 340.

Elgin, Kane Co.,

1—St. Joseph, (1887) (German-Spanish), Rev. Michael E. Morrisey; Deacons John Sauceda; Armando Martinez.
Res., 272 Division St., 60120. Tel: 847-931-2800; Fax: 847-931-2810.
School—274 Division St., Tel: 847-931-2804. Mrs. Mary Beth Mitchell, Prin.
Lay Teachers 10; Students 263.
Catechesis/Religious Programs—Tel: 847-931-2808.
Students 615.

2—St. Laurence, (1929), Rev. Joseph F. Kulak.
Office: 226 Orchard St., 60123. Tel: 847-468-6900; Fax: 847-468-6904.
Res., 1213 Oakdale Dr., 60123. Tel: 847-468-6105.
School—572 Standish St., 61203. Tel: 847-468-6100; Fax: 847-468-6104. Mrs. Phyllis Jensen, Prin.
Lay Teachers 13; Students 270.
Catechesis/Religious Programs—Tel: 847-468-6900.
Students 230.

3—St. Mary, (1851), Rev. Thomas J. Dempsey.
Parish Office—397 Fulton St., 60120. Tel: 847-888-2828; Fax: 847-888-2883.
Res., 390 Fulton St., 60120. Tel: 847-888-0502.

School—103 S. Gifford St., Tel: 847-695-6609; Fax: 847-695-6623. Mr. Carl Macaione, Prin.
Lay Teachers 10; Students 236.
Catechesis/Religious Programs—Tel: 847-888-2718. Lesli Wiseman, D.R.E.
Students 257.

4—St. Thomas More, (1959), Revs. Richard M. Russo; Louis F. Tosto; Deacons Thaddeus Ciochon; William Joynt; Robert Plazewski.
Office: 215 Thomas More Dr., 60123. Tel: 847-888-1682; Fax: 847-888-3198. [JC]
School—1625 W. Highland Ave., Tel: 847-742-3959. Mr. David Knott, Prin.
Lay Teachers 13; Students 290.
Catechesis/Religious Programs—Tel: 847-888-4887. Mr. Ron Becker, D.R.E.
Students 500.

Elizabeth, Jo Daviess Co., St. Mary (1886), Rev. Ronald J. Conro.
Res., 112 E. Washington St., Box 246, 61028. Tel: 815-858-3422; Fax: 815-858-2622. [CEM]
Catechesis/Religious Programs—Students 105.

Freeport, Stephenson Co.,

1—St. Catherine. Closed. For inquiries for parish records contact the Chancery.

2—St. Joseph, (1862) (German), Rev. John W. Cahill. In res., Rev. Michael J. Bolger.
Res., 229 W. Washington Pl., 61032. Tel: 815-232-7622; Fax: 815-235-4690. [CEM]
School—Freeport Catholic Elementary School, 202 W. Pleasant St., Tel: 815-232-6416. Mrs. Kathy Runte, Prin.; Mr. Randall Musser, Admin. Prin.
Lay Teachers 12; Students 254.
Catechesis/Religious Programs—Tel: 815-235-4324.
Students 78.

3—St. Mary, (1846), Rev. Joseph L. Lutz.
Office: 813 S. State Ave., 61032. Tel: 815-235-7544; Fax: 815-232-8561.
Res., 704 S. State Ave., 61032. [CEM]
Catechesis/Religious Programs—Students 69.

4—St. Thomas Aquinas, (1921), Very Rev. P. William McDonnell; Deacon H. Donald Brunette.
Res., 1400 Kiwanis Dr., 61032. Tel: 815-232-3225. [JC]
Catechesis/Religious Programs—Mary L. Gerbode, D.R.E.
Students 241.

Fulton, Whiteside Co., Immaculate Conception (1863), Rev. Kenneth J. Anderson.
Res., 703 12th Ave., 61252. Tel: 815-589-3542.
Mission—Albany, Whiteside Co., St. Patrick, 1445 Waller Rd., 61230. Tel: 309-887-4072.
Catechesis/Religious Programs—Students 110.

Galena, Jo Daviess Co., St. Mary (1851) (German), Rev. Daniel D. Tranel; Miss Socorro Vasquez de Velasco, Pastoral Assoc.
Res., 406 Franklin St., 61036. Tel: 815-777-0134. [CEM]
Catechesis/Religious Programs—Tel: 815-777-2219. Patricia Schuler, D.R.E.
Students 159.

St. Michael (1832) (Irish), Rev. Daniel D. Tranel, Admin.
Res., 227 S. Bench St., 61036. Tel: 815-777-2053. [CEM]
Catechesis/Religious Programs—Tricia Tranel, D.R.E.
Students 172.

Geneva, Kane Co., St. Peter (1912), Revs. Joseph F. Jarmoluk; Anthony Pantyra; Deacon Joseph McCafferty; Mrs. Lois Bushman, Pastoral Assoc. In res., Rev. Mark Campobello.
Office: 1891 Kaneville Rd., 60134. Tel: 630-232-0124; Fax: 630-232-9262.
Res., 1771 Kaneville Rd., 60134. Tel: 630-208-1625. [JC]
School—1881 Kaneville Rd., Tel: 630-232-0476; Fax: 630-208-5681. Mrs. Deborah Bray, Prin.
Lay Teachers 12; Students 352.
Catechesis/Religious Programs—Tel: 630-232-7659. Sr. Mary Stella Schellenberger, S.S.C.M, D.R.E.
Students 1,123.
Convent—Tel: 630-879-2921.

Genoa, DeKalb Co., St. Catherine of Genoa (1912), Rev. Harold L. Nilges; Sr. Marianne Nilges, O.S.F., Pastoral Assoc.
Res., 340 S. Stott St., 60135. Tel: 815-784-2355. [CEM]
Catechesis/Religious Programs—Tel: 815-784-2045. Janet Elwer, D.R.E.
Students 270.

Hampshire, Kane Co., St. Charles Borromeo (1878), Rev. Thomas E. Brantman.
Res., 297 E. Jefferson St., P.O.Box 505, 60140-0505. Tel: 847-683-2391; Fax: 847-683-7499. [CEM]
School—(Grades PreK-8) 288 E. Jefferson St., P.O. Box 699, Tel: 847-683-3450. Mrs. Kimberly Kohler Freitag, Prin.
Lay Teachers 11; Students 138.
Catechesis/Religious Programs—297 E. Jefferson, P.O. Box 815, Tel: 847-683-1536. Sandra Iwanski, D.R.E.
Students 288.

Hanover, Jo Daviess Co., St. John the Evangelist, Rev. Michael A. Librandi.
Res., 103 Savanna Rd., 61041. Tel: 815-591-2258; 244-2577; Fax: 815-244-3974.

Harmon, Lee Co., St. Flannen (1898), Rev. Thomas P. Dolan.
Res., P.O. Box 130, 61042. Tel: 815-359-7819. [CEM]

Hartland, McHenry Co., St. Patrick (1837), Rev. Lawrence M. Urbaniak; Deacon Arthur Holt.
Res., 15012 St. Patrick Rd., Woodstock, 60098. Tel: 815-338-7883. [CEM]
Catechesis/Religious Programs—Students 72.

Harvard, McHenry Co., St. Joseph (1866), Rev. Richard R. Kramer; Sr. Alice Lamping, C.S.C., Pastoral Assoc.
Res., 206 E. Front St., 60033. Tel: 815-943-6406; Fax: 815-943-1604. [CEM]
School—201 N. Division St., Tel: 815-943-6933. Mrs. Marilyn Knapp, Prin.
Lay Teachers 7; Students 126.
Catechesis/Religious Programs—Tel: 815-943-1644. Beverly O'Leary, D.R.E.
Students 211.

Huntley, McHenry Co., St. Mary (1873), Rev. Robert M. Garrity.
Res., 10911 N. Woodstock St., P.O. Box 835, 60142. Tel: 847-669-3137. [CEM]
Catechesis/Religious Programs—Students 200.

Johnsburg, McHenry Co., St. John the Baptist (1841), Rev. Robert A. Balog.
Res., 2302 W. Church St., McHenry, 60050. Tel: 815-385-1477; Fax: 815-363-3333. [CEM]
School—Tel: 815-385-3959; Fax: 815-363-3337. Pamela Dvonch, Prin.
Sisters 1; Lay Teachers 17; Students 227.
Catechesis/Religious Programs—Tel: 815-385-4870. Sr. Clara Bauman, O.P., D.R.E.
Students 469.

Lee, Lee Co., St. James (1878), Rev. Louis J. Pesut.
Res., P.O. Box 108, 60530. Tel: 815-824-2053. [CEM]
Catechesis/Religious Programs—Students 70.

Lena, Stephenson Co., St. Joseph (1870), Rev. Salvatore J. Guagliardo.
Res., 410 W. Lena St., 61048. Tel: 815-369-2810. [CEM]
Catechesis/Religious Programs—Tel: 815-443-2892. Louise Kloepping, D.R.E.
Students 126.

Loves Park, Winnebago Co., St. Bridget (1946), Rev. Msgr. John J. Mitchell; Rev. Michael J. Fuller. In res., Rev. John J. Calkins.
Res., 600 Clifford Ave., 61111. Tel: 815-633-6311; Fax: 815-633-6314.
School—604 Clifford Ave., 61111. Tel: 815-633-8255. Sr. Mary Ann Hettel, S.S.C.M., Prin.
Lay Teachers 20; Students 450.
Catechesis/Religious Programs—Tel: 815-633-4006.
Students 357.

McHenry, McHenry Co., Church of Holy Apostles (1989), Rev. Robert N. Sherry; Deacon Joseph Phelan.
Church—5211 W. Bull Valley Rd., 60050. Tel: 815-385-5673; Fax: 815-385-6045.
Catechesis/Religious Programs—Tel: 815-385-4273. Jeanne Fraser, D.R.E.
Students 660.

St. Mary (1894) (German), Rev. Thomas E. Burr; Sr. Eleanor King, S.S.S.F., Pastoral Assoc.
Res., 1401 N. Richmond Rd., 60050. Tel: 815-385-0024; Fax: 815-385-7809. [CEM]
School—Montini-Middle Grades, 1405 N. Richmond Rd., 60050. Tel: 815-385-1022.
Lay Teachers 9; Students 214. School Sisters of St. Francis, Tel: 815-385-0407. Mrs. Sheila Murphy, Prin.
Catechesis/Religious Programs—Tel: 815-385-2959. Anne Chrzan, D.R.E.
Students 384.

St. Patrick (1840) (Irish), Rev. James V. McKitrick; Deacon John H. Waterman.
Res., 3500 W. Washington St., 60050. Tel: 815-385-0025; Fax: 815-385-0861. [CEM 2]
School—Montini Primary Center, Tel: 815-385-5380; Fax: 815-385-5017. Mrs. Sheila Murphy, Prin.; Mrs. Luann Gavula, Asst. Prin.
Sisters 1; Lay Teachers 25; Students 525.
Catechesis/Religious Programs—Tel: 815-385-2959. Anne Chrzan, D.R.E.
Students 364.

Maple Park, DeKalb Co., St. Mary (1850), Rev. William J. Clausen.
Res., 123 S. Sycamore, P.O. Box 280, 60151. Tel: 815-827-3218; Fax: 815-827-3218.
Novak Center: 205 S. Sycamore St., Tel: 815-827-3205. [CEM 2]
Catechesis/Religious Programs—Students 82.

Marengo, McHenry Co., Sacred Heart (1902), Rev. Msgr. Philip E. O'Neil.
Res., 323 N. Taylor St., 60152. Tel: 815-568-7878; Fax: 815-568-7929. [CEM]
Catechesis/Religious Programs—Tel: 815-568-6230. D.R.E.: Robert Olsen; Christine Murphy.
Students 425.

Maytown, Lee Co., St. Patrick (1840), Rev. Thomas P. Dolan.
Res., P.O. Box 130, Harmon, 61042. Tel: 815-359-7819. [CEM]

Menominee, Jo Daviess Co., Nativity of the Blessed Virgin Mary (1864), Rev. Bernard F. Dittman, Admin.
Res., 15406 W. Creek Valley Rd., East Dubuque P.O., 61025. Tel: 815-747-3676. [CEM]
School—15390 W. Creek Valley Rd., Tel: 815-747-3670. Sr. Janette Wicker, O.P., Prin.
Sisters 1; Lay Teachers 4; Students 96.

Morrison, Whiteside Co., St. Mary (1904), Very Rev. Leo J. Bartel.
Office: 126 E. Lincolnway, P.O. Box 248, 61270. Tel: 815-772-3095; Fax: 815-772-4890.
Res., 611 Greenwood Dr., 61270. Tel: 815-772-3095.
Catechesis/Religious Programs—Tel: 815-772-4890; Fax: 815-772-4890.
Students 131.

Mount Carroll, Carroll Co., SS. John and Catherine (1923). Attended by Savanna. Rev. Timothy J. Seigel.
Res., 314 S. Main St., P.O. Box 193, 61053. Tel: 815-244-1835 (Church).
Catechesis/Religious Programs—Students 77.

North Aurora, Kane Co., Blessed Sacrament (1970), Rev. Msgr. Edward S. Wright, V.F.; Sr. Rose Marie Weber, O.S.F., Pastoral Assoc. & D.R.E.
Res., 801 Oak St., 60542-1063. Tel: 630-897-1029; Fax: 630-897-1062.
Catechesis/Religious Programs—Students 295.

Oregon, Ogle Co., St. Mary (1862), Rev. William A. Budden.
Mailing Address: P.O. Box 419, 61061. Tel: 815-732-7383; Fax: 815-732-4742.
Res., 303 N. Fourth St., 61061. Tel: 815-732-2234; Fax: 815-732-6332. [CEM]
Catechesis/Religious Programs—Students 162.

Pecatonica, Winnebago Co., St. Mary (1872) (Irish-German), Rev. Robert J. Sweeney; Deacon Warren LaMont.
Res., 126 W. Fifth St., P.O. Box 656, 61063. Tel: 815-239-1271. [CEM]
Catechesis/Religious Programs—Students 134.

Polo, Ogle Co., St. Mary's (1856), Rev. Donald F. Smithes; Deacon John Gilmour.
Res., 211 N. Franklin Ave., 61064. Tel: 815-946-2535. [CEM]
Catechesis/Religious Programs—Students 93.

Prophetstown, Whiteside Co., St. Catherine (1917), Rev. Daniel E. Peters, Admin.
Res., 308 E. Third St., 61277. Tel: 815-537-2077.
Catechesis/Religious Programs—Doris Cox, D.R.E.
Students 50.
Mission—Erie, Whiteside Co., St. Ambrose.

Richmond, McHenry Co., St. Joseph (1930), Rev. Joseph W. Kaiser; Deacon Lawrence Geinosky.
Res., 10519 Main St., 60071. Tel: 815-678-7421. [CEM]
Catechesis/Religious Programs—Tel: 815-678-6961. Patricia Donovan, D.R.E.
Students 123.

Rochelle, Ogle Co., St. Patrick (1868), Pastoral Team: Very Rev. Francis P. Kennedy; Sr. Judith Hermann, R.S.M.; Deacon Higinio Perez.
Res., 250 Kelley Dr., 61068. Tel: 815-562-2370; Fax: 815-562-5250. [CEM]
Catechesis/Religious Programs—Tel: 815-562-7677. Judy Snyder, D.R.E.
Students 449.

Rock Falls, Whiteside Co., St. Andrew (1950), Rev. Msgr. Thomas L. Dzielak.
Res., 708 10th Ave., 61071. Tel: 815-625-4508; Fax: 815-625-1569. [JC]
School—701 11th Ave., 61071. Tel: 815-625-1456. Mr. Philip D. Bellini, Prin.
Lay Teachers 7; Students 109.
Catechesis/Religious Programs—Tel: 815-625-4508.
Students 161.

St. Charles, Kane Co., St. John Neumann (1977), Very Rev. Robert B. Hoffman; Rev. Robert W. Jones; Deacons Martin Hetzel; Paul Iwanski; Ronald Williams.
Res., 2900 E. Main St., 60174. Tel: 630-377-2797; Fax: 630-377-2834.
Catechesis/Religious Programs—Tel: 630-377-2803. Karen Dix, D.R.E.
Students 1,360.

St. Patrick (1851), Revs. Joseph B. Linster; Joseph P. Nicolosi; Sr. Dorothy Dempsey, Pastoral Assoc. In res., Rev. David A. Peck.
Res. & Church Address: 408 Cedar St., 60174. Tel: 630-584-0092; Fax: 630-513-2246.
School—State St. & Fifth St., Tel: 630-584-6367; Fax: 630-584-9759. Mr. Joseph Battisto, Prin.
Sisters 1; Lay Teachers 24; Students 540.
Catechesis/Religious Programs—Tel: 630-513-2247. Sr. Joelyn Hayes, D.R.E.
Students 1,500.
Mission—St. Charles, Kane Co., St. Patrick, 6N491 Crane Rd., 60175.

Sandwich, DeKalb Co., St. Paul (1925), Rev. John A. Kraemer.
Res., 110 N. Eddy St., 60548. Tel: 815-786-9266. [CEM]
Catechesis/Religious Programs—Tel: 815-786-8964.
Students 228.

Savanna, Carroll Co., St. John the Baptist (1884), Rev. Timothy J. Seigle.
Res., 318 Chicago Ave., 61074. Tel: 815-273-3961; Fax: 815-273-3503. [CEM]
Catechesis/Religious Programs—Tel: 815-273-3582.
Students 101.

Scales Mound, Jo Daviess Co., Holy Trinity (1863), Rev. Ronald J. Conro.
Mailing Address: 112 E. Washington, Box 246, Elizabeth, 61028. Tel: 815-858-3422; Fax: 815-858-2622. [CEM 2]
Catechesis/Religious Programs—Students 97.

Shannon, Carroll Co., St. Wendelin (1870). Attended by St. Mary, Freeport. Rev. Joseph L. Lutz.
18 S. Linn St., P.O. Box 23, 61078. Tel: 815-864-2548 (Church). [CEM]
Catechesis/Religious Programs—Students 60.

Somonauk, DeKalb Co., St. John the Baptist (1865), Rev. Donald D. DeSalvo.
Res., 320 S. Depot St., Box 276, 60552. Tel: 815-498-2010. [CEM]
Catechesis/Religious Programs—Tel: 815-498-2627.
Students 250.

South Beloit, Winnebago Co., St. Peter (1909), Rev. Msgr. Thomas C. Brady; Rev. Carlos Hoffner, M.S.; Deacon Peter Calgaro, Pastoral Assoc.
Res., 620 Blackhawk Blvd., 61080. Tel: 815-389-2024; Fax: 815-389-2024.
School—320 Elmwood Ave., Tel: 815-389-3193. Sr. David Ennis, C.S.A., Prin.
Lay Teachers 14; Students 129.
Catechesis/Religious Programs—Tel: 815-389-9091. Jeanne Pulkrabek, D.R.E.
Students 260.
Mission—Roscoe, Winnebago Co., Church of the Holy Spirit, P.O. Box 478, Roscoe, 61073. Tel: 815-623-8742.

Spring Grove, McHenry Co., St. Peter (1900) (German), Rev. Andrew J. Plesa.
Church—2206 Main St., P.O. Box 129, 60081. Tel: 815-675-2288; Fax: 815-675-6774. [CEM]
Catechesis/Religious Programs—Tel: 815-675-2576.
Students 324.

Sterling, Whiteside Co., Sacred Heart (1870), Rev. Paul C. White.
Res., 2224 Avenue J, 61081. Tel: 815-625-0631; 625-1134; Fax: 815-625-1138. [CEM]
Catechesis/Religious Programs—Students 131.

St. Mary (1898), Very Rev. Thomas E. Bales; Deacon John Kellen; Jane Olson, Pastoral Assoc. In res., Rev. John P. Earl.
Res., 507 Ave. B, 61081. Tel: 815-625-0640; Fax: 815-625-1684. [CEM]
School—6 W. Sixth St., Tel: 815-625-2253; Fax: 815-625-8942. Mrs. Rebecca Scmitt Tel: 815-284-2926.
Lay Teachers 19; Students 221.
Catechesis/Religious Programs—600 Ave. B, 61081. Tel: 815-625-6688.
Students 333.

Stockton, Jo Daviess Co., Holy Cross (1893) (German), Rev. Aloysius J. Neumann.
Res., 216 E. Benton Ave., 61085. Tel: 815-947-2545. [CEM]
Catechesis/Religious Programs—Students 150.

Sublette, Lee Co., Our Lady of Perpetual Help, Rev. Edward R. Hughes.
Mailing Address: Box 80, West Brooklyn, 61378. Tel: 815-628-3901. [CEM]
Catechesis/Religious Programs—Students 89.

Sycamore, De Kalb Co., St. Mary (1885), Rev. Frank John Timar, M.S.C.
Res., 244 Waterman St., 60178. Tel: 815-895-3275; Fax: 815-895-4561. [CEM]
School—222 Waterman St., Tel: 815-895-5215. Ms. Janine M. Bolchazy, Prin.
Lay Teachers 10; Students 172.
Catechesis/Religious Programs—Tel: 815-895-3726.
Students 320.

Tampico, Whiteside Co., St. Mary (1875), Very Rev. F. James Larson, Admin.
Res., 105 Benton St., P.O. Box 159, 61283. Tel: 815-438-5425. [CEM]

Virgil, Kane Co., SS. Peter and Paul (1909), Rev. Thomas W. Neville; Deacon Clark Reynolds.
Res., 5 N. 939 Meredith Rd., P.O. Box 26, 60182. Tel: 630-365-6618. [CEM]
Catechesis/Religious Programs—Students 117.

Walton, Lee Co., St. Mary (1913), Rev. Thomas P. Dolan.
Res., P.O. Box 130, Harmon, 61042. Tel: 815-359-7819. [CEM]

Warren, Jo Daviess Co., St. Ann, Rev. Everett J. Hiller.
Res., 608 Railroad St., P.O. Box 665, 61087. Tel: 815-745-2312. [CEM]
Catechesis/Religious Programs—Students 94.

West Brooklyn, Lee Co., St. Mary, Rev. Edward R. Hughes.
Mailing Address: P.O. Box 80, 61378. Tel: 815-628-3901. [CEM]

Wonder Lake, McHenry Co., Christ the King (1949), Rev. Dorrance E. Tranel.
Res., 5006 E. Wonder Lake Rd., 60097. Tel: 815-653-2561. [CEM]
Catechesis/Religious Programs—Tel: 815-653-2581. Ms. Maureen Mclain, D.R.E.
Students 283.

Woodstock, McHenry Co., Resurrection (1978), Rev. Eugene Majewski, C.R.
Mailing Address: 2918 S. Country Club Rd., 60098. Tel: 815-338-7330; Fax: 815-338-7365.
Res., 6022 Shenandoah Dr., Crystal Lake, 60012. Tel: 815-356-5834.
Catechesis/Religious Programs—Nancy Neumeister, D.R.E.
Students 136.

St. Mary (1853), Revs. James W. McLoughlin; Christopher J. Kuhn; Deacon Eugene Wedoff.
Res., 312 Lincoln Ave., 60098. Tel: 815-338-3377; Fax: 815-338-3497. [CEM]
School—313 Tryon St., Tel: 815-338-3598; Fax: 815-338-3408. Mrs. Susan Rancak, Prin.
Lay Teachers 22; Students 398.
Catechesis/Religious Programs—Tel: 815-338-3413. Mrs. Connie Soucek, D.R.E.
Students 392.

Chaplains of Public Institutions

ELGIN. *Elgin State Hospital*. Vacant. 750 S. State St., 60123.

MOOSEHEART. *School of the Loyal Order of Moose* 301 Fifth Ave., 60539. Rev. John T. Heraty, Chap.

ST. CHARLES. *Illinois State Youth Center*. Records kept at St. Patrick, St. Charles. Chapel of the Immaculate Conception.

Special Assignment:
Reverend Monsignors—
Binsfeld, Michael A., Vice-Chancellor, Vicar for Clergy and Religious, 1226 N. CHurch St., Rockford, IL 61103. Tel: 815-965-5767
Kagan, David D., Vicar Gen./Moderator of the Curia, 1245 N. Court St., P.O. Box 7044, Rockford, IL 61126. Tel: 815-962-3709
McNamee, Charles W., Chancellor, 1245 N. Court St., P.O. Box 7044, Rockford, 61103. Tel: 815-962-3709
Reverend Fathers—
Jones, Ronald A., Education Sabbatical
Larson, F. James, Vicar for Catholic Education, 1260 N. Church St., Rockford, IL 61103
Nelson, Glenn L., Secretary to the Bishop, 1245 N. Court St., P.O. Box 7044, Rockford, IL 61126. Tel: 815-962-3709
Schuessler, William R., Vicar for Ministry to Hispanics, 921 W. State St., Rockford, IL 61102. Tel: 815-962-8042

Active Outside the Diocese:
Reverend Fathers—
Donahugh, Donald E., 100 Gifford Pond Ln., Port Arthur, TX 77642
Falcone, Emilio, Chap., PSC 02, Box 7192, APO AE, NY 09012
Myers, William F., St. Joachim, 19150 S.W.-117th Ave., Miami, FL 33117. Tel: 305-247-8268
Simonini, Michael F., St. Bernard, 1617 W. Pine St., Appleton, WI 54914. Tel: 414-739-0331
Swarthout, James E., St. Francis de Sales, 277 E. Main St., Lake Zurich, IL 60047. Tel: 847-438-6622

On Health Leave:
Reverend Fathers—
Holdren, John C.

On Disability Leave:
Reverend Fathers—
Fitzgibbons, Al L.
Joffe, William I.
Vlasz, Melvyn J.

Absent on Leave:
Reverend Fathers—
Tripodi, Frank J.
Waser, Frank A.

Retired:
Reverend Monsignors—
Healey, Joseph T., 2505 Whitehall Circle, Rockford, IL 61107. Tel: 815-399-8579
Reverend Fathers—
Becker, Anthony J., Cor Mariae Center, 3330 Maria Linden Dr., Rockford, IL 61114
Calkins, John J., 600 Clifford Ave., Loves Park, IL 61111. Tel: 815-633-6311
Draude, Frank C., 7 Sabadell Ln., Hot Springs Village, AR 71909. Tel: 501-922-1109
Gorinas, Vytautas, 605 Park Ave., Beloit, WI 53511
Knott, William P., 15528 W. Sky Hawk Dr., Sun City West, AZ 85375. Tel: 602-214-2520
Kriegsmann, William A., 1439 Rohde, Berkeley, IL 60163. Tel: 708-544-3039
London, Lawrence, Vianney Oaks, 7712 E. McGregor Rd., Rockford, IL 61102. Tel: 815-963-4820
McCarren, Charles K., 5208 East Dr., Loves Park, IL 61111. Tel: 815-877-2702
McGowan, John J., Health Center, 5100 John Ryan Blvd., #108, San Antonio, TX 78245. Tel: 512-677-8855
Peterson, William F., 147 Shadowood Dr., Martinez, GA 30907. Tel: 706-860-4738
Petit, Edmund P., 616 Redwood Dr., Aurora, IL 60506. Tel: 630-897-8052
Ratazak, Bernard A., Vianney Oaks, 7712 E. McGregor Rd., Rockford, IL 61102. Tel: 815-965-0910
Regnier, William H., Cor Mariae Center, 3330 Maria Linden Dr., Rockford, IL 61114. Tel: 815-633-4573
Rennell, Albert F., 1060 N. Farnsworth Ave., Apt. 1104, Aurora, IL 60505. Tel: 708-898-0664
Richter, Norbert M., Vianney Oaks, 7712 E. McGregor Rd., Rockford, IL 61102. Tel: 815-965-4112
Schlade, Joseph F., 1109 N. Ashland Ave., Chicago, IL 60622. Tel: 312-384-7967
Sherman, Charles E., Vianney Oaks, 7712 E. McGregor Rd., Rockford, IL 61102. Tel: 815-962-6731
Thennes, Clarence J., 659 E. Jefferson St., Freeport, IL 61032. Tel: 815-232-6181
Verstynen, Robert J., 1094 Tulip Ln., #5, Rockford, IL 61107. Tel: 815-394-0447

Permanent Deacons:
Anchor, Robert, Sacred Heart, Marengo
Bach, John, St. Monica, Carpentersville
Balsamo, Robert, St. Mary, Elgin
Barone, Frank, St. Anthony of Padua, Rockford
Battista, James, Holy Cross, Mesa, AZ
Berard, Samuel, St. Parick, Dixon
Boyes, Eugene, St. Mary, DeKalb
Bracken, Robert, Holy Family, Rockford
Brandenburg, Robert, St. Patrick, Dixon
Brunette, Donald J., St. Thomas, Freeport
Buga, John, Port Richey, FL
Burch, Michael, St. Rita, Rockford
Calgaro, Peter, St. Peter, South Beloit; Church of the Holy Spirit, Roscoe
Callahan, Donald J., St. James, Belvidere
Callahan, Patrick, St. John the Baptist, Johnsburg
Cassaro, Sam, St. Anthony of Padua, Rockford
Ciochon, Thaddeus, St. Thomas More, Elgin
Cooper, Charles, St. Peter Cathedral, Rockford
Cordes, Luke, Holy Angels, Aurora
Cristoforo, Michael, St. Rita, Rockford
Czerniewski, Martin, St. Peter Cathedral, Rockford

Dean, William, St. James, Rockford
Demming, Robert, Lake Wales, FL
Devine, John E., Houston, TX
Dolan, Robert J., St. Mary, Woodstock
Dombek, James, Christ the Teacher, DeKalb
Ferolo, James, St. Anne, Dixon
Frazier, J. Michael, St. Monica, Carpentersville
Freund, Walter, McHenry
Garber, Dennis, St. Monica, Carpentersville
Geinosky, Lawrence, St. Joseph, Richmond
Gerdeman, Richard, St. Bernadette, Rockford
Giambalvo, Michael, St. Laurence, Elgin
Gilmour, John, St. Mary, Polo
Goetz, Claude E., Manitowoc, WI
Graw, Ronald, St. Patrick, Rockford
Groom, Richard, Sacred Heart and St. Mary, Aurora
Grossmayer, Simon, St. Margaret Mary, Algonquin
Hainchek, Alex J., St. Rita, Rockford
Hawksworth, Thomas, Holy Angels, Aurora
Hetzel, Martin, St. John Neumann, St. Charles
Hoefler, Ben, Springfield
Holt, Arthur, St. Patrick, Hartland
Hurley, Dan A., Surprise, AZ
Iwanski, Paul, St. John Neumann, St. Charles
Johnson, Raymond R., Annunciation, Aurora
Joynt, William, St. Thomas More, Elgin
Kellen, John, St. Mary, Sterling
Kohler, John, St. Catherine, Genoa
LaMont, Warren R., St. Mary, Pecatonica
LaPlante, Joseph A.
Linstad, Richard E., Sr., Moutain Home, AK
Magee, Ronald, St. James, Rockford
Maher, Patrick, St. Margaret Mary, Algonquin
Martin, Richard, St. Rita of Cascia, Aurora
Martin, Robert H., St. Rita, Rockford
Martinez, Armondo, St. Joseph, Elgin
McCafferty, Joseph, St. Peter, Geneva
McElroy, Robert D., Safety Harbor, FL
Milano, Robert, St. Patrick, Amboy
Mosley, William
Muehler, Gerald, St. Mary, Huntley
Mulcahey, Richard, St. Mary, Durand
Murphy, Melvin J., Dixon
Nebel, Robert E., St. Thomas the Apostle, Crystal Lake
Olson, James D., St. James, Belvidere
Patton, James, St. Elizabeth Ann Seton, Crystal Lake
Perez, Higinio, St. Patrick, Rochelle
Phelan, Joseph, Church of Holy Apostles, McHenry
Plazewski, Robert, St. Thomas More, Elgin
Porter, John, Rockford
Poss, Harold, Annunciation of the B.V.M., Aurora
Prendergast, John, Schoolcraft, MI
Real, Robert, St. Laurence, Elgin
Rees, William, St. Mary, Aurora
Reilly, Eugene, St. Edward, Rockford
Reynolds, Clark, S.S. Peter and Paul, Virgil
Sauceda, John, St. Joseph, Elgin
Schaffer, Stephen, St. Thomas the Apostle, Crystal Lake
Smith, Daniel, St. James, Belvidere
Smits, Robert, St. Mary, Byron
Statter, Ralph, Crystal Lake
Steinhable, George C., Jr., Chicago
Stredde, John C., Montgomery
Szudarski, Norbert, St. Joseph, Aurora
Trost, Ray, Hampshire
Valesano, James J., Our Lady of Good Counsel, Aurora
Verstynen, Lambert, St. Edward, Rockford
Vondra, Edward
Ward, Richard
Washburn, Dale C., Orlando, FL
Waterman, John, St. Patrick, McHenry
Wedoff, Eugene, St. Mary, Woodstock
Welch, Thomas, SS. Peter and Paul, Cary
White, Thomas, Holy Angels, Aurora
Whitehead, William, Jr., St. Catherine of Siena, Dundee
Williams, Ronald, St. John Neumann, St. Charles
Zitkus, Lawrence, St. Catherine of Genoa, Genoa

INSTITUTIONS LOCATED IN THE DIOCESE

[A] SEMINARIES, RELIGIOUS OR SCHOLASTICATES

AURORA. *Marmion Abbey*, Butterfield Rd., 60504. Tel: 630-897-7215.
Web site: www.marmion.org
Rt. Rev. Vincent Bataille, O.S.B., Abbot; Very Rev. Kenneth Theisen, O.S.B., Prior. Priests 33; Brothers 12.

WOODSTOCK. *Resurrection Center Retreat House*, 2710 S. Country Club Rd., 60098. Tel: 815-338-1032; Fax: 815-338-1017.
E-mail: rescenter@stans.com
Mr. James F. Ivers, Dir.; Rev. Richard Grek, C.R., Coord., Adult Programs in Spirituality. Priests 2; Lay Staff 8.

[B] HIGH SCHOOLS, DIOCESAN

ROCKFORD. *Boylan Central Catholic High School*, 4000 St. Francis Dr., 61103. Tel: 815-877-0531; Fax: 815-877-2544.
E-mail: boylan@bossnet.com
Sr. M. Anthony Marelli, O.P., Prin.; Mr. Vincent E. McGuire, Asst. Prin., Student Affairs; Rev. F. William Etheredge, Spiritual Dir. & Chm., Dept. of Religious Studies; Mr. William C. Thumm, Dean of Students; Mr. Howard Willis, Guidance Dir. Priests 6; Sisters 2; Lay Teachers 82; Students 1,344.

AURORA. *Aurora Central Catholic High School*, 1255 N. Edgelawn Dr., 60506. Tel: 630-907-0095; Fax: 630-907-1076. Mr. Robert Stewart, Dir. of Institutional Advancement; Mr. Randolph Thomas, Prin.; Rev. Mark A. Compobello, Asst. Prin., Spiritual Dir. Priests 2; School Sisters of St. Francis 1; Lay Teachers 27; Students 455.

ELGIN. *St. Edward Central Catholic High School*, 335 Locust St., 60123. Tel: 847-741-7535; Fax: 847-741-8658. Dr. George D. Laird, Supt.; Richard W. Sollenberger, Prin.; Mr. Thomas Rapp, Asst. Prin. & Dean; Rev. David A. Peck, Asst. Prin. & Spiritual Dir. Priests 3; Lay Teachers 38; Students 553.

FREEPORT. *Aquin Central Catholic Junior-Senior High School*, 1419 S. Galena Ave., 61032. Tel: 815-235-3154. Kathleen Runte, Supt. Prin.; Rev. Michael J. Bolger, Asst. Prin. & Chm. Religious Studies Dept. Priests 1; Lay Teachers 14; Students 210.

STERLING. *Newman Central Catholic High School*, 1101 St. Mary's Rd., 61081-9002. Tel: 815-625-0500; Fax: 815-625-8444.
E-mail: newman@cin.net
Mr. Philip Bellini, Supt.; Mr. Donald E. Loftus, Prin.; Rev. Daniel E. Peters, Asst. Prin./Spiritual Dir. Priests 2; Lay Teachers 25; Students 261.

WOODSTOCK. *Marian Central Catholic High School*, 1001 McHenry Ave., 60098. Tel: 815-338-4220; Fax: 815-338-4253. Mr. Thomas E. Landers, Supt.; Mr. Charles Rakers, Prin.; Rev. Paul M. Lipinski, Asst. Prin. & Spiritual Dir.; Mr. James Dvorak, Dean of Students; Mr. Vito C. DeFrisco, Development Dir. Priests 5; Sisters 1; Lay Teachers 38; Students 719.

[C] HIGH SCHOOLS, PRIVATE

AURORA. *Marmion Academy*, 1000 Butterfield Rd., 60504. Tel: 630-897-6936; Fax: 630-897-7086.
Web site: www.marmion.org
Boarding and Day School. Rt. Rev. Vincent Bataille, O.S.B., Abbot & Pres.; Rev. Basil Yender, O.S.B., Headmaster. Benedictines 18; Lay Teachers 33; Students 470.

Rosary High School, 901 N. Edgelawn Ave., 60506. Tel: 630-896-0831; Fax: 630-896-8372. Sr. M. Megan Farrelly, O.P., Prin.; Sr. Mary Joseph Weigand, O.P., Asst. Prin.; Sr. Elizabeth Wrenn, O.P., Chm., Religious Studies. Sisters of St. Dominic 10; Lay Teachers 27; Girls 418.

[D] GENERAL HOSPITALS

ROCKFORD. *Saint Anthony College of Nursing*, 5658 E. State St., 61108. Tel: 815-395-5090
For a complete listing, refer to the Hospitals section.

Saint Anthony Medical Center, 5666 E. State St., 61108. Tel: 815-226-2000
For a complete listing, refer to the Hospitals section.

AURORA. *Mercy Health Corporation*, 1325 N. Highland Ave., 60506. Tel: 630-859-2222; Fax: 630-859-9014
For a complete listing, refer to the Hospitals section.

BELVIDERE. *Saint Joseph Hospital*, 1005 Julien St., 61008. Tel: 815-544-3411; Fax: 815-547-5977
For a complete listing, refer to the Hospitals section.

ELGIN. *St. Joseph Hospital*, 77 N. Airlite St., 60123. Tel: 847-695-3200
For a complete listing, refer to the Hospitals section.

[E] SCHOOLS FOR EXCEPTIONAL ADOLESCENTS AND ADULTS

FREEPORT. *St. Vincent's Community Living Facility and Supported Living Arrangement*, 659 E. Jefferson St., 61032. Tel: 815-232-6181; Fax: 815-232-6143. Ms. Deb Clicquennoi, Program Dir.; Rev. Clarence J. Thennes, Chap. Sisters 2. Patients assisted annually 30.

[F] SCHOOLS FOR EXCEPTIONAL CHILDREN

FREEPORT. *Saint Francis School for Exceptional Children*, 1209 S. Walnut Ave., 61032. Tel: 815-235-3174; Fax: 815-232-4667. Mr. John McCoy, L.C.S.W., Admin. Students 46.

[G] HOMES FOR AGED AND ADULT DAY CARE CENTERS

ROCKFORD. *Cor Mariae Center*, 3330 Maria Linden Dr., 61114
For a complete listing, refer to the Special Care Facilities section.

St. Anne Center, 4405 Highcrest Rd., 61107. Tel: 815-229-1999
For a complete listing, refer to the Special Care Facilities section.

St. Anne Place, 4444 Brendenwood Rd., 61107. Tel: 815-399-6167
For a complete listing, refer to the Special Care Facilities section.

Vianney Oaks, 7712 E. McGregor Rd., 61102. Tel: 815-965-0910
For a complete listing, refer to the Special Care Facilities section.

AURORA. *Fox Knoll (Retirement Community)*, 421 N. Lake St., 60506. Tel: 630-844-0380
For a complete listing, refer to the Special Care Facilities section.

McAuley Manor, 400 W. Sullivan Rd., 60506. Tel: 630-859-3700; Fax: 630-264-1862
For a complete listing, refer to the Special Care Facilities section.

FREEPORT. *St. Joseph Adult Day Care Center*, 659 E. Jefferson St., 61032. Tel: 815-232-6181; Fax: 815-232-6143
For a complete listing, refer to the Special Care Facilities section.

St. Joseph Center, 659 E. Jefferson St., 61032. Tel: 815-232-6181; Fax: 815-232-6143
For a complete listing, refer to the Special Care Facilities section.

[H] MONASTERIES AND RESIDENCES OF PRIESTS AND BROTHERS

AURORA. *Marmion Abbey-St. Augustine's Abbey*, Butterfield Rd., 60504. Tel: 630-897-7215; Fax: 630-897-0393. Legal Title: *Marmion*. Rt. Revs. Vincent Bataille, O.S.B., Abbot; Gerald Benkert, O.S.B., Abbot Emeritus; David J. Cyr, O.S.B., Abbot Emeritus; Very Rev. Kenneth Theisen, O.S.B., Prior; Revs. Barnabas Lundergan, O.S.B.; Andrew Wahmhoff, O.S.B.; Bede Stocker, O.S.B.; Alcuin Deck, O.S.B.; Bro. Anselm Mangano, O.S.B., Subprior; Revs. Luke Bohr, O.S.B.; Augustine Jones, O.S.B.; Martin Witting, O.S.B.; Hugh Schuck, O.S.B.; Terence Stanton, O.S.B.; Matthias Zinkan, O.S.B.; Bernard Schaefer, O.S.B.; Gregory Obee, O.S.B.; Philip Kremer, O.S.B.; Mario Pedi, O.S.B.; Francis Daleiden, O.S.B.; David Palmatier, O.S.B.; Charles Reichenbacher, O.S.B.; Basil Yender, O.S.B.; Joel Rippinger, O.S.B.; Carlos Quintana, O.S.B.; Christian Pusateri, O.S.B.; Michael Burrows, O.S.B.; John Brahill, O.S.B.; Thomas McLaughlin, O.S.B.; Matthew F. Kowalski, O.S.B.; Rene Otzoy Colaj, O.S.B.; Cristobal Coche Quic; George Glover, O.S.B.; Frederick Peterson, O.S.B. Priests 33; Brothers 12.

Missionaries of the Sacred Heart Community, 305 S. Lake St., 60507. Tel: 630-892-2371; Fax: 630-892-1678.
E-mail: PROMSC@aol.com
Provincial Administrative Office of the Missionaries of the Sacred Heart. Very Rev. David Faxen, M.S.C., Prov. Supr.; Revs. Edward Ball, M.S.C.; Thomas Cain, M.S.C.; James Campbell, M.S.C.; Peter E. Campbell, M.S.C.; Robert Cell, M.S.C.; Raymond Diesbourg, M.S.C.; Ronald Leinen, M.S.C.; Joseph Muller, M.S.C.; Thomas Murphy, M.S.C.; Gerald Paul, M.S.C.; Leo Petit, M.S.C.; Frank Timar, M.S.C.; Bros. James Hall, M.S.C.; Eugene Thomas, M.S.C.; Nicholas Lanese, M.S.C.; Michael Tomcics, M.S.C. Priests 13; Brothers 4.
Priests of the Province Serving Elsewhere - In Bogota, Colombia: Very Rev. Howard Fath, M.S.C., Sectional Supr.; Revs. Javier Bautista, M.S.C.; German Barona, M.S.C.; Tito Medina, M.S.C.; Michael Miller, M.S.C.; Wilson Tascon, M.S.C. In Papua New Guinea: Very Rev. Joseph Gleixner, M.S.C., Regional Supr.; Revs. Steve Boland, M.S.C.; David DeLuca, M.S.C.; Henry Einhaus, M.S.C.; Hilary Fischer, M.S.C.; Anthony Gendusa, M.S.C.; Bernard Miller, M.S.C.; Leon Weisenberger, M.S.C.; Bros. Anton Freitas, M.S.C.; James Miller, M.S.C.; Patrick O'Hara, M.S.C.; Joseph Tesar, M.S.C.; Daniel Rakow, M.S.C. In Namibia: Rev. Francis Westhoff, M.S.C.

MCHENRY. *Villa Desiderata Retreat House*, 3015 N. Bayview Ln., 60050. Tel: 815-385-2264. Bro. Patrick Drohan, C.S.V., Facilities Mgr.

[I] CONVENTS AND RESIDENCES FOR SISTERS

ROCKFORD. *The Poor Clares of Rockford*, Corpus Christi Monastery, 2111 S. Main St., 61102. Tel: 815-963-7343. Franciscan Colettine Poor Clares. Mother Mary Annette Lepine, P.C.C., Abbess; Rev. Msgr. Al F. Harte, Chap., Res., 2223 S. Main St., 61102. Tel: 815-964-7606. Cloistered Sisters 22; Extern Sisters 1.

AURORA. *McAuley Convent*, 400 W. Sullivan Rd., 60506. Tel: 630-859-3700. Sisters of Mercy. Mrs. Mary A. Burnell, Admin.; Sr. Nadine Hargadon, R.S.M., Coord. of Sisters. Bed Capacity 27.

BATAVIA. *Holy Heart of Mary Novitiate*, 717 N. Batavia Ave., 60510. Tel: 630-879-1296.
E-mail: hatton@inil.com
Web site: www@inil.com/users/hatton
Servants of the Holy Heart of Mary. Sr. Linda K. Hatton, S.S.C.M., Supr. & Formation Dir. Professed Sisters 7; Candidate 1; Novices 1.

ST. CHARLES. *Our Lady of Creek Bend*, 37 W. 584 Dean St., 60175. Tel: 630-584-5699. Felician Sisters Residence. Sisters 4.

[J] COMMUNITY SERVICES

ROCKFORD. *Fourth Street Bridge Youth Shelter*, 405 S. Fourth St., 61104. Tel: 815-965-1234; Fax: 815-965-0324. Gloria Hulbert, Program Supv.; Jerry T. Fox, L.C.S.W., Program Admin. Tel: 815-965-0623. Total Staff 14; Total assisted 431.

Martin House, 1020 S. Main St., 61101. Tel: 815-963-6967. Mr. Thomas McKenna, Admin.; Rev. William P. Collins, Chap.

St. Elizabeth's Community Center, 1536 S. Main St., 61102. Tel: 815-969-6526. Mr. Thomas McKenna, Admin. Total Staff 22; Total assisted 25,028.

AURORA. *Hesed House, Inc.*, 659 S. River St., 60506. Tel: 630-897-2156. Sr. Rose Marie Lorentzen, B.V.M., Exec. Dir. Ecumenical Center for ministry to the poor. Total assisted 228,977.

Public Action to Deliver Shelter, Inc. (PADS), 659 S. River St., 60506. Tel: 630-897-2165. Sr. Rose Marie Lorentzen, B.V.M., Exec. Dir. Ecumenical advocacy, overnight and transitional shelters and daytime drop-in center for homeless persons. Total assisted 32,661.

[K] RETREAT HOUSES

ROCKFORD. *Bishop Lane Retreat Center*, 7708 E. McGregor Rd., 61102. Tel: 815-965-5011; Fax: 815-965-5811. Don & Lorrie Gramer, Admins.

[L] FOUNDATIONS

ROCKFORD. *Boylan Educational Foundation, Inc.*, 4000 St. Francis Dr., 61103; Fax: 815-877-2544.

The Catholic Foundation for the People of the Diocese of Rockford, 921 W. State St., 61102. Tel: 815-964-6711. Mr. John Sentovich, Exec. Dir.

AURORA. *Aurora Catholic Education Foundation*, P.O. Box 234, 60507.

Mercy Services Foundation of Aurora, 1325 N. Highland Ave., 60506. Tel: 630-801-2663. Ms. Joann S. Rebeck, Exec. Dir.

CRYSTAL LAKE. *St. Thomas the Apostle School Foundation, Inc.*, 272 King St., 60014.

DEKALB. *Newman Center of Northern Illinois University Educational Program*, 512 Normal Rd., 60115; Fax: 815-753-2053. Legal Title: *Newman Center of Northern Illinois University Educational Program and Development Fund, Inc.* Total Staff 16.

ELGIN. *St. Edward Central Catholic High School Education Foundation*, 100 Perry St., 60123. Bradley T. Freeman, Foundation Pres.

FREEPORT. *Education Through the 90's Foundation*, 1419 S. Galena Ave., 61032. The foundation provides financial support for the Freeport Catholic School System.

Freeport Catholic Education Foundation, 1419 S. Galena Ave., 61032. The foundation provides financial support for the Freeport Catholic School System.

STERLING. *Sauk Valley Catholic Education Foundation*, 1101 St. Mary's Rd., 61081.

Sauk Valley Area Religious Education Center, 1101 St. Mary Rd., 61081.

SYCAMORE. *St. Mary's of Sycamore Foundation, Ltd.*, 244 Waterman St., 60178.

WOODSTOCK. *McHenry County Catholic Education Foundation*, 1005 McHenry Ave., 60098. Mr. Thomas Landers, Exec. Officer.

[M] NEWMAN CENTERS

DEKALB. *Newman Foundation for Catholic Students of Northern Illinois University*, 512 Normal Rd., 60115. Tel: 815-758-6667. Rev. Stephen J. Knox. Pastoral Assocs.: Mr. Terry Beer; Ms. Rose Drance; Ms. Andrea Rusin; Mrs. Sandy Kowalkowski, Dir., Alumni Devel. Assoc.

[N] MISCELLANEOUS

ROCKFORD. *Catholic Office of the Deaf*, 1245 N. Court St., P.O. Box 7044, 61126. Tel: 815-962-3709 (Voice); 962-2994 (TTY).

The Vineyard Books and Gifts, Highcrest Centre, 1638 N. Alpine Rd., 61107. Tel: 815-398-4030; Fax: 815-398-8477.
E-mail: vineyard.org@catholic.connect
Joann Toti, Mgr. Total Staff 13.

AURORA.

**Joseph Corporation of Illinois, Inc.*, P.O. Box 525, 60507. Tel: 630-820-7400; Fax: 630-820-7402. (Ecumenical not-for-profit housing developer). MaryAnn Shanley, Exec. Dir.; Sr. Mary Catherine Daly, R.S.M., Admin. Asst.; Sr. Margaret Barrett, R.S.M., Project Dir.; Sr. Kathleen Braun, S.S.S.F., Housing Counselor.

MOUNT CARROLL. *Samaritan Homecare/Hospice*. Sponsor: Mercy Health Services, Sisters of Mercy, Regional Community of Detroit, 102 E. Washington St., 60153. Tel: 815-244-2749. Katherine McCann, R.N., Supvr.; Joan Noe, Dir.; Tom Hesselmann, Pres.

ST. CHARLES. *Queen of Americas Guild*, 345 Kautz Rd., P.O. Box 851, 60174. Tel: 630-584-1822; Fax: 630-584-0648. Most Rev. Joseph J. Madera, M.Sp.S., Bishop for the Archdiocese for the Military Services, USA, Episcopal Moderator; Mr. Frank Smoczynski, Pres.; Mr. Stephen Banaszak, Vice Pres.; Mr. Alan Napleton, Sec.; Beverly Smoczynski, Treas. & Dir.
Board of Directors: Revs. Christopher Rengers, O.F.M.Cap.; Jacob Joerger, O.P.; George M. Hastrich; Sr. M. Theresa Alonso, M.C.M.; Mrs. Ruth Sloan.

STERLING. *St. Vincent DePaul Society*. St. Mary's Conference, 600 Ave. B, 61081. Total Staff 16; Total assisted 2,719.

STOCKTON. *Christ in the Wilderness*, 7500 S. Randecker Rd., 61085-8922. Sr. Lorraine Mark, C.S.J., Dir., Center of Solitude and Prayer.

RELIGIOUS INSTITUTES OF MEN REPRESENTED IN THE DIOCESE

For further details refer to the corresponding bracketed number in the Religious Institutes of Men or Women section.

[0200]—*Benedictine Monks*. (Marmion Abbey, Aurora).—O.S.B.
[1320]—*Clerics of St. Viator*.—C.S.V.
[1080]—*Congregation of the Resurrection*. (Chicago Prov.).—C.R.
[0480]—*Conventual Franciscans*. (St. Bonaventure Province).—O.F.M.Conv.
[0520]—*Franciscan Friars*. (Assumption of the B.V.M. Prov.).—O.F.M.
[]—*Institute of Christ the King Sovereign Priest (Provincial House-Italy)*.
[0690]—*Jesuit Fathers-Chicago Province of the Society of Jesus*.—S.J.
[0720]—*The Missionaries of Our Lady of La Salette*.—M.S.
[1110]—*Missionaries of the Sacred Heart*.—M.S.C.

RELIGIOUS INSTITUTES OF WOMEN REPRESENTED IN THE DIOCESE

[]—*Auxiliaries of the Blessed Sacrament*.—A.S.B.
[0230]—*Benedictine Sisters*.—O.S.B.
[0350]—*Carmelite Sisters (Corpus Christi)*.—O.Carm.
[2100]—*Congregation of the Humility of Mary*.—C.H.M.
[1920]—*Congregation of the Sisters of the Holy Cross*.—C.S.C.
[1710]—*Congregation of the Third Order of St. Francis of Mary Immaculate*.—O.S.F.
[1070-02]—*Dominican Sisters*.—O.P.
[1070-03]—*Dominican Sisters*.—O.P.
[1070-10]—*Dominican Sisters*.—O.P.
[1070-13]—*Dominican Sisters*.—O.P.
[1070-01]—*Dominican Sisters of St. Catharine*.—O.P.
[1170]—*Felician Sisters*.—C.S.S.F.
[2575]—*Institute of the Sisters of Mercy of the Americas*. (Chicago, IL).—R.S.M.
[]—*Mexican Passionist Sisters*.—C.F.P.
[2865]—*Missionaries of the Sacred Heart & Our Lady of Guadalupe*.—M.S.C.Gpe.
[2790]—*Missionary Servants of the Most Blessed Trinity*.—M.S.B.T.
[3760]—*Poor Clare Colettines*.—P.C.C.
[2970]—*School Sisters of Notre Dame*.—S.S.N.D.
[1680]—*School Sisters of St. Francis*.—O.S.F.
[3520]—*Servants of the Holy Heart of Mary*.—S.S.C.M.
[0430]—*Sisters of Charity of the Blessed Virgin Mary*.—B.V.M.
[2360]—*Sisters of Loretto at the Foot of the Cross*.—S.L.
[2450]—*Sisters of Mary of the Presentation*.—S.M.P.
[3360]—*Sisters of Providence of Saint Mary-of-the-Woods, Indiana*.—S.P.
[3710]—*Sisters of St. Agnes*.—C.S.A.
[1760]—*Sisters of St. Francis*.—O.S.F.
[1705]—*The Sisters of St. Francis of Assisi*.—O.S.F.
[1640]—*Sisters of St. Francis of Perpetual Adoration*.—O.S.F.
[1570]—*Sisters of St. Francis of the Holy Family*.—O.S.F.
[1660]—*Sisters of St. Francis of the Providence of God*.—O.S.F.
[3830-02]—*Sisters of St. Joseph*.—C.S.J.
[3830-15]—*Sisters of St. Joseph*.—C.S.J.
[3930]—*Sisters of St. Joseph of the Third Order of St. Francis*.—S.S.J.-T.O.S.F.
[1970]—*Sisters of the Holy Family of Nazareth*.—C.S.F.N.
[2350]—*Sisters of the Living Word*.—S.L.W.
[1770]—*Sisters of the Third Order of St. Francis*. (Peoria, Illinois).—O.S.F.
[3530]—*Spirit Missionary Sisters*.—S.Sp.S.

DIOCESAN CEMETERIES

ROCKFORD. *Calvary-St. Mary's/St. James*.
AURORA. *Mount Olivet*.
BATAVIA. *Geneva-St. Charles Resurrection*.
ELGIN. *Mount Hope*.

NECROLOGY

† Petit, Clement P., (Retired). —Died Sept. 4, 1997.

Diocese of Rockville Centre

(Dioecesis Petropolitana In Insula Longa)

Most Reverend

JOHN R. MCGANN, D.D.

Bishop of Rockville Centre; ordained June 3, 1950; appointed Titular Bishop of Morosbisdus and Auxiliary to the Bishop of Rockville Centre November 12, 1970; ordained Bishop January 7, 1971; appointed Bishop of Rockville Centre May 3, 1976; installed June 24, 1976. *Res., St. Agnes Cathedral, 29 Quealy Pl., Rockville Centre, NY, 11570.* Tel.: 516-766-0205.

Most Reverend

JAMES J. DALY, D.D.

Retired Auxiliary Bishop of Rockville Centre and Vicar General; ordained May 22, 1948; appointed Titular Bishop of Castra Nova and Auxiliary to the Bishop of Rockville Centre February 28, 1977; ordained Bishop May 9, 1977. *Res., 25 Lanes Rd., Blue Point, NY, 11715.* Tel.: 516-363-6672; Fax: 516-363-5150.

Most Reverend

EMIL A. WCELA, D.D.

Auxiliary Bishop of Rockville Centre and Episcopal Vicar of Eastern Vicariate; appointed Titular Bishop of Filaca and Auxiliary to the Bishop of Rockville Centre October 21, 1988; ordained Bishop December 13, 1988. *Res., Eastern Vicariate - Diocese of Rockville Centre, P.O. Box 780, Riverhead, NY, 11901.* Tel.: 516-369-0071.

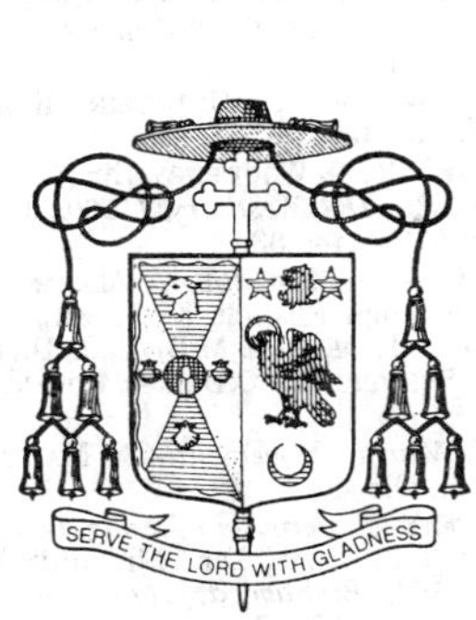

Most Reverend

JOHN C. DUNNE, D.D.

Auxiliary Bishop of Rockville Centre and Episcopal Vicar of Central Vicariate; appointed Titular Bishop of Abercorn and Auxiliary to the Bishop of Rockville Centre October 21, 1988; ordained Bishop December 13, 1988. *Res., Central Vicariate - Diocese of Rockville Centre, P.O. Box 39, Farmingdale, NY, 11735-0039.* Tel.: 516-249-1700.

ESTABLISHED APRIL 6, 1957.

Square Miles 1,222.

THE ROMAN CATHOLIC DIOCESE OF ROCKVILLE CENTRE, NEW YORK.

Comprises the Counties of Nassau and Suffolk (excepting Fishers Island) in the State of New York.

For legal titles of parishes and diocesan institutions, consult the Chancery Office.

Chancery Office: 50 N. Park Ave., Rockville Centre, NY, 11570. Tel.: 516-678-5800; Fax: 516-678-1786.

STATISTICAL OVERVIEW

Personnel	
Bishop	1
Auxiliary Bishops	2
Retired Bishops	1
Priests: Diocesan Active in Diocese	308
Priests: Active Outside Diocese	25
Priests: Diocesan in Foreign Missions	1
Priests: Retired, Sick or Absent	115
Number of Diocesan Priests	449
Religious Priests in Diocese	74
Extern Priests in Diocese	59
Ordinations:	
Transitional Deacons	1
Permanent Deacons	7
Permanent Deacons in Diocese	197
Total Brothers	99
Total Sisters	1,487
Parishes	
Parishes	134
With Resident Pastor:	
Resident Diocesan Priests	131
Resident Religious Priests	3
Without Resident Pastor:	
Professional Ministry Personnel:	
Brothers	6
Sisters	143
Lay Ministers	350
Welfare	
Catholic Hospitals	4
Total Assisted	755,760
Homes for the Aged	4
Total Assisted	6,394
Residential Care of Children	4
Total Assisted	8,499
Day Care and Extended Day Care Centers	103
Total Assisted	4,723
Specialized Homes	3
Total Assisted	1,084
Special Centers for Social Services	26
Total Assisted	222,586
Residential Care of Disabled	1
Total Assisted	18
Other Institutions	85
Total Assisted	221,000
Educational	
Seminaries, Diocesan	1
Students from This Diocese	21
Students from Other Diocese	29
Students Religious	4
Total Seminarians	25
Colleges and Universities	2
Total Students	4,913
High Schools, Diocesan and Parish	4
Total Students	3,817
High Schools, Private	9
Total Students	7,134
Elementary Schools, Diocesan and Parish	63
Total Students	28,848
Elementary Schools, Private	4
Total Students	1,132
Non-residential Schools for the Disabled	3
Total Students	295
Catechesis/Religious Education:	
High School Students	4,140
Elementary Students	109,114
Total Students Under Catholic Instruction	159,418
Teachers in the Diocese:	
Priests	11
Brothers	60
Sisters	225
Lay Teachers	1,762
Vital Statistics	
Receptions into the Church:	
Infant Baptism Totals	21,582
Adult Baptism Totals	638
Received into Full Communion	442
First Communions	19,034
Confirmations	16,497
Marriages:	
Catholic	5,945
Interfaith	1,239
Total Marriages	7,184
Deaths	12,926
Total Catholic Population	1,372,111
Total Population	2,899,195

Former Bishops—Most Rev. WALTER P. KELLENBERG, D.D., first Bishop of Rockville Centre; ord. June 2, 1928; appt. Titular Bishop of Joannina and Auxiliary Bishop of New York, Aug. 25, 1953; cons. Oct. 5, 1953; appt. Bishop of Ogdensburg, Jan. 19, 1954; appt. first Bishop of Rockville Centre, April 16, 1957; installed May 27, 1957; died Jan. 11, 1986.

Vicar General—Most Rev. EMIL A. WCELA, D.D.

Episcopal Vicars—Rev. Msgr. JOHN A. ALESANDRO, S.T.L., J.C.D., J.D., Western Vicariate; Most Rev. EMIL A. WCELA, D.D., Eastern Vicariate; Most Rev. JOHN C. DUNNE, D.D., Central Vicariate.

Chancery—50 N. Park Ave., Rockville Centre, 11570. Tel: 516-678-5800; Fax: 516-678-1786(Building); 516-764-3316(Chancery).

Chancellor—Rev. Msgr. FRANCIS J. SCHNEIDER, J.C.D.

Vice-Chancellors—Sr. LUCY M. BLYSKAL, C.S.J., M.A., J.C.D.; Rev. Msgr. ALAN J. PLACA, J.D.; Rev. ROBERT J. BRENNAN, M.Div.

Secretary to the Bishop—Rev. Msgr. ROBERT J. BRENNAN, M.Div.

Diocesan Tribunal—50 N. Park Ave., Rockville Centre, 11570.

Officialis—Rev. Msgr. MICHAEL MANZELLI, S.T.L., J.C.D., M.A.

Vice-Officiales—Revs. THOMAS V. ARNAO, J.C.L.; ROBERT O. MORRISSEY, J.C.D.; Rev. Msgr. EDWARD A. SWEENEY, J.C.D.Cand.; Revs. JAMES A. MILLER, J.C.L.; JAMES F. PEREDA, J.C.D.

Diocesan Judges—Sr. LUCY BLYSKAL, C.S.J., J.C.D.; Rev. Msgr. THOMAS D. CANDREVA, S.T.L., J.C.D.; Rev. RICHARD P. KOPINSKI, M.A., M.S.; Rev. Msgr. JOHN C. NOSSER, M.S.; Rev. Msgr. GEORGE P. GRAHAM, J.C.D., Ph.D.; Rev. Msgr. THOMAS E. MOLLOY, S.T.B., J.C.D.; Rev. Msgr. RICHARD C. BAUHOFF, J.C.D.; Rev. Msgr. CHARLES A. GUARINO, J.C.D.; Rev. Msgr. FRANCIS S. MIDURA, M.Ch.A.; Rev. JOHN C. TUTONE, J.C.D.

Promoter of Justice—Rev. DONALD F. DIEDERICH, J.C.D.

Defender of the Bond—Sr. LOIS KELLER, R.S.M., J.C.L.

Adjunct Defender of the Bond—Rev. ABRAHAM PORUNNOLIL, J.C.L.

Post Annulment Counseling Coordinator—Mrs. MARGARET WILSON, M.A.

Medical Experts—Dr. CHRISTOPHER DEEG, Ph.D.; Dr. FRANK GENOVESE, Ph.D.; Dr. MAUREEN M. KALEY, Ph.D.; Dr. JOHN M. MCDONAGH, Ph.D.; Dr. SIMEON RYAN, Ph.D.

Procurator-Advocates—Deacon JOSEPH T. BARTOLOTTO;

MARIAN BOPP; Deacon EDWARD BILLIA; Rev. WILLIAM G. BRESLAWSKI; Deacon ROBERT P. BROYLES; Sr. MARY JANE BRUSTMAN, C.I.J.; Sr. IMELDA BUETOW, R.G.S.; Mrs. BARBARA BUTLER; Mr. JAMES BUTLER; Sr. HELEN BYRNE, C.S.J.; Deacon FRANCISCO CALES; Mrs. VIRGINIA CONLIN; Sr. MIRIAM HONORA CORR, C.S.J.; Rev. THOMAS C. COSTA; Deacon FRANK COVE; Deacon ANTHONY CUSEO; Sr. LUCILLE D'AMELIO, O.P.; Deacon GREGORY D'ANGELO; Mr. RICHARD J. DEMARCO; Rev. JOHN DERASMO; Ms. ANITA DOS SANTOS; Rev. Msgr. JOHN R. DREASEN; Rev. LAWRENCE T. DUNCKLEE; Rev. JOHN J. FITZGERALD; Deacons ANDREW GARGIULO; RONALD J. GILLETTE; Sr. MARGARET GERARD, O.P.; Sr. MONA GUERRETTE, D.W.; Sr. MARGARET ANN HARTIGAN, R.S.M.; Deacon ROBERT HESCHL; Sr. ANN HORN, O.P.; Sr. BONNIE KELLY, C.S.J.; Sr. JANE LYONS, C.I.J.; Rev. JAMES P. MANNION, JR.; Deacon SALVATORE MARINO; Mr. JAMES J. MAUNE; Rev. Msgr. JAMES M. MCDONALD; Sr. PATRICIA A. MCDONNELL, C.S.J.; Mr. STEVE MCGIFF; Deacon JAMES MCQUADE; Sr. ALICE MEEHAN, C.S.J.; Rev. Msgr. JOHN J. MIRECKI; Revs. JOSEPH MIRRO; JOHN R. MOORE; Mrs. NANCY NEWBERT; Mrs. MARY ANN O'CONNOR; Mr. THOMAS O'CONNOR; Sr. MAUREEN O'DONNELL, O.P.; Rev. VITALIS B. PEDZIK; Sr. MERCY POSTHAUER, O.P.; Mr. JOSEPH PUMA; VILMA RIVERA; Sr. MARY RONALD, C.S.F.N.; Deacon PETER SCHULTZ; Revs. THOMAS J. ST. PIERRE; ANTHONY STANGANELLI; Sr. MARIA STAPLETON, C.S.J.; Rev. JOSEPH W. STAUDT; Mrs. ANN-MARY STRIEDER; Sr. KATHLEEN T. SULLIVAN, C.S.J.; Deacon GARY SWANE; EILEEN TRACY; Sr. EUGENIA A. TRAVERS, O.P.; Rev. Msgr. EDMOND J. TRENCH; Sr. PATRICIA TURLEY, C.S.J.; Rev. MICHAEL VETRANO; Sr. ELLEN ZAK, C.S.F.N.; Rev. ANDRZEJ ZGLEJSZEWSKI.

Notaries—Sr. RUTH BORGERSEN, R.S.M., M.A.; Mrs. C. GATZ; Sr. MARGARET GERARD VON ACHEN, O.P., M.A., M.S., In-Take Sec.; Mrs. H. HOWE; Mrs. G. ROHE; Mrs. T. TUZZOLINO.

Archives—Ms. JEAN WASSONG.

College of Consultors—Most Rev. JOHN R. MCGANN, D.D.; Most Rev. JOHN C. DUNNE, D.D.; Most Rev. EMIL A. WCELA, D.D.; Rev. Msgr. JOHN A. ALESANDRO; Rev. Msgr. DANIEL E. FAGAN; Rev. Msgr. ROBERT E. FAGAN; Rev. Msgr. FRANCIS J. SCHNEIDER; Rev. Msgr. JOHN J. SKELLY; Rev. Msgr. DANIEL J. HURLEY; Revs. WILLIAM G. BRESLAWSKI; BRIAN MCKEON; BRIAN J. MCNAMARA; FREDERICK J. PELLEGRINI, S.J.

Senate of Priests—Most Rev. JOHN R. MCGANN, D.D.; Most Rev. JOHN C. DUNNE, D.D.; Most Rev. EMIL A. WCELA, D.D.; Rev. Msgr. JOHN A. ALESANDRO; Rev. Msgr. ROBERT EMMET FAGAN; Revs. WILLIAM BRESLAWSKI; WILLIAM E. KOENIG; Rev. DANIEL E. FAGAN; Rev. Msgr. DANIEL J. HURLEY; Rev. Msgr. WILLIAM W. JABLONSKI; Rev. Msgr. JAMES M. MCDONALD; Revs. BRIAN A. MCKEON; BRIAN J. MCNAMARA; FREDERICK PELLEGRINI, S.J.; Rev. Msgr. FRANCIS J. SCHNEIDER; Rev. Msgr. JOHN J. SKELLY.

Deans—Deanery 1, Rockville Centre: Rev. Msgr. DONALD T. BENNETT,
Deanery 2, North Hempstead: Rev. Msgr. JOHN J. SKELLY,
Deanery 3, Oyster Bay: Rev. Msgr. JOHN J. MCCANN,
Deanery 4, Belmont: Rev. Msgr. JOHN R. DREASEN,
Deanery 5, Hicksville: Rev. Msgr. JAMES E. BOESEL,
Deanery 6, Five Towns: Rev. Msgr. CHARLES R. FINK,
Deanery 7, Seaford: Rev. Msgr. ROBERT E. GUGLIELMONE,
Deanery 8, Huntington: Rev. Msgr. PATRICK J. ARMSHAW,
Deanery 9, Babylon: Rev. Msgr. ROBERT J. SACCACIO,
Deanery 10, Islip: Rev. Msgr. JOHN J. ROWAN,
Deanery 11, North Brookhaven: Rev. Msgr. JOHN A. MCGUIRE,
Deanery 12, South Brookhaven: Rev. Msgr. JAMES MCDONALD,
Deanery 13, Peconic: Rev. Msgr. JOHN P. SULLIVAN,
Deanery 14, Smithtown; Rev. Msgr. CHARLES A. GUARINO.

Diocesan Offices and Directors

Director of Administration—Mr. HENRY DWYER. Tel: 516-678-5800.

Apostleship of Prayer—Rev. Msgr. JAMES M. MCDONALD, Dir.

Catholics of African Ancestry—VANESSA BAIRD STREETER.

Building Office—Mr. CHESTER STRZEPEK, Dir.

Diocesan Building Commission—Rev. Msgr. JOHN A. ALESANDRO, Chm.; Rev. Msgr. RONALD HAYDE; Rev. Msgr. DANIEL A. PICCIANO; Rev. Msgr. BRENDAN P. RIORDAN; Mr. EDWARD FITZPATRICK; Mr. JOSEPH MCCORMACK; Mr. EUGENE SOUTHER, ESQ.; Mr. CHESTER STRZEPEK; Mr. CHARLES V. VACHRIS.

Campus Ministry—Rev. JOSEPH D'ANGELO, Diocesan Dir./Pastor, Campus Parish, *50 N. Park Ave., Rockville Centre, 11510.* Tel: 516-678-5800.

Office of Catechesis—GEORGE RAND, Dir.; Sr. ANNE MARIE DEAN, C.S.J., Central Vicariate, Catechetical Coord., DRE Personnel Service; Sr. JOAN MARY FINN, O.P., Coord. Pastoral Ministry for the Deaf; Sr. SALLY RYAN, R.S.M., Western Vicariate, Catechetical Coord. Pastoral Ministry for persons with Disabilities; Ms. DIANE VELLA, Eastern Vicariate, Catechetical Coord. Adult Catechesis. Secretarial Staff: Mrs. THERESA ALBANESE; Mrs. MARGARET DEROSA; Mrs. ELEANOR SHERIDAN; Ms. PATRICIA DALY, Office Mgr.

Office of Worship—Rev. Msgr. RONALD E. HAYDE, M.A., M.Div., Dir.; Sr. SHEILA BROWNE, R.S.M., Coord., Catechumenate and Liturgical/Musical Support Svcs. Secretarial Staff: Mrs. MARION HAWKEY; Mrs. MICHELE KASHUBA; Mrs. CAROL QUARANTO; Ms. PATRICIA DALY, Office Mgr.

Catholic Charities—Rev. Msgr. JOHN D. GILMARTIN, Diocesan Dir., *90 Cherry Ln., Hicksville, 11801-6232.* Tel: 516-733-7000.

Catholic Press Association of the Diocese of Rockville Centre, Inc., Publisher of "The Long Island Catholic"—ELIZABETH O'CONNOR, Editor, *99 N. Village Ave., P.O. Box 9009, Rockville Centre, 11571-9009.* Tel: 516-594-1000.

Catholic Relief Services—Sr. CATHERINE KELLY, S.S.J. Tel: 516-678-5800, Ext. 513.

Cemeteries—Mrs. ELLEN WOODBURY, Dir., *Catholic Cemeteries, P.O. Box 182, Westbury, 11590.* Tel: 516-334-7998; Fax: 516-334-4383.

Censors of Books—Rev. Msgr. JOHN A. ALESANDRO, S.T.L., J.C.D.; Rev. Msgr. FRANCIS X. GLIMM, S.T.L.; Rev. Msgr. GEORGE P. GRAHAM, M.Div., J.C.D.; Rev Msgr. FRANCIS J. SCHNEIDER, J.C.D.; Rev. ROBERT J. SMITH, S.T.D.

Ministry to the Marian Movement—Sr. MARCELLA PURPURA, C.S.J., Dir.

Charismatic Renewal Services of Long Island, Inc.—Mr. STEPHEN BENTHAL, Dir.; Mr. JOHN BOUCHER, *P.O. Box 1301, Brentwood, 11717.* Tel: 516-952-7400; Fax: 516-952-7403.

Haitian Ministry—Rev. MOISE AIME, Dir. Tel: 516-868-8076.

Justice and Peace Commission—Board Members: Mrs. ALICE BOYLE; Mr. ROB SMITH; Rev. Msgr. JOHN D. GILMARTIN, Chm.; Mrs. MARGARET MELKONIAN; Rev. BRUCE REED; Rev. Msgr. DENNIS M. REGAN, Consultant; Sr. ROSE SHERIDAN, C.S.J., Staff; Rev. JOHN W. WHITE; Rev. GERALD S. TWOMEY; Dr. CHARLES KERNER; Mrs. JOANN CAIN. Tel: 516-733-7077.

Commission on Parish Boundaries—Rev. Msgr. JOHN F. BENNETT, Chm.; Rev. WILLIAM GILL; Rev. Msgr. JOHN A. MCGUIRE; Rev. Msgr. FRANCIS J. SCHNEIDER; Rev. Msgr. THOMAS SPADARO; Mr. CHET STRZEPEK, Exec. Sec.

Consultation Service for Religious Personnel—Sr. THOMAS MORE, R.G.S., Exec. Dir., *984 N. Village Ave., Box 467, Rockville Centre, 11571.* Tel: 516-678-2135.

Office of Bishop's Annual Appeal—JOHN J. KELLY, Dir.

Office of Development—JOHN J. KELLY, Dir.

Stewardship Office—M. DANIEL HENRY, Ph.D., Dir., *P.O. Box 532, Rockville Centre, 11571.* Tel: 516-763-6795; Fax: 516-763-6799.

Office of Religious Retirement Fund—JOHN J. KELLY, Dir.

Office of Deacons—Deacon GERARD WILSON, Dir.; Deacon GEORGE RIEGGER, Coord., Diaconate Formation; Mrs. MARGARET WILSON, Coord., Diaconate Wives.

Diocesan Commodities, Corp.—Mr. CHET STRZEPEK, Gen. Mgr. Tel: 516-764-2130.

Diocese of Rockville Centre Protected Self Insurance Program—50 N. Park Ave., Rockville Centre, 11570. Tel: 516-678-5800.

Diocesan Campaign for Human Development—Rev. Msgr. JOHN D. GILMARTIN, Dir.

Due Process Committee (Conciliation-Arbitration)—Sr. LUCY BLYSKAL, C.S.J., J.C.D., Admin.

Ecumenism, Office of Ecumenical & Interreligious Affairs—50 N. Park Ave., Rockville Centre, 11570. Tel: 516-678-5800, Ext. 614. Rev. Msgr. DONALD M. BECKMANN, D.Min., Dir.

Education Dept.—Sr. JOANNE CALLAHAN, O.S.U., M.A., P.D., Supt., Schools; JOANNE O'BRIEN, M.A., M.Ed., Ed.D., Assoc. Supt., Schools; Sr. KATHLEEN M. EAGAN, C.S.J., M.A., Asst. Supt., Public Policy & Government Programs; ROSEMARY DAMM, M.A., Dir., Curriculum & Instruction; Mr. BIAGIO M. ARPINO, M.S., P.D., Dir., Teacher Personnel; Sr. TERESA RORKE, C.S.J., M.S., P.D., Dir., Regional School Planning; Sr. CATHERINE STARE, S.C., M.S., M.A., Dir., Curriculum & Testing; Sr. ANTOINETTE DE AVEIRO, O.P., M.S., Dir., Early Childhood Programs; PAUL J. LYNCH, M.A., Dir., Technology.

Finance Council—Mr. HARRY DWYER, Chm.; Rev. Msgr. JOHN ALESANDRO; Rev. Msgr. JAMES KELLY; Mr. D. DESMOND MCCARTHY; Mr. KEVIN MURPHY; Rev. Msgr. JOHN ROWAN.

Health Care Ministry—Rev. Msgr. ALAN J. PLACA, Sec. to the Bishop for Health Affairs. Tel: 516-678-5800. Sr. PATRICIA HARTIGAN, O.P., Dir., Pastoral Planning, , Ext. 248.

Chaplaincy Services & Pastoral Health Ministries—Sr. EILEEN DONOVAN, O.P., Dir. Tel: 516-678-5800, Ext. 521.

Diocesan Medical Ethics Commission—Rev. Msgr. ALAN J. PLACA, Exec. Sec. *Members*—Rev. Msgr. DENNIS M. REGAN, S.T.D., Chm.; Rev. Msgr. JOHN A. ALESANDRO, J.C.D.; Sr. ALICE O'SHAUGHNESSY, M.D.; Sr. EILEEN DONOVAN, O.P.; DAVID J. FLEMING, ESQ.; Rev. Msgr. GEORGE P. GRAHAM, J.C.D.; Sr. AUDREY HARSEN, O.P.; Mr. JAMES CONNOLLY; Mrs. DONNA M. O'BRIEN; Bro. CAMPION LALLY, O.S.F.; Rev. EUGENE F. MURPHY; Mr. BARRY ZEMAN; Rev. VINCENT RUSH; Mr. LEWIS GROSSMAN; Rev. ROBERT S. SMITH, S.T.D.; JAMES B. TORMEY, M.D.; ROBERT F. VIZZA, Ph.D.; DANIEL P. WALSH; ROBERT J. SMITH, Chm.

Family Ministry, Office of—Vacant; Dir. Coords.: Dr. NANCY BENVENGA; Ms. PATRICIA MCDONOUGH; Sr. JUDITH O'BRIEN; Mrs. MAUREEN RUSSELL.

Respect Life Coordinator—Vacant.

Finance Office—Mr. KEVIN T. MURPHY, Chief Fiscal Officer; Mr. DENNIS J. MEEKINS, Dir., Diocesan Accounting.

Holy Childhood Association—Sr. CATHERINE G. KELLY, S.S.J.

Holy Name Societies, Diocesan Union of—Rev. JOHN P. HALPIN, Spiritual Dir.

Information Bureau—JOANNE NOVARRO, Dir., Communications, *P.O. Box 9009, Rockville Centre, 11571.* Tel: 516-594-1000, Ext. 38.

Manager of Employee Benefits—JOHN CALAMARI. Tel: 516-678-5800, Ext. 523.

Manager of Property and Casualty Insurance—Vacant. Tel: 516-678-5800, Ext. 261.

Lawyers' Guild—Rev. Msgr. GEORGE P. GRAHAM, M.Div., Moderator/Dir.

Pastoral Formation—Mrs. PATRICIA MEGALE, Dir.; Sr. LAUREN HANLEY, C.S.J., Assoc. Dir.; Sr. MAUREEN JESSNIK, R.S.M., Coord., Instruction & Ministry Track Devel.; Ms. ROSE S. VINAS, Coord., Spiritual Formation Programs.

Legion of Mary—Rev. JAMES MANNING, S.M.M.

Nocturnal Adoration Society—Rev. Msgr. JAMES M. MCDONALD.

Physicians' Guild—Rev. EUGENE F. MURPHY.

Director for Priest Personnel—Rev. Msgr. FRANCIS J. CALDWELL, M.S.W.

Priests Personnel Assignment Board—Most Rev. JOHN R. MCGANN, D.D.; Most Rev. JOHN C. DUNNE, D.D.; Most Rev. EMIL A. WCELA, D.D.; Rev. Msgr. JOHN A. ALESANDRO, D.D., J.C.D.; Rev. Msgr. RICHARD C. BAUHOFF, J.C.D.; Rev. Msgr. FRANCIS J. CALDWELL, M.S.W.; Rev. Msgr. RONALD A. RICHARDSON; Rev. Msgr. EDMOND J. TRENCH; Revs. BRIAN J. INGRAM; CHARLES E. PAPA; KENNETH H. WINKLER.

Priests Personnel Policy Board—Rev. Msgr. FRANCIS J. CALDWELL, M.S.W.; Rev. Msgr. FRANCIS S. MIDURA; Revs. JOSEPH DEGROCCO; PAUL F. RAHILLY; ANTHONY M. STANGANELLI; Rev. JOHN WHITE, Chm.

Ministry to Priests-Internship Program-Sabbatical—Rev. Msgr. FRANCIS J. CALDWELL, M.S.W., Dir.

St. Pius X Priests' Residence and Vicar for Senior Priests—Rev. ROBERT BLYMAN, M.D.

Vocations Office—Rev. THOMAS J. HAROLD.

Priests' Sickness, Disability and Retirement Board—Most Rev. JOHN R. MCGANN, D.D., Chm.; Most Rev. JOHN C. DUNNE, D.D.; Rev. Msgr. JOHN A. ALESANDRO; Rev. Msgr. CHARLES A. GUARINO; Rev. Msgr. ROBERT GUGLIELMONE; Revs. ROBERT Y. BLYMAN; ROBERT J. CLERKIN; THOMAS W. GROENEWOLD; Rev. Msgr. JOHN P. MARTIN; Rev. Msgr. FRANCIS J. CALDWELL, Dir., Priest Personnel; Rev. Msgr. THADDEUS ROONEY; Rev. Msgr. JAMES SWIADER.

Prison Ministry and Criminal Justice, Office of—Pastoral Team: Bro. JOHN MOYLAN, O.S.F., Dir.; Sr. VIRGINIA WATERS, F.S.P.; Bro. WILLIAM CAWLEY, S.C.; Rev. RALPH FERRO; Deacons CHRIS VIGLIOTTA; JOHN SULLIVAN; Sr. MICHELLE BREMER, C.S.F.N., *26 S. Saxon Ave., Bay Shore, 11706.* Tel: 516-969-0837. Tel: 516-242-8631. For individual institutions see separate listing.

Mission Office—Sr. CATHERINE G. KELLY, S.S.J., Dir., , Ext. 513.

Telicare of the Diocese of Rockville Centre—Rev. Msgr. THOMAS J. HARTMAN, Dir.; Mr. MICHAEL O'LEARY, Gen. Mgr., *1200 Glenn Curtiss Blvd., Uniondale, 11553.* Tel: 516-538-8700.

Research & Planning, Diocesan Office of—Mr. CHESTER J. STRZEPEK, M.S., P.D., Dir.

Resettlement Council (Immigration Matters)—Catholic Charities-See separate listing.

Seminary of the Immaculate Conception Board of Governors—Most Rev. JOHN R. MCGANN, D.D., Chm.; Most Rev. EMIL A. WCELA, D.D., Vice Chm.; Most Rev. IGNATIUS A. CATANELLO, D.D.; Dr. TONY H. BONAPARTE; Mrs. HILDA BROSKY; Rev. Msgr. OCTAVIO CISNEROS; Mr. HENRY W. DWYER; Rev. Msgr. VINCENT F. FULLAM; Rev. THOMAS J. HAROLD; Dr.

JUDITH S. HEALY, Ph.D.; Dr. IRENE IMPELLIZZERI; Very Rev. JOSEPH L. LEVESQUE, C.M.; Mr. JAMES T. MCCARTHY; Mr. KEVIN T. MURPHY; Rev. Msgr. FRANCIS J. SCHNEIDER, S.T.L., J.C.D.; Revs. MICHAEL G. TEDONE; ANDREW J. VACCARI; Sr. REGINA WILSON, I.H.M.

Shrines and Pilgrimages—Rev. Msgr. RONALD E. HAYDE, Liaison.

Spanish Apostolate, Diocesan—Sr. MARGARET MAYCE, O.P., Dir.

Vicar for Hispanics—Rev. Msgr. PABLO M. RODRIQUEZ.

Vicars for Religious—Sr. MARIA REGINA LOURES, I.H.M.; Bro. PATRICK MURPHY, O.S.F.

Women's Commission—JOSEPHINE E. MISCIOSCIA, Co-Chm. MARY J. WEILER, Co-Chm.; Rev. Msgr. VINCENT T. RUSH, Sec. CONSTANCE LA SALA; PATRICIA MIZZI; MARY ANN O'CONNOR; PATRICIA A. RIEGGER; ANITA L. YOUNG.

Youth Ministries, Office of—Mr. MICHAEL G. MCCARTHY, Dir.; Rev. KEVIN SMITH, Chap., Scouting; Mr. AUSTIN CANNON, Prog. Coord., Scouting; Mrs. MARIANNE COLLINS, Prog. Coord., C.Y.O. -Support.

Young Adult Ministry—MARY BETH REYNOLDS, Prog. Coord.

CLERGY, PARISHES, MISSIONS AND PAROCHIAL SCHOOLS

VILLAGE OF ROCKVILLE CENTRE (Nassau County)

1—ST. AGNES CATHEDRAL (1894), Rev. Msgr. James P. Kelly, Rector; Most Rev. John R. McGann, D.D.; Revs. German Villabon, O.S.A.; William E. Koenig; Thomas W. Groenewold; Deacons Thomas McDaid; Vincent Smyth. In res., Rev. Msgr. Frank J. Caldwell; Rev. Msgr. Ronald E. Hayde; Rev. Msgr. Robert J. Brennan.
Res., 29 Quealy Pl., 11570. Tel: 516-766-0205; Fax: 516-763-0745.
School—Tel: 516-678-5550; Fax: 516-678-0437. Sr. Kathleen Carlin, Prin.
Sisters of St. Dominic 3; Lay Teachers 41; Students 906.
Catechesis/Religious Programs—Tel: 516-678-2306. Mrs. Donna Eschenauer, D.R.E.
Students 1,250.

2—CAMPUS PARISH OF LONG ISLAND (1972), Rev. Joseph J. D'Angelo, M.Div.,M.S.,CASAC,M.A.C.
Office Address—(For details, please refer to Campus Ministries and Newman Centers under the Institution section.) 50 N. Park Ave., 11570. Tel: 516-678-5800, Ext. 614; Fax: 516-763-1078.

OUTSIDE VILLAGE OF ROCKVILLE CENTRE

Amityville, Suffolk Co., St. Martin's (1897), Rev. Msgr. Robert J. Saccacio; Revs. Richard T. Stelter; Francis Sang.
Res., 37 Union Ave., 11701. Tel: 516-264-0124; Fax: 516-264-0139.
School—Tel: 516-264-7166.
Sisters of St. Dominic (Union Ave.) 4; Lay Teachers 21; Students 524.
Catechesis/Religious Programs—Tel: 516-691-1617.
Students 388.

Babylon, Suffolk Co., St. Joseph's (1877), Rev. Msgr. Ronald A. Richardson; Revs. John R. Moore; Thomas G. McCormick; Thomas P. Maloney; Deacons Michael J. Leyden; John F. Sullivan. In res., Rev. John J. Gorman.
Res., 39 N. Carll Ave., 11702-2701. Tel: 516-669-0068; Fax: 516-669-9175. [CEM]
Catechesis/Religious Programs—Tel: 516-587-4717. Marianne Mione, D.R.E.
Students 1,423.
Missions—Oak Beach, Suffolk Co. (Summer) 11702.; West Gilgo Beach, Suffolk Co. (Summer) 11702.

Baldwin, Nassau Co., St. Christopher (1915), Rev. Msgr. John F. Bennett; Rev. Msgr. Joseph F. Lawlor, Pastor Emeritus; Revs. Gennaro DiSpigno; William R. Logan; Deacons Charles Muscarnera; Joseph Pellegrino.
Res., 11 Gale Ave., 11510. Tel: 516-223-0723; Fax: 516-867-5678.
School—21 Pershing Blvd., 11510. Tel: 516-223-4404. Sr. Dolores McLaughlin, Prin.
Sisters of St. Joseph 4; Lay Teachers 18; Students 419.
Catechesis/Religious Programs—Tel: 516-223-5813. D.R.E.: Mrs. Julianne Markey; Mrs. Gail Milne.
Students 1,173.

Bay Shore, Suffolk Co., St. Patrick's (1883), Rev. Msgr. Robert Emmet Fagan; Revs. Robert Giuntini; Thomas M. Coogan; Deacons Joseph Peralta; Michael Mahoney. In res., Rev. Msgr. James F. Coffey, Pastor Emeritus; Rev. Msgr. Richard P. Hendel, (Retired).
Res., 9 N. Clinton Ave., 11706. Tel: 516-665-4911; Fax: 516-665-8388. [CEM]
School—6 N. Clinton Ave., 11706. Tel: 516-665-0569. Ms. Cathleen Quinn, Prin.
Lay Teachers 22; Students 500.
Catechesis/Religious Programs—Tel: 516-665-4914.
Students 1,475.

Bayville, Nassau, St. Gertrude's (1959), Revs. Peter Kaczmarek; Martin W. Curley.
Res., 28 School St., 11709. Tel: 516-628-1113; Fax: 516-628-9032.
Catechesis/Religious Programs—Tel: 516-628-2432.
Students 520.

Bellmore, Nassau Co., St. Barnabas the Apostle (1912), Rev. Peter C. Dooley; Rev. Msgr. Daniel J. Potterton, Pastor Emeritus; Revs. Edward J. Muhs, Pastor Emeritus; Brian Ingram; Robert Petekiewicz; Deacon Bernard Sherlock.
Res., 2320 Bedford Ave., 11710. Tel: 516-785-0054; Fax: 516-221-7789.
Schools—St. Elizabeth Ann Seton Regional School, Bellmore Campus, 2341, Washington Ave., Tel: 516-785-5709; Fax: 516-785-4468.; St. Elizabeth Ann Seton Regional School, East Meadow Campus, 600 Newbridge Road, East Meadow, Tel: 516-785-7006; Fax: 516-784-7008. See Regional Schools under Institutions Located in the Diocese.
Catechesis/Religious Programs—Tel: 516-785-0130.
Students 1,450.

Bellport, Suffolk Co., Mary Immaculate (1905), Rev. Msgr. Bernard J. Ryan; Rev. Constantino Nieva; Deacon Arthur J. Dooling.
Res., 16 Brown's Ln., 11713. Tel: 516-286-0154; Fax: 516-286-2937.
School—Holy Angels Regional School, Patchogue, Tel: 516-475-0422; Fax: 516-475-2641. See Regional Schools under Institutions Located in the Diocese.
Catechesis/Religious Programs—Tel: 516-286-3504.
Students 425.

Bethpage, Nassau Co., St. Martin of Tours (1923), Revs. Raymond Collins, C.SS.R.; Thomas Schmidt, C.SS.R.; Kevin MacDonald, C.SS.R.; Vincent Crotty, C.SS.R.; Deacons James A. Biggin; Eugene Campobianco.
Res., 40 Seaman Ave., 11714. Tel: 516-931-0818; Fax: 516-931-0559.
School—St. John Baptist de LaSalle Regional School, Bethpage/Farmingdale. See Regional Schools under Institutions Located in the Diocese. Tel: 516-931-0983.
Catechesis/Religious Programs—208 Broadway, 11714. Tel: 516-822-9768; Fax: 516-932-8454. Mrs. Elizabeth Lukaschek, D.R.E.
Students 1,200.

Blue Point, Suffolk Co., Our Lady of the Snow (1917), Revs. Diarmuid F. McGann; Richard M. Scanlon, Pastor Emeritus; Deacons Robert Gronenthal; Steve Kramer; Frank Hartmann.
Res., 175 Blue Point Ave., 11715. Tel: 516-363-6385; Fax: 516-363-7394.
School—Prince of Peace Regional School, Sayville, Tel: 516-589-3426. See Regional Schools under Institutions Located in the Diocese.
Catechesis/Religious Programs—Tel: 516-363-6394; Fax: 516-589-3426.
Students 900.

Bohemia, Suffolk Co., St. John Nepomucene (1919), Revs. James L. Wood; Louis L. Reuss, Pastor Emeritus; Charles N. Mangano; Sr. Phyllis Esposito, C.S.J., Pastoral Assoc.; Deacon James Bohuslaw. In res., Rev. Bartholomew J. Galvin, M.M.
Res., 1140 Locust Ave., 11716. Tel: 516-589-0540; Fax: 516-244-8086. [CEM]
School—Prince of Peace Regional School, Sayville. See Regional Schools under Institutions Located in the Diocese. Tel: 516-589-0422.
Catechesis/Religious Programs—1150 Locust Ave., 11716. Tel: 516-567-1765. D.R.E. Margaret Foote; Doris Petrocelli.
Students 1,450.

Brentwood, Suffolk Co., St. Anne's (1895), Revs. Thomas J. St. Pierre; Gerald S. Twomey; James J. Hannon; Jean Gerard LaGuerre (Haiti); Deacons Jesus Alvarado; Juan Diaz; Terence A. Rasanen; Thomas R. Samson.
Res., 88 Second Ave., 11717. Tel: 516-273-8113; Fax: 516-436-7914.
School—Our Lady of Providence Regional School, Central Islip, Tel: 516-234-6324; Fax: 516-234-6360. See Regional Schools under Institutions Located in the Diocese.
Catechesis/Religious Programs—Tel: 516-231-7344. Ms. Virginia Conzo, D.R.E.
Students 1,400.

St. Luke (1965), Revs. Lawrence Duncklee; Camilo Lugo; Deacons John Trodden; Richard A. Luken.
Res., 266 Wicks Rd., 11717. Tel: 516-273-1110; Fax: 516-951-2779. [JC]
School—Our Lady of Providence Regional School, Central Islip, Tel: 516-234-6535. See Regional Schools under Institutions Located in the Diocese.
Catechesis/Religious Programs—Tel: 516-273-4333.
Students 912.

Bridgehampton, Suffolk Co., Queen of the Most Holy Rosary (1922), Rev. Patrick J. Callan.
Mailing Address: P.O. Box 3035, 11932. Tel: 516-537-0156; Fax: 516-537-7116.
School—Stella Maris Regional School, Sag Harbor, Tel: 516-725-2525; Fax: 516-725-4587. See Regional Schools under Institutions Located in the Diocese.

Brookville, Nassau Co., St. Paul the Apostle (1962), Revs. Mario Costa; Arthur C. Anderson.
Res., Cedar Swamp Rd., Brookville, Glen Head, 11545. Tel: 516-935-1880; Fax: 516-938-3683.
Catechesis/Religious Programs—Tel: 516-938-4531. D.R.E.: Sr. Regina Kraft; Mr. Len Tufaro.
Students 464.

Carle Place, Nassau Co., Church of Our Lady of Hope (1987), Rev. Msgr. Francis S. Midura; Deacons Lawrence V. Hammel; John T. Hickey; Thomas B. Rich; Raymond J. Tirelli.
Church—Cherry Ln. & Broadway, P.O. Box 352, 11514-0352. Tel: 516-334-6288; Fax: 516-997-4622.
School—St. Brigid/ Our Lady of Hope Regional School, 101 Maple Ave., Westbury, 11590. Tel: 516-333-0580; Fax: 516-333-0590.
Catechesis/Religious Programs—Tel: 516-334-4781. Margaret V. Cecere, D.R.E.
Students 778.

Cedarhurst, Nassau Co., St. Joachim (1894), Rev. Paul Rahilly; Deacon Frank J. Bono. In res., Rev. Patrick Nsionu (Nigeria).
Res., 614 Central Ave., 11516. Tel: 516-569-1845; Fax: 516-569-0117.
School—620 Central Ave., 11516. Tel: 516-569-2290; Fax: 516-374-5158.
Sisters of St. Joseph 3; Lay Teachers 11; Students 236.
Catechesis/Religious Programs—Tel: 516-295-0878.
Students 210.

Centereach, Suffolk Co., Assumption of the Blessed Virgin Mary (1955), Rev. Msgr. Joseph K. Curley; Revs. William F. Shean; Paul J. Mijas.
Res., 20 Chestnut St., 11720. Tel: 516-585-8760; Fax: 516-585-3601.
Catechesis/Religious Programs—Tel: 516-588-6408. Mrs. Miriam Selig, D.R.E.
Students 1,294.

Center Moriches, Suffolk Co., St. John the Evangelist (1898), Rev. Msgr. James M. McDonald, Pastor; Revs. John J. Corcoran, Pastor Emeritus; Kevin W. Gruber, Assoc. Pastor; Deacons Galvin Murphy; Chris Vigliotta.
Res., 25 Ocean Ave., 11934. Tel: 516-878-0009; Fax: 516-874-2466.
School—Our Lady, Queen of Apostles Regional School, Center Moriches. See Regional Schools under Institutions Located in the Diocese. Tel: 516-878-1033; Fax: 516-878-1059.
Catechesis/Religious Programs—Tel: 516-878-4141.
Students 1,600.

Centerport, Suffolk Co., Our Lady Queen of Martyrs (1966), Rev. Msgr. T. Peter Ryan; Rev. Harold J. Heindel; Sr. Eileen Corcoran, O.P. In res., Rev. Msgr. Joseph F. Colligan, Pastor Emeritus.
Res., Prospect and Mill Dam Rds., P.O. Box 609, 11721. Tel: 516-757-8184; Fax: 516-262-0155.
School—Trinity Regional School, East Northport, Tel: 516-261-5130; Fax: 516-266-5345. See Regional Schools under Institutions Located in the Diocese.
Catechesis/Religious Programs—Tel: 516-757-0720. Margaret Dritto, D.R.E.
Students 1,052.

Central Islip, Suffolk Co., St. John of God (1904), Revs. Joseph P. Granata; Gerald F. Di Giralamo, S.A. Pastoral Assocs.: Sr. Catherine Peluso, O.P.; Sr. Agnes Claudia Allen, C.S.J., (Spanish Apostolate); Deacon Ronald J. Gillette. In res., Revs. Augustine J. Sheehan, Chap. Northport Veterans' Hospital; John P. Halpin, Chap., Pilgrim Psychiatric Center.
Res., 84 Carleton Ave., 11722. Tel: 516-234-6535; Fax: 516-234-7474. [CEM]
School—Our Lady of Providence Regional School, Central Islip. See Regional Schools under Institutions Located in the Diocese. Tel: 516-234-6324.

Catechesis/Religious Programs—Tel: 516-234-4040. Sr. Diane Morgan, O.P., D.R.E.
Students 539.
Parish Outreach Office—Tel: 516-234-1884. Sr. Julianne Spiess, S.S.N.D.
Convent—330 St. John St., 11722. Tel: 516-234-6533. Sisters of St. Joseph

Commack, Suffolk Co., Christ the King (1959), Revs. Joseph W. Staudt; Simon Fernando; Jeffrey J. Madley.
Res., Indian Head Rd., P.O. Box 284, 11725. Tel: 516-864-1623; Fax: 516-732-8978.
School—Holy Family Regional School, Commack, Tel: 516-543-0202; Fax: 516-543-0203. See Regional Schools under Institutions Located in the Diocese.
Catechesis/Religious Programs—Tel: 516-864-3696. Mrs. Viola Fusco, D.R.E.
Students 1,020.

Copiague, Suffolk Co., Our Lady of the Assumption (1928), Revs. Michael Flynn; Peter Karpiel; Edward Sullivan.
Res., Molloy St., 11726. Tel: 516-842-5211; 842-5476; Fax: 516-789-5326.
Catechesis/Religious Programs—Ruth Durago, D.R.E.
Students 920.

Coram, Suffolk Co., St. Frances Cabrini (1953), Revs. Nicholas J. Figliola; Siby J. Alenchery; Deacon Carmen L. Pagrotta.
Res., 134 Middle County Rd., 11727. Tel: 516-732-8445; Fax: 516-732-8978.
School—Holy Angels Regional School, Patchogue, Tel: 516-475-0422. See Regional Schools under Institutions Located in the Diocese.
Catechesis/Religious Programs—Tel: 516-698-3149. Sr. Dorothy Schnell, C.S.J., D.R.E.
Students 879.

Cutchogue, Suffolk Co., Sacred Heart (1901), Revs. Peter A. Allen; John P. Henry, Pastor Emeritus; Sr. Anne Lynch, R.S.M., Pastoral Assoc.; Deacon John Bopp.
Res., 27700 Main Rd., P.O. Box 926, 11935-0926. Tel: 516-734-6722; Fax: 516-734-7906. [CEM]
School—Our Lady of Mercy Regional School, Tel: 516-734-5166. See Regional Schools under Institutions Located in the Diocese.
Catechesis/Religious Programs—Tel: 516-734-2568.
Students 405.
Mission—Mattituck, Suffolk Co., Our Lady of Good Counsel, Main Rd., 11952.

Our Lady of Ostrabrama (1909) (Polish), Rev. Wladyslaw Rudnicki, Admin.
Res., Depot Ln., Box 997, 11935. Tel: 516-734-6446; Fax: 516-734-4117.
School—North Fork Regional Catholic School, Cutchogue, Tel: 516-734-5166. See Regional Schools under Institutions Located in the Diocese.
Catechesis/Religious Programs—Students 85.

Davis Park, Fire Island Suffolk Co., Most Precious Blood (1962). (Summer Mission). Rev. Msgr. Donald M. Beckmann, D.Min., Admin.; Rev. Edward C. Fitzpatrick.
Mailing Address: St. Martha's, 546 Greengrove Ave., Uniondale, 11553. Tel: 516-481-2550.
Res., Spindrift Walk, Fire Island, 11728. Tel: 516-597-6525.

Deer Park, Suffolk Co., SS. Cyril and Methodius (1956), Rev. Msgr. Brendan P. Riordan; Revs. Joseph Baidoo; Forrest T. Parkinson; Donald C. Hayden. In res., Rev. Msgr. Alan J. Placa.
Res., 125 Half Hollow Rd., 11729-4288. Tel: 516-667-4044; Fax: 516-667-6237.
School—(Grades K-8). Tel: 516-667-6229.
Sisters of St. Joseph 2; Lay Teachers 27; Students 640; Nursery 70.
Catechesis/Religious Programs—Tel: 516-667-6264.
Students 598.

Dix Hills, Suffolk Co., St. Matthew (1965), Rev. Msgr. Saverio C. Mattei; Rev. Msgr. Leo J. Goggin, Pastor Emeritus; Revs. Lawrence A. Chadwick; William G. Dailey; Bonaventure Thekkeveetil; Robert Kayser; Deacons James M. McQuade; Arnold Quaranta; Frank Gariboldi.
Res., 35 N. Service Rd., 11746. Tel: 516-499-8520; Fax: 516-499-1530.
School—Holy Family Regional School. See Regional Schools under Institutions Located in the Diocese. Tel: 516-453-0202.
Catechesis/Religious Programs—Tel: 516-499-8521. Mr. Anthony C. D'Amico, D.R.E.
Students 1,384.

East Hampton, Suffolk Co., Most Holy Trinity (1894), Rev. Donald J. Desmond, Pastor; Rev. Msgr. Christopher Huntington, Pastor Emeritus; Sr. Eileen Marie Connor, O.P., D.R.E.
Res., 57 Buell Ln., 11937. Tel: 516-324-0134; Fax: 516-329-3552. [CEM]
School—Stella Maris Regional School, Sag Harbor. See Regional Schools under Institutions Located in the Diocese. Tel: 516-725-2525; Fax: 516-725-4587.
Catechesis/Religious Programs—Tel: 516-324-7994; Fax: 516-329-3552.
Students 462.
Convent—79 Buell Ln., 11937. Tel: 516-324-1444.
Mission—Amagansett, Suffolk Co., St. Peter the Apostle, Main St., Amagansett, 11930. Tel: 516-324-0134; Fax: 516-329-3552.

East Islip, Suffolk Co., St. Mary's (1898), Rev. Steven J. Peterson; Rev. Msgr. Peter A. Chiara, Pastor Emeritus; Revs. Lucian Fernandes; Vincent Marteja; Deacon Gerard R. Wilson; Dorothy Horstmann, Pastoral Assoc.
Res., 20 Harrison Ave., 11730. Tel: 516-581-4266; Fax: 516-581-0112.
School—Tel: 516-581-3423; Fax: 516-581-7509. Biagio Arpino, Prin.
Lay Teachers 47; Students 950.
Catechesis/Religious Programs—Tel: 516-581-3304. D.R.E.: Susan Fullam; Sr. Kati Hamm.
Students 1,300.

East Meadow, Nassau Co., St. Raphael (1941), Revs. Thomas J. Haggerty; Aaron Vellaramparampil; Joseph E. Nohs; Sr. Judith Enterlin, C.S.J., Pastoral Assoc.
Res., 600 Newbridge Rd., 11554. Tel: 516-785-0236; Fax: 516-783-9578.
School—St. Elizabeth Ann Seton Regional School, East Meadow Campus. See Regional Schools under Institutions Located in the Diocese. Tel: 516-785-7006; Fax: 516-785-7008.
Catechesis/Religious Programs—Tel: 516-221-9096. D.R.E.: Sr. Elizabeth Mc Neill, R.S.M.; Sr. Karen Kaelin, C.S.J.
Students 1,455.

East Northport, Suffolk Co., St. Anthony of Padua (1951), Revs. Richard P. Hoerning; James Atkins; James M. Kissane; Deacons Robert Braun; Martin W. Duggan. In res., Rev. James A. Kirrane (BRK).
Res., 20 Cheshire Pl., 11731-2591. Tel: 516-261-1077; Fax: 516-757-0572.
School—Trinity Regional School, East Northport. See Regional Schools under Institutions Located in the Diocese. Tel: 516-261-5130.
Catechesis/Religious Programs—Tel: 516-261-1306. D.R.E.: Mrs. Judith Corbellini; Mrs. Eileen Schlee; Mrs. Marguerite Goglia.
Students 1,544.

East Patchogue, Suffolk Co., St. Joseph the Worker (1955), Revs. Thomas March, O.F.M.Cap.; William Winters, O.F.M.Cap.; Joseph Shea, O.F.M.Cap.
Res., 510 Narragansett Ave., 11772. Tel: 516-286-9133; Fax: 516-286-9145.
School—Holy Angels Regional School, Patchogue. See Regional Schools under Institutions Located in the Diocese. Tel: 516-475-0422; Fax: 516-475-2036.
Catechesis/Religious Programs—Mrs. Therese Marsh, D.R.E.
Students 652.

East Rockaway, Nassau Co., St. Raymond's (1909), Rev. Msgr. William W. Jablonski; Rev. William V. Singleton, Pastor Emeritus. Pastoral Assocs.: Revs. Antonio S. Pascual; Michael A. Carroll; Deacons Robert C. Campbell; Richard W. LaRossa; Gregory D'Angelo; Guy Donza. In res., Rev. James P. Moyna.
Res., 263 Atlantic Ave., 11518. Tel: 516-593-5000; Fax: 516-887-0554.
School—Tel: 516-593-9010; Fax: 516-593-0986.
Sisters, Servants of the Immaculate Heart of Mary 4; Lay Teachers 18; Students 403.
Catechesis/Religious Programs—Tel: 516-593-9075. Mrs. Evelyn Contaldi, D.R.E.
Students 923.

Elmont, Nassau Co., St. Boniface, Rev. Msgr. John R. Dreasen, V.F.; Revs. Mathew Kottaram (India); Douglas Dower; George Punti; Joseph Lainesca (Haiti); Sr. Evelyn Lamoureux, D.W., Human Svcs. In res., Rev. Francis Odufuye (Nigeria).
Res., 631 Elmont Rd., 11003. Tel: 516-354-0715; Fax: 516-354-0446.
School—Tel: 516-354-6084; Fax: 516-437-5554. Mrs. Christine Faber, Prin.
Sisters of St. Dominic 2; Lay Teachers 18; Students 318.
Catechesis/Religious Programs—Tel: 516-437-7112. Sr. Margaret Fanning, C.S.J., D.R.E.
Students 770.

St. Vincent de Paul (1951), Revs. Joseph M. Hickey, M.A., M.S.Ed., P.D.; Augustine Fernando; Bruce Reed, M.Div. In res., Rev. Msgr. Francis J. Schneider, J.C.D., M.Div.; Deacon Thomas Divita.
Res., 1500 DePaul St., 11003. Tel: 516-352-2127; Fax: 516-352-2358.
Catechesis/Religious Programs—Tel: 516-352-2265. Ms. Mary Alice Burchell, M.A., D.R.E.
Students 765.

Farmingdale, Nassau Co., St. Kilian (1896), Rev. Msgr. Charles W. Swiger; Rev. Msgr. John P. Martin; Revs. Angel V. Resultay (Philippines); Gerard J. Gentleman, Jr.; Leo Peter Prengaman, S.J.; Deacons Frank D. Barone; Lucio Cotone; Herman Rodenburg; Donald Zirkel. In res., Most Rev. John C. Dunne.
Res., 485 Conklin St., 11735. Tel: 516-249-0127; Fax: 516-249-7131.
School—St. John Baptist de LaSalle Regional School, Bethpage/Farmingdale. See Regional Schools under Institutions Located in the Diocese. Tel: 516-931-0983 (Bethpage); 516-694-3610 (Farmingdale); Fax: 516-931-1502 (Bpg); 516-694-3614 (Fmdl).
Catechesis/Religious Programs—Tel: 516-694-0633; Fax: 516-454-8612. Mrs. Joanne Kolasa, D.R.E.
Students 1,325.
Parish Social Ministy/Outreach—Tel: 516-756-9656. Lisa Molluso, Dir.

Farmingville, Suffolk Co., Church of the Resurrection (1988), Rev. Thomas F. Mulvanerty; Deacons Daniel Macellaro; Walter Williams.
Church—50 Granny Rd., 11738. Tel: 516-696-0232; Fax: 516-696-0271.
Catechesis/Religious Programs—Tel: 516-696-0270.
Students 698.

Floral Park, Nassau Co., St. Hedwig's (1902) (Polish), Revs. Francis E. Filmanski; Chester Diadia.
Res., One Depan Ave., 11001. Tel: 516-354-0042; Fax: 516-327-2458.
Catechesis/Religious Programs—Students 200.

Our Lady of Victory (1921), Rev. Msgr. Charles J. Nosser; Revs. Thomas Moriarty; Charles N. Srion (Thailand); Deacon Lawrence P. Mulligan.
Res., 2 Floral Pkwy., 11001-3198. Tel: 516-354-0482; 354-0479; Fax: 516-354-7450.
School—2 Bellmore St., 11001. Tel: 516-352-4466; 354-2150; Fax: 516-352-4467. Sr. Maria Wittenborn, S.C., Prin.
Religious 3; Lay Teachers 25; Students 466.
Catechesis/Religious Programs—Tel: 516-352-0510. Sr. Barbara Kaiser, C.S.J., D.R.E.
Students 1,131.

Franklin Square, Nassau Co., St. Catherine of Sienna (1908), Rev. Msgr. William Costello; Revs. Edward J. Walsh; Marian Bicz; Dennis Whelan.
Res., 33 New Hyde Park Rd., 11010. Tel: 516-352-0146; Fax: 516-326-7427.
School—Holzhimer, Tel: 516-437-2733. Mrs. Diane Staudinger, Prin.
Sisters of St. Dominic 2; Lay Teachers 25; Students 397.
Catechesis/Religious Programs—Tel: 516-354-4554.
Students 1,425.

Freeport, Nassau Co., Our Holy Redeemer (Hispanic), Revs. Richard Figliozzi; Sabbas Rodriguez; Gonzalo Betancur. In res., Revs. Michael Manzelli; William Henesy; Deacons James Dunne; Francisco Cales; Bruce A. Burnham.
Res., 37 S. Ocean Ave., 11520. Tel: 516-378-0665; Fax: 516-546-1416.
Catechesis/Religious Programs—Tel: 516-546-1057; Fax: 516-546-1416.
Students 712.

Garden City, Nassau Co., St. Joseph's (1901), Rev. Msgr. Donald T. Bennett; Revs. Richard F. Delaney; Steven P. Scarmozzino. In res., Rev. Msgr. John A. Alesandro.
Res., 130 Fifth St., 11530. Tel: 516-747-3535; Fax: 516-746-0719.
School—450 Franklin Ave., 11530. Tel: 516-747-2730. Sr. Mary O'Donnell, O.P., Prin.; Ms. Florence Puff, Asst. Prin.
Lay Teachers 25; Students 434.
Catechesis/Religious Programs—Tel: 516-741-7787. Susan Mirabella, D.R.E.
Students 978.

St. Anne (1929), Revs. Brian A. McKeon; Richard R. Donovan; Deacons Edward Cunningham; Jack McGowan. In res., Rev. James C. Miller.
Res., 35 Dartmouth St., 11530. Tel: 516-352-5904; Fax: 516-352-1360.
School—25 Dartmouth St., 11530. Tel: 516-352-1205. Miss Jacqueline Lucarelli, Prin.
Religious of the Sacred Heart of Mary 3; Lay Teachers 22; Students 479.
Catechesis/Religious Programs—Tel: 516-488-1032. Sr. Kathleen Corr, O.P., D.R.E.
Students 767.

Glen Cove, Nassau Co., St. Patrick's (1856), Rev. Msgr. John J. McCann; Revs. Thomas J. McCarthy; Robert J. Coyle; Henry I. Benack, Hospital Chap.; Sr. Frances Gritte, S.C.H., Pastoral Assoc. In res., Rev. Rodrigo Velasquez.
Res., 235 Glen St., 11542. Tel: 516-676-0276; Fax: 516-674-9137. [CEM]
School—All Saints Regional Catholic School, Glen Cove. See Regional Schools under Institutions Located in the Diocese. Tel: 516-676-0762; Fax: 516-676-0660.

Catechesis/Religious Programs—Tel: 516-671-7223. Ms. Catherine Bilquin, D.R.E.
Students 413.

St. Rocco (1937) (Italian), Rev. Msgr. Domenick T. Graziadio.
Res., 18 Third St., 11542. Tel: 516-676-2482; Fax: 516-676-2117.
School—All Saints Regional Catholic School, Glen Cove. See Regional Schools under Institutions Located in the Diocese. Tel: 516-676-0762; Fax: 516-676-0660.
Catechesis/Religious Programs—Students 290.

Glen Head, Nassau Co., St. Hyacinth (1909) (Polish), Revs. Richard Kopinski; Francis Podgorski; Joseph P. Kozlowski, Pastor Emeritus; Deacon Robert J. Heintz.
Res., 319 Cedar Swamp Rd., 11545. Tel: 516-676-0361; Fax: 516-674-4728.
School—All Saints Regional Catholic School, Glen Cove. See Regional Schools under Institutions Located in the Diocese. Tel: 516-671-3033.
Catechesis/Religious Programs—Tel: 516-674-2269. Miss Eileen Meserole, D.R.E.
Students 200.

Great Neck, Nassau Co., St. Aloysius (1876), Revs. Thomas Candreva, S.T.L., J.C.D.; John Seung Chi Baek (Korea).
Res., 592 Middle Neck Rd., 11023. Tel: 516-482-2770; Fax: 516-829-3504.
Catechesis/Religious Programs—Tel: 516-482-5660.
Students 258.

Greenlawn, Suffolk Co., St. Francis of Assisi (1966) (Haitian), Rev. Msgr. Patrick J. Armshaw; Rev. Thomas W. Coby. In res., Rev. Malachy C. Flaherty, O.F.M.Cap.; Deacon Allan Longo.
Res., 29 Northgate Dr., 11740. Tel: 516-757-7435; Fax: 516-757-0469.
School—Trinity Regional School, East Northport. See Regional Schools under Institutions Located in the Diocese. Tel: 516-261-5130; Fax: 516-266-5345.
Catechesis/Religious Programs—Tel: 516-754-6436. Mrs. Theresa DeMayo, D.R.E.
Students 650.

Greenport, Suffolk Co., St. Agnes (1886), Rev. Msgr. John P. Sullivan; Sr. Sheila Molloy, O.S.U.
Res., Front St., 11944. Tel: 516-477-0048; Fax: 516-477-8519. [CEM]
School—Our Lady of Mercy, Cutchogue. See Regional Schools under Institutions Located in the Diocese. Tel: 516-734-5166.
Catechesis/Religious Programs—Tel: 516-477-1422.
Students 168.

Hampton Bays, Suffolk Co., St. Rosalie's (1901), Revs. William J. Gill; Patrick A. Bergin, M.M.
Res., 31 Montauk Hwy., 11946. Tel: 516-728-9461; Fax: 516-728-2559.
School—Our Lady of the Hamptons Regional School. See Regional Schools under Institutions Located in the Diocese. Tel: 516-283-9140.
Catechesis/Religious Programs—Tel: 516-728-9461. Sarah Cunliffe, D.R.E.
Students 508.
Mission—East Quogue, Suffolk Co., 31 Montauk Hwy., 11946. Tel: 516-653-4471.

Hauppauge, Suffolk Co., St. Thomas More (1967), Revs. Ellsworth R. Walden; Michael Boyle; Deacons Alfred Pankus; Robert Weisz. In res., Rev. Ralph Sommer.
Res., 115 Kings Hwy., 11788. Tel: 516-234-5551; Fax: 516-234-6412.
School—Holy Family Regional School, Commack. See Regional Schools under Institutions Located in the Diocese. Tel: 516-678-5800.
Catechesis/Religious Programs—119 Kings Hwy., 11788. Tel: 516-234-0397. D.R.E.: Mrs. Mary Ellen Carroll; Mrs. Patricia Chapin.
Students 1,090.

Hempstead, Nassau Co., Our Lady of Loretto (1870), Rev. Msgr. Pablo M. Rodriguez; Rev. Fruto Rosales; Sr. Teresa Logue, S.C., Pastoral Assoc.; Sr. Mary Therese Von Holdt, B.V.M.; Deacon Jose Roa; Mr. Kevin Hickson; Mrs. Peggy Bischof.
Res., 104 Greenwich St., 11550. Tel: 516-489-3675; Fax: 516-485-8371.
School—St. Martin de Porres Regional School, Uniondale. See Regional Schools under Institutions Located in the Diocese. Tel: 516-481-3303.
Catechesis/Religious Programs—Tel: 516-489-3675.
Students 324.

St. Ladislaus (1915) (Polish), Rev. Msgr. Edward Wawerski. In res., Rev. John Siebor.
Res., 18 Richardson Pl., 11550. Tel: 516-489-0368; Fax: 516-292-9193.
School—St. Martin de Porres Regional School, Uniondale. See Regional Schools under Institutions Located in the Diocese.

Hewlett, Nassau Co., St. Joseph's (1872), Rev. Msgr. Charles R. Fink; Deacons Thomas Costello; Pat Acquafredda. In res., Rev. Eugene J. McManus.
Res., 1346 Broadway, 11557. Tel: 516-374-0290; Fax: 516-374-2598.
Catechesis/Religious Programs—1355 Noel Ave., 11557. Tel: 516-569-6080. Frances Acquafredda, D.R.E.
Students 429.

Hicksville, Nassau Co., St. Ignatius Loyola (1859), Rev. Msgr. Edward L. Tarrant; Revs. Frederic J. Harrer, Pastor Emeritus; James Carmody; Gerard A. Gordon.
Res., 129 Broadway, 11801. Tel: 516-931-0056; Fax: 516-939-0852.
School—20 Cherry St., 11801. Tel: 516-931-0831; Fax: 516-933-6528. Ms. Jacqueline Burdi, Prin.
Lay Teachers 23; Students 342.
Catechesis/Religious Programs—Tel: 516-935-6873. Jane E. Schreiber, D.R.E.
Students 630.

Holy Family (1951), Rev. Msgr. Edward J. Donnelly; Revs. Jeffrey W. Johnston; Julian Cassar.
Res., 5 Fordham Ave., 11801. Tel: 516-938-3846; Fax: 516-938-6241.
School—Tel: 516-938-3881; Fax: 516-938-5041. Sr. Eileen McMahon, O.P., Prin.
Sisters of Saint Dominic 3; Lay Teachers 23; Students 593.
Catechesis/Religious Programs—Tel: 516-938-3854. Mrs. Carol Nealon, D.R.E.
Students 1,044.

Our Lady of Mercy, Rev. Msgr. James E. Boesel; Revs. Charles A. Gartner, (Retired); Basil C. Colasito; Robert S. Hewes.
Res., 500 S. Oyster Bay Rd., 11801. Tel: 516-931-4351; Fax: 516-433-8702.
School—Tel: 516-433-7040; Fax: 516-433-6809. Sr. Mary Joanne Deegan, R.S.M., Prin.
Sisters of Mercy 8; Lay Teachers 23; Students 675.
Catechesis/Religious Programs—Tel: 516-681-1228. Sr. Suzanne LePre, D.R.E.
Students 748.
Youth Ministry—Tel: 516-935-2444.
Lay Teachers 10; Students 60.

Holbrook, Suffolk Co., Good Shepherd (1970), Revs. Thomas L. Spadaro; Paul J. Rogers; Robert C. Scheckenback; Deacon Robert Hernandez.
Res., 1370 Grundy Ave., 11741. Tel: 516-588-7689; Fax: 516-588-7603.
School—Prince of Peace Regional School, Sayville. See Regional Schools under Institutions Located in the Diocese.
Catechesis/Religious Programs—Tel: 516-981-3889. D.R.E.: Sr. Lillian Delorme, O.P.; Sr. Margaret Mary Caulson, I.H.M.
Students 2,500.

Huntington, Suffolk Co., St. Patrick's (1849), Rev. John Denniston; Rev. Msgr. Martin J. Flynn, Pastor Emeritus; Rev. Msgr. James B. Richter; Revs. Thomas Edamattam (India); Ernest E. Robinson; Deacons Robert R. Maro; Jules Gagnon. In res., Rev. Owen Shelley, O.F.M.Cap., Chap.
Res., 400 Main St., 11743-3298. Tel: 516-673-5320; Fax: 516-673-4102. [CEM]
School—360 Main St., 11743-3298. Tel: 516-673-5325. Sr. Maureen McDade, Prin.
Sisters 2; Lay Teachers 24; Students 600.
Catechesis/Religious Programs—Tel: 516-673-5323. D.R.E.: Sr. Frances Viola; Sr. Peggy Ford.
Students 1,300.

Huntington Station, Suffolk Co., St. Hugh of Lincoln (1913), Rev. Msgr. Vincent Rush; Revs. Joseph Arevalo; Joseph V. Davanzo; Deacons Edward W. Billia; Vito B. Taranto; Thomas Reilly.
Res., 21 E. Ninth St., 11746. Tel: 516-427-0638; Fax: 516-427-1319.
Parish Center—1450 New York Ave., 11746.
School—Trinity Regional School, East Northport. See Regional Schools under Institutions Located in the Diocese. Tel: 516-261-5130; Fax: 516-266-5345.
Catechesis/Religious Programs—Tel: 516-271-6081. Miss Eileen McNamara, D.R.E.
Students 1,136.

Inwood, Nassau Co., Our Lady of Good Counsel (1910), Rev. Peter A. Libasci.
Res., 68 Wanser Ave., 11096. Tel: 516-239-0953; Fax: 516-239-0386.
Catechesis/Religious Programs—Sr. Kathleen Schaetzle, C.S.J., D.R.E.
Students 355.

Island Park, Nassau Co., Sacred Heart (1938), Rev. John J. Tutone.
Res., 282 Long Beach Rd., 11558. Tel: 516-432-0655; Fax: 516-897-7567.
Catechesis/Religious Programs—Tel: 516-431-7877. Mrs. Carmel Caracciolo, D.R.E.
Students 360.

Islip Terrace, Suffolk Co., St. Peter the Apostle (1962), Revs. Gerard A. Ringenback; Felix Weerasinghe, Pastoral Assoc.
Res., 94 Valley Stream St., 11752. Tel: 516-277-9448; Fax: 516-224-1594.
School—Our Lady of Providence Regional School, Central Islip. See Regional Schools under Institutions Located in the Diocese.
Catechesis/Religious Programs—Tel: 516-581-5715. Sr. Ellen Zak, C.S.F.N., D.R.E.
Students 800.

Kings Park, Suffolk Co., St. Joseph's (1888), Rev. Msgr. Alex F. Manly; Revs. Francis P. Vattakudiyil; Paul A. Dolan; Deacon W. Donald Bennettson.
Parish Center—59 Church St., 11754. Tel: 516-269-6635; Fax: 516-269-7508.
School—Holy Family Regional School, Commack. See Regional Schools under Institutions Located in the Diocese. Tel: 516-543-0202; Fax: 516-543-0203.
Catechesis/Religious Programs—Tel: 516-269-4383.
Students 1,750.

Lake Ronkonkoma, Suffolk Co., St. Elizabeth Ann Seton (1988), Rev. Patrick J. Whitney; Deacons Robert Gaudioso; Joseph Gioglio.
Res., 800 Portion Rd., 11779. Tel: 516-737-4388; Fax: 516-737-4389.
Catechesis/Religious Programs—Tel: 516-737-8915. Mrs. Michelle Hahn, D.R.E.
Students 1,000.

Levittown, Nassau Co., St. Bernard (1948), Rev. Msgr. George P. Graham, J.C.D., Ph.D.; Revs. Paul G. Driscoll, M.A.; Tony Lacson, J.C.D.; Orsete Dias, Ed.D. In res., Rev. Martin J. Hall, M.A.
Res., 3100 Hempstead Tpke., 11756. Tel: 516-731-4220; Fax: 516-731-4355.
School—Tel: 516-731-4322.
Lay Teachers 15; Students 350.
Catechesis/Religious Programs—Tel: 516-731-8511.
Students 1,364.

Lindenhurst, Suffolk Co., Our Lady of Perpetual Help (1871), Rev. Msgr. Daniel S. Hamilton; Revs. Vitalis B. Pedzik; Edward M. Seagriff; Richard F. Kammerer; Damian L. Cooper.
Res., 210 S. Wellwood Ave., 11757-4989. Tel: 516-226-7725; Fax: 516-225-9597.
School—Tel: 516-226-0208.
Sisters of St. Dominic 2; Lay Teachers 27; Students 691.
Catechesis/Religious Programs—Tel: 516-226-2384. Diana Castellano, Coord. Program Admin.; Biagio Arpino, Coord. Teaching Training & Curriculum Planning.
Students 2,117.

Long Beach, Nassau Co., St. Ignatius Martyr (1926), Revs. Thomas P. O'Donnell; Richard A. Nilsson, Pastoral Assoc. In res., Rev. Msgr. Edward A. Sweeny.
Res., 721 W. Broadway, 11561. Tel: 516-432-0045; Fax: 516-432-0358.
School—Long Beach Regional Catholic School, Long Beach. See Regional Schools under Institutions Located in the Diocese. Tel: 516-432-8900; Fax: 516-432-8926.
Catechesis/Religious Programs—Tel: 516-432-6788.
Students 600.

St. Mary of the Isle (1915), Rev. Thomas E. Donohoe; Deacon John P. Dunlop; Sr. Frances Monuszko, O.P., Dir. St. Mary of the Isle Community Center.
Res., 315 E. Walnut St., 11561. Tel: 516-432-0157; Fax: 516-897-0566.
School—Long Beach Regional Catholic School, Long Beach. See Regional Schools under Institutions Located in the Diocese. Tel: 516-432-8900.
Catechesis/Religious Programs—Claire Schirtzer, M.A., D.R.E.
Students 421.

Lynbrook, Nassau Co., Our Lady of Peace (1941), Revs. Lawrence M. Penzes; Mark P. Rowan; Deacon Aniello Squitieri. In res., Rev. Antony Asir.
Res., 25 Fowler Ave., 11563. Tel: 516-599-6414; Fax: 516-596-1847.
School—Tel: 516-593-4884.
Sisters of Mercy 1; Lay Teachers 16; Students 342.
Catechesis/Religious Programs—Tel: 516-593-5150.
Students 620.

Malverne, Nassau Co., Our Lady of Lourdes (1926), Revs. Donald M. Baier; Edwin J. Collins, Pastor Emeritus; John F. Whelan; John F. Wymes, M.M.; John F. Meade (NY); Deacon Frank Cove.
Res., 65 Wright Ave., 11565. Tel: 516-599-1269; Fax: 516-887-9517.
School—76 Park Blvd., 11565. Tel: 516-599-7328. Mr. John A. McQuillan, Prin.
Lay Teachers 18; Students 321.

Catechesis/Religious Programs—Tel: 516-599-7222; Fax: 516-599-2256. Mrs. Margaret DeStefano, D.R.E.
Students 484.

Manhasset, Nassau Co., St. Mary's (1853), Rev. Msgr. John J. Skelly; Rev. Msgr. John J. Wiest, Pastor Emeritus; Revs. Joseph D. Casaclang; Kevin M. Smith; Anthony E. Refalo.
Res., 1300 Northern Blvd., 11030. Tel: 516-627-0385; Fax: 516-627-6070.
School—1340 Northern Blvd., 11030. Tel: 516-627-0184; Fax: 516-627-3795.
Sisters of the Immaculate Heart of Mary 4; Lay Teachers 33; Students 440.
High Schools—(Coed) 25 Second St., 11030. Tel: 516-627-2092; Fax: 516-627-4383.; 51 Clapham Ave., 11030. Tel: 516-627-2711; Fax: 516-627-3209.
Sisters of the Immaculate Heart of Mary 6; Marist Brothers 5; Lay Teachers 51; Students 860.
Catechesis/Religious Programs—Tel: 516-627-4028.
Students 1,037.

Manorhaven, Nassau Co., Our Lady of Fatima (1948), Revs. Kenneth T. Nee; Joseph Minturn. In res., Rev. Lino S. Gonsalves (GOA).
Res., 6 Cottonwood Pl., Port Washington, 11050. Tel: 516-767-0781; Fax: 516-767-2981.
Catechesis/Religious Programs—Tel: 516-944-8322.
Students 440.

Manorville, Suffolk Co., St. Peter & Paul (1912), Rev. John J. McGratty; Deacons Joseph Guntert; John C. Pettorino; Eda Lorello, Pastoral Assoc.
Res., 781 Wading River Rd., P.O. Box 207, 11949. Tel: 516-369-1273; Fax: 516-369-1273.

Massapequa, Nassau Co., St. Rose of Lima (1952), Rev. Msgr. Daniel J. Hurley; Revs. Lawrence A. Sheehan, S.J.; John M. Derasmo; Thomas P. Tuite; Deacons Thomas J. Forbes; Thomas J. Quinn; Frank J. Flood; Francis B. McGuiness; Dennis R. O'Connor.
Res., 2 Bayview Ave., 11758-7299. Tel: 516-798-4992; Fax: 516-795-7836.
School—Tel: 516-541-1546. Sr. Kathleen Gallina, Prin.
Sisters of St. Dominic 3; Lay Teachers 29; Students 461.
Catechesis/Religious Programs—Tel: 516-541-1712.
Students 2,095.

Massapequa Park, Nassau Co., Our Lady of Lourdes (1955), Revs. Robert E. Mason; Thomas J. Reynolds; Anthony J. Heinlein; Deacons Domenick Valdano; Steve Delligatti.
Res., 855 Carmans Rd., 11762. Tel: 516-541-3270; Fax: 516-797-9851.
School—Tel: 516-798-7926.
Lay Teachers 21; Students 390.
Catechesis/Religious Programs—379 Linden St., 11762. Tel: 516-799-5179.
Students 715.

Mastic Beach, Suffolk Co., St. Jude (1949), Revs. Joseph A. Mirro; Steven A. Berbig; Anthony Iaconis; Franklin Salazar; Deacons Thomas Gross; Thomas Gillen; Luis Giraldo.
Res., 89 Overlook Dr., 11951. Tel: 516-281-5743; Fax: 516-395-5786.
School—Our Lady, Queen of Apostles Regional School, Center Moriches. See Regional Schools under Institutions Located in the Diocese.
Catechesis/Religious Programs—Tel: 516-281-2835. Virginia Struckhoff, D.R.E.
Students 1,911.
Parish Human Services Center—89 Overlook Dr., 11951. Tel: 516-281-5634. Helen Mahon, Coord.

Medford, Suffolk Co., St. Sylvester (1948), Revs. Charles E. Papa; Michael F. Holzmann; Edward J. Kealey; Deacons George J. Riegger; Francis P. Roettinger.
Res., 68 Ohio Ave., P.O. Box 336, 11763. Tel: 516-475-4506; Fax: 516-475-1057.
School—Holy Angels Regional School, Patchogue. See Regional Schools under Institutions Located in the Diocese. Tel: 516-475-0422; Fax: 516-475-2038.
Catechesis/Religious Programs—Tel: 516-475-8191. Mrs. Patricia A. Desmond, D.R.E.
Students 1,350.

Melville, Suffolk Co., St. Elizabeth (1962), Revs. Bruce J. Powers; Michael A. Vetrano; Deacons Richard Johnston; Joseph Mercolino.
Res., 181 Wolf Hill Rd., 11747. Tel: 516-271-4455; Fax: 516-271-1415.
School—Trinity Regional School, East Northport. See Regional Schools under Institutions Located in the Diocese. Tel: 516-261-5130; Fax: 516-266-5345.
Catechesis/Religious Programs—Students 800.

Merrick, Nassau Co., Cure of Ars (1926), Rev. Msgr. James P. Swiader; Rev. Robert A. Romeo; Sr. Miriam Michael Joos, O.P., Pastoral Assoc. In res., Revs. Thomas V. Arnao; John P. Murray.
Res., 2323 Merrick Ave., 11566. Tel: 516-623-1400; Fax: 516-623-1107.
School—St. Elizabeth Ann Seton Regional School, Bellmore/East Meadow. See Regional Schools under Institutions Located in the Diocese. Tel: 516-679-1990; Fax: 516-679-2082.

Mineola, Nassau Co., Corpus Christi (1901) (Portuguese), Revs. Kenneth H. Winkler; Tomaz Gomide; Robert J. Batule; Rev. Msgr. Eugene F. Murphy; Rev. Thomas F. Murphy; Deacon John C. Reinhart. In res., Rev. Msgr. Lawrence D. Costello, Pastor Emeritus.
Res., 155 Garfield Ave., 11501. Tel: 516-746-1223; Fax: 516-294-5311.
School—120 Searing Ave., 11501. Tel: 516-746-2966. Sr. Laura Helbig, O.P., Prin.
Sisters of St. Dominic 2; Lay Teachers 19; Students (Nursery to 8th) 443.
Catechesis/Religious Programs—Tel: 516-294-0631. D.R.E.: Mrs. Ursula Bordonaro; Mrs. Joan O'Brien.
Students 724.

Montauk, Suffolk Co., St. Therese of Lisieux (1950), Rev. Msgr. John C. Nosser, M.S.
Res., 55 S. Etna Ave., P.O. Drawer 5027, 11954. Tel: 516-668-2200; Fax: 516-668-2384.
School—Stella Maris Regional School, Sag Harbor. See Regional Schools under Institutions Located in the Diocese. Tel: 516-725-2525.
Day Care/Nursery School—Tel: 516-668-5353. Children (3 & 4 years old) 38.
Catechesis/Religious Programs—Students 90.

Nesconset, Suffolk Co., Church of the Holy Cross (1988), Pastoral Team: Revs. Joseph M. Schlafer; William G. Breslawski; Sr. Jane Halligan, S.S.N.D., Pastoral Assoc.
Res., 95 Old Nichols Rd., 11767. Tel: 516-265-2200; Fax: 516-265-2229.
Catechesis/Religious Programs—Mrs. Judith Pickel, D.R.E.
Students 858.

New Hyde Park, Nassau Co., Holy Spirit (1893), Rev. Msgr. John T. Heinlein; Revs. Charles P. Romano; John T. Daley. In res., Rev. Robert O. Morrissey.
Res., 500 Jericho Tpke., 11040. Tel: 516-354-0359; Fax: 516-354-2611 (Rectory).
School—13 S. Sixth St., 11040. Tel: 516-354-5566. Sr. Angela LiVecchi, O.P., Prin.
Sisters of St. Dominic (Amityville) 4; Lay Teachers 27; Students 510.
Catechesis/Religious Programs—13 S. 6th St., 11040. Tel: 516-354-2363.
Students 480.

Notre Dame (1941), Revs. Peter Pflomm; John Murray, Pastor Emeritus; William T. Slater; Stephen H. Donnelly; Anthony Kim (Korea); Sr. Judith A. Golden, O.P., Pastoral Assoc.; Deacon Gilbert McGaffney.
Res., 45 Mayfair Rd., 11040. Tel: 516-352-7203; Fax: 516-326-7988.
School—Tel: 516-354-5618; Fax: 516-354-5952. Sr. Lorraine McDonald, O.P., Prin.
Sisters of St. Dominic (Amityville) 5; Lay Teachers 28; Students 585.
Catechesis/Religious Programs—25 Mayfair Rd., 11040. Tel: 516-437-5604. D.R.E.: Sr. Mary Jane Coleman, R.S.M.; Sr. Alice Reichmeider, O.P.
Students 944.

North Merrick, Nassau Co., Sacred Heart (1952), Revs. Thomas G. Gallagher; James F. Drew; Deacon Daniel J. Delargy. In res., Rev. Brian J. Brinker, Chap. at Nassau County Medical Center.
Res., 1921 Old Mill Rd., 11566. Tel: 516-379-1356; Fax: 516-379-1610.
School—Tel: 516-378-5797; Fax: 516-378-5797. Sr. Mary Morrin, C.S.J., Prin.
Sisters of St. Joseph 8; Lay Teachers 16; Students 315.
Catechesis/Religious Programs—Tel: 516-868-9406. Mrs. Cecelia Lerro, D.R.E.
Students 1,058.

Northport, Suffolk Co., St. Philip Neri (1894), Revs. Peter J. Garry; Michael J. O'Farrell; Anthony M. Stanganelli; Deacons John F. Burkart; Andrew Schneider. In res., Rev. Thomas J. Colgan.
Res., 344 Main St., 11768. Tel: 516-261-7753; Fax: 516-261-7420. [CEM]
School—Trinity Regional School, East Northport. See Regional Schools under Institutions Located in the Diocese. Tel: 516-261-8520; Fax: 516-261-8560.
Catechesis/Religious Programs—Tel: 516-261-7800. Lorraine Cortina, D.R.E.
Students 510.

Ocean Beach, (Fire Island) Suffolk Co., Our Lady of the Magnificat (1921), Rev. Msgr. Ronald E. Hayde; Rev. Robert Morrissey.
Mailing Address: P.O. Box 445, 11770. Tel: 516-583-5868.

Oceanside, Nassau Co., St. Anthony (1927), Revs. Kirk R. Reynolds, S.J.; Frederick J. Pellegrini, S.J.; Conrad R. Dietz; Martin F. Kirby; Pierce A. Brennan, S.J.; Matthew F. Roche, S.J.; Sr. Gena Travers, O.P., Pastoral Assoc.; Deacon James W. Flannery; Anna Maria Sirianni, Parish Outreach Coord., Tel: 516-764-9257.
Res., 110 Anchor Ave., 11572. Tel: 516-764-0048; 764-0665; Fax: 516-764-7726.
Catechesis/Religious Programs—Tel: 516-678-3388. Pam Shannon, D.R.E.
Students 700.

Oyster Bay, Nassau Co., St. Dominic's (1895), Rev. Msgr. Charles A. Ribaudo; Rev. Msgr. James E. Collins, Pastor Emeritus; Revs. Malcolm J. Burns; Paul F. Butler.
Res., 96 Anstice St., 11771. Tel: 516-922-4488; Fax: 516-922-9491.
School—35 School St., 11771. Tel: 516-922-4233; Fax: 516-624-7613.
Sisters of the Immaculate Heart of Mary 2; Lay Teachers 18; Students 344.
High School—110 Antice St., 11771. Tel: 516-922-4888; Fax: 516-922-4898.
Sisters 2; Lay Teachers 42; Students 488.
Catechesis/Religious Programs—Tel: 516-922-7788.
Students 640.

Patchogue, Suffolk Co., St. Francis de Sales (1888) (Hispanic), Rev. Robert J. Clerkin; Deacons Martin McIndoe; Fernando J. Quinones; Francisco Diaz-Granados.
Res., 7 Amity St., 11772. Tel: 516-475-0161; Fax: 516-475-1481. [CEM]
School—Holy Angels Regional School, Patchogue. See Regional Schools under Institutions Located in the Diocese. Tel: 516-475-0422.
Catechesis/Religious Programs—Tel: 516-289-4339.
Students 450.

Our Lady of Mt. Carmel, Revs. Robert J. O'Connell; Alexander L. Sledzaus, Pastor Emeritus; Deacon Joseph Mystkowski. In res., Rev. Edward J. Werring.
Res., 495 New North Ocean Ave., 11772. Tel: 516-475-4739; Fax: 516-447-1030.
School—Holy Angels Regional School, Patchogue. See Regional Schools under Institutions Located in the Diocese.
Catechesis/Religious Programs—Tel: 516-289-7327. Kathleen Reid, M.A., D.R.E.
Students 800.

Plainview, Nassau Co., St. Pius X (1955), Rev. Hugh D. Cannon. In res., Revs. Brian J. McNamara, Chap. St. Anthony's High School; Jose Simon Palliparambil, Chap., North Shore University Hospital at Plainview; Moise Aime; Robert A. McGuire, S.J., Dir. Spirit Life Center, Tel: 516-938-7119.
Res., One St. Pius Ct., 11803. Tel: 516-938-3959; Fax: 516-433-6138.
School—St. John Baptist de LaSalle Regional School, Bethpage/Farmingdale. See Regional Schools under Institutions Located in the Diocese. Tel: 516-931-0983 (Bethpage); 516-694-3610 (Farmingdale); Fax: 516-931-1502 (Bthpg.); 694-3614 (Fmgdl.).
Catechesis/Religious Programs—Tel: 516-822-0919. Elaine D. Hallisey, D.R.E.
Students 312.

Point Lookout, Nassau Co., Our Lady of the Miraculous Medal (1937) (Irish), Revs. William Gomes; Andrew J. Gallagher, Pastor Emeritus.
Res., 75 Parkside Dr., 11569. Tel: 516-431-2772; Fax: 516-432-8669.
School—Long Beach Regional Catholic School, Long Beach. See Regional Schools under Institutions Located in the Diocese. Tel: 516-432-8900; Fax: 516-432-8926.

Port Jefferson, Suffolk Co., Infant Jesus 1903, Rev. Msgr. Dennis M. Regan; Revs. Abraham Z. Porunnolil; Michael J. Rieder; Deacons Patrick C. Gerace; William J. Powers; Richard E. Waldmann.
Res., 110 Myrtle Ave., 11777. Tel: 516-473-0165; Fax: 516-331-8094.
School—Our Lady of Wisdom Regional School, Port Jefferson. See Regional Schools under Institutions Located in the Diocese. Tel: 516-473-1211; Fax: 516-473-1064.
Catechesis/Religious Programs—Tel: 516-928-0447. Mrs. Barbara Saulino, D.R.E.
Students 1,400.

St. Gerard Majella (1968), Co-Pastors: Revs. William A. Hanson; Christopher J. Heller; Deacon Thomas O'Connor.
Res., 300 Terryville Rd., Port Jefferson Station, 11776. Tel: 516-473-2900; Fax: 516-473-0015.
School—Our Lady of Wisdom Regional School, Port Jefferson. See Regional Schools under Institutions Located in the Diocese.
Catechesis/Religious Programs—Tel: 516-928-2550. Alice Meyer, D.R.E.
Students 1,157.

Port Washington, Nassau Co., St. Peter of Alcantara (1901), Rev. Msgr. Walter E. Simmons; Revs. William O'Rourke, Ph.D.; Eugene C. Vollmer.
Res., 1327 Port Washington Blvd., 11050. Tel: 516-883-6675; Fax: 516-944-7461.
School—Tel: 516-944-3772; Fax: 516-767-8075.
Sisters 8; Lay Teachers 19; Students 620.
Catechesis/Religious Programs—Tel: 516-883-5584. Mrs. Elizabeth Eleanor Miller, D.R.E.
Students 410.
Convent—1317 Port Washington Blvd., 11050. Tel: 516-762-1282. Sisters, Servants of the Immaculate Heart of Mary (Scranton, PA)

Riverhead, Suffolk Co., St. John the Evangelist (1861), Revs. Thomas S. Kane; Paul R. Bie. In res., Most Rev. Emil A. Wcela; Rev. Msgr. John Lovett; Rev. Msgr. Martin Bowe.
Res., 546 St. John's Pl., 11901. Tel: 516-727-2030. [CEM]
School—Tel: 516-727-4144.
Sisters of St. Dominic (Amityville) 1; Lay Teachers 9; Students 254.
Catechesis/Religious Programs—Tel: 516-727-6774.
Students 468.

St. Isidore's (1903) (Polish), Rev. Msgr. John Mirecki; Rev. Joseph Walas (Poland) Pastoral Assoc.
Res., 622 Pulaski St., 11901. Tel: 516-727-2114; Fax: 516-369-3566. [CEM]
School—515 Marcy Ave., 11901. Tel: 516-727-1650; Fax: 516-727-3945. Sr. Linda Joseph Chichi, C.S.F.N., Prin.
Sisters of the Holy Family of Nazareth 3; Lay Teachers 8; Students 252.
Catechesis/Religious Programs—Students 93.

Rocky Point, Suffolk Co., St. Anthony of Padua (1948), Revs. Joseph C. Coschignano; Michael Maffeo.
Res., 614 Rte. 25A, 11778. Tel: 516-744-2609; Fax: 516-744-5782.
Catechesis/Religious Programs—Tel: 516-821-0872.
Students 1,100.

Ronkonkoma, Suffolk Co., St. Joseph's (1910), Revs. Donald R. Shane; Caetano F.X. Costa; Raymond H. Nugent; Angelo Ditta; Peter T. Liu; Deacons James Altonji; Michael J. DeBellis; Joseph Dougherty; John Erdman; Joseph Maffeo.
Res., 45 Church St., 11779. Tel: 516-588-8456; Fax: 516-471-2569.
School—25 Church St., 11779. Tel: 516-588-4760. Mrs. Marie Salvietti, Prin.
Lay Teachers 26; Students 541.
Catechesis/Religious Programs—Tel: 516-981-1805. Linda Cussen, D.R.E.
Students 1,526.

Roosevelt, Nassau Co., Queen of the Most Holy Rosary (1919), Rev. Msgr. Thomas E. Molloy, J.C.D.; Sr. Kathleen O'Donnell, S.C., Pastoral Assoc.; Deacon Louis Sandberg. In res., Rev. Ralph Ferro.
Res., 196 W. Centennial Ave., 11575. Tel: 516-378-1315; Fax: 516-378-5754.
Catechesis/Religious Programs—200 W. Centennial Ave., 11575. Tel: 516-623-1391. Mrs. Ellen Zaffonte, D.R.E.
Students 335.

Roslyn, Nassau Co., St. Mary's (1871), Rev. Msgr. Richard C. Bauhoff; Deacon Edward M. Case.
Res., 110 Bryant Ave., P.O. Box 387, 11576-0387. Tel: 516-621-2222; Fax: 516-621-7892.
School—All Saints Regional Catholic School, Glen Cove. See Regional Schools under Institutions Located in the Diocese. Tel: 516-676-0762.
Catechesis/Religious Programs—Tel: 516-621-6798. Sr. Frances Birmingham, O.P., D.R.E.
Students 306.

Sag Harbor, Suffolk Co., St. Andrew's (1859), Rev. Andrew P. Blake; Sr. Lucille D'Amelio, O.P., Pastoral Assoc.
Res., 122 Division St, 11963-3154. Tel: 516-725-0123; Fax: 516-725-3310. [CEM]
School—Stella Maris Regional School, Sag Harbor. See Regional Schools under Institutions Located in the Diocese. Tel: 516-725-2525; Fax: 516-725-4587.
Catechesis/Religious Programs—Tel: 516-725-5805.
Students 176.

St. James, Suffolk Co., SS. Philip and James (1907), Rev. Msgr. Charles A. Guarino, V.F.; Revs. Daniel P. Sheridan; Brian D. McQuade; Deacons Charles Brown; Kenneth Maher; Frank Crivello; Robert Heschl. In res., Rev. Ladislaus Cser, S.J.
Res., One Carow Pl., 11780. Tel: 516-584-5454; Fax: 516-862-9675.
School—(Grades PreK-8). Tel: 516-584-7896; Fax: 516-584-3258. Mr. Anthony Giordano, Prin.
Lay Teachers 17; Students 429.
Catechesis/Religious Programs—Tel: 516-584-5486. Sr. Mary Regina Tierney, O.P., D.R.E.
Students 1,175.

Saltaire, Suffolk Co., Our Lady Star of the Sea, Mission Chapel. (Summer Mission). Rev. Richard R. Viladesau, S.T.D., Admin.
Res., St. Anastasia Church, 45-14 245th St., Douglaston, 11362. Tel: 718-631-4454.

Sayville, Suffolk Co., St. Lawrence the Martyr (1895), Rev. Msgr. John Rowan; Revs. Sean J. Gann; Ronald Rebaldo; Deacons Edward W. Smith; William F. Fullam, Jr.
Res., 27 Handsome Ave., 11782. Tel: 516-589-0042; 589-8135; 589-3887; Fax: 516-589-5318. [CEM]
School—Prince of Peace Regional School, Sayville. See Regional Schools under Institutions Located in the Diocese. Tel: 516-589-3926.
Catechesis/Religious Programs—Tel: 516-589-3160. Mrs. Lorraine Gallagher, D.R.E.
Students 1,200.

Sea Cliff, Nassau Co., St. Boniface Martyr (1898), Rev. Michael J. Torpey; Sr. Kathleen P. Murphy, O.P., Pastoral Assoc.
Res., 12 Main Ave., 11579-1312. Tel: 516-676-0676; Fax: 516-674-6742.
School—All Saints Regional Catholic School, Glen Cove. See Regional Schools under Institutions Located in the Diocese.
Catechesis/Religious Programs—Tel: 516-671-0418. Julia Byrne, D.R.E.
Students 380.

Seaford, Nassau Co., St. William, the Abbot (1928), Rev. Msgr. Thomas G. Leavey; Revs. John Hien; Steven Camp; Peter Dugandzic; Deacons William Brennan; Thomas Buchenberger; Michael Metzdorff. In res., Rev. James F. Pereda, J.C.D.
Res., 2000 Jackson Ave., 11783. Tel: 516-785-1266; Fax: 516-785-4824.
School—2001 Jackson Ave., 11783. Tel: 516-785-6784. Mrs. Anna Guardino, Prin.
Ursuline Sisters 2; Lay Teachers 23; Students 566.
Catechesis/Religious Programs—Tel: 516-679-9558. D.R.E.: Mrs. Georgette Levesque; Mrs. Susan Martin.
Students 1,260.

Maria Regina (1954), Revs. James A. Brassil; John Malone; Andrew L. Millar; Lawrence B. Rafferty; Deacons Gerald F. Whitfield; John A. Weigel. In res., Rev. Francis M. Casey.
Res., 3945 Jerusalem Ave., 11783. Tel: 516-798-2415; Fax: 516-798-7493.
School—4045 Jerusalem Ave., 11783. Tel: 516-541-1229; Fax: 516-541-1235.
Sisters of Mercy 3; Lay Teachers 25; Students 568.
Catechesis/Religious Programs—3945 Jerusalem Ave., 11783. Tel: 516-541-0921; Fax: 516-795-2510. Maureen Morea, D.R.E.
Students 1,520.

St. James (1951), Revs. Daniel A. Picciano; Francis Samuel; Richard P. Whitney; Deacons Robert J. Haley, (Retired); James G. Beirne; John G. Leahy.
Res., 80 Hicksville Rd., 11783. Tel: 516-731-3710; Fax: 516-731-4828.
School—St. John Baptist de LaSalle Regional School, Bethpage/Farmingdale. See Regional Schools under Institutions Located in the Diocese. Tel: 516-931-0983; Fax: 516-931-1502.
Catechesis/Religious Programs—Tel: 516-796-2979; Fax: 516-731-4828. Sr. Rosemary Traynor, D.R.E.
Students 1,638.

Selden, Suffolk Co., St. Margaret of Scotland (1948), Revs. Christopher Aridas; John J. Mullen, Pastor Emeritus; Donald Hanson; Deacons William E. Kogler; Biagio Muratore; Phil Paolicelli; Joseph Scollan.
Res., 81 College Rd., 11784. Tel: 516-732-3131; Fax: 516-732-8827.
School—Holy Angels Regional School, Patchogue. See Regional Schools under Institutions Located in the Diocese. Tel: 516-475-0422.
Catechesis/Religious Programs—Tel: 516-698-0798; Fax: 516-732-8827. D.R.E.: Cathy DePasquale; Barbara Mahon; Marilynne Schaefer; Peggy Scheiner.
Students 2,100.

Setauket, Suffolk Co., St. James (1949), Revs. Donald Diederich, J.C.D.; John Barrett, Ph.D.; John Fitzgerald; Thomas F. McGlade, Pastor Emeritus; Philip J. Reehil, Pastor Emeritus; Deacons Gerry Coates; Thomas Owens; Joseph Ingulli.
Res., 429 Rte. 25-A, 11733. Tel: 516-941-4141; Fax: 516-751-6607. [CEM]
School—Our Lady of Wisdom Regional School, Port Jefferson. See Regional Schools under Institutions Located in the Diocese. Tel: 516-473-1211.
Catechesis/Religious Programs—Tel: 516-751-7287. Catherine Roberts, D.R.E.
Students 1,004.

Shelter Island, Suffolk Co., Our Lady of the Isle, Rev. Charles Dougherty, C.P. In res., Revs. Blaine Brezinski, C.P.; Malcolm Cornwell, C.P.
Res., Shelter Island Heights, Box 3027, 11965. Tel: 516-749-0001; Fax: 516-749-4218. [CEM]
School—Stella Maris Regional School, Sag Harbor. See Regional Schools under Institutions Located in the Diocese.

Shoreham, Suffolk Co., St. Mark (1973), Revs. Theodore J. Howard; William E. McCarthy; Deacons Albert Vigliotta; Donald Donovan.
Res., 105 Randall Rd., 11786. Tel: 516-744-2800; Fax: 516-821-1628.
Catechesis/Religious Programs—Tel: 516-821-0550. Sr. Virginia Dunne, D.W., D.R.E.
Students 828.

Smithtown, Suffolk Co., St. Patrick (1952) (Irish/Italian), Revs. Paul Walsh; Vincent Liu; Frank J. Parisi; Deacons Richard Sanders; Fred Jackman.
Res., 280 E. Main St., 11787. Tel: 516-265-2271; Fax: 516-360-0381. [CEM]
School—Tel: 516-724-0285; Fax: 516-724-4958. Mrs. Eileen Sadicario, Prin.
Sisters of St. Joseph 5; Lay Teachers 21; Students 674.
Catechesis/Religious Programs—Tel: 516-724-7454. Paula Billyard, D.R.E.
Students 1,452.

Sound Beach, Suffolk Co., St. Louis de Montfort (1971), Rev. Msgr. John A. McGuire; Rev. Thomas P. Murray; Deacons Joseph T. Bartlotto; Peter F. Schultz; Gary F. Swane; Montford D. Naylor.
Mailing Address: P.O. Box 923, 11789. Tel: 516-744-8566; Fax: 516-744-8611.
Res., New York Ave., 11764.
School—Our Lady of Wisdom Regional School, Port Jefferson. See Regional Schools under Institutions Located in the Diocese. Tel: 516-473-1211.
Catechesis/Religious Programs—Tel: 516-744-9515. Mr. John McNamara, D.R.E.
Students 2,010.

Southampton, Suffolk Co., Sacred Hearts of Jesus and Mary (1896), Rev. Msgr. Edmond J. Trench; Deacon John W. McGauvran.
Res., 168 Hill St., 11968. Tel: 516-283-0097; Fax: 516-283-3836. [CEM]
School—Our Lady of the Hamptons Regional School. See Regional Schools under Institutions Located in the Diocese. Tel: 516-283-9140.
Catechesis/Religious Programs—Students 360.

Our Lady of Poland (1918) (Polish), Rev. Stanley Kondeja.
Res., 35 Maple St., 11968. Tel: 516-283-0667; Fax: 516-287-4146.
School—Our Lady of the Hamptons Regional School. See Regional Schools under Institutions Located in the Diocese. Tel: 516-283-9140; Fax: 516-287-3958.
Catechesis/Religious Programs—Tel: 516-283-5230; Fax: 516-283-5230.
Students 282.

Southold, Suffolk Co., St. Patrick's (1865), Revs. George J. Michell; Martin J. Osborne, Pastor Emeritus.
Res., Main Rd., P.O. Box 1117, 11971-1401. Tel: 516-765-3442; Fax: 516-765-9631. [CEM]
School—Our Lady of Mercy, Cutchogue. See Regional Schools under Institutions Located in the Diocese. Tel: 516-734-5166.
Catechesis/Religious Programs—Tel: 516-765-2338.
Students 240.

Syosset, Nassau Co., St. Edward Confessor (1952), Revs. Joseph C. McComiskey; Anthony Refalo.
Res., 205 Jackson Ave., 11791-4218. Tel: 516-921-0756; Fax: 516-921-4549.
School—2 Teibrook Ave., 11791. Tel: 516-921-7767; Fax: 516-496-0001. Sr. Margaret A. Hartigan, R.S.M., Prin.
Sisters of Mercy (Brooklyn) 2; Lay Teachers 16; Students 270.
Parish Social Ministry Office:—Tel: 516-921-5628; Fax: 516-364-7326. Ms. Dawn Ravella, Dir.
Youth Ministry Office—Tel: 516-921-7631. Mr. Frank Maiello.
Catechesis/Religious Programs—Tel: 516-364-1790. Mrs. Mary Jane Mastrodomenico, D.R.E.
Students 738.

Uniondale, Nassau Co., St. Martha (1949), Rev. Edward Fitzpatrick. In res., Revs. Zachary Callahan; George Vadakethayil.
Res., 546 Greengrove Ave., 11553. Tel: 516-481-2550; Fax: 516-564-4552.
School—St. Martin de Porres Regional School, Uniondale. See Regional Schools under Institutions Located in the Diocese. Tel: 516-481-3303; Fax: 516-483-4138.
Catechesis/Religious Programs—Tel: 516-481-6608. Sr. Eileen Curley, R.S.M., D.R.E.
Students 251.

Valley Stream, Nassau Co., Holy Name of Mary (1902), Rev. Msgr. Daniel E. Fagan; Revs. Theodore J. LeTure, Pastor Emeritus; James L. Maltese; Stephen J. Brigandi, Jr.; Deacon Anthony Cuseo.
Res., 55 E. Jamaica Ave., 11580. Tel: 516-825-1450; Fax: 516-825-1906.

School—90 S. Grove St., 11580. Tel: 516-825-4009. Sr. Elizabeth Marie Lynch, C.S.J., Prin.
Lay Teachers 18; Students 315.
Catechesis/Religious Programs—90 Grove St., 11580. Tel: 516-825-1810. Sr. Barbara Shea, O.P., D.R.E.
Students 1,175.
Parish Outreach—90 Grove St., 11580. Tel: 516-825-0177; Fax: 516-825-5092. Sr. Margie Kelly, C.S.J., Dir.

Blessed Sacrament (1950), Revs. Gregory J. Cappuccino; Frank M. Nelson; Aloysius P. Pakianather (Sri Lanka); Deacons Anthony M. Cedrone; Salvatore A. Marino; Sr. Josann Gallagher, Dir. Family Svcs.
Res., 201 N. Central Ave., 11580. Tel: 516-568-1027; Fax: 516-872-1499.
School—50 Rose Ave., 11580. Tel: 516-825-7334. Melanie Maione, Prin.
Sisters of St. Joseph 2; Lay Teachers 16; Students 376.
Catechesis/Religious Programs—Tel: 516-561-1407. D.R.E.: Lucille Vavosa; Neil Griffin.
Students 1,011.

Wading River, Suffolk Co., St. John Baptist (1922), Revs. Joseph T. Mundy; John P. Vitsas, Pastor Emeritus; Deacons Frederick Finter; Gregory Senholzi.
Res., 1488 North Country Rd., 11792. Tel: 516-929-4339; Fax: 516-369-6961.
Catechesis/Religious Programs—Students 552.

Wantagh, Nassau Co., St. Frances de Chantal (1952), Rev. Msgr. Robert E. Guglielmone; Revs. Joseph DeGrocco; James Mannion; Deacons Robert O'Donovan; Thomas Bast. In res., Rev. David G. Farley, (Retired).
Res., 1309 Wantagh Ave., 11793. Tel: 516-785-2333; Fax: 516-826-7645.
School—St. Elizabeth Ann Seton Regional School, Bellmore/East Meadow. See Regional Schools under Institutions Located in the Diocese. Tel: 516-785-5709; Fax: 516-785-4468.
Catechesis/Religious Programs—Judith Brady, D.R.E.
Students 1,675.

West Babylon, Suffolk Co., Our Lady of Grace, Rev. Msgr. James McNamara; Revs. Thomas Saloy; Gerald Cestare; Deacons Peter DiGiuseppe, Pastoral Assoc.; John Morrow; Charles Graff.
Res., 702 Albin Ave., 11704. Tel: 516-587-5185; Fax: 516-587-1427.
Catechesis/Religious Programs—Tel: 516-661-9353. D.R.E.: Sr. Janet Whelan; Sr. Ann Higgins; Lee Abseck.
Students 2,109.

Westbury, Nassau Co., St. Brigid (1850), Revs. Thomas C. Costa; Claude J. D'Souza; Martin Klein; Francis X. Gaeta; Deacons Robert P. Broyles; William F.X. Byrne; John Falls; Felix Matheis; James Morris.
Res., 75 Post Ave., 11590. Tel: 516-334-0021; Fax: 516-334-0082.
School—St. Brigid/ Our Lady of Hope Regional School, 101 Maple Ave., 11590. Tel: 516-333-0580; Fax: 516-333-0590. Paul P. Clagnaz, Prin.
School Sisters of Notre Dame 1; Lay Teachers 28; Students 402.
Catechesis/Religious Programs—Tel: 516-333-9434. D.R.E.: Stephanie Clagnaz; Jennifer Gallagher.
Students 800.

Westhampton Beach, Suffolk Co., Immaculate Conception (1891), Rev. Msgr. Joseph Murray.
Res., 580 Main Rd., 11978. Tel: 516-288-1423; Fax: 516-288-5498.
School—Our Lady, Queen of Apostles Regional School, Center Moriches. See Regional Schools under Institutions Located in the Diocese.
Catechesis/Religious Programs—Tel: 516-288-4188. Sr. Virginia Baeder, D.R.E.
Students 450.

West Hempstead, Nassau Co., St. Thomas, the Apostle (1931), Rev. Msgr. James P. Lisante; Revs. Brian Patrick Barr; Andrzej Zglejszewski; Thomas M. Fusco. In res., Rev. Msgr. Francis Maniscalco.
Res., 24 Westminster Rd., 11552. Tel: 516-489-8585; Fax: 516-292-2651.
School—12 Westminster Rd., 11552. Tel: 516-481-9310; Fax: 516-481-8769. Sr. Mary Casey, O.P., Prin.
Sisters 3; Lay Teachers 22; Students 404.
Catechesis/Religious Programs—Tel: 516-538-7460. Mrs. Marilyn Meehan, D.R.E.
Students 875.
Mission—Lakeview, Nassau Co., Chapel, Nassau Blvd. & Hempstead Ave., 11552. Tel: 516-483-4091.

West Islip, Suffolk Co., Our Lady of Lourdes (1956), Revs. Joseph C. Lukaszewski; Francis X. Eisele; Michael Hands; Deacons Richard Barry; John Teufel. In res., Rev. James C. Vlaun.
Res., 455 Hunter Ave., 11795. Tel: 516-661-3224; Fax: 516-661-7143.
School—44 Toomey Rd., 11795. Tel: 516-587-7200. Regina A. Cioffi, Prin.
Lay Teachers 15; Students 340.
Catechesis/Religious Programs—Tel: 516-661-5440. D.R.E.: Sr. Diane Liona; Sr. Nancy Campkin.
Students 1,616.

Williston Park, Nassau Co., St. Aidan's (1929), Revs. Robert L. Hayden; Donald E. Babinski; Stephen Pietrowski; Rev. Msgr. Charles E. Bermingham, Pastor Emeritus; Rev. Msgr. Robert J. Kirwin, Pastor Emeritus; Deacons Herman J. Determann; Richard T. Blake; Salvatore Villani. In res., Rev. Thomas J. Harold.
Res., 505 Willis Ave., 11596. Tel: 516-746-6585; Fax: 516-746-6055.
Schools—(Grades Nursery-3) 525 Willis Ave., 11596. Tel: 516-746-6270.; (Grades 4-8) 510 Willis Ave., 11596. Tel: 518-747-6150. Eileen Oliver, Prin.
Sisters 3; Lay Teachers 25; Students 584.
Catechesis/Religious Programs—Tel: 516-747-3272. D.R.E.: Sr. Jo Ann Bonauro, S.C.; Sr. Mary Sullivan, S.H.C.J.
Students 1,035.
Convent—16 Pembroke St., 11596. Tel: 518-741-6869. Sisters of Charity

Woodbury, Nassau Co., Holy Name of Jesus (1962), Rev. Msgr. Anthony J. Savastano; Rev. Msgr. Donald Beckman, D.Min., Admin.
Res., 690 Woodbury Rd., 11797-2504. Tel: 516-921-2334; Fax: 516-921-2408.
Catechesis/Religious Programs—Sr. Laboure D.R.E.
Students 178.

Wyandanch, Suffolk Co., Our Lady of the Miraculous Medal (1934), Rev. John I. Cervini; Deacons Bernard Taylor; Richard Lamb. In res., Rev. Msgr. John D. Gilmartin.
Res., 1434 Straight Path, 11798. Tel: 516-643-7568; Fax: 516-643-5935.
Gerald Ryan Outreach Center, Inc.—Tel: 516-643-7591; Fax: 516-491-7285. Mrs. Ann Druckenmiller, Dir.; Sr. Elizabeth Myles, C.S.J., Religious Education & Youth Ministry, Tel: 516-643-3364.

Chaplains of Public Institutions

ROCKVILLE CENTRE. *Mercy Medical Center* 50 North Park Ave., Tel: 516-678-5800, Ext. 521. Sr. Eileen Donovan, O.P., Dir., Chaplaincy, Chaplains: Revs. Denis J. Sheridan; Asir Antony; Sr. Mary Alice Aschenbach, C.I.J., Dir.; Sr. Mary Morrow, D.W.; Sr. Norma Jean Lokcinski, C.I.J.; Sr. Bernadette Foley, C.I.J; Sr. Elizabeth Scanlan, R.S.M.; Deacon Robert Walsh,
Mercy Hospice, Tel: 516-255-2360. Sr. Dolores Castellano.

AMITYVILLE. *Brunswick Hospital* 366 Broadway, 11701. Tel: 516-789-7000; 264-0124; 842-8488. Rev. Robert A. Hyatt.
South Oaks Psychiatric Hospital Sunrise Hwy., 11701. Tel: 516-264-4000. Rev. Robert A. Hyatt, Res., Our Lady of Consolation Home, Tel: 516-598-0497.

BAY SHORE. *Southside Hospital* Montauk Hwy., 11706. Tel: 516-435-3484. Revs. Harold E. McBride, S.M.M.; Peter J. McCrann, S.M.M.

BETHPAGE. *Mid-Island Hospital* Tel: 516-520-0222. Rev. Vincent Crotty, C.S.S.R.

EAST MEADOW. *Nassau County Medical Center* 2201 Hempstead Tpke., 11554. Tel: 516-572-3195; 542-2069. Revs. Brian J. Brinker; John P. Murray; Sr. Maureen Chase.
Nassau County Police Department. Rev. Msgr. John A. Alesandro; Rev. Joseph J. D'Angelo.
Nassau County, Fire Chiefs, Council of. Rev. Vincent A. Kennedy.

GLEN COVE. *North Shore Community Hospital at Glen Cove* Tel: 516-676-5000. Rev. Henry I. Benack.

HUNTINGTON. *Huntington Hospital* 11743. Tel: 516-351-2000. Rev. Owen Shelley, O.F.M.Cap.

MANHASSET. *North Shore Univ. Hospital* 1554 Northern Blvd., 11030. Tel: 516-562-0100. Revs. Antony Xavier; Isaac Mensah, Res., North Shore Hospital, Tel: 516-562-4713.

MELVILLE. *Long Island Developmental Center* Box 788, 11747. Tel: 516-385-2700. Rev. Malachy C. Flaherty, O.F.M.Cap., Res., St. Francis of Assisi, 29 Northgate Dr., Greenlawn, 11740. Tel: 516-751-7435.

MINEOLA. *Winthrop Hospital* First St., 11501. Tel: 516-663-0333. Rev. Msgr. Eugene F. Murphy; Rev. Thomas Murphy, Res., Corpus Christi, 155 Garfield Ave., 11501-2583. Tel: 516-746-1223.

NESCONSET. *Nesconset Nursing Home*. Vacant. 11767. Tel: 516-361-8800.

NORTHPORT. *Veteran's Hospital* 11768. Tel: 516-261-4400. Revs. Eugene T. Jarcynski, C.S.C.; Charles L. Mockevicius; Augustine J. Sheehan; Gerald DiGiralamo.

OCEANSIDE. *South Nassau Communities Hospital* Tel: 516-763-2030. Deacon Charles Muscarnera.

PATCHOGUE. *Brookhaven Memorial Hospital* 100 Hospital Rd., 11772. Tel: 516-654-7100. Bro. James Maloney, O.F.M.Cap.

PLAINVIEW. *North Shore Hospital at Plainview* 888 Old Country Rd., 11083. Tel: 516-681-8900. Rev. Jose Simon Palliparambil, Res., St. Pius X, 1 St. Pius Ct., 11803-4023. Tel: 516-938-3959.

PORT JEFFERSON. *Maryhaven Center of Hope* 11777. Tel: 516-474-3400. Sr. Maryaline Zierle, O.P.
Mather Memorial Hospital 11777. Tel: 516-473-1320, Ext. 4007. Rev. Thomas Jones; Mrs. Valerie Rohrecker.
St. Charles Hospital, Port Jefferson, New York 11777. Tel: 516-474-6000. Revs. Thomas Jones; Andrew Nirrengarten; Sr. Martha Winum, D.W.; Sr. Mona Guerrette, D.W.; Sr. Josefita Rodriguez.

ROSLYN. *St. Francis Hospital* 11576. Sr. Lois Ann Van Delft, F.M.M., Dir.; Revs. Gabriel Miah; Joseph Maniangatt; Sr. Rita Sculti, O.P.; Sr. Nancy Exconde, F.M.M.; Bro. John Lesica, C.F.X.; Sr. Mari Garesche, F.M.M.; Sr. Noreen O'Malley, F.M.M.

ST. JAMES. *St. James Nursing Home* 11780. Tel: 516-862-8000. Rev. Aidan Neenan, O.F.M.Cap.

SAYVILLE. *Good Samaritan Nursing Home* 11782. Tel: 516-567-6600. Sr. Elizabeth Toohig, S.C.; Rev. Francis B. Nuss.

SMITHTOWN. *St. John Ambulatory Surgery Center* Smithtown By-Pass, Rte. 111, 11787. Tel: 516-979-9800. Deacon Fred Jackman.
St. John's Episcopal Hospital 11787. Tel: 516-360-2000. Rev. Frederick Hill, O.F.M.Cap., Res., St. Patrick, 280 E. Main St., 11787. Tel: 516-862-3000; 979-1292.

STONY BROOK. *L.I. State Veterans' Home* Tel: 516-444-8500. Rev. Charles F. Kohli.
Stony Brook University Hospital SUNY at Stony Brook, 11790. Tel: 516-444-2765. Revs. John Keegan, M.M.; Anthony Ewherido; Sr. Marjorie Devlin.

UNIONDALE. *Holly Patterson Geriatric Center* 875 Jerusalem Ave., 11553. Tel: 516-572-1500. Revs. Michael Reid; John H. McCabe, Res., Holy Trinity High School, Hicksville. Tel: 516-433-2900.

VALLEY STREAM. *Franklin Medical Center Hospital* 11580. Tel: 516-256-6000. Rev. Francis Odufuye; Mrs. Carol Breslin, Res., St. Boniface Rectory, 631 Elmont Rd., Elmont, 11003-4028. Tel: 516-825-8800.

WEST BRENTWOOD. *Pilgrim Psychiatric Center* P.O. Box A, 11717. Tel: 516-434-5134. Rev. Lawrence J. O'Leary; Sr. Mary Summerville, C.S.J.; Rev. John P. Halpin.

WEST ISLIP. *Consolation Nursing Home* 11795. Tel: 516-587-1600. Rev. Robert A. Hyatt; Sr. M. Alicia Lanni, O.P.
Good Samaritan Hospital Medical Center 11795. Tel: 516-376-3000. Revs. Lawrence Bellew, C.P.; Bernard M. Blood, S.M.M.; Vincent P. Cunningham, S.M.M.; Paul Dahn; Sr. Gertrude O'Brien, D.W.; Sr. Ellen Moore, O.P.; Sr. Felicia Moore, R.G.S.; Sr. Betty Keegan, F.M.M.,
Good Samaritan Hospice Program, 175 Beach Dr., 11795. Tel: 516-376-3850. Sr. Dorothy Monks; Sr. Joyce Osgood.

Prison Ministry

DEER PARK. *Office of Prison Ministry and Criminal Justice Affairs* 1767 Deer Park Ave., 11729. Tel: 516-242-8631. Bro. John Moylan, O.S.F., Pastoral Team.

HICKSVILLE. *Nassau County Correctional Center*. Vacant. C.S. 1072, 11802. Tel: 516-572-4145; 572-3621.

RIVERHEAD. *Suffolk County Correctional Facility*. Vacant. One Center Dr., 11901. Tel: 516-852-2294.

YAPHANK. *Suffolk County Minimum Security Facility*. Vacant. Box 69, 11980. Tel: 516-852-4713.

Absent on Leave:
Reverend Fathers—
Ball, Matthew J.
Dillon, John
Flaherty, Kevin S.
Gabriele, John J.
Gress, Warren
Hart, James
Heenan, Michael F.
Houghton, Timothy
Huneke, Robert D.
Lennon, Charles
Mann, Peter
McDonnell, Stephen
Meyer, John D.
Morrelly, Leonard
Passamonte, Philip B.
Petriano, Thomas

Priests Released from Diocesan Assignment:
Reverend Monsignors—
Maniscalco, Francis

Reverend Fathers—
Alarcon, Felix
Bogert, James
Bowman, James
Carlo, Raymond
DeVita, Thomas F.
Duvelsdorf, Peter L.
Ehrhart, Charles, Chap. Major
Gallagher, William G.
Hanson, Donald M.
Mahoney, John F.
McMullen, Francis R.
Miraglia, Salvatore J.
Morris, Stephen P.
Newman, Louis I.
Trapani, Anthony, Lt., CHC, USNR
Viladesau, Richard R.
Walsh, Kevin

Military Chaplains:
Reverend Fathers—
Bowman, James C.
Erhart, Charles M., U.S.M.C.A.-N.B.G.
Trapini, Anthony

Graduate Studies:
Reverend Monsignors—
Sweeny, Edward, St. Paul's, Ottawa, Canada
Reverend Fathers—
Miller, James C., Catholic University, Washington, DC
Pereda, James F., Rome, Italy

Sick Leave:
Reverend Monsignors—
Mott, John D.
Reverend Fathers—
Hagan, Vincent
Joseph, Ramon A.
Quesada, Manuel
Staiger, Charles

Retired:
Reverend Monsignors—
Ballweg, Lawrence
Bermingham, Charles E.
Chiara, Peter A.
Coffey, James F.
Colligan, Joseph F.
Collins, James E.
Costello, Lawrence D.
Cwalina, John F.
Flynn, Martin J.
Glimm, Francis X.
Goggin, Leo J.
Hendel, Richard P.
Huntington, Christopher
Kane, Arthur J.
Kirwin, Robert J.
Lawlor, Joseph F.
Margiotta, Vincent S.
McCarren, Edgar P.
Potterton, Daniel J.
Rooney, Thaddeus
Soave, Alfred
Stegmann, Raymond V.
Villar, Demetrio
Wiest, John J.
Reverend Fathers—
Barry, Ronald
Branigan, Patrick G.
Brendel, John A.
Buckley, Harold P.
Byrne, John J.
Casey, Francis M.
Collins, Edwin
Corali, Serafino A.
Cser, Ladislaus, S.J.
Curley, Robert
Curry, Thomas P.
Daley, John T.
De Vita, James C.
Delaney, William I.
Dolan, James J.
Drab, John
Farley, David G.
Flaherty, Malachy, O.F.M.Cap.
Flaherty, William H.
Flynn, Edward J.
Gallagher, Andrew J.
Gartner, Charles A.
Gfroerer, Gerard J.
Gorman, John J.
Govern, William H.
Hall, Martin
Harrer, Frederic J.
Henesy, William
Henry, John P.
Hourihane, Francis
Kayser, Robert
Kennedy, Vincent A.
Korycki, Walter R.
Kozlowski, Joseph P.
LeTure, Theodore J.
Loy, Vincent P.
McGlade, Thomas F.
McManus, Eugene J.
Meade, James C.
Mockevicius, Charles L.
Monteleone, Raphael D.
Muhs, Edward J.
Mullen, John J.
Murphy, William T.
Murray, John E.
Navarroli, Frederick
O'Brien, Denis J.
O'Farrell, Michael J.
Osborne, Martin J.
Pai, Simon
Parrini, Warren
Pazo, John T.
Power, Virgil
Powers, Vincent J.
Reehil, Philip J.
Reidy, Martin F.
Reuss, Louis L.
Scanlon, Richard M.
Serrano, John J.
Shanahan, Edward J.
Sheehan, Lawrence A., S.J.
Singleton, William
Sledzaus, Alexander L.
Spinner, Hubert
Swiatocha, Bruno
Tortora, Raymond
Traynor, John
Vitsas, John P.
Wickman, Robert
Wilutis, John P.
Wodziak, Michael
Yang, Paul

Permanent Deacons:
Acquafredda, Patrick, St. Joseph, Hewlett
Altonji, James F., St. Joseph, Ronkonkoma
Alvarado, Jesus, St. Anne, Brentwood
Ashe, James C., Our Lady of Poland, Southampton
Barone, Frank D., St. Kilian, Farmingdale
Barry, Richard C., Our Lady of Lourdes, West Islip
Bartolotto, Joseph T., St. Louis De Montfort, Sound Beach
Bast, Thomas J., St. Frances de Chantal, Wantagh
Bedell, Paul, St. Barnabas Apostle, Bellmore
Beirne, James G., St. James, Seaford
Bennettson, Donald W., St. Joseph's, Kings Park
Biggin, James A., St. Martin of Tours, Bethpage
Billia, Edward W., St. Hugh of Lincoln, Huntington Station
Blake, Richard T., St. Aidan, Williston Park
Bohuslaw, James, St. John Nepomucene, Bohemia
Bono, Frank J., St. Joachim, Cedarhurst
Bopp, John T., Sacred Heart, Cutchogue
Bowe, Martin J., St. John the Evangelist, Riverhead
Braun, Robert G., St. Anthony of Padua, East Northport
Brennan, William V., St. William the Abbot, Seaford
Brown, Charles, SS. Philip & James, St. James
Broyles, Robert, St. Bridgid, Westbury
Buchenberger, Thomas E., St. William the Abbot, Seaford
Burkart, John F., St. Philip Neri, Northport
Burnham, Bruce A., Our Holy Redeemer, Freeport
Byrne, William F., St. Brigid, Westbury
Cales, Francisco, Our Holy Redeemer, Freeport
Campbell, Robert, St. Raymond, East Rockaway
Capobianco, Eugene, St. Martin of Tours, Bethpage
Case, Edward M., St. Mary, Roslyn
Cavallaro, John, Outreach Project, Brentwood
Cedrone, Anthony M., Blessed Sacrament, Valley Stream
Cepeda, Jose A., Our Lady of Assumption, Copiague
Coates, Gerard, St. James, Setauket
Coleman, Thomas, St. Barnabas the Apostle, Bellmore
Connolly, George P., Our Lady of Perpetual Help, Lindenhurst
Costello, Thomas P., St. Joseph, Hewlett
Cotone, Louis, St. Kilian, Farmingdale
Cove, Francis K., Our Lady of Lourdes, Malverne
Crivello, Frank, Sts. Philip & James, St. James
Cunningham, Edward F., St. Anne, Garden City
Cuseo, Anthony W., Holy Name of Mary, Valley Stream
D'Angelo, Gregory R., St. Raymond, East Rockaway
DeBellis, Michael J., St. Joseph, Ronkonkoma
Deignan, Thomas F., SS. Cyril and Methodius, Deer Park
Dejewski, Robert, St. John the Evangelist, Riverhead
Delargy, Daniel, Sacred Heart, North Merrick
Determann, Herman J., St. Aidan, Williston Park
Diaz, Juan, St. Anne, Brentwood
Diaz-Granados, Francisco, St. Francis de Sales, Patchogue
DiGiovanna, James R., St. Catherine of Siena, Franklin Square
DiGiuseppe, Peter A., Our Lady Grace, West Babylon
DiVita, Thomas, St. Vincent de Paul, Elmont
Donovan, Donald T., St. Mark, Shoreham
Donza, Gaetano, St. Raymond, East Rockaway
Dooling, Arthur J., Mary Immaculate, Bellport
Dougherty, Joseph M., St. Joseph, Ronkonkoma
Duggan, Martin, St. Anthony of Padua, East Northport
Dunlop, John P., St. Mary of the Isle, Long Beach
Dunne, James A., Our Holy Redeemer, Freeport
Erdman, John P., St. Joseph, Ronkonkoma
Evers, Jeffrey, SS. Cyril & Methodius, Deer Park
Falls, John D., St. Brigid, Westbury
Ferri, Richard, St. Martin of Tours, Amityville
Finter, Frederick E., St. John the Baptist, Wading River
Flannery, James W., St. Anthony, Oceanside
Flood, Frank J., St. Rose of Lima, Massapequa
Fodale, John E., St. Catherine of Siena, Franklin Square
Forbes, Thomas J., St. Rose of Lima, Massapequa
Fullam, William F., Jr., St. Lawrence the Martyr, Sayville
Gagnon, Jules O. A., St. Patrick, Huntington
Gargiulo, Andrew T., Our Lady of Perpetual Help, Lindenhurst
Gariboldi, Frank, St. Matthew, Dix Hills
Gaudioso, Robert, St. Elizabeth Ann Seton, Lake Ronkonkoma
Gerace, Patrick C., Infant Jesus, Port Jefferson
Giambalvo, Anthony M., Ss. Cyril and Methodius, Deer Park
Gillen, Thomas J., St. Jude's, Mastic Beach
Gillette, Ronald J., St. John of God, Central Islip
Giraldo, Luis D., St. Jude, Mastic Beach
Graff, Charles J., Our Lady of Grace, West Babylon
Gronenthal, Robert W., Our Lady of Snow, Blue Point
Gross, Thomas A., Jr., St. Jude, Mastic Beach
Guntert, Joseph F., Ss. Peter and Paul, Manorville
Hammel, Lawrence V., Our Lady of Hope, Carle Place
Hartmann, Frank C., Our Lady of the Snow, Bluepoint
Heintz, Robert, St. Hyacinth, Glen Head
Hernandez, Robert, Good Shepherd, Holbrook
Heschl, Robert J., Sts. Philip & James, St. James
Hickey, John, Our Lady of Hope, Carle Place
Huber, Charles F., SS. Cyril & Methodius, Deer Park
Ingulli, Joseph, St. James, Setauket
Jackman, Frederick, St. Patrick, Smithtown
Johnston, Richard J., St. Elizabeth, Melville
Kogler, William E., St. Margaret of Scotland, Selden
Kramer, Steven L., Our Lady of the Snow, Blue Point
Lamb, Richard W., Our Lady of the Miraculous Medal, Wyandanch
LaRossa, Richard W., St. Raymond, East Rockaway
Leahy, John G., St. James, Seaford
Lewis, Clinton, St. Martha, Uniondale
Leyden, Michael J., St. Joseph, Babylon
Logsdon, Patrick B., Queen of the Most Holy Rosary, Roosevelt
Longo, Allan D., St. Francis of Assisi, Greenlawn
Lovett, John J., St. John the Evangelist, Riverhead
Luken, Richard A., St. Luke, Brentwood
Macellaro, Daniel A., Resurrection, Farmingdale
Maffeo, Joseph R., St. Joseph, Ronkonkoma
Maher, Kenneth, SS. Philip & James, St. James
Mahoney, Michael A., St. Patrick, Bay Shore
Marino, Salvatore A., Blessed Sacrament, Valley Stream
Maro, Robert R., St. Patrick, Huntington
Matheis, Felix J., St. Brigid, Westbury
McDaid, Thomas P., St. Agnes, Rockville Centre
McGaffney, Gilbert, Notre Dame, New Hyde Park
McGauvran, John W., Sacred Hearts of Jesus and Mary, Southampton
McGowan, John, St. Anne, Garden City
McGuinness, Francis B., St. Rose of Lima, Massapequa
McGuirk, Eugene G., St. Hedwig, Floral Park
McIndoe, Martin B., St. Francis de Sales, Patchogue
McKenna, Michael A., St. Boniface, Elmont
McQuade, James J., St. Matthew, Dix Hills
Mercolino, Joseph T., St. Elizabeth, Melville
Metzdorff, Michael C., St. William the Abbot, Seaford
Micucci, Raymond R., St. Boniface, Elmont
Mildeberger, William H., Jr., St. Boniface, Elmont

Montesano, Joseph A., Our Lady Queen of Martyrs, Centerport
Morris, James P., St. Brigid, Westbury
Morrow, John W., Our Lady of Grace, West Babylon
Mulligan, Lawrence P., Our Lady of Victory, Floral Park
Muratore, Biagio V., St. Margaret of Scotland, Selden
Murphy, Galvin C., St. John the Evangelist, Center Moriches
Muscarnera, Charles, St. Christopher, Baldwin
Mystkowski, Joseph J., Our Lady of Mt. Carmel, Patchogue
Naylor, Montford D., St. Louis de Montfort, Sound Beach
O'Connor, Dennis R., St. Rose of Lima, Massapequa
O'Connor, Thomas F., St. Gerard Majella, Port Jefferson Station
O'Donovan, Robert S., St. Frances de Chantal, Wantagh
Odin, Frank A., Our Lady Perpetual Help, Lindenhurst
Owens, Thomas F., St. James, Setauket
Pagnotta, Carmen, St. Frances Cabrini, Coram
Pankus, Alfred, St. Thomas More, Hauppauge
Paolicelli, Philip, St. Margaret of Scotland, Selden
Pellegrino, Joseph C., St. Christopher, Baldwin
Peralta, Joseph F., St. Patrick, Bay Shore
Pettorino, John C., SS. Peter and Paul, Manorville
Powers, William J., Infant Jesus, Port Jefferson
Quaranta, Arnold T., St. Matthew, Dix Hills
Quinn, Thomas J., St. Rose of Lima, Massapequa
Quinones, Fernando J., St. Francis de Sales, Patchogue
Rasanen, Terence A., St. Anne, Brentwood
Reilly, Thomas J., St. Hugh of Lincoln, Huntington Station
Reinhart, John C., Corpus Christi, Mineola
Rich, Thomas B., Our Lady of Hope, Carle Place
Riegger, George J., St. Sylvester, Medford
Rivera, Wenceslao, St. Luke, Brentwood
Roa, Jose, Our Lady of Loretto, Hempstead
Rodenburg, Herman I., St. Kilian, Farmingdale
Roettinger, Francis P., St. Sylvester, Medford
Samson, Thomas R., St. Anne, Brentwood
Sandberg, Louis C., Queen of the Most Holy Rosary, Roosevelt
Sanders, Richard W., St. Patrick's, Smithtown
Schneider, Andrew M., St. Philip Neri, Northport
Schultz, Peter F., St. Louis de Montfort, Sound Beach
Scollan, Joseph M., St. Margaret of Scotland, Selden
Senholzi, Gregory B., St. John the Baptist, Wading River
Sherlock, Bernard F., St. Barnabas Apostle, Bellmore
Shortell, Michael V., St. Martha, Uniondale
Smith, Edward W., St. Lawrence the Martyr, Sayville
Smith, Robert, St. Rosalie, Hampton Bays
Smyth, Vincent P., St. Agnes, Rockville Centre
Squiteri, Aniello, Our Lady of Peace, Lynbrook
Stampfli, William J., St. Martin of Tours, Amityville
Sullivan, John F., St. Joseph, Babylon
Sullivan, Kenneth R., St. Martha, Uniondale
Swane, Gary, St. Louis de Montfort, Sound Beach
Taranto, Vito, St. Hugh, Huntington Station
Taylor, Bernard H., Our Lady Miraculous Medal, Wyandanch
Teufel, John G., Our Lady of Lourdes, West Islip
Tirelli, Raymond J., Our Lady of Hope, Carle Place
Trodden, John E., St. Luke, Brentwood
Valdaro, Dominick, Our Lady Lourdes, Massapequa Park
Vargas, Daniel E., Our Lady of Assumption, Copiague
Vigliotta, Albert C., St. Mark, Shoreham
Vigliotta, Crescenzo T., St. John the Evangelist, Center Moriches
Villani, Salvatore B., St. Aidan, Williston Park
Waldmann, Richard E., Infant Jesus, Port Jefferson
Walsh, Robert P., Mercy Hospital, Rockville Centre
Weigel, John A., Maria Regina, Seaford
Weisz, Robert D., St. Thomas More, Hauppauge
Wetzel, Edward V., St. Martin of Tours, Amityville
Whitfield, Gerard F., Maria Regina, Seaford
Williams, Walter B., Jr., Resurrection, Farmingville
Wilson, Gerard R., St. Mary, East Islip
Zirkel, Donald E., St. Kilians, Farmingdale

INSTITUTIONS LOCATED IN THE DIOCESE

[A] SEMINARIES, DIOCESAN

HUNTINGTON. *Diocesan Seminary of the Immaculate Conception*, 440 West Neck Rd., 11743. Tel: 516-423-0483; Fax: 516-423-2346. Most Rev. John R. McGann, D.D., Chm., Board of Governors; Rev. Msgr. Vincent F. Fullam, J.D. (BRK), Rector; Revs. Robert J. Smith, S.T.L.; S.T.D., Vice Rector & Academic Dean; Edward R. D'Andrea, M.Div., Dir. Spiritual Formation; Thomas M. Fusco, M.Div., Dir. Pastoral Formation & Dean of Seminarians; Sr. Kieran Hartigan, R.S.M., P.D., Assoc. Dean; Jiri Lipa, Ph.D., Library Dir.; Mrs. Bernadette M. Grodman, Business Officer; Mrs. Joan Innvar, Registrar; Revs. William T. Donavan, S.T.B.; Roland Faley, T.O.R., S.T.D., Moderator of Liturgy; Joseph R. Gibino, Ph.D. (BRK); Katherine M. Hayes, Ph.D.; Rev. Gerard H. Luttenberger, C.M., S.T.D.; Sr. Maria Pascuzzi, C.S.J., S.S.L., S.T.D.; Sr. Mary Alice Piil, C.S.J., Ph.D.; Rev. Peter I. Vaccari, S.T.L. (BRK). Priests 9; Sisters 3; Lay Professor 1; Seminarians 43; M.A. Students 101; D.Min. Students 10.

[B] COLLEGES AND UNIVERSITIES

ROCKVILLE CENTRE. *Molloy College*, 1000 Hempstead Ave., 11571-5002. Tel: 516-678-5000; 888-4-MOLLOY.
Web site: http://molloy.edu
For a complete listing, refer to the Colleges and Universities section.

PATCHOGUE. *St. Joseph's College*, 155 W. Roe Blvd., 11772-2399. Tel: 516-447-3200; Fax: 516-654-1782
For a complete listing, refer to the Colleges and Universities section.

[C] HIGH SCHOOLS, DIOCESAN

NASSAU COUNTY

HICKSVILLE. *Holy Trinity*, 98 Cherry Ln., 11801. Tel: 516-433-2900. Mr. James J. Boglioli, Prin.; Rev. Joseph J. Nixon, Chap. In res. Rev. Msgr. Thomas J. Hartman; Revs. John H. McCabe; Michael Reid. Sisters 13; Lay Teachers 80; Students 1,500.

SUFFOLK COUNTY

WEST ISLIP. *St. John the Baptist*, 1170 Montauk Hwy., 11795. Tel: 516-587-8000. Walter D. Lace, Prin.; Rev. James C. Vlaun, Chap. Sisters 14; Priests 2; Lay Teachers 57; Students 925.

[D] HIGH SCHOOLS, PRIVATE

BRENTWOOD. *Academy of St. Joseph.* Independent; (Coed school grades PreK-6; Girl's school grades 7-12), Brentwood Rd., 11717. Tel: 516-273-2406; 273-4023; Fax: 516-231-4155. Directed by the Sisters of St. Joseph. Sr. Valerie Scholl, C.S.J., Dir.; Sr. Joanne Forker, C.S.J., Prin. Sisters of St. Joseph 20; Lay Teachers 33; Students 450.

HEMPSTEAD. *Sacred Heart Academy.* College preparatory-girls, 47 Cathedral Ave., 11550. Tel: 516-483-7383; Fax: 516-483-1016.
E-mail: sha@li.net
Web site: www.li.net/~sha
Sr. Jeanne Marie Ross, C.S.J., Prin. Sisters 22; Lay Teachers 53; Students 812.

MINEOLA. *Chaminade High School (Boys).* Directed by the Society of Mary (Marianists), 11501. Tel: 516-742-5555.
E-mail: flyers@iii.com
Web site: http://www.chaminade-hs.org
Bros. George E. Endres, S.M., Pres.; Michael J. McAward, S.M., Prin.; Mr. Salvatore Trentacoste, Asst. Prin.; Bros. Michael J. Gillen, S.M., Dir. Guidance; Thomas J. Cleary, S.M., Dean of Students; James W. Conway, S.M., Dir. Student Svcs.; Rev. Garrett J. Long, S.M., Chap. Brothers 20; Priests 3; Lay Teachers 49; Students 1,600.

OAKDALE. *LaSalle, A Global Learning Community.* (Grades PreK-12), 500 Montauk Hwy., 11769. Tel: 516-589-0900; Fax: 516-589-1830. Directed by the De La Salle Christian Brothers. Mr. Donald Puleio, Comptroller; Rosemary Barone, Dir. of Admissions. Brothers 11; Sisters 2; Lay Teachers 40; Students: Upper School 285; Middle School 65; Primary School 175; Pre-School 60.

RIVERHEAD. *Mercy High School.* (Coed), 1225 Ostrander Ave., 11901. Tel: 516-727-5900.
E-mail: mercy@northeast.com
Directed by the Sisters of Mercy. Sr. Mary Elaine, R.S.M., Prin.; Mr. Thomas Taylor, R.S.M., Dean of Students; Sr. Mary Christi, R.S.M., Asst. Prin. Sisters of Mercy (Brooklyn) 13; Other Sisters 3; Lay Teachers 27; Students 375.

SOUTH HUNTINGTON. *St. Anthony's High School.* College Prep. 275 Wolf Hill Rd., 11747-1394. Tel: 516-271-2020. Directed by the Franciscan Brothers of Brooklyn. Bro. Shane Burke, O.S.F., Ed.D., Prin. Brothers 21; Priests 1; Intercommunity Sisters 14; Lay Teachers 92; Students 2,200.

SYOSSET. *Our Lady of Mercy Academy.* Girls-day students. 815 Convent Rd., 11791. Tel: 516-921-1047. Directed by the Sisters of Mercy. Sr. Virginia Bertschi, R.S.M., Prin. Sisters of Mercy 15; Lay Teachers 26; Students 405.

UNIONDALE. *Kellenberg Memorial High School*, 1400 Glenn Curtiss Blvd., 11553.
E-mail: kmhs@li.net
Web site: www.kellenberg.org
Directed by the Society of Mary. Rev. Philip K. Eichner, S.M., Pres.; Bros. Kenneth M. Hoagland, S.M., Prin.; Richard Hughes, Asst. Prin. Academics; Mr. Kenneth Conrade, Asst. Prin. Admissions; Rev. Albert Bertoni, S.M., Asst. Prin. Guidance; Ms. Maria Korzekwinski, Asst. Prin. Latin School; Bro. Roger Poletti, S.M., Asst. Prin. Activities; Rev. Thomas A. Cardone, S.M., Chap.; Mrs. Marina Trentacoste, Dean of Students; Mr. Edward Solosky, Dean of Men; Mr. Kevin A. Hearn, Athletic Dir.; Mr. Richard Kotlarz, Supvr. of Building Maintenance and Landscaping; Bro. Donald Nussbaum, S.M.; Mr. James Jones, Supvr. Cleaning Maintenance; Mrs. Catherine Zabrouski, Financial Supvr. Priests 3; Brothers 8; Lay Teachers 73; Students 1,700.

[E] REGIONAL SCHOOLS

BELLMORE. *St. Elizabeth Ann Seton Regional School.* Supported by the following parishes: St. Barnabas, Bellmore; St. Raphael, East Meadow; Cure of Ars, Merrick; St. Frances de Chantal, Wantagh.
Bellmore Campus, 2341 Washington Ave., 11710. Tel: 516-785-5709. Dr. Eileen Kilbride, Prin. Sisters 1; Lay Teachers 24; Students 560.
East Meadow Campus, 600 Newbridge Ave., East Meadow, 11554. Tel: 516-785-7006. Sr. William Noreen, S.C.H., Prin. Sisters 4; Lay Teachers 24; Students 550.

BETHPAGE. *St. John Baptist de LaSalle Regional School.*
E-mail: Lasallet@aol.com
Supported by the following parishes: St. Martin of Tours, Bethpage; St. Kilian, Farmingdale; St. Pius X, Plainview; St. James, Seaford.
Bethpage Campus, Central Ave., 11714. Tel: 516-931-0983. Dr. Victor Lana, Headmaster. Lay Teachers 20; Students 298.
Farmingdale Campus, 50 Cherry St., Farmingdale, 11735. Tel: 516-694-3610. Mrs. Susan Anaischik, Prin. Sisters 1; Lay Teachers 25; Students 395.

CENTER MORICHES. *Our Lady, Queen of Apostles Regional School*, 2 St. Johns Pl., 11934. Tel: 516-878-1033. Sr. Eileen Martin, S.C., Prin. Lay Teachers 16; Students 342. Supported by the following parishes: St. John Evangelist, Center Moriches; St. Jude, Mastic Beach; Immaculate Conception, Westhampton Beach; Ss. Peter & Paul, Manorville.

CENTRAL ISLIP. *Our Lady of Providence Regional School*, 82 Carleton Ave., 11722. Tel: 516-234-1113; 234-6324; Fax: 516-234-6360. Sr. Judith Burchyns, C.S.J., Prin.-Upper School; Sr. Stephen Mary Puglisi, C.S.J., Prin.-Lower School. Sisters 4; Lay Teachers 30; Students 620. Supported by the following parishes: St. Anne, Brentwood; St. Luke, Brentwood; St. John of God, Central Islip; St. Peter the Apostle, Islip Terrace.

COMMACK. *Holy Family Regional School*, Indian Head Rd., P.O. Box 729, 11725. Tel: 516-543-0202. Ms. Agatha Cavoli, Prin. Sisters 4; Lay Teachers 17; Students 445. Supported by the following parishes: Christ the King, Commack; St. Matthew, Dix Hills; St. Thomas More, Hauppauge; St. Joseph, Kings Park.

CUTCHOGUE. *Our Lady of Mercy Regional School*, P.O. Box 970 - Main St., 11935. Tel: 516-734-5166. Sr. Mary Christi, Prin. Lay Teachers 8; Students 144. Supported by the following parishes: Sacred Heart, Cutchogue; Our Lady of Ostrabrama, Cutchogue; St. Agnes, Greenport; and St. Patrick, Southold.

EAST NORTHPORT. *Trinity Regional School*, 1025 Fifth Ave., 11731. Tel: 516-261-5130. Ms. Jeanne Morcone, Prin. Sisters 6; Lay Teachers 40; Students 850. Supported by the following parishes: Our Lady Queen of Martyrs, Centerport; St. Anthony of Padua, East Northport; St. Francis of Assisi, Greenlawn; St. Hugh of Lincoln, Huntington Station; St. Elizabeth, Melville; St. Philip Neri, Northport.
Satellite campuses exist at: 1450 New York Ave., Huntington Station, 11746. Tel: 516-549-7450. 364 Main St., Northport, 11768. Tel: 516-261-8520.

GLEN COVE. *All Saints Regional Catholic School*, 12 Pearsall Ave., 11542-3052. Tel: 516-676-0762. Sisters 1; Lay Teachers 25; Students 388. Supported by the following parishes: St. Boniface, Sea Cliff; St. Hyacinth, Glen Head; St. Mary, Roslyn; St. Patrick, Glen Cove; St. Rocco, Glen Cove.
Primary School. (Grades Nursery-3), 319 Cedar Swamp Rd., Glen Head, 11545-2298. Tel: 516-671-3033.
Upper Campus. (Grades 4-8), 12 Pearsall Ave., 11542-3052. Tel: 516-676-0762. Sr. Maureen Vellon, R.S.H.M., Prin.

LONG BEACH. *Long Beach Catholic Regional School.* (Grades PreK-8), 735 W. Broadway, 11561. Tel:

516-432-8900. Sr. Patricia Koehler, O.P., Prin. Sisters 3; Lay Teachers 19; Students 389. Supported by the following parishes: St. Ignatius, Long Beach; St. Mary of the Isle, Long Beach, and Our Lady of the Miraculous Medal, Point Lookout.

PATCHOGUE. *Holy Angels Regional School.* (Grades K-8), Division St., 11772. Tel: 516-475-0422.
E-mail: angels@li.net
Sr. Elise Bier, R.S.M., Prin. Sisters 2; Lay Teachers 15; Students 380. Supported by the following parishes: Mary Immaculate, Bellport; St. Frances Cabrini, Coram; St. Joseph the Worker, E. Patchogue; St. Sylvester, Medford; Our Lady of Mount Carmel, Patchogue; St. Frances de Sales, Patchogue, and St. Margaret of Scotland, Selden.

PORT JEFFERSON. *Our Lady of Wisdom Regional School,* 114-116 Myrtle Ave., 11777. Tel: 516-473-1211. Mrs. Angela Orofino, Prin. Lay Teachers 18; Students 323. Supported by the following parishes: Infant Jesus, Port Jefferson; St. Louis de Montfort, Sound Beach; St. James, Setauket; St. Gerard Majella, Port Jefferson Station.

SAG HARBOR. *Stella Maris Regional School,* Division St., 11963. Tel: 516-725-2525. Judith Curtin, Prin. Sisters 2; Lay Teachers 22; Students 250. Supported by the following parishes: St. Therese of Lisieux, Montauk; Most Holy Trinity, East Hampton; St. Andrew, Sag Harbor; Queen of the Most Holy Rosary, Bridgehampton; Our Lady of the Isle, Shelter Island.

SAYVILLE. *Prince of Peace Regional School,* 200 Main St., 11782. Tel: 516-589-3426. Sr. Mary Kelly, S.S.N.D., Prin. Sisters 2; Lay Teachers 14; Students 325. Supported by the following parishes: Our Lady of Snow, Blue Point; St. John Nepomucene, Bohemia; Good Shepherd, Holbrook; St. Lawrence, Sayville.

SOUTHAMPTON. *Our Lady of the Hamptons Regional School.* (Grades K-8), 160 N. Main St., 11968. Tel: 516-283-9140.
E-mail: olh@hamptons.com
Web site: http://www.webhampton.com/olh
31 Montauk Hwy., Hampton Bays, 11946. Tel: 516-723-3740. Nursery and PreK. Sr. Kathryn Schlueter, C.S.J., Prin. Sisters 3; Lay Teachers 17; Students 379. Supported by the following parishes: St. Rosalie, Hampton Bays; Our Lady of Poland, Southampton, and Sacred Hearts Jesus Mary, Southampton.

UNIONDALE. *St. Martin de Porres Regional School,* 530 Hempstead Blvd., 11553. Tel: 516-481-3303. Lay Teachers 20; Students 315. Supported by the following parishes: Our Lady of Loretto, Hempstead; St. Ladislaus, Hempstead; St. Martha, Uniondale.

[F] ELEMENTARY SCHOOLS, PRIVATE

MANHASSET. *Our Lady of Grace Montessori School and Center.* (Grades PreK-1), 29 Shelter Rock Rd., 11030. Tel: 516-365-9832; Fax: 516-365-9329. Sisters, Servants of the Immaculate Heart of Mary 5; Lay Teachers 13; Students 200.

OLD WESTBURY. *Old Westbury School of the Holy Child.* (Grades PreK-8), 25 Store Hill Rd., 11568. Tel: 516-626-9300. Mrs. Grace Cavallo, Head of School; Beth Ann Raymond, Dir. Upper Grades; Gail Walker, Dir. Lower Grades. Lay Teachers 26; Students 170.

[G] SPECIALIZED CHILD CARE AGENCIES

NESCONSET. *Cleary Deaf Child Center, Inc.,* 301 Smithtown Blvd., 11767. Tel: 516-588-0530 (Voice and TTY); Fax: 516-588-0016.
E-mail: CatherineF@ClearySchool.org
For a complete listing, refer to the Special Care Facilities section.

PORT JEFFERSON. *Maryhaven Center of Hope,* Myrtle Ave., 11777. Tel: 516-474-4100; Fax: 516-474-4110
For a complete listing, refer to the Special Care Facilities section.

SYOSSET. *St. Mary's Children and Family Services,* 525 Convent Rd., 11791-3864. Tel: 516-921-0808
For a complete listing, refer to the Special Care Facilities section.

WADING RIVER. *Little Flower Children's Services of New York,* 11792. Tel: 516-929-6200
For a complete listing, refer to the Special Care Facilities section.

[H] CATHOLIC CHARITIES

HICKSVILLE. *Catholic Charities Central Administration,* 90 Cherry Ln., 11801-6299. Tel: 516-733-7000; Fax: 516-733-7099. Rev. Msgr. John D. Gilmartin, Ph.D., Diocesan Dir. Tel: 516-733-7013; Laura A. Cassell, Chief Operating Officer. Tel: 516-733-7012; David P. Nelson, Chief Ministries Officer & Dir. Parish Social Min. Tel: 516-789-5230; William McNamara, Special Asst. Tel: 516-733-7023; Daniel J. Keane, Special Asst. Tel: 516-733-7093; Jerry O'Sullivan, Dir. Finance. Tel: 516-733-7015; Michael S. H. Young, Dir. Admin./Aids Services. Tel: 516-733-7040; Ann Russo, Dir. Behavioural Health Services. Tel: 516-623-4305; Robert A. Murphy, Dir. Housing. Tel: 516-733-7075; Paul Engelhart, Dir. Public Affirs & Development. Tel: 516-733-7084; Sr. Geraldine Bowes, O.P., Dir. Human Services. Tel: 516-789-9550; James E. Claffey, Dir. Immigrant Services. Tel: 516-789-5224; Rev. John W. White, Dir. Education & Training. Tel: 516-733-7044.

Administrative Services, 90 Cherry Ln., 11801-6299. Tel: 516-733-7000. Edward Moore, Human Resource Admin. Tel: 516-733-7005; Carol Ann Radziewicz, Human Resource Coord. Tel: 516-733-7005; Robert J. Manfredi, MIS Admin. Tel: 516-733-7003; John Gonta, Purchasing/Facilities Admin. Tel: 516-733-7090.

Finance, 90 Cherry Ln., 11801-6299. Tel: 516-733-7000. Jo Ann Parda, Financial Admin. Tel: 516-733-7017; Maureen Angelillo, Payroll Mgr. Tel: 516-733-7030.

Behavioral Health Services, 333 N. Main St., Freeport, 11520. Tel: 516-623-7400.

Office of Mental Health Residences. Tel: 516-665-5092. Esther Lowengart, Program Coord.
Residence for people who are psychiatrically impaired:

Siena Residence, 12 Mechanicsville Rd., Bay Shore, 11706. Tel: 516-968-8807. Anita Dimatteo, Contact.
Residences for children who are seriously emotionally disturbed:

Teaching Family Home Program. 759 Stewart Ave., Bethpage, 11714. Tel: 516-938-2338. Bobby & April Walsh, Contacts, 4 Pleasant Ave., Farmingdale, 11735. Tel: 516-293-3153. Toinette & Tony Wheeler, Contacts, 2280 Sunrise Hwy., 11751. Tel: 516-581-6760. Mary & Bill Toomey, Contacts.

Maternity Services, 29 Kirkwood Ave., Merrick, 11566. Tel: 516-223-7888. Sr. Lesley Block, Prog. Mgr.

Mentoring of Moms/Case Management, 29 Kirkwood Ave., Merrick, 11566. Tel: 516-223-7888. Gudelia Miranda, Case Mgmt. Contact; Carole Hendler, Mentoring for Moms Contact.
Residence for Pregnant Women:

Regina Residence, 29 Kirkwood Ave., Merrick, 11566. Tel: 516-223-7888. Sr. Leslie Block, Contact.
Residence for Mothers and Babies:

Malta House, 39 Spruce St., Brentwood, 11717. Tel: 516-223-7888.

Alcohol & Substance Abuse Services, 155 Indian Head Rd., Commack, 11725. Tel: 516-543-6200. Kathleen Ayers, Program Admin.
Outpatient Clinics: P.O. Box 156, 119 Main St., Bridgehampton, 11932. Tel: 516-537-1159. Wayne Cavaliere, Contact, 155 Indian Head Rd., Commack, 11725. Tel: 516-543-6200. Simone Tomassoni, Contact, Talbot House Alcohol Crisis Center, 30-C Carlough Rd., Bohemia, 11716. Tel: 516-589-4144. Robert Howard, Contact.

Mental Health Services, 333 N. Main St., Freeport, 11520. Tel: 516-623-7400. Ann Russo, Dir. Tel: 516-623-7400.
Community Support Services (For deinstitutionalized people with chronic mental illness): 269 W. Main St., Bay Shore, 11706. Tel: 516-665-5320. Kate Bishop, Contact, 1729 N. Ocean Ave., Medford, 11763. Tel: 516-654-2944. Denis Demers, Contact.
Mental Health Clinics (Suffolk): 29 Fourth Ave., Bay Shore, 11706. Tel: 516-665-6707. Adelaide Corvelle, Contact, 1727 N. Ocean Ave., Medford, 11763. Tel: 516-654-1919. Ann Easparro, Contact.
St. Anthony's Guidance Clinics (Nassau): 124 Greenwich St., Hempstead, 11550. Tel: 516-292-8280. Phyllis Friedlin, Contact, 259 Mineola Blvd., Mineola, 11501. Tel: 516-248-7100. Patricia Quinn, Contact.

Administrative/AIDS Services, 333 N. Main St., Freeport, 11520. Tel: 516-623-7400. Charles McCarron, Program Admin.; Rev. James Nunes, Pastoral Care Admin.

Special Dental Services Program, 333 N. Main St., Freeport, 11520. Tel: 516-623-7400. Dr. Frank Heravi, Program Admin.

AIDS Adult Day Health Care Program, 333 N. Main St., Freeport, 11520. Tel: 516-623-7400.

Housing Services, 90 Cherry Ln., 11801-6299. Tel: 516-733-7000. James Verity, Pastoral Care Coord. Tel: 516-733-7082; Lynn Reddy, Housing Coord. Tel: 516-733-7081.

Senior Housing: St. Agnes Village, 100 St. Agnes Rd., Uniondale, 11553. Tel: 516-485-4721. St. Joseph's Village, 2000 Boyle Rd., Selden, 11784. Tel: 516-736-0524. Bishop Kellenberg Gardens, 2477 Long Beach Rd., Oceanside, 11572. Tel: 516-766-0777. Peternana Terrace, 45 Wallace St., Freeport, 11520. Tel: 516-378-4072. Bishop Ryan Village, 10 Squiretown Rd., Hampton Bays, 11946. Tel: 516-728-2413. St. Paul's Gardens. George Link Jr. Apts., George Link Jr. Cir., Coram, 11727. Tel: 516-732-6878. Mary's Manor, 60 Doughty Blvd., Inwood, 11696. Tel: 516-239-4291. Msgr. Henry J. Reel, 590 Christopher Ct., Medford, 11763. Tel: 516-475-6504.

Human Services, 143 Schleigel Blvd., Amityville, 11701. Tel: 516-789-9550.

Food and Nutrition (FAN) Program, 143 Schleigel Blvd., Amityville, 11701. Tel: 516-789-9542. Robert H. Horn, Program Admin. Tel: 516-789-9533. Food Center Locations: 66 N. 19th St., Wyandanch, 11798. Tel: 516-491-4166. 61-C Brightside Ave., Central Islip, 11722. Tel: 516-232-2797. 127 Bedell St., Hempstead, 11550. Tel: 516-489-9660. St. Hugh of Lincoln, 21 E. Ninth St., Huntington Station, 11746. Tel: 516-549-5606. 23A Nassau Ave., Inwood, 11696. Tel: 516-371-5640. Blanco Dr., Mastic Beach, 11951. Tel: 516-399-5141. 400 Hallett Ave., Riverhead, 11901. Tel: 516-369-9246.
Health Services:

Office for Persons with Disabilities, 143 Schleigel Blvd., Amityville, 11701. Tel: 516-789-5219. Bro. Alan J. Thomas, O.F.M., Contact, Services for Persons Blind/Visually Impaired. Tel: 516-789-5213. Paul Sauerland, Contact, Services for Persons Deaf and Hard of Hearing. Tel: 516-789-5219. Bro. Alan J. Thomas, O.F.M., Contact.

Residential Services, 269 W. Main St., Bay Shore, 11706. Tel: 516-665-3434. Diane Ammirati, Program Admin.
Community residences for people who are developmentally disabled: Alhambra House, 3 Forest Pl., Huntington Station, 11746. Tel: 516-673-5240. Sr. Dolores Lawson, Contact, Caritas Residence, P.O. Box 2383, 4 Hilton Ct., Aqueboque, 11931. Tel: 516-722-5366. James Denning, Contact, Christopher Residence, 70 McKeon Ave., Valley Stream, 11580. Tel: 516-825-8282. Lynn Baumgarten, Contact, Msgr. R. Emmet Fagan Residence, 1504 DePaul St., Elmont, 11003. Tel: 516-358-2559. LeRoy Grant, Contact, Rev. Thomas Helfrick Residence, 1 E. Moriches Blvd., East Moriches, 11940. Tel: 516-878-2965. Deborah Gladden, Contact, Mako Residence, 380 Ed's Rd., Southold, 11971. Tel: 516-675-1783. Deborah Gladden, Contact, Neumann Residence. (For Deaf Adults), 30 Brinkerhoff Ln., Mahasset, 11030. Tel: 516-627-5038. Sr. Jane Mullen, Contact, Bishop Ryan Residence, 258 Deauville Blvd., Copiague, 11726. Tel: 516-691-2126. Sr. Clare Romeo, Contact, Seton Residence, 3 Lombardi Pl., Amityville, 11701. Tel: 516-598-8216. Sr. Margaret Stadelman, Contact, Ted Hansler Residence, 24 Gardiners Ln., Hampton Bays, 11946. Tel: 516-728-8125. John T. Garvey, Contact, Joseph Virdone Residence, 27 North Carll Ave., Babylon, 11702. Tel: 516-661-2826. Sr. Ursula Sheridan, Contact.

Senior Services, 90 Cherry Ln., 11801-6299. Tel: 516-733-7000. Liivia Westervelt, Program Admin. Tel: 516-733-7057.

Bi-County Alliance of Senior Clubs, 90 Cherry Ln., 11801-6299. Tel: 516-733-7074. Liivia Westervelt, Contact.

Link-Age Case Management, 90 Cherry Ln., 11801-6299. Tel: 516-733-7057. Esther Green, Contact, Meals-On-Wheels (Nassau). (For Seniors and People with AIDS), 124 Greenwich St., Hempstead, 11550. Tel: 516-485-7555. Jackie Blount, Contact, Meals-On-Wheels (Suffolk), 555 Albany Ave., Amityville, 11701. Tel: 516-842-4123. Mary-Ann McGrenra, Contact.
Senior Community Service Centers: 555 Albany Ave., Amityville, 11701. Tel: 516-842-7331. Dennis Sullivan, Contact, 379 Linden St., Massapequa Park, 11762. Tel: 516-797-5357. Marline Evangelista, Contact, 619 Fenworth Blvd., P.O. Box 183, Franklin Square, 11010. Tel: 516-481-3322. Susan Weilhoefer, Contact, P.O. Box 243, 25 Nassau Ln., Island Park, 11558. Tel: 516-432-3388. Marie Frangella, Contact, 80 Anchor Ave., Oceanside, 11572. Tel: 516-764-9792. Margaret Keffel, Contact, P.O. Box 524, 2197 Jackson Ave., Seaford, 11783. Tel: 516-679-8373. Patricia Nadeau, Contact.

Immigrant Services, 143 Schleigel Blvd., Amityville, 11701-1399. Tel: 516-789-5210. Carmen Maquilon, Legal Svcs. Tel: 516-789-5212; Gloria Jordan, M.S.W., Social Svcs. Tel: 516-789-5212.

New Neighbors, 1729 N. Ocean Ave., Medford, 11763. Tel: 516-654-0385.

Parish Social Ministry, 90 Cherry Ln., 11801. Tel: 516-733-7000. Richard Koubec, Public Policy Network Coord. Tel: 516-733-7037; Judy Mazzarella, Developer; Specialist. Tel: 516-733-7037; Brian Paradine, Employment Services.

Ministry of Health, 90 Cherry Ln., 11801. Tel: 516-733-7045. Mary Ann Scibetta, Contact.
Parish Social Ministry Developers:
Western Vicariate: Patricia Oliviero, Deanery 1 & 5; Bridget Sheehan, Deanery 2 & 3; John Bingham, Deanery 4 & 6; Nancy Healy, Deanery 7, 9 & 10; Tom Burns, Deanery 8 & 14.

Eastern Vicariate: Sr. Mary Anne Owens, Deanery 11, 12 & 13; Chris Reimann, Developer Special Projects; Sr. Rose Sheridan, Developer Special Projects.

[I] DIOCESAN HOSPITALS

NASSAU COUNTY

ROCKVILLE CENTRE. *Catholic Health Services of Long Island, Inc.*, 50 N. Park Ave., 11570. Tel: 516-678-5800, Ext. 528

For a complete listing, refer to the Hospitals section.

Catholic Healthcare Network of Long Island, 50 N. Park Ave., 11570. Tel: 516-678-5800

For a complete listing, refer to the Hospitals section.

Mercy Medical Center, 1000 N. Village Ave., 11570. Tel: 516-255-0111

For a complete listing, refer to the Hospitals section.

ROSLYN. *St. Francis Hospital*, 100 Port Washington Blvd., 11576. Tel: 516-562-6000

For a complete listing, refer to the Hospitals section.

SUFFOLK COUNTY

PORT JEFFERSON. *St. Charles Hospital, Port Jefferson, New York*, 11777. Tel: 516-474-6000

For a complete listing, refer to the Hospitals section.

WEST ISLIP. *Good Samaritan Hospital Medical Center*, 1000 Montauk Hwy., 11795. Tel: 516-376-4001

For a complete listing, refer to the Hospitals section.

[J] RESIDENCES FOR AGED

AMITYVILLE. *Dominican Village, Inc.*, 565 Albany Ave., 11701. Tel: 516-842-6091

For a complete listing, refer to the Special Care Facilities section.

HUNTINGTON. *St. Joseph's Guest Home for the Aged, Inc.*, 350 Cuba Hill Rd., 11743. Tel: 516-368-9528

For a complete listing, refer to the Special Care Facilities section.

WEST ISLIP. *Our Lady of Consolation Geriatric Care Center*, 111 Beach Dr., 11795. Tel: 516-587-1600; Fax: 516-587-5960

For a complete listing, refer to the Special Care Facilities section.

[K] HOSPICES

SAYVILLE. *Good Samaritan Nursing Home*, 11782. Tel: 516-244-2400

For a complete listing, refer to the Special Care Facilities section.

UNIONDALE. *Mercy Hospice*, St. Pius X Service Center, 122 Front St., 11553. Tel: 516-485-3060

For a complete listing, refer to the Special Care Facilities section.

WEST ISLIP. *Good Samaritan Hospice*, 1000 Montauk Hwy., 11795. Tel: 516-376-4001

For a complete listing, refer to the Special Care Facilities section.

[L] SOCIETY OF ST. VINCENT DE PAUL

BETHPAGE. *Central Council*, Diocese of Rockville Centre, 249 Broadway, 11714. Tel: 516-822-3132. Rev. Msgr. Patrick J. Armshaw, Spiritual Dir.; James J. Reilly, Pres.; Robert S. Ellis, Exec. Dir. Total Assisted 41,776; Total Staff 96; Volunteers 864.

[M] HOME HEALTH SERVICES

HAMPTON BAYS. *Dominican Sisters Family Health Service*, 103 W. Montauk Hwy., P.O. Box 209, 11946. Tel: 516-728-0181; Fax: 516-728-2943. Montauk Hwy. & Cross Hwy., P.O. Box 866, 11930. Tel: 516-267-1090. Mrs. Joanna O'Connell, R.N., B.S., Admin. Suffolk Offices.

WESTBURY. *Nursing Sisters Home Visiting Service, Inc.* Administrative Office, 1600 Stewart Ave., 11590. Tel: 516-683-1370. Sr. Agnes Stumpf, C.I.J., Exec. Dir.; Sr. Dolores Wisniewski, C.I.J., Assoc. Exec. Dir., Corporate Office, 310 Prospect Park W., Brooklyn, 11215. Tel: 516-683-1370. Sr. Mary Nadine Casey, C.I.J., Pres.

Nursing Service Offices: Kings County, 310 Prospect Park W., Brooklyn, 11215. Tel: 718-965-7339. Mrs. Elise Mattia, Mgr. Patient Services, Nassau County, 1600 Stewart Ave., 11590. Tel: 516-683-1300. Ms. Roslyn Brown, Mgr. Patient Services, Suffolk County, 3241 Rte. 112, Medford, 11763. Tel: 516-696-1002. Mrs. Janet Kennedy, Mgr. Patient Services.

[N] MONASTERIES AND RESIDENCES OF PRIESTS AND BROTHERS

BAY SHORE. *Montfort Missionaries*, 26 S. Saxon Ave., 11706. Tel: 516-666-7500.

E-mail: PRETRE@worldnet.att.net

Montfort Spiritual Center and Headquarters of magazine "Queen of All Hearts" and "Montfort Publications". Tel: 516-665-0726. Revs. Roger M. Charest, S.M.M., Mng. Editor; J. Patrick Gaffney, S.M.M., Assoc. Edit. & Preaching Team; George J. Werner, S.M.M., Supr., Preaching Team; Bernard M. Blood, S.M.M., Preaching Team; William M. Dilgen, S.M.M., Marriage Encounter; Maurice A. Landry, S.M.M.; Ronald L. Lloyd, S.M.M. (England); James Manning, S.M.M., Preaching Team; Eugene J. Moynihan, S.M.M.; Francis J. Allen, S.M.M., Preaching Team; Frank A. Setzer, S.S.M., (Retired); Francis Pizzarelli, S.M.M., Hope House Ministry. Hospital Chaplains: Revs. Vincent P. Cunningham, S.M.M.; Harold E. McBride, S.M.M.; Peter J. McCrann, S.M.M.; Theodore Murphy, S.M.M. Priests 14.

Montfort Missionaries - Retreat Center, 26 S. Saxon Ave., 11706.

EASTPORT. *Shrine of Our Lady of the Island*, Montfort Misionaries; Eastport-Manor Rd., 11941. Tel: 516-325-0661. Revs. William J. Vigliotta, S.M.M., Dir.; Raymond Graham, S.M.M.; Bro. Christopher Golla, S.M.M.

GLEN COVE. *St. Josaphatis Monastery, Novitiate and Retreat House*, East Beach Dr., 11542. Tel: 516-671-0545; Fax: 516-676-7465.

E-mail: Mpopadiuk@aol.com

Basilian Fathers. Revs. Mauricio Popadiuk, O.S.B.M. (Brazil), Supr. & Master of Novices; Hilarion Bebedik, O.S.B.M.; Theodosius Ilnicki, O.S.B.M., Asst. Master of Novices; Julian Katrij, O.S.B.M.; Atanasius B. Pekar, O.S.B.M.

MINEOLA. *Provincial Residence and Novitiate*, 240 Emory Rd., 11501. Tel: 516-742-5555.

E-mail: president@chaminade-hs.org

Society of Mary (Marianists). Bro. George E. Endres, S.M., Prov.; Rev. Thomas A. Cardone, S.M., Asst. Prov. & Asst. Religious Life; Bro. Kenneth M. Hoagland, S.M., Asst. Education; Rev. Philip K. Eichner, S.M., Asst. Temporalities; Bro. Michael J. Gillen, S.M., Councilor; Rev. Francis T. Keenan, S.M., Councilor; Bro. Michael J. McAward, S.M., Councilor. In res. Revs. Ernest P. Lorfanfant, S.M.; Garrett J. Long, S.M.; Francis T. Keenan, S.M.

OYSTER BAY. *St. Francis Monastery, Novitiate and Apostolic Center*, Planting Fields Rd., R.F.D. 1, Box 1365, 11771-1302. Tel: 516-922-3545. Franciscan Brothers. Bros. Patrick Murphy, Co-Vicar for Religious, Diocese of Rockville Centre. Tel: 516-922-3886; Roman Morris, O.S.F., Dir., St. Francis Center. Tel: 516-922-3708. Brothers 8.

Vincentian Community, 104 Anstice St., 11771. Revs. Gerard H. Luttenberger, C.M.; Timothy J. Lyons, C.M.

POINT LOOKOUT. *Franciscan Friars*, 128 Hewlett Ave., P.O. Box 211, 11569. Tel: 516-432-3719.

UNIONDALE. *St. Pius X Residence*, 1220 Front St., 11553. Tel: 516-485-4200. Rev. Robert Y. Blyman, Vicar for Senior Priests. In res. Revs. Serafino A. Corali; Edward J. Flynn; John J. Serrano; Edward D. Shillito; John P. Wilutis; Gerard J. Gfroerer; John P. Vitsas; Thomas P. Curry; Hubert Spinner; Rev. Msgr. Alfred Soave; Rev. Msgr. John J. Byrne; Rev. Msgr. Arthur J. Kane.

WEST HEMPSTEAD. *Maryknoll Residence*, 813 Myrna Dr., 11552. Tel: 516-489-7799. Rev. Alphonse A. Schiavone, M.M., Dir.

[O] CONVENTS AND RESIDENCES FOR SISTERS

ROCKVILLE CENTRE. *Villa St. Joseph*, 984 N. Village Ave., 11570. Tel: 516-823-3800; Fax: 516-594-0476. Congregation of the Infant Jesus (Nursing Sisters of the Sick Poor). Professed Sisters 65.

AMITYVILLE. *Queen of the Rosary, Motherhouse*, 555 Albany Ave., 11701-1197. Tel: 516-842-6000; Fax: 516-842-0240.

E-mail: Prioress@juno.com

Sisters of St. Dominic. Legal Titles: *Dominican Sisters Community Support Corporation.*; *Amityville Dominican Sisters, Inc.* Sr. Mary Hughes, O.P., Prioress; Sr. Helen Zalak, Admin.; Rev. Msgr. Domenick J. Adessa, Chap. Total in Residence 141.

BAY SHORE. *New Jerusalem*, 106 N. Penataquit Ave., 11706-6939. Tel: 516-968-8859. Sisters 6.

BLUE POINT. *Ursuline Sisters, St. Ursula Center*, Middle Rd., P.O. Box 86, 11715. Tel: 516-363-6544. Congregation of Tidonk. Sr. Philomena O'Brien, O.S.U., Retreat Dir.; Sr. Ursula Liebold, O.S.U., Coord.

BRENTWOOD. *Maria Regina Convent*, 1725 Brentwood Rd., Bldg. 1, 11717-5589. Tel: 516-273-4500. Sisters of St. Joseph. Sr. Marie de Montfort Shields, C.S.J., Local Supr. Sisters 150.

Saint Joseph Convent, Motherhouse, Brentwood Rd., 11717. Tel: 516-273-4531; Fax: 516-273-1345.

E-mail: BrentCSJ@aol.com

Sisters of Saint Joseph Generalate. Sr. Angela Gannon, Gen. Supr.; Sr. Miriam Lucille Montella, Gen. Sec.; Sr. Joan Larkin, Gen. Treas.; Sr. Edna McKeever, C.S.J., Community Archivist. Sisters 942.

Saint Joseph Novitiate, Brentwood Rd., 11717. Tel: 516-273-1187, Ext. 42. Sr. Maryann Rogers, C.S.J., Coord.

CORAM. *Daughters of Wisdom*, 2 Welling Way, 11727-1005. Sisters 3.

DIX HILLS. *Contemplative Sisters of the Good Shepherd*, 151 Burrs Ln., P.O. Box 8020, 11746-9020. Tel: 516-643-1071. Sr. Helen Lussier, Supr. Sisters 17.

Sisters of the Good Shepherd, 151 Burrs Ln., P.O. Box 8020, 11746-9020. Tel: 516-491-6850. Coordinators: Sr. Yvette Arnold; Sr. Karen Keegan. Sisters 28. Legal Title: *Sisters of the Good Shepherd, Huntington, NY, Inc.*

FRANKLIN SQUARE. *Spiritual Life Center*, 1031 Mosefan St., 11010. Tel: 516-328-7438. Sisters of St. Dominic. Sr. Kathleen Murphy, O.P., Dir. Sisters 2.

HAMPTON BAYS. *St. Joseph's Villa Retreat and Renewal Center*, 81 Lynn Ave., 11946. Tel: 516-728-6447. Sisters of St. Joseph 2.

HUNTINGTON. *Missionary Sisters of St. Benedict*, 350 Cuba Hill Rd., 11743. Tel: 516-368-9528; Fax: 516-266-1015. Sr. M. Bernarda Krajewska, O.S.B., Supr. Sisters 22.

ISLIP. *Daughters of Wisdom (Administration)*, 385 Ocean Ave., 11751-4600; Fax: 516-277-3274.

E-mail: 105521-1133@compuserve.com

Sr. Evelyn Eckhardt, D.W., Prov. Administration Offices. Sisters 3.

Daughters of Wisdom Islip Community, 385 Ocean Ave., 11751-4600.

E-mail: 105521-1133@compuserve.com

Sisters 5.

MEDFORD. *Inter-Community*, 97 Robinson Ave., 11763. Sisters 2.

OCEANSIDE. *St. Anthony's Parish House*, 111 Anchor Ave., 11572. Dominican Sisters (Amityville).

OLD WESTBURY. *Sisters of the Holy Child Jesus*, 25 Store Hill Rd., 11568; Fax: 516-626-7914. 28 Central Dr., 11545.

RONKONKOMA. *Religious of Our Lady of the Retreat in the Cenacle*, 310 Cenacle Rd., 11779-2203.

Provincial House, P.O. Box 2429, 11779-2203. Tel: 516-471-6270. Sr. Marian Hahn, Prov. Professed Sisters 3.

Cenacle Retreat House. Tel: 516-588-8366. Sr. Emma K. Finkbohner, Admin. Coord. Professed Sisters in Residence 60.

Cenacle Formation House, 312 Cenacle Rd., 11779-2203. Tel: 516-737-8491. Professed Sisters 2; Novices in Residence 3.

ROOSEVELT. *Oblate Sisters of the Most Holy Redeemer*, Mother of Good Counsel Home, 290 Babylon Tpke., P.O. Box 329, 11575-0329. Tel: 516-223-1013; Fax: 516-223-4254. Sr. Celina Ardila, O.SS.R., Exec. Dir. Mother of Good Counsel Home is a small group home for pregnant and parenting teenage mothers and their infants.

SEAFORD. *Sisters of St. Joseph*, 2316 Hampton Ave., 11783. Tel: 516-826-1773. Sisters 5.

SELDEN. *Providence Newman Center*, 76 College Rd., 11784. Sr. Grace Maria Dolan, C.S.J.

SOUND BEACH. *Our Lady of Perpetual Help Convent*, 49 Hilltop Dr., Box 926, 11789. Tel: 516-744-2477. Sr. Alice Benedict, D.W., Admin./Coord. Daughters of Wisdom 23.

[P] RETREAT HOUSES

BLUE POINT. *St. Ursula Retreat Center, Inc.*, Middle Rd. and Blue Point Ave., P.O. Box 86, 11715-0086. Tel: 516-363-6544; 363-2422 (Retreat Center). Directed by Ursuline Sisters of Tildonk. Sr. Philomena O'Brien, O.S.U., Retreat Dir. Weekend retreats; private retreats; directed retreats; days and evenings of prayer. Sr. Ursula Liebold, O.S.U., Coord. of Sisters. Total in residence 14.

MANHASSET. *St. Ignatius Retreat House, Inisfada*, Box 756, 11030. Tel: 516-621-8300. The Society of Jesus. Revs. Leo J. Daly, S.J., Dir.; Timothy A. Curtin, S.J.; James J. Dinneen, S.J.; Peter F. O'Brien, S.J.; Vincent J. Ritchie, S.J.; Bernard E. Shannon, S.J. Sisters 2; Total Staff 12; Total in Residence 9.

MELVILLE. *St. Joseph's Prayer Center*, 167 Wolf Hill Rd., 11747. Tel: 516-421-3369. Sr. Mary Dymphna Murray, R.S.M., Admin. Dir.; Rev. James J. Wheeler, S.J., Apostolic Dir. Total Staff 20.

MOUNT SINAI. *House of the Holy Innocents, Inc.*, 722 Mt. Sinai-Coram Rd., Box 174, 11766. Tel: 516-331-1745.

OYSTER BAY. *St. Francis Center, Inc.*, R.F.D. No. 1, Box 1365, Planting Fields Rd., 11771-1302. Tel: 516-922-3708. Directed by Franciscan Bros. of Brooklyn. Bro. Roman Morris, O.S.F., Dir.

RONKONKOMA. *Cenacle Retreat House*, 310 Cenacle Rd., 11779-2203. Tel: 516-588-8366. Religious of the Cenacle. Sr. Mary Jane Laffan, Ministry Coord. Ministry Staff 12.

SAG HARBOR. *Cormaria Retreat House*, 11963. Tel: 516-725-4206. Directed by the Religious of the Sacred Heart of Mary. Sr. Ann Thaddeus Marino, R.S.H.M., Retreat Dir. Religious of the Sacred Heart of Mary 5; Total Staff 11.

SHELTER ISLAND HEIGHTS. *St. Gabriel's Youth House*, 64 Burns Rd., P.O. Box 3015, 11965. Tel: 516-749-0850; Fax: 516-749-3154. A Youth Retreat Ministry directed by the Passionists. Retreats available for youth and young adult; women, men and married couples. Private retreats available at 3 bedroom, waterfront, "Star of the Sea" House of Prayer. Mr. Robert A. Scott, Retreat Dir.; Sr. Maureen Kervick, S.S.J., Dir. Admin. Retreat Team: Ms. Patricia Krupski; Rev. Blaine Brezinski, C.P.

WATER MILL. *Siena Spirituality Center*, 615 Montauk Hwy., 11976. Tel: 516-726-4740; Fax: 516-726-1930. Mailing Address: P.O. Box, 11976. Sr. Peggy Tully, O.P. Dominican Sisters O.P. 8. Center offers Sabbatical in the Dominican tradition, recollection days, private/directed retreats, spiritual formation, and hermitage.

[Q] CAMPUS MINISTRIES AND NEWMAN CENTERS

ROCKVILLE CENTRE. *The Campus Parish of Long Island*, Office of Campus and Young Adult Ministry, 50 N. Park Ave., 11570. Tel: 516-678-5800, Ext. 614; Fax: 516-763-1068. Rev. Joseph J. D'Angelo, M.Div., M.S., C.A.S.A.C., Pastor & Dir. Canonical Institute of Non-territorial Campus Parishes.

Adelphi University, Rm. 316, University Center, Chaplain's Center, Garden City, 11530. Tel: 516-877-3116. Sr. Marilyn Nichols, S.S.J.

Hofstra University. Chaplains' Office, Student Center 213, Hempstead, 11550. Tel: 516-463-6920. Rev. Joseph J. D'Angelo, M.Div., M.S., C.A.S.A.C.; Sr. Kathleen Riordan, O.P.

Nassau Community College. Stewart Avenue-Nursing Department, Garden City, 11530-6793. Tel: 516-572-7234. Deacon Thomas Rich.

LIU/C.W. Post College and New York Institute of Technology - Old Westbury. Interfaith Center, Brookville, 11548. Tel: 516-299-2229. Rev. Edward J. Brown, M.S.

Southampton Campus of Long Island University. Box 301, East Quogue, 11942. Tel: 516-728-2022. Ms. Sally McGuire.

Suffolk Community College. 533 College Rd., Selden, 11784. Tel: 516-451-4369. Sr. Grace Dolan, C.S.J.

SUNY at Farmingdale. Memorial Hall, Rm. 211, Melville Rd., Farmingdale, 11735. Tel: 516-420-2638. Rev. Edward J. Werring.

SUNY at Old Westbury. Vacant. Box 210, Old Westbury, 11568. Tel: 516-876-3000, Ext. 3380.

SUNY at Stony Brook - Catholic Campus Ministry. Interfaith Center, 158 Humanities, Stony Brook, 11794-8033. Tel: 516-632-6562. Sr. Margaret Ann Landry, R.S.H.M.; Rev. John Fitzgerald.

Dowling College. Drama Dept., Oakdale, 11769. Tel: 516-286-6865. Bro. Benilde Montgomery, O.S.F., Dir.

Young Adult Ministry. 50 N. Park Ave., 11570. Tel: 516-678-5800, Ext. 616. Ms. Mary Beth Reynolds.

[R] MISCELLANEOUS

ROCKVILLE CENTRE.
**Women Helping Women*, 255 Merrick Rd., 11570.

AMITYVILLE. *Amityville Dominican Sisters, Inc.*, 555 Albany Ave., 11701. Tel: 516-842-6000. Sr. Mary Hughes, O.P., Pres.; Sr. Francis Ann Gorman, O.P., Vice Pres.; Sr. Barbara C. Suessmann, O.P., Sec. & Treas.

Benincasa Family Services, Inc., 555 Albany Ave., 11701. Tel: 516-842-6949. Sr. Margaret A. Krajci, O.P., Contact.

Dominican Sisters Community Support Corp., 555 Albany Ave., 11701. Tel: 516-842-6000. Sr. Mary Hughes, O.P., Pres.; Sr. Francis Ann Gorman, O.P., Vice Pres.; Sr. Barbara C. Suessmann, O.P., Sec. & Treas.

BAY SHORE. *Pronto of Long Island, Inc.*, 128 Pine Aire Dr., 11706. Tel: 516-231-8290. Contact Persons: Sr. Mary Schramm, O.S.U.; Mrs. Nilda Alvarez.

BELLMORE. *Damien-Dutton Society for Leprosy Aid, Inc.*, 616 Bedford Ave., 11710. Tel: 516-221-5829; 800-448-6166; Fax: 516-221-5909.
Web site: www.damien-dutton.org
Howard E. Crouch, Pres.; Betty Campbell, Vice Pres.

BRENTWOOD. *Thomas I. Conerty Outreach Center of Brentwood, Inc.*, 88 Second Ave., 11717. Tel: 516-273-8113. Michael O'Keefe, Contact Person.

BROOKVILLE. *Sisters, Lovers of the Holy Cross*. St. Paul's Cottage, Cedar Swamp Rd., 11545. Sr. Maria Lien Tran, Pres.

CENTERPORT. *Mt. Alvernia, Inc.*, Prospect Rd., P.O. Box 301, 11721. Tel: 516-261-5730. Directed by the Franciscan Brothers.
Camp Alvernia.
Mt. Alvernia Center for Retreats.

DEER PARK. *Aid to the Church in Need*. United States Office.
Web site: www.ChurchInNeed.org
Mailing Address: P.O. Box 576, 11729. Tel: 800-628-6333; 516-242-8321; Fax: 516-243-1922. 2017 Deer Park Ave., 11729. Mr. Robert W. Lulley, Nat'l Dir.

FARMINGVILLE. *Religious Computer Systems*, P.O. Box 508, 11738-0508. Tel: 516-732-7270; Fax: 516-732-6591.
E-mail: rcsjane@compuserve.com
Sr. Jane Muller, O.P. Social Security and computer services for Religious institutions under sponsorship of the Amityville Dominicans.

HICKSVILLE. *Hope Community of Hicksville, Inc.*, 46 Miller Rd., 11801. Total Assisted 50.

ISLIP. *Wisdom Charitable Trust*, 385 Ocean Ave., 11751. Tel: 516-277-2660.
E-mail: 105521.1133@compuserve.com

NEW HYDE PARK. *Apostleship of Prayer, National Office for the U.S.* (Directed by the Society of Jesus), 3 Stephen Ave., 11040-3130. Tel: 516-328-9777; Fax: 516-328-6039.
E-mail: aposprayer@aol.com
Rev. John H. Rainaldo, S.J., Nat'l Dir. Total Staff 3.

OAKDALE. *Saint John Baptist De La Salle of New York, Inc.*, 500 Montauk Hwy., 11769. Tel: 401-789-0244. Bro. William Mann, F.S.C.

RONKONKOMA. *Catholic Press Association of the United States and Canada, Inc.*, 3555 Veterans Memorial Hwy., Unit O, 11779. Tel: 516-471-4730.
E-mail: CathJourn@aol.com
Web site: http://www.catholicpress.org/index.htm
Mr. Christopher J. Gunty, Pres.; Mr. Owen P. McGovern, Exec. Dir.

UNIONDALE. *TELIcare of the Diocese of Rockville Centre*. 1200 Glenn Curtiss Blvd., 11553. Michael P. O'Leary, Gen. Mgr.

WEST BABYLON. *Christa House, Inc.*, P.O. Box 1633, 11704. Tel: 516-376-0114. Sr. Patricia A. Ryan, C.S.J.

WYANDANCH. *Gerald J. Ryan Outreach Center, Inc.*, 1434 Straight Path, 11798; Fax: 516-491-7285. Total Assisted 15,600; Total Staff 3.

The Opening Word Program, Inc., 1434 Straight Path, 11798. Tel: 516-643-0541. Directed by the Sisters of St. Dominic & Sisters of St. Joseph. Sr. Mary Ryan, O.P., Exec. Dir.; Sr. Kathleen Carberry, C.S.J., Treas.; Sr. Mary Hughes, O.P., Chairperson.

RELIGIOUS INSTITUTES OF MEN REPRESENTED IN THE DIOCESE

For further details refer to the corresponding bracketed number in the Religious Institutes of Men or Women section.

[0330]—*Brothers of the Christian Schools*.—F.S.C.
[1100]—*Brothers of the Sacred Heart*. (Province of New York).—S.C.
[0470]—*The Capuchin Friars*. (St. Mary Prov.).—O.F.M.Cap.
[1330]—*Congregation of the Mission-Vincentians*. (Eastern Prov.).—C.M.
[1000]—*Congregation of the Passion*. (Prov. of St. Paul of the Cross).—C.P.
[0490]—*Franciscan Brothers of Brooklyn*.—O.S.F.
[0690]—*Jesuit Fathers and Brothers*. (N.Y. Prov.).—S.J.
[0770]—*The Marist Brothers*.—F.M.S.
[0800]—*Maryknoll*.—M.M.
[0720]—*Missionaries of Our Lady of La Salette*.—M.S.
[0870]—*Montfort Missionaries*.—S.M.M.
[0430]—*Order of Preachers-Dominicans*.—O.P.
[1070]—*Redemptorist Fathers*.—C.SS.R.
[0760]—*Society of Mary*. (Provs. of NY; Meribah).—S.M.
[0560]—*Third Order Regular of St. Francis*. (Provice of the Most Sacred Heart of Jesus).—T.O.R.

RELIGIOUS INSTITUTES OF WOMEN REPRESENTED IN THE DIOCESE

[3110]—*Congregation of Our Lady of the Retreat in the Cenacle*.—R.C.
[1920]—*Congregation of the Sisters of the Holy Cross*.—C.S.C.
[0960]—*Daughters of Wisdom*.—D.W.
[1070-05]—*Dominican Sisters*.—O.P.
[1070-11]—*Dominican Sisters*.—O.P.
[1070-15]—*Dominican Sisters*.—O.P.
[1070-16]—*Dominican Sisters*.—O.P.
[1370]—*Franciscan Missionaries of Mary*.—F.M.M.
[1180]—*Franciscan Sisters of Allegany, New York*.—O.S.F.
[1425]—*Franciscan Sisters of Peace*.—F.S.P.
[2575]—*Institute of the Sisters of Mercy of the Americas*. (Brooklyn, NY).—R.S.M.
[0210]—*Missionary Benedictine Sisters*.—O.S.B.
[3030]—*Oblate Sisters of M.H. Redeemer*.—O.S.S.R.
[2070]—*Religious of the Holy Union of the Sacred Hearts*.—S.U.S.C.
[3465]—*Religious of the Sacred Heart of Mary*.—R.S.H.M.
[2970]—*School Sisters of Notre Dame*.—S.S.N.D.
[2970]—*School Sisters of Notre Dame*. (Northeastern & Dallas Provinces).—S.S.N.D.
[0640]—*Sisters of Charity of St. Vincent de Paul*. (Halifax).—S.C.
[0650]—*Sisters of Charity of St. Vincent de Paul, of New York*.—S.C.
[0430]—*Sisters of Charity of the Blessed Virgin Mary*.—B.V.M.
[2575]—*Sisters of Mercy of the Americas*. (Dallas Region).—R.S.M.
[2990]—*Sisters of Notre Dame de Namur*.—S.N.D.
[3000]—*Sisters of Notre Dame de Namur*. (Baltimore & Base Communities Provinces).—S.N.D.deN.
[3830]—*Sisters of St. Joseph*.—C.S.J.
[3830-16]—*Sisters of St. Joseph*. (Springfield, MA.—S.S.J.
[3840]—*Sisters of St. Joseph of Carondelet*. (Province of Albany).—C.S.J.
[3880-3]—*Sisters of St. Joseph of Chestnut Hill*. (Philadelphia, PA).—S.S.J.
[3830-11]—*Sisters of St. Joseph of Nazareth*.—S.S.J.
[2980]—*Sisters of the Congregation de Notre Dame*.—C.N.D.
[3180]—*Sisters of the Cross and the Passion*.—C.P.
[1830]—*Sisters of the Good Shepherd*.—R.G.S.
[1970]—*Sisters of the Holy Family of Nazareth*.—C.S.F.N.
[2240]—*Sisters of the Infant Jesus*.—C.I.J.
[2160]—*Sisters, Servants of the Immaculate Heart of Mary*.—I.H.M.
[4060]—*Society of the Holy Child Jesus*.—S.H.C.J.
[4130]—*Ursuline Sisters of the Congregation of Tildonk, Belgium*.—O.S.U.

DIOCESAN CEMETERIES

CENTRAL ISLIP. *Queen of All Saints*, 115 Wheeler Rd., 11722. Tel: 516-234-8297.

CORAM. *Holy Sepulchre*, 3443 Rte. 112, 11727. Tel: 516-732-3460.

WESTBURY. *Holy Rood*, Old Country Rd., Box 182, 11590. Tel: 516-334-7990.

NECROLOGY

† Brendel, John A., (Retired). —Died March 25, 1997.
† Cwalina, Rev. Msgr. John F., (Retired). —Died April 11, 1997.
† David, Raymond J., (Retired). —Died Sept. 25, 1997.
† Hein, George J., Commack, NY, Christ the King. —Died June 22, 1997.
† Kennedy, Vincent A., (Retired). —Died Feb. 22, 1997.
† Murphy, Kenneth G., Great Neck, NY, St. Aloysius. —Died Feb. 2, 1997.
† Shanahan, Edward J., (Retired). —Died Nov. 15, 1996.
† Shillito, Edward D., (Retired). —Died Oct. 20, 1997.
† Tunny, John V., Hicksville, NY, St. Ignatius Loyola. —Died June 23, 1997.

Diocese of Sacramento

(Dioecesis Sacramentensis)

Most Reverend

WILLIAM K. WEIGAND, D.D.

Bishop of Sacramento; ordained May 25, 1963; appointed Bishop of Salt Lake City September 3, 1980; ordained and installed November 17, 1980; appointed Bishop of Sacramento November 30, 1993; installed January 27, 1994. *Mailing Address: Diocesan Pastoral Center, Office of the Bishop, 2110 Broadway, Sacramento, 95818-2541.* Tel.: 916-733-0200; Fax: 916-733-0215.

Most Reverend

RICHARD J. GARCIA, D.D.

Auxiliary Bishop of Sacramento; ordained June 15, 1973; appointed Titular Bishop of Bapara and Auxiliary Bishop of Sacramento November 1997. *Office: Diocesan Pastoral Center, 2110 Broadway, Sacramento, CA, 95818-2541.* Tel.: 916-733-0200.

Most Reverend

FRANCIS A. QUINN, D.D., ED.D.

Retired Bishop of Sacramento; ordained June 15, 1946; appointed Titular Bishop of Numana and Auxiliary Bishop of San Francisco April 28, 1978; Episcopal ordination June 29, 1978; appointed Bishop of Sacramento December 18, 1979. *Office: 2110 Broadway, Sacramento, CA, 95818-2541.* Tel.: 916-733-0200 (Office).

ERECTED BY HIS HOLINESS, LEO XIII, MAY 28, 1886.

Square Miles 42,597.

Legal Title: "Roman Catholic Bishop of Sacramento, A Corporation Sole".

Comprises the Counties of Amador, Butte, Colusa, El Dorado, Glenn, Lassen, Modoc, Nevada, Placer, Plumas, Sacramento, Shasta, Sierra, Siskiyou, Solano, Sutter, Tehama, Trinity, Yolo and Yuba in the State of California.

CO-PATRONS OF DIOCESE: St. Patrick; Our Lady of Guadalupe.

For legal titles of parishes and diocesan institutions, consult the Diocesan Pastoral Center.

Diocesan Pastoral Center: 2110 Broadway, Sacramento, CA, 95818-2541. Tel.: 916-733-0100 (General); Fax: 916-733-0195.

Web site address: http://www.diocese-sacramento.org

E-mail address: Sacdiocese@aol.com

STATISTICAL OVERVIEW

Personnel	
Bishop	1
Auxiliary Bishops	1
Retired Bishops	1
Abbots	1
Priests: Diocesan Active in Diocese	114
Priests: Active Outside Diocese	7
Priests: Retired, Sick or Absent	40
Number of Diocesan Priests	161
Religious Priests in Diocese	72
Extern Priests in Diocese	31
Ordinations:	
Transitional Deacons	2
Permanent Deacons in Diocese	102
Total Brothers	30
Total Sisters	201
Parishes	
Parishes	98
With Resident Pastor:	
Resident Diocesan Priests	88
Resident Religious Priests	9
Without Resident Pastor:	
Administered by Priests	1
Missions	42
Pastoral Centers	2
Professional Ministry Personnel:	
Sisters	35
Lay Ministers	64
Welfare	
Catholic Hospitals	8
Total Assisted	367,137
Health Care Centers	3
Total Assisted	13,751
Homes for the Aged	1
Total Assisted	118
Residential Care of Children	2
Total Assisted	21
Day Care and Extended Day Care Centers	3
Total Assisted	372
Special Centers for Social Services	7
Total Assisted	950,000
Educational	
Diocesan Students in Other Seminaries	29
Seminaries, Religious	2
Students Religious	8
Total Seminarians	37
High Schools, Diocesan and Parish	4
Total Students	1,658
High Schools, Private	3
Total Students	2,348
Elementary Schools, Diocesan and Parish	48
Total Students	13,544
Catechesis/Religious Education:	
High School Students	2,182
Elementary Students	14,390
Total Students Under Catholic Instruction	34,159
Teachers in the Diocese:	
Priests	13
Scholastics	3
Brothers	7
Sisters	16
Lay Teachers	501
Vital Statistics	
Receptions into the Church:	
Infant Baptism Totals	8,742
Adult Baptism Totals	667
Received into Full Communion	649
First Communions	6,479
Confirmations	4,732
Marriages:	
Catholic	1,093
Interfaith	597
Total Marriages	1,690
Deaths	2,649
Total Catholic Population	432,300
Total Population	2,882,000

Former Bishops—Rt. Rev. EUGENE O'CONNELL, D.D., cons. Titular Bishop of Flaviopolis and appt. Vicar Apostolic of Marysville, Feb. 3, 1861; appt. First Bishop of Grass Valley, March 22, 1868; resigned March 17, 1884 and appt. Titular Bishop of Joppa; died Dec. 4, 1891.—Rt. Rev. PATRICK MANOGUE, D.D., cons. Titular Bishop of Ceremos, Coadjutor to Bishop O'Connell of Grass Valley, Jan. 16, 1881; succeeded to the See of Grass Valley on Bishop O'Connell's resignation, March 17, 1884; became the first Bishop of Sacramento, May 1886; died Feb. 27, 1895.—Rt. Rev. THOMAS GRACE, D.D., cons. June 16, 1896; died Dec. 27, 1921.—Rt. Rev. PATRICK J. KEANE, D.D., ord. June 20, 1895; cons. Bishop of Samaria, Dec. 14, 1920; appt. to See of Sacramento, March 17, 1922; died Sept. 1, 1928.—Most Rev. ROBERT J. ARMSTRONG, D.D., Litt.D., ord. Dec. 10, 1910; cons. March 12, 1929; died Jan. 14, 1957.—Most Rev. JOSEPH T. MCGUCKEN, D.D., S.T.D., LL.D., ord. Jan. 16, 1928; cons. Titular Bishop of Sanavo and Auxiliary Bishop of Los Angeles, March 19, 1941; Coadjutor Bishop of Sacramento, Oct. 26, 1955; succeeded to Jan. 14, 1957, as Bishop of Sacramento; promoted to the See of San Francisco, Feb. 21, 1962; died Oct. 6, 1983.—Most Rev. ALDEN J. BELL, D.D., M.S.S.W., ord. May 14, 1932; appt. Titular Bishop of Rhodopolis and Auxiliary Bishop of Los Angeles, April 18, 1956; cons. June 4, 1956; appt. Bishop of Sacramento, March 30, 1962; retired March 15, 1979; died Aug. 28, 1982.—Most Rev. JOHN S. CUMMINS, D.D., ord. Jan. 24, 1953; appt. Titular Bishop of Lambesi and Auxiliary Bishop of Sacramento, Feb. 26, 1974; cons. May 26, 1974; appt. Bishop of Oakland, May 3, 1977.—Most Rev. FRANCIS A. QUINN, D.D., Ed.D., ord. June 15, 1946; appt. Titular Bishop of Numana and Auxiliary Bishop of San Francisco, April 28, 1978; Episcopal Ordination, June 29, 1978; appt. Bishop of Sacramento, Dec. 18, 1979; retired Nov. 30, 1993.—Most Rev. ALPHONSE GALLEGOS, O.A.R., D.D., ord. May 24, 1958; appt. Titular Bishop of Sassabe and Auxiliary Bishop of Sacramento, Sept. 1, 1981; cons. Nov. 4, 1981; died Oct. 6, 1991.—Most Rev. WILLIAM K. WEIGAND, D.D., ord. May 25, 1963; appt. Bishop of Salt Lake City, Sept. 3, 1980; ord.

Bishop, Nov. 17, 1980; appt. Bishop of Sacramento, Nov. 30, 1993.

Diocesan Pastoral Center—2110 Broadway, Sacramento, 95818-2541. Office Hours: Mon.-Fri. 8:30-4:30. Tel: 916-733-0100; Fax: 916-733-0195.

Vicar General and Moderator of the Curia—Rev. ROBERT P. WALTON, Diocesan Pastoral Center. Tel: 916-733-0200; Fax: 916-733-0215.

Chancellor—Sr. EILEEN ENRIGHT, R.S.M.

Vicar Episcopal for Theological and Canonical Affairs—Rev. CHARLES S. MCDERMOTT, S.T.D., *2110 Broadway, Sacramento, 95818-2541.* Tel: 916-733-0200; Fax: 916-733-0215.

Vicar for Priests—Rev. MICHAEL CORMACK, *615 Vine Ave., Roseville, 95678.* Tel: 916-783-5211.

Vicar for Religious—Sr. MAUREEN MCINERNEY, O.P., *2110 Broadway, Sacramento, 95818-2541.*

Vicar for Deacons—Deacon GERALD PAULY, *2110 Broadway, Sacramento, 95818-2541.* Tel: 916-733-0244.

Vicars Forane—Revs. AIDAN O'REILLY, (Siskiyou); MICHAEL CANNY, (Shasta); THOMAS SEABRIDGE, (Lower Valley West); BRENDAN MCKEEFRY, (Lower Valley East); BERNARD BURNS, (Ridge); JOHN MOLUMBY, (Northern Mines); Rev. Msgr. JAMES C. KIDDER, (Southern Mines); Revs. DANIEL LOONEY, (Yolo); MICHAEL DOWNEY, (Solano); NICHOLAS DUGGAN, (Southern Suburbs); T. BRENDAN O'SULLIVAN, (Center Suburbs); LEO MCALLISTER, (American River); MICHAEL CORMACK, (Northern Suburbs); VINCENT BRADY, (City).

Vicar for Hispanics—Rev. HUMBERTO GOMEZ, *2110 Broadway, Sacramento, 95818-2541.* Tel: 916-733-0177; Fax: 916-733-0195.

Diocesan Tribunal—Please direct all requests to the Tribunal. Mailing Address: *2110 Broadway, Sacramento, 95818-2541.* Tel: 916-733-0225; Fax: 916-733-0295.

Judicial Vicar—Rev. DAVID L. DEIBEL, J.D., J.C.L.

Pro-Synodal Judges—Rev. Msgr. PATRICK M. NOLAN; Rev. Msgr. ALBERT G. O'CONNOR; Revs. CESAR AGEAS, J.C.L.; RODOLFO DELGADO, J.C.L.; LIAM MACCARTHY; CORNELIUS O'DONNELL, J.C.B.; KRYSTYNA AMBORSKI, J.C.L.

Promotor of Justice—Rev. CHARLES S. MCDERMOTT, S.T.D.

Defenders of the Bond—Rev. Msgr. JAMES C. KIDDER; Revs. JOHN BOLL; BRENDAN MCKEEFRY; JOHN CANTWELL; JOHN FOLMER, J.C.D.; KIERAN MCMAHON, J.C.L.

Approved Advocates—SUSAN BOONE; JOANNE FANKHAUSER; CAROL SCOTT.

Notaries—CAROL CHEEVER; EVA GREINER.

Civil Law—LOUIS N. DESMOND, ESQ., Diocesan Attorney.

College of Consultors—Rev. Msgr. JAMES CHURCH; Revs. MICHAEL J. CORMACK; HUMBERTO GOMEZ; POLYCARPO GUMAPO; MICHAEL KIERNAN; PATRICK O'CONNOR; ROBERT P. WALTON.

Diocesan Offices and Directors

AIDS, Ministry to—Rev. JOHN HEALY, Coord., *832 41st St., Sacramento, 95819-2747.* Tel: 916-453-4753.

Alcoholism Advisory Board—Revs. MICHAEL CORMACK. Tel: 916-783-5211. THOMAS MAGUIRE. Tel: 209-274-4911. Dr. WILLIAM MERZ. Tel: 916-353-6623.

Apostleship of Prayer—Rev. RICHARD DOHENY, Dir., *P.O. Box 1180, Fair Oaks, 95628.* Tel: 916-967-1229.

Archives—Rev. WILLIAM BREAULT, S.J., Pro-Tem Archivist, *2110 Broadway, Sacramento, 95818-2541.* Tel: 916-733-0100.

Black Catholic Council—CHARLES FARRELL, *Office, 2110 Broadway, Sacramento, 95818-2541.* Tel: 916-733-0160; Fax: 916-733-0195.

Building Committee—Direct inquiries to: Mr. THOMAS MCNAMARA, Staff, *Diocesan Pastoral Center, 2110 Broadway, Sacramento, 95818-2541.* Tel: 916-733-0277; Fax: 916-733-0295.

California Catholic Conference—1010 - 11th St., Ste. 200, Sacramento, 95814. Tel: 916-443-4851; Fax: 916-443-5629. Most Rev. SYLVESTER C. RYAN, Pres.; Most Rev. WILLIAM K. WEIGAND, Vice Pres.; Most Rev. MICHAEL DRISCOLL, Sec./Treas.; Mr. EDWARD "NED" E. DOLEJSI, Exec. Dir.; Mr. DAVID A. POLLARD, Assoc. Dir., Legislative and Public Policy; Mr. ROBERT TEEGARDEN, Assoc Dir., Education; CAROL HOGAN, Assoc. Dir., Communications; Rev. ALEJANDRO CASTILLO, S.V.D., Assoc. Dir., Hispanic Affairs; Mr. RICHARD MOCKLER, Exec. Dir., Catholic Charities of California, Inc.

California Association of Catholic Hospitals—1121 L St., 409, Sacramento, 95814. Tel: 916-444-3386.

Campus Ministry—Rev. MICHAEL NEWMAN, S.D.S., Diocesan Dir., *Newman Catholic Ctr., 346 Cherry St., Chico, 95926.* Tel: 530-342-5180; Fax: 530-342-3016.

Catholic Faith Formation—Sr. MAURA POWER, R.S.M., Dir., *2110 Broadway, Sacramento, 95818-2541.* Tel: 916-733-0123; Fax: 916-733-0195.

Catholic Charities of Sacramento, Inc.—DONALEE HALLENBECK, Pres. & Chm. of Board of Directors; JAMES F. RODGERS, Exec. Dir., *5890 Newman Ct., Sacramento, 95819.* Tel: 916-452-4621; Fax: 916-736-0282.

Cemeteries—Rev. Msgr. PATRICK M. NOLAN, Dir., *6700 21st Ave., Sacramento, 95820.* Tel: 916-452-5951., *P.O. Box 245346, Sacramento, 95824-5346.*

Censor Librorum—Rev. CHARLES S. MCDERMOTT, S.T.D., *2110 Broadway, Sacramento, 95818-2541.* Tel: 916-733-0200.

Communications and Media—Rev. JAMES T. MURPHY, Dir., *2110 Broadway, Sacramento, 95818-2541.* Tel: 916-733-0258; Fax: 916-733-0295.

Council of Priests—Most Rev. WILLIAM K. WEIGAND, D.D., Pres. Please direct all inquiries to: Rev. MICHAEL KIERNAN, Chm. Tel: 916-365-8573. Rev. Msgr. JAMES CHURCH; Revs. JOHN BOLL; RONAN BRENNAN; MICHAEL CORMACK; HUMBERTO GOMEZ; POLYCARPO GUMAPO; MICHAEL KIERNAN; ERIC LOFGREN; THOMAS MAGUIRE; KIERAN MCMAHON; JULIAN MEDINA; MARTIN MORONEY; PATRICK O'CONNOR; BRENDAN O'SULLIVAN; GILBERTO PENA; ROBERT P. WALTON; CARLTON WHITTEN, S.J.; Deacon WILLIAM RIEHL, Deacon Observor Direct all correspondence to: *2110 Broadway, Sacramento, 95818-2541.*

Deaf and Hard of Hearing (Office of Catholic Faith Formation)—JEAN NELSON, Coord. of Support Services; JAMES ANDERSON, Pastoral Minister for Deaf and Hard of Hearing, *2110 Broadway, Sacramento, 95818-2541.* Tel: 916-733-0123; TDD 733-0144.

Detention Service—Rev. LIAM P. MCSWEENEY, *CA Youth Authority, 3001 Ramona Ave., Sacramento, 95826.* Tel: 916-733-2356.

Development—MIMI SCHERBER, Diocesan Dir., *2110 Broadway, Sacramento, 95818-2541.* Tel: 916-733-0266; Fax: 916-733-0295.

Diocesan Pastoral Council—Please direct all inquiries to: Rev. EDWARD LEWIS, Staff. Tel: 707-644-8396. or Office of the Bishop:Tel: 916-733-0200. VIDA RYAN, Staff; GIL AZEVEDO; Mr. ANTONIO BARBOSA; Mrs. EVELIA BERUMEN; Mr. HENRY BOYER; Mrs. BARBARA COELHO; Mrs. BELEN "BEL" CORPUZ; Mr. EUGENE EVEN; Mr. CHARLES FARRELL; Mrs. TILLIE FERNANDEZ; Sr. MAUREEN FITZGERALD; Mr. ROBERT GILBRIDE; Revs. HUMBERTO GOMEZ; POLYCARPO GUMAPO; Rev. EDWARD LEWIS; Sr. NANCY MCINERNEY; Mr. HAROLD MYERS; Mr. JOHN ROE; Mrs. MARY ROSE; Ms. VIDA RYAN; Mrs. JESSIE SHIELDS; Rev. ROBERT P. WALTON; Rev. PHILIP WELLS; Ms. MARY ANN WESLEY; Most Rev. WILLIAM K. WEIGAND, D.D.

Diocesan Priests' Trust Fund—Most Rev. WILLIAM K. WEIGAND, D.D., Pres. Ex Officio Direct inquiries to: Rev. Msgr. MURROUGH WALLACE, Treas., *St. Theresa Church, 1041 Lyons Ave., South Lake Tahoe, 96150.* Tel: 530-544-3533; Fax: 916-544-4662.

Disability Ministry—Mr. ROBERT BRENNER, *2110 Broadway, Sacramento, 95818-2541.* Tel: 916-733-0123; Fax: 916-733-0195.

Divorced and Separated, Ministry to—Direct inquiries to: *Family Life Office, 2110 Broadway, Sacramento, 95818-2541.* Tel: 916-733-0155; Fax: 916-733-0195.

Due Process Conciliation, Council of—Rev. Msgr. MURROUGH WALLACE, Chm.; Rev. ALFRED KASTER; Dr. WILLIAM MARIANO; ELAINE MASSEY; Sr. MAURA POWER, R.S.M.,Direct all correspondence to: Rev. CHARLES S. MCDERMOTT, S.T.D., *2110 Broadway, Sacramento, 95818-2541.* Tel: 916-733-0200.

Office of Arbitration—Revs. CHARLES S. MCDERMOTT, Chm. DANIEL CASEY; MICHAEL CORMACK; FRED OLIVER; Mrs. SHEILA NOLAN, Office: *2110 Broadway, Sacramento, 95818-2541.* Tel: 916-733-0200.

Eastern Catholic Churches—Rev. CHARLES S. MCDERMOTT, Liaison Officer, *2110 Broadway, Sacramento, 95818-2541.* Tel: 916-733-0200.

"Ecclesia Dei" Community (Latin Mass)—JOHN RIZZO, F.S.S.P., Chap., *St. Rose Parish, 5961 Franklin Blvd., P.O. Box 5037 Oak Park Station, Sacramento, 95824.* Tel: 916-421-1414; Fax: 916-421-0460.

Ecumenism—Rev. Msgr. JAMES C. KIDDER, *5145 Golden Foothill Pkwy., #100, El Dorado Hills, 95762.* Tel: 916-933-6532.

Evangelization (Office of Catholic Faith Formation)—THOMAS FAUSONE, *2110 Broadway, Sacramento, 95818-2541.* Tel: 916-733-0123.

Family Life—JOHN RIESCHICK, Dir., *2110 Broadway, Sacramento, 95818-2541.* Tel: 916-733-0155.

Finance Council—Members: Sr. M. MICHAEL MURPHY, R.S.M.; Rev. MICHAEL CORMACK; ROBERT GRANUCCI, ESQ.; ANNE HECK LONG; Mr. MICHAEL PROFUMO; ROBERT SLAKEY; Mr. CHARLES SYLVA; Mr. PETE PADILLA; Ms. JULIE NAUMAN. Ex Officio: Rev. ROBERT P. WALTON; Mr. THOMAS J. MCNAMARA, *Chancery Office, 2110 Broadway, Sacramento, 95818-2541.* Tel: 916-733-0277.

Investment Review Committee—Direct inquiries to: Mr. THOMAS MCNAMARA, *2110 Broadway, Sacramento, 95818-2541.* Tel: 916-733-0277; Fax: 916-733-0295.

Finance Office—Mr. THOMAS MCNAMARA, Dir., *2110 Broadway, Sacramento, 95818-2541.* Tel: 916-733-0277; Fax: 916-733-0295.

Gospel Justice Resource Ctr., Catholic Reg. Commission—Vacant, *2110 Broadway, Sacramento, 95818-2541.*

Hispanic Apostolate—Rev. HUMBERTO GOMEZ, Vicar for Hispanics, *2110 Broadway, Sacramento, 95818-2541.* Tel: 916-733-0177; Fax: 916-733-0195.

Holy Childhood Association—Mr. THOMAS BUTLER, *2110 Broadway, Sacramento, 95818-2541.* Tel: 916-733-0110; Fax: 916-733-0120.

Hospitals, Diocesan Liaison for Catholic—Rev. JOHN J. HEALY, *832 41st St., Sacramento, 95819-2747.* Tel: 916-453-4753.

Lay Ministry—Sr. ANITA MINIHANE, R.S.M., *2110 Broadway, Sacramento, 95818-2541.* Tel: 916-733-0250; Fax: 916-733-0295.

Marriage Preparation—JOHN RIESCHICK, Dir., Family Life Office, *2110 Broadway, Sacramento, 95818-2541.* Tel: 916-733-0155.

Newspapers—"Catholic Herald" and "El Heraldo Catolico"; Ms. JULIE SLY, Editor; RICARDO OLVERA, Editor, El Heraldo, Office: *5890 Newman Ct., Sacramento, 95819-2608.* Tel: 916-452-3344; Fax: 916-452-2945.

Ongoing Education of Clergy—Rev. T. BRENDAN O'SULLIVAN, Dir., *St. Anthony Church, 660 Florin Rd., Sacramento, 95831.* Tel: 916-428-5678.

Opus Sanctorum Angelorum—Rev. J. DERMOT DWYER, Spiritual Dir., *P.O. Box 752, Colfax, 95713.* Tel: 916-346-2286.

Permanent Diaconate Program—Sr. PAULINA HURTADO, O.P., Dir. Asst. Directors: Deacon WILLIAM RIEHL; Sr. STEPHANA O'LEARY, S.S.S., Office: *2110 Broadway, Sacramento, 95818-2541.* Tel: 916-733-0244.

Priests' Diocesan Aid Society—Ex-Officio Officer: Most Rev. WILLIAM K. WEIGAND, D.D.,Please direct inquiries to: Rev. Msgr. JAMES F. CHURCH, Sec./Treas., *2428 Bell St., Sacramento, 95825.* Tel: 916-455-3001.

Priests' Personnel Board, Diocesan—Please direct all inquiries to: Rev. VINCENT BRADY, Sec., *1017 11th St., Sacramento, 95814.* Tel: 916-444-3071. Revs. ROY DONER; LEON JUCHNIEWICZ; WILLIAM KINANE, Chm. PATRICK MCGRATH; JULIAN MEDINA; GERALD RYLE; ROBERT P. WALTON.

Propagation of the Faith—Rev. Msgr. JAMES CHURCH, Dir., *2110 Broadway, Sacramento, 95818-2541.* Tel: 916-733-0200; Fax: 916-733-0215.

Properties Committee—Please direct all inquiries to: Mr. THOMAS MCNAMARA, Staff, *2110 Broadway, Sacramento, 95818-2541.* Tel: 916-733-0277.

Radio and Television—See Communications and Media.

Research and Planning—Sr. EILEEN ENRIGHT, R.S.M., Chancellor, *2110 Broadway, Sacramento, 95818-2541.* Tel: 916-733-0200; Fax: 916-733-0215.

Respect Life—MARIE SHEAHAN BROWN, Diocesan Coord., *Family Life Office, 2110 Broadway, Sacramento, 95818-2541.* Tel: 916-733-0155.

Schools—Mr. THOMAS BUTLER, Supt.; Mr. DOMINIC PUGLISI, Assoc. Supt., *2110 Broadway, Sacramento, 95818-2541.* Tel: 916-733-0110; Fax: 916-733-0120.

Vocations—Revs. JAMES T. MURPHY, Dir. HUMBERTO GOMEZ, Dir., Hispanic Seminarians; Sr. MAUREEN MCINERNEY, O.P., Asst. Dir., *2110 Broadway, Sacramento, 95818-2541.* Tel: 916-733-0258.

Worship, Office of—Rev. KIERAN MCMAHON, Interim Dir., *2110 Broadway, Sacramento, 95818-2541.* Tel: 916-733-0220.

Lay Organizations—

Beginning Experience—STEVEN HILLBLOM, Pres., *P.O. Box 161761, Sacramento, 95816.* Tel: 916-535-5057. GARY CRABBE, Pub. Rels.

Catholic Alumni Club—ERIC PATTON, Pres., *P.O. Box 1777, Carmichael, 95609-1777.* Tel: 916-427-6396; 863-3040.

Catholic Daughters of the Americas—SHIRLEY GODFREY, *6600 Greenhaven Dr., Sacramento, 95831.* Tel: 916-428-5044.

Charismatic Renewal—Rev. Msgr. ANDREW V. COFFEY, Diocesan Liaison; Deacon JERRY PAULY, Assoc. Diocesan Liaison. Tel: 916-451-3738. Mr. MICHAEL DONEEN, Treas.

Cursillo Movement—Office: *2110 Broadway, Sacramento, 95818-2541.* Tel: 916-733-0181.

Daughters of Isabella—STELLA POST, Regent, *9814 Pringle Ave., Galt, 95632.* Tel: 209-744-1802.

Diocesan Council of Catholic Nurses—Mrs. ELEANOR HAVEY, *4935 61st St., Sacramento, 95820.* Tel: 916-457-8649.

Diocesan Council of Catholic Women—Rev. Msgr. EDWARD J. KAVANAGH, Moderator; Mrs. LUCILLE TURLIS, Pres., *3925 El Ricon Way, Sacramento, 95864.* Tel: 916-483-1087.

Handicapables—BOB KNAPIK. Tel: 916-422-5011.

Italian Catholic Federation—Rev. MARTIN BRUSATO, Chap., *P.O. Box 276, Galt, 95632.* Tel: 916-446-6310. HELEN PIERSON, Dist. Pres., *1266 Ridgeway Dr., Sacramento, 95822.* Tel: 209-745-1389.

Knights of Peter Claver and Ladies Aux.—Mr. FRED MCLAURIN, Sacramento, Area Deputy, *P.O. Box 13471, Sacramento, 95813.* Tel: 916-971-4954. Mrs. NOELLA M. FRANCIS, Area Deputy, Ladies Div., *7375 Putnam Way, Sacramento, 95822.* Tel: 916-427-7041.

Knights of Columbus—Mr. JOHN H. STEVENS, Northern California Chapter Pres., *2221 Emerson Pl., Fairfield, 94533.* Tel: 707-425-1692.

Legion of Mary Comitium—Rev. Msgr. CORNELIUS P. HIGGINS, *3027 Olive Glen Ct., Sacramento, 95821.* Tel: 916-487-9493. HORTENCIA MORALES, Pres., *6415 Longridge Way, Sacramento, 95831.* Tel: 916-421-1227. Three Curiae attached: Marysville-Yuba City, North Sacramento, Solano.

Marriage Encounter Worldwide—Contact Family Life Office, *2110 Broadway, Sacramento, 95818-2541.* Tel: 916-733-0155.

Scouting, Catholic Committee on—Rev. ROBERT MARSICEK, S.D.S., Diocesan Chap., *9079 Greenback Ln., Orangevale, 95662-4703.* Tel: 916-989-7400.

Secular Franciscan Order—

Grass Valley-St. Patrick Parish—San Damiano Fraternity; CARMEN M. BROOKE, SFO. Tel: 916-273-2347.

Loomis-Mount St. Joseph Novitiate—Little Portion Fraternity; DONNA RIETZ, SFO. Tel: 916-652-9552.

Sacramento-St. Francis of Assisi Parish—Fraternidad De San Juan Bautista (Spanish); GENARO GONZALEZ, SFO. Tel: 916-392-9632. St. Francis of Assisi Fraternity (English); BILL TURNER, SFO. Tel: 916-447-4637.

Secular Order of Discalced Carmelites—HAROLD HUNT, Pres., *P.O. Box 25, Rancho Cordova, 95741.* Tel: 916-362-5631.

Serra Club of Sacramento—YOUNG D. STEWART, Pres., *5903 Via Casitas, Carmichael, 95608.* Tel: 916-332-8732.

Young Ladies Institute—Mrs. PATRICIA CARVO, District 21 Deputy, *2768 Lincoln Rd., Yuba City, 95993.* Tel: 916-673-7147.

St. Thomas More Society—HERB BOLZ, Pres. Tel: 916-753-6094. Rev. CHARLES S. MCDERMOTT. Tel: 916-733-0200.

CLERGY, PARISHES, MISSIONS AND PAROCHIAL SCHOOLS

CITY OF SACRAMENTO
(Sacramento County)

1—CATHEDRAL OF THE BLESSED SACRAMENT (1889), Most Rev. William K. Weigand; Revs. Vincent Brady, Rector; Michael McKeon; Deacons Don De Haven; John Masla.
Res., 1017 Eleventh St., 95814. Tel: 916-444-3071; Fax: 916-443-2749. Catechetical Center Cathedral Parish Hall Conducted by parish CCD and Daughters of Charity of Canossa.
Res., 1949 North Ave., 95838. Tel: 916-925-4001.
Social Service Center—Tel: 916-444-3070.
Catechesis/Religious Programs—Tel: 916-444-5364.
Students 140.

2—ALL HALLOWS (1942), Rev. Polycarpo Gumapo; Deacons Michael Donovan; George Kriske. In res., Rev. Vincent Lenehan.
Res., 5500 13th Ave., 95820. Tel: 916-456-7206; Fax: 916-456-7325.
School—5700 13th Ave., 95820. Tel: 916-457-5621. Stephanie C. Jones, Prin.
Lay Teachers 10; Students 319.
Catechesis/Religious Programs—Tel: 916-736-0204.
Students 47.
Station—California State Youth Authority Center, 3001 Ramona Ave., 95820. Tel: 916-733-2350; Fax: 916-227-2511. Rev. William P. McSweeney, Chap.

3—HOLY SPIRIT (1940), Rev. Charles Brady; Deacon Bernard J. Weeks.
Res., 3159 Land Park Dr., 95818. Tel: 916-443-5442; Fax: 916-446-9015.
School—3920 W. Land Park Dr., 95822. Tel: 916-448-5663. Sr. Jean Marie Gorman, R.S.M., Prin.
Sisters 1; Lay Teachers 11; Students 315.
Convent—Tel: 916-448-3578. Sisters of Mercy (Auburn, CA)
Catechesis/Religious Programs—Tel: 916-448-8257.
Students 115.

4—IMMACULATE CONCEPTION (1909), Rev. Mark L. Mosher; Deacon Gerald Pauly.
Parish Office: 3263 First Ave., 95817. Tel: 916-452-6866; Fax: 916-452-3879.
Res., 2549 32nd St., 95817. Tel: 916-452-6866.
School—3263 First Ave., 95817. Tel: 916-452-7308. Lee Roark, Prin.
Sisters 1; Lay Teachers 8; Students 90.
Catechesis/Religious Programs—Students 62.

5—OUR LADY OF GUADALUPE SHRINE (1958) (Hispanic), Revs. Rodolfo Delgado, Admin.; Roberto Jaramillo.
Res., 711 T St., 95814. Tel: 916-442-3211; Fax: 916-442-3679.
Catechesis/Religious Programs—730 S St., 95814. Tel: 916-446-3500.
Students 619.

6—OUR LADY OF LOURDES (1957), Rev. Anthony Traynor; Deacon James Lalonde.
Res., 1951 North Ave., 95838. Tel: 916-925-5313; Fax: 916-922-0625.
Catechesis/Religious Programs—Students 150.
Convent—1949 North Ave., 95838. Tel: 916-925-4001; Fax: 916-925-8897. Daughters of Charity of Cannosa

7—PRESENTATION OF THE BLESSED VIRGIN MARY (1961), Revs. Simon D. Twomey; Michael Carroll. In res., Rev. Msgr. Cornelius P. Higgins, Pastor Emeritus; Rev. William Feeser.
Mailing Address: P.O. Box 214208, 95821-0208.
Res., 4123 Robertson Ave., 95821. Tel: 916-481-7441; Fax: 916-481-2841.
School—3100 Norris Ave., 95821. Tel: 916-482-0351; Fax: 916-482-0377. Theresa Altieri, Prin.
Lay Teachers 13; Students 329.
Parish Center—3110 Norris Ave., 95821.
Catechesis/Religious Programs—Tel: 916-482-8883. Susan B. McLeod.
Students 70.

8—SACRED HEART OF JESUS (1926), Rev. Michael O'Hara; Sr. Mary Martin, R.S.M., Pastoral Assoc., Tel: 916-452-4830; Deacons Gilbert Parra; William Riehl.
Res., 1040 39th St., 95816. Tel: 916-452-4136.
School—Sacred Heart, 3933 I St., 95816. Tel: 916-456-1576; Fax: 916-456-4773. Maureen Douglass, Prin.
Sisters of Mercy (Auburn, CA) 1; Lay Teachers 11; Students 312.
Catechesis/Religious Programs—Tel: 916-454-3640. Sr. O'Meara, R.S.M., D.R.E.
Students 40.

9—ST. ANNE (1961), Revs. Januarius E. Rodrigues; Patrick J. Lee; Deacons Pedro Manriquez; Modesto Chavarria. In res., Rev. Enrique Sanchez.
Res., 7724 24th St., 95832. Tel: 916-422-8380; Fax: 916-422-7538.
School—7720 24th St., 95832. Tel: 916-422-3142. Mr. Francis T. McNamara, Prin.
Religious 1; Lay Teachers 8; Students 232.
Catechesis/Religious Programs—Tel: 916-422-2419.
Students 197.

10—ST. ANTHONY (1974), Rev. T. Brendan O'Sullivan; Deacons James Healy; Richard Koppes; Michael Crowley.
Res., 660 Florin Rd., 95831. Tel: 916-428-5678; Fax: 916-428-0312.
Catechesis/Religious Programs—Tel: 916-392-6362.
Students 260.

11—ST. CHARLES BORROMEO (1960), Revs. Michael McFadden; Cesar Ageas; Alvaro Alzate; Deacon Manuel Ocon. In res., Rev. James T. Murphy.
Res., 7584 Center Pkwy., 95823. Tel: 916-421-5177; Fax: 916-392-4831.
School—7580 Center Pkwy., 95823. Tel: 916-421-6189; Fax: 916-421-3954. Sr. Maureen Fitzgerald, Prin.
Sisters 4; Lay Teachers 10; Students 319.
Catechesis/Religious Programs—Students 319.
Convent—(Motherhouse, Hamden, CT). Tel: 916-421-7174. Apostles of the Sacred Heart of Jesus

12—ST. ELIZABETH (1909) (Portuguese), Rev. Eduino Silveira.
Res., 1817 12th St., 95814. Tel: 916-442-2333.

13—ST. FRANCIS OF ASSISI (1894), Rev. Richard Juzix, O.F.M.; Deacon Richard Driggs.
1066 26th St., 95816. Tel: 916-443-8084; Fax: 916-443-7356.
School—2500 K St., 95816. Tel: 916-442-5494; Fax: 916-442-1390. Ms. Barbara O'Donnell, Prin.
Lay Teachers 17; Students 340.
Catechesis/Religious Programs—Students 205.

14—ST. IGNATIUS OF LOYOLA (1954), Revs. Christopher M. Cartwright, S.J.; Paul F. Belcher, S.J.; David W. MacDonald, S.J.; Peter K.C. Siu, S.J.; Deacon Jackson Gualco. In res., Rev. Gerald H. Robinson, S.J., Dir., Ignatian Institute for Family Life.
Res., 3235 Arden Way, 95825-2014. Tel: 916-482-9666; Fax: 916-482-6573.
School—3245 Arden Way, 95825. Tel: 916-488-3907. Cassandra Saenz, Prin.
Lay Teachers 15; Students 354.
Catechesis/Religious Programs—Students 150.
Ignatian Institute for Family Life—.

15—ST. JEONG-HAE ELIZABETH, Rev. John Hee-Wan Jeong.
Res., 9354 Kiefer Blvd., 95826. Tel: 916-368-9204.

16—ST. JOSEPH'S (1924), Revs. Robert A. Copsey; Andrew Koziczuk (Poland); Sr. Ellen Philbin, R.S.M., Parish Min.; Deacon Henry Garcia.
Res., 1717 El Monte Ave., 95815. Tel: 916-925-3584; Fax: 916-925-1045.
School—1718 El Monte Ave., 95815. Tel: 916-925-1465; Fax: 916-925-0963. Mrs. Marsha J.B. Cornelius, Prin.
Sisters of Mercy (Auburn, CA) 1; Lay Teachers 8; Students 297.
Catechesis/Religious Programs—Tel: 916-924-8541.
Students 140.

17—ST. MARY (1906) (Italian), Rev. Philip Massetti, O.S.J.; Deacon Luigi Del Gaudio.
Res., 1333 58th St., 95819. Tel: 916-452-0296; Fax: 916-452-3908.
School—5815 N St., 95819. Tel: 916-452-1100; Fax: 916-452-3908. Sr. Joan O'Sullivan, P.B.V.M., Prin.
Sisters 1; Lay Teachers 10; Students 327.
Convent—5801 N St., 95819. Tel: 916-451-5881. Sisters of the Presentation of the Blessed Virgin Mary (Monastereven, Ireland)
Catechesis/Religious Programs—Tel: 916-452-4115.
Students 480.

18—ST. PAUL (1958), Rev. Nicholas Duggan; Deacon Charles Morrison.
Res., 7200 Gardner Ave., P.O. Box 292280, 95829. Tel: 916-381-5200; Fax: 916-381-0332.
Catechesis/Religious Programs—Students 240.

19—ST. PETER (1955), Revs. Sidney Peter Hall; Malachy Conway; Deacons Deogracia "Ray" Ramos; Alejandro Reynoso.
Res., 6210 McMahon Dr., 95824. Tel: 916-455-3001; Fax: 916-455-4721.
School—6200 McMahon Dr., 95824. Tel: 916-455-2915; Fax: 916-455-2915.
Sisters 4; Lay Teachers 8; Students 300.
Catechesis/Religious Programs—Students 197.
Convent—5870 62nd St., 95824. Tel: 916-457-0182. Sisters Servants of the Blessed Sacrament (Guadalajara, Mexico)

20—ST. PHILOMENE (1948), Rev. Msgr. James F. Church; Rev. Msgr. Patrick M. Nolan, Pastor Emeritus; Rev. Terry A. Fulton; Deacons Charles Cheever; Keith Burke.
Res., 2428 Bell St., 95825. Tel: 916-481-6757; Fax: 916-481-1603.
School—2320 El Camino Ave., 95825. Tel: 916-489-5466; Fax: 916-489-2642. Debra Mosbaucker, Prin.
Lay Teachers 13; Students 296.
Catechesis/Religious Programs—Tel: 916-488-6091.
Students 127.

21—ST. ROBERT (1955), Rev. Kieran M. McMahon; Deacon Martin Rodriguez.
Res., 2243 Irvin Way, 95822. Tel: 916-451-1475.
School—2251 Irvin Way, 95822. Tel: 916-452-2111; Fax: 916-452-5765. Gail Sherman, Prin.
Lay Teachers 10; Students 310.

22—ST. ROSE (1942), Rev. Msgr. Edward J. Kavanagh; Rev. Francis Lawlor. In res., Rev. Charles S. McDermott.
Res., P.O. Box 5037, Oak Park Station, 95817. Tel: 916-421-1414; Fax: 916-421-0460.
School—St. Patrick, 5945 Franklin Blvd., 95824. Tel: 916-421-4963; Fax: 916-421-3849. Dave Hoffman, Prin.
Lay Teachers 15; Students 373.
Catechesis/Religious Programs—Tel: 916-392-5679.
Students 483.

23—VIETNAMESE CATHOLIC MARTYRS (Vietnamese), Rev. Jude Ban Nguyen, C.M.C.; Deacon Anthony Huy Nguyen.
Res., 10371 Jackson Rd., 95827. Tel: 916-366-3162.
Catechesis/Religious Programs—Students 664.

OUTSIDE THE CITY OF SACRAMENTO

Alturas, Modoc Co., Sacred Heart (1883), Rev. Rodney L. Hall.
Res., 507 E. Fourth St., 96101. Tel: 530-233-2119.
Catechesis/Religious Programs—Students 25.
Mission—Cedarville, Modoc Co., St. James, Bonner St. & Garfield St., Cedarville, 96104.

Anderson, Shasta Co., Sacred Heart (1949), Rev. Michael F. Kiernan; Deacon Michael Evans.
Res., 3141 St. Stephen's Dr., P.O. Box 547, 96007. Tel: 530-365-8573; Fax: 530-365-9544.

School—(Grades PreK-5) 3167 St. Stephen's Dr., 96007. Tel: 530-365-1429. Mrs. Margaret Heyfron, Prin.
Lay Teachers 7; Students 170.
St. Francis Middle School, 21945 Old 44 Dr., Palo Cedro, 96073.
Students 133.
Catechesis/Religious Programs—Students 190.
Missions—Cottonwood, Shasta Co., St. Anne, 2nd St. & Main St., Cottonwood, 96022.; Shingletown, Shasta Co., Mary Queen of Peace, Shingletown Ridge Rd., Shingletown, 96088. Tel: 916-474-1870.

Antelope, Sacramento Co., St. Clare (1992), Rev. Colin MacDonald.
Res., 4313 Shandwick Dr., 95843. Tel: 916-721-4771; Fax: 916-721-4288. [JC]
Catechesis/Religious Programs—Tel: 916-722-8721.
Students 84.

Auburn, Placer Co., St. Joseph (1861), Revs. John Molumby, (Sabbatical); Thomas A. Bland, Admin.; Glenn Dare; Deacon Ed Morgado.
Res., 1162 Lincoln Way, 95603. Tel: 530-885-2956; Fax: 530-823-6676. [CEM]
School—11610 Atwood Rd., 95603. Tel: 530-885-4490; Fax: 530-885-0182. Mrs. Joan Walthers, Prin.
Sisters 1; Lay Teachers 14; Students 297.
Catechesis/Religious Programs—Tel: 530-885-0362.
Students 289.
Mission—Auburn, Placer Co., St. Teresa of Avila, (1994) 11600 Atwood Rd., 95603.
Station—Forest Hill.

Benicia, Solano Co., St. Dominic (1854), Revs. Victor Cavalli, O.P.; Dominic DeLay, O.P.; Eugene Sousa, O.P.; Deacon Ed Lazarek. In res., Rev. John Morris, O.P.
Res., 475 E. I St., P.O. Box 756, 94510. Tel: 707-747-7220; Fax: 707-745-5642. [CEM]
School—935 E. 5th St., 94510. Tel: 707-745-1266. Mr. Mark Donnelly, Prin.
Lay Teachers 13; Students 342.
Catechesis/Religious Programs—433 E. I St., 94510. Tel: 707-747-7240.
Students 520.

Burney, Shasta Co., St. Francis of Assisi (1949), Rev. Eric D. Lofgren.
Res., 37464 Juniper Ave., P.O. Drawer 160, 96013. Tel: 530-335-2372.
Catechesis/Religious Programs—Students 68.
Missions—Bieber, Lassen Co., St. Stephen, Hwy. 299, Bieber, 96009.; Fall River Mills, Shasta Co., Our Lady of the Valley, 43434 Main St., Fall River Mills, 96028.

Carmichael, Sacramento Co., Our Lady of the Assumption (1952), Rev. Leo McAllister; Deacons Michael Tateishi; Thomas Ferreira; James Meucci. In res., Revs. Antony B. Warnakula; William Broderick, (Retired).
Res., 5057 Cottage Way, 95608. Tel: 916-481-5115; Fax: 916-481-4026.
School—5055 Cottage Way, 95608. Tel: 916-489-8958. Sr. Mary Ellen Beck, I.B.V.M., Prin.
Sisters 1; Lay Teachers 9; Students 307.
Catechesis/Religious Programs—Tel: 916-488-4626.
Students 303.
Convent—Tel: 916-488-8188. Ladies of Loretto (Toronto, Canada)

St. John the Evangelist (1960), Revs. John Lagomarsino, S.S.C., Parochial Admin.; Ambrose Ugwuegbu; Sr. Eileen Mary O'Connor, R.S.M., Pastoral Assoc.; Deacon James Weeks, (Retired). In res., Rev. Patrick O'Rafferty.
Res., 5751 Locust Ave., 95608. Tel: 916-483-8454; Fax: 916-481-8326.
School—5701 Locust Ave., 95608. Tel: 916-481-8845. Dr. Jacqueline Pajda, Prin.
Lay Teachers 14; Students 294.
Catechesis/Religious Programs—Tel: 916-483-4628. Sr. Celine Heneghan, R.S.M., D.R.E.
Students 215.

Chico, Butte Co., Our Divine Savior (1967), Revs. Roy R. Doner; Joseph Huyen Van Nguyen.
Office: 566 E. Lassen Ave., 95973. Tel: 530-343-4248; Fax: 530-343-3538.
Catechesis/Religious Programs—Tel: 530-345-6201.
Students 225.

St. John the Baptist (1878), Revs. Gilberto Pena-Martinez; Brent Nall; Michael Hebda; Deacons Antonio Ramirez; Jesus Campos Padilla; James Burkett; Stephen Schwartz.
Res., 435 Chestnut St., 95928. Tel: 530-343-8741; Fax: 530-345-8602.
School—(Grades K-8) 435 Hazel St., 95928. Tel: 530-342-2502; Fax: 530-342-6292. Colleen Waugh, Prin.
Lay Teachers 13; Students 300.
Catechesis/Religious Programs—Students 460.
Mission—Durham, Butte Co., St. James, P.O. Box 562, Durham, 95938. [JC]

Citrus Heights, Sacramento Co., Holy Family (1949), Revs. John Cantwell; Jose Karikattil; Rev. Msgr. Vito F. Mistretta, Pastor Emeritus; Deacon William Lubinsky.
Res., 7817 Old Auburn Rd., 95610. Tel: 916-723-2494; Fax: 916-723-0199.
School—Tel: 916-722-7788; Fax: 916-722-5297. Sr. Arlene Connelly, I.B.V.M., Prin.
Lay Teachers 21; Students 617.
Preschool—Patricia Peterson, Preschool Dir., Tel: 916-722-4620.
Lay Teachers 7; Students 72.
Catechesis/Religious Programs—Tel: 916-726-7217. Linda Pulido, D.R.E.
Students 300.

Clarksburg, Yolo Co., St. Joseph (1893), Rev. Daniel Madigan.
Res. & Church Address—32890 S. River Rd., 95612. Tel: 530-665-1132; Fax: 530-665-9264.

Colfax, Placer Co., St. Dominic (1951), Rev. Dermot Dwyer, Admin.
Res., 58 E. Oak St., P.O. Box 752, 95713. Tel: 530-346-2286; Fax: 530-346-2286. [CEM]
Catechesis/Religious Programs—Students 140.

Colusa, Colusa Co., Our Lady of Lourdes (1870), Rev. Edward Pepka, Admin.
Res., 745 Ware Ave., 95932. Tel: 530-458-4170; Fax: 530-458-8728. Rev. Guillermo Rodriguez.; Res., 627 8th St., P.O. Box 1346, Williams, 95987. Tel: 530-473-3200. Deacon Miguel Fernandez.
Church—4th St., 95932. Tel: 530-458-7901.
School—(Grades PreK-8). Tel: 530-458-8208. Mrs. Barbara Genera, Prin.
Lay Teachers 11; Students 120.
Catechesis/Religious Programs—Students 90.
Mission—Princeton, Colusa Co., St. Joseph, 1st St. & Center St., Princeton, 95970.
Station—Sycamore, Our Lady of Sorrows. [CEM]

Corning, Tehama Co., Immaculate Conception (1947), Revs. Miguel Silva; Thomas L. Seabridge.
Res., 814 Solano St., 96021. Tel: 530-824-5879. [JC]
Catechesis/Religious Programs—Tel: 530-824-2619; Fax: 530-824-1102.
Students 92.
Mission—Tehama, Tehama Co., St. Stanislaus, 4th St. & D St., Tehama, 96090.

Davis, Yolo Co., St. James (1912), Rev. Daniel A. Looney; Rev. Msgr. Andrew V. Coffey, Pastor Emeritus; Rev. Richard J. Blinn, S.J.; Deacons Paul Taloff; Sam Colenzo.
Res., 200 W. 14th St., 95616. Tel: 530-756-3636; Fax: 530-756-5342. [JC]
School—1215 B St., 95616. Tel: 530-756-3946; Fax: 530-753-9765. Mary Kay Bolz, Prin.
Lay Teachers 14; Students 297.
Catechesis/Religious Programs—Tel: 916-756-9000. Linda O'Hara, D.R.E.
Students 240.
Newman Center—514 C St., 95616. Tel: 916-753-7393; Fax: 916-753-2794. Rev. Tongele Ngbatana.

Dixon, Solano Co., St. Peter (1877), Revs. Maurice O'Brien; John J. Kyne, Pastor Emeritus; Deacons Robert H. Ikelman; John King.
Res., 105 S. 2nd St., 95620. Tel: 707-678-9424; Fax: 707-678-9432.
Catechesis/Religious Programs—Students 230.

Downieville, Sierra Co., Immaculate Conception (1853), Rev. Godwin Xavier.
Res., Flume St., P.O. Box 48, North San Juan, 95960. Tel: 530-292-3227.
Church—Church St., 95936. Tel: 530-289-3102. [CEM][JC]
Missions—North San Juan, Nevada Co., St. John, 10047 Flume St., North San Juan, 95960.; Sierra City, Sierra Co., St. Thomas, 108 Butte Aly, Sierra City, 96125.; Challenge, Yuba Co., St. Anthony, La Porte Rd., Challenge, 95925. Tel: 530-675-2001. Deacon George Lucas.

Dunsmuir, Siskiyou Co., St. John the Evangelist (1900), Rev. Cornelius O'Donnell.
Res., 5605 Shasta Ave., 96025. Tel: 530-235-4705; Fax: 530-235-4759. [JC]

El Dorado Hills, El Dorado Co., Holy Trinity (1992), Rev. Msgr. James C. Kidder; Deacon Charles Rasmussen.
Church—5145 Golden Foothill Pkwy. #100, 95762. Tel: 916-933-6532; Fax: 916-933-6532.
Catechesis/Religious Programs—Students 370.

Elk Grove, Sacramento Co., St. Joseph (1962), Rev. Msgr. Albert G. O'Connor. In res., Rev. Robert Walton; Deacon Paul Imrisek.
Res., 9961 Elk Grove-Florin Rd., 95624. Tel: 916-685-3681; Fax: 916-685-7254.
Catechesis/Religious Programs—Tel: 916-685-5636.
Students 540.
Mission—Rancho Murieta, P.O. Box 552, 95683.

Good Shepherd Catholic Church (1993), Rev. Philip Wells.
Res., 6310 Thresher Ct., 95758. Tel: 916-684-5722; Fax: 916-684-4472.
Catechesis/Religious Programs—Students 285.

Fairfield, Solano Co., Holy Spirit (1950) (Spanish), Revs. Michael Downey; Luciano Valenzuela (Philippines); Umberto Penunuri. Pastoral Assocs.: Sr. Maura O'Sullivan; Sr. Elizabeth Curtis, C.H.F.
Res., 1050 N. Texas St., P.O. Box X, 94533. Tel: 707-425-3138; Fax: 707-425-2029. [CEM]
School—(Grades K-8). Tel: 707-422-5016. Sr. Mairead Langley, C.H.F., Prin.
Sisters 3; Lay Teachers 12; Students 360.
Catechesis/Religious Programs—Tel: 707-425-9042. Suselia Hernandez, D.R.E.
Students 604.
Convent—Tel: 707-425-3572. Sisters of the Holy Faith (Dublin, Ireland)

Our Lady of Mount Carmel, (1979). (Carmelite Fathers). Revs. Sebastian Meyer, O.Carm.; Neal McNanna, O.Carm.; Deacon Len Trueworthy.
Parish Office—Tel: 707-422-7767; Fax: 707-422-7946.
Res., 698 Berkeley Way, 94533. Tel: 707-426-3639.
Church—2700 Dover Ave., 94533.
Catechesis/Religious Programs—Tel: 707-422-2814.
Students 334.

Fair Oaks, Sacramento Co., St. Mel (1948), Revs. Richard Doheny; Carroll Keating, S.J.; Rev. Msgr. William Horgan, Pastor Emeritus; Deacon Patrick Henning.
Res., 4745 Pennsylvania Ave., P.O. Box 1180, 95628. Tel: 916-967-1229; Fax: 916-967-5659.
School—Tel: 916-967-2814. Janet Nagel, Prin.
Lay Teachers 15; Students 308.
Catechesis/Religious Programs—Tel: 916-966-4314.
Students 227.

Folsom, Sacramento Co., St. John the Baptist (1857), Revs. Ignatius Haran; Alfredo Tamayo; Deacons Leslie White; Dennis Merino.
Office & Mailing Address—307 Montrose Dr., 95630. Tel: 916-985-2065; Fax: 916-985-7579.
Res., 107 Joseph Way, 95763-0235. Tel: 916-351-1939. [CEM]
School—St. John's-Notre Dame, Tel: 916-985-4129. Jim Gabrielli, Prin.
Lay Teachers 16; Students 325.
Catechesis/Religious Programs—Tel: 916-985-7338.
Students 484.
Station—Folsom State Prison, P.O. Box W, Represa, 95671. Tel: 916-985-2561. Rev. Thomas Maguire, Chap.
Mailing Address: Folsom State Prison, P.O. Box 29, Represa, 95671. Tel: 916-985-8610, Ext. 6425. Deacon Dennis Merino, Chap.

Fort Jones, Siskiyou Co., Sacred Heart (1921), Rev. John Lawrence.
Res., 101 Carlock St., P.O. Box 126, 96032-0126. Tel: 916-468-2605; Fax: 916-468-5577.
Missions—Etna, Siskiyou Co., St. Mary, 386 Center St., Etna, 96027.; Happy Camp, Siskiyou Co., All Saints, 1321 Indian Creek Rd., Happy Camp, 96093.; Sawyer's Bar, Siskiyou Co., St. Joseph, Sawyer's Bar Rd., Etna, 96027.

Galt, Sacramento Co., St. Christopher (1885), Rev. Martin Brusato; Deacon Thomas McGill.
Res., 526 Third St., P.O. Box 276, 95632. Tel: 209-745-1389.
Catechesis/Religious Programs—Students 373.

Grass Valley, Nevada Co., St. Patrick (1855), Revs. Nicholas Phelan; Alfred D. Kaster; Sr. Geneva Paluka, R.S.M., Pastoral Min.; Deacons Carlos Astesana; James Chatigny; Milton Stackhouse; Brian Moore.
Res., 235 Chapel St., 95945. Tel: 530-273-2347. [CEM]
School—Mt. St. Mary's, Tel: 530-273-4694; Fax: 530-273-1724. Charles Suarez, Prin.
Lay Teachers 11; Students 212.
Preschool/Day Care—Tel: 530-273-6244.
Lay Teachers 2; Students 24.
Catechesis/Religious Programs—Students 304.

Gridley, Butte Co., Sacred Heart (1926), Rev. Julian Medina.
Res., 1560 Hazel St., P.O. Box 205, 95948. Tel: 530-846-2140; Fax: 530-846-5615.
Catechesis/Religious Programs—Tel: 530-846-5091.
Students 190.
Convent—1515 Hazel St., 95948.
Mission—Live Oak, Sutter Co., Our Lady of Guadalupe, 9660 Broadway, Live Oak, 95953.

Ione, Amador Co., Sacred Heart (1932), Rev. Thomas Relihan.
Res., Church and Washington Sts., P.O. Box 4, 95640. Tel: 209-274-2158. [CEM][JC]

Catechesis/Religious Programs—Students 45.
Missions—Ione, Amador Co., Preston School of Industry, California Youth Authority, 201 Waterman Rd., 95640. Tel: 209-274-4771, Ext. 250. Rev. Paul Schloeder; Ione, Amador Co., Mule Creek State Prison, P.O. Box 409099, 95640. Tel: 209-274-4911.

Isleton, Sacramento Co., St. Therese's (1953), Rev. Mario Nunez, Ph.L.
Res., P.O. Box 697, 95641. Tel: 916-777-6871.
Church—4th St. & Jackson Blvd., 95641.
Catechesis/Religious Programs—Students 79.

Jackson, Amador Co., St. Patrick's (1864), Rev. Paul C. Ricks; Deacons William Thompson; Don Gercich.
Res., 115 Court St., P.O. Box 923, 95642. Tel: 209-223-0168; Fax: 209-223-2548. [CEM 2]
Catechesis/Religious Programs—170 New York Ranch Rd., 95642. Tel: 209-223-2145.
Students 150.
Missions—Buckhorn, Amador Co., Our Lady of the Pines, Tiger Creek Rd., Pioneer, 95660.; Volcano, Amador Co., St. Bernard, Plug-Emigrant St., Volcano, 95689.

Knights Landing, Yolo Co., St. Paul (1949), Rev. Thomas A. Batch; Rev. Msgr. Cornelius P. Higgins, Pastor Emeritus; Deacon Antonio Gonzalez.
Res., 222 Sycamore Way, P.O. Box 176, 95645. Tel: 530-735-6478.
Catechetical Center—6th & Locust Sts., 95645.
Mission—Zamora, Yolo Co., St. Agnes, 95645.

Lincoln, Placer Co., St. Joseph (1892) (Hispanic), Revs. Julian Medina; James Rockenstein, O.F.M.; Deacons Jesus Rodriguez; Roberto Ruiz; Kenneth Boone.
Res., 585 D St., 95648. Tel: 916-645-2102; Fax: 916-645-1422. [JC]
Catechesis/Religious Programs—412 6th St., 95648. Tel: 916-645-7754.
Students 160.
Missions—Nicolaus, Sutter Co., St. Boniface, 1028 Marcum Rd., Nicolaus, 95659. Tel: 916-656-2368; Wheatland, Yuba Co., St. Daniel, 214 Main St., Wheatland, 95692. Tel: 916-633-0344.
Shrine—Our Lady of Guadalupe, 3rd and K Sts., 95648.

Marysville, Yuba Co., St. Joseph (1852), Rev. Leon Juchniewicz; Deacons Juan Perez; Jesus Munoz; David Perez.
Mailing Address: Office, 223 Eighth St., 95901.
Res., 319 Seventh St., 95901. Tel: 530-742-6461; Fax: 530-742-0346. [CEM]
School—(Grades K-8) 715 C St., 95901. Tel: 530-743-4484. Mrs. Janet Wales, Prin.
Lay Teachers 9; Students 242.
Catechesis/Religious Programs—Tel: 530-742-7100.
Students 310.
Mission—Dobbins, Yuba Co., Sacred Heart Church, P.O. Box 208, Dobbins, 95953.

Maxwell, Colusa Co., Sacred Heart (1881), Revs. John Myles; Heriberto Serrano.
Res., 45 Elm St., P.O. Box 607, 95955. Tel: 530-438-2432. [CEM]
Missions—Arbuckle, Colusa Co., Holy Cross, 408 Laurel St., Arbuckle, 95912.; Williams, Colusa Co., Annunciation, 617 8th St., Williams, 95987. Tel: 530-473-2925; Stonyford, Colusa Co., St. Mary of the Mountain, 2nd St. & Geary St., Stonyford, 95979.

McCloud, Siskiyou Co., St. Joseph (1933), Rev. Cornelius O'Donnell.
213 Colombero Dr., P.O. Box 518, 96057. Tel: 530-235-4705.
Res., 5605 Shasta Ave., Dunsmuir, 96025. Tel: 530-235-4705. [JC]

Mount Shasta, Siskiyou Co., St. Anthony (1954), Rev. Aidan O'Reilly.
Res., P.O. Box 467, 96067. Tel: 530-926-4477.
Church—Pine St. & Alma St., 96067.
Catechesis/Religious Programs—Tel: 530-926-3061.
Students 71.

Nevada City, Nevada Co., St. Canice (1851), Revs. James McKnight; Edward Mello, Pastor Emeritus.
Res., 317 Washington St., P.O. Box 1597, 95959. Tel: 530-265-2049. [CEM]
Church—Coyote St., 95959.
Catechesis/Religious Programs—Tel: 916-265-2712; Fax: 530-265-8119.
Students 140.

North Highlands, Sacramento Co., St. Lawrence (1955), Rev. Gerald Ryle; Deacon Gary Fracolli.
Res., 4325 Don Julio Blvd., 95660. Tel: 916-332-4777; Fax: 916-332-8325.
School—(Grades K-8) 4325 Don Julio Blvd., 95660. Tel: 916-332-4779. Mr. John Ruport, Prin.
Religious 1; Lay Teachers 10; Students 295.
Catechesis/Religious Programs—Tel: 916-332-4777.
Students 444.

Orangevale, Sacramento Co., Divine Savior (1987), Revs. Robert R. Marsicek, S.D.S.; Neil W. Seidl, S.D.S. In res., Rev. J. Patrick Ritter, S.D.S.
Office: 9079 Greenback Ln., 95662. Tel: 916-989-7400; Fax: 916-989-7410.
Res., 8680 Hickory Leaf Pl., 95662. Tel: 916-989-5425.
Catechesis/Religious Programs—Tel: 916-989-7407.
Students 406.
Counseling Center—Tel: 916-989-7414.

Orland, Glenn Co., St. Dominic (1919), Revs. Thomas L. Seabridge; Miguel Silva.
Res., 822 A St., P.O. Box 816, 95963. Tel: 530-865-4550; 865-7080 (Spanish Tel.); Fax: 530-865-8451.
Catechesis/Religious Programs—Tel: 530-865-7115.
Students 40.
Mission—Hamilton City, Glenn Co., St. Mary, 400 Los Robles, 95951.

Oroville, Butte Co., St. Thomas the Apostle (1864), Rev. Troy David Powers.
Res., 1330 Bird St., 95965. Tel: 530-533-0262; Fax: 530-533-1148.
School—1380 Bird St., 95965. Tel: 530-534-6969. Mr. Paul Weber, Prin.
Lay Teachers 8; Students 157.
Catechesis/Religious Programs—Students 60.

Paradise, Butte Co., St. Thomas More (1949), Rev. Brendan McKeefry.
Res., 767 Elliott Rd., 95969. Tel: 530-877-4501; Fax: 530-877-5633.
School—771 Elliott Rd., 95969. Tel: 530-877-5328; Fax: 530-877-1485. Ms. Suellen Grenko, Prin.
Lay Teachers 9; Students 144.
Catechesis/Religious Programs—Tel: 530-877-6023.
Students 105.

Placerville, El Dorado Co., St. Patrick's (1855), Revs. John Sullivan; Robert H. Taylor, S.J.; Deacon Stan S. Rudger.
Res., 3109 Sacramento St., 95667. Tel: 530-622-0373; Fax: 530-621-7770. [CEM]
Catechesis/Religious Programs—Tel: 530-622-7692; Fax: 530-621-7771.
Students 535.
Convent—3122 Sacramento St., 95667. Tel: 530-622-1983. Sr. Thomas Marie Heavey, S.A., Supr. & Pastoral Assoc.
Mission—Georgetown, El Dorado Co., St. James, 2831 Harkness St., Georgetown, 95634. Tel: 530-333-9432.

Portola, Plumas Co., Holy Family (1929), Rev. Bernard J. Burns.
Res., 108 Taylor Ave., P.O. Box 1077, 96122. Tel: 530-832-5006; Fax: 530-832-5520.
Catechesis/Religious Programs—Students 77.
Mission—Loyalton, Sierra Co., Holy Rosary, 4th St., 96118.

Quincy, Plumas Co., St. John (1947), Rev. Walter Deo Burke.
Res., 170 Lawrence St., P.O. Box 510, 95971. Tel: 530-283-0890; Fax: 530-283-4204.
Catechesis/Religious Programs—Students 90.
Mission—Greenville, Plumas Co., St. Anthony.
Station—Buck's Lake, Quincy.

Rancho Cordova, Sacramento Co., St. John Vianney (1958), Rev. Martin J. Moroney; Deacons Walter Little; Phil Moseley. In res., Rev. John Folmer.
Res., 10497 Coloma Rd., 95670. Tel: 916-362-1385; Fax: 916-361-8102.
School—10499 Coloma Rd., 95670. Tel: 916-363-4610; Fax: 916-363-3243. Mrs. Vicky Andrews, Prin.
Lay Teachers 12; Students 321.
Catechesis/Religious Programs—Tel: 916-362-3827.
Students 175.

Red Bluff, Tehama Co., Sacred Heart (1867), Rev. Sean O'Leary.
Res., 515 Main St., 96080. Tel: 530-527-2209; Fax: 530-529-2586. [CEM]
Parish Hall: 2355 Monroe St., 96080. Tel: 530-527-1351.
School—2255 Monroe St., 96080. Tel: 530-527-6727. Mrs. Victoria Wilson, Prin.
Lay Teachers 9; Students 196; Preschool 70.
Catechesis/Religious Programs—Students 170.

Redding, Shasta Co., Our Lady of Mercy (1980), Rev. Michael Canny; Deacon Anthony Short.
Office: 2600 Shasta View Dr., 96002. Tel: 530-222-3424; Fax: 530-221-5717.
School—St. Francis Middle School, 21945 Old 44 Dr., Palo Cedro, 96073.
Students 133.
Catechesis/Religious Programs—Tel: 530-222-2497.
Students 237.

St. Joseph (1907), Rev. Msgr. Russell G. Terra; Deacons David Gasman; Frank Lopez; Michael Mangas.
Res., 2040 Walnut Ave., 96001. Tel: 530-243-3463; Fax: 530-243-2747. [CEM]
Schools—2460 Gold St., 96001. Tel: 530-243-2302; Fax: 530-243-2747. Mr. Tom Schwerdt, Prin.
Lay Teachers 14; Students 327; St. Francis Middle School, 21945 Old 44 Dr., Palo Cedro, 96073.
Students 133.
Catechesis/Religious Programs—Tel: 530-243-7999.
Students 60.
Mission—Shasta Lake City, Shasta Co., St. Michael, 3440 Shasta Dam Blvd., 96019.

Rio Vista, Solano Co., St. Joseph (1885), Revs. Patrick J. McGrath; William K. Walsh, Pastor Emeritus.
Res., 130 S. 4th St., 94571. Tel: 707-374-2155. [CEM 2]
Catechesis/Religious Programs—Tel: 707-374-5071.
Students 116.

Rocklin, Placer Co., SS. Peter and Paul (1981), Rev. Michael J. Dillon.
Res., 4450 Granite Dr., P.O. Box 824, 95677. Tel: 916-624-5827; Fax: 916-624-5924.
Catechesis/Religious Programs—Tel: 916-624-3093.
Students 720.

Roseville, Placer Co., St. Rose of Lima (1907), Revs. Daniel J. Casey; Robert Brooks; Deacons William H. Boudier; Peter M. Silott; Juan Tamayo. In res., Rev. Michael J. Cormack, Pastor Emeritus.
Res., 615 Vine Ave., 95678. Tel: 916-783-5211; Fax: 916-783-5212.
School—633 Vine Ave., 95678. Tel: 916-782-1161; Fax: 916-782-7862. Marie Giorgi, Prin.
Sisters 1; Lay Teachers 14; Students 314.
Catechesis/Religious Programs—Tel: 916-786-0650.
Students 491.

South Lake Tahoe, El Dorado Co., St. Theresa (1951), Rev. Msgr. Murrough C. Wallace; Revs. Michael O'Reilly; John J. Grace, Pastor Emeritus.
Res., 1041 Lyons Ave., 96150. Tel: 530-544-3533; Fax: 530-544-4662.
School—1081 Lyons Ave., 96150. Tel: 530-544-8944. Dr. Jeannette Holmes, Prin.
Catechesis/Religious Programs—Tel: 530-544-4788; Fax: 530-544-8909.
Students 200.
Mission—Camp Sacramento, El Dorado Co., Our Lady of the Sierras.

Susanville, Lassen Co., Sacred Heart (1912), Rev. Noel Lynch.
Res., 120 N. Union St., P.O. Box 501, 96130. Tel: 530-257-3230; Fax: 530-257-9213.
Catechesis/Religious Programs—Msgr. Moran Hall, 140 N. Weatherlow St., 96130. Tel: 530-257-8008.
Students 95.
Station—Herlong.

Sutter Creek, Amador Co., Immaculate Conception (1864), Revs. Liam MacCarthy; Ronan P. Brennan, Pastor Emeritus.
Res., 130 Spanish St., P.O. Box 127, 95685. Tel: 209-267-5602; Fax: 209-267-1278. [CEM 4]
Catechesis/Religious Programs—Spanish & Amelia Sts., 95685. Tel: 209-267-0447.
Students 90.
Mission—Plymouth, Amador Co., St. Mary of the Mountains, Church St., Plymouth, 95669.

Tahoe City, Placer Co., Corpus Christi (1961), Rev. Patrick J. O'Connor.
Church & Res.—905 W. Lake Blvd., Hwy. 89 S., P.O. Box 1878, 96145. Tel: 530-583-4409; Fax: 530-583-1408.
Catechesis/Religious Programs—Tel: 530-583-4637.
Students 112.
Mission—Olympic Valley, Placer Co., Queen of the Snows, 1550 Squaw Valley Rd., 96145.
Station—Tahoma.

Truckee, Nevada Co., Assumption of the Blessed Virgin Mary (1870), Revs. Stanley Poltorak; Francisco Hernandez-Tovar; Deacon Ray Craig.
Res., 10124 E. St., Hwy. 267 N., P.O. Box 34014, 96160. Tel: 530-587-3595; Fax: 530-582-8648.
Catechesis/Religious Programs—Students 235.
Mission—Kings Beach, Placer Co., Our Lady of the Lake, 8363 Steelhead, Kings Beach, 96143. Tel: 530-546-2291.

Tulelake, Siskiyou Co., Holy Cross (1949), Rev. Patrick Henry, Admin.
Res., 765 First St., 96134. Tel: 530-667-2727.
Church—P.O. Box 266, 96134.
Mission—Dorris, Siskiyou Co., Our Lady of Good Counsel, W. 3rd St., Dorris, 96023.

Vacaville, Solano Co., St. Joseph (1992), Rev. Vincent O'Reilly.
Res., 1771 Marshall Rd., 95687. Tel: 707-447-2354; Fax: 707-447-9322.
School—Notre Dame, 1781 Marshall Rd., 95687. Tel: 707-447-1460; Fax: 707-447-1498. Maryalice Clare, Prin.
Catechesis/Religious Programs—Students 285.

St. Mary (1947), Revs. Benedict DeLeon; Eugenio Lopez; Lawrence A. Ryan, Pastor Emeritus; Deacon Domingo Cabrera.
Res., 350 Stinson Ave., 95688. Tel: 707-448-2390; Fax: 707-448-2818.
Catechesis/Religious Programs—Tel: 707-446-1881.
Students 615.
Catechetical Center—300 Hemlock St., 95688. Tel: 707-446-1881.
Students 633.

Vallejo, Solano Co., St. Basil (1941), Rev. William P. Storan; Deacon Michael Carlomagno.
Res., 1200 Tuolumne St., 94590. Tel: 707-644-5251; Fax: 707-644-1423.
School—1230 Nebraska St., 94590. Tel: 707-642-7629; Fax: 707-642-8635. Mrs. Susan M. Hill, Prin.
Lay Teachers 12; Students 346; Preschool 92.
Catechesis/Religious Programs—Tel: 707-644-8309.
Students 313.

St. Catherine of Siena (1964), Revs. William P. Kinane; Jesus Soriano.
Res., 3450 Tennessee St., P.O. Box 5390, 94591. Tel: 707-553-1355; Fax: 707-557-6896.
School—(Grades K-8) 3460 Tennessee St., 94591. Tel: 707-643-6691; Fax: 707-647-4441. Mrs. Flavia R. Lorega, Prin.
Lay Teachers 14; Students 339.
Catechesis/Religious Programs—Tel: 707-643-1951.
Students 365.

St. Vincent Ferrer (1855), Revs. Edward J. Lewis; Erwin Mesiona; Gerardo Rubio (Tijuana, Mexico); Tobias Vereker.
Res., 925 Sacramento St., 94590. Tel: 707-644-8396; Fax: 707-644-1330.
School—420 Florida St., 94590. Tel: 707-642-4311; Fax: 707-642-1329. Mrs. Susan Fulton, Prin.
Lay Teachers 11; Students 556.
Catechesis/Religious Programs—Tel: 707-643-0188.
Students 430.
Mission—South Vallejo, Solano Co., St. Louis Bertrand. Fax: 707-644-8396.

Walnut Grove, Sacramento Co., St. Anthony (1931), Rev. Edward Mello.
Res., 14012 Walnut Ave., P.O. Box 436, 95690. Tel: 916-776-1330.

Weaverville, Trinity Co., St. Patrick (1853), Rev. Keith Canterbury; Deacon Everett Layne.
Res., P.O. Box 1219, 96093. Tel: 916-623-4383.
Church—102 Church St., 96093.
Missions—Hayfork, Trinity Co., Holy Trinity; Lewiston, Trinity Co., St. Gilbert.

Weed, Siskiyou Co., Holy Family (1933), Rev. John Hannan.
Res., 1051 N. Davis Ave., P.O. Box 248, 96094. Tel: 530-938-2076.
Catechesis/Religious Programs—Tel: 530-938-4334.
Students 64.

West Sacramento, Yolo Co., Holy Cross (1913), Revs. John Kouba, S.D.S.; Chad C. Puthoff, S.D.S., Vicar; Bro. William Hoefgen, S.D.S.; Deacon Raul Leon.
Res., 1321 Anna St., 95605. Tel: 916-371-1211; Fax: 916-371-9277.
School—800 Todhunter Ave., 95605. Tel: 916-371-1313. Mrs. Julie Brehl, Prin.
Sisters 2; Lay Teachers 7; Students 236.
Catechesis/Religious Programs—Students 160.
Convent—Tel: 916-371-1931; 933-0971. Sisters of Mercy (Auburn, CA)

Our Lady of Grace (1949), Rev. Edward O'Hara.
Res., 911 Park Blvd., 95691. Tel: 916-371-4814.
School—1990 Linden Rd., 95691. Tel: 916-371-9416; Fax: 916-371-1319. Sr. Michael Henry Moulin, D.H.S., Prin.
Sisters 1; Lay Teachers 9; Students 260.
Catechesis/Religious Programs—Students 50.
Convent—Tel: 916-371-9715.

Westwood, Lassen Co., Our Lady of the Snows (1929), Rev. Thomas Carrigan.
Res., 307 Fifth St., P.O. Box 905, 96137. Tel: 530-256-3344; Fax: 530-256-3344.
Church—425 Cedar St., 96137.
Catechesis/Religious Programs—Tel: 530-596-4261.
Students 78.
Mission—Chester, Plumas Co., Christ the King, Melissa St., Chester, 96020. Tel: 530-258-3151.

Willows, Glenn Co., St. Monica (1877), Revs. Matthias J. O'Callaghan; Heriberto Serrano.
Res., 1129 W. Wood St., 95988. Tel: 530-934-3314; Fax: 530-934-3205. [CEM]
Catechesis/Religious Programs—Tel: 530-934-2239; Fax: 530-934-2253.
Students 190.
Catechetical School—1151 W. Wood St., 95988. Tel: 530-934-5916.
Students 190.

Winters, Yolo Co., St. Anthony (1913), Rev. Joseph P. Ternullo; Deacons Alejandro Arroyo; Colby Smith.
Res., 303 Main St., P.O. Box 986, 95694. Tel: 530-795-2230; Fax: 530-795-5470.
Church—301 Main St., 95694.
Parish Center—511 Main St., 95694.
Catechesis/Religious Programs—Sr. Anne Chester, R.S.M., D.R.E.
Students 190.
Mission—Esparto, Yolo Co., St. Martin, 25633 Grafton Rd., Esparto, 95627. Tel: 530-787-3750.

Woodland, Yolo Co., Holy Rosary (1871), Revs. John E. Boll; Colm O'Kelly; Francisco J. Saenz (Colombia); Charles D. Nguyen (Vietnam); Deacons Edward Kull; Gonzalo Chavez; Antonio Fernandez.
Res., 318 Court St., 95695. Tel: 530-662-2805; Fax: 530-662-0796. [CEM]
School—505 California St., 95695. Tel: 530-662-3494; Fax: 530-668-2442. Jeanni Venturini, Prin.
Lay Teachers 11; Students 285.
Catechesis/Religious Programs—Tel: 530-662-5394. Nancy Johnson.
Students 730.
Mission—Yolo, Yolo Co., Our Lady of Guadalupe, 318 Court St., 95695.

Yreka, Siskiyou Co., St. Joseph (1855), Rev. William Hold.
Res., 314 Fourth St., P.O. Box 570, 96097. Tel: 530-842-3842.
Catechetical Center—308 Fourth St., 96097. Tel: 530-842-4874.
Catechesis/Religious Programs—Tel: 530-842-4874.
Students 72.
Mission—Hawkinsville, Siskiyou Co., Immaculate Conception.

Yuba City, Sutter Co., St. Isidore (1952), Revs. Manuel Soria; Joseph Huong Nguyen. In res., Revs. Joseph E. Bishop, Pastor Emeritus; Vincent A. Meskenas (BEL).
Res., 222 Clark Ave., 95991. Tel: 530-673-1573; Fax: 530-673-2512.
School—200 Clark Ave., 95991. Tel: 530-673-2217; Fax: 530-673-2217. Miss Sheila S. Garlock, Prin.
Lay Teachers 11; Students 283.
Catechesis/Religious Programs—Students 450.

Chaplains of Public Institutions

SACRAMENTO. *California Youth Authority* Northern Reception Center-Clinic, 3001 Ramona Ave., 95826. Tel: 916-739-2104. Rev. Liam P. McSweeney, Res., 929 Fulton Ave., No. 441, 95825. Tel: 916-488-4149; 733-2356.
Mule Creek State Prison. P.O. Box 409099, Ione, 95640. Tel: 209-274-4911. Rev. Thomas Maguire, Res., P.O. Box 578, Plymouth, 95669. Tel: 209-245-4331.
Sutter General Hospital 2801 L St., 95816. Tel: 916-454-2222. Rev. James P. Sheets.
Sutter Memorial Hospital 52nd & F Sts., 95819. Tel: 916-454-3333. Rev. James P. Sheets.
University of California, Davis Medical Center 2315 Stockton Blvd., 95817. Tel: 916-453-2011. Rev. William J. Dinelli, Res., 4315 Martin Luther King Jr. Blvd., 95820.

FOLSOM. *Folsom State Prison Annex*. Vacant. P.O. Box 29, Represa, 95671.
State Prison. Vacant. P.O. Box W, Represa, 95671. Tel: 916-985-2561. Res., 1521 Lake Vista Ln., 95630. Tel: 916-933-4980.

PRESTON. *School of Industry* California Youth Authority, Tel: 209-274-8000, Ext. 8250. Rev. Paul Schloeder.

SUSANVILLE. *California Correctional Center*. Attended by Lassen County. P.O. Box 790, 96130. Tel: 916-257-2181, Ext. 1180. Deacon Ramon Vega.
Sierra Army Depot. Attended by Army & Navy Chaplains and Sacred Heart Parish.

VACAVILLE. *California Medical Facility, Solano Co* P.O. Box 4000, 95696. Tel: 707-448-6841, Ext. 2378. Rev. Innocent Emechete, Chap., Res., 105 S. Second St., Dixon, 95620.
California Medical Facility, South P.O. Box 4000, 95696. Tel: 707-448-6841, Ext. 3137. Rev. Paul Schloeder, Chap.

Special Assignment:
Reverend Fathers—
O'Callaghan, Matthias J., Chap. to Police Officers, St. Monica Parish, 1129 W. Wood St., Willows, CA 95988
O'Halloran, Michael, O.P., Chap. for Law Enforcement, 201 Waterman Rd., Ione, CA 95640
Seabridge, Thomas L., Liaison for Arts and Shrines, St. Dominic Parish, P.O. Box 816, Orland, CA 95963. Tel: 916-865-4550
Silveira, Eduino, Chap. to Sheriff Deputies, St. Elizabeth Church, 1817 12th St., Sacramento, CA 95814
Traynor, Anthony, Chap. to Firefighters & Sacramento Metro Airport, Our Lady of Lourdes Church, 1951 North Ave., Sacramento, CA 95838

On Duty Outside the Diocese:
Reverend Fathers—
Dermody, Thomas, San Diego
Leslie, Patrick J., Santa Rosa

Military Chaplains:
Reverend Fathers—
Higgins, Richard B., U.S. Air Force
Mennis, James F., U.S. Navy
Stevenson, Francis R., U.S. Army

Graduate Studies:
Reverend Fathers—
Richards, Mark, 206 Caldwell Hall, Catholic University of America, Washington, DC

Awaiting Assignment:
Reverend Fathers—
Walsh, Michael

Absent on Leave:
Reverend Fathers—
Dermody, Michael
Garcia, Javier
Harlan, Anthony Vern
Moreno, Jorge
Steinauer, Carl J.

Retired and in Senior Ministry:
Reverend Monsignors—
Coffey, Andrew V., 520 C St., Davis, CA 95616
Higgins, Cornelius P., 3027 Olive Glen Ct., Sacramento, CA 95821
Horgan, William, Carrigan Wood, Brosna, Tralee, Co. Kerry, Ireland
Mistretta, Vito F., 7760 Woodchuck Way, Citrus Heights, CA 95610
Nolan, Patrick, P.O. Box 215231, Sacramento, CA 95821
O'Neill, Patrick J., 350 Locust Dr., Apt. #L-104, Vallejo, CA 94591
Peters, Roy V., 469 Ena Rd. #3010, Honolulu, HI 96815
Schons, Gerard, 627 3rd St., Galt, CA 95632
Terwilliger, John G., 3865 J St., Apt. #354, Sacramento, CA 95816
Reverend Fathers—
Albrecht, Walter H., 722 State St., Aberdeen, WA 98520
Brennan, Ronan P., 2007 Country Villa, Auburn, CA 95603
Broderick, William, 5057 Cottage Way, Carmichael, CA 95608
Connelly, Robert J., P.O. Box 5037, Oak Park Sta., Sacramento, CA 95817
Cormack, Michael J., 7413 Timberrose, Roseville, CA 95747
Delahunty, Thomas P., 3247 Sandhurst Ct., Cameron Park, CA 95682
Grace, John J., 3035 Berkeley Ave., South Lake Tahoe, CA 96150
Gurnell, Anthony, P.O. Box 627, Cayucos, CA 93430
Kyne, John J., Box 143, Corning, CA 96021
Lanigan, Patrick J., 1182 Hartford Pl., Fairfield, CA 94533
Lenehan, Vincent, 2251 Northrop Ave., Sacramento, CA 95825
Lyons, Vincent, 1147-A Porter St., Vallejo, CA 94590
Maio, Anthony V., 110 Village Ct., Vacaville, CA 95687
Mello, Edward, 3250 Blue Oaks Dr., #203, Auburn, CA 95602
Moloney, Sean
O'Brien, Thomas, 30 Woodlawn Park, Killarney, Co. Kerry, Ireland
O'Dowd, Brendan
O'Rafferty, Patrick, 5751 Locust Ave., Carmichael, CA 95608
Ramos, Cipriano, 338 Elm St., Roseville, CA 95678
Ryan, Lawrence A., P.O. Box 8050, Santa Cruz, CA 95061
Walsh, William K., 50 River Rd., #30, Rio Vista, CA 94571
Wdowiak, Boleslaw, c/o Alta Sierra, 11564 Tammy Way, Grass Valley, CA 95949

Permanent Deacons:
Adams, James V., Chatsworth, CA
Arroyo, Alejandro, St. Anthony, Winters
Astesana, Carlos, St. Patrick's, Grass Valley
Boone, Kenneth, St. Joseph, Lincoln
Boudier, William, St. Rose, Roseville
Burke, Keith, St. Philomene, Sacramento
Burkett, James, St. John, Chico
Cabrera, Domingo, St. Mary, Vacaville
Carlomagno, Michael, St. Basil, Vallejo
Cavanagh, Paul, St. Vincent Ferrer, Vallejo
Chatigny, James, St. Patrick, Grass Valley
Chavarria, Modesto, St. Anne, Sacramento
Chavez, Gonzalo, Holy Rosary, Woodland
Cheever, Charles, St. Philomene, Sacramento
Christiansen, George, Unassigned
Colenzo, Sam, St. James, Davis
Craig, Ray, Assumption, Truckee
Crowley, Michael, St. Anthony, Sacramento
DeHaven, Donald, Cathedral of the Blessed Sacrament, Sacramento
Del Gaudio, Lou, St. Mary, Sacramento
Donovan, Michael, All Hallows, Sacramento
Driggs, Richard, St. Francis of Assisi, Sacramento
Duvernay, Anthony, Newman Catholic Community, Chico
Evans, Michael, Sacred Heart, Anderson
Fernandez, Antonio, Holy Rosary, Woodland
Fernandez, Miguel, Our Lady of Lourdes, Colusa
Ferreira, Thomas, Our Lady of Assumption, Carmichael
Fracolli, Gary, St. Lawrence, North Highlands
Garcia, Henry, St. Joseph, Sacramento
Gasman, David H., St. Joseph, Redding
Gercich, Don, St. Patrick, Jackson
Godinez, Rafael, Unassigned
Gonzalez, Antonio, St. Paul, Knights Landing
Gualco, Jack, St. Ignatius, Sacramento
Healy, James, St. Anthony's, Sacramento
Helgeson, Raymond, Stubenville, OH
Henning, Patrick, St. Mel, Fair Oaks
Hernandez, Jesus, Holy Spirit, Fairfield
Ikelman, Robert, St. Peter, Dixon
Imrisek, Paul, St. Joseph, Elk Grove
King, John, St. Peter, Dixon
Koppes, Richard, St. Anthony, Sacramento
Kriske, George, All Hallows, Sacramento
Kull, Carl Ed, Holy Rosary, Woodland
LaLonde, James, Our Lady of Lourdes, Sacramento
Layne, Everett H., Holy Trinity (Mission of Weaverville)
Lazarek, Edward, St. Dominic, Benicia
Leon, Raul, Holy Cross, West Sacramento
Lewandowski, Daniel, Unassigned
Link, Robert, Holy Rosary, Woodland
Little, Walter, St. John Vianney, Rancho Cordova
Lobo, Pete, St. Catherine, Vallejo
Lopez, Frank, St. Joseph, Redding
Lubinsky, William, Holy Family, Citrus Heights
Lucas, George, Immaculate Conception, North San Juan
Mangas, Michael, St. Joseph, Redding
Mangoba, Leo, St. Vincent Ferrer, Vallejo
Manriquez, Pedro, St. Anne, Sacramento
Masla, John, Cathedral of the Blessed Sacrament, Sacramento
McGill, Thomas, Unassigned
McSwain, Gary, ID
Merino, Dennis, St. John the Baptist, Folsom
Meucci, James, Our Lady of the Assumption, Carmichael
Moore, Brian, St. Patrick, Grass Valley
Morgado, Edwin, St. Joseph, Auburn
Morris, Douglas, Austin, TX
Morrison, Charles, St. Paul, Sacramento
Moseley, Philip, St. John Vianney, Rancho Cordova
Munoz, Jesus, St. Joseph, Marysville
Nguyen, Anthony, Vietnamese Catholic Martyrs, Sacramento
Niekamp, Lawrence, Our Divine Savior, Orangevale
Padilla, Jesus, St. John the Baptist, Chico
Parra, Gilbert, Sacred Heart, Sacramento
Pauly, Gerald, Immaculate Conception, Sacramento; Vicar for Deacons
Perez, Ben, St. Catherine, Vallejo
Perez, David, St. Joseph's, Marysville
Ramirez, Antonio, St. John, Chico
Ramirez, Jose, Unassigned
Ramos, Ray, St. Peter, Sacramento
Rasmussen, Charles, Holy Trinity, El Dorado Hills
Redling, Ralph, Kelseyville, CA
Reyna, Pedro, Sacred Heart, Maxwell
Reynoso, Alejandro, St. Peter, Sacramento
Riehl, William, Sacred Heart, Sacramento
Rodriquez, Jesus, St. Joseph, Lincoln
Rodriquez, Martin, St. Robert, Sacramento
Rudger, Stanley, St. Patrick, Placerville
Ruiz, Roberto, St. Joseph's, Lincoln
Sanchez, Miquel, Holy Spirit, Fairfield
Schaeffer, William, Abbey of New Clairvaux, Vina
Schwartz, Steve, St. John, Chico
Sheldon, Lawrence, San Diego, CA
Shields, Floyd, McClellan Air Force Base
Short, Sam, Our Lady of Mercy, Redding
Silott, Peter, St. Rose of Lima, Roseville
Sims, Robert, St. Vincent Ferrer, Vallejo
Smith, Colby, St. Anthony, Winters
Stackhouse, Milton, St. Patrick, Grass Valley
Symkowick, Joseph, Newman Catholic Community, CSUS, Sacramento
Taloff, Paul, St. James, Davis
Tamayo, Juan, St. Rose of Lima, Roseville
Tateishi, Michael, Our Lady of the Assumption, Carmichael
Thompson, William, St. Patrick, Jackson
Trueworthy, Len, Our Lady of Mt. Carmel, Fairfield
Vega, Ramon, Chap. California Correctional Center, Susanville, CA
Weeks, Bernard J., Holy Spirit, Sacramento
Weeks, James, St. John the Evangelist, Carmichael
White, Les, St. John the Baptist, Folsom
Wortman, Richard, St. Philip (Byzantine), Sacramento
Wroblicky, Theodore, St. Andrew the Apostle (Ukrainian)
Yang, Gnia, Hmong Community
Zellmer, Gary, Washington

INSTITUTIONS LOCATED IN THE DIOCESE

[A] SEMINARY, RELIGIOUS

LOOMIS. *Mount St. Joseph Novitiate and Seminary*, 6530 Wells Ave., P.O. Box 547, 95650. Tel: 916-652-6336. Novitiate of Oblates of St. Joseph. Revs. John C. Warburton, O.S.J., Rector; Brian Crawford, O.S.J.; Bro. Marcello DiNardo, O.S.J. Priests 2; Brothers 1.

VINA. *Abbey of New Clairvaux, Trappist Seminary*, P.O. Box 80, 96092. Tel: 916-839-2161; Fax: 916-839-2332.
E-mail: txd@maxinet.com
Web site: www.maxinet.com/trappist/
Rt. Rev. Thomas X. Davis, O.C.S.O., J.C.L., Abbot. In res. Revs. Timothy VanderVennet, O.C.S.O., S.T.L.; Lawrence A. Glaser, O.C.S.O.; Joseph Wittbrod, O.C.S.O.; Paul Jerome Konkler, O.C.S.O.; Harold K. Meyer, O.C.S.O.; Anthony R. Bellesorte, O.C.S.O.; Mark A. Scott, O.C.S.O., S.S.L.; John Baptist Porter, O.C.S.O.; Paul Mark Schwan, O.C.S.O.; Maurus Pei, O.C.S.O. Seminarians 2.

[B] HIGH SCHOOLS, DIOCESAN

SACRAMENTO. *St. Francis High School*. (Girls), 6051 M St., 95819. Tel: 916-452-3461; Fax: 916-452-1591.
E-mail: sfhssac@connect.com
Web site: www.saintfrancishs.org
Apostles of the Sacred Heart of Jesus (Hamden, CT). Sr. Catherine Sedgeman, A.S.C.J., Prin. Sisters 5; Lay Teachers 53; Girls 782.

PALO CEDRO. *Bishop Quinn High School*, 21893 Old 44 Dr., 96073. Tel: 916-547-2900; Fax: 916-547-5349.
E-mail: BQSF@connect.com
Dr. Raymond L. John, Principal.

RED BLUFF. *Mercy High School*, 233 Riverside Way, 96080. Tel: 916-527-8313. Michael J. Steinbrecher, Ed.D., Prin. Lay Teachers 13; Students 152.

VALLEJO. *St. Patrick-St. Vincent High School*, 1500 Benicia Rd., 94591. Tel: 707-644-4425; Fax: 707-644-3107.
E-mail: spsvhs@connectinc.com
Sr. Sue Pixley, O.P., Principal. Sisters 3; Lay Teachers 41; Students 630.

[C] HIGH SCHOOLS, PRIVATE

SACRAMENTO. *Christian Brothers High School of Sacramento, Inc.*, 4315 Martin Luther King Jr. Blvd., 95820. Tel: 916-733-3630. Mr. Mark L. Warren, Pres.; Tom J. Rutten, Prin. Brothers 5; Sisters 2; Lay Teachers 58; Students 909.

Jesuit High School. Mailing Address: P.O. Box 254647, 95865-4647. Tel: 916-482-6060. 1200 Jacob Ln., Carmichael, 95608. (Boys). Revs. Edwin B. Harris, S.J., Pres.; Alfred E. Naucke, S.J., Rector; Reynold J. Gatto, S.J.; Francis G. Hernandez, S.J.; Richard L. McCurdy, S.J.; John P. McGarry, S.J.; Charles R. Olsen, S.J.; Lorenzo J. Palafox, S.J.; John T. Quinn, S.J.; A. Francis Stiegeler, S.J., Prin.; William K. Stolz, S.J.; George V. Wanser, S.J.; Carlton E. Whitten, S.J. Jesuit Priests 13; Brothers 3; Scholastics 3; Lay Teachers 55; Boys 1,016.

Loretto High School. (Girls), 2360 El Camino Ave., 95821. Tel: 916-482-7793.
E-mail: LorettoHS@aol.com
Web site: www.Loretto.Room.Net
Religious of the Institute of the Blessed Virgin Mary. Sr. Helen Timothy, I.B.V.M., Prin. Sisters 2; Lay Teachers 46; Girls 425.

[D] DAY NURSERY AND CHILD CARE HOMES

SACRAMENTO. *Grace Day Home*, 1909 7th St., 95814. Tel: 916-442-6557.
E-mail: graceday@pacbell.net
Ms. Nancy DeArmond, Exec. Dir. Lay Staff 34; Children 150.

St. Patrick Children's Home, Inc., 5945 Franklin Blvd., 95824. Tel: 916-421-1620. Rev. Msgr. Edward J. Kavanagh, Exec. Dir.; Colleen Maloney, Financial Officer.
Two Residential Group Homes for Boys and Girls: Veda Cannon, Dir., Lopresti, 5036 Lemon Hill Ave., 95828. McMahon, 8529 Florin Rd., 95828. Total Residents 16; Total Assisted 21; Total Staff 42.
St. Patrick's Child Care Centers, 5945 Franklin Blvd., 95824. Tel: 916-422-0123. Sandra Patitucci, Dir. Children (ages 2-5) 68; Children in after school care program 32; Total Assisted 101.
St. Patrick's Infant Toddler Program, 5945 Franklin Blvd., 95824. Tel: 916-422-0123. Children (ages 6 weeks-2 years) 24; Total Assisted 27.
St. Patrick's Infant-Toddler Program, 8201 Florin Rd., 95828. Tel: 916-383-3254. Sandra Patitucci, Dir. Children (ages 6 weeks-2 years 9 months) 34; Total Assisted 94. State funded for low income families-12 children ages 2-5. Private care: non-state funded.
St. Patrick's Foster Care Program. Stephen Isbell, Dir. Tel: 916-421-3714. Families providing care 22; Children 42; Total Staff 5.

[E] HOMES FOR SENIOR CITIZENS

SACRAMENTO. *Mercy-McMahon Terrace*, 3865 J St., 95816. Tel: 916-733-6510; Fax: 916-733-6515
For a complete listing, refer to the Special Care Facilities section.

[F] GENERAL HOSPITALS

SACRAMENTO. *Mercy General Hospital*, 4001 J St., 95819. Tel: 916-453-4545
For a complete listing, refer to the Hospitals section.

CARMICHAEL. *Mercy American River/Mercy San Juan Hospital/Mercy American River Campus*, 4747 Engle Rd., 95608. Tel: 916-484-2222
For a complete listing, refer to the Hospitals section.

FOLSOM. *Mercy Hospital of Folsom*, 1650 Creekside Dr., 95630. Tel: 916-983-7400.
E-mail: cgrittner@chw.edu.
For a complete listing, refer to the Hospitals section.

MT. SHASTA. *Mercy Medical Center*, 914 Pine St., P.O. Box 239, 96067. Tel: 916-926-6111.
Web site: ntmhn1.mercy.org
For a complete listing, refer to the Hospitals section.

RANCHO CORDOVA. *Mercy Healthcare Sacramento*, 10540 White Rock Rd., 95670. Tel: 916-851-2000
For a complete listing, refer to the Hospitals section.

RED BLUFF. *St. Elizabeth Community Hospital Mercy Healthcare North*, 2550 Sr. Mary Columba Dr., 96080-4397. Tel: 916-529-8000; Fax: 916-529-8009
For a complete listing, refer to the Hospitals section.

REDDING. *Mercy Medical Center*, Clairmont Heights, P.O. Box 496009, 96049. Tel: 916-225-6000
For a complete listing, refer to the Hospitals section.

SUSANVILLE. *Lassen Community Hospital*, 560 Hospital Ln., 96130. Tel: 916-257-5325
For a complete listing, refer to the Hospitals section.

[G] MONASTERIES AND RESIDENCES OF PRIESTS AND BROTHERS

CARMICHAEL. *Jesuit High School Community of Sacramento.*
(California Prov., Los Gatos). Mailing Address: P.O. Box 254647, Sacramento, 95865. Tel: 916-482-6060. 1200 Jacob Ln., 95608. Revs. Alfred E. Naucke, S.J., Rector; Michael C Barber, S.J.; William F. Breault, S.J.; Reynold J. Gatto, S.J.; Edwin B. Harris, S.J.; Francis G. Hernandez, S.J.; David F. Klein, S.J.; Richard L. McCurdy, S.J.; John P. McGarry, S.J.; Charles R. Olsen, S.J.; Lorenzo J. Palafox, S.J.; John T. Quinn, S.J.; A. Francis Stiegeler, S.J.; William K. Stolz, S.J.; George V. Wanser, S.J.; Carlton E. Whitten, S.J.; Bros. Justin DeChance, S.J.; Charles Onorato, S.J.; James Sanders, S.J.; Mr. Michael Taylor, S.J. Priests 16; Brothers 3; Scholastics 2.

CITRUS HEIGHTS. *Christ the King Retreat*, 6520 Van Maren Ln., 95621. Tel: 916-969-0685; Fax: 916-725-4812. The Passionists (Chicago, IL). A community residence for the Passionist priests and brothers who conduct missions and retreats. Very Rev. Donald A. Webber, C.P., Supr.; Revs. Neil J. Parsons, C.P.; Thomas More Newbold, C.P.; James G. Strommer, C.P.; Joseph O. Mitchell, C.P., Retreat Dir.; James Busch, C.P.; Cedric Pisegna, C.P.; Raymond McDonough, C.P.; Bro. Carl Hund, C.P. Priests 8; Brothers 1.

VINA. *Abbey of New Clairvaux, Trappist*, P.O. Box 80, 96092. Tel: 916-839-2161; Fax: 916-839-2332.
E-mail: txdavis@maxinet.com
Web site: www.maxinet.com/trappist/
Cistercian Abbey, Cistercians of the Strict Observance. Rt. Rev. Thomas X. Davis, O.C.S.O., J.C.L., Abbot; Revs. Joseph J. Wittbrod, O.C.S.O., Prior; Timothy VanderVennett, O.C.S.O., S.T.L.; Lawrence A. Glaser, O.C.S.O.; Paul Jerome Konkler, O.C.S.O.; Harold K. Meyer, O.C.S.O.; Anthony R. Bellesorte, O.C.S.O.; Mark A. Scott, O.C.S.O.; John Baptist Porter, O.C.S.O.; Paul Mark Schwan, O.C.S.O., Trappist Monastery, Lantao Island, P.O. 5, Peng Chau, Hong Kong. Rev. Maurus Pei, O.C.S.O. Priests 10; Professed Brothers 13.

[H] CONVENTS AND RESIDENCES FOR SISTERS

SACRAMENTO. *Apostles of the Sacred Heart of Jesus*, St. Francis High School Convent, 5945 M St., 95819. Tel: 916-457-1768; Fax: 916-452-1591.
Web site: www.saintfrancishs.org
Sisters 5. St. Charles Borromeo Convent, 7580 Center Pkwy., 95823. Tel: 916-421-7174; Fax: 916-421-3954. Sisters 4.

Canossian Daughters of Charity, Our Lady of Lourdes Convent, 1949 North Ave., 95838. Tel: 916-925-4001. Sisters 4.

Presentation Sisters, St. Mary's Convent, 5801 N St., 95819. Tel: 916-451-5881. Sisters 3.

Religious of the Cenacle, 1964 Ethan Way #15, 95825. Tel: 916-924-3913; 971-1777 (Office).

Religious of the Virgin Mary, 1123 W St., 95818. Tel: 916-447-7008. Sisters 4.

Sister Servants of the Blessed Sacrament, St. Peter's Convent, 5870 62nd St., 95824. Tel: 916-457-0182. Sisters 6.

Sisters of Social Service, 1181 Fulton Ave. #51, 95825. Other Locations: 6016 Homesweet Way, Carmichael, 95608. Tel: 916-489-0803. 5349 Sedona Ct., Carmichael, 95608. Tel: 916-489-3714. Jericho, 926 J St., Ste 410, 95814. Catholic Social Service.

Sisters of St. Dominic, 381 Bell Ave., #30, 95838. Tel: 916-929-4375. Sisters 1.

Sisters of St. Francis of Penance and Christian Charity, 2245 Woodside Ln., 95825.
Other Locations: St. Francis Manor, 2515 J. St. #608, 95816.

Sisters of the Holy Rosary of Fatima, 1708 U St., 95818. Tel: 916-442-8646. Sisters 3.

Sisters of the Sacred Hearts of Jesus & Mary, St. Paul's Convent, P.O. Box 292280, 95829. Tel: 926-381-5200. Sisters 2.

AUBURN. *Institute of the Sisters of Mercy of the Americas*.
Auburn Regional Community. Motherhouse: 535 Sacramento St., 95603-5699. Tel: 530-887-2000; Fax: 530-885-6581. Sr. Susan McCarthy, R.S.M., Pres. Sisters in Community 23; Sisters in Diocese 83.

Russell House, 2223 L St., Sacramento, 95816-4926. Tel: 916-446-9251. Sisters 5.

McAuley Convent, 3846 H St., Sacramento, 95816-4613. Tel: 916-455-2843. Sisters 3.

Sisters of Mercy, 5625 Frontier Way, Carmichael, 95608. Tel: 916-489-0844. Sisters 5.

Our Lady of Fatima Convent, 1715 El Monte Ave., Sacramento, 95815-2904. Tel: 916-924-8541. Sisters 3.

Holy Spirit Convent, 3920 W. Land Park Dr., Sacramento, 95822-1123. Tel: 916-448-3578. Sisters 6.

Mercy Convent, 750 41st St., Sacramento, 95819-2738. Tel: 916-457-8274. Sisters 8.

Mercy San Juan, 6620 Oakbrook Dr., Fair Oaks, 95628. Tel: 916-962-7144. Sisters 8.

Mercy Convent, 2254 Gold St., Redding, 96001-2420. Tel: 530-225-7590. Sisters 3.

Mercy Residence, 8637 Posadera Ave., Orangevale, 95662-3329. Tel: 916-987-1436. Sisters 2.

Holy Cross Convent, 800 Todhunter Ave., West Sacramento, 95605-2299. Tel: 916-371-1931. Sisters 5.

Sisters of Mercy, 212 Bittercreek Dr., Folsom, 95630-2353. Tel: 916-983-9268. Sisters 2.

Sisters of Mercy, 848 39th St., Sacramento, 95816. Tel: 916-454-1723. Sisters 2.

Sisters of Mercy, 1396 Oakwood Ave., Vallejo, 94591. Tel: 707-552-9882. Sisters 2.

Sisters of Mercy, 2101 Shoreline Dr., #146, Alameda, 94501. Tel: 510-521-7756. Sr. Brenda O'Keeffe, 1100 39th St., #214, Sacramento, 95816-5527. Tel: 916-457-5509. Sr. Teresa Gahan.

Franciscan Center, 1784 LaCross Ave., St. Paul, MN, 55119-4808. Tel: 612-739-7953. Sr. Mary Corita Keane, (Sept.-Dec.).

Sisters of Mercy, 800 41st St., Sacramento, 95819. Tel: 916-454-3658. Sr. Caritas Cunningham, P.O. Box 1522, Mt. Shasta, 96067-9510. Tel: 916-926-6644. Sr. Mary Virginia Sullivan, 1180 Matmore Rd., #32, Woodland, 95776-6341. Tel: 916-662-6840. Sr. Sally Dominic Torres, 4740 Appian Way, #10, El Sobrante, 94803. Tel: 510-222-8415. Sr. Frances Walshe.

CARMICHAEL. *Dominican Sisters*, 8633 Fair Oaks Blvd., #30, 95608-2592. Congregation of the Most Holy Rosary, Sinsinawa, WI. Sisters 2.

Religious of the Institute of the Blessed Virgin Mary, Assumption Convent, 5055 Cottage Way, 95608. Tel: 916-488-8188. Sisters 5.
Other Locations: 3606 Chadsworth Way, Sacramento, 95821. Tel: 916-485-6384. Sisters 5. 2904 Cottage Way, #2, Sacramento, 95825. Tel: 916-487-1589. Sisters 1.

FAIR OAKS. *Sisters of Mercy of Cashel*, St. Mel's Convent, P.O. Box 1180, 95628. Tel: 916-967-9504. Sisters 2.

FAIRFIELD. *Sisters of the Holy Faith*, Holy Spirit Convent, 1050 N. Texas St., 94533. Tel: 707-425-3572. Sisters 5.

GEORGETOWN. *Discalced Carmelite Nuns*, P.O. Box 1720, 95634. Tel: 916-333-1617. Carmel of the Holy Family and Saint Therese. Sisters 16.

PLACERVILLE. *Franciscan Sisters of the Atonement*, Sr. Thomas Marie Heavey, S.A., 3158 Big Cut Rd. #2, 95667. Tel: 916-622-1983.
E-mail: tmheavey@innercite.com

POLLOCK PINES. *Ursuline Sisters*, 6305 Sierra Springs Dr., 95726. Tel: 916-644-3319.

WEST SACRAMENTO. *Daughters of the Holy Spirit*, Our Lady of Grace Convent, 1990 Linden Rd., 95691. Tel: 916-371-9715. Sisters 2.

[I] RETREAT HOUSES

SACRAMENTO. *Pendola Center*, 2110 Broadway, 95818-2541. Tel: 916-733-0123; 916-PEN-DOLA; Fax: 916-733-0195.
E-mail: campenoola@aol.com
Web site: http://www.geocitius.com/yosemite/1038
Center located in Sierra-Nevada foothills near Camptonville. Summer camp for boys and girls 7-16. Available for teenage and young adult retreats, school midweek retreats, field trips. Contact: Stephen Tholcke, Dir. of Pendola Center, Dept. of Catholic Faith Formation.

APPLEGATE. *Our Lady of the Oaks Villa*, P.O. Box 128, 95703. Tel: 916-878-2776. For Jesuit Fathers, Brothers and Scholastics. Rev. Gerald H. Robinson, S.J., Dir. Tel: 916-482-9666; Bro. James Sanders, S.J., Asst. Dir. Tel: 916-482-6060.

AUBURN. *Marian Retreat Center*, 535 Sacramento St., 95603. Tel: 916-887-2019. Sr. Katherine Doyle, R.S.M., Dir.

CITRUS HEIGHTS. *Christ the King Retreat Center*, 6520 Van Maren Ln., 95621. Tel: 916-969-4706. Rev. Joseph O. Mitchell, C.P., Dir. Associate Directors: Revs. Raymond McDonough, C.P.; Donald A. Webber, C.P.; Bro. Carl Hund; Mr. Thomas Borkowski, Admin.

[J] CAMPUS MINISTRIES AND NEWMAN CENTERS

CHICO. *Director of Campus Ministry*, 346 Cherry St., 95928. Tel: 916-342-5180; Fax: 916-342-3016. Rev. Michael J. Newman, S.D.S.

California State University (Sacramento), Newman Catholic Community. Rev. D. Joseph McCarthy, Dir., 5900 Newman Ct., Sacramento, 95819. Joseph Symkowick, Deacon; Ms. Mary Ann Williams, Admin. Asst., Tel: 916-454-4198; Fax: 916-454-4180.

California State University (Chico), Newman Catholic Community. Rev. Michael J. Newman, S.D.S., Diocesan Dir. of Campus Ministry; Anthony Duvernay, Deacon; Ms. Marge Flynn, Sec., 346 Cherry St., 95928. Tel: 916-342-5180; Fax: 916-342-3016.

University of California (Davis), Newman Catholic Community, 514 C St., Davis, 95616. Tel: 916-753-7393; Fax: 916-753-2794. Rev. Tongele Ngbatara, Dir.; Ms. Cyndi Smit, Sec.

[K] CATHOLIC SOCIAL WELFARE ACTIVITIES

SACRAMENTO. *Catholic Charities of Sacramento, Inc.* Diocese of Sacramento. 5890 Newman Ct., 95819. Tel: 916-452-4621; Fax: 916-736-0282. Roman Catholic Bishop of Sacramento, A Corporation Sole. Donalee Hallenbeck, Pres. & Chm. Bd. of Dirs.; James F. Rodgers, Exec. Dir.

Adult Reading Program, 3300 3rd Ave., 95817. Tel: 916-456-7323.

Clothing Program, 3333 Third Ave., 95817.

Food Distribution Center Program, 3333 Third Ave., 95817. Tel: 916-456-1980.

Homeless Haven (Transitional Housing Program), 3333 Third Ave., 95817. Tel: 916-456-1980.

Mother-Baby Program, 3333 Third Ave., 95817. Tel: 916-456-1980.

Sacramento Food Bank Services, Inc., 3333 Third Ave., 95817. Tel: 916-456-1980; 452-3663.

Catholic Social Service, Sacramento, Central Office, 5890 Newman Ct., 95819-2608. Tel: 916-452-7481. Richard Mata, Pres., Bd. of Dirs.; Adrienne F. Rogers, Exec. Dir.

Sacramento, Camellia City Senior Center, 1121 - Ninth St., 95814. Tel: 916-442-9014. Denise Nelson, Center Dir. Day Center, In-Home Visiting, Money management program, meals, housing assistance, health screening, information and referral.

New Pathways, Counseling Services, School-Based Counseling Program, 5890 Newman Ct., 95819-2608. Peter Caldwell, M.F.C.C., Dir., Counseling Dept. Tel: 916-452-7481.

Sacramento, Centro Guadalupe. Advocacy, Information and Referral, Licensed Bilingual Counseling, Bilingual Food Closet, Parenting Classes, Employment Assistance, Adult Homeless Education Program. Sylvia Villalobos, Center Dir., 730 S St., 95814. Tel: 916-443-5367.

Immigration Services & Citizenship Dept., 5890 Newman Ct., 95819. Tel: 916-452-7481. Adela Avila, Program Dir. Total Staff 49; Total Assisted 113,112.

Grand Council, Catholic Ladies Relief Society of the Sacramento Diocese, Shirley Godfrey, Grand President, 6600 Greenhaven Dr., 95831.

Mercy Education Resource Center, 6007 Folsom Blvd. #200, 95819. Tel: 916-737-6026. Sponsored by the Sisters of Mercy Auburn Regional Community. Provides Marriage counseling and individual counseling, and psycho-educational assessment. Sr. Anne Sekul, R.S.M., Dir.

Society of St. Vincent de Paul, Sacramento District Council, 95609-0564. Mailing Address: P.O. Box 1040, Carmichael, 95609-0564. Main Office: 2620 Fulton Ave., 95821. Tel: 916-972-1253. Phil Niederberger, Pres.

St. Vincent de Paul Thrift Store, 2620 Fulton Ave., 95821. Tel: 916-972-1212. Virginia C. Pennington, Mgr.

REDDING. *Northern Valley Catholic Social Service*, 1020 Market St., 96001. Tel: 916-241-0552. Jan Maurer Watkins, Exec. Dir. Foster family agency; adolescent family life programs; counseling program; housing programs; independent living skills for foster youth; foster care education; family support and preservation; HIV/AIDS program; Stillwater learning program; Community Alternatives to Violence; Volunteer Program.

Pine Street Place (Transitional Shelter).

Wilshire Place (Developmentally Disabled Housing).

Hartford Place (Developmentally Disabled Housing).

Second Time Around Thrift Store, 872 N. Market St., 96001.
Offices: 1020 Market St., 96001. 1051 Mangrove, Chico, 95926. 2445 Oroville Dam Blvd., Ste.5, Oroville, 95965.

ROSEVILLE. *Society of St. Vincent DePaul*, 139 Riverside, 95678. Tel: 916-781-3303; (dining room & thrift store) 781-3368; (food locker) 781-3335. Mr. Dave Sorensen, Pres.

VALLEJO. *Catholic Social Service of Solano County*, Central Office, 745 Georgia St., 94590. Tel: 707-644-8909. Caroline Kieffer. Sisters of Social Service 1; Lay Workers 10; Total Assisted 3,648.
Outreach Offices: 2700 Dover Ave., Fairfield, 94533. Tel: 707-422-3466. 40 Eldrige Ave., Ste. 9A, Vacaville, 95688. Tel: 707-453-0844.

Society of St. Vincent de Paul Solano District Council, P.O. Box 931, 94590. Mr. Michael Hayes, Pres.

[L] YOUTH AND YOUNG ADULT MINISTRIES

SACRAMENTO. *Department of Catholic Faith Formation*, 2110 Broadway, 95818. Tel: 916-733-0123. Sr. Maura Power, R.S.M., Dir.; Linda Shumate, Asst. Admin. for Catechetics; Sr. Maria Padilla, R.S.M., Consultant, Hispanic Catechesis; Ms. Milagros Calvetti, Coord. Hispanic Youth/Young Adult Ministry; Mrs. Cheryl Tholcke, Coord. Youth Ministry. Program Coordinators: James Anderson; Jean Nelson; Mr. Stephen Tholcke, Dir. Pendola Center; Mr. Robert Brenner, Coord. For The Ministry To Persons With Disabilitites; Mr. John Donahoe, Coord. Camp Recreation; Mr. Thomas Fausone, Coord. Evangelization.

ORANGEVALE. *Catholic Committee on Scouting*, 9079 Greenback Ln., 95662.
E-mail: fatherbob@divinesavior.com
Web site: http://www.divinesavior.com
Rev. Robert R. Marsicek, S.D.S., Diocesan Chap.

[M] CAMPS

SACRAMENTO. *Pendola Center*, Office, 2110 Broadway, 95818-2541. Tel: 916-733-0123; 736-3652; Fax: 916-733-0195.
E-mail: campendola@aol.com
Web site: http://www.geocities.com/yosemite/1038
Located at Camptonville, Yuba County. Mr. Stephen F. Tholcke, Dir. Diocesan youth & young adult retreat center (September-April). Summer camp for boys and girls 7-16 (June, July, August). Outdoor

school (September, October, November), available for parish youth and young adult retreats, school field trips and retreats.

[N] MISSIONARY ORGANIZATIONS

SACRAMENTO. *Friends of Leprosy Patients*, P.O. Box 2655, 95812-2655. National Headquarters. Most Rev. William K. Weigand, D.D., Ed.D., Bishop of Sacramento, Honorary Chm.; R.B. Roberts, Pres.

[O] MISCELLANEOUS

SACRAMENTO. *Catholic Charities of California, Inc.*, Cathedral Sq., 1010 11th St., Ste. 200, 95814. Tel: 916-443-4851; Fax: 916-443-4731. Mr. Frank Hudson, Pres.; Sr. Ray Monda DuVall, Vice Pres.; Rev. Msgr. Gregory A. Cox, Sec. & Treas.; Richard Mockler, Exec. Dir.

**Loaves & Fishes*, P.O. Box 2161, 95812.

Loaves & Fishes Dining Room, 1321 N. C St., 95814. Tel: 916-446-0874. LeRoy Chatfield, Exec. Dir.

Mustard Seed.

Brother Martin's Courtyard.

Maryhouse, 1321 N. C St., #32, 95814. Tel: 916-446-4961. Joan Burke, Dir.

MercyClinic, 1321 N. C St., 95814. Tel: 916-446-3345.

Friendship Park, 1300 N. C St., 95814. Tel: 916-443-7378. Rev. Chris Hartmire.

**Stanford Settlement*, 450 W. El Camino, 95833-2299. Tel: 916-927-1303; Fax: 916-922-1694. Sr. Jeanne Felion, S.S.S., Dir. Assisted annually 10,000.

RELIGIOUS INSTITUTES OF MEN REPRESENTED IN THE DIOCESE

For further details refer to the corresponding bracketed number in the Religious Institutes of Men or Women section.

[]—*Assumptionist Fathers.*—A.A.

[0330]—*Brothers of the Christian Schools.* (Moraga, CA).—F.S.C.

[0270]—*Carmelite Fathers & Brothers.* (Barrington, IL).—O.Carm.

[0350]—*Cistercians Order of the Strict Observance-Trappists.*—O.C.S.O.

[0370]—*Columban Fathers.*—S.S.C.

[]—*Congregation of Mother Coredemptrix.*—C.M.C.

[1000]—*Congregation of the Passion.* (Chicago, IL).—C.P.

[0520]—*Franciscan Friars.* (Prov. of St. Barbara).—O.F.M.

[0690]—*Jesuit Fathers and Brothers.* (California Prov., Los Gatos, CA).—S.J.

[0930]—*Oblates of St. Joseph.* (Santa Cruz, CA).—O.S.J.

[0430]—*Order of Preachers-Dominicans.* (Oakland).—O.P.

[1200]—*Society of the Divine Savior.* (Milwaukee, WI).—S.D.S.

[]—*Society of the Most Holy Trinity.*—S.O.L.T.

RELIGIOUS INSTITUTES OF WOMEN REPRESENTED IN THE DIOCESE

[0130]—*Apostles of the Sacred Heart of Jesus.* (Hamden, CT).—A.S.C.J.

[3110]—*Congregation of Our Lady of the Retreat in the Cenacle.* (Chicago, IL).—R.C.

[1940]—*Congregation of the Sisters of the Holy Faith.*—C.H.F.

[0730]—*Daughters of Charity of Canossa.*—Fd.CC. (Rome, Italy).

[0820]—*Daughters of the Holy Spirit.* (Putnam, CT).—D.H.S.

[0420]—*Discalced Carmelite Nuns.*—O.C.D.

[1070-03]—*Dominican Sisters.* (Sinsinawa, WI).—O.P.

[1070-04]—*Dominican Sisters.* (San Rafael, CA).—O.P.

[1190]—*Franciscan Sisters of the Atonement.* (Garrison, NY).—S.A.

[2370]—*Institute of the Blessed Virgin Mary (Loretto Sisters).*—I.B.V.M.

[2575]—*Institute of the Sisters of Mercy of the Americas.*—R.S.M.

[]—*Religious of the Virgin Mary.* (Quezon City, Philippines).—R.V.M.

[3499]—*Sister Servants of the Blessed Sacrament.*—S.S.B.S.

[]—*Sisters of Mercy of Cashel.*—S.M.

[4080]—*Sisters of Social Service of Los Angeles, Inc.*—S.S.S.

[1630]—*Sisters of St. Francis of Penance and Christian Charity.* (Redwood City, CA).—O.S.F.

[]—*Sisters of St. Joseph of Carondelet.*—C.S.J.

[1960]—*Sisters of the Holy Family.* (San Jose, CA).—S.H.F.

[]—*Sisters of the Holy Name of Jesus & Mary.*—S.N.J.M.

[]—*Sisters of the Holy Rosary of Fatima.* (Salvatierra, Mexico).—H.R.F.

[3680]—*Sisters of the Sacred Hearts of Jesus and Mary.* (Essex).—S.H.J.M.

[]—*Society of the Holy Child Jesus.*—S.H.C.J.

[3330]—*Union of the Sisters of the Presentation of the Blessed Virgin Mary.*—P.B.V.M.

[4110]—*Ursuline Nuns.*—O.S.U.

DIOCESAN CEMETERIES

SACRAMENTO. *St. Joseph*, 2615 21st St., 95818. Tel: 916-455-8324.

St. Mary's Cemetery & Mausoleum, 6700 21st Ave., 95820. Tel: 916-452-4831.

CITRUS HEIGHTS. *Calvary Cemetery & Mausoleum*, 7101 Verner Ave., P.O. Box 41303, 95841. Tel: 916-969-6541.

VALLEJO. *All Souls Cemetery & Mausoleum*, Glen Cove Rd., 94590. Tel: 707-644-5209.

St. Vincent, 550 Glen Cove Rd., 94590. Tel: 707-644-5209.

NECROLOGY

† Degnan, Rev. Msgr. Paul, (Retired). —Died Aug. 16, 1997.

† Poole, Rev. Msgr. James D., (Retired). —Died Nov. 10, 1997.

† Snellenberg, John Van, (Retired). —Died Oct. 24, 1997.

Diocese of Saginaw

(Dioecesis Saginavensis)

Most Reverend

KENNETH E. UNTENER, S.T.D., D.D.

Bishop of Saginaw; ordained June 1, 1963; ordained and installed as Bishop of Saginaw November 24, 1980. *Res., 5800 Weiss St., Saginaw, MI, 48603-2799.*

ESTABLISHED FEBRUARY 26, 1938.

Square Miles 6,955.

Comprises the following Counties in the State of Michigan: Arenac, Bay, Clare, Gladwin, Gratiot, Huron, Isabella, Midland, Saginaw, Sanilac and Tuscola.

For legal titles of parishes and diocesan institutions, consult the Chancery Office.

Chancery: 5800 Weiss St., Saginaw, MI, 48603-2799. Tel.: 517-799-7910; Fax: 517-797-6670.

Web site address: http://www.dioceseofsaginaw.org

STATISTICAL OVERVIEW

Personnel	
Bishop	1
Priests: Diocesan Active in Diocese	78
Priests: Active Outside Diocese	4
Priests: Diocesan in Foreign Missions	3
Priests: Retired, Sick or Absent	34
Number of Diocesan Priests	119
Religious Priests in Diocese	15
Extern Priests in Diocese	7
Ordinations:	
Diocesan Priests	1
Permanent Deacons in Diocese	17
Total Brothers	1
Total Sisters	143
Parishes	
Parishes	110
With Resident Pastor:	
Resident Diocesan Priests	75
Resident Religious Priests	8
Without Resident Pastor:	
Administered by Priests	13
Administered by Permanent Deacons	1
Administered by Women Religious	11
Administered by Lay People	2
Welfare	
Catholic Hospitals	1
Total Assisted	123,620
Health Care Centers	1
Total Assisted	10,330
Homes for the Aged	1
Total Assisted	100
Residential Care of Children	3
Total Assisted	96
Day Care and Extended Day Care Centers	7
Total Assisted	151
Specialized Homes	1
Total Assisted	47
Special Centers for Social Services	5
Total Assisted	1,246
Educational	
Diocesan Students in Other Seminaries	4
Total Seminarians	4
High Schools, Diocesan and Parish	3
Total Students	935
Elementary Schools, Diocesan and Parish	31
Total Students	5,744
Catechesis/Religious Education:	
High School Students	3,191
Elementary Students	11,263
Total Students Under Catholic Instruction	21,137
Teachers in the Diocese:	
Priests	1
Sisters	22
Lay Teachers	329
Vital Statistics	
Receptions into the Church:	
Infant Baptism Totals	2,245
Adult Baptism Totals	276
Received into Full Communion	301
First Communions	2,194
Confirmations	4,650
Marriages:	
Catholic	573
Interfaith	388
Total Marriages	961
Deaths	1,514
Total Catholic Population	139,876
Total Population	685,532

Former Bishops—Most Rev. WILLIAM F. MURPHY, S.T.D., J.C.L., LL.D., ord. June 13, 1908; appt. first Bishop of Saginaw, March 17, 1938; cons. May 17, 1938; died Feb. 7, 1950.—Most Rev. STEPHEN S. WOZNICKI, D.D., second Bishop; ord. Dec. 22, 1917; appt. Titular Bishop of Pelte and Auxiliary Bishop of Detroit, Dec. 13, 1937; cons. Jan. 25, 1938; transferred to Saginaw, March 28, 1950 Assistant at the Pontifical Throne, Dec. 22, 1967; resigned and transferred to the Titular See of Tiava, Oct. 30, 1968; died Dec. 10, 1968.—Most Rev. FRANCIS F. REH, S.T.L., J.C.D., third Bishop; ord. Dec. 8, 1935; appt. Bishop of Charleston, June 4, 1962; cons. June 29, 1962; transferred to the Titular See of Macrinna in Mauretania; Rector Pontifical North American College in Rome, Sept. 5, 1964; transferred to Saginaw, Dec. 18, 1968; installed Feb. 26, 1969; retired April 29, 1980; died Nov. 14, 1994.

Delegate to Senior Priests—Rev. Msgr. EUGENE A. FORBES, P.A., S.T.L., J.C.D., *4699 S. 11 Mile Rd., Auburn, 48611-9535.* Tel: 517-662-6480.

Vicars General—Rev. JAMES F. GAVIT, J.C.D., *2872 N. Euclid Ave., Bay City, 48706-1342.* Tel: 517-684-1523. Rev. THOMAS E. SUTTON, *84 W. Midland Rd., Auburn, 48611.* Tel: 517-662-6861.

Episcopal Vicars—

Vicar for Hispanics—MARIA CEPEDA, Pastoral Minister, Coord., *Our Lady of Guadalupe Chapel & Center, 1619 Broadway, Bay City, 48708-8538.* Tel: 517-894-0661.

Vicar for Religious—Sr. JANET FULGENZI, O.P., Ph.D., *5800 Weiss St., Saginaw, 48603-2799.* Tel: 517-799-7910.

Vicar of Administration—Rev. THOMAS E. SUTTON, *c/o 5800 Weiss St., Saginaw, 48603-2799.*

Vicar for Canonical Affairs—Rev. JAMES F. GAVIT, J.C.D., *c/o 5800 Weiss St., Saginaw, 48603-2799.*

Vicars for Vicariates—Revs. ROBERT SHINE, Vicariate 1; WILLIAM GRUDEN, Vicariate 2; RICHARD BOKINSKIE, Vicariate 3; GEORGE SEROUR, Vicariate 4; FREDERICK J. KAWKA, Vicariate 5; JOHN SARGE, Vicariate 6; ROBERT H. BYRNE, Vicariate 7; JAMES HELLER, Vicariate 8; DONALD DUEWEKE, Vicariate 9; STEPHEN FILLION, Vicariate 10; LEONARD WILKUSKI, Vicariate 11; THOMAS KOWALCZYK, Vicariate 12.

Chancery—*5800 Weiss St., Saginaw, 48603-2799.* Tel: 517-799-7910; Fax: 517-797-6670.

Chancellor—THOMAS P. SCHROEDER.

Administrative Assistant to the Chancellor—CONNIE HUISKENS WOJDA.

Administrative Assistant to the Bishop—LEONA JONES.

Director of Finance—Mr. LEONARD A. MELESKI.

Administrative Assistant—BARBARA PINE.

General Accountant—MARY JANE TACEY.

Accounting Assistant—JOSEPHINE MENDOZA.

Finance Council—THOMAS OUELLETTE, Chm.

Catholic Services Appeal—ADRIENNE JESCHKE, Coord., *5800 Weiss St., Saginaw, 48603-2799.* Tel: 517-799-7910.

Diocesan Building Commission—CLEMENT RICHTER, Chm., *5800 Weiss St., Saginaw, 48603-2799.* Tel: 517-799-7910.

Tribunal—*5800 Weiss St., Saginaw, 48603-2799.* Tel: 517-799-7910.

Judicial Vicar—Rev. RICHARD M. FILARY, J.C.L.

Defenders of the Bond—Very Rev. JAMES F. GAVIT, J.C.D.; Rev. ROBERT J. DELAND, J.C.L.

Judges—Revs. THOMAS E. SUTTON, J.C.L.; EUGENE A. FORBES, J.C.D.; ROBERT J. MEISSNER; ROBERT W. DAVEY, M.A.; RICHARD M. FILARY, J.C.L.

Promoter of Justice—Rev. JAMES F. GAVIT, J.C.D.

Notary—PATRICIA D. PRESTON.

Advocate—Rev. ROBERT W. DAVEY, M.A.

Diocesan Council—JESSE ZAMORA, Chm., *5800 Weiss, Saginaw, 48603-2799.* Tel: 517-799-7910.

Diocesan Presbyteral Council—Rev. JAMES HELLER, Chm., *P.O. Box 1092, Bay City, 48706-1092.*

Diocesan Consultors—Revs. ROBERT S. GOHM; PETER J. GASPENY; JAMES HELLER; RANDY J. KELLY; LEONARD WILKUSKI; JACK HAMMER.

Clergy Personnel Board—Rev. WILLIAM TAYLOR, Chm., *1525 S. Washington, Saginaw, 48601-2895.* Tel: 517-755-8020.

Diocesan Council of Catholic Women—Mrs. BETTY LAFAVE, Pres., *754 Frank St., Caro, 48723.* Rev. DONALD J. EPPENBROCK, Moderator, *5366 Main St., Box 399, Lexington, 48450-0399.* Tel: 313-359-8101.

Office of Communication—Mrs. CATHERINE HAVEN, Dir., *5800 Weiss St., Saginaw, 48603-2799.* Tel: 517-797-6666.

Mission Office—Rev. ROBERT W. DAVEY, Dir. & Vicar for Missions; IRENE G. ALVA, Assoc. Dir., *5800 Weiss St., Saginaw, 48603-2799.* Tel: 517-797-6631.

Office of Education-Formation—Dr. MARIAN MIKOLAIZYK, Supt. of Schools, *5800 Weiss St., Saginaw, 48603-2799.* Tel: 517-797-6651. DANIEL GAST, Dir. Religious Education Formation; MARIAN MIKOLAIZYK, Schools Consultant.

Director of Family-Youth Ministry—PEGGY MCCOURTNEY.

Family Life Ministry—Refer to: Catholic Family Service, *5800 Weiss St., Saginaw, 48603-2799.* Tel: 517-797-6638.

Evangelization Ministry—Contact Office of Education.

Black Catholic Concerns—Mr. RICK NIX, *5800 Weiss St., Saginaw, 48603-2799.* Tel: 517-799-7910.

Ecumenism Ministry—Rev. GEORGE SEROUR, *8370 Unionville Rd., Sebewaing, 48759-9553.* Tel: 517-883-2746.

Ministry to Charismatic Renewal—MARGE FOBEAR, Dir., *Charismatic Renewal Center, 127 N. Warren St., P.O. Box 1287, Saginaw, 48606-1287.* Tel: 517-754-9351.

Ministry to Priests—Rev. ROBERT S. GOHM,Saginaw Diocesan Center, *5800 Weiss St., Saginaw, 48603-2799.* Tel: 517-799-7910.

Office of Church Ministries—Rev. ROBERT S. GOHM, Dir. of Church Ministries Office, Ministry to Priests Program, Continuing Education for Priests; Rev. THOMAS MOORE, O.S.F.S., Dir. Seminarians & Vocation Dir.; Sr. ROBERTA KOLASA, S.J., Dir., Diocesan Ministries Institute; Sr. JOSEPHINE GAUGIER, O.P., English Language Lay Ministry Program.

Office of Christian Service—CHRISTINE DOBY, Dir., *5800 Weiss St., Saginaw, 48603-2799.* Tel: 517-797-6672.

Office of Liturgy—MARY SELLARS MALLOY, Dir., *5800 Weiss St., Saginaw, 48603-2799.* Tel: 517-797-6664.

Catholic Family Services—THOMAS CONKLIN, Exec. Dir., *5800 Weiss St., Saginaw, 48603-2799.* Tel: 517-797-6636.

Saginaw Counseling Center—THOMAS CONKLIN, Dir., *710 N. Michigan Ave., Saginaw, 48602-4372.* Tel: 517-753-8446.

Bad Axe Counseling Center—123 Scott St., Bad Axe, 48413-1329. Tel: 517-269-7931.

Bay City Counseling Center—512 N. Lincoln St., Bay City, 48708-6615. Tel: 517-892-2504.

Midland Counseling Center—220 W. Main St., Midland, 48640-5165. Tel: 517-631-4711.

Mt. Pleasant Counseling Center—120 S. University St., Mt. Pleasant, 48858-2305. Tel: 517-773-9328.

Caro Counseling Center—124 E. Burnside St., Caro, 48723-1213. Tel: 517-673-5352.

Sandusky Counseling Center—119 E. Sanilac, Sandusky, 48471-1147. Tel: 810-648-2304.

Hispanic Ministries Cultural Center—MARIA CEPEDA, Dir.; Mr. GILBERTO GUEVARA, Dir. of Social Awareness, Youth & Immigration, *405 Hayes St., Saginaw, 48602.* Tel: 517-755-4477.

St. Francis Home (for elderly)—Sr. JANE MARIE LEBIEDZINSKI, C.S.S.F., Admin., *915 N. River Rd., 48609-6865.* Tel: 517-781-3150.

St. Vincent Home-Boysville of Michigan (for children)—Mr. RICK L. BOONE, M.S.W., North Reg. Dir., *925 N. River Rd., 48609-6866.* Tel: 517-781-0490.

St. Vincent de Paul Store—Mr. THOMAS M. SCHREMS, Mgr., *122 S. Hamilton St., Saginaw, 48602-2013.* Tel: 517-793-9585.

Organizations and Services—

Association of Saginaw Priests—Rev. JOHN A. EDERER, Pres., *2168 N. Winn Rd., Mt. Pleasant, 48858-9730.*

Catholic Cemeteries—Mr. JOSEPH LUGHERMO, Dir., *5800 Weiss St., Saginaw, 48603-2799.* Tel: 517-797-6627.

Catholic Newspaper—KATHLEEN A. SOCHA, Editor, *1520 Court St., P.O. Box 1405, Saginaw, 48605-1405.* Tel: 517-793-7661.

Censor—Rev. Msgr. FRANCIS J. MURRAY, *5965 W. Michigan Ave., Saginaw, 48603-7500.* Tel: 517-791-5002.

Clergy Benefit Society—Rev. ROBERT BYRNE, *1035 N. River Rd., Saginaw, 48609-6864.* Tel: 517-868-4081.

Conciliation-Arbitration—THOMAS SCHROEDER, Conciliation Clerk, *5800 Weiss, Saginaw, 48603.*

Holy Childhood Association—Rev. ROBERT W. DAVEY, *5800 Weiss St., Saginaw, 48603-2799.*

Marriage Encounter—Rev. JOSEPH A. SCHABEL, Spiritual Dir. Tel: 517-753-8446.

St. Vincent de Paul Society—Mr. DONALD RUBIS, Pres., *523 Michigan Ave., Bay City, 48708.* Tel: 517-893-5772.

Office of Stewardship / Development—ANNETTE O'BRIEN, *5800 Weiss St., Saginaw, 48603-2799.* Tel: 517-797-6679.

CLERGY, PARISHES, MISSIONS AND PAROCHIAL SCHOOLS

CITY OF SAGINAW
(Saginaw County)

1—ST. MARY CATHEDRAL (1853), Sr. Honora Remes, D.C., Pastoral Admin.; Rev. Thomas Moore, O.S.F.S.
Res., 615 Hoyt Ave., 48607-1713. Tel: 517-752-8119; Fax: 517-752-2165. [CEM]

2—HOLY FAMILY, Rev. William R. Taylor.
Res., 1525 S. Washington Ave., 48601-2895. Tel: 517-755-8020. [CEM]

3—HOLY ROSARY. Closed. For inquiries for parish records contact SS. Simon and Jude Parish, Saginaw.

4—SS. SIMON AND JUDE, Rev. Robert Schramm, O.S.F.S.; Sr. Teresita Weind, S.N.D.deN., Pastoral Assoc. In res., Revs. John S. Mancini, O.S.F.S.; Thomas M. Moore, O.S.F.S.
Res., 2395 S. Outer Dr., 48601-6643. Tel: 517-752-7424; Fax: 517-753-8601.

5—OUR LADY HELP OF CHRISTIANS. Closed. For inquiries for parish records contact SS. Simon and Jude Parish, Saginaw.

6—OUR LADY OF MOUNT CARMEL. Closed. For inquiries for parish records contact SS. Simon and Jude Parish, Saginaw.

7—SACRED HEART. Closed. For inquiries for parish records contact SS. Simon and Jude Parish, Saginaw.

8—ST. ANDREW, Rev. Donald L. Christensen.
Res., 612 N. Michigan Ave., 48602-4387. Tel: 517-754-0487; Fax: 517-754-0308.

9—ST. ANTHONY OF PADUA, Rev. Walter Balduck, O.F.M.Cap.
Res., 3680 S. Washington Rd., 48601-4997. Tel: 517-752-1971; Fax: 517-752-1441. [JC]

10—ST. CASIMIR, Rev. John S. Sarge.
Res., 2122 S. Jefferson Ave., 48601-3498. Tel: 517-752-6648; Fax: 517-752-6691. [JC]

11—ST. GEORGE, Rev. John S. Sarge; Nanette Navarre, Pastoral Assoc.
Res., 2120 Erie St., 48601-4497. Tel: 517-753-3865; Fax: 517-753-6903. [JC]

12—ST. HELEN, Rev. Emmet L. Marceau.
Res., 2445 N. Charles St., 48602-5096. Tel: 517-793-0618; Fax: 517-793-5487. [JC]
School—Sr. Corinne Weiss, S.J., Prin. Servants of Jesus 1; Lay Teachers 11; Students 283.

13—ST. JOHN VIANNEY, Rev. Loren M. Kalinowski.
Church—6400 McCarty Rd., 48603-9621. Tel: 517-790-5086; Fax: 517-790-1681.
Res., 4477 McCarty Rd., 48603. Tel: 517-792-6582.

14—ST. JOSEPH, Rev. Daniel Anholzer, O.F.M.Cap. In res., Rev. Arthur Cooney, O.F.M.Cap.
Res., 910 N. Sixth Ave., 48601-1103. Tel: 517-753-4418; Fax: 517-755-1090.
Convent—903 N. Seventh St., 48601. Tel: 517-752-5470.
Sisters 6.

15—SS. PETER AND PAUL, Rev. Robert J. DeLand; Sr. Janet Brown, O.P., Pastoral Assoc.
Res., 4735 W. Michigan Ave., 48603-6370. Tel: 517-799-5448; Fax: 517-799-1495.
School—Sr. Anne Breitag, O.P., Prin. Sisters 1; Lay Teachers 11; Students 210.

16—ST. RITA. Closed. For inquiries for parish records contact the Chancery.

17—ST. STEPHEN, Revs. Patrick Jankowiak; Patrick C. O'Connor.
Res., 2711 Mackinaw St., 48602-3146. Tel: 517-799-2334; Fax: 517-793-3611.
School—Barbara Geary, Prin. Lay Teachers 23; Students 518.

18—ST. THOMAS AQUINAS, Revs. Robert Konopa, O.F.M.; Leonard Stunek, O.F.M.
Res., 5376 State Rd., 48603-3771. Tel: 517-799-2460; Fax: 517-799-2464. [JC]
School—Bernardine Sisters of Third Order of St. Francis. (Farmington, MI). Sr. Ann De Guise, O.S.F., Prin.
Sisters 2; Lay Teachers 20; Students 463.

OUTSIDE THE CITY OF SAGINAW

Albee, Saginaw Co., St. Mary, Rev. Kenneth E. Yaroch.
Res., 5661 Fergus Rd., Rte. 2, St. Charles, 48655-9624. Tel: 517-770-4453.

Alma, Gratiot Co., St. Mary, Rev. David Parsch.
Res., 517 N. Prospect Ave., 48801-1694. Tel: 517-463-5370; Fax: 517-463-8297.
School—220 W. Downie St., 48801. Tel: 517-463-4579. Mrs. Mary Jo Fachting, Prin.
Lay Teachers 9; Students 208.

Argyle, Sanilac Co., St. Joseph, Rev. William J. Gruden.
Res., 4960 N. Ubly Rd., 48410-0007. Tel: 517-658-8145; Fax: 517-658-8105. [CEM]
Mission—Freiburg, Sanilac Co., St. Ignatius.

Auburn, Bay Co., St. Joseph, Rev. Thomas E. Sutton.
Res., 84 W. Midland Rd., 48611. Tel: 517-662-6861; Fax: 517-662-0064.
School—Area School. Sr. Lucy Ann Quinn, Prin.

AuGres, Arenac Co., St. Mark, Rev. Noel T. Rudy.
Res., 415 S. Court St., 48703-9598. Tel: 517-876-7925; Fax: 517-876-7778.

Bad Axe, Huron Co., Sacred Heart, Rev. Jack J. Leipert.
Res., 311 Whitelam St., 48413-1205. Tel: 515-269-7729; Fax: 517-269-4010. [CEM]

Bannister, Gratiot Co., St. Cyril, Rev. R.K. LeFleur.
Res., 517 E. Main St., 48807-9762. Tel: 517-862-5270; Fax: 517-862-4534.

Bay City, Bay Co.,

1—HOLY TRINITY, Rev. Michael G. Dunckel.
Res., 1008 S. Wenona Ave., 48706-5094. Tel: 517-893-4073; Fax: 517-893-7087.
School—Tel: 517-892-3018. Sally Preston, Prin.
Lay Teachers 12; Students 156.

2—ST. BONIFACE, Rev. Dale A. Orlik.
Res., 510 N. Lincoln Ave., 48708-6694. Tel: 517-893-4851; Fax: 517-893-1781.

3—ST. HEDWIG, Rev. Richard M. Filary.
Res., 1504 S. Kiesel, 48706-5240. Tel: 517-893-1072; Fax: 517-893-4710.

4—ST. HYACINTH, Rev. Gerald F. Kukla.
Res., 1515 Cass Ave., 48708-8740. Tel: 517-895-5581; Fax: 517-895-5583. [CEM]
School—Sr. Alice Ann Gradowski, C.S.S.F., Prin. Felician Sisters (Livonia, MI) 1; Lay Teachers 6; Students 82.
Convent—1507 Michigan Ave., 48708.

5—ST. JAMES, (1983), Rev. Peter J. Gaspeny.
Res., 710 Columbus Ave., 48708-6483. Tel: 517-893-4693; Fax: 517-893-1504. [CEM]
School—Sr. Maureen Donovan, S.C., Prin. Sisters of Charity of Cincinnati, OH 3; Lay Teachers 13; Students 222.
Convent—200 S. Farragut St., 48708.

6—ST. JOSEPH, Rev. Raymond S. Fron.
Res., 1005 Third St., 48708-6006. Tel: 517-895-5783; Fax: 517-895-8837.

7—ST. MARIA GORETTI, Rev. James F. Gavit.
Res., 2872 N. Euclid Rd., 48706-1342. Tel: 517-684-1523; Fax: 517-684-8286.

8—ST. MARY, Rev. James Heller.
Res., 501 N. Walnut St., P.O. Box 1092, 48706-1092. Tel: 517-892-6031; Fax: 517-892-4005.

9—ST. STANISLAUS, Revs. William J. Rutowski; Francis Arthur.
Res., 1503 Kosciuszko Ave., Ste. 100, 48708-8027. Tel: 517-893-6421; Fax: 517-893-3985.
School—Sr. Mary Elise Milostan, C.S.S.F., Prin. Felician Sisters (Livonia, MI) 2; Lay Teachers 10; Students 147.

10—ST. VINCENT DE PAUL, Rev. Robert J. Meissner.
Res., 4505 Two Mile Rd., 48706-2799. Tel: 517-684-1170; Fax: 517-684-4925.

11—OUR LADY OF GUADALUPE CHAPEL AND CENTER, Mrs. Maria Cepeda, Vicar for Hispanics.
Res., 1619 Broadway, 48708-8538. Tel: 517-894-0661.

12—OUR LADY OF THE VISITATION, Rev. Gerald E. Balwinski.
Res., 1106 State St., 48706-3697. Tel: 517-684-5184; Fax: 517-684-5189.
School—Visitation Academy, 1110 State St., 48706. John Leaman, Prin.
Lay Teachers 13; Students 75.

Beal City, Isabella Co., St. Joseph the Worker, Rev. John F. Cotter.
Res., 2163 N. Winn Rd., Mount Pleasant, 48858-9730. Tel: 517-644-2041; Fax: 517-644-2026. [CEM]
School—Sr. Jean Birkman, O.P., Prin. Sisters 1; Lay Teachers 6; Students 122.

Beaver, Bay Co., St. Valentine, Rev. Richard C. Ratajczak.
Res., 999 S. 9 Mile Rd., Kawkawlin, 48631-9756. Tel: 517-662-6843; Fax: 517-662-0152. [CEM]
School—1010 S. 9 Mile Rd., Kawkawlin, 48631. Tel: 517-662-6966; Fax: 517-662-0152. Sr. Mary Agnestine Rosinski, C.S.S.F., Prin.
Felician Sisters (Livonia, MI) 2; Lay Teachers 3; Students 64.

Birch Run, Saginaw Co., Sacred Heart, Rev. Mason L. Vaughn.
Res., 12157 Church St., 48415-8706. Tel: 517-624-9098; Fax: 517-624-9427.

Bridgeport, Saginaw Co., Assumption of the Blessed Virgin Mary, Rev. Daniel Nowak, O.F.M.
Res., 7945 Bell Rd., P.O. Box 602, 48722-0602. Tel: 517-777-1200; Fax: 517-777-6280.
St. Christopher, Rev. Robert W. Davey.
Res., 3926 Williamson Rd., Saginaw, 48601-5839. Tel: 517-777-2605; Fax: 517-777-9691.

Caro, Tuscola Co., Sacred Heart, Rev. Michael J. Bell.
Res., 140 Atwood, 48723-1742. Tel: 517-673-2346. [CEM]
Convent—919 W. Frank St., 48723. Tel: 517-673-7813.

Carrollton, Saginaw Co., St. John the Baptist, Rev. J.J. Fleming; Sr. Virginia Scally, S.N.D.deN., Pastoral Admin.
Res., 545 Maple Ridge, P.O. Box 248, 48724-0248. Tel: 517-752-9350; Fax: 517-753-4943.
St. Josaphat, Rev. Richard E. Jozwiak.
Res., 469 Shattuck Rd., Saginaw, 48604-2391. Tel: 517-753-2497; Fax: 517-753-2498.
School—Betty MacArthur, Prin. Lay Teachers 13; Students 217.

Caseville, Huron Co., St. Roch, Rev. Dennis Kucharczyk.
Res., 6253 Main St., 48725. Tel: 517-856-4933.

Cass City, Tuscola Co., St. Pancratius, Rev. Paul W. Bala.
Res., 4292 S. Seeger St., 48726-1423. Tel: 517-872-3336; Fax: 517-872-1852.

Chesaning, Saginaw Co., Our Lady of Perpetual Help, Rev. Joseph M. Griffin.
Res., 404 S. Wood, 48616-1399. Tel: 517-845-6894; Fax: 517-845-7787. [CEM]
School—802 Lockwood St., 48616. Carol Klemko, Prin.
Lay Teachers 9; Students 133.

Clare, Clare Co., St. Cecilia, Rev. Joseph Ryan.
Res., 902 N. McEwan St., 48617-1297. Tel: 517-386-7681. [CEM]
School—Pam Dickerson, Prin. Lay Teachers 5; Students 123.

Coleman, Midland Co., St. Philip Neri, Rev. James W. Bessert.
Res., 5199 W. Shaffer Rd., P.O. Box M, 48618-0512. Tel: 517-465-1768; Fax: 517-465-6311.
Mission—Edenville, Gladwin Co., St. Anne.

Croswell, Sanilac Co., St. Patrick, Rev. Wolfgang Streichardt.
Res., 105 W. Sanborn Ave., 48422-1399. Tel: 810-679-3849; Fax: 810-679-3903. [CEM]
Mission—Peck, Sanilac Co., St. John. [CEM]

Essexville, Bay Co., St. John the Evangelist, Rev. John W. Mullet. In res., Rev. Michael H. Wolf.
Res., 1600 Hudson St., 48732-1377. Tel: 517-892-1893; Fax: 517-894-5558.
School—619 Main St., 48732. Sue Grzegorczyk, Prin.
Lay Teachers 8; Students 105.

Fisherville, Bay Co., St. Anthony, Rev. Msgr. Eugene A. Forbes, J.C.D., V.G., P.A.
Res., 4699 S. 11 Mile Rd., Auburn, 48611-9535. Tel: 517-662-6480; Fax: 517-662-4335. [CEM]
School—Auburn Area Catholic, West Campus, 1492 W. Midland Rd., Auburn, 48611-9560. Tel: 517-662-6581; Fax: 517-662-4335.

Frankenmuth, Saginaw Co., Blessed Trinity, Rev. Frederick J. Kawka.
Res., 958 E. Tuscola Rd., 48734-9770. Tel: 517-652-3259; Fax: 517-652-2206.

Freeland, Saginaw Co., St. Agnes, Rev. Lawrence M. Pashak.
Res., 335 Johnson, 48623-9006. Tel: 517-695-5652; Fax: 517-695-6275.

Gagetown, Tuscola Co., St. Agatha, Rev. George A. Serour, Sacramental Min.; Sr. Joan Maher, M.Ss.P., Admin.
Res., 4618 South St., Box 139, 48735-0139. Tel: 517-665-9966.

Gladwin, Gladwin Co., Sacred Heart, Rev. Julius A. Spleet.
Res., 300 N. Silverleaf St., 48624-1697. Tel: 517-426-7154; Fax: 517-426-0896.
School—Sr. Mary Elizabeth Klier, O.S.F., Prin. Bernardine Sisters of Third Order of St. Francis (Farmington, MI) 1; Lay Teachers 6; Students 100.

Harbor Beach, Huron Co., Our Lady of Lake Huron, Rev. Edward J. Konieczka; Sr. Eileen Houlihan, I.H.M., Pastoral Assoc.
Res., 413 S. First St., 48441-1325. Tel: 517-479-3393. [CEM]
School—Mr. Lawrence E. Kish, II, Prin. Lay Teachers 10; Students 168.
Convent—406 S. First St., 48441.

Harrison, Clare Co., St. Athanasius, Rev. Stephen J. Fillion.
Res., 1010 Byfield Dr., P.O. Box 528, 48625-0528. Tel: 517-539-6232.

Helena, Huron Co., St. Anthony, Rev. James Krasman, O.F.M.
Res., 4190 Parisville Rd., Ruth, 48470-9759. Tel: 517-479-6781. [CEM]

Hemlock, Saginaw Co., St. Mary, Rev. Robert S. Gohm.
Res., 151 St. Mary's Dr., 48626-9614. Tel: 517-642-5606; Fax: 517-642-5240. [CEM]
St. Mary Center—245 St. Mary's Dr., 48626.

Ithaca, Gratiot Co., St. Paul the Apostle, Rev. John F. Ederer.
Res., 621 E. Center St., 48847-1596. Tel: 517-875-3654; Fax: 517-875-7027.
Mission—Perrinton, Gratiot Co., St. Martin De Porres.

Kawkawlin, Bay Co., Sacred Heart, Rev. Chester J. Pilarski.
Res., 2510 S. Fraser Rd., 48631-9115. Tel: 517-684-1402; Fax: 517-684-0038.

Kinde, Huron Co., St. Mary-St. Edward, Rev. Kevin Kerbawy.
Res., 1709 Moeller Rd., P.O. Box 68, 48445-0068. Tel: 517-874-4744.

Lexington, Sanilac Co., St. Denis, Rev. Donald J. Eppenbrock.
Res., 5366 Main St., P.O. Box 399, 48450-0399. Tel: 810-359-5400; Fax: 810-359-5833. [CEM]

Linwood, Bay Co., St. Anne, Rev. Thomas M. Kowalczyk.
Res., 315 Center St., P.O. Box 397, 48634-0397. Tel: 517-697-4443.
School—Tel: 517-697-3100. Sr. Rose Ellen Dzwieleski, O.S.F., Prin.
Bernardine Sisters of Third Order of St. Francis (Farmington, MI) 3; Lay Teachers 8; Students 164.

Maple Grove, Saginaw Co., St. Michael, Rev. Donald G. Dueweke.
Res., 17994 Lincoln Rd., New Lothrop, 48460-9600. Tel: 517-845-7011; Fax: 517-845-4729. [CEM]

Marlette, Sanilac Co., St. Elizabeth, Rev. Richard Bokinskie.
Res., 6785 W. Marlette St., 48453-1296. Tel: 517-635-7581; Fax: 517-635-5808.

Mayville, Tuscola Co., St. Joseph, Rev. Richard Bokinskie; Sr. Ruth Adamites, O.P., P.A.
Mailing Address: 315 Ohmer Rd., P.O. Box 283, 48744-0283. Tel: 517-843-6565; Fax: 517-683-2556.

Merrill, Saginaw Co., Sacred Heart, Rev. Craig L. Albrecht.
Res., 419 S. Midland St., 48637-0099. Tel: 517-643-5366. [CEM]

Midland, Midland Co., Assumption Blessed Virgin Mary, Rev. Henry P. DuRussel.
Res., 3516 Monroe, Rd. 8, 48642. Tel: 517-631-4447; Fax: 517-631-4323.
Blessed Sacrament, Revs. John R. Johnson; Steven M. Gavit.
Res., 3109 Swede Ave., 48642-3888. Tel: 517-835-6777; Fax: 517-835-2451.
School—Lay Teachers 12; Students 242.
St. Brigid, Rev. Leonard F. Wilkuski.
Res., 207 Ashman St., 48640-5185. Tel: 517-835-7121; Fax: 517-835-9141.
School—130 W. Larkin St., 48640-6579. Tel: 517-835-9481; Fax: 517-835-9141. Christine Szatkowski, Prin.
Lay Teachers 18; Students 130.

Mount Pleasant, Isabella Co., Sacred Heart, Rev. Thomas J. McNamara. In res., Rev. Donald E. Henkes (MEM).
Res., 302 S. Kinney, 48858-2773. Tel: 517-772-1385; Fax: 517-773-9118. [CEM]
School—(Grades PreK-6) 200 S. Franklin St., 48858-2275. Christine Siwik, Prin.
Sisters 1; Lay Teachers 18; Students 294.
High School—Sacred Heart Academy, (Grades 7-12) 316 E. Michigan, 48858-2640. Tel: 517-772-1457. Virginia Chamberlain, Prin.
Priests 1; Sisters 1; Lay Teachers 18; Students 277.
St. Mary University Parish, Rev. Jeffrey Donner.
Res., 1405 S. Washington, 48858-4280. Tel: 517-773-3931.

Munger, Bay Co., St. Norbert, Rev. James R. Carlson.
Res., 126 W. Munger Rd., 48747-9767. Tel: 517-659-2193; Fax: 517-659-3417.

Nine Mile, Bay Co., St. Mary, Rev. Joseph K. Miller.
Res., 739 W. Cody-Estey Rd., Pinconning, 48650-8925. Tel: 517-879-5596; Fax: 517-879-6151. [CEM]

Oakley, Saginaw Co., St. Michael, Rev. Peter Nickels, O.F.M. Conv.
Res., Box 75, 48649-0075. Tel: 517-845-3545; Fax: 517-845-5499. [CEM]

Palms, Sanilac Co., St. Patrick, Rev. Ronald F. Wagner, Sacramental Min.; Sr. Theresa Carlow, S.N.D.deN., Pastoral Admin.
Res., 1801 Palms Rd., 48465. Tel: 810-376-4853; Fax: 517-864-3526.

Parisville, Huron Co., St. Mary, Rev. James Krasman, O.F.M.
Res., 4190 Parisville Rd., Ruth, 48470-9759. Tel: 517-864-3523; Fax: 517-864-3164. [CEM]

Pigeon, Huron Co., St. Francis Borgia, Rev. Malcolm Maloney; Sr. Theresa Fox, O.P., P.A.
Res., 25 Moeller St., Box U, 48755. Tel: 517-453-2151. [CEM]

Pinconning, Bay Co., St. Agnes, Rev. Joseph K. Miller, Sacramental Min.; Barbara J. Walker, Pastoral Admin.
Res., 216 E. Fifth St., P.O. Box 325, 48650-0325. Tel: 517-879-2151; Fax: 517-879-2583. [CEM]
St. Michael, Rev. Ramon Matuszewski.
Res., 225 Jennings St., 48650-9408. Tel: 517-879-2141; Fax: 517-879-6633.
School—Joan Turmell, Prin. Lay Teachers 9; Students 173.

Pinnebog, Huron Co., St. Felix, Rev. Dennis Kucharczyk, Sacramental Min.; Sr. Mary Schwartz, S.S.J., Pastoral Min.
Res., 3515 Limerick, Kinde, 48445-9723. Tel: 517-874-5833. [CEM]

Port Austin, Huron Co., St. Michael, Rev. Robert W. Shine.
Res., 8637 Garfield, P.O. Box 298, 48467-0298. Tel: 517-738-7521; Fax: 517-738-5886. [CEM]
Parish Center—8661 Independence Ave., P.O. Box 350, 48467.

Port Sanilac, Sanilac Co., St. Mary, Rev. Ronald J. Dombrowski.
Res., 7066 W. Main St., P.O. Box 467, 48469-0467. Tel: 810-622-9904; Fax: 810-622-7953. [CEM]
Mission—Forestville, Sanilac Co., St. John Chrysostom.

Rapson, Huron Co., St. Joseph, Rev. John Weis.
Res., 3455 Rapson Rd., Rte. 3, Bad Axe, 48413-9149. Tel: 517-269-8084. [CEM]
Mission—Smiths Corners, Hurenco Co., Holy Trinity. [CEM]

Reese, Tuscola Co., St. Elizabeth, Rev. James R. Carlson.
Res., 12835 E. Washington, 48757-9712. Tel: 517-868-4081; Fax: 517-868-9785. [CEM]
School—Robin Andress, Prin. Lay Teachers 6; Students 102.

Rosebush, Isabella Co., St. Henry, Sr. Ellen McDonald, O.P., Pastoral Admin.; Rev. Thomas J. McNamara, Sacramental Min.
Res., P.O. Box 67, 48878-0067. Tel: 517-433-2229. [CEM]
School—James Cardon, Prin. Lay Teachers 5; Students 54.
Mission—Leaton, Isabella Co., St. Charles.

Ruth, Huron Co., SS. Peter and Paul, Rev. Ronald F. Wagner.
Res., 7115 Atwater Dr., P.O. Box 55, 48470-0055. Tel: 517-864-3650. [CEM]
School—Richard Smith, Prin. Lay Teachers 8; Students 118.

Ryan, Midland Co., St. Patrick, Sr. Elaine Raymond, M.S.S.P., Pastoral Admin.; Rev. Craig L. Albrecht, Sacramental Min.
Res., 4708 N. Meridian Rd., Rte. 2, Merrill, 48637-9546. Tel: 517-643-5652; Fax: 517-643-5652, Ext. 111. [CEM]

St. Charles, Saginaw Co., Immaculate Conception, Rev. Joseph J. Kearns.
Res., 708 Sanderson St., 48655-1895. Tel: 517-865-9460. [CEM]
School—H. Ross Klemko, Prin. Lay Teachers 6; Students 51.
Convent—712 Sanderson St., 48655. Tel: 517-865-6166.

St. Louis, Gratiot Co., St. Joseph, Rev. John E. Hammer.
Office: 605 S. Franklin, 48880-1747. Tel: 517-681-5080; Fax: 517-681-2887.
Res., 409 Butternut St., 48880-1747.
Mission—Irishtown, Gratiot Co., St. Patrick. [CEM]

Sandusky, Sanilac Co., St. Joseph, Rev. Stanislaus Surman.
Res., 511 N. Sandusky Rd., P.O. Box 249, 48471-0249. Tel: 810-648-4293.

Sanford, Midland Co., St. Agnes, Rev. Francis Voris, O.F.M.Cap.
Res., 2500 W. River Rd., 48657-9497. Tel: 517-687-5657; Fax: 517-687-2450.

Sebewaing, Huron Co., Holy Family, Rev. George J. Serour.
Res., 8370 Unionville Rd., 48759-9553. Tel: 517-883-2746; Fax: 517-883-3117. [CEM]

Shepherd, Isabella Co., St. Vincent De Paul, Rev. Robert J. Howe.
Res., 168 Wright, 48883-9079. Tel: 517-828-5720; Fax: 517-828-4652. [CEM]
School—Gail Schmidt, Prin. Lay Teachers 7; Students 146.
Mission—Winn, Isabella Co., St. Leo. [CEM]

Shields, Saginaw Co., Holy Spirit, Rev. Robert H. Byrne.
Res., 1035 N. River Rd., Saginaw, 48609-6864. Tel: 517-781-2457; Fax: 517-781-5518.

Standish, Arenac Co., Resurrection of the Lord, Rev. James M. Fitzpatrick.
Res., 423 Cedar, Box 306, 48658-0306. Tel: 517-846-9565; Fax: 517-846-9566. [CEM]

Ubly, Huron Co., St. Columbkille, Rev. Randy Kelly.
Res., 4470 Washington St., 48475. Tel: 517-658-8824; Fax: 517-658-2088. [CEM]
St. John the Evangelist, Rev. Randy Kelly.
Res., 4470 Washington St., 48475. Tel: 517-658-8824; Fax: 517-658-2088. [CEM]

Vassar, Tuscola Co., St. Frances Xavier Cabrini, Rev. Richard T. Szafranski.
Res., 165 W. Maple St., 48768-1203. Tel: 517-823-2911; Fax: 517-823-2999.
Mission—Millington, Tuscola Co., St. Bernard.

Wilmot, Tuscola Co., St. Michael, Rev. Paul Bala; Sr. Ruth Adamites, O.P., Pastoral Admin.
Res., 1951 Kingston Rd., Deford, 48729. Tel: 517-683-2475; Fax: 517-683-2556. [CEM]

Zilwaukee, Saginaw Co., St. Matthew, Rev. Thomas J. Fleming.
Res., 511 W. Cornell, Saginaw, 48604-1311. Tel: 517-755-7336; Fax: 517-755-4228.

Chaplains of Public Institutions

BAY CITY. *Bay Medical Center and Bay Osteopathic Hospital* 1201 S. Erie, 48706. Sr. Beth Pero, S.S.J.

On Duty Outside the Diocese:
Reverend Fathers—
Falsey, James E., P.O. Box 89, Nulato, AK 99765
Friske, Joseph P., Damaschkestr. 20, 8000 Munchen 82, Germany
Loos, Frederick C., Ave. Naucalpan #84, Col. La Canada, Naucalpan, Mexico, C.P. 53570
Sikorski, Harold R., Recife, Brazil

Retired:
Reverend Monsignors—
Murdick, Olin J.
Murray, Francis
Reverend Fathers—
Bauer, Joseph O.
Boucher, Edward F.
Bur, Stanislaus
Eickholt, Henry C.
Favara, Joseph F.
Frego, Max
Ganley, Charles
Greiner, Lawrence
Hart, Harry J.
Hoogterp, John P.
Howard, T. Cyril
Janowicz, Barney J.
Klimas, George H.
Kryszak, Marian
LaMarre, Theodore E.
Maher, Michael L.
McEachin, Cornelius
Navarre, Robert G.
Rabideau, Richard L.
Roach, Joseph W., S.A.G.
Schabel, Joseph A.
Sierminski, Vernon
Sikorski, Harold R.
Skornia, Bernard L.
Thome, John J.
Torok, Bela E.
Trombley, J. Edward
Van Mullekom, Richard
Welna, Floyd
Welsmiller, Francis F.
Wolf, Michael H.
Woloszyk, Ignatius J.

Permanent Deacons:
Alex, Frank, St. Anne, Edenville; & St. Philip Neri, Coleman
Arnold, Michael, St. Valentine Church, Beaver
Belanger, Stanley, (Retired)
Belmer, Floyd, Holy Family Church, Saginaw
Cremin, John J., St. Mary, Alma
DeNeut, Gerard H., St. Matthew, Zilwaukee
Emmeot, Dale, Blessed Sacrament Church, Midland
Fussman, Lawrence, Sacred Heart Church, Mount Pleasant
Hudson, Francis W., St. Brigid, Midland
Jankowiak, Michael, Blessed Sacrament, Midland
Kasprzyk, David, On Duty Outside the Diocese
Kebblish, Edward, Assumption B.V.M., Midland
Keller, George, Bay County Jail Ministry
Kuhr, Lambert, Jr., (Retired), Out of the Diocese
Masserang, Lawrence, Blessed Trinity, Frankenmuth
Middleton, Allan, St. Cecilia, Clare
Moeggenberg, John, St. Brigid, Midland
Stilwell, Lee, St. Norbert, Munger
Wilberding, John, St. Vincent dePaul, Shepherd
Winkler, Frank, (Retired)

INSTITUTIONS LOCATED IN THE DIOCESE

[A] HIGH SCHOOLS, INTER-PAROCHIAL

SAGINAW. *Nouvel Catholic Central High School*, 2555 Wieneke Rd., 48603. Stanley DeVoir, Prin.; John Cuhbertson, Asst. Prin.; Sharon Jordan, Campus Min. Lay Teachers 35; Students 525.

BAY CITY. *All Saints Central High School*, 217 S. Monroe St., 48708; Fax: 517-892-7188. Thomas Grange, Prin. Lay Teachers 14; Students 212.

[B] MIDDLE SCHOOLS

BAY CITY. *Holy Family Middle School*, 1503 Kosciuszko Ave., Ste. 200, 48708. Tel: 517-892-8332. Barbara Rakowski, Prin.; Sr. Anne LaHaie, R.S.M., Pastoral Counselor. Sisters 1; Lay Teachers 11; Students 145.

[C] ELEMENTARY SCHOOLS, PRIVATE

SAGINAW. *Francis F. Reh Academy*, 2201 Owen St., 48601. Tel: 517-753-2349. Sr. Diane Hoffman, O.P., Prin. Religious 2; Lay Teachers 7; Students 141.

AUBURN. *Auburn Area Catholic Schools*, East Campus: 114 Midland Rd., 48611. Tel: 517-662-6431. West Campus: 1492 W. Midland Rd., 48611. Tel: 517-662-6581. Sr. Lucy Ann Quinn, O.P., Prin. Sisters 1; Lay Teachers 7; Students 137.

[D] CHILDREN'S HOMES

SAGINAW. *St. Vincent Home-Boysville of Michigan, Inc.*, 925 N. River Rd., 48609. Tel: 517-781-2780; Fax: 517-781-5422
For a complete listing, refer to the Special Care Facilities section.

[E] GENERAL HOSPITALS

SAGINAW. *St. Mary's Medical Center of Saginaw, Inc.*, 830 S. Jefferson Ave., 48601-2594
For a complete listing, refer to the Hospitals section.

[F] HOMES FOR AGED

SAGINAW. *St. Francis Nursing Home*, 915 N. River Rd., 48609 Fax: 517-781-3791
For a complete listing, refer to the Special Care Facilities section.

[G] MONASTERIES AND RESIDENCES OF PRIESTS AND BROTHERS

SAGINAW. *Queen of Angels Friary and Retreat House*, 3400 S. Washington Rd., P.O. Box 2026, 48605. Tel: 517-755-2149. Capuchin Friars of the Province of St. Joseph (Detroit) of the Capuchin Order of Friars Minor Capuchin.
Retreat Team: Revs. Robert Malloy, O.F.M.Cap., Dir.; Walter Balduck, O.F.M.Cap.; Francis Voris, O.F.M.Cap.; Bro. James Gleason, O.F.M.Cap. In res. Rev. Vernon Wagner, O.F.M.Cap. Priests 4.

[H] CONVENTS AND RESIDENCES FOR SISTERS

SAGINAW. *Franciscan Poor Clare Nuns, O.S.C.*, 4875 Shattuck Rd., 48603-2962. Tel: 517-797-0593; Fax: 517-797-0527. Sr. Dianne Doughty, O.S.C., Supr./Abbess. Sisters 4.
Motherhouse and Novitiate of the Mission Sisters of the Holy Spirit, 1030 N. River Rd., 48609. Tel: 517-781-0934. Sr. Margo Tafoya, M.S.Sp., Community Coord. Sisters 12.

ALMA. *Motherhouse and Novitiate of the Religious Sisters of Mercy of Alma, Michigan*, 1835 Michigan Ave., P.O. Box 564, 48801. Tel: 517-463-6035. Mothers Mary Quentin Sheridan, R.S.M.; Mary McGreevy, R.S.M., Vicar. Sisters 16.

[I] MISCELLANEOUS LISTINGS

SAGINAW. *Emmaus House*, 733 S. 14th St., 48601. Tel: 517-755-7538. Co-Directors, Emmaus House: Sr. Marietta Fritz, S.N.D.deN.
Jail Ministry, 1325 Cherry St., 48601. Tel: 517-755-3305. Sr. Mary Ruth Rault, D.C., Chap.
Holy Spirit Sisters Charitable Trust, 1030 N. River Rd., 48609. Sr. Margo Tafoya, M.S.Sp., Pres.
St. Mary's Medical Center of Saginaw, Inc., 830 S. Jefferson Ave., 48601.
Seton Health Corporation of East Central Michigan, 830 S. Jefferson Ave., 48601. Fred Fraizer, Pres. & CEO.

ALMA. *Religious Sisters of Mercy of Alma Corporation*, 1835 Michigan Ave., 48801. Tel: 517-463-6035. Mothers Mary Quentin Sheridan, R.S.M., Pres.; Mary McGreevy, R.S.M., Vice Pres.
Sacred Heart Mercy Health Care Center, 7320 N. Alger Rd., 48801. Tel: 517-463-3451; 463-8464. Sr. Mary Judith O'Brien, R.S.M.

BAY CITY. *Bay County Jail Ministry*, 1100 Stanton St., 48708. Tel: 517-893-7985. Deacon George F. Keller, Chap.
Retrouvaille Program of the Saginaw Diocese, 915 Columbus Ave., 48708. Tel: 517-684-5206. Dave & Vickie Murray, Contact Persons.
Society of St. Vincent de Paul, 523 Michigan Ave., 48708. Mr. Donald Rubis, Pres.
Member Conferences: Bay City-Holy Trinity, St. Hyacinth, St. James, St. Joseph's, St. Mary, St. Stanislaus, Visitation, St. Vincent de Paul; Essexville-St. John.

RELIGIOUS INSTITUTES OF MEN REPRESENTED IN THE DIOCESE

For further details refer to the corresponding bracketed number in the Religious Institutes of Men or Women section.

[0470]—*The Capuchin Friars.* (St. Joseph Prov.).—O.F.M.Cap.
[0480]—*Conventual Franciscans.*—O.F.M.
[0520]—*Franciscan Friars.* (Assumption Prov.).—O.F.M.
[0920]—*Oblates of St. Francis De Sales.*—O.S.F.S.

RELIGIOUS INSTITUTES OF WOMEN REPRESENTED IN THE DIOCESE

[1810]—*Bernadine Sisters of Third Order of St. Francis.*—O.S.F.
[0760]—*Daughters of Charity of St. Vincent de Paul.* (Evansville).—D.C.
[1070-03]—*Dominican Sisters.* (Sinsinawa, WI).—O.P.
[1070-09]—*Dominican Sisters.* (Racine, WI).—O.P.
[1070-13]—*Dominican Sisters.* (Adrian, MI).—O.P.
[1070-14]—*Dominican Sisters.* (Grand Rapids).—O.P.
[1070-26]—*Dominican Sisters.* (Oxford, MI).—O.P.
[1170]—*Felician Sisters.*—C.S.S.F.
[]—*Franciscan Sisters of St. Clare.*—F.S.S.C.
[2740]—*Mission Sisters of the Holy Spirit.*—M.S.Sp.
[3130]—*Our Lady of Victory Missionary Sisters.* (Huntington, IN).—O.L.V.M.
[3560]—*Servants of Jesus.*—S.J.
[0440]—*Sisters of Charity of Cincinnati, Ohio.*—S.C.
[2519]—*Sisters of Mercy of Alma, Michigan.*—R.S.M.
[2575]—*Sisters of Mercy of the Americas.* (Detroit, MI).—R.S.M.
[3000]—*Sisters of Notre Dame de Namur.* (Boston, MA; Cincinnati, OH).—S.N.D.deN.
[1570]—*Sisters of St. Francis of the Holy Family.* (Dubuque, IA).—O.S.F.
[3830-11]—*Sisters of St. Joseph.* (Nazareth, MI).—S.S.J.
[1030]—*Sisters of the Divine Savior.* (Milwaukee, WI).—S.D.S.
[1990]—*Sisters of the Holy Name of Jesus and Mary.* (Spokane, WA).—S.N.J.M.
[3260]—*Sisters of the Precious Blood (Dayton, Ohio).*—C.PP.S.
[2150]—*Sisters, Servants of the Immaculate Heart of Mary.* (Monroe).—I.H.M.

DIOCESAN CEMETERIES

SAGINAW. *St. Andrew's, Mt. Olivet & Calvary.*
BAY CITY. *St. Patrick's, Calvary & St. Stanislaus.*
MIDLAND. *Calvary.*

NECROLOGY

† Gentner, John F., Essexville, MI, St. John the Evangelist. —Died May 4, 1997.
† O'Neil, Charles H., Auburn, MI, St. Joseph. —Died April 5, 1997.

Diocese of St. Augustine

(Dioecesis Sancti Augustini)

Most Reverend

JOHN J. SNYDER, D.D.

Bishop of St. Augustine; ordained June 9, 1951; appointed Titular Bishop of Forlimpopuli December 19, 1972; consecrated February 2, 1973; appointed Bishop of St. Augustine October 2, 1979; installed December 5, 1979. *Res., Cathedral-Basilica of Saint Augustine, 35 Treasury St., St. Augustine, FL, 32084.* Tel.: 904-824-2806; Fax: 904-260-8736. *Please address all official mail to: Catholic Center, P.O. Box 24000, Jacksonville, FL, 32241-4000.* Tel.: 904-262-3200; Fax: 904-260-8736.

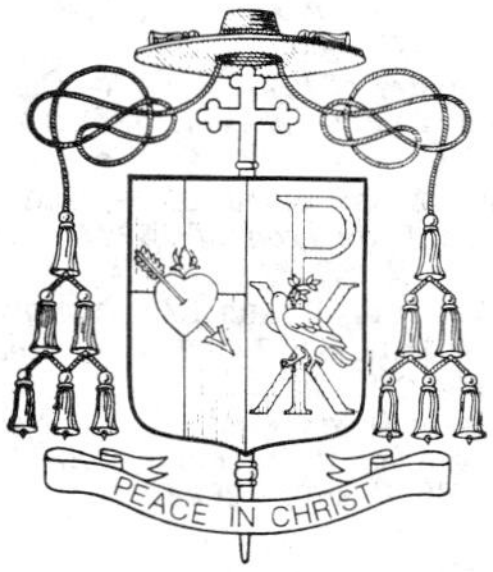

Square Miles 11,032.

Florida, east of the Apalachicola River, was erected by Pope Pius IX into a Vicariate-Apostolic in the year 1857, and in 1870 into the Diocese of St. Augustine.

Comprises all of the northeastern Counties of the State of Florida including Alachua, Baker, Bradford, Clay, Columbia, Dixie, Duval, Flagler, Gilchrist, Hamilton, Lafayette, Levy, Nassau, Putnam, St. Johns, Suwannee and Union Counties.

For legal titles of parishes and diocesan institutions, consult the Catholic Center.

Catholic Center: P.O. Box 24000, Jacksonville, FL, 32241-4000. Tel.: 904-262-3200; Fax: 904-262-0698.

Web site address: http://staugustine.ml.org/diocese

E-mail address: krb9953@aol.com

STATISTICAL OVERVIEW

Personnel	
Bishop	1
Priests: Diocesan Active in Diocese	70
Priests: Active Outside Diocese	13
Priests: Retired, Sick or Absent	7
Number of Diocesan Priests	90
Religious Priests in Diocese	26
Extern Priests in Diocese	20
Permanent Deacons in Diocese	23
Total Brothers	2
Total Sisters	111
Parishes	
Parishes	50
With Resident Pastor:	
Resident Diocesan Priests	46
Resident Religious Priests	4
Without Resident Pastor:	
Missions	9
Welfare	
Catholic Hospitals	1
Total Assisted	192,700
Homes for the Aged	2
Total Assisted	702
Special Centers for Social Services	6
Total Assisted	50,000
Residential Care of Disabled	4
Total Assisted	21
Other Institutions	4
Total Assisted	234
Educational	
Diocesan Students in Other Seminaries	21
Total Seminarians	21
High Schools, Diocesan and Parish	2
Total Students	1,867
Elementary Schools, Diocesan and Parish	21
Total Students	7,118
Non-residential Schools for the Disabled	1
Total Students	110
Catechesis/Religious Education:	
High School Students	1,106
Elementary Students	7,919
Total Students Under Catholic Instruction	18,141
Teachers in the Diocese:	
Priests	2
Sisters	17
Lay Teachers	434
Vital Statistics	
Receptions into the Church:	
Infant Baptism Totals	2,022
Adult Baptism Totals	333
Received into Full Communion	439
First Communions	2,317
Confirmations	1,834
Marriages:	
Catholic	420
Interfaith	365
Total Marriages	785
Deaths	931
Total Catholic Population	124,669
Total Population	1,528,377

Former Bishops—Rt. Rev. AUGUSTIN VEROT, S.S., D.D., cons. April 25, 1858; Vicar-Apostolic of Florida; translated to the See of Savannah in July, 1861; appt. Bishop of St. Augustine March, 1870; died June 10, 1876.—Rt. Rev. JOHN MOORE, D.D., cons. May 13, 1877; died July 30, 1901.—Rt. Rev. WILLIAM JOHN KENNY, D.D., ord. Jan. 15, 1879; cons. May 18, 1902; died Oct. 23, 1913.—Rt. Rev. M. J. CURLEY, D.D., cons. June 30, 1914; promoted to See of Baltimore Aug. 10, 1921; died May 16, 1947.—Most Rev. PATRICK BARRY, D.D., ord. June 9, 1895; appt. Feb. 22, 1922; cons. May 3, 1922; died Aug. 13, 1940.—Most Rev. JOSEPH P. HURLEY, D.D., ord. May 25, 1919; appt. Aug. 16, 1940; cons. Oct. 6, 1940 Received Personal title of Archbishop Aug. 18, 1950; died Oct. 30, 1967.—Most Rev. PAUL F. TANNER, D.D., ord. May 30, 1931; appt. Titular Bishop of Lamasba, Oct. 18, 1965; appt. Bishop of Saint Augustine, Feb. 21, 1968; retired April 21, 1979 Remained as Administrator to Dec. 4, 1979; died July 29, 1994.

Catholic Center—11625 Old St. Augustine Rd., Jacksonville, 32258., Mailing Address: P.O. Box 24000, Jacksonville, 32241-4000. Office Hours: Mon.-Fri. 9-4:30. Tel: 904-262-3200; Fax: 904-262-0698.

Vicar General and Moderator of Curia—Rev. Msgr. VINCENT J. HAUT, V.G., M.S.W.

Chancellor—Rev. KEITH R. BRENNAN, J.C.D.

Secretary to the Bishop—NANCY KELLY.

Secretary to the Chancellor—JUDY T. PINSON.

Fiscal Office—IRENE G. PULEO, Fiscal Mgr.

Diocesan Tribunal—P.O. Box 24000, Jacksonville, 32241-4000. Tel: 904-262-3200.

Judicial Vicar—Rev. JOHN R. REYNOLDS, J.C.L.

Associate Judges—Rev. Msgr. DANIEL B. LOGAN; Rev. PETER H. COLASURDO, J.C.L.

Defenders of the Bond—Revs. JAMES R. BODDIE, JR.; KEITH R. BRENNAN, J.C.D.; RALPH L. BESENDORFER, J.C.D.

Advocates—Revs. GREGORY J. FAY; DONAL SULLIVAN.

Promoter of Justice—Rev. Msgr. PATRICK M. MADDEN, S.T.L.

Executive Secretary—VERONICA DOSKOCIL.

Secretary—MARY C. SLEEPER.

Diocesan Consultors—Rev. Msgr. JOHN J. LENIHAN, M.S.W.; Rev. Msgr. EUGENE C. KOHLS, P.A., J.C.D.; Rev. Msgr. VINCENT HAUT, V.G., M.S.W.; Revs. ROBERT J. BAKER, S.T.D., V.F.; JAMES R. BODDIE, JR.; DANIEL CODY; ROLAND M. JULIEN, V.F.; MICHAEL J. LARKIN.

Diocesan Pastoral Council—Sr. EILEEN DONOGHUE, D.C., Chm., *Diocese of St. Augustine Catholic Center, P.O. Box 24000, Jacksonville, 32241-4000.* Tel: 904-262-3200; Fax: 904-262-0698.

Presbyteral Council—Revs. PAUL V. DONNELLY, Chm. TIMOTHY LINDENFELSER, Vice Chm. KEITH R. BRENNAN, J.C.D., Chancellor & Treas. WILLIAM HOCHHEIM, Sec.; Rev. Msgr. VINCENT J. HAUT, V.G., M.S.W.; Rev. Msgr. DANIEL B. LOGAN; Revs. JOHN PHILLIPS; NOEL COX, C.S.Sp.; WILLIAM A. KELLY, V.F.; JAMES O. NEAL; ROLAND M. JULIEN, V.F.; JAMES R. BODDIE, JR.; THOMAS SULLIVAN, V.F.

Deans—Rev. DONAL SULLIVAN, V.F., St. Augustine Deanery; Rev. ROLAND M. JULIEN, V.F., Gainesville Deanery; Rev. THOMAS SULLIVAN, V.F., North Jacksonville Deanery; Rev. WILLIAM A. KELLY, V.F., South Jacksonville Deanery.

Building Commission—Most Rev. JOHN J. SNYDER, Chm.; Rev. Msgr. VINCENT J. HAUT, V.G., M.S.W., Vice Chm.; Rev. KEITH R. BRENNAN, J.C.D., Chancellor; Rev. Msgr. DANIEL B. LOGAN; Rev. THOMAS CODY; ARTHUR TODD; Revs. MICHAEL J. LARKIN; GREGORY J. FAY.

Catholic Foundation of Diocese of St. Augustine—Most Rev. JOHN J. SNYDER; Rev. Msgr. VINCENT J. HAUT, V.G., M.S.W.; Rev. Msgr. JOHN J. LENIHAN, M.S.W.; Rev. KEITH R. BRENNAN, J.C.D., Chancellor; Dr. GASTON ACOSTA-RUA; JOHN CRAWFORD; KAY ZAMBETTI; PETER STRAIN; RICARDO MORALES; FRANCIS SCHOLTZ; MARTHA BARRETT; S. P. BRAUD, III; JACK DEMETREE; PHIL SMITH; ERNEST P. BONO; DIANNE T. RICE; DENIS PLUMB; IRENE G. PULEO, Fiscal Mgr., *P.O. Box 24000, Jacksonville, 32241-4000.* Tel: 904-262-3200.

Finance Committee—Dr. GASTON ACOSTA-RUA; ROBERT A. DEVEREUX; CLYDE E. LOWER; Rev. Msgr. MORTIMER DANAHER; Rev. Msgr. VINCENT J. HAUT, V.G., M.S.W.; Revs. KEITH R. BRENNAN, J.C.D.; LUKE MCLOUGHLIN; IRENE G. PULEO, Fiscal Mgr. PATRICIA JEREMIAH; MARY ALICE PHELAN; TIMOTHY LANE; MARIA ALLEN; FRANCIS N. SCHOLTZ, *P.O. Box 24000, Jacksonville, 32241-4000.* Tel: 904-262-3200.

Health Insurance Committee, Diocesan—Rev. KEITH R. BRENNAN, J.C.D.; Rev. Msgr. VINCENT J. HAUT, V.G., M.S.W.; Rev. MICHAEL R. HOULE; PATRICIA A. TIERNEY; WILLIAM J. TIERNEY; IRENE G. PUELO; JANET P. MORTON; SANDRA WARD; Sr. MAUREEN KELLEY, O.P., *P.O. Box 24000, Jacksonville, 32241-4000.* Tel: 904-262-3200.

Stewardship Council, Diocesan—Most Rev. JOHN J. SNYDER; Rev. ROBERT MCDERMOTT; Rev. JAMES R. BODDIE, JR.; Rev. Msgr. JAMES J. HESLIN; Rev. JOSEPH FINLAY; DANIEL L. TALAGA; FRANCIS SCHOLTZ; DENIS M. PLUMB; ROBERT ARMSTRONG; Rev. JOSEPH MEEHAN; GERALD WEEDON; PAT THOMAS; MICHAEL

CASCONE, JR.; BETSY BERGMAN; JOHN WOMBOUGH; KENNETH DAVIDSON, *P.O. Box 24000, Jacksonville, 32241-4000.* Tel: 904-262-3200.

Diocesan Offices and Directors

Alcohol and Other Drug Abuse Commission—WILLIAM J. TIERNEY, Convener, *P.O. Box 24000, Jacksonville, 32241-4000.* Tel: 904-262-3200.

Apostleship of the Sea—Deacon DALE WAMSTAD, O.F.M., *Providence Center, 134 E. Church St., Jacksonville, 32202-3130.* Tel: 904-356-3104.

Archives of Diocese—Rev. KEITH R. BRENNAN, J.C.D., Chancellor, *P.O. Box 24000, Jacksonville, 32241-4000.* Tel: 904-262-3200.

Assisted Suicide Task Force—T. JAMES GALLAGHER, M.D., Chm., *P.O. Box 24000, Jacksonville, 32241-4000.* Tel: 904-262-3200.

Bioethics Commission—T. JAMES GALLAGHER, M.D., Chm., *P.O. Box 24000, Jacksonville, 32241-4000.* Tel: 904-262-3200.

Black, African, Caribbean and Native American Ministries—Rev. JAMES R. BODDIE, JR., Vicar of the Black Apostolate; ELLA SIMMONS, Dir., *P.O. Box 24000, Jacksonville, 32241-4000.* Tel: 904-262-3200.

Campaign for Human Development—Rev. EDWARD K. ROONEY, Dir., *1606 Blanding Blvd., Middleburg, 32068.* Tel: 904-282-0439.

Campus Ministry—Ms. CINDEE CASE, Dir. PETER W. MORGAN, Campus Minister, *Jacksonville University, Jacksonville, 32211.* Tel: 904-744-3950, Ext. 2258; 646-2638.

Christian Formation—Sr. LUCILLE CLYNES, D.W, Dir., *P.O. Box 24000, Jacksonville, 32241-4000.* Tel: 904-262-3200.

Catholic Burse Endowment Fund, Inc.—(Education of Priests), *P.O. Box 24000, Jacksonville, 32241-4000.* Tel: 904-262-3200.

Catholic Charities Bureau, Inc.—WILLIAM J. TIERNEY, Exec. Dir., *P.O. Box 24000, Jacksonville, 32241-4000.* Tel: 904-262-3200. See Separate Listing for more details.

Catholic Relief Services—WILLIAM J. TIERNEY, Dir., *P.O. Box 24000, Jacksonville, 32241-4000.* Tel: 904-262-3200.

Catholic Women, Council of—Rev. LUKE MCLOUGHLIN, Spiritual Moderator, *St. Matthew Church, 1773 Blanding Blvd., Jacksonville, 32210.* Tel: 904-388-8698.

Charismatic Renewal—Rev. Msgr. HAROLD F. JORDAN, Diocesan Coord., *Mission of Nombre de Dios, 30 Ocean Ave., St. Augustine, 32084.* Tel: 904-824-3045.

Civil Institutions—Rev. JOSEPH MANIANGAT, M.A., *St. Mary Parish, P.O. Box 1120, Macclenny, 32063.* Tel: 904-259-6414.

Communications Commission—ART MARSHALL, Chm., *P.O. Box 24000, Jacksonville, 32241-4000.* Tel: 904-262-3200.

Communications, Office of—KATHLEEN BAGG-MORGAN, Dir., *P.O. Box 24000, Jacksonville, 32241-4000.* Tel: 904-262-3200.

Continuing Education for Priests—Rev. Msgr. R. JOSEPH JAMES, Dir., *9401 Staples Mill Rd., Jacksonville, 32244.*

Cursillos de Cristiandad—Rev. Msgr. R. JOSEPH JAMES, Spiritual Dir., *Mary Queen of Heaven, 9401 Staples Mill Rd., Jacksonville, 32244.* Tel: 904-777-3168. Rev. TIMOTHY R. LOZIER, Asst. Spiritual Dir., *St. Augustine Parish, P.O. Box 13888, Gainesville, 32604.* Tel: 904-372-3533.

Disabilities, Ministry of Persons with—DAN JOHNSON, Dir., *P.O. Box 24000, Jacksonville, 32241-4000.* Tel: 904-262-3200.

Ecumenism—Rev. Msgr. JOHN J. LENIHAN, M.S.W., Chm., *3619 Toledo Rd., Jacksonville, 32217.* Tel: 904-733-1630.

Educational Services—PATRICIA A. TIERNEY, M.S.Ed., Supt. Schools, *P.O. Box 24000, Jacksonville, 32241-4000.* Tel: 904-262-3200.

The Guardian of Dreams—Mr. LOUIS WALSH, Chm., *P.O. Box 24000, Jacksonville, 32241-4000.* Tel: 904-262-3200; Fax: 904-262-0698.

Family Life, Diocesan Center for—NANCY C. FISHER, R.N., Dir.; Rev. DANIEL CODY, Consultant, *P.O. Box 24000, Jacksonville, 32241-4000.* Tel: 904-262-3200. Regional Office: Baptist/St. Vincent's Health System. Tel: 904-308-7474.

Farmworker Services Program—Mrs. CHIQUI MALDONADO, Dir., *40 Sanford St., St. Augustine, 32084.* Tel: 904-829-6300.

Florida Catholic Conference—D. MICHAEL MCCARRON, Ph.D., Exec. Dir., *890 Tallahassee Bank Bldg., P.O. Box 1638, Tallahassee, 32302-1638.* Tel: 904-222-3803.

Health Care Task Force—LEONARD SPILLANE, Chm., *P.O. Box 24000, Jacksonville, 32241-4000.* Tel: 904-262-3200.

Hispanic Ministry—Rev. LUIS FLOREZ, Dir.; Deacon JAMES SWANSON, Coord., *P.O. Box 53257, Jacksonville, 32201.* Tel: 904-262-3200; 353-3243.

Holy Childhood Association, The—Rev. BRIAN EBURN, Dir., *P.O. Box 24000, Jacksonville, 32241-4000.* Tel: 904-262-3200.

Holy Name Societies—Rev. Msgr. PATRICK M. MADDEN, S.T.L., Spiritual Dir., *Sacred Heart Rectory, 5752 Blanding Blvd., Jacksonville, 32244.* Tel: 904-771-2152.

Investment Commission—Rev. Msgr. VINCENT J. HAUT, M.S.W., V.G.; Rev. KEITH R. BRENNAN, J.C.D., Chancellor; IRENE G. PUELO, Fiscal Mgr. JAMES DOLAN; THOMAS TIERNEY; TIMOTHY LANE; ROBERT A. DEVEREAUX.

Justice and Peace Commission—ELIZABETH O'BRIEN, Chm., *P.O. Box 24000, Jacksonville, 32241-4000.* Tel: 904-262-3200.

Justice and Reconciliation, Ministry for—Sr. DOROTHEA MURPHY, R.S.M., Coord.; Rev. GROVER B. TIPTON, Chap., *1717 N.E. 9th, Suite 123, Gainesville, 32609.* Tel: 904-372-6006.

Legalization—NANCY VALDIVIESO, Dir., *P.O. Box 24000, Jacksonville, 32241-4000.* Tel: 904-272-3200., *Providence Center, P.O. Box 53257, Jacksonville, 32201.* Tel: 904-354-5904.

Legion of Mary—Rev. JOSE MANIYANGAT, Spiritual Dir., *P.O. Drawer 5040, Jacksonville, 32247-5040.* Tel: 904-398-1963.

Liturgy Office—Rev. THOMAS WILLIS, Chm. LUCILLE BARRETT, Vice-Chm.; Dr. GLENN KUHNEL, Exec. Sec., *P.O. Box 24000, Jacksonville, 32241-4000.* Tel: 904-262-3200.

Planned Giving Office—Mrs. DENIS PLUMB, Dir., *P.O. Box 24000, Jacksonville, 32241-4000.* Tel: 904-262-3200.

Marriage Encounter—NANCY C. FISHER, R.N., Exec. Dir. Exec. Team: SUSAN SHIELDS; BILL SHIELDS, *1851 King St., Room 103, Jacksonville, 33204.* Tel: 904-308-7474.

Parish Social Ministry—Sr. MARLENE PAYETTE, S.S.J., Dir., *Providence Center, 134 E. Church St., Jacksonville, 32202-3130.* Tel: 904-354-3416.

Priests' Spirituality Committee—Rev. DONAL P. SULLIVAN, *P.O. Box 276, Green Cove Springs, 32043.* Tel: 904-284-3811.

Propagation of the Faith—Rev. BRIAN EBURN, Dir., *P.O. Box 24000, Jacksonville, 32241-4000.* Tel: 904-262-3200.

Refugee Resettlement—WILLIAM C. BEITZ, Dir., *Providence Center, 134 E. Church St., Jacksonville, 32202-3130.* Tel: 904-354-3416.

Respect Life Activities—BONNIE SEAVER, Dir.; Rev. THOMAS S. WILLIS, Spiritual Moderator, *P.O. Box 24000, Jacksonville, 32241-4000.* Tel: 904-262-3200.

Rural Life Director—Rev. MICHAEL PENDERGRAFT, *P.O. Box 863, Chiefland, 32626.* Tel: 904-493-1561.

St. Vincent de Paul Societies—Rev. Msgr. MORTIMER DANAHER, Moderator. Tel: 904-262-3200.

Scouts—Revs. JAMES R. BODDIE, JR., Chap. EDWARD MURPHY, Asst. Chap., *P.O. Box 24000, Jacksonville, 32241-4000.* Tel: 904-262-3200.

Seminarians—Rev. JOHN H. TETLOW, Dir., *P.O. Box 24000, Jacksonville, 32241-4000.* Tel: 904-262-3200.

Stewardship, Office of—FRANCIS N. SCHOLTZ, Dir., *P.O. Box 24000, Jacksonville, 32241-4000.* Tel: 904-262-3200.

Vicar for Clergy—Rev. RALPH L. BESENDORFER, J.C.D., *P.O. Box 24000, Jacksonville, 32241-4000.* Tel: 904-262-3200.

Vicar for Religious—Sr. MAUREEN KELLEY, O.P., *P.O. Box 24000, Jacksonville, 32241-4000.* Tel: 904-262-3200.

Vicar for Senior Priests—Rev. Msgr. EUGENE C. KOHLS, P.A., J.C.D., *P.O. Box 5040, Jacksonville, 32247-5040.* Tel: 904-387-2554.

Vocations—Rev. JOHN H. TETLOW, Dir., *P.O. Box 24000, Jacksonville, 32241-4000.* Tel: 904-262-3200.

Youth and Young Adult Ministry—Ms. CINDEE CASE, Dir., *P.O. Box 24000, Jacksonville, 32241-4000.* Tel: 904-262-3200.

CLERGY, PARISHES, MISSIONS AND PAROCHIAL SCHOOLS

CITY OF ST. AUGUSTINE
(St. Johns County)

1—CATHEDRAL OF ST. AUGUSTINE (1565). (A Minor Basilica). Revs. Jeremiah F. Lambe, C.S.Sp.; Timothy M. Lindenfelser, Admin.; Edward N. Booth; Patrick Doody, C.S.Sp.; Deacons Thomas Richards; John Pelletier. In res., Rev. Msgr. Harold F. Jordan; Revs. Rene Robert, Chap. to the Catholic Deaf; Terry Smith, C.S.Sp.

Res., 35 Treasury St., 32084. Tel: 904-824-2806; Fax: 904-824-0761. [CEM]

School—Cathedral Parish School, (Grades K-8) 259 St. George St., 32084. Tel: 904-824-2861; Fax: 904-824-2862. Sr. Mary Victor Azar, S.S.J., Prin. Sisters 1; Lay Teachers 26; Students 401.

Cathedral Parish Early Education Center—(Preschool and After School Care) 10 San Sabastian Ave., 32084. Tel: 904-829-2933. Kathleen Tiews, Dir.

Lay Teachers 5; Students 45.

Catechesis/Religious Programs—Tel: 904-829-3338.

Students 220.

Missions—St. Augustine, St. Johns Co., Prince of Peace, San Marco Ave., 32084.; St. Augustine, St. Johns Co., St. Benedict the Moor, Martin Luther King Ave., 32084.

2—MISSION OF NOMBRE DE DIOS AND SHRINE OF OUR LADY OF LA LECHE (1565), Rev. Msgr. Harold F. Jordan, Dir.

Office: 30 Ocean Ave., 32084. Fax: 904-829-0819.

Res., 35 Treasury St., 32084. Tel: 904-824-3045; Fax: 904-824-0761.

3—ST. ANASTASIA (1988), Rev. Seamus O'Flynn; Sr. Enda Egan, Pastoral Assoc.; Deacon Bob Lucian.

Mailing Address: 5205 A1A S., 32084-7107.

Res., 5319 Fifth St., 32084. Tel: 904-471-3747; 471-5364 (Office); Fax: 904-471-7448.

Catechesis/Religious Programs—Susan Seasholtz, D.R.E.

Students 127.

4—SAN SEBASTIAN (1968), Revs. Peter Colasurdo; Gerald A. Vallee; Deacon James Swanson.

Res., 1112 State Rd. 16, 32095. Tel: 904-824-6625; Fax: 904-829-0459.

Catechesis/Religious Programs—Students 74.

OUTSIDE THE CITY OF ST. AUGUSTINE

Atlantic Beach, Duval Co., St. John the Baptist (1967), Rev. Joseph Meehan; Deacon Harold Brodeur. In res., Rev. D. Terrence Morgan.

Mailing Address: P.O. Drawer 330005, 32233. Tel: 904-246-6014; Fax: 904-246-1219.

Catechesis/Religious Programs—Carole Fuchs, D.R.E.

Students 297.

Branford, Suwannee Co., San Juan Mission (1980). Unassigned.

Mailing Address: P.O. Box 949, 32008. Tel: 904-935-2632; 752-4470; Fax: 904-935-2632.

Bunnell, Flagler Co., St. Stephen (1957), Rev. Frederick Parke.

Mailing Address: 4600 Belle Terre Pkwy., Palm Coast, 32164.

Res., Rte. 100, 32110. Tel: 904-445-2246; Fax: 904-445-7808.

Callahan, Nassau Co., Our Lady of Consolation (1974), Rev. Ralph L. Besendorfer, J.C.D.

Res., 11625 Old St. Augustine Rd., Jacksonville, 32258. Tel: 904-262-3200; Fax: 904-262-0698.

Catechesis/Religious Programs—Edith Tasso, D.R.E.

Students 71.

Chiefland, Levy Co., St. John the Evangelist (1981), Rev. Michael Pendergraft.

Res., P.O. Box 863, 32644-0863. Tel: 352-493-1561; Fax: 352-493-9258.

Catechesis/Religious Programs—Students 59.

Mission—Cross City, Dixie Co., Holy Cross, Cross City, 32628. Tel: 352-498-5671.

Crescent City, Putnam Co., St. John the Baptist (1910), Rev. Brian Eburn; Sr. Bridie Ryan, Pastoral Assoc.

Res., P.O. Box 908, 32112. Tel: 904-698-2055; Fax: 904-698-4146. [CEM]

Catechesis/Religious Programs—Tel: 904-698-4334.

Students 59.

Elkton, St. John Co., St. Ambrose (1875) (Minorcan), Rev. Patrick Carroll, C.S.Sp., Admin.

Res., 6070 Church Rd., 32033. Tel: 904-692-1366; Fax: 904-692-1136. [CEM]

Mission—Bakersville, St. Johns Co., Our Lady of Good Counsel, 5005 Church Rd., Bakersville, 32092. [CEM]

Fernandina Beach, Amelia Island, Nassau Co., St. Michael's (1872), Revs. Mark S. Waters; Neil Cornelli.

Res., 505 Broome St., 32034. Tel: 904-261-3472; Fax: 904-321-1901. [JC]

Catechesis/Religious Programs—Janice Balota, Pastoral Assoc.

Students 250.

Flagler Beach, Flagler Co., Santa Maria Del Mar (1970), Rev. John O'Flaherty; Deacon Charlie Karr.
Res., 801 N. Central Ave., P.O. Box 130, 32136. Tel: 904-439-2791; Fax: 904-439-2791. [CEM]

Gainesville, Alachua Co.,

1—St. Patrick's, (1887), Revs. Roland M. Julien; Paul V. Donnelly; Michael Thompson.
Res., 500 N.E. 16th Ave., 32601. Tel: 352-372-4641; 376-0575; Fax: 352-376-0575.
School—Tel: 352-376-9878; Fax: 352-371-6177. Elaine Baumgartner, Prin.
Lay Teachers 28; Students 520.
Catechesis/Religious Programs—Tel: 352-376-9878, Ext. 60. Diane St. Onge, D.R.E.
Students 80.
Mission—Hawthorne, Alachua Co., St. Philip Neri, U.S. 301 S., Hawthorne, 32640.

2—Holy Faith, (1973), Revs. Michael S. Williams; Ignatius J. Plathanam.
Res., 700 N.W. 39 Rd., 32607. Tel: 352-376-5405; Fax: 352-375-7568.
Catechesis/Religious Programs—Tel: 352-374-4708; Fax: 352-375-7568. Carmen M. Delgado, D.R.E.
Students 315.

3—Queen of Peace, (1987), Rev. Jeffrey A. McGowan.
Church—10900 S.W. 24th Ave., 32607. Tel: 352-332-6279; Fax: 352-331-7347. [JC]
Catechesis/Religious Programs—Dan Talaga, D.R.E.
Students 415.

4—St. Augustine, (1923), Revs. John D. Gillespie; John M. Phillips; Timothy R. Lozier.
Res., 1738 W. University Ave., P.O. Box 13888, 32604. Tel: 352-372-3533; Fax: 352-378-9010.
Catechesis/Religious Programs—Kelli Brew, D.R.E.
Students 323.

Green Cove Springs, Clay Co., Sacred Heart (1874), Rev. Donal Sullivan.
Res., 614 W. Bay St., P.O. Box 276, 32043. Tel: 904-284-3811.
Catechesis/Religious Programs—Mrs. Sherry Latta-Raines, D.R.E.
Students 138.

High Springs, Alachua Co., St. Madeleine Sophie Parish (1925), Rev. Noel Cox, C.S.Sp.
Mailing Address: P.O. Box 892, 32655-0892.
Res., 3330 E. Martin Luther King Blvd., 32643. Tel: 904-454-2358; Fax: 904-454-4985.
Catechesis/Religious Programs—Students 81.

Interlachen, Putnam Co., St. John's Mission (1968), Revs. James E. O'Neal, S.A.; John J. Heerey (BRK) Pastor Emeritus.
Res., P.O. Box 207, 32148. Tel: 904-684-2528. [JC]
Catechesis/Religious Programs—Students 50.

Jacksonville, Duval Co.,

1—Assumption, (South Jacksonville) (1913), Rev. Msgr. Eugene C. Kohls; Revs. Jose Maniyangat; Raymond J. Carlo. In res., Rev. Luis Florez, Dir., Hispanic Apostolate.
Res., 2403 Atlantic Blvd., P.O. Box 5040, 32247-5040. Tel: 904-398-1963; Fax: 904-398-6115.
School—Tel: 904-398-1774; Fax: 904-398-6712. Mrs. Maureen Matthes, Prin.
Lay Teachers 31; Students 631.
Catechesis/Religious Programs—Sr. Lyn Payette, S.S.J., D.R.E.
Students 80.

2—Blessed Trinity, (1957), Rev. Denis O'Regan.
Res., 10472 Beach Blvd., P.O. Box 16466, 32245. Tel: 904-641-1414; Fax: 904-641-1414.
Catechesis/Religious Programs—Tel: 904-641-0515. Mrs. Joanne Davis, D.R.E.
Students 223.

3—Christ the King, (1954), Revs. Robert Baker; Brian Carey, C.S.Sp.; Thanh T. Nguyen. In res., Rev. John H. Tetlow.
Res., 742 Arlington Rd., 32211. Tel: 904-724-0080; Fax: 904-721-2326.
School—Tel: 904-724-2954; Fax: 904-721-8004. Mrs. Janet Morton, Prin.
Sisters 1; Lay Teachers 125; Teachers Aids 8; Students 975.
Catechesis/Religious Programs—Deacon Dave McNamara, D.R.E.
Students 169.

4—Crucifixion, (1974) (African American), Rev. Cletus M. Watson, T.O.R.
Mailing Address: 454 W. 63rd St., 32208. Tel: 904-768-0261.
Church of the Crucifixion Rectory: 6079 Bagley Rd., 32209-1800. Tel: 904-765-5284; Fax: 904-765-1680.

5—Holy Family, (1974), Rev. Msgr. Daniel B. Logan; Sr. Helen Marie Kling, D.C., Pastoral Assoc.
Office: 9800 Baymeadows Rd., 32256. Tel: 904-641-5838; Fax: 904-641-9704.
Catechesis/Religious Programs—Sr. Martha Costello, O.P., D.R.E.
Students 190.

6—Holy Rosary, (1921), Revs. Glenn D. Parker, C.SS.R.; Alfred A. Sieradski, C.SS.R.
Res., 746 W. 41st St., 32206. Tel: 904-764-3241; Fax: 904-765-4995.
School—Sisters of Notre Dame. (Toledo Prov.) 4920 Brentwood Ave., 32206. Tel: 904-765-6522; 353-6933. Sr. Patricia Marie McClain, S.N.D., Prin.
Sisters 4; Lay Teachers 9; Students 145.

7—Holy Spirit, (1966), Rev. Msgr. James J. Heslin; Deacon Gjet Bajraktari.
Res., 11665 Fort Caroline Rd., 32225. Tel: 904-641-7244; Fax: 904-641-7266.
School—(Grades PreK-6). Tel: 904-642-9165. Therese Moore, Prin.
Lay Teachers 10; Students 204.
Catechesis/Religious Programs—Judy Altmiller, D.R.E.
Students 352.

8—Immaculate Conception, (1854), Revs. Antonio Leon; Warren Keene; Richard E. Powers, S.J.
Res., 121 E. Duval St., P.O. Box 100, 32201. Tel: 904-359-0331; Fax: 904-356-8133. [CEM][JC]

9—Mary Queen of Heaven, (1988), Rev. Msgr. R. Joseph James.
Res., 9401 Staples Mill Dr., 32244. Tel: 904-777-1272.
Catechesis/Religious Programs—Tel: 904-777-3168; Fax: 904-778-7691.
Students 96.

10—Most Holy Redeemer, (1962), Rev. Thomas S. Willis.
Res., 8523 Normandy Blvd., 32221-6701. Tel: 904-786-1192; Fax: 904-786-4224.
Catechesis/Religious Programs—Sharon Tomore, D.R.E.
Students 111.

11—Our Lady of the Angels, (1917), Rev. Joseph Notarpole.
Res., 430 Crystal St., 32254. Tel: 904-389-4878; Fax: 904-389-4878. [CEM]

12—Prince of Peace, (1970), Rev. Michael J. Larkin.
Res., 6320 Bennett Rd., 32216. Tel: 904-733-6860; Fax: 904-367-0215.
Catechesis/Religious Programs—Tel: 904-733-6018.
Students 82.

13—Resurrection, (1959), Revs. Thomas Cody; Daniel Shashy.
Res., 3383 University Blvd. N., 32277. Tel: 904-744-0833; Fax: 904-744-7235.
School—Tel: 904-744-1266. Katherine Boice, Prin.
Lay Teachers 16; Students 300.
Catechesis/Religious Programs—Tel: 904-744-5800. Noreen Thurson, D.R.E.
Students 235.

14—Sacred Heart, (1959), Rev. Msgr. Patrick M. Madden; Revs. Victor Z. Narivelil, C.M.I.; Conrad Cowart.
Res., 5752 Blanding Blvd., 32244. Tel: 904-771-2152; Fax: 904-573-8816.
School—Sisters of Mercy (Clonakilty, Ireland), Tel: 904-771-5800. Sr. Josephine O'Leary, R.S.M., Prin.
Sisters 1; Lay Teachers 28; Students 609.
Catechesis/Religious Programs—Sr. Mary of Mercy, D.R.E.
Students 215.

15—St. Francis Choe Chapel, Rev. Park Seong Yeol Thomas.
Res., 8051 Rampart Rd., 32244. Tel: 904-573-1833.

16—St. Joseph's, (1883), Revs. Daniel Cody; Patrick Soares, C.S.Sp.
Res., 11730 Old St. Augustine Rd., 32258-2002. Tel: 904-268-5422; Fax: 904-292-0248. [CEM]
School—Tel: 904-268-6688; Fax: 904-268-8989. Mrs. Carolyn Backherms, Prin.
Lay Teachers 26; Students 602.
Catechesis/Religious Programs—Carole Ginzl, D.R.E.
Students 638.

17—St. Matthew's, (Lake Shore) (1949), Revs. Luke McLoughlin; Patrick Cooke, C.S.Sp. In res., Rev. John R. Reynolds, J.C.L.
Res., 1773 Blanding Blvd., 32210. Tel: 904-388-8698; Fax: 904-384-1233.
School—Tel: 904-387-4401; Fax: 904-388-4404. David Yazdiya, Prin.
Lay Teachers 16; Students 322.
Catechesis/Religious Programs—Tel: 904-388-1207. Onie Rodriguez, D.R.E.
Students 150.

18—St. Patrick, (1959), Rev. Robert T. McDermott.
Res., 1429 Broward Rd., 32218. Tel: 904-768-2593; Fax: 904-786-2144.
School—Sisters of Mercy, (Grades K-8). Tel: 904-768-6323; Fax: 904-768-2144. Sr. Carmel O'Callahan, C.S.M., Prin.
Lay Teachers 14; Students 305.
Catechesis/Religious Programs—Tel: 904-757-4720.
Students 59.

19—St. Paul's, (1923), Revs. Thomas K. Sullivan; James J. Corry, C.S.Sp.
Res., 2609 Park St., P.O. Box 40705, 32203. Tel: 904-387-2554; Fax: 904-388-6871.
School—Tel: 904-387-2841; Fax: 904-387-1781. Mrs. Ana Voss, Prin.
Lay Teachers 12; Students 238.
Catechesis/Religious Programs—Students 25.

20—St. Pius the Fifth, (1919) (African American), Rev. James R. Boddie, Jr.
Res., 2110 Blue Ave., 32209. Tel: 904-354-1501; Fax: 904-354-7240.
School—1470 W. 13th St., 32209. Tel: 904-354-2613; Fax: 904-356-4522. Sr. Elise Kennedy, S.S.J., Prin.
Sisters 2; Lay Teachers 10; Students 202.
Catechesis/Religious Programs—Tel: 904-354-1501; Fax: 904-354-7240.
Students 63.

21—San Jose, (1959), Rev. Msgr. John J. Lenihan; Revs. Thomas Walsh; Anthony P. Palazzolo; Rodolfo Godinez Fuentes.
Res., 3619 Toledo Rd., 32217. Tel: 904-733-1630; Fax: 904-733-7973.
School—Sisters of Mercy, Tel: 904-733-2510. Sr. Eithne Lowther, R.S.M., Prin.
Sisters 2; Lay Teachers 24; Students 556.
Catechesis/Religious Programs—Tel: 904-733-1630, Ext. 19. Nancy Cronin, D.R.E.
Students 289.

22—Syriac Antiochian-Rite Mission St. Ephrem, (1986). Closed. For inquiries for parish records contact the Chancery.

Jacksonville Beach, Duval Co., St. Paul's (1930), Revs. William A. Kelly; Robert L. Napier; Wayne Price.
Res., 224 N. Fifth St., 32250. Tel: 904-249-2600; Fax: 904-249-0422.
School—Tel: 904-249-5394; Fax: 904-241-2911. Mrs. Rosemary Spraggins, Prin.
Lay Teachers 26; Students 528.
Catechesis/Religious Programs—Tel: 904-249-2660. Mary Coleman, D.R.E.
Students 545.

Keystone Heights, Clay Co., St. William (1948), Rev. Moises Palaroan.
Res., P.O. Box 721, 32656. Tel: 352-473-4136; Fax: 352-473-4119. [JC]
Catechesis/Religious Programs—Tel: 904-473-4223.
Students 145.

Korona, Flagler Co., St. Mary's (1914) (Polish), Revs. John O'Flaherty; Walter C. Bayer (Poland); Deacon Charlie Karr.
Mailing Address: P.O. Box 1537, Bunnell, 32110-1537. Tel: 904-437-5098 (Tues. & Thurs., 9:00am - 12:00pm).
Res., 801 N. Central Ave., P.O. Box 130, Flagler Beach, 32036. Tel: 904-439-2791. [CEM]

Lake City, Columbia Co., Epiphany (1965), Revs. Anthony G. Sebra; Patrick Murphy, S.J.; Sr. Mary Esther Flanagan, S.S.J., Pastoral Assoc.
Res., Malone Dr., Rte. 10, Box 161-B, 32025. Tel: 904-752-4470; Fax: 904-752-4652.
School—Tel: 904-752-2320; Fax: 904-755-1799. Mr. Mark Akerman, Prin.
Lay Teachers 8; Students 128.
Catechesis/Religious Programs—Tel: 904-752-3018.
Students 61.

Live Oak, Suwannee Co., St. Francis Xavier, Rev. Michael E. Morse.
Res., P.O. Box 1179, 32060. Tel: 904-364-1108; Fax: 904-364-1836.
Catechesis/Religious Programs—Tel: 904-362-7287. Nancy Roberts, D.R.E.
Students 86.
Mission—Jasper, Hamilton Co., St. Therese of Lisieux, P.O. Box 890, Jasper, 32052. Tel: 904-364-1108.

Macclenny, Baker Co., St. Mary's (1960), Rev. Joseph Maniangat.
Res., 104 Jacqueline Cir., P.O. Box 1120, 32063. Tel: 904-259-6414; Fax: 904-259-6414. [JC]
Catechesis/Religious Programs—Tel: 904-259-3217. Janet DeBoe, D.R.E.
Students 57.
Chaplaincy—Northeast Florida State Hospital, Macclenny; Union Correctional Institute, Raiford; and Florida State Prison, Starke.

Middleburg, Clay Co., St. Luke's (1982), Rev. Edward Rooney.
Res., 1606 Blanding Blvd., 32068. Tel: 904-282-0439; Fax: 904-291-9711.
Catechesis/Religious Programs—Students 341.

Orange Park, Clay Co., St. Catherine's (1877), Rev. Msgr. Vincent J. Haut, V.G.; Revs. Alex Ducci; Ronald A. Camarda; Felicien K. Houndjame; William Butler, C.S.Sp.

Res., 1649 Kingsley Ave., 32073. Tel: 904-264-0577; Fax: 904-264-7999.

Catechesis/Religious Programs—Tel: 904-264-2470. Bro. Dominic M. O'Brien, F.M.S., D.R.E. Students 1,010.

Mission—Orange Park, Clay Co., Moosehaven Chapel, 1700 Park Ave., 32073. Tel: 904-278-1210.

Palatka, Putnam Co., St. Monica's (1873), Rev. Joseph F. Finlay.

Office: 114 S. 4th St., 32177. Tel: 904-325-9777; Fax: 904-329-1960. [CEM]

Catechesis/Religious Programs—Tel: 904-325-7777. Rev. Joseph F. Finlay, D.R.E.

Students 84.

Palm Coast, Flager Co., St. Elizabeth Ann Seton (1979), Revs. Frederick Parke; Edward Murphy; Sr. Mary Ryan, I.H.M., Pastoral Min.; Deacons Richard Arsenault; James Casapulla; Robert McDermott. In res., Rev. Jose Panthaplamthottiyil.

Res., 4600 Belle Terre Pkwy., 32164. Tel: 904-445-2246; Fax: 904-445-7808.

Catechesis/Religious Programs—Tel: 904-446-5854. D.R.E. Mrs. Rosaire Downey; Mrs. Dee Casapulla.

Students 30.

Ponte Vedra Beach, St. John Co., Our Lady Star of the Sea (1972), Rev. Msgr. T. Leo Danaher.

Mailing Address: 545 Hwy. A1A N., 32082. Tel: 904-285-2698; Fax: 904-285-2502.

Catechesis/Religious Programs—Tel: 904-273-0590.

Students 488.

St. Augustine Shores, St. John Co., Corpus Christi (1975), Rev. William C. Mooney; Deacon Joseph Cross.

Res., P.O. Box 3064, St. Augustine, 32085. Tel: 904-797-4842; Fax: 904-797-2746.

Catechesis/Religious Programs—Students 200.

Starke, Bradford Co., St. Edward's (1941), Rev. William A. Hochheim.

Res., 441 N. Temple Ave., 32091-3207. Tel: 904-964-6155.

Catechesis/Religious Programs—Students 33.

Switzerland, St. John Co., San Juan Del Rio (1977), Rev. Gregory J. Fay.

Res., 1714-3 State Rd., No. 13, 32259. Tel: 904-287-1589; 287-0519 (Office); Fax: 904-287-0519.

Catechesis/Religious Programs—Tel: 904-287-2270.

Students 235.

Williston, Levy Co., Holy Family (1970), Rev. James T. Moss.

Res., 17353 NE 27 A, 32696. Tel: 352-528-2893; Fax: 352-528-6002.

Catechesis/Religious Programs—Students 89.

Mission—Inglis, Levy Co., St. Anthony the Abbot, P.O. Box 1070, Inglis, 34449. Tel: 352-447-3630; Fax: 352-447-4573.

Special Assignment:
Reverend Fathers—
Brennan, Keith R., Chancellor, The Catholic Center, P.O. Box 24000, Jacksonville, FL 32241-4000. Tel: 904-262-3200
Foley, Patrick H.
Revilla, Francisco
Tipton, Grover B., Chap. of Prison Ministry

Graduate Studies:
Reverend Fathers—
Glisson, Nicholas J.

On Duty Outside the Diocese:
Reverend Monsignors—
Conesa, Diego, Diocese of St. Petersburg
Reverend Fathers—
Brown, Raymond E., S.S., 418 N.E. 105th St., Miami Shores, FL 33138
Fernandez, Marcellus
Moore, Frederick Thomas, Pensacola, FL
Morgan, D. Terrence, North American College, Rome, Italy
Russo, Caesar, P.O. Box 343, Bronx, NY 10470
Walsh, Flannan J.
Young, Dennis M., Chap., V.A. Medical Center, Augusta, GA

Military Chaplains:
Reverend Fathers—
Bower, Alan E.
Dux, John H.

Absent on Sick Leave:
Reverend Fathers—
Gagan, Philip R.
Pollard, John L.

Retired:
Reverend Monsignors—
Danaher, Mortimer, 7843 Fawn Oaks Ct., Jacksonville, FL 32256
Dawson, Joseph, 301 Elizabeth, Folkston, GA 31537
Reverend Fathers—
Barry, Joseph A., Presbyterian Apartments, 1045 Oak St., Apt. #206, Jacksonville, FL 32204
Couture, Fernand, Hwy. 17, Orange Park, FL 32073
Haryasz, Francis S., 397 Village Drive St., Augustine, FL 32095

INSTITUTIONS LOCATED IN THE DIOCESE

[A] HIGH SCHOOLS, DIOCESAN

ST. AUGUSTINE. *St. Joseph Academy*, 155 State Rd. 207, 32095. Tel: 904-824-0431.
E-mail: carlucci2@juno.com
Day School. Mr. John R. Carlucci, Prin. Lay Teachers 17; Students 280.

JACKSONVILLE. *Bishop Kenny High School*, 1055 Kingman Ave., P.O. Box 5544, 32247. Tel: 904-398-7545; Fax: 904-398-5728. Rev. Michael R. Houle, M.A., M.Ed., M.Div., Pres.; Miss Jane Marnett, M.S., Prin.; Robert West, M.Ed., Vice Prin. & Athletic Dir.; Ms. Deborah Coffey, M.Ed., Academic Dean; Dave Williams, M.Ed., Dean of Students. Priests 2; Sisters 1; Lay Teachers 87; Students 1,584.

San Juan del Rio Catholic School, 1714-2 State Rd. 13, 32259. Tel: 904-287-8081.
E-mail: SJDelRio@juno.com
Lay Teachers 6; Students 132.

[B] ELEMENTARY SCHOOLS, INTERPAROCHIAL

MIDDLEBURG. *Annunciation School.* (Grades PreK-6), 1610 Blanding Blvd., 32068.
E-mail: spowell3@juno.com
Interparish school composed of students from Sacred Heart, Green Cove Springs; St. Catherine's, Orange Park; and St. Luke, Middleburg. Susan Powell, Prin. Students 230.

[C] CATHOLIC CHARITIES

ST. AUGUSTINE. *Catholic Charities Regional Office*, 225 W. King St., P.O. Box 543, 32085. Tel: 904-829-6300. Rebecca Stringer, Exec. Dir.

GAINESVILLE. *Catholic Charities Regional Office*, 1717 N.E. 9th St., 32609. Tel: 352-372-0294. Leonard Spillane, Dir.

JACKSONVILLE. *Catholic Charities Bureau, Inc.*, 11625 Old St. Augustine Rd., P.O. Box 24000, 32241-4000.
E-mail: charities@CXP.COM
Mr. William J. Tierney, Diocesan Dir. Tel: 904-262-3200.

Catholic Charities Regional Office, 134 E. Church St., 32202. Tel: 904-354-4846; Fax: 904-354-4718. William C. Beitz, Dir. Provides counseling services for substance abuse, marriage, families, maternity & aging. Also, emergency financial assistance for housing/utilities, food pantry, & adoption programs.

New Hope Program, 134 East Church St., 32202. Tel: 904-354-3464. Deacon Stanley Grenn, Dir. Total Assisted 300.

Office of Aging Services, 134 E. Church St., 32202. Tel: 904-354-4846; Fax: 904-354-4718. Ms. Kathryn Strayer, L.C.S.W., Dir. Office of Aids Ministry, 134 East Church St., 32202. Tel: 904-354-4718. Sr. Marlene Payette, S.S.J., Dir.

Office of Justice and Peace, 134 E. Church St., 32202-3130. Tel: 904-358-7409; 7410. Delena Stephens, Dir.

[D] SPECIAL APOSTOLATES

ST. AUGUSTINE. *Religious Education for Catholic Deaf and Blind*, 207 N. San Marco Ave., 32084. Tel: 904-823-4407 (Voice/TDD). Rev. Rene Robert, Chap. Tel: 904-825-0359 (Voice/TDD); Kathy Waller, Pastoral Worker and Teacher. Tel: 904-823-4407. Florida School for the Deaf and Blind.

JACKSONVILLE. *L'Arche Harbor House I, II, III, and IV*, 700 Arlington Rd., 32211. Tel: 904-744-4435; Fax: 904-744-4470. Dorothy B. Klein, Exec. Dir. Total Staff 15; Total in Residence 21. A community residence with mentally retarded adults.

Morning Star School, 725 Mickler Rd., 32211. Mrs. Teri Aschliman, Prin. A school for exceptional children. Lay Teachers 11; Students 110.

[E] GENERAL HOSPITALS

JACKSONVILLE. *St. Vincent's Medical Center, Inc.*, 1800 Barrs St., P.O. Box 2982, 32203. Tel: 904-308-7300.
Web site: www.Baptist-Stvincents.com/
For a complete listing, refer to the Hospitals section.

[F] HOMES FOR AGING

JACKSONVILLE. *All Saints Home*, 5888 Blanding Blvd., 32246
For a complete listing, refer to the Special Care Facilities section.

St. Catherine Laboure Manor, 1750 Stockton St., 32204. Tel: 904-308-4700
For a complete listing, refer to the Special Care Facilities section.

[G] CATHOLIC CHARITIES OFFICE OF HOUSING

JACKSONVILLE. *Housing Association of the Diocese of Saint Augustine*, 134 E. Church St., 32202-3130. Tel: 904-632-1244; Fax: 904-632-2135. Sandra B. Bonna, Dir. Management; Leo V. Rabuck, Dir. Devel.; Alma C. Ballard, Admin. Asst.

Jacksonville, Family Housing Management Co., 134 E. Church St., 32202. Tel: 904-632-1255. Sandra B. Bonna, Dir., Jacksonville, Office of Housing Development, 134 E. Church St., 32202. Tel: 904-632-1255. Leo V. Rabuck, Dir.

Hurley Manor I, 3333 University Blvd. N., 32277. Tel: 904-744-6022. Norma Sullivan, Res. Mgr.
Parent Co., Catholic Charities Housing Association of Jacksonville, Inc. T. William Glocker, Pres.

Hurley Manor II, 3335 University Blvd. N., 32277. Tel: 904-744-9348. Norma Sullivan, Res. Mgr.
Parent Co., Diocesan Housing Bureau, Inc. Alton W. Yates, Pres.

Barry Manor, 1000 Husson Ave., Palatka, 32277. Tel: 904-328-5137. Mary Geer, Res. Mgr.
Parent Co., Palatka Retirement Villas, Inc. Bernice Trotman, Pres.

St. Clare House, 2064 Dellwood Ave., 32204.

Providence Center, 134 E. Church St., 32202. Tel: 904-632-1255.

[H] MONASTERIES AND RESIDENCES OF PRIESTS AND BROTHERS

JACKSONVILLE. *Maryknoll Fathers & Brothers*, 2243 Saragossa Ave., 32217-2685. Tel: 904-739-1112.
E-mail: mklflorida@igc.apc.org
In res. Revs. John King, M.M.; Henry Murphy, M.M. Total in Residence 2.

[I] CONVENTS AND RESIDENCES FOR SISTERS

ST. AUGUSTINE. *Motherhouse of the Sisters of St. Joseph of St. Augustine, Florida*, 241 St. George St., P.O. Box 3506, 32085.
E-mail: ssjfl@aol.com
Sr. Florence Bryan, S.S.J., Gen. Supr. Professed Sisters 110.

The Sisters of St. Joseph Continuing Community Support Trust Fund.

[J] RETREAT HOUSES

BUNNELL. *Discalced Carmelite Fathers of Florida*, HC 1 Box 70 - Korona, 32110. Revs. Joseph F. Zawada, O.C.D., Prior; Benedict Jurkiewicz; Augustyn Kwiatkowski; Bro. Anthony Gemmato. Total Staff 5.

JACKSONVILLE. *Loretto House of Prayer*, 4118 Loretto Rd., 32223. Sr. Eileen Marie Flanagan, Dir.

Marywood Center for Spirituality and Ministry, 1714-5 State Rd. 13, 32259. Tel: 904-287-2525; Fax: 904-287-9738.
E-mail: marywoodctr@ilnlc.com
Mr. David E. Nowak, Dir.; Ms. Patricia McHugh, Conference Coord.; Sr. Kathleen Power, Prog. Coord.; Mr. Tim Kennedy, Plant Mgr. Total Staff 10; Total in Residence 1.

[K] MISCELLANEOUS

GAINESVILLE. *The Center for the Study of the Passion of Christ and the Holy Shroud*, 1738 W. University, 32603. Mrs. Gerry DeGraff, Exec. Sec.

JACKSONVILLE. *The Florida Catholic AIDS Network*, Catholic Charities, 134 E. Church St., 32202-3130. Tel: 904-354-4846, Ext. 229; Fax: 904-354-4718. Sr. Marlene Payette, S.S.J., Contact.

[L] NEWMAN CENTERS

ST. AUGUSTINE. *Flagler College Newman Center*, c/o Cathedral of St. Augustine, 35 Treasury St., 32084. Rev. Timothy Lindenfelser.

GAINESVILLE. *University of Florida-St. Augustine Parish and Student Center*, 1738 W. University Ave., P.O. Box 13888, 32604. Tel: 904-372-3533. Revs. John D. Gillespie; Timothy R. Lozier; John M. Phillips.

JACKSONVILLE. *Jacksonville Univ. & Univ. of North Florida Catholic Campus Ministry*, 32211. Tel: 904-744-3950, Ext. 7258.
E-mail: pmorgan@mail.ju.edu
Web site: http://www.unf.edu/groups/ccm/
Mr. Pete Morgan, Dir. Catholic Campus Ministry.

RELIGIOUS INSTITUTES OF MEN REPRESENTED IN THE DIOCESE

For further details refer to the corresponding bracketed number in the Religious Institutes of Men or Women section.

[0275]—*Carmelites of Mary Immaculate.*—C.M.I.
[1330]—*Congregation of the Mission.*—C.M.
[0260]—*Discalced Carmelite Friars.*—O.C.D.
[0650]—*Holy Ghost Fathers.*—C.S.Sp.
[0690]—*Jesuit Fathers and Brothers.*—S.J.
[0770]—*Marist Brothers.*—F.M.S.
[0780]—*Marist Fathers.*—S.M.
[0800]—*Maryknoll.*—M.M.
[1070]—*Redemptorist Fathers.*—C.SS.R.
[1190]—*Salesians of Don Bosco.*—S.D.B.
[0560]—*Third Order Regular of St. Francis.*—T.O.R.

RELIGIOUS INSTITUTES OF WOMEN REPRESENTED IN THE DIOCESE 0760; Daughters of Charity of St. Vincent de Paul; (Eastern Prov.); D.C.

[0230]—*Benedictine Sisters of Pontifical Jurisdiction.*—O.S.B.
[2515]—*Cashel Mercy Sisters.*—C.M.S.
[0960]—*Daughters of Wisdom.*—D.W.
[1070-13]—*Dominican Sisters.*—O.P.
[2490]—*Medical Mission Sisters.*—M.M.S.
[2720]—*Mission Helpers of the Sacred Heart.*—M.H.S.H.
[2170]—*Servants of the Immaculate Heart of Mary.*—I.H.M.
[]—*Sisters for Christian Community.*—S.F.C.C.
[2517]—*Sisters of Mercy.*—S.M.
[2600]—*Sisters of Mercy.* (Cork and Ross).—S.M.
[2990]—*Sisters of Notre Dame.* (Toledo Prov.).—S.N.D.
[3900]—*Sisters of St. Joseph of St. Augustine, FL.*—S.S.J.
[1530]—*Sisters of St. Francis of the Congregation of Our Lady of Lourdes, Sylvania, OH.*—O.S.F.

NECROLOGY

(No Deaths)

Diocese of St. Cloud

(Dioecesis S. Clodoaldi)

Most Reverend

JOHN F. KINNEY, D.D., J.C.D.

Bishop of St. Cloud; ordained February 2, 1963; appointed Titular Bishop of Caorle and Auxiliary Bishop of St. Paul and Minneapolis November 16, 1976; consecrated January 25, 1977; appointed Bishop of Bismarck June 28, 1982; installed August 23, 1982; appointed Bishop of St. Cloud May 9, 1995; installed July 6, 1995. *Office: 214 Third Ave. S., P.O. Box 1248, St. Cloud, MN, 56302-1248.* Tel.: 320-251-2340.

Most Reverend

GEORGE H. SPELTZ

Former Bishop of St. Cloud; ordained June 2, 1940; appointed Auxiliary Bishop of Winona and Titular Bishop of Claneus February 13, 1963; consecrated March 25, 1963; appointed Coadjutor of St. Cloud April 4, 1966; succeeded January 31, 1968; resigned January 13, 1987. *Res., 224 Third Ave. S., St. Cloud, MN, 56302.* Tel.: 320-251-3871.

Chancery: 214 Third Ave. S., P.O. Box 1248, St. Cloud, MN, 56302. Tel.: 320-251-2340; Fax: 320-251-0470.

Corporate Title: *"The Diocese of St. Cloud."*

ERECTED AS THE VICARIATE OF NORTHERN MINNESOTA, FEBRUARY 12, 1875.

CREATED AS THE DIOCESE OF ST. CLOUD, SEPTEMBER 22, 1889.

Square Miles 12,251.

Comprises the Counties of Stearns, Sherburne, Benton, Morrison, Mille Lacs, Kanabec, Isanti, Pope, Stevens, Traverse, Grant, Douglas, Wilkin, Otter Tail, Todd and Wadena in the State of Minnesota.

For legal titles of parishes and diocesan institutions, consult the Chancery Office.

STATISTICAL OVERVIEW

Personnel	
Bishop	1
Retired Bishops	1
Abbots	1
Retired Abbots	1
Priests: Diocesan Active in Diocese	99
Priests: Active Outside Diocese	4
Priests: Diocesan in Foreign Missions	2
Priests: Retired, Sick or Absent	38
Number of Diocesan Priests	143
Religious Priests in Diocese	113
Extern Priests in Diocese	2
Ordinations:	
Diocesan Priests	1
Permanent Deacons	5
Permanent Deacons in Diocese	35
Total Brothers	71
Total Sisters	562
Parishes	
Parishes	141
With Resident Pastor:	
Resident Diocesan Priests	87
Resident Religious Priests	15
Without Resident Pastor:	
Administered by Priests	39
Professional Ministry Personnel:	
Sisters	15
Lay Ministers	66
Welfare	
Catholic Hospitals	4
Total Assisted	164,957
Homes for the Aged	14
Total Assisted	1,402
Residential Care of Children	1
Total Assisted	104
Day Care and Extended Day Care Centers	2
Total Assisted	28
Specialized Homes	1
Total Assisted	36
Special Centers for Social Services	8
Total Assisted	34,412
Residential Care of Disabled	7
Total Assisted	68
Other Institutions	7
Total Assisted	702
Educational	
Diocesan Students in Other Seminaries	9
Seminaries, Religious	1
Students Religious	1
Total Seminarians	10
Colleges and Universities	2
Total Students	3,803
High Schools, Diocesan and Parish	1
Total Students	579
High Schools, Private	1
Total Students	216
Elementary Schools, Diocesan and Parish	33
Total Students	6,193
Non-residential Schools for the Disabled	1
Total Students	25
Catechesis/Religious Education:	
High School Students	8,890
Elementary Students	16,263
Total Students Under Catholic Instruction	35,979
Teachers in the Diocese:	
Priests	24
Brothers	5
Sisters	29
Lay Teachers	567
Vital Statistics	
Receptions into the Church:	
Infant Baptism Totals	2,521
Adult Baptism Totals	81
Received into Full Communion	222
First Communions	2,816
Confirmations	2,838
Marriages:	
Catholic	780
Interfaith	350
Total Marriages	1,130
Deaths	1,436
Total Catholic Population	145,702
Total Population	470,105

Former Bishops—Rt. Rev. RUPERT SEIDENBUSCH, O.S.B., D.D., cons. Bishop of Halia, Vicar-Apostolic of Northern Minnesota, May 30, 1875; resigned Nov. 15, 1888; died June 2, 1895.—Rt. Rev. OTTO ZARDETTI, D.D., cons. Oct. 20, 1889; transferred to Bucharest, Roumania, and raised to the Archiepiscopal Dignity, Feb. 23, 1894; died May 9, 1902.—Rt. Rev. MARTIN MARTY, O.S.B., D.D., cons. Bishop of Tiberias, Feb. 1, 1880; Bishop of Sioux Falls, 1889; transferred to St. Cloud, Jan. 21, 1895; died Sept. 19, 1896.—Rt. Rev. JAMES TROBEC, D.D., ord. Sept. 8, 1865; cons. Bishop of St. Cloud, Sept. 21, 1897; resigned April 15, 1914 and; Titular Bishop of Lycopolis; died Dec. 14, 1921.—Most Rev. JOSEPH F. BUSCH, D.D., ord. July 28, 1889; appt. Bishop of Lead, S. D., April 9, 1910; cons. May 19, 1910; transferred to See of St. Cloud, Jan. 19, 1915; died May 31, 1953.—Most Rev. PETER W. BARTHOLOME, D.D., ord. June 12, 1917; appt. Titular Bishop of Lete and Coadjutor Bishop of St. Cloud "cum jure successionis", Dec. 6, 1941; cons. March 3, 1942; succeeded to See May 31, 1953; appt. Assistant at the Pontificial Throne July 23, 1954; resigned Jan. 31, 1968; died June 17, 1982.—Most Rev. GEORGE H. SPELTZ, D.D., Ph.D., appt. Auxiliary Bishop of Winona and Titular Bishop of Claneus February 13, 1963; cons. March 25, 1963; appt. Coadjutor of St. Cloud April 4, 1966 succeeded Jan. 31, 1968; resigned Jan. 13, 1987.—Most Rev. JEROME HANUS, O.S.B., D.D., appt. Bishop of St. Cloud, July 6, 1987; ord. and installed Aug. 24, 1987; appt. Coadjutor Archbishop of Dubuque, IA, Aug. 23, 1994.

Chancery—*P.O. Box 1248, 214 Third Ave. S., St. Cloud, 56302.* Tel: 320-251-2340; 251-7801(after hours); Fax: 320-251-0470. Office Hours: Mon.-Fri. 9-12 & 1-4:30.

Vicar General—Rev. Msgr. DANIEL J. TAUFEN, S.T.L.

Chancellor—Rev. ROBERT ROLFES, J.C.L.

Assistant Chancellor—Sr. MARY MANDERNACH, O.S.B.

Diocesan Tribunal—*316 Seventh Ave. N., St. Cloud.* All marriage cases are to be directed to: *The Tribunal, Box 576, St. Cloud, 56302.* Tel: 320-251-6557.

Judicial Vicar—Rev. VIRGIL HELMIN, J.C.L.

Adjutant Judicial Vicar—Revs. ROBERT E. ROLFES, J.C.L.; WILLIAM VOUK, III, J.C.L.

Promoter Justitiae—Rev. Msgr. DANIEL J. TAUFEN, S.T.L.

Defensor Vinculi—Revs. NICHOLAS LANDSBERGER; ALFRED HELTEMES; GREGORY LIESER; THOMAS OLSON.

Judges—Revs. ROBERT C. HARREN, J.C.L.; ROBERT E. ROLFES, J.C.L.; PAUL SCHMELZER; ROBERT LANDSBERGER; WILLIAM VOUK, III, J.C.L.; JONATHAN LICARI, O.S.B.

Notaries—Revs. VIRGIL HELMIN, J.C.L.; ROBERT E. ROLFES, J.C.L.; WILLIAM VOUK, III, J.C.L.; JILL LENTNER; DIANA SKAJA.

Advocates—Revs. JOSEPH KORF; MARVIN ENNEKING; LEON SLOMINSKI.

Marriage Counseling—Caritas Family Services, *Pastoral Center, Diocese of St. Cloud, 305 N. Seventh Ave., St. Cloud, 56303.* Tel: 320-252-4121.

Diocesan Consultors—Rev. Msgr. DANIEL J. TAUFEN, S.T.L.; Revs. TIMOTHY BALTES; GERALD DALSETH; RAYMOND DONNAY; JAMES HAHN; JOSEPH KORF; RICHARD LEISEN; VINCENT LIESER; KENNETH RIEDEMANN; DAVID RIEDER; EBERHARD SCHEFERS; RAYMOND STEFFES, O.S.C.

Deans—Rev. TIMOTHY BALTES, St. Cloud; Rev. VINCENT LIESER, Melrose; Rev. KENNETH RIEDEMANN, Alexandria; Rev. JOHN CASKEY, Cold Spring; Rev. JOSEPH KORF, Fergus Falls; Rev. FRANCIS BRITZ, Foley; Rev. LAURN VIRNIG, Little Falls; Rev. RALPH ZIMMERMAN, St. Joseph; Rev. ARLIE SOWADA, Morris; Rev. MARK OSTENDORF, Princeton; Rev. BERNARD KAHLHAMER, Sauk Centre; Rev. DAVID RIEDER, Wadena.

Diocesan Corporate Board—Most Rev. JOHN KINNEY, Pres.; Rev. Msgr. DANIEL J. TAUFEN, S.T.L., Vice Pres.; Revs. ROBERT ROLFES, Sec. ROBERT C. HARREN, J.C.L.; ALFRED HELTEMES.

Diocesan Finance Council—DANIEL WARNEKE, Finance Officer; Rev. Msgr. DANIEL J. TAUFEN, S.T.L.; Rev. ROBERT E. ROLFES, J.C.L.; Mr. LEE TORBORG; Sr. KATHLEEN KALINOWSKI, O.S.B.; Mr. JOHN LEISEN; Mr. RICHARD GRUBER; Mr. THOMAS REIF; Mrs. SHARON HESS; Mrs. LUANN POPP; Mr. LOREN LIESEMEYER.

Due Process Service—Rev. ROBERT C. HARREN, J.C.L., Chm.

Presbyteral Council—Revs. TIMOTHY BALTES, Chm. JOHN CASKEY, Vice Chm. RALPH ZIMMERMAN, Sec. KENNETH RIEDEMANN; FRANCIS BRITZ; JOSEPH KORF; MARK OSTENDORF; LLOYD HAUPT; BERNARD KAHLHAMER; VINCENT LIESER; GREGORY MASTEY; DAVID RIEDER; ARLIE SOWADA; DOMINIC RUIZ, O.S.B.; LAURN VIRNIG; Rev. Msgr. DANIEL J. TAUFEN, S.T.L.,Address correspondence to: *Presbyteral Council of the Diocese of St. Cloud, Church of St. Paul, 1125 N. 11th Ave., St. Cloud, 56303.*

Pastoral Council—MARY THERESE ANDERSON, Chm.; Revs. KENNETH RIEDEMANN; GREGORY MASTEY; ROGER KASPERICK, O.S.B.; Deacon BERNARD GRUENES; Sr. MARIE DONAHUE, S.S.N.D.; Sr. MARITERESE WOIDA, O.S.B.; ROSEMARY BORGERT; Mrs. MARCELLA BRIOL; Mrs. JEAN COOL; CHARLOTTE KREBS; JEROME FISCHER; CAROL STEIDL; NANCY HENDRICKX; KATIE HENNEMANN; HELEN HEISICK; KATHY MOELLER; PAT QUACKENBUSH; JENNIFER SCHNEIDER; ALFRED SCHWALBE; VIRGINIA TERHAAR; Mrs. LEMAY BECHTOLD, Exec. Sec.

Diocesan Offices and Programs

Apostleship of Prayer and Enthronement of the Sacred Heart—Rev. RICHARD WEY, Dir., *11 Eighth Ave. S., St. Cloud, 56301.*

Boy Scouts—Rev. LEROY SCHEIERL, Dir., *St. Francis DeSales, P.O. Box 69, Belgrade, 56312-0069.*

Building Commission—Revs. EBERHARD SCHEFERS, Chm. THOMAS OLSON; Sr. COLLEEN HAGGERTY, O.S.B.; JEANNE CHRISTIANSON; DONALD KAINZ,Address correspondence to: BRADLEY FORBROOK, *113 5th Ave. S., St. Cloud, 56301.* Rev. EBERHARD SCHEFERS, *Church of St. Francis Xavier, P.O. Box 150, Sartell, 56377-0150.*

Campaign for Human Development—Rev. Msgr. DANIEL J. TAUFEN, S.T.L., Dir., *P.O. Box 1248, St. Cloud, 56302.*

Campus Ministry—Rev. KEVIN ANDERSON, *Newman Center, 396 First Ave. S., St. Cloud, 56301.*

Catholic Charities—Mr. STEVEN BRESNAHAN, Dir., *1730 Seventh Ave. S., St. Cloud, 56301.* Tel: 320-252-0412. Caritas Family Services: Adoption, Counselling (Individual, Family, Financial, Pregnancy), Food Shelf and Women's Guild Clothing, P.M.I.'s, Refugee Resettlement, Services to Widowed and Divorced. Supervisors: JAMES WAGNER, *207 Seventh Ave. N., St. Cloud, 56303.* Tel: 320-252-1280. DONNA JOHNSON, *305 Seventh Ave. N., St. Cloud, 56303.* Tel: 320-252-4121.

Women's Guild—JOYCE STOCK, Coord., *207 Seventh Ave. N., St. Cloud, 56303.* Tel: 320-253-3454.

Catholic Relief Services—Rev. RICHARD LEISEN, Dir., *P.O. Box 39, Paynesville, 56362.* Tel: 320-252-0412.

Catholic Women, Council of—Rev. HAROLD J. KOST, Moderator, *Holy Family Church, Belle Prairie, Rte. 4, Little Falls, 56345.* PAT EIKMEIER, Pres., *23515 Co. Rd. 8, Cold Spring, 56320.*

Cemeteries Assumption-Calvary—Rev. WILLIAM GARDING, Operations Mgr., *2341 Roosevelt Rd., St. Cloud, 56301.* Tel: 320-251-5511.

Censores Librorum—Revs. PAUL ZYLLA, S.T.D.; ROBERT C. HARREN, J.C.L.; Rev. Msgr. DANIEL J. TAUFEN, S.T.L.

Charismatic Renewal, Bishop's Liaison To—Rev. GERALD MISCHKE, *St. Mary's Parish, P.O. Box 308, Holdingford, 56340-0308.*

Clerical Aid Association—Most Rev. JOHN F. KINNEY, Pres.; Rev. Msgr. DANIEL J. TAUFEN, S.T.L., Sec.; Revs. ROBERT ROLFES, Treas. Directors: SYLVESTER KLEINSCHMIDT; RICHARD LEISEN; ALEXANDER LUDWIG; EUGENE DOYLE; EUGENE MEEMKEN; SILVERIUS SCHMITT, Address mail to: *The Chancery, P.O. Box 1248, St. Cloud, 56302.*

Commission for the Catholic Mission Among the Black and Indian Mission—Rev. RAYMOND STEFFES, O.S.C., Dir., *P.O. Star Route, Onamia, 56359.*

Communications Office—(Radio, Television, Public Information, CTNA Affiliate), ROSEMARY BORGERT, Dir., *Pastoral Center, Diocese of St. Cloud, 305 N. Seventh Ave., St. Cloud, 56303.* Tel: 320-251-0558.

Continuing Formation of Priests—Rev. RALPH ZIMMERMAN, Dir., *St. John Seminary, Collegeville, 56321.*

Development Office—Mr. MARK LEASE, Dir. Devel.

Diocesan Education Council—Sr. KATHERINE KALLHOFF, S.S.N.D.; Deacon GREGORY STEELE; JOAN HEIPER; AIMEE BATES; NOELLA FATH; GERALYN NATHE-EVANS; JOANNE KRAVA.

Office of Catholic Education Ministries—Sr. CATHERINE KALLHOFF, S.S.N.D., Supt. Education; LINDA KAISER, School Consultant; LORI DAHLHOFF, Consultant for Ministries/Persons with Disabilities and Cathechist Formation; JAN HAARMAN, Consultant Religious Education and Faith Formation; TIMOTHY WELCH, Consultant Media/Computer and Ministry Formation Program; PAT MALOVRH, Office Coord. JEFFREY KASTER, Consultant for the Formation of Youth; CLAIRE CAUCCI, Media Coord., Address all correspondence to: *Catholic Education Ministries, Pastoral Center, Diocese of St. Cloud, 305 N. Seventh Ave., St. Cloud, 56303.* Tel: 320-251-0111.

Diocesan Ecumenical Commission—Rev. ALBERT HOLMES, Chm., Address all correspondence to: *514 1st St. S.E., Wadena, 56482.*

Diocesan Planning Council—Mr. THOMAS KEAVENY, Dir.; Revs. ALBERT HOLMES; JONATHAN LICARI, O.S.B.; ANTHONY OELRICH; LEROY SCHOLZ; Sr. ADELA GROSS, O.S.F.; Sr. LINDA WALL, O.S.F.; Sr. MARITERESE WOIDA, O.S.B.; Deacon STAN HENNEN; Mr. ROBERT BARRETT; Ms. MARY JO COBB; Mr. MEL EUTENEUER; Dr. BERNARD EVANS.

Diocesan Priests Pension Plan Trustees—Most Rev. JOHN KINNEY; Rev. Msgr. DANIEL J. TAUFEN, S.T.L.; Revs. RICHARD LEISEN; ALEXANDER LUDWIG; KENNETH BRENNY; SILVERIUS SCHMITT; ROBERT ROLFES; STANLEY WIESER; LLOYD HAUPT.

Eucharistic League—Rev. RAYMOND SCHULZETENBERG, Dir., *S.S. Peter & Paul Church, Gilman, 56333.*

Family Life Bureau—CHRISTINE CODDEN, Dir., *Pastoral Center, Diocese of St. Cloud, 305 N. Seventh Ave., St. Cloud, 56303.* Tel: 320-252-4721.

Health Ministry Coordinator—Sr. MICHAEA BYRON, O.S.F., *214 3rd Ave. S., St. Cloud. 56301.* Tel: 320-252-7644.

Holy Childhood Association—Rev. RICHARD WEY, Dir., *11-Eighth Ave., S., St. Cloud, 56301.*

Koinonia Program of Central Minnesota—Rev. DAVID MACIEJ, *P.O. Box 188, Rice, 56367.*

Legion of Decency—Rev. ROBERT E. ROLFES, J.C.L., *P.O. Box 1248, St. Cloud, 56302.*

Legion of Mary—Rev. RAYMOND STEFFES, O.S.C., *Crosier Monastery, Onamia, 56359.*

Natural Family Planning—Mrs. KAY EK, Dir., *316 Seventh Ave. N., St. Cloud, 56303.* Tel: 320-252-2100.

Newspaper "St. Cloud Visitor"—Sr. NANCY BAUER, O.S.B., Editor & Business Mgr., *Pastoral Center, Diocese of St. Cloud, 305 N. Seventh Ave., Box 1068, St. Cloud, 56302.*

Permanent Diaconate Program—Deacon MICHAEL KEABLE, Dir.; Rev. LEROY KREMER, Vicar for Permanent Deacons, *Our Lady of Lourdes Church, 208 W. Broadway, Little Falls, 56345.* Deacon STEPHEN YANISH, Pres., Diaconal Community, *305 Seventh Ave. N., St. Cloud, 56303.* Tel: 612-252-4721.

Personnel Committee—Revs. GREGORY LIESER, Dir., *930 31st Ave. N., St. Cloud, 56303.* JONATHAN LICARI, O.S.B.; MARVIN ENNEKING; LEROY KREMER; DAVID RIEDER; LEROY SCHOLZ; Rev. Msgr. DANIEL J. TAUFEN.

Respect Life Program—JANE MARRIN, *316 7th Ave N., St. Cloud, 56303.* Tel: 320-259-0976.

Propagation of the Faith—Rev. RICHARD WEY, Dir., *11 Eighth Ave. S., St. Cloud, 56301.* Tel: 320-251-1100; Fax: 320-251-2061.

Rural Life Program—*214 3rd Ave. S., St. Cloud, 56301.* Tel: 320-251-2340.

Spanish Migrant Program—*214 3rd Ave. S., St. Cloud, 56301.* Tel: 320-251-2340.

TEC (Central Minnesota TEC) (Together Encountering Christ)—Rev. KENNETH OPAT, O.S.C., Coord., *516 School St., Anoka, 55303.* Tel: 612-323-8178; Fax: 612-421-4230.

Vocations—Rev. DONALD WAGNER, Dir., *305 Seventh Ave. N., St. Cloud, 56303.* Tel: 320-251-5001.

Worship, Office of—Mr. GARY FELDHEGE, Dir., *Pastoral Center, Diocese of St. Cloud, 305 N. Seventh Ave., St. Cloud, 56303.* Tel: 320-255-9068.

CLERGY, PARISHES, MISSIONS AND PAROCHIAL SCHOOLS

CITY OF ST. CLOUD

(Benton, Stearns, Sherburne Counties)

1—ST. MARY'S CATHEDRAL OF ST. CLOUD, Rev. Steven Binsfeld.
Res., 25 Eighth Ave., S., 56301. Tel: 320-251-1840; Fax: 320-253-5001.
School—Tel: 320-252-2740; Fax: 320-252-5360.
School Sisters of Notre Dame 3; Lay Teachers 6; Students 134.

2—HOLY ANGELS. Closed. For inquiries for parish records contact the Chancery.

3—HOLY SPIRIT, Rev. Virgil A. Helmin.
Office: 2405 Walden Way, 56301. Tel: 320-251-3764; Fax: 320-252-5143.
School—St. Elizabeth Ann Seton. Inter-Parochial school. See separate listing.

4—ST. ANTHONY OF PADUA, Revs. Robert C. Harren; David P. Grundman.
Res., 33 24th Ave., N., 56303. Tel: 320-251-5966; Fax: 320-251-0664.
School—St. Elizabeth Ann Seton Inter-Parochial School. See separate listing.

5—ST. AUGUSTINE, Rev. Simon Bischof, O.S.B.; Deacon Jeff Hennes.
Office: 443 Second St., S.E., 56304. Tel: 320-251-8335; Fax: 320-251-8364.
Res., 210 Fifth Ave., S.E., 56304.
School—Tel: 320-251-2376.
Lay Teachers 13; Students 208.

6—ST. JOHN CANTIUS, Rev. Peter Snyers; Deacon Fred Reker.
Res., 1515 N. Third St., 56303. Tel: 320-251-4455; Fax: 320-240-1238.

7—ST. MICHAEL, Rev. Edwin J. Kraemer; Deacon Bernard Gruenes.
Res., 1036 Co. Rd. 4, 56303. Tel: 320-251-6923; Fax: 320-202-1104.
School—Sts. Peter & Paul & Michael Inter-Parochial School. See separate listing.

8—ST. PAUL, Rev. Timothy Baltes; Deacons Michael Keable; Todd Warren; David Lindmeier. In res., Rev. Christopher Trussel.
Res., 1125 11th Ave., N., 56303. Tel: 320-251-4831; Fax: 320-251-2648.
School—Sts. Peter & Paul & Michael Inter-Parochial School. See separate listing.

9—ST. PETER, Rev. Gregory Lieser.
Res., 930 31st Ave., N., 56303. Tel: 320-252-2113.
School—Sts. Peter & Paul & Michael Inter-Parochial School. See separate listing.

10—CHRIST CHURCH, Rev. Kevin Anderson.
Res., 396 S. First Ave., 56301. Tel: 320-251-2712; Fax: 320-251-3261.

OUTSIDE THE CITY OF ST. CLOUD

Albany, Stearns Co., Seven Dolors, Rev. Corwin Collins, O.S.B.
Res., Box 277, 56307. Tel: 320-845-2705. [CEM]
School—Tel: 320-845-2011.
Lay Teachers 8; Students 120.

Alexandria, Douglas Co., St. Mary's, Revs. Alexander P. Ludwig; Gregory J. Mastey.
Res., 411 Hawthorne St., P.O. Box 669, 56308. Tel: 320-763-5781; Fax: 320-763-4833. [CEM]
School—Tel: 320-763-5861.
Lay Teachers 11; Students 194.

Avon, Stearns Co., St. Benedict's, Rev. James Reichert, O.S.B.
Church—P.O. Box 98, 56310. Tel: 320-356-7121. [CEM]

Battle Lake, Otter Tail Co., Our Lady of the Lake, Rev. Paul Folsom.
Res., 409 Lake Ave., N., P.O. Box 671, 56515. Tel: 218-864-5619.

Becker, Sherbune Co., Immaculate Conception, Rev. Mark G. Ostendorf; Deacon Gregory Steele.
Res., 12100 Sherburne Ave., Box 426, 55308. Tel: 612-261-4242.

Belgrade, Stearns Co., St. Francis De Sales, Rev. LeRoy Scheierl.
Res., 541 Martin Ave., P.O. Box 69, 56312. Tel: 320-254-8218. [CEM]

Belle Prairie, Morrison Co., Holy Family, Rev. Harold J. Kost.
Res., R.R. 4, Little Falls P.O., 56345. Tel: 320-632-5720. [CEM]

Belle River, Douglas Co., St. Nicholas, Rev. Jeff Ethen.
Church—9473 County Rd. 3, N.E., Carlos, 56319. Tel: 612-852-7041. [CEM]

Bertha, Todd Co., St. Joseph's, Rev. LeRoy Maus.
Res., 56437. Tel: 218-924-2605. [CEM]

Big Lake, Sherburne Co., Our Lady of the Lake, Rev. Nicholas Dressen.
Res., 55309. Tel: 320-263-2863; Fax: 320-263-3187. [CEM]

BlueGrass, Wadena Co., St. Hubert's, Rev. Peter K. Kirchner, Jr.
Res., 20 Brown St., N., P.O. Box C, Verndale, 56481. Tel: 218-445-5786.

Bluffton, Otter Tail Co., St. John the Baptist, Rev. Kevin Schwartz.
Res., 56518. Tel: 218-385-2608. [CEM]

Bowlus, Morrison Co., St. Stanislaus Kostka, Rev. Silverius J. Schmitt.
Res., 428 Main St., 56314. Tel: 320-584-5313. [CEM]

Braham, Isanti Co., St. Peter & Paul, Rev. Nicholas M. Zimmer.
Res., 55006. Tel: 320-396-3105.

Brandon, Douglas Co., Church of St. Ann, Rev. Eugene Lemm. In res., Rev. Richard J. Heid.
Res., P.O. Box 256, 56315. Tel: 320-524-2462. [CEM]

Breckenridge, Wilkin Co., St. Mary of the Presentation, Rev. Leo Moenkedrick.
Res., 221 N. Fourth St., 56520-1496. Tel: 218-643-5173. [CEM 2]
School—Tel: 218-643-5443.
Lay Teachers 11; Students 140.

Brennyville, Benton Co., St. Elizabeth, Rev. Thomas F. Olson.
Res., 16426 125 Ave., N.E., Foley, 56329. Tel: 320-355-2454. [CEM]

Brooten, Stearns Co., St. Donatus, Rev. James Statz.
Res., 33932 County Rd. 18, Sauk Centre, 56378. Tel: 320-352-2521; 346-2431.

Browerville, Todd Co., Christ the King, Rev. Kenneth Thielman; Deacon Vincent Leisen.
Res., 56438. Tel: 320-594-2291. [CEM]
School—Tel: 320-594-6114.
Lay Teachers 6; Students 72.

Brown's Valley, Traverse Co., St. Anthony's, Rev. Arlie Sowada.
Res., Box 359, 56219. Tel: 320-695-2621. [CEM]

Buckman, Morrison Co., St. Michael's, Rev. Ronald Dockendorf.
Res., 56317. Tel: 320-468-2316. [CEM]

Butler, Otter Tail Co., Holy Cross, Rev. Kevin Schwartz.
Res., P.O. Box 36, Bluffton, 56518. Tel: 218-385-2608.

Cambridge, Isanti Co., Christ the King, Rev. James David Hahn.
Res., 227 N. Fern, 55008. Tel: 612-689-1221. [CEM]

Chokio, Stevens Co., St. Mary's, Rev. Jerome G. Nordick.
Res., 56221. Tel: 320-324-2680. [CEM]

Clarissa, Todd Co., St. Joseph, Rev. Eugene A. Meemken.
Res., 107 S. John St., P.O. Box 5, 56440. Tel: 218-756-2205. [CEM]

Clear Lake, Sherburne Co., St. Marcus, Rev. LeRoy Scholz.
Res., 55319. Tel: 320-743-2481. [CEM]

Cold Spring, Stearns Co., St. Boniface, Rev. Cletus Connors, O.S.B.; Deacons John Salchert; Bruce Maltzen.
Res., 418 Main St., 56320. Tel: 320-685-3280; Fax: 320-685-7792. [CEM]
School—Tel: 320-685-3541.
Lay Teachers 13; Students 232.

Collegeville, Stearns Co., St. John the Baptist, Rev. Jonathan Licari, O.S.B.
Res., 56321. Tel: 320-363-2765. [JC]

Dent, Otter Tail Co., Sacred Heart, Rev. Leo Otto.
Res., 56528. Tel: 218-758-2700. [CEM]

Donnelly, Stevens Co., St. Theresia. Closed. For inquiries for parish records contact the Chancery.

Duelm, Benton Co., St. Lawrence's, Rev. Elmer J. Torborg.
Res., 10915 Duelm Rd., N.E., Foley, 56329. Tel: 320-968-7502. [CEM]

Dumont, Traverse Co., St. Peter's, Rev. Tony Salzbrunn.
Res., 201 Ninth St., S., Wheaton, 56296. Tel: 320-563-4421.

Eden Valley, Stearns Co., The Church of the Assumption, Rev. Virgil Braun.
Res., 55329. Tel: 320-453-2788. [CEM]

Elbow Lake, Grant Co., St. Olaf, Rev. Andrew Marthaler.
Res., 18 Sixth Ave., N., 56531. Tel: 218-685-4318. [CEM]

Elizabeth, Otter Tail Co., St. Elizabeth, Rev. Alan Wielinski.
Res., 56533. Tel: 218-736-5230. [CEM]

Elk River, Sherburne Co., The Church of St. Andrew, Rev. Robert J. Kieffer; Deacon Frederick St. Jean.
Res., 566 Fourth St., 55330. Tel: 612-441-1483; Fax: 612-441-1485. [CEM]
School—Tel: 320-441-3202; Fax: 320-441-2262.
Lay Teachers 13; Students 295.

Elmdale, Morrison Co., St. Edward's, Rev. Todd Schneider.
Res., P.O. Box 188, Upsala, 56384. Tel: 320-573-2975. [CEM]

Elrosa, Stearns Co., SS. Peter and Paul, Rev. LeRoy Scheierl. In res., Rev. Lawrence Botz.
Res., 56325. Tel: 320-697-5541. [CEM]

Farming, Stearns Co., St. Catherine's, Rev. Gunther Rolfson, O.S.B.
Res., Rte. 1, Richmond P.O., 56368. Tel: 320-548-3467. [CEM]

Fergus Falls, Otter Tail Co., Our Lady of Victory, Rev. Joseph Korf.
Res., 207 Vine St., N., 56537. Tel: 218-736-2429; Fax: 218-736-4407. [JC]
School—Tel: 218-736-6661; Fax: 218-736-4407.
Lay Teachers 8; Students 143.

Flensburg, Morrison Co., Sacred Heart, Rev. Anthony Kroll.
Res., 56328. Tel: 320-632-6930. [CEM 2]

Foley, Benton Co., St. John's, Rev. Alfred J. Heltemes.
Res., 56329. Tel: 320-968-7913. [CEM]
School—St. John's Area School. Consolidation of the following parishes: St. John's, Foley; St. Lawrence, Dvelm; St. Elizabeth, Brennyville; St. Joseph, Morrill; SS. Peter & Paul, Gilman; St. Patrick of Minden Township. Tel: 320-968-7972.
Lay Teachers 7; Students 115.

Foreston, Mille Lacs Co., St. Louis Bertrand, Rev. James Cashman, O.S.C.
Res., P.O. Box 128, 56330. Tel: 320-294-5460; Fax: 320-294-5588. [CEM]

Foxhome, Wilkin Co., St. Joseph. Closed. For inquiries for parish records contact the Chancery.

Freeport, Stearns Co., Sacred Heart, Rev. Roger Klassen, O.S.B.
Res., 56331. Tel: 320-836-2143. [CEM]
School—Tel: 320-836-2591.
Lay Teachers 6; Students 69.

Gilman, Benton Co., SS. Peter and Paul, Rev. Raymond A. Schulzetenberg.
Res., 56333. Tel: 320-387-2255. [CEM]
School—St. John's. (Foley) Area School. Tel: 320-968-7972.

Glenwood, Pope Co., Sacred Heart, Rev. Thomas G. Becker; Deacon Frank Schmainda.
Res., 105 N. Franklin, 56334. Tel: 320-634-3813. [CEM]

Greenwald, Stearns Co., St. Andrew's, Rev. Kenneth J. Popp.
Res., 56335. Tel: 612-987-3160. [CEM]
School—Tel: 320-987-3133.
Lay Teachers 2; Students 22.

Grey Eagle, Todd Co., St. Joseph's, Rev. Joel Nathe.
Res., P.O. Box 366, 56336. Tel: 320-285-2545. [CEM]

Harding, Morrison Co., Holy Cross, Rev. Roger Thoennes.
Res., P.O. Rte. 4, Pierz, 56364. Tel: 320-277-3701. [CEM]

Henning, Otter Tail Co., Church of St. Edward of Henning, Rev. LeRoy Maus.
Res., 56551. Tel: 218-583-2490. [CEM]

Herman, Grant Co., St. Charles, Rev. Jerome G. Nordick.
Res., P.O. Box 187, Chokio, 56221. Tel: 320-324-2680. [CEM]

Hillman, Morrison Co., St. Rita's, Rev. Nathan Packard.
Res., Rte. 2, Box 308, 56338. Tel: 320-277-3807. [CEM]

Holdingford, Stearns Co., St. Hedwig's, Co-Pastors: Revs. Gerald Mischke; Anthony Oelrich; Deacon Jeffrey Fromm.
Res., 56340. Tel: 320-746-2231; Fax: 320-746-2884. [CEM]

St. Mary's, Co-Pastors: Revs. Gerald Mischke; Anthony Oelrich; Deacon Jeffrey Fromm.
Res., 56340. Tel: 320-746-2231; Fax: 320-746-2884. [CEM]

Isanti, Isanti Co., St. Elizabeth Ann Seton, Rev. Richard McGuire.
Res., 109 Fifth Ave., S., 55040. Tel: 320-444-5226. [CEM]

Jacob's Prairie, Wakefield Township, Stearns Co., St. James, Rev. Julian Schmiesing, O.S.B.
Res., 25042 County Rd. 2, Cold Spring, 56320. Tel: 320-685-3479. [CEM]

Kensington, Grant Co., Our Lady of the Runestone, Rev. Kenneth Riedemann.
Res., R.R. 2, Box 31, Lowry, 56349-9519. Tel: 320-283-5273.

Kent, Wilkin Co., St. Thomas, Rev. Stanley Wieser.
Res., 56553. Tel: 218-557-8312. [CEM]

Kimball, Stearns Co., Church of Saint Anne, Rev. Frank S. Tomasiewicz; Deacon Stephen Yanish.
Res., P.O. Box 99, 55353. Tel: 320-398-3860. [CEM]

Lake Henry, Stearns Co., St. Margaret's, Rev. Leo Leisen. In res., Rev. Walter Bednark.
Res., Roscoe, 56371. Tel: 320-243-4574. [CEM]

Lake Reno, Pope Co., St. John Nepomuk, Rev. Kenneth Riedemann.
Res., R.R. #2, Box 31, Lowry, 56349. Tel: 320-283-5273. [CEM]

Lastrup, Morrison Co., St. John Nepomuk, Rev. Roger Thoennes.
Res., 56344. Tel: 320-468-2111. [CEM]

Little Falls, Morrison Co., St. Mary, Rev. Nicholas Landsberger.
Res., 305 Fourth St., S.E., 56345. Tel: 320-632-5640. [CEM 3]
School—See Inter-Parochial Schools under Institutions Located in the Diocese.

Our Lady of Lourdes, Rev. Leroy M. Kremer; Deacon Bruce Geyer.
Res., 208 W. Broadway, 56345. Tel: 320-632-8243; Fax: 320-616-2129. [CEM]
School—See Inter-Parochial Schools under Institutions Located in the Diocese.

Long Prairie, Todd Co., St. Mary of Mt. Carmel, Rev. Mark Stang.
Res., 56347. Tel: 320-732-2635; Fax: 320-732-2025. [CEM][JC]
School—Tel: 320-732-3478; Fax: 320-732-3894.
Sisters of St. Benedict 1; Lay Teachers 7; Students 117.

Luxemburg, Stearns Co., St. Wendelin's, Rev. Leon Slominski.
Res., 22714 State Hwy. 15, St. Cloud, 56301. Tel: 320-251-6944. [CEM]
School—Tel: 612-251-9175.
Sisters 1; Lay Teachers 5; Students 100.

Maine, Otter Tail Co., Church of Saint James at Maine, Rev. Paul Folsom.
Res., 409 Lake Ave., N., P.O. Box 671, Battle Lake, 56515. Tel: 218-864-5619. [CEM]

Mayhew Lake, Benton Co., Annunciation, Rev. Francis Britz.
Res., 9965 Mayhew Lake Rd., N.E., Sauk Rapids, 56379. Tel: 320-252-1729. [CEM]

Meire Grove, Stearns Co., St. John's, Rev. Kenneth J. Popp.
Res., Greenwald, 56335. Tel: 320-987-3160. [CEM]
School—Tel: 612-987-3491.
Lay Teachers 3; Students 41.

Melrose, Stearns Co., St. Mary's, Revs. Vincent Lieser; Paul Ryan, O.P.
Res., 211 S. Fifth Ave., E., 56352-1427. Tel: 320-256-4207; Fax: 320-256-4208. [CEM]
School—Tel: 320-256-4257.
Lay Teachers 13; Students 192.

Menahga, Wadena Co., The Church of the Assumption of Our Lady of Menahga, Rev. Kevin Schwartz.
Res., St. John the Baptist, Bluffton, 56518. Tel: 218-385-2608. [CEM]

Milaca, Mille Lacs Co., St. Mary's, Rev. Richard John, O.S.C.
Res., 625 3rd Ave. S.E., 56353. Tel: 320-983-3255. [CEM]

Millerville, Douglas Co., Seven Dolors, Rev. Eugene Lemm.
Res., 16921 County Rd. 7, N.W., Brandon, 56315. Tel: 320-876-2240. [CEM]

Mora, Kanabec Co., St. Mary's, Rev. Eugene G. Belair.
Res., 55051. Tel: 320-679-1593. [CEM]
Mission—Ogilvie, Kanabec Co., St. Kathryn.

Moran, Todd Co., St. Isidore, Rev. Eugene A. Meemken.
Res., St. Joseph's Church, P.O. Box 5, Clarissa, 56440. Tel: 218-756-2205. [CEM]

Morrill, Morrison Co., St. Joseph's, Rev. Thomas F. Olson.
Res., 33009 Nature Rd., Foley, 56329. Tel: 320-355-2585. [CEM]

Morris, Stevens Co., Assumption of the Blessed Virgin Mary, Rev. Gerald Dalseth; Deacon Stan Hennen.
Res., 207 E. Third, Box 287, 56267. Tel: 320-589-3003. [CEM]
School—Tel: 320-589-1704.
Lay Teachers 7; Students 102.

Motley, Morrison Co., St. Michael's, Rev. Robert Landsberger.
Res., 56466. Tel: 218-352-6143.

New Munich, Stearns Co., Immaculate Conception, Rev. Roger Klassen, O.S.B.
Res., Freeport, 56331. Tel: 320-836-2143. [CEM]

North Prairie, Morrison Co., Holy Cross, Rev. Silverius J. Schmitt.
Res., Bowlus, 56314. Tel: 320-584-5313. [CEM]

Ogilvie, Kanabec Co., St. Kathryn's, Rev. Eugene Belair.
Res., 201 Forest Ave., E., Mora, 55051. Tel: 320-679-1593.

Onamia, Mille Lacs Co., The Church of the Holy Cross of Onamia, Rev. William T. McNiff, O.S.C.
Res., 56359. Tel: 320-532-3122. [CEM]

Opole, Stearns Co., Our Lady of Mt. Carmel, Co-Pastors: Revs. Gerald Mischke; Anthony Oelrich; Deacon Jeffrey Fromm.
Res., St. Mary's Rectory, Holdingford, 56340. Tel: 320-746-2231. [CEM]

Osakis, Douglas Co., Immaculate Conception, Rev. Victor Kinzer.
Res., 56360. Tel: 312-859-2390. [CEM]
School—St. Agnes, Tel: 320-859-2130.
Lay Teachers 5; Students 81.

Padua, Stearns Co., Church of St. Anthony of Padua, Rev. James Statz.
Res., 33932 County Rd. 18, Sauk Centre, 56378. Tel: 320-352-2521. [CEM]

Parkers Prairie, Otter Tail Co., Church of St. William, Rev. Jeff Ethen.
Res., 56361. Tel: 218-338-2761.

Paynesville, Stearns Co., St. Louis, Rev. Richard Leisen.
Res., 505 Burr St., Box 39, 56362. Tel: 320-243-4413. [CEM]

Pearl Lake, Stearns Co., Holy Cross, Rev. John Caskey; Deacon Andrew Kunkel.
Res., 10651 County Rd. 8, Kimball, 55353. Tel: 320-398-7986. [CEM]
School—Tel: 320-398-7885.
Lay Teachers 4; Students 57.

Pelican Rapids, Otter Tail Co., St. Leonard's, Rev. Alan Wielinski.
Res., 56572. Tel: 218-863-5161. [CEM]

Perham, Otter Tail Co., St. Henry's, Rev. David J. Rieder; Deacon Donald Tzinski.
Res., Box 216, 56573. Tel: 218-346-4240; Fax: 218-346-4240. [CEM]
School—Area School, Tel: 218-346-6190; Fax: 218-346-6190.
Lay Teachers 8; Students 100.
St. Stanislaus, Rev. David J. Rieder; Deacon Donald Tzinski.
Res., P.O. Box 216, 56573. Tel: 218-346-4240. [CEM]

Pierz, Morrison Co., St. Joseph's, Rev. Kenneth Brenny. In res., Rev. Charles Padathuruthy.
Res., 56364. Tel: 320-468-6033; Fax: 320-468-2296. [CEM]
School—See Inter-Parochial School under Institutions Located in the Diocese.

Princeton, Mille Lacs Co., St. Edward's, Rev. Mark Willenbring.
Res., 804-S. Seventh Ave., 55371. Tel: 612-389-2115. [CEM]

Randall, Morrison Co., St. James, Rev. Alvin Quade.
Res., Box 225, 56475. Tel: 320-749-2720. [CEM]

Rice, Benton Co., Immaculate Conception, Rev. David Maciej.
Res., 130 First Ave., N.E., P.O. Box 189, 56367. Tel: 320-393-2725. [CEM]

Richmond, Stearns Co., SS. Peter and Paul's, Rev. Dominic Ruiz, O.S.B.; Deacon Joe Stefancin.
Res., P.O. Box 69, 56368. Tel: 320-597-2575. [CEM]
School—Tel: 612-597-2565.
Lay Teachers 7; Students 124.

Rockville, Stearns Co., Mary of the Immaculate Conception, Rev. Robert E. Rolfes.
Res., 56369. Tel: 320-251-7801. [CEM]

Roscoe, Stearns Co., St. Agnes, Rev. Leo Leisen.
Res., 56371. Tel: 320-243-4574. [CEM]

Royalton, Morrison Co., Holy Trinity, Rev. Laurn Virnig.
Res., 56373. Tel: 320-584-5484. [CEM]

Rush Lake, Otter Tail Co., St. Lawrence, Rev. Leo Otto.
Res., Rte. 1, Box 1, Dent, 56528. Tel: 218-758-2700. [CEM]

St. Anna, Stearns Co., Immaculate Conception, Co-Pastors: Revs. Gerald Mischke; Anthony Oelrich; Deacon Jeffrey Fromm.
Res., St. Mary's Rectory, Holdingford, 56340. Tel: 320-746-2231. [CEM]

St. Anthony, Stearns Co., St. Anthony's, Rev. William Vouk, III.
Res., 24328 Trobec St., Albany, 56307. Tel: 320-845-2416. [CEM]

St. Augusta, Stearns Co., St. Mary Help of Christians, Rev. Robert D. Schmainda.
Res., 24588 County Rd. 7, St. Cloud, 56301. Tel: 320-252-1799; Fax: 320-252-1992. [CEM]
School—Tel: 320-251-3937.
Sisters of St. Benedict 2; Lay Teachers 5; Students 157.

St. Francis, Stearns Co., St. Francis of Assisi, Rev. William Vouk, III.
Res., 44055 State Hwy. 238, Freeport P.O., 56331. Tel: 320-573-2203. [CEM]

St. Joseph, Stearns Co., St. Joseph's, Rev. Florian Muggli, O.S.B.
Res., 12 W. Minnesota St., 56374. Tel: 320-363-7505. [CEM]
School—Tel: 320-363-7769.
Lay Teachers 9; Students 154.

St. Martin, Stearns Co., St. Martin's, Rev. Michael Kwatera, O.S.B.
Res., 119 Maine St., Box 290, 56376. Tel: 320-548-3550. [CEM]

St. Nicholas, Stearns Co., St. Nicholas, Rev. John Caskey.
Res., 15862 County Rd. 165, Watkins, 55389. Tel: 320-398-7986; 764-7345. [CEM]

St. Rosa, Stearns Co., St. Rose of Lima, Rev. Arthur H. Hoppe.
Res., 28905 County Rd. 17, Freeport P.O., 56331-9610. Tel: 320-836-2151. [CEM]

St. Stephen, Stearns Co., St. Stephen's, Rev. John Miller.
Res., 56375. Tel: 320-251-1520. [CEM]

St. Wendel, Stearns Co., St. Columbkille's, Co-Pastors: Revs. Gerald Mischke; Anthony Oelrich; Deacon Jeffrey Fromm. In res., Rev. Donald Wagner.
Res., St. Mary's Rectory, Holdingford, 56340. Tel: 320-746-2231. [CEM]

Sartell, Stearns Co., St. Francis Xavier, Rev. Eberhard Schefers; Deacon Jerome Schwarzbauer.
Res., P.O. Box 150, 56377. Tel: 320-252-1363; Fax: 320-259-7090. [CEM]
School—Tel: 320-252-9940.
Lay Teachers 14; Students 197.

Sauk Centre, Stearns Co., Our Lady of the Angels, Rev. Bernard Kahlhamer; Deacon Lawrence Kaas.
Res., 211 S. Seventh, 56378. Tel: 320-352-3502. [CEM]
St. Paul's, Rev. Timothy Wenzel.
Res., 304 Sinclair Lewis Ave., 56378. Tel: 320-352-2196.
School—Holy Family School. Inter-Parochial School: St. Paul's Sauk Centre, Our Lady of Angels, Sauk Center. 231 Sinclair Lewis Ave., 56378. Tel: 320-352-6535.
Lay Teachers 19; Students 398.

Sauk Rapids, Benton Co., Sacred Heart, Revs. Eugene Doyle; James Herzing.
Res., 308 Third Ave., S., 56379. Tel: 320-251-8115; Fax: 320-251-8115. [CEM]
School—324 Third Ave., S., 56379. Tel: 320-251-2854; Fax: 320-251-0705.
Sisters 2; Lay Teachers 15; Students 287.
St. Patrick, Rev. Elmer J. Torborg.
Res., 7286 Duelm Rd., N.E., 56379. Tel: 320-252-2069. [CEM]

Sedan, Pope Co., Immaculate Conception Church, Rev. Frank Poncelet.
Res., Rte. 3, Box 78, Glenwood, 56334. Tel: 320-634-5489; Fax: 320-634-5489. [CEM]

Sobieski, Morrison Co., St. Stanislaus, Rev. Raymond N. Donnay.
Res., P.O. R.F.D. 3, Little Falls, 56345. Tel: 320-632-5086. [CEM]

Spring Hill, Stearns Co., St. Michael's, Rev. Leo Leisen. In res., Rev. Edward Ramacher.
Res., 100 Lillie Ave., Roscoe, 56371. Tel: 320-243-4574. [CEM]

Staples, Todd Co., Sacred Heart, Rev. Lauren A. Germann; Deacon Robert Shaffer.
Res., 310 Fourth St. N.E., Box 177, 56479. Tel: 218-894-2296. [JC]
School—Tel: 218-894-2077.
Lay Teachers 7; Students 131.

Swanville, Morrison Co., St. John the Baptist, Rev. Thomas C. Meyer.
Res., 22 1st. St., P.O. Box 68, 56382. Tel: 320-547-2920; Fax: 320-547-2578. [CEM]

Tintah, Traverse Co., St. Gall's, Rev. Andrew Marthaler.
Res., 56583. Tel: 218-369-2188. [CEM]

Upsala, Morrison Co., St. Mary, Rev. Todd Schneider.
Res., 308 S. Main St., P.O. Box 188, 56384. Tel: 320-573-2132. [CEM]

Urbank, Otter Tail Co., Sacred Heart, Rev. Jeff Ethen.
Res., Rte. 2, Box 133, P.O. Parkers Prairie, 56361. Tel: 218-267-2661. [CEM]

Verndale, Wadena Co., St. Frederick's, Rev. Peter K. Kirchner, Jr.
Res., 56481. Tel: 218-445-5786. [CEM]

Villard, Pope Co., St. Bartholomew's, Rev. Joseph Vandeberg.
Res., St. Alexius Church, West Union, 56389. Tel: 320-352-2563. [CEM]

Vineland, Mille Lacs Co., St. Therese, Little Flower Indian Mission, Rev. Raymond Steffes, O.S.C.
Res., P.O. Onamia, 56359. Tel: 320-532-3614. [CEM]

Wadena, Wadena Co., St. Ann's, Rev. Albert Holmes.
Res., 514 First St., S.E., 56482. Tel: 218-631-1593; Fax: 218-631-7149. [CEM]
School—Tel: 218-631-2631.
Lay Teachers 7; Students 105.

Wahkon, Mille Lacs Co., Sacred Heart, Rev. Nathan Packard.
Res., 56386. Tel: 320-495-3324.

Waite Park, Stearns Co., St. Joseph's, Rev. Ronald Weyrens; Deacon Richard Midas. In res., Rev. Susainathan Michael.
Res., 106 Seventh Ave., N., 56387. Tel: 320-251-5231; Fax: 320-251-3010. [CEM]
School—Tel: 320-251-4741, Ext. 1.
Lay Teachers 8; Students 145.

Ward Springs, Todd Co., St. Bernard's, Rev. Joel Nathe.
Res., P.O. Box 366, Grey Eagle, 56336. Tel: 320-285-2544.

West Union, Todd Co., St. Alexius, Rev. Joseph Vandeberg.
Res., 56389. Tel: 320-352-2563. [CEM]
Mission—Villard, Pope Co., St. Bartholomew.

Wheaton, Traverse Co., Ave Maria, Rev. Tony Salzbrunn.
Res., 201 Ninth St. S., 56296. Tel: 320-563-4421. [JC]

Zimmerman, Sherburne Co., St. Pius X, Rev. Antonio Marfori.
Res., Box 152, 55398. Tel: 320-856-4401.

Chaplains of Public Institutions

ST. CLOUD. *Minnesota State Reformatory for Men.* Rev. Joel Kelly, O.S.B., Res., St. John's Abbey, Collegeville, 56321.
U.S. Veteran's Hospital 56301. Rev. Alfred Stangl.
CAMBRIDGE. *Cambridge State School and Hospital.* Vacant. 55008.
FERGUS FALLS. *State Hospital Chapel.* Vacant. 56537.
SAUK CENTRE. *State Home School for Girls.* Rev. Kenneth Thielman.

Special Assignment:
Reverend Fathers—
Eccleston, John
Garding, William
Stangl, Alfred
Taufen, Daniel, V.G.
Thoennes, James
Trussel, Christopher
Wagner, Donald
Zimmerman, Ralph G.

On Duty Outside the Diocese:
Reverend Fathers—
Enneking, Marvin, 175 Main St., Ottawa, K1S 1C3 Canada
Kalkman, Richard, 23 Diaz Ave., San Francisco, CA 94132
Knoblach, Thomas, 6303 Nottingham Ave., St. Louis, MO 63109
Majerus, Daniel, 8722 Timberbriar, San Antonio, TX 78250
Vos, William, Maryknoll Fathers, P.O. Box 578, Musoma, Tanzania, Africa
Walz, Richard, Apartado 3008 Las Acacias, Avenida 9(El Pinonal) Calle 15, Maracay 400, Aragua, Venezuela

---

Retired:
Reverend Monsignors—
Kleinschmidt, Anthony, Josephinum College, Worthington, OH 43085
Reverend Fathers—
Bednark, Walter, 23189 State Hwy. 4, Paynesville, MN 56362

Botz, Lawrence, Box 95, Elrosa, MN 56325
Ebner, Frank, 10339 Parrish Ave. N.E., Elk River, MN 55330
Ekman, Robert, St. Benedict's Center, 1810 S.E. Minnesota Blvd., St. Cloud, MN 56304
Fadrowski, Stanislaus, 1934 Michigan Ave., Englewood, FL 34224
Finnegan, Roscoe L., 715 Farney Rd., Las Cruces, NM 88005
Fridgen, Joseph, P.O. Box 364, Grey Eagle, MN 56336-0366
Furlan, William, 320 Fourth Ave. S., Sauk Rapids, MN 56379
Gall, Sylvester, 520 First St. N.E., Apt. 80, Sartell, MN 56377
Haupt, Lloyd, 929 Brenda Lee Dr., St. Cloud, MN 56303
Heid, Richard, Box 256, Brandon, MN 56315
Illies, Wilfred, 2000 15th Ave. S.E., St. Cloud, MN 56304
Kleinschmidt, Sylvester, 412 First St. S., Apt. 1, Sauk Centre, MN 56378
Kloeckner, William, 10540 Co. Rd. 34 N.W., Alexandria, MN 56308
Lang, Raymond, 1615 15th Ave. S.E. #342, St. Cloud, MN 56304
Minette, James, 101 Enterprise Dr., Apt. 163, Rohnert Park, CA 94928
Morslander, Edward, 500 Third St. S. #164, Waite Park, MN 56387
Otto, Leo, R.R. 3, Box 118, Perham, MN 56573
Pavelis, Harold, Box 88, Concord, CA 94522
Pecovnik, Karel, Parkers Prairie, MN 56361
Peterka, Theodore, Russell Arms 209, 315 Division St., Sauk Rapids, MN 56379
Podrosky, Alfred, 117 Bechwood Dr., Monongahela, PA 15063
Ramacher, Edward, 102 St. Michael Ave., N. Spring Hill RQI, Melrose, MN 56352
Rieder, Donald, 1615 15th Ave., S.E., Apt. 328, St. Cloud, MN 56304
Riley, Patrick, 3034 Fulton Cir., Clearwater, MN 55320
Santo, Vincent, 907 Sinclair Lewis Ave., Sauk Centre, MN 56378
Sauer, Alban, 1120 11th Ave. N., St. Cloud, MN 56303
Schmelzer, Paul, 213 Third St., S., St. Cloud, MN 56301
Schwieters, Severin, 207-3rd. St. S., St. Cloud, MN 56301
Schwinghammer, Claude, Park Gardens, 114 First St. N., Apt. 219, Waite Park, MN 56387
Sobieck, Elmer, P.O. Box 281, St. Joseph, MN 56374
Speiser, Allan, 101 Riverside Dr. S.E. Apt. 224, St. Cloud, MN 56304
Vogel, Arthur, 617 Pinecone Rd., Apt. 308, Sartell, MN 56377
Vogrin, Joseph, Parkers Prairie, MN 56361
Wey, Richard, Rte. 1, Box 31A, Cushing, MN 56443
Wiersgalla, Joseph, St. Benedict's Center, 1810 S.E. Minnesota Blvd., St. Cloud, MN 56304
Zylla, Paul, 1615-15th Ave., S.E. #251, St. Cloud, MN 56304

Permanent Deacons:
Adams, Cecil, St. Henry's Monticello
Anderberg, George, Qwatonna
Bates, Kenneth, Country Manor, Sartell
Bobertz, Charles, Holy Spirit, St. Cloud
Eichers, Elmer, (Retired)
Fromm, Jeffrey, St. Mary's, Holdingford
Geyer, Bruce, Our Lady of Lourdes, Little Falls
Gruenes, Bernard, St. Michael, St. Cloud
Hackett, Russell, Immaculate Conception, Rice
Hennen, Stanley, Assumption, Morris
Hennes, James C., St. Augustine, St. Cloud
Kaas, Lawrence, Our Lady of the Angels, Sauk Centre
Kaebs, Brian, St. Benedict, Avon
Keable, Michael, St. Paul, St. Cloud
Kosiba, Leo, St. Mary, St. Cloud
Krebs, Brian, St. Joseph, Waite Park
Kruchten, Kenneth R., (Retired)
Kunkel, Andrew, Holy Cross, Pearl Lake
Leisen, Vincent, Christ the King, Browerville
Lindmeier, David, St. Paul, St. Cloud
Maltzen, Bruce, St. Boniface, Cold Spring
Midas, Richard, St. Joseph, Waite Park
Reker, Fred, St. John Cantius, St. Cloud
Roth, Jerome
Salchert, John, St. Boniface, Cold Spring
Schmainda, Frank, Sacred Heart, Glenwood
Schwarzbauer, Jerome, St. Francis Xavier, Sartell
Scott, John W., (Retired)
Shaffer, Robert, Sacred Heart, Staples
St. Jean, Fred, St. Andrew, Elk River
Steele, Gregory J., Immaculate Conception, Becker
Tzinski, Donald, St. Henry and St. Stanislaus, Perham
Warren, Todd, St. Paul, St. Cloud
Weinhandl, Thomas, St. Michael, Motley
Woods, John, St. Peter, St. Cloud
Yanish, Stephen, St. Anne's, Kimball

INSTITUTIONS LOCATED IN THE DIOCESE

[A] SEMINARIES, RELIGIOUS OR SCHOLASTICATES

COLLEGEVILLE. *St. John's Seminary*, 56321. Tel: 320-363-2100; Fax: 320-363-2504. Revs. Robert Pierson, O.S.B., Rector; Jonathan Licari, O.S.B., Vice Rector; Ralph Zimmerman, Dir. Spiritual Formation. Students 25. Legal Title: *St. John's Seminary*.

[B] COLLEGES AND UNIVERSITIES

COLLEGEVILLE. *St. John's University*, (1857), 56321-2000. Tel: 320-363-2011; Fax: 320-363-2504.
Web site: http://www.csbsju.edu
For a complete listing, refer to the Colleges and Universities section.

ST. JOSEPH. *College of St. Benedict*, (1913) 37 S. College Ave., 56374-2099. Tel: 320-363-5407 (Public Affairs); Fax: 320-363-5136 (Public Affairs)
For a complete listing, refer to the Colleges and Universities section.

[C] HIGH SCHOOLS, DIOCESAN

ST. CLOUD. *Cathedral High and John XXIII Middle School*, 312 Seventh Ave. N. Box 1579, 56302. Tel: 320-251-3421; Fax: 320-253-5576. Mr. James McConnell, Chief Admin.; Mr. Raymond Aafedt, Prin.; Mr. Thomas P. Raiche, Middle School Coord.; Rev. Christopher Trussel. Priests 1; Sisters 1; Lay Teachers 53; Students 795.
Cathedral High School Education Foundation, 312 Seventh Ave. N. P.O. Box 1579, 56302. Jeannette Stack, Chm.

[D] HIGH SCHOOLS, PRIVATE

COLLEGEVILLE. *St. John's Preparatory School*. College Preparatory. P.O. Box 4000, 56321. Tel: 320-363-3315; Fax: 320-363-3513. Rev. Mark Thamert, O.S.B., Pres. Students 176.

[E] INTER-PAROCHIAL SCHOOLS

ST. CLOUD. *St. Elizabeth Ann Seton School*. (Grades K-3), Primary: 1615 Eleventh Ave. S., 56301. Tel: 320-251-1988. Bonnie Massmann, Prin. Lay Teachers 10; Students 160. Middle: (Grades 4-6), 2410 First St. N., 56303. Tel: 320-251-6231. Dan Hollenhorst, Prin. Lay Teachers 8; Students 119. Consolidation of schools of the following parishes: Holy Spirit, St. Cloud; St. Anthony, St. Cloud.
Sts. Peter, Paul and Michael School. (Grades K-4), Primary: 925 N. 30th Ave., 56303. Tel: 320-251-4737. Principals: Mrs. Sharon Bichler; Phyllis Schlagel. Lay Teachers 25. Middle: (Grades 5-8), 1215 N. 11th Ave., 56303. Tel: 320-251-5295. Lay Teachers 24; Students 675. Consolidation of the following parishes: St. Michael; St. Paul; St. Peter, St. Cloud.

FOLEY. *St. John's Area School*. (Grades K-6), 215 7 Ave. South, 56329. Tel: 320-968-7972. Susan Burris, Prin. Consolidation of the following parishes: St. John of Foley; St. Lawrence, Duelm; St. Elizabeth, Brennyville; St. Joseph, Morrill; SS. Peter and Paul, Gilman; St Louis, Foreston; St. Patrick of Minden Township. Lay Teachers 8; Students 118.

LITTLE FALLS. *Mary of Lourdes Elementary and Middle School*. (Grades K-4), Primary: 307 Fourth St., S.E., 56345. Tel: 320-632-5408. Janet Stone, Prin. Benedictine Sister 1; Lay Teachers 12; Students 193; Preschool Students 40. Middle: (Grades 5-8), 205 N.W. Third St., 56345. Tel: 320-632-6742. Debra J. Meyer, Prin. Lay Teachers 9; Students 125. Consolidation of following parishes: St. Mary, Little Falls and Our Lady of Lourdes, Little Falls.

PIERZ. *Holy Trinity School*, Box 427, 56364. Tel: 320-468-6446. Mrs. Julia Barten, Admin. Prin.; Rev. Kenneth Brenny, Pres.-Corporate Board. Lay Teachers 13; Students 177. Consolidation of the following parishes: St. Michael's, Buckman; Holy Cross, Harding; St. John Nepomuk, Lastrup; St. Joseph, Pierz.

SAUK CENTRE. *Holy Family School*. (Grades K-6), 231 Sinclair Lewis Ave., 56378. Tel: 320-352-6535.
E-mail: holyts@saukherald.com
Lynn Peterson, Prin. Consolidation of the following parishes: St. Paul's, Sauk Centre; Our Lady of the Angels, Sauk Centre. Lay Teachers 19; Students 356.

[F] HOMES FOR EMOTIONALLY DISTURBED AND HANDICAPPED

ST. CLOUD. *Caritas Family Services, Catholic Charities Community Services*, 305 N. Seventh Ave., 56303. Tel: 320-252-4121; Fax: 320-259-8761
For a complete listing, refer to the Special Care Facilities section.
Community Services of Catholic Charities, 205 Seventh Ave. N., 56303. Tel: 320-259-8757; Fax: 320-240-3339
For a complete listing, refer to the Special Care Facilities section.
Day Treatment Services, 1712 Seventh Ave. S., 56301. Tel: 320-251-3647
For a complete listing, refer to the Special Care Facilities section.
In-Home Family Services, Catholic Charities Community Services, 700 Mall Germain, 56302. Tel: 320-251-1404; Fax: 320-252-8180
For a complete listing, refer to the Special Care Facilities section.
LaPaz Community Inc., 1730 Seventh Ave., S., 56301. Tel: 320-253-9470
For a complete listing, refer to the Special Care Facilities section.
St. Cloud Children's Home of the Diocese of St. Cloud, 1726 Seventh Ave. S., 56301. Tel: 320-251-8811; Fax: 320-251-3198
For a complete listing, refer to the Special Care Facilities section.
St. Elizabeth Home, 306 15th Ave., N., 56301. Tel: 320-252-8350
For a complete listing, refer to the Special Care Facilities section.

COLD SPRING. *Mother Teresa Home*, 101 Tenth Ave., 56320. Tel: 320-685-8626
For a complete listing, refer to the Special Care Facilities section.
St. Ann's Home, 103 10th Ave. N., 56320. Tel: 320-685-7898
For a complete listing, refer to the Special Care Facilities section.
St. Luke's Home, 411 Eighth Ave. N., 56320. Tel: 320-685-7750
For a complete listing, refer to the Special Care Facilities section.

COLD SPRINGS. *Bethany Home*, 13 8th Ave. S., 56320. Tel: 320-685-7899
For a complete listing, refer to the Special Care Facilities section.

FERGUS FALLS. *Catholic Charities Intensive Treatment Unit*, Box 1006, 56538-1006. Tel: 218-739-9325; Fax: 218-739-2242
For a complete listing, refer to the Special Care Facilities section.

LITTLE FALLS. *St. Camillus Place*, 1100 S.E. Fourth St., 56345. Tel: 320-632-1212
For a complete listing, refer to the Special Care Facilities section.

WAITE PARK. *St. Francis Home*, 25 Second St. N., 56387. Tel: 320-251-7630
For a complete listing, refer to the Special Care Facilities section.

[G] GENERAL HOSPITALS

ST. CLOUD. *St. Cloud Hospital*, 1406 Sixth Ave. N., 56303. Tel: 320-251-2700
For a complete listing, refer to the Hospitals section.

ALBANY. *Albany Area Hospital*, 300 Third Ave., 56307. Tel: 320-845-2121
For a complete listing, refer to the Hospitals section.

BRECKENRIDGE. *St. Francis Medical Center*, 415 Oak St., 56520. Tel: 218-643-3000
For a complete listing, refer to the Hospitals section.

LITTLE FALLS. *St. Gabriel's Hospital*, 815 S.E. Second St., 56345. Tel: 320-632-5441; Fax: 320-632-1190
For a complete listing, refer to the Hospitals section.

[H] HOMES FOR AGED

ST. CLOUD. *St. Benedict's Center*, 1810 Minnesota Blvd., S.E., 56304. Tel: 320-252-0010; Fax: 320-654-2351
For a complete listing, refer to the Special Care Facilities section.

ALBANY. *Mother of Mercy Nursing Home and Retirement Center*, Box 676, 56307. Tel: 320-845-2195
For a complete listing, refer to the Special Care Facilities section.

BRECKENRIDGE. *St. Francis Home*, 56520. Tel: 218-643-7661
For a complete listing, refer to the Special Care Facilities section.

COLD SPRING. *Assumption Court*, 615 1st St. N., 56320. Tel: 320-685-4110
For a complete listing, refer to the Special Care Facilities section.
Assumption Home, 715 N. First St., 56320. Tel: 320-685-3693; Fax: 320-685-7044

For a complete listing, refer to the Special Care Facilities section.

John Paul Apartments, 200 Eighth Ave. N., 56320. Tel: 320-685-4429
For a complete listing, refer to the Special Care Facilities section.

LITTLE FALLS. *Alverna Apartments*, 300 Eighth Ave., S.E., 56345. Tel: 320-632-1246
For a complete listing, refer to the Special Care Facilities section.

St. Otto's Care Center, 920 S.E. 4th St., 56345. Tel: 320-632-9281; Fax: 320-632-1120
For a complete listing, refer to the Special Care Facilities section.

MORRIS. *Villa of St. Francis Nursing Home*, 1001 Scott Ave., 56267. Tel: 320-589-1133
For a complete listing, refer to the Special Care Facilities section.

PARKERS PRAIRIE. *St. William's Living Center*, P.O. Box 30, 56361. Tel: 218-338-4671; Fax: 218-338-5917
For a complete listing, refer to the Special Care Facilities section.

PIERZ. *St. Mary's Villa Inc.*, 56364. Tel: 320-468-6405
For a complete listing, refer to the Special Care Facilities section.

STAPLES. *Mary Rondorf Retirement Home of Sacred Heart Parish*, 56479. Tel: 218-894-2124
For a complete listing, refer to the Special Care Facilities section.

[I] MONASTERIES AND RESIDENCES OF PRIESTS AND BROTHERS

COLLEGEVILLE. *St. John's Abbey, of the Order of St. Benedict.* and St. John's University, School of Theology, Seminary, Preparatory School and Novitiate. P.O. Box 2015, 56321-2015. Tel: 612-363-2011. Rt. Rev. Timothy Kelly, O.S.B., Abbot and Chancellor; Very Revs. Geoffrey Fecht, O.S.B., Prior; Douglas Mullin, O.S.B., Subprior; Revs. Henry Anderl, O.S.B.; Knute Anderson, O.S.B.; Thomas Andert, O.S.B.; Alexander Andrews, O.S.B.; Burkard Arnheiter, O.S.B.; Timothy Backous, O.S.B., College Chap.; Rudolph Baumberger, O.S.B.; Peregrin Berres, O.S.B.; Luigi Bertocchi, O.S.B.; Michael Bik, O.S.B.; Paschal Botz, O.S.B.; Allan Bouley, O.S.B.; Silvan Bromenshenkel, O.S.B.; Alto Butkowski, O.S.B.; Jerome Coller, O.S.B.; Cletus Connors, O.S.B.; Alberic Culhane, O.S.B.; Cosmas Dahlheimer, O.S.B.; Godfrey Diekmann, O.S.B.; Arnold Dittberner, O.S.B.; Ian Dommer, O.S.B.; Nicholas Doub, O.S.B.; Daniel Durken, O.S.B.; John Patrick Earls, O.S.B.; Richard Eckroth, O.S.B.; Gall Fell, O.S.B.; Melchior Freund, O.S.B.; Bernard Friedl, O.S.B.; Cyril Gorman, O.S.B.; Nathanael Hauser, O.S.B.; Henry Bryan Hays, O.S.B.; William G. Heidt, O.S.B.; Francis Hoefgen, O.S.B., Guestmaster; Eric Hollas, O.S.B., HMML Dir.; Roger Kasprick, O.S.B.; Philip Kaufman, O.S.B.; Joel Kelly, O.S.B.; Emmanuel Kelsch, O.S.B.; Chrysostom Kim, O.S.B.; John Klassen, O.S.B., Formation Dir.; Roger Klassen, O.S.B.; Jude Koll, O.S.B.; Robert Koopmann, O.S.B.; John Kulas, O.S.B.; Michael Kwatera, O.S.B.; Dale Launderville, O.S.B., Dean at the School of Theology, Rector of Seminary; Emeric Lawrence, O.S.B.; Donald LeMay, O.S.B.; Nathan Libaire, O.S.B.; Jonathan Licari, O.S.B.; Luke Mancuso, O.S.B.; Omer Maus, O.S.B.; Brennan Maiers, O.S.B.; J. Patrick McDarby, O.S.B.; Finian McDonald, O.S.B.; Kilian McDonnell, O.S.B.; Rene McGraw, O.S.B.; Aloysius Michels, O.S.B.; Dustan Moorse, O.S.B.; Michael Naughton, O.S.B., Dir. Liturgical Press; Benedict Nordick, O.S.B.; Virgil O'Neill, O.S.B.; Michael Patella, O.S.B.; Roman Paur, O.S.B.; Raymond Pedrizetti, O.S.B.; Robert Pierson, O.S.B., Rector of Seminary; Anthony Ruff, O.S.B., Study Leave; Dominic Ruiz, O.S.B.; Jan Santich, O.S.B.; Bartholomew Sayles, O.S.B.; Sebastian Schramel, O.S.B.; Paul Schwietz, O.S.B.; Kevin Seasoltz, O.S.B.; Gregory Sebastian, O.S.B.; Cyprian Seitz, O.S.B.; Gervase Soukup, O.S.B.; Gregory Soukup, O.S.B.; Luke Steiner, O.S.B.; Columba Stewart, O.S.B.; James Studer, O.S.B.; Edwin Stueber, O.S.B.; Benjamin Stein, O.S.B.; Don Talafous, O.S.B.; Allen Tarlton, O.S.B.; Donald Tauscher, O.S.B.; Gordon Tavis, O.S.B.; Vincent Tegeder, O.S.B.; Mark Thamert, O.S.B., Pres., St. Johns Preparatory School; Wilfred Theisen, O.S.B.; Hilary Thimmesh, O.S.B.; Simeon Thole, O.S.B.; Thomas Thole, O.S.B.; James Tingerthal, O.S.B., Dir. Special Events; Jerome Tupa, O.S.B.; Blane Wasnie, O.S.B.; Magnus Wenninger, O.S.B.; Robert Wieber, O.S.B., Study Leave; Andrew Winczewski, O.S.B.; Hugh Witzmann, O.S.B.; Bruce Wollmering, O.S.B.; Angelo Zankl, O.S.B.; Germain Loeber, O.S.B.
On Special Assignments: Rev. Burton Bloms, O.S.B., St. Theresa Home, 8000 Bass Lake Rd., New Hope, 55428. Tel: 612-531-5040. Rev. Gerard Farrell, O.S.B., 302 Nassau St., Princeton, NJ, 08540. Tel: 609-924-5638. Rev. Barnabas Laubach, O.S.B., St. Bernardine Hospital, 2101 N. Waterman Ave., San Bernardino, CA, 92404. Tel: 909-883-8711. Rev. Stanley Roche, O.S.B., St. Theresa Southwest, Apt. 102, 1011 Feltl Court, Hopkins, 55343. Tel: 612-933-3333. Rev. Paul Marx, O.S.B., Leave of Exclaustration.
Priests of the Abbey Serving Abroad: Revs. George Wolf; Anthony Hellenberg, O.S.B.; Francisco Schulte, O.S.B.; Daniel Ward, O.S.B., St. Augustine Monastery, Box N-3940, Nassau, Bahamas. Tel: 809-364-1331; Fax: 809-364-1265. Very Rev. Mel Taylor, O.S.B.; Rev. Fintan Bromenshenkel, O.S.B., St. Augustine Monastery, Box N-3940, Nassau, Bahamas. Tel: 809-364-1511; Fax: 809-364-1265. Mary Mother of the Church Abbey, 12617 River Rd., Richmond, VA, 23233. Rev. Theophile Brown, O.S.B., St. Anselm Priory, 6-22, 4-Chome, Kamiosaki, Shinagawa-Ku, Tokyo, Japan, 141. Revs. Neal Henry Lawrence, O.S.B.; Thomas Wahl, O.S.B., St. Anselm Priory, 6-22, 4-Chome, Kamiosaki, Shinagawa-Ku, Tokyo, Japan, 141. Rev. Peter Kawamura, O.S.B.; Very Rev. Kieran Nolan, O.S.B., Prior; Rev. William Skudlarek, O.S.B. Japan, St. Anselm Priory, 6-22, 4-Chome, Kamiosaki, Shinagawa-Ku, Tokyo, Japan, 141. Rev. Cyprian Weaver, O.S.B., Benedictine Wimmer Priory, 1 Lane 96, Ming Chih Rd., Sec. 3, Taishan, Taipei, Hsien Republic of China, Taiwan, 24302. Rev. Aelred Tegels Germany. Community Priests 149; Professed Brothers 62; Novices 3; Claustral Oblate 1.

ONAMIA. *Crosier Monastery*, 56359. Tel: 320-532-3103; Fax: 320-532-3103, Ext. 214. Legal Title: *Crosier Fathers of Onamia.* Very Rev. Raymond A. Steffes, O.S.C., Prior.; Revs. William T. McNiff, O.S.C., Sub Prior; Joseph Brennan, O.S.C.; Bernard Mischke, O.S.C.
Priests Elsewhere: Revs. Clement N. Gustin, O.S.C., Buhl; James Cashman, O.S.C., Foreston; John J. Fleischhacker, O.S.C., McGregor; Richard T. John, O.S.C., Milaca; Henry A. Miller, O.S.C., Fort Ripley-St. Mathias; Frank Trenkenschuh, O.S.C.
The National Shrine of St. Odilia is sponsored and maintained by the Crosier Fathers of Onamia. Priests in Residence 4; Priests Elsewhere 6; Brothers in Residence 7.

[J] CONVENTS AND RESIDENCES FOR SISTERS

LITTLE FALLS. *St. Francis Convent*, 116 Eighth Ave., S.E., 56345. Tel: 320-632-2981. Motherhouse of Franciscan Sisters of Little Falls, MN. Sr. Rose Margaret Schneider, Community Min.; Rev. John Eccleston, Chap. Sisters 85; Total in Community 254.

ST. JOSEPH. *Congregation of the Sisters of the Holy Cross (C.S.C.)*, 12543 Old Collegeville Rd., 56374. Sr. Kathleen Moroney, C.S.C., Treas.

St. Benedict's Monastery, 104 Chapel Ln., 56374-0220. Tel: 320-363-7100. Motherhouse and Formation House for all but the Dependent Priories of the Sisters of the Order of Saint Benedict. Sr. Ephrem Hollermann, O.S.B., Prioress; Sr. Theresa Schumacher, O.S.B., Coord. Eucharistic Presiders. Sisters 144; Total in Community 421.

SAUK RAPIDS. *St. Clare's Monastery*. Major Papal Cloister, 56379. Tel: 320-251-3556. Franciscan Poor Clare Nuns. Mother Mary Peter, O.S.C, Abbess. Cloistered Nuns: Solemn Professed 14; Extern Sisters: Perpetual Professed 3; Novices 1.

[K] RETREAT HOUSES

ST. FRANCIS. *Pacem in Terris Center for Spirituality*, Hermitage Retreats, P.O. Box 418, 55070. Tel: 612-444-6408; Fax: 612-444-9649. Mrs. Shirley Wanchena, S.F.O., Dir.

[L] NEWMAN CENTERS

ST. CLOUD. *Newman Center, Inc.*, 396 First Ave., S., 56301. Tel: 320-251-3260; 251-2712 (Home).
E-mail: bgraber@stcloudstate.edu
Web site: www.stcloudstate.edu/.~newman
Rev. Kevin Anderson.

MORRIS. *Newman Catholic Student Center*, 306 E. Fourth St., 56267. Tel: 320-589-1947.
E-mail: catholic@ida.mrs.umn.edu
Directors of Campus Ministry: Jeff Schaffer; Carol Schaffer.

[M] MISCELLANEOUS

ST. CLOUD. *Domus Transitional Housing of Catholic Charities*, 217 Sixth Ave., N., 56301. Tel: 320-259-9270. 321 & 323 Fourteenth Ave., 56301. Mr. Steven P. Bresnahan; Harvey Schmitt.

Key Row Community, Inc.; Key Row-Little Falls, Inc.; Key Row-Milaca, Inc., 1730 Seventh Ave., S., 56301. Tel: 320-253-9470. Organizations providing low-cost housing to Elderly and Families Little Falls, Milaca, Morris, Wheaton and St. Cloud. Mr. Steven P. Bresnahan, Exec. Dir.; Harvey Schmitt, Dir. Housing Svcs.

Sacred Music Inc. of the Diocese of St. Cloud, Box 1248, 56302.

St. Joseph's Apartment, Inc. Located in St. Joseph and Sauk Centre, MN. 1730 Seventh Ave., S., 56301. Tel: 320-253-9470. Mr. Steven P. Bresnahan, Exec. Dir.; Harvey Schmitt, Dir. Housing Svcs.

St. Therese Center for Special Ministry, 823 First St., S., 56301. Tel: 320-251-8064. Rev. John H. McManus, O.M.I.; Sr. Georganne Burr, O.S.B.; Nan Figge; Mary Lou Dinndorf.

Services to Aging of Catholic Charities, 1252 Thirty-Second Ave., N., 56303. Tel: 320-252-2048; Fax: 320-253-7464. Mr. Steven P. Bresnahan, Exec. Dir.; Sr. Grace Donovan, O.S.B., Dir. Aging Svcs. Legal Title: *Services to Aging of Catholic Charities: Senior Dining / Meals on Wheels, Caregivers, Share-A-Home, Foster Grandparent Program.*

The Society of the Homeless Orphan of the Diocese of St. Cloud, St. Cloud Children's Home, 1730 Seventh Ave., S., 56301. Tel: 320-252-0412.

Valley Vista Apartments of Browns Valley Inc., 1730 Seventh Ave., S., 56301. Tel: 320-253-9470. Mr. Steven P. Bresnahan, Exec. Dir.; Harvey Schmitt, Dir. Housing Svcs.

ALEXANDRIA. *Carmelite Hermits of Adoration, Inc.*, 7005 E. State Hwy. 27, 56308. Sr. Imelda, Prioress. Sisters 2.

BROWNS VALLEY.
**Browns Valley Health Center*, S. Jefferson St., R.R.1 Box 182 D., 56219; Fax: 320-695-2166.

LITTLE FALLS. *Franciscan Sisters Health Care, Inc.*, 116 Eighth Ave. S.E., 56345-2981. Tel: 320-632-3601. Sr. Rose Margaret Schneider, O.S.F., Pres.

Franciscan Sisters of Little Falls, MN Charitable Trust, 116 Eighth Ave. S.E., 56345. Tel: 320-632-2981.

MORRIS. *St. Francis Health Services*, 801 Nevada, Ste. 100, 56267. Tel: 320-589-2004.
**Prairie Community Services.*

ONAMIA. *National Shrine of St. Odilia*, 56359. Tel: 320-532-3103. Sponsored and maintained by The Crosiers of Onamia.

ST. JOSEPH. *Monastic Interreligious Dialogue*, St. Benedict's Convent, 104 Chapel Ln., 56374-2020. Sr. Katherine Howard, O.S.B., Contact Person.

RELIGIOUS INSTITUTES OF MEN REPRESENTED IN THE DIOCESE

For further details refer to the corresponding bracketed number in the Religious Institutes of Men or Women section.

[0200]—*Benedictine Monks.* (Collegeville, MN).—O.S.B.

[0400]—*Canons Regular of the Order of the Holy Cross.* (Province of St. Odilia).—O.S.C.

RELIGIOUS INSTITUTES OF WOMEN REPRESENTED IN THE DIOCESE

[0230]—*Benedictine Sisters of Pontifical Jurisdiction.*—O.S.B.

[1920]—*Congregation of the Sisters of the Holy Cross.*—C.S.C.

[1310]—*Franciscan Sisters of Little Falls, Minnesota.*—O.S.F.

[3760]—*Order of St. Clare.*—O.S.C.

[2970]—*School Sisters of Notre Dame.* (Northwestern Prov.).—S.S.N.D.

[1710]—*Sisters of St. Francis of Mary Immaculate.*—O.S.F.

[1570]—*Sisters of St. Francis of the Holy Family.*—O.S.F.

NECROLOGY

† Kampsen, Frederick, (Retired). —Died Nov. 7, 1997.

Archdiocese of St. Louis

(Archidioecesis S. Ludovici)

His Eminence

JOHN JOSEPH CARDINAL CARBERRY, D.D., S.T.D., J.C.D., PH.D.

Former Archbishop of St. Louis; ordained July 28, 1929; appointed Titular Bishop of Elis and Coadjutor of Lafayette in Indiana May 3, 1956; consecrated July 25, 1956; succeeded to See November 20, 1957; transferred to Columbus January 16, 1965; appointed Archbishop of St. Louis February 17, 1968; installed March 25, 1968; created Cardinal April 28, 1969.; retired July 31, 1979. *All communications to His Eminence should be addressed to: The Catholic Center, 4445 Lindell Blvd., St. Louis, MO, 63108-2497.*

Most Reverend

GEORGE J. GOTTWALD, D.D.

Former Auxiliary Bishop of St. Louis; ordained June 9, 1940; appointed Titular Bishop of Cedamusa and Auxiliary Bishop of St. Louis June 10, 1961; consecrated August 8, 1961; retired August 1, 1988. *All communications should be addressed to: The Catholic Center, 4445 Lindell Blvd., St. Louis, MO, 63108-2497.*

Most Reverend

JUSTIN F. RIGALI, J.C.D.

Archbishop of St. Louis; ordained April 25, 1961; appointed Titular Archbishop of Bolsena June 8, 1985; ordained Bishop September 14, 1985; appointed Archbishop of St. Louis January 25, 1994; installed March 16, 1994

The Catholic Center: 4445 Lindell Blvd., St. Louis, MO, 63108-2497. Tel.: 314-533-1887; Fax: 314-533-1889.

Most Reverend

EDWARD K. BRAXTON, PH.D, S.T.D.

Auxiliary Bishop of St. Louis; ordained May 13, 1970; appointed Titular Bishop of Macomades Rusticiana and Auxiliary Bishop of St. Louis March 28, 1995; consecrated May 17, 1995. *Res., 4431 Lindell Blvd., St. Louis, MO, 63108.*

Most Reverend

JOSEPH F. NAUMANN, D.D.

Auxiliary Bishop of St. Louis; ordained May 24, 1975; appointed Titular Bishop of Caput Cilla and Auxiliary Bishop of St. Louis July 9, 1997; consecrated September 3, 1997. *Res., 8900 Clayton Rd., Richmond Heights, MO, 63117.*

Most Reverend

MICHAEL J. SHERIDAN, D.D.

Auxiliary Bishop of St. Louis; ordained May 29, 1971; appointed Titular Bishop of Thibiuca and Auxiliary Bishop of St. Louis July 9, 1997; consecrated September 3, 1997. *Res., 6047 Bishops Place, St. Louis, MO, 63109.*

DIOCESE JULY 18, 1826; ARCHDIOCESE JULY 20, 1847.

Square Miles 5,968.

Comprises that portion of the State of Missouri bounded on the north by the northern line of the County of Lincoln; on the west by the western lines of the Counties of Lincoln, Warren, Franklin and Washington; on the south by the southern lines of the Counties of Washington, St. Francois and Perry; on the east by the Mississippi River.

Heavenly Patrons—Saint Louis, King, Saint Vincent de Paul and Saint Rose Philippine Duchesne.

For legal titles of parishes and archdiocesan institutions, consult the Catholic Center.

STATISTICAL OVERVIEW

Personnel	
Retired Cardinals	1
Archbishop	1
Auxiliary Bishops	3
Retired Bishops	2
Abbots	1
Retired Abbots	1
Priests: Diocesan Active in Diocese	374
Priests: Active Outside Diocese	4
Priests: Diocesan in Foreign Missions	7
Priests: Retired, Sick or Absent	91
Number of Diocesan Priests	476
Religious Priests in Diocese	373
Extern Priests in Diocese	6
Ordinations:	
Diocesan Priests	7
Religious Priests	3
Transitional Deacons	5
Permanent Deacons	17
Permanent Deacons in Diocese	209
Total Brothers	179
Total Sisters	2,230
Parishes	
Parishes	227
With Resident Pastor:	
Resident Diocesan Priests	202
Resident Religious Priests	25
Without Resident Pastor:	
Missions	8
Welfare	
Catholic Hospitals	12
Total Assisted	1,278,393
Homes for the Aged	17
Total Assisted	28,602
Residential Care of Children	10
Total Assisted	2,771
Day Care and Extended Day Care Centers	16
Total Assisted	1,348
Specialized Homes	14
Total Assisted	6,182
Special Centers for Social Services	24
Total Assisted	275,292
Residential Care of Disabled	1
Total Assisted	58
Educational	
Seminaries, Diocesan	2
Students from This Diocese	31
Students from Other Diocese	44
Diocesan Students in Other Seminaries	3
Seminaries, Religious	5
Students Religious	36
Total Seminarians	70
Colleges and Universities	2
Total Students	13,902
High Schools, Diocesan and Parish	14
Total Students	6,638
High Schools, Private	15
Total Students	8,846
Elementary Schools, Diocesan and Parish	147
Total Students	41,260
Elementary Schools, Private	6
Total Students	2,334
Non-residential Schools for the Disabled	8
Total Students	220
Catechesis/Religious Education:	
High School Students	511
Elementary Students	22,374
Total Students Under Catholic Instruction	96,155
Teachers in the Diocese:	
Priests	40
Scholastics	3
Brothers	17
Sisters	197
Lay Teachers	3,484
Vital Statistics	
Receptions into the Church:	
Infant Baptism Totals	7,546
Adult Baptism Totals	939
Received into Full Communion	726
First Communions	7,938
Confirmations	7,239
Marriages:	
Catholic	2,827
Interfaith	1,237
Total Marriages	4,064
Deaths	4,236
Total Catholic Population	573,000
Total Population	2,072,868

Former Bishops—Rt. Rev. JOSEPH ROSATI, C.M., Bishop of St. Louis; cons. Bishop of the Titular See of Tenagra and constituted Coadjutor of Bishop DuBourg of Louisiana at Donaldsville, LA, March 25, 1824. When the See of Louisiana was divided Bishop Rosati was made Bishop of St. Louis and Administrator of New Orleans. He died while on business in Rome on September 25, 1843.—Most Rev. LOUIS WILLIAM VALENTINE DUBOURG, Archbishop of the Cardinalatial See of Besancon; cons. in Rome, Sept. 24, 1815, Bishop of Louisiana, Upper and Lower, took his first residential seat in St. Louis, Jan. 6, 1818. On July 18, 1826, the Diocese of Louisiana was divided and the Sees of St. Louis and New Orleans erected. Bishop DuBourg, having resigned the See of Louisiana, was transferred to the Diocese of Montauban in France, Aug. 13, 1826, and made Archbishop of the Cardinalatial See of Besancon, Feb. 15, 1833, where he died Dec. 12 of the same year.—Most Rev. PETER RICHARD KENRICK, D.D., Archbishop of St. Louis; cons. Nov. 30, 1841, Bishop of Drasa and Coadjutor to.—Rt. Rev. BISHOP ROSATI, Bishop of St. Louis, 1843; Archbishop, 1847; Titular Archbishop of Marcianopolis, May 21, 1895; died March 4, 1896.—Most Rev. JOHN JOSEPH KAIN, D.D., Archbishop of St. Louis; cons. Bishop of Wheeling, WV on May 23, 1875; Titular Archbishop of Oxyrynchia and Coadjutor "cum jure successionis" of Archbishop of St. Louis, 1893; Administrator of Archdiocese of St. Louis, Dec. 14, 1893; created Archbishop of St. Louis on May 21, 1895; died Oct. 13, 1903.—His Eminence JOHN CARDINAL GLENNON, D.D., Archbishop of St. Louis; born June 14, 1862; ord. Dec. 20, 1884; appt. Titular Bishop of Pinara and Coadjutor to the Bishop of Kansas City, March 14, 1896; cons. June 29, 1896; transferred to St. Louis, April 27, 1903, as Coadjutor to the Archbishop of St. Louis "cum jure successionis"; Archbishop of St. Louis, Oct. 13, 1903; Pallium received May 14, 1905; Assistant at the Pontifical Throne, June 21, 1921; created Cardinal Priest, Feb. 18, 1946; died March 9, 1946.—His Eminence JOSEPH CARDINAL RITTER, D.D., Archbishop of St. Louis; born July 20, 1892; ord. May 30, 1917; appt. Titular Bishop of Hippo, Feb. 3, 1933 and Auxiliary Bishop of Indianapolis; cons. March 28, 1933; appt. Archbishop of Indianapolis, Nov. 11, 1944; appt. Archbishop of St. Louis, July 20, 1946 assistant at the Pontifical Throne, Oct. 5, 1956; created Cardinal, Priest Jan. 16, 1961; died June 10, 1967.—His Eminence JOHN JOSEPH CARDINAL CARBERRY, D.D., S.T.D., J.C.D., Ph.D., Archbishop of St. Louis; ord. July 28, 1929; appt. Titular Bishop of Elis and Coadjutor of Lafayette in Indiana, May 3, 1956; cons. July 25, 1956; succeeded to See, Nov. 20, 1957; transferred to Columbus, Jan. 16, 1965; appt. Archbishop of St. Louis, Feb. 17, 1968; installed March 25, 1968; created Cardinal, April 28, 1969; retired July 31, 1979.—Most Rev. JOHN L. MAY, D.D., Archbishop of St. Louis; ord. May 3, 1947; appt. Auxiliary Bishop of Chicago, June 21, 1967; cons. Aug. 24, 1967; transferred to Mobile, Oct. 8, 1969; installed as Bishop of Mobile, Dec. 10, 1969; appt. Archbishop of St. Louis, Jan. 29, 1980; installed March 25, 1980; resigned Dec. 9, 1992; died March 24, 1994.

The Catholic Center—4445 Lindell Blvd., St. Louis, 63108-2498. Tel: 314-533-1887; Fax: 314-533-1889. Office Hours: Mon.-Fri. 8:30-4.

Vicars General—Most Rev. EDWARD K. BRAXTON, Ph.D., S.T.D., V.G.; Most Rev. JOSEPH F. NAUMANN, V.G.; Most Rev. MICHAEL J. SHERIDAN, V.G.; Rev. Msgr. RICHARD F. STIKA, V.G.

Moderator of the Curia—Rev. Msgr. RICHARD F. STIKA, V.G.

Chancellor—Rev. Msgr. RICHARD F. STIKA, V.G., *4445 Lindell Blvd., St. Louis, 63108.* Tel: 314-533-1887.

Secretary to the Archbishop—Rev. HENRY J. BREIER.

Masters of Ceremonies to the Archbishop—Revs. HENRY J. BREIER; MARK S. RIVITUSO.

Master of Ceremonies to the Cathedral of St. Louis—Rev. PAUL J. NIEMANN.

Chief Financial Officer—Mr. VINCENT M. JONES.

Metropolitan Tribunal—4445 Lindell Blvd., St. Louis, 63108. Tel: 314-533-1887; Fax: 314-533-0049.

Judicial Vicar—Rev. JOHN B. SHAMLEFFER, J.C.L., M.C.L.

Adjutant Judicial Vicar—Rev. MARK S. RIVITUSO, J.C.L., M.C.L.

Judges—Deacon J. GERARD QUINN, J.C.L.; Rev. MICHAEL P. JOYCE, C.M., J.C.D.; Sr. CHARLOTTE RIGALI, C.S.J., J.C.D.

Defenders of the Bond—Revs. JAMES J. RAMACCIOTTI, J.C.L.; JEROME D. BILLING, J.C.L.

Director of Advocate Services—Rev. CHARLES C. DEISTER.

Auditors—Revs. MICHAEL P. BOEHM; MATTHEW L. O'TOOLE.

Promoter of Justice—Rev. JEROME D. BILLING, J.C.L.

Notaries—Mrs. ELIZABETH KWIATKOWSKI; Mrs. JOYCE KOETTING; Mrs. PATRICIA LANASA.

Archdiocesan Consultors—Most Rev. EDWARD K. BRAXTON, Ph.D., S.T.D., V.G.; Most Rev. JOSEPH F. NAUMANN, V.G.; Most Rev. MICHAEL J. SHERIDAN, V.G.; Rev. Msgr. ROBERT P. JOVANOVIC; Rev. Msgr. GEORGE J. LUCAS, V.G.; Rev. Msgr. RICHARD F. STIKA, V.G.; Rev. Msgr. WALTER M. WHITED; Rev. Msgr. JOHN J. LEYKAM.

Deaneries / Deans—Rev. Msgr. JAMES T. TELTHORST, V.F., North St. Louis; Very Rev. DENNIS E. DOERHOFF, V.F., South St. Louis; Very Rev. DONALD R. WESTER, V.F., Northeast County; Very Rev. ROBERT J. HERMANN, V.F., Northwest County; Rev. Msgr. JAMES E. PIEPER, V.F., Southwest County; Rev. Msgr. ROBERT P. JOVANOVIC, V.F., Southeast County; Very Rev. MICHAEL L. DONALD, V.F., Festus; Very Rev. DONALD C. SCHRAMM, V.F., St. Charles; Rev. Msgr. JAMES E. HANSON, V.F., Ste. Genevieve; Very Rev. ROBERT L. HEIMOS, V.F., Washington.

Vicar for Administration—Rev. Msgr. JOHN R. MAGUIRE.

Vicar for Planning—Rev. Msgr. TED WOJCICKI.

Co-Vicar for Religious—Sr. EVA MARIA ACKERMAN, O.S.F.

Archdiocesan Offices and Directors

Archdiocesan Archives—Rev. Msgr. RICHARD F. STIKA, V.G., Chancellor; Sr. TERESA MARIA EGAN, C.S.J.; ELAINE SNYDER, *7800 Kenrick Rd., St. Louis, 63119.* Tel: 314-961-4320, Ext. 101.

Archdiocesan Board of Conciliation and Arbitration—Rev. Msgr. DONALD E. RAU, Chm.; Ms. EILEEN SEARLS, Sec.; Mr. JAMES BURTON, Treas.; Rev. BERNARD NIENHAUS; Mr. BERNARD HUGER; Sr. JOAN MARIE GLEASON, C.S.J.

Archdiocesan Building and Boundary Commission—Rev. Msgr. RICHARD J. GALLAGHER, Exec. Sec.; Rev. Msgr. RICHARD J. LUBELEY; Rev. Msgr. ROBERT J. MUESENFECHTER.

Catholic Family Service—Mr. RICHARD E. HENNICKE, A.C.S.W., Exec. Dir., *7800 Kenrick Rd., St. Louis, 63119.* Tel: 314-968-8010. See MISCELLANEOUS section for more information.

Archdiocesan Development Appeal—See MISCELLANEOUS section for more information; MARY MORFELD, Exec. Dir., *4140 Lindell Blvd., St. Louis, 63108.* Tel: 314-371-4980.

Catholic Information Center—Rev. VALENTINE YOUNG, O.F.M.Cap., Dir. Tel: 314-621-6555; 231-9991. See MISCELLANEOUS section for more information.

Catholic Office of Disability Ministry—LORRAINE FAHEY, Dir., *7800 Kenrick Rd., St. Louis, 63119.* Tel: 314-961-4320, Ext. 190; Fax: 314-918-0878. Also see MISCELLANEOUS section.

Catholic Relief Services—Rev. Msgr. BERNARD H. SANDHEINRICH, Dir., *4140 Lindell Blvd., St. Louis, 63108.* Tel: 314-371-4980.

Catholic Cemeteries of St. Louis—Rev. Msgr. ROBERT MCCARTHY, Dir., *6901 Mackenzie Rd., St. Louis, 63123.* Tel: 314-352-5300. See CEMETERIES section for more information.

Central Purchasing—Rev. Msgr. RICHARD J. GALLAGHER, Dir., *7800 Kenrick Rd., St. Louis, 63119.* Tel: 314-961-4320, Ext. 163.

Catholic Charities—Mr. JOHN LALLY, Pres. JOHN W. MCCARTHY, Assoc. Dir., Finance, *4532 Lindell Blvd., St. Louis, 63108.* Tel: 314-367-5500; Fax: 314-367-6927. See MISCELLANEOUS section for more information.

Cardinal Ritter Institute-Archdiocesan Office for Services to the Elderly—JOHN M. LALLY, CEO; ARTHUR J. KORTE, COO-Svcs. MICHAEL J. LALLY, COO-Residences, *4483 Lindell Blvd., St. Louis, 63108.* Tel: 314-652-3600. See SERVICES FOR THE ELDERLY section for more information.

Catholic Commission on Housing—Rev. RICHARD J. QUIRK, Exec. Dir., *4140 Lindell Blvd., St. Louis, 63108.* Tel: 314-371-4980. See MISCELLANEOUS section for more information.

Catholic Community Services—Sr. BETTY BRUCKER, F.S.M., Exec. Dir., *325 N. Newstead, St. Louis, 63108.* Tel: 314-531-0511. See MISCELLANEOUS section for more information.

Archdiocesan Deaf Ministry—Rev. VICTOR A. BARNHART, Dir.; See MISCELLANEOUS section for more information.

Archdiocesan Orphan Board-(Managers of the Roman Catholic Orphan Asylums)—Mr. JOHN SIMON, JR., Pres., *4532 Lindell Blvd., St. Louis, 63108.* Tel: 314-367-5500.

Catholic Services for Children and Youth—WILLIAM J. MURPHY, Admin., *4140 Lindell Blvd., St. Louis, 63108.* Tel: 314-371-4980. See MISCELLANEOUS section for more information.

Archdiocesan Data Center—Mr. GERALD F. LAWLER, Dir. Mgmt. Information Systems, *4140 Lindell Blvd., St. Louis, 63108.* Tel: 314-371-0124.

Office for Ecumenical & Interreligious Affairs—Rev. VINCENT A. HEIER, Dir., *462 N. Taylor, St. Louis, 63108.* Tel: 314-531-9700; Fax: 314-531-2269.

Archdiocesan Office of Worship—Rev. PAUL J. NIEMANN, *7800 Kenrick Rd., St. Louis, 63119.* Tel: 314-961-4320, Ext. 117.

Archdiocesan Liturgical Commission—Sr. CATHY DOHERTY, S.S.N.D.; Mrs. ANA ANITA ATOK; Deacon GEORGE BEINKE; Dr. GLENN BYER; Rev. DONALD CAREY; Mrs. ELIZABETH COFFMAN; Deacon RICHARD COFFMAN; Mr. JIM COMBS; Ms. RUBY DOUTHET; Mrs. KATHY GIBLER; Mrs. SHARON MCGINNIS; Mrs. MARGE MEYER.

Archdiocesan Sacred Music Commission—Mr. JEFF BUSH; Mrs. MARY KAY CHRISTIAN; Ms. BECKY GAUGHAN; Ms. JOAN MAHER; Mr. CHRISTOPHER ORF; Sr. VIRGINIA MARIE PERKINS, O.S.U.; Mr. JOHN A. ROMERI; Ms. BRENDA SOBOLESKI.

Archdiocesan Sacred Art Commission—Mr. ROBERT BARRINGER; Bro. STEVE ERSPAMER, S.M.; Sr. GABRIEL MARY HOARE, S.L.; Ms. LEA KOESTERER; Ms. BETH PILLARSKI; Sr. GABRIELLA ROGENSKI, C.D.P.

Archdiocesan Human Rights Office / HRO System—Mr. THOMAS M. NOLAN, Dir.; Rev. Msgr. JOHN A. SHOCKLEE, M.A., Dir., Emeritus, *462 N. Taylor, St. Louis, 63108.* Tel: 314-652-6100; Fax: 314-531-2269.

Commission on Human Rights—

Domestic Social Development Divisions—

Black & Native American Missions Program—

International Justice & Peace Division—

Campaign for Human Development—

Parish Social Concerns & Social Concerns Education—

Committee on Women in the Church—

Black Catholic Congress / African American Catholics—

Catholic Legal Assistance Ministry—Tel: 314-454-6964.

Immigration Law Project—Tel: 314-454-6867.

General & Management—

Council of Catholic Youth—Mr. MICHAEL P. KALIST, Exec. Dir., *4140 Lindell Blvd., St. Louis, 63108.* Tel: 314-371-4980, Ext. 110.

Holy Childhood, Pontifical Association—Rev. Msgr. BERNARD H. SANDHEINRICH, Dir., *4140 Lindell Blvd., St. Louis, 63108.* Tel: 314-371-4980.

Holy Name Society—Rev. MARVIN C. KOPFF, Spiritual Dir.; Mr. JOSEPH A. RYAN, SR., Pres., *Mailing Address: Holy Name Society, P.O. Box 109435, St. Louis, 63119-6435.*

Latin American Apostolate, Archdiocese of St. Louis—Rev. Msgr. BERNARD H. SANDHEINRICH, Dir., *4140 Lindell Blvd., St. Louis, 63108.* Tel: 314-371-4980.

The Legion of Mary—JEAN M. LEONHARDT, Pres., *324 Algonquin Dr., Ballwin, 60311.* Tel: 314-230-0347. Spiritual Dirs.: Revs. ROBERT C. LISS; EDWARD HILGEMAN.

Pan y Amor—Rev. Msgr. BERNARD H. SANDHEINRICH, Dir., *4140 Lindell Blvd., St. Louis, 63108.* Tel: 314-371-4980.

Archdiocesan Newspaper "The St. Louis Review"—Rev. Msgr. DENNIS M. DELANEY, Editor; Mr. PAUL P. PENNICK, Mng. Editor; Mr. THOMAS L. COURTAWAY, Comptroller & Circulation Mgr., *462 N. Taylor, St. Louis, 63108.* Tel: 314-531-9700; Fax: 314-531-2269.

Archdiocesan Office of Stewardship & Development—Mr. FRANK J. COGNATA, JR., Chief Devel. Officer, *4445 Lindell Blvd., St. Louis, 63108.* Tel: 314-533-1887.

Archdiocesan Charitable Bequest Council—See MISCELLANEOUS section for more information.

Office for the Continuing Formation of Priests—Rev. ROBERT W. FINN, Dir., *7800 Kenrick Rd., St. Louis, 63119.* Tel: 314-961-4320, Ext. 428.

Priests' Mutual Benefit Society—Rev. Msgr. JOHN R. MAGUIRE, Pres.; Rev. Msgr. JOHN T. RONQUEST, Exec. Sec.; Rev. MARVIN KOPFF, Archbishop's Rep.-Retired Priests.

Priests' Purgatorial Society—Rev. Msgr. RICHARD F. STIKA, V.G., Pres.

Pro-Life—Mrs. MOLLY CORCORAN KERTZ, Dir./Coord., *462 N. Taylor Ave., St. Louis, 63108.* Tel: 314-531-3666.

Regina Cleri—Sr. GERALDINE VOGEL, Admin.; Rev. MARVIN KOPFF, Archbishop's Rep., *7850 Kenrick Rd., St. Louis, 63119.* Tel: 314-968-2240.

Society for the Propagation of the Faith—Rev. Msgr. BERNARD H. SANDHEINRICH, Dir., *4140 Lindell Blvd., St. Louis, 63108.* Tel: 314-371-4980.

Today and Tomorrow Education Foundation—BRIDGET FLOOD, Exec. Dir., *4140 Lindell Blvd., St. Louis, 63108.* Tel: 314-371-4980, Ext. 269.

Criminal Justice Ministry—1408 S. Tenth St., St. Louis, 63104. Tel: 314-241-8062.

Office of Communications—Rev. Msgr. DENNIS DELANEY, Dir., *462 N. Taylor Ave., St. Louis, 63108.* Tel: 314-531-9700; Fax: 314-531-2269.

St. Vincent de Paul Society of St. Louis—Mr. ROBERT J. O'REILLY, II, Pres.; Mr. ROBERT GRONEMEYER, Pres. Emeritus; Mr. ROBERT E. O'DONNELL, Exec. Sec.; Mr. RICHARD KLOHR, III, Vice Pres.; Mr. GLENNON CURRAN, Treas.; Rev. JAMES CORMACK, C.M., Spiritual Advisor; ROSE MARIE VOELKER, Sec., Office: *4141 Forest Park Blvd., St. Louis, 63108.* Tel: 314-531-2183; Fax: 314-531-6712.

Society of St. Vincent de Paul, Council of the United States—(Territory: United States)—Most Rev. J. TERRY STEIB, S.V.D., Bishop of Memphis, Spiritual Advisor; JOSEPH H. MUELLER, Pres. RITA W. PORTER, Exec. Sec./Dir., *58 Progress Pkwy., Hazelwood, 63043-3706.* Tel: 314-576-3993; Fax: 314-576-6755. See MISCELLANEOUS section for more information.

Schools / Catholic Education Office—Mr. GEORGE HENRY, Supt., *4140 Lindell Blvd., St. Louis, 63108.* Tel: 314-371-4980. See SCHOOLS section for more information.

St. Louis Roman Catholic Theological Seminaries, Inc.—Rev. Msgr. RICHARD F. STIKA, V.G., Sec., *4445 Lindell Blvd., St. Louis, 63108.* Tel: 314-533-1887.

Kenrick-Glennon Seminary (St. Louis Roman Catholic Theological Seminary-Kenrick School of Theology)—Rev. Msgr. GEORGE J. LUCAS, Pres./Rector.

Cardinal Glennon College—Rev. EDWARD M. RICE, Dir., *5200 Glennon Dr., St. Louis, 63119.* Tel: 314-644-0266. See SEMINARIES section for more information.

Archdiocesan Vocation Office—Rev. MICHAEL T. BUTLER, Dir.; Sr. JEANETTE HEMMER, C.PP.S, *5200 Glennon Dr., St. Louis, 63119.* Tel: 314-647-5270.

Archdiocesan Pastoral Council—In transition—

Archdiocesan Council of Priests—Most Rev. JUSTIN RIGALI, Pres.; Most Rev. EDWARD K. BRAXTON, V.G.; Most Rev. JOSEPH F. NAUMANN, V.G.; Most Rev. MICHAEL J. SHERIDAN, V.G.; Rev. Msgr. RICHARD F. STIKA, V.G., Chancellor Ex Officio; Rev. Msgr. GEORGE J. LUCAS, Rector, Kenrick Glennon Seminary; Revs. PETER BLAKE, Washington Deanery; RICHARD BOCKSKOPF, Northwest County Deanery; JOHN J. BRENNELL, Southwest County Deanery; JOHN G. DEMPSEY, Dir., Priests' Personnel Ex Officio; NORBERT A. ERNST, Festus Deanery, Exec. Comm. ROBERT W. FINN, Dir., Continuing Formation of Priests Sec. & Ex Officio; MICHAEL L. HENNING, St. Charles Deanery, Chm. JOHN M. SEPER, Ste. Genevieve Deanery; BRIAN P. SMITH, Northeast County Deanery; DENNIS R. STEHLY, Southeast County Deanery, Vice Chm. & Treas. GERALD T. WILL, North City Deanery; DALE P. WUNDERLICH, South City Deanery; JAMES H. BAKER, S.J., Religious-Teaching; JAMES B. CORMACK, C.M., Religious-Parish, Exec. Comm. ROBERT A. LILLY, M.M., Religious-Other.

Office of Priests' Personnel—Rev. JOHN G. DEMPSEY, Dir., *4532 Lindell Blvd., St. Louis, 63108.* Tel: 314-367-5530.

Archdiocesan Priests' Personnel Board—Rev. JOHN G. DEMPSEY, Personnel Dir.; Rev. Msgr. CHARLES J. FORST; Rev. Msgr. WILLIAM A. DRENNAN; Rev. Msgr. JAMES T. TELTHORST; Rev. Msgr. JAMES E. PIEPER; Revs. H. JOHN REIKER; PAUL J. ROTHSCHILD.

Archdiocesan Office of Urban and Community Affairs—Rev. Msgr. SALVATORE E. POLIZZI, Dir. Consultors: Dr. GEORGE D. WENDEL; LOUIS G. BERRA, *6052 Waterman, St. Louis, 63112.* Tel: 314-721-6340.

Archdiocesan Office of the Permanent Diaconate—Deacon MARTIN TOWEY, Ph.D., Dir., *7800 Kenrick Rd., St. Louis, 63119.* Tel: 314-961-4320, Ext. 401. Committee: Deacons ROBERT C. RIEGEL; STANLEY M. PETERSON, JR.; JOSEPH PEACOCK; E. RAYMOND KIELY; Mrs. BONNIE FORSTER; Mr. RICHARD HENNICKE; Mrs. ANGELA MENARD; Mrs. CAROL HERDLER; Mrs. JOAN DEISNER; Rev. PHILIP G. KRAHMAN.

Archdiocesan Office of Laity and Family Life—Mrs. SUSAN EDWARDS, Dir., *7800 Kenrick Rd., St. Louis, 63119.* Tel: 314-961-4320, Ext. 404.

Catholic Services Agencies Building—Mr. ROBERT J. FAHEY, Admin. & Bldg. Mgr., *4140 Lindell Blvd., St. Louis, 63108.* Tel: 314-371-4980.

Archdiocesan Pastoral Center—Deacon ROBERT SNYDER, Admin., *7800 Kenrick Rd., St. Louis, 63119.* Tel: 314-961-4320, Ext. 114.

CLERGY, PARISHES, MISSIONS AND PAROCHIAL SCHOOLS

CITY OF ST. LOUIS
(St. Louis County)

1—CATHEDRAL BASILICA OF ST. LOUIS (1896), Rev. Msgr. James T. Telthorst. In res., Most Rev. Edward K. Braxton, V.G.; Revs. Bryan M. Kuchar; Paul J. Niemann.
Res., 4431 Lindell Blvd., 63108. Tel: 314-533-2824; Fax: 314-533-2844.
School—Tel: 314-531-3375. Mary Lou Storment, Prin.
Lay Teachers 12; Students 221.
Catechesis/Religious Programs—Students 265.

2—EPIPHANY OF OUR LORD (1911), Revs. Dale P. Wunderlich; Patrick J. Christopher; Deacon Edward Flint.
Res., 6596 Smiley Ave., 63139. Tel: 314-781-1199; Fax: 314-645-8760.
School—Tel: 314-781-5626. Mr. Tom Archer, Prin.
Sisters of St. Dominic 1; Lay Teachers 21; Students 400.
Catechesis/Religious Programs—Students 427.

3—HOLY FAMILY (1898), Revs. Robert G. Leibrecht; Michael Freymuth.
Res., 4125 Humphrey St., 63116. Tel: 314-772-8292.
School—Tel: 314-771-2007. Mary Ann Kauffman, Prin.
Lay Teachers 12; Students 205.
Catechesis/Religious Programs—Students 200.

4—HOLY GUARDIAN ANGELS. Closed. For inquiries for parish records contact the Chancery.

5—HOLY INNOCENTS (1893), Revs. George P. Brennan; Vincent A. Heier; Deacon Fred Hummel.
Res., 4923 Odell St., 63139. Tel: 314-776-6440; Fax: 314-776-6441.
School—Tel: 314-771-2188.
Lay Teachers 12; Students 136.

6—IMMACULATE CONCEPTION-ST. HENRY (1865), Rev. John Gavin, O.S.A.; Deacon James McGrath. In res., Rev. Francis Lawlor, O.S.A.
Res., 3120 Lafayette Ave., 63104. Tel: 314-776-1333.

7—IMMACULATE HEART OF MARY (1951), Revs. H. John Reiker; Robert H. Babka. In res., Rev. Msgr. Dennis M. Delaney.
Res., 4092 Blow St., 63116. Tel: 314-481-7543; Fax: 314-481-6316.
School—4070 Blow St., 63116. Tel: 314-832-1678. Mrs. Christina Cheak, Prin.
Lay Teachers 21; Students 356.
Catechesis/Religious Programs—Students 360.

8—MOST BLESSED SACRAMENT (1907), Rev. Michael J. Witt; Deacon Cliff Gholston.
Res., 5017 Northland Ave., 63113. Tel: 314-367-5244.
School—Bishop Healy School, 2727 N. Kingshighway, 63113. Tel: 314-361-5696.
Sisters 1; Lay Teachers 22; Students 412.

9—MOST HOLY NAME OF JESUS. Merged with Most Holy Trinity.

10—MOST HOLY ROSARY (1891). Closed. See St. Elizabeth, Mother of John the Baptist.

11—MOST HOLY TRINITY (1848), Rev. Richard H. Creason; Deacon Robert S. Smerek; Sr. Joyelle Proot, S.S.N.D., Pastoral Assoc.
Res., 3519 N. Fourteenth St., 63107-3796. Tel: 314-241-9165; Fax: 314-436-9291.
School—1435 Mallinckrodt St., 63107-3796. Tel: 314-231-9014. David Chiodini, Prin.
Sisters 1; Lay Teachers 12; Students 157.
Convent—Tel: 314-621-6835.
Sisters 1.

12—OUR LADY OF MOUNT CARMEL. Closed. For inquiries for parish records contact the Chancery.

13—OUR LADY OF PERPETUAL HELP. Merged with Most Holy Trinity.

14—OUR LADY OF SORROWS (1907), Revs. Michael Campbell; Mitchell Doyen; John R. Vien; Rev. Msgr. James J. Holland, Senior Priest; Deacons Robert Wertz; Robert H. Schnable.
Res., 5020 Rhodes Ave., 63109. Tel: 314-351-1600; Fax: 314-351-1602.
School—S. Kingshighway, 63109. Tel: 314-353-1451.
Sisters of Notre Dame 2; Lay Teachers 38; Students 525.
Catechesis/Religious Programs—Students 550.

15—OUR LADY OF THE HOLY CROSS (1864), Rev. Patrick K. Hambrough; Deacon Donald Driscoll.
Res., 8115 Church Rd., 63147. Tel: 314-381-0323.
School—1018 Baden Ave., 63147. Tel: 314-383-4782; Fax: 314-383-5982.
Sisters 3; Lay Teachers 8; Students 120.

16—RESURRECTION OF OUR LORD (1930), Revs. Thomas W. Wyrsch; Robert W. Argent.
3900 Meramec St., 63116. Tel: 314-832-7023.
School—3800 Meramec St., 63116. Tel: 314-772-6745; Fax: 314-772-6745. Ms. Kathy Sodlacek, Prin.
Sisters 2; Lay Teachers 9; Students 173.

17—VISITATION-ST. ANN'S SHRINE (1881) (African American), Rev. Timothy R. Cook.
Res., 4515 Evans Ave., 63113. Tel: 314-535-8804.
School—Bishop Healy at Blessed Sacrament, Tel: 314-367-5696.

18—ST. ADALBERT/ST. PHILIP NERI. See St. Simon of Cyrene.

19—ST. AGATHA (1871), Rev. James Rodis.
Res., 3239 S. 9th St., 63118. Tel: 314-772-1603; Fax: 314-772-7609.

20—ST. AGNES. Closed. For inquiries for parish records contact the Chancery.

21—ST. ALOYSIUS GONZAGA (1892) (Italian), Revs. John Blomberg; Ralph E. Stroot, Senior Priest; Deacon Richard C. Lake.
Res., 5608 N. Magnolia Ave., 63139. Tel: 314-647-2541; Fax: 314-647-2011. [JC]
School—5628 N. Magnolia Ave., 63139. Tel: 314-647-7056. Sr. Michele Intravia, O.S.U., Prin.
Sisters 2; Lay Teachers 11; Students 164.
Preschool—5625 S. Magnolia, 63139. Tel: 314-645-2363.
Extended Day Care—.
Lay Teachers 5; Students 50.

22—ST. ALPHONSUS LIGUORI (1867) (African American), Revs. Maurice Nutt, C.SS.R.; Richard Potts, C.SS.R.; Deacons Leslie A. Johnson; Henry Buckner. In res., Bro. Terrance Burke, C.SS.R.
Res., 1118 N. Grand Blvd., 63106. Tel: 314-533-0304; Fax: 314-533-4260.

23—ST. AMBROSE (1903) (Italian), Revs. Thomas J. Santen; James J. Ramacciotti; Sr. Patricia Kofron, A.S.C.J., Pastoral Assoc.; Deacon John J. Stoverink.
Res., 5130 Wilson Ave., 63110. Tel: 314-771-1228; Fax: 314-771-0454.
School—5110 Wilson Ave., 63110. Tel: 314-772-1437; Fax: 314-771-4560. Sr. Patricia Brady, A.S.C.J., Prin.
Apostles of the Sacred Heart of Jesus 5; Lay Teachers 19; Students 344.
Catechesis/Religious Programs—Students 344.

24—ST. ANN, MOTHER B.V.M.. Closed. For inquiries for parish records contact the Chancery.

25—ST. ANTHONY OF PADUA (1863), Revs. Benet A. Fonck, O.F.M.; Kenneth Rosswog, O.F.M. Pastoral Assocs.: Bros. Loyola Freightman, O.F.M.; Richard Baranski, O.F.M.
Res., 3140 Meramec St., 63118. Tel: 314-353-7470; Fax: 314-353-0958.
School—4235 Compton Ave., 63118. Tel: 314-752-3397; Fax: 314-752-4384. Ms. Joan Feldmann, Prin.
Lay Teachers 11; Students 161.

26—ST. BARBARA. Closed. See St. Augustine for details.

27—ST. AUGUSTINE (1992), Rev. Robert J. Gettinger. Center: 1371 Hamilton Ave., 63112. Tel: 314-385-1934; Fax: 314-385-2949. Consolidation of St. Barbara, St. Rose of Lima, St. Edward, St. Mark and Notre Dame de Lourdes (Wellston).

28—ST. BONIFACE (1859) (German), Rev. Thomas M. Begley; Deacon Earl Tresch.
Res., 7622 Michigan Ave., 63111. Tel: 314-638-1438; Fax: 314-638-1438.

29—ST. BRIDGET OF ERIN (1853) (African American), Rev. Msgr. Richard A. Buchheit.
Res., 2401 Carr St., 63106. Tel: 314-231-8870; Fax: 314-231-3780.
School—Central Catholic/St. Nicholas School, 1106 N. Jefferson Ave., 63106. Tel: 314-231-6254.
Sisters 2; Lay Teachers 14; Students 309.

30—ST. CECILIA (1906), Rev. Francis X. Blood. In res., Rev. Gregory G. Kirsch.
Res., 5418 Louisiana Ave., 63111. Tel: 314-351-1318; Fax: 314-351-3372.
Church—Eiler & Alaska Ave., 63111.
School—906 Eichelberger Ave., 63111. Tel: 314-353-2455. Sr. Suzanne Laughlin, O.P., Prin.
Lay Teachers 11; Students 220.

31—ST. CRONAN (1878), Revs. Joseph D. Ross; James A. Krings.
Res., 1203 S. Boyle Ave., 63110. Tel: 314-289-9545; Fax: 314-289-9546.

32—ST. EDWARD, KING. Closed. See St. Augustine for details.

33—ST. ELIZABETH, MOTHER OF JOHN THE BAPTIST (1891) (African American), Rev. Carl J. Scheble; Deacons Nathaniel E. Shipp; Jesse Bell.
Res., 4330 Shreve Ave., 63115. Tel: 314-381-4145; Fax: 314-381-2212.
School—St. Engelbert "FOCUS" Consolidated School, 4720 Carter Ave., 63115. Tel: 314-389-0401. Ms. Barbara Soete, Prin.
Religious 4; Lay Teachers 9; Students 212.
St. Engelbert "FOCUS" Day Care Ctr.—4746 Carter Ave., 63115. Tel: 314-389-0720. Ms. Belinda Palmer, Dir.
Lay Teachers 18; Students 105.

34—ST. FRANCIS DE SALES (1867) (German), Rev. John D. Bolderson; Deacon Thomas A. Buhr. In res., Rev. John P. Comer.
Res., 2653 Ohio Ave., 63118. Tel: 314-771-3100; Fax: 314-771-3295.
School—2647 Ohio Ave., Tel: 314-776-0883.

35—ST. FRANCIS XAVIER (1841). (College). Rev. Leonard E. Kraus, S.J.; Deacon Bro. Anthony I. Messineo, T.O.R.S.Carm.
3628 Lindell Blvd., 63108. Tel: 314-977-7300; Fax: 314-977-7315.
Catechesis/Religious Programs—Students 156.

36—ST. GABRIEL THE ARCHANGEL (1934), Revs. Charles E. Burgoon; C. Eugene Morris; Edwin J. Burmester; Deacons Phillip Gerdes; James Volansky.
Res., 6303 Nottingham Ave., 63109. Tel: 314-353-6303; Fax: 314-353-7704.
School—4700 Tamm Ave., 63109. Tel: 314-353-1229.
Lay Teachers 30; Students 554.

37—ST. HEDWIG (1904), Rev. Msgr. Joseph W. Baker.
Res., 3202 Pulaski St., 63111. Tel: 314-481-2486.

38—ST. JAMES THE GREATER (1860) (Irish-Italian), Rev. Msgr. Edward J. Deutschmann; Rev. David E. Rauch.
Res., 6401 Wade Ave., 63139. Tel: 314-645-0167; Fax: 314-645-0168.
School—1360 Tamm Ave., 63139. Tel: 314-647-5244; Fax: 314-647-8237. Ms. Karen Battaglia, Prin.
Lay Teachers 13; Students 204.
Catechesis/Religious Programs—Students 287.

39—ST. JOAN OF ARC (1941), Rev. Msgr. Lawrence J. Walsh; Rev. Bradley E. Modde; Deacons Daniel H. Henroid; Wayne Bryant; Gregory Klump. In res., Rev. Msgr. Richard J. Gallagher; Rev. John G. Dempsey.
Res., 5800 Oleatha St., 63139. Tel: 314-832-2838; Fax: 314-352-9350.
School—Tel: 314-752-4171. Mrs. Judy Talleur, Prin.
Lay Teachers 30; Students 490.

40—ST. JOHN THE APOSTLE AND EVANGELIST (1847), Rev. John J. Johnson.
Res., 15 Plaza Sq., 63103. Tel: 314-421-3467.

41—ST. JOHN THE BAPTIST (1914), Revs. John J. Ghio; Edward R. Goldian, S.J.; Bro. Padraic Campbell, O.S.F. In res., Rev. Jeffrey N. Knight.
4200 Delor St., 63116. Tel: 314-353-1255.
School—4170 Delor St., 63116. Tel: 314-481-6654.
Sisters of the Most Precious Blood, O'Fallon 1; Lay Teachers 21; Students 404.
High School—5021 Adkins St., 63116. Tel: 314-351-5604; Fax: 314-351-3050. Bro. David A. Migliorino, O.S.F., Prin.
Sisters 3; Lay Teachers 29; Students 440.
Catechesis/Religious Programs—Students 844.

42—ST. JOHN NEPOMUK (1854) (Czech), Rev. Joseph J. Portucheck.
Res., 1625 S. 11th St., 63104. Tel: 314-231-0141.

43—SHRINE OF ST. JOSEPH, CAPUCHIN FATHERS (1844) (German). Unassigned.
Res., 1220 N. 11th St., 63106. Tel: 314-231-9407; Fax: 314-231-0802.

44—ST. JOSEPH (1904) (Croatian), Revs. Joseph M. Abramovic, O.F.M.; Ivo Sivric, O.F.M.
Res., 2112 S. 12th St., 63104. Tel: 314-771-0958.

45—ST. LIBORIUS. Closed. For inquiries for parish records contact the Chancery.

46—BASILICA OF ST. LOUIS, THE KING (1770), Rev. Msgr. Bernard H. Sandheinrich; Revs. Michael L. Seidel; Richard J. Quirk.
Res., 209 Walnut St., 63102. Tel: 314-231-3250; Fax: 314-231-4280.

47—ST. MARGARET OF SCOTLAND (1899), Rev. Kenneth Brown.
Res., 3854 Flad Ave., 63110. Tel: 314-776-0363.
School—3864 Castlemen, 63110. Tel: 314-776-7837.
Sisters 5; Lay Teachers 13; Students 256.

48—ST. MARK, EVANGELIST. Closed. See St. Augustine for details.

49—ST. MARY MAGDALEN (1919), Very Rev. Dennis E. Doerhoff, V.F.; Rev. Thomas C. Bryon; Deacon J. Gerard Quinn. In res., Rev. Mark Rivituso.
Res., 4924 Bancroft Ave., 63109. Tel: 314-352-2111; Fax: 314-481-7661.
School—4911 Sutherland Ave., 63109. Tel: 314-832-3360; Fax: 314-481-7661.
Lay Teachers 16; Students 246.

50—SS. MARY AND JOSEPH (1821), Rev. Robert L. Szydlowski; Rev. Msgr. Fenton J. Runge, Senior Priest.
Res., 6304 Minnesota Ave., 63111. Tel: 314-481-6304.

51—ST. MARY OF VICTORIES, Rev. Msgr. Donald E. Rau.
Res., 744 S. 3rd St., 63102. Tel: 314-231-9062.

52—ST. MATTHEW, APOSTLE (1893), Revs. Matthew D. Ruhl, S.J.; Jeffrey D. Harrison, S.J.; Dirk Dunfee, S.J.; Robert J. Luchi, S.J.
Res., 2715 N. Sarah St., 63113. Tel: 314-531-6443. [CEM]

53—ST. NICHOLAS (1865), Rev. Richard R. Andrus, S.V.D.; Deacon Stanley Peterson. Pastoral Assocs.: Sr. Antona Ebo, F.S.M.; Ms. Ella L. Scott.
Res., 701 N. 18th St., 63103. Tel: 314-231-2860; Fax: 314-231-9823.
School—Central Catholic/St. Nicholas School, 1805 Lucas St., 63103. Tel: 314-421-1822.
Lay Teachers 40; Students 400.
Chapel—Christ the King.

54—ST. PATRICK (1981), Revs. Valentine Young, O.F.M.Cap.; Simon R. Conrad, O.F.M.Cap.; Canice Froelich, O.F.M.Cap.; Simeon Gallagher, O.F.M.Cap.
Res., 1000 N. 7th St., 63101. Tel: 314-231-9991.
Shrine—Shrine of St. Joseph, Tel: 314-231-9407.

55—SS. PETER AND PAUL (1849), Rev. Bruce H. Forman; Deacons Joseph T. Haefner; Thomas Gorski.
Res., 1919 S. 7th Blvd., 63104. Tel: 314-231-9923; Fax: 314-231-9923.

56—ST. SIMON OF CYRENE (1993), Rev. Gerald T. Will; Deacons Raymond V. Mroczkowski; Fred Dodson.
Res., 5076 Durant Ave., 63115. Tel: 314-385-0068; Fax: 314-385-5339.

57—ST. PIUS THE FIFTH (1905) (Irish), Rev. Michael J. Lydon; Deacon Walter W. Christ. Pastoral Assocs.: Sr. Paulette Weindell, C.PP.S.; Sr. Dorothy Ann Katke, C.PP.S. In res., Rev. Hyacinth Okwara (Nigeria).
Res., 3310 S. Grand Blvd., 63118. Tel: 314-772-1525; Fax: 314-772-5615.
School—3530 Utah, 63118. Tel: 314-773-8770. Sr. Barbara Siderewicz, O.S.F., Prin.
Sisters 3; Lay Teachers 9; Students 166.

58—ST. RAPHAEL THE ARCHANGEL (1950), Rev. Msgr. William A. Drennan; Rev. Matthew L. O'Toole. In res., Most Rev. Michael J. Sheridan, V.G.
Res., 6047 Bishops Pl., 63109. Tel: 314-352-8100; Fax: 314-353-6603.
School—Tel: 314-352-9474. Mrs. Susan Brown, Prin.
Sisters 1; Lay Teachers 12; Students 186.
Catechesis/Religious Programs—Students 289.

59—ST. ROCH, Rev. Msgr. Salvatore E. Polizzi; Rev. Lawrence A. Herzog. In res., Rev. Msgr. Adrian I. Dwyer.
Res., 6052 Waterman Ave., 63112. Tel: 314-721-6340; Fax: 314-721-1656.
School—6040 Waterman Ave., 63112. Tel: 314-721-2595. Mrs. Gloria Openlander, Prin.
Lay Teachers 15; Students 195.

60—ST. ROSE OF LIMA. Closed. See St. Augustine for details.

61—ST. SEBASTIAN (1953), Rev. Msgr. Richard J. Gallagher Temp. Admin.; Deacon Herbert L. Ehrhard.
Res., 9950 Glen Owen Dr., 63136. Tel: 314-868-0730; Fax: 314-868-0731.
School—1826 Chambers Rd., 63136. Tel: 314-869-1923.
Lay Teachers 10; Students 155.

62—ST. STANISLAUS KOSTKA (1880) (Polish), Rev. Msgr. Ted L. Wojcicki; Rev. Wesley Kozlowski (Poland).
Res., 1413 N. 20th St., 63106. Tel: 314-421-5948.

63—ST. STEPHEN, PROTOMARTYR (1926), Revs. Charles Barthel; Ronald Chochol, Senior Assoc.
Res., 3949 Wilmington Ave., 63116. Tel: 314-481-1133; Fax: 314-481-6036.
School—3929 Wilmington Ave., 63116. Tel: 314-752-4700. Sr. Mary Eschbacher, C.S.J., Prin.
Lay Teachers 14; Students 265.

64—ST. TERESA OF AVILA (1865), Rev. Robert E. Zinser.
Res., 3636 N. Market St., 63113. Tel: 314-371-1190; Fax: 314-531-1047.
Missionaries of Charity—3629 Cottage, 63113. Tel: 314-533-2777.

65—ST. THOMAS OF AQUIN (1882), Rev. Chau Pham, S.V.D.
Res., 3949 Iowa Ave., 63118. Tel: 314-772-2644; Fax: 314-776-4639.

66—ST. VINCENT DE PAUL (1841), Rev. James B. Cormack, C.M.; Sr. Jackie Toben, S.S.N.D., Pastoral Assoc.; Mr. Dennis Wells, Pastoral Assoc. In res., Rev. William E. Hartenbach, C.M.
Res., 1408 S. Tenth St., 63104. Tel: 314-231-9328; Fax: 314-621-2232.

67—ST. WENCESLAUS (1895) (Bohemian), Very Rev. Joseph Paul Roelke, M.S.F.; Deacon George W. Miller. In res., Rev. Eugene Ronan, M.S.F.; Bro. Kenneth J. Schwartz, M.S.F.
Res., 3014 Oregon Ave., 63118-1498. Tel: 314-865-1020; Fax: 314-664-8260.
Catechesis/Religious Programs—Notre Dame Elementary School, 3022 Oregon Ave., 63118-1498. Tel: 314-776-0883.
Students 164.

CHURCHES IN ST. LOUIS COUNTY

Affton, St. Dominic Savio (1956), Revs. Edward F. Feuerbacher; Richard J. Heman; Deacon James L. Murphy.
Res., 6120 Pebble Hill Dr., 63123. Tel: 314-353-7629; Fax: 314-481-2908.
Church—7748 MacKenzie Rd., 63123.
School—Tel: 314-832-4161. Sr. Ann Gregory Bischof, O.P., Prin.
Lay Teachers 16; Students 236.

St. Timothy (1958), Rev. David A. Walter; Deacons Philip Caruana; Gene Hoffmann.
Res., 816 Union Rd., St. Louis, 63123. Tel: 314-631-4244; Fax: 314-631-4250.
School—824 Union Rd., St. Louis, 63123. Tel: 314-631-0991; 638-4557. Michael Talleur, Prin.
Lay Teachers 12; Students 249.
Catechesis/Religious Programs—Students 265.

Seven Holy Founders (1927), Revs. Timothy M. Kremen, O.S.M.; Francis Martin, O.S.M.; John Fontana, O.S.M.; Deacon Charles Lombardo.
Office: 6820 Aliceton Ave., St. Louis, 63123. Tel: 314-638-3938; Fax: 314-638-0613.
Church—6741 Rock Hill Rd., St. Louis, 63123. Tel: 314-631-3938.
School—6737 Rock Hill Rd., St. Louis, 63123. Tel: 314-631-8149. Miss Barbara Peach, Prin.
Lay Teachers 35; Students 509.
Catechesis/Religious Programs—Tel: 314-631-2333.
Students 164.

Ballwin, Holy Infant (1954), Rev. Msgr. Jerome J. Buchheit; Revs. Joseph G. Kempf; Joseph R. Monahan; Deacons John A. O'Leary; Kenneth C. Clemens.
Res., 627 Dennison Dr., 63021. Tel: 314-227-7440; Fax: 314-227-4548.
School—Tel: 314-227-0802; Fax: 314-227-9184. Sr. Rosario Delaney, R.S.M., Prin.
Sisters of Mercy (Meath Mercy Generalate, Ireland) 4; Lay Teachers 29; Students 820.
Catechesis/Religious Programs—Students 630.

Bellefontaine Neighbors, Our Lady of Good Counsel (1951), Revs. Donald R. Wester; John E. Vogler.
Res., 1160 St. Cyr Rd., St. Louis, 63137. Tel: 314-867-1441; Fax: 314-867-1442.
School—1134 St. Cyr Rd., St. Louis, 63137. Tel: 314-867-2400; Fax: 314-867-3776. Sr. Barbara Thomas, A.S.C.J., Prin.
Sisters 5; Lay Teachers 9; Students 204.
Convent—1142 St. Cyr Rd., St. Louis, 63137. Tel: 314-868-3067.

Bel-Ridge, St. Thomas More (1955), Rev. Norbert A. Mersinger; Deacons Singleton Harris; Edward C. Fronick.
Res., 3425 St. Thomas More Pl., St. Louis, 63121. Tel: 314-428-7900.

Berkeley, Holy Ghost (1923), Rev. Aloysius A. Forst.
Res., 6314 Garfield Ave., 63134. Tel: 314-522-1200.

Bissell Hills, St. Jerome (1952), Rev. Mark A. Dolan.
Res., 10235 Ashbrook Dr., St. Louis, 63137. Tel: 314-868-2310; Fax: 314-868-3919.
School—Tel: 314-867-2100.
Lay Teachers 21; Students 318.

Brentwood, St. Mary Magdalen (1912), Revs. Bernard J. Wilkins; Clark B. Maes; Deacon Leroy Martin.
Res., 2618 Brentwood Blvd., 63144. Tel: 314-961-8400; Fax: 314-961-7019.
School—8762 Magdalen Ave., 63144. Tel: 314-961-0149; Fax: 314-961-7208. Mrs. Pamela Brown, Prin.
Sisters 1; Lay Teachers 12; Students 180.
Catechesis/Religious Programs—Students 180.

Bridgeton, St. Mary (1852), Rev. William J. Baier.
Res., 4603 Long Rd., 63044. Tel: 314-731-0593. [CEM]
School—4601 Long Rd., 63044. Tel: 314-731-3147.
Lay Teachers 14; Students 125.

St. Lawrence the Martyr (1960), Rev. James E. Murphy; Deacons Wm. Walbridge; Simon Bachu; R. Fielding Harrison.
Res., 4335 DuPage Dr., 63044. Tel: 314-739-0496; Fax: 314-739-2768.
School—4329 DuPage Dr., 63044. Tel: 314-739-3123.

Chesterfield, Ascension (1923), Rev. Msgr. Joseph Pins; Revs. Richard Nelke; Jeffrey G. Vomund; R. John Schwaig; Deacons Larry Hutti; Frank Chauvin; William P. Wunderlich; Robert Brooks; Robert Keeney.
Res., 230 Santa Maria Dr., 63005. Tel: 314-532-3304; Fax: 314-532-3518.
Preschool: Ascension Early Childhood Center—63005. Tel: 314-532-3375.
School—238 Santa Maria Dr., 63005. Tel: 314-532-1151; Fax: 314-532-6502. Mrs. Laurie Ann O'Connor, Prin.
Lay Teachers 23; Students 540.
Catechesis/Religious Programs—Tel: 314-532-1136; 532-9344 (Adult Education).
Students 690.

Incarnate Word (1965), Revs. Robert J. Hermann; Eugene E. Utrup; Mark S. Bozada; Deacons Jerome Toohey; Glennon Bourbon.
Res., 13416 Olive Blvd., 63017. Tel: 314-576-5366; Fax: 314-576-2046.
School—Tel: 314-878-3207. Lucia Signorelli, Prin.
Sisters 2; Lay Teachers 21; Students 429.
Catechesis/Religious Programs—Tel: 314-878-0442. Mrs. Denise DeFord, D.R.E.
Students 225.

Clayton, St. Joseph (1842), Rev. Msgr. Jerome F. Wilkerson; Rev. Gerald J. Kleba; Deacon Albert Williams.
Res., 106 N. Meramec Ave., 63105. Tel: 314-726-1221; Fax: 314-721-5110.

Catechesis/Religious Programs—Tel: 314-727-2271. Mrs. Kathleen Wolfersberger, D.R.E.
Students 125.

Concord Village, St. Simon the Apostle (1959), Revs. William B. Ahrens; James B. Wilke; Rev. Msgr. John T. Ronquest; Deacon Carl Beckman.
Res., 11011 Mueller Rd., St. Louis, 63123. Tel: 314-842-3848; Fax: 314-842-9829.
Preschool—11015 Mueller Rd., St. Louis, 63123. Tel: 314-842-3435.
School—11019 Mueller Rd., St. Louis, 63123. Tel: 314-842-0181; Fax: 414-842-7206.
Lay Teachers 24; Students 487.
Catechesis/Religious Programs—Students 145.

Crestwood, St. Elizabeth of Hungary (1956), Rev. Thomas J. Haley; Deacons Robert Snyder; Robert Kiechlin. In res., Revs. Donald J. Hoffman; John M. Kilcullen.
Res., 1420 S. Sappington Rd., 63126. Tel: 314-968-0760; Fax: 314-968-8023.
School—1414 S. Sappington Rd., 63126. Tel: 314-962-9698. Sr. Charlotte Flarlong, Prin.
Sisters 1; Lay Teachers 13; Students 197.
Catechesis/Religious Programs—Students 90.
Convent—1405 S. Sappington Rd., 63126. Tel: 314-961-2630.

Creve Coeur

1—St. Anselm (1966), Revs. Gerard Garrigan, O.S.B.; R. Benedict Allin, O.S.B.; D. Ralph Wright, O.S.B.; Deacon William J. McKenna; Miss Barbara Peiffer, Pastoral Assoc.
Res., 530 S. Mason Rd., St. Louis, 63141. Tel: 314-878-2120; Fax: 314-878-2199.
Catechesis/Religious Programs—Students 235.

2—St. John Bosco (1972), Rev. Patrick J. O'Laughlin. In res., Rev. Msgr. Rowland Gannon; Rev. David T. Thomas; Deacon Charles W. Georges.
Res., 12934 Marine Ave., St. Louis, 63146. Tel: 314-434-1312; Fax: 314-434-1315.
Catechesis/Religious Programs—Tel: 314-878-6492.
Students 221.

3—St. Monica (1872), Rev. Msgr. Nicholas A. Schneider; Rev. Raymond D. Hager; Deacons John W. Baker; Michael H. Dalton; Robert K. Gamache; Millard R. Miller. In res., Rev. Charles C. Deister.
Res., 12136 Olive Blvd., 63141-6629. Tel: 314-434-4211; Fax: 314-434-5978. [CEM]
School—12132 Olive Blvd., 63141-6698. Tel: 314-434-2173; Fax: 314-434-7689. Mrs. Susan E. Rohman, Prin.
Lay Teachers 26; Students 425.

4—Our Lady of the Pillar (1938), Rev. James M. Tobin, S.M.; Deacon Norman B. Werner. In res., Rev. J. Donald Cahill, S.M.
Res., 401 S. Lindbergh Blvd., St. Louis, 63131. Tel: 314-993-2280; Fax: 314-993-6462.
School—Tel: 314-993-3353; Fax: 314-993-2172.
Franciscan Sisters of Our Lady of Perpetual Help 3; Lay Teachers 24; Students 213.
Convent—403 S. Lindbergh Blvd., St. Louis, 63131. Tel: 314-993-3666.

5—St. Richard (1963), Rev. C. Robert Dorhauer. In res., Rev. Msgr. Vernon E. Gardin.
Res., 11223 Schuetz Rd., St. Louis, 63146. Tel: 314-432-6224; Fax: 314-432-6030.
School—11211 Schuetz Rd., St. Louis, 63146. Tel: 314-872-3152; Fax: 314-872-7326. Mr. Michael R. Corley, Prin.
Sisters 2; Lay Teachers 14; Students 168.

Des Peres, St. Clement (1951), Rev. Msgr. James E. Pieper; Rev. Mark G. Whitman. In res., Rev. William H. Thurmer.
Res., 1510 Bopp Rd., St. Louis, 63131. Tel: 314-965-0709; Fax: 314-965-1486.
School—1508 Bopp Rd., St. Louis, 63131. Tel: 314-822-1903; Fax: 314-822-8371. Mary Christina Reichardt, Prin.
Lay Teachers 30; Students 435.

Ellisville, St. Clare of Assisi (1963), Revs. Richard E. Hanneke; Charles M. Frankey.
Res., 15642 Clayton Rd., 63011. Tel: 314-394-7307; Fax: 314-394-6264.
School—Tel: 314-227-8654. Mrs. Denny Bram, Prin.
Sisters 1; Lay Teachers 18; Students 358.
Catechesis/Religious Programs—Tel: 314-394-4368.
Students 456.

Eureka, Sacred Heart (1889), Rev. Alexander R. Anderson.
Res., 350 E. Fourth St., 63025. Tel: 314-938-5048.
School—Tel: 314-938-4602. Patricia J. Corley, Prin.
Sisters 1; Lay Teachers 11; Students 260.
Catechesis/Religious Programs—Students 213.

Fenton, St. Paul (1878), Rev. Richard F. Everding; Rev. Msgr. Robert J. Muesenfechter; Deacon John Weatherholt.
Res., 15 Forest Knoll, 63026. Tel: 314-343-1234; Fax: 314-343-4809. [CEM]
School—465 New Smizer Mill Rd., 63026. Tel: 314-343-4333.
Religious 2; Lay Teachers 23; Students 418.
Catechesis/Religious Programs—Tel: 314-343-1678.
Students 525.

Ferguson, Good Shepherd (1958), Rev. Gregory R. Mikesch.
Res., 921 Smith Ave., 63135. Tel: 314-521-1008; Fax: 314-521-1034.
School—1050 Smith Ave., 63135. Tel: 314-524-4332.
Sisters 2; Lay Teachers 12; Students 230.

Sts. John and James (1882), Rev. Timothy M. Foley; Deacon L. Jerome Marren.
Res., 140 N. Elizabeth Ave., 63135. Tel: 314-522-0275.
School—150 N. Elizabeth Ave., 63135. Tel: 314-522-3888.
Catechesis/Religious Programs—Students 310.

Our Lady of Guadalupe (1954), Rev. A. John Schuler.
Res., 17 Hawkesbury Dr., 63121. Tel: 314-522-9264; Fax: 314-522-8461.
School—1115 S. Florissant Rd., 63121. Tel: 314-524-1948.
Lay Teachers 9; Students 180. Principals: Sharon J. Morgenthaler; Kathryn Sedlacek.
Catechesis/Religious Programs—Students 37.

Florissant

1—North American Martyrs (1954), Rev. James J. Byrnes; Deacons Robert J. Powers; Peter Gounis.
Res., 1400 S. Lafayette St., 63031. Tel: 314-837-9304; Fax: 314-837-9305.
School—Tel: 314-831-2440; Fax: 314-831-2398.
Lay Teachers 13; Students 170.

2—Our Lady of Fatima (1950), Rev. Thomas J. Schaab; Deacon Andrew Neimeyer.
Res., 4550 Washington St., 63033. Tel: 314-837-9366; Fax: 314-837-9367.
School—4500 Washington St., 63033. Tel: 314-921-0437.
Lay Teachers 12; Students 215.
Catechesis/Religious Programs—Students 220.

3—St. Angela Merici (1962), Revs. Ferdinand J. Wesloh; James W. Dyer.
Res., 14005 Davey Dr., 63034. Tel: 314-838-6565; Fax: 314-838-6566.
School—3860 N. Hwy. 67, 63034. Tel: 314-831-8012.
Lay Teachers 24; Students 440.

4—St. Christopher (1967), Rev. Donald L. Dyer; Deacons Kenneth M. Potzman; George A. Graham; George Blase.
Res., 11575 Old Halls Ferry Rd., 63033. Tel: 314-839-2427; Fax: 314-839-2428.

5—St. Dismas (1956), Rev. Robert W. Burkemper; Deacon Herbert B. Gettemeier.
Res., 2650 Parker Rd., 63033. Tel: 314-837-3410; Fax: 314-837-6628.
School—1220 Paddock Dr., 63033. Tel: 314-837-0369.
Lay Teachers 14; Students 215.
Catechesis/Religious Programs—St. Thomas the Apostle, 500 St. Catherine, 63033. Tel: 314-921-3023; Fax: 314-921-6724.
Students 60.

6—St. Ferdinand (1788), Revs. Gary Gebelein; Michael G. Murphy; Glennon Goellner; Deacon Raymond C. Hennicke.
Res., 1765 Charbonier Rd., 63031. Tel: 314-837-3165; Fax: 314-837-3166.
School—Tel: 314-921-2201; Fax: 314-921-2253.
Sisters of Loretto at the Foot of the Cross 1; Sisters of the Most Precious Blood 1; Franciscan 1; Lay Teachers 17; Students 314.
Catechesis/Religious Programs—Students 380.

7—Sacred Heart (1866) (German), Revs. John Paul Hess; Thomas C. Miller.
Res., 751 N. Jefferson St., 63031. Tel: 314-837-3757; Fax: 314-837-8897.
School—501 St. Louis St., 63031. Tel: 314-831-3372; Fax: 314-831-7310. Ms. Clare Ortmeier, Prin.
Religious 2; Lay Teachers 24; Students 460.

8—St. Norbert (1965), Revs. Michael E. Turek; Brian P. Smith; Deacons Robert Klostermann; Len Sisul.
Res., 16455 New Halls Ferry Rd., 63031. Tel: 314-831-3874; Fax: 314-831-3875.
School—Tel: 314-839-0948. Sr. Agnes Marie Keena, B.V.M., Prin.
Sisters 2; Lay Teachers 25; Students 481.
Catechesis/Religious Programs—Tel: 314-830-0841. Sr. Therese Flerlage, O.S.F., D.R.E.
Students 290.

9—St. Sabina (1960), Revs. Robert J. Samson; John S. Sieffert; Deacons Harold A. Strauss; Joseph Marcinkiewicz, Jr.; Alvin Dietz; Paul Porterfield.
Res., 1365 Harkee Dr., 63031. Tel: 314-837-1365; Fax: 314-837-7680.
School—1625 Swallow Dr., 63031. Tel: 314-837-6524. Sr. Joan Galli, C.S.J., Prin.
Sisters 2; Lay Teachers 11; Students 221.
Catechesis/Religious Programs—Students 310.

10—St. Thomas the Apostle (1960), Rev. Vincent Bommarito; Deacons Joseph Morris; Charles Holmes.
Res., 500 Clemens Dr., 63033. Tel: 314-838-4017; Fax: 314-921-6724.
School—3500 St. Catherine St., 63033. Tel: 314-921-7313. Colleen MacKin, Prin.
Lay Teachers 21; Students 339.

11—Transfiguration (1965), Rev. Joseph W. Banden; Deacon Joseph Peacock.
Res., 6685 Lakeside Hills Dr., 63033. Tel: 314-741-2309; Fax: 314-355-7527.
School—12555 Partridge Run Dr., 63033. Tel: 314-741-0413. Carol Werner, Prin.
Lay Teachers 10; Students 176.
Convent—12613 Partridge Run Dr., 63033. Tel: 314-741-6568.

Gardenville, St. George (1915), Revs. Harold H. Voelker; Joseph J. Adragna; Deacons Roy E. Schulze; Robert Penberthy.
Res., 4980 Heege Rd., St. Louis, 63123. Tel: 314-352-3544.
School—4974 Heege Rd., St. Louis, 63123. Tel: 314-832-6432.
Lay Teachers 25; Students 261.

Glasgow Village, St. Pius X (1954), Rev. James C. Marshall; Deacon Tom Dowd.
Res., 335 Shepley Dr., St. Louis, 63137. Tel: 314-867-1139.

Glen Owen, St. Sebastian. See St. Sebastian, St. Louis County.

Grantwood, Our Lady of Providence (1954), Revs. Robert F. Johnston; Glennon Doherty, Pastoral Assoc.; Deacons Gerald Prives; Christian Winkelmann. In res., Rev. John P. Heil.
Res., 8866 Pardee Rd., St. Louis, 63123. Tel: 314-843-3570; Fax: 314-843-8033.
School—8874 Pardee Rd., St. Louis, 63123. Tel: 314-842-2073. Mary Jo Masterson, Prin.
Lay Teachers 13; Students 240.

Glencoe, St. Alban Roe (1980), Rev. Msgr. Edmund O. Griesedieck; Rev. Charles Robert Manning; Sr. Mary Whited, C.PP.S., Pastoral Assoc.; Deacons Anthony D. Falbo; Thomas L. Eultgen.
Res., 2001 Shepard Rd., 63038. Tel: 314-458-2977; Fax: 314-273-5425.
Catechesis/Religious Programs—Tel: 314-458-2460. Jill McKendry, D.R.E.
Students 840.

Hathaway Manor, St. Casimir. Closed. For inquiries for parish records contact the Chancery.

Hazelwood, St. Bartholomew (1959), Rev. David M. Novak.
Res., 8370 Latty Ave., 63042. Tel: 314-524-4422; Fax: 314-524-7036.

Our Lady of Mercy (1964), Rev. Gregory J. Lockwood; Deacon Robert De Pyper.
Res., 1607 Ville-Maura Ln., 63042. Tel: 314-739-9369; Fax: 314-739-1242.

St. Martin de Porres (1962), Revs. G. Timothy Vowels; Martin J. Mulvihill.
Res., 615 Dunn Rd., 63042. Tel: 314-895-1100; Fax: 314-895-5992.
School—631 Undercliff, 63042. Tel: 314-895-3600.
Lay Teachers 13; Students 210.
Kinderhaus—627 Undercliff, 63042.

Jennings

1—Corpus Christi/St.Lucy (1915), Revs. James J. Foster; William J. Wigand; Deacons Harry Nieman; Raymond Audrain.
Res., 8449 Corpus Christi Ln., St. Louis, 63136. Tel: 314-388-0123; Fax: 314-868-2401.
School—2120 Switzer Ave., St. Louis, 63136. Tel: 314-388-0468; Fax: 314-388-3855.
Sisters 1; Lay Teachers 9; Students 246.

2—St. Frances Xavier Cabrini (1965), Rev. Msgr. Robert L. McCarthy.
Res., 8450 Lucas-Hunt Rd., 63136. Tel: 314-385-0009; Fax: 314-385-0009.

3—St. Louise de Marillac (1935), Rev. James J. Foster.
Res., 8449 Jennings, St. Louis, 63136. Tel: 314-388-0123; Fax: 314-868-0123.

4—St. Lucy. See Corpus Christi/St. Lucy, Jennings for details.

Kinloch, Holy Angels (1931) (African American), Rev. Edward J. Schramm; Deacon Frank Nesbitt; Judy Brown, Pastoral Assoc.
Res., 8122 Scott St., 63140. Tel: 314-522-0863; Fax: 314-521-3208.
School—Tel: 314-521-0877.
Lay Teachers 8; Students 104.

Kirkwood, St. Peter (1832), Revs. John J. Brennell; Michael P. Boehm; Deacons Joseph Sulze; Richard Hesse. In res., Rev. Theodore Burghoff.

Res., 243 W. Argonne Dr., 63122. Tel: 314-966-8600; Fax: 314-966-5721. [CEM]
School—215 N. Clay St., 63122. Tel: 314-821-0460. Lay Teachers 33; Students 457.
Catechesis/Religious Programs—Tel: 314-822-1347. Linda Doyle, D.R.E. Students 239.

St. Gerard Majella (1955), Revs. Herbert C. Hauck; Matthew M. Mitas; Deacons Timothy Dolan; James Burton.
Res., 1969 Dougherty Ferry Rd., 63122. Tel: 314-965-3985; Fax: 314-965-7650.
School—2005 Dougherty Ferry Rd., 63122. Tel: 314-822-8844. Jane Koberlein, Prin.
Lay Teachers 17; Students 304.
Catechesis/Religious Programs—Tel: 314-822-4814.
Students 306.

Ladue, Church of the Annunziata (1929), Rev. Msgr. Robert M. Krawinkel; Rev. Jerome R. Keaty.
Res., 925 Cella Rd., St. Louis, 63124. Tel: 314-993-4422; Fax: 314-994-7877.
Catechesis/Religious Programs—Students 181.

Lemay

1—Mary Queen of the Universe (1956), Revs. William M. McCumber; Lawrence C. Brennan; Deacon Eugene Czarnecki.
Res., 4230 Ripa Ave., St. Louis, 63125. Tel: 314-638-3030; Fax: 314-638-5353.
School—4220 Ripa Ave., St. Louis, 63125. Tel: 314-638-2520.
Lay Teachers 17; Students 185.
Catechesis/Religious Programs—Students 185.

2—Most Precious Blood (1961), Rev. Msgr. Charles Forst; Rev. Patrick D. Ryan; Deacon Allen Boedeker.
Res., 3635 Union Rd., St. Louis, 63125. Tel: 314-487-6456; Fax: 314-487-5358.
School—Tel: 314-892-5349. Roseanne Burgoon, Prin.
Lay Teachers 12; Students 171.
Catechesis/Religious Programs—Sr. Rose Dobelman, C.PP.S., D.R.E.
Students 171.

3—St. Andrew (1905), Revs. Edward J. Hilgeman; Paul J. Spielman; Deacon Robert Karsznia.
Res., 309 Hoffmeister Ave., St. Louis, 63125. Tel: 314-631-0691.
School—Sisters of Notre Dame, 321 Hoffmeister Ave., St. Louis, 63125. Tel: 314-631-5135; 631-2010. Robert S. Cowell, Prin.
Catechesis/Religious Programs—317 Hoffmeister Ave., St. Louis, 63125. Tel: 314-631-5135.
Students 190.

4—St. Bernadette (1947), Rev. Mark S. Ebert; Deacon Michael Coppage.
Res., 68 Sherman Rd., Jefferson Barracks, 63125. Tel: 314-892-6882; Fax: 314-892-7716.
School—74 Kearney St., Jefferson Barracks, 63125. Tel: 314-892-8379; Fax: 314-892-4281.
Sisters of Notre Dame 1; Lay Teachers 8; Students 134.

5—St. Martin of Tours (1937), Revs. Kevin G. Callahan; Nicholas Smith; Deacon Terry McNamee; Mrs. Leslie Walrath, Pastoral Assoc.
Res., 610 W. Ripa Ave., 63125. Tel: 314-544-5664; Fax: 314-631-3118.
School—618 W. Ripa Ave., 63125. Tel: 314-544-5793. Mrs. Joanne Geels, Prin.
Lay Teachers 11; Students 215.

6—St. Matthias (1959), Rev. William J. Kester; Deacons John F. Smith; Joseph Hercules; Gary J. Kuenz.
Res., 796 Buckley Rd., St. Louis, 63125. Tel: 314-892-5109.
School—800 Buckley Rd., St. Louis, 63125. Tel: 314-892-7500.
Lay Teachers 14; Students 194.
Convent—798 Buckley Rd., St. Louis, 63125.

Manchester, St. Joseph (1865), Revs. Gerard R. Welsch; John J. Wetmore; Rickey J. Valleroy.
Res., 567 St. Joseph Ln., 63021. Tel: 314-227-5247; Fax: 314-391-8393. [CEM]
School—555 St. Joseph Ln., 63021. Tel: 314-391-1253. Phyllis Fredrickson, Prin.; Milissa Milan, Asst. Prin.
Sisters of Notre Dame 1; Lay Teachers 36; Students 657.
Catechesis/Religious Programs—Tel: 314-391-1404.
Students 650.

Christ, Prince of Peace (1971), Revs. Joseph E. Wormek; Robert Corbett.
Res., 415 Weidman Rd., 63011. Tel: 314-391-1307; Fax: 314-391-1319.
School—417 Weidman Rd., 63011. Tel: 314-394-6840. Sr. Kathleen Donnelly, O.P., Prin.
Dominican Sisters 2; Lay Teachers 23; Students 384.
Catechesis/Religious Programs—Tel: 314-391-1560.
Students 221.

Maplewood, Immaculate Conception (1904), Rev. Thomas J. Ripper, M.S.; Sr. Georgeann Hanson, S.L., Pastoral Assoc.; Deacon Edwin Dingman.
Res., 2934 Marshall Ave., 63143. Tel: 314-645-3307; Fax: 314-645-0672. [JC]
Additional Residence for Priests—2900 Marshall, 63143. Tel: 314-645-5904. Revs. Joseph C. Shea, M.S.; Peter D. Kohler.

Maryland Heights, St. Blaise (1961), Revs. Richard J. Bockskopf; Stephen G. Puricell; Deacons Jacob W. Dorhauer; Jerry McGuire.
Res., 3130 Parkwood Ln., 63043. Tel: 314-739-0230; Fax: 314-739-0237.
School—Tel: 314-739-1934.
Sisters 3; Lay Teachers 12; Students 249.
Catechesis/Religious Programs—Tel: 314-739-9796. Donna Wright, D.R.E.
Students 300.

Mattese, Assumption (1839), Rev. Msgr. Thomas J. Dempsey, V.F.; Revs. Francis F. Koeninger; Richard J. Schilli; Deacons Frederick J. Mueller, Jr.; Richard B. Levac.
Res., 4725 Mattis Rd., St. Louis, 63128. Tel: 314-487-7970; Fax: 314-892-5513. [CEM]
School—Tel: 314-487-6520; Fax: 314-487-3598. Margaret Adams, Prin.
Lay Teachers 21; Students 446.
Catechesis/Religious Programs—Tel: 314-487-2149. Evelyn Tucker, D.R.E.
Students 205.

Mary, Mother of the Church (1971), Rev. Msgr. Edward Reilly; Rev. Steve Robeson; Deacons Eugene W. Caton; Michael Esswein.
Res., 5901 Kerth Rd., St. Louis, 63128. Tel: 314-894-1373; Fax: 314-894-3801.
Catechesis/Religious Programs—Ed Lewandowski, D.R.E.
Students 372.

Mehlville, St. Margaret Mary Alacoque (1962), Revs. Dennis Stehly; Thomas G. Keller. In res., Rev. Alan J. Knaup, (Retired).
4900 Ringer Rd., St. Louis, 63129. Fax: 314-487-4475.
Res., 5056 Faust Ct., St. Louis, 63129. Tel: 314-487-2522.
School—Tel: 314-487-1666.
Lay Teachers 32; Students 700.
Catechesis/Religious Programs—Students 427.

Normandy, Ascension-St. Paul (1955), Rev. Stephen G. Joyce; Deacon Albert Bernsen.
Res., 7005 Ascension Dr., 63121. Tel: 314-385-6750; Fax: 314-385-6965.
School—3801 Nelson Dr., 63121. Tel: 314-261-1592. Jo Ann Gaynor, Prin.
Lay Teachers 18; Students 320.

St. Ann (1854), Rev. James T. Edwards; Deacon Norman Jansen.
Res., 7530 Natural Bridge Rd., 63121. Tel: 314-385-5090; Fax: 314-385-6527. [CEM]
School—Tel: 314-381-0113. Sr. Gloria Clapperton, Prin.
Lay Teachers 15; Students 253.

Oakville, St. Francis of Assisi (1927), Revs. Robert Behnen, O.F.M.; Blane O'Neill, O.F.M.; Aloys Jost, O.F.M.; Deacons Alan Ecker; George R. Fink; Lawrence Kelly. In res., Revs. Silas Musholt, O.F.M.; Valerian Schott, O.F.M.; Ermin Micka, O.F.M.; Charles Reuter, O.F.M.
Res., 4556 Telegraph Rd., St. Louis, 63129. Tel: 314-487-5736; Fax: 314-487-3701.
School—4550 Telegraph Rd., St. Louis, 63129. Tel: 314-892-3918; Fax: 314-892-3918. Marlyne Huenneke, Prin.
Franciscan Sisters of Our Lady of Perpetual Help 2; Lay Teachers 34; Students 720.
Catechesis/Religious Programs—Students 270.

Queen of All Saints (1972), Rev. Msgr. Robert P. Jovanovic, M.Ed.; Revs. John L. Hallemann, Senior Assoc.; Edward J. Stanger; Deacon Richard W. Coffman.
Res., 6603 Christopher Dr., 63129-4919. Tel: 314-846-8207; Fax: 314-846-0636.
School—6611 Christopher Dr., 63129-4919. Tel: 314-846-0506. Sr. JoDonna Grimes, S.S.N.D., Prin.
Students 700.
Catechesis/Religious Programs—Tel: 314-846-8126. Marge Schumer, D.R.E.
Students 400.

Overland, All Souls, Revs. Paul J. Rothschild; Frank D'Amico; Deacon Arnold Krieger.
Res., 9550 Tennyson Ave., 63114. Tel: 314-427-0442; Fax: 314-427-3872.
School—9600 Tennyson Ave., 63114. Tel: 314-429-5319.
Sisters of Notre Dame 1; Lay Teachers 12; Students 165.

Our Lady of the Presentation (1915), Rev. Dennis R. Port.
Res., 8860 Tudor Ave., St. Louis, 63114. Tel: 314-427-0486; Fax: 314-423-3020.
School—8840 Tudor Ave., St. Louis, 63114. Tel: 314-428-8191; Fax: 314-423-1213.
Lay Teachers 24; Students 305.

Pagedale, St. Catherine of Siena (1909), Rev. Victor A. Barnhart.
Res., 6815 Page Ave., St. Louis, 63133-1505. Tel: 314-721-3069 (Voice); 727-2747 (TDD); Fax: 314-727-2747.

Pine Lawn, St. Paul the Apostle. Merged to form Ascension-St. Paul, Normandy.

Richmond Heights, Immacolata (1945), Revs. John M. Seper; Gary J. Faust; Louis Roedig. In res., Most Rev. Joseph F. Naumann, V.G.
Church—8900 Clayton Rd., 63117. Tel: 314-991-5700; Fax: 314-991-4769.
School—8910 Clayton Rd., 63117. Tel: 314-991-1924. Mr. Salvatore Latragna, Prin.
Lay Teachers 20; Students 272.

Little Flower, St. Teresa of the Infant Jesus (1926), Revs. James J. Benz; Philip G. Krahman; Deacon Stephen Murray.
Res., 1264 Arch Terrace, 63117. Tel: 314-645-1445; Fax: 314-645-3258.
School—1275 Boland Pl., 63117. Tel: 314-781-4995. Mrs. Deborah Marino, Prin.
Sisters 3; Lay Teachers 13; Students 201.

St. Luke the Evangelist (1914), Revs. Richard L. Stoltz; William G. Kempf; Rev. Msgr. John J. Kennedy; Deacon Thomas O. Murphy.
Res., 7230 Dale Ave., St. Louis, 63117. Tel: 314-644-2144; Fax: 314-644-4624.
School—1414 Bellevue Ave., St. Louis, 63177. Tel: 314-781-2072; Fax: 314-781-7411.
Lay Teachers 13; Students 164.

Riverview Gardens, St. Catherine of Alexandria (1921), Revs. Thomas M. Robertson; John L. Eckhard; Deacon Edwin Schulte.
Res., 351 Chambers Rd., St. Louis, 63137. Tel: 314-867-8515.
School—10014 Diamond Dr., St. Louis, 63137. Tel: 314-869-0515. Sr. Patricia Dalton, S.S.N.D., Prin.
Sisters 2; Lay Teachers 10; Students 186.

St. Ann, St. Gregory (1942), Rev. John I. Caffe. In res., Deacon William F. Priesmeyer.
Res., 3500 St. Luke Ln., 63074. Tel: 314-428-3346.
School—3400 St. Gregory Ln., 63074. Tel: 314-429-0964.
Lay Teachers 6; Students 89.

St. Kevin (1953), Revs. John J. Leykam; Andrew J. O'Connor.
Res., 10909 St. Henry Ln., 63074. Tel: 314-427-6336; Fax: 314-427-5333.
School—10901 St. Henry Ln., 63074. Tel: 312-427-7074. Margaret Fortner, Prin.
Lay Teachers 16; Students 282.

Sappington, St. Catherine Laboure (1953), Rev. Patrick J. Keeley, C.M. Pastoral Assocs.: Rev. Raymond Ross, C.M.; Deacon George Tichacek. In res., Rev. Richard J. Janson, C.M.
Res., 9740 Sappington Rd., St. Louis, 63128. Tel: 314-843-3245; Fax: 314-843-3196.
School—9750 Sappington Rd., St. Louis, 63128. Tel: 314-843-2819; Fax: 314-843-7687. William Braun, Prin.
Lay Teachers 26; Students 476.
Catechesis/Religious Programs—Tel: 314-843-2996.
Students 138.

Shrewsbury, Cure' of Ars (1966), Rev. Clarence P. Good. In res., Rev. Msgr. John R. Maguire.
Res., 670 S. Laclede Station Rd., St. Louis, 63119. Tel: 314-962-5883.

St. Michael (1895), Revs. Edmond J. Fitzgibbon; Jerome D. Billings, J.C.L.; Bernard Suellentrop; Deacon Stephen Arnold.
Res., 7622 Sutherland Ave., St. Louis, 63119. Tel: 314-647-5611; Fax: 314-781-9211.
School—7630 Sutherland Ave., St. Louis, 63119. Tel: 314-647-7159.
Sisters 1; Lay Teachers 15; Students 214.

Spanish Lake, St. Aloysius (1871), Rev. Gerald T. Nienhaus; Deacon Walter J. Ruegg.
Res., 12110 Larimore Rd., St. Louis, 63138. Tel: 314-741-3690; Fax: 314-741-6468.
School—12122 Larimore Rd., St. Louis, 63138. Tel: 314-741-0294.
Sisters 1; Lay Teachers 8; Students 114.
Catechesis/Religious Programs—Trinity School of Religion (Combined with Our Lady of Loretto and Transfiguration), Tel: 314-741-2583.
Students 170.

Our Lady of Loretto (1959), Revs. Stephen Gira, C.R.; Steven R. Thoma, C.R.; Deacons Francis Droesch; James Michael Buckley.
Res., 11725 Bellefontaine Rd., St. Louis, 63138. Tel: 314-741-7700; Fax: 314-741-7700.
School—1650 Redman Ave., St. Louis, 63138. Tel: 314-741-0400. Mrs. Marie Moritz, Prin.

Sisters of Notre Dame 1; Lay Teachers 13; Students 197.
Catechesis/Religious Programs—Tel: 314-741-2583.
Students 200.

Sunset Hills, St. Justin Martyr (1964), Revs. Bernard J. Schloemer; Leo T. Lewis.
Res., 11962 Bardmont Dr., St. Louis, 63126. Tel: 314-843-8482; Fax: 314-843-8507.
School—11914 Eddie and Park Rd., St. Louis, 63126. Tel: 314-843-6447; Fax: 314-843-9257. Sr. Ann Martinek, Prin.
Sisters of St. Francis of Clinton, Iowa 2; Lay Teachers 11; Students 242.

University City

1—ALL SAINTS (1901), Rev. Donald Molitor; Deacon Franklin J. Fick.
Res., 6403 Clemens Ave., 63130. Tel: 314-721-6403.

2—CHRIST THE KING (1927), Rev. John A. Ditenhafer. In res., Rev. John Jay Hughes; Deacon E. Ray Kiely.
Res., 7316 Balson Ave., 63130. Tel: 314-721-8737; Fax: 314-721-8738.
School—7324 Balson Ave., 63130. Tel: 314-725-5855; Fax: 314-725-5981. Sr. Rosella McNamee, R.S.M., Prin.
Sisters of Mercy 1; Lay Teachers 14; Students 211.

3—OUR LADY OF LOURDES (1916), Rev. Msgr. Edward J. Sudekum; Rev. Msgr. Norbert J. Dietz; Rev. Gary P. Wolken; Deacon Albert X. Vaughn.
Res., 7148 Forsyth Blvd., 63105. Tel: 314-726-6200; 6201; Fax: 314-726-1602.
School—7157 Northmoor Ave., 63105. Tel: 314-726-3352.
Lay Teachers 19; Students 243.

4—ST. PATRICK (1940), Rev. Eugene Bendel.
Res., 8665 Olive Blvd., 63132. Tel: 314-993-1277.

Valley Park, Sacred Heart (1903), Revs. Robert T. Rosebrough; Robert A. Marshall; Sr. Donna Fischer, S.S.N.D., Pastoral Assoc.; Deacons Ewald Winker; Larry Damato; Allen F. Love.
Res., 17 Ann Ave., 63088. Tel: 314-225-5268; Fax: 314-225-6969. [CEM]
School—12 Ann Ave., 63088. Tel: 314-225-3824; Fax: 314-225-8941. Sharon Baumgartner, Prin.
Lay Teachers 22; Students 321.
Catechesis/Religious Programs—Tel: 314-225-0341.
Students 453.

Vinita Park, St. Rita (1919), Rev. David L. Wichlan; Deacon Louis J. Reynoso.
Res., 8240 Washington St., St. Louis County, 63114. Tel: 314-428-4845.

Warson Woods, Ste. Genevieve Du Bois (1956), Rev. Msgr. Paul G. Anthony; Rev. John B. Shamleffer. In res., Rev. Msgr. John P. Holland, Senior Priest.
Res., 1575 N. Woodlawn Ave., 63122. Tel: 314-966-3780; Fax: 314-966-4687.
School—Tel: 314-821-4245. Helen Petropoulos, Prin.
Sisters 1; Lay Teachers 12; Students 228.

Webster Groves, Annunciation (1950), Revs. Denny M. Schaab; John G. Klocker, Senior Priest; Deacon Tom Forster Tel: 314-631-5440.
Res., 12 W. Glendale Rd., 63119. Tel: 314-962-5955; Fax: 314-961-0643.
School—16 W. Glendale, 63119. Tel: 314-961-7712. Mrs. Ann Cleeland, Prin.
Lay Teachers 15; Students 243.

Holy Redeemer (1886), Revs. Joseph M. Simon; Richard J. Rath; Deacon Richard Wessels.
Res., 17 Joy Ave., 63119. Tel: 314-962-0038; Fax: 314-962-2084.
School—341 E. Lockwood, 63119. Tel: 314-962-8989. Cynthia Hasten, Prin.
Lay Teachers 14; Students 222.
Catechesis/Religious Programs—Tel: 314-962-1487.
Students 180.

Mary, Queen of Peace (1922), Rev. Gerald A. Meier; Rev. Msgr. Richard J. Lubeley, Senior Priest; Rev. John J. Borcic; Deacons Robert C. Riegel; Paul McKee; Bill Weiss.
Res., 676 W. Lockwood Blvd., 63119. Tel: 314-962-2311; Fax: 314-968-9885.
School—680 W. Lockwood Ave., 63119. Tel: 314-961-2891. Mrs. Tozia George, Prin.
Sisters of Loretto at the Foot of the Cross 1; Lay Teachers 28; Students 525.
Catechesis/Religious Programs—Students 115.

Wellston, Notre Dame De Lourdes. Closed. See St. Augustine, St. Louis for details.

West Overland, St. Jude (1953), Rev. Joseph L. Parisi.
Res., 2218 N. Warson Rd., St. Louis, 63114. Tel: 314-428-2262.

Woodson Terrace, St. William (1953), Rev. Eugene P. Selzer; Deacons John J. Buckley; Dave Bolderson.
Res., 9311 Stansberry Ave., 63134. Tel: 314-428-7371; Fax: 314-428-1158.
School—9330 Stansberry Ave., 63134. Tel: 314-427-6444.
Lay Teachers 5; Students 70.

CHURCHES OUTSIDE ST. LOUIS CITY AND ST. LOUIS COUNTY

Apple Creek, Perry Co., St. Joseph's (1828) (German), Rev. Terry J. Borgerding.
Res., 139 St. Joseph Ln., 63775. Tel: 314-788-2330. [CEM][JC 2]
School—(Grades K-8). Tel: 314-788-2320.
Lay Teachers 4; Students 52. Principals: Nancy Heberlie; Michelle Huffman.

Arnold, Jefferson Co., Immaculate Conception (1840), Revs. Earl R. Meyer, O.F.M.Cap.; Gilmary Tallman, O.F.M.Cap.; Deacons Joseph C. Streckfuss; Bradford M. Buchek.
Res., 2300 Church Rd., P.O. Box 217, 63010. Tel: 314-296-5289. [CEM]
School—Holy Child School. Consolidated with St. David, Arnold. Tel: 314-296-0055; Fax: 314-296-5639. Mrs. Marlene DiMaggio, Prin.
Lay Teachers 24; Students 369.
Catechesis/Religious Programs—Tel: 314-296-5598. Joyce Ott, D.R.E.
Students 396.

St. David (1963), Rev. Thomas Schmidt; Deacon Thomas G. Politte.
Res., 2334 Tenbrook Rd., 63010. Tel: 314-296-5485; Fax: 314-296-5526.
School—Holy Child Consolidated School. See Immaculate Conception for details. Tel: 314-296-0055.
Catechesis/Religious Programs—Students 200.

Augusta, St. Charles Co., Immaculate Conception (1851), Rev. Msgr. Charles G. Clavenna.
Res., 5912 Hwy. 94 S., 63332. Tel: 314-482-4455; Fax: 314-228-4529. [CEM]

Belgique, Perry Co., Nativity of the Blessed Virgin Mary. Closed. For inquiries for parish records contact the Chancery.

Berger, Franklin Co., St. Paul (1853) (German), Rev. Daniel E. Mosley.
Res., 603 Miller St., New Haven, 63068. Tel: 573-237-3372. [CEM]

Biehle, Perry Co., St. Maurus (1870) (German), Rev. Terry J. Borgerding.
Res., Rte. 7, Box 237, Perryville, 63775. Tel: 573-547-5246. [CEM][JC]

Bloomsdale, Ste. Genevieve Co., St. Agnes (1835), Rev. Raymond J. Oge.
Res., P.O. Box 124, 63627. Tel: 573-483-2555; Fax: 573-483-9497. [CEM]
School—Tel: 573-483-2506. Sr. Donna Marie Kist, C.PP.S., Prin.
Sisters of the Most Precious Blood (O'Fallon, MO) 1; Lay Teachers 10; Students 167.

Bonne Terre, St. Francois Co., St. Joseph's (1872), Rev. John H. Schneider; Deacon Ronald Kreff.
Res., 15 St. Joseph St., 63628. Tel: 573-358-2112; Fax: 573-358-4233. [CEM]
School—(Grades K-6). Tel: 573-358-5947. William Martim, Prin.
Lay Teachers 4; Students 44.
Mission—French Village, St. Francois Co., St. Anne, P.O. Box 307 French Village, 63036. Tel: 573-358-2112.

Brewer, Perry Co., Christ the Savior (1907), Rev. Felipe J. Martinez, C.M.
Res., 57 Shady Ln., Perryville, 63775. Tel: 573-547-2677.

Catawissa, Franklin Co., St. James (1913), Rev. Hubert E. Creason.
Res., 1107 Summit Dr., 63015. Tel: 314-271-6038. [CEM]
Mission—Armagh, Franklin Co., St. Patrick, Hwy. NN & Rock Church Rd., 63015. [CEM]

Clover Bottom, Franklin Co., St. Ann's (1883) (Polish-German), Rev. John E. Majewski.
Res., Clover Bottom, 7851 State Rd. YY, Washington, 63090-9627. Tel: 314-239-3222. [CEM]

Coffman, Ste. Genevieve Co., St. Catherine of Alexandria (1929). Attended by River Aux Vases. Rev. F. Joseph Reilly.
Res., 18411 RAV Church Rd., Ste. Genevieve, 63670. Tel: 314-883-2923. [CEM]

Concord Hill, Warren Co., St. Ignatius (1857) (German), Rev. Finbarr Dowling, O.S.B.
Res., 701 Mill Rd., Marthasville, 63357. Tel: 314-932-4445. [CEM 2]
School—703 Mill Rd., 63357. Tel: 314-932-4444. Barbara McDermott, Prin.
Sisters of Notre Dame 1; Sisters of Mercy 1; Lay Teachers 2; Students 54.

Cottleville, St. Charles Co., St. Joseph (1873), Rev. Msgr. Walter M. Whited; Revs. Erich A. Fechner; Timothy P. Cronin; Deacons Ronald Bachista; Gary MeyerKord; Glennon Schultheis.
Res., 1355 Motherhead Rd., St. Charles, 63304. Tel: 314-441-0055; Fax: 314-926-7341. [CEM]
School—1351 Motherhead Rd., St. Charles, 63304. Tel: 314-441-7978; Fax: 314-441-9932. Ms. Mary Ellen Schraeder, Prin.; Mrs. Charlotte Litzinger, Asst. Prin.
Sisters 1; Lay Teachers 39; Students 764.
Catechesis/Religious Programs—Tel: 314-447-5239. D.R.E.: Mrs. Barbara Blackburn; Mrs. Laura Lucas.
Students 988.

Crystal City, Jefferson Co., Sacred Heart (1881), Rev. Michael L. Donald; Deacon Gerard G. Stoverink.
Res., 555 Bailey Rd., 63019-1798. Tel: 314-937-4662; Fax: 314-931-0422. [CEM]
School—Tel: 314-931-5701.
Lay Teachers 11; Students 144.
Catechesis/Religious Programs—Students 199.

Dardenne, St. Charles Co., Immaculate Conception (1880), Revs. Robert J. Reiker; K. Robert Smoot; Emmanuel Ogunnaike, M.S.P. (Nigeria); Deacons Don Schiffman; Charles Drayton.
Res., 7701 Hwy. N, O'Fallon, 63366. Tel: 314-561-4459; Fax: 314-561-3883. [CEM]
School—Tel: 314-561-4450.
Lay Teachers 12; Students 255.
Catechesis/Religious Programs—Tel: 314-561-1974.
Students 751.

De Soto, Jefferson Co., St. Rose of Lima (1885), Revs. Ronald J. Hopmeir; Robert J. Suit; Deacon Edward J. Boyer.
Res., 504 S. Third St., 63020. Tel: 314-337-2212; Fax: 314-337-2394. [CEM]
School—Tel: 314-586-3594; 337-7855. Sr. Margaret Schmidt, S.N.D., Prin.
Sisters 2; Lay Teachers 8; Students 112.
Catechesis/Religious Programs—Students 150.

Dutzow, Warren Co., St. Vincent de Paul (1856), Rev. Stephen F. Bauer.
Res., 7602 S. Hwy. 94, Marthasville, 63357. Tel: 314-433-2678; Fax: 314-433-2924. [CEM]
School—Tel: 314-433-2466.
Lay Teachers 10; Students 149.

Elsberry, Lincoln Co., Sacred Heart (1905), Rev. James P. Grady.
Res., 714 Lincoln St., 63343. Tel: 573-898-2202; Fax: 573-898-2652.

Farmington, St. Francois Co., St. Joseph (1890), Revs. Eugene Robertson; Thomas J. Wissler; Deacons William J. Greif; Albin A. Gegg.
Res., 5 S. Carleton, 63640. Tel: 573-756-4250; Fax: 573-756-6938. [CEM 2][JC]
School—501 Ste. Genevieve Ave., 63640. Tel: 573-756-6312; Fax: 573-756-0783.
Students 163.

Festus, Jefferson Co., Our Lady, Rev. John V. Kerber; Sr. Pat Murray, O.S.F., Pastoral Min.
Res., 1550 St. Mary Ln., 63028. Tel: 314-937-5513; 931-4702 (toll-free).
School—Fax: 314-937-5008.
Sisters of Notre Dame 2; Lay Teachers 8; Students 200.

Flint Hill, St. Charles Co., St. Theodore (1883), Rev. Albert A. Mattler.
Res., P.O. Box 246, 63346. Tel: 314-332-9269. [CEM]
School—Tel: 314-332-9465.
Lay Teachers 6; Students 93.

Gildehaus, Franklin Co., St. John the Baptist (1839), Rev. William J. Leach.
Res., 5567 Gildenhaus Rd., Gildenhaus, 63089. Tel: 314-583-2488; Fax: 314-583-6114. [CEM]
School—Tel: 314-583-2392. Ruth O. Himmelberg, Prin.
Lay Teachers 8; Students 195.

Hawk Point, Lincoln Co., St. Mary (1919) (Bohemian), Rev. Bernard Nienhaus.
Res., P.O. Box 205, 63349. Tel: 314-338-4331. [CEM 2]

Herculaneum, Jefferson Co., Church of the Assumption of B.V.M. (1916), Rev. Robert F. Fleiter.
Res., 329 Station St., 63048-1328. Tel: 314-475-5305. [CEM]

High Ridge, Jefferson Co., St. Anthony of Padua (1921), Revs. Eugene R. Sinz; Richard H. Suren; Deacons Bill Gearon; Paul Crafts; Dick Shelby; Joe Otzenberger.
Res., 3009 High Ridge Blvd., 63049. Tel: 314-677-4868; Fax: 314-677-2781.
School—3005 High Ridge Blvd., 63049. Tel: 314-677-3585. Mr. Thomas McKenna, Prin.
Lay Teachers 11; Students 162.
Catechesis/Religious Programs—Students 132.

Hillsboro, Jefferson Co., Church of the Good Shepherd (1934), Rev. Michael E. Dieckmann.
Res., 703 Third St., 63050-4342. Tel: 314-789-3356; Fax: 314-789-9986. [CEM]

School—Tel: 314-789-2300. Mrs. Michel Wendell, Prin.
Lay Teachers 9; Students 86.

House Springs, Jefferson Co., Our Lady, Queen of Peace (1961), Revs. Norbert A. Ernst; Larry T. Huber, Jr.; Deacon Thomas Gerling.
Res., 4696 Notre Dame Ln., 63051. Tel: 314-671-3062; Fax: 314-671-0003. [CEM 2]
School—Tel: 314-671-0247. Mrs. Marietta Stiebler, Prin.
Sisters 2; Lay Teachers 7; Students 211.
Catechesis/Religious Programs—Students 240.

Imperial, Jefferson Co., St. John Lateran (1869), Rev. Edward L. Heim.
Res., 4525 Old Hwy. 21, 63052. Tel: 314-296-8061; Fax: 314-296-8067. [CEM]
School—Tel: 314-296-8112. Mrs. Vicky Meadows Yochum, Prin.
Lay Teachers 10; Students 160.

Josephville, St. Charles Co., St. Joseph, Rev. Timothy P. Ekriott.
Res., 1390 Josephville Rd., Wentzville, 63385. Tel: 314-332-6676. [CEM]
School—1410 Josephville Rd., Wentzville, 63385. Tel: 314-327-7174. Barbara Rygelski, Prin.
Lay Teachers 4; Students 92.

Kimmswick, Jefferson Co., St. Joseph's (1905), Rev. Andrew J. Sigmund; Deacons Kenneth A. Henning; Glennon P. Politte, Sr.
Res., 63053. Tel: 314-464-1013; Fax: 314-461-0411. [CEM]
School—Tel: 314-464-9027. Pat Kirk, Prin.
Students 230.
Catechesis/Religious Programs—Students 240.

Krakow, Franklin Co., St. Gertrude's (1845), Rev. Dennis B. Zacheis.
Res., 6535 State Rd. YY, Washington, 63090. Tel: 314-239-4216; Fax: 314-451-0221. [CEM]
School—Tel: 314-239-2347; Fax: 314-239-3722. Mike Newbanks, Prin.
Lay Teachers 20; Students 314.

Lawrenceton, Ste. Genevieve Co., St. Lawrence's (1872). Attended by St. Agnes Rectory. Rev. Raymond J. Oge.
Bloomsdale, 63627. Tel: 573-483-2555; Fax: 573-483-9497. [CEM]

Luebbering, Franklin Co., St. Francis of Assisi (1874), Rev. John B. McEntee.
Res., 100 Luebbering Rd., 63061-9705. Tel: 314-629-1717. [CEM]

Millwood, Lincoln Co., St. Alphonsus (1850), Rev. John L. Mayer.
Res., 29 St. Alphonsus, Silex, 63377. Tel: 573-384-6223. [CEM]
School—Tel: 573-384-5305.
Lay Teachers 5; Students 80.
Catechesis/Religious Programs—Students 35.

Moselle, Franklin Co., St. Mary's (1905) (German), Rev. Lawrence J. Schieber.
Res., 1587 Hwy. AM, Villa Ridge, 63089. Tel: 314-451-4685. [CEM]

Neier, Franklin Co., St. Joseph's (1881), Rev. Gerald T. Simpson.
Res., 2401 Neier Rd., Union, 63084. Tel: 314-583-2806. [CEM]

New Haven, Franklin Co., Assumption (1892) (German), Rev. Daniel E. Mosley.
Res., 63068. Tel: 314-237-3372. [CEM]

New Melle, St. Charles Co., Immaculate Heart of Mary (1945), Rev. Joseph A. Weber; Deacon Lonnie Weishaar; Shawn Mueller, Pastoral Assoc.
Res., 26 W. Hwy. D, Box 100, 63365. Tel: 314-398-5270; Fax: 314-398-5577. [CEM]
Catechesis/Religious Programs—Sandra Robor, D.R.E.
Students 200.

O'Fallon, St. Charles Co., Assumption (1871) (German), Revs. Robert D. Boisaubin; Ronald J. Rubbelke. In res., Revs. Edmund C. Igboanusi, C.M.F. (Nigeria); Paul Link, C.PP.S.
Res., 115 W. Third St., 63366. Tel: 314-240-3721; Fax: 314-240-3722. [CEM]
School—Tel: 314-240-4474. Sr. Patricia Cody, O.P., Prin.
Lay Teachers 25; Students 431.
Catechesis/Religious Programs—Tel: 314-978-3857.
Students 354.

St. Barnabas (1961), Rev. Daniel M. Hogan.
Res., 1415 N. Main St., 63366. Tel: 314-272-4555; Fax: 314-978-3358.

Old Mines, Washington Co., St. Joachim's (1723), Rev. Theodore X. Pieper; Deacon Steven Politte.
Res., Rte. 1, P.O. Box 1110, Cadet, 63630. Tel: 573-438-6181; Fax: 573-438-6181. [CEM]
School—Tel: 573-438-3973. Joyce Politte, Prin.
Lay Teachers 7; Students 61.

Old Monroe, Lincoln Co., Immaculate Conception (1857), Rev. Gregory L. Schmidt; Deacon Anthony Trautman.
Res., 110 Maryknoll Rd., 63369. Tel: 314-661-5002. [CEM]
School—120 Maryknoll Rd., 63369. Tel: 314-665-5463. Sr. Kathleen Eggleston, Prin.
Sisters of the Third Order Regular of St. Francis (Oldenburg, IN) 1; Lay Teachers 8; Students 170.
Convent—122 Maryknoll Rd., Tel: 314-665-5303.

Ozora, Ste. Genevieve Co., Sacred Heart (1898), Rev. James W. Schoefer.
Res., 17742 State Rte. N., St. Mary, 63673. Tel: 573-543-2209. [CEM]
School—Tel: 573-543-2997. Mrs. Kathleen Grither, Prin.
Sisters of the Most Precious Blood 1; Lay Teachers 3; Students 36.

Pacific, Franklin Co., St. Bridget Church (1841) (Irish), Rev. Richard V. Coerver.
Res., 111 W. Union St., 63069. Tel: 314-271-3993. [CEM]
School—Tel: 314-271-4533.
Lay Teachers 7; Students 102.

Park Hills, St. Francois Co., Immaculate Conception (1903), Rev. James R. French.
Res., Box 66, 63601-0066. Tel: 573-431-2427; Fax: 573-431-4060. [CEM][JC]
Mission—Bismarck, St. Francois Co., St. John, (1879) Maple St. & Walnut St., 63624. [CEM][JC]

Perryville, Perry Co., St. Vincent De Paul (1818), Revs. Kevin P. Fausz, C.M.; Gerard P. Kelly, C.M.
Res., 1000 Rosati Court, 63775. Tel: 573-547-4591; Fax: 573-547-4145. [CEM 4]
Parish Center—1010 Rosati Ct., 63775.
School—Tel: 573-547-6503. Robert Rousseau, Prin.
Daughters of Charity of St. Vincent de Paul 1; Lay Teachers 20; Students 331.
Junior-Senior High School—Tel: 573-547-2560. Sr. Mary Bryan Owens, S.S.N.D., Prin.
Daughters of Charity of St. Vincent de Paul 1; Lay Teachers 21; Students 283.
Catechesis/Religious Programs—Parish School of Religion, 63775.
Students 231.
Missions—Highland, Perry Co., St. Joseph, 1701 W. St. Joseph, Perryville, 63775. Tel: 314-547-6533; Fax: 573-547-2204; Crosstown, Perry Co., St. James, c/o St. Vincent De Paul Parish, Perryville, 63775.
Catechesis/Religious Programs—Parish School of Religion, 63775. Tel: 314-547-4503.
Students 285.

Portage Des Sioux, St. Charles Co., St. Francis (1799) (French-German), Rev. Michael J. Sandweg.
Res., P.O. Box 128, 63373. Tel: 314-899-0906; Fax: 314-899-0909. [CEM]
Mission—West Alton, St. Charles Co., Immaculate Conception, 14060 Hwy. 94 N., West Alton, 63386.
Catechesis/Religious Programs—Students 7.

Port Hudson, Franklin Co., Holy Family (1872), Rev. James M. Sullivan.
Res., 124 Holy Family Church Rd., New Haven, 63068. Tel: 573-459-6441. [CEM]
Catechesis/Religious Programs—Students 130.
Mission—Gerald, Franklin Co., St. Gerald, 63068.

Potosi, Washington Co., St. James (1829), Rev. George Galovich.
Res., 201 N. Missouri Ave., 63664. Tel: 314-438-4686; 1-800-533-8163 (toll-free); Fax: 314-438-2100. [CEM][JC 2]

Richwoods, Washington Co., St. Stephen's (1841), Rev. Robert C. Liss.
Res., H.C.R. 63, Box 1, 63071-9701. Tel: 573-678-2207. [CEM]

River Aux Vases, Ste. Genevieve Co., SS. Phillip and James (1840), Rev. F. Joseph Reilly.
Res., 18411 RAV Church Rd., Ste. Genevieve, 63670. Tel: 314-883-2923. [CEM]

St. Charles, St. Charles Co.,

1—St. Charles Borromeo, (1792), Revs. Richard J. Tillman; Xavier R. Albert; Rev. Msgr. Bernard H. Boessen.
Res., 601 N. 4th St., 63301. Tel: 314-946-6370; 946-1893.
School—431 Decatur, 63301. Tel: 314-946-2713.
Sisters of Notre Dame 2; Lay Teachers 19; Students 334.
Catechesis/Religious Programs—Tel: 314-946-2916.
Students 94.
Chapel—Convent of the Sacred Heart, Regis Hall, Tel: 314-946-6456.

2—St. Cletus, (1965), Revs. James P. Callahan; Dennis M. Doyle; Donald E. Henke; Deacon Frank Prideaux.
Res., 2705 Zumbehl Rd., 63301. Tel: 314-946-6327; Fax: 314-946-6466.
School—Tel: 314-946-7756.
Lay Teachers 24; Students 288.
Catechesis/Religious Programs—Tel: 314-946-5936.
Students 260.

3—St. Elizabeth Ann Seton, (1975), Revs. Kevin J. Mahoney; Jeffrey A. Maasen; Donald L. Neuner.
Res., 2 Seton Ct., 63303. Tel: 314-946-6717; Fax: 314-946-9263.
School—Tel: 314-946-6716.
Sisters 2; Lay Teachers 37; Students 713.
Catechesis/Religious Programs—Tel: 314-949-3833. Nancy Burian, D.R.E.
Students 500.

4—Sts. Joachim and Ann, (1981), Revs. Dennis J. Doyle; James L. Gahan; John A. Keenoy.
Mailing Address: 4112 McClay Rd., 63304. Tel: 314-441-7503.
School—(Grades K-8) 4110 McClay Rd., 63304. Tel: 314-441-4835; Fax: 314-441-9534. Sr. Kathleen Eilers, C.S.J., Prin.
Sisters 1; Lay Teachers 29; Students 585.
Catechesis/Religious Programs—Tel: 314-926-0021.
Students 735.

5—St. Peter, (1850), Revs. Arthur F. Bromschwig; Donald D. Carey; Deacon Thomas J. Willbrand. In res., Rev. Msgr. Raymond A. Hampe.
Res., 324 S. Third St., 63301. Tel: 314-946-6641; Fax: 314-946-9789. [CEM]
School—222 Jackson St., 63301. Tel: 314-947-9669.
Lay Teachers 20; Students 326.

6—St. Robert Bellarmine, (1964), Revs. Fred A. Meyer; Tony Dattilo.
Res., 1424 First Capitol Dr., S., 63303. Tel: 314-946-6799; Fax: 314-946-4792.
School—Tel: 314-946-1474. Ken Morr, Prin.; Sue Finley, Asst. Prin.
Lay Teachers 8; Students 183.
Catechesis/Religious Programs—Students 211.

St. Clair, Franklin Co., St. Clare, Rev. Paul E. Telken.
Res., Box 526, 63077. Tel: 314-629-0315. [CEM]
School—Sisters of Notre Dame 1; Lay Teachers 5; Students 102.

Ste. Genevieve, Ste. Genevieve Co., Ste. Genevieve's (1759), Revs. John J. Johnson; John C. Deken; John P. Day, C.P.; Deacon George Wood.
Res., 49 Du Bourg Pl., 63670. Tel: 573-883-2731; Fax: 573-883-2907. [CEM]
School—40 N. Fourth St., 63670. Tel: 573-883-2403.
Lay Teachers 21; Students 308.
High School—Valle High School, Tel: 573-883-7496.
Sisters 1; Lay Teachers 14; Students 164.

St. Mary's, Ste. Genevieve Co., Immaculate Conception, Rev. Richard C. Kasznel.
Res., P.O. Box 27, 63673. Tel: 573-543-2536. [CEM]

St. Paul, St. Charles Co., St. Paul (1850), Rev. Msgr. John J. Hickel.
Rectory: Tel: 314-978-1400.; Parish Center: Tel: 314-978-1900.
Res., P.O. Box 66069, 63366. [CEM]
School—P.O. Box 66070, 63366. Mary Price, Prin.
Lay Teachers 13; Students 200.

St. Peters, St. Charles Co., All Saints (1815), Revs. Michael L. Henning; James M. Mitulski; Robert C. Lane; Deacon Gerald Knobbe.
Res., 7 McMenemy Rd., 63376. Tel: 314-397-1440; Fax: 314-397-1421. [CEM]
School—Tel: 314-397-1477. Rae Ann Kielty, Prin.
Lay Teachers 28; Students 430.
Catechesis/Religious Programs—Tel: 314-397-6995. Ms. Marya Pohlmeier, D.R.E.
Students 570.

Sereno, Perry Co., Our Lady of Victory (1908), Rev. Francis H. Agnew, C.M.
Res., 172 PCR 920, Perryville, 63775. Tel: 314-547-6812. [JC]

Silver Lake, Perry Co., St. Rose of Lima (1885), Rev. Kevin P. Fausz, C.M.
Res., 1010 Rosati Ct., Perryville, 63775. Tel: 573-547-4591; Fax: 573-547-4145. [CEM]

Sullivan, Franklin Co., St. Anthony (1891), Rev. Theodore J. Brunnert; Deacons Michael Sabo; Allen Kaufman.
Res., 201 W. Springfield Ave., 63080. Tel: 573-468-6101; Fax: 573-468-8584. [CEM]
School—101 W. Springfield Ave., 63080. Tel: 573-468-4423. Barbara Kelley, Prin.
Lay Teachers 6; Students 90.

Church of the Holy Martyrs of Japan (1879), Rev. James J. Pavlik, Admin.
Church—8244 Hwy. AE, 63080. Tel: 573-627-3378. [CEM 2]

Tiff, Washington Co., St. Joseph's (1723), Rev. Theodore X. Pieper, Admin.
Res., R.R.I. Box 1110, Cadet, 63630. Tel: 573-438-6181; Fax: 573-438-6181. [CEM]

Troy, Lincoln Co., Sacred Heart (1891), Rev. Donald C. Schramm; Sr. Mary Ann Fisher, C.S.J., Pastoral Min.; Deacon Thomas Burkemper.
Res., 80 Main St., 63379. Tel: 314-528-8219; Fax: 314-528-3983. [CEM]
School—Tel: 314-528-6684. Sr. Jeannette Fennewald, S.S.N.D., Prin.
Lay Teachers 10; Students 227.
Catechesis/Religious Programs—Students 223.

Union, Franklin Co., Immaculate Conception (1866), Revs. Peter M. Blake; Kevin V. Schmittgens.
Res., 100 N. Washington Ave., 63084. Tel: 314-583-5144; Fax: 314-583-7784. [CEM]
School—6 W. State St., 63084. Tel: 314-583-2641.
Sisters 1; Lay Teachers 12; Students 251.

Warrenton, Warren Co., Holy Rosary (1868), Rev. Eugene P. Brennan.
Res., 724 E. Booneslick Rd., 63383. Tel: 314-456-3698; Fax: 314-456-5560. [CEM]
School—716 E. Booneslick Rd., 63383. Tel: 314-456-2882. Sr. Mary Ann Boes, Prin.
Sisters of St. Joseph of Carondelet 1; Lay Teachers 9; Students 155.
Catechesis/Religious Programs—Students 155.

Washington, Franklin Co., St. Francis Borgia (1834) (German), Revs. John M. Costello; Michael E. Oslance; Deacons Gilbert Holtmeyer; Leon Noelker.
Res., 311 W. Second St., 63090. Tel: 314-239-6701; Fax: 314-938-3267. [CEM]
School—225 Cedar St., 63090. Tel: 314-239-2590.
Lay Teachers 25; Students 422.

Our Lady of Lourdes (1958), Very Rev. Robert L. Heimos, V.F.
Res., 1014 Madison Ave., 63090. Tel: 314-239-3520; Fax: 314-239-7682.
School—950 Madison Ave., 63090. Tel: 314-239-5292.
Sisters of Notre Dame 1; Lay Teachers 18; Students 307.
Catechesis/Religious Programs—Students 463.

Weingarten, Ste. Genevieve Co., Our Lady Help of Christians (1872), Rev. John Suren.
Res., 13370 Hwy. 32, Ste. Genevieve, 63670-9402. Tel: 314-883-3796. [CEM]

Wentzville, St. Charles Co., St. Patrick (1905), Revs. Leo J. Spezia; Donald A. Glastetter; Deacon Paul H. Chavaux.
Res., 405 S. Church St., 63385. Tel: 314-332-9225; Fax: 314-332-6998. [CEM]
School—701 Church St., 63385. Tel: 314-332-9913. Mrs. Janice Ward, Prin.
Lay Teachers 16; Students 225.
Catechesis/Religious Programs—Tel: 314-332-9036.
Students 250.

West Alton, St. Charles Co., Immaculate Conception. Closed. See St. Francis, Portage des Sioux.

Zell, Ste. Genevieve Co., St. Joseph (1845), Rev. Msgr. James E. Hanson.
Res., 11824 Zell Rd., Ste. Genevieve, 63670. Tel: 573-883-3481. [CEM]
School—Tel: 573-883-5097.
Adorers of the Blood of Christ (Ruma, IL) 1; Lay Teachers 4; Students 62.

Korean Ministry

Ellisville, St. Andrew Kim Korean Catholic Community Church (Korean), Rev. Joseph Mun, Byung Hak (South Korea).
Res., P.O. Box 453, 63011. Tel: 314-230-9601.

Chaplains of Public Institutions

ST. LOUIS. *Christian Hospital Northeast-Northwest* 11133 Dunn Rd., 63136. Tel: 314-355-2300. Rev. James L. Winzerling, Res. Chap.
Lammert International Airport. Vacant.
Regional Hospital 5535 Delmar Blvd., 63112. Tel: 314-361-1212. Rev. Francis J. Shine, C.M., Chap.
St. Anthony Medical Center Tel: 314-525-1000. Rev. Donald J. Hoffman Tel: 314-968-0760.
St. John's Mercy Medical Ctr Tel: 314-569-6470. Rev. Philip G. Krahman Tel: 314-645-1445.
Saint Louis University Hospital Tel: 314-525-1000. Rev. Gregory G. Kirsch Tel: 314-351-1318.
St. Mary's Health Ctr Tel: 314-768-8000. Revs. James A. Krings Tel: 314-289-9545; James N. Rutkowski.

KIRKWOOD. *St. Joseph Hospital* Tel: 314-966-1596. Rev. Mark L. Fuller Tel: 314-962-0038.

ST. CHARLES. *St. Joseph Health Center* Tel: 314-947-5000. Rev. Msgr. Raymond A. Hampe Tel: 314-946-6641.

WASHINGTON. *St. John's Hospital* Tel: 314-239-8000. Rev. Timothy J. Toohey Tel: 314-239-8081.

Special Assignment:
Reverend Monsignors—
Lucas, George J., Pres. & Rector, Kenrick-Glennon Seminary, 5200 Glennon Dr., St. Louis, MO 63119. Tel: 314-644-0266
O'Brien, Joseph M., Mktg. & Devel., Catholic Family Services, 7800 Kenrick Rd., St. Louis, MO 63119. Tel: 314-968-8010
Stika, Richard F., V.G., Chancellor, 4510 Lindell, St. Louis, MO 63108. Tel: 314-367-4437
Reverend Fathers—
Aten, Robert L., Contemplative Heart of Mary Hermitage, Centerville, MO. Tel: 573-648-2467
Dalton, Donald T., Ursuline Provincialate, 210 Glennon Heights Rd., Crystal City, MO 63019. Tel: 314-937-6206
Mannion, Martin K., St. Vincent Home, 7401 Florissant Rd., St. Louis, MO 63121. Tel: 314-261-3246

On Duty Outside the Archdiocese:
Reverend Monsignors—
Dolan, Timothy M., Rome, Italy
Ratermann, David A., Cochabamba, Bolivia
Reverend Fathers—
Blattner, Joseph H., Benedicta, ME
Fidler, W. Larch, IV, Brunswick, ME
Hayden, Patrick T., La Paz, Bolivia
Kopfensteiner, Thomas R., Fordham University, Bronx, NY
Lampert, Robert E., Oblate School of Theology, San Antonio, TX
Means, David A., Anchorage, AK
Menner, Robert J., Riberalta, Bolivia
Michler, James, La Paz, Bolivia
Schmidt, Dennis C., Columbia, MO
Siebert, Anthony G., Belize, Central America
Somos, Joseph, Chicago, IL
Stretch, Daniel P., La Paz, Bolivia
Tichacek, Charles P., La Paz, Bolivia
Vollmer, Gary l., Las Vegas, NV

Graduate Studies:
Reverend Fathers—
Bene, Philip J., M.A., M.Div., Rome, Italy
Brockland, John A., Rome, Italy

Military Chaplains:
Reverend Fathers—
Banken, Robert L., Lt.
Breig, Gary R.
Kovalcin, John A.
Swetnam, R. William
Zinzer, Walter A.

Absent on Sick Leave:
Reverend Fathers—
Brinkman, Don G.
Christian, Norman H.
Fitzgerald, Alfred J.
Haberkern, Thomas A.
Knight, Robert D.
Valentine, Leroy A.

Retired:
Reverend Monsignors—
Behrmann, Elmer H., 2012 Clermont Crossing Dr., Apt. G, St. Louis, MO 63146
Boessen, Bernard H., Regina Cleri, 7850 Kenrick Rd., St. Louis, MO 63119
Byrne, Henry L., No. 7, Newberry Ct., St. Peters, MO 63376
Byrne, John T., 13900 Clayton Rd., Manchester, MO 63011
Chiodini, Jasper J., Regina Cleri, 7850 Kenrick Rd., St. Louis, MO 63119
Dwyer, Adrian I., 6052 Waterman, St. Louis, MO 63112
Finley, James J., 4607 Poepping, St. Louis, MO 63123
Gannon, Rowland E., 12934 Marine Ave., St. Louis, MO 63146-2234
Glynn, Gerard N., 9814a Greenery Ln., St. Louis, MO 63132
Hartnett, James R., 2013 Trailcrest Ln., St. Louis, MO 63122
Hesseldenz, Clarence H., 5126 Shaw Pl. #A, Waldorf, MD 20602-1519
Holland, James J., 5020 Rhodes Ave., St. Louis, MO 63109-3589
Holland, John P., 1575 N. Woodland Ave., St. Louis, MO 63122-1462
Kennedy, John J., 665 S. Skinker #10E, St. Louis, MO 63105
Krieger, Wilfred L., 4286 Putting Green Dr., San Antonio, TX 78217
Marschner, Aloysius J., Regina Cleri, 7850 Kenrick Rd., St. Louis, MO 63119
Meyer, Louis F., 4908 Sutherland, St. Louis, MO 63109
Molloy, Patrick J., Regina Cleri, 7850 Kenrick Rd., St. Louis, MO 63119
Nibberich, Lawrence C., Regina Cleri, 7850 Kenrick Rd., St. Louis, MO 63119
O'Brien, Joseph T., P.O. Box 54764, St. Petersburg, FL 33739
O'Connell, James P., 60 Plaza Sq., Apt. 1207, St. Louis, MO 63103
Obmann, Russell J., 5851 Itaska Ave., St. Louis, MO 63109-3117
Overman, Robert F., 1711 Parkhaven, San Antonio, TX 78232
Peet, Arthur V., Regina Cleri, 7850 Kenrick Rd., St. Louis, MO 63119
Regan, Michael F., 4335 DuPage Dr., Bridgeton, MO 63044-1606
Ronquest, John T., St. Simon Rectory, 11011 Mueller Rd., St. Louis, MO 63123
Rotrige, Henry J., 2143 Crownhill Rd., San Diego, CA 92109
Schilly, Adolph M., Regina Cleri, 7850 Kenrick Rd., St. Louis, MO 63119
Shocklee, John A., 3225 N. Florissant Ave., St. Louis, MO 63107
Sommer, Jerome, Regina Cleri, 7850 Kenrick Rd., St. Louis, MO 63119
Sullivan, Donald E., Regina Cleri, 7850 Kenrick Rd., St. Louis, MO 63119
Reverend Fathers—
Althoff, Arthur J., Regina Cleri, 7850 Kenrick Rd., St. Louis, MO 63119
Bell, Ira J., Regina Cleri, 7850 Kenrick Rd., St. Louis, MO 63119
Boul, Walter, Regina Cleri, 7850 Kenrick Rd., St. Louis, MO 63119
Britt, William J., Regina Cleri, 7850 Kenrick Rd., St. Louis, MO 63119
Bukauskas, Anthony, 11 Bertha Ln., Union, MO 63084
Burmester, Edwin J., St. Gabriel, 6303 Nottingham, St. Louis, MO 63109
Campbell, John R., 5375 Kenrick Park Dr., St. Louis, MO 63119
Cooper, Thomas T., Regina Cleri, 7850 Kenrick Rd., St. Louis, MO 63119
Deutsch, Bernard F., 101 Winter Harbor Rd., Ocean City, MD 21842
Figge, Edwin H., 753 Rozier, Apt. 10, Ste. Genevieve, MO 63670
Gambon, John A., 300 Eastlane Dr., Washington, MO 63090
Gerst, Lawrence G., 1371 Hamilton, St. Louis, MO 63112
Gibson, Michael P., 665 S. Skinker Blvd., St. Louis, MO 63105
Haar, George B., Regina Cleri, 7850 Kenrick Rd., St. Louis, MO 63119
Hrdlicka, Lambert A., 4243 LaSalette Dr., St. Louis, MO 63123
Huhn, Donald W., 303-107 Racquet Club Rd., Fort Lauderdale, FL 33326
Julius, James A., 1800 Beach Dr., Gulf Port, MS 39507
Kersgieter, Paul J., 2605 Mullanphy Ln., Florissant, MO 63031
Knoll, Urban H., 628 S. Fourth St., St. Charles, MO 63301
Kraus, Robert J., 318 Jefferson St., Apt. 25, Jefferson City, MO 65101
Lessard, Joseph P., P.O. Box 322, Prairie DuRocher, IL 62277
Matyas, Francis B., Regina Cleri, 7850 Kenrick Rd., St. Louis, MO 63119
McLain, J. Clyde, Regina Cleri, 7850 Kenrick Rd., St. Louis, MO 63119
Mersinger, Arthur J., Regina Cleri, 7850 Kenrick Rd., St. Louis, MO 63119
Morse, John A., 525 Mill rd., Marthasville, MO 63357
Noser, J. Homer, 7677 Watson Rd., Apt. 302, St. Louis, MO 63119
Ottoline, Robert A., Regina Cleri, 7850 Kenrick Rd., St. Louis, MO 63119
Phelan, John R., Regina Cleri, 7850 Kenrick Rd., St. Louis, MO 63119
Rehme, Albert A., 362 Rue Bonne Terre (TDL), Bonne Terre, MO 63628
Ruff, Charles R., Regina Cleri, 7850 Kenrick Rd., St. Louis, MO 63119
Ryan, Joseph J., 1526 Chevy Chase, Sun City Center, FL 33573
Scheer, Joseph O., 2800 Olive St., Apt. 4M, St. Louis, MO 63103
Schlattmann, Edward B., Regina Cleri, 7850 Kenrick Rd., St. Louis, MO 63119
Schmaltz, Albert F., 1279 Josephville Rd., Wentzville, MO 63385
Schneider, John G., 1607 Tomkins St., St. Charles, MO 63301
Sommer, Jerome, Regina Cleri, 7850 Kenrick Rd., St. Louis, MO 63119
Thurmer, William H., 1510 Bopp Rd., St. Louis, MO 63131-4137
Unterreiner, Glennon T., 6825 Natural Bridge, St. Louis, MO 63121

Vogler, John E., 7530 Natural Bridge, Normandy, MO 63121
Wetzel, William I., Col., 770 Carolyn Ave., Summerland Key, FL 33042-5646
Wolf, Joseph B., 1970 Greenpoint Dr., Apt. 103, St. Louis, MO 63122

Permanent Deacons:
Arnold, Steven J.
Audrain, Raymond J.
Bachista, Ronald J.
Bachu, Simon W.
Baker, John W., M.D.
Bansbach, Paul, On Duty Outside the Archdiocese
Barron, Eugene D.
Basler, James H.
Bauwens, Gerard, On Duty Outside the Archdiocese
Beckman, Carl H.
Beinke, George A.
Bell, Jesse H.
Bernsen, Albert B.
Blase, George A.
Boedeker, C. Allen
Boland, Richard J.
Bolderson, David A.
Bourbon, Glennon L., Sr.
Boyer, Edward J.
Brooks, Robert A.
Bryant, Wayne T.
Buchek, Bradford M.
Buckley, James Mike
Buckley, John J.
Buckner, Henry A., Sr.
Buhr, Thomas A.
Burkemper, Thomas B.
Burton, James L.
Caruana, Philip P.
Casseau, William U.
Caton, Eugene W.
Chauvin, Charles Frank
Chavaux, Paul H.
Chitwood, Dennis M.
Christ, Walter W.
Clemens, Kenneth C., Jr.
Coffman, Richard W.
Coppage, Michael J., Jr.
Cox, Joseph E.
Crafts, R. Paul
Czarnecki, Eugene J.
Dalton, Michael H.
Damato, Larry (PAT)
Davanzo, Charles R.
DePyper, Robert R.
Dickerson, Raymond A.
Dietz, Alvin J.
Dingman, Edwin H.
Dodson, Fred
Dolan, Timothy C.
Dorhauer, Jacob W.
Dowd, Thomas L.
Drayton, Charles E.
Driscoll, Donald L.
Droesch, Francis A.
Dunning, John W., On Duty Outside the Archdiocese
Ecker, Alan E.
Efken, Donald C.
Ehrhard, Herbert L.
Esswein, Leo F.
Eultgen, Thomas L.
Falbo, Anthony D. (HRT)
Fick, Franklin J.
Fink, George Russ
Flint, Edward G.
Forster, Thomas E.
Fronick, Edward C.
Gabbert, William L.
Gamache, Robert K. (DEN)
Gawedzinkski, Norbert L.
Gearon, William A.
Gegg, Albin A.
Geiser, Gerald J.
Georges, Charles W.
Gerdes, Philip J.
Gerling, Thomas J. (JC)
Gettemeier, Herbert B.
Gholston, Clifford
Gorski, Thomas (ARL)
Gounis, Peter E.
Graham, George A.
Grant, Maurice A., Sr.
Greif, William J.
Gunsaullus, Roland J.
Haefner, Joseph Tom
Hanses, Eugene J.
Harris, Singleton L.
Harrison, R. Fielding
Heitert, Donald C.
Hengen, Philip R.
Hennicke, Raymond C.
Henning, Kenneth A.
Henroid, Daniel H.
Hercules, Joseph E.
Hesse, Richard P.
Hirtz, Frederick J., On Duty Outside the Archdiocese
Hoffmann, Eugene A.
Holmes, Charles E.
Holtmeyer, Gilbert C.
Hummel, Fred J.
Hutti, Lawrence J., Jr.
Janson, Norman F.
Johnson, Leslie A.
Jurek, Thomas F., On Duty Outside the Archdiocese
Karsznia, Robert A.
Kaufman, Allen G.
Keeney, Robert J.
Kelly, Lawrence C.
Kennedy, Joseph M.
Kenney, T. Michael, III
Kiechlin, Robert J., Jr.
Kiely, E. Ray
Klempert, Michael L.
Klostermann, Robert, Sr.
Knobbe, Gerald E.
Kreft, Ronald J.
Krieger, Arnold F.
Kuenz, Gary J.
Lake, Richard C.
Levac, Richard B.
Lombardo, Charles W.
Longmeyer, Harold
Love, Allen F.
Luke, Herbert, M.D.
Macauley, Edward C.
Marcinkiewicz, Joseph, Jr.
Marren, L. Jerome
Martin, Leroy A., Jr.
McGrath, James E.
McGuire, Jerry N.
McInnis, J. Kevin
McKee, Paul R.
McKenna, William J.
McNamee, George W., On Duty Outside the Archdiocese
McNamee, Terrance M.
Menard, Louis A.
Messineo, Anthony L.
MeyerKord, Gary A.
Miller, George W.
Miller, Millard Ray
Morris, Joseph C.
Mroczkowski, R. V.
Mueller, Frederick J.
Murphy, James L.
Murphy, Thomas P.
Murphy, Thomas O.
Murray, Stephen L.
Nesbitt, Frank E.
Nieman, Harry
Niemeyer, Andrew C.
Noelker, Leon R.
O'Leary, John A.
Otzenberger, Joseph M.
Peacock, Joseph C.
Penberthy, Robert S.
Peterson, Stanley M., Jr.
Politte, Glennon P., Sr.
Politte, Stephen A.
Politte, Thomas G.
Porterfield, Paul D.
Potzman, Kenneth M.
Powers, Robert J.
Prideaux, Frank W.
Priesmeyer, W., Jr.
Prives, Gerald J.
Quinn, J. Gerard
Reynoso, Louis J.
Riegel, Robert C.
Roberson, Robert L.
Roderick, Walter L.
Ruegg, Walter J.
Sabo, Michael C.
Schiffman, Donald J.
Schnable, Robert H.
Schuld, Gerald C.
Schulte, Edwin
Schultheis, Glennon J.
Schulze, Roy E.
Shelby, Richard L.
Shipp, Nathaniel E.
Sinak, William S.
Sisul, Leonard A.
Smerek, Robert S.
Smith, James R.
Smith, John F.
Snyder, Robert J.
Snyder, Robert C.
Stoverink, Gerard G.
Stoverink, John J.
Strauss, Harold A.
Streckfuss, Joseph C.
Suden, Michael E., D.D.S.
Sulze, Joseph W.
Sutton, Ronald L.
Tichacek, George A.
Toohey, Jerome V.
Towey, Martin G.
Trautman, Anthony G.
Tresch, Earl K.
Vaughn, Albert X.
Volansky, James M.
Walbridge, William F.
Weatherholt, Harold J.
Weishaar, Lonnie G.
Weiss, William G.
Werner, Norman B.
Wertz, Robert E.
Wessels, Richard H.
Willbrand, Thomas J.
Williams, Albert C.
Winkelmann, Christian H.
Winker, Ewald
Wood, George F.
Wunderlich, William P.
Wussler, Donald A.

INSTITUTIONS LOCATED IN THE ARCHDIOCESE

[A] SEMINARIES, ARCHDIOCESAN

ST. LOUIS. *Kenrick-Glennon Seminary*. (St. Louis Roman Catholic Theological Seminary). Rev. Msgr. George J. Lucas, M.A., Rector.

Kenrick School of Theology, 5200 Glennon Dr., 63119. Tel: 314-644-1645; Fax: 314-644-3079. Rev. Msgr. George J. Lucas, M.A., Rector; Revs. Thomas M. Molini, M.A., Vice Rector & Dean Formation; Lawrence C. Brennan, S.T.D., Academic Dean; James E. Swift, C.M., S.T.D., Dir. of Spiritual Life; Rev. Msgr. William J. Lyons, S.T.L., Dir. Pre-Theology; Mr. William J. Matula, B.A., Business Officer; Mr. Peter S. Maher, J.D., LL.M., Dir. Devel.; Revs. John F. Clark, C.M., M.A.; Robert F. Coerver, C.M., S.T.D., Prof. Emeritus; Glennon C. Doherty, M.A.; John P. Heil, S.S.D.; Gregory J. Lockwood, S.T.D. (Candidate); Donald F. Molitor, M.A.; James J. Ramacciotti, J.C.L.; Edward J. Richard, M.S., S.T.D.; Rev. Msgr. Edward C. Eichor, M.A.; Sr. Zoe Glenski, D.C., Ph.D.; Susanne M. Harvath, Ph.D.; Anne Marie Kitz, Ph.D.; Glenn C.J. Byer, S.L.D.; Andrew J. Sopko, Ph.D.; Lawrence J. Welch, Ph.D.; Mr. Peter F. Hesed, M.A.; Deacon George W. Miller, B.S.; Rabbi Howard M. Graber, Ph.D.; Ms. Lucille M. Trujillo-Tiroch, M.A. Priests 16; Sisters 2; Students 58; St. Louis Students 21. Permanent Staff: Priests 16; Sisters 2; Lay Staff 10.

Cardinal Glennon College, 5200 Glennon Dr., 63119. Tel: 314-644-0266; Fax: 314-644-3079. Rev. Edward M. Rice, Dir.; Rev. Msgr. Edward C. Eichor, Assoc. Dir.; Rev. Msgr. William J. Lyons, Spiritual Dir.; Sr. Pat Dalton, S.S.N.D.; Sr. M. Johanna Paruch, O.S.F.; Mr. Robert Meyer; Mrs. Jeanine Burton; Ms. Helen Marx, Exec. Sec. Priests 3; Sisters 2; Lay Teachers 3; Students 18; St. Louis Students 11; Belize Students 1; Belleville Students 1; Birmingham, AL Students 2; Peoria, IL Students 3. Permanent Staff: Priests 15; Sisters 8; Lay Teachers 11.

[B] SEMINARIES, RELIGIOUS, OR SCHOLASTICATES

ST. LOUIS. *Aquinas Institute of Theology*, 3642 Lindell Blvd., 63108. Tel: 314-977-3882; Fax: 314-977-7225.
E-mail: aquinas@slu.edu
Web site: www.op.org/aquinas/
Rev. Charles E. Bouchard, O.P., Pres.; Sr. Diane Kennedy, O.P., Dean; Rev. Albert G. Glade, O.P., Business Mgr. & Dir. Student Affairs; Eileen Wickham, Inst. Advancement; Ron Knapp, Admissions and Public Rels.; Revs. Richard A. Peddicord, O.P.; Joseph P. Gillespie, O.P.; Donald Goergen, O.P.; Gregory J. Heille, O.P.; Thomas Esselman, C.M.; Harry M. Byrne, O.P.; Frank C. Quinn, O.P.; George Boudreau, O.P.; Sr. Marygrace Peters, O.P.; Sr. Joan Delaplane, O.P.; Sr. Mary Margaret Pazdan, O.P.; Sr. Carla Mae Streeter, O.P.; Sr. Catherine Vincie, R.S.H.M. Priests 10; Sisters 9; Lay Teachers 4; Seminarians 22; Total Enrollment 197.

St. John Neumann House. Redemptorist College Seminary Residence, 3737 Washington Blvd., 63108. Tel: 314-531-2777; Fax: 314-531-5726. Revs. Gary Lauenstein, C.Ss.R., Rector and Superior; Joseph Nolen, C.Ss.R., Dir. of Formation; David Polek, C.Ss.R., Vocation Dir.; Wm. Emmett Collins, C.Ss.R.; Jack Hacker, C.Ss.R. Priests 5; Seminarians 11.

[C] COLLEGES AND UNIVERSITIES

ST. LOUIS. *Fontbonne College*, 6800 Wydown Blvd., 63105. Tel: 314-862-3456.
E-mail: sking@fontbonne.edu
Web site: www.fontbonne.edu
For a complete listing, refer to the Colleges and Universities section.

Saint Louis University, 221 N. Grand Blvd., DB 261, 63103-2097. Tel: 314-977-2222
For a complete listing, refer to the Colleges and Universities section.

[D] RELIGIOUS EDUCATION

ST. LOUIS. *Paul VI Institute of Catechetical and Pastoral Studies*, 4140 Lindell Blvd., 63108. Tel: 314-371-4980, Ext. 74; Fax: 314-371-0267.
E-mail: stlpaul@connectinc.com
Rev. Msgr. John M. Unger, Dir.; Sr. Marianne Almon, S.S.N.D., Admin. Total Enrollment 2,000.

[E] HIGH SCHOOLS, ARCHDIOCESAN

ST. LOUIS. *Bishop DuBourg High School*, 5850 Eichelberger St., 63109. Tel: 314-832-3030. A Co-Educational School Staffed by Diocesan Priests, Religious and Lay Teachers. Mr. Thomas Jokerst, Prin. Associate Principals: Dr. Gerald Gruszka; Ms. Cathy Fetter. Priests 4; Sisters 4; Lay Teachers 54; Students 898.

Cardinal Ritter College Prep, 5421 Thekla Ave., 63120. Tel: 314-381-7980; Fax: 314-381-8050. Co-Educational High School Staffed by Religious and Laity. Mrs. Carmele U. Hall, Pres. & Prin. Sisters 1; Lay Teachers 19; Students 258.

Rosati-Kain High School, 4389 Lindell Blvd., 63108. Tel: 314-533-8513.
E-mail: archstl808@connectinc.com
Conducted for Girls by Diocesan Priest, the Sisters of St. Joseph and the School Sisters of Notre Dame. Sr. Joan Andert, S.S.N.D., Prin.; Patrice Johannes, Assoc. Prin. Priests 1; Sisters 4; Lay Teachers 22; Girls 429.

Saint Mary's High School, 4701 S. Grand Blvd., 63111. Tel: 314-481-8400.
E-mail: archstl809@connectinc.com
For Boys, Staffed by Brothers of Mary and Archdiocesan Priests. Rev. Mitchell Doyen, Admin.; Mr. Kevin Hacker, B.A., M.Ed., Prin. Priests 3; Brothers 1; Sisters 1; Lay Teachers 30; Total Enrollment 482.

FESTUS. *St. Pius X High School*, 1030 St. Pius Dr., 63028. Tel: 314-937-3695; 931-7487. A Co-Educational High School Conducted by Diocesan Priests and Lay Faculty. Mrs. Gayle Rogan, Prin. Priests 3; Lay Teachers 28; Students 454.

FLORISSANT. *St. Thomas Aquinas-Mercy High School*, 845 Dunn Rd., 63031. Tel: 314-837-1144. A Co-Educational High School Conducted by One Diocesan Priest, a Vincentian Priest, and Lay Men and Women. Mr. Paul Frein, Prin.; Patricia Moore, Asst. Prin. Priests 2; Lay Teachers 30; Students 515.

MANCHESTER. *John F. Kennedy Catholic High School*, 500 Woods Mill Rd., 63011. Tel: 314-227-5900.
E-mail: archstl804@connectinc.com
A Co-Educational High School Staffed by Diocesan Priests. Randy Berzon, Prin. Priests 1; Lay Teachers 30; Students 462.

O'FALLON. *St. Dominic High School*, 31 St. Dominic Dr., 63366. Tel: 314-240-8303; Fax: 314-240-9884. A Co-Educational High School Conducted by Diocesan Priests and Sisters of the Third Order of St. Dominic. Sr. Mary H. Bender, S.S.N.D., Admin.; Sr. Carolyn, O.P., Prin. Priests 2; Sisters 2; Lay Teachers 39; Students 645.

ST. CHARLES. *Duchesne High School*, 2550 Elm St., 63301-1494. Tel: 314-946-6767.
E-mail: archstl821@connectinc.com
Web site: www.duchesne-hs.org
A Co-Educational College Prep High School Conducted by Archdiocesan Priests and Catholic Lay Staff. Under the Auspices of the Catholic Education Office. Sponsored by Seven Parishes in and around St. Charles, MO. Mr. Charles L. Nolan, Admin.; Mr. Donald C. Burkhart, Prin.; Revs. James L. Gahan; Donald E. Henke. Priests 2; Sisters 1; Lay Teachers 42; Students 622.

SPANISH LAKE. *Rosary High School*, 1720 Redman Ave., 63138. Tel: 314-741-1333. A Co-Educational High School Staffed by Archdiocesan Priests, Religious and Lay Teachers. Daniel J. Matusiak, Ed.D., Prin.; Sr. Geraldine Neier, S.S.N.D., Asst. Prin.; Mr. Richard Barrett, Asst. Prin. Priests 1; Sisters 2; Lay Teachers 32; Students 546.

WASHINGTON. *St. Francis Borgia Regional High School*, 1000 Borgia Dr., 63090. Tel: 314-239-7871; Fax: 314-239-1198.
Web site: http://www.borgia.com
A Co-Educational High School Staffed by Diocesan Priests and School Sisters of Notre Dame and dedicated lay faculty. Marilyn Traffas, Admin.; Mr. George Wingbermuehle, Prin. Priests 1; Sisters 2; Lay Teachers 42; Students 629.

[F] HIGH SCHOOLS, PRIVATE

ST. LOUIS. *Christian Brothers College High School (C.B.C.)*, 6501 Clayton Rd., 63117. Tel: 314-721-1200; Fax: 314-721-2471.
E-mail: archstl852@connectinc.com
Bro. Lawrence Humphrey, F.S.C., Pres.; Mr. James B. Gerdes, Prin. Brothers 10; Lay Teachers 60; Students 967.

Cor Jesu Academy, 10230 Gravois, 63123. Tel: 314-842-1546.
E-mail: soneill@corjesu.pvt.k12.mo.us
Web site: http://www.corjesu.pvt.k12.mo.us
Apostles of the Sacred Heart. Sr. Sheila O'Neill, A.S.C.J., Prin. Priests 1; Sisters 10; Lay Teachers 30; Students 535.

De Smet Jesuit High School, 233 N. New Ballas Rd., 63141. Tel: 314-567-3502. Dr. Gregory A. Densberger, Ph.D., Prin.; Rev. Richard L. Bailey, S.J., Pres. Priests 9; Sisters 2; Brothers 1; Lay Teachers 68; Students 1,230.

Incarnate Word Academy, 2788 Normandy Dr., 63121. Tel: 314-725-5850; Fax: 314-725-2308. Sisters of Charity of Incarnate Word of San Antonio. Mrs. Nancy Repking, Prin. Lay Teachers 38; Support Staff 16; Students 482.

Notre Dame High School, 320 E. Ripa Ave., 63125. Tel: 314-544-1015; Fax: 314-544-8003.
E-mail: archstl875@connectinc.com
Sr. Michelle Emmerich, S.S.N.D., Prin. Sisters 10; Lay Teachers 44; Girls 509.

St. Elizabeth Academy, 3401 Arsenal St., 63118. Tel: 314-771-5134. Sisters of the Most Precious Blood. Sr. Theresa Austin, C.PP.S., Pres.; Sr. Timothy Ann Timmek, C.PP.S., Prin. Sisters 5; Lay Teachers 19; Students 235.

St. Joseph's Academy, 2307 S. Lindbergh Blvd., 63131. Tel: 314-965-7205; Fax: 314-965-9114. Sr. Nancy Folkl, C.S.J., Prin. Sisters of St. Joseph of Carondelet 7; Lay Teachers 44; Girls 608.

St. Louis University High School, George H. Backer Memorial, 4970 Oakland Ave., 63110. Tel: 314-531-0330.
Web site: http://www.sluh.org.
Revs. Richard E. Hadel, S.J.; Paul G. Sheridan, S.J., Pres.; Martin Hagan, S.J.; Jeffrey D. Harrison; James G. Knapp, S.J., Supr.; Ralph D. Houlihan, S.J.; Bros. Thomas C. Thornton, S.J.; Richard H. Witzofsky, S.J. In res. Very Rev. Frank E. Reale, S.J.; Rev. Philip G. Steele, S.J. Priests 6; Brothers 2; Scholastics 1; Admin. 4; Lay Teachers 76; Students 1,026.

CREVE COEUR. *Chaminade College Preparatory School Inc.*, 425 S. Lindbergh Blvd., 63131-2799. Tel: 314-993-4400; Fax: 314-993-4403. Residents and Day Students. Society of Mary. Rev. Ralph A. Siefert, S.M., Pres.; James E. Gerker, Prin.; Michael Thro, Campus Min. Priests 2; Brothers 4; Lay Teachers 61; Students 525.

St. Louis Priory School, 500 S. Mason Rd., 63141-8500. Tel: 314-434-3690; Fax: 314-576-7088.
Web site: http://www.priory.org.
Rev. J. Gregory Mohrman, O.S.B., Headmaster; Rt. Rev. W. Thomas Frerking, O.S.B.; Revs. Christopher Hanson, O.S.B.; M. Paul Kidner, O.S.B.; J. Laurence Kriegshauser, O.S.B.; Joseph Marino, O.S.B.; Bede Price, O.S.B.; D. Ralph Wright, O.S.B. Priests 8; Brothers 4; Lay Teachers 39; High School Students 228; Students Grades 7-8 146.

FRONTENAC. *Villa Duchesne/Oak Hill*, 801 S. Spoede Rd., 63131. Tel: 314-432-2021.
(Girls: PreK-12; Boys: PreK-6). Religious of the Sacred Heart. Mrs. Renee Allen, Prin. (7-12); Dr. Harry Trumfio, Prin. (PreK-6); Sr. Ann Caire, R.S.C.J., Headmistress. Sisters 6; Lay Faculty 78; Elementary School Students (PreK-6) 396; High School Students (7-12) 390.

KIRKWOOD. *Ursuline Academy*, 341 S. Sappington Rd., 63122. Tel: 314-966-4556.
E-mail: archstl879@connectinc.com
Ursuline Nuns of the Roman Union. Dr. Patricia Hensley, Prin. Sisters 3; Lay Teachers 50; Students 609.

Vianney High School, 1311 S. Kirkwood Rd., 63122. Tel: 314-965-4853; Fax: 314-965-1950.
E-mail: archstl856@connectinc.com
Conducted for Boys by the Society of Mary (Marianists). Revs. Richard Wosman, S.M., Pres.; J. Donald Cahill, S.M.; Robert R. Osborne, S.M. Priests 3; Brothers 6; Lay Teachers 42; Students 700.

TOWN AND COUNTRY. *Visitation Academy*, 3020 N. Ballas Rd., 63131. Tel: 314-432-5353; Fax: 314-432-7210.
E-mail: archstl871@connectinc.com
Web site: www.inlink.com/~viz
William Gallop, Head of School; Maxine Adlersfluegel, Ph.D., Prin. (Grades 7-12); Barbara McMullen, Asst. Prin. Visitation Sisters 6; Precious Blood Sisters 1; Lay Teachers 53; Students 396.

WEBSTER GROVES. *Nerinx Hall High School*, 530 E. Lockwood, 63119. Tel: 314-968-1505; Fax: 314-962-6556.
E-mail: cwinkler@nerinxhs.org
Web site: www.nerinxhs.org
Sr. Barbara Roche, S.L., Pres.; Dr. Mary Schenkenberg, Prin.; Mrs. Jane Kosash, Assoc. Prin. Sisters of Loretto at the Foot of the Cross 6; Religious 3; Lay Teachers 43; Students 579.

[G] ELEMENTARY SCHOOLS, PRIVATE

CHESTERFIELD. *Linda Vista Catholic School*, 1633 Kehrs Mill Rd., 63005. Tel: 314-532-3315. Conducted by the Sisters of the Most Precious Blood.
Preschool Classes for 3-6 Year Olds, Grades 1-6. Lay Teachers 30; Students 252.

CREVE COEUR. *Chaminade College Preparatory*. (Middle School), Residents and Day Students, 425 S. Lindbergh Blvd., 63131. Tel: 314-993-4400; Fax: 314-993-4403.
(Boys Grades 7-12). Society of Mary. Rev. Ralph A. Siefert, S.M., Pres.; Mr. Michael T. Bander, Prin. Priests 2; Lay Teachers 24; Students 260.

St. Louis Priory School, 500 S. Mason Rd., 63141-8500. Tel: 314-434-3690; Fax: 314-576-7088.
(Boys Grades 7-8).
Corporate Title: The Abbey of St. Mary and St. Louis. Rev. J. Gregory Mohrman, O.S.B., Headmaster. Priests 3; Brothers 2; Lay Teachers 24; Students 135.

FRONTENAC. *Oak Hill School*, 801 S. Spoede Rd., 63131. Tel: 314-432-2021.
E-mail: acaire@vdoh.org
Web site: www.sofie.org/villa/web
(Grades PreK-6) (Coed). Dr. Harry Trumfio, Prin.; Sr. Ann Caire, R.S.C.J., Headmistress. Sisters 2; Lay Teachers 34; Students 400.

Villa Duchesne. Tel: 314-432-2021. (Girls 7-12). Mailing Address: 801 S. Spoede Rd., St. Louis, 63131-2699. Mrs. Renee Allen, Prin.; Sr. Ann Caire, R.S.C.J., Headmistress. Sisters 6; Lay Teachers 48; Girls 384.

ST. CHARLES. *Academy of the Sacred Heart*. (Coed), 619 N. 2nd St., 63301. Tel: 314-946-6127; Fax: 314-949-6659.
Web site: http://www.i1.net/~nsh03ed.
Religious of the Sacred Heart. Sr. Margaret Caire, Headmistress; Mrs. Kathy Hopper, Prin. Sisters 11; Lay Teachers 48; Students 689.

TOWN AND COUNTRY. *Visitation Academy*, 3020 N. Ballas Rd., 63131. Tel: 314-432-5353.
E-mail: mrath@visitation.com
Web site: www.inlink.com/~viz
Mr. William Gallop, Head of School; Mary Rath, Prin. (PreK-6). Visitation Sisters 3; Lay Teachers 20; Students 254.

[H] DEPARTMENT OF SPECIAL EDUCATION

ST. LOUIS. *Catholic Guidance Center*, 4472 Lindell Blvd., 63108. Tel: 314-533-3454. Psycho-Educational Testing Facility and also Administrative Office for the Archdiocesan Department of Special Education, Serving Children with Developmental Disabilities, Mental Retardation or Learning Disabilities. Rev. Msgr. Vernon E. Gardin, Ph.D., Exec. Dir.
Special Ungraded Day Classes, Schools and Residential School, PSR for Disabled and with Mental Retardation Children or Major Learning Disabilities (ages 5-16). Located in the Following Parish Schools: Holy Innocents (2 LD Classes); Sacred Heart (2 MR Classes); St. Christopher (5 LD Classes); Our Lady of Guadalupe (1 LD Class); Annunziata (6 LD Classes); St. John the Baptist (3 LD Classes); St. George (3 LD Classes); St. Gregory (2 LD Classes). Total Number of Children Served 270.

St. Mary's Special Services, 5341 Emerson Ave., 63120. Tel: 314-261-8533; Fax: 314-381-2002. Legal Title: *St. Mary's Special School for Exceptional Children*. Rev. Msgr. Vernon E. Gardin, Exec. Dir. A Residential Facility for children with mental retardation & other developmental disabilities (ages 5-21); Early Intervention Prog. for children (ages 0-35 months) with developmental disabilities; Independent Supported living Prog. serving clients with mental retardation & other developmental disabilities (age 14 & up); Vocational Placement Svcs. for clients (age 16 & up). Lay Staff 64; Clients 97.

Special Religious Education Ministry, 4472 Lindell Blvd., 63108. Tel: 314-533-3454. Department of Special Education. Mary Beth Schulte, Coord. Provides catholic religious education for children with disabilities in public special programs. (ages 7-21) & for adults with disabilities living in institutions or in their own homes. Lay Teachers 35; Total Enrollment 105.

UNIVERSITY CITY. *St. Joseph Institute for the Deaf*, 1483 82nd Blvd., 63132. Tel: 314-993-1507 (Voice/TDD); Fax: 314-993-9890. School for the Deaf (School for Handicapped). J. Michael Keller, Pres.; Marietta Paterson, Ph.D., Prin. Sisters 12; Lay Teachers 27; Students 110. Audio/oral day & residential school for hearing-impaired children from birth-8th grade. Early intervention therapy for children 0-5; pre- & elementary school offering intense speech & academic prog.

[I] SERVICES FOR THE ELDERLY

ST. LOUIS. *Cardinal Ritter Institute*, 4483 Lindell Blvd., 63108. Tel: 314-652-3600. Archdiocesan Office Provides Social Services, Health Services and Housing Services for the Elderly. Legal Title: *Cardinal Ritter Institute, Inc.* Mr. John M. Lally, CEO; Arthur J. Korte, COO. Total Clients Served 27,726.

Cardinal Ritter Institute Residential Services, Inc., 4483 Lindell Blvd., 63108. Tel: 314-652-3600. Provides housing Mgmt. & other svcs. for residential facilities for the elderly. Mr. John M. Lally, CEO; Michael J. Lally, COO.

Alexian Court Apartments. (Legal Title: Alexian Brothers Services, Inc.), 2636 Chippewa St., 63118. Tel: 314-771-5604.
Sponsored by Alexian Brothers of Missouri, Inc., Managed by Cardinal Ritter Institute.

St. John Neumann Apartments, Inc., 8424 Lucas Hunt Rd., 63136. Tel: 314-385-0707.

St. Joseph Apartments, Inc., 7677 Watson Rd., 63119. Tel: 314-962-0969.

St. Patrick Apartments, Inc. A part of Cardinal Carberry Living Center. 555 Bluff Parks Dr., 63031. Tel: 314-839-3212.

San Luis Apartments, Inc., 4483 Lindell Blvd., 63108. Tel: 314-534-4730.

Santa Ana Apartments, Inc., 3737 Ashby Rd., 63074. Tel: 314-428-7385.

Visitation Senior Apartments, Inc., 1911 N. Taylor Ave., 63113. Tel: 314-652-3600.

Holy Infant Apartments, Inc. A part of Cardinal Carberry Living Center. 7663 Watson Rd., 63119. Tel: 314-962-7878.

St. Agnes Apartments, Inc., 2840 Wisconsin, 63118. Tel: 314-664-1255. St. Peter Residence for Seniors, 333 S. Second St., St. Charles, 63301-6401. Tel: 314-947-7004. Property of St. Peter Parish, Managed by Cardinal Ritter Institute. Santa Maria Apartments, 12565 Santa Maria Ct., Hazelwood, 63042. Tel: 314-739-7220.

Pope John Paul II Apartments, Inc., 6325 Waterways Dr., 63033.

Cardinal Ritter Institute Residential Services Corp., 4483 Lindell Blvd., 63108. Tel: 314-652-3600. Provides Housing Management and Other Services for Residential Facilities for the Elderly. Mr. John M. Lally, CEO; Michael J. Lally, Dir. and COO.

Corporate Action for the Care of the Elderly, Inc., 7601 Watson Rd., 63119. Tel: 314-961-8485. Association Composed of Representatives of 14 Religious Communities and The Cardinal Ritter Institute. Corporal Work of Mercy in the Metro St. Louis Area. Bro. Thomas Keusenkothen, C.F.A., Pres.

St. Elizabeth Adult Day Care Center, 3401 Arsenal St., 63118. Tel: 314-772-5107; Fax: 314-772-3674. Conducted by the Sisters of the Most Precious Blood to Provide Day Care for the Elderly and handicapped. Sr. John Antonio Miller, C.PP.S., Dir.

St. Elizabeth East Adult Day Care Center, 3227 S. Ninth St., 63118. Tel: 314-771-1591.

St. Elizabeth West Adult Day Care Center, 7240 Anna, 63143. Tel: 314-644-6585.

St. Elizabeth North Adult Day Care Center, 2545 Dorwood, 63136. Tel: 314-867-6511.

St. Elizabeth / Visitation Adult Day Care Center, 1421 N. Taylor, 63113. Tel: 314-531-2985. For all: Total Assisted 210; Total Staff 48.

[J] CHILD GUIDANCE

ST. LOUIS. *Central Intake*, 4140 Lindell Blvd., 63108. Tel: 314-371-0047; 371-0051; 371-0053 (Managed Care Ref. only).
E-mail: cscy@stl.unitedway.org
Sally Nelson, A.C.S.W., L.C.S.W., Dir. of Central Intake. Provides evaluation & referral svcs. for Child Help (formerly Catholic Charities Children's Network or Catholic Charities Children's Services Network) & handles managed care referrals for entire Catholic Charities Federation of St. Louis. Total Assisted 2,794; Total Staff 2.

Child Center of Our Lady, 7900 Natural Bridge Rd., 63121. Tel: 314-383-0200; Fax: 314-383-6334. Psychiatric Treatment Center. Donna Coble, Exec. Dir. Legal Title: *Child Center of Our Lady of Grace, Inc.* Patients assisted annually 200 (Children, Adolescents, Parents and Families); Total Staff 48.

[K] GENERAL HOSPITALS

ST. LOUIS. *Alexian Brothers Hospital*, 3933 S. Broadway, 63118. Tel: 314-865-3333
For a complete listing, refer to the Hospitals section.

Lafayette Grand Hospital, 3545 Lafayette, 63104. Tel: 314-865-6500; Fax: 314-865-6526
For a complete listing, refer to the Hospitals section.

St. Anthony's Medical Center, 10010 Kennerly Rd., 63128. Tel: 314-525-1000.
E-mail: solamsestlo.smhs.com
For a complete listing, refer to the Hospitals section.

Saint Louis University Hospital, 3635 Vista Ave., P.O. Box 15250, 63110-0250. Tel: 314-577-8000, Ext. 8066; Fax: 314-577-8003 (Exec. Office)
For a complete listing, refer to the Hospitals section.

St. Mary's Health Center, 6420 Clayton Rd., 63117. Tel: 314-768-8000; Fax: 314-768-8011
For a complete listing, refer to the Hospitals section.

BRIDGETON. *De Paul Health Center*, 12303 De Paul Dr., 63044. Tel: 314-344-6000
For a complete listing, refer to the Hospitals section.

CREVE COEUR. *St. John's Mercy Medical Center*, 615 S. New Ballas Rd., 63141. Tel: 314-569-6000; Fax: 314-569-6910
For a complete listing, refer to the Hospitals section.

KIRKWOOD. *St. Joseph Hospital of Kirkwood*, 525 Couch Ave., 63122. Tel: 314-966-1601
For a complete listing, refer to the Hospitals section.

LAKE ST. LOUIS. *St. Joseph Hospital West*, 100 Medical Plaza, 63367. Tel: 314-625-5200; Fax: 314-625-5314
For a complete listing, refer to the Hospitals section.

ST. CHARLES. *St. Joseph Health Center*, 300 First Capitol Dr., 63301. Tel: 314-947-5000; Fax: 314-947-5090
For a complete listing, refer to the Hospitals section.

WASHINGTON. *St. John's Mercy Hospital*, 200 Madison Ave., 63090. Tel: 314-239-8000
For a complete listing, refer to the Hospitals section.

[L] SPECIAL HOSPITALS

ST. LOUIS. *Cardinal Glennon Children's Hospital*, 1465 S. Grand Blvd., 63104. Tel: 314-577-5600; Fax: 314-268-6468
For a complete listing, refer to the Special Care Facilities section.

SSM Rehab, 6420 Clayton Rd., #600, 63117. Tel: 314-768-5300; Fax: 314-768-5355
For a complete listing, refer to the Special Care Facilities section.

[M] PROTECTIVE INSTITUTIONS

Day Care Centers

ST. LOUIS. *Guardian Angel Settlement Association*, Mailing Address: P.O. Box 2055, 63158. Tel: 314-231-3188. Fonda Fantroy, Exec. Dir. Founded by the Daughters of Charity of St. Vincent de Paul. Child Day Care Services.

DeSales Day Care, 2652 Ohio, 63118. Tel: 314-771-6417.

St. Patrick's Day Care, 1200 N. 6th St., 63106. Tel: 314-421-2816.

Social Services, 1401 La Salle St., 63104. Tel: 314-231-3188. Casework & Case Mgmt.; Emergency Svcs.; Senior Prog., Summer Youth Employment Prog.; Neighborhood Activities; Art, Gardening & Environmental Prog.; Paralegal on staff. For all: Total Assisted 14,964; Total Staff 40.

Sacred Heart Villa, 2108 Macklind Ave., 63110. Tel: 314-771-2224.
E-mail: SHVilla@aol.com
Web site: http://members.aol.com/shvilla
Sr. Barbara Ann Matazzaro, A.S.C.J., Dir. Full-Time Care From 6:30-5:30 for Children 3-5 Years Old. Conducted by the Apostles of the Sacred Heart of Jesus. Total Assisted 125; Total Staff 22.

Stella Maris Child Center, 5654 Delmar Blvd., 63112. Tel: 314-367-7950. Ann Bingham, Dir. Conducted by a Board of Directors and Staff of Lay Teachers. Licensed Capacity 132; Total Assisted 200; Total Staff 50.

Visitation Child Development Center, 1421 N. Taylor, 63113. Tel: 314-533-8411. E. Nancy Norman, Dir. Learning Center and Day Care Service for 2-6 Year Old Children; Kindergarten Included. Conducted by Visitation Parish. Total Assisted 2; Total Staff 5.

FERGUSON. *Villa St. Joseph Child Care and Education Center*, 205 Brotherton Ln., 63135. Tel: 314-521-4424. Brenda Thomas, Dir. Operated by the Franciscan Sisters of Our Lady of Perpetual Help. Total Assisted 60; Total Staff 14.

IMPERIAL. *Queen of Apostles Center*, 800 Montebello Camp Rd., 63052. Tel: 314-464-0163. Apostles of the Sacred Heart of Jesus 4; Total Staff 10; Children 65.

KINLOCH. *St. Martin's Child Center*, 8140 Scott Ave., P.O. Box 9722, 63140. Tel: 314-524-4719. Ms. Lula Stallings, Exec. Dir. Day care for children 2-6 years, 2-12 Summer only. Legal Title: *St. Martin Child Center, Inc.* Bed Capacity 63; Total Assisted 100; Total Staff 13.

KIRKWOOD. *Carmelite Child Development Center*, 1111 N. Woodlawn Ave., 63122.
E-mail: stagnes@primary.net
Web site: http://www.carmelitedcj.org
Provides child development, child care and child education and services. Full Day 106; Kindergarten 31; Total Staff 15.

St. Joseph Educational Child Care Center, 1132 S. Glenwood Ave., 63122. Tel: 314-821-6636. Operated by the St. Joseph Hospital in Kirkwood.

[N] HOMES FOR CHILDREN

ST. LOUIS. *Boys Hope / Girls Hope of St. Louis, Inc.*, 755 S. New Ballas Rd., Ste. 120, 63141. Tel: 314-692-7477; Fax: 314-692-7810
For a complete listing, refer to the Special Care Facilities section.

Marian Hall Agencies, 1340 Partridge Ave., 63130. Tel: 314-726-3339
For a complete listing, refer to the Special Care Facilities section.

Marian Hall Emergency Shelter, 325 N. Newstead, 63108. Tel: 314-531-0511
For a complete listing, refer to the Special Care Facilities section.

St. Joseph's Home for Boys, 4753 S. Grand Blvd., 63111-1459. Tel: 314-481-9121; Fax: 314-481-5605.
E-mail: stjoehome@stl.unitedway.org
For a complete listing, refer to the Special Care Facilities section.

FLORISSANT. *Father Dunne's News Boys Home*, 853 Dunn Rd., 63031. Tel: 314-837-0513
For a complete listing, refer to the Special Care Facilities section.

Marygrove Services, Inc., 2705 Mullanphy Ln., 63031. Tel: 314-837-1702; Fax: 314-830-6258.
E-mail: mgrove@swb.net
For a complete listing, refer to the Special Care Facilities section.

NORMANDY. *St. Vincent Home for Children*, 7401 Florissant Rd., 63121. Tel: 314-261-6011
For a complete listing, refer to the Special Care Facilities section.

[O] HOMES FOR AGED

ST. LOUIS. *Alexian Brothers Lansdowne Village*, 4624 Lansdowne, 63116. Tel: 314-351-6888; Fax: 314-351-5825
For a complete listing, refer to the Special Care Facilities section.

Alexian Brothers Sherbrooke Village, 4005 Ripa Ave., 63125. Tel: 314-544-1111; Fax: 314-544-5134
For a complete listing, refer to the Special Care Facilities section.

Chariton Apartments, 4249 Michigan Ave., 63111. Tel: 314-352-7600
For a complete listing, refer to the Special Care Facilities section.

Fusz Pavilion, 3601 Lindell Blvd., 63108. Tel: 314-534-1201
For a complete listing, refer to the Special Care Facilities section.

Little Sisters of the Poor, Home for the Aged, 3225 N. Florissant Ave., 63107. Tel: 314-421-6022
For a complete listing, refer to the Special Care Facilities section.

Mary Queen and Mother Center, 7601 Watson Rd., 63119. Tel: 314-961-8485
For a complete listing, refer to the Special Care Facilities section.

Mary, Queen and Mother Nursing Center, 7601 Watson Rd., 63119
For a complete listing, refer to the Special Care Facilities section.

Mother of Good Counsel Home, 6825 Natural Bridge Rd., (St. Louis Co.), 63121. Tel: 314-383-4765
For a complete listing, refer to the Special Care Facilities section.

Mother of Perpetual Help Residence, 7609 Watson Rd., 63119. Tel: 314-961-8000
For a complete listing, refer to the Special Care Facilities section.

Our Lady of Life Apartments, Inc., 7655 Watson Rd., 63119. Tel: 314-968-9447
For a complete listing, refer to the Special Care Facilities section.

Regina Cleri Residence, 7850 Kenrick Rd., 63119. Tel: 314-968-2240
For a complete listing, refer to the Special Care Facilities section.

EUREKA. *Price Memorial*, Forby Rd., P.O. Box 476, 63025. Tel: 314-587-3200
For a complete listing, refer to the Special Care Facilities section.

St. Joseph Hill Infirmary, Inc., St. Joseph Rd., 63025. Tel: 314-587-3661
For a complete listing, refer to the Special Care Facilities section.

KIRKWOOD. *St. Agnes Home for the Elderly*, 10341 Manchester Rd., 63122. Tel: 314-965-7616; Fax: 314-965-3179
For a complete listing, refer to the Special Care Facilities section.

MEHLVILLE. *Nazareth Living Center*, 2 Nazareth Ln., 63129. Tel: 314-487-3950
For a complete listing, refer to the Special Care Facilities section.

ST. CHARLES. *St. Joseph Carmelite Home*, 723 First Capitol Dr., 63301. Tel: 314-946-4140.
E-mail: stjoseph@primary.net
For a complete listing, refer to the Special Care Facilities section.

[P] MONASTERIES AND RESIDENCES OF PRIESTS AND BROTHERS

ST. LOUIS. *The Abbey of St. Mary and St. Louis*, 500 S. Mason Rd., 63141-8500. Tel: 314-434-2557; Fax: 314-434-0795.
Web site: http://www.priory.org.
Benedictines of the English Congregation. Rt. Rev. W. Thomas Frerking, O.S.B., Abbot; Very Rev. M. Paul Kidner, O.S.B., Prior; Rt. Rev. J. Luke Rigby, O.S.B.; Very Rev. Timothy Horner, O.S.B.; Revs. D. Ralph Wright, O.S.B.; R. Benedict Allin, O.S.B.; P. Finbarr Dowling, O.S.B.; J. Laurence Kriegshauser, O.S.B.; J. Gregory Mohrman, O.S.B.; Gerard Garrigan, O.S.B.; Joseph Marino, O.S.B.; Christopher Hanson, O.S.B.; Bede Price, O.S.B. Priests 13; Brother Monks 6; Oblates 1; Total Staff 21.

Bellarmine House of Studies, 3737 Westminster, 63108-3407. Tel: 314-652-8862. Jesuit Residence for Students in the College of Philosophy and Letters of St. Louis University. Rev. Ralph G. Huse, S.J., Rector; Bro. Pablo Hernandez, S.J., Treas.; Revs. Timothy S. Godfrey, S.J.; William T. Oulvey, S.J.; Bro. Thomas Naughton, S.J., Asst. Rector. Priests 3; Brothers 3; Students 13; Total Staff 3.

De Smet Jesuit High School Community, 233 N. New Ballas Rd., 63141. Tel: 314-567-3500. Revs. John D. Arnold, S.J., Rector; Richard L. Bailey, S.J.; John J. Bergin, S.J.; Robert E. Bosken, S.J.; John V. Craig, S.J.; Michael H. Durso, S.J.; Charles F. Ferrara, S.J.; Bro. Donald E. Lee, S.J.; Revs. Michael A. Marchlewski, S.J.; Thomas F. McQueeny, S.J.; William J. Snyders, S.J.; Bro. Henry E. Welch, S.J.; Rev. Martin J. Whealen, S.J. Total in Residence 13; Total Staff 1.

Dominican Community of St. Louis. St. Louis Bertrand Priory - Province of St. Albert the Great. 97 Waterman St., 63112. Tel: 314-361-4445. Revs. Kevin David O'Rourke, O.P.; Benedict M. Ashley, O.P.; Ralph A. Powell, O.P.; Joseph P. Gillespie, O.P.; Eric A. Reiran, O.P.; Stanley A. Drongowski, O.P.
Assigned but living elsewhere: Rev. Charles E. Bouchard, O.P., 2001 26th Ave. S., Nashville, TN, 37212. Tel: 615-297-9686.

Franciscan Brothers. Saint John's Friary, 5167 Dresden Ave., 63116. Tel: 314-832-6061. Religious Brothers of the Third Order Regular of Saint Francis (Generalate, Saint Francis Monastery, Brooklyn, New York). Bro. Padraic Campbell, O.S.F., Coord. Brothers in Congregation 125; Brothers in Archdiocese of Saint Louis 2.

Franciscan Friary of St. Anthony of Padua. (Franciscan Province of the Sacred Heart-Provincial Headquarters), 3140 Meramec St., 63118-4339. Tel: 314-353-7470. Legal Title: *The Franciscan Friars of the State of Missouri*. Co-sponsor of the 8th Day Center for Justice in Chicago. Very Rev. Kurt Hartrich, O.F.M., Prov. Minister; Rev. John Doctor, O.F.M., Prov. Vicar; Bro. Richard Baranski, O.F.M., Pastoral Assoc.; Revs. Maynard Billig, O.F.M., Priest's Confessor; Michael Crosby, O.F.M., Dir. of Office of Friar Formation; Allan DaCorte, O.F.M., Prov. Treas.; Bro. Patrick Darnell, O.F.M.; Revs. David Eckelkamp, O.F.M., Province Ministry to Retired Friars; Benet A. Fonck, O.F.M., Admin.; Thomas Gardner, O.F.M., Prov. Promotor for Missions, Commissary of the Holy Land & Exec. Dir. Franciscan O.F.M. Conference; Bro. Loyola Freightman, O.F.M. Co-Directors, Franciscan Connection: Bro. Leo Geurts, O.F.M.; Rev. Pio Jackson; Bros. James Hickey, O.F.M., Devel. Office; Donald Lachowicz, O.F.M., Dir. St. Jane Catholic Community Center; Christopher Lambert, O.F.M., Province Sec.; Rev. Andrew Lewandowski, O.F.M., Chap. for Benedictine Nuns; Bros. Damian Pfeifer, O.F.M.; Dennis Pryor, O.F.M.; Revs. John Rausch, O.F.M., Chap., St. Louis University Hospital; Kenneth Rosswog, O.F.M., Parochial Vicar; Bros. David Schulte, O.F.M.; William Schulte, O.F.M., Dir. Office of Public Rels. & Devel.; Revs. Floribert Veverka, O.F.M., Sen. Parochial Vicar; Martin Wolter, O.F.M., Chap. Little Portion, Eureka Springs, AR. Priests 13; Brothers 11.
Military Chaplains: Rev. Joseph Carlos, CHC, USNR, 810 E. OceanView Ave., #305, Norfolk, VA, 23503. Rev. Charles E. Gunti, O.F.M., (Lt. Col.) Chap., 806 N. Pitt St., Carlisle, PA, 17013.
Friars of Sacred Heart Province Serving Abroad: Rev. Gilberto Cavazos, O.F.M., Antonianum, Via Merulana 124, Rome, Italy, 00185. Rev. Albert Haase, Beijing 2nd Foreign Language Institute. Foreign Experts Building #403, 1 Dingfu Zhuang Rd., Chaoyang District, Beijing 100024, People's Republic of. Bro. Jeffrey Haller, O.F.M., Franciscan Friary, 133 Waterloo Rd., Kowloon, Hong Kong. Rev. Basil Tsung-Li-Chuen, O.F.M., Catholic Mission Church, Kanchuang Rd. 305, Tashi Taoyuan, Taiwan, ROC. Revs. Francis Li-Chung-Lun, O.F.M.; Louis Antl, O.F.M., Penitenzieri, Pazza S. Giovanni in Laterano, 4, Vatican City, Italy, 00120. Rev. James Perluzzi, O.F.M., Curia Generalizia dei Frati Minori, Via Santa Maria Mediatrice, 25, Rome, Italy, 00165.
Friars Attached to the Province but Residing Elsewhere: Rev. Edd Anthony, O.F.M., Franciscan Canticle, 370 W. Arenas Rd., Palm Springs, CA, 92262. Rev. Bernon Gensert, O.F.M., Good Shepherd Manor, 10127 Guadalupe Tr., N.W., P.O. Box 10248, Albuquerque, NM, 87184. Rev. Bernadine Hahn, O.F.M., St. Thomas More Parish, 4804 Grover St., Omaha, NE, 68106. Revs. Michael Hill, O.F.M., Pastor; John J. Abts, O.F.M., Parochial Vicar, Co-Cathedral of St. Theresa, 712 N. School St., Honolulu, HI, 96817-3099. Rev. Kenneth Kieffer, O.F.M., 1782 Troy Ln., Oceanside, CA, 92054. Rev. Michael Lanning, O.F.M., Holy Trinity Rectory, 213 W. 82nd St., New York, NY, 10024. Rev. Leon Reuter, O.F.M., St. Joseph, 125 E. Broadway, Shelbyville, IN, 46176. Bro. Ronald Witkewitz, O.F.M., 10030 Clifton Pk., Evergreen Park, IL, 60642. Rev. Allan Wolter, O.F.M., Old Mission, 2201 Laguna St., Santa Barbara, CA, 93105-3697. Rev. Eric Kahn, O.F.M., House of Prayer, 648 S. Assisi Way, Republic, 65738. Rev. Theodosius Schelich, O.F.M., Chap. St. Francis Hospital, 1215 E. Union, Litchfield, IL, 62056. Rev. Gary German, O.F.M., Parochial Vicar, Saint Joseph Church, P.O. Box 1000, Laguna, NM, 87026.

Hallahan House, 4511 W. Pine Blvd., 63108-2191. Tel: 314-361-7765 (day); 758-7125 (night). Revs. Robert F. Weiss, S.J., Supr.; Gregory H. Jacobsmeyer, S.J., Min.; J. David Corrigan, S.J.; James J. Dougherty, S.J.; Thomas J. Hogan, S.J.; L. Gene Martens, S.J.; Raymond M. Tully, S.J.; Ralph E. Vonderhaar, S.J.; Bro. Julius F. Petrk, S.J. Total in Residence 9; Total Staff 4.

Jesuit Community Corporation at St. Louis University - Jesuit Hall, 3601 Lindell Blvd., 63108-3393. Tel: 314-658-2588; Fax: 314-535-0402.
E-mail: obrienec@slu.edu
Revs. A. James Blumeyer, S.J., Rector; John A. Apel, S.J.; Robert J. Araudo, S.J.; James H. Baker, S.J.; Lawrence H. Biondi, S.J.; John E. Blewett, S.J.; Harold C. Bradley; Joseph E. Brown, S.J.; Robert A. Brungs, S.J.; J. Richard Burtschi, S.J.; Thomas J. Casey, S.J.; Lucius F. Cervantes, S.J.; Maria Joseph Christie, S.J. (India); Francis X. Cleary, S.J.; J. Eugene Coomes, S.J.; Anthony C. Daly, S.J.; Denis E. Daly, S.J.; Lowrie J. Daly, S.J.; Terrence E. Dempsey, S.J.; Philip T. Derrig, S.J.; Everett A. Diederich, S.J.; Michael J. Doody, S.J.; William B. Faherty, S.J.; Robert S. Flack, S.J.; David L. Fleming; Philip C. Fischer, S.J.; John B. Foley, S.J.; William B. Foley; Ignatius Futo, S.J.; Chester E. Gaiter, S.J.; Michael J. Garanzini, S.J.; Eugene E. Grollmes, S.J.; Francis J. Guentner, S.J.; Martin Hagan, S.J.; Garth L. Hallett, S.J.; Marcus A. Haworth, S.J.; W. Charles Heiser, S.J.; John F. Kavanaugh, S.J.; George V. Kennard, S.J.; John J. Killoren; E. Edward Kinerk, S.J.; Harry R. Klocker, S.J.; Gregory N. Konz, S.J.; Leonard E. Kraus, S.J.; Philip D. Kraus, S.J.; Thomas N. Lay, S.J.; Gerhardt B. Lehmkuhl, S.J.; Edwin L. Lisson, S.J.; Michael W. Maher, S.J.; Michael K. May, S.J.; John L. McCarthy, S.J.; J. Barry McGannon, S.J.; Frederick G. McLeod, S.J.; Maurice B. McNamee, S.J.; John J. Mueller, S.J.; William L. Mugan, S.J.; Peter G. Neeley, S.J.; Edward C. O'Brien, S.J.; Martin D. O'Keefe, S.J.; Walter J. Ong, S.J.; John W. Padberg, S.J.; Claude N. Pavur, S.J.; Robert L. Phillips, S.J.; Robert Poirier; L. Michael Pope, S.J.; Nicholas F. Pope, S.J.; Paul C. Reinert, S.J.; Raymond H. Reis, S.J.; Ralph C. Renner, S.J.; Anthony J. Rochel, S.J.; Albert C. Rotola, S.J.; John C. Ruoff, S.J.; Albert H. Schulz, S.J.; James A. Sebesta, S.J.; Gerald E. Sheahan, S.J.; John F.X. Sheehan, S.J.; John F. Snyder, S.J.; Paul V. Stark, S.J.; William V. Stauder, S.J.; Linus J. Thro, S.J.; John G. Valenta; James V. Veltrie, S.J.; John J. Walsh, S.J.; Laurence E. Walsh, S.J.; Raymond L. Windle, S.J. Priests 85; Brothers 2; Scholastics 1.

The Jesuits of the Missouri Province, 4511 W. Pine Blvd., 63108-2191. Tel: 314-361-7765.
E-mail: misjesuits@aol.com
Missouri Province of the Society of Jesus. Very Rev. Frank Reale, S.J., Prov.; Revs. Philip G. Steele, S.J., Socius & Asst. Secondary Educ.; Robert F. Weiss, S.J., Treas.; John A. Apel, S.J., Asst. for Jesuits in Pastoral & Intl. Apostolates; William T. Oulvey, S.J., Asst. for Province Planning & Vocation Dir.; L. Gene Martens, S.J., Assoc. Dir. Jesuit Devel. Office; David L. Fleming, S.J., Editor, The Jesuit Bulletin; William B. Faherty, S.J., Prov. Archivist. Priests 277; Students in Major Seminary 24; Novices 7; Brothers 32.
Missouri Province Jesuit Priests Not Listed Elsewhere: Rev. John R. Daly, S.J., 2426 Alto Cerro Cir., San Diego, CA, 92109-1501. Tel: 619-274-0057. Rev. Joseph L. Herbert, S.J., 1085 Zang, Golden, CO, 80401. Tel: 303-233-3046. Rev. William J. Kane, S.J., St. Clement Hospital, 325 Spring St., Red Bud, IL, 62278. Tel: 618-282-3831. Rev. Urban J. Kramer, S.J., St. Francis Hospital, 6161 S. Yale Ave., Tulsa, OK, 74139. Tel: 918-494-2200. Rev. John F. O'Shea, S.J., 220 W. 10th St., Casa Grande, AZ, 85222. Tel: 520-316-0021. Rev. Frederick E. Schuller, S.J., Saints Peter & Paul Church, 1436 N. 67th Ave. E., Tulsa, OK, 74115-5666. Tel: 918-838-0646. Total in Residence 180; Total Staff 9.

La Salette Missionaries, 4650 S. Broadway, 63111-1398. Tel: 314-353-5000; Fax: 314-353-4582. Missionaries of Our Lady of La Salette, Province of Mary Queen. Very Rev. Dennis J. Meyer, M.S., Prov. Supr.; Rev. Joseph C. Shea, M.S., Mission Awareness. Tel: 314-353-5000.
Provincial Vocation Office. Tel: 314-353-5000.
La Salette Ministries Development Center. Tel: 314-752-0760. Rev. Edward J. Brunnert, M.S., Dir.
La Salette Spirituality Center. Tel: 314-353-5000. Revs. James R. Dunphy, M.S.; Dennis J. Meyer, M.S.; Edward Richard, M.S.; Edward J. Brunnert, M.S.; Laval L. Landry, M.S., (Retired); Louis L. VanDane, M.S.; Bros. Roman Wilbers, M.S.; Thomas Murphy, M.S.
Priests and Brothers of the Province Serving in the Foreign Missions:
Diocese of Morondava, Madagascar: Rev. Arthur A. Lueckenotto, M.S.
Diocese of Cordoba, Argentina: Revs. John M. Garvey, M.S.; John M. McCarthy, M.S.
Rome, Italy: Generalate, Missionari di N.S. de La Salette, Piazza Madonna della Salette, 3. Tel: (06) 53-04-51. Very Rev. Isidro Perin, M.S.; Revs. Raphael Rakatonocliarimanana, M.S., Vicar Gen.; Gerald Lebanowski, General Councillor & Gen. Sec.; Antoni Skalb, Gen. Councillor; Rene Gelinas, Gen. Councillor; Orlando Sapuay; Bolivar Hauck, M.S., Gen. Treas.; Jean Stern, M.S., Procurator to Holy See. Priests 36; Brothers 5; Oblates 2; Total Staff 4.

Leo Brown Jesuit Community, 5047 Washington Pl., 63108. Tel: 314-367-8013. Revs. Albert Agresti, S.J.; Michael D. Barber, S.J.; Thomas E.J. Kelly, S.J., Supr.; Donald W. Reck, S.J.; Lars Reuter; Bro. Donald R. Schlichter. Total in Residence 6.

Marianist Community. P.O. Box 718, Eureka, 63025. Tel: 314-938-5470. Rev. Jose Ramirez, S.M., Dir. Priests 2; Brothers 5.

Maryknoll House, 4542 W. Pine Blvd., 63108. Tel: 314-361-7729.
E-mail: mklstl@igc.org
Revs. Stephen L. Schroeppel, M.M.; Robert A. Lilly, M.M.; John C. Ganly, M.M.

Provincialate of the Society of Mary, Province of St. Louis, P.O. Box 23130, 63156-3130. Tel: 314-367-0390; Fax: 314-361-3131.
E-mail: stlprov@mo.net
Web site: http://www.neosoft.com/~csjga
4538 Maryland Ave., 63108-1911. Rev. Timothy Dwyer, S.M.; Bros. Jerome Bommer, S.M., Asst. Prov.; Richard Dix, S.M., Temporalities; Revs. Alvin McMenamy, S.M., Rel. Life; John Moder, S.M., Councillor.
Priests of the Province on Special Assignment: Rev. Edward M. Jach, S.M., 1600 Madison Rd., Cincinnati, OH, 45206-1815. Rev. Bernard M. Rochon, S.M., St. Timothy Parish, 1515 Saltillo St., San Antonio, TX, 78207-6898. Rev. Adolf M. Windisch, S.M., 300 College Park, Dayton, OH, 45469-0300. Rev. David Paul, S.M., 911 B. Geyer Ave., 63104-3921. Rev. Lawrence Doersching, S.M., 175 Phelan Ave., San Francisco, CA, 94112-1897. Rev. George Montague, S.M., 2107 Davy Crockett, San Antonio, TX, 78238-5109.
Priests of the Province Serving Outside the USA: Rev. David Fleming, S.M., Supr. Gen., Marianisti, Via Latina 22, Rome, Italy, 00179.
Priests of the Province Serving in the Missions: Rev. William A. Christensen, S.M., IIRD, House #5/10, Rd. Number 48, Block-E, Lalmatia, Bangladesh, Dhaka-1207. Rev. James Schimelpfening, S.M., Nirmal Deep, P.B. 144, Ranchi 834 001, Bihar, India. Rev. Lawrence E. Jordan, S.M., Colegio San Jose Obrero, Apartado 459, Trujillo, Peru. Rev. William J. Morris, S.M., Universidad Santa Maria, Apartado 1350, Arequipa, Peru. Rev. Michael Barber, S.M., Comunidad Marianista Sagrado Corazon, Apartado 839, 96400 Coatzacoalcos, Veracruz, Mexico. Rev. Quentin Hakewerth, S.M.,

Noviciado Marianista, Apartado 1152 - Adm. 1, Queretaro, QRO, Mexico, 76000.
Special Status: Revs. Anthony Pogorelc, S.M.; Gregory Benkowski, S.M.; Paul Donoghue, S.M. Total in Residence 53; Total Staff 12.

Redemptorist Fathers, 3626 S. Utah Pl., 63116. Tel: 314-776-7326; Fax: 314-771-5804. Revs. Thomas M. Santa, C.SS.R.; Paul J. Coury, C.SS.R. Priests 2; Brothers 1.

St. Alphonsus Rectory of the Redemptorist, 1118 N. Grand Blvd., 63106. Tel: 314-533-0304. Revs. Maurice Nutt, C.SS.R.; Richard Potts, C.SS.R. In res. Rev. Gary Ziuraitis, C.SS.R.; Bro. Terrance Burke, C.SS.R. Total Staff 4.

St. Bonaventure Friary (Province of Our Lady of Consolation), 4012 Washington Blvd., 63108. Tel: 314-533-3179. Revs. David Lenz, O.F.M.Conv., Guardian; Formation Dir.; Wayne Hellmann, O.F.M.Conv.; Angelus LaFleur, O.F.M.Conv. Solemn Profession: Bros. Steven McMichael, O.F.M.Conv.; Paul Clark, O.F.M.Conv. Priests 3; Solemn Professed 5; Candidates 2.

St. Crispin's Friary, 3731 Westminster Pl., 63108. Tel: 314-531-4406.
E-mail: blaineb@slu.edu
Web site: http://www.feefhs.org/lfs/frg-lfs.html
Revs. Christopher Popravak, O.F.M.Cap.; Blaine Burkey, O.F.M.Cap., Guardian; Jeff Ernst, O.F.M.Cap., Vicar; Didacus Joseph Dunn, O.F.M.Cap. Priests 4; Postulants 1.

St. Dominic Priory, 3601 Lindell Blvd., 63108. Tel: 314-977-2588.
Web site: http://www.op.org/stlouis
Revs. Richard A. Peddicord, O.P., Prior; Charles R. Malatesta, O.P.; Arthur L. Kinsella, O.P.; Albert S. Moraczewski, O.P.; Philip J. Lamberty, O.P.; Albert G. Glade, O.P.; Gregory J. Heille, O.P.; George R. Boudreau, O.P.; Michael A. Mascari, O.P., Subprior; Thomas M. Condon, O.P.; Patrick F. Norris, O.P.; Rodney T. Adams, O.P. Total in Residence 33.

St. Louis University High School Jesuit Community, #3 Lawn Pl., 63110. Tel: 314-652-5425; Fax: 314-531-8446. Revs. James G. Knapp, S.J., Supr.; Richard E. Hadel, S.J.; Ralph D. Houlihan, S.J.; Frank E. Reale, S.J.; Paul G. Sheridan, S.J.; Philip G. Steele, S.J.; Bros. C. Thomas Thornton, S.J.; Richard H. Witzofsky, S.J.; Barton T. Geger, S.J. Priests 6; Brothers 2; Scholastics 1.

St. Matthew Jesuit Community, 2715 N. Sarah St., 63113-2940. Tel: 314-531-6443. Revs. Matthew D. Ruhl, S.J., Supr.; Jeffrey D. Harrison, S.J.; Dirk Dunfee, S.J.

St. Patrick Friary, 1000 N. 7th St., 63101. Tel: 314-231-9991. Revs. Valentine Young, O.F.M.Cap., Supr.; Simon R. Conrad, O.F.M.Cap.; Canice Froehlich, O.F.M.Cap.; Simeon Gallagher, O.F.M.Cap.; Julian Haas; Bro. Eugene Pellegrino. Priests 4.

Servants of the Paraclete, St. Michael's Community, 13270 Maple Dr., 63127. Tel: 314-965-0860; Fax: 314-965-7202.
Web site: www.theservants.org
Revs. Mario D'Agostini, S.P.; Joseph McNamara, S.P.; Richard Brown, S.P., St. John Vianney Renewal Center; Michael Foley, S.P., Fr. Servant, Clinical Prog. Dir., Eime Rd., 63023. Tel: 314-677-1828; Fax: 314-285-5895. Priests 3.

Vincentian Bellerive Residence, 73 Bellerive Acres, 63121. Tel: 314-389-4394. Very Rev. Lawrence F. Asma, C.M., Supr.; Revs. James T. Beighlie, C.M.; Edward J. Virgets, C.M.; Jules G. Yallaly, C.M.; John V. Farris, C.M.

Vincentian Henrietta Residence, 42 Henrietta Pl., 63104. Tel: 314-776-6148. Very Rev. Romain G. Morales, C.M., Supr.; Revs. John A. Shaughnessy, C.M.; Francis J. Shine, C.M.; Wilbert H. Bruns, C.M.; Joseph E. Begue, C.M.; Daniel P. Kearns, C.M.; Bro. Dave Goodman, C.M.

Vincentian Residence, 2904 Arsenal St., 63118. Tel: 314-773-7633. Rev. James E. Swift, C.M.; Bro. F. Joseph Hess, C.M.; Revs. Michael P. Joyce, C.M.; Daniel A. Ricci, C.M.; Ronald W. Ramson, C.M., Supr.
Attached But Not In Residence: Revs. Glennon E. Figge, C.M., Daughters of Charity, Mater Dei Prov. House, Evansville, IN; Daniel E. Harris, C.M., St. John's Seminary Theologate, Camarillo, CA 93012; Patrick J. McDevitt, C.M., Loyola Univ., Baltimore, MD; John E. Rybolt, C.M., Paris, France; P. Vincent Aherne, C.M., Vista, CA; Philip M. Floersh, C.M., Flagstaff, AZ. Priests 4; Brothers 1.

Vincentian-St. Lazare Residence, 2912 Arsenal St., 63118. Tel: 314-771-1869; Fax: 314-771-2410. Revs. John F. Clark, C.M., Supr.; William A. Bogel, C.M.; Bro. James E. Donlevy, C.M.; Revs. J. Dennis Martin, C.M.; Thomas E. Esselman, C.M.

White House Retreat Jesuit Community, 7400 Christopher Dr., 63129-5799. Tel: 314-846-2575. Office, 3601 Lindell Blvd., 63108-3393. Tel: 314-533-8903. Rev. Luke J. Byrne, S.J., Dir. & Supr.; Bro. George R. Hale, S.J., Min. & Treas. Associate Directors: Revs. Robert A. Doyle, S.J.; Robert L. Holmes, S.J.; David W. Koesterer, S.J.; William H. Runde, S.J.

ARNOLD. *Immaculate Conception Friary*, 2300 Church Rd., P.O. Box 217, 63010. Tel: 314-296-5301.
E-mail: iceal@juno.com
Revs. Gilmary Tallman, O.F.M.Cap., Vicar; Earl R. Meyer, O.F.M.Cap., Supr. In res. Rev. John Schmeidler, O.F.M.Cap.

CENTERVILLE. *Contemplative Heart of Mary Hermitage*. Rev. Robert L. Aten, Mailing Address: R.R. #1 309-C, Lesterville, 63654. Tel: 573-648-2467.

EARTH CITY. *Congregation of the Mission Midwest Province (Vincentians)*, 13663 Rider Tr. N., 63045-1512. Tel: 314-344-1184; Fax: 314-344-2989.
E-mail: cmstlouis@aol.com
Very Rev. William E. Hartenbach, C.M., Prov.; Revs. Michael P. Joyce, C.M.; David J. Nygren, C.M.; Christopher S. Robinson, C.M.; Bro. F. Joseph Hess, C.M., Treas.

Vincentian Foreign Mission Society, 13663 Rider Tr. N., 63045-1512. Tel: 314-344-1184. Office for Vincentian Foreign Missions' Personnel and Projects. Rev. James P. Graham, C.M., Dir.

EUREKA. *Franciscan Brothers House of Studies*, Forby Rd., P.O. Box 129, 63025. House of Studies of Franciscan Missionary Brothers of the Sacred Heart of Jesus. Bro. John Spila, O.S.F., Dir. Brothers 3.

Our Lady of the Angels Monastery, St. Joseph Rd., 63025; Fax: 314-938-4960. Generalate of Franciscan Missionary Brothers of the Sacred Heart of Jesus. Bros. Matthew Gallagher, O.S.F., Dir. General; Damien DeBraekeleer, O.S.F., Asst. Dir.; Rev. Josef Lukaszczyk, Chap. Professed Brothers 13.
Apostolate: Price Memorial Nursing Home and St. Joseph's Hill Infirmary/Black Madonna Shrine, Adult Boarding Facility at Camilus Hall Boarding Home, Merkle Knipprath Nursing home, Joliet Diocese and Countryside Villas Retirement Center, Clifton, IL 60927.

HIGH RIDGE. *Society of Our Mother of Peace*, Sons of Our Mother of Peace, Maria Fonte Solitude, 6150 Antire Rd., 63049-2100. Tel: 314-677-3235. Rev. Placid Guste, S.M.P., Supr. Priests 2; Brothers 4; Total in Residence 6; Total Staff 3.

LIGUORI. *Alphonsian Foundation Office*, One Liguori Dr., 63057-9999. Tel: 314-464-2500; Fax: 314-464-8449.
E-mail: 104705.3434@compuserve.com
Web site: http://www.alponsiana.edu
Purpose: to provide public relations and financial support for the Alphonsian Academy of Moral Theology in Rome. Victor L. Ottenlips, Devel. Dir.; Rev. John C. Vargas, C.SS.R., Exec. Dir.

Liguori Mission House/Redemptorists, Ten Liguori Dr., 63057. Tel: 314-464-6999; Fax: 314-464-6765.
E-mail: william@jcnl.com
Web site: www.jcnl.com/william
Very Rev. Norman J. Muckerman, C.SS.R.; Revs. Charles C. Bueche, C.SS.R.; Thomas Cosgrove, C.SS.R.; Thomas Duggan, C.SS.R.; Paul Farrell, C.SS.R.; James Gleason; James J. Higgins, C.SS.R.; William Hogan, C.SS.R.; Victor Karls, C.SS.R.; Harry Korte, C.SS.R.; William McKee, C.SS.R.; Bro. Gabriel Medic, C.SS.R.; Revs. James Patterson, C.SS.R.; Allan Weinert, C.SS.R.; Henry McKeever, C.SS.R.; Robert Rossbach, C.SS.R. Priests 15; Brothers 1.

Redemptorists Foundation Office, One Liguori Dr., 63057-9999. Tel: 314-464-2500; Fax: 314-464-8449.
E-mail: 75424.1416@compuserve.com
Conducted by the Redemptorist/Denver Province in the Archdiocese of St. Louis. Purpose: supports the religious and charitable purposes of the Redemptorists. Victor L. Ottenlips, Exec. Dir.

St. Clement Health Care Center, 300 Liguori Dr., 63057. Tel: 314-464-3666; Fax: 314-464-4717. The Redemptorists. Revs. Edmund T. Langton, C.SS.R., Rector; George J. Corbett, C.SS.R.; Francis A. Flanagan, C.SS.R.; Albert A. Fuytinck, C.SS.R.; Evan B. Gautreau, C.SS.R.; Robert M. Gaydos, C.SS.R.; James S. Kelly, C.SS.R.; Arthur B. Klyber, C.SS.R.; Bruno V. Lischwe, C.SS.R.; Orville C. Mailloux, C.SS.R.; Dwaine J. Marsch, C.SS.R.; Thomas E. Monaghan, C.SS.R.; Henry F. Porten, C.SS.R.; Gerard F. Resch, C.SS.R.; Henry A. Schultz, C.SS.R.; Paul E. Schwarz, C.SS.R.; Anthony A. Stuebben, C.SS.R.; Raymond F. Walter, C.SS.R.; Alvin O. Billimek, C.SS.R.; Norbert E. Delort, C.SS.R.; Francis J. Ryan, C.SS.R.

OAKVILLE. *St. Francis Friary*, 4556 Telegraph Rd., 63129. Tel: 314-487-5736. Franciscan Fathers. Revs. Robert Behnen, O.F.M.; Blane O'Neill, O.F.M.; Charles Reuter, O.F.M., Chap. Poor Clare Monastery; Valerian Schott, O.F.M., (Retired); Ermin Micka, O.F.M., (Retired); Aloys Jost, O.F.M.; Silas Musholt, O.F.M.

PERRYVILLE. *Congregation of The Mission*, St. Mary's Seminary, 63775-1599. Tel: 314-547-6533; Fax: 314-547-2204. U.S. Motherhouse of the Congregation of the Mission (Vincentian Fathers, Prov. of the Midwest). Very Rev. Arthur L. Trapp, C.M., Supr.; Revs. Charles T. Herbst, C.M.; Charles F. Rice, C.M.; Robert J. Brockland, C.M.; Clarence J. Bogetto, C.M.; Francis A. Byrne, C.M.; John P. Tackaberry, C.M.; Willis F. Darling, C.M.; Alphonse X. Hoernig, C.M.; Charles F. Shelby, C.M.; Gilmore H. Guyot, C.M.; Charles D. Saunders, C.M.; Kenneth E. Grass, C.M.; Francis Germovnik, C.M.; Nicholas E. Persich, C.M.; Robert J. Zimney, C.M.; Louis J. Derbes, C.M.; James P. Graham, C.M.; John F. Zimmerman, C.M.; Oscar Lukefahr, C.M.; James A. Fischer, C.M.; C. William Stein, C.M.; Edward J. Mullin, C.M.; John F. Gagnepain, C.M.; Bros. Peter Baxter, C.M.; Harvey Goertz, C.M.; Richard A. Hermann, C.M.; Mark Howard Argus, C.M.; John Mangogna, C.M.; Matthew J. Teel, C.M.; Raymond J. Tochtrop, C.M.; Richard Zoellner, C.M. Fathers 24; Professed Brothers 8; Total Staff 4.

[Q] PERSONAL PRELATURES

KIRKWOOD. *Opus Dei*. (Legal Name: Prelature of the Holy Cross and Opus Dei), Wespine Study Center, 100 E. Essex Ave., 63122. Tel: 314-821-1608; Fax: 314-821-4722.
E-mail: WespineSTL@aol.com
Revs. Michael E. Giesler; Mark S. Mannion.

[R] CONVENTS AND RESIDENCES FOR SISTERS

ST. LOUIS. *Augustinian Nuns of Contemplative Life*. Mother of Good Counsel Convent, 4328 Westminster Pl., 63108. Tel: 314-533-2054. Legal Title: *Augustinian Cloistered Nuns, Inc.* Total in Residence 5.

Benedictine Convent of Perpetual Adoration, 8300 Morganford Rd., 63123. Tel: 314-638-6427; Fax: 314-638-2028 (Community); 638-7360.
E-mail: cathleen@icon-stl.net
Web site: http://www.icon-stl.net/~congbspa/index.html
Generalate, Novitiate and Healthcare Community of Benedictine Sisters of Perpetual Adoration, under Pontifical Jurisdiction. Sr. Mary Jane Romero, Prioress Gen.
Four other interdependent monasteries: Clyde, MO; Tucson, AZ; Sand Springs, OK; and Dayton, WY. Membership in St. Louis Community 57; Total in Congregation 134; Novices 2.

Congregation of Mary, Queen of the World Community, 4540 Lindell Blvd., 63108. Tel: 314-361-8211. Sr. Jacinta Tran, C.M.R., Local Supr.

Daughters of Our Mother of Peace, 5587 Page Blvd., 63112. Tel: 314-382-2592. Sr. Maryjoy Lambert, S.M.P., Supr. Sisters 3.

Daughters of St. Paul Convent, 9804 Watson Rd., 63126. Tel: 314-965-3571. Sisters 4.

Franciscan Sisters of Mary Administration, 1100 Bellevue Ave., 63117-1883. Tel: 314-768-1824; Fax: 314-768-1880.
E-mail: fsmst12@aol.com
Offices of the Franciscan Sisters of Mary & Convent. Sr. Jacqueline Motzel, F.S.M., Pres.; Rev. Pio Jackson, O.F.M., Chap. Professed Sisters in Archdiocese 146; In Residence 98.

Franciscan Sisters of Mary Novitiate, 1100 Bellevue Ave., 63117-1883. Tel: 314-768-1703; Fax: 314-768-1880.
E-mail: fsmstldv@aol.com

Franciscan Sisters of Our Lady of Perpetual Help, 201 Brotherton Ln., 63135. Tel: 314-522-6800; Fax: 314-521-7179. Motherhouse and Novitate of Franciscan Sisters of Our Lady of Perpetual Help. Sr. Monica Marie Laws, O.S.F., Supr. Gen.; Rev. Larry Nickels, O.F.M., Res. Chap. Total Sisters in the Community 151; In Residence 17; Total Staff 9.

Heart of Mary Center, 5306 Winona Ave., 63109. Tel: 314-351-4049. Sr. Anita Baird, D.H.M., Supr. Daughters of the Heart of Mary 4.

Incarnate Word Sisters, 7800 Natural Bridge Rd., 63121. Tel: 314-385-8739. Regional House of the St. Louis Province of the Sisters of Charity of the Incarnate Word of San Antonio. Sr. Kathleen Coughlin, C.C.V.I., Prov. Supr.; Sr. Rose Mary Politte, C.C.V.I., Coord. Sisters 3.

Loretto Center, 590 E. Lockwood, 63119-3279. Tel: 314-968-1887. Sr. Anthony Mary Sartorius, S.L., Coord. Sisters 30; Total Staff 24.

Medical Mission Sisters, 2800 Olive St. #3C, 63103. Sr. Joan Coughlin, Local Contact.

Missionaries of Charity, 3629 Cottage, 63113. Tel: 314-533-2777. Sr. M. Manorama, M.C., Supr. Sisters 6; Total Assisted 22,237.
Missionaries of Charity also in: Peoria, IL; Chicago, IL; Detroit, MI; Memphis, TN; Dallas, TX; Little Rock, AR; Baton Rouge, LA; Lafayette, LA.

Monastery of St. Clare of the Immaculate Conception, 200 Marycrest Dr., 63129-4813. Tel: 314-846-2618. Poor Clare Nuns. Mother Mary Leo Hoffman, O.S.C., Abbess. Cloistered Nuns 9.

Mount Grace Convent and Chapel of Perpetual Adoration, 1438 E. Warne Ave., 63107. Tel: 314-381-2654. Sister Servants of the Holy Spirit of Perpetual Adoration (Generalate, Bad Driburg, Germany). Sr. Mary Gemma, Supr., 1438 E. Warne

Ave., 63107. Attended by Divine Word Fathers. 1446 E. Warne Ave., 63107. Sisters 28.

Provincial House, Society of the Sacred Heart-United States Province, 4389 W. Pine Blvd., 63108. Tel: 314-652-1500; Fax: 314-534-6800.
E-mail: rscjph@aol.com
Web site: http://www.rscj.org
Total in Residence 7; Total Staff 4. Province Corporations: California Province of the Society of the Sacred Heart, Inc.; Ladies of the Sacred Heart of St. Louis, Missouri; Society of the Sacred Heart, Chicago Province, Inc.; Religious of the Sacred Heart, Washington Province, Inc.; Religious of the Sacred Heart, New York Province, Inc.; Religious of the Sacred Heart in Massachusetts, Inc.

St. Joseph's Convent of Mercy, 611 S. New Ballas Rd., 63141. Sr. Michael Marie Flannery, R.S.M., Coord. Sisters of Mercy of the Americas. Sisters 47.

St. Joseph's Provincial House, 6400 Minnesota Ave., 63111-2899. Tel: 314-481-8800; Fax: 314-481-2366; 351-3111.
E-mail: bldreher@aol.com
Web site: www.fontbonne.edu/csjsl.html
Prov. House of the Sisters of St. Joseph of Carondelet. Sr. Barbara Dreher, C.S.J., Prov. Dir. Co-Administrators: Sr. Eileen Hoffer, C.S.J.; Sr. Catherine Lucien Mattler, C.S.J. Sisters in Province 622; In Archdiocese 410.

School Sisters of Notre Dame, Sancta Maria in Ripa, 320 E. Ripa Ave., 63125-2897. Tel: 314-544-0455; Fax: 314-544-6754. Motherhouse of the School Sisters of Notre Dame, St. Louis Province. Sr. Kathleen Wegman, Prov. Leader; Rev. John M. Unger, Chap. Sisters in Diocese 415.

Interprovincial Novitiate for School Sisters of Notre Dame, 4950 Heege Rd., 63123. Tel: 314-481-8634. Sisters 10.

Liturgical Fabric Arts.

Maria Center.

Resource Development.

Sisters of Mercy of the Americas, Regional Community of St. Louis, 2039 N. Geyer Rd., 63131-3399. Tel: 314-966-4313.
E-mail: jarvin@somh.smhs.com
Sr. Richard Mary Burke, R.S.M., Reg. Pres. Regional Sisters in Archdiocese 98.
Convent Corporations:
Sisters of Mercy of the St. Louis Regional Community, Inc.
St. Joseph's Convent of Mercy of St. Louis.
Education Institutions:
Sisters of Mercy Education System, St. Louis, Inc., Begin Literacy Program.
Sisters of Mercy - ARISE, Las Milpas, Inc.
Health Institutions:
Sisters of Mercy Health System, St. Louis, Inc.
Other: Mercy Center, Conference/Renewal Ministry.

Sisters of St. Francis of the Martyr St. George. Mother of Good Counsel Home, 6825 Natural Bridge Rd., 63121. Tel: 314-383-4765; Fax: 314-383-7256. Sisters 15.

Society of the Helpers of the Holy Souls, 3432A Crittenden, 63118. Tel: 314-771-7482.
E-mail: hottingp@slu.edu
Sr. Patricia A. Hottinger, S.H.
Spiritual direction, Parish Weeks of Guided Prayer. Sr. Mary Funge, S.H., Contact, 3817 McDonald Ave., 63116. Tel: 314-776-6917.

Villa Gesu, 11755 Riverview Dr., 63138. Tel: 314-741-6830. School Sisters of Notre Dame. Health Care and Retirement Center for Sisters of the St. Louis Province. Sr. Marina Langhorst, S.S.N.D., Supr.; Sr. Joan DiProspere, S.S.N.D., Admin.; Rev. Elvan Maschmann, O.F.M., Chap. Sisters 90.

CHESTERFIELD. *Missionary Sisters of St. Peter Claver*, 667 Woods Mill Rd., S., P.O. Box 401, 63006-0401. Tel: 314-434-8084. Sr. M. Irene Brahmakulath, S.S.P.C., Supr. Sisters 7.

CRYSTAL CITY. *Ursuline Provincialate*, 210 Glennon Heights Rd., 63019. Tel: 314-937-6206; Fax: 314-937-7627. Central Province of the Ursuline Nuns of the Roman Union. Sr. Pauline Lorch, O.S.U., Prov. Prioress. Sisters: In Province 216; In the Archdiocese 41; In residence 12.
Other Locations: 512 S. Third St., DeSoto, 63020. Tel: 314-337-2854. Sisters 3. 6344 Garesche Ave., St. Louis, 63136. Tel: 314-385-0899; Fax: 314-385-0605. Sr. Mary June Jun, O.S.U., Prioress, Sisters 6. 353 S. Sappington Rd., St. Louis, 63122. Tel: 314-821-2150; Fax: 314-821-5827. Sr. Darlene Fulgenzi, O.S.U., Prioress, Sisters 14. 4900 Reber Pl., St. Louis, 63139. Tel: 314-773-4829; Fax: 314-773-3982. Sr. Mary Jacqueline Pratt, O.S.U., Prioress. Sisters 6.

ELLISVILLE. *Immaculate Conception Monastery Passionist Nuns*, 15700 Clayton Rd., 63011-2300. Tel: 314-227-5275. Mother Mary Salvador, C.P., Supr. Professed Religious 14. Cloistered Contemplatives.

FLORISSANT. *Contemplative Sisters of the Good Shepherd*, 2711 Mullanphy Ln., 63031. Tel: 314-837-1719. Sr. Magdalen Clark, C.G.S. Sisters 25.

Pallottine Missionary Sisters-Queen of Apostles Province, 15270 Old Halls Ferry Rd., 63034-1661. Tel: 314-837-7100. Provincialate & novitiate & renewal center of the Missionary Sisters of the Catholic Apostolate. Sr. Elisabeth Heptner, S.A.C., Prov. Professed Sisters 5; Novices 1; Total Staff 12. Convent Frascati, 1932 W. Linda Ln., Lonedell, 63060-9739. Tel: 314-629-5610. Professed Sisters 3; Total Staff 3.

FRONTENAC. *Congregational Office of the Sisters of St. Joseph of Carondelet*, 2307 S. Lindbergh Blvd., 63131. Tel: 314-966-4048.
E-mail: congctrcsj@aol.com
Congregational Leadership Team: Sr. Marie Damien Adams, C.S.J.; Sr. Maureen Freeman, C.S.J.; Sr. Mary McGlone, C.S.J.; Sr. Virginia Webb, C.S.J.; Sr. Helene Wilson, C.S.J. Sisters 5.

Religious of the Sacred Heart Convent, 801 S. Spoede Rd., 63131. Sisters 7.

HIGH RIDGE. *Society of Our Mother of Peace, Daughters of Our Mother of Peace*, Maria Fonte Solitude, 6150 Antire Rd., 63049-2100. Tel: 314-677-3235. Sr. Mary Perpetua Spranger, S.M.P. Sisters 14; Total in Residence 8.

KIRKWOOD. *Carmelite Sisters of the Divine Heart of Jesus Provincial House and Novitiate*, 10341 Manchester Rd., 63122. Tel: 314-965-1638; Fax: 314-822-3154. Sr. M. Angelina Finnell, Prov. Supr. Sisters 10; Postulants 3. We are a house of formation where young women are taught to be religious. Besides our child care center we have St. Agnes Home, a nursing home.

LADUE. *Carmel of St. Joseph*, 9150 Clayton Rd., 63124-1898. Tel: 314-993-6899; Fax: 314-993-5039. Discalced Carmelites.
Chapel of the Precious Blood. Mother Mary Joseph, O.C.D., Prioress; Rev. Kevin D. Horrigan, Res. Chap. Professed 8; Extern Sisters 1.

LIGUORI. *Monastery of St. Alphonsus*, 200 Liguori Dr., 63057-9999. Tel: 314-464-1093. Order of the Most Holy Redeemer (Redemptoristine Nuns). Professed 16; Postulants 1.

LONEDELL. *Pallottine Missionary Sisters-Frascati Community*, 1932 W. Linda Ln., 63060-9739.
E-mail: pallotti@mail.usmo.com
Sisters 3.

NORMANDY. *Convent of the Immaculate Heart*, 7626 Natural Bridge Rd., 63121. Tel: 314-383-0300. A residence for aged & infirm Good Shepherd Sisters of the St. Louis Prov.

Good Shepherd Provincialate, 7654 Natural Bridge Rd., 63121. Tel: 314-381-3400. Sr. M. Nora Patricia O'Flannigan, R.G.S., Prov. Sisters 8; Total Staff 6.

Pelletier Trust, a Charitable Trust of the Sisters of the Good Shepherd.

Marillac Provincial House, 7800 Natural Bridge Rd., 63121-4694. Tel: 314-382-2800; Fax: 314-382-8392.
E-mail: srrita@marillac.dcnhs.org
Daughters of Charity of St. Vincent de Paul. Provincial House and Place of Retirement for Daughters of Charity. Sr. Nannette Gentile, D.C., Visitatrix; Sr. Germaine Price, D.C., Asst.; Very Rev. William A. Bogel, C.M., Dir. Sisters in Archdiocese 99; In Residence 74.

Mount Providence, 8351 Florissant Rd., 63121. Tel: 314-524-3803; Fax: 314-524-7203. Motherhouse of the Sisters of Divine Providence of the St. Louis Prov. Sr. Janet Folkl, C.D.P., Prov. Legal Titles: *Sisters of Divine Providence of Missouri.; Sisters of Divine Providence of Missouri Charitable Trust.* Sisters 59.

O'FALLON. *St. Mary's Institute*, 204 N. Main St., 63366-2299. Tel: 314-240-3420; 240-6010; Fax: 314-272-5031.
E-mail: andreef@aol.com
Motherhouse of the Sisters of the Most Precious Blood.
Chapel of St. Joseph. Sr. Andree Fries, C.PP.S., Supr. Gen. Sisters in Archdiocese 252.

ST. CHARLES. *Franciscan Sisters of Mary*, 567 Jackson St., 63301-2667. Tel: 314-946-7258. Sisters 3.

Religious of the Sacred Heart, 301 Decatur St., 63301; Fax: 314-949-6659.
E-mail: mmmunch@rscj.org
Sisters 4.

Religious of the Sacred Heart, 800 N. 5th St., 63301.
Web site: http://www.rscj.org
Sisters 5.

Religious of the Sacred Heart-Regis, 221 Decatur St., 63301. Tel: 314-946-6456; 946-6527.
E-mail: regis211@aol.com
Sisters 7.

ST. LOUIS COUNTY. *Religious of the Sacred Heart*, 13644 Conway Rd., 63141. Tel: 314-434-7687. Sisters 2. 13648 Conway Rd., 63141. Tel: 314-878-1882. Sisters 5.

Religious of the Sacred Heart, 541 S. Mason Rd., 63141. Tel: 314-878-6705. Sisters 5.

TOWN AND COUNTRY. *Monastery of the Visitation, St. Louis*, 3020 N. Ballas Rd., 63131. Tel: 314-432-5353.
E-mail: vhmsam@inlink.com
Web site: www.inlink.com/~vhmstl/.
Sr. Anne Madeleine Godefroy, V.H.M., Supr. Residence of Visitation Nuns Teaching or Living at the Monastery of the Visitation. Sisters 25.

[S] HOMES FOR MEN AND WOMEN

ST. LOUIS. *Cathedral Tower*, 325 N. Newstead Ave., 63108. Tel: 314-531-0511
For a complete listing, refer to the Special Care Facilities section.

Father Dempsey's Hotel, Inc., 3427 Washington Ave., 63103
For a complete listing, refer to the Special Care Facilities section.

Father Jim's Home, 3427 Washington Ave., 63103. Tel: 314-535-7221
For a complete listing, refer to the Special Care Facilities section.

Queen of Peace Center, 325 N. Newstead Ave., 63108. Tel: 314-531-0511
For a complete listing, refer to the Special Care Facilities section.

Rosati Group Home, Inc., 4532 Lindell Blvd., 63108. Tel: 314-367-5500
For a complete listing, refer to the Special Care Facilities section.

Rosati Stabilization Center, 4224 N. Grand Ave., 63107. Tel: 314-534-6624
For a complete listing, refer to the Special Care Facilities section.

St. Martha's Hall, P.O. Box 4950, 63108. Tel: 314-533-1313
For a complete listing, refer to the Special Care Facilities section.

St. Philippine Duchesne Shelter, 1015 Goodfellow Blvd., 63112. Tel: 314-454-1012
For a complete listing, refer to the Special Care Facilities section.

Villa Maria Center, 8351 Florissant Rd., 63121. Tel: 314-521-2255
For a complete listing, refer to the Special Care Facilities section.

NORMANDY. *Maria Droste Residence*, 7660 Natural Bridge Rd., 63121. Tel: 314-383-5553
For a complete listing, refer to the Special Care Facilities section.

[T] RETREAT HOUSES

ST. LOUIS. *Caroline Conference and Retreat Center*, 320 E. Ripa Ave., 63125. Tel: 314-544-0455; Fax: 314-544-6754. Sr. Marie Kevin Brothers, S.S.D.N.

The Cenacle, 7654 Natural Bridge Rd., 63121-4989. Tel: 314-381-7070. Congregation of Our Lady of the Retreat in the Cenacle. Sr. Mary Westhues, R.C., Supr. Sisters 6.

Mercy Center, 2039 N. Geyer Rd., 63131. Tel: 314-966-4686.
E-mail: mkaletta@somh.smhs.com
Mary Ann Kaletta, Admin. Conference and Renewal Ministry. Operated by the Sisters of Mercy of the Americas, Province St. Louis.

White House Retreat, Office: 3601 Lindell Blvd., Ste. 204, 63108. Tel: 314-533-8903. 7400 Christopher Dr., 63129. Tel: 314-846-2575. Rev. Luke J. Byrne, S.J., Dir. Associate Directors: Revs. William H. Runde, S.J.; Robert A. Doyle, S.J.; Robert L. Holmes, S.J.; David W. Koesterer, S.J.; Bro. George R. Hale, S.J. Total in Residence 6; Total Staff 6.

DITTMER. *Il Ritiro-The Little Retreat*, Eime Rd., P.O. Box 38, 63023. Tel: 314-285-3759; Toll Free from St. Louis: 274-0554; Fax: 314-274-2380. Operated by the Franciscan Friars. Revs. Bertin Miller, O.F.M., Exec. Dir.; Nathan McNally, O.F.M., Retreat Dir.; Dismas Bonner, O.F.M.; Gavin Griffith, O.F.M.; Damien Dougherty, O.F.M.; Leonard Paskert, O.F.M.; Michael Crosby, O.F.M. Total in Residence 11; Total Staff 6.

Vianney Renewal Center, 6476 Eime Rd., P.O. Box 130, 63023. Tel: 314-274-5226; 677-1828; Fax: 314-274-1430.
Web site: www.theservants.org
Operated by the Servants of the Paraclete. Rev. Richard Brown, S.P., Dir. of Prog. Total in Residence 16; Total Staff 8.

EUREKA. *Marianist Retreat & Conference Center*, P.O. Box 718, 63025. Tel: 314-938-5390. Center for Formation and Growth in the Christian Life. Conducted by the Society of Mary. Revs. Joseph Uvietta, S.M., Dir.; Jose Ramirez, S.M. Total in Residence 5; Total Staff 18.

FLORISSANT. *Pallottine Renewal Center*, 15270 Old Halls Ferry Rd., 63034. Tel: 314-837-7100. Pallottine Missionary Sisters. Sr. Bernadita Peterson, S.A.C., Admin. Total in Residence 6; Total Staff 12.

GLENCOE. *La Salle Institute*, 2101 Rue de la Salle, 63038. Tel: 314-938-5374; Fax: 314-587-9792. Community: Tel: 314-938-6142. Bro. Marvin Becker, Dir. Community 5; Total in Residence 4; Total Staff 7.

HIGH RIDGE. *Society of Our Mother of Peace-Maria Fonte Solitude*, 6150 Antire Rd., 63049-2100. Tel: 314-677-3235. Sr. Mary Perpetua, S.M.P.; Rev. Placid Guste, S.M.P.

[U] CAMPS AND COMMUNITY CENTERS

HILLSBORO. *Don Bosco Camp*, 9607 Msgr. Meyer Rd., 63050. J. Kevin McInnis, Dir.

[V] NEWMAN CENTERS

ST. LOUIS. *University of Missouri, St. Louis, Newman House*, 63121. Tel: 314-385-3455. Deacon Dennis Chitwood, Dir.

Washington University Newman Centers, Washington University Newman Chapel, 6352 Forsyth Blvd., 63105-2269. Tel: 314-725-3358; Fax: 314-727-6053. Rev. Gary G. Braun, Archdiocesan Dir. of Campus Ministries. In res. Rev. Msgr. William J. Lyons. Total in Residence 2; Total Staff 15.

[W] MISCELLANEOUS

ST. LOUIS. *Alexian Brothers of Missouri, Inc.*

Alexian Brothers of St. Louis, Inc.

Alexian Brothers Services, Inc.

Almost Home, 203 Brotherton Lane, 63135-3105. Tel: 314-521-3832. Transitional living prog. for teenage mothers & their children who are homeless. Sr. Irene Radtke, F.S.M., Exec. Dir. Total Assisted 126; Total Staff 10.

**American Academy of Natural Family Planning*, 615 S. New Ballas Rd., 63141. Tel: 314-991-5766. Mrs. Diane Daly.

Anna House, 1100 Bellevue Ave., 63117-1883. Tel: 314-768-1827; Fax: 314-768-1880.
E-mail: fsmstl2@aol.com
Supports the religious and charitable purposes of the Daughters of Charity and the Franciscan Sisters of Mary.

Anna Trust, 6400 Minnesota Ave., 63111. A Charitable Trust Fund Established to Support the Religious and Charitable Purposes of the Sisters of St. Joseph of Carondelet, St. Louis Province.

Archdiocesan Charitable Bequest Council, 4445 Lindell Blvd., 63108. Tel: 314-533-1887; Fax: 314-533-1889. Mr. Frank J. Cognata, Jr., Chief Devel. Officer;Mr. Roger E. Cammon; Mr. David T. Keifer; Mr. Timothy Wichmer; Mr. James G. Blase; Ms. Christi S. Fingal; Rev. Richard E. Hanneke, Archbishop's Rep., Planned Giving; Mr. T. Jack Challis; Ms. Susan Christensen; Mr. Robert Edler; Mr. Timothy Hammett; Mr. Michael Heck; Mr. Gene Morgenthaler; Mr. Douglas Rothermich; Ms. Teresa Schlafly; Mr. Dennis Schleper.

Archdiocesan Development Appeal, 4140 Lindell Blvd., 63108. Tel: 314-371-4980, Ext. 166. Mary Morfeld, Exec. Dir.

Archdiocesan Stewardship Education Committee, 4445 Lindell Blvd., 63108. Tel: 314-533-1887; Fax: 314-533-1889. Mr. Frank J. Cognata, Chief Devel. Officer; Mrs. Teresa R. Manna, Assoc. Dir.; Mrs. Kimberly Sapa; Mr. Bob Barrett; Ms. Mary Weiskopf; Rev. Michael Boehm; Mr. Tom Coerver; Revs. Dennis Doerhoff; Michael L. Henning.

Aware, Inc., St. Anthony's Medical Center, 10010 Kennerly Rd., 63128. Tel: 314-525-1622. Donna Kallal, Pres.; Mrs. Colleen George, Vice Pres.

B.R.E.M. Catholic Social Ministry, 1371 Hamilton Ave., 63112. Tel: 314-383-4666; Fax: 314-383-5366. Ms. Dorothy Kastigar, Dir. Provides Employment Counseling and Referrals, Health Outreach, and Referrals for Food, Clothing and Housing. Also Provides Community Education, Leadership Development, Family Support and Community Development Services. Total Assisted 2,500; Total Staff 2.

Birthright, 2206 S. Brentwood Blvd., 63144. Tel: 314-962-5300.
Web site: www.birthright.org
Shirley E. Ducey, Admin. Dir.
Branch Offices: 215 Clarkson Exec. Pkwy., 63011. Tel: 314-227-2266. 6500 Chippewa, 63109. Tel: 314-962-3653. 3435A Bridgeland, 63044. Tel: 314-227-8775. 205 N. 5th St., St. Charles, 63301. Tel: 314-724-1200. 4144 Lindell, 63108. Tel: 314-946-4900.

Boys Hope-Girls Hope, 12120 Bridgeton Square Dr., 63044. Tel: 314-298-1250; Fax: 314-298-1251.
E-mail: BoysHope-GirlsHope@charitiesusa.com
Web site: www.BoysHopeGirlsHope.org
John L. Doman, Pres. & CEO. A College Preparatory Residential Child Care Agency Serving Abandoned, Abused and Neglected Children. Founded in 1977. Total Assisted 3,600; Total Staff 109.
With affiliated programs in: Baton Rouge; Chicago; Cincinnati; Denver; Detroit; Jacksonville; Nevada; New Orleans; New York; Northeast Ohio; Orange County, CA; Phoenix; Pittsburgh; St. Louis.

Cardinal Glennon Children's Hospital Foundation, 1465 S. Grand Blvd., 63104. Tel: 314-577-5605. Member of SSM Health Care.

Caritas. Ladies of Charity Service Center, 7500 Natural Bridge Rd., 63121. Tel: 314-383-4207. Legal Title: *Ladies of Charity Service Center*. Aid for the Needy. Sr. Louise Scheessele, D.C., Dir. Total Assisted 26,310; Total Staff 54.

The Caroline Trust, 320 E. Ripa Ave., 63125-2897. Tel: 314-544-0455; Fax: 314-544-6754. Supports the Religious and Charitable Purposes of the School Sisters of Notre Dame and Provides Support for the Aged, Infirm and Disabled Sisters of the Province.

Carondelet Health System, 13801 Riverport Dr., Ste. 300, 63043-4810. Tel: 314-770-0333; Fax: 314-770-0444. Gary F. Christiansen, Pres. Tel: 314-770-0333.

Catholic Charities Foundation, 4532 Lindell Blvd., 63108. Tel: 314-367-5500. Mr. John M. Lally, M.S.W., L.C.S.W., CEO. A Charitable Fund Established to Support the Activities of Catholic Charities.

Catholic Charities Volunteer Department, 4532 Lindell Blvd., 63108. Tel: 314-367-5500.
E-mail: volsvcs@swbell.net
The Recruiting and Referral Office for Volunteers Serving the Needs of the Various Programs Affiliated with Catholic Charities in Conjunction with the St. Vincent Pallotti Center for Apostolic Development which Develops and Enhances Lay Volunteer Ministry by Bringing Together Clergy, Religious and Laity.

Catholic Commission on Housing, 4140 Lindell Blvd., 63108. Tel: 314-371-0138. Rev. Richard J. Quirk, Exec. Dir. An Agency of the Catholic Charities Federation that Assists Low and Moderate Income Families in Buying their First Home.

Catholic Community Services Administration, 325 N. Newstead, 63108-2728. Tel: 314-531-0511. Sr. Betty Brucker, F.S.M., Exec. Dir. An Agency of the Catholic Charities Federation. A Consolidation of Catholic Charities Outreach Services, Catholic Health Outreach Program and the Archbishop's Commission on Community Health.

Midtown Catholic Community Services, 1202 S. Boyle Ave., 63110-3814. Tel: 314-534-1180.

Jefferson County Catholic Community Services, P.O. Box 668, Festur, 63028-0668. Tel: 314-931-5859.

Rural Catholic Community Services, Rte. 1, Box 1110, Cadet, 63630-9717. Tel: 573-438-6182.

Father Tolton Catholic Community Services, 2011 E. Linton Ave., 63107-1134. Tel: 314-534-5323.

St. Jane Catholic Community Services, 7005 Ascension Dr., 63121-3427. Tel: 314-383-6539.

St. Joseph Catholic Community Services, 6322 Minnestoa, 63111-2553. Tel: 314-351-6407.

Southside Catholic Community Services, 2647 Ohio, 63118. Tel: 314-773-6100.

St. Charles County Catholic Community Services, 1101 S. Service Rd. (E. Hwy. 40), Ste. 255, Wentzville, 63385-4845. Tel: 314-332-6889.

Vietnamese Health Center, 2651 Keokuk St., Bldg. A, 63118-4624. Tel: 314-664-8990. 3535 S. Jefferson, Ste. 111, 63118-3907.

Catholic Community Services - Friends of Moms. At Joint Neighborhood Ministry, 2911 McNair Ave., 63118-1632. Tel: 314-771-3987. For all: Total Assisted 55,886; Total Staff 49.

Catholic Deaf Ministry, 6815 Page Ave., 63133-1505. Tel: 314-721-3069; 727-2747 (TDD). Provides Services for Deaf and Hearing Impaired Persons.

Catholic Family Services, 7800 Kenrick Rd., 63119. Tel: 314-968-8010. Richard Hennicke, Exec. Dir. Provides professional counseling (individual & small groups) to individuals & families experiencing stress. Family Life Outreach & Parent Education available. Fees based on ability to pay.
District Offices:

South, 7800 Kenrick Rd., 63119. Tel: 314-968-8010.

Northwest, 4450 Washington, Florissant, 63033. Tel: 314-831-1533.

West County, 504 Woods Mill Rd., Manchester, 63011. Tel: 314-391-9966.

St. Charles, 1360 S. Fifth, St. Charles, 63302. Tel: 314-946-6014.

North City, Monsanto YMCA, 63112. Tel: 314-367-4646.

Crystal City/Festus, 305 W. Main, Festus, 63028. Tel: 314-937-2157; 937-2163; 1-800-652-8055.

Franklin Warren Counties, P.O. Box 342, Union, 63084. Tel: 314-583-1800.

St. Vincent Church, 1000 Rosati Ct., Perryville, 63775. Tel: 314-547-4591; 1-800-652-8055. For all: Total Assisted 12,562; Total Staff 49.

The Catholic Health Association of the United States, 4455 Woodson Rd., 63134. Tel: 314-427-2500; Fax: 314-427-0029.
Established June 24, 1915. John E. Curley, Jr., Pres. & CEO.

Catholic High School Association, 4140 Lindell Blvd., 63108. Tel: 314-371-4980.
E-mail: archstlceo@connectinc.com
Mr. George Henry, Supt.

Focus Foundation (Federation of Catholic Urban Schools), 4140 Lindell Blvd., 63108. Tel: 314-371-4980. Sr. Margaret McCulloch, B.V.M., Dir.

Today and Tomorrow Educational Foundation, 4140 Lindell Blvd., 63108. Tel: 314-371-4980. Bridgett Flood, Dir.

Catholic Education Office, 4140 Lindell Blvd., 63108. Tel: 314-371-4980.

Catholic Information Center, 1000 N. Seventh St., 63101. Tel: 314-621-6555; 231-9991. Rev. Valentine Young, O.F.M.Cap., Dir.

Catholic Kolping Society of America, 4035 Keokuk St., 63116. Tel: 314-776-5312. Otto J. Eichhorn, Treas.

Catholic Leadership Development, 4140 Lindell Blvd., 63108. Tel: 314-727-2350. Mailing Address: 43 Aberdeen Pl., 63105. Gerty O'Leary, Dir.
Participants are nominated by pastors and Catholic leaders and are committed to learning and active project work.

Catholic Office of Disability Ministry, 7800 Kenrick Rd., 63119-5004. Tel: 314-961-4320, Ext. 190; Fax: 314-918-0878. Lorraine Fahey, Dir.

Catholic Services for Children and Youth, 4140 Lindell Blvd., 63108. Tel: 314-371-4980. William J. Murphy, M.S.W., Dir. Child Welfare Agency Providing Adoption, Foster Family Care, Outreach Counseling in Own Home, Social Services for Residential Treatment Centers and Services for Unmarried and Single Parents. Total in Residence 3,400; Total Staff 60.

Central Bureau of the CCUA, 3835 Westminster Pl., 63108-3472. Tel: 314-371-1653. Rev. John H. Miller, C.S.C., Dir. and Editor of the Social Justice Review.

Chiara Corporation, 1100 Bellevue, 63117. Tel: 314-768-1817; Fax: 314-768-1880. Mr. John O'Shaughnessy, Contact Person. Ministries that promote, enhance and provide for the spiritual, religious, physical or mental well-being of members of society in accordance with the religious and charitable purposes of the Franciscan Sisters of Mary.

Child Center Foundation, 7900 Natural Bridge Rd., 63121; Fax: 314-383-6334. William L. Meyer, Chm. Bd.
Child Center Foundation provides financial support to the Child Center of Our Lady, a residential, day treatment, and outpatient services facility serving severely emotionally disturbed children and their families.

Daughters of Charity Healthcare Foundation of St. Louis, 7806 Natural Bridge Rd., 63121-4626. Tel: 314-679-1520. Sr. Joan Kuester, Exec. Dir.

Daughters of Charity National Health System, P.O. Box 45998, 63145-5998.
E-mail: dbrennan@national.dcnhs.org
4600 Edmundson Rd., 63134. Tel: 314-253-6888; Fax: 314-253-6407. Donald A. Brennan, Pres./CEO.
The Daughters of Charity National Health System is sponsored by four of the United States Provinces of the Daughters of Charity: Northeast Prov., Albany, NY; Southeast Prov., Emmitsburg, MD; East Central Prov., Evansville, IN; and West Central Prov., St. Louis, MO.

Daughters of Charity National Health System-West Central Inc., 7806 Natural Bridge Rd., 63121. Tel: 314-679-1500. Dennis J. Eike, Regl. Exec. & CEO.

Daughters of Charity West Central Region Foundation, 7806 Natural Bridge Rd., 63121-4626. Tel: 314-679-1500. Sr. Joan Kuester, D.C., Contact Person. Provides funds for the poor & underserved; will fund projects related to health education, wellness & prevention, primary medical svcs. & social svcs.

Dial Help, 325 N. Newstead, 63108. Tel: 314-371-4357; 800-666-9990. Mrs. Mary Carroll, Dir.; Sr. Cunegunda Mueller, Admin. Total Assisted 23,009; Total Staff 2. Information and Referral Service Operated by Catholic Charities.

Dismas House of St. Louis, 5025 Cote Brilliante Ave., 63113. Tel: 314-361-2802; Fax: 314-361-8780. Rev. Joseph M. Kohler, Exec. Dir. Total in Residence 154; Total Staff 53.

Elizabeth House, 1100 Bellevue Ave., 63117-1883. Tel: 314-768-1827; Fax: 314-768-1880.
E-mail: fsmstl2@aol.com
Purpose: provides retirement housing and services to members of religious congregations and laity.

Eucharistic Missionaries of St. Theresa, 4431 Lindell Blvd., 63108. Tel: 314-533-2824. Sr. Theresa Caracheo Espinal, M.E.S.T.

Franciscan Sisters of Mary, 1100 Bellevue Ave., 63117-1883. Tel: 314-768-1824; Fax: 314-768-1880.
E-mail: fsmstl2@aol.com

Good Shepherd Programs, Inc., 7654 Natural Bridge Rd., 63121. Operates the Maria Droste Residence.

Gregorian University Foundation, 3601 Lindell Blvd., 63108. Tel: 314-977-2598; Fax: 314-977-7211. Rev. John F. Snyder, S.J., Vice Chm. Bd. of Trustees.

Hispanic Ministry of the Archdiocese of St. Louis, 5418 Louisiana, 63111. Tel: 314-351-7009. Sr. Alicia Alvarado, O.P., Coord.; Rev. Luis Moreno, Contact Person. Total Staff 2.

Institute for Theological Encounter with Science & Technology (ITEST), 221 N. Grand Blvd., 63103. Tel: 314-977-2703; Fax: 314-977-7264.
E-mail: postigm@wpogate.slu.edu
Web site: http://ITEST.slu.edu
Rev. Robert A. Brungs, S.J., Dir.

Institute of Jesuit Sources, 3700 W. Pine St., 63108. Tel: 314-977-7257; Fax: 314-977-7263. Rev. John W. Padberg, S.J., Dir.

Intercommunity Housing Association, 3407 Lafayette Ave., 63104-1313. Provides safe, affordable housing & supportive svcs. for economically disadvantaged & working poor families in St. Louis.

The Jesuits of the Missouri Province, Office of Development: 4517 W. Pine Blvd., 63108. Tel: 314-361-7765; Fax: 314-758-7163.
E-mail: misdvelop@jesuit-mis.com
Web site: http://www.jesuit-mis
Mr. Ray Markham, Dir.; Rev. L. Gene Martens, S.J., Assoc. Dir. Legal Title: *The Jesuits of the Missouri Prov.*

Ladies of Charity of St. Catherine Laboure, 12160 Leelaine Dr., 63126. Affiliate with Ladies of Charity of the United States & the Assoc. of Intl. Charities of St. Vincent de Paul. Susan Tumminia, Pres.

Ladies of Charity of St. Vincent-Guardian Angel. St. Vincent's Church, 1408 S. Tenth St., 63104. Affiliate with Ladies of Charity of the United States & the Assoc. of Intl. Charities of St. Vincent de Paul. Natalie Cox, Pres.

Ladies of Charity of the United States of America, P.O. Box 31697, 63131-1697. Doris C. Hoag, National Pres.
LCUSA continues, expands, and improves the charitable works of the local associations of the LCUSA, which number 79.

Mary and Joseph Trust, 1100 Bellevue Ave., 63117-1883. Tel: 314-768-1817.

McAuley Charitable Trust, 2039 N. Geyer Rd., 63131-3399. Tel: 314-966-4313.
E-mail: kglosenger@somh.smhs.com
The Sisters of Mercy of the Americas, Regional Community of St. Louis. Sr. Katherine Marie Glosenger, R.S.M., Contact Person.

Migration and Refugee Services, 2840 Wisconsin Ave., 63118. Tel: 314-771-2570; Fax: 314-771-6406.
E-mail: ccrs1@stlnet.com
To Facilitate the Settlement of Refugees.

The Missionaries of Our Lady of La Salette, Provincialate, 4650 S. Broadway, 63111-1398. Total in Residence 11; Total Staff 4.

Missionaries of the Kingship of Christ, P.O. Box 2234, 63109. Tel: 314-353-5002.
E-mail: clmaley@inlink.com
Rev. Msgr. Louis F. Meyer, Spiritual Dir. Total in Residence 1. Madonna House, 4908 Sutherland Ave., 63109. Tel: 314-352-5822.
A Pontifical Secular Institute.

The Museum of Western Jesuit Missions, 700 Howdershell Rd., Box 1095, 63031. Rev. William B. Faherty, S.J., Curator. Total in Residence 1; Total Staff 10.

National Christian Life Community of the United States of America (CLC), 3601 Lindell Blvd., Rm. 202 (Jesuit Hall), 63108-3393. Tel: 314-977-7370. Joan Felling, Pres. Founded c. 1540 & approved 1584, a public, intl. assn. of the Faithful of Pontifical Right which builds small Faith-Communities for mission & Svc. to the church. It uses the Spiritual Exercises of Saint Ignatius of Loyola as its specific source & characteristic instrument for its spirituality. Membership equally open to primarily catholic christian men, women, youth & young adults, clergy, brothers & sisters.

Network of Sacred Heart Schools, Inc., 4389 W. Pine Blvd., 63108. Tel: 314-652-1500; Fax: 314-534-6800.
E-mail: nshoffice@sofie.org
Web site: http://www.sofie.org
Sr. Barbara Dawson, Prov.

Notre Dame Ministry Corporation, 320 Ripa Ave., 63125. Tel: 314-544-0455. Sr. Barbara Marie McInturff, S.S.N.D. Includes: Notre Dame High School, Notre Dame Preschool, Notre Dame Travel & Notre Dame Tutorial Center.

Oblate House of Studies, 3741 Laclede Ave., 63108-3317. Tel: 314-534-2451. Rev. Allen Maes, O.M.I.

Our Lady's Inn, 4223 S. Compton, 63111. Tel: 314-351-4590. Julie Peetz, Contact Person. Total Assisted 200; Total Staff 15. A residential shelter for pregnant women who have no home, who are being abused, who have no one who cares, and/or who are being pressured to abort their baby. We provide living facilities, food, clothing, counseling, and vocational guidance.

Perpetual Help Charitable Trust, 201 Brotherton Ln., 63135; Fax: 314-521-7179. Established by the Franciscan Sisters of Our Lady of Perpetual Help to Support the Religious and Charitable Purposes of the Franciscan Sisters of Our Lady of Perpetual Help.

Pope John Paul II Apartments, Inc., 4483 Lindell Blvd., 63108. Tel: 314-652-3600. Purpose: to provide facilities and services specifically designed to meet the physical, social and psychologial needs of elderly persons or handicapped persons.

Review for Religious, 3601 Lindell Blvd., Rm. 428, 63108. Tel: 314-977-7363; Fax: 314-977-7362.
E-mail: foppema@slu.edu
Total Staff 6.

Sacred Heart Program, Inc., 3900 Westminster Pl., 63108. Tel: 314-533-0320. Gary Kolarcik, Exec. Dir. Total Staff 8. The Sacred Heart Program produces "Contact," an international broadcast designed to help society's "strugglers" - the spiritually, physically or financially impoverished. The organization also offers Sacred Heart devotional items.

St. Charles Lwanga Center, 5021 Northland Ave., 63113-1014. Tel: 314-367-7929; Fax: 314-367-4134. Provides spiritual formation and leadership development with evangelization and youth outreach for the Black Catholic Community, those working in the community and all interested persons in the Archdiocese of St. Louis and throughout the United States. Gloria N. Green, Dir. Total Staff 5.

St. Francis de Sales Association, 228 Chestnut Ave., 63119. Mrs. Martha Smith, Western Regl. Dir. Promotes Christian Living of the Baptismal Commission According to the Spirituality of St. Francis de Sales.

St. Francis Home Care, Inc., 477 N. Lindbergh, 63141. Tel: 314-994-7800.

St. John's Mission, 4517 W. Pine Blvd., 63108. Tel: 314-361-7765; Fax: 314-758-7163.
E-mail: misjesuits@aol.com

St. Louis Catholic Charismatic Renewal, 7800 Kenrick Rd., 63119. Tel: 314-961-3420, Ext. 418; Fax: 314-961-4320, Ext. 444. Rev. Dennis Chitwood, Liaison; Barbara Thompson, Sec., Healing & Deliverance Ministry. Tel: 314-961-3420, Ext. 416. Overflowing Joy Ministry. Tel: 314-961-3420, Ext. 410. Tree House Healing Ministry. Tel: 314-961-3420, Ext. 413. Heart to Heart Scripture Study. Tel: 314-838-9024. Theo Tokes Ministry, 4311 S. Compton, 63111. Tel: 314-351-6061. Center with books & tapes, prayer time, ministry times, retreats for parishes, leaders training, small faith groups, conferences, special events & days of renewal.

St. Louis Roman Catholic Landmark Corp., 4445 Lindell Blvd., 63108. Maintains, Supports, Repairs and Preserves the St. Louis Roman Catholic Cathedral Located at Lindell and Newstead.

St. Martha's Hall, P.O. Box 4950, 63108. Tel: 314-533-1313. Provides Emergency Shelter, Counseling, Advocacy to Abused Women and their Children. Michelle Schiller-Baker, Dir. Total Assisted 340; Total Staff 10.

St. Mary's Health Center Foundation, 6420 Clayton Rd., 63117. Tel: 314-768-8067. Member of SSM Health Care.

St. Patrick Center, 1200 N. 6th St., 63106. Tel: 314-621-1283. An Agency in Downtown St. Louis, Housing a Wide Range of Social Services for Mentally Ill and/or Chemically Dependent Homeless Persons and for Residents in the Area at Risk of Becoming Homeless. Total Assisted 7,000; Total Staff 55.

St. Paul Books and Media, 9804 Watson Rd., 63126. Tel: 314-965-3512; Fax: 314-821-8401. Total in Residence 4.

St. Vincent de Paul Educational Foundation Perryville, 1010 A Rosati Ct., 63775. Develops, Promotes and Sustains Catholic Education in Perry County. Rev. Kevin P. Fausz, C.M., Moderator.

St. Vincent Pallotti Center for Apostolic Development, 4532 Lindell Blvd., 63108. Tel: 314-367-5500.
E-mail: volsvcs@swbell.net
Support for lay volunteers in full-time service. (See Catholic Charities Volunteer Department).

The Sarah Community, 1100 Bellevue Ave., 63117-1883. Tel: 314-768-1827; Fax: 314-768-1880.
E-mail: fsmstl2@aol.com
Purpose: provides retirement housing and services to members of religious congregations and laity.

Seminar on Jesuit Spirituality, 3700 W. Pine St., 63108. Tel: 314-977-7257; Fax: 314-977-7263. Rev. John W. Padberg, S.J., Chm. Total Staff 3.

Sisters of Mercy Education System, Inc., 2039 N. Geyer Rd., 63131; Fax: 314-966-2298.
Serves the Mission of the Sisters of Mercy in its Charitable Ministry and Education Services.

Society of St. Vincent DePaul, Council of the United States, 58 Progress Pkwy., 63043-3706.
E-mail: svdpus@aol.com
Most Rev. J. Terry Steib, S.V.D., Bishop of Memphis, Spiritual Advisor; Joseph H. Mueller, Pres.; Rita W. Porter, Exec. Sec./Dir., Tel: 314-576-3993; Fax: 314-576-6755.

SSM Health Care Central Region, 477 N. Lindbergh, 63141. Tel: 314-994-7800. Member of SSM Health Care.

SSM Health Care Corporation, 477 N. Lindbergh, 63141. Tel: 314-994-7800. Member of SSM Health Care.

SSM Rehabilitation Institute Foundation, 6420 Clayton Rd. #600, 63117. Tel: 314-768-5300. Member of SSM Health Care.

Theology Digest, 3634 Lindell Blvd., 63108. Total Staff 2.

Veronica House, 1100 Bellevue Ave., 63117-1883. Tel: 314-768-1827; Fax: 314-768-1880.
E-mail: fsmstl2@aol.com
Purpose: provides retirement housing and services to members of religious congregations and laity.

The Vincentian Press Religious Supply, 1405 S. Ninth St., 63104. Rev. Joseph E. Begue, C.M., Dir. Total Staff 3.

We & God Spirituality Center, 3601 Lindell Blvd., 63108. Tel: 314-977-2696.

**Women for Faith and Family*, P.O. Box 8326, 63132.
E-mail: 72223.3601@compuserve.com
Mrs. Helen Hull Hitchcock, Pres.

ARNOLD. *AJT, Inc.*, 320 E. Ripa Ave., 63125. 2488 Birch Ln., 63010. Tel: 314-296-1882. Sr. Alene Faul, S.S.N.D., Ph.D., Pres.; Rev. J. Patrick Gaffney, S.M.M., Vice Pres.; Betty A. Studley, Sec.-Treas. Exclusively Religious, Literary Educational and Charitable Related to the Integration of Religious, Charitable and Educational Service Resources to Provide Materials to Existing Religious Instruction, Specifically the Development of Bible Study Computer Study Computer Software Programs.

BRIDGETON. *DePaul Health Center Foundation*, 12303 DePaul Dr., 63044. Tel: 314-344-7477.
E-mail: cbell@ssmhc.com
Member of SSM Health Care. The mission of the foundation is to develop the financial, in-kind and volunteer resources of the community in support of DePaul's ministry: making a positive difference in the lives and health status of the individuals we serve with particular concern for maintaining the respect and dignity of the poor, the elderly and those less fortunate.

CADET. *Rural Parish Workers of Christ the King*, R.R. 1, Box 1667, 63630. Tel: 314-586-5171. Miss Natalie Villmer, Gen. Dir. A Secular Institute of the Archdiocese of St. Louis. Workers 5; Total Assisted 2,500; Total in Residence 6; Total Staff 7.

EARTH CITY. *Congregation of the Mission International Fund*, 13663 Rider Tr. N., 63045-1512. Tel: 314-344-1184; Fax: 314-344-2989.
E-mail: cmstlouis@aol.com
Bro. F. Joseph Hess, C.M.

Lazarist Trust Fund, 13663 Rider Tr. N., 63045-1512. Tel: 314-344-1184; Fax: 314-344-2989.
E-mail: cmstlouis@aol.com

EUREKA. *Providence Trust*, Our Lady of the Angels Monastery, St. Joseph Rd., 63025. Purpose: supports the religious and charitable purposes of the Franciscan Missionary Brothers of the Sacred Heart.

FLORISSANT. *Marygrove, Inc.*, 2705 Mullanphy, 63031.
E-mail: mgrove@swb.net
Total Assisted 2,689; Total Staff 125.

KIRKWOOD. *St. Joseph Hospital of Kirkwood Foundation*. A member of SSM Health Care. 525 Couch Ave., St. Louis, 63122. Tel: 314-966-1644.

LIGUORI. *Redemptorists Fathers dba Liguori Publications*, One Liguori Dr., 63057. Tel: 314-464-2500; Fax: 314-464-8449.
Web site: www.liguori.org
Rev. Thomas M. Santa, C.SS.R.

O'FALLON. *Centers for Professional and Pastoral Services*, 204 N. Main St., 63366. Tel: 314-240-6010. Sponsored by Sisters of the Most Precious Blood of O'Fallon, MO. Sr. Andree Fries, C.PP.S. Centers 5; Total Assisted 461; Total Staff 5.

Charitable Trust, Sisters of the Most Precious Blood of O'Fallon, MO, 204 N. Main St., 63366. Trust fund for support of retired Sisters of the Most Precious Blood.

St. Dominic Endowment Fund, St. Dominic High School, 31 St. Dominic Dr., 63366. Tel: 314-240-8303; Fax: 314-240-9884. Sr. Mary H. Bender, S.S.N.D., Treas.

PERRYVILLE. *The Association of the Miraculous Medal*, 1811 W. St. Joseph St., 63775. Tel: 573-547-8343; Fax: 573-547-1389.
E-mail: amml@amm.org
Web site: http://www.amm.org
Rev. Charles F. Shelby, C.M., Dir.

Catholic Home Study Service, P.O. Box 363, 63775. Tel: 573-547-4084.
E-mail: 102036.3005@compuserve.com
Web site: http://www.amm.org/chss.htm
Rev. Oscar Lukefahr, C.M., Dir.
Offers free correspondence courses on the Catholic Faith.

Ladies of Charity of St. Vincent de Paul Parish, 1010 Rosati Ct., 63775. Affiliate with Ladies of Charity of the United States & the Assoc. of Intl. Charities of St. Vincent de Paul. Dorothy Barry, Pres. Total Assisted 750.

PEVELY. *Vision of Peace Ministries,* Abby Ln., P.O. Box 69, 63070. Tel: 314-475-3697. Mrs. James Ruth Muskopf. Total in Residence 2; Total Staff 2.

ST. CHARLES. *Duchesne High School Endowment Fund Inc.,* 2550 Elm St., 63301. Tel: 314-946-6767. Mr. Charles L. Nolan, Admin. Receives Bequests and Gifts from Various Donors for the Express Purpose of Aiding and Benefitting Duchesne High School, St. Charles, and by Investment and Use of Such Bequests and Gifts and Income therefrom Aids and Benefits the High School in Fulfilling its Educational Purposes.

St. Joseph Health Center and St. Joseph Hospital West Foundation, 300 First Capitol Dr., 63301. Tel: 314-947-5612; Fax: 314-947-5090. Member of SSM Health Care.

RELIGIOUS INSTITUTES OF MEN REPRESENTED IN THE ARCHDIOCESE

For further details refer to the corresponding bracketed number in the Religious Institutes of Men or Women section.

[0120]—*Alexian Brothers.* (Chicago).—C.F.A.
[0140]—*The Augustinians. (Prov. of Our Mother of Good Counsel).*—O.S.A.
[0200]—*Benedictine Monks. (English, Swiss American Congregation).*—O.S.B.
[0330]—*Brothers of the Christian Schools. (St. Louis Prov.).*—F.S.C.
[0600]—*Brothers of the Congregation of Holy Cross.*—C.S.C.
[0470]—*The Capuchin Friars.* (Kansas City, MO).—O.F.M.Cap.
[1330]—*Congregation of the Mission. (Midwest Prov.).*—C.M.
[0630]—*Congregation of the Missionaries of the Holy Family.* (Europe).—M.S.F.
[1000]—*Congregation of the Passion. (Western Prov. of Holy Cross).*—M.S.F.
[1130]—*Congregation of the Priests of the Sacred Heart.*—S.C.J.
[1080]—*Congregation of the Resurrection.* (Rome, Italy).—C.R.
[0480]—*Conventual Franciscans. (Our Lady of Consolation Prov.).*—O.F.M.Conv.
[0520]—*Franciscan Friars. (Croatian Franciscan Commissariat, Sacred Heart Prov.).*—O.F.M.
[0540]—*Franciscan Missionary Brothers of the Sacred Heart of Jesus.* (Eureka, MO).—O.S.F.
[0690]—*Jesuit Fathers and Brothers.* (Missouri Prov.).—S.J.
[0800]—*Maryknoll.*—M.M.
[0830]—*Mill Hill Missionaries.*—M.H.M.
[0720]—*The Missionaries of Our Lady of La Salette.*—M.S.
[0870]—*Monfort Missionaries.*—S.M.M.
[0910]—*Oblates of Mary Immaculate.*—O.M.I.
[0430]—*Order of Preachers.*—O.P.
[0610]—*Priests of the Congregation of Holy Cross.*—C.S.C.
[1070]—*Redemptorist Fathers.* (St. Louis Prov.).—C.SS.R.
[0700]—*St. Joseph's Society of the Sacred Heart.*—S.S.J.
[1230]—*Servants of the Paraclete.*—s.P.
[1240]—*Servites.* (Chicago).—O.S.M.
[0760]—*Society of Mary.* (St. Louis Prov.).—S.M.
[0420]—*Society of the Divine Word.* (Northern Prov.).—S.V.D.
[]—*Sons of Our Mother.*—S.M.P.

RELIGIOUS INSTITUTES OF WOMEN REPRESENTED IN THE ARCHDIOCESE

[0100]—*Adorers of the Blood of Christ.* (Ruma, IL; Wichita, KS).—A.S.C.
[0130]—*Apostles of the Sacred Heart of Jesus.*—A.S.C.J.
[0160]—*Augustinian Cloistered Nuns.*—O.S.A.
[0230]—*Benedictine Sisters of Pontifical Jurisdiction.* (Atchison; Columbia; Fort Smith; Olivetan; Yankton).—O.S.B.
[0360]—*Carmelite Sisters of the Divine Heart of Jesus.* (Carmel).—D.C.J.
[3110]—*Congregation of Our Lady of the Retreat in the Cenacle.*—R.C.
[0220]—*Congregation of the Benedictine Sisters of Perpetual Adoration of Pontifical Jurisdiction.*—O.S.B.
[0460]—*Congregation of the Sisters of Charity of the Incarnate Word.*—C.C.V.I.
[]—*Daughters of Calvary.*—C.M.F.C.
[0760]—*Daughters of Charity of St. Vincent de Paul.*—D.C.
[]—*Daughters of Our Mother of Peace.*—S.M.P.
[0810]—*Daughters of the Heart of Mary.*—D.H.M.
[0420]—*Discalced Carmelite Nuns.*—O.C.D.
[1070-01]—*Dominican Sisters.*—O.P.
[1070-11]—*Dominican Sisters.* (Sparkill).—O.P.
[1070-13]—*Dominican Sisters.* (Akron).—O.P.
[1070-28]—*Dominican Sisters.* (Akron).—O.P.
[]—*Eucharist Missionaries of St. Theresa.*—M.E.S.T.
[1370]—*Franciscan Missionaries of Mary.*—F.M.M.
[1310]—*Franciscan Sisters of Little Falls, Minnesota.*—O.S.F.
[1415]—*Franciscan Sisters of Mary.*—F.S.M.
[1430]—*Franciscan Sisters of Our Lady of Perpetual Help.*—O.S.F.
[2340]—*Little Sisters of the Poor.*—L.S.P.
[2470]—*Maryknoll Sisters of St. Dominic.*—M.M.
[2490]—*Medical Mission Sisters.*—S.C.M.M.
[2710]—*Missionaries of Charity.*—M.C.
[0390]—*Missionary Carmelites of St. Teresa.*—C.M.S.T.
[3990]—*Missionary Sisters of St. Peter Claver.*—S.S.P.C.
[3040]—*Oblate Sisters of Providence.*—O.S.P.
[3760]—*Order of St. Clare.*—O.S.C.
[2010]—*Order of the Most Holy Redeemer.*—O.SS.R.
[0950]—*Pius Society Daughters of St. Paul.*—F.S.P.
[3170]—*Religious of the Passion of Jesus Christ.*—C.P.
[3465]—*Religious of the Sacred Heart of Mary.*—R.S.H.M.
[2970]—*School Sisters of Notre Dame.*—S.S.N.D.
[0500]—*Sisters of Charity of Nazareth.*—S.C.N.
[0590]—*Sisters of Charity of St. Elizabeth, Convent Station.*—S.C.
[0630]—*Sisters of Charity of St. Vincent de Paul.*—S.V.Z.
[0430]—*Sisters of Charity of the Blessed Virgin Mary.*—B.V.M.
[0660]—*Sisters of Christian Charity.*—S.C.C.
[]—*Sisters of Christian Community.*—S.F.C.C.
[0990]—*Sisters of Divine Providence.*—C.D.P.
[2360]—*Sisters of Loretto at the Foot of the Cross.* (St. Louis Prov.).—S.L.
[2570]—*Sisters of Mercy.*—R.S.M.
[2580]—*Sisters of Mercy of the Americas.*—R.S.M.
[2630]—*Sisters of Mercy of the Holy Cross.*—S.C.S.C.
[3000]—*Sisters of Notre Dame de Namur.*—S.N.D.deN.
[1540]—*Sisters of Saint Francis, Clinton, Iowa.*—O.S.F.
[1540]—*Sisters of St. Francis of the Martyr St. George.*—O.S.F.
[3830]—*Sisters of St. Joseph.*—C.S.J.
[1830]—*Sisters of the Good Shepherd.*—R.G.S.-C.G.S.
[2350]—*Sisters of the Living Word.*—S.L.W.
[3270]—*Sisters of the Most Precious Blood.* (O'Fallon, MO).—C.PP.S.
[3150]—*Sisters of the Pallottine Missionary Society.*—S.A.C.
[3540]—*Sisters Servants of the Holy Spirit of Perpetual Adoration.*—S.Sp.S.deA.P.
[2150]—*Sisters, Servants of the Immaculate Heart of Mary.*—I.H.M.
[]—*Society of Helpers of the Holy Souls.*—S.H.
[4070]—*Society of the Sacred Heart.*—R.S.C.J.
[4110]—*Ursuline Nuns.*—O.S.U.
[4120-05]—*Ursuline Nuns, of the Congregation of Paris.* (Maple Mount).—O.S.U.
[4190]—*Visitation Nuns.*—V.H.M.

ARCHDIOCESAN CEMETERIES

ST. LOUIS. *Calvary,* 5239 W. Florissant Ave., 63115. Tel: 314-381-1313.
Resurrection, 7301 Watson Rd., 63119.
SS. Peter and Paul, 7030 Gravois Ave., 63116.
CREVE COEUR. *St. Monica,* Olive Street Rd., 63141.
DARDENNE. *Our Lady of the Miraculous Medal,* Freymuth & Orf Rd., 63366.
FLORISSANT. *Sacred Heart,* Graham Rd., 63033.
St. Ferdinand, Graham Rd., 63031.
GLENCOE. *Holy Cross,* 16200 Manchester Rd., 63038.
KIRKWOOD. *St. Peter,* Geyer & W. Monroe Ave., 63122.
LEMAY. *Mount Olive,* 3906 Mount Olive St., 63125.
ST. CHARLES. *St. Charles Borromeo,* Randolph St., 63301.

NECROLOGY

† Brug, Theodore R., University City, MO, St. Patrick's. —Died Dec. 20, 1996.
† Byrne, John H., (Retired). —Died Dec. 26, 1996.
† Dierker, Louis P., Florissant, MO, St. Christopher. —Died April 19, 1997.
† Flynn, James, (Retired). —Died April 2, 1997.
† Huels, Vincent P., (Retired). —Died July 7, 1997.
† Kurtz, Rev. Msgr. George, (Retired). —Died June 20, 1997.
† Leibinger, Arthur, (Retired). —Died April 2, 1997.
† O'Brien, Joseph A., (Retired). —Died June 23, 1997.
† Regan, William, (Retired). —Died Feb. 18, 1997.
† Siesle, John W., Lemay, MO, Mary, Queen of the Universe. —Died April 21, 1997.
† Winkler, Clarence E., (Retired). —Died Dec. 3, 1996.

Archdiocese of St. Paul and Minneapolis

(Archidioecesis Paulopolitana et Minneapolitana)

Most Reverend

HARRY J. FLYNN, D.D.

Archbishop of Saint Paul and Minneapolis; ordained May 28, 1960; appointed Coadjutor of Lafayette April 19, 1986; consecrated June 24, 1986; appointed Bishop of Lafayette May 13, 1989; appointed Coadjutor Archbishop of Saint Paul and Minneapolis February 22, 1994; appointed Archbishop of Saint Paul and Minneapolis September 8, 1995

Most Reverend

J. RICHARD HAM, M.M., D.D.

Retired Auxiliary Bishop of Saint Paul and Minneapolis; ordained June 12, 1948; appointed Titular Bishop of Putzia of Numidia and Auxiliary Bishop of Guatemala November 28, 1967; consecrated January 6, 1968; appointed Auxiliary Bishop of Saint Paul and Minneapolis October 7, 1980; resigned October 30, 1990. *Res., St. Teresa Residence,, Maryknoll, NY, 10545.*

Most Reverend

JOHN R. ROACH, D.D.

Retired Archbishop of Saint Paul and Minneapolis; ordained June 8, 1946; appointed Titular Bishop of Cenae and Auxiliary Bishop of Saint Paul and Minneapolis July 12, 1971; consecrated September 8, 1971; appointed Archbishop of Saint Paul and Minneapolis May 21, 1975; installed July 16, 1975; resigned September 8, 1995. *Office: 226 Summit Ave., St. Paul, MN, 55102.* Tel.: 612-291-4400.

Chancery: 226 Summit Ave., St. Paul, MN, 55102. Tel.: 612-291-4400; Fax: 612-290-1629.

Web site address: http://www.mtn.org/archcom/

E-mail address: archcom@archspm

Most Reverend

LAWRENCE H. WELSH, D.D.

Auxiliary Bishop of Saint Paul and Minneapolis; ordained May 26, 1962; appointed Bishop of Spokane November 7, 1978; consecrated November 14, 1978; resigned April 17, 1990; appointed Titular Bishop of Aulona and Auxiliary Bishop of Archdiocese of Saint Paul and Minneapolis November 5, 1991. *Office: 226 Summit Ave., St. Paul, MN, 55102.* Tel.: 612-291-4400.

DIOCESE ESTABLISHED, JULY 19, 1850. ARCHDIOCESE ESTABLISHED, MAY 4, 1888.

Square Miles 6,187.

Comprises the following twelve Counties of the State of Minnesota: Ramsey, Hennepin, Anoka, Carver, Chisago, Dakota, Goodhue, Le Sueur, Rice, Scott, Washington and Wright.

Corporate Title: The Archdiocese of Saint Paul and Minneapolis.

For legal titles of parishes and archdiocesan institutions, consult the Chancery.

STATISTICAL OVERVIEW

Personnel	
Archbishop	1
Retired Archbishops	1
Bishop	1
Auxiliary Bishops	1
Retired Bishops	1
Priests: Diocesan Active in Diocese	235
Priests: Active Outside Diocese	12
Priests: Diocesan in Foreign Missions	4
Priests: Retired, Sick or Absent	99
Number of Diocesan Priests	350
Religious Priests in Diocese	148
Extern Priests in Diocese	35
Ordinations:	
Diocesan Priests	7
Permanent Deacons	9
Permanent Deacons in Diocese	170
Total Brothers	55
Total Sisters	1,093
Parishes	
Parishes	222
With Resident Pastor:	
Resident Diocesan Priests	180
Resident Religious Priests	28
Without Resident Pastor:	
Administered by Priests	14
Missions	5
Pastoral Centers	4
Closed Parishes	1
Professional Ministry Personnel:	
Brothers	3
Sisters	83
Lay Ministers	508
Welfare	
Catholic Hospitals	3
Total Assisted	141,444
Homes for the Aged	4
Total Assisted	693
Residential Care of Children	1
Total Assisted	4,000
Specialized Homes	4
Special Centers for Social Services	5
Educational	
Seminaries, Diocesan	2
Students from This Diocese	104
Students from Other Diocese	159
Total Seminarians	104
Colleges and Universities	3
Total Students	15,288
High Schools, Diocesan and Parish	7
Total Students	4,498
High Schools, Private	4
Total Students	2,380
Elementary Schools, Diocesan and Parish	88
Total Students	27,375
Elementary Schools, Private	1
Total Students	261
Catechesis/Religious Education:	
High School Students	21,618
Elementary Students	64,230
Total Students Under Catholic Instruction	135,754
Teachers in the Diocese:	
Priests	2
Brothers	11
Sisters	91
Lay Teachers	2,375
Vital Statistics	
Receptions into the Church:	
Infant Baptism Totals	11,606
Adult Baptism Totals	416
Received into Full Communion	1,267
First Communions	11,725
Confirmations	7,413
Marriages:	
Catholic	2,400
Interfaith	1,371
Total Marriages	3,771
Deaths	4,865
Total Catholic Population	747,660
Total Population	2,720,413

Former Bishops—Rt. Rev. JOSEPH CRETIN, D.D., cons. Jan. 26, 1851; died Feb. 22, 1857.—Most Rev. THOMAS L. GRACE, O.P., D.D., cons. July 24, 1859; resigned July 31, 1884; named Titular Bishop of Menith, and later, Titular Archbishop of Siunia; died Feb. 22, 1897.—Most Rev. JOHN IRELAND, D.D., cons. Dec. 21, 1875; Bishop of Maronea, and Coadjutor to.—Most Rev. THOMAS L. GRACE, O.P., D.D., succeeded to the See of St. Paul, July 31, 1884; appt. Archbishop, May 15, 1888; died Sept. 25, 1918.—Most Rev. AUSTIN DOWLING, D.D., Archbishop of St. Paul; ord. June 24, 1891; appt. Bishop of Des Moines, Iowa, Jan. 31, 1912; cons. April 25, 1912 Nominated Archbishop of St. Paul, Feb. 1, 1919; died Nov. 29, 1930.—Most Rev. JOHN GREGORY MURRAY, S.T.D., ord. April 14, 1900; appt. Titular Bishop of Flavias, Auxiliary to the Bishop of Hartford, Nov. 15, 1919; cons. April 28, 1920; transferred to the Diocese of Portland, May 29, 1925; appt. Archbishop of St. Paul, Oct. 29, 1931; died Oct. 11, 1956.—Most Rev. WILLIAM O. BRADY, D.D., Archbishop of St. Paul; ord. Dec. 21, 1923; appt. Bishop of Sioux Falls, June 10, 1939; cons. Aug. 24, 1939; appt. Titular Archbishop of Selymbria and Coadjutor "cum jure successionis" of St. Paul, June 16, 1956; succeeded to See, Oct. 11, 1956; died Oct. 1, 1961.—Most Rev. LEO C. BYRNE, D.D., Coadjutor Archbishop "cum jure successionis" of Saint Paul and Minneapolis; ord. June 10, 1933; appt. titular Bishop of Sabidia and Auxiliary of St. Louis, May 21, 1954; cons. June 29, 1954; transferred to Wichita, "cum jure successionis" 1961; appt. Apostolic Administrator of Wichita, Feb. 25, 1963; promoted to St. Paul and Minneapolis, Aug. 2, 1967; died Oct. 21, 1974.—Most Rev. LEO BINZ, D.D., ord. March 15, 1924; appt. Titular Bishop of Pinara and Coadjutor Bishop of Winona, Nov. 21, 1942; cons. Dec. 21, 1942; Titular Archbishop of Silyum and Coadjutor to the Archbishop of Dubuque "cum jure successionis," Oct. 15, 1949; Archbishop of Dubuque, Dec. 2, 1954; appt. Archbishop of Saint Paul, Dec. 16, 1961; resigned May 21, 1975; died Oct. 9, 1979.—Most Rev. JOHN R. ROACH, D.D., Archbishop of St. Paul and Minneapolis; ord. June 8, 1946; appt. Titular Bishop of Cenae and Auxiliary Bishop of St. Paul and Minneapolis, July 12, 1971; cons. Sept. 8, 1971; appt. Archbishop of St. Paul and Minneapolis, May 21, 1975; resigned Sept. 8, 1995.

Chancery—226 Summit Ave., St. Paul, 55102. Tel: 612-291-4400; Fax: 612-290-1629. Office Hours: Mon.-Fri. 9-5 All Official business should be directed to this office.
Vicar General and Moderator of the Curia—Rev. KEVIN M. MCDONOUGH, J.C.D.
Vicar General—Most Rev. LAWRENCE H. WELSH.
Chancellor for Civil Affairs—Mr. WILLIAM S. FALLON, J.D.
Chancellor for Canonical Affairs—Sr. M. DOMINICA BRENNAN, O.P., J.C.L.
Vice Chancellor—Rev. AUSTIN T. WARD.
Assistant Chancellor—Bro. VINCENT H. CHAMPINE, O.P.
Delegate for Marriage Dispensations—Bro. VINCENT H. CHAMPINE, O.P.
Episcopal Vicars—
For Eastern Vicariate—Rev. KEVIN M. MCDONOUGH, J.C.D.
For Western Vicariate—Most Rev. LAWRENCE H. WELSH.
For Southern Vicariate—Most Rev. HARRY J. FLYNN.
For Hispanic Vicariate—Most Rev. LAWRENCE H. WELSH.
For Canonical Affairs—Rev. KEVIN M. MCDONOUGH, J.C.D.
For African-American Catholics—Rev. KEVIN M. MCDONOUGH, J.C.D.
For Retired Priests—Rev. CHARLES M. EGGERT.
For Marriages—Revs. KEVIN M. MCDONOUGH, J.C.D.; AUSTIN T. WARD.
Co-Vicars for Religious—Sr. DOMINICA BRENNAN, O.P.; Sr. FRAN DONNELLY, B.V.M.
Archdiocesan Divisions—
Administration and Financial Services—Rev. AUSTIN T. WARD, Dir.
Christian Formation and Education—THOMAS MCCARVER, Dir.
Ministry Personnel—
Outreach—Mrs. JANET KROCHESKI, Dir.
Community Services—Rev. Msgr. J. JEROME BOXLEITNER, Dir.
Resource Development—JAMES MULLIN, Dir.
Due Process Dir.—Sr. M. DOMINICA BRENNAN, O.P., J.C.L.
Administrative Asst. to the Vicar General and to the Moderator of the Curia—Mrs. JUDY DELANEY.
Special Asst. to Archbishop Flynn—Mr. MERTON J. LASSONDE.
Archivist—Mr. STEVEN T. GRANGER; Mr. PATRICK ANZELC, Asst.
Controller—Mr. THOMAS J. BAKER.
Assistant Controller—Mr. SCOTT J. DOMEIER.
Department of Human Resources, Pension Plan, General Insurance Program and Personnel Director—Deacon WILLIAM G. UMPHRESS.
Metropolitan Tribunal—328 W. Kellogg Blvd., St. Paul, 55102-1997. Tel: 612-291-4466.
Judicial Vicar—Rev. JOSEPH L. WAJDA, J.C.L.
Adjutant Judicial Vicars—Revs. RONALD J. BOWERS, J.C.D; KEVIN M. MCDONOUGH, J.C.D.
Associate Judges—Rev. Msgr. WILLIAM BAUMGAERTNER; Rev. Msgr. ELLSWORTH KNEAL, J.C.D.; Revs. LEO J. TIBESAR, M.A.; MICHAEL V. TEGEDER; Deacon PAUL W. CARLSON; Sr. DOMINICA BRENNAN, O.P., J.C.L.; Mrs. RUTH DUHAMEL, J.C.L.; Mrs. MARILIES YOUNG, J.U.D.
Defenders of the Bond—Revs. JEROME W. FEHN; LAWRENCE R. JOHNSON; ROBERT B. WELLISCH; Deacon JOHN J. SALCHERT; Bro. VINCENT H. CHAMPINE, O.P.; Mr. ROBERT MANUELE, J.D.
Advocates—Mr. VINCENT D. MCGRAW; Mr. MICHAEL D. REISBIG, J.D.; Mr. MERLIN N. ROERS, M.Div.
Ecclesiastical Notaries—Mrs. LINDA BOTKIN; Mrs. KAREN NEDEAU.
Archdiocesan Consultors—Most Rev. LAWRENCE H. WELSH; Rev. Msgr. RICHARD E. PATES; Revs. GEORGE J. GRAFSKY; KEVIN M. MCDONOUGH, J.C.D.; JOSEPH J. ARACKAL, V.C.; A. MICHAEL SAUBER; ROBERT T. CASSIDY; PETER C. WITTMAN.
Presbyteral Council—Most Rev. HARRY J. FLYNN; Most Rev. LAWRENCE H. WELSH; Rev. Msgr. RICHARD E. PATES; Revs. KEVIN M. MCDONOUGH, J.C.D.; JOHN R. ESTREM, Exec. Dir. MICHAEL J. KRENIK; JEROME F. KEISER; JOSEPH H. HITPAS, O.M.I.; THOMAS H. BRIOSCHI; FREDERICK F. CAMPBELL; JOSEPH J. ARACKAL, V.C.; GEORGE J. GRAFSKY; THOMAS M. KOMMERS; ROBERT T. CASSIDY; CHARLES L. FROEHLE; HAROLD J. TASTO; STEPHEN J. LACANNE; LEO J. TIBESAR; GREGORY T. WELCH; PETER F. CHRISTENSEN; KEVIN FINNEGAN; JOHN L. UBEL; JOSEPH T. GANNON; RICHARD J. WOLTER; JEFFREY H. HUARD; TIMOTHY F. NOLAN; EUGENE MCGLOTHLIN, O.S.B.
Corporate Board—Most Rev. HARRY J. FLYNN; Most Rev. LAWRENCE H. WELSH; Revs. KEVIN M. MCDONOUGH, J.C.D.; AUSTIN T. WARD; Rev. Msgr. RICHARD E. PATES; THOMAS HOLLORAN; MARY FREY; CHERYL O'SHAUGHNESSY; JERRY HALLORAN; WILLIAM S. FALLON.
Censores Librorum—Rev. FREDERICK F. CAMPBELL, Chm., Bd., *St. John the Evangelist, Hopkins, 55343.* Rev. Msgr. RICHARD J. SCHULER; Revs. DENNIS J. DEASE; CHARLES L. FROEHLE; JAMES A. LAVIN; DAVID W. SMITH; ARTHUR L. KENNEDY.

Archdiocesan Offices and Directors

Advisory Board on Natural Family Planning—Deacon JAMES F. BASKFIELD, Liaison, *328 W. Kellogg Blvd., St. Paul, 55102.* Tel: 612-291-4438.
Allocations Committee—Rev. AUSTIN T. WARD, Dir., *226 Summit Ave., St. Paul, 55102.* Tel: 612-291-4400.
Apostleship of Prayer—Rev. Msgr. CLARENCE J. STEINER, *324 S. Prior Ave., St. Paul, 55105.*
Archbishop Ireland Educational Fund, Inc.—Most Rev. HARRY J. FLYNN, D.D., Pres., *226 Summit Ave., St. Paul, 55102.*
Archdiocesan AIDS Ministry Office—Sr. JOANNE LUCID, B.V.M., Dir., *Riverside Medical Center, Riverside at 25th Ave. S., Minneapolis, 55454.* Tel: 612-672-4345.
Archdiocesan Council of Catholic Women—Rev. Msgr. JAMES D. HABIGER, Moderator; ELAINE MONITOR, Pres., *328 W. Kellogg Blvd., St. Paul, 55102.* Tel: 612-291-4545.
Archdiocesan Director of Youth—Mr. GREGORY WEINAND.
Archdiocesan Finance Council—Deacon THOMAS DOLAN, Chm., *226 Summit Ave., St. Paul, 55102.* Tel: 612-291-4492.
Building Commission—Rev. AUSTIN T. WARD, Coord., *226 Summit Ave., St. Paul, 55102.*
Campus Ministry—Rev. JEFFREY H. HUARD, Dir., *University of St. Thomas, 2115 Summit Ave., P.O. Box 5028, St. Paul, 55105.*
Catholic Youth Ministry Services—Mr. GREGORY WEINAND, Dir., *328 W. Kellogg Blvd., St. Paul, 55102.* Tel: 612-290-1644.
Catholic Center for the Separated and Divorced—STEVE KING, Dir., *215 Old Sixth St., St. Paul, 55102.* Tel: 612-222-3001.
Catholic Charities—Rev. Msgr. J. JEROME BOXLEITNER, Dir.; Rev. LARRY SNYDER, Assoc. Dir., *404 S. 8th St., Minneapolis, 55404.* Tel: 612-340-7500.
Catholic Commission on Social Justice—JULIE SMENDZIOL-O'BRIEN, Chm. RON KRIETEMEYER, Dir., *328 W. Kellogg Blvd., St. Paul, 55102.* Tel: 612-291-4477.
Catholic Committee on Scouting—Deacon DONALD RINKENBERGER, Church of St. Joseph the Worker: *Maple Grove, 55369.* Tel: 612-559-9178.
Catholic Education and Formation Ministries—THOMAS MCCARVER, Dir., *328 W. Kellogg Blvd., St. Paul, 55102.* Tel: 612-291-4500.
Cemeteries—Mr. JOHN CHEREK, Dir., *400 Selby Ave., St. Paul, 55102.* Tel: 612-228-9991.
Center for Ministry—Sr. FRAN DONNELLY, B.V.M., Dir., *244 Dayton Ave., St. Paul, 55102.* Tel: 612-290-1616.
Charismatic Renewal Office—COLIN LAVERGNE, Dir., *3927 E. Lake, Minneapolis, 55406.* Tel: 612-721-2543.
Christ Child Services, Inc.—226 Summit Ave., St. Paul, 55102. Tel: 612-291-4400.
Christian Sharing Fund—SARA MCGRATH JOHNSON, *328 W. Kellogg Blvd., St. Paul, 55102.* Tel: 612-291-4477.
Commission on Bio-Medical Ethics—Dr. RICHARD BERQUIST, Chm., *University of St. Thomas, 2115 Summit Ave., St. Paul, 55105.* Tel: 612-647-5000.
Commission on Chemical Health—Rev. BRYAN O'ROURKE, Chm., *Church of St. Mary of the Lake, 105 N. Forestview Ln., Plymouth, 55441.* Tel: 612-545-1447.
Commission on Women—PHYLLIS A. WILLERSCHEIDT, Exec. Coord., *328 W. Kellogg Blvd., St. Paul, 55102.* Tel: 612-291-4495.
Commission for Black Catholics—HERBERT GIBBS, Chm.; Sr. SHARON M. HOWELL, C.S.J., Exec. Sec., *2115 Summit Ave., Mail #5006, St. Paul, 55105.* Tel: 612-962-6462.
Commission for Ecumenism and Interreligious Affairs—Rev. ARTHUR L. KENNEDY, Chm., *University of St. Thomas, 2115 Summit Ave., P.O. Box 5022, St. Paul, 55105.* Tel: 612-647-5300.
Commission on Pastoral Health Care—Sr. MARY HEINEN, C.S.J., Chm., *1884 Randolph Ave., St. Paul, 55105.* Tel: 612-690-7028.
Commission on Ministry—PATTI BRADY, Chm., *244 Dayton Ave., St. Paul, 55102.* Tel: 612-290-1616.
Common Bond Communities—Mr. JOSEPH A.L. ERRIGO, JR., Pres., *328 W. Kellogg Blvd., St.Paul, 55102.* Tel: 612-291-1750.
Communications Office—TIMOTHY ANDERSON, Dir., *226 Summit Ave., St. Paul, 55102.* Tel: 612-291-4411.
Council of Religious—Sr. FRAN DONNELLY, B.V.M., Ex Officio, *244 Dayton Ave., St. Paul, 55102.*
Cursillo—Rev. EUGENE POULIOT, Spiritual Advisor; AL SCHROEDER, Lay Dir. MARY SCHROEDER, Lay Dir., *1575 W. 200th St., Jordan, 55352.* Tel: 612-492-6257.
Holy Childhood, Pontifical Association—Deacon LAWRENCE J. SWIRTZ, Dir., *328 W. 6th St., St. Paul, 55102.*
Legion of Mary—St. Paul Curia and Comitium, Rev. Msgr. RICHARD J. SCHULER, *548 Lafond Ave., St. Paul, 55103.* Tel: 612-293-1710. North Minneapolis Curia, Rev. FRANCIS L. FRIED, *1315 2nd St. N.E., Minneapolis, 55413.* Tel: 612-379-9736. South Minneapolis Curia, Rev. MICHAEL SAUBER, *535 S. Lewis St., Shakopee, 55379.* Tel: 612-445-1319.
Marriage Encounter—JEANNE STOESSEL, Exec. Dir., *953 Lake Dr., St. Paul, 55120.* Tel: 612-454-3238.
Marriage and Family Life Office—KATHLEEN M. LAIRD, Dir., *328 W. Kellogg Blvd., St. Paul, 55102.* Tel: 612-291-4438.
Migration and Refugee Services—Mr. THOMAS KOSEL, Admin., *215 Old Sixth St., St. Paul, 55102.* Tel: 612-222-3001.
Ministry to Hmong—Rev. ROBERT B. WELLISCH; Deacon VA THAI LO, *Twin Cities Hmong Catholic Community, 68 W. Exchange St., St. Paul, 55102.* Tel: 612-771-4644.
Ministry to Koreans—Rev. ANDREW LIM, *Church of St. Andrew Kim, 1449 Cleveland Ave., St. Paul, 55108.* Tel: 612-642-9822.
Ministry to Vietnamese—Rev. MATTHIAS CHUONG, C.M.C., *Church of St. Joseph Hien, 1800 Dupont Ave. N., Minneapolis, 55411.* Tel: 612-522-5006.
Nazareth Hall College and Seminary, Inc.—Most Rev. HARRY J. FLYNN, D.D., Pres.
Newman Centers—University of Minnesota, Minneapolis and St. Paul Campus, THOMAS MCCARVER, Acting Dir., *1701 University Ave. S.E., Minneapolis, 55414.* Tel: 612-331-3437. Hamline University, Macalster College, St. Olaf College, Rev. DAVID HASCHKA, S.J., Campus Min., *1550 Summit Ave., St. Paul, 55105.* Tel: 612-644-9041.
Newspaper—*"The Catholic Bulletin"*; Mr. DENNIS W. HEANEY, Publisher/Gen. Mgr.; Mr. ROBERT ZYSKOWSKI, Editor, *244 Dayton Ave., St. Paul, 55102.* Tel: 612-291-4444.
Office of the Deaf—Rev. WILLIAM J. KENNEY, *701 Fillmore St. N.E., Minneapolis, 55413.* Tel: 612-623-4019; 378-1344 (TTD).
Office of Indian Ministry—Rev. JAMES C. NOTEBAART, Dir., *3045 Park Ave., Minneapolis, 55407.* Tel: 612-824-7616.
Office for Social Justice—Mr. RON KRIETEMEYER, Admin., *328 W. Kellogg Blvd., St. Paul, 55102.* Tel: 612-291-4477.
Office of Due Process—Sr. M. DOMINICA BRENNAN, O.P., J.C.L., Dir., *226 Summit Ave., St. Paul, 55102.* Tel: 612-291-4437.
Office of Ecumenism—Rev. ARTHUR L. KENNEDY, Ecumenical Officer, *University of St. Thomas, 2115 Summit Ave., P.O. Box 5022, St. Paul, 55105.* Tel: 612-962-5050.
Office of Evangelization—Vacant, *328 W. Kellogg Blvd., St. Paul, 55102.* Tel: 612-291-4488.
Office of Human Resources—Deacon WILLIAM G. UMPHRESS, Dir., *328 W. Kellogg Blvd., St. Paul, 55102.* Tel: 612-291-4499.
Office of Pastoral Planning—Mr. ROBERT J. BURKE, Dir., *328 W. Kellogg Blvd., St. Paul, 55102.* Tel: 612-291-4544.
Office of Presbyteral Personnel Resources—Rev. PAUL JAROSZESKI, Exec. Sec., *226 Summit Ave., St. Paul, 55102.* Tel: 612-291-4430.
Parish Pastoral Council Assistance Center—Mr. ROBERT J. BURKE, Dir., *328 W. Kellogg Blvd., St. Paul, 55102.* Tel: 612-291-4544.
Pastoral Council—Most Rev. HARRY J. FLYNN, D.D., Chm.; Mr. MERTON J. LASSONDE, Exec. Sec., *226 Summit Ave., St. Paul, 55102.* Tel: 612-291-4400.
Permanent Deacon Assembly—Deacon DANIEL D. KIRCHOFFNER, Pres., *2220 Summit Ave., St. Paul, 55105.* Tel: 612-962-6875.
Permanent Deacon Office—Deacon PETER A. D'HEILLY, Dir., *2220 Summit Ave., St. Paul, 55105.* Tel: 612-962-6875.
Presbyteral Council—Rev. JOHN R. ESTREM, Exec. Dir., *226 Summit Ave., St. Paul, 55102.* Tel: 612-291-4400.
Propagation of the Faith—ALICIA KELLY, Acting Dir., *328 W. Kellogg Blvd., St. Paul, 55102.* Tel: 612-222-6556.
Resource Development Office—Mr. JAMES MULLIN, Dir., *328 W. Kellogg Blvd., St. Paul, 55102.* Tel: 612-290-1610.
Annual Catholic Appeal—MARY NICHOLSON, Dir.
Endowment Campaign—Mr. JAMES MULLIN, Consultant.
Respect Life—Mrs. JANET KROCHESKI, Dir., *328 W. Kellogg Blvd., St. Paul, 55102.* Tel: 612-291-4505.
Rural Life Conference—Mr. DALE R. HENNEN, *105 3rd St. N.W., Montgomery, 56069.* Tel: 612-364-7323.

Sacerdotal Union of Daily Adoration—Rev. ALBERT F. BYRNE, *2590 Margaret St., North St. Paul, 55109.*

Seton Center—MICHELLE BAILEY, Admin., *Spruce Tree Center, Ste. 400, 1600 University Ave., St. Paul, 55104.* Tel: 612-641-1180. Outpatient social and medical services for unwed women and young couples.

Society of St. Vincent De Paul, Archdiocesan Council—Ms. BERNICE MARUSKA, Pres., *1008 Arcade St., St. Paul, 55102.* Tel: 612-771-0358.

To Encounter Christ (TEC)—PAM GEEMSCHEID DEMORETT, Coord., *1201 S.E. 5th St., Minneapolis, 55414.* Tel: 612-331-3644.

Venezuelan Missions—Revs. PATRICK J. RYAN; DENNIS DEMPSEY; PAUL L. MAGEE; GREGORY J. SCHAFFER, *El Buen Pastor Parroquia San Francisco de Asis, Apartado 272, Puerto Ordaz, Estado Bolivar, Venezuela, 8015.*

Vocation Office—Dir., Vocations: Revs. STAN P. MADER; JOHN L. UBEL, *2260 Summit Ave., St. Paul, 55105.* Tel: 612-962-6890.

Worship Board—Mr. FRANK WINKELS, Chm., *244 Dayton Ave., St. Paul, 55102.* Tel: 612-290-1625.

Worship Center—VICKI KLIMA, Dir.; Mr. MICHAEL SILHAVY, Assoc. Dir., Music, *244 Dayton Ave., St. Paul, 55102.* Tel: 612-290-1625.

CLERGY, PARISHES, MISSIONS AND PAROCHIAL SCHOOLS

METROPOLITAN ST. PAUL
(Ramsey County)

1—CATHEDRAL OF ST. PAUL (1850), Revs. John Estrem, Rector; Andrew H. Cozzens.
Res., 239 Selby Ave., 55102. Tel: 612-228-1766; Fax: 612-228-9942.

2—ASSUMPTION (1856) (German), Rev. John M. Malone.
Res., 51 W. Seventh St., 55102. Tel: 612-224-7536; Fax: 612-224-8514.

3—BLESSED SACRAMENT (1916), Revs. Thomas R. McDonough; Orlando Tatel.
Res., 1801 La Crosse Ave., 55119. Tel: 612-735-3707; Fax: 612-578-1125.
School—1800 Ames Ave., 55119. Tel: 612-735-3676. Lay Teachers 13; Students 205.
Catechesis/Religious Programs—977 E. 5th St., 55106. Tel: 612-771-9152; Fax: 612-771-9152. Students 164.

4—HOLY CHILDHOOD (1946), Rev. Gordon M. Doffing.
Res., 1457 Midway Pkwy., 55108. Tel: 612-644-7495.
School—1435 Midway Pkwy., 55108. Tel: 612-644-2791; Fax: 612-917-8797. Sharon Brennan, Prin. Sisters 5; Lay Teachers 9; Students 160.
Catechesis/Religious Programs—Tel: 612-644-5645. Sr. Thelma Vetsch, S.S.N.D., D.R.E. Students 15.

5—HOLY SPIRIT (1936), Rev. Michael L. Papesh; Deacons William Umphress; W. Richard Barrett.
Res., 512 S. Albert St., 55105. Tel: 612-698-3353; Fax: 612-698-1605.
School—Tel: 612-698-7233. Jody Biedrzycki, Faith Formation Dir.
Catechesis/Religious Programs—Tel: 612-699-7258; Fax: 612-698-1605. Students 424.

6—THE IMMACULATE HEART OF MARY (1949), Rev. Charles F. Burns, S.J.; Sr. Mary Claire Inhofer, O.S.B., Pastoral Assoc. In res., Revs. David J. Haschka, S.J. Tel: 612-644-9041; Richard M. Rice, S.J. Tel: 612-644-9024; Robert F. O'Connor, S.J. Tel: 612-644-9018; Philip Dreckman, S.J. Tel: 612-646-2938; Frederick Maples, S.J. Tel: 612-645-0136.
Res., 1543 Summit Ave., 55105. Tel: 612-644-5458; 699-7722 (Office).
School—IHM-St. Luke. See St. Luke, St. Paul for details. Tel: 612-224-4836.

7—MATERNITY OF THE BLESSED VIRGIN (1949), Revs. John G. Donahue; Francis R. Dudley.
Res., 1414 N. Dale St., 55117. Tel: 612-489-8825; Fax: 612-488-4055.
School—Maternity of Mary-St. Andrew, 592 Arlington Ave., 55117. Tel: 612-489-1459; Fax: 612-489-3560.
Sisters 2; Lay Teachers 25; Students 342.
Catechesis/Religious Programs—Tel: 612-489-8827; Fax: 612-488-4055. Mary Weyandt, D.R.E. Students 188.

8—THE NATIVITY OF OUR LORD (1922), Rev. Patrick D. Lannan; Rev. Msgr. Clarence J. Steiner; Revs. John W. Kelley; William Baer; Deacon Gerald L. Devine.
Office: 1900 Wellesley, 55105. Tel: 612-696-5401; Fax: 612-696-5458.
School—1900 Stanford Ave., 55105. Tel: 612-699-1311; Fax: 612-696-5420.
Sisters of St. Joseph 1; Lay Teachers 38; Students 810. Principals: Mrs. Margo Weiberg; Kate Wollan.
Catechesis/Religious Programs—Tel: 612-696-5454; Fax: 612-696-5458. Students 100.

9—OUR LADY OF GUADALUPE (1931) (Mexican), Rev. Hugo L. Montero (Ecuador).
Res., 401 Concord Street, 55107. Tel: 612-228-0506.
Catechesis/Religious Programs—Students 212.

10—SACRED HEART (1881) (German), Revs. John Dombrowski, O.F.M.; Salvador Valdez, O.F.M.; Deacon Wayne Wittman. In res., Revs. Fabian F. Burdiek, O.F.M.; Nicholas W. Meyer, O.F.M.; Michael Cusato, O.F.M.; Bros. Gary Jeriha, O.F.M.; Francis Gonser, O.F.M.; Lester Kochlin, O.F.M.; Michaek Luke Ubben, O.F.M.
Res., 840 E. Sixth St., 55106. Tel: 612-776-2741; Fax: 612-776-2759.
School—Trinity Catholic School. Collaborative School with St. Patrick & St. Casimir Parishes in St. Paul. 835 E. Fifth St., 55106. Tel: 612-776-2763; Fax: 612-776-2764.
Catechesis/Religious Programs—Tel: 612-774-7505. Kim Smith, D.R.E. Students 236.
Mission—St. Paul, Ramsey Co., Hispanic Ministry. Deacon Carlos Valdez.

11—ST. ADALBERT (1881) (Polish-Vietnamese-Mexican), Rev. Timothy J. Kernan; Maggie Rein, Pastoral Assoc.; Deacons Kao Yang; Bill Falvey. In res., Rev. Michael J. Stevens.
Res., 265 Charles Ave., 55103. Tel: 612-228-9002.
Catechesis/Religious Programs—Students 85.
Frogtown Resource Center—262 Edmund Ave., 55103. Tel: 612-293-1931.

12—ST. AGNES (1887) (German), Rev. Msgr. Richard J. Schuler; Rev. Robert J. Altier; Deacons Jerome J. Bilder; Harold Hughesdon; Bernard Pedersen.
Res., 548 Lafond Ave., 55103. Tel: 612-293-1710; Fax: 612-227-4229.
School—530 Lafond Ave., 55103. Tel: 612-227-1886. Mr. John Boone, Prin.
Sisters of Notre Dame 2; Lay Teachers 14; Students 230.
High School—Tel: 612-228-1161. Mr. William Peper, Prin.
Sisters of Notre Dame 1; Lay Teachers 22; Students 290.
Catechesis/Religious Programs—Students 70.

13—ST. AMBROSE (1915) (Italian), Rev. Thomas J. Pingatore.
Res., 711 Bradley St., 55101. Tel: 612-776-4957.
Catechesis/Religious Programs—Tel: 612-483-1910. Jeanne Kelcher, D.R.E. Students 33.

14—ST. ANDREW (1895), Rev. Roger F. Carroll; Deacon Thomas Konkel.
Res., 1051 Como Ave., 55103. Tel: 612-488-6775.
School—Maternity of Mary/St. Andrew. Consolidated. See Maternity of the Blessed Virgin for details. Tel: 612-489-1459; Fax: 612-489-3560.

15—ST. ANDREW KIM (1990) (Korean), Rev. Dong Chun John Kim (Korea).
Res., 1449 N. Cleveland Ave., 55108. Tel: 612-642-9822; Fax: 612-642-0140. [JC]

16—ST. BERNARD (1890) (German), Revs. Michael F. Anderson; Jose Gutierrez; Robert E. Wiley; Deacon Sonny Laqui.
Res., 197 W. Geranium Ave., 55117. Tel: 612-488-6733; Fax: 612-488-9466.
School—(Grades PreK-8) 180 W. Rose Ave., 55117. Tel: 612-489-8086. Jennifer Cassidy, Prin.
Lay Teachers 17; Students 265.
High School—170 W. Rose Ave., 55117. Tel: 612-489-1338. John O'Neill, Prin.
Lay Teachers 24; Students 342.

17—ST. CASIMIR (1892) (Polish), Rev. Patrick T. Casey; Tony Schreiner, Business Mgr.
Res., 934 E. Geranium Ave., 55106. Tel: 612-774-0365; Fax: 612-774-0508.
School—Trinity Catholic School. Collaborative School with St. Patrick & Sacred Heart Parishes in St. Paul. 835 E. Fifth St., 55106. Tel: 612-776-2763; Fax: 612-776-2764.
Students 270; Preschool 45.
Catechesis/Religious Programs—Tel: 612-776-5641. Students 143.

18—ST. CECILIA (1912), Rev. Paul A. Jaroszeski.
Res., 2357 Bayless Pl., 55114. Tel: 612-644-4502; Fax: 612-647-1445.

19—ST. COLUMBA, Revs. Paul A. LaFontaine; Thomas Tam (Vietnam).
Res., 1327 Lafond Ave., 55104. Tel: 612-645-9179; Fax: 612-645-9170.
School—1330 Blair Ave., 55104. Tel: 612-644-1807. Lay Teachers 12; Students 250.

20—ST. FRANCIS DE SALES (1884) (German), Rev. James P. Burns. In res., Rev. Karl M. Wittman, (Retired).
Res., 650 Palace Ave., 55102-3593. Tel: 612-228-1169; Fax: 612-224-7744.
School—St. Francis-St. James United School, 426 S. Osceola St., 55102. Tel: 612-228-1167; Fax: 612-228-0169.
Sisters of Notre Dame 4; Lay Teachers 16; Students 239.

21—ST. GREGORY THE GREAT (HIGHLAND CATHOLIC COMMUNITY) (1951). (A formation of the following: St. Gregory the Great, St. Paul; St. Leo, St. Paul and St. Therese, St. Paul). Revs. Thomas P. Hunstiger, Co-Pastor; Gerald G. Grieman, Co-Pastor; Deacon Gerald Scherkenbach.
Mailing Address: 2055 Bohland Ave., 55116.
Church—1668 Montreal Ave., 55116-2499.
Parish Center: Tel: 612-698-5581; Fax: 612-698-9526.
School—Highland Catholic School. See listing under Institutions located in the Archdiocese for details. Tel: 612-690-2477; Fax: 612-699-1869.
Catechesis/Religious Programs—Highland Catholic Community, 1668 Montreal Ave., 55116. Students 282.

22—ST. JAMES (1887), Rev. James P. Burns.
Res., 496 View St., 55102. Tel: 612-227-7029.
School—St. Francis-St. James United School, (Grades K-8). See St. Francis De Sales for details. Tel: 612-228-1167; Fax: 612-228-0169.
Catechesis/Religious Programs—Tel: 612-228-1169; Fax: 612-228-1169; 224-7744. Students 233.

23—ST. JOHN OF ST. PAUL (1886) (Irish), Rev. Joseph P. Fink. In res., Rev. Richard M. Hogan.
Res., 977 E. Fifth St., 55106. Tel: 612-771-3690; Fax: 612-771-7919.
Catechesis/Religious Programs—Blessed Sacrament School. Blessed Sacrament and St. John's combine religious education. 1801 Lacrosse Ave., 55119. Tel: 612-771-9152. Students 166.

24—ST. LEO (HIGHLAND CATHOLIC COMMUNITY) (1945). (A formation of the following: St. Gregory the Great, St. Paul; St. Leo, St. Paul; St. Therese, St. Paul). Revs. Gerald G. Grieman, Co-Pastor; Thomas P. Hunstiger, Co-Pastor; Deacon Gerald Scherkenbach.
Office: 2055 Bohland Ave., 55116. Tel: 612-698-5581; Fax: 612-698-9526.
School—Highland Catholic School. See listing under Institutions located in the Archdiocese for details. Tel: 612-690-2477; Fax: 612-699-1869.
Catechesis/Religious Programs—Highland Catholic Community, 1668 Montreal Ave., Tel: 612-698-5583; Fax: 612-698-9526. Students 282.

25—ST. LOUIS KING OF FRANCE (1868) (French), Revs. Paul F. Morrissey, S.M.; James D. Duffy, S.M.
Res., 506 Cedar St., 55101. Tel: 612-224-3379; Fax: 612-224-0017.

26—ST. LUKE (1888), Rev. David J. Haschka, S.J.; Deacon Thomas Dzik.
Center: 1079 Summit Ave., 55105. Tel: 612-227-7669; Fax: 612-227-0847.
School—IHM-St. Luke, 1065 Summit Ave., 55105. Tel: 612-224-4836; Fax: 612-224-0097.
Sisters 2; Lay Teachers 25; Students 406.
Catechesis/Religious Programs—Students 146.

27—ST. MARK (1889), Revs. Jerome F. Keiser; Stan Mader; Deacon Robert Conlin. In res., Rev. Anthony Andrade, O.S.B.
Res., 2001 Dayton Ave., 55104. Tel: 612-645-5717; Fax: 612-644-0011.
School—1983 Dayton Ave., 55104. Tel: 612-644-3380; Fax: 612-644-1923.
Sisters 2; Lay Teachers 22; Students 425.

28—ST. MARY (1865), Revs. Joseph Hitpas, O.M.I.; Daniel Taillez, O.M.I., (France) Hmong Chap.; Donald Dummer, O.M.I., Chap., Regions Hospital; Joseph Menker, O.M.I., Chap., Regions Hospital. In res., Rev. Robert Allie, O.M.I.
Res., 261 E. 8th St., 55101. Tel: 612-222-2619.

29—ST. MATTHEW (1886) (German), Revs. Stephen J. Adrian; Martin L. Warren (England); Deacon John Murphy.
Office: 490 Hall Ave., 55107.
Church—510 Hall Ave, 55107. Tel: 612-224-9793; Fax: 612-228-9448.
Res., 507 Hall Ave., 55107. Tel: 612-224-1037; Fax: 612-292-0925.
School—497 Humboldt Ave., 55107. Tel: 612-224-6912. Sr. Leonius Skarr, O.P., Prin.
Sisters 1; Lay Teachers 14; Students 234.

30—St. Pascal Baylon (1946), Rev. Thomas H. Brioschi; Deacons Joseph Schmitz; Richard Pashby.
Res., 1757 Conway St., 55106. Tel: 612-774-1585; Fax: 612-774-9152.
School—1770 E. 3rd St., 55106. Tel: 612-776-0092; Fax: 612-776-2365.
Sisters 1; Lay Teachers 21; Students 434.
Catechesis/Religious Programs—Tel: 612-774-0655.
Students 190.

31—St. Patrick (1884), Rev. Jerome B. Hackenmueller.
Res., 1095 De Soto St., 55101. Tel: 612-774-8675; Fax: 612-774-9106.
School—Trinity Catholic School - North & South Campus. Collaborative School with St. Patrick, St. Casimir & Sacred Heart Parishes in St. Paul. Tel: 612-776-2763 (South); 776-5169 (North); Fax: 612-774-9943 (North); 776-2764 (South).

32—St. Peter Claver (1892) (African American), Rev. Kevin M. McDonough.
Res., 375 N. Oxford St., 55104. Tel: 612-646-1797; Fax: 612-646-3021.

33—St. Stanislaus (1872) (Czech), Rev. John C. Clay.
Res., 398 Superior St., 55102. Tel: 612-292-0303.
Catechesis/Religious Programs—395 Superior St., 55102. Tel: 612-292-1913.
Students 65.

34—St. Therese (Highland Catholic Community) (1926). (A formation of the following: St. Gregory the Great, St. Paul; St. Leo, St. Paul; and St. Therese, St. Paul). Revs. Thomas P. Hunstiger, Co-Pastor; Gerald G. Grieman, Co-Pastor; Deacon Gerald Scherkenbach.
Mailing Address: 1850 Mississippi River Blvd., S., 55116-2644.
Office: 2055 Bohland Ave., 55116.
Parish Center—Tel: 612-698-5581; Fax: 612-698-9526.
School—Highland Catholic School. See listing under Institutions located in the Archdiocese for details. Tel: 612-690-2477; Fax: 612-699-1869.
Catechesis/Religious Programs—Highland Catholic Community, 16681 Montreal Ave., 55116. Tel: 612-698-5583.
Students 282.

35—St. Thomas The Apostle (1954), Rev. Richard P. Wirth; Deacon Ervin Barrett.
Res., 2119 Stillwater Ave., 55119. Tel: 612-738-0677; Fax: 612-738-6492.
Catechesis/Religious Programs—Tel: 612-738-2995.
Students 210.

36—St. Vincent de Paul (1888), Rev. Chue Ying Vang; Deacon Va Thai Lo.
Res., 651 Virginia St., 55103. Tel: 612-488-6737; Fax: 612-487-6790. [CEM]

OUTSIDE METROPOLITAN ST. PAUL

Cottage Grove, Washington Co., St. Rita (1966), Rev. Thomas P. Fitzgerald; Deacons Jack Nicklay; Steve Koop.
8694 80th St. S., 55016. Tel: 612-459-4596; Fax: 612-459-5364.
Catechesis/Religious Programs—Students 768.

Lake Elmo, Washington Co., Guardian Angels (1885), Rev. Mark J. Underdahl; Sr. Dorothy Mrock, O.S.F.; Deacon Larry Murphy.
Res., 8260 Hudson Blvd., Oakdale, 55128. Tel: 612-738-2223; Fax: 612-738-2453. [CEM]
Catechesis/Religious Programs—Roy Dick, D.R.E.
Students 1,252.

Little Canada, Ramsey Co., St. John the Evangelist (1851), Rev. Robert J. Fitzpatrick; Sr. Anne Becker, S.S.N.D., Dir. Pastoral Ministry.
Res., 380 Little Canada Rd., St. Paul, 55117. Tel: 612-484-2708; Fax: 612-484-0567. [CEM]
Preschool:—.
Lay Teachers 2; Students 80.
School—2621 McMenemy St., 55117. Tel: 612-484-3038; Fax: 612-484-3187. Mary Kay Rowan, Prin.
Lay Teachers 18; Students 254.
Catechesis/Religious Programs—Tel: 612-484-0048. Jean Conant Winter, D.R.E.
Students 560.

Mahtomedi, Washington Co., St. Jude of the Lake (1939), Rev. Jerry C. Vandrovec.
Res., 700 Mahtomedi Ave., 55115. Tel: 612-426-3245; Fax: 612-653-3554.
School—600 Mahtomedi Ave., 55115. Tel: 612-426-2562. Ann Austin McCormick, Prin.
Lay Teachers 11; Students 234.
Catechesis/Religious Programs—Tel: 612-426-4469.
Students 641.

Maplewood, Ramsey Co., Holy Redeemer (1880) (Italian), Rev. Austin T. Ward.
Res., 2555 Hazelwood Ave., St. Paul, 55109. Tel: 612-777-1321.
Presentation of the Blessed Virgin Mary (1946), Revs. Charles V. Lachowitzer; David A. Barrett; Deacon Jack Veiman.
Res., 1725 Kennard St., 55109. Tel: 612-777-8116; Fax: 612-777-8743.
School—1695 Kennard St., 55109. Tel: 612-777-5877.
Lay Teachers 22; Students 422.
Catechesis/Religious Programs—Tel: 612-777-6041; Fax: 612-777-8743.
Students 275.
St. Jerome (1940), Rev. Kenneth F. Ludescher.
1894 McMenemy Rd., 55117. Tel: 612-771-1928.
Church—380 Roselawn Ave. E., 55117. Tel: 612-771-1209; Fax: 612-771-3623.
School—384 E. Roselawn Ave., 55117. Tel: 612-771-8494.
Lay Teachers 11; Students 245.

Mendota, Dakota Co., St. Peter (1840) (Native American-French-English), Rev. Kevin I. Clinton; Deacon Jim Seaton. In res., Rev. Gilbert J. Gustafson.
Res., P.O. Box 50679, 55150. Tel: 612-452-4030; Fax: 612-456-0646. [CEM]
Catechesis/Religious Programs—Tel: 612-452-4551; Fax: 612-456-0646. Ellen Casey, D.R.E.
Students 339.

New Brighton, Ramsey Co., St. John the Baptist (1906) (Polish), Revs. William Murtaugh; James M. Grogan; Deacons Joseph McPherson; Russel Evans.
Parish Center:—835 2nd Ave., N.W., 55112. Tel: 612-633-8333; Fax: 612-633-7404.
Res., 812 1st Ave., N.W., 55112. [CEM]
School—845 2nd Ave., N.W., 55112. Tel: 612-633-1522; Fax: 612-633-1522.
Sisters 1; Lay Teachers 19; Students 403.
Catechesis/Religious Programs—Tel: 612-633-1540; Fax: 612-633-7404.
Students 1,041.

North St. Paul, Ramsey Co., St. Peter (1888), Revs. Albert F. Byrne; Stanley Maslowski; George Kolath (India); Deacon James Hepp.
Res., 2590 N. Margaret St., 55109. Tel: 612-777-8304; Fax: 612-777-0497. [CEM]
Preschool:—.
Lay Teachers 2; Students 80.
School—2602 N. Margaret St., 55109. Tel: 612-777-3091; Fax: 612-777-7750.
Lay Teachers 20; Students 436.
Catechesis/Religious Programs—Students 534.

Oakdale, Washington Co., Transfiguration (1939), Revs. James D. Smith; Michael A. Reding; Deacon Dan Kirchoffner.
Res., 6133 15th St. N., 55128. Tel: 612-738-2646; Fax: 612-578-8816.
School—935 Ferndale Ave., Maplewood, 55119. Tel: 612-739-0550; Fax: 612-578-2782. Ted Zarembski, Prin.
Lay Teachers 12; Students 258.
Catechesis/Religious Programs—Tel: 612-738-3276. Susan Brady, D.R.E.
Students 850.

Roseville, Ramsey Co., Corpus Christi (1939), Rev. Robert C. Nygaard.
Res., 2131 N. Fairview Ave., 55113-5499. Tel: 612-639-8888; Fax: 612-639-8288.
Catechesis/Religious Programs—D.R.E.: Colleen Ciaccio; Alisa Weber.
Students 254.
St. Rose of Lima (1939), Revs. Walter L. Sochacki; Minh Xuan Vu.
Res., 2048 N. Hamline Ave., 55113. Tel: 612-645-9389; Fax: 612-646-4187.
School—2072 Hamline Ave. N., 55113. Tel: 612-646-3832.
Sisters 3; Lay Teachers 19; Students 333.
Catechesis/Religious Programs—Tel: 612-646-8029. Deb McPherson, D.R.E.
Students 300.

Shoreview, Ramsey Co., St. Odilia (1960), Revs. Richard McGuire, O.S.C.; Jerome Schik, O.S.C.; Marven Tellers, O.S.C.; Deacons John Flood; Jerome Ciresi.
3495 N. Victoria St., 55126. Tel: 612-484-6681; Fax: 612-484-0780.
School—(Grades K-8). Tel: 612-484-3364; Fax: 612-484-0780. Mr. Robert Grose, Prin.
Lay Teachers 33; Students 668.
Catechesis/Religious Programs—Tel: 612-484-2777. Katie Gebhard, D.R.E.
Students 1,464.

West St. Paul, Dakota Co., St. Joseph (1942), Revs. Frederick F. Campbell; Michael J. Miller.
Res., 1154 Seminole Ave., 55118. Tel: 612-457-2781; Fax: 612-451-1272.
School—1138 Seminole Ave., 55118. Tel: 612-457-8550; Fax: 612-451-1272.
Lay Teachers 44; Students 790.
Catechesis/Religious Programs—Tel: 612-457-8841.
Students 295.
St. Michael (1879), Rev. Gerald L. Dvorak.
Res., 337 E. Hurley, 55118. Tel: 612-457-2334; Fax: 612-451-1668.
School—E. Haskell & Sperl, 55118. Tel: 612-457-2510.
Sisters 6; Lay Teachers 9; Students 220.

White Bear Lake, Ramsey Co., St. Mary of the Lake (1881), Rev. Roger P. Pierre; Deacons Sherm Stromen; Joe Thill.
Res., 4741 Bald Eagle Ave., 55110. Tel: 612-429-7771; Fax: 612-429-9539. [CEM]
School—4690 Bald Eagle Ave., 55110. Tel: 612-429-5378. Mary Kane, Prin.
Lay Teachers 10; Students 298.
Catechesis/Religious Programs—Tel: 612-429-8001. D.R.E.: Helen Welter; Mary Beth Jambor.
Students 800.
St. Pius X (1954), Revs. Michael J. Krenik; Mark Shane Wasinger; Deacon Edward F. Feffer.
Res., 3878 Highland Ave., 55110. Tel: 612-429-5337; Fax: 612-429-9359.
School—Tel: 612-429-5338.
Lay Teachers 21; Students 324.
Catechesis/Religious Programs—Tel: 612-429-5994.
Students 388.

METROPOLITAN MINNEAPOLIS
(Hennepin County)

1—The Basilica of St. Mary Co-Cathedral (1907), Revs. Michael O'Connell, Rector; Dale J. Korogi; Deacons George H. Babcock; Del Ferguson; Roger Carlson.
Mailing Address: P.O. Box 50010, 55405-0010.
Res., 88 N. 17th St., 55403-1295. Tel: 612-333-1381; Fax: 612-333-7230. [CEM]
Catechesis/Religious Programs—Students 420.

2—All Saints (1916) (Polish), Rev. George J. Kovalik.
Res., 435 4th St., N.E., 55413. Tel: 612-379-4996.
School—Northeast Regional Catholic School. See Elementary Schools, Consolidated, Parochial under Institutions located in the Archdiocese for details. Tel: 612-789-8851.

3—Annunciation (1922), Rev. Kenneth J. Pierre.
Res., 509 W. 54th St., 55419. Tel: 612-824-0787; Fax: 612-823-8467.
School—525 W. 54th St., 55419. Tel: 612-823-4394; Fax: 612-824-9915.
Sisters 1; Lay Teachers 23; Students 380.

4—Ascension (1890), Revs. Robert L. Hazel; Lawrence E. Hubbard. In res., Rev. Luke Mikschl, S.T.
Res., 1723 Bryant Ave., N., 55411. Tel: 612-529-9684; Fax: 612-529-7618.
School—1726 Dupont Ave., N., 55411. Tel: 612-521-3609; Fax: 612-522-3862.
Sisters 2; Lay Teachers 11; Students 240.

5—Christ the King (1938), Rev. John M. Hofstede.
5029 Zenith Ave., S., 55410. Tel: 612-920-5030; Fax: 612-920-1179. [JC]
School—Cooperative program with St. Thomas the Apostle, Minneapolis. Tel: 612-927-8673; 920-9075; Fax: 612-927-7426.

6—Holy Cross (1886) (Polish), Revs. David T. Ostrowski, O.S.B.; Jan Karpowicz, S.Ch.
Res., 1621 University Ave., N.E., 55413. Tel: 612-789-7238; Fax: 612-789-5769.
School—Northeast Regional Catholic School. See Elementary Schools, Consolidated, Parochial under Institutions located in the Archdiocese for details. Tel: 612-789-8851; Fax: 612-789-8773.

7—Holy Name (1916), Rev. Ronald E. Clubb.
Res., 3637 11th Ave., S., 55407. Tel: 612-724-5465; Fax: 612-724-5466.
School—Risen Christ Catholic School. See Elementary Schools, Consolidated, Parochial under Institutions located in the Archdiocese for details. Tel: 612-822-5329.

8—Holy Rosary (1878), Revs. Charles M. Santoro, O.P.; Edward W. Leahy, O.P.; Sr. Martha Wiegand, O.P., Pastoral Assoc.; Deacon Thomas E. Dolan.
Res., 2424 18th Ave., S., 55404. Tel: 612-724-3651; Fax: 612-728-8944.
School—Risen Christ Catholic School. See Elementary Schools, Consolidated, Parochial under Institutions located in the Archdiocese for details. Tel: 612-822-5329.
Convent—1614 E. 24th St., 55404. Tel: 612-724-2620.
Dominican Sisters (Sinsinawa, WI) 8.

9—Incarnation (1909), Rev. Robert Monaghan.
Res., 3817 Pleasant Ave., 55409-1296. Tel: 612-822-2101; Fax: 612-822-7928.
School—Risen Christ Catholic School. See Elementary Schools, Consolidated, Parochial under Institutions located in the Archdiocese for details. Tel: 612-822-5329; Fax: 612-822-5903.
Catechesis/Religious Programs—Students 479.

10—OUR LADY OF LOURDES (1877) (French-Canadian), Rev. William J. Ward.
Res., One Lourdes Pl., 55414. Tel: 612-379-2259.

11—OUR LADY OF MOUNT CARMEL (1938) (Italian), Rev. William J. Kenney.
Res., 701 Fillmore St., N.E., 55413. Tel: 612-331-1746; Fax: 612-378-1344.
School—Northeast Regional Catholic School. See Elementary Schools, Consolidated, Parochial under the Institutions located in the Archdiocese for details.

12—OUR LADY OF PEACE (1991), Rev. Msgr. Richard E. Pates; Deacons Jack Weiland; Michael Friesen.
Res., 5425 11th Ave., S., 55417. Tel: 612-823-8253; Fax: 612-823-5102.
School—5435 11th Ave., S., 55417. Tel: 612-824-3455.
Lay Teachers 23; Students 412.
Catechesis/Religious Programs—Students 160.

13—OUR LADY OF PERPETUAL HELP. Closed. For inquiries for parish records contact the Chancery.

14—OUR LADY OF VICTORY (1945), Rev. Terrence M. Hayes.
Res., 5155 Emerson Ave., N., 55430. Tel: 612-529-7788; Fax: 612-529-3343.
Church—52nd and Fremont Aves., 55430.
School—St. Elizabeth Seton, 5140 Fremont Ave., N., 55430. Tel: 612-529-7781.
Sisters 2; Lay Teachers 22; Students 311.
Catechesis/Religious Programs—Tel: 612-287-9180.
Students 90.

15—ST. ALBERT THE GREAT (1935), Rev. Thomas R. Poulsen, O.P. In res., Revs. Brendan J. McMullen, O.P.; James R. Motl, O.P.; John G. O'Connell, O.P.; C. A. Kilroy, O.P.; Robert M. Kelly, O.P.; Jay M. Harrington, O.P.; Joseph E. Bidwill, O.P.; Edward W. Leahy, O.P.; Charles M. Santoro, O.P.; Bro. Vincent H. Champine, O.P.
Res., 2833 32nd Ave., S., 55406. Tel: 612-724-3644; Fax: 612-724-5057.
Parish Center—2836 33rd Ave., S., 55406. Tel: 612-724-3643; Fax: 612-722-9726.
School—Risen Christ Catholic School. See Elementary Schools, Consolidated, Parochial under Institutions located in the Archdiocese for details. Tel: 612-822-5329.

16—ST. ANNE (1884) (French), Rev. Michael G. Monogue.
Res., 2627 Queen Ave., N., 55411. Tel: 612-529-0503; Fax: 612-529-5860.
School—St. Elizabeth Seton. (Consolidated). 5140 Fremont Ave., N., 55430-3496. Tel: 612-529-7781; Fax: 612-529-3343.

17—ST. ANTHONY OF PADUA (1849), Rev. Joseph G. Kivel.
Res., 804 Second St., N.E., 55413. Tel: 612-379-2324.
School—Northeast Regional Catholic School. See Elementary Schools, Consolidated, Parochial under the Institutions located in the Archdiocese for details. Tel: 612-789-8851.

18—ST. AUSTIN (1937), Rev. Gregory T. Welch; Deacon James C. Dondelinger.
Res., 4050 Upton Ave., N., 55412. Tel: 612-529-9561; Fax: 612-529-8787.
School—St. Elizabeth Seton, 5140 Fremont Ave., N., 55430. Tel: 612-529-7781; Fax: 612-529-3343.
Sisters 1; Lay Teachers 19; Students 360.

19—ST. BONIFACE (1858) (German), Rev. Mathias Spier, O.S.B.
Res., 629 Second St., N.E., 55413. Tel: 612-379-2761.
School—Northeast Regional Catholic School. See Elementary Schools, Consolidated, Parochial under the Institutions located in the Archdiocese for details. Tel: 612-789-8851.

20—ST. BRIDGET (1915), Rev. Killian J. Perry, T.O.R. In res., Revs. Vincent J. Spinos, T.O.R.; J. Patrick Quinn, T.O.R.
Res., 3811 Emerson Ave., N., 55412. Tel: 612-529-7779; Fax: 612-529-8451.
School—5140 Fremont Ave., N., 55430-3497. Tel: 612-529-7781; Fax: 612-529-3343. Joyce Klevens, Prin.
Sisters 1; Lay Teachers 20; Students 360.

21—ST. CHARLES BORROMEO (1938), Revs. Francis R. Kittock; Mark A. Huberty; Deacon Dennis Neumann.
Res., 2420 St. Anthony Blvd., 55418. Tel: 612-781-6529; Fax: 612-781-9723.
School—2727 Stinson Blvd., 55418. Tel: 612-781-2643; Fax: 612-788-7768.
Lay Teachers 25; Students 376.

22—ST. CLEMENT (1902), Rev. Earl C. Simonson.
Res., 911 24th Ave., N.E., 55418. Tel: 612-789-3533.
School—Northeast Regional Catholic School. See Elementary Schools, Consolidated, Parochial under the Institutions located in the Archdiocese for details. Tel: 612-789-8851.

23—SS. CYRIL & METHODIUS (1891) (Slovak), Rev. Joseph Kivel, Temp. Admin.
Res., 1315 2nd St., N.E., 55413. Tel: 612-379-9736.
School—Northeast Regional Catholic School. See Elementary Schools, Consolidated, Parochial under the Institutions located in the Archdiocese for details. Tel: 612-789-8851.

24—ST. FRANCES CABRINI (1946), Rev. Leo J. Tibesar; Marie Rossa, Admin.
Res., 1500 Franklin Ave., S.E., 55414-3697. Tel: 612-339-3023; Fax: 612-339-0734.
Catechesis/Religious Programs—Students 153.

25—ST. HEDWIG (1914) (Polish), Rev. Theodore C. Guminga.
Res., 129 29th Ave., N.E., 55418. Tel: 612-789-4830.
School—Northeast Regional Catholic School. See Elementary Schools, Consolidated, Parochial under the Institutions located in the Archdiocese for details.

26—ST. HELENA (1913), Rev. Richard R. Villano.
3204 E. 43rd St., 55406. Tel: 612-729-7344.
Res., 4320 33rd Ave., S., 55406. Tel: 612-729-2252; Fax: 612-724-8695.
School—3200 E. 44th St., 55406. Tel: 612-729-9301.
Lay Teachers 13; Students 187.

27—ST. JOAN OF ARC (1946), Rev. George P. Wertin.
Res., 4537 3rd Ave., S., 55409. Tel: 612-823-8205; Fax: 612-825-7028.
Catechesis/Religious Programs—Kathy Itzin, D.R.E.
Students 575.

28—ST. JOSEPH HIEN, Revs. Andrew Dolinh Sang, C.M.C. (Vietnam); Joachim Ngo Choi, C.M.C. (Vietnam); Deacon Joseph Nhac Phuc Nguyen.
Res., 1814 Dupont Ave., N., 55411. Tel: 612-522-5006.

29—ST. LAWRENCE (1887), Revs. James F. Wiesner, C.S.P.; John J. Behnke, C.S.P.; Deacon Paul Carlson. In res., Revs. Charles A. Martin, C.S.P.; Wilfred A. Brimley, C.S.P.
Res., 1201 5th St., S.E., 55414. Tel: 612-331-7941; Fax: 612-378-1771.

30—ST. LEONARD OF PORT MAURICE (1941) (African American), Rev. James DeBruycker.
Res., 3949 Clinton Ave., 55409. Tel: 612-825-5811; 347-2260.

31—ST. OLAF (1941), Revs. John E. Forliti; Peter A. Laird; Kevin T. Kenney; Leon F. Klimczyk, S.J.; Deacon Stephen Boatwright.
Res., 215 S. 8th St., 55402. Tel: 612-332-7471; Fax: 612-332-3412.

32—ST. PHILIP (1906) (Polish), Rev. Gregory Tolaas.
Res., 2507 Bryant Ave., N., 55411. Tel: 612-529-3125; Fax: 612-287-9133.

33—ST. STEPHEN (1885), Revs. Patrick E. Griffin; Lawrence E. Hubbard.
Parish Center—2211 Clinton Ave., 55404. Tel: 612-874-0311; Fax: 612-874-0313.
School—Risen Christ Catholic School. See Elementary Schools, Consolidated, Parochial under Institutions located in the Archdiocese for details. Tel: 612-822-5329.

34—ST. THOMAS THE APOSTLE (1908), Rev. Stephen R. O'Gara.
Res., 2914 W. 44th St., 55410. Tel: 612-922-0041; Fax: 612-922-1921.
School—Combined program with Christ the King, Minneapolis. 2900 W. 44th St., 55410. Tel: 612-920-9075; Fax: 612-927-7426.
Lay Teachers, Both Campuses; 29; Students 421.

35—VISITATION (1946), Rev. Francis A. Pouliot; Deacon Peter A. D'Heilly.
Res., 4500 Lyndale Ave., S., 55409. Tel: 612-822-3139.
School—4530 Lyndale Ave., S., 55409. Tel: 612-827-3861.
Sisters of St. Benedict 1; Lay Teachers 7; Students 121.

OUTSIDE METROPOLITAN MINNEAPOLIS

Blaine, Anoka Co., St. Timothy's (1943), Rev. Harold J. Tasto; Deacons Bernie Dols; Kevin Jents.
Res., 707 89th Ave., N.E., 55434. Tel: 612-784-1329; Fax: 612-784-0652.
Catechesis/Religious Programs—Students 870.

Bloomington, Hennepin Co., Nativity of the Blessed Virgin Mary (1949), Revs. Robert E. Johnson; Brendan J. McMullen, O.P.; Deacons James McLaughlin; Rob Warhol.
Office: 9900 Lyndale Ave., S., 55420. Tel: 612-881-8671; Fax: 612-881-8692.
School—9901 Bloomington Fwy., 55420. Tel: 612-881-8160; Fax: 612-881-3032.
Lay Teachers 20; Students 434.
Catechesis/Religious Programs—Tel: 612-881-1451; Fax: 612-881-8671. Rose Ann Stans, D.R.E.
Students 230.

St. Bonaventure (1959), Revs. Bernard Zajdel, O.F.M.Conv.; Joseph West, O.F.M.Conv.; Deacon Patrick Casey. In res., Rev. Urban S. Wagner, O.F.M.Conv.
Res., 901 E. 90th St., S., 55420. Tel: 612-854-4733.
Catechesis/Religious Programs—Tel: 612-854-7062.
Students 419.

St. Edward (1967), Revs. Martin B. Shallbetter; J. Kevin Finnegan; Deacon Willard F. Dornfeld.
Res., 9401 Nesbitt Ave., S., 55437. Tel: 612-835-9220; Fax: 612-835-0156.
Catechesis/Religious Programs—Tel: 612-835-3272.
Students 710.

Brooklyn Center, Hennepin Co., St. Alphonsus (1959), Revs. Thomas Donaldson, C.SS.R.; Arthur Rossie, C.S.S.R.; Martin Stillmock, C.SS.R.; Edward Monroe, C.SS.R.; Deacons Jerome H. Bisek; Bobby May; David Holst; Bro. Raymond Bowersox, C.SS.R. In res., Rev. David Shannon, C.SS.R.
Res., 7025 Halifax Ave., N., 55429. Tel: 612-561-5100; Fax: 612-561-0336.
School—Benedictine Sisters, 7031 Halifax Ave., N., 55429. Tel: 612-561-5101.
Lay Teachers 17; Students 286.
Catechesis/Religious Programs—4111 71st Ave., N., 55429. Tel: 612-561-5102. Barbara Walhood, D.R.E.
Students 1,018.

Brooklyn Park, Hennepin Co., St. Gerard (1970), Revs. Anthony Criscitelli, T.O.R.; Bradley Baldwin, T.O.R.
Res., 9600 Regent Ave., N., 55443. Tel: 612-424-8770; Fax: 612-424-4327.
Catechesis/Religious Programs—Tel: 612-424-8600; Fax: 612-424-4327. Brian Richards, D.R.E.
Students 715.

Burnsville, Dakota Co., Mary, Mother of the Church (1965), Revs. James C. Zappa, Jr.; William G. Pelant; Deacons Peter Huberty; George Nugent; Barry Haller, Business Admin.
Church—3333 Cliff Rd., 55337. Tel: 612-890-0045; Fax: 612-890-0789.
Catechesis/Religious Programs—Al Rocklage, D.R.E.
Students 1,116.

Church of the Risen Savior (1970), Revs. Thomas H. Sieg; James Gorman; Deacon Richard Stevens; Lawrence Blake, Admin.
Office: 1501 E. County Rd. 42, 55306. Tel: 612-431-5222; Fax: 612-431-5221.
Catechesis/Religious Programs—D.R.E.: Karen Fitzpatrick; Barbara Skierecki; Susan Ford.
Students 1,443.

Columbia Heights, Anoka Co., Immaculate Conception (1923), Rev. Paul G. Moudry; Deacon Larry Palkert.
Res., 4030 Jackson St., N.E., 55421. Tel: 612-788-9062; Fax: 612-788-0202.
School—4053 N.E. Quincy, 55421. Tel: 612-788-9065.
Sisters of St. Francis 3; Lay Teachers 14; Students 321.
Catechesis/Religious Programs—Tel: 612-788-9067.
Students 269.

Coon Rapids, Anoka Co., Church of the Epiphany (1964), Revs. Bernard A. Reiser; Thomas W. Wilson; James E. Holl; James L. Lamm, Admin.
Res., 1900 111th Ave., N.W., 55433. Tel: 612-755-1020; Fax: 612-755-8069. [CEM]
School—11001 Hanson Blvd., 55433. Tel: 612-754-1750. Michael Strauss, Prin.
Lay Teachers 43; Students 800.
Catechesis/Religious Programs—11001 Hanson Blvd., 55433. Tel: 612-755-5010.
Students 1,604.

Crystal, Hennepin Co., St. Raphael (1951), Revs. Mark R. Juettner; John Zuhlsdorf; Thomas Rayer (India).
Res., 7301 Bass Lake Rd., 55428. Tel: 612-537-8401; Fax: 612-537-4878.
School—Tel: 612-537-6242; Fax: 612-537-4878.
Sisters 1; Lay Teachers 22; Students 488.
Catechesis/Religious Programs—Tel: 612-533-3770; Fax: 612-537-8401, Ext. 211. Paulette Schatz, D.R.E.
Students 430.

Eagan, Dakota Co., St. Thomas Becket (1989), Rev. Thomas M. Kommers; Deacon Paul Tatone.
Res., 4455 S. Robert Tr., 55123. Tel: 612-683-0689; 683-9808 (Parish Center); Fax: 612-683-0361.
Catechesis/Religious Programs—Students 350.

St. John Neumann (1977), Revs. Robert M. Schwartz; John J. Mitchell.
Res., 4030 Pilot Knob Rd., 55122. Tel: 612-454-2079; Fax: 612-454-0860.
Catechesis/Religious Programs—Students 1,553.

Eden Prairie, Hennepin Co., Pax Christi (1981), Rev. J. Timothy Power; Deacon Mike Gerdts.
Res., 12100 Pioneer Tr., 55347. Tel: 612-941-3150; Fax: 612-941-7942.

Catechesis/Religious Programs—Tel: 612-941-6007; Fax: 612-941-7942.
Students 1,575.

Edina, Hennepin Co., Our Lady of Grace (1946), Revs. Robert T. Cassidy; Robert L. Valit; Deacon Donald Pendergast. In res., Rev. Jerome W. Fehn.
Res., 5071 Eden Ave., 55436. Tel: 612-929-3317; Fax: 612-929-4612.
School—5051 Eden Ave., 55436. Tel: 612-929-5463; Fax: 612-929-8170.
Lay Teachers 28; Students 512.
Catechesis/Religious Programs—Students 370.

St. Patrick (1857) (Irish), Rev. Ambrose J. Mahon.
Res., 6820 St. Patrick's Ln., 55439. Tel: 612-941-3164; Fax: 612-941-7371.
Catechesis/Religious Programs—Tel: 612-941-1407. Sue Kelley, D.R.E.
Students 666.

Fridley, Anoka Co., St. William (1963), Rev. Patrick A. Kennedy, Admin.; Deacon Jim Wagner.
Res. and Admin. Center: 6120 5th St., N.E., 55432. Tel: 612-571-5600; Fax: 612-571-6924.
Catechesis/Religious Programs—Students 225.

Golden Valley, Hennepin Co., Good Shepherd (1946), Rev. Theodore C. Campbell.
Res., 145 Jersey Ave., S., 55426. Tel: 612-544-0649; Fax: 612-544-9896. [JC]
School—Tel: 612-545-4285; Fax: 612-545-1896.
Lay Teachers 18; Students 319.
Catechesis/Religious Programs—Students 150.

St. Margaret Mary (1946), Rev. Richard J. Huber.
Res., 2301 Zenith Ave., N., 55422. Tel: 612-588-9466; Fax: 612-588-0190.
Catechesis/Religious Programs—Students 137.

Ham Lake, Anoka Co., Saint Paul (1981), Rev. Timothy F. Nolan; Deacons Bill Beck; Don McPhee.
Res., 1740 Bunker Lake Blvd., N.E., 55304. Tel: 612-757-6910; Fax: 612-757-6920.
Catechesis/Religious Programs—Bob Peach, D.R.E.
Students 825.

Lino Lakes, Anoka Co., St. Joseph (1891), Revs. Timothy Morin; Kenneth G. LaVan.
Office: 171 Elm St., 55014. Tel: 612-784-3015; Fax: 612-784-3699. [CEM]
Catechesis/Religious Programs—D.R.E.: Shirley Gormley; Christine Kroner; Kenneth Schaan; Jeanne Degerstrom.
Students 1,128.

New Hope, Hennepin Co., St. Joseph (1858), Rev. Donald J. Piche.
Res., 8701 36th Ave., N., 55427. Tel: 612-544-3352. [CEM]
Parish Center & Office—Fax: 612-544-3435.
Catechesis/Religious Programs—D.R.E.: Mary Greving; Christopher Briggs; Larry Thomas.
Students 686.

Plymouth, Hennepin Co., St. Mary of the Lake (1935), Rev. Bryan A. O'Rourke; Deacon William Schiller.
Res., 105 Forestview Ln., N., 55441. Tel: 612-545-1443; Fax: 612-797-0996.
Catechesis/Religious Programs—Students 214.

Richfield, Hennepin Co., Assumption of the B.V.M. (1876), Rev. Michael Tix; Deacon Robert Smith.
Res., 305 E. 77th St., 55423. Tel: 612-866-5019; Fax: 612-866-5274.
School—Blessed Trinity Nicollet & Penn Campus, Tel: 612-869-5200 (Trinity); 866-6906 (Penn); Fax: 612-869-0277;866-5080.
Students 452.
Catechesis/Religious Programs—Students 127.

St. Peter (1943), Rev. Rodger R. Bauman.
Res., 6740 Nicollet Ave., S., 55423. Tel: 612-866-5089; Fax: 612-866-5080.
School—Consolidation of Assumption, St. Peter & St. Richard. 6720 Nicollet Ave., S., 55423. Tel: 612-869-5200.
Lay Teachers 21; Students 444.
Catechesis/Religious Programs—Tel: 612-866-3257.
Students 197.

St. Richard (1952), Rev. Gregory L. Esty; Deacons William J. Berghoff; Byron Rudolphi.
Office: 7540 Penn Ave., S., 55423. Tel: 612-869-2426; Fax: 612-869-0277.
Res., 7601 Penn Ave., S., 55423.
School—Blessed Trinity Catholic School. Consolidation of Assumption, St. Peter & St. Richard. Tel: 612-866-6906.
Lay Teachers 22; Students 403.
Catechesis/Religious Programs—Students 292.

Robbinsdale, Hennepin Co., Sacred Heart (1911), Rev. Robert E. Zasacki; Deacon Thomas Coleman.
Office: 4087 W. Broadway, 55422. Tel: 612-537-4561; Fax: 612-537-5426.
Res., 4510 40-1/2 Ave., N., 55422.
School—4050 Hubbard, 55422. Tel: 612-537-1329; Fax: 612-537-1486.
Lay Teachers 20; Students 248.
Catechesis/Religious Programs—Cyrilene Brouillard, D.R.E.
Students 194.

St. Louis Park, Hennepin Co., Most Holy Trinity (1943), Rev. Dennis Thompson, O.F.M.Conv.
Res., 4017 Utica Ave., 55416. Tel: 612-926-7516; Fax: 612-926-2222.
School—3946 Wooddale Ave., 55416. Tel: 612-926-2222.
Lay Teachers 9; Students 102.

Holy Family (1926), Rev. Thomas W. Dufner; Deacon Alfred R. Kattar.
Res., 5900 W. Lake St., 55416. Tel: 612-929-0113; Fax: 612-915-1474.
School—Park Valley Catholic School, Tel: 612-545-4285. Joint Venture with Good Shepherd, Golden Valley.
Catechesis/Religious Programs—Tel: 612-929-0113.
Students 300.

OUTSIDE TWIN-CITY METROPOLITAN AREA

Albertville, Wright Co., St. Albert (1904), Rev. Robert R. Harrer, O.M.I.
Mailing Address: P.O. Box 127, 55301. Tel: 612-497-2474. [CEM]
Catechesis/Religious Programs—P.O. Box 67, 55301. Tel: 612-497-3782.
Students 246.

Annandale, Wright Co., St. Ignatius (1882), Rev. Stanley Kozlak.
Res., 55302. Tel: 320-274-8828. [CEM]
Catechesis/Religious Programs—Tel: 320-274-5064.
Students 276.

Anoka, Anoka Co., St. Stephen (1856), Revs. Michael Paquet, O.S.C.; Michael Van Sloun, O.S.C.; William Deziel; Dale Ettel, O.S.C.; Deacons Peter Bednarczyk; Dominic Ehrmantraut. In res., Revs. David E. Gallus, O.S.C.; Edward Greiwe, O.S.C.; Kenneth Opat, O.S.C.; Eugene D. Plaisted, O.S.C.
Office: 2020 Fifth Ave., N., 55303. Tel: 612-421-2471; Fax: 612-421-4230. [CEM]
School—506 Jackson, 55303. Tel: 612-421-3236.
Sisters 1; Lay Teachers 24; Students 457.
Catechesis/Religious Programs—Students 1,309.

Bayport, Washington Co., St. Charles (1943), Rev. Jonathan P. Shelley.
Res., 409 N. 3rd St., 55003. Tel: 612-439-4511; Fax: 612-430-9717. [CEM]
School—St. Croix Catholic School. See Elementary Schools, Consolidated, Parochial under Institutions located in the Archdiocese for details. Tel: 612-439-5581.

Bellechester, Goodhue Co., St. Mary (1860) (Luxembourgian), Rev. Peter Njoku (Nigeria) Admin.
Res., 223 Chester Ave., 55027. Tel: 612-923-4305. [CEM]

Belle Creek, Goodhue Co., St. Columbkill (1860), Rev. Bruce Peterson.
Res., Goodhue Rte. 2, Box 90, 55027. Tel: 612-258-4307. [CEM]
Mission—Goodhue, Goodhue Co., Holy Trinity, Rte. 2, P.O. Box 90, 55027. Tel: 612-923-4472.

Belle Plaine, Scott Co., Our Lady of the Prairie (1972), Rev. Thomas McCabe.
Res., 212 N. Chestnut St., 56011. Tel: 612-873-2323; Fax: 612-873-2323. [CEM 2]
School—Tel: 612-873-6564; Fax: 612-873-6564.
Lay Teachers 5; Students 63.
Catechesis/Religious Programs—Fax: 612-873-2008. Rev. Thomas McCabe, D.R.E.
Students 400.

Buffalo, Wright Co., St. Francis Xavier (1915), Rev. Charles L. Froehle; Deacon Richard Boisclair.
Res., 9 N.W. 3rd St., 55313. Tel: 612-682-1183; Fax: 612-682-0485. [CEM 2]
School—Tel: 612-682-1295. Dianna Vossen, Prin.
Lay Teachers 12; Students 225.
Catechesis/Religious Programs—Sharon Kelly, D.R.E.
Students 500.

Cannon Falls, Goodhue Co., St. Pius V (1856), Rev. Roger J. Hessian, Admin.
Res., 410 W. Colvill Ave., P.O. Box 367, 55009-0367. Tel: 507-263-2578; Fax: 507-263-8005. [CEM]
Catechesis/Religious Programs—Tel: 507-263-4800 (Grades PreK-8); 263-4680 (Grades 9-12).
Students 328.

Carver, Carver Co., St. Nicholas (1868) (German), Rev. Gerard J. Rowan.
Res., 412 W. Fourth St., Box 133, 55315. Tel: 612-448-2345. [CEM 2]

Cedar, Anoka Co., St. Patrick (1894), Rev. Michael J. Kennedy; Thomas Patricia Orzechowski, Parish Admin.; Deacon Terry Scherer.
Res., 19921 Nightingale St., N.W., Oak Grove, 55011-9243. Tel: 612-753-2011; Fax: 612-753-9803. [CEM]
Catechesis/Religious Programs—Tel: 612-753-2036. Doris Murphy, D.R.E.
Students 536.

Cedar Lake, Scott Co., St. Patrick (1856) (Irish), Rev. Sebastien Bakatuinamina, C.I.C.M.
Res., Cedar Lake Twp., 24425 Old Hwy. 13 Blvd., Jordan, 55352. Tel: 612-492-6276; Fax: 612-492-6276. [CEM]
Catechesis/Religious Programs—Tel: 612-492-6290; Fax: 612-492-6290.
Students 221.
Mission—Spring Lake Twp., Scott Co., St. Catherine, (1865) 4500 E. 220th St., Prior Lake, 55372. Tel: 612-447-2180. [CEM]

Centerville, Anoka Co., St. Genevieve (1854) (French Canadian), Rev. Richard J. Wolter.
Res., 7087 Goiffon Ave., 55038. Tel: 612-429-7937. [CEM]
Catechesis/Religious Programs—Tel: 612-426-1818.
Students 190.

Chanhassen, Carver Co., St. Hubert (1865) (German), Revs. Stephen D. Ulrick; Joseph G. Gallatin; Deacons Timothy Helmeke; Robert Wagner.
Res., 8102 Main St., 55317. Tel: 612-934-9106; Fax: 612-934-8209. [CEM]
School—Tel: 612-934-6003.
Lay Teachers 30; Students 400.
Catechesis/Religious Programs—Students 846.

Chaska, Carver Co., Guardian Angels (1858), Rev. Timothy Rudolphi.
Res., 218 W. 2nd St., 55318. Tel: 612-448-4100; Fax: 612-448-3076. [CEM]
School—Tel: 612-448-2562; Fax: 612-448-3281.
Lay Teachers 13; Students 221.
Catechesis/Religious Programs—Tel: 612-448-3478.
Students 212.

Clearwater, Wright Co., St. Luke (1870), Rev. Ramon J. Buckley.
Mailing Address: P.O. Box 249, 55320-0249.
Res., 425 Spring St., 55320. Tel: 612-558-6341. [CEM]

Cleveland, Le Sueur Co., Church of the Nativity of the Blessed Virgin Mary (1865) (Irish-German), Rev. Glen T. Jenson.
Res., 56017-0187. Tel: 507-931-5409. [CEM]

Coates, Dakota Co., St. Agatha (1870), Rev. James W. Whalen, Temp. Admin.
Res., University of St. Thomas, 2115 Summit Ave., St. Paul, 55105. Tel: 612-645-2400. [CEM]

Cologne, Carver Co., St. Bernard (1859), Rev. George Thoomkuzhy (India) (Ujjain).
Res., 212 Church St., E., 55322. Tel: 612-466-2031. [CEM]
School—300 Church St., E., 55322. Tel: 612-466-5917.
Sisters of Notre Dame 2; Lay Teachers 4; Students 63.

Corcoran, Hennepin Co., St. Thomas the Apostle (1896), Rev. George R. Kinney.
Res., 20,000 County Rd. 10, Hamel, 55340. Tel: 612-420-2385; Fax: 612-420-4710. [CEM 4][JC 4]
Catechesis/Religious Programs—Tel: 612-420-2385; Fax: 612-420-4710. D.R.E.: Lori Palmode; Pam Dombeck; Linda Stanton.
Students 300.

Dayton, Hennepin Co., St. John the Baptist (1862) (French Canadian), Rev. Dale Ettel, O.S.C.
Res., 55327. Tel: 612-428-2828. [CEM 2][JC]
Catechesis/Religious Programs—Tel: 612-856-3122.
Students 150.

Deephaven, Hennepin Co., St. Therese (1946), Rev. John M. Bauer; Deacon James F. McDonald.
Res., 18323 Minnetonka Blvd., 55391. Tel: 612-473-4422; Fax: 612-473-2685.
School—18325 Minnetonka Blvd., 55391. Tel: 612-473-4355.
Sisters 5; Lay Teachers 12; Students 268.
Catechesis/Religious Programs—Tel: 612-473-2891; 473-5455. Margaret Stimmler, D.R.E.
Students 698.

Delano, Wright Co., St. Joseph (1902) (Polish), Rev. Thomas G. Boedy, S.J.; Deacon Joseph Frederick.
Church—401 River St., P.O. Box 470, 55328-0470. Tel: 612-972-2077; Fax: 612-972-6177. [CEM]
School—Delano Catholic Elementary School, Tel: 612-972-2528.
Catechesis/Religious Programs—Tel: 612-972-2976.
Students 113.

St. Mary of Czestochowa (1884) (Polish), Rev. James T. Livingston.
Office & Res.: 1867 95th St., S.E., 55328. Tel: 612-955-1139. [CEM]

St. Peter (1865) (German), Rev. Thomas G. Boedy, S.J.; Deacon Joseph Frederick.
Offices: 204 River St., 55328. Tel: 612-972-2077; Fax: 612-972-6177. [CEM 2]
School—Tel: 612-972-2528.
Lay Teachers 10; Students 112.
Catechesis/Religious Programs—235 S. 2nd St., 55328. Tel: 612-972-2976; Fax: 612-972-6177.
Students 227.

Elysian, Le Sueur Co., St. Andrew Holy Trinity, Waterville, MN (1894), Rev. Michael W. Ince, Admin.
Church—Box 261, 56028. Tel: 507-267-4928.

Excelsior, Lake Minnetonka, Hennepin Co., St. John the Baptist (1903), Rev. Mark B. Dosh; Deacons John MacKenzie; James Baskfield; Gary Hoffman.
Res., 680 Mill St., 55331. Tel: 612-474-8868; Fax: 612-474-5962. [CEM]
School—Tel: 612-474-5812.
Lay Teachers 10; Students 119.
Catechesis/Religious Programs—Students 250.

Faribault, Rice Co., Immaculate Conception (1856), Rev. George J. Freeman; Deacon R. Daniel Wesley.
Res., 4 Second Ave., S.W., 55021-6029. Tel: 507-334-2266. [CEM]
School—Catholic School of Faribault. See Elementary Schools, Consolidated, Parochial under Institutions located in the Archdiocese for details. Tel: 507-334-7704.
Catechesis/Religious Programs—Tel: 507-334-9142.
Students 320.

Fairbault, Rice Co., Sacred Heart (French-German). Merged with St. Lawrence, Fairbault, and renamed Sacred Heart - St. Lawrence of Fairbault in 1996.

Faribault, Rice Co., St. Lawrence (1869) (German). Merged with Sacred Heart, Fairbault, and renamed Sacred Heart - St. Lawrence of Fairbault in 1996.

Sacred Heart - St. Lawrence of Fairbault. Sacred Heart, Fairbault, and St. Lawrence, Fairbault, were merged and renamed in 1996. Rev. David W. Kohner.
Res., 520 4th Ave., N.W., 55021-4227.
Catechesis/Religious Programs—Students 180.

Farmington, Dakota Co., St. Michael, Rev. Eugene A. Pouliot.
Res., 622 5th St., 55024-0227. Tel: 612-463-3360; Fax: 612-463-2339.
Center: 421 Walnut, P.O. Box 227, 55024.
Church—412 Spruce, 55024. Tel: 612-463-7078. [CEM]
Catechesis/Religious Programs—Students 383.

Forest Lake, Washington Co., St. Peter (1904), Revs. Robert J. Sipe; Jerome C. Kern; Deacons Gary Houle; Ralph L'Allier, Pastoral Min.
Res., 1250 S. Shore Dr., 55025. Tel: 612-464-3578; Fax: 612-464-5494. [CEM]
School—Tel: 612-464-2610. Sharon Tomlin, Prin.
Lay Teachers 23; Students 304.
Catechesis/Religious Programs—Tel: 612-464-7557. D.R.E.: Judy Foster; Susan Fast.
Students 1,000.

Hamel, Hennepin Co., St. Anne (1879), Rev. Allen J. McIntrye.
Res., 200 Hamel Rd., Box 256, 55340. Tel: 612-478-6644; Fax: 612-478-9141. [CEM]

Hampton, Dakota Co., St. Mathias (1900), Rev. Valerius U. Messerich, O.F.M.
Res., 23315 Northfield Blvd., 55031-9701. Tel: 612-437-9030; Fax: 612-437-5848. [CEM]
School—(Grades K-5). Tel: 612-437-5282.
Lay Teachers 7; Students 72.

Hancock Township, Carver Co., Assumption. Closed. For inquiries for parish records contact the Chancery.

Hassan Township, Hennepin Co., St. Walburga (1857), Rev. Lawrence R. Johnson; Deacon Dominic Ehrmentrant.
Res., 12020 Fletcher Ln., Rogers, 55374. Tel: 612-428-2081; Fax: 612-428-4032. [CEM 2]

Hastings, Dakota Co., St. Elizabeth Ann Seton (1987), Revs. Eugene J. McGlothlin, O.S.B.; Landelin A. Robling, O.S.B.; Stephen G. Beauclair, O.S.B.; Deacon Michael A. Humbert.
Res., 2035 W. Fifteenth St., 55033. Tel: 612-437-4254; Fax: 612-438-2948. [CEM][JC]
School—Tel: 612-437-3098; Fax: 612-438-3377. Barbara Vergenz, Prin.
Lay Teachers 24; Students 460.
Catechesis/Religious Programs—Tel: 612-437-9191; Fax: 612-437-9785.
Students 960.

Hazelwood, Rice Co., Annunciation of the B.V.M. (1863), Rev. Dennis D. Evenson.
Res., 4996 Hazelwood Ave., Northfield, 55057. Tel: 612-652-2625. [CEM]

Heidelberg, Le Sueur Co., St. Scholastica (1856) (German-Czech), Rev. Richard P. Roedel.
Res., Rte. 1, Box 218, New Prague, 56071. Tel: 612-758-4292. [CEM]

Hopkins, Hennepin Co., St. John the Evangelist (1950), Rev. Ralph J. Goman.
Res., 6 Interlachen Rd., 55343. Tel: 612-935-5536.
School—John Ireland Schools. See Elementary Schools, Consolidated, Parochial under Institutions located in the Archdiocese for details. Tel: 612-938-3442.

St. Joseph's (1926), Rev. John M. Long; Deacon Francis J. Tangney.
Res., 1310 Main St., 55343. Tel: 612-935-0111; Fax: 612-935-4539. [CEM]
School—John Ireland Schools. See Elementary Schools, Consolidated, Parochial under Institutions located in the Archdiocese for details. Tel: 612-938-3442; Fax: 612-938-3457.
Catechesis/Religious Programs—Tel: 612-935-7004; 935-5059.
Students 259.

Hugo, Washington Co., St. John the Baptist (1902), Rev. Daniel W. Friberg; Deacon Thomas Barrett.
Res., 14383 N. Forest Blvd., 55038. Tel: 612-426-1004. [CEM]
Catechesis/Religious Programs—Tel: 612-429-9170. Alice Christiansen, D.R.E.
Students 237.

Inver Grove Heights, Dakota Co., St. Patrick (1856) (Irish), Rev. Michael M. Arms; Deacon Harlan Christensen.
Res., 3535 72nd St., E., 55076. Tel: 612-455-6624; Fax: 612-455-8984. [CEM]
Catechesis/Religious Programs—Tel: 612-455-5900.
Students 531.

Jordan, Scott Co., St. John the Baptist (1858), Rev. James M. Perkl.
Res., 313 E. 2nd St., P.O. Box 97, 55352. Tel: 612-492-2640. [CEM][JC]
School—215 E. 2nd St., 55352. Tel: 612-492-2030; Fax: 612-492-3211.
Lay Teachers 14; Students 202.
Catechesis/Religious Programs—Students 320.

Kenyon, Goodhue Co., St. Michael (1944), Rev. Dennis C. Kampa, Admin.
Church—108 Bullis St., 55946. Tel: 507-789-6120.
Res., 451 5th St., S.W., Box 368, Pine Island, 55963. Tel: 507-356-4944. [CEM]

Kilkenny, Le Sueur Co., St. Canice (1858) (Irish), Rev. Ronald W. Dahlheimer.
Res., 56052. Tel: 507-595-2561. [CEM]

Lake St. Croix Beach, Washington Co., St. Francis Of Assisi (1938), Rev. Thomas J. Hallsten, O.S.B.
Res., 16770 13th St., 55043. Tel: 612-436-7817; Fax: 612-436-6524.
Catechesis/Religious Programs—Tel: 612-436-6527; Fax: 612-436-6527.
Students 278.

Lakeville, Dakota Co., All Saints (1889), Revs. Eugene W. Tiffany; Donald E. DeGrood.
Res., P.O. Box 518, 55044. Tel: 612-469-4481; Fax: 612-469-4484. [CEM]
School—Tel: 612-469-3332. Jackie Sauber, Prin.
Lay Teachers 10; Students 222.
Catechesis/Religious Programs—20965 Holyoke Ave., 55044. Tel: 612-469-6461. Joan Williamson, D.R.E.
Students 1,450.

Le Center, Le Sueur Co., St. Mary (1899), Rev. Raymond G. Monsour.
Res., 165 N. Waterville Ave., 56057. Tel: 507-357-4838. [CEM]
Catechesis/Religious Programs—Tel: 507-357-6633.
Students 268.

Le Sueur, Le Sueur Co., St. Anne (1852), Rev. Kenneth L. O'Hotto.
Res., 217 N. 3rd St., 56058. Tel: 612-665-2047. [CEM 2]
School—Tel: 612-665-2489.
Lay Teachers 9; Students 98.
Catechesis/Religious Programs—503 N. 4th St., 56058. Tel: 612-665-3811.
Students 130.

Lexington, Le Sueur Co., St. Joseph (1903) (Polish), Rev. Richard P. Roedel.
Res., Rte. 1, Box 218, New Prague, 56071. Tel: 612-758-4292. [CEM]

Lindstrom, Chisago Co., St. Bridget of Sweden (1948), Rev. Charles A. Brambilla.
Res., Box 754, 55045. Tel: 612-257-2474; Fax: 612-257-1498.
Catechesis/Religious Programs—Students 575.

Long Lake, Hennepin Co., St. George (1917), Rev. Timothy Dolan; Deacon John Reed.
Church—133 N. Brown Rd., 55356. Tel: 612-473-1247. [CEM]
Res., Tel: 612-473-1248.

Lonsdale, Rice Co., Immaculate Conception (1903), Rev. A. Michael Sauber.
Res., 55046-0169. Tel: 507-744-2829. [CEM]
School—Lonsdale, New Market, Veseli Area School. See Elementary Schools, Consolidated, Parochial under Institutions located in the Archdiocese for details. Tel: 507-744-2394.
Catechesis/Religious Programs—Students 105.

Loretto, Hennepin Co., SS. Peter and Paul (1867). Unassigned.
Mailing Address: P.O. Box 96, 55357. Tel: 612-479-0535; Fax: 612-479-4383.
Res., 125 Railway St., 55357. Tel: 612-479-0537. [CEM]
School—Tel: 612-479-0540; Fax: 612-479-4046.
Lay Teachers 10; Students 150.
Catechesis/Religious Programs—Tel: 612-479-0538.
Students 200.

Maple Grove, Hennepin Co., St. Joseph the Worker (1870), Rev. John F. Parkos; Deacon Donald S. Rinkenberger.
Church—7180 Hemlock Ln., 55369-5597. Tel: 612-425-6505; Fax: 612-425-6587.
Catechesis/Religious Programs—Tel: 612-425-9801. Stephen R. Robach, D.R.E.
Students 1,100.

Maple Lake, Wright Co., St. Timothy (1882), Rev. Michael J. McGlauchlin; Deacon Ron Freeman.
Res., 8 N. Oak Ave., Box 281, 55358. Tel: 320-963-3726. [CEM 3]
School—Tel: 320-963-3417. Mr. Frank Mazzuca, Sr., Prin.
Lay Teachers 6; Students 70.
Catechesis/Religious Programs—Students 225.

Marysburg, Le Sueur Co., Immaculate Conception (1857) (Irish), Rev. Glen T. Jenson.
Res., Rte. 1, Box 196, Madison Lake, 56063. Tel: 507-243-4157. [CEM]

Marystown, Scott Co., St. Mary of the Purification (1855), Rev. John R. Gilbert.
Res., 15850 Marystown Rd., Shakopee, 55379-9138. Tel: 612-445-3469. [CEM]
Parish Center: Tel: 612-445-2647; Fax: 612-445-2647.
School—Shakopee Area Catholic School. See Elementary Schools, Consolidated, Parochial under Institutions located in the Archdiocese for details.

Miesville, Dakota Co., St. Joseph (1873) (German-Irish), Rev. Marvin J. Klaers. In res., Rev. Michael F. O'Connor.
Office: 23955 Nicolai Ave., E., 55033-9650.
Res., 8433 239th St., E., 55033. Tel: 612-437-5520. [CEM]
Church—55033. Tel: 612-437-3526.
Catechesis/Religious Programs—Tel: 612-437-3506.
Students 171.

Minnetonka, Hennepin Co., Immaculate Heart of Mary (1946), Revs. Patrick J. Hipwell; Timothy Cloutier; Deacon David Huibregtse.
Res., 13505 Excelsior Blvd., 55345. Tel: 612-935-1432; Fax: 612-935-0474.
Catechesis/Religious Programs—Tel: 612-935-7077. D.R.E. Sr. Arlene Pomje, C.S.J.; Patricia Byrd.
Students 438.

Montgomery, Le Sueur Co., Holy Redeemer (1881), Revs. George J. Grafsky; Glen T. Jenson.
Res., 206 Vine Ave., W., 56069. Tel: 507-364-7981; Fax: 507-364-8660. [CEM]
School—205 Vine Ave., W., 56069. Tel: 507-364-7383.
Sisters of St. Benedict 1; Lay Teachers 12; Students 151.
Catechesis/Religious Programs—Students 153.

Monticello, Wright Co., St. Henry (1904), Rev. Marc T. Maus; Deacon Cecil Adams.
Office: 501 W. 4th St., 55362. Tel: 612-295-2402; Fax: 612-295-6333. [CEM]
Catechesis/Religious Programs—Tel: 612-295-2345. D.R.E.: Gary Russell; Karen Jendro.
Students 951.
Convent—Sisters of the Presentation.

Mound, Hennepin Co., Our Lady of the Lake (1909), Rev. Michael V. Tegeder.
Res., 2385 Commerce Blvd., 55364. Tel: 612-472-1284; Fax: 612-472-1216. [CEM]
Preschool:—.
Students 61.
School—Tel: 612-472-3400. Miss Kim Doyle, Prin.
Lay Teachers 19; Students 171.
Catechesis/Religious Programs—Tel: 612-472-4848.
Students 295.

New Market, Scott Co., St. Nicholas (1893) (German), Rev. George A. Welzbacher.
Res., 51 Church St., P.O. Box 9, 55054-0009. Tel: 612-461-2403. [CEM]
School—Lonsdale, New Market, Veseli Area School. See Elementary Schools, Consolidated, Parochial under Institutions located in the Archdiocese for details. Tel: 507-744-2394.

New Prague, Scott Co., St. Wenceslaus (1857), Rev. William J. Paron; Deacon Leonard J. Shanbour.
Res., 215 E. Main St., 56071. Tel: 612-758-3225. [CEM]
School—Tel: 612-758-3133. John Harty, Prin.
Lay Teachers 21; Students 329.
Catechesis/Religious Programs—Tel: 612-758-2276. Sr. Gayle Volz, P.B.V.M., D.R.E.
Students 370.

New Trier, Dakota Co., St. Mary (1856), Rev. Marvin J. Klaers.
Res., 8433 239th St., E., Hampton, 55031. Tel: 612-437-5520. [CEM]
School—Tel: 612-437-5546.
Lay Teachers 3; Students 33.

North Branch, Chisago Co., St. Gregory (1874), Rev. James T. Schoenberger; Deacon Thomas P. Langlois; Elizabeth R. Langlois, Pastoral Min.
Res., P.O. Box 609, 55056. Tel: 612-674-4056. [CEM]
Catechesis/Religious Programs—Tel: 612-674-7382.
Students 320.

Northfield, Rice Co., St. Dominic (1869), Revs. Francis L. Fried; Timothy L. Norris; Deacon Len Gruber.
Office: 216 N. Spring St., 55057. Tel: 507-645-8816; Fax: 507-645-8818.
Res., 116 N. Linden, 55057. Tel: 507-663-0154. [CEM]
School—Tel: 507-645-8136.
School Sisters of Notre Dame 1; Students 215.
Catechesis/Religious Programs—Students 477.

Norwood, Carver Co., Ascension (1859) (German), Rev. Paul C. Ardolf.
Res., 55368. Tel: 612-467-3351. [CEM 2]
Catechesis/Religious Programs—Students 99.

Osseo, Hennepin Co., St. Vincent de Paul (1855) (French), Revs. Curtis F. Lybarger; Robert A. Patterson; Deacon Sherman H. Otto.
Res., 9100 93rd Ave., N., Brooklyn Park, 55445-1407. Tel: 612-425-2210; Fax: 612-425-7898. [CEM]
School—Tel: 612-425-3970; Fax: 612-425-2674.
Lay Teachers 11; Students 250.
Catechesis/Religious Programs—D.R.E.: Arlys Lingen; Renee Paske; Bruce Baumann; Carol Ekstrom.
Students 1,500.

Pine Island, Goodhue Co., St. Michael (1878), Rev. Dennis C. Kampa.
Res., 55963. Tel: 507-356-4944. [CEM]
Catechesis/Religious Programs—Tel: 507-356-4280.
Students 261.
Mission—Kenyon, Goodhue Co., St. Michael, 108 Bullis St., Kenyon, 55946. Tel: 507-789-6120.

Prior Lake, Scott Co., St. Michael (1912), Rev. Richard Banker.
Res., 16311 Duluth Ave., S.E., 55372. Tel: 612-447-2491; Fax: 612-447-2489. [CEM 2]
Preschool:—.
Lay Teachers 2; Students 72.
School—(Grades K-8). Tel: 612-447-2124; Fax: 612-447-2124 (call before sending).
Sisters 1; Lay Teachers 21; Students 380.
Catechesis/Religious Programs—Tel: 612-447-2486; Fax: 612-447-2489. D.R.E.: Janel Boegeman; Tom Donlon; Margaret Breunig.
Students 580.

Red Wing, Goodhue Co., St. Joseph (1865), Rev. Thomas J. Walker.
Res., 426 8th St., 55066. Tel: 612-388-1133; Fax: 612-388-5294. [CEM]
School—Tel: 612-388-9493. Marion Willis, Prin.
Lay Teachers 6; Students 80.
Catechesis/Religious Programs—Tel: 612-388-6000.
Students 530.

Rogers, Hennepin Co., St. Martin (1912), Rev. Lawrence R. Johnson.
Office: 21304 Church Ave., 55374-9445. Tel: 612-428-2585. [CEM]
School—Tel: 612-428-2355.
Lay Teachers 9; Students 117.
Catechesis/Religious Programs—Students 160.

Rosemount, Dakota Co., St. Joseph (1865), Rev. Thomas F. Hill, O.F.M.Cap.
Res., 14375 S. Robert Tr., 55068. Tel: 612-423-4402; Fax: 612-423-4403. [CEM]
School—Tel: 612-423-1658.
Sisters 1; Lay Teachers 9; Students 237.
Catechesis/Religious Programs—Tel: 612-423-3131. Sr. Mary Louise McKenna, D.R.E.
Students 650.

Rush City, Chisago Co., Sacred Heart (1872) (Irish), Rev. Ralph F. Huar.
Res., P.O. Box 45, 55069. Tel: 320-358-4370; Fax: 320-358-4729. [CEM]

St. Benedict, Scott Co., St. Benedict, Rev. Elgar Bockenfeld, O.F.M.
Res., Rte. 1, P.O. Box 93, New Prague, 56071. Tel: 612-738-4642. [CEM][JC]

St. Bonifacius, Hennepin Co., St. Boniface (1859) (German), Rev. James T. Livingston.
Res., 4025 Main St., P.O. Box 68, 55375. Tel: 612-446-1054; Fax: 612-446-1158. [CEM]

St. Henry, Le Sueur Co., Church of St. Henry, Rev. Frederick C. Meyer.
Mailing Address: P.O. Le Sueur, R.R. No. 1, Box 52, 56058. Tel: 507-357-4990. [CEM]

St. Michael, Wright Co., St. Michael (1857), Rev. Leonard Siebenaler; Deacons Maynard Warne; Donald Becker.
Res., 55376. Tel: 612-497-2745; Fax: 612-497-2745. [CEM]
School—Tel: 612-497-3887.
Sisters 1; Lay Teachers 10; Students 225.
Catechesis/Religious Programs—Students 480.

St. Paul Park, Washington Co., St. Thomas Aquinas (1885), Rev. Timothy J. Wozniak.
Res., 920 Holly Ave., 55071. Tel: 612-459-2131; Fax: 612-459-8765. [CEM]
Catechesis/Religious Programs—Fax: 612-459-8756.
Students 325.

St. Thomas, Le Sueur Co., St. Thomas (1858) (Irish), Rev. Richard P. Ruedel.
Res., Rte. 1, Box 218, New Prague, 56071. Tel: 612-758-4292. [CEM]

Savage, Scott Co., St. John the Baptist (1854), Revs. Peter C. Wittman; Rinaldo B. Custodio; Deacon Tom Michaud.
Res., 55378. Tel: 612-890-9465; Fax: 612-890-3006. [CEM]
School—Tel: 612-890-6604.
Lay Teachers 30; Students 730.
Catechesis/Religious Programs—Tel: 612-890-9434. D.R.E.: Amy Kusber; Andi Little.
Students 1,034.

Shakopee, Scott Co., St. Mark (1856) (German), Rev. William F. Stolzman; Deacon Alan Schroeder.
Res., 350 S. Atwood St., 55379-1238. Tel: 612-445-1229; Fax: 612-445-9639. [CEM][JC]
School—Shakopee Area Catholic School. See Elementary Schools, Consolidated, Parochial under Institutions located in the Archdiocese for details. Tel: 612-445-3387.
Catechesis/Religious Programs—305 S. Scott St., 55379. Tel: 612-445-3488.
Students 435.

St. Mary (1865), Rev. James P. McConville; Deacon James L. Thornton.
Res., 535 S. Lewis St., 55379. Tel: 612-445-1319; 445-3234; Fax: 612-445-0511. [CEM][JC]
School—Shakopee Area Catholic School. See Elementary Schools, Consolidated, Parochial under Institutions located in the Archdiocese for details. Tel: 612-445-3387; 445-3159; Fax: 612-445-7256.
Catechesis/Religious Programs—Shakopee Area Religious Education. This is a consolidation of three parish programs. 305 S. Scott St., 55379. Tel: 612-445-3488. D.R.E.: Laura Shupe; Karen Martin.
Students 582.

Shieldsville, Rice Co., St. Patrick (1856) (Irish-Czech), Revs. Clarence Vowra; George J. Grafsky.
Res., 7525 Dodd Rd., Faribault, 55021. Tel: 507-334-6002. [CEM]

South St. Paul, Dakota Co., Holy Trinity (1918) (Polish), Rev. John M. LeVoir.
Res., 752 5th Ave., S., 55075. Tel: 612-455-1228.
Office: 749 6th Ave., S., 55075. Tel: 612-455-1302; Fax: 612-455-6004.
School—745 6th Ave., S., 55075. Tel: 612-455-8557.
Lay Teachers 22; Students 381.
Catechesis/Religious Programs—Tel: 612-455-6004.
Students 191.

St. Augustine (1896), Rev. Raymond J. Zweber.
Res., 302 5th Ave., N., 55075. Tel: 612-451-1212.
Catechesis/Religious Programs—Tel: 612-451-1560; 451-0685. Sr. Bernadine Frischmon, O.S.B., D.R.E.
Students 168.

St. John Vianney (1946), Rev. Martin A. Beckman; Deacon Fred de los Reyes.
Res., 789 17th Ave., N., 55075. Tel: 612-451-1863; Fax: 612-451-1864.
School—1815 Bromley, 55075. Tel: 612-451-8395.
Lay Teachers 12; Students 202.
Catechesis/Religious Programs—Students 288.

Stillwater, Washington Co., St. Mary (1865), Rev. William A. Brown; Deacons Ronald Getz; Peter Bellavance.
Res., 407 S. 5th St., 55082. Tel: 612-439-1270; Fax: 612-439-7705. [JC]
Church and Office:—611 S. Third St., 55082.
School—St. Croix Catholic School. See Elementary Schools, Consolidated, Parochial under Institutions located in the Archdiocese for details. Tel: 612-439-5581.
Catechesis/Religious Programs—Tel: 612-439-7142.
Students 125.

St. Michael (1853), Revs. Michael C. Skluzacek; Michael S. Creagan.
Res., 611 S. Third St., 55082. Tel: 612-439-4400; Fax: 612-430-3271. [JC]
School—St. Croix Catholic School. See Elementary Schools, Consolidated, Parochial under Institutions located in the Archdiocese for details. Tel: 612-439-5581. Martin Weisbeck, Prin.
Catechesis/Religious Programs—Tel: 612-439-7142; Fax: 612-439-7705. William Klein, D.R.E.
Students 900.

Taylors Falls, Chisago Co., St. Joseph's (1873), Rev. Albert J. Shanley, M.S.; Deacon Kevin Madden.
Res., 500 River St., 55084. Tel: 612-465-7345. [CEM][JC]
Mission—Franconia, Chisago Co., St. Francis Xavier, 55084.

Union Hill, Le Sueur Co., St. John the Evangelist, Rev. Elgar Bockenfeld, O.F.M.
Res., Rte. 1, P.O. Box 93, New Prague, 56071. Tel: 612-758-4642. [CEM]

Vermillion, Dakota Co., St. John the Baptist (1881), Rev. Joseph J. Arackal, V.C.
Res., 106 W. Main St., 55085. Tel: 612-437-5652; Fax: 612-437-1933. [CEM]
School—111 W. Main St., 55085. Tel: 612-437-2644.
Franciscan Clarist Sisters 2; Lay Teachers 5; Students 84.

Veseli, Rice Co., Most Holy Trinity (1874) (Czech), Rev. John G. Lapensky.
Res., 9845 Main St., 55046. Tel: 507-744-2823; Fax: 507-744-2823. [CEM 2]
School—Lonsdale, New Market, Veseli Area School. See Elementary Schools, Consolidated, Parochial under Institutions located in the Archdiocese for details. Tel: 507-744-2394; Fax: 507-744-2395.
Catechesis/Religious Programs—Students 204.

Victoria, Carver Co., St. Victoria (1856) (German), Rev. Robert L. White.
Res., 8228 Victoria Dr., 55386. Tel: 612-443-2661; Fax: 612-443-3866. [CEM]
Catechesis/Religious Programs—Tel: 612-443-3536.
Students 92.

Waconia, Carver Co., St. Joseph (1859), Rev. Martin J. Siebenaler.
Res., 32 E. 1st St., 55387. Tel: 612-442-2384; Fax: 612-442-4500. [CEM]
School—Tel: 612-442-4500.
Lay Teachers 11; Students 180.
Catechesis/Religious Programs—Tel: 612-442-4871.
Students 210.

Watertown, Carver Co., Immaculate Conception (1863) (German-Irish), Rev. Frank J. Wampach.
Res., 109 Angel Ave., N.W., P.O. Box 548, 55388. Tel: 612-955-1458; Fax: 612-955-1211. [CEM]
Catechesis/Religious Programs—113 Angel Ave., N.W., Tel: 612-955-1777. Deb Kennedy, D.R.E.
Students 264.

Waterville, Le Sueur Co., Holy Trinity (1892), Rev. Michael W. Ince.
Res., 506 Common St., 56096. Tel: 507-362-4311. [CEM]
Catechesis/Religious Programs—Tel: 507-362-8396.
Students 123.

Waverly, Wright Co., St. Mary (1884), Rev. William F. Martin.
Res., P.O. Box 278, 55390. Tel: 612-658-4319. [CEM][JC 3]
Catechesis/Religious Programs—Tel: 612-658-4118.
Students 290.

Wayzata, Hennepin Co., Holy Name (1865), Rev. Arnold Weber, O.S.B.; Deacons Joe Wierschem; Nelson Hickman; Terry Schneider.
Res., 155 County Rd., 24, 55391. Tel: 612-473-9620 (rectory); Fax: 612-473-8678. [CEM]
School—Tel: 612-473-3675; Fax: 612-473-4715.
Lay Teachers 22; Students 371.
Catechesis/Religious Programs—Tel: 612-473-7901.
Students 1,037.

St. Bartholomew (1916), Rev. Stephen J. LaCanne.
Office: 630 E. Wayzata Blvd., 55391. Tel: 612-473-6601; Fax: 612-473-0980.

School—(Grades PreK-6). Tel: 612-473-6189.
Lay Teachers 12; Students 242.
Catechesis/Religious Programs—Students 260.

Zumbrota, Goodhue Co., St. Paul (1900), Rev. Peter Njoku (Nigeria).
Office: 749 S. Main St., 55903. Tel: 507-732-5324. [CEM][JC]
Res., 223 Chester Ave., Bellechester, 55027. Tel: 612-923-4305.
Catechesis/Religious Programs—Students 150.

Chaplains of Public Institutions

ST. PAUL. *Bethesda Medical Center.* Deacon Jerome J. Bilder.
Gillette Children's Hospital. Revs. Joseph Menker, O.M.I.; Robert Allie, O.M.I.
HealthEast, Inc. Rev. Gerald K. Foley (CR).
Midway Hospital. Attended by Church of St. Mark, St. Paul.
Ramsey County Correctional Facilities. Rev. Edward J. Flahavan.
Ramsey County Home. Vacant. 1735 Kennard St., 55109.
St. John's Hospital. (Lutheran) 840 E. 6th St., 55106. Rev. Fabian F. Burdiek, O.F.M.
St. Paul-Ramsey Hospital 261 E. 8th St., 55101. Revs. Joseph Menker, O.M.I.; Robert Allie, O.M.I.
United Hospitals, Inc. Vacant.

MINNEAPOLIS. *Abbot-Northwestern Hospital* 3617 38th Ave., S., 55066. Revs. Robert A. Patterson; Clement J. Burke (DUB).
Hennepin County Courts. Rev. James Jackson, 2055 Bohland Ave., St. Paul, 55116.
Hennepin County Medical Center 2421 Third Ave., S., 55404. Rev. James R. DeBruycker.
Metropolitan Medical Center. Rev. James Cassidy, Chap.
Minneapolis Children's Medical Center 3617 38th Ave., S., 55406. Rev. Robert A. Patterson.
Minnesota Soldiers' Home. Rev. Eugene J. Abbott.
Riverside Medical Center 2450 Riverside Ave., 55454. Rev. Leo J. Tibesar.
University of Minnesota Hospitals. Rev. Meinrad Dindorf, O.S.B., Chap., 2001 Dayton Ave., St. Paul, 55104.
Veterans Administration Medical Center 54th and 48th Aves., S., 55417. Rev. William K. Gamber.

ANOKA. *Anoka State Hospital.* Vacant. 516 School St., 55303.

EDINA. *Fairview-Southdale Hospital.* Rev. Jerome W. Fehn, Chap.

FARIBAULT. *Faribault State School and Hospital.* Attended by Immaculate Conception Parish. Braille and Sight Saving School, Minnesota School for the Deaf, (Retardation).

GOLDEN VALLEY. *North Memorial Hospital.* Rev. Leo D. Krautkremer, 4003 Bryant Ave., N., Minneapolis, 55412.

LINO LAKES. *Minnesota Correctional Facility.* Rev. Msgr. J. Jerome Boxleitner, Chap., 1121 E. 46th St., Minneapolis, 55407.

ST. LOUIS PARK. *Methodist Hospital.* Rev. Jerome W. Fehn, Chap.

SHAKOPEE. *Women's State Reformatory.* Rev. James T. Schoenberger, Church of St. Gregory, North Branch.

STILLWATER. *Minnesota State Prison.* Rev. Gregory A. Skrypek.

Special Assignment:
Reverend Fathers—
Abbott, Eugene J.
Flahavan, Edward J., Chap., Ramsey County Correctional Facilities
Gamber, William K., Chap., V.A. Medical Center
Hubbard, Lawrence E., Hispanic Ministry
Jackson, James, Chap., Hennepin County Courts
Jeub, Richard H., Chancery, Pro Tem.
Kapoun, Robert E., Chancery Pro Tem
Lepak, Roy C., Hermit, Cotton, MN
McConville, James P., Chancery Pro Tem.
Notebaart, James C., Office of Indian Ministry
Snyder, Larry J., Catholic Charities
Stevens, Michael J., Catholic Education Center
Wajda, Joseph L., Tribunal
Walsh, Harry A., Chancery, Pro Tem.

On Duty Outside the Archdiocese:
Reverend Monsignors—
Namie, James B., Maronite Chancery, P.O. Box 280036 - Dyker Heights Station, Brooklyn, NY 11228-0002
Reverend Fathers—
Brandes, John F., Parroquia San Lucas Toliman, Dept. Solola 07013, Guatemala
Bury, Harold J., P.O. Box 20310, Cleveland, OH 44120
Dempsey, Dennis K., El Buen Pastor Parroquia San Francisco de Asis, Apartado 272, Puerto Ordaz, Estado Bolivar, 8015 Venezuela
Magee, Paul L., El Buen Pastor Parroquia San Francisco de Asis, Apartado 272, Puerto Ordaz, Estado Bolivar, 8015 Venezuela
O'Connell, Marvin R., University of Notre Dame, IN
Ryan, Patrick J., El Buen Pastor Parraquia San Francisco de Asis, Apartado 272, Puerto Ordaz, Estado Bolivar, 8015 Venezuela
Schaffer, Gregory J., El Buen Pastor Parraquia San Francisco de Asis, Apartado 22, Puerto Ordaz, Estado Bolivar 8015 Venezuala
Slusser, Michael S., Dept. of Theology, Duquesne Univ., Pittsburgh, PA 15282

Military Chaplains:
Reverend Fathers—
Himmelsbach, James R., U.S. Army
Smith, John B., U.S. Army
Vakoc, Henry T., U.S. Army

Graduate Studies:
Reverend Fathers—
Byron, J. Michael
Conlin, Daniel C.

Retired:
Reverend Monsignors—
Baumgaertner, William L., 2190 Summit Ave., St. Paul, MN 55105
Dillon, David A., 1011 Feltl Ct., No. 910, Hopkins, MN 55343
DuLac, Henri J., 1011 Feltl Ct., No. 628, Hopkins, MN 55343
Fleming, Francis J., 2115 Summit Ave., Mail #4337, St. Paul, MN 55105
Hessian, Patrick J., P.O. Box 7598, Silver Spring, MD 20907
Kneal, Ellsworth, 2260 Summit Ave., St. Paul, MN 55105
Lavin, James M., 2115 Summit Ave., St. Paul, MN 55105
Murphy, Terrance J., 2115 Summit Ave., St. Paul, MN 55105
Probst, Robert L., College of St. Thomas, 2115 Summit Ave., St. Paul, MN 55105
Sankovitz, John P., 2115 Summit Ave., St. Paul, MN 55105
Srnec, Stanley J., Leo Byrne Residence, St. Paul, MN
Steiner, Clarence J., 324 Pior Ave. S., St. Paul, MN 55105
Sweeney, John A., 60 S. Mississippi River Blvd., #227, St. Paul, MN 55105
Reverend Fathers—
Abbott, Eugene J., 1241 Edgcumbe Rd., St. Paul, MN 55105
Barthelme, Frederick J., 1204 W. Linden St., Stillwater, MN 56071
Berg, Richard V., 60 S. Mississippi River Blvd., St. Paul, MN 55105
Bigot, Ross G., 2190 Summit Ave., St. Paul, MN 55105
Blais, Melvin J., Gallery Towers-Unit 703, 26 W. 10th St., St. Paul, MN 55102
Boller, Robert J., 1435 Hampshire S., St. Louis Park, MN 55426
Brown, John T., Box 10, Cannon Falls, MN 55009
Buchanan, John J., 2190 Summit Ave., St. Paul, MN 55105
Burns, Donald W., 2067 Sheperd Rd. #205, St. Paul, MN 55116
Cody, Nicholas A., P.O. Box 22, Cross Lake, MN 56442
Colon, Vincent A., 2350 Springside Dr., Maplewood, MN 55119
Conroy, Thomas J., 2115 Summit Ave., Mail 4042, St. Paul, MN 55105
Decowski, Frank J., 3308 Bayshore Cir, Isanti, MN 55040
DeSutter, Gilbert J., 24571 W. Cedar Lake Dr., Jordan, MN 55352
Dobihal, Robert F., 2067 Shepard Rd., Apt. 202, St. Paul, MN 55116
Dolan, Leo A., 2190 Summit Ave., St. Paul, MN 55105
Dudley, Francis R., Maternity of B.V.M., St. Paul, MN
Dufresne, Oliver J., P.O. Box 3848, Minneapolis, MN 55403
Dunn, John P., 1926 Norfolk Ave., St. Paul, MN 55116
Dynes, Leo J., 627 Linden Ave., Kilkenny, MN 56052
Egan, Harvey F., 121 S. Washington, No. 512, Minneapolis, MN 55401
Eggert, Charles M., 2190 Summit Ave., St. Paul, MN 55105
Endres, Gilbert J., 13100 318th St., Lot 158, Lindstrom, MN 55045
Fitzpatrick, John P., Rte. 1, P.O. Box 825, Ogilvie, MN 56358
Flahavan, Edward J., 811 Portland Ave., St. Paul, MN 55104
Fleming, Martin M.P., 383 Portland Ave., St. Paul, MN 55104
Gamber, William K.
Gannon, Joseph T., 2190 Summit Ave., St. Paul, MN 55105
Garvey, Thomas J., 1041 16th Ave., S.E., Minneapolis, MN 55414
Gessner, Henry E., 433 W. 5th St., Waconia, MN 55387
Grzeskowiak, Edward S.
Guillemette, Joseph H., 330 S. Exchange St., St. Paul, MN 55102
Hamel, Robert F., 2136 Reaney, St. Paul, MN 55119
Hayes, Francis R., 1500 Douglas Dr., N., Minneapolis, MN 55422
Hermes, Roger J., 2329 N. Recker Rd., #117, Mesa, AZ
Holl, James E., 1800-111th Ave., N.W., Coon Rapids, MN 55433
Houle, Cecil T., 4368 Buckingham Ct., Vadnais Heights, MN 55110
Howley, Leo W., 1101 Sibley Memorial Hwy., Unit 111, St. Paul, MN 55118
Huber, Leo R.
Janski, Jerome J., 16551 S. Temple Dr., St. Paul, MN 55345
Jenniges, Leonard J., RR. 2, Sanborn, MN 56083
Jirik, Charles C., 1422 Emerson Ave., N., Minneapolis, MN 55411
Joyce, John E., Rt. 1, Henderson, MN 56044
Jude, Robert J., P.O. Box 219, Maple Lake, MN 55358
Karels, Agdus S., 513 N.W. 4th St., Ortonville, MN 56278
Keane, Robert E., 5921 14th Ave. S., Minneapolis, MN 55417
Keefe, Gerald E.
Keller, Lawrence E., 1212 Larpenteur Ave., E., St. Paul, MN 55109
Klein, Bernard C.
Kolar, Thomas F., 2750 N. Victoria St., Room 225, Roseville, MN 55113
Kubat, Alphonse M., 2190 Summit Ave., St. Paul, MN 55105
Larkin, Richard
Mahoney, Richard J.
McGrade, William H., 6541 Golden Valley Rd. #302, Golden Valley, MN 55427
Mertz, Frederick A., 391 Laurel Ave., #102, St. Paul, MN 55102
Mertz, William H., 4115 Beaver Dam Rd., Eagan, MN 55152
Mitchell, John E., 1824 Eleanor Ave., St. Paul, MN 55116
Moorman, Raymond J., 3220 S. Yosemite Ave., S., St. Louis Park, MN 55416
Moudry, Richard P., 11113 Hyland Ter., Eden Prairie, MN 55344
Mycue, Gordon E., 5805 Winnetka Ave., N., New Hope, MN 55428
Payant, Remi J., 2190 Summit Ave., St. Paul, MN 55105
Reidy, James E., University of St. Thomas, C301, Mail 4066, St. Paul, MN
Remes, James A.
Riley, John F., 2190 Summit Ave., St. Paul, MN 55105
Roach, Francis J., 2132 Bard Ct., P.O. Box 1064, Faribault, MN 55021
Robertson, Thomas J., 2154 Upper Roy Lake, Nisswa, MN 56468
Russell, J. Christopher, Leo Byrne Residence, St. Paul, MN
Ryan, T. Kenneth, c/o Catholic Digest, P.O. Box 3090, St. Paul, MN 55165
Schmitzer, Richard C., El Mirage Park, #322, 305 S. Val Vista, Mesa, AZ 85204
Schnitzius, Donald J., 2190 Summit Ave., St. Paul, MN 55105
Seefeldt, Wilbert T., 15442 Red Oaks Rd., S.E., Prior Lake, MN 55372
Siebenaler, John M., Leo Byrne Residence, St. Paul, MN
Streff, Joseph N.
Stromberg, James S.
Thurner, Robert M., Chancery, Pro Tem., 2190 Summit Ave., St. Paul, MN 55105
Vrana, Francis R., 14840 62nd St., N., No. 205, Stillwater, MN 55082
Wagner, Alfred S., 2190 Summit Ave., St. Paul, MN 55105
Westhoff, Donald F., 20 E. Exchange B-208, St. Paul, MN 55101
Whalen, James W., University of St. Thomas
Wirth, John J., 330 S. Exchange, St. Paul, MN 55102
Wittman, Karl M.
Zweber, Clement J., P.O. Box 962, Lakeville, MN 55044

Permanent Deacons:
- Asenbrenner, Francis
- Babcock, George H., (Retired)
- Backmann, Howard, St. Anthony of Padua, MN
- Barrett, Ervin F., St. Thomas the Apostle, St. Paul
- Barrett, Thomas F., St. John the Baptist, Hugo
- Barrett, W. Richard, Holy Spirit, St. Paul
- Baskfield, James F., St. John the Baptist, Excelsior
- Beck, William E., St. Paul, Ham Lake
- Becker, Donald L., St. Michael, St. Michael
- Beckfeld, William F., St. Bartholomew, Wayzata
- Bednarczyk, Peter, St. Stephen, Anoka
- Bellavance, Peter G., St.Mary, Stillwater
- Berghoff, William J., St. Richard, Richfield
- Bernard, Charles V., On Leave of Absence
- Bilder, Jerome J., St. Agnes, St. Paul
- Bisek, Jerome H., St. Alphonsus, Brooklyn Center and AIDS Ministry
- Blissenbach, Gerald, On Medical Leave of Absence
- Boatwright, Stephen, St. Olaf, Minneapolis
- Boisclair, A. Richard, St. Francis, Buffalo
- Bramwell, Robert, St. Thomas, Corcoran
- Brown, Fredrick L., (Retired)
- Campbell, Kevin A., On Leave of absence
- Carlson, Paul, St. Lawrence, Minneapolis and Metropolitan Tribunal
- Carlson, Roger B., Unassigned
- Casey, Patrick J., St. Bonaventure, Bloomington
- Cate, Allan, On Leave of Absence
- Christensen, Harlan L., St. Patrick, Inver Grove Heights
- Ciresi, Jerome D., St. Odilia, Shoreview
- Coleman, Thomas F., Sacred Heart, Robbinsdale
- Conlin, Robert E., St. Mark, St. Paul
- D'Heilly, Peter, Dir., Center for Diaconate and Visitation, Minneapolis
- DeLosReyes, Alfredo L., St. John Vianney, South St. Paul
- Devine, Gerald L., Nativity, St. Paul
- DeVinney, Charles A., Unassigned
- Dinzeo, Anthony J., Sabbatical
- Dolan, Thomas E., Holy Rosary, Minneapolis
- Dols, Bernard R., St. Timothy, Blaine
- Dondelinger, James, St. Austin, Minneapolis
- Donnelly, Patrick T., (Retired)
- Dornfeld, Willard, St. Edward, Bloomington
- Dubay, Frank X., Diocese of Venice, FL
- Dzik, Thomas W., St. Luke, St. Paul
- Ehrmantraut, Dominic, St. Stephen, Anoka and St. Walburga, Fletcher
- Erpenbach, William L., Sacred Heart, St. Lawrence, Faribault
- Evans, Russell, St. John the Baptist, New Brighton
- Falvey, William E., St. Adalbert, St. Paul
- Feffer, Edward F., St. Pius X, White Bear Lake
- Ferguson, Delmar F., Basilica, Minneapolis
- Fidler, Donald, Holy Name, MN
- Flood, John J., St. Odilia, Shoreview
- Frederick, Joseph J., Delano Catholic Community
- Freeman, Ronald, St. Timothy, Maple Lake
- Friesen, Michael, Our Lady of Peace, MN
- Gerdts, Michael G., Pax Christi, Eden Prairie
- Getz, Ronald L., Retired
- Giesen, Robert F., On Leave of Absence
- Gruber, Leonard L., St. Dominic, Northfield
- Hanten, Nick, (Retired)
- Hathaway, Donald F., (Retired)
- Heidenreich, Michael, Diocese of Las Vegas, NV
- Helmeke, Timothy, St. Hubert, Chanhassen
- Hepp, James E., St. Peter, N. St. Paul
- Hickman, Nelson, Holy Name, Medina
- Hoffman, Gary, St. John Excelsior
- Holst, David, St. Alphonsus, Brooklyn Park
- Houle, Gary J., St. Peter, Forest Lake
- Huberty, Peter J., Mary, Mother of the Church, Burnsville
- Hughesdon, Harold, St. Agnes, St. Paul
- Huibregtse, David, Immaculate Heart of Mary, Minnetonka, AIDS Ministry
- Humbert, Michael, St. Elizabeth Ann Seton, Hastings; Cretin-Derham Hall High School, St. Paul
- Janes, Edward, St. Peter, Richfield
- Jents, Kevin, St. Timothy, Blaine
- Johnson, Fred, St. Peter, St. Paul
- Kasbohm, Thomas F., (Retired)
- Kattar, Alfred R., Holy Family, St. Louis Park
- Kenney, Joseph G., Assumption, Richfield
- Keys, Thomas, St. John the Evangelist, Little Canada
- Kirchoffner, Daniel D., Transfiguration, Maplewood
- Konkel, Thomas A., St. Andrew, St. Paul
- Koop, Steven E., St. Rita, Cottage Grove
- Kuebler, Myon, St. Michael, Pine Island
- Kuhns, James C., (Retired)
- L'Allier, Ralph, St. Peter, Forest Lake
- La Qui, Marciano I., St. Bernard, St. Paul
- Langlois, Thomas, St. Gregory the Great, North Branch
- Lee, Joseph, Office of Indian Ministry
- Lo, Va Thai, Hmong Community, St. Vincent de Paul, St. Paul
- Lukach, George, St. Henry, Monticello
- MacKenzie, John M., St. John the Baptist, Excelsior
- Madden, Kevin, St. Joseph, Taylors Falls; St. Francis, Franconia
- Maltzen, Bruce H., Diocese of St. Cloud
- Mangan, John T., Minnesota Veteran's Home
- Mann, George A., On Leave of Absence
- Mantel, James F., Immaculate Conception, Watertown
- May, Bobby, St. Alphonsus, Brooklyn Center
- McDonald, James F., St. Therese, Deephaven
- McLaughlin, James, Nativity, Bloomington
- McPhee, Don, On Medical Leave of Absence
- McPherson, Joseph T., St. John the Baptist, New Brighton
- Medlicott, James V., (Retired)
- Michaud, Thomas P., St. John, Savage
- Murphy, James W., St. John, Hopkins
- Murphy, John L., St. Matthew, St. Paul
- Murphy, Lawrence J., Guardian Angels, Lake Elmo
- Neumann, Dennis J., St. Charles Borromeo, St. Anthony
- Nicklay, John, St. Rita, Cottage Grove
- Nicolosi, Dr. Charles, On Leave of Absence
- Nugent, George J., Mary, Mother of the Church, Burnsville
- O'Connor, Robert, United Hospital
- O'Keefe, Clyde, (Retired)
- Otto, Sherman H., St. Vincent de Paul, Osseo
- Palkert, Lawrence, Immaculate Conception, Columbia Heights
- Pashby, Richard E., St. Pascal, St. Paul
- Pasko, Anthony, Our Lady of Grace, Edina
- Pederson, Bernard A., St. Agnes, St. Paul
- Pendergast, Donald, Our Lady of Grace, Edina
- Rajcich, G. Michael, St. Bridget, Lindstrom
- Reed, John A., St. George, Long Lake
- Rinkenberger, Donald, St. Joseph the Worker, Maple Grove
- Rollings, Virgil, (Retired)
- Rudolphi, Byron W., Jr., St. Richard, Richfield
- Scherer, Terrance P., St. Patrick, Cedar
- Scherkenbach, Gerald A., St. Leo, St. Paul
- Schiller, William C., St. Mary of the Lake, Plymouth
- Schmitz, Joseph, Woodbury Health Care Center
- Schneider, Frank J., St. Jerome, Maplewood
- Schneider, Terrence, Holy Name, Medina
- Schramer, Joseph J., Campus Ministry, University of St. Thomas
- Schroeder, Allan, St. Mark, Shakopee
- Seaton, James B., St. Peter, Mendota
- Semlak, Thomas L., St. Casimir, St. Paul
- Shambour, Leonard, St. Wenceslaus, New Prague
- Shupe, Russell, St. Michael, Prior Lake
- Smith, James, (Retired)
- Smith, Robert B., Assumption, Richfield
- Stickney, Stephen S., Sabbatical
- Stiles, Thomas G., St. Columba, St. Paul
- Stipe, Bruce, On Leave of Absence
- Straub, Arthur J., On Leave of Absence
- Stromen, Sherman, St. Mary of the Lake, White Bear Lake
- Swirtz, Lawrence, (Retired)
- Tangney, Francis J., St. Joseph, Hopkins
- Tatone, Paul M., St. Thomas Becket, Eagan
- Thell, Frank J., St. Paul Police Chap.
- Thill, Joseph, St. Mary of the Lake, White Bear Lake
- Thornton, James, St. Mary, Shakopee
- Tift, J. Neil, Cathedral, St. Paul
- Trombley, Robert, On Leave of Absence
- Umphress, William G., Holy Spirit, St. Paul
- Urbanski, Roger G., (Retired)
- Valdez, Carl R., Hispanic Ministry
- Veiman, John, Presentation, Maplewood
- Vivier, Louis J., On Leave of Absence
- Wagner, James M., St. William, Fridley
- Wagner, Robert C., St. Hubert, Chanhassen
- Warhol, Robert W., Nativity of B.V.M., Bloomington
- Warne, Maynard E., St. Michael, St. Michael
- Weiland, John D., Our Lady of Peace, MN
- Wesley, R. Daniel, Immaculate Conception, Faribault
- Wierschem, Joseph G., Holy Name, Medina
- Wilkinson, Delvin L., On Leave of Absence
- Williams, Merlin J., St. Walburga, Fletcher; St. Martin, Rogers
- Winkelman, John W., Ascension, Minneapolis
- Winn, Luther E., (Retired)
- Wirtz, Howard, St. Joseph's Home for Children
- Wittman, Wayne C., Sacred Heart, St. Paul
- Witucki, Richard P., St. Bartholomew, Wayzata
- Yaeger, Loren, On Leave of Absence
- Yang, Naokao, St. Adalbert, St. Paul
- Yekaldo, Fred D., St. Ambrose, St. Paul

INSTITUTIONS LOCATED IN THE ARCHDIOCESE

[A] SEMINARIES, ARCHDIOCESAN

ST. PAUL. *St. John Vianney Seminary*, 2115 Summit Ave., 55105. Tel: 612-962-6825; Fax: 612-962-6835.
E-mail: pfchristense@stl
Rev. Peter F. Christensen, Rector. Spiritual Directors-Counselors: Revs. Paul D. Sirba; John Ubel, Counselor; Mrs. Theresa Thurmes, Apostolic Life Coord.; John Daniewicz, D.R.E.; Rev. Kevin T. Connor, Spiritual Dir. Priests 4; Lay Teachers 2; Students 92.

The Saint Paul Seminary, School of Divinity of the University of St. Thomas, 2260 Summit Ave., 55105. Tel: 612-962-5050; Fax: 612-962-5790.
E-mail: vjklimoski@stthomas.edu
Web site: www.stthomas.edu/www/sod_http/seminary/index.htm
Legal Title: *The Saint Paul Seminary*. Rev. Phillip J. Rask, Ph.D., Rector; Mrs. Jan Viktora, M.A., Asst. Academic Dean; Revs. Dominic Serra, S.L.D.; Thomas Krenik, D.Min., Spiritual Dir.; Jerome M. Dittberner, S.T.D.; Paul F. Feela, M.A., Dir. Worship; Peter E. Feldmeier, Ph.D.; Ms. Mary Martin, M.A., Theological Librarian; Revs. James R. Motl, O.P., Ph.D.; Ronald Bowers, J.C.D., Vice Rector; Dr. Thomas Fisch, Ph.D.; Dr. Victor J. Klimoski, Ph.D., Academic Dean; Rev. John Echert, S.S.L.; Sr. Christine Athans, B.V.M., Ph.D.; Dr. Gene Scapanski, S.T.D.; Rev. William C. McDonough, S.T.D.; Sr. Carol Rennie, O.S.B., M.A., Dir. Student Life; Dr. David Jenkins, D.Mus., Dir. Liturgical Music; Sr. Paul Therese Saiko, S.S.N.D., M.A.; Sr. Katarina Schuth, O.S.F., Ph.D.; Rev. Douglas E. Dandurand. MDIV/Seminarians 79; MDIV/non-Sems 4; Pastoral Studies Division 59; Pastoral Studies (non-degree) 6; Doctor of Ministry 29 ; Priests 13; Sisters 4; Lay Staff 23.

[B] SEMINARIES, RELIGIOUS, OR SCHOLASTICATES

ST. PAUL. *Jesuit Novitiate*, 1035 Summit Ave., 55105. Tel: 612-224-5593; Fax: 612-224-4734.
E-mail: mhartersj@compuserve.com
Revs. Michael G. Harter, S.J., Supr. and Novice Director; John M. Paul, S.J., Novice Dir.; Bro. John J. Masterson, S.J., Asst. to Novice Dir. Priests 2; Brothers 1; Novices 22.

[C] COLLEGES AND UNIVERSITIES

ST. PAUL. *College of St. Catherine*, 2004 Randolph Ave., 55105. Tel: 612-690-6000.
Web site: www.stkate.edu
For a complete listing, refer to the Colleges and Universities section.

University of St. Thomas, 2115 Summit Ave., 55105. Tel: 612-962-5000; Fax: 612-962-6504
For a complete listing, refer to the Colleges and Universities section.

MINNEAPOLIS. *The College of St. Catherine-Minneapolis*, 601 25th Ave. S., 55454. Tel: 612-690-7702.
E-mail: dajohnson@stkate.edu
Web site: http://www.stkate.edu
For a complete listing, refer to the Colleges and Universities section.

[D] HIGH SCHOOLS, PAROCHIAL

ST. PAUL. High Schools are maintained in the following parishes (for particulars refer to the individual parish). City of St. Paul: St. Agnes, St. Bernard.

[E] HIGH SCHOOLS, ARCHDIOCESAN

ST. PAUL. *Hill-Murray School*. (Grades 7-12), 2625 Larpenteur Ave. E., 55109-5098; Fax: 612-770-5262. Joseph M. Peschges, Pres. Lay Teachers 58; Students 888.

The Saint Thomas Academy, 55120. Tel: 612-454-4570.
E-mail: jgreving@eta.k12.mn.us
Web site: www.cadets.com
Mr. John B. Greving, Headmaster. Lay Professors 64; Students 683.

MINNEAPOLIS. *DeLaSalle High School*, Christian Brothers, One De La Salle Dr., 55401.
E-mail: info@delasalle.com
Web site: www.delasalle.com
Bro. Michael Collins, F.S.C., Pres.; Barry C. Lieske, Prin. Priests 1; Brothers 6; Sisters 1; Lay Teachers 24; Students 410.

Totino-Grace High School, 1350 Gardena Ave., N.E., 55432. Tel: 612-571-9116.
Web site: http://www.eta.k12.mn.us/~wmtotino/

Bro. Milton Barker, F.S.C., Pres.; Kathleen M. Murphy, Prin. Brothers 2; Lay Teachers 62; Students 1,050.

ST. LOUIS PARK. *Benilde-St. Margaret's School*, 2501 Hwy. 100 S., 55416. Tel: 612-927-4176.
Web site: http:www.bsm.pvt.k12.mn.us
Mr. James F. Hamburge, Pres.; Mr. Robert C. Tift, Prin.; Mary Andersen, Asst. Prin. Sisters 1; Lay Teachers 70; Students 980.

[F] HIGH SCHOOLS, PRIVATE

ST. PAUL. *Convent of the Visitation School.* Day School for Girls grades 7-12; coed grades PreK-6. 2455 Visitation Dr., 55120. Tel: 612-683-1700; Fax: 612-454-7144.
E-mail: adoffice@etz.k12.ma.us
K. Michele Clarke, Head of School. Sisters 3; Lay Teachers 60; Students 537.

Cretin-Derham Hall, 550 S. Albert St., 55116. Tel: 612-690-2443; Fax: 612-696-3393. Co-Sponsors: Brothers of the Christian Schools and Sisters of St. Joseph of Carondelet. Richard Engler, Pres. & Prin. Sisters 2; Brothers 1; Lay Teachers 71; Students 1,260.

EXCELSIOR. *The Southwest Metro Catholic High School*, 34 Water St., Ste. #2, 55331. Tel: 612-559-4443. Robert J. Roy, Chm.; Theo Chalgren, Vice Chm.; Dianna Goebel, Sec.; Sr. Ann Ganley, Prin.

FARIBAULT. *Bethlehem Academy*, 55021. Tel: 507-334-3948. Sisters 2; Lay Teachers 16; Students 200.

Faribault B.A., Inc., 55021. Tel: 507-334-3948. Sisters of St. Dominic (Sinsinawa, WI). Sisters 2; Lay Teachers 16; Students 200.

RICHFIELD. *Academy of Holy Angels*, 6600 Nicollet Ave., S., 55423-2498. Tel: 612-798-2600; Fax: 612-798-2610.
E-mail: jmacneil@holyangels.pvt.k12-mn.us
Dr. Jill M. Reilly, Prin. Priests 1; Sisters 3; Lay Teachers 50; Students 700.

[G] ELEMENTARY SCHOOLS, PRIVATE

MENDOTA HEIGHTS. *Convent of the Visitation School*, 2455 Visitation Dr., 55120. Tel: 612-454-6474; Fax: 612-454-7144. K. Michele Clarke, Head of School. Sisters of The Visitation of Holy Mary 1; Lay Teachers 29; Students 244.

[H] ELEMENTARY SCHOOLS, CONSOLIDATED, PAROCHIAL

ST. PAUL. *Highland Catholic School.* (Grades K-8), 2017 Bohland Ave., 55116.
E-mail: highland@winternet.com
Lay Teachers 25; Students 487. Serving the parishes of St. Leo, St. Therese and St. Gregory.

IHM/St. Luke's Consolidated School. (Grades PreK-8), 1065 Summit Ave., 55105. Tel: 612-224-4836; Fax: 612-224-0097. Sisters 2; Lay Teachers 25; Students 405. Serving the parishes of Immaculate Heart of Mary and St. Luke.

Trinity Catholic School, 835 E. Fifth St., 55106. Sisters 2; Lay Teachers 17; Students 314. Serving the parishes of Sacred Heart, St. Casimir and St. Patrick.

MINNEAPOLIS. *Northeast Regional Catholic School*, 1630 Fourth St, N.E., 55413; Fax: 612-789-8773. Sisters 2; Lay Teachers 15; Students 229. Serving the parishes of St. Cyril & Methodius, Holy Cross, St. Anthony, All Saints, Our Lady of Lourdes, St. Hedwig, St. Clement, St. Boniface, St. Maron, St. Constantine, Our Lady of Mt. Carmel and St. Lawrence.

Risen Christ Catholic School. (Grades K-2), East Campus: 1120 E. 37th St., 53407. Tel: 612-729-2336. Sisters 1; Lay Teachers 8; Students 199. (Grades 3-8), West Campus: 3800 Pleasant Ave., 55409. Tel: 612-822-5329. Sisters 1; Lay Teachers 14; Students 276. Serving the parishes of Holy Name, Holy Rosary, Incarnation, St. Albert the Great and St. Stephen.

EAGAN. *Faithful Shepherd Catholic School*, 4030 Pilot Knob Rd., 55122. Tel: 612-452-4550; Fax: 612-452-4550. Revs. Kevin I. Clinton, Pres.; Robert M. Schwartz, Vice Pres.; Margie Judd, Sec.; Robert Cass, Treas. Serving the parishes of St. Peter, St. John Neumann and St. Thomas Becket.

FARIBAULT. *Consolidated Catholic School of Faribault.* (Grades PreK-6), 15 S.W. Third Ave., 55021. Lay Teachers 20; Students 368. Serving the parishes of Immaculate Conception, St. Lawrence and Sacred Heart.

HASTINGS. *St. Elizabeth Ann Seton School*, 600 Tyler St., 55033. Mrs. Barbara Vergenz, Admin. Lay Teachers 24; Students 475.

HOPKINS. *John Ireland Schools.* (Grades PreK-8), 1320 Main Street, 55343. Tel: 612-938-3442. Sisters 2; Lay Teachers 21; Students 244. Serving the parishes of St. John the Evangelist, St. Joseph and Immaculate Heart of Mary.

LONSDALE. *Lonsdale, New Market, Veseli Area Catholic School*, 108 First Ave., S.E., P.O. Box 10, 55046. Sisters 1; Lay Teachers 11; Students 198. Serving the parishes of Veseli, New Market and Lonsdale.

RICHFIELD. *Blessed Trinity Catholic School of Richfield, Minnesota*, 7540 Penn Ave., S., 55423. Tel: 612-866-6906. Rev. Gregory L. Esty, Pres. Lay Teachers 20; Students 450. Serving the parishes of Assumption, St. Peter's and St. Richard's.

SHAKOPEE. *Shakopee Area Catholic School.* (Grades PreK-8), 305 S. Scott, 55379. Tel: 612-445-3387. Notre Dame Sisters 1; Lay Teachers 21; Students 509. Serving the parishes of St. Mark, St. Mary, St. Mary of the Purification.

STILLWATER. *St. Croix Catholic Educational Programs*, 611 S. 3rd St., 55082. Tel: 612-439-4400. Rev. Michael C. Skluzacek, Pres. Lay Teachers 21; Students 391. Serving the parishes of St. Michael's, St. Mary's, and St. Charles.

St. Croix Catholic School. (Grades K-8), 621 S. Third St., 55082. Tel: 612-439-5581. Mr. Marty Weisbeck, Prin. Lay Teachers 21; Students 397. Serving the parishes of St. Charles, Bayport; St. Mary, Stillwater; St. Michael, Stillwater.

[I] HOMES FOR CHILDREN

MINNEAPOLIS. *St. Joseph's Home for Children*, 1121 E. 46th St., 55407. Tel: 612-827-6241
For a complete listing, refer to the Special Care Facilities section.

[J] GENERAL HOSPITALS

HASTINGS. *Regina Medical Center*, 1175 Nininger Rd., 55033. Tel: 612-480-4100
For a complete listing, refer to the Hospitals section.

NEW PRAGUE. *Queen of Peace Hospital*, 302 Second St., N.E., 56071. Tel: 612-758-4431; Fax: 612-758-5009.
Web site: http://www.np.k12.mn.us/~qofp.htm
For a complete listing, refer to the Hospitals section.

SHAKOPEE. *St. Francis Regional Medical Center*, 1455 St. Francis Ave., 55379. Tel: 612-403-3000; Fax: 612-403-3820
For a complete listing, refer to the Hospitals section.

[K] SPECIAL HOSPITALS AND SANATORIA FOR INVALIDS

ST. PAUL. *Our Lady of Good Counsel Home*, 2076 St. Anthony Ave., 55104. Tel: 612-646-2797
For a complete listing, refer to the Special Care Facilities section.

[L] SOCIAL SERVICE AGENCIES

ST. PAUL. *Home of the Good Shepherd*, 5100 Hodgson Rd., 55126. Tel: 612-484-0221; Fax: 612-486-1616. Helen Chargo, Admin. Diversified programs providing services for women and children. Sisters 6; Lay Staff 23.

[M] HOMES FOR AGED

ST. PAUL. *Bethany Convent for Retired Sisters*, 1870 Randolph, 55105. Tel: 612-690-7050
For a complete listing, refer to the Special Care Facilities section.

Franciscan Health Community, 1925 Norfolk Ave., 55116. Tel: 612-696-8400
For a complete listing, refer to the Special Care Facilities section.

Holy Family Residence, 330 S. Exchange St., 55102. Tel: 612-227-0336
For a complete listing, refer to the Special Care Facilities section.

HASTINGS. *Regina Convalescent and Nursing Care and Retirement Center*, 55033. Tel: 612-480-4333
For a complete listing, refer to the Special Care Facilities section.

[N] MONASTERIES AND RESIDENCES OF PRIESTS AND BROTHERS

ST. PAUL. *Oblate Provincial Offices*, 267 E. Eighth St., 55101. Tel: 612-292-8622; Fax: 612-292-8769. Revs. David A. Kalert, O.M.I., Prov.; Thomas J. Singer, O.M.I., Personnel Dir.; Robert F. Moosbrugger, O.M.I., Treas. Total Staff 3.

Oblate Residence, 104 N. Mississippi River Blvd., 55104. Tel: 612-645-3560. Bro. Gerald Decker, O.M.I., Dir. of House; Revs. William P. Clark, O.M.I.; Edward C. Coleman, O.M.I.; James L. Datko, O.M.I.; Donald L. Dietz; Rene P. DuFour, O.M.I.; Terence J. Figel, O.M.I.; William E. Hagen, O.M.I.; Thomas J. Hayes, O.M.I.; Michael J. Hussey, O.M.I.; Maynard C. Kegler, O.M.I.; Thomas M. Killeen, O.M.I.; Charles Prass, O.M.I.; John F. Louis, O.M.I.; Leo M. Miller, O.M.I.; William E. Nadeau, O.M.I.; James J. Pillar, O.M.I.; Dale M. Schlitt, O.M.I.; John A. Weissler, O.M.I.; Jerome A. Ward, O.M.I.; Paul W. Wilhelm, O.M.I.; James J. Wynne, O.M.I. In res. Revs. David A. Kalert, O.M.I., Prov.; Thomas J. Singer, O.M.I.; Paul Ischler, O.M.I.; John E. Pilaczynski, O.M.I.; Stanley Sergot, O.M.I.; Robert F. Moosbrugger, O.M.I.

Special Assignments: Military Chaplains: Rev. Terence J. Figel, O.M.I., Chaplaincy, 1461 Starlifter Cir., Scott AFB, IL, 62225.

MINNEAPOLIS. *La Storta Jesuit Community*, 2201 Pillsbury Ave., S., 55404. Tel: 612-871-1612; Fax: 612-871-0947. Revs. Dennis R. Karamitis, S.J.; Robert H. Fitzgerald, S.J.; Matthew L. Linn, S.J., Supr.; Robert P. Neenan, S.J.; Joseph N. Pershe, S.J.; Aloysius F. Schmitz, S.J.; Francis J. Burke, S.J.; Thomas G. Boedy, S.J.; Leon F. Klimczyk, S.J.; John A. Mazzitello, S.J.; John M. Ginsterblum, S.J.; Bro. Lee A. McNamee, S.J.

Maryknoll Fathers and Brothers, Catholic Foreign Mission Society of America, 10345 Portland Ave. S., 55420. Tel: 612-884-7743; Fax: 612-884-7744. Rev. Dennis T. Dunne, Dir.

Paulist Fathers, 1201 Fifth St., S.E., 55414. Tel: 612-331-7941; Fax: 612-378-1771. Revs. John J. Behnke, C.S.P.; Wilfred A. Brimley, C.S.P., (Retired); Charles A. Martin, C.S.P.; James F. Wiesner, C.S.P. Total in Residence 4.

St. Albert the Great Priory, 2833 32nd Ave., S., 55406. Tel: 612-724-3644; Fax: 612-724-5057.
E-mail: domcom@mn.uswest.com
Rev. Charles M. Santoro, O.P., Prior. Order of Preachers (Dominicans). Province of St. Albert the Great. Total in Residence 11.

ANOKA. *Crosier Community of Anoka*, 516 School St., 55303-2349. Tel: 612-421-7115. In res. Revs. William Deziel, O.S.C.; Dale Ettel, O.S.C.; David E. Gallus, O.S.C.; Edward Greiwe, O.S.C.; Kenneth Opat, O.S.C., Supr.; Michael Paquet, O.S.C.; Eugene D. Plaisted, O.S.C.; Michael Van Sloun, O.S.C., St. Mary's International School, 1-6-19, Seta Setagaya-Ku, Tokyo, 158, Japan. Tel: 81-3-3707-3416. In res. Revs. Lyle Ehmke, O.S.C.; Jim Hermann, O.S.C. Total in Residence 8; Total Staff 10.

SHOREVIEW. *Crosier Community of Shoreview*, 3500 Vivian Ave., 55126-3852. Tel: 612-490-3352.
E-mail: crosier.org
Revs. Jerome Schik, O.S.C.; Dale Ehrman, O.S.C.; Marven Tellers, O.S.C.; Richard McGuire, O.S.C.; Thomas O'Brien, O.S.C.; Thomas Carkhuff, O.S.C.; Kermit Holl, O.S.C.

Crosier Provincial House Province of St. Odilia, 3470 Vivian Ave., 55126. Tel: 612-787-0832.
E-mail: jneville@crosier.org
In res. Very Rev. John J. Neville, O.S.C., Prov.

[O] CONVENTS AND RESIDENCES FOR SISTERS

ST. PAUL. *Contemplative Sisters of the Good Shepherd*, 5104 Hodgson Rd., 55126-1229. Tel: 612-482-5240. Sr. Teresita Mater, Supr. Sisters 15.

Convent of the Good Shepherd, 5100 Hodgson Rd., 55126-1297. Tel: 612-484-0221; Fax: 612-486-1600. Sr. Joan Spiering, Pres. Sisters of the Good Shepherd 36. Contemplative Sisters of the Good Shepherd, 5104 Hodgson Rd., 55126-1229. Tel: 612-482-5240; Fax: 612-486-1600. Sisters 23.

Franciscan Sisters of Little Falls, MN (O.S.F.), 727 E. Margaret St., 55106. Tel: 612-772-1740. Sr. Jean Schwieters, O.S.F., Formation Min. Professed 3; Novices 1.

Franciscan Sisters of St. Paul, Franciscan Regional Center, 1388 Prior Ave., S., 55116. Tel: 612-690-1501; Fax: 612-690-2509. Sr. Antonice Delury, O.S.F., Reg. Dir. Sisters 12.

Monastery of the Visitation, 2455 Visitation Dr., 55120. Tel: 612-683-1700. Sr. Mary Denise Villaume, V.H.M., Supr. Visitation Nuns 20.

St. Mary's Mission House, 265 Century Ave., 55125. Tel: 612-738-9704. Missionary Sisters of St. Peter Claver. Sr. Maria Moryl, S.S.P.C., Supr. Sisters 13; Novices 1.

St. Paul's Monastery, 2675 Larpenteur Ave., E., 55109-5097. Tel: 612-777-8181; Fax: 612-777-4442.
E-mail: mfujan@usinternet.com
Benedictine Sisters of Pontifical Jurisdiction. Sr. Marie Fujan, O.S.B., Prioress; Sr. Mary Lou Dummer, O.S.B., Subprioress. Sisters 89.

Sisters of St. Joseph of Carondelet, 1884 Randolph Ave., 55105. Tel: 612-690-7000; Fax: 612-690-7039. Province Leadership Team: Sr. Margaret Belanger, C.S.J.; Sr. Margaret L. Kvasnicka, C.S.J.; Sr. Ann V. Walton, C.S.J. Sisters of Province 473; Total Staff 91.

Carondelet Center; St. Joseph School of Music; Suzuki Talent Education School for Strings; Editorial Development Associates; Project One-Fifty; Sisters Care; Free Store; Derham Community; Vineyard; Carondelet LifeCare Ministries/St. Mary's Health Clinics; Youth & Family Center, Inc.; Holy Family Hospital; Carondelet LifeCare Corporation; Sisters of St. Joseph of Carondelet Ministries Foundation, St. Paul Province; Learning in Style; INSTEP, Women at the Well; Adult Literacy; The College of St. Catherine; Minnesota Center for Health Care Ethics; Wisdom Ways: A Resource Center for Spirituality.

Sisters of the Good Shepherd - St. Paul Province, 5100 Hodgson Rd., 55126. Tel: 612-484-0221; Fax: 612-486-1611. Sr. Joan Spiering, Prov. Supr.

MINNEAPOLIS. *Congregation of the Handmaids of the Holy Child Jesus*, 1707 Bryant Ave., S., 55411. Tel: 612-521-3127. Sr. Mary Angela Ihiat, Pres.; Sr. Rosemary I. Essien, Vice Pres.; Sr. Regina Nworah, Sec. & Treas.; Sr. Geraldine Inyang; Sr. Anne Egen. Total in Residence 5.

St. Clare's Monastery of the Infant Jesus, 8650 Russell Ave. S., 55431-1998. Tel: 612-881-4766.
E-mail: mmewhorter@juno.com
Sr. Helen Weier, O.S.C., Abbess. Franciscan Poor Clare Nuns. Professed Nuns 13.

Visitation Monastery of Minneapolis, 1527 Fremont Ave., N., 55411. Tel: 612-521-6113. Sr. Mary Francis Reis, V.H.M., Supr.

LAKE ELMO. *Carmel of Our Lady of Divine Providence*, 8251 De Montreville Tr. N., 55042-9547. Tel: 612-777-3882. Sr. Paula of the Eucharist, O.C.D., Prioress; Rev. John M. Burns, Chap. Discalced Carmelite Nuns. Professed 10; Postulants 1; Novices 3.

WAYZATA. *Franciscan Clarist Congregation, F.C.C.*, Vimala Province, Convent of St. Therese House, 17931 Minnetonka Blvd., 55391. Tel: 612-473-4771. Sr. Mary Vandanakara, Coord. Total in Residence 6.

[P] SECULAR INSTITUTES

ST. PAUL. *Missionaries of the Kingship of Christ*, The Chancery, 226 Summit Ave., 55102. Tel: 612-291-4400. Sr. M. Dominica Brennan, O.P. Secular Institute of Pontifical Right for women and men founded in Italy in 1919.

[Q] RETREAT HOUSES AND CENTERS OF SPIRITUALITY

ST. PAUL. *Benedictine Center - St. Paul's Monastery*, 2675 E. Larpenteur Ave., 55109. Tel: 612-777-7251; Fax: 612-777-4442. Patricia Roberts, Dir. Total Staff 6.

Catholic Youth Ministry Services, 328 W. Kellogg, 55102. Tel: 612-291-4500. Mr. Gregory T. Weinand, Dir.

Loyola, 389 N. Oxford St., 55104. Tel: 612-641-0008. Revs. Richard M. Rice, S.J.; Frederic A. Maples, S.J.; Sr. Elizabeth Kerwin, C.S.J., Dir. Total Staff 8.

Maryhill, 1988 Summit Ave., 55105. Tel: 612-696-2970. Daughters of the Heart of Mary Sisters 14; Total in Residence 3; Total Staff 4.

BUFFALO. *Christ the King Retreat Center*, 621 First Ave., S., 55313. Tel: 612-682-3453. Revs. Aloysius Svobodny, O.M.I.; John H. McManus, O.M.I.; Raymond R. Kirtz, O.M.I.; James D. Deegan, O.M.I., Dir.; Don Joseph Paris, O.M.I.; Bro. Anthony Szklarski, O.M.I., Bus. Mgr. Total in Residence 6; Total Staff 24.

FRONTENAC. *Villa Maria Center*, 29847 County Blvd. 2, 55026. Tel: 612-345-4582.
E-mail: villajam@aol.com
Sr. Carolyn Marie Brockland, O.S.U., Prioress; Sr. Chabanel Mathison, O.S.U., Dir. Ursuline Sisters of the Roman Union 14.

LAKE ELMO. *Jesuit Retreat House*, 8243 Demontreville Tr., N., 55042-9546. Tel: 612-777-1311. Revs. Gerald E. Goetz, S.J., Dir.; Edward S. Sthokal, S.J., Asst. Total in Residence 2; Total Staff 5.

MARINE ON ST. CROIX. *Christian Brothers Retreat Center*, 15525 St. Croix Tr., N., 55047. Tel: 612-433-2486. Bro. Charles Kelly, F.S.C., Admin. Total in Residence 7; Total Staff 12.

PRIOR LAKE. *Franciscan Retreat House*, 16385 Saint Francis Ln., 55372. Tel: 612-447-2182. Revs. Ken Bartsch, O.F.M.Conv., Guardian & Retreat Dir.; Mark F. Mindrup, O.F.M.Conv.; Ambrose Finnegan, O.F.M.Conv.; Simeon Yates, O.F.M.Conv.; Ronald Mrozinski, O.F.M.Conv.; Francisco Gomez, O.F.M.Conv.; Thomas Smith, O.F.M.Conv.

WAYZATA. *Cenacle Retreat House*, 1221 Wayzata Blvd., 55391-1942. Tel: 612-473-7308. Sr. Laura Koberlein, r.c., Supr.; Sr. Mary Peters, r.c., Coord. of Ministry; Rev. Matthew L. Linn, S.J. Cenacle Religious 4; Lay Directors 50.

[R] HOMES FOR DISABLED

ST. PAUL. *Our House of Minnesota, Inc. I*, 1846 Dayton Ave., 55104. Tel: 612-644-6650
For a complete listing, refer to the Special Care Facilities section.

Our House of Minnesota, Inc. II, 1846 Portland, 55104. Tel: 612-644-2411
For a complete listing, refer to the Special Care Facilities section.

WEST ST. PAUL. *Guild Incorporated*, 1025 Dodd Rd., 55118. Tel: 612-450-2220
For a complete listing, refer to the Special Care Facilities section.

[S] MINNESOTA CATHOLIC CONFERENCE (M.C.C.)

ST. PAUL. *Minnesota Catholic Conference*, 475 University Ave. W., Ste. B, 55103. Tel: 612-227-8777; Fax: 612-227-2675.
E-mail: mmmm@connectinc.com
Rev. David F. McCauley (FAR), Exec. Dir.; Thomas J. Pearson, Dir. Education Dept.; Timothy J. Rudnicki, Dir. Social Concerns Dept. Total Staff 7. The M.C.C. is a Minnesota Corporation, the purpose of which is to promote the general welfare of the people of the State of Minnesota. All Catholic Bishops of the State of Minnesota constitute Ex Officio the Board of Directors.

[T] ASSOCIATIONS OF THE FAITHFUL

ST. PAUL. *The Companions of Christ*, 2137 Marshall Ave., 55104. Tel: 612-642-5933.
E-mail: frcozzens@msn.com
Jeffrey Huard, Mod. Total in Residence 14.

Franciscan Brothers of Peace, Inc., Queen of Peace Friary, 1289 Lafond Ave., 55104. Tel: 612-646-8586. Bros. Michael Gaworski, F.B.P., Founder; Paul O'Donnell, F.B.P., Guardian Overall. Total Assisted 20; Total in Residence 10; Total Staff 2.

LAKE ELMO. *Hermits of the Most Blessed Virgin Mary of Mount Carmel*, 8249 De Montreville Tr., N., 55042-9545. Tel: 612-779-7351. Carmel of the Blessed Virgin Mary. Revs. John M. Burns, Prior; Joseph V. Vaccaro. Priests 2; Brothers 4.

WEST ST. PAUL. *Community of Christ the Redeemer*, 110 Crusader Ave., 55118. Tel: 612-451-6114. Mr. James C. Kolar, Pres.

NET Ministries, Inc., 110 Crusader Ave., W., 55118-4427. Tel: 612-450-6833; Fax: 612-450-9984.
E-mail: ministry@netusa.org
Mr. Mark Berchem, Exec. Dir. Total Staff 24.

[U] CAMPS AND COMMUNITY CENTERS

ST. PAUL. *Catholic Youth Ministry Services*, 328 W. Kellogg, 55102. Tel: 612-290-1644. Mr. Gregory T. Weinand, Dir.

MCGREGOR. *Catholic Youth Camps, Inc.* Mailing Address: Administrative Office: 2131 Fairview Ave. N., Ste. 200, Roseville, 55113. Tel: 612-636-1645.
E-mail: cyccamp@juno.com
Mr. Jerome J. Meeds, Camp. Dir., Location: HCR 3, Box 655, 55760. Tel: 218-426-3383. Total Assisted 1,535; Total Staff 55.

[V] NEWMAN CENTERS

MINNEAPOLIS. *University of Minnesota Newman Center and Chapel*, 1701 University Ave., S.E., 55414. Tel: 612-331-3437.
E-mail: newmancc@tc.umn.edu
Web site: http://umn.edu/home/newmancc/
Rev. Charles A. Martin, C.S.P., Dir.; Rose Mary Boyd, Admin. Campus Ministers: Sr. Jeri Cashman, O.P.; Bro. Fintan Moore, C.F.C.; Tom Conry. Total Staff 5.

[W] MISCELLANEOUS LISTINGS

ST. PAUL. *Carondelet Lifecare Ministries/St. Mary's Health Clinics*, 1884 Randolph Ave., 55105-1700. Tel: 612-690-7020. Sr. Mary Madonna Ashton, Pres. Neighborhood Clinics 11; Patient visits 4,413; Total Staff 11.

**Catholic Community Foundation in the Archdiocese of St. Paul and Minneapolis*, 328 W. Kellogg Blvd., 55102. Tel: 612-290-1613; Fax: 612-290-1609.
E-mail: ccfendow@archspm.org
Mr. James Mullin, Exec. Dir.

Christian Brothers Youth Home, 1540 Lincoln Ave., 55105. Tel: 612-699-0736. Bro. Michael Lee Anderson, F.S.C., Dir.; Mr. Pat McGuire. Total Assisted 12; Total Staff 2.

The Highland Catholic Community, 2055 Bohland Ave., 55116. Tel: 612-698-5581. Rev. Gerald G. Grieman, Pres.; Thomas P. Hunstiger, Vice Pres.; Mr. John Hannahan, Sec.

Missionary Oblates of Mary Immaculate, 267 E. Eighth St., 55101. Tel: 612-292-8622. Legal Title: *Missionary Oblates of Mary Immaculate Central United States Province - Continuity of Care Charitable Trust.*

Nativity of Our Lord Endowment Fund, 1900 Wellesley Ave., 55105. Tel: 612-699-0309; Fax: 612-696-5458. Rev. Patrick D. Lannan, Vice Pres. Total Assisted 2,000; Total Staff 15.

Oblate Media and Communication Corporation, 267 E. Eighth St., 55101. Tel: 612-292-8622. Rev. David A. Kalert, O.M.I., Pres. Oblates of Mary Immaculate, Central U.S. Province.

St. Joseph's Hospital Sponsor, Inc., 1884 Randolph Ave., 55105. Sr. Mary Madonna Ashton, C.S.J., Pres.

Sisters of St. Joseph of Carondelet Ministries Foundation, St. Paul Province, 1884 Randolph Ave., 55105. Tel: 612-690-7026. Sr. Irene O'Neill, C.S.J., Exec. Dir.

Trinity Catholic School, 835 E. 5th St., 55106.

MINNEAPOLIS. *Catholic Eldercare, Inc.*, 817 Main St., N.E., 55413. Tel: 612-379-1370. Michael J. Shasky, COO.
Skilled Nursing Facility, 150 Beds; Assisted Living Apartments for Elderly Adults, 52 Units; Home Health Care for the Elderly, 250 Assisted. Total Assisted 500; Total Staff 300.

**Samaritan Homes, Inc.*, 4639 Blaisdell Ave., S., 55409. Tel: 612-824-2911. Bros. Paul O'Donnell, F.B.P., Pres.; Anthony Sweere, F.B.P., Vice Pres. & Sec.; Dominic Marie Hart, F.B.P., Guardian.

To Encounter Christ of the Archdiocese of St. Paul-Minneapolis, Minnesota, Inc., 1201 S.E. Fifth St., 55414. Tel: 612-331-3644. Pam Germscheid DeMorett, Prog. Coord. Total Staff 1.

Twin Cities Catholic Alumni Club, Mailing Address: P.O. Box 581321, 55458-1321. Tel: 612-338-1288. Teddi Tri, Club Pres.

Youth and Family Center Inc., 4405 E. Lake St., 55406. Sr. Martha Merriman, C.S.J., Dir.; Sr. Betty Wurm, C.S.J., Dir. Counseling Center. Total Assisted 50; Total Staff 3.

MAPLEWOOD. *Maple Tree: Priory Childcare Center*, 1695 Century Ave., N., 55109. Tel: 612-770-0766. Sr. Marie Fujan, Prioress - St. Paul Priory; Sr. Mary Lou Dummer, Pres. Total Assisted 67; Total Staff 21.

SHAKOPEE. *St. Gertrude's Health Center*, 1850 Sarazin St., 55379. Tel: 612-403-3499. Ron Gilsrud, Admin.; Barry J. Halm, CEO; David H. Amundson, Treas.

SHOREVIEW. *Crosier Missions*, 3510 Vivian Ave., 55126-3852. Tel: 612-486-7456.
E-mail: dgallus@crosier.org
Rev. David E. Gallus, O.S.C., Dir. Total Staff 1.

WEST ST. PAUL. *St. Paul's Outreach, Inc.*, 110 Crusader Ave., 55118. Tel: 612-451-6114. Mr. Gordon C. DeMarais, Pres.; Dr. James C. Kolar, Vice Pres.; Patrick D. Menke, Sec. & Treas.

RELIGIOUS INSTITUTES OF MEN REPRESENTED IN THE ARCHDIOCESE

For further details refer to the corresponding bracketed number in the Religious Institutes of Men or Women section.

[0200]—*Benedictine Monks.* (St. John's Abbey).—O.S.B.
[0330]—*Brothers of the Christian Schools.* (Winona Province).—F.S.C.
[0400]—*Canons Regular of the Order of the Holy Cross.*—O.S.C.
[0470]—*The Capuchin Fathers.* (Prov. of St. Joseph).—O.F.M.Cap.
[0480]—*Conventual Franciscans.* (Prov. of Our Lady of Consolation).—O.F.M.Conv.
[0520]—*Franciscan Friars.* (Prov. of Sacred Heart).—O.F.M.
[0690]—*Jesuit Fathers and Brothers.* (Wisconsin Prov.).—S.J.
[0780]—*Marist Fathers.* (American Prov.).—S.M.
[0800]—*Maryknoll.*—M.M.
[0720]—*The Missionaries of Our Lady of La Salette.*—M.S.
[0910]—*Oblate Fathers of Mary Immaculate.* (Central Prov.).—O.M.I.
[0430]—*Order of Preachers (Dominicans).* (Prov. of St. Albert the Great).—O.P.
[1030]—*Paulist Fathers.*—C.S.P.
[1070]—*Redemptorist Fathers.* (St. Louis Prov.).—C.SS.R.
[1060]—*Society of the Precious Blood.* (Cincinnati Prov.).—C.PP.S.
[0560]—*Third Order Regular of St. Francis.* (Prov. of the Immaculate Conception).—T.O.R.
[]—*Vincentian Congregation.* (India).—V.C.

RELIGIOUS INSTITUTES OF WOMEN REPRESENTED IN THE ARCHDIOCESE

[0230]—*Benedictine Sisters of Pontifical Jurisdiction.* (Crookston, St. Paul, St. Joseph, Duluth, MN).—O.S.B.
[3110]—*Congregation of Our Lady of the Retreat in the Cenacle.*—R.C.
[3710]—*Congregation of the Sisters of St. Agnes.*—C.S.A.
[1780]—*Congregation of the Sisters of the Third Order of St. Francis of Perpetual Adoration.* (Eastern Region).—F.S.P.A.
[0810]—*Daughters of the Heart of Mary.*—D.H.M.
[0420]—*Discalced Carmelite Nuns.*—O.C.D.
[1070-03]—*Dominican Sisters.*—O.P.
[1070-10]—*Dominican Sisters.*—O.P.
[1070-23]—*Dominican Sisters.*—O.P.
[1170]—*Felician Sisters.*—C.S.S.F.
[1310]—*Franciscan Sisters of Little Falls, Minnesota.*—O.S.F.
[1485]—*Franciscan Sisters of St. Paul, MN.*—O.S.F.

[2575]—*Institute of the Sisters of Mercy of the Americas.* (Dubuque, IA; Detroit, MI; Omaha, NE).—R.S.M.
[2340]—*Little Sisters of the Poor.*—L.S.P.
[3990]—*Missionary Sisters of St. Peter Claver.*—S.S.P.C.
[3760]—*Order of St. Clare.*—O.S.C.
[3230]—*Poor Handmaids of Jesus Christ.*—P.H.J.C.
[2970]—*School Sisters of Notre Dame.*—S.S.N.D.
[1680]—*Schools Sisters of St. Francis.*—O.S.F.
[3590]—*Servants of Mary (Servite Sisters).*—O.S.M.
[3520]—*Servants of the Holy Heart of Mary.*—S.S.C.M.
[0520]—*Sisters of Charity of Our Lady, Mother of Mercy.*—S.C.M.M.
[0430]—*Sisters of Charity of the Blessed Virgin Mary.*—B.V.M.
[0660]—*Sisters of Christian Charity.*—S.C.C.
[1705]—*The Sisters of St. Francis of Assisi.*—O.S.F.
[1530]—*Sisters of St. Francis of the Congregation of Our Lady of Lourdes, Sylvania, Ohio.*—O.S.F.
[1570]—*Sisters of St. Francis of the Holy Family.*—O.S.F.
[3840]—*Sisters of St. Joseph of Carondelet.*—C.S.J.
[3880]—*Sisters of St. Joseph of Medaille.*—C.S.J.
[3930]—*Sisters of St. Joseph of the Third Order of St. Francis.*—S.S.J.-T.O.S.F.
[1020]—*Sisters of the Divine Redeemer.*—S.D.R.
[1830]—*The Sisters of the Good Shepherd.*—R.G.S.
[3320]—*Sisters of the Presentation of the B.V.M.* (Dubuque, IA; Sioux Falls, SD).—P.B.V.M.
[1720]—*Sisters of the Third Order Regular of St. Francis of the Congregation of Our Lady of Lourdes.*—O.S.F.
[2150]—*Sisters, Servants of the Immaculate Heart of Mary.*—I.H.M.
[4110]—*Ursuline Nuns (Roman Union).*—O.S.U.
[4190]—*Visitation Nuns.*—V.H.M.

ARCHDIOCESAN CEMETERIES

ST. PAUL. *Calvery.*
The Catholic Cemeteries, Central Office, 244 Dayton Ave., 55102. Tel: 612-227-6543.

MINNEAPOLIS. *St. Anthony & St. Mary.*

MENDOTA HEIGHTS. *Resurrection.*

NEW HOPE. *Assumption & Gethsemane.*

PARISH CEMETERIES

SHAKOPEE, MN. *Catholic Cemeteries of Shakapee, Minnesota, Inc.* A corporation formed by the Church of St. Mark and the Church of St. Mary, both of Shakopee, to consolidate separate cemeteries. 535 S. Lewis St., 55379.

NECROLOGY

† Baglio, Joseph L., (Retired). —Died Aug. 23, 1997.
† Broker, Ralph H., (Retired). —Died June 3, 1997.
† Gilligan, Francis J., (Retired). —Died April 6, 1997.
† Guillemette, Joseph H., (Retired). —Died Dec. 2, 1997.
† Hayden, Ambrose V., (Retired). —Died June 24, 1997.
† Louis, Anthony M., (Retired). —Died May 2, 1997.
† McNulty, William C., (Retired). —Died May 26, 1997.
† Salt, Donald L., (Retired). —Died Feb. 7, 1997.

Diocese of St. Petersburg

(Dioecesis Sancti Petri in Florida)

Most Reverend

ROBERT N. LYNCH

Fourth Bishop of St. Petersburg; ordained May 13, 1978; appointed Fourth Bishop of St. Petersburg December 5, 1995; consecrated and installed January 26, 1996. *Office: P.O. Box 40200, St. Petersburg, FL, 33743-0200.*

Most Reverend

W. THOMAS LARKIN, D.D.

Retired Bishop of St. Petersburg; ordained May 15, 1947; appointed Second Bishop of St. Petersburg April 24, 1979; ordained Bishop May 27, 1979; installed June 28, 1979; retired November 28, 1988.

ESTABLISHED JUNE 17, 1968.

Square Miles 3,177.

Comprises the Counties of Citrus, Hernando, Hillsborough, Pasco and Pinellas in the State of Florida.

For legal titles of parishes and diocesan institutions, consult the Chancery.

Chancery: P.O. Box 40200, St. Petersburg, FL, 33743-0200. Tel.: 813-344-1611; Fax: 813-345-2143.

STATISTICAL OVERVIEW

Personnel	
Bishop	1
Retired Bishops	2
Retired Abbots	1
Priests: Diocesan Active in Diocese	98
Priests: Active Outside Diocese	8
Priests: Retired, Sick or Absent	24
Number of Diocesan Priests	130
Religious Priests in Diocese	147
Extern Priests in Diocese	66
Ordinations:	
Diocesan Priests	3
Permanent Deacons	20
Permanent Deacons in Diocese	86
Total Brothers	49
Total Sisters	359
Parishes	
Parishes	72
With Resident Pastor:	
Resident Diocesan Priests	62
Resident Religious Priests	10
Without Resident Pastor:	
Missions	5
Pastoral Centers	1
Welfare	
Catholic Hospitals	2
Total Assisted	2,343,257
Health Care Centers	7
Total Assisted	39,007
Homes for the Aged	7
Total Assisted	1,592
Day Care and Extended Day Care Centers	13
Total Assisted	1,456
Specialized Homes	3
Total Assisted	1,219
Special Centers for Social Services	8
Total Assisted	14,981
Educational	
Diocesan Students in Other Seminaries	13
Total Seminarians	13
Colleges and Universities	1
Total Students	7,124
High Schools, Diocesan and Parish	3
Total Students	1,927
High Schools, Private	2
Total Students	989
Elementary Schools, Diocesan and Parish	40
Total Students	11,006
Elementary Schools, Private	4
Total Students	1,298
Non-residential Schools for the Disabled	2
Total Students	141
Catechesis/Religious Education:	
High School Students	2,380
Elementary Students	19,479
Total Students Under Catholic Instruction	44,357
Teachers in the Diocese:	
Priests	13
Scholastics	1
Brothers	4
Sisters	61
Lay Teachers	831
Vital Statistics	
Receptions into the Church:	
Infant Baptism Totals	4,451
Adult Baptism Totals	713
Received into Full Communion	592
First Communions	5,016
Confirmations	3,417
Marriages:	
Catholic	1,072
Interfaith	906
Total Marriages	1,978
Deaths	4,325
Total Catholic Population	354,699
Total Population	2,364,659

Former Bishops—Most Rev. CHARLES B. MCLAUGHLIN, D.D., ord. June 6, 1941; appt. Titular Bishop of Risinium and Auxiliary of Raleigh, Jan. 13, 1964; appt. First Bishop of St. Petersburg, May 8, 1968; installed June 17, 1968; died in Office, Dec 14, 1978.—Most Rev. W. THOMAS LARKIN, D.D., ord. May 15, 1947; Second Bishop of St. Petersburg; appt. April 24, 1979; ord. Bishop, May 27, 1979; installed June 28, 1979; retired Nov. 28, 1988.—Most Rev. JOHN C. FAVALORA, D.D., Third Bishop of St. Petersburg; ord. Dec. 20, 1961; appt. Bishop of Alexandria, June 16, 1986; ord. and installed July 29, 1986; appt. Third Bishop of St. Petersburg, March 7, 1989; installed May 16, 1989; installed Third Archbishop of Miami, Dec. 20, 1994.

Diocesan Offices

Chancery—6363 Ninth Ave. N., St. Petersburg, 33710. Tel: 813-344-1611; Fax: 813-345-2143., *Mailing Address: P.O. Box 40200, St. Petersburg, 33743-0200.*

Notre Dame Building—6533 Ninth Ave. N., St. Petersburg, 33710. Tel: 813-345-3338; Fax: 813-347-6508., *Mailing Address: P.O. Box 43022, St. Petersburg, 33743-3022.*

Tribunal—905 S. Prospect Ave., Clearwater, 33756. Tel: 813-446-2326; 442-8884; Fax: 813-446-4287.

Catholic Media Center—2816 Morrison Ave., Tampa, 33629. Tel: 813-289-4562 (Hillsborough); 823-5346 (Pinellas)., *Mailing Address: P.O. Box 18081, Tampa, 33679.*

WBVM Radio—Tampa. Tel: 813-289-8040.

Office of the Bishop; Most. Rev. ROBERT N. LYNCH

Executive Secretary—Mrs. SUE TULLY.

Diocesan Curia

Vicar General and Moderator of the Curia—Rev. Msgr. BRENDAN MULDOON, V.G.; Mrs. JOAN MORGAN, Sec.

Chancellor—Rev. ROBERT C. GIBBONS, J.C.L.; Mrs. SOPHIE CARROLL, Sec. & Notary; Mrs. LISA MOBLEY, Archivist.

Judicial Vicar—Very Rev. DACIAN DEE, J.C.D.

Tribunal Staff—Rev. WILLIAM SWENGROS, J.C.L., Vice Judicial Vicar; Revs. STEPHEN DAMBRAUSKAS, J.C.L.; RONALD B. AUBIN, J.C.L., Defender of the Bond; ROBERT C. GIBBONS, J.C.L., Promoter of Justice; WALTER BUECHE, C.SS.R., Judge; Mr. ANTHONY ELLUL, J.C.D., Judge; Deacon KAZIMIEREZ MIELCAREK, Ph.D., Auditor. Notaries: Mrs. SARAH DURST; Mrs. LOUISE KNOCHELMANN; Mrs. MARY SUE OLIVER.

Vicar for Clergy—Rev. Msgr. JOHN NEFF, *St. Paul Church, 12708 N. Dale Mabry Hwy., Tampa, 33624.* Tel: 813-961-3023.

Personnel Board—Revs. ARTHUR PROULX, Chm. DENNIS HUGHES; ROBERT MORRIS; Rev. Msgr. J. BERNARD CAVERLY. Ex Officio: Rev. Msgr. JOHN NEFF; Rev. Msgr. BRENDAN MULDOON; Rev. ROBERT C. GIBBONS, J.C.L.

Incardination Commission—Rev. Msgr. JOHN NEFF, Chm.; Rev. ROBERT C. GIBBONS, J.C.L., Exec. Sec.; Revs. THOMAS EARNER; JOSEPH PELLEGRINO, V.F.; Rev. Msgr. BRENDAN MULDOON, V.G.; Rev. MICHAEL LYDON.

Vocations Office—Rev. MICHAEL O'BRIEN, Dir. Vocations, *Notre Dame Building.* Asst. Dirs.: Revs. LEONARD PIOTROWSKI; ARTHUR PROULX; Sr. PHYLLIS SHAUGHNESSY, O.S.C.

Permanent Diaconate Office—Revs. ALAN WEBER, Dir., *Notre Dame Building;* Deacon VINCENT ALTERIO, Asst. Dir.

Vicar for Religious—Very Rev. JUDE DUFFY, O.F.M.Cap., *Most Holy Redeemer Church, 10110 Central Ave., Tampa, 33612.* Tel: 813-933-2859. Sr. EUGENE MARIE SCHNEIDER, O.S.F., Sec., *Notre Dame Building.*

Our Lady of Good Counsel Camp—Rev. JAMES JOHNSON, Dir., *8888 E. Gobbler Dr., Floral City, 32636.* Tel: 904-726-2198.

Department of Apostolates

Executive Director—Rev. ROBERT C. GIBBONS, J.C.L.

Black Catholics, Office of—Rev. CALLIST NYAMBO, Dir.; Ms. YVONNE NELLUM, Coord., *Catholic Media Center.*

Charismatic Renewal, Office of—Dr. RONALD NOVOTNY, Coord., *709 Bayview Ave., Clearwater, 34619.* Tel: 813-797-3311. Rev. ANTONIO DIEZ, Spanish Speaking Spiritual Moderator, *6819 Krycul Ave., P.O. Box 418, Riverview, 33569.* Tel: 813-677-2175.

Cursillo—Rev. Msgr. JOHN MCNULTY, P.A., Moderator, *Notre Dame Building.* Tel: 813-345-3338.

Spanish Cursillo—Deacon JOHN SIERRA, Dir., *St. Paul Church, 12708 N. Dale Mabry Hwy., Tampa, 33624.* Tel: 813-961-3023.

Cursillo Center—1706 11th Ave., Tampa, 33675. Tel: 813-248-3942.

Ecumenical and Inter-Religious Affairs—Rev. Msgr. J. BERNARD CAVERLY, *St. Raphael Church, 1376 Snell Isle Blvd. N.E., St. Petersburg, 33704.* Tel: 813-821-7989.

Evangelization, Office of—Rev. Msgr. JOHN SCULLY, P.A., Dir., *Chancery.*

Haitian Apostolate—Rev. CHRISTOPHER FITZGERALD, I.C., Dir., *P.O. Box 1218, Seffner, 33584.* Tel: 813-682-9115.

Hispanic Apostolate—Rev. DEMETRIO LORDEN, Co-Dir., *P.O. Box 16397, Temple Terrace, 33687.* Tel: 813-988-1593. Rev. CHRISTOPHER FITZGERALD, I.C., Co-Dir., *P.O. Box 1218, Seffner, 33584.* Tel: 813-682-9115. Deacon JUAN SIERRA, Assoc. Dir., *2021 E. Busch Blvd., Tampa, 33612.* Tel: 813-931-3005.

St. Casimir Lithuanian Apostolate—Rev. STEPHEN ROPOLAS, O.F.M., Dir., *555 68th Ave., St. Petersburg Beach, 33706.* Tel: 813-367-2408.

Miserere Guild, Inc.—Rev. Msgr. J. BERNARD CAVERLY, Dir., *St. Raphael Church, 1376 Snell Isle Blvd. N.E., St. Petersburg, 33704.* Tel: 813-821-7989.

Calvary Catholic Cemetery—Mr. GREG TSCHIDERER, Mgr., *11801 U.S. Hwy. 19 N., Clearwater, 34624-7407.* Tel: 813-572-4355.

Prison and Jail Ministry—Rev. JOSE FURTADO, O.deM., Dir., *Notre Dame Bldg.* Tel: 813-345-3338.

Propagation of the Faith—Rev. Msgr. JOHN SCULLY, P.A., Diocesan Dir., *Chancery Building.*

Rural Life Ministry—Very Rev. CHRISTOPHER FITZGERALD, I.C., Dir., *P.O. Box 1218, Seffner, 33584.* Tel: 813-681-9115.

Sea, Apostleship of the—

Port of St. Petersburg—Rev. BERNARDINE SMITH, T.O.R., Chap., *515 4th St., St. Petersburg, 33701.* Tel: 813-896-2191.

Port of Tampa—Rev. THOMAS STOKES, S.M., *Our Lady of Perpetual Help Church, 1711 E. 11th Ave., Tampa, 33605.* Tel: 813-248-5701.

Department of Catholic Formation and Education

Executive Director—Dr. BARBARA MCCONVILLE, Ph.D., *Notre Dame Building.*

Catholic Schools Office—Rev. ROBERT KROLL, O.F.M., Supt.; Ms. MARY BRYAN, Assoc. Supt. for Curriculum.

Family Life Office—Deacon JOE GROTE, Dir.

Spanish Marriage Encounter—Rev. DEMETRIO LORDEN, Coord. Tel: 813-988-1593 (Tampa).

Library, Father William F. Balfe Memorial—Mrs. CLARA BLOWERS, Coord.

Religious Education Office—Mr. BRIAN A. LEMOI, Dir.

Respect Life Office—Mrs. SHARON ILER, Coord.; Rev. Msgr. JOHN MCNULTY, P.A., Bishop's Delegate to Pro-Life Activities.

Scouting Office—Revs. ANTON DECHERING, Dir., *1600 54th Ave. S., St. Petersburg, 33712.* Tel: 813-867-3663. JAMES JOHNSON, Assoc. Dir. Tel: 352-726-1670.

Worship, Office of—Rev. JOHN TAPP, Dir.; Mr. DOUGLAS REATINI, Assoc. Dir.

Youth Ministry Office—Mr. THOMAS J. MIKLUSICAK, Dir.

Department of Communications

Executive Director—Mr. WILLIAM J. URBANSKI, *Chancery.*

Catholic Television Mass—MARY JO MURPHY, Producer.

Diocesan Radio - WBVM 90.5 FM & WLMS 88.3 FM—Mr. THOMAS DERZYPOLSKI, Station Mgr., *Media Center, Tampa.* Tel: 813-289-8040; 800-223-WBVM.

"The Florida Catholic" Newspaper—Mr. STEPHEN SIMS, Editor, *Notre Dame Building, St. Petersburg.* Tel: 813-345-3338.

Circulation & Subscription—P.O. Box 3551, Orlando, 32802. Tel: 407-423-3438.

Department of Temporal Affairs

Department of Temporal Affairs—Chancery Building; Rev. ROBERT C. GIBBONS, Chief Financial Officer; Mr. PAUL A. WARD, JR., Exec. Dir.; Mr. JOSEPH CORSETTI, Asst. to the Exec. Dir.; Mr. JOSEPH G. GABAY, Controller; Mrs. CHARLOTTE MYERS, Personnel; Mr. ZBIGNIEW GAWIENCZUK, Data Processing; Mrs. CAROL PILARSKI, Data Processing.

Finance Council—Mr. THEO CHIVE, Chm.; Mr. C. DAVID CARLEY; Rev. Msgr. BRENDAN MULDOON; Mr. JAMES QUINLAN, SR.; Mrs. LAURA KRUEGER BROCK; Revs. JACOB MONTELEONE; ROBERT C. GIBBONS; Mr. FRED DOBBINS; Mr. GREGORY C. JEWELL; Mr. WILLIAM G. TAPP; Mr. PATRICK WALSH.

Insurance, Health & Welfare Administration—Mr. DONALD BRASIER, Insurance Mgr.; Mrs. KAE YAUCHLER, Admin. Asst.

Department of Real Estate

Chancery Building—Mr. JAMES A. SEBESTA, Exec. Dir.; Mr. RONALD G. BENTO, Real Estate Mgr.; Mr. STEVE B. ZIENTEK, Real Estate Planning.

Department of Facilities and Construction Management

Notre Dame Building—Mrs. DENISE DIGRUCCIO, Dir.

Department of Social Ministries

Notre Dame Building—6533 Ninth Ave. N., St. Petersburg, 33710. Tel: 813-345-3338., *Mailing Address: P.O. Box 43022, St. Petersburg, 33743-3022.* Mr. ARNOLD ANDREWS, Exec. Dir.

Pastoral Offices and Consultative Bodies to the Diocesan Curia

Presbyteral Council—Most Rev. ROBERT N. LYNCH, Pres.; Rev. Msgr. BRENDAN MULDOON, V.G., Vice Pres.; Very Rev. RALPH ARGENTINO, V.F., Chm.; Rev. Msgr. JOHN NEFF; Rev. ROBERT GIBBONS, J.C.L.; Very Revs. DACIAN DEE, J.C.D.; ROBERT DONLAN, V.F.; JUDE DUFFY, O.F.M.Cap., V.F.; JAMES JOHNSON, V.F.; JAMES LARA, V.F.; JOSEPH PELLEGRINO, V.F.; GERARD POWERS, V.F.; Revs. RICHARD ALLEN; JOHN CIPPEL; JOSEPH DOYLE, S.J.; BRENDAN LAWLOR; THOMAS MADDEN; JACOB MONTELEONE; ROBERT MORRIS; MICHAEL MUHR; ERIC PETERS; ROBERT SCHNEIDER; WILLIAM SWENGROS; GREGG TOTTLE.

College of Consultors—Rev. Msgr. BRENDAN MULDOON, V.G.; Rev. ROBERT C. GIBBONS, J.C.L., Sec.; Rev. Msgr. JOHN NEFF; Very Rev. DACIAN DEE, J.C.D.; Revs. RALPH ARGENTINO, V.F.; ROBERT DONLAN, V.F.; JUDE DUFFY, O.F.M.Cap., V.F.; JAMES JOHNSON, V.F.; JAMES LARA, V.F.; JOSEPH PELLEGRINO, V.F.; GERARD POWERS, V.F.; GREGG TOTTLE.

Vicars Forane—Very Revs. RALPH ARGENTINO, V.F., Lower Pinellas Deanery; JOSEPH PELLEGRINO, V.F., Upper Pinellas Deanery; JUDE DUFFY, O.F.M.Cap., V.F., West Hillsborough Deanery; JAMES LARA, V.F., East Hillsborough Deanery; GERARD POWERS, V.F., Pasco Deanery; ROBERT DONLAN, V.F., Hernando Deanery; JAMES JOHNSON, V.F., Citrus Deanery.

Cemetery Board—Rev. Msgr. J. BERNARD CAVERLY, Chm.; Mr. TERRENCE BRETT; Mrs. ELEANOR KIRBY; Mr. CHARLES MARSICANO; Mr. GREG TSCHIDERER.

Committees for Priestly Life & Ministry—

Continuing Formation—Appointed Members: Revs. MICHAEL O'BRIEN, Chm. LEONARD PLAZEWSKI; ARTHUR PROULX; JOHN CIPPEL; JAMES MERKEL; Rev. Msgr. JOHN NEFF, Ex Officio.

Commission for Women Religious—Sr. PATRICIA CAULFIELD, O.P.; Sr. DOROTHY DWYER, O.S.F.; Sr. MARY RENETTA GRAFF, S.N.D.; Sr. MARY DAVID HYDRO, O.S.B.; Sr. MARGARET MCGINLEY, I.H.M.; Sr. PHYLLIS SHAUGHNESSY, O.S.C.; Sr. JOSEPHINE MARIE STREVA, O.S.F.; Sr. VIRGINIA TURNER, S.N.D.; Sr. MARY CHARLES PRINCE, O.S.M.; Sr. JOHN EUDES DUFFY, S.O.L.C.; Very Rev. JUDE DUFFY, O.F.M.Cap., Ex Officio.

Diocesan Liturgical Commission—Rev. JOHN TAPP, Chm.; Revs. DAVID DEJULIO; COLMAN COOKE; LEONARD PLAZEWSKI; ROBERT SCHNEIDER; Deacon JOSEPH KRZANOWSKI; Mr. CLARK BOKOR; Ms. MARIA ESPINOSA; Dr. WILLIAM PICHER; Mr. DOUGLAS REATINI; Mr. CHRISTOPHER BERKE; Sr. LISA-JUDENE ERAZMUS, O.S.B.; Ms. MARCY SCHWABENBAUER.

Diocesan Board of Catholic Formation & Education—Mrs. JUDY FLYNN; Mr. STEVE CHUMBRIS; Rev. GERARD POWERS; Sr. ADELE LUBER, S.S.N.D.; Mrs. JOANN WHITE; Mrs. ROSANNE M. SMITHWICK; Mr. CHUCK SULLIVAN; Mr. EDWARD TAYLOR; Mrs. MARIE HOUGH; Dr. BARBARA MCCONVILLE; Rev. Msgr. BRENDAN MULDOON, V.G.; Dr. DUKE STERN; Mr. JOSEPH BROWN; Mr. AUGIE MONTEJO; Rev. ROBERT SCHNEIDER; Rev. COLMAN MCGARRIL, T.O.R.

Permanent Diaconate Board—Rev. Msgr. JOHN F. NEFF; Revs. JACOB MONTELEONE; ALAN WEBER; Deacons VINCENT ALTERIO; JERRY CRALL; AUGUSTIN ORTIZ; Mrs. PAT KRZANOWSKI.

Realty Advisory Board—Rev. Msgr. BRENDAN MULDOON, V.G.; Mr. RONALD G. BENTO; E. THOMAS FISHER, JR., Esq.; Mr. EUGENE MOHLER; Mr. JAMES A. SEBESTA; Mr. STEVE B. ZIENTEK; Mr. JERRY GANEY; Mr. ROBERT E. SCHWEIGER; Mr. VERNON SHEA.

Organizations Serving the Diocese

Archdiocese of Miami, Diocese of St. Petersburg, and Diocese of Venice Pension Plan—

Pension Plan Administrator—Gabriel, Roeder, Smith & Co., 301 E. Las Olas Blvd., Ste. 200, Fort Lauderdale, 33301. Tel: 954-527-1616; Fax: 954-525-0083.

Catholic Charities, Diocese of St. Petersburg, Inc.

Central Services—6533 Ninth Ave. N., St. Petersburg, 33710. Tel: 813-893-1313; 800-260-2294 (Evenings & Weekends). Mr. ARNOLD ANDREWS, Exec. Dir.

Pious Foundations

Catholic Education Foundation, Inc.—6363 Ninth Ave. N., St. Petersburg, 33710. Tel: 813-344-1611., *Mailing Address: P.O. Box 40200, St. Petersburg, 33743.*

Organizations of the Catholic Faithful

Catholic Daughters of America—Mrs. ROSE TOMASSI, National Dir. Tel: 813-360-8508. Mrs. ROSE MONCHECOURT, State Regent. Tel: 813-934-6209.

Diocesan Council of Catholic Women—Rev. HAROLD BUMPUS, Diocesan Moderator. Tel: 352-489-4889.

Deanery Chaplains—Revs. ROBERT SCHAEUFELE, Lower Pinellas; Rev. AIDEN FOYNES, Upper Pinellas; Revs. PATRICK IRWIN, East Hillsborough; MICHAEL MUHR, West Hillsborough; FELIX SANCHEZ, Pasco; Vacant; Hernando; THOMAS MORGAN, Citrus.

Family of St. Jerome, "Familian Sancti Hieronymi"—Mr. JAN G. HALISKY, P.A., Praeses Generalis, *507 S. Prospect Ave., Clearwater, 33756.*

Knights of Columbus—Rev. PAUL HERVEY, Chap. Tel: 813-885-7861.

Society of St. Vincent de Paul—

Council of St. Petersburg Diocese—P.O. Box 13938, Tampa, 33681-0938. Tel: 813-832-5486. Mr. MARVIN ROPERT, Pres.

Hernando/Citrus St. Vincent de Paul Society District Council—Mr. CESAR LANDAETA, Pres. Tel: 904-688-9070.

Hillsborough District Council—Mr. JOSEPH LATINA, Pres. Tel: 813-985-1012.

Ozanam District Council (Pasco Deanery)—Mr. DENNIS HOLT, Pres. Tel: 813-966-2046.

Lower Pinellas District Council—Mr. WILLIAM REAGOR, Pres. Tel: 813-345-0212.

Upper Pinellas District Council—Mr. WALTER HAINS, Pres. Tel: 813-442-7370.

CLERGY, PARISHES, MISSIONS AND PAROCHIAL SCHOOLS

CITY OF ST. PETERSBURG
(Pinellas County)

1—CATHEDRAL OF ST. JUDE THE APOSTLE (1950), Very Rev. David T. DeJulio, Rector; Revs. Joel M. Kovanis; Marino Frascati, O.de.M.; Sr. Jean Charles Birney, O.P., Pastoral Assoc.; Deacon David Sirrianna.

Res., 5815 Fifth Ave. N., P.O. Box 40928, 33743. Tel: 813-347-9702; Fax: 813-343-8370.

School—Tel: 813-347-8622; Fax: 813-343-0305. Sr. Patricia Caulfield, O.P., Prin.

Sisters 3; Lay Teachers 28; Students 501.

Catechesis/Religious Programs—Tel: 813-345-8780; Fax: 813-343-8370. Sr. Joseph Eilese Hukle, O.P., D.R.E.

Students 282.

2—BLESSED TRINITY (1960), Revs. Anton Dechering; Mathew Pathilchirayil, M.Afr.; Sr. Jean Barrett, O.S.F., Pastoral Assoc.

Res., 1600 54th Ave. S., 33712. Tel: 813-867-3663; Fax: 813-864-2679.

School—St. Paul Interparochial School. See Elementary Schools, Interparochial under Institutions Located in the Diocese. Tel: 813-823-6144; Fax: 813-896-0609.

Catechesis/Religious Programs—Tel: 813-867-2421; Fax: 813-864-2679.

Students 211.

3—HOLY CROSS (1965), Revs. Robert L. Schaeufele; Gerald Hendry; Deacons Richard Brady; Richard Nagle, Jr.; Barry Wallace. In res., Rev. Michael O'Brien.

Res., 7851 54th Ave. N., 33709. Tel: 813-546-3315; 541-2242; Fax: 813-547-2005.
Catechesis/Religious Programs—Tel: 813-547-2004; Fax: 813-547-2005.
Students 275.

4—HOLY FAMILY (1959), Revs. Robert J. Schneider; Jerome E. Diffley, Pastor Emeritus; Paul Pecchie; Sr. Jamesann McCue, I.H.M., Dir., Pastoral Assoc.; Deacons Michael Columbus; Gene Loffredo.
Res., 200 78th Ave., N.E., 33702. Tel: 813-526-5783; Fax: 813-521-2545.
School—250 78th Ave., N.E., 33702. Tel: 813-526-8194; Fax: 813-527-6567. Sr. Florence Ann Marino, I.H.M.; Sr. Electa Schmidt, I.H.M.
Sisters 2; Lay Teachers 15; Students 233.
Catechesis/Religious Programs—Anne P. Perez, D.R.E. (Adult and Elementary).
Students 327.

5—ST. JOSEPH (1922), Rev. Callist Nyambo. In res., Rev. Peter Young.
Res., 2624 Union St., S., 33712. Tel: 813-822-2153; Fax: 813-823-5820.
Preschool—Immaculate Conception, Tel: 813-822-2156; Fax: 813-553-9133.
Lay Teachers 6; Students 188.
Catechesis/Religious Programs—Tel: 813-822-8427.
Students 60.
Mission—St. Petersburg, Pinellas Co., Vietnamese Martyrs Mission, Tel: 813-822-7344.

6—ST. MARY OUR LADY OF GRACE (1921), Revs. Bernardine J. Smith, T.O.R.; Brian J. Miller, T.O.R.; Thomas M. Scanlon, T.O.R.
Res., 515 Fourth St., S., 33701. Tel: 813-896-2191; Fax: 813-895-6279.
St. Mary's Center—.

7—ST. PAUL (1929), Revs. Robert C. Gibbons; Paul Mizener.
Res., 1800 12th St. N., 33704. Tel: 813-822-3481; Fax: 813-822-1754.
School—St. Paul Interparochial School. See Elementary Schools, Interparochial under Institutions Located in the Diocese. Tel: 813-823-6144; Fax: 813-896-0609.
Catechesis/Religious Programs—Tel: 813-822-3481; Fax: 813-822-1754.
Students 109.
Mission—St. Petersburg, The Mercy of God Polish Mission, 1358 20th Ave. N., 33704. Tel: 813-823-6997; Fax: 813-821-8242. Rev. Wiktor Dziedziech.

8—ST. RAPHAEL (1961), Rev. Msgr. J. Bernard Caverly; Rev. Kenneth Malley; Deacon Joseph Grote. In res., Rev. Jose Gonzalez.
Res., 1376 Snell Isle Blvd., N.E., 33704. Tel: 813-821-7989; Fax: 813-823-8824.
School—Tel: 813-821-9663. Mrs. Carole Huff, Prin.
Lay Teachers 14; Students 291.
Catechesis/Religious Programs—Tel: 813-821-7989. Rhona Beettam, D.R.E.
Students 204.

9—TRANSFIGURATION (1959), Revs. John Bolger; John Gerth. Deacons: Revs. Gerald McGory; Raphael Quiles.
Res., 4000-43 St. N., 33714. Tel: 813-525-0262; Fax: 813-522-1328.
School—Tel: 813-527-2880; Fax: 813-522-1328. Mrs. Joanne Claire, Prin.
Lay Teachers 12; Students 222.
Catechesis/Religious Programs—Students 65.

OUTSIDE THE CITY OF ST. PETERSBURG

Beverly Hills, Citrus Co., Our Lady of Grace (1966), Revs. Henry J. Riffle; Nehmatallah El-Hayek; Deacon Romulo Postadan. In res., Rev. Jorge Gonzalez.
Res., 6 Roosevelt Blvd., 34465. Tel: 352-746-2144; Fax: 352-746-6892.
School—Central Catholic School of Citrus County, Lecanto. See Elementary Schools, Interparochial under Institutions Located in the Diocese. Tel: 352-746-2020; Fax: 352-746-3448.
Catechesis/Religious Programs—Tel: 352-746-2144; Fax: 352-746-6892. Maryann Gajos, D.R.E.
Students 86.

Brandon, Hillsborough Co., Church of the Nativity (1960), Revs. James C. Lara; George Rozycki; Edward P. Nichols, Jr.; Deacons Jim Pescatore; Richard Beaudry; John Koppennaal.
Church—705 E. Brandon Blvd., 33511. Tel: 813-681-4608; Fax: 813-653-9482.
Res., 805 Westbrook, 33511. Tel: 813-684-0256. [JC]
School—Tel: 813-689-3395; Fax: 813-681-5406. Sr. Irene St. Jean, C.S.C., Prin.
Sisters of Holy Cross (Pittsfield, NH) 2; Lay Teachers 33; Students 758.
Catechesis/Religious Programs—Tel: 813-689-3395; Fax: 813-681-5406. Ann Marie Sullivan, D.R.E.
Students 753.

Brooksville, Hernando Co., St. Anthony (1892), Rev. Robert R. Donlan; Sr. Loretta Lonsdorf, O.S.M., Pastoral Asst.; Deacon Manuel Carreiro.
Res., 20428 Cortez Blvd., 34601-5601. Tel: 352-796-2096; Fax: 352-796-7144.
School—Notre Dame Interparochial School. See Elementary Schools, Interparochial under Institutions Located in the Diocese. Tel: 352-683-0755; Fax: 352-683-3924.
Catechesis/Religious Programs—Tel: 352-796-4434, Ext. 20; Fax: 352-796-7144. Sr. Patricia Saunders, O.P., D.R.E.
Students 202.
Mission—Ridge Manor, Hernando Co., St. Anne, 4142 Treiman Blvd., Ridge Manor, 33525. Tel: 352-583-2550; Fax: 352-583-0300. Rev. Gerard Murphy.

Citrus Springs, Citrus Co., St. Elizabeth Ann Seton (1976), Rev. Harold Bumpus; Rev. Msgr. George Cummings, Pastor Emeritus; Deacon Thomas Metty.
Res., 1460 W. St. Elizabeth Pl., 34434. Tel: 352-489-4889.
School—Central Catholic School of Citrus County. See Elementary Schools, Interparochial under Institutions Located in the Diocese. Lecanto, Tel: 352-746-2020; Fax: 352-746-3448.
Catechesis/Religious Programs—Tel: 352-489-4889. Mrs. Claire Mangine, D.R.E.
Students 41.

Clearwater, Pinellas Co.,

1—ALL SAINTS, (1987), Rev. Gregory J. Andrews.
Office: 2801 Curlew Rd., 33761. Tel: 813-789-1025; Fax: 813-784-8025.
School—Guardian Angels Interparochial School. See Elementary Schools, Interparochial under Institutions Located in the Diocese. Tel: 813-799-6724.
Catechesis/Religious Programs—Students 154.

2—LIGHT OF CHRIST, (1966), Revs. Timothy J. Allman; Ronald Poirier; Deacon James Hassett. In res., Rev. Keith McKee (Canada).
Mailing Address: P.O. Box 6115, 33758. Tel: 813-441-4545; Fax: 813-441-8771.
Res., 2176 Marilyn St., 33765.
School—St. Cecelia Interparochial School. See Elementary Schools, Interparochial under Institutions Located in the Diocese. Tel: 813-461-1200; Fax: 813-446-9140.
Pre-School—Tel: 813-442-4797; Fax: 813-441-8771. Mrs. Barbara Barko, Dir.
Lay Teachers 16; Students 120.
Catechesis/Religious Programs—Tel: 813-442-7081. William Woodard, D.R.E.
Students 604.

3—ST. BRENDAN, (1978), Rev. Edward J. Mulligan.
Res., 245 Dory Passage, 33767. Tel: 813-443-5485; Fax: 813-442-5896.
School—St. Cecelia Interparochial School. See Elementary Schools, Interparochial Under Institutions Located in the Diocese. Tel: 813-447-3494; Fax: 813-442-4810.

4—ST. CECELIA, (1924), Revs. Aiden Foynes; Kenneth Bischko, T.O.R.; Francis X. Sarjeant, S.J. In res., Rev. Eduardo Wal; Deacon Kazimierez Mielcarek.
Res., 820 Jasmine Way, 33756. Tel: 813-447-3494; Fax: 813-442-4810.
School—St. Cecelia Interparochial School. See Elementary Schools, Interparochial under Institutions Located in the Diocese. Tel: 813-461-1200; Fax: 813-446-9140.
Catechesis/Religious Programs—Mrs. Mary M. Thomas, D.R.E.
Students 347.

5—ST. MICHAEL THE ARCHANGEL, (1980), Revs. Colman M. Cooke; Ted Costello; Nino Viviano; Sr. Theresa Betz, S.N.D., Pastoral Assoc.
Res., 2281 State Rd. 580, 33763. Tel: 813-797-2375; Fax: 813-791-8287.
Catechesis/Religious Programs—Mrs. Katie White, D.R.E.
Students 391.

Crystal River, Citrus Co., St. Benedict (1953), Revs. James Merkel; Edward De Russy, S.J.; Deacon James Pullar.
Mailing Address: 455 S. Suncoast Blvd., 34429. Tel: 352-795-4478; 4479; Fax: 352-795-4160.
School—Central Catholic School of Citrus County. See Elementary Schools, Interparochial under Institutions Located in the Diocese. Lecanto, Tel: 352-746-2020; Fax: 352-746-3448.
Catechesis/Religious Programs—Deacon James Pullar, D.R.E.
Students 136.

Dade City, Pasco Co., St. Rita (1912) (Hispanic), Rev. Felix Sanchez. In res., Rev. Anselm Harry Morrison, A.A.
Mailing Address: P.O. Box 944, 33526-0944.
Office: 14404 14th St., 33523. Tel: 352-567-2894; Fax: 352-523-0039.
Res., 14325 13th St., 33523. Tel: 352-521-3145.
School—St. Anthony Interparochial School. See Elementary Schools, Interparochial under Institutions Located in the Diocese. San Antonio, Tel: 352-588-3041; Fax: 352-588-3142.
Catechesis/Religious Programs—Lillie Dennard, D.R.E.
Students 425.

Dunedin, Pinellas Co., Our Lady of Lourdes (1958), Revs. Thomas L. Madden; Thomas M. Conmy, C.S.C. In res., Rev. William Swengros.
Res., 750 San Salvador Dr., 34698. Tel: 813-733-3606; Fax: 813-733-8305.
School—Tel: 813-733-3776; Fax: 813-733-3776. Mrs. Janice Metz.
Sisters of Notre Dame (Chardon Ohio) 1; Lay Teachers 17; Students 333.
Catechesis/Religious Programs—Tel: 813-733-0872; Fax: 813-733-8305. Sr. Mary Deborah Carlin, S.N.D., D.R.E.
Students 490.

Gulfport, Pinellas Co., Most Holy Name of Jesus (1960), Revs. Raymond O'Neill; Patrick Rebel; Deacon Glenn Pickart.
Res., 5800 15th Ave., S., 33707. Tel: 813-347-9989; Fax: 813-343-6420.
School—Tel: 813-347-1774. Sr. M. Francis Elizabeth, O.P., Prin.
Sisters 2; Lay Teachers 15; Students 191.
Catechesis/Religious Programs—Tel: 813-347-7803. Sr. Jean Clemenger, O.P., D.R.E.
Students 101.

Holiday, Pasco Co., St. Vincent De Paul (1969), Revs. Paul Goudreau; Emil Styczen; Sr. Josephine Rooney, O.S.C., Pastoral Assoc.
Res., 4843 Mile Stretch Dr., P.O. Box 3865, 34690. Tel: 813-938-1974; Fax: 813-938-1975.
School—Bishop Larkin Interparochial School. See Elementary Schools, Interparochial under Institutions Located in the Diocese. Hudson, Tel: 813-862-6981.
Catechesis/Religious Programs—Tel: 813-934-8035. Sr. Christa Rowe, O.S.C., D.R.E.
Students 212.

Homosassa, Citrus Co., St. Thomas the Apostle (1987), Rev. David A. Banks; Deacon Richard Meyer.
Res., 7040 S. Suncoast Blvd., 34446. Tel: 352-628-7000; Fax: 352-628-4723.
School—Central Catholic School of Citrus County. See Elementary Schools, Interparochial under Institutions Located in the Diocese. Lecanto.
Catechesis/Religious Programs—Students 63.

Hudson, Pasco Co., St. Michael (1971), Revs. Desmond Daly; Thomas Dieter; Seamus Collins, O.P.; Deacon Robert Simpson.
Res., 8014 State Rd. #52, 34667. Tel: 813-868-5276; Fax: 813-862-9187.
School—Bishop Larkin Catholic Interparochial School. See Elementary Schools, Interparochial under Institutions Located in the Diocese. Tel: 813-862-6981; Fax: 813-869-9893.
Catechesis/Religious Programs—Tel: 813-863-9742. Mary Alber, D.R.E.
Students 502.

Indian Rocks Beach, Pinellas Co., St. Jerome (1956), Very Rev. Msgr. Brendan Muldoon, V.G.; Revs. Leonard Piotrowski; Sean O'Sullivan, I.C.; Deacon William Mahood; Cathie Darnauer, Admin. Pastoral Assocs.: Sr. Lucia Brady, O.S.C.; Sr. Cecilia McDonnell, O.S.C. In res., Very Rev. Dacian Dee, J.C.D., V.E.
Mailing Address: P.O. Box 100, 33785.
Res., 10895 Hamlin Blvd., Largo, 33774. Tel: 813-595-4610; Fax: 813-596-6792.
Early Childhood Center: Denise Roach, Dir.
Catechesis/Religious Programs—Tel: 813-595-3100. Sandra Bonilla, D.R.E.
Students 843.

Inverness, Citrus Co., Our Lady of Fatima (1955), Revs. James B. Johnson; Vincent R. Morton; Desmond Gill, Pastor Emeritus; Deacon Steve Kurylowicz.
Mailing Address: 550 U.S. Hwy. 41 S., 34450. Tel: 352-726-1670; Fax: 352-344-8384.
Res., 518 Desota Ave., 34450. Tel: 352-726-1670.
School—Central Catholic School of Citrus County. See Elementary Schools, Interparochial under Institutions Located in the Diocese. Tel: 352-746-2020; Fax: 352-746-3448.
Catechesis/Religious Programs—D.R.E.: Sr. Mary Charia Ripple, S.S.N.D.; Sr. Constance Coulter, S.S.N.D.
Students 303.

Land O'Lakes, Pasco Co., Our Lady of the Rosary (1952), Rev. Ronald B. Aubin; Deacons Augustin Ortiz; Eric Wells.
Res., P.O. Box 1229, 34639. Tel: 813-949-4565; Fax: 813-948-1981.

School—Most Holy Redeemer Interparochial School. See Elementary Schools, Interparochial under Institutions Located in the Diocese. Tampa, Tel: 813-933-4750; Fax: 813-933-3181.
Catechesis/Religious Programs—Tel: 813-949-2699; Fax: 813-948-1981.
Students 368.

Largo, Pinellas Co.,

1—ST. CATHERINE OF SIENA, (1976), Revs. Michael J. Finnegan; Matthew Arackal, M.C.B.S (BIS); John O'Donovan (Ireland). Pastoral Assocs.: Tel: 813-531-1690. Sr. Ann Gertrude, S.S.J.; Sr. Therese Ganly, S.S.J.; Deacon Michael Slattery.
Res., 1955 S. Belcher Rd., Clearwater, 34624. Tel: 813-531-7721; Fax: 813-531-7723.
School—St. Cecelia Interparochial School. See Elementary Schools, Interparochial under Institutions Located in the Diocese. Tel: 813-461-1200.
Catechesis/Religious Programs—Sr. Frances Hance, S.S.J., D.R.E.
Students 402.

2—ST. JUSTIN MARTYR, (1987), Rev. Michael Lydon; Sr. Kathleen Francis Honc, O.S.F., Pastoral Asst.
Res., 10725 Ridge Rd., 34648. Tel: 813-397-3312; Fax: 813-392-6653.
Catechesis/Religious Programs—Rosemary Mandery, D.R.E.
Students 153.

3—ST. MATTHEW, (1985), Rev. Thomas Spillett; Deacon John DiVito.
Mailing Address: P.O. Box 10097, 33773.
Office: 9111 90th Ave., N., 33777. Tel: 813-393-1288; Fax: 813-398-2683.
Catechesis/Religious Programs—Ruth Appel, D.R.E.
Students 343.

4—ST. PATRICK, (1958), Rev. Msgr. John M. McCall; Rev. Richard Jankowski.
Res., 2121 16th Ave. S.W., P.O. Box 167, 34640. Tel: 813-584-2318; Fax: 813-586-5413.
School—Tel: 813-581-4865; Fax: 813-581-7842. Mrs. Patricia Coyle, Prin.
Lay Teachers 17; Students 250.
Catechesis/Religious Programs—Tel: 813-584-6697. Annetta Wallace, D.R.E.
Students 315.

Lecanto, Citrus Co., St. Scholastica (1987), Rev. Thomas Morgan; Deacons Terrence E. Knox; Leo Borkowicz; Stephen Sablone.
Res., 4301 W. Homosassa Trail, 34461-9106. Tel: 352-746-9422; 563-2296; Fax: 352-746-2335.
School—Central Catholic School of Citrus County. See Elementary Schools, Interparochial under Institutions Located in the Diocese. Tel: 352-746-2020; Fax: 352-746-3448.
Catechesis/Religious Programs—Tel: 352-746-9422; Fax: 352-746-2335. D.R.E.: Sr. Mary Loyola Mathia, S.C.; Judi Bescher.
Students 302.

Masaryktown, Pasco Co., St. Mary, Our Lady of Sorrows (1931), Rev. James A. Bucaria.
Mailing Address: P.O. Box 9675, 34609-0106. Tel: 352-796-2792; Fax: 352-544-0398.
School—Notre Dame Interparochial School. See Elementary Schools, Interparochial under Institutions Located in the Diocese. Spring Hill, Tel: 352-683-0755.

New Port Richey, Pasco Co., Our Lady Queen of Peace (1913), Revs. Gerard E. Powers, V.F.; Kenneth Slattery; John Anoia (SPR); Deacons Roger Lind (RVC); John Liggan (NY).
Res., 5340 High St., 34652. Tel: 813-849-7521; Fax: 813-849-4814.
School—Bishop Larkin Interparochial School. See Elementary Schools, Interparochial under Institutions Located in the Diocese. Hudson, Tel: 813-862-6981; Fax: 813-869-9893.
Catechesis/Religious Programs—Tel: 813-842-9396.
Students 473.

St. Thomas Aquinas (1980), Revs. Thomas F. Earner; Raymond A. Lettre.
Res., 8320 State Rd. #54, 34653. Tel: 813-372-8600; Fax: 813-376-7204.
St. Thomas Early Childhood Development Center—Tel: 813-376-2330.
School—Bishop Larkin Interparochial School. See Elementary Schools, Interparochial under Institutions Located in the Diocese. Hudson, Tel: 813-862-6981; Fax: 813-862-9187.
Catechesis/Religious Programs—Tel: 813-376-1622. Sr. Sabrina Burton, D.R.E.
Students 638.

Palm Harbor, Pinellas Co., St. Luke the Evangelist (1985), Revs. Donald F. Leininger; Michael O'Neill. Pastoral Assocs.: Sr. Madeleine Donnelly; Sr. Bridget Mulligan; Sr. Bridget Finn; Deacon James Blaney.
Res., 2757 Alderman Rd., 34684. Tel: 813-786-3648; Fax: 813-789-9556.
St. Luke Early Childhood Center—Tel: 813-787-2914.
School—Guardian Angels Interparochial School. See Elementary Schools, Interparochial under Institutions Located in the Diocese. Clearwater, Tel: 813-799-6724.
Students 136.
Catechesis/Religious Programs—Tel: 813-787-2845. Sr. Madeleine Donnelly, O.S.C., D.R.E.
Students 915.

Pinellas Park, Pinellas Co., Sacred Heart (1910), Revs. Ralph Argentino; Peter Busch, T.O.R.; Thomas Anastasia; Deacons Louis Izzo; L. Roger Cartier.
Res., 8001 46th St., N., 34665. Tel: 813-541-4447; Fax: 813-541-2073.
School—7951 46th Way N., 34665. Tel: 813-544-1106; Fax: 813-541-2073. Mrs. JoEllen Caldwell, Prin.
Sisters 1; Lay Teachers 16; Students 259.
Catechesis/Religious Programs—Ms. Lynn Edmonds, D.R.E.
Students 275.

Plant City, Hillsborough Co., St. Clement (1912), Revs. Hugh F. Lagan; Seamus Hatton, C.SS.R.; Oscar Kozyra, O.de.M.
Res., 1104 Alexander St., 33566. Tel: 813-752-8251; Fax: 813-759-2721.
Catechesis/Religious Programs—Jo Ann Parolini, D.R.E.
Students 274.

Port Richey, Pasco Co., St. James the Apostle (1984), Rev. Michael Devine; Deacon Paul G. Metilly.
Res., 8400 Monarch Dr., 34668. Tel: 813-869-3130; Fax: 813-869-8886.
School—Bishop Larkin Interparochial School. See Elementary Schools, Interparochial under Institutions Located in the Diocese. Hudson, Tel: 813-862-6981.
Catechesis/Religious Programs—Tel: 813-869-3132. Mrs. Carole Lutz, D.R.E.
Students 281.

Ridge Manor, Hernando Co., St. Anne (1965),
Res., 4142 Tremain Blvd., Hwy. 301, 33525. Tel: 352-583-2550. Rev. Gerard Murphy.

Riverview, Hillsborough Co., Resurrection (1983), Rev. Antonio Diez.
Mailing Address: P.O. Box 418, 33568.
Res., 6819 Krycul Ave., 33569. Tel: 813-677-2175; Fax: 813-671-7844.
Catechesis/Religious Programs—Students 73.

Ruskin, Hillsborough Co., St. Anne (1956), Revs. Tim Uniac, C.R.; Nelson Carvajal, C.R. In res., Rev. Msgr. Augustine Ndeukoya.
Office: 106 11th Ave., N.E., 33570. Tel: 813-645-1714; Fax: 813-645-5570.
Catechesis/Religious Programs—D.R.E.: Sr. Maureen Smith, O.S.F.S.; Sr. Marian Stenken, S.C.N.; Mrs. Cindy Cyman.
Students 500.
Mission—Wimauma, Our Lady of Guadalupe, P.O. Box 1022, Wimauma, 33598.

Safety Harbor, Pinellas Co., Espiritu Santo (1960), Revs. Gregg Tottle; Timothy Sherwood. Pastoral Assocs.: Sr. Phyllis Shaughnessy, O.S.C.; Sr. Paulamarie Lacy, S.N.D.; Sr. Nanette Herman, S.N.D.; Deacons Dominic P. Friscia; Vincent Alterio; Robert McElroy.
Res., 2405 Philippe Pkwy., P.O. Box 176, 34695. Tel: 813-726-8477; Fax: 813-799-2062.
School—St. Cecelia Interparochial School. See Elementary Schools, Interparochial under Institutions Located in the Diocese. Clearwater, Tel: 813-461-1200.
Catechesis/Religious Programs—Tel: 813-726-6742.
Students 786.

St. Joseph, Pasco Co., Sacred Heart (1888), Rev. Arthur M. Villemaire; Deacon William Connors.
Res., 32145 St. Joe Rd., Dade City, 33525. Tel: 352-588-3641; Fax: 352-588-5299. [CEM]
School—St. Anthony Interparochial School. See Elementary Schools, Interparochial under Institutions Located in the Diocese. San Antonio, Tel: 352-588-3041; Fax: 352-588-3142.
Catechesis/Religious Programs—Students 108.
Sacred Heart Child Care Center—32245 St. Joe Rd., Dade City, 33525. Tel: 352-588-4060; Fax: 352-588-4311. Mrs. Toni Watkins.

St. Pete Beach, Pinellas Co., St. John (1939), Revs. John C. Murphy; Julio B. Rivero, T.O.R.; Deacon Karl A. Boehme. In res., Rev. Msgr. Patrick Trainor, P.A.; Rev. George A. Reskey.
Res., 445 82nd Ave., 33706. Tel: 813-360-1147; Fax: 813-367-4418.
School—500 84th Ave., 33706. Tel: 813-360-1113; Fax: 813-367-8734. Sr. Joan Brennan, S.C., Prin.
School Sisters of Notre Dame (Baltimore, MD) 1; Lay Teachers 14; Students 255.
Catechesis/Religious Programs—D.R.E.: Robert Davis; Sharon Davis.
Students 90.

San Antonio, Pasco Co., St. Anthony of Padua (1884), Rev. Dennis E. Hughes.
Res., 32832 Massachusetts Ave., P.O. Box 578, 33576. Tel: 352-588-3081; Fax: 352-588-5070. [CEM]
School—St. Anthony Interparochial School. See Elementary Schools, Interparochial under Institutions Located in the Diocese. Tel: 352-588-3041; Fax: 352-588-3142.
Catechesis/Religious Programs—Tel: 352-588-3081.
Students 104.

Seffner, Hillsborough Co., St. Francis of Assisi (1987), Very Rev. Christopher Fitzgerald, I.C., V.F.; Rev. Dai Viet Mai, I.C.; Deacons Joseph Brown; Jerome Thomas.
Res., P.O. Box 1218, 33583. Tel: 813-681-9115; Fax: 813-689-4148.
Catechesis/Religious Programs—Joan McCollum, D.R.E.
Students 279.

Seminole, Pinellas Co., Blessed Sacrament (1959), Revs. James Gordon, I.C.; G. Richard Pilger, I.C.; Michael Ferran, I.C.
Res., 11565 66th Ave. N., 33772. Tel: 813-391-4661.
School—Tel: 813-391-4060; Fax: 813-391-5638. Jane Moerschbacher, Prin.
Lay Teachers 21; Students 305.
Catechesis/Religious Programs—Students 160.

Spring Hill, Hernando Co., St. Theresa (1969), Rev. Msgr. John Scully; Rev. Francis Ferrara; Deacon Gerard Uzzi.
Res., 1107 Commercial Way, 34606. Tel: 352-683-2849; Fax: 352-683-3437.
School—Notre Dame Interparochial School. See Elementary Schools, Interparochial under Institutions Located in the Diocese.
Catechesis/Religious Programs—Margaret Uhl, D.R.E.
Students 225.

St. Frances Xavier Cabrini (1980), Revs. John A. Cippel; Merrell Dickey. In res., Rev. Andrew Beaudoin, S.S.S.
Mailing Address: 5030 Mariner Blvd., 34609. Tel: 352-683-9666; Fax: 352-688-2660.
School—Notre Dame Interparochial School. See Elementary Schools, Interparochial under Institutions Located in the Diocese. Tel: 352-683-0755.
Catechesis/Religious Programs—Charles R. Payne, D.R.E.
Students 862.

Saint Joan of Arc (1988), Rev. Philip Scott.
Res., 13485 Spring Hill Dr., 34609. Tel: 352-688-0663; Fax: 352-688-0663, Ext. 34.
School—Notre Dame Interparochial School. See Elementary Schools, Interparochial under Institutions Located in the Diocese.

Sun City Center, Hillsborough Co., Prince of Peace (1970), Rev. Msgr. Diego Conesa; Rev. Hilarios Aranjaniyil, V.C.; Deacon Angelo Pignataro.
Res., 1002 Fordham Dr., 33573. Tel: 813-634-2328; Fax: 813-633-9244.
Mailing Address: 702 Valley Forge Blvd., 33573-5353. Tel: 813-634-2328.
Catechesis/Religious Programs—Students 17.
Mission—Wimauma, Hillsborough Co., Our Lady of Guadalupe Catholic Mission, P.O. Box 1022, Wimauma, 33598. Tel: 813-633-2384. Rev. Nelson Carajal, C.R.

Tampa, Hillsborough Co.,

1—BLESSED SACRAMENT, (1960) (Spanish), Rev. Marciano G. Martin, C.PP.S.
Res., 1205 Windermere Way, 33619. Tel: 813-626-2984; Fax: 813-626-2984.
Catechesis/Religious Programs—1603 Carnegie Cir., 33619. Tel: 813-626-9564.
Students 86.

2—CHRIST THE KING, (1941), Revs. Michael Muhr; Edwin Palka; Timothy Moffatt, T.O.R.; Deacons William E. Diaz; Michael Solomon.
Res., 821 S. Dale Mabry Hwy., P.O. Box 10395, 33679-0395. Tel: 813-876-5841; Fax: 813-873-2426.
School—Tel: 813-876-8770; Fax: 813-879-0315. Sr. Patricia Roche, F.M.A., Prin.
Daughters of Mary Help of Christians 3; Lay Teachers 29; Students 538.
Catechesis/Religious Programs—Tel: 813-870-2509. D.R.E.: Linda A. Waggoner; Linda B. Edge, (Adult).
Students 564.

3—EPIPHANY, (1963), Rev. Ignatius Tuoc; Deacons Richard McIntosh; Maximo E. Montayre.
Mailing Address: P.O. Box 11246, 33680. Tel: 813-258-3440.
Res., 2510 E. Hanna Ave., 33610. Tel: 813-238-5060; 234-8693.
Catechesis/Religious Programs—Tel: 813-238-1751. Suzy Mackey, D.R.E.
Students 89.

Mission—Tampa, Hillsborough Co., St. Joseph Vietnamese Mission, 2510 E. Hanna Ave., 33610. Tel: 813-238-5060.

4—GOOD SHEPHERD, (1966), Rev. Richard Allen.
Res., 6410 E. Hillsborough Ave., 33610. Tel: 813-626-7588; Fax: 813-626-5882.
Catechesis/Religious Programs—Tel: 813-626-9991.
Students 60.

5—INCARNATION, (1962), Revs. Eric Hunter; Felician Napoli, O.F.M.; Paul Hervey; Deacon Joseph Krzanowski.
Res., 5124 Gateway Dr., 33615. Tel: 813-885-7861; Fax: 813-886-3624.
School—Tel: 813-884-4502; Fax: 813-885-3743. Mrs. Carolyn Goslee, Prin.
Lay Teachers 28; Students 576.
Catechesis/Religious Programs—Tel: 813-887-5110; Fax: 813-884-3624. Barbara Catineau, D.R.E.
Students 644.

6—MOST HOLY REDEEMER, (1937), Revs. Jude Duffy, O.F.M.Cap.; John V. Salvas, O.F.M.Cap. Pastoral Assocs.: Bro. John Paul Russo, O.F.M.Cap.; Deacons Lowell L. Hecht, Jr.; J. Manuel Rodriguez.
Res., 10110 Central Ave., 33612. Tel: 813-933-2859; Fax: 813-933-8258.
School—See Elementary Schools, Interparochial under Institutions Located in the Diocese. Tel: 813-933-4750; Fax: 813-933-3181.
Catechesis/Religious Programs—Fax: 813-931-8258. Miss Marie O'Driscoll, D.R.E.
Students 150.

7—OUR LADY OF PERPETUAL HELP, (1890) (Hispanic-Haitian), Revs. Thomas A. Stokes, S.M.; Robert Fahey, S.M.; Richard Colbert, S.M.; John Jazwiecki, S.M.
Res., 1711 11th Ave., 33605. Tel: 813-248-5701; Fax: 813-241-4128. [JC]
Catechesis/Religious Programs—Students 81.

8—SACRED HEART, (1860), Revs. C. Kirk Mansell, S.J.; Michael F. Kennelly, S.J., Pastor Emeritus; Paul V. Osterle, S.J.; Robert Nilon, S.J.; Bro. J. Fillmore Elliot, S.J.
P.O. Box 1524, 33601. Tel: 813-229-1595; Fax: 813-221-2350.
School—Tel: 813-229-0618; Fax: 813-223-7667. Mrs. Madeline O'Dea, Prin.
Sisters 1; Lay Teachers 19; Students 271.
Catechesis/Religious Programs—Students 38.

9—ST. JOSEPH, (1896) (Hispanic), Revs. James H. Geiger, C.SS.R.; Joseph Gorney, C.SS.R.; Jerome A. Murphy, C.SS.R.; George Phillips, C.SS.R.
Mailing Address: P.O. Box 4298, 33677.
Res., 3012 Cherry St., 33607. Tel: 813-877-5729; Fax: 813-877-5720.
School—Tel: 813-879-7720; Fax: 813-873-0804. Daughters of Mary Help of Christians (Paterson, NJ) 4; Lay Teachers 14; Students 266.
Catechesis/Religious Programs—Students 60.

10—ST. LAWRENCE, (1959), Rev. Msgr. Laurence E. Higgins, P.A.; Reverend Fathers Edward C. Keating, O.F.M.; Alberto Bueno, T.O.R.
Mailing Address: 5225 N. Himes Ave., 33614.
Res., 3407 W. Ellicott Ave., 33614. Tel: 813-875-4040; Fax: 813-876-0491.
School—Tel: 813-879-5090; Fax: 813-879-6886.
Lay Teachers 35; Students 633.
Catechesis/Religious Programs—Students 231.

11—ST. MARK THE EVANGELIST, (1996), Rev. Austin M. Mullen.
Res., 15349 Amberly Dr., 33647-2144. Tel: 813-907-9717; Fax: 813-907-9617.
Catechesis/Religious Programs—Tel: 813-615-1866; Fax: 813-615-1860.
Students 301.

12—ST. MARY, (1966), Revs. Robert Morris; Robert Young; Sr. Nancy Christopher, O.S.F., Pastoral Care; Deacon Stanley Gould.
Res., 15520 North Blvd., 33613. Tel: 813-961-1061; Fax: 813-961-3782.
School—Most Holy Redeemer Interparochial School. See Elementary Schools, Interparochial under Institutions Located in the Diocese. Tel: 813-933-4750.
Catechesis/Religious Programs—Tel: 813-963-2079. Sr. Eileen Derrick, O.S.F., D.R.E.
Students 314.

13—ST. PATRICK, (1958), Revs. Colman McGarrill, T.O.R.; Robert Conlin, T.O.R.; Angelus Migliore, T.O.R.; Deacon John M. Edgerton.
Parish Office: 4212 Fair Oaks Ave., 33611. Tel: 813-839-5337; Fax: 813-831-2778. [JC]
School—4518 S. Manhattan Ave., 33611. Tel: 813-839-5056; Fax: 813-832-5907. Mr. Robert Kenel, Prin.
Lay Teachers 18; Students 343.
Catechesis/Religious Programs—Tel: 813-839-4958. Marcia Seheult, D.R.E.
Students 240.

14—ST. PAUL, (1963), Rev. Msgr. John F. Neff; Revs. Terrance Sowada; Ramon Hernandez (Cuba); Deacons John Alvarez; Greg Lambert; Greg Kovalesky, Pastoral Assoc.; Juan Sierra; Ron Rojas.
Mailing Address: 12708 N. Dale Mabry, 33618. Tel: 813-961-3023; Fax: 813-962-8780.
School—Most Holy Redeemer Interparochial School. See Elementary Schools, Interparochial under Institutions Located in the Diocese. Tel: 813-933-4750; Fax: 813-933-3181.
Catechesis/Religious Programs—Tel: 813-961-3023, Ext. 230. Sr. Barbara Jean Rosswurm, D.R.E.
Students 890.

15—ST. PETER CLAVER, (1893) (African American), Rev. Edward Lamp.
Res., 1203 N. Nebraska Ave., 33602. Tel: 813-223-7098; Fax: 813-223-6520.
School—(Grades PreK-6). Tel: 813-224-0865; Fax: 813-223-1982. Sr. Thomas Joseph McGoldrick, S.S.J., Prin.
Lay Teachers 8; Students 133.

16—ST. TIMOTHY, (1985), Revs. John G. Tapp; Eric Peters; Deacon Jerry L. Crall.
Res., 4015 Ragg Rd., 33624. Tel: 813-968-1077; Fax: 813-961-9429.
School—Most Holy Redeemer Interparochial School. See Elementary Schools, Interparochial under Institutions Located in the Diocese. Tel: 813-933-4750; Fax: 813-933-3181.
Catechesis/Religious Programs—Tel: 813-961-1716; Fax: 813-961-9429. Mary Olson, D.R.E.
Students 650.

Tarpon Springs, Pinellas Co., St. Ignatius (1956), Very Rev. Joseph A. Pellegrino, V.F.; Revs. John J. Blum; Louis DeTommaso, O.F.M.
Mailing Address: P.O. Box 1306, 34688-1306.
Res., 715 E. Orange St., 34689. Tel: 813-937-4050; Fax: 813-943-0676.
School—Guardian Angels Interparochial School, Clearwater. See Elementary Schools, Interparochial under Institutions Located in the Diocese. Tel: 813-799-6724; Fax: 813-724-9018.
Catechesis/Religious Programs—Tel: 813-934-4163. Diane Magoulis, D.R.E.
Students 705.

Temple Terrace, Hillsborough Co., Corpus Christi (1958), Revs. Brendan Lawlor; Demetrio L. Lorden; Leonard J.M. Plazewski; Deacon Thomas Shiel.
Res., 9715 N. 56th St., 33617. Tel: 813-988-1593; Fax: 813-985-3583.
School—Tel: 813-988-1722. Margaret A. Penn, Prin.
Lay Teachers 15; Students 297.
Catechesis/Religious Programs—Paul F. Archer, D.R.E.
Students 517.

Valrico, Hillsborough Co., St. Stephen (1987), Revs. Patrick Irwin; Jaroslaw Sztybel.
Church—5049 Bell Shoals Rd., 33594. Tel: 813-689-4900; Fax: 813-661-9619.
Catechesis/Religious Programs—Tel: 813-689-7174. Joyce Morgan, D.R.E.
Students 922.

Zephyrhills, Pasco Co., St. Joseph, Revs. Jacob A. Monteleone; John Hays. In res., Rev. Robert Rittmeyer; Deacon Raymond A. Haberle.
Church—5316 11th St., 33540. Tel: 813-782-2813; Fax: 813-788-1036.
School—St. Anthony Interparochial School, San Antonio. See Elementary Schools, Interparochial under Institutions Located in the Diocese. Tel: 352-588-3041; Fax: 352-588-3142.
Catechesis/Religious Programs—Tel: 813-788-2510. Mrs. Patricia Knopp, D.R.E.
Students 181.

On Duty Outside the Diocese:
Reverend Fathers—
Galan, Juan Cerro
Garcia, Avelino
Londono, Antonio
McDonough, Donat Michael
Plourde, Peter
Waters, Joseph

Graduate Studies:
Reverend Fathers—
Toups, David, Rome, Italy

Absent on Leave:
Reverend Fathers—
Lau, William
Schweitzer, Peter

Military Chaplains:
Reverend Fathers—
McCahon, Joseph F.S., U.S.A.F.
Plourde, John, U.S.A.F.

Retired:
Reverend Monsignors—
Cummings, George
DuBois, William
Trainor, Patrick
Reverend Fathers—
Colgan, John
Cottrell, James
D'Angelo, Rocco
Dambrauskas, Stephen
Dauss, Francis
Diffley, Jerome E.
Estibalez, Inocencio
Gardner, Simeon
Gill, Desmond
Goodman, Frank
Jozwiak, Zygmunt
Kearney, William
Mahony, John
Malin, George
O'Toole, Charles
Obert, Martin
Rinaldo, Alexander
Rittmeyer, Robert
Simon, Bernard
Szymusiak, Bruno

Permanent Deacons:
Alterio, Vincent
Alvarez, John
Anctil, Edmond
Andre, Peter
Beaudry, Richard
Bevvino, Frank J., Jr., On Duty Outside the Diocese
Blaney, James (RVC)
Boehme, Karl
Brady, Richard
Brennan, Lee
Breznak, Charles
Brown, Joseph
Buga, John (PSC)
Buttles, Edward
Cajaio, Henry
Carreiro, Manuel
Cartier, Roger L. (NOR)
Ciarciaglino, Joseph (PSC)
Columbus, Michael
Connors, William
Crall, Jerry
Culkin, John (ALB)
Desjardins, Roland (ORL)
Diaz, William
DiVito, John
Dunphy, Melvin (WOR)
Edgerton, John (NY)
Evans, Forrest, On Duty Outside the Diocese
Friscia, Dominic
Gould, Stanley
Grote, Joseph
Haberle, Raymond
Hassett, James
Hecht, Lowell, Jr.
Izzo, Louis
Knox, Terrence (MIA)
Koppenaal, John
Kovalesky, George
Krzanowski, Joseph
Kurylowicz, Stephen
Lambert, Greg
Liggan, John (NY)
Lind, Roger F. (RVC)
Loffredo, Eugene E. (HRT)
Lyons, John
Mahood, William
Marini, Anthony (ROC)
McElroy, Robert (RCK)
McGory, Gerald
McIntosh, Richard
Metilly, Paul (FR)
Metty, Thomas
Meyer, Richard (TR)
Montayre, Maximo
Moschetto, Samuel (BO)
Nagle, Richard
Ortiz, Samuel
Pescatore, James (RVC)
Pickart, Glenn
Pignatoro, Angelo
Polcari, Joseph (MIA)
Postadan, Romulo (NEW)
Powell, Eugene
Pullar, James
Quiles, Rafael (CLV)
Rodriguez, Manuel
Rojas, Ronald (PCE)
Sablone, Stephen
Schott, Thomas (OKL)
Shiel, Thomas (NY)
Sierra, John

Simpson, Robert C. (RVC)
Sirrianna, David
Slattery, Michael
Solomon, Michael
Thomas, Jerome
Tibbetts, Albert
Uzzi, Gerard (PAT)
Vance, Ronald, On Duty Outside the Diocese
Wallace, Barry
Wells, Eric
Yarawsky, William
Zeitler, Richard

INSTITUTIONS LOCATED IN THE DIOCESE

[A] COLLEGES

ST. LEO. *Saint Leo College* Mailing Address: P.O. Box 6665, 33574. Tel: 352-588-8200.
For a complete listing, refer to the Colleges and Universities section.

[B] HIGH SCHOOLS, DIOCESAN

ST. PETERSBURG. *St. Petersburg Catholic High School*, 6333 Ninth Ave., N., 33710. Tel: 813-344-4065. Ms. Barbara A. Rusin, Interim Prin.; Rev. Gerald Hendry, Chap. Priests 3; Sisters 2; Lay Teachers 35; Students 505.

CLEARWATER. *Clearwater Central Catholic High School*, 2750 Haines Bayshore Rd., 33760. Tel: 813-531-1449; Fax: 813-535-7034. Sr. Mary Dion Horrigan, S.N.D., Prin. Priests 1; Sisters of Notre Dame (Chardon, Ohio) 3; Sisters of Providence (Indiana) 1; Lay Teachers 45; Students 661.

TAMPA. *Tampa Catholic High School*, 4630 N. Rome Ave., 33603. Tel: 813-870-0860. Rev. Richard Colbert, S.M., Dir. Pastoral Svcs.; Bro. James J. MacDonald, C.F.C., Prin. Priests 1; Congregation of Christian Brothers (New Rochelle, NY) 4; Sisters 1; Lay Teachers 52; Students 800.

[C] HIGH SCHOOLS, PRIVATE

TAMPA. *Academy of the Holy Names High School*, 3319 Bayshore Blvd., 33629. Tel: 813-839-5371; Fax: 813-839-1486. Dr. Claire M. Helm, Pres.; Mrs. Mary Johnson, Prin. Legal Titles: *Academy of the Holy Names of Florida, Inc.*; *Academy of the Holy Names Foundation, Inc.* Sisters 7; Lay Teachers 31; Students 329.

Jesuit High School, 4701 N. Himes Ave., 33614. Tel: 813-877-5344; Fax: 813-872-1853. Revs. Paul Deutsch, S.J., Rector; Joseph Doyle, S.J., Chap. & Pres.; Mr. Michael D. Trainor, Prin.; Bro. A. Joseph Martin, S.J., Minister; Revs. Richard G. Hartnett, S.J., Alumni Chap.; John Kaack, S.J.; John J. Cazenavette, S.J.; Rodney T. Kissinger, S.J.; Michael E. Chesney, S.J.; Donald E. Saunders, S.J. Legal Titles: *Jesuit High School of Tampa, Inc., FKA.*; *St. Louis Catholic, Benevolent and Educational Association, Inc.*; *Jesuit High School Foundation, Inc.* Priests 8; Brothers 1; Scholastics 1; Lay Teachers 47; Students 678.

[D] ELEMENTARY SCHOOLS, INTERPAROCHIAL

ST. PETERSBURG. *St. Paul Interparochial School.* (Grades PreK-8), 1900 12th St. N., 33704. Tel: 813-823-6144; Fax: 813-896-0609. Sr. Kathleen Stagnaro, O.S.F., Prin. Serving Blessed Trinity and St. Paul. Sisters 2; Lay Teachers 14; Students 297.

CLEARWATER. *Guardian Angels Catholic School.* (Grades K-6), 2270 Evans Rd., 33763. Tel: 813-799-6724. Cindy H. Mann, Prin. Serving All Saints, St. Ignatius, St. Luke and St. Michael the Archangel. Lay Teachers 17; Students 323.

St. Cecelia Interparochial School. (Grades K-8), 400 S. Hillcrest Ave., 34616. Tel: 813-461-1200. Mrs. Helen S. Marston, Prin. Serving Espiritu Santo, Light of Christ, St. Brendan, St. Catherine of Siena and St. Cecelia. Lay Teachers 55; Students 779.

HUDSON. *Bishop Larkin Interparochial School.* (Grades K-6), 8014 State Rd. 52, 34677. Tel: 813-862-6981. Serving Our Lady Queen of Peace, St. James, St. Michael the Archangel, St. Thomas Aquinas and St. Vincent de Paul. Lay Teachers 17; Students 270.

LECANTO. *Central Catholic School of Citrus County*, 4341 W. Homosassa Trail, 34461. Tel: 352-746-2020. Penelope N. Howell, Prin. Serving Our Lady of Fatima, Our Lady of Grace, St. Benedict, St. Elizabeth Ann Seton, St. Scholastica and St. Thomas the Apostle. Lay Teachers 16; Students 245.

SAN ANTONIO. *St. Anthony Interparochial School.* (Grades K-8), 32902 Massachusetts Ave., P.O. Box 847, 33576-0847. Tel: 352-588-3041. Concetta A. Rizzo, Prin. Serving Sacred Heart, St. Anthony, St. Joseph and St. Rita. Sisters 1; Lay Teachers 12; Students 205.

SPRING HILL. *Notre Dame Interparochial School.* (Grades PreK-8), 1117 Suzanne Dr., 34607. Tel: 352-683-0755.
Web site: http://home.imsweb.net/~notredmei
Maureen Wickert, Prin. Serving St. Anne Mission, St. Anthony, St. Frances Xavier Cabrini, St. Joan of Arc, St. Mary and St. Theresa. Sisters 4; Lay Teachers 18; Students 416.

TAMPA. *Most Holy Redeemer Interparochial School.* (Grades K-8), 302 E. Linebaugh Ave., 33612. Tel: 813-933-4750. Fred Coffaro, Prin.; Marcella Walker, Asst. Prin. Serving Most Holy Redeemer, Our Lady of the Rosary, St. Mary, St. Paul and St. Timothy. Lay Teachers 25; Students 497.

[E] ELEMENTARY SCHOOLS, PRIVATE

TAMPA. *Academy of the Holy Names Elementary.* (Grades PreK-8), 3319 Bayshore Blvd., 33629. Tel: 813-839-5371; Fax: 813-837-5710. Dr. Claire Helm, Pres. Principals: Sr. Ann Regan, S.N.J.M.; Dr. Carmen Caltagirone. Legal Titles: *Academy of the Holy Names of Florida, Inc.*; *Academy of the Holy Names Foundation, Inc.* Sisters of the Holy Names of Jesus and Mary (Albany) 8; Lay Teachers 34; Students 531.

Mary Help of Christians School. (Grades 6-8). (Boys), 6400 E. Chelsea St., 33610-5699. Tel: 813-626-6191.
E-mail: sf9tof@scfn.thpl.lib.fl.us
Salesians of St. John Bosco. (Resident and Day School). Revs. William F. Keane, S.D.B., Dir.; John Nazzaro, S.D.B., Prin.; Kenneth Germaine, S.D.B., Admin.; Lawrence Urban, S.D.B., Youth Dir.; August P. Bosio, S.D.B.; August Bruce Craig, S.D.B.; Bernard Justen, S.D.B.; Bros. Dominic Casaraghi, S.D.B.; John Versaggi, S.D.B.; Joseph Ackroyd, S.D.B.; Salvatore Sammarco, S.B.D. Legal Title: *Salesian Society, Inc.* Priests 5; Brothers 2; Lay Teachers 7; Students 120.

Villa Madonna School, 315 W. Columbus Dr., 33602. Tel: 813-229-1322. Sr. Liz Ryan, F.M.A., Prin. Legal Title: *Salesian Sisters of Tampa, Inc.* Daughters of Mary Help of Christians 9; Lay Teachers 28; Students 580.

[F] PRESCHOOLS AND DAY CARE CENTERS

ST. PETERSBURG. *Immaculate Conception Pre-School.* Ages 1-5, Extended Care. Lower Pinellas Deanery, 2100 26th Ave. S., 33712. Tel: 813-822-2156; Fax: 813-553-9133. Mrs. Rita A. Jackson, Dir.; Mrs. Mary Calloway, Asst. Dir.; Rev. Callist N. Nyambo. Lay Teachers 16; Children 180; Total Staff 26.

CLEARWATER. *Light of Christ Preschool.* Ages 2-5, Extended Care. Upper Pinellas Deanery, 2176 Marilyn St., 34625. Tel: 813-442-4797. Mrs. Barbara Barko, Sunday School & Preschool Dir.; Rev. Timothy J. Allman, Pastor. Lay Teachers 8; Students 90.

Little Nazareth Early Childhood Center. Ages 3-4. Upper Pinellas Deanery, 820 Jasmine Way, 33756. Tel: 813-447-3494. Mrs. Sandra A. Barbeau, Dir.; Very Rev. Aiden Foynes. Lay Teachers 2; Children 32.

DADE CITY. *Sacred Heart Child Care Center.* Infant-PreK, Extended Care. Pasco Deanery, 32245 Saint Joe Rd., 33525. Tel: 904-588-4060. Mrs. Toni Watkins, Dir.; Rev. Arthur M. Villemaire. Children 150.

LARGO. *St. Jerome Early Childhood Center.* Ages 3-4. 10895 Hamlin Blvd., 33774. Tel: 813-596-9491. Denise Roach, Dir.; Rev. Msgr. Brendan Muldoon, V.G. Children 100.

NEW PORT RICHEY. *St. Thomas Aquinas Early Childhood Center*, 8320 State Rd. 54, 34653. Tel: 813-376-2330. Mrs. Cindy McKallip, Dir.; Rev. Thomas F. Earner; Pamela Bruno, Sec. Lay Teachers 6; Children 100.

PALM HARBOR. *St. Luke Early Childhood Center.* Ages 2-4, Extended Care. 2757 Alderman Rd., 34684. Tel: 813-787-2914; Fax: 813-789-9556. Ms. Carol Hussin, Dir.; Rev. Donald F. Leininger. Children 175; Total Staff 20.

SAN ANTONIO. *Holy Name Academy Child Care Center dba Bendictine Sisters of Florida.* (aka Holy Name Academy, Inc.) Ages 2-5, Extended Care. 12117 Wichers Rd., 33576. Tel: 352-588-8325; Fax: 352-588-3331. Sr. Roberta Bailey, O.S.B., Admin. Sisters 1; Lay Teachers 8; Children 70.

TAMPA. *St. Paul Preschool.* Ages 3-4. 12708 N. Dale Mabry Hwy., 33618-2802. Tel: 813-961-3023, Ext. 241. Mrs. Maureen Miller, Dir.; Rev. Msgr. John F. Neff. Lay Teachers 8; Children 120.

St. Timothy Catholic Early Childhood Learning Center, 4015 Ragg Rd., P.O. Box 340129, 33694-0129. Tel: 813-960-4857. Mrs. Charlotte Blackburn, Dir.; Rev. John G. Tapp. Students 118.

TARPON SPRINGS. *St. Ignatius Early Childhood Center.* Ages 2-6. 725 E. Orange St., P.O. Box 1306, 34688-1306. Tel: 813-934-4163. Ms. Jean Lanes, Dir.; Rev. Joseph A. Pellegrino, V.F. Lay Teachers 6; Children 54.

[G] SCHOOLS FOR EXCEPTIONAL CHILDREN

PINELLAS PARK. *Morning Star School*, 4661 80th Ave., N., 33781. Tel: 813-544-6036. Ms. Mary Lou Giacobbe, Prin. Lay Teachers 9; Students 55.

TAMPA. *Morning Star School*, 210 E. Linebaugh Ave., 33612. Tel: 813-935-0232; 932-2321. Miss Jeanette Friedheim, Prin. Lay Teachers 10; Students 86.

[H] SCHOOLS FOR THEOLOGICAL AND SPIRITUAL TRAINING

ST. PETERSBURG. *St. Petersburg Diocesan Library*, 6533 Ninth Ave. N., 33710. Mailing Address: P.O. Box 43022, 33743-3022. Tel: 813-345-3338. Rev. Msgr. Frank Mouch, Exec. Dir. Diocesan Library.

CLEARWATER. *The Cenacle of Our Lady of Divine Providence.* School of Spirituality. 702 Bayview Ave., 33759. Tel: 813-724-9505; Fax: 813-724-9421.
E-mail: cenacle@ix.netcom.com
Web site: divineprovidence.org
Ronald W. Novotny, Ph.D., Dir. Lay Teachers 3; Total Staff 9; Total Enrollment 500.

[I] DAY CARE CENTERS

TAMPA. *Peter Claver Day Care Center, Inc.*, 1431 Tampa Park Plaza, 33605. Tel: 813-229-7632. Total Staff 15; Total Assisted 82.

[J] CATHOLIC CHARITIES

ST. PETERSBURG. *Catholic Charities, Diocese of St. Petersburg, Inc.* Mailing Address: 6533 Ninth Ave., N., Ste. 1, E., 33710. Tel: 813-893-1313. Provides Counseling Services to Individuals, Families and Children; Pregnancy Related Services; Adoption Placement; Daystar Life Centers; Foster Home Placement; Family Life Education; Gerontology Services; Refugee and Immigration Services; Child Care Services; Basic Education Program; Emergency Care Services; AIDS Volunteer; Campaign for Human Development; Catholic Relief Services; Disabilities Services.
Pinellas County Regional Offices:
Central Services, 6533 Ninth Ave., N., 33710. Tel: 813-893-1313. Mr. Arnold Andrews, Exec. Dir.

[K] GENERAL HOSPITALS

ST. PETERSBURG. *St. Anthony's Hospital, Inc.*, 1200 Seventh Ave., N., 33705. Tel: 813-825-1100
For a complete listing, refer to the Hospitals section.

TAMPA. *St. Joseph's Hospital, Inc.*, 3001 W. Martin Luther King Blvd., 33607
For a complete listing, refer to the Hospitals section.

[L] RETIREMENT AND HEALTH CARE CENTERS

*ST. PETERSBURG. *Bon Secours-Maria Manor Nursing Care Center, Inc.*, 10300 Fourth St., N., 33716. Tel: 813-576-1025
For a complete listing, refer to the Hospitals section.

CLEARWATER. *The Tepeyac Corporation dba/La Clinica Guadalupana*, 1215 Drew St., Ste. 7B, 34615. Tel: 813-461-7730.
E-mail: laclinica@compuserve.com
For a complete listing, refer to the Hospitals section.

[M] RETIREMENT HOUSING

ST. PETERSBURG. *Holy Cross Housing dba Casa Santa Cruz*, 7825 54th Ave. N., 33709
For a complete listing, refer to the Hospitals section.

CLEARWATER. *St. Michael's Housing Corporation dba Casa Miguel*, 2285 State Rd. #580, 33763. Tel: 813-797-8551
For a complete listing, refer to the Hospitals section.

TAMPA. *Christ the King Housing II, Inc. dba Kings Manor*, 2946 W. Columbus Dr., 33607. Tel: 813-875-0139; Fax: 813-875-6061
For a complete listing, refer to the Hospitals section.

Christ the King Housing, Inc. dba Kings Arms, 4125 N. Lincoln Ave., 33607. Tel: 813-873-0234
For a complete listing, refer to the Hospitals section.

St. Patrick's Housing Corporation dba Patrician Arms, 4516 S. Manhattan Ave., 33611. Tel: 813-835-8227
For a complete listing, refer to the Hospitals section.

[N] SENIOR CENTERS

LARGO. *Bethlehem Centre, Inc.*, 10895 Hamlin Blvd., 34644. Tel: 813-596-9394. Senior Center Offering Daily Programming of a Social, Educational, Remedial, and Religious Nature; Luncheon on Tuesday and Friday, Counseling; Alzheimer's Support Group. Jean L. Matus, Dir. Total Staff 3.

[O] MONASTERIES AND RESIDENCES OF PRIESTS AND BROTHERS

ST. PETERSBURG. *Missionaries of Africa*, 5757 Seventh Ave. N., 33710. Tel: 813-343-1001; Fax: 813-343-4395. Rev. Paul J. Heon, M.Afr.; Bro. Philip J. Nadeau, M.Afr.; Revs. Jean C. Robitaille, M.Afr.,

Coord.; Joseph E. Hebert, M.Afr., Asst. Coord.; Constant H. Durette, M.Afr.; Joseph Sys, M.Afr.; Charles Tardiff, M.Afr.; Aime F. Lacasse, M.Afr.; Charles E. Lebel, M.Afr.

Notre Dame Residence, 1101 66th St. N., 33710. Tel: 813-384-0546.

St. Anthony Friary. Franciscan Residence and Retirement Community. 357 Second St., N., 33701; Fax: 813-821-8067. Revs. Roch A. Coogan, O.F.M., Guardian; Roy Gasnick, O.F.M., Vicar; Venard Murphy, O.F.M.; Bros. Richard James, O.F.M.; Michael Madden, O.F.M.; Marion Ressel, O.F.M., (Retired); Valerian Vaverchack, O.F.M.
Full-time Active Ministry: Revs. James Jones, O.F.M.; Arthur Murray, O.F.M.; Thomas K. Murphy, O.F.M.
Retirement Community: Revs. Patrick Adams, O.F.M.; Edward Burke, O.F.M.; Declan Bailey, O.F.M.; Theodore A. Blackowski, O.F.M.; Arnold Brown, O.F.M.; Simeon Capizzi, O.F.M.; Peter Carr, O.F.M.; Paul Feichter, O.F.M.; Louis Foley, O.F.M.; Martin A. Hanhauser; Laurence A. Hardy, O.F.M.; Clement Healy; Leonard E. Lencewicz; Neil Padden, O.F.M.; Alexis P. Morris; James P. Mulhern, O.F.M.; Columba Murphy, O.F.M.; James Schwantner, O.F.M.; Bernard Weinholtz, O.F.M.; Guy Morgan, O.F.M., (Retired); Bros. John V. Krieg, O.F.M.; John Reeder, O.F.M.; Francis X. Tokar, O.F.M.; Mathias Will, O.F.M. Total in Residence 34; Total Staff 6.

St. Peter Nolasco Residence, 5650 Seventh Ave. N., 33710-7112. Tel: 813-345-4766; Fax: 813-347-5345. Revs. Marion Frascati, O.de.M., Local Supr.; Steven M. Roszczewski, O.de.M.; Benedict Ptacek, O.de.M.; Oscar Kozyra, O.de.M.; Jose A. Furtado, O.de. M.; Bro. Richard Henry, O.de.M. Total Staff 6; Total in Residence 6.

BELLEAIR BLUFFS. *St. James Friary*, 2433 Indian Ave., 33770-2032. Tel: 813-585-2521; Fax: 813-585-2460. Franciscan Friars Ministry of the Word (New York). Revs. Edward Flanagan, O.F.M.; Roderic Petrie, O.F.M.; Martin Bednar, O.F.M.

PINELLAS PARK. *Priests of the Sacred Heart*, 6701 82nd Ave., N., 34665. Tel: 813-541-2661; Fax: 813-547-0408.
E-mail: timothy@juno.com
Bro. Timothy Murphy, S.C.J., Coord.; Most Rev. Joseph A. DePalma, S.C.J., Retired Bishop of DeAar, S.Africa; Revs. Joseph Poirier, S.C.J., (Staff); Joseph Doscher, S.C.J., (Staff); Thomas Simcox, S.C.J., (Retired); Leonard Tadyszak, S.C.J., (Retired); Raymond Vega, S.C.J., (Retired); Kenneth Mitchell, S.C.J., (Retired); Michael van der Peet, S.C.J., (Retired); Bros. Paul Schneeberger, S.C.J., (Retired); Gabriel Kersting, S.C.J., (Retired). Total Staff 3; Total in Residence 11.

ST. LEO. *St. Leo Abbey*, 33574. Tel: 352-588-8626; 588-8623; Fax: 352-588-8623. Very Rev. Simeon J. Thole, O.S.B., Apostolic Admin.; Rt. Rev. Marion Bowman, O.S.B., Retired Abbot; Revs. Andrew Metzger, O.S.B.; Paul Romfh, O.S.B.; Gregory Traeger, O.S.B.; Damian Duquesnay, O.S.B.; Richard Hugli, O.S.B.
On Duty Outside the Monastery: Rt. Rev. Patrick Shelton, O.S.B., Retired Abbot; Revs. James Hoge, O.S.B.; Robert Velten, O.S.B.; Jude Krogol, O.S.B.; David Draim, O.S.B.; Francis A. Flood, O.S.B.; Vincent Morton, O.S.B. Priests 13; Brothers 18; Internal Oblates 1.

ST. PETE BEACH. *Franciscan Friary*, 555 - 68th Ave., 33706. Tel: 813-367-2408.

SEMINOLE. *Capuchin Franciscan Residence*, 7171 128th St. N., 33776. Tel: 813-397-0011. Rev. Joseph Testagrossa, O.F.M.Cap., Admin.

[P] CONVENTS AND RESIDENCES FOR SISTERS

ST. PETERSBURG. *St. Anthony Hospital Convent*, 631 11th St. N., 33705. Tel: 813-825-1142. Franciscan Sisters of Allegany (Allegany, NY). Total in Residence 11.

FORT MYERS, 138 Coconut Drive, Rte. 10, 33908. Tel: 941-466-8139. Sisters 1.

HOLIDAY. *St. Clare's Convent*, 2109 Tilogia Court, 34690. Sr. Lucia Brady, O.S.C., Regl. Supr.
St. Clare Sisters Retreat Ministry. Tel: 813-786-3821. Total in Residence 18.

ST. LEO. *Holy Name Monastery*, P.O. Box 2450, 33574-2450. Mailing Address: P.O. Box 2450, 33574-2450. Tel: 352-588-8320; Fax: 352-588-8319.
E-mail: mgelis@saintleo.edu
Motherhouse and Novitiate of the Benedictine Sisters of Florida. Legal Title: *Holy Name Academy, Inc.* Sr. Germaine Bevans, O.S.B., Prioress. Professed Sisters 26; Temporary Promises 1; Novices 2.

TAMPA. *Franciscan Sisters of Mary*, 8501 Anglers Pointe Dr., 33637-1833. Tel: 813-988-0893. Sisters 1.
St. Clare Convent, 2924 Curtis St., 33614. Tel: 813-870-4272. Franciscan Sisters of Allegany (Allegany, NY).
St. Elizabeth Convent, 3000 Perry Ave., 33603. Tel: 813-229-1978. Franciscan Sisters of Allegany. Total Staff 5; Total in Residence 24.
Villa Madonna Convent, 2611 N. Massachusetts Ave., 33602. Tel: 813-223-2209.
E-mail: fmavilla@aol.com
Daughters of Mary Help of Christians (Haledon, NJ). Total Staff 10; Total in Residence 10.

[Q] RETREAT CENTERS

CLEARWATER. *Our Lady of Divine Providence, House of Prayer, Inc.*, 702 Bayview Ave., 34619. Tel: 813-797-7412.
Ministries of the Marian Servants of Divine Providence:
Our Lady of Divine Providence House of Prayer.
Our Lady's House of Peace. Retreat House.
Providence House. Retreat House.
The Cenacle of Our Lady of Divine Providence School of Spirituality. Affiliated with Franciscan University of Steubenville.
Living His Life Abundantly. Media Ministry.

ST. LEO. *St. Leo Abbey Retreat Center*, P.O. Box 2350, 33574. Tel: 352-588-2009. Bro. Dennis McCarthy, O.S.B., Dir.

TAMPA. *Franciscan Center, Retreat House*, 3010 Perry Ave., 33603. Tel: 813-229-2695.
E-mail: FranCntr@AOL.com
Web site: www.Lourdesnet.Org/FranciscanCenter/start.htm
Franciscan Sisters of Allegany. Sr. Catherine Cahill, O.S.F., Admin.; Sr. Colleen Brady, O.S.F.; Sr. Mary Fleming, O.S.F.; Sr. Regina Kane, O.S.F.; Sr. Patrice McCabe, O.S.F.; Sr. Juliana Mohr, O.S.F.; Sr. Margaret Rumsey, O.S.F.; Sr. Jo Marie Streva, O.S.F. Total Staff 17.

[R] SUMMER CAMPS

ST. PETERSBURG. *Our Lady of Good Counsel Camp*. Mailing Address: 8888 E. Gobbler Dr., Floral City, 34436. Tel: 352-726-2198; Fax: 352-726-3212.
E-mail: gcccamp@citrus.infi.net
Rev. James Johnson, Dir., Our Lady of Fatima Church, 550 US Hwy 41, S., Inverness, 34450. Tel: 352-726-1910; Fax: 352-344-8384.

[S] CAMPUS MINISTRY

ST. PETERSBURG. *Eckerd College - Campus Ministry*, c/o 5650 7th Ave., N., 33710-7112. Tel: 813-864-8470; Fax: 813-384-9073. Bro. Richard Henry, O.de.M., Chap.

TAMPA. *Catholic Student Center, University of South Florida*, 13005 N. 50th St., 33617. Tel: 813-988-3727. Rev. Alan Weber, Chap.
University of Tampa, 401 West Kennedy St., 33606. Tel: 813-229-1595.
E-mail: admissions@alpha.utampa.edu
Web site: http://www.utampa.edu
Rev. Kirk Mansell, S.J.

[T] MISCELLANEOUS

ST. PETERSBURG. *Catholic Charities Housing, Inc.*, 6533 Ninth Ave. N., 33710.
E-mail: ccsp@citicom.com
Web site: http://www.ccsp.org/
Chancery Office, 6363 Ninth St., 33743. For detailed information on the following listings contact the Chancery Office.
Allegany Health System Foundation, Inc.
Catholic Charities Housing, Inc.
Catholic Education Foundation, Inc.
Catholic Media Ministry, Inc.
Christopher Assurance, Inc.
Franciscan Sisters of Allegany Health System, Inc.
Regis Manor, Inc.
WBVM, 90.5 FM, Inc., Clearwater.
Catholic Charities Foundation of Tampa Bay, Inc.
Magnificat Inc., Lower Pinellas Deanery Chapter of the Diocese of St. Petersburg, Florida, 1448 83rd Ave., N., 33702.

PALM HARBOR. *St. Vincent Ministry to Priests, Inc.*, 970 Pine Hill Rd., 34683-3013. Tel: 813-784-6462; Fax: 813-787-3741. Rev. Kevin Scallon, C.M.

TAMPA. *Epiphany Housing of Tampa, Inc.*, 2514 E. Hanna Ave., 33601. Hector Buria, Pres.

RELIGIOUS INSTITUTES OF MEN REPRESENTED IN THE DIOCESE

For further details refer to the corresponding bracketed number in the Religious Institutes of Men or Women section.

[0140]—*The Augustinians*. (Villanova, PA).—O.S.A.
[0190]—*Basilian Salvatorian Fathers*. (Methuen, MA).—B.S.O.
[0200]—*Benedictine Monks*. (St. Leo, FL).—O.S.B.
[1350]—*Brothers of St. Francis Xavier*. (Ellicott City, MD).—C.F.X.
[0470]—*The Capuchin Friars*. (White Plains, NY; Union City, NJ).—O.F.M.Cap.
[0350]—*Cistercians Order of the Strict Observance (Trappists)*. (Spencer, MA).—O.C.S.O.
[1320]—*Clerics of St. Viator*. (Arlington Heights, IL).—C.S.V.
[0310]—*Congregation of Christian Brothers*. (New Rochelle, NY).—C.F.C.
[0220]—*Congregation of the Blessed Sacrament*. (Cleveland, OH).—S.S.S.
[0630]—*Congregation of the Missionaries of the Holy Family*. (Santiago, Chile).—M.S.F.
[1130]—*Congregation of the Priests of the Sacred Heart*. (Hales Corner, WI).—S.C.J.
[0520]—*Franciscan Friars*. (New York, NY; Pulaski, WI; Kennebunkport, ME; Dublin, Ireland).—O.F.M.
[0530]—*Franciscan Friars of the Atonement*. (Garrison, NY).—S.A.
[0650]—*Holy Ghost Fathers*. (Dublin, Ireland).—C.S.Sp.
[0300]—*Institute of Charity*. (Peoria, IL).—I.C.
[0690]—*Jesuit Fathers and Brothers*. (New Orleans, LA; Baltimore, MD).—S.J.
[0780]—*Marist Fathers*. (Washington, DC).—S.M.
[0800]—*Maryknoll*.—M.M.
[0850]—*Missionaries of Africa*. (Washington, DC).—M.Afr.
[0910]—*Oblates of Mary Immaculate*. (Washington, DC; St. Paul, MN).—O.M.I.
[0970]—*Order of Our Lady of Mercy*. (Cleveland, OH).—O.deM.
[0430]—*Order of Preachers (Dominicans)*. (Dublin, Ireland).—O.P.
[0610]—*Priests of the Congregation of the Holy Cross*. (Notre Dame, IN; Bridgeport, CT).—C.S.C.
[1060]—*Redemptorist Fathers*. (New York, NY).—C.SS.R.
[0700]—*St. Joseph's Society of the Sacred Heart*. (Baltimore, MD).—S.S.J.
[1190]—*Salesians of Don Bosco*. (New Rochelle, NY).—S.D.B.
[]—*Scarboro Foreign Missions*. (Scarboro, Ontario, Canada).—S.F.M.
[1060]—*Society of the Precious Blood*. (Dayton, OH).—C.PP.S.
[0560]—*Third Order Regular of Saint Francis*. (Pittsburgh, PA).—T.O.R.

RELIGIOUS INSTITUTES OF WOMEN REPRESENTED IN THE DIOCESE

[0130]—*Apostles of the Sacred Heart of Jesus*. (Hamden, CT).—A.S.C.J.
[0230]—*Benedictine Sisters of Pontifical Jurisdiction*. (St. Leo, FL).—O.S.B.
[3110]—*Congregation of Our Lady of Retreat in the Cenacle*. (Lake Ronkonkoma, NY).—R.C.
[3710]—*Congregation of the Sisters of St. Agnes*.—C.S.A.
[1920]—*Congregation of the Sisters of the Holy Cross*.—C.S.C.
[1730]—*Congregation of the Sisters of the Third Order of St. Francis, Oldenburg, IN*.—O.S.F.
[0850]—*Daughters of Mary Help of Christians*. (Haledon, NJ).—F.M.A.
[]—*Daughters of Mary Immaculate*. (Vietnam).—F.M.I.
[1070-01]—*Dominican Sisters*.—O.P.
[1070-02]—*Dominican Sisters*.—O.P.
[1070-05]—*Dominican Sisters*.—O.P.
[1070-11]—*Dominican Sisters*.—O.P.
[1070-13]—*Dominican Sisters*.—O.P.
[1120]—*Dominican Sisters of the Roman Congregation*.—O.P.
[1140]—*Eucharistic Missionaries of St. Dominic*.—O.P.
[1370]—*Franciscan Missionaries of Mary*.—F.M.M.
[1180]—*Franciscan Sisters of Allegany, New York*.—O.S.F.
[1310]—*Franciscan Sisters of Little Falls, Minnesota*.—O.S.F.
[1370]—*Franciscan Sisters of Mary*. (Bronx, NY).—F.M.M.
[1415]—*Franciscan Sisters of Mary*. (St. Louis, MO).—F.S.M.
[]—*Handmaids of the Holy Child Jesus*. (Nigeria).—H.H.C.J.
[2575]—*Institute of the Sisters of Mercy of the Americas*. (Merion, PA; Chicago, IL; New York, NY; Detroit, MI).—R.S.M.
[2420]—*Marist Missionary Sisters (Missionary Sisters of the Society of Mary)*.—S.M.S.M.
[2470]—*Maryknoll Sisters of St. Dominic*.—M.M.
[2490]—*Medical Mission Sisters*. (Philadelphia, PA).—S.C.M.M.
[2480]—*Medical Missionaries of Mary*.—M.M.M.
[2720]—*Mission Helpers of the Sacred Heart*. (Baltimore, MD).—M.H.S.H.
[]—*Missionarias Hijas de la Madre de la Luz*. (Mexico).—M.H.M.L.

[1360]—*Missionary Franciscan Sisters of the Immaculate Conception.* (Newton, MA).—O.S.F.
[0242]—*Missionary Sisters of the Society of Mary.*—S.M.S.M.
[3760]—*Order of St. Clare.* (Evansville, IN; Greenville, SC).—O.S.C.
[3770]—*Order of St. Clare.*—O.S.C.
[4180]—*Religious Venerini Sisters.*—M.P.V.
[2970]—*School Sisters of Notre Dame.* (Baltimore, MD; Wilton, CT).—S.S.N.D.
[1680]—*School Sisters of St. Francis.* (Milwaukee, WI).—S.S.S.F.
[3590]—*Servants of Mary (Servite Sisters).*—O.S.M.
[0440]—*Sisters of Charity of Cincinnati, Ohio.* (Mt. St. Joseph, OH).—S.C.
[0500]—*Sisters of Charity of Nazareth.*—S.C.N.
[0590]—*Sisters of Charity of Saint Elizabeth, Convent Station.*—S.C.
[0570]—*Sisters of Charity of Seton Hill.* (Greensberg, PA).—S.C.
[0650]—*Sisters of Charity of St. Vincent dePaul.*—S.C.
[1930]—*Sisters of Holy Cross.* (Pittsfield, NH).—C.S.C.
[]—*Sisters of Mary, Mother of God.* (Tampa, FL).—S.M.M.G.
[2575]—*Sisters of Mercy of The Americas.*—R.S.M.
[2990]—*Sisters of Notre Dame.* (Chardon, OH).—S.N.D.
[3000]—*Sisters of Notre Dame de Namur.* (Boston, MA).—S.N.D.deN.
[3360]—*Sisters of Providence.* (St. Mary of the Woods, IN.).—S.P.
[3893]—*Sisters of Saint Joseph of Chestnut Hill, Philadelphia.*—S.S.J.
[3720]—*Sisters of St. Anne.*—S.S.A.
[]—*Sisters of St. Anne Bangalore.*—S.A.B.
[3750]—*Sisters of St. Chretienne.* (Wrentham, MA).—S.S.Ch.
[3770]—*Sisters of St. Clare.*—O.S.C.
[1510]—*Sisters of St. Francis.*—O.S.F.
[1630]—*Sisters of St. Francis of Penance and Christian Charity.*—O.S.F.
[1650]—*Sisters of St. Francis of Philadelphia.*—O.S.F.
[1570]—*Sisters of St. Francis of the Holy Family.*—O.S.F.
[3830-11]—*Sisters of St. Joseph.*—S.S.J.
[3830-14]—*Sisters of St. Joseph.*—S.S.J.
[3840]—*Sisters of St. Joseph of Carondelet.* (St. Louis, MO).—C.S.J.
[3880]—*Sisters of St. Joseph of Medaille.*—C.S.J.
[3890]—*Sisters of St. Joseph of Peace.* (Englewood Cliffs, NJ).—C.S.J.P.
[3900]—*Sisters of St. Joseph of St. Augustine, Florida.*—S.S.J.
[1970]—*Sisters of the Holy Family of Nazareth.* (Philadelphia, PA).—C.S.F.N.
[1990]—*Sisters of the Holy Names of Jesus and Mary.* (Albany, NY).—S.N.J.M.
[3730]—*Sisters of the Order St. Basil the Great.* (Uniontown, PA).—O.S.B.M.
[1490]—*Sisters of the Third Franciscan Order.*—O.S.F.
[2150]—*Sisters, Servants of the Immaculate Heart of Mary.*—I.H.M.
[2160]—*Sisters, Servants of the Immaculate Heart of Mary.*—I.H.M.
[4190]—*Visitation Nuns.* (Wheeling, WV; Washington, DC).—V.H.M.

DIOCESAN CEMETERIES

CLEARWATER. *Calvary Catholic,* 11801 U.S. Hwy. 19 N., 33764-7407.

NECROLOGY

(No Deaths)

Diocese of Salina

(Dioecesis Salinensis)

Most Reverend

GEORGE K. FITZSIMONS, D.D.

Bishop of Salina; ordained March 18, 1961; appointed Titular Bishop of Pertusa and Auxiliary Bishop of Kansas City-St. Joseph May 27, 1975; Episcopal ordination July 3, 1975; appointed Bishop of Salina March 22, 1984; installed May 29, 1984. *Address all official communications to: P.O. Box 980, Salina, KS, 67402.*

Chancery Office: 103 N. Ninth, P.O. Box 980, Salina, KS, 67402-0980. Tel.: 785-827-8746; Fax: 785-827-6133.

E-mail address: chancery@midusa.net

FORMERLY DIOCESE OF CONCORDIA.

ESTABLISHED AUGUST 2, 1887.

SEE TRANSFERRED TO SALINA DECEMBER 23, 1944.

Square Miles 26,685.

(New boundaries established by Apostolic Letters dated July 1, 1897).

Bounded on the west by Colorado, on the north by Nebraska, on the east by the east lines of Washington, Riley, Geary and Dickinson Counties, and on the south by the south lines of Dickinson, Saline, Ellsworth, Russell, Ellis, Trego, Gove, Logan and Wallace Counties in the State of Kansas.

For legal titles of parishes and diocesan institutions, consult the Chancery Office.

STATISTICAL OVERVIEW

Personnel	
Bishop	1
Retired Bishops	1
Priests: Diocesan Active in Diocese	49
Priests: Active Outside Diocese	3
Priests: Diocesan in Foreign Missions	1
Priests: Retired, Sick or Absent	16
Number of Diocesan Priests	69
Religious Priests in Diocese	16
Ordinations:	
Diocesan Priests	1
Total Brothers	1
Total Sisters	207
Parishes	
Parishes	92
With Resident Pastor:	
Resident Diocesan Priests	42
Resident Religious Priests	5
Without Resident Pastor:	
Administered by Priests	40
Administered by Women Religious	4
Administered by Lay People	1
Welfare	
Homes for the Aged	3
Total Assisted	238
Educational	
Diocesan Students in Other Seminaries	4
Total Seminarians	4
High Schools, Diocesan and Parish	4
Total Students	402
High Schools, Private	1
Total Students	305
Elementary Schools, Diocesan and Parish	12
Total Students	1,953
Catechesis/Religious Education:	
High School Students	2,383
Elementary Students	6,124
Total Students Under Catholic Instruction	11,171
Teachers in the Diocese:	
Priests	8
Sisters	8
Lay Teachers	203
Vital Statistics	
Receptions into the Church:	
Infant Baptism Totals	1,005
Adult Baptism Totals	141
Received into Full Communion	185
First Communions	959
Confirmations	1,264
Marriages:	
Catholic	311
Interfaith	223
Total Marriages	534
Deaths	589
Total Catholic Population	53,060
Total Population	331,427

Former Bishops—Rt. Rev. RICHARD SCANNELL, D.D., cons. in Nashville, Tenn., Nov. 30, 1887; transferred to Omaha, Jan. 30, 1891; died Jan. 8, 1916.—Rt. Rev. JOHN J. HENNESSY, D.D., Apostolic Administrator, 1891-98, Bishop of Wichita.—Rt. Rev. THADDEUS BUTLER, D.D., Bishop-elect; died July 17, 1897.—Rt. Rev. JOHN F. CUNNINGHAM, D.D., cons. Sept. 21, 1898; died June 23, 1919.—Most Rev. FRANCIS J. TIEF, D.D., cons. Mar. 30, 1921; retired and appointed Titular Bishop of Nisa, June 11, 1938; died Sept. 22, 1965.—Most Rev. FRANK A. THILL, D.D., cons. Oct. 28, 1938; transferred to Salina, Dec. 23, 1944; died May 21, 1957.—Most Rev. FREDERICK W. FREKING, D.D., cons. Nov. 30, 1957; transferred to LaCrosse, Dec. 30, 1964.—Most Rev. CYRIL J. VOGEL, D.D., ord. Bishop, June 17, 1965; died Oct. 4, 1979.—Most Rev. DANIEL W. KUCERA, O.S.B., Ph.D., D.D., ord. May 26, 1949; appt. Titular Bishop of Natchez and Auxiliary Bishop of Joliet, June 6, 1977; cons. July 21, 1977; appt. Bishop of Salina, March 11, 1980; installed May 7, 1980; transferred to Archbishop of Archdiocese of Dubuque, February 23, 1984.

Chancery Office—103 N. Ninth, P.O. Box 980, Salina, 67402-0980. Tel: 785-827-8746; Fax: 785-827-6133.

Vicar General and Chancellor—Rev. Msgr. JAMES E. HAKE, J.C.L., *Res., Sacred Heart Cathedral, 118 N. 9th, Salina, 67401.*

Diocesan Finance Officer—Rev. JEROME L. MORGAN, *Res., St. Wenceslaus, Box 528, Wilson, 67490.* Mr. GREG LUST, Asst. Finance Officer & Business Mgr., *P.O. Box 980, Salina, 67402-0980.* Rev. Msgr. GILBERT LANDOLL, Financial Consultant.

Diocesan Office of Planning—Sr. DORIS DURANT, O.S.M., Dir.

Diocesan Tribunal—103 N. Ninth, P.O. Box 980, Salina, 67402-0980. Tel: 785-827-8746; Fax: 785-827-6133.

Judicial Vicar-Officialis—Rev. KENNETH LOHRMEYER, J.C.L.

Associate Judges—Rev. Msgr. ARMAND GIRARD, J.C.L.; Rev. Msgr. JAMES E. HAKE, J.C.L.; Revs. KENNETH P. LOHRMEYER, J.C.L.; DANIEL SCHEETZ, J.C.L.

Defenders of the Bond—Rev. Msgr. ARMAND GIRARD, J.C.L.; Rev. Msgr. JAMES E. HAKE, J.C.L.; Revs. KENNETH P. LOHRMEYER, J.C.L.; DANIEL SCHEETZ, J.C.L.

Auditors-Notaries—MARY ANN HUFFMAN; JENNY KEELER; FRANCES SCHNEIDER; DARLENE STREIT.

Promoter of Justice and Guardians—Rev. DANIEL SCHEETZ, J.C.L.; Rev. Msgr. GILBERT LANDOLL.

Procurators and Advocates—Revs. ROGER K. MEITL; JEROME L. MORGAN; WILLIAM SURMEIER; JOHN WOLESKY; Sr. MARY LOU ROBERTS, C.S.J.

Diocesan Finance Council—Most Rev. GEORGE K. FITZSIMONS, D.D.; Rev. JEROME L. MORGAN; BILL BECKMEYER; DONALD P. DIEDERICH; JOHN GRAHAM; GREG LUST; JOHN GRAHAM; ROBERT SCHMIDT.

College of Consultors—Rev. Msgr. JAMES E. HAKE, J.C.L.; Revs. MERLIN KIEFFER; MELVIN LONG; JEROME L. MORGAN; DONALD D. ZIMMERMAN.

Episcopal Vicars—Rev. JAMES HOOVER, Western District; Rev. DONALD D. ZIMMERMAN, West Central District; Rev. JEROME L. MORGAN, East Central District; Rev. LOUIS MATTAS, Eastern District.

Council of Priests—Revs. WILLIAM SURMEIER, Chm. MERLIN KIEFFER; JOSEPH POPELKA, Recording Sec.; Rev. Msgr. JAMES E. HAKE, J.C.L.; Revs. FRANK COADY; FRANK GRINKO, O.F.M.Cap., Sec. KENNETH LOHRMEYER; ALLEN SCHEER, Treas. FRED GATSCHET; JAMES HOOVER; MELVIN LONG; JEROME L. MORGAN; DONALD D. ZIMMERMAN, Vice-Chm.

Diocesan Pastoral Council—Most Rev. GEORGE K. FITZSIMONS, D.D.; PAT SCHMIDTBERGER, Chm.; Sr. MARY LOU ROBERTS, C.S.J., Moderator; DEBORAH JOHNSTON, Vice Chm.; Revs. JEROME L. MORGAN; JOSEPH POPELKA; MERLIN KIEFFER; LOUIS MATTAS; WILLIAM SURMEIER; Sr. CAROLYN JUENEMANN, C.S.J.; Sr. DORIS DURANT, O.S.M.; Sr. MARY CATHERINE GRIEF, C.S.A.; Sr. KENNETH STRUCKHOFF, C.S.A.; Sr. MARY JO THUMMEL, C.S.J. Laity: JOHN BROBERG; MARITA CAMPBELL, Sec. TERRY CHAPUT; MONICA DUSIN; ROSANN FELDER; ALICE FOX; KATHY GANSEL; RANDY HUSER; STANLEY KRIER; RON LAGER; LARRY LARSON; ROXANNA MARTIN; MARLENE MONTGOMERY; DENNIS PAHLS; LEE PLOUSSARD; ED WALDSCHMIDT; JOAN WESSEL.

Personnel Board—Most Rev. GEORGE K. FITZSIMONS, D.D.; Revs. HENRY BAXA; AL BRUNGARDT; FRANK COADY; AL DWYER; JEROME MORGAN; Rev. Msgr. JAMES E. HAKE, J.C.L., Ex Officio.

Seminary Board—Most Rev. GEORGE K. FITZSIMONS, D.D.; Revs. STEVE HEINA; GALEN LONG; LEROY METRO; KEITH WEBER; KEVIN WEBER; JOHN WOLESKY.

Diocesan Offices and Directors

Art and Architecture Commission—Rev. JEROME L. MORGAN, Chm.; Rev. Msgr. JAMES E. HAKE, J.C.L., Vice Chm.; Rev. Msgr. JOHN GEORGE WEBER; Revs. FRANK COADY; JOHN MOEDER; DONALD D. ZIMMERMAN; Mr. GREG LUST; Mr. STEVE HOLKE.

Continuing Formation Committee—Revs. MELVIN LONG, Chm. KEN LOHRMEYER; MARK WESELY. Ex-Officio: Most Rev. GEORGE K. FITZSIMONS; Rev. Msgr. JAMES HAKE.

Catholic Charities, Inc. & Family Life, Board—Most Rev. GEORGE K. FITZSIMONS, D.D.; Revs. ALOYSIUS BRUNGARDT; RON GILARDI, O.F.M.Cap.; DAMIAN RICHARDS; Sr. MARY LOU ROBERTS, C.S.J., L.B.S.W.; MIKE STOTTMANN, Pres. DARLENE STOTTMANN; JIM LEDUC; SUSAN LEDUC; RICHARD BACHAMP, Vice Pres. TONYA BACHAMP; RENZIE POE; LULA POE; RON RIPPE,

Sec. DEBI RIPPE; GUY STEIER; JULIE STEIER; Dr. BILL SIBILLA; JUDY SIBILLA; BOB SCHUMACHER; BERNIE SCHUMACHER.

Catholic Charities Outreach Office—JOAN PERKINS, Sec. JANET RUSSELL, L.S.C.S.W., Adoption Counselor; Rev. WILLIAM SURMEIER, M.S., Pastoral Counselor; Sr. ANN WALTERS, C.S.A., M.S., Pastoral Counselor, *2707 Vine #17, P.O. Box 811, Hays, 67601.* Tel: 785-625-2644; Fax: 785-625-6497.

Catholic Charities of Salina, Inc.—Sr. MARY LOU ROBERTS, C.S.J., L.B.S.W., Social Worker; BONNIE FREY, L.S.C.S.W., Adoption Worker; BILL WHITE, L.S.C.S.W., Counselor; BONNIE OTEY, Sec., *425 W. Iron, P.O. Box 1366, Salina, 67401.* Tel: 785-825-0208; Fax: 785-826-9708.

Catholic Community Annual Appeal—*P.O. Box 980, Salina, 67402-0980;* Fax: 785-827-6133.

Office of Catholic Formation—Rev. Msgr. JAMES E. HAKE, J.C.L., Dir., *103 N. Ninth, P.O. Box 825, Salina, 67402.* Tel: 785-827-8746; Fax: 785-827-6133.

Coordinator of Office of Catholic Formation—Sr. BARBARA ELLEN APACELLER, C.S.J.

Director of Religious Education—Sr. BARBARA ELLEN APACELLER, C.S.J.

Superintendent of Schools—Sr. CLARISSA TENBRINK, A.S.C.

Consultant for Religious Education & Media—(Grades K-8), PEGGY HERBERT.

Consultant for Religious Education—(Grades 9-12), Sr. BARBARA ELLEN APACELLER, C.S.J.

Director of Adult Education—Rev. FRANK COADY.

Valuing Your Sexuality—PEGGY HEBERT, Dir.

Audio-Visual—PEGGY HEBERT.

Catholic Youth Organization and Youth Ministry—Sr. BARBARA ELLEN APACELLER, C.S.J., *P.O. Box 980, Salina, 67402.*

Office of Communications—*P.O. Box 980, Salina, 67402.*

Diocesan Council of Education—NADINE KARLIN, Pres.; Sr. MARY JO THUMMEL, C.S.J.; PAT BRECKUNITCH, Sec. JERRY CASEY; STEVE JUENEMANN; ARVILLA JUENEMANN, Vice Pres. MARY POPELKA; ANGIE BAALMAN; MARTHA BRUNGARDT; Revs. HENRY BAXA; GALEN LONG. Ex Officio from Chancery Staff: Rev. Msgr. JAMES E. HAKE, J.C.L.; Sr. BARBARA APACELLER, C.S.J.; Sr. CLARISSA TENBRINK, A.S.C.

Due Process Board—Revs. KENNETH P. LOHRMEYER, J.C.L., Chm.; Sr. BETH STOVER, C.S.J.; Mr. NICK COMPAGNONE; MARY JO HEATH; Mr. LEROY HERRMAN; Rev. Msgr. JAMES E. HAKE, J.C.L., Clerk.

Family Life Office—Sr. MARY LOU ROBERTS, C.S.J., Acting Dir.; Rev. ALOYSIUS BRUNGARDT, Moderator.

Family Ministry Advisory Board—Sr. MARY LOU ROBERTS, C.S.J.; Revs. ALOYSIUS BRUNGARDT; MERLIN KIEFFER; LOREN WERTH; Sr. CAROLYN JUENEMANN; SHEILA MARCOTTE, Sec.

Holy Childhood, Pontifical Association—Rev. Msgr. JAMES E. HAKE, J.C.L., Dir., *P.O. Box 980, Salina, 67402.*

Office of Liturgy—Rev. FRANK COADY, Dir., *P.O. Box 980, Salina, 67402.* Tel: 785-827-8746; Fax: 785-827-6133.

Newspaper—*"The Register, Northwestern Kansas Edition";* Rev. Msgr. RAYMOND MENARD, Editor; Mr. GREG LUST, Business Mgr., *P.O. Box 1038, Salina, 67402.*

Priests' Continuing Formation Committee—Revs. MELVIN LONG, Chm. KENNETH P. LOHRMEYER, J.C.L.; KERRY NINEMIRE; MARK WESELY. Ex Officio: Most Rev. GEORGE K. FITZSIMONS, D.D.; Rev. Msgr. JAMES E. HAKE, J.C.L.

Propagation of the Faith—Rev. Msgr. JAMES E. HAKE, J.C.L., Dir., *P.O. Box 980, Salina, 67402.* Tel: 785-827-8746.

Rural Life Conference—Rev. Msgr. JOHN GEORGE WEBER, Dir., *926 E. Republic, Salina, 67432.* Tel: 785-823-1322.

Salina Diocesan Clergy Health and Retirement Association, Inc.—Board of Trustees: Most Rev. GEORGE K. FITZSIMONS, D.D., Pres., *103 N. Ninth, P.O. Box 980, Salina, 67402-0980.* Revs. AL BRUNGARDT; ROGER HOUGH; LOREN WORTH; LOUIS MATTAS; RALPH ASCHENBRENNER; FRED GATSCHET. Ex-Officio: Rev. JEROME MORGAN; Mr. GREG LUST.

Salina Diocesan Council of Catholic Women (S.D.CC.W.)—ALICE FOX, Pres., *2326 Glen Circle, Salina, 67401.* Rev. KEVIN WEBER, Moderator, *St. Mary's Church, 703 Monroe St., Ellis, 67637.*

Scouting—Rev. DONALD P. MCCARTHY, *625 Freeman Ave., Oakley, 67748.*

Vocations—

Diocesan Director of Vocations—Rev. KEVIN WEBER.

Spiritual Formation for Newly Ordained Priests—Rev. FRANK COADY.

Spiritual Dir. for Seminarians & Newly Ordained Priests—Rev. LEROY METRO.

CLERGY, PARISHES, MISSIONS AND PAROCHIAL SCHOOLS

CITY OF SALINA
(Saline County)

1—CATHEDRAL OF THE SACRED HEART (1876), Rev. Msgr. James E. Hake; Rev. Fred Gatschet; Sr. Mary Augustine, C.S.J., Pastoral Assoc. In res., Rev. Msgr. Raymond Menard.
Res., 118 N. Ninth St., 67401. Tel: 785-823-7221. [JC]
School—(Grades PreK-6) 406 W. Iron Ave., 67401. Tel: 785-825-4798. Pat Breckunitch, Prin.
Sisters of St. Joseph 1; Lay Teachers 10; Students 169.
Catechesis/Religious Programs—Tel: 785-823-2713. Peggy Hebert, D.R.E.
Students 146.

2—ST. ELIZABETH ANN SETON (1982), Rev. Frank Coady, Priest Supvr.; Sr. Rose Walters, C.S.A., Parish Dir. & Pastoral Admin.
Res., 1000 Burr Oak Ln., 67401. Tel: 785-825-5282. [JC]
Catechesis/Religious Programs—D.R.E.: Beverly Carlin; Melaney Melander.
Students 165.

3—ST. MARY'S (1959), Revs. Kerry Ninemire; John Wolesky.
Res., 230 E. Cloud St., 67401. Tel: 785-827-5575; Fax: 913-827-8997. [JC]
School—(Grades PreK-6) 304 E. Cloud St., 67401. Tel: 913-827-4200. Mr. Nick Compagnone, Prin.
Lay Teachers 20; Students 406.
Catechesis/Religious Programs—Mrs. Nancy Main, D.R.E.
Students 367.

OUTSIDE THE CITY OF SALINA

Abilene, Dickinson Co., St. Andrew's (1874), Rev. Louis S. Mattas.
Res., 102 N.W. 4th, P.O. Box 398, 67410. Tel: 785-263-1570. [CEM]
School—(Grades PreK-5). Tel: 785-263-2453. Dennis McCall, Prin.
Lay Teachers 6; Students 64.
Catechesis/Religious Programs—Tel: 785-263-1570. Alice Bartow, D.R.E.
Students 145.

Angelus, Sheridan Co., St. Paul's (German). Attended by St. Joseph's Church, Oakley.
Mailing Address: 625 Freeman Ave., Oakley, 67748. Tel: 785-672-3828.
Church—Tel: 785-824-3256. [CEM]
Catechesis/Religious Programs—Students 49.

Antonino, Ellis Co., Our Lady Help of Christians (1905). Attended by St. Joseph, Hays.
Mailing Address: P.O. Drawer 1000, Hays, 67601. Tel: 785-625-7356; Fax: 785-625-7394.

Atwood, Rawlins Co., Sacred Heart (1879), Rev. Damian Richards.
Res., Sacred Heart, 508 N. Railroad Ave., 67730. Tel: 785-626-3335. [CEM][JC 3]
Catechesis/Religious Programs—Tel: 785-626-3431. Sharon McDougal, D.R.E.
Students 148.

Aurora, Cloud Co., St. Peter's (1884), Rev. Henry Kieffer; Rev. Msgr. James E. Hake, Parish Dir. & Pastoral Admin.
Res., Tel: 785-464-3754. [CEM][JC]
Catechesis/Religious Programs—Tel: 785-464-3461.
Students 57.

Beardsley, Rawlins Co., St. John's,
Mailing Address: P.O. Box 1170, St. Francis, 67756.
Church—Atwood, 67730. [CEM]
Catechesis/Religious Programs—Students 38.

Belleville, Republic Co., St. Edward's (1901), Rev. John A. Moeder.
Res., 1827 Q St., P.O. Box 99, 66935. Tel: 785-527-5559. [CEM]
Catechesis/Religious Programs—Sacred Hearts Center, 1813 Q St., 66935. Tel: 785-527-5819. Bev Lapo, D.R.E.
Students 166.

Beloit, Mitchell Co., St. John the Baptist (1869), Rev. Henry R. Baxa; Sr. Mary Stanislaus Porter, Pastoral Assoc.
Res., 701 E. Court St., 67420. Tel: 785-738-2851. [CEM]
School—(Grades PreK-6). Tel: 785-738-3941. William F. Orth, Prin.
Sisters of St. Joseph 1; Lay Teachers 8; Students 143.
High School—(Grades 7-12). Tel: 785-738-2942; Fax: 785-738-4462. Bertha Johnson, Prin.
Priests 1; Lay Teachers 11; Students 83.
Catechesis/Religious Programs—Tel: 785-738-2851.
Students 103.

Bird City, Cheyenne Co., St. Joseph's (1911). Attended by St. Francis, St. Francis. Rev. Mark Wesely.
Church—67731. Tel: 785-332-2680.
Catechesis/Religious Programs—Students 33.

Brookville, Saline Co., St. Joseph's (1884). Attended by Sacred Heart Cathedral, Salina.
Mailing Address: 118 N. 9th, Salina, 67401.
Church—67425. [CEM]

Catharine, Ellis Co., St. Catherine's (1892), Rev. Ronald Gilardi, O.F.M.Cap.
Mailing Address: P.O. Box 18, 67627. Tel: 785-625-5091. [CEM]

Cawker City, Mitchell Co., SS. Peter and Paul (1878) (German). Attended by St. Boniface, Tipton. Jeanie Munsch, Pastoral Assoc.
Church—Tel: 785-781-4319; 373-4455. [CEM]
Catechesis/Religious Programs—1202 Holly, 67430. Tel: 785-781-4835.
Students 54.

Chapman, Dickinson Co., St. Michael's (1883), Carolyn Juenemann, C.S.J., Parish Dir./Pastoral Admin.; Rev. Richard E. Lutgen.
Res., P.O. Box 217, 67431. Tel: 785-922-6509. [CEM]
Catechesis/Religious Programs—Tel: 785-922-6509. Loretta Fisher, D.R.E.
Students 102.

Claudell, Smith Co., St. Francis (1914). Attended by SS. Philip & James, Phillipsburg.
Mailing Address: R.R. #3, Box 144A, Phillipsburg, 67661. Tel: 785-543-5367.

Clay Center, Clay Co., SS. Peter and Paul (1879), Rev. Loren J. Werth.
Res., 730 Court St., 67432. Tel: 785-632-5011. [CEM]
Catechesis/Religious Programs—Tel: 913-632-3204. Cyndy Schwensen, D.R.E.
Students 135.

Clifton, Washington Co., St. Mary's (French-German). Attended by St. John the Baptist, Clyde.
Mailing Address: 204 N. High, Clyde, 66938. Tel: 785-446-3474; Fax: 785-446-2268.
Church—Tel: 913-455-3384. [CEM]
Catechesis/Religious Programs—Tel: 913-455-2291. Mrs. Linda Kantack, D.R.E.
Students 60.

Clyde, Cloud Co., St. John the Baptist's (1880) (French-German), Rev. LeRoy Metro; Brenda Koch, Pastoral Assoc. & D.R.E.
Res., 204 N. High, 66938. Tel: 785-446-3474; Fax: 785-446-2268. [CEM]
Catechesis/Religious Programs—Students 108.

Colby, Thomas Co., Sacred Heart, Rev. Galen Long; Sr. Rosalyn Juenemann, C.S.J., Pastoral Assoc. & D.R.E.
Res., 585 N. French Ave., 67701. Tel: 785-462-2179. [CEM]
School—(Grades PreK-5). Tel: 785-462-2813. Mr. Ladislado Hernandez, Prin.
Lay Teachers 6; Students 104.
Catechesis/Religious Programs—Students 333.

Collyer, Trego Co., St. Michael's (1893) (German), Rev. Basil Torrez.
Res., Ainslie Ave., Box 174, 67631. Tel: 785-769-5272. [CEM][JC]
Catechesis/Religious Programs—Melissa Metcalf, D.R.E.
Students 73.

Concordia, Cloud Co., Our Lady of Perpetual Help (1887), Rev. Steven Heina.
Office: 232 E. Fifth, P.O. Box 608, 66901. Tel: 785-243-1099.
Res., 420 Kansas, P.O. Box 608, 66901. Tel: 785-243-4658. [CEM]
Catechesis/Religious Programs—Tel: 785-243-1410. Laura Jo Meyer, D.R.E.
Students 339.

Cuba, Republic Co., St. Isidore's (1873) (Czech). Attended by St. Edward, Belleville.
Mailing Address: P.O. Box 99, Belleville, 66935. [CEM]

Damar, Rooks Co., St. Joseph's (1912). Attended by Immaculate Heart of Mary, Hill City.
Mailing Address: 10 N. 10th Ave., Hill City, 67642. Tel: 785-839-4343. [CEM]
Catechesis/Religious Programs—Tel: 785-839-4360. Gil Berland, D.R.E.
Students 78.

Delphos, Ottawa Co., St. Paul's. Attended by Immaculate Conception, Minneapolis.
Church—67436.

Densmore, Norton Co., St. Mary's. Closed. For inquiries for parish records contact the Chancery.

Dorrance, Russell Co., St. Joseph's (1902) (German-Irish). Attended by St. Wenceslaus, Wilson. Rev. Jerome Morgan.
Mailing Address: P.O. Box 528, Wilson, 67490. Tel: 785-658-3361. [CEM]
Catechesis/Religious Programs—Tel: 785-666-4419. Susan Thielen, D.R.E.
Students 68.

Downs, Osborne Co., St. Mary's (1903). Attended by St. Aloysius, Osborne.
Mailing Address: P.O. Box 267, Osbourne, 67473.
Church—1312 Prentice, 67437. Tel: 785-454-3551.
Catechesis/Religious Programs—Students 59.

Ellis, Ellis Co., St. Mary's (1870), Rev. Kevin Weber; Sr. Doris M. Flax, Pastoral Assoc.
Church—703 Monroe, 67637. Tel: 785-726-4522.
School—(Grades PreK-6). Tel: 913-726-3185. Mrs. Annie Diedrich, Prin.
Sisters of St. Joseph 2; Lay Teachers 8; Students 72.
Catechesis/Religious Programs—Mary Reiter, D.R.E.
Students 137.

Ellsworth, Ellsworth Co., St. Bernard's (1909), Rev. Daniel L. Scheetz.
Res., 911 Kansas St., 67439. Tel: 785-472-3136.
Catechesis/Religious Programs—Students 90.

Elmo, Dickinson Co., St. Columba's. Attended by St. John the Evangelist, Herington.
712 N. Broadway, Herington, 67449. [CEM]

Esbon, Jewell Co., Sacred Heart (1887). Attended by St. Theresa's, Mankato.
Mailing Address: P.O. Box 265, Mankato, 66956.
Church—Tel: 785-378-3939. [CEM]

Fort Riley, Riley Co., Fort Riley Catholic Community. Attended by Archdiocese for the Military Services.

Glasco, Cloud Co., St. Mary's. Attended by St. Patrick, Lincoln.
Mailing Address: P.O. Box 327, Lincoln, 67455.
Church—301 E. First St., P.O. Box 554, 67445. [CEM]

Goodland, Sherman Co., Our Lady of Perpetual Help (1887), Rev. Daryl Olmstead.
Church—307 W. 13th, 67735. Tel: 785-899-7205.
Catechesis/Religious Programs—Tel: 785-899-5407. John Eisenbart, D.R.E.
Students 178.

Gorham, Russell Co., St. Mary's (1984), Rev. Daniel L. Scheetz, Supvr.; Sr. Mary Jo Thummel, C.S.J., Admin.
Res., Box 135, 67640. Tel: 785-637-5241. [CEM]
Catechesis/Religious Programs—St. Mary's Parish Center, 161 Chicago, 67640. Tel: 785-637-5224. Pam Novak, D.R.E., Tel: 785-637-5273.
Students 69.

Grainfield, Gove Co., St. Agnes (1910) (German). Attended by Sacred Heart, Park. Rev. Mark Berland.
Mailing Address: P.O. Box 78, Park, 67751-0078. Tel: 785-673-4684. [JC]
Catechesis/Religious Programs—Tel: 785-673-5510. Kathryn Kraus, D.R.E.
Students 66.

Greenleaf, Washington Co., Sacred Heart (1890). Attended by St. John the Baptist, Hanover. Rev. Edward J. Oen, C.PP.S. Pastoral Assocs.: Lawrence Hogan; James Donigan.
Mailing Address: P.O. Box 395, Hanover, 66945. Tel: 785-337-2207.
Church—Tel: 785-747-2862. [CEM]

Grinnell, Gove Co., Immaculate Conception (1888) (German). Attended by St. Joseph's Oakley. Rev. Roger K. Meitl, Parish Dir./Pastoral Admin.
Mailing Address: 625 Freeman Ave., Oakley, 67748. [CEM]
Catechesis/Religious Programs—Fax: 785-824-3388. Sr. Kenneth Struckhoff, D.R.E.
Students 66.

Gypsum, Saline Co., St. Patrick's. Attended by Immaculate Conception, Solomon. Rev. John Lahey. Parish Directors/Pastoral Administrators: Mr. James Karber; Mrs. Alan (Debie) Martin.

Hanover, Washington Co., St. John the Baptist (1868) (Bohemian), Rev. Edward J. Oen, C.PP.S.
Res., Box 395, 66945. Tel: 785-337-2207. [CEM]
School—(Grades 1-8). Tel: 785-337-2782. Sr. Vivian Boucher, C.S.J., Prin.
Sisters of St. Joseph 1; Lay Teachers 8; Students 93.
Catechesis/Religious Programs—Students 53.

Hays, Ellis Co., Immaculate Heart of Mary (1967), Revs. Donald D. Zimmerman; Beryl Gibson. Pastoral Assocs.: Sr. Rosalia Costello, C.S.A.; Betty Lou Whalen.
Res., 1805 Vine, 67601. Tel: 785-625-7339. [JC]
Catechesis/Religious Programs—D.R.E.: Dorothy Jacobs; Pat Legleiter.
Students 729.

St. Joseph's (1885), Revs. Michael Scully, O.F.M.Cap.; Michael Suchnieki, O.F.M.Cap.; Earl Befort, O.F.M.Cap.; Paulinus I. Karlin, O.F.M.Cap. In res., Most Rev. Firmin Schmidt, O.F.M.Cap., (Retired); Revs. Curtis Carlson, O.F.M.Cap.; Bennett Collucci.
Res., P.O. Drawer 1000, 67601. Tel: 785-625-7356; Fax: 785-625-7394. [JC]
School—(Grades K-5). Tel: 785-625-3131. Dolores McKibbin, Prin.
Lay Teachers 16; Students 234.
Catechesis/Religious Programs—Tel: 785-628-2311. D.R.E.: Martha A. Brungardt; Jerry Michaud; Renee Michaud.
Students 256.

St. Nicholas of Myra (1983), Arvilla Juenemann, Admin.; Rev. William J. Surmeier.
Office: 2901 E. 13th, P.O. Box 932, 67601. Tel: 785-628-1446; Fax: 785-628-6627.
Res., 2405 A Henry Dr., 67601. Tel: 785-628-6658.
Catechesis/Religious Programs—Tel: 785-628-2188. Sr. Martina Stegman, O.P., D.R.E.
Students 243.

Herington, Dickinson Co., St. John the Evangelist, Rev. Donald F. Pfannenstiel.
Res., 712 N. Broadway, 67449. Tel: 785-258-2013. [CEM]
Catechesis/Religious Programs—D.R.E.: Linda Polston; Beth Blackwell.
Students 70.

Herndon, Rawlins Co., Assumption (1880). Attended by Sacred Heart, Atwood. Rev. Damian Richards.
Mailing Address: 508 N. Railroad Ave., Atwood, 67730.
Church—Box 247, 67739. Tel: 785-322-5560. [CEM]
Catechesis/Religious Programs—Students 42.

Hill City, Graham Co., Immaculate Heart of Mary (1958), Rev. Donald P. McCarthy.
Res., 10 N. 10th Ave., 67642. Tel: 785-421-2535.
Catechesis/Religious Programs—Tel: 785-421-2665. Joyce Tauber, D.R.E.
Students 127.

Holyrood, Ellsworth Co., St. Mary's (1886). Attended by St. Bernard's, Ellsworth. Rev. Daniel L. Scheetz.
Mailing Address: 911 Kansas, Ellsworth, 67439. Tel: 785-472-3136.

Hope, Dickinson Co., St. Phillip's. Attended by St. John's, Herington.
Mailing Address: 712 N. Broadway, Herington, 67449.
Church—67451. Tel: 785-366-7353.

Hoxie, Sheridan Co., St. Frances Xavier Cabrini (1949), Rev. Merlin Kieffer.
Res., 924 N. 17th, Box 38, 67740. Tel: 785-675-3300. [CEM]
Catechesis/Religious Programs—Verlene Feldt, D.R.E.
Students 159.

Jamestown, Cloud Co., St. Mary's (1873). Closed. For sacramental records contact Our Lady of Perpetual Help, Concordia.

Junction City, Geary Co., St. Francis Xavier's, Revs. Aloysius Brungardt; Albert Dwyer.
Res., 218 N. Washington, P.O. Box 399, 66441. Tel: 785-238-2998; Fax: 785-238-4731. [CEM]
School—(Grades PreK-8) 280 N. Jefferson St., 66441. Tel: 913-238-2841. Mr. John Rodriguez, Prin. (Elementary & High School).
Priests 1; Lay Teachers 11; Students 185.
High School—Lay Teachers 11; Students 77.
Catechesis/Religious Programs—Students 127.

Kanopolis, Ellsworth Co., St. Ignatius Loyola (1947) (Mexican). Attended by St. Bernard's, Ellsworth. Rev. Daniel L. Scheetz.
Mailing Address: 911 Kansas, Ellsworth, 67439.
Church—Tel: 785-472-4628. [JC]

Kimeo, Washington Co., St. Michael's. Closed. For inquiries for parish records contact the Chancery.

Leoville, Decatur Co., Immaculate Conception (1885). Attended by Sacred Heart Parish, Selden.
Mailing Address: P.O. Box 57, Selden, 67757. Tel: 785-386-4496.
Church—Tel: 785-386-4409. [CEM]
Catechesis/Religious Programs—Jill Reichert, D.R.E.
Students 80.

Lincoln, Lincoln Co., St. Patrick's (1870), Rev. Ralph L. Aschenbrenner.
Res., 206 N. Fifth, Box 327, 67455. Tel: 785-524-4823. [CEM 2]
Catechesis/Religious Programs—Tel: 785-524-3043. Linda Workman, D.R.E.
Students 64.

Logan, Phillips Co., St. John's (1888). Attended by St. Thomas, Stockton. Rev. James P. Grennan.
Mailing Address: 722 Main St., Stockton, 67669. [CEM]
Catechesis/Religious Programs—Jean Kiser, D.R.E.
Students 54.

Manhattan, Riley Co., Seven Dolors (1880), Revs. Lawrence E. Grennan; David Metz; Sr. Janis Wagner, C.S.J., Pastoral Assoc.
Res., 731 Pierre St., Box 844, 66502. Tel: 785-565-5000; Fax: 785-565-5003.
School—(Grades PreK-8) 306 S. Juliette, 66502. Tel: 785-565-5050. Tom Schmitz, Prin.
Lay Teachers 19; Students 263.
Catechesis/Religious Programs—D.R.E.: Connie Ranker; Mike Ryan; Maggie Haag.
Students 253.

St. Isidore (1963), Rev. Keith Weber.
Res., 711 Denison St., 66502. Tel: 785-539-7496; Fax: 785-539-0220.

St. Thomas More Parish (1981), Rev. Melvin T. Long.
Church Office—2900 Kimball Ave., 66502. Tel: 785-776-5151.
Catechesis/Religious Programs—Tel: 785-776-1398.
Students 397.

Mankato, Jewell Co., St. Theresa of Infant Jesus (1949), Rev. Allen Scheer.
Res., 422 N. Commercial, Box 265, 66956. Tel: 785-378-3939. [CEM]

McDowell, Geary Co., St. Joseph. Closed. For inquiries for parish records contact the Chancery.

Meredith, Cloud Co., St. Peter's. Closed. Sacramental records are located at St. Peter.

Miltonvale, Cloud Co., St. Anthony's. Attended by SS. Peter and Paul, Clay Center.
Mailing Address: 730 Court St., Clay Center, 67432. Tel: 785-632-5011.
Church—Tel: 785-427-2253.

Minneapolis, Ottawa Co., Immaculate Conception of the Blessed Virgin Mary, Rev. Kenneth Lohrmeyer.
Res., 216 Cherry St., Box 167, 67467. Tel: 785-392-2079; 392-2013 (Church Hall).
Catechesis/Religious Programs—Students 89.

Morrowville, Washington Co., SS. Peter and Paul (1887). Attended by St. Augustine's, Washington.
410 B St., Washington, 66968. Tel: 785-325-2346. [CEM]

Munden, Republic Co., St. George's (1887) (Czech). Attended by St. Edward's, Belleville.
Mailing Address: P.O. Box 99, Belleville, 66935. [CEM]

Munjor, Ellis Co., St. Francis of Assisi (1876), Rev. William J. Surmeier.
Mailing Address: P.O. Box 932, Hays, 67601.
Church—883 Moscow, 67601. Tel: 785-625-5314. [CEM]

New Almelo, Norton Co., St. Joseph's (1878). Attended by St. Francis of Assisi, Norton. Sr. Olive Geiger, O.S.B., Pastoral Assoc.
Res., 67652. Tel: 785-567-4875. [CEM]

Niles, Ottawa Co., Sacred Heart. Closed. Sacramental records are located at Immaculate Conception.

Norton, Norton Co., St. Francis of Assisi (1878), Rev. John Walsh.
Res., 108 S. Wabash, Box 148, 67654. Tel: 785-877-2234.
Catechesis/Religious Programs—Cathy Hanchett, D.R.E.
Students 118.
Mission—New Almelo, Norton Co., St. Joseph's Church, HC-1 Box 175, New Almelo, 67652. Tel: 785-567-4875.

Oakley, Logan Co., St. Joseph's (1890), Rev. Roger K. Meitl.
Res., 625 Freeman Ave., 67748. Tel: 785-672-3828. [CEM]
School—(Grades K-5) 725 Freeman Ave., 67748. Tel: 785-672-4451. Mr. Robert Sattler, Prin.
Priests 1; Lay Teachers 7; Students 80.
Catechesis/Religious Programs—St. Joseph Parish Annex, 405 E. Seventh, 67748. Tel: 785-672-4443. Phyllis Temaat, D.R.E.
Students 107.

Oberlin, Decatur Co., Sacred Heart (1888), Rev. James F. Hoover; Sr. Marilyn Wall, C.S.J., Pastoral Admin. & Dir.
Res., 210 E. Washington, 67749. Tel: 785-475-3103. [JC]
Catechesis/Religious Programs—Angela Corcoran, D.R.E.
Students 86.

Ogden, Riley Co., St. Patrick's (1866). Attended by Seven Dolors, Manhattan.
Res., P.O. Box A, 66517. Tel: 785-565-5090. [CEM]

Osborne, Osborne Co., St. Aloysius (1881), Rev. Roger W. Hough.
Res., Box 267, 67473. Tel: 785-346-5582. [CEM]

Catechesis/Religious Programs—Rhonda Reed, D.R.E.
Students 146.
Mission—Downs, Osborne Co., St. Mary's.

Park, Gove Co., Sacred Heart (1898) (German), Rev. Mark Berland.
Res., P.O. Box 78, 67751. Tel: 785-673-4684. [CEM]
Catechesis/Religious Programs—D.R.E.: Gloria Pfannenstiel; Pam Nemechek.
Students 114.

Pfeifer, Ellis Co., Holy Cross. Closed. For sacramental records contact St. Fidelis, Victoria.

Phillipsburg, Phillips Co., SS. Philip and James (1875), Rev. Alvin Werth.
Res., R.R. #3, Box 144A, 67661. Tel: 785-543-5577; 543-5367.
Catechesis/Religious Programs—Janie Harger, D.R.E.
Students 102.
Mission—Claudell, Phillips Co., St. Francis.

Plainville, Rooks Co., Sacred Heart (1890), Rev. Joseph Popelka.
Res., 206 N. Washington, P.O. Box 100, 67663. Tel: 785-434-4658. [CEM]
School—Tel: 785-434-2157.
Sisters 1; Lay Teachers 7; Students 140.
Catechesis/Religious Programs—Students 107.

Russell, Russell Co., St. Mary's (1886), Rev. Charles Steier; Sr. Clarene Kennedy, C.S.J., Pastoral Assoc.
Res., 28 N. Kansas St., 67665. Tel: 785-483-2871. [CEM]
Catechesis/Religious Programs—Tel: 785-483-4359. Kim Boxberger, D.R.E.
Students 194.

St. Francis, Cheyenne Co., St. Francis (1912) (German). Unassigned.
Res., 625 S. River St., P.O. Box 1170, 67756. Tel: 785-332-2680.
Catechesis/Religious Programs—Myra Douthit, D.R.E.
Students 43.
Missions—Bird City, Cheyenne Co., St. Joseph's, 203 N. Bird, Bird City, 67731. Tel: 785-734-2287; Beardsley, Rawlins Co., St. John's, Rte. 2, 67756. Tel: 785-626-3946.

St. Joseph, Cloud Co., St. Joseph's. Closed. For sacramental records contact St. John the Baptist, Clyde.

St. Peter, Graham Co., St. Anthony's (1894) (German). Attended by St. Michael's, Collyer. Rev. Basil Torrez; Sr. Clarice Richmeier, C.S.J., Pastoral Assoc.
Mailing Address: Box 174, Collyer, 67631. Tel: 785-769-5272. [CEM]

Schoenchen, Ellis Co., St. Anthony's (1877). Attended by St. Joseph's, Hays.
Res., 215 W. 13th, P.O. Drawer 1000, Hays, 67601. Tel: 785-625-7356; Fax: 785-625-7394. [CEM]

Seguin, Sheridan Co., St. Martin's (1910). Attended by St. Frances Xavier Cabrini, Hoxie.
Mailing Address: P.O. Box 38, Hoxie, 67740. Tel: 785-675-3300. [CEM]

Selden, Sheridan Co., Sacred Heart (1906), Rev. James F. Hoover.
Res., Box 57, 67757. Tel: 785-386-4496. [CEM]
Catechesis/Religious Programs—Students 61.

Sharon Springs, Wallace Co., Holy Ghost (1907), Rev. Francis Stuart, O.S.B.
Res., 403 N. Main St., 67758. Tel: 785-852-4984.
Catechesis/Religious Programs—Shirley Blaesi, D.R.E.
Students 60.
Mission—Wallace, Wallace Co., St. Peter.

Smith Center, Smith Co., St. Mary's (1959). Attended by St. Theresa, Mankato.
403 W. Hwy. 6, Box 263, 66967. Tel: 785-282-6888.
Catechesis/Religious Programs—Mrs. Stacey Rempe, D.R.E.
Students 48.

Solomon, Dickinson Co., Immaculate Conception (1886), Rev. John Lahey.
Res., 3599 N. Field Rd., 67480. Tel: 785-655-2221. [CEM]
Catechesis/Religious Programs—Marcia Storer, D.R.E.
Students 78.

Stockton, Rooks Co., St. Thomas (1878), Rev. James P. Grennan.
Res., 722 Main St., 67669. Tel: 785-425-6656. [CEM]
Catechesis/Religious Programs—Cindy Kriley, D.R.E.
Students 89.

Tipton, Mitchell Co., St. Boniface's (1874), Rev. Albert DeSanctis.
Res., Box 87, 67485. Tel: 785-373-4455. [CEM]
High School—Tel: 785-373-5635.
Priests 1; Lay Teachers 6; Students 32.
Catechesis/Religious Programs—Students 93.

Victoria, Ellis Co., St. Fidelis (1876), Rev. Frank X. Grinko, O.F.M.Cap.
Church Office—601 10th St., 67671. Tel: 785-735-2777.
Res., 900 Cathedral Ave., 67671. Tel: 785-735-2777; 735-9456; Fax: 785-735-9455. [CEM]
Catechesis/Religious Programs—Tel: 785-735-9244. Eugenie Ricklefs, D.R.E.
Students 255.

Vincent, Ellis Co., St. Boniface (1908) (German-Russian). Attended by St. Fidelis, Victoria. Rev. Frank X. Grinko, O.F.M.Cap.
601 10th St., Victoria, 67671. Tel: 785-735-2777; 735-9456. [CEM]

WaKeeney, Trego Co., Christ the King (1933), Rev. Joseph H. Scheetz.
Res., 412 N. Ninth St., 67672. Tel: 785-743-2330. [CEM]
Catechesis/Religious Programs—Tel: 785-743-2339. Verna Flax, D.R.E.
Students 212.

Walker, Ellis Co., St. Ann's (1904) (German-Russian). Attended by St. Fidelis, Victoria.
Mailing Address: 601 10th St., Victoria, 67671. Tel: 785-735-2777.

Wallace, Wallace Co., St. Peter's (1877). Attended by Holy Ghost Church, Sharon Springs.
Mailing Address: P.O. Box 190, 67761.

Washington, Washington Co., St. Augustine's, Rev. Paul Becquet, C.PP.S.
Res., 410 B St., 66968. Tel: 785-325-2346. [JC]
Catechesis/Religious Programs—Marilyn Pachta, D.R.E.
Students 52.

Wilson, Ellsworth Co., St. Wenceslaus (1882) (Slovak), Rev. Jerome Morgan.
Res., P.O. Box 528, 67490. Tel: 913-658-3361. [CEM]
Catechesis/Religious Programs—Tel: 913-658-3474. Mrs. Mary Ellen Stoppel, D.R.E.
Students 69.
Mission—Dorrance, Russell Co., St. Joseph.

Zurich, Rooks Co., St. Ann's. Attended by Sacred Heart, Plainville. Rev. Joseph Popelka.
Res., P.O. Box 8, 67676. Tel: 785-662-3212. [CEM]

On Duty Outside the Diocese:
Reverend Fathers—
Dallen, James, W. 818 21st Ave., Spokane, WA 99203
Dlabal, Norbert F., In Mission in Peru, P.O. Box 551, Jefferson City, MO 65102

Educational Leave of Absence:
Reverend Fathers—
Brinkman, Barry, Studying Canon Law, Edifice Deschatelets, 175 Rue Main, Ottawa, Ontario Canada K1S 1C3

Leave of Absence:
Reverend Fathers—
Sterrett, Brad

Retired:
Reverend Monsignors—
Girard, Armand, 2150 Westchester, Manhattan, KS 66503
Hecker, Adolph J., St. John's New Horizon, 2225 Canterbury, Apt. 107, Hays, KS 67601
Kruse, Clement, 205 E. 25th St. Terrace, Hays, KS 67601
Landoll, Gilbert J., 507 N. Broadway, Apt. G., P.O. Box 475, Abilene, KS 67410
Lemoine, Vincent P., P.O. Box 141, Winterset, IA 50273
Sinner, Emil E., 209 24th St., Box 549, Wilson, KS 67490
Wasinger, Alfred J., Nazareth Motherhouse, Box 279, Concordia, KS 66901
Weber, John George, 926 E. Republic, Salina, KS 67401
Reverend Fathers—
Conklin, Christopher J., Mailing Address: P.O. Box 454, Concordia, KS 66901
Dion, Maurice B., 214 E. North St., Hanover, KS 66945
Kilian, William T., St. Joseph Church, P.O. Box 68, Damar, KS 67632
Kramer, Carl, 513 E. 19th, Hays, KS 67601
Kuhn, Herbert C., Catholic Care Center, 6700 E. 45th St. N., Wichita, KS 67226
Moeder, August L., P.O. Box 74, 217 Grant, Quinter, KS 67752
Pierce, Larry E., P.O. Box 237, Oakley, KS 67748

INSTITUTIONS LOCATED IN THE DIOCESE

[A] HIGH SCHOOLS, INTER-PAROCHIAL

SALINA. *Sacred Heart Junior-Senior High School*, 230 E. Cloud, 67401. Tel: 785-827-4422. John Krajicek, Prin. Sisters 2; Lay Teachers 22; Total 210.

[B] HIGH SCHOOLS, PRIVATE

HAYS. *Thomas More Prep-Marian*, 1701 Hall, 67601. Tel: 785-625-6577; Fax: 785-625-3912. Rev. Michael Scully, O.F.M.Cap., Pres. Legal Title: *Thomas More Prep-Marian Inc.* Four-year Catholic High School, with college preparatory programs conducted by Capuchin Friars and Sisters of St. Agnes; residency programs for boys and girls; special program for candidates for Priesthood and Religious Life. Capuchin Friars 3; Lay Teachers 27; Students 305.
Endowment Foundation of Thomas More Prep-Marian, Inc. Dennis Bieker, Pres.

[C] HOMES FOR AGED

CONCORDIA. *Mount Joseph Senior Community*, 66901. Tel: 785-243-1347; Fax: 785-243-1907
For a complete listing, refer to the Special Care Facilities section.

HAYS. *St. John's New Horizons*, 2225 Canterbury, 67601. Tel: 785-628-8742
For a complete listing, refer to the Special Care Facilities section.

MANHATTAN. *St. Joseph Senior Community, Inc.*, 2423 Kimball Ave., 66502. Tel: 785-539-7671.
Web site: www.talk2u.com/sjsc
For a complete listing, refer to the Special Care Facilities section.

VICTORIA. *St. John's Rest Home*, 701 Seventh St., 67671. Tel: 785-735-2208
For a complete listing, refer to the Special Care Facilities section.

[D] MONASTERIES AND RESIDENCES OF PRIESTS AND BROTHERS

HAYS. *St. Joseph's Friary*, P.O. Drawer 1000, 67601. Tel: 913-625-7356. Revs. Michael Scully, O.F.M.Cap.; Michael Suchnicki, O.F.M.Cap.; Paulinus I. Karlin, O.F.M.Cap.; Earl Befort, O.F.M.Cap. In res. Rev. Fidelis McManus, O.F.M.Cap.; Most Rev. Firmin Schmidt, O.F.M.Cap., (Retired); Revs. Bennett Collucci, O.F.M.Cap.; Curtis Carlson, O.F.M.Cap.

VICTORIA. *St. Fidelis Friary*, 67671. Tel: 785-735-9456; Fax: 785-735-9455. Revs. Christian Fey, O.F.M.Cap.; Felix Petrovsky, O.F.M.Cap.; Ronald Gilardi, O.F.M.Cap., Vicar; Berard Tomassetti, O.F.M.Cap.; Frank X. Grinko, O.F.M.Cap., Pastor & Guardian; Harold Vogler, O.F.M.Cap., (Retired); Bro. Augustine Rohde, O.F.M.Cap. Total in Residence 7.

[E] CONVENTS AND RESIDENCES FOR SISTERS

SALINA. *Medaille Center*, 148 N. Oakdale St., 67401. Tel: 785-827-3685. Sisters of St. Joseph. Sr. Rose Beatrice Dreiling, C.S.J., Coord. Sisters 14.

CONCORDIA. *Nazareth Motherhouse for the Sisters of St. Joseph, Concordia*, Administration Offices, 215 Court St., P.O. Box 279, 66901. Tel: 785-243-2149.
E-mail: csjcenter@theonramp.net
Rev. Curtis Van Del, S.J., Chap.; Sr. Christine Doman, C.S.J., Pres. Professed Sisters 243; Postulants 4; In Community 247.
Saint Joseph Foundation for Apostolic and Charitable Purposes.

[F] RETREAT CENTERS

CONCORDIA. *Manna House of Prayer*, 323 E. Fifth St., Box 675, 66901. Tel: 785-243-4428. Sr. Bette Moslander, C.S.J., Dir. Total Staff 10; Total in Residence 10.

VICTORIA. *Capuchin Center for Spiritual Life*, 900 Cathedral Ave., 67671. Tel: 913-735-9393; Fax: 913-735-9455.
E-mail: frron@compuserve.com
Rev. Ronald Gilardi, O.F.M.Cap.

[G] NEWMAN CENTERS

HAYS. *Comeau Catholic Campus Center at Fort Hays State University*, Office: 506 W. Sixth, 67601. Tel: 913-625-7396. Rev. Curtis Carlson, O.F.M.Cap., Chap. Total Staff 5.

MANHATTAN. *St. Isidore's Catholic Student Center.* Kansas State University. 711 Denison, 66502. Tel: 785-539-7496. In res. Rev. Keith Weber, Chap. Total Staff 4; Total in Residence 1.

[H] MISCELLANEOUS

SALINA. *Marymount Diocesan Activities Center, Inc.*, P.O. Box 980, 67402-0980. Tel: 785-827-8746; Fax: 785-827-6133. Rev. Msgr. James E. Hake, Pres.

Marymount Memorial Educational Trust Fund, P.O. Box 980, 67402-0980. Tel: 785-827-8746; Fax: 785-827-6133. Most Rev. George K. Fitzsimons, D.D., Trustee.

Sacred Heart Junior-Senior School Endowment Fund, P.O. Box 6318, 67401. Tel: 785-825-4011. E-mail: heart@midusa.net Web site: sacredheart@knights.org

Salina Catholic Diocese Education Endowment, Inc., 103 N. Ninth St., P.O. Box 980, 67402-0980. Tel: 785-827-8746; Fax: 785-827-6133.

Salina Catholic Diocese Gift & Annuity Fund, Inc., 103 N. Ninth St., P.O. Box 980, 67402-0980. Tel: 785-827-8746; Fax: 785-827-6133.

Salina Catholic Diocese Seminary Burses, Inc., 103 N. Ninth St., P.O. Box 980, 67402-0980. Tel: 785-827-8746; Fax: 785-827-6133.

Salina Diocesan Clergy Health and Retirement Association, Inc., Diocese of Salina, P.O. Box 980, 67402-0980. Tel: 785-827-8746. Most Rev. George K. Fitzsimons, Pres.

RELIGIOUS INSTITUTES OF MEN REPRESENTED IN THE DIOCESE

For further details refer to the corresponding bracketed number in the Religious Institutes of Men or Women section.

[0470]—*The Capuchin Friars*. (Province of Mid-America).—O.F.M.Cap.

[0200]—*Monks of St. Benedict*. (Conception, MO).—O.S.B.

[1060]—*Society of the Precious Blood*. (Kansas City Prov.).—C.PP.S.

RELIGIOUS INSTITUTES OF WOMEN REPRESENTED IN THE DIOCESE

[0100]—*Adorers of the Blood of Christ*.—A.S.C.

[3710]—*Congregation of the Sisters of Saint Agnes*.—C.S.A.

[1070-24]—*Dominican Sisters*.—O.P.

[3580]—*Servants of Mary*.—O.S.M.

[]—*Sisters of St. Benedict*.—O.S.B.

[3830-15]—*Sisters of St. Joseph*.—C.S.J.

NECROLOGY

(No Deaths)

Diocese of Salt Lake City

(Dioecesis Civitatis Lacus Salsi)

Most Reverend

GEORGE H. NIEDERAUER, D.D., PH.D.

Bishop of Salt Lake City; ordained April 30, 1962; appointed Bishop of Salt Lake City November 3, 1994; ordained January 25, 1995. *Office: 27 C St., Salt Lake City, UT, 84103.* Tel.: 801-328-8641, Ext. 304; Fax: 801-328-0324.

Most Reverend

JOSEPH LENNOX FEDERAL, D.D.

Retired Bishop of Salt Lake City; ordained December 8, 1934; appointed Auxiliary Bishop of Salt Lake City February 5, 1951; consecrated Titular Bishop of Appiaria April 11, 1951; made Coadjutor Bishop of Salt Lake City, *cum jure successionis*, May 8, 1958; succeeded to the See, March 31, 1960; retired April 1980. *Mailing Address: 451 Bishop Federal Lane, Salt Lake City, UT, 84115.*

ESTABLISHED AS A VICARIATE-APOSTOLIC ON NOV. 23, 1886.

ERECTED A DIOCESE ON JANUARY 27, 1891.

Square Miles 84,990.

Originally comprised all Utah and the Counties of Eureka, Lander, Lincoln, White Pine, Nye, Elko and Clark in the State of Nevada. By Apostolic Constitution dated March 27, 1931, the Nevada section was separated from the Salt Lake Diocese and incorporated in the Reno Diocese. The name was changed to Diocese of Salt Lake City on March 31, 1951.

Comprises the State of Utah.

Patron of the Diocese of Salt Lake City: St. Mary Magdalene.

For legal titles of parishes and diocesan institutions, consult the Chancery Office.

Diocesan Offices and Organizations: 27 C St., Salt Lake City, UT, 84103. Tel.: 801-328-8641; Fax: 801-328-9680.

Web site address: www.utahcatholicdiocese.org

E-mail address: dioslc@xmission.com

STATISTICAL OVERVIEW

Personnel	
Bishop	1
Retired Bishops	1
Abbots	1
Priests: Diocesan Active in Diocese	41
Priests: Active Outside Diocese	5
Priests: Diocesan in Foreign Missions	1
Priests: Retired, Sick or Absent	8
Number of Diocesan Priests	55
Religious Priests in Diocese	29
Extern Priests in Diocese	10
Ordinations:	
Diocesan Priests	1
Permanent Deacons in Diocese	24
Total Brothers	14
Total Sisters	65
Parishes	
Parishes	43
With Resident Pastor:	
Resident Diocesan Priests	29
Resident Religious Priests	8
Without Resident Pastor:	
Administered by Priests	5
Administered by Lay People	1
Missions	19
Professional Ministry Personnel:	
Brothers	14
Sisters	65
Lay Ministers	39
Welfare	
Homes for the Aged	1
Total Assisted	723
Day Care and Extended Day Care Centers	7
Total Assisted	324
Special Centers for Social Services	2
Total Assisted	209,274
Educational	
Diocesan Students in Other Seminaries	6
Total Seminarians	6
High Schools, Diocesan and Parish	2
Total Students	1,159
Elementary Schools, Diocesan and Parish	10
Total Students	2,767
Catechesis/Religious Education:	
High School Students	1,287
Elementary Students	6,656
Total Students Under Catholic Instruction	11,875
Teachers in the Diocese:	
Priests	2
Brothers	1
Sisters	5
Lay Teachers	239
Vital Statistics	
Receptions into the Church:	
Infant Baptism Totals	2,213
Adult Baptism Totals	359
Received into Full Communion	248
First Communions	1,758
Confirmations	1,269
Marriages:	
Catholic	302
Interfaith	174
Total Marriages	476
Deaths	628
Total Catholic Population	94,700
Total Population	2,200,362

Former Bishops—Rt. Rev. LAWRENCE SCANLAN, D.D., ord. June 24, 1868; appt. Vicar-Apostolic of Utah, Jan. 25, 1887; cons. Titular Bishop of Larandum, June 29, 1887; named first Bishop of Salt Lake, Jan. 30, 1891; died May 10, 1915.—Rt. Rev. JOSEPH S. GLASS, C.M., D.D., LL.D., second Bishop; ord. Aug. 15, 1897; cons. Aug. 24, 1915; died Jan. 26, 1926.—Most Rev. JOHN J. MITTY, D.D., third Bishop; ord. Dec. 22, 1906; cons. Sept. 8, 1926; made Coadjutor Archbishop of San Francisco, cum jure successionis, Feb. 4, 1932; Titular Archbishop of Egina; succeeded to the See, March 5, 1935.—Most Rev. JAMES E. KEARNEY, D.D., ord. Sept. 19, 1908; appt. July 4, 1932; cons. Oct. 28, 1932; appt. Bishop of Rochester, July 31, 1937; installed Nov. 11, 1937.—Most Rev. LEO J. STECK, D.D., ord. June 8, 1924; appt. Auxiliary Bishop of Salt Lake, March 3, 1948; cons. Titular Bishop of Ilium, May 20, 1948; died June 19, 1950.—Most Rev. DUANE G. HUNT, D.D., LL.D., ord. June 27, 1920; appt. Aug. 6, 1937; cons. Oct. 28, 1937; appt. assistant at the Pontifical Throne; appt. May 25, 1946; died March 31, 1960.—Most Rev. WILLIAM KEITH WEIGAND, D.D., ord. May 25, 1963; appt. Sept. 3, 1980; ord. Bishop, Nov. 17, 1980; transferred to the See of Sacramento; installed Jan. 27, 1994.

Diocesan Pastoral Center—27 C. St., Salt Lake City, 84103. Tel: 801-328-8641; Fax: 801-328-9680.

Office of the Bishop—SHIRLEY MARES, Sec. Tel: 801-328-8641, Ext. 304; Fax: 801-328-0324.

Vicar General and Moderator of the Curia—Rev. Msgr. J. TERRENCE FITZGERALD, Ext. 305.

Chancellor—Deacon SILVIO MAYO, Ext. 315.

Diocesan Offices

African American, Hmong, Korean, Native American—Sr. LORRAINE MASTERS, O.L.V.M., Dir., Ext. 335.

Apostleship of Prayer—Rev. MATTHEW O. WIXTED, Dir., *15 S. 7th St., Tooele, 84074.* Tel: 801-882-3860.

Archives—Mrs. BERNICE MOONEY, Dir., Ext. 346. Rev. Msgr. JEROME STOFFEL, Dir., Emeritus.

Campus Ministry—Sr. MARILYN MARK, O.S.B., *795 N. 800 East, Logan, 84321.* Tel: 801-752-1478.

Catholic Community Services—Sr. MARGO CAIN, C.S.C., Exec. Dir., *2300 W. 1700 S., Salt Lake City, 84104.* Tel: 801-977-9119; Fax: 801-977-9224. FRANK LEONARD, Bd. Pres.

Catholic Foundation of Utah—Mrs. NANCY GILES, Pres.; Mr. KURT SIMPSON, Exec. Dir., Ext. 306.

Catholic Relief Services—Deacon SILVIO MAYO, Ext. 315.

Catholic Schools Offices—Rev. JOSEPH MAYO, Supt., Ext. 330.

Cemetery—Mount Calvary—JENNINGS H. MEASE, Dir. Tel: 801-355-2476.

Chancery—LINDA MARTINEZ, Sec., Ext. 317.

College of Consultors—Rev. Msgr. ROBERT J. BUSSEN; Rev. Msgr. J. TERRENCE FITZGERALD; Rev. Msgr. JOHN J. HEDDERMAN; Rev. Msgr. M. FRANCIS MANNION; Rev Msgr. ROBERT R. SERVATIUS; Rev. Msgr. JOHN J. SULLIVAN; Rev. VICTOR G. BONNELL.

Communications Media Office—JO LEE HEATON, , Ext. 344. MARY MAYO, Volunteer, Ext. 333.

Cursillo—FLORENTINO J. VALLES, *P.O. Box 1801, Salt Lake City, 84110*. Tel: 801-484-9068.

Deans—Rev. Msgr. ROBERT R. SERVATIUS, Wasatch Deanery; Rev. WILLIAM WHEATON, Southeastern Deanery; Rev. VICTOR G. BONNELL, Northern Deanery; Rev. GERALD P. LYNCH, Salt Lake Deanery; Rev. MICHAEL WINTERER, Southwestern Deanery.

Diaconate Formation—Sr. ELLEN MARY TAYLOR, C.S.C., Dir., Ext. 320. Sr. MARIA MOLINA, S.N.D.deN., Assoc. Dir., Ext. 338.

Diocesan Development Drive—Mr. KURT SIMPSON, Dir., Ext. 306.

Diocesan Lay Volunteers—Sr. ELLEN MARY TAYLOR, C.S.C., Dir., Ext. 320.

Development Office—KURT SIMPSON, Dir., Ext. 306.

Diocesan Office for Persons with Disabilities—BIBIAN J. RENDON, Ext. 345.

Diocesan Pastoral Council—VERNIE HEENEY, Pres.

Ecunemical Commission—Rev. Msgr. M. FRANCIS MANNION, Chm. Tel: 801-328-8941. Revs. CASSIAN LEWINSKI, O.P.; VICTOR BONNELL.

Engaged Encounter—MARY RAKOWSKI; ROGER RAKOWSKI. Tel: 801-280-6839.

Family Life-Natural Family Planning—Mrs. VEOLA MARTINEZ-BURCHETT, Ext. 337.

Finance Council—Most Rev. GEORGE H. NIEDERAUER, Ex Officio; Rev. Msgr. J. TERRENCE FITZGERALD; Rev. Msgr. JOHN J. HEDDERMAN; Rev. COLIN F. BIRCUMSHAW; CAROL BROCKMAN; O. YOGI GILLILAND; MICHAEL JOSEPH; Deacon SILVIO MAYO; JILL MORBY; JOSEPH ZVONEK; BARBARA WOODBURY; GEORGE BEATON.

Finance Office—BARBARA WOODBURY, Comptroller, Ext. 309.

Government Liaison—DEE ROWLAND, Ext. 336.

Hispanic Evangelization & Leadership Formation—Sr. MARIA MOLINA, S.N.D.deN., Ext. 338.

Hispanic Affairs—JUANCARLOS R. QUESADACESPEDES, Ext. 361.

Holy Childhood Association—Deacon SILVIO MAYO, Dir., Ext. 315.

Lay Ministries—Sr. ELLEN MARY TAYLOR, C.S.C., Ext. 320. Sr. MARIA MOLINA, S.N.D.deN., Assoc. Dir., Ext. 338.

Liturgy Office—MAXINE KAISER, Ext. 321.

Liturgical Commission—Rev. COLIN F. BIRCUMSHAW, Chm. Tel: 801-399-5627.

Marriage Encounter—MIKE FULTON; NANCY FULTON. Tel: 801-576-0418.

Ministry to Correctional Institutions—Revs. JAMES E. BLAINE, Dir., *P.O. Box 142, American Fork, 84003*. Tel: 801-756-7771. MICHAEL ARKINS, S.S.S. Tel: 801-968-2369. JOSEPH KOCH. Tel: 801-485-5610. FRANCIS B. PELLIGRINO. Tel: 801-966-5111. MICHAEL SCIUMBATO. Tel: 801-896-5539.

Ministry to Priests Program—Clergy Continuing Education, Rev. WILLIAM H. FLEGGE, Dir., *172 North 500 West Provo, Utah, 84601*. Tel: 801-314-5001. Team: Revs. MICHAEL ARKINS, S.S.S.; CLARENCE SANDOVAL; ANDRZEJ SKRZYPIEC; ROBERT MORIARTY.

Newspaper—"Intermountain Catholic", BARBARA S. LEE, Editor, , Ext. 340. ERIKA MARTINEZ, Staff Writer; LON SCHIFFBAUER, Business Mgr.

Peace and Justice Commission—DEE ROWLAND, Dir., Ext. 336.

People's Eucharistic League—Blessed Sacrament Fathers.

Diaconate—Co-Dirs.: Deacons SILVIO MAYO, Ext. 315. DOUGLAS SLIGER. Tel: 801-479-8815.

Presbyteral Council—Revs. WILLIAM H. FLEGGE, Pres. GERALD P. LYNCH, Vice Pres. TERENCE M. MOORE, Sec.

Priests' Mutual Benefit Society (Retirement)—Most Rev. GEORGE H. NIEDERAUER, Chm. Ex Officio; Bd. of Dirs.: Rev. VICTOR G. BONNELL, Vice Chm.; Rev. Msgr. JOHN J. HEDDERMAN, Sec./Treas.; Rev. Msgr. JOHN J. SULLIVAN; Revs. JOSEPH M. MAYO; TERENCE M. MOORE; COLIN BIRCUMSHAW.

Priests' Personnel Board—Most Rev. GEORGE H. NIEDERAUER; Rev. Msgr. JOHN J. HEDDERMAN; Rev. Msgr. J. TERRENCE FITZGERALD; Revs. WILLIAM WHEATON; GERALD P. LYNCH; DONALD E. HOPE; ANDREW SKIZYPIEC, Ext. 304.

Real Estate Office—RICHARD SALVITTI, Ext. 360.

Religious Education—DAN JOHN, Dir., Ext. 326.

Respect Life—Mrs. VEOLA MARTINEZ-BURCHETT, Ext. 337.

Retreat Movement—Sr. DANILE KNIGHT, O.S.B., Dir., *1794 Lake St., Ogden, 84401*. Tel: 801-392-9231.

Retrouvaille—JIM AUMEN; LAUREN AUMEN. Tel: 801-262-8023.

Sisters' Council—Executive Team: Sr. GEORGITA CUNNINGHAM, R.S.M.; Sr. JUDINE SUTER, O.S.B.; Sr. MARIANNE ROHRER, S.A.; Sr. CATHERINE KAMPHAUS, C.S.C.; Sr. CLAUDE CRINNION, S.H.F.; Sr. LORRAINE MASTERS, O.L.V.M.

Society for the Propagation of the Faith—Deacon SILVIO MAYO, Dir., Ext. 315.

Tribunal—

Judicial Vicar—Rev. Msgr. JOHN J. HEDDERMAN, J.C.L., Ext. 318.

Secretary & Notary—VIOLA MCGEHEE, Ext. 316.

Adjutant Judicial Vicars—Revs. ROBERT T. MORIARTY, Ext. 319. GERALD P. LYNCH, Ext. 324. LANGES SILVA, Ext. 312.

Promotor of Justice—Rev. COLIN F. BIRCUMSHAW.

Defenders of the Bond—Rev. Msgr. J. TERRENCE FITZGERALD; Rev. Msgr. ROBERT R. SERVATIUS; Rev. Msgr. JOHN J. SULLIVAN; Rev. JOSEPH M. MAYO.

Judges—Rev. Msgr. JOHN J. HEDDERMAN; Revs. GERALD P. LYNCH; ROBERT T. MORIARTY; WALTER RIENDEAU, S.S.S.; LANGES SILVA.

Vocation Office—Rev. GERALD P. LYNCH, Dir.; Sr. JEREMIA JANUSCHKA, O.S.B., Assoc. Dir., Ext. 324.

Youth Ministry—MARY FASIG, Dir., Ext. 313.

CLERGY, PARISHES, MISSIONS AND PAROCHIAL SCHOOLS

SALT LAKE CITY
(Salt Lake County)

1—CATHEDRAL OF THE MADELEINE (1866), Rev. Msgr. M. Francis Mannion, Rector. In res., Rev. Henry J. Piacitelli, C.M.

Res., 331 E. S. Temple St., 84111. Tel: 801-328-8941; Fax: 801-328-9680.

School—Madeleine Choir School, Tel: 801-323-9850; Fax: 801-323-0581. Betsy Hunt, Prin.

Lay Teachers 14; Students 112.

Catechesis/Religious Programs—Tel: 801-328-1241; Fax: 801-364-6504.

Students 55.

2—OUR LADY OF GUADALUPE (1944) (Hispanic), Rev. Kenneth L. Vialpando.

Res., 715 W. 300 N., 84116. Tel: 801-364-2019; Fax: 801-363-2709.

Catechesis/Religious Programs—Students 178.

3—OUR LADY OF LOURDES (1913), Rev. James Semple.

Res., 1085 E. Seventh S. St., 84102. Tel: 801-322-3330; Fax: 801-363-6007. [CEM]

School—1065 E. Seventh S. St., 84102. Tel: 801-364-5624; Fax: 801-364-0925. Edward Campos, Prin.

Sisters of the Holy Cross 1; Lay Teachers 14; Students 270.

Catechesis/Religious Programs—Students 60.

4—SACRED HEART (1917) (Hispanic), Rev. Hernando Diaz. In res., Rev. Stanislaw Dudek.

Res., 948 S. 2nd East St., 84111. Tel: 801-363-8632; Fax: 801-363-1539.

Catechesis/Religious Programs—174 E. 900 S., 84111.

Students 230.

5—ST. AMBROSE (1948), Rev. Msgr. John J. Hedderman; Rev. Joseph Koch.

Res., 2315 Redondo Ave., 84108. Tel: 801-485-5610; 484-3642.

School—J. E. Cosgriff Memorial School, 2335 Redondo Ave., 84108. Tel: 801-486-3197; Fax: 801-484-8270. Mrs. Judith Puhe, Prin.

Lay Teachers 19; Students 290.

Catechesis/Religious Programs—Tel: 801-485-9324; Fax: 801-484-1065.

Students 377.

6—ST. ANN (1917), Rev. Msgr. John J. Sullivan; Deacon Mansueto Flaim. In res., Rev. Reyes G. Rodriguez.

Res., 2119 S. 400 E., 84115. Tel: 801-487-1000.

School—430 E. 2100 S., 84105. Tel: 801-486-0741; Fax: 801-486-0742. Kathleen Hood, Prin.

Daughters of Charity 1; Lay Teachers 12; Students 290.

Catechesis/Religious Programs—Tel: 801-261-5943.

Students 150.

7—ST. CATHERINE OF SIENA (1981), Revs. Cassian Lewinski, O.P.; Bartholomew Hutcherson, O.P.

Res., 170 S. University, 84102. Tel: 801-359-6066; Fax: 801-359-4547.

Catechesis/Religious Programs—Students 130.

8—ST. PATRICK'S (1892) (Hispanic-Tongan-Korean), Rev. Gerald P. Lynch.

Res., 1058 W. 400 S., 84104-1261. Tel: 801-596-7233; Fax: 801-363-3743. [CEM]

Catechesis/Religious Programs—Tel: 801-596-7255. Sr. Georgita Cunningham, R.S.M., D.R.E.

Students 125.

9—ST. THOMAS MORE (1981), Rev. Terence M. Moore.

Res. & Parish Center: 3015 E. Creek Rd., Sandy, 84093. Tel: 801-942-5285 (Office); 942-7678 (Rectory); Fax: 801-942-5287.

Catechesis/Religious Programs—Students 381.

10—ST. VINCENT DE PAUL (1925), Rev. George F. Davich. In res., Rev. Thomas J. Kaiser.

Res., 1375 E. Spring Ln., 84117. Tel: 801-272-9216; Fax: 801-273-1156.

School—(Grades PreK-8) 1385 E. Spring Ln., 84117. Tel: 801-277-6702. Antoinette Houston, Prin.

Lay Teachers 15; Students 359.

Catechesis/Religious Programs—Tel: 801-272-2132.

Students 270.

SUBURBAN SALT LAKE CITY

1—IMMACULATE CONCEPTION, Salt Lake Co., (1890). Unassigned.

Res., P.O. Box 151, Copperton, Bingham Canyon, 84006. Tel: 801-569-2706.

2—ST. FRANCIS XAVIER, Salt Lake Co., (1955), Revs. Joseph M. Mayo; Francisco Gomez; Deacon Mel Sanchez.

Res., P.O. Box 18631, 84118. Tel: 801-968-2123; Fax: 801-966-1639.

School—See separate listing under Elementary Schools, Regional in the Diocese. Fax: 801-966-1369.

Catechesis/Religious Programs—Students 525.

3—OUR LADY OF LOURDES, Salt Lake Co., (1916) (English), Rev. Andrzej Skrzypiec (Poland).

Res., P.O. Box 38, 84044. Tel: 801-250-6349; Fax: 801-250-3860. [CEM]

Catechesis/Religious Programs—8585 W. 3010 S., 84044. Tel: 801-250-6052.

Students 70.

4—ST. THERESE OF THE CHILD JESUS, Salt Lake Co., (1925), Revs. Stanislaw Herba; Mario Arbelaez; Deacon Stanley Stott.

Office: 112 S. Allen St., 84047. Tel: 801-255-3721.

Res., 130 S. Allen St., 84047. Tel: 801-255-0340.

Catechesis/Religious Programs—Tel: 801-561-0431.

Students 225.

5—ST. JUDE, Salt Lake Co., (1975) (Maronite Rite), Rev. Gebran Bou-Merhi.

Res., 4893 Wasatch St., 84107. Tel: 801-268-2820.

6—BLESSED SACRAMENT, Salt Lake Co., (1972), Rev. Msgr. Robert R. Servatius; Rev. James Janda; Deacon Russell Langner.

Res., 9757 S. 1700 E., 84092. Tel: 801-571-5517; Fax: 801-571-2071.

School—1745 E. 9800 S., 84092. Tel: 801-572-5311; Fax: 801-572-0251. Sr. Catherine Kamphaus, C.S.C., Prin.

Holy Cross Sisters 1; Lay Teachers 15; Students 395.

Catechesis/Religious Programs—1745 E. 9800 S., 84092. Tel: 801-571-2071.

Students 417.

Mission—Draper, Salt Lake Co., St. John the Baptist, 9757 S. 1700 E., 84092. Tel: 801-571-8594.

Station—Alta, Our Lady of the Snows.

7—ST. MARTIN DE PORRES, Salt Lake Co., (1982), Rev. Michael J. Arkins, S.S.S.; Bro. David Phelan, S.S.S. In res., Rev. Joe Roy, S.S.S.

Mailing Address: 4976 Valois Cir., 84118. Tel: 801-969-8857; Fax: 801-966-9675.

Church—4914 S. 2200 W., 84118. Tel: 801-968-2369.

Catechesis/Religious Programs—Students 150.

8—ST. JOSEPH THE WORKER, Salt Lake Co., (1969), Rev. John B. Hart.

Res., P.O. Box 98, 84084. Tel: 801-255-8902; Fax: 801-255-5003.

Catechesis/Religious Programs—Tel: 801-961-4062.
Students 321.

9—SS. PETER AND PAUL, Salt Lake Co., (1972), Rev. Francis B. Pellegrino; Deacon Lynn Johnson.
Res., P.O. Box 70308, 84170. Tel: 801-966-5111; 966-5119.
Catechesis/Religious Programs—Tel: 801-969-7116; Fax: 801-966-2114.
Students 260.

OUTSIDE SALT LAKE CITY

American Fork, Utah Co., St. Peter's (1969), Rev. James E. Blaine, Parochial Admin.
Res., 626 N. 600 East, 84003. Tel: 801-756-7771.
Catechesis/Religious Programs—Tel: 801-756-2747.
Students 80.

Bountiful, Davis Co., St. Olaf (1944), Rev. Rudolph A. Daz.
Res., 276 E. 1700 South, 84010. Tel: 801-295-3621; Fax: 801-295-8261.
School—1793 S. Orchard Dr., 84010. Tel: 801-295-5341; Fax: 801-295-5915.
Lay Teachers 10; Students 214.
Catechesis/Religious Programs—Students 153.

Brigham City, Box Elder Co., St. Henry (1950), Revs. F. Warren Schoeppe, S.J.; Francisco Pires (Brazil); Deacons Bob Bambrick; Dick Werling.
Res., P.O. Box 872, 84302. Tel: 435-723-2941.
Catechesis/Religious Programs—Tel: 801-723-1215.
Students 188.
Mission—Tremonton, Box Elder Co., Santa Ana, 760 W. 600 N., Tremonton, 84337.

Cedar City, Iron Co., Christ the King (1934), Rev. Michael J. Winterer.
Res., 70 N. 200 West, P.O. Box 626, 84720. Tel: 801-586-8298; Fax: 801-865-5960.
Catechesis/Religious Programs—Students 80.
Missions—Panguitch, Garfield Co., St. Gertrude, S. Main St., Panguitch, 84759. Tel: 801-676-8406; Bryce Canyon, Garfield Co., St. Dominic, P.O. Box 1626, 84721.
Stations—Beryl Junction.; Brian Head. (Winter).

East Carbon, Carbon Co., Good Shepherd (1947), Rev. Joseph W. Morris, S.J.
Res., P.O. Box 99, 84520. Tel: 435-888-3306.
Mission—Green River, Emery Co., St. Michael, 140 N. Long St., Green River, 84525. Tel: 801-564-3320.

Eureka, Juab Co., St. Patrick's (1885) (Irish), Rev. Walter A. Riendeau, S.S.S.
Res., P.O. Box 387, Payson, 84651. Tel: 801-465-4782.

Helper, Carbon Co., St. Anthony's (1944), Rev. Erik J. Richtsteig.
Res., 5 S. Main, 84526. Tel: 435-472-5661. [JC]
Catechesis/Religious Programs—Students 120.

Huntsville, Weber Co., St. Florence Catholic Community (1990), Rev. Charles T. Cummins, Admin.
Mailing Address: 514-24th St., Ogden, 84401-1594. Tel: 801-399-9531.
Church: Tel: 801-745-5673.
Catechesis/Religious Programs—Students 50.

Kanab, Kane Co., St. Christopher's (1953), Rev. Anthony L. Vollmer, C.PP.S.
Res., 39 W. 200 S., 84741. Tel: 801-644-5652; Fax: 801-644-3413.
Station—North Rim, Grand Canyon.

Layton, Davis Co., St. Rose of Lima (1948), Revs. Victor G. Bonnell; Langes L. Silva; Deacons Robert Quintana, (Retired); John Weis.
Mailing Address: 210 South Chapel St., P.O. Box 557, 84041. Tel: 801-544-4269.
Res., 321 Whitesides St., 84041. Tel: 801-546-2541.
Catechesis/Religious Programs—400 E. 500 N., 84041. Tel: 801-544-5425.
Students 354.

Logan, Cache Co., St. Thomas Aquinas (1941), Rev. Clarence J. Sandoval; Sr. Marilyn Mark, O.S.B., Pastoral Assoc.
Res., 795 N. 800 E., 84321. Tel: 435-752-1478.
Catechesis/Religious Programs—Students 207.

Milford, Beaver Co., St. Bridget (1948), Rev. David Bittmenn.
Res., 210 S. 1st West, P.O. Box 785, 84751. Tel: 801-387-2732.
Missions—Delta, Millard Co., St. John Bosco, P.O. Box 924, Delta, 84624. Tel: 801-364-3710; Fillmore, Millard Co., Holy Family, 390 N. Main St., Fillmore, 84631.

Moab, Grand Co., St. Pius X (1955), Rev. Julio Sanchez.
Res., 122 W. 400 North, P.O. Box 357, 84532. Tel: 801-259-5211.
Catechesis/Religious Programs—Tel: 801-259-0384.
Students 70.
Mission—LaSal, Grand Co., Sacred Heart, Hwy. 46/Main, 84530. Tel: 801-686-2255.

Monticello, San Juan Co., St. Joseph (1935) (Spanish), Rev. Julio Sanchez.
Res., P.O. Box 518, 84535. Tel: 801-587-2322. [JC]
Catechesis/Religious Programs—Students 61.
Station—Blanding, Halls Crossing.

Ogden, Weber Co.,

1—HOLY FAMILY, (1979), Rev. Lawrence P. Sweeney.
Res., P.O. Box 3070, 84409. Tel: 801-479-1112; Fax: 801-479-1126. [JC]
Catechesis/Religious Programs—Students 203.

2—ST. JAMES, (1966), Rev. Donald E. Hope; Deacons Bud J. Wardle; Tony Lopez.
Res., 495 N. Harrison Blvd., 84404. Tel: 801-782-5393.
Catechesis/Religious Programs—Tel: 801-782-7372.
Students 391.

3—ST. JOSEPH'S, (1875), Revs. Colin F. Bircumshaw; Gustavo A. Vidal; Charles E. Cummins; Deacons John Conniff; Thomas Buller.
Res., 514 24th St., 84401. Tel: 801-399-5627; Fax: 801-399-5918.
School—See separate listing under Elementary Schools, Regional Located in the Diocese. Tel: 801-393-6051; Fax: 801-393-6086. R. Louise Price, Prin.
Catechesis/Religious Programs—Tel: 801-621-3602.
Students 371.
Mission—Huntsville, Weber Co., St. Florence, 6481 E. Hwy. 39, 84317. Tel: 801-745-5673.

4—ST. MARY'S, (1957), Revs. Martin Rock, S.J.; Neale W. Herrlich, S.J.; John Ferguson, S.J.
Res., P.O. Box 9196, 84409. Tel: 801-621-7961; Fax: 801-394-1244.
Catechesis/Religious Programs—Tel: 801-621-2274.
Students 333.

Park City, Summit Co., St. Mary of the Assumption (1881), Revs. Robert J. Bussen; Reyes Rodriquez; Deacon Lowell Palm.
Res., P.O. Box 669, 84060. Tel: 801-649-9676; Fax: 801-647-9678.
Catechesis/Religious Programs—Students 270.
Mission—Heber City, Wasatch Co., St. Lawrence, 1st West Center, Heber City, 84032. Tel: 801-654-4035.

Payson, Utah Co., San Andres (1986), Rev. Walter A. Riendeau, S.S.S.
Mailing Address: P.O. Box 387, 84651. Tel: 801-465-4782.
Church—315 E. 100 N., 84651.
Catechesis/Religious Programs—Students 91.
Missions—Nephi, Utah Co., Our Lady of Victory Mission, c/o San Andres, 84651.; Eureka, Utah Co., St. Patrick Parish, c/o San Andres, 84651.

Price, Carbon Co., Notre Dame de Lourdes (1918), Rev. William Wheaton.
Res., 160 N. Carbon Ave., 84501. Tel: 801-637-1846; Fax: 801-637-6338. [JC]
Catechesis/Religious Programs—Tel: 801-637-7917.
Students 30.
Mission—Huntington, Emery Co., San Rafael.

Provo, Utah Co., St. Francis of Assisi (1892), Revs. William Flegge; Javier G. Virgen.
Res., 172 N. 500 West St., 84601. Tel: 801-374-5001; Fax: 801-375-4751.
Catechesis/Religious Programs—Students 469.
Mission—American Fork, Utah Co., St. Peter's, 634 N. 600 E., American Fork, 84003. Tel: 801-756-7771.

Richfield, Sevier Co., St. Elizabeth's (1947), Rev. Michael R. Sciumbato; Deacon James McElfresh.
Res., 5995 N. Hwy. 89, Monroe, 84754. Tel: 801-896-5539.
Catechesis/Religious Programs—Students 28.
Missions—Torrey, Wayne Co., St. Anthony of the Desert, Sandcreek Rd., Torrey, 84775. Tel: 801-425-3319; Ephraim, Sanpete Co., St. Jude, 160 E. Center St., Ephraim, 84627. Tel: 801-283-6242.
Stations—Marysvale.; Central Utah Correctional Facility, Gunnison, Tel: 801-528-6000; Fax: 801-528-6259. [JC]

Roosevelt, Duchesne Co., St. Helen's (1940) (Native American), Rev. Thomas L. Culleton.
Res., 433 E. 200 North, P.O. Box 415, 84066. Tel: 801-722-2975; Fax: 801-722-0525. [CEM]
Missions—Duchesne, Duchesne Co., Holy Spirit; Fort Duchesne, Uintah Co., Blessed Kateri Tekakwitha, P.O. Box 533, 84026. Tel: 801-722-4734.

St. George, Washington Co., St. George's (1955), Rev. Leonadis Lopez; Deacon John O'Brien.
Mailing Address: P.O. Box 188, 84771. Tel: 801-673-2604; Fax: 801-688-2704.
Res., 165 N. 200 West, 84770. Tel: 801-673-7354.
Catechesis/Religious Programs—Students 170.
Station—Zion National Park. (Lodge). Tel: 801-772-3256.

Tooele, Tooele Co., St. Marguerite's (1910), Revs. Matthew O. Wixted; Hernando Diaz; Sr. Marianne Rohrer, Pastoral Assoc.; Deacon James Garcia.
Res., 15 S. 7th St., 84074. Tel: 801-882-3860; Fax: 801-882-3866.
Pre-School—Tel: 801-882-0081. Mrs. Janet Barbiero, Coord.
Catechesis/Religious Programs—Students 230.
Mission—Wendover, Tooele Co., San Felipe, 606 E. Aria Blvd., Wendover, 84083. Tel: 801-665-7710; 665-2339.

Vernal, Uintah Co., St. James the Greater (1948), Rev. Jan Bednarz.
Res., 138 N. 100 West St., 84078. Tel: 801-789-3016; Fax: 801-789-3016. [JC]
Catechesis/Religious Programs—Tel: 801-789-3034.
Students 95.
Station—Dutch John, Flaming Gorge.

Wendover, Tooele Co., Mission San Felipe, Rev. Eugenio Yance.
Res., 606 E. Aria Blvd., P.O. Box 1270, 84083. Tel: 801-665-7710.
Catechesis/Religious Programs—Students 140.

Chaplains of Public Institutions

SALT LAKE CITY. *County Youth Detention Center*. Rev. Michael Arkins, S.S.S.
Decker Lake Youth Center. Rev. Francis B. Pellegrino.
Oxbow Correctional Facility. Rev. Joseph Koch.
Salt Lake County Jail. Rev. Reyes G. Rodriguez.
Veterans Administration Hospital 500 Foothill Dr., 84113. Tel: 801-581-2121. Rev. Gebran Bou-Mehri; Sr. Julie Maher.

DRAPER. *State Penitentiary*. Rev. James E. Blaine, P.O. Box 142, American Fork, 84003. Tel: 801-756-7771.

GUNNISON. *State Penitentiary*. Rev. Javier G. Virgen.

On Duty Outside the Diocese:
Reverend Fathers—
Curran, Patrick J., 872 Farmington Ave., Hartford, CT 06119
Gaeta, David R., 102 Gilmore Dr., Kelly AFB, TX 78241-5813
Govorchin, Vincent, 240 Nice Ln. #203, Newport Beach, CA 92663
Tkach, Norman A., 858 N. 6th St., Banning, CA 92220

Retired:
Reverend Monsignors—
Kenny, James T.
Pollock, Robert C.
Stoffel, Jerome C.
Reverend Fathers—
Curnutte, William G.
Fischer, Louis A.
Fogarty, James
Kaiser, Thomas J.
Spellen, Lawrence M.

Permanent Deacons:
Aguilar, James, Sabbatical
Bambrick, Robert W., St. Henry's, Brigham City
Buller, Thomas M., St. Joseph's, Ogden
Conniff, John J., St. Joseph's, Ogden
Flaim, Mansueto, St. Ann's, Salt Lake City
Foote, Deane L., (Retired)
Garcia, James D., St. Marguerite's, Tooele
Glodowski, Robert J., On Duty Outside the Diocese
Herron, Dan, St. Patrick, Salt Lake City
Johnson, Lynn R., Sts. Peter and Paul, Salt Lake City
Kirts, Steven W., On Medical Leave of Absence
Lopez, Anthony J., St. James, Ogden
Mayo, Silvio, Chancellor
McElfresh, James L., St. Elizabeth, Richfield
O'Brien, John, St. George, St. George
O'Connell, Charles L., On Duty Outside the Diocese
Otero, Tranquilino, Unassigned
Palm, Lowell L., St. Lawrence, Heber
Quintana, Robert J., (Retired)
Reed, Joseph W., On Duty Outside the Diocese
Roscoe, Lt. Col. John H., On Duty Outside the Diocese
Sanchez, Mel J., St. Francis Xavier
Sliger, Douglas R., Hill Air Force Base
Stott, Stanley L., St. Therese, Midvale
Wardle, Bud J., St. James, Ogden
Weis, John C., St. Rose of Lima, Layton
Werling, Richard E., St. Henry's, Brigham City

INSTITUTIONS LOCATED IN THE DIOCESE

[A] SEMINARIES, RELIGIOUS, OR SCHOLASTICATES

HUNTSVILLE. *Abbey of Our Lady of the Holy Trinity*, 1250 S. 9500 E., 84317. Tel: 801-745-3784.
E-mail: hta@xmission.com
Web site: http:www.xmission.com/~hta
Rt. Rev. Leander Dosch, O.C.S.O., Abbot and Dir. of Studies; Bro. Lawrence Baumbach, O.C.S.O., Novice Master. Priests 14; Brothers 10; Oblate 1.

[B] HIGH SCHOOLS, DIOCESAN

SALT LAKE CITY. *Judge Memorial Catholic High School*, 650 S. 11th E., 84102. Tel: 801-363-8895.
Web site: http://www.utw.com/~judge
Day School. (Coed). Rev. John Norman, Pres.; Ms. Renee Genereux, Prin.; Rev. James P. McHugh, O.S.F.S. Priests 2; Lay Teachers 74; Students 968.

OGDEN. *St. Joseph Catholic High School*, 1790 Lake St., 84401. Tel: 801-394-1515. Bro. Harold Hathaway, C.S.C., Admin. & Prin. Brothers 1; Lay Teachers 17; Students 175.

[C] ELEMENTARY SCHOOLS, REGIONAL

KEARNS. *St. Francis Xavier Regional School*, 4501 W. 5215 S., 84118. Tel: 801-966-1571. Revs. Joseph M. Mayo; Francisco Gomez; Jim Mello, Prin. Lay Teachers 15; Students 282.

OGDEN. *St. Joseph Regional School*. (Grades PreK-8), 2980 Quincy St., 84401. Tel: 801-393-6051. Revs. Colin F. Bircumshaw; Gustavo A. Vidal; R. Louise Price, Prin. Lay Teachers 24; Students 507.

PRICE. *Notre Dame Regional School*. (Grades PreK-9), 210 N. 6th E., 84501. Tel: 801-637-2850. Daughters of Charity. Rev. William Wheaton, Admin.; Sr. Stella J. Burns, D.C., Prin. Sisters 2; Lay Teachers 10; Students 205.

[D] FOUNDATIONS

MURRAY. *Holy Cross Ministries* Mailing Address: P.O. Box 57672, 84157-0672.
For a complete listing, refer to the Hospitals section.

OGDEN. *The St. Benedict's Foundation*, 319 E. Ridgeline Dr., 84405-6925. Tel: 801-479-1800; Fax: 801-479-3216
For a complete listing, refer to the Hospitals section.

[E] HOMES FOR AGED

SALT LAKE CITY. *St. Joseph Villa*, 451 Bishop Federal Ln., 84115-2295. Tel: 801-487-7557
For a complete listing, refer to the Special Care Facilities section.

[F] MONASTERIES AND RESIDENCES OF PRIESTS AND BROTHERS

SALT LAKE CITY. *Oblate House*, 554 E St., 84103. Tel: 801-359-8201.
E-mail: jimmac4@ixnetcom
Oblates of St. Francis de Sales. Rev. James P. McHugh, O.S.F.S., Contact Person. Total in Residence 2.

HUNTSVILLE. *Abbey of Our Lady of the Holy Trinity of the Order of Cistercians*, 1250 S. 9500 E., 84317. Tel: 801-745-3784.
E-mail: hta@xmission.com
Web site: http:www.xmission.com/~hta
Rt. Rev. Leander Dosch, O.C.S.O., Abbot; Revs. David Altman, O.C.S.O.; Casimir Bernas, O.C.S.O.; Patrick Boyle, O.C.S.O.; Charles Cummings, O.C.S.O.; Malachy Flaherty, O.C.S.O.; Bartholomew Gottemoller, O.C.S.O.; Brendan Hanratty, O.C.S.O.; Alan Hohl, O.C.S.O.; David Kinney, O.C.S.O.; Thomas Porter, O.C.S.O.; Joseph Schroer, O.C.S.O.; Baldwin Shea, O.C.S.O.; Emmanuel Spillane, O.C.S.O. Priests 14; Brothers 11; Total in Community 25. Legal Title: *Abbey of Our Lady of the Holy Trinity of the Order of Cistercians of the Strict Observance*.
Residing Elsewhere: Revs. Cletus Dollinger, O.C.S.O.; Gregory Santos, O.C.S.O.

[G] CONVENTS, MONASTERIES AND RESIDENCES FOR SISTERS

SALT LAKE CITY.
**Carmel of the Immaculate Heart of Mary Monastery*, 5714 Holladay Blvd., 84121. Tel: 801-277-6075; Fax: 801-277-4263.
E-mail: carmelslc@worldnet.att.net
Web site: http://www.carmelslc.org
Mother Margaret Mary Miller, O.C.D., Prioress. Professed Cloistered Sisters 6; Professed Out-Sisters 1.
Convent of Mary Queen of Peace, 347 E. S. Temple, 84111. Tel: 801-364-7535. Our Lady of Victory Missionary Sisters 2; Our Lady of China Sisters 1.
Our Lady of Lourdes Convent, 675 S. 11th E., 84102. Tel: 801-583-1204. Sisters of the Holy Cross 4.
Our Lady of the Wasatch Convent, 2335 Redondo Ave., 84108. Tel: 801-467-4984. Sisters of the Holy Cross 3.
Queen of Peace Convent, 1583 S. 19th E., 84108. Tel: 801-583-4661. Legal Title: *Sisters of the Holy Cross, Inc.* Sisters 3.
St. Joseph Villa Convent, 451 Bishop Federal Ln., 84115-2295. Tel: 801-487-7557. Congregation of Sisters of Charity of the Incarnate Word 5.
St. Vincent de Paul Convent, 1385 E. Spring Ln., 84117-6797. Tel: 801-277-7890. Sisters of the Holy Family 1; Sisters of the Holy Cross 1; Sisters for Christian Community 1.
Sisters of Notre Dame de Namur, 27 C St., 84103. Tel: 801-328-8641. Sr. Maria Molina, S.N.D., Dir. Office of Hispanic Ministry & Assoc. Dir. Diaconate, 5306 Cobble Creek Rd., #15-I, 84117.

HELPER. *St. Anthony Convent*, 30 S. Main St., 84526. Tel: 801-472-5468. Total Assisted 1,000.

OGDEN. *Mount Benedict Priory*, Shalom Convent, 309 E. 5450 S., 84405. Tel: 801-479-6030.
E-mail: mbp6@juno.com
Sisters of St. Benedict 3. St. Benedict's Convent, 5462 S. 200 E., 84405. Tel: 801-479-8107. Sisters 4. St. Benedict's Convent, 665 S. 1100 E., Salt Lake City, 84102. Tel: 801-582-1042. Our Lady of the Mountains Convent, 1794 Lake St., 84401. Tel: 801-392-1476. Sisters 2. 484 N. 300 E., Logan, 84321. Tel: 801-753-7445.

PRICE. *Home of the Daughters of Charity*, 48 W. 200 N., 84501. Tel: 801-637-0163. Daughters of Charity. Sr. Ellen Van Zandt, D.C., Sr. Servant. Sisters 2.

WEST JORDAN. *St. Joseph the Worker Convent*, 7405 S. Redwood Rd., 84084. Tel: 801-561-4090.

[H] NEWMAN CENTERS

SALT LAKE CITY. *University of Utah, Newman Center*. St. Catherine of Siena University Parish. 170 S. University, 84102. Tel: 801-359-6066. Revs. Cassian Lewinski, O.P.; Bartholomew Hutcherson, O.P. Total Students in Residence 10; Total Staff 5.

EPHRAIM. *St. Jude Catholic Center*, 160 E. Center, 84627. Tel: 801-283-6242. Rev. Michael R. Sciumbato, Pastoral Admin. Total Staff 2.

LOGAN. *St. Thomas Aquinas, Newman Center*. (Utah State University), 795 N. 800 E., 84321. Tel: 801-752-1478. Rev. Clarence J. Sandoval; Sr. Marilyn Mark, O.S.B., Campus Min. Total in Residence 1; Total Staff 2.

OGDEN. *Weber State University, Newman Center*, 3738 Custer Ave., 84403. Tel: 801-399-9531. Rev. Charles T. Cummins, Dir. Total in Residence 3; Total Staff 1.

PRICE. *College of Eastern Utah, Newman Club*, 454 E. 400 North, 84501. Tel: 801-637-6785. Rev. William Wheaton. Total Staff 1.

ST. GEORGE. *Dixie College, Newman Center*. Tel: 801-673-2604; 673-7354. Mailing Address: St. George Church, P.O. Box 188, 84771. Rev. Leo Lopez, Dir., 165 N. 200 W., 84770.

[I] RETREAT HOUSES

OGDEN. *Our Lady of the Mountains*, 1794 Lake St., 84401. Tel: 801-392-9231.
E-mail: olmrh@juno.com
Sr. Danile Knight, O.S.B., Dir. Total Staff 6; Total in Residence 1.

[J] CATHOLIC COMMUNITY SERVICES

SALT LAKE CITY. *Catholic Community Services*, 2300 W. 1700 S., 84104. Tel: 801-977-9119; Fax: 801-977-8227; 977-9224. Frank Leonard, Board Pres.; Sr. Margo Cain, C.S.C., Exec. Dir. Total Assisted 200,623; Total Staff 71. Northern Utah Office: 622 23rd St., Ogden, 84401. Tel: 801-394-5944; Fax: 801-394-5948. Mr. Matthew M. Minkevitch, B.A., Dir.
Marillac House, 2300 W. 1700 S., 84104. Tel: 801-977-9119; Fax: 801-363-3621. Sr. Susan Shaw, C.S.C., Dir. Tel: 801-359-0830.
St. Mary's Home For Men, 1206 W. 200 S., Box 941, 84110. Tel: 801-328-1894; Fax: 801-328-1895. Three daily family style meals. 40 beds for homeless, fundless, sober men. Work obligation, Inc., non-profit organization, 1972. Mr. John G. Bash, Dir.
St. Vincent de Paul Center, 437 W. 200 S., 84101. Tel: 801-534-1500; Fax: 801-596-8532. Mr. Robert D. Mayo, Dir.
Marillac Transitional Housing Services, Inc., 2300 W. 1700 S., 84104. Sr. Susan Shaw, C.S.C., Dir.
William K. Weigand Resource Center, 235 Rio Grande St., 84101. Tel: 801-363-7710; Fax: 801-363-7647. Mr. Robert D. Mayo, Dir.
Villa Maria, 2300 W. 1700 S., 84104. Sr. Susan Shaw, C.S.C., Dir. Tel: 801-359-0830. Home for Single Pregnant Women.
Shelter Plus Housing, 622 23rd St., Ogden, 84401. Matthew M. Minkevitch, B.A., Dir. Housing for people with AIDS/HIV.
Additional Programs:
Refugee Resettlement and Immigration Services, 2300 W. 1700 S., 84104. Lina Alabbas, Dir. Tel: 801-977-9119.
Family and Counseling Services, 2300 W. 1700 S., 84104. Pam Sanders, Dir. Tel: 801-977-9119.
Adoption Services, 2300 W. 1700 S., 84104. Pam Sanders, Dir. Tel: 801-977-9119.
Refugee Foster Care, 2300 W. 1700 S., 84104. Pam Sanders, Dir. Tel: 801-977-9119.

RELIGIOUS INSTITUTES OF MEN REPRESENTED IN THE DIOCESE

For further details refer to the corresponding bracketed number in the Religious Institutes of Men or Women section.

[0600]—*Brothers of the Congregation of the Holy Cross.*—C.S.C.
[0220]—*Congregation of the Blessed Sacrament.*—S.S.S.
[1330]—*Congregation of the Mission*. (Province of the West).—C.M.
[1000]—*Congregation of the Passion.*—C.P.
[0690]—*Jesuit Fathers*. (California Prov.).—S.J.
[0920]—*Oblates of St. Francis de Sales.*—O.S.F.S.
[0350]—*Order of Cistercians of the Strict Observance (Trappists).*—O.C.S.O.
[0430]—*Order of Preachers (Dominicans)*. (Western Province).—O.P.
[1060]—*Society of the Precious Blood.*—C.PP.S.

RELIGIOUS INSTITUTES OF WOMEN REPRESENTED IN THE DIOCESE

[0230]—*Benedictine Sisters of Pontifical Jurisdiction.*—O.S.B.
[0470]—*Congregation of the Sisters of Charity of the Incarnate Word, Houston, Texas.*—C.C.V.I.
[3935]—*The Congregation of the Sisters of St. Louis, Juilly-Monaghan.*—S.S.L.
[1920]—*Congregation of the Sisters of the Holy Cross.*—C.S.C.
[0760]—*Daughters of Charity of St. Vincent de Paul*. (Province of the West).—D.C.
[0420]—*Discalced Carmelite Nuns.*—O.C.D.
[1070-09]—*Dominican Sisters.*—O.P.
[1190]—*Franciscan Sisters of the Atonement.*—S.A.
[2575]—*Institute of the Sisters of Mercy of the Americas.*—R.S.M.
[3130]—*Our Lady of Victory Missionary Sisters.*—O.L.V.M.
[]—*Sisters for Christian Community.*—S.F.C.C.
[2575]—*Sisters of Mercy of the Americas.*—R.S.M.
[3000]—*Sisters of Notre Dame de Namur.*—S.N.D.deN.
[3840]—*Sisters of St. Joseph of Carondelet.*—C.S.J.
[1960]—*Sisters of the Holy Family.*—S.H.F.

DIOCESAN CEMETERIES

SALT LAKE CITY. *Mount Calvary Catholic*, Office, 275 U St., 84103. Tel: 801-355-2476. Mr. Jennings H. Mease, Dir.; Harriet Malloy, Sec.

NECROLOGY

† Mobley, William M., (Retired). —Died Dec. 24, 1996.

Diocese of San Angelo

(Dioecesis Angeliana)

Most Reverend

MICHAEL D. PFEIFER, O.M.I.

Bishop of San Angelo; ordained December 21, 1964; consecrated and installed Bishop of San Angelo July 26, 1985. *Res., P.O. Box 1829, San Angelo, TX, 76902.*

ESTABLISHED OCTOBER 16, 1961.

Square Miles 37,433.

Comprises 29 Counties in the State of Texas as follows: Andrews, Brown, Callahan, Coke, Coleman, Concho, Crane, Crockett, Ector, Glasscock, Howard, Irion, Kimble, McCulloch, Martin, Menard, Midland, Mitchell, Nolan, Pecos, Reagan, Runnells, Schleicher, Sterling, Sutton, Taylor, Terrell, Tom Green and Upton.

For legal title of parishes and diocesan institutions, consult the Chancery Office.

The Chancery: P.O. Box 1829, San Angelo, TX, 76902. Tel.: 915-651-7500; Fax: 915-651-6688.

Web site address: http://wcc2.wcc.net~/catholic

E-mail address: mdpomi@aol.com

STATISTICAL OVERVIEW

Personnel	
Bishop	1
Priests: Diocesan Active in Diocese	27
Priests: Active Outside Diocese	9
Priests: Retired, Sick or Absent	14
Number of Diocesan Priests	50
Religious Priests in Diocese	19
Extern Priests in Diocese	3
Permanent Deacons in Diocese	41
Total Sisters	43
Parishes	
Parishes	49
With Resident Pastor:	
Resident Diocesan Priests	23
Resident Religious Priests	11
Without Resident Pastor:	
Administered by Priests	9
Administered by Permanent Deacons	1
Administered by Women Religious	2
Administered by Lay People	1
Administered by Pastoral Teams, etc.	2
Missions	24
Professional Ministry Personnel:	
Sisters	14
Lay Ministers	7
Welfare	
Educational	
Diocesan Students in Other Seminaries	7
Total Seminarians	7
Elementary Schools, Diocesan and Parish	3
Total Students	843
Catechesis/Religious Education:	
High School Students	4,462
Elementary Students	8,808
Total Students Under Catholic Instruction	14,120
Teachers in the Diocese:	
Sisters	4
Lay Teachers	53
Vital Statistics	
Receptions into the Church:	
Infant Baptism Totals	1,966
Adult Baptism Totals	142
Received into Full Communion	139
First Communions	1,964
Confirmations	1,667
Marriages:	
Catholic	449
Interfaith	102
Total Marriages	551
Deaths	587
Total Catholic Population	82,500
Total Population	696,093

Former Bishops—Most Rev. THOMAS J. DRURY, D.D., LL.D., ord. June 2, 1935; appt. Oct. 16, 1961; cons. and installed Jan. 24, 1962; transferred to Corpus Christi, July 19, 1965; died July 22, 1992.—Most Rev. THOMAS TSCHOEPE, D.D., ord. May 30, 1943; appt. Bishop Jan. 12, 1966; cons. March 9, 1966; transferred to Dallas, Aug. 27, 1969.—Most Rev. STEPHEN A. LEVEN, D.D., ord. June 10, 1928; cons. Feb. 8, 1956, Auxiliary of San Antonio; appt. to San Angelo Oct. 22, 1969; retired April 16, 1979; died June 28, 1983.—Most Rev. JOSEPH A. FIORENZA, ord. May 29, 1954; appt. Sept. 4, 1979; ord. and installed October 25, 1979; transferred to Galveston-Houston, Dec. 18, 1984.

Vicar General—Rev. Msgr. TIMOTHY J. MURPHY, J.C.L.

Chancery Office—804 Ford, San Angelo, 76905. Tel: 915-651-7500; Fax: 915-651-6688. Office Hours: Mon.-Fri. 9-12 & 1-5, *Mailing Address: Box 1829, San Angelo, 76902.*

Chancellor—Rev. Msgr. LARRY J. DROLL, J.C.L.

Diocesan Tribunal—P.O. Box 1829, San Angelo, 76902.

Judicial Vicar—Rev. Msgr. TIMOTHY J. MURPHY, J.C.L., *P.O. Box 1829, San Angelo, 76902.*

Judges—Revs. WILLIAM DUBUISSON, O.M.I., J.C.L., Adjutant Judicial Vicar; TOM BARLEY, J.C.L.; Very Rev. MAURICE J. VOITY.

Promotor Justitiae—Rev. JAMES PLAGENS.

Defensores Vinculi—Rev. Msgr. LARRY J. DROLL, J.C.L.; Rev. CHARLES GREENWELL; Rev. MARK WOODRUFF.

Diocesan Consultors—Rev. Msgr. LARRY J. DROLL; Rev. BERNARD L. GULLY; Rev. MARK WOODRUFF; Rev. Msgr. TIMOTHY J. MURPHY; Revs. WILLIAM DU BUISSON, O.M.I.; TOM BARLEY.

Priests' Personnel Committee—Rev. Msgr. LARRY J. DROLL, Chm.

Presbyteral Council—Rev. TOM BARLEY, J.C.L., Chm.; Rev. Msgr. TIMOTHY J. MURPHY; Rev. Msgr. LARRY J. DROLL; Revs. TERENCE BRENON; JAMES PLAGENS; MARK WOODRUFF; WILLIAM DU BUISSON, O.M.I.; Revs. JAMES BRIDGES; STEPHEN KENNELLY; JOSEPH UECKER, C.PP.S.

Vicar for Women Religious—Sr. MALACHY GRIFFIN, O.P.

Diocesan Offices and Directors

Accounting Office—KAREN MAYRAND.

Office of Parish Pastoral Leadership—Rev. JAMES PLAGENS.

Campaign for Human Development—Mr. LES MAIMAN.

Catholic Relief Services—Mr. LES MAIMAN.

Catholic University, Friends of—Rev. Msgr. TIMOTHY J. MURPHY.

Communications Office—Rev. MAURICE J. VOITY.

Continuing Education of the Clergy—Rev. JAMES PLAGENS.

Cursillos de Cristiandad—Rev. BERNARD GULLY.

Deans—Revs. CHARLES GREENWELL, San Angelo Deanery: MARK WOODRUFF, Midland-Odessa Deanery: FRED NAWARSKAS, Abilene Deanery:

Diocesan Liturgical Commission—Rev. JAMES PLAGENS.

Holy Childhood, Pontifical Association—Miss MARY SUE BREWER.

Newspaper—"West Texas Angelus"; Rev. MAURICE J. VOITY, Editor.

Office of Education and Formation—Sr. JOAN MARKUS, S.S.N.D.

Permanent Deacon Director—Deacon ALAN NEFF.

Priests' Pension Plan—Board of Directors: Rev. Msgrs. TIMOTHY J. MURPHY; LARRY J. DROLL; Very Rev. CHARLES GREENWELL; Rev. Msgr. FRED NAWARSKAS; Rev. BENEDICT ZIENTEK.

Propagation of the Faith—Rev. Msgr. TIMOTHY J. MURPHY.

Rural Life—Deacon LEROY BEACH, Dir.

Schools—Sr. ELIZABETH ANN SWARTZ, S.S.N.D., Supt.

Vocations—Rev. DAVID ESPITIA, Dir.

CLERGY, PARISHES, MISSIONS AND PAROCHIAL SCHOOLS

CITY OF SAN ANGELO
(Tom Green County)

1—CATHEDRAL OF THE SACRED HEART (1884), Rev. Maurice Voity, Rector; Deacon Jerry Trevino, Pastoral Assoc.
Office: 19 S. Oakes St., 76903. Tel: 915-658-6567; Fax: 915-659-0588.
School—Angelo Catholic School, Sacred Heart Campus, (Grades 2-6). Tel: 915-655-3325; Fax: 915-655-1286. Mr. Charles Guenat, Prin.
Lay Teachers 10; Students 290.
Catechesis/Religious Programs—Sr. Carol Markus, S.S.N.D., D.R.E.
Students 290.
Sacred Heart Cathedral-Parish Educational Endowment Fund, Inc.—Tel: 915-658-6567.

2—HOLY ANGELS (1961), Rev. Charles C. Greenwell; Sr. Georgia Ann Fucik, C.D.P., Pastoral Assoc.
Parish Office: 2202 Rutgers Ave., 76904. Tel: 915-949-3308; 944-8967; Fax: 915-223-8153.
School—Angelo Catholic School, (Grades PreK-1).

Holy Angels Campus 2315 A & M Ave., Tel: 915-655-3325. Mr. Charles Guenat, Prin.
Lay Teachers 4; Students 72.
Catechesis/Religious Programs—Tel: 915-942-8192. Mrs. Judy Feist, D.R.E., (Grades 1-6).
Students 399.

3—ST. MARGARET (1967), Deacons Ray Smith, Pastoral Coord.; Dan Pena.
Office: 2619 Era St., 76905. Tel: 915-651-4633.
Catechesis/Religious Programs—Dee Ann Kemp, D.R.E.
Students 108.

4—ST. MARY'S (1930), Rev. Terence Brenon; Deacons Lazaro Sevier; Mario Torres; Roy Ibarra. In res., Rev. George Fey, C.PP.S.
Res., 7 West Ave. N., 76903. Tel: 915-655-6278; Fax: 915-653-7517.
Catechesis/Religious Programs—Minnie Ibarra, D.R.E.
Students 361.

5—ST. JOSEPH (1942), Rev. Joe S. Vasquez; Deacons Manuel Maldonado; John Munoz. In res., Rev. Miguel Dinio, O.P.
Res., 301 W. 17th, 76903. Tel: 915-653-5006; Fax: 915-659-2795.
Catechesis/Religious Programs—Tel: 915-658-8759. Michael R. Wyse, D.R.E.
Students 575.

OUTSIDE THE CITY OF SAN ANGELO

Abilene, Taylor Co.,

1—SACRED HEART, (1891), Rev. Robert Bush; Deacon William Smith.
Res., 837 Jeanette St., 79602. Tel: 915-677-7951; Fax: 915-677-7710.
Catechesis/Religious Programs—Tel: 915-673-0697. D.R.E.: Sr. Mary Rose Keegan, S.M.; Penny Pope.
Students 509.
Mission—Clyde, Callahan Co., Sts. Joachim and Ann. Deacon Peter Ballaro. [CEM]

2—HOLY FAMILY, (1976), Rev. Msgr. Frederick Nawarskas; Sr. Dolores Siebenmorgen, S.S.N.D., Pastoral Assoc.; Deacons Paul Klein; Gerald Schwalb.
Res., 5410 Buffalo Gap Rd., P.O. Box 5970, 79606. Tel: 915-692-1820; Fax: 915-698-5131.
Catechesis/Religious Programs—Sr. Marie de Loudres Unterreiner, S.S.N.D., D.R.E.
Students 385.

3—ST. FRANCIS OF ASSISI, (1906), Revs. Joseph H. Uecker, C.PP.S.; David Matz, C.PP.S.; Deacon Jose Sanchez.
Office: 826 Cottonwood St., 79601. Tel: 915-672-6695.
Catechesis/Religious Programs—D.R.E.: Virginia Camacho; Norma Collazo.
Students 152.

4—ST. VINCENT PALLOTTI, (1963), Revs. Joseph H. Uecker, C.PP.S. Tel: 915-673-7048; David Matz, C.PP.S; Sr. Rebecca Otter, O.P., Pastoral Assoc., Tel: 915-672-5933.
Res., 2525 Westview, 79603. Tel: 915-672-1794.
Catechesis/Religious Programs—D.R.E.: Ofilia Rodriguez; Minerva Garcia.
Students 376.

Andrews, Andrews Co., Our Lady of Lourdes (1957), Rev. Bernard L. Gully.
Res., 1109 N.E. 2nd St., 79714. Tel: 915-523-4215.
Catechesis/Religious Programs—Tel: 915-524-2789. Sr. Helen Riva, C.D.P., D.R.E.
Students 621.

Ballinger, Runnels Co., St. Mary Star of the Sea (1885), Rev. Hubert Wade, Jr.; Deacons Henry Martinez; D.J. Goetz.
Res., 608 Sixth St., 76821. Tel: 915-365-2687. [JC]
Catechesis/Religious Programs—D.R.E.: Shawn Nagel; Dolly Martinez.
Students 280.
Missions—Bronte, Coke Co., St. James, Bronte, 76933.; Robert Lee, Coke Co., Our Lady of Guadalupe.

Big Lake, Reagan Co., St. Margaret of Cortona (1949), Rev. Barry McLean, O.F.M.
107 First St., 76932. Tel: 915-884-2645.
Res., Drawer G, McCamey, 79752. Tel: 915-884-2645. [JC]
Catechesis/Religious Programs—Tel: 915-884-6874. Linda Lozano, D.R.E.
Students 179.
Mission—Rankin, Upton Co., St. Thomas.

Big Spring, Howard Co., Immaculate Heart of Mary (1961), Revs. Jeremiah McCarthy, M.S.C.; Jeremiah Murphy, M.S.C.; Deacons Wayne Rock; David King.
Res., 1009 Hearn St., 79720. Tel: 915-267-4124; Fax: 915-267-7844.
Catechesis/Religious Programs—Mrs. Ruth Salazar, D.R.E.
Students 275.
Mission—Coahoma, St. Joseph, Coahoma, 79511.

Sacred Heart (1948), Rev. Cornelius J. Scanlan, O.M.I.
Res., 508 N. Aylford, 79720. Tel: 915-263-7884; Fax: 915-263-3621.
Mailing Address: P.O. Box 2101, 79721-2101.
Catechesis/Religious Programs—Tel: 915-267-9092. Margie Rodriguez, D.R.E.
Students 206.

St. Thomas (1887), Rev. Cornelius J. Scanlan, O.M.I. In res., Rev. Adolfo L. Valenzuela.
Res., 605 N. Main St., P.O. Box 627, 79721. Tel: 915-263-2864; Fax: 915-263-3621.
Catechesis/Religious Programs—Miss Mary Chavez, D.R.E.
Students 150.

Brady, McCulloch Co., St. Patrick's (1876), Mr. Noe Rocha, Pastoral Coord.
Res., P.O. Box 1188, 76825. Tel: 915-597-2324.
Catechesis/Religious Programs—Mercy James, D.R.E.
Students 208.
Mission—Melvin, McCullogh Co., St. Francis Xavier.

Brownwood, Brown Co., St. Mary's (1896), Rev. Msgr. Benedict Zientek; Deacon John Specht.
Res., 1105 Main Ave., 76801. Tel: 915-646-7455.
Catechesis/Religious Programs—Tel: 915-646-9630. Bryan Scott Boyce, D.R.E.
Students 318.

Carlsbad, Tom Green Co., St. Therese of the Child Jesus (1957), Sr. Mary Kay Bailey, Pastoral Coord.
Mailing Address: P.O. Box 416, 76934-0416. Tel: 915-465-8062.
Catechesis/Religious Programs—Students 66.
Mission—Sterling City, Sterling Co., St. Paschal Baylon.
Station—San Angelo State School for the Mentally Retarded.

Coleman, Coleman Co., Sacred Heart (1950), Rev. Lawrence S. Cyr, C.PP.S.; Sr. Guadalupe Rodriguez, C.C.V.I., Pastoral Assoc. In res., Rev. Austin C. Herrmann, C.PP.S.
Res., 303 E. College, 76834. Tel: 915-625-5773; Fax: 915-625-3320.
Catechesis/Religious Programs—201 San Saba, 76834. Tel: 915-625-2031.
Students 163.

Colorado City, Mitchell Co., St. Ann's (1943), Rev. Ray Wilhelm, O.M.I.; Sr. Ruth Barron, S.C.L., Pastoral Assoc. & D.R.E.
Res., P.O. Box 966, 79512. Tel: 915-728-3252; Fax: 915-728-3252.
Catechesis/Religious Programs—Tel: 915-728-5865.
Students 258.
Mission—Loraine, Mitchell Co., San Jose.

Crane, Crane Co., Good Shepherd, Rev. Barry McLean; Sr. Josephine Glessner, S.S.N.D., Pastoral Coord.; Deacons Julio Carrasco; Apolonio Gutierrez.
Mailing Address: P.O. Box 1294, 79731.
Res., 1109 S. Virginia St., 79731. Tel: 915-558-2718.
Church—9th & S. Virginia St., 79731.
Catechesis/Religious Programs—D.R.E.: Sr. Carol Markus, S.S.N.D; Theresa Figuora.
Students 137.

Eden, Concho Co., St. Charles (1927), Rev. Michael Rodriguez; Deacons Leroy Beach; Joe Lopez.
Res., P.O. Box 575, 76837. Tel: 915-869-8311.
Catechesis/Religious Programs—Students 72.
Missions—Millersview, Concho Co., Our Lady of Guadalupe; Eola, Concho Co., St. Philip.

Eldorado, Schleicher Co., Our Lady of Guadalupe (1924), Rev. Michael Dwyer, M.S.C.
Res., P.O. Box 211, 76936. Tel: 915-853-2663.
Catechesis/Religious Programs—Tel: 915-853-3366. D.R.E.: Sylvia Belman; Nell Edmiston; Rosie Diaz; Martha Acosta; Lucy Rodriguez; Patty Furr.
Students 289.
Missions—Knickerbocker, Tom Green Co., Immaculate Conception, P.O. Box 36, Knickerbocker, 76939. Tel: 915-944-2820; Mertzon, Irion Co., St. Peter's, 324 N. Commerce, P.O. Box 772, Tel: 915-835-2000.

Fort Stockton, Pecos Co., St. Joseph's (1875), Rev. James Chaumont; Deacon Cosme Ureta, Jr.
Res., 403 S. Main, 79735. Tel: 915-336-5027. [CEM]
Catechesis/Religious Programs—Tel: 915-336-5037. Elizabeth C. Rojo, D.R.E.
Students 340.

St. Agnes (1953), Rev. Charles Geller; Sr. Miriam Tracey, M.S.H.R., Pastoral Assoc.; Sr. Maria O'Connor, M.S.H.R.; Deacon Simon Franco.
Mailing Address: Rte. 1, Box 105, 79735. Tel: 915-336-2724; Fax: 915-336-6950. [CEM]
Catechesis/Religious Programs—D.R.E.: Lillian Subia; Arabella Granado.
Students 385.
Missions—Coyanosa, Pecos Co., St. Isidore; Imperial, Pecos Co., Our Lady of Lourdes. Deacon Jose Esparza.

Junction, Kimble Co., St. Theresa of the Child Jesus (1959), Rev. Quirino H. Cornejo.
Res., P.O. Box 486, 76849. Tel: 915-446-3393; Fax: 915-396-2076.
Catechesis/Religious Programs—Students 42.

McCamey, Upton Co., Sacred Heart (1935), Rev. Barry L. McLean.
Res., Drawer G, 79752. Tel: 915-652-8216; Fax: 915-652-3219.
Catechesis/Religious Programs—Tel: 915-652-8810.
Students 292.
Mission—Iraan, Pecos Co., St. Francis of Assisi, Tel: 915-652-8216. Deacon James Bacon.

Menard, Menard Co., Sacred Heart (1873), Rev. Quirino H. Cornejo.
Res., P.O. Box 788, 76859. Tel: 915-396-4906; Fax: 915-396-2076.
Catechesis/Religious Programs—Students 84.

Midland, Midland Co.,

1—ST. ANN'S, (1896), Rev. Msgr. Timothy J. Murphy; Deacon Hubert Collins. Pastoral Assocs.: Sr. Mary Brian Overfield, S.S.N.D.; Mr. Thomas Burke.
Res., 1908 W. Texas Ave., 79701. Tel: 915-682-6303; 6304; 682-6694; 682-8905; Fax: 915-684-4528.
School—(Grades PreK-6) 2000 W. Texas Ave., Tel: 915-684-4563; Fax: 915-687-2468. Mrs. Barbara Ransbottom, Prin.
Religious 1; Lay Teachers 30; Students 401.
Catechesis/Religious Programs—Tel: 915-687-0941. Marge Hellinghausen, D.R.E.
Students 826.

2—OUR LADY OF GUADALUPE, (1960), Revs. Robert Vreteau, O.M.I.; Jerome Burnet, O.M.I.; Gilbert Rodriguez; Deacon Jesse Guajardo, Pastoral Assoc.
Res., 1401 E. Garden Ln., P.O. Box 7, 79702. Tel: 915-682-2581; Fax: 915-682-9364.
Catechesis/Religious Programs—Tel: 915-683-8908. D.R.E.: Sr. Regina Javier, O.N.D.; Sr. Luisita Iglesias, O.N.D.
Students 904.

3—OUR LADY OF SAN JUAN DE LOS LAGOS, (1984), Rev. Thomas Kelley.
Res., 1008 W. New Jersey, 79701. Tel: 915-570-0952.
Catechesis/Religious Programs—Tel: 915-682-2100; Fax: 915-687-5082. D.R.E.: Isabel Rey; Isabel Gonzales; Carla Repman.
Students 511.

4—ST. STEPHEN'S, (1982), Rev. James P. Bridges.
Mailing Address: 4601 Neely Ave., 79707. Tel: 915-520-7394; Fax: 915-520-7395.
Parish Office: 4601 Neely Ave., 79707.
Catechesis/Religious Programs—Tel: 915-520-3065. Karla Blake, D.R.E.
Students 301.

Miles, Runnels Co., St. Thomas (1962), Rev. Stephen Kennelly (Ireland); Sr. Madeleine Zimmerer, C.D.P., Pastoral Assoc.
Res., P.O. Box 306, 76861. Tel: 915-468-3171.
Catechesis/Religious Programs—Tel: 915-442-4021.
Students 154.

Odessa, Ector Co.,

1—HOLY REDEEMER, (1961), Rev. Frank Chavez; Deacons Ignacio Cisneros; Antonio Gonzales.
Res., 2633 Conover, 79763. Tel: 915-580-4295; Fax: 915-332-6631.
Catechesis/Religious Programs—Tel: 915-332-9231. D.R.E.: Anita Diaz; Isabel Garza, (Elementary).
Students 1,093.

2—ST. ANTHONY, (1948), Revs. David Lee Herrera; Luis Zepeda; Sr. Jovita Perez, Pastoral Assoc.; Deacon Barney Rodriguez.
Office: 1321 W. Monahans St., 79763. Tel: 915-337-6314; Fax: 915-333-3631.
Catechesis/Religious Programs—Tel: 915-337-0241. D.R.E.: Belinda Urias; Yolanda Chavarria; Irene Nunez.
Students 321.

3—ST. ELIZABETH ANN SETON, (1982), Rev. Mark Woodruff; Deacons Alan Neff, Pastoral Assoc.; Manuel Luevano; Pedro Santoya.
Office: 4251 Candy Ln., 79762. Tel: 915-367-4657; Fax: 915-367-0700.
Res., 1506 Alpine, 79762. Tel: 915-366-8629.
Catechesis/Religious Programs—Tel: 915-367-4668. Rebecca McIlwain, D.R.E.
Students 359.
Mission—Odessa, Ector Co., Our Lady of San Juan, 905 Edgeport, 79765.

4—ST. JOSEPH, (1948), Revs. David Lee Herrera; Luis Zepeda; Sr. Jovita Perez; Deacons Abel Campos; Eufracio Hernandez; Jesus Mercado.

Res., 907 S. Dixie St., 79761. Tel: 915-337-2213; Fax: 915-333-3631.
Catechesis/Religious Programs—Tel: 915-337-4734. D.R.E.: Monica Lopez; Mary Rivas; Polo Ramirez.
Students 526.
Mission—Odessa, Ector Co., St. Martin de Porres, 2821 E. Hammett, 79766.

5—St. Mary's, (1938), Rev. Francis Frey.
Res., 612 E. 18th St., 79761. Tel: 915-332-5334.
School—(Grades PreK-6) 1703 N. Adams, 79761. Tel: 915-337-6052. Sr. Kathleen Murray, D.C., Prin. Sisters 3; Lay Teachers 14; Students 207.
Catechesis/Religious Programs—Tel: 915-332-1844. Sr. Doris Moore, D.C., D.R.E.
Students 323.

Olfen, Runnels Co., St. Boniface (1901), Rev. Stephen Kennelly; Rev. Msgr. Kevin J. Heyburn.
Res., P.O. Box 96, Rowena, 76875-0096. Tel: 915-442-2893. [CEM]
Church—1118 County Rd. 234, Rowena, 76875.

Ozona, Crockett Co., Our Lady of Perpetual Help (1929), Rev. Henry Laenen, O.M.I.
Res., P.O. Box 1069, 76943. Tel: 915-392-3063; Fax: 915-392-3353.
Catechesis/Religious Programs—Tel: 915-392-3429. D.R.E.: Juanita Delgado; Mabel Hernandez.
Students 291.
Mission—Sheffield, Pecos Co., Good Shepherd.

Rowena, Runnels Co., St. Joseph's (1906), Rev. Stephen Kennelly; Rev. Msgr. Kevin J. Heyburn; Sr. Madeleine Zimmerer, C.D.P., Pastoral Assoc.
Res., P.O. Box 96, 76875. Tel: 915-442-3521; Fax: 915-442-4602. [CEM]
Catechesis/Religious Programs—Mrs. Ina Albarado, D.R.E.
Students 136.

St. Lawrence, Glasscock Co., St. Lawrence (1948), Rev. Tom Barley.
Res., 2400 FM 2401, Garden City, 79739. Tel: 915-397-2300. [CEM]
Catechesis/Religious Programs—Tel: 915-397-2777. Deborah Pelzel, D.R.E.
Students 330.
Mission—Midkiff, Upton Co., St. Thomas.

Sanderson, Terrell Co., St. James (1916), Rev. James Chaumont.
Res., 409 N. Second St., P.O. Box 520, 79848. Tel: 915-345-2354.
Catechesis/Religious Programs—Tel: 915-345-2354. Lee Warrington, D.R.E.
Students 95.

Sonora, Sutton Co., St. Ann's (1927), Very Rev. William Du Buisson, O.M.I.
Office: 311 W. Plum St., P.O. Box 1397, 76950. Tel: 915-387-2278; Fax: 9115-387-2278.
Res., 105 Oakwood, Box 1397, 76950. Tel: 915-387-5966.
Catechesis/Religious Programs—Students 280.

Stanton, Martin Co., St. Joseph's (1882), Sr. Laureana Perez, D.C., Pastoral Coord.; Deacon Ernie Sanchez.
Res., P.O. Box 846, 405 N. Convent St., 79782-0846. Tel: 915-756-3743.
Catechesis/Religious Programs—Nestor Hernandez, D.R.E.
Students 222.
Mission—Lenorah, Martin Co., St. Isidore.

Sweetwater, Nolan Co., Holy Family (1885), Revs. Michael Goode, C.PP.S.; Timothy Guthridge, C.PP.S.
Mailing Address: P.O. Box 847, 79556.
Res., 507 Crane St., 79556. Tel: 915-235-2694; Fax: 915-235-3483.
Catechesis/Religious Programs—D.R.E.: Margaret Torres; Mary Petrie; Diane Miller.
Students 65.
Mission—Merkel, Taylor Co., Our Mother of Mercy, P.O. Box 206, Merkel, 79536. Tel: 915-928-5239.
Immaculate Heart of Mary (1962), Revs. Michael Goode, C.P.P.S.; Timothy Guthridge, C.P.P.S.
Res., 511 W. Alabama, 79556. Tel: 915-235-5271; 235-3318 (Office); Fax: 915-235-0258.
Catechesis/Religious Programs—Students 135.
Mission—Roscoe, Nolan Co., St. Albert the Great.

Wall, Tom Green Co., St. Ambrose (1941), Rev. Msgr. Larry J. Droll.
Res., P.O. Box 228, 76957. Tel: 915-651-7551; Fax: 915-651-6605. [CEM]
Catechesis/Religious Programs—D.R.E.: Dolores Gully; Mary Kay Ripple; Sylvia Chappa.
Students 308.
Mission—Mereta, Tom Green Co., Holy Family, Tel: 915-468-3101. Sr. Maria Geheb, O.P., Pastoral Assoc.

Winters, Runnels Co., Our Lady of Mt. Carmel (1962), Rev. Sam F. Homsey, C.PP.S.
Res., 119 W. College, 79567. Tel: 915-754-4626.
Catechesis/Religious Programs—Tel: 915-754-4893. Dinell Jacob, D.R.E.
Students 98.

On Special or Other Diocesan Assignment:
Reverend Fathers—
Espitia, David, Box 1829, San Angelo, TX 76902
Plagens, James, Box 1829, San Angelo, TX 76902

On Duty Outside the Diocese:
Reverend Fathers—
Chengazcheril, George
Esquivez, Miguel
Lynes, James F.
McCaffrey, Daniel
Regan, Richard

Military Chaplains:
Reverend Fathers—
Diab, Thomas, 2 BW/HC, 275 Barksdale Blvd., E., Barksdale AFB, LA 71710-2121
Hicks, Steven, 15th NEU, Box 555365, Camp Pendleton, CA 92055-5365

Retired:
Reverend Fathers—
Aaron, James R., Catholic Care Center, 6700 E. 45th, Wichita, KS 67226
Braun, Serran R., 4908 Blue Ridge, San Angelo, TX 76904
Colacicco, Frank, St. Isidore Church, 445 LaGanda, CA 94526
Coleman, James, Padua Place, 100 Peter Baque Rd., San Antonio, TX 78209
Diersing, Leo, 102 Hamilton, Ballinger, TX 76821
Droll, Louis J., 132 Betama Dr., Georgetown, TX 78626
Femenia, Nicholas, P.O. Box 37056, San Antonio, TX 78237
Gallagher, Raymond, 2801 Wildflower Rd., Rocky River, OH 44116
Kelly, Robert M., Box 601, Center Moriches, NY 11934
Larue, Charles, Padua Place, 80 Peter Baque Rd., San Antonio, TX 78209
Schultz, Russell, 80 Peter Baque Rd., San Antonio, TX 78209
Vergauwen, Peter, 80 Peter Baque, San Antonio, TX 78209

Permanent Deacons:
Bacon, James, Sacred Heart, McCamey
Ballaro, Peter, Sts. Joachim & Ann Mission, Clyde
Ballero, Peter, Sacred Heart, Abilene
Beach, Leroy, Our Lady of Guadalupe, Millersview
Beach, Leroy, St. Charles, Eden
Camacho, Isaac, Holy Family, Abilene
Campos, Abel, San Jose, Odessa
Carrasco, Julio, Good Shepherd, Crane
Cisneros, Ignacio, Holy Redeemer Church, Odessa
Collins, Hubert, St. Ann's Church, Midland
Crochet, Larry, Austin
Decuir, Harold, On Duty Outside the Diocese
Esparza, Jose, Our Lady Of Lourdes, Imperial
Franco, Simon, St. Agnes, Ft. Stockton
Giovannitti, Thomas
Goetz, D. J., St. Mary's, Ballinger
Gonzales, Antonio, Holy Redeemer Church, Odessa
Guajardo, Jesse, Our Lady of Guadalupe, Midland
Gutierrez, Apolonio, Good Shepherd, Crane
Hernandez, Andres, St. Agnes Church, Ft. Stockton
Hernandez, Eufracio, San Jose, Odessa
Ibarra, Roy, St. Mary, San Angelo
King, David, Immaculate Heart of Mary Church, Big Spring
Klein, Paul, Holy Family Church, Abilene
Lopez, Joseph, St. Philip's Church, Eola
Luevano, Manuel, St. Elizabeth, Odessa
Maldonado, Manuel, St. Joseph, San Angelo
Martinez, Enrique, St. James, Bronte
Mercado, Jesus, San Jose, Odessa
Munoz, John, St. Joseph, San Angelo
Neff, Alan, St. Elizabeth Ann Seton, Odessa
Pena, Daniel, On Duty Outside the Diocese
Rock, Wayne, Immaculate Heart of Mary Church, Big Spring
Rodriguez, Barney, St. Anthony's Church, Odessa
Rodriguez, Damian
Saldivar, Audon Stanton
Samaniego, Enemencio, St. Ann, Sonora
Sanchez, Ernie, St. Joseph Church, Stanton
Sanchez, Pedro, St. Francis, Abilene
Santoya, Pedro, St. Elizabeth, Odessa
Schwalb, Gerald, Holy Family, Abilene
Sevier, Lazaro, St. Mary, San Angelo
Smith, Raymond, St. Margaret, San Angelo
Smith, William, Sacred Heart Church, Abilene
Specht, John, St. Mary, Brownwood
Torres, Mario, St. Mary, San Angelo
Trevino, Jerry, Sacred Heart, San Angelo
Ureta, Cosme, St. Joseph Church, Ft. Stockton
Yanez, Horacio, St. Thomas, Big Spring
Youngblood, Jack C., Worcester Diocese

INSTITUTIONS LOCATED IN THE DIOCESE

[A] MONASTERIES AND RESIDENCES OF PRIESTS & BROTHERS

Christoval. *Mount Carmel Hermitage*, Box 337, 76935-0337. Tel: 915-896-2249. Hermits of the Most Blessed Virgin Mary of Mt. Carmel. Rev. Fabian Maria Rosette, H.O.Carm. Hermits 4.

[B] CONVENTS AND RESIDENCES FOR SISTERS

San Angelo. *Carmelite Nuns of the Ancient Observance*, Monastery of Our Lady of Grace, One Saint Joseph Pl., 76905. Tel: 915-651-4959.
Dominican Sisters, 3526 Juanita, 76901. Tel: 915-944-7605. Congregation of the Most Holy Rosary. Sinsinawa Dominicans. Total in Residence 1; Total Staff 1. 2113 N. 7th, Abilene, 76903.
School Sisters of St. Francis, 1217 Lester Lane, 76903.
Sisters of Charity of the Incarnate Word, Mailing Address: 555 Smith Blvd., 76905. Tel: 915-655-3294. Sisters 1.
Sisters of the Living Word, 3111 W. Beauregard, Apt. B, 76904-4901.

Abilene. *Marist Sisters*, 810 Peach, 79602.
School Sisters of Notre Dame, P.O. Box 5970, 79605. 2627 Era St., San Angelo, 76905.

Ft. Stockton. *Missionary Sisters of the Lady of the Holy Rosary*, Rte. 1, Box 105, 79735. 1111 W. 13th St., #14, Odessa, 79763.

Midland. *Congregation of the Humility of Mary, CHM*, 1109-A N. Carrizo, #A, 79701.
Oblates of Notre Dame, 1400 Garden Ln., 79701.

Odessa. *Daughters of Charity*, 3525 Oakridge Dr., 79762. Tel: 915-362-7358.
Missionary Catechists of Divine Providence, 1321 W. Monahans, 79761.

Rowena. *Sisters of Divine Providence*, Mailing Address: P.O. Box 132, 76875. Tel: 915-442-4021. 3301B Moss St., Midland, 79701. 1717 Idlewild St., Abilene, 79602. Sisters 1.

[C] ST. VINCENT DE PAUL SOCIETY

San Angelo. *Catholic Outreach Services*, 102 N. Chadbourne, 76903. Tel: 915-658-4124. Thrift Store Social Services.

Abilene. *St. Vincent De Paul Society*, 1241 Walnut, 79601. Tel: 915-677-6871.
St. Vincent De Paul Thrift Store. Total Assisted 12,000; Total Staff 3.

Big Spring. *St. Vincent De Paul Society*, 1009 Hearn, 79720.
Food Distribution. Families 663; People 1,953.

Midland. *St. Vincent De Paul Society*. Mailing Address: P.O. Box 711, 79702-0711. Total Staff 2.

Odessa. *Catholic Charities Community Services Odessa, Inc.*, 606 W. 10th, 79761. Tel: 915-332-1387.

Stanton. *St. Vincent De Paul Society*. Mailing Address: P.O. Box 158, 79782.

[D] CAMPUS MINISTRY

San Angelo. *Catholic Newman Center*, 2451 Dena Dr., 76904. Tel: 915-949-8033. Sr. Marie Malachy Griffin, O.P., Campus Min. Total Staff 1.

[E] MISCELLANEOUS

San Angelo. *Christ the King Retreat Center*, 802 Ford, 76905. Tel: 915-651-5352; 651-5358; Fax: 915-651-5667. Rev. Andy Wueste, O.M.I., Dir. Tel: 915-651-5472; Sr. Maria Geheb, O.P., Asst. Dir. Total in Residence 1; Total Staff 11.

RELIGIOUS INSTITUTES OF MEN REPRESENTED IN THE DIOCESE

For further details refer to the corresponding bracketed number in the Religious Institutes of Men or Women section.

[1110]—*Missionaries of the Sacred Heart*. (Cork Ireland Prov.).—M.S.C.

[0910]—*Oblates of Mary Immaculate*. (Southern American Prov.).—O.M.I.

[]—*Order of Preachers (Dominicans).* (Philippines).—O.P.

[1060]—*Society of the Precious Blood.* (Kansas City Prov.).—C.PP.S.

RELIGIOUS INSTITUTES OF WOMEN REPRESENTED IN THE DIOCESE

[0320]—*Carmelite Nuns of the Ancient Observance.*—O.Carm.

[1010]—*Congregation of Divine Providence of San Antonio, Texas.*—C.D.P.

[0460]—*Congregation of Sisters of Charity of the Incarnate Word.*—C.C.V.I.

[]—*Congregation of the Humility of Mary.*—C.H.M.

[1070-13]—*Congregation of the Most Holy Rosary.*—O.P.

[0760]—*Daughters of Charity of St. Vincent De Paul.*—D.C.

[1070-03]—*Dominican Sisters.*—O.P.

[1070-24]—*Dominican Sisters.*—O.P.

[2430]—*Marist Sisters / Congregation of Mary.*—S.M.

[2690]—*Missionary Catechists of Divine Providence, San Antonio, Texas.*—M.C.D.P.

[2730]—*Missionary Sisters of Our Lady of the Holy Rosary.*—M.S.H.R.

[2960]—*Oblates of Notre Dame.*—O.N.D.

[]—*Oblates of Notre Dame.* (Midland, TX).

[]—*Oblates of Notre Dame, Philippines.*

[]—*Order of St. Ursula.*—O.S.U.

[2970]—*School Sisters of Notre Dame.* (St. Louis & Dallas Provinces).—S.S.N.D.

[1690]—*School Sisters of the Third Order of St. Francis.* (Pittsburgh, PA).—O.S.F.

[]—*Sisters of Charity of Leavenworth.*—S.C.L.

[1570]—*Sisters of St. Francis of the Holy Family.*—O.S.F.

[2350]—*Sisters of the Living Word.*—S.L.W.

NECROLOGY

† Valladares, Herman, (Retired). —Died Sept. 22, 1997.

Archdiocese of San Antonio

(Archidioecesis Sancti Antonii)

Most Reverend

PATRICK F. FLORES, D.D.

Archbishop of San Antonio; ordained May 26, 1956; appointed Titular Bishop of Italica and Auxiliary of San Antonio March 18, 1970; consecrated May 5, 1970; appointed Bishop of El Paso April 4, 1978; installed May 29, 1978; promoted Archiepiscopal See of San Antonio August 28, 1979; installed October 13, 1979. *Res., 2600 W. Woodlawn Ave., San Antonio, TX, 78228. All official communications to the Most Reverend Archbishop should be addressed to the Chancery Office, P.O. Box 28410, San Antonio, TX, 78228-0410.* Tel.: 210-734-2620.

Most Reverend

BERNARD F. POPP, D.D.

Retired Auxiliary Bishop of San Antonio; ordained February 24, 1943; appointed Titular Bishop of Capsus and Auxiliary Bishop of San Antonio June 7, 1983; consecrated July 25, 1983. *Res., 4535 Lord Rd., San Antonio, TX, 78220. Mailing Address: P.O. Box 28410, San Antonio, TX, 78228-0410.* Tel.: 210-734-2620.

ESTABLISHED AUGUST 28, 1874.

CREATED AN ARCHBISHOPRIC, AUGUST 3, 1926.

Square Miles 27,841.

The San Antonio Archdiocese comprises Atascosa, Bandera, Bexar, Comal, Dimmit, Edwards, Frio, Gillespie, Gonzales, Guadalupe, Karnes, Kendall, Kerr, Kinney, La Salle (that part of La Salle County north of the Nueces River), Maverick, McMullen (that part of McMullen County north of the Nueces River), Medina, Real, Uvalde, Val Verde, Wilson and Zavala.

For legal titles of parishes and archdiocesan institutions, consult the Chancery Office.

Chancery Office: 2718 W. Woodlawn Ave., P.O. Box 28410, San Antonio, TX, 78228-0410. Tel.: 210-734-2620; Fax: 210-734-0231.

STATISTICAL OVERVIEW

Personnel	
Archbishop	1
Retired Bishops	1
Priests: Diocesan Active in Diocese	117
Priests: Active Outside Diocese	13
Priests: Retired, Sick or Absent	23
Number of Diocesan Priests	153
Religious Priests in Diocese	213
Extern Priests in Diocese	53
Ordinations:	
Diocesan Priests	1
Religious Priests	1
Transitional Deacons	1
Permanent Deacons	11
Permanent Deacons in Diocese	252
Total Brothers	93
Total Sisters	980
Parishes	
Parishes	144
With Resident Pastor:	
Resident Diocesan Priests	91
Resident Religious Priests	44
Without Resident Pastor:	
Administered by Priests	8
Administered by Lay People	1
Missions	39
Pastoral Centers	2
Professional Ministry Personnel:	
Brothers	5
Sisters	37
Lay Ministers	140
Welfare	
Catholic Hospitals	5
Total Assisted	170,068
Health Care Centers	2
Total Assisted	12,410
Homes for the Aged	8
Total Assisted	522
Residential Care of Children	2
Total Assisted	90
Day Care and Extended Day Care Centers	13
Total Assisted	1,932
Specialized Homes	5
Total Assisted	3,099
Special Centers for Social Services	8
Total Assisted	323,161
Other Institutions	1
Total Assisted	80
Educational	
Seminaries, Diocesan	1
Students from This Diocese	7
Students from Other Diocese	32
Diocesan Students in Other Seminaries	5
Seminaries, Religious	10
Students Religious	51
Total Seminarians	63
Colleges and Universities	4
Total Students	11,346
High Schools, Diocesan and Parish	2
Total Students	738
High Schools, Private	7
Total Students	2,440
Elementary Schools, Diocesan and Parish	38
Total Students	11,578
Elementary Schools, Private	4
Total Students	1,631
Catechesis/Religious Education:	
High School Students	12,006
Elementary Students	37,440
Total Students Under Catholic Instruction	77,242
Teachers in the Diocese:	
Priests	40
Scholastics	1
Brothers	32
Sisters	161
Lay Teachers	1,712
Vital Statistics	
Receptions into the Church:	
Infant Baptism Totals	13,960
Adult Baptism Totals	660
Received into Full Communion	716
First Communions	9,927
Confirmations	5,280
Marriages:	
Catholic	2,281
Interfaith	597
Total Marriages	2,878
Deaths	4,636
Total Catholic Population	663,257
Total Population	1,869,329

Former Bishops—Rt. Rev. ANTHONY DOMINIC PELLICER, D.D., cons. Dec. 8, 1874; died April 14, 1880.—Rt. Rev. JOHN C. NERAZ, D.D., cons. May 8, 1881; died Nov. 15, 1894.—Rt. Rev. JOHN ANTHONY FOREST, D.D., cons. Oct. 28, 1895; died March 11, 1911.—Most Rev. JOHN W. SHAW, D.D., Coadjutor Bishop of San Antonio; appt. Feb. 7, 1910; cons. Titular Bishop of Castabala, April 14, 1910; succeeded to the See of San Antonio, March 11, 1911; made assistant at the Pontifical Throne, Sept., 1916; promoted to the See of New Orleans, Jan. 25, 1918; died Nov. 2, 1934.—Most Rev. ARTHUR JEROME DROSSAERTS, D.D., LL.D., Bishop of San Antonio; appt. July 18, 1918; cons. Dec. 8, 1918; named Archbishop, Aug. 3, 1926; assistant at the Pontifical Throne, Aug. 19, 1934; died Sept. 8, 1940.—Most Rev. ROBERT E. LUCEY, S.T.D., Bishop of Amarillo; appt. February 10, 1934; cons. May 1, 1934; promoted to the Archiepiscopal See of San Antonio, Jan. 23, 1941; died Aug. 1, 1977.—Most Rev. FRANCIS J. FUREY, Titular Bishop of Temnus and Auxiliary of Philadelphia; appt. Aug. 24, 1960; cons. Dec. 22, 1960; promoted to Coadjutor and Apostolic Administrator "sede plena" of San Diego, July 25, 1963; promoted to Archiepiscopal See of San Antonio, June 4, 1969; Pallium conferred, Dec. 15, 1969; died April 23, 1979.

Vicar General and Moderator of the Curia—Rev. Msgr. LAWRENCE STUEBBEN, V.G.

Chancery Office—2718 W. Woodlawn Ave., P.O. Box 28410, San Antonio, 78228-0410. Tel: 210-734-2620; Fax: 210-734-0231. Office Hours: Mon.-Fri. 8:30-5.

Chancellor and Judicial Vicar—Rev. Msgr. TERENCE NOLAN, J.C.L.

Archives—Bro. EDWARD J. LOCH, S.M., Archivist.

Administrative Asst. to the Archbishop—Rev. Msgr. LAWRENCE J. STUEBBEN, V.G.

Office of the Archbishop—Secretaries to the Archbishop: MYRTLE G. SANCHEZ; CARMEN IRUEGAS, *2718 W. Woodlawn Ave., P.O. Box 28410, San Antonio, 78228-0410.*

Office of the Synod—Sr. JANET MARIE ABBACCHI, S.S.N.D., Coord., *P.O. Box 28410, San Antonio, 78228-0410.* Tel: 210-734-2620; Texas: 1-800-SYNOD-98.

College of Consultors—Most Rev. BERNARD F. POPP, D.D., V.G.; Most Rev. JOHN W. YANTA, D.D., V.G.; Rev. Msgr. LAWRENCE STUEBBEN, V.G.; Rev. Msgr. JOHN FLYNN, V.U.; Rev. Msgr. THOMAS FLANAGAN; Rev. Msgr. EUGENE O'CALLAGHAN; Revs. DAVID GARCIA; STUART JULEEN.

Deans—In Metropolitan Area: Very Rev. GERALD HAMMEL, S.M., V.U., North; Rev. Msgr. BALTHASAR JANACEK, V.U., Central; Rev. WALTER D'HEEDENE, C.I.C.M. V.U., Northwest; Rev. JOHN O'DONOGHUE, V.U., Northeast; Very Rev. GILBERT OBIN, C.I.C.M., Western; Very Rev. LAWRENCE BRUMMER, O.F.M., V.U., Southwest; Very Rev. LAWRENCE JANEZIC, O.F.M., V.U., Southeast; In Rural Area: Very Rev. RAMIRO CORTEZ, O.M.I., Del Rio; Very Rev. WILLIAM MCNAMARA, V.F., Floresville; Very Rev. MICHAEL BOULETTE, V.F., Fredericksburg; Very Rev. WALLIS STILES, V.F., Hondo; Very Rev. MICHAEL YARBROUGH, V.F., Pleasanton; Rev. JAMES WASSER, M.S.F., V.F., Seguin; Very Rev. PABLO SILICIA, V.F., Uvalde.

Vicars for Religious—Rev. Msgr. THOMAS FRENCH, *Incarnate Word Residence, 4515 Broadway, San Antonio, 78209.* Tel: 210-822-0385. Sr. CHARLENE WEDELICH, C.D.P., *P.O. Box 28410, San Antonio, 78228-0410.* Tel: 210-734-2620.

Vicar for Priests—Vacant.

Vicar for Retired Priests—Rev. Msgr. ALEXANDER WANGLER.

Archdiocesan Presbyteral Council—Most Rev. PATRICK F. FLORES, D.D.; Most Rev. BERNARD F. POPP, D.D., V.G.; Rev. Msgr. TERENCE NOLAN, J.C.L.; Rev. EDWARD BERNAL, Chm.; Rev. Msgr. LAWRENCE STUEBBEN, V.G.; Very Rev. JOHN O'DONOGHUE, V.U.; Very Rev. GERALD HAMMEL, S.M., V.U.; Very Rev. WALLIS STILES, V.F.; Rev. JAMES WASSER, M.S.F., V.F; Rev. WALTER D'HEEDENE, C.I.C.M., V.F.; Rev. Msgr. BALTHASAR JANACEK, V.U.; Very Rev. GILBERT OBIN, C.I.C.M., V.F.; Very Rev. LAWRENCE JANEZIC, O.F.M., V.U.; Very Rev. LAWRENCE BRUMMER, O.F.M., V.U.; Very Rev. RAMIRO CORTEZ, O.M.I., V.F.; Very Rev. MICHAEL BOULETTE, V.F.; Very Rev. WILLIAM MCNAMARA, V.F.; Very Rev. MICHAEL YARBROUGH, V.F.; Rev. Msgr. PABLO SILICIA, V.F.; Rev. MICHAEL DEGEROLAMI.

Women's Commission—Mrs. MARTHA BRINKMANN, Chm., *P.O. Box 28410, San Antonio, 78228-0410.*

Archdiocesan Tribunal—*P.O. Box 28410, San Antonio, 78228-0410.* Tel: 210-734-2620, Ext. 135.

Judicial Vicar—Rev. Msgr. TERENCE NOLAN, J.C.L.

Assistant Director—Mrs. MARY DELATTE.

Judges—Rev. Msgr. JOHN FLYNN; Rev. Msgr. BERNARD MULLANEY; Rev. Msgr. TERENCE NOLAN, J.C.L.; Rev. Msgr. JAMES HENKE; Rev. Msgr. JAMES JANISH; Revs. EMMET CAROLAN; MICHAEL KENNY; JOSEPH LOPEZ.

Promotor Justitiae—Rev. Msgr. J. L. MANNING, J.C.D., P.A.

Defenders of the Bond—Revs. KEVIN RYAN; DENNIS DARILEK; PATRICK CRONIN; PAUL CLEARY; ROGELIO MARTINEZ; JOHN MAKOTHAKAT, J.C.D.; ADOLFO VALDIVIA, J.C.L.; Rev. Msgr. THOMAS MURPHY.

Approved Advocates—Rev. Msgr. J. L. MANNING, J.C.D., P.A.; Rev. Msgr. CHARLES PUGH; Rev. Msgr. JOSEPH DEANE; Rev. Msgr. LAMBERT BILY, V.U.; Revs. JOHN O'DONOGHUE, M.Ed.; STEVE GENGENBACHER; Mrs. CARMEN MASON; Sr. BERNICE A. LINDSEY, O.S.B.; Mrs. ADRIAN FERRARO SEAWRIGHT; Mrs. EDNA BONO, M.S.W.

Notaries—Mrs. MARY DELATTE; Mrs. SUE FORBRICH; Mrs. CLAUDIA MENCK; Mrs. LORETTA REYES; Mrs. JANENE TIJERINA.

Interdiocesan Appellate Court—*P.O. Box 28410, San Antonio, 78228-0410.* Tel: 210-736-9444; 736-2620, Ext. 145, 147.

Moderator—Most Rev. PATRICK F. FLORES, D.D.

Judicial Vicar—Rev. FRED SACKETT, O.M.I., J.C.D.

Judges—Revs. LESLIE A. VANCE, J.C.L.; ALBERT HUBERTUS; TIMOTHY A. GOLLOB (DAL); Sr. MARGARET A. RAMSDEN, S.F.C.C., J.C.L.

Defenders of the Bond—Revs. RAY WILHELM, O.M.I., J.C.L.; WARREN A. BROWN, O.M.I., J.C.L.; ANH Q. TRAN, J.C.L. (FTW); RICHARD F. VAUGHAN (AMA); JAMES M. KOTARA; Ms. DENISE J. DOYLE, J.C.D., Ph.D.; Ms. LAURA L. LEFAVE, J.C.L.

Notary—DONNA MILLS.

Due Process: Councils of Conciliation and Arbitration—Mr. GEORGE VOLZ, K.C.S.G., Chm., *503 Mary Louise Dr., San Antonio, 78201.* Tel: 210-732-5670.

Diocesan Administration

Administrative Services Department—Rev. Msgr. LAWRENCE J. STUEBBEN, V.G., Dir., *P.O. Box 28410, San Antonio, 78228-0410.* Tel: 210-734-2620.

Archives—Bro. EDWARD J. LOCH, S.M., *P.O. Box 28410, San Antonio, 78228-0410.* Tel: 210-734-2620.

Archdiocesan Business Manager and Finance Officer—Mr. DAVID CASTILLEJA, *P.O. Box 28410, San Antonio, 78228-0410.* Tel: 210-734-2620; Fax: 210-734-2774.

Archdiocesan Development Office—Mr. CHRIS GRASSO, Dir., *P.O. Box 28410, San Antonio, 78228-0410.* Tel: 210-734-2620; Fax: 210-734-0231.

Archdiocesan Finance Council—Mrs. CARMEN RIVERO; Mr. C. J. KRAUSE; Mr. JOHN FENSKE; Mr. TIM BRANIFF; Mr. ROGER CUMPIAN; Mr. JEFF PRUETT; Mr. DENNIS BIEDIGER; Mrs. MARY LOU BENAVIDES; Mr. LAWRENCE ERNST; Mr. AUGUST LUBANSKI; Deacon ROBERT KUSENBERGER; Mrs. JILL LEWIS; Mr. DARREL GRECO.

Archdiocesan Debt Review Committee—Mr. DAVID CASTILLEJA, Sec.; Mr. ALEX HINOJOSA; Mr. LOUIS SANCHEZ; Mr. GEORGE VOLZ; Mr. ALEX STEWART; Mr. JOHN D. SPECIA; Mr. S. F. DANYSH; Mrs. JENNITA POSTON; Mrs. DORA ANN VERDE; Mr. JOHN F. KRAMER.

Building Board—Mr. EDWARD TSCHOEPE; Mr. COSMO F. GUIDO; Mr. JIM RODRIGUEZ; Mr. DAN CERNA; Mr. STEVE PERSYN.

Lay Pension Plan—Mr. RENE WILKES, Mgr., *P.O. Box 28410, San Antonio, 78228-0410.* Tel: 210-734-2620.

Archdiocesan Cemeteries Office—Most Rev. BERNARD F. POPP, D.D., V.G., Dir.; Mr. ALBERT J. SANCHEZ, Supt., *746 Castroville Rd., San Antonio, 78207.* Tel: 210-432-2303.

Computer Center—CHUCK HUGHES, *P.O. Box 28410, San Antonio, 78228-0410.* Tel: 210-734-2620.

Director of Accounting—DELIA THOMAS, *P.O. Box 28410, San Antonio, 78228-0410.* Tel: 210-734-2620.

Parish Accounting System—Ms. ROSE RODRIGUEZ. Tel: 210-734-2420.

Print/Mail Room—MARIA HINJOSA. Tel: 210-734-2620; Fax: 210-734-0231.

Department of Educational Services—Sr. THERESE SAN MIGUEL, O.S.F., Dir., *P.O. Box 28410, San Antonio, 78228-0410.* Tel: 210-734-2620.

Archdiocesan Schools Office—Mr. DALE HOYT, Supt., *P.O. Box 28410, San Antonio, 78228-0410.* Tel: 210-734-2620.

Archdiocesan Catechetical-Religious Education Center—BONNIE LE MELLE ABADIE, Dir., *P.O. Box 28410, San Antonio, 78228-0410.* Tel: 210-734-2620.

Office of Catholic Youth Ministry-CYO—Mr. PAT PERILLO, Dir., *P.O. Box 28410, San Antonio, 78228-0410.* Tel: 210-734-2620.

Catholic Committee on Scouting (Boys)—Rev. PATRICK GITZEN, O.M.I., Chap. ALBERT REITER, Chm., *13023 El Marro, San Antonio, 78233-5835.* Tel: 210-653-5404.

Catholic Committee on Girl Scouting—Deacon BOB HENNESSY, Chap. FRAN POTEET, Chm., *4807 Lambeth Dr., San Antonio, 78228.* Tel: 210-734-7960.

Campus Ministry (Newman Apostolate)—Sr. GLORIA URRABAZO, M.C.D.P., Dir. SAC, St. Philip's, UTSA, UTSA Downtown, Palo Alto, Texas Lutheran, Schreiner College, Kerrville, Trinity, UT Health Science Center, S.W. Texas Junior College-Uvalde. *Catholic Student Center, 312 Courtland, San Antonio, 78212.* Tel: 210-736-3752.

Family Life Office—Mr. STEVE GENGENBACHER, Dir., *P.O. Box 28140, San Antonio, 78228-0410.* Tel: 210-734-2620.

Life Concerns Ministry—Mr. GENE TOWNSEND, Life Concerns Advocate, *P.O. Box 28140, San Antonio, 78228-0410.* Tel: 210-734-2620.

Natural Family Planning Office—Mrs. HENRIETTA O'CONNOR, Dir., *P.O. Box 28410, San Antonio, 78228.* Tel: 210-734-2620.

Office of Worship—Rev. Msgr. JAMES HENKE, Chm., Liturgy Commission; DOLORES MARTINEZ, Dir., *P.O. Box 28410, San Antonio, 78228-0410.* Tel: 210-734-2620.

Missions Awareness Office—(Holy Childhood Pontifical Assn.; Propagation of the Faith); MARY WISNIEWSKI, Dir., *P.O. Box 28410, San Antonio, 78228-0410.* Tel: 210-734-2620.

Catholic Adult Faith Enrichment (C.A.F.E.)—Bro. JOSEPH ESPARZA, C.S.C., Consultant, *P.O. Box 28140, San Antonio, 78228-0410.* Tel: 210-734-2620.

Department of Personnel Services—Vacant.

Priests Personnel Board—Rev. Msgr. BALTHASAR JANACEK, V.U.; Rev. Msgr. LIAM BROSNAM; Revs. FRANK MACIAS; NORMAN ERMIS; Rev. Msgr. ALBERT HUBERTUS; Rev. Msgr. DERMOT BROSNAN; Revs. STUART JULEEN; ANTHONY CUMMINS; PHILLIP HENNING; JOE LOPEZ.

Office for Priests—Vacant.

Catholic Consultation Center—LILLIAN YONKERS, Exec. Dir., *11103 West Ave., Ste. 202, San Antonio, 78213.* Tel: 210-377-1133; Fax: 210-377-1230.

Assumption-St. John's Seminary—Rev. DAVID CRUZ, (LUB) '86; *P.O. Box 28240, San Antonio, 78284.* Tel: 210-734-5137.

Permanent Diaconate Program—Rev. JOHN O'DONOGHUE, Dir., *2600 W. Woodlawn Ave., P.O. Box 28240, San Antonio, 78284-2701.* Tel: 210-734-0114.

Vocation Office—Rev. CARLOS VELAZQUEZ, Dir.; Sr. MARY FAGAN, S.H.S.P., Assoc. Dir., *2600 W. Woodlawn Ave., P.O. Box 28240, San Antonio, 78228-0410.* Tel: 210-734-0553.

Pro-Life Office—Mr. PETER MONOD DE FROIDVILLE, Interim. Dir., *P.O. Box 28410, San Antonio, 78228-0410.* Tel: 210-734-2620; Fax: 210-734-0231.

Catholic Television of San Antonio—(CTSA) Channel 22; Mr. PAT ROGERS, Dir., . Fax: 210-734-2939.

Today's Catholic Newspaper—Mrs. MARTHA PACK BRINKMAN, Editor, . Fax: 210-734-2939.

Department of Social and Community Services—Rev. MICHAEL DEGEROLAMI, Dir., *P.O. Box 28410, San Antonio, 78228-0410.* Tel: 210-734-2620.

Office of Social Concerns—Rev. MICHAEL DEGEROLAMI, Dir. CARMEN BADILLO, Assoc. Dir., *P.O. Box 28410, San Antonio, 78228-0410.* Tel: 210-734-2620.

Campaign for Human Development—Mrs. IRMA CARDENAS, Dir. Tel: 210-734-2620.

Ministry to Hearing Impaired—CHERYL VAN LEEUWEN RIOS, *223 E. Summit, San Antonio, 78212.* Tel: 210-731-8404 (Voice); 731-9208 (TDD).

Ministry to Persons with Disabilities—BECKY VILLARREAL, *815 McDougal, San Antonio, 78223.* Tel: 210-533-3120.

Bexar County Detention Ministries—Sr. MARGARET CAREW, C.C.V.I. Tel: 210-270-6328. Sr. TERESA CARTER, C.S.B. Tel: 210-270-6329. Deacon GILBERT PRATT. Tel: 210-270-6457. Revs. LEN BRONIAK, C.SS.R.; DAVID CURRAN, C.I.C.M. Tel: 210-270-6320., *200 N. Comal, San Antonio, 78207.* Rev. KEVIN MANION, (Mexico), *600 Mission Rd., San Antonio, 78210.* Tel: 210-531-1189. Deacon A. C. CAMERO; FABIAN DOMINGUEZ, *State Jail, 6535 Cagnon Rd., San Antonio, 78252.* Tel: 210-675-6620. Each works in a different area of the jails.

St. Peter and Joseph's Home—(See Protective Institutions).

Seton Home—(See Protective Institutions).

Health Ministry Committee—Rev. MICHAEL DEGEROLAMI.

Catholic Charities, Archdiocese of San Antonio—VALERIE TREVINO, Exec. Dir., *2903 W. Salinas St., San Antonio, 78207.* Tel: 210-475-9011; Fax: 210-475-0456.

Refugee Resettlement Services—ALBA BALTODANO. Tel: 210-433-3256.

Director Immigration Services—ELAINE DAMIAN, *2903 W. Salinas St., San Antonio, 78207.* Tel: 210-433-3256.

Diocesan Offices And Directors

Apostleship of Prayer—Vacant.

Archdiocesan Council of Catholic Women—Mrs. MARGARET ROEL, *8702 Village Dr. #143, San Antonio, 78217.* Tel: 210-656-8049. Rev. JOE AVILES, V.U., *1710 Clower, San Antonio, 78201-3597.* Tel: 210-735-5269.

Catholic Center for Charismatic Renewal—Rev. THOMAS FLANAGAN, Dir., Liaison, *1707 S. Flores, San Antonio, 78204.* Tel: 210-226-7545; 7546.

Catholic Lawyers Guild—Rev. Msgr. TERENCE NOLAN, J.C.L., Spiritual Moderator, *P.O. Box 28410, San Antonio, 78228-0410.* Tel: 210-734-2620.

Catholic Physicians Guild—Rev. JOHN A. LEIES, S.M., S.T.D.; MIGUEL BEDOLLA, M.D., Ph.D., Pres., *520 Fordham Ln., San Antonio, 78228.* Tel: 210-436-3227.

Censores Librorum—Rev. FRED SACKETT, O.M.I.

Movimiento de Apostolado Familiar & Marriage Encounter (Rural)—Rev. ABRAHAM LA TORRE, (Colombia), *3107 N. St. Mary's St., San Antonio, 78212.* Tel: 210-732-6295.

Movimiento Familiar Cristano (Urban)—Presidents: CHELO MEDINA; JOSE MEDINA, *9215 Brink, San Antonio, 78221.* Tel: 210-924-2972.

Christian Life Communities—Vacant.

Black Catholic Apostolate—Deacon THOMAS WHITE, Dir., *1819 Nevada, San Antonio, 78203.* Tel: 210-532-5358.

Cursillo Movement (Spanish)—Mr. JOE BERRELEZ, *419 S. Moreno, Pearsall, 78061.* Tel: 210-334-4876.

Cursillo Movement (English)—Sr. BERNICE LINDSEY, O.S.B., *416 W. Highland Dr., Boerne, 78006.* Tel: 210-816-8504; 210-922-4061.

Ecumenical Affairs—Rev. J. WILLIS LANGLINAIS, S.M., Dir., *One Camino Santa Maria, P.O. Box 18, San Antonio, 78228-8518.* Tel: 210-436-3092.

Holy Childhood, Pontifical Association—MARY WISNIEWSKI, *P.O. Box 28410, San Antonio, 78228-0410.* Tel: 210-734-2620.

Holy Name Society—Isidro Leos, Jr., *363 Pinewood, San Antonio, 78216.* Tel: 210-828-1089.

Pre-Seminary Program—Rev. Carlos Velazquez, Dir., *Assumption Seminary, P.O. Box 28240, San Antonio, 78284.* Tel: 210-735-0553.

Priests Eucharistic League—Rev. Thomas Flanagan, Dir., *6097 Kitchener, San Antonio, 78240.* Tel: 210-696-0896.

Propagation of the Faith—Mary Wisniewski, *P.O. Box 28410, San Antonio, 78228-0410.*

Public Relations Council—Col. Joseph B. McShane, *1410 Treasure Way, San Antonio, 78209.* Tel: 210-826-3361.

Retreats, Men—Rev. Kevin Collins, O.M.I., Dir., *Oblate Renewal Center, 127 Oblate Dr., San Antonio, 78216.* Tel: 210-349-4173.

Respect Life Program—Rev. Sherrill Smith, Moderator, *8520 Cross Mountain Tr., #201, San Antonio, 78255.* Tel: 210-698-8819.

Rural Life Conference—Vacant.

St. Vincent de Paul Society—Ms. Nell Sharrock, Pres., Mailing Address: *928 W. Commerce, San Antonio, 78207.* Tel: 210-225-7837.

CLERGY, PARISHES, MISSIONS AND PAROCHIAL SCHOOLS

CITY OF SAN ANTONIO

1—Cathedral of San Fernando (1731) (Hispanic), Revs. David Garcia; Jose Arturo Cepeda; James L. Emperur, S.J.; Deacons Albert Garza; Doroteo E. Pedroza; Enrique Barrera.
Res., 115 Main Plaza, 78205. Tel: 210-227-1297; Fax: 210-271-0149.
Catechesis/Religious Programs—Sr. Clara Ruiz, H.C.G., D.R.E.
Students 898.
Mission—San Antonio, Bexar Co., San Francesco di Paola, 205 Piazza Italia, 78207. Tel: 210-227-0548. Rev. Msgr. Balthasar J. Janacek.

2—Blessed Sacrament (1956), Rev. John O'Donoghue; Deacons Joe Fertitta; Wayne Chycinski; Joseph Jorgensen.
Office: 600 Oblate Dr., 78216. Tel: 210-824-7231; Fax: 210-822-2144.
School—Tel: 210-824-3381. Sr. Eileen Gurecky, Prin.
Sisters of Incarnate Word and Blessed Sacrament 1; Lay Teachers 12; Students 290; Day Care 123.
Catechesis/Religious Programs—Students 297.

3—Christ the King (1928) (Hispanic), Rev. Richard Pena; Esther Rodriguez, Admin.; Deacon Rudy Pena.
Res., 2623 Perez St., 78207. Tel: 210-433-6301; Fax: 210-435-2736.
Catechesis/Religious Programs—Ms. Patricia R. Garcia, D.R.E.
Students 239.

4—Divine Providence (1981) (Hispanic), Rev. P. John Mannion; Deacons Jose Suniga; Juan G. Martinez.
Church—5667 Old Pearsall Rd., 78242-2335. Tel: 210-623-3970; Fax: 210-623-3978.
Catechesis/Religious Programs—Sr. Eileen Howley, P.B.V.M., D.R.E.
Students 559.

5—Holy Family (1963) (Hispanic), Rev. James Kotara; Deacons Manuel Carranza; Javier Tamez.
Res., 152 Florencia, 78228-5899. Tel: 210-433-8216.
Catechesis/Religious Programs—Tel: 210-433-3006. Ester Mango, D.R.E.
Students 325.

6—Holy Name (1961) (Polish/Hispanic), Rev. Franciszek Kurzaj; Deacon David L. Herbert.
Res., 3814 Nash Blvd., 78223. Tel: 210-333-5020; 5021.
School—Tel: 210-333-7356; Fax: 210-333-7642. Mrs. Miriam Christiansen, Prin.
Lay Teachers 23; Students 331.
Catechesis/Religious Programs—Tel: 210-333-3613; Fax: 210-333-5021. Margaret Miksch, D.R.E.
Students 290.

7—Holy Redeemer (1910) (African American), Rev. Augustine Amanzeh (Nigeria); Deacon Thomas White. In res., Rev. Kevin Manion (Mexico).
Res., 1819 Nevada, 78203. Tel: 210-532-5358.

8—Holy Rosary (1948) (Hispanic), Revs. John J. Manahan, S.M.; Bernard Meyer, S.M. Pastoral Assocs.: Bros. James Droste, S.M.; James McCaffrey, S.M.; Robert Hatesohl, S.M.; Deacons Felipe Barajas; Earl Colley.
Res., 159 Camino Santa Maria, 78228. Tel: 210-433-3241; Fax: 210-433-2133.
School—155 Camino Santa Maria, 78228. Tel: 210-433-4312. Sr. Bernice Mallory, S.H.Sp., Prin.
Sisters 2; Deacons 1; Lay Teachers 16; Students 237.
Catechesis/Religious Programs—Sr. Marcy Loehrlein, F.M.I., D.R.E.
Students 181.

9—Holy Spirit (1964), Rev. Anthony Pesek; Deacons Joe Krupa; Sonny Staudt.
Res., 758 W. Ramsey Rd., 78216. Tel: 210-341-1395; Fax: 210-341-8438.
School—770 W. Ramsey Rd., 78216. Tel: 210-349-1169; Fax: 210-349-1247. Mrs. Joann Gawlik, Prin.
Lay Teachers 46; Students 437.
Catechesis/Religious Programs—Tel: 210-341-1397. Pat Keene, D.R.E.
Students 644.

10—Holy Trinity (1987), Rev. Douglas Fater; Deacon Jerry Micek.
Res., 20523 Huebner Rd., 78258. Tel: 210-497-4200; Fax: 210-497-4285.
Catechesis/Religious Programs—Jolene Waun, D.R.E.
Students 397.

11—Immaculate Conception (1933) (Hispanic), Rev. Msgr. Leo Martinez; Deacons Ignacio T. Martinez; Antonio R. Munoz; Jose Hernandez.
Res., 314 Merida St., 78207. Tel: 210-225-2986; Fax: 210-225-2987.
Catechesis/Religious Programs—Students 130.

12—Immaculate Heart of Mary (1912) (Hispanic), Revs. Ignacio Blanco, C.M.F.; Robert Alvarado, C.M.F.; Deacons Jorge Bonilla-Valentin; Alfredo Cervantes. In res., Revs. Michael Cecere, C.M.F.; George Sturm, C.M.F.; Richard Trevino, C.M.F.; Martin Sanz.
Res., 617 S. Santa Rosa Blvd., 78204. Tel: 210-226-8268; 8269; Fax: 210-222-1479.
Catechesis/Religious Programs—Linda Trevino, D.R.E.
Students 115.

13—Our Lady of the Angels (1947) (Hispanic), Revs. Mauricio A. Lopez (Columbia); Jose Antonio Villanueva (Spain); Deacon Albert Ramirez.
Res., 1214 Stonewall St., 78211. Tel: 210-924-6591; Fax: 210-924-6593.
Catechesis/Religious Programs—Mary Jessie Rodriguez, D.R.E.
Students 678.

14—Our Lady of the Atonement Catholic (1983). (A Personal Parish for the Anglican Common Identity). Rev. Christopher G. Phillips; Deacon James P. Orr.
Res., 8015 Shady Hollow Ln., 78255. Tel: 210-695-3332.
Church—15415 Red Robin Rd., 78255. Tel: 210-695-2944; Fax: 210-695-9679.
School—Atonement Academy, Tel: 210-695-2240.
Lay Teachers 8; Students 103.

15—Our Lady of Good Counsel (1952) (Hispanic), Revs. Paul Van Coillie, C.I.C.M., D.R.E.; Celestin Tongotani, C.I.C.M.
Res., 1204 Castroville Rd., 78237. Tel: 210-432-0873.
Catechesis/Religious Programs—Remolino Center, 107 Remolino, 78237.
Students 335.

16—Our Lady of Grace (1938), Rev. Msgr. Lawrence Walsh; Rev. Thomas Kavanaugh, C.M.; Deacon Robert Schonhoff.
Res., 223 E. Summit Ave., 78212. Tel: 210-734-7285; Fax: 210-734-8334.

17—Our Lady of Guadalupe (1911) (Hispanic), Revs. James L. Lambert, S.J.; Martin L. Elsner, S.J.; Samuel Rosales, S.J.; Bro. Alexander Gussio, S.J.; Deacons Joe Camero; Robert Galvan; Leon Kattengell; Carlos Sandoval.
Res., 1321 El Paso St., 78207. Tel: 210-226-4064; Fax: 210-226-4973.
Catechesis/Religious Programs—Mr. Michael Bouzigard, S.J.
Students 100.
Mission—San Antonio, Bexar Co., Santa Cruz, 1303 Tampico, 78207.

18—Our Lady of Mt. Carmel and St. Therese, Discalced Carmelite Fathers National Shrine of the Little Flower (1926) (Hispanic), Revs. John Magdalene Suenram, O.C.D., Supr.; Ralph Reyes, O.C.D.; Michael Okuroski, O.C.D.; Louis Scagnelli, O.C.D.; Christopher Timoney, O.C.D.; James A. Curiel, O.C.D.; Deacon Dan Cisneros.
Res., 906 Kentucky Ave., 78201-6097. Tel: 210-735-9126; Fax: 210-735-1389 (parish); 738-0818 (res.).
School—905 Kentucky Ave., 78201. Tel: 210-732-9207; Fax: 210-732-3214. Sr. Eileen Mannion, S.H.Sp., Prin.
Sisters of the Holy Spirit 4; Brothers 1; Lay Teachers 17; Students 257.
Catechesis/Religious Programs—Sr. Dympna Clark, S.H.Sp., D.R.E.
Students 364.

19—Our Lady Of Perpetual Help (1913) (Hispanic), Rev. John R. Cody, C.SS.R. Pastoral Assocs.: Sr. Teresa Ledesma, M.P.S.; Sr. Gina Brillantes, M.P.S.
Res., 618 S. Grimes St., 78203. Tel: 210-532-7031; Fax: 210-534-1280.
Catechesis/Religious Programs—Tel: 210-534-7193.
Students 102.

20—Our Lady of Sorrows (1915) (Hispanic), Rev. Lambert S. Bily; Deacon Jesse Fraga. In res., Revs. Abraham LaTorre; Marian Piekarczyk, S.D.S., (Poland) Dir. Polish Catholic Mission.
Res., 3107 N. St. Mary's St., 78212. Tel: 210-732-6295; 736-6719 (Polish).
Catechesis/Religious Programs—Donna Salas, D.R.E.
Students 160.

21—Prince of Peace (1980), Rev. Patrick Cronin; Deacons Robert Garza; Scott Imburgia; Pino Sanabria; Tom Neal; William Thornberry.
Res., 7893 N. Grissom Rd., 78251. Tel: 210-681-8330; Fax: 210-681-2286.
Catechesis/Religious Programs—Tel: 210-681-5063. Shirley Jones, D.R.E.
Students 1,408.

22—Resurrection of the Lord (1981), Rev. Paul A. Raaz; Deacon Thomas Swift.
Offices & Mailing Address: 7990 W. Military Dr., 78227. Tel: 210-675-1470.
Res., 7151 Cypress Grove, 78227.
Catechesis/Religious Programs—Students 501.

23—Sacred Heart (1899) (Belgium), Revs. Walter O. D'heedene, C.I.C.M.; Romo Olivares, C.I.C.M. (Phillipines); Deacon Valentine Gallegos.
Res., 2114 W. Houston St., 78207-3496. Tel: 210-227-5059; Fax: 210-227-6209.
Catechesis/Religious Programs—Tel: 210-227-9763. Sr. Juanita Ramirez, D.R.E.
Students 200.

24—St. Agnes (1923) (Hispanic), Rev. Msgr. Peter O'Callaghan; Deacon Leon Guerrero. In res., Very Rev. Lawrence Stuebben, V.G.
Res., 804 Ruiz St., 78207. Tel: 210-227-8258.
Catechesis/Religious Programs—Tel: 210-226-4441. Sr. Margaret Mary Barrett, D.R.E.
Students 713.

25—St. Alphonsus (1925) (Hispanic), Rev. Jose Luis Sandoval; Sr. Adele Massaro, Pastoral Assoc.
Res., 2004 Chihuahua St., 78207. Tel: 210-433-9365; Fax: 210-433-9365.
Catechesis/Religious Programs—Tel: 210-432-3176.
Students 52.

26—St. Ann (1912) (Hispanic), Revs. Richard B. Williams, O.P.; Cayet Mangiaracina, O.P.; Vincente M. Pena, O.P.; Rafael Proneza, O.P. (Cuba); Deacon Richard Hormachea.
Res., 210 St. Ann St., 78201. Tel: 210-734-6687; Fax: 210-738-1755.
School—Tel: 210-735-2341. David Fernandez, Prin.
Sisters 1; Lay Teachers 6; Students 100.
Catechesis/Religious Programs—Tel: 210-733-9681.
Students 355.

27—St. Anthony Mary Claret (1988), Rev. Albert Hubertus.
Res., 6150 Roft Rd., 78253. Tel: 210-688-9033; Fax: 210-688-3575.
Catechesis/Religious Programs—Linda Burrage, D.R.E.
Students 526.

28—St. Anthony of Padua (1957), Rev. William J. Collins, M.S.C.; Sr. Dorothea O'Meara, C.S.B., Admin.; Deacon Gilbert Wiessler.
Res., 102 Lorenz Rd., 78209. Tel: 210-824-1743; Fax: 210-824-3242.
Catechesis/Religious Programs—Tel: 210-824-6740. Mrs. Carmen Ortiz, D.R.E.
Students 287.

29—St. Benedict (1958) (Polish/Hispanic), Rev. Edward A. Pavlicek, Jr.; Most Rev. Bernard F. Popp, D.D.; Deacon Dan Kearns.
Res., 4535 Lord Rd., 78220. Tel: 210-648-0123; Fax: 210-648-1722.
School—Tel: 210-648-1611. Mrs. Frances Grams, Prin.
Lay Teachers 13; Students 160.
Catechesis/Religious Programs—Tel: 210-648-4632. Deborah Desjean, D.R.E.
Students 255.

30—St. Bonaventure (1959) (Hispanic), Revs. Raymond Schuster; Toby Guerrero; Deacons Fidel Hinojosa; Amador Gonzalez; Edward Patino.
Res., 1918 Palo Alto Rd., 78211. Tel: 210-922-1685; Fax: 210-922-7821.
Catechesis/Religious Programs—Tel: 210-922-1882. Mrs. Diane Guerra, D.R.E.
Students 495.

31—St. Brigid (1972), Revs. Thomas Flanagan; Francis M. Landwermeyer, S.J.; Jeannette Easley, Pastoral Admin.; Deacons Thomas Billimek; Pasquale M. Benigno; George G. Alberty, Jr.; Roy Amo; Peter Gutierrez.
Res., 6907 Kitchener Rd., 78240. Tel: 210-696-0896; Fax: 210-696-7319.
Catechesis/Religious Programs—Charlene Staedtler, D.R.E.
Students 437.

32—St. Cecilia (1919), Rev. Msgr. Joseph Deane; Phyllis Evans, Pastoral Assoc.; Deacon Fred Quarles.
Res., 125 W. Whittier St., 78210-2897. Tel: 210-533-7109; Fax: 210-532-2599.
School—Tel: 210-534-2711; Fax: 210-533-8284. Mr. Albert M. Casillas, Prin.
Sisters 5; Lay Teachers 9; Students 235.
Catechesis/Religious Programs—Tel: 210-532-1994. Rose M. Luera, D.R.E.
Students 203.
Mission—San Antonio, Bexar Co., Purisima Concepcion, 807 Mission Rd., 78210.

33—St. Clare (1968) (Hispanic), Rev. Jeffery Salwach, O.F.M.; Deacons Florencio Moreno, Jr.; Charles F. Pope, Sr.
Res., 7701 Somerset Rd., 78211. Tel: 210-924-5252.
Catechesis/Religious Programs—Tel: 210-922-6458. Mercedes G. Cortez, D.R.E.
Students 250.

34—St. Dominic (1971), Rev. Paul Cleary; Deacons Henry Medina; Lionel Garza; Alan Fitzpatrick; Ree Stockton; Jimmie Trevino; Bert Stewart.
Res., 5919 Ingram Rd., 78228. Tel: 210-435-6211; 435-0114; Fax: 210-435-1732.
Catechesis/Religious Programs—Tel: 210-435-9267. Sue Graves, D.R.E.
Students 530.

35—St. Francis of Assisi (1980), Rev. Msgr. James Henke; Deacons Tom Franklin; Anton Svatek; Gilbert Pratt; Bruce Bellg.
Res., 4201 De Zavala Rd., 78249-2000. Tel: 210-492-4600; Fax: 210-492-8128.
Education Office—Tel: 210-492-4683.
Catechesis/Religious Programs—Pat Hanavan, D.R.E.
Students 490.

36—St. Gabriel (1958) (Hispanic), Revs. Louis Jaspers, C.I.C.M. (Belgium); David Curran, C.I.C.M.; Carmen Morales, Admin.; Deacon Frank Castellano.
Res., 747 S.W. 39th St., 78237. Tel: 210-433-3689.
Catechesis/Religious Programs—Tel: 210-433-3354. Mavis Montemayor, D.R.E.
Students 199.

37—St. Gerard Majella (1911), Revs. Gerard F. Siebold, C.SS.R.; Carl Schindler, C.SS.R.; Robert Ruhnke, C.SS.R.
Res., 1523 Iowa St., 78203. Tel: 210-533-0161 (Church Office); Fax: 210-533-0558.
School—1619 Iowa St., 78203. Tel: 210-533-9541; Fax: 210-533-4196. Mrs. Peggy Burt, Prin.
Sisters 1; Lay Teachers 10; Students 200.
High School—Archdiocesan Regional, 521 S. New Braunfels Ave., 78203. Tel: 210-533-8061; Fax: 210-533-3697. Maurice Abadie, Prin.
Sisters 1; Lay Teachers 21; Students 215.
Catechesis/Religious Programs—Students 133.

38—St. Gregory's (1955), Rev. Michael B. O'Gorman (Ireland). Pastoral Assocs.: Sr. M. Carmel O'Callaghan, P.B.V.M.; Sr. Luz Valdez, M.C.M.; Deacons Don Novian; Fred Campos, Jr.
Res., 700 Dewhurst, 78213. Tel: 210-342-5271; Fax: 210-342-0542.
School—Tel: 210-342-0281. Joyce Z. Burc, Prin.
Lay Teachers 32; Students 605.
Catechesis/Religious Programs—Tel: 210-342-3826. Allison Baez, D.R.E.
Students 414.

39—St. Helena (1974), Rev. Leo M. Dolan; Deacons Harrold De Cuir; Michael D'Agostino; Joseph De Leon; Rose Marden, Pastoral Asst.
Office: 14714 Edgemont, 78247. Tel: 210-653-3316; Fax: 210-653-3163.
Res., 14527 Angora, 78247. Tel: 210-653-3850.
Catechesis/Religious Programs—Tel: 210-653-3316. D.R.E.: Suzan Roy; Joan Raymond.
Students 832.

40—St. Henry (1904) (Hispanic), Rev. Msgr. Emil J. Wesselsky.
Res., 1619 S. Flores St., 78204. Tel: 210-225-6877; Fax: 210-225-6878.
Catechesis/Religious Programs—Tel: 210-227-1585. Sr. Diana O. Rodriguez, H.C.G., D.R.E.
Students 306.

41—St. James the Apostle (1954) (Hispanic), Rev. Emmit Carolan; Onofre Toscano, Pastoral Assoc.; Deacon John McDonald.
Res., 907 W. Theo Ave., 78225. Tel: 210-922-2136; Fax: 210-923-0940.
School—Tel: 210-924-1201; Fax: 210-924-0201. Sr. Josephine Ochoa, F.M.A., Prin.
Daughters of Mary Help of Christians 4; Lay Teachers 19; Students 410.
Catechesis/Religious Programs—Tel: 210-922-4061. Mary Toscano, D.R.E.
Students 664.

42—St. John, the Evangelist (1956), Rev. Edward Kelly; Deacons Rosendo Urrabazo; Evan Wittig; Hugo Chavez.
Res., 102 S. Audubon Dr., 78212. Tel: 210-828-2201; Fax: 210-738-0599.
School—128 S. Audubon Dr., 78212. Tel: 210-735-3526. Mrs. Linda Murphy, Prin.
Sisters 2; Lay Teachers 11; Students 284.
Catechesis/Religious Programs—D.R.E.: Gloria Chavez; Lisa Flores.
Students 165.

43—St. John Berchmans (1910) (Hispanic), Revs. Edward M. Bernal; James M. Hynes (Peru); Deacons Jose Diaz; James T. Raso; Librado Cena.
Res., 1147 Cupples Rd., 78226. Tel: 210-434-3247; Fax: 210-432-0431.
School—Tel: 210-433-0411; Fax: 210-433-2335. Ms. Deborah Goering, Prin.
Lay Teachers 18; Students 387.
Catechesis/Religious Programs—Tel: 210-433-2121. Marta Lucia S. Garcia, D.R.E.
Students 481.

44—St. John Neumann (1977), Rev. Robert Silverman.
Church—6680 Crestway Dr., 78239. Tel: 210-654-1643; Fax: 210-654-1645.
Catechesis/Religious Programs—Tel: 210-654-3707.
Students 353.

45—St. Joseph (Downtown) (1868) (German), Rev. Thomas J. Fitzgerald, S.S.S. In res., Bro. Martin Hayes, S.S.S.
Res., 623 E. Commerce St., 78205. Tel: 210-227-0126; Fax: 210-227-7690. [CEM]

46—St. Joseph (South San) (1935) (Hispanic), Revs. Eugene Michel, O.F.M.; Lawrence Brummer, O.F.M.; Deacons Leon Mueller; Genaro Herrera. In res., Revs. Michael Haney, O.F.M.; Jeffery Salwach, O.F.M.; Bro. Joseph Middleton, O.F.M.
Res., 535 New Laredo Hwy., 78211-1900. Tel: 210-924-4383.
School—2372 W. Southcross St., 78211. Tel: 210-922-0193; 923-7910. Mrs. Margaret Schlueter, Prin.
Lay Teachers 14; Students 211.
Catechesis/Religious Programs—Tel: 210-924-4383. Mrs. Imelda Morales, D.R.E.
Students 525.

47—St. Jude (1954) (Hispanic), Rev. Jose A. Giganto, O.S.A. In res., Rev. Leonidas Fresno, O.S.A.
Res., 130 S. San Augustine Ave., 78237. Tel: 210-432-8044; Fax: 210-432-1760.
Catechesis/Religious Programs—Tel: 210-432-5786. Rosalinda F. Rodriguez, D.R.E.
Students 411.
Mission—San Antonio, Santa Maria Goretti.

48—St. Lawrence (1959) (Hispanic), Rev. Adolfo A. Valdivia; Deacons Alois Keller; Richard Gonzalez.
Res., 236 E. Petaluma, 78221. Tel: 210-924-4401; Fax: 210-924-4401.
Catechesis/Religious Programs—Students 790.

49—St. Leo (1919) (Hispanic), Revs. Enda McKenna; James Kammerer. Pastoral Assocs.: Sr. Joanne Whalen; Deacons John Landez; Alvino Pacheco; Thomas Torres; Jose Almanza.
Res., 123 Octavia Pl., 78214. Tel: 210-533-9108; Fax: 210-533-0643.
School—119 Octavia Pl., 78214. Tel: 210-532-3166; Fax: 210-532-5997. Carol Johnson, Prin.
Lay Teachers 13; Students 212.
Catechesis/Religious Programs—Tel: 210-532-7317. Lupe Sielski, D.R.E.
Students 350.

50—St. Leonard's (1966) (Hispanic), Revs. Michael Haney, O.F.M.; Jesus Aguirre-Garza, O.F.M.; Deacon Carlos Salinas.
Res., 8510 S. Zarzamora, 78224-2099. Tel: 210-924-6000; Fax: 210-924-5552.
Catechesis/Religious Programs—Students 500.

51—St. Luke (1959), Rev. Patrick J. Ragsdale.
Office: 4603 Manitou, 78228-1889. Tel: 210-433-2777; Fax: 210-433-2778.
Res., 6014 Horizon, 78228.
School—Tel: 210-434-2011. Dr. Harold A. Kreger, Prin.
Lay Teachers 28; Students 574.
Catechesis/Religious Programs—Tel: 210-436-0339; Fax: 210-433-2778. Kathy Hill, D.R.E.
Students 475.

52—St. Margaret Mary (1955) (Hispanic), Revs. Michael Kenny; Anthony Cowan; Deacons Wilfred Lamb; Gerardo Mechler; Zeke Moczygemba.
Res., 1314 Fair Ave., 78223. Tel: 210-532-6309; Fax: 210-532-6333.
School—Tel: 210-534-6137. Miss Susan Bukala, Prin.
Felician Sisters 2; Lay Teachers 18; Students 470.
Catechesis/Religious Programs—Theresa Pawelek, Prin.
Students 334.
Mission—San Antonio, St. Catherine.

53—St. Mark the Evangelist (1976), Rev. Kevin E. Ryan; Dorothea G. Hamlin, Pastoral Admin.; Deacons Ernest Zepeda; Loni Lugo.
Res., 1602 Thousand Oaks Dr., 78232-2398. Tel: 210-494-1606; 1607; Fax: 210-494-4957.
Catechesis/Religious Programs—Tel: 210-494-7434.
Students 1,208.

54—St. Martin de Porres (1964) (Hispanic), Rev. Gilbert Obin, C.I.C.M.; Deacons Jose Menchaca; Anthony Patlan.
Res., 1730 Dahlgreen St., 78237. Tel: 210-432-5203.
Catechesis/Religious Programs—Tel: 210-436-2071.
Students 284.

55—St. Mary (1852), Rev. Michael Levy, O.M.I.
Res., 202 N. St. Mary's St., 78205. Tel: 210-226-8381; Fax: 210-226-8440.
School—207 N. St. Mary's St., 78205. Tel: 210-223-8581; Fax: 210-223-5672. Mrs. Beatrice Aleman, Prin.
Sisters 3; Lay Teachers 10; Students 170.

56—St. Mary Magdalen (1940) (Hispanic), Revs. Joe Aviles; Dennis A. Jarzombek.
Res., 1710 Clower St., 78201. Tel: 210-735-5269; Fax: 210-738-0698.
School—Tel: 210-735-1381. Sr. Patricia O'Sullivan, Prin.
Presentation Sisters 4; Lay Teachers 10; Students 224.
Catechesis/Religious Programs—Tel: 210-735-5284. Linda Froboese, D.R.E.
Students 757.

57—St. Matthew's (1968), Rev. Msgr. John F. Flynn; Revs. Don C. Shepanski; James G. Galvin; Jeffery Pehl; Deacons Tom Fox; Wilbur Hoelschler; Horacio Tudon; Keith Werner.
Res., 10703 Wurzbach Rd., 78230. Tel: 210-696-4161; Fax: 210-696-8858.
School—Tel: 210-696-7433; Fax: 210-696-7624. Cynthia Salinas, Prin.
Sisters 2; Lay Teachers 34; Students 619.
Catechesis/Religious Programs—Fax: 210-696-8858. Sr. Therese Gleitz, D.R.E.
Students 1,523.

58—St. Michael (1866) (Hispanic), Rev. Jesus Murugarren, O.S.A. (Spain); Lillie P. Ramirez, Admin. Pastoral Assocs.: Juan Garcia; Alice Olivera; Nicholas Farley.
Res., 418 Indiana, 78210. Tel: 210-532-3707; Fax: 210-532-3707. [CEM]
Catechesis/Religious Programs—Students 95.

59—St. Patrick (1893) (Hispanic), Rev. Walter E. Ebarb (SHP). In res., Rev. Thomas McSwiggan.
Res., 1114 Willow St., 78208. Tel: 210-226-5223; Fax: 210-227-8616.
Catechesis/Religious Programs—Tel: 210-227-5478. Sr. Alicia Drone, A.S.C., D.R.E.
Students 361.

60—St. Paul (1954) (Hispanic), Revs. Dennis Darilek; Jimmy D. Drennan; Deacons Clayton Mangold; Daniel Muriada. In res., Rev. Michael DeGerolami.
Res., 350 Sutton Dr., 78228-3199. Tel: 210-733-7152; Fax: 210-733-0929.
School—307 John Adams, 78228. Tel: 210-732-2741; Fax: 210-732-7702. Sr. Virginia Huser, C.D.P., Prin.
Religious Sisters 1; Lay Teachers 27; Students 451.
Catechesis/Religious Programs—Virginia Valenzuela, D.R.E.
Students 360.

61—St. Peter Prince of the Apostles (1923), Rev. Msgr. Thomas Murphy; Teresa Berg, Admin.; Deacons John Dunn; John Spitzer; Raymond Cross.
Res., 111 Barilla Pl., 78209. Tel: 210-822-3367; Fax: 210-828-5826.
School—112 Marcia Pl., 78209. Tel: 210-824-3171; Fax: 210-822-4504. Leslie Kvapil, Prin.
Lay Teachers 26; Students 473.
Catechesis/Religious Programs—Tel: 210-822-1605. Alma Small, D.R.E.
Students 275.

62—St. Philip of Jesus (1914) (Hispanic), Revs. Robert Bovenzi, C.P.; Mario Cardenas (Columbia); Deacons G. T. Zapata; Jose Sanchez.
Res., 131 Bank St., 78204. Tel: 210-226-5024.
School—134 E. Lambert St., 78204. Tel: 210-222-2872; Fax: 210-229-1829. Sr. Celly Ann Amparo, S.S.N.D., Prin.

Sisters 2; Lay Teachers 13; Aides 3; Students 263.
Catechesis/Religious Programs—Tel: 210-225-6622. Sr. Marian Sturm, I.W.B.S., D.R.E.
Students 219.

63—St. Pius X (1957), Rev. Msgr. Liam P. Brosnan; Deacon Thomas Crowley.
Office: 3303 Urban Crest, 78209. Tel: 210-824-0139; Fax: 210-829-5125.
Res., 654 Cave Ln., 78209. Tel: 210-826-4064.
School—(Grades PreK-8) 7734 Robin Rest Dr., 78209. Tel: 210-824-6431; Fax: 210-824-7454. Celeste Bonsignore, Prin.
Lay Teachers 35; Students 397.
Catechesis/Religious Programs—Tel: 210-824-4533. Diana Carpenter, D.R.E.
Students 505.

64—St. Rose of Lima (1981), Revs. Juan Alfaro; Virgil Elizondo; Deacons Rey Jasso; Anthony Lira; Chester Ostaszewski.
Res., 9883 Marbach Rd., 78245. Tel: 210-675-1920; Fax: 210-675-6067.
Catechesis/Religious Programs—D.R.E.: Mr. Jesse Mauricio; Ms. Yvonne Diaz.
Students 940.

65—St. Stephen (1965) (Hispanic), Rev. Luis Ruiz; Deacon Henry Dillard.
Res., 2127 S. Zarzamora St., 78207. Tel: 210-224-8474; Fax: 210-224-8474.

66—St. Thomas More (1964), Rev. John M. Makothakat; Deacon Jerome Ciarrocchi.
Res., 4411 Moana, 78218. Tel: 210-655-5070; Fax: 210-655-8446.
School—4427 Moana, 78218. Tel: 210-655-2882; Fax: 210-655-9603. Mrs. Mary Jane Regel, Prin.
Presentation Sisters 1; Lay Teachers 11; Students 249.
Catechesis/Religious Programs—Tel: 210-654-6824. Mrs. Carol McGuire, D.R.E.
Students 275.

67—St. Timothy's (1953) (Hispanic), Rev. Bernard M. Rochon, S.M.; Deacons Pedro M. Soriano; Rudy Medrano; Antonio Caballero; Tomas Alvarado.
Res., 1515 Saltillo St., 78207. Tel: 210-434-2391; Fax: 210-434-4828.

68—St. Vincent de Paul (1961), Rev. Jose Luis De La Rosa.
Res., 4222 S.W. Loop 410, 78227-4495. Tel: 210-674-1200; Fax: 210-674-1640.
Catechesis/Religious Programs—Tel: 210-674-4291. Cathy Canty, D.R.E.
Students 575.

69—San Francisco de la Espada (1731) (Hispanic), Rev. Lawrence Janezic, O.F.M.
Res., 10040 Espada Rd., 78214. Tel: 210-627-2064; Fax: 210-627-2064.
Catechesis/Religious Programs—Hope Esparza, D.R.E.
Students 190.
Mission—San Antonio, St. Francis Cabrini, 1606 San Casimiro, 78214. Tel: 210-627-9263.

70—San Jose y San Miguel (1720) (Hispanic), Revs. Herbert Jones, O.F.M.; Thomas Shaughnessy, O.F.M.; Sr. Immaculata Kelly, P.B.V.M., Pastoral Assoc.; Deacon Santiago Rodriguez. In res., Revs. Jesus M. Aguirre-Garza, O.F.M.; Daniel Reed, O.F.M.; Bros. Ben Eastman, O.F.M.; Thomas Eisenmenger, O.F.M.; Ducam Pham, O.F.M.
Res., 701 E. Pyron Ave., 78214. Tel: 210-922-0543.
Catechesis/Religious Programs—Kathleen Rollow, D.R.E.
Students 181.

71—San Juan Capistrano (1731) (Hispanic), Rev. Jorge Baistra.
Mailing Address: 9101 Graf Rd., 78214.
Church—78214. Tel: 210-534-3161.
Mission—Southton, Bexar Co., St. Ann.

72—San Juan De Los Lagos (1952) (Hispanic), Rev. Tom Ovalle, O.M.I.; Deacons Albert Salinas; Eleodoro Vasquez.
Res., 3231 El Paso St., 78207. Tel: 210-433-9722.
Catechesis/Religious Programs—Tel: 210-433-2411.
Students 175.

73—Senyor Santo Nino de Cebu (1993) (Filipino), Rev. Gilbert Obin, C.I.C.M.; Mr. Robert Lewis, Parish Council Chair, Tel: 210-599-4828.
Mailing Address: P.O. Box 33514, 78265. Tel: 210-648-1705.

74—Vietnamese Martyers Catholic Center (1976), Rev. Dominic Luong, S.S.S.
Centers—1210 S. W.W. White, P.O. Box 28023, 78208. Tel: 210-359-5923.

OUTSIDE THE CITY OF SAN ANTONIO

Asherton, Dimmit Co., Immaculate Conception (1918) (Hispanic), Rev. Miguel Arango (Columbia).
Res., P.O. Box 8, 78827. Tel: 830-468-3343.
Catechesis/Religious Programs—Tel: 830-468-3713. Mrs. Ignacia Sanchez, D.R.E.
Sisters 4; Students 120.
Missions—Big Wells, Dimmit Co., St. Michael; Catarina, Dimmit Co., St. Henry.

Bandera, Bandera Co., St. Stanislaus (1855) (Polish), Rev. Msgr. Michael G. McManus.
Res., Box 757, 78003-0757. Tel: 830-460-4712; Fax: 830-796-7641. [CEM]
Catechesis/Religious Programs—Tel: 210-796-3573. Elouise Mangold, D.R.E.
Students 220.
Mission—Medina Lake, Bandera Co., St. Victor's Chapel, Park Rd. 37, Lakehills, 78063. Tel: 830-612-3012.

Boerne, Kendall Co., St. Peter the Apostle (1866) (German), Rev. Anthony O. Cummins; Mary Ann Chandler, Admin.
Mailing Address: 119 Kronkosky, 78006. Tel: 830-816-2233; Fax: 830-816-2143.
Catechesis/Religious Programs—D.R.E.: Val Marko; Rebecca Cash; Jeanette Belter.
Students 613.

Brackettville, Kinney Co., St. Mary Magdalen (1875), Rev. James Cashin; Deacon Robert W. Nelson, D.R.E.
Res., Box 95, 78832. Tel: 830-563-2487. [CEM]
Catechesis/Religious Programs—James Bader, D.R.E.
Students 185.
Mission—Spofford Junction, Kinney Co., St. Blaise.

Canyon Lake, Comal Co., St. Thomas the Apostle (1967), Rev. Patrick J. Palmer.
Res., 180 St. Thomas Dr., 78133-4131. Tel: 830-964-3497.

Carrizo Springs, Dimmit Co., Our Lady of Guadalupe (1881) (Hispanic), Rev. Msgr. Pablo A. Sicilia; Deacons Jose F. Perez; Genaro Ramon; Juan Sauceda.
Res., 1107 N. Eighth St., 78834. Tel: 830-876-2239; Fax: 830-876-2172.
Catechesis/Religious Programs—Tel: 830-876-5150.
Students 326.

Castroville, Medina Co., St. Louis (1844) (Alsatian), Rev. James Conway; Jeri White, Pastoral Assoc.; Deacon Gene Ebner.
Res., 610 Madrid, 78009. Tel: 830-931-9016. [CEM]
School—Tel: 830-931-3544. Vickie Tschirhart, Prin.
Lay Teachers 14; Students 189.
Catechesis/Religious Programs—Tel: 830-931-2556. Jeri White, D.R.E.
Students 440.
Mission—Mico, Medina Co., St. Francis of Assisi (Medina Lake Chapel).

Cestohowa, Karnes Co., Nativity of the Blessed Virgin Mary (1873) (Polish), Revs. Damian Tomiczek, S.D.S.; Gregory Sawicki, S.D.S.
Res., Rte. 1, Box 20, 78113. Tel: 830-745-2633. [CEM]

Charlotte, Atascosa Co., St. Rose of Lima (1909) (Hispanic), Rev. John Wagner.
Mailing Address: P.O. Box 69, 78011. Tel: 830-277-1242.
Catechesis/Religious Programs—Students 151.
Mission—Tilden, McMullen Co., St. Joseph, Tel: 830-274-3374.

Comfort, Kendall Co., Sacred Heart (1949), Rev. Joseph P. Petsch.
Church—510 Broadway, 78013. Tel: 830-995-3708; Fax: 830-995-2952.
Res., 104 Daniel St., 78013. Tel: 830-995-3501.
Mailing Address: P.O. Box 599, 78013-0599. Tel: 830-995-3708.
Catechesis/Religious Programs—Students 135.

Converse, Bexar Co., St. Monica (1959), Rev. Msgr. Patrick J. Flanagan (Ireland).
Res., 501 North St., P.O. Box 429, 78109. Tel: 210-658-3816.
School—Tel: 210-658-6701; Fax: 210-658-6945. James Mollicone, Prin.
Lay Teachers 18; Students 543; Day Care 228.
Catechesis/Religious Programs—Tel: 210-658-7920. Janice Van Slambrouck, D.R.E.
Students 358.

Cotulla, La Salle Co., Sacred Heart (1884) (Hispanic), Rev. John van Lare, C.M. (Holland); Deacon Jose Patterson.
Res., P.O. Box 560, 78014. Tel: 830-879-2658. [CEM]
Catechesis/Religious Programs—Tel: 830-879-3196. Sr. Petra Salgado, D.R.E.
Students 400.

Crystal City, Zavala Co., Sacred Heart (1917) (Hispanic), Rev. Msgr. Jose Maria Guevara (Peru); Deacons Jose L. Lopez; Jose G. Garza.
Res., 115 E. Kinney St., 78839. Tel: 830-374-3148; Fax: 830-374-2211.
Catechesis/Religious Programs—Tel: 830-374-5547. Deacon Jose G. Garza, D.R.E.
Students 257.

Del Rio, Val Verde Co., Our Lady of Guadalupe (1906) (Hispanic), Revs. Jose Caracoza Perez, M.N.M.; Armando Guerrero Mendoza, M.N.M.; Deacons Eliesar Hernandez; Adrian Falcon.
Res., 509 Garza St., 78840. Tel: 830-775-3713; Fax: 830-775-9161.
Catechesis/Religious Programs—Tel: 830-775-2178. Rev. Armando Guerrero Mendoza, M.N.M., D.R.E.
Students 669.

Sacred Heart (1895), Rev. Gerard Barrett, O.M.I.; Deacons John C. Graf; Robert C. Kusenberger; David B. Scarbo.
Mailing Address: P.O. Box 1503, 78841.
Office: 302 E. Greenwood, 78840.
Res., 411 Spring St., 78840. Tel: 830-775-2143; Fax: 830-775-2143. [CEM]
Church—304 Mill St., 78840.
School—209 E. Greenwood, 78840. Tel: 830-775-3274. Mrs. Terri Barrera, Prin.
Lay Teachers 23; Students 277.
Catechesis/Religious Programs—Sr. Theresa P. Hereford, D.R.E.
Students 236.

St. Joseph's (1927) (Hispanic), Rev. Roberto Pena, O.M.I.; Deacons Filomeno Salazar; Federico Cuellar.
Res., 510 Wernett St., P.O. Box 1455, 78840. Tel: 830-775-4753; Fax: 830-775-5200.
Catechesis/Religious Programs—Tel: 830-775-5200. D.R.E.: Raymundo Mendoza; Yolanda Mendoza.
Students 774.
Mission—Comstock, Valverde Co., Mary, Queen of the Universe.

Devine, Medina Co., St. Joseph's (1897), Rev. Clement De Meersman, C.I.C.M.
Res., 108 S. Washington Dr., 78016. Tel: 830-663-2244. [CEM]
Catechesis/Religious Programs—Janie Saucedo, D.R.E.
Students 208.

D'Hanis, Medina Co., Holy Cross (1847) (Hispanic), Rev. Wallis Stiles.
Res., P.O. Box 426, 78850. Tel: 830-363-7268. [CEM]
Catechesis/Religious Programs—Students 170.
Mission—Yancy, Medina Co., Immaculate Heart of Mary.

Dilley, Frio Co., St. Joseph's (1899) (Hispanic), Rev. Salvador Pedroza.
Res., 114 E. Frio, P.O. Box N, 78017. Tel: 830-965-1926.
Catechesis/Religious Programs—Josefa Canales, D.R.E.
Students 120.
Mission—Dilley, Frio Co., St. Mary.

Eagle Pass, Maverick Co., Our Lady of Refuge (1859) (Hispanic), Revs. Richard Beck, O.M.I.; Patricio Dominguez, O.M.I.; Deacon Efren Maldonado.
Office: Box 909, 78853-0909. Tel: 830-773-8451.
Res., 810 Ceylon St., Box 909, 78853. Tel: 830-773-8421. [CEM]
School—Tel: 830-773-3531. Sr. Elizabeth Orr, Prin.
Sisters of Charity of the Incarnate Word 1; Lay Teachers 13; Students 160.
Catechesis/Religious Programs—Tel: 830-773-6011. Sr. Irene Mejia, D.R.E.
Students 265.
Missions—Seco Mines, Maverick Co., Our Lady of Lourdes, Tel: 210-773-8288; Quemado, Maverick Co., Our Lady of Guadalupe, Tel: 210-758-1888.

Sacred Heart (1967) (Hispanic), Revs. Ramiro Cortez, O.M.I.; David Tarlizzo, O.M.I.; Domingo Estrada, O.M.I.; Deacons Manuel Cardona; Placido Zavala.
Res., 2055 William St., P.O. Box 806, 78852. Tel: 830-773-2451; Fax: 830-758-1023.
Catechesis/Religious Programs—Tel: 830-773-5013 (Parish Hall); Fax: 830-758-1023. Carmen S. Garcia, D.R.E.
Students 1,248.
Mission—El Indio, Maverick Co., Our Lady of San Juan.

St. Joseph's (1967) (Hispanic), Rev. John McGrath, O.M.I. Administrators: Jesus de la Garza; Graciela T. Gonzalez.
Res., P.O. Box 246, 78852. Tel: 830-773-6114.
Catechesis/Religious Programs—Tel: 830-773-6515; 773-6536. Mrs. Gloria R. Cantu, D.R.E.
Students 298.

Elmendorf, Bexar Co., St. Anthony (1896) (Hispanic), Rev. William McNamara; Deacons John K. Miller; Armando J. Scott.
Res., P.O. Box 248, 78112. Tel: 210-635-8539; Fax: 210-635-8644. [CEM]
Catechesis/Religious Programs—Anita Casillas, D.R.E.
Students 200.
Mission—Saspamco, Bexar Co., Our Lady of Perpetual Help. [CEM]

Falls City, Karnes Co., Holy Trinity (1902) (Polish), Rev. Jan Piotr Klak (Poland).
Res., Box 158, 78113. Tel: 830-254-3539; Fax: 830-254-3530. [CEM]
Catechesis/Religious Programs—Rose Lee Moczygemba, D.R.E.
Students 196.

Floresville, Wilson Co., Sacred Heart (1882), Rev. Victor Carrillo; Rose Marie Pennartz, Admin.; Deacons Scott Donaho; Mike Perez.
Res., 1009 Trail St., 78114. Tel: 830-393-6117. [CEM]
School—Tel: 830-393-2117. Bro. Joseph Ballard, C.S.C., Prin.
Sisters 2; Lay Teachers 9; Students 118.
Catechesis/Religious Programs—Debbie Leal, D.R.E.
Students 265.

Fredericksburg, Gillespie Co., St. Mary's (1846) (German), Revs. Phillip D. Henning; Eduardo D. Morales; Deacons Gregorio Martinez, Jr.; Francisco De La Torre; Louis Loth.
Mailing Address: P.O. Box 152, 78624.
Res., 306 W. San Antonio St., 78624. Tel: 830-997-9523; Fax: 830-997-1037. [CEM]
School—Tel: 830-997-3914; 997-2203; Fax: 830-997-2382. Billy Pahl, Prin.
Lay Teachers 21; Students 347.
Catechesis/Religious Programs—Tel: 830-997-7487. Sr. Lucille Ann Fritsch, C.D.P., D.R.E.
Students 294.
Mission—Fredericksburg, Gillespie Co., Our Lady of Guadalupe.

Gonzales, Gonzales Co., St. James (1885), Revs. Francisco A. Macias; Ubaldo Santos, C.M.F.; Deacon Alfonso Moreno.
Res., 417 N. College St., 78629. Tel: 830-672-2945; Fax: 830-672-1058. [CEM]
Catechesis/Religious Programs—Tel: 830-672-6291.
Students 425.
Missions—Gonzales, Gonzales Co., Sacred Heart; Waelder, Gonzales Co., St. Patrick.
Stations—Gonzales, Care Inn of Gonzales.; Ottine, Warm Springs Rehabilitation Hospital, Tel: 830-672-6592.

Harper, Gillespie Co., St. Anthony's (1909), Rev. David C. Meurer.
Res., Box 318, 78631. Tel: 830-864-4026. [CEM]

Helotes, Bexar Co., Our Lady of Guadalupe (1942), Revs. Gerald Hammel, S.M.; Gerald Pleva, S.M.; Deacon Timothy Houlihan.
Res., P.O. Box 639, 78023. Tel: 210-695-8791; Fax: 210-695-9957. [CEM]
Catechesis/Religious Programs—D.R.E.: Nancy Drymala; Jan Growney; Cindy Tejeda; Mary Shrader.
Students 825.

Hobson, Karnes Co., St. Boniface (1901) (Polish), Revs. Damian Tomiczek, S.D.S. (Poland); Gregory Sawicki, S.D.S.
Res., P.O. Box 135, 78117. Tel: 830-780-3559. [CEM]

Hondo, Medina Co., St. John the Evangelist (1892), Rev. Msgr. Vincent Fecher; Deacon Albert Villa; Martina Saathoff, Admin.
Res., 2102 Avenue J, 78861. Tel: 830-741-2236; Fax: 830-426-3339. [CEM]
Catechesis/Religious Programs—Tel: 830-426-2565. Norma Villa, D.R.E.
Students 640.

Jourdanton, Atascosa Co., St. Matthew's (1912) (Hispanic), Rev. Michael H. Yarbrough, Admin.; Deacons Eusebio Guevara; Welton Fiedler, Jr.
Mailing Address: Box 670, 78026.
Res., 1700 Campbell, 78026. Tel: 830-769-3687; Fax: 830-769-2861. [CEM]
Catechesis/Religious Programs—D.R.E.: Sr. Karen Schwane, O.S.U.; Lydia Brown; Judy Hooge.
Students 126.
Mission—Christine, Ataseosa Co., St. Ignatius.

Karnes City, Karnes Co., St. Cornelius (1917), Rev. Stuart Juleen.
Res., 605 E. Calvert St., 78118. Tel: 830-780-3947.
Catechesis/Religious Programs—Tel: 830-780-3949. Sr. Rose Anthony McClosky, O.L.V.M., D.R.E.
Students 280.
Mission—Fashing, Atascosa Co., St. Elizabeth.

Kenedy, Karnes Co., Our Lady of Peace (1959), Revs. Patrick P. Bergin (CC); John Flanagan, M.S.F.
Res., One Notre Dame Pl., 78119. Tel: 830-583-2417.
Catechesis/Religious Programs—Tel: 830-583-2247. Janie Hernandez, D.R.E.
Students 364.

Kerrville, Kerr Co., Notre Dame (1889), Revs. Michael J. Boulette; Anthony Vilano.
Res., 909 Main St., 78028. Tel: 830-257-5961; Fax: 830-257-5961.
School—923 Main St., 78028. Tel: 830-257-6707; Fax: 830-792-4348. Sr. Conchessa Johnston, C.C.V.I., Prin.
Sisters of Charity of the Incarnate Word 5; Dominican Sisters 1; Lay Teachers 10; Students 263.
Catechesis/Religious Programs—Tel: 830-896-4233. Mrs. Lou Chamberlain, D.R.E.
Students 465.

Kirby, Bexar Co., St. Joan of Arc (1971), Rev. Leslie A. Vance; Deacons John Buchanan; Robert Galan, Jr.; John X. Huttinger; Joseph P. Nash.
Res., 2829 Ackermann Rd., San Antonio, 78219. Tel: 210-661-5277; Fax: 210-661-5735.
Catechesis/Religious Programs—Tel: 210-661-2220. Mrs. Paulette Petron, D.R.E.
Students 362.

Kosciuszko, Wilson Co., St. Ann's (1898) (Polish), Rev. Edward Wanat, S.D.S.
Res., 8161 FM 541-E, Stockdale, 78160. Tel: 830-745-2541; Fax: 830-745-2434. [CEM]

LaCoste, Medina Co., Our Lady of Grace (1911) (Hispanic), Rev. Msgr. Thomas M. Palmer.
Res., P.O. Box 39, 78039. Tel: 210-985-3346; 762-3334. [CEM]
Catechesis/Religious Programs—Mary Ann Mangold, D.R.E.
Students 321.

La Pryor, Zavala Co., St. Joseph (1917) (Hispanic), Rev. Jose Luis Balderas; Deacons Gene Corrigan; Juan Gallegos.
Res., P.O. Box 436, 78872. Tel: 830-365-4107.
Mission—Batesville, Zavalaco Co., St. Patrick.

La Vernia, Wilson Co., St. Ann (1917), Rev. Peter McKenna.
Mailing Address: P.O. Box 256, 78121.
Res., 78121. Tel: 830-779-3131; Fax: 830-779-1749.
Catechesis/Religious Programs—D.R.E.: Chickie McManus; Robin Thompson; Sandra Burg; Irene Martinez; Clay Bordner.
Students 261.

Leon Springs, Bexar Co., St. Elizabeth Ann Seton (1961), Rev. Patrick L. Marron.
Res., 7655 Curres Creek Cir., Boerne, 78015-6503. Tel: 210-698-1941; 698-1983.
Catechesis/Religious Programs—Dr. Chela Gonzalez, D.R.E.
Students 165.

Losoya, Bexar Co., El Carmen Catholic Church (1898) (Hispanic). (Our Lady of Mt. Carmel). Rev. Richard J. McCarthy, C.M., Admin. In res., Rev. Oscar J. Miller, C.M.
Res., 18555 Leal Rd. (Losoya), San Antonio, 78221. Tel: 210-626-2333.
Catechesis/Religious Programs—Tel: 210-626-1063. D.R.E.: Emily Ortiz; Mary Esther Rodriguez.
Students 402.

Lytle, Atascosa Co., St. Andrew (1904), Rev. Francis Vanhee, C.I.C.M.
Res., P.O. Box 326, 78052. Tel: 830-709-4287. [CEM]
Catechesis/Religious Programs—Students 342.
Missions—Natalia, Medina Co., St. John Bosco; Coal Mine, Atascosa Co., Immaculate Conception.

Macdona, Bexar Co., Our Lady Queen of Heaven (1944) (Hispanic), Rev. Rudolph T. Carrola, Jr.
Res., 9961 Aliann, 78054.
Mailing Address: P.O. Box 94, 78054-0094. Tel: 210-622-3282; Fax: 210-622-3282.

Martinez, Bexar Co., St. Jerome (1925), Rev. Thomas J. O'Brien; Deacon Joe Champagne.
Res., 7955 Real Rd., San Antonio, 78263. Tel: 210-648-2694; Fax: 210-648-3690. [CEM]
Catechesis/Religious Programs—Tel: 210-648-0336. Shirley Bordovsky, D.R.E.
Students 250.

New Braunfels, Comal Co., Holy Family (1964) (Hispanic), Rev. James Wasser; Amelia Lankford, Pastoral Assoc.
Res., 245 S. Hidalgo, 78130. Tel: 830-609-5320; Fax: 830-609-5322.
Catechesis/Religious Programs—Tel: 210-608-9615. Loraine Blount, D.R.E.
Students 350.

Our Lady of Perpetual Help (1926), Rev. Richard Oberstar, M.S.F.; Deacons Cayetano Morales; Ramond Ybarra.
Res., 138 W. Austin St., 78130. Tel: 830-625-3534; Fax: 830-625-3566.
Catechesis/Religious Programs—Elizabeth Martinez, D.R.E.
Students 225.
Mission—Hunter, Comal Co., St. John. [CEM]

SS. Peter and Paul (1845), Rev. Msgr. Eugene O'Callaghan, V.F.; Rev. Msgr. Edward Bily; Deacons Fred Fey; Ray Kaufman; Ben Wehman; Frank Fikac; William Schroeder; James Behling.
Res., 386 N. Castell St., 78130. Tel: 830-625-4531; Fax: 830-606-5461. [CEM]
School—Tel: 830-625-3233; Fax: 830-625-3246. Sr. Geraldine Bienek, Prin.
Lay Teachers 19; Students 270.
Catechesis/Religious Programs—386 N. Castell, 78130. Tel: 830-625-1519. Bill Smith, D.R.E.
Students 730.
Mission—Comal, Comal Co., St. Joseph.

Nixon, Gonzales Co., St. Joseph's (1915), Rev. David G. Zumaya; Deacons Dimas Medina; Daniel Medina, Sr.; Ciriaco V. Barron, Jr.
Res., 207 S. Washington Ave., 78140-2920. Tel: 830-582-1127. [CEM]
Catechesis/Religious Programs—Students 72.

Panna Maria, Karnes Co., Immaculate Conception of the Blessed Virgin Mary (1854) (Polish), Rev. Robert Ploch (Poland).
Res., P.O. Box 9, 78144. Tel: 830-780-2748. [CEM]
Mission—Helena, Karnes Co., St. Helena.

Pearsall, Frio Co., Immaculate Heart of Mary (1891), Rev. Andrew Kafara, S.J. (Poland); Deacon Manuel Carrizales.
Res., 422 W. Brazos, P.O. Box AK, 78061. Tel: 830-334-2382. [CEM]
Catechesis/Religious Programs—Tel: 210-334-4879. Esther Martinez, D.R.E.
Students 415.

Pleasanton, Atascosa Co., St. Andrew (1913), Rev. Carlos Davalos; Deacons Norman Phillips; Jose Valenzuela.
Res., 626 Market St., 78064-2747. Tel: 830-569-3356; Fax: 830-281-4902. [CEM]
Catechesis/Religious Programs—Sr. Dorothy Moczygemba, C.S.S.F., D.R.E.
Students 459.
Mission—Campbellton, Atascosa Co., Sacred Heart.

St. Luke-Loire (1859), Rev. James Hoelscher; Deacons Jose Trevino; Richard Gonzalez.
Res., 3930 FM 536, 78064. Tel: 830-393-6021.
Catechesis/Religious Programs—Students 175.
Mission—Leming, Atascosa Co., Our Lady of Guadalupe. [CEM]

Poteet, Atascosa Co., St. Philip Benizi (1897) (Hispanic), Rev. Felix A. Avau, C.I.C.M.
Res., P.O. Box 348, 78065. Tel: 830-742-3796. [CEM]
Catechesis/Religious Programs—Beatrice Bermudez, D.R.E.
Students 230.

Poth, Wilson Co., Blessed Sacrament (1910) (Hispanic/Polish), Rev. Samuel Heitkamp; Deacon Alan Crosby.
Res., P.O. Box 339, 78147. Tel: 830-484-3302. [CEM]
Catechesis/Religious Programs—Tel: 830-484-3303. Megan Rotter, D.R.E.
Students 251.

Rocksprings, Edwards Co., Sacred Heart of Mary (1900) (Hispanic), Rev. John M. Pagel (CHL).
Res., P.O. Box 887, 78880. Tel: 830-683-2165.
Missions—Camp Wood, Real Co., St. Mary Magdalen; Leakey, Real Co., St. Raymond of Pennafort.

Runge, Karnes Co., St. Anthony's (1901) (Polish), Revs. Paschal Bergin (CC) Admin.; John Flanagan, M.S.F.
Mailing Address: P.O. Box 188, 78151.
Res., Arsenso St., 78151. Tel: 830-239-4146. [CEM 2]

Sabinal, Uvalde Co., St. Patrick's (1884), Rev. Einer R. Ochoa.
Res., Box 117, 78881. Tel: 830-988-2255.
Missions—Knippa, Uvalde Co., St. Joseph; Vanderpool, Bandera Co., St. Mary.

St. Hedwig, Bexar Co., Annunciation of the Blessed Virgin Mary (1857) (Polish), Rev. Bill Zadora, S.D.S. (Poland).
Res., P.O. Box 100, 78152. Tel: 210-667-1232; Fax: 210-667-1232. [CEM]
Catechesis/Religious Programs—Sr. Luz Moreno, D.R.E.
Students 300.

Schertz, Guadalupe Co., Church of the Good Shepherd (1972), Rev. Roger P. Robbins; Mrs. Micki Christy, Admin.; Deacons John J. Gorman; Paul La Combe.
Res., P.O. Box 929, 78154. Tel: 830-658-4350.
Catechesis/Religious Programs—Tel: 830-658-6188. D.R.E.: Mrs. Gerry Stift; Mrs. Joan Smith.
Students 375.
Mission—Marion, Guadalupe Co., Immaculate Conception.

Seguin, Guadalupe Co., Our Lady of Guadalupe (1908) (Hispanic), Revs. Gerard Mackin, M.S.F.; James E. Wuerth, M.S.F.; Deacons Nick Carillo; Juan Garza.

Res., 409 W. Krezdorn, 78155-4429. Tel: 830-379-4338; Fax: 830-303-1002. [CEM]
Catechesis/Religious Programs—Tel: 210-379-2818. Mr. George Oliva, D.R.E.
Students 800.

St. James (1873), Rev. Gerald Hubertus.
Res., 510 S. Camp St., 78155. Tel: 830-379-1796; Fax: 830-379-1796. [CEM]
School—507 S. Camp St., 78155. Tel: 830-379-2878; Fax: 830-379-2878. Janice Jessen, Prin.
Sisters 1; Lay Teachers 12; Students 241.
Catechesis/Religious Programs—Sr. Pat Crehan, S.H.Sp., D.R.E.
Students 261.

Selma, Bexar Co., Our Lady of Perpetual Help (1897) (German), Rev. Conor McGrath; Deacons Clifford Friesenhahn; Robert Thayer.
Res., 16075 N. Evans Rd., 78154-3824. Tel: 210-651-6913; Fax: 210-651-5272.
School—Tel: 210-651-6811; Fax: 210-651-6811. Sr. Evelyn Korenek, I.W.B.S., Prin.
Sisters of Incarnate Word and Blessed Sacrament 3; Lay Teachers 19; Students 372.
Catechesis/Religious Programs—Verneanne Wong, D.R.E.
Students 687.

Smiley, Gonzales Co., St. Philip Benizi (1963) (Hispanic), Rev. David G. Zumaya; Deacons Frank Rojas Pastoral Admin.; John J. Moreno.
Res., P.O. Box 32, 78159-0032. Tel: 830-587-6258.

Somerset, Bexar Co., St. Mary's (1920), Rev. Paul M. Newhouse, C.I.C.M. (Belgium); Deacon Walter Mushalla.
Res., Box 295, 78069. Tel: 830-429-3645. [CEM]
Catechesis/Religious Programs—Mrs. Rebecca Martinez, D.R.E.
Students 240.

Spring Branch, Comal Co. (Honey Creek), St. Joseph (1876), Rev. James Janish; Sandy Strange, Pastoral Assoc.; Deacons Johnny Gass; James Legendre. In res., Rev. Mark A. Garrett, O.S.A.
Res., 25781 Hwy. 46 W., 78070-3613. Tel: 830-980-2268; Fax: 830-980-3184. [CEM]
Catechesis/Religious Programs—Sandy Strange, D.R.E.
Students 355.

Stockdale, Wilson Co., St. Mary (1895) (Polish), Rev. Wieslaw Iwaniec.
Res., Box 535, 78160. Tel: 830-996-3415.
Catechesis/Religious Programs—Venice Grantham, D.R.E.
Students 163.

Stonewall, Gillespie Co., St. Francis Xavier (1945), Rev. Joseph G. De La Garza.
Res., Ranch Rd. 1, H.C. 1, Box 425, 78671. Tel: 830-644-2368.

Uvalde, Uvalde Co., Sacred Heart (1883), Revs. Kenneth M. Dakin; Joseph Pena; Deacons Hector V. Garcia; Ernest Gonzales; Antonio Hinojosa; Fortunato Hinojosa; Gonzalo Uriegas.
Res., 408 Fort Clark St., 78801. Tel: 830-278-3448; Fax: 830-278-2835. [CEM]
School—Tel: 830-278-2661. Sr. Dolores Aviles, S.T.J., Prin.
Teresian Sisters 3; Lay Teachers 15; Students 198.
Catechesis/Religious Programs—Tel: 830-278-3060. Linda Milam, D.R.E.
Students 1,121.

Von Ormy, Bexar Co., Sacred Heart (1935) (Hispanic), Rev. Rudolph T. Carrola, Jr.
13466 IH 35 S., 78073-3302. Tel: 210-622-3457; 622-3282; Fax: 210-622-3457.
Catechesis/Religious Programs—Denise Barker, D.R.E.
Students 100.
Res., P.O. Box 94, Macdona, 78054-0094. Tel: 210-622-3282; Fax: 210-622-3282.

St. Peter the Fisherman (1987) (Hispanic), Rev. Msgr. Charles Pugh.
Res., 17534 N. State Hwy. 16, 78073. Tel: 830-276-8778.
Catechesis/Religious Programs—Students 300.
Missions—Moore, Frio Co., St. Augustine; Bigfoot, Frio Co., Our Lady of Mt. Carmel.

KOREAN APOSTOLATE

San Antonio, Korean Catholic Community (1991), Rev. Andrew Yong Min Im (Korea); Deacon Philip C. Kim.
Res., 6831 Leyland, 78239. Tel: 210-655-3373.
Church—St. Pius X, 3303 Urban Crest, 78209. Tel: 210-824-0139.

OLD SPANISH MISSIONS

San Antonio, Old Spanish Missions, Rev. Msgr. Balthasar J. Janacek, Dir.
Mailing Address: c/o Catholic Chancery, P.O. Box 28410, 78228.
Purisima Concepcion—807 Mission Rd., 78210.
San Francisco de la Espada—10040 Espada Rd., 78214.
San Juan Capistrano—9101 Graf Rd., 78214.
San Jose—701 E. Pyron Rd., 78214.

Chaplains of Public Institutions

SAN ANTONIO. *Audie Murphy VA Hospital* 7400 Merton Minter, 78229. Tel: 210-617-5308. Revs. Harry Martin; George Evans, O.C.S.O.
Baptist Memorial Hospital 111 Dallas St., 78205. Tel: 210-222-8431. Rev. Edward Murray, O.M.I.; Mrs. Pat Sammis.
Brooke Army Medical Center P.O. Box 15097, 78212. Tel: 210-650-5518. Rev. James Schellenberg.
Methodist Hospital 7700 Floyd Curl, 78229. Tel: 210-692-4030. Revs. Aaron Arce, O.P.; Stefan Wiera; Marian Piekarczyk.
St. Luke's Baptist Hospital; University Hospital 4502 Medical Dr., 78229. Tel: 210-680-2635 (Residence). Revs. George F. Healy, C.S.Sp.; Nicholas Brown, S.C.J.
San Antonio State Hospital 6711 S. New Braunfels, 78223. Tel: 210-532-8811. Rev. Augustine Amanzeh.
Santa Rosa Hospital System 519 W. Houston, 78207. Tel: 210-704-2021. Rev. Mark Scheffler, C.Ss.R.; Mr. Richard Woodley.
Southwest General Hospital Tel: 210-921-2000. Deacon Leon Mueller.

KERRVILLE. *Veterans' Administration Hospital*. Vacant. Tel: 210-896-2020.

Special Assignment:
Reverend Fathers—
Horan, Michael

On Duty Outside the Archdiocese:
Reverend Fathers—
Dillane, Maurice, Ireland
Garret, Sean, 110 St. Mary St., S.W., Fort Walton Beach, FL 32548. Tel: 904-243-3742
Keane, John F.
Kownacki, Robert, 7224 Balmoral, Chicago, IL 60656. Tel: 312-775-7315
Martinez, Manuel, Federal Bureau of Prisons, 320 1st St. N.W., HOLC Bldg. 254, Washington, DC 20534
Rubaj, Leon, Incarnate Word Sister's Convent, 1101 N.E. Water St., Victoria, TX 77901

Military Chaplains:
Reverend Fathers—
Barlow, James P., Chaplain Major, 8539 Odyssey Dr., Universal City, TX 78148
Gonzalez, George G., Chap. Major, 6726 Widgeon Dr., Midland, GA 31820
Hernandez, Alfred Ricardo, Col. Catholic Chap., 3240 Old Lawley Toll Rd., Calistoga, CA 94515
Nee, Eugene O., A.P.O., PFE 50, Box RET 667, APO, AE 09494
Tellez, Jairo, Major, U.S.A.F., Germany

On Educational Leave of Absence:
Reverend Fathers—
Watson, Douglas, S.C.J., 11800 Braesview, Apt. 2203, San Antonio, TX 78213. Tel: 210-341-4893

Absent on Sick Leave:
Reverend Fathers—
Busteed, Francis

On Leave:
Reverend Fathers—
Crane, Jeff
Currie, Donald
Davila, Johnny
De La Rosa, Vincent
Dietz, Xavier Ortiz
Duran, Jorge
O'Sullivan, Michael
Ruiz, Enrique

Retired:
Reverend Monsignors—
Costantino, Anthony J., 80 Peter Baque Rd., San Antonio, TX 78209. Tel: 210-826-7721
Garcia, Raymond, 7458 Louis Pasteur Dr., San Antonio, TX 78229
Goertz, Alois J., 8520 Cross Mountain Tr., #100, San Antonio, TX 78255. Tel: 210-698-9067
Manning, J. Leroy, 8520 Cross Mountain Tr. #1102, San Antonio, TX 78255. Tel: 210-698-3183
Matocha, John L., Box 158B, Mathis, TX 78368. Tel: 512-547-9859
Mullaney, Bernard C., 8520 Cross Mountain Tr. #402, San Antonio, TX 78255. Tel: 210-698-3975
Rihn, Roy, 8520 Cross Mountain Tr. #301, San Antonio, TX 78255. Tel: 210-698-0287
Smith, Sherill, 8520 Cross Mountain Tr., #201, San Antonio, TX 78255. Tel: 210-698-8819
Stuebben, George, 314 Cave Ln., San Antonio, TX 78209. Tel: 210-829-0238
Wangler, Alex, 6701 Blanco Rd., Apt. 110, San Antonio, TX 78216-6111. Tel: 210-342-6063
Reverend Fathers—
Femenia, Nicholas, Mailing Address: P.O. Box 37056, San Antonio, TX 78237
Gitter, Aloysius A., Mailing Address: P.O. Box 98, Harper, TX 78631. Tel: 210-864-4131
Goebel, Bernard M., 150 Beethoven St., San Antonio, TX 78210. Tel: 210-359-9034
Johnston, Robert F., 601 Van Ness Ave., #1052, San Francisco, CA 94102. Tel: 415-674-3572
Martinez, Rogelio, 8520 Cross Mountain Tr. #1101, San Antonio, TX 78255. Tel: 210-698-2243
O'Callaghan, Patrick, Mailing Address: P.O. Box 34413, San Antonio, TX 78265
Paniagua, Pablo, 8520 Cross Mountain Trail, #401, San Antonio, TX 78255. Tel: 210-698-8036

Permanent Deacons:
Alberty, George G., Jr., St. Brigid's, San Antonio
Almanza, Jose M., St. Leo's, San Antonio
Alvarado, Thomas, St. Timothy's, San Antonio
Amo, Ernest Roy, St. Brigid, San Antonio
Baker, Robert L., On Duty Outside the Archdiocese
Barajas, Felipe, Holy Rosary, San Antonio
Barrera, Enrique, San Fernando, San Antonio
Barron, Cyriaco, Jr., St. Joseph's, Nixon
Bautista, Teofilo, Annunciation of BVM, St. Hedwig
Behling, James, Ss. Peter and Paul, New Braunfels
Bellg, Bruce J., St. Francis of Assisi, San Antonio
Bemrich, Richard, (Retired)
Benigno, Pasquale, St. Brigid's, San Antonio
Billimek, Thomas E., St. Brigid's, San Antonio
Bonilla-Valentin, Jorge, Immaculate Heart of Mary, San Antonio
Bozek, Edwin J., Jr., St. Francis of Assisi, San Antonio
Brumley, Denson C., On Leave
Buchanan, John, (Retired)
Caballero, Antonio, St. Timothy, San Antonio
Callaway, George, Jr., St. Anthony Mary Claret, San Antonio
Camero, A. C., Our Lady of Guadalupe & Jail Ministry, San Antonio
Campos, Fred, Jr., St. Gregory the Great, San Antonio
Cardona, Manuel, Sacred Heart, Eagle Pass
Carranza, Manuel G., Jr., Holy Family, San Antonio
Carrillo, Nick L., Our Lady of Guadalupe, Seguin
Carrillo, Victor, Jr., On Duty Outside the Archdiocese
Carrizales, Manuel, Immaculate Heart of Mary, Pearsall
Carroll, Bernard, On Leave
Casanova, Ismael G., St. Mary Magdalen, San Antonio
Castellano, Frank V., St. Gabriel, San Antonio
Cena, Librado, St. John Berchmans, San Antonio
Cervantes, Alfredo, Immaculate Heart of Mary, San Antonio
Champagne, Joseph, St. Jerome, Martinez
Chavez, Hugo V., St. John the Evangelist, San Antonio
Chycinski, Wayne, Blessed Sacrament, San Antonio
Ciarrochi, Jerome, St. Thomas More, San Antonio
Cisneros, Daniel, Our Lady of Mt. Carmel & St. Therese (aka Little Flower), San Antonio
Clancey, Patrick, The Patrician Movement, San Antonio
Colley, Earl M., Holy Rosary, San Antonio
Corrigan, Gene, St. Joseph, La Pryor
Crosby, Alan, Blessed Sacrament, Poth
Cross, Raymond, St. Peter Prince of Apostles, San Antonio
Crowley, Thomas, St. Pius X, San Antonio
Cruz, Robert, On Leave
Cuellar, Federico, On Leave
D'Agostino, Michael, St. Helena, San Antonio
De la Torre, Francisco, St. Mary's, Fredericksburg
DeCuir, Harold, St. Helena, San Antonio
DeLaGarza, Gustavo, On Leave
DeLauter, Paul, On Duty Outside the Archdiocese
DeLeon, Joseph L., St. Helena, San Antonio
Diaz, Jose G., St. John Berchman, San Antonio
Dillard, Henry, St. Stephen, San Antonio
Donaho, Scott, Jr., Sacred Heart, Floresville
Donias, Justo, Jr., Catholic Charities, Fort Wayne, IN
Droll, Victor, St. Elizabeth's, Pflugerville
Dunn, John N., St. Peter Prince of Apostles, San Antonio
Ebner, Eugene, St. Louis, Castroville
Elliot, Robert R., St. James, Seguin
Enriquez, Marcos, On Leave
Espinosa, Jose R., On Leave
Estrada, Melchor, On Leave
Falcon, Adrian, Our Lady of Guadalupe, Del Rio

Fertitta, J. V., Sr., Blessed Sacrament, San Antonio
Fey, Fred, Sts. Peter & Paul, New Braunfels
Fiedler, Welton J., St. Matthew, Jourdanton, TX
Fikac, Frank J., Sts. Peter & Paul, New Braunfels
Fitzpatrick, Alan, St. Dominic, San Antonio
Fox, Thomas J., St. Matthew's, San Antonio
Fraga, Jesse, Our Lady of Sorrows, San Antonio
Franklin, Thomas M., St. Francis of Assisi, San Antonio
Friesenhahn, Clifford, Our Lady of Perpetual Help, Selma
Galan, Roberto L., Jr., St. Joan of Arc, Kirby
Gallegos, Juan, St. Joseph, La Pryor
Gallegos, Valentine, Sacred Heart, San Antonio
Galvan, Robert, Our Lady of Guadalupe, San Antonio
Garcia, Hector, Sacred Heart, Uvalde
Garcia, Roberto, St. Bernard of Clairvaux, Dallas
Garza, Albert G., San Fernando Cathedral, San Antonio
Garza, Jose, Sacred Heart, Crystal City
Garza, Juan, Our Lady of Guadalupe, Seguin
Garza, Lionel, Jr., St. Dominic, San Antonio
Garza, Robert M., Prince of Peace, San Antonio
Gass, Johnny J., St. Joseph, Honey Creek, Spring Branch
Gonzales, Ernest L., Sacred Heart, Uvalde
Gonzalez, Richard, St. Luke-Loire, Pleasanton
Gorman, John J., Good Shepherd, Schertz
Gorton, Everett D., St. Vincent De Paul, San Antonio
Graf, John E., Sacred Heart, Del Rio
Guerrero, Leon, St. Agnes, San Antonio
Guevara, Eusebio, St. Matthew's, Jourdanton
Gutierrez, Pedro, St. Brigid, San Antonio
Hansbauer, Eugene, On Leave
Hennessy, Robert, St. Luke's, San Antonio
Henson, Archibald, St. Louis, Castroville
Herbert, David L., Holy Name, San Antonio
Hernandez, Elieser, Our Lady of Guadalupe, Del Rio
Hernandez, Jose D., St. Lawrence, San Antonio
Herrera, Genaro M., St. Joseph's (South San), San Antonio
Herrera, Ramon, On Leave
Hinojosa, Antonio, Sacred Heart, Uvalde
Hinojosa, Fidel, St. Bonaventure, San Antonio
Hinojosa, Fortunado, Sacred Heart, Uvalde
Hobbs, John R., San Francisco di Paola, San Antonio
Hoelscher, Wilbur L., St. Matthew's, San Antonio
Hollstein, Albert, (Retired)
Holmstrom, Joseph, On Leave
Hormachea, Richard, St. Ann's, San Antonio
Houlihan, Timothy, Our Lady of Guadalupe, Helotes, TX
Hunsucker, Paul, St. Thomas the Apostle, Canyon Lake
Huttinger, John X., St. Joan of Arc, San Antonio
Imburgia, Scott, Permanent Diaconate Office, San Antonio
Jasso, Reynaldo, St. Rose of Lima, San Antonio
Jorgensen, J. D., Blessed Sacrament, San Antonio
Joslin, Wayne L., March A.F.B. Chapel, Military
Kasavage, Richard, (Retired)
Kattengell, Leon E., Our Lady of Guadalupe, San Antonio
Kaufman, Raymond, (Retired)
Kearns, W. Daniel, St. Benedict, San Antonio
Keller, Alois, Jr., St. Lawrence, San Antonio
Kim, Philip C., Korean Community, San Antonio
Knopp, Kenneth P., (Retired)
Krupa, Joseph, Church of the Holy Spirit, San Antonio
Kusenberger, Robert, Sacred Heart, Del Rio
La Combe, Paul B., Church of Good Shepherd, Schertz, TX
Lamm, Wilfred, St. Margaret Mary, San Antonio
Landez, John, St. Leo & Permanent Diaconate Office, San Antonio
Legendre, James F., St. Joseph, Honey Creek, Spring Branch
Link, John Dennis, On Leave
Lira, Antonio, St. Rose of Lima, San Antonio
Lira, Rodolfo, Toledo, OH
Lopez, Jose Luis, Sacred Heart, Crystal City
Loth, Louis E., St. Mary's, Fredricksburg
Ludolph, Anthony, Schoenstatt Rep., San Antonio
Lugo, Loni G., St. Mark, San Antonio
Maldonado, Efren, Our Lady of Lourdes, Seco Mines
Mangold, Clayton, St. Paul, San Antonio
Marin, Arturo, On Leave
Marques, Steven J., On Leave
Martinez, Gregorio, Jr., St. Mary, Fredricksburg
Martinez, Ignacio, (Retired)
Martinez, Juan G., Divine Providence, San Antonio
McDonald, John, On Leave
Mechler, Gerardo A., St. Margaret Mary, San Antonio
Medina, Damacio, St. Joseph, Nixon
Medina, Daniel G., St. Joseph, Nixon
Medina, Henry, St. Dominic, San Antonio
Medina, Ricardo, On Duty Outside the Archdiocese
Medrano, Rudy C., St. Timothy, San Antonio
Menchaca, Jose, St. Martin De Porres, San Antonio
Merlin, Joseph, On Leave
Meyers, Joseph L., On Duty Outside the Archdiocese
Micek, Jerome, Holy Trinity, San Antonio
Miller, John K., St. Anthony, Elmendorf
Miller, Mark C., Indiana
Moczygemba, Zafirin, St. Margaret Mary, San Antonio
Morales, Cayetano, Our Lady of Perpetual Help, New Braunfels
Moreno, Alfonso, Sacred Heart, Gonzales
Moreno, Florencio, Internship, El Paso, TX
Moreno, John J., St. Philip's, Smiley
Mueller, Leon, (Retired)
Munoz, Antonio, Immaculate Conception, San Antonio
Muraida, Daniel, St. Paul's & Permanent Diaconate Office, San Antonio
Mushalla, Walter A., St. Mary's, Somerset
Nash, Joseph, St. Joan of Arc, Kirby, TX
Navarro, Ruben W., St. Raymond Pennafort, Leakey
Neal, Thomas R., Prince of Peace, San Antonio
Nelson, Robert W., On Duty Outside the Archdiocese
Neville, Richard F., Jr., Randolph, A.F.B., San Antonio
Novian, Donald, St. Gregory, San Antonio
O'Sullivan, Ridge, Jr., St. Anthony of Padua, San Antonio
Olivares, Jesse, On Leave
Orr, James, Our Lady of Atonement, San Antonio
Ortega, Sylvester, St. Jude, San Antonio
Ortiz, Antonio H., St. Jude, San Antonio
Ostaszewski, Chester R., St. Rose of Lima, San Antonio
Pacheco, Alvino, St. Leo, San Antonio
Paiz, Gabriel, (Retired)
Patino, Edward, St. Agnes, San Antonio
Patlan, Antonio, St. Martin de Porres, San Antonio
Patterson, Jose, Sacred Heart, Cotulla, TX
Pedroza, Doroteo E., San Fernando, San Antonio
Pena, Rudy, Christ the King, San Antonio
Perez, Jose F., Our Lady of Guadalupe, Carrizo Springs
Perez, Julio T., American Embassy, Luanda, Angola, Africa
Perez, Miguel, Jr., Sacred Heart, Floresville
Pettengill, Howard W., Jr., St. Pius X, San Antonio
Phillips, Norman D., St. Andrew, Pleasanton
Pope, Charles F., Sr., St. Clare, San Antonio
Pratt, Gilbert, St. Francis of Assisi & Jail Ministry, San Antonio
Prevott, Raymond, (Retired)
Pruneda, Esmeraldo, St. Jude, San Antonio
Quarles, Fred J., St. Cecilia, San Antonio
Ramirez, Albert, Our Lady of Angels, San Antonio
Ramirez, Victor, Our Lady of the Angels, San Antonio
Ramon, Genaro, Sr., Our Lady of Guadalupe, Carrizo Springs
Raso, James, St. John Berchman, San Antonio
Reyes, Ramiro, Ligonier, IN
Riojas, Francisco, St. Philip, Smiley
Risk, Ralph F., Unassigned
Rodriguez, Santiago, San Jose Mission, San Antonio
Rodriguez, Severo, Jr., On Leave
Salazar, Filomeno, St. Joseph, Del Rio
Salinas, Alberto, San Juan DeLos Lagos, San Antonio
Salinas, Carlos, On Leave
Sanabria, Agripino, Prince of Peace, San Antonio
Sanchez, Jose H., St. Philip of Jesus, San Antonio
Sandoval, Carlos, Our Lady of Guadalupe, San Antonio
Sauceda, Juan, Our Lady of Guadalupe, Carrizo Springs
Scarbo, David B., Sacred Heart, Del Rio
Schonhoff, Robert L., Our Lady of Grace, San Antonio
Schroeder, William, Sts. Peter and Paul, New Braunfels
Scott, Armando, St. Anthony, Elmendorf
Sekinger, Eugene, Military Parochial, Brooks Air Force Base
Seymour, Warren V., (Retired)
Shoemake, William, Christ the King, Belton
Soriano, Pedro, St. Timothy, San Antonio
Spitzer, John L., On Leave
Staudt, Milton N., Church of the Holy Spirit, San Antonio
Stewart, Wilbert, St. Dominic, San Antonio
Stockton, Ree, St. Dominic, San Antonio
Stokes, Leslie, On Duty Outside the Archdiocese
Suniga, Jose A., Divine Providence, San Antonio
Svatek, Anton, (Retired)
Swift, Thomas N., Resurrection of the Lord, San Antonio
Tamez, Javier, Holy Family, San Antonio
Thayer, Robert, Our Lady of Perpetual Help, Selma
Thornberry, William, Prince of Peace, San Antonio
Tijerina, Salvador, On Leave
Torres, Thomas, St. Leo, San Antonio
Trevino, Jimmie, St. Dominic, San Antonio
Trevino, Jose S., St. Luke-Loire, Pleasanton
Trujillo, Jose M., Mission San Juan Capistrano, San Antonio
Tudon, Horacio R., St. Matthew's, San Antonio
Uriegas, Gonzalo, Sacred Heart, Uvalde
Urrabazo, Rosendo, St. John the Evangelist, San Antonio
Valenzuela, Jose J., (Retired)
Vasquez, Eleodore, San Juan de Los Lagos, San Antonio
Villa, Albert G., St. John the Evangelist, Hondo, TX
Wasniewski, Michael, On Leave
Wehman, Ben, St. Peter and Paul, New Braunfels
Weissler, Gilbert, St. Anthony of Padua, San Antonio
Werner, Keith N., St. Matthew's, San Antonio
White, George, (Retired)
White, Thomas, St. Clair, Holy Redeemer, San Antonio
Wittig, Evan, St. John Evangelist, San Antonio
Wright, Michael, On Duty Outside the Archdiocese
Ybarra, Ray, Our Lady of Perpetual Help, New Braunfels
Zapata, Gumercindo, St. Philip of Jesus, San Antonio
Zapata, Thomas, On Leave
Zavala, Placido, Sacred Heart, Eagle Pass
Zepeda, Ernest, (Retired)
Zizke, William, On Leave

INSTITUTIONS LOCATED IN THE ARCHDIOCESE

[A] SEMINARIES, ARCHDIOCESAN

SAN ANTONIO. *The Assumption-St. John's Seminary*, 2600 W. Woodlawn Ave., P.O. Box 28240, 78228. Tel: 210-734-5137; Fax: 210-734-2324. Legal Title: *The Seminary of the Assumption of the Blessed Virgin Mary-St. John of San Antonio, TX.* Revs. David R. Cruz (LUB), Rector, Admissions & Devel., Admin.; Norman Ermis, Vice Rector & Assoc. Dir. Internship, Admissions, Community Life; Gerald McBrearity, S.S., Dir. Spiritual Formation, Coord. Pre-Theology Program, Liason with O.S.T. Academic Affairs.; Sr. Mary Teresa Cullen, C.S.B., Dir. Pastoral Formation, Coord. Cultural Prog., Coord. Language Prog., Assoc. Dir. Internship Prog.; Sr. Addie Walker, S.S.N.D., Dir. Liturgical Formation, Co-Coord. Cultural Program; Revs. John Kemper, S.S., Dir. Internship Prog., Spiritual Dir. In Residence; Jose A. Lopez, Spiritual Dir. In Res. Priests 5; Sisters 2; Seminarians 39; Domestic Dept.: Josephine Sisters (Mexico City, Mexico) 9.

Diaconate Program, 2600 W. Woodlawn, P.O. Box 28240, 78284-2701. Tel: 210-734-0114. Rev. John O'Donoghue, Dir. Assistant Directors: Deacons John Landez; George White; Joe Fertitta.

[B] SEMINARIES, RELIGIOUS OR SCHOLASTICATES

SAN ANTONIO. *Congregation of Holy Cross - Formation Community*, Bro. Charles Andersen Residence, 320 Brahan Blvd., 78215-1020. Tel: 210-233-9117. Bro. Michael Winslow, C.S.C., Co-Dir.; Rev. Lawrence A. LeVasseur, C.S.C., Co-Dir. Brothers 1; Seminarians 3.

Dominican Priory of Juan Macias, 210 St. Ann St., 78201. Tel: 210-734-6687; Fax: 210-738-1755. E-mail: st-ann@juno.com

Revs. Richard B. Williams, O.P., Prior; Aaron Arce, O.P.; Cayet Mangiaracina, O.P.; Vicente M. Pena, O.P.; Joseph Determan, O.P.; Rafael Proenza, O.P.; John Raymond Corr, O.P.

Franciscan Formation Program in San Jose Friary (Casa Juan Diego), 701 E. Pyron Ave., 78214. Tel: 210-922-4976.

E-mail: casa@aol.com

Revs. Herbert Jones, O.F.M., Dir.; Jesus Aguirre-Garza, O.F.M., Asst. Dir. Seminarians 3.

George Sexton House of Studies. (Theology), 314 E. King's Hwy., 78212. Tel: 210-735-7318.

E-mail: demazenod1@aol.com

Missionary Oblates of Mary Immaculate, United States Region. Revs. Robert E. Wright, O.M.I., Supr.; James Brobst, O.M.I. Scholastics 13.

Immaculate Heart Claretian Seminary, 617 S. Santa Rosa Blvd., 78204. Tel: 210-222-9406; Fax: 210-222-1479. Revs. Lawrence Christian, C.M.F., Formation Dir.; Richard DeTore, C.M.F., Dir. Seminarians 8.

Joseph Gerard House of Studies, 318 Oblate Dr., 78216. Tel: 210-377-3640; 377-0142. Revs. Patrick Guidon, Dir.; Rufus J. Whitley, O.M.I., Assoc. Dir.
Missionhurst Formation Community, 1147-A Cupples Rd., 78226. Tel: 210-434-5347. Rev. William Quigley, C.I.C.M., Dir. Formation. Theology 8.
MSF Formation Community, 104 Cas-Hills Dr., 78213-3322. Tel: 210-344-9145. Rev. Alberto T. Trevino, Jr., M.S.F., Dir. Seminarians 6.
Priests of the Sacred Heart- House of Formation, 133 Thelma Dr., 78212-2517. Tel: 210-826-6091; 6092; Fax: 210-826-8019. Revs. Stephen Huffstetter, S.C.J., Dir. Formation; Nicholas Brown, S.C.J.; Bro. Peter Mankins, S.C.J., Dir. In res. Rev. Ralph Intranuovo, S.C.J. Students 4.
Redemptorist Formation Program, 1523 Iowa, 78203-1817. Tel: 210-533-0442, 0443; Fax: 210-533-0558.
E-mail: 75224.3213@compuserve.com
Rev. Byron Miller, C.Ss.R., Dir., Vice-Prov. of New Orleans. Students 3.
St. Anthony Mary Claret Seminary, 402 John Adams Dr., 78228-4231. Tel: 210-734-2678; Fax: 210-733-8732.
E-mail: sksherwood@aol.com
Web site: www.home.earthlink.net/~cmfftex/
Revs. Stephen K. Sherwood, C.M.F., Dir.; Daryld Olds, C.M.F.; Steven Niskanen, C.M.F., Voc. Dir. Seminarians 4.
San Damiano Friary, 1104 Kentucky Ave., 78201. Tel: 210-734-4962. Conventual Franciscans Friars Minor Conventual. Rev. Miguel Briseno, O.F.M.Conv.; Bro. Timothy Unser, O.F.M.Conv., Guardian of House of Formation. Seminarians 5.

[C] COLLEGES AND UNIVERSITIES

SAN ANTONIO. *Oblate School of Theology*, (1903) 285 Oblate Dr., 78216-6693. Tel: 210-341-1366; Fax: 210-341-4519
For a complete listing, refer to the Colleges and Universities section.
Our Lady of the Lake University, 411 S.W. 24th, 78207-4689. Tel: 210-434-6711; Fax: 210-436-0824.
E-mail: mahos@lake.OLLUSA.edu
For a complete listing, refer to the Colleges and Universities section.
St. Mary's University of San Antonio, Texas, (1852) One Camino Santa Maria, 78228-8572. Tel: 210-436-3011.
E-mail: jmoder@alvin.stmarytx.edu
Web site: www.stmarytx.edu
For a complete listing, refer to the Colleges and Universities section.
The United Colleges of San Antonio, 285 Oblate Dr., 78216
For a complete listing, refer to the Colleges and Universities section.
University of the Incarnate Word, 4301 Broadway, 78209. Tel: 210-829-6000
For a complete listing, refer to the Colleges and Universities section.

[D] HIGH SCHOOLS, ARCHDIOCESAN

SAN ANTONIO. *Antonian College Preparatory High School*. (Coed), 6425 West Ave., 78213. Tel: 210-344-9265. Mr. Gilbert L. Saenz, Prin.; Revs. Francis M. Lanwermeyer, S.J.; Richard Detore, C.M.F. Priests 2; Deacons 1; Lay Teachers 33; Students 525.

[E] HIGH SCHOOLS, REGIONAL

SAN ANTONIO. *St. Gerard Catholic High School*, 521 S. New Braunfels Ave., 78203. Tel: 210-533-8061. Maurice Abadie, Prin. Sisters 1; Lay Teachers 18; Students 215.

[F] HIGH SCHOOLS, PRIVATE

SAN ANTONIO. *Blessed Sacrament Academy*, 1135 Mission Rd., 78210. Tel: 210-532-4731. Sr. M. Odilia Korenek, I.W.B.S., Dir. & Supr.
Second Chance High School, Texas Charter School. Sisters of the Incarnate Word and Blessed Sacrament 2; Lay Teachers 10; Other Sisters 2; Students 180.
Child Development Center. Sisters of the Incarnate Word and Blessed Sacrament 2; Lay Teachers 17; Students 121.
Central Catholic High School, 1403 N. St. Mary's St., 78215-1785. Tel: 210-225-6794.
E-mail: asacscentmhs
Web site: www.cchs.pvt.sa.tx.us.
Rev. Joseph A. Tarrillion, S.M., Pres.; Dr. Paul M. Sullivan, Ed.D., Prin.; Revs. Donald Cowie, S.M.; Joseph G. Rasky, S.M. Priests 3; Brothers 6; Lay Teachers 33; Students 454.
Healy-Murphy Center, Inc., 618 Live Oak St., 78202. Tel: 210-223-2944. Sr. Veronica Cahill, S.H.Sp., Prin. & Exec. Dir. Day School for High School Students. Provides an alternative to the Regular School System. Sisters 5; Lay Teachers 45; Counselors 2; Nurses 1; Students 300; Child Development Department: Six weeks-5 yrs 110; On Campus Clinic: Nurse 1; Doctor 1.
Holy Cross High School, 426 N. San Felipe, 78228. Tel: 210-433-9395.
E-mail: saholycross@worldnet.ATT.net
Web site: www.onr.com/user/holycross/
Brothers of the Holy Cross. Rev. B. Patrick Foley, C.S.C.; Bro. Stanley Culotta, C.S.C., Prin. Priests 1; Brothers 8; Sisters 2; Lay Teachers 21; Students 464.
Incarnate Word High School, 727 E. Hildebrand Ave., 78212-2598. Tel: 210-829-3100; Fax: 210-829-3120. Mr. Roger Labat, Prin. Sisters 10; Brothers 1; Lay Teachers 50; Students 575.
Providence High School, 1215 N. St. Mary's St., 78215-1787. Tel: 210-224-6651; Fax: 210-224-6214. Sr. Ramona Bezner, C.D.P., Prin. Sisters 4; Lay Teachers 34; Students 507.
St. Anthony Catholic High School, 3200 McCullough Ave., 78212-3099. Tel: 210-731-2500; Fax: 210-731-2515. Revs. Patrick Gitzen, O.M.I.; Richard Hall, O.M.I.; Raul Salas, O.M.I.
Boys boarding department. Dr. Gary L. Short, Prin. Priests 3; Sisters 1; Lay Teachers 18; Students 240.
St. Francis Academy, 1807 Centennial Ave., 78211. Tel: 210-923-1421. Sr. Jeanne Marie Ulica, O.S.F., Prin. School Sisters of St. Francis 6; Lay Teachers 14; Students 197.

[G] ELEMENTARY SCHOOLS, PRIVATE

SAN ANTONIO. *Mount Sacred Heart School*. (Grades PreK-8), 619 Mount Sacred Heart Rd., 78216. Tel: 210-342-6711. Coed Montessori. Mrs. Sylvia D. Herrera, Prin.; Rev. James Hubert, C.I.C.M., Chap. Sisters 5; Lay Teachers 30; Students 425.
St. Anthony's School, 205 W. Huisache St., 78212. Tel: 210-732-8801; Fax: 210-732-5968. Robert C. Niehoff, Prin. Lay Teachers 17; Students 250.
St. John Bosco School. (Grades K-8), 5630 W. Commerce St., 78237. Tel: 210-432-8011. Day School. Institute of the Daughters of Mary Help of Christians (Salesian Sisters of St. John Bosco). Sr. Theresa Sironi, F.M.A., Supr.; Mary Anne Oehler, Prin. Sisters 19; Lay Teachers 29; Students 670.
St. Martin Hall, Our Lady of the Lake University of San Antonio, 411 S.W. 24th St., 78207. Tel: 210-434-6711, Ext. 308. Sr. Rita Louise Petsch, C.D.P., Prin. Campus Laboratory School, Preschool Kindergarten and Elementary. Sisters 3; Lay Teachers 19; Students 295.
Westside Catholic Interparish School. (Grades K-8), Mailing Address: P.O. Box 830513, 78283-0513. 314 Merida St., 78207. Tel: 210-224-2450. Mrs. Marianne Mongiollo. Sisters 2; Seminarians 1; Lay Teachers 6; Students 145.

[H] GENERAL HOSPITALS

SAN ANTONIO. *Incarnate Word Health System*, 9311 San Pedro #1250, 78216-4496. Tel: 210-524-4100.
E-mail: iwhs@iwhs.org
Web site: www.incarnatewordhealth.org
For a complete listing, refer to the Hospitals section.
Santa Rosa Children's Hospital, 519 W. Houston St., 78207-3198. Tel: 210-704-2011
For a complete listing, refer to the Hospitals section.
Santa Rosa Health Care System, 519 W. Houston St., 78207-3198. Tel: 210-704-2011.
Web site: www.santarosahealth.org
For a complete listing, refer to the Hospitals section.
Santa Rosa Hospital, 519 W. Houston St., 78207-3198. Tel: 210-704-2011
For a complete listing, refer to the Hospitals section.
Santa Rosa Northwest Hospital, 2827 Babcock Rd., 78229. Tel: 210-705-6300
For a complete listing, refer to the Hospitals section.
Santa Rosa Skilled Nursing Facility, 519 W. Houston St., 78207-3198. Tel: 210-704-2011
For a complete listing, refer to the Hospitals section.

[I] PROTECTIVE INSTITUTIONS

SAN ANTONIO. *Father Flanagan's Boys' Town of San Antonio*, 503 Urban Loop, 78204. Tel: 210-271-1010
For a complete listing, refer to the Special Care Facilities section.
Providence Home & Family Services, Inc., 2650 Castroville Rd., 78237. Tel: 210-434-2111; Fax: 210-433-2806
For a complete listing, refer to the Special Care Facilities section.
St. Peter & Joseph Childrens Home, 919 Mission Rd., 78210. Tel: 210-533-1203
For a complete listing, refer to the Special Care Facilities section.
Seton Home for Homeless, Pregnant Young Women, 1115 Mission Rd., 78210. Tel: 210-533-3504
For a complete listing, refer to the Special Care Facilities section.
Visitation Hospitality House of San Antonio, Texas and La Posada Transitional Housing, 945 W. Huisache, 78201. Tel: 210-735-6910
For a complete listing, refer to the Special Care Facilities section.
BOERNE. *Childrens' Inn*, 216 W. Highland, 78006. Tel: 830-249-9456
For a complete listing, refer to the Special Care Facilities section.

[J] DAY CARE CENTERS AND KINDERGARTENS

SAN ANTONIO. *Blessed Sacrament Learning Center*, 222 W. Cevallos St., 78204. Tel: 210-223-5013. Sisters of Mercy of the Blessed Sacrament. Sr. Rita Pinedo, H.M.S.S., Dir. Sisters 4; Children 40.
Carmelite Learning Center, 2006 Martin Luther King Dr., 78203. Tel: 210-533-0651. Sr. Fatima Cardoza, Carmel,D.C.J., Dir. Carmelite Sisters of the Divine Heart of Jesus 4; Lay Staff 15; In Day Care 120. Attended from St. Patrick's Church.
Immaculate Conception Kindergarten and Nursery, 2407 W. Travis St., 78207. Tel: 210-226-3934. Sr. Maria Del Carmen Sanchez, A.P.G., Dir. Sisters 4; Lay Staff 17; Kindergarten & Nursery Children 95.
St. Anthony Day Care Learning Center; Infant and Toddler Center, 1707 Centennial Blvd., 78211. Tel: 210-924-4443. Sr. Mary Ann Domagalski, M.S.S.A., Admin.; Sr. Lucelia Sanchez, M.S.S.A., Dir. Sisters 2; Lay Staff 23; Children 135.
St. Brigid's Kindergarten, 5118 Loma Linda Dr., 78201. Tel: 210-733-0037. Sr. Stephenie Deegan, C.S.B., Dir. Children 30.
BOERNE. *St. Albert Hall dba St. Albert Early Learning Center*, 216 W. Highland Dr., 78006. Tel: 210-816-2059; 2060; Fax: 210-816-2060. Sr. Sylvia Ahr, O.S.B., Exec. Dir. Children 252; Staff 45.

[K] HOMES FOR AGED

SAN ANTONIO. *Casa De Padres*, 8520 Cross Mountain Tr., 78255
For a complete listing, refer to the Special Care Facilities section.
Incarnate Word Motherhouse and Retirement Center, 4707 Broadway, 78209. Tel: 210-829-7561
For a complete listing, refer to the Special Care Facilities section.
Marianist Residence: Skilled Nursing, 520 Fordham Ln., 78228-4821. Tel: 210-436-3771 (Nurses' Station)
For a complete listing, refer to the Special Care Facilities section.
Oblate Madonna Residence, 5722 Blanco Rd., 78216. Tel: 210-341-2350
For a complete listing, refer to the Special Care Facilities section.
Padua Place, 80 Peter Baque Rd., 78209. Tel: 210-826-7721
For a complete listing, refer to the Special Care Facilities section.
St. Francis Nursing Home, 630 W. Woodlawn, 78212. Tel: 210-736-3177; Fax: 210-783-2221
For a complete listing, refer to the Special Care Facilities section.
The South Texas Catholic Retirement Center, Inc., P.O. Box 6290, 78209-0290. Tel: 210-829-7561; Fax: 210-826-6280
For a complete listing, refer to the Special Care Facilities section.
KENEDY. *John Paul II Nursing Home*, 209 S. 3rd St., P.O. Box 359, 78119. Tel: 830-583-9841
For a complete listing, refer to the Special Care Facilities section.

[L] BOARDING HOMES

SAN ANTONIO. *Seraphic Sisters Boarding Home for the Aged*, 619 W. Craig Pl., 78212. Tel: 210-736-3177. Sr. Elizabeth Dubicka, S.O.L.S., Dir. Guests 8.

[M] MONASTERIES AND RESIDENCES OF PRIESTS AND BROTHERS

SAN ANTONIO. *Casa Maria Marianist Community*, St. Mary's University, One Camino Santa Maria, 78228-8518. Tel: 210-436-3066. Revs. Chris Janson, S.M. Tel: 210-436-3273; J. Willis Langlinais, S.M. Tel: 210-436-3705; Bros. Joseph Barrett, S.M. Tel: 210-436-3228; Roger Bau, S.M. Tel: 210-431-2269; Terrence O'Connor, S.M. Tel: 210-436-3231; Fred A. Stoval, S.M., Dir. Tel: 210-436-3242; Michael Sullivan, S.M. Tel: 210-436-3258.
Casa Pasionista Guadalupe, 700 Waverly, 78201. Tel: 210-736-5228; Fax: 210-737-6549. Revs. G. Alexander Steinmiller, C.P.; Robert Bovenzi, C.P.; Clemente Barron, C.P.
Casa San Juan Marianist Community, 2107 Davy Crockett, 78238. Tel: 210-521-5507. Revs. George T. Montague, S.M., Dir.; Robert E. Hogan, S.M. Aspirants 2.
Central Catholic Marianist Community, 1403 N. St. Mary's St., 78215-1785. Tel: 210-225-1112. Revs. Donald Cowie, S.M., Dir.; Joseph G. Rasky, S.M. Sacred Heart of Jesus Brothers 1; Brothers 9.
Chaminade Community House, 10910 Wild Grape, 78230-3459. Tel: 210-641-6354. Marianists. Revs. Conrad J. Kaczkowski, S.M., Supr.; Joseph A. Tarrillion, S.M.; Charles H. Miller, S.M.

De Mazenod House. (Faculty Residence), 7707 Madonna Dr., 78216. Tel: 210-349-8572. Missionary Oblates of Mary Immaculate. Revs. Ken Hannon, O.M.I., Supr.; Warren Brown, O.M.I.; Vaughn Fayle, O.M.I.; Jan Heemrood, O.M.I.; William Morrell, O.M.I.; Fredrick Sackett. Priests 7.

Discalced Carmelites (Prov. of St. Therese), 906 Kentucky Ave., 78201-6097. Tel: 210-735-9126. Revs. Ralph Reyes, O.C.D., Supr.; John Magdalene Suenram, O.C.D.; Louis Scagnelli, O.C.D.; Michael Okuroski, O.C.D.; James Anthony Curiel, O.C.D.; Christopher Timoney, O.C.D.; Bros. Bernard O'Neil, O.C.D.; Patrick Byrd, O.C.D. Priests 6; Brothers 2.

Harcar House, 6111 Walking Gait, 78240. Tel: 210-680-3685.

Hospital Ministry: Revs. George F. Healy, C.S.Sp.; Nicholas Brown, S.C.J.

Holy Cross Community, 426 N. San Felipe St., 78228. Tel: 210-434-9100. Bro. Stanley Culotta, C.S.C., Dir.; Rev. Patrick Foley, C.S.C. Priests 1; Brothers 6.

Brothers of the Holy Cross, 800 Babcock Rd., Apt. G-1, 78201. Tel: 210-734-8602. Bro. Terrence Muehlenkamp, C.S.C.

Bro. Charles Andersen Residence, 320 Brahan Blvd., 78215. Tel: 210-223-9117. Rev. Lawrence A. LeVasseur, C.S.C., Dir.; Bro. Michael Winslow, C.S.C., Co-Dir. Priests 1; Brothers 3; Seminarians 3.

Holy Cross Fathers, 5714 Prentiss Dr., 78204. Tel: 210-684-6818. Rev. Thomas E. Hewitt, C.S.C.

Villas of Castle Hills, 1000 Jackson-Keller Rd., #604, 78213. Tel: 210-377-3997. Bro. David Fitzgerald, C.S.C.

Holy Cross Brothers, 1000 Jackson-Keller Rd., #1101, 78213. Bro. Edward Libber, C.S.C. Tel: 210-340-7024.

Holy Cross Brothers, 181 W. Hermine, 78212. Bro. Joseph Esparza, C.S.C. Tel: 210-828-9545.

Holy Cross Brothers, 3601 Magic Dr., #1202, 78229-5456. Tel: 210-525-9423. Bro. Peter Mullett, C.S.C.

Holy Cross Brothers, 2519 Broadway, 78215. Bro. William Dooling, C.S.C.

Sacred Heart School, 1007 Trail St., Floresville, 78114. Bro. Joseph Ballard, C.S.C. Tel: 830-393-2117.

Holy Rosary Marianist Community, 159 Camino Santa Maria, 78228-4997. Tel: 210-433-6137; Fax: 210-433-2133. Rev. John J. Manahan, S.M.; Bros. James Droste, S.M., Dir.; James Facette, S.M.; Robert Hatesol, S.M.; James McCaffery, S.M.

LaRisa Apartments Marianist Community, 800 Babcock Rd., #252, 78201. Tel: 210-735-5952.
E-mail: socmat@stmarytx.edu
Brothers 2.

Marianist Residence, St. Mary's University, 520 Fordham Ave., 78228-4821. Tel: 210-436-3744; Fax: 210-436-3747. Bro. Joseph Greishaber, S.M., Dir. Tel: 210-436-3745; Revs. John A. Leies, S.M. Tel: 210-436-3227; Bernard Meyer, S.M. Tel: 210-436-3761; John Rechtien, S.M. Tel: 210-431-2092; Paul Ryan, S.M. Tel: 210-436-3766; W. Franz Schorp, S.M. Tel: 210-431-2259. Priests 5; Brothers 15.

Marianist Vocation Ministry, One Camino Santa Maria, 78228-8556. Tel: 210-431-2193; Fax: 210-436-3724.
E-mail: mumikevax@stmarytx.edu
Bro. Michael Sullivan, S.M., Dir.

Marianist Woodlawn Community, 3303 W. Woodlawn Ave., 78228. Tel: 210-436-0182. Bro. Paul Metzger, S.M., Dir.; Revs. Rudy Vela, S.M.; John Moder, S.M.; Norbert Brockman, S.M.; William J. Meyer, S.M. Priests 4; Brothers 6.

Missionaries of the Sacred Heart. Sectional Headquarters of the Irish Province for California and Southern States. 237 W. Magnolia, 78212-2916. Tel: 210-737-6394; Fax: 210-737-0327. Revs. Christopher Coleman, M.S.C., Supr.; Patrick O'Shea, M.S.C.; Augustine Kim, M.S.C.; Stephen White, M.S.C.; Mark Coffey, M.S.C., P.O. Box 250, Spring Branch Rd., 78070. Tel: 210-885-4853. Sunray Apartments, 7600 Blanco Rd., #508, 78216. Tel: 210-308-8235. Rev. John Finn, M.S.C.

Miscellaneous: Rev. Patrick Stenson, M.S.C., Religious Activities Office, 3700 N. Capitol St. N.W., Washington, DC, 20317. Tel: 202-882-1888. Rev. L. Aidan O'Donovan, M.S.C., 907 Colony Ridge, Irving, 75061. Tel: 972-590-8512; Fax: 972-986-1322.

Missionhurst Community Residence, 1746 Donaldson, 78228. Tel: 210-432-1384; 435-4210. Revs. David Curran, C.I.C.M.; Pieter Van Der Paalen, C.I.C.M. Other Addresses: 6534 Kings Crown, 78233. Tel: 210-653-0832. Revs. Francis Van Hee, C.I.C.M.; James Meuree, C.I.C.M., 7600 Blanco Rd., Apt. 1605, 78216. Tel: 210-344-3813. Rev. Ralph Nuyten, C.I.C.M.

MSF Center & Provincialate, 210 El Rancho Way, 78209. Tel: 210-826-9815. Congregation of the Missionaries of the Holy Family. Very Revs. Robert E. O'Hara, M.S.F., Prov.; John Dowling, M.S.F., Prov. Treas. In res. Rev. Gary Perret, M.S.F.

Oblate Benson Residence (Southern Prov.), 334 W. Kings Hwy., 78212. Tel: 210-732-5162. Missionary Oblates of Mary Immaculate. Very Rev. Salvatore DeGeorge, O.M.I., Vicar Prov.; Revs. Gerard Weber, O.M.I. Tel: 210-732-8024; Edward Murray, O.M.I.; William O'Conner, O.M.I. Tel: 210-733-7833; Charles Borgers, O.M.I. Tel: 210-731-9894.

Provincial Administration Office, Oblates of Mary Immaculate (Southern Prov.), 7711 Madonna Dr., 78216-6696. Tel: 210-349-1475; Fax: 210-349-7411.
E-mail: provinc@connecti.com
Very Rev. Charles Banks, O.M.I., Prov.; Revs. Salvatore F. DeGeorge, O.M.I., Vicar Prov.; Rufus Whitley, O.M.I., Prov. Treas.

Chaplains Not Listed Elsewhere: Rev. Donald McNally, O.M.I., Chap., Texas Department of Corrections, Jester III Unit, Rte. 2, Richmond, 77469. Tel: 713-277-7000. Rev. Donald Burnet, O.M.I., PSC Box 1289, Scott A.FB, IL, 62225. Tel: 916-643-6021. Rev. Clifford Blackburn, O.M.I., Santa Rosa Hospital, 519 W. Houston St., 78207. Rev. Edward Murray, O.M.I., Audie Murphy VA Hospital, 7400 Merton Minter, 78229. Tel: 210-617-5300. Baptist Memorial Hospital, 111 Dallas St., 78205. Tel: 210-222-8431.

Redemptorists of Texas- San Antonio #1, 1617 Iowa St., 78203. Tel: 201-534-4351. (Vice Province of New Orleans). Revs. Thomas Picton, C.SS.R., Supr.; John Cody, C.SS.R.; Jose Chavez, C.SS.R.; Mark Sheffler, C.SS.R.; Leonard Broniak, C.SS.R., Deaf Ministry Team.

St. Anthony Catholic High School House, 3200 McCullough Ave., 78212. Tel: 210-731-8724. Revs. Raul Salas, O.M.I.; Patrick Gitzen, O.M.I.; Richard Hall, O.M.I.; Leo Perez, O.M.I.

San Damiano Friary, 1104 Kentucky Ave., 78201. Tel: 210-734-4962. Friars Minor Conventual. Conventual Franciscans. Revs. Miguel Briseno, O.F.M.Conv.; Mark Tegmeyer, O.F.M.Conv.; Bro. Tim Unser, O.F.M.Conv.

[N] CONVENTS AND RESIDENCES FOR SISTERS

SAN ANTONIO. *Bernadine Franciscan Sisters,* 445 Burr Rd., 78209. Tel: 210-805-8698. Sisters 2. 500 N. Santa Rosa Blvd., 78207. Tel: 210-271-3091. Sisters 1. 1234 E. Mullberry, #219, 78209. Tel: 210-828-9409. Sr. Therese San Miguel, O.S.F., Coord.

Blessed Sacrament Convent, 222 W. Cevallos St., 78204. Tel: 210-223-5013. Sisters of Mercy of the Blessed Sacrament. Sr. Guadalupe Barcena, H.M.S.S., Supr. Sisters 12.

Blessed Sacrament Convent, 118 Melba, 78216. Tel: 210-828-0155. Sisters of the Incarnate Word and Blessed Sacrament. Sr. Mary Eileen Gurecky, Supr. Sisters 3.

Carmelite Convent, 2006 Martin Luther King Dr., 78203. Tel: 210-533-0651. Carmelite Sisters of the Divine Heart of Jesus. Sr. Maria Fatima, Carmel, D.C.J., Supr. Sisters 4.

Cordi-Marian Missionary Sisters, Cordi-Marian Villa, 11624 FM 471, 78253. Tel: 210-688-3099; 688-3889. Convent, Provincial House and Retreat Center. Sr. Catalina Marquez, M.C.M., Prov. Supr.; Sr. Celina Martin, M.C.M., Supr. Sisters 12.

Cordi-Marian Missionary Sisters Convent and Formation House, 2902 Morales St., 78207. Tel: 210-433-5064. Sr. Mary Elia Jaime, M.C.M., Supr. Sisters 3.

Daughters of Charity Convent, 7603 Somerset Rd., 78211. Tel: 210-927-2795; Fax: 210-922-0332. Daughters of Charity of St. Vincent de Paul. Sr. Patricia Connolly, D.C., Supr. Sisters 5.

The Daughters of St. Paul Convent. (Pontifical F.S.P.), 114 Main Plaza, 78205. Tel: 210-224-8101. Sr. Susan Miriam Wolf, F.S.P., Supr. Sisters 4.

El Carmen Sister's Residence, 1835-1 Martinez-Losoya, 78221. Tel: 210-626-2024. Daughters of Charity of St. Vincent de Paul. Sr. Aileen Marek, D.C., Supr. Sisters 4.

Eucharistic Franciscan Missionary Sisters, 558 Cumberland, 78204. Tel: 210-224-7993. Sr. Flora Ramirez, M.E.F., Supr. Sisters 4.

Felician Sisters, 3910 Meadow Ridge, 78210. Tel: 210-532-3433. Sr. Dorothy Moczygemba, C.S.S.F., Supr. Sisters 3.

Other Residences:
5518 King Richard Dr., 78229. Tel: 210-520-9767. Sr. Lucy Korzekwa, C.S.S.F., Supr. Sisters 4.
Cestohowa Rte. 1, Box 19, Falls City, 78113-9502. Tel: 830-745-2632. Sisters 2.
510B S. Austin St., Seguin, 78155. Tel: 830-379-1239. Sisters 2.

Franciscan Sisters of Little Falls, MN, 6900 No. Vandiver, Apt. D201, 78209. Tel: 210-822-1074. Sr. Mary Dumonceaux, O.S.F.

Hermanas Catequistas Guadalupanas Convent, 4110 S. Flores St., 78214. Tel: 210-532-9344. Sr. Laura Sanchez, H.C.G., Supr. Sisters 6. 115 Arlington Ct., 78210. Tel: 210-533-2968. Sr. Sofia Arredondo, H.C.G., Supr. Sisters 4.

Holy Rosary Convent, 543 Westminister, 78228. Tel: 210-433-1108. Sr. Joyce des Jardins, S.S.N.D., Correspondent. Sisters 4.

Holy Spirit Motherhouse, 301 Yucca St., 78203. Tel: 210-533-5149. Motherhouse of the Sisters of the Holy Spirit and Mary Immaculate. Sr. Anne Finnerty, S.H.Sp., Gen. Supr. Sisters 57.

Incarnate Word and Blessed Sacrament Convent, 1135 Mission Rd., 78210. Tel: 210-534-8005. Sisters of the Incarnate Word and Blessed Sacrament. Sr. M. Odilia Korenek, Supr. Sisters 8.

Incarnate Word Generalate (1869), 4503 Broadway, 78209-6297. Tel: 210-828-2224; Fax: 210-828-9741. General Administration of the Congregation of Sisters of Charity of the Incarnate Word. Sr. Teresa Stanley, C.C.V.I., Supr. Gen. Total in Congregation 533; Total in U.S. Province 316.

Incarnate Word Motherhouse and Retirement Community, U.S. Provincilate, 4707 Broadway, 78209-6200. Tel: 210-820-0987, (Motherhouse); 829-7561 (Retirement Community); Fax: 210-830-3743. Sr. Kathleen Coughlin, C.C.U.I., Prov. Supr. Sisters in Extended Care 40; Sisters Independent Living 91; Lay Independent Living 77.

Institute of the Daughters of Mary Help of Christians, Province of Mary Immaculate, 6019 Buena Vista St., 78237. Tel: 210-432-0089; 0090; Fax: 210-432-4016. Salesian Sisters of St. John Bosco. Sr. Martina Ponce, F.M.A., Prov. Supr.

Missionary Catechists of Divine Providence, St. Andrew's Convent, 2318 Castroville Rd., 78237. Tel: 210-432-0113. Casa Benitia, 4650 Eldridge Ave., 78237. Tel: 210-433-5259. Sisters 3. Catholic Student Center, 312 Courtland St., 78212. Tel: 210-736-3752. Casa Providencia, 203 Tansyl Dr., 78213. Tel: 210-348-6534. Sisters 3. St. Mary's Catholic School, 207 N. St. Mary's St., 78205. Tel: 210-223-1151. House of Studies of the Missionary Catechists of Divine Providence & House of Administration. Sr. Carmen Therese Lazo, M.C.D.P., Supr. Gen., House of Initial Formation. Tel: 210-435-4626. Students 3. Sisters 9.

Monastery of the Discalced Carmelite Nuns, 6301 Culebra & St. Joseph Way, 78238-4909. Tel: 210-680-1834.
E-mail: saocdnun@dcci.com
Rev. Mother Therese Leonard, O.C.D., Prioress. Sisters 10.

Mount Sacred Heart Convent, 5922 Blanco Rd., 78216. Tel: 210-344-4805; 344-4193. Provincial House of Sisters of the Sacred Heart of Jesus. Sr. Laura Gonzalez, S.S.C.J., Prov. Sisters 39.

North American Union, Sisters of Our Lady of Charity, 1900 Montana, P.O. Box 10443, 78210. Tel: 210-534-1231. Sr. Deana Kohlman, O.L.C., Supr. Sisters 8.

Our Lady of Czestochowa, Grotto Shrine and Convent, 138 Beethoven St., 78210. Tel: 210-333-4582; 337-8193 (Convent). Seraphic Sisters of Our Lady of Sorrows. Sr. Helen Haladyna, S.O.L.S., Supr.; Rev. Bernard M. Goebel, Chap. Sisters 4.

Our Lady of the Lake Convent, 515 S.W. 24th St., 78207. Tel: 210-434-1866; Fax: 210-431-9965. Sisters of Divine Providence. Sr. Eugenia Ann Stell, C.D.P., Coord. Professed Sisters 48. O.L.L. Convent Home for retired Sisters of Divine Providence. Coordinators: Sr. Madonna Sangalli, C.D.P.; Sr. Anna-Lee Prather, C.D.P., McCullough Hall Nursing Center and Regan Hall, 603 S.W. 24th St., 78207. Tel: 210-433-6011. Home for retired Sisters of Divine Providence. Sisters 82.

Our Lady of the Pillar Convent, 251 W. Ligustrum Dr., 78228. Tel: 210-433-5501.
E-mail: eescobar@st.marytx.edu
Centralhouse of the Congregation of the Daughters of Mary Immaculate. Marianist Sisters. Sr. Evangeline Escobar, F.M.I., Prov.; Sr. La Von Kampf, F.M.I., Dir. of Sisters. Sisters 7.

Our Lady of Victory Missionary Sisters Convent, 1114 San Carlos, 78207-6727. Tel: 210-223-5005. Sisters 2.

Presentation Convent, 8931 Callaghan Rd., 78230-4570. Tel: 210-342-2503. Residence of the Community of the Union of the Sisters of the Presentation of the B.V.M. Sr. Mary F. O'Driscoll, P.B.V.M., Supr. Sisters 17.

Religious of Mary Immaculate Convent, 719 Augusta St., 78215. Tel: 210-226-0025; Fax: 210-226-3305. Religious of Mary Immaculate Sisters. Sr. Clara Echeverria, R.M.I., Local Supr. Sisters 12.

St. Anthony Convent, 100 Peter Baque Rd., 78209. Tel: 210-824-4553. Motherhouse and Novitiate of the Missionary Servants of St. Anthony. Sr. Mary Ann Domagalski, M.S.S.A., Supr. Sisters 5.

St. Brigid's Convent, 5118 Loma Linda Dr., 78201. Tel: 210-733-0701; 736-1671; Fax: 210-733-3145; 737-3683. Regional House. Sr. Teresa Carter, C.S.B., Regional Coord.

Address matters connected with congregation to the Regional Coord. Sisters 18.

St. James Convent, 402 Nunes, 78225. Tel: 210-533-9659. Daughters of Mary Help of Christians (Salesian Sisters of St. John Bosco). Sr. Josephine Ochoa, F.M.A., Supr. Sisters 4.

St. John Bosco Convent, 5630 W. Commerce St., 78237. Tel: 210-432-8011; Fax: 210-434-8559. Daughters of Mary Help of Christians. Sr. Theresa Sirioni, F.M.A., Supr. Sisters 18.

St. Joseph's Convent - S.S.N.D. House of Formation, 2372 W. Southcross, 78211-1898. Tel: 210-923-2364. Sr. Judy Schaefer, S.S.N.D., Coord. Sisters 3.

St. Teresa's Convent, 138 Fair Ave., 78223-1014. Tel: 210-533-5330; Fax: 210-533-2532. Sr. Carmelina Guzman, S.T.J., Coord. Society of St. Teresa of Jesus 19.

School Sisters of Notre Dame, 155 N. Josephine Tobin Dr., 78201. Tel: 210-737-3104; Fax: 210-737-2279. Sr. Carol George, S.S.N.D., Coord. Sisters 3.

School Sisters of Notre Dame, Convents: Caroline House, 3415 W. Woodlawn, 78228. Tel: 210-435-3234. Sr. M. Emiliana Fecher, S.S.N.D., Correspondent. Sisters 4.

Seraphic Franciscan Sisters of Our Lady of Sorrows Convent. (Grotto Shrine of Our Lady of Czestochowa), 138 Beethoven St., 78210. Tel: 210-337-8193. Sr. Helen Haladyna, O.L.S., Dir. Seraphic Sisters of Our Lady of Sorrows 4.

Seraphic Sisters of Our Lady of Sorrows Convent, 621 W. Woodlawn Ave., 78212. Tel: 210-734-3364. Sr. Emilia Rzeznik, Supr. Sisters 6.

The Sisters of Perpetual Adoration Convent, 2403 W. Travis St., 78207. Tel: 210-227-5546. Sr. Maria Conception Quesada-Aguirre, A.P.G., Supr. Sisters 7.

The Sisters of the Holy Cross, 404 Faith, 78228. Tel: 210-433-6408. Sisters 3.

Sisters, Servants of the Immaculate Heart of Mary, 5440 Babcock, #10, 78240. Tel: 210-641-7400. Sr. Virginia Celmer, I.H.M., Ph.D., L.C.D.C.

Stella Maris Convent, 2702 Castroville Rd., 78237. Tel: 210-434-1314. Congregation of Divine Providence, Inc. Sisters 4.

Ursuline Residences, 4812 Vance Jackson Rd., 78230. Tel: 210-344-1800. Ursuline Nuns.
Other Residences Located At: 3500 Oakgate, 78230. Tel: 210-694-5054. 1207 Olive, Jourdanton, 78026. Tel: 830-769-2015. Sisters 7.

BIG WELLS. *Carmelitas del Sagrado Corazon-OCD*, P.O. Box 266, 78830. Tel: 830-457-2693. Sr. Maria Guadalupe Esparza, O.C.D., Supr. Sisters 3.

BOERNE. *St. Scholastica Monastery*, 416 W. Highland, 78006. Tel: 830-249-2645; 210-816-8504. Congregation of Benedictine Sisters, Monastery, Novitiate and Omega Retreat Center. Sr. Mary Agnes Zinni, O.S.B., Prioress. Sisters 23.

HELOTES. *Generalate of the Congregation of Divine Providence*, P.O. Box 197, 78023. Tel: 210-695-8721. Sr. Lora Ann Quinonez, C.D.P., Supr. Gen. Sisters 6.

UVALDE. *Society of St. Teresa of Jesus*. (Teresian Sisters), Mailing Address: 343 N. Crisp St., 78801. Tel: 210-278-6724. Sisters 3.

[O] RETREAT HOUSES

SAN ANTONIO. *Oblate Renewal Center*, Mailing Address: 5700 Blanco Rd., 78216-6615. Tel: 210-349-4173; Fax: 210-349-4821. Revs. Kevin Collins, O.M.I.; John Joyce, O.M.I., Assoc. Dir.; Sr. Theresa O'Toole, S.H.Sp.; Ms. Shirley Russell, Hospitality Dir.

BOERNE. *Omega Retreat Center*, 216 W. Highland Dr., 78006. Tel: 830-816-8471 (San Antonio); 249-3894 (Boerne). Mr. Andrew Anderson, Dir.

CASTROVILLE. *Moye Center*, 600 London, 78009. Tel: 830-931-2227. Center for Retreats and Renewal. Under the direction of the Sisters of Divine Providence. Sisters 3.

NEW BRAUNFELS. *Spiritan Renewal Center*, 19440 IH 35 N., 78132-4839. Tel: 830-609-1200.
E-mail: jgaglione@aol.com
Rev. Joseph Gaglione, C.S.Sp., Dir.

[P] CATHOLIC CHARITABLE ORGANIZATIONS AND CLINICS

SAN ANTONIO. *Catholic Charities, Archdiocese of San Antonio*, Main Office, 2903 W. Salinas St., 78207. Tel: 210-433-3256; Fax: 210-433-0851. Valerie J. Trevino, Exec. Dir., North Side Office, 811 E. Mistletoe, 78212. Tel: 210-734-5054; Fax: 210-734-5346. Adolescent Pregnancy Prog., Adoption, Counseling. West Side Office, 2300 W. Commerce, Ste. 200, 78207. Tel: 210-475-9011; Fax: 210-475-0436. Location of Dir. Devel. and Dir. Professional Svcs. See Curia Section - Department of Social & Community Services.

Daughters of Charity Services of San Antonio, 7607 Somerset Rd., 78211-3752. Tel: 210-921-0071; Fax: 210-922-0332. Mr. Donald Moore, Exec. Dir. Daughters of Charity Svcs.
This corporation operates centers at two locations: De Paul Family Center, 7603 Somerset, 78211. Tel: 210-924-5903. El Carmen Center, 18555-1 Leal Rd., 78221. Tel: 210-626-2121. Sisters 4.

Society of St. Vincent de Paul, 928 W. Commerce, 78207. Tel: 210-225-7837; Fax: 210-225-8878. Ms. Nell Sharrock, Pres.; Mary M. Armstrong, Exec. Dir.

[Q] NEWMAN CENTERS

SAN ANTONIO. *Catholic Campus Ministry*, Catholic Student Center, 312 W. Courtland Pl., 78212-3906. Tel: 210-736-3752. Sr. Gloria Urrabazo, M.C.D.P., Dir. Archdiocesan Campus Ministry: Bob Gonzales, San Antonio College; Sr. Imelda Phelan, C.S.B., Palo Alto College & UTSA Downtown Campus; Carol F. White, St. Phillip's College; Rev. Thomas Ovalle, O.M.I., Trinity University; Sr. M. Carmen Salas, M.H.S.H., Palo Alto College and Southwest Texas Junior College,Uvalde.; Mario Macias, University of Texas at San Antonio.
St. Anthony Catholic Student Center, 14523 Roadrunner Way, 78249. Tel: 210-699-9594. Mrs. Beatriz M. Garcia.
Southwest Texas Junior College, 2401 Garner Field Rd., Uvalde, 78801-6297. Tel: 210-278-4401.
Texas Lutheran College, 1000 W. Court St., Seguin, 78155-5999. Tel: 210-372-8000.
Schreiner College, 2100 Memorial Blvd., Kerrville, 78028-5697. Tel: 210-896-5411.
Both Texas Lutheran and Schreiner Colleges are served by Sr. Gloria Urrabazo, M.C.D.P.

[R] PERSONAL PRELATURES

SAN ANTONIO. *Opus Dei (Prelature of the Holy Cross and Opus Dei)*, 345 E. Summit, 78212. Tel: 210-732-3065.
E-mail: info@opusdei.org
Web site: www.opusdei.org
Rev. Jose Gomez.

[S] FOUNDATIONS, ENDOWMENTS AND TRUSTS

SAN ANTONIO. *The Archbishop Charity Fund*, P.O. Box 28410, 78228. Tel: 210-734-2620.

Archbishop Flores Charity Fund, P.O. Box 28410, 78228. Tel: 210-734-2620.

Archdiocesan Endowment Fund, P.O. Box 28410, 78228-0410. Tel: 210-734-2620. Most Rev. Patrick Flores.

Assumption Seminary Endowment Fund, P.O. Box 28410, 78228-0410. Tel: 210-734-2620. Most Rev. Patrick Flores.

Casa de Padres Endowment Fund, P.O. Box 28410, 78228-0410. Tel: 210-734-2620. Most Rev. Patrick Flores.

Holy Spirit Sisters' Trust, 301 Yucca St., 78203. Tel: 210-533-8142. Sisters of the Holy Spirit. Sr. Anne Finnerty, Pres.

Missionary Oblates of Mary Immaculate of Texas Continuing Care Foundation, 7711 Madonna Dr., 78216-6696. Tel: 210-349-1475. Rev. Rufus Whitley, O.M.I., Treas.

National Foundation for Mexican-American Vocations, P.O. Box 7367, 78207-0367. Tel: 210-227-0548. A nonprofit organization to help financially Mexican American Seminarians. Rev. Msgr. Balthasar J. Janacek, Chm.

St. Peter and Joseph Childrens' Home Endowment Fund, P.O. Box 28410, 78228-0410. Tel: 210-734-2620. Most Rev. Patrick Flores.

Seton Home Endowment Fund, P.O. Box 28410, 78228-0410. Tel: 210-734-2620. Most Rev. Patrick Flores.

HELOTES. *Providence Trust*, P.O. Box 197, 78023. Tel: 210-695-8721.
Congregation of Divine Providence, Inc. Charitable Trust. Trustees: Sr. Imelda Gonzalez, C.D.P.; Sr. John Martin Ebrom, C.D.P.; Sr. Madonna Sangalli, C.D.P.

[T] MISCELLANEOUS

SAN ANTONIO. *"Today's Catholic"*, Mailing Address: P.O. Box 28410, 78228-0410. 2718 W. Woodlawn Ave., 78228. Tel: 210-734-2620; Fax: 210-734-2939. Official Catholic newspaper of the Archdiocese of San Antonio. Owned and operated by the San Antonio Archdiocesan Publishing Society. Most Rev. Patrick F. Flores, Publisher; Mrs. Martha Pack Brinkmann, Editor.

Archdiocesan Union of Holy Name Societies, 2610 Perez St., 78207. Tel: 210-433-6301. Rev. Richard Pena, Spiritual Dir.

Benedictine Resource Center, 530 Bandera Rd., 78228-5525. Tel: 210-735-4988; Fax: 210-735-2615. Sr. Mary Agnes Zinni, O.S.B., Pres.; Arturo Chavez, CEO.

Benitia Family Center, 4650 Eldridge Ave., 78237-2600. Tel: 210-433-9300; 432-0113; Fax: 210-432-6739. Sr. Carmen M. Sanchez, M.C.D.P., Dir. Sisters 3.

The Blue Army, 6680 Crestway, 78239. Tel: 210-654-1643. Rev. Robert Silverman, Archdiocesan Chap.

Catholic Eastside Apostolate. Healy-Murphy Center Inc. See High Schools, Private. 618 Live Oak, 78202. Tel: 210-223-2944.

Daughters of Mary Help Development Office, 6019 Buena Vista St., 78237-1700. Tel: 210-432-0089; Fax: 210-432-4016.
E-mail: fmasuopt@aol.com
Sr. Gloria Mar, F.M.A., Dir. Coordinates Volunteers internationally dedicated to the education and promotion of socially at risk Youth and Women. (VIDES-YW) A Christian service organization in collaboration with the Daughters of Mary Help (F.M.A.).

Directors: Sr. Kathleen Kean, S.S.J.; Marilyn Haider. Provide foster care for children with special needs in a holistic setting.

Federation of Catholic Parent Teacher Clubs of the Archdiocese of San Antonio, 506 Burcham, 78221. Tel: 210-923-7615. Blanche Vera, Pres.

Focolare Movement, Mailing Address: P.O. Box 15726, 78212; Fax: 210-341-2535. (Work of Mary) (Men and Women), Founded in Trent, Italy, in 1943. International Headquarters is in Rome. Women's Branch, Texas, 10714 Mt. Tipton, 78213. Tel: 210-341-8445. Marigen Lohla, Men's Branch, Texas, 9315 Overton Rd., 78217. Tel: 210-590-8812; Fax: 210-590-8921. Mr. Joe Ting.

Hispanic Telecommunications Network, Inc., 1405 N. Main, #240, 78212. Tel: 210-227-5959; Fax: 210-554-0822. Mr. Jose Roberto Gutierrez, Pres.
Principal Activity is the production of Nuestra Familia, the National Catholic evangelization television series for U.S. Hispanics.

Ladies of Charity of El Carmen, 18555 Leal Rd., 78221. Tel: 210-626-1861. Rosalinda Puente, Pres.

Las Hermanas U.S.A., P.O. Box 15792, 78212-8992. Tel: 210-434-0947. Promotes the leadership role of Hispanic Women in the church and society. Dolores Florez.

Madonna Neighborhood Center, 1906 Castroville Rd., 78237. Tel: 210-432-2374. Norma J. Funari, Dir. Casework, Day Care, After School Care, Social Services, Adult & Youth Socialization Programs. Emergency Food Pantry, Clothing, Furniture, Counseling, Evening Meal, Summer Recreation.

Marian Center of San Antonio, P.O. Box 831001, 78283-1001. Tel: 210-225-6279; Fax: 210-225-0044. Ms. Therese H. Palacios, Pres.

Marianist Lay Network, 218 S. Josephine Tobin Dr., 78201-5941. Tel: 210-735-0212.
Web site: www.MLNNA.com
Rita J. Bordano, Treas.

Merced Housing Texas, 3120 W. Ashby St., 78228. Tel: 210-732-5667; Fax: 210-732-2309.
E-mail: merced@netxpress.com
Susan R. Sheeran, Regl. Pres. A consortium of religious orders to provide quality, affordable, service orientated housing for the economically poor, to strengthen families and promote healthy communities.

Missionaries of Pastoral Charity Society, 1135 Mission Rd., 78210-4598. Tel: 210-534-8005; Fax: 210-534-6568. Rev. Kenneth C. Myers (El Salvador), Dir.; Sr. Claudia Klesel, I.W.B.S., Office Mgr.

Oblate Lourdes Grotto Shrine of the Southwest, 5722 Blanco Rd., 78216-6615. Tel: 210-342-9864. Revs. Richard A. Houlahan, O.M.I., Grotto Dir.; Gerald Weber, O.M.I., Activities Dir.

Oblate Missions, 2503 Blanco Rd., 78212-1859.
E-mail: omsa@connecti.com
Mailing Address: P.O. Box 96, 78291. Tel: 210-736-1685; Fax: 210-736-1314. Mailing Address: P.O. Box 2904, 78299-2904. Missionary Association of Mary Immaculate; Island of Lepers; Isles of Hope; Children of the Mountain. Most Rev. Philip F. Smith, O.M.I., D.D. (Philippines); Revs. Richard A. Houlahan, O.M.I., Dir.; Saturnino Lajo, O.M.I. (Spain), Spanish Consultant; Edward J. Cronin, O.M.I., Dir. Emeritus.

The Patrician Movement, Main Office: La Villita de San Patricio, 222 E. Mitchell St., 78210. Tel: 210-532-3126.
Field Offices: 1249 S. St. Mary St., 78210. Tel: 210-533-9191. 278 E. Mitchell, 78210. Tel: 210-533-2507. 528 S. Polaris, 78203. Tel: 210-534-4029. 215 Claudia, 78210. Tel: 210-533-0226. A non-profit corporation chartered under the laws of the State of Texas. Rev. Msgr. Dermot N. Brosnan, Exec. Dir.; Deacon Patrick M. Clancey, Ed.D., Admin.; Patrick M. Clancey, Admin. & Contact Person. Provides comprehensive, Residential and Outpatient Substance Abuse Treatment Services. Accredited by the Joint Commission on Accreditation of Healthcare Organizations. Licenced by the Texas Commission on Alcohol and Drug Abuse. 222 E. Mitchell, 78210. Total Assisted 1,750.

Pauline Book and Media Center, 114 Main Plaza, 78205. Tel: 210-224-8101; Fax: 210-224-0938. E-mail: fspsatx@aol.com

Sr. Susan Miriam Wolf, F.S.P., Supr. Daughters of St. Paul 4.

Pilgrim Center of Hope - Evangelization Center, 7680 Joe Newton, 78251. Tel: 210-521-3377; Fax: 210-521-0288. Directors: Deacon Tom Fox; Mrs. Mary Jane Fox; Rev. Jasper Mauss, O.F.M.

Pillars of San Fernando Cathedral, 115 Main Plaza, 78205. Tel: 210-734-2620. An organization of benefactors that promotes and helps finance the oldest cathedral-sanctuary in the United States. Rev. Msgr. Balthasar Janacek.

Polish American Priest Association (P.A.P.A.), 5035 Bernadine, 78220. Tel: 210-648-1991. Rev. Peter Zendzian (BRK).

Religious of Mary Immaculate. (Pontifical), Villa Maria, 719 Augusta St., 78215. Tel: 210-226-0025; Fax: 210-226-3305. Sr. Clara Echeverria, R.M.I., Local Supr. Residence for Students and Working Girls. Apostolic Work: Counseling & guidance of young women of good moral conduct of any race or religion. Sisters 12; Girls 139.

St. Monica's Guild (1929), 6515 Broadway, 78209. Tel: 210-828-9266. Mrs. Celeste Barron, Pres. Elect. A social, civic, and charitable group.

San Antonio Community Law Center, 322 W. Woodlawn Ave., 78212. Tel: 210-271-9595; Fax: 210-734-4410. Provides legal assistance to the working poor. Attorneys: Bro. William Dooling, C.S.C.; Charles E. Montemayor.

San Antonio Intercommunity Finance Office, 5922 Blanco Rd., 78216. Tel: 210-341-8884. E-mail: saifo@juro.com

Sr. Susan Welsby, A.S.C., Dir.

Santa Rosa Family Practice Residency Program, 519 W. Houston St., 78207. Tel: 210-704-2535. Dr. James Martin, M.D., Dir.

Serra Club of San Antonio, Inc., 5107 Merlin, 78218-2745. Tel: 210-653-2093. Mr. Eugene Gittinger, Pres.

Teleton Navideno, 2903 W. Salinas, 78207. Tel: 210-433-3256. Christmas Telethon-Branch of Catholic Charities of San Antonio, Inc. Mr. Olegario G. Tijerina, Volunteer Admin. Coord.

FAIR OAKS RANCH. *Secular Franciscan Order*, 29623 Double Eagle Cir., 78015. Tel: 830-981-9623. Mr. George Irving.

MOUNTAIN HOME. *Camp Tecaboca*, P.O. Box 69, 78058. Tel: 830-866-3425. Texas Catholic Boy's Camp. Operated by the Society of Mary, Province of St. Louis.

RELIGIOUS INSTITUTES OF MEN REPRESENTED IN THE ARCHDIOCESE

For further details refer to the corresponding bracketed number in the Religious Institutes of Men or Women section.

[0140]—*The Augustinians*. (Prov. of Castile).—O.S.A.
[0600]—*Brothers of the Congregation of Holy Cross*.—C.S.C.
[0350]—*Cistercian Order of the Strict Observance*.—O.C.S.O.
[0360]—*Claretian Missionaries*. (Western Prov.).—C.M.F.
[0220]—*Congregation of the Blessed Sacrament*.—S.S.S.
[1330]—*Congregation of the Mission*. (Southern Prov.).—C.M.
[0630]—*Congregation of the Missionaries of the Holy Family*.—M.S.F.
[1000]—*Congregation of the Passion*.—C.P.
[1130]—*Congregation of the Priests of the Sacred Heart*.—S.C.J.
[0480]—*Conventual Franciscans*.—O.F.M.Conv.
[0260]—*Discalced Carmelite Fathers*.—O.C.D.
[0520]—*Franciscan Friars*. (Sacred Heart Prov.).—O.F.M.
[0650]—*Holy Ghost Fathers*. (Western Prov.).—C.S.Sp.
[0690]—*Jesuit Fathers and Brothers*. (New Orleans Prov.).—S.J.
[]—*Missionaries of the Nativity of Mary*. (Mexico).—M.N.M.
[1110]—*Missionaries of the Sacred Heart*.—M.S.C.
[0860]—*Missionhurst Congregation of the Immaculate Heart of Mary*.—C.I.C.M.
[0910]—*Oblates of Mary Immaculate*. (Southern Prov.).—O.M.I.
[0430]—*Order of Preachers (Dominican)*. (New Orleans Prov.).—O.P.
[0610]—*Priests of the Congregation of Holy Cross*.—C.S.C.
[1070]—*Redemptorist Fathers*.—C.SS.R.
[0760]—*Society of Mary (Marianists)*.—S.M.
[1200]—*Society of the Divine Savior*.—S.D.S.
[1060]—*Society of the Precious Blood*.—C.PP.S.

RELIGIOUS INSTITUTES OF WOMEN REPRESENTED IN THE ARCHDIOCESE

[0100]—*Adorers of the Blood of Christ*.—A.S.C.
[0230]—*Benedictine Sisters of the Pontifical Jurisdiction*.—O.S.B.
[1810]—*Bernardine Sisters of the Third Order of St. Francis*.—O.S.F.
[]—*Carmelitas del Sagrado Corazon*.—O.C.D.
[0360]—*Carmelite Sisters of the Divine Heart of Jesus*.—Carmel.D.C.J.
[0460]—*Congregation of Sisters of Charity of the Incarnate Word*.—C.C.V.I.
[3735]—*Congregation of St. Brigid*.—C.S.B.
[0870]—*Congregation of the Daughters of Mary Immaculate (Marianist Sisters)*.—F.M.I.
[2200]—*Congregation of the Incarnate Word and Blessed Sacrament*.—I.W.B.S.
[0725]—*Cordi-Marian Sisters*.—M.C-M.
[0760]—*Daughters of Charity of St. Vincent de Paul*.—D.C.
[0850]—*Daughters of Mary Help of Christians*.—F.M.A.
[0420]—*Discalced Carmelite Nuns*.—O.C.D.
[1070-13]—*Dominican Sisters*.—O.P.
[1070-19]—*Dominican Sisters*.—O.P.
[1150]—*Eucharistic Franciscan Missionary Sisters*.—E.F.M.S.
[1170]—*Felician Sisters*.—C.S.S.F.
[1310]—*Franciscan Sisters of Little Falls, MN*.
[1900]—*Hermanas Catequistas Guadalupanas*.—H.C.G.
[1910]—*Hermanas Josefinas*.—H.J.
[2590]—*Hermanas Mercedarias Del Santisimo Sacramento*.—H.M.S.S.
[2720]—*Mission Helpers of the Sacred Heart*.—M.H.S.H.
[2770]—*Missionaries of Jesus, Mary and Joseph*.—M.J.M.J.
[2690]—*Missionary Catechists of Divine Providence, San Antonio, Texas*.—M.C.D.P.
[2890]—*Missionary Servants of St. Anthony*.—M.S.S.A.
[]—*Missionary Sisters of Our Lady of Perpetual Help*.—M.P.S.
[2760]—*Missionary Sisters of the Immaculate Conception of the Mother of God*.—S.M.I.C.
[3070]—*North American Union of the Sisters of Our Lady of Charity*.—O.L.C.
[]—*Oblate Missionaries of Mary Immaculate*.—O.M.M.I.
[3130]—*Our Lady of Victory Missionary Sisters*.—O.L.V.M.
[0950]—*Pious Society Daughters of St. Paul*.—F.S.P.
[3460]—*Religious of Mary Immaculate*.—R.M.I.
[2970]—*School Sisters of Notre Dame*.—S.S.N.D.
[1680]—*School Sisters of St. Francis. WI*.—S.S.S.F.
[1690]—*School Sisters of the Third Order of St. Francis*.—O.S.F.
[]—*Seraphic Franciscan Sisters of Our Lady of Sorrows*. (Poland).—O.L.S.
[0480]—*Sisters of Charity of Leavenworth, KS*.—S.C.L.
[1010]—*Sisters of Divine Providence of San Antonio, Texas*.—C.D.P.
[2360]—*Sisters of Loretto At the Foot of the Cross*.—S.L.
[3000]—*Sisters of Notre Dame de Namur*.—S.N.D.deN.
[3195]—*Sisters of Perpetual Adoration*.—A.P.G.
[3460]—*Sisters of Providence of Saint Mary-of-the-Woods, Indiana*.—S.P.
[1570]—*Sisters of St. Francis of the Holy Family*.—O.S.F.
[1930]—*Sisters of the Holy Cross*.—C.S.C.
[1960]—*Sisters of the Holy Family*.—S.H.F.
[2050]—*Sisters of the Holy Spirit and Mary Immaculate*.—S.H.Sp.
[2110]—*Sisters of the Humility of Mary*.—H.M.
[3320]—*Sisters of the Presentation of the B.V.M.*—P.B.V.M.
[3670]—*Sisters of the Sacred Heart of Jesus*.—S.S.C.J.
[2150]—*Sisters, Servants of the Immaculate Heart of Mary*.—I.H.M.
[4020]—*Society of St. Theresa of Jesus*.—S.T.J.
[4110]—*Ursuline Nuns (Roman Union)*.—O.S.U.

ARCHDIOCESAN CEMETERIES

SAN ANTONIO. *Holy Cross*.
San Fernando No. 1.
San Fernando No. 2.
San Fernando No. 3 (Roselawn).

NECROLOGY

† Collins, Rev. Msgr. Thomas J., (Retired). —Died July 13, 1997.

† Martin, Rev. Msgr. William C., San Antonio, TX, St. Pius X. —Died Sept. 17, 1997.

† Murray, Rev. Msgr. Patrick J., (Retired). —Died March 28, 1997.

† Reyna, Joseph A., Pearsall, TX, Immaculate Heart of Mary. —Died June 28, 1997.

Diocese of San Bernardino

DIOCESE ESTABLISHED NOVEMBER 6, 1978.

Square Miles 27,293.

Comprises the Counties of San Bernardino and Riverside.

Legal Titles:

The Roman Catholic Bishop of San Bernardino, a Corporation Sole (Churches, Rectories, Halls, Catechetical Centers, etc.).

Diocese of San Bernardino Education and Welfare Corporation (Schools, Convents, Newman Facilities, etc.).

Diocese of San Bernardino Catholic Charities.

St. Bernardine Plaza.

La Paz Dev. Corp. (Senior Citizens Housing).

San Gorgonio Villa.

Caritas Telecommunications.

A California Non-profit Corporation.

Most Reverend

GERALD R. BARNES

Bishop of San Bernardino; ordained December 20, 1975; appointed Titular Bishop of Montefiascone and Auxiliary of San Bernardino January 27, 1992; succeeded to the See, December 28, 1995; installed as Second Bishop of San Bernadino March 12, 1996. *Office: 1201 E. Highland Ave., San Bernardino, CA, 92404.*

Chancery: 1201 E. Highland Ave., San Bernardino, CA, 92404. Tel.: 909-475-5300; Fax: 909-475-5155.

STATISTICAL OVERVIEW

Personnel	
Bishop	1
Priests: Diocesan Active in Diocese	85
Priests: Active Outside Diocese	4
Priests: Retired, Sick or Absent	48
Number of Diocesan Priests	144
Religious Priests in Diocese	87
Extern Priests in Diocese	7
Ordinations:	
Diocesan Priests	5
Permanent Deacons in Diocese	83
Total Brothers	21
Total Sisters	158
Parishes	
Parishes	97
With Resident Pastor:	
Resident Diocesan Priests	61
Resident Religious Priests	30
Without Resident Pastor:	
Administered by Priests	2
Administered by Women Religious	3
Administered by Lay People	1
Missions	13
Professional Ministry Personnel:	
Lay Ministers	42
Welfare	
Catholic Hospitals	2
Educational	
Seminaries, Diocesan	1
Students from This Diocese	7
Students from Other Diocese	1
Diocesan Students in Other Seminaries	7
Total Seminarians	14
High Schools, Diocesan and Parish	2
Total Students	902
Elementary Schools, Diocesan and Parish	34
Total Students	8,370
Catechesis/Religious Education:	
High School Students	10,776
Elementary Students	32,326
Total Students Under Catholic Instruction	52,388
Teachers in the Diocese:	
Lay Teachers	372
Vital Statistics	
Receptions into the Church:	
Infant Baptism Totals	10,306
Adult Baptism Totals	1,348
Received into Full Communion	917
First Communions	9,817
Confirmations	3,468
Marriages:	
Catholic	1,517
Interfaith	369
Total Marriages	1,886
Deaths	2,703
Total Catholic Population	779,504
Total Population	3,784,000

Former Bishop—Most. Rev. PHILLIP F. STRALING D.D., Bishop of San Bernardino; ord. March 19, 1959; appt. July 18, 1978; cons. Nov. 16, 1978; transferred to See of Reno, June 29, 1995.

Vicar General/Chancellor/Moderator of Curia—Rev. Msgr. DONALD S. WEBBER., J.C.L., V.G, *1201 E. Highland Ave., San Bernardino, 92404.* Tel: 909-475-5120; 796-6448.

Vice Chancellor—Sr. MARY JO NELSON, O.L.V.M., Dir., Diocesan Planning Process, *1201 E. Highland Ave., San Bernardino, 92404.* Tel: 909-475-5100.

Bishops Secretary—Mrs. MARIA ECHEVERRIA, *1201 E. Highland Ave., San Bernardino, 92404.* Tel: 909-475-5110; Fax: 909-475-5109.

Chancery—*1201 E. Highland Ave., San Bernardino, 92404.* Tel: 909-475-5300; Fax: 909-475-5155. Office Hours: Mon.-Fri. 8:30-4:30.

The Ministry of Administrative Services—

Human Resources (Personnel/Payroll)—*1201 E. Highland Ave., San Bernardino, 92404-4607.* Tel: 909-475-5170; Fax: 909-475-5189. JAMES PESTA, M.P.A., M.P.S., Chief Administrative Officer & Dir., Human Resources. Tel: 909-475-5177.

Presbyteral Council—Most Rev. GERALD R. BARNES; Rev. Msgr. DONALD S. WEBBER, J.C.L., V.G.; Very Rev. GEORGE GONZALES; Rev. EFREN MUSGNI, M.S.; Rev. Msgr. PHILIP BEHAN; Rev. MARK KOTLARCZYK; Very Rev. MICHAEL BROOKS, SS.CC.; Rev. RAFAEL PARTIDA; Rev. Msgr. PETER LUQUE; Rev. THOMAS BURDICK; Very Rev. RENO AIARDI, I.M.C.; Rev. KENNETH JENKINS; Very Rev. STEPHEN PORTER; Revs. JOSEPH KRAH; ARTURO BALAGAT; VINCENT CONNOR; ANTHONY FERRERO; FRED GAGLIA.

Diocesan Curia—Most Rev. GERALD R. BARNES; Rev. Msgr. DONALD S. WEBBER, J.C.L., V.G.; Sr. MARY JO NELSON, O.L.V.M.; Deacon GEORGE SCHMIT; JIM PESTA; PETER BRADLEY; CLARE COLELLA; MARIA ACOSTA; Rev. ROMEO SELECCION, M.S.; Sr. GEORGIANNA CAHILL, S.S.S.; Sr. CECILIA CALVA, S.N.I.M.; Sr. ALICE MOLINA, R.S.H.M.

College of Consultors—Rev. Msgr. PHILIP BEHAN; Rev. Msgr. PETER LUGUE; Rev. Msgr. DONALD S. WEBBER, J.C.L., V.G.; Very Rev. RENO AIARDI, I.M.C.; Very Rev. MICHAEL BROOKS, SS.CC.; Very Rev. VINCENT CONNOR; Very Rev. GEORGE GONZALES; Very Rev. STEPHEN PORTER; Revs. ARTURO BALAGAT; FRED GAGLIA.

Council of Religious—Council Members: Revs. DAVID FARRUGIA, O.P.; ERIC VARGAS, S.V.D.; Bro. GARY HILL, O.H.; Sr. SUSAN DE GUIDE, R.S.M.; Sr. CAROLYN GRIES, O.S.B.; Sr. MARY HOWARD MORIARTY, I.B.V.M.; Sr. ELIZABETH SCULLY, O.S.F.; Sr. SARAH SHREWSBURY, O.S.C.; Sr. MARVE WATKINS-KING, O.D.N.

Finance Council—Deacon GEORGE SCHMIT, Chm., *1201 E. Highland Ave., San Bernardino, 92404-4607.* Tel: 909-475-5151.

Finance Council Members—Most Rev. GERALD R. BARNES; Rev. Msgr. MALACHY MCGINN; Rev. Msgr. DONALD S. WEBBER, J.C.L., V.G.; Very Rev. STEVEN C. PORTER, S.T.L., V.F.; Rev. HOWARD LINCOLN; Sr. MARY JO NELSON, O.L.V.M.; Deacon GEORGE SCHMIT; MARION ASHLEY; LINDA BORBA; WILLIAM J. Brunick; PHILLIP BURBACH; RICHARD GRANILLO; TERRY GRAY; WILFRID C. LEMANN; JOYCE LEON; MARTIN MATICH; MICHAEL V. MCINTIRE; RONALD MERAZ; ALBERTO NEIRA; PETER ROELL; JEFFERY G. ROLLERT; THOMAS STULL; JOHN VAN DAELE; MARYROSE WALLACE.

Diocesan Boards and Committees

Priests' Personnel Board—*1201 E. Highland Ave., San Bernardino, 92404-4607.* Tel: 909-475-5120. Personnel Board Memebers: Most Rev. GERALD R. BARNES; Rev. Msgr. DONALD S. WEBBER, J.C.L., V.G.; Very Rev. ROBERT MILLER; Very Rev. RAFAEL PARTIDA; Revs. PETER COVAS; MICHAEL LAMA.

Building Committee—Deacon JOHN SKORA, Construction Project Mgr., *1201 E. Highland Ave., San Bernardino, 92404.* Tel: 909-475-5305. Deacon JOHN SKORA, Committee Coord. Committee Members: Rev. GERALD DELUNEY; RON CARDUCCI; DON GARDNER; DALE KLEIN. Staff Members: Deacon GEORGE SCHMIT, Chief Financial Officer.

Diocesan Planning Council—Members: Rev. JACK BARKER; Rev. ROMEO SELECCION; Sr. CECILIA CALVA, S.N.J.M.; Sr. MAUREEN CHICOINE, R.S.C.J.; Sr. MAURA REDDINGTON, R.S.M.; KATHERINE A. HALDER; REGINA HEREDIA; MICHAEL M. KARPMAN; LUIS E. LOPEZ; JAMES PESTA; JOSEPH SAMPSON.

Diocesan Planning Team—Very Rev. ROBERT L. MILLER; Sr. MARY JO NELSON, O.L.V.M.; PETER BRADLEY; Mrs. FRANCESCA COVER.

Diocesan Seminary Board—Ex Officio Members: Most Rev. GERALD R. BARNES; Rev. Msgr. DONALD S. WEBBER, J.C.L., V.G.; Rev. JOSE SANZ; Sr. SARAH SHREWSBURY, O.S.C. Members: Revs. DAVID ANDEL; MIGUEL CEJA; GERARDO MENDOZA; BRIAN ROGAN; ROMEO SELECCION, M.S.; Sr. BETTY MCGOVERN, R.S.M.; THELMA BLEDSOE; Dr. RAY BURIEL; HERMINE LEE; STEPHAN WAGNER.

Parish Staffing Committee—Very Rev. ROBERT MILLER; Rev. ARTURO BALAGAT; Sr. MARY JO NELSON, O.L.V.M.; Deacon WALTER MELENDREZ; MONICA ARCE-ARCHULETTA; PETER BRADLEY, Chm. KATHY JEFFRIES; JIM PESTA; PAT WOODS.

Diocesan Tribunal—*1201 E. Highland Ave., San Bernardino, 92404-4607.* Tel: 909-475-5320; Fax: 909-475-5330.

Judicial Vicar—Rev. Msgr. ROBERT E. LAWRENCE, J.C.L.

Adjutant Judicial Vicar—Rev. Msgr. DONALD S. WEBBER, J.C.L., V.G.

Defenders of the Bond—Rev. Msgr. PHILIP BEHAN, J.C.L., V.F.; Rev. Msgr. DONALD S. WEBBER, J.C.L., V.G.; Revs. ARTHUR CARRILLO, J.C.L.; ANTHONY T. FERRERO, J.C.L.; THOMAS WALLACE; FRANCIS WIESER, J.C.D.

Pro-Synodal Judges—Rev. Msgr. LOURENCO AVILA; Rev. Msgr. PHILIP A. BEHAN, J.C.L., V.F.; Rev. Msgr. CORNELIUS O'LEARY, Ph.D., Col./Chap; Rev. Msgr. DONALD S. WEBBER, J.C.L., V.G.; Very Rev. GEORGE GONZALES; Revs. ADRIAN BRINN; ROBERT ERICKSON; ANTHONY T. FERRERO, J.C.L.; KENNETH JENKINS; FRANCIS WIESER, J.C.D.

Lay Advocates—Sr. PATRICIA HAIRE, C.S.J., Ph.D.; Sr. DEANNA O'NEIL, O.S.B.; Sr. ELIZABETH SCULLY, O.S.F.; Deacons BUD BURRIS; MARLIN FILIPEK; LLOYD S. HAWES; PHILIP KERMOTT; WALTER MELENDREZ; GEORGE SCHMIT; SANDRA BOYD; CONSTANCE BROWN; CLARE COLELLA; SHARON DONOVAN; FRANCES FITZGERALD; JOHN FITZGERALD; DAVID A. HATCHER, JR.; MARGARET HAWES; ALVIN KELLY; PHYLLIS KOLBY; JOAN MCNELIS; MARY MYERS; DEE A. OGDEN, Ph.D.; JAMES E. PESTA; YOLANDA REGALADO; JODY SANCHEZ; WALDO SANCHEZ; STEPHEN SCARPITTA; ROGER C. SCHERER; BETTY SCHMIT; MARY SULLIVAN-TANSEY; CAROLINA P. TORRES; PATRICIA WOODS.

Secretaries & Diocesan Notaries—GWENDOLYN GIFFORD; GINA GRADIAS; IRENE MARTINEZ.

Vicar for Deacons—Vacant. Tel: 909-475-5160.

Vicar General—Rev. Msgr. DONALD S. WEBBER, J.C.L., V.G., *1201 E. Highland Ave., San Bernardino, 92404-4607*. Tel: 909-475-5120; Fax: 909-475-5109.

Judicial Vicar—Rev. Msgr. ROBERT E. LAWRENCE, J.C.L., *1201 E. Highland Ave., San Bernardino, 92404-4607*. Tel: 909-475-5320.

Vicar for Ethnic Affairs—Vacant, *1201 E. Highland Ave., San Bernardino, 92404-4607*. Tel: 909-475-5104.

Vicar for African-Americans—Very Rev. RICHARD MCGEE, C.R., *St. Joseph Church, 17080 Arrow Blvd., Fontana, 92335*. Tel: 909-822-0566.

Vicar for Clergy—Rev. RON LARKIN, M.S.C., *1201 E. Highland Ave., San Bernardino, 92404-4607*. Tel: 909-475-5455; 5458.

Director for the Office of Hispanic Affairs—Sr. CECILIA CALVA, S.N.J.M., *1201 E. Highland Ave., San Bernardino, 92404-4607*. Tel: 909-475-5360; Fax: 909-475-5457.

Vicar for Native Americans—Very Rev. RAFAEL PARTIDA, *Our Lady of Perpetual Help Church, P.O. Box BB, Indio, 92201-2527*. Tel: 760-347-3507.

Vicar for Priests in Special Works—Very Rev. VINCENT CONNOR, *1201 E. Highland Ave., San Bernardino, 92404-4607*. Tel: 909-475-5341.

Director for the Office for Men and Women Religious—Sr. CAROLYN GRIES, O.S.B., *1201 E. Highland Ave., San Bernardino, 92404-4607*. Tel: 909-475-5345; Fax: 909-475-5354.

Vicar for Retired Priests—Rev. Msgr. THOMAS MEAGHER, *1011 St. Andrew St., Upland, 91766*.

Vicars Forane—Very Rev. GEORGE GONZALES, Hemet Vicariate. Tel: 909-674-6881. Rev. Msgr. PHILIP A. BEHAN, V.F., High Desert Vicariate. Tel: 760-244-9180. Very Rev. MICHAEL BROOKS, SS.CC., V.F., Lower Desert Vicariate. Tel: 760-328-2398. Rev. Msgr. PETER H. LUQUE, V.F., Riverside Vicariate. Tel: 909-737-6432. Very Rev. RENO AIARDI, I.M.C., V.F., San Bernardino Vicariate. Tel: 909-475-5130. Very Rev. STEVEN PORTER, V.F., West End Vicariate. Tel: 909-899-1049.

The Ministry of Communications—*1201 E. Highland Ave., San Bernardino, 92404-4607*. Tel: 909-475-5350; Fax: 909-475-5357.

Caritas Telecommunications—*1201 E. Highland Ave., San Bernardino, 92404-4607*. Tel: 909-475-5350; Fax: 909-475-5357. CLARE COLELLA, Dir. Tel: 909-475-5351.

Newspaper—*"Inland Catholic"*, STEVEN BARRIE, Editor, *1201 E. Highland Ave., San Bernardino, 92404-4607*. Tel: 909-475-5420; Fax: 909-475-5155.

Information Systems/Computer Services/Purchasing—*1201 E. Highland Ave., San Bernardino, 92404-4607*. Tel: 909-475-5400. JOE BOGDANSKI, Dir. Tel: 909-475-5401.

Office of Construction and Real Estate—*1201 E. Highland Ave., San Bernardino, 92404-4607*. Tel: 909-475-5310. Deacon JOHN SKORA, Dir., Tel: 909-475-5312, JUDY A. JUAREZ-FLORES, Oper. Mgr. Tel: 909-475-5313.

Diocesan Archivist—BRUCE HARLEY, Ph.D., *1201 E. Highland Ave., San Bernardino, 92404-4607*. Tel: 909-475-5399.

The Ministry of Ecclesial Services—

Vicar for Clergy—Rev. RON LARKIN, M.S.C., *1201 E. Highland Ave., San Bernardino, 92404-4607*. Tel: 909-475-5458; Fax: 909-475-5343.

Committee for the Continuing Education of Priests—Rev. RON LARKIN, M.S.C., *1201 E. Highland Ave., San Bernardino, 92404-4607*. Tel: 909-475-5458; Fax: 909-475-5343.

Clerical Personnel—Rev. Msgr. DONALD S. WEBBER, J.C.L., V.G., Dir., *1201 E. Highland Ave., San Bernardino, 92404-4607*. Tel: 909-475-5120; Fax: 909-475-5109.

Seminarains—Rev. JOSE SANZ, D.L.P., Dir. Tel: 909-788-9931; Fax: 909-781-9031.

Office for Men and Women Religious—Sr. CAROLYN GRIES, O.S.B., Dir., *1201 E. Highland Ave., San Bernardino, 92404-4607*. Tel: 909-475-5345; Fax: 909-475-5354.

Office of Vocations—*1201 E. Highland Ave., San Bernardino, 92404-4607*. Tel: 909-475-5470; Fax: 909-475-5475. Sr. SARAH SHREWSBURY, O.S.C., Vocations Coord. Tel: 909-475-5471.

Serra International, District 157, San Bernardino—HOWARD C. LITTLEFIELD, Governor, *758 W. 24th St., San Bernardino, 92405*. Tel: 909-882-7146; Fax: 909-882-0907.

Palm Springs Chapter—THOMAS LINEHARD, Pres., *314 Castellana St., Palm Desert, 92260*. Tel: 760-340-1660.

Riverside Chapter—PHIL MASTRAMICO, Pres., *9558 Pebble Brook Dr., Moreno Valley, 92577*. Tel: 909-781-6200.

San Bernardino Chapter—LORENE SPONSLER, Pres., *3171 N. Valencia Ave., San Bernardino, 92404*. Tel: 909-883-9324.

Murrieta Chapter—MARVIN J. HAYES, Pres., *44611 La Paz Rd., Temecula, 92592*. Tel: 909-676-4804.

Blessed Junipero Serra House of Formation—Revs. JOSE SANZ, D.L.P., Rector; ROLANDO FONSECA, D.L.P., Vice Rector, *3325 13th St., Riverside, 92501*. Tel: 909-788-9931; Fax: 909-781-9031. For seminarians call: Tel: 909-683-8749.

Permanent Diaconate Office—MARIE ACOSTA, Dir. DOTTIE FILIPEK, Ministry Service Analyst, *1201 E. Highland Ave., San Bernardino, 92404-4607*. Tel: 909-475-5160; Fax: 909-475-5155.

The Ministry of Educational Services—Sr. ALICE MOLINA, R.S.H.M., Dir., *1201 E. Highland Ave., San Bernardino, 92404-4607*. Tel: 909-475-5450; Fax: 909-475-5457.

The Office of Catholic Schools—*1201 E. Highland Ave., San Bernardino, 92404-4607*. Tel: 909-475-5437; Fax: 909-475-5477. THOMAS J. HEDING, Supt. of Catholic Schools; Sr. SARA KANE, C.S.J., Dir., School Svcs. TRISH BOGDANSKI, Admin. Asst. Diocesan School Board; ELDON HEASTON, Pres. AUSTIN CONLEY, III; CHARLES WILLIAMS; RALPH CASTRO; MARIETTA WILLIAMS; CONNIE PADILLA.

Campus Ministry—Rev. NED REIDY, C.S.C., Dir., *Christ of the Desert Newman Center, 73441 Fred Waring Dr., #3, Palm Desert, 92260*. Tel: 760-346-0089.

Missions Office of the Diocese of San Bernardino—Offices: *1201 E. Highland Ave., San Bernardino, 92404-4607*. Tel: 909-475-5130; Fax: 909-475-5135. *Mailing Address: P.O. Box 1416, San Bernardino, 92402-1416*. Very Rev. RENO AIARDI, I.M.C., V.F., Dir.; Sr. ROSALINE O'CONNOR, R.S.M., Coord., Holy Childhood Association.

Diocesan Media Center—MARCIA HANINGER, Dir. Tel: 909-475-5391.

The Office of Religious Education and Formation—*1201 E. Highland Ave., San Bernardino, 92404-4607*. Tel: 909-475-5450; Fax: 909-475-5457.

Vicariate Pastoral Centers—

Center A: San Bernardino/High Desert—*1201 E. Highland Ave., San Bernardino, 92404-4607*. Sr. ALICE MOLINA, R.S.H.M., Dir. ROSE LUCERO, Consultant. Tel: 909-475-5384.

Center B: Hemet/Low Desert—*1612 First St., Coachella, 92236*. BERTHA BAZALDUA, Consultant; Sr. NADINE MCGUINNESS, C.S.J., Consultant. Tel: 760-398-0606.

Center C: Riverside/West End—*6974 Brockton Ste. 102, Riverside, 92506*. Sr. M. DOMINIC REANTASO, SS.CC., Consultant; ROLANDO ROSALES, Consultant. Tel: 909-682-9131.

Ministry Formation Institute—

Evangelization & Catechesis—LYNN ZUPAN, Program Coord. Tel: 909-475-5385.

Youth & Young Adult Ministry—GRACE CASSETTA, Program Coord. Tel: 909-475-5383.

Leadership Formation—STEVE VALENZUELA, Program Coord. Tel: 909-475-5382.

The Ministry of Ethnic Affairs—

Diocesan African-American Catholic Commission and Assembly—*1201 E. Highland Ave., San Bernardino, 92404-4607*. Tel: 909-475-5194. EFFIE SHARPE, Chm. MAUDRY OWINGS, Coord.; Very Rev. RICHARD MCGEE, C.R., Vicar, *St. Joseph Church, 17080 Arrow Blvd., Fontana, 92335*. Tel: 909-822-0566.

Arab-American Ministry—Rev. LABIB KOBTI, *St. Joseph Church, 1150 W. Holt Ave., Pomona, 91768*. Tel: 909-865-6895.

Asian-Pacific Islander Ministry—Rev. ROMEO SELECCION, M.S., Dir., *St. Christopher Church, 25075 Cottonwood Ave., Moreno Valley, 92553*. Tel: 909-924-1968.

Filipino Ministry—Rev. ARTURO BALAGAT, Diocesan Dir., *St. Mel Church, P.O. Box 700, Norco, 91760-0700*. Tel: 909-737-7144.

Hmong Ministry—JOHN YING YANG, *248 Allview Dr., Banning, 92220*. Tel: 909-849-7908.

Indonesian Ministry—LANI FUKUMOTO, Dir., *33785 Date Palm Dr., Cathedral City, 92234*. Tel: 760-324-7740.

Korean Ministry—PETER CHUNG, Diocesan Liaison, *6739 Laurelbrook Dr., Riverside, 92506*. Tel: 909-787-3906. Rev. PAUL KIM, *St. Andrew Kim Korean Catholic Community, 4110 Corona Ave., Norco, 91760*. Tel: 909-372-9932.

Native American Ministry—Deacon FRANK ALANIZ, Chm., *10727 Duncan Rd., Phelan, 92371*. Tel: 760-949-0696. Very Rev. RAFAEL PARTIDA, Vicar, *Our Lady of Perpetual Help Church, P.O. Box BB, Indio, 92201*. Tel: 760-347-3507; Fax: 760-347-8367.

Tongan Ministry—KAPILILI POMEE; NITA POMEE, *1268 1/2 Berkeley St., San Bernardino, 92405*. Tel: 909-387-8140. *St. Joseph Church, Upland.*

Vietnamese Ministry—*Congregation of the Mother Coredemptrix, Shrine of Presentation, 1775 S. Main St., Corona, 91720*. Tel: 909-737-4125; Fax: 909-340-9880.

The Ministry of Hispanic Affairs—*1201 E. Highland Ave., San Bernardino, 92404-4607*. Tel: 909-475-5451; Fax: 909-475-5457. Sr. CECILIA CALVA, S.N.J.M., Dir., Office of Hispanic Affairs.

Valley Missionary Program, Shrine of Our Lady of Guadalupe—Rev. JOSEPH "JOSE" PAWLICKI, C.S.C., Dir. DAVID FAJARDO, Coord., *52-565 Oasis Palm, Coachella, 92236*. Tel: 760-398-9277; Fax: 760-398-9281. DAVID FAJARDO, Retreats Coord.

The Ministry of Financial Affairs—*1201 E. Highland Ave., San Bernardino, 92404-4607*. Tel: 909-475-5150. Deacon GEORGE M. SCHMIT, Chief Fin. Officer.Tel: 909-475-5151.

Accounting Services—*1201 E. Highland Ave., San Bernardino, 92404-4607*. Tel: 909-475-5480. MARY-ROSE WALLACE, Dir. Tel: 909-475-5481.

Parish Assistance Program—BARB LOGGINS, Supvr./Internal Auditor. Tel: 909-475-5491. JOHN HAGMANN, Accountant. Tel: 909-475-5492.

Development Office—*1201 E. Highland Ave., San Bernardino, 92404-4607*. Tel: 909-475-5460. PETER ROELL, Dir. Tel: 909-475-5461.

Catholic Mutual Insurance Group—*1201 E. Highland Ave., San Bernardino, 92404-4607*. Tel: 909-475-5140. TAMAR BRINKERHOFF, Claims/Risk Mgr. Tel: 909-475-5141.

The Ministry of Pastoral Services—*1201 E. Highland Ave., San Bernardino, 92404-4607*. Tel: 909-475-5340. PETER BRADLEY, Dir. Tel: 909-475-5341.

Office of Worship—LINDA VALDIVIA, Sec. Tel: 909-475-5335.

Charismatic Renewal—Rev. MICHAEL BARRY, SS.CC., Dir., *150 E. Olive St., Colton, 92324*. Tel: 909-824-6897; Fax: 909-824-5481.

Refugee and Immigration Services—MY-HANH LUU, Dir.

Yucca Valley Regional Center—*56300 Twentynine Palms Hwy., Yucca Valley, 92285*. ANTHONY MOLLICA, Program Dir. Tel: 760-369-7444; Fax: 760-369-0622., *Cathedral City Regional Center, 67-625 E. Palm Canyon Dr., A-5, Cathedral City, 92234*. CATHERINE MCMILLAN, Assoc. Dir. ARLENE BRANDT, Sec. Tel: 760-202-1222; Fax: 760-202-1230.

Nightengale Manor Emergency Shelter—CATHERINE MCMILLAN, Contact. Tel: 760-202-1222.

HIV/AIDS Programs—CATHERINE MCMILLAN, Contact. Tel: 760-202-1222.

Indio Regional Center—*45149 Smurr St., Indio, 92201*. NORMA MILLER, Regl. Coord. Tel: 760-347-1188; Fax: 760-347-8388.

Farm Worker Resource Program—

Moreno Valley Regional Center—*23700 Sunnymead Blvd., P.O. Box 119, Moreno Valley, 92556-0119*. MARTA MELENDEZ, Regl. Coord. Tel: 909-485-2185; Fax: 909-485-2188.

Caritas Counseling—*1437 N. LaCadena Dr., Colton, 92324*. SUSAN KLESZEWSKI, M.S.W., L.C.S.W., Dir. KEN SAWA, M.A., M.S.W., Program Admin. Tel: 909-370-1293; Fax: 909-370-4679., Corona Office:: Tel: 909-734-8831; Fax: 909-734-8518., Lake Elsinore Office: Tel: 909-245-4850.

Affiliated Programs:—

Campaign for Human Development—JEANETTE ARNQUIST, *1450 N. D St., San Bernardino, 92405*. Tel: 909-388-1239.

Desert Manna—*209 N. First Ave., Barstow, 92311*. Tel: 760-256-7797; Fax: 760-256-4043.

Detention Ministry—MIKE KENNEDY, Coord. Tel: 909-388-1239; Fax: 909-384-1130.

Commissions/Committees—

Children and Family Council—JEANETTE ARNQUIST, Coord., *1450 N. D St., San Bernardino, 92405*. Tel: 909-388-1239.

Natural Family Planning—Deacon RALPH PARTIDA, *5927 Kimball Ave., Chino, 91710*. Tel: 909-597-1002.

Pro-Life Catholic Ministries—MARIE WIDMANN, Coord., *2879 Burnt Oak Dr., Chino Hills, 91709*. Tel: 909-393-9498.

Catholic Organizations in the Diocese—

Catholic Daughters of America—BETTY TICICH, *11461 Courtside St., Victorville, 92392-9048.* Tel: 760-949-4056.

Cursillo—HANK ESPINOZA, English Language Dir. Tel: 909-683-5956. Rev. ARTURO BALAGAT, Filipino Dir. Tel: 909-737-7144. DAVID CHUN, Korean Dir. Tel: 909-883-0880. Dr. ANGEL GARCIA, Spanish Dir. Tel: 909-864-2374. TAM VAN DO, Vietnamese Dir. Tel: 909-272-3446.

Council of Catholic Women—NANCY TICICH, *P.O. Box 291399, Phelan, 92329.* Tel: 760-868-6219.

Equestrian Order of Holy Sepulchre of Jerusalem—MARY HUMANN, *1605 Laurel Ave., Upland, 91784.* Tel: 909-982-7206.

Italian Catholic Federation—MARGUERITE HALSTED, Corresponding Office Sec., *4159 Largewood Pl., Riverside, 92506.* Tel: 909-683-1994.

Knights of Columbus—TOM SULLIVAN, Contact Person, *3321 N. Erwin Ave., San Bernardino, 92404.* Tel: 909-886-1964.

World Apostolate of Fatima (Blue Army)-San Bernardino Division—FERNE C. SCHMITT, Pres., *P.O. Box 361, Rialto, 92377-0361.* Tel: 909-875-2894.

Ministry for Special Needs—

Engaged Encounter (English)—Coords.: BILL SHANNON; CLAUDIA SHANNON. Tel: 909-465-1434.

Engaged Encounter (Spanish)—Coords.: ALBERTO SANTANA; MONICA SANTANA. Tel: 909-872-0738.

Pre-Cana Marriage Preparation—Deacon JAMES DALE, *St. Frances de Sales Church, 4268 Lime St., Riverside, 92501.* Tel: 909-686-4004 (Church); 689-4411 (Work); 684-4623 (Residence).

Pre-Marital Instruction in Spanish—Deacon RALPH PARTIDA. Tel: 909-597-1002.

Marriage Enrichment—

Marriage Encounter—DAN QUAM; THERESA QUAM, *1421 Francine Court, San Jacinto, 92583.* Tel: 909-487-9325.

Marriage Enrichment—CHRIS STEVENSON; CHERYL STEVENSON, *St. Joseph Church, 877 N. Campus Ave., Upland, 91730.* Tel: 909-989-1893.

Catholic Committee on Scouting—(Boy Scouts and Girl Scouts); PHILIP COLELLA, Chm., *4862 Pershing Ave., San Bernardino, 92407.* Tel: 909-882-6372.

CLERGY, PARISHES, MISSIONS AND PAROCHIAL SCHOOLS

CITY OF SAN BERNARDINO
(San Bernardino County)

1—OUR LADY OF THE ROSARY CATHEDRAL, Revs. Robert Miller; Lorenzo Paz.
Office: 265 W. 25th St., 92405. Tel: 909-883-8991; Fax: 909-882-2061.
Res., 2525 Arrowhead Ave., 92405. Tel: 909-881-1588.
School—2620 Arrowhead Ave., 92405. Tel: 909-886-1088.
Lay Teachers 13; Students 308.
Catechesis/Religious Programs—Students 145.

2—CHRIST THE KING (1934), Rev. Miguel Urrea.
Res., 272 E. Rialto Ave., 92408. Tel: 909-885-1476; Fax: 909-885-3926.

3—OUR LADY OF THE ASSUMPTION (1954), Rev. Michael L. Sturn; Deacon G. Dale Plein.
Res., 796 W. 48th St., 92407. Tel: 909-882-2931; Fax: 909-883-4851.
School—Tel: 909-881-2416. Sr. Maura Redington, Prin.
Sisters of Mercy 3; Lay Teachers 9; Students 310.
Catechesis/Religious Programs—Students 210.

4—OUR LADY OF FATIMA (1952), Rev. Edmund Gomez; Sr. Marita Beumer, C.PP.S., Pastoral Coord.
Office: 1000 N. Valencia Ave., 92410. Tel: 909-885-0948; Fax: 909-384-0576.
Catechesis/Religious Programs—Students 105.

5—OUR LADY OF GUADALUPE (1925) (Hispanic), Revs. Ramon Rosales; Martin S. Rodriguez, O.R.C.; Rev. Msgr. Adolphus Chavez.
Res., 1430 W. Fifth St., 92411. Tel: 909-888-0044; 884-8010; Fax: 909-888-4428.
Catechesis/Religious Programs—1475 W. 7th St., 92411. Tel: 909-381-1628.
Students 711.

6—ST. ANNE (1938), Revs. Gerald Leonard, S.V.D.; Matthias Nguyen H. Chuong.
Res., 6885 Del Rosa Ave., 92404. Tel: 909-884-6375; Fax: 909-884-8976.
School—6886 Del Rosa Ave., 92404. Tel: 909-885-7472; Fax: 909-884-5870.
Lay Teachers 9; Students 128.
Catechesis/Religious Programs—Tel: 909-884-5400.
Students 198.

7—ST. ANTHONY (1948), Revs. Eric P. Vargas, S.V.D.; Paul Vung Le, S.V.D.
Res., 1640 Western Ave., 92411. Tel: 909-887-3810; Fax: 909-880-0982.
School—1510 W. 16th St., 92411. Tel: 909-887-5413; Fax: 909-887-5413.
Sisters of Mercy 5; Lay Teachers 6; Students 268.
Catechesis/Religious Programs—Students 267.

8—ST. BERNARDINE (1862), Rev. Edmund Gomez; Sr. Marita Beumer, C.PP.S., Pastoral Coord.
Res., 531 North F St., 92410. Tel: 909-884-0104; Fax: 909-885-4634.
Catechesis/Religious Programs—Students 150.

9—ST. PHILLIP THE APOSTLE. Unassigned. (Melkite-Greek Catholic Mission).
Res., 923 W. Congress, 92410.

10—ST. THERESA. Closed. For inquiries for parish records contact the Chancery.

OUTSIDE THE CITY OF SAN BERNARDINO

Adelanto, San Bernardino Co., Christ the Good Shepherd (1962), Rev. Antonio Das Neves.
Res., 17900 Jonathan, P.O. Box 579, 92301. Tel: 760-246-7083; Fax: 760-246-4603.
Catechesis/Religious Programs—Students 140.

Alta Loma, San Bernardino Co., St. Peter & St. Paul (1970), Very Rev. Peter Covas; Rev. Jaime Hamame.
Mailing Address: P.O. Box 248, 91701. Tel: 909-987-9312; Fax: 909-980-9404.
School—9135 Banyan Ave., 91701. Tel: 909-987-7908.
Lay Teachers 9; Aides 5; Students 116.
Catechesis/Religious Programs—Tel: 909-980-9423. Dot Flagg, D.R.E.
Students 1,700.
Youth Ministry—Tel: 909-944-8483. Carol Michaud.
Students 300.

Anza, Riverside Co., Sacred Heart (1993), Rev. Bernard J. Carr.
Mailing Address: P.O. Box 390118, 92539.
Res., 56250 Cahuilla Rd., Hwy. 371, 92539. Tel: 909-763-5636; Fax: 909-763-0236.
Catechesis/Religious Programs—Ms. Linda Bahash, D.R.E.
Students 160.
Missions—Anza, Riverside Co., Our Lady of the Snows Cahuilla Indian Reservation,; Anza, Cahuilla Indian Reservation; Riverside Co., Santa Rosa Indian Mission, Santa Rosa Reservation, Tel: 909-659-2708; Santa Rosa Reservation.

Apple Valley, San Bernardino Co., Our Lady of the Desert (1974), Revs. Maurice Cardinal; Vimencio Ignacio; Deacons Carlos Reyes; Robert Rittman.
Office: 18386 Corwin Rd., 92307. Tel: 760-242-4427; Fax: 760-242-1195.
Catechesis/Religious Programs—Tel: 760-242-5819.
Students 300.

Banning, Riverside Co., Precious Blood (1890), Rev. Michael Lama; Deacon Ralph Sepulveda.
Res., 157 W. Nicolet St., 92220. Tel: 909-849-2434; Fax: 909-849-8698.
School—P.O. Box 458, 92220. Tel: 909-849-2433; Fax: 909-849-0843.
Lay Teachers 7; Students 162.
Missions—Banning, Riverside Co., St. Mary, 92220. Tel: 909-849-2434; Morongo Reservation, Riverside Co., Indian Mission, North of Fields Rd., 92220.
Catechesis/Religious Programs—117 W. Nicolet St., Tel: 909-849-1897.
Students 142.

Barstow, San Bernardino Co., St. Joseph (1914), Revs. Gerard Lopez; Joseph Anthony Borba; Deacons Francis Roman; Margarito Saenz; Donald Burgett.
Res., 505 E. Mountain View Ave., 92311. Tel: 760-256-6818; Fax: 760-256-8307.
School—555 E. Mountain View Ave., 92311. Tel: 760-256-2397.
Sisters of Mercy of the Blessed Sacrament 3; Lay Teachers 8; Students 185.
Mission—Baker, San Bernardino Co., Our Lady of the Desert, 92311.
Catechesis/Religious Programs—Students 370.

St. Philip Neri Church (1979), Rev. Joseph Nacu, M.S.
Mailing Address: 909 Armory #409, 92311. Tel: 760-253-5412; Fax: 760-253-2021. [JC]
Catechesis/Religious Programs—Students 75.

Beaumont, Riverside Co., San Gorgonio (1908), Rev. John Robert Domas. In res., Revs. John Yates, C.SS.P.; Michael A. Krelovich.
Res., 1234 Palm Ave., P.O. Box 155, 92223. Tel: 909-845-2849; Fax: 909-845-9259.
Catechesis/Religious Programs—Students 220.

Big Bear Lake, San Bernardino Co., St. Joseph (1931), Rev. Lawrence F. Grajek.
Res., 42242 N. Shore Dr., P.O. Box 1709, 92315. Tel: 909-866-3030; Fax: 909-866-5087. [JC]
Catechesis/Religious Programs—Tel: 909-866-4581.
Students 125.

Bloomington, San Bernardino Co., St. Charles Borromeo (1939) (Hispanic), Rev. Richard Humphrys.
Office: 11342 Spruce St., Box 248, 92316. Tel: 909-877-0792; Fax: 909-877-4304.
Res., 11368 Spruce St., 92316.
Catechesis/Religious Programs—Students 445.

Blythe, Riverside Co., St. Joan of Arc, Rev. Tom Wallace.
Res., 875 E. Chanslorway, 92225. Tel: 760-922-3261; Fax: 760-922-5279.

Cathedral City, Riverside Co., St. Louis (1948), Revs. Michael J. Brooks, SS.CC.; Paul Granilla.
Res., 37-220 Glenn Ave., 92234. Tel: 760-328-2398; Fax: 760-770-4598. [CEM]
Catechesis/Religious Programs—Students 118.

Chino, San Bernardino Co., Our Lady of Guadalupe (1902) (Hispanic), Rev. Anthony T. Ferrero.
Res., 5048 D St., 91710. Tel: 909-591-9402; Fax: 909-591-9404.
Catechesis/Religious Programs—Tel: 909-628-3615.
Students 486.

St. Margaret Mary (1947), Revs. Thomas F. Gillespie; Omer-Luzolo Lwa-Lu Zombe, O.P. (Zaire); Deacon Pat Martinez.
Res., 12686 Central Ave., 91710. Tel: 909-627-8466; Fax: 909-627-8049. [JC]
School—12664 Central Ave., 91710. Tel: 909-591-8419.
Sisters of St. Francis 1; Lay Teachers 13; Students 306.
Catechesis/Religious Programs—Tel: 909-591-7408.
Students 950.

Chino Hills, San Bernardino Co., St. Paul the Apostle (1986), Revs. Michael N. Maher, SS.CC.; David Farrugia, O.P.; Sr. Mary Mackessy, S.N.J.M., Pastoral Assoc.
Office: 14085 Peyton Dr., 91709. Tel: 909-465-5503; Fax: 909-465-1683.
Res., 14860 Cherry Dr., 91709. Tel: 909-597-6154.
Catechesis/Religious Programs—Tel: 909-465-5503, Ext. 16. Lori Muniz, D.R.E.
Students 1,650.

Coachella, Riverside Co., Our Lady of Soledad, Revs. Robert J. Nogosek, C.S.C.; John S. Connor, C.S.C. In res., Rev. Joseph Pawlicki, C.S.C.
Res., 52-525 Oasis Palm, 92236. Tel: 760-398-5577; Fax: 760-398-1783.
Catechesis/Religious Programs—Judy Hoy, D.R.E.
Students 500.

Colton, San Bernardino Co., Immaculate Conception (1943), Rev. Michael R. McNally; Deacon Wayn Joslin.
Office: 1106 N. La Cadena Dr., 92324. Tel: 909-825-5110; Fax: 909-825-0912.
Res., 1090 N. La Cadena Dr., 92324. Tel: 909-825-3004. [JC]
Catechesis/Religious Programs—Students 475.

San Salvador (1893) (Hispanic), Rev. Pierre Deglaire, C.S.Sp.
Parish Center: 178 W. K St., 92324. Tel: 909-825-3481; Fax: 909-825-4473.
Church—Seventh St. & L St., 92324.
Catechesis/Religious Programs—Students 451.

Corona, Riverside Co.,

1—CORPUS CHRISTI CHURCH, (1994), Rev. Gerald C. Deluney.
Office: 107 N. McKinley #109, 91719. Tel: 909-272-9043; Fax: 909-272-6821.
Catechesis/Religious Programs—Students 375.

2—ST. EDWARD, (1896), Rt. Rev. Peter Lugue; Revs. Timothy Jernejcic; John S. Vieira.
Res., 605 W. Fifth St., 91720. Tel: 909-737-6432; Fax: 909-737-7259.
School—500 S. Merrill St., 91720. Tel: 737-2530.
Lay Teachers 23; Students 517.
Catechesis/Religious Programs—Tel: 909-737-5060.
Students 776.

3—ST. MARY MAGDALENE, (1989), Sr. Maureen Chicoine, R.S.C.J., Pastoral Coord.
Church—8540 Weirick Rd., 91719. Tel: 909-277-1801; Fax: 909-277-2513.
Catechesis/Religious Programs—Students 200.

4—St. Matthew, (1973), Rev. John Wagner; Sandra Boyd, Pastoral Assoc.
Res., 2140 W. Ontario, 91720. Tel: 909-737-1621; Fax: 909-737-9715.
Catechesis/Religious Programs—Lou Ann Tannaz, D.R.E.
Students 775.

Crestline, San Bernardino Co., St. Frances Xavier Cabrini (1946), Rev. John R. Hindman.
Res., 23079 Crest Forest Dr., P.O. Box 3817, 92325. Tel: 909-338-2303; Fax: 909-338-2383.
Catechesis/Religious Programs—Students 75.

Desert Hot Springs, Riverside Co., St. Elizabeth of Hungary (1946), Rev. Edward McGuiness.
Res., 66700 E. Pierson Blvd., 92240. Tel: 760-329-8794; Fax: 760-329-6760.
Catechesis/Religious Programs—Tel: 760-251-9268.
Students 135.

Fontana, San Bernardino Co.,

1—Church of the Resurrection, (1953), Revs. Leonard Krzywda, C.R.; Ted Wicki, C.R. In res., Rev. Humphrey Ruszel, C.R.
Res., 7650 Tamarind, 92336. Tel: 909-822-4732; Fax: 909-822-0620.
School—17434 Miller Ave., 92335. Tel: 909-822-4431; Fax: 909-822-0617.
Lay Teachers 10; Students 243.
Catechesis/Religious Programs—Tel: 909-822-2502.
Students 575.

2—St. George, (1954), Rev. Philip A. O'Carroll.
Res., 17895 San Bernardino Ave., 92335. Tel: 909-877-1531; Fax: 909-877-6531.
Catechesis/Religious Programs—Students 350.

3—St. Joseph, (1930), Revs. Richard F. McGee, C.R.; Henry Ruszel, C.R.; Deacon Michael Juback.
Office: 17080 Arrow Blvd., 92335. Tel: 909-822-0566; Fax: 909-829-1739.
School—8460 Mango Ave., 92335. Tel: 909-822-5423.
Daughters of Divine Charity 2; Lay Teachers 9; Students 261.
Catechesis/Religious Programs—Tel: 909-822-3411.
Students 387.

4—St. Mary, (1939), Rev. Clif Marquis, S.T.; Deacons Mario Gutierrez; Roberto Cardenas.
Church—14798 Slover Ave., 92337. Tel: 909-822-5670 (English) 909-356-8398 (Spanish) 909-822-1830; Fax: 909-822-6672.
Catechesis/Religious Programs—Tel: 909-822-1830.
Students 645.

5—St. Nicholas, (Byzantine Rite), Rev. Kurt Burnette, Admin.
Res., 9112 Oleander Ave., 92335-5599. Tel: 909-822-9917.

Grand Terrace, San Bernardino Co., Christ the Redeemer (1980), Rev. Robert Tomkins.
Res., 12770 Oriole, 92313. Tel: 909-783-3811; Fax: 909-783-4689.
Catechesis/Religious Programs—Students 175.

Guasti, San Bernardino Co., San Secondo d'Asti (1926) (Italian), Rev. Louis Marx.
Res., 250 N. Turner Ave., P.O. Box 1056, 91743. Tel: 909-390-0011; Fax: 909-390-9919.
Catechesis/Religious Programs—Students 119.

Hemet, Riverside Co., Holy Spirit Parish (1991), Rev. Silvio D'Ostilio, C.S.Sp.; Jamie Allred, Youth Ministry; Joyce Frichtel, Pastoral Assoc.
Res., 26340 Soboba Ave., Box 5268, 92544. Tel: 909-927-8544; Fax: 909-927-8546.
Catechesis/Religious Programs—Students 190.

Our Lady of the Valley (1946), Revs. James H. Burnie, C.S.Sp.; Clement Lachowsky, C.S.Sp.; Wayne Epperley, C.S.Sp.; Deacon Jack Henke.
Mailing Address: P.O. Box 2446, 92546.
Res., Parish Office, 780 S. State St., 92543. Tel: 909-929-6131; Fax: 909-929-8009.
Catechesis/Religious Programs—Tel: 909-658-7436. Tim Smith, D.R.E.
Students 573.

Hesperia, San Bernardino Co., Holy Family, Rev. Msgr. Philip A. Behan; Rev. Robert Guerrero.
Res., 9974 I Ave., 92345. Tel: 760-244-9180; Fax: 760-244-1959.

Highland, San Bernardino Co., St. Adelaide (1956), Rev. John Ryan; Sr. Maura Feely, Admin. Assoc.
Res., 27457 E. Baseline, 92346. Tel: 909-862-8669; Fax: 909-862-1603.
School—27487 E. Baseline, 92346. Tel: 909-862-5851; Fax: 909-862-2877.
Lay Teachers 11; Students 315.
Catechesis/Religious Programs—Tel: 909-862-8184.
Students 400.
Mission—East Highlands, San Bernardino Co., St. John Bosco, 28991 Merris St., Highland, 92346. Tel: 909-425-0931. Rev. John Ryan.

Idyllwild, Riverside Co., Queen of Angels, Rev. Charles Devine.
Res., 54525 N. Circle Dr., P.O. Box 1106, 92549. Tel: 909-659-2708; Fax: 909-659-0208.

Indio, Riverside Co., Our Lady of Perpetual Help (1937), Revs. Rafael A. Partida; Richard Casillas, S.V.D.
Office: 82-450 Bliss St., 92201. Tel: 760-347-3507; Fax: 760-347-8367.
Res., 45-119 Park St., P.O. Box BB, 92201. Tel: 760-347-5661 (Rectory).
School—82-470 Bliss St., 92201. Tel: 760-347-3786; Fax: 760-347-7207.
Lay Teachers 9; Students 176.
Catechesis/Religious Programs—Tel: 760-347-0594.
Students 447.

Joshua Tree, San Bernardino Co., St. Christopher of the Desert (1960), Rev. Ignatius Rasquinha, Admin.
Res., 61350 Wahl Terr., 92252. Tel: 760-366-8710; Fax: 760-366-2690.
Church—Parish Center, 61261 Sunburst Dr., 92252. Tel: 760-366-8810.

Lake Arrowhead, San Bernardino Co., Our Lady of the Lake (1938), Rev. Timothy F. Keppel, C.R.
Res., 27642 Rim of the World Dr., P.O. Box 7, Crest Park, 92326. Tel: 909-337-2333; Fax: 909-337-5041. [CEM]
Catechesis/Religious Programs—Students 220.

Lake Elsinore, Riverside Co., St. Frances of Rome (1887), Revs. George Gonzalez; Jose P. Kuruvila, O.I.C.; Deacon Bud Burris.
Res., 21591 Lemon St., Wildomar, 92595. Tel: 909-674-6881; Fax: 909-674-6443.
Catechesis/Religious Programs—Students 450.

Lake Tamarisk, Riverside Co., St. Augustine. Unassigned.
Mailing Address: P.O. Box 768, Desert Center, 92239. Tel: 619-227-3191; Fax: 619-328-8392.
Res., 43960 Shasta Dr., 92239.

La Quinta, Riverside Co., St. Francis of Assisi (1974), Rev. Jack D. Barker.
Res., 47-225 Washington, P.O. Box 1503, 92253. Tel: 760-564-1255; Fax: 760-564-0763.
Catechesis/Religious Programs—Tel: 760-564-2069.
Students 378.

Loma Linda, San Bernardino Co., St. Joseph the Worker (1944), Rev. Paul R. Gill.
Res., 10816 Mt. View Ave., 92354. Tel: 909-796-2605; Fax: 909-796-0755.
Catechesis/Religious Programs—Tel: 909-796-4308.
Students 185.

Lucerne Valley, San Bernardino Co., St. Paul (1963), Rev. John Benjamin, Admin.
Res., 8973 Mesa Rd., P.O. Box 588, 92356. Tel: 760-248-7410; Fax: 760-248-2559.

Mecca, Riverside Co., Our Lady of Guadalupe Shrine (1927), Revs. Jose Varela, O.R.C.; Saul Ayala.
Mailing Address: 2858 Ninth Street, Riverside, 92507. Tel: 909-684-0279. [JC]
Church—65-100 Dale Killer Rd., 92254.
Res., 91-110 5th St., 92254.
Catechesis/Religious Programs—Tel: 909-684-0279; Fax: 909-684-0390.
Students 500.

Montclair, San Bernardino Co., Our Lady of Lourdes, Rev. Robert J. Donat.
Res., 10191 Central Ave., 91763. Tel: 909-626-7278; Fax: 909-626-0562.
School—5303 Orchard St., 91763. Tel: 909-621-4418; 624-5164; Fax: 909-626-0318.
Sisters of the Presentation 3; Lay Teachers 10; Students 280.
Catechesis/Religious Programs—Sr. Angela Callanan, D.R.E.
Students 579.

Moreno Valley, Riverside Co., St. Christopher (1959), Revs. Efren Musngi, M.S.; Enrique La Puebla, M.S.; Romeo Seleccion, M.S.; Deacon Samual Sanchez.
Res., 25075 Cottonwood Ave., 92553. Tel: 909-924-1968; Fax: 909-247-6477.
Catechesis/Religious Programs—D.R.E.: Elizabeth Scretchings; Pat Garza, (High School); Mirca Sanchez, (Spanish).
Students 2,000.

Murrietta, Riverside Co., St. Martha's (1992), Rev. Ponciano M. Ramos, S.V.D.
Church—37200 Whitewood Rd., 92563. Tel: 909-698-8180; Fax: 909-698-7353.
Catechesis/Religious Programs—Students 850.

Needles, San Bernardino Co., St. Ann (1888), Rev. William M. Brunner, S.S.C.
Res., 218 D St., P.O. Box 175, 92363. Tel: 760-326-2721; Fax: 760-326-3068. [JC]
Catechesis/Religious Programs—Students 105.

Norco, Riverside Co., St. Mel (1959), Rev. Arturo Balagat.
Res., 4200 Corona Ave., P.O. Box 700, 91760. Tel: 909-737-7144; Fax: 909-735-8332.

Ontario, San Bernardino Co., Our Lady of Guadalupe (1948) (Hispanic), Revs. Sacramento Perez, O.de.M.; Adrian Ochoa, O.de.M.; Deacon Guiseppe Raspa.
Res., 710 S. Sultana St., 91761. Tel: 909-986-6154; Fax: 909-984-1541.
Catechesis/Religious Programs—Students 838.

St. George (1905), Revs. Joseph Krah; Santos Leonel Ortega; Sr. Danielle Daran, R.N., Pastoral Assoc. In res., Rev. Msgr. Timothy Lawlor.
Res., 325 W. E St., 91762. Tel: 909-983-2637; Fax: 909-395-9707. [JC]
School—322 W. D St., 91762. Tel: 909-984-9123.
Lay Teachers 9; Students 303.
Catechesis/Religious Programs—Students 290.

St. Elizabeth Ann Seton (1980), Rev. Msgr. Lourenco Avila; Rev. Amaro Saumell.
Res., 2713 S. Grove Ave., 91761. Tel: 909-947-2956; Fax: 909-947-2946.
Catechesis/Religious Programs—Tel: 909-947-5436.
Students 626.

Palm Desert, Riverside Co., Christ of the Desert (1986). (Newman Center). Rev. Ned Reidy, C.S.C.
Res., 73441 Fred Waring Dr., 92260. Tel: 760-346-0089; Fax: 760-340-2245.

Sacred Heart (1956), Revs. Anthony J. Timlin; Peter McCormick, S.P.
Res., 43-775 N. Deep Canyon Rd., 92260. Tel: 760-346-6502; Fax: 760-773-4873.
School—Tel: 760-346-3513. Sr. Joan Griffin, O.S.F., Prin.
Lay Teachers 9; Religious Teachers 2; Students 270.
Catechesis/Religious Programs—Tel: 760-340-0143.
Students 165.

Palm Springs, Riverside Co., Our Lady of Guadalupe (1912) (Cahuilla Indian), Rev. Eugene Speno.
Res., 204 S. El Segundo, P.O. Box 1947, 92263. Tel: 760-325-5809; Fax: 760-327-2049.

Our Lady of Solitude (1929) (Hispanic), Revs. Miguel Ceja; Cirilo Bailon; Deacon John Skora.
Res., 151 W. Alejo Rd., 92262. Tel: 760-325-3816; Fax: 760-325-5316. [JC]
Catechesis/Religious Programs—Students 225.

St. Theresa, Rev. Msgr. Malachy M. McGinn; Rev. David Andel.
Res., 2800 E. Ramon Rd., 92264. Tel: 760-323-2669; Fax: 760-322-8581.
School—455 S. Compadre, 92262. Tel: 760-327-4919.
Sisters 2; Lay Teachers 10; Students 320.

Perris, Riverside Co., St. James (1907), Rev. William D. Erstad. In res., Rev. John Niessen.
Office: 269 W. Third St., 92570.
Res., 260 W. Third St., 92570. Tel: 909-657-2380; Fax: 909-943-7290.
School—250 W. Third St., 92570. Tel: 909-657-5226; Fax: 909-657-1793.
Irish Sisters of Mercy 3; Lay Teachers 10; Students 300.
Catechesis/Religious Programs—Tel: 909-657-8809. Sr. Noreen O'Connor, D.R.E.
Students 989.

Phelan, San Bernardino Co., Blessed Junipero Serra Church (1989), Rev. Patrick V. Kirsch.
Mailing Address: P.O. Box 292570, 92329-2570.
Rectory Office: 4471 Sunrise Blvd., 92371. Tel: 760-868-4342; Fax: 760-249-3438.
Catechesis/Religious Programs—Students 172.

Rancho Cucamonga, San Bernardino Co., Our Lady of Mount Carmel (1905), Rev. Francisco Cabarello, O.de.M.
Res., 10079 Eighth St., P.O. Box 303, 91729-0303. Tel: 909-987-2717; Fax: 909-987-3818.
Catechesis/Religious Programs—Students 410.

Sacred Heart (1953), Very Rev. Stephen C. Porter; Deacon Charles Fultz.
Res., 12704 Foothill Blvd., 91739. Tel: 909-899-1049; Fax: 909-899-3229.
School—Tel: 909-899-1601.
Lay Teachers 11; Students 300.
Catechesis/Religious Programs—Students 340.

Redlands, San Bernardino Co., Sacred Heart (1894), Revs. Joseph F. Felker, Admin.; Frank T. Dicristina; Deacons William Keough; Richard Cover.
Res., 115 W. Olive Ave., 92373. Tel: 909-793-2469; Fax: 909-335-1719.
School—215 S. Eureka St., 92373. Tel: 909-792-3958.
Lay Teachers 20; Students 289.

Catechesis/Religious Programs—Tel: 909-798-4167. Dr. Sarah Elder, D.R.E.
Students 490.

St. Mary (1941) (Latino), Rev. Jose Maria Cima.
Res., 1214 Columbia St., 92374. Tel: 909-792-3695; Fax: 909-798-2665. [JC]
Catechesis/Religious Programs—Students 330.

Rialto, San Bernardino Co., St. Catherine of Siena (1949), Rev. Howard A. Lincoln; Deacons Joseph F. Rios; Edwin Chamberlayne; Gonzalo Sotelo. Pastoral Assoc.: Kay Halder; Steve Valenzuela; Horacio Cortez. In res., Rev. Ciro Libanati.
Res., 339 N. Sycamore, 92376-3517. Tel: 909-875-1360; Fax: 909-875-2822.
School—335 N. Sycamore Ave., 92376. Tel: 909-875-7821.
Lay Teachers 9; Students 300.
Catechesis/Religious Programs—Students 280.

St. Thomas More, Rev. Edward A. Dubel, C.R.
Res., 222 E. Easton, P.O. Box 367, 92376. Tel: 909-421-7030; Fax: 909-421-1374.

Riverside, Riverside Co.,

1—Our Lady of Guadalupe Shrine, Rev. Jose Varlea, O.R.C.; Deacon Rudy Ybarra. In res., Rev. Martin S. Rodriguez.
Res., 2858 Ninth St., 92507. Tel: 909-684-0279; Fax: 909-684-0390.

2—Our Lady of Perpetual Help, Revs. Ignatius Rodrigues; Cristian Mier, D.L.P.; Deacons Joe Gomeck; Ysidro, Gurrola; Larry Quilliam.
Res., 5250 Central Ave., 92504. Tel: 909-689-8921; Fax: 909-689-3619.
School—6686 Streeter Ave., 92504. Tel: 909-689-2125.
Lay Teachers 12; Students 283.

3—Queen of Angels, Revs. Ronald Rocky, O.F.M.Conv.; Anthony Howard, O.F.M.Conv.
Res., 4824 Jones Ave., 92505. Tel: 909-689-3674; Fax: 909-687-6146.
School—Tel: 909-689-1992.
Lay Teachers 15; Students 240.

4—Sacred Heart, (1945), Rev. Edward J. Connolly.
Res., 9935 Mission Blvd., 92509. Tel: 909-685-5058; Fax: 909-685-1056.
Catechesis/Religious Programs—Tel: 909-685-8510.
Students 980.

5—St. Anthony, (1923), Rev. Eliseo Hernandez.
Res., 3074 Madison St., 92504. Tel: 909-352-8393; Fax: 909-352-8816.

6—St. Catherine of Alexandria, (1946), Rev. Thomas J. Burdick.
Res., 7050 Brockton Ave., 92506. Tel: 909-683-0800; Fax: 909-683-4114.
School—3728 Arlington Ave., 92506. Tel: 909-684-1091; Fax: 909-684-4936.
Lay Teachers 16; Students 361.
Catechesis/Religious Programs—Tel: 909-684-6519. Sr. Claudine Wietecha, D.R.E.
Students 512.

7—St. Francis de Sales, (1886), Revs. Vincent Salemi, I.M.C.; Reno Aiardi, I.M.C.; Luigi Inveraradi, I.M.C.; Deacon James Dale.
Res., 4268 Lime St., 92501. Tel: 909-686-4004; Fax: 909-686-3948. [JC]
School—Tel: 909-683-5083; Fax: 909-683-0249.
Religious 2; Lay Teachers 15; Students 340.
Catechesis/Religious Programs—Tel: 909-784-0987.
Students 335.

8—St. John the Evangelist, (1956), Rev. Michael Fredericks. In res., Rev. Msgr. Edward T. Cronin.
Res., 3980 Opal St., 92509. Tel: 909-684-6864; Fax: 909-684-3115.
Mission—Rubidoux, Riverside Co., Our Lady of Guadalupe, 2518 Hall Ave., P.O. Box 3024, Riverside, CA 92509. Tel: 909-788-1464.
Catechesis/Religious Programs—Tel: 909-686-5181.
Students 608.

9—St. Patrick, Rev. James McLaughlin.
Mailing Address: 10915 Pigeon Pass Rd., Moreno Valley, 92557. Tel: 909-485-6673; Fax: 909-485-3834.
Church—6296 Rivercrest Dr., 92507. Tel: 909-697-7727; Fax: 909-697-7729.

10—St. Andrew's Newman Center. Serving Riverside Community College & UCR. Revs. David Geib, O.P.; Francis Goode.
105 W. Big Springs Rd., 92507. Tel: 909-682-8751; Fax: 909-682-3513.
Res., 872 Spruce St., 92507. Tel: 909-784-0160.
Catechesis/Religious Programs—Fax: 909-784-0160. Frances Hodgkinson, D.R.E.
Students 120.

11—St. Thomas the Apostle, (1903), Rev. Robert M. Herbst, O.F.M.Conv.; Bro. Gerald Villanueva, O.F.M.Conv., Pastoral Assoc. In res., Rev. Victor Abegg, O.F.M.Conv.
Res., 3774 Jackson St., 92503. Tel: 909-689-1131; Fax: 909-354-7402.
School—9136 Magnolia Ave., 92503. Tel: 909-689-1981; Fax: 909-689-1985.
Sisters 1; Lay Teachers 10; Students 349.
Catechesis/Religious Programs—Tel: 909-689-7180. Nancy Corbitt, D.R.E.
Students 600.
Mission—Riverside, Our Lady of Guadalupe, 9398 Indiana Ave., 92503. Rev. Robert M. Herbst, O.F.M.Conv.

Running Springs, San Bernardino Co., St. Anne in the Mountains (1963), Rev. Adrian Brinn.
Res., 30480 Fredalba Rd., P.O. Box 2400, 92382. Tel: 909-867-2832; Fax: 909-867-2832.

San Jacinto, Riverside Co., St. Anthony (1890), Rev. Charles Devine; Mr. Chuck Stroud, Pastoral Assoc.
Res., 630 S. Santa Fe Ave., 92583. Tel: 909-654-7911; Fax: 909-654-2309.
School—St. Hyacinth Academy, Tel: 909-654-2013.
Sisters 2; Lay Teachers 11; Students 224.
Catechesis/Religious Programs—Tel: 909-654-3311.
Students 250.

Soboba Indian Reservation, Riverside Co., St. Joseph (1888) (American Indian), Rev. Francis Neiser; Mr. Michael Madrigal, Admin.
Mailing Address: P.O. Box 1027, San Jacinto, 92581. Tel: 909-654-2086; Fax: 909-654-2086. [CEM]

Sun City, Riverside Co., St. Vincent Ferrer (1965), Rev. Gerard J. McGuinness; Deacon Ronald Rehaume. In res., Rev. Michael O'Day.
Res., 27931 Murrieta Rd., 92586-2320. Tel: 909-679-4531; Fax: 909-679-7521.
Catechesis/Religious Programs—Tel: 909-672-4019.
Students 295.

Temecula, Riverside Co., St. Catherine (1979), Revs. Anthony M. DiLeo; Charles Patron; Deacon John Barth.
Res., 41875 C St., 92592. Tel: 909-676-4403; Fax: 909-695-6659.
Catechesis/Religious Programs—Kathleen Igo, D.R.E.
Students 1,006.

Thermal, San Bernardino Co., San Felipe de Jesus, Revs. Bob Nogosek; John Connor, C.S.C.
Church—67-305 Hwy. 86, 92274. Tel: 760-398-5577; Fax: 760-398-1783.

Trona, San Bernardino Co., St. Madeleine Sophie Barat, Rev. William J. Kiefer.
Res., 83395 Trona Rd., 93562. Tel: 760-372-4717.

Thousand Palms, San Bernardino, St. Philip the Apostle, Rev. Joseph Mawicke.
Res., 31-525 Via Pared, P.O. Box 405, 92276. Tel: 760-343-1911; Fax: 760-343-3211.
Catechesis/Religious Programs—Students 76.

Twentynine Palms, San Bernardino Co., Blessed Sacrament, Rev. Baldwin Beyer, O.F.M.Cap., Admin.
Office: 6785 Sage Ave., 92277. Tel: 760-367-3343; Fax: 760-367-0543.
School—6755 Sage Ave., 92277. Tel: 760-367-3341.
Lay Teachers 8; Students 122.
Catechesis/Religious Programs—Virginia Harris, D.R.E.
Lay Teachers 9; Students 120.

Upland, San Bernardino Co., St. Joseph (1922), Revs. John Kavcak, M.S.C.; Tom Burns, M.S.C.; Joseph Jablonski, M.S.C.; Deacons Charles Pobjoy; Frank Simoni; John Kim.
Res., 877 N. Campus Ave., 91786. Tel: 909-981-8110; Fax: 909-949-8090.
School—905 Campus Ave., 91786. Tel: 909-920-5185; Fax: 909-920-5190.
Sisters of the Presentation 3; Lay Teachers 13; Students 356.
Catechesis/Religious Programs—Tel: 909-982-9518. Liliana Moore, D.R.E.
Students 627.

St. Anthony (1974), Rev. Edmond G. O'Donnell; Deacon Eugene Bello.
Res., 2110 N. San Antonio Ave., P.O. Box 608, 91785. Tel: 909-985-2803; Fax: 909-982-8643.
Church—2110 N. San Antonio Ave., 91785.
Catechesis/Religious Programs—Tel: 909-981-7080. Susan Breen, D.R.E.
Students 450.

Victorville, San Bernardino Co., Holy Innocents (1992), Rev. Mark E. Kotlarczyk.
Mailing Address: 15384 Tamarack Rd., 92392. Tel: 760-955-6010; Fax: 760-955-2100.
Catechesis/Religious Programs—Tel: 760-955-6262.
Students 394.

St. Joan of Arc (1922), Revs. Gerardo Mendoza; John Fahnestock.
Res., 15512 Sixth St., 92392. Tel: 760-245-7674; Fax: 760-245-7077.
Catechesis/Religious Programs—15503 5th St., 92392.
Students 491.

Wrightwood, San Bernardino Co., Our Lady of the Snows (1946), Rev. Patrick V. Kirsch.
Mailing Address: P.O. Box 292570, Phelan, 92329. Tel: 760-868-4342; Fax: 760-868-2171.
Rectory Office: 4471 Sunrise Blvd., Phelan, 92371.
Catechesis/Religious Programs—Students 74.

Yucaipa, San Bernardino Co., St. Frances Xavier Cabrini (1953), Rev. Kenneth Jenkins.
Res., 12687 California St., 92399. Tel: 909-797-2533; Fax: 909-790-5803.
Catechesis/Religious Programs—Students 150.

Yucca Valley, San Bernardino Co., St. Mary of the Valley, Rev. Charles E. Miller.
Res., 7495 Church St., 92284-3247. Tel: 760-365-2287; Fax: 760-369-0622.
Catechesis/Religious Programs—Students 150.

Chaplains of Public Institutions

San Bernardino. *San Bernardino City and County Jails.* Vacant.
San Bernardino Community Hospital 1500 W. 17th St., 92411. Tel: 909-884-6333; 881-4053. Rev. John Gorman.
San Bernardino County Medical Center 780 E. Gilbert St., 92404. Tel: 909-387-8111. Rev. Dennis Flynn, S.V.D.
San Bernardino Juvenile Hall & Verdemont Boys Ranch. Catholic Charities, 1450 N. D St., 92405. Tel: 909-388-1239. Michael Kennedy, Detention Ministry.
San Bernardino Medical Center 2101 N. Waterman Ave., 92404. Tel: 909-883-8711. Rev. Barnabas Laubach, O.S.B.

Blythe. *Chuckawalla Valley State Prison* P.O. Box 2289, 92226. Tel: 760-243-7243. Rev. John Rusk.

Chino. *California Institute for Men* P.O. Box 128, 91710. Tel: 909-681-6497; 597-1821, Ext. 2289; 2689. Rev. Chester Kopec, O.P.
California Youth Authority. P.O. Box 800, Ontario, 91761. Tel: 909-597-1861, Ext. 395. Rev. Vincent Connor, Chap.
Camp Prado. Vacant.
Southern Conservation Center P.O. Box 128, 91710. Tel: 909-597-1821, Ext. 2289. Rev. Michael Bucaro.

Fontana. *Kaiser Permanente Hospital* 9961 Sierra Ave., 92335. Tel: 909-829-5850; 829-5000 (Emergency). Rev. William Marcotte.

Frontera. *California Institute for Women* 16756 Chino-Corona Rd., 91720. Tel: 909-597-1771. Rev. Neil D. Fuller, S.V.D., Chap.

Loma Linda. *Jerry Pettis Memorial Hospital* 11201 Benton St., 92354. Tel: 909-825-7084. Rev. Msgr. Adolphus Chavez, (Hispanics); Mr. Stephen Elias.
Loma Linda Community Hospital 25333 Barton Rd., 92354. Tel: 909-796-7311, Ext. 4367. Rev. Leonard Mestas.
Loma Linda University Medical Center Barton Rd. and Anderson St., 92354. Tel: 909-824-0800. Rev. Leonard Mestas.

Norco. *California Rehabilitation Center* Western & Fifth Sts., P.O. Box 1841, 91760. Tel: 909-737-2683, Ext. 4305. Rev. Msgr. Cosimo Corciulo.

Patton. *Patton State Hospital.* Rev. Bernard Donaghey.

Pilot Rock. *Crestline.* Vacant. Tel: 909-338-2303.

Riverside. *Riverside Community Hospital.* Rev. Martin S. Rodriguez.
Riverside General Hospital 9851 Magnolia Ave., 92503. Tel: 909-358-7100; 689-3674. Bro. Dario Garcia, O.F.M.Conv.
Riverside Juvenile Hall. Vacant.

On Duty Outside the Diocese:
Reverend Fathers—
Buchanan, Robert, Our Lady of Snows, 1138 Wright St., Las Vegas, NV 89509
Frankovich, Frank, Companions of the Cross, 100 Young St., Ottawa, Ontario, Canada KIY 3P7
Kurilec, Robert, USN, 3908 Roebling Ln., Virginia Beach, VA 23452
Lowe, Frank, Capt., Chap., 42 ABWHC, 331 West Dr., Maxwell A.F.B., AL 36112-6023

Military Chaplains:
Reverend Fathers—
Jasinski, John B., Office of the Chaplain, MCLB, Barstow, CA 92311-5000. Tel: 619-269-2630
Menz, Anthony, National Training Center, Center Chapel, P.O. Box 10007, Fort Irwin, CA 92310. Tel: 619-386-3562
Schnipke, Eugene, 831 CSG-HC, George AFB, CA 92394. Tel: 619-269-2630

On Leave:
Reverend Fathers—
Gil, Rudi
Stauber, James

Retired:
Reverend Monsignors—
Andreatta, Tullio, 2245 Fort Stockton Rd., San Diego, CA 92103
Bradley, John J., 3066 Ladera Dr., San Bernardino, CA 92405
Lawlor, Timothy, 325 W. E St., Ontario, CA 91762
Meagher, Thomas, 1011 St. Andrews #4, Upland, CA 91786
Nightengale, Francis, 6458 N. Via Divina, Tucson, AZ 85715-0973
O'Leary, Cornelius, 25098 Jaclyn Ave., Moreno Valley, CA 92543
Slattery, John T., P.O. Box 588, Lucerne Valley, CA 92356
Reverend Fathers—
Baseford, Paul, 485 Foxenwood Dr., Santa Maria, CA 92355
Battle, Lawrence, 73450 Country Club Dr. #190, Palm Desert, CA 92260
Bonacum, Thomas, 124 Box Garner Valley Rd., Mountain Center, CA 92561
Casey, Donald A., 546 Reliance Ave., Henderson, NV 89015-9690
Coslowsky, Marion, 733 Belinda Ave., Barstow, CA 92311
Cronin, Edward, 3980 Opal St., Riverside, CA 92509
DePasquale, Dominic, 4673 Braemar Pl., Riverside, CA 92501
Dien, Vincent, 5186 Homestead Pl., Riverside, CA 92504
Dietrich, Edward, 2034 Chia, Palm Springs, CA 92262
Diezel, Joseph J., 5734 N. McVickor, Chicago, IL 60646
Downey, Robert, P.O. Box 292629, Phelan, CA 92329
Fitzwilliam, Ivan, 388 Reposo St., San Jacinto, CA 92582
Ganahl, James, 15767 Tuscola Rd., Apt. 1, Apple Valley, CA 92307
Greiner, Lawrence, 197 Via Lola, Apt. 10, Palm Springs, CA 92262
Guillen, Manuel R., 1535 Third Ave., San Diego, CA 92101
Guillen, Patricio, 2002 S. Magnolia Ave., Ontario, CA 91762
Jalbert, Marcel, 25714 Mesa Ct., San Bernardino, CA 92404
Jazbec, Stanley, 6784 Outpost Rd., Joshua Tree, CA 92252
Kiefer, William J., 83395 Trona Rd., Trona, CA 93562
Leahy, Anthony, P.O. Box 4027, Oceanside, CA 92051
Leissler, Joseph L., 45-803 Hwy. 74, Palm Desert, CA 92260
Lenoir, Jean, 79-925 Camelback Dr., Bermuda Dunes, CA 92201
Nagler, Robert, 1945 Illion St., San Diego, CA 92110
O'Day, Michael, 28710 Olympia Way, Sun City, CA 92586
O'Keeffe, Patrick, 1201 E. Highland Ave., San Bernardino, CA 92404
O'Sullivan, Brendan, 1001 Encinitas Blvd., San Diego, CA 92024
Roach, Joseph W., S.A.G., 9466 Navajo Tr., Morongo Valley, CA 92256
Scanlan, Patrick J., 6333 Rancho Mission Rd., San Diego, CA 92108
Schilly, Joseph, 2772 Sterling Ave., San Benardino, CA 92404
Strancar, Ignatius, 6333 Rancho Mission Rd., San Diego, CA 92108
Trong, Joseph, 12772 Louise Cir., Garden Grove, CA 92643
Valdes, Luis, 1775 Pennsylvania, Riverside, CA 92507
Vehovec, Valentine, 6333 Rancho Mission Rd., #104, San Diego, CA 92108
Wadell, John, Cl. Fra. Pere Fornes, 13, Muro, Mallorca, Spain 07440
Walters, Vincent, 565 Wisconsin St., San Francisco, CA 94107
Waterfall, Richard A., P.O. Box 409, Palm Springs, CA 92263
White, Kris, 11171 Oakwood Dr., I-305, Loma Linda, CA 92354
Wieser, Francis, 10831 Deerfield Dr., Cherry Valley, CA 92223
Yahn, George, P.O. Box 167, Songnor, Nandi Hills District, Kenya, East Africa
Zaratti, Elio, 6333 Rancho Mission Rd., San Diego, CA 92108

Permanent Deacons:
Acosta, Joseph, Highland
Aguilera, Santos, Hesperia
Alaniz, Frank, Hesperia
Basoco, Raymond, On Duty Outside the Diocese
Bello, Eugene, Upland
Borne, Edward, Perris
Brannick, Thomas, Rialto
Burger, Joseph, Ontario
Burgett, Donald, Barstow
Burns, Charles, La Quinta
Burns, Jim, On Duty Outside the Diocese
Burris, Bud, Lake Elsinore
Campbell, Gerald, Cathedral City
Chamberlayne, Edwin, Rialto
Clinton, Jack, Upland
Cohoon, Kenneth, Corona
Conrad, Jack, Alta Loma
Cover, Richard, Redlands
Dale, James R., Riverside
Everard, Ed, On Duty Outside the Diocese
Freeman, Russ, On Duty Outside the Diocese
Fultz, Charles, Upland
Garcia, Joseph, Norco
Gomeck, Joseph, Riverside
Gomez, Manuel, Apple Valley
Gonzalez, Victor, Bermuda Dunes
Grandon, Walter, Anza
Grandon, Wayne, On Duty Outside the Diocese
Gurrola, Ysidro, Riverside
Haproff, David, Corona
Hawes, Lloyd, Chino
Henke, John A., San Jacinto
Heredia, Juan, Palm Desert
Hodnick, Mark, Alta Loma
Hoy, Wayne, Coachella
Jacobs, Gary, Apple Valley
Joslin, Wayne, Moreno Valley
Kafka, Gene, San Bernardino
Keough, William, Redlands
Kermott, Philip P., Banning
Key, Joseph, San Bernardino
Kilbourn, Austin, Moreno Valley
Kim, John, Upland
Meader, James, Twentynine Palms
Melendrez, Walter, Alta Loma
Melton, Harold, Lake Elsinore
Michel, Jesse, Desert Hot Springs
Millen, Arthur, Riverside
Mirci, Philip, Redlands
Neufell, James, Riverside
Olivas, Manuel, Riverside
Ortiz, Joseph, Riverside
Partida, Ralph, Jr., Chino
Plein, Dale, San Bernardino
Pobjoy, Charles, Cucamonga
Quilliam, Lawrence, Riverside
Ramirez, Raymond, Indio
Rehaume, Ronald J., Sun City
Reyes, Carlos, Apple Valley
Rios, Joseph, Redlands
Rittman, Robert, Apple Valley
Robicheaux, Paul, Norco
Rodriquez, Jose, On Duty Outside the Diocese
Roman, Francis, Barstow
Saenz, Margarito, Barstow
Saladin, Jerry, On Duty Outside the Diocese
Salinas, Arcadio, Jr., Cathedral City
Sanchez, Samuel, Moreno Valley
Schmit, George, Upland
Sepulveda, Ralph, Banning
Shalhoub, William J., Yucaipa
Silva, Francisco, Mecca
Simoni, Frank, Upland
Simpson, Jerry, Running Springs
Skora, John, Palm Springs
Soper, Leonard, On Duty Outside the Diocese
Sotelo, Gonzalo, Rialto
Spinney, Don, On Duty Outside the Diocese
Vasquez, Sergio, Coachella
Vital, Ernesto, Upland
Von Ins, Paul, Alta Loma
Wagner, Tom, On Duty Outside the Diocese
Ybarra, Rudy, Riverside
Zambrano, Jose, Corona

INSTITUTIONS LOCATED IN THE DIOCESE

[A] SEMINARIES, RELIGIOUS OR SCHOLASTICATES

RIVERSIDE. *Blessed Junipero Serra House of Formation*, 3325 13th St., 92501. Tel: 909-788-9931; Fax: 909-781-9031. Revs. Jose Sanz, Rector; Rolando Fonsela, Vice Rector.

Divine Word Seminary, 11316 Cypress Ave., 92505. Tel: 909-689-4858; Fax: 909-785-0327. Revs. Walt Miller, S.V.D., Rector; Richard Casillas, S.V.D.; Joseph Fertal, S.V.D.; Clifton Etienne, S.V.D.; Michael Manning; John McHenry, S.V.D.; Cosmas A. Meyer, S.V.D.; John Shevlin, S.V.D.; Richard Winters, S.V.D.; Bros. Bernard Dorade, S.V.D.; Daniel Yunck, S.V.D.; Robert Zalikowski, S.V.D.

[B] HIGH SCHOOLS, DIOCESAN

SAN BERNARDINO. *Aquinas High School*. (Coed), 2772 Sterling Ave., 92404. Tel: 909-886-4659; Fax: 909-886-7717.
E-mail: AquinasHS@connectinc.com
Rev. Andrew Sotelo, S.J., Prin. Priests 1; Sisters 1; Lay Teachers 18; Students 295.

RIVERSIDE. *Notre Dame High School*. (Coed), 7085 Brockton Ave., 92506. Tel: 909-369-2810; Fax: 909-781-9020. Mr. Stephen T. Krup, Prin.; Rev. Richard Parker. Priests 1; Sisters 2; Lay Teachers 43; Students 576.

[C] HOMES FOR SENIOR CITIZENS

SAN BERNARDINO. *St. Bernardine Plaza*, 550 W. Fifth St., 92401. Tel: 909-888-0153; Fax: 909-381-1589
For a complete listing, refer to the Special Care Facilities section.

PALM DESERT. *La Paz Villas*, P.O. Box 1962, 92261. Tel: 619-346-6033
For a complete listing, refer to the Special Care Facilities section.

[D] GENERAL HOSPITALS AND CLINICS

SAN BERNARDINO. *St. Bernardine Medical Center*, 2101 N. Waterman Ave., 92404. Tel: 909-883-8711; Fax: 909-881-4546
For a complete listing, refer to the Hospitals section.

APPLE VALLEY. *St. Mary Regional Medical Center*, 18300 Hwy. 18, P.O. Box 7025, 92307. Tel: 760-242-2311; Fax: 760-242-9750
For a complete listing, refer to the Hospitals section.

[E] MONASTERIES AND RESIDENCES OF PRIESTS AND BROTHERS

APPLE VALLEY. *Hospitaller Brothers St. John of God*, P.O. Box 1664, 92307. Tel: 760-242-2783; Fax: 760-241-8911. Bro. Gary Hill, O.H., Prior. Brothers 6.

CORONA. *Congregation of the Mother Coredemptrix*, 1775 S. Main St., 91720-4961. Tel: 909-737-4125; 340-9880.
Shrine of Presentation (Den Thanh Duc Me Dang Con). Revs. Pius M. Nguyen Dan, C.M.C., Dir.; Leo M. Vu Dinh Huyen, C.M.C.; Matthias M. Nguyen Huy Chuong, C.M.C.; Aloysius M. Tran Ngoc Thoai, C.M.C.; Francis Hoang-Anh-Thang, C.M.C.; Luke M. Do Binh Dinh, C.M.C.

HEMET. *Congregation of the Sacred Hearts, SS.CC.*, Western U.S. Province, 32481 Sage Rd., 92544. Tel: 909-767-9436.

Holy Ghost Fathers, 309 E. Whittier Ave., 92543. Tel: 909-658-2241. Revs. Louis G. Perreault, C.S.Sp., Novitiate; Matthew Evanstock, C.S.Sp.; Edmond J. Leonard, C.S.Sp.; Edward Bernacki, C.S.Sp.; Richard Kissane, C.S.Sp.; Kitira Gabriel, C.S.Sp.; Joseph G. Tobin, C.S.Sp.; Kenneth F. Milford, C.S.Sp., 1600-177 San Jacinto St., 92383-5146. Tel: 909-654-7010. San Gorgonio Church, P.O. Box 155, Beaumont, 92223-0155. Tel: 909-845-2849; Fax: 909-845-9259. Rev. Daniel C. Murphy.

MORONGO VALLEY. *St. Michael's of Morongo Valley, Inc.*, 9466 Navajo Tr., 92256. Tel: 760-363-6617. Retirement Facility. In res. Revs. Gerald F. Clune (ALB) (Retired); Aloysius A. Lucking, (Retired); Richard S. Bradley, S.J., (Retired); Joseph Buttimer (LOA); Gino G. Rive, (Retired); Joseph W. Roach, SAG, (Retired).

RIVERSIDE. *Operarios Del Reino De Cristo, O.R.C.*, 2858 Ninth St., 92507. Tel: 909-684-0279; Fax: 909-684-0309. Revs. Jose Varela, O.R.C., Local Contact; Edwardo Carmona (Mexico), Regl. Dir.

St. Vincent Ferrer House, 872 Spruce St., 92507. Tel: 909-784-0160; Fax: 909-682-3513. Dominicans. Revs. Lawrence Farrell, O.P.; Francis Goode.

[F] CONVENTS AND RESIDENCES FOR SISTERS

SAN BERNARDINO. *Congregation of the Sisters of Mercy*, 4825 H St., 92407.

CALIMESA. *Missionary Sisters of the Immaculate Conception*, 1271 Nugget Ct., 92320; Fax: 909-795-8128. Madonna of the Community 2.

COACHELLA. *Our Lady of Victory Missionary Sisters*, Office: 52-525 Oasis Palm Ave., 92236. Tel: 619-398-5577. Res., 81-860 Shadow Palm, #48, 92201. Tel: 619-347-7034.

GRAND TERRACE. *Sisters of St. Benedict, Holy Spirit Monastery*, 22791 Pico St., 92313-5750. Tel: 909-783-4446. Sr. Carolyn Gries, O.S.B., Prioress. Sisters 13.

REDLANDS. *Sisters of Mercy, U.S. Province*, 1075 Bermuda Dr., 92374. Tel: 909-809-4747; Fax: 909-798-5300. Sr. Teresa O'Connell, R.S.M., Prov.

TUSTIN. *Sisters of the Company of Mary (O.D.N.)*, 16791 E. Main St., 92780. Tel: 714-541-3125; Fax: 714-835-0648. Sr. Ernestine Velarde, O.D.N., Maj. Sup. Convent. Vina de Lestonnac Ministry Center-Retreat, 39300 De Portola Rd., Temecula, 92592. Tel: 909-695-1076.

Vina de Lestonnac Ministry Center, 39300 De Portola Rd., Temecula, 92592. Tel: 909-695-2186; Fax: 909-695-1509.

St. Jeanne de Lestonnac Preschool/Kindergarten - Second Grade, 39300 De Portola Rd., Temecula, 92692. Tel: 909-695-3396. Sr. Enedina Badillo, O.D.N.; Sr. Cheryl Hebestreit, O.D.N.; Sr. Zina Choro, O.D.N.; Sr. Andrea Calderon, O.D.N.; Sr. Maria de la Torre, O.D.N.; Sr. Josephine Diaz, O.D.N.; Sr. Raphael Garcia, O.D.N.; Sr. Justine Gonzales, O.D.N.; Sr. Manuela Hernandez, O.D.N.; Sr. Patricia Huber, O.D.N.; Sr. Catalina Ponce, O.D.N.; Sr. Lupe Romero, O.D.N.; Sr. Victoria Ruiz, O.D.N.; Sr. Marve Watkins-King, O.D.N.

YUCAIPA. *Our Lady of Victory Missionary Sisters*, 12755 California St., 92399. Tel: 909-797-6369. Sr. Mary Matilda Spetter, O.L.V.M., D.R.E.; Sr. Elizabeth Hann, O.L.V.M., Ministry to Elderly. Sisters 2.

[G] CAMPS & RETREATS

ARROW BEAR LAKE. *Camp Don Bosco*. (Boys), Near Running Springs Office, 13640 Bellflower Blvd., 92382. Salasian Fathers.

BIG BEAR. *Sacred Heart Retreat Camp*, 896 Cienega Rd., P.O. Box 1795, 92315. Tel: 909-866-5696.

CHERRY VALLEY. *Servants of the Paraclete Guadalupe Retreat Center*, 39100 Orchard Ave., 92223-3797. Tel: 909-845-7777; Fax: 909-845-6271. Revs. Salvatore L. Busca, s.P., Sec. Gen. & Supr.; Gregory McCormick, s.P., Asst. Supr.

LOS ANGELES. *Camp Mariastella, Inc.* Camp for girls. 2303 S. Figueroa Way, 90007. Tel: 213-745-7870; Fax: 213-747-4499. P.O. Box 99, Wrightwood, 92394. Founded by the Sisters of Social Service.

REDLANDS. *El Carmelo Retreat House*, 926 E. Highland Ave., P.O. Box 446, 92373. Tel: 909-792-1047. Rev. Patrick Sugrue, O.C.D., Sup.; Bro. Fernando Pinto, O.C.D.; Revs. Dominic O'Callaghan, O.C.D.; Thomas Koller; Richard Mandoli, O.C.D.; Bro. Boniface Scheerer, O.C.D. Priests 4; Brothers 2; Sisters 4.

RIVERSIDE. *Divine Word Retreat Center*, 11316 Cypress Ave., 92505. Tel: 909-689-4858. Bro. Robert Zalikowski, S.V.D.

RUNNING SPRINGS. *St. Joachin & St. Anne Retreat Center*, P.O. Box 1760, 92382. Tel: 909-867-7362. Robert Fredericks, Guestmaster.

[H] NEWMAN CENTERS

SAN BERNARDINO. *Newman Catholic Fellowship*, 265 W. 25th St., 92405. Tel: 909-883-8991; Fax: 909-882-2061. Rev. Gilles Allard, I.M.C.

PALM DESERT. *Christ of the Desert Newman Center*, 73441 Fred Waring Dr., 92260. Tel: 760-346-0089; Fax: 760-340-2245. Rev. Ned Reidy, C.S.C., Dir.

REDLANDS. *University of Redlands Newman Community*, 1200 E. Colton Ave., Box 3080, 92373-0999. Tel: 909-335-4006. Rev. Thomas Koller, O.C.D.

RIVERSIDE. *St. Andrews Newman Center*, 105 W. Big Springs Rd., 92507. Tel: 909-682-8751. Directors: Revs. David Geib, O.P.; Frances Goode, O.P. Serving Riverside Community College and University of California at Riverside.

[I] MISCELLANEOUS

SAN BERNARDINO.
**Caritas Telecommunications*, 1201 E. Highland Ave., 92404. Clare Colella, Dir.

RIVERSIDE.
**Wordnet, Inc.*, Divine Word Seminary, 11316 Cypress Ave., Ste. 9, 92505. Tel: 909-689-4885. Rev. Michael Manning, S.V.D.

VICTORVILLE. *Casa Venegas*, 16694 Allen St., 92392-3511. Tel: 760-241-6607. Home for homeless.

RELIGIOUS INSTITUTUES OF MEN REPRESENTED IN THE DIOCESE

For further details refer to the corresponding bracketed number in the Religious Institutes of Men or Women section.

[0200]—*Benedictine Monks.* (MN; WA).—O.S.B.
[0470]—*Capuchin Franciscans.*—O.F.M.Cap.
[]—*Congregation of Mother Coredemptrix.*—C.M.C.
[1080]—*Congregation of the Resurrection.*—C.R.
[1140]—*Congregation of the Sacred Hearts of Jesus and Mary.* (Western Prov.).—SS.CC.
[0390]—*Consolata Missionaries.*—I.M.C.
[0480]—*Conventual Franciscans.* (St. Joseph Cupertino Prov.).—O.F.M.Conv.
[0260]—*Discalced Carmelite Friars.* (Western Prov.).—O.C.D.
[0520]—*Franciscan Friars.*—O.F.M.
[0650]—*Holy Ghost Fathers.*—C.S.Sp.
[0670]—*Hospitaller Brothers of St. John of God.*—O.H.
[0690]—*Jesuit Fathers and Brothers.*—S.J.
[0720]—*Missionaries of Our Lady of La Salette.*—M.S.
[1110]—*Missionaries of the Sacred Heart.*—M.S.C.
[0920]—*Oblates of St. Francis de Sales.*—O.S.F.S.
[]—*Operarios del Reino de Cristo.*—O.R.C.
[0970]—*Order of Our Lady of Mercy.*—O.de.M.
[0430]—*Order of Preachers (Dominicans).* (Holy Name Prov.).—O.P.
[0610]—*Priests of the Congregation of Holy Cross.*—C.S.C.
[1230]—*Servants of the Paraclete.*—s.P.
[0760]—*Society of Mary.*—S.M.
[0420]—*Society of the Divine Word.* (Western Prov.).—S.V.D.
[]—*Western Dominican Fathers and Brothers.*—O.P.

RELIGIOUS INSTITUTES OF WOMEN REPRESENTED IN THE DIOCESE

[0230]—*Benedictine Sisters of Pontifical Jurisdiction.* (Grand Terrace, CA).—O.S.B.
[0700]—*Company of Mary.*—O.D.N.
[3690]—*Congregation of the Sacred Hearts and of Perpetual Adoration.*—SS.CC.
[]—*Congregation of the Sacred Hearts of Jesus and Mary.*—SS.CC.
[0470]—*Congregation of the Sisters of Charity of the Incarnate Word.* Houston, Texas.—C.C.V.I.
[]—*Consolation Sisters.* (Highland CA).—O.S.F.
[0790]—*Daughters of Divine Charity.*—F.D.C.
[0880]—*Daughters of Mary and Joseph.*—D.M.J.
[1070-10]—*Dominican Sisters.*—O.P.
[1070-13]—*Dominican Sisters.*—O.P.
[1070-15]—*Dominican Sisters.*—O.P.
[1070-19]—*Dominican Sisters.*—O.P.
[1070-20]—*Dominican Sisters.*—O.P.
[1070-26]—*Dominican Sisters.*—O.P.
[1230]—*Franciscan Sisters of Christian Charity.*—O.S.F.
[]—*Immaculate Heart Community.*—I.H.M.
[2370]—*Institute of the Blessed Virgin Mary (Loretto Sisters).*—I.B.V.M.
[2575]—*Institute of the Sisters of Mercy of the Americas.* (Burlington, VT; Hartford, CT).—R.S.M.
[2760]—*Missionary Sisters of the Immaculate Conception of the Mother of God.*—S.M.I.C.
[]—*Oblates of Santa Marta.*—O.S.M.
[3130]—*Our Lady of Victory Missionary Sisters.*—O.L.V.M.
[]—*Religious of the Good Shepherd.*—R.G.S.
[2970]—*School Sisters of Notre Dame.*—S.S.N.D.
[1680]—*School Sisters of St. Francis.*—O.S.F.
[0430]—*Sisters of Charity of the Blessed Virgin Mary.*—B.V.M.
[2360]—*Sisters of Loretto at the Foot of the Cross.*—S.L.
[2549]—*Sisters of Mercy.* (Sligo, Ireland).—R.S.M.
[2590]—*Sisters of Mercy of the Blessed Sacrament.*—H.M.S.S.
[1540]—*Sisters of Saint Francis.* Clinton, Iowa.—O.S.F.
[]—*Sisters of St. Benedict.*—O.S.B.
[3770]—*Sisters of St. Clare.*—O.S.C.
[1720]—*Sisters of St. Francis.*—O.S.F.
[1650]—*The Sisters of St. Francis of Philadelphia.*—O.S.F.
[1550]—*Sisters of St. Francis of the Holy Cross.*—O.S.F.
[3830-03]—*Sisters of St. Joseph.*—C.S.J.
[3840]—*Sisters of St. Joseph of Carondolet.*—C.S.J.
[1990]—*Sisters of the Holy Names of Jesus and Mary.*—S.N.J.M.
[3320]—*Sisters of the Presentation of the B.V.M.*—P.B.V.M.
[4050]—*Sisters of the Society Devoted to the Sacred Heart.*—S.D.S.H.
[2150]—*Sisters, Servants of the Immaculate Heart of Mary.*—I.H.M.
[4070]—*Society of the Sacred Heart.*—R.S.C.J.

NECROLOGY

† Humphrey, Robert, Riverside, CA, St. Catherine of Alexandria. —Died Nov. 1, 1997.

† Nolan, Rev. Msgr. Michael, (Retired). —Died March 23, 1997.

† Snoj, Joseph, (Retired). —Died June 30, 1997.

† Stadler, Joseph, (Retired). —Died Sept. 20, 1997.

Diocese of San Diego

(Dioecesis Sancti Didaci)

Most Reverend

ROBERT H. BROM, D.D.

Bishop of San Diego; ordained December 18, 1963; appointed Bishop of Duluth March 25, 1983; consecrated and installed May 23, 1983; appointed Coadjutor Bishop of San Diego April 22, 1989; appointed Bishop of San Diego July 10, 1990. *Office: P.O. Box 85728, San Diego, CA, 92186-5728.* Tel.: 619-490-8200.

Most Reverend

GILBERT E. CHAVEZ, D.D.

Auxiliary Bishop of San Diego and Titular Bishop of Magarmel; ordained March 19, 1960; appointed April 19, 1974; Episcopal ordination June 21, 1974. *Res., 1535 Third Ave., San Diego, CA, 92101.*

ESTABLISHED JULY 11, 1936.

Square Miles 8,852.

Legal Titles: *The Roman Catholic Bishop of San Diego, a Corporation Sole*—(Churches, Rectories, Halls, Catechetical Centers, etc.) Diocese of San Diego.

Comprises the Counties of Imperial and San Diego in the State of California.

For legal titles of parishes and diocesan institutions, consult the Diocesan Office.

Pastoral Center: P.O. Box 85728, San Diego, CA, 92186-5728. Tel.: 619-490-8200; Fax: 619-490-8272.

Web site address: www.diocese-sdiego.org

STATISTICAL OVERVIEW

Personnel	
Bishop	1
Auxiliary Bishops	1
Abbots	1
Retired Abbots	1
Priests: Diocesan Active in Diocese	125
Priests: Active Outside Diocese	10
Priests: Retired, Sick or Absent	75
Number of Diocesan Priests	210
Religious Priests in Diocese	96
Extern Priests in Diocese	75
Ordinations:	
Diocesan Priests	1
Permanent Deacons in Diocese	86
Total Brothers	22
Total Sisters	361
Parishes	
Parishes	98
With Resident Pastor:	
Resident Diocesan Priests	85
Resident Religious Priests	13
Without Resident Pastor:	
Missions	19
Pastoral Centers	2
Professional Ministry Personnel:	
Brothers	2
Sisters	55
Lay Ministers	222
Welfare	
Catholic Hospitals	1
Total Assisted	341,695
Homes for the Aged	5
Total Assisted	716
Residential Care of Children	1
Total Assisted	120
Specialized Homes	8
Total Assisted	1,051
Special Centers for Social Services	21
Total Assisted	283,227
Residential Care of Disabled	1
Total Assisted	52
Other Institutions	3
Total Assisted	312
Educational	
Seminaries, Diocesan	1
Students from This Diocese	7
Students from Other Diocese	11
Diocesan Students in Other Seminaries	7
Total Seminarians	14
Colleges and Universities	1
Total Students	6,694
High Schools, Diocesan and Parish	3
Total Students	1,850
High Schools, Private	2
Total Students	1,326
Elementary Schools, Diocesan and Parish	43
Total Students	13,134
Elementary Schools, Private	1
Total Students	351
Non-residential Schools for the Disabled	1
Total Students	184
Catechesis/Religious Education:	
High School Students	6,565
Elementary Students	27,202
Total Students Under Catholic Instruction	57,320
Teachers in the Diocese:	
Priests	12
Sisters	56
Lay Teachers	1,066
Vital Statistics	
Receptions into the Church:	
Infant Baptism Totals	11,794
Adult Baptism Totals	487
Received into Full Communion	637
First Communions	9,691
Confirmations	3,654
Marriages:	
Catholic	1,743
Interfaith	540
Total Marriages	2,283
Deaths	2,935
Total Catholic Population	716,602
Total Population	2,798,114

Former Bishops—Most Rev. CHARLES F. BUDDY, D.D., S.T.D., Ph.D., ord. Sept. 19, 1914; appt. Oct. 31, 1936; cons. Dec. 21, 1936; named Asst. at Pontifical Throne, Jan. 12, 1964; died March 6, 1966.—Most Rev. FRANCIS J. FUREY, D.D., Ph.D., LL.D., ord. March 15, 1930; appt. Auxiliary Bishop of Philadelphia, Aug. 24, 1960; cons. Dec. 22, 1960; succeeded to the See of San Diego, March 6, 1966; translated to Archbishop of San Antonio, June 4, 1969; died April 23, 1979.—Most Rev. LEO T. MAHER, D.D., Bishop of San Diego; ord. Dec. 18, 1943; First Bishop of Santa Rosa; appt. Feb. 21, 1962; cons. April 5, 1962; translated to San Diego, Aug. 27, 1969; retired July 10, 1990; died Feb. 23, 1991.

Pastoral Center—3888 Paducah Dr., San Diego, 92117., Mailing Address: P.O. Box 85728, San Diego, 92186-5728. Tel: 619-490-8200; Fax: 619-490-8272. Office Hours: Mon.-Fri. 8:30-4:30.

Auxiliary Bishop and Vicar General—Most Rev. GILBERT E. CHAVEZ, D.D., *1535 Third Ave., San Diego, 92101-3192.* Tel: 619-239-0229.

Chancellor/Moderator of the Diocesan Offices—Rev. Msgr. DANIEL J. DILLABOUGH. Tel: 619-490-8310.

Assistants to Bishop Robert H. Brom—Rev. EDWARD P. MCNULTY. Tel: 619-490-8300. Mr. RODRIGO VALDIVIA. Tel: 619-490-8301.

Temporal Affairs—Rev. Msgr. DANIEL J. DILLABOUGH, Dir. Tel: 619-490-8310.

Diocesan Tribunal

Judicial Vicar—Rev. Msgr. MARK A. CAMPBELL, B.A., M.Ed., J.C.L.

Adjutant Judicial Vicar—Rev. DAVID N. CROISETIERE, J.C.L., M.C.L.

Promotor of Justice—Rev. Msgr. DANIEL J. DILLABOUGH, S.T.D., J.C.L.

Defenders of the Bond—Rev. Msgr. DANIEL J. DILLABOUGH; Very Rev. STEVEN CALLAHAN, J.C.L.

Diocesan Judges—Rev. Msgr. MARK A. CAMPBELL, B.A., M.Ed., J.C.L.; Revs. DAVID CROISETIERE, J.C.L., M.C.L.; BRIAN HAYES, J.C.L.; DANIEL MURRAY, J.C.L.; Miss MARY O'GARA, J.C.L; Miss MARY JO GRETSINGER, S.T.L., J.C.L.; EDWARD PETERS, J.D., J.C.D.

Auditor—Rev. LOUIS I. NEWMAN, B.A.

Notaries—Mrs. CONNIE NOEL; Mrs. INES ANDREWS.

Consultants—Rev. JOHN HOWARD, C.J.M., Ph.D.; PETER MCDADE, Ph.D.

Diocesan Offices and Directors

Archivist—Contact, *Chancellor's Office.* Tel: 619-490-8310.

Canonical Affairs—EDWARD PETERS, J.D., J.C.D., Dir. Tel: 619-490-8314.

Catholic Charities—Sr. RAYMONDA DUVALL, C.H.S., Exec. Dir., *349 Cedar St., San Diego, 92101.* Tel: 619-231-2828.

Cemetery Committee—Rev. Msgr. W. FRANCIS PATTISON, Dir., *Holy Cross Cemetery, 4470 Hilltop Dr., San Diego, 92102.* Tel: 619-264-3127.

Censores Librorum—Rev. Msgr. RICHARD F. DUNCANSON, S.T.D.; Rev. Msgr. JOHN R. PORTMAN, S.T.D.; Revs. DENNIS W. KROUSE, S.T.D.; NORBERT J. RIGALI, S.J., Ph.D.; Mr. TERRY MCGOLDRICK, S.T.D.

Civil Affairs—VINCENT WHELAN, Esq., Dir. Tel: 619-490-8277. EDWARD PETERS, Esq. of Counsel.

Computer Services—Ms. JENNA SEMER, Dir. Tel: 619-490-8222.

Ecumenical and Interreligious Affairs—Rev. DENNIS MIKULANIS, S.T.D., Vicar, *990 Saturn Blvd., San Diego, 92154.* Tel: 619-423-0242.

Education—Sr. CLAIRE PATRICE FITZGERALD, C.S.J., Dir. Pro Tem. Tel: 619-490-8241.

San Diego Diocesan Institute for Adult Education and Formation for Ministry—TERRY MCGOLDRICK, S.T.D., Dir. Tel: 619-490-8212.

Evangelization & Catechetical Ministry—Mrs. GINGER INFANTINO, Dir. Tel: 619-490-8232. Sr. M. CRISTINA GONZALEZ, C.V.I., Asst. Dir. for Hispanic Catechesis. Tel: 619-490-8233.

Schools—Sr. CLAIRE PATRICE FITZGERALD, C.S.J., Dir. Tel: 619-490-8241. Sr. TIMOTHEA KINGSTON, C.S.C., Personnel Dir. Tel: 619-490-8243. Mrs. PATRICIA BANNON, Curriculum Dir. Tel: 619-490-8244.

Youth and Young Adult Ministry—MONIQUE MUTHER, M.F.C.C., Dir. Tel: 619-490-8261.

Hispanic Evangelization—Sr. GLORIA GALVAN-GRIMALDO, M.G.S.S., Assoc. Dir. for Hispanic Evangelization. Tel: 619-490-8214.

Finance—Mr. H.L. "HAL" GARDNER, Finance Officer. Tel: 619-490-8284. Ms. KAREN TISI, Accounting Supr. Tel: 619-490-8207.

Hispanic Affairs—ENRIQUE MENDEZ, Dir. Tel: 619-490-8249.

Human Resources—Mr. STEVEN WOOLLEY, Dir. Tel: 619-490-8282.

Liturgy and Spirituality—Mrs. MARY ANN FALLON, Dir. Tel: 619-490-8290.

Marriage and Family Life—Rev. WILLIAM ORTMANN, Dir. Tel: 619-490-8295.

Missions—Rev. Msgr. RAYMOND C. KIRK, Dir. Tel: 619-490-8250.

Multicultural Affairs—Mr. RODRIGO VALDIVIA, Dir. Tel: 619-490-8301.

Permanent Diaconate—Deacon JAMES KEELEY, Dir. Assocs.: Deacons THOMAS DOUGHERTY; LOUIS ROCHA. Tel: 619-490-8216.

Seminary—St. Francis—Very Rev. STEVEN CALLAHAN, Rector, *1667 Santa Paula Dr., San Diego, 92111.* Tel: 619-291-7446.

Social Ministry—Mr. KENT PETERS, Dir. Tel: 619-490-8324.

"Southern Cross"—(Diocesan Newspaper)—Tel: 619-490-8269.

Stewardship—Mrs. JENNIFER TURCK, Dir. Tel: 619-490-8280.

Women Religious—Sr. NANCY KANE, R.S.C.J., Vicar. Tel: 619-490-8289.

Advisory Bodies

Clergy Personnel Board—Rev. Msgr. DANIEL J. DILLABOUGH, Chm. Tel: 619-490-8310.

College of Consultors—Most Rev. GILBERT E. CHAVEZ; Rev. Msgr. DANIEL J. DILLABOUGH; Rev. Msgr. JOHN A. DICKIE; Rev. Msgr. W. FRANCIS PATTISON; Rev. Msgr. JOHN PORTMAN; Rev. Msgr. LAWRENCE PURCELL; Very Rev. STEVEN CALLAHAN.

Diocesan Pastoral Council—Mr. RODRIGO VALDIVIA, Exec. Coord. Tel: 619-490-8301.

Finance Council—Most Rev. ROBERT H. BROM, Chm.; Mr. KAREN TISI, Recording Sec.; Rev. Msgr. DANIEL J. DILLABOUGH; Rev. Msgr. THOMAS PRENDERGAST; Sr. MARY JO ANDERSON; Mr. ROBERT BAKER; Mr. THOMAS BLAKE; Mr. JOHN T. BLANKINSHIP JR.; Mr. JOHN D. BOYCE; Mr. JOHN FOWLER; Mr. OSCAR PADILLA; Mr. DAVID SCHAEFER; Mr. BARRY SHILLITO.

Presbyteral Council—Most Rev. ROBERT H. BROM; Most Rev. GILBERT E. CHAVEZ; Rev. Msgr. W. FRANCIS PATTISON, Chm.; Rev. EDWARD P. MCNULTY, Exec. Sec.; Rev. Msgr. JOHN DICKIE; Rev. Msgr. DANIEL J. DILLABOUGH; Rev. Msgr. LAWRENCE PURCELL; Revs. STEVEN CALLAHAN; JOHN DOLAN; JAIME ESCOBEDO; PATRICK MULCAHY; MICHAEL MURPHY; PETER NAVARRA; ROBERT D. NIKLIBORC; BRUCE ORSBORN; FRANCIS PENKO; JOHN PROCTOR; JAMES RAFFERTY; MATTHEW SPAHR; ROQUE VANO,Liaison for Military Chaplains: Rev. MICHAEL DIAZ, CHC, USNR Retired Priests Representative: Rev. Msgr. JOHN PORTMAN.

Vicars Forane—Cathedral: Rev. KENNETH DEL PRIORE, El Cajon: Rev. RAYMOND O'DONNELL, Escondido: Rev. CHARLES FULD, La Jolla: Rev. NICHOLAS DEMPSEY, Oceanside: Rev. RAMON MARRUFO, University: Rev. Msgr. MARK CAMPBELL, El Centro: Rev. JOSEPH MASAR, South Bay: Rev. Msgr. RICHARD DUNCANSON.

Miscellaneous

Apostleship of the Sea—Rev. DANIEL WALSH, C.S.Sp., Port Chap., *1140 Evergreen St., San Diego, 92106.* Tel: 619-223-2200.

Charismatic Renewal—SHAWN QUINN, Admin., *4202 Genesee St., Ste. 102, San Diego, 92117.* Tel: 619-627-0180.

Hispanic Charismatic Renewal Center—NARCISCO GUZMAN, Coord. Tel: 619-482-2201.

Christ Child Society—Rev. NICHOLAS DEMPSEY, Spiritual Advisor. Tel: 619-223-2200.

Cursillo—Deacon JAMES SCULL, Spiritual Advisor; JIM ZAWADZKI, Lay Dir. Tel: 619-460-3171.

Filipino—JESSE TRAPSE, Lay Dir. Tel: 619-484-6959.

Hispanic—RICARDO DEL ROSARIO, Pres. Secretariat. Tel: 619-656-1132.

Vietnamese—Rev. BIEN QUANG DO, Spiritual Adv. NGHI VU, Lay Dir. Tel: 619-272-9356.

Holy Childhood Association—Rev. Msgr. RAYMOND KIRK, Dir., *P.O. Box 711011, San Diego, 92171-1011.* Tel: 619-490-8250.

Propagation of the Faith—Rev. Msgr. RAYMOND KIRK, Dir.; Sr. KATHY SCHMITTGENS, S.S.N.D., Assoc. Dir., *P.O. Box 711011, San Diego, 92171-1011.* Tel: 619-490-8250.

CLERGY, PARISHES, MISSIONS AND PAROCHIAL SCHOOLS

CITY OF SAN DIEGO
(San Diego County)

1—ST. JOSEPH CATHEDRAL, Most Rev. Gilbert E. Chavez, D.D.; Revs. Frank Theriault, C.S.C. (Canada); Robert Campbell, O.P. In res., Revs. Paul Balio (Philippines); William Ortmann.
Res., 1535 Third Ave., 92101-3192. Tel: 619-239-0229; Fax: 619-239-3788.
Catechesis/Religious Programs—Students 100.

2—ASCENSION (1980), Rev. James Sassone; Deacon Jim Scull.
Res., 11292 Clairemont Mesa Blvd., 92124-1524. Tel: 619-279-2735; Fax: 619-279-1023.
Catechesis/Religious Programs—Tel: 619-279-2752. Susan Paul, D.R.E.
Students 210.

3—BLESSED SACRAMENT (1938), Revs. William F. Rowland, C.J.M.; Louis Levesque, C.J.M.; James Burson, C.J.M.; Deacon Louis Principe. In res., Rev. Jerry Hamperzonian; Deacon Tony Albers.
Res., 4540 El Cerrito Dr., 92115. Tel: 619-582-5722.
School—Tel: 619-582-3862; Fax: 619-265-9310. Ms. Theodora Furtado, Prin.
Lay Teachers 21; Students 504.
Catechesis/Religious Programs—Tel: 619-582-4633.
Students 152.
Mission—San Diego, San Diego Co., SDSU Newman Center, 5855 Hardy Ave., 92115. Tel: 619-583-9181.

4—CHRIST THE KING (1938), Revs. Eduardo A. Samaniego, S.J.; Wayne Negrete, S.J. In res., Revs. Gilbert J. Gentile, S.J.; Joe Speiler, S.J.
Res., 29 N. 32nd St., 92102. Tel: 619-231-8906; Fax: 619-238-7060.
Catechesis/Religious Programs—Students 118.

5—GOOD SHEPHERD (1970), Revs. Fernando Ramirez; Earl Edward Eggleston; Cavana Wallace; Deacon Alberto Paras.
Res., 8200 Gold Coast Dr., 92126-3699. Tel: 619-271-0207; Fax: 619-271-0748.
School—8180 Gold Coast Dr., 92126. Tel: 619-693-1522; Fax: 619-271-0207. Mrs. Chris Corpora, Prin.
Lay Teachers 13; Students 315.
Catechesis/Religious Programs—Tel: 619-271-8769. Mr. Charles McGuire, D.R.E.
Lay Teachers 78; Students 1,215.

6—HOLY FAMILY (Linda Vista) (1942), Revs. Bruce Orsborn; Joseph Khuyen Van Lai; Andrew Wang; Deacons Thomas Dougherty; Paul Davidson.
Res., 1957 Coolidge St., 92111-7098. Tel: 619-277-0404; Fax: 619-277-7978.
School—Tel: 619-277-0222; Fax: 619-277-0224.
Lay Teachers 15; Students 243.
Catechesis/Religious Programs—Tel: 619-268-0557.
Students 130.

7—HOLY SPIRIT (1952), Rev. Msgr. Roger A. Lechner; Rev. Doan Van Lai.
Res., 2725-55th St., 92105-5094. Tel: 619-262-2435; Fax: 619-262-8718.
Catechesis/Religious Programs—Students 318.

8—IMMACULATA (1958), Most Rev. Robert H. Brom; Rev. Msgr. Daniel J. Dillabough; Sr. Priscilla Lemire, Pastoral Assoc.
Res., U.S.D. Campus, Alcala Park, 92110. Tel: 619-574-5700; Fax: 619-574-5707.
Catechesis/Religious Programs—Students 104.

9—IMMACULATE CONCEPTION (1849), Rev. Msgr. Alphonsus Moloney.
Res., 2540 San Diego Ave., 92110-2840. Tel: 619-295-4148; Fax: 619-297-6916.

10—MISSION BASILICA SAN DIEGO DE ALCALA (1769). (California's First Mission). Rev. Msgr. Thomas Prendergast; Rev. William A. Springer; Deacons Bill Vasquez; Ernest Grosso; Larry Sheldon. In res., Rev. Mark A. Campbell.
Res., 10818 San Diego Mission Rd., 92108-2498. Tel: 619-283-7319; Fax: 619-283-7762.
Catechesis/Religious Programs—Tel: 619-624-0900.
Students 180.

11—OUR LADY OF ANGELS (1906) (Hispanic), Rev. Kenneth Del Priore.
Res., 656 24th St., 92102-2911. Tel: 619-239-1231; Fax: 619-234-5520.
School—Our Lady's School-North Campus, Tel: 619-233-8888; Fax: 619-234-5520.
Sisters 2; Lay Teachers 9; Students 256.
Catechesis/Religious Programs—Sr. Dina Marie Garcia, D.R.E.
Students 400.

12—OUR LADY OF GUADALUPE (1919) (Mexican), Revs. Richard H. Brown, S.J.; James I. Rasura, S.J.; Augusto Berrio, S.J. In res., Rev. Max Oliva, S.J.
Res., 1770 Kearny Ave., 92113-1128. Tel: 619-233-3838; Fax: 619-233-3252.
School—Our Lady's School-South Campus, 744 Beardsley, 92113. Tel: 619-233-8888.
Religious 2; Lay Teachers 3; Students 135.
Catechesis/Religious Programs—Tel: 619-233-3838; Fax: 619-233-3252. Veronica Lopez, D.R.E.
Students 200.

13—OUR LADY OF MT. CARMEL (Rancho Penasquitos) (1976), Rev. Msgr. Henry F. Fawcett; Rev. Paul Palmitessa; Deacons Bernard Yeatts; John Phelps; H. Thomas Jones.
Res., 13541 Stoney Creek Rd., 92129. Tel: 619-566-3550; 484-1070; Fax: 619-484-6157.
Catechesis/Religious Programs—Students 1,372.

14—OUR LADY OF REFUGE (Pacific Beach), Rev. Msgr. William E. Elliott.
Res., 4226 Jewell St., 92109. Tel: 619-274-9670; Fax: 619-274-9671.
Catechesis/Religious Programs—Tel: 619-274-2959. Martin Magana, D.R.E.
Students 124.

15—OUR LADY OF THE ROSARY (1925) (Italian), Revs. Steven M. Grancini, C.R.S.P.; Louis M. Solcia, C.R.S.P.
Res., 1659 Columbia St., 92101-2584. Tel: 619-234-4820; Fax: 619-234-3559.
Catechesis/Religious Programs—Tel: 619-234-4820. Esther Leuzzi, D.R.E.
Students 129.

16—OUR LADY OF THE SACRED HEART (1911), Revs. Richard L. Perozich; Joseph Phen Van Pham; Deacon Peter Can Nguyen.
Res., 4177 Marlborough Ave., 92105-1412. Tel: 619-280-0515; Fax: 619-280-0517.
School—Tel: 619-284-1715; Fax: 619-284-8332. Sr. Linda Lutz, Prin.
Lay Teachers 8; Students 150.
Catechesis/Religious Programs—Tel: 619-283-9262; Fax: 619-283-0159. Sr. Mary Jo Maes, D.R.E.
Students 475.

17—OUR MOTHER OF CONFIDENCE (University City) (1964), Rev. Msgr. Donal C. Sheahan; Deacons William Klopchin; Arnold Hess. In res., Rev. Brian Hayes.
Res., 3131 Governor Dr., 92122. Tel: 619-453-0222; Fax: 619-453-2547.
Catechesis/Religious Programs—Tel: 619-453-3554. D.R.E.: Cathy Whelan; Sr. Frances Franey, S.N.J.M.
Students 339.

18—SACRED HEART (Ocean Beach) (1911), Revs. Ronald Hebert; Daniel Murray; Deacon Giles Schmitt.
Res., 4776 Saratoga, 92107-9990. Tel: 619-224-2746; Fax: 619-224-0459.
School—Tel: 619-222-7252; Fax: 619-222-2836. Mr. Robert Hamm, Prin.
Lay Teachers 12; Students 287.

Catechesis/Religious Programs—Tel: 619-223-4594. Ed Nolan, D.R.E.
Students 100.

19—St. Agnes (Pt. Loma) (1932), Revs. Nicholas Dempsey; Daniel Walsh, C.S.Sp.; Deacon William Pollock.
Res., 1140 Evergreen St., 92106. Tel: 619-223-2200; Fax: 619-226-4009.
Catechesis/Religious Programs—Tel: 619-223-9748. Mrs. Robert Spondike, D.R.E.
Students 112.

20—St. Anne (1921), Rev. Robert D. Nikliborc.
Res., 621 Sicard St., 92113-2334. Tel: 619-239-8253.
Catechesis/Religious Programs—Tel: 619-232-5903.
Students 200.

21—St. Brigid (Pacific Beach) (1940), Rev. Peter Escalante; Rev. Msgr. Sean Murray, Pastor Emeritus.
Res., 4735 Cass St., 92109-2698. Tel: 619-483-3030; Fax: 619-483-7131.
Catechesis/Religious Programs—Tel: 619-483-3032. D.R.E.: Sr. Hilda McDonagh, R.S.M.; Sr. Josephine Breen.
Students 180.

22—St. Catherine Laboure (1964), Rev. Msgr. William Cuddihy; Rev. Msgr. Fernando Gutierrez.
Res., 4026 Mt. Abraham Ave., 92111. Tel: 619-277-3133; Fax: 619-277-9181.
Catechesis/Religious Programs—Tel: 619-279-0587. Patricia Doyle, D.R.E.
Students 272.

23—St. Charles (1946), Revs. Dennis Mikulanis; Michael Dean Robinson; Deacon Seodello Martinez.
Res., 990 Saturn Blvd., 92154. Tel: 619-423-0242; Fax: 619-423-1966.
School—Tel: 619-423-3701; Fax: 619-423-5331.
Sisters of Mercy 1; Lay Teachers 14; Students 300.
Catechesis/Religious Programs—Tel: 619-575-2240.
Students 494.

24—St. Charles Borromeo (1946), Revs. Michel Froidurot; David N. Croisetiere.
Res., 2802 Cadiz St., 92110-4813. Tel: 619-225-8157; Fax: 619-225-2288.
School—Tel: 619-223-8271.
Sisters 2; Lay Teachers 12; Students 259.
Catechesis/Religious Programs—Tel: 619-224-4455.
Students 90.

25—St. Columba (1955), Rev. Msgr. Patrick J. Mullarkey; Rev. Noel S. Ryan, S.S.C.; Deacons Louis X. Ball; Nick Santiago. In res., Rev. Louis Newman.
Res., 3327 Glencolum Dr., 92123. Tel: 619-277-3863; Fax: 619-279-9053.
School—(Grades PreK-8). Tel: 619-279-1882; Fax: 619-279-1653.
Lay Teachers 13; Students 300.
Catechesis/Religious Programs—Tel: 619-277-3861.
Students 140.

26—St. Didacus (1926), Rev. Scott J. McColl. In res., Rev. Gary M. Holtey, Chap.
Res., 4772 Felton St., 92116. Tel: 619-284-3472; Fax: 619-284-3484.
School—4630 34th St., 92116. Tel: 619-284-8730; Fax: 619-284-1764.
Lay Teachers 13; Students 280.
Catechesis/Religious Programs—Tel: 619-284-7050. Mrs. Mary J. Curtis, D.R.E.
Students 65.

27—St. Gregory the Great (1985), Rev. James N. Poulsen; Deacon L. Ferris Bell.
Mailing Address: P.O. Box 261699, 92196. Tel: 619-695-6799; Fax: 619-695-6639.
Res., 10403 Avenida Magnifica, 92131.
Parish Center: 10650 Treena St., 92131.
Catechesis/Religious Programs—Tel: 619-695-0272.
Students 397.

28—St. Jerome (1985), Rev. James V. Caldwell; Deacons Kenneth E. Montoya; Joseph Delano.
Office: 2515 Beyer Blvd., 92154-1502. Tel: 619-423-0405; Fax: 619-423-9363.
Res., 4485 Murrieta Cir., 92154-1713. Tel: 619-428-7978.
Catechesis/Religious Programs—Tel: 619-423-5302. Sr. Roberta Collins, C.S.J.P., D.R.E.
Students 328.

29—St. John the Evangelist (1913), Rev. Msgr. Anthony A. Giesing. In res., Rev. Manuel Ediza (Philippines).
Res., 1638 Polk Ave., 92103. Tel: 619-291-1660.
Catechesis/Religious Programs—Tel: 619-460-0340.
Students 98.

30—St. Jude (1946), Revs. Jose Castillo; Henry Rodriguez; Deacon Manuel Nunez.
Res., 1129 S. 38th St., 92113-3210. Tel: 619-264-2195; Fax: 619-264-8528.
School—1228 S. 38th St., 92113. Tel: 619-264-3154; Fax: 619-264-8050.
Religious 1; Lay Teachers 10; Students 320.
St. Jude's Child Care and Development Center—1129 S. 38th St., 92113.
St. Jude's Senior Nutrition Program—.
Catechesis/Religious Programs—Tel: 619-264-5651. D.R.E.: Susy Maldonado, (Spanish); Eddie Johnson, (English).
Students 300.

31—St. Mary Magdalene (Clairemont) (1953), Rev. Msgr. John A. Dickie. In res., Revs. Robert J. Nagler (SB) (Retired); Michael T. White, C.S.Sp.
Res., 1945 Illion St., 92110. Tel: 619-276-1041; Fax: 619-276-0144.
School—Tel: 619-276-6545.
Lay Teachers 33; Students 570.
Catechesis/Religious Programs—Tel: 619-276-6814. Mrs. Phyllis Alcaraz, D.R.E.
Students 114.

32—St. Maximilian Kolbe Mission (1971) (Polish). Unassigned. (Quasi Parish).
Res., 1735 Grand Ave., 92109. Tel: 619-668-0485; Fax: 619-272-7655.
Catechesis/Religious Programs—Students 55.

33—St. Michael (1957) (Filipino), Revs. Joseph Mel Collier; Joselito Tiongson (Philippines).
Res., 2643 Homedale St., 92139. Tel: 619-470-1977; Fax: 619-470-6357.
School—2637 Homedale St., 92139. Tel: 619-470-4880.
Sisters 1; Lay Teachers 16; Students 332.
Catechesis/Religious Programs—Tel: 619-470-2291. Mr. Louis Costa, D.R.E.
Students 1,024.

34—St. Patrick (1921), Revs. Thomas J. McLaughlin, O.S.A.; James P. Retzner, O.S.A.; Bro. Michael T. Bube, O.S.A.
Res., 3585 30th St., 92104. Tel: 619-295-2157; Fax: 619-688-1225.
School—Tel: 619-297-1314.
Lay Teachers 10; Students 250.
Catechesis/Religious Programs—Tel: 619-284-5063. Mary Jo Waggoner, D.R.E.
Students 108.
Chapel—St. Augustine, 3266 Nutmeg St., 92104. Tel: 619-282-2028; Fax: 619-282-1203.

35—St. Rita (1941), Rev. Msgr. Francis Pattison; Rev. Juvencio D. Ricafort. In res., Rev. Msgr. Joseph A. Carroll.
Res., 5124 Churchward St., 92114-3797. Tel: 619-264-3165; Fax: 619-264-2907.
School—Tel: 619-264-0109.
Sisters 1; Lay Teachers 12; Students 292.
Catechesis/Religious Programs—Tel: 619-264-4399. Margaret Castro, D.R.E.
Students 515.

36—St. Therese (1956), Rev. Msgr. Frederick J. Florek; Rev. John Cuddigan, S.J.; Deacons Leo Dube; Robert Ekhaml.
Res., 6016 Camino Rico, 92120-3099. Tel: 619-582-3716; Fax: 619-582-2535.
School—St. Therese Academy, Tel: 619-583-6270; Fax: 619-583-6271.
Sisters 4; Lay Teachers 13; Students 350.
Catechesis/Religious Programs—Tel: 619-582-2585. Sr. Damien Peters, D.F.C., D.R.E.
Students 211.

37—St. Vincent de Paul (1910), Revs. Nicholas P. Clavin; James Rankin, (Retired).
Res., 4077 Ibis St., 92103-1899. Tel: 619-299-3881; Fax: 619-299-9509.
School—Tel: 619-296-2222; Fax: 619-296-2763.
Sisters of Mercy 2; Lay Teachers 9; Students 275.
Catechesis/Religious Programs—Students 76.

38—San Rafael (Rancho Bernardo) (1974), Rev. Msgr. Lloyd V. Bourgeois; Rev. Ralph Poirier, C.S.Sp.
Res., 17252 Bernardo Center, 92128. Tel: 619-487-4314; Fax: 619-487-1498.
Catechesis/Religious Programs—Tel: 619-674-1145. D.R.E.: Mary Jane Heggeness; Sr. Joan Derry, S.H.F.
Students 800.

OUTSIDE THE CITY OF SAN DIEGO

Alpine, San Diego Co., Queen of Angels (1950), Rev. Matthew D. Spahr.
Res., 2569 Victoria Dr., 91901-3662. Tel: 619-445-2145; Fax: 619-445-9682.
Catechesis/Religious Programs—Students 203.

Bonita, San Diego Co., Corpus Christi (1984), Rev. John G. Proctor, Jr.; Deacon James H. Hitch.
Mailing Address: P.O. Box 1349, 91908.
Res., 2934 Degen Dr., 91902. Tel: 619-482-3954; Fax: 619-482-7236. [CEM]
Church—450 Corral Canyon Rd., 91902.
Catechesis/Religious Programs—Tel: 619-482-3957; Fax: 619-482-7236. Deacon James H. Hitch, D.R.E.
Students 500.

Borrego Springs, San Diego Co., St. Richard (1954), Rev. Simon Lefebvre, C.S.V.
Res., P.O. Box 1128, 92004-1128. Tel: 760-767-5701. [CEM]
Catechesis/Religious Programs—Students 120.

Brawley, Imperial Co., Our Lady of Perpetual Help (1956) (Hispanic), Rev. Jorge Moreno.
Res., 1250 B St., P.O. Box 1283, 92227. Tel: 760-344-2226; Fax: 760-344-1557.
Catechesis/Religious Programs—Tel: 760-344-5787. Rosie Romero, D.R.E.
Students 291.

Sacred Heart (1908), Rev. Joseph G. Masar; Deacon Donald L. Spinney.
Res., 402 S. Imperial St., 92227. Tel: 760-344-3171; Fax: 760-344-3171.
School—(Grades K-8). Tel: 760-334-2662; Fax: 760-344-1910.
Lay Teachers 7; Students 146.
Catechesis/Religious Programs—Sr. Dawnna Spinney, D.C.M.
Students 160.

St. Margaret Mary (1934) (Hispanic), Rev. Roque P. Vano.
Res., 620 S. 10th St., 92227. Tel: 760-344-3571; Fax: 760-344-3598.
Catechesis/Religious Programs—Students 350.

Calexico, Imperial Co., Our Lady of Guadalupe (1907), Revs. Bernard A. Rapp; Patrick J. Mulcahy.
Res., 124 E. Fifth St., 92231. Tel: 760-357-1822; Fax: 760-357-0115.
School—Our Lady of Guadalupe Academy, Tel: 760-357-1986; Fax: 760-357-3282.
Sisters, Servants of the Blessed Sacrament 6; Lay Teachers 23; Students 602.
Catechesis/Religious Programs—Tel: 760-357-2532. Sr. Maria Teresa Bandera, C.V.I., D.R.E.
Students 482.

Calipatria, Imperial Co., St. Patrick (1919), Revs. Amador Lopez, O.M.I.; James Kernan, O.M.I.
Res., 133 E. Church St., P.O. Box 238, 92233. Tel: 760-348-2733; Fax: 760-348-2733.
Catechesis/Religious Programs—Tel: 760-348-2454.
Students 195.
Mission—Niland, Imperial Co., Immaculate Heart of Mary, 19 Sixth St., P.O. Box 160, Niland, 92257. Tel: 760-359-0464.

Carlsbad, San Diego Co., St. Elizabeth Seton (1997), Rev. Donald E. Coleman.
Res., 6628 Santa Isabel St., 92009-5148. Tel: 760-438-3393; Fax: 760-438-7739.
Catechesis/Religious Programs—Tel: 760-438-3438. Larry Broding, D.R.E.
Students 290.

St. Patrick (1943) (Spanish), Revs. Stephen P. McCall; Joseph E. Mullen, S.J.; Patrick Joseph Murphy.
Res., 3821 Adams St., 92008-0249. Tel: 760-729-2866; Fax: 760-434-3325.
School—3820 Pio Pico, 92008. Tel: 760-729-1333. Ms. Jean Panno, Prin.
Lay Teachers 17; Students 360.
Catechesis/Religious Programs—Tel: 760-729-8442.
Students 815.

St. Thomas More (1985), Rev. Peter McGuine.
Mailing Address: P.O. Box 4415, 92018-4415.
Res., 2256 Cameo Rd., 92008. Tel: 760-599-1980; Fax: 760-599-1982.
Church—1910 Shadowridge Dr., Ste. 107, Vista, 92083.
Catechesis/Religious Programs—Students 125.

Chula Vista, San Diego Co.,

1—Most Precious Blood, (1957), Revs. Frank Wagner, O.M.I.; Ernest Sylvestre, O.M.I.
Res., 1245 4th Ave., 91911-3012. Tel: 619-422-2100; Fax: 619-422-1375.
Catechesis/Religious Programs—Tel: 619-422-2159. Sr. Camille Crabbe, C.V.I., D.R.E.
Students 360.

2—Our Lady of Guadalupe, (1945) (Hispanic), Rev. Mario Vesga; Deacons Daniel Parra; Margarito Lozoya; Raul Hernandez.
Res., 345 Anita St., 91911-4198. Tel: 619-422-3977; Fax: 619-422-1056.
Catechesis/Religious Programs—Tel: 619-427-2774.
Students 301.

3—St. Pius X, (1955), Rev. Msgr. Donald R. Kulleck; Rev. Paul Bauer; Deacon Dan De Pozo. In res., Rev. James J. Kinzig.
Res., 36 E. Naples St., 91911-2298. Tel: 619-420-9193.
School—37 E. Emerson, 91911. Tel: 619-422-2015; Fax: 619-422-0048. Eileen Hanson, Prin.
Lay Teachers 10; Students 410.
Catechesis/Religious Programs—Tel: 619-426-2263. Lois Richards, D.R.E.
Students 622.

4—St. Rose of Lima, (1913), Rev. Msgr. Richard F. Duncanson; Rev. Msgr. Charles P. Young, Pastor Emeritus; Revs. Michael X. Tran; Andre Ramos; Deacons Oscar Alvarez; Joe Arismendez.
Res., 293 H St., 91910. Tel: 619-427-0230; Fax: 619-427-5786.
School—473 Third Ave., 91910. Tel: 619-422-1121; Fax: 619-422-8007.
Lay Teachers 15; Religious 1; Students 339.
Catechesis/Religious Programs—Tel: 619-426-6717. Sr. Margaret Ann Altmiller, O.L.V.M., D.R.E.
Students 1,165.

Coronado, San Diego Co., Sacred Heart (1897), Rev. Michael F. Murphy; Rev. Msgr. John R. Portman, Pastor Emeritus. In res., Rev. Msgr. Jeremiah O'Sullivan, Pastor Emeritus; Rev. John Wheeler.
Res., 655 C Ave., 92118-2299. Tel: 619-435-3167; Fax: 619-437-1572.
School—Tel: 619-437-4431; Fax: 619-437-1559.
Benedictine Sisters 1; Lay Teachers 8; Students 255.
Catechesis/Religious Programs—Tel: 619-435-4858.
Students 190.

Del Mar, San Diego Co., St. William of York (1985), Rev. George Byrne.
Res., P.O. Box 2726, 92014-5726. Tel: 619-481-3232; Fax: 619-481-3573.
Catechesis/Religious Programs—Tel: 619-481-4061. Sr. Catherine Osimo, C.S.C., D.R.E.
Students 226.

Descanso, San Diego Co., Our Lady of Light (1935), Rev. Gerald F. Palcheck.
Res., 9136 Riverside Dr., P.O. Box 219, 91916. Tel: 619-445-3620.
Catechesis/Religious Programs—Claire Donivan, D.R.E.
Students 60.
Mission—Descanso, San Diego Co., Our Lady of the Pines, 9136 Riverside Dr., 91916.

El Cajon, San Diego Co.,

1—Holy Trinity, (1903), Revs. Brian M. Corcoran; William A. Kernan; Deacons C. Edwin Donivan; Louis Rocha.
Res., 405 Ballard St., 92019. Tel: 619-444-9425; Fax: 619-444-9426.
School—Tel: 619-444-7529; Fax: 619-444-3721.
Lay Teachers 16; Students 301.
Catechesis/Religious Programs—Tel: 619-444-5043.
Students 396.

2—Our Lady of Grace, (1954), Rev. Msgr. Michael J. Gallagher; Revs. Burt Boudoin; Joseph Bien Quang Do; Omer LeBlanc, C.J.M.; Deacons R. Walt Woznicki; George Shea; Sr. Carmel Lohan, S.M., Pastoral Asst.
Res., 2766 Navajo Rd., 92020-2183. Tel: 619-469-0133; Fax: 619-469-0575.
School—Tel: 619-466-0055.
Sisters 2; Lay Teachers 15; Students 306.
Catechesis/Religious Programs—Tel: 619-466-5656. D.R.E.: Doris Hertzig; Stephanie Hagenburger.
Students 423.

3—St. Kieran, (1958), Rev. Francis G. Penko; Deacon John Trumble.
Mailing Address: P.O. Box 2428, 92021-0428.
Office: 1510 Greenfield Dr., 92021-0428. Tel: 619-588-6881; Fax: 619-588-5274.
School—1347 Camillo Way, Tel: 619-588-6398. Miss Michaele Durant, Prin.
Lay Teachers 12; Students 194.
Catechesis/Religious Programs—Tel: 619-447-2424.
Students 195.

4—St. Louise de Marillac, (1944), Rev. Louis A. Salca.
Res., 2005 Crest Dr., 92021-4309. Tel: 619-444-3076.

5—St. Luke, (1985), Rev. Raymond G. O'Donnell; Deacon John Snyder.
Res., 1980 Hillsdale Rd., 92019. Tel: 619-442-1697; Fax: 619-442-2293.
Catechesis/Religious Programs—Tel: 619-442-2515. D.R.E.: Rosalie Camacho, (K-6); Jane Alfano, (7-12).
Students 307.

El Centro, Imperial Co., Our Lady of Guadalupe (1946), Rev. Eduardo Gudino.
Res., 153 E. Brighton Ave., 92243. Tel: 760-352-5535; Fax: 760-352-8003.
Catechesis/Religious Programs—Tel: 760-352-5554. Victor Hernandez, D.R.E.
Students 452.

St. Mary (1907), Rev. Msgr. Thomas J. Vidra.
Res., 795 LaBrucherie, P.O. Box 3425, 92244. Tel: 760-352-4211; Fax: 760-352-7397. [JC]
School—Tel: 760-352-7285; Fax: 760-352-9726.
Sister Servants of the Blessed Sacrament 4; Lay Teachers 10; Students 285.
Catechesis/Religious Programs—Tel: 760-353-8260.
Students 295.

Encinitas, San Diego Co., St. John the Evangelist (1946), Rev. Msgr. Timothy Harnett; Rev. Michael G. Ortiz.
Res., 1001 Encinitas Blvd., 92024-0457. Tel: 760-753-6254; Fax: 760-753-7118.
School—Tel: 760-753-1893.
Lay Teachers 22; Students 408.
Catechesis/Religious Programs—Tel: 760-436-0664.
Students 510.

Escondido, San Diego Co., Church of the Resurrection (1970), Revs. Charles Fuld; Jose Edmundo Zarate-Suarez; Deacons James Kostick; Lawrence Michaels; Leopoldo Valdivia.
Res., 1445 Conway Dr., 92027. Tel: 760-747-2322; Fax: 760-747-7079.
Catechesis/Religious Programs—Tel: 760-747-4550. Margaret Butkis, D.R.E.
Students 1,050.
Comunidad Hispana—Tel: 760-747-4553.

Church of St. Timothy (1985), Rev. James E. Rafferty.
Res. and Offices: 3110 Quiet Hills Dr., 92029-7304. Tel: 760-489-1200; Fax: 760-489-2731.
Church—2960 Canyon Rd., 92029.
Catechesis/Religious Programs—Tel: 760-489-0482. Josie Piranio, D.R.E.
Students 178.

St. Mary (1890), Revs. Peter Navarra; Victor Maristela.
Res., 1160 S. Broadway Ave., 92025-5815. Tel: 760-745-1611; Fax: 760-745-1238.
School—Tel: 760-743-3431; Fax: 760-743-6808.
Sisters of the Precious Blood 2; Lay Teachers 13; Students 309.
Catechesis/Religious Programs—130 E. 13th Ave., 92025. Tel: 760-745-8255. Sharon Twilliger, D.R.E.
Students 677.

Fallbrook, San Diego Co., St. Peter (1946), Rev. Edward Kaicher.
Res., 450 S. Stage Coach Ln., 92028. Tel: 760-728-7034; Fax: 760-723-4050.
School—St. Peter's Catholic School, Tel: 760-728-6961; Fax: 760-723-4050.
Lay Teachers 13; Students 172.
Catechesis/Religious Programs—Tel: 760-728-3412.
Students 620.

Holtville, Imperial Co., St. Joseph (1911), Rev. Cecilio T. Moraga.
Res., 560 Maple Ave., 92250. Tel: 619-356-2147; Fax: 760-356-1985.
Catechesis/Religious Programs—Tel: 619-356-5738. Eleanor Valenzuela, D.O.M., D.R.E.
Students 354.

Imperial, Imperial Co., St. Anthony of Padua (1948), Revs. Firmo Mantovani, C.S. (Brazil); Guillermo Garcia, C.S. (Mexico).
Res., 210 W. Seventh St., 92251. Tel: 619-355-1347; Fax: 619-355-1226.
Catechesis/Religious Programs—Tel: 619-355-1304. Martha P. Rubalcava, D.R.E.
Students 220.
Missions—Heber, Sacred Heart, 46 E. Main St., Heber, 92249. Tel: 619-353-6987; Seeley, Holy Spirit, 1798 Rio Vista, Tel: 619-352-3811.

Jacumba, San Diego Co., St. Mary Magdalene (1947), Rev. George A. Carroll, S.J.
Res., 44686 Calexico Ave., P.O. Box 406, 91934-0406. Tel: 619-766-4661.
Catechesis/Religious Programs—Debbie Hebert, D.R.E.
Students 15.
Missions—Cameron Corner, St. Adelaide; Campo Indian Reservation, Our Lady of Mount Carmel.

Jamul, San Diego Co., St. Pius X (1956), Rev. Scott Burnia; Deacons H. B. Cody; A. R. McDaniel.
Res., 14107 Lyons Valley Rd., P.O. Box 369, 91935. Tel: 619-669-0085; Fax: 619-669-0087.
Catechesis/Religious Programs—Tel: 619-669-0086. Terry Salvatore, D.R.E.
Students 128.

Julian, San Diego Co., St. Elizabeth (1949), Rev. Donal C. Walsh.
Res., P.O. Box 366, 92036-0366. Tel: 760-765-0613; Fax: 760-765-0552.
Catechesis/Religious Programs—Students 60.

La Jolla, San Diego Co., All Hallows (1959), Rev. Msgr. Patrick Fox. In res., Rev. Thomas Thompson.
Res., 6602 La Jolla Scenic Dr. S., 92037-5799. Tel: 619-459-2975; Fax: 619-459-9712.
School—2390 Nautilus, 92037. Tel: 619-459-6074; Fax: 619-459-4602.
Sisters 2; Lay Teachers 11; Students 288.
Catechesis/Religious Programs—Patricia Stewart, D.R.E.
Students 135.

Mary, Star of the Sea (1906), Rev. Msgr. Eamonn F. Lyng; Rev. Msgr. James M. Gilfillan, Pastor Emeritus; Deacon William Dalzell.
Res., 7727 Girard Ave., 92037-4480. Tel: 619-454-2631; Fax: 619-454-5968.
School—Stella Maris Academy, 7654 Herschel Ave., 92037. Tel: 619-454-2461; Fax: 619-454-4913.
Lay Teachers 16; Students 243.
Catechesis/Religious Programs—Tel: 619-454-1714. Sr. Christian Koch, D.R.E.
Students 301.

Lakeside, San Diego Co., Blessed Kateri Tekakwitha (1982) (Native American), Rev. Anthony C. May; Deacon Bill Clarke.
Res., 1054 Barona Rd., 92040-1502. Tel: 619-443-3412.
Catechesis/Religious Programs—Tel: 619-445-8333. Betty Alto, D.R.E.
Students 140.
Missions—Lakeside, Barona, 1054 Barona Rd., 92040-1502. Tel: 619-443-3412; Alpine, Viejas; El Cajon, Sycuan.

Our Lady of Perpetual Help (1947), Rev. Msgr. Neal T. Dolan; Rev. Barry Vinyard; Deacon Anthony L. Gasparovic.
Res., 13208 Lakeshore Dr., 92040. Tel: 619-443-1412; Fax: 619-443-1733.
School—Tel: 619-443-1440. Mr. Richard Scherer, Prin.
St. Joseph of Carondelet Sisters 1; Lay Teachers 12; Students 230.
Catechesis/Religious Programs—Tel: 619-443-5018. D.R.E.: Joan Lopez, (Jr. High School); Carol Lane, (Adult Ed.).
Students 492.

La Mesa, San Diego Co., St. Martin of Tours (1921), Revs. John M. Sproul; Edward P. McNulty. In res., Rev. Msgr. Patrick O'Neill; Deacon Timothy Treadwell.
Res., 7710 El Cajon Blvd., 91941. Tel: 619-465-5334; Fax: 619-465-7297.
School—Tel: 619-466-3241; Fax: 619-466-0285.
Lay Teachers 14; Students 310.
Catechesis/Religious Programs—Tel: 619-698-8434. Christine Davis, D.R.E.
Students 290.

Lemon Grove, San Diego Co., St. John of the Cross (1939), Rev. Msgr. Edward Brockhaus; Rev. Jorge A. Soria; Deacons Ralph Robbins; Peter Corrao; Frank Santoyo; Martin Villafana. In res., Rev. Donald Buchanan, (Retired).
Res., 8086 Broadway, 91945-2598. Tel: 619-466-3209; Fax: 619-466-9276.
School—8175 Lemon Grove Way, 91945. Tel: 619-466-8624; Fax: 619-466-3732. Sr. Guadalupe Mier Y Teran, H.M.S.S., Prin.
Sisters 2; Lay Teachers 7; Students 350.
Catechesis/Religious Programs—Tel: 619-461-2681. Karen Dey, D.R.E.
Students 660.
Convent—8171 Lemon Grove Way, 91945. Tel: 619-460-4271.
Sisters of Mercy of the Blessed Sacrament 5.

National City, San Diego Co., St. Anthony of Padua (1910) (Hispanic), Rev. Willaim T. Lawson. In res., Rev. Peter Borda.
Res., 1816 Harding Ave., P.O. Box 1507, 91951-1507. Tel: 619-477-4520; Fax: 619-477-8708.
Catechesis/Religious Programs—Angelina Sampo, D.R.E.
Students 356.

St. Mary (1926), Revs. Dionisio Macalintal (PH); Jose Castillo (Columbia).
Res., 411 E. Eighth St., 91950-2395. Tel: 619-474-1501; Fax: 619-474-1502.
Catechesis/Religious Programs—Tel: 619-474-5777.
Students 972.

Oceanside, San Diego Co., St. Margaret (1977), Rev. William F. Gold; Deacon Lewis Beatty.
Res., 4300 Oceanside Blvd., 92056-2999. Tel: 760-941-5560; Fax: 760-941-1857.
Catechesis/Religious Programs—Tel: 760-941-5561. Sr. Yvonne Hawker, O.S.F., D.R.E.
Students 400.

St. Mary Star of the Sea (1937) (Hispanic), Revs. John P. Dolan; Humberto C. Zanetti, O.F.M. (Italy). Res., 609 Pier View Way, 92054-2861. Tel: 760-722-1688; Fax: 760-722-2653.
School—Tel: 760-722-7259; Fax: 760-722-0862.
Lay Teachers 24; Students 337.
Catechesis/Religious Programs—Tel: 619-722-1000.
Students 230.

Pala, San Diego Co., Mission San Antonio de Pala (1816) (Native American), Rev. Paul Marconi, C.R.S.P.
Res., P.O. Box 70, 92059-0070. Tel: 760-742-3317; Fax: 760-742-3040.
Catechesis/Religious Programs—Tel: 760-742-1714.
Students 90.
Convent—Tel: 760-742-1714.
Franciscan Sisters of Philadelphia 3.
Chapels—Rincon Indian Reservation, St. Bartholomew.; Pauma, El Centro Guadalupano, Tel: 760-742-4559; La Jolla Indian Reservation, Our Lady of Refuge.; Pauma Indian Reservation, St. James.

Poway, San Diego Co., St. Gabriel (1973), Rev. Joseph Brady.
Res., 13734 Twin Peaks Rd., 92074-0867. Tel: 619-748-5348; Fax: 619-748-5764.
Catechesis/Religious Programs—Tel: 619-748-7475. Sr. Carlene Galuan, D.C.M., D.R.E.
Students 675.

St. Michael (1959), Rev. Msgr. Joseph L. Finnerty; Rev. William Mooney; Deacon Franz Schultz.
Res., 15546 Pomerado Rd., 92064-2404. Tel: 619-487-4755; Fax: 619-487-5937.
School—15542 Pomerado Rd., 92064. Tel: 619-485-1303; Fax: 619-485-5059.
Sisters of Mercy of Sligo 2; Lay Teachers 13; Students 318.
Catechesis/Religious Programs—Tel: 619-487-0360. Kathy Wood, D.R.E.
Students 1,050.

Ramona, San Diego Co., Immaculate Heart of Mary (1947), Rev. Michael J. Sinor; Deacons A. R. McDaniel; Modesto M. Perez.
Res., 537 E St., 92065. Tel: 760-789-0583; Fax: 760-789-3875.
Catechesis/Religious Programs—Tel: 760-789-6151. Eileen Morgan, D.R.E.
Students 410.

Rancho Santa Fe, San Diego Co., Church of the Nativity (1985), Rev. Msgr. Dennis R. Clark.
Mailing Address: P.O. Box 8770, 92067-8770.
Res., 6309 El Apajo Rd., 92067. Tel: 619-756-1911; Fax: 619-756-9562.
Catechesis/Religious Programs—Tel: 619-756-0937. Mrs. Anne Lonnecker, D.R.E.
Students 287.

San Luis Rey, San Diego Co., Mission San Luis Rey de Francia (1798), Revs. Michel Gagnon, O.F.M.; Vincent Hughes, O.F.M.; Armando Lopez, O.F.M.
Res., 4070 Mission Ave., Oceanside, 92057-6497. Tel: 619-757-3250; Fax: 619-757-3299.
Catechesis/Religious Programs—Students 626.

San Marcos, San Diego Co., St. Mark (1963), Rev. Msgr. Thomas P. Healy; Rev. Aurelio P. Crisologo; Deacons Sam Hunt; Dick Jansing.
Res., 1147 Discovery, 92069. Tel: 760-744-1540; Fax: 760-744-3828.
Catechesis/Religious Programs—Tel: 760-744-1130.
Students 480.

Santa Ysabel, San Diego Co., Santa Ysabel Indian Mission (1818) (Native American), Rev. William P. Stevenson.
Res., 23013 Hwy. 79, P.O. Box 129, 92070-1010. Tel: 619-765-0810; Fax: 619-765-0810. [CEM]
Missions—Warner Springs, San Diego Co., St. Francis, Hwy. 79, Warner Springs, 92086.; Los Coyotes Reservation, San Diego Co., St. Isadore.

Santee, San Diego Co., Guardian Angels (1962), Revs. Michael A. Cunnane; Michael L. Baumgardner.
Res., 9310 Dalehurst Rd., 92071-1010. Tel: 619-448-1213; Fax: 619-448-2980.
Catechesis/Religious Programs—9310 Dalehurst, 92071. Tel: 619-448-1274. Sr. Mary Potter, R.S.M., D.R.E.
Students 520.

San Ysidro, San Diego Co., Our Lady of Mt. Carmel (1927) (Hispanic), Revs. Emmet L. Farrell; Ricardo Mejia, Admin.
Res., 2020 Alaquinas Dr., 92173-2107. Tel: 619-428-1415; Fax: 619-428-5626.
School—Tel: 619-428-2091; Fax: 619-428-8324. Sr. Rebeca Munoz, Prin.
Sisters of the Most Blessed Sacrament 5; Lay Teachers 9; Students 345.
Catechesis/Religious Programs—Tel: 619-428-3686.
Students 178.

Solana Beach, San Diego Co., St. James (Del Mar) (1911), Rev. Msgr. Lawrence M. Purcell; Deacons John Gallagher; John Brice; Ted Bear. In res., Rev. John Howard, C.J.M.
Office: 625 S. Nardo Ave., 92075-2398. Tel: 619-755-2545; Fax: 619-755-3845.
School—Tel: 619-755-1777; Fax: 619-755-3124.
Lay Teachers 16; Students 257.
Catechesis/Religious Programs—Tel: 619-755-2545. Sr. Shaun Marie Larkin, S.B.L., Prin.; Robert Kidd, D.R.E.
Students 353.
Mission—Solana Beach, San Diego Co., St. Leo, 936 Genevieve, 92075. Tel: 619-481-6788.

Spring Valley, San Diego Co., Santa Sophia (1956), Revs. Michael Ratajczak; Joseph Viet Hoang; Deacons Francis DeMoor; James Keeley. In res., Rev. Gary Holtey.
Res., 9800 San Juan St., 91977. Tel: 619-463-6629; Fax: 619-463-8101.
School—Tel: 619-463-0488; Fax: 619-668-5469.
Lay Teachers 11; Students 296.
Catechesis/Religious Programs—Tel: 619-463-6011. Sr. Alyce Waters, D.R.E.
Students 410.

Valley Center, San Diego Co., St. Stephen (1981), Rev. Michael A. Booth.
Res., P.O. Box 1015, 31020 Cole Grade Rd., 92082. Tel: 760-749-3324; Fax: 760-749-6684.
Catechesis/Religious Programs—Tel: 760-749-3352. Penny Phillips, D.R.E.
Students 251.

Vista, San Diego Co., St. Francis of Assisi (1941), Revs. Ramon R. Marrufo; George A. Dunkley; Peter Nguyen (Vietnamese); Deacons Robert P. Mueller; Michael Collins; Frank Mercardante; Ronald Arnold; Pedro Enciso.
Res., 525 W. Vista Way, 92083-5974. Tel: 760-945-8000; Fax: 760-945-8036.
School—Tel: 760-630-7960; Fax: 760-726-2910. Linda McCotter, Prin.
Lay Teachers 15; Students 392.
Catechesis/Religious Programs—Tel: 760-945-8010. Susan Ferraris, D.R.E.
Students 775.

Westmorland, St. Joseph (1939) (Mexican-American), Rev. Manuel Mesa, O.M.I.
Res., 300 N. Center St., P.O. Box 627, 92281. Tel: 619-344-5267; 344-3721 (Parish Hall).
Catechesis/Religious Programs—Students 110.

Winterhaven, Imperial Co., St. Thomas (1780). (Indian Mission). Rev. Duncan W. Monohan.
Res., P.O. Box 1176, 92283-1176. Tel: 760-572-0283; Fax: 760-572-0283.
Mission—Winterhaven, Imperial Co., St. Mary, 92283.

Eastern Churches

San Diego, San Diego Co., Our Lady of Perpetual Help. (Ukrainian Catholic). Rev. Andrew Mykyta.
Res., 4014 Winona Ave., 92105. Tel: 619-282-9538.

El Cajon, San Diego Co., St. Peter. (Chaldean Eastern Catholic). Rev. Michael J. Bazzi; Faik Tominna, Admin.
Res., 1627 Jamacha Way, 92019. Tel: 619-579-7913; 588-9921; Fax: 619-588-8281.
Catechesis/Religious Programs—Tel: 619-447-4842. Khelood Allos, D.R.E.
Students 650.
Convent—1591 Jamacha Way, 92019. Tel: 619-447-4842. Chaldean Sisters

Chaplains of Public Institutions

Hospitals

SAN DIEGO. *Alvarado, Grossmont and Kaiser Hospitals.* Revs. James Burson, C.J.M. Tel: 619-287-3270; Gary M. Holtey.
Children's Hospital. Rev. Manuel Ediza.
Mercy Hospital. Revs. Benjamin Bachmeier; Francis W. McDonnell Tel: 619-260-7020; Robert White.
Scripps Hospital. Rev. Thomas Thompson Tel: 619-457-4123.
Sharp Memorial Hospital. Revs. Manuel Ediza Tel: 619-541-3475; James V. Corrigan, O.S.A., Clinical Pastoral Ed.
UCSD Medical Center. Rev. Paul Balio Tel: 619-543-6737.

LA JOLLA. *Veterans Administration Hospital* Tel: 619-552-8585. Rev. Jerry Hamperzonian.

OCEANSIDE. *Tri City Hospital.* Rev. Walter Kersey Tel: 760-724-8411.

Retirement Homes

SAN DIEGO. *Nazareth House.* Revs. Willian Wilson Tel: 619-563-0480; Harry Murphy.

LA MESA. *Little Flower Haven.* Rev. Philip Bronk, S.T. Tel: 619-466-3163.

Detention Ministries

SAN DIEGO. *Calipatria State Prison* Tel: 619-236-3011. Rev. Thomas Dermody.
Central Detention Facility and San Diego City Jail. Rev. James I. Rasura, S.J. Tel: 619-236-3011.
East Mesa Detention Facility Tel: 619-661-2608. Deacon Sam Martinez.
George F. Bailey Maximum Security Facility Tel: 619-661-2620.
Juvenile Hall. Monique Muther Tel: 619-694-4365.
Metropolitan Correction Center. Deacon Nicholas Santiago Tel: 619-232-4311.
R.J. Donovan Correctional Facility. Rev. Ron Chiasson, O.M.I. Tel: 619-661-6500.

CHULA VISTA. *South Bay Detention Facility.* Rev. James V. Caldwell.

EL CENTRO. *El Centro Juvenile Hall.* Diana Espinoza Tel: 760-339-6229.
Imperial County Jail. Julia Ulloa Tel: 760-339-6367.

SANTEE. *Las Colinas Women's Detention Facility.* Deacon George Shea Tel: 619-258-3176.

VISTA. *Vista Detention Facility.* Deacon Jesse Pagliard Tel: 760-940-4473.

State Conservation Camps

SAN DIEGO. *Rainbow Work Camp.* Deacon George Paulicivic Tel: 760-728-7492.

Special Assignment:
Reverend Fathers—
Dunn, Stephen
Mort, Ernest C., C.S.P., University Admin. of U.S.C.D.
Oliva, George M., S.J., Retreat Ministry

On Duty Outside the Diocese:
Reverend Fathers—
Cordileone, Salvatore
Cribbin, James
Flynn, Edward R., 98 San Marino Dr., San Rafael, CA 94901
Parrales, Napoleon J., Cementerio Nuevo, Barquisimeto, Venezuela
Reilly, John (Ireland)

Military Chaplains:
Reverend Fathers—
Buchmiller, Ronald J., Ch.C., USN
Diaz, Michael, CHC, USN
Jennings, Tommie, CHC, USNR
Merris, Christopher

Unassigned:
Reverend Monsignors—
Higgins, Michael K., P.O. Box 87225, San Diego, CA 92138. Tel: 619-280-7500; 280-8400 (fax)
Reverend Fathers—
Foley, Patrick J.
Gomes-Kelly, John R.
Langille, Justin
Merris, Christopher
Polizzi, Daniel
Ryland, Raymond
Stanonik, Anthony

Absent on Sick Leave:
Reverend Fathers—
Moffo, James
Twarog, Theodore S.

Leave of Absence:
Reverend Fathers—
Buttimer, Joseph J.
Conwill, Giles A.
Dunleavy, Steven
Huggins, Michael L.
Kennedy, James
Kothuis, Hans
Mason, James H.
Sweeney, Lawrence

Retired:
Reverend Monsignors—
Aldasoro, Francisco
Balderas, Luis G.
Bergin, William A.
Bolger, William
Brennan, Joseph F.
Briody, Thomas
Campion, John J.
Chylewski, Anthony
Coughlan, Michael J.
Creighton, Edward
Dollen, Charles
Galindo, Rudolph
Gilfillan, James M.
Hanley, Andrew W.
Kearney, Patrick J.
Kraft, William A.
McDermott, Thomas J.

Mimnagh, Peter F.
Moore, J. Raymond
Murray, Sean
O'Donoghue, James P.
O'Neill, Patrick J.
O'Sullivan, Jeremiah
Portman, John R.
Rhatigan, John
Topping, Joseph
Young, Charles P.
Reverend Fathers—
Anderson, Arthur Edward
Borda, Peter Paul
Buchanan, Donald
Chase, Maurice
Fischer, Eugene
Goce, Lauro
Holland, Kilian
Houck, Richard
Keenan, John J.
Keith, John C.
Lorenz, Vincent E.
Lucev, John
McDonnell, Francis W.
McDonnell, Joseph T.
McManus, Martin
Nesbitt, John B.
O'Curneen, Hugh
Quinn, John T.
Rankin, James
Roll, David H.
Russell, Richard J.
Ryan, Alphonsus
Salada, Urbano
Sheslo, Charles
Sierra, Francis A.
Smith, Aquinas
Smith, Michael
Sostrich, John L.
Thompson, J. Noel
Tindall, Harold
Uboldi, Victor
Ullman, Earl L.
Wheeler, John
Wilson, William

Permanent Deacons:
Albers, Tony, Blessed Sacrament, San Diego
Arias, Luciano, St. Mary, El Centro
Arismendez, Joe, St. Rose of Lima, Chula Vista
Arnold, Ron, St. Francis, Vista
Ball, Lou, St. Columba, San Diego
Bear, Ted, St. James, Del Mar
Beatty, Lewis, St. Margaret, Oceanside
Bell, L. Ferris, St. Gregory, San Diego
Brice, John, St. James, Solona Beach
Chia, Henry, St. Elizabeth Seton, Carlsbad
Clarke, William G., Blessed Kateri Tekakwitha, Jamul
Cody, Henry B., St. Pious X, Jamul
Collins, Michael, Saint Francis, Vista
Corder, Richard G., St. John, Encinitas
Corrao, Jack P., (Retired)
Corrao, Peter T., St. John of the Cross, Lemon Grove
Costello, John M., (Retired)
Dalzell, William, (Retired)
Davidson, Paul, Holy Family, San Diego
Dean, Ben, St. Peter, Fallbrook
Delano, Joe, St. Jerome, Chula Vista
DeMoor, Francis, (Retired)
DePozo, Daniel, St. Pius X, Chula Vista
Diem, Ronald H., Unassigned
Donivan, Ed, (Retired)
Dougherty, Thomas P., Holy Family, San Diego
Dube, Leo, (Retired)
Early, John M., St. Mary, Escondido
Ekhaml, Robert T., St. Therese, San Diego
Enciso, Pedro, St. Francis, Vista
Finn, Kenneth, St. Mary, Escondido
Frazee, Mike, St. Patrick, Carlsbad
Gallagher, John V., (Retired)
Gasparovic, Anthony L., Our Lady of Perpetual Help, Lakeside
Graff, Albert P., (Retired)
Grosso, Ernest, Mission San Deigo de Alcala, San Diego
Gullotta, Daniel, Lakeside, MT
Hernandez, Raul, Our Lady of the Angels, San Diego
Hess, Arnie, Our Mother of Confidence, San Diego
Hitch, James, Corpus Christi, Bonita
Hunt, Sam, St. Mark, San Marcos
Jansing, Dick, (Retired)
Jones, Thom, Our Lady of Mt. Carmel, San Diego
Keeley, Jim, Santa Sophia, Spring Valley
Klopchin, Bill, Our Mother of Confidence, San Diego
Kostick, Jim, Resurrection, Escondido
Kutler, Harold, St. Mary, Star of the Sea, Oceanside
Leach, Dave, San Luis Obispo
Lozoya, Margarito, Our Lady of Guadalupe, Chula Vista
Mackey, Bob, (Retired)
Maher, Thomas M., Jr., St. Mary, Escondido
Martinez, Seodello A., St. Charles, San Diego
Mather, Dick, St. Patrick, Carlsbad
McDaniel, Al, Immaculate Heart of Mary, Ramona
Mercardante, F., St. Francis, Vista
Michaels, Larry, Resurrection, Escondido
Montoya, Ken, St. Jerome, San Diego
Mueller, Robert, St. Francis, Vista
Nevins, William J., (Retired)
Nguyen, Peter Can, Our Lady of the Sacred Heart, San Diego
Nunez, Manuel, St. Jude, San Diego
Osgood, Franklin B., Unassigned
Pagliaro, Jesse, St. Thomas More, Carlsbad
Parra, Daniel, Our Lady of Guadalupe, Chula Vista
Paulicivic, George, Sr., Murrieta
Perez, Modesto, Immaculate Heart of Mary, Ramona & St. Mary, Escondida
Phelps, John, Our Lady of Mt. Carmel, San Diego
Pollock, William, (Retired)
Principe, Louis, Blessed Sacrament
Robbins, Ralph, St. John of the Cross, Lemon Grove
Robles, Manny, Holy Spirit, San Diego
Rocha, Louis, Holy Trinity, El Cajon
Rondeau, Dick, Belpre, KS
Roy, James, Klamath Falls, OR
Santiago, Nicholas M., St. Columba, San Diego
Santoyo, Juan, St. John of the Cross, Lemon Grove
Schmitt, Giles V., Sacred Heart, San Diego
Scull, James, Ascension, San Diego
Shea, George, Our Lady of Grace, El Cajon
Shelton, Carl, St. John the Evangelist, San Diego
Shockley, Gordon E., Louisville, KY
Skupnik, Ray, Long Beach
Snyder, John A., St. Luke, El Cajun
Threatt, Marvin, Unassigned
Treadwell, Timothy, St. Martin of Tours, La Mesa
Trumble, John, St. Kieran, El Cajon
Valdivia, Leopoldo, Resurrection, Escondido
Vasquez, Bill, Mission San Diego de Alcala, San Diego
Vecchitto, Glenn, Our Lady of Mt. Carmel, San Ysidro
Villafana, Martin, St. John of the Cross, San Diego
Vivio, Bill, Glendale, AZ
Walling, Robert, Bend, OR
Wood, Joseph, All Hallows, La Jolla
Woznicki, Walter, Our Lady of Grace, El Cajon
Yeatts, Bernard, Our Lady of Mt. Carmel, San Diego

INSTITUTIONS LOCATED IN THE DIOCESE

[A] SEMINARIES, DIOCESAN

SAN DIEGO. *St. Francis Seminary*, 1667 Santa Paula Dr., 92111. Tel: 619-291-7446; Fax: 619-291-7011. Very Rev. Steven Callahan, Rector; Revs. Jaime Escobedo; Richard Huston. Priests 3; Students 19.

[B] COLLEGES AND UNIVERSITIES

SAN DIEGO. *Austin House - House of Formation*, 1605 28th St., 92102. Tel: 619-233-9141 (Prov. Office). E-mail: osagartII@aol.com
For a complete listing, refer to the Colleges and Universities section.

University of San Diego, 5998 Alcala Park, 92110-2492. Tel: 619-260-4600
For a complete listing, refer to the Colleges and Universities section.

[C] HIGH SCHOOLS, DIOCESAN

SAN DIEGO. *Academy of Our Lady of Peace.* (Grades 9-12), 4860 Oregon St., 92116. Tel: 619-297-2266; Fax: 619-297-2473. (Girls). Sr. Dolores Anchondo, C.S.J., Prin. Sisters of St. Joseph of Carondelet 3; Lay Teachers 40; Students 725.

Marian Catholic High School, 1002 18th St., 92154. Tel: 619-423-2121; Fax: 619-423-6910. (Coed). Mrs. Estelle Kassebaum, Prin. Religious 2; Lay Teachers 27; Students 325.

St. Augustine High School, 3266 Nutmeg St., 92104-5199. Tel: 619-282-2184; Fax: 619-282-1203. Conducted By the Augustinians. (Boys). Revs. John R. Sanders, O.S.A., Prin.; Timothy Lamm, O.S.B.; Harry M. Neely, O.S.A.; Walter P. Vogel, O.S.A.; Bro. Stephen McKenna, O.S.A.; Deacon Richard Hardick, O.S.A.

(For information concerning the monastery see separate listing under Monasteries). Priests 4; Brothers 1; Deacons 1; Sisters 1; Lay Teachers 30; Students 600.

University of San Diego High School. (Coed), 5961 Linda Vista Rd., 92110-1947. Tel: 619-298-8277; Fax: 619-260-1696. Richard E. Kelly, Ph.D., Prin.; Rev. Michael White, C.S.Sp. Priests 1; Lay Teachers 73; Students 1,360.

CALEXICO. *Vincent Memorial High.* (Grades 9-12), 525 W. Sheridan, 92231. Tel: 760-357-3461; Fax: 760-357-0902. (Coed). Conducted by Sisters Servants of the Blessed Sacrament. Sisters 2; Lay Teachers 11; Students 166.

[D] SPECIAL SCHOOLS

EL CAJON. *St. Madeleine Sophie's Center for Developmentally Disabled Adults*, 2119 E. Madison Ave., 92019-1111. Tel: 619-442-5129; Fax: 619-442-2590. Frances S. Glasser, Exec. Dir. Sisters 1; Lay Teachers 50; Enrollment 180.

[E] PROTECTIVE INSTITUTIONS

SAN DIEGO. *Nazareth House*, 6333 Rancho Mission Rd., 92108. Tel: 619-563-0480
For a complete listing, refer to the Special Care Facilities section.

SPRING VALLEY. *Noah Homes*, 12526 Campo Rd., 91978. Tel: 619-660-6200; Fax: 619-660-1481. E-mail: NoahHomes@Juno.com
For a complete listing, refer to the Special Care Facilities section.

[F] GENERAL HOSPITALS AND CLINICS

SAN DIEGO. *Mercy Hospital and Medical Center dba Mercy Healthcare San Diego*, 4077 Fifth Ave., 92103. Tel: 619-294-8111; Fax: 619-686-3530. E-mail: sisterJ@Mercvsd.com
For a complete listing, refer to the Hospitals section.

[G] HOMES FOR SENIOR CITIZENS

SAN DIEGO. *Cathedral Plaza*, 1551 Third Ave., 92101. Tel: 619-234-0093
For a complete listing, refer to the Special Care Facilities section.

Guadalupe Plaza, 4142 42nd St., 92105. Tel: 619-584-2414
For a complete listing, refer to the Special Care Facilities section.

Nazareth House Retirement Home, 6333 Rancho Mission Rd., 92108. Tel: 619-563-0480
For a complete listing, refer to the Special Care Facilities section.

St. John's Plaza 8150 Broadway Lemon Grove, 91945. Tel: 619-466-5354.
For a complete listing, refer to the Special Care Facilities section.

LA MESA. *Little Flower Haven*, 8585 La Mesa Blvd., 91941. Tel: 619-466-3163
For a complete listing, refer to the Special Care Facilities section.

[H] MONASTERIES AND RESIDENCES OF PRIESTS AND BROTHERS

SAN DIEGO. *Augustinian Community*, 3266 Nutmeg St., 92104. Tel: 619-282-2028; Fax: 619-282-1203. Revs. John R. Sanders, O.S.A., Prin.; John D. Keller, O.S.A.; Peter J. Marron, O.S.A.; Thomas P. Garrett, O.S.A.; James E. Hannan, O.S.A.; Harry M. Neely, O.S.A., Prior; James A. Mott, O.S.A., Prov.; Stephen Ochoa; James Retzner; William H. Sullivan, O.S.A.; Bros. J. Stephen McKenna, O.S.A., Procurator; Michael Bube, O.S.A., 1605 28th St., 92102. Revs. Walter P. Vogel, O.S.A., Prior; John Blethen; Jerome Bevilacqua, O.S.A.; Deacon Richard Hardick.

Monica House - Augustinian Community, 1621 28th St., 92104.

BOULEVARD. *Cedar Pines - Augustinian Community*, 1371 Tierra del Sol Rd., 91905-4694.

OCEANSIDE. *Prince of Peace Abbey, Benet Hill*, 92054. Tel: 760-430-1305; 1306. Benedictine Fathers. Rt. Revs. Charles Wright, O.S.B., Abbot; Claude Ehringer, O.S.B., (Retired), Abbot; Revs. David Carvalho, O.S.B.; Luke Dougherty, O.S.B.; Sharbel Ewen, O.S.B.; Anselm Fister, O.S.B.; Alexis Foyo, O.S.B.; Basil Mattingly, O.S.B.; Aquinas Nichols, O.S.B.; Herbert Palmer, O.S.B.; Stephanos Pedrano, O.S.B.; Bros. Peter Aslin, O.S.B.; Joseph Black, O.S.B.; Thomas Cimini, O.S.B.; Anselm Clark, O.S.B.; Anthony Green, O.S.B.; Blaise Heuke, O.S.B.; Clement Kennedy, O.S.B.; Benedict Menezes, O.S.B.; Raphael Meyer, O.S.B.; Michael Pham; Mario Quizon, O.S.B.; Daniel Sokol, O.S.B.; Meinrad Taylor, O.S.B.; Gabriel Williams; Timothy Balk, O.S.B., Bro. Oblate. Priests 11; Brothers 15; Novices 2.

SAN LUIS REY. *Mission San Luis Rey*, 4050 Mission Ave., 92068. Tel: 760-757-3651.
Web site: www.sanluisrey.org
Franciscan Friars. Rev. Ben R. Innes, O.F.M., Guardian; Bros. Ed Dunn; Conrad Duran, O.F.M.; Bede McKinnon, O.F.M.; Maurice Peltier, O.F.M.; Roch Schwab, O.F.M.; Thomas Thing, O.F.M.; Revs. Michel Gagnon, O.F.M.; Anthony Garibaldi, O.F.M.; William Haney, O.F.M.; Vincent Hughes, O.F.M.; Paul Lee, O.F.M.; Armando Lopez, O.F.M.; Mel Bucher, O.F.M. Priests 8; Brothers 6.

[I] CONVENTS AND RESIDENCES FOR SISTERS

SAN DIEGO. *Carmelite Monastery of San Diego, California*. (Discalced), 5158 Hawley Blvd., 92116-1934. Tel: 619-280-5425. Sr. Yvonne Hanke, O.C.D. Sisters 15.
Community of the Holy Spirit, 6151 Rancho Mission Rd., #205, 92108. Tel: 619-584-0809.
E-mail: chsmurrieta@connect.com
Sr. Sara Murrietta. Sisters 17.
Daughters of Divine Charity, 10294 Eagle Rock Ave., 92126. Tel: 619-271-1451. Sisters 3.
Maryknoll Sisters, 2227 31st St., 92104. Tel: 619-283-5678. Sisters 4.
Missionaries of Charity, 3877 Boston Ave., 92113. Tel: 619-263-9566. Sisters 5.
Poor Sisters of Nazareth, 6330 Rancho Mission Rd., 92108. Tel: 619-563-0480. Sisters 8.
Religious of Jesus and Mary, 1510 Third Ave., 92101. Tel: 619-234-0556. Sisters 10.
Religious of the Sacred Heart. Casa Maria Community, Univ. of San Diego, 5998 Alcala Park, 92110-2492. Tel: 619-299-3639. Sisters 5.
School Sisters of Notre Dame, 5202 Santa Margarita Ave., 92114. Tel: 619-264-7011. Sisters 4.
Sisters of Loretto, 6528 Bradford St., 92115. Tel: 619-287-8388. Sisters 2.
Sisters of Mercy (Ireland & South Africa), 10726 Caminito Cascara, #15, 92108. Tel: 619-284-1027. Sisters 2.
Sisters of Mercy of the Americas (Burlingame), 4216 Albatross Dr., 92103. Tel: 619-260-8047. Sisters 2.
Sisters of Social Service, 3525 Third Ave., 92103-4908. Tel: 619-295-1896. Sisters 3.
Sisters of St. Francis (Philadelphia), 17155 Ruette Compana, 92128. Tel: 619-451-2649. Sisters 2.
Sisters of St. Joseph of Carondelet, 4860 Oregon St., 92116. Tel: 619-295-2891; 295-2887. Sisters 4.
Sisters of St. Joseph of Peace, 2880 Caulfield Dr., 92154. Tel: 619-423-7360. Sisters 2.
Sisters of the Holy Family, 6333 College Grove Way, B9, 92115. Tel: 619-286-3371.
Sisters of the Precious Blood, 4202 58th St., 92115. Tel: 619-229-1817. Sisters 2.
Society of the Holy Child Jesus, 6243 Caminito Telmo, 92111. Tel: 619-277-0309.
E-mail: corneliasd@aol.com
Sisters 3.

CALEXICO. *Sister Servants of the Blessed Sacrament*, 536 Rockwood, 92231. Tel: 760-357-1046. Sisters 9.

CARLSBAD. *Sisters of Charity of the Blessed Virgin Mary*, 2409 La Pluma Ln., 92009. Tel: 760-633-1315. Sr. Mary Kay Dun, Reg. Supr. Sisters 3.
Sisters of St. Francis (Rochester), 7216 San Lucas, 92009. Tel: 760-438-5443.

CHULA VISTA. *Benedictine Sisters of Glendora*, 236 Alvarado, 91910-3610. Tel: 619-422-3610. Sisters 2.
Religious of the Incarnate Word, 153 Rainier Ct., 91911. Tel: 619-420-0231; Fax: 619-691-5939. Sisters 4.

EL CAJON. *Sisters of Mercy (Ireland & South Africa)*, 2766 Navajo Rd., 92020. Tel: 619-465-2233.
E-mail: carmel48@aol.com
Sisters 3.

EL CENTRO. *Our Lady of Victory Convent*, 604 El Centro Ave., 92243. Tel: 760-353-6416. Our Lady of Victory Missionary Sisters 3.
Religious of the Incarnate Word, 102 W. Holt, 92243. Tel: 760-353-4146. Sisters 3.

LA JOLLA. *Dominican Sisters of Adrian*, 6570 La Jolla Scenic Dr., 92037. Tel: 619-459-3681.
E-mail: clausenk@connect
Sisters 2.
Sisters of the Holy Cross, 1001 Kline St., 92037-4426. Tel: 619-454-2861. Sisters 3.

LA MESA. *Carmelite Sisters of the Divine Heart of Jesus*, 8585 La Mesa Blvd., 91941. Tel: 619-466-3163; Fax: 619-466-9642. Sr. M. Angela Therese Lovato, Prov. Supr.; Sr. Mary Alice Prieto, Supr. Sisters 11; Novices 2.
Medical Mission Sisters. (Western District). Mailing Address: 4817 Palm Ave., Ste. M, 91941. Tel: 619-789-7000.
E-mail: mmscalsd@juno.com
Web site: http://www.libertynet.org/~mmsl
Legal Title: *Society of Catholic Medical Missionaries, Inc.* Sr. Justine Church, M.M.S., Western Dist. Coord., 5673 Marne Ave., San Diego, 92120. Tel: 619-286-6880. Sisters 4. 211 N. Citrus, #123, Escondido, 92027. Tel: 619-480-1372. Sisters 2. 636 Mariposa Cir., Chula Vista, 91911-2511. Tel: 619-482-3109. Sisters 3. 2675 Fletcher Pkwy. #27, El Cajon, 92020. Tel: 619-465-6545. 8585 La Mesa Blvd., 91941. Tel: 619-697-5880. Sisters 2. 4601 Schaumberg Pl., Bonita, 91902. Tel: 619-267-1954. Sisters 2. 4142 42nd St. #501, San Diego, 92105. Tel: 619-584-8221. 8150 Broadway #127, Lemon Grove, 91945. Tel: 619-462-3888.
Religious of Jesus and Mary, 4197 S. Tropico Dr., 91941-6866. Tel: 619-465-0158. Sr. Rosemary Nicholson, R.J.M., Reg. Supr. Sisters 4.

LAKE SAN MARCOS. *Daughters of Mary and Joseph*, 1545 Via Brisa del Lago, 92069. Tel: 760-744-6578.

LEMON GROVE. *Sisters of Mercy of the Blessed Sacrament*, 8171 Lemon Grove Way, 91945. Tel: 619-460-4271. Sisters 5.

NATIONAL CITY. *Sisters of the Heart of Jesus in the Blessed Sacrament*, 912 Arcadia Pl., 91950. Tel: 619-267-4342. Sisters 3.

OCEANSIDE. *Sisters of the Precious Blood*, 4070 Mission Ave., 92057. Tel: 760-757-2155. Sisters 4.

PALA. *Sisters of St. Francis (Philadelphia)*, P.O. Box M, 92059. Tel: 760-742-1714. Sisters 3.

SAN YSIDRO. *Medical Missionaries of Mary*, 438 Blackshaw Ln., 92173. Tel: 619-690-9237.
E-mail: mmmsy@aol.com
Sisters 7.
Sister Servants of the Blessed Sacrament, 333 W. Park Ave., 92173. Tel: 619-428-1314. Sisters 6.
Sisters of St. Dominic (Tacoma), 1868 Via las Tonadas, 92173. Tel: 619-428-1629. Sisters 3.

SOLANA BEACH. *Sisters of St. Joseph of Carondelet*, 409 Santa Domingo, 92075. Tel: 619-755-6446. Sr. Suzanne Steffen, Regl. Supr. Sisters 3.

SPRING VALLEY. *Sisters of St. Joseph of Orange*, 10771 Del Rio Rd., 91978. Tel: 619-670-9663. Sisters 3.

VISTA. *Sisters of St. Clare*, 326 Santa Clara Dr., 92083. Tel: 760-945-8025. Sisters 4.

[J] SOCIAL SERVICES

SAN DIEGO.
**Bayside Settlement House*, 2202 Comstock St., 92111-6502. Tel: 619-278-0771; Fax: 619-278-6193. Grover Diemert, Exec. Dir.
Catholic Charities, 349 Cedar St., 92101. Tel: 619-231-2828; Fax: 619-234-2272. Sr. RayMonda DuVall, C.H.S., Exec. Dir.
Emergency Services—Main Office: Tel: 619-231-2828. St. Francis Center—Vista. Tel: 760-631-2819. Counseling Services. Peter McDade, Ph.D., Dir. Tel: 619-231-2828, Pregnancy, Parenting, and Adoption. Tel: 619-231-2828. Refugee & Immigrant Services—San Diego. Tel: 619-287-9454. La Posada de Guadalupe de Carlsbad. Tel: 619-929-2322. El Centro—Imperial Valley Services, 250 W. Orange, El Centro, 92243. Tel: 760-353-6822. House of Hope—Imperial Valley, Emergency Shelter. Tel: 760-352-1182. Our Lady of Guadalupe Shelter. Tel: 760-357-2894. Homeless Women's Services.
Rachel's Women's Center—San Diego. Tel: 619-696-0873. Women's Bean Project. Tel: 619-230-1151.
Joan of Arc Residence, 1510 Third Ave., 92101. Tel: 619-239-2663. Residence for Employed Young Women and College Students 18-62 Years. Sr. Margaret Mary Doucet, R.J.M., Supr. Religious 10; Permanent Residents 60; Capacity 71.
St. Vincent de Paul Management Inc.
St. Vincent de Paul Village, 3350 E St., 92102. Tel: 619-687-1000; Fax: 619-687-1010. Rev. Msgr. Joseph A. Carroll, Pres. Total Staff 292; Total Assisted Annually 151,432.
Joan Kroc Homeless Center, 1501 Imperial Ave., 92101. Tel: 619-233-8500. Mary Case, Vice Pres.
Bishop Maher Men's Center, 1501 Imperial Ave., 92101. Tel: 619-233-8500.
SHARE Southern California, 3350 E St., 92101. Tel: 619-525-2200.
Josue AIDS Centers, 3350 E St., 92102. Tel: 619-466-4827.
Paul Mirabile Center—Mirabile Housing Inc., 1501 Imperial Ave., 92101. Tel: 619-233-8500.
Toussaint Teen Center, 633 State St., 92101. Tel: 619-233-8500, Ext. 3399. Patricia Dean, Village Place, 32-17th St., 92102. Tel: 619-687-1000.
Thrift Stores, 815 33rd St., 92102. Tel: 619-687-1021. Keith McKay, Vice Pres.
SHARE Southern California, 3350 E St., 92101. Tel: 619-525-2200.
Josue AIDS Centers, 3350 E St., 92102. Tel: 619-466-4827. Paul Mirabile Center, 1501 Imperial Ave., 92101. Tel: 619-233-8500.
Toussaint Teen Center, 633 State St., 92101. Tel: 619-233-8500, Ext. 3399. Patricia Dean, Village Place, 32-17th St., 92101. Tel: 619-687-1000.
Thrift Stores, 815 33rd St., 92102. Tel: 619-687-1021. Keith MacKay, Vice Pres.

[K] RETREATS

SAN DIEGO. *Spiritual Ministry Center*, 4822 Del Mar Ave., 92107-3407. Tel: 619-224-9444.

ALPINE. *La Providencia Spiritual Renewal Center*, 641 N. Glen Oaks Dr., 91901-2736. Tel: 619-445-4570. Sr. Patricia Hanson, C.S.J.O.

OCEANSIDE. *Prince of Peace Retreat Center*, 92054. Tel: 760-430-1305; 1306. Benedictine Fathers-Benet Hill. Rev. Sharbel Ewen, O.S.B., Guest Master.

PALA. *Pala Rey Youth Camp & Retreat Center*, 10779 Pala Rd., 92059. Tel: 760-742-8767. Mr. Roy Alvarado, Contact Person.

SAN LUIS REY. *Mission San Luis Rey Retreat*.
Web site: www.sanluisrey.org
Mailing Address: P.O. Box 409, 92068. Tel: 760-757-3659; Fax: 760-757-8025. Revs. William Haney, O.F.M., Retreat Master; Mel Bucher, O.F.M., Retreat Mgr.; Ben Innes, O.F.M., Retreat Dir.

[L] CAMPS

SAN DIEGO. *Whispering Winds Catholic Conference Center*, P.O. Box 608054, 92160-8054. Tel: 619-277-9963. Don Kojis, Exec. Dir.

DESCANSO.
**Camp Oliver*. Summer Resident Camp for Girls & Boys ages 6-14. Directed by Sisters of Social Service. (June-Aug.; Available Sept.-June for rental groups). P.O. Box 712525, 2202 Comstock St., Ste. 2, San Diego, 92171. Tel: 619-492-9171. Sr. Ellen Hunter, S.S.S., Dir.

[M] NEWMAN CENTERS

SAN DIEGO. *San Diego State University Newman Center*, 5855 Hardy Ave., 92115. Tel: 619-583-9181; Fax: 619-265-9310. Revs. Cesar Rubiano, C.J.M., Dir.; Angus Beaton, C.J.M., Assoc. Dir.
University of California at San Diego (Campus Ministry), 3115 Bremerton Pl., 92037. Tel: 619-534-2521 (Office); 453-1855 (Res.). Revs. James W. Moran, C.S.P.; Peter M. Abdella, C.S.P.

[N] MISCELLANEOUS

SAN DIEGO.
**Catholic Answers, Inc.*, P.O. Box 17490, 92177. Tel: 619-541-1131; Fax: 619-541-1154. Karl Keating, Pres.
This Rock. (A magazine of Catholic apologetics and evagelization).
Catholic Committee on Scouting, 3350 E St., 92102. Tel: 619-687-1000. Rev. Msgr. Joseph A. Carroll, Scout Chap.; Jim Fallon, Coord.; Steve Rostart, Chm.
Central San Diego Magnificat, 13106 Roundup Ave., 92129. Tel: 619-484-1058. Mary Ann Silva.
Pauline Book and Media Center, 5945 Balboa Ave., 92111. Tel: 619-565-9181. Daughters of St. Paul. Sr. Sean Marie David, F.S.P., Supr. Sisters 2.
San Diego Catholic Worker, P.O. Box 127244, 92112. Tel: 619-233-0519. Mike Jennings, Pres.

EL CAJON. *Kraemer Endowment Foundation, Inc.*, 2119 E. Madison Ave., 92019-1111. Tel: 619-442-5129.

ESCONDIDO.
**Benedictus*, 1555 Glenna Dr., 92025. Tel: 760-743-8453. Deacon Kenneth J. Finn, Contact Person.

RELIGIOUS INSTITUTES OF MEN REPRESENTED IN THE DIOCESE

For further details refer to the corresponding bracketed number in the Religious Institutes of Men or Women section.

[0140]—*The Augustinians*.—O.S.A.
[0200]—*Benedictine Monks*.—O.S.B.
[0270]—*Carmelite Fathers*.—O.Carm.
[1320]—*Clerics of St. Viator*.—C.S.V.
[0160]—*Clerics Regular of St. Paul*.—C.R.S.P.
[0450]—*Congregation of Jesus and Mary*.—C.J.M.
[1130]—*Congregation of the Priests of the Sacred Heart*.—S.C.J.
[0520]—*Franciscan Friars*.—O.F.M.
[0650]—*Holy Ghost Fathers*.—C.S.Sp.
[]—*Holy Ghost Fathers of Ireland*.—C.S.Sp.
[0690]—*Jesuit Fathers and Brothers*.—S.J.
[0800]—*Maryknoll Fathers*.—M.M.
[1210]—*Missionaries of St. Charles (Scalabrinians)*.—C.S.
[0840]—*Missionary Servants of the Most Holy Trinity*.—S.T.
[0910]—*Oblates of Mary Immaculate*.—O.M.I.
[0430]—*Order of Preachers (Dominicans)*.—O.P.
[1030]—*Paulist Fathers*.—C.S.P.
[0610]—*Priests of the Congregation of Holy Cross*.—C.S.C.
[1260]—*Society of Christ*.—S.Ch.
[0370]—*Society of St. Columban*.—S.S.C.

RELIGIOUS INSTITUTES OF WOMEN REPRESENTED IN THE DIOCESE

[0100]—*Adorers of the Blood of Christ.*
[0370]—*Carmelite Sisters of Most Sacred Heart.*
[0360]—*Carmelite Sisters of the Divine Heart of Jesus.*—Carmel.D.C.J.
[2020]—*Community of the Holy Spirit.*—C.H.S.
[1920]—*Congregation of the Sisters of the Holy Cross.*—C.S.C.
[1940]—*Congregation of the Sisters of the Holy Faith.*—C.H.F.
[1710]—*Congregation of the Third Order of St. Francis of Mary Immaculate, Joliet, IL.*—O.S.F.
[0790]—*Daughters of Divine Charity.*—F.D.C.
[0880]—*Daughters of Mary and Joseph.*—D.M.J.
[0420]—*Discalced Carmelite Nuns.*—O.C.D.
[1070-03]—*Dominican Sisters.*—O.P.
[1070-11]—*Dominican Sisters.*—O.P.
[1070-13]—*Dominican Sisters.*—O.P.
[1070-20]—*Dominican Sisters.*—O.P.
[1070-21]—*Dominican Sisters.*—O.P.
[2470]—*Maryknoll Sisters of St. Dominic.*—M.M.
[2490]—*Medical Mission Sisters.*—M.M.S.
[2480]—*Medical Missionaries of Mary.*—M.M.M.
[2710]—*Missionaries of Charity.*—M.C.
[1845]—*Missionary Cathechists Guadalupanas of the Holy Spirit (Mexico).*—M.G.Sp.S.
[3070]—*North American Unions of Sisters of Our Lady of Charity.*—N.A.U.-O.L.C.
[3190]—*Nuns of the Perpetual Adoration of Blessed Sacrament.*—A.P.
[3130]—*Our Lady of Victory Missionary Sisters.*—O.L.V.M.
[0950]—*Pious Society Daughters of St. Paul.*—F.S.P.
[3242]—*Poor Sisters of Nazareth.*—P.S.N.
[3450]—*Religious of Jesus and Mary.*—R.J.M.
[3449]—*Religious of the Incarnate Word.*—C.V.I.
[3465]—*Religious of the Sacred Heart of Mary.*—R.S.H.M.
[2970]—*School Sisters of Notre Dame.*—S.S.N.D.
[1680]—*School Sisters of St. Francis.*—O.S.F.
[3499]—*Sister Servants of the Blessed Sacrament.*—S.J.S.
[0480]—*Sisters of Charity of Leavenworth, KS.*
[0520]—*Sisters of Charity of Our Lady, Mother of Mercy.*—S.C.M.M.
[0430]—*Sisters of Charity of the Blessed Virgin Mary.*—B.V.M.
[2360]—*Sisters of Loretto At the Foot of the Cross.*—S.L.
[2549]—*Sisters of Mercy of Ireland & U.S. Province.*—R.S.M.
[2575]—*Sisters of Mercy of The Americas.* (Burlingame, CA; Omaha, NE; Cincinnati, OH).—R.S.M.
[2590]—*Sisters of Mercy of the Blessed Sacrament.*—H.M.S.S.
[1540]—*Sisters of Saint Francis, Clinton, Iowa.*—O.S.F.
[4080]—*Sisters of Social Service of Los Angeles, Inc.*—S.S.S.
[3770]—*Sisters of St. Clare.*—O.S.C.
[1705]—*The Sisters of St. Francis of Assisi.*—O.S.F.
[1630]—*Sisters of St. Francis of Penance and Christian Charity.*—O.S.F.
[1650]—*Sisters of St. Francis of Philadelphia.*—O.S.F.
[3830-03]—*Sisters of St. Joseph.*—C.S.J. (Orange).
[3840]—*Sisters of St. Joseph of Carondelet.* (Los Angeles, CA; St. Louis, MO).—C.S.J.
[3890]—*Sisters of St. Joseph of Peace.* (Bellevue, WA).—C.S.J.P.
[]—*Sisters of the Heart of Jesus in the Blessed Sacrament.*
[1960]—*Sisters of the Holy Family.*—S.H.F.
[1990]—*Sisters of the Holy Names of Jesus and Mary.*—S.N.J.M.
[3260]—*Sisters of the Precious Blood (Dayton, Ohio).*—C.PP.S.
[3320]—*Sisters of the Presentation of the Blessed Virgin Mary.*—P.B.V.M.
[1720]—*Sisters of the Third Order Regular of St. Francis of The Congregation of Our Lady of Lourdes.*—O.S.F.
[1490]—*Sisters of Third Franciscan Order.*—O.S.F.
[4060]—*Society of the Holy Child Jesus.*—S.H.C.J.
[4070]—*Society of the Sacred Heart.*—R.S.C.J.

DIOCESAN CEMETERIES

SAN DIEGO. *Holy Cross, El Campo, Mission San Diego de Alcala.*
DEL MAR. *Calvary.*
JACUMBA. 3 Indian Reservation cemeteries.
PALA INDIAN MISSIONS. 6 separate Indian burial grounds.
SAN LUIS REY. *Mission San Luis Rey.*
SANTA YSABEL INDIAN MISSIONS. 15 separate Indian burial grounds.

NECROLOGY

† Beatty, John M., (Retired). —Died July 17, 1997.
† Eagen, Rev. Msgr. Isaac Brent, San Diego, CA, University of San Diego. —Died Oct. 14, 1997.
† England, Robert Ellis, (Absent on Sick Leave). —Died Jan. 31, 1997.

Archdiocese of San Francisco

(Archidioecesis Sancti Francisci)

Most Reverend

JOHN R. QUINN, D.D.

Archbishop Emeritus of San Francisco; ordained July 19, 1953; appointed Auxiliary Bishop of San Diego and Titular Bishop of Thisiduo October 21, 1967; Episcopal ordination December 12, 1967; transferred to Oklahoma City and Tulsa November 18, 1971; appointed as Archbishop of the Archdiocese of Oklahoma City on February 6, 1973; appointed Archbishop of San Francisco February 22, 1977; installed as Archbishop of San Francisco April 26, 1977; resigned December 27, 1995.

Most Reverend

WILLIAM J. LEVADA, S.T.D.

Archbishop of San Francisco; ordained December 20, 1961; appointed Titular Bishop of Capri and Auxiliary Bishop of Los Angeles March 29, 1983; Episcopal ordination May 12, 1983; appointed Archbishop of Portland in Oregon July 1, 1986; installed as Archbishop of Portland in Oregon September 21, 1986; appointed Coadjutor Archbishop of San Francisco August 17, 1995; succeeded to See December 27, 1995. *Office: 445 Church St., San Francisco, CA, 94114.*

Most Reverend

PATRICK J. MC GRATH, D.D., J.C.D.

Auxiliary Bishop of San Francisco and Titular Bishop of Allegheny; ordained June 7, 1970; appointed December 6, 1988; Episcopal ordination January 25, 1989. *Office: 445 Church St., San Francisco, CA, 94114.*

ESTABLISHED JULY 29, 1853.

Square Miles 1,012.

Legal Title: *The Roman Catholic Archbishop of San Francisco, a Corporation Sole*

Code Address: *Roman, San Francisco.*

Comprises the Counties of San Francisco, San Mateo and Marin in the State of California.

PATRONS OF THE ARCHDIOCESE OF SAN FRANCISCO: St. Francis of Assisi, October 4; St. Patrick, March 17.

For legal titles of parishes and archdiocesan institutions, consult the Chancery Office.

The Chancery Office: 445 Church St., San Francisco, CA, 94114. Tel.: 415-565-3600; Fax: 415-565-3649.

Web site address: www.sfarchdiocese.org

E-mail address: ezappia@sfarchdiocese.org

STATISTICAL OVERVIEW

Personnel	
Archbishop	1
Retired Archbishops	1
Auxiliary Bishops	1
Retired Bishops	1
Priests: Diocesan Active in Diocese	152
Priests: Active Outside Diocese	11
Priests: Diocesan in Foreign Missions	1
Priests: Retired, Sick or Absent	63
Number of Diocesan Priests	222
Religious Priests in Diocese	187
Extern Priests in Diocese	50
Ordinations:	
Diocesan Priests	2
Religious Priests	8
Transitional Deacons	4
Permanent Deacons in Diocese	53
Total Brothers	38
Total Sisters	884
Parishes	
Parishes	89
With Resident Pastor:	
Resident Diocesan Priests	75
Resident Religious Priests	14
Without Resident Pastor:	
Missions	7
Pastoral Centers	3
Professional Ministry Personnel:	
Brothers	3
Sisters	66
Lay Ministers	105
Welfare	
Catholic Hospitals	3
Total Assisted	515,000
Homes for the Aged	9
Total Assisted	7,051
Residential Care of Children	2
Total Assisted	334
Day Care and Extended Day Care Centers	2
Total Assisted	120
Specialized Homes	6
Total Assisted	215
Special Centers for Social Services	35
Total Assisted	73,000
Residential Care of Disabled	4
Total Assisted	88
Other Institutions	11
Total Assisted	875,375
Educational	
Seminaries, Diocesan	1
Students from This Diocese	11
Students from Other Diocese	42
Diocesan Students in Other Seminaries	4
Students Religious	6
Total Seminarians	21
Colleges and Universities	3
Total Students	11,062
High Schools, Diocesan and Parish	4
Total Students	3,574
High Schools, Private	9
Total Students	4,255
Elementary Schools, Diocesan and Parish	60
Total Students	19,417
Elementary Schools, Private	6
Total Students	1,701
Catechesis/Religious Education:	
High School Students	4,452
Elementary Students	12,691
Total Students Under Catholic Instruction	57,173
Teachers in the Diocese:	
Priests	35
Scholastics	4
Brothers	10
Sisters	128
Lay Teachers	1,759
Vital Statistics	
Receptions into the Church:	
Infant Baptism Totals	7,078
Adult Baptism Totals	464
Received into Full Communion	262
First Communions	4,648
Confirmations	2,588
Marriages:	
Catholic	1,283
Interfaith	446
Total Marriages	1,729
Deaths	2,861
Total Catholic Population	422,000
Total Population	1,700,000

Former Bishops—Rt. Rev. FRANCIS GARCIA DIEGO Y MORENO, O.F.M., D.D., cons. Bishop of both Californias, Oct. 4, 1840; died in Santa Barbara, April 30, 1846.—Most Rev. JOSEPH SADOC ALEMANY, O.P., D.D., cons. Bishop of Monterey, June 30, 1850; appt. first Archbishop of San Francisco, July 29, 1853; resigned and appt. Titular Archbishop of Pelusio, Dec. 28, 1884; died in Valencia, Spain, April 14, 1888.—Most Rev. PATRICK WILLIAM RIORDAN, D.D., cons. Titular Archbishop of Cabasa and appt. Coadjutor Archbishop of San Francisco *cum jure successionis* Sept. 16, 1883; succeeded to Dec. 28, 1884; died in San Francisco, Dec. 27, 1914.—Most Rev. GEORGE MONTGOMERY, D.D., cons. Titular Bishop of Tmui and appt. Coadjutor Bishop of Monterey and Los Angeles *cum jure successionis* April 8, 1894; succeeded to May 6, 1896; appt. Titular Archbishop of Osimo and Coadjutor Archbishop of San Francisco *cum jure successionis* March 27, 1903; died in San Francisco, Jan. 10, 1907.—Most Rev. EDWARD J. HANNA, D.D., cons. Titular Bishop of Titopolis and appt. Auxiliary Bishop of San Francisco Dec. 4, 1912; appt. Archbishop of San Francisco, June 1, 1915; resigned and; appt. Titular Archbishop of Gortyna, March 2, 1935; died July 10, 1944.—Most Rev. JOHN JOSEPH MITTY, D.D., cons. Bishop of Salt Lake City, June 21, 1926; appt. Coadjutor Archbishop of San Francisco *cum jure successionis,* Jan. 29, 1932; succeeded to March 2, 1935; died Oct. 15, 1961.—Most Rev. JOSEPH T. MCGUCKEN, S.T.D., appt. Auxiliary of Los Angeles, Feb. 4, 1941; cons. Titular Bishop of Sanavo March 19, 1941; appt. Coadjutor Bishop of Sacramento *cum jure successionis,* Oct. 26, 1955; succeeded to Jan. 14, 1957; appt. Archbishop of San Francisco, Feb. 21, 1962; appt. Assistant at the Pontifical

Throne, March 19, 1966; retired Feb. 22, 1977; died Oct. 26, 1983.—Most Rev. JOHN R. QUINN, D.D., appt. Auxiliary Bishop of San Diego, Oct. 21, 1967; cons. Titular Bishop of Thisiduo, Dec. 12, 1967; transferred to Oklahoma City and Tulsa, Nov. 18, 1971; appt. Archbishop of the Archdiocese of Oklahoma City, Feb. 6, 1973; appt. Archbishop of San Francisco, April 26, 1977; resigned Dec. 27, 1995.

The Chancery Office—445 Church St., San Francisco, 94114. Tel: 415-565-3600; Fax: 415-565-3649. Open Mon.-Fri. All applications for dispensations, faculties, etc., and all correspondence should be addressed: The Chancery Office.

Vicar General and Moderator of the Curia—Most Rev. PATRICK J. MCGRATH, V.G.

Vicar for Parishes—Most Rev. PATRICK J. MCGRATH, V.G.

Vicar for Administration—Rev. Msgr. ROBERT W. MCELROY, V.G.

Vicar for Clergy—Rev. Msgr. JOHN C. WESTER.

Chancellor Pro-Tempore—Rev. GREGORY INGELS, J.C.D.

Administrative Assistant to the Archbishop—Rev. THOMAS S. MERSON.

College of Consultors—Most Rev. PATRICK J. MCGRATH, V.G.; Rev. Msgr. ROBERT W. MCELROY, V.G.; Rev. Msgr. JAMES P. MCKAY; Revs. MAURICE M. MCCORMICK; WILLIAM P. QUINN; ALBERT C. VUCINOVICH.

Deans—Rev. WILLIAM P. QUINN, Deanery 1 (San Francisco); Rev. BRUCE A. DREIER, Deanery 2 (San Francisco); Rev. Msgr. JOHN J. O'CONNOR, Deanery 3 (San Francisco); Rev. Msgr. FRED A. BITANGA, Deanery 4 (San Francisco); Rev. PETER J. SAMMON, Deanery 5 (San Francisco); Rev. EUGENE D. TUNGOL, Deanery 8 (San Mateo Co.); Rev. VINCENT RING, Deanery 9 (San Mateo Co.); Rev. JAMES H. MACDONALD, Deanery 10 (San Mateo Co.); Rev. JOHN P. PENEBSKY, Deanery 11 (San Mateo Co.); Rev. RICHARD S. DEITCH, Deanery 12 (Marin Co.); Rev. ALBERT P. VUCINOVICH, Deanery 13 (Marin Co.).

Council of Priests—Rev. JOHN P. PENEBSKY, Chm.; Mrs. MARY ELLEN HOFFMAN, Admin. Asst. Tel: 415-565-3670.

Censores Librorum—Rev. Msgr. WARREN HOLLERAN, S.T.D.; Revs. GERALD D. COLEMAN, S.S., S.T.L., Ph.D.; MILTON T. WALSH, S.T.D.

Metropolitan Tribunal

San Francisco Metropolitan Tribunal—445 Church St., San Francisco, 94114. Tel: 415-565-3690; Fax: 415-565-3696.

Judicial Vicar and Director—Rev. STEVEN A. MERIWETHER, J.C.L.

Adjutant Judicial Vicars—Revs. JOSE CHAVARIN, J.C.L.; GREGORY INGELS, J.C.D.

Assoc. Director of Tribunal—Sr. NANCY REYNOLDS, S.P., J.C.L.

Promoter of Justice—Rev. Msgr. RICHARD S. KNAPP.

Defenders of the Bond—Rev. MAURICE MCCORMICK, J.C.L.; Sr. LYNN JARRELL, O.S.U., J.C.D.

Judges—Sr. NANCY REYNOLDS, S.P., J.C.L.; Rev. Msgr. IGNATIUS WANG, J.C.D.; Revs. RANDOLPH R. CALVO, J.C.D.; WILLIAM E. DUGGAN, J.C.L.

Tribunal Auditors—Sr. RAYA HANLON, O.P.; Sr. MARIANNE RASMUSSEN, O.S.F.

Notaries and Secretaries to the Tribunal—Ms. ANNETTE GOLEY; Mrs. REINA A. PARADA; Mrs. ROBYN CARRANZA.

Department of the Moderator of the Curia

Moderator of the Curia—Most Rev. PATRICK J. MCGRATH, V.G.

Archives—Dr. JEFFREY BURNS, Dir.; Rev. JOHN J. REILLY, Assoc. Dir.; Sr. CATHERINE ANN CURRY, P.B.V.M., Asst. Archivist, *320 Middlefield Rd., Menlo Park, 94025.* Tel: 650-328-6502; Fax: 650-322-0997.

Campaign for Human Development—(See the Catholic Charities listing under Institutions located in the Archdiocese for details and information.).

Catholic Relief Services—(See the Catholic Charities listing under Institutions located in the Archdiocese for details and information.).

Cemeteries, Office of—Mrs. KATHERINE ATKINSON, Gen. Mgr., *P.O. Box 1577, Colma, 94014.* Tel: 650-756-2060; Fax: 650-994-8147.

Communications, Office of—Mr. MAURICE HEALY, Dir., *441 Church St., San Francisco, 94114.* Tel: 415-565-3630; Fax: 415-565-3633.

Ecumenism and Interreligious Affairs, Office of—Rev. P. GERARD O'ROURKE, Dir. Tel: 415-565-3645; Fax: 415-565-3633.

Mission Office—(San Francisco Society for Propagation of the Faith); Rev. Msgr. IGNATIUS WANG, Dir. Tel: 415-565-3676; Fax: 415-565-3677.

Public Policy and Social Concerns, Office of—Mr. GEORGE WESOLEK, Dir. Tel: 415-565-3673; Fax: 415-565-3648.

Respect Life Office—Directors, Respect Life Commission: MARY ANNE SCHWAB; ALICE ASTURIAS; Rev. LAWRENCE C. GOODE, Chm. Tel: 415-565-3672.

Department of the Vicar for Clergy

Vicar for Clergy—Rev. Msgr. JOHN C. WESTER; TERESITA GALANG, Adm. Asst., *445 Church St., San Francisco, 94114.* Tel: 415-565-3605.

Priests Personnel Board—Rev. Msgr. JOHN C. WESTER, Chm. Tel: 415-565-3605.

Priests Personnel, Office of—Rev. Msgr. JOHN C. WESTER, Dir. Tel: 415-565-3605.

Clergy Education, Office of—Rev. JOSEPH WALSH, Dir., *St. Stephen Church, 601 Eucalyptus Dr., San Francisco, 94132.* Tel: 415-681-2444. TERESITA GALANG, Admin. Asst., *445 Church St., San Francisco, 94114.* Tel: 415-565-3605.

Permanent Diaconate, Office of—Deacon LEON KORTENKAMP, Dir. Tel: 415-565-3620.

Vocations Office—Rev. CRAIG FORNER, Dir. Tel: 415-565-3618.

Vicar for Religious—Rev. ANDREW F. MAGINNIS, S.J. Tel: 415-565-3656.

Vicar for Priests—Rev. ANTHONY E. MCGUIRE, *St. Anne Parish, 850 Judah St., San Francisco, 94122.* Tel: 415-665-1600. *415-665-1603.*

Priests Retirement Board—Rev. Msgr. JOHN C. WESTER, Chm. Tel: 415-565-3658. Rev. WILLIAM WORNER, Archbishop's Liaison to Retired Priests, *Serra Clergy House, 455 W. 20th Ave., San Mateo, 94403.* Tel: 415-358-1566.

Department of the Vicar for Administration

Vicar for Administration—Rev. Msgr. ROBERT W. MCELROY, V.G.

Director of Finance/Finance Officer—Mr. RICHARD P. HANNON.

Director of Real Estate—Mr. LES MCDONALD.

Director of Stewardship—Rev. HARRY G. SCHLITT.

Director of Development—Mr. MICHAEL DE NUNZIO.

Director of Human Resources—Mr. CARL FEIL. Tel: 415-565-3627.

In-House Legal Counsel—Mr. JACK M. HAMMEL.

Pastoral Center Facilities Manager—Mr. LES MCDONALD.

Finance Council—Rev. Msgr. ROBERT W. MCELROY, V.G., Chm.; Mr. DONALD BAIRD; Rev. Msgr. CHARLES J. DURKIN; Mrs. CECILIA HERBERT; Mr. RICHARD HANNON; Mr. JOHN HITCHCOCK, JR.; Mr. FRANK HUDSON; Deacon HENRY JACQUEMET, JR.; Mr. JAMES JENSEN; Deacon GARY WEST.

Investment Committee—Mrs. CECILIA HERBERT, Chm.; Rev. JACQUES DIDIER, M.E.P.; Mr. VICTOR BARRIOS; Mr. JOHN KELLER; Mr. PETER MAIER; Mr. I. P. SICOTTE, JR.

Building and Maintenance Committee—Rev. Msgr. EDWARD MCTAGGART, Chm.; Rev. Msgr. JAMES P. MCKAY, V.G.; Rev. RICHARD S. DEITCH; Mr. JAMES HAGEN; Mr. RICHARD HANNON; Mr. DONALD JUNKIN; Mr. BEN MURPHY; Mr. RALPH MARCHESE. Ex Officio: Mr. CHARLES BARBERINI; Mr. STEVEN BOWERS; Mr. LES MCDONALD.

Real Estate Committee—Rev. Msgr. ROBERT W. MCELROY; Mr. DONALD BAIRD; Mr. JOHN A. CATTALINI; Mr. BILL HALEY; Mr. RICK HANNON; Mr. TERRENCE E. O'BRIEN; Mr. RALPH MARCHESE; Mr. LES MCDONALD; Mr. JOHN WEINGERTHER. Tel: 415-565-3600.

Department of the Vicar for Parishes

Vicar for Parishes—Most Rev. PATRICK J. MCGRATH, V.G.

Ethnic Ministries, Office of—Ms. NOEMI CASTILLO, Dir. Tel: 415-565-3622.

Chinese Ministry—Sr. MARIA HSU, Fd.CC., Coord. Tel: 415-565-3680.

Hispanic Ministry—Mrs. CECILIA ARIAS-RIVAS, Coord. Tel: 415-565-3668.

Japanese Mission—Mr. HARRY YASUMURA, Liaison, *St. Francis Xavier Church, 1801 Octavia St., San Francisco, 94109.* Tel: 415-346-7309.

Arab-American Roman Catholic Community Mission—Rev. LABIB KOBTI, *St. Anne Church, 850 Judah St., San Francisco, 94122.* Tel: 415-564-3211; Fax: 415-665-1603.

Polish Mission and Croatian-Slovene Mission—Rev. CZESLAW RYBACKI, S.Ch., Coord., *245 Linden St., San Francisco, 94102.* Tel: 415-252-5799.

St. Michael Korean Church—Rev. STEPHANUS CHEOL SOO LEE, Pastor, *32 Broad St., San Francisco, 94112.* Tel: 415-333-1194; Fax: 415-333-1196.

Tongan Ministry—Rev. SAIMONE MOALA, Coord., *St. Timothy Church, 1515 Dolan Ave., San Mateo, 94401.* Tel: 650-342-2470; Fax: 650-342-8156.

Vietnamese Catholic Ministry—Rev. JOSEPH NGUYEN DUC TRONG, Coord., *3240 Lawton St., San Francisco, 94122.* Tel: 415-759-4293; Fax: 415-664-9775.

Evangelization/Renew, Office of—Sr. ANTONIO HEAPHY, P.B.V.M., Dir. Tel: 415-565-3600.

Family Life, Office of—CARMEN DE LA VEGA NEAFSEY, Dir. Tel: 415-565-3650.

Parish Life, Office of—Rev. DAVID M. PETTINGILL, Dir. Tel: 415-565-3600.

Religious Education, Office of—Sr. CELESTE ARBUCKLE, S.S.S., Dir. Tel: 415-565-3652.

School of Pastoral Leadership—Dr. KEN WEARE, Ph.D., Dir., *475 Eucalyptus Dr., San Francisco, 94132.* Tel: 415-242-9087; Fax: 415-242-9089.

Worship, Office of—Rev. JOHN TALESFORE, Dir. Tel: 415-565-3600.

Young Adults, Office of—Vacant.

Youth Ministry—(Coordinated by Catholic Youth Organization); Rev. DAVID A. GHIORSO, Exec. Dir. (See separate category under Institutions located in the Archdiocese for details and information.), *Youth Ministry Services, One St. Vincent's Dr., San Rafael, 94903.* Tel: 415-507-2000; Fax: 415-491-0842. Parish-based youth leadership training Program and Services.

Department of Catholic Schools

Superintendent—Sr. GLENN ANNE MCPHEE, O.P.; Mr. PAUL BERGEZ, Assoc. Supt. Planning & Devel.; Sr. MARIANNE VIANI, S.N.J.M., Assoc. Supt. Curriculum; LOIS BAUER, Asst. Supt. Administrative Svcs.; Sr. MARCELLA HOLIAN, C.S.J., Asst. Supt. Personnel & Staff Devel. MARILYN LYNCH, Asst. Supt. for Staff Devel./Improvement, *443 Church St., San Francisco, 94114-1792.* Tel: 415-565-3660.

Archdiocesan Board of Education—Most Rev. WILLIAM J. LEVADA; Sr. KATHRYN CAMACHO, S.N.D., Chm. SUSAN BURNS; GERALD BURRONI; Revs. BERNARD DABBENE, S.D.B.; BRUCE DREIER; CATHY GEE; Rev. PIERS LAHEY; LUPITA MONROY; GERALYN O'MAHONEY; MOLLY O'SHEA; JOHN PICETTI.

Roman Catholic Welfare Corporation of San Francisco—Most Rev. WILLIAM J. LEVADA, Pres.; Most Rev. PATRICK J. MCGRATH, Vice Pres.; Rev. Msgr. ROBERT W. MCELROY, Vice Pres.-Sec.; Rev. JOSE A. RODRIGUEZ; Rev. Msgr. JOHN C. WESTER; Revs. JAMES H. MACDONALD; RANDOLPH R. CALVO, J.C.D.; Mr. PAUL BERGEZ; Rev. Msgr. FRED A. BITANGA; Sr. GLENN ANNE MCPHEE, O.P., Asst. Sec.; Mr. RICHARD HANNON, Treas.; Rev. GREGORY INGELS, Asst. Treas. Tel: 415-565-3660.

CLERGY, PARISHES, MISSIONS AND PAROCHIAL SCHOOLS

CITY OF SAN FRANCISCO

(San Francisco County)

1—CATHEDRAL OF ST. MARY (ASSUMPTION) (1891), Rev. Msgr. John J. O'Connor; Revs. Lee Kaylor; Michael Martin; Deacon Joseph Borg. In res., Rev. Jose Chavarin.

Cathedral Office: 1111 Gough St., 94109. Tel: 415-567-2020; Fax: 415-567-2040.

2—ST. AGNES (1893), Revs. Russell J. Roide, S.J.; Joseph Specht, S.J.; Sr. Michaela O'Connor, S.H.F., D.R.E.

Res., 1025 Masonic Ave., 94117. Tel: 415-487-8560; Fax: 415-487-8575.

3—ALL HALLOWS (1886). Closed. For sacramental records please contact Our Lady of Lourdes, San Francisco.

4—ST. ANNE (1904), Revs. Anthony McGuire; Dominic Savio Lee; Deacon John Dupre. In res., Revs. Labib Kobti (Latin Patriarchy of Jerusalem); Thomas S. Merson.

Res., 850 Judah St., 94122. Tel: 415-665-1600; Fax: 415-665-1603.

School—1320 14th Ave., 94122. Tel: 415-664-7977. Sisters 1; Lay Teachers 28; Students 600.

Catechesis/Religious Programs—Students 80.

5—ST. ANTHONY (1893), Revs. Michael Weldon, O.F.M.; Francisco Reyes, O.F.M.; Robert Pfisterer, O.F.M.; Salvador Parisi, O.F.M.; Guglielmo Lauriola, O.F.M. In res., Revs. Floyd A. Lotito, O.F.M., Guardian; Anthony Baumann, O.F.M.; Finian McGinn, O.F.M.; Bro. David Cobian, O.F.M.

Res., 3215 Cesar Chavez St., 94110. Tel: 415-647-2704; Fax: 415-647-7282.

Chapel—Immaculate Conception Chapel. Under the care and administration of the pastor of St. Anthony of Padua parish. 3255 Folsom St., 94110. Tel: 415-824-1762; Fax: 415-824-0129.

High School—St. Anthony, 299 Precita Ave., 94110. Tel: 415-648-2008. Sr. John Ellen Turner, O.P., Prin.

Sisters 5; Lay Teachers 13; Students 290.

School—Immaculate Conception Elementary School, 1550 Treat Ave., 94110. Tel: 415-824-6860; Fax: 415-824-0129.
Sisters of the Third Order of St. Dominic, Congregation of the Queen of the Holy Rosary 4; Lay Teachers 11; Students 251.

6—ST. BENEDICT PARISH AT ST. FRANCIS XAVIER CHURCH (1913) (Japanese). (Founded 1962 for Deaf and Hearing Impaired). Rev. Daniel Adams.
Res., 1801 Octavia, 94109. Tel: 415-567-9855; 567-0438 (TDD); Fax: 415-567-0916.
Masses for the Hearing Impaired:—.
St. Anthony: 3500 Middlefield Rd., Menlo Park, 94025. Tel: 650-366-4692; 675 Sir Francis Drake Blvd., Kentfield, 94904. Tel: 415-461-8844.

7—ST. BONIFACE (1860) (German), Revs. Louis Vitale, O.F.M.; Terence Cronin, O.F.M.; John Luat Nguyen, O.F.M. Pastoral Assocs.: Rev. Sergio Santos; Bros. Didacus Clavel, O.F.M.; Simon Scanlon. In res., Revs. Joaquin Moreno, O.F.M.; Stephen Tan Nguyen, O.F.M.; Stephan Kain, O.F.M.; Bros. Regan Chapman, O.F.M.; Robert Brady, O.F.M.; Angelo Cardanalli, O.F.M.; Kelly Cullen, O.F.M.; Dennis Duffy, O.F.M.; Kurt Rawhauser, O.F.M.; Jorge Hernandez, O.F.M.
Res., 133 Golden Gate Ave., 94102. Tel: 415-863-0111; Fax: 415-863-7602.
Catechesis/Religious Programs—Students 180.

8—ST. BRENDAN (1929), Rev. Msgr. Edward P. McTaggart; Rev. William P. Crowley, C.S.Sp. In res., Most Rev. Patrick J. McGrath; Rev. Joseph Thannickal, S.D.B.
Res., 29 Rockaway Ave., 94127. Tel: 415-681-4225; Fax: 415-681-3976.
School—234 Ulloa St., 94127. Tel: 415-731-2665; Fax: 415-731-7207.
Sisters of St. Dominic, Adrian, MI 2; Lay Teachers 20; Students 353.

9—ST. BRIGID (1863). Closed. For sacramental records please contact St. Vincent de Paul, San Francisco.

10—ST. CECILIA (1917), Revs. Michael D. Harriman; Lodovico Joseph Landi; Thuan Van Hoang. In res., Rev. Msgr. John T. Foudy; Rev. Heribert Duquet, M.E.P.
Res., 2555 17th Ave., 94116. Tel: 415-664-8481; Fax: 415-661-2957.
School—660 Vicente St., 94116. Tel: 415-731-8400.
Sisters of the Holy Names 5; Lay Teachers 16; Students 581.
Catechesis/Religious Programs—Students 51.

11—ST. CHARLES BORROMEO (1887), Revs. Jose A. Rodriguez; Victorio Balagapo.
Res., 713 S. Van Ness Ave., 94110. Tel: 415-824-1700; Fax: 415-824-0844.
School—3250 18th St., 94110. Tel: 415-861-7652.
Dominican Sisters of the Most Holy Rosary (Philippines) 5; Lay Teachers 6; Students 298.
Catechesis/Religious Programs—Students 269.

12—CORPUS CHRISTI (1898), Revs. Bernard J. Dabbene, S.D.B.; Armand Oliveri, S.D.B.; Hugo Santucci, S.D.B.; Aloysius Pestun, S.D.B.
Res., 62 Santa Rosa Ave., 94112. Tel: 415-585-2291; Fax: 415-585-0773.
School—75 Francis St., 94112. Tel: 415-587-7014; Fax: 415-587-1575.
Salesian Sisters of St. John Bosco (Daughters of Mary Help of Christians) 5; Lay Teachers 8; Students 314.
Catechesis/Religious Programs—Tel: 415-585-3240.
Students 150.

13—ST. DOMINIC (1873), Revs. Roberto Corral, O.P.; Timothy Conlan, O.P.; Xavier M. Lavagetto, O.P.; Bro. Mark Gorski, O.P.; Deacon Fred Swanson. In res., Revs. Reginald Martin, O.P., Prior; Gregory H. Anderson, O.P.; Felix F. Cassidy, O.P.; John J. Klaia, O.P.; Thomas J. Hayes, O.P.; Brian T. Mullady, O.P.; Paul Raftery, O.P.; Terrence J. Reilly, O.P.; Bros. Gregory Lira, O.P.; Peter Yost, O.P.; Robert F. Christian, O.P.; Samuel R. Parsons, O.P.; Gerald A. Buckley, O.P.; James S. Jenner, O.P.
Res., 2390 Bush St., 94115. Tel: 415-567-7824; Fax: 415-567-1608.
School—2445 Pine St., 94115. Tel: 415-346-9500; Fax: 415-346-8001.
Sisters of the Third Order of St. Dominic, Congregation of the Most Holy Name 4; Sisters of the Holy Names of Jesus and Mary 1; Lay Teachers 7; Students 274.

14—ST. EDWARD (1916). Closed. For sacramental records please contact Star of the Sea, San Francisco.

15—ST. ELIZABETH (1912), Revs. Edwin W. Farrugia; Benjamin Nombrado; Edward Phelan.
Res., 449 Holyoke Ave., 94134. Tel: 415-468-0820; Fax: 415-468-1457.
School—450 Somerset St., 94134. Tel: 415-468-3247; Fax: 415-468-1804.
Lay Teachers 11; Students 288.
Catechesis/Religious Programs—Tel: 415-468-0423.
Students 150.

16—ST. EMYDIUS (1913), Rev. William J. Brady. Pastoral Assocs.: Deacon John W. Hutzler; Barbara Loughrey. In res., Rev. David M. Pettingill.
Res., 286 Ashton Ave., 94112. Tel: 415-587-7066; Fax: 415-587-6690.
School—301 DeMontfort Ave., 94112. Tel: 415-333-4877. Miss Nell Jeffrey, Prin.
Lay Teachers 11; Students 195.
Catechesis/Religious Programs—Students 55.

17—CHURCH OF THE EPIPHANY (1914), Revs. Bruce A. Dreier; Mark V. Taheny; Rolando Caverte; Manuel Estrada; Deacons Manuel Ocon; Ding Viray.
Res., 827 Vienna St., 94112. Tel: 415-333-7630; Fax: 415-333-1803.
School—600 Italy Ave., 94112. Tel: 415-337-4030; Fax: 415-337-8583.
Sisters 2; Lay Teachers 23; Students 570.
Catechesis/Religious Programs—Tel: 415-333-5051.
Students 335.

18—ST. FINN BARR (1926), Revs. Lawrence C. Goode; Cyril O'Sullivan.
Res., 415 Edna St., 94112. Tel: 415-333-3627; Fax: 415-333-4090.
School—419 Hearst Ave., 94112. Tel: 415-333-1800; Fax: 415-452-0177.
Dominican Sisters of the Holy Rosary (Philippines) 4; Lay Teachers 7; Students 343.

19—ST. FRANCIS OF ASSISI MISSION. Closed. For sacramental records please contact SS. Peter and Paul, San Francisco.

20—ST. GABRIEL (1941), Revs. Harry G. Schlitt; Thomas Moran. In res., Rev. P. Gerard O'Rourke.
Res., 2535 40th Ave., 94116. Tel: 415-731-6161; Fax: 415-731-1270.
School—2550 41st Ave., 94116. Tel: 415-566-0314.
Lay Teachers 23; Students 510.
Catechesis/Religious Programs—Students 137.

21—HOLY CROSS (1887) (Korean). Closed. For sacramental records please contact St. Michael, San Francisco.

22—HOLY FAMILY CHINESE MISSION (1921). (aka St. Mary's Chinese Catholic Center—1903). Rev. Daniel E. McCotter, C.S.P.; Sr. Prisca Hui, S.N.J.M., Pastoral Assoc.; Ms. Lisa Tom French, Admin.
Res., 660 California St., 94108. Tel: 415-421-5636; Fax: 415-929-4698.
School—St. Mary Chinese School, 910 Broadway, 94133. Tel: 415-929-4690; Fax: 415-929-4699. Jerry DiNoto, Prin.
Sisters 5; Lay Teachers 15; Students 340.
Chinese Language School—Tel: 415-929-4694. Stephen Woon Wah Tang, Prin.
Students 650; Chinese Teachers 15; Elementary Students 600; High School Students 50.
Holy Family Association—Fax: 415-929-4698. Katy Sid, Pres.

23—HOLY NAME OF JESUS (1925), Revs. William P. Quinn; Raym J. Zohlen; Edward Ludeman. In res., Rev. Msgr. Ignatius Wang; Rev. Trong Duc Nguyen; Deacon Dennis Rivera.
Res., 3240 Lawton St., 94122. Tel: 415-664-8590; Fax: 415-664-9775.
School—1560 40th Ave., 94122. Tel: 415-731-4077; Fax: 415-731-3328.
Sisters 2; Lay Teachers 24; Students 610.
Catechesis/Religious Programs—Students 100.

24—ST. IGNATIUS (1855), Revs. Charles R. Gagan, S.J.; Albert A. Grosskopf, S.J.; Thomas G. Piquado, S.J.
Res., 650 Parker Ave., 94118. Tel: 415-422-2188; Fax: 415-387-1867.

25—IMMACULATE CONCEPTION (1912) (Italian). Closed. For sacramental records please contact St. Anthony of Padua, San Francisco.

26—ST. JAMES (1888), Rev. Daniel E. Carter.
Res., 1086 Guerrero St., 94110. Tel: 415-824-4232; Fax: 415-824-0605.
School—321 Fair Oaks St., 94110. Tel: 415-647-8972; Fax: 415-647-0166.
Sisters of the Third Order of St. Dominic, Congregation of Queen of the Holy Rosary 2; Lay Teachers 9; Students 225.
Catechesis/Religious Programs—Students 70.

27—ST. JOHN THE EVANGELIST (1893), Rev. James E. Myers, S.S.; Sr. Louise O'Reilly, S.N.D., Pastoral Assoc. In res., Rev. Anthony Lobo, S.S.
Res., 19 St. Mary's Ave., 94112-1098. Tel: 415-334-4646; Fax: 415-334-0891.
Parish Center: 98 Bosworth St., 94112. Tel: 415-334-4646; Fax: 415-334-0891.
School—925 Chenery St., 94131. Tel: 415-584-8383; Fax: 415-584-8359.
Lay Teachers 8; Students 286.
Catechesis/Religious Programs—Students 78.

28—ST. JOHN OF GOD (1967), Revs. Alex L. Legaspi; James Stump, O.F.M.Cap., Hospital Chap., (UCSF).
Res., 1290 Fifth Ave., 94122. Tel: 415-566-5610; Fax: 415-566-5073.
Catechesis/Religious Programs—Tel: 415-664-9850. Phil Warren, D.R.E.
Students 76.

29—ST. JOSEPH (1861). Closed. For sacramental records please contact St. Patrick, San Francisco.

30—ST. KEVIN (1922), Rev. Clifford A. Martin; Deacon Dan Rosen; Suzanne Hockel, Pastoral Assoc.
Res., 704 Cortland Ave., 94110. Tel: 415-648-5751; Fax: 415-648-4441.
Catechesis/Religious Programs—Tel: 415-282-0277.
Students 105.

31—OLD ST. MARY'S CATHEDRAL (1854), Revs. John J. Foley, C.S.P.; Thomas J. Dove, C.S.P.; Peter G. Shea, C.S.P. In res., Revs. Philip Cunningham, C.S.P., (Retired); Charles A. Donovan, C.S.P., (Retired); Daniel E. McCotter, C.S.P.; John A. Carr, C.S.P., (Retired); Joseph M. Hanly, C.S.P., (Retired); Edward A. Maher, C.S.P., (Retired).
Res., 660 California St., 94108. Tel: 415-288-3800; Fax: 415-288-3838.

32—ST. MICHAEL KOREAN CHURCH (1898) (Korean), Rev. Stephanus Cheol Soo Lee.
Res., 32 Broad St., 94112. Tel: 415-333-1194; Fax: 415-333-1196.

33—MISSION DOLORES BASILICA (1776). (San Francisco de Asis). Revs. Maurice M. McCormick; Santos Rodriguez; Deacon Vicente Cervantes.
Res., 3321 16th St., 94114. Tel: 415-621-8203; Fax: 415-621-2294. [CEM]
School—3371 16th St., 94114. Tel: 415-861-7673; Fax: 415-861-7620. Andreina Gualco, Prin.
Sisters 3; Lay Teachers 8; Students 270.
Catechesis/Religious Programs—Students 81.

34—ST. MONICA (1911), Revs. Warren L. Woods; Simeon Chang; Jonathan Paala. In res., Revs. John Kavanaugh; Didacus Ma.
Res., 470 24th Ave., 94121. Tel: 415-751-5275; Fax: 415-751-0440.
School—5920 Geary Blvd., 94121. Tel: 415-751-9564; Fax: 415-751-0781.
Sisters of the Holy Names of Jesus and Mary 3; Lay Teachers 7; Students 354.
Catechesis/Religious Programs—Students 72.

35—MOST HOLY REDEEMER (1900), Revs. Zachary J. Shore; Thomas J. Hayes, O.M.I. In res., Rev. William W. Young.
Res., 100 Diamond St., 94114-2414. Tel: 415-863-6259; Fax: 415-552-8786.

36—NATIVITY (1902) (Polish and Croatian-Slovene), Rev. Czeslaw Rybacki, S.Ch.
Res., 245 Linden St., 94102. Tel: 415-252-5799.

37—NOTRE DAME DES VICTOIRES (1856) (French), Revs. Etienne Siffert, S.M.; Phillip d'Auby, S.M.
Res., 566 Bush St., 94108. Tel: 415-397-0113; Fax: 415-397-3217.
School—659 Pine St., 94108. Tel: 415-421-0069. Mary K. Ghisolfo, Prin.
Sisters of St. Joseph of Orange 2; Lay Teachers 16; Students 300.

38—OUR LADY OF FATIMA BYZANTINE CATHOLIC CHURCH (1954). Catholic Russian Center (Byzantine). Rev. Steven A. Armstrong, S.J.; Deacon Gerald F. Sondergaard.
Res., 101 20th Ave., 94121-1398. Tel: 415-752-2052; Fax: 415-752-6073.

39—OUR LADY OF GUADALUPE. Closed. For sacramental records please contact SS. Peter and Paul, San Francisco.

40—OUR LADY OF LOURDES (1942), Rev. Kirk Ullery.
Res., 1715 Oakdale Ave., 94124. Tel: 415-285-3377; Fax: 415-285-2191.

41—ST. PATRICK (1851), Rev. Msgr. Fred A. Bitanga; Revs. Herny J. Trainor; Antonio Lambino, S.J.; Raymund Reyes; Deacons Tom Buenavista; Virgil Capati.
Res., 756 Mission St., 94103. Tel: 415-421-3730; Fax: 415-512-9730.
Catechesis/Religious Programs—Students 125.

42—ST. PAUL (1880), Revs. Mario P. Farana; Mamerto Sigaran; Mary Tan, Pastoral Assoc. In res., Rev. Msgr. Daniel P. Cahill.
Res., 221 Valley St., 94131. Tel: 415-648-7538; Fax: 415-648-4740.
School—180 Fair Oaks St., 94110. Tel: 415-648-2055; Fax: 415-648-1920. Sr. Ann Cronin, B.V.M., Prin.; Patricia Esling, Vice Prin.
Sisters 1; Lay Teachers 9; Students 265.
Catechesis/Religious Programs—1660 Church St., 94131. Tel: 415-826-4484.
Students 115.
Convent—316 29th St., 94131. Tel: 415-647-1889. Novitiate of the Missionaries of Charity

43—St. Paul of the Shipwreck (1915), Rev. John Heinz, O.F.M. Conv. In res., Revs. Stephen Gross, O.F.M.Conv.; Kevin Schindler-McGraw, O.F.M.Conv.
Res., 3350 Jennings St., 94124. Tel: 415-468-3434; Fax: 415-468-1400.
School—St. Paul of the Shipwreck Academy, 1060 Key Ave. at Third St., 94124. Tel: 415-467-1798; Fax: 415-467-0569.
Lay Teachers 8; Students 168.

44—St. Peter (1867), Revs. Daniel J. Maguire; Gustavo Perez; Francis MacPeck, S.J.; Deacons Roger Hernandez; David Gamarra. In res., Revs. Edmund M. Shipp; Zosimo C. Alvar, Jr.
Res., 1200 Florida St., 94110. Tel: 415-282-1652; Fax: 415-282-6097.
School—1266 Florida St., 94110. Tel: 415-647-8662; Fax: 415-647-4618. Vicki Butler, Prin.
Sisters 3; Lay Teachers 11; Students 520.

45—SS. Peter and Paul (1884) (Italian), Revs. David T. Purdy, S.D.B.; Austin Conterno, S.D.B.; Salvatore Giacomini, S.D.B.; John Lam, S.D.B.; John O'Brien, S.D.B.; Jerry Bonjean, S.D.B.; Steve Whelan, S.D.B. In res., Revs. Anthony F. Di Falco, S.D.B.; Gabriel J. Zavattaro, S.D.B.
Res., 666 Filbert St., 94133. Tel: 415-421-0809; Fax: 415-421-0217.
School—632 Filbert St., 94133. Tel: 415-421-5219; Fax: 415-421-1831. Sr. Sandra Neaves, F.M.A., Prin.
Salesian Sisters 4; Lay Teachers 9; Students 300.

46—St. Philip the Apostle (1910), Rev. Michael J. Healy. In res., Rev. Brendan McBride.
Res., 725 Diamond St., 94114. Tel: 415-282-0141; Fax: 415-282-8962.
School—4174 24th St., 94114. Tel: 415-824-8467. Peg Rybicki, Prin.
Lay Teachers 10; Students 250.

47—Sacred Heart (1885), Rev. Kenneth M. Westray. In res., Rev. Daniel Adams.
Res., 546 Fillmore St., 94117. Tel: 415-861-5460; Fax: 415-861-7839.
School—735 Fell St., 94117. Tel: 415-621-8035; Fax: 415-861-7039. Eileen Murphy, Prin.
Lay Teachers 7; Students 114.
Catechesis/Religious Programs—Students 114.

48—Star of the Sea (1894), Rev. Msgr. Charles J. Durkin; Revs. Benedict Chang; Greg Aherne, S.J. In res., Rev. Calixto Armas.
Res., 4420 Geary Blvd., 94118. Tel: 415-751-0450; Fax: 415-368-5651.
School—360 Ninth Ave., 94118. Tel: 415-221-8558; Fax: 415-221-7118. Sr. Rosemarie Carroll, C.S.J., Prin.
Sisters 4; Lay Teachers 6; Students 320.
Convent—4350 Geary Blvd., 94118. Tel: 415-752-6050. Sisters of St. Joseph of Carondelet
Catechesis/Religious Programs—Tel: 415-221-3758.
Students 61.

49—St. Stephen (1950), Revs. Joseph R. Walsh; Sean Corcoran, C.S.S.P.; John L. Greene; Deacon Gary West. In res., Rev. Joseph P. O'Reilly.
Res., 451 Eucalyptus Dr., 94132. Tel: 415-681-2444; Fax: 415-681-7843.
School—401 Eucalyptus Dr., 94132. Tel: 415-664-8331. Sr. Paulinea Simms, R.S.M., Prin.
Sisters of Mercy 2; Lay Teachers 10; Students 310.
Catechesis/Religious Programs—Sr. Toni Lynn Gallagher, R.S.M., D.R.E.
Students 46.

50—St. Teresa (1880), Rev. Peter J. Sammon. Pastoral Assocs.: Sr. Kathleen Healy, P.B.V.M.; Sr. Lucia Lodolo, P.B.V.M.; Deacon Charles Allen.
Res., 390 Missouri St., 94107. Tel: 415-285-5272; Fax: 415-285-8510.
Church—19th & Connecticut Sts., 94107.
Catechesis/Religious Programs—Students 51.

51—St. Thomas, The Apostle (1922), Revs. Kirby C. Hanson; Charles J. Sullivan; Stanley Wu. In res., Rev. Francis Filice.
Res., 3835 Balboa St., 94121. Tel: 415-387-5545; Fax: 415-221-0868.
School—3801 Balboa St., 94121. Tel: 415-221-2711; Fax: 415-221-8611.
Lay Teachers 10; Students 291.

52—St. Thomas More (1950), Rev. Jerome P. Foley, Chap. In res., Revs. Steven E. Davies; John Talesfore.
Res., 1300 Junipero Serra Blvd., 94132. Tel: 415-452-9634; Fax: 415-452-9653.

53—St. Vincent de Paul (1901), Revs. John K. Ring; Joseph Bradley; Lewis B. O'Neil, S.J.; Sr. M. Sheila Donegan, P.B.V.M., Pastoral Assoc., Dir. of Religious Formation.
Res., 2320 Green St., 94123. Tel: 415-922-1010; Fax: 415-922-7203.
School—2350 Green St., 94123. Tel: 415-346-0970. Claude Gibney, Prin.
Lay Teachers 10; Students 261.

54—Visitacion, Church of the (1907), Revs. Thomas L. Seagrave; Gabriel R. Flores, M.C.C.J.
Res., 655 Sunnydale Ave., 94134. Tel: 415-239-5950; Fax: 415-239-0538.
School—Our Lady of the Visitacion, 785 Sunnydale Ave., 94134. Tel: 415-239-7840. Sr. Lois Lapeyre, D.C., Prin.
Daughters of Charity of St. Vincent de Paul 4; Lay Teachers 7; Students 278.
Mission—Brisbane, Our Lady of Guadalupe, 285 Alvarado St., Brisbane, 94005.
Catechesis/Religious Programs—Tel: 415-239-6723.
Students 169.

OUTSIDE THE CITY OF SAN FRANCISCO

Belmont, San Mateo Co., Immaculate Heart of Mary (1947), Revs. James H. MacDonald; Jose Superiaso; Deacons Steven Hackett; Henry Jacquemet. In res., Rev. Msgr. John J. Kenny.
Res., 1040 Alameda de las Pulgas, 94002. Tel: 650-593-6157; Fax: 650-593-1665.
School—1000 Alameda de las Pulgas, 94002. Tel: 650-593-4265. Dr. Margaret Purcell, Prin.
Lay Teachers 12; Students 305.
Catechesis/Religious Programs—Mrs. Genny Pereira, D.R.E.
Students 356.

St. Mark (1965), Rev. Floro B. Arcamo. In res., Revs. Miles O'Brien Riley; William J. Flanagan.
Res., 325 Marine View Ave., 94002. Tel: 650-591-5937; Fax: 650-591-7645.
Catechesis/Religious Programs—Tel: 650-591-7072.
Students 139.

Burlingame, San Mateo Co., St. Catherine of Siena (1908), Rev. James W. Aylward.
Res., 1310 Bayswater Ave., 94010. Tel: 650-344-6884; Fax: 650-344-1022.
School—1300 Bayswater Ave., 94010. Tel: 650-344-7176; Fax: 650-344-7426. Sr. Antonella Manca, M.S.C., Prin.
Sisters of the Sacred Side of Jesus 5; Lay Teachers 15; Students 324.
Catechesis/Religious Programs—Students 190.

Our Lady of Angels (1926), Revs. Michael Mahoney, O.F.M.Cap.; Evangelist Kelly, O.F.M.Cap.; Michael Ronayne, O.F.M.Cap. In res., Revs. Emilian Meade, O.F.M.Cap.; Donal O'Mahony, O.F.M.Cap.; Eugene Ludwig, O.F.M.Cap.
Res., 1721 Hillside Dr., 94010. Tel: 650-347-7768; Fax: 650-347-3550.
School—1328 Cabrillo Ave., 94010. Tel: 650-343-9200; Fax: 650-343-5260. Joan Marino, Prin.
Lay Teachers 18; Students 314.
Catechesis/Religious Programs—Tel: 650-347-3671. Mrs. Kathryn Jones, D.R.E.
Students 311.

Colma, San Mateo Co., Holy Angels (1914), Revs. John J. Cloherty; Arturo Albano; Deacons John Ruiz; Lernito Prudenciado.
Res., 107 San Pedro Rd., 94014. Tel: 650-755-0478; Fax: 650-755-7653.
School—20 Reiner St., 94014. Tel: 650-755-0220.
Sisters 2; Lay Teachers 8; Students 262.
Catechesis/Religious Programs—Tel: 650-992-5539.
Students 430.

Daly City, San Mateo Co., St. Andrew (1968) (Filipino), Revs. Frank R. Piro; Roberto Andrey; Sr. Nancy McLaughlin, P.B.V.M., Pastoral Assoc.; Deacon Felix Amora.
Church—1571 Southgate Ave., 94015. Tel: 650-756-3223; Fax: 650-756-0251.
Rectory: One Ridgefield Ave., 94015. Tel: 650-756-3223; Fax: 650-756-0251.
Catechesis/Religious Programs—Tel: 650-991-2937. Michele Bussey, D.R.E.
Students 315.

Our Lady of Mercy (Westlake) (1954), Revs. Manuel Curso; John F. Glogowski.
Res., One Elmwood Dr., 94015. Tel: 650-755-2727.
School—15 Elmwood Dr., 94015. Tel: 650-756-3395. Arlene Fife, Prin.
Sisters 5; Lay Teachers 21; Students 611.
Catechesis/Religious Programs—Tel: 650-755-7353.
Students 206.

Our Lady of Perpetual Help (Westlake) (1925), Rev. Msgr. John R. Pernia; Rev. Antonio Petilla.
Res., 60 Wellington Ave., 94014. Tel: 650-755-9786.
School—80 Wellington Ave., 94014. Tel: 650-755-4438. James Costello, Prin.
Religious 1; Lay Teachers 8; Students 320.
Catechesis/Religious Programs—Tel: 650-755-4010. Sr. Hermina F. Coquia, F.M.M., D.R.E.
Students 320.

East Palo Alto, San Mateo Co., St. Francis of Assisi (1951), Rev. Joseph A. Gordon; Deacon Louis Dixon.
Res., 1425 Bay Rd., 94303. Tel: 650-322-2152; Fax: 650-322-7319.
Catechesis/Religious Programs—Tel: 650-325-6236.
Students 300.

Fairfax, Marin Co., St. Rita (1930), Rev. Albert Vucinovich; Deacon Peter Kehrlein. In res., Rev. Paul A. Perlite.
Res., 100 Marinda Dr., 94930. Tel: 415-456-4815; Fax: 415-456-3677.
School—102 Marinda Dr., 94930. Tel: 415-456-1003; Fax: 415-456-7946. Maureen Cassidy, Prin.
Lay Teachers 11; Students 233.
Catechesis/Religious Programs—Tel: 415-456-1867.
Students 96.

Foster City, San Mateo Co., St. Luke (1970), Revs. Edward K. Murray, Ed.D.; Irenio Ramoso; Deacon Mar Tano.
Res., 1111 Beach Park Blvd., 94404. Tel: 650-345-6660; Fax: 650-345-8167.
Catechesis/Religious Programs—Tel: 650-574-9191; 573-7409.
Students 268.

Greenbrae, Marin Co., St. Sebastian (1951), Revs. Thomas M. Parenti; W. Paul O'Dell.
Res., 373 Bon Air Rd., 94904. Tel: 415-461-0704; Fax: 415-461-2018.
Catechesis/Religious Programs—Students 59.

Half Moon Bay, San Mateo Co., Our Lady of the Pillar (1868), Revs. Domingo Orimaco; Agnel Jose de Heredia; Fabio Medina; Deacon John McGhee.
Res., 400 Church St., 94019. Tel: 650-726-4674; Fax: 650-726-0980. [CEM]
Catechesis/Religious Programs—Tel: 650-726-5587. Sr. Teresa Walsh, C.S.J., D.R.E.
Students 475.
Missions—Pescadero, San Mateo Co., St. Anthony, P.O. Box 277, Pescadero, 94060. Tel: 650-879-0750; La Honda, San Mateo Co., Our Lady of Refuge, La Honda, 94060. Tel: 650-879-0750.

Lagunitas, Marin Co., St. Cecilia (1937), Rev. Thomas A. Daly.
Rectory: Box 289, 94938. Tel: 415-488-9799; Fax: 415-488-1963.
High School—Marin Catholic, 675 Sir Francis Drake Blvd., Kentfield, 94904. Tel: 415-461-8844; Fax: 415-461-7161.
Mission—Nicasio, St. Mary.

Larkspur, Marin Co., St. Patrick (1915), Rev. John D. Shanahan. In res., Rev. Joseph Eagan, S.J.
Res., 114 King St., 94939. Tel: 415-924-0600; Fax: 415-924-3617.
School—120 King St., 94939. Tel: 415-924-0501; Fax: 415-924-3554. Ann Kalajian, Prin.
Lay Teachers 9; Students 270.
Catechesis/Religious Programs—Students 150.

Menlo Park, San Mateo Co.,

1—St. Anthony, (1951), Revs. James L. Garcia; Eduardo Mendoza; Deacon Jose Solano.
Res., 3500 Middlefield Rd., 94025. Tel: 650-366-4692; Fax: 650-366-4135.
Catechesis/Religious Programs—Tel: 650-365-6071. Gladys Fields, D.R.E.
Students 800.
Mission—Redwood City, San Mateo Co., St. Joseph the Workman, 400 Heller St., Redwood City, 94063.

2—St. Denis, (1853; Restored 1961), Rev. Msgr. John F. Rodriguez.
Res., 2250 Avy Ave., 94025. Tel: 650-854-5976; Fax: 650-854-3754.
Chapel—Our Lady of the Wayside, 930 Portola Rd., Portola Valley, 94028. Tel: 650-851-5085; Fax: 650-851-1019. Rev. George L. Thomas.
Catechesis/Religious Programs—Tel: 650-854-3754.
Students 333.

3—The Church of the Nativity, (1877), Revs. Clement A. Davenport; William J. Queenan, S.S (TR); Donald S. D'Angelo. In res., Rev. John J. Reilly, Assoc. Dir., Archives, Tel: 650-328-6502.
Res., 210 Oak Grove Ave., 94025. Tel: 650-323-7914; Fax: 650-323-3231.
School—1250 Laurel St., 94025. Tel: 650-325-7304; Fax: 650-325-3841.
Sisters 3; Lay Teachers 12; Students 270.
Catechesis/Religious Programs—Tel: 650-327-2319. Sr. Carmel Silva, P.B.V.M., D.R.E.
Students 270.

4—St. Raymond, (1950), Revs. Patrick T. Michaels; Edward A. Bohnert.
Office: 1100 Santa Cruz Ave., 94025. Tel: 650-323-1755.
Res., 1231 Arbor Rd., 94025. Tel: 650-321-1339; Fax: 650-323-3206.
School—1211 Arbor Rd., 94025. Tel: 650-322-2312; Fax: 650-322-2910. Sr. Ann Bernard O'Shea, C.S.J., Prin.

Sisters 2; Lay Teachers 13; Students 253.
Catechesis/Religious Programs—Tel: 650-323-6353; Fax: 650-323-3206. Sr. Rita McCloskey, D.R.E. Students 176.

Millbrae, San Mateo Co., St. Dunstan (1940), Revs. Dermon Kavanagh, C.S.Sp.; Finnbar Horrigan, C.S.Sp.; Francis Mulloy, C.S.Sp. In res., Rev. William Doolin, C.S.Sp.
Res., 1133 Broadway, 94030. Tel: 650-697-4730; Fax: 650-697-5203.
School—1150 Magnolia Ave., 94030. Tel: 650-697-8119; Fax: 650-697-9295. Bonnie Davis, Prin.
Lay Teachers 14; Students 311.
Catechesis/Religious Programs—Tel: 650-697-7451.
Students 366.

Mill Valley, Marin Co., Our Lady of Mt. Carmel (1910), Revs. Joseph O'Connell; Paul Perry; Deacon Bruce Hall. In res., Rev. William E. Duggan.
Res., 3 Oakdale Ave., 94941. Tel: 415-388-4190; Fax: 415-388-4197.

Novato, Marin Co., St. Anthony of Padua (1968), Revs. Kevin P. Gaffey; Toan Nguyen; Deacon Joseph Brumbaugh. In res., Rev. James E. O'Malley.
Res., 1000 Cambridge St., 94947. Tel: 415-883-2177; Fax: 415-883-4049.
Catechesis/Religious Programs—Tel: 415-883-9000. Judith Ann Ross, D.R.E.
Students 386.

Our Lady of Loretto (1892), Revs. John J. O'Neill; Martin Avila; Gerard J. O'Donnell; Deacon William Mitchell. In res., Rev. Msgr. Richard K. Knapp; Rev. William Myers.
Res., 1806 Novato Blvd., 94947. Tel: 415-897-2171; Fax: 415-897-8251.
School—1811 Virginia Ave., 94947. Tel: 415-892-8621. Ms. Clare Menezes, Prin.
Lay Teachers 13; Students 272.
Catechesis/Religious Programs—Tel: 415-897-6714. D.R.E.: Betty McDonald; Mary Ann Hudick.
Students 370.

Olema, Marin Co., Sacred Heart (1967), Rev. Joseph A. Bravo.
Res., P.O. Box 70, 94950. Tel: 415-663-1139; Fax: 415-663-9660. [CEM]
Mission—Bolinas, St. Mary Magdalen.

Pacifica, San Mateo Co., Good Shepherd (1951), Rev. Piers M. Lahey.
Res., 901 Oceana Blvd., 94044. Tel: 650-355-2593; Fax: 650-355-1832.
School—909 Oceana Blvd., 94044. Tel: 650-359-4544. Patricia Volan, Prin.
Lay Teachers 14; Students 343.
Catechesis/Religious Programs—Sr. Eleanor Maloney, S.N.J.M., D.R.E.
Students 200.

St. Peter (1956), Rev. Leonard J. Calegari; Deacon Peter Solan. In res., Rev. Msgr. John C. Webster.
Res., 700 Oddstad Blvd., 94044. Tel: 650-359-6313; Fax: 650-359-2262.
Catechesis/Religious Programs—Tel: 650-359-5000. D.R.E.: Mrs. Barbara Malone; Ms. Judy Martin.
Students 620.

Portola Valley, San Mateo Co., Our Lady of the Wayside (1941). See St. Denis, Menlo Park.

Redwood City, San Mateo Co., Our Lady of Mount Carmel (1887), Revs. Randolph Calvo; Charito Suan; Deacon Paul Moriarty. In res., Rev. Msgr. William M. Roche; Rev. Msgr. Dominique Desjardins (Ottawa) (Retired).
Res., 347 Grand St., 94062. Tel: 650-366-3802; Fax: 650-366-1421.
Parish Center—300 Fulton St., 94062.
School—301 Grand St., 94062. Tel: 650-366-6127; Fax: 650-366-0902.
Lay Teachers 12; Students 298.
Catechesis/Religious Programs—Tel: 650-368-8237.
Students 150.

St. Matthias (1961), Rev. Msgr. James B. Flynn. In res., Rev. Thomas E. Lacey.
Res., 1685 Cordilleras Rd., 94062. Tel: 650-366-9544; Fax: 650-366-4817.
St. Matthias Day Care Center—533 Canyon Rd., 94062. Tel: 650-366-7085; 367-1320; Fax: 650-366-1049; 366-4817.
Students 85.
Catechesis/Religious Programs—Students 73.

St. Pius (1951), Rev. Msgr. Peter G. Armstrong; Revs. William E. Brown; John P. Penebsky; Deacon Steve Michaelson. In res., Rev. Msgr. James J. Haggarty; Rev. Anthony Chung.
Res., 1100 Woodside Rd., 94061. Tel: 650-361-1411; Fax: 650-369-3641.
School—Tel: 650-368-8327; Fax: 650-368-7031. Rita Carroll, Prin.
Lay Teachers 13; Students 313.
Catechesis/Religious Programs—Tel: 650-368-0429. Joyce Wickstrom, D.R.E.
Students 255.

San Anselmo, Marin Co., St. Anselm (1907), Revs. Peter McDonald; Neal Healy; Deacon Bernard O'Halloran. In res., Revs. Dennis McManus, C.S.Sp.; Richard Bain.
Res., Shady Ln. & Bolinas Ave., 94960. Tel: 415-453-2342; Fax: 415-453-8713.
School—40 Belle Ave., 94960. Tel: 415-454-8667; Fax: 415-454-4730. Marilyn Dineen, Prin.
Lay Teachers 17; Students 258.
Catechesis/Religious Programs—Tel: 415-457-5910. Tom Kavanaugh, D.R.E.
Students 186.

San Bruno, San Mateo Co., St. Bruno (1912), Revs. Rene J. Gomez; Ronald A. Burke; Deacon Joseph Lavulo. In res., Rev. Thomas Matthew.
Res., 555 San Bruno Ave., W., 94066. Tel: 650-588-2121; Fax: 650-588-6087.
Catechesis/Religious Programs—Tel: 650-588-4509. Mrs. Gloria Flores, D.R.E.
Students 305.

St. Robert (1958), Revs. Vincent D. Ring; James H. Morris; Deacon Rusty Duffey. In res., Rev. Joseph J. Marini.
Res., 1380 Crystal Springs Rd., 94066. Tel: 650-589-2800; Fax: 650-588-3628.
School—345 Oak Ave., 94066. Tel: 650-583-5065.
Lay Teachers 14; Students 316.
Catechesis/Religious Programs—Tel: 650-588-0477.
Students 574.

San Carlos, San Mateo Co., St. Charles (1928), Revs. John A. Ryan; Feliciano Mofan; Francis Murray; Sr. Pat Hunter, Pastoral Assoc.; Deacon Roy Twitty.
Res., 880 Tamarack Ave., 94070. Tel: 650-591-7349; Fax: 650-637-1968.
School—850 Tamarack Ave., 94070. Tel: 650-593-1629; Fax: 650-593-9723. Arlene Bertellotti, Prin.
Lay Teachers 17; Students 315.
Catechesis/Religious Programs—Joanne Thompson, D.R.E.
Students 660.

San Mateo, San Mateo Co.,

1—St. Bartholomew, (1955), Rev. Daniel T. Keohane; Deacon John Sequeira. In res., Revs. William R. Lowery; George R. Meyer.
Res., 300 Alameda de las Pulgas, 94402. Tel: 650-347-0701; Fax: 650-347-2429.
Catechesis/Religious Programs—Tel: 650-348-3412; Fax: 650-347-3429. Karen Melko, D.R.E.
Students 446.

2—St. Gregory, (1941), Rev. Msgr. Robert W. McElroy; Revs. Kevin J. Longworth, S.P.S.; Robert Cipriano; Deacon Fred Iskander.
Res., 2715 Hacienda St., 94403. Tel: 650-345-8506; Fax: 650-345-9329.
School—2701 Hacienda St., 94403. Tel: 650-573-0111; Fax: 650-573-6548. Patricia Teilh, Prin.
Lay Teachers 10; Students 304.

3—St. Matthew, (1863), Rev. Msgr. James McKay; Revs. William J. Ahlbach; Terence J. Horan; Aquino Padilla; Te Van Nguyen; Deacon Gerald Pera.
Res., One Notre Dame Ave., 94402. Tel: 650-344-7622; Fax: 650-344-4830.
School—901 S. El Camino Real, 94402. Tel: 650-343-1373; Fax: 650-343-2046. Mr. Kenneth F. Boegel, Prin.
Lay Teachers 24; Students 545.
Catechesis/Religious Programs—Tel: 650-344-7622.
Students 378.

4—St. Timothy, (1954), Revs. Kieran J. McCormick; Jorge del Real; Deacons Angel Aguilar; Nicolas Rodriguez. In res., Revs. Craig Forner; Saimone Moala.
Res., 1515 Dolan Ave., 94401. Tel: 650-342-2468; Fax: 650-342-8156.
School—Tel: 650-342-6567; Fax: 650-342-5913. Mrs. Evelyn Nordberg, Prin.
Lay Teachers 9; Students 273.
Catechesis/Religious Programs—Tel: 650-579-0901. Mrs. Irl Bolin, D.R.E.
Students 248.

San Rafael, Marin Co.,

1—Blessed Sacrament, (1951). Closed. For sacramental records please contact St. Isabella, San Rafael.

2—St. Isabella, (Terra Linda) (1961), Revs. Michael J. Keane; Tony LaTorre; Rory Murphy; Deacon Jerry Friedman. In res., Rev. William L. Knapp.
Res., One Trinity Way. P.O. Box 6166, 94903. Tel: 415-479-1560; Fax: 415-479-8303. [CEM]
School—P.O. Box 6188, 94903. Tel: 415-479-3727. Sr. Jeanne Marie, O.P., Prin.
Sisters 2; Lay Teachers 13; Students 252.
Catechesis/Religious Programs—Tel: 415-479-1222; Fax: 415-479-9961. Sharon Grant, D.R.E.
Students 435.

3—St. Raphael, (Terra Linda) (1817), Revs. Paul J. Rossi; Agustin Escalante; Joseph Hung; William L. Vaughan. Pastoral Assocs.: Sr. Dianne Nixon, S.N.J.M.; Sr. Mary Helen Jathas, S.H.F.
Res., 1104 Fifth Ave., 94901. Tel: 415-454-8141; Fax: 415-454-8193.
School—1100 Fifth Ave., 94901. Tel: 415-454-4455; Fax: 415-454-5927. Sr. Anne Marie Mullin, O.P., Prin.
Sisters of the Third Order of St. Dominic, Congregation of the Most Holy Name 2; Lay Teachers 12; Students 240.
Station—San Quentin, State Prison.
Catechesis/Religious Programs—Students 240.

4—St. Sylvester, (1961). Closed. For sacramental records please contact St. Raphael, San Rafael.

Sausalito, Marin Co., St. Mary Star of the Sea (1881), Rev. Richard S. Deitch. In res., Rev. Eugene F. Duggan.
Res., 180 Harrison Ave., 94965. Tel: 415-332-1765; Fax: 415-332-4962.

South San Francisco, San Mateo Co.,

1—All Souls, (1913), Revs. William J. Justice; Raphael de Avila; Sr. Martha Vega, S.S.S., Pastoral Assoc.; Deacon Alex Aragon.
Res., 315 Walnut Ave., 94080. Tel: 650-871-8944; Fax: 650-871-5806.
School—479 Miller Ave., 94080. Tel: 650-583-3562; Fax: 650-952-1167. Eileen Gorman, Prin.
Priests 2; Lay Teachers 13; Students 330.
Catechesis/Religious Programs—Tel: 650-573-5356. Maureen Galeotti, D.R.E.
Students 425.

2—Mater Dolorosa, (1961), Revs. Hugh O'Donnell; Eduardo Dura. In res., Rev. Stephen A. Meriwether.
Res., 307 Willow Ave., 94080. Tel: 650-583-4131; Fax: 650-761-2232.
School—1040 Miller Ave., 94080. Tel: 650-588-8175. William Kovacich, Prin.
Sisters 1; Lay Teachers 10; Students 251.
Catechesis/Religious Programs—Tel: 650-589-4448. Sr. Bernard Joseph, P.B.V.M., D.R.E.
Students 152.

3—St. Augustine, (1970), Revs. Eugene D. Tungol; Jed Sumampong; Felix S. Namocatcat; Deacons Robert Bertolani; Frank Almeida.
Res., 3700 Callan Blvd., 94080. Tel: 650-873-2282; Fax: 650-873-1356.
Catechesis/Religious Programs—Tel: 650-873-2878. Sr. Nona Barairo, D.R.E.
Students 566.

4—St. Veronica, (1951), Revs. Wilton S. Smith; Lawrence Finegan; Deacon Roger Beaudry. In res., Revs. Edward Cleary; Richard Kalkman.
Res., 434 Alida Way, 94080. Tel: 650-588-1455; Fax: 650-588-1481.
School—Tel: 650-589-3909; Fax: 650-589-2826. Joan Coleman, Prin.
Lay Teachers 13; Students 334.

Tiburon, Marin Co., St. Hilary (1951), Rev. James Tarantino; Rev. Msgr. Robert J. Plocki; Deacon Russell H. Holm. In res., Rev. Msgr. Francis A. Lacey, P.A., Pastor Emeritus.
Res., 761 Hilary Dr., 94920-1498. Tel: 415-435-1122; Fax: 415-435-1862.
School—765 Hilary Dr., 94920. Tel: 415-435-2224; Fax: 415-435-5895. Mrs. Theresa Canizzaro, Prin.
Lay Teachers 18; Students 285.
Catechesis/Religious Programs—Tel: 415-435-1639; Fax: 415-435-1639. Elsie Peregrin, D.R.E.
Students 132.

Tomales, Marin Co., Church of the Assumption (1860), Rev. Robert K. White.
Res., 26825 Shoreline Hwy., P.O. Box 82, 94971-0082. Tel: 707-878-2208; Fax: 707-878-2208. [CEM]
Mission—Marshall, Marin Co., St. Helen, (1902) P.O. Box 82, 94971-0082.

Woodside, San Mateo Co., St. Marcella Mission. Closed. For sacramental records please contact St. Denis, Menlo Park.

Chaplains of Public Institutions

San Francisco. *County Jail, Redwood City.* Deacon Paul Moriarty, St. Vincent De Paul Prison Chap.
Kaiser Hospital Redwood City. Revs. Francis Murray; Anthony Chung.
Kaiser Hospital San Francisco. Rev. Steven E. Davies.
Knights of Malta. The Sovereign Military Order of Malta (Western U.S.A. Association of the Sovereign Military Hospitaller Order of St. John of Jerusalem of Rhodes and of Malta—a Nonprofit Corporation). Revs. Egon J. Javor, O.S.B.; John P. Kavanaugh; Milton T. Walsh.
Laguna Honda Home. Rev. Timothy Enright, C.S.Sp.
Laguna Honda Home. Deacon Pete Palimiano.

St. Mary's Medical Center. Revs. Richard A. Lopez, Contact; Edward K. Murray.
St. Thomas More Society. (Lawyers). Rev. Jose' Chavarin.
San Francisco Fire Department. Rev. John L. Greene.
San Francisco General Hospital. Revs. Edmund M. Shipp; Zosimo Alvar.
San Francisco Police Department. Rev. Msgr. John P. Heaney; Rev. Thomas A. Daly.
Sequoia Hospital. Revs. Francis Murray; Anthony Chung.
Serra Club of San Francisco (Downtown). Rev. Craig Forner.
Serra Club of San Francisco (Golden Gate). Rev. Msgr. Edward P. McTaggart.
Sheriff's Honor Camp and Medium Security Facility. Served by St. Vincent de Paul volunteers, Redwood City.
Young Ladies' Institute. Rev. Msgr. Edward P. McTaggart, Moderator-ACCW.
Youth Guidance Center. Rev. Daniel E. Carter.
MARIN. *Serra Club of Marin.* Rev. Paul Rossi.
NOVATO. *Serra Club of Marin.* Rev. Piers M. Lahey.
SAN MATEO. *Serra Club of El Camino Real.* Rev. James J. Ward.
Serra Club of San Mateo. Rev. Msgr. James McKay.
Seton Medical Center. Deacon Richard J. Olsen.
Sheriff's Honor Camp and Medium Security Facility. Served by St. Vincent de Paul volunteers, Redwood City.
SAN QUENTIN. *California State Prison.* Rev. Dennis McManus, C.S.Sp.

Special Assignment:
Reverend Monsignors—
Holleran, J. Warren, St. Patrick Seminary
McElroy, Robert W., Vicar for Admin.
Otellini, Steven, Pres., Marin Catholic High School
Reilly, John J., Asst. Dir., Archives
Wang, Ignatius, Dir. Propagation of the Faith
Wester, John, Vicar for Clergy
Reverend Fathers—
Bain, Richard, Dir. Healing Ministry
Brennan, Bernard, Chap. Ft. Mason
Chung, Anthony, Chap., Kaiser and Sequoia Hospitals, Redwood City
Daly, Thomas A., Marin Catholic High School
Davies, Steven E., Chap., Kaiser Hospital
Foley, Jerome, Vocations, San Francisco State University
Forner, Craig, Vocations
Ghiorso, David A., Catholic Youth Organization
Haberman, Robert, Dominican College
Howell, Stephen H., Junipero Serra High School
Ingels, Gregory, Chancellor pro-tempore
Madden, Thomas, Vallombrosa Center
McCain, William, Studies, North American College, Rome
Meriwether, Stephen A., Judicial Vicar, Metropolitan Tribunal, San Francisco
Merson, Thomas S., Admin. Asst. to the Archbishop
Murray, Francis, Kaiser and Sequoia Hospitals, Redwood City
Nguyen, Trong Duc, Coord., Vietnamese Ministry
O'Rourke, P. Gerard, Ecumenical & Interreligious Affairs
Padazinski, C. Michael, Studies, North American College, Rome
Pettingill, David M., Dir., Office of Parish Life
Riley, Miles O'Brien, Communications
Sanchez, Joseph, Chap. St. Anne's Home
Schipper, Carl A., St. Patrick's Seminary
Schlitt, Harry G., Archdiocesan Dir. of Stewardship
Smith, Raymond K., Silver Penny Farm
Talesfore, John, Dir., Office of Worship
Walsh, Joseph, Dir., Clergy Education
Worner, William H., Serra Clergy House

On Duty Outside the Archdiocese:
Reverend Fathers—
Belleza, John A., Diocese of San Jose
Bonsor, Jack, University of Santa Clara, Diocese of San Jose
Coleman, John, VA Hospital, Palo Alto
Fredericks, James L., Loyola-Marymount, Los Angeles
Hagan, James, Mexico
Jocson, Salvador, Portugal
McElligott, Thomas J., Berkeley
Ochylski, Ronald S., Society of St. Sulpice
Richard, Joseph E., Diocese of Reno
Smith, Raymond K., Silver Penny Farm, Petaluma

Absent on Leave:
Reverend Monsignors—
O'Shea, Patrick J.
Reverend Fathers—
Balleza, John
Bravo, Joseph
Conley, John
Ervin, Thomas
Hoenisch, Richard
Keegan, A. Peter
Leach, Jerome
Young, William

Retired:
Reverend Monsignors—
Cahill, Daniel R.
Foudy, John T.
Gallagher, Eugene A.
Heuring, Alvan P. (DUB)
Keane, James P.
Kennedy, Edwin J.
Kennedy, Thomas I.
Kenny, John J.
Murphy, John J.
Plocki, Robert
Reverend Fathers—
Armas, James
Atkins, James
Bitangjol, Albert P.
Burns, Thomas J.
Chang, Simeon
Cleary, Edward M.
Decker, Raymond G.
Duggan, Eugene F.
Duggan, Paul E.
Duggan, William
Flanagan, William J.
Foudy, Denis D.
Greenlaw, Martin F.
Hurley, Mark J., (SR)
Jaszovsky, Joseph
Keane, Patrick J.
Knapp, William L.
Lacey, Thomas E.
Lee, Joseph Chun Yuan
Lowery, William R.
Marini, Joseph J.
McCaffrey, James L.
McCarthy, Patrick P.
McDonnell, Donald C.
Meyer, George R.
Mihovilovich, John B.
O'Connell, William A.
O'Malley, James E.
O'Reilly, Joseph P.
Ojeda, Filemon G.
Perlite, Paul A.
Pyne, Donald E.
Quinn, John R.
Raimondi, Michele
Robello, Louis J.
Rodriguez, Guillermo
Thomas, George L.
Walsh, David I.
Ward, John J.
Worner, William H.
Zoph, John L

Permanent Deacons:
Aguilar, Angel, St. Timothy, San Mateo
Allen, Charles, St. Teresa, San Francisco
Almeida, Frank, St. Augustine, South San Francisco
Amora, Felix, St. Andrew, Daly City
Aragon, Alex, All Souls, South San Francisco
Beaudry, Roger, St. Veronica, South San Francisco
Bertolani, Robert, St. Augustine, South San Francisco
Borg, Joseph, St. Mary Cathedral, San Francisco
Brumbaugh, Joseph, St. Anthony of Padua, Novato
Buenavista, Tom, St. Patrick, San Francisco
Capati, Bill, St. Patrick, San Francisco
Cervantes, Vicente, Mission Dolores, San Francisco
Dixon, Louis, St. Francis of Assisi, East Palo Alto
Duffey, Rusty, St. Robert, San Bruno
Dupre, John, St. Anne, San Francisco
Friedman, Jerome, Nazareth House/St. Isabella, San Rafael
Gamarra, David, St. Peter, San Francisco
Hackett, Steven, Immaculate Heart of Mary, Belmont
Hall, J. Bruce (NEW), Our Lady of Mt. Carmel, Mill Valley
Hernandez, Roger, St. Peter, San Francisco
Holm, Russell, (Retired)
Hutzler, John, St. Emydius, San Francisco
Ilao, Thomas, Corpus Christi, San Francisco
Iskander, Fred, St. Gregory, San Mateo
Jacquemet, Henry, Immaculate Heart of Mary, Belmont
Jee, John, Sabbatical, San Francisco
Kehrlein, Peter, St. Rita, Fairfax
Kortenkamp, Leon, Dir., Permanent Diaconate
Lavulo, Joseph, St. Bruno, San Bruno
McGhee, John, Our Lady of Refuge, La Honda
Michaelson, Steven, St. Pius, Redwood City
Mitchell, William, Archdiocesan Communications Office, San Francisco
Moriarty, Paul K. (RIC), St. Vincent de Paul, San Francisco; Detention Ministry, San Mateo County
O'Halloran, Bernard, St. Anselm, San Anselmo
Ocon, Manuel, Epiphany, San Francisco
Olsen, Richard (SEA), Seton Medical Center
Pelimiano, Pete, Good Shepherd, Pacifica
Pera, Gerald, St. Matthew, San Mateo
Prudenciado, Lernito, Holy Angels, Colma
Rivera, Dennis, Holy Name of Jesus, San Francisco
Rodriguez, Nicolas, St. Timothy, San Mateo
Rosen, Dan, St. Kevin, San Francisco
Ruiz, Juan, Holy Angels, Colma
Sequeira, John, St. Bartholomew, San Mateo
Solan, Peter, St. Peter, Pacifica
Solano, Jose, St. Anthony of Padua, Menlo Park
Soo, Felix, (Retired)
Swanson, Fred, St. Dominic, San Francisco
Tano, Mar, St. Luke, Foster City
Twitty, Roy, St. Charles, San Carlos
Viray, Ricardo, Epiphany, San Francisco
West, Gary, St. Stephen, San Francisco

INSTITUTIONS LOCATED IN THE ARCHDIOCESE

[A] SEMINARIES, ARCHDIOCESAN

MENLO PARK. *St. Patrick Seminary* (1889), 320 Middlefield Rd., 94025. Tel: 650-325-5621; 321-5655 (Library); Fax: 650-322-0997.
E-mail: info@stpatricksseminary.org
Web site: www.stpatricksseminary.org
Major Seminary of the Archdiocese of San Francisco, under the direction of the Society of St. Sulpice. Legal Title: *(1891, 1944): The Roman Catholic Seminary of San Francisco.* Most Rev. William J. Levada, Chancellor; Revs. Gerald D. Coleman, S.S., Ph.D., Pres. & Rector; James P. Oberle, S.S., Ph.D., Vice Rector; Carl A. Schipper, Ed.D., Academic Dean; Milton Walsh, S.T.D., Dean of Students; Sr. Dorothea M. Ross, C.S.J., Dir. Field Educ. & Pastoral Year; Dr. Cecil White, Ph.D., Librarian; Ms. Dorothy Tully, D.A., Registrar.
Faculty in Residence: Rev. Msgr. J. Warren Holleran, S.T.D.; Revs. Frederick J. Cwiekowski, S.S., S.T.D.; Robert V. Gavin, S.S.; Frank B. Norris, S.S., S.T.D.; Ronald D. Witherup, S.S., Ph.D. Priests 8; Religious 2; Lay Teachers 2; Students 61.

[B] SEMINARIES, RELIGIOUS OR SCHOLASTICATES

SAN FRANCISCO. *Capuchin House of Studies,* San Buenavista Friary, 750 Anza St., 94118. Tel: 415-387-7005. Revs. Julian Gonzalez-Montenegro, O.F.M.Cap., Guardian; James Stump, O.F.M.Cap; Dale Trunk, CPE Student; Bros. Francis Driscoll, O.F.M.Cap., Hospital Chap.; Mark Ortega, Instructor. Priests 3; Brothers 2.
Marianist Seminary, 175 Phelan Ave., 94112. Tel: 415-239-0841; Fax: 415-239-0848. Rev. John McEnhill, S.M., Rector. Priests 1; Brothers 2.
St. Peter Chanel Seminary, College Division, 625 Pine St., 94108. Tel: 415-398-3543. Very Rev. John F. McGregor, S.M., Prov. & Supr.; Bro. Patrick Souza, S.M., Admin. In res. Revs. James L. Pratt, S.M.; Patrick Coyle, S.M.; Francis Springer, S.M.; Bro. John Hunt, S.M.

[C] COLLEGES AND UNIVERSITIES

*SAN FRANCISCO. *University of San Francisco,* 2130 Fulton St., 94117-1080. Tel: 415-422-5555; Fax: 415-422-2303
For a complete listing, refer to the Colleges and Universities section.
BELMONT. *College of Notre Dame,* 1500 Ralston Ave., 94002. Tel: 650-593-1601; Fax: 650-637-0493.
Web site: www.cnd.edu
For a complete listing, refer to the Colleges and Universities section.
SAN RAFAEL. *Dominican College,* 50 Acacia Ave., 94901-2298. Tel: 415-457-4440; Fax: 415-485-3205
For a complete listing, refer to the Colleges and Universities section.

[D] HIGH SCHOOLS, ARCHDIOCESAN

SAN FRANCISCO. *Archbishop Riordan High School (Boys),* 175 Phelan Ave., 94112. Tel: 415-586-8200.
Web site: www.riordan.pvt.k12.ca.us
Rev. Timothy M. Kenney, S.M., Prin. Priests 1; Brothers 10; Lay Teachers 39; Students 700.

Sacred Heart Cathedral Preparatory (Coed), 1055 Ellis St., 94109. Tel: 415-775-6626.
E-mail: shcp.edu
Bro. Christopher Brady, F.S.C., Prin. Brothers 5; Sisters 3; Lay Teachers 77; Students 1,210.

KENTFIELD. *Marin Catholic College Preparatory (Coed)*, 675 Sir Francis Drake Blvd., 94904. Tel: 415-461-8844; Fax: 415-461-7161. Mr. William G. Isetta, Prin.; Rev. Msgr. Steven D. Otellini, Pres.; Rev. Thomas A. Daly, Chap. In res. Rev. John J. Ward, (Retired). Priests 3; Dominican Sisters of San Jose 1; Franciscan Sisters 1; Lay Teachers 59; Students 748.

SAN MATEO. *Junipero Serra High School (Boys)*, 451 W. 20th Ave., 94403-1385. Tel: 650-345-8207; Fax: 650-573-6638.
Web site: www.serrans.com
Rev. Stephen H. Howell, Pres.; Mr. C. Michael Peterson, Prin.; Rev. John L. Zoph. Priests 2; Lay Teachers 55; Students 902.

[E] HIGH SCHOOLS, PRIVATE

SAN FRANCISCO. *Convent of the Sacred Heart, High School (Girls)*, 2222 Broadway, 94115. Tel: 415-563-2900. Religious of the Sacred Heart. Dr. Mary Magnano Smith, Dir.; Mr. Douglas Grant, Prin. Religious 1; Lay Teachers 27; Students 196.

Immaculate Conception Academy, (Girls), 3625 24th St., 94110. Tel: 415-824-2052. Sr. Mary Catherine Antczak, O.P., Prin. Sisters 5; Lay Teachers 23; Students 270.

Mercy High School (Girls), 3250 19th Ave., 94132. Tel: 415-334-0525. Ms. Dorothy McCrea, Prin. Sisters 4; Lay Teachers 39; Students 557.

St. Ignatius College Preparatory (Coed), 2001 37th Ave., 94116. Tel: 415-731-7500; Fax: 415-731-9704.
Web site: www.siprep.org
Revs. Mark F. Toohey, S.J., Rector; Anthony P. Sauer, S.J., Pres.; Samuel P. Bellino, S.J.; Paul F. Capitolo, S.J.; Harry V. Carlin, S.J., Exec. Vice Pres.; Edward S. Fassett, S.J.; A. Francis Frugoli, S.J.; Gregory M. Goethals, S.J.; Charles A. Hofmann, S.J.; Gerald F. Hudson, S.J.; Michael J. Kotlanger, S.J.; Stephen C. Nejasmich, S.J., Prin.; Gregory L. Miller, S.J.; Michael R. Moodie, S.J.; Warren J. Wright, S.J. Priests 15; Scholastics 3; Brothers 6; Lay Teachers 90; Students 1,464.

ATHERTON. *Sacred Heart Preparatory (Convent of the Sacred Heart)(Girls)*, 94027. Tel: 650-322-1866. Religious of the Sacred Heart. Mr. Milton Werner, Ed.D., Dir. Sacred Heart Schools; Mr. Richard Dioli, Prin. Religious 2; Lay Teachers 56; Students 375.

BELMONT. *Notre Dame High School (Girls)*, 1540 Ralston Ave., 94002. Tel: 650-595-1913; Fax: 650-595-2116. Ms. Rita Gleason, Prin. Lay Teachers 50; Students 673.

BURLINGAME. *Mercy High School (Girls)*, 2750 Adeline Dr., 94010-5597. Tel: 650-343-3631. Sr. Rosann Fraher, R.S.M., Prin. Sisters 3; Lay Teachers 29; Students 387.

PORTOLA VALLEY. *Woodside Priory School*. (Coed, Boarding). 302 Portola Rd., 94028. Tel: 650-851-8221.
E-mail: woodsidepriory.com
Web site: www.woodsidepriory.com
Mr. Tim Molak, Headmaster. Priests 4; Brothers 1; Lay Teachers 40; Students 250. Legal Title: *Benedictine Fathers of the Priory, Inc.*

SAN ANSELMO. *San Domenico School*. (Grades 1-8, Coed; Grades 9-12, Girls. Boarding and Day Students.), 1500 Butterfield Rd., 94960-1099. Tel: 415-454-0200; Fax: 415-454-6604.
E-mail: rgray@marin.k12.ca.us
Web site: www.sandomenico.com
Sr. Gervaise Valpey, O.P., Head of School; John Bowermaster, Upper School Prin. Chaplains 1; Lay Teachers 25; Students 133.

[F] ELEMENTARY SCHOOLS, ARCHDIOCESAN

SAN FRANCISCO. *St. Brigid Elementary School*. (Grades K-8), 2250 Franklin St., 94109. Tel: 415-673-4523. Sr. Encarnacion Ortega, R.C.M., Prin. Sisters 5; Lay Teachers 10; Students 318.

St. Thomas More School. (Grades K-8), 50 St. Thomas More Way, 94132. Tel: 415-337-0100. Joseph T. Elsbernd, Prin. Lay Teachers 10; Students 330.

[G] ELEMENTARY SCHOOLS, PRIVATE

SAN FRANCISCO. *Schools of the Sacred Heart, Convent of the Sacred Heart Elementary School*. (Grades K-8), 2222 Broadway, 94115. Tel: 415-563-2900. Dr. Mary Magnano Smith, Dir.; Pamela Hayes, Head. Lay Teachers 53; Students 327.

Schools of the Sacred Heart, Stuart Hall For Boys. (Grades K-8), 2222 Broadway, 94115. Tel: 415-563-2900. Schools of the Sacred Heart. Dr. Mary Magnano Smith, Dir.; Mr. Thomas G. Lengel, Headmaster. Sisters 1; Lay Teachers 22; Students 312.

ATHERTON. *St. Joseph's School*. (Grades PreK-8), 50 Emilie Ave., 94027. Tel: 415-322-9931.
Web site: www.shschools.org
Dr. Milton Werner, Dir.; Mr. John Miller, Prin. Sisters 2; Lay Teachers 61; Students 512.

BELMONT. *C.N.D. Early Learning Center*. (Preschool), 1500 Ralston Rd., 94002. Tel: 650-508-3519. Sisters of Notre Dame de Namur. Mrs. Mary O'Keeffe, Dir. Lay Teachers 9; Children 72.

Notre Dame Elementary School, 1500 Ralston Ave., 94002. Tel: 650-591-2209. Sr. Dolores Quigg, S.N.D-.deN., Prin. Sisters 4; Lay Teachers 21; Students 260.

SAN ANSELMO. *San Domenico Early Education and Middle School*, 1500 Butterfield Rd., 94960-1099. Tel: 415-454-0200; Fax: 415-454-6604. Sr. Gervaise Valpey, O.P., Head of School; Mathew Heersche, Middle School Prin. (Grades 6-8); Carole Chase, Primary School Prin. (PreK-5). Sisters 2; Chaplains 1; Lay Teachers (Middle and Lower School) 18; (Early Education) 15; Students 434.

[H] ST. VINCENT DE PAUL SOCIETY

SAN FRANCISCO. *Society of St. Vincent de Paul Archdiocesan Council*, 1825 Mission St., 94103. Tel: 415-621-5305; Fax: 415-340-9210.
E-mail: vincent@vincent.org
Web site: http://www.vincent.org/
Deborah Payne, Pres.

San Francisco District Council of the St. Vincent de Paul Society, 425 Fourth St., 94107. Tel: 415-977-1270; Fax: 415-977-1271. Jack Noonan, Pres.; Michael J. Romo, Exec. Dir.

Thrift Stores:
425 Fourth St., 94107. Tel: 415-908-0250 (For information or pick-up).
1519 Haight St., 94117. Tel: 415-863-3615. 1529 Haight St., 94117. 186 W. Portal Ave., 94127. Tel: 415-664-7119. 5424 Geary Blvd., 94121. Tel: 415-666-0299.

Thrift Store Pickups. Tel: 888-637-7837.
Vehicle Donations. Tel: 1-800-YES-SVDP.
Vehicle Sales. Tel: 415-908-0250.

Vincentian Villa, 1825 Mission St., 94103. Tel: 415-621-5305. Housing project for fixed income seniors and handicapped. Capacity 124.

Arlington Residence, 480 Ellis St., 94102. Tel: 415-673-9600. A safe and sober residential, low cost hotel for men and women in recovery. Rooms 172.

Ozanam Center, 1175 Howard St., 94103. Tel: 415-864-3057. Detox and counseling services for drop-in clients and 3-day stay.

Reception Center. Tel: 415-621-6471; 621-6427.

Rosalie House, 3543 18th St. #4, 94110. Tel: 415-255-2754. An eight week emergency shelter for victims of domestic violence. Beds 20.

San Francisco Vincentian Life, 425 Fourth St., 94107. Tel: 415-977-1270. Supports and develops membership of the Society through parish conferences and involvement in the programs.

South of Market Multi-Service Center, 525 Fifth St., 94103. Tel: 415-597-7970. A 24-hour shelter for homeless men, offering social, physical and counseling services. Beds 200.

Brennan House. Tel: 415-255-2894; 255-0165 (Crisis Hotline). Transitional housing program for the survivors of domestic violence. Program provides in-depth counseling, job rehabilitation, education, children's programs, and support groups. Beds 15.

Riley Center Community Office, 2543 18th St., #4, 94110. Tel: 415-552-2943. Provides drop-in counseling and follow up services for survivors of domestic abuse. Community outreach available.

San Francisco Vincentian Desk, 425 Fourth St., 94107. Tel: 415-908-0250. Sr. Mary Loretta, Contact. Homeless help desk operated out of the San Francisco store.

SAN MATEO. *San Mateo County District Council*. Main Office, St. Vincent de Paul Society. 50 N. B St., 94401. Tel: 650-343-4405; Fax: 650-343-9495. Joe Marchetti, Pres.; Lorraine Moriary, Exec. Dir.
Thrift Stores:
113 S. B St., 94401. Tel: 650-347-5101.
344 Grand Ave., South San Francisco, 94080. Tel: 650-589-8445.
6298 Mission St., Daly City, 94014. Tel: 650-871-6844.
2406 El Camino Real, Redwood City, 94063. Tel: 650-369-5898.

Thrift Store Pickups:
South San Francisco. Tel: 650-871-6844.
Tel: 650-342-1860.
Redwood City. Tel: 650-369-2837.
Vehicle Sales. Tel: 650-593-8447.

St. Vincent de Paul Dining Room at St. Francis of Assisi Church. Monday evenings 5-6:30pm, 1425 Bay Rd., East Palo Alto, 94303. Tel: 650-322-2152; Fax: 650-322-7319.

San Mateo Vincentian Life, 50 N. B St., 94401. Tel: 650-343-4403.

Services for the Incarcerated - Hope in Action Ministry, 50 N. B St., 94401. Tel: 650-330-8937. Deacon Paul Moriarty, Chap.

Homeless Services:
Central County. M-F, 10am-12noon, 50 N. B St., 94401. Tel: 650-343-4403; Fax: 650-343-9495.
North County. M-F, 10am-12noon, 344 Grand Ave., South San Francisco, 94080. Tel: 650-589-9039.
South County. M-F, 1:00pm-2:00pm, 2600 Middlefield Rd., Redwood City, 94063. Tel: 650-780-7260; Fax: 650-780-7217.

SAN RAFAEL. *St. Vincent de Paul Society Marin County District Council*, 820 B St., P.O. Box 150527, 94915. Tel: 415-454-3303; Fax: 415-454-3406. Bob Kunst, Pres.

St. Vincent de Paul Dining Room, 820 B St., 94901-3003. Tel: 415-454-0336.

Marin County Vincentian Desk, 820 B. St., 94915. Tel: 415-454-3303.

[I] DAY NURSERIES

SAN FRANCISCO. *Holy Family Day Home*, 299 Dolores St., 94103. Tel: 415-861-5361; Fax: 415-398-1925. Legal Title: *Holy Family Day Home, Inc.* Donna M. Kraves, Exec. Dir. Religious 2; Lay Staff 23; Capacity 100.

[J] GENERAL HOSPITALS

SAN FRANCISCO. *St. Mary's Medical Center*, 450 Stanyan St., 94117. Tel: 415-668-1000
For a complete listing, refer to the Hospitals section.

DALY CITY. *Seton Medical Center*, 1900 Sullivan Ave., 94015. Tel: 650-992-4000
For a complete listing, refer to the Hospitals section.

MOSS BEACH. *Seton Medical Center Coastside*, 600 Marine Blvd., 94038. Tel: 650-728-5521
For a complete listing, refer to the Hospitals section.

[K] SENIOR CITIZEN RESIDENCES

SAN FRANCISCO. *Alexis Apartments of St. Patrick's Parish*, 390 Clementina St., 94103
For a complete listing, refer to the Special Care Facilities section.

Home for the Aged of the Little Sisters of the Poor, St. Anne's Home, 300 Lake St., 94118. Tel: 415-751-6510; Fax: 415-751-0650
For a complete listing, refer to the Special Care Facilities section.

Madonna Residence, 1055 Pine St., 94109. Tel: 415-928-0743
For a complete listing, refer to the Special Care Facilities section.

Mercy Terrace Corporation Apartments, 333 Baker St., 94117. Tel: 415-931-2325.
E-mail: mercyterrace@msn.com
For a complete listing, refer to the Special Care Facilities section.

SAN RAFAEL. *Nazareth House*, 245 Nova Albion Way, 94903. Tel: 415-479-8282
For a complete listing, refer to the Special Care Facilities section.

[L] RESIDENTIAL GROUP HOMES

SAN FRANCISCO. *The Good Shepherd Gracenter*, 1310 Bacon St., 94134. Tel: 415-586-2822
For a complete listing, refer to the Special Care Facilities section.

Mount St. Joseph-St. Elizabeth, (1976) 100 Masonic Ave., 94118. Tel: 415-567-8370; Fax: 415-292-5531
For a complete listing, refer to the Special Care Facilities section.

[M] RETREAT HOUSES

BURLINGAME. *Mercy Center, Spirituality and Conference Center*, 2300 Adeline Dr., 94010. Tel: 650-340-7474; Fax: 650-340-1299. Carlo Busby, Dir.; Michael Lane, Mgr. of Conference Services; Sue Thourson, Reservation Coord. Staff 21; Overnight capacity 93; Daytime use 300.

MENLO PARK. *Vallombrosa Center* (1946), 250 Oak Grove Ave., 94025. Tel: 650-325-5614.
E-mail: host@vallombrosa.org
Web site: www.vallombrosa.org
Rev. J. Thomas Madden, Live-in Dir. Legal Title: *Vallombrosa Center, Conference and Retreat Center of the Archdiocese of San Francisco*.

PETALUMA. *Silver Penny Farm Retreat Center*, 5215 Old Lakeville Rd., No. 1, 94954. Tel: 707-762-1498. Rev. Raymond K. Smith, Dir.

REDWOOD CITY. *Mount Alverno Conference and Retreat Center*, 3910 Bret Harte Dr., Box 1028, 94064. Tel: 650-369-0798.
E-mail: mt.alverno@aol.com
Web site: www.mountalverno.com

SAN RAFAEL. *Santa Sabina Center*, 25 Magnolia, 94901. Tel: 415-457-7727; Fax: 415-457-2310.
E-mail: sntasabina@aol.com

Sr. Susannah Malarkey, O.P., Dir. Dominican Sisters Retreat and Conference Center.

[N] MONASTERIES AND RESIDENCES OF PRIESTS AND BROTHERS

SAN FRANCISCO. *Jesuit Community at St. Ignatius College Preparatory*, 2001 37th Ave., 94116-1165. Tel: 415-731-7500; Fax: 415-731-9408. Revs. Mark F. Toohey, S.J.; Samuel P. Bellino, S.J.; Paul F. Capitolo; Harry V. Carlin; Edward S. Fassett; A. Francis Frugoli; Gregory M. Goethals; Rev. Charles A. Hofmann, S.J.; Revs. Gerald F. Hudson; Michael J. Kotlanger; Stephen C. Nejasmich; David J. Robinson; Anthony P. Sauer; Warren J. Wright; Bros. Douglas E. Draper; Louis A. Bueler; Thomas J. Koller; Arthur W. Lee; John E. Maloney; Daniel J. Peterson. Priests 14; Brothers 6; Scholastics 4.

Jesuit Community at University of San Francisco. (Corporate Title: Jesuit Community at University of San Francisco), 650 Parker Ave., 94118-4267. Tel: 415-422-4200; Fax: 415-387-1867.
E-mail: stackpoole@usfca.edu
Revs. Edward V. Stackpoole, S.J., Rector; William J. Wood, S.J., Asst. Rector; Joseph T. Angilella, S.J.; Steven A. Armstrong, S.J.; Paul J. Bernadicou, S.J.; Cornelius M. Buckley, S.J.; Francis J. Buckley, S.J.; Albert Chan, S.J. (Hong Kong); Denis E. Collins, S.J.; Albert C. Corcoran, S.J.; Robert F. Curran, S.J.; Geoffrey R. Dillon, S.J. (NO); Charles W. Dullea, S.J.; Joseph D. Fessio, S.J.; Charles R. Gagan, S.J.; Albert A. Grosskopf, S.J.; Richard A. Hill, S.J.; R. Daniel Kendall, S.J.; Francis E. King, S.J.; John P. Koepling, S.J.; John J. LoSchiavo, S.J.; Thomas M. Lucas, S.J.; Andrew F. Maginnis, S.J.; Edward J. Malatesta, S.J.; Robert L. Maloney, S.J.; John H. Martin, S.J.; Edwin J. McDermott, S.J.; Everett J. Mibach, S.J.; Richard E. Mulcahy, S.J.; Robert L. Niehoff, S.J. (ORE); Stephen Olivo, S.J.; Daniel A. O'Sullivan, S.J.; Antonio Pabayo, S.J. (Philippines); Thomas G. Piquado, S.J.; Robert B. Plushkell, S.J.; Thomas J. Powers, S.J.; Luis H. Quihuis, S.J.; Thomas A. Reed, S.J.; William O. Richardson, S.J.; David C. Robinson, S.J.; Vernon J. Ruland, S.J.; Donald B. Sharp, S.J.; John P. Schlegel, S.J.; Alden J. Stevenson, S.J.; Theodore T. Taheny, S.J.; Peter J. Togni, S.J.; George M. Twigg-Porter, S.J.; Eric Velandria, S.J. (Philippines); Eugene R. Zimmers, S.J.; Michael J. Zimmers, S.J.; Bros. John F. Graham, S.J.; John Keck, S.J. Priests 50; Brothers 2.

Marianist Community, 175 Phelan Ave., 94112. Tel: 415-586-8082. Bro. Thomas Redmond, S.M., Supr.; Revs. Lawrence Doersching, S.M.; Timothy M. Kenney, S.M.; Bros. Thomas Deasy, S.M.; Paul Fennelly, S.M.; Thomas Jalbert, S.M.; David McGuigan, S.M.; James Leahy, S.M.; Patrick McMahon, S.M.; Richard Olsen, S.M.; Kevin Thomas, S.M.; John Thompson, S.M. Priests 4; Brothers 11.

Maryknoll Fathers and Brothers, Catholic Foreign Mission Society of America, Inc., 2555 Webster St., 94115. Tel: 415-921-1100.
E-mail: mkls@igc.org
Web site: www.maryknoll.org
Revs. Gerald J. Nagle, M.M., Dir.; Arthur H. Wille, M.M.; Bro. James J. Fahy, M.M. Priests 5; Brothers 1.

Casa Maryknoll, 453 Miller Ave., South San Francisco, 94080. Tel: 415-952-5500. Revs. Manuel J. Mejia, M.M., Co-Dir.; Juan M. Zuniga, M.M., Co-Dir.; Richard T. Ouellette, M.M.

Paris Foreign Mission Society Residence, 930 Ashbury St., 94117. Tel: 415-664-6747. Revs. Jacques R. Didier, M.E.P., Dir.; Maurice J. Duhart, M.E.P.; Heribert Duquet, M.E.P. Priests 3.

Provincial Residence. San Francisco Province of the Society of Mary (Marist Fathers), 625 Pine St., 94108. Tel: 415-398-3543; Fax: 415-781-4937. Very Rev. John F. McGregor, S.M., Prov. & Supr.; Revs. James L. Pratt, S.M.; Patrick J. Coyle, S.M.; Francis Springer, S.M.; Bros. Patrick Souza, S.M.; John Hunt, S.M. Priests 4; Deacons 2; Brothers 6; Scholastics 3.

St. Dominic Priory, 2390 Bush St., 94115. Tel: 415-567-7824; Fax: 415-567-1608.
Web site: www.stdominics.org
Very Rev. Reginald E. Martin, O.P., Prior; Revs. Gregory H. Anderson, O.P.; Gerald A. Buckley, O.P.; Felix F. Cassidy, O.P.; Robert F. Christian, O.P.; Timothy Conlan, O.P.; Roberto Corral, O.P.; Thomas J. Hayes, O.P.; James S. Jenner, O.P.; John J. Klaia, O.P.; Xavier M. Lavagetto, O.P.; Samuel R. Parsons, O.P.; Paul Raftery, O.P.; Terrence J. Reilly, O.P.; Paul Connor, O.P.; Salvatore DiNardo, O.P.; Brian T. Mullady, O.P.; Bros. Mark A. Gorski, O.P.; Gregory R. Lira, O.P.; Peter A. Yost, O.P. Priests 15; Brothers 3.

Salesian Provincial Residence, 1100 Franklin St., 94109. Tel: 415-441-7144; Fax: 415-563-5394.
E-mail: suosec@aol.com
Revs. Nicholas J. Reina, S.D.B., Prov.; Thomas Prendiville, S.D.B., Dir.; Bro. Joseph R. Lockwood, S.D.B., Prov. Treas.; Rev. Roger Luna, S.D.B. In res. Revs. Joseph Scanagatta, S.D.B.; James Collins, S.D.B.; George Hacker, S.D.B.; Larry Lorenzoni, S.D.B.; Richard A. Voight, S.D.B. Priests 8; Brothers 1.
Military Chaplain: Rev. Robert Delis, S.D.B., Hq. MAG-12, 1st MAW, 96603-8725.

Verbum Dei Community, 1618 Howard St., #B, 94103. Tel: 415-861-8406. Rev. Rodolfo DLC Llamas, V.D.C. Priests 1; Brothers 1.

BURLINGAME. *Capuchin Provincial House*, 1345 Cortez Ave., 94010. Tel: 650-342-1489.
E-mail: ofmcap@aol.com
Revs. Ronald Talbott, O.F.M.Cap., Prov.; Enda Heffernan, O.F.M.Cap.; Richard Lopes, O.F.M.Cap.; Bertram Mulligan, O.F.M.Cap.; Camillus MacRory, O.F.M.Cap.; Flavian Welstead, O.F.M.Cap.

PORTOLA VALLEY. *Woodside Priory*, 302 Portola Rd., 94028. Tel: 650-851-8220. Very Revs. William J. Sullivan, O.S.B., Prior; Martin J. Mager, O.S.B., Subprior; Revs. Pius L. Horvath, O.S.B.; Egon J. Javor, O.S.B.; Maurus B. Nemeth, O.S.B. Priests 6; Brothers 2. Legal Title: *Benedictine Fathers of the Priory, Inc.*

[O] CONVENTS AND RESIDENCES FOR SISTERS

SAN FRANCISCO. *Carmelite Monastery of Cristo Rey, Discalced Carmelite Nuns*, 721 Parker Ave., 94118-4297. Mother Mary Joseph Chavez, O.C.D., Prioress. Professed Nuns 16.

Daughters of St. Paul, 46 Geary St., 94108. Tel: 415-781-5180. Sr. Laura Rhoderica, F.S.P., Supr. Sisters 4.

Franciscan Missionaries of Mary (F.M.M.), St. Joseph Convent, 46 Harrington St., 94112. Tel: 415-587-8359. Sisters 5.

Missionaries of Charity. (India), 1596 Fulton St., 94117. Tel: 415-563-9446. Sisters 7. Noviciate, 312 29th St., 94131. Tel: 415-647-1889. Sisters 4; Novices 45. 55 Sadowa St., 94117. Tel: 415-566-3449. Sisters 4.

Monastery of Perpetual Adoration, Nuns of Perpetual Adoration, 771 Ashbury St., 94117. Tel: 415-566-2743; Fax: 415-564-4469. Mother Rosalba Vargas, A.P., Supr. Cloistered Nuns 23.

Presentation Convent, Motherhouse of the Sisters of the Presentation of B.V.M., 2340 Turk Blvd., 94118. Tel: 415-751-0406.
E-mail: admoffice@aol.com
Sr. Rosina Conrotto, P.B.V.M., Pres. Sisters in Archdiocese 92; Total in congregation 143.

St. Francis Convent of Mercy (Sisters of Mercy-Burlingame), 826 30th Ave., 94121. Sisters 2.

Shalom Convent, 416 Stanyan St., 94117. Tel: 415-750-5545. Sisters of Mercy (Burlingame, CA) 4.

Sisters of Social Service, 1850 Ulloa St., 94116. Tel: 415-681-9219. Sisters 4.

Sisters of St. Joseph of Orange, 544 Bush St., 94108. Tel: 415-398-7383. Sisters 5.

Sisters of St. Joseph of Orange, 1737 Silliman St., 94134. Tel: 415-585-0159. Sisters 3.

Sisters of the Good Shepherd, 1310 Bacon St., 94134. Tel: 415-586-2822; Fax: 415-586-0355. Sisters 8.

Sisters of the Holy Family, 174 Stanyan St., Flat #2, 94118. Tel: 415-221-7704. Sisters 4.

Sisters of the Precious Blood, 326 Ewing Ter., 94118. Sisters 2.

Sisters of the Visitation of Japan, 604 Cabrillo St., 94118. Tel: 415-751-5067. Sisters 4. Serving the Archdiocese in Japanese Bible Study and visiting the elderly and sick.

Society of Helpers (Helpers of the Holy Souls), 855 Lincoln Way, 94122. Tel: 415-661-6316. Sr. Veronica Donlon, Local Supr. Sisters 7.

Verbum Dei Community. (Apostolic Institute: Instituto Apostolico Verbum Dei, Loeches, Madrid), 1239 Howard St., 94103. Tel: 415-863-4469. Prayer and ministry of the Word, working with youth, young adults & adults. Sr. Maria Teresa Pasadas, V.D.C., Supr.; Sr. Raquel Mora, V.D.C.; Sr. Guadalupe Medrano, V.D.C.; Sr. Bella Rodas, V.D.C.; Sr. Maureen Blackburn, V.D.C.; Sr. Ellen Hess, V.D.C.; Sr. Mary Gomez, V.D.C.; Sr. Tania Echegaray, V.D.C.

ATHERTON. *Religious of the Sacred Heart Oakwood*, 140 Valparaiso Ave., 94027; Fax: 650-326-2251. Sr. Catherine Baxter, R.S.C.J., Dir. Sisters 37. Infirmary for elderly Religious of the Sacred Heart.

BURLINGAME. *Regional Community of the Sisters of Mercy of the Americas*, 2300 Adeline Dr., 94010-5599. Tel: 650-340-7410; Fax: 650-347-2550.
E-mail: sombur@aol.com
Sisters 57; Total in congregation 215; Total in Archdiocese 127.

DALY CITY. *Quinhon Missionary Sisters of the Holy Cross*, 298 Southgate Ave., 94015. Tel: 650-992-1560. Sisters 10; Novices 7; Postulants & Aspirants 10.

MENLO PARK. *Corpus Christi Monastery*, 215 Oak Grove Ave., 94025. Tel: 650-322-1801; Fax: 650-322-6816.
E-mail: mchrist774@aol.com
Nuns of the Order of Preachers. Sr. Mary of the Holy Family, Prioress. Cloistered Religious 22; Extern Sisters 2.

REDWOOD CITY. *Casa Chiara Community*, 3910 Bret Harte Dr., Box 685, 94064-0685. Tel: 650-366-3968. Franciscan Sisters. Sisters 5.

Provincial House of the Sisters of St. Francis of Penance and Christian Charity, 3910 Bret Harte Dr., P.O. Box 1028, 94064. Tel: 650-369-1725.
E-mail: alverno@juno.com
Legal Titles: *Sisters of St. Francis-Mount Alverno; Sisters of St. Francis Charitable Trust.* Sr. Maria Elena Martinez, O.S.F., Prov. Min. Sisters 16; Total in Province 106.

SAN RAFAEL. *Carmelite Monastery of the Mother of God, Discalced Carmelite Nuns*, 530 Blackstone Dr., 94093. Tel: 415-479-6872; Fax: 415-491-4964. Mother Anna Marie Vanni, O.C.D., Prioress. Sisters 5.

Dominican Sisters of San Rafael Generalate & Convent, 1520 Grand Ave., 94901-2236. Tel: 415-453-8303; Fax: 415-453-8367.
Web site: sanrafaelop.org
Sr. Patricia Simpson, O.P., Prioress Gen. Total in Community 158; Total in Archdiocese 96.

Dominican Convent, 1540 Grand Ave., 94901. Tel: 415-454-9221. Sisters 26.

Our Lady of Lourdes Convent (Infirmary), 77 Locust Ave., 94901. Tel: 415-457-3171. Sisters 22.

Our Lady of Mercy Convent, 15 Elmwood Dr., Daly City, 94015. Tel: 650-756-3457. Sisters 5.

Our Lady of Mt. Carmel Convent, 34 Buena Vista Ave., Mill Valley, 94941. Tel: 415-389-0328. Sisters 6.

San Domenico Convent, 1500 Butterfield Rd., San Anselmo, 94960. Tel: 415-453-9172. Sisters 12.

Sacred Heart Convent, 660 Oak St., San Francisco, 94117. Tel: 415-431-2881. Sisters 9.

St. Dominic Convent, 1851 Pierce St., San Francisco, 94115. Tel: 415-922-8817. Sisters 5.

St. Catherine of Siena Convent, 14 Roger Dr., 94901. Tel: 415-453-4330. Sisters 4.

SOUTH SAN FRANCISCO. *Holy Family Convent*, 381 Avalon Dr., 94080. Tel: 650-588-3471. Sisters 3.

[P] SECULAR INSTITUTES

SAN FRANCISCO. *Missionaries of the Kingship of Christ*, 3215 Cesar Chavez St., 94110. Tel: 415-647-2704. A Franciscan secular institute for women.

The Society of Our Lady of the Way, 147 Dorado Ter., 94112. Tel: 415-585-3319. A secular institute for women. Sr. Yvonne Claire Artigues, S.O.L.W., Local Contact, 726 Geneva Ave., 94112-3327. Tel: 415-585-7967.

[Q] CATHOLIC CHARITIES

SAN FRANCISCO. *Catholic Charities of the Archdiocese of San Francisco*, 814 Mission St., 3rd Fl., 94103. Tel: 415-281-1200; Fax: 415-281-1394.
Web site: www.ccasf.org
Mr. Frank C. Hudson, CEO; Mr. Joseph Kavingada, CFO; Mr. David B. Lloyd, COO; Mrs. Sophie L. Aldrich, Exec. Dir. Devel. & Mktg.; Sr. Irma L. Dillard, Dir. of Human Resources/Volunteers.

Campaign for Human Development, 814 Mission St., 3rd Fl., 94103. Tel: 415-442-6844; Fax: 415-281-1394. Francis C. Hudson, Archdiocesan Dir.

Catholic Relief Services, 814 Mission St., 3rd Fl., 94103. Tel: 415-442-6844; Fax: 415-281-1394.

Mercy/Charities Housing California, 1028A Howard St., 94103. Tel: 415-487-6825; Fax: 415-487-6834. Ms. Jane Graf, Pres.

MENTAL HEALTH AND CLINICAL SERVICES: Charles King, Ph.D., Dir.

Marin Counseling, 179 Los Ranchitos Rd., San Rafael, 94903. Tel: 415-499-1470, Ext. 24; Fax: 415-479-2667.

San Francisco Counseling, 814 Mission St., 5th floor, 94103.

Daly City Counseling, 6755 Mission St., Daly City, 94014. Tel: 650-922-4222; Fax: 650-922-7867.

San Mateo Counseling. Tel: 650-579-0277.

Pregnancy Counseling / Adoption Services / Foster Care, 814 Mission St., 5th floor, 94103. Tel: 415-778-6111; Fax: 415-284-0682. Tel: 1-800-CARE-002 Hotline (state-wide).

Grief Care, 2559 40th Ave., 94116. Tel: 415-564-7882; Fax: 415-731-1270.

CHILDREN AND FAMILY SERVICES. Bonita Davenport, Svc. Dir.

San Francisco Family Services, 812 Mission St., Mezzanine, 94103. Tel: 415-281-1200; Fax: 415-281-1230. Hearing Impaired, 1801 Octavia St., 94109. Tel: 415-749-3812; Fax: 415-567-0916.

Peninsula Family Resource Center (PFRC), 520 S. El Camino Real, Ste. 204, San Mateo, 94402. Tel: 650-696-1255; Fax: 650-696-1257.

Richmond Hills Family Center, 6324 Geary Blvd., 94121. Tel: 415-750-5080; Fax: 415-750-5085.

Guerrero House, 899 Guerrero St., 94110. Tel: 415-550-4478; Fax: 415-550-4481.

West Marin Social Services, 11315 State Rte. 1, Point Reyes Station, 94956. Tel: 415-663-1252; Fax: 415-663-1319.
Marin Family Services, 179 Los Ranchitos Rd., San Rafael, 94903. Tel: 415-499-1470, Ext. 14; Fax: 415-479-2667.
SOCIAL MINISTRY AND COMMUNITY OUTREACH:
Citizenship Services, 814 Mission St., Mezzanine, 94103. Tel: 415-281-1200; Fax: 415-281-1230. 179 Los Ranchitos Rd., San Rafael, 94903. Tel: 415-499-1470; Fax: 415-479-2667.
Detention Ministries, 814 Mission St., 3rd floor, 94103. Tel: 415-442-5207; Fax: 415-281-1394.
St. Joseph's Village, 220 10th St., 94103. Tel: 415-575-4920; Fax: 415-575-4925.
HIV Community Housing and Services: Ms. Tiffany Mock-Goeman, Svc. Dir.
HIV Direct Services, 814 Mission St., Mezzanine, 94103. Tel: 415-281-1200; Fax: 415-281-1230.
Leland Avenue Project, 141 Leland Ave., 94134. Tel: 415-405-2000.
HIV Money Management, 814 Mission St., Mezzanine, 94103. Tel: 415-281-1200; Fax: 415-281-1230.
HIV Housing Services, 814 Mission St., Mezzanine, 94103. Tel: 415-281-1200; Fax: 415-281-1230.
**Peter Claver Community*, 1340 Golden Gate Ave., 94115. Tel: 415-749-3800; Fax: 415-563-3153.
Belmont House Aids Hospice, 730 El Camino Real, Belmont, 94002. Tel: 650-802-9426; Fax: 650-802-8385.
Derek Silva Community, 1594 Market St., 94102. Tel: 415-553-8700; Fax: 415-575-3729.
HIV Food & Emergency Services, 600 Columbia Dr., San Mateo, 94402. Tel: 650-579-7490; Fax: 650-343-0413.
AGING SERVICES: Bea Lopez, Dir.
San Francisco Senior Services, 812 Mission St., 94103. Tel: 415-281-1200; Fax: 415-281-1230.
Meals on Wheels, 600 Columbia Dr., San Mateo, 94002. Tel: 650-579-0277, Ext. 3340; Fax: 650-343-0413.
Ombudsman, 600 Columbia Dr., San Mateo, 94402. Tel: 650-579-0277, Ext. 3312; Fax: 650-343-0413.
San Carlos Adult Day Care, 787 Walnut St., San Carlos, 94070. Tel: 650-595-9325; Fax: 650-593-2316.
Noriega Adult Day Support Center, 3601 Noriega St., 94122. Tel: 415-242-8015; Fax: 415-242-8017.
OMI Senior Center, 446 Randolph St., 94132. Tel: 415-587-1443; Fax: 415-586-7960.
Marin Senior Services, 179 Los Ranchitos, San Rafael, 94903. Tel: 415-499-1470, Ext. 16; Fax: 415-479-2667.
AUXILIARIES:
Auxiliary of Little Children's Aid, P.O. Box 31040, 94131.
Little Children's Aid, Junior Auxiliary, P.O. Box 27336, 94131.
Catholic Charities Auxiliary of San Mateo, 600 Columbia Dr., San Mateo, 94402. Tel: 650-597-0277.
Primrose House of Catholic Charities of San Mateo, 307 Primrose Rd., San Mateo, 94010. Tel: 650-343-1920.

[R] CATHOLIC YOUTH ORGANIZATIONS

SAN RAFAEL. *Catholic Youth Organization of the Archdiocese of San Francisco*, 1 St. Vincent Dr., 94903. Tel: 415-507-2000; Fax: 415-491-0842. Rev. David A. Ghiorso, Exec. Dir.; Stewart Clark, Archdiocesan Youth Dir.
CYO Archbishop McGucken Youth Retreat and Conference Center. Location of CYO Camp Armstrong, and CYO Caritas Creek Environmental Education Program. 2136 Bohemian Hwy., Occidental, 95465. Tel: 707-874-0210. Steve Grant, Dir.
CYO Sports & Recreation, 1 St. Vincent Dr., 94903. Tel: 415-507-4290. Provides a variety of organized team sports programs throughout the year for elementary school age children.
CYO Camp Armstrong, 2136 Bohemian Hwy., Occidental, 95465. Tel: 415-507-2000. Paula M. Pardini, Dir. Summer camp located at Archbishop McGucken Youth Center.
CYO Caritas Creek Environmental Education Program, 1 St. Vincent Dr., 94903. Tel: 415-507-2000. Paula Pardini, Dir. An environmental education program located at Archbishop McGucken Youth Center, serving children grades 5-8.
CYO Mission Day Care, 180 Fair Oaks St., San Francisco, 94110. Tel: 415-826-6880. Liliana Carnero-Rossi, Dir. Provides after-school services for children, summer day camps, and holiday recess camps.
CYO San Francisco Boys and Girls Home, P.O. Box 210399, San Francisco, 94121-0399. Tel: 415-750-5300. Kent Eagleson, Exec. Dir. Since 1915. Residential treatment, special education and home-based services for emotionally, behaviorally, and educationally disadvantaged abused children ages 10-18 at residential group homes. Individual psychotherapy and family counseling provided.
St. Vincent's School for Boys, 1 St. Vincent Dr., 94903. Tel: 415-507-2000. Mr. Kent Eagleson, Exec. Dir. Since 1855. Residential treatment, special education, foster care, day treatment, and home-based services for emotionally, behaviorally, and educationally disadvantaged boys.
CYO Transportation Services, 699 Serramonte Blvd., Ste. 210, Daly City, 94015. Tel: 650-757-2110. Martin Rea, Dir. Provides school bus transportation for all CYO-related programs and for other nonprofit school and community organizations.
CYO Youth Ministry Services, 1 St. Vincent Dr., 94903. Tel: 415-507-2000. Parish-based youth leadership training programs and services.

[S] NEWMAN CENTERS

SAN FRANCISCO. *Newman Center, San Francisco State University*, St. Thomas More Church, 1300 Junipero Serra Blvd., 94123. Tel: 415-452-9634; Fax: 415-452-9653.
E-mail: stmchurch@hotmail.com
Web site: www.re.net/sanfrancisco/stm
Rev. Jerome P. Foley, Chap. In res. Revs. John J. Talesfore; Steven E. Davies.
Newman Center, University of California Medical Center, 1290 Fifth Ave., 94122. Tel: 415-566-5610. Revs. Alex L. Legaspi; James Stump, O.F.M.Cap.

[T] PERSONAL PRELATURES

SAN FRANCISCO. *Opus Dei*. (Prelature of the Holy Cross and Opus Dei) Delegate Vicariate. 765 14th Ave., 94118. Tel: 415-386-0431. Very Rev. George M. Rossman, Delegate Vicar; Revs. Torlach C. Delargy; Arne A. Panula.
Other Priests in the Archdiocese: Rev. Salvador V. Serrano, 1835 Bay Laurel, Menlo Park, 94025. Tel: 650-327-1675. Rev. Jose P. Ruisanchez, 108 Kipling Dr., Mill Valley, 94941. Tel: 415-388-4531.

[U] MISCELLANEOUS LISTINGS

SAN FRANCISCO.
**All Hallows Community, Inc.*, c/o Mercy Services Corp., 1035 Folsom St., 94103.
Apostleship of Prayer, 650 Parker Ave., 94118-4287. Tel: 415-422-4200. Rev. George M. Twigg-Porter, S.J., Dir.
Archdiocesan Council of Catholic Women, 445 Church St., 94114. Tel: 415-565-3600. Cathy Mibach, Pres.
Association of Ladies of Charity of St. Vincent de Paul, 2570 Ocean Ave., P.O. Box 194, 94132. Tel: 650-369-6287; Fax: 650-639-6290. Lauren Santucci, Pres. Tel: 650-592-2160; Linda Ramelot, Vice-Pres.; Nina Smith, Sec.; Hilda Barradas, Recording Sec.; Marilyn Christen, Treas.; Charlotte Kiesel, Founding Pres. The purpose of the Association is to make known the spirit of St. Vincent de Paul, St. Louise de Marillac and St. Elizabeth Ann Seton by performing corporal works of mercy for the poor and needy of the San Francisco Archdiocese.
California Handicapables, Inc. (1965), 1311 Montgomery St., 94133-3521. Tel: 415-474-3821.
E-mail: saltooley@aol.com
Miss Nadine Calligiuri, Founder; Sally Tooley, Treas. Provides transportation & lunch along with Mass on the 2nd Saturday of every month at St. Mary's Cathedral, San Francisco for shut-ins & handicapped.
Catholic Healthcare West, 1700 Montgomery St., Ste. 300, 94111. Tel: 415-438-5500.
E-mail: tstevens@chw.edu
Mr. Richard J. Kramer, Pres./CEO. A nonprofit corporation. CHW is a multi-congregational Health System co-sponsored by the Auburn Regional Community of the Sisters of Mercy; the Burlingame Regional Community of the Sisters of Mercy; the Sisters of St. Dominic of the Congregation of the Most Holy Rosary, Adrian, MI; the Daughters of Charity of St. Vincent de Paul, Province of the West; the Sisters of the Third Order of St. Dominic, Congregation of the Most Holy Name, San Rafael, CA; the Congregation of the Sisters of St. Catherine of Siena of Kenosha, WI; Franciscan Sisters of the Sacred Heart of Frankfurt, IL; Sisters of St. Francis of Penance and Christian Charity of Redwood City, CA. There are 37 affiliated hospitals, retirement homes, long-term care facilities, and related corporations, located in California, Arizona, and Nevada. This organization provides centralized management and support functions for the following affiliated nonprofit organizations in the Archdiocese of San Francisco (other affiliates are listed in their respective dioceses): CHW West Bay, which includes St. Mary's Medical Center, San Francisco; Seton Medical Center, Daly City; Seton Medical Center, Coastside, Moss Beach; Seton Health Services Foundation; Mercy Terrace Corporation; MSC Psychiatric Services Corporation; San Francisco Heart Institute.
Catholic Kolping Society, 440 Taraval St., 94116. Hubert Brinkman, Pres., 1738 Quesada Way, Burlingame, 94010. Catherine Vennemeyer, Treas., 2733 Trousdale Dr., Burlingame, 94010.
Catholics for Truth & Justice, P.O. Box 26756, 94126-0756. Tel: 415-693-2TRU. Rev. John P. Penebsky, Chap.
Charismatic Movement, Charismatic Board, 2555 17th Ave., 94116. Tel: 415-664-8481; Fax: 415-661-2957.
E-mail: sfccr@slip.net
Web site: sfspirit.com
Rev. L. Joseph Landi, Chm.
Equestrian Order of the Holy Sepulchre of Jerusalem - Northwest Lieutenancy, 3050 24th Ave., 94132. Tel: 415-664-6565; Fax: 415-664-5069. Albert E. Maggio.
Father Raphael Piperni Charitable Trust, 1100 Franklin St., 94109. Tel: 415-441-7144.
E-mail: suosec@aol.com
(The FRPC (R) Trust).
Filipino Cursillo Secretariat, P.O. Box 881601, 94188-1601. Deacon Mar Tano, Spiritual Advisor.
Franciscan Friars of California, Provincial Office of Communications, 135 Golden Gate Ave., 94102-3809. Tel: 415-241-2636; Fax: 415-863-8240. Rev. Floyd A. Lotito, O.F.M., Dir.
Holy Childhood Pontifical Association, 445 Church St., 94114. Tel: 415-565-3676; Fax: 415-565-3677. Rev. Msgr. Ignatius Wang, Dir.
Italian Catholic Federation, 1801 Van Ness Ave., Ste. 330, 94109. Tel: 415-673-8240. Rev. Msgr. Charles Durkin, Chap.
Legion of Mary, 415 Edna St., 94112. Tel: 415-333-3627. Rev. Lawrence C. Goode, Dir.
Mercy / Charities Housing California, 1028 A Howard St., 94103. Housing development for low-income families, elderly, and singles.
Mercy Family Plaza, c/o Mercy/Charities Housing California, 1028 A Howard St., 94103. Thirty-six affordable units for families.
MSC Psychiatric Services. Provides certain psychiatric patient care services.
Mercy Terrace Corporation. Housing project for low- and moderate-income persons and families; also multi-services for residents and community.
Pauline Books & Media, 46 Geary St., 94108. Tel: 415-781-5180.
E-mail: fspsanfran@aol.com
Web site: www.pauline.org
Daughters of St. Paul. Sr. Karen Marie, F.S.P., Supr. Sisters 5.
Philip Rinaldi Charitable Trust, P.O. Box 640009, 94164-0009. Tel: 415-441-7144. For the care of needy youth and for the formation needs of Salesians of St. John Bosco. Thomas Prendiville, Sec.
Religious Trust (RETA), Box 7443, 94120. A nonprofit multiple, religious employer health plan with trust fund.
The Ricci Institute for Chinese-Western Cultural History at the Center for the Pacific Rim, University of San Francisco, 2130 Fulton St., 94117-1080. Tel: 415-422-6401; Fax: 415-422-2291.
E-mail: ricci@usfc.edu
Web site: www.usfca.edu/ricci
Revs. Edward J. Malatesta, S.J., Dir.; Albert Chan, S.J., Ph.D., Senior Research Fellow; Mark Mir, Research Fellow and Chinese Library Cataloguer; Xiao Wu-Xin, Ed.D., Assoc. Dir./Research Fellow.
St. Anthony Foundation, 121 Golden Gate Ave., 94102. Tel: 415-241-2600; Fax: 415-252-1635.
E-mail: kathryn@stanthonyfdn.org
Web site: www.stanthonyfdn.org
Rev. Dan Lackie, O.F.M. A nonprofit, charitable corporation assisting the homeless and low-income.
St. Benedict Center for Deaf and Hearing Impaired at St. Francis Xavier Church.
St. Rose Academy Corporation, Rose Court, 2507 Pine St., 94109. Tel: 415-921-3584.
Shrine of St. Jude Thaddeus, 2390 Bush St., 94115. Rev. Reginald E. Martin, O.P., Dir.
Sisters of the Presentation Community Support Trust Fund, 2340 Turk Blvd., 94118. Tel: 415-751-0406.
E-mail: admoffice@aol.com
Trust used for the religious and charitable needs of the Sisters of the Presentation of the Blessed Virgin Mary. Trustees: Sr. Joanna Bruno, P.B.V.M.; Sr. Pamela Chiesa, P.B.V.M.; Sr. Patricia Anne Cloherty, P.B.V.M.; Sr. Roberta Green, P.B.V.M.; Sr. Adele Hancock, P.B.V.M.; Sr. Patricia Marie Mulpeters, P.B.V.M.; Sr. Rose Therese Sousa, P.B.V.M.
Spiritual Programs and Retreats, 704 Cortland Ave., 94110. Rev. Clifford Martin, Dir.
**The Ordinary Mutual, RRG*, P.O. Box 191867, 94119-1867. Tel: 415-536-8440; Fax: 415-536-8513. Dennis Mulqueeney, Underwriting Mgr.; Rev. Msgr. Thomas J. Keys, Pres. A Risk Retention Group Corporation, incorporated in Vermont, serving the Dioceses of Boise, Tucson, Fresno, Monterey, Oakland, Orange, Sacramento, San Jose, Santa Rosa, and Stockton, and the Archdioceses of Los Angeles and San Francisco.

Together in the Mission of Education (T.I.M.E.), 98 Bosworth St., 94112. Tel: 415-334-4334.
E-mail: together@sirius.com
Thomas E. Weiss, Devel. Dir.

BURLINGAME. *Music at Kohl Mansion, Inc.*, 2750 Adeline Dr., 94010. Tel: 650-343-8463; Fax: 650-343-2316. Carol Eggers, Contact Person. To develop and promote public knowledge and appreciation of musical arts by sponsoring chamber music concerts and other public performances of music, as well as music education activities.

DALY CITY. *Association of Catholic Student Councils*, 242 Greenview Dr., 94014. Tel: 415-584-9877. Marilyn Thickett, Exec. Dir.

LOS ANGELES. *Christian Live Communities (Sodalities)*, P.O. Box 45041, 90045. Tel: 310-338-7445; Fax: 310-338-3002. Rev. James D. Earps, S.J.

MENLO PARK. *St. Joseph's-St. Patrick's College Alumni Association*, St. Patrick's Seminary, 320 Middlefield Rd., 94025. Tel: 650-327-8956. Mr. Donald C. Carroll, Contact.

Vatican II Institute for Clergy Formation, 320 Middlefield Rd., 94025. Tel: 650-325-9122; Fax: 650-325-6765. Revs. Eugene J. Konkel, S.S., Dir.; Jeremiah Farrell, S.S., Assoc. Dir.

MOUNTAIN VIEW. *Hospital and Health Services Liaison*, St. Joseph's College, P.O. Box 7009, 94039. Tel: 650-694-1400. Rev. Gerald D. Coleman, S.S., Ph.D.

PACIFICA. *Cursillo*, 901 Oceana Blvd., 94044. Tel: 415-355-2593; Fax: 415-355-1832. Rev. Maurice M. McCormick, Chap., Gen. Secretariat.

REDWOOD CITY. *The Catholic Worker Community*, 545 Cassia St., 94063. Tel: 650-366-4415. Lawrence P. Purcell. A foster home for teenagers.

SAN RAFAEL. *Catholic Scouting*, 1 St. Vincent Dr., 94903. Tel: 415-507-2000; Fax: 415-491-0842. Rev. David A. Ghiorso.

**Center Interfaith Housing*, 164 N. San Pedro Rd., 94903; Fax: 415-453-8367.

Mission Holding Corporation, 1520 Grand Ave., 94901. Web site: sanrafaelop.org
Governing Board: Sr. Sharon Cross, O.P.; Sr. Patricia Simpson, O.P.; Sr. Anne Bertain, O.P.; Sr. Katherine Hamilton, O.P.; Sr. Abby Newton, O.P.

Third Order of St. Dominic Support and Charitable Trust Fund, 1520 Grand Ave., 94901. Tel: 415-453-8303; Fax: 415-453-8367.
Web site: sanrafaelop.org
Legal Title: *Third Order of St. Dominic, Congregation of the Most Holy Name, Support and Charitable Trust Fund.* Trust used for the religious and charitable needs of the Sisters of the Third Order of St. Dominic, Congregation of the Most Holy Name. Trustees: Sr. Patricia Boss, O.P.; Sr. Patricia Simpson, O.P.; Sr. Sharon Cross, O.P.; Sr. Pamela Chiesa, O.P.; Rev. Msgr. Richard Knapp; Dr. Dennis Burke; Mr. Thomas Bertelsen.

[V] CLOSED INSTITUTIONS

SAN FRANCISCO. *All Hallows Church.* For sacramental records please contact Our Lady of Lourdes, 1715 Oakdale Ave., San Francisco 94124. Tel: 415-285-3377; Fax: 415-285-2191.

Holy Cross Korean Church. For sacramental records please contact St. Michael, 32 Broad St., San Francisco, 94112. Tel: 415-333-1194; Fax: 415-333-1196.

Immaculate Conception Church. For sacramental records please contact St. Anthony of Padua, 3215 Cesar Chavez St., San Francisco, 94110. Tel: 415-647-2704; Fax: 415-647-7282.

Our Lady of Guadalupe Church. For sacramental records please contact SS. Peter and Paul, 666 Filbert St., San Francisco, 94133. Tel: 415-421-0809; Fax: 415-421-0217.

St. Brigid Church. For sacramental records please contact St. Vincent de Paul, 2320 Green St., San Francisco 94123. Tel: 415-992-1010; Fax: 415-922-7203.

St. Edward the Confessor Church. For sacramental records please contact Star of the Sea, 4420 Geary Blvd., San Francisco, 94118. Tel: 415-751-0450; Fax: 415-368-5651.

St. Francis of Assisi Church. For sacramental records please contact SS. Peter and Paul, 666 Filbert St., San Francisco, 94133. Tel: 415-421-0809; Fax: 415-421-0217.

St. Joseph Church. For sacramental records please contact St. Patrick, 756 Mission St., San Francisco, 94103. Tel: 415-421-0547; 415-512-9730.

SAN RAFAEL. *Blessed Sacrament Church.* For sacramental records please contact St. Isabella, One Trinity Way, San Rafael, 94901. Tel: 415-479-1560; Fax: 415-479-8303.

St. Sylvester Church. For sacramental records please contact St. Raphael, 1104 Fifth Ave., San Rafael, 94901. Tel: 415-453-2314; Fax: 415-453-5402.

WOODSIDE. *St. Marcella Mission.* For sacramental records please contact St. Denis, 2250 Avy Ave., Menlo Park, 94025. Tel: 650-854-5976; Fax: 650-854-3754.

RELIGIOUS INSTITUTES OF MEN REPRESENTED IN THE ARCHDIOCESE

For further details refer to the corresponding bracketed number in the Religious Institutes of Men or Women section.

[0200]—*Benedictine Monks.* (Hungary).—O.S.B.
[0330]—*Brothers of the Christian Schools.* (Prov. of San Francisco).—F.S.C.
[0470]—*The Capuchin Franciscans.* (Irish Prov.).—O.F.M.Cap.
[0520]—*Franciscan Friars.* (Santa Barbara Prov.).—O.F.M.
[0650]—*Holy Ghost Fathers.*—C.S.Sp.
[0690]—*Jesuit Fathers and Brothers.* (California Prov.).—S.J.
[0780]—*Marist Fathers.* (American Prov.).—S.M.
[0800]—*Maryknoll.*—M.M.
[0910]—*Oblates of Mary Immaculate.*—O.M.I.
[0430]—*Order of Preachers (Dominicans).* (Western Prov.).—O.P.
[0897]—*Paris Foreign Mission Society.*—M.E.P.
[1030]—*Paulist Fathers.*—C.S.P.
[1170]—*St. Patrick Missionary Society.*—S.P.S.
[1190]—*Salesian Don Bosco.*—S.D.B.
[1260]—*Society of Christ.* (Chicago Prov.).—S.Ch.
[0760]—*Society of Mary (Marianists).* (Prov. of the Pacific).—S.M.
[1200]—*Society of the Divine Savior.*—S.D.S.
[0420]—*Society of the Divine Word.* (Western Prov.).—S.V.D.
[1290]—*Society of the Priests of Saint Sulpice.* (American Prov.).—S.S.
[]—*Verbum Dei Community.*—V.D.C.

RELIGIOUS INSTITUTES OF WOMEN REPRESENTED IN THE ARCHDIOCESE

[]—*Announcers of the Lord.*—S.A.L.
[]—*Benedictine Sisters of Perpetual Adoration.*—O.S.B.
[]—*Bernardine Franciscan Sisters.*—O.S.F.
[]—*Congregation of Divine Providence.*
[1920]—*Congregation of the Sisters of the Holy Cross.* (Notre Dame, IN).—C.S.C.
[1940]—*Congregation of the Sisters of the Holy Faith.*—C.H.F.
[1710]—*Congregation of the Third Order of St. Francis of Mary Immaculate, Joliet, IL.*—O.S.F.
[0730]—*Daughters of Charity of Canossa.*—F.D.C.C.
[0760]—*Daughters of Charity of St. Vincent de Paul.* (Prov. of the West).—D.C.
[0880]—*Daughters of Mary and Joseph.*—D.M.J.
[0850]—*Daughters of Mary Help of Christians.*—F.M.A.
[0420]—*Discalced Carmelite Nuns.*—O.C.D.
[1050]—*Dominican Contemplative Nuns.*—O.P.
[1070-03]—*Dominican Sisters.*—O.P.
[1070-13]—*Dominican Sisters.*—O.P.
[1370]—*The Franciscan Missionaries of Mary.*—F.M.M.
[1390]—*Franciscan Missionaries Sisters of Our Lady of Sorrows.*—O.S.F.
[]—*Franciscan Missionaries, Our Lady of Peace.*—M.F.P.
[1415]—*Franciscan Sisters of Mary.*—F.S.M.
[]—*Las Hermanas Misioneras.*—M.S.C.Gpe.
[2340]—*Little Sisters of the Poor.*—L.S.P.
[2390]—*Lovers of the Holy Cross Sisters.*—L.H.C.
[]—*Maryknoll Missionary Sisters.*—M.M.
[2720]—*Mission Helpers of the Sacred Heart.*—M.H.S.H.
[2710]—*Missionary Sisters of Charity.*—M.C.
[]—*Missionary Sisters of the Sacred Side.*—M.C.S.
[3190]—*Nuns of the Perpetual Adoration of the Blessed Sacrament.*—A.P.
[]—*Oblates of Jesus the Priest.*—O.S.J.
[0950]—*Pious Society Daughters of St. Paul.*—F.S.P.
[3242]—*Poor Sisters of Nazareth.*—P.S.N.
[3465]—*Religious of the Sacred Heart of Mary.*—R.S.H.M.
[0440]—*Sisters of Charity of Cincinnati, Ohio.*—S.C.
[0430]—*Sisters of Charity of the Blessed Virgin Mary.*—B.V.M.
[]—*Sisters of Mercy (Galaway).* (Loughrea, Ireland).—S.M.
[2575]—*Sisters of Mercy of the Americas.* (Burlingame, CA).—R.S.M.
[2580]—*Sisters of Mercy of the United States of America.*—R.S.M.
[3000]—*Sisters of Notre Dame de Namur.* (Prov. of CA).—S.N.D.deN.
[3360]—*Sisters of Providence of Saint Mary-of-the-Woods, Indiana.*—S.P.
[4080]—*Sisters of Social Service of Los Angeles, Inc.*—S.S.S.
[1570]—*Sisters of St. Francis of Holy Family.*—O.S.F.
[1630]—*Sisters of St. Francis of Penance and Christian Charity.*—O.S.F.
[3840]—*Sisters of St. Joseph of Carondelet.* (Los Angeles Prov.).—C.S.J.
[3930-03]—*Sisters of St. Joseph of Orange.*—C.S.J.O.
[3890]—*Sisters of St. Joseph of Peace.*—C.S.J.P.
[1830]—*The Sisters of the Good Shepherd.*—R.G.S.
[1960]—*Sisters of the Holy Family.* (San Francisco, CA).—S.H.F.
[1990]—*Sisters of the Holy Names of Jesus and Mary.* (Provs. of CA; Oregon; Washington).—S.N.J.M.
[2130]—*Sisters of the Immaculate Conception.* (Prov. of Madrid).—R.C.M.
[3260]—*Sisters of the Precious Blood (Dayton, Ohio).*—C.PP.S.
[3320]—*Sisters of the Presentation of the B.V.M.*—P.B.V.M.
[1720]—*Sisters of the Third Order Regular of St. Francis of the Congregation of Our Lady of Lourdes.*—O.S.F.
[1890]—*Society of Helpers.*—H.H.S.
[]—*Society of Our Lady of the Way.*—S.O.L.W.
[4070]—*Society of the Sacred Heart.*—R.S.C.J.
[3330]—*Union Sisters of the Presentation of the Blessed Virgin Mary.*—P.B.V.M.
[4110]—*Ursuline Nuns (Roman Union).*—O.S.U.
[]—*Ursuline Sisters of the Immaculate Conception.* (Louisville,KY).—O.S.U.
[]—*Verbum Dei Community.* (Valencia, Spain).—V.D.C.
[4190]—*Visitation Nuns.*—V.H.M.

ARCHDIOCESAN CEMETERIES AND MAUSOLEUMS

SAN FRANCISCO. *Holy Cross Cemetery and Mausoleum.* Mailing Address: P.O. Box 577, Colma, 94014. Tel: 650-756-2060.

MENLO PARK. *Holy Cross.* Mailing Address: P.O. Box 577, Colma, 94014. Tel: 650-756-2060.

SAN RAFAEL. *Mount Olivet*, Box 4368, 94903. Tel: 415-479-9020.

NECROLOGY

✠ Scanlon, Most Rev. John J., (Retired). —Died Jan. 31, 1997.

† Fitzpatrick, Joseph, (Retired). —Died Dec. 1997.

† Gluszek, W. Adalbert, (Retired). —Died Feb. 22, 1997.

† Lee, Joseph, (Retired). —Died May 13, 1997.

† Uglesic, Leopold, (Retired). —Died Nov. 14, 1997.

Diocese of San Jose in California

(Dioecesis Sancti Josephi in California)

Most Reverend

PIERRE DUMAINE, D.D., PH.D.

First Bishop of San Jose; ordained June 15, 1957; appointed Auxiliary Bishop of San Francisco and Titular Bishop of Sarda April 28, 1978; Episcopal ordination June 29, 1978; appointed Bishop of San Jose January 27, 1981; installed as Bishop of San Jose March 18, 1981. *Office: Diocese of San Jose, 900 Lafayette St., Ste. 301, Santa Clara, CA, 95050-4966.*

Diocese of San Jose: 900 Lafayette St., Ste. 301, Santa Clara, CA, 95050-4966. Tel.: 408-983-0100; Fax: 408-983-0295.

Web site address: www.dsj.org

E-mail address: chancellor@dsj.org

ESTABLISHED JANUARY 27, 1981.

Square Miles 1,300.

Legal Title: The Roman Catholic Bishop of San Jose, a Corporation Sole.

The Diocese of San Jose comprises the County of Santa Clara in the State of California.

PATRONS OF THE DIOCESE OF SAN JOSE: St. Joseph, Husband of Mary, March 19; St. Clare of Assisi, August 11.

For legal titles of parishes and diocesan institutions, consult the Chancery Office.

STATISTICAL OVERVIEW

Personnel	
Bishop	1
Priests: Diocesan Active in Diocese	82
Priests: Active Outside Diocese	2
Priests: Retired, Sick or Absent	28
Number of Diocesan Priests	112
Religious Priests in Diocese	185
Extern Priests in Diocese	30
Ordinations:	
Diocesan Priests	1
Permanent Deacons in Diocese	8
Total Brothers	40
Total Sisters	407
Parishes	
Parishes	48
With Resident Pastor:	
Resident Diocesan Priests	40
Resident Religious Priests	7
Without Resident Pastor:	
Administered by Priests	1
Missions	4
Pastoral Centers	1
New Parishes Created	3
Professional Ministry Personnel:	
Brothers	4
Sisters	30
Lay Ministers	154
Welfare	
Catholic Hospitals	3
Total Assisted	273,515
Health Care Centers	1
Total Assisted	85
Homes for the Aged	1
Total Assisted	47
Day Care and Extended Day Care Centers	1
Total Assisted	250
Special Centers for Social Services	47
Total Assisted	140,953
Residential Care of Disabled	1
Total Assisted	4
Other Institutions	2
Total Assisted	185
Educational	
Diocesan Students in Other Seminaries	17
Total Seminarians	17
Colleges and Universities	1
Total Students	7,863
High Schools, Diocesan and Parish	2
Total Students	1,742
High Schools, Private	4
Total Students	3,996
Elementary Schools, Diocesan and Parish	30
Total Students	10,710
Elementary Schools, Private	1
Total Students	152
Catechesis/Religious Education:	
High School Students	2,391
Elementary Students	14,636
Total Students Under Catholic Instruction	41,507
Teachers in the Diocese:	
Priests	53
Scholastics	9
Brothers	5
Sisters	50
Lay Teachers	1,173
Vital Statistics	
Receptions into the Church:	
Infant Baptism Totals	9,208
Adult Baptism Totals	586
Received into Full Communion	410
First Communions	5,654
Confirmations	2,582
Marriages:	
Catholic	1,452
Interfaith	408
Total Marriages	1,860
Deaths	1,918
Total Catholic Population	398,901
Total Population	1,599,604

Diocese of San Jose—900 Lafayette St., Ste. 301, Santa Clara, 95050-4966. Tel: 408-983-0100; Fax: 408-983-0295.

Vicar General—Rev. MICHAEL J. MITCHELL, V.G., Moderator, *Diocese of San Jose, 900 Lafayette St., Ste. 301, Santa Clara, 95050-4966.* Tel: 408-983-0240.

Episcopal Vicars—

Vicar for Canonical Affairs—Rev. MAURICE F. SHEA, S.T.L., J.C.D., *Diocese of San Jose, 900 Lafayette St., Ste. 301, Santa Clara, 95050-4966.* Tel: 408-983-0219.

Vicar for Clergy—Rev. RICHARD GARCIA, *Diocese of San Jose, 900 Lafayette St., Ste. 301, Santa Clara, 95050-4966.* Tel: 408-983-0149.

Vicar for Parish—Rev. PHILIP MCCRILLIS. Tel: 408-983-0129.

Vicar for Pastoral Ministry—Sr. PATRICIA MARIA MULPETERS. Tel: 408-983-0120.

Vicar for Religious—Rev. DAVID H. SCHUYLER, S.M., S.T.L., J.C.D., *Diocese of San Jose, 900 Lafayette St., Ste. 301, Santa Clara, 95050-4966.* Tel: 408-983-0219.

Chancellor—LINDA BEARIE, *Diocese of San Jose, 900 Lafayette St., Ste. 301, Santa Clara, 95050-4966.* Tel: 408-983-0160.

Diocesan Tribunal—Diocese of San Jose, 900 Lafayette St., Ste. 301, Santa Clara, 95050-4966. Tel: 408-983-0219.

Judicial Vicar—Rev. DAVID H. SCHUYLER, S.M., S.T.L., J.C.D.

Adjutant—Rev. MAURICE F. SHEA, S.T.L., J.C.D.

Judges—Revs. DAVID H. SCHUYLER, S.M., S.T.L., J.C.D.; MAURICE F. SHEA, S.T.L., J.C.D.; HEIN MINH NGUYEN, J.C.D.

Defender of the Bond—Rev. FRANCIS V. CILIA.

Advocates—Sr. M. JUDE RISTEY, P.B.V.M. Tel: 408-983-0221. NANCY STEVENS, J.C.L. Tel: 408-983-0223. Sr. ANN MARGUERITE SOUZA, C.S.J., J.C.L. Tel: 408-983-0224.

Notary and Secretary to the Tribunal—Mrs. BELVA M. DICAROLIS. Tel: 408-983-0219.

Bishop's Executive Committee—Most Rev. PIERRE DUMAINE, D.D, Ph.D.; Revs. MICHAEL J. MITCHELL, V.G.; PHILIP MCCRILLIS; RICHARD GARCIA; Sr. PATRICIA MARIE MULPETERS, P.B.V.M.; Sr. MARY CLAUDE POWER, P.B.V.M.; LINDA BEARIE.

Diocesan Consultors—Revs. LUDWIG ANDRE; J. PATRICK BROWNE; BERNARD K. FREYNE; JOSEPH J. MILANI; MICHAEL J. MITCHELL, V.G.; FRANCIS CILIA; ALEXANDER LARKIN; TERRENCE J. SULLIVAN.

Council of Priests—Most Rev. PIERRE DUMAINE, D.D., Ph.D.; Revs. RICHARD GARCIA, Liaison; MICHAEL J. MITCHELL, V.G.; HIEN NGUYEN; J. PATRICK BROWNE; BARRY FREYNE; NORMAN SEGOVIA; JOHN SANDERSFELD; MATTHEW STANLEY; PHILIP MCCRILLIS; JOSEPH MILANI; LUDWIG ANDRE; MICHAEL O'CONNOR; ROBERT LEGER; FRANCIS CILIA; WARWICK JAMES; PETER LUC PHAN; ANGEL MARIANO, S.J.; ANTONIO DE ANGELIS, C.S.; CHARLES MACEDO; TERRENCE SULLIVAN, Chm. JEFFREY LABELLE, S.J.; MATEO SHEEDY.

Council of Religious—Revs. ALBERT BUNSIC, O.C.D.; DAVID H. SCHUYLER, S.M., S.T.L., J.C.D., Liaison; PETER FILICE, S.J.; Bro. RALPH KUDER, C.S.C.; Sr. AILEEN DONOHUE, S.N.D.; Sr. PAULE FREEBURG, D.C.; Sr. MARY PETER MCCUSKER, R.S.M.; Sr. MARGARET MCGRAW, C.S.J.; Sr. BARBARA NIXON, S.N.J.M.; Sr. GISELA ENRIQUEZ, M.E.s.s.T., *Diocese of San Jose, 900 Lafayette St., Ste. 301, Santa Clara, 95050-4966.* Tel: 408-983-0161.

Deans—Rev. JEFFREY LABELLE, S.J., Northern Deanery; Rev. TERRENCE J. SULLIVAN, Northwestern Deanery; Rev. WARWICK JAMES, Northeastern Deanery; Rev. FRANCIS CILIA, Southwestern Deanery; Rev. J. PATRICK BROWNE, Central Deanery; Rev. TERRENCE SULLIVAN, Southeastern Deanery.

Apostleship of Prayer—Rev. JOHN J. SWEENY, *2800 Mission College Rd., Santa Clara, 95051.*

Archives—Mr. TONY MCGILTON, Records Management, *Diocese of San Jose, 1068 The Alameda Suite 4, San Jose, 95126.* Tel: 408-292-7128.

Building Committee—Mr. ROBERT E. SUMMERS; Revs. FRANCIS V. CILIA; MARK CATALANA; DANIEL DERRY; ROBERT GRAY; MICHAEL J. MITCHELL, V.G.; THOMAS F. MURRAY; STEPHEN E. PERATA; Mr. CHARLES F. BUCKLEY, Consultant.

Canonical Affairs—Rev. MAURICE F. SHEA, S.T.L., J.C.D., *Diocese of San Jose, 900 Lafayette St., Ste. 301, Santa Clara, 95050-4966.* Tel: 408-983-0219.

Charismatic Communities—Revs. ANTHONY PEREIRA, S.D.B.; ANGEL MARIANO, S.J.; Deacon JOSE ALVAREZ, *Charismatic Renewal Center, 3000 El Camino Real, Santa Clara, 95051.* Tel: 408-378-4646.

Catholic Charities—Catholic Charities of Santa Clara County. MICHAEL CUMMINS, Acting Interim CEO, *2625 Zanker Rd., Ste. 200, San Jose, 95134.* Tel: 408-468-0100; Fax: 408-944-0275.

Management Information System—TOM ACKERSON, Mgr., *900 Lafayette St., Ste. 301, Santa Clara, 95050-4966.* Tel: 408-983-0163.

Cursillo Movement—Rev. ROBERT LEGER, Chap., *St. Frances Cabrini, 15333 Woodard Rd., San Jose, 95124.* Tel: 408-377-3090.

Permanent Diaconate—Rev. RICHARD GARCIA, Dir., *Diocese of San Jose, 900 Lafayette St., Ste. 301, Santa Clara, 95050-4966.* Tel: 408-983-0149.

Education Department—Sr. MARY CLAUDE POWER, P.B.V.M., Supt. of Schools. Asst. Supt. of Schools: Mr. JIM BRENNAN; MARIAN STUCKEY, *Diocese of San Jose, 900 Lafayette St., Ste. 301, Santa Clara, 95050-4966.* Tel: 408-983-0185.

Continuing Education & Ministry to Priests Committee—*Diocese of San Jose, 900 Lafayette St., Ste. 301, Santa Clara, 95050-4966.* Revs. TIMOTHY KIDNEY, Chm. GEORGE MANCHA; DAVID MERCER; JOSEPH DELGADO; RICK RODONI; ROBERT HAYES; KEVIN JOYCE; HIEN NGUYEN.

Diocesan Development Office—VALLYN TURNER, Dir., *Diocese of San Jose, 900 Lafayette St., Ste. 301, Santa Clara, 95050-4966.* Tel: 408-983-0245.

Evangelization Committee—Rev. PHILIP MCCRILLIS, Chm., *Diocese of San Jose, 900 Lafayette St., Ste. 301, Santa Clara, 95050-4966.*

Finance Office—Rev. MICHAEL J. MITCHELL, V.G., Dir.; Mr. CHARLES TULLY, Controller/Deputy Dir.

Finance Council—Bishop PIERRE DUMAINE; Rev. MICHAEL J. MITCHELL, V.G.; Mr. ROBERT MCADAMS; Mr. MATTHEW O'ROURKE; Mr. EUGENE TOOMEY; DONALD WAITE; Mr. ROBERT E. SUMMERS.

Health Affairs—Sr. PATRICIA MARIE MULPETERS, P.B.V.M., Liaison.

Human Concern Commission—Rev. TIMOTHY KIDNEY, Pres. Tel: 408-983-0137. *Diocese of San Jose, 900 Lafayette St., Ste. 301, Santa Clara, 95050-4966.* Tel: 408-983-0121.

Italian Catholic Federation—Rev. GEORGE ARANHA, Chap., *200 O'Connor Dr., San Jose, 95128.* Tel: 408-294-8953.

Knights of Columbus—ANTHONY J. PERRELLA, Pres., *931 Brookgrove Ln., Cupertino, 95014.* Tel: 408-255-5399.

Legion of Mary—Rev. JOHN J. SWEENY, *Our Lady of Peace, 2800 Mission College Blvd., Santa Clara, 95051.* Tel: 408-988-4585.

Vicar of Pastoral Ministry—Sr. PATRICIA MARIE MULPETERS, Ministry Institute; ANNE GRYCZ, Assoc. Dir. Scripture & Liturgy; THERESA MAES, Assoc. Dir. Family Life & Pastoral Care; JEANNINE LEICHNER, Assoc. Dir. Catechetical Ministry; CHARMAINE WARMENHOVEN, Assoc. Dir. Special Pastoral Ministries; VINCENT NIMS, Assoc. Dir. Youth & Young Adult Ministry; TERRIE IACINO, Assoc. Dir. Sec. Human Concerns; ROBERT DELANEY, Assoc. Dir. Hispanic Ministry.

Diocesan Clergy Personnel—Most Rev. PIERRE DUMAINE, Ex Officio; Revs. FRANCIS CILID, Chm. RICHARD GARCIA; MARK CATALANA; BERNARD FREYNE; PHILIP MCCRILLIS; EUGENE O'DONNELL.

Pastoral Care Advisory Committee—Liaisons: THERESA MAES; CHARMAINE WARMENHOVEN, *Diocese of San Jose, 900 Lafayette St., Ste. 301, Santa Clara, 95050-4966.* Tel: 408-983-0126.

Pastoral Resource Committee for Ministry to the Homosexual—Sr. PATRICIA MARIE MULPETERS, P.B.V.M., Chm., *Diocese of San Jose, 900 Lafayette St., Ste. 301, Santa Clara, 95050-4966.* Tel: 408-983-0160.

Advisory Committee for Ministry with the Deaf and Persons with Disabilities—CHARMAINE WARMENHOVEN, Liaison, *Diocese of San Jose, 900 Lafayette St., Ste. 301, Santa Clara, 95050-4966.* Tel: 408-983-0141 (Voice); 408-983-0292 (TDD).

Personnel Office—LINDA BEARIE, Dir. MARY ANN ARNOLD, Asst. Dir., *Diocese of San Jose, 900 Lafayette St., Ste. 301, Santa Clara, 95050-4966.* Tel: 408-983-0149.

Propagation of the Faith-Holy Childhood Association-Catholic Relief Service—MARGARET COAKER, Dir. Tel: 408-983-0166., *Diocese of San Jose, 900 Lafayette St., Ste. 301, Santa Clara, 95050-4966.* Tel: 408-983-0166.

Research and Planning—Sr. PATRICIA MARIE MULPETERS, P.B.V.M., Liaison, *Diocese of San Jose, 900 Lafayette St., Ste. 301, Santa Clara, 95050-4966.* Tel: 408-983-0160.

Respect Life Program—TERRIE IACINO, Assoc. Dir., *Diocese of San Jose, 900 Lafayette St., Ste. 301, Santa Clara, 95050-4966.* Tel: 408-983-0137.

Clergy Retirement Board—Revs. ARTHUR HARRISON, Chm. MICHAEL J. MITCHELL, V.G.; RICHARD GARCIA; BERNARD FREYNE; THOMAS AHERN; ROBERT KIEFER; CHARLES MACEDO; Mr. GEORGE DELUCCHI; Prof. JOHN WHALEN.

Catholic Telemedia Network—SHIRLEY CONNOLLY, Gen. Mgr., *324 Middlefield Rd., Menlo Park, 94025.* Tel: 415-326-7850; Fax: 415-326-4605.

Vocation Office—Rev. STEVEN BROWN, Dir., *Diocese of San Jose, 900 Lafayette St., Ste. 301, Santa Clara, 95050-4966.* Tel: 408-983-0149.

Women in the Church Office—Sr. PATRICIA MARIE MULPETERS, P.B.V.M.; EHMIE SHICK, Sec., *Diocese of San Jose, 900 Lafayette St., Ste. 301, Santa Clara, 95050-4966.* Tel: 408-983-0160.

Liturgical Commission—ANNE E. GRYCZ, Liaison; Sr. FRANCIS ALLEN; Sr. PATRICIA DAVIS, P.B.V.M.; Rev. JOSEPH DELGADO; TONY EIRAS; Sr. BETTE GAMBONINI, B.V.M.; BLESSIE LASCOLA; ELIZABETH LILLY, Chm.; Sr. SHARON MCMILLAN, S.N.D.; RAUL MENDOZA; BARBARA MOUNT; BERNIE NOJADERA; JAY SOMERA; Rev. MATTHEW STANLEY; JUDY SWAZEY.

"The Valley Catholic" (Diocesan Newspaper)—ROBERTA WARD, Editor; JOHN GALARHEAU, Business Mgr., *Diocese of San Jose, 900 Lafayette St., Ste. 301, Santa Clara, 95050-4966.* Tel: 408-983-0260.

Consultation Processes: Diocesan and Parish—Rev. PHILIP MCCRILLIS, *Diocese of San Jose, 900 Lafayette, Ste. 301, Santa Clara, 95050-4966.* Tel: 408-983-0160.

Ecumenical and Interreligious Affairs—Rev. JOSE RUBIO, Dir., *Diocese of San Jose, 900 Lafayette St., Ste. 301, Santa Clara, 95050-4966.* Tel: 408-983-0161.

CLERGY, PARISHES, MISSIONS AND PAROCHIAL SCHOOLS

CITY OF SAN JOSE

1—CATHEDRAL BASILICA OF ST. JOSEPH (1849), Revs. J. Patrick Browne; Abel Lopez. In res., Revs. Fausto Lopez; Rick Rodoni; Jon Pedigo.
Res. and Church—80 S. Market St., 95113. Tel: 408-283-8100; Fax: 408-283-8110.
Catechesis/Religious Programs—Susan Olsen, D.R.E.
Students 253.

2—ST. PATRICK PROTO-CATHEDRAL (1871), Revs. Timothy Kidney; Walter Mallo.
Res., 389 E. Santa Clara St., 95113. Tel: 408-294-8120; Fax: 408-291-6277.
School—51 N. 9th St., 95112. Tel: 408-283-5858; Fax: 408-291-6277. John Bracco, Prin.
Lay Teachers 10; Students 332.
Catechesis/Religious Programs—Tel: 408-291-6279; Fax: 408-291-6277. Irma Rangel, D.R.E.
Students 213.

3—ST. FRANCIS OF ASSISI (1997), Rev. John Sandersfeld.
Res., 4100 San Felipe Rd., 95135. Tel: 408-223-1562; Fax: 408-223-1759.
Catechesis/Religious Programs—Vito Perrone, D.R.E.
Students 170.

4—CHRIST THE KING (1997), Revs. Norman Segovia; Lieu Vu.
Res., 5278 B Monterey Rd., 95111. Tel: 408-362-9958; Fax: 408-362-9695.
Catechesis/Religious Programs—Students 60.

5—FIVE WOUNDS PORTUGUESE NATIONAL CHURCH (1914) (Portuguese), Rev. Leonel C. Noia. In res., Revs. Jack La Rocca; Robert Gray.
Res., 1375 E. Santa Clara St., 95116. Tel: 408-292-2123; Fax: 408-292-0201.
School—1390 Five Wounds Ln., 95116. Tel: 408-293-0425; Fax: 408-971-7607. Gary Meegan, Prin.
Priests 1; Sisters 2; Lay Teachers 12; Students 279.
Catechesis/Religious Programs—Joanne Dobrzynski, D.R.E.
Students 626.

6—ST. FRANCES CABRINI (1955), Revs. G. Robert Leger; Robert Kiefer; Patrick Kilcoyne. In res., Rev. Don Flickinger (FRS).
Res., 15333 Woodard Rd., 95124. Tel: 408-879-1120; Fax: 408-377-3587.
School—15325 Woodard Rd., 95124. Tel: 408-377-6545; Fax: 408-377-8491. Yvonne Gomez, Prin.
Sisters 1; Lay Teachers 31; Students 674.
Catechesis/Religious Programs—Barbara Ross, D.R.E.
Students 252.

7—HOLY CROSS (1911) (Italian), Revs. Antonio DeAngelis, C.S.; Jesus Olivares, C.S.
Res., 580 E. Jackson St., 95112. Tel: 408-294-2440; Fax: 408-294-8609.
Catechesis/Religious Programs—Bro. Charles Muscat, C.S., D.R.E.
Students 500.

8—HOLY FAMILY (1905), Revs. Francis V. Cilia; Gregory Kimm; Anthony Mancuso; Sr. Bette Gamboni, Pastoral Assoc.
Res., 4848 Pearl Ave., 95136. Tel: 408-265-4040; Fax: 408-978-9979.
School—4850 Pearl Ave., Tel: 408-978-1355; Fax: 408-978-0290. Kay Ingalls, Prin.
Lay Teachers 21; Students 655.
Catechesis/Religious Programs—Tel: 408-265-6201. Virginia Silvers, D.R.E.
Students 480.

9—HOLY SPIRIT (1963), Rev. Paul P. Weisbeck.
Res., 1200 Redmond Ave., 95120. Tel: 408-997-5101; Fax: 408-997-5102.
Catechesis/Religious Programs—Tel: 408-997-5115. Joy Hill, D.R.E.
Students 222.

10—ST. ANTHONY (1982), Rev. George Mancha. In res., Rev. Anthony Mancuso.
Mailing Address: 20101 McKean Rd., 95120. Tel: 408-997-4800; Fax: 408-997-4801.
Catechesis/Religious Programs—Joann Maier, D.R.E.
Students 188.

11—ST. CHRISTOPHER (1951), Revs. James Walsh; Christopher Bennett.
Office: 2278 Booksin Ave., 95125. Tel: 408-269-2226; Fax: 408-269-2784.
School—Tel: 408-723-7223; Fax: 408-978-5458. Arlene Ernst, Prin.
Sisters of the Presentation 2; Lay Teachers 34; Students 626.
Catechesis/Religious Programs—Tel: 408-264-8764; Fax: 408-978-5458. Sr. Felicia Gross, O.S.F., D.R.E.
Students 285.

12—ST. JOHN VIANNEY (1952), Revs. Lawrence Hendel; Joseph Delgado; Deacon Joseph Alvarez.
Res., 4609 Alum Rock Ave., 95127. Tel: 408-258-7832; Fax: 408-258-6152.
School—4601 Hyland Ave., 95127. Tel: 408-258-7677; Fax: 408-258-5997. Sr. Michele Anne Murphy, P.B.V.M., Prin.
Sisters of the Presentation B.V.M. 3; Lay Teachers 22; Students 624.
Catechesis/Religious Programs—Tel: 408-251-0657; Fax: 408-272-1045. Lily Tenes, D.R.E.
Students 648.

13—ST. JULIE (1974), Rev. Richard C. Fry; Rev. Msgr. Jose V. Suarez (Philippines). In res., Rev. John Balleza.
Res., 366 St. Julie Dr., 95119. Tel: 408-629-3030; Fax: 408-629-3343.
Catechesis/Religious Programs—Tel: 408-226-3595. Jeanine Jensen, D.R.E.
Students 163.

14—ST. LEO THE GREAT (1923), Rev. Francisco Rios, I.V.E. In res., Revs. Maurice F. Shea; Matthew Koo.
Res., 88 Race St., 95126. Tel: 408-293-3503; Fax: 408-293-3516.
School—Tel: 408-293-4846; Fax: 408-293-5855. Phyllis Taurosa, Prin.
Lay Teachers 10; Students 298.
Catechesis/Religious Programs—Tel: 408-293-1662. Gayle Morrissette, D.R.E.
Students 198.

15—ST. MARIA GORETTI (1961), Revs. Kevin Joyce; Arthur Yabes, S.V.D.; Gerardo Menchaca.
Res., 2980 Senter Rd., 95111. Tel: 408-363-2300; Fax: 408-363-2305.
Catechesis/Religious Programs—Tel: 408-363-2310. Jeanne Gaffney, D.R.E.
Students 604.

16—ST. MARTIN OF TOURS (1914), Revs. David Mercer; William Pegnan, O.F.M.Cap. In res., Revs. Patrick Ryan; John Legerski.
Res., 200 O'Connor Dr., 95128. Tel: 408-294-8953; Fax: 408-294-2624.

School—300 O'Connor Dr., 95128. Tel: 408-287-3630; Fax: 408-287-4313. Kevin Eagelson, Prin.
Lay Teachers 33; Students 362.
Catechesis/Religious Programs—Arlene Golden, D.R.E.
Students 148.

17—MOST HOLY TRINITY (1961) (Hispanic-Filipino), Revs. Jeffrey LaBelle, S.J.; Angel Mariano, S.J.; Deacons Salvador Alvarez; Vincente Perez.
Res., 2040 Nassau Dr., 95122. Tel: 408-729-0101; Fax: 408-258-4131.
School—Aurora Quevedo, Prin. Sisters 3; Lay Teachers 10; Students 308.
Catechesis/Religious Programs—Clara R. Morales, D.R.E.
Students 375.

18—OUR LADY OF GUADALUPE (1962) (Hispanic), Revs. Damian Gamboa, O.F.M.; Javier Alvarez, O.F.M.; Pedro Vasquez, O.F.M.
Office: 2020 E. San Antonio St., 95116. Tel: 408-258-7057; Fax: 408-258-8249.
Catechesis/Religious Programs—Tel: 408-258-0544. Connie Torres, D.R.E.
Students 723.

19—ST. THOMAS OF CANTERBURY (1967), Rev. Walter M. McMahon.
Res., 1522 McCoy Ave., 95130. Tel: 408-378-1595; Fax: 408-378-1215.
Catechesis/Religious Programs—Students 93.

20—QUEEN OF APOSTLES (1960), Revs. James J. Mifsud, S.M.; Robert Hughes, S.M. In res., Bros. William McCall, S.M.; T. William Bolts, S.M.
Res., 4911 Moorpark Ave., 95129. Tel: 408-253-7560; Fax: 408-253-9530.
School—Tel: 408-252-3659. Marianna Willis, Prin.
Lay Teachers 13; Students 310.
Catechesis/Religious Programs—Patricia Sarria, D.R.E.
Students 370.

21—OUR LADY QUEEN OF MARTYRS, VIETNAMESE MISSION (1985) (Vietnamese), Revs. Dominic Do van Dinh, Admin.; Peter Chinh Pham; Joseph N. Vanthu; Vincent Kien Nguyen.
Office: 389 E. Santa Clara St., 95113. Tel: 408-291-6280; Fax: 408-291-6289.
Catechesis/Religious Programs—Tel: 408-291-6282. Bro. Fortunat Tran Trong An Phong, F.S.C., D.R.E.
Students 1,520.

22—SACRED HEART OF JESUS (1920), Revs. Mateo E. Sheedy; Robert S. Brocato. In res., Rev. Jose Rubio.
Res., 325 Willow St., 95110. Tel: 408-292-0146; Fax: 408-292-0172.
Catechesis/Religious Programs—Tel: 408-292-0146. Maria Guadalupe Vital, D.R.E.
Students 300.

23—SANTA TERESA (1967), Rev. Raymond G. Kenny.
Res., 794 Calero Ave., 95123. Tel: 408-629-7777; Fax: 408-629-5260.
Catechesis/Religious Programs—Tel: 408-227-5915; Fax: 408-629-5260. Sandy Mory, D.R.E.
Students 190.

24—CHURCH OF THE TRANSFIGURATION (1965), Rev. George Aranha.
Mailing Address: 4325 Jarvis Ave., 95118. Tel: 408-264-3600; Fax: 408-266-2745.
Catechesis/Religious Programs—Tel: 408-266-2745. Paula Ramos, D.R.E.
Students 92.

25—ST. VICTOR (1961), Revs. Stephen F. Perata; Robert R. Taheny, S.J.; Candido O. Lim, S.J. (Philippines).
Res., 3108 Sierra Rd., 95132. Tel: 408-251-7055; Fax: 408-251-5528.
School—Tel: 408-251-1740; Fax: 408-251-1492. Sr. Sharon Breden, C.S.J., Prin.
Sisters of St. Joseph of Carondelet 2; Lay Teachers 11; Students 317.
Catechesis/Religious Programs—Tel: 408-251-0154; Fax: 408-251-5528. Angela Giampaoli, D.R.E.
Students 493.

26—ST. MARY OF THE ASSUMPTION (1975). (Croatian Mission). Rev. Dujo Boban, O.F.M. In res., Rev. Joseph Mikulich, O.F.M.
Res., 901 Lincoln Ave., 95126. Tel: 408-279-0279; Fax: 408-292-5868.
Catechesis/Religious Programs—Students 35.
Croatian Franciscan Fathers Corporation—Tel: 408-279-0279; Fax: 408-292-5868.
Franciscan Fathers—Tel: 408-276-0279; Fax: 408-292-5868.

OUTSIDE THE CITY OF SAN JOSE

Alviso, Santa Clara Co., Our Lady, Star of the Sea (1985) (Mexican-American), Rev. Steven P. Brown; Deacon James Nunez, Admin.
Mailing Address: P.O. Box 426, 95002.
Res., 1385 Michigan Ave., 95002. Tel: 408-263-2121; Fax: 408-263-1182.
Catechesis/Religious Programs—Tel: 408-263-6637; Fax: 408-263-1182. Sr. Josefina Mantalro, R.S.C.J., D.R.E.
Students 622.

Campbell, Santa Clara Co., St. Lucy (1947), Revs. Terrence J. Sullivan; Joseph M. Benedict. In res., Rev. Robert Passalacqua.
Res., 2350 Winchester Blvd., 95008. Tel: 408-378-2464; Fax: 408-378-5548.
School—76 Kennedy Ave., 95008. Tel: 408-378-7454; Fax: 408-378-4945. Sr. Jolene Schmitz, C.H.S., Prin.
Sisters 3; Lay Teachers 15; Students 319.
Catechesis/Religious Programs—Tel: 408-379-5900; Fax: 408-378-5548. Sr. Fidelma Heeran, R.S.M., D.R.E.
Students 309.

Cupertino, Santa Clara Co., St. Joseph of Cupertino (1913), Revs. Robert Hayes; Mark Catalana; Peter Luc Phan; Deacon Don McLaughlin. In res., Revs. Michael J. Mitchell; Joseph J. Milani.
Res., 10110 N. DeAnza Blvd., 95014. Tel: 408-252-7653; Fax: 408-252-5263.
School—10120 N. DeAnza Blvd., 95014. Tel: 408-252-6441. Mary Lyons, Prin.
Lay Teachers 13; Students 318.
Catechesis/Religious Programs—Tel: 408-253-0660. Donna Brock, D.R.E.
Students 358.

Gilroy, Santa Clara Co., St. Mary (1865), Revs. Daniel Derry; Jeronimo Guitierrez (Mexico). In res., Rev. John Coleman.
Res., 11 First St., 95020. Tel: 408-847-5151; Fax: 408-847-4851. [CEM]
School—7900 Church St., 95020-4499. Tel: 408-842-2827; Fax: 408-847-7679. Christa Hanson, Prin.
Religious 1; Lay Teachers 14; Students 314.
Catechesis/Religious Programs—7950 Church St., 95020. Tel: 408-847-2652; Fax: 408-847-4851. D.R.E.: Carrie Rauch; Hilda Porcella.
Students 1211.

Los Altos, Santa Clara Co., St. Nicholas (1947), Rev. Gary R. Thomas.
Res., 473 Lincoln Ave., 94022. Tel: 650-948-2158; Fax: 408-948-8566.
School—12816 S. El Monte Ave., Los Altos Hills, 94022. Tel: 650-941-4056; Fax: 650-941-3842. Sr. Barbara Nixon, S.N.J.M., Prin.
Sisters of Mercy 1; Lay Teachers 9; Students 286.
Catechesis/Religious Programs—Tel: 650-941-7622. Jan Cicoletti, D.R.E.
Students 200.
Station—Seven Oaks, Residential Park for the Aged, 1174 Los Altos Ave., 94022. Tel: 650-948-7337.

St. Simon (1955), Revs. Ludwig M. Andre; Alexander Affonso. In res., Revs. Thomas Murray; Randy Benas.
Res., 1860 Grant Rd., 94024. Tel: 650-967-8311; Fax: 650-967-8876.
School—1840 Grant Rd., 94024. Tel: 650-968-9952. Sr. Mary Glackin, I.H.M., Prin.
Sisters, Servants of the Immaculate Heart of Mary (Immaculata, PA) 2; Lay Teachers 23; Students 611.
Catechesis/Religious Programs—Tel: 650-961-5469. Sr. Pauline Komrska, C.S.J., D.R.E.
Students 130.

St. William (1959), Rev. Michael J. Burns.
Res., 611 S. El Monte Ave., 94022-4058. Tel: 650-948-8169; Fax: 650-948-8508.
Catechesis/Religious Programs—Tel: 650-941-1460; Fax: 650-948-8508. Ann Piazzon, D.R.E.
Students 109.

Los Gatos, Santa Clara Co., St. Mary of the Immaculate Conception (1912), Revs. Justin Zawadzki; Anthony Pereira.
Res., 219 Bean Ave., 95030. Tel: 408-354-3726; Fax: 408-354-9302.
School—30 Lyndon Ave., 95030. Tel: 408-954-3944; Fax: 408-395-9151. Sr. Nicki Thomas, S.N.J.M., Prin.
Sisters of the Holy Names of Jesus and Mary 3; Lay Teachers 20; Students 282.
Catechesis/Religious Programs—Tel: 408-354-4061; Fax: 408-354-9302. Terrie Trotter, D.R.E.
Students 420.

Milpitas, Santa Clara Co., St. Elizabeth (1968), Rev. Edward Samy. In res., Rev. Hien Minh Nguyen.
Res., 750 Sequoia Dr., 95035. Tel: 408-262-8100; Fax: 408-946-8703.
Catechesis/Religious Programs—Tel: 408-263-1995. Laura Riffle, D.R.E.
Students 313.

St. John the Baptist (1877), Revs. Charles F. Dougherty; Hao Dinh.
Res., 279 S. Main St., 95035. Tel: 408-262-2546; Fax: 408-263-2564.
School—360 S. Abel St., 95035. Tel: 408-262-8110; Fax: 408-262-0814. Judy Perkowski, Prin.
Augustinian Recollect Sisters 2; Lay Teachers 11; Students 340.
Catechesis/Religious Programs—Tel: 408-262-3955; Fax: 408-262-3955. Linda Jo White, D.R.E.
Students 300.

Morgan Hill, Santa Clara Co., St. Catherine of Alexandria (1909), Revs. Eugene P. O'Donnell; Enrico A. Hernadez.
Res., 17400 Peak Ave., 95037. Tel: 408-779-3959; Fax: 408-779-0289.
School—Tel: 408-779-9950. Sr. Ann Therese Lynch, P.B.V.M., Prin.; Jeanne Smith, Vice Prin.
Lay Teachers 16; Students 306.
Catechesis/Religious Programs—Tel: 408-779-9604. Mrs. Wendy Scherbart, D.R.E.
Students 940.

Mountain View, Santa Clara Co., St. Athanasius (1959), Revs. Diarmuid Casey, C.S.Sp. (Ireland); Kevin B. Corrigan, C.S.Sp. (Ireland). In res., Rev. Desmond McGlade, C.S.Sp. (Ireland).
Res., 160 N. Rengstorff Ave., 94043. Tel: 650-961-8600; Fax: 650-968-5633.
Catechesis/Religious Programs—Tel: 650-967-7900; Fax: 650-968-5633. Margery Ryan, D.R.E.
Students 296.

St. Joseph the Worker (1901), Revs. Oscar D. Tabujara; Robert B. Moran.
Res., 582 Hope St., 94041. Tel: 415-967-3831; Fax: 415-691-1522.
School—1120 Miramonte Ave., 94041. Tel: 415-967-1839; Fax: 415-691-1530. Leonor Bolle, Prin.
Lay Teachers 13; Students 288.
Catechesis/Religious Programs—Sr. Elizabeth Daly, O.P., D.R.E.
Students 110.

Palo Alto, Santa Clara Co.,

1—ST. THOMAS AQUINAS, (1901), Revs. Barry Freyne; Matthew Stanley; Charles Macedo; Daniel Kiriti.
Office: 3290 Middlefield Rd., 94306. Tel: 650-494-2496; Fax: 650-494-3780.
School—St. Elizabeth Seton Catholic Community School, 1095 Channing Ave., 94306. Tel: 650-326-9004; Fax: 650-326-2949. Joan Casey, Prin.
Priests 1; Sisters 2; Lay Teachers 12; Students 252.
Catechesis/Religious Programs—Tel: 650-494-3097. Mary Ann Sztaba, D.R.E.
Students 302.

2—ST. ALBERT THE GREAT, (1961). Merged with St. Thomas Aquinas Parish.

3—ST. ANN CHAPEL, (1951). Merged with St. Thomas Aquinas Parish.

4—OUR LADY OF THE ROSARY, (1959). Merged with St. Thomas Aquinas Parish.

Santa Clara, Santa Clara Co.,

1—CHINESE CATHOLIC COMMUNITY, Rev. Matthew Koo.
Res., 900 Layfayette St., Ste. 301, 95050-4966. Tel: 408-983-0211; Fax: 408-983-0212.

2—ST. CLARE, (1777), Revs. John M. Martin, S.J.; Gerald J. Phelan, S.J.; Paul Devot, S.J.; Gregg Servis, S.J. In res., Rev. Thomas H. Smolich, S.J.
Mailing Address: 725 Washington St., 95050-4935. Tel: 408-248-7786; Fax: 408-248-8150.
School—Tel: 408-246-6797. Sr. Virginia Crilly, B.V.M., Prin.
Sisters 4; Lay Teachers 10; Students 200.
Catechesis/Religious Programs—Tel: 408-241-0252. Mrs. Diane Madruga, D.R.E.
Lay Teachers 12; Aides 16; Students 196.
Station—Convalescent Hospital. (Mission skilled Nursing Home). Tel: 408-248-3736.

3—ST. JUSTIN, (1951), Revs. Jose Galang; Terrence Davis; Joseph Prendergast.
Res., 2655 Homestead Rd., 95051. Tel: 408-296-1193; Fax: 408-244-9437.
School—Tel: 408-248-1094. Kathy Almazol, Prin.
Lay Teachers 17; Students 311.
Catechesis/Religious Programs—Tel: 408-296-3483. Dorothy Carlson, D.R.E.
Students 276.

4—ST. LAWRENCE THE MARTYR, (1959), Rev. V. Warwick James (South Africa). In res., Rev. Victor L. Wilkiemeyer, Pastor Emeritus.
Res., 1971 St. Lawrence Dr., 95051. Tel: 408-296-3000; Fax: 408-296-3100.
Schools—(Grades PreK-5) 1977 St. Lawrence Dr., 95051. Tel: 408-296-2260; Fax: 408-296-1068. Priscilla Murphy, Prin.
Lay Teachers 10; Students 255; (Grades 6-8). Tel: 408-296-3013. Priscilla Murphy, Prin.
Sisters 2; Lay Teachers 8; Students 196; (Grades 9-12) 2000 Lawrence Ct., 95051. Tel: 408-296-3013; Fax: 408-296-3794. Ron Madeste, Prin.
Sisters 3; Lay Teachers 25; Students 310.
Catechesis/Religious Programs—Genny Hall, D.R.E.
Students 205.

5—Our Lady of Peace, (1961), Rev. John J. Sweeny. In res., Rev. Msgr. Edgar P. McCarren (RVC); Rev. Camilo P. Villanueva.

Res., 2800 Mission College Blvd., 95054. Tel: 408-988-4585; Fax: 408-988-0679.

Catechesis/Religious Programs—Tel: 408-988-7543. Richard Hernandez, D.R.E. Students 622.

Saratoga, Santa Clara Co., Sacred Heart (1951), Revs. Alexander C. Larkin; Kenneth Silvia, C.S.C. In res., Deacon Thomas Combellick.

Res., 13724 Saratoga Ave., 95070. Tel: 408-867-3634; Fax: 408-867-5339.

School—13718 Saratoga Ave., 95070. Tel: 408-867-9241. Jane Daigle, Prin.

Sisters of Notre Dame de Namur 1; Lay Teachers 17; Students 300.

Catechesis/Religious Programs—Tel: 408-867-1530. Janice LaMotta, D.R.E. Students 282.

Church of the Ascension (1964), Rev. Paul Duong. In res., Rev. Raymund Field, C.S.V.

Res., 12033 Miller Ave., 95070. Tel: 408-725-3939; Fax: 408-725-3932.

Catechesis/Religious Programs—Tel: 408-725-3930. Charleen Kennedy, D.R.E. Students 170.

Stanford, Catholic Community at Stanford, Revs. Patrick LaBelle, O.P.; John Paul Forte, O.P.; Mary Jeanne Gralen, Admin.

P.O. Box 2301, 94309. Tel: 650-725-0080; Fax: 650-723-6797.

Sunnyvale, Santa Clara Co.,

1—St. Albert Chmielowski Polish Catholic Pastoral Mission, (1986) (Polish), Rev. Pawel Bandurski, S.Ch. (Poland).

Res., Mass held at St. Cyprian Church. 1133 W. Washington Ave., 94086. Tel: 408-735-9160; Fax: 408-735-9160.

Catechesis/Religious Programs—Students 70.

2—Sts. Andrew and Paul Korean Catholic Mission of San Jose, (1981), Rev. James Park.

Res., 531 E. Weddell Dr., 94089-2162. Tel: 408-734-9721; Fax: 408-734-9723.

Catechesis/Religious Programs—John Choi, D.R.E. Students 200.

3—St. Cyprian, (1961), Revs. Mark J. Neary; Raymund J. Field, C.S.V. In res., Revs. Pawel Bandurski, S.Ch.; Wilfred D'Souza, S.D.B.

Res., 1133 W. Washington, 94086. Tel: 408-739-8506; Fax: 408-739-2815.

School—195 Leota Ave., 94086. Tel: 408-738-3444; Fax: 408-733-3730. Sr. Marie Renee Murphy, I.H.M., Prin.

Sisters of the Immaculate Heart of Mary (Westchester, PA) 3; Lay Teachers 8; Students 263.

Catechesis/Religious Programs—Tel: 408-739-9417. Loretta Fennell, D.R.E. Students 60.

4—St. Martin, (1916), Revs. Benito O. Manding; Antonio Medina, M.G. In res., Rev. Richard Garcia.

Res., 590 Central Ave., 94086. Tel: 408-736-3725; Fax: 408-736-4968.

School—597 Central Ave., 94086. Tel: 408-736-5534. Rosemary Griggs, Prin.

Lay Teachers 13; Students 341.

Catechesis/Religious Programs—Tel: 408-736-0967. Judy Kelch, D.R.E. Students 246.

5—Church of The Resurrection, (1963), Rev. Michael J. O'Connor. In res., Revs. Nicholas E. Farana; Joseph C. Rich; Bede Marandu (Kenya) (Kakamega).

Res., 725 Cascade Dr., 94087. Tel: 408-245-5554; Fax: 408-245-5589.

Church—1399 Hollenbeck Ave., 94087.

School—1395 Hollenbeck Ave., 94087. Tel: 408-245-4571; Fax: 408-733-7301. Virginia Mirrione, Prin. Religious 1; Lay Teachers 12; Students 293.

Catechesis/Religious Programs—Students 207.

Chaplains of Public Institutions

San Jose. *Agnews State Hospital*. Rev. Thomas J. Byrne, S.J. Tel: 408-294-9224.

Alexian Brothers Hospital. Rev. Arturo Mateo, M.S.C. Tel: 408-259-5000.

Catholic Scouting. Rev. Paul Soukup, S.J. Tel: 408-554-4124.

Detention Ministry for Juveniles. Rev. Jack LaRocca Tel: 408-280-7744.

Notre Dame Villa. Rev. Leonard Traverso Tel: 408-867-3212.

O'Connor Hospital. Revs. Toribio Ives Aniban Tel: 408-947-2500; Robert Carey, C.S.V. Tel: 408-947-2500.

St. Louise Hospital. Rev. Walter Johnson, M.M., Chap.

Santa Clara County Jail. Revs. Francisco Rios Tel: 408-293-3503; Juan Carranco; Patrick Kilcoyne.

Santa Clara County Women's Facility. Ms. Marilu Eder.

Los Gatos. *Presentation Center*. Rev. Antonio Medina, M.G. Tel: 408-354-2346.

Milpitas. *Elmwood Rehabilitation Center*. Revs. Patrick Kilcoyne Tel: 408-629-3030; Joseph Okorie Tel: 415-948-1685; Francisco Rios Tel: 408-293-3503.

Stanford Medical Center. Rev. John Hester Tel: 415-723-4000.

Palo Alto. *Children's Hospital at Stanford*. Vacant. Tel: 415-961-2118.

Veterans Administration Medical Center. Revs. John William Murray; John Coleman.

Santa Clara. *Santa Clara Valley Medical Center*. Revs. Lenox C. Day, S.J. Tel: 408-294-9224; Eugene J. Corbett, S.J. Tel: 408-294-9224.

Saratoga. *Our Lady of Fatima Villa*. Rev. Leonard Traverso Tel: 408-867-3212.

Special Assignment:
Reverend Fathers—
Brown, Steven, Dir. Vocations
Garcia, Richard J., Vicar for Clergy
Gray, Robert, Finance Dept.
McCrillis, Philip, Vicar for Parish
Mitchell, Michael J., Vicar General
Rubio, Jose, Dir. Ecumenical & Interreligious Affairs
Schuyler, David, S.M., Judicial Vicar & Vicar for Religious
Shea, Maurice F., Vicar for Canonical Affairs
Tribunal, Hien Nguyen
Tucker, James, S.S., Pastoral Services

On Duty Outside the Diocese:
Reverend Fathers—
Keulman, Kenneth P., New Orleans, LA
Tinh, Joseph Nguyen, Heimback-Vlatten, West Germany

Military Chaplains:
Reverend Fathers—
Hendel, Lawrence, Army National Guard. Tel: 408-252-7653

Retired:
Reverend Monsignors—
Maher, James
McCarren, Edgar
O'Brien, Timothy
Powers, John
Reverend Fathers—
Ahern, Thomas
Baltazar, Ayala
Blandino, Salvatore
Boyle, Eugene J.
Coleman, John
Cottrell, Frank
Farana, Nicholas E.
Field, Raymund
Harrison, Arthur
Hofmann, Arthur
Kelly, Alfred
Largente, Laurent
Leininger, William
Lenane, William
Macedo, Charles
Maher, Raymond
Milani, Joseph J.
Murray, Thomas
O'Connor, William
Passalacqua, Robert
Peace, John
Re, Angelo
Shea, Thomas
Spika, Anthony L.
Suarez, Jose
Wilkiemeyer, Victor L.

Permanent Deacons:
Alvarez, Jose, St. John Vianney
Alvarez, Salvador, Most Holy Trinity
Bunje, Carl, St. Thomas Aquinas
Chavez, Eloy, Our Lady of Guadalupe
Combellick, Thomas, Sacred Heart, Saratoga
McLaughlin, Donald, St. Joseph of Cupertino
Perez, Vincente, Most Holy Trinity

INSTITUTIONS LOCATED IN THE DIOCESE

[A] SHRINES

Santa Clara. *Shrine of Our Lady of Peace*, 2800 Mission College Blvd., 95054. Tel: 408-988-4585; Fax: 408-988-0679. Rev. John J. Sweeny, Dir.
Staff: Mary Jean Kula; Kathryn Dwyer.
Our Lady of Peace Gift Shop. Tel: 408-980-9825.

[B] COLLEGES AND UNIVERSITIES

Santa Clara. *Santa Clara University*, 500 El Camino Real, 95053-0001. Tel: 408-554-4764; Fax: 408-554-2700.
E-mail: username@mailer.scu.edu
Web site: www.scu.edu
For a complete listing, refer to the Colleges and Universities section.

[C] HIGH SCHOOLS, DIOCESAN

San Jose. *Archbishop Mitty High School*. (Coed), 5000 Mitty Ave., 95129. Tel: 408-252-6610; Fax: 408-252-0518.
E-mail: Tim_Brosnan@mitty.com
Web site: Mitty.com
Mr. Timothy Brosnan, Prin.; Rev. Rick Rodini, Campus Chap. Priests 1; Sisters 1; Lay Teachers 81; Students 1,432; Total Staff 118.

Santa Clara. *Saint Lawrence Academy*. (Grades 7-12), 2000 Lawrence Ct., 95051. Tel: 408-296-3013. College Prep Coed. Ron Modeste, Prin.; Gail Harrell, Assoc. Prin. Sisters 3; Lay Teachers 26; Students 315.

[D] HIGH SCHOOLS, PRIVATE

San Jose. *Bellarmine College Preparatory*, 850 Elm St., 95126-1899. Tel: 408-294-9224; Fax: 408-294-1894.
Web site: www.bcp.org
Society of Jesus.
Non-Resident Students: Revs. Gerald T. Wade, S.J., Supr. & Contact; William H. Muller, S.J., Pres.; James E. Morse, S.J., Treas.; John D. Murphy, S.J., Prin.; Raymond P. Allender, S.J.; Mario L. Capitolo, S.J.; Matthew E. Carnes, S.J.; Ronald M. Clemo, S.J.; Eugene J. Corbett, S.J.; Lenox C. Day, S.J.; Ralph J. Drendel, S.J.; John F. Dullea, S.J.; John L. Flynn, S.J.; Doan T. Hoang, S.J.; Gerald J. Lentz, S.J.; Robert B. Mathewson, S.J.; Edward J. McFadden, S.J.; Michael G. Scully, S.J.; Robert J. Shinney, S.J.; Francis J. Silva, S.J.; Bros. Raymond P. Koeplin, S.J.; Edmund W. Ryan, S.J.; Stephen J. Corder, S.J., Scholastics; Paul T. Mariani, S.J. Priests 20; Scholastics 3; Brothers 2; Lay Teachers 77; Students 1,350.

Notre Dame High School, 596 S. Second St., 95112. Tel: 408-294-1113; Fax: 408-293-9779. Sisters of Notre Dame de Namur.
Non-Resident Students. Anne A. Koch, Prin. Sisters 3; Lay Teachers 31; Students 490.

Presentation High School, 2281 Plummer Ave., 95125. Tel: 408-264-1664; Fax: 408-266-3028.
Web site: http://www.Pres-Net.com
Sisters of the Presentation. Priests 1; Sisters 1; Lay Teachers 38; Teachers 56; Students 696; Total Staff 57.

Mountain View. *St. Francis High School*, 1885 Miramonte Ave., 94040. Tel: 650-968-1213; Fax: 650-968-3241. Brothers of Holy Cross. Mr. Kevin Makley, Pres.; Mr. Michael Speckman, Dir. of Activities; Mrs. Patty Tennant, Prin.; Angelo Aguiar, Exec. Dir. Devel.; Rev. Salvatore M. DiNardo, O.P. Brothers 2; Lay Teachers 77; Students 1,460; Total Staff 127.

[E] ELEMENTARY SCHOOLS, PRIVATE

Los Gatos. *Casa Maria Montessori, Preschool & Kindergarten*, 200 Prospect Ave., 95030. Tel: 408-354-8475. Cindy Acker, Admin. Sisters 2; Lay Teachers 12; Students 152; Total Staff 14.

[F] THE CATHOLIC CHARITIES OF THE DIOCESE OF SAN JOSE

San Jose. *Catholic Charities of Santa Clara County*, 2625 Zanker Rd., 95134. Tel: 408-468-0100; Fax: 408-944-0275. Michael J. Cummins, Acting Interim CEO & CFO; Gisela Bushey, Dir. of Devel.; Marilou Cristina, Dir. of Family Svcs.; Sr. Marilyn Lacey, Dir. of Immigration, Refugee & Employment Svcs.; Kitty Mason, Dir. Managed Care; Chris Block, Dir. of Housing Devel. & Svcs., 195 E. San Fernando, 95112. Tel: 408-282-1125.
FAMILY SERVICES: Ron Ober, Assoc. Dir. Clinical Svcs.

Children's Counseling Center. Tel: 408-944-0469. Number Assisted 3,509.

Community Counseling & Education Svcs., 2625 Zanker Rd., 95134. Tel: 408-944-0469. Number Assisted 3,247.

Focus for Work, 2625 Zanker Rd., Ste. 101, 95134. Tel: 408-944-0591. Eila Latif, Prog. Dir. Number Assisted 15,046.

Oasis. (Older Adult Mental Health Team), 2625 Zanker Rd., 95134. Tel: 408-955-9170. Number Assisted 5,594.

COMMUNITY SERVICES:

Foster Grandparent Program, 2625 Zanker Rd., 95134. Tel: 408-944-0668. Jane Contois, Prog. Dir. Foster Grandparents 85; at-risk Foster Grandchildren 3,000.

Martha's Kitchen, 311 Willow St., 95110. Tel: 408-293-6111. Bro. Joseph Nuuanu, Dir.

Independent Aging Program, 195 E. San Fernando St., 95112. Tel: 408-282-8600. Number Assisted 7,034. (Respite Care, Case Management, Direct Services).

Long Term Care Ombudsman Program, 2625 Zanker Rd., 95134. Tel: 408-944-0567. Donna DiMinico, Prog. Dir. Number Assisted 7,890.

OLDER ADULT SERVICES:

Multi-Service Senior Center Programming, Eastside Neighborhood Ctr., 2150 Alum Rock Ave., 95112. Tel: 408-251-0215.

John XXIII Multiservice Center, 195 E. San Fernando St., 95112. Tel: 408-295-4116.

Volunteer Services, 2625 Zanker Rd., 95134. Tel: 408-944-0282. Susan Alberto, Mgr.

HOUSING DEVELOPMENT & SERVICE:

Shared Housing Program, 195 E. San Fernando St., 95112. Tel: 408-282-1144. Chris Block, Dir. Number Assisted 1,227.

IMMIGRATION, REFUGEE & YOUTH SERVICES:

Immigration Program, 2625 Zanker Rd., 95134. Tel: 408-944-0691; Fax: 408-944-0347.
E-mail: imm@ccsj.org
Number Assisted 53,128. Second Immigration Program Site, 7950 Church St., Gilroy, 95020. Tel: 408-842-4808.

Employment and Education Program & Career Center, 2625 Zanker Rd., 95134. Tel: 408-944-0362; Fax: 408-944-0347.
E-mail: emp@ccsj.org
Jane Hills, Dir.

USCC Refugee Resettlement, 2625 Zanker Rd., 95134. Tel: 408-944-0362.
E-mail: res@ccsj.org
Sr. Marilyn Lacey, Dir.

Y.E.S. Youth Programs, 645 Wool Creek Rd., 95112. Tel: 408-283-6150; Fax: 408-283-6152.
E-mail: yes@ccsj.org
Akemi Flynn, Dir. Numbers Assisted 1,867.

NEIGHBORHOOD SERVICE CENTERS:

Eastside Neighborhood Center, 2150 Alum Rock Ave., 95116. Tel: 408-251-0215. Ellen Hertel, Prog. Coord.

John XXIII Neighborhood Center, 195 E. San Fernando St., 95112. Tel: 408-295-4116. Marion Johnson, Prog. Coord. Number Assisted 16,079.

NUTRITION SERVICES:

Senior Nutrition Services, 2625 Zanker Rd., 95134. Tel: 408-944-0100, Ext. 103. Judd Ingram, Prog. Mgr.

Burbank Nutrition Site, 2400 Clove Dr., 95128. Tel: 408-293-0623.

Eastside Nutrition Site, 2150 Alum Rock Ave., 95116. Tel: 408-251-0215.

Gilroy Nutrition Site, 7371 Hanna St., Gilroy, 95020. Tel: 408-842-4200.

John XXIII Nutrition Site, 195 E. San Fernando, 95112. Tel: 408-295-6940.

Morgan Hill Nutrition Site, 17666 Crest Ave., Morgan Hill, 95037. Tel: 408-779-1413. All Nutrition Sites: Number Assisted 2,665; Meals 116,367.

HANDICAPABLES PROGRAM:

Handicapables Program, 4353 Payne Avenue #705, 95114. Tel: 408-243-3160.

AUXILIARIES:

Palo Alto/Los Altos Auxiliary. Tel: 650-948-3425. Patricia A. Sykes, Pres.

[G] DAY NURSERIES

SAN JOSE. *St. Elizabeth's Day Home*, 1544 McKinley Ave., 95126. Tel: 408-295-3456; Fax: 408-295-5917.
E-mail: ewillet@aol.com
Emili Willet, Exec. Dir. & Contact. Lay Staff 50; Children 250.

[H] GENERAL HOSPITALS

SAN JOSE. *Alexian Brothers Hospital*, 225 N. Jackson Ave., 95116. Tel: 408-259-5000
For a complete listing, refer to the Hospitals section.

O'Connor Hospital, 2105 Forest Ave., 95128. Tel: 408-947-2500
For a complete listing, refer to the Hospitals section.

MORGAN HILL. *O'Connor Hospital dba Saint Louise Hospital & Health Center*, Admin. Office, 18500 Saint Louise Dr., 95037. Tel: 408-779-1500
For a complete listing, refer to the Hospitals section.

[I] SPECIAL SANATORIUM AND HOSPITALS

CAMPBELL. *Susan House*, 100 El Caminito Ave., 95008-3412. Tel: 408-374-8684
For a complete listing, refer to the Special Care Facilities section.

SARATOGA. *Our Lady of Fatima Villa*, 20400 Saratoga-Los Gatos Rd., 95070. Tel: 408-741-2950; Fax: 408-741-4930.
E-mail: ourlady@earthlink.com
For a complete listing, refer to the Special Care Facilities section.

[J] HOTEL, SENIOR CITIZENS RESIDENCE

SAN JOSE. *Giovanni Center, Inc.*, 85 S. Fifth St., 95112. Tel: 408-288-7436.
E-mail: EdnCarol@aol.com
For a complete listing, refer to the Special Care Facilities section.

Jeanne d'Arc Manor, 85 S. Fifth St., 95112. Tel: 408-288-7421; Fax: 408-288-7264
For a complete listing, refer to the Special Care Facilities section.

[K] HOMES FOR THE AGED

MOUNTAIN VIEW. *Villa Siena*, 1855 Miramonte Ave., 94040. Tel: 415-961-6484
For a complete listing, refer to the Special Care Facilities section.

[L] RETREATS

LOS ALTOS. *Jesuit Retreat House*, 300 Manresa Way, 94022. Tel: 415-948-4491; Fax: 415-948-0640.
E-mail: elretiro@retreat.scu.edu
Web site: http://retreat.scu.edu/jesuit/
Revs. Gerald P. McCourt, S.J., Supr. & Contact; Philip C. Blake, S.J.; Bernard J. Bush, S.J.; Robert J. Fabing, S.J.; Terence E. Koch, S.J.; Dave J. Morgan, S.J.; James R. Hanley, S.J.; Joseph P. Logan, S.J.; Timothy J. Meier, S.J.; Bro. Lawrence Thoo, S.J. Priests 9; Brothers 1.

LOS GATOS. *Presentation Education and Retreat Center*, 19480 Bear Creek Rd., 95030-9519. Tel: 408-354-2346; Fax: 408-354-5226. Retreat and Conference Center for Religious and Laity. Sr. Virginia Pfluger, O.P., Exec. Dir. & Contact. Capacity 112; Staff 22.

Villa Holy Names, 82 Prospect Ave., 95032. Tel: 408-354-2312. Sr. Jacquelyn Slater, S.N.J.M. Total Staff 2.

[M] MONASTERIES AND RESIDENCES OF PRIESTS AND BROTHERS

SAN JOSE. *Carmelite Monastery, Novitiate*, P.O. Box 3420, 95156-3420. Tel: 408-251-1361. Very Rev. Albert Bunsic, O.C.D., Prior & Contact; Revs. Michael Buckley, O.C.D.; Ailbe Doolan, O.C.D.; Donald Kinney, O.C.D., Subprior, Novice Master; Pascal Pierini, O.C.D.; Jan Lundberg, O.C.D.; Bros. Michael Villagomez, O.C.D.; James Kennedy, O.C.D.; Thomas Kryst; Hadi Gunawan; Lawrence Poncini; Adam Gonzales; Gary Villanueva; Mario Catumgal; Jose Luis Ferroni; Anthony Flores. Priests 6; Brothers 1; Novices 7.

Marianist Community, 10381 Singleton Rd., 95111. Tel: 408-972-2716. Bros. Ronald Allen, S.M.; William Farrell, S.M., Contact. Priests 2; Brothers 3.

CUPERTINO. *The Marianist Mission*, 22825 San Juan Rd., P.O. Box 1775, 95015-1775. Tel: 408-253-4841. Rev. Donald F. Bracht, S.M., Dir.

Marianist Provincial Residence. Legal Title: *Marianist Province of the Pacific*. Mailing Address: P.O. Box 1775, 95015-1775. Tel: 408-253-4841; Fax: 408-253-5280. Res., 22825 San Juan Rd., 95014. Tel: 408-253-4841; Fax: 408-253-5280. Rev. John Russi, S.M., Prov.; Bros. Gary E. Morris, S.M., Asst. Prov. & Dir. Education & Community Dir.; John Haster, S.M., Asst. for Temporalities & Community Dir.; Rev. Joseph Stefanelli, S.M., Prov. Councilor. In res. Rev. John Rielly, S.M.; Bros. Stanley Murakami, S.M.; James Riley, S.M. Priests 4; Brothers 4.
Priests of the Pacific Province Working at Other Locations: Rev. Rodney De Martini, S.M., 12500 Dupont Rd., Sebastopol, 95472. Rev. Thomas Havel, S.M., 334 State St., #106, Los Altos, 94022. Rev. Jorge da Silva, 461 Monterey Ave., Los Altos, 95030-5302. Rev. Francis Nakagawa, S.M., 1184 Bishop St., Honolulu, HI, 96813-2857. Rev. Theodore Ley, S.M., Assoc. Pastor, Maria Regina Church, 2150 W. 135th St., Gardena, 90249.
On Sabbatical: Rev. Timothy Eden, S.M., 800 Polhemus Rd. #7, San Mateo, 94402. Rev. John McEnhill, S.M., 1456 Barry Ave. #4, Los Angeles, 90025. Retreat Center 1; Lay Staff Only 22.

Marianist Novitiate Corporation, P.O. Box 1775, 95015-1775.

Marianist Retreat Center, 22622 Marianist Way, 95014. Tel: 408-253-6279; Fax: 408-253-1834. Ms. Mimi Latno, Dir. Retreat Center 2; Staff 12; Total Assisted 50,000 Adults.

Villa Saint Joseph, 22840 Mercedes Rd., 95014-3920. Tel: 408-257-4427. Marianist Retirement Home. Rev. Stephen Tutas, S.M., Dir. Priests 2; Brothers 11; Total in Residence 13.

LOS ALTOS. *Maryknoll*, 23000 Cristo Rey Dr., 94024. Tel: 650-967-3822; Fax: 650-965-3473. Retirement House for Priests and Brothers. In res. Revs. Edward F. Moore, M.M., Admin.; James A. Bodenstedt, M.M.; George M. Buckley, M.M.; James C. Connell; Clyde F. Davis, M.M.; Gilbert J. DeRitis, M.M.; John J. Drew, M.M.; Joseph E. Early, M.M.; James E. Ebbe, M.M., (Non-Retired Resident); Thomas F. Foley, M.M.; James F. Habenicht, M.M.; Donald J. Haren, M.M.; Leon A. Harter, M.M.; Walter W. Johnson; Thomas S. Keane, M.M.; Wenceslaus F. Knotek, M.M.; John J. McCabe, M.M.; Joseph J. O'Neill, M.M.; John J. Ridyard, M.M.; Michael J. Ruck, M.M.; Norbert M. Verhagen, M.M.; John J. Vinsko, M.M.; James R. Whitmore, M.M.; Bros. Thomas A. Hickey, Asst. Admin.; John Brown, M.M.; Gordon M. Burns, M.M.; Conrad Fleisch, M.M.; Charles A. Heschele, M.M. Priests 34; Brothers 5.

LOS GATOS. *California Province of the Society of Jesus, Jesuit Provincial Office*, P.O. Box 519, 95031. Tel: 408-354-6143.
E-mail: calprovsj@aol.com
Very Rev. John A. Privett, S.J., Regl. Prov.; Revs. John T. Mitchell, S.J., Exec. Asst. & Contact; Gerdenio M. Manuel, S.J.; Robert L. St. Clair, S.J.

Marianists, 461 Monterey Ave., 95030. Tel: 408-395-1816.
E-mail: jorgeda@aol.com
Rev. Jorge da Silva, S.M.; Bro. Jerome Gorg, S.M.

Sacred Heart Jesuit Center, Box 128, 95031. Tel: 408-354-9240; Fax: 408-354-1773. Legal Title: *California Province of the Society of Jesus dba Sacred Heart Jesuit Center*. Rev. John A. Privett, S.J., Prov., Life's Journey, P.O. Box 40168, Phoenix, AZ, 85067. Rev. Leo J. Hombach, S.J., Supr. & Contact; Bro. Joseph Avila; Revs. Philip L. Bourret, S.J. (China); Edward T. Burke, S.J.; Thomas H. Byrne, S.J.; J. Ripley Caldwell; James N. Chevedden, S.J.; Joseph M. Costa, S.J.; Eugene J. Colosimo; Bro. Charles L. Connor, S.J.; Revs. George L. Crain, S.J.; Patrick D. Doherty, S.J.; Thomas M. Donohoe, S.J.; John D. Dryden, S.J.; Bro. Howard C. Ellis, S.J.; Revs. Thomas P. Finsterbach, S.J.; David Fitch, S.J.; Francis J. Gallagher, S.J.; John C. Geary, S.J.; Robert E. Griffin, S.J.; Bro. Jack Hughes, S.J.; Rev. Pierre P. Jacobs, S.J.; Bro. Raymond F. Keefe, S.J.; Rev. George J. Koch, S.J.; Bro. Norbert J. Korte, S.J.; Revs. Robert R. Leonard, S.J.; William F. Lester, S.J.; William J. Maring, S.J.; Bro. Thomas A. Marshall, S.J.; Revs. Joseph L. Martin, S.J.; Roger D. McAuliffe, S.J.; James P. McCauley, S.J.; Bro. Paul I. McElligott, S.J.; Revs. Joseph F. Meehan, S.J.; John R. Moholy, S.J.; Cornelius J. Monacell, S.J.; James Monaghan, S.J.; Alfred G. Playoust, S.J.; Bro. Edward J. Rethers, S.J.; Rev. Leo P. Rock, S.J.; Bro. Theodore C. Rohrer, S.J.; Revs. Arthur F. Rutledge, S.J.; Arthur J. Schenk, S.J.; Donald F. St. Sure, S.J.; Bro. Leonard J. Sullivan, S.J.; Revs. Edward J. Thylstrup, S.J.; Francis X. Wang, S.J. (China); Bro. Lee H. Williams, S.J.; Revs. Ronald D. Wolf, S.J.; George Wong, S.J. (China); John C. Wright, S.J., Villa Serra #336, 1320 Padre Dr., Salinas, 93901. Rev. Michael J. Zimmers, S.J.
Priests of the Province residing elsewhere: Revs. Thomas G. Allender, S.J., San Francisco; Ernesto Arbelaez, S.J., Tracy, CA; Bernard Brannon, S.J., Bakersfield, CA; Raymond A. Devlin, S.J., Pacifica, CA; Thomas W. Foster, S.J., Capitola, CA; Francis D. MacPeck, S.J., San Francisco. Priests 38; Brothers 12.

SANTA CLARA. *Marianist Community*, 319 Pineview Dr., 95050. Tel: 408-241-7110. Bro. Robert G. Hoppe, S.M., Dir. Priests 1; Brothers 3.

SARATOGA. *St. Patrick's Missionary Society*. (St. Patrick Fathers), 19536 Eric Dr., 95070. Tel: 408-253-3135. Revs. Christopher Byrne, S.P.S., Supr.; Eamonn Hayden, S.P.S. Priests 2.

[N] CONVENTS AND RESIDENCES FOR SISTERS

SAN JOSE. *Community of the Holy Spirit*, 1275 Naglee Ave., 95126. Tel: 408-275-1710.

Daughters of Charity of St. Vincent de Paul, O'Connor Hospital, Sisters' Residence, 350 O'Connor Dr., 95128. Tel: 408-289-9215. Sr. Carol Padilla, D.C., Contact. Sisters 12.

Dominican Sisters, Congregation of the Sacred Heart, Houston, 1092 W. San Fernando St., 95126. Tel: 408-294-7151. Sr. Clarice Sparkman, O.P., Contact.

Eucharistic Missionaries of the Most Holy Trinity, 815 S. Daniel Way, 95128. Tel: 408-243-3157. Sr. Gisela Enriquez, Supr. Sisters 5.

Pious Disciples of the Divine Master, 2076 Lincoln Ave., 95125. Tel: 408-265-8105. Sr. Connie Marletta, P.D.D.M., Supr. Sisters 4.

Quinhon Missionary Sisters of the Holy Cross, 1050 St. Elizabeth Dr., 95126. Tel: 408-287-8385.

St. Joseph's Novitiate, Franciscan Hospitaller Sisters of the Immaculate Conception, 300 S. 17th St., 95112-2245. Tel: 408-998-2896; Fax: 408-998-3407. E-mail: confhic@worldnet.att.net
Sr. Lucinda Dias Fonseca, F.H.I.C., Regl. Supr. Sisters 7.

Sinsinawa Dominican Congregation of the Most Holy Rosary, 613 S. Clover Ave., 95128. Sisters 7. 952 Carrabelle Way, 95120.

Sisters of Charity of Nazareth, 3208 Neal Ave., 95117. Tel: 408-244-4206. Sr. Rose Mary Maguire, S.C.N., Contact.

Sisters of LaSalle, 3867 Silver Creek Rd., 95121-1969. Tel: 408-238-9351. Sr. Theresa Claire Nguyen Thi Sang, Supr. Sisters 13.

Sisters of Loretto at the Foot of the Cross, 635 Bolton Ct., No. 1, 95129. Tel: 408-255-4875. Sr. Ann Virginia Tigh, S.L., Contact. Sisters 2.

Sisters of Mercy of Americas (Burlingame), 256 LaPala Dr., #14, 95127. Tel: 408-929-7383. Sr. Maria Juanita Van Bommel, R.S.M., Local Contact. Sisters 7.

Sisters of the Holy Family, Holy Family Convent, 1050 St. Elizabeth Dr., 95126. Tel: 408-287-8385. Sisters 11. St. Elizabeth's Day Home Day Care Center. Children 230.

Society of Helpers, 612 N. 3rd St., #8, 95112. Tel: 408-275-8309. Sr. Ascension Higuera, H.H.S.

Society of the Sacred Heart, 362 N. Seventh St., 95112. Tel: 408-297-3634.
Web site: http://www.sofie.org/rscj/
Rosemary Statt, Contact. Sisters 2.

ALVISO. *Society of the Sacred Heart*, P.O. Box 962, 95002. Tel: 408-262-7539. Sr. Josefina Montalvo, R.S.C.J.

CUPERTINO. *Blessed Virgin Missionaries of Carmel (B.V.M.C.)*, 10130 N. Deanza Blvd., 95014. Tel: 408-257-1022. Sr. Adelpha Luminate, B.V.M.C., Supr. Sisters 3.

Intercommunity Convent, 10351 S. Blaney Ave., 95014-3122. Tel: 408-725-0898; Fax: 408-252-4848.
E-mail: J96write@aol.com
Web site: http://insyte-inc.com
Sr. Harriet Dow, O.S.F. Sisters 2.

Medical Mission Sisters, 10150 Torre Ave., Apt. 236, 95014-2156; Fax: 408-446-4913.
Web site: www.Libertynet.org/mms/
Sr. Mary Pritchard, M.M.S., Area Contact. Sisters 6.

GILROY. *Maryknoll Missioners*, 10230-B New Ave., 95020. Tel: 408-847-1055.
E-mail: nthomas@hotcity.com

LOS ALTOS HILLS. *Daughters of Charity of St. Vincent de Paul (Laboure Residence), Seton Provincialate*, 26000 Altamont Rd., 94022. Tel: 415-941-4490; Fax: 415-949-3874. Sr. Joyce Weller, D.C., Prov.; Rev. Joseph V. Haley, C.M., Dir. Sisters 37; Total in Province 157; Total in Diocese 49.

Immaculate Heart Monastery of the Poor Clares, 28210 Natoma Rd., 94022. Tel: 415-948-2947. Mother Maura, P.C.C., Abbess. Sisters 20.

LOS GATOS. *Sisters of the Holy Names of Jesus & Mary*, P.O. Box 907, 95031.
E-mail: snjmcdsec@connectinc.com
Sr. Sally Slyngstad, S.N.J.M., Prov. Supr. & Contact; Ms. Julie Harrigan, Admin.; Sr. Carol Nicklas, S.N.J.M., Community Life Coord. Total in Province 273; Total in Diocese 95. Convent, 200 Prospect Ave., 95032. Mailing Address: P.O. Box 1906, 95031-1906. Tel: 408-354-1730.

MOUNTAIN VIEW. *Dominican Sisters of Oakford (Dedicated to St. Catherine of Siena)*, 1855 Miramonte Ave., 94040. Tel: 650-965-1903. Sr. Ursula Bomholt, O.P., Regl. Supr. Sisters 6; Total in province 19; Total in Diocese 9. Dominican Sisters of Oakford, St. Catherine's Convent, 749 San Diego Ave., Sunnyvale, 94086. Tel: 408-734-3210. Sisters 3.

SANTA CLARA. *Carmelite Monastery of the Infant Jesus, Discalced Carmelite Nuns*, 1000 Lincoln St., 95050. Tel: 408-296-8412. Sr. Emmanuel, O.C.D., Prioress. Sisters 17.

Dominican Sisters of San Rafael, 1565 Main St. #5, 95050. Tel: 408-248-5748. 1156 Santa Clara St. #11, 95050. Tel: 408-554-6431.

Sisters of Charity of the Blessed Virgin Mary, 807 Washington St., 95050. Tel: 408-249-0773. Sr. Ann Marie Dress, B.V.M., Contact. Sisters 11.

SARATOGA. *Our Lady of Fatima Villa Convent*, 20400 Saratoga-Los Gatos Rd., P.O. Box 442, 95070. Tel: 408-867-9542. Dominican Sisters of St. Catherine of Siena. Miscellaneous: We operate an 85-bed nursing home for lay retired relgious. Sisters 2.

Sisters of Notre Dame de Namur, 14800 Bohlman Rd., 95070. Tel: 408-741-0324; Fax: 408-741-5809. Sr. Barbara Thiella, S.N.D., Team Liaison for Diocese. Sisters in Province 174; Sisters in Diocese 63.

[O] NEWMAN CENTERS

SAN JOSE. *The Newman Center/Catholic Campus Ministry*, San Jose State University, 195 E. San Fernando St., 95112. Tel: 408-938-1610; Fax: 408-938-1612. Mailing Address: Catholic Campus Ministry/SJSU, The Newman Community, P.O. Box 720204, 95172-0204. Rev. Jose Rubio, Chap.; Ms. Ginny Hinkle, Dir.

[P] MISCELLANEOUS LISTINGS

SAN JOSE. *Charities Housing Development Corporation of Santa Clara County*, 195 E. San Fernando St., 95112. Tel: 408-282-1125. Mr. Chris Block.

St. Vincent de Paul Society, District Council of Santa Clara County, 2040 S. 7th St., 95112. Tel: 408-993-9500; Fax: 408-993-0885.
E-mail: help@svdp.org
Mr. Stephen J. Pehanich, Exec. Dir. Total Assisted 30,000; Total Staff 27.

San Tomas/Charities Housing Corporation, 195 E. San Fernando St., 95112. Tel: 408-282-1125. Mr. Chris Block.

Serra Clubs District 31, 1558 Monteval Ln., 95120. Mr. Fred Mollerus, Contact.

Vietnamese Youth and Culture Association, La Salle Vietnam House, 1103 Maxey Ct., 95132. Tel: 408-926-4665. Brothers of the Christian Schools (San Francisco Prov.). Bro. Tran Trong An Phong, F.S.C., Dir.

LOS ALTOS. *Jesuit Institute for Family Life*, 300 Manresa Way, 94022. Tel: 415-948-4854. Rev. Robert J. Fabing, S.J., Dir.

St. Joseph the Worker Center, 4898 El Camino Real, Ste. 300, 94022. Tel: 650-962-1902. Day Worker Center. Elizabeth Fitting Keller, Exec. Dir. Total Assisted 400.

MENLO PARK. *Catholic Communications Corp.* The Catholic Telemedia Network of the Bay Area. 324 Middlefield Rd., 94025. Tel: 415-326-7850; Fax: 415-326-4605. Legal Title: *Roman Catholic Communications Corporation of the Bay Area.* Most Revs. John S. Cummins, Chm.; Pierre DuMaine, Vice Chm.; Shirley Connolly, Gen. Mgr.

SANTA CLARA. *The Roman Catholic Welfare Corporation of San Jose*, 900 Lafayette St., Ste. 301, 95050-4966. Tel: 408-983-0240; Fax: 408-983-0295. Rev. Michael J. Mitchell, Contact Person.

St. Joseph Seminary Corporation, 900 Lafayette St., Ste. 301, 95050-4966. Tel: 408-983-0237; Fax: 408-983-0295. Rev. Michael J. Mitchell, Contact Person.

San Jose Cathedral Foundation. (A nonprofit, charitable, public-benefit California corporation.), 900 Lafayette St., Ste. 301, 95050-4966. Tel: 408-983-0100. Most Rev. Pierre DuMaine, Chm. of Bd. & Pres.

SARATOGA. *Notre Dame Plaza Corporation*, 14800 Bohlman Rd., 95070-6399. Tel: 408-741-0324; Fax: 408-741-5809.

RELIGIOUS INSTITUTES OF MEN REPRESENTED IN THE DIOCESE

For further details refer to the corresponding bracketed number in the Religious Institutes of Men or Women section.

[0120]—*Alexian Brothers.*—C.F.A.
[0330]—*Brothers of the Christian Schools.*—F.S.C.
[0600]—*Brothers of the Congregation of Holy Cross (Eastern Province).*—C.S.C.
[0600]—*Brothers of the Congregation of the Holy Cross (Southwest Province).*—C.S.C.
[0470]—*Capuchin Friars, The.*—O.F.M.Cap.
[1320]—*Clerics of St. Viator.*—C.S.V.
[1330]—*Congregation of the Mission (Vincentians).*—C.M.
[0260]—*Discaled Carmelite Friars.*—O.C.D.
[0520]—*Franciscan Friars (Province of St. Barbara).*—O.F.M.
[0650]—*Holy Ghost Fathers.*—C.S.Sp.
[]—*Institute of Incarnate Word.* (Argentina).—I.V.E.
[0690]—*Jesuit Fathers and Brothers (Society of Jesus) (California Province).*—S.J.
[0760]—*Marianists (Society of Mary).*—S.M.
[0800]—*Maryknoll (Catholic Foreign Mission Society of America, Inc.).*—M.M.
[1210]—*Missionaries of St. Charles - Scalabrinians (Province of St. John Baptist).*—C.S.
[1110]—*Missionaries of the Sacred Heart.*—M.S.C.
[0430]—*Order of Preachers (Province of the Most Holy Name of Jesus-Western Dominican Province).*—O.P.
[1260]—*St. Patrick's Missionary Society.*—S.P.S.
[1260]—*Society of Christ.*—S.Ch.
[0420]—*Society of the Divine Word.*—S.V.D.
[1290]—*Society of the Priests of St. Sulpice.*—S.S.

RELIGIOUS INSTITUTES OF WOMEN REPRESENTED IN THE DIOCESE

[]—*Augustinian Recollects.*—A.R.
[]—*Blessed Virgin Missionaries of Carmel.*—B.V.M.C.
[]—*Caritas Sisters of Miyazaki.*—C.S.M.
[2020]—*Community of the Holy Spirit.*—C.H.S.
[1070-25]—*Congregation of the Dominican Sisters of Saint Catherine of Siena of Kenosha.*—O.P.
[1070-04]—*Congregation of the Most Holy Name (Dominican Sisters of San Rafael).*—O.P.
[2100]—*Congregation of the Humility of Mary.*—C.H.M.
[1070-13]—*Congregation of the Most Holy Rosary (Dominican Sisters).*—O.P.
[1070-12]—*Congregation of the Queen of the Holy Rosary (Dominican Sisters).*—O.P.
[1780]—*Congregation of the Sisters of the Third Order of St. Francis of Perpetual Adoration.*—E.S.P.A.
[0760]—*Daughters of Charity of St. Vincent De Paul.*—D.C.
[0420]—*Discaled Carmelite Nuns.*—O.C.D.
[1070-19]—*Dominican Sisters of Houston, Texas (Congregation of the Sacred Heart).*—O.P.
[1070-30]—*Dominican Sisters of Oakford.*—O.P.
[]—*Eucharistic Missionaries of the Most Holy Trinity.*—M.E.S.S.T.
[1270]—*Franciscan Hospitaller Sisters of the Immaculate Conception.*—F.H.I.C.
[2470]—*Maryknoll Sisters.*—M.M.
[2490]—*Medical Mission Sisters.*—M.M.S.
[2715]—*Missionary Sisters of Christ the King.*—M.S.C.K.
[2900]—*Missionary Sisters of St. Charles Borromeo (Scalabrini Sisters).*—M.S.C.S.
[3760]—*Order of St. Clare (Immaculate Heart Monastery of Poor Clares).*—P.C.C.
[0980]—*Pious Disciples of the Divine Master.*—P.D.D.M.
[0980]—*Quinhon Missionary Sisters of the Holy Cross.*—Q.M.H.C.
[3465]—*Religious of the Sacred Heart of Mary (West American Province).*—R.S.H.M.
[1070-03]—*Sinsinawa Dominican Congregation of the Most Holy Rosary.*—O.P.
[0500]—*Sisters of Charity of Nazareth (Southern Region).*—S.C.N.
[0430]—*Sisters of Charity of the Blessed Virgin Mary.*—B.V.M.
[]—*Sisters of LaSalle.*—L.S.
[2360]—*Sisters of Loretto at the Foot of the Cross.*—S.L.
[2516]—*Sisters of Mercy (Ireland).*—R.S.M.
[2570]—*Sisters of Mercy of the Americas (Regional Community of Burlingame).*—R.S.M.
[3000]—*Sisters of Notre Dame de Namur (California Province).*—S.N.D.
[3840]—*Sisters of St. Joseph of Carondelet (Province of Los Angeles).*—C.S.J.
[3840]—*Sisters of St. Joseph of Carondelet (Province of St. Louis).*—C.S.J.
[1960]—*Sisters of the Holy Family.*—S.H.F.
[1990]—*Sisters of the Holy Names of Jesus and Mary (California Province).*—S.N.J.M.
[3320]—*Sisters of the Presentation of the Blessed Virgin Mary.*—P.B.V.M.
[1760]—*Sisters of the Third Order of Saint Francis of Penance and of Charity.*—O.S.F.
[2170]—*Sisters, Servants of the Immaculate Heart of Mary.*—I.H.M.
[2150]—*Sisters, Servants of the Immaculate Heart of Mary, Monroe, Michigan.*—I.H.M.
[1890]—*Society of Helpers (American Province).*—H.H.S.
[4070]—*Society of the Sacred Heart.*—R.S.C.J.
[4110]—*Ursuline Nuns (Roman Union, Western Province).*—O.S.U.

DIOCESAN CEMETERIES AND MAUSOLEUMS

SAN JOSE. *Calvary.* (Santa Clara Co.), 2655A Madden Ave., 95126. Tel: 408-258-2940; Fax: 408-258-5614. Robert E. Summers, Dir.

LOS ALTOS. *Gate of Heaven*, 22555 Cristo Rey Dr., 94024. Tel: 415-428-3730; Fax: 415-428-3733. Robert E. Summers, Dir.

NECROLOGY

† Hayden, Guy B., (Retired). —Died May 31, 1997.

† Pavalkis, Victor, Milpitas, CA, St. John the Baptist. —Died Dec. 4, 1996.

† Rooney, Leo J., Cupertino, CA, St. Joseph of Cupertino. —Died Jan. 14, 1997.

Archdiocese of Santa Fe

(Archidioecesis Sanctae Fidei)

Most Reverend

MICHAEL J. SHEEHAN, S.T.L., J.C.D.

Archbishop of Santa Fe; ordained July 12, 1964; consecrated and installed as First Bishop of Lubbock June 17, 1983; appointed Apostolic Administrator of Santa Fe April 6, 1993; installed as Eleventh Archbishop of Santa Fe September 21, 1993. *Res., Catholic Center, 4000 St. Joseph Pl., N.W., Albuquerque, NM, 87120.*

Archdiocese of Santa Fe Catholic Center: 4000 St. Joseph Pl., N.W., Albuquerque, NM, 87120. Tel.: 505-831-8100.

ESTABLISHED IN 1850.

CREATED AN ARCHBISHOPRIC IN 1875.

Solemnly consecrated to the Immaculate Heart of Mary on October 7, 1945.

Square Miles 61,142.

Comprises the Counties of Colfax, Curry, DeBaca, Guadalupe, Harding, Los Alamos, Mora, Quay, Roosevelt, San Miguel, Santa Fe, Socorro, Taos, Torrance and Union with a part of Bernalillo, Sandoval, Rio Arriba and Valencia Counties.

PATRON OF THE ARCHDIOCESE: St. Francis of Assisi.

For legal titles of parishes and archdiocesan institutions, consult the Chancery Office.

STATISTICAL OVERVIEW

Personnel	
Archbishop	1
Retired Archbishops	1
Abbots	2
Priests: Diocesan Active in Diocese	67
Priests: Active Outside Diocese	3
Priests: Retired, Sick or Absent	36
Number of Diocesan Priests	106
Religious Priests in Diocese	104
Extern Priests in Diocese	8
Ordinations:	
Diocesan Priests	2
Religious Priests	1
Transitional Deacons	1
Permanent Deacons	1
Permanent Deacons in Diocese	135
Total Brothers	89
Total Sisters	287
Parishes	
Parishes	91
With Resident Pastor:	
Resident Diocesan Priests	60
Resident Religious Priests	25
Without Resident Pastor:	
Administered by Permanent Deacons	3
Administered by Women Religious	2
Administered by Lay People	1
Missions	216
Pastoral Centers	4
Professional Ministry Personnel:	
Brothers	3
Sisters	57
Lay Ministers	181
Welfare	
Catholic Hospitals	4
Total Assisted	17,508
Health Care Centers	1
Total Assisted	5,000
Homes for the Aged	3
Total Assisted	183
Day Care and Extended Day Care Centers	2
Total Assisted	1,218
Specialized Homes	3
Total Assisted	774
Special Centers for Social Services	5
Total Assisted	236,389
Residential Care of Disabled	1
Total Assisted	16
Educational	
Seminaries, Diocesan	1
Students from This Diocese	3
Students from Other Diocese	31
Diocesan Students in Other Seminaries	22
Total Seminarians	25
Colleges and Universities	1
Total Students	1,417
High Schools, Diocesan and Parish	1
Total Students	1,003
High Schools, Private	2
Total Students	895
Elementary Schools, Diocesan and Parish	17
Total Students	4,515
Catechesis/Religious Education:	
High School Students	5,712
Elementary Students	18,387
Total Students Under Catholic Instruction	31,954
Teachers in the Diocese:	
Priests	4
Brothers	5
Sisters	34
Lay Teachers	386
Vital Statistics	
Receptions into the Church:	
Infant Baptism Totals	6,599
Adult Baptism Totals	268
Received into Full Communion	293
First Communions	5,508
Confirmations	2,831
Marriages:	
Catholic	1,156
Interfaith	231
Total Marriages	1,387
Deaths	2,707
Total Catholic Population	271,698
Total Population	1,036,297

Former Archbishops—Most Rev. J. B. LAMY, cons. Nov. 24, 1850; created first Archbishop, 1875; resigned July 18, 1885; died Feb. 13, 1888.—Most Rev. J. B. SALPOINTE, D.D., second Archbishop; cons. Bishop of Doryla and Vicar Apostolic of Arizona, June 20, 1869; appt. Coadjutor of Santa Fe "cum jure successionis", April, 22, 1884; promoted to the Titular Archiepiscopal See of Anazarba, Oct. 11 of same year; succeeded to the See of Santa Fe, July 18, 1885; resigned Jan. 7, 1894; Titular Archbishop of Tomi; died July 15, 1898.—Most Rev. P. L. CHAPELLE, cons. Nov. 1, 1891; Archbishop of Santa Fe, Jan 7, 1894; transferred to New Orleans, Dec. 1, 1897; died Aug. 9, 1905.—Most Rev. PETER BOURGADE, D.D., cons. May 1, 1885; Bishop of Thaumacum and Vic. Ap. of Arizona; Bishop of Tucson, May 8, 1897; transferred to Santa Fe, Jan. 7, 1899; died May 17, 1908.—Most Rev. J. B. PITAVAL, D.D., cons. Titular Bishop of Sora and Auxiliary of Santa Fe, July 25, 1902; promoted to the See of Santa Fe, Jan. 3, 1909; resigned Feb., 1918; appt. Titular Archbishop of Amida, July 29, 1918; died May 23, 1928.—Most Rev. ALBERT T. DAEGER, O.F.M., D.D., cons. May 7, 1919; died Dec. 2, 1932.—Most Rev. RUDOLPH ALOYSIUS GERKEN, D.D., cons. Bishop of Amarillo, April 26, 1927; appt. Archbishop of Santa Fe, June 2, 1933; installed as Archbishop of Santa Fe, Aug. 23, 1933; died March 2, 1943.—Most Rev. EDWIN V. BYRNE, D.D., cons. Bishop of Ponce, P.R. transferred to Diocese of San Juan, P.R. promoted to Archbishop of Santa Fe, June 15, 1943; died July 25, 1963.—Most Rev. JAMES P. DAVIS, D.D., cons. Bishop of San Juan, P.R., Oct. 6, 1943; promoted to Archbishop, April 30, 1960; transferred to Archdiocese of Santa Fe, Jan. 3, 1964; retired Oct. 1974; died March 4, 1988.—Most Rev. ROBERT F. SANCHEZ, cons. 10th Archbishop of Santa Fe, July 25, 1974; resigned April 6, 1993.—

All offices are located at the *Archdiocese of Santa Fe Catholic Center, 4000 Saint Joseph Pl., N.W., Albuquerque, NM 87120. Tel. 505-831-8100, unless otherwise indicated.*

Office of the Archbishop

Vicar-General—Very Rev. LEO LUCERO, V.G., *1120 Canyon Rd., Santa Fe, 87501.* Tel: 505-983-8528.

Secretary to the Archbishop—Mrs. JULIE ROMERO. Tel: 505-831-8120.

Office of the Chancellor

Chancellor—Rev. RICHARD OLONA. Tel: 505-831-8158. Vice Chancellors: Sr. NANCY KAZIK, O.S.F. Tel: 505-831-8188. Rev. DONALD STARKEY. Tel: 505-831-8348.

Archivist and Artistic Patrimony—Mrs. MARINA OCHOA, *213 Cathedral Pl., Santa Fe, 87501.* Tel: 505-983-3811, *Albuquerque Office at the Catholic Center.* Tel: 505-831-8174.

Attorney for the Archdiocese—Mr. CHARLES P. REYNOLDS, *201 12th St., N.W., Albuquerque, 87102.* Tel: 505-842-8177.

Communications-Media—Ms. MARY RYLAND, Dir. Tel: 505-831-8180.

Ecumenical Commission and Inter-Religious Affairs—Rev. ERNEST FALARDEAU, S.S.S., Dir., *St. Charles Borromeo Church, 1818 Coal S.E., Albuquerque, 87106.* Tel: 505-242-3462.

Madonna Retreat and Conference Center—Sr. MARIE VIRGINIA LOVATO, S.C., Dir., *4040 St. Joseph Pl., N.W., Albuquerque, 87120.* Tel: 505-831-8196.

Newspaper, Archdiocesan "People of God"—Most Rev. MICHAEL J. SHEEHAN, Publisher; Sr. NANCY KAZIK, O.S.F., Editor, *4000 St. Joseph Pl., N.W., Albuquerque, 87120.* Tel: 505-831-8188.

Parish Bulletin Service, "The Catholic Communicator"—JENNY CHILSON, *P.O. Box 93244, Albuquerque, 87199-3244.* Tel: 505-856-0333; Fax: 505-822-5589.

Human Resources—Mr. WALTER DUGUAY, Dir. Tel: 505-831-8130.

Canonical Services Division

Judicial Vicar—Rev. Msgr. JOSEPH A. PEPE, J.C.D. Tel: 505-831-8177.

College of Consultors—Very Revs. LEO LUCERO, V.G.; GILBERT SCHNEIDER, O.F.M.; Rev. Msgr. SIPIO SALAS; Revs. RAMON ARAGON; JUAN MENDEZ; RICHARD OLONA; FRANCIS EGGERT; MIKE SHEA.

Council of Men & Women Religious—Vacant.

Holy Childhood Association—See Mission Office.

Immaculate Heart of Mary Seminary—Rev. ARTURO MEZA, Rector, *Mt. Carmel Rd., Santa Fe, 87501.* Tel: 505-988-1975.

Mission Office—Rev. ARKAD BICZAK, Dir. Propagation of the Faith; Holy Childhood; Catholic Relief Svcs., *John XXIII Catholic Community, 4831 Tramway Ridge Dr. N.E., Albuquerque, 87111.* Tel: 505-293-0088.

Office of Religious—Sr. NANCY KAZIK, O.S.F., Dir. Tel: 505-831-8188.

Permanent Diaconate Program—Deacon DONATO LUCERO, Dir., *Immaculate Heart of Mary, 3700 Canyon Rd., Los Alamos, 87544.* Tel: 505-662-6193.

Pilgrimage for Vocations—Rev. EDMOND SAVILLA, Dir., *P.O. Box 888, Taos, 87571.* Tel: 505-758-9208.

Presbyteral Council of the Archdiocese of Santa Fe—Most Rev. MICHAEL J. SHEEHAN, Pres.; Rev. RICHARD OLONA, Ex-Officio; Very Rev. LEO LUCERO, V.G., Ex-Officio; Revs. RON CARRILLO, Chm. TIM MARTINEZ, Sec. Exec. Committee Exec. Board Members: Rev. LAMBERT LUNA; Rev. Msgr. DOUG RAUN.

Propagation of the Faith—See Mission Office.

Vicars Forane (Deans)—Very Revs. JUAN MENDEZ, Santa Fe Deanery: LAMBERT LUNA, Albuquerque-Deanery A: RONALD BRUCKNER, Albuquerque-Deanery B: Rev. JOHNNY LEE CHAVEZ, Albuquerque-Deanery C: Very Revs. VIRGIL FURFARO, Southwest Deanery: CHARLES BROWN, Northwest Deanery: VINCENT DEFAZIO, Northeast Deanery: ANTHONY MARTINEZ, Southeast Deanery:

Tribunal—Tel: 505-831-8177.

Judicial Vicar—Rev. Msgr. JOSEPH A. PEPE, J.C.D.

Adjutant Judicial Vicar—Vacant.

Promoter of Justice—Rev. JEROME MARTINEZ Y ALIRE, J.C.L.

Defenders of the Bond—Revs. SOTERO SENA; MIKE SHEA; RICK ZERWAS; ROBERT MALLOY; DOUGLAS RAUN.

Associate Judges—Revs. RAMON ARAGON; C. JOHN BRASHER; CRISPIN C. BUTZ, O.F.M.; JOHN R. CONWAY; ARTHUR J. ESPELAGE, O.F.M., J.C.D.; NORMAN R. FALARDEAU, S.S.S.; LUIS JARAMILLO, J.C.L.; ROYCE R. THOMAS, J.C.L.; MANUEL VIERA, O.F.M., J.C.L.; BOB COUGHLAN.

Notaries—Mrs. LEDIA APODACA; Ms. PAULA DUVALL; Ms. HELEN WILLS.

Delegate for Matrimonial Dispensations—Rev. Msgr. JOSEPH A. PEPE, J.C.D.; DONALD J. STARKEY, Reverend Deans.

Appeal Court—Tel: 505-831-8177.

Vocation Director—Rev. JOHN CARNEY, Dir. Tel: 505-831-8143. Rev. RICK ZERWAS, Assoc. Dir.; Deacon RUDY ZAMORA, Asst. Dir.

Finance Division

Executive Director of Finance—Mr. TONY SALGADO, C.P.A. Tel: 505-831-8132.

Annual Catholic Appeal—Archdiocesan Annual Appeal Program, Mrs. LINDA J. GARCIA, Operations Mktg. Mgr. Tel: 505-831-8155.

Archdiocese of Santa Fe Catholic Foundation—MARY P. DUNN, Exec. Dir., *2201 San Pedro N.E., Bldg. 2, Ste. 211, Albuquerque, 87110.* Tel: 505-872-2901. Non-profit corporation for financial support of Archdiocese of Santa Fe.

Finance Council—Most Rev. MICHAEL J. SHEEHAN, Pres.; Mr. WILLIAM GRADY, Chm.; Very Revs. GILBERT SCHNEIDER, O.F.M.; LEO LUCERO, V.G.; Revs. RICHARD OLONA; JOHN CONWAY; Mr. GIG BRUMMEL; Mr. TONY SALGADO, C.P.A.; Mr. TIM SHEEHAN; Ms. JENNIFER CANTRELL; Sr. NANCY KAZIK, O.S.F.

Property Managers and Construction Contract Coord.—Mr. JOHN HUCHMALA. Tel: 505-831-8136.

Pastoral Ministries

Executive Director—Ms. FRANCES VOGEL, *4000 St. Joseph Pl., N.W., Albuquerque, 87120.* Tel: 505-831-8151.

AIDS/HIV Ministry of the Archdiocese of Santa Fe—JEFF STROBEL, Dir., *P.O. Box 4231, Albuquerque, 87196.* Tel: 505-243-3203; 800-497-2450.

Campaign for Human Development—Mrs. JOAN LEAHIGH, Coord., *4000 St. Joseph Pl., N.W., Albuquerque, 87192.* Tel: 505-831-8167.

Catholic Committee on Scouting—(Boy Scouts and Girl Scouts). Rev. ROBERT MALLOY, Dir. Scouting, *Queen of Heaven, 5311 Phoenix N.E., Albuquerque, 87110.* Tel: 505-881-1772.

Catholic Schools Office—Sr. MICHELLE MICEK, O.S.F., Supt. Tel: 505-831-8173. Mrs. CELINE RADIGAN, Dir. Program and Fund Devel.

Catholic Social Services of Albuquerque—GREGORY R. KEPFERLE, M.A., M.Div., Exec. Dir., *2010 Bridge S.W., Albuquerque, 87105., Mailing Address: P.O. Box 25405, Albuquerque, 87125.* Tel: 505-247-9521.

Catholic Social Services of Santa Fe, Inc.—GREGORY R. KEPFERLE, M.A., M.Div., Exec. Dir., *138 Park Ave., Santa Fe, 87501., Mailing Address: P.O. Box 443, Santa Fe, 87504.* Tel: 505-982-0441.

Cursillo Movement—Rev. CHRYSTOSTOM PARTEE, O.F.M., Coord., *San Diego Friary, P.O. Box 79, Jemez Pueblo, 87024.* Tel: 505-834-7300.

Ministry to the Disabled—Ms. PATRICIA STEFFES, Dir. Tel: 505-831-8174.

Hospital Ministry—Ms. PATRICIA STEFFES, Coord. Tel: 505-831-8151.

Prison & Detention Ministry—PATRICIA STEFFES, Dir. Tel: 505-831-8174.

Archdiocesan Network for Catholic Legislative Advocacy—Mrs. JOAN LEAHIGH. Tel: 505-831-8167.

Liturgical Commission—Most Rev. MICHAEL J. SHEEHAN, Pres. GENE VARELA, Chm., *2307 Camino Artista, Santa Fe, 87505.* Tel: 505-827-7640.

Marriage and Family Life Office—Mrs. REMEDIOS (HEDDY) LONG, Dir. Tel: 505-831-8117.

Ministry to Spanish Speaking—Deacon JUAN BARAJAS. Tel: 505-831-8152.

African American Ministry—Ms. BRENDA DABNEY. Tel: 505-831-8243.

Native American Ministry—Mr. MIKE VALDO. Tel: 505-831-8243.

Newman Centers—

ALBQ: Aquinas Newman Center—Rev. ROBERT KELLER, O.P., Dir., *Univ. of New Mexico, 1815 Las Lomas Rd. N.E., Albuquerque, 87106.* Tel: 505-247-1095.

LAS VEGAS: Newman Center—Rev. GEORGE SALAZAR, Coord., *Highlands University, 811 Sixth St., Las Vegas, 87701.* Tel: 505-425-9295.

PORTALES: St. Thomas Moore Newman Center—Very Rev. ANTHONY MARTINEZ, Chap., *Eastern New Mexico University, P.O. Box 2253, Portales, 88130.* Tel: 505-356-5615.

SANTE FE: College of Santa Fe—Rev. JAMES CRONIN, Dir., *St. Michael's Dr., Santa Fe, 87501.* Tel: 505-473-6011.

Office of Worship—Rev. THOMAS MAYEFSKE, Dir. Tel: 505-831-8194.

Peace Pilgrimage—Deacon JOHN LEAHIGH, Coord. Tel: 505-831-8167.

Pro Life Commission—JOAN LEAHIGH, Dir., *4000 St. Joseph Pl., N.W., Albuquerque, 87120.* Tel: 505-831-8167.

RCIA—Rev. THOMAS MAYEFSKE. Tel: 505-831-8194.

Religious Education—Ms. CATHERINE ABEYTA, Dir. Tel: 505-831-8127. Ms. MARYANN HOLLAND, Dir. Catachetical Support, *4000 St. Joseph Pl., N.W., Albuquerque, 87120.* Tel: 505-831-8128.

Schools of Lay Ministry Formation—

Albuquerque Deanery A,B,C, "Emmaus Journey"—FRANCES VOGEL, Coord., *4000 St. Joseph Pl. N.W., Albuquerque, 87120.* Tel: 505-831-8151.

Northwest Deanery—Ms. MARY ANN HOLLAND, Coord., *Ojo Sarco, 87550.* Tel: 505-689-2457.

Santa Fe Deanery—(Jornada de Fe). JUANITA MONTOYA, Coord., *St. John the Baptist, 1301 Osage Ave., Santa Fe, 87505.* Tel: 505-983-5034.

St. Vincent de Paul Council—Rev. PAUL BACA, Spiritual Dir., *Community of the Risen Savior, 7701 Wyoming N.E., Albuquerque, 87109.* Tel: 505-821-1571.

Social Justice—Mrs. JOAN LEAHIGH. Tel: 505-831-8167.

Stewardship and Evangelization—Deacon JUAN BARAJAS, Dir. Tel: 505-831-8152.

Youth and Young Adult Ministry—Mrs. BERNADETTE JARAMILLO, Dir. Tel: 505-831-8145.

Ministry Resource Center—Mrs. PATRICIA MCINTIRE, Dir. Tel: 505-831-8187.

CLERGY, PARISHES, MISSIONS AND PAROCHIAL SCHOOLS

CITY OF SANTA FE
(Santa Fe County)

1—THE CATHEDRAL OF SAN FRANCISCO DE ASIS (1610), Revs. Salvador Aragon, O.F.M., Rector; Godfrey Blank, O.F.M.; Wayne Gibbeaut, O.F.M.; Cecil Kleber, O.F.M.; Manuel Viera, O.F.M.; Deacons Charles Bates; William Kollasch. In res., Rev. Antonio Valdez, O.F.M.
Res., P.O. Box 2127, 87504. Tel: 505-982-5619; Fax: 505-989-1952. [CEM]
School—Tel: 505-982-0331. Sr. Josephine Macias, C.D.P., Prin.
Sisters 1; Lay Teachers 9; Students 179.
Catechesis/Religious Programs—Tel: 505-982-3625. Maria Comito, D.R.E.
Students 156.
Missions—Santa Clara, Rio Arriba Co., Indian Pueblo, 87504-2127.; San Ildefonso, Sante Fe Co., Indian Pueblo, 87504-2127.; Tesuque, Sante Fe Co., Indian Pueblo, 87504-2127.

2—OUR LADY OF GUADALUPE (1882) (Hispanic American), Rev. William E. Sanchez; Deacons Anthony Trujillo; Carlos F. Pacheco; Oswaldo Montoya.
Res., 417 Agua Fria St., 87501. Tel: 505-983-8868; Fax: 505-983-4304. [CEM][JC]
Catechesis/Religious Programs—Tel: 505-988-3336. Connie Smith, D.R.E.
Students 561.
Missions—Tesuque, Santa Fe Co., San Ysidro, 87574; Rio en Medio, Sante Fe Co., Our Lady of Sorrows, 87574.

3—CRISTO REY (1940), Rev. Leo E. Lucero, V.G.; Deacon Randy Rodriguez.
Res., 1120 Canyon Rd., 87501. Tel: 505-983-8528; Fax: 505-983-8528. [JC]
School—Tel: 505-983-8411. Terry Lopez, Prin.
Lay Teachers 6; Students 138.
Mission—Canada de Los Alamos, Santa Fe Co., Our Lady of Guadalupe, 1120 Canyon Rd., 87501.
Catechesis/Religious Programs—Students 65.

4—ST. ANNE'S (1942), Rev. R. E. Coughlan.
Res., 511 Alicia, 87501. Tel: 505-983-4430; Fax: 505-983-7483. [JC]
School—Tel: 505-982-3712. Sr. Phyllis Stowell, S.C.L., Prin.
Sisters 2; Lay Teachers 3; Students 81.
Catechesis/Religious Programs—Students 211.

5—ST. JOHN BAPTIST (1953), Revs. Juan Mendez; Nathan Libaire, O.S.B.; Deacons Andres Carrillo; Tony Rodriguez.
Res., 1301 Osage Ave., 87505. Tel: 505-983-5034; Fax: 505-983-1861.
Catechesis/Religious Programs—D.R.E.: Sr. Rebecca Wolf, Elementary; Juanita Montoya, Confirmation & Adult.
Students 441.

6—SAN ISIDRO (1835) (Hispanic), Rev. Franklin D. Pretto.
Res., Rte. 6, Box 111, 87501. Tel: 505-471-0710; Fax: 505-471-9034. [CEM 2]
Catechesis/Religious Programs—Sr. Lorraine Delisle, S.C., D.R.E.
Students 216.
Mission—La Cienega, Santa Fe Co.

7—SANTA MARIA DE LA PAZ CATHOLIC COMMUNITY (1990), Rev. Jerome J. Martinez y Alire. Pastoral Assocs.: Sr. Emelia Atencio, O.P.; Sr. Paula Gallagher, I.H.M.; Sr. Colleen Shanahan, O.S.F.; Deacon Facundo R. Rodriguez.
Res., 11 College Ave., 87505. Tel: 505-473-4330; 473-4200 (Office); Fax: 505-473-1602.
Catechesis/Religious Programs—Mrs. Patricia Lopez, D.R.E.
Students 667.

OUTSIDE THE CITY OF SANTA FE

Abiquiu, Rio Arriba Co., St. Thomas Apostle (1745) (Hispanic), Rev. Don J. Chavez.
Res., P.O. Box 117, 87510. Tel: 505-685-4462. [CEM 5]
Catechesis/Religious Programs—Tel: 505-685-4462 (All Missions). Sr. Melanie Persche, O.L.V.M., D.R.E.
Students 150.
Missions—Canones, Rio Arriba Co.,; Medanales, Rio Arriba Co.; Youngsville, Rio Arriba Co., 87064; Coyote, Rio Arriba Co., 87012; Mesa de Poleo, Rio Arriba Co.; Capulin, Rio Arriba Co.; Gallina, Rio Arriba Co., 87017.

Alameda, Bernalillo Co., Nativity of the Blessed Virgin Mary (1911), Rev. Michael J. Shea; Deacons Robert Contreras; Enrique Padilla.
Res., 9502 Fourth St., N.W., 87114. Tel: 505-898-5253. [CEM][JC 2]
Catechesis/Religious Programs—Tel: 505-898-1441. Mary Duneman, D.R.E.
Students 493.
Mission—Alameda, Bernalillo Co., Our Lady of Mount Carmel, 7807 Etith, 87114.

Albuquerque, Bernalillo Co.,

1—ANNUNCIATION, (1959), Rev. Ronald L. Bruckner; Deacons Harry Gogan; Victor J. Bachechi. In res., Rev. Msgr. Joseph A. Pepe, J.C.D.
Res., 2600 Vermont N.E., 87110. Tel: 505-293-5462; 298-7553.
Office: 2532 Vermont N.E., 87110. Tel: 505-298-7553; Fax: 505-294-7418.
School—2610 Utah N.E., 87110. Tel: 505-299-6783. Sr. Rose Therese Wich, S.C., Prin.
Lay Teachers 35; Students 533.

Catechesis/Religious Programs—Tel: 505-296-0411. Sr. Sharon Brannen, Fd.C.C., D.R.E.
Students 318.

2—ASCENSION, (1962), Rev. Anthony P. Bolman; Deacons Jesus Medina; Bill Hoefler.
Res., 2150 Raymac Rd., S.W., 87105. Tel: 505-877-8550. [CEM 2]
Catechesis/Religious Programs—Tel: 505-877-8144. Sr. Connie Martinez, Fd.C.C., D.R.E.
Students 303.

3—COMMUNITY OF THE RISEN SAVIOUR, (1979), Revs. Paul M. Baca; Antonio Mondragon; Sr. Marie Luisa Vasquez, O.P., Pastoral Assoc.
Church—7701 Wyoming, N.E., 87109. Tel: 505-821-1571; Fax: 505-857-0065.
Catechesis/Religious Programs—Ann Bazen, D.R.E.
Students 975.
Mission—Albuquerque, Bernalillo Co., Prince of Peace, 12500 Carmel, N.E., 87122. Tel: 505-856-7657.

4—HOLY FAMILY, (1953) (Hispanic), Rev. Jack Clark Robinson, O.F.M.; Deacons Santos Abeyta; Robert Paiz; Eddie Blea. In res., Rev. Nils Francis Thompson, O.F.M.; Bro. Peter Forton, O.F.M.
Res., 562 Atrisco Dr., S.W., P.O. Box 12127, 87105. Tel: 505-842-5426; Fax: 505-842-9767.
Catechesis/Religious Programs—Tel: 505-842-5448. Patricia Furlong, D.R.E.
Students 135.

5—HOLY GHOST, (1953), Rev. Joe D. Vigil; Deacons Pat Kneafsey; Robert Stromberg; Ubaldo Chavez.
Res., 833 Arizona Ave., S.E., 87108. Tel: 505-265-5957; Fax: 505-265-5958.
School—Tel: 505-256-1563; Fax: 505-262-9635. Noreen Copeland, Prin.
Sisters 2; Lay Teachers 17; Students 228.
Catechesis/Religious Programs—Tel: 505-265-1975; Fax: 505-265-1975. Bro. Bruce Michalek, D.R.E.
Students 172.

6—IMMACULATE CONCEPTION, (1883) (Hispanic), Revs. Francis E. Renfroe, S.J.; William King, S.J.; John J. Heaney, S.J.; Richard Rodriguez, S.J.; Deacons Gilbert Valverde; George Sandoval; Tom Perez.
Res., 619 Copper Ave., N.W., 87102. Tel: 505-247-4272; Fax: 505-243-0402.
School—St. Mary, 227 Seventh St., 87102. Tel: 505-242-6271; Fax: 505-242-4837. Sr. Marianella Domenici, S.C., Prin.
Sisters 2; Lay Teachers 35; Students 604.
Catechesis/Religious Programs—Tel: 505-247-2555.
Students 164.

7—OUR LADY OF FATIMA, (1949), Revs. Francis X. Eggert; Ted J. Hunt, (Retired); Deacons Thomas Jones; Frank See; Hugh Hackett; Sandy Hall. In res., Rev. Vidal Martinez.
Res., 4020 Lomas, N.E., 87110. Tel: 505-265-5868; Fax: 505-268-0680.
School—Tel: 505-255-6391. Linda Honeyfield, Prin.
Lay Teachers 23; Students 277.

8—OUR LADY OF GUADALUPE, (1954) (Hispanic), Rev. Ramon Aragon; Deacons Manuel Facio; Jim Delgado; George Valverde.
Res., 1860 Griegos, N.W., 87107. Tel: 505-345-4596; Fax: 505-342-2984.
Catechesis/Religious Programs—Tel: 505-344-7153. Molly C. De Baca, D.R.E.
Students 400.

9—OUR LADY OF LAVANG, (1986) (Vietnamese), Rev. Tin Mahn Bui.
Mailing Address: 2115 Inez, N.E., 87110. Tel: 505-275-3079.
Church—8600 Gonzales Rd., S.W., 87105. Tel: 505-839-4738.

10—OUR LADY OF THE ASSUMPTION, (1954), Revs. Luis D. Jaramillo; Michael Cimino; Deacons James Baca; Rue White.
Office: 811 Guaymas, N.E., 87108. Tel: 505-256-9818; 256-9877; Fax: 505-256-3131.
Res., 8030 Fruit, N.E., 87108. Tel: 505-255-5727.
School—817 Guaymas, N.E., 87108. Tel: 505-256-3167. Robert M. Kaiser, Prin.
Lay Teachers 19; Students 196.
Catechesis/Religious Programs—Robert Shields, D.R.E.
Students 275.

11—OUR LADY OF MOST HOLY ROSARY, (1950) (Hispanic), Revs. Joel P. Garner, O.Praem.; John Beall, O.Praem.; Deacons Juan Barajas; Harry Beare; Charles Johnson; Ricardo Mishler; Frank Perez; Gene Tuma.
Office: 5415 Fortuna Rd., N.W., 87105. Tel: 505-836-5011; Fax: 505-836-7562.
Res., Santa Maria de la Vid Priory, 5825 Coors S.W., 87121. Tel: 505-873-4399; Fax: 505-873-4388.
Catechesis/Religious Programs—Tel: 505-831-2525. D.R.E.: Michael Doyle; Sr. Evangeline Salazar, O.S.B.
Students 810.

12—QUEEN OF ANGELS NATIVE AMERICAN CENTER AND ARCHDIOCESAN SHRINE TO KATERI TEKAKWITHA, (1952) (Native American), Rev. Paul Juniet, O.F.M.
Res., I 40 & 12 St., N.W., P.O. Box 6881, 87197. Tel: 505-243-0835.

13—QUEEN OF HEAVEN, (1952), Rev. Robert P. Malloy; Deacons Ruben Barela; Larry Cleveland; Pilar Garcia; Dan Lopez; Julian Padilla. In res., Revs. Stephen A. Sanchez; John W. Fitz Gerald, (Retired).
Office: 5311 Phoenix, N.E., 87110. Tel: 505-881-1772; 881-6719 (Rectory); Fax: 505-883-5222.
School—Tel: 505-881-2484; Fax: 505-837-1123. Mary Cunning, Prin.
Sisters 4; Lay Teachers 37; Students 398.
Catechesis/Religious Programs—Tel: 505-881-0715. Donna Arellanes, D.R.E.
Students 588.

14—SACRED HEART, (1903), Rev. Enrique Bravo, C.S.B.; Deacon Alfonso Montoya, (Retired).
Res., 412 Stover Ave., S.W., 87102. Tel: 505-242-0561. [JC]
Catechesis/Religious Programs—Tel: 505-247-8930. JoAnn Garcia, D.R.E.
Students 150.

15—SAINT JOSEPH ON THE RIO GRANDE, (1986), Rev. Frank Prieto; Deacons Don Bruckner; Frank Lucero.
Office: 4080 Saint Joseph Pl., N.W., 87120. Tel: 505-831-8265; Fax: 505-831-8264.
Catechesis/Religious Programs—Tel: 505-831-8346. Harv Weakland, D.R.E.
Students 442.

16—SAN FELIPE DE NERI, (1703) (Hispanic), Rev. Lambert Joseph Luna; Deacons Jose Lucero; Gerald Hietpas; James Robert (Bob) Lewis.
Res., P.O. Box 7007, 87194. Tel: 505-243-4628; Fax: 505-224-9495.
School—2000 Lomas Blvd., N.W., 87104. Tel: 505-242-2411; Fax: 505-242-7355. Sr. Carmel M. Purcell, B.V.M., Prin.
Sisters 1; Lay Teachers 11; Students 212.
Catechesis/Religious Programs—Tel: 505-247-2041. Silvia O. Zapata, D.R.E.
Students 90.
Mission—Albuquerque, Bernalillo Co., San Jose de los Duranes, 2110 Los Luceros Rd., N.W., 87104.

17—SAN IGNACIO, (1916) (Hispanic), Deacon Merce Villareal, Admin.
Res., 1300 Walter, N.E., 87102. Tel: 505-243-4287.
Catechesis/Religious Programs—Students 54.

18—SAN JOSE, (1938), Revs. Joseph A. Farias, S.D.B.; Paul Tran, S.D.B.; Deacons Charles Lucero; Paul Nguyen.
Res., 2401 Broadway, S.E., 87102. Tel: 505-242-3658; Fax: 505-248-0810.
Catechesis/Religious Programs—Sr. Bernice Garcia, O.P., D.R.E.
Students 370.

19—SANTUARIO SAN MARTIN DE PORRES, (1979), Rev. Daniel L. Farris; Deacons Patricio Santistevan; Sotero Montoya.
Res., 8321 Camino San Martin, S.W., 87121. Tel: 505-836-4676.
Catechesis/Religious Programs—Renee Ortiz, D.R.E.
Students 150.

20—SANGRE DE CRISTO, (1972), Rev. Albert J. Podvin; Deacon Lloyd Martinez.
Res., 8901 Candelaria, N.E., 87112. Tel: 505-293-2327; Fax: 505-292-0590.
Catechesis/Religious Programs—Tel: 505-293-2328.
Students 250.

21—ST. ANNE, (1929) (Armijo), Rev. Msgr. Joaquin Bazan; Deacons Tibo Chavez; Rene Greivel.
Res., 1400 Arenal Rd., S.W., 87105. Tel: 505-877-3121; Fax: 505-877-0084.
Catechesis/Religious Programs—Tel: 505-873-2188. D.R.E.: Sr. Marcella Campos, C.S.J.; Sr. Gemella Casey, C.S.J.
Students 550.

22—ST. BERNADETTE, (1959), Revs. Thomas A. Zotter; James P. Moore; Deacons Alfred McLane; J. Robert Martinez.
Res., 1800 Martha, N.E., 87112. Tel: 505-298-7557; Fax: 505-271-8099.
Catechesis/Religious Programs—Tel: 505-293-7779; Fax: 505-298-2412. Sr. Necy Guan, Fd.CC., D.R.E.
Students 623.

23—ST. CHARLES BORROMEO, (1934), Revs. Robert Chabot, S.S.S.; Roger Bourgeois, S.S.S.; Normand R. Falardeau, S.S.S.; Ernest Falardeau, S.S.S.; Julian Rousseau, S.S.S.; Dennis Ruane, S.S.S.; Robert Stark, S.S.S.; Joseph Thai Minh Tran, S.S.S.; Bro. Peter Mahady, S.S.S.; Deacons Lorenzo Castillo; John Leahigh.
Res., 1818 Coal Pl., S.E., 87106. Tel: 505-242-3462; Fax: 505-247-1292. [JC]
School—Tel: 505-243-5788; Fax: 505-764-8842. Mr. James Ochoa, Prin.
Sisters 2; Lay Teachers 20; Students 350.
Catechesis/Religious Programs—Tel: 505-268-9197. Juanita Gonzales, D.R.E.
Students 182.

24—ST. EDWIN, (1965) (Hispanic), Rev. Jose Hernandez; Deacons Nestor Garcia; Desiderio Luna; Bill Grossman.
Res., 2105 Barcelona, S.W., 87105. Tel: 505-877-2967. [CEM]
Catechesis/Religious Programs—Tel: 505-877-3727.
Students 435.

25—ST. FRANCIS XAVIER, (1928) (Hispanic), Deacon Andrew Chavez, Parish Life Coord.
Res., 4602 Inspiration Dr., S.E., 87108. Tel: 505-243-5201; 265-8983. [JC]
Catechesis/Religious Programs—817 Arno, S.E., 87102.
Students 88.

26—ST. JOHN THE APOSTLE, (1984). (John XXIII Catholic Community). Revs. Arkad Biczak; Paul Johnson, O.P.; Deacons John Russo; Charles Allen; John Wertz; Alex Trujillo.
Res., 4831 Tramway Ridge Dr., N.E., 87111. Tel: 505-293-0088; Fax: 505-293-7276.
Catechesis/Religious Programs—Tel: 505-293-7756. Kyle Kemp, D.R.E.
Students 426.

27—ST. JUDE THADDEUS, (Paradise Hills) (1968), Rev. John R. Conway; Deacon Robert Aragon.
Mailing Address: P.O. Box 67710, 87193. Tel: 505-898-0826 (Church); 897-0391 (Res.).
Catechesis/Religious Programs—Tel: 505-897-4006.
Students 405.

28—ST. THERESE OF THE INFANT JESUS SHRINE OF THE LITTLE FLOWER, Rev. John Plans, S.F.; Deacons Patrick M. Cooney; Esequiel Torres, (Retired); Manuel Montoya.
Res., 300 Mildred, N.W., 87107. Tel: 505-344-8050.
School—Tel: 505-344-4479; Fax: 505-344-3349. Antoinette Crump, Prin.
Lay Teachers 14; Students 270.
Catechesis/Religious Programs—Tel: 505-344-7643.
Students 270.

29—ST. THOMAS AQUINAS UNIVERSITY PARISH, (1954). (Serving the University of New Mexico). Revs. Robert J. Keller, O.P.; Steven F. Kuhlmann, O.P.; Deacon Bruce Eklund. In res., Revs. John Vincent Blake, O.P.; Michael T. Demkovich, O.P.; Paul J. Johnson, O.P.
Res., 1815 Las Lomas Rd., N.E., 87106-3803. Tel: 505-247-1094; Fax: 505-247-2933.
Catechesis/Religious Programs—Carole A. Everton, D.R.E.
Students 265.

Anton Chico, Guadalupe Co., San Jose (1857) (Hispanic), Rev. Patrick S. Duffy, O.C.S.O.
Res., Box 99, 87711. Tel: 505-427-1164. [CEM][JC 5]
Catechesis/Religious Programs—Tel: 505-427-1211.
Students 24.
Missions—Dilia, Guadalupe Co.; Dahlia, Guadalupe Co.; Tecolotito, San Miguel Co.

Arroyo Seco, Taos Co., Holy Trinity (1834) (Spanish), Rev. Vincent P. Chavez; Deacons Patrick DeLozier; Michael L. Kittredge.
Res., Box 189, 87514. Tel: 505-776-2273; Fax: 505-776-2273. [CEM]
Catechesis/Religious Programs—Students 120.
Missions—Arroyo Hondo, Taos Co.; Valdez, Taos Co.; Las Colonias, Taos Co.; San Cristobal, Taos Co.

Belen, Valencia Co., Our Lady of Belen (1793), Rev. David Gallegos, O.S.M.; Allen Sanchez, Pastoral Assoc.; Deacons Felix Barela; Manuel Gallegos; Norbert Sanchez; Robert Sanchez; Rudy Zamora.
Res., 101-A N. 10th St., 87002. Tel: 505-864-8043; Fax: 505-861-0969. [CEM][JC]
School—Tel: 505-864-4724. Dr. Rebecca Lutz, Prin.
Sisters 1; Lay Teachers 8; Students 210.
Catechesis/Religious Programs—Tel: 505-864-7869.
Students 560.
Missions—Los Chavez, Valencia Co., 20 Thresher Ln., 87002. Tel: 505-864-9297; Jarales, Valencia Co., P.O. Box 29, Jarales, 87023. Tel: 505-864-4231; Pueblitos, Valencia Co., 7 Wood Dr., 87002. Tel: 505-864-6267; Bosque, Valencia Co., P.O. Box 159, Bosque, 87006. Tel: 505-864-2192.

Bernalillo, Sandoval Co., Our Lady of Sorrows (1699) (Indio-Hispanic), Rev. Virgil Furfaro; Deacon Paul Maestas.
Office: P.O. Box 607, 87004. Tel: 505-867-5252; Fax: 505-867-0267.
Res., 301 Camino del Pueblo, 87004. Tel: 505-867-0585. [CEM 3]
Catechesis/Religious Programs—Ursulita Perez, D.R.E.
Students 586.
Missions—Placitas, Sandoval Co.; Algodones, Sandoval Co.; Sandia Indian Pueblo, Sandoval Co.

Cerrillos, Santa Fe Co., St. Joseph (1850), Rev. Donnan Herbe, O.F.M.
Res., Box 98, 87010. Tel: 505-471-1562. [CEM 4]
Catechesis/Religious Programs—Students 47.
Missions—Golden, Santa Fe Co.; Galisteo, Santa Fe Co.

Chama, Rio Arriba Co., St. Patrick (1963), Rev. Clarence Maes.
Res., 247 Pine St., Box 36, 87520-0036. Tel: 505-756-2926.
Missions—Cebolla, Santo Nino; Canjilon, St. Juan Nepumoceno.

Chimayo, Rio Arriba Co., Holy Family (1955) (Hispanic), Revs. Miguel Mateo, S.F.; Casimiro Roca, S.F.; Deacon Jose Lopez.
Res., P.O. Box 235, 87522. Tel: 505-351-4360; Fax: 505-351-4698. [CEM][JC 2]
Catechesis/Religious Programs—Tel: 505-351-4131. D.R.E.: Sr. Marilyn Schata, O.L.V.M.; Sr. Priscilla Wilke, O.L.V.M.; Sr. Carol Virnig, O.S.F.
Students 243.
Missions—Truchas, Rio Arriba Co., Holy Rosary; Trampas, Taos Co., San Jose de Gracia; Cundiyo, Rio Arriba Co., Santo Domingo; Cordova, Rio Arriba Co., San Antonio; Rio Chiquito, Rio Arriba Co., Sagrado Corazon; Ojo Sarco, Rio Arriba Co., Santo Tomas; El Valle, Taos Co., San Miguel Archangel; El Santuario, Santa Fe Co., El Santuario Shrine, Tel: 505-351-4889.

Cimarron, Colfax Co., Immaculate Conception Church (1864) (Hispanic-Mexican), Rev. C. John Bresler; Sr. Hildegard Smith, S.C.C., Pastoral Assoc.
Res., Rte. 1, Box 11, 87714. Tel: 505-483-2775. [JC]
Catechesis/Religious Programs—Tel: 505-376-9028. D.R.E.: Mrs. Gloria Martinez; Mr. James Doherty.
Students 113.
Convent—Tel: 505-376-2553. Sisters of Christian Charity
Missions—Eagle Nest, Colfax Co., St. Mel, 200 Willow Creek, Eagle Nest, 87718. Tel: 505-376-2553; Black Lake, Colfax Co., St. Anthony.

Clayton, Union Co., St. Francis Xavier (1937), Rev. George Silva; Deacon P. Louis Montoya.
Res., 115 N. First St., 88415. Tel: 505-374-9500.
Catechesis/Religious Programs—118 N. 2nd St., 88415. Tel: 505-374-2477. Addie Montoya, D.R.E.
Students 125.
Missions—Des Moines, Union Co., Our Lady of Guadalupe, Des Moines, 88418; Folsom, Union Co., St. Joseph, Folsom, 88419; Moses, Union Co., Sacred Heart, Seneca, 88437; Hayden, Quay Co., Holy Trinity, Nara Visa, 88430.

Clovis, Curry Co., Sacred Heart (1908), Rev. Carlos Chavez.
Res., 921 Merriwether St., 88101. Tel: 505-763-6947; Fax: 505-762-5557.
Catechesis/Religious Programs—Mary Ann Lingnau, D.R.E.
Students 250.
Mission—Melrose, Curry Co., P.O. Box 375, Melrose, 88124.

Our Lady of Guadalupe (1945), Rev. Daniel Balizan.
Res., 108 Davis St., 88101. Tel: 505-763-4445; Fax: 505-763-0261. [JC]
Catechesis/Religious Programs—Tel: 505-762-7343. D.R.E.: Helen Gauna; Lindy Esquibel; Sally Romero; Manuel Torres.
Students 380.
Mission—Texico, Curry Co., Box 122, 88135.

Corrales, Sandoval Co., San Ysidro (1966), Rev. Clarence F. Galli; Deacon Faustin Archuleta.
Res., Box 460, 87048. Tel: 505-898-1779. [CEM]
Catechesis/Religious Programs—Tel: 505-899-0276. Kathy M. Carr, D.R.E.
Students 123.

Dixon, Rio Arriba Co., St. Anthony (1934), Rev. Adam Lee Ortega y Ortiz; Joanne M. Dupont, Parish Life Coord.
Res., 5 Church St., P.O. Box 39, 87527-0039. Tel: 505-579-4389; Fax: 505-579-4389. [CEM 2]
Catechesis/Religious Programs—Students 105.
Missions—Velarde, Rio Arriba Co., Nuestra Senora de Guadalupe; Pilar, Taos Co., Nuestra Senora de los Dolores; Lyden, Rio Arriba Co., San Jose.

El Rito, Rio Arriba Co., San Juan Nepomuceno (1832) (Spanish), Rev. Patrick J. Chavez; Deacon Fabian Garcia.
Res., 87530. Tel: 505-581-4714. [CEM][JC 9]
Catechesis/Religious Programs—Students 80.
Missions—La Madera, Rio Arriba Co., Gen. Del., La Madera, 87539; Las Tablas, Taos Co., Gen. Del., Las Tablas, 87539; Ojo Caliente, Rio Arriba Co., Gen. Del., Ojo Caliente, 87549; Petaca, Taos Co., Gen. Del., Petaca, 87539; Servilleta, Taos Co., Gen. Del., Servilleta, 87539; Vallecitos, Rio Arriba Co., Gen. Del., Vallecitos, 87581.; Canon de Vallecitos, Rio Arriba Co., Gen. Del., Canon de Vallecitos, 87581.; Tres Piedras, Taos Co., Gen. Del., Tres Piedras, 87579.; Placitas, Rio Arriba Co., P.O. Box 7, Placitas, 87530.

Espanola, Rio Arriba Co., Sacred Heart (1950) (Hispanic), Rev. Augustine Moore; Sr. Rosemary Schwer, S.C.C., Pastoral Assoc. & D.R.E.; Sr. Marianne Schwer, S.C.C.; Deacons Ralph Vigil; Diego Herrera; Benjie Lopez.
Res., P.O. Box 69, 87532. Tel: 505-753-4225; Fax: 505-753-3312. [CEM 2]
Catechesis/Religious Programs—Tel: 505-753-9413; Fax: 505-753-1695.
Students 242.
Missions—Hernandez, Rio Arriba Co., 87532. Tel: 505-753-3312; Chili, Rio Arriba Co., 87532; El Guache, Rio Arriba Co., 87532; Guachupanque, Rio Arriba Co., 87532; El Duende, Rio Arriba Co., 87532.

Fort Sumner, De Baca Co., St. Anthony (1958) (Hispanic). Attended by St. Rose of Lima, Santa Rosa. Rev. Sotero A. Sena.
Res., 114 W. Richard Ave., P.O. Box 370, 88119. Tel: 505-355-2320. [CEM]
Catechesis/Religious Programs—Students 75.

Isleta, Pueblo Bernalillo Co., St. Augustine (1613) (Native American), Rev. Nicholas E. Nirschl, O.Praem.
Res., P.O. Box 463, 87022. Tel: 505-869-3398; 873-4399.
Catechesis/Religious Programs—Sr. Stella Negri, Fd.CC., D.R.E.
Students 120.

Jemez Pueblo, Sandoval Co., San Diego Indian Missions (1608) (Native American-Spanish), Revs. Chrysostom Partee, O.F.M.; Gino Correa, O.F.M.
Res., P.O. Box 79, 87024. Tel: 505-834-7300. [CEM]
School—Indian Mission School, Tel: 505-834-7419. Sr. Barbara Tylkowski, O.S.F., Prin.
Sisters 2; Lay Teachers 7; Students 85.
Catechesis/Religious Programs—Gail Madalena, D.R.E.
Students 60.
Missions—Canyon, Sandoval Co., Canyon; Ponderosa, Sandoval Co.; San Ysidro, Sandoval Co.; Santa Ana, Sandoval Co.; Zia, Sandoval Co.

Jemez Springs, Sandoval Co., Our Lady of the Assumption (1947), Very Rev. Liam Hoare, s.P.
Res., 87025. Tel: 505-829-3586; Fax: 505-829-3592. [CEM]

La Joya, Socorro Co., Our Lady of Sorrows (1930) (Spanish), Rev. Vincent A. Nicosia, S.O.L.T.; Deacon Alfred Edwin Esquibel.
Mailing Address: 19 Calle de la Iglesia, 87028. Tel: 505-864-4461; Fax: 505-861-3552.
Res., 1249 Hwy. 304, Veguita, 87062. Tel: 505-864-0745. [CEM 6]
Missions—Abeytas, Socorro Co., San Antonio, 87006; Contreras, Socorro Co., San Jose, 87028; Las Nutrias, Socorro Co., San Isidro, Veguita, 87062; Veguita, Socorro Co., San Juan, Veguita, 87062; Sabinal, Socorro Co., San Antonio, Sabinal, 87006.
Catechesis/Religious Programs—Students 70.

Las Vegas, San Miguel Co., Immaculate Conception (1885), Rev. George V. Salazar.
Res., 811 Sixth St., 87701. Tel: 505-425-7791; Fax: 505-425-6991. [CEM]
Catechesis/Religious Programs—Tel: 505-454-0685. D.R.E.: Rosa de Aragon; Salomon Maese; Carol Corbin.
Students 472.
Mission—San Antonio, San Miguel Co., Los Vigiles (Our Lady of Refuge), 811 6th, 87701.

Our Lady of Sorrows Church (1851) (Hispanic), Rev. Vincent G. DeFazio; Deacons Jose Leroy Martinez; Macedon Montoya, Jr.
Res., 403 Valencia St., 87701. Tel: 505-454-1469; Fax: 505-454-1460. [CEM][JC 2]
Catechesis/Religious Programs—Tel: 505-425-6823. Mrs. Rosa de Aragon, D.R.E.
Students 318.
Missions—Sapello, San Miguel Co., Our Lady of Guadalupe, HC 68, Box 11, Sapello, 87745. Tel: 505-425-8084; Trujillo, San Miguel Co., San Isidro, HC 32 Box 26, 87701. Tel: 505-641-5367; Variadero, San Miguel Co., Holy Family, Box 1020, Garita, 88421. Tel: 505-641-5339; Rociada Abajo, San Miguel Co., Santo Nino, HC 69 Box 4, Rociada, 87742. Tel: 505-425-8251; Gallinas, San Miguel Co., Santo Nino, Box 63 El Porvenir Rte., Montezuma, 87731. Tel: 505-425-6015.
Chapels—Christ the King, 2609 Encino St., 87701. Tel: 505-425-6894; Montezuma; San Antonio, Rte. Box 90, El Porvenir, 87731. Tel: 505-425-8010; San Ignacio, HC 68 Box 15, Sapello, 87745. Tel: 505-425-3092; 454-1139; Our Lady of Sorrows, Box 39 Anton Chico Rte., 87701. Tel: 505-421-5599; San Geronimo, Box 310 Mineral Hill Rte., 87701. Tel: 505-425-3011; San Antonio, P.O. Box 85, 87701. Tel: 505-425-3405; Lourdes; San Jose, HC 69 Box 12A, Rociada, 87742. Tel: 505-425-2809; San Rafael, c/o Al Sanchez Jr., General Delivery, Trementina, 88439. Tel: 505-641-5384; Santo Nino de Atocha, Anton Chico Rte. Box 20, 87701. Tel: 505-425-8014; Ojitos Frios; Manuelitas; Santo Nino, Tel: 505-454-0409.

Los Alamos, Los Alamos Co., Immaculate Heart of Mary (1946), Rev. Charles C. Brown; Deacons Charles Pacheco; Gerald Langner; Don Lucero; Tony Porto; Ray Alcouffe.
Mailing Address: 3700 Canyon Rd., 87544.
Res., 3694 Canyon Rd., 87544. Tel: 505-662-6193.
Catechesis/Religious Programs—Tel: 505-662-7773. Karen McLoughlin, D.R.E.
Students 450.
Mission—White Rock, Los Alamos Co., 196 Meadow, 87544. Tel: 505-672-1270.

Los Lunas, Valencia Co., St. Clement (1961), Rev. Rick Zerwas; Deacons Edward Espinosa; John O'Hare.
Res., P.O. Box 147, 87031. Tel: 505-865-7385; Fax: 505-865-8323. [CEM][JC]
Catechesis/Religious Programs—Tel: 505-865-3018. Sr. Charlotte Moser, O.P., D.R.E.
Students 447.
Mission—Los Lentes, Valencia Co., 87031.

Los Ojos, Rio Arriba Co., San Jose (1883) (Spanish), Rev. Sean Murnan, O.F.M.
Res., Box 6, 87551. Tel: 505-588-7473. [CEM][JC 2]
Catechesis/Religious Programs—Students 69.
Missions—Ensenada, Rio Arriba Co.; La Puente, Rio Arriba Co.; Plaza Blanca, Rio Arriba Co.

Mora, Mora Co., St. Gertrude (1851), Rev. Timothy A. Martinez; Bercy Espinoza, Pastoral Assoc.
Res., P.O. Box 599, 87732. Tel: 505-387-2336; Fax: 505-387-5786. [CEM][JC 9]
Catechesis/Religious Programs—Mary Romero, D.R.E.
Students 420.
Missions—Le Doux, Mora Co., 87732; El Carmen, Mora Co., 87732; Lucero, Mora Co., 87732; Santiago-Talco, Mora Co., 87732; Ojo Feliz, Mora Co., 87732; Buenavista, Mora Co., 87732; Golondrinas, Mora Co., 87732; Rainsville, Mora Co., 87732; Chacon, Mora Co., 87732; Holman, Mora Co., 87732; Cleveland, Mora Co., 87732; Guadalupita, Mora Co., 87732; Monte Aplanado, Mora Co., 87732; Turquillo, Mora Co., 87732; La Cueva, Mora Co., 87732; Holman, Mora Co., 87732.

Moriarty, Torrance Co., Estancia Valley Catholic Parish (1972), Rev. Johnny Lee Chavez; Deacon Juan S. Lucero.
Res., Box 129, 87035. Tel: 505-832-6655. [CEM][JC]
Catechesis/Religious Programs—Corriene Lucero, D.R.E.
Students 1,007.
Missions—Estancia, Torrance Co.; Tajique, Torrance Co.; Tapia, San Miguel Co.; Edgewood, Santa Fe Co.

Mountainair, Torrance Co., St. Alice. Unassigned.
Res., P.O. Box 206, 87036. Tel: 505-847-2264. [CEM 5][JC]
Catechesis/Religious Programs—Tel: 505-847-0190. Prescilla Quintana, D.R.E.
Students 180.
Missions—Abo, Torrance Co., 87036; Punta de Agua, Torrance Co., 87036; Manzano, Torrance Co., 87036; Torreon, Torrance Co., Torreon, 87061; Willard, Torrance Co., Willard, 87063.

Pecos, San Miguel Co., St. Anthony (1862), Rev. Bennett J. Voorhies.
Res., HC 70, Box 23, 87552. Tel: 505-757-6345. [CEM 5]
Catechesis/Religious Programs—Tel: 505-757-6305.
Students 357.
Missions—Canoncito, Santa Fe Co., 87552; Las Colonias, San Miguel Co., 87552; Glorieta, Santa Fe Co., 87552; Rowe, San Miguel Co., 87552; El Macho, San Miguel Co., 87552.

Pena Blanca, Sandoval Co., Nuestra Senora De Guadalupe (Hispanic-Native American), Revs. Hilaire Valiquette, O.F.M.; Joseph Redinbo, O.F.M.; Deacon Albert Arquero.
Res., P.O. Box 1270, 87041. Tel: 505-465-2226. [CEM 3]
Catechesis/Religious Programs—Tel: 505-465-3011. Sr. Jeanne Tranel, O.P., D.R.E.
Students 265.

Missions—Cochiti, Sandoval Co., Indian Pueblo; San Felipe, Sandoval Co., Indian Pueblo; Santo Domingo, Sandoval Co., Indian Pueblo; Sile, Sandoval Co.; La Bajada, Sandoval Co.

Penasco, Taos Co., San Antonio de Padua (1866), Rev. Adam Lee Ortega y Ortiz.
Res., 14079 N. Hwy. 75, P.O. Box 460, 87553-0460. Tel: 505-587-2188; 587-2111 (Office); Fax: 505-587-2188. [CEM]
Catechesis/Religious Programs—Tel: 505-587-2216. Joyce Kilgore, D.R.E.
Students 189.
Missions—Chamisal, Taos Co., Santa Cruz Mission; Llano Largo, Taos Co., San Acacio Mission; Rio Lucio, Taos Co., Sagrado Corazon Mission; Vadito, Taos Co., Nuestra Senora de los Dolores Mission; Picuris Indian Pueblo, Taos Co., San Lorenzo Mission; Llano San Juan, Taos Co., San Juan Nepomuceno Mission; Placita, Taos Co., Nuestra Senora de la Asuncion Mission; Rodarte, Taos Co., Santa Barbara Mission.

Peralta, Valencia Co., Our Lady of Guadalupe (1970), Rev. Albert Gallegos, O.S.M.; Deacon Joe Trujillo.
Res., P.O. Box 288, 87042. Tel: 505-869-2189; Fax: 505-869-5850. [CEM]
Catechesis/Religious Programs—Tel: 505-869-6993. D.R.E.: Marlene Monteith; Margaret Trujillo.
Students 356.
Station—Peralta, Valencia.

Pojoaque, Santa Fe Co., N.S. de Guadalupe del Valle de Pojoaque (1959) (Spanish), Rev. Jose Flavio Santillanes; Deacons John Archuleta; Pedro Garcia.
Res., Rte. 5, Box 216 D, Santa Fe, 87501. Tel: 505-455-2472; Fax: 505-455-3849. [JC]
Catechesis/Religious Programs—Tel: 505-455-2267. Gregory Reynolds, D.R.E.
Students 262.
Missions—Nambe, Santa Fe Co., Nambe Indian Pueblo; El Rancho, Santa Fe Co.

Portales, Roosevelt Co., St. Helen (1952), Rev. Anthony L. Martinez.
Office: Tel: 505-356-4241; Fax: 505-359-1721.
Res., 1600 S. Avenue O, 88130. Tel: 505-359-1557.
Catechesis/Religious Programs—Tel: 505-356-4241. Debbie Walker, D.R.E.
Students 203.
Mission—Portales, Roosevelt Co., University Catholic Center, 88130.

Questa, Taos Co., St. Anthony (1841), Rev. William E. Young (NY).
Res., Box 200, 87556. Tel: 505-586-0470; 0471; Fax: 505-586-1755. [CEM 6]
Catechesis/Religious Programs—Tel: 505-586-0388.
Students 124.
Missions—Cerro, Taos Co.; Red River, Taos Co.; Costilla, Taos Co.; Amalia, Taos Co.

Ranchos De Taos, Taos Co., San Francisco de Asis (1936) (Hispanic), Rev. John M. Tourangeau.
Res., Box 72, 87557. Tel: 505-758-2754; Fax: 505-758-8022. [CEM]
School—(Grades K-6) P.O. Box 463, 87557. Tel: 505-758-1236. Sr. Grace Aufderbeck, Prin.
Sisters of Charity of Cincinnati 2; Lay Teachers 6; Students 150.
Catechesis/Religious Programs—D.R.E.: Sr. Catherine Mary Cohara; Nora Perea.
Students 225.
Missions—Talpa, Taos Co., N.S. de San Juan de Los Lagos; Llano Quemado, Taos Co., N.S. del Carmel; Los Cordovas, Taos Co., San Isidro.

Raton, Colfax Co., St. Patrick/St. Joseph (1891), Rev. James L. Vance; Deacon Thomas Alderette.
Res., 105 Buena Vista St., Box 278, 87740. Tel: 505-445-9763. [CEM]
School—401 S. Fourth St., 87740. Tel: 505-445-3862.
Sisters 1; Lay Teachers 7; Students 113.
Catechesis/Religious Programs—104 Buena Vista St., 87740. Tel: 505-445-9563.
Students 217.
St. Patrick's. Consolidated with St. Joseph's to form St. Patrick/St. Joseph.
St. Joseph's. Consolidated with St. Patrick's to form St. Patrick/St. Joseph.

Ribera, San Miguel Co., San Miguel Del Vado (1804) (Hispanic-Native American), Rev. Vincent DeFazio.
Res., HCR 72, Box 187, San Miguel, 87560. Tel: 505-421-2405; 421-2780 (Office). [CEM]
Catechesis/Religious Programs—Students 114.
Missions—San Isidro Norte, San Miguel Co., Ilfield, 87538. [JC]
San Jose, San Miguel Co., San Jose, 87565. [JC]
San Juan, San Miguel Co., San Jose, 87565. [JC]
Santa Rita, San Miguel Co., Serafina, 87569. [JC]
El Pueblo, San Miguel Co., San Antonio de Padua, 87560. [JC]
La Lagunita, San Miguel Co., Serafina, 87569. [JC]
San Isidro Sur, San Miguel Co., Ilfield, 87538. [JC]

Rio Rancho, Sandoval Co., St. Thomas Aquinas (1974), Rev. Msgr. Douglas A. Raun; Rev. Tien Tri Nguyen; Deacon Aston Bailey.
Res., 1502 Sara Rd., S.E., 87124. Tel: 505-892-1511; Fax: 505-891-3044.
Catechesis/Religious Programs—Tel: 505-892-1497.
Students 1,400.
Missions—Rio Rancho, Sandoval Co., Church of the Incarnation, 87124.; Rio Rancho, Sandoval Co., St. John Vianney, 87124.

Roy, Harding Co., Holy Family-St. Joseph (1918) (Hispanic), Rev. Francisco "Paco" Vallejos; Deacon Raynaldo A. Cordova.
Res., P.O. Box 37, 87743.
Tel: 505-485-2579. [CEM 4]
Missions—Bueyeros, Harding Co.; Gallegos, Harding Co.; Clayton, St. Francis Xavier; Sabinoso, San Miguel Co.; Mosquero, Harding Co.

San Juan Pueblo, Rio Arriba Co. (Indian Pueblo), St. John the Baptist (Hispanic-Native American), Deacon Eloy E. Martinez.
Res., P.O. Box 1075, 87566. Tel: 505-852-4179.
Catechesis/Religious Programs—Sr. Clarita Trujillo, D.R.E. & Pastoral Assoc.
Students 358.
Missions—Alcalde, Rio Arriba Co., 87566.; Chamita, Rio Arriba Co., 87566.; El Guique, Rio Arriba Co., 87566.; Ranchitos, Rio Arriba Co., 87566.; Estaca, Rio Arriba Co., 87566. [CEM]
Shrine—Our Lady of Lourdes. Pilgrimage shrine.

Santa Cruz, Santa Fe Co., Holy Cross (1695) (Hispanic), Revs. Ron Carrillo, S.F.; Jose Maria Blanch, S.F.
Res., P.O. Box 1228, 87567. Tel: 505-753-3345; Fax: 505-753-7401. [CEM]
School—Tel: 505-753-4644. Sr. Lucille Leannah, O.P., Prin.
Sisters 3; Lay Teachers 13; Students 244.
Catechesis/Religious Programs—Tel: 505-753-4567; Fax: 505-753-7401. D.R.E.: Sr. Angelina Gonzales, O.P., (Elementary); Mrs. Lynda Martinez, (Junior & Senior High).
Students 1,110.
Convent—Box 1137, 87567. Tel: 505-753-3340.
Missions—Cuarteles; La Mesilla; La Puebla; San Pedro; Santo Nino.

Santa Rosa, Guadalupe Co., St. Rose of Lima (1907) (Hispanic), Rev. Sotero A. Sena; Deacon Pat Houlihan, (Retired).
Res., 439 Third St., 88435. Tel: 505-472-3724; Fax: 505-472-3724. [CEM]
Catechesis/Religious Programs—Tel: 505-472-3992. D.R.E.: Sr. Helen Halligan; Sr. Ann Kaufmann.
Students 335.
Missions—Puerto de Luna, Guadalupe Co., 88435; San Ignacio, Guadalupe Co., 88435; Borica, Guadalupe Co., 88435; Cuervo, Guadalupe Co., 88435; Newkirk, Guadalupe Co., 88435; Colonias, Guadalupe Co., 88435; Pintada, Guadalupe Co., 88435; Milagro, Guadalupe Co., 88435.

Socorro, Socorro Co., San Miguel (1615), Rev. Domingo B. Gumpal; Deacons Alfred Gilbert; James Alexander Elsberg.
Res., 403 El Camino Real, N.W., 87801. Tel: 505-835-1620; Fax: 505-835-2750. [CEM 8][JC]
School—Tel: 505-835-3661; Fax: 505-835-4343. Gerry Klinglesmith, Prin.
Lay Teachers 8; Students 84.
Catechesis/Religious Programs—Tel: 505-835-2891. Stella C. Castillo, D.R.E.
Students 280.
Missions—Lemitar, Socorro Co., 87801; Polvadera, Socorro Co., 87801; Luis Lopez, Socorro Co., 87801; San Antonio, Socorro Co., 87801; Alamillo, Socorro Co., 87801; Magdalena, Socorro Co., 87801; Kelly, Socorro Co., 87801; Riley, Socorro Co., 87801.

Springer, Colfax Co., St. Joseph (1882) (Hispanic), Rev. C. John Brasher; Deacon Edward Olona.
Res., 605 Fifth St., P.O. Box 516, 87747. Tel: 505-483-2775. [JC]
Catechesis/Religious Programs—Martha Lopez, D.R.E.
Students 65.
Missions—Palo Blanco, Colfax Co.; Maxwell, Colfax Co., 87728; Tinaja, Colfax Co.
Station—New Mexico Boys' School. (Detention Facility). Tel: 505-483-2775. Rev. Jacob McLeroy, Chap.

Taos, Taos Co., Nuestra Senora De Guadalupe (1801), Rev. Edmund Savilla; Deacon Donald Martinez.
Res., P.O. Box 888, 87571. Tel: 505-758-2095; Fax: 505-758-2745. [CEM]
Catechesis/Religious Programs—Tel: 505-758-8451. Patricia Davidson, D.R.E.
Students 297.
Missions—Taos, Taos Co., St. Jerome; Taos Pueblo.
Chapels—El Prado, St. Theresa; Canon, Our Lady of Sorrows; Ranchitos, Immaculate Conception; La Loma, San Antonio; Taos Indian Pueblo.

Tierra Amarilla, Rio Arriba Co., Santo Nino (1966) (Spanish), Rev. Sean Murnan, O.F.M.
Mailing Address: Box 193, 87575. Tel: 505-588-7463. [JC]

Tijeras, Bernalillo Co., Holy Child (1962), Rev. John F. Carney; Deacon Jose Escandon.
Res., Box 130, 87059. Tel: 505-281-1502; 281-2297 (Office); Fax: 505-281-7794. [CEM 9]
Catechesis/Religious Programs—Students 177.
Missions—Carnuel, Bernalillo Co., Holy Child; Chilili, Bernalillo Co., San Juan de Nepumoceno; Escobosa, Bernalillo Co., San Isidro; San Antonio, Bernalillo Co.; Sedillo, Bernalillo Co., San Isidro; Canoncito, San Lorenzo; Tijeras, San Antonito.

Tome, Valencia Co., Immaculate Conception (1750) (Spanish), Rev. Carl Feil, O.S.M.
Res., P.O. Box 100, 87060-0100. Tel: 505-865-7497; Fax: 505-865-7497. [CEM]
Catechesis/Religious Programs—7 Church Loop, Juan Diego Hall.
Students 207.
Mission—Casa Colorada, Valencia Co., State Hwy. 304 South, 87002.

Tucumcari, Quay Co., St. Anne (1910), Rev. John C. Daniel; Deacon Robert Welch.
Res., 306 W. High St., 88401. Tel: 505-461-2515; Fax: 505-461-3058. [JC]
Catechesis/Religious Programs—Tel: 505-461-3568. Nancy Arias, D.R.E.
Students 362.
Missions—Logan, Quay Co., San Antonio, Logan, 88426.; Nara Visa, Quay Co., Sacred Heart, Nara Visa, 88430.; San Jon, Quay Co., Our Lady of Guadalupe, San Jon, 88434.

Vaughn, Guadalupe Co., St. Mary (1936), Rev. Patrick Duffy, O.C.S.O.; Sr. Elena Carney, O.L.V.M., Parish Life Coord.
Res., P.O. Box 276, 88353.
Tel: 505-584-2954. [CEM][JC]
Catechesis/Religious Programs—Students 64.
Missions—Encino, Torrance Co.; Duran, Torrance Co.; Pastura, Guadalupe Co.; Pinos Wells, Torrance Co.

Villanueva, Our Lady of Guadalupe (1830) (Hispanic), Rev. Vincent DeFazio.
Mailing Address: P.O. Box 39, 87583. Tel: 505-421-2548. [CEM]
Catechesis/Religious Programs—Students 65.
Missions—Sena, San Miguel Co., 87533; Cerrito, San Miguel Co., 87533; Gonzales Ranch, San Miguel Co., 87533; Leyba, San Miguel Co., 87533; Aurora, San Miguel Co., 87533.

Wagon Mound, Mora Co., Santa Clara (1882) (Hispanic). Attended by Immaculate Conception, Las Vegas.
Res., P.O. Box 186, 87752. Tel: 505-666-2478. [CEM]
Catechesis/Religious Programs—Students 60.
Missions—Ocate, Mora Co.; Los Hueros, Mora Co.; Los Le Febres, Mora Co.; Watrous, Mora Co.

Priests Serving Private and Public Institutions

SANTA FE. *New Mexico State Penitentiary*. Rev. Ricardo Russo, O.F.M.
St. Vincent's Hospital. Rev. Arthur Jakobiak, Chap.

ALBUQUERQUE. *Lovelace Hospital*. Rev. Steve Sanchez.
Presbyterian Hospital. Revs. David Klein, C.S.B.; Reinaldo Davila, O.F.M.
St. Joseph Medical Center. Revs. Christian T. O'Brien, O.Praem.; James Huth, O.Praem.
U.S.P.H. Indian Hospital. Rev. Nils Francis Thompson, O.F.M.
University Hospital. Revs. Millan J. Garcia; Reinaldo Davila, O.F.M.
Veterans Administration Medical Center. Rev. Julian Rousseau, S.S.S.

LAS VEGAS. *State Hospital*. Attended by Immaculate Conception Parish.

LOS LUNAS. *Correctional Facility (State)*. Deacon Lorenzo Castillo.

SPRINGER. *New Mexico Boys School*. Attended by St. Joseph Parish, Springer.

On Duty Outside the Archdiocese:
Reverend Fathers—
Berg, Timothy
Plotkowski, Jerome

Military Chaplains:
Reverend Fathers—
Flaska, John, U.S. Army

Awaiting Assignment:
Reverend Fathers—
Skelly, Stephen

Absent on Leave:
Reverend Fathers—
Ortega, Eduardo

Retired:
Reverend Monsignors—
Burns, Bernard
Hill, Peter J.
McNiff, James
Stadtmueller, Fred
Reverend Fathers—
Alvarez, Manuel
Amiro, Raymond M.
Anstiss, Arthur
Auman, Robert
Bayer, Leonard
Beach, Robert
Cuesta, Benedicto
Cushing, Alan
Debaenst, Emmanuel
Dennis, Clay
Fitzgerald, John W.
Galli, Clarence
Hendren, Lucien
Hendriks, Boniface
Homola, William B.
Hunt, Ted
Kapitz, Donald
Montoya, Ernest
Rebold, John
Rivera, Guadalupe
Salas, Sipio
Savard, Wilfred

Permanent Deacons:
Abeyta, Santos, Holy Family, Albuquerque
Aird, Gordon, Community of the Risen Savior, Albuquerque
Alcouffe, Raymond, Immaculate Heart of Mary, Los Alamos
Alderette, Thomas, St. Joseph-St. Patrick, Raton
Allen, Charles, John XXIII, Albuquerque
Aragon, Robert, St. Jude Thaddeus, Paradise Hills
Archuleta, Faustin, Our Lady of Fatima, Albuquerque
Archuleta, John, Our Lady of Guadalupe, Pojoaque
Armijo, Vicente, Immaculate Conception, Las Vegas
Arquero, Albert, Nuestra Senora de Guadalupe, Pene Blanca
Baca, James, Estancia Valley Parish, Moriarty
Bachechi, Victor, Annunciation, Albuquerque
Bailey, Aston, St. Thomas Aquinas, Rio Rancho
Ballard, Alphonse L., St. Joseph on the Rio Grande, Albuquerque
Barajas, Juan, Holy Rosary, Albuquerque, Stewardship
Bates, Charles, St. Francis Cathedral, Santa Fe
Beare, Harry, St. Thomas Aquinas, Rio Rancho
Black, Joseph, NM National Guard, Santa Fe
Blea, Edward, Holy Family, Albuquerque
Bouffard, Raymond, Holy Child, Tijeras
Braune, Oscar, Our Lady of Fatima, Albuquerque
Bruckner, Donald G., St. Joseph on the Rio Grande, Albuquerque
Carrillo, Andres, St. John the Baptist, Santa Fe
Castillo, Lorenzo, St. Charles, Albuquerque
Chavez, Andrew, St. Francis Xavier, Albuquerque
Chavez, Tiburci, St. Anne, Albuquerque
Chavez, Ubaldo, Holy Ghost, Albuquerque
Cleveland, Larry, Queen of Heaven; Ministry to Deaf, Santa Fe
Contreras, Robert, Nativity of Blessed Virgin Mary, Alameda
Cooney, Patrick, St. Therese, Albuquerque
Cordova, Raynaldo A., Our Lady of Sorrows, Las Vegas
Cullen, Charles, Queen of Heaven, Albuquerque
Delgado, James P., Our Lady of Guadalupe, Albuquerque
Delozier, Patrick, Holy Trinity, Arroyo Seco
Dimas, Claudio, New Mexico State Penitentiary
Duran, Charles, Our Lady of Fatima, Albuquerque
Eklund, Bruce, St. Thomas Aquinas Newman Center, Albuquerque
Elliott, Robert, Community of the Risen Savior, Albuquerque
Escandon, Jose, St. Bernadette, Albuquerque
Espinosa, Edward, San Clemente, Los Lunas
Esquibel, A. Edwin, Our Lady of Sorrows, La Joya
Facio, Manuel, Our Lady of Guadalupe, Albuquerque
Gagnon, Fabian, St. Joseph on the Rio Grande, Albuquerque; Office of Handicappable, Santa Fe
Gallegos, Manuel A., Our Lady of Belen, Belen
Garcia, Fabian A., San Juan Nepomuceno, El Rito
Garcia, Nestor, St. Edwin, Albuquerque
Garcia, Pedro, Our Lady of Guadalupe, Pojoaque
Garcia, Pilar, Queen of Heaven, Albuquerque
Gilbert, Alfred, San Miguel, Socorro
Gogan, Harry L., Annunciation, Albuquerque
Gonzales, Raymond, St. Jude Thaddeus, Paradise Hills
Greivel, Rene, St. Anne, Albuquerque
Grossman, William L., St. Edwin, Albuquerque
Hackett, Hugh, Our Lady of Fatima, Albuquerque
Hall, Sandy, Our Lady of Fatima, Albuquerque
Herrera, Diego A., Sacred Heart, Espanola
Hietpas, Gerald M., San Felipe de Neri, Albuquerque
Hoefler, William C., Ascension, Albuquerque
Houlihan, William, St. Rose of Lima, Santa Rosa
Johnson, Charles V., Holy Rosary, Albuquerque
Jones, Thomas E., Our Lady of Fatima, Albuquerque
Kazek, Chester, Leave of Absence
Kittredge, Michael, Holy Trinity, Arroyo Seco
Kneafsey, John, Holy Ghost, Albuquerque
Langner, Gerald, Immaculate Heart of Mary, Los Alamos
Leahigh, John, St. Charles, Albuquerque
Lewis, Bob, San Felipe de Neri, Albuquerque
Lopez, Benjamin, Sacred Heart, Espanola
Lopez, Demetrio, Queen of Heaven, Albuquerque
Lopez, Jose O., Holy Family, Chimayo
Lovato, Frank, San Felipe de Neri, Albuquerque
Lucero, Charles
Lucero, Donato, Immaculate Heart of Mary, Los Alamos
Lucero, Frank, St. Joseph on the Rio Grande, Albuquerque
Lucero, John S., St. Joseph-St. Patrick, Raton
Lucero, Jose E., San Felipe de Neri, Albuquerque
Lucero, Juan S., Estancial Valley Parish, Estancia
Luna, Desiderio, St. Edwin, Albuquerque
Maestas, Pablo, Our Lady of Sorrows, Bernalillo
Martinez, Donald J., Our Lady of Guadalupe, Taos
Martinez, Eloy, San Juan, San Juan Pueblo
Martinez, J. Robert, St. Bernadette, Albuquerque
Martinez, Jose Leroy, Our Lady of Sorrows, Las Vegas
Martinez, Lloyd, Sangre de Cristo, Albuquerque
McLane, Alfred, St. Bernadette, Albuquerque
Medina, Jesus, San Jose, Albuquerque
Meyrick, Earl, John XXIII, Albuquerque
Mishler, Richard, Holy Rosary, Albuquerque
Montoya, Alfonso, Sacred Heart, Albuquerque
Montoya, Macedon, Jr., Our Lady of Sorrows, Las Vegas
Montoya, Oswaldo, Our Lady of Guadalupe, Santa Fe
Montoya, P. Louis, St. Francis Xavier, Clayton
Montoya, Sotero, Santuario de San Martin, Albuquerque
Nguyen, Dung (Paul), San Jose, Albuquerque
Nunez, Salvador, Our Lady of the Assumption, Albuquerque
O'Hare, John J., Our Lady of Belen, Belen
Olona, Edward, St. Joseph, Springer
Pacheco, Carlos Felix, Our Lady of Guadalupe, Santa Fe
Pacheco, Charles, Immaculate Heart of Mary, Los Alamos
Padilla, Daniel F., St. John the Baptist, Santa Fe
Padilla, Julian, Queen of Heaven, Albuquerque
Paiz, Robert, Holy Family, Albuquerque
Perez, Frank, Holy Rosary, Albuquerque
Perez, Tomas, Immaculate Conception, Albuquerque
Prentiss, Richard, Kirtland AFB Chapel, Albuquerque
Rodriguez, Antonio, St. John the Baptist, Santa Fe
Rodriguez, Facundo, Santa Maria de la Paz, Santa Fe
Rodriguez, Juan
Rodriguez, Randall, Cristo Rey, Santa Fe
Russo, John L., John XXIII Catholic Community, Albuquerque
Sanchez, Norbert C., Our Lady of Belen, Belen
Sanchez, Robert, Our Lady of Belen, Belen
Sandoval, Alberto, San Antonio de Padua, Penasco
Sandoval, George, Immaculate Conception, Albuquerque
Santistevan, Patrick, San Martin de Porres, Albuquerque
Santistevan, Peter, Our Lady of Sorrows, Bernalillo
Schwenn, Charles E., St. Joseph, Cerrillos
See, Frank C., Our Lady of Fatima, Albuquerque
Stromberg, Robert, Holy Ghost, Albuquerque
Torres, H. Esequiel, St. Therese, Albuquerque
Toya, Patrick, San Diego Mission, Jemez Pueblo
Trujillo, Alex, John XXIII, Albuquerque
Trujillo, Anthony, Our Lady of Guadalupe, Santa Fe
Trujillo, Joseph, Our Lady of Guadalupe, Peralta
Tuma, Eugene, St. Jude Thaddeus, Albuquerque
Vallarreal, Robert, Immaculate Heart of Mary, Los Alamos
Valverde, George, Our Lady of Guadalupe, Albuquerque
Vigil, Ralph, Sacred Heart, Espanola
Villareal, Merce A., Admin., Sacred Heart, Espanola
Welch, Robert, St. Anne, Tucumcari
White, Rue, Our Lady of the Assumption, Albuquerque; Worship, Santa Fe
Zamora, Rudy R., Our Lady of Belen, Belen; Vocations Office, Santa Fe

PILGRIMAGE SHRINES

CHIMAYO. *Santuario de Chimayo.* Attended by Holy Family, Chimayo. 87522.

SAN JUAN. *Our Lady of Lourdes.* (San Juan Pueblo P.O.) P.O. Box 1075, 87566.

INSTITUTIONS LOCATED IN THE ARCHDIOCESE

[A] SEMINARIES, ARCHDIOCESAN

SANTA FE. *Immaculate Heart of Mary Seminary,* College Seminary, Mt. Carmel Rd., 87501. Tel: 505-988-1975. Rev. Arturo Meza (AMA), Rector.
Staff Members: Rev. Fernando Rubio-Boitel, Spiritual Dir.; Sr. Maria Armijo, S.F.C.C., Dean of Academics. Seminarians 34.

[B] SEMINARIES, RELIGIOUS OR SCHOLASTICATES

SANTA FE. *Sangre de Cristo Center,* Rte. 4, 87501. Tel: 505-983-7291; Fax: 505-983-7291.
E-mail: SANGRE@roadrunner.com; bLoCoco@roadrunner.com
Bro. Bernard LoCoco, F.S.C., Dir. Associate Directors: Bro. Joseph Schmidt, F.S.C.; Sr. Patrice Kerin, O.S.F.; Bro. John Kidd, F.S.C.; Sr. Julie McCole, O.S.F. Program of refoundation for religious and priests, under the administration of the Christian Brothers. Participants 68 annually. Total Staff 7.

[C] COLLEGES AND UNIVERSITIES

SANTA FE. *College of Santa Fe,* (1947), 87501. Tel: 505-473-6011
For a complete listing, refer to the Colleges and Universities section.

[D] HIGH SCHOOLS, ARCHDIOCESAN AND PAROCHIAL

ALBUQUERQUE. *St. Pius X High School,* 5301 St. Joseph Dr., N.W., 87120. Tel: 505-831-8400. Revs. Ronald G. Schwenzer, C.S.B., Prin.; Donald F. Hyatt, C.S.B.; Samuel J. Falbo. Priests 3; Religious 1; Lay Teachers 69; Students 1,003.

[E] HIGH SCHOOLS, PRIVATE

SANTA FE. *St. Catherine Indian Boarding School, Inc., Junior-Senior High Boarding School.* (Coed), 801-A Griffin St., 87501. Tel: 505-982-1889. Sr. Patrick Marie Dempsey, Prin. Lay Teachers 16; Sisters 4; Students 206.

St. Michael's High School. (Grades 7-12). (Coed Day School), 100 Siringo Rd., 87505. Tel: 505-983-7353; Fax: 505-982-8722. Bro. Richard Kovatch, F.S.C., Prin. Brothers of the Christian Schools 5; Sisters 1; Lay Teachers 34; Students 688.

[F] GENERAL HOSPITALS

ALBUQUERQUE. *St. Joseph Healthcare System.*
E-mail: ConeM@SJHS.ORG
Mailing Address: P.O. Box 25555, 87125-0555.
For a complete listing, refer to the Hospitals section.

St. Joseph Medical Center.
E-mail: ConeM@SJHS.ORG
Mailing Address: P.O. Box 25555, 87125-0555.
For a complete listing, refer to the Hospitals section.

St. Joseph Northeast Heights Hospital.
E-mail: ConeM@SJHS.ORG
Mailing Address: P.O. Box 25555, 87125-0555.
For a complete listing, refer to the Hospitals section.

St. Joseph Rehabilitation Hospital.
E-mail: ConeM@SJHS.ORG
Mailing Address: P.O. Box 25555, 87125-0555.
For a complete listing, refer to the Hospitals section.

St. Joseph West Mesa Hospital.
E-mail: ConeM@SJHS.ORG
Mailing Address: P.O. Box 25555, 87125-0555.
For a complete listing, refer to the Hospitals section.

[G] SPECIAL HOSPITALS AND SANATORIA FOR INVALIDS

SANTA FE. *Villa Therese Catholic Clinic*, 219 Cathedral Pl., 87501. Tel: 505-983-8561
For a complete listing, refer to the Special Care Facilities section.

[H] SHELTER CARE HOMES

ALBUQUERQUE. *Good Shepherd Center, Inc.*, 218 Iron St., S.W., P.O. Box 749, 87103. Tel: 505-243-2527
For a complete listing, refer to the Special Care Facilities section.

Good Shepherd Manor, 10127 Guadalupe Tr., N.W., P.O. Box 10248, 87184. Tel: 505-898-0177
For a complete listing, refer to the Special Care Facilities section.

Marie Amadea Shelter for Unwed Mothers, P.O. Box 708, 87103. Tel: 505-242-1516
For a complete listing, refer to the Special Care Facilities section.

[I] CARE HOMES FOR PHYSICALLY AND MENTALLY HANDICAPPED

ALBUQUERQUE. *Casa Angelica*, 5629 Isleta Blvd., S.W., 87105. Tel: 505-877-5763
For a complete listing, refer to the Special Care Facilities section.

[J] MONASTERIES AND RESIDENCES OF PRIESTS AND BROTHERS

ABIQUIU. *Monastery of Christ in the Desert*, 87510. Tel: 505-470-4515. Subiaco Congregation. Rt. Rev. Philip Lawrence, O.S.B., Abbot; Revs. Christian Leisy, O.S.B., Sub Prior; Bernard Cranor, O.S.B.; Ezequiel Bas Luna, O.S.B.; Luis Regalado, O.S.B. Monks 38.

ALBUQUERQUE. *Bethany on the Rio Grande*, 2508 Pajarito Rd., S.W., 87105. Tel: 505-873-1487. House of Rest and Recreation for Priests. Mr. Tom Schellenbach, Dir.

Little Brothers of the Good Shepherd, Villa Mathias-Foundation House, 901 Bro. Mathias Pl., N.W., P.O. Box 389, 87103. Tel: 505-243-4238; Fax: 505-764-9721. Brothers 9; Total Staff 2.

San Antonio Provincial Friary Franciscan Friars, 1350 Lakeview Rd., S.W., Box 12315, 87105. Tel: 505-877-5425; Fax: 505-877-2591.
E-mail: GSCHNEI134
Very Rev. Gilbert Schneider, O.F.M., Prov.; Revs. Salvador Aragon, O.F.M., Vicar Prov.; Donald Billiard, O.F.M., Treas. of Prov.; Bro. Gerald Grantner, Archivist; Rev. Lawrence Schreiber, O.F.M., Sec. of Prov. Priests 68; Brothers 18; Temporary Professed 2; Postulants 1; Novices 1. Legal Titles: *San Antonio Provincial Friary Franciscan Friars - Province of Our Lady of Guadalupe.*; *The Province of Our Lady of Guadalupe of Friars Minor, Inc.*; *Southwest Franciscan Services, Inc.*; *Southwest Franciscan Missions, Inc.*

Santa Maria de la Vid Priory, 5825 Coors Rd., S.W., 87121-6700. Tel: 505-873-4399. Canons Regular of Premontre (Norbertine Community). Very Rev. Joel P. Garner, O.Praem., Prior & Vocation Dir.; Revs. Vincent J. DeLeers, O.Praem.; James Huth, O.Praem.; Stan N. Joppe, O.Praem.; Nicholas E. Nirschl, O.Praem.; Francis Dorff, O.Praem; Christian T. O'Brien, O.Praem.; John Beall, O.Praem.; Bro. Dennis Butler. Priests 7.
Sponsor of "Center for Spiritual Life".

BERNALILLO. *Southwest Marian Divine Mercy Center*, 161 Sheriffs Posse Rd., P.O. Box 1840, 87004-1840.
E-mail: TRRN71A@Prodigy.com
Rev. Richard J. Drabik, M.I.C., Spiritual Dir. Total in Residence 2; Total Staff 2.

JEMEZ SPRINGS. *The Jemez Program, Our Lady of Lourdes Novitiate*, 87025-0010. Tel: 505-829-3586. Motherhouse for Servants of the Paraclete and Treatment Center for Priests and Brothers. Retreat House. Very Rev. Liam Hoare, s.P., Servant General & Supr.; Revs. James Sampson, s.P. Tel: 505-829-3004; Ray Gunzel, s.P.; Paul Valley, s.P.; Fernand Couture; Bros. J. Paul Pelletier, s.P.; Conrad Rydelek, Formation House. Rev. Benedict Livingston, s.P., Dir. of Formation. Novices: Mr. Antony Licata; Mr. Philip Taylor. Priests 6; Brothers 2.

[K] CONVENTS AND RESIDENCES FOR SISTERS

SANTA FE. *Discalced Carmelite Monastery*, 49 Mount Carmel Rd., 87501-4597. Tel: 505-983-7232. Mother Rose Teresa, O.C.D., Prioress; Revs. Anderson E. Bakewell, S.J., Chap.; Mathias O'Connor, O.P.; Solemn Professed Nuns 7; Novices 1; Postulants 2; Extern Sisters 3; Extern Novices 1.

ABIQUIU. *Monastery of Our Lady of the Desert*, P.O. Box 1040, 87510.

ALBUQUERQUE. *Cristo Rey Provincial House*, 5625 Isleta Blvd., S.W., 87105. Tel: 505-873-2854; Fax: 505-873-0678.
E-mail: fdccabq@Rt66.com
Canossian Daughters of Charity. Sr. Elizabeth Chambers, Prov. Supr. Sisters 15.

JEMEZ SPRINGS. *Cor Jesu Monastery*, 87025. Tel: 505-829-3906; Fax: 505-829-3423. Motherhouse and Novitiate of the Handmaids of the Precious Blood. Rev. Mother John Paul, H.P.B., Mother Prioress. Perpetually Professed Sisters 33; First Professed Sisters 1.

RIO RANCHO. *Felician Sisters*, Provincial House & Novitiate, 4210 Meadowlark Ln., S.E., P.O. Box 15096, 87124-1021. Tel: 505-892-8862; Fax: 505-891-3893. Assumption of the Blessed Virgin Mary. Sr. Rosemarie Goins, C.S.S.F., Prov. Min. In res. Rev. Paul Schneider, O.F.M., Chap. Residents 43; Professed Sisters of Province 77; Total Assisted per Month 6,000; Total Staff 65; Postulants 1; Novices 1.

[L] RETREAT HOUSES

ALBUQUERQUE. *Dominican Retreat House*, 2348 Pajarito Rd., S.W., 87105. Tel: 505-877-4211. Center for Retreats. Dominican Sisters (Elkins Park, PA). Sisters 3; Total Staff 3.

Madonna Retreat and Conference Center, 4040 St. Joseph Pl., N.W., 87120. Tel: 505-831-8196; Fax: 505-831-8103. Sr. M. Virginia Lovato, S.C., Dir. Total in Residence 2; Total Staff 3.

PECOS. *Our Lady of Guadalupe Benedictine Abbey*, 87552. Tel: 505-757-6415; Fax: 505-757-2285.
E-mail: guestmaster@juno.com
Web site: www.pecosabbey.org
Monastery. Rt. Revs. James Liprie, O.S.B., Delegated Supr.; Andrew Miles, O.S.B., Resigned Abbot; Very Rev. Paul Meaden, O.S.B., Claustral Prior; Revs. Samuel Dennis, O.S.B.; Robert Lussier, O.S.B.; Bernard Lebiedz, O.S.B.; Colman Heffern, O.S.B.; Michael Leek, O.S.B.; Wilfrid Tunink, O.S.B.; Mark Norris, O.S.B. Priests 10; Brothers 6; Novices 1; Monastic Oblate Sisters 8; Novices 1; Postulants 2; Total in Residence 28.

[M] NEWMAN CENTERS

ALBUQUERQUE. *St. Thomas Aquinas*, 1815 Las Lomas Rd., N.E., 87106. Tel: 505-247-1094. Revs. Robert Keller, O.P.; Paul Wierenga, O.P. Total in Residence 5; Total Staff 10.

LAS VEGAS. *Highlands University Newman Center*, 909 Eighth St., 87701. Tel: 505-454-6050.
E-mail: Quintanas@meclin.nmhu.edu
Attended by Immaculate Conception Parish, Las Vegas. Rev. George V. Salazar, Chap.

PORTALES. *University Catholic Center - St. Thomas More Chapel*, P.O. Box 2253, E.N.M.U., 88130. Tel: 505-356-5615.
E-mail: Tony.Martinez@ENMU.Edu
Web site: htttp://wwwstd.ENMU.EDU/Martinet/Cathcntr/Home.htm
Rev. Anthony L. Martinez, Chap. Total Staff 3.

[N] MISCELLANEOUS LISTINGS

SANTA FE. *Medjugorje Group*, Rte. 2, Box 305-41, 87501. Tel: 505-471-1928. Mr. Armando Carrillo, Contact Person.

St. Michael's High School Foundation, 2209 Brothers Rd., Ste. 220, 87505. Tel: 505-988-2264. Mr. Eugene I. Zamora, Pres.

ALBUQUERQUE. *Annual Catholic Appeal Foundation of the Archdiocese of Santa Fe*, 4000 St. Joseph Pl., N.W., 87120. Tel: 505-831-8155.
E-mail: asfaca@flash.net
Linda J. Garcia, C.F.R.E., Exec. Dir.

Archbishop's School Fund, 4000 St. Joseph Pl., N.W., 87120. Tel: 505-831-8173. Carol Lonski, Pres.

Archdiocese of Santa Fe Catholic Foundation, 2201 San Pedro, N.E., Bldg. 2, Ste. 211, 87110. Tel: 505-872-2901; Fax: 505-872-2905. Mary P. Dunn, Contact Person.

Brother Mathias Barrett, Inc., dba Good Shepherd Manor, P.O. Box 10248, 87184. Total Assisted 40; Total Staff 21.

Brothers of the Good Shepherd Inc. of New Mexico, 901 Brother Mathias Pl., N.W., P.O. Box 389, 87102-7103. Tel: 505-243-4238; Fax: 505-764-9721. Total in Residence 9; Total Staff 2.

Caritas Deus Inc., P.O. Box 389, 87103. Tel: 505-243-2527; Fax: 505-247-2207. Property management nonprofit corporation.

Catholic Charismatic Center, 1412 Fifth St., N.W., 87102. Tel: 505-247-0398. Sr. Martha Jean McGarry, I.H.M., Dir.

Center for Action and Contemplation, P.O. Box 12464, 87195. Tel: 505-242-9588. Rev. Richard Rohr, O.F.M., Founder & Animator. Co-Directors: Wendy Corry; Shari Wightman. Total in Residence 3; Total Staff 7.

Charity Unlimited, Inc., P.O. Box 389, 87103. Tel: 505-243-4238; Fax: 505-764-9721. Property management nonprofit corporation.

Dominican Ecclesial Institute, 1815 Las Lomas, N.E., 87106. Tel: 505-243-0525.
E-mail: lumen@sprynet.com
Web site: mac.the'amp.net/domcentral/study/dei.htm
Rev. Michael T. Demkovich, O.P.

Fraternidad Piadosa de Nuestro Padre Jesus Nazareno, 4000 St. Joseph Pl., N.W., 87120. Rev. Jerome J. Martinez y Alire, Chap.

Good Shepherd Center, Inc. of New Mexico, 218 Iron St., N.W., P.O. Box 749, 87103. Tel: 505-243-2527; Fax: 505-247-2207. Total Staff 8.

Norbertine Community of New Mexico, Inc., 5825 Coors Rd., N.W., 87121-6700. Tel: 505-873-4399. Rev. Joel Garner, O.Praem.

St. Francis Gardens Nursing Home.
E-mail: ConeM@SJHS.ORG
Chaplains/Priests Available 1; Beds 135; Total Staff 133. Mailing Address: P.O. Box 25555, 87125-0555. 904 Las Lomas Rd., NE, 87102. Tel: 505-727-2804; Fax: 505-727-2814.
Affiliate of Catholic Health Initiatives. Mary Lou Coors, Admin.; Sr. Marie Raphael Morell, O.P., Dir. Spiritual Care.

St. Pius X High School Foundation, Inc., 5301 St. Joseph Dr., N.W., 87120. Tel: 505-831-8406. Nonprofit corporation for the financial support of St. Pius X High School. Rev. Ronald G. Schwenzer, C.S.B.

**St. Bernadette Institute of Sacred Art*, P.O. Box 8249, 87198. Tel: 505-265-9126; Fax: 505-266-4678.
E-mail: bernadette@usa.net
Web site: www.stbernadette-abq.org/
Dan Paulos, Contact Person.

Villa Mathias Inc., P.O. Box 389, 87103. Tel: 505-243-4238; Fax: 505-764-9721.

JEMEZ SPRINGS. *Fitzgerald Charitable Trust*, P.O. Box 10, 87025. Tel: 505-829-3586. Rev. Benedict Livingstone, s.P.

RIO RANCHO. *St. Felix Pantry, Inc.*, 4020 Barbara Loop, 87124-1021. Tel: 505-891-8075. Sr. Seraphine Moynier, Contact Person. Total Assisted per Month 6,000; Total Staff 65.

RELIGIOUS INSTITUTES OF MEN REPRESENTED IN THE ARCHDIOCESE

For further details refer to the corresponding bracketed number in the Religious Institutes of Men or Women section.

[0170]—*Basilian Fathers.*—C.S.B.
[0200]—*Benedictine Monks.* (Our Lady of Guadalupe Abbey, Pecos; Abbey of Christ in the Desert, Abiquiu).—O.S.B.
[1350]—*Brothers of St. Francis Xavier.*—C.F.X.
[0330]—*Brothers of the Christian Schools.* (Baltimore, Midwest & De La Salle Provinces).—F.S.C.
[0580]—*Brothers of the Good Shepherd.*—B.G.S.
[0900]—*Canons Regular of Premontre.* (Norbertine Fathers of De Pere, Wisconsin).—O.Praem.
[0350]—*Cistercian Order of the Strict Observance.* (GA).—O.C.S.O.
[0740]—*Congregation of Marians of the Immaculate Conception.* (St. Stanislaus Kostka Prov.).—M.I.C.
[0220]—*Congregation of the Blessed Sacrament.*—S.S.S.
[0520]—*Franciscan Friars.* (Our Lady of Guadalupe, St. John the Baptist & St. Barbara Provinces).—O.F.M.
[0430]—*Order of Preachers-Dominicans.* [St. Albert the Great & Southern Dominican (New Orleans) Provinces].—O.P.
[0610]—*Priests of the Congregation of the Holy Cross.*
[1190]—*Salesians of Don Bosco.* (San Francisco Province).—S.D.B.
[1230]—*Servants of the Paraclete.*—s.P.
[1240]—*Servites.* (Eastern Prov.).—O.S.M.
[0690]—*Society of Jesus.* (New Orleans Prov., Oregon Prov., Missouri Prov.).—S.J.
[]—*Society of Our Lady of the Most Holy Trinity.*—S.O.L.T.
[0640]—*Sons of the Holy Family.* (Silver Spring, MD).—S.F.

RELIGIOUS INSTITUTES OF WOMEN REPRESENTED IN THE ARCHDIOCESE

[0200]—*Benedictine Sisters.* (Pecos and Abiquiu, NM).—O.S.B.
[0730]—*Canossian Daughters of Charity.* (Albuquerque, NM).—Fd.C.C.
[1282]—*Congregation of Divine Providence, Allison Park, Texas.*—C.D.P.
[1730]—*Congregation of the Sisters of the Third Order of St. Francis.* (Oldenburg, IN).—O.S.F.
[1780]—*Congregation of the Sisters of the Third Order of St. Francis of Perpetual Adoration.* (La Crosse, WI).—F.S.P.A.
[0420]—*Discalced Carmelite Nuns.* (Santa Fe, NM).—O.C.D.
[1070-02]—*Dominican Sisters.* (Columbus, OH).—O.P.
[1070-03]—*Dominican Sisters.* (Sinsinawa, WI).—O.P.
[1070-09]—*Dominican Sisters.* (Racine, WI).—O.P.

[1070-13]—*Dominican Sisters.* (Adrian, MI).—O.P.
[1070-14]—*Dominican Sisters.* (Grand Rapids, MI).—O.P.
[1070-17]—*Dominican Sisters.* (Elkins Park, PA).—O.P.
[1070-21]—*Dominican Sisters.* (Edmonds, PA).—O.P.
[1170]—*Felician Sisters.* (Congregation of Sisters of St. Felix of Cantalice).—C.S.S.F.
[1500]—*Franciscan Sisters of Mary Immaculate of the Third Order of St. Francis of Assisi.* (Amarillo, TX).—F.M.I.
[1430]—*Franciscan Sisters of Our Lady of Perpetual Help.* (St. Louis, MO).—O.S.F.
[1860]—*Handmaids of the Precious Blood.* (Jemez Springs, NM).—H.P.B.
[1820]—*Hospital Sisters of the Third Order of St. Francis.* (Springfield, IL).
[3130]—*Our Lady of Victory Missionary Sisters.* (Huntington, IN).—O.L.V.M.
[2519]—*Religious Sisters of Mercy of Alma, Michigan.*—R.S.M.
[1680]—*School Sisters of St. Francis.* (Milwaukee, WI).—O.S.F.
[]—*Sisters for Christian Community.* (Cincinnati).—S.F.C.C.
[0440]—*Sisters of Charity of Cincinnati, Ohio.* (Mt. St. Joseph, OH).—S.C.
[0480]—*Sisters of Charity of Leavenworth, Kansas.*—S.C.L.
[0590]—*Sisters of Charity of St. Elizabeth of New Jersey.*—S.C.
[0430]—*Sisters of Charity of the Blessed Virgin Mary.* (Dubuque, IA).—B.V.M.
[0660]—*Sisters of Christian Charity.* (Wilmette, IL).—S.C.C.
[2360]—*Sisters of Loretto at the Foot of the Cross.* (Denver, CO).—S.L.
[0230]—*Sisters of Pontifical Jurisdiction.* (Colorado Springs, CO).—O.S.B.
[1705]—*The Sisters of St. Francis of Assisi.* (Milwaukee, WI).—O.S.F.
[1630]—*Sisters of St. Francis of Penance and Christian Charity.* (Sacred Heart and Holy Name Provinces).—O.S.F.
[1640]—*Sisters of St. Francis of Perpetual Adoration.* (St. Joseph Province, Colorado Springs, CO).—O.S.F.
[1650]—*Sisters of St. Francis of Philadelphia.* (Aston, PA).—O.S.F.
[1530]—*Sisters of St. Francis of the Congregation of Our Lady of Lourdes, Sylvania, Ohio.*—O.S.F.
[1570]—*Sisters of St. Francis of the Holy Family.* (Dubuque, IA).—O.S.F.
[3830-01]—*Sisters of St. Joseph.* (Boston, MA).—C.S.J.
[3830-11]—*Sisters of St. Joseph.* (Kalamazoo, MI).—S.S.J.
[0260]—*Sisters of the Blessed Sacrament for Indians and Colored People.* (Bensalem, PA).—S.B.S.
[3320]—*Sisters of the Presentation of B.V.M.* (Aberdeen, SD).—P.B.V.M.
[3670]—*Sisters of the Sacred Heart of Jesus.* (San Antonio, TX).—S.S.C.J.
[1760]—*Sisters of the Third Order of St. Francis of Penance and Charity.* (Tiffin, OH).—O.S.F.
[1780]—*Sisters of the Third Order of St. Francis of Perpetual Adoration.* (LaCross, WI).
[1720]—*Sisters of the Third Order Regular of St. Francis of the Congregation of Our Lady of Lourdes.* (Rochester, MN).—O.S.F.
[2150-60]—*Sisters, Servants of the Immaculate Heart of Mary.* (Monroe, MI; Scranton, PA).—I.H.M.
[]—*Society of Our Lady of the Most Holy Trinity.* (Robstown, TX).—S.O.L.T.
[4120]—*Ursuline Nuns, of the Congregation of Paris.* (Maple Mount, KY).—O.S.U.

ARCHDIOCESAN CEMETERIES

ALBUQUERQUE. *Archdiocesan Cemetery Association,* 4000 St. Joseph Pl., N.W., 87120. Tel: 505-831-8100. Operates Rosario Cemetery, Santa Fe; Mount Calvary & Gate of Heaven, Albuquerque.
Catholic Cemetery Association, 4000 St. Joseph Pl., N.W., 87120. Tel: 505-831-8100.

NECROLOGY

† Klister, Irving, Springer, NM, St. Joseph. —Died April 19, 1997.
† Martinez, Armando, Santa Rosa, NM, St. Rose of Lima. —Died May 3, 1997.
† Niemeyer, Elmer, Albuquerque, NM, St. Therese. —Died Feb. 19, 1997.

Diocese of Santa Rosa in California

(Dioecesis Sanctae Rosae in California)

Most Reverend

G. PATRICK ZIEMANN, D.D.

Bishop of Santa Rosa; ordained April 29, 1967; appointed Titular Bishop of Obba and Auxiliary of Los Angeles on December 29, 1986; ordained Bishop on February 23, 1987; appointed Bishop of Santa Rosa July 14, 1992.

ESTABLISHED FEBRUARY 21, 1962.

Square Miles 11,711.

Comprises six Counties in the State of California-viz., Del Norte, Humboldt, Lake, Mendocino, Napa and Sonoma.

Legal Titles: "The Roman Catholic Bishop of Santa Rosa, a Corporation Sole" and "The Roman Catholic Welfare Corporation of Santa Rosa."

For legal titles of parishes and diocesan institutions, consult the Chancery Office.

Chancery Office: 560 Ninth St., P.O. Box 1297, Santa Rosa, CA, 95402. Tel.: 707-545-7610; Fax: 707-542-9702.

STATISTICAL OVERVIEW

Personnel	
Bishop	1
Retired Bishops	1
Priests: Diocesan Active in Diocese	58
Priests: Active Outside Diocese	4
Priests: Retired, Sick or Absent	23
Number of Diocesan Priests	85
Religious Priests in Diocese	20
Extern Priests in Diocese	21
Ordinations:	
Transitional Deacons	2
Permanent Deacons in Diocese	19
Total Brothers	45
Total Sisters	98
Parishes	
Parishes	43
With Resident Pastor:	
Resident Diocesan Priests	39
Resident Religious Priests	4
Without Resident Pastor:	
Missions	20
Pastoral Centers	13
Professional Ministry Personnel:	
Sisters	5
Lay Ministers	31
Welfare	
Catholic Hospitals	4
Total Assisted	325,009
Homes for the Aged	1
Total Assisted	54
Residential Care of Children	1
Total Assisted	107
Day Care and Extended Day Care Centers	2
Total Assisted	80
Specialized Homes	1
Total Assisted	45
Special Centers for Social Services	13
Total Assisted	12,500
Residential Care of Disabled	2
Total Assisted	12
Educational	
Diocesan Students in Other Seminaries	12
Total Seminarians	12
High Schools, Diocesan and Parish	3
Total Students	1,055
High Schools, Private	3
Total Students	1,012
Elementary Schools, Diocesan and Parish	13
Total Students	3,001
Elementary Schools, Private	1
Total Students	30
Catechesis/Religious Education:	
High School Students	1,198
Elementary Students	5,842
Total Students Under Catholic Instruction	12,150
Teachers in the Diocese:	
Priests	4
Sisters	11
Lay Teachers	309
Vital Statistics	
Receptions into the Church:	
Infant Baptism Totals	2,852
Adult Baptism Totals	196
Received into Full Communion	182
First Communions	2,135
Confirmations	1,014
Marriages:	
Catholic	496
Interfaith	327
Total Marriages	823
Deaths	1,108
Total Catholic Population	139,513
Total Population	772,859

Former Bishops—Most Rev. LEO T. MAHER, D.D., ord. Dec. 18, 1943; appt. First Bishop of Santa Rosa, Feb. 21, 1962; cons. April 5, 1962; translated San Diego, Aug. 27, 1969; died Feb. 23, 1991.—Most Rev. MARK J. HURLEY, D.D., Ph.D., J.C.B., L.L.D., ord. Sept. 23, 1944; appt. Titular Bishop of Thunusuda and Auxiliary of San Francisco, Oct. 12, 1967; cons. Jan. 4, 1968; translated Santa Rosa, Nov. 9, 1969; appt. member of the Vatican Secretariat for Non-Believers, consultor to the Congregation for Catholic Education; resigned as Bishop of Santa Rosa, April 15, 1986.—Most Rev. JOHN T. STEINBOCK, D.D., ord. May 1, 1963; Titular Bishop of Midila and Auxiliary Bishop of Orange; appt. May 29, 1984; translated Santa Rosa, March 31, 1987; translated Fresno, Nov. 25, 1991.

Vicar General—Rev. LOREN ALLEN, *560 Ninth St., P.O. Box 1297, Santa Rosa, 95402.* Tel: 707-545-7610.

Deans—Rev. DAVID SHAW, Sonoma-North; Rev. Msgr. JOHN J. BRENKLE, Napa; Rev. STEPHEN J. CANNY, Sonoma-South; Rev. THOMAS K. DIAZ, Mendocino-Lake; Rev. MICHAEL M. KELLY, Humboldt-Del Norte.

Chancery Office—560 Ninth St., P.O. Box 1297, Santa Rosa, 95402. Tel: 707-545-7610; Fax: 707-542-9702. Office Hours: Mon.-Fri. 9-5 All applications for dispensations, faculties, etc., and all correspondence should be addressed to the Chancery Office.

Moderator of Curia—Rev. LOREN ALLEN.

Members of the Curia—Rev. Msgr. THOMAS J. KEYS, V.G.; Rev. Msgr. JAMES E. PULSKAMP; Rev. Msgr. JOHN J. BRENKLE; Revs. DAVID SHAW; STEPHEN J. CANNY; THOMAS K. DIAZ; MICHAEL M. KELLY; DANIEL P. WHELTON.

Chancellor—Rev. Msgr. JAMES E. PULSKAMP.

Vice-Chancellor—Sr. PATRICIA BRANDMEIR, S.N.J.M.

Vicar of Finance—Rev. Msgr. THOMAS J. KEYS, V.G.

Secretary to the Bishop—GUADALUPE GUERRERO . Fax: 707-545-3810.

Diocesan Tribunal—P.O. Box 1297, Santa Rosa, 95402. Tel: 707-542-9014.

Judicial Vicar—Rev. DANIEL P. WHELTON, J.C.L.

Adjutant Judicial Vicar—Rev. Msgr. JOHN J. BRENKLE, J.C.D.

Promoter of Justice—Rev. STEPHEN J. CANNY.

Defender of the Bond—Rev. DAVID SHAW.

Diocesan Judges—Rev. Msgr. JOHN J. BRENKLE, J.C.D.; Rev. Msgr. JAMES P. GAFFEY; Revs. JOHN CREWS; DANIEL WHELTON, J.C.L.; Mrs. MARGUERITE B. STEIN, J.C.L., J.D.

Advocates—Revs. MICHAEL M. KELLY; FERGAL MCGUINNESS; WALTER ROGINA; Sr. MAURA MURPHY, O.S.U.; Deacon RODRIGO AGUDELO; STELLA AGUDELO.

Advocate-Auditor—Sr. ROSE MARY KUKLOK, O.S.B.

Notary—Rev. Msgr. JAMES E. PULSKAMP.

Board of Consultors—Rev. Msgr. THOMAS J. KEYS, V.G.; Rev. Msgr. JAMES E. PULSKAMP; Rev. Msgr. JOHN J. BRENKLE; Revs. DAVID SHAW; STEPHEN J. CANNY; THOMAS K. DIAZ; MICHAEL M. KELLY.

Ministries Board—Rev. Msgr. THOMAS J. KEYS, V.G.; Rev. Msgr. JAMES E. PULSKAMP; Revs. SEAN MURRAY, C.SS.R.; XAVIER OCHOA; ANGELITO PERIES, C.SS.R.; ALVIN VILLARUEL; Deacons ALLAN BOHNER; JOSEPH REMLEY; Sr. OLIVE MURPHY, S.M.; Sr. ANN PATRICIA O'CONNOR, C.S.J.; GUADALUPE GUERRERO, Sec. MICHELLE HEALY; NANCY MARSDEN; LINDA REMLEY; MAUREEN SHAW; ED BYROM; STANLEY CORDERO; MICHAEL KAMPLAIN.

Diocesan Priests' Council—Rev. Msgr. THOMAS J. KEYS, V.G.; Rev. Msgr. JAMES E. PULSKAMP; Rev. Msgr. JOHN J. BRENKLE; Rev. Msgr. JAMES P. GAFFEY; Revs. ANDRE BERNARD; STEPHEN J. CANNY; THOMAS K. DIAZ; DONALD EAGLESON; MICHAEL M. KELLY; ANDREW METCALF; SEAN MURRAY, C.Ss.R.; XAVIER OCHOA; DAVID G. SHAW; PATRICK STEPHENSON.

Finance Committee—Rev. Msgr. THOMAS J. KEYS, V.G.; Mr. CONO DI PIETRO; Mr. JOHN KLEIN.

Diocesan Offices and Directors

AIDS Ministry Outreach—NANCY MARSDEN, *P.O. Box 11574, Santa Rosa, 95406.* Tel: 707-528-3887.

Archivist—Rev. Msgr. JAMES E. PULSKAMP, *560 Ninth St., P.O. Box 1297, Santa Rosa, 95402.* Tel: 707-545-7610.

Attorney for the Diocese—Mr. JOHN KLEIN, *P.O. Box 1845, Santa Rosa, 95402.* Tel: 707-546-6767.

Boy Scouts—STANLEY CORDERO, *P.O. Box 11574, Santa Rosa, 95406.* Tel: 707-571-8647.

Building Committee—Rev. Msgr. THOMAS J. KEYS, V.G., Chm.; Rev. MICHAEL J. CLEARY; DON LINDSAY; JOHN RYAN; THOMAS FELLENZ; JOHN KLEIN; JOHN MILES; CLYDE SMITH.

Catholic Charities, Central Admin. Office—MAUREEN E. SHAW, A.C.S.W., Diocesan Dir., *2325 Montgomery Dr., P.O. Box 4900, Santa Rosa, 95402.* Tel: 707-528-8712.

Catholic Youth Organization—Rev. Msgr. THOMAS J. KEYS, V.G., Dir., Office: *560 Ninth St., P.O. Box 3268, Santa Rosa, 95402.* Tel: 707-545-7610.

Cemeteries—Rev. Msgr. GERARD FAHEY, Dir., Office: *P.O. Box 2098, 2930 Bennett Valley Rd., Santa Rosa, 95404*. Tel: 707-546-6290.

Clergy Formation—Chancery Office, 560 Ninth St., P.O. Box 1297, Santa Rosa, 95402. Tel: 707-545-7610.

Detention Ministry, Adult—24A Ursuline Rd., Santa Rosa, 95403. Tel: 707-544-9080.

Detention Ministry, Juvenile—ED BYROM, Dir., *155 N. Pythian Rd., Santa Rosa, 95409*. Tel: 707-537-6300, Ext. 6248.

Development—Rev. Msgr. THOMAS J. KEYS, V.G., Dir., *560 Ninth St., P.O. Box 1297, Santa Rosa, 95402*. Tel: 707-545-7610.

Disabled—Chancery Office, 560 Ninth St., P.O. Box 1297, Santa Rosa, 95402. Tel: 707-545-7610.

Ecumenical and Interreligious Affairs—Rev. THOMAS W. DEVEREAUX, Dir., *208 Matheson St., Healdsburg, 95448*. Tel: 707-433-5536.

Health Affairs—MICHAEL GOSPE, M.D., Liaison, *170 Sotoyome, Santa Rosa, 95405*. Tel: 707-546-6948.

Hispanic Ministry—Rev. XAVIER OCHOA, Dir., *Centro Pastoral Hispano, 81 W. Cotati Ave., Cotati, 94931*. Tel: 707-795-0578.

Cursillos De Cristiandad—Rev. MANUEL CHAVEZ, Spiritual Dir., *8460 Alden Ln., Windsor, 95492*. Tel: 707-837-8962.

Los Jovenes—Centro Pastoral Hispano, 81 W. Cotati Ave., Cotati, 94931. Tel: 707-795-0578.

Movimiento Familiar Cristiano—Deacon RODRIGO AGUDELO, Spiritual Dir., *3727 View Ct., Santa Rosa, 95403*. Tel: 707-526-4892.

Renovacion Carismatica Catolica—Rev. JOSE GONZALEZ, Dir., *408 Matheson St., Healdsburg, 95448*. Tel: 707-433-5536.

Leadership Development—MICHAEL KAMPLAIN, *151 Faught Ct., Santa Rosa, 95403*. Tel: 707-545-5236.

National Council of Catholic Women—Sr. ANTONIA KILLIAN, S.M., Spiritual Dir., *1100 High School Rd., Sebastopol, 95472*. Tel: 707-824-1851.

Native American Affairs—Rev. RALPH MONTEIRO, O.S.A., Liaison, *P.O. Box 429, Hoopa, 95546*. Tel: 916-625-4415.

Newspaper—"Redwood Crozier", Deacon ALLAN BOHNER, Editor, *560 Ninth St., P.O. Box 1297, Santa Rosa, 95402*. Tel: 707-545-7610.

Parish Priest Consultors—Rev. Msgr. WILLIAM HYNES; Rev. Msgr. GERARD FAHEY; Revs. MICHAEL J. CLEARY; THOMAS W. DEVEREAUX.

Parish Social Ministry—NANCY MARSDEN, *P.O. Box 11574, Santa Rosa, 95406*. Tel: 707-528-3887.

Permanent Diaconate—Directors: Deacon JOSEPH REMLEY; LINDA REMLEY, *560 Ninth St., P.O. Box 1297, Santa Rosa, 95402*. Tel: 707-545-7610.

Pontifical Association of Holy Childhood—Deacon RICHARD NAUMANN, *560 Ninth St., P.O. Box 1297, Santa Rosa, 95402*. Tel: 707-545-7610.

Priests' Health and Retirement Board—Rev. Msgr. THOMAS J. KEYS, V.G.; JAMES P. GAFFEY; Revs. APOLINAR HERNANDEZ; GEORGE RISDEN.

Priests' Personnel Committee—Rev. Msgr. THOMAS J. KEYS, V.G.; Rev. Msgr. JAMES E. PULSKAMP; Rev. Msgr. JAMES P. GAFFEY; Revs. GERARD GORMLEY; DANIEL P. WHELTON.

Propagation of the Faith—Deacon RICHARD NAUMANN, *560 Ninth St., P.O. Box 1297, Santa Rosa, 95402*. Tel: 707-545-7610.

Property Committee—Rev. Msgr. THOMAS J. KEYS, V.G., Chm.; Mr. CONO DI PIETRO; Mr. LAWRENCE GIOVANNONI; Mr. HAROLD LOCKWOOD.

Council for Religious—Sr. PATRICIA CARSON, R.S.M.; Sr. JEAN HOPMAN, O.S.U.; Sr. ANTONIA KILLIAN, S.M.; Sr. JOYCE POESCHL, O.P.; Bros. JONATHAN CORD, F.S.C.; RAFAEL WILLEKE, F.S.C.

Religious Education—Sr. OLIVE MURPHY, S.M., Dir. MARIA DE JESUS CERVANTES, Hispanic Catechetical Ministry, *P.O. Box 11574, Santa Rosa, 95406*. Tel: 707-525-8440. MICHELLE HEALY, Assoc. D.R.E. & Coord. of Ministries (North), *222 Dollison St., Eureka, 95501*. Tel: 707-444-3627.

Respect Life—JOSEPH OLSEN; NORA OLSEN, *4525 Heath Cir., Rohnert Park, 94928*. Tel: 707-586-3009.

Schools—Sr. ANN PATRICIA O'CONNOR, C.S.J., Supt. of Schools; Sr. MARION IRVINE, O.P., Asst. Supt. of Schools; Sr. FRANCIS MARIE HANSEN, C.S.J., Consultant, Office: *P.O. Box 6654, Santa Rosa, 95406*. Tel: 707-525-9525.

Serra Club—Rev. HANS RUYGT, Chap., *900 S. Oak St., Ukiah, 95482*. Tel: 707-642-1431.

Vocations—Rev. HANS RUYGT, Dir., *900 S. Oak St., Ukiah, 95482*. Tel: 707-642-1431. Rev. ALVIN VILLARUEL, Assoc. Dir. of Vocations & Seminarians.

Youth Ministry / Young Adult Ministry—STANLEY CORDERO, Dir., *P.O. Box 11574, Santa Rosa, 95406*. Tel: 707-571-8647. AGNES BAILEY, Dir., Humboldt & Del Norte Counties, *222 Dollison St., Rm. 212, Eureka, 95501*. Tel: 707-445-1006.

CLERGY, PARISHES, MISSIONS AND PAROCHIAL SCHOOLS

CITY OF SANTA ROSA
(Sonoma County)

1—CATHEDRAL OF ST. EUGENE (1950), Rev. Msgr. James P. Gaffey; Revs. Walter Rogina, Jr.; Bruce Lamb; Jerald F. Thomas; Deacons Richard Naumann; W. Everett Woodruff. In res., Rev. Msgr. Patrick McCoy (England).
Res., 2323 Montgomery Dr., 95405. Tel: 707-542-6984; Fax: 707-542-1621. [CEM]
School—300 Farmers Ln., 95405. Tel: 707-545-7252; Fax: 707-545-2594. Mrs. Barbara Gasparini, Prin.
Lay Teachers 13; Students 357.
Catechesis / Religious Programs—Diane Drew, D.R.E. Students 250.

2—HOLY SPIRIT (1964), Rev. Msgr. James E. Pulskamp; Rev. Roger Lamoureux. In res., Rev. Daniel P. McCarthy, Pastor Emeritus.
Res., 1244 St. Francis Rd., 95409. Tel: 707-539-4495.
Catechesis / Religious Programs—Tel: 707-539-3343. Bernard Ciernick, D.R.E.
Students 125.

3—ST. ROSE OF LIMA (1877), Revs. Denis A. O'Sullivan; Gerard Gormley; David Villalobos. In res., Rev. Msgr. Thomas J. Keys.
Res., 398 10th St., 95401. Tel: 707-542-6448; Fax: 707-542-3359.
School—4300 Old Redwood Hwy., 95403. Tel: 707-545-0379; Fax: 707-545-7150. Kathy Ryan, Prin.
Lay Teachers 14; Students 361.
Catechesis / Religious Programs—Tel: 707-542-3080. Sr. Shelia Coffey, S.M., D.R.E.
Students 260.

4—RESURRECTION (1967), Rev. David Shaw; Deacon Rodrigo Agudelo.
Res., 303 Stony Point Rd., 95401. Tel: 707-544-7272; Fax: 707-544-2901.
Catechesis / Religious Programs—Tel: 707-544-0708. Betty Kovanis, D.R.E.
Students 460.

5—STAR OF THE VALLEY (1981), Rev. Msgr. Gerard Fahey. In res., Rev. Patrick J. Leslie (SAC).
Res., 615 Wild Oak Dr., 95409. Tel: 707-538-2387; Fax: 707-539-8620.

OUTSIDE CITY OF SANTA ROSA

American Canyon, Holy Family, Rev. Patrick Stephenson; Deacon Michael Simmons.
Res., 402 Donaldson Way, 94589. Tel: 707-645-9331; Fax: 707-645-0424.
Catechesis / Religious Programs—Lia Estupin, D.R.E.
Students 96.

Arcata, Humboldt Co., St. Mary's (1883), Rev. Michael M. Kelly; Deacon John Gai. In res., Rev. Hector Flores, M.S.S.
Res., 1690 Janes Rd., 95521. Tel: 707-822-7696; Fax: 707-822-6931. [CEM]
School—1730 Janes Rd., 95521. Tel: 707-822-3877. Sr. Gretchen Krueger, O.P., Prin.
Sisters 1; Lay Teachers 6; Students 77.
Catechesis / Religious Programs—Patricia Heavilin, D.R.E.
Students 130.
Mission—Blue Lake, St. Joseph.

Boyes Hot Springs, Sonoma Co., St. Leo (1966), Rev. Msgr. John J. O'Hare; Rev. Aurelio Villa, O.F.M.
Res., 601 Agua Caliente Rd., Sonoma, 95476. Tel: 707-996-8422; Fax: 707-996-3984.
Church—P.O. Box 666, 95416.
Catechesis / Religious Programs—Tel: 707-996-7503. Cindy Vrooman, D.R.E.
Students 287.

Calistoga, Napa Co., Our Lady of Perpetual Help (1915), Rev. J. Lawrence Carolan.
Res., 901 Washington St., 94515. Tel: 707-942-6894.
Catechesis / Religious Programs—D.R.E.: Laverne Oyarzo; Teresa Olguin.
Students 39.

Clearlake, Lake Co., Our Lady, Queen of Peace (1967), Rev. Louis J. Nichols (SY) Admin.
Res., P.O. Box 460, 95422. Tel: 707-994-6618.
Catechesis / Religious Programs—Lela Davis-Cagnacci, D.R.E.
Students 80.

Cloverdale, Sonoma Co., St. Peter's (1917), Rev. Robert Blake; Deacon Rodolfo Silagan. In res., Rev. Henry L. Faucher, Pastor Emeritus.
Res., 491 S. Franklin St., 95425. Tel: 707-894-2535.
Catechesis / Religious Programs—Debbi Davis, D.R.E.
Students 131.
Mission—Asti, Our Lady of Mt. Carmel.

Cotati, Sonoma Co., St. Joseph (1913), Rev. Stephen J. Canny.
Res., 150 St. Joseph Way, 94931-4117. Tel: 707-795-4807; Fax: 707-795-7851.
Catechesis / Religious Programs—Tel: 707-795-7678. Georgette Parry, D.R.E.
Students 488.

Crescent City, Del Norte Co., St. Joseph (1869), Rev. Diego C. Baptista.
Res., 319 E St., 95531. Tel: 707-465-1762; Fax: 707-465-1763. [CEM]
School—300 E St., 95531. Tel: 707-464-3477.
Sisters 2; Lay Teachers 2; Students 47.
Catechesis / Religious Programs—Rev. Diego Baptista, D.R.E.
Students 100.
Mission—Klamath, St. Robert and Ann.
Station—Smith River, Our Lady of Guadalupe.

Eureka, Humboldt Co., St. Bernard (1864), Rev. Michael Cloney.
Res., P.O. Box 169, 95502. Tel: 707-442-6466. [CEM]
School—115 Henderson St., 95502. Tel: 707-443-2226. Mrs. Marguerite Meyer, Prin.
Lay Teachers 10; Students 220.
Catechesis / Religious Programs—Debbie Kamberg, D.R.E.
Students 70.
Mission—Eureka, St. Joseph.

Sacred Heart (1963), Rev. Donald W. Eagleson; Ann Lynch, Pastoral Assoc.; Deacons James Hercher; Anthony Viegas.
Res., 2085 Myrtle Ave., 95501. Tel: 707-443-8429; Fax: 707-443-8420.
Catechesis / Religious Programs—Marianne Keesee, D.R.E.
Students 135.

Ferndale, Humboldt Co., Church of the Assumption (1878), Rev. Denis Doyle.
Res., 546 Berding St., P.O. Box 1097, 95536. Tel: 707-786-9551. [CEM]
Catechesis / Religious Programs—Maura Eastman, D.R.E.
Students 77.
Mission—Petrolia, St. Patrick.

Fort Bragg, Mendocino Co., Our Lady of Good Counsel (1890), Revs. Thomas K. Diaz; Apolinar Hernandez.
Res., 255 S. Harold St., 95437. Tel: 707-964-0229.
Catechesis / Religious Programs—Tel: 707-964-5727. D.R.E.: Toni Clark; Caryn Brady.
Students 157.

Fortuna, Humboldt Co., St. Joseph (1909), Rev. Norman J. Simoneau (MAN) Admin.; Deacon Thomas Silva. In res., Revs. James Thottapally (India); Hector Flores, M.S.S., (Hispanic Ministry).
Res., P.O. Box 430, 95540. Tel: 707-725-1148; Fax: 707-725-5678. [CEM]
Catechesis / Religious Programs—2292 Newburg Rd., 95540. Tel: 707-725-1216.
Students 150.
Mission—Loleta, St. Patrick.

Garberville, Humboldt Co., Our Lady of the Redwoods (1950), Rev. Thomas Gowing, Admin.
Res., 515 Maple Ln., 95542. Tel: 707-923-7864.
Mission—Leggett, St. Cecilia, (1954).

Guerneville, Sonoma Co., St. Elizabeth (1916), Rev. Philip J. Ryan, Admin.
Res., 14095 Woodland Dr., 95446-9553. Tel: 707-869-2107.
Catechesis / Religious Programs—Tel: 707-923-7864.
Students 29.
Missions—Monte Rio, St. Catherine; Cazadero, St. Colman.

Healdsburg, Sonoma Co., St. John the Baptist (1884), Revs. Thomas W. Devereaux; Jose Gonzalez (Mexico); Rose Marie Woodruff, Pastoral Assoc. & D.R.E.
Res., 208 Matheson St., 95448. Tel: 707-433-5536; Fax: 707-433-1813.
School—217 Fitch St., 95448. Tel: 707-433-2758; Fax: 707-433-0353. Sandra Blasser, Prin.
Lay Teachers 17; Students 309.
Catechesis / Religious Programs—Tel: 707-433-5112.
Students 350.

Hoopa, Humboldt Co., Mission of Blessed Kateri Tekakwitha (1986), Rev. Ralph Monteiro, O.S.A., Admin.
Res., P.O. Box 429, 95546. Tel: 530-625-4415; Fax: 530-625-4530.
Tekakwitha Center—P.O. Box 845, 95546. Tel: 530-625-4464. Sr. Patricia Carson, R.S.M., Dir.

Lakeport, Lake Co., St. Mary (1871), Rev. Ted Oswald.
Res., 801 N. Main St., 95453. Tel: 707-263-4401. [CEM]

School—Holy Family School, 95453. Tel: 707-262-1954.
Sisters 1; Lay Teachers 1; Students 25.
Catechesis/Religious Programs—Tel: 707-263-0606. Hedy Griego, D.R.E.
Students 160.
Missions—Lucerne, Queen of the Rosary; Kelseyville, St. Peter. [CEM]

McKinleyville, Humboldt County, Christ the King (1967), Rev. Stephen MacPherson.
Res., P.O. Box 2367, 95519. Tel: 707-839-2911; Fax: 707-839-3441.
Catechesis/Religious Programs—Alouez Linehan, D.R.E.
Students 125.
Missions—Trinidad, Holy Trinity; Orick, St. Thomas.

Mendocino, Mendocino Co., St. Anthony (1864), Rev. John J. Martin, M.M., Admin.
Res., P.O. Box 665, 95460. Tel: 707-937-5808. [CEM]

Middletown, Lake Co., St. Joseph (1894), Rev. Andrew Metcalf, Admin.
Res., P.O. Box 1350, 95461. Tel: 707-987-3676.
Mission—Loch Lomond, Our Lady of the Lake.
Station—Forest Lake, Our Lady of the Pines.

Napa, Napa Co., St. Apollinaris (1957), Rev. Michael J. Cleary. In res., Rev. Fergal McGuinness.
Res., 3700 Lassen St., 94558. Tel: 707-257-2555; Fax: 707-257-3552.
School—Tel: 707-224-6525. Patricia Granucci, Prin.
Sisters 1; Lay Teachers 14; Students 320.
Catechesis/Religious Programs—Tel: 707-255-7200. Sr. Peggy Cruise, S.M., D.R.E.
Students 352.

St. John the Baptist (1859), Revs. Timothy J. O'Sullivan; Luis Martinez; Joseph Nolan (Ireland).
Res., Box 178, 94559. Tel: 707-226-9379; Fax: 707-254-9262.
School—983 Napa St., 94559. Tel: 707-224-8388; Fax: 707-224-0236.
Principals: Charles Stanton; Judy Stanton.
Sisters 1; Lay Teachers 11; Students 229.
Catechesis/Religious Programs—Tel: 707-255-3533. D.R.E.: Charles Stanton; Judy Stanton.
Students 250.
Station—Imola, State Hospital, St. Luke's Chapel.

St. Thomas Aquinas (1964), Rev. Msgr. Gerard J. Brady. In res., Rev. Gary Sumpter.
Res., 2725 Elm St., 94558. Tel: 707-255-2949.
Catechesis/Religious Programs—Students 160.

Occidental, Sonoma Co., St. Philip (1964), Rev. Daniel P. Whelton.
Res., P.O. Box 339, 95465. Tel: 707-874-3812.
Catechesis/Religious Programs—Judy Van Gorder, D.R.E.
Students 59.
Mission—Bodega, St. Teresa. [CEM]

Petaluma, Sonoma Co., St. James (1964), Rev. Michael A. Culligan; Deacons Ray Noll; Ken Manz. In res., Rev. Msgr. Joseph Alzugaray.
Res., 125 Sonoma Mt. Pky., 94954. Tel: 707-762-4256.
Catechesis/Religious Programs—Tel: 707-762-9063.
Students 673.

St. Vincent de Paul (1857), Rev. Gary Lombardi; Rev. Msgr. Joseph Alzugaray; Revs. Ramon Pons, O.A.R.; Chinh Nguyen.
Res., 35 Liberty St., 94952. Tel: 707-762-4278; Fax: 707-763-8188.
School—Howard & Union Sts., 94952. Tel: 707-762-6426; Fax: 707-762-6791. Sue Kernan, Prin.
Lay Teachers 11; Students 312.
High School—849 Keokuk, P.O. Box 517, 94953. Tel: 707-763-1032; Fax: 707-763-9448. Mr. Edward Kavanaugh, Prin.
Priests 1; Lay Teachers 25; Students 357.
Catechesis/Religious Programs—Camilla Edwards, D.R.E.
Students 420.

Philo, Mendocino Co., St. Elizabeth Seton, Rev. Michaelraj Philominsamy, C.PP.S., Admin.
Res., P.O. Box 248, 95466. Tel: 707-895-2690.

Point Arena, Mendocino Co., St. Aloysius (1950), Rev. Thomas P. O'Sullivan (SAC) Admin.
Res., P.O. Box 66, 95468. Tel: 707-882-2277; Fax: 707-882-2277. [CEM]
Missions—Elk, Blessed Sacrament, (1880); Gualala, Mary, Star of the Sea.

Rohnert Park, Sonoma Co., St. Elizabeth Seton (1981), Rev. John Griffin; Deacon Paul Bromham.
Res., 4595 Snyder Ln., 94928. Tel: 707-585-3708; Fax: 707-585-1201.
Catechesis/Religious Programs—Tel: 707-585-8821. Moira Bromham, D.R.E.
Students 230.

Saint Helena, Napa Co., St. Helena (1887), Rev. Msgr. John J. Brenkle; Rev. Oscar Diaz.
Res., 1340 Tainter St., 94574. Tel: 707-963-1228; Fax: 707-963-2894. [CEM]
School—1255 Oak Ave., 94574. Tel: 707-963-4677; Fax: 707-963-4677. Sr. Mary Dorothea Quinn, C.S.J., Prin.
Sisters 2; Lay Teachers 8; Students 133.
Catechesis/Religious Programs—Tel: 707-963-8290. D.R.E.: Sr. Kathleen O'Shea, C.S.J.; Maria Conroy Phelps.
Students 97.

Scotia, Humboldt Co., St. Patrick (1930), Rev. Andre Bernard, Admin.
Res., P.O. Box 98, 95565. Tel: 707-764-5446.

Sebastopol, Sonoma Co., St. Sebastian (1898), Rev. Msgr. William Hynes; Rev. George Aziz, S.J.; Deacon Harry Martin.
Res., 7983 Covert Ln., 95472. Tel: 707-823-2208; Fax: 707-823-1098.
Catechesis/Religious Programs—Tel: 707-823-4966. Barbara Schliemann, D.R.E.
Students 171.

Sonoma, Sonoma Co., St. Francis Solano (1878), Revs. James McSweeney; Robert Castro; Aurelio Villa, O.F.M.; Mario Munari.
Res., 469 Third St., W., 95476. Tel: 707-996-6759; Fax: 707-939-8128. [CEM]
School—342 W. Napa St., 95476. Tel: 707-996-4994. Dr. Lydia Treadwell-Blecksmith, Prin.
Lay Teachers 25; Students 360.
Catechesis/Religious Programs—Tel: 707-996-1578. Will Roll, D.R.E.
Students 409.

Ukiah, Mendocino Co., St. Mary of the Angels (1887), Revs. Hans Ruygt; Perfecto Nacional (Philippines); Mary Leittem-Thomas, Pastoral Assoc.
Res., 900 S. Oak St., 95482. Tel: 707-462-1431; Fax: 707-462-2879. [CEM]
School—991 S. Dora St., 95482. Tel: 707-462-3888; Fax: 707-462-6014. Mary Jo Hons, Prin.
Lay Teachers 12; Students 251.
Catechesis/Religious Programs—Tel: 707-462-1131; Fax: 707-467-0980. Sr. Jane Kelly, P.B.V.M., D.R.E.
Students 107.
Mission—Hopland, St. Francis.

Willits, Mendocino Co., St. Anthony (1923), Rev. Gary W. Logan, Admin.; Deacon Allan G. Bohner.
Res., 61 W. San Francisco Ave., 95490. Tel: 707-459-2252; Fax: 707-459-9070.
Catechesis/Religious Programs—Donna Jara, D.R.E.
Students 76.
Mission—Covelo, Queen of Peace. [CEM]

Windsor, Sonoma Co., Our Lady of Guadalupe (1969), Revs. Angelito Peries, C.Ss.R., Admin.; Manuel Chavez; Marge Bailly, Pastoral Assoc.
Mailing Address: 8460 Alden Ln., 95492. Tel: 707-837-8962; Fax: 707-837-9157.
Catechesis/Religious Programs—Tel: 707-837-7617. Louis Gonzalez, D.R.E.
Students 150.

Yountville, Napa Co., St. Joan of Arc (1920), Rev. Mathew Ittiyappara; Deacon Jerry Cain.
Res., Box 2009, 94599. Tel: 707-944-2461.
Catechesis/Religious Programs—Students 52.
Mission—Rutherford, Holy Family.

Chaplains of Public Institutions

CRESCENT CITY. *Pelican Bay State Prison.* Rev. Joseph Vallooran.

ELDRIDGE. *Sonoma Developmental Center.* Rev. Patrick J. Leslie (SAC) Chap.

IMOLA. *Napa State Hospital* 94558. Rev. James Lantsberger, O.M.I., Chap.

PETALUMA. *U.S. Coast Guard Training Center.* Rev. James A. Ingram (ORL) Chap.

YOUNTVILLE. *Veterans Administration Home.* Rev. Paul F. Ledermann (OG) Chap.

Special Assignment:
Reverend Fathers—
Allen, Loren
Kalil, Gordon, O.P.
Ochoa, Xavier

Military Chaplains:
Reverend Fathers—
Serban, Ron

Unassigned:
Reverend Fathers—
Talcott, Peter

On Duty Outside the Diocese:
Reverend Fathers—
Boettcher, John
Rioux, Raymond

Graduate Studies:
Reverend Fathers—
Gramajo, Rodolfo
Hume, Jorge
Kelly, Michael E.

On Leave:
Reverend Fathers—
Donahue, William

On Sick Leave:
Reverend Fathers—
O'Neill, Vincent

Retired:
Reverend Monsignors—
Fleming, Vincent A.
Monaghan, George D.
Serado, William
Tillman, Clyde F.
Tournier, Andre
Reverend Fathers—
Hanratty, Brendan
Healy, John
Keffer, Thomas
Keogh, Thomas
McAllister, Alex
McCarthy, Daniel P.
McIntyre, Justin
Sheehy, Wilfred
Tracy, Charles

Permanent Deacons:
Agudelo, Rodrigo, Santa Rosa
Bohner, Allan G., Willits
Bond, Ken, Arcata
Bromham, Paul, Rohnert Park
Cain, Jerry B., Yountville
Gai, John, Aracata
Glendinning, Ralph, Clearlake
Hercher, James, Eureka
Manz, Kenneth, Petaluma
Martin, Harry, Sebastopol
Naumann, Richard, Santa Rosa
Noll, Ray, Petaluma
Remley, Joseph, Rohnert Park
Ross, Norman, Santa Rosa
Silva, Thomas, Fortuna
Viegas, Anthony, Eureka
Woodruff, W. Everett, Santa Rosa

INSTITUTIONS LOCATED IN THE DIOCESE

[A] SEMINARIES, RELIGIOUS, OR SCHOLASTICATES

NAPA. *Mont La Salle Novitiate*, 4405 Redwood Dr., 94558. Mailing Address: P.O. Box 3470, 94558. Tel: 707-252-3821. Brothers of the Christian Schools. Bro. Richard Moratto, Dir.

[B] HIGH SCHOOLS, DIOCESAN

SANTA ROSA. *Cardinal Newman High School*, 50 Ursuline Rd., 95403. Tel: 707-546-6470. Mr. Thomas C. Beecher, Prin.; Rev. Alvin M. Villaruel. Priests 1; Lay Teachers 29; Students 468.

EUREKA. *St. Bernard's High School*, 222 Dollison St., 95501. Tel: 707-443-2735; Fax: 707-443-4723. Jeffery A. Jacobs, Prin.; Rev. Loren Allen; Craig Brown, Campus Min. Priests 1; Lay Teachers 19; Students 230.

[C] HIGH SCHOOLS, PRIVATE

SANTA ROSA.

**Ursuline High School*, 90 Ursuline Rd., 95403. Tel: 707-524-1130; Fax: 707-542-0131. Ursuline Sisters of the Roman Union. Legal Title: *Santa Rosa Ursuline Corporation.* Sr. Dianne Baumunk, O.S.U., Prin. Sisters 3; Lay Teachers 37; Students 416.

**Ursuline Parent Association of Santa Rosa.*

**Ursuline Memorial Scholarship Fund.*

NAPA. *Justin-Siena High School*, 4026 Maher St., 94558. Tel: 707-255-0950; Fax: 707-255-0334. Joseph W. Bracco, Pres. & CEO; Gregory J. Schmitz, Prin.; Dennis Ruggiero, Vice Prin. Dean Studies; Bruce Halverson, Chair Guidance Dept.; Rev. Fergal McGuinnerss. Priests 1; Sisters 1; Lay Teachers 46; Students 592.

**Justin-Siena High School Corporation, Inc.*

**Justin-Siena High School Foundation, Inc.*

**Kolbe Academy for Boys and Girls.* (High School). 1600 F St., 94559. Tel: 707-255-6412. Mr. Francis Crotty, Admin.; Diane Muth, Prin. Lay Teachers 3; Students 4.

[D] ELEMENTARY SCHOOLS, PRIVATE

NAPA.
Kolbe Academy for Boys and Girls, 1600 F St., 94559. Tel: 707-255-6412. Mr. Francis Crotty, Admin.; Diane Muth, Prin. Lay Teachers 6; Students 30.

[E] CATHOLIC CHARITIES

SANTA ROSA.
Diocese of Santa Rosa, Catholic Charities.
Central Administrative Offices, 2325 Montgomery Dr., P.O. Box 4900, 95402. Tel: 707-528-8712. Maureen E. Shaw, A.C.S.W., Diocesan Dir.; Mary Ann McGee, R.N., Assoc. Dir. Programs; Sharon McCarty, Dir. Admin. Svcs./Human Resources; Lia Boatman, Dir. Accounting Svcs.; Frances Caballo, Development Dir.
Family Support Center, 465 A St., 95401. Tel: 707-542-5426. Mailing Address: P.O. Box 4900, 95402. Daniel Richardi, Prog. Dir.
Homeless Service Center, 600 Morgan St., 95401. Tel: 707-525-0226. Mailing Address: P.O. Box 4900, 95402. Nick Baker, Program Dir.
Professional Foster Care, 3295 Claremont Way, Ste. #1, Napa, 94558. Tel: 707-224-3191. Anna Shetka, Program Dir.
I'm Home Alone, 2325 Montgomery Dr., 95405. Tel: 707-528-8712. Mailing Address: P.O. Box 4900, 95402. Michele Osmon, Prog. Dir.
Immigration Services, 516 Morgan St., 95401. Tel: 707-578-6000. Mailing Address: P.O. Box 4900, 95402.
Interfaith Volunteer Caregiver Program, 9470 Mendenhall Ave., Upper Lake, 95485. Tel: 707-275-9161. Mailing Address: P.O. Box 925, Upper Lake, 95485. Louis P. Denny, Prog. Dir.
Rural Food Program, 2325 Montgomery Dr., 95405. Tel: 707-528-8712. Mailing Address: P.O. Box 4900, 95402. Sharon Malm Read, Program Dir.
Phone Friend, 2325 Montgomery Dr., 95405. Tel: 707-528-8712. Mailing Address: P.O. Box 4900, 95402. Michele Osmon, Program Dir.
Alzheimer's Respite/Resource Center, 398 Tenth St., 95401. Tel: 707-528-8712. 1000 N. Gravenstein Hwy., Sebastopol, 95472. Tel: 707-528-8712. Mailing Address: P.O. Box 4900, 95402. Scott Hale, Program Dir.
Professional Counseling Services of Humboldt/Del Norte, 2936 J St., Eureka, 95501. Tel: 707-444-9611. 1151 Main St., Fortuna, 95540. Tel: 707-725-3389. Sr. Patricia Carson, R.S.M., Regional Dir.
Housing Options, 3295 Claremont Way, Ste. #1, Napa, 94558. Tel: 707-224-4403. Danda Winford, M.A., Prog. Dir.
Teen Mom Program, 3295 Claremont Way, Ste. #1, Napa, 94558. Tel: 707-224-3191. Marjorie Lewis, Prog. Dir.
Free-To-Be, 2325 Montgomery Dr., 95405. Tel: 707-528-8712. Mailing Address: P.O. Box 4900, 95402. Sue Bisbee, Program Dir.
Social Justice, 2325 Montgomery Dr., 95405. Tel: 707-528-8712. Mailing Address: P.O. Box 4900, 95402. David Hinkley, Program Dir.
Rainbow House, 1209 Jefferson St., Napa, 94559. Tel: 707-258-0260. Jane Ries, Prog. Dir.
Counseling Referral, 3295 Claremont Way, Ste. #1, Napa, 94558. Tel: 707-224-4403. Danda Winford, Prog. Dir.
Parish/Family Services, 2325 Montgomery Dr., 95405. Tel: 707-528-8712. Mailing Address: P.O. Box 4900, 95402. Ann McGee, Prog. Dir.
Phase Two - Housing Development, 2325 Montgomery Dr., 95405. Tel: 707-528-8712. Mailing Address: P.O. Box 4900, 95402. Sr. Teresita Poulin, B.V.M., Prog. Dir.
Phase Two - Supportive Services, 516 Morgan St., 95401. Tel: 707-577-7696. American Romero, Prog. Dir.

[F] VOLUNTEER SERVICES

EUREKA. *Society of St. Vincent de Paul, District Council of the Redwood Region*, 212 G St., 95501. Tel: 707-443-8676. C. M. Weisel, Pres.

NAPA. *Society of St. Vincent de Paul, District Council of Napa County*, P.O. Box 187, 94558. Tel: 707-253-0445. Hillman Brooks, Pres.

ROHNERT PARK. *Society of St. Vincent de Paul, District Council of Sonoma County*, P.O. Box 1095, 94928. Tel: 800-584-1579. Mr. Bob Solak, Pres.; Mr. Paul Bromham, Exec. Dir.; Rev. Msgr. Thomas J. Keys, Spiritual Dir.

[G] GENERAL HOSPITALS

SANTA ROSA. *Santa Rosa Memorial Hospital*, 1165 Montgomery Dr., 95405. Tel: 707-546-3210
For a complete listing, refer to the Hospitals section.

EUREKA. *St. Joseph Hospital of Eureka*, 2700 Dolbeer St., 95501. Tel: 707-445-8121
For a complete listing, refer to the Hospitals section.

FORTUNA. *Redwood Memorial Hospital*, 3300 Renner Dr., 95540. Tel: 707-725-3361; Fax: 707-725-7212
For a complete listing, refer to the Hospitals section.

NAPA. *Queen of the Valley Hospital of Napa*, 1000 Trancas St., 94558. Tel: 707-252-4411; Fax: 707-257-4073
For a complete listing, refer to the Hospitals section.

[H] RESIDENTIAL TREATMENT CENTERS

ARCATA.
Butler Valley, Inc., Administrative Office, 380 12th St., 95521. Tel: 707-822-0301; Fax: 707-822-3589. 3971 F St., Eureka, 95501. Tel: 707-442-7313. Robert Clayton, Exec. Dir. Staff 23; Residents 12.

SONOMA. *Hanna Boys Center*, P.O. Box 100, 95476. Tel: 707-996-6767; Fax: 707-996-4742. Legal Title: *Hanna Boys Center.* For underprivileged, emotionally disturbed and pre-delinquent boys, ages 9 to 18 years. Revs. John S. Crews, Ed.D., Exec. Dir.; Gregory Klaas; George Risden. Priests 3; Sisters 1; Staff 136; Students 107.

[I] HOMES FOR SENIOR CITIZENS

*SANTA ROSA. *Vigil Light Apartments (The Vigil Light, Inc.)*, 1945 Long Dr., 95405. Tel: 707-544-2810
For a complete listing, refer to the Special Care Facilities section.

[J] CAMPS AND COMMUNITY CENTERS

DUNCAN MILLS. *St. Joseph Camp.* Brothers of the Christian Schools. Mailing Address: P.O. Box 198, 95430-0198. Tel: 707-865-9941; Fax: 707-865-1025. Bro. Bede Van Duren, F.S.C., Dir. Tel: 707-252-3857.

LEGGETT. *Camp St. Michael.* (Boys - Girls). Mailing Address: P.O. Box 287, Eureka, 95502. Office: 222 Dollison St., Rm. 212, Eureka, 95501. Tel: 707-445-1006 (Business Office); 925-6471 (Campsite Office). Mrs. Agnes J. Bailey, Dir.

MIDDLETOWN. *Camp Salesian*, 95461. Office, Salesian High School, 2851 Salesian Ave., Richmond, 94804. Tel: 510-234-4433, Ext. 58.
Conducted by the Salesians of St. John Bosco.

[K] NEWMAN CENTERS

ARCATA. *Newman Community, Humboldt State University*, 700 Union St., 95521. Tel: 707-822-6057; Fax: 707-822-6057. Rev. Louis Coddaire, O.S.B.Cam.; Deacon Kenneth M. Bond.

PENNGROVE. *Newman Hall, Sonoma State University, Intercollegiate Catholic Ministries*, 1798 E. Cotati Ave., 94951. Tel: 707-794-7957. Rev. Stephen Frost (ORG).

[L] HOUSES OF PRAYER AND RETREAT HOUSES

SANTA ROSA. *Angela Center*, 535 Angela Dr., 95403. Tel: 707-528-8578. Sr. Christine Van Swearingen, O.S.U., Dir.
Cardinal Newman Retreat Center, 24 Ursuline Rd., 95403. Tel: 707-579-9200; 525-8440. Sr. Olive Murphy, S.M., Dir.

NAPA. *Christian Brothers Retreat and Conference Center.* Mailing Address: 4401 Redwood Rd., P.O. Box 3720, 94558. Tel: 707-252-3810; 3811; Fax: 707-252-3818. Linda Lewis, Dir.; Charlotte Horne, Sec.

OAKVILLE. *Carmelite House of Prayer*, P.O. Box 347, 94562. Tel: 707-944-2454. Rev. James Geohegan, O.C.D., Dir.

SEBASTOPOL. *Diocesan House of Prayer*, 1100 High School Rd., 95472. Tel: 707-824-8936. Rev. Sean Murray, C.SS.R.; Sr. Antonia Killian, S.M.

[M] MONASTERIES AND RESIDENTS FOR PRIESTS AND BROTHERS

NAPA. *De La Salle Institute/Provincial Office*, 4401 Redwood Rd., 94558. Tel: 707-252-0222; Fax: 707-252-0407. Mailing Address: P.O. Box 3720, 94558. Brothers of the Christian Schools. Bro. David Brennan, F.S.C., Pres.
Lasallian Education Corporation.
District of San Francisco Christian Brothers Charitable Trust.
Holy Family Community, 4405 Redwood Rd., 94558-9708. Tel: 707-252-3768. Brothers of the Christian Schools. Bros. Jonathan Cord, F.S.C., Dir.; James Riordan, F.S.C., Sub. Dir. Brothers 20.
Justin Community, 4026 Maher St., 94558-2297. Tel: 707-256-4450. Brothers of the Christian Schools. Brothers 10.
Provincialate Community, 4403 Redwood Rd., 94558. Tel: 707-252-0802; Fax: 707-252-7046. Brothers of the Christian Schools. Bros. David Brennan, F.S.C., Prov.; Stanislaus Campbell, F.S.C., Asst. Prov.; Raphael Willeke, F.S.C., Dir.; Rev. David L. Deibel, Chap. Brothers 9.

OAKVILLE. *Carmelite House of Prayer.* Mailing Address: P.O. Box 347, 94562. Tel: 707-944-2454; 944-2460; Fax: 707-944-8533. Discalced Carmelite Friars. Revs. James Geoghegan, O.C.D., Supr.; Mark Kristy, O.C.D.; John Lysaght, O.C.D.; John R. McSweeney, O.C.D.; Bro. Roger Larre, O.C.D. Priests 4; Brothers 1.

[N] CONVENTS AND RESIDENCES FOR SISTERS

SANTA ROSA. *Memorial Hospital Convent*, 271 Doyle Park Dr., 95405. Tel: 707-525-5235. Sister St. Joseph of Orange. Sisters 7.
Provincialate of Ursuline Nuns, 639 Angela Dr., 95403. Tel: 707-545-6811; Fax: 707-579-8571. Ursulines of the Roman Union - Western Province. Sr. Francis Xavier Porter, O.S.U., Prov.

ARCATA. *St. Mary's Convent*, 1710 Janes Rd., 95521. Tel: 707-822-4293.

CRESCENT CITY. *Holy Family Convent*, 440 Third St., 95531. Tel: 707-464-3450. Sisters St. Francis of Holy Family. Sisters 2.

EUREKA. *St. Bernard's Convent*, 255 Henderson St., 95501-4313. Tel: 707-442-2454. Sisters St. Joseph of Orange. Sisters 3.

FORTUNA. *Redwood Memorial Hospital Convent*, 3300 Renner Dr., 95540. Tel: 707-725-3361. Sisters St. Joseph of Orange. Sisters 3.

HEALDSBURG. *Ursuline Residence*, 8730 Middlecreek Rd., 95448. Ursuline Nuns.

NAPA. *Queen of the Valley Convent*, 1000 Trancas St., 94558. Tel: 707-255-6169; Fax: 707-257-4192. Sisters St. Joseph of Orange. Sisters 7.
St. Apollinaris Convent, 3700 Lassen St., P.O. Box 3012, 94558. Tel: 707-255-2185. Congregation of the Sisters of Mercy - The United States Province. Sisters 3.
Siena Convent, 4038 Maher St., 94558. Tel: 707-255-6110. Dominican Sisters of San Rafael. Sisters 7.

ST. HELENA. *St. Helena Convent*, 1229 Oak Ave., 94574. Tel: 707-963-5530. Sisters St. Joseph of Carondelet. Sisters 4.

SEBASTOPOL. *Hermitage of Christ the King*, 6501 Orchard Station Rd., 95472. Tel: 707-795-8555. Sisters of Christ the King. Sr. Michael Bird, S.C.K., Supr. Sisters 2; Assoc. Sisters 5.

WHITETHORN. *Our Lady of the Redwoods Abbey*, 18104 Briceland-Thorn Rd., 95589. Tel: 707-986-7419. Cistercian Nuns of the Strict Observance. Sr. Rosemary Durcan, O.C.S.O., Supr. Ad Nutum; Rev. Roger De Ganck, O.C.S.O., Chap. Priests 1; Sisters 9.

WINDSOR. *Ursuline Residence*, 9248 Lakewood Dr., 95492. Tel: 707-838-4973. Ursuline Nuns. Sisters 2.

[O] MISCELLANEOUS

SANTA ROSA. *Apostolic Endowment Trust*, P.O. Box 1297, 95402. Tel: 707-545-7610. Rev. Msgr. Thomas J. Keys, Dir.
**Catholic Community Foundation*, P.O. Box 1297, 95402. Tel: 707-942-8262. James McN. Dillon, Exec. Dir.
Loyola Institute, 5213 El Mercado Pkwy., 95403. Tel: 707-526-1167. Robert Dalzell, Dir.

SEBASTOPOL. *National Catholic AIDS Network*, 12500 Dupont Rd., 95472. Tel: 707-874-3013; Fax: 707-874-1433. Rev. Rodney J. DeMartini, S.M., Exec. Dir.

RELIGIOUS INSTITUTES OF MEN REPRESENTED IN THE DIOCESE

For further details refer to the corresponding bracketed number in the Religious Institutes of Men or Women section.

[0140]—*Augustinians.*—O.S.A.
[0330]—*Brothers of the Christian Schools.* (San Francisco Prov.).—F.S.C.
[]—*Camadolese Hermits.*—O.S.B.Cam.
[0480]—*Conventual Franciscans.*—O.F.M.Conv.
[0260]—*Discalced Carmelite Friars.* (Anglo-Irish Prov.).—O.C.D.
[0520]—*Franciscan Friars.*—O.F.M.
[0690]—*Jesuit Fathers.*—S.J.
[0825]—*Missionaries of the Blessed Sacrament.*—M.S.S.
[0910]—*Oblates of Mary Immaculate.*—O.M.I.
[0430]—*Order of Preachers.*—O.P.
[1070]—*Redemptorist Fathers.*—C.SS.R.
[1060]—*Society of the Precious Blood.*—C.PP.S.

RELIGIOUS INSTITUTES OF WOMEN REPRESENTED IN THE DIOCESE

[0670]—*Cistercian Nuns of the Strict Observance.*—O.C.S.O.
[1070-03]—*Dominican Sisters.*—O.P.
[1070-04]—*Dominican Sisters.*—O.P.
[1070-13]—*Dominican Sisters.*—O.P.
[2575]—*Institute of the Sisters of Mercy of the Americas.*—R.S.M.
[2470]—*Maryknoll Sisters of St. Dominic.*—M.M.
[1680]—*School Sisters of St. Francis.* (Holy Name Prov.).—O.S.F.
[0430]—*Sisters of Charity of the Blessed Virgin Mary.* (Dubuque, IA).—B.V.M.
[]—*Sisters of Christ the King.*—S.C.K.
[2516]—*Sisters of Mercy.*—S.M.
[0230]—*Sisters of St. Benedict.*—O.S.B.

[1570]—*Sisters of St. Francis of the Holy Family.* (Dubuque IA).—O.S.F.

[3830-03]—*Sisters of St. Joseph.*—C.S.J.

[3840]—*Sisters of St. Joseph of Carondelet.*—C.S.J.

[1990]—*Sisters of the Holy Names of Jesus and Mary.*—S.N.J.M.

[3320]—*Sisters of the Presentation of the B.V.M..*—P.B.V.M.

[1705]—*Sisters of the Third Order of St. Francis of Assisi.*—O.S.F.

[4110]—*Ursuline Nuns.* (Western Prov.).—O.S.U.

DIOCESAN CEMETERIES

SANTA ROSA. *Calvary Catholic.*

EUREKA. *St. Bernard.*

PETALUMA. *Calvary Catholic.*

ST. HELENA. *Holy Cross.*

SONOMA. *St. Francis Solano.*

NECROLOGY

† Tappe, Rev. Msgr. Walter J., Santa Rosa, CA, St. Rose. —Died July 28, 1997.

Diocese of Savannah

(Dioecesis Savannensis)

Most Reverend

J. KEVIN BOLAND, D.D.

Bishop of Savannah; ordained June 14, 1959; appointed Bishop of Savannah February 7, 1995; ordained and installed April 18, 1995.

Most Reverend

RAYMOND W. LESSARD, D.D.

Retired Bishop of Savannah; ordained December 16, 1956; appointed March 5, 1973; consecrated and installed April 27, 1973. *Catholic Pastoral Center: 601 E. Liberty St., Savannah, GA, 31401-5196.* Tel.: 912-238-2320.

ESTABLISHED AS DIOCESE OF SAVANNAH JULY 3, 1850. NAME CHANGED TO DIOCESE.OF SAVANNAH-ATLANTA JAN. 5, 1937; REDESIGNATED NOV. 8, 1956.

Square Miles 37,038.

Comprises 90 Counties in the southern part of the State of Georgia.

PATRONS OF THE DIOCESE: I. ST. JOHN THE BAPTIST; II. OUR LADY OF PERPETUAL HELP. This diocese was solemnly consecrated to the Sacred Heart of Jesus, May 7, 1872, and on Dec. 8, 1943, it was solemnly consecrated to the Immaculate Heart of Mary.

For legal titles of parishes and diocesan institutions, consult the Chancery.

Chancery: Catholic Pastoral Center, 601 E. Liberty St., Savannah, GA, 31401-5196. Tel.: 912-238-2320; Fax: 912-238-2335.

Web site address: http://www.interpath.net/mdoyle/svhhom.html

E-mail address: Diosav@msn.com

STATISTICAL OVERVIEW

Personnel	
Bishop	1
Retired Bishops	1
Priests: Diocesan Active in Diocese	44
Priests: Active Outside Diocese	10
Priests: Retired, Sick or Absent	12
Number of Diocesan Priests	66
Religious Priests in Diocese	33
Extern Priests in Diocese	9
Ordinations:	
Diocesan Priests	3
Permanent Deacons in Diocese	37
Total Brothers	18
Total Sisters	133
Parishes	
Parishes	53
With Resident Pastor:	
Resident Diocesan Priests	37
Resident Religious Priests	16
Without Resident Pastor:	
Missions	28
Professional Ministry Personnel:	
Brothers	18
Sisters	111
Welfare	
Catholic Hospitals	3
Total Assisted	241,423
Health Care Centers	8
Total Assisted	166,200
Residential Care of Children	1
Total Assisted	42
Specialized Homes	1
Total Assisted	22
Special Centers for Social Services	19
Total Assisted	358,746
Educational	
Diocesan Students in Other Seminaries	7
Total Seminarians	7
High Schools, Diocesan and Parish	2
Total Students	613
High Schools, Private	3
Total Students	1,800
Elementary Schools, Diocesan and Parish	15
Total Students	4,731
Catechesis/Religious Education:	
High School Students	935
Elementary Students	4,316
Total Students Under Catholic Instruction	12,402
Teachers in the Diocese:	
Priests	6
Brothers	1
Sisters	29
Lay Teachers	386
Vital Statistics	
Receptions into the Church:	
Infant Baptism Totals	1,363
Adult Baptism Totals	233
Received into Full Communion	446
First Communions	1,194
Confirmations	1,046
Marriages:	
Catholic	156
Interfaith	209
Total Marriages	365
Deaths	496
Total Catholic Population	74,716
Total Population	2,440,868

Former Bishops—Rt. Rev. FRANCIS X. GARTLAND, D.D., first bishop; cons. Nov. 10, 1850; died Sept. 20, 1854.—Rt. Rev. JOHN BARRY, D.D., second bishop; cons. Aug. 2, 1857; died Nov. 21, 1859.—Rt. Rev. AUGUSTIN VEROT, S.S., D.D., cons. April 25, 1858; Vic. Ap. of Florida; transferred to Savannah, July, 1861; returned to Florida as first Bishop of St. Augustine, 1870; died June 10, 1876.—His Eminence IGNATIUS CARDINAL PERSICO, D.D., transferred to this See March 11, 1870; resigned 1872; created Cardinal 1893; died 1895.—Rt. Rev. W. H. GROSS, C.SS.R., D.D., cons. April 27, 1873; promoted to Oregon 1885; died Nov. 14, 1898.—Rt. Rev. THOMAS A. BECKER, D.D., cons. Bishop of Wilmington, Aug. 16, 1868; transferred to Savannah 1886; died July 29, 1899.—Rt. Rev. BENJAMIN J. KEILEY, D.D., cons. June 3, 1900; resigned Feb. 13, 1922; appt. Titular Bishop of Scillium, March 24, 1922; died June 17, 1925.—Most Rev. MICHAEL J. KEYES, S.M., D.D., cons. Oct. 18, 1922; resigned Sept. 23, 1935; appt. Titular Bishop of Areopolis and Assistant at the Pontifical Throne; died July 31, 1959.—Most. Rev. GERALD P. O'HARA, D.D., J.U.D., appt. Titular Bishop of Heliopolis and Auxiliary Bishop of Philadelphia April 26, 1929; cons. May 20, 1929; transferred to See of Savannah, Nov. 16, 1935 received personal title of Archbishop July 12, 1950; appt. Apostolic Nuncio to Ireland, 1951; appt. Apostolic Delegate to Great Britain, 1954; resigned Nov. 11, 1959; died July 16, 1963.—Most Rev. THOMAS J. McDONOUGH, D.D., J.C.D., cons. April 30, 1947; transferred as Auxiliary from St. Augustine to Savannah, Jan. 2, 1957; succeeded to See, March 2, 1960; promoted to Archbishop of Louisville, March 1, 1967; resigned Sept. 29, 1981.—Most Rev. GERARD L. FREY, D.D., cons. Aug. 8, 1967; transferred to Bishop of Lafayette, Nov. 7, 1972; retired May 13, 1989.—Most Rev. RAYMOND W. LESSARD, D.D., cons. April 27, 1973; resigned Feb. 7, 1995.

Vicar General—Rev. FRANCIS J. NELSON, J.C.L., *Catholic Pastoral Center, 601 E. Liberty St., Savannah, 31401-5196.* Tel: 912-238-2320.

Chancery—*Catholic Pastoral Center, 601 E. Liberty St., Savannah, 31401-5196.* Tel: 912-238-2320; Fax: 912-238-2335.

Chancellor—Sr. MARY FAITH McKEAN, R.S.M.

Business Manager—DONALD W. FREW.

Diocesan Tribunal—*Catholic Pastoral Center, 601 E. Liberty St., Savannah, 31401-5196.* Tel: 912-238-2320.

Officialis—Rev. JEREMIAH J. McCARTHY, J.C.L.

Tribunal Judges—Revs. DOUGLAS K. CLARK, S.T.L.; FRANCIS J. NELSON, J.C.L.; HERBERT J. WELLMEIER.

Defender of the Bond—Rev. J. GERARD SCHRECK, J.C.D.

Promoter of Justice—Rev. Msgr. DANIEL J. BOURKE, P.A.

Notaries—CAROLE BARRAS; KATHLEEN TRAHAN.

Censor Librorum—Rev. DOUGLAS K. CLARK, S.T.L.

Archivist—Sr. MARY OF VICTORY O'BRIEN, I.H.M., *Catholic Pastoral Center, 601 E. Liberty St., Savannah, 31401-5196.* Tel: 912-238-2320.

Georgia Catholic Conference—Mr. CHEATHAM HODGES, Exec. Sec., *3200 Deans Bridge Rd., Augusta, 30906.* Tel: 706-798-1719.

Legal Counsel—JOHN BRENNAN, *Catholic Pastoral Center, 601 E. Liberty St., Savannah, 31401-5196.* Tel:

912-238-2320.

Finance Board—Most Rev. J. KEVIN BOLAND; Revs. P. JAMES COSTIGAN; FRANCIS J. NELSON; Sr. MARY FAITH MCKEAN, R.S.M.; FERNANDO ARGUELLES; DONALD FREW; JOHN M. BRENNAN; JOSEPH P. BRENNAN; EMMET BOYD; LULA L. HUFF; E. J. MADDOCKS; FRED MILLER; GREGORY H. SMITH.

Investment Committee—Most Rev. J. KEVIN BOLAND; Rev. P. JAMES COSTIGAN; Mr. DONALD FREW; Mr. ODILO BLANCO; Mr. EDWARD J. BROWN, JR.; Sr. MARY FAITH MCKEAN, R.S.M.

Building Committee—Most Rev. J. KEVIN BOLAND; Rev. FRANCIS J. NELSON; DONALD W. FREW; Revs. P. JAMES COSTIGAN; GABRIEL CUMMINGS; Mr. RONALD A. JACOBS; M. SCOTT CLARK; RICHARD SIMMONS; LEON M. HOBBS, III; ROY HUSSEY; JAMES BANNON.

Catholic Cemetery Board—Rev. JAMES M. MAYO; Mr. JOHN M. SCHRODER, SR.; Mrs. GERALDINE WILLIAMS; Mr. DAVID BLANTON; Mr. SCOTT CLARK; Mr. DONALD FREW.

Deans—

Savannah Deanery: Rev. JOHN A. KENNEALLY, V.F., *18412 Whitfield Ave., Savannah, 31406.* Tel: 912-355-1523.

Augusta Deanery: Rev. ALLAN J. MCDONALD, V.F., *P.O. Box 2446, Augusta, 30903.* Tel: 706-722-4944.

Albany Deanery: Rev. FINBARR P. STANTON, V.F., *421 Edgewood Ln., Albany, 31707.* Tel: 912-439-2302.

Columbus Deanery: Rev. FRANK PATTERSON, V.F., *320 12th St., Columbus, 31901.* Tel: 706-323-6908.

Macon Deanery: Rev. JOHN CUDDY, V.F., *830 Poplar St., Macon, 31201.* Tel: 912-745-1631.

Statesboro Deanery: Rev. MICHAEL SMITH, V.F., *201 Telfair Ave., McRae, 31055.* Tel: 912-868-2002.

Valdosta-Brunswick Deanery: Rev. JOHN O'BRIEN, *800 Gornto Rd., Valdosta, 31602.* Tel: 912-876-4364.

College of Consultors—Current Consultors: Revs. JOHN J. FITZPATRICK; WILLIAM LEAHY; JAMES M. MAYO; FRANCIS J. NELSON, J.C.L.; J. GERARD SCHRECK, J.C.D.; FINBARR P. STANTON; HERBERT J. WELLMEIER.

Council of Priests—Revs. BRETT A. BRANNEN; ROBERT CHANEY; JOHN FITZPATRICK; FREDERICK A. GREEN; JAMES KIRCHNER; BRIAN LABURT; JEREMIAH MCCARTHY; FRANCIS J. NELSON, J.C.L., V.G.; GERALD RAGAN; CHARLES ROLAND; J. GERARD SCHRECK, J.C.D.; VICTOR SEIDEL, S.T.

Council of Religious—Sr. CARMEL TURSI, S.B.S., Pres.; Bro. WALTER GLUHM, C.S.C., Vice Pres.

Religious Vicar—Vacant.

Temporal Affairs Vicar—Rev. P. JAMES COSTIGAN, *1420 Monte Sano Ave., Augusta, 30904.* Tel: 706-733-6627.

Diocesan Offices and Directors

Newspaper—"The Southern Cross"; Rev. DOUGLAS K. CLARK, Editor, Business Office: *Catholic Pastoral Center, 601 E. Liberty St., Savannah, 31401-5196.* Tel: 912-238-2320; Fax: 912-238-3339., Printing Office: *601 E. 6th St., Waynesboro, 30830.*

Director of Communications—Mrs. BARBARA KING, *Catholic Pastoral Center, 601 E. Liberty St., Savannah, 31401-5196.* Tel: 912-238-2320; Fax: 912-236-0848.

Superintendent of Schools—Sr. MARY FRANCES SOBCZAK, C.D.P., *Catholic Pastoral Center, 601 E. Liberty St., Savannah, 31401-5196.* Tel: 912-238-2320; Fax: 912-238-2339.

Director of African American Ministry—Deacon FRANK MATHIS, *Catholic Pastoral Center, 601 E. Liberty St., Savannah, 31401-5196.* Tel: 912-238-2320.

Director of Campus Ministry—Rev. MICHAEL SMITH, *201 Telfair Ave., McRae, 31055.* Tel: 912-868-2002.

Director of Youth Ministry—Mr. JULIAN HEYMAN, *Catholic Pastoral Center, 601 E. Liberty St., Savannah, 31401-5196.* Tel: 912-238-2320.

Director of Ecumenism and Interreligious Affairs—Deacon FRETWELL G. CRIDER, *P.O. Box 57, Tybee Island, 31328.* Tel: 912-786-8217.

Director of Family Life—Vacant, *Catholic Pastoral Center, 601 E. Liberty St., Savannah, 31401-5196.* Tel: 912-238-2320.

Director of Home Missions—Rev. LAWRENCE A. LUCREE, *332 S. Lee St., Americus, 31709.* Tel: 912-924-3495.

Director of Hispanic Ministry—Rev. MICHAEL H. SMITH, *201 Telfair Ave., McRae, 31055.* Tel: 912-868-2002.

Director of Social Ministry—Sr. MARIA CIESLINSKI, M.S.B.T., *601 E. Liberty St., Savannah, 31401-5196.* Tel: 912-238-2320; Fax: 912-238-2339.

Director of Vocations—Rev. BRETT A. BRANNEN, *4937 Bloomfield Rd., Macon, 31206.* Tel: 912-788-6386; Fax: 912-788-2837.

Director of Vocations—Irish Seminarians; Rev. JOHN O'BRIEN, V.F., *800 Gornto Rd., Valdosta, 31602-1699.* Tel: 912-244-2430; Fax: 912-244-5352.

Diocesan Departments and Agencies

Apostleship of the Sea—Rev. K. D. XAVIER, *112 Fell St., Savannah, 31401.* Tel: 912-236-7716.

Campaign for Human Development—Sr. MARIA CIESLINSKI, M.S.B.T., *Catholic Pastoral Center, 601 E. Liberty St., Savannah, 31401-5196.* Tel: 912-238-2320.

Catholic Cemetery Advisory Board—Board Members: DONALD W. FREW; M. SCOTT CLARK; Rev. JAMES M. MAYO; GERALDINE WILLIAMS; DAVID BLANTON; JOHN M. SCHRODER, SR., *601 E. Liberty St., Savannah, 31401-5196.* Tel: 912-238-2320.

Catholic Relief Services—Sr. MARY FAITH MCKEAN, Dir., *Catholic Pastoral Center, 601 E. Liberty St., Savannah, 31401-5196.* Tel: 912-238-2320.

Clergy Welfare Board—Rev. ROBERT GIRARDEAU, *8412 Whitfield Ave., Savannah, 31406.* Tel: 912-355-1523.

Council of Catholic Women—Rev. JOHN O'BRIEN, Chap., *800 Gornto Rd., Valdosta, 31602-1699.* Tel: 912-244-2430. Mrs. ROSALIE SUGRUE, Pres., *P.O. Box 7574, Warner Robins, 31095.*

Diocesan Communications Commission—Mrs. BARBARA KING, Contact Person, *Catholic Pastoral Center, 601 E. Liberty St., Savannah, 31401-5196.* Tel: 912-238-2320; Fax: 912-236-0848.

Diocesan Liturgical Commission—Vacant, *Catholic Pastoral Center, 601 E. Liberty St., Savannah, 31401-5196.* Tel: 912-238-2320; Fax: 912-238-2335.

Diocesan Scout Chairman—Mr. JULIAN HEYMAN, *Catholic Pastoral Center, 601 E. Liberty St., Savannah, 31401-5196.* Tel: 912-238-2320.

Holy Childhood Association—Sr. MARY FRANCES SOBCZAK, C.D.P., Dir., *Catholic Pastoral Center, 601 E. Liberty St., Savannah, 31406-5196.* Tel: 912-238-2346.

Lay Ministry Formation—Ms. ANN PINCKNEY, *Catholic Pastoral Center, 601 E. Liberty St., Savannah, 31406-5196.* Tel: 912-238-2320.

Natural Family Planning—Mrs. SALLY KENNEDY, Dir. JAMES ROUTON, M.D., Medical Consultant, *601 E. Liberty St., Savannah, 31401-5196.* Tel: 912-238-2320.

Permanent Diaconate—Deacon GEORGE H. FOSTER, *4568 Betty's Branch Way, Evans, 30809.* Tel: 404-860-2379.

Propagation of the Faith—Ms. ANN PINCKNEY, *Catholic Pastoral Center, 601 E. Liberty St., Savannah, 31401-5196.* Tel: 912-238-2320.

Refugee Resettlement—Vacant, *601 E. Liberty St., Savannah, 31401-5196.* Tel: 912-238-2320.

Religious Education—Ms. ANN PINCKNEY, *Catholic Pastoral Center, 601 E. Liberty St., Savannah, 31401-5196.* Tel: 912-238-2320; Fax: 912-238-2339.

Stewardship and Development—Ms. PATRICIA SIGNS, Dir., *Catholic Pastoral Center, 601 E. Liberty St., Savannah, 31401-5196.* Tel: 912-238-2320.

CLERGY, PARISHES, MISSIONS AND PAROCHIAL SCHOOLS

CITY OF SAVANNAH
(Chatham County)

1—CATHEDRAL OF ST. JOHN THE BAPTIST, Revs. William O. O'Neill; Douglas K. Clark; Kim Son Nguyen; Bro. Robert Sokolowski, S.M., Pastoral Assoc.; Deacon Dewain Smith. In res., Rev. Msgr. Felix G. Donnelly.
Res., 222 E. Harris St., 31401. Tel: 912-233-4709; Fax: 912-233-8229.
School—Notre Dame Academy, Tel: 912-232-5473.
Sisters 2; Lay Teachers 11; Students 113.

2—ST. ANTHONY'S, Rev. Robert E. Chaney; Deacon Fretwell G. Crider. In res., Rev. Xavier Kumbalaparambil.
Res., 112 Fell St., 31401. Tel: 912-232-5258.

3—ST. BENEDICT THE MOOR, Rev. James M. Mayo; Deacon Prince A. Jackson, Jr.
Res., 556 E. Gordon St., 31401. Tel: 912-232-7147; Fax: 912-238-0184.

4—MOST BLESSED SACRAMENT, Revs. Jeremiah J. McCarthy; Robert T. Hand; Deacon Michael F. Daly. In res., Rev. Msgr. Daniel J. Bourke.
Res., 1003 E. Victory Dr., 31405-2499. Tel: 912-356-6980.
School—Tel: 912-356-6987; Fax: 912-356-6988. Miss Mary Anne Butler, Prin.
Lay Teachers 28; Students 366.

5—MOST PURE HEART OF MARY, Rev. Michael O'Keeffe; Deacon Frank Mathis.
Mailing Address: P.O. Box 24308, 31403-4308.
Res., 902 W. 36th St., 31401. Tel: 912-232-4751.

6—SACRED HEART OF JESUS, Rev. John Lyons. Pastoral Assocs.: Sr. Ann Walker, O.S.F.; Sr. Lida Bulf, O.S.F.
Res., 1707 Bull St., 31401. Tel: 912-232-0792; Fax: 912-236-0065.

7—ST. FRANCES XAVIER CABRINI, Rev. Francis J. Nelson; Deacon Louis J. Andruzzi. In res., Rev. Joseph F. Ware.
Res., 11500 Middleground Rd., 31419-1227. Tel: 912-925-4725; Fax: 912-925-1379.

8—ST. JAMES, Revs. John A. Kenneally, V.F.; Robert A. Girardeau.
Res., 8412 Whitfield Ave., 31406. Tel: 912-355-1523; Fax: 912-353-7226.
School—Tel: 912-355-3132. Sr. Joan Felicia, I.H.M., Prin.
Sisters 5; Lay Teachers 17; Students 608.
Mission—Isle of Hope, Our Lady of Good Hope.

9—ST. PETER THE APOSTLE CHURCH, Revs. Patrick O'Brien; Gabriel Cummings.
Mailing Address: 7020 Concord Rd., P.O. Box 30859, 31410.
Res., 302 Bryson Dr., 31410. Tel: 912-897-5156; Fax: 912-897-7924.
School—Tel: 912-897-5224. Sr. Assunta Desposito, R.S.M., Prin.
Lay Teachers 16; Students 290.

10—STS. PETER AND PAUL. (Vietnamese Mission). Rev. Kim Son Nguyen, Admin.
Res., P.O. Box 8307, 31412. Tel: 912-231-1180.

OUTSIDE THE CITY OF SAVANNAH

Albany, Dougherty Co., St. Teresa, Revs. Finbarr P. Stanton; James P. Dalton.
Res., 421 Edgewood Ln., 31707. Tel: 912-432-0891; 439-2302 (office); Fax: 912-439-0516.
School—417 Edgewood Ln., 31707. Tel: 912-436-0134. Mrs. Grace Ledwitch, Prin.
Lay Teachers 36; Students 432.

Americus, Sumter Co., St. Mary, Rev. Lawrence A. Lucree.
Res., 332 S. Lee St., 31709. Tel: 912-924-3495.
Missions—Montezuma, Macon Co., St. Michael; Buena Vista, Marion Co., St. Mary Magdalen.

Augusta, Richmond Co.,

1—CHURCH OF THE MOST HOLY TRINITY, Revs. Allan J. McDonald; Andrew T. Doris; Daniel Munn; Deacons Joseph F. Colbert; Donald R. McArdle; Ephraim J. Williams. Pastoral Assocs.: Sr. Bridget Lennon, O.S.F.; Mr. Fletcher R. Bingham.
Mailing Address: P.O. Box 2446, 30903. Tel: 706-722-4944; Fax: 706-722-7774.
Res., 303 Broad St., 30901. Tel: 706-724-4367.
School—Immaculate Conception School, Tel: 706-722-9964. Sr. Una Toomey, Prin.
Sisters 5; Lay Teachers 11; Students 202. Missionary Franciscan Sisters of the Immaculate Conception.
Convent & Chapel—Immaculate Conception, 1018 Laney Walker Blvd., 30901. Tel: 706-722-2380.

2—ST. JOSEPH'S, Rev. Sam Zebron, O.F.M.Conv.; Deacon Gregory L. Bernard.
Res., 2607 Lumpkin Rd., 30906. Tel: 706-798-1920.

3—ST. MARY ON THE HILL, Rev. P. James Costigan; Deacons Donald G. Cisick; James J. O'Connell.
Res., 1420 Monte Sano Ave., 30904. Tel: 706-733-6627; Fax: 706-733-4887.
School—1220 Monte Sano Ave., 30904. Tel: 706-733-6193; Fax: 706-737-7985. Ms. Joyce Connelly, Prin.
Lay Teachers 24; Students 480.
Convent—1210 Monte Sano Ave., 30904. Tel: 706-733-4101. Sisters of St. Joseph of Carondelet
Chapels—St. Joseph Hospital; St. Mary on the Hill Convent; Aquinas High School.

4—ST. TERESA OF AVILA, Rev. Walter L. DiFrancesco; Deacon William L. Johnson.
Res., 117 Pleasant Home Rd., 30907-3517. Tel: 706-863-4956; Fax: 706-863-5001.

Bainbridge, Decatur Co., St. Joseph's, Rev. Joel S. Bladt, S.T.; Deacon William N. Halbohn.
Res., 822 Ramsey St., P.O. Box 192, 31717. Tel: 912-248-0030.
Mission—Donalsonville, Seminole Co., Church of the Incarnation.

Blakely, Early Co., Holy Family, Rev. Conrad Schmitt, S.T.
Mailing Address: Box 425, 31723.
Res., 109 Arlington St., P.O. Box 425, 31723. Tel: 912-723-3339.
Mission—Cuthbert, Randolph Co., St. Luke.

Brunswick, Glynn Co., St. Francis Xavier, Revs. Wilfrid Logsdon, O.F.M.Conv.; Cletus Pifher, O.F.M.Conv.; Bro. Michael Wright, O.F.M.Conv.; Deacons Ntungwa Maasha; George F. Ruehling, III.
Res., 729 Union St., 31520. Tel: 912-265-3249.
School—Tel: 912-265-9470; Fax: 912-265-9471. Ms. Jane O'Day, Prin.
Lay Teachers 12; Students 288.
Mission—Darien, McIntosh Co., Nativity of Our Lady.

Claxton, Evans Co., St. Christopher, Revs. Laurence B. Goulding, Glmy.; Robert Healy, Glmy.; Sr. Janet Fischer, F.S.P.A., Pastoral Assoc.
Res., 402 S. River St., P.O. Box 890, 30417-0890. Tel: 912-739-3913.
Convent—402 S. River St., 30417. Tel: 912-739-2275. Franciscan Sisters of Perpetual Adoration
Missions—Glennville, Tattnall Co., St. Jude, P.O. Box 772, Glennville, 30427. Tel: 912-654-1908. Bro. Charles Kennedy, Glmy., Pastoral Assoc.; Pembroke, Bryan Co., Holy Cross, P.O. Box 890, 30417-0890.

Columbus, Muscogee Co.,

1—HOLY FAMILY, Revs. Frank Patterson, V.F.; Arthur Weltzer, Pastor Emeritus.
Res., 320 12th St., 31901. Tel: 706-323-6908; Fax: 706-323-2043.

2—OUR LADY OF LOURDES, Rev. George Gonzalez; Deacon Francis P. Benyo.
Res., 1953 Torch Hill Rd., 31903. Tel: 706-689-5720; Fax: 706-687-9579.
School—1973 Torch Hill Rd., 31903. Tel: 706-689-5644. Mr. Larry Rousseau, Prin.
Lay Teachers 12; Students 171.

3—ST. ANNE, Revs. Joseph Gerard Schreck; Joseph A. Smith.
Res., 3544 Trinity Dr., P.O. Box 6606, 31907. Tel: 706-561-8678; Fax: 706-568-0179.
School—3550 Trinity Dr., 31907. Tel: 706-561-8232. Mrs. Patricia Nobes, Prin.
Lay Teachers 17; Students 317.
Mission—Pine Mountain, Harris Co., Christ the King, P.O. Box 32, Hamilton, 31811. Tel: 706-628-5158. Sr. Philomena Fogarty, F.M.M., Pastoral Assoc.
Chapels—St. Francis Hospital.; Pacelli High School.

4—ST. BENEDICT THE MOOR, Rev. Paul T. Brick, S.D.S.
Church—2930 Thomas St., P.O. Box 5705, 31906.
Res., 2939 Ninth St., 31906. Tel: 706-323-8300; Fax: 706-324-7099.
Parish Hall—2935 Ninth St., 31906. Tel: 706-324-1749.

Cordele, Crisp Co., St. Theresa, Rev. Raul Perez.
Res., 807 Third St., S., 31015. Tel: 912-273-3446.

Douglas, Coffee Co., St. Paul's, Rev. Daniel O'Connell.
Res., 523 E. Ward St., 31533. Tel: 912-384-3560; Fax: 912-383-7649.
Missions—Fitzgerald, Ben Hill Co., St. William; Willacoochee, Atkinson Co., Holy Family.

Dublin, Laurens Co., Immaculate Conception, Revs. Gerald Ragan; Charles Hughes.
Res., 204 N. Church St., 31021. Tel: 912-272-0266.
Chapel—Dublin, VA Hospital.
Mission—Sandersville, Washington Co., St. William.

Hazlehurst, Jeff Davis Co., Good Shepherd, Rev. Herbert Graf, O.F.M.Conv.
Mailing Address: P.O. Box 1468, 31539. Tel: 912-375-5948.
Mission—Baxley, Appling Co., St. Rose of Lima.

Hinesville, Liberty Co., St. Stephen, First Martyr, Rev. Gerard Herman, O.F.M.Conv.
Res., 399 Woodland Ave., 31313. Tel: 912-876-4364; Fax: 912-876-4368.

Jesup, Wayne Co., St. Joseph, Rev. John Curran, O.F.M.Conv.
Res., 1048 E. Cherry St., P.O. Box 176, 31598. Tel: 912-427-9239.

Lakeland, Lanier Co., Queen of Peace, Rev. Christian LeFrois, O.S.B, Admin.
Res., 1332 S. Mill St., P.O. Box 26, 31635. Tel: 912-482-3555.
Missions—Nashville, Berrien Co., St. Mary; Adel, Cook Co., St. Margaret Mary.

Macon, Bibb Co., St. Joseph's, Revs. John Cuddy, V.F.; Timothy P. McKeown.
Res., 830 Poplar St., 31201. Tel: 912-745-1631; Fax: 912-745-2254.
School—Sisters of Mercy 1; Lay Teachers 19; Students 357.

Holy Spirit, Rev. Brett A. Brannen; Sr. Catherine France, D.C., Pastoral Assoc.; Deacon Daniel W. Bish, Jr.
Res., 4937 Bloomfield Rd., 31206. Tel: 912-784-0178; Fax: 912-788-2837.
Parish Center—4074 Chambers Rd., 31206. Tel: 912-788-6386.

St. Peter Claver, Rev. James B. Walker.
Res., 131 Ward St., 31204. Tel: 912-743-1454.
School—133 Ward St., 31204. Tel: 912-743-3985. Sr. Donna Marie Coward, R.S.M., Prin.
Sisters 2; Lay Teachers 13; Students 206.

McRae, Telfair Co., Holy Redeemer, Rev. Michael H. Smith, V.F.; Sr. Fran Trochta, C.D.P., Pastoral Assoc.
Res., 201 Telfair, 31055. Tel: 912-868-2002; Fax: 912-868-2939.
Convent—804 Anson St., Eastman, 31023. Tel: 912-374-4031. Congregation of Divine Providence Sisters
Mission—Eastman, Dodge Co., St. Mark, P.O. Box 4304, Eastman, 31023. Tel: 912-374-0238.

Moultrie, Colquitt Co., Immaculate Conception, Revs. Edward R. Frank; Lorenzo Garcia; Deacon Philip J. Walsh.
Res., 202 Hillcrest Ave., S.E., 31768. Tel: 912-985-8949.
Mission—Camilla, Mitchell Co., St. John Vianney, P.O. Box 391, Camilla, 31730. Tel: 912-336-8685.

Perry, Houston Co., St. Patrick, Rev. Thomas J. Murphy; Deacons Ralph H. McAtee; Ken Hutnick.
Res., I-75 at 341 S., P.O. Box 612, 31069. Tel: 912-987-4213.
Mission—Fort Valley, Peach Co., St. Juliana.

Port Wentworth, Chatham Co., Our Lady of Lourdes, Rev. Michael J. Kavanaugh.
Res., 501 S. Coastal Hwy., Rte. U.S. 17, P.O. Box 4056, 31407. Tel: 912-964-0219.
Mission—Springfield, St. Boniface, P.O. Box 927, Springfield, 31329. Tel: 912-754-7473. Sr. Rose Ballantine, O.S.F., Pastoral Assoc.

Richmond Hill, Bryan Co., St. Anne, Rev. Herbert J. Wellmeier.
Res., P.O. Box 648, 31324. Tel: 912-756-3338.

St. Marys, Camden Co., Our Lady Star of the Sea, Rev. William J. Leahy.
Res., P.O. Box 290, 31558. Tel: 912-882-4718.
Mission—Folkston, Charlton Co., St. Francis of Assisi, 1609 N. 2nd St., Folkston, 31537. Tel: 912-496-3219.

St. Simons Island, Glynn Co., St. Williams, Revs. Germain Belen, O.F.M.Conv.; George Schroeder, O.F.M.Conv.
Res. & Mailing Address: 2300 Frederica, 31522. Tel: 912-638-2647.

Statesboro, Bulloch Co., St. Matthew's, Rev. David Stachurski, O.F.M.Conv.
Res., 221 John Paul Ave., 30458. Tel: 912-681-6726; 681-2445; Fax: 912-681-6727.

Swainsboro, Emanuel Co., Holy Trinity, Rev. Michael Langell.
Res., 928 W. Main St., 30401. Tel: 912-237-8722.
Mission—Metter, Candler Co., Holy Family, P.O. Box 231, Metter, 30439. Tel: 912-685-5811. Sr. Paul Marie Westlake, R.S.M., Pastoral Assoc.

Sylvania, Screven Co., Our Lady of the Assumption, Rev. Edward V. Gorny, Glmy.
Res., 121 Ridgecrest Dr., 30467. Tel: 912-564-2312.
Mission—Millen, Jenkins Co., St. Bernadette, P.O. Box 616, Millen, 30442. Tel: 912-982-1445.
Chapel—Bay Branch, St. Joseph.

Thomasville, Thomas Co., St. Augustine's, Rev. Victor Seidel, S.T.; Deacon Howard G. Halladay.
Res., 211 N. Pinetree Blvd., 31792. Tel: 912-226-3624.
Mission—Cairo, Grady Co., St. Elizabeth Ann Seton, 11th Ave. N.W., Cairo, 31728. Tel: 912-377-6996.

Thunderbolt, Chatham Co., Nativity of Our Lord, Rev. Francis C. Higgins.
Mailing Address: P.O. Box 3855, Savannah, 31414.
Res., 3115 E. Victory Dr., 31404. Tel: 912-354-4014; Fax: 912-352-1048.
Chapel—Thunderbolt, St. Mary's Home.

Tifton, Tift Co., Our Divine Saviour, Rev. James A. Kirchner.
Res., 1205 Love Ave., P.O. Box 212, 31793. Tel: 912-382-4600.
Mission—Alapaha, Berrien Co., St. Ann, Tel: 912-532-2216.

Tybee Island, Chatham Co., St. Michael's, Rev. John J. Fitzpatrick; Deacon Charles J. Hosti.
Res., 802 Lovell Ave., P.O. Box 38, 31328. Tel: 912-786-4505; Fax: 912-786-6653.
School—808 Lovell Ave., P.O. Box 740, 31328. Tel: 912-786-4507. Ms. Glynn M. Poole, Prin.
Lay Teachers 11; Students 121.

Valdosta, Lowndes Co., St. John the Evangelist, Rev. John O'Brien.
Church Office: 800 Gornto Rd., 31602-1699. Tel: 912-244-2430; Fax: 912-244-5352.
Res., 2402 Berkley Dr., 31602. Tel: 912-244-9920.
Newman Center—412 Baytree Rd., 31602. Tel: 912-247-6707.
School—Sisters of St. Joseph, Tel: 912-244-2556; 244-0050 (Convent); Fax: 912-244-0865. Sr. Pauline Oetgen, C.S.J., Prin.
Sisters 4; Lay Teachers 22; Students 291.

Vidalia, Toombs Co., Sacred Heart, Rev. Mark J. Ross; Deacons Clayton J. Burke, Jr.; Joseph P. Claroni.
Mailing Address: P.O. Box 1086, 30474. Tel: 912-537-7709; Fax: 912-537-4691.
Res., 3119 E. North St., 30474. Tel: 912-537-7709.
Mission—Reidsville, Tattnall Co., St. Andrew the Apostle.

Warner Robins, Houston Co., Sacred Heart, Revs. Fred J. Nijem; Michael C. Lubinsky; Sr. Teresa Baugh, P.B.V.M., Pastoral Assoc.; Deacons Harold P. Kimball; Dennis A. Arcand.
Mailing Address: P.O. Box 5052, 31099. Tel: 912-923-0124; Fax: 912-328-3078.
School—Sisters of Presentation. Mrs. Bonnie Solinsky, Prin.
Sisters 1; Lay Teachers 23; Students 280.

Waycross, Ware Co., St. Joseph's, Rev. Charles W. Roland; Sr. Mary Robers, S.C., Pastoral Assoc.
Res., 2011 Darling Ave., 31501. Tel: 912-283-7700; Fax: 912-283-1944.
Mission—Alma, Bacon Co., St. Raymond.

Waynesboro, Burke Co., Sacred Heart, Rev. Brian LaBurt.
Res., 115 S. Liberty St., 30830. Tel: 706-554-2535.
Mission—Louisville, Jefferson Co., St. Joan of Arc, Tel: 912-625-3433.

Special Assignment:
Reverend Fathers—
Brown, Wayland Y., 8920 Old Montgomery Rd., Savannah, GA 31406
Canty, Richard J., Memorial Medical Center & Candler General Hospital
Cushing, Robert A., 3890 Russell St., Smyrna, GA 30082-3533. Tel: 404-436-0610
Lopez, Juan, Migrant Ministry. Tel: 912-557-6570
Ryan, Timothy K., 1310 Primrose Dr., Roswell, GA 30076. Tel: 404-667-1313; 667-6305 (Fax)

On Duty Outside the Diocese:
Reverend Fathers—
Healy, Thomas, St. Kilian's Parish, Irishe Katholische Mission, Landsberger Strasse 39, 80339 Munich, Germany. Tel: 0.11.49.89.5003580
Keohane, Donal
Pachence, Ronald A., University of San Diego, San Diego, CA 92110
Schreck, Christopher J., St. Charles Borromeo Seminary, 1000 E. Wynnewood Rd., Wynnewood, PA 19096-3099. Tel: 215-667-3394

Military Chaplains:
Reverend Fathers—
Cerrone, Michael J., U.S.A.
Madden, Ronald, U.S.N.
Minch, Richard, U.S.A.
Quang, John, U.S.N.

Retired:
Reverend Monsignors—
Bourke, Daniel J., P.A., Blessed Sacrament Church, 1003 E. Victory Dr., Savannah, GA 31405. Tel: 912-356-6980
Donnelly, Felix G., Cathedral of St. John the Baptist, P.O. Box 8307, Savannah, GA 31412. Tel: 912-233-4709
LeFrois, Marvin J., 800 Gornto Rd., Valdosta, GA 31602-1699. Tel: 912-253-0041
Reverend Fathers—
Barry, Francis, c/o Mrs. John Blainey, Ross Tara, County Meath, Republic of Ireland
Campbell, Thomas E., 206 W. Gen. Stewart Way, Hinesville, GA 31313. Tel: 912-876-3731
Doris, Andrew T., 2346 McDowell St., Augusta, GA 30904. Tel: 706-736-0593
Dowling, William P.
Payne, Thomas H., P.O. Box 24683, St. Simons Island, GA 31522. Tel: 912-634-9189
Weltzer, Arthur, 320 12th St., Columbus, GA 31901

Permanent Deacons:
Andruzzi, Louis J., St. Frances Cabrini, Savannah
Arcand, Dennis A., Sacred Heart, Warner Robins
Benyo, Francis P., Our Lady of Lourdes, Columbus
Bernard, Gregory L., St. Joseph's, Augusta
Bish, Daniel W., Jr., Holy Spirit, Macon
Burke, Clayton J., Jr., Sacred Heart, Vidalia
Cisick, Donald G., St. Mary's on the Hill, Augusta
Claroni, Joseph P., Sacred Heart, Vidalia
Colbert, Joseph L., Holy Trinity, Augusta
Crider, Fretwell G., St. Anthony, Savannah
Daly, Michael F., Blessed Sacrament, Savannah
Fleury, Philippe D., Windmeadows Apts., 2712 S.W. 34th St., Apt. 137, Gainesville, FL 32608
Foley, Michael F., P.O. Box 324, Tybee Island, GA 31328
Foster, George H., St. Michael, Fort Gordon
Halbohn, William N., St. Joseph Church, Bainbridge
Halladay, Howard G., St. Augustine, Thomasville
Hosti, Charles J., St. Michael, Tybee Island
Houghton, Arthur A., Good Shepherd, Hazlehurst
Hutnick, Kenneth P., St. Juliana Church, Perry
Jackson, Prince A., Jr., St. Benedict the Moor, Savannah
Johnson, William L., St. Teresa of Avila, Augusta
Kimball, Harold P., Sacred Heart, Warner Robins
Maasha, Ntungwa, St. Francis Xavier, Brunswick

Mathis, Frank, Most Pure Heart of Mary, Savannah
McArdle, Donald R., Holy Trinity, Augusta
McAtee, Ralph H., St. Patrick, Perry
O'Connell, James J., 1215-10 Monte Sano Ave., Augusta, GA 30904
O'Neill, Robert, Unassigned
Pierce, Raymond G., 1225 Weston Way, Pooler, GA 31322
Rowe, John A., Unassigned
Ruehling, George F., III, St. Francis Xavier, Brunswick
Sanchez, Aurelio, Holy Trinity Church, Swainsboro
Smith, Dewain E., Cathedral of St. John the Baptist, Savannah
Walsh, Philip J., Immaculate Conception, Moultrie
White, George H., 4 Dolan Dr., Savannah, GA 31406
Williams, Ephraim J., Holy Trinity, Augusta

INSTITUTIONS LOCATED IN THE DIOCESE

[A] HIGH SCHOOLS, DIOCESAN

AUGUSTA. *Aquinas High School*, 1920 Highland Ave., 30904-5305. Tel: 706-736-5516; Fax: 706-736-2678. Mr. John Albert, Prin.; Mrs. Penny Jackson, Asst. Prin. Sisters 1; Lay Teachers 23; Students 284.

COLUMBUS. *Pacelli Catholic High School*, 3556 Trinity Dr., 31907. Tel: 706-561-8243; Fax: 706-561-3243. Mr. John Cobis, Prin.; Revs. Carey Lahrs, S.D.S.; J. Gerard Schreck, Diocesan Moderator. Priests 1; Lay Teachers 24; Students 295.

[B] HIGH SCHOOLS, PRIVATE

SAVANNAH. *Benedictine Military School*. (Grades 9-12), 6502 Seawright Dr., P.O. Drawer 13577, 31416. Tel: 912-356-3500; Fax: 912-356-3527. Secondary school conducted by the Dependent Priory of Benedictine Monks of St. Vincent Archabbey, Latrobe, PA. Rev. John Murtha, O.S.B., Pres.; Ms. Kelly Burke, Prin.; Revs. Wilfred M. Dumm, O.S.B.; Albert Bickerstaff, O.S.B.; Ronald P. Gatman, O.S.B.; Anthony P. Wesolowski, O.S.B.; Jeffrey S. Nyardy, O.S.B.; Bros. Gerard J. Klaric, O.S.B.; Timothy J. Brown, O.S.B.; Francis G. Ehnat, O.S.B. Priests 7; Brothers 1; Lay Teachers 27; Boys 449.

Convent and Academy of St. Vincent de Paul, 207 E. Liberty St., 31401. Tel: 912-236-9541; Fax: 912-236-7877. Sisters of Mercy of the Americas. Sr. Helen Marie Buttimer, R.S.M., Prin. Sisters 9; Lay Teachers 25; Girls 362.

MACON. *Mount de Sales Academy*. (Grades 7-12), 851 Orange St., 31201. Tel: 912-751-3240; Fax: 912-751-3241. Sisters of Mercy of the Americas. Sr. Mary Rosina Bayliss, R.S.M., Pres.; Mr. Terrence G. Mermann, Prin. Sisters 2; Lay Teachers 44; Students 620.

[C] CHILD CARE HOMES

SAVANNAH. *St. Mary's Home*, E. Victory Dr., P.O. Box 3627, Sta. B, 31404. Tel: 912-236-7164; Fax: 912-236-9699

For a complete listing, refer to the Special Care Facilities section.

[D] RESIDENCES FOR SINGLE PREGNANT WOMEN

MACON. *Nazareth Home, Residence for Single Pregnant Women*, 538 Orange St., P.O. Box 204, 31202-0204. Tel: 912-746-9803. Sr. Carol Durkin, D.C., Dir.

[E] GENERAL HOSPITALS

SAVANNAH. *St. Joseph's Hospital*, 11705 Mercy Blvd., P.O. Box 60129, 31419-1791. Tel: 912-925-4100

For a complete listing, refer to the Hospitals section.

AUGUSTA. *St. Joseph Center For Life, Inc.*, 2260 Wrightsboro Rd., 30910

For a complete listing, refer to the Hospitals section.

St. Joseph Hospital, Augusta, GA, Inc., 2260 Wrightsboro Rd., 30910. Tel: 706-481-7400; Fax: 706-481-7599

For a complete listing, refer to the Hospitals section.

COLUMBUS. *St. Francis Hospital*, 2122 Manchester Expwy., P.O. Box 7000, 31908-7000. Tel: 706-596-4000

For a complete listing, refer to the Hospitals section.

[F] MONASTERIES AND RESIDENCES OF PRIESTS

SAVANNAH. *The Benedictine Priory*, 6502 Seawright Dr., 31406. Tel: 912-356-3520. Dependent Priory of St. Vincent Archabbey, Latrobe, PA. Revs. Wilfred M. Dumm, O.S.B.; Anthony P. Wesolowski, O.S.B.; Ronald P. Gatman, O.S.B.; John Murtha, O.S.B.; Jeffrey S. Nyardy, O.S.B.; Albert Bickerstaff, O.S.B.; Very Rev. Meinrad J. Lawson, O.S.B., Prior; Bros. Gerard J. Klaric, O.S.B.; Timothy Brown, O.S.B.; Francis Ehnat, O.S.B.

[G] CONVENTS AND RESIDENCES FOR SISTERS

SAVANNAH. *Carmelite Monastery*, 11 W. Back St., 31419. Tel: 912-925-8505; Fax: 912-925-8506. Sr. Angela Collins, O.C.D., Prioress. Professed Nuns 5.

Mercy Convent, 11801 McAuley Dr., 31419. Tel: 912-925-3800.

[H] NEWMAN CENTERS

SAVANNAH. *Armstrong Atlantic State University Newman Group*, 402 Willow Rd., 31419. Tel: 912-925-5993. Mr. Mathew Daly, Campus Min.

Savannah State University Newman Group, 4 Indigo Ct., 31406. Tel: 912-925-5477. Mrs. Ann Lipsey, Campus Min.

MACON. *Mercer University, Wesleyan College Newman Center*, 2737 Gwinette Dr., 31204. Tel: 912-741-7522. Sr. Catherine France, D.C., Campus Min.

STATESBORO. *Georgia Southern University Newman Center*, 221 John Paul Ave., 30458. Tel: 912-681-6728. Ms. Jane Hall, Campus Min.

VALDOSTA. *Valdosta State College Newman Center*. Mailing Address: 800 Gornto Rd., 31602. 412 Baytree Rd., 31602. Tel: 912-247-6707. Mr. Carl Hand, Campus Min.

[I] MISCELLANEOUS

SAVANNAH. *Office of Social Ministry*, 601 E. Liberty St., 31401-5196. Tel: 912-238-2320; Fax: 912-238-2339. Sr. Maria Cieslinski, M.S.B.T., L.I.C.S.W., Dir.

Social Apostolate, 502 E. Liberty St., P.O. Box 8703, 31412. Tel: 912-233-1877. Sr. Mary Therese Brown, O.S.F., Dir.

ALBANY. *St. Clare's Evangelization-Community Center*, 2005 Martin Luther King Dr., P.O. Box 4123, 31706. Tel: 912-883-2566; Fax: 912-883-9116. Sr. Deborah Driscoll, O.S.F., Contact Person.

AUGUSTA. *Catholic Social Services*, 1419 Arsenal Ave., P.O. Box 2823, 30904. Tel: 706-733-8332; Fax: 706-733-7749. Mr. Richard Tuchscherer, Dir.

BRUNSWICK. *Society of St. Vincent de Paul*, 1217 Newcastle St., 31520. Tel: 912-262-6027. Mrs. Pamela Kesegi, Pres.

CLAXTON. *Clothesbasket*, 402 S. River St., 30417. Tel: 912-739-2275. Sr. Janet Fischer, F.S.P.A., Dir.

COLUMBUS. *Holy Family Soup Kitchen*, 320 12th St., 31901. Tel: 706-322-8102; Fax: 706-327-8191. Mrs. Frances Cummings, Dir.

Our Lady of Lourdes, 1953 Torch Hill Rd., 31903. Tel: 706-689-5720. Mrs. Judie Huff, Dir.

St. Benedict Social Concerns, 2935 Ninth St., 31906. Tel: 706-323-8300.

St. Vincent de Paul, St. Anne Conference, 2000 Kay Cir., 31907. Tel: 706-568-1592. Paul and Claire Arrington, Dirs.

HAMILTON. *Christ the King (FOCUS)*, Hwy. 27, Box 32, 31811. Tel: 706-628-5158. Sr. Philomena Fogarty, F.M.M., Dir.

MACON. *Macon Social Apostolate (SERVE)*, 570 High Pl., 31201. Tel: 912-745-7165; Fax: 912-745-2254. Ms. Deloris Bailey, Dir.

MILLEN. *Catholic Thrift Shop*, P.O.Box 616, 30442. Tel: 912-554-5842. Sr. Mary Ellen Barrette, Dir.

VALDOSTA. *St. Francis Center*, P.O. Box 1331, 31601. Tel: 912-242-8656.

WARNER ROBINS. *Sacred Heart Christian Service Center*, P.O. Box 5052, 31099-5052. Tel: 912-929-3897.

RELIGIOUS INSTITUTES OF MEN REPRESENTED IN THE DIOCESE

For further details refer to the corresponding bracketed number in the Religious Institutes of Men or Women section.

[0200]—*Benedictine Monks*. (St. Vincent Archabbey).—O.S.B.
[0600]—*Brothers of the Congregation of Holy Cross*.—C.S.C.
[0480]—*Conventual Franciscans*. (Prov. of Our Lady of Consolation & St. Anthony of Padua).—O.F.M.Conv.
[0570]—*Glenmary Home Missioners*. (Glendale, OH).—Glmy.
[0770]—*The Marist Brothers*. (Poughkeepsie, NY).—F.M.S.
[0780]—*Marist Fathers*. (Washington Prov.).—S.M.
[0840]—*Missionary Servants of Most Holy Trinity*. (Dublin).—S.T.
[0610]—*Priests of the Congregation of Holy Cross*.—C.S.C.
[1200]—*Society of the Divine Savior*. (American Prov.).—S.D.S.

RELIGIOUS INSTITUTES OF WOMEN REPRESENTED IN THE DIOCESE

[1780]—*Congregation of the Sisters of the Third Order of St. Francis of Perpetual Adoration*.—F.S.P.A.
[0760]—*Daughters of Charity of St. Vincent De Paul*. (Emmitsburg, MD).—D.C.
[0420]—*Discalced Carmelite Nuns*.—O.C.D.
[1070-13]—*Dominican Sisters*.—O.P.
[1370]—*Franciscan Missionaries of Mary*.—F.M.M.
[1470]—*Franciscan Sisters of St. Joseph*.—F.S.S.J.
[2080]—*Home Mission Sisters of America*.
[1360]—*Missionary Franciscan Sisters of the Immaculate Conception*.—O.S.F.
[2790]—*Missionary Servants of the Most Blessed Trinity*.—M.S.B.T.
[3230]—*Poor Handmaids of Jesus Christ*. (Indiana).—P.H.J.C.
[0440]—*Sisters of Charity of Cincinnati*.—S.C.
[1000]—*Sisters of Divine Providence of Kentucky*.—C.D.P.
[1010]—*Sisters of Divine Providence of San Antonio, Texas*.—C.D.P.
[2575]—*Sisters of Mercy of the Americas*. (Baltimore, Erie, Portland).—R.S.M.
[3950]—*Sisters of Saint Mary of Namur*.—S.S.M.N.
[1070-18]—*Sisters of St. Dominic of the American Congregation of the Sacred Heart of Jesus*.—O.P.
[3893]—*Sisters of St. Joseph*. (Chestnut Hill, PA).—S.S.J.
[3840]—*Sisters of St. Joseph of Carondelet*. (St. Louis, MO).—C.S.J.
[0260]—*Sisters of the Blessed Sacrament for Indians and Colored People*.—S.B.S.
[1720]—*Sisters of the Third Order Regular of St. Francis of the Congregation of Our Lady of Lourdes*.—O.S.F.
[2170]—*Sisters, Servants of the Immaculate Heart of Mary*.—I.H.M.
[3330]—*Union of the Sisters of the Presentation of the Blessed Virgin Mary*.—P.B.V.M.

DIOCESAN CEMETERIES

SAVANNAH. *Catholic Cemetery and Properties*. Mr. Donald W. Frew, Dir.

Catholic Pastoral Center, 601 E. Liberty St., 31401-5196. Tel: 912-238-2320.

AUGUSTA. *Catholic Cemetery*. Rev. Allan J. McDonald.

Holy Trinity Church, 720 Telfair St., P.O. Box 2446, 30903. Tel: 706-722-4944.

DOUGLAS. *St. Paul's*, c/o 523 Ward St., 31533. Tel: 912-384-3560.

SYLVANIA. *Catholic Cemetery*. Rev. Edward V. Gorny, Glmy.

Our Lady of the Assumption Church, 121 Ridgecrest Dr., 30467. Tel: 912-564-2312.

WILLACOOCHEE. *Catholic Cemetery*. Rev. Daniel P. O'Connell.

NECROLOGY

† Ring, Michael J., Augusta, GA, St. Joseph. —Died July 13, 1997.

Diocese of Scranton

(Dioecesis Scrantonensis)

Most Reverend

JAMES C. TIMLIN, D.D.

Bishop of Scranton; ordained July 16, 1951; appointed Titular Bishop of Gunugo and Auxiliary Bishop of Scranton August 3, 1976; consecrated September 21, 1976; succeeded to See of Scranton April 24, 1984; installed June 7, 1984. *Office: 300 Wyoming Ave., Scranton, PA, 18503.* Tel.: 717-346-8910.

Most Reverend

JOHN M. DOUGHERTY, D.D., V.G.

Auxiliary Bishop of Scranton; ordained June 15, 1957; appointed Titular Bishop of Sufetula and Auxiliary Bishop of Scranton February 7, 1995; Episcopal ordination received March 7, 1995. *Office: 300 Wyoming Ave., Scranton, PA, 18503.* Tel.: 717-346-8910.

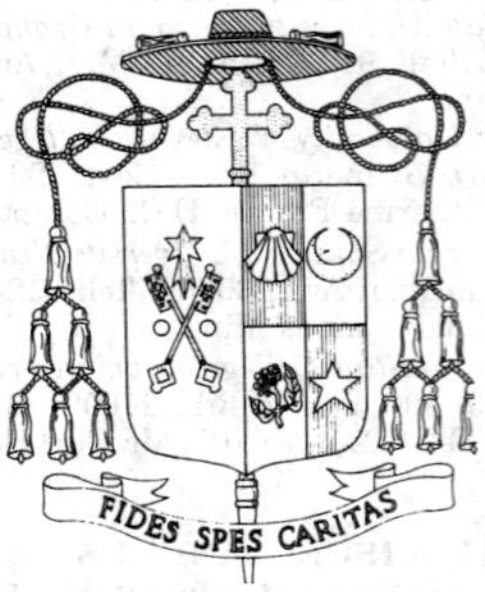

Chancery Office: 300 Wyoming Ave., Scranton, PA, 18503. Tel.: 717-346-8910.

ESTABLISHED MARCH 3, 1868.

Square Miles 8,847.

Comprises the Counties of Luzerne, Lackawanna, Bradford, Susquehanna, Wayne, Tioga, Sullivan, Wyoming, Lycoming, Pike and Monroe in Pennsylvania.

For legal titles of parishes and diocesan institutions, consult the Chancery Office.

STATISTICAL OVERVIEW

Personnel	
Bishop	1
Auxiliary Bishops	1
Priests: Diocesan Active in Diocese	252
Priests: Active Outside Diocese	13
Priests: Retired, Sick or Absent	90
Number of Diocesan Priests	355
Religious Priests in Diocese	108
Extern Priests in Diocese	9
Ordinations:	
Diocesan Priests	1
Religious Priests	1
Transitional Deacons	3
Permanent Deacons in Diocese	37
Total Brothers	9
Total Sisters	843
Parishes	
Parishes	200
With Resident Pastor:	
Resident Diocesan Priests	190
Resident Religious Priests	7
Without Resident Pastor:	
Administered by Priests	3
Missions	85
Pastoral Centers	25
Professional Ministry Personnel:	
Sisters	65
Lay Ministers	10
Welfare	
Catholic Hospitals	7
Total Assisted	780,171
Health Care Centers	3
Total Assisted	98,235
Homes for the Aged	7
Total Assisted	750
Residential Care of Children	9
Total Assisted	1,176
Day Care and Extended Day Care Centers	8
Total Assisted	313
Specialized Homes	9
Total Assisted	1,478
Special Centers for Social Services	13
Total Assisted	168,213
Residential Care of Disabled	1
Total Assisted	142
Educational	
Seminaries, Diocesan	1
Students from This Diocese	17
Students from Other Diocese	8
Diocesan Students in Other Seminaries	15
Seminaries, Religious	1
Students Religious	54
Total Seminarians	86
Colleges and Universities	4
Total Students	11,442
High Schools, Diocesan and Parish	9
Total Students	3,395
High Schools, Private	2
Total Students	747
Elementary Schools, Diocesan and Parish	50
Total Students	17,418
Non-residential Schools for the Disabled	1
Total Students	15
Catechesis/Religious Education:	
High School Students	12,835
Elementary Students	31,101
Total Students Under Catholic Instruction	77,039
Teachers in the Diocese:	
Priests	7
Sisters	152
Lay Teachers	971
Vital Statistics	
Receptions into the Church:	
Infant Baptism Totals	4,737
Adult Baptism Totals	463
Received into Full Communion	540
First Communions	5,711
Confirmations	7,958
Marriages:	
Catholic	1,533
Interfaith	580
Total Marriages	2,113
Deaths	5,489
Total Catholic Population	351,188
Total Population	1,054,814

Former Bishops—First Bishop: Rt. Rev. WILLIAM O'HARA, D.D., cons. July 12, 1868; died Feb. 3, 1899.—*Second Bishop:* Rt. Rev. MICHAEL J. HOBAN, D.D., cons. Coadjutor, March 22, 1896; succeeded to See, Feb. 3, 1899; died Nov. 13, 1926.—*Third Bishop:* Most Rev. THOMAS C. O'REILLY, D.D., ord. June 4, 1898; elected Dec. 19, 1927; cons. Feb. 16, 1928; installed March 8, 1928; died March 25, 1938.—*Fourth Bishop:* Most Rev. WILLIAM J. HAFEY, D.D., ord. June 16, 1914; appt. First Bishop of Raleigh, April 6, 1925; cons. June 24, 1925; transferred to Scranton as Coadjutor *cum jure successionis* and Apostolic Administrator, Oct. 2, 1937; succeeded to See, March 25, 1938; died May 12, 1954.—*Fifth Bishop:* Most Rev. JEROME D. HANNAN, D.D., ord. May 22, 1921; appt. August 17, 1954; cons. Sept. 21, 1954; died Dec. 15, 1965.—*Sixth Bishop:* Most Rev. J. CARROLL M. MCCORMICK, D.D., ord. July 10, 1932; appt. Titular Bishop of Ruspae and Auxiliary of Philadelphia, Jan. 11, 1947; cons. April 23, 1947; appt. Bishop of Altoona-Johnstown, June 25, 1960; transferred to the See of Scranton, March 4, 1966; installed May 25, 1966; retired Feb. 15, 1983; died Nov. 2, 1996.—*Seventh Bishop:* Most Rev. JOHN J. O'CONNOR, D.D., ord. Dec. 15, 1945; appt. Titular Bishop of Cuzola and Auxiliary Bishop to the Military Vicar April 24, 1979; cons. May 27, 1979; appt. Bishop of Scranton, May 10, 1983; installed June 29, 1983; transferred to the See of New York, Jan. 31, 1984.

Vicar General—Most Rev. JOHN M. DOUGHERTY, D.D., V.G., *300 Wyoming Ave., Scranton, 18503.* Tel: 717-346-8910.

Chancery Office—300 Wyoming Ave., Scranton, 18503. Tel: 717-346-8910.

Moderator of the Curia—Most Rev. JOHN M. DOUGHERTY, D.D., V.G. Tel: 717-346-8910.

Chancellor—Mr. JAMES B. EARLEY. Tel: 717-346-8910; 346-8908.

Secretary to Bishop Timlin—Rev. ANDREW W. KILPATRICK. Tel: 717-346-8910; 346-8956; 344-7231 (After 5 P.M.).

Diocesan Financial Office—JAMES M. QUINN, Dir. Tel: 717-346-8965.

Diocesan Tribunal—300 Wyoming Ave., Scranton, 18503. Tel: 717-346-8944; Fax: 717-346-8991.

Judicial Vicar—Rev. PATRICK J. PRATICO, J.C.D.

Coordinator—JOSEPH V. FOX.

Judges—Very Rev. EDWARD R. LIPTOCK, V.F.; Rev. JOSEPH C. BAMBERA, J.C.L.; CHARLES J. REID, J.D., J.C.L.; Rev. PATRICK J. PRACTICO, J.C.D.; LINDA E. PRICE, J.C.L.; Revs. DAVID M. O'CONNELL, C.M., J.C.L.; JOHN L. SULLIVAN, J.C.L.

Defenders of the Bond—Very Rev. JOSEPH G. QUINN, J.D., J.C.L., V.F.; Rev. JOHN A. BERGAMO, J.C.L.; Very Rev. RICHARD A. BURKE, C.P., J.C.L.; Rev.

JAMES J. WALSH, J.C.L.
Promotor of Justice—Rev. JOHN A. BERGAMO, J.C.L.
Auditors—JOSEPH A. BARRETT, Ph.D.; JOSEPH V. FOX; Revs. JOHN A. BERGAMO, J.C.L.; CYRIL D. EDWARDS, M.Div.; BERNARD P. EVANOFSKI; JOSEPH ELSTON; MICHAEL J. SULLIVAN.
Procurator / Advocate—JOSEPH V. FOX.
Psychological Expert—JOSEPH A. BARRETT, Ph.D.
Notaries—ANN WALSH; PATRICIA WALTON; JOSETTE JORDAN.

Diocesan Finance Council—Most Rev. JOHN M. DOUGHERTY, D.D., V.G.; Rev. Msgr. JOHN J. BENDIK; Mrs. ELLEN DERMODY; JOHN D. MCCARTHY; JAMES E. O'BRIEN, JR., ESQ.; MARY THERESA PATERSON, ESQ.; Rev. Msgr. NEIL J. VAN LOON, V.F.; JAMES M. QUINN; JAMES B. EARLEY; THOMAS MEDICO; Sr. JEAN MOHL, S.C.C.

Diocesan Consultors—Most Rev. JAMES C. TIMLIN, D.D.; Rev. Msgr. F. ALLAN CONLAN; Rev. Msgr. PETER P. MADUS, V.F.; Rev. Msgr. NEIL J. VAN LOON, V.F.; Very Rev. FRANCIS J. CASTELLANO, V.F.; Very Rev. JOSEPH G. QUINN, V.F.; Revs. JOSEPH M. ZIOBRO; WILLIAM J. FELDCAMP; PATRICK J. PRATICO; BERNARD A. TOLOCZKO. Ex-Officio: Most Rev. JOHN M. DOUGHERTY, D.D., V.G.; Revs. JOSEPH C. BAMBERA; ANDREW W. KILPATRICK, Sec.

Diocesan Pastoral Council—Contact: ELLEN C. DERMODY, Diocesan Dir., Pastoral Planning. Tel: 717-346-8932.

Deans—Rev. Msgr. LEONARD J. NOVAK, V.F., Scranton-South; Very Rev. PAUL P. COTTONE, V.F., Scranton-West; Rev. Msgr. PETER P. MADUS, V.F., Scranton-North; Very Rev. JOSEPH G. QUINN, V.F., Scranton-Central; Very Rev. PETER V. HERHENREADER, V.F., Carbondale; Very Rev. JOSEPH M. BOLES, V.F., Abingtons; Very Rev. EDWARD R. LIPTOCK, V.F., Dunmore; Very Rev. MICHAEL J. PICCOLA, V.F., Freeland; Very Rev. GIRARD F. ANGELO, V.F., Hazleton; Rev. Msgr. NEIL J. VAN LOON, V.F., Kingston; Very Rev. JAMES E. MCGAHAGAN, V.F., Nanticoke; Very Rev. JOSEPH F. CIPRIANO, V.F., Old Forge; Rev. Msgr. STANLEY W. PIORKOWSKI, V.F., Olyphant; Very Rev. JAMES J. PAISLEY, V.F., Pittston; Rev. Msgr. VINCENT J. GRIMALIA, V.F., Plymouth; Very Rev. DANIEL D. HITCHKO, V.F., West Pittston; Rev. Msgr. FRANCIS J. CALLAHAN, V.F., Wilkes-Barre Central/South; Very Rev. E. FRANCIS KELLY, V.F., Wilkes-Barre Plains; Very Rev. RONALD J. HUGHES, V.F., Bradford and Sullivan; Very Rev. FRANCIS J. CASTELLANO, V.F., Lycoming; Very Rev. JOHN B. BOYLE, V.F., Monroe; Rev. Msgr. WILLIAM P. WARD, V.F., Pike; Very Rev. THOMAS A. CAPPELLONI, V.F., Susquehanna; Very Rev. BERT S. KOZEN, V.F., Tioga; Very Rev. EDWARD R. SCOTT, V.F., Wayne; Very Rev. THOMAS J. O'MALLEY, V.F., Ashley-Mountain Top.

Presbyteral Council—Most Rev. JAMES C. TIMLIN, D.D., Pres.; Revs. JOHN K. MANNO, Chm. J. PETER CRYNES, Vice Chm. JOHN M. LAPERA, Sec.; Rev. Msgr. JOHN J. BENDIK; Rev. Msgr. GEORGE R. DEMUTH; Rev. Msgr. PETER P. MADUS, V.F.; Rev. Msgr. NEIL J. VAN LOON, V.F.; Very Rev. JOSEPH G. QUINN, V.F.; Rev. JOSEPH M. ZIOBRO; Very Rev. FRANCIS J. CASTELLANO, V.F.; Revs. PHILIP A. ALTAVILLA; JOHN A. BERGAMO; JOHN J. CHMIL; JOSEPH ELSTON; WILLIAM J. FELDCAMP; GREGORY FINN, O.S.J.; WILLIAM J. FLYNN, S.S.; GERARD M. GANNON; LOUIS T. KAMINSKI; ANDREW W. KILPATRICK; JOSEPH R. KOPACZ; JAMES J. MCGARRY; THOMAS D. MCLAUGHLIN; PAUL M. MULLEN; PATRICK J. PRATICO; JOSEPH A. SIDERA, C.S.C.; ROBERT M. TIMCHAK; BERNARD A. TOLOCZKO; JOSEPH O. WEBER; DONALD J. WILLIAMS. Ex-Officio: Most Rev. JOHN M. DOUGHERTY, D.D., V.G.; Rev. JOSEPH C. BAMBERA.

Diocesan Building Commission—All plans for building should be sent to Chancery Office, *300 Wyoming Ave., Scranton, 18503.* Most Rev. JOHN M. DOUGHERTY, D.D., V.G.; MICHAEL A. BARBETTI; Rev. Msgr. JOHN J. BENDIK; WILLIAM J. BURKAVAGE; Rev. WILLIAM J. FELDCAMP; Rev. Msgr. ANTHONY C. MARRA; JOSEPH M. O'CONNOR; PAUL S. ROTELLA, ESQ.; Rev. Msgr. NEIL J. VAN LOON, V.F.; JAMES B. EARLEY; DONALD J. WOLFF.

Vicar for Canonical Services—Rev. PATRICK J. PRACTICO, J.C.D., *300 Wyoming Ave., Scranton, 18503.* Tel: 717-346-8944.

Vicar for Priests—Rev. JOSEPH C. BAMBERA, *300 Wyoming Ave., Scranton, 18503.* Tel: 717-346-8939; 563-8515.

Vicars for Religious—Most Rev. JOHN M. DOUGHERTY, D.D., V.G., *300 Wyoming Ave., Scranton, 18503.* Tel: 717-346-8910. Sr. M. GABRIEL KANE, I.H.M. Tel: 717-346-8947.

Diocesan Offices and Directors

Blue Army of Our Lady of Fatima—Rev. JOHN S. MARINKO, Diocesan Spiritual Dir., *120 Willow Ave., Olyphant, 18447.* Tel: 717-489-2023.

Campaign for Human Development Director—Rev. WILLIAM B. PICKARD, *300 Wyoming Ave., Scranton, 18503.* Tel: 717-346-8968.

Campus Ministry—Sr. CATHERINE ANN GILVARY, I.H.M., Dir., *Lycoming College, 700 College Pl., Box 149, Williamsport, 17701.* Tel: 717-321-4111.

Catholic Charismatic Renewal—Rev. RICHARD J. LOCH, Spiritual Advisor; ROBERT VALIANTE, Coord., *P.O. Box 3306, Scranton, 18505.* Tel: 717-344-2214.

Catholic Health Care Facilities Director and Representative to Catholic Institutions of Higher Learning—Rev. Msgr. ANDREW J. MCGOWAN, *Mercy Hospital, Scranton, 18501.* Tel: 717-348-7010.

Catholic Relief Services—JAMES B. EARLEY, Chancellor, *300 Wyoming Ave., Scranton, 18503.* Tel: 717-346-8910.

Catholic Social Services—Diocesan Dir., *400 Wyoming Ave., Scranton, 18503.* Tel: 717-346-8935.

Lackawanna County Branch—
Scranton Office—Mr. STEPHEN R. NOCILLA, M.A., Exec. Dir., *400 Wyoming Ave., Scranton, 18503.* Tel: 717-346-8936; Fax: 717-341-1293.
Carbondale Office—39 S. Main St., Carbondale, 18407. Tel: 717-282-0460.

Luzerne County Branch—
Wilkes-Barre Office—Mr. NED DELANEY, M.A., Exec. Dir., *33 E. Northampton St., Wilkes-Barre, 18701.* Tel: 717-822-7118; Fax: 717-829-7781.
Hazleton Office—Mr. NEIL OBERTO, M.A., Exec. Dir., *81 S. Church St., Hazleton, 18201.* Tel: 717-455-1521; Fax: 717-455-2707.

Lycoming County Branch—
Williamsport Office—Mr. ROBERT MAKOS, L.S.W., Exec. Dir., *1015 Washington Blvd., Williamsport, 17701.* Tel: 717-322-4220; Fax: 717-322-4276.

Wyoming County Branch—
Tunkhannock Office—Ms. JOANNE DONATO, L.S.W., *102 Warren Ave., Tunkhannock, 18657-0704.* Tel: 717-836-1101; Fax: 717-836-3765.

Monroe County Branch—
Stroudsburg Office—Mrs. MARY LOU MALLOY, L.S.W., Exec. Dir., *411 1/2 Main St., Stroudsburg, 18360.* Tel: 717-476-6460; Fax: 717-476-6466.

Pike County Branch—
Milford Office—Mr. DONALD BROWN, L.S.W., *Rte. 6, P.O. Box 1195, Milford, 18337.* Tel: 800-916-1913; 717-296-1054; Fax: 717-296-9227.

Tioga County Branch—
Wellsboro Office—Mr. BERN MAKOS, L.S.W., *109 East Ave., Wellsboro, 16901.* Tel: 717-724-2734; Fax: 717-724-5855.

Natural Family Planning Coordinator—ELLEN DERMODY, Diocesan Coord., *400 Wyoming Ave., Scranton, 18503.* Tel: 717-346-8932.

Diocesan Board of Education—Rev. Msgr. WILLIAM P. WARD, V.F., Pres.; Sr. KATHRYN CLAUSS, I.H.M., Vice Pres. RUTH A. CONNOLLY, Exec. Sec. JANE QUINN, Sec.

Cemeteries—Mr. WALTER BENNETT, Dir., *1708 Oram St., Scranton, 18504.* Tel: 717-346-8923.

Censor Librorum—Rev. Msgr. DAVID A. BOHR, S.T.D., *St. Pius X Seminary, Dalton, 18414.* Tel: 717-563-1131.

Continuing Education of Priests—Rev. JOSEPH C. BAMBERA, Dir., *300 Wyoming Ave., Scranton, 18503.* Tel: 717-346-8939; 563-8515.

Cursillo Movement—Rev. JAMES R. NASH, Spiritual Moderator, *60 S. Main St., Montrose, 18801.* Tel: 717-278-1504.

Diocesan Commission on Ethics for Catholic Health Care Facilities—Rev. Msgr. DAVID A. BOHR, S.T.D., Chm.; Sr. JOANNE BEDNAR, S.C.C.; Deacon THOMAS M. CESARINI; Sr. JEAN COUGHLIN, I.H.M.; Sr. VINCENTIA DORSEY, I.H.M.; Rev. JAMES J. DOYLE, C.S.C.; PATRICK J. FERRARO, M.D.; Rev. ANDREW W. KILPATRICK; Rev. Msgr. ANDREW J. MCGOWAN; JAMES MCKENNA, M.D.; JOANNE ORLOSKI, M.D.; Revs. JAMES A. RAFFERTY, S.T.L.; ROBERT J. SIMON; WILLIAM P. SMEDLEY, M.D.; Rev. JOSEPH B. WILSON, Ph.D.; GLEN YANIK, ESQ.

Diocesan Commission on Ecumenism and Inter-Faith Matters—Rev. PHILIP A. ALTAVILLA, Diocesan Dir.

Diocesan Director of Public Relations—Sr. MARIANNE ADDY, I.H.M., Dir., *300 Wyoming Ave., Scranton, 18503.* Tel: 717-346-8931.

Diocesan Engineer—Mr. TERRY K. STEPHENS, *300 Wyoming Ave., Scranton, 18503.* Tel: 717-341-1287; 341-1295; Fax: 717-346-8992.

Diocesan Historian—Rev. CHARLES P. CONNOR, Ph.D., *1403 Jackson St., Scranton, 18504.* Tel: 717-344-2679.

Diocesan Office for Communications—Mrs. MARIA ORZEL, Exec. Dir., *400 Wyoming Ave., Scranton, 18503.* Tel: 717-346-8953; 800-246-0288; Fax: 717-346-8958.

Diocesan Office of Religious Education—SANDRA CZYZYK, Dir.

Ministry for Persons with Disabilities—MARY RYAN, Dir.

Ministry with Deaf and Hard of Hearing—Sr. MARY BETH MAKUCH, SS.C.M., Dir., *400 Wyoming Ave., Scranton, 18503.* Tel: 717-346-8961., Audio-Visual Resource Center. Tel: 717-346-8911.

Diocesan Office of Development—ANTHONY SHIPULA, Dir., *300 Wyoming Ave., Scranton, 18503.* Tel: 717-346-8903.

Diocesan Office of Ecumenism—Rev. PHILIP A. ALTAVILLA, Dir., *300 Wyoming Ave., Scranton, 18503.* Tel: 717-344-2679.

Diocesan Office of Parish Ministries—Rev. ROBERT J. SIMON, Exec. Dir.; Sr. CATHERINE E. MULKERRIN, C.S.J., Parish Structures Dir. JOAN TUREL, Worship Dir. KATHY YAKLIC, Youth and Young Adult Ministry Dir. MARY ANN PAULUKONIS, Family Life Dir. MARTIN A. KEARNEY, Social Concerns Dir., *300 Wyoming Ave., Scranton, 18503.* Tel: 717-346-8914.

Diocesan Pro-Life Office—Rev. ROBERT J. SIMON, Diocesan Dir., *300 Wyoming Ave., Scranton, 18503.* Tel: 717-346-8904.

Holy Childhood Association—Rev. Msgr. JOHN A. ESSEFF, Dir., *300 Wyoming Ave., Scranton, 18503.* Tel: 717-346-8933.

Holy Name Society—Rev. SCOTT P. STEROWSKI, Spiritual Moderator, *300 Wyoming Ave., Scranton, 18503.* Tel: 717-346-8914; 489-0752.

Legion of Mary—Rev. CHARLES P. CONNOR, Ph.D., Diocesan Spiritual Dir., *1403 Jackson St., Scranton, 18504.* Tel: 717-344-2679.

Liturgical Commission—Rev. Msgr. DALE R. RUPERT, Chm.; Rev. ROBERT J. SIMON, Vice Chm. JOAN TUREL, Diocesan Worship Dir.

Marriage Encounter—Rev. JOHN S. MARINKO, S.T.L., Spiritual Advisor, *120 Willow Ave., Olyphant, 18447.* Tel: 717-489-2023.

D.C.C.M.—Rev. SCOTT P. STEROWSKI, Spiritual Moderator, *300 Wyoming Ave., Scranton, 18503.* Tel: 717-489-0752; 346-8914.

D.C.C.W.—Rev. Msgr. FRANCIS J. CALLAHAN, V.F., Spiritual Moderator, *300 Wyoming Ave., Scranton, 18503.* Tel: 717-346-8921; 822-1075.

Newspaper—"The Catholic Light"; Mr. JEROME M. ZUFELT, Editor, *300 Wyoming Ave., Scranton, 18503.* Tel: 717-346-8918.

Office of Pastoral Planning—ELLEN C. DERMODY, Exec. Dir., *300 Wyoming Ave., Scranton, 18503-1279.* Tel: 717-346-8932.

Diocesan Television Station-CTV—Mrs. MARIA ORZEL, Exec. Dir. JAMES BRENNAN, Mgr., *400 Wyoming Ave., Scranton, 18503.* Tel: 717-346-8953.

Permanent Diaconate Office—Rev. Msgr. DAVID A. BOHR, Dir., *St. Pius X Seminary, 1000 Seminary Rd., Dalton, 18414.* Tel: 717-563-1131.

Pilgrimages—Rev. ANDREW S. HVOZDOVIC, Diocesan Dir., *118 Kendall Ave., Jersey Shore, 18705.* Tel: 717-398-2557.

Priests Purgatorial Society—Rev. JOSEPH C. BAMBERA, Sec., *300 Wyoming Ave., Scranton, 18503.* Tel: 717-346-8939; 563-8515.

Priests' Retirement Advisory Board—Most Rev. JOHN M. DOUGHERTY, D.D., V.G.; Rev. Msgr. JOHN J. O'BRIEN; JAMES M. QUINN; Revs. JOHN J. KILPATRICK; RICHARD J. LOCH; RICHARD J. POLMOUNTER; JOSEPH C. BAMBERA; JAMES B. EARLEY.

Propagation of the Faith—Rev. Msgr. JOHN A. ESSEFF, Dir., *300 Wyoming Ave., Scranton, 18503.* Tel: 717-346-8933; Fax: 717-346-8948.

Pastoral Formation Institute—Rev. Msgr. DAVID A. BOHR, S.T.D., Dir., *St. Pius X Seminary, 1000 Seminary Rd., Dalton, 18414.* Tel: 717-563-8501.

Renewal—Fatima Center—Mr. JEFFREY SEYMOUR, M.A., *1000 Seminary Rd., Dalton, 18414.* Tel: 717-563-8500.

Retirement Fund for Religious—Dirs.: Sr. MARIANNE ADDY, I.H.M.; Sr. M. GABRIEL KANE, I.H.M. Tel: 717-346-8931; 346-8947.

Schools—RUTH A. CONNOLLY, Ed.D., Supt., *300 Wyoming Ave., Scranton, 18503.* Tel: 717-346-8942. PATRICK G. CAWLEY, Asst. Supt., Curriculum and Staff Devel. Tel: 717-346-8943. DANIEL F. DONOVAN, Asst. Supt., Personnel. Tel: 717-346-8941. Rev. DAVID L. TRESSLER, Asst. Supt., Christian Formation. Tel: 717-455-9431. JOSEPH S. HAGGERTY, Fiscal Mgr.

Scouts of America—Rev. RICHARD E. FOX, Diocesan Chap., *801 Taylor Ave., Scranton, 18510.* Tel: 717-961-5211.

Council of Women Religious—Contact: Sr. M. GABRIEL KANE, I.H.M., Vicar for Religious.

Christian Life Communities—Sr. MARYLA FARFOUR, I.H.M., Coord., *333 Wyoming Ave., Scranton, 18503.* Tel: 717-344-9725. Rev. ROBERT J. SIMON, Spiritual Advisor, *2523 Jackson St., Scranton, 18504.* Tel: 717-344-9745.

Vocations—Rev. DONALD J. WILLIAMS, Dir.; Sr. M. GABRIEL KANE, I.H.M., Assoc. Dir., *300 Wyoming Ave., Scranton, 18503.* Tel: 717-346-8997.

CLERGY, PARISHES, MISSIONS AND PAROCHIAL SCHOOLS

CITY OF SCRANTON
(Lackawanna County)

1—ST. PETER'S CATHEDRAL (1853), Very Rev. Joseph G. Quinn, V.F.; Revs. Jeffrey J. Walsh; Andrew W. Kilpatrick. In res., Most Rev. James C. Timlin, D.D.
Res., Tel: 717-344-7231; Fax: 717-344-4749.

2—ST. ANN'S BASILICA PARISH (1901), Revs. Roger Elliott, C.P.; Patrick Geinzer, C.P.
Res., 1250 St. Ann St., 18504. Tel: 717-342-5166; Fax: 717-348-3750.
School—1228 St. Ann St., 18504. Tel: 717-348-3753; Fax: 717-348-3758.
Lay Teachers 12; Students 249.

3—ST. ANTHONY OF PADUA (1913) (Italian), Rev. Michael A. Penn. In res., Rev. Robert J. Barone.
Res., 1402 Short Ave., 18508. Tel: 717-342-4190.

4—ST. DAVID'S (1946), Rev. Robert J. Simon, Admin.
Res., 2523 Jackson St., 18504. Tel: 717-344-9745.

5—ST. FRANCIS (1920) (Italian), Rev. Msgr. Philip A. Gray.
Res., 630 Genet St., 18505. Tel: 717-346-0797; Fax: 717-346-7187.

6—HOLY CROSS (1897). Merged with St. Patrick's, Scranton.

7—HOLY FAMILY (1891), Rev. Msgr. Constantine V. Siconolfi.
Res., 510 Gibson St., 18509. Tel: 717-342-8548; Fax: 717-342-2581. [CEM]

8—HOLY NAME (1938), Rev. John J. Kilpatrick.
Res., 1414 E. Elm St., 18505. Tel: 717-346-3859; Fax: 717-346-3859.

9—HOLY ROSARY (1871), Rev. Msgr. Joseph P. Kelly.
Res., 316 William St., 18508. Tel: 717-342-4881.
School—312 William St., 18508.
Priests 1; Sisters of the I.H.M. 4; Lay Teachers 12; Students 300.
Missions—Scranton, Lackawanna Co., St. Stanislaus; St. Stephen's.

10—IMMACULATE CONCEPTION (1967), Revs. William D. Campbell; Joseph F. Orloski; Richard E. Fox; Edward F. Barrett.
Res., 801 Taylor Ave., 18510. Tel: 717-961-5211.

11—ST. CLARE (1967), Rev. Msgr. Joseph A. Fadden.
Res., 2301 N. Washington Ave., 18509. Tel: 717-344-9884.
School—2215 N. Washington Ave., 18509. Tel: 717-343-2790.
Sisters of the I.H.M. 4; Lay Teachers 17; Students 272.

12—ST. JOHN THE BAPTIST (1885) (German). Merged with St. Patrick's, Scranton.

13—ST. JOHN THE EVANGELIST (1886), Rev. Eugene R. Carr.
Res., 516 Fig St., 18505. Tel: 717-343-6026.

14—ST. JOSEPH'S (1894) (Lithuanian), Rev. Msgr. Peter P. Madus, V.F.
Res., 116 Theodore St., 18508. Tel: 717-342-4339; Fax: 717-342-4245. [CEM]

15—ST. JOSEPH'S (1872), Rev. John M. Lapera. In res., Rev. Conan Conaboy, C.P.
Res., 312 Davis St., 18505. Tel: 717-344-1724; Fax: 717-344-1787. [CEM]

16—ST. LUCY'S (1901) (Italian), Very Rev. Paul P. Cottone; Rev. Salvatore A. Bentivegna, O.S.J.
Res., 949 Scranton St., 18504. Tel: 717-347-9421.

17—ST. MARY OF THE ASSUMPTION (1854) (German), Revs. Richard J. Loch; Patrick D. Healey. In res., Rev. M. Jones Jayaraj.
Res., 430 Pittston Ave., 18505. Tel: 717-961-2297; Fax: 717-961-1468. [CEM]
School—430 River St., 18505. Tel: 717-342-9700; Fax: 717-341-7664.
Sisters of Christian Charity 4; Lay Teachers 17; Students 290.

18—ST. MARY'S (1904) (Polish), Rev. Albert E. Oldfield. In res., Rev. P. Lawrence Homer.
Res., 3335 Greenwood Ave., Moosic, 18507. Tel: 717-343-4024. [CEM]
School—Lay Teachers 6; Students 80.

19—ST. MICHAEL'S (1914) (Lithuanian), Revs. Louis J. Campbell, F.S.S.P.; Dennis Duvelius, F.S.S.P.
Res., 1703 Jackson St., 18504. Tel: 717-961-1205; Fax: 717-961-2284.

20—NATIVITY OF OUR LORD (1903), Rev. Joseph R. Kopacz. In res., Revs. John C. Ruth; Gustavo Aldolfo Tenorio Pena.
Res., 633 Orchard St., 18505. Tel: 717-344-6159.
School—638 Hemlock St., 18505. Tel: 717-346-9922; Fax: 717-346-9482.
Sisters of the I.H.M. 3; Lay Teachers 23; Students 500.

21—ST. PATRICK'S (1870), Revs. Paul F. Leonard; Charles P. Connor; Philip A. Altavilla; Thomas Yuen.
Res., 1403 Jackson St., 18504. Tel: 717-344-2679; 343-4353; Fax: 717-343-2835.
School—122 S. Summer Ave., 18504. Tel: 717-343-8114.
Sisters of the I.H.M. 2; Lay Teachers 20; Students 531.
Missions—Scranton, Lackawanna Co., Holy Cross; Scranton, Lackawanna Co., St. John the Baptist.
Chapel—Scranton, Immaculate Heart of Mary.

22—ST. PAUL'S (1887), Rev. Msgr. Paul J. Purcell. In res., Rev. William B. Pickard.
Res., 1510 Penn Ave., 18509. Tel: 717-961-1549; Fax: 717-343-0069.
School—1527 Penn Ave., 18509. Tel: 717-343-7880; Fax: 717-343-0069.
Sisters of the I.H.M. 1; Lay Teachers 12; Students 250.

23—SS. PETER AND PAUL (1910) (Polish), Rev. Edward J. Shoback.
Res., 1309 W. Locust St., 18504. Tel: 717-343-7015; Fax: 717-343-7023. [CEM]

24—SACRED HEARTS OF JESUS AND MARY (1885) (Polish), Rev. Msgr. Leonard J. Novak, V.F. In res., Revs. Emil M. Hussack; Walter L. Ferrett.
Res., 1217 Prospect Ave., 18505. Tel: 717-343-6420. [CEM]

25—ST. STANISLAUS (1915) (Polish). Merged with Holy Rosary, Scranton.

26—ST. VINCENT DE PAUL (1925), Rev. Eugene L. Gunning.
Res., 1201 Providence Rd., 18508. Tel: 717-346-9739; Fax: 717-347-3250.

OUTSIDE THE CITY OF SCRANTON

Archbald, Lackawanna Co., St. Thomas Aquinas (1858), Revs. Gerard M. Gannon; Edward P. Lyman.
Res., 411 Church St., 18403. Tel: 717-876-1701; Fax: 717-876-3617. [CEM]

Ashley, Luzerne Co., Holy Rosary (1900) (Slovak), Rev. John F. Samson.
Res., 60 Charles St., 18706. Tel: 717-822-7543.
St. Leo's (1887), Very Rev. Thomas J. O'Malley, V.F.
Res., 33 Manhattan St., 18706. Tel: 717-825-6669; Fax: 717-823-3714.

Athens, Bradford Co., St. Joseph (1852). Merged with St. John the Evangelist, South Waverly.

Avoca, Luzerne Co., St. Mary's (1871), Rev. Leo J. McKernan.
Res., 715 Hawthorne St., 18641. Tel: 717-655-8218; 457-3412; Fax: 717-655-8218. [CEM]
School—742 Spring St., 18641. Tel: 717-457-9700; 457-9600.
Lay Teachers 10; Students 184.
SS. Peter and Paul (1909) (Polish), Rev. Mark J. Bochinski.
Res., 912 Vine St., 18641. Tel: 717-457-2483; 457-9806. [CEM]

Bastress, Lycoming Co., Immaculate Conception (1838) (German), Rev. Robert T. Busteed.
Res., R.R. No. 3, Box 122, Williamsport, 17701. Tel: 717-745-3301. [CEM]
School—R.R. No. 3, P.O. Box 120, Williamsport, 17701. Tel: 717-745-3320; Fax: 717-745-3723.
Sisters of Christian Charity 3; Lay Teachers 6; Students 115.

Bear Creek Township, Luzerne Co., St. Christopher (1962). Merged with Holy Saviour, Wilkes-Barre.
St. Elizabeth (1938), Rev. Anthony M. Urban.
Res., P.O. Box 25, 18602. Tel: 717-472-3061; Fax: 717-472-3061.
Mission—Thornhurst, Luzerne Co., St. Mark.

Bentley Creek, Bradford Co., St. Ann's (1843), Rev. Richard G. Ghezzi.
Res., R.R. No. 3, Box 138A, Gillett, 16925. Tel: 717-596-2109. [CEM]
Mission—Ridgebury, Bradford Co., Our Lady of Perpetual Help.

Blakeslee, Monroe Co., Christ the King (1976), Rev. Raymond L. Deviney.
Res., P.O. Box 171, 18610. Tel: 717-646-8990.

Blossburg, Tioga Co., St. Andrew's. Merged with St. Mary, Blossburg.
St. Mary's (1874) (Polish), Rev. Kenneth M. Seegar.
Res., 138 St. Mary's St., 16912. Tel: 717-638-3241; Fax: 717-638-2952. [CEM]
Missions—Arnot, Tioga Co., St. Stanislaus Kostka; Morris Run, Tioga Co., St. Joseph; Blossburg, Tioga Co., St. Andrew, (1851).

Brodheadsville, Monroe Co., Our Lady Queen of Peace (1968), Rev. William J. McCawley.
Res., P.O. Box 38, 18322. Tel: 610-681-6137; Fax: 610-681-6139.

Buttonwood, Luzerne Co., Exaltation of the Holy Cross (1917) (Polish), Very Rev. James E. McGahagan, V.F.
Res., 420 Main Rd., Buttonwood, Wilkes-Barre, 18702. Tel: 717-823-6242; Fax: 717-829-4732. [CEM]

Canadensis, Monroe Co., St. Bernadette (1967), Rev. Alfred J. Vito.
Res., P.O. Box 14, 18325. Tel: 717-595-2139; 595-7622 (Maloney Hall); Fax: 717-595-6235.
Mission—Promised Land, Monroe Co., Our Lady of Fatima.

Canton, Bradford Co., St. Michael (1853), Very Rev. Bert S. Kozen, V.F.; Deacon William H. Graham.
Res., 24 N. Washington St., 17724. Tel: 717-673-5253; Fax: 717-673-5630. [CEM]
Missions—Troy, Bradford Co., St. John Nepomucene, Tel: 717-297-4405. [CEM]
Ralston, Lycoming Co., St. Aloysius.

Carbondale, Lackawanna Co., Our Lady of Mt. Carmel (1882) (Italian), Rev. Russell E. Motsay. In res., Rev. Michael P. Litcheck.
Res., 15 Fallbrook St., 18407. Tel: 717-282-5172. [CEM]
School—29 Fairview St., 18407. Tel: 717-282-0340.
Lay Teachers 14; Students 119.
St. Rose of Lima (1830), Revs. William J. Feldcamp; Daniel J. Doherty; James A. Rafferty.
Res., 6 N. Church St., 18407. Tel: 717-282-2991; Fax: 717-282-7580. [CEM]
School—86 Terrace St., 18407. Tel: 717-282-7930.
Priests 3; Sisters of the I.H.M. 11; Lay Teachers 10; Students 178.

Carverton, Luzerne Co., St. Frances Cabrini (1947), Rev. Joseph O. Weber.
Res., 585 Mt. Olivet Rd., Wyoming, 18644-9333. Tel: 717-696-3737.
Mission—Centermoreland, Luzerne Co., Blessed Sacrament.

Clarks Green, Lackawanna Co., St. Gregory (1974), Rev. Msgr. John H. Louis.
Res., 330 N. Abington Rd., 18411. Tel: 717-587-4808.

Clarks Summit, Lackawanna Co., Our Lady of the Snows (1911), Revs. James J. McGarry; Thomas J. Major; John K. Schaal.
Res., 301 S. State St., 18411. Tel: 717-586-1741; Fax: 717-586-2504.
Mission—Newton, Lackawanna Co., St. Benedict.

Conyngham, Luzerne Co., St. John Bosco (1964), Rev. John K. Manno; Sr. Judy Baldino, S.S.J., Pastoral Assoc.
Res., 2 Charles Ave. P.O. Box 919, 18219. Tel: 717-788-1997; Fax: 717-788-6667.
Parish Center—Tel: 717-788-9933.

Dallas, Luzerne Co., Gate of Heaven (1951), Rev. John C. Lambert; Deacon Thomas M. Cesarini.
Res., Machell Ave., 18612. Tel: 717-675-2121.

Dalton, Lackawanna Co., Our Lady of the Abingtons (1967), Very Rev. Joseph M. Boles, V.F.
Res., W. Main St., 18414. Tel: 717-563-1622.

Dickson City, Lackawanna Co., St. Thomas the Apostle. Merged with Visitation of the Blessed Virgin Mary (Polish), Dickson City.
Visitation of the Blessed Virgin Mary (1890) (Polish), Rev. Msgr. Stanley W. Piorkowski, V.F.; Rev. Patrick L. Albert.
Res., St. Mary's Square, P.O. Box 9038, 18519. Tel: 717-489-2091. [CEM]
School—Tel: 717-489-0061.
Bernardine Sisters of St. Francis 2; Lay Teachers 10; Students 215.
Mission—Dickson City, Lackawanna Co., St. Thomas Apostle, (1889).

Dorrance, Luzerne Co., Our Lady Help of Christians (Polish), Rev. Mark G. Balczeniuk.
Res., R.R. No. 1, Box 263, (Dorrance), Wapwallopen, 18660-9801. Tel: 717-868-5855. [CEM]

Drums, Luzerne Co., Church of the Good Shepherd (1940), Very Rev. Michael J. Piccola, V.F.
Res., P.O. Box 430, 18222. Tel: 717-788-3141; Fax: 717-788-2953.

Dunmore, Lackawanna Co.,

1—ALL SAINTS, (1905) (Slovak), Very Rev. Edward R. Liptock, V.F.
Res., 324 Ward St., 18512. Tel: 717-342-6468. [CEM]

2—CHRIST THE KING, (1949), Rev. John F. Poplawski.
Res., 1214 Quincy Ave., 18510. Tel: 717-343-2777.

3—ST. ANTHONY OF PADUA, (1894) (Italian), Rev. Msgr. Anthony C. Marra.
Res., 303 Smith St., 18512. Tel: 717-344-1209.
School—208 Smith St., 18512. Tel: 717-342-1182.
Sisters 2; Lay Teachers 9; Students 172.
Convent—215 Franklin St., 18512. Tel: 717-343-1422. Religious Teachers Filippini

4—ST. CASIMIR, (Polish). Merged with St. Mary of Mount Carmel, Dunmore.

5—St. Mary of Mount Carmel, (1856), Revs. John A. Doris; Michael B. Harris.
Res., 322 Chestnut St., 18512. Tel: 717-346-7429; Fax: 717-346-0523. [CEM]
School—325 Chestnut St., 18512. Tel: 717-346-4429.
Sisters of the I.H.M. 2; Priests 1; Lay Teachers 14; Students 292.
Mission—Dunmore, Lackawanna Co., St. Casimir, (1929).

6—St. Rocco's, (1905) (Italian), Rev. Anthony R. Tombasco.
Res., 118 Kurtz St., 18510-1539. Tel: 717-344-1239.

Dupont, Luzerne Co., Sacred Heart of Jesus (1902) (Polish), Rev. Daniel D. Olszewski.
Res., 215 Lackawanna Ave., 18641. Tel: 717-654-3713. [CEM]
School—217 Lackawanna Ave., 18641. Tel: 717-654-8822.
Lay Teachers 11; Students 170.

Duryea, Luzerne Co., Holy Rosary (1893) (Polish), Rev. Charles W. Rokosz.
Res., 127 Stephenson St., 18642. Tel: 717-457-3502. [CEM]
School—110 1/2 Stephenson St., 18642. Tel: 717-457-2553; Fax: 717-457-3537.
Bernardine Sisters 1; Lay Teachers 10; Students 271.

Sacred Heart of Jesus (1889) (German), Rev. Albert M. Liberatore.
Res., 529 Stephenson St., 18642. Tel: 717-457-2253.
Mission—Duryea, Luzerne Co., St. Joseph's, (1909).

St. Joseph's (1909) (Lithuanian). Merged with Sacred Heart of Jesus, Duryea. [CEM].

Dushore, Sullivan Co., St. Basil's (1838), Rev. Patrick J. McLaughlin.
Res., P.O. Box 307, 18614. Tel: 717-928-8865. [CEM]
Missions—Cummiskey, Sullivan Co., St. Francis of Assisi; Overton, Sullivan Co., St. Francis Xavier; Mildred, Sullivan Co., St. Francis of Assisi, (1894). [CEM]
Laporte, Sullivan Co., Sacred Heart; Eagles Mere, Sullivan Co., St. Francis of Assisi.
Shrine—Sugar Ridge, SS. Philip and James Church-St. John Neumann Shrine.

East Stroudsburg, Pike Co., St. John (1986), Rev. Msgr. Kevin P. O'Neill.
Mailing Address: 5171 Milford Rd., 18301. Tel: 717-223-9144; Fax: 717-223-9146.

St. Matthew's, Monroe Co., (1902), Revs. John A. Bergamo; Thomas J. Sokolowski.
Res., 200 Brodhead Ave., 18301. Tel: 717-421-2342; Fax: 717-421-8414.

Edwardsville, Luzerne Co., SS. Cyril and Methodius (1900) (Slovak). Merged with St. Anthony's, Larksville.

Elkland, Tioga Co., St. Thomas the Apostle (1907), Rev. Joseph P. Kutch.
Res., 111 First St., 16920. Tel: 814-258-5121; Fax: 814-258-5122.
Mission—Westfield, Tioga Co., St. Catherine.

Elmhurst, Lackawanna Co., St. Eulalia (1950), Rev. Msgr. F. Allan Conlan, Ph.D.
Res., P.O. Box 143, 18416. Tel: 717-842-7656; Fax: 717-842-7193.

Exeter, Luzerne Co., St. Anthony of Padua (1928) (Italian), Revs. Gregory T. Finn, O.S.J.; Raymond Tabon, O.S.J.
Res., 28 Memorial Ave., Exeter Boro, Pittston, 18643. Tel: 717-654-2103; Fax: 717-654-8621.

St. Cecilia (1900), Very Rev. Daniel D. Hitchko, V.F.
Res., 1700 Wyoming Ave., 18643. Tel: 717-654-2133; Fax: 717-654-3449. [CEM]
Convent—1690 Wyoming Ave., 18643. Tel: 717-655-8119.

St. John the Baptist (1898) (Polish). Merged with St. Cecilia, Exeter.

Eynon, Lackawanna Co., St. Mary's Czestochowa (1915) (Polish), Rev. Patrick J. Pratico.
Res., 417 Main St., 18403. Tel: 717-876-2223.
Mission—Eynon, Lackawanna Co., St. Mary of Vilna, (1901).

St. Mary of Vilna (Lithuanian). Merged with St. Mary's Czestochowa, Eynon.

Fairmount Springs, Luzerne Co., St. Martha's (1966). Merged with Our Lady of Mt. Carmel, Lake Silkworth.

Forest City, Susquehanna Co., Sacred Heart of Jesus (1904) (Polish), Rev. Richard J. Cirba.
Res., 612 Hudson St., 18421. Tel: 717-785-3838.
Missions—Forest City, Susquehanna Co., St. Anthony; Forest City, Susquehanna Co., St. Michael; Forest City, Susquehanna Co., St. Agnes.

St. Joseph's (1904) (Slovenian). Merged with Sacred Heart of Jesus, Forest City.

Freeland, Luzerne Co.,

1—St. Ann's, (1862), Revs. Cyril D. Edwards; Edward J. Williams; Deacon Cyril J. Kowalchick.
Office: 898 Centre St., 18224. Tel: 717-636-3035; Fax: 717-636-1743. [CEM]
Res., 420 Vine St., 18224. Tel: 717-636-2192.
Missions—Freeland, Luzerne Co., St. Anthony's, (1901). [CEM]
Freeland, Luzerne Co., St. Casimir's, (1886). [CEM]
Freeland, Luzerne Co., St. John Nepomucene, (1892). [CEM]

2—St. Anthony's. Merged with St. Ann's, Freeland.

3—St. Casimir's. Merged with St. Ann's, Freeland.

4—St. John Nepomucene. Merged with St. Ann's, Freeland.

Friendsville, Susquehanna Co., St. Francis Xavier's (1831), Rev. William J.P. Langan.
Res., 18818. Tel: 717-553-2288. [CEM 3]
Missions—Middletown, Susquehanna Co., St. Patrick; Little Meadows, Susquehanna Co., St. Thomas the Apostle, (1887).

St. Joseph's (1829), Rev. Joseph J. Manarchuck.
Res., Quinn Rd., R.R. #1, Box 1402, 18818. Tel: 717-553-2300. [CEM 2][JC]
Mission—Silver Lake, Susquehanna Co., St. Augustine.

Glen Lyon, Luzerne Co., St. Adalbert's (1889) (Polish), Rev. Carl T. Prushinski.
Res., 31 S. Market St., 18617. Tel: 717-736-6372. [CEM]
Missions—Glen Lyon, Luzerne Co., St. Denis; Glen Lyon, Luzerne Co., St. Michael's, (1909). [CEM]

St. Michael's. Merged with St. Adalbert's, Glen Lyon.

Gouldsboro, Wayne Co., St. Rita (1975), Rev. Martin M. Boylan, Ph.D.
Res., P.O. Box 537, 18424. Tel: 717-842-4995; Fax: 717-842-5413.
Missions—South Sterling, Wayne Co., St. Mary Magdalene; Newfoundland, Wayne Co., St. Anthony of Padua.

Great Bend, Susquehanna Co., St. Lawrence's (1872), Rev. John J. Kulavich.
Res., 506 Franklin St., 18821. Tel: 717-879-2392. [CEM]
Mission—New Milford, Susquehanna Co., St. John. [CEM]

Harding, Luzerne Co., Church of the Holy Redeemer (1952), Rev. Thomas E. McCann.
Res., R.D. 1, Pittston, 18643. Tel: 717-388-6300.

Harleigh, Luzerne Co., Sacred Heart of Jesus (1903), Very Rev. Girard F. Angelo, V.F.
Res., One Church Pl., 18225. Tel: 717-455-1162; Fax: 717-455-1162.
Shrines—National Shrine of the Sacred Heart, (1975).; Men of the Sacred Heart, National Office, (1977), Tel: 717-455-1162.

Harveys Lake, Luzerne Co., Our Lady of Victory (1969), Rev. Joseph P. Rafferty; Deacon William A. Dervinis.
Res., R.D. #1, Box 309, 18618. Tel: 717-639-1535; Fax: 717-639-1294.

Hawley, Wayne Co., Blessed Virgin Mary, Queen of Peace (1852), Rev. William B. Healey; Deacon Frank Kujawa.
Res., 314 Chestnut Ave., 18428. Tel: 717-226-3183; Fax: 717-226-2126. [CEM]
Mission—Lake Wallenpaupack, Pike Co., St. Veronica.

Hazleton, Luzerne Co.,

1—St. Gabriel's, (1855), Revs. Michael J. Delaney; John C. O'Bell.
Res., 122 S. Wyoming St., 18201. Tel: 717-454-0212; Fax: 717-459-5187. [CEM]

2—Church of the Most Precious Blood, (1885) (Italian), Revs. Maurice L. Raymond; James J. Alco. In res., Rev. Austin E. Flanagan.
Res., 131 E. Fourth St., 18201. Tel: 717-454-8714; Fax: 717-454-8754.

3—Holy Rosary, (1916) (Italian), Rev. Patrick J. Genello.
Res., 240 S. Poplar St., 18201. Tel: 717-454-6693.

4—Holy Trinity, (1887) (German), Rev. David L. Tressler, Admin. In res., Rev. Joseph J. Ferrara.
Res., 123 W. Oak St., 18201. Tel: 717-454-5394. [CEM]
School—35 N. Church St., 18201. Tel: 717-455-9645.
Sisters of Christian Charity 1; Lay Teachers 10; Students 213.
Mission—Hazleton, Luzerne Co., Our Lady of Mount Carmel, (1905).

5—Holy Trinity, (1907) (Slovak), Rev. Leonard M. Butcavage; Deacon Louis Smolinsky.
Res., 178 N. Wyoming St., 18201. Tel: 717-454-3233; Fax: 717-454-0237. [CEM]

6—St. Joseph's, (1882) (Slovak), Rev. Msgr. Francis J. Beeda; Rev. Stephen Krawontka; Deacon Leonard G. Kassick.
Res., 604 N. Laurel St., 18201. Tel: 717-454-0881; Fax: 717-454-1285. [CEM]
School—600 N. Laurel St., 18201. Tel: 717-454-4411.
Sisters of SS. Cyril and Methodius 4; Lay Teachers 8; Students 211.
Mission—Hazleton, Luzerne Co., St. Ladislaus.

7—Our Lady of Grace, (1910) (Italian), Rev. Neil O. Gugliemelli. In res., Rev. Francis P. Skitzki.
Res., 750 N. Vine St., 18201. Tel: 717-454-8797. [CEM]

8—Our Lady of Mount Carmel, (1905) (Tyrolese). Merged with Holy Trinity (German), Hazleton.

9—SS. Peter and Paul, (1887) (Lithuanian). Merged with Transfiguration, West Hazleton.

10—St. Stanislaus, (1893) (Polish), Rev. Louis S. Garbacik.
Res., 652 Carson St., 18201. Tel: 717-454-0662. [CEM]

Honesdale, Wayne Co., St. John the Evangelist (1842), Revs. Kevin P. Mulhern; Wieslaw Ziebacz; Sr. Mary Rose Mitchell, Pastoral Min.; Deacon Mark S. Jennings.
Res., 150 Terrace St., 18431. Tel: 717-253-4561; Fax: 717-253-1058. [CEM 3]
Mission—Rileyville, Wayne Co., St. Joseph.
Chapel—Honesdale, St. Mary Magdalene, (1853).

Hudson, Luzerne Co., St. Joseph's (1889) (Polish), Rev. Richard J. Kvedrovicz.
Res., 25 Oak St., (Hudson), Wilkes-Barre, 18705. Tel: 717-823-0238; Fax: 717-822-0394. [CEM]

Hughestown, Luzerne Co., Blessed Sacrament (1945), Rev. Joseph D. Verespy.
Res., 65 Rock St., P.O. Pittston, 18640. Tel: 717-654-6553.

Inkerman, Luzerne Co., St. Mark's (1900), Rev. Edward M. Masakowski.
Res., 1 St. Mark Ln., 18640. Tel: 717-654-0033.

Jackson, Susquehanna Co., St. Martin of Tours (1940), Very Rev. Thomas A. Cappelloni, V.F.
Res., P.O. Box 20, 18825. Tel: 717-756-2541; Fax: 717-756-2105.
Mission—Starrucca, Wayne Co., St. Paul.

Jermyn, Lackawanna Co., Sacred Heart of Mary (1889), Rev. James J. Walsh.
Res., 624 Madison Ave., 18433. Tel: 717-876-1061. [CEM]

Jersey Shore, Lycoming Co., St. Luke's (1902), Rev. Andrew S. Hvozdovic.
Res., 118 Kendall Ave., 17740. Tel: 717-398-2557.

Jessup, Lackawanna Co., St. Mary's Assumption (1904) (Italian), Rev. Andrew R. Gallia.
Res., 516 Third Ave., 18434. Tel: 717-489-4726. [CEM]

St. James (1899), Rev. William B. Blake. In res., Rev. Joseph A. Matz; Deacon John Hatala.
Res., 605 Church St., 18434. Tel: 717-489-2252; Fax: 717-489-2527. [CEM]
Missions—Jessup, Lackawanna Co., St. Michael, (1911); Jessup, Lackawanna Co., St. Stanislaus.

Kingston, Luzerne Co., St. Hedwig's (1901) (Polish), Rev. Richard A. Zavacki.
Res., 207 Zerbey Ave., 18704. Tel: 717-287-5634; Fax: 717-287-8566. [CEM]
School—16 Pulaski St., 18704. Tel: 717-288-6051.
Lay Teachers 8; Students 132.

St. Ignatius (1885), Rev. Msgr. Neil J. VanLoon, V.F.; Rev. David W. Cramer.
Res., 339 N. Maple Ave., 18704. Tel: 717-288-6446. [CEM]
Chapel—St. Ann's, Tel: 717-288-5919.

St. Mary's Annunciation (1902) (Lithuanian), Rev. Joseph J. Lasky.
Res., 258 Zerbey Ave., 18704. Tel: 717-287-5096.

Laflin, Luzerne Co., St. Maria Goretti (1967), Very Rev. James J. Paisley, V.F.
Res., 42 Redwood Dr., 18702. Tel: 717-655-8956; Fax: 717-655-1746.

Lake Ariel, Wayne Co., St. Thomas More (1941), Very Rev. Edward R. Scott, V.F.
Mailing Address: Box 188, 18436. Tel: 717-698-5584; Fax: 717-698-8468. [CEM]
Mission—Ledgedale, Wayne Co., St. Mary.

Lake Silkworth, Luzerne Co., Our Lady of Mount Carmel (1923), Rev. Thomas R. Hudak; Deacon Frank J. Sehn.
Res., R.R. 2, Box 265, Lake Silkworth, Hunlock Creek, 18621. Tel: 717-477-5040. [CEM]
Mission—Fairmount Springs, Luzerne Co., St. Martha's, (1966).

Lake Winola, Wyoming Co., St. Mary of the Lake (1986), Rev. Msgr. Dale R. Rupert, Admin.; Deacon Raymond A. Pieretti.
Res., P.O. Box 1, Fairview Rd., 18625. Tel: 717-378-2181; Fax: 717-378-3948.

Larksville, Luzerne Co., St. Anthony of Padua (1908) (Slovak), Rev. Bernard P. Evanofski.

Res., 1 Wilson St., 18704. Tel: 717-287-4018. [CEM]
Mission—Edwardsville, Luzerne Co., SS. Cyril and Methodius, (1900). [CEM]

Lattimer Mines, Luzerne Co., St. Mary's (1903) (Italian). Merged with St. Nazarius, Pardeesville.

Little Meadows, Susquehanna Co., St. Thomas the Apostle (1887). Merged with St. Francis Xavier, Friendsville.

Lords Valley, Pike Co., St. John Neumann (1976), Rev. Charles J. Cummings; Deacon John Nash.
Res., Lords Valley, HC8, Box 8390, Hawley, 18428.
Mission—Blooming Grove, Good Shepherd.

Luzerne, Luzerne Co., Sacred Heart (1893) (German), Rev. Robert P. Arnold.
Res., 535 Charles St., P.O. Box 125, 18709. Tel: 717-287-6600.
School—469 Miller St., 18709. Tel: 717-287-3431. Sisters of Christian Charity 2; Lay Teachers 6; Students 161.
St. Ann's (1924) (Lithuanian). Merged with Sacred Heart, Luzerne.
St. John Nepomucene (1907) (Slovak). Merged with Sacred Heart, Luzerne.

Mansfield, Tioga Co., Holy Child (1953), Rev. Louis T. Kaminski.
Res., 237 S. Main St., 16933. Tel: 717-662-3568; 662-2113.
Mission—Tioga, Tioga Co., St. Mary.

Matamoras, Pike Co., St. Joseph's (1892), Rev. John J. Turi.
Res., 309 Ave. F, 18336. Tel: 717-491-2618.
Mission—Mill Rift, Pike Co., Holy Family.

Mayfield, Lackawanna Co., Sacred Heart of Jesus (1904) (Polish), Rev. Joseph S. Sitko.
Res., 420 Hudson St., 18433. Tel: 717-876-1950. [CEM]

Meshoppen, Wyoming Co., St. Joachim's (1873), Rev. Patrick D. McDowell.
Res., P.O. Box 67, 18630. Tel: 717-833-2114; Fax: 717-833-2115. [CEM]
Mission—Auburn, Susquehanna Co., St. Bonaventure. [CEM]

Mildred, Sullivan Co., St. Francis of Assisi (1894). Merged with St. Basil, Dushore.
Missions—Eagles Mere, Sullivan Co., St. Francis of Assisi; Laporte, Sullivan Co., Sacred Heart.

Milford, Pike Co., St. Patrick's (1946), Rev. Gerald F. Mullally.
Res., 111 E. High St., P.O. Box W, 18337. Tel: 717-296-7451.
St. Vincent de Paul (1976), Rev. Msgr. William P. Ward; Deacon Albert W. Perreault.
Res., R.R. 3, Box 240, 18337. Tel: 717-686-4545.

Mocanaqua, Luzerne Co., St. Mary, Our Lady of Perpetual Help (1904) (Polish), Rev. Gerard M. McGlone.
Res., 150 Main St., 18655. Tel: 717-542-4157. [CEM]
Mission—Mocanaqua, Luzerne Co., Ascension.

Montdale, Lackawanna Co., Corpus Christi (1942), Rev. William J. Flynn, S.S.
Res., R.R. 1, Box 389, Olyphant, 18447. Tel: 717-254-9502.

Montoursville, Lycoming Co., Our Lady of Lourdes (1942), Rev. Thomas P. Shoback.
Res., 800 Mulberry St., 17754. Tel: 717-368-8598.

Montrose, Susquehanna Co., Holy Name of Mary (1898), Rev. James R. Nash.
Res., 60 S. Main St., 18801. Tel: 717-278-1504; Fax: 717-278-1504. [CEM]

Moscow, Lackawanna Co., St. Catherine of Siena (1861), Rev. Michael E. Finn; Deacon John J. Franceschelli.
Res., Church St., 18444. Tel: 717-842-4561; Fax: 717-842-6648.

Mount Pocono, Monroe Co., St. Mary of the Mount (1909), Rev. Msgr. Arthur J. Kaschenbach.
Res., 27 Fairview Ave., 18344. Tel: 717-839-7138.
Mission—Pocono Summit, Monroe Co., St. Joan of Arc.

Mountaintop, Luzerne Co., St. Jude's (1953), Revs. Paul M. Mullen; Joseph J. Evanko.
Res., 422 S. Mountain Blvd., 18707. Tel: 717-474-6315; Fax: 717-474-0775.
School—Tel: 717-474-5803.
Sisters 2; Lay Teachers 20; Students 436.
Missions—Solomon's Gap, Luzerne Co., St. Catherine; Nuangola, Luzerne Co., St. Ann.

Muncy, Lycoming Co., Resurrection (1941), Rev. David P. Cappelloni. In res., Rev. Sergio Bicomong.
Res., 526 S. Main St., 17756. Tel: 717-546-3900.

Nanticoke, Luzerne Co.,

1—Holy Child, (1942) (Polish). Merged with Holy Trinity (Polish), Nanticoke.

2—Holy Trinity, (1894) (Polish), Revs. Bernard A. Tboloczko; Patrick J. Naughton.
Res., 520 S. Hanover St., 18634. Tel: 717-735-4833; Fax: 717-735-2281. [CEM]
Mission—Nanticoke, Luzerne Co., Holy Child, (1942).

3—St. Francis of Assisi, (1872), Rev. Msgr. John W. Jordan.
Res., 173 E. Green St., 18634. Tel: 717-735-6903; 735-7011; Fax: 717-735-6903.

4—St. Joseph's, (1888) (Slovak), Rev. Leo M. Gardzalla.
Res., 107 E. Noble St., 18634. Tel: 717-735-0331. [CEM]

5—St. Mary of Czestochowa, (1901) (Polish), Rev. John S. Krafchak.
Res., 1030 S. Hanover St., 18634. Tel: 717-735-6911. [CEM]

6—St. Stanislaus, (1875) (Polish), Rev. Joseph R. Kakareka.
Res., 38 W. Church St., 18634. Tel: 717-735-0313. [CEM]

Nicholson, Wyoming Co., St. Patrick's (1888), Rev. John V. Polednak.
Res., Main and High Sts., 18446. Tel: 717-942-6602. [CEM]

Old Forge, Lackawanna Co.,

1—St. Lawrence O'Toole, (1895), Rev. Michael J. Kirwin; Deacon Carmine Mendicino.
Res., 620 S. Main St., 18518. Tel: 717-457-2032.

2—St. Mary's, (1897) (Italian), Very Rev. Joseph F. Cipriano, V.F.; Rev. Stanley J. Kurash.
Res., 123 W. Grace St., 18518. Tel: 717-457-5900.
School—216 W. Grace St., 18518. Tel: 717-457-6750.
Sisters 3; Lay Teachers 10; Students 191.

3—St. Michael's, (1905) (Polish), Rev. Joseph M. Brozena.
Res., 236 Vine St., 18518. Tel: 717-457-3353.

4—St. Stanislaus, (1903) (Polish), Rev. Cyril J. Rable.
Res., 1267 Franklin St., 18518. Tel: 717-457-5103. [CEM]

Olyphant, Lackawanna Co., Holy Ghost (1888) (Slovak), Rev. John S. Marinko.
Res., 120 Willow Ave., 18447. Tel: 717-489-2023. [CEM]
Convent—126 Willow Ave., 18447. Tel: 717-489-0792. Sisters of SS. Cyril and Methodius
St. Michael the Archangel (1909) (Polish), Rev. Kenneth G. Kizis.
Res., 132 Lincoln St., 18447. Tel: 717-489-0623. [CEM]
St. Patrick's (1875), Revs. Phillip J. Sladicka; Scott P. Sterowski.
Res., 200 Delaware Ave., 18447. Tel: 717-489-0752. [CEM]

Pardeesville, Luzerne Co., St. Nazarius (1966) (Italian), Rev. Joseph W. Bucolo.
Res., R.D. 2, P3D3, Hazleton, 18201. Tel: 717-454-2469.
Mission—Lattimer Mines, Luzerne Co., St. Mary, (1903). Tel: 717-454-4975.

Peckville, Lackawanna Co., Sacred Heart of Jesus (1946), Rev. Santino J. Fanucci; Deacon Frank A. Earley.
Res., 1101 Willow St., 18452. Tel: 717-383-3244.

Pittston, Luzerne Co.,

1—Our Lady of Mt. Carmel, (1904) (Italian), Rev. Paul A. McDonnell, O.S.J.
Res., 237 William St., 18640. Tel: 717-654-6902.

2—St. Casimir's, (1890) (Lithuanian). Merged with St. John the Evangelist, Pittston.

3—St. John the Baptist, (1892) (Slovak), Rev. Andrew F. Strish; Rev. Msgr. Joseph J. Super, Pastor Emeritus.
Res., 16 William St., 18640. Tel: 717-654-2112; Fax: 717-654-4210. [CEM 2]
School—12 William St., 18640. Tel: 717-654-0845. Robert Kaluzavich, Prin.
Lay Teachers 9; Students 241.

4—St. John the Evangelist, (1854), Rev. Msgr. John J. Bendik; Revs. Frank S. Homets; Gerard L. Hawley. In res., Rev. Hugh H. McGroarty.
Res., 35 William St., 18640. Tel: 717-654-0053; Fax: 717-654-3751. [CEM]

5—St. Joseph's, (1909) (Polish). Merged with St. John the Evangelist, Pittston.

6—St. Mary, Help of Christians, (1851), Rev. Richard J. Polmounter; Deacon Joseph J. Gowarty.
Res., 535 N. Main St., 18640. Tel: 717-654-0263. [CEM]
Mission—Pittston, Luzerne Co., St. Mary of the Assumption, (1863).

7—St. Mary's Assumption, (1863) (German). Merged with St. Mary, Help of Christians, Pittson.
School—41 Carroll St., 18640. Tel: 717-654-8313; Fax: 717-654-8320.
Sisters of Christian Charity 3; Lay Teachers 9; Students 287.

8—St. Rocco, (1919) (Italian), Rev. Nicholas J. Dininni, O.S.J.
Res., 62 W. Oak St., 18640. Tel: 717-654-2914. [CEM]

Plains, Luzerne Co., Sacred Heart (1883), Rev. Robert E. Burnett.
Res., 115 N. Main St., 18705. Tel: 717-823-3830. [CEM]
SS. Peter and Paul (1898) (Polish), Rev. Joseph A. Greskiewicz. In res., Rev. Michael J. Kloton.
Res., 13 Hudson Rd., 18705. Tel: 717-825-6663; Fax: 717-823-4556. [CEM]
School—15 Hudson St., 18705. Tel: 717-824-9433. Bernardine Sisters of St. Francis 2; Lay Teachers 8; Students 183.

Pleasant Mount, Wayne Co., St. James (1887), Rev. Richard W. Beck.
Res., P.O. Box 53, 18453. Tel: 717-448-2211.
Missions—Hill Top, Wayne Co., St. Cecilia; Lake Como, Wayne Co., Assumption of the B.V.M.; Rock Lake, Wayne Co., St. Juliana's.

Plymouth, Luzerne Co.,

1—Nativity of the Blessed Virgin Mary, (1885) (Polish), Rev. Msgr. Vincent J. Grimalia, V.F.; Rev. Samuel T. Perrins; Deacon Leo R. Thompson.
Res., 66 Willow St., 18651. Tel: 717-779-5324; Fax: 717-779-4921. [CEM 2]

2—St. John the Baptist, (1899) (Polish), Rev. Msgr. John C. Masakowski.
Res., 126 Nesbitt St., (Larksville), 18651. Tel: 717-779-9620. [CEM]

3—St. Stephen's, (1886) (Slovak). Merged with Nativity of the Blessed Virgin Mary, Plymouth.

4—St. Vincent de Paul, (1872), Rev. Joseph F. Houston; Deacon Peter G. Smith.
Res., 101 Church St., 18651. Tel: 717-779-9508; Fax: 717-779-2332. [CEM]

Pocono Pines, Monroe Co., Our Lady of the Lake (1985), Rev. Thomas J. Maloney.
Res., P.O. Box 0, 18350. Tel: 717-646-6424; Fax: 717-646-1047.

Rock Lake, Wayne Co., St. Juliana's (1838). Merged with St. James, Pleasant Mount.
R.R. 1, Box 117, Pleasant Mount, 18453. Tel: 717-448-2211.

Royal, Susquehanna Co., St. Pius X (1967), Very Rev. Peter V. Herhenreader, V.F.
Res., Box 64, Clifford, 18413. Tel: 717-222-4209.

Sayre, Bradford Co., Church of the Epiphany (1888), Revs. William J. Karle; Glenn E. McCreary.
Res., 304 S. Elmer Ave., 18840. Tel: 717-888-9641.
School—627 Stevenson St., 18840. Tel: 717-888-5802.
Sisters of I.H.M. 2; Lay Teachers 10; Students 213.

Shavertown, Luzerne Co., St. Therese (1926), Rev. J. Peter Crynes.
Res., 64 Davis St., 18708. Tel: 717-696-1144; Fax: 717-696-1210.

Shohola, Pike Co., St. Ann's (1928), Rev. Michael F. Quinnan.
Res., P.O. Box 86, 18458. Tel: 717-559-7642; Fax: 717-559-7499. [CEM]
Missions—Lackawaxen, Pike Co., St. Mary; Greeley, Pike Co., Sacred Heart.

Simpson, Lackawanna Co., St. Michael's (1903), Rev. Hilary L. Malinowski.
Res., 46 Midland St., 18407. Tel: 717-282-2161. [CEM]
Mission—Simpson, Lackawanna Co., Holy Trinity.

South Waverly, Bradford Co., St. John the Evangelist (1902), Rev. Vincent F. Langan.
Res., 85 Division St., 18840. Tel: 717-888-2123.

South Williamsport, Lycoming Co., St. Lawrence's (1931), Rev. Francis L. Pauselli.
Res., 344 Winthrop St., 17701. Tel: 717-322-0403; Fax: 717-322-4335.

Stroudsburg, Monroe Co., St. Luke's (1968), Revs. Thomas D. McLaughlin; Carmen J. Perry.
Office: 818 Main St., 18360. Tel: 717-421-9097; 421-9863; Fax: 717-421-6015.
Res., 906 Main St., 18360. Tel: 717-421-8460.

Sugar Notch, Luzerne Co., Holy Family (1901) (Polish), Rev. John S. Terry; Deacon Philip Harris.
Office: 828 Main St., 18706. Tel: 717-822-8983; Fax: 717-822-6016. [CEM]
Mission—Sugar Notch, Luzerne Co., St. Charles Borromeo.
SS. Peter and Paul (1847) (Lithuanian). Merged with Holy Family, Sugar Notch.

Susquehanna, Susquehanna Co., St. John the Evangelist (1847), Rev. Michael J. Pulicare.
Res., 101 Jackson Ave., 18847. Tel: 717-853-4634; Fax: 717-853-3356. [CEM]

Swoyersville, Luzerne Co.,

1—Holy Name of Jesus, (1905). Merged with St. Mary of Czestochowa, Swoyersville.

2—Holy Name/St. Mary's, Revs. Louis A. Grippe; Joseph J. Fanti; Deacon Peter J. Hoegen.
Res., 283 Shoemaker St. (P.O. Kingston), 18704. Tel: 717-287-2139; Fax: 717-287-6474. [CEM]

3—Holy Trinity, (1895) (Slovak), Rev. Michael J. Zipay.
Res., 116 Hughes St. (P.O. Kingston), 18704. Tel: 717-287-6624. [CEM]

4—St. Mary of Czestochowa, (1909). Merged with Holy Name of Jesus, Swoyersville.

Tannersville, Monroe Co., Our Lady of Victory (1968), Rev. Henry E. Zapotocki.
Res., Rte. 611, 18372. Tel: 717-629-4572; Fax: 717-629-0335.

Taylor, Lackawanna Co., Immaculate Conception (1898), Rev. Joseph D. Flannery.
Res., 202 Church St., 18517. Tel: 717-562-2390.
St. John the Baptist (1904) (Slovak), Rev. Joseph J. Mattey.
Res., 408 N. Main St., 18517. Tel: 717-562-1341. [CEM]

Throop, Lackawanna Co., St. Anthony's (1911) (Polish). Merged with St. John the Baptist, Throop. Rev. August A. Ricciardi.
Office: 215 Rebecca St., 18519. Tel: 717-489-1963. [CEM]
Res., 520 Charles St., 18512. Tel: 717-489-1682.
St. Bridget's (1916). Merged with St. John the Baptist & St. Anthony's, Throop. Rev. August A. Ricciardi.
Office: 520 Sanderson St., 18512. Tel: 717-489-1682.
Res., 520 Charles St., 18512.
St. John the Baptist (1905) (Slovak). Merged with St. Anthony's, Throop. Rev. August A. Ricciardi.
Office: 520 Sanderson St., 18512. Tel: 717-489-1822. [CEM]
Res., 520 Charles St., 18512. Tel: 717-489-1682.
Missions—Throop, Lackawanna Co., St. Bridget; St. Mary.

Tobyhanna, Monroe Co., St. Ann (1923), Very Rev. John B. Boyle, V.F.; Deacon Michael Squillante.
Res., Main St., P.O. Box 188, 18466-0188. Tel: 717-894-8018; Fax: 717-894-9619. [CEM 2]

Towanda, Bradford Co., SS. Peter and Paul (1841), Very Rev. Ronald J. Hughes.
Res., 106 Third St., 18848. Tel: 717-265-2113; Fax: 717-265-2114. [CEM 3]
School—St. Agnes, 102 Third St., 18848. Tel: 717-265-6803; Fax: 717-265-2114.
Lay Teachers 12; Students 250.
Mission—Ulster, Bradford Co., Immaculate Conception.

Tunkhannock, Wyoming Co., Nativity of Blessed Virgin Mary (1884), Rev. Joseph F. Sica.
Res., 99 E. Tioga St., 18657. Tel: 717-836-3275. [CEM 2]

Wanamie, Luzerne Co., St. Mary's (1906) (Lithuanian), Rev. Gerald J. Gurka.
Res., 203 Bellas Rd., Wanamie, Nanticoke, 18634. Tel: 717-735-2153. [CEM]
Mission—Nanticoke, Luzerne Co., St. Joseph.

Waymart, Wayne Co., St. Mary's (1915), Rev. John T. Albosta.
Res., 242 Carbondale Rd., P.O. Box 160, 18472. Tel: 717-488-6440; Fax: 717-488-7440. [CEM]
Mission—Canaan, Wayne Co., St. Patrick.
Station—Wayne Co., Farview State Prison.

Wellsboro, Tioga Co., St. Peter's (1879), Rev. Michael J. Sullivan; Deacon Robert A. Scheib.
Res., 38 Central Ave., 16901. Tel: 717-724-3371; Fax: 717-724-6322. [CEM]
Mission—Morris, Tioga Co., Sacred Heart.

West Hazleton, Luzerne Co., St. Francis of Assisi (1940), Rev. Connell A. McHugh.
Res., 544 N. Broad St., 18201. Tel: 717-454-3072.
Mission—Harwood, Luzerne Co., St. Michael.
Transfiguration (1907) (Polish), Rev. Richard E. Czachor.
Res., 213 W. Green St., 18201. Tel: 717-454-3933; Fax: 717-454-8326. [CEM]
School—217 W. Green St., 18201. Tel: 717-454-6131.
Bernardine Sisters of St. Francis 1; Lay Teachers 9; Students 189.
Mission—Hazleton, Luzerne Co., SS. Peter and Paul.

Weston, Luzerne Co., Sacred Heart (1888), Rev. Joseph P. Bonner.
Res., 18256. Tel: 717-384-4121. [CEM]
Mission—Nuremberg, Luzerne Co., St. Joseph.

West Pittston, Luzerne Co., Immaculate Conception (1910), Rev. Joseph J. Adonizio.
Res., 605 Luzerne Ave., 18643. Tel: 717-654-2753; Fax: 717-654-9244.

West Wyoming, Luzerne Co., Our Lady of Sorrows (1953), Rev. Michael J. Rafferty.
Res., 363 W. 8th St., 18644. Tel: 717-693-1991.

White Haven, Luzerne Co., St. Patrick's (1874), Rev. Stephen J. Stavoy.
Res., 580 Elmira St., 18661. Tel: 717-443-9944. [CEM]
Station—White Haven Center, Tel: 717-453-9564.

White Mills, Wayne Co., St. Joseph's (1968), Rev. Michael H. Marchetti.
Mailing Address: Box 153, 18473. Tel: 717-253-0307; Fax: 717-253-0314.
Mission—Beach Lake, Wayne Co., St. Bernard, Tel: 717-729-7247.

Wilkes-Barre, Luzerne Co.,

1—St. Aloysius, (1898), Rev. Msgr. Donald A. McAndrews; Revs. Thomas D. Skotek; Paul E. Miller.
Res., 143 W. Division St., 18702. Tel: 717-823-3791; Fax: 717-826-0233.
School—321 Barney St., 18702. Tel: 717-824-6131; Fax: 717-824-1643.
Lay Teachers 16; Students 251.

2—Blessed Sacrament, (1917), Rev. Joseph A. Kearney.
Res., 213 E. Main St., 18705. Tel: 717-822-9561.
Missions—Wilkes-Barre, Luzerne Co., St. Francis of Assisi; Wilkes-Barre, Luzerne Co., St. John the Baptist.
Station—Wilkes-Barre, Geisinger Wyoming Valley Hospital, Tel: 717-826-7300.

3—St. Boniface, (1896) (German), Rev. T. Timothy Delaney; Deacon Francis J. Bradigan.
Res., 225 Blackman St., 18702. Tel: 717-822-8330; Fax: 717-819-4125.

4—St. Casimir's, (1889) (Lithuanian), Revs. James F. Boyle, C.S.C.; Joseph F. Callahan, C.S.C. In res., Rev. James B. Mannis, C.S.C.
Res., 301 Delaney St., Lyndwood, Wilkes-Barre, 18702. Tel: 717-825-2598. [CEM]

5—St. Dominic, (1882), Rev. William R. Culnane.
Res., 155 Austin Ave., 18705. Tel: 717-822-8871.

6—St. Francis of Assisi, (1913) (Lithuanian). Merged with Blessed Sacrament, Wilkes-Barre.

7—Holy Rosary, (1906) (Italian), Rev. Peter D. Menghini.
Res., 363 Park Ave., 18702. Tel: 717-822-1183.

8—Holy Saviour, (1895), Very Rev. E. Francis Kelly, V.F.; Rev. Robert M. Timchak; Deacon Carl J. Orbon.
Res., 54 Hillard St., 18702. Tel: 717-822-1186; Fax: 717-822-1074.
Mission—Bear Creek Township, Luzerne Co., St. Christopher.

9—Holy Trinity, (1893) (Lithuanian), Rev. Theodore L. Obaza.
Res., 416 E. South St., 18702. Tel: 717-823-1081. [CEM 2]

10—St. John the Evangelist, (1927). Merged with Sacred Heart of Jesus, Wilkes-Barre.

11—St. John the Baptist, (1924) (Slovak). Merged with Blessed Sacrament, Wilkes-Barre.

12—St. Joseph, (Georgetown) (1898), Revs. Raymond J. Lynch, O.F.M.; Alvin Black, O.F.M. In res., Rev. Benjamin J. Foerch, O.F.M.
Res., St. Joseph's Friary, 783 E. Northampton St., 18702. Tel: 717-822-8023; Fax: 717-822-2891.

13—St. Joseph's, (1927) (Slovak). Merged with St. Mary's Church of the Immaculate Conception, Wilkes-Barre.

14—St. Mary's Church of the Immaculate Conception, (1845), Rev. Msgr. Thomas V. Banick; Rev. Vincent Dang.
Res., P.O. Box 348, 134 S. Washington St., 18703. Tel: 717-823-4168; Fax: 717-822-3477. [CEM]
Mission—Wilkes-Barre, Luzerne Co., St. Joseph.

15—Maternity of the Blessed Virgin Mary, (1885) (Polish), Rev. Msgr. Alexander T. Kulik.
Res., 40 Park Ave., 18702. Tel: 717-824-7832. [CEM 2]

16—St. Nicholas, (1856) (German), Rev. Msgr. Joseph G. Rauscher; Rev. John J. Chmil.
Res., 226 S. Washington St., 18701-2897. Tel: 717-823-7736; 823-5842; Fax: 717-823-0256. [CEM]

17—St. Patrick's, (1920), Rev. J. Duane Gavitt; Deacon Florian J. Gyza.
Res., 316 Parrish St., 18702. Tel: 717-823-1948.

18—Sacred Heart of Jesus, (1896) (Slovak), Revs. John J. Sempa; Gerard F. Safko; Deacon Joseph F. DeVizia. In res., Rev. Joseph T. Gilbert.
Res., 601 N. Main St., 18705. Tel: 717-823-4988; Fax: 717-823-5932. [CEM]
School—607 N. Main St., 18705. Tel: 717-824-0818.
Sisters of SS. Cyril and Methodius 3; Lay Teachers 13; Students 278.
Mission—Wilkes-Barre, Luzerne Co., St. John the Evangelist.

19—St. Stanislaus Kostka, (1908) (Polish), Rev. Joseph M. Horanzy.
Res., 666 N. Main St., 18705. Tel: 717-822-8026. [CEM]

20—St. Therese's, (1929), Rev. Msgr. Francis J. Callahan, V.F. In res., Rev. George A. Jeffrey.
Res., 25 Old River Rd., 18702. Tel: 717-822-1075; 824-3052; Fax: 717-829-4147.

Williamsport, Lycoming Co.,

1—Annunciation, (1865), Rev. Msgr. William J. Fleming; Rev. Joseph Elston; Deacon J. Morris Smith.
Res., 410 Walnut St., 17701. Tel: 717-323-9456; 693-0289; Fax: 717-323-3728. [CEM]
School—711 W. Edwin St., 17701. Tel: 717-322-6036, 322-2754.
Sisters of I.H.M. 4; Lay Teachers 6; Students 154.

2—Ascension, (1907), Rev. Joseph B. Wilson, Ph.D., Admin.
Office: 2100 Linn St., 17701. Tel: 717-326-4922.
Res., 2111 Linn St., 17701. Tel: 717-326-4922; Fax: 717-327-1196.

3—St. Boniface's, (1853) (German), Revs. Stephen D. McGough; Jacek Bialkowski; Anthony Boothali; Deacon Clair J. Raisch.
Res., 326 Washington Blvd., 17701. Tel: 717-326-1544; Fax: 717-326-6746.
School—710 Franklin St., 17701. Tel: 717-326-3738.
Sisters of Christian Charity 1; Lay Teachers 8; Students 206.

4—Holy Rosary, (1915) (Polish), Rev. Andrew J. Krusinski.
Res., 313 Arch St., 17701. Tel: 717-323-6316.

5—Mater Dolorosa, (1908) (Italian), Very Rev. Francis J. Castellano, V.F.
Res., 635 Hepburn St., 17701. Tel: 717-326-9769; Fax: 717-327-8141.

6—St. Ann's, (1959), Rev. Andrew Kurovsky.
Res., 1220 Northway Rd., 17701. Tel: 717-322-5935; Fax: 717-322-2451.
School—1225 Northway Rd., 17701. Tel: 717-323-0500.
Sisters of Christian Charity 1; Lay Teachers 8; Students 200.
Mission—Cascade, Lycoming Co., Assumption of the B.V.M.

Wyalusing, Bradford Co., St. Mary's Assumption (1950), Rev. Thomas J. McDermott.
Res., R.R. 4, Box 3, 18853. Tel: 717-746-1006.
Mission—Stowell, Wyoming Co., St. Anthony.

Wyoming, Luzerne Co., St. Joseph's (1914) (Polish), Rev. Walter F. Skiba.
Res., 97 E. Sixth St., 18644. Tel: 717-693-0510. [CEM]

Chaplains of Public Institutions

Clarks Summit. *Clarks Summit State Hospital* 18411. Tel: 717-586-1741. Rev. Thomas J. Major.

Dallas. *State Correctional Institution* 18612. Tel: 717-675-1101. Deacon Jose A. Munoz.

East Stroudsburg. *East Stroudsburg State University* P.O. Box 331, 18301. Tel: 717-476-0321. Sr. Ann Newell, I.H.M., Campus Min.

La Plume. *Keystone Junior College*. Rev. John K. Schaal, Clarks Summit. Tel: 717-586-1741.

Mansfield. *Mansfield University*. Ms. Laurie Grab, 4899 Lambscreek Rd., Apt. 3, 16933. Tel: 717-662-4431; Fax: 717-662-2113.

Muncy. *Muncy Prison* Tel: 717-546-3900. Rev. David P. Cappelloni, Chap.

Wilkes-Barre. *Geisinger Wyoming Valley Hospital* Tel: 717-822-9561. Rev. Joseph A. Kearney.
Veteran's Administration Hospital Tel: 717-824-3521. Rev. Benjamin J. Foerch, O.F.M., Chap.

Williamsport. *Lycoming College* 17701. Tel: 717-321-4111. Sr. Catherine Ann Gilvary, I.H.M., Campus Min.

On Special or Other Diocesan Assignment:
Reverend Monsignors—
McGowan, Andrew J., Dir., Catholic Health Care Facilities & Rep., Catholic Institutions of Higher Learning, Mercy Hospital, Scranton, PA 18501. Tel: 717-348-7010
Reverend Fathers—
Ensey, Eric
Finn, Edward S., Chap., R.D. #1, Box 310A, Equinunk, PA 18417. Tel: 717-224-4380
Fullerton, Daniel, P.O. Box 183, Elmhurst, PA 18416. Tel: 717-842-9511; Fax: 717-842-9507
Roberts, Marshall
Urrutigoity, Carlos
Yaszcz, Thomas A., 52 W. Grove St., Nanticoke, PA 18634. Tel: 717-735-8754, Ext. 315

On Duty Outside the Diocese:
Reverend Monsignors—

Kline, Robert R., Mt. St. Mary's College, Emmitsburg, MD 21727. Tel: 301-447-6122
Yarrish, Bernard E., North American College, 00120 Vatican City State. Tel: 011-39-6-684-931

Reverend Fathers—
Fives, Carl J., Mt. St. Mary's College, Emmitsburg, MD 21727. Tel: 301-447-6122
Gabuzda, Richard J., Kenefick #1208, 320 N. 20th St., Omaha, NE 68178. Tel: 402-449-6384
McGee, James J., S.S., Society of St. Sulpice
Plominski, Walter J., Diocese of Rochester, NY
Purta, Jerome J., St. Vincent Archabbey, 300 Fraser-Purchase Rd., Latrobe, PA 15650
Rossi, Walter R., Assoc. Rector & Dir., Pilgrimages, Basilica of the National Shrine of the Immaculate Conception, Washington, DC
Silvestri, Luke A., 2106 W. Yukon Dr., Phoenix, AZ 85027
Walsh, John A., 258 Acorn Dr., Longwood, FL 32750. Tel: 407-330-4966
Waznak, Robert J., S.S., Society of St. Sulpice
Wysocki, Joseph A., 5424 Burling Rd., Bethesda, MD 20014
Yenkevich, Daniel J.

Military Chaplains:
Reverend Fathers—
Dormer, David J., Chap., U.S. Army, 1305-B Bastogne Ct., Ft. Wainwright, AK 99703
Ferretti, Samuel J., Chap., U.S.N.R., 3516 Sale Dr., Virginia Beach, VA 23464-1830
Hochreiter, Robert S., Chap., Major, U.S. Air Force, PSC Box 1348, Scott Air Force Base, IL 62225
Kelly, Brian F., Chap., U.S. Navy, 2047 San Remo Dr., Oceanside, CA 92056
Motsay, Joseph R., Chap., U.S.A.F., 9409 B Washington St., Ellsworth Air Force Base, SD 57706. Tel: 605-923-6066
Petruska, William M., CHC, U.S.N., 307 Saddle Ridge Rd., Annapolis, MD 21403

Unassigned or Leave of Absence:
Reverend Fathers—
Gibson, Robert J.
Jacobs, James J.
Kringe, Charles J., 708 N. Broad St. W., West Hazleton, PA 18201. Tel: 717-454-1380
Kulik, Francis J.
Rossetti, Mark T.
Tamalis, John J.
Ziobro, Joseph M.

Retired:
Reverend Monsignors—
Burns, Gerald J., Villa St. Joseph Residence, Dunmore, PA 18509. Tel: 717-343-7161
Casey, George T., P.O. Box 1578, Hollywood, FL 33022. Tel: 954-920-0681
Cawley, Thomas J., Villa St. Joseph Residence, Dunmore, PA 18509. Tel: 717-343-2254
Clarke, James T., Villa St. Joseph Residence, Dunmore, PA 18509. Tel: 717-969-1235
Demuth, George R., Holy Family Pavilion, 2510 Adams Ave., Apt. 303, Scranton, PA 18509-1597. Tel: 717-344-3719
Donovan, William L., Villa St. Joseph Residence, Dunmore, PA 18509. Tel: 717-963-9383
Gajewski, Chester A., Villa St. Joseph Residence, Dunmore, PA 18509. Tel: 717-347-1851
Gallagher, John P., Ph.D., 1026 Wheeler Ave., Scranton, PA 18510. Tel: 717-342-1991
Harvan, Michael S., 185 Hickory Rd., Bear Creek Township, Wilkes-Barre, PA 18702. Tel: 717-472-3072
Horan, Thomas C., 137 S. Church St., Carbondale, PA 18407. Tel: 717-282-4291; 698-5366
Kane, Francis A., Holy Family Residence, 2500 Adams Ave., Scranton, PA 18509. Tel: 717-346-2501
Law, Joseph A., Hemlock Farms, Box 2170, Hawley, PA 18428. Tel: 717-775-0912
Mecca, Mark A., St. Mary's Villa, Elmhurst, PA 18416. Tel: 717-842-7621
Meier, Joseph F., 175 N. Vine St., Apt. 2E, Hazleton, PA 18201. Tel: 717-454-8970
Norkunas, Anthony J., 253 S. Meade St., Wilkes-Barre, PA 18702. Tel: 717-824-6490
O'Brien, John J., Villa St. Joseph Residence, Dunmore, PA 18509. Tel: 717-961-1865
Ozalas, Michael C., 106 Venard Rd., Clarks Summit, PA 18411. Tel: 717-587-5149
Pakutka, William J., Villa St. Joseph Residence, Dunmore, PA 18509. Tel: 717-341-9168
Penkala, Edmund S., Villa St. Joseph Residence, Dunmore, PA 18509. Tel: 717-344-6288
Sullivan, Edward T., Villa St. Joseph Residence, Dunmore, PA 18509. Tel: 717-341-9203
Super, Joseph J., 16 William St., Pittston, PA 18640. Tel: 717-654-2112

Reverend Fathers—
Alisauskas, Peter J., Indian Lake, P.O. Box 106, White Haven, PA 18661. Tel: 717-472-3360
Bocianski, Andrew B., St. Mary's Villa, Elmhurst, PA 18416. Tel: 717-842-7621
Breslin, Joseph W., Villa St. Joseph Residence, Dunmore, PA 18509. Tel: 717-341-3315
Brogus, Albert G., 43 James St., Plains, PA 18705
Casey, John W., P.O. Box 1578, Hollywood, FL 33022. Tel: 954-920-0681
Conboy, Joseph T., Villa St. Joseph Residence, Dunmore, PA 18509. Tel: 717-941-9405
Cortese, Patrick S., P.O. Box 366, Mildred, PA 18632. Tel: 717-928-7230
Dacey, Martin J., St. Mary's Villa, Elmhurst, PA 18416. Tel: 717-842-7621
Domnick, Alphonsus, T.O.R., Villa St. Joseph Residence, Dunmore, PA 18509. Tel: 717-341-9176
Everling, Robert M., Villa St. Joseph Residence, Dumore, PA 18509. Tel: 717-343-4925
Fabian, John L., Villa St. Joseph, Dunmore, PA 18509. Tel: 717-348-0728
Ferrara, Joseph J., 123 W. Oak St., Hazleton, PA 18201. Tel: 717-455-2188
Flynn, Thomas A., Villa St. Joseph, Dunmore, PA 18509. Tel: 717-348-0589
Fox, Joseph F., 1706 Delaware St., Dunmore, PA 18509. Tel: 717-343-5522
Gaiardo, Martin J., Mulberry Tower, 499 Mulberry St., Apt. 1216, Scranton, PA 18503. Tel: 717-347-4826
Gallagher, Edward F., Villa St. Joseph Residence, Dunmore, PA 18509. Tel: 717-348-6873
Hines, William F., 2461 S.W. 82nd Ave., Bldg. 2-Apt. 105, Ft. Lauderdale, FL 33324. Tel: 305-423-9301
Hlopko, John J., Lake Rd., P.O. Box 67, Bear Creek, PA 18602. Tel: 717-472-3483
Kalinowski, Stainslaus J., 3020 Cedar Ave., Scranton, PA 18505
Kelley, John J., Candlewood Park, 12 Hunter Rd., Hazleton, PA 18201. Tel: 717-450-0131
Langan, James J., 2420 S.W. 81st Ave., Arrowhead Condominium, Bldg. 7, Apt. 402, Davie, FL 33324
Lewis, Harry J., Villa St. Joseph Residence, Dunmore, PA 18509. Tel: 717-343-5499
Madaj, John A., Fox Manor, R.D. 1, Box 309, Hazleton, PA 18201. Tel: 717-455-0634
Makowski, Edward J., Little Flower Manor, 200 South Meade St., Wilkes-Barre, PA 18702
Maloney, Andrew P., P.O. Box 583, Mountainhome, PA 18342. Tel: 717-595-7679
Markowski, Clement A., Villa St. Joseph Residence, Dunmore, PA 18509. Tel: 717-343-0555
McCarthy, Daniel A., St. Mary's Villa, Elmhurst, PA 18416. Tel: 717-842-7621
Mikus, Frank P., Villa St. Joseph Residence, Dunmore, PA 18509. Tel: 717-342-2728
Mulrooney, Charles F., Villa St. Joseph Residence, Dunmore, PA 18509. Tel: 717-969-1305
Mulrooney, F. Harold, 1203 Schlager St., Scranton, PA 18504. Tel: 717-343-8704
Noviello, Anthony A., 385 Montgomery Pike, South Williamsport, PA 17701. Tel: 717-323-6552
O'Haire, John A., Villa St. Joseph Residence, Dunmore, PA 18509. Tel: 717-342-6865
Pace, William J., Villa St. Joseph Residence, Dunmore, PA 18509. Tel: 717-961-5856
Plevyak, Valentine R., Villa St. Joseph Residence, Dunmore, PA 18509. Tel: 717-969-9109
Purcell, William F., Villa St. Joseph Residence, Dunmore, PA 18509. Tel: 717-348-0695
Rusin, Joseph C., 199 East Ave., Bear Creek Twp., Gouldsboro, PA 18424. Tel: 717-472-2229
Ryan, Joseph F., P.O. Box 77, Pocono Summit, PA 18346. Tel: 717-839-9260
Saltry, Joseph A., Holy Family Residence, Rm. 256, 2500 Adams Ave., Scranton, PA 18509. Tel: 717-341-1549
Sammons, Joseph F., 101 Queen Esther Dr., Sayre, PA 18840. Tel: 717-888-7821
Sokolowski, Edward V., 3 Regina Dr., Mountaintop, PA 18707. Tel: 717-474-2269
Stalavicz, George P., Little Flower Manor, 200 S. Meade St., Wilkes-Barre, PA 18702
Ulrich, Carl G., Villa St. Joseph Residence, Dunmore, PA 18509. Tel: 717-341-5898
Wayda, Henry A., St. Mary's Villa, Elmhurst, PA 18416. Tel: 717-842-7621
Zawadzki, Victor C., 5 O'Donnell St., Wilkes-Barre, PA 18702. Tel: 717-819-1692
Zawodniak, Edward J., R.R. #2, Box 355, Hickory Tree Rd., Loyalville, Dallas, PA 18612. Tel: 717-477-2086

INSTITUTIONS LOCATED IN THE DIOCESE

[A] SEMINARIES, DIOCESAN

DALTON. *Saint Pius X Seminary.* (Collaborative College/Pre-Theology Seminary), 1000 Seminary Rd., 18414. Tel: 717-563-1131; Fax: 717-563-8520. Rev. Msgr. David A. Bohr, S.T.D., Rector; Rev. Msgr. John A. Esseff, D.Min., M.A., S.T.L., Dir., Apostolic Formation; Rev. Msgr. Dale R. Rupert, Spiritual Dir. & Dir., Liturgical Formation; Rev. Joseph C. Bambera, M.Div., J.C.L., Formation Advisor.
Non-Resident Faculty: Revs. Robert J. Barone, S.T.D.; Albert M. Liberatore; James A. Rafferty, S.T.L., Academic Dean; Deacon J. Morris Smith, M.A., Th.D.; Mr. Edward G. Mathews, Jr., M.A., M.Phil., Ph.D. Seminarians 25.

[B] SEMINARIES, RELIGIOUS

PITTSTON. *St. Joseph's Oblate Seminary*, R.R. 4, Box 4, 18640. Tel: 717-654-7542. Revs. Mario S. Buttini, O.S.J., Rector; Gregory T. Finn, O.S.J., Dir. Formation & Vocation.

[C] COLLEGES AND UNIVERSITIES

SCRANTON. *Marywood University*, 18509. Tel: 717-348-6211.
E-mail: mreap@ac.marywood.edu
Web site: http://www.marywood.edu
For a complete listing, refer to the Colleges and Universities section.
University of Scranton, 18510. Tel: 717-941-7533.
Web site: http://www.uofs.edu
For a complete listing, refer to the Colleges and Universities section.

DALLAS. *College Misericordia*, 18612. Tel: 717-674-6400.
Web site: www.miseri.edu
For a complete listing, refer to the Colleges and Universities section.

*WILKES-BARRE. *Kings College*, 18711. Tel: 717-826-5900.
Web site: http://www.kings.edu
For a complete listing, refer to the Colleges and Universities section.

[D] HIGH SCHOOLS, DIOCESAN

SCRANTON. *Bishop Hannan High School*, 330 Wyoming Ave., 18503. Tel: 717-346-4643. Mr. James P. Marcks, Prin.; Rev. Jeffrey J. Walsh, Dir., Religious Formation; Mr. Matthew Rakauskas, Asst. Prin. Priests 3; Sisters Servants of the Immaculate Heart of Mary 5; Lay Teachers 30; Students 406.

CARBONDALE. *Sacred Heart Junior/Senior High School*, 44 S. Church St., 18407. Tel: 717-282-2790. Sr. Margo McCormick, I.H.M., Prin.; Rev. James A. Rafferty, Dir., Religious Formation. Priests 1; Sisters 4; Lay Teachers 12; Students 150.

DUNMORE. *Bishop O'Hara High School*, 501 E. Drinker St., 18512. Tel: 717-346-7541. Joseph Casciano, Prin.; Rev. Scott P. Sterowski, Dir., Religious Formation. Sisters, Servants of the Immaculate Heart of Mary; Sisters of SS. Cyril and Methodius. Priests 1; Sisters 5; Lay Teachers 25; Students 380.

EAST STROUDSBURG. *Notre Dame Junior/Senior High School*, 60 Spangenburg Ave., 18301. Tel: 717-421-0466; Fax: 717-476-0629. Jeffrey N. Lyons, Prin.; Rev. John A. Bergamo, Dir., Religious Formation; John D. Gormley, Dean of Students. Priests 2; Sisters, Servants of the Immaculate Heart of Mary 1; Lay Teachers 24; Students 352.

HAZLETON. *Bishop Hafey Junior/Senior High School*, 1700 W. 22nd St., 18201. Tel: 717-455-9431.
E-mail: bhafey@ptd.net
Rev. David L. Tressler, M.S., M.Ed., Prin. & Procurator; Mrs. Kathleen Stark, Exec. Vice Prin.; Mr. Richard Smith, Vice Prin.; Mr. Michael Stofko, Coord. of Student Affairs; Mr. Thomas A. Kostic, Dir., Religious Formation; Sr. Roberta Peters, I.H.M., Dir., Guidance; Mrs. Miriam Jamelli, Jr. High Guidance Counselor; Mr. Thomas Cipriano, Asst. Procurator / Development Dir. Priests 2; Religious 4; Lay Teachers 38; Students 650.

KINGSTON. *Bishop O'Reilly High School*, 316 N. Maple Ave., P.O. Box 1346, 18704. Tel: 717-288-1404.
E-mail: boreilly@liul8.K12.pa.us
Web site: http://www.liul8.K12.pa.us:80/~oreilly4
Mrs. Anita M. Sirak, Prin.; Sr. Carol Makravitz, S.C.C., Vice Prin.; Rev. Michael J. Kloton, Dir., Religious Formation & Asst. Prin.; Mrs. Linda Prawdzik, Dir., Guidance; Mr. Ralph Mancuso, Business Mgr. Priests 1; Sisters 2; Lay Teachers 29; Students 443.

PITTSTON. *Seton Catholic High School*, 37 William St., 18640. Tel: 717-654-4831; 655-0208; Fax: 717-654-2599. James J. Redington, Prin.; Rev. Frank S. Homets, Dir., Religious Formation. Sisters 3; Lay Teachers 21; Students 275.

WILKES-BARRE. *Bishop Hoban High School*, 159 S. Penna Blvd., 18701-3394. Tel: 717-829-2424.
E-mail: hoban@liv18.K12.pa.us
Mr. Frank Majikes, Prin.; Sr. Mary Ann Cody,

I.H.M., Asst. Prin.; Sr. Leonita Duhoski, R.S.M., Dir. of Devel.; Sr. Catherine Ann Morris, SS.C.M., Dir. of Guidance; Sr. Ellen Maroney, I.H.M., Dean of Students; Rev. Robert M. Timchak, Dir., Religious Formation. Priests 2; Sisters 14; Lay Teachers 30; Students 550.

WILLIAMSPORT. *Bishop Neumann Junior/Senior High School*, 901 Penn St., 17701. Tel: 717-323-9953. Dr. Thomas O'Rourke, Prin.; Sr. Carmelita Smith, S.C.C., Vice Prin.; Sr. Minnette Welding, I.H.M., Dir., Religious Formation; Rev. Andrew Kurovsky, Chap. Priests 1; Sisters 4; Lay Teachers 17; Students 220.

[E] HIGH SCHOOLS, PRIVATE

SCRANTON.

**Scranton Preparatory School*, 1000 Wyoming Ave., 18509. Tel: 717-941-7737. Society of Jesus. Revs. Herbert B. Keller, S.J., Pres.; Brendan G. Lally, S.J., Rector; Richard S. McCouch, S.J., Chap.
Faculty: Revs. Michael A. Hricko, S.J.; Leonard A. Martin, S.J.; William J. McGrath, S.J.; Bro. James C. Lemon, S.J. Priests 5; Brothers 1; Lay Teachers 47; Students 686.

MOSCOW. *St. Gregory's Academy*, R.R. 8, Box 8214, 18444. Tel: 717-842-8112; Fax: 717-842-4513. Priestly Fraternity of St. Peter. Rev. Paul Carr, F.S.S.P., Chap.; Alan Hicks, Headmaster. Lay Teachers 10; Students 60.

[F] INTER-PAROCHIAL ELEMENTARY SCHOOLS

CLARKS GREEN. *Our Lady of Peace Elementary School*, 410 N. Abington Rd., 18411. Tel: 717-587-4152. I.H.M. Sisters 1; Lay Teachers 19; Students 452.

Saint Gregory Early Childhood Center, 330 N. Abington Rd., 18411. Tel: 717-587-4808; Fax: 717-586-4515.
E-mail: jlouis3662@aol
Web site: http://www.NVDS.com.STGREGORY.html
Rev. Msgr. John H. Louis, Acting Prin. Lay Teachers 3; Students 75.

CRESCO. *Monsignor McHugh Elementary School*, 18326. Tel: 717-595-7463; Fax: 717-595-9639. Sr. Rosemarie Mozzachio, I.H.M., Prin. Sisters, Servants of the Immaculate Heart of Mary 5; Lay Teachers 14; Students 413.

Immaculate Heart of Mary Convent, R.R. 1, Box 568, 18326. Tel: 717-595-7548.

DALLAS. *Gate of Heaven Elementary School*, 40 Machell Ave., 18612. Tel: 717-675-6566; Fax: 717-674-0198. Mrs. Mary Tigue, Prin. Lay Teachers 22; Students 513.

EAST STROUDSBURG. *Notre Dame Elementary School*, 78 Ridgeway St., 18301. Tel: 717-421-3651. Sr. Mary Alice Kane, I.H.M., Prin. I.H.M. Sisters 3; Lay Teachers 21; Students 400.

EXETER. *Wyoming Area Catholic Elementary School*, 1690 Wyoming Ave., 18643. Tel: 717-654-7982. Sr. Dorothy Kibler, I.H.M., Prin. I.H.M. Sisters 3; Lay Teachers 10; Students 244.

FORTY FORT. *Regis Elementary School*, 1133 Wyoming Ave., 18704. Tel: 717-288-5558; Fax: 717-288-5560. Mr. Michael Booth, Prin. Lay Teachers 10; Students 250.

HAZLETON. *Holy Spirit Academy*, 225 E. Fourth St., 18201. Tel: 717-459-0054. Mrs. Alice Flynn, Prin. Priests 3; Sisters 2; Lay Teachers 13; Students 309.

HONESDALE. *Saint Vincent Elementary School*, 329 Cliff St., 18431. Tel: 717-253-1074. Mrs. Sue Delling, Prin. Lay Teachers 10; Students 256.

JESSUP. *La Salle Academy*, 309 First Ave., 18434. Tel: 717-489-2010. Sr. Christopher Godlewski, SS.C.M., Prin. Sisters 3; Lay Teachers 26; Students 517.

NANTICOKE. *Pope John Paul II Elementary School*, 518 S. Hanover St., 18634. Tel: 717-735-7935. Mr. James A. Jones, Prin. Lay Teachers 15; Students 305.

PLYMOUTH. *Holy Child Elementary School*, 119 Willow St., 18651. Tel: 717-779-2843. Sr. Carole Griffin, I.H.M., Prin. Sisters 3; Lay Teachers 8; Students 165.

SWOYERSVILLE. *Regis Academy*, 112 Hughes St., 18704. Tel: 717-287-3133. Robert Hines, Prin. Lay Teachers 12; Students 184.

WILKES-BARRE. *Saint Boniface Elementary School*, 221 Blackman St., 18702. Tel: 717-823-0939. Sr. John Marie Hickl, S.C.C., Prin. S.C.C. Sisters 3; Lay Teachers 9; Students 265.

Saint Nicholas-Saint Mary Elementary School, 242 S. Washington St., 18701. Tel: 717-823-8089.
E-mail: snsm@epix.net
Sr. Mary Catherine Slattery, S.C.C., Prin. S.C.C. Sisters 4; Lay Teachers 21; Students 503.

[G] PRESCHOOLS AND CHILD CARE CENTERS

SCRANTON. *Immaculate Care Preschool*, 800 Taylor Ave., 18510. Tel: 717-344-4380. Ann Marie McDonald, Prin.

Marywood Early Childhood Center. Marywood College. 2300 Adams Ave., 18509. Tel: 717-343-7762. Sr. Marilyn Muro, I.H.M., Dir.

MILFORD. *St. Patrick Preschool*, 111 E. High St., P.O. Box W, 18337. Tel: 717-296-4721. Rita Straka, Teacher.

St. Vincent de Paul Preschool, R.R. #3, Dingman Hills, Box 240, 18337. Tel: 717-686-3493. Diane C. Quintiliani, Teacher.

MOSCOW. *St. Catherine Preschool*, P.O. Box 250, 18444. Tel: 717-842-4561. Kathy LoRusso, Dir.

MOUNT POCONO. *St. Mary Playschool*, 27 Fairview Ave., 18344. Tel: 717-839-1718. Halina Lombardy, Dir.

MUNCY. *Resurrection Early Childhood Center*, 526 S. Main St., 17756. Tel: 717-546-5272. Laura Osenbach, Dir.

PITTSTON. *St. Mary's Early Childhood Learning Center*, 535 N. Main Ave., 18640-2244. Tel: 717-654-8188. Sr. Anne Therese Peach, S.C.C., Prin.

[H] RENEWAL CENTERS

CRESCO. *The Immaculate Heart of Mary Spiritual Renewal Center*, R.R. 1, Box 568, 18326. Tel: 717-595-7548; 7549. Sr. Anne Mary Boslett, I.H.M., Dir.

DALTON. *Fatima Renewal Center*, 1000 Seminary Rd., 18414. Tel: 717-563-8500. Diocesan Renewal Center. Jeff Seymour, Retreat Coord.

NANTICOKE. *Holy Family Spiritual Renewal Center*, 151 Newport St., 18634-1300. Martin J. Hudak, Dir.

[I] GENERAL HOSPITALS

SCRANTON. *Mercy Hospital*, 746 Jefferson Ave., 18501. Tel: 717-348-7100
For a complete listing, refer to the Hospitals section.

CARBONDALE. *Marian Community Hospital*, 100 Lincoln Ave., 18407. Tel: 717-281-1000; Fax: 717-281-7177
For a complete listing, refer to the Hospitals section.

Marian Community Hospital Foundation, 100 Lincoln Ave., 18407. Tel: 717-281-1000
For a complete listing, refer to the Hospitals section.

Maxis Medical Services, 100 Lincoln Ave., 18407. Tel: 717-281-1000
For a complete listing, refer to the Hospitals section.

HAZLETON. *Hazleton-Saint Joseph Medical Center*, 687 N. Church St., 18201. Tel: 717-459-4444.
E-mail: pward@ptd.net
Web site: www.ghha.org
For a complete listing, refer to the Hospitals section.

MUNCY. *Muncy Valley Hospital*, 215 E. Water St., 17756. Tel: 717-546-4242.
E-mail: Lcioffi:@shscares.org
For a complete listing, refer to the Hospitals section.

NANTICOKE. *Mercy Special Care Hospital*, 128 W. Washington St., 18634. Tel: 717-735-5000; Fax: 717-740-5220
For a complete listing, refer to the Hospitals section.

WILKES-BARRE. *Mercy Hospital*, 25 Church St., P.O. Box 658, 18765. Tel: 717-826-3100; Fax: 717-831-8989
For a complete listing, refer to the Hospitals section.

Mercy Med-Care, Inc., 25 Church St., Box 658, 18765. Tel: 717-826-3100
For a complete listing, refer to the Hospitals section.

WILLIAMSPORT. *Divine Providence Hospital of the Sisters of Christian Charity*, 1100 Grampian Blvd., 17701. Tel: 717-320-7007.
E-mail: Lcioffi@shscares.org
For a complete listing, refer to the Hospitals section.

**Grampian Health Services, Inc.*, 1201 Grampian Blvd., 17701. Tel: 717-326-8214
For a complete listing, refer to the Hospitals section.

Providence Foundation, 1100 Grampian Blvd., 17701. Tel: 717-321-5467.
E-mail: gharrington@shscares.org
Web site: www.shscares.org
For a complete listing, refer to the Hospitals section.

Providence Health System, Inc., 1100 Grampian Blvd., 17701. Tel: 717-320-7007.
E-mail: Lcioffi@shscares.org
Web site: www.shscares.org
For a complete listing, refer to the Hospitals section.

Sisters of Christian Charity Healthcare Corporation, 1100 Grampian Blvd., 17701. Tel: 717-326-8181.
E-mail: Lcioffi@shscares.org
Web site: www.shscares.org
For a complete listing, refer to the Hospitals section.

**Susquehanna Regional Home Health & Services*, 1201 Grampian Blvd., 17701. Tel: 717-323-9891.
E-mail: Lcioffi@shscares.org
Web site: www.shscares.org
For a complete listing, refer to the Hospitals section.

[J] SPECIAL HOSPITALS

SCRANTON. *St. Joseph's Center*, 2010 Adams Ave., 18509. Tel: 717-342-8379; 961-1549
For a complete listing, refer to the Special Care Facilities section.

NANTICOKE. *Mercy Health Care Center*, Newport St., 18634. Tel: 717-735-7300
For a complete listing, refer to the Special Care Facilities section.

[K] SPECIAL EDUCATION SCHOOLS

CLARKS GREEN. *Lourdesmont*, 537 Venard Rd., 18411. Tel: 717-587-4741. Legal Title: *Good Shepherd Corporation of Clarks Summit, PA.* Sr. Mary Joanne Getzendaner, R.G.S., Supr.; Kathleen Serafin, M.S., Prin.; John A. Antognoli, Ed.D., Exec. Dir. Sisters of the Good Shepherd 5; Staff 106; Total Assisted 503.

FALLS. *St. Michael's Group Home*, Box 405A, 18615. Tel: 717-378-2560. Total Assisted 28; Total Staff 5.

HOBAN HEIGHTS. *St. Michael's School*, Box 370, 18657. Tel: 717-388-6155; Fax: 717-388-6979. Mr. James F. Huff, M.S.W., Dir. Students Assisted 374; Total Staff 169.

PINE GROVE. *St. Michael's Group Home*, 25 Oak Grove Rd., 17963. Tel: 717-345-1160. Total Assisted 39; Total Staff 8.

TUNKHANNOCK. *St. Michael's Group Home*, 17 Chestnut St., 18657. Tel: 717-836-6360. Total Assisted 15.

St. Michael's Group Home, 28 Putnam St., 18657. Tel: 717-836-4911. Total Assisted 15; Total Staff 4.

WEST PITTSTON. *St. Michael's Group Home*, 225/227 Damon St., 18643. Tel: 717-655-9370. Total Assisted 14; Total Staff 4.

WILLIAMSPORT. *St. Michael's Group Home*, 119 E. Fourth St., 17701. Tel: 717-322-0561. Total Assisted 25; Total Staff 6.

[L] HOMES FOR AGED

SCRANTON. *Home for Aged of the Little Sisters of the Poor, Holy Family Residence*, 2500 Adams Ave., 18509. Tel: 717-343-4065; 346-5788; Fax: 717-347-1941
For a complete listing, refer to the Special Care Facilities section.

DALLAS. *Mercy Center Nursing Unit, Inc.*, Lake St., Box 370, 18612. Tel: 717-675-2131; Fax: 717-674-5658
For a complete listing, refer to the Special Care Facilities section.

ELMHURST. *St. Mary's Villa Nursing Home*, 18416. Tel: 717-842-7621; Fax: 717-842-2953
For a complete listing, refer to the Special Care Facilities section.

WILKES-BARRE. *Little Flower Manor of the Diocese of Scranton*, 200 S. Meade St., 18702. Tel: 717-823-6131
For a complete listing, refer to the Special Care Facilities section.

[M] MONASTERIES AND RESIDENCES OF PRIESTS AND BROTHERS

SCRANTON. *Saint Ann's Passionist Monastery*, 1230 St. Ann St., 18504. Tel: 717-347-5691. Congregation of the Passion.
Chaplaincies: St. Gabriel's Convent, Clarks Summit, 18411. Very Rev. Richard Burke, C.P., Rector, Monastery & Shrine; Revs. Berard Tierney, C.P.; Vincent Boney, C.P.; Conan Conaboy, C.P.; Roger Elliott, C.P.; Patrick Geinzer, C.P.; Nicolas Gill, C.P.; Peter A. Grace, C.P.; Richard Nalepa, C.P.; Cassian J. Yuhaus, C.P., Exec. Dir., Ministry for Religious Research & Consultancy. Tel: 717-586-9099; Bro. Daniel Turner, C.P. Priests 10; Brothers 1.

St. Gregory's Priory (Priestly Fraternity of St. Peter), 819 N. Webster Ave., 18510. Tel: 717-342-1271; Fax: 717-347-7073. Rev. Arnaud J. Devillers, F.S.S.P., District Supr.

BRODHEADSVILLE. *Salesian Monastery*, HC 1, Frantz Rd., Box 455, 18322. Tel: 717-992-0230 (Monastery); 992-3448 (Abbot's Office).
E-mail: monk@epix.net
Bro. Bernard Seif, S.M.C., Abbot.

ELMHURST. *Priestly Fraternity of St. Peter (F.S.S.P.), North American District Headquarters*, Griffen Rd., P.O. Box 196, 18416. Tel: 717-842-4000; Fax: 717-842-4001. Revs. Arnaud J. Devillers, F.S.S.P., District Supr.; Paul S. Carr, F.S.S.P., Faculty & Chap., St. Gregory's Academy; Daniel W. Oppenheimer, F.S.S.P., (On Duty Outside the Diocese).

Our Lady of Guadalupe Seminary, Griffen Rd., P.O. Box 188, 18416. Tel: 717-842-6711. Revs. Karl Pikus, F.S.S.P., Rector; Charles Van Vliet, F.S.S.P., Vice-Rector; Dennis Duvelius, F.S.S.P., Registrar, Dir. of Admissions; James B. Buckley, F.S.S.P., Dir., Spirituality; Michel R. Berger, F.S.S.P., Faculty; James McLucas, F.S.S.P., Faculty; John Berg, F.S.S.P., (On Duty Outside the Diocese); Nathan R. Vail, F.S.S.P., (On Duty Outside the Diocese); Deacons Alfredo Reyes-Barrios, F.S.S.P.; Philip Creurer, F.S.S.P. Priests 27; Seminarians 46; Novices 17.
Priests Working Elsewhere: Rev. Louis J. Campbell, F.S.S.P., St. Michael's Church, 1703 Jackson St., Scranton, 18504. Tel: 717-961-1205. Rev. Carlos S. Casavantes, F.S.S.P. (CC), St. Michael the Archangel Latin Mass Community, 2233 Waldron Rd., Corpus Christi, TX, 78418. Tel: 512-854-2997; 854-9481 (Chap. direct); Fax: 512-939-7774. Rev. Pablo Alvarez, F.S.S.P. (LR), Community of St. John the Baptist, 2414 N. Tyler, Apt.312, Little

Rock, AR, 72207. Tel: 501-280-9155. Rev. Gary Dilley, F.S.S.P., Queen of the Holy Rosary Parish, 291 Scoville Dr., Vienna, OH, 44473. Tel: 330-856-4204. Revs. Peter J. Gee, F.S.S.P. (KCK); Edouard de Mentque, F.S.S.P., 208 Sunset Ln., P.O. Box 98, Maple Hill, KS, 66507. Tel: 785-256-4727. Revs. James W. Jackson, F.S.S.P. (TLS); George Gabet, 1720 E. Apache, Tulsa, OK, 74148. Tel: 918-425-0486. Rev. Chad Ripperger, F.S.S.P. (PH), 1404 Castelar St., Omaha, NE, 68108. Tel: 402-341-1305. Rev. Michael T. Irwin, F.S.S.P., 522 Columbus St., Rapid City, SD, 57701. Tel: 605-341-1578. Rev. Karl Claver (DAL), 6228 Winton St., Dallas, TX, 75214. Tel: 214-823-7934. Rev. Joseph P. Terra, F.S.S.P. (PAT), Our Lady of Fatima Chapel, 32 W. Franklin Ave., Pequannock, NJ, 07440. Tel: 201-694-6727. Rev. Jose' Salgado, F.S.S.P., Our Lady of Mt. Carmel Community, 4697 Field St., Wheat Ridge, CO, 80033-3050. Tel: 303-425-3273. Rev. Mark Fischer, F.S.S.P., 3400 Old Alabama Rd., Alpharetta, GA, 30022. Tel: 770-442-2511. Rev. Paul Petko, F.S.S.P., P.O. Box 47334, Indianapolis, IN, 46227. Tel: 317-791-9923.

LITTLE MEADOWS. *St. Joseph's House*, R.R. 1, Box 1418, 18830. Tel: 717-395-3639. Rev. Vincent J. Young, O.M.V., Dir.

MOUNT POCONO. *Diocesan Oratory of Saint Philip Neri - Newman House*, 21 Fairview Ave., 18344. Tel: 717-839-2185. Revs. Peter M.J. Stravinskas, Ph.D., S.T.D., Provost; Nicholas L. Gregoris. Priests 2; Seminarians 2.

PITTSTON. *Eastern Province of the Oblates of St. Joseph*, Rte. 315, R.D. 4, 18640. Tel: 717-654-7542; Fax: 717-654-8621. Very Rev. Joseph D. Sibilano, O.S.J., Prov.; Revs. Gregory Finn, O.S.J., 1st Councilor; Paul A. McDonnell, O.S.J., 2nd Councilor; Joseph L. Iannuzzi, O.S.J. Priests 12.

WILKES-BARRE. *Moreau House*. (House of Formation for the Congregation of Holy Cross - C.S.C.), 415 N. Main St., 18702. Tel: 717-824-8820. Revs. Charles Kociolek, C.S.C.; Thomas P. Looney, C.S.C.

St. Joseph's Friary, 783 E. Northampton St., 18702. Tel: 717-822-8023. Revs. Raymond J. Lynch, O.F.M., Guardian; Alvin Black, O.F.M.; Benjamin J. Foerch, O.F.M. Priests 3.

[N] DIOCESAN RESIDENCE FOR RETIRED PRIESTS

DUNMORE. *Villa St. Joseph*, 1600 Green Ridge St., 18509. Tel: 717-343-4791. Most Rev. John M. Dougherty, D.D., V.G. Tel: 717-344-3272. In res. Rev. Msgr. Gerald J. Burns. Tel: 717-343-7161; Rev. Msgr. Thomas J. Cawley. Tel: 717-343-2254; Rev. Msgr. James T. Clarke. Tel: 717-969-1235; Rev. Msgr. William L. Donovan. Tel: 717-963-9383; Rev. Msgr. Chester A. Gajewski. Tel: 717-347-1851; Rev. Msgr. John J. O'Brien. Tel: 717-961-1865; Rev. Msgr. William J. Pakutka. Tel: 717-341-9168; Rev. Msgr. Edmund S. Penkala. Tel: 717-344-6288; Rev. Msgr. Edward T. Sullivan. Tel: 717-341-9203; Revs. Joseph W. Breslin. Tel: 717-341-3315; Joseph T. Conboy. Tel: 717-941-9405; Alphonsus M. Domnick, T.O.R. Tel: 717-341-9176; Robert M. Everling. Tel: 717-343-4925; John L. Fabian. Tel: 717-348-0728; Thomas A. Flynn. Tel: 717-348-0589; Edward F. Gallagher. Tel: 717-348-6873; Alex J. Hazzouri. Tel: 717-343-2859; Harry J. Lewis. Tel: 717-343-5499; Clement A. Markowski. Tel: 717-343-0555; Joseph F. Meighan. Tel: 717-941-0509; Frank P. Mikus. Tel: 717-342-2728; Charles F. Mulrooney. Tel: 717-969-1305; John A. O'Haire. Tel: 717-342-6865; William J. Pace. Tel: 717-961-5856; Valentine R. Plevyak. Tel: 717-969-9109; William F. Purcell. Tel: 717-969-0695; Carl G. Ulrich. Tel: 717-341-5898.

[O] CONVENTS AND RESIDENCES FOR SISTERS

SCRANTON. *Immaculate Heart of Mary Center, Marywood*, 2300 Adams Ave., 18509. Tel: 717-342-6850. Sisters, Servants of the Immaculate Heart of Mary. Sr. Anne Munley, I.H.M., Congregation Admin.; Sr. Therese O'Rourke, I.H.M., Asst. to Congregation Admin. & Dir., Apostolic Planning. Tel: 717-346-5401; Sr. Catherine Luxner, I.H.M., Dir., Spiritual Renewal. Tel: 717-346-5402; Sr. Mary Persico, I.H.M., Dir., Temporal Affairs. Tel: 717-346-5405; Sr. Mary Martha Gardiner, I.H.M., Councilor at Large. Tel: 202-529-5654; Sr. Theresa Jordan, I.H.M., Business Mgr. Tel: 717-346-5406; Sr. Annmarie Sanders, I.H.M., Dir., Communications. Tel: 717-346-5404 Ext. 508; Sr. Beatrice Caulson, I.H.M., Dir., Novices/Candidates. Tel: 717-346-5414; Sr. Kathryn Kurdziel, I.H.M., Dir., Vocations. Tel: 717-346-5413; Sr. Amy Zychal, I.H.M., Dir., Devel. Tel: 717-346-5431 Ext. 599; Rev. Robert J. Barone, S.T.D., Chap. Professed Sisters 675.

Marian Convent, Marywood, 18509. Tel: 717-346-1752.
E-mail: marian@ac.marywood.edu
Sr. St. Mel Wright, I.H.M., Coord. Tel: 717-346-1752; Sr. Rosemary Goulet, I.H.M., Admin. Tel: 717-346-1752. Sisters, Servants of the Immaculate Heart of Mary 150.

Parish Visitors of Mary Immaculate, 410 S. Main Ave., 18504. Tel: 717-343-7841. Sr. Dolores Marie, P.V.M.I., Supr. Sisters 4.

CLARKS SUMMIT. *St. Gabriel's Monastery*, 631 Griffin Pond Rd., 18411. Tel: 717-586-2791.
E-mail: cpnuns@intiques.com
Web site: http://www.intiques.con/cpnuns/
Religious of the Passion of Jesus Christ; Passionist Nuns (Contemplative). Sr. Helen V. Gallagher, C.P., Supr.; Sr. Colette Greder, C.P., Vicar; Sr. Gail Worcelo, C.P., Councilor. Professed Sisters 15.

DALLAS. *Mercy Center*, Lake St., 18612. Tel: 717-675-2131. Sr. Sara Sweeney, R.S.M., Admin.; Sr. Ruth Ann Fox, R.S.M., Coord. Sisters 127.

Mercy Center Convent, 18612. Tel: 717-675-2131. Sr. Sara Sweeney, R.S.M., Admin.; Sr. Ruth Ann Fox, R.S.M., Coord.; Louise Christofor, R.N., Dir. of Nursing; Rev. Francis G. Kulig, Chap. Sisters 115.

Sisters of Mercy of the Americas Regional Community of Dallas, 18612. Tel: 717-675-1966; Fax: 717-675-9051.
E-mail: som@epix.net
Sr. Maureen McCann, R.S.M., Pres.; Sr. Catherine McGroaty, R.S.M., Assoc. Tel: 717-675-2048. Sisters 5.

MOUNTAINTOP. *Saint Jude Convent*, 6 Colony Dr., 18707.

[P] RETREAT HOUSES

CLARKS SUMMIT. *St. Gabriel's Retreat Center*, 631 Griffin Pond Rd., 18411. Tel: 717-586-4957.
E-mail: cpnuns@intiques.com
Web site: http://www.intiques.com/cpnuns/
Religious of the Passion of Jesus Christ; Passionist Nuns (Contemplative).

MOUNT POCONO. *Villa Our Lady Retreat House*, HCR 1, Box 41, 18344-9714. Tel: 717-839-7217; Fax: 717-839-7553. Sr. M. Bonaventa, O.S.F., Supr. Bernadine Sisters 9.

[Q] CAMPS AND COMMUNITY CENTERS

SCRANTON. *Catholic Youth Center*, 500 Jefferson Ave., 18510. Tel: 717-347-3311. Mr. John J. O'Connor, Exec. Dir.; Rev. Cyril D. Edwards, Spiritual Moderator.

TUNKHANNOCK. *Camp St. Andrew*, P.O. Box 679, 18657. Tel: 717-836-2975. Off-Season Mailing Address: 316 William St., 18508. Tel: 717-341-1290. Rev. Msgr. Joseph P. Kelly, Exec. Dir. Regular Camp, Basketball Clinics 1,000 children.

WILKES-BARRE. *Catholic Youth Center*, 36 S. Washington St., 18702. Tel: 717-823-6121. Rev. John S. Terry, Dir.; Mr. Anthony D. English, Jr., Exec. Dir.

[R] MISCELLANEOUS LISTINGS

SCRANTON.

**Aid to the Church in Russia*, 300 Wyoming Ave., 18503-1279. Tel: 717-842-5422. Deacon Frank A. Earley, Dir., Scranton Office.

The Catherine McAuley Center, 747 Madison Ave., 18510. Tel: 717-342-1342; Fax: 717-341-8108. Sr. Therese Marie Marques, R.S.M., Exec. Dir.

The Catherine McAuley Center - Bridge Program, 747 Madison Ave., 18510. Tel: 717-342-1342; Fax: 717-341-8108. Sr. Therese Marie Marques, R.S.M., Exec. Dir.

The Catherine McAuley Center - Maple Street House, 1030 Maple St., 18505. Tel: 717-342-1342. Sr. Therese Marie Marques, R.S.M., Exec. Dir.

The Catherine McAuley Center - Swetland Street House, 747 Madison Ave., 18510. Tel: 717-342-1342. Sr. Therese Marie Marques, R.S.M., Exec. Dir.

The Catherine McAuley House Annex, 115 Ferdinand St., 18508. Tel: 717-342-1342; Fax: 717-341-8108. Sr. Therese Marie Marques, R.S.M., Exec. Dir.

Cross Apartments, 507 Broadway, 18505. Tel: 717-342-1342. Sr. Therese Marie Marques, R.S.M., Exec. Dir.; Sr. Marise Fabie, R.S.M., Dir., Housing.

Frances Warde House, 1646 Capouse Ave., 18509. Tel: 717-342-6962. Sr. Therese Marie Marques, R.S.M., Exec. Dir.; Sr. Marise Fabie, R.S.M., Dir., Housing.

The Guild Studios. Religious Store, 400 Wyoming Ave., 18503. Tel: 800-367-6610. Mrs. Michele D. Keating, Gen. Mgr.

I.H.M. Congregation Charitable Trust, 2300 Adams Ave., 18509. Tel: 717-342-6850. Congregation of the Sisters, Servants of the Immaculate Heart of Mary.

ISECP, Inc., 1105 Cornell St., 18504-3008. Tel: 717-344-7295; Fax: 717-941-6340.
E-mail: Judyr@isecp.org
Web site: www.isecp.org
Rev. George J. Schemel, S.J., Dir.

Saint Ann's Media, Inc., 1230 St. Ann St., 18504. Tel: 717-941-0100; Fax: 717-941-0185. Rev. Peter A. Grace, C.P., Dir. Sponsored by the Passionist Fathers.

St. Anthony's Haven, 409 Olive St., 18509. Tel: 717-969-0753.

St. Francis of Assisi Kitchen, 500 Penn Ave., 18509. Tel: 717-342-5556. Rev. Msgr. Constantine V. Siconolfi, M.S., Dir.

CLARKS SUMMIT. *Ministry for Religious Research and Consultancy*, 631 Griffin Pond Rd., 18411. Tel: 717-586-9099; Fax: 717-586-9203. Rev. Cassian J. Yuhaus, C.P., Exec. Dir.

DALLAS. *Stoneview Studio*, Mercy Center, 18612. Tel: 675-1361. Producers of Art: Paintings, Sculpture and Other Media. Sr. Benedicta San Antonio, R.S.M., Dir.

Studio I, Mercy Center, Box 370, 18612. Tel: 717-675-2131; 675-1865. Designing and handcrafting fine jewelry and sculpture. Workshops in jewelry making using the lost wax casting technique: A. Couples - wedding bands/engagement rings. B. All ages interested in learning the art of jewelry making. Sr. Regina Kiel, R.S.M., Designer & Artist.

HARLEIGH. *National Shrine of the Sacred Heart*, 1 Church Pl., 18225. Tel: 717-455-1162; Fax: 717-455-0306. National Office: Men of the Sacred Heart, P.O. Box 500, 18225. Tel: 717-455-1162.

NANTICOKE. *Lay Missionaries of the Passion (Passionist Secular Institute)*, P.O. Box 269, 18634. Tel: 717-735-1889. Frances Davis. Professed Members 7; In Formation 10.

People of God Community of Northeastern PA, 151 Newport St., 18634. Tel: 717-735-2599. Martin J. Hudak, Pres.

PITTSTON. *The Gabriel House*, 13 William St., 18640. Tel: 717-654-7157. Anne Marie McCawley, Project Coord.
Residence for low income women.

PLYMOUTH. *The Catherine McAuley House*, 121 Church St., 18651. Tel: 717-779-2801. Sr. Therese Marie Marques, R.S.M., Exec. Dir.; Sr. Marie Larkin, P.B.V.M., Case Mgr.

WILKES-BARRE. *Project REMAIN*, Valley View Terrace, 215 High St., Apt. 100, 18702. Tel: 717-829-5373. Sr. Miriam Francis Stadulis, R.S.M., Dir.; Sr. Gertrude Marie Bogdan, R.S.M., Co-Dir.

St. Vincent De Paul Kitchen, 39 E. Jackson St., 18701. Tel: 717-829-7796; Fax: 717-829-7721. Ned Delaney, M.A., Exec. Dir.

RELIGIOUS INSTITUTES OF MEN REPRESENTED IN THE DIOCESE

For further details refer to the corresponding bracketed number in the Religious Institutes of Men or Women section.

[0470]—*The Capuchin Friars.*—O.F.M.Cap.
[1000]—*Congregation of the Passion.* (Union City, NJ).—C.P.
[0520]—*Franciscan Friars.* (Prov. of the Most Holy Name of Jesus).—O.F.M.
[0690]—*Jesuit Fathers and Brothers.* (Maryland Prov.).—S.J.
[0920]—*Oblates of St. Francis de Sales.*—O.S.F.S.
[0930]—*Oblates of St. Joseph.* (Asti, Italy).—O.S.J.
[1065]—*Priestly Fraternity of St. Peter.*—F.S.S.P.
[0610]—*Priests of the Congregation of Holy Cross.* (Wilkes-Barre, PA).—C.S.C.
[1290]—*Society of the Priests of St. Sulpice.*—S.S.
[0560]—*Third Order Regular of St. Francis.*—T.O.R.

RELIGIOUS INSTITUTES OF WOMEN REPRESENTED IN THE DIOCESE

[1810]—*Bernardine Sisters of the Third Order of St. Francis.*—O.S.F.
[0330]—*Carmelite Sisters of the Aged and Infirm.*—O.Carm.
[2980]—*Congregation of Notre Dame.*—C.N.D.
[3830-01]—*Congregation of the Sisters of St. Joseph.* (Boston).—C.S.J.
[3830-05]—*Congregation of the Sisters of St. Joseph.* (Brentwood).—C.S.J.
[0890]—*Daughters of Our Lady of Mercy.*—D.M.
[0960]—*Daughters of Wisdom.*—D.W.
[]—*Dominican Sisters of St. Catherine de Ricci.*—O.P.
[1180]—*Franciscan Sisters of Allegany, N.Y.*—O.S.F.
[1310]—*Franciscan Sisters of Little Falls, Minnesota.*—O.S.F.
[2575]—*Institute of the Sisters of Mercy of the Americas.*—R.S.M.
[2340]—*Little Sisters of the Poor.*—P.S.D.P.
[3040]—*Oblate Sisters of Providence.*—O.S.P.
[3160]—*Parish Visitors of Mary Immaculate.*—P.V.M.I.
[3240]—*Poor Sisters of Jesus Crucified and the Sorrowful Mother.*—C.J.C.
[3170]—*Religious of the Passion of Jesus Christ.*—C.P.
[3430]—*Religious Teachers Filippini.*—M.P.F.
[1700]—*School Sisters of the Third Order of St. Francis.* (Bethlehem, PA).—O.S.F.
[0570]—*Sisters of Charity of Seton Hill, Greensburg, PA.*—S.C.
[0660]—*Sisters of Christian Charity.*—S.C.C.

[2990]—*Sisters of Notre Dame.* (Ohio).—S.N.D.
[3780]—*Sisters of Saints Cyril and Methodius.*—SS.C.M.
[3840]—*Sisters of St. Joseph of Carondelet.*—C.S.J.
[3893]—*Sisters of St. Joseph of Chestnut Hill.*—S.S.J.
[1830]—*Sisters of the Good Shepherd.*—R.G.S.
[1970]—*Sisters of the Holy Family of Nazareth.*—C.S.F.N.
[2160]—*Sisters, Servants of the Immaculate Heart of Mary.*—I.H.M.

DIOCESAN CEMETERIES

SCRANTON. *Cathedral,* 1708 Oram St., 18504. Tel: 717-347-9251; Fax: 717-347-4354.
Diocesan Cemeteries Office, 1708 Oram St., 18504. Tel: 717-346-8923; Fax: 717-347-4354. Walter Bennett, Dir.

CARVERTON. *Mount Olivet,* P.O. Box 257, 18644. Tel: 717-696-3636.

DRUMS. *Calvary,* P.O. Box 485, 18222. Tel: 717-788-2150.

MOSCOW. *St. Catherine's,* Main St., P.O. Box 114, 18444. Tel: 717-842-8411; Fax: 717-842-8406.

OLD FORGE. *Holy Cross,* 18518. Tel: 717-347-9251; Fax: 717-347-4354.

WILLIAMSPORT. *Resurrection,* P.O. Box 12, 17754. Tel: 717-368-2727.

NECROLOGY

† Augustyn, Albert J., Inkerman, PA, St. Mark. —Died July 29, 1997.
† Crotti, Rev. Msgr. William A., Dunmore, PA, St. Anthony of Padua. —Died Dec. 13, 1996.
† Cusick, William F., Dallas, PA, Gate of Heaven. —Died May 1, 1997.
† Lowry, Rev. Msgr. James M., Scranton, PA, St. Vincent de Paul. —Died Aug. 13, 1997.
† Merkel, Francis J., Scranton, PA, St. John the Baptist. —Died July 30, 1997.
† Shilala, Robert N., Dorrance, PA, Our Lady Help of Christians. —Died Aug. 26, 1997.
† Smith, Arnold R., Luzerne, PA, Sacred Heart of Jesus. —Died Feb. 1, 1997.
† Sulicki, Casimir F., Forest City, PA, St. Joseph (Slovenian). —Died Dec. 10, 1996.

Archdiocese of Seattle

Archidioecesis Seattlensis

Most Reverend

ALEXANDER J. BRUNETT, PH.D.

Archbishop of Seattle; ordained July 13, 1958; appointed Bishop of Helena April 19, 1994; consecrated and installed July 6, 1994; appointed Archbishop of Seattle October 28, 1997; installed December 18, 1997. *Res., Connolly House, 1104 Spring St., Seattle, WA, 98104.* Tel.: 206-623-2625; Fax: 206-682-9661.

Most Reverend

RAYMOND G. HUNTHAUSEN, D.D.

Retired Archbishop of Seattle; ordained June 1, 1946; appointed Bishop of Helena, Montana July 8, 1962; consecrated August 30, 1962; appointed Archbishop of Seattle February 25, 1975; installed May 22, 1975; retired August 21, 1991. *Office: 910 Marion St., Seattle, WA, 98104.* Tel.: 206-382-4884; Fax: 206-382-3495.

Legal Title: *"Corporation of the Catholic Archbishop of Seattle"*

ESTABLISHED MAY 31, 1850. NAME CHANGED TO SEATTLE, SEPTEMBER 11, 1907.

CREATED ARCHDIOCESE, JUNE 23, 1951.

Square Miles 24,834.

Comprises the Counties of Clallam, Clark, Cowlitz, Grays Harbor, Island, Jefferson, King, Kitsap, Lewis, Mason, Pacific, Pierce, San Juan, Skagit, Skamania, Snohomish, Thurston, Wahkiakum and Whatcom in the State of Washington.

For legal titles of parishes and archdiocesan institutions, consult The Chancery.

Chancery Office: 910 Marion St., Seattle, WA, 98104. Tel.: 206-382-4560; Fax: 206-382-4840.

Web site address: http://www.seattlearch.org

STATISTICAL OVERVIEW

Personnel	
Archbishop	1
Retired Archbishops	1
Abbots	1
Retired Abbots	2
Priests: Diocesan Active in Diocese	122
Priests: Active Outside Diocese	6
Priests: Retired, Sick or Absent	58
Number of Diocesan Priests	186
Religious Priests in Diocese	141
Extern Priests in Diocese	16
Ordinations:	
Diocesan Priests	3
Transitional Deacons	3
Permanent Deacons in Diocese	86
Total Brothers	33
Total Sisters	652
Parishes	
Parishes	138
With Resident Pastor:	
Resident Diocesan Priests	82
Resident Religious Priests	16
Without Resident Pastor:	
Administered by Priests	31
Administered by Permanent Deacons	1
Administered by Women Religious	5
Administered by Lay People	3
Missions	30
Pastoral Centers	7
Professional Ministry Personnel:	
Brothers	33
Sisters	40
Lay Ministers	425
Welfare	
Catholic Hospitals	9
Total Assisted	985,981
Homes for the Aged	11
Total Assisted	809
Residential Care of Children	1
Total Assisted	48
Day Care and Extended Day Care Centers	5
Total Assisted	1,854
Specialized Homes	8
Total Assisted	163
Special Centers for Social Services	35
Total Assisted	92,200
Residential Care of Disabled	2
Total Assisted	18
Other Institutions	25
Total Assisted	182,148
Educational	
Diocesan Students in Other Seminaries	27
Students Religious	11
Total Seminarians	38
Colleges and Universities	2
Total Students	7,510
High Schools, Diocesan and Parish	3
Total Students	2,231
High Schools, Private	6
Total Students	3,042
Elementary Schools, Diocesan and Parish	53
Total Students	15,689
Elementary Schools, Private	2
Total Students	670
Catechesis/Religious Education:	
High School Students	5,875
Elementary Students	28,050
Total Students Under Catholic Instruction	63,105
Teachers in the Diocese:	
Priests	27
Brothers	15
Sisters	25
Lay Teachers	1,458
Vital Statistics	
Receptions into the Church:	
Infant Baptism Totals	6,653
Adult Baptism Totals	1,262
Received into Full Communion	769
First Communions	5,807
Confirmations	2,255
Marriages:	
Catholic	1,036
Interfaith	1,038
Total Marriages	2,074
Deaths	2,939
Total Catholic Population	374,800
Total Population	4,277,700

Former Bishops—Rt. Rev. A. M. A. BLANCHET, cons. Bishop of Walla Walla, Sept. 27, 1846; transferred to Nesqually, May 31, 1850; resigned 1879; made Bishop of Ibora; died Feb. 25, 1887.—Rt. Rev. AEGIDIUS JUNGER, D.D., cons. Oct. 28, 1879; died Dec. 26, 1895.—Most Rev. EDWARD JOHN O'DEA, D.D., cons. Bishop of Nesqually, Sept. 8, 1896; See transferred to Seattle, Sept. 11, 1907; died Dec. 25, 1932.—Most Rev. GERALD SHAUGHNESSY, S.M., S.T.D., Bishop of Seattle; appt. July 1, 1933; cons. Sept. 19, 1933; died May 18, 1950.—Most Rev. THOMAS A. CONNOLLY, D.D., cons. Aug. 24, 1939; succeeded, May 18, 1950; retired Feb. 25, 1975; died April 18, 1991.—Most Rev. RAYMOND G. HUNTHAUSEN, D.D., ord. June 1, 1946; appt. Bishop of Helena, Montana, July 8, 1962; cons. Aug. 30, 1962; appt. Archbishop of Seattle, Feb. 25, 1975; installed May 22, 1975; retired Aug. 21, 1991.—Most Rev. THOMAS J. MURPHY, D.D., S.T.D., ord. April 12, 1958; appt. Bishop of Great Falls, July 5, 1978; appt. Coadjutor Archbishop of Seattle, May 26, 1987; succeeded to See Aug. 21, 1991; died June 26, 1997.

Office of the Archbishop

Chancery Office—910 Marion St., Seattle, 98104. Tel: 206-382-4560; Fax: 206-382-3495.

Vicar General—Very Rev. GEORGE L. THOMAS, Ph.D., V.G., *910 Marion St., Seattle, 98104.* Tel: 204-382-4888.

Chancellor—Very Rev. GEORGE L. THOMAS, Ph.D., V.G., *910 Marion St., Seattle, 98104.* Tel: 206-382-4888.

Episcopal Vicar for Parishes and Faith Communities—Very Rev. JAMES D. PICTON, V.G., J.D., *910 Marion St., Seattle, 98104.* Tel: 206-382-4288; Fax: 206-382-2069.

Canonical Consultant—Rev. ANTHONY E. BAWYN, J.C.L.; Sr. BEVERLY DUNN, S.P., J.C.D., *910 Marion St., Seattle, 98104.* Tel: 206-382-4565; Fax: 206-654-4654.

Notaries—Ms. CHRISTINE TAYLOR. Tel: 206-382-4357. Rev. ANTHONY E. BAWYN, J.C.L. Tel: 206-382-4565. Sr. JOYCE COX, B.V.M. Tel: 206-382-4829.

Coordinator for Religious—Sr. JOYCE COX, B.V.M., *910 Marion St., Seattle, 98104.* Tel: 206-382-4829; Fax: 206-654-4654.

Administrative Assistant to the Archbishops—Mrs. MARILYN MADDEFORD, *910 Marion St., Seattle, 98104.* Tel: 206-382-4886; Fax: 206-382-3495.

College of Consultors—Very Rev. GEORGE L. THOMAS, Ph.D., V.G.; Very Rev. JAMES D. PICTON, V.G.,

J.D., and Very Reverend Deans.

Deans—Very Rev. GARY MORELLI, Northern: Very Rev. OLIVER DUGGAN, Snohomish: Very Rev. JOSEPH P. MITCHELL, Peninsula: Very Rev. JOHN MCMULLAN, North Seattle: Very Rev. HORACIO YANEZ, Eastside: Very Rev. LESTER MCCLOSKEY, South Seattle: Very Rev. PETER DUGGAN, South King: Very Rev. MICHAEL MCDERMOTT, Pierce: Very Rev. ROGER SMITH, South Sound: Very Rev. HANS OLSON, Southern:

Assistant to the Archbishop for Administration and Finance—Mr. PATRICK SURSELY, Dir., *910 Marion St., Seattle, 98104.* Tel: 206-382-4588; Fax: 206-382-4279.

Assistant to the Archbishop for Chancery Management & Pastoral Planning—Mr. DENNIS J. O'LEARY, *910 Marion St., Seattle, 98104.* Tel: 206-382-4834.

Metropolitan Tribunal

Judicial Vicar—Very Rev. JOSEPH H. DOOGAN, J.C.L., *910 Marion St., Seattle, 98104.* Tel: 206-382-4830; Fax: 206-382-2071.

Adjunct Judicial Vicar—Rev. JAMES A. WILLIAMS, J.C.L.

Judges—Rev. ANTHONY BAWYN, J.C.D. Cand.; JAMES L. BROOKS, M.Ed.; CHARLENE CRAM, J.C.L.; Rev. Msgr. JOHN P. DOOGAN, M.Ed.; Very Rev. JOSEPH H. DOOGAN, J.C.L.; Sr. BEVERLY DUN, S.P., J.C.D.; Revs. JAMES EBLEN, S.T.L., Ph.D.; BERNARD A. KONDA, J.C.D.; Deacon JOHN LARUSSA; Rev. PHILIP LUCID, S.J., J.D.; Deacon LAWRENCE J. SULLIVAN; Revs. WILLIAM VARVARO, J.C.D.; JAMES A. WILLIAMS, J.C.L.

Defenders of the Bond—CHARLOTTE S. EDMAN; DONALD R. ESPEN, J.C.D.; KAREN GIFFIN; Sr. ANNE HERKENRATH, S.N.J.M.; Sr. GAIL MILHOLLAND, S.N.J.M.; Very Rev. JAMES D. PICTON, J.D.; Hon. JOHN F. WILSON, J.D.

Notaries—VALERIE BLESENER; IRENE DELVILLAR; KAREN LEZCANO.

Archdiocesan Offices and Directors

African / American Ministry—SHARON PITRE-WILLIAMS, Dir., *910 Marion St., Seattle, 98104.* Tel: 206-382-2061; Fax: 206-382-2069.

AIDS Ministry—Rev. DAVID JAEGER, Chap., *910 Marion St., Seattle, 98104.* Tel: 206-382-4942; Fax: 206-382-3493.

Adult and Religious Education—Ms. CARLA CALDWELL, *910 Marion St., Seattle, 98104.* Tel: 206-382-4268; Fax: 206-382-4840.

Archdiocesan Council of Catholic Women—Sr. JOYCE COX, B.V.M., Liaison, *910 Marion St., Seattle, 98104.* Tel: 206-382-4829; Fax: 206-654-4654.

Archdiocesan Liturgical Commission—Mr. DENNIS LUCEY, Chm., *910 Marion St., Seattle, 98104.* Tel: 206-382-4878.

Archdiocesan Pastoral Council—Ms. CARLA CALDWELL, Exec. Sec., *910 Marion St., Seattle, 98104.* Tel: 206-382-4268; Fax: 206-382-4840.

Archives—Ms. CHRISTINE TAYLOR, *910 Marion St., Seattle, 98104.* Tel: 206-382-4857; Fax: 206-382-4840.

Asian / Pacific Island Ministry—VERONICA LEASIOLAGI BARBER, Dir., *910 Marion St., Seattle, 98104.* Tel: 206-382-4828; Fax: 206-382-2069.

Campaign for Human Development—Mr. J. L. DROUHARD, Dir., *910 Marion St., Seattle, 98104.* Tel: 206-382-4869; Fax: 206-382-3487.

Campus Ministry—Rev. THOMAS DEMAN, O.P., *Newman Center, U of W, 4502 20th Ave., N.E., Seattle, 98105.* Tel: 206-527-5072.

Catholic Community Services of Western Washington—Mr. MICHAEL REICHERT, Dir., *100 23rd Ave. S., Seattle, 98144.* Tel: 206-328-5696; Fax: 206-328-5699.

Catholic Relief Services—J.L. DROUHARD, Dir., *910 Marion St., Seattle, 98104.* Tel: 206-382-4583.

Catholic Schools—Mr. HARRY PURPUR, Supt., *910 Marion St., Seattle, 98104.* Tel: 206-382-4855.

Catholic Youth Organization—Dr. STEPHEN MCAULIFFE, Dir., *910 Marion St., Seattle, 98104.* Tel: 206-382-4562; Fax: 206-382-2071.

Cemeteries—Mr. RICHARD PETERSON, Dir., *910 Marion St., Seattle, 98104.* Tel: 206-382-9281.

Censores Librorum—Revs. PETER CHIRICO, S.S., S.T.D.; WILLIAM TREACY; MICHAEL RASCHKO, Ph.D.

Chinese, Ministry to—Rev. Msgr. JOHN CHI, Chap., *1531 Bradner Pl., S., Seattle, 98144.* Tel: 206-324-8521.

Planned Giving Office—Mr. PAUL LEBLANC, Dir., *910 Marion St., Seattle, 98104.* Tel: 206-382-4836.

Due Process, Office for—Ms. JESSIE DYE, Admin., *910 Marion St., Seattle, 98104.* Tel: 206-382-4592; Fax: 206-382-3495.

Ecumenical and Interreligious Affairs—Sr. JOYCE COX, B.V.M., *910 Marion St., Seattle, 98104.* Tel: 206-382-4829; Fax: 206-654-4654.

Events Planning—Mr. DAVID JONES, *910 Marion St., Seattle, 98104.* Tel: 206-382-4882; Fax: 206-382-4840.

Hispanic Ministry—MARIA ESTHER BAZAN, Dir., *910 Marion St., Seattle, 98104.* Tel: 206-382-4825; Fax: 206-382-2069.

Formation and Training—Dr. MARY CROSS, *910 Marion St., Seattle, 98104.* Tel: 206-382-4835. JOHN REID.

Holy Childhood, Pontifical Association of the—J.L. DROUHARD, Dir., *910 Marion St., Seattle, 98104.* Tel: 206-382-4583.

Human Resources—COLLEEN BRANAGAN, *910 Marion St., Seattle, 98104.* Tel: 206-382-3920; Fax: 206-382-4267.

Inclusion Ministry—KATHY SMALLEY, Dir., *910 Marion St., Seattle, 98104.* Tel: 206-382-2014.

Justice and Peace Office—Mr. J. L. DROUHARD, Dir., *910 Marion St., Seattle, 98104.* Tel: 206-382-4869; Fax: 206-382-3487.

Koreans, Ministry to—Rev. AUGUSTINE YOO, *7912 Golden Given Rd. E., Tacoma, 98404.* Tel: 206-536-8660. MICHAEL AHN, *11700 1st Ave., N.E., Seattle, 98125.* Tel: 206-362-2492; 362-2278.

Marriage Encounter—Rev. JOHN D. MCCLUSKEY, S.J., Spiritual Dir., *9460 N.E. 14th, Bellevue, 98004.* Tel: 206-454-9536.

Ministry to Priests, Program of—Sr. JOYCE COX, B.V.M., *910 Marion St., Seattle, 98104.* Tel: 206-382-4829; Fax: 206-654-4654.

Native American Ministry—Rev. PATRICK TWOHY, S.J.; Sr. JULIE CODD, C.S.J.P., *P.O. Box A, LaConner, 98257.* Tel: 206-466-4680.

Newspaper "The Catholic Northwest Progress"—Ms. KAY LAGRIED, Exec. Editor; DAN MADDEN, Mng. Editor, *910 Marion St., Seattle, 98104.* Tel: 206-382-4827; Fax: 206-382-3487.

Permanent Diaconate Program—Vacant, *910 Marion St., Seattle, 98104.* Tel: 206-382-3482.

Personnel Director for Priests—Rev. PAUL MAGNANO, *910 Marion St., Seattle, 98104.* Tel: 206-382-7317; Fax: 206-654-4654.

Polish Speaking, Ministry to—Revs. PIOTR DZIKOWSKI, S.Ch., *3422 Portland Ave., Tacoma, 98404.* Tel: 206-272-5232. JOZEF CALIK, S.Ch., *3221 14th Ave., W., Seattle, 98119.* Tel: 206-282-1804.

Presbyteral Council—Most Rev. ALEXANDER J. BRUNETT, D.D., Ph.D., Pres.

Priests' Eucharistic League—Rev. DESMOND MCMAHON, Dir., *910 Marion St., Seattle, 98104.* Tel: 206-382-4886.

Priests' Health Plan—Most Rev. ALEXANDER J. BRUNETT, D.D., Ph.D., Pres.; Rev. SEAN FOX, Chm.

Priests' Pension Plan—Most Rev. ALEXANDER J. BRUNETT, D.D., Ph.D.; Rev. SEAN FOX, Chm.

Detention Ministry—KEVIN GLACKIN COLEY, *910 Marion St., Seattle, 98104.* Tel: 206-382-4868.

Propagation of the Faith, Society for the—J.L. DROUHARD, Dir., *910 Marion St., Seattle, Wa, 98104.* Tel: 206-382-4583.

Public Affairs Office—Mr. JAMES F. BRITT, Dir., *910 Marion St., Seattle, 98104.* Tel: 206-382-4862; Fax: 206-382-3487.

Resettlement Dir.—Mr. DENNY HUNTHAUSEN, *5410 N. 44th, Tacoma, 98407.* Tel: 206-752-2455.

Sacramental Resources—Ms. CAROLYN LASSEK, *910 Marion St., Seattle, 98104.* Tel: 206-382-4838.

Seminarians, Vocation Discernment and Formation—Rev. CLAYTON MEYER, Ph.D., *910 Marion St., Seattle, 98104.* Tel: 206-382-4880.

Sisters' Council—Sr. SHARON PARK, O.P., *22010 S.E. 35th St., Issaquah, 98027.* Tel: 206-391-4493.

Special Ministries: Blessed Margaret Guild for the Blind—Rev. ANTHONY HAYCOCK, *10240 12th Ave. S., Seattle, 98168.* Tel: 206-762-3343. *International Catholic Deaf Assoc.*, Seattle Chapter No. 62, Rev. RICHARD HAYATSU, Chap., *406 S. 4th, Renton, 98055.* Tel: 206-255-3132. *Ministry to Mentally Retarded*, Rev. JAMES BOYLE, *204 6th Ave. S.W., Puyallup, 98371.* Tel: 206-841-3923.

Theological Resources—Revs. PETER CHIRICO, S.S., S.T.D., *804 9th Ave., Seattle, 98104.* Tel: 206-628-3920. JAMES EBLEN, S.T.L., Ph.D., *408 Bellevue Ave. E., Seattle, 98102.* Tel: 206-329-5692. CLAYTON MEYER, Ph.D., *P.O. Box 1763, Bellevue, 98009.* Tel: 206-382-4880. MICHAEL RASCHKO, Ph.D., *910 Marion St., Seattle, 98104.* Tel: 206-382-4276.

Telecommunication—Ms. KATHRYN JOHNSON, *910 Marion St., Seattle, 98104.* Tel: 206-382-4827.

Vietnamese, Representative for—Rev. PHUONG DUC TRAN (Vietnam), *1230 E. Fir, Seattle, 98122.* Tel: 206-325-5626.

Vocations Office—Mr. RICHARD SHIVELY, *910 Marion St., Seattle, 98104.* Tel: 206-382-4595.

Worship, Resources—Ms. CAROLYN LASSEK, *910 Marion St., Seattle, 98104.* Tel: 206-382-4838.

CLERGY, PARISHES, MISSIONS AND PAROCHIAL SCHOOLS

CITY OF SEATTLE
(King County)

1—ST. JAMES CATHEDRAL, Very Rev. Michael G. Ryan; Rev. Richard Ward. In res., Most Rev. Raymond Hunthausen; Rev. Peter F. Chirico, S.S.
Res., 804 Ninth Ave., 98104. Tel: 206-622-3559; Fax: 206-622-5303.
Convent—907 Columbia St., 98104. Tel: 206-682-1308.
Sisters 7.

2—ST. ALPHONSUS, Rev. James Gandrau. In res., Revs. Timothy Moynihan; George Limbani (Malawi, Africa).
Res., 5816 15th Ave., N.W., 98107. Tel: 206-784-6464; Fax: 206-789-5709.
School—Mrs. Donna DeFrancesco, Prin. Lay Teachers 15; Students 200.

3—ST. ANNE, Rev. Robert Camuso.
Res., 1411 1st Ave. W., 98119. Tel: 206-282-0223; Fax: 206-217-9541.
School—101 W. Lee St., 98119. Tel: 206-282-3538; Fax: 206-284-4191. Mrs. Pat Durand, Prin.
Sisters of the Holy Names of Jesus and Mary 1; Lay Teachers 13; Students 214.

4—ST. BENEDICT, Rev. Paul Waldie, O.M.I. In res., Revs. Gerard Clenaghan, O.M.I.; Edward T. McHugh, O.M.I.; Denis Pringle, S.A.
Res., 1805 N. 49th St., 98103. Tel: 206-632-1475; Fax: 206-632-2167.
School—4811 Wallingford N., 98103. Tel: 206-633-3375. Charles Secrest, Prin.
Sisters 2; Lay Teachers 12; Students 247.

5—ST. BERNADETTE, Rev. James Williams, Admin.
Res., 861 S.W. 126th St., 98146. Tel: 206-242-7370; Fax: 206-242-7371.
School—1028 S.W. 128th St., 98146. Tel: 206-244-4934; Fax: 206-243-6010. Sr. Marie Colarossi, Prin.
Sisters 2; Lay Teachers 12; Students 252.

6—ST. BRIDGET, Rev. Harold Quigg; Deacon Dennis Duffell.
Res., 4900 N.E. 50th, 98105. Tel: 206-523-8787; Fax: 206-528-7511.

7—ST. CATHERINE, Revs. David White, Admin.; Peter Duggan.
Res., 8610 8th Ave., N.E., 98115. Tel: 206-524-8800.
School—8524 8th Ave., N.E., 98115. Tel: 206-525-0581. Ms. Noel Mishler, Prin.
Lay Teachers 13; Students 262.

8—ST. EDWARD, Revs. Joseph Tyson; John Nwanze, O.P. (Nigeria).
Res., 4213 S. Orcas St., 98118. Tel: 206-722-7888; Fax: 206-722-7895.
School—4212 S. Mead St., 98118. Tel: 206-725-1774. Sr. Nancy Anderson, S.N.J.M., Co-Prin.; Ms. Patty Mitchell, Co-Prin.
Lay Teachers 12; Students 127.

9—ST. GEORGE, Revs. Joseph Tyson, Pastor; John Nwanze, O.P. (Nigeria).
Res., 5306 13th Ave. S., 98108. Tel: 206-762-7744; Fax: 206-762-4207.
School—5117 13th Ave. S., 98108. Tel: 206-762-0656; Fax: 206-763-3220. Bernadette Mahoney, Prin.
Sisters 1; Lay Teachers 12; Students 251.

10—ST. JOHN, Rev. William A. McKee.
Office: 121 N. 80th St., 98103. Tel: 206-782-2810; Fax: 206-782-0242.
School—Tel: 206-783-0337. Dan Sherman, Prin.
Lay Teachers 27; Students 440.

11—ST. JOSEPH, Revs. Craig Boly, S.J.; Lee Kapfer, S.J.
Res., 732 18th Ave., E., 98112. Tel: 206-324-2522; Fax: 206-329-5698.
School—700 18th Ave., E., Tel: 206-329-3260; Fax: 206-324-7773. George Hofbauer, Prin.
Lay Teachers 39; Students 620.

12—ST. LUKE, Rev. Roger O'Brien.
Res., 322 N. 175th St., 98133. Tel: 206-546-2451; Fax: 206-546-0328.
School—17533 St. Luke Pl., N., 98133. Tel: 206-542-1133; Fax: 206-546-8693. Mr. John Allen, Prin.
Sisters of St. Dominic 2; Lay Teachers 25; Students 425.

13—ST. MARGARET OF SCOTLAND, Rev. Robert Camuso. In res., Rev. Joseph Calik, S.Ch., Polish Ministry.
Res., 3221 14th Ave., W., 98119. Tel: 206-282-1804; Fax: 206-282-6461.

14—ST. MARK, Rev. Dennis Kemp.
Res., 18033 15th Pl., N.E., 98155. Tel: 206-364-7900; Fax: 206-367-3919.
School—Tel: 206-364-1633. Kathryn Palmquist-Keck, Prin.
Lay Teachers 14; Students 240.

15—ST. MARY, Rev. Anthony J. Haycock, Admin.
Res., 611 20th Ave., S., 98144. Tel: 206-324-7100; Fax: 206-329-4596.

Convent—2021 S. Weller St., 98144. Tel: 206-324-1535. Religious of the Sacred Heart of Jesus.

16—ST. MATTHEW, Rev. Gordon Douglas; Very Rev. John E. McMullan; Sr. Kathleen Buzard, S.N.J.M., Pastoral Life Dir.
Res., 1240 N.E. 127th St., 98125. Tel: 206-363-6767; Fax: 206-362-4863.
School—1230 N.E. 127th St., 98125. Tel: 206-362-2785. Sr. Monica Moffat, S.N.J.M., Prin.
Lay Teachers 13; Students 263.

17—ST. PATRICK, Very Rev. Lester J. McCloskey; Rev. James Eblen; Ms. Victoria Ries, Pastoral Life Dir.
Res., 2702 Broadway E., 98102. Tel: 206-329-2960; Fax & TTY: 206-329-2961.

18—ST. PAUL, Revs. Joseph Tyson, Co-Pastor; John Nwanze, O.P. (Nigeria).
Res., 5600 S. Ryan St., 98178. Tel: 206-725-2050; Fax: 206-725-7476.
School—10001 57th Ave., S., 98178. Tel: 206-725-0780. Mary Buza-Sims, Prin.
Lay Teachers 13; Students 217.

19—ST. PETER, Rev. Clayton Meyer, Admin.
Res., 2807 15th Ave., S., 98144. Tel: 206-324-2290.

20—ST. THERESE, Very Rev. Lester J. McCloskey; Ms. Patricia Repikoff, Pastoral Life Dir.; Rev. Joseph O. McGowan, S.J.
Res., 3416 E. Marion St., 98122. Tel: 206-325-2711; Fax: 206-329-8373.
School—900-35th Ave., 98122. Tel: 206-324-0460; Fax: 206-324-8464. Mrs. Eileen Gray, Prin.
Sisters of Providence 1; Lay Teachers 13; Students 212.

21—ASSUMPTION, Deacon John La Russa, Pastoral Life Dir.; Rev. Michael Angelovic; Very Rev. John E. McMullan.
Res., 3214 N.E. 62nd St., 98115. Tel: 206-522-7674; Fax: 206-522-7675.
School—Tel: 206-524-7452; Fax: 206-524-6757. Michael Foy, Prin.
Sisters 1; Lay Teachers 24; Students 530.

22—BLESSED SACRAMENT, Revs. Joseph Bradshaw, O.P.; Patrick O'Neil, O.P. In res., Revs. Leo Thomas, O.P.; Joseph Fulton, O.P.
Res., 5041 Ninth Ave., N.E., 98105. Tel: 206-547-3020; Fax: 206-547-6371.

23—CHRIST THE KING, Rev. Joseph R. Stocking, S.J., Parochial Vicar.
Res., 405 N. 117th St., 98133. Tel: 206-362-1545; Fax: 206-364-8325.
School—415 N. 117th, 98133. Tel: 206-364-6890.
Lay Teachers 15; Students 224.

24—HOLY FAMILY, Rev. Phillip Bloom.
Res., 9622 20th Ave., S.W., 98106. Tel: 206-767-6220; Fax: 206-767-0374.
School—Tel: 206-767-6640. Dr. Robert Scripko, Prin.
Sisters 1; Lay Teachers 13; Students 241.

25—HOLY ROSARY, Rev. Jeffery L. Sarkies.
Res., 4139 42nd Ave., S.W., 98116. Tel: 206-935-8353; Fax: 206-935-4303.
School—Tel: 206-937-7255. Kristi Brown, Prin.
Sisters 1; Lay Teachers 27; Students 407.

26—IMMACULATE CONCEPTION, Rev. Armando Guzman, Admin. In res., Rev. Jaime Tolang.
Res., 820 18th Ave., 98122. Tel: 206-322-5970; Fax: 206-322-9417.

27—OUR LADY OF FATIMA, Rev. Thomas Quinn. In res., Rev. Joseph H. Doogan.
Res., 3218 W. Barrett, 98199. Tel: 206-283-1456; Fax: 206-283-5788.
School—3301 W. Dravus St., 98199. Tel: 206-283-7031; Fax: 206-283-7696. Susan Burdett, Prin.
Lay Teachers 21; Students 272.

28—OUR LADY OF GUADALUPE, Rev. William Hallahan, O.M.I.
Res., 7000-35th Ave. S.W., 98126. Tel: 206-935-0358; Fax: 206-935-1230.
School—3401 S.W. Myrtle, 98126. Tel: 206-935-0651; Fax: 206-938-3695. Barbara Heneghan, Ed.D., Prin.
Lay Teachers 12; Students 225.

29—OUR LADY OF THE LAKE, Very Rev. John E. McMullan.
Res., 8900 35th Ave., N.E., 98115. Tel: 206-523-6776; Fax: 206-524-0848.
School—3520 N.E. 89th St., 98115. Tel: 206-525-9980; Fax: 206-523-2858. Mrs. Maureen Blum, Prin.
Lay Teachers 18; Students 206.

30—OUR LADY OF LOURDES, Rev. Gerald L. Mayovsky.
Res., 10240 12th Ave. S., 98168. Tel: 206-762-3343; Fax: 206-768-1507.

31—OUR LADY OF MOUNT VIRGIN (Italian), Very Rev. Lester J. McCloskey; Rev. Pasquale M. Spoletini, S.J. In res., Rev. Msgr. John Chi (Taipei); Bro. Fred Mercy, S.J.
Res., 1531 Bradner Pl. S., 98144. Tel: 206-324-8521.

32—SACRED HEART OF JESUS, Revs. Gregory Schmitt, C.SS.R., Admin.; Michael Logan, C.SS.R.; Lyle Konen, C.SS.R. In res., Revs. Bernard Mulligan, C.SS.R.; Anthony Slane, C.SS.R.; Bernard Vanhoomissen, C.SS.R.
Res., 205 2nd Ave. N., P.O. Box 9040, Queen Anne Sta., 98109. Tel: 206-284-4680; Fax: 206-284-3161.

OUTSIDE THE CITY OF SEATTLE

Aberdeen, Grays Harbor Co., St. Mary's, Sr. Deanna Carr, B.V.M., Pastoral Life Dir.; Revs. Patrick McDermott; Scott Connolly; Stephen Roman; Very Rev. James Picton.
Res., 306 E. Third St., 98520. Tel: 360-532-8300; Fax: 360-538-9987.
School—518 N. H St., 98520. Tel: 360-532-1230; Fax: 360-532-1209. Sr. Angela McCarthy, C.S.J.P., Prin.
Lay Teachers 10; Students 191.
Mission—Westport, St. Paul, P.O. Box 332, Westport 98585. Tel: 206-268-0665. In res., Rev. Stephen Roman.

SS. Peter and Paul (Polish), Sr. Deanna Carr, B.V.M., Pastoral Life Dir.; Revs. Patrick McDermott; Scott Connolly; Stephen Roman; Very Rev. James Picton; Rev. Joseph A. Dominic, Pastor Emeritus.
Res., 306 E. Third St., 98520. Tel: 360-532-8300; Fax: 360-538-9987.

Anacortes, Skagit Co., St. Mary's, Rev. William R. Harris.
Res., 4001 St. Mary's Dr., 98221. Tel: 360-293-2101; Fax: 360-293-2102.

Arlington, Snohomish Co., Immaculate Conception, Rev. Richard J. Spicer.
Res., 1200 E. Fifth, P.O. Box 69, 98223. Tel: 360-435-8565; Fax: 360-435-3781.
Mission—Darrington, Snohomish Co., St. John Mary Vianney, 1150 Riddle St., Darrington, 98241.

Auburn, King Co., Holy Family, Rev. Phuong Hoang.
Res., 505 17th St., S.E., P.O. Box B, 98071. Tel: 253-833-5130; Fax: 253-833-3421.
School—(Grades K-8) 505 17th St., S.E., 98002. Tel: 253-833-8688; Fax: 253-833-9311. Kathleen Cowin, Prin.
Sisters 1; Lay Teachers 15; Students 230.

Bainbridge Island, Kitsap Co., St. Cecilia's, Rev. Patrick Godley.
Res., 1310 Madison Ave. N., 98110. Tel: 206-842-3594; Fax: 206-842-6988.

Battle Ground, Clark Co., Sacred Heart, Rev. Franklin Lott, Admin.
Mailing Address: P.O. Box 38, 23505 N.E. 132nd Ave., 98604. Tel: 360-687-4515; Fax: 360-687-3322.
Mission—Yacolt, Clark Co., St. Joseph the Workman, 200 Jones St., Yacolt, 98675.

Bellevue, King Co., Sacred Heart, Rev. Marlin Connole. In res., Rev. John D. McCluskey, S.J.
Res., 9460 N.E. 14th St., 98004. Tel: 206-454-9536; Fax: 206-450-3909.
School—9450 N.E. 14th St., 98004. Tel: 206-451-1773; Fax: 206-454-9538. Dr. Karen Matthews, Prin.
Lay Teachers 30; Students 457.

St. Louise, Very Rev. Horacio V. Yanez; Rev. William Finn.
Res., 141 156th Ave., S.E., 98007. Tel: 206-747-4450; Fax: 206-644-3678.
School—133 156th Ave., S.E., 98007. Tel: 206-746-4220. Dan Fitzpatrick, Prin.
Lay Teachers 23; Students 467.

St. Madeleine Sophie, Rev. John Renggli; Deacon Eugene R. Vanderzanden.
Res., 4400 130th Pl., S.E., 98006-2014. Tel: 206-747-6770; Fax: 206-747-6349.

Bellingham, Whatcom Co., Assumption B.V.M., Revs. Joseph A. De Folco; Patrick Freitag.
Res., 2116 Cornwall Ave., 98225. Tel: 360-733-1380; Fax: 360-733-5644.
School—Tel: 360-733-6133; Fax: 360-733-3601. Ms. Anne Brand, Prin.
Lay Teachers 14; Students 306.

Sacred Heart, Revs. Joseph A. De Folco; Patrick Freitag.
Res., 1111 14th St., 98225. Tel: 360-734-2850; Fax: 360-734-0947. [JC]

Black Diamond, King Co., St. Barbara, Rev. M. Charles Palluck.
Res., Sixth Ave. near Baker, P.O. Box 189, 98010. Tel: 360-886-2229.

Bothell, King Co., St. Brendan, Rev. Steven Sallis.
Res., 10051 N.E. 195th, 98011-2931. Tel: 425-483-9400; Fax: 425-483-2839.
School—Tel: 425-483-8300; Fax: 425-486-9735. Arlene Sullivan, Prin.
Lay Teachers 16; Students 262.
Catechesis/Religious Programs—Students 530.

St. Elizabeth Ann Seton, Snohomish Co., Very Rev. Oliver F. Duggan.
Res., P.O. Box 12429, Mill Creek, 98082-0429. Tel: 206-481-0303; Fax: 206-485-8510.
Catechesis/Religious Programs—Mavis Kalbrener, D.R.E.
Students 534.

Bremerton, Kitsap Co., Our Lady, Star of the Sea, Very Rev. Joseph P. Mitchell; Rev. David Mayovsky; Deacon James Bemis.
Office: 1513-6th St., 98337. Tel: 360-479-3777; Fax: 360-479-3155.
School—1516-5th St., 98337. Tel: 360-373-5162. Jill Metcalf, Prin.
Lay Teachers 12; Students 206.

Holy Trinity, Rev. Jack Buckalew; Deacon Robert Rupno.
Mailing Address: P.O. Box 910, Tracyton, 98393.
Res., 4215 Pine Rd., 98310. Tel: 360-377-7674; Fax: 360-377-6181.

Buckley, Pierce Co., St. Aloysius, Rev. Hervey Vanasse.
Res., 211 W. Mason St., P.O. Box H, 98321. Tel: 360-862-6014.
Mission—Wilkeson, Pierce Co., Our Lady of Lourdes.

Burlington, Skagit Co., St. Charles, Revs. Paul A. Magnano; J. Michael Holland.
Res., 935 Peterson Rd., 98233. Tel: 360-757-0128; Fax: 360-757-0418.

Camas, Clark Co., St. Thomas, Rev. Ronald H. Belisle.
Res., 324 N.E. Oak, 98607. Tel: 360-834-2126; Fax: 360-834-5106. [CEM]
Mission—Stevenson, Skamania Co., Star of the Sea, P.O. Box 901, Stevenson, 98648. Tel: 509-427-8478.

Castle Rock, Cowlitz Co., St. Mary, Rev. Robert L. Evenson.
Mailing Address: P.O. Box 960, 98611-0960.
Rectory—635 Buland Ave., 98611-0960. Tel: 360-274-7404; Fax: 360-274-7404.
Church—120 Powell Rd., 98611-0960.

Centralia, Lewis Co., St. Mary's, Rev. Tuan Nguyen.
Res., 225 N. Washington Ave., 98531. Tel: 360-736-4356.

Chehalis, Lewis Co., St. Joseph's, Rev. Tuan Nguyen.
Mailing Address: 157 S.W. 6th St., 98532.
Res., 682 S.W. Cascade Ave., 98532. Tel: 360-748-4953; Fax: 360-748-3149.
School—123 S.W. 6th St., 98532. Tel: 360-748-0961; Fax: 360-748-3149. Laurie Heinz, Prin.
Sisters 1; Lay Teachers 9; Students 145.

Des Moines, King Co., St. Philomena, Rev. Martin Bourke, S.S.C.
Res., 1790 S. 222nd St., 98198. Tel: 206-878-8709; Fax: 206-824-3480.
School—1815 S. 220th, 98198. Tel: 206-824-4051; Fax: 206-878-4664. Karen Tarabochia, Prin.
Lay Teachers 14; Students 258.

Edmonds, Snohomish Co., Holy Rosary, Revs. Kenneth Haydock; David Brant.
Res., 630 7th Ave., N., P.O. Box 206, 98020. Tel: 425-778-3122; Fax: 425-672-4909.
School—770 Aloha St., 98020. Tel: 425-778-3197. Tim Blair, Prin.
Lay Teachers 14; Students 253.

Elma, Grays Harbor Co., St. Joseph's, Rev. John McLaughlin.
Res., 510 W. Waldrip St., P.O. Box AA, 98541. Tel: 206-482-3190. [CEM]
Mission—Montesano, Grays Harbor Co., St. John, Broadway and Church St., Montesano, 98563. Tel: 206-249-5766.

Enumclaw, King Co., Sacred Heart of Jesus, Rev. Gary M. Zender.
Res., 1614 Farrelly St., 98022. Tel: 360-825-3759; Fax: 360-825-6832.
Station—Crystal Springs, Crystal Mountain Chapel.

Everett, Snohomish Co., Immaculate Conception, Rev. Dennis E. Robb.
Mailing Address: 2619 Cedar St., 98201.
Res., 2430 Hoyt Ave., 98201. Tel: 425-349-7014; Fax: 425-349-7015. [JC]
School—2508 Hoyt Ave., 98201. Tel: 425-349-7777; Fax: 425-349-7048. Sr. Dolores Crosby, S.N.J.M., Prin.
Sisters 1; Lay Teachers 19; Students 438.

Our Lady of Perpetual Help, Rev. Dennis E. Robb.
Res., 2619 Cedar St., 98201. Tel: 425-349-7014; Fax: 425-349-7015. [JC]

St. Mary Magdalen, Revs. Joseph M. Marquart; Reynaldo Yu.
Res., 8717 7th Ave., S.E., 98208. Tel: 206-353-1211; Fax: 206-348-0458.
School—8615 7th Ave., S.E., 98208. Tel: 206-353-7559; Fax: 206-356-2687. Sr. Joanne McCauley, O.P., Prin.
Sisters 2; Lay Teachers 22; Students 454.
Mission—Mukilteo, Snohomish Co., St. John Evangelist.

Federal Way, King & Pierce Cos., St. Theresa, Rev. Kevin Moran, Admin.
Res., 3939 S.W. 331st, 98023. Tel: 206-838-5924;

Fax: 206-838-6825.
St. Vincent De Paul, King Co., Revs. Thomas L. Vandenberg; Anthony Lan Tran (Vietnam).
Res., 30525 8th Ave., S., 98003. Tel: 253-839-2320; Fax: 253-839-1819.
School—30527 8th Ave., S., 98003. Tel: 253-839-3532; Fax: 253-839-1819. Wanda Stewart, Prin.
Lay Teachers 16; Students 278.

Ferndale, Whatcom Co., St. Joseph, Rev. Timothy J. Sauer.
Res., 5781 Hendrickson Ave., 98248. Tel: 360-384-3651; Fax: 360-384-1879.
Missions—Blaine, Whatcom Co., St. Anne, 608 H. St., Blaine, 98230. Tel: 360-332-8048; Lummi, Whatcom Co., St. Joachim (Indian Reservation), Kwina & Lummi, Lummi, 98226. Tel: 360-734-2044.

Forks, Clallam Co., St. Anne Parish, Rev. Gerald O. Brunet, O.M.I.
Res., 511-5th Ave., P.O. Box 2359, 98331. Tel: 360-374-9184.
Mission—Clallam Bay, Clallam Co., St. Thomas the Apostle.

Friday Harbor, San Juan Co., St. Francis, Rev. James Meehan.
Res., 425 Price St., P.O. Box 1489, 98250. Tel: 360-378-2910 (Office); 378-6603 (Rectory).
Stations—Eastsound, St. Francis, Baker Rd. & N. Beach Rd., Eastsound, 98245. Tel: 360-376-6301; 378-2910; Lopez Island.; San Juan Island, Roche Harbor.

Gig Harbor, Pierce Co., St. Nicholas, Rev. Gary Weisenberger.
Res., 3510 Rosedale St., P.O. Box 220, 98335. Tel: 253-851-8850; Fax: 253-851-8823.

Hoquiam, Grays Harbor Co., Our Lady of Good Help, Sr. Deanna Carr, B.V.M., Pastoral Life Dir.; Revs. Scott Connolly; Patrick McDermott; Stephen Roman; Very Rev. James Picton.
Res., 200 L St., 98550. Tel: 360-532-6103; Fax: 360-533-9012.
Mission—Quinault, Grays Harbor & Jefferson Cos., Our Lady of the Olympics, Box 165, Quinault, 98575. Tel: 360-288-2802.

Issaquah, King Co., Mary, Queen of Peace, Rev. J. Paul Dalton; Deacon William Taube.
Res., 1121 228th Ave., S.E., 98029. Tel: 425-391-1178; 868-8251; Fax: 425-391-7979.
St. Joseph, Rev. Patrick S. Clark.
Res., 220 Mt. Park Blvd., S.W., P.O. Box 200, 98027. Tel: 425-392-5516; Fax: 425-392-2722.

Kelso, Cowlitz Co., St. Mary, Rev. Robert L. Evenson.
Res., 2200 Allen St., 98626. Tel: 360-423-3650; Fax: 360-423-4165.

Kent, King Co., Holy Spirit Parish, Rev. Michael J. Ryan.
Res., 310 3rd Ave., S., 98032. Tel: 253-859-0444; Fax: 253-859-5974. [CEM]
St. John the Baptist, Rev. Jack Walmesley.
Church—25810 156th Ave., S.E., 98042. Tel: 253-630-0701; Fax: 253-630-3174.

Kirkland, King Co., Holy Family, Revs. Gary Movelli; Emil Anderson.
Res., 7355 120th Ave., N.E., 98033. Tel: 425-822-0295; Fax: 425-827-0648.
School—Tel: 425-827-0444. Sue Ford Clausen, Prin.
Lay Teachers 17; Students 330.
St. John Mary Vianney, Rev. William Heric; Deacon Edward F. White, Sr.
Res., 12600 84th Ave., N.E., 98034. Tel: 425-823-0787; Fax: 425-814-2115.

LaConner, Skagit Co., Sacred Heart, Rev. Paul A. Magnano; Deacon George Peterson, Pastoral Assoc.
Res., P.O. Box 757, 98257-0757. Tel: 360-466-3967; Fax: 360-466-3942.
St. Paul (Swinomish), Revs. Paul A. Magnano; Patrick Twohy, S.J., Parochial Vicar.
Mailing Address: P.O. Box 2100, 98257. Tel: 360-466-5737.
Church—1742 Pioneer Pkwy. Rd., 98257.

Lacey, Thurston Co., Sacred Heart of Jesus, Rev. Richard Parle.
Res., P.O. Box 3805, 98509-3805. Tel: 360-491-0890; Fax: 360-456-1028.

Langley, Island Co., St. Hubert, Rev. Gerald Moffat.
Mailing Address: P.O. Box 388, 98260.
Res., 815 Saratoga Ave., 98260. Tel: 360-221-5383; Fax: 360-221-2011.

Longview, Cowlitz Co., St. Rose de Viterbo, Rev. Lawrence Mender, O.S.B., Admin.
Mailing Address: 701-26th, 98632.
Res., 2571 Nichols Blvd., 98632. Tel: 360-425-4660; Fax: 360-577-5820.
School—727 25th Ave., 98632. Kay Purcell, Prin.
Lay Teachers 16; Students 192.
Mission—Cathlamet, Wahkiakum Co., St. Catherine, 400 Columbia St., Cathlamet, 98612. Tel: 360-795-8725.

Lynden, Whatcom Co., St. Joseph's, Rev. Richard McCallister.
Res., 205 Twelfth St., 98264. Tel: 360-354-2334; Fax: 360-354-5889.
Mission—Deming, Whatcom Co., St. Peter, 6210 Mt. Baker Hwy., Deming, 98244. [CEM]

Lynnwood, Snohomish Co., St. Thomas More, Rev. James Dalton.
Res., 6511-176th S.W., Lynwood, 98037. Tel: 206-743-2929; Fax: 206-743-3652.
School—Tel: 206-743-4242. Patrick White, Prin.
Sisters 1; Lay Teachers 15; Students 254.

Marysville, Snohomish Co., St. Mary's, Rev. John Bulger.
Res., 4200 88th St, N.E., 98270. Tel: 360-653-9400; Fax: 360-658-7439. [CEM]
Mission—Tulalip, Snohomish Co., Tulalip Indian Reservation, St. Anne, 7213 Totem Beach Rd., Tulalip, 98271.

Mercer Island, King Co., St. Monica, Rev. John Bowman; Deacon Jack Warfield. In res., Rev. John Horan.
Res., 4301 88th S.E., P.O. Box 730, 98040. Tel: 206-232-2900; Fax: 206-232-7875.
School—4320 87th S.E., 98040. Tel: 206-232-5432; Fax: 206-232-7875. Ken Dorsett, Prin.
Lay Teachers 19; Students 230.

Monroe, Snohomish Co., St. Mary of the Valley, Rev. Philip Fitzsimons.
Res., 601 W. Columbia, P.O. Box 279, 98272. Tel: 360-794-8945; Fax: 360-489-1409.

Morton, Lewis Co., Sacred Heart, Very Rev. Roger J. Smith.
Res., 7th and W. Adams Sts., P.O. Box 880, 98356. Tel: 360-496-5456; Fax: 360-496-5616.
Mission—Harmony, Lewis Co., St. Yves. [CEM]
Station—Packwood.

Mountlake Terrace, Snohomish Co., St. Pius X, Revs. Sean P. Fox; Richard Roach, S.J.
Res., 22106 56th W., 98043. Tel: 206-775-7545; Fax: 206-775-8744.
School—22105 58th W., 98043. Tel: 206-778-9861. Mrs. Terri McDermott, Prin.
Lay Teachers 13; Students 220.

Mount Vernon, Skagit Co., Immaculate Conception, Revs. Paul A. Magnano; John Schwartz, S.J., Parochial Vicar.
Res., 110 S. Fifth St., 98273. Tel: 360-336-6622; Fax: 360-336-5203.
School—1321 E. Division St., 98273. Tel: 360-428-3912; Fax: 360-424-8838. Mary Schau, Prin.
Lay Teachers 18; Students 285.

Oak Harbor, Island Co., St. Augustine, Rev. G. Barry Ashwell.
Res., 185 N. Oak Harbor St., 98277. Tel: 360-675-2303; Fax: 360-675-9490.
Mission—Coupeville, Island Co., St. Mary, 207 N. Main, 98239. Tel: 360-678-6536.

Ocean Shores, Grays Harbor Co., St. Jerome, Sr. Deanna Carr, B.V.M., Pastoral Life Dir.; Revs. Patrick McDermott; Scott Connolly; Stephen Roman; Very Rev. James Picton; Deacon Bruce MacPherson.
Res., P.O. Box 143, 98569. Tel: 360-289-2838; Fax: 360-289-0163.

Olympia, Thurston Co., St. Michael's, Revs. James Lee; James Northrop.
Res., 1021 S. Boundary, P.O. Box 766, 98507. Tel: 360-754-4666; Fax: 360-754-0628. [CEM]
School—1203 E. 10th, 98501. Tel: 360-754-5131. Thomas Ward, Prin.
Lay Teachers 13; Students 250.

Pe Ell, Lewis Co., St. Joseph's, Rev. Timothy Berg.
Res., Main and Pe Ell Ave., P.O. Box 235, 98572. Tel: 360-291-3434. [CEM]
Mission—Frances, Pacific Co., Holy Family.

Port Angeles, Clallam Co., Queen of Angels, Rev. John Wilkie.
Res., 209 W. 11th St., 98362. Tel: 360-452-2351; Fax: 360-452-1447.
School—1107 S. Oak, 98362. Tel: 360-457-6903; Fax: 360-457-6866. Mrs. Theresa Sekac, Prin.
Lay Teachers 16; Students 200.

Port Orchard, Kitsap Co., St. Gabriel's, Rev. Dennis C. Sevilla.
Res., 1150 Mitchell Ave., 98366-4499. Tel: 360-876-2762; Fax: 360-876-6085.
Mission—Belfair, Kitsap Co., Prince of Peace, N.E. 1171 Sand Hill Rd., P.O. Box 517, Belfair, 98528. Tel: 360-275-8760; Fax: 360-275-8760.

Port Townsend, Jefferson Co., St. Mary's, Star of the Sea, Rev. Raymond J. Heffernan.
Res., 1335 Blaine St., 98368. Tel: 360-385-3700; Fax: 360-379-1989. [CEM]

Poulsbo, Kitsap Co., St. Olaf, Rev. Hung Nguyen; Deacon Carl Moyer.
Res., 18943 Caldart Ave., N.E., P.O. Box 907, 98370. Tel: 360-779-4291; Fax: 360-598-5888.
Mission—Suquamish, Kitsap Co., St. Peter.

Puyallup, Pierce Co., All Saints, Revs. Robert Riler; Ronald Knudsen; Deacon Michael McGillicuddy. In res., Rev. James Boyle Tel: 253-841-3923.
Res., 204 6th S.W., 98371. Tel: 253-845-7521; Fax: 253-845-3105.
Schools—504 2nd S.W., 98371. Tel: 206-845-5025. Alice Milam, Prin.
Lay Teachers 12; Students 147; St. Martin of Tours School (Satellite School), (Grades PreK-2) 2323 54th Ave., E., Fife, 98424. Tel: 253-922-5360. Alice Milam, Prin.
Lay Teachers 7; Students 155.
Holy Disciples, Rev. Gary Southerton.
Res., 15012 Meridian Ave., E., Ste. 4, 98373. Tel: 253-845-0828; Fax: 253-845-0930.
Mission—Eatonville, Pierce Co., Our Lady of Good Counsel, 229 Antonie Ave., N., Eatonville, 98328.

Raymond, Pacific Co., St. Lawrence, Rev. Richard Gallagher, Admin.
Res., 1112 Blake St., P.O. Box 31, 98577. Tel: 360-942-3000; Fax: 360-942-3000.

Redmond, King Co., St. Jude, Rev. Gerald F. Lovett.
Res., 10526 166th N.E., 98052. Tel: 425-883-7685; Fax: 425-881-2207.

Renton, King Co., St. Anthony's, Revs. Richard Hayatsu; Gerald Woodman; Deacon Richard Combs.
Res., 314 S. 4th St., 98055. Tel: 425-255-3132; Fax: 425-271-4729.
School—336 Shattuck Ave., S., 98055. Tel: 425-255-0059; Fax: 425-235-6555. Doug Arthur, Prin.
Sisters 2; Lay Teachers 25; Students 510.
St. Stephen the Martyr, Rev. John C. Madigan.
Res., 13055 S.E. 192nd St., 98058. Tel: 253-631-1940; Fax: 253-255-2943.

Seahurst, King Co., St. Francis of Assisi, Revs. Philip D. Wallace; Lester McCloskey.
Res., 15236 21st Ave., S.W., P.O. Box 929, 98062. Tel: 206-242-4575; Fax: 206-242-1957.
School—P.O. Box 870, 98062. Tel: 206-243-5690; Fax: 206-433-8593. Sheila Keaton, Prin.
Lay Teachers 26; Students 401.

Seaview, Pacific Co., St. Mary, Rev. Richard J. Gallagher.
Res., P.O. Box 274, 98644. Tel: 360-642-2002.
Station—McGowan.

Sedro Woolley, Skagit Co., Immaculate Heart of Mary, Revs. Paul A. Magnano; Victor Olvida, Parochial Vicar.
Res., 719 Ferry St., 98284. Tel: 360-855-0077; 855-2282; Fax: 360-855-2282.
Mission—Concrete, Skagit Co., St. Catherine, 239 Limestone, Concrete, 98237. Tel: 360-853-8941.

Sequim, Clallam Co., St. Joseph, Rev. Thomas Beattie.
Res., 121 E. Maple, P.O. Box 1209, 98382. Tel: 360-683-6076; Fax: 360-683-4674.

Shelton, Mason Co., St. Edward's, Rev. Dominic D. Hahn, O.S.B.
Res., 321 N. 3rd St., P.O. Box 758, 98584. Tel: 360-426-6134; Fax: 360-426-6231.

Snohomish, Snohomish Co., St. Michael's, Rev. Dennis V. Champagne.
Res., 1512 Pine Ave., 98290. Tel: 360-568-0821; Fax: 360-568-6426.
Mission—Granite Falls, Snohomish Co., Holy Cross, Tel: 360-691-5945.

Snoqualmie, King Co., Our Lady of Sorrows, Rev. Jan Larson.
Res., 39025 S.E. Alpha St., P.O. Box 909, 98065. Tel: 425-888-2974; Fax: 425-888-7098.
Missions—Carnation, King Co., St. Anthony, P.O. Box 175, Carnation, 98014. Tel: 425-333-4930; Duvall, King Co., Holy Innocents, P.O. Box 850, Duvall, 98109. Tel: 425-788-1400; 775-1477. Very Rev. George Thomas.
Station—Snoqualmie Summit, St. Bernard's Chapel, Tel: 206-454-6161.

Stanwood, Snohomish Co., St. Cecilia's, Rev. Matthew Williams, O.C.D. In res., Rev. Colm Stone, O.C.D.
Res., 26900 78th Ave., N.W., P.O. Box 1002, 98292. Tel: 360-629-3737.

Sumner, Pierce Co., St. Andrew, Rev. Thomas A. Belleque.
Res., 704 Kincaid Ave., 98390. Tel: 253-863-2253; Fax: 253-863-3567.
Mission—Orting, Pierce Co., SS. Cosmas and Damian, 213 W. Leber St., Orting, 98360.

Tacoma, Pierce Co.,

1—St. Ann, Revs. Vincent Pastro; Patrick O'Neill, Parochial Vicar. Administrators: Revs. C. Vincent Peterson; Emmanuel Iweh (Nigeria).
Res., 7001 S. Park Ave., 98408. Tel: 253-472-1360.

2—St. Charles Borromeo, Revs. Patrick J. Ritter; Kurt Nagle.
Res., 7112 S. 12th St., 98465. Tel: 253-564-5185; Fax: 253-565-0936.
School—Tel: 253-581-2908. Patrick Feist, Prin.
Sisters of St. Francis of Philadelphia 3; Lay

Teachers 23; Students 512.

3—St. Frances Cabrini, Rev. James P. Coyne.
Res., 5505 108th St., S.W., 98499. Tel: 253-588-2141; Fax: 253-582-5351.
School—Tel: 253-584-3850; Fax: 253-582-5351. Stephanie Van Leuven, Prin.
Sisters 1; Lay Teachers 14; Students 267.

4—St. John Bosco, Rev. Ralph Carney, O.F.M., Admin.
Res., 10508 112 St., S.W., 98498. Tel: 253-582-1028; Fax: 253-584-0633.
Mission—Steilacoom, Pierce Co., Immaculate Conception.

5—St. John of the Woods, Revs. Vincent Pastro; Patrick G. O'Neill, Parochial Vicar; C. Vincent Peterson; Emmanuel Iweh (Nigeria).
Res., 9903 24th Ave., E., 98445. Tel: 253-537-8551.

6—St. Joseph's, (Slovak), Revs. Richard S. Cebula, O.S.B., Admin.; John E. Koehler; Deacon Jack W. Buck.
Res., 608 S. 34th St., 98408. Tel: 253-472-2489.

7—St. Leo the Great, Rev. John D. Fuchs, S.J.; Deacon Thomas Horlander.
Res., 710 S. 13th St., 98405. Tel: 253-272-5136; Fax: 253-272-6285.

8—St. Martin of Tours, Rev. Patrick K. O'Brien.
Res., 2303-54th Ave., E., 98424. Tel: 253-922-7882.

9—St. Patrick's, Rev. Seamus Laverty.
Res., 1001 N. J St., 98403. Tel: 253-383-2783; Fax: 253-627-5396.
School—1112 N. G St., 98403. Tel: 253-272-2297. Larry Di Palma, Prin.
Sisters 3; Lay Teachers 27; Students 457.

10—SS. Peter & Paul, (Polish), Rev. Piotr Dzikowski, S.Ch.
Res., 3422 Portland Ave., 98404. Tel: 253-272-5232; Fax: 253-627-7848.

11—St. Rita, Rev. Carmine J. Sacco, S.J.
Res., 1403 S. Ainsworth, 98405. Tel: 253-627-4851.

12—Holy Cross, Rev. Robert Rekofke, S.J.
Res., 5510 N. 44th St., 98407. Tel: 253-759-3368.

13—Holy Rosary, Revs. Richard S. Cebula, O.S.B.; John E. Koehler.
Res., 512 S. 30th St., 98402. Tel: 253-383-4549.
School—504 S. 30th, 98402. Tel: 253-272-7012. Sr. Catherine Lendosky, Prin.
Sisters 2; Lay Teachers 8; Students 205.
Convent—424 S. 30th, 98402.

14—Our Lady, Queen of Heaven, Rev. Michael McDermott; Deacon Robert R. Dardis.
Res., 14601 A St. S., 98444. Tel: 253-537-3252; Fax: 253-536-2662.

15—Sacred Heart, Revs. Vincent Pastro; Patrick O'Neill, Parochial Vicar; C. Vincent Peterson; Emmanuel Iweh (Nigeria).
Res., 4520 McKinley Ave., 98404. Tel: 253-472-7738.

16—Visitation, Rev. David Gese.
Res., 3314 S. 58th St., 98409. Tel: 253-473-4960; Fax: 253-474-8378.
School—3306 S. 58th St., 98409. Imelda Mead, Prin.
Lay Teachers 9; Students 222.

Toledo, Lewis Co., St. Francis Xavier, Rev. Timothy Berg, Admin.
Res., 139 Spencer Rd., 98591. Tel: 360-864-4126. [CEM]

Tukwila, King Co., St. Thomas, Rev. Gerald L. Mayovsky.
Res., 4415 S. 140th St., 98168. Tel: 206-242-5501; Fax: 206-244-9387.

Vancouver, Clark Co.,

1—Our Lady of Lourdes, Revs. Robert Dell, C.O., Admin.; Clarence Jones, C.O.; Deacon Robert Tomich.
Res., 4723 Franklin St., N.W., 98663. Tel: 360-695-1366; Fax: 360-695-7966.
School—Tel: 360-696-2301. Ms. Shirley Loesch, Prin.
Lay Teachers 14; Students 259.

2—St. James, Rev. Anthony Ton.
Res., 218 W. 12th St., 98660. Tel: 360-693-3052; Fax: 360-693-3077. [CEM]

3—St. John, Rev. Michael C. OBrien.
Res., 8701 N.E. 119 St., 98662. Tel: 360-573-3325; Fax: 360-573-3344. [CEM]
Station—Larch Mountain Corrections Center.

4—St. Joseph, Revs. Hans Olson; Michael Wright.
Res., 6600 Highland Dr., 98661. Tel: 360-696-4407; Fax: 360-696-3959.
School—6500 Highland Dr., 98661. Tel: 360-696-2586; Fax: 360-696-3959. Teri Stegman, Prin.
Lay Teachers 23; Students 370.

Vashon, King Co., St. John Vianney, David Giusti, Pastoral Life Dir.; Very Rev. Lester J. McCloskey.
Res., P.O. Box 308, 98070. Tel: 206-567-4149; Fax: 206-567-4198.
Mission—Dockton, King Co., St. Patrick, Tel: 206-463-3224.

Winlock, Lewis Co., Sacred Heart, Rev. Timothy Berg, Admin.; Deacon Clay Hartzell.
Res., P.O. Box 69, 98596. Tel: 360-864-4126.
Station—St. Urban.

Woodland, Cowlitz Co., St. Philip's, Rev. Joseph O'Shea.
Res., 430 Bozarth, Box 177, 98674. Tel: 360-225-8308; Fax: 360-225-8866.
Missions—Kalama, Cowlitz Co., St. Joseph, 4th & Elm, Kalama, 98625. Tel: 360-673-4682; Ridgefield, Clark Co., St. Mary of Guadalupe, 28309 N.W. 11th, Ridgefield, 98642. Tel: 360-887-8194.

Yelm, Thurston Co., St. Columban, Rev. Terence J. Wager, O.S.B.
Res., P.O. Box 956, 98597. Tel: 360-458-3031; Fax: 360-458-4094.
Mission—Tenino, Thurston Co., St. Peter, P.O. Box 744, Sussex & Keithan St., Tenino, 98589. Tel: 360-264-2124.

Chaplains of Public Institutions

Seattle. *U.S. Public Health Hospital.* Attended by St. Peter's Church.
Veterans Administration Medical Center. Rev. Thomas Park, O.S.B.
Youth Service Center. Sr. Anne Davis, C.S.J., Pastoral Min.

Buckley. *Rainier School.* Rev. James Boyle.
Western State Custodial School. Attended from St. Aloysius Church.

Chehalis. *State Training School for Boys.* Rev. Tuan Nguyen.

Gig Harbor. *Washington Corrections Center for Women.* Rev. John Haas.

McNeil Island. *McNeil Island Correction Center.* Rev. Thomas Suss.

Monroe. *Washington State Reformatory.* Pastoral Ministers: Pat Hoban; Jose Contreras.

Orting. *U.S. Soldiers' Home.* Rev. Thomas A. Belleque.

Retsil. *Washington Veterans Home Hospital.* Rev. Dennis C. Sevilla.

Shelton. *Washington Corrections Center* P.O. Box 900, 98584. Sr. Esperanza Cintron, Pastoral Min.

Snoqualmie. *Echo Glen School.* Rev. Jan Larson.

Steilacoom. *Western State Hospital.* Rev. Robert Tino.

Tacoma. *Veterans Admin. Medical Center.* Rev. David W. Prebula, O.S.B.

Vancouver. *Veterans Administration Hospital.* Attended from St. James.
Washington State School for the Blind. Attended from St. James.
Washington State School for the Deaf. Attended from St. Joseph.

Special Assignment:
Reverend Fathers—
Ahn, Michael, Peace of Christ Korean Center, 11700 1st Ave., Seattle, WA 98125
Bawyn, Anthony, American College, University of Louvain, Naamestraat 100, 3000 Leuven, Belgium
Eblen, James, Theologian, 910 Marion St., Seattle, WA 98104. Tel: 206-382-4593
Fewing, Ross, Seattle Hospital Ministry, 910 Marion, Seattle, WA 98104
Hart, Brian, Box R-PFE 59, APO, AE 9624
Jaeger, David, AIDS Ministry, 910 Marion St., Seattle, WA 98104
Meyer, Clayton, Coord. for Discernment & Formation of Seminarians, P.O. Box 1763, Bellevue, WA 98009
Picton, James, Episcopal Vicar, 910 Marion St., Seattle, WA 98104
Raschko, Michael, Theologian, 1614 Summit, #602, Seattle, WA 98122
Rowan, Stephen, Seattle University, Res., P.O. Box 51029, Seattle, WA 98115
Snyder, Brian, Seattle Hospital Ministry, 910 Marion, Seattle, WA 98104
Stehly, Mark, Seattle Hospital Ministry, 910 Marion St., Seattle, WA 98104
Thomas, George, Episcopal Vicar, 910 Marion St., Seattle, WA 98104
Yoo, Augustine, Korean Ministry, 7912 Golden Given Rd. E., Tacoma, WA 98404

On Duty Outside the Archdiocese:
Reverend Fathers—
Larrivee, Leo J., S.S., 4210 N. Charles St. #3, Baltimore, MD 21218
Pins, Herbert, Diocese of Helena
Rogerson, Daniel, Mount Angel Abbey, St. Benedict, OR 97373

Military Chaplains:
Reverend Fathers—
Bailey, Lawrence, 15 ABG/HC, 180 Kuntz Ave., Hickam AFB, HI 96853-5112
McKenna, Timothy J., 435 Logistic SUPSQ AW/HC, PSC 5 Box 2311 APO, AE 09097

Unassigned:
Reverend Fathers—
Clark, John, 910 Marion St., Seattle, WA 98104
Gonzales, Emilio, 910 Marion St., Seattle, WA 98104
Jonientz, Bernard, 4231 S. Juneau, Seattle, WA 98118
Lesnick, Richard, 910 Marion St., Seattle, WA 98104
Salazar, Felipe, 910 Marion St., Seattle, WA 98104
Tucker, Michael, 910 Marion St., Seattle, WA 98104
Vega (Vega-Montalbo), Jose (Giuseppe), 910 Marion St., Seattle, WA 98104

Medical Leave:
Reverend Fathers—
MacDonald, Fabian, 23501-112th Ave., S.E., G-102, Kent, WA 98031
McMahon, Desmond, 1115 North I St., #104, Tacoma, WA 98403
Naumes, Matthew, 1100 University, 11J, Seattle, WA 98101
Sondergeld, Theodore, 2627 S. 310th, Federal Way, WA 98003
Wood, Dennis, 23526-55th Ave. S., Kent, WA 98032

Retired:
Reverend Monsignors—
Doogan, John P., 500 Wall St. #314, Seattle, WA 98121
Reverend Fathers—
Aspiras, Jose, Station Rita East, Agoo, La Union Philippines
Auer, Paul, 1208 7th St., Anacortes, WA 98221
Buck, James, 1701 18th Ave. S., Seattle, WA 98144
Cloquet, Victor, P.O. Box 1232, Allyn, WA 98524-1232
Cody, Michael, 910 Marion St., Seattle, WA 98104
Crosse, Charles, 8539 Zircon Dr. S.W., Tacoma, WA 98498
Delahunty, Thomas, 7320C 142nd Ave., E., Summer, WA 98390
Domandich, Anthony, 2600 N.E. Minnehaha St., #105, Vancouver, WA 98665
Dominic, Joseph A., 3333 Ensign Rd., N.E., Olympia, WA 98506
Donohoe, John P., 2500 S. 370th St., #252, Federal Way, WA 98003
Doogan, Joseph H., 3218 W. Barrett, Seattle, WA 98199
Gallagher, William E., 6108 N. Park, Tacoma, WA 98407
Hamilton, James, 4831 35th Ave., S.W., Seattle, WA 98126
Harrington, Cornelius, 1156 Alki Ave. S.W., Seattle, WA 98116
Heneghan, Jarlath, 9460 N.E. 44th, Bellevue, WA 98004
Heneghan, Sean, 12450 20th Ave. S., Seattle, WA 98168
Horan, John, P.O. Box 730, Mercer Island, WA 98040
Jennings, John A., 2430 S. 371st St., Federal Way, WA 98003
Kramis, Joseph, 2009 Walker Park Rd., Shelton, WA 98584
Lane, William, 20826 70th Ave. W., #6, Lynnwood, WA 98036
Linehan, David, 515 S. 136th St., Seattle, WA 98168
Lukas, Michael, 495 Toutle Rd., Apt. 4, Castle Rock, WA 98611
Lynch, Ibar, 1427 3rd Ave. W., #19, Seattle, WA 98119
Mallahan, James, 949 N. 35th St., #103, Seattle, WA 98103
McEnnis, Thomas, 10343 W. Cameo Dr., Sun City, AZ 85351
McGreal, James, 910 Marion St., Seattle, WA 98104
Moore, Gerald T., 2810 W. Hayes, Seattle, WA 98199
Moynihan, Timothy, 5816 15th Ave. N.W., Seattle, WA 98107
Murray, Maximillian, P.O. Box 402, Bremerton, WA 98310
O'Callaghan, Thomas, P.O. Box 346, Suquamish, WA 98392
O'Neil, Michael, 1065 N. American Ln., Coupeville, WA 98239
O'Neill, Patrick, 9903 24th Ave. E., Tacoma, WA 98445
Petosa, Joseph, 22404-59th Ave. W, Mountlake Terrace, WA 98403
Phelan, Thomas, 1601 S. Jackson, Tacoma, WA 98465
Rafalowski, Leonard, 2137 Washington, #4, Port Townsend, WA 98368

Rice, John A., 1208-6455 Willingdon Ave., Burnaby, B.C. V5H 4E4
Rink, George, 1828 S.W. 318th Pl., Unit D, Federal Way, WA 98023
Slate, William, P.O. Box 4258, Kent, WA 98032
Szeman, Stephen, 12611 S.E. 30th, #1, Bellvue, WA 98005
Tolang, Jaime, 820 18th Ave., Seattle, WA 98122
Treacy, William, 9460 N.E. 14th, Bellevue, WA 98004
Welch, Paul, S.S., St. Charles Villa, 603 Maiden Choice Ln., Baltimore, MD 21228

Permanent Deacons:
Alexander, Richard
Allen, Daniel
Anderson, Carl
Anderson, David
Bemis, James
Benedict, Nathan
Bentley, Ernest
Burkholder, Thomas, On Leave
Cavanaugh, Robert
Cliffton, Glenn
Crandall, Charles
Curtis, Joseph
Dardis, Robert
Denby, Marshall
Dodson, Arthur, On Leave
Dolan, Robert
Dorr, LuVerne
Duffell, Denny
Dunne, Joseph, Unassigned
Edtl, Lee
Ellis, Rolland
Erskine, Thomas
Ficken, George
Frost, Harold
Hanika, Donald
Hartzell, Clay
Hawkins, Tom
Henn, Thomas, Richland
Ho, Bernard, San Jose, CA
Hoover, Delbert
Horlander, Tom
Huelett, William
Kim, Duk
Krempl, Joseph
La Russa, John
Lane, Loren
MacPherson, Bruce
Magnuson, John
Maher, Dean, Walla Walla
Majeau, Henrie, On Leave
Marcell, Terrance
Marshall, Norman, On Leave
McGary, Fred, On Leave
McGary, Robert, On Leave
McGillicuddy, Michael
Michalak, William, On Leave
Miller, Robert L., Jackson, WY
Minetti, Bernard, Tucson, AZ
Monuteaux, Lawrence
Moyer, Carlton
Moynihan, Patrick
Murdy, Don, Inactive
Myer, Philip
Nathe, Richard
O'Loane, Phil
O'Neill, Richard, Inactive
Olsen, Richard, S. San Francisco, CA
Origenes, Maurice
Parsons, Eamon D.
Pellegrino, Joseph
Peterson, George
Pioli, Albert, On Leave
Ricciardi, John
Ruiz, Nehemias, Thornton, CO
Rupno, Robert
Sarver, Richard, Las Vegas, NV
Shields, Walter J.
Snider, Lloyd
Stenson, Mark
Stromberg, Alton L., Seaside, OR
Tanasse, William
Taube, William
Tomich, Robert
Townsend, William
Vanderzanden, Gene
Warfield, Jack
Warmuth, David
Wiese, Ted
Wilson, Howard
Zipp, Frank
Zuanich, Matthew

INSTITUTIONS LOCATED IN THE ARCHDIOCESE

[A] COLLEGES AND UNIVERSITIES

SEATTLE. *Seattle University*, 900 Broadway, 98122. Tel: 206-296-6000.
Web site: http://www.seattleu.edu
For a complete listing, refer to the Colleges and Universities section.

LACEY. *St. Martin's College*, 5300 Pacific Ave., S.E., 98503. Tel: 360-491-4700
For a complete listing, refer to the Colleges and Universities section.

[B] HIGH SCHOOLS, ARCHDIOCESAN

SEATTLE. *Blanchet High School*. (Coed), 8200 Wallingford Ave. N., 98103. Tel: 206-527-7711; Fax: 206-527-7712. Dr. Joseph R. Haggerty, Prin.; Rev. Gordon Douglas. Sisters 2; Lay Teachers 58; Students 990.

John F. Kennedy Memorial High School. (Coed), 140 S. 140th, 98168. Tel: 206-246-0500; Fax: 206-242-0831. Mr. John Schuster, Prin.; Rev. Michael J. Batterberry. Priests 1; Sisters 1; Lay Teachers 55; Students 760.

O'Dea High School. (Boys), 802 Terry Ave., 98104. Tel: 206-622-6596; Fax: 206-340-4110.
Conducted by the Congregation of Christian Brothers. Bro. Dominic Murray, C.F.C., Prin. Brothers 9; Lay Teachers 23; Students 465.

[C] HIGH SCHOOLS, PRIVATE

SEATTLE. *Holy Names Academy*. (Girls), 728 21st Ave. E., 98112. Tel: 206-323-4272.
Web site: http://www.holynamessea.org
Sisters of the Congregation of the Holy Names of Jesus and Mary. Ms. Elizabeth Swift, Prin. Sisters 10; Lay Teachers 32; Students 485.

Seattle Preparatory School, 2400 11th E., 98102. Tel: 206-324-0400; Fax: 206-323-6509. Mr. Robert P. Graby, Ed.D., Pres.; Mr. Christopher P. Conroy, Prin. Priests 2; Lay Teachers 70; Students 645.

BELLEVUE. *Eastside Catholic High School*. (Coed), 11650 S.E. 60th, 98006. Tel: 206-644-7737. Glen T. Lutz, Interim Prin.; Rev. Richard Basso. Priests 1; Sisters 1; Lay Teachers 45; Students 585.

Forest Ridge School of the Sacred Heart. (Grades 5-12). (Girls), 4800 139th Ave. S.E., 98006. Tel: 425-641-0700.
Web site: http://www.forestridge.org
Sr. Suzanne Cooke, R.S.C.J., Prin. Religious of the Sacred Heart 5; Lay Teachers 50; Students 325.

EVERETT. *Holy Cross High School*. (Coed), 2617 Cedar St., 98201. Tel: 425-252-6203; Fax: 425-252-3581.
Web site: http://www.holycrosshs.org
Dr. Kristine Brynildsen-Smith, Prin. Students 192; Lay Teachers 16.

TACOMA. *Bellarmine Preparatory School*. (Coed), 2300 S. Washington, 98405. Tel: 253-752-7701; Fax: 253-756-3887.
Owned by the Jesuit Fathers. Board of Directors: 5 members of the Jesuit order and 12 others. Very Rev. Gerard E. Chapdelaine, S.J., Rector; Mr. Jack Peterson, Pres. In res. Revs. Frederick P. Mayovsky, S.J.; William J. Bichsel, S.J.; James E. Poole, S.J.; Thomas Sexton, S.J.; Francis Walsh, S.J.; Daniel C. Weber, S.J.; Bros. Paul Cawthorne, S.J.; Patrick Flannigan, S.J.; Michael Richards, S.J.; William Yam, S.J., Ministry to Street People, 1419 1/2 G St., 98405. Tel: 206-627-4347. Priests 6; Brothers 4; Sisters 1; Lay Teachers 70; Students 990.

[D] ELEMENTARY SCHOOLS, PRIVATE

SEATTLE. *Villa Academy*. (Grades K-8). (Coed), 5001 N.E. 50th St., 98105. Tel: 206-524-8885.
Web site: www.thevilla.org
Mary Frances Thomas, Head of School. Lay Teachers 47; Students 485.

LACEY. *Holy Family School*. (Grades PreK-8), 2606 Carpenter Rd., S.E., P.O. Box 3700, 98503. Tel: 360-491-7060; Fax: 360-456-3725. Mr. John Oliver, Prin. Lay Teachers 11; Students 184.

[E] CATHOLIC SOCIAL SERVICES OF THE ARCHDIOCESE OF SEATTLE

SEATTLE. *Catholic Community Services of Western Washington*, 100 23rd Ave. S., 98144-2302. Tel: 206-328-5696; Fax: 206-328-5699. Michael L. Reichert, Pres.

Archdiocesan Housing Authority (AHA), 1902 Second Ave., 98101. Tel: 206-448-3360; Fax: 206-448-8495. Michael L. Reichert, Pres.

Josephinum Housing Institute, 1902 Second Ave., 98102. Tel: 206-448-8500. Michael L. Reichert, Pres.

Redmond Elderly Housing Association, 7960-169th Ave, N.E., Redmond, 98053. Tel: 425-869-2424. Michael L. Reichert, Pres.

AHA-Pierce County Association, 112 S. 127th, Tacoma, 98444. Tel: 253-845-3557. Michael L. Reichert, Pres.

St. Martin's Housing Institute, 2008 Westlake Ave., 98121. Tel: 206-340-0410. Michael L. Reichert, Pres.

Catholic Community Services of Western Washington Long Term Care System. Tacoma Office, 1323 S. Yakima St., Tacoma, 98405. Tel: 253-502-2716; Fax: 253-272-6356. Olympia Office, P.O. Box 7845, Olympia, 98507. Tel: 425-704-3394; Fax: 425-357-8823. Seattle Office, P.O. Box 22416, 98122. Tel: 206-322-3637; Fax: 206-328-6850. Gary Church, CCSWW Long Term Care Dir.

Catholic Community Services Northwest. Bellingham Office, P.O. Box 5704, Bellingham, 98227. Iowa St. Location. Tel: 360-733-5800; Fax: 360-676-0778. Douglas St. Location. Tel: 360-733-5804; Fax: 360-647-0302. Everett Office, 1918 Everett Ave., Everett, 98201. Tel: 425-259-9188; Fax: 425-252-7599. Thomas MacIntyre, Agency Dir.

Catholic Community Services of King County, 100-23rd Ave. S., 98144-2302. Tel: 206-323-6336; (TDD: 328-5646); Fax: 206-324-4835. Josephine Tamayo Murray, Agency Dir.

Catholic Community Services Southwest, 1323 S. Yakima St., Tacoma, 98405. Tel: 253-383-3697; Fax: 253-502-2750. Eugene Matsusaka, Agency Dir.

[F] DAY CARE CENTERS

SEATTLE. *Martin Luther King. Jr., Day Home Center*, 1855 S Ln., 98144. Tel: 206-328-5670. Mr. Michael L. Koetje, Dir.

Our Place Day Care, 717 20th Ave. S., 98144. Tel: 206-328-5724. Terri Yaffe, Dir.

EVERETT. *Child Space*, 10110 19th Ave. S.E., #R100, 98208. Tel: 206-316-0728; Fax: 206-337-6586. Sherrie Winicky, Dir.

OLYMPIA. *St. Mike's Tikes*, 1010 Eastside St., 98501. Tel: 360-943-3080. Marsha Brown, Dir.

POULSBO. *St. Olaf's Daycare*, P.O. Box 907, 98370. Tel: 360-779-5791; Fax: 360-598-5888. Doreen Valverde, Dir.

[G] GENERAL HOSPITALS

SEATTLE. *Providence Seattle Medical Center*, 500 17th Ave., Box 34008, 98124. Tel: 206-320-2000.
Web site: www.proups.org
For a complete listing, refer to the Hospitals section.

BELLINGHAM. *St. Joseph Hospital*, 2901 Squalicum Pkwy., 98225. Tel: 360-734-5400; Fax: 360-738-6393
For a complete listing, refer to the Hospitals section.

CENTRALIA. *Providence Centralia Hospital*, 914 S. Scheuber Rd., 98531. Tel: 360-736-2803
For a complete listing, refer to the Hospitals section.

EVERETT. *Providence General Medical Center*, 14th & Colby, P.O. Box 1147, 98206. Tel: 206-261-2000
For a complete listing, refer to the Hospitals section.

FEDERAL WAY. *St. Francis Hospital of Federal Way*, 3415 9th Ave. S., 98003. Tel: 206-927-9700; 838-9700
For a complete listing, refer to the Hospitals section.

LAKEWOOD. *St. Clare Hospital*, 11315 Bridgeport Way S.W., 98499. Tel: 206-588-1711; Fax: 206-584-3001
For a complete listing, refer to the Hospitals section.

LONGVIEW. *Peace Health, St. John Medical Center*, 1614 E. Kessler Blvd., 98632. Tel: 360-423-1530; Fax: 360-414-7550
For a complete listing, refer to the Hospitals section.

OLYMPIA. *Providence St. Peter Hospital*, 413 Lilly Rd., N.E., 98506. Tel: 360-491-9480
For a complete listing, refer to the Hospitals section.

TACOMA. *St. Joseph Medical Center*, 1717 S. J St., 98401-2197. Tel: 253-627-4101
For a complete listing, refer to the Hospitals section.

[H] HOMES FOR CHILDREN

BELLINGHAM. *The Martin Center*, 2806 Douglas, 98225. Tel: 206-733-5804
For a complete listing, refer to the Special Care Facilities section.

[I] NURSING HOMES

SEATTLE. *Providence Mount St. Vincent*, 4831 35th Ave. S.W., 98126. Tel: 206-937-3700; Fax: 206-938-8999
For a complete listing, refer to the Special Care Facilities section.

ISSAQUAH. *Providence Marianwood*, 3725 Providence Point Dr., S.E., 98027. Tel: 425-391-2800; Fax: 425-391-5440
For a complete listing, refer to the Special Care Facilities section.

[J] HOSPICES

SEATTLE. *Providence Home Services*, 425 Pontius Ave., N., Ste. 300, 98109. Tel: 206-320-4848
For a complete listing, refer to the Special Care Facilities section.

EVERETT. *Providence Home Care and Hospice of Snohomish County*, 2731 Wetmore Ave., #520, 98201.

Tel: 206-261-4800
For a complete listing, refer to the Special Care Facilities section.

OLYMPIA. *Providence Mother Joseph Care Center*, 3333 Ensign Rd., N.E., 98506. Tel: 360-493-4900; Fax: 360-493-4948
For a complete listing, refer to the Special Care Facilities section.

Providence Sound Home Care and Hospice, 3706 Griffin Ln., S.E., 98501. Tel: 800-869-7062; 360-459-8311
For a complete listing, refer to the Special Care Facilities section.

[K] RESIDENCES FOR ELDERLY OR DISABLED

SEATTLE. *Chancery Place*, 910 Marion, 98104. Tel: 206-343-9415
For a complete listing, refer to the Special Care Facilities section.

The Franciscan, 15237 21st Ave. S.W., 98166. Tel: 206-431-8001
For a complete listing, refer to the Special Care Facilities section.

The Josephinum, 1902 2nd Ave., 98101. Tel: 206-448-8500
For a complete listing, refer to the Special Care Facilities section.

Providence Mount St. Vincent, 4831 35th Ave. S., 98126. Tel: 206-937-3700
For a complete listing, refer to the Special Care Facilities section.

Vincent House, 1423 First Ave., 98101. Tel: 206-682-9307
For a complete listing, refer to the Special Care Facilities section.

The Westlake, 2008 Westlake Ave., 98121. Tel: 206-340-0410
For a complete listing, refer to the Special Care Facilities section.

BELLEVUE. *Champion House*, 1800 145th Pl. S.E., 98007. Tel: 206-644-4477
For a complete listing, refer to the Special Care Facilities section.

Elbert House, 16000 N.E. 8th St., 98008. Tel: 206-747-5111
For a complete listing, refer to the Special Care Facilities section.

Halcyon, 1200 134th Ave. N.E., 98005. Tel: 206-643-780; Fax: 206-746-0438
For a complete listing, refer to the Special Care Facilities section.

BOTHELL. *Franciscan Health System West dba FHS Care Center at Bothell*, 10909 N.E. 185th St., 98011. Tel: 206-486-7174; 483-9905; Fax: 206-487-1313
For a complete listing, refer to the Special Care Facilities section.

CHEHALIS. *Providence Place*, 350 S.E. Washington Ave., 98532. Tel: 360-740-8389
For a complete listing, refer to the Special Care Facilities section.

REDMOND. *Emma McRedmond Manor*, 7960 169th N.E., 98052. Tel: 206-869-2424
For a complete listing, refer to the Special Care Facilities section.

TACOMA. *Franciscan Health System West dba FHS Care Center at Tacoma*, 6220 S. Alaska, 98408. Tel: 253-473-2273
For a complete listing, refer to the Special Care Facilities section.

Norm Fournier Court, 112 S. 127th, 98444. Tel: 253-531-5087
For a complete listing, refer to the Special Care Facilities section.

TUMWATER. *Tumwater Apartments*, 5701 6th Ave., S.W., 98501. Tel: 206-352-4321
For a complete listing, refer to the Special Care Facilities section.

[L] SOCIAL SERVICES

SEATTLE. *Catholic Seamen's Club*, 2330 1st Ave., 98121. Tel: 206-441-4773. Rev. Anthony J. Haycock, Chap., St. Mary Church, 611 20th Ave. S., 98144. Tel: 206-324-7100.

Providence Hospitality House, P.O. Box 22382, 98122. Tel: 206-322-2107. Sisters of Providence - Pariseau Association.

St. Francis House, 169 12th Ave., 98122. Tel: 206-621-0945. Third Order of St. Francis, Sponsor. Mary Lou Newman, Admin.

Sojourner Place, P.O. Box 95892, 98105. Tel: 206-545-4200. Sisters of Providence - Pariseau Association.

AUBURN. *Store and Workshop*, 926 Auburn Way N., 98002. Tel: 206-833-0400.

BELLEVUE. *Association for Catholic Childhood*, 15726 N.E. 4th, 98008. Tel: 425-746-6751. Mrs. Sharon Haggerty Anderson.

Society of St. Vincent de Paul - Archdiocesan Council, 10638 N.E. 13th, 98004. Tel: 425-454-2392. Mrs. Patricia A. Meehan, Pres.

Society of St. Vincent de Paul District - Council of Seattle Area, 5950 4th Ave. S., Seattle, 98108-3208. Tel: 206-767-6449. Mrs. Maureen Allenback, Pres.

Society of St. Vincent de Paul - Stores. No. 1, 17712 15th Ave. N.E., Seattle, 98155. Tel: 206-364-1492. No. 2, 9835 16th Ave., S.W., Seattle, 98106. Tel: 206-763-2130. No. 3, 13445 1st Ave., S., Seattle, 98166. Tel: 206-243-6370. No. 4, 2825 Sunset Blvd., N.E., Renton, 98056. Tel: 425-226-9426. No. 5, 5950 4th Ave. S., Seattle, 98108-3208. Tel: 206-767-3835. Mr. Donald Stephens, Gen. Mgr., No. 6, 4501 Tolt Ave., S., Carnation, 98014.

BREMERTON. *St. Vincent dePaul Assistance Office*, 1137 N. Callow, 98312. Tel: 360-479-7017. Thrift Store, 1117 N. Callow, 98312. Tel: 360-377-2929.

EVERETT. *Society of St. Vincent de Paul*, Council of Snohomish County, 5303 Evergreen Way, 98203. Tel: 206-355-3525; Fax: 206-513-6051. Mr. Chuck Seider, Pres.; Mr. William Cramer, Exec. Dir., Store, 6430 S. Broadway, 98203. Tel: 206-355-3504; 3505.

MANCHESTER. *Society of St. Vincent de Paul and Related Stores*, District Council of Olympic Peninsula, Box 24. 203 Grant Rd., Sequim, 98382. Tel: 360-683-6097.

OLYMPIA. *Sunshine House*, 413 N. Lilly Rd., 98506. Tel: 206-493-7900. Legal Title: *Sisters of Providence in Washington*.

TACOMA. *Society of St. Vincent de Paul - Particular Council of Tacoma*, 4009 S. 56th, 98409. Joan Christnacht, Pres.

Society of St. Vincent de Paul Stores and Workshop. No. 1, 4009 S. 56th St., 98409. Tel: 253-474-0519. No. 2, 3805-07 S. Yakima Ave., 98408. Tel: 253-472-7334. No. 3, 113 Meeker W., 98371. Tel: 253-848-5637. St. Vincent de Paul Emergency Office, 4009 S. 56th St., 98409. Tel: 253-472-1783.

[M] MONASTERIES AND RESIDENCES OF PRIESTS AND BROTHERS

SEATTLE. *Congregation of Christian Brothers*. (Irish Christian Brothers), 1021 Columbia St., 98104-2018. Tel: 206-622-2639. Bros. J. Hugh Greenan, C.F.C., Supr.; James R. McDonald, C.F.C.; Jerome A. Heustis, C.F.C.; Robert A. Koppes, C.F.C.; T. Kieran Lawler, C.F.C.; D. Clement Mahoney, C.F.C.; D. Peter Ryan, C.F.C.; G. Gregory Lindeman, C.F.C.; D Dominic Murray, C.F.C.; John A. Pettit, C.F.C.; D. Thomas LeJeune, C.F.C. Brothers 11.

Jesuit Community, 2838 Broadway E., 98102. Tel: 206-324-0329. Revs. L. Paul Fitterer, S.J., Supr.; John J. Ludvik, S.J.; John D. McCluskey, S.J.; Mark D. McGregor, S.J.; Richard D. Perry, S.J.; Joseph W. Conyard, S.J.

Jesuit House, Seattle, 621 17th Ave. E., 98112. Tel: 206-324-7496. Revs. Robert J. Egan, S.J., Supr.; Alexander F. McDonald, S.J.; Joseph P. O'Connell, S.J.; Pasquale M. Spoletini, S.J.; William J. Rimes, S.J.

Maryknoll Fathers, Catholic Foreign Mission Society of America, 958 16th Ave. E., 98112. Tel: 206-322-8831. Revs. Thomas J. Marti, M.M.; Brian V. Allbright, M.M.; Bro. William T. Raible, M.M.

LACEY. *St. Martin's Abbey*. Order of St. Benedict, College, and Novitiate, 98503. Tel: 206-491-4700. Rt. Revs. Neal G. Roth, O.S.B., Abbot & Dir. Vocations; Conrad R. Rausch, O.S.B., Novice Master & Resigned Abbot; Adrian J. Parcher, O.S.B., Resigned Abbot; Very Revs. Urban Feucht, O.S.B., Prior; Nicholas Rausch, O.S.B., Subprior; Revs. Alfred J. Hulscher, O.S.B., Treas. & Dir. Fiscal Affairs; William A. Maat, O.S.B.; Arnold J. Fox, O.S.B.; Luke N. O'Donnell, O.S.B.; Killian Malvey, O.S.B.; Richard S. Cebula, O.S.B.; David W. Prebula, O.S.B.; Michael Feeney, O.S.B.; Clement H. Pangratz, O.S.B.; Timothy J. Lamm, O.S.B.; Placidus G. Reischman, O.S.B.; Thaddaeus R. Arledge, O.S.B.; George J. Seidel, O.S.B.; Alfred J. Hulscher, O.S.B.; Dominic D. Hahn, O.S.B.; Kieran P. Cunningham, O.S.B.; Thomas R. Park, O.S.B.; Terence Wagner, O.S.B.; Justin D. McCreedy, O.S.B.; Gerard D. Kirsch, O.S.B.; John Scott, O.S.B.; Killian Malvey, O.S.B.; Edward R. Receconi, O.S.B., Junior Master; Harvey J. Wingfield, O.S.B.; Benedict L. Auer, O.S.B.; Sean R. Malvey, O.S.B. Priests 29; Brothers 19.

[N] CONVENTS AND RESIDENCES FOR SISTERS

SEATTLE. *St. Joseph's Carmelite Monastery*. 2215 N.E. 147th, Shoreline, 98155. Sr. Michael Marie, O.C.D., Prioress. Discalced Carmelites 8; In Formation 2.

St. Joseph's Residence, 4800 37th Ave. S.W., 98126. Tel: 206-937-4600. Sr. Shirley Smith, S.P., Supr.; Rev. John A. Jennings, Chap. Sisters of Providence 54; Dominican Sisters 5; Daughters of Mary 2; Benedictines 2; Carmelites 1.

Sisters of St. Joseph of Peace, 1104 21st Ave., E., 98112. Tel: 206-324-1529. Sisters 5.

BELLEVUE. *St. Mary's House of Studies*, 1663 Killarney Way, P.O. Box 1763, 98009. Tel: 425-451-1833; Fax: 425-462-9760. Sr. Elizabeth Ann Brennan. Sisters of St. Joseph of Peace 40.

Our Lady's Province.

St. Mary's Provincialate, 1663 Killarney Way, Box 248, 98009-0248. Tel: 425-451-1770. Sr. Kathleen Pruitt, C.S.J.P., Prov. Sisters of St. Joseph of Peace, Our Lady Province.

EDMONDS. *Rosary Heights*. (Motherhouse of the Dominican Sisters Congregation of Holy Cross), 23120 Woodway Park Rd., P.O. Box 280, 98020. Tel: 425-542-7511. Sr. Judy Byron, O.P., Prioress.

LACEY. *St. Placid Priory*, 500 College St., N.E., 98516. Tel: 360-438-1771. Sr. Sharon McDonald, O.S.B., Prioress. Sisters of St. Benedict 30.

SHAW ISLAND. *Franciscan Sisters of the Eucharist*, P.O. Box 455, 98286. Mother Helen Jean Brinkman, F.S.E., Supr. Sisters 4.

Our Lady of the Rock Priory. (Cloistered), P.O. Box 425, 98286. Benedictine Nuns. Rev. Mother Therese Critchley, O.S.B., Supr. Professed Nuns 7; Novices 1.

TACOMA. *III Order of St. Dominic*, Tacoma Dominican Center, 935 Fawcett Ave., S., 98402. Tel: 253-272-9688. Sr. Agnes Huck, O.P., Pres.
(Congregation of St. Thomas Aquinas), Sisters of Saint Dominic of Tacoma Charitable Trust - Tacoma Dominican Center.

Sister of St. Francis of Philadelphia, St. Ann Retirement Convent, 6602 S. Alaska St., 98408. Tel: 253-474-8319; 475-0791; Fax: 253-474-0734. Serra House, 6602 S. Alaska St., 98408. Tel: 253-474-8026. Evergreen House, 6602 S. Alaska St., 98408. Tel: 253-474-9803. Olympus House, 6602 S. Alaska St., 98408. Tel: 253-474-8573. Marian House, 6802 47th St. W., 98466. Tel: 253-564-1816. LaVerna, 701 North K St. #12, 98403. Tel: 253-272-2232.

[O] RETREAT HOUSES, CONFERENCE CENTERS AND CAMPS

SEATTLE. *Camp Don Bosco*, Contact C.Y.O., 910 Marion, 98104. Tel: 206-382-4562.

Still Point, 1111 Harvard Ave., 98122. Tel: 206-322-8006. Sr. Carol Deschane, Dir.

EDMONDS. *Dominican Reflection Center*, 23120 Woodway Park Rd., P.O. Box 280, 98020. Tel: 425-542-3740; 546-6561. Co-Directors: Sr. Kathleen Logan, O.P.; Sr. Mary White, O.P.

FEDERAL WAY. *Palisades Retreat House*, Palisades Retreat Association, P.O. Box 3739, 98063. Tel: 206-838-9583; 927-9621 (Tacoma); Fax: 206-927-9624. Rev. Richard Ochiltree, C.Ss.R., Dir.; Bro. William Roberts, C.Ss.R., Admin.; Rev. Raymond Maiser, C.S.Sp., Dir.

MONROE-DUVALL. *Camp Hamilton*, 25405 Lake Frontal Rd., 98272. Contact C.Y.O., 910 Marion, Seattle, 98104. Tel: 360-382-4562.

TOLEDO. *St. Mary Conference Center*, 107 Spencer Rd., 98591. Tel: 360-864-6464; Fax: 360-864-6465.

[P] NEWMAN CENTERS

SEATTLE. *Office of Campus and Young Adult Ministry*, 910 Marion St., 98104. Tel: 206-527-5072. Rev. Thomas De Man, O.P., Dir., Seattle University, Campus Ministry, Broadway & E. Madison, 98122. Tel: 206-626-5900. Mary Romer Cline, Dir., University of Washington, Catholic Newman Center, 4502 20th Ave. N.E., 98105. Tel: 206-527-5072. Rev. Thomas De Man, O.P., Dir., Western Washington University (Bellingham). Campus Christian Ministry. 102 Highland Dr., Bellingham, 98225. Tel: 206-733-3400. Shirley Osterhaus, St. Martin's College (Lacey). Campus Ministry, Lacey, 98503. Tel: 360-491-4700.

[Q] MISCELLANEOUS

SEATTLE. *Catholic Hospital Ministries*, 910 Marion St., 98104. Revs. Brian Snyder; Mark Stehly; Ross Fewing. Hospitals served include: Harborview, Virginia Mason, Fred Hutchinson Cancer Center, Swedish Medical Center.

CHANNEL Program, 9641 20th Ave., S.W., 98106. Tel: 206-768-9250; Fax: 206-768-9253. Stephen Hueffed, Dir.

Cursillo Movement, P.O. Box 68803, 98168-0803. Tel: 206-361-9901. Mr. Ed Schaefer. Tel: 206-361-5579.

Intercommunity Housing, 150 12th Ave., #3, 98122. Tel: 206-223-1051. Sr. Charlotte Davenport, C.S.J.P., Contact Person.

Intercommunity Housing Ferndale, 150 12th Ave., 98122. Tel: 206-223-1051; Fax: 206-621-7046. Sr. Charlotte Davenport, C.S.J.P., Pres./Exec. Dir.

Intercommunity Ministry Volunteer Program, 150 12th, #3, 98122. Tel: 206-442-4268. Sr. Honora Notty, O.P., Pres.

**Intercommunity Peace & Justice Center*, 150 12th Ave. #3, 98122. Tel: 206-223-1138; 328-5307. Sr. Linda Haydock, S.N.J.M., Exec. Dir.

Intercommunity Properties, 150 12th Ave., 98122. Tel: 206-223-1051. Sr. Charlotte Davenport, C.S.J.P., Exec. Dir.

The Rosary, P.O. Box 33762, 98133. Mrs. Pauline Coveny, Pres.

St. Mary's Food Bank, 611 20th Ave., S., 98144. Tel: 206-324-0050. Bonnie Baker, Dir.

Seattle, Vietnamese Catholic Center, 1230 E. Fir St., 98122. Tel: 206-325-5626. Rev. Phuong Duc Tran (Vietnam).

Sisters of Providence Health System, 520 Pike Tower, P.O. Box 11038, 98111-9038. Tel: 206-464-3355. Sisters of Providence in Oregon, Sisters of Providence in Washington, Sisters of Providence in California, Sisters of Providence Pariseau Association, and Provincial Offices for Sacred Heart Province. Sr. Roberta Rorke, S.P., Prov. Supr. For detailed information on corporate holdings for the Sisters of Providence, please refer to Religious Institutes of Women in the back of the directory.

Washington State Catholic Conference, 508-2nd Ave. W., 98119. Tel: 206-301-0556. Sr. Sharon Park, O.P., Exec. Dir.

BELLEVUE. *Sisters of St. Joseph of Peace, Our Lady Province, Charitable Trust*, 1663 Killarney Way, P.O. Box 248, 98009-0248. Tel: 206-451-1770. Sheila Lemieux, C.S.J.P., Prov. Leader.

Sisters of St. Joseph of Peace, PeaceHealth, Corporate Center, 15325 S.E. 30th Pl., Ste. 300, 98007. Tel: 206-747-1711; Fax: 206-649-3825. Sr. Monica F. Heeran, C.S.J.P., Pres.

EDMONDS. *Edmonds Dominicans, Holy Angels Alumnae Assoc.* 942 N.W. 60th, Seattle, 98107. Tel: 206-782-1181.

LACONNER. *Skagit Valley Regional Ministry*, P.O. Box 1260, 98257. Tel: 360-336-6622; Fax: 360-424-8838. Rev. Paul A. Magnano.

TACOMA. *Catholic Pastoral Care-Hospital Tacoma Ministry*, 911 S. Fifth St., 98405. Rev. Michael E. Walsh, S.J., Dir.

Pierce County Association of Catholic Educators (PACE), 2300 S. Washington, 98405. Tel: 253-756-7830.

Pierce County Deanery, 1001 N. J St., 98403. Tel: 253-383-3496. Deacon Del Hoover, Admin.

VANCOUVER. *Vancouver Oratorian Community*, 4723 N.W. Franklin St., 98663. Tel: 360-696-3725. Revs. Robert Dell, C.O.; Clarence Jones, C.O.

RELIGIOUS INSTITUTES OF MEN REPRESENTED IN THE ARCHDIOCESE

For further details refer to the corresponding bracketed number in the Religious Institutes of Men or Women section.

[0200]—*Benedictine Monks*. (Olympia, WA).—O.S.B.
[0310]—*Congregation of Christian Brothers*. (Western U.S.).—C.F.C.
[0260]—*Discalced Carmelite Friars*. (California Prov.).—O.C.D.
[0520]—*Franciscan Friars*. (Prov. of Santa Barbara).—O.F.M.
[0690]—*Jesuit Fathers and Brothers*. (Oregon Province).—S.J.
[0800]—*Maryknoll*.—M.M.
[0910]—*Oblates of Mary Immaculate*. (Western Province).—O.M.I.
[]—*Oratorian Community*.
[0430]—*Order of Preachers (Dominicans)*. (San Francisco, CA).—O.P.
[1070]—*Redemptorist Fathers*. (Oakland Province).—C.SS.R.
[1250]—*Society of Christ*. (American-Canadian Prov.).—S.Ch.
[0370]—*Society of St. Columban*.—S.S.C.
[1290]—*Society of the Priests of Saint Sulpice*.—S.S.

RELIGIOUS INSTITUTES OF WOMEN REPRESENTED IN THE ARCHDIOCESE

[0180]—*Benedictine Nuns of the Primitive Observance*.—O.S.B.
[0230]—*Benedictine Sisters of Pontifical Jurisdiction*. (Lacey, WA; Duluth, MN).—O.S.B.
[]—*Carmelite*.—O.L.
[]—*Congregation of Divine Province*.—C.D.P.
[2100]—*Congregation of the Humility of Mary*.—C.H.M.
[1920]—*Congregation of the Sisters of the Holy Cross*.—C.S.C.
[1780]—*Congregation of the Sisters of the Third Order of St. Francis of Perpetual Adoration*. (Western Region).—F.S.P.A.
[0420]—*Discalced Carmelite Nuns*.—O.C.D.
[1070-03]—*Dominican Sisters*. (Edmonds).—O.P.
[1070-04]—*Dominican Sisters*. (Tacoma).—O.P.
[1070-13]—*Dominican Sisters*. (San Rafael).—O.P.
[1070-19]—*Dominican Sisters*. (Sinsinawa).—O.P.
[1070-20]—*Dominican Sisters*. (Adrian).—O.P.
[1070-21]—*Dominican Sisters*. (Houston).—O.P.
[]—*Franciscan Sisters of Rochester*.—O.S.F.
[]—*Franciscan Sisters of St. Mary of the Angels*.—F.S.M.A.
[1250]—*The Institute of the Franciscan Sisters of the Eucharist*.—F.S.E.
[2860]—*Missionary Sisters of the Sacred Heart*.—M.S.C.
[1830]—*Religious of the Good Shepherd*.—R.G.S.
[4070]—*Religious of the Sacred Heart*.—R.S.C.J.
[]—*Religious Sisters of Mercy*.—R.S.M.
[2970]—*School Sisters of Notre Dame*.—S.S.N.D.
[3500]—*Servants of the Blessed Sacrament*.—S.B.S.
[]—*Sisters for Christian Community*.—S.F.C.C.
[0480]—*Sisters of Charity of Leavenworth, Kansas*.—S.C.L.
[0430]—*Sisters of Charity of the Blessed Virgin Mary*.—B.V.M.
[3000]—*Sisters of Notre Dame De Namur*.—S.N.D.deN.
[3350]—*Sisters of Providence*.—S.P.
[]—*Sisters of Social Service*.—S.S.S.
[1705]—*The Sisters of St. Francis of Assissi*.—O.S.F.
[1630]—*Sisters of St. Francis of Penance and Christian Charity*.—O.S.F.
[1650]—*The Sisters of St. Francis of Philadelphia*.—O.S.F.
[3830-08]—*Sisters of St. Joseph at Cleveland*.—C.S.J.
[3840]—*Sisters of St. Joseph of Carondelet*. (California Prov.).—C.S.J.
[]—*Sisters of St. Joseph of Carondelet*. (St. Paul, MN Prov.).—C.S.J.
[3890]—*Sisters of St. Joseph of Peace*.—C.S.J.P.
[3960]—*Sisters of St. Mary of Oregon*.—S.S.M.O.
[1990]—*Sisters of the Holy Names of Jesus and Mary*.—S.N.J.M.
[]—*Sisters of the Holy Names of Jesus and Mary*. (Oregon Prov.).—S.N.J.M.
[]—*Sisters of the Holy Names of Jesus and Mary*. (California Prov.).—S.N.J.M.

ARCHDIOCESAN CEMETERIES

Central Office: 910 Marion, 98104. Tel: 206-382-9281

SEATTLE. *Calvary*, 5041 35th Ave. N.E., 98105. Tel: 206-522-0996.

Holyrood, 205 N.E. 205th, 98155. Tel: 206-363-8404.

FEDERAL WAY. *Gethsemane*, 37600 Pacific Hwy. S., 98003. Tel: 206-838-2240.

NECROLOGY

✠ Murphy, Most Rev. Thomas J., Archbishop of Seattle. —Died June 26, 1997.
† Bullwinkel, Andrew, Seattle, WA, Christ the King. —Died Oct. 19, 1997.
† Lane, Thomas, (Retired). —Died Aug. 11, 1997.
† Mattie, Rev. Msgr. John G., (Retired). —Died May 6, 1997.
† van Gogh, James, (Retired). —Died Feb. 27, 1997.

Diocese of Shreveport

(Dioecesis Sreveportuensis in Louisiana)

Most Reverend

WILLIAM B. FRIEND, D.D.

Bishop of Shreveport; ordained May 7, 1959; appointed Titular Bishop of Pomaria and Auxiliary Bishop of Alexandria-Shreveport August 31, 1979; ordained Bishop October 30, 1979; appointed Bishop of Alexandria-Shreveport November 23, 1982; installed January 11, 1983; appointed Bishop of Shreveport June 16, 1986. *Address all communications to: Catholic Center, 2500 Line Ave., Shreveport, LA, 71104-3043.* Tel.: 318-222-2006; Fax: 318-222-2080.

Chancery Office: Catholic Center, 2500 Line Ave., Shreveport, LA, 71104-3043. Tel.: 318-222-2006; Fax: 318-222-2080.

Web site address: http://www.dioshpt.org

ESTABLISHED AND CREATED A DIOCESE JUNE 16, 1986.

Comprises the Counties (parishes) of Bienville, Bossier, Caddo, Claiborne, DeSoto, East Carroll, Jackson, Lincoln, Morehouse, Ouachita, Red River, Richland, Sabine, Union, Webster and West Carroll.

For legal titles of parishes and diocesan institutions, consult the Chancery Office.

STATISTICAL OVERVIEW

Personnel	
Bishop	1
Priests: Diocesan Active in Diocese	29
Priests: Active Outside Diocese	4
Priests: Retired, Sick or Absent	8
Number of Diocesan Priests	41
Religious Priests in Diocese	12
Extern Priests in Diocese	4
Ordinations:	
Diocesan Priests	1
Permanent Deacons in Diocese	7
Total Sisters	62
Parishes	
Parishes	31
With Resident Pastor:	
Resident Diocesan Priests	22
Resident Religious Priests	8
Without Resident Pastor:	
Administered by Priests	1
Missions	14
Pastoral Centers	2
Professional Ministry Personnel:	
Sisters	4
Lay Ministers	30
Welfare	
Catholic Hospitals	3
Total Assisted	191,594
Health Care Centers	1
Total Assisted	30,163
Homes for the Aged	1
Total Assisted	132
Day Care and Extended Day Care Centers	1
Total Assisted	130
Specialized Homes	2
Total Assisted	20
Special Centers for Social Services	21
Total Assisted	19,100
Residential Care of Disabled	1
Total Assisted	184
Other Institutions	2
Total Assisted	1,425
Educational	
Diocesan Students in Other Seminaries	4
Total Seminarians	4
High Schools, Diocesan and Parish	2
Total Students	735
Elementary Schools, Diocesan and Parish	10
Total Students	2,407
Catechesis/Religious Education:	
High School Students	751
Elementary Students	2,323
Total Students Under Catholic Instruction	6,220
Teachers in the Diocese:	
Sisters	7
Lay Teachers	210
Vital Statistics	
Receptions into the Church:	
Infant Baptism Totals	521
Adult Baptism Totals	102
Received into Full Communion	318
First Communions	564
Confirmations	641
Marriages:	
Catholic	92
Interfaith	123
Total Marriages	215
Deaths	341
Total Catholic Population	40,436
Total Population	772,938

Vicar General—Rev. Msgr. J. CARSON LACAZE, V.G.

Vicars Forane—Rev. Msgr. EARL V. PROVENZA, V.F., Western Deanery; Very Rev. J. ROBERT INZINA, V.F., Eastern Deanery; Very Rev. WILLIAM H. CAREY, K.C.H.S., Southern Deanery.

Chancery Office—Catholic Center, 2500 Line Ave., Shreveport, 71104-3043. Tel: 318-222-2006; Fax: 318-222-2080.

Chancellor—Sr. MARGARET DAUES, C.S.J., Ph.D.

Archives—Mrs. CHRISTINE RIVERS.

Diocesan Tribunal—2500 Line Ave., Shreveport, 71104-3043. Tel: 318-222-2006; Fax: 318-222-2080.

Judicial Vicar—Rev. PETER B. MANGUM, J.C.L.

Secretary—Ms. PATTY S. WHEELER.

Judges—Rev. PETER B. MANGUM, J.C.L., J.V.; Rev. Msgr. FRANZ GRAEF, S.T.D.; Rev. ROTHELL PRICE, J.C.L.

Defenders of the Bond—Rev. PHILIP F. MICHIELS; Very Rev. WILLIAM H. CAREY, V.F.; Rev. EDMUND A. "LARRY" NIEHOFF.

Promotor of Justice—Very Rev. WILLIAM H. CAREY, V.F.

Advocates—Rev. Msgr. EDMUND J. MOORE; Rev. Msgr. FRANZ GRAEF, S.T.D.

Notaries—PATTY S. WHEELER; DEBBY STEINMILLER.

Corporate Council—Most Rev. WILLIAM B. FRIEND, D.D.; Rev. Msgr. J. CARSON LACAZE, V.G.; Sr. MARGARET DAUES, C.S.J., Ph.D.

College of Consultors—Very Rev. WILLIAM H. CAREY, V.F.; Rev. TIMOTHY C. HURD; Very Rev. J. ROBERT INZINA, V.F.; Rev. JOHN D. KENNEDY; Rev. Msgr. J. CARSON LACAZE, V.G., Ex Officio; Rev. Msgr. EDMUND J. MOORE; Revs. EDMUND A. "LARRY" NIEHOFF; RICHARD NORSWORTHY; ROTHELL PRICE, J.C.L.; Rev. Msgr. EARL V. PROVENZA, V.F.; Rev. WILLIAM SPENCER, O.F.M.

Finance Council—Most Rev. WILLIAM B. FRIEND, D.D.; Rev. Msgr. J. CARSON LACAZE, V.G., Ex Officio; Sr. MARGARET DAUES, C.S.J., Ex Officio; Rev. Msgr. WILLIAM O'HANLON; MARY A. BROWN; DAVID CATTAR; JOAN FISHER; JOHN HUSSEY, Chm.; Dr. JAMES ROBERT MICHAEL; LYNN ROOS; NICHOLAS ROPPOLO; LAWRENCE H. RUSSO, III; WILLIAM STAAB; EALIE THORNTON.

Presbyteral Council—Very Rev. WILLIAM H. CAREY, V.F., Ex Officio; Rev. Msgr. J. CARSON LACAZE, V.G., Ex Officio; Most Rev. WILLIAM B. FRIEND; Rev. TIMOTHY C. HURD; Very Rev. J. ROBERT INZINA, V.F., Ex Officio; Rev. JOHN D. KENNEDY; Rev. PETER B. MANGUM, J.C.L., J.V.; Revs. EDMUND A. "LARRY" NIEHOFF, Chm. RICHARD NORSWORTHY, Ex Officio; ROTHELL PRICE; Rev. Msgr. EARL V. PROVENZA, V.F., Ex Officio; Revs. DAVID T. RICHTER, Vice Chm. WILLIAM SPENCER, O.F.M.; LAVERNE (PIKE) THOMAS, Sec.

Diocesan Pastoral Council—Dr. JOSEPH FELDHAUS, Monroe; Mr. DAVID FOLEY, Shreveport; Mrs. SOPHIE FONSECA, Monroe; Mr. TOM GUANELLA, Bossier City; Mrs. LINDA HOLYFIELD, Monroe; Mrs. BESSIE MCKINNEY, Grambling; Mrs. ALICE PRUDHOMME, Mansfield; Mrs. LUCY A. RIVERO, Shreveport; Mr. CHARLES SCOTT, Monroe; Mr. STEVE VASKO, Keithville; Mrs. TAMMY YATCKO, Minden; Dr. ELIZABETH ZIPPI, Shreveport; Sr. MARGARET DAUES, Shreveport.

Priests' Retirement Board—Rev. Msgr. J. CARSON LACAZE, V.G., Chm.; Rev. EARL G. BEAULIEU; WADE DUPUIS; Very Rev. J. ROBERT INZINA, V.F.; Rev. EDMUND A. "LARRY" NIEHOFF; NICHOLAS ROPPOLO; Rev. Msgr. EARL V. PROVENZA, V.F.; Rev. DANIEL M. WALSH.

The Catholic Foundation of North-Central Louisiana, Inc.—P.O. Box 8021, Alexandria, 71306-1021. Tel: 318-487-9222.

Diocesan Offices and Directors

Black Catholic Commission—Rev. ROTHELL PRICE, Chap., *Catholic Center, 2500 Line Ave., Shreveport, 71104-3043.* Tel: 318-222-2006.

Business Affairs—Mr. E. MICHAEL SCHOFIELD, C.P.A., *Catholic Center, 2500 Line Ave., Shreveport, 71104-3043.* Tel: 318-222-2006.

Campaign for Human Development—Address Communications to: Office of Community and Family Life Ministries: *Catholic Center, 2500 Line Ave., Shreveport, 71104-3043.* Tel: 318-222-2006.

Campus Ministry—Sr. EILEEN MCGRORY, S.C., Coord., *Catholic Center, 2500 Line Ave., Shreveport, 71104-3043.* Tel: 318-222-2006.

Catechetics and Worship—Mrs. MARY MCGILL, M.A., *Catholic Center, 2500 Line Ave., Shreveport, 71104-3043.* Tel: 318-222-2006.

Catholic Relief Services—Address Communications to: Office of the Vicar General; Very Rev. WILLIAM H. CAREY, V.F., *Catholic Center, 2500 Line Ave., Shreveport, 71104-3043.* Tel: 318-222-2006.

Cemeteries—Mr. E. MICHAEL SCHOFIELD, C.P.A., *Catholic Center, 2500 Line Ave., Shreveport, 71104-3043.* Tel: 318-222-2006.

Censor of Books—Rev. Msgr. FRANZ GRAEF, S.T.D.

Charismatic Movement—Mr. JOHN J. GUERRIERO, JR., *2316 Sauvelle Dr., Monroe, 71201-2953.* Mr. THOMAS HARLAN, *9536 Pitch Pine, Shreveport, 71118-4527.*

Church Vocations—Revs. ROTHELL PRICE, Dir. TIMOTHY C. HURD, Assoc. Dir., *2500 Line Ave., Shreveport, 71104-3043.* Tel: 318-222-2006.

Church Vocations Board—Mr. LAWRENCE W. PETTIETTE, JR., Chm.; Revs. ROTHELL PRICE, Dir. TIMOTHY C. HURD, Assoc. Dir. CHARLES GLORIOSO; PHILIP F. MICHIELS; Sr. MAVIS CHAMPAGNE, O.L.S.; Sr. EILEEN MCGRORY, S.C.; Mrs. SHARON CHANEY; Mrs. ANNE JONES; Mr. DON ANZELMO; Mr. SAM GILLIAM; Mr. BRIAN D. LANDRY; Mr. MACK MILES, JR. Ex-Officio Member: Most Rev. WILLIAM B. FRIEND; Rev. Msgr. J. CARSON LACAZE, V.G.

Continuing Education for the Clergy—Rev. RICHARD NORSWORTHY, Dir., *St. Jude Church, 3800 Viking Dr. East, Bossier City, 71111-7403.* Tel: 318-746-2508.

Development and Public Relations—Mr. JOHN MARK WILLCOX, Dir., *Catholic Center, 2500 Line Ave., Shreveport, 71104-3043.* Tel: 318-222-2006.

Diocesan Publications—Ms. POLLY VOORHIES, Editor, *Catholic Center, 2500 Line Ave., Shreveport, 71104-3043.* Tel: 318-222-2006.

Ecumenism and Interreligious Affairs—Rev. Msgr. CARSON J. LACAZE, V.G., *Our Lady of the Holy Rosary Church, 1755 Corbitt St., Shreveport, 71108-3098.* Tel: 318-636-3530.

Community and Family Life Ministries—Vacant, *Catholic Center, 2500 Line Ave., Shreveport, 71104-3043.* Tel: 318-222-2006.

Greco Institute—Mr. DONALD R. EMGE, Ph.D., *Catholic Center, 2500 Line Ave., Shreveport, 71104-3043.* Tel: 318-222-2006.

Health Ministry—Very Rev. WILLIAM H. CAREY, V.F., Coord., *St. John the Baptist Church, 1130 E. San Antonio Ave., Many, 71449-3226.* Tel: 318-256-5689.

Hispanic Community—Mrs. ELISA MILAZZO, Coord., *Catholic Center, 2500 Line Ave., Shreveport, 71104-3043.* Tel: 318-222-2006. Rev. RIGOBERTO BETANCURT, O.S.M., Chap.

Holy Childhood—Mr. GARY GELO, M.E., Contact Person, *Catholic Center, 2500 Line Ave., Shreveport, 71104-3043.* Tel: 318-222-2006.

Human Resources—Mrs. CHRISTIE WEEKS, Dir., *Catholic Center, 2500 Line Ave., Shreveport, 71104-3043.* Tel: 318-222-2006; Fax: 318-222-2080.

Information Systems Management—Ms. PATRICIA PILLORS, Dir., *Catholic Center, 2500 Line Ave., Shreveport, 71104-3043.* Tel: 318-222-2006.

Jail-Prison Ministry—Rev. DANIEL WALSH, Coord., *St. Clement Church, 819 N. Pine St., Vivian, 71082-3354.* Tel: 318-375-2789.

Diocesan Liturgy Commission—JODI TOLIVER; SUSAN GIBSON; MICHAEL KENNEY; Rev. ROTHELL PRICE; JO KAUFMAN; Rev. DAVID RICHTER; MARY CUNNINGHAM; ARCHIE PERRY; Rev. PHILIP F. MICHIELS; CAROLE MOON; JIM SPANN; PAM FOWLER; VONNY JAUBERT; DEBI POINT; RON MORRIS; JOE JARZABEK; MARY MCGILL, Ex Officio.

Mission Director—Very Rev. WILLIAM H. CAREY, V.F., *Catholic Center, 2500 Line Ave., Shreveport, 71104-3043.* Tel: 318-222-2006.

Permanent Deacon Coordinator—Rev. PHILIP F. MICHIELS, *St. Mary of the Pines Church, 1050 Bert Kouns Industrial Loop, Shreveport, 71118-3499.* Tel: 318-687-5121. Deacon CLARY NASH, Dean Permanent Deacons, *St. John Berchmans Cathedral, 939 Jordan St., Shreveport, 71101-4391.* Tel: 318-221-5296.

Propagation of the Faith—Very Rev. WILLIAM H. CAREY, V.F., *Catholic Center, 2500 Line Ave., Shreveport, 71104-3043.* Tel: 318-222-2006.

Religious Education—Mrs. MARY MCGILL, M.A., Dir., *Catholic Center, 2500 Line Ave., Shreveport, 71104-3043.* Tel: 318-222-2006.

Religious-Advisory Council—Sr. ANNA MARIA IANNETTI, O.L.S.

Schools—Mr. GARY GELO, M.E., Supt., *Catholic Center, 2500 Line Ave., Shreveport, 71104-3043.* Tel: 318-222-2006.

Child Nutrition Program—Mrs. LAVON G. PRUITT, M.S., R.D., *2500 Line Ave., Shreveport, 71104-3043.* Tel: 318-222-2055.

Scouting—Rev. DAVID RICHTER, Coord., *St. Joseph Church, P.O. Box 8, Zwolle, 71486-0008.* Tel: 318-645-9852; 645-6155.

Spanish-Speaking Ministers—Rev. Msgr. C. MURRAY CLAYTON, *Sacred Heart of Jesus Church, P.O. Box 19467, Shreveport, 71149-0467.* Revs. RIGOBERTO BETANCURT, O.S.M., *St. Joseph Church, P.O. Box 1203, Monroe, 71210-1203.* JUAN GARCIA, *Cathedral of St. John Berchmans, 939 Jordan St., Shreveport, 71101-4391.*

St. Catherine Community Center—Mr. ROBERT ALFORD, Dir., *331 E. 71st St., Shreveport, 71106-4305.* Tel: 318-865-9817.

St. Vincent de Paul Society—Mrs. SHEILA FRITZ, Contact Person, *Catholic Center, 2500 Line Ave., Shreveport, 71104-3043.* Tel: 318-222-2006.

The Beginning Experience—MILDRED COLLINS, Shreveport. Tel: 318-861-3878.

Youth and Young Adult Ministry—Sr. EILEEN MCGRORY, S.C., Dir., *Catholic Center, 2500 Line Ave., Shreveport, 71104-3043.* Tel: 318-222-2006; Fax: 318-222-2080.

CLERGY, PARISHES, MISSIONS AND PAROCHIAL SCHOOLS

CITY OF SHREVEPORT
(Caddo Parish)

1—ST. JOHN BERCHMANS CATHEDRAL (1902), Revs. Juan F. Garcia; Charles Glorioso; Deacon Clary Nash. In res., Revs. Rothell Price; Earl Johnson, S.J.
Res., 939 Jordan St., 71101-4391. Tel: 318-221-5296; Fax: 318-221-8076.
School—Tel: 318-221-6005; Fax: 318-425-0648. Miss Marie R. Rinaudo, Prin.
Lay Teachers 21; Students 307.
Catechesis/Religious Programs—947 Jordan St., 71101. Tel: 318-424-2317.
Students 141.

2—HOLY TRINITY (1856), Rev. Msgr. William O'Hanlon.
Res., 315 Marshall St., P.O. Box 144, 71161-0144. Tel: 318-221-5990.

3—OUR LADY OF THE BLESSED SACRAMENT (1923) (African American), Rev. Richard K. Pusch.
Res., 1558 Buena Vista St., 71101-2448. Tel: 318-222-3790.
School—2932 Murphy St., 71103-2241. Tel: 318-222-5051. Dr. Thomas C. Archey, Prin.
Sisters of the Holy Spirit and Mary Immaculate 2; Lay Teachers 13; Students 272.

4—OUR LADY OF THE HOLY ROSARY (1952), Rev. Msgr. J. Carson LaCaze.
Res., 1755 Corbitt St., 71108-3098. Tel: 318-636-3530; Fax: 318-632-4955.
School—1730 Cox St., 71108. Tel: 318-636-3826; Fax: 318-636-9123. Sr. Sandra Norsworthy, O.L.S., Prin.
Sisters of Our Lady of Sorrows 5; Lay Teachers 16; Students 197.

5—SACRED HEART OF JESUS (1966), Rev. Msgr. C. Murray Clayton.
Res., 4736 Lyba St., P.O. Box 19467, 71149-0467. Tel: 318-635-2121; Fax: 318-635-5226.

6—ST. CATHERINE OF SIENA (1938), Rev. William Spencer, O.F.M.
Res., 331 E. 71st St., 71106-4305. Tel: 318-868-6506; Fax: 318-861-6177.

7—ST. ELIZABETH ANN SETON (1984), Revs. LaVerne Thomas, III; Mark A. Watson; Deacon William Long.
Res., 522 E. Flournoy-Lucas Rd., 71115-2073. Tel: 318-798-1887; Fax: 318-797-7302.

8—ST. JOSEPH (1949), Revs. Richard J. Lombard; Curtis Woods; Karl J. Daigle.
Res., 228 Patton Ave., P.O. Box 5188, 71135-5188. Tel: 318-865-3581; Fax: 318-865-5125.
School—1210 Anniston Ave., 71135. Tel: 318-865-3585; Fax: 318-868-1859. Mrs. Carmen Heflin, Prin.
Lay Teachers 36; Students 530.
Catechesis/Religious Programs—Students 262.

9—ST. MARY OF THE PINES (1973), Rev. Philip F. Michiels. In res., Rev. Andre McGrath, O.F.M.
Res., 1050 Bert Kouns Industrial Loop, 71118-3499. Tel: 318-687-5121; Fax: 318-687-5124. [CEM]
Catechesis/Religious Programs—Students 360.
Mission—Stonewall, DeSoto Parish, St. Ann, Hwy. 171, Stonewall, 71078. Tel: 318-925-0591.

10—ST. PIUS X (1955), Rev. John D. Pardue.
Res., 4300 N. Market St., 71107-2953. Tel: 318-222-2165.

11—ST. THERESA. Consolidated with St. John Berchmans Cathedral.

OUTSIDE THE CITY OF SHREVEPORT

Bastrop, Morehouse Parish, St. Joseph (1943), Rev. Joseph Robert Inzina.
Res., 217 Harrington Ave., 71220-3025. Tel: 318-281-4327. [CEM]
School—Tel: 318-281-5894. Angie Druhan, Prin.
Lay Teachers 10; Students 181.
Our Lady Help of Christians. Consolidated with St. Joseph, Bastrop.

Bossier City, Bossier Parish, Christ the King (1939), Rev. Msgr. Earl V. Provenza; Rev. Ron Matthews (ALX); Deacon David Ludke. In res., Rev. Msgr. Norman Buvens.
Res., 425 McCormick St., 71111-4692. Tel: 318-221-0238; Fax: 318-425-0011.
School—1000 Ogilvie St., 71111. Tel: 318-222-8934; Fax: 318-424-7002. Dr. Julia Johnson, Prin.
Lay Teachers 17; Students 219.
Catechesis/Religious Programs—Students 220.
Missions—Doyline, Webster Parish, Mary, Queen of the Holy Rosary, Tel: 318-747-9496; Caplis, Bossier Parish, Mary, Queen of Peace.
St. Jude (1964), Rev. Richard Norsworthy; Deacon John J. Finnorn, Jr.; Mrs. Twyla Satterthwaite, Parish Life Coord.
Res., 3800 Viking Dr., E., 71111-7403. Tel: 318-746-2508; Fax: 318-742-4526.
Catechesis/Religious Programs—Students 428.
Mission—Benton, Mary, Queen of Heaven.

Grambling, Lincoln Parish, St. Benedict the Black (1966) (African American), Rev. Adrian Fischer, O.F.M.
Res., 471 Main St., 71245-3088. Tel: 318-247-6734.

Hodge, Jackson Parish, St. Lucy (1935), Rev. Joseph B. Hagen, O.F.M.
Res., Second St., P.O. Drawer 100, 71247-0100. Tel: 318-259-2326. [CEM]

Lake Providence, East Carroll Parish, St. Patrick (1870), Rev. Joseph Martina.
Res., P.O. Box 351, 71254-0351. Tel: 318-559-1276. [CEM]

Mansfield, DeSoto Parish, St. Joseph (1907), Rev. Edmund A. Niehoff.
Res., 305 Jefferson St., P.O. Box 760, 71052-0760. Tel: 318-872-1158; Fax: 318-872-1161. [CEM 3]
Catechesis/Religious Programs—Students 122.
Mission—Coushatta, Red River Parish, St. George, 1811 Ashland Rd., P.O. Box 937, Coushatta, 71019-0937. Tel: 318-932-3733.

Many, Sabine Parish, St. John the Baptist (1871), Rev. William H. Carey.
Res., 1130 E. San Antonio Ave., 71449-3226. Tel: 318-256-5680; 256-5689; Fax: 318-256-9177. [CEM]
Mission—Many, Sabine Parish, St. Terence, Hwy. 191 & 476, 1130 E. San Antonio Ave., 71449. Tel: 318-586-7444.

Minden, Webster Parish, St. Paul (1942), Rev. Peter Mangum.
Res., 414 Fincher Rd., P.O. Box 799, 71058-0799. Tel: 318-377-5364; Fax: 318-377-5119.
Missions—Ringgold, Bienville Parish, Blessed Sacrament, Hwy. 7 at Hwy. 4, Ringgold, 71068.; Homer, Claiborne Parish, St. Margaret, 600 E. 2nd St., Homer, 71040. Tel: 316-927-2865; Springhill, Webster Parish, Sacred Heart, 304 Gaisser St., Springhill, 71075. Tel: 318-539-4919.

Monroe, Ouachita Parish,

1—JESUS THE GOOD SHEPHERD, (1958), Rev. Timothy C. Hurd. In res., Rev. Msgr. Edmund J. Moore, (Retired).
Office: 2510 Emerson St., 71201-2699. Tel: 318-325-7549; Fax: 318-322-6969.; Priest's Residence: 804 Marquette St., 71201. Tel: 318-325-6956.
School—900 Good Shepherd Ln., 71201. Tel: 318-325-8569.
Religious 1; Lay Teachers 13; Students 252.
Catechesis/Religious Programs—Students 85.

2—LITTLE FLOWER OF JESUS, (1940) (African American), Rev. Carroll Mizicko, O.F.M.
Res., 600 S. 16th St., 71201. Tel: 318-322-1224; Fax: 318-322-1261.
School—610 S. 16th St., 71201. Tel: 318-322-7379. Mrs. Roylene Jones, Prin.
Lay Teachers 9; Students 100.

3—OUR LADY OF FATIMA, (1952), Revs. John D. Kennedy; Thomas Kizito Nwachukwu (Nigeria).
Res., 3205 Concordia, P.O. Box 4136, 71211-4136. Tel: 318-325-7595.
School—3202 Franklin St., 71211. Tel: 318-387-1851. Sherry Fontana, Prin.
Lay Teachers 11; Students 191.
Catechesis/Religious Programs—Students 75.
Mission—Swartz, St. Lawrence, 203 School Rd., P.O. Box 554, Swartz, 71281.

4—ST. JOSEPH, (1956), Rev. Rigoberto Betancurt, O.S.M. (Colombia).
Res., 506 Benton Ave., P.O. Box 1203, 71210-1203. Tel: 318-325-4527.

5—ST. MATTHEW, (1856), Rev. Joseph Puthuppally (India).
Res., 121 Jackson St., P.O. Box 33, 71210-0033. Tel: 318-323-8878; 8879; Fax: 318-323-8878. [CEM]

Noble, Sabine Parish, St. Ann (1955), Rev. Kenneth Williams.
Res., 5272 Hwy. 482, 71462. Tel: 318-645-9419. [CEM]

Catechesis/Religious Programs—Tel: 318-645-7033.
Students 93.
Mission—Noble, Sabine Parish, St. Catherine, 71462. Tel: 318-645-2711. [CEM]

Oak Grove, West Carroll Parish, Sacred Heart (1947), Rev. Joseph A. Martina, Jr.
Church—203 Purvis St., P.O. Box 419, 71263-0419. Tel: 318-428-2683.

Rambin, DeSoto Parish, St. Mary. Consolidated with St. Joseph, Mansfield.

Rayville, Richland Parish, Sacred Heart (1920), Rev. Thomas J. Flynn, C.S.Sp.
Res., 716 Francis St., P.O. Box 717, 71269-0717. Tel: 318-728-2445.
Mission—Delhi, Richland Parish, St. Theresa, 420 Main St., P.O. Box 363, Delhi, 71232-0363. Tel: 318-878-3484.

Ruston, Lincoln Parish, St. Thomas Aquinas (1941), Rev. Jerome Thelen, O.F.M.; Deacon John J. Serio.
Res., 810 Carey Ave., 71270-4915. Tel: 318-255-2870; Fax: 318-254-8319.

Vivian, Caddo Parish, St. Clement (1945), Rev. Daniel M. Walsh.
Office: 819 N. Pine, 71082-3354. Tel: 318-375-2789.

West Monroe, Ouachita Parish, St. Paschal (1940), Rev. Robert Leonhardt, O.F.M. In res., Rev. Donatus Grunloh, O.F.M.
Res., 711 N. Seventh St., 71291-4211. Tel: 318-323-1631; Fax: 318-361-0527. [CEM]
School—102 Wilson St., 71291. Tel: 318-322-8246; Fax: 318-322-8477. Catherine Letendre, Prin.
Lay Teachers 13; Students 158.
Missions—Calhoun, St. Francis of Assisi, Tel: 318-322-1487; Farmerville, Our Lady of Perpetual Help, Tel: 318-368-9239. Rev. Adrian Fischer, O.F.M., Admin.
Res., 471 Main St., Grambling, 71245-3088. Tel: 318-247-6734.

Zwolle, Sabine Parish, St. Joseph (1881), Rev. David T. Richter; Mr. Ronald J. Morris, Pastoral Assoc.
Res., P.O. Box 8, 71486-0008. Tel: 318-645-9852. [CEM]

Chaplains of Public Institutions

SHREVEPORT. *Overton Brooks Veteran's Administration Medical Center* 510 E. Stoner Ave., 71101. Rev. Philip F. Michiels, Chap. Emergencies, Res., St. Mary of the Pines Church, 1050 Bert Kouns Industrial Loop, 71118-3499. Tel: 318-687-5121; 687-1818.

MONROE. *Swanson Correctional Center for Youth.* (Formerly Louisiana Training Institute) 4701 S. Grand, 71202-6499. Tel: 318-323-4406. Rev. Joseph Robert Inzina.

On Duty Outside the Diocese:
Reverend Monsignors—
Graef, Franz, Notre Dame Seminary, New Orleans, LA
Reverend Fathers—
Ebarb, Walter E., St. Patrick, San Antonio, TX
Howard, Joseph, Jr., Queen of Peace, LaMarque, TX
Madden, Patrick, St. Mary Seminary and University, Baltimore, MD

Awaiting Assignment:
Reverend Fathers—
Scully, Patrick A.

Retired:
Reverend Monsignors—
Moore, Edmund J.
Reverend Fathers—
Barker, Harry O.
Beaulieu, Earl
Binh, John Phan Cong
Fuoco, Armando
Germain, Jean M.
McMullen, Roger
Richardson, J.W. Albert (HT)
Tremblay, Leger

Permanent Deacons:
Cummings, John
Finnorn, John J., Jr.
Long, William R.
Ludke, David
Nash, Clary
Serio, John J.
Wisdom, Clarence, Inactive

INSTITUTIONS LOCATED IN THE DIOCESE

[A] HIGH SCHOOLS, DIOCESAN

SHREVEPORT. *Loyola College Prep*, 921 Jordan St., 71101-4390. Tel: 318-221-2675; Fax: 318-221-2678.
E-mail: loyola@prysm.net
Mrs. Mary Ann Whited, Prin. Sisters 1; Lay Teachers 29; Students 370.

MONROE. *St. Frederick High School*, 3300 Westminster, 71201-3299. Tel: 318-323-9636.
E-mail: stfred@iamerica.net
Franciscan Sisters of Our Lady of Perpetual Help. Mr. Grady Jones, Prin.; Rev. John D. Kennedy, Chap. Sisters 1; Lay Teachers 26; Students 365.

[B] GENERAL HOSPITALS

SHREVEPORT. *Schumpert Medical Center*, (1907) One St. Mary Pl., P.O. Box 21976, 71120-1976. Tel: 318-681-4500
For a complete listing, refer to the Hospitals section.

MONROE. *St. Francis Medical Center*, P.O. Box 1901, 71210-1901. Tel: 318-327-4000; Fax: 318-327-4142
For a complete listing, refer to the Hospitals section.

**St. Francis Specialty Hospital*, (1995) 309 Jackson St., P.O. Box 1532, 71210. Tel: 318-327-4600.
E-mail: ryanm@stfran.com
Web site: http://www.specialtyhospital.com
For a complete listing, refer to the Hospitals section.

[C] PROTECTIVE INSTITUTIONS

SHREVEPORT. *Holy Angels Residential Facility*, 10450 Ellerbe Rd., 71106-7712. Tel: 318-797-8500; 797-9070; Fax: 318-798-0159
For a complete listing, refer to the Special Care Facilities section.

[D] HOMES FOR AGED

MONROE. *St. Joseph Home*, 2301 Sterlington Rd., P.O. Box 6057, 71211-6057. Tel: 318-323-3426
For a complete listing, refer to the Special Care Facilities section.

[E] SPECIAL CENTERS FOR SOCIAL SERVICES & ASSISTANCE

SHREVEPORT. *St. Catherine Community Center*, 331 E. 71st St., 71106-4305. Tel: 318-865-9817.
E-mail: RAlford318@aol.com
Afterschool Enrichment, Summer Day Camp, Parenting, Literacy, Arts. Mr. Robert Alford, Dir. Total Assisted 800; Total Staff 26.

[F] CONVENTS AND RESIDENCES FOR SISTERS

SHREVEPORT. *Motherhouse of the Daughters of the Cross in America*, 1000 Fairview St., 71104-4182. Tel: 318-869-3482. Sr. Mary Louise Parisy, D.C., Supr.; Rev. Govie Moraus, Chap. Sisters 9.
Religious House of Formation and Retirement-Our Lady of Sorrows, 9894 Norris Ferry Rd., 71106-7724. Tel: 318-797-0213; Fax: 318-797-7003. Sr. Mavis Champagne, O.L.S., Supr. Sisters 8.

[G] NEWMAN CENTERS

GRAMBLING. *Student Center*, 471 S. Main St., 71245-3088. Tel: 318-247-6288; 247-6734 (Office). Rev. Adrian Fischer, O.F.M., Campus Min.

MONROE. *Catholic Campus Ministry at Northeast Louisiana University*, 911 University Ave., P.O. Box 7250, 71211-7250. Tel: 318-343-4897. Rev. John D. Kennedy, Chap.

RUSTON. *E. Donn Piatt Catholic Student Center at Louisiana Tech University*, 600 S. Thornton St., 71270-4946. Tel: 318-251-0793.
E-mail: ediths@bayou.com
Web site: http://members.tripod.com~aquinas/
Rev. Jerome Thelen, O.F.M.; Sr. Edith Schnell, O.P.

RELIGIOUS INSTITUTES OF MEN REPRESENTED IN THE DIOCESE

For further details refer to the corresponding bracketed number in the Religious Institutes of Men or Women section.

[0275]—*Carmelites of Mary Immaculate (India).*—C.M.I.
[0520]—*Franciscan Friars.* (Sacred Heart Prov.).—O.F.M.
[0520]—*Franciscan Friars.* (Prov. of St. John the Baptist).—O.F.M.
[0650]—*Holy Ghost Fathers of Ireland.* (Louisiana Prov.).—C.S.Sp.
[0690]—*Jesuit Fathers and Brothers.* (New Orleans Prov.).—S.J.
[1240]—*Order of Friar Servants of Mary.*—O.S.M.
[0560]—*Third Order Regular of St. Francis (Spanish Province of Immaculate Conception).*—T.O.R.

RELIGIOUS INSTITUTES OF WOMEN REPRESENTED IN THE DIOCESE

[0470]—*Congregation of the Sisters of Charity of the Incarnate Word, Houston, Texas.*—C.C.V.I.
[0770]—*Daughters of the Cross.*—D.C.
[1070-14]—*Dominican Sisters.*—O.P.
[1380]—*Franciscan Missionaries of Our Lady.*—O.S.F.
[1180]—*Franciscan Sisters of Allegany.* New York.—O.S.F.
[1430]—*Franciscan Sisters of Our Lady of Perpetual Help.*—O.S.F.
[1530]—*Franciscan Sisters of Sylvania.* Ohio.—O.S.F.
[2420]—*Marist Missionary Sisters (Missionary Sisters of the Society of Mary Inc.).*—S.M.S.M.
[2970]—*School Sisters of Notre Dame, St. Louis Province.*—S.S.N.D.
[0650]—*Sisters of Charity of St. Vincent de Paul of New York.*—S.C.
[3120]—*Sisters of Our Lady of Sorrows.*—O.L.S.
[3840]—*Sisters of St. Joseph of Carondelet.*—C.S.J.
[2050]—*Sisters of the Holy Spirit and Mary Immaculate.*—S.H.Sp.

DIOCESAN CEMETERIES

SHREVEPORT, LA. *St. Joseph*, Catholic Center, 2500 Line Ave., 71104-3034. Tel: 318-222-2006; Fax: 318-222-2080. Mr. E. Michael Schofield, C.P.A., Contact Person.

NECROLOGY

† Martinez, Rev. Msgr. George W., Monroe, LA, St. Matthew. —Died June 23, 1997.
† Pierce, William Jean, (Retired). —Died Nov. 5, 1996.
† Scanlan, John, Lake Providence, LA, St. Patrick. —Died March 18, 1997.

Diocese of Sioux City

(Dioecesis Siopolitana)

Most Reverend

LAWRENCE D. SOENS, D.D.

Bishop of Sioux City; ordained May 6, 1950; appointed Bishop of Sioux City June 15, 1983; consecrated and installed August 17, 1983. *Address all correspondence to: P.O. Box 3379, Sioux City, IA, 51102-3379; Fax: 712-233-7598.*

Most Reverend

DANIEL N. DINARDO, D.D.

Coadjutor Bishop of Sioux City; ordained July 16, 1977; appointed Coadjutor Bishop of Sioux City August 19, 1997; consecrated October 7, 1997. *Address all correspondence to: P.O. Box 3379, Sioux City, IA, 51102-3379; Fax: 712-233-7598.*

Corporate Title: *"The Diocese of Sioux City."*

ESTABLISHED JANUARY 15, 1902.

Square Miles 14,518.

Comprises 24 Counties in the northwest part of Iowa, west of Winnebago, Hancock, Wright, Hamilton and Story Counties, and north of Harrison, Shelby, Audubon, Guthrie and Dallas Counties.

For legal titles of parishes and diocesan institutions, consult the Chancery.

Chancery: Administrative Offices, 1821 Jackson St., P.O. Box 3379, Sioux City, IA, 51102-3379. Tel.: 712-255-7933; 233-7512; Fax: 712-233-7598.

STATISTICAL OVERVIEW

Personnel	
Bishop	1
Auxiliary Bishops	1
Priests: Diocesan Active in Diocese	115
Priests: Active Outside Diocese	8
Priests: Retired, Sick or Absent	50
Number of Diocesan Priests	173
Ordinations:	
Diocesan Priests	2
Transitional Deacons	2
Permanent Deacons in Diocese	35
Total Sisters	114
Parishes	
Parishes	123
With Resident Pastor:	
Resident Diocesan Priests	95
Without Resident Pastor:	
Administered by Priests	24
Administered by Pastoral Teams, etc.	4
Missions	10
Professional Ministry Personnel:	
Sisters	14
Lay Ministers	6
Welfare	
Catholic Hospitals	3
Total Assisted	315,780
Homes for the Aged	3
Total Assisted	259
Specialized Homes	1
Special Centers for Social Services	4
Total Assisted	6,142
Educational	
Diocesan Students in Other Seminaries	7
Total Seminarians	7
Colleges and Universities	1
Total Students	1,011
High Schools, Diocesan and Parish	8
Total Students	2,802
Elementary Schools, Diocesan and Parish	28
Total Students	6,353
Catechesis/Religious Education:	
High School Students	3,516
Elementary Students	7,586
Total Students Under Catholic Instruction	21,275
Teachers in the Diocese:	
Priests	8
Sisters	26
Lay Teachers	521
Vital Statistics	
Receptions into the Church:	
Infant Baptism Totals	1,691
Adult Baptism Totals	124
Received into Full Communion	358
First Communions	1,892
Confirmations	1,412
Marriages:	
Catholic	397
Interfaith	281
Total Marriages	678
Deaths	1,146
Total Catholic Population	92,309
Total Population	472,307

Former Bishops—Most Rev. PHILIP J. GARRIGAN, D.D., ord. June 11, 1870; appt. March 21, 1902; cons. May 25, 1902; died Oct. 14, 1919.—Most Rev. EDMOND HEELAN, D.D., ord. June 24, 1890; cons. April 8, 1919; died Sept. 20, 1948.—Most Rev. JOSEPH M. MUELLER, D.D., ord. June 14, 1919; cons. Oct. 16, 1947; died Aug. 9, 1981.—Most Rev. FRANK H. GRETEMAN, D.D., ord. Dec. 8, 1932; appt. Titular Bishop of Vissalsa April 14, 1965; cons. May 26, 1965; appt. Bishop of Sioux City Oct. 20, 1970; installed Dec. 9, 1970; retired Aug. 17, 1983; died March 21, 1987.

Vicar-General—Most Rev. DANIEL N. DINARDO, V.G., *P.O. Box 3379, Sioux City, 51102.* Tel: 712-233-7512. Rev. Msgr. ROGER J. AUGUSTINE, V.G., *Immaculate Conception Church, 419 Jones St., P.O. Box C, Moville, 51039-0802.* Tel: 712-873-3745.

Chancery—Administrative Offices, 1821 Jackson St., P.O. Box 3379, Sioux City, 51102-3379. Tel: 712-255-7933; 233-7512; Fax: 712-233-7598.

Chancellor—Rev. KEVIN C. MCCOY, S.T.D., *Res., 2514 Leech Ave., Sioux City, 51107-1244.* Tel: 712-276-7368.

Vice Chancellor—Rev. R. MARK DUCHAINE, J.C.L., *Res., Our Lady of Good Counsel Church, 513 Mueller St., Holstein, 51025-9802.* Tel: 712-368-4755.

Diocesan Tribunal—Address all marriage related materials to: *Diocesan Tribunal, P.O. Box 3379, Sioux City, 51102-3379.* Tel: 712-233-7533; Fax: 712-233-7588.

Judicial Vicar—Rev. R. MARK DUCHAINE, J.C.L., *1821 Jackson St., P.O. Box 3379, Sioux City, 51102-3379., Res., Our Lady of Good Counsel Church, 513 Mueller St., Holstein, 51025-9802.* Tel: 712-368-4755.

Promotor of Justice—Rev. KEVIN C. MCCOY, S.T.D.; Rev. Msgr. RICHARD E. ZENK, J.C.D.

Defender of the Bond—Revs. ROBERT P. BROWN, S.T.L.; KEVIN C. MCCOY, S.T.D.; Rev. Msgr. RICHARD E. ZENK, J.C.D.; Rev. EUGENE ULSES, J.C.L.

Judges—Rev. Msgrs. MICHAEL D. SERNETT, J.C.D.; ROGER AUGUSTINE, V.G.; Revs. PAUL-LOUIS ARTS; JEROME COSGROVE; MARK J. STOLL, J.C.L.

Notary—JUDY E. PUETZ.

Diocesan Corporate Board—Most Rev. LAWRENCE D. SOENS, D.D., Pres.; Most Rev. DANIEL N. DINARDO, Coadjutor Bishop; Rev. Msgr. ROGER J. AUGUSTINE, V.G., Vice Pres.; Rev. KEVIN C. MCCOY, Sec. Directors: Revs. THOMAS E. GEELAN; ROGER J. LINNAN; Mr. WILLIAM C. METZ; Mr. MICHAEL J. MOELLER; Mr. JEFFREY R. MOHRHAUSER; Mrs. SUSAN H. PIERCE; Dr. DANIEL J. SHEY; Sr. MARGARET WICK.

Diocesan Legal Counsel—Mr. JAMES M. COSGROVE-,(Shull, Cosgrove, Hellige & Lundberg Law Firm, Sioux City). Refer all legal matters to The Chancery.

Presbyteral Council—Most Rev. DANIEL N. DINARDO; Rev. Msgr. ROGER J. AUGUSTINE, V.G.; Revs. PAUL-LOUIS ARTS; STEVEN W. BRODERSEN; R. MARK DUCHAINE; PAUL F. EISELE; THOMAS E. GEELAN; TIMOTHY A. JOHNSON; JAMES C. MCALPIN; HARRY D. MCALPINE; KEVIN C. MCCOY; VICTOR R. RAMAEKER; ROBERT J. SCHIMMER; MERLIN J. SCHRAD; JAMES TIGGES.

Diocesan Consultors—Rev. Msgr. ROGER J. AUGUSTINE, V.G.; Revs. PAUL-LOUIS ARTS; JAMES C. MCALPIN; THOMAS E. GEELAN; KEVIN C. MCCOY; A. E. MCCOY; ROBERT J. SCHIMMER.

Deans—Very Revs. ROBERT J. SCHIMMER, V.F., Southwestern Deanery; MERVIN J. HOOD, V.F., Central Deanery; PAUL KELLY, V.F., South Central Deanery; DONALD C. RIES, V.F., Southeastern Deanery; ALBERT O. GRENDLER, V.F., Northeastern Deanery; Rev. TIMOTHY J. HOGAN, V.F., Northwestern Deanery.

Diocesan Offices and Directors

Board of Education—Most Rev. LAWRENCE D. SOENS, D.D., Ex Officio Chm.; Mr. EUGENE MEISTER, Pres.; Revs. THOMAS E. GEELAN, Vice Pres. PAUL-LOUIS

ARTS; WILLIAM A. SCHREIBER; GERALD F. FEIERFEIL; SR. MARY CLARENITA FROEHLICH, P.B.V.M.; SR. MARY ANN HELLE, O.S.F.; SR. ELENA HOYE, P.B.V.M.; SR. JOAN STOFFEL, O.S.F.; SR. ELAINE TWOREK, S.L.W.; DR. KEITH GUY; MRS. KATHLEEN HANSEN; MR. NEVEN MULHOLLAND; MRS. SHERRY NILLES; MR. PATRICK RINKER.

Building Commission—Most Rev. LAWRENCE D. SOENS, D.D., Chm.; Revs. CLAIR L. BOES; JEROME DEGEN; BRIAN C. HUGHES.

Catholic School Foundation of the Diocese of Sioux City—Most Rev. LAWRENCE D. SOENS, D.D., Pres., *1821 Jackson St., P.O. Box 3379, Sioux City, 51102.*

Archives—Sr. KEVIN CUMMINGS, P.B.V.M., *1821 Jackson St., P.O. Box 3379, Sioux City, 51102-3379.* Tel: 712-233-7525.

Catholic Youth Organization—Rev. CRAIG A. COLLISON, Dir., *St. Mary Church, R.R.1, Box 57A, Carroll, 51401-9726.* Tel: 712-792-4516.

Office of Religious Education and Youth Ministry—Mr. PATRICK RINKER, Dir., *1821 Jackson St., P.O. Box 3379, Sioux City, 51102-3379.*

Censor Librorum—Rev. Msgr. JAMES K. LAFFERTY, Ph.D., *St. John Church, P.O. Box 23, Arcadia, 51430-0023.* Tel: 712-689-2595.

Catholic Charities—Mr. BRUNO FINOCCHIARIO, M.S.W., Dir., *1601 Military Rd., Sioux City, 51103.* Tel: 712-252-4547. Fort Dodge Office: *3 N. 16th, Fort Dodge, 50501.* Tel: 515-576-4156. Carroll Office: *409 1/2 W. 7th St., P.O. Box 13, Carroll, 51401.* Tel: 712-792-9597.

Office of Youth Ministry and Catechesis—Directors: Mr. PATRICK RINKER; Sr. ELENA HOYE, *1821 Jackson St., P.O. Box 3379, Sioux City, 51102-3379.* Tel: 712-233-7520.

Continuing Education for Priests—Rev. ROGER J. LINNAN, Ph.D., Dir., *St. Francis of Assisi Church, 744 Main St., Rockwell City, 50579-1399.* Tel: 712-297-8263.

Council of Catholic Women—Rev. EUGENE T. SCHUMACHER, Moderator, *Holy Name Church, R.R. 2, Box 71, Rock Rapids, 51246-9529.* Tel: 712-472-3248.

Ecumenical Commission—Rev. Msgr. FRANK J. BRADY, Chm.; Revs. ROBERT W. GRALAPP; JOSEPH KERWIN; JAMES C. MCALPIN; ALFRED E. MCCOY.

Episcopal Representative for Religious—Sr. ROSALIE ERDMANN, S.L.W., *1812 Jackson St., Sioux City, 51105-1054.* Tel: 712-258-2579.

Episcopal Representative for Hospitals and Health Care—Rev. KEVIN C. MCCOY, S.T.D., *1821 Jackson St., P.O. Box 3379, Sioux City, 51102-3379.*

Family Life Office And Adult Ministries—Mrs. KAY MORRISSEY, Dir., *1821 Jackson St., P.O. Box 3379, Sioux City, 51102-3379.* Tel: 712-233-7530.

Holy Childhood Association—Rev. Msgr. RICHARD E. ZENK, J.C.D., Dir., *P.O. Box 3379, Sioux City, 51102-3379.*

Liturgy Commission—Mrs. MONICA PEARSON, Chm.; Revs. STEVE BRODERSEN; TIM FITZGERALD; BRUCE LAWLER; HARRY MCALPINE; Sr. JULIE MARSH, P.B.V.M.; Sr. JANICE HOFFMAN, O.S.F.; Sr. M. ARNOLD STAUDT, O.S.F.; Mr. RICHARD CAREY; Mrs. MARLENE FITZPATRICK; Mr. BERNARD KENINGER; Ms. KRIS MUELLER; Mrs. MARJORIE KRAFT.

Office Of Communications—"The Globe"—Deacon JOSEPH F. MAHER, Mgr., *1825 Jackson St., P.O. Box 5079, Sioux City, 51102-5079.* Tel: 712-255-2550. Editorial Office; Circulation.

Office of Catholic Education—Tel: 712-233-7589. Sr. JOAN STOFFEL, Supt., *1821 Jackson, P.O. Box 3379, Sioux City, 51102-3379.*

Permanent Diaconate—Rev. ARMAND J. BERTRAND, Co-Dir., *Our Lady of Good Counsel Church, P.O. Box 306, Fonda, 50540-0306.* Tel: 712-288-6480. Deacon RONALD M. FORREST, Co-Dir., *1821 Jackson St., P.O. Box 3379, Sioux City, 51102-3379.*

Priests' Eucharistic League—Rev. MERVIN J. HOOD, Dir., *Early, 50535.*

Priests' Personnel Board—Rev. Msgr. ROGER J. AUGUSTINE, V.G., Bishop's Liaison; Revs. PAUL EISELE; THOMAS GEELAN; ANDREW W. HOFFMAN; JOHN J. MCGUIRK.

Priests' Pension Plan - Board of Trustees—Most Rev. LAWRENCE D. SOENS, D.D.; Rev. KEVIN C. MCCOY; Rev. Msgr. FRANK J. BRADY; Mr. WILLIAM C. METZ; Mr. RICHARD L. BILLINGS; Mr. PATRICK D. KUEHL; Mr. MICHAEL J. MOELLER; Mr. JEFFREY R. MOHRHAUSER; Mr. ROBERT V. WILLIAMS.

Priests' Provident Society—Most Rev. LAWRENCE D. SOENS, D.D., Pres.

Propagation of the Faith, Association of the Holy Childhood, Catholic Students' Mission Crusade—Rev. Msgr. RICHARD E. ZENK, J.C.D., Dir., *1821 Jackson St., P.O. Box 3379, Sioux City, 51102-3379.*

Radio and Television—Deacon JOSEPH F. MAHER, Dir., *P.O. Box 5079, Sioux City, 51102-5079.*

Rural Life Conference—MARILYN MURPHY, Dir., *1601 Military Rd., Sioux City, 51103.* Tel: 712-252-4547.

St. Joseph Student Aid Society—(Diocesan Seminarian Board). Most Rev. LAWRENCE D. SOENS, D.D., Honorary Pres.; Rev. PAUL-LOUIS ARTS, Exec. Sec., *P.O. Box 2817, Sioux City, 51106-2817.* Tel: 712-276-4821.

Vocations—Rev. BRIAN C. HUGHES, *3303 Rebecca St., Sioux City, 51104-2340.* Tel: 712-233-7523; 279-5461.

CLERGY, PARISHES, MISSIONS AND PAROCHIAL SCHOOLS

CITY OF SIOUX CITY
(Woodbury County)

1—CATHEDRAL OF THE EPIPHANY (1867), Revs. Edward M. Girres; Randy J. Guerdet; Hieu Nguyen (Vietnam); Verne P. Stapenhorst; Don Slaven.
Res., 1011 Douglas St., 51105-1399. Tel: 712-255-1637; Fax: 712-255-4194.
School—Holy Family Epiphany Center. (Grades 6-8) 1000 Douglas St., 51105. Tel: 712-252-3181.
Sisters 1; Lay Teachers 24; Students 85.
Catechesis/Religious Programs—Students 157.

2—BLESSED SACRAMENT (1922), Revs. Thomas E. Geelan; Joseph A. Dillinger; Deacons John Hefferman; James Sands; Fred Karpuk; George Spellman.
Res., 3012 Jackson St., 51104-2799. Tel: 712-277-2949; Fax: 712-277-2963.
School—3030 Jackson St., 51104. Tel: 712-277-4739; Fax: 712-277-8592.
Priests 1; Lay Teachers 28; Students 435.
Catechesis/Religious Programs—Patricia Walsh, D.R.E.
Students 445.

3—ST. BONIFACE (1906), Rev. Marvin J. Boes. In res., Rev. Richard A. Sitzmann.
Res., 703 W. Fifth St., 51103-3799. Tel: 712-255-3577. [JC]
School—Holy Family, (Grades K-5) 700 W. Sixth St., 51103. Tel: 712-258-9464.
Sisters of the Living Word 1; Lay Teachers 5; Students 84.
Catechesis/Religious Programs—Students 104.

4—ST. CASIMIR (1915) (Lithuanian), Revs. Paul-Louis Arts; Daniel M. Greving; Deacon Ron Forrest.
Mailing Address: P.O. Box 2817, 51107.
Res., Clustered with Immaculate Conception, Sioux City. 1212 Morningside Ave., 51106. Tel: 712-276-4821; Fax: 712-276-1321. [JC]

5—ST. FRANCIS OF ASSISI (1907) (Polish), Revs. Paul-Louis Arts; Daniel M. Greving; Deacon Ron Forrest.
Mailing Address: P.O. Box 2817, 51106. Tel: 712-276-4821.
Res., Clustered with Immaculate Conception, Sioux City. 1212 Morningside Ave., P.O. Box 2817, 51106. Tel: 712-276-4821; Fax: 712-276-1321. [JC]

6—IMMACULATE CONCEPTION (1905), Revs. Paul-Louis Arts; Daniel M. Greving; Deacon Ron Forrest.
Res., P.O. Box 2817, 51106-2817. Tel: 712-276-4821; Fax: 712-276-1321. [JC]
School—3719 Ridge Ave., 51106. Tel: 712-276-6216; Fax: 712-274-1221.
Priests 2; Lay Teachers 23; Students 227.
Catechesis/Religious Programs—Students 225.

7—ST. JOSEPH (1887), Rev. Robert J. Schimmer; Deacons Jerome Reicks; Ronald Pietz; Patrick McCruden.
Res., 1112 Eighth St., 51105-1899. Tel: 712-258-3813. [JC]
School—Holy Family, (Grades K-5). Consolidated with St. Francis, Cathedral of the Epiphany and St. Boniface. 709 Iowa St., 51105. Tel: 712-258-4962.
Lay Teachers 6; Students 100.
Catechesis/Religious Programs—Tel: 712-258-5944.
Students 65.

8—ST. MICHAEL (1907), Rev. Lawrence L. McCarty; Deacons Larry Sitzman; William Berger; Sr. Jean Ann Rausch, F.S.P.A., Pastoral Min.
Res., 2223 Indian Hills Dr., 51104-1605. Tel: 712-239-2411; Fax: 712-239-4710. [JC]
School—4106 Van Buren St., 51104. Tel: 712-239-1090; Fax: 712-239-8546.
Sisters of the Blessed Virgin Mary 3; Lay Teachers 14; Students 254.
Catechesis/Religious Programs—Students 155.

9—NATIVITY OF OUR LORD JESUS CHRIST (1966), Rev. Msgr. Michael D. Sernett.
Res., 4242 Natalia Way, 51106-4099. Tel: 712-276-3022.
School—Mater Dei School, (Grades 6-8). Consolidated with Immaculate Conception Parish. Tel: 712-274-0268; Fax: 712-274-0377.
Catechesis/Religious Programs—Tel: 712-274-0497.
Students 380.

10—SACRED HEART (1907), Rev. James A. Bruch.
Res., 5000 Military Rd., 51103-1564. Tel: 712-233-1652; Fax: 712-255-3056. [JC]
School—5010 Military Rd., 51103. Tel: 712-233-1624.
Sisters 1; Lay Teachers 12; Students 207.
Catechesis/Religious Programs—Students 107.

OUTSIDE SIOUX CITY

Akron, Plymouth Co., St. Patrick's (1988), Rev. Richard E. Zenk.
Res., 650 Dakota Ave., P.O. Box 317, 51001-0317. Tel: 712-568-3292. [CEM]
Catechesis/Religious Programs—Students 104.

Algona, Kossuth Co., St. Cecelia (1892), Rev. Steven W. Brodersen; Deacon Joseph Straub.
Res., P.O. Box 633, 50511-0633. Tel: 515-295-3435; Fax: 515-295-9290. [CEM]
School—Seton Elementary. Consolidation of St. Cecelia, Algona, St. Benedict, St. Joseph, Wesley, St. Joseph, Bode. Tel: 515-295-3509; Fax: 515-295-7739.
Presentation Sisters 5; Lay Teachers 25; Students 271.
Catechesis/Religious Programs—Students 587.

Alton, Sioux Co., St. Mary's (1870), Rev. James Tigges.
Res., 609 10th St., 51003-0181. Tel: 712-756-4224. [CEM]
School—Spalding Catholic, (Grades 4-6). Consolidation of Alton, Hospers and Granville. Tel: 712-756-4532.
Lay Teachers 3; Students 67.
Catechesis/Religious Programs—Cluster of St. Mary, St. Anthony's, and St. Joseph's.
Students 60.

Anthon, Woodbury Co., St. Joseph's (1890), Rev. David Hogan; Sr. Mary Clare Walling, Pastoral Min.
Res., P.O. Box 285, 51004-0285. Tel: 712-373-5573. [CEM]
Catechesis/Religious Programs—Tel: 712-373-5011.
Students 130.

Arcadia, Carroll Co., St. John the Baptist (1875), Rev. Msgr. James K. Lafferty.
Res., P.O. Box 23, 51430-0023. Tel: 712-689-2595; Fax: 712-689-2282. [CEM]
Catechesis/Religious Programs—Tel: 712-689-1491.
Students 72.

Armstrong, Emmet Co., St. Mary's (1892), Rev. Thomas C. Nash.
Office: 404 Fifth Ave., 50514-9301. Tel: 712-864-3160. [CEM][JC]
Catechesis/Religious Programs—Students 72.

Ashton, Osceola Co., Our Lady of Perpetual Help (1880), Rev. Timothy J. Hogan.
Res., P.O. Box 157, 51232-0157. Tel: 712-724-6411. [CEM]
Catechesis/Religious Programs—2191 Nettle Ave., 51232. Tel: 712-724-6297. Mrs. Nancy Marnach, D.R.E.
Students 37.

Auburn, Sac Co., St. Mary's (1893) (German), Rev. Mark E. Harrington.
Res., P.O. Box H, 51433. Tel: 712-688-2845. [CEM][JC]
Catechesis/Religious Programs—Students 43.

Bancroft, Kossuth Co., St. John the Baptist's (1891), Rev. John M. Thomas; Deacon Philip Doocy.
Res., P.O. Box 195, 50517-0195. Tel: 515-885-2462; Fax: 515-885-2462. [CEM]
School—St. John's Elementary School, Tel: 515-885-2580.
Lay Teachers 7; Students 65.
Catechesis/Religious Programs—Students 188.

Barnum, Webster Co., St. Joseph's (1891), Rev. Dale E. Reiff.
Res., P.O. Box 105, Clare, 50524-0105. Tel: 515-546-4505. [CEM]
Catechesis/Religious Programs—Students 51.

Boone, Boone Co., Sacred Heart (1868), Revs. Gerald F. Feierfeil; Steven J. McLoud.
Res., 921 12th St., 50036-2295. Tel: 515-432-1971; Fax: 515-433-0103. [CEM]
School—Sacred Heart Elementary, Tel: 515-432-4124; Fax: 515-432-4124.
Lay Teachers 13; Students 200.
Catechesis/Religious Programs—Tel: 515-432-2884.
Students 145.

Breda, Carroll Co., St. Bernard's, Rev. James R. Smith.
Res., P.O. Box 39, 51436-0031. Tel: 712-673-2351. [CEM]
School—Christ the King Elementary. Consolidation of Breda, Lidderdale, Maple River and Mt. Carmel. Tel: 712-673-2582.
Lay Teachers 12; Students 185.
High School—Kuemper High School, Carroll.
Students 40.

Carroll, Carroll Co., St. Lawrence (1914), Revs. Laurence J. Burns; Douglas Michael Klein; Deacons Robert Bruner; Louis Westendorf.
Res., 1607 N. West St., 51401-4198. Tel: 712-792-9244; Fax: 712-792-9245. [JC]
School—(Grades K-8) 1519 N. West St., 51401. Tel: 712-792-2123; Fax: 712-792-8072.
Franciscan Sisters of Perpetual Adoration 1; Lay Teachers 42; Students 285.
Catechesis/Religious Programs—Tel: 712-792-0513. Sr. Judith Myers, D.R.E.
Students 133.

Holy Spirit (1964), Revs. James D. McCormick; Peter Duc Hung Nguyen; Deacon Anthony Reuter.
Res., 421 E. Bluff St., 51401-3099. Tel: 712-792-4386; Fax: 712-792-8038. [JC]
School—Kuemper Catholic Grade Schools, Tel: 712-792-3610; Fax: 712-792-8072.
Franciscan Sisters of Perpetual Adoration 1; Lay Teachers 42; Students 191.
Catechesis/Religious Programs—Tel: 712-792-0513. Sr. Judith Myers, D.R.E.
Students 107.

Charter Oak, Crawford Co., St. Boniface (1883) (German-Irish), Rev. Benjamin E. Jensen.
Res., P.O. Box 317, Dow City, 51528. Tel: 712-678-3449. [CEM]
Mission—Ute, Monona Co., St. Mary's, c/o Box 317, 51528. [CEM]
Catechesis/Religious Programs—Tel: 712-674-3329.
Students 76.

Cherokee, Cherokee Co., Immaculate Conception (1870), Rev. Timothy R. Schott; Deacon Leroy Rupp.
Res., 709 W. Cedar St., P.O. Box 658, 51012-0658. Tel: 712-225-4606. [CEM]
Catechesis/Religious Programs—7th & Willow, 51012. Tel: 712-225-4466.
Students 359.

St. Dymphna (1960). (Mental Health Institute, Chapel for Patients). Rev. Eugene E. Sitzmann.
Res., 1251 W. Cedar Loop, 975 540th St., 51012. Tel: 712-225-6929; Fax: 712-225-6925.

Churdan, Greene Co., St. Columbkille's (1886) (German-Irish), Rev. Dennis W. Meinen.
Res., P.O. Box 128, 50050-0128. Tel: 515-389-3625; Fax: 515-389-3795. [JC]
Catechesis/Religious Programs—Tel: 515-389-3156.
Students 79.

Clare, Webster Co., St. Matthew's (1886), Rev. Dale E. Reiff.
Res., P.O. Box 105, 50524-0105. Tel: 515-546-4505. [CEM]
Catechesis/Religious Programs—Students 71.

Coon Rapids, Carroll Co., Annunciation (1891), Rev. Paul Kelly.
Res., P.O. Box 76, 50058-0076. Tel: 712-684-2823. [CEM]
Catechesis/Religious Programs—Students 161.

Danbury, Woodbury Co., St. Mary's (1897), Rev. David Hogan.
Res., P.O. Box 318, 51019-0318. Tel: 712-883-2406. [CEM]
School—Danbury Elementary, Tel: 712-883-2244.
Priests 1; Sisters 2; Lay Teachers 4; Students 59.
Catechesis/Religious Programs—Students 87.

Dayton, Webster Co., Christ the King (1950), Rev. Thomas J. Munn. Pastoral Ministers: Sr. Mary Lois Lehmann, P.B.V.M.; Sr. Mary Bernard Mauss, P.B.V.M.
Res., P.O. Box 528, Ogden, 50530-0528. Tel: 712-275-2580. [CEM]
Catechesis/Religious Programs—Tel: 515-547-2743.
Students 61.

Dedham, Carroll Co., St. Joseph's (1892), Rev. Terry A. Roder.
Res., P.O. Box 47, 51440-0047. Tel: 712-683-5744. [CEM]
School—Kuemper Catholic Grade Schools. Consolidation of Dedham, Willey Elementary, Holy Spirit and St. Lawrence. Tel: 712-792-2123; Fax: 712-792-3365.

Denison, Crawford Co., St. Rose of Lima (1872), Rev. Andrew W. Hoffmann.
Res., 1008 2nd Ave. S., P.O. Box 280, 51442-0280. Tel: 712-263-2152. [CEM]
School—Tel: 712-263-5408.
Lay Teachers 8; Students 108.
Catechesis/Religious Programs—Students 418.

Dow City, Crawford Co., St. Mary's (1947) (German-Irish), Rev. Benjamin E. Jensen.
Res., 215 Clark St., P.O. Box 317, 51528-0317. Tel: 712-674-3329.
Catechesis/Religious Programs—Students 59.

Duncombe, Webster Co., St. Joseph's (1880), Rev. Timothy J. Boekelman.
Res., P.O. Box 135, Moorland, 50566-0135. Tel: 515-549-3556. [CEM]

Early, Sac Co., Sacred Heart (1882), Very Rev. Mervin J. Hood; Rev. Eriberto DaCosta.
Res., P.O. Box 378, 50535-0378. Tel: 712-273-5482; Fax: 712-273-5798. [CEM]
Catechesis/Religious Programs—Tel: 712-273-5577.
Students 70.

Emmetsburg, Palo Alto Co., Holy Family (1870) (Irish), Rev. Eugene L. Murray.
Res., 2001 S. Broadway, P.O. Box 322, 50536-0322. Tel: 712-852-3187. [CEM]
School—Emmetsburgh Catholic School, (Grades 1-8). Tel: 712-852-3464. Sr. Lucille Hass, O.S.F., Prin.
Lay Teachers 12; Students 126.
Catechesis/Religious Programs—Mary Freeman, D.R.E.
Students 125.

St. Thomas. Closed. For sacramental records contact Holy Family, Emmetsburg.

Estherville, Emmet Co., St. Patrick's (1891), Rev. Thomas C. Nash.
Res., P.O. Box 383, 51334-0383. Tel: 712-362-5851; Fax: 712-362-5852. [CEM]
Catechesis/Religious Programs—Duhigg Center, 902 Central Ave., 51334. Tel: 712-362-4172.
Students 307.

Fonda, Pocahontas Co., Our Lady of Good Counsel (1884), Rev. Armand J. Bertrand; Deacon J. R. Hogan.
Res., P.O. Box 306, 50540-0306. Tel: 712-288-6480. [CEM]
School—Tel: 712-288-4465.
Sisters 1; Lay Teachers 6; Students 74.
Catechesis/Religious Programs—Students 54.

Fort Dodge, Webster Co., Corpus Christi (1856), Very Rev. Donald C. Ries, V.F.; Rev. Brian Danner.
Res., 430 N. 8th St., P.O. Box 994, 50501-0994. Tel: 515-573-3616; Fax: 515-573-4556. [JC]
School—Tel: 515-576-0522.
Lay Teachers 20; Students 310.
Catechesis/Religious Programs—Students 144.

Holy Rosary (1946), Rev. Thomas J. Topf.
Res., 2401 9th Ave. S., 50501-6246. Tel: 515-573-3162 (Res.); 573-2018 (Church). [JC]
School—2406 9 1/2 Ave. S., 50501. Tel: 515-576-0574.
Lay Teachers 7; Students 117.
Catechesis/Religious Programs—Students 57.

Sacred Heart (1897), Rev. Harry D. McAlpine.
Res., 1321 Second Ave. S., 50501-4925. Tel: 515-573-7617. [JC]
School—214 S. 13th St., 50501. Tel: 515-576-0563.
Lay Teachers 15; Students 121.
Catechesis/Religious Programs—Students 123.

Gilmore City, Pocahontas Co., St. John's (1889), Rev. Timothy J. Fitzgerald.
Res., P.O. Box 262, 50541-0262. Tel: 515-373-6016. [CEM]
Catechesis/Religious Programs—Students 46.

Graettinger, Palo Alto Co., Immaculate Conception (1891), Rev. Msgr. Thomas M. Donahoe.
Res., P.O. Box 448, 51342-0448. Tel: 712-859-3327; Fax: 712-859-3327. [CEM]
Catechesis/Religious Programs—Tel: 712-859-3990.
Students 94.

Grand Junction, Greene Co., St. Brigid's (1873) (Irish), Rev. Daniel C. Guenther.
Res., 50107. Tel: 515-738-2684. [CEM]
Catechesis/Religious Programs—St. Brigid Parish Center, 602 Hager St. E., 50107. Tel: 515-738-2254.
Students 58.

Granville, Sioux Co., St. Joseph (1886), Rev. Clem W. Currans.
Res., P.O. Box 127, 51022-0127. Tel: 712-727-3551. [CEM]
School—Spalding Catholic School, (Grades 7-8). Consolidation of Alton, Hospers and Granville. Tel: 712-727-3451; Fax: 712-727-3455.
Lay Teachers 2; Students 45.
High School—Spalding Catholic High School.
Priests 1; Sisters 1; Lay Teachers 14; Students 90.

Halbur, Carroll Co., St. Augustine's (1904), Rev. Gary B. Snyder.
Res., P.O. Box 13, 51444-0013. Tel: 712-658-2464. [CEM]
School—Holy Trinity Elementary. Consolidation of Halbur, Templeton and Roselle. Tel: 712-669-3346.
Lay Teachers 4; Students 60.
High School—Kuemper High School.
Students 22.
Catechesis/Religious Programs—Tel: 712-792-0513 (Carroll); 653-2131 (Mannina).
Students 21.

Hawarden, Sioux Co., St. Mary's (1887), Rev. Kevin M. Richter; Deacon Joseph Maher.
Res., P.O. Box 271, 51023-0271. Tel: 712-551-1501. [JC]
Catechesis/Religious Programs—Students 129.

Holstein, Ida Co., Our Lady of Good Counsel (1884), Rev. R. Mark Duchaine.
Res., 513 Mueller St., 51025-9802. Tel: 712-368-4755; Fax: 712-368-2470. [CEM]
Catechesis/Religious Programs—Tel: 712-368-2504.
Students 123.
Mission—Quimby, Cherokee Co., St. John the Baptist, 208 E. Railway, Quimby, 51049. Tel: 712-445-2256.

Hornick, Woodbury Co., St. Philip's (1900). Closed. For inquiries for parish records contact the Chancery.

Hospers, Sioux Co., St. Anthony's (1877), Rev. James Tigges.
Res., 506 Elm, P.O. Box 86, 51238-0086. Tel: 712-752-8784. [CEM]
School—Spalding Elementary, (Grades K-3). Consolidation of Alton, Hospers and Granville. Tel: 712-752-8286.
Lay Teachers 4; Students 94.

Humboldt, Humboldt Co., St. Mary's (1878), Rev. Eugene J. Ulses.
Res., 311 Fourth St. N., 50548-1647. Tel: 515-332-2856. [CEM]
School—Tel: 515-332-2134.
Sisters 1; Lay Teachers 11; Students 207.
Catechesis/Religious Programs—Students 131.

Ida Grove, Ida Co., Sacred Heart (1878), Rev. Gerald M. Fisch.
Res., 800 N. Main, P.O. Box 244, 51445-1297. Tel: 712-364-2718. [CEM]
Catechesis/Religious Programs—Tel: 712-364-3628.
Students 181.

Jefferson, Greene Co., St. Joseph's (1875), Rev. Daniel C. Guenther.
Res., 503 N. Chestnut St., 50129-1507. Tel: 515-386-2638; Fax: 515-386-3672.
Catechesis/Religious Programs—501 N. Locust, 50129. Tel: 515-386-4010.
Students 205.

Kingsley, Plymouth Co., St. Michael's (1888), Rev. James E. Fangman.
Res., P.O. Box 486, 51028-0486. Tel: 712-378-2722. [CEM]
Catechesis/Religious Programs—Tel: 712-378-2021.
Students 170.

Lake City, Calhoun Co., St. Mary's (1894), Rev. Dennis L. Sefcik; Deacon Don Kunecke.
Res., P.O. Box 131, 51449-0131. Tel: 712-464-3395. [CEM]
Catechesis/Religious Programs—Students 150.

Larchwood, Lyon Co., St. Mary (1898) (German-Dutch), Rev. Francis J. Nemmers; Deacon Jeffrey F. Gallagher.
Res., P.O. Box 37, 51241-0037. Tel: 712-477-2273. [JC]
Catechesis/Religious Programs—Tel: 712-477-2403.
Students 177.

Laurens, Pocahontas Co., Sacred Heart (1893), Rev. Msgr. Leonard M. Ziegmann.
Res., P.O. Box 171, 50554-0171. Tel: 712-845-4596. [CEM]
Catechesis/Religious Programs—Tel: 712-843-5683.
Students 122.

Ledyard, Kossuth Co., Sacred Heart (1887), Rev. John M. Thomas.
Mailing Address: P.O. Box 67, 50556-0067. Tel: 515-646-2525.
Res., 204 S. Summit Ave., P.O. Box 195, Bancroft, 50517. Tel: 515-885-2462. [CEM]

Le Mars, Plymouth Co., St. Joseph's (1875) (German), Revs. Jerome P. Cosgrove; William A. Schreiber; Rev. Msgr. Gerald F. Lyon, (Retired).
Res., 20 Sixth Ave. N.E., 51031-3714. Tel: 712-546-5223; Fax: 712-546-8346. [CEM][JC]

School—Gehlen Catholic School, Plymouth St. S.E., 51031.
Catechesis/Religious Programs—Tel: 712-546-6038.
Students 111.

St. James (1883), Rev. Richard S. Ries; Deacon Donald Kunkel.
Res., 109 Sixth Ave. S.W., 51031-3434. Tel: 712-546-5201. [JC]
School—Gehlen Catholic Elementary, Tel: 712-546-5126.
Lay Teachers 23; Students 411.
High School—Gehlen Catholic High School, Tel: 712-546-4181.
Lay Teachers 25; Students 203.
Catechesis/Religious Programs—20 Sixth Ave. N.E., 51031. Tel: 712-546-6038.
Students 210.

Lidderdale, Carroll Co., Holy Family (1914) (German), Rev. Merlin Schrod.
Res., P.O. Box 160, 51452-0160. Tel: 712-822-5522. [CEM]
School—Christ the King Elementary. Consolidation of Breda, Lidderdale, Maple River and Mt. Carmel. Tel: 712-673-2582.
Catechesis/Religious Programs—Carroll, 51401. Tel: 712-792-0513.
Students 178.

Livermore, Humboldt Co., Sacred Heart (1881), Rev. Eugene J. Ulses.
Res., 311 Fourth St. N., Humboldt, 50548-1647. Tel: 515-332-2856. [CEM]
Catechesis/Religious Programs—Tel: 515-379-2508.
Students 65.

Lohrville, Calhoun Co., St. Joseph's (1885), Rev. Dennis L. Sefcik.
Res., N. Lloyd St., P.O. Box 131, Lake City, 51449. Tel: 712-464-3395. [CEM]
Catechesis/Religious Programs—Students 79.

Madrid, Boone Co., St. Malachy's (1923), Rev. Msgr. Louis H. Kollasch; Deacon Frank Milani.
Res., 207 Gerald St., 50156-1464. Tel: 515-795-2731.
Church—405 Gerald St., 50156. Tel: 515-795-2613.
Catechesis/Religious Programs—Students 180.

Mallard, Palo Alto Co., St. Mary's (1889), Rev. Peter J. Fransco.
Res., P.O. Box 236, 50562-0236. Tel: 712-425-3359. [CEM]
Catechesis/Religious Programs—Students 47.

Manilla, Crawford Co., Sacred Heart (1887), Rev. Robert W. Gralapp.
Res., 269 6th St., P.O. Box 339, 51454-0339. Tel: 712-654-9511. [CEM]
Catechesis/Religious Programs—Students 143.

Manning, Carroll Co., Sacred Heart (1916) (German), Rev. James C. McAlpin.
Res., 203 Sue St., 51455-1399. Tel: 712-653-3804. [CEM]
Catechesis/Religious Programs—Tel: 712-653-2933.
Students 259.

Manson, Calhoun Co., St. Thomas (1885), Rev. Jerome A. Degen.
Res., P.O. Box 99, 50563-0099. Tel: 712-469-3743. [CEM]
Catechesis/Religious Programs—Students 103.

Maple River, Carroll Co., St. Francis of Assisi (1907) (German), Rev. Robert Brown.
Res., 19481 140th St., Carroll, 51401-9499. Tel: 712-792-3934. [CEM]
School—Christ the King Elementary. Consolidation of Breda, Lidderdale, Maple River and Mt. Carmel. Tel: 712-792-3977.
Lay Teachers 9.
Catechesis/Religious Programs—Tel: 712-792-9422.
Students 9.

Mapleton, Monona Co., St. Mary's (1894), Rev. Edmund Tiedeman. In res., Rev. Gerald Zensen.
Res., 703 Heisler St., 51034-1222. Tel: 712-827-4467. [CEM][JC]
Catechesis/Religious Programs—Tel: 712-882-1780.
Students 128.
Mission—Oto, Woodbury Co., St. Mary's, 620 State St., Box 67, Oto, 51044-6007.

Marcus, Cherokee Co., Holy Name (1877), Rev. Richard R. Remmes.
Res., 110 N. Elm St., P.O. Box 366, 51035-0366. Tel: 712-376-2628. [CEM]
Catechesis/Religious Programs—Tel: 712-376-2625.
Students 171.

Maryhill, Cherokee Co., Visitation of the B.V.M. (1895), Rev. Eugene E. Sitzmann.
Res., 975-540th St., Cherokee, 51012-7151. Tel: 712-225-2131. [CEM]
Catechesis/Religious Programs—Students 75.

Merrill, Plymouth Co., Assumption Church (1893), Rev. Richard D. Ball.
Res., P.O. Box 175, 51038-0175. Tel: 712-938-2236. [CEM]
Catechesis/Religious Programs—Tel: 712-239-2845. Cindy Palmer, D.R.E.
Students 113.
Mission—Ellendale, Plymouth Co., St. Joseph's.

Milford, Dickinson Co., St. Joseph's (1884), Rev. John A. Vakulskas, Jr.; Deacon M. Peter Hart.
Res., 1413 Okoboji Ave., 51351-1232. Tel: 712-338-2172 (Res.); 338-2274 (Office); Fax: 712-338-2191. [CEM]
Catechesis/Religious Programs—Patricia Scott, D.R.E.
Students 250.

Moorland, Webster Co., Our Lady of Good Counsel (1902), Rev. Timothy J. Boekelman.
Res., P.O. Box 135, 50566-0135. Tel: 515-549-3556. [CEM]
Catechesis/Religious Programs—Students 86.

Mount Carmel, Carroll Co., Our Lady of Mt. Carmel (1869) (German), Rev. Robert Brown.
Res., 19481 140th St., Carroll, 51401-9499. Tel: 712-792-3934. [CEM]
School—Christ the King Elementary. Consolidation of Breda, Lidderdale, Maple River and Mt. Carmel. Tel: 712-792-3977.
Lay Teachers 6; Students 182.

Moville, Woodbury Co., Immaculate Conception (1892), Rev. Msgr. Roger J. Augustine, V.G.
Res., P.O. Box C, 51039-0802. Tel: 712-873-3745. [CEM]
Catechesis/Religious Programs—Tel: 712-873-3644.
Students 178.

Neptune, Plymouth, St. Joseph (Hinton) (1880), Rev. Mark J. Stoll.
Res., 28172 Nature Ave., Hinton, 51024-8553. Tel: 712-546-8228. [CEM]
Catechesis/Religious Programs—St. Joseph Church, 20 6th Ave. NE, LeMars, 51031. Tel: 712-546-5223.
Students 86.

Odebolt, Sac Co., St. Martin's (1877), Rev. Allan Reicks.
Res., P.O. Box 500, 51458-0500. Tel: 712-668-2690. [CEM]
Catechesis/Religious Programs—Students 130.

Ogden, Boone Co., St. John's (1896), Rev. Thomas J. Munn. Pastoral Ministers: Sr. Mary Lois Lehman, P.B.V.M.; Sr. Mary Bernard Mauss, P.B.V.M.
Res., P.O. Box J, 50212-0810. Tel: 515-275-2580. [CEM]
Catechesis/Religious Programs—Tel: 800-796-2722.
Students 59.
Mission—Dayton, Webster Co., Christ the King.

Onawa, Monona Co., St. John's (1900), Rev. Alfred E. McCoy.
Res., 1009 13th St., 51040-0417. Tel: 712-423-2656.
Catechesis/Religious Programs—Students 136.
Mission—Blencoe, Monona Co., St. Bernard's.

Oyens, Plymouth Co., St. Catherine's (1900), Rev. Randy L. Schon.
Res., P.O. Box 538, 51045-0538. Tel: 712-546-4588. [CEM]
School—St. Catherine-St. Mary's Elementary. (Oyens, Remsen). Tel: 712-786-2764.
Lay Teachers 13; Students 231.
Catechesis/Religious Programs—321 Fulton St., Remsen, 51050. Tel: 712-786-1160.
Students 186.

Pocahontas, Pocahontas Co., Church of the Resurrection (1973), Rev. Merle F. Kollasch.
Res., 21 3rd St. S.W., 50574-0157. Tel: 712-335-3242; Fax: 712-335-3919. [CEM]
School—Pocahontas Catholic Elementary, Tel: 712-335-3603.
Sisters 1; Lay Teachers 7; Students 102.
Catechesis/Religious Programs—Students 94.

Pomeroy, Calhoun Co., St. Mary's (1881), Rev. Richard J. Macke; Deacon Robert Lenz.
Res., P.O. Box 57, 50575-0057. Tel: 712-468-2473. [CEM]
Catechesis/Religious Programs—Tel: 712-468-2248.
Students 52.
Mission—Palmer, Pocahontas Co., St. Joseph's, 502 Meade St., Palmer, 50571.

Remsen, Plymouth Co., St. Mary's (1889), Rev. Thomas J. Hart; Deacon Allan Wieler.
Res., Box #509, 51050. Tel: 712-786-1437; 786-1444. [CEM]
School—St. Catherine-St. Mary's. (Oyens-Remsen). Tel: 712-786-1160.
Sisters 1; Lay Teachers 18; Students 234.
High School—Tel: 712-786-1433; Fax: 712-786-2499.
Priests 1; Sisters 1; Lay Teachers 16; Students 122.
Catechesis/Religious Programs—Tel: 712-786-2376; Fax: 712-786-1167.
Students 186.

Rock Rapids, Lyon Co., Holy Name (1871) (Irish), Rev. Eugene T. Schumacher.
Res., 1108 S. Carroll St., 51246-9529. Tel: 712-472-3248. [CEM]
Catechesis/Religious Programs—Students 94.

Rock Valley, Sioux Co., St. Mary's (1895), Rev. Dale George.
Res., 1821 14th St., 51247-0098. Tel: 712-476-2060. [CEM]
Catechesis/Religious Programs—Totals include Sacred Heart, Sioux Center and Christ the King, Sioux Center. Tel: 712-476-2007.
Students 132.
Mission—Alvord, Lyon Co., Sacred Heart, Alvord, 51230. Tel: 712-473-2215. [CEM]

Rockwell City, Calhoun Co., St. Francis of Assisi (1899) (German), Rev. Richard Kielbasa.
Res., 744 Main St., 50579-1399. Tel: 712-297-8263. [CEM]
Catechesis/Religious Programs—Tel: 712-297-7183.
Students 105.

Rolfe, Pocahontas Co., St. Margaret's (1895), Rev. Timothy J. Fitzgerald.
Res., St. John's Rectory, P.O. Box 262, Gilmore City, 50541-0262. Tel: 515-373-6016. [CEM]
Catechesis/Religious Programs—Students 52.

Roselle, Carroll Co., Holy Angels (1874), Rev. Gary B. Snyder.
Res., Box 13, Halbur, 51444-0013. Tel: 712-658-2464. [CEM]
School—Holy Trinity Elementary, Tel: 712-669-3346.
Students 19.
High School—Kuemper Catholic High School.
Students 14.
Catechesis/Religious Programs—Tel: 712-792-0513 (Carroll); 653-2131 (Mennina).
Students 11.

Royal, Clay Co., St. Louis (1923) (French-German), Rev. Anthony P. Pick.
Res., P.O. Box 49, 51357-0049. Tel: 712-933-2667; Fax: 712-933-2356.
Catechesis/Religious Programs—Tel: 712-933-2604.
Students 102.
Mission—Everly, Clay Co., St. Mary's, P.O. Box 49, 51357. Tel: 712-834-2681.

Ruthven, Palo Alto Co., Sacred Heart (1888), Rev. Donald Slaven.
Church—P.O. Box 400, 51358-0400. Tel: 712-837-5240. [CEM]
Catechesis/Religious Programs—Students 71.
Mission—Ayrshire, Palo Alto Co., Sacred Heart, P.O. Box 207, Ayrshire, 50515. Tel: 515-426-3260.

Sac City, Sac Co., St. Mary's (1892) (German-Irish), Rev. Mark E. Harrington.
Res., P.O. Box 324, 50583-0324. Tel: 712-662-7240. [CEM]
Catechesis/Religious Programs—Students 142.

St. Benedict, Kossuth Co., St. Benedict's (1877), Rev. Lynn Bruch.
Res., 2003 190th St., Algona, 50511-9801. Tel: 515-679-4165. [CEM]
School—Seton Elementary. Consolidation of St. Cecelia, Algona, St. Benedict and St. Joseph, Wesley. Tel: 515-295-3509; Fax: 515-295-7739.
Catechesis/Religious Programs—St. Cecelia, 715 E. North St., Algona, 50511.
Students 8.

St. Joseph, Kossuth Co., St. Joseph's (1876), Rev. Paul F. Eisele.
Res., 1023 Hwy. 169, Bode, 50519. Tel: 515-379-1470. [CEM]
Catechesis/Religious Programs—Students 85.

Salix, Woodbury Co., St. Joseph's (1869), Rev. Bruce A. Lawler.
Res., P.O. Box 270, 51052-0270. Tel: 712-946-5635. [CEM][JC]
Catechesis/Religious Programs—Students 146.

Sanborn, O'Brien Co., St. Cecilia's (1882), Rev. David A. Hemann.
Res., P.O. Box 326, 51248-0326. Tel: 712-729-3423. [CEM]
Catechesis/Religious Programs—Students 141.
Mission—Hartley, O'Brien Co., St. Joseph's, Tel: 712-728-2626.

Schaller, Sac Co., St. Joseph's (1891), Rev. Francis Higgins.
Res., P.O. Box 457, 51053-0457. Tel: 712-275-4238. [CEM]
Catechesis/Religious Programs—Students 70.

Scranton, Greene Co., St. Paul's (1926) (German-Irish), Rev. Dennis W. Meinen.
Res., P.O. Box 215, 51462-0215. Tel: 712-652-3448; Fax: 712-652-3795. [JC]
Catechesis/Religious Programs—Tel: 515-389-3625; Fax: 515-389-3795.
Students 51.

Sheldon, O'Brien Co., St. Patrick's (1873) (Irish), Rev. John McGuirk.
Res., 310 10th St., 51201-1530. Tel: 712-324-3220. [CEM]
School—Tel: 712-324-3181.
Sisters 1; Lay Teachers 11; Students 116.
Catechesis/Religious Programs—Tel: 712-324-4588.
Students 143.

Sibley, Osceola Co., St. Andrew's (1896), Rev. Timothy J. Hogan.
Res., 716 Eighth St., P.O. Box 130, 51249-0130. Tel: 712-754-3311. [CEM]
Catechesis/Religious Programs—Tel: 712-754-2739.
Students 183.

Sioux Rapids, Buena Vista Co., St. Joseph's (1886), Rev. J. Charles Yetmar.
Res., P.O. Box 450, 50585-0450. Tel: 712-283-2765. [CEM]
Catechesis/Religious Programs—Students 70.

Spencer, Clay Co., Sacred Heart (1883), Rev. Roger Linnan.
Res., 1111 4th Ave. W., P.O. Box 817, 51301-0817. Tel: 712-262-3047.
School—Tel: 712-262-6428.
Lay Teachers 11; Students 167.
Catechesis/Religious Programs—Students 249.

Spirit Lake, Dickinson Co., St. Mary's (1914), Rev. Albert O. Grendler.
Res., P.O. Box 354, 51360-0354. Tel: 712-336-1742; Fax: 712-336-0546. [CEM]
Catechesis/Religious Programs—Students 223.

Storm Lake, Buena Vista Co., St. Mary's (1872), Revs. Clair L. Boes; Michael J. Erpelding.
Res., Third & Seneca Sts., P.O. Box 1106, 50588-1106. Tel: 712-732-3110. [CEM]
School—Elementary & High School, Tel: 712-732-1856 (Elem.); 732-4166 (H.S.); Fax: 712-732-4590.
Sisters of the Presentation 2; Lay Teachers 26; Students 383.
Catechesis/Religious Programs—Students 208.

Struble, Plymouth Co., St. Joseph's (1903), Rev. Timothy A. Friedrichsen.
Res., 430 Main St., P.O. Box H, 51057-9999. Tel: 712-562-6401. [CEM 2]
Catechesis/Religious Programs—Tel: 712-546-5223.
Students 39.

Sutherland, O'Brien Co., Sacred Heart (1883), Rev. Gerald L. Zeman.
Res., P.O. Box 70, 51058-0070. Tel: 712-446-3742. [CEM]
Catechesis/Religious Programs—Students 119.
Mission—Primghar, O'Brien Co., St. Anthony of Padua, 375 S. Green St., Primghar, 51245. Tel: 712-757-3735. [CEM]

Templeton, Carroll Co., Sacred Heart (1882), Rev. Gary B. Snyder.
Res., Box 13, Halbur, 51444. Tel: 712-669-3345. [CEM]
School—Holy Trinity Elementary. Consolidation of Halbur, Templeton and Roselle. Tel: 712-669-3341.
Students 59.
High School—Kuemper Catholic High School.
Students 23.
Catechesis/Religious Programs—Tel: 712-792-0513 (Carroll); 653-2131 (Mannina).
Students 16.

Vail, Crawford Co., St. Ann's (1878), Rev. Victor F. Ramaeker.
Res., P.O. Box 158, 51465-0158. Tel: 712-677-5556; Fax: 712-677-2727. [CEM]
School—Holy Cross Elementary, Tel: 712-677-5555.
High School—Interparochial Catholic High School, Tel: 712-792-3596; Fax: 712-792-8070.
Students 16.
Sisters of St. Francis of Clinton: Tel: 712-689-2589.
Lay Teachers 4; Students 46.
Catechesis/Religious Programs—Tel: 712-677-5514.
Students 96.

Varina, Pocahontas Co., St. Columbkille's (1882), Rev. Armand J. Bertrand.
Res., Box 306, Fonda, 50540-0306. Tel: 712-288-6480. [CEM]

Wall Lake, Sac Co., St. Joseph's (1878), Rev. Leo L. Riesberg.
Res., P.O. Box L, 51466-0607. Tel: 712-664-2915.
Catechesis/Religious Programs—Tel: 712-664-2910.
Students 158.

Wesley, Kossuth Co., St. Joseph's (1891), Rev. Paul D. Bormann.
Res., P.O. Box 38, 50483-0038. Tel: 515-679-4279; 679-4135. [CEM]
School—Seton Elementary. Consolidation of St. Cecelia, Algona, St. Benedict, St. Joseph, Wesley, St. Michael's, Whittemore, and St. Joseph, Bode. Tel: 515-295-3509.
Students 69.
High School—Bishop Garrigan High School.
Students 23.

West Bend, Palo Alto Co., SS. Peter and Paul (1888), Rev. Bruce A. Lefebvre; Deacon Gerald Streit.
Res., P.O. Box 316, 50597-0316. Tel: 515-887-3333; Fax: 515-887-3333. [CEM]
School—Tel: 515-887-4542.
Lay Teachers 8; Students 70.
Catechesis/Religious Programs—Tel: 515-887-4058.
Students 102.

Whittemore, Kossuth Co., St. Michael's (1889), Rev. Edward G. Murray; Deacon Joseph Straub.
Res., P.O. Box 337, 50598-0337. Tel: 515-884-2669. [CEM]

Willey, Carroll Co., St. Mary's, Rev. Craig A. Collison.
Res., 201 Olympic Ave., Carroll, 51401-9726. Tel: 712-792-4516. [CEM]
School—Consolidation of Holy Spirit, Dedham, Willey and St. Lawrence Elementary. Tel: 712-792-3610.
Students 50.
High School—Kuemper Catholic High School.
Students 22.
Catechesis/Religious Programs—Tel: 712-792-4386.
Students 21.

Woodward, Boone Co., St. John of God (1965). (State Hospital and School). Rev. Msgr. Louis H. Kollasch; Deacon Frank Milani.
Res., 207 Gerald St., Madrid, 50156-1464. Tel: 515-795-2731.

Chaplains of Public Institutions

Sioux City. *Marian Health Center*. Rev. Richard A. Sitzmann.

Carroll. *St. Anthony Regional Hospital*. Rev. Robert L. Leiting.

Cherokee. *State Mental Health Institute*. Rev. Eugene E. Sitzmann.

Fort Dodge. *Trinity Regional Hospital*. Revs. P. Joseph Nooney; Eugene F. Walding.

Rockwell City. *Calhoun County State Reformatory, Minimum Security for Men*. Rev. Roger J. Linnan, Chap.

Woodward. *Woodward State Hospital and School*. Rev. Msgr. Louis H. Kollasch.

Special Assignment:
Reverend Fathers—
Friedrichsen, Timothy A., Briar Cliff College, 3303 Rebecca St., Sioux City, IA 51104-2340. Tel: 712-279-1704; 712-562-6401 (Res.)
Guredet, Randy J., Co-Dir., Minorities & Human Development, 1011 Douglas St., Sioux City, IA 51105-1399
Seuntjens, LeRoy L., Chap., Holy Spirit Retirement Home, 1701 W. 25th St., Sioux City, IA 51103-1799. Tel: 712-252-2726
Stone, Stanley R., Chap., Sioux City Nursing Homes, 1122 Grandview Blvd., Apt. 7, Sioux City, IA 51103-4398. Tel: 712-258-5202

On Duty Outside the Diocese:
Reverend Monsignors—
Schnurr, Dennis M., General Secretary, National Conference of Catholic Bishops, St. John's Hall, 4001 14th St. N.E., Washington, DC 20017
Reverend Fathers—
Barrett, Miles J., USS Kitty Hawk (CV-63), Chaplain's Office, FPO AP, 96634-2770
Dandurand, Douglas E., Archdiocese of St. Paul and Minneapolis, MN
Farrell, Emmett L., 2020 Alaquinas Dr., San Ysidro, CA 92173
Flanagan, Thomas J., Pfarrer-Bendel-Weg 2, D-61462 Koenigstein-Mammolshain, Germany. Tel: 011-496-1734-169
Holland, Thomas D., U.S. Air Force, 4050 Harbors Dr., Apt. 244, Las Vegas, NV 89121
Kurzak, John, U.S. Air Force, 2685 S. Dayton Way #205, Denver, CO 80231. Tel: 303-676-6480
Larkin, Michael T.
O'Kane, Patrick J.
Seifried, Kenneth A., 6 W. Staff Row, Atlanta, GA 30310. Tel: 404-755-1487
Van Oosbree, Christian J.

Absent on Leave:
Reverend Fathers—
Adam, Richard A.
Waters, Robert J.

Retired:
Reverend Monsignors—
Behrens, A.W., P.O. Box 94, Marcus, IA 51035-0094. Tel: 712-376-4788
Brady, Frank J., 1703 W. 25th St., Apt. B208, Sioux City, IA 51103-1799. Tel: 712-255-9343
Lilly, E. C., 1701 W. 25th St., Bldg. B, Apt. 205, Sioux City, IA 51103-1799. Tel: 712-255-5423
Lyon, Gerald F., 20-6th Ave., NE, LeMars, IA 51031. Tel: 712-546-3714
Quinn, Robert J., P.O. Box 1346, Imperial Beach, CA 91933-1346. Tel: 619-437-0180
Ruba, Nicholas J., 403 Cleveland Ct., Remsen, IA 51050. Tel: 712-786-2719
Walker, Dean P., P.O. Box 2142, Sioux City, IA 51104-2142
Reverend Fathers—
Adams, Edmond F., Sacred Heart Church, 1321 2nd Ave. S., Fort Dodge, IA 50501-4925. Tel: 515-573-7617
Alvey, J. Paul, 7791 E. Via Del Futuro, Scottsdale, AZ 85258
Beacom, Vincent L., R.R. 3, Arnolds Park, IA 51331-9803
Becker, Nicholas J., January thru March: 10360 N. 76th Dr., Peoria, AZ., P.O. Box 633, Algona, IA 50511-0633
Brennan, C. John, 1703 W. 25th, Apt. 204, Sioux City, IA 51103-1799. Tel: 712-277-8981
Bruch, Walter L., 110 Peeble Ln., Apt. 16, Carroll, IA 51401. Tel: 712-792-6251
Cain, John F., P.O. Box 34, Larchwood, IA 51241-0034. Tel: 605-338-9329
Calkins, Raymond J., 326 Green Chase Cir., Montgomery, AL 36117. Tel: 334-215-1813
Carpenter, Edward V., 1122 Grandview Blvd., Apt. #5, Sioux City, IA 51105-4398. Tel: 712-252-2338
Ceperley, Eugene F., Marian Village, Apt. 102, 2320 6th Ave. N., Fort Dodge, IA 50501
Condon, Robert M., 2300 Indian Hills Dr., Apt. 2-201, Sioux City, IA 51104
Cooper, Harold V., 2507-33rd. St., Sioux City, IA 51105. Tel: 712-239-2880
Fangman, Robert M., 422 E. 7th St., Apt. 23, Carroll, IA 51401
Friedman, Cecil H., 1021 E. Call St., Algona, IA 50511
Greving, Louis H., Grotto of the Redemption, P.O. Box 376, West Bend, IA 50597-0376. Tel: 515-887-2371
Holland, Thomas D., 4050 Pacific Harbors Dr., #244, Las Vegas, NV 89121
Kerwin, Joseph A., 229 Courtyard Blvd., Apt. 104, Sun City Center, FL 33573-5768. Tel: 813-634-4813
Koster, Dale F., P.O. Box 264 W. 1st St., Apt. 8, Auburn, IA 51433
Lisowski, Jan, 1122 Grandview Blvd., Apt. 3, Sioux City, IA 51103-4398. Tel: 716-549-0372
Lynch, Daniel C., 407 S. 13th St., Sac City, IA 50583. Tel: 712-662-4801
McFadden, George B., 1122 Grandview Blvd., Apt. 2, Sioux City, IA 51105-4398. Tel: 712-255-0827
Meyer, Henry H., 1414 N. West St., Carroll, IA 51401-1442. Tel: 712-792-2368
Montag, Bernard J., P.O. Box 73, West Bend, IA 50597-0073. Tel: 515-887-6874
Nemmers, Reinhard E., Plymouth Manor, 954 7th Ave., S.E., LeMars, IA 51031
Nooney, Patrick J., Trinity Regional Hospital, S. Kenyond Rd., Fort Dodge, IA 50501-5795
O'Rourke, Gabriel A., Holy Spirit Retirement Home, 1701 W. 25th St., Sioux City, IA 51103-1798
Reinhart, Ralph W., 312 Elm St., Apt. 2, Manning, IA 51455
Schissel, John G., 605 N. 11th St., Cherokee, IA 51012-1526
Schumacher, Leo C., Apt. A-2, 2320 6th Ave. N., Fort Dodge, IA 50501-3561. Tel: 515-955-2275
Smith, Donald R., 3929 Winona Way, Apt. 4, Sioux City, IA 51104-4447. Tel: 712-239-5865
Thiele, Robert A., 101 N. Earl, Lake City, IA 51449
Thom, Elmer D., 1122 Grandview Blvd., Apt. 9, Sioux City, IA 51103-4398. Tel: 712-277-3954
Waite, Patrick J., 5682 Tulane St., San Diego, CA 92122-3244
White, Lloyd W., 130 Peeble Ln., Apt. 6, Carroll, IA 51401-3020. Tel: 712-792-5633
Wieling, Raymond P., 3015 Chicago Ave., Sioux City, IA 51106-1259. Tel: 712-276-7065
Wingert, D. William, 4014 Yellow Ave., Hartley, IA 51346-7606

Wingert, Gerald R., 216 W. Nebraska, Algona, IA 50511-2608. Tel: 515-295-3123
Young, Edward J., 1122 Grandview Blvd., Apt. 1, Sioux City, IA 51103-4398. Tel: 712-277-4638
Zensen, Gerald F., P.O. Box 67, Oto, IA 51044-0067

Permanent Deacons:
Berger, William J., St. Michael's, Sioux City
Bertrand, Gerald L., Holy Name, Marcus
Bruner, Robert S., St. Lawrence, Carroll
Doocy, Philip F., St. John the Baptist, Bancroft
Dunn, Francis M., Immaculate Conception Church, Graettinger
Easter, Jack L., Sacred Heart, Spencer
Forrest, Ronald M., Associate Dir., Permanent Diaconate, Sioux City
Gallagher, Jeffrey F., St. Mary Church, Larchwood
Hand, Michael J., Church of the Nativity, Sioux City
Hart, M. Peter, St. Joseph, Milford
Heffernan, John J., Blessed Sacrament Church, Sioux City
Hogan, Joseph R., Our Lady of Good Counsel Church, Fonda
Karpuk, Fred P., Blessed Sacrament Church, Sioux City
Kelley, Richard C.
Kunecke, Donald L., St. Mary's Church, Lake City
Kunkel, Donald M., St. Joseph Church, LeMars
Lenz, Robert D., St. Mary's Church, Pomeroy
Lester, Jary
MacDonald, W. B., St. Cecelia Church, Algona
Maher, F. Joseph, St. Mary's Church, Hawarden
McCruden, Patrick J., St. Joseph Church, Sioux City, IA
Milani, Frank J., St. Malachy's Church, Madrid
Pietz, Ronald C., St. Joseph Church, Sioux City
Portz, Ray, St. Patrick, Sheldon
Reicks, Jerome A., St. Joseph Church, Sioux City
Reuter, Anthony C., Holy Spirit Church, Carroll
Rupp, J. LeRoy, Immaculate Conception Church, Cherokee
Sands, James H.
Sitzman, Larry K., St. Michael's Church, Sioux City
Spellman, George G., Ph.D., Marian Health Center and Blessed Sacrament Church, Sioux City
Straub, Joseph J., St. Michael's Church, Whittmore
Streit, Gerald B., Sts. Peter & Paul Church, West Bend
Weiler, Allan A., St. Mary's Church, Remsen
Westendorf, Louis B., M.D., St. Lawrence Church, Carroll
Wiskus, Robert A., Sacred Heart Church, Sioux City

INSTITUTIONS LOCATED IN THE DIOCESE

[A] COLLEGES AND UNIVERSITIES

SIOUX CITY. *Briar Cliff College*, 3303 Rebecca St., P.O. Box 2100, 51104-2100. Tel: 712-279-5321; Fax: 712-279-5410.
E-mail: rasmuss@briar-cliff.edu
Web site: www.briar-cliff.edu
For a complete listing, refer to the Colleges and Universities section.

[B] HIGH SCHOOLS, INTER-PAROCHIAL

SIOUX CITY. *Bishop Heelan Catholic High School*, 1021 Douglas St., 51105. Tel: 712-252-0573.
E-mail: connectdioscheelan
Web site: http://www.avalon.net/~hlnlang/
Serving the parishes of the Siouxland area. Rev. Alfred E. McLoy, Pres. Pro Tem; Joe Malsam, Prin.; Rev. Verne P. Stapenhorst. Priests 2; Sisters 2; Lay Teachers 45; Students 752.

ALGONA. *Bishop Garrigan Catholic High School*, 1224 N. McCoy St., 50511. Tel: 515-295-3521.
Serving the parishes at Algona, St. Benedict, Bode, Wesley, and Whittemore. Mr. Eugene Meister, Pres. Priests 2; Sisters 2; Lay Teachers 23; Students 253.

CARROLL. *Kuemper Catholic High School*, 109 S. Clark St., 51401. Tel: 712-792-3596.
Serving the thirteen parishes of Carroll-Holy Spirit and St. Lawrence Parishes; Arcadia; Dedham; Halbur; Lidderdale-Glidden; Maple River; Mount Carmel; Roselle; Templeton; Vail; Willey and Breda. Rev. Merlin J. Schrad, Pres.; Dr. Keith Guy, Prin.; Revs. Craig A. Collison; Terry A. Roder, Spiritual Dir. Priests 3; Sisters 1; Lay Teachers 36; Students 515.

FORT DODGE. *St. Edmond High School*, 501 N. 22nd St., 50501. Tel: 515-955-5850; Fax: 515-955-8473. Rev. Patrick R. Walsh, Pres.; Mr. Michael G. Kavars, Prin.; Mr. Thomas Mikio, Dir. Devel.; Sr. Dominic Church, P.B.V.M. Priests 1; Sisters 1; Lay Teachers 28; Students 324.

GRANVILLE. *Spalding Catholic High School*, 51022. Tel: 712-727-3451.
Serving the parishes of Granville; Alton and Hospers. Revs. Clem Currans, Pres.; Tim Johnson, Religion Teacher. Priests 3; Sisters 1; Lay Teachers 15; Students 90.

LE MARS. *Gehlen Catholic School*, 709 Plymouth St. N.E., 51031. Tel: 712-546-4181.
E-mail: gehlen@pionet.net
Web site: http://www.pionet.net/~gehlen
Serving the two parishes of LeMars; Assumption, Merrill; St. Joseph's, Ellendale; St. Joseph's, Neptune; St. Joseph's, Struble. Revs. William A. Schreiber, Admin.; Richard D. Ball. Priests 2; Sisters 2; Lay Teachers 48; Students 652.

REMSEN. *St. Mary's High School*, 523 Madison, 51050. Sr. Elaine Tworek, S.L.W., Prin. Priests 1; Sisters 1; Lay Teachers 14; Students 122.

STORM LAKE. *St. Mary's High School*, 50588.
Serving St. Mary's. Priests 1; Sisters 1; Lay Teachers 15; Students 94.

[C] ORPHANAGES

SIOUX CITY. *St. Anthony's Orphanage* Mailing Address: Catholic Charities of the Diocese of Sioux City, 1601 Military Rd., P.O. Box 2025, 51104. Tel: 712-252-4547.
For a complete listing, refer to the Special Care Facilities section.

[D] GENERAL HOSPITALS

SIOUX CITY. *Marian Health Center*, 801 Fifth St., 51101. Tel: 712-279-2010; Fax: 712-279-2034.
E-mail: mccrudep@mercyhealth.com
Web site: www.mercyhealth.com arian
For a complete listing, refer to the Hospitals section.

CARROLL. *St. Anthony Regional Hospital*, 51401. Tel: 712-792-3581
For a complete listing, refer to the Hospitals section.

ESTHERVILLE. *Holy Family Hospital*, 826 N. Eighth St., 51334. Tel: 712-362-2631
For a complete listing, refer to the Hospitals section.

[E] HOMES FOR THE AGED

SIOUX CITY. *Holy Spirit Retirement Home*, 1701 W. 25th St., 51103. Tel: 712-252-2726
For a complete listing, refer to the Special Care Facilities section.

CARROLL. *St. Anthony Nursing Home*, 406 E. Anthony St., 51401. Tel: 712-792-3581
For a complete listing, refer to the Special Care Facilities section.

FORT DODGE. *The Marian Home*, 2400 Sixth Ave. N., 50501
For a complete listing, refer to the Special Care Facilities section.

[F] CONVENTS AND RESIDENCES FOR SISTERS

SIOUX CITY. *Monastery of the Discalced Carmelite Nuns*, 2901 S. Cecelia St., 51106-3299. Tel: 712-276-1680.
E-mail: SrTherese@aol.com
Mother Therese of the Spirit of Love, O.C.D., Prioress. Chaplains: Revs. Gerald Hartz; Patrick J. O'Kane. Solemn Professed 13.

[G] SECULAR INSTITUTES

POCAHONTAS. *Opus Spiritus Sancti*, 21 SW 3rd St., 50574. Tel: 712-335-3242. Rev. Merle F. Kollasch, Regl. Coord. Community Activities & Member Secular Institute of Priests.

[H] MISCELLANEOUS

SIOUX CITY. *The Catholic Schools Foundation of the Diocese of Sioux City*, 1821 Jackson St., 51105.
Diocese of Sioux City Priests' Welfare Foundation, 1821 Jackson St., 51102-3379. Rev. Kevin C. McCoy, Contact Person.
Holy Spirit Retirement Home Foundation, Inc., 1701 W. 25th St., 51103. Tel: 712-252-2726. Lawrence D. Soens, Pres. Directors: Roger J. Augustine; Patrick J. Tomscha.

CARROLL. *Orchard View, Inc.*, S. Clark St., 51401. Tel: 712-792-3581. Franciscan Sisters of Perpetual Adoration. Gary P. Riedmann, Admin. Total in Residence 56.
St. Anthony Foundation, S. Clark St., 51401. Tel: 712-792-3581. Mr. Gary P. Reidmann.

WEST BEND. *Grotto of the Redemption.*
E-mail: grotto@ncn.net
Web site: www.okobaji.com/Attractions/Grotto
Mailing Address: P.O. Box 376, 50597. Tel: 515-887-2371. Gerald Streit, Dir.

RELIGIOUS INSTITUTES OF WOMEN REPRESENTED IN THE DIOCESE

For further details refer to the corresponding bracketed number in the Religious Institutes of Women section.

[0230]—*Benedictine Sisters of the Pontifical Jurisdiction.*—O.S.B.
[1780]—*Congregation of the Sisters of the Third Order of St. Francis of Perpetual Adoration.* (Central Prov.).—F.S.P.A.
[0420]—*Discalced Carmelite Nuns.*—O.C.D.
[]—*Opus Spiritus Sancti.*—O.S.S.
[2970]—*School Sisters of Notre Dame.* (Mankato Province).—S.S.N.D.
[2970]—*School Sisters of Notre Dame.* (Milwaukee Province).—S.S.N.D.
[2970]—*School Sisters of Notre Dame.* (St. Louis Province).—S.S.N.D.
[3580]—*Servants of Mary.* (American Province).—O.S.M.
[]—*Sisters For Christian Community.*—S.F.C.C.
[0430]—*Sisters of Charity of the Blessed Virgin Mary.*—B.V.M.
[2575]—*Sisters of Mercy of the Americas.* (Cedar Rapids Regional Community).—R.S.M.
[]—*Sisters of St. Benedict.* (Taegu, Korea).—O.S.B.
[1540]—*Sisters of St. Francis, Clinton, Iowa.*—O.S.F.
[1570]—*Sisters of St. Francis of the Holy Family.*—O.S.F.
[2350]—*Sisters of the Living Word.*—S.L.W.
[3270]—*Sisters of the Most Precious Blood (O'Fallon, MO).*—C.PP.S.
[3320]—*Sisters of the Presentation of the B.V.M.*—P.B.V.M.
[1720]—*Sisters of the Third Order Regular of St. Francis of the Congregation of Our Lady of Lourdes.*—O.S.F.

DIOCESAN CEMETERIES

SIOUX CITY. *Calvary*, Office, 1821 Jackson St., P.O. Box 3379, 51102-3379. Tel: 712-233-7511.

NECROLOGY

† Birdsall, Richard W., (Retired). —Died July 11, 1997.
† Carel, William L., (Retired). —Died June 10, 1997.
† Hoffmann, Edward D., (Retired). —Died Nov. 22, 1996.
† Kevane, Rev. Msgr. M. Eugene, (Retired). —Died Nov. 20, 1996.
† McClintock, Robert J., Odebolt, IA, St. Martin. —Died Aug. 29, 1997.
† Morkunas, Rev. Msgr. Simon, (Retired). —Died July 5, 1997.
† Phillips, Robert W., (Retired). —Died Dec. 7, 1996.
† Staber, Francis H., (Retired). —Died July 22, 1997.

Diocese of Sioux Falls

(Dioecesis Siouxormensis)

Most Reverend

ROBERT J. CARLSON

Bishop of Sioux Falls; ordained May 22, 1970; appointed Titular Bishop of Aviocala and Auxiliary Bishop of Saint Paul and Minneapolis November 22, 1983; consecrated January 11, 1984; appointed Coadjutor Bishop of Sioux Falls, 1994; succeeded to the See, March 21, 1995

Most Reverend

PAUL V. DUDLEY, D.D.

Retired Bishop of Sioux Falls; ordained June 2, 1951; appointed Titular Bishop of Ursona and Auxiliary Bishop of St. Paul and Minneapolis November 16, 1976; Episcopal ordination January 25, 1977; appointed Bishop of Sioux Falls September 26, 1978; installed December 13, 1978; retired March 21, 1995. *Res., 2500 W. 320th St., Northfield, MN, 55057.* Tel.: 507-663-1145.

"Jesus is Lord"

ESTABLISHED NOVEMBER 12, 1889.

Square Miles 35,091.

Comprises that part of the State of South Dakota East of the Missouri River.

For legal titles of parishes and diocesan institutions, consult the Chancery Office.

Chancery Office: 523 N. Duluth Ave., Sioux Falls, SD, 57104. Tel.: 605-334-9861; Fax: 605-333-3346.

Web site address: Diocese-of-Sioux-Falls.org

E-mail address: jklein@iw.net

STATISTICAL OVERVIEW

Personnel	
Bishop	1
Retired Bishops	1
Abbots	1
Retired Abbots	2
Priests: Diocesan Active in Diocese	80
Priests: Active Outside Diocese	3
Priests: Retired, Sick or Absent	36
Number of Diocesan Priests	119
Religious Priests in Diocese	39
Extern Priests in Diocese	10
Ordinations:	
Diocesan Priests	1
Transitional Deacons	5
Permanent Deacons in Diocese	24
Total Brothers	22
Total Sisters	449
Parishes	
Parishes	157
With Resident Pastor:	
Resident Diocesan Priests	70
Resident Religious Priests	17
Without Resident Pastor:	
Administered by Priests	55
Administered by Permanent Deacons	2
Administered by Professed Men Religious	1
Administered by Women Religious	4
Administered by Pastoral Teams, etc.	3
Completely Vacant	2
Professional Ministry Personnel:	
Brothers	4
Sisters	36
Lay Ministers	28
Welfare	
Catholic Hospitals	9
Total Assisted	485,000
Homes for the Aged	9
Total Assisted	1,500
Day Care and Extended Day Care Centers	1
Total Assisted	50
Specialized Homes	2
Total Assisted	145
Special Centers for Social Services	5
Total Assisted	112,000
Residential Care of Disabled	1
Total Assisted	15
Educational	
Diocesan Students in Other Seminaries	29
Total Seminarians	29
Colleges and Universities	2
Total Students	2,350
High Schools, Diocesan and Parish	3
Total Students	986
Elementary Schools, Diocesan and Parish	23
Total Students	4,196
Catechesis/Religious Education:	
High School Students	7,882
Elementary Students	10,811
Total Students Under Catholic Instruction	26,254
Teachers in the Diocese:	
Priests	1
Sisters	12
Lay Teachers	282
Vital Statistics	
Receptions into the Church:	
Infant Baptism Totals	1,961
Adult Baptism Totals	101
Received into Full Communion	319
First Communions	2,164
Confirmations	1,949
Marriages:	
Catholic	365
Interfaith	359
Total Marriages	724
Deaths	997
Total Catholic Population	121,811
Total Population	503,000

Former Bishops—Rt. Rev. MARTIN MARTY, O.S.B., D.D., appt. Bishop of Tiberias, Aug. 8, 1879; appt. Vicar Apostolic of Dakota, Aug. 12, 1879; cons. Feb. 1, 1880; Bishop of Sioux Falls, 1889; transferred to St. Cloud, MN, 1894; died Sept. 19, 1896.—Rt. Rev. THOMAS O'GORMAN, D.D., appt. Jan. 24, 1896; cons. April 19, 1896; died Sept. 18, 1921.—Most Rev. BERNARD J. MAHONEY, D.D., appt. May 22, 1922; cons. June 29, 1922; died March 20, 1939.—Most Rev. WILLIAM O. BRADY, S.T.D., D.D., appt. Bishop of Sioux Falls, June 10, 1939; cons. Aug. 24, 1939; appt. Coadjutor of St. Paul, June 21, 1956; succeeded to the See, Oct. 11, 1956; died Oct. 1, 1961.—Most Rev. LAMBERT A. HOCH, D.D., Former Bishop of Sioux Falls; ord. May 30, 1928; Bishop of Bismarck; appt. Jan. 23, 1952; cons. March 25, 1952; transferred to Sioux Falls, Nov. 27, 1956; retired June 13, 1978; died June 27, 1990.—Most Rev. PAUL V. DUDLEY, D.D., Bishop of Sioux Falls; ord. June 2, 1951; appt. Sept. 26, 1978; installed Dec. 13, 1978; retired March 21, 1995.

Vicar General—Rev. Msgr. RICHARD MAHOWALD, P.A., V.G., *523 N. Duluth Ave., Sioux Falls, 57104.*

Chancery Office—523 N. Duluth Ave., Sioux Falls, 57104. Tel: 605-334-9861; Fax: 605-333-3346. Refer all official business to this address.

Chancellor—JEROME KLEIN, *523 N. Duluth Ave., Sioux Falls, 57104.* Tel: 605-333-3345.

Vice Chancellor—JAY CONZEMIUS, *523 N. Duluth Ave., Sioux Falls, 57104.*

Diocesan Theologian—STEPHEN A. HIPP, *523 N. Duluth Ave., Sioux Falls, 57104.*

Diocesan Tribunal—523 N. Duluth Ave., Sioux Falls, 57104. Tel: 605-333-3357. (Address all rogatory commissions to this address).

Tribunal Judges—Revs. AL KRZYZOPOLSKI; RODNEY FARKE; LEONARD FOX; DONALD IMMING; THOMAS RYAN, Presiding Judge; GARY TERNES; Sr. LYNN MARIE WELBIG, P.B.V.M., J.C.L.

Defenders of the Matrimonial Bond—Revs. JAMES ENGLERT; GREGORY TSCHAKERT, J.C.L.; Mr. JAY CONZEMIUS, J.C.L.

Promoters of Justice—Rev. GREGORY TSCHAKERT, J.C.L.

Judges of the Appellate Court—Revs. JIM FRIEDRICH; JEROME KOPEL; KENNETH KOSTER; JOHN LANTSBERGER; JOSEPH MARDIAN; PIUS MARDIAN; CHARLES CIMPL; JEROME RANEK.

Defender of the Bond-Appellate Tribunal—Rev. CHARLES MANGAN, J.C.L.

Judicial Vicar—Rev. DONALD KETTLER, J.C.L.

Executive Coordinator of Matrimonial Tribunal—Mrs. VICKIE BEACH.

Director—Sr. LYNN MARIE WELBIG, P.B.V.M., J.C.L.

Diocesan Consultors—Rev. Msgr. RICHARD MAHOWALD, V.G.; Revs. TERRY ANDERSON; DENIS MEIER; RICHARD CASHEL; JOSEPH FORCELLE; JOSEPH SHORT; DARRELL LAMBERTY; GREGORY TSCHAKERT; JOSEPH RIPP.

Consilium Administrationis—Most Rev. Bishop, Vicar General, Chancellor.

Deans—Revs. TERRY ANDERSON; DENIS MEIER; RICHARD CASHEL; JOSEPH FORCELLE; JOSEPH SHORT; DARRELL LAMBERTY; GREGORY TSCHAKERT; JOSEPH RIPP.

Presbyteral Council—Most Rev. ROBERT J. CARLSON; Rev. Msgr. RICHARD MAHOWALD, V.G.; Revs. TERRY ANDERSON; DENIS MEIER; RICHARD CASHEL; JOSEPH FORCELLE; DARRELL LAMBERTY; THOMAS HILLENBRAND, O.S.B.; MICHAEL KELLY; JOSEPH SHORT; CHESTER MURTHA; GREGORY TSCHAKERT; JOSEPH RIPP.

Diocesan Offices and Directors

Apostleship of Prayer—Rev. CHARLES M. MANGAN, Dir., *P.O. Box 285, Gettysburg, 57442-0305.*

Pastoral Ministry with Disabled Persons—Vacant, *Catholic Pastoral Center, 523 N. Duluth Ave., Sioux Falls, 57104.* Tel: 605-333-3365.

Bishop's Bulletin—Rev. MICHAEL GRIFFIN, Exec. Editor; Mr. KENYON GLEASON, Mgr. Editor, *523 N. Duluth Ave., Sioux Falls, 57104.*

Building Commission—JEROME KLEIN, Chancellor, *Catholic Chancery Office, 523 N. Duluth Ave., Sioux Falls, 57104.*

Catholic Charities—JAMES MASON, Dir., *523 N. Duluth Ave., Sioux Falls, 57104.* Tel: 605-333-3351; Fax: 605-333-3346.

Catholic Foundation for Eastern South Dakota—MARK CONZEMIUS, Exec. Dir., *523 N. Duluth Ave., Sioux Falls, 57104.*

Catholic Relief Services—JEROME KLEIN, Chancellor, *523 N. Duluth Ave., Sioux Falls, 57104.*

Catholic Family Services—SR. MARY CAROLE CURRAN, O.S.B., Exec. Dir., *523 N. Duluth Ave., Sioux Falls, 57104.* Tel: 605-333-3375.

Catholic Family Sharing Appeal—TIM BENZ, Dir., *523 N. Duluth Ave., Sioux Falls, 57104.* Tel: 605-333-3387.

Censor Librorum—Rev. CHARLES MANGAN, *523 N. Duluth Ave., Sioux Falls, 57104.*

Communications Office—DARYL THURINGER, *523 N. Duluth Ave., Sioux Falls, 57104.* Tel: 605-333-3390.

Cursillo—Rev. ROD FARKE, *P.O. Box 689, Yankton, 57078.*

Development Office—MARK CONZEMIUS, Dir., *523 N. Duluth Ave., Sioux Falls, 57104.* Tel: 605-333-3384.

Diocesan Archivist—JEROME KLEIN, Chancellor, *523 N. Duluth Ave., Sioux Falls, 57104.* Tel: 605-334-9861.

Diocesan Office of Education—Sr. NATHALIE MEYER, O.P., Ph.D., Supt. of Schools; KEITH BORCHERS, Dir. Education, *523 N. Duluth Ave., Sioux Falls, 57104.* Tel: 605-333-3366.

Ecumenical Commission—Rev. JAMES ANDRASCHKO, *3601 E. Dudley Ln., Sioux Falls, 57103.*

Family Life Ministry—STEPHAN PATTON, *523 N. Duluth Ave., Sioux Falls, 57104.*

Finance Officer—MICHAEL BANNWARTH, *523 N. Duluth Ave., Sioux Falls, 57104.* Tel: 605-333-3359; Fax: 605-333-3346.

Good Shepherd Center—Deacon JAMES WALDEN, *300 N. Main, Sioux Falls, 57102.* Tel: 605-335-3321.

Worldwide Marriage Encounter—Rev. JAMES M. JOYCE, *P.O. Box 80, Brandon, 57005.* Tel: 605-582-6902.

Newman Apostolate—Rev. JOSEPH VOGEL, Coord., *310 15th Ave. S.E., Aberdeen, 57401.*

Office of Worship—Rev. DALE SIEVERDING, S.L.D., *523 N. Duluth Ave., Sioux Falls, 57104.* Tel: 605-334-9861.

Permanent Diaconate Council—Deacon JAMES WALDEN, *523 N. Duluth Ave., Sioux Falls, 57104.* Tel: 605-334-9861.

Personnel Board—Most Rev. ROBERT J. CARLSON, Chm.

Propagation of the Faith—Rev. JOSEPH HOLZHAUSER, Dir., *P.O. Box 98, Hoven, 57450-0098.*

Respect Life Office—MARCELLA EFFERTZ, Dir., *523 N. Duluth Ave., Sioux Falls, 57104.* Tel: 605-335-3321.

Search—*523 N. Duluth Ave., Sioux City, 57104.* Tel: 605-334-9861.

Spanish-Speaking Apostolate—Rev. JOHN RADER, *1220 E. 8th St., Sioux Falls, 57103.*

Teens Encounter Christ—*523 N. Duluth Ave., Sioux Falls, 57104.*

Vocations—KEVIN MILES, Exec. Dir., *523 N. Duluth Ave., Sioux Falls, 57104.* Tel: 605-333-3372.

Youth Ministry—NANCY WERNER, *523 N. Duluth Ave., Sioux Falls, 57104.* Tel: 605-333-3385.

CLERGY, PARISHES, MISSIONS AND PAROCHIAL SCHOOLS

CITY OF SIOUX FALLS
(Minnehaha County)

1—ST. JOSEPH CATHEDRAL, Rev. Msgr. Stephen T. Barnett; Rev. Dale Sieverding; Deacon Mike Huntington.
Res., 504 N. Summit Ave., 57104. Tel: 605-336-7390; Fax: 605-330-0416. [JC]
School—See separate listing under Inter-Parochial Schools in the Institution section. Tel: 605-338-3159; Fax: 605-338-2647.
Catechesis/Religious Programs—Students 229.

2—CHRIST THE KING (1949), Rev. Msgr. Richard Mahowald, P.A.; Rev. Brian Simon; Deacon James J. Walden.
Res., 1501 W. 26th St., 57105. Tel: 605-332-5477; Fax: 605-332-0552.
School—See separate listing under Inter-Parochial Schools in the Institution section. Tel: 605-338-5103; Fax: 605-335-1231.
Catechesis/Religious Programs—Students 151.

3—HOLY SPIRIT (1988), Rev. Msgr. James F. Andraschko; Deacon John Cole.
Res., 3601 E. Dudley Ln., 57103. Tel: 605-371-2320; Fax: 605-371-1957.
Catechesis/Religious Programs—Students 452.

4—OUR LADY OF GUADALUPE (1996), Rev. John S. Rader.
Res., 1220 E. 8th St., 57103-1702. Tel: 605-338-8126; Fax: 605-338-0419. [JC]
Catechesis/Religious Programs—Students 100.

5—ST. LAMBERT (1957), Rev. Msgr. Donald Kettler; Rev. David Krogman; Deacons Ralph C. Counter; Jerome F. Wathen.
Res., 1000 S. Bahnson Ave., 57103. Tel: 605-336-8808; Fax: 605-339-4389.
School—See separate listing under Inter-Parochial Schools in the Institution section. Tel: 605-338-7042; Fax: 605-336-8727.
Catechesis/Religious Programs—Students 451.

6—ST. MARY (1947), Revs. James Michael Doyle; Gary Ternes; Deacon Henry Knapp.
Res., 2109 S. Fifth Ave., 57105. Tel: 605-332-6391; Fax: 605-338-2953.
School—See separate listing under Inter-Parochial Schools in the Institution section. Tel: 605-334-9881; Fax: 605-334-9224.
Catechesis/Religious Programs—Students 203.

7—ST. MICHAEL (1979), Revs. Michael G. Wensing; Chester Murtha.
Res., 1600 S. Marion Rd., 57106. Tel: 605-361-1600; Fax: 605-361-4350. [JC]
School—See separate listing under Inter-Parochial Schools in the Institution section. Tel: 605-361-0021; Fax: 605-361-0094.
Catechesis/Religious Programs—Tel: 605-361-1317.
Students 1,134.

8—ST. THERESE (1917), Rev. Charles L. Cimpl; Deacon Michael Conrads.
Res., 1301 N. Dubuque Ave., 57110-6450. Tel: 605-338-2433; Fax: 605-339-2203.
School—See separate listing under Inter-Parochial Schools in the Institution section.
Catechesis/Religious Programs—Students 164.

OUTSIDE THE CITY OF SIOUX FALLS

Aberdeen, Brown Co., Sacred Heart (1882), Revs. John R. Lantsberger; Thomas Clement.
Res., 409 3rd Ave., S.E., 57401. Tel: 605-225-7065. [CEM]
Catechesis/Religious Programs—Students 374.
St. Mary, Revs. Robert Vinslauski; Mark Lichter; Deacon Truman Stevens.
Res., 215 N. Arch St., 57401. Tel: 605-229-4422; Fax: 605-226-4908. [CEM]
Catechesis/Religious Programs—Students 666.

Alexandria, Hanson Co., St. Mary of Mercy (1880) (German), Rev. Robert J. Fox.
Res., P.O. Box 158, 57331. Tel: 605-239-4532; Fax: 605-239-4532. [CEM]
Catechesis/Religious Programs—Students 110.

Andover, Day Co., All Saints (1880). Attended by Groton.
Mailing Address: Box 407, Groton, 57445. Tel: 605-397-8448.

Arlington, Kingsbury Co., St. John the Evangelist. Attended by Ramona.
Mailing Address: Box 128, Ramona, 57054.
Catechesis/Religious Programs—Students 68.

Armour, Douglas Co., St. Paul the Apostle (1886), Rev. William Hamak.
Res., Box 400, 57313. Tel: 605-724-2191.
Catechesis/Religious Programs—Tel: 605-724-2121.
Students 83.

Artesian, Sanborn Co., St. Charles. Attended by St. Wilfrid, Woonsocket.
Mailing Address: Box 266, Woonsocket, 57385. [JC]
Catechesis/Religious Programs—Students 55.

Athol, Spink Co., St. Mary (1885). Closed. For inquiries for parish records contact All Saints, Mellette.

Aurora, Brookings Co., St. William (1881). Attended by Elkton.
Mailing Address: Box E, Elkton, 57026. [CEM]
Catechesis/Religious Programs—Students 30.

Beresford, Union Co., St. Teresa of Avila (1885), Rev. Denis Meier.
Res., 903 S. Third, 57004. Tel: 605-763-2028; 763-5159 (Church.). [CEM]
Catechesis/Religious Programs—Students 137.

Big Bend, Hughes Co., St. Catherine (1950). Attended by Fort Thompson.
Box 47, Fort Thompson, 57339. Tel: 605-245-2350. [CEM]

Big Stone City, Grant Co., St. Charles (1882), Rev. Raymond Otto, O.S.B.
Res., P.O. Box 68, 57216. Tel: 605-862-8485. [CEM]
Catechesis/Religious Programs—Students 62.

Blunt, Hughes Co., Holy Spirit. Closed. For inquiries for parish records contact the Chancery.

Bowdle, Edmunds Co., St. Augustine (1894), Rev. Paul T. Josten. Also serves: Holy Trinity, Hosmer; St. Thomas, Roscoe. Box 310, 57428. Tel: 605-285-6466. [CEM]

Brandon, Minnehaha Co., Risen Savior (1979), Rev. James M. Joyce; Deacon Edwin Gruhot.
Res., 309 N. Needles, P.O. Box 80, 57005-0080. Tel: 605-582-6902. [JC]
Catechesis/Religious Programs—Tel: 605-582-2292.
Students 401.

Bridgewater, McCook Co., St. Stephen (1880), Rev. Paul Offerman.
Res., Box 49, 57319. Tel: 605-729-2505. [CEM]
Catechesis/Religious Programs—Students 65.

Bristol, Day Co., St. Anthony (1885), Sr. Karen La Follette, P.B.V.M., Admin.
Res., Box 336, 57219. Tel: 605-492-3135; Fax: 605-492-3135. [CEM]

Britton, Marshall Co., St. John de Britto (1888), Rev. Joseph Forcelle.
Res., Box 108, 57430. Tel: 605-448-5379; Fax: 605-448-5388. [JC]
Catechesis/Religious Programs—Students 72.

Brookings, Brookings Co., St. Thomas More (1904), Rev. Thomas A. Heck.
Res., 924 Fourth St., 57006. Tel: 605-692-4361; Fax: 605-692-6176. [CEM]
Catechesis/Religious Programs—Tel: 605-692-6941.
Students 538.

Bryant, Hamlin Co., St. Mary (1881). Attended by St. Thomas, De Smet.
Res., Box 15, De Smet, 57231. Tel: 605-854-3564. [CEM]

Canton, Lincoln Co., St. Dominic, Rev. Lawrence A. Jonas, S.J.; Deacon Edward B. Oliver.
Res., 800 E. Walnut, 57013. Tel: 605-987-5640.
Catechesis/Religious Programs—Students 142.

Castlewood, Hamlin Co., St. John (1885). Attended by Kranzburg.
Mailing Address: Box 166, Kranzburg, 57245. Tel: 605-886-9166; Fax: 605-886-9166. [JC]
Catechesis/Religious Programs—Students 72.

Cavour, Beadle Co., St. Patrick (1883). Attended by Church of the Resurrection, Huron.
Mailing Address: 400 20th St. S.W., Huron, 57350. Tel: 605-352-3403. [CEM]

Centerville, Turner Co., Good Shepherd (1888). Attended by Beresford.
P.O. Box 98, 57014. Tel: 605-563-2220. [JC]
Catechesis/Religious Programs—Students 85.

Chamberlain, Brule Co., St. James (1891), Rev. Anthony Kelly, S.C.J.
Res., 400 S. Main, 57325. Tel: 605-734-6122; Fax: 605-734-6729. [JC]
Catechesis/Religious Programs—Tel: 605-734-6122; Fax: 605-734-6729.
Students 228.

Chelsea, Faulk Co., Sacred Heart. Attended by Mellette.
Mailing Address: P.O. Box 46, Mellette, 57461. Tel: 605-887-3414; Fax: 605-887-3414.

Clark, Clark Co., St. Michael (1887), Rev. Ken Bain.
Res., 110 N. Idaho St., 57225. Tel: 605-532-3855. [CEM]
Catechesis/Religious Programs—112 N. Idaho St., 57225. Tel: 605-532-3776.
Students 116.

Clear Lake, Deuel Co., St. Mary (1900), Rev. Joseph Short.
Res., 408 Third St. W., Box 589, 57226. Tel: 605-874-2080.
Catechesis/Religious Programs—Students 131.

Colman, Moody Co., St. Peter (1905), Rev. David Roehrich; Deacon Robert Cross.
Res., Box J, 57017. Tel: 605-534-3612. [CEM]
Catechesis/Religious Programs—Students 127.

Conde, Spink Co., St. John the Baptist (1906) (German), Rev. Mathew Vazhappily, C.M.I. (India).
Res., P.O. Box 228, 57434. Tel: 605-382-5902. [CEM]

Dante, Charles Mix Co., Assumption B.V.M. (1909). Attended by T.O.R. Team Ministry.
P.O. Box 36, 57329-0036. Tel: 605-384-5155. [CEM]
Catechesis/Religious Programs—Students 107.

Dell Rapids, Minnehaha Co., St. Mary's (1898), Rev. Hal L. Barber.
Res., 608 8th St., 57022. Tel: 605-428-3390. [CEM][JC]
School—Tel: 605-428-3459.
Sisters of the Presentation B.V.M. 2; Lay Teachers 9; Students 191.
High School—Tel: 605-428-5591; Fax: 605-428-5377.
Priests 1; Sisters 1; Lay Teachers 9; Students 68.
Catechesis/Religious Programs—Tel: 605-428-3597.
Students 196.

De Smet, Kingsbury Co., St. Thomas Aquinas, Rev. David A. Janes.
Res., Box 15, 57231. Tel: 605-854-3564. [CEM]
Catechesis/Religious Programs—Students 84.

Dimock, Hutchinson Co., SS. Peter and Paul (1885) (German), Rev. Richard Cashel.
Res., R.R. 1, Box 14 A, 57331. Tel: 605-928-3883. [CEM]
Catechesis/Religious Programs—Students 85.

Doland, Spink Co., St. Joseph of Doland (1909). Attended by Conde.
P.O. Box 393, 57436-0393. Tel: 605-635-6301; Fax: 605-635-6411.
Catechesis/Religious Programs—Students 52.

Duncan, Buffalo Co., St. Placidus (1887). Wessington Springs.
510 N. Wallace, P.O. Box N, Wessington Springs, 57382-0348. [CEM]

Eden, Marshall Co., Sacred Heart (1917), Rev. Paul Pathiyamoola.
Res., Box 15, 57232. Tel: 605-486-4702. [CEM]
Catechesis/Religious Programs—Students 82.

Elk Point, Union Co., St. Joseph (1901), Rev. John C. Rasmussen.
Res., Box 340, 605 E. Main St., 57025. Tel: 605-356-2693; Fax: 605-356-3284. [CEM]
Catechesis/Religious Programs—Students 136.

Elkton, Brookings Co., Our Lady of Good Counsel (1879), Sr. Marlene Konrady, O.S.B., Admin.
Res., Box E, 57026. Tel: 605-542-8221. [CEM]
Catechesis/Religious Programs—P.O. Box 192, 57026. Tel: 605-542-3121. Diane Baker, D.R.E.
Students 125.

Emery, Hanson Co., St. Martin (1884), Rev. Joseph Thalanany, V.C. (India).
Res., Box 312, 57332. Tel: 605-449-4374. [CEM]
Catechesis/Religious Programs—Students 85.

Epiphany, Hanson Co., Church of the Epiphany (1896) (German), Rev. Leo C. Pospichal.
Res., R.R. 1, Box 107, Canova, 57321. Tel: 605-523-2640. [CEM]
Catechesis/Religious Programs—Students 75.

Estelline, Hamlin Co., St. Francis de Sales (1884). Attended by Clear Lake.
Res., Box B, 57234. Tel: 605-873-2254. [CEM]
Catechesis/Religious Programs—Students 41.

Ethan, Davison Co., Holy Trinity (1889). Attended by Dimock.
R.R. 1, Box 14A, Dimock, 57331. Tel: 605-928-3883. [CEM]
Catechesis/Religious Programs—Tel: 605-227-4666. Mrs. Glen Erpenback, D.R.E.
Students 77.

Eureka, McPherson Co., St. Joseph (1896) (German). Attended by Herreid.
Mailing Address: P.O. Box 37, Herreid, 57632. Tel: 605-437-2614.
Catechesis/Religious Programs—Students 48.

Farmer, Hanson Co., St. Peter (1889). Attended by Epiphany.
Mailing Address: Rte. 1, Canova, 57321-9417.
Church—57336. Tel: 605-523-2640.

Faulkton, Faulk Co., St. Thomas the Apostle (1903), Rev. Terence Anderson; Deacon Arvid Holsing.
Res., P.O. Box 394, 57438. Tel: 605-598-6590. [CEM]
Catechesis/Religious Programs—Deb Clement, D.R.E.
Students 86.

Flandreau, Moody Co., SS. Simon and Jude (1882), Rev. David Roehrich.
Res., 105 S. Bates, 57028. Tel: 605-997-2610. [CEM]
Catechesis/Religious Programs—Students 167.

Florence, Codington Co., Blessed Sacrament, Rev. Gregory Frankman.
Res., Box 6, 57235. Tel: 605-758-2271. [CEM]
Catechesis/Religious Programs—Students 65.

Fort Thompson, Buffalo Co., St. Joseph (1889), Rev. Yvon Sheehy, S.C.J., Moderator.
Mailing Address: Box 47, 57339. Tel: 605-245-2350. [CEM]
Catechesis/Religious Programs—Students 164.

Frankfort, Spink Co., St. Ann (1884). Attended by Redfield.
Mailing Address: 213 E. 6th Ave., Redfield, 57469. Tel: 605-472-2500.

Garretson, Minnehaha Co., St. Rose of Lima (1898), Rev. John Riedman; Deacon Pete Cheskie.
Res., Drawer O, 57030. Tel: 605-594-3750. [CEM]
Catechesis/Religious Programs—Students 111.

Garryowen, Union Co., St. Mary. Closed. For sacramental records contact St. Joseph, Elk Point.

Gary, Deuel Co., St. Peter (1900). Attended by Clear Lake.
408 3rd St. W., Box 589, Clear Lake, 57226. Tel: 605-874-2080.

Geddes, Charles Mix Co., St. Ann (1902). Attended by Platte.
Mailing Address: P.O. Box 335, Platte, 57369-0335. Tel: 605-337-2465; 337-3710. [CEM][JC]
Catechesis/Religious Programs—Students 60.

Gettysburg, Potter Co., Sacred Heart (1905), Rev. Charles Mangan.
Res., Box 285, 57442. Tel: 605-765-2161; Fax: 605-765-9293. [CEM]
Catechesis/Religious Programs—Students 128.

Grenville, Day Co., St. Joseph. Attended by Immaculate Conception, Waubay. Rev. Basil Maduike (Nigeria).
Res., Box 759, 57239. Tel: 605-947-4540. [CEM]
Catechesis/Religious Programs—Students 66.

Groton, Brown Co., St. Elizabeth Ann Seton (1883). (formerly St. John the Baptist). Rev. Marvin E. McPhee.
Res., 107 E. 7th Ave., 57445. Tel: 605-397-8448. [CEM]
Catechesis/Religious Programs—Students 97.

Grover, Codington Co., St. Peter. Attended by Blessed Sacrament, Florence.
Mailing Address: P.O. Box 6, Florence, 57235. Tel: 605-758-2271.

Harrold, Hughes Co., St. John the Evangelist. Attended by Highmore.
Box 457, Highmore, 57345. Tel: 605-852-2733. [CEM]

Hartford, Minnehaha Co., St. George (1882), Rev. Gregory Tschakert; Sr. Muriel Spartz, O.S.B., Pastoral Assoc.
Res., 102 N. Mundt, Box 377, 57033. Tel: 605-528-3426. [CEM]
Catechesis/Religious Programs—St. George Center, 207 S. Main Ave., 57033. Tel: 605-528-3902.
Students 242.

Hecla, Brown Co., St. Anthony (1904). Attended by St. John, Britton.
Box 108, Britton, 57430. Tel: 605-448-5379. [JC]

Henry, Codington Co., St. Henry. Florence.
Mailing Address: P.O. Box 6, Florence, 57235. Tel: 605-758-2271.
Catechesis/Religious Programs—Students 58.

Herreid, Campbell Co., St. Michael (1895), Rev. Jim D. Friedrich.
Res., Box 37, 57632. Tel: 605-437-2614. [CEM]
Catechesis/Religious Programs—Students 96.

Highmore, Hyde Co., St. Mary, Rev. Ivo Martini, Admin.
Res., Box 457, 57345. Tel: 605-852-2733. [CEM]
Catechesis/Religious Programs—Students 75.

Hosmer, Edmunds Co., Holy Trinity. Attended by Bowdle.
Res., P.O. Box 46, 57448. Tel: 605-283-2275. [CEM]

Hoven, Potter Co., St. Anthony of Padua (1887), Rev. Joseph Holzhauser.
Res., Box 98, 57450. Tel: 605-948-2451. [CEM]
School—Tel: 605-948-2245.
Lay Teachers 5; Students 61.
Catechesis/Religious Programs—Students 83.

Howard, Miner Co., St. Agatha (1882), Rev. Michael Schneider.
Res., Box H, 57349. Tel: 605-772-5564. [CEM]
Catechesis/Religious Programs—Students 153.

Humboldt, Minnehaha Co., St. Ann (1912) (German), Rev. Terry Weber; Deacon Francis Graff; Sr. Mildred Nikolas, O.S.B.
Res., 204 S. Jefferson, 57035. Tel: 605-363-3330. [CEM]
Catechesis/Religious Programs—Tel: 605-363-5068.
Students 123.

Huntimer, Minnehaha Co., St. Joseph the Workman (1889). Unassigned.
Mailing Address: 3100 W. 41st St., Sioux Falls, 57105. Tel: 605-334-9861. [CEM]
Catechesis/Religious Programs—Students 136.

Huron, Beadle Co., Church of the Resurrection (1969), Rev. J. E. Murphy.
Res., 400 20th St., S.W., 57350. Tel: 605-352-3403. [JC]
Catechesis/Religious Programs—Tel: 605-352-2237.
Students 142.

St. Martin (1881), Rev. Michael D. Kelly.
Res., 133 5th St., S.E., 57350. Tel: 605-352-2203; Fax: 605-352-2203. [CEM]
School—Tel: 605-352-9344.
Lay Teachers 10; Students 198.
Catechesis/Religious Programs—Students 215.

Idylwilde, Turner Co., St. Boniface (1885). Attended by Parker.
Box 610, Parker, 57053. Tel: 605-297-4983. [CEM]
Catechesis/Religious Programs—Students 74.

Ipswich, Edmunds Co., Holy Cross (1886), Rev. Edward P. Burian. In res., Rev. Raymond G. Mowry.
Res., Box 67, 57451. Tel: 605-426-6967; Fax: 605-426-6967. [CEM]
School—Tel: 605-426-6222.
Lay Teachers 4; Students 51.
Catechesis/Religious Programs—Students 215.

Iroquois, Kingsbury Co., St. Paul. Attended by St. Thomas Aquinas, De Smet.
Box 15, De Smet, 57231. Tel: 605-854-3564. [CEM]

Jefferson, Union Co., St. Peter (1867), Rev. Andrew K. Swietochowski.
Res., P.O. Box 188, 57038-0188. Tel: 605-966-5716; Fax: 605-966-5492. [CEM]
School—P.O. Box 98, 57038-0098. Tel: 605-966-5529.
Lay Teachers 7; Students 61.
Catechesis/Religious Programs—Students 80.

Kimball, Brule Co., St. Margaret (1884), Rev. Daniel Manning.
Res., Box 137, 57355. Tel: 605-778-6420; Fax: 605-778-6487. [CEM]
Catechesis/Religious Programs—Tel: 605-778-6487.
Students 200.

Kranzburg, Codington Co., Holy Rosary (1879), Rev. Richard Baumberger.
Res., Box 166, 57245. Tel: 605-886-9166; Fax: 605-886-9166. [CEM]
School—(Grades K-6). Tel: 605-886-8114.
Lay Teachers 3; Students 41.
Catechesis/Religious Programs—Students 128.

Lake Andes, Charles Mix Co., St. Mark (1904), Rev. David Tickerhoof, T.O.R.
Res., Box 250, 57356. Tel: 605-487-7300. [CEM]
Catechesis/Religious Programs—Students 64.

Lake City, Marshall Co., St. Joseph (1919). Attended by Eden.
Box 15, Eden, 57232. Tel: 605-486-4702. [CEM]

Lennox, Lincoln Co., St. Magdalen. Attended by St. Nicholas, Tea.
Mailing Address: Box 136, 57039. Tel: 605-647-2187. [CEM]
Catechesis/Religious Programs—Students 114.

Leola, McPherson Co., Our Lady of Perpetual Help (1891), Rev. Edward P. Burian.
Res., P.O. Box 67, Ipswich, 57451. Tel: 605-426-6967; Fax: 605-426-6967. [CEM]
Catechesis/Religious Programs—Students 58.

Lesterville, Yankton Co., St. John the Baptist (1904). Attended by St. Wenceslaus, Tabor. Rev. William Osborn.
Mailing Address: Box 168, 57040. Tel: 605-364-7581. [CEM]
Catechesis/Religious Programs—Students 58.

Letcher, Sanborn Co., St. Scholastica. Closed. For inquiries for parish records contact the Chancery.

Lily, Day Co., St. Joseph. Closed. For sacramental records contact St. Anthony, Bristol.

Madison, Lake Co., St. Thomas Aquinas (1881), Rev. Anthony Opem.
Res., 217 N.W. Fourth St., 57042. Tel: 605-256-2304. [CEM]
School—Tel: 605-256-4419.
Lay Teachers 9; Students 114.
Catechesis/Religious Programs—Students 256.

Marion, Turner Co., Our Lady of Perpetual Help (1880). Attended by Parker.
Res., Box 610, Parker, 57053. Tel: 605-297-4983. [CEM]
Catechesis/Religious Programs—Students 57.

Marty, Charles Mix Co., St. Paul's Church (1913). Attended by T.O.R. Team Ministry, Lake Andes. Sr. Miriam Shindelar, O.S.B.S., Admin.; Deacon Edward P. Zephier.
Res., P.O. Box 266, 57361. Tel: 605-384-3234; 487-7300. [CEM]
Catechesis/Religious Programs—Tel: 605-384-3234.
Students 96.

Mayfield, Yankton Co., St. Columba (1884) (Irish), Rev. Leonard Kayser.
1105 W. Eighth St., Yankton, 57078. Tel: 605-668-1236. [CEM]
Catechesis/Religious Programs—Students 47.

Mellette, Spink Co., All Saints, Rev. Antonio W. Ramos.
Box 46, 57461. Tel: 605-887-3414; Fax: 605-887-3414. [CEM]
Catechesis/Religious Programs—Students 76.

Milbank, Grant Co., St. Lawrence (1882), Rev. Denis Quinkert, O.S.B.
Res., 101 6th St., S., 57252. Tel: 605-432-5353. [CEM]
School—Tel: 605-432-5673.
Sisters 1; Lay Teachers 7; Students 130.
Catechesis/Religious Programs—Tel: 605-432-5353.
Students 264.

Miller, Hand Co., St. Ann (1884), Rev. Donald J. Molumby.
Res., 709 E. 4th, 57362. Tel: 605-853-2207. [CEM]
Catechesis/Religious Programs—Students 169.

Mitchell, Davison Co., Holy Family (1880), Rev. Edward J. Pierce.
Res., 321 E. 3rd Ave., 57301. Tel: 605-996-3639; Fax: 605-995-0378. [CEM]
School—Holy Family/Holy Spirit-Mitchell Catholic Schools, Tel: 605-996-2365.
Lay Teachers 16; Students 280.
Catechesis/Religious Programs—200 N. Kimball St., 57301. Tel: 605-996-3842.
Students 298.

Holy Spirit (1962), Rev. Richard Fox.
Res., 1412 W. Cedar Ave., 57301. Tel: 605-996-7424.
School—Holy Family/Holy Spirit-Mitchell Catholic Schools. See Holy Family for details. Tel: 605-996-2365; Fax: 605-996-6964.
Catechesis/Religious Programs—Tel: 605-996-3842.
Students 265.

Mobridge, Walworth Co., St. Joseph (1912), Rev. Jerome M. Ranek.
Res., 514 W. Second Ave., 57601. Tel: 605-845-2100; Fax: 605-845-2100. [JC]
Catechesis/Religious Programs—614 W. Second Ave., 57601. Tel: 605-845-2646.
Students 206.

Montrose, McCook Co., St. Patrick (1904), Rev. Terry Weber.
211 S. Church, P.O. Box 158, 57048. Tel: 605-363-5068; Fax: 605-363-3856. [CEM]
Catechesis/Religious Programs—Students 124.

Mount Vernon, Davison Co., St. Michael. Attended by Plankinton.
Box 430, Plankinton, 57368.
Catechesis/Religious Programs—Students 71.

New Effington, Roberts Co., Sacred Heart (1913). Attended by Rosholt.
P.O. Box 45, Rosholt, 57260. Tel: 605-537-4583.

Oldham, Kingsbury Co., St. Catherine of Sienna. Attended by Ramona.
P.O. Box 128, Ramona, 57054.

Onaka, Faulk Co., St. John the Baptist (1906). Attended by St. Anthony of Padua, Hoven.
P.O. Box 98, Hoven, 57450. Tel: 605-948-2451. [CEM]

Onida, Sully Co., St. Pius X (1959). Attended by Sacred Heart, Gettysburg. Rev. Charles Mangan; Sr. Veronica Haag, O.S.B., Pastoral Min.
P.O. Box 13, 57564. Tel: 605-258-2336. [CEM]
Catechesis/Religious Programs—Students 71.

Orient, Faulk Co., St. Joseph (1884). Attended by Polo.
17985 354th Ave., 57467.

Parker, Turner Co., St. Christina (1887), Deacon William Frankman, Admin.
Res., P.O. Box 610, 57053. Tel: 605-297-4983. [CEM]
Catechesis/Religious Programs—Students 56.

Parkston, Hutchinson Co., Sacred Heart (1887), Rev. Robert V. Krantz; Deacon Barry Wagner.
Res., Box 460, 57366. Tel: 605-928-3676. [CEM 2]
Catechesis/Religious Programs—Students 231.

Pierre, Hughes Co., SS. Peter and Paul (1882), Revs. Darrell V. Lamberty; Gary Lantz, S.C.J.
Res., 304 N. Euclid, 57501. Tel: 605-224-2483; Fax: 605-224-1483. [CEM]
School—Tel: 605-224-7185.
Benedictine Sisters 3; Lay Teachers 8; Students 158.
Catechesis/Religious Programs—Students 548.

Plankinton, Aurora Co., St. John, Rev. Alex Bombera, T.O.R.
Res., Box 430, 57368. Tel: 605-942-7125.
Catechesis/Religious Programs—Students 105.

Platte, Charles Mix Co., St. Peter the Apostle (1904), Rev. Donald R. Imming.
Res., Box 335, 57369. Tel: 605-337-3710, 337-2465. [CEM]
Catechesis/Religious Programs—Students 87.

Polo, Hand Co., St. Liborius (1904), Sr. Mary Myles Schwahn, S.S.N.D., Admin.
Res., 17985 354th Ave., Orient, 57467. Tel: 605-392-2440. [CEM]
Catechesis/Religious Programs—Students 47.

Pukwana, Brule Co., St. Anthony. Attended by Chamberlain.
400 S. Main, Chamberlain, 57325. Tel: 605-734-6122; Fax: 605-734-6729.

Ramona, Lake Co., St. William of Vercelli, Rev. Jose Edayadiyil, V.C (India).
Res., Box 128, 57054. Tel: 605-482-8214. [CEM]
Catechesis/Religious Programs—Students 52.

Redfield, Spink Co., St. Bernard (1884), Rev. John Fischer.
Res., 213 E. 6th Ave., 57469-1249. Tel: 605-472-2500. [CEM]
Catechesis/Religious Programs—Tel: 605-472-1482.
Students 244.

Revillo, Grant Co., Annunciation, Rev. Ray Otto, O.S.B.
Res., P.O. Box 128, Milbank, 57252. Tel: 605-623-4541; 432-5438; Fax: 605-432-5412. [CEM]
Catechesis/Religious Programs—Students 54.

Roscoe, Edmunds Co., St. Thomas Apostle. Attended by Bowdle. Rev. Paul T. Josten.
Res., P.O. Box 257, 57471. Tel: 605-285-6466. [JC]
Catechesis/Religious Programs—Students 39.

Rosholt, Roberts Co., St. John the Baptist (1911), Rev. Dennis Deis, O.M.I.
Res., Box 45, 57260. Tel: 605-537-4583. [CEM]
Catechesis/Religious Programs—Students 61.

Salem, McCook Co., St. Mary (1885) (German), Rev. Joseph Ripp. In res., Rev. Ladislaus Dudek, (Retired).
Res., Box 308, 340 N. Idaho, 57058. Tel: 605-425-2600; Fax: 605-425-2600. [CEM]
School—Lay Teachers 10; Students 97.
Catechesis/Religious Programs—Students 88.

Scotland, Bon Homme Co., St. George, Rev. John Maliyekal, V.C. (India).
Res., Box 449, 57059. Tel: 605-583-4318; Fax: 605-583-4318. [CEM]
Catechesis/Religious Programs—Tel: 605-583-4696.
Students 88.

Selby, Walworth Co., St. Anthony. Attended by Herreid.
Catechesis/Religious Programs—Students 50.

Seneca, Faulk Co., St. Boniface (1903). Attended by St. Thomas the Apostle, Faulkton.

Sigel, Yankton Co., St. Agnes (1885) (German), Rev. Leonard Kayser.
R.R. 1 Box 26, Utica, 57067. Tel: 605-665-5358. [CEM]

Sisseton, Roberts Co., St. Catherine (1962), Revs. Mietek Bajek, O.M.I.; Gari Ruthenberg, O.M.I.
Office: 120 E. Chestnut, 57262. Tel: 605-698-7414; Fax: 605-698-7236. [CEM 2]
Mission—Veblen, Marshall Co., St. Matthew.

St. Peter (1899), Revs. Mietek Bajek, O.M.I.; Gari Ruthenberg, O.M.I.
Office: 120 E. Chestnut, 57262. Tel: 605-698-7414; Fax: 605-698-7236. [CEM]
Catechesis/Religious Programs—Students 148.

Spencer, McCook Co., St. Mary (1906). Attended by Bridgewater.
Box 49, Bridgewater, 57319. Tel: 615-729-2505.

Springfield, Bon Homme Co., St. Vincent. Attended by Tyndall.

Stephan, Hyde Co., Immaculate Conception (1886), Revs. Yvon Sheehy, S.C.J., Moderator; James Walters, S.C.J.
Res., 57346. Tel: 605-852-2216. [CEM][JC]

Stickney, Aurora Co., St. Mary (1908). Attended by Armour.
Box 400, Armour, 57313. Tel: 605-724-2191. [CEM]

Tabor, Bon Homme Co., St. Wenceslaus (1872), Rev. William Osborn; Deacon David Kostel.
Res., 205 N. Lidice St., 57063-2005. Tel: 605-463-2336. [CEM]
Catechesis/Religious Programs—Students 102.

Tea, Lincoln Co., St. Nicholas (1905), Rev. Kenneth Koster; Deacon Steven Beaubien.
Res., 510 W. Maple, P.O. Box 116, 57064. Tel: 605-368-5449. [JC]
Church—200 Maple St., 57064. Tel: 605-368-5449.
Catechesis/Religious Programs—Students 140.

Tripp, Hutchinson Co., Holy Rosary. Attended by Parkston.

Turton, Spink Co., St. Joseph (1888). Attended by Conde.
Mailing Address: P.O. Box 127, 57477. Tel: 605-382-5902. [CEM][JC]

Tyndall, Bon Homme Co., St. Leo (1890), Rev. Jerry Kopel.
Res., Box 47, 57066. Tel: 605-589-3504; Fax: 605-589-3392. [CEM]
Catechesis/Religious Programs—Students 140.
Station—Springfield Correctional Facility, Tel: 605-369-2201. Bro. Placid Hellman, O.S.B., Chap.

Veblen, Marshall Co., St. John Nepomucene. Attended by Catholic Community, Sisseton.

Vermillion, Clay Co., St. Agnes (1860), Rev. Leonard D. Fox.
Res., 416 Walker St., 57069. Tel: 605-624-4479. [CEM 2][JC 3]
School—909 E. Lewis St., 57069. Tel: 605-624-4144.
Lay Teachers 7; Students 141.
Catechesis/Religious Programs—Tel: 605-624-5161.
Students 251.

Vodnany, Bon Homme Co., SS. Cyril and Methodius (1886). Attended by Scotland.
Mailing Address: P.O. Box 102, Kaylor, 57354. [CEM]

Wagner, Charles Mix Co., St. John the Baptist (1903), Pastoral Team: Revs. Joseph Glancy, T.O.R.; Jordan Hite, T.O.R.; David Tickerhoof, T.O.R.; Bro. Martin Zatsick, T.O.R.; Deacon Albert J. Kocer.
Res., Box 637, 57380. Tel: 605-384-5518; Fax: 605-384-5518. [CEM]
Catechesis/Religious Programs—Tel: 605-384-5314.
Students 128.

Wakonda, Clay Co., St. Patrick (1904), Deacon Thomas Vogel.
Res., Box 386, 57073. Tel: 605-267-2676. [CEM 2]
Catechesis/Religious Programs—Tel: 605-267-2676.
Students 60.

Watertown, Codington Co., Holy Name (1955), Rev. Jerome J. Holtzman.
Res., 1009 Skyline Dr., 57201. Tel: 605-886-2628; Fax: 605-886-2142. [JC]
Catechesis/Religious Programs—Tel: 605-886-3368; Fax: 605-886-2141.
Students 449.

Immaculate Conception (1887), Revs. Roger Geditz; Randy Phillips.
Res., 309 Second Ave. S.E., 57201. Tel: 605-886-4049. [CEM]
School—Tel: 605-886-3883.
Lay Teachers 10; Students 179.
Catechesis/Religious Programs—103 Third St. S.E., 57201. Tel: 605-886-2772.
Students 546.

Waubay, Day Co., Immaculate Conception (1894), Rev. Basil Maduike (Nigeria).
Res., Box 77, 57273. Tel: 605-947-4540. [CEM]
Catechesis/Religious Programs—Students 83.

Waverly, Codington Co., St. Joseph (1889). Attended by Kranzburg.
Box 166, Kranzburg, 57245. Tel: 605-886-9166; Fax: 605-886-9166. [CEM]

Webster, Day Co., Christ the King, Rev. John M. Garvey.
Res., 1101 E. 1st St., 57274. Tel: 605-345-3447; Fax: 605-345-4871. [CEM]
Catechesis/Religious Programs—Students 177.

Wellington, Minnehaha Co., St. Joseph. Closed. For sacramental records contact St. Ann, Humboldt.

Wessington, Beadle Co., St. Joseph. Attended by Miller.

Wessington Springs, Jerauld Co., St. Joseph (1906), Rev. Augustine Belinda, T.O.R.
Mailing Address: P.O. Box N, 510 N. Wallace, 57382. Tel: 605-539-9569. [JC]
Catechesis/Religious Programs—Students 96.

Westport, Brown Co., Sacred Heart of Westport (1889), Rev. Joseph Vogel.
Mailing Address: Box 85, 57481. Tel: 605-229-1011. [CEM]
Catechesis/Religious Programs—Students 60.

White, Brookings Co., St. Paul Attended (1898). Brookings Student Center. Rev. Michael Griffin.
Box 7019, University Sta., Brookings, 57007. Tel: 605-692—9461. [JC]
Catechesis/Religious Programs—Students 49.

White Lake, Aurora Co., St. Peter (1883), Rev. Arnold Petrosky, T.O.R.
Res., Box 277, 57383. Tel: 605-249-2700. [CEM]
Catechesis/Religious Programs—Students 108.

Willow Lake, Clark Co., St. James (1895). Attended by St. Michael, Clark.
110 N. Idaho St., Clark, 57225. Tel: 605-532-3855.

Wilmot, Roberts Co., St. Mary (1886), Rev. John McMullen, O.S.B.
Res., Box 204, 57279. Tel: 605-938-4289; Fax: 605-432-4754. [CEM]
Catechesis/Religious Programs—Students 88.

Woonsocket, Sanborn Co., St. Wilfrid (1884), Rev. Gerald Thury.
Res., Box 266, 57385. Tel: 605-796-4666. [CEM]
Catechesis/Religious Programs—Students 122.

Worthing, Lincoln Co., St. Edward (1908). Attended by St. Dominic, Canton.
800 E. Walnut, Canton, 57013. Tel: 605-987-5640. [CEM]

Yankton, Yankton Co., St. Benedict (1993), Rev. Rodney Farke.
Res., 1500 St. Benedict Dr., 57078. Tel: 605-665-6214; Fax: 605-665-2305. [JC]
Catechesis/Religious Programs—1500 St. Benedict Dr., 57078. Tel: 605-665-6214.
Students 287.

Sacred Heart (1871), Revs. James I. Bream; Lawrence Regynski; Deacon Thomas Healy.
Res., 509 Capitol St., 57078. Tel: 605-665-3655. [CEM]
School—Tel: 605-665-5841.
Sisters 1; Lay Teachers 12; Students 203.
Catechesis/Religious Programs—Students 365.

Zell, Hand Co., St. Mary. Attended by Mellette.
Catechesis/Religious Programs—Students 64.

Chaplains of Public Institutions

SIOUX FALLS. *South Dakota State Penitentiary & Minnehaha County Jail*. Rev. Bernard Ashfeld.
State School for the Deaf. Vacant. 3100 W. 41st St., 57105.

FLANDREAU. *Government Indian School*. Attended by SS. Simon & Jude, Flandreau.

PLANKINTON. *State Training School*. Attended by St. John Church, Plankinton. Rev. Alex Bombera, T.O.R.

REDFIELD. *State Hospital and State School, SD*. Attended by St. Bernard Church, Redfield.

SPRINGFIELD. *State Prison*. Attended by Tyndall. Bro. Placid Hellman, O.S.B.

YANKTON. *State Hospital*. Rev. Leonard Kayser.

On Duty Outside the Diocese:
Reverend Monsignors—
Gullickson, Thomas E., Apostolic Nunciature, Postfach 200152, D-53131, Bonn, Germany

Military Chaplains:
Reverend Fathers—
Wagner, Joseph, HQ AIA/HC, Kelly AFB, TX 87505

Awaiting Assignment:
Reverend Fathers—
Wolfgram, Daniel

On Leave of Absence:
Reverend Fathers—
Dobitz, Roger
Johnson, Douglas
McCormick, James
McNeil, Frank J.

Retired:
Reverend Monsignors—
Duraczynski, Jerome A., 1041 Singer Ln., Norristown, PA 19403
Foley, Andrew E., 1265 4th St., N.W., Watertown, SD 57201-1128
Hermann, Carlton P., 505 Burgess Rd., Yankton, SD 57078-1819
McEneaney, John P.A., 423 N. Duluth, Sioux Falls, SD 57104
Zwinger, Leonard, 500 S. 4th Ave., #101, Sioux Falls, SD 57104

Reverend Fathers—
Anderson, Joseph R., R.R. 1 Box 75-A, Corona, SD 57227
Brady, John, 509 Broadway, Yankton, SD 57078
Burns, Thomas, 411 Vander Horck, P.O. Box 297, Britton, SD 57430
Carroll, Howard, 4701 S. Oxbow Ave., #320, Sioux Falls, SD 57106
Connolly, Thomas, 3109 Corona Dr., Holiday, FL 34690
Dudek, Ladislaus, 330 N. Idaho, Salem, SD 57058. Tel: 605-425-2031
Duman, Charles J., P.O. Box 24-A, Huntington, NE 68739
Duraczynski, Walter, 2007 New Hope St., Norristown, PA 19401
Fox, Leo, P.O. Box 1441, Watertown, SD 57201
Friedrich, Lawrence, 4510 S. Prince of Peace Pl., Apt. #213, Sioux Falls, SD 57103. Tel: 605-371-4537
Keating, David, 4500 S. Prince of Peace Pl., Sioux Falls, SD 57103
Krzyzopolski, Al, 4700 S. Cliff Ave., #210, Sioux Falls, SD 57103
MacArthur, Bruce, P.O. Box 416, Clint, TX 79836
Marbach, Lawrence J., 617 Maple St., Yankton, SD 57078-3823
Mardian, Joseph P., 4510 S. Prince of Peace Pl., #205, Sioux Falls, SD 57103
Mardian, Pius, 4510 S. Prince of Peace Pl. #120, Sioux Falls, SD 57103
McMahon, Marvin J., 509 Broadway Ave., Yankton, SD 57078
McPhillips, Thomas J., Bishop Hoch Villa, 500 S. Ohlman, Box 430, Mitchell, SD 57301
Mociun, Casimir T., 1320 Cedar Ave., Scranton, PA 18505
Morgen, Paul, 4510 S. Prince of Peace Pl. #210, Sioux Falls, SD 57103
Mowry, Raymond G., Holy Cross Rectory, P.O. Box 67, Ipswich, SD 57451-0067
Murray, John I., 912 Missoula Ave., Helena, MT 59601
Ortmeier, Richard J., Mother of God Monastery, 110 28th Ave., S.E., Watertown, SD 57201
Petrucci, Dominic, 1417 W. Ash Ave., Mitchell, SD 57301
Ryan, Thomas J., 609 W 5th St., Sioux Falls, SD 57104-2734
Wolf, James, 215 N. Arch, Aberdeen, SD 57401

Permanent Deacons:
Beaubien, Steven, St. Nicholas, Tea
Bierer, Richard B., St. Mary, Sioux Falls
Cheskie, Pete, St. Rose, Garretson
Cole, John M., Holy Spirit, Sioux Falls
Conrads, Michael, St. Therese, Sioux Falls
Counter, Ralph, St. Lambert, Sioux Falls
Cross, Robert, St. Peter, Colman
Frankman, William, Admin., St. Christina, Parker
Graff, Francis, St. Ann, Humboldt
Gruhot, Edward, Risen Savior, Brandon
Healy, Thomas, Sacred Heart, Yankton
Holsing, Arvid, St. Thomas the Apostle, Faulkton
Huntington, Michael, St. Joseph Cathedral, Sioux Falls
Knapp, Henry J., St. Mary's, Sioux Falls
Kocer, Albert, St. John the Baptist, Wagner
Kostel, David, SS. Peter and Paul, Pierre
Oliver, Edward B., St. Dominic, Canton
Pardew, Harold, Hospital Chap.
Stevens, Truman, St. Mary, Aberdeen
Vogel, Thomas, St. Patrick, Wakonda
Wagner, Barry, Sacred Heart, Parkston
Walden, James I., Christ the King Parish, Sioux Falls
Wathen, Jerome F., St. Lambert, Sioux Falls
Zephier, Edward P., Jr., St. Paul Parish

INSTITUTIONS LOCATED IN THE DIOCESE

[A] COLLEGES AND UNIVERSITIES

ABERDEEN. *Presentation College*, 57401. Tel: 605-225-1634; Fax: 605-229-8430
For a complete listing, refer to the Colleges and Universities section.

YANKTON. *Mount Marty College*, 1105 W. 8th St., 57078 Fax: 605-668-1357
For a complete listing, refer to the Colleges and Universities section.

[B] EDUCATION CENTERS, PRIVATE

CHAMBERLAIN. *St. Joseph Indian School*, N. Main, 57326. Tel: 605-734-3300; Fax: 605-734-3480. Revs. Joseph Haselbauer, S.C.J.; T. Anthony Kluckman, S.C.J.; Bro. David Nagel, S.C.J., Exec. Dir. Brothers 1; Lay Teachers 24; Students 224.

WATERTOWN. *Harmony Hill Center-Mt. Marty Branch Campus*, 57201. Tel: 605-886-6777; Fax: 605-886-2108. Conducted by Benedictine Sisters (Mother of God Monastery, Watertown). Sr. Ramona Fallon, O.S.B., Admin. Sisters 2; Lay Teachers 25; Students 300.

[C] INTER-PAROCHIAL SCHOOLS

SIOUX FALLS. *Sioux Falls Catholic School System*, 3201 S. Kiwanis Ave., 57105. Tel: 605-336-6241. Dr. Thomas Lorang, Supt.
O'Gorman High School, 3201 S. Kiwanis Ave., 57105. Tel: 605-336-3644; Fax: 605-336-9272. Brett Bradfield, Prin.; Rev. Gregory Tschakert, Chap. Priests 1; Sisters 2; Lay Teachers 47; Students 705.
St. Joseph Cathedral Elementary, 601 W. 4th St., 57104. Tel: 605-338-1359; Fax: 605-338-2647. John Bradbury, Prin. Lay Teachers 20; Students 362.
Sioux Falls Catholic Junior High. (Grades 7-8), 3100 W. 41st St., 57105. Colley Broveliet, Prin.
St. Mary Elementary, 2001 S. 5th Ave., 57105. Tel: 605-334-9881; Fax: 605-334-9224. Courtney Tielke, Prin. Sisters 1; Lay Teachers 24; Students 471.
Christ the King Elementary School, 1801 S. Lake Ave., 57105. Tel: 605-338-5103; Fax: 605-335-1231. Nancy Clarey, Prin. Benedictine Sisters 1; Lay Teachers 18; Students 353.
St. Lambert Elementary School, 1000 S. Bahnson Ave., 57103. Tel: 605-338-7042; Fax: 605-336-8727. Elsie Baye, Prin. Lay Teachers 15; Students 263.
St. Michael Elementary School, 1600 S. Marion Rd., 57106. Tel: 605-361-0021. Lisa Huemoeller, Prin. Lay Teachers 4; Students 90.

ABERDEEN. *Aberdeen Catholic Schools Education Office*, 1400 N. Dakota St., S.E., 57401. Tel: 605-226-2100; Fax: 605-226-0616. Mr. Don Meyer, Supt.
Roncalli Elementary School. (Grades PreK-2), 424 Second Ave. N.E., 57401. Tel: 605-225-3460. Nancy A. Zenk, Prin. Sisters 1; Lay Teachers 8; Students 183.
Roncalli High School, 1400 N. Dakota St., 57401. Tel: 605-225-7440; Fax: 605-226-0616. (Junior and Senior High School). Donald Meyer, Supt. Lay Teachers 23; Students 347.
Roncalli Middle School. (Grades 3-6), 505 Third Ave. S.E., 57401. Tel: 605-229-4100. Nancy A. Zenk, Prin. Lay Teachers 10; Students 191.

[D] GENERAL HOSPITALS

SIOUX FALLS. *McKennan Hospital*, 57110-5045. Tel: 605-322-8000
For a complete listing, refer to the Hospitals section.

ABERDEEN. *St. Luke's Midland Regional Medical Center*, 57401. Tel: 605-622-5000
For a complete listing, refer to the Hospitals section.

GETTYSBURG. *Gettysburg Medical Center*, 57442. Tel: 605-765-2488
For a complete listing, refer to the Hospitals section.

MILBANK. *St. Bernard Providence Hospital*, 57252. Tel: 605-432-4538.
E-mail: sbphosp@tnics.com
For a complete listing, refer to the Hospitals section.

MITCHELL. *Queen of Peace Hospital*, 525 N. Foster, 57301. Tel: 605-995-2000; Fax: 605-995-2441
For a complete listing, refer to the Hospitals section.

PARKSTON. *St. Benedict Health Care Center; Bormann Manor; Parkston Supervised Living*, 57366. Tel: 605-928-3311
For a complete listing, refer to the Hospitals section.

PIERRE. *Maryhouse Residential Nursing Facility*, 800 E. Dakota, P.O. Box 1023, 57501
For a complete listing, refer to the Hospitals section.
Parkwood Retirement Apartments, 400 Parkwood Dr., 57501
For a complete listing, refer to the Hospitals section.
St. Mary's Foundation, 800 E. Dakota, 57501. Tel: 605-224-3451.
E-mail: StMary'sSD@aol.com
Web site: www.ST-Marys.com
For a complete listing, refer to the Hospitals section.
St. Mary's Healthcare Center of Pierre, South Dakota, 800 E. Dakota, P.O. Box 1023, 57501. Tel: 605-224-3100
For a complete listing, refer to the Hospitals section.

TYNDALL. *St. Michael's Hospital*, 57066. Tel: 605-589-3341
For a complete listing, refer to the Hospitals section.

YANKTON. *Sacred Heart Health Services*, 501 Summit, 57078. Tel: 605-668-8000
For a complete listing, refer to the Hospitals section.

[E] HOMES FOR AGED

SIOUX FALLS. *Prince of Peace Retirement Community, Inc.*, 4500 Prince of Peace Pl., 57103. Tel: 605-371-0700
For a complete listing, refer to the Special Care Facilities section.

ABERDEEN. *Aberdeen Living Center* 1700 N. Hwy. 281, 57401. Tel: 605-225-7315.
For a complete listing, refer to the Special Care Facilities section.
Mother Joseph Manor, Nursing Care Facility, 1002 N. Jay St., 57401. Tel: 605-622-5850
For a complete listing, refer to the Special Care Facilities section.

MILBANK. *St. William Home for the Aged*, 57252. Tel: 605-432-4538; Fax: 605-432-5412
For a complete listing, refer to the Special Care Facilities section.

MITCHELL. *Queen of Peace Hospital dba Brady Memorial Home*, 500 S. Ohlman, 57301. Tel: 605-966-7701; Fax: 605-996-5726
For a complete listing, refer to the Special Care Facilities section.

SISSETON. *Tekakwitha Nursing Center, Inc.*, 6 E. Chestnut, 57262. Tel: 605-693-7693; Fax: 605-698-3091
For a complete listing, refer to the Special Care Facilities section.

[F] MONASTERIES AND RESIDENCES OF PRIESTS AND BROTHERS

CHAMBERLAIN. *Priests of the Sacred Heart.* P.O. Box 89, 57325. Tel: 605-734-3300; 734-3325. Rev. Joseph Haselbauer, S.C.J.; Bro. David Nagel, S.C.J., Admin. Priests 1; Brothers 2.
St. Joseph Indian School.

EMERY. *Vincentian Congregation.* North American Headquarters, Vincentian House, P.O. Box 252, 57332-0252. Rev. Joseph Thalanany, V.C., Regl. Coord.

MARVIN. *Blue Cloud Abbey.*
E-mail: Abbey@BlueCloud.org
Web site: www.BlueCloud.org
P.O. Box 98, 57251. Tel: 605-432-5528; Fax: 605-432-4754. Rt. Revs. Thomas Hillenbrand, O.S.B.; Alan Berndt, O.S.B., Retired Abbot; Denis Quinkert, O.S.B., Retired Abbot; Revs. George Lyon, O.S.B., Prior; Daniel Madlon, O.S.B.; Stanislaus Maudlin, O.S.B.; Julius Armbruster, O.S.B.; Thomas Roznowski, O.S.B.; Odo Gogel, O.S.B.; Lawrence Kratz, O.S.B.; Guy Gau, O.S.B.; Peter Schwartz, O.S.B.; Bede Roman, O.S.B.; John McMullen, O.S.B.; Raymond Otto, O.S.B.; Basil Dilger, O.S.B.; Cletus Miller, O.S.B.; Odilo Burkhardt, O.S.B.; Bernardine Ness, O.S.B.; Theophane Gonnelly, O.S.B.; Larry Barnett, O.S.B.; Christopher Uehlein, O.S.B.; Wilfrid Lambertz, O.S.B.; Pedro Choc, O.S.B.; Francisco Arrivillaga Lemus, O.S.B. Priests 25; Brothers 17.

[G] CONVENTS AND RESIDENCES FOR SISTERS

ABERDEEN. *Presentation Convent*, 57401. Tel: 605-225-0420; Fax: 605-229-8412.
E-mail: vvetter@nrctv.com
Motherhouse and Novitiate of the Sisters of the Presentation of the B.V.M. Sr. Joyce Meyer, P.B.V.M., Pres. Final Professed Sisters 166.

ALEXANDRIA. *Monastery of Our Mother of Mercy, Discalced Carmelite Nuns*, 221 5th St. W., P.O. Box 67, 57311-0067. Tel: 605-239-4382. Mother Marie Therese of the Child Jesus, O.C.D., Mother Prioress.

MARTY. *Motherhouse Oblate Sisters of the Blessed Sacrament.* St. Sylvester's Convent, Box 217, 57361-0217. Tel: 605-384-3305; Fax: 605-384-5886.
E-mail: osbs@charles-mix.com
Sr. Patricia Mylott, O.S.B.S. Professed Sisters 7.

MITCHELL. *Sisters of St. Francis of Our Lady of Guadulupe*, 1417 W. Ash, 57301. Private Association of the Faithful. Sr. Marita Pfau, Sister Leader. Professed Sisters 6.

WATERTOWN. *Mother of God Monastery*, 110 28th Ave., S.E., 57201-8418.
E-mail: monastery@icontrol.net
Web site: http://www.icontrol.net/monastery
Motherhouse and Novitiate of Benedictine Sisters. Sr. Sandra Meek, O.S.B., Prioress. Sisters 82.

YANKTON. *Sacred Heart Monastery*, 1005 W. Eighth St., 57078. Tel: 605-668-1011; Fax: 605-668-1559. Motherhouse and Novitiate of the Benedictine Sisters. Sr. Jacquelyn Ernster, O.S.B., Prioress; Rev. Mel Patton, O.S.B., Chap. Sisters 168.

[H] NEWMAN CENTERS

ABERDEEN. *Aquinas Student Center.*
E-mail: nsunewman@index.com
Northern State University, 310 15th Ave. S.E., 57401. Tel: 605-229-1011. Rev. Joseph Vogel, Chap.; Michala Heller, Campus Min.
Diocesan Newman Apostolate, 310 15th Ave. S.E., 57401-7505. Rev. Joseph Vogel, Coord.

BROOKINGS. *Pius XII Student Center.* Our Lady of Wisdom Chapel. South Dakota State University, Box 7019 University Station, 57007. Tel: 605-692-9461. Rev. Michael Griffin. Mission. St. Paul, White, 57276.

MADISON. *Dakota State University Newman Club Office.* Attended by St. Thomas Parish, Madison. Trojan Center #101, 57042. Tel: 606-256-5061.

VERMILLION. *St. Thomas More Catholic Newman Center.* University of South Dakota, 320 Cherry St., 57069. Tel: 605-624-2697. Sr. Rosemarie Maly, O.S.B., Assoc. Dir.; Brian Begley, Activities Coord.

[I] MISCELLANEOUS LISTINGS

SIOUX FALLS. *The Banquet*, 300 N. Main Ave., 57102. Tel: 605-335-7066. Carolyn Downs, Exec. Dir. Total Staff 8; Total Assisted 84,283.
The Berakkah House, 400 Western Ave. N., 57104. Tel: 605-332-4017. Rev. Howard Carroll, Dir. Total Assisted 13.
The Catholic Foundation for Eastern South Dakota, 3100 W. 41st St., 57105. Mark Conzemius, Exec. Dir.
Community Outreach, 431 N. Cliff Ave., 57103. Jerry Bohnhoff, Dir. Total Staff 2; Total families assisted annually 1,407.
Good Shepherd Center, 300 N. Main Ave., 57102. Deacon Jim Walden, Dir.
Holy Family Child Care Center, 217 N. Sherman, 57103. Tel: 605-357-9227. Shannon Miles, Dir.
Kateri Indian Center, 300 N. Main Ave., 57104. Tel: 605-335-3321. Marlene Worth, Dir.
Little Flower of Jesus School Foundation, Inc., 1301 N. Dubuque Ave., 57110-6450.
St. Francis House, 1301 E. Austin St., 57103. Tel: 605-334-3879. Rev. Steve Wohlfeil, Dir. Total Staff 6; Total Assisted 8,468.
St. Joseph Catholic Housing, Inc., Catholic Chancery Office, 3100 W. 41st St., 57105. Tel: 605-334-9861. Mr. James Mason, Dir., Catholic Charities.
St. Joseph Catholic Housing - Rolling Hills, Inc.
St. Joseph Catholic Housing - West Creek Woods, Inc.
St. Joseph Catholic Housing - Northridge, Inc.
St. Joseph Catholic Housing - Heritage, Inc.
St. Joseph Catholic Housing - Split Rock, Inc.
St. Vincent de Paul Store, 431 N. Cliff Ave., 57103. Tel: 605-335-5823. Nick Feyerisen, Mgr. Staff 6.
Sioux Falls Catholic School Corporation, 3201 S. Kiwanis, 57105; Fax: 605-373-1035. Total staff 11; Total Assisted 80.

ALEXANDRIA. *Fatima Family Apostolate*, St. Mary of Mercy Church, P.O. Box 158, 57311. Tel: 605-239-4532.
E-mail: fatimafambks@basec.net
Web site: www.tot.com
Rev. Robert J. Fox, Dir.

MARVIN. *Blue Cloud Abbey Retirement Trust*, P.O. Box 98, 57251-0098. Tel: 605-432-5528.
E-mail: 76354,1337@compuserve.com
Rev. John McMullen, O.S.B., Treas.

SISSETON. *Tekakwitha Adolescent Treatment Center*, R.R. 2, Box 187, 57262. Tel: 605-698-3935; 800-658-4727. Clayton R. Houff, Exec. Dir. Total Assisted 150.
Tekakwitha Housing Corp, 711 Veteran's Ave., 57262.
Tekakwitha Indian Mission, Inc., 120 E. Chestnut, 57262. Tel: 605-698-7414.
Tekekwitha Fine Arts Center, 401 S. 8th Ave. W., P.O. Box 208, 57262. Tel: 605-698-7058. Harold D. Moore, Curator. Staff 3.

WATERTOWN. *Immaculate Conception School Foundation, Inc.*, 309 2nd Ave. S.E., 57201.
Retirement Trust, Mother of God Monastery, 110 28th Ave. S.E., 57201.
St. Ann's Corporation, Mother of God Monastery, 110 28th Ave. S.E., 57201. Tel: 605-882-6600. Barbara Faller, Gen. Mgr.
Benet Place. Independent Living. 100 28th Ave., S.E., 57201. Tel: 605-886-9177. Units 39; Staff 3.
Evergreen Assisted Living, 90 28th Ave., S.E., 57201. Tel: 605-882-8555. Units 10; Staff 7.

YANKTON. *Benedictine Center, Inc.*, 1005 W. 8th, 57078.
Benedictine Health Foundation, Inc., 1017 W. Fifth, 57078. Kelly Kathol, Exec. Dir.
Benedictine Health System, 1005 W. 8th St., 57078. Tel: 605-668-1505; Fax: 605-668-1559.
The House of Mary Shrine, Inc., Box 455, Lewis & Clark Lake, 57078-0455. Russell Weller, Pres. Bd. Dirs.; Rev. Rodney Farke, Spiritual Dir.

RELIGIOUS INSTITUTES OF MEN REPRESENTED IN THE DIOCESE

For further details refer to the corresponding bracketed number in the Religious Institutes of Men or Women section.

[0200]—*Benedictine Monks.* (Aurora, IL; Marvin, SD).—O.S.B.
[]—*Carmelite.* (India).
[1130]—*Congregation of the Priests of the Sacred Heart.* (Hales Corners, WI).—S.C.J.
[0690]—*Jesuit Fathers and Brothers.* (Wisconsin Prov.).—S.J.
[0910]—*Oblates of Mary Immaculate.* (Central Prov.).—O.M.I.
[0560]—*Third Order Regular of Saint Francis.* (Loretto, PA).—T.O.R.
[1335]—*Vincentian.* (India).—V.C.

RELIGIOUS INSTITUTES OF WOMEN REPRESENTED IN THE DIOCESE

[0230]—*Benedictine Sisters of Pontifical Jurisdiction.* (Yankton, Watertown, SD).—O.S.B.
[0940]—*Daughters of St. Mary of Providence.*—D.S.M.P.
[1070-14]—*Dominican Sisters.* Grand Rapids.—O.P.
[1310]—*Franciscan Sisters of Little Falls, MN.*—O.S.F.
[3010]—*Oblate Sisters of the Blessed Sacrament.*—O.S.B.S.
[3320]—*Sisters of the Presentation of the B.V.M.*—P.B.V.M.
[1720]—*Sisters of the Third Order Regular of St. Francis of the Congregation of Our Lady of Lourdes.*—O.S.F.

INTER-PAROCHIAL CEMETERIES

SIOUX FALLS. *St. Michael*, 3001 N. Cliff, 57104. Tel: 605-338-3376.

NECROLOGY

† Bachman, Paul, (Retired). —Died April 16, 1997.
† Kasch, John, Howard, SD, St. Agatha. —Died March 15, 1997.
† Latterell, Glenn F., (Retired). —Died July 20, 1997.
† Liepold, Donald F., (Retired). —Died June 15, 1997.
† Martin, Rev. Msgr. Myron, (Retired). —Died Jan. 28, 1997.
† Patrick, Maurice C., (Retired). —Died Oct. 20, 1997.
† Presinell, Joseph C., (Retired). —Died Aug. 8, 1997.
† Stanton, Leonard F., (Retired). —Died April 3, 1997.

Diocese of Spokane

(Dioecesis Spokanensis)

Most Reverend

WILLIAM S. SKYLSTAD, D.D.

Bishop of Spokane; ordained May 21, 1960; appointed Bishop of Yakima February 22, 1977; consecrated and installed May 12, 1977; transferred to Spokane April 17, 1990; succeeded to the See April 27, 1990. *Office: W. 1023 Riverside Ave., P.O. Box 1453, Spokane, WA, 99210-1453. Res., W. 1025 Cleveland, Spokane, WA, 99205-3320.*

Catholic Pastoral Center: W. 1023 Riverside Ave., P.O. Box 1453, Spokane, WA, 99210-1453. Tel.: 509-358-7300.

Web site address: www.dioceseofspokane.org

E-mail address: cathdio@gntech.net

Solemnly consecrated to the Immaculate Heart of Mary on December 8, 1948.

ESTABLISHED DECEMBER 17, 1913.

Square Miles 24,356.

Corporate Title: *"The Catholic Bishop of Spokane, a Corporation Sole."*

Comprises the following Counties in the State of Washington: Okanogan, Ferry, Stevens, Pend Oreille, Lincoln, Spokane, Adams, Whitman, Franklin, Walla Walla, Columbia, Garfield and Asotin.

For legal titles of parishes and diocesan institutions, consult the Chancery Office.

STATISTICAL OVERVIEW

Personnel	
Bishop	1
Retired Bishops	1
Retired Abbots	1
Priests: Diocesan Active in Diocese	48
Priests: Active Outside Diocese	1
Priests: Diocesan in Foreign Missions	1
Priests: Retired, Sick or Absent	35
Number of Diocesan Priests	85
Religious Priests in Diocese	97
Extern Priests in Diocese	4
Ordinations:	
Religious Priests	2
Transitional Deacons	1
Permanent Deacons in Diocese	45
Total Brothers	15
Total Sisters	338
Parishes	
Parishes	78
With Resident Pastor:	
Resident Diocesan Priests	43
Resident Religious Priests	4
Without Resident Pastor:	
Administered by Priests	28
Administered by Pastoral Teams, etc.	3
Missions	3
Pastoral Centers	1
Professional Ministry Personnel:	
Sisters	2
Lay Ministers	6
Welfare	
Catholic Hospitals	7
Total Assisted	324,781
Health Care Centers	2
Total Assisted	16,114
Homes for the Aged	11
Total Assisted	1,619
Day Care and Extended Day Care Centers	14
Total Assisted	911
Specialized Homes	2
Total Assisted	198
Special Centers for Social Services	4
Total Assisted	16,113
Other Institutions	1
Total Assisted	684
Educational	
Seminaries, Diocesan	1
Students from This Diocese	19
Students from Other Diocese	5
Diocesan Students in Other Seminaries	11
Seminaries, Religious	1
Students Religious	18
Total Seminarians	48
Colleges and Universities	1
Total Students	4,370
High Schools, Diocesan and Parish	1
Total Students	191
High Schools, Private	1
Total Students	950
Elementary Schools, Diocesan and Parish	16
Total Students	3,325
Catechesis/Religious Education:	
High School Students	1,921
Elementary Students	4,692
Total Students Under Catholic Instruction	15,497
Teachers in the Diocese:	
Priests	18
Scholastics	1
Brothers	14
Sisters	5
Lay Teachers	86
Vital Statistics	
Receptions into the Church:	
Infant Baptism Totals	1,291
Adult Baptism Totals	383
Received into Full Communion	121
First Communions	796
Confirmations	392
Marriages:	
Catholic	302
Interfaith	161
Total Marriages	463
Deaths	1,793
Total Catholic Population	79,323
Total Population	710,789

Former Bishops—Most Rev. A. F. SCHINNER, D.D., cons. Bishop of Superior, July 25, 1905; resigned from that See, Jan. 15, 1913; appt. first Bishop of Spokane, March 18, 1914; resigned Dec. 17, 1925, and made Titular Bishop of Sala; died Feb. 7, 1937.—Most Rev. CHARLES D. WHITE, D.D., ord. Sept. 24, 1910; appt. Dec. 20, 1926; cons. Feb. 24, 1927; died Sept. 25, 1955.—Most Rev. BERNARD J. TOPEL, D.D., Ph.D., appt. coadjutor Bishop Aug. 9, 1955; cons. Sept. 21, 1955; succeeded to to the See Sept. 25, 1955; retired April 11, 1978; died Oct. 22, 1986.—Most Rev. LAWRENCE H. WELSH, D.D., ord. May 26, 1962; appt. Bishop of Spokane Nov. 7, 1978; cons. and installed Dec. 14, 1978; resigned April 17, 1990; appt. Auxiliary of St. Paul-Minneapolis, Nov. 5, 1991.

Vicar General—Rev. Msgr. JOHN M. STEINER, *P.O. Box 1453, Spokane, 99210-1453.* Tel: 509-358-7303; 466-0220; 326-8748.

Catholic Pastoral Center—W. 1023 Riverside Ave., P.O. Box 1453, Spokane, 99210-1453. Tel: 509-358-7300; Fax: 509-358-7302. Office Hours: Mon.-Fri. 9-5.

Moderator of the Curia—Rev. Msgr. JOHN M. STEINER, *P.O. Box 1453, Spokane, 99210-1453.* Tel: 509-358-7303.

Chancellor—Rev. MARK PAUTLER, *P.O. Box 1453, Spokane, 99210.* Tel: 509-358-7336.

Archivists—Revs. EDWARD J. KOWRACH; THEODORE BRADLEY, *P.O. Box 1453, Spokane, 99210-1453.* Tel: 509-358-7300.

Diocesan Tribunal—W. 1023 Riverside Ave., P.O. Box 1453, Spokane, 99210. Tel: 509-358-7336.

Judicial Vicar—Rev. MARK PAUTLER, J.C.L.

Defensor Vinculi—Rev. JOHN M. STEINER; JUDY ELLIFRITT, Sec.

Diocesan Consultors/Presbyteral Council—Rev. Msgr. JOHN M. STEINER; Rt. Rev. ADRIAN PARCHER, O.S.B.; Revs. DARRIN CONNALL; THOMAS KHUE; OTTO KOLTZENBURG; JAMES MANGAN; JAMES KUHNS; ROBERT LYONS, S.J.; JAMES MCGREEVY; MARK PAUTLER; JOHN SAND; EUGENE TRACY; JAKE MORTON, S.J.

Pastoral Council—Rev. Msgr. JOHN M. STEINER; Revs. MARTY MARKARIAN; TERENCE TULLY; Sr. ANNE BOSSERMAN, S.N.J.M.; Sr. MAUREEN HEALY, O.P.; MIKE CAREY; JUDY DAVIS; JUANITA CONTRERAS; KENNETH DUNLAP; ANN FIGENSHOW; AL GILMORE; PAUL KIENBAUM; JULIE KIENBAUM; JON MCFARLAND; ROB MITCHELL; GERALD MOSMAN; LORETTA MOSMAN; LUISA ORELLENA-WESTBROOK; SHIRLEY PANTALEO; AMY PRY; MARY BETH RAUCH; TRACEY RICE; PATTI VAN HEEL; GEORGE VASIL; JOHN VLAHOVICH; JAMES WYNNE.

Diocesan Offices and Directors

Administrative Division: Diocesan Business Affairs—Sr. BERNADETTE BOTCH, S.P., Bishop Sec., *W. 1023 Riverside Ave., P.O. Box 1453, Spokane, 99210.* Tel: 509-358-7300; Fax: 509-358-7302.

Director of Fiscal Services—MERRILIN FULTON, *P.O. Box 1453, Spokane, 99210-1453.* Tel: 509-358-7320.

Catholic Foundation-Development Office—STEVEN C. KOCHARHOOK, Ph.D, *P.O. Box 1453, Spokane, 99210.* Tel: 509-358-4280.

Computer Office—JERRY M. DUFRESNE, *P.O. Box 1453, Spokane, 99210-1453.* Tel: 509-358-7346.

Administrative Division: Catholic Schools—Bishop's Secretary: Mr. DUANE SCHAFER, Supt., *Office of Education, P.O. Box 1453, Spokane, 99210.* Tel: 509-358-7330.

Administrative Division: Evangelization and Ministries Formation—BETTY NEWSTROM, Bishop's Sec., *P.O. Box 1453: Spokane, 99210-1453.* Tel: 509-358-7311.

Parish Services Office—BETTY NEWSTROM, Dir., *P.O. Box 1453, Spokane, 99210.* Tel: 409-358-7311.

Communications Office—ERIC MEISFJORD, Dir. & Editor, *Inland Register, P.O. Box 1453, Spokane, 99210-1453.* Tel: 509-358-7340. NANCY LOBERG, Advertising Mgr. Tel: 509-358-7343.

Charismatic Renewal—Rev. DANIEL WETZLER, *St. Paschal Parish, 7404 E. Marietta Ave., Spokane, 99212.* Tel: 509-924-4871.

Ecumenical Relations—Rev. THOMAS CASWELL, *Sacred Heart Parish, N.E. 440 Ash St., Pullman, 99163.* Tel: 509-332-5312.

Spanish Speaking Apostolates—Rev. HELIODORO LUCATERO, *Sacred Heart Parish, P.O. Box 548, Brewster, 98812.* Tel: 509-689-2931.

Vietnamese Apostolate—Vietnamese Catholic Community of the Diocese of Spokane, Revs. JOACHIM L. HEIN; TOM KHUE, *St. Patrick Parish, 5021 N. Nelson St., Spokane, 99207-6161.* Tel: 509-487-1325.

Vocation Director—Rev. RICHARD ROOT, *Bishop White Seminary, 429 E. Sharp, Spokane, 99202.* Tel: 509-487-6363.

Diocesan Liturgical Commission—Rev. STEVE DUBLINSKI, St. Mary Parish: *304 S. Adams Rd., Spokane, 99216-3112.* Tel: 509-928-3210.

Permanent Deaconate Formation—Dr. JOHN BYRNE, Ph.D., Dir., *E. 502 Boone Ave., Spokane, 99258.* Tel: 509-328-4220.

Deacon Council—Deacon JOHN SICILIA, *4515 N. Alberta St., Spokane, 99205.* Tel: 509-456-7119.

Catholic Committee on Scouting—Rev. TERENCE TULLY, Chap., *221 E. Rockwood Blvd., Apt.308, Spokane, 99202-1200.* Tel: 509-458-7674.

Bishop White Seminary—Rev. RICHARD ROOT, Dir. Seminarians & Rector, *E. 429 Sharp Ave., Spokane, 99202.* Tel: 509-326-3255.

Administrative Division: Social Ministries—Mrs. DONNA HANSON, Bishop's Sec., *W. 1023 Riverside, P.O. Box 1453, Spokane, 99210-1453.* Tel: 509-358-4250.

Catholic Family Services—MICHAEL T. RYAN, Dir., *W. 1023 Riverside, P.O. Box 1453, Spokane, 99210-1453.* Tel: 509-358-4260.

St. Vincent de Paul Society—*E. 2901 Trent Ave., Spokane, 99202.* Tel: 509-535-2491.

Censor Liborum—Rev. MICHAEL SAVELESKY, Ph.D., *St. Patrick Church Rectory, 408 W. Poplar St., Walla Walla, 99362-2831.* Tel: 509-525-1602.

Continuing Education of Priests—Rev. JAMES KUHNS, Chm., *Our Lady of Fatima Parish, 1517 E. 33rd, Spokane, 99203.* Tel: 509-747-7213.

Detention Ministry—Sr. MYRTA ITURRIAGA, S.P., *P.O. Box 1453, Spokane, 99210.* Tel: 509-358-7315.

Director of Cemeteries—DENNIS FAIRBANK, *Catholic Cemeteries of Spokane, P.O. Box 18006, Spokane, 99208-0006.* Tel: 509-467-5496.

Holy Childhood, Pontifical Association—Rev. MARK PAUTLER, *W. 1023 Riverside Ave., P.O. Box 1453, Spokane, 99210.* Tel: 509-358-7336.

Immaculate Heart Retreat Center—Sr. K.C. YOUNG, O.P., Dir., *S. 6910 Ben Burr Rd., Spokane, 99223.* Tel: 509-448-1224.

Priests' Personnel Board—Revs. THOMAS CASWELL, Chm. MARK PAUTLER, Sec. AL GRASHER; JOHN ROMPA; JOSEPH PASH; TOM MELE, *P.O. Box 1453, Spokane, 99210-1453.* Tel: 509-358-7336.

Propagation of the Faith—Rev. MARK PAUTLER, *W. 1023 Riverside Ave., P.O. Box 1453, Spokane, 99210.* Tel: 509-358-7336.

CLERGY, PARISHES, MISSIONS AND PAROCHIAL SCHOOLS

CITY OF SPOKANE
(Spokane County)

1—CATHEDRAL OF OUR LADY OF LOURDES, Rev. Msgr. James M. Ribble, Ph.D.; Deacon J. Andrew Phelps, M.D.
Res., 1115 W. Riverside Ave., 99201. Tel: 509-358-4292; Fax: 509-358-4277.

2—ASSUMPTION OF THE BLESSED VIRGIN MARY, Rev. Joseph W. Bell.
Office: 3624 W. Indian Trail Rd., 99208. Tel: 509-326-0144; 326-6951.
School—Tel: 509-328-1115; Fax: 509-328-1449. Sally Merriwether, Prin.
Lay Teachers 16; Students 330.
Station—Tum Tum, Our Lady of the Lake, Tel: 509-276-6165.

3—MARY QUEEN, Rt. Rev. Adrian Parcher, O.S.B.
Res., E. 3423 Carlisle Ave., 99207. Tel: 509-483-4384.

4—OUR LADY OF FATIMA, Rev. James Kuhns; Deacons John Byrne; Walter Weid.
Office: E. 1517-33rd Ave., 99203. Tel: 509-747-7213; Fax: 509-747-7217.
School—All Saints Interparochial, (Grades 5-8). Tel: 509-624-5712; Fax: 509-624-7752. Ms. Kathy Hicks, Prin.
Lay Teachers 12; Students 180.

5—SACRED HEART, Rev. George Haspedis; Deacon Dan Ritchie.
Res., E. 219 Rockwood Blvd., 99202. Tel: 509-747-5810.

6—ST. ALOYSIUS, Mr. Donald Weber, Parochial Admin.; Revs. L. Patrick Carroll, S.J.; J.K. Adams, S.J.; Deacons Jack Back; James E. Murphy; Jack McLain, S.J.
Res., 330 E. Boone Ave., 99202. Tel: 509-484-6496.
School—E. 611 Mission, 99202. Tel: 509-489-7825. Richard Shea, Prin.
Montessori Education Center—Susan Boughton, Dir.
Lay Teachers 14; Students 266.

7—ST. ANN, Linda Kobe-Smith, Admin.; Rev. James Dallen.
Church—E. 2120 First Ave., 99202. Tel: 509-535-3031.

8—ST. ANTHONY, Rev. Msgr. John Donnelly.
Res., N. 2320 Cedar St., 99205. Tel: 509-327-1162; Fax: 509-328-8728.
School—Trinity Interparochial School. Serving St. Anthony and St. Joseph. Tel: 509-327-9369. Mike Trudeau, Prin.
Lay Teachers 8; Students 135.
Educare Center—.
Lay Teachers 8; Students 30.

9—ST. AUGUSTINE, Rev. Msgr. Robert A. Pearson; Deacons Kenneth Dunlap; Gary Cooper, Pastoral Assoc.
Res., 428 W. 19th Ave., 99203. Tel: 509-747-4421.
School—Cataldo Catholic Interparochial, Tel: 509-624-8759; Fax: 509-747-9086.
Lay Teachers 22; Students 365.

10—ST. CHARLES, Rev. Heini Joachim Le Quang; Deacon John F. Sicilia.
Res., N. 4515 Alberta St., 99205. Tel: 509-327-9573.
School—Tel: 509-327-9575; Fax: 509-328-4575. Marquita Yriarte, Prin.
Lay Teachers 18; Students 311.

11—ST. FRANCIS OF ASSISI, FRIARS, Revs. Brian V. Flynn, O.F.M.; Sebastian Drake, O.F.M.; Bro. Franklin Fong, O.F.M.; Deacon Stephen Barnufsky, Sr.
Res., W. 1104 Heroy Ave., 99205. Tel: 509-325-1321.

12—ST. FRANCIS XAVIER, Rev. Paul Vevik.
Office: 3715 N. Standard St., 99207. Tel: 509-487-6363; Fax: 509-482-2770.
School—Tel: 509-487-1571. Mr. Richard Winkler, Prin.
Lay Teachers 6; Students 98.

13—ST. JOHN VIANNEY, Rev. Tyrone J. Schaff; Deacon Derwood Braungardt. In res., Rev. Charles D. Skok.
Office: 503 N. Walnut Rd., 99206. Tel: 509-926-5428; Fax: 509-922-5282.
School—(Grades PreK-8) N. 501 Walnut Rd., 99206. Tel: 509-926-7987. Dr. Judith Morbeck, Prin.
Lay Teachers 14; Students 218.

14—ST. JOSEPH, Sr. Ann Pizelo, S.N.J.M., Parish Admin.; Rev. Mark Pautler.
Res., W. 1503 Dean Ave., 99201. Tel: 509-328-4841.
School—Trinity Interparochial School. (See listing under St. Anthony).

15—ST. MARY, Revs. Steven L. Dublinski; Edward Borchardt; Deacons Richard Malone; James Blaine; Don Bentley.
Res., S. 304 Adams Rd., 99216. Tel: 509-928-3210; Fax: 509-926-9550.
School—14601 E. 4th Ave., 99216. Tel: 509-924-4300. Mrs. Carol Speltz, Prin.
Lay Teachers 14; Students 236.

16—ST. PASCHAL, Rev. Daniel E. Wetzler; Deacon John Crandall.
Res., 7404 E. Marietta Ave., 99212. Tel: 509-924-4871; Fax: 509-924-8731.
School—N. 2521 Park Rd., 99212. Tel: 509-924-5090; Fax: 509-924-6106. Sr. Loretta Giampietri, F.S.P.A., Prin.
Sisters 1; Lay Teachers 5; Students 83.
Educare Center—Tel: 509-922-7616. Dawn Davis, Dir. & Prog. Supr.
Lay Teachers 5; Students 73.

17—ST. PATRICK, Rev. Thomas L.T. Khve; Deacons John Gross; Mike Samuels.
Res., N. 5021 Nelson St., 99207. Tel: 509-487-1325.
School—Tel: 509-487-2830. Ms. Joanne Duffy, Prin.
Sisters 1; Lay Teachers 8; Students 200.
Convent—N. 5008 Lacey St., 99207. Tel: 509-487-1166.

18—ST. PETER, Rev. Eugene Tracy.
Res., 3520 E. 18th Ave., 99223-3814. Tel: 509-534-2227; Fax: 509-534-5522.
School—All Saints Interparochial, (Grades K-4). Tel: 509-534-1098; Fax: 509-534-1529. Ms. Kathy Hicks, Prin.
Lay Teachers 10; Students 238.

19—ST. THOMAS MORE, Rev. Msgr. John M. Steiner.
Res., N. 8112 Howard Dr., 99208. Tel: 509-466-0220; Fax: 509-466-0220.
School—Tel: 509-466-3811; Fax: 509-466-3316. Ann Doherty, Prin.
Lay Teachers 10; Students 270.

OUTSIDE THE CITY OF SPOKANE

Brewster, Okanogan Co., Sacred Heart, Rev. Pat Kerst.
Res., Box 548, 98812. Tel: 509-689-2931.

Cheney, Spokane Co., St. Rose of Lima, Rev. James Severyn Westbrook.
Res., N. 460 Fifth St., 99004. Tel: 509-235-6229.

Chewelah, Stevens Co., St. Mary of the Rosary, Rev. Albert Grasher, Jr.
Res., P.O. Box 26, 99109. Tel: 509-937-2452.
Church—E. 504 Main Ave., Box 26, 99109. Tel: 509-935-8028. [CEM]

Clarkston, Asotin Co., Holy Family, Rev. Leonard Forsmann.
Res., 917 Chestnut St., 99403. Tel: 509-758-6102; Fax: 509-758-4997. [CEM]
School—(Grades PreK-6). Tel: 509-758-6621. Mrs. Sharon Clizer, Prin.
Lay Teachers 8; Students 137.
Educare Preschool—.
Students 55.

Clayton, Stevens Co., St. Joseph, Rev. Edward F. Caffrey.
Mailing Address: N. 316 Main St., P.O. Box 749, Deer Park, 99006. Tel: 509-276-2948.

Colbert, Spokane Co., St. Joseph, Rev. Michael Kwiatkowski.
Res., 3720 E. Colbert Rd., 99005. Tel: 509-466-4991.

Colfax, Whitman Co., St. Patrick, Rev. Felix P. Lorge.
Res., S. 1108 Main St., 99111. Tel: 509-397-3921.

Colton, Whitman Co., St. Gall, Rev. Patrick MacMahon.
Res., P.O. Box 108, 99113. Tel: 509-229-3548. [CEM]
School—Guardian Angel-St. Boniface Interparochial, Tel: 509-299-3579. Mr. Walter O'Neill, Prin.
Lay Teachers 5; Students 58.

Colville, Stevens Co., Immaculate Conception, Rev. Darrin Connall.
Res., 320 N. Maple St., 99114. Tel: 509-684-6223; Fax: 509-684-8084.

Connell, Franklin Co., St. Vincent, Rev. Richard Poole.
Res., Box 1030, 99326. Tel: 509-234-2262; Fax: 509-234-0295.

Coulee Dam, Okanogan Co., St. Benedict. Closed. Sacramental records maintained at St. Henry's, Grand Coulee (Diocese of Yakima).
Mailing Address: 509 Grand Ave. W., Box 108, Grand Coulee, 99133. Tel: 509-633-1180.

Curlew, Ferry Co., St. Patrick, Rev. George Morbeck.
Res., Box 333, Republic, 99166. Tel: 509-775-3935.

Cusick, Kalispel Indian Reservation, Our Lady of Sorrows, Rev. Edward Marier.
Res., W. 612 First St., Box C, Newport, 99156. Tel: 509-447-4231.

Davenport, Lincoln Co., Immaculate Conception, Rev. John P. Krier (GF).
Res., 1310 Adams, P.O. Box 910, 99122. Tel: 509-725-1761. [CEM]

Dayton, Columbia Co., St. Joseph, Rev. John P. Sand; Deacon Dale Shaeffer.
Res., 112 S. First St., 99328-1307. Tel: 509-382-2311.

Deer Park, Spokane Co., St. Mary's Presentation, Rev. Edward F. Caffrey.
Res., N. 316 Main St., P.O. Box 749, 99006. Tel: 509-276-2948. [CEM]

Eltopia, Franklin Co., St. Paul, Rev. Richard Poole.
Res., 14181 Glade North Rd., 99330. Tel: 509-297-4371.

Ford, Stevens Co., St. Philip Benizi, Rev. Jake Morton, S.J.
Res., Indian-Spokane Reservation, Box 214, Wellpinit, 99040. Tel: 509-258-7233.

Harrington, Lincoln Co., St. Francis of Assisi, Rev. John P. Krier (GF).
Res., P.O. Box 166, 99134. Tel: 509-253-4310.

Inchelium, Ferry Co., St. Michael's Mission, Rev. Jake Morton, S.J.; Jenny-Ann Edgen, Admin.
Res., Box 122, 99138. Tel: 509-722-4592.

Ione, Pend Oreille Co., St. Bernard, Rev. Edward Marier.
Mailing Address: Box 731, 99139. Tel: 509-447-4231.
Res., W. 612 First St., Box C, Newport, 99156. Tel: 509-447-4231.

Keller, Ferry Co., St. Rose of Lima, Rev. Robert Erickson, S.J.; Deacon Archie Arnold.
Res., Box 70, Nespelem, 99155. Tel: 509-634-4249.

Kettle Falls, Stevens Co., Sacred Heart, Rev. Darrin Connall.
Mailing Address: Box 303, 99141. Tel: 509-738-2356.

Lacrosse, Whitman Co., St. Joseph, Rev. Felix P. Lorge.
Res., St. Patrick Parish, S. 1018 Main St., Colfax, 99111. Tel: 509-397-3921.

Lind, Adams Co., St. Ambrose, Rev. James V. McGreevy.
Res., E. 404 Fifth Ave., Ritzville, 99169. Tel: 509-659-0437.

Medical Lake, Spokane Co., St. Anne, Rev. Tom Mele; Deacon Robert King.
Res., E. 708 Lake St., Box 125, 99022. Tel: 509-299-3585.

Metaline Falls, Pend Oreille Co., St. Joseph, Rev. Edward Marier.
Mailing Address: P.O. Box 417, 99153. Tel: 509-446-2651.
Res., W. 612 First St., Box C, Newport, 99156. Tel: 509-447-4231.

Nespelem, Okanogan Co., Sacred Heart Mission, Rev. Robert Erickson, S.J.
Res., Box 70, 99155. Tel: 509-634-4249. [CEM]

Newport, Pend Oreille Co., St. Anthony, Rev. Edward Marier.
Res., W. 612 First St., Box C, 99156. Tel: 509-447-4231.

Northport, Stevens Co., Pure Heart of Mary, Rev. Darrin Connall.
Res., Box 29, 99157. Tel: 509-732-4552.

Oakesdale, Whitman Co., St. Catherine of Alexandria, Rev. Eugene Glatt.
Res., Box 8, Rosalia, 99170. Tel: 509-523-4011.

Odessa, Lincoln Co., St. Joseph, Rev. W. Roy Floch.
Res. & Mailing Address—P.O. Box 106, Wilbur, 99185. Tel: 509-647-2380.

Okanogan-Omak, Okanogan Co., Our Lady of the Valley, Rev. Robert D. Turner.
Res., Rte. 2, N. 2511 Elmway, Okanogan, 98840. Tel: 509-422-5049; Fax: 509-422-5817.

Omak, Okanogan Co., St. Mary Mission, Rev. Charles Peterson, S.J.; Bettejo Passalaqua, Pastoral Assoc.
Res., Rte. 2, Box 66A, 98841. Tel: 509-826-6401. [CEM]

St. Joseph, Rev. Charles Peterson, S.J.
Mailing Address: 6th & Jackson, Rte. 2, P.O. Box 12, 98841.
Res., 323 Edmonds, 98841. Tel: 509-826-6401.

Oroville, Okanogan Co., Immaculate Conception, Rev. Kevin Codd.
Res., 1715 Main St., Box 340, 98844. Tel: 509-476-2110; Fax: 509-476-2110.

Othello, Adams Co., Sacred Heart, Rev. Heliodoro Lucatero; Deacons Antonio Beraza; Joel Pruneda.
Res., E. 616 Juniper St., 99344. Tel: 509-488-5653.

Otis Orchards, Spokane Co., St. Joseph, Rev. James Mangan.
Res., 4521 N. Arden Rd., 99027-9358. Tel: 509-926-7133; Fax: 509-926-9454.

Pasco, Franklin Co., St. Patrick, Rev. Msgr. Pedro Ramirez-Alejos; Revs. John Bieh; Rory Pitstick; Deacons Andres Espinoza; Robert Kalinowski; Gary Franz; Juanita Contreras, Pastoral Assoc.
Res., 1320 W. Henry, 99301. Tel: 509-547-8841; Fax: 509-547-8841, Ext. 22.
School—1016 N. 14th Ave., 99301. Tel: 509-547-7261. David-Paul Zuber, Prin.
Lay Teachers 9; Students 220.

Pomeroy, Garfield Co., Holy Rosary, Rev. John P. Sand.
Mailing Address: Rte. 1, Box 4, 99347-9702.
Res., 634 High St., 99347. Tel: 509-843-3801. [CEM]

Pullman, Whitman Co., Sacred Heart, Rev. Thomas C. Caswell.
Office: N.E. 440 Ash St., 99163. Tel: 509-332-5312; Fax: 509-332-5312.

Reardan, Lincoln Co., St. Michael, Rev. John P. Krier (GF).
Mailing Address: P.O. Box 451, Rearden, 99029. Tel: 509-725-1761.
Res., 455 Cottonwood, 99029.

Republic, Ferry Co., Immaculate Conception, Rev. George H. Morbeck.
Res., 756 S. Portland, 99166. Tel: 509-775-3935.

Ritzville, Adams Co., St. Agnes, Rev. James V. McGreevy.
Res., E. 404 Fifth Ave., 99169. Tel: 509-659-0437.

Rockford, Spokane Co., St. Joseph, Rev. Steven L. Dublinski.
Res., Box 54, 99030. Tel: 509-291-3481.

Rosalia, Whitman Co., Holy Rosary, Rev. Eugene Glatt.
Res., P.O. Box 8, N. 600 Whitman Ave., 99170. Tel: 509-523-4011.

St. John, Whitman Co., Our Lady of Perpetual Help, Rev. Eugene Glatt.
Mailing Address: P.O. Box 325, 99171.
Res., P.O. Box 8, Rosalia, 99170. Tel: 509-523-4011.

Sprague, Lincoln Co., Mary Queen of Heaven, Rev. James V. McGreevy.
Res., E. 404 Fifth Ave., Ritzville, 99160. Tel: 509-659-0437. [CEM]

Springdale, Stevens Co., Sacred Heart, Rev. Albert Grasher, Jr.
Res., P.O. Box 188, Valley, 99181. Tel: 509-937-2452.

Tekoa, Whitman Co., Sacred Heart, Rev. Eugene Glatt.
Res., P.O. Box 8, Rosalia, 99170. Tel: 509-523-4011. [CEM]

Tonasket, Okanogan Co., Holy Rosary, Rev. Kevin Codd.
Res., 1715 Main St., Box 340, Oroville, 98844. Tel: 509-476-2110; Fax: 509-476-2110.

Twisp, Okanogan Co., St. Genevieve, Rev. Pat Kerst.
Res., P.O. Box 6, 98856. Tel: 509-997-4201.

Uniontown, Whitman Co., St. Boniface, Rev. Patrick MacMahon.
Res., P.O. Box 108, Colton, 99113. Tel: 509-229-3548. [CEM]
School—Guardian Angel-St. Boniface Interparochial. See St. Gall, Colton.

Usk, Pend Oreille Co., St. Jude, Rev. Edward Marier.
Res., W. 612 First St., Box C, Newport, 99156. Tel: 509-447-4231.

Valley, Stevens Co., Holy Ghost, Rev. Albert Grasher, Jr.
Res., P.O. Box 188, 99181. Tel: 509-937-2452.
Station—Jump-off Joe, Stevens Co., St. Joseph.

Waitsburg, Walla Walla Co., St. Mark, Rev. John P. Sand; Deacon Dale Shaeffer.
Res., 112 S. First St., Dayton, 99328-1307. Tel: 509-382-2311.

Walla Walla, Walla Walla Co., Assumption of the Blessed Virgin Mary, Rev. Otto Koltzenburg.
Res., 2098 E. Alder St., 99362. Tel: 509-525-8163.
School—Assumption Interparochial, Tel: 509-525-9283. Mrs. Michele Acock, Prin.
Lay Teachers 13; Students 204.

St. Francis of Assisi, Revs. Michael Savelesky, Ph.D.; Timothy Hays; Sr. Sharon Bongiorno, F.S.P.A., Pastoral Min.
Res., 722 W. Alder St., 99362. Tel: 509-525-1663; Fax: 509-529-7849.
Sisters 2.

St. Patrick, Revs. Michael Savelesky, Ph.D.; Timothy Hays. Pastoral Assocs.: Sr. Karen Dunham; Deacons Olegario Reyes; Bob Dalecki.
Office: 425 W. Alder St., 99362-2811.
Res., 408 W. Poplar St., 99362. Tel: 509-525-1602.

Washtunca, Adams Co., Holy Trinity, Rev. James V. McGreevy.
Res., E. 404 Fifth St., Ritzville, 99169. Tel: 509-659-0437.

Wellpinit, Stevens Co., Sacred Heart, Rev. Jake Morton, S.J.
Res., Indian-Spokane Reservation, Box 214, 99040. Tel: 509-258-7233. [CEM]

Westend, Stevens Co., Our Lady of Lourdes, Rev. Jake Morton, S.J.
Res., Indian-Spokane Reservation, P.O. Box 214, Wellpinit, 99040. Tel: 509-258-7233.

Wilbur, Lincoln Co., Sacred Heart, Rev. W. Roy Floch.
Res., P.O. Box 106, 99185. Tel: 509-647-2380.

Chaplains of Public Institutions

SPOKANE. *U.S. Veterans Hospital*. Rev. Theodore F.X. Bradley.

WALLA WALLA. *U.S. Veterans Hospital*. Vacant.
Washington State Penitentiary. Served by priests of Walla Walla.

Special Ministry:
Reverend Fathers—
Birk, John, Our Lady of Lourdes Health Center, Pasco
Venneri, Michael D., Sacred Heart Medical Center, Spokane

On Duty Outside the Diocese:
Reverend Fathers—
Baronti, David
McGrann, John

Absent on Leave:
Reverend Fathers—
Boulden, Garry
Hemenway, Richard

Retired:
Reverend Monsignors—
Bach, Frank J.
Mertens, Arthur, 221 E. Rockwood Blvd., No. 320, Spokane, WA 99202
Rosage, David E., 221 E. Rockwood Blvd., No. 222, Spokane, WA 99202
Reverend Fathers—
Barry, Bernard J., 221 E. Rockwood Blvd., No. 318, Spokane, WA 99202
Beaver, Reinard W., 1101 Powell St., Steilacoon, WA 98388
Bradley, Theodore F.X., 700 W. 7th Ave., Apt. 801, Spokane, WA 99204
Brennan, William J., 2030 Delaware, Walla Walla, WA 99362
Breznikar, Victor, 1018 Whitman St., #111, Walla Walla, WA 99362-3475
Donnelly, Sean, 1 Parkview, Freshford Rd., Kilkenny, Ireland
Dugan, William M., 272 Kennedy St., No. 48, Chula Vista, CA 92011
Eis, Charles, 9202 Irvington Ave., San Diego, CA 92123-3129
Flour, Anton, 14819 E. Mission, Spokane, WA 99216-1960
Grant, James, 217 W. Spokane Falls, No. 1802, Spokane, WA 99201
Hanley, William, Killula, Newmarket-on-Fergus, Claire Co., Ireland
Helfenstein, Maurice R., 14819 E. Mission, Spokane, WA 99216-1960
Hullings, Clifford, 3110 E. Chattaroy Rd. #43, Chattaroy, WA 99003
Kelley, Joseph, 221 E. Rockford Blvd., No. 104, Spokane, WA 99202-1200
Kelley, N. F., 629 S. Main St., #7, Fond du Lac, WI 54935
Kowrach, Edward, 530 Flora Rd., Veradale, WA 99037
McCabe, George V., S.J., 12016 E. Cataldo Ave., Spokane, WA 99206-4963
O'Brien, John P., P.O. Box 1808, Santa Rosa, CA 95402
O'Dea, John W., Ballingaddyworth, Kilmallock, Limerick Co., Ireland
O'Malley, James J., Kilsallagh, Westport, Mayo Co., Ireland
Pash, Joseph, 221 E. Rockwood Blvd., No. 204, Spokane, WA 99202
Rompa, John, 4423 S. Sunny Creek Dr., Spokane, WA 99204-8460
Schoffelmeer, Arnold L., Box 36123, N. Findlay Rd., Deer Park, WA 99006
Schwemin, Ralph H., 3915 N. Washington St., Spokane, WA 99205
Tully, Terence, 221 E. Rockwood Blvd., No. 308, Spokane, WA 99202
Verdoon, Cornelius, P.O. Box 280, Odessa, WA
Wenning, Paul A., 7423 N. Laurelhurst Dr., Spokane, WA 99208
Wietensteiner, Joseph M., P.O. Box 8087, Spokane, WA 99203

Permanent Deacons:
Arnold, Archie, St. Rose of Lima, Keller
Arnoux, Richard
Back, Jack, St. Aloysius, Spokane
Barnufsky, Stephen, St. Francis of Assisi, Spokane
Bentley, Donald, St. Francis Assisi, Spokane
Beraza, Antonio, Sacred Heart, Othello
Braungardt, Derwood, St. John Vianney, Spokane
Buckman, Thomas, Kateri Institute
Byrne, John, Our Lady of Fatima, Spokane
Cooper, Gary, St. Augustine, Spokane
Crandall, John, St. Paschal, Spokane
Crow, John, Assumption Parish, Spokane
Dalecki, Robert
Dunlap, Kenneth, St. Augustine, Spokane
Espinoza, Andres, St. Patrick, Pasco
Farrell, Daniel, St. Henry, Grand Coulee
Fosmire, Charles
Franz, Gary, St. Patrick, Pasco
Gress, John, St. Patrick's Parish, Spokane
Kalinowski, Robert, St. Patrick, Pasco
King, Robert, St. Anne, Medical Lake
Mackin, Francis, Sitka, AL
Maher, Dean, Washington State Penitentiary, Walla Walla
Malone, Richard, St. Mary, Spokane
Martinez, Gonzalo, St. Mary's, Spokane
Murphy, James E., Sacred Heart Medical Center, Spokane
Phelps, J. Andrew, Our Lady of Lourdes, Spokane

Polensky, Hugh, Sacred Heart Medical Center, Spokane
Pruneda, Joel, Sacred Heart, Othello
Reyes, Olegario, St. Patrick, Walla Walla
Ritchie, Dan, Sacred Heart, Spokane
Samuel, Mike, St. Patrick's, Spokane
Sando, William
Schuster, Donald, St. Peter's, Spokane
Schutt, David, Immaculate Conception, Davenport
Shaeffer, Dale, St. Joseph, Dayton
Sicilia, John F., St. Charles, Spokane
Weid, Walter, Our Lady of Fatima, Spokane
Wilson, Charles, Port Angeles
Yenko, David

INSTITUTIONS LOCATED IN THE DIOCESE

[A] SEMINARIES, DIOCESAN

SPOKANE. *Bishop White Seminary*, E. 429 Sharp Ave., 99202. Tel: 509-326-3255; Fax: 509-326-3761.
E-mail: sembw@spkn.uswest.net
Rev. Richard Root, Rector. Students 12.

[B] SEMINARIES, RELIGIOUS, OR SCHOLASTICATES

SPOKANE. *St. Michael's Institute*, Gonzaga University, N. 1107 Astor St., 99202. Tel: 509-328-4220; Fax: 509-324-5820. Very Rev. Joseph E. LIngan, S.J. (Maryland), Rector; Revs. Kenneth J. Rudnick, S.J. (California), Dean; Richard J. Comboy, S.J. (Missouri), Min. Scholastics; Joseph F. Conwell, S.J., Scholar in Res.; Ms. Anita Foreman, Admin. Asst. Fathers 6; Scholastics 18; Brothers 1.

[C] COLLEGES AND UNIVERSITIES

SPOKANE. *Gonzaga University*, 99258. Tel: 509-328-4220
For a complete listing, refer to the Colleges and Universities section.
Mater Dei Institute, E. 405 Sinto Ave., 99202. Tel: 509-328-8332; Fax: 509-325-4011
For a complete listing, refer to the Colleges and Universities section.

[D] HIGH SCHOOLS, INTERPAROCHIAL

WALLA WALLA. *Walla Walla Catholic School System.* (Grades Educare-12), E. 919 Sumach, 99362. Tel: 509-525-3030.
E-mail: desales@wwics.com
Mrs. Michele Acock, Prin. (Grades K-5); Mr. Robert R. Wehde, Admin & Prin. (Grades 6-12). Lay Teachers 29; Students: Elementary 225; High School 191.

[E] HIGH SCHOOLS, PRIVATE

SPOKANE. *Gonzaga Preparatory School*, E. 1224 Euclid Ave., 99207. Tel: 509-483-7737.
E-mail: gonzaga@mail.gntech.com
Mr. John Traynor, Pres.; Mr. Al Falkner, Prin.; Revs. Michael Tyrrell, S.J., Rector; J.K. Adams; Thomas A. Colgan, S.J.; Steven Dillard, S.J.; Robert A. Goebel, S.J.; Kevin P. McGinley, S.J.; Richard R. Mercy, S.J.; Joseph Showutter, S.J.; Thomas Lamanna, S.J. Priests 9; Lay Teachers 60; Students 950.

[F] INTERPAROCHIAL GRADE SCHOOLS

SPOKANE. *All Saints School.* (Grades 5-8), E. 1428 33rd Ave., 99203. Tel: 509-624-5712.
E-mail: allsaint@spkn.uswest.net
Kathy Hicks, Prin.
All Saints Primary. (Grades K-4), E. 3406 18th Ave., 99223. Tel: 509-534-1098. Kathy Hicks, Prin. Serving St. Peter, St. Ann, and Our Lady of Fatima Parishes. Lay Teachers 23; Students 392.
Cataldo Catholic School. (Grades K-8), W. 455-18th Ave., 99203. Tel: 509-624-8759.
E-mail: cataldoc@spokane.net
Mr. Richard Pelkie, Prin. Serving St. Augustine, Sacred Heart, and Our Lady of Lourdes Parishes. Lay Teachers 24; Students 365.
St. Francis School. (Grades K-8), E. 544 Providence, 99207. Tel: 509-487-1571. Mr. Richard Winkler, Prin. Serving St. Francis of Assisi and St. Francis Xavier Parishes. Lay Teachers 6; Students 98.
Trinity School. (Grades K-8), W. 1306 Montgomery Ave., 99205. Tel: 509-327-9369. Mr. Michael S. Trudeau, Prin.
Serving St. Anthony and St. Joseph Parishes. Lay Teachers 7; Students 138.
COLTON. *Guardian Angel-St. Boniface School*, P.O. Box 48, 99113. Tel: 509-229-3579. Mr. Walt O'Neill, Prin.
Serving St. Gall and St. Boniface Parishes. Lay Teachers 4; Students 67.
WALLA WALLA. *Assumption Elementary School.* (Grades K-5), E. 2066 Alder St., 99362. Tel: 509-525-9283.
E-mail: assumption@wwics.com
Mrs. Michele Acock, Prin. & Bldg. Admin.
Serving Assumption, St. Francis of Assisi, and St. Patrick Parishes. Lay Teachers 13; Students 225.
Walla Walla Catholic School System. See listing under High Schools, Interparochial.

[G] GENERAL HOSPITALS

SPOKANE. *Holy Family Hospital*, N. 5633 Lidgerwood St., 99207. Tel: 509-482-0111
For a complete listing, refer to the Hospitals section.
Holy Family Hospital Adult Day Health c/o Dominican Network, N. 5633 Lidgerwood, 99207. Tel: 509-482-2475.
For a complete listing, refer to the Hospitals section.
Sacred Heart Medical Center, W. 101 Eighth Ave., TAF-C9, 99220. Tel: 509-455-3131
For a complete listing, refer to the Hospitals section.
CHEWELAH. *St. Joseph's Hospital of Chewelah*, E. 500 Webster, 99109. Tel: 509-935-8211
For a complete listing, refer to the Hospitals section.
COLVILLE. *Mount Carmel Hospital*, 982 E. Columbia, Box 351, 99114. Tel: 509-684-2561
For a complete listing, refer to the Hospitals section.
DEER PARK. *Deer Park Health Center and Hospital* Mailing Address: 5633 N. Lidgerwood Spokane, 99207.
For a complete listing, refer to the Hospitals section.
PASCO. *Our Lady of Lourdes Health Center*, 520 N. Fourth Ave., P.O. Box 2568, 99302. Tel: 509-547-7704
For a complete listing, refer to the Hospitals section.
WALLA WALLA. *St. Mary Medical Center*, 401 W. Poplar St., 99362. Tel: 509-525-3320
For a complete listing, refer to the Hospitals section.

[H] PROTECTIVE INSTITUTIONS
(Catholic Social Service)

SPOKANE. *Catholic Charities, Inc.*, W. 1023 Riverside Ave., P.O. Box 1453, 99210-1453. Tel: 509-358-4250
For a complete listing, refer to the Special Care Facilities section.
Catholic Family Service, W. 1023 Riverside Ave., P.O. Box 1453, 99210-1453. Tel: 509-358-4260
For a complete listing, refer to the Special Care Facilities section.
Guse Summit View, 820 N. Summit Blvd., 99201.
E-mail: sumview@gntech.net
For a complete listing, refer to the Special Care Facilities section.
House of Charity, W. 9 Main Ave., P.O. Box 1453, 99210-1453. Tel: 509-624-7821
For a complete listing, refer to the Special Care Facilities section.
Miryam's House, W. 1805 Ninth St., 99204
For a complete listing, refer to the Special Care Facilities section.
St. Anne's Children's Home, N. 707 Cedar St., 99201-1999. Tel: 509-325-7672
For a complete listing, refer to the Special Care Facilities section.
St. Joseph's Counseling Center, N. 1016 Superior St., 99202. Tel: 509-483-6495.
E-mail: sjfc@icehouse.net
For a complete listing, refer to the Special Care Facilities section.
St. Margaret's Shelter, P.O. Box 1453, 99210. Tel: 509-624-7624
For a complete listing, refer to the Special Care Facilities section.
St. Vincent de Paul Social Service Office, E. 2901 Trent Ave., 99202. Tel: 509-534-2824 (Social Svc.); 535-2491 (Main Store & Office)
For a complete listing, refer to the Special Care Facilities section.
St. Vincent de Paul Society, E. 2901 Trent Ave., 99202. Tel: 509-534-2824
For a complete listing, refer to the Special Care Facilities section.
Transitional Living Center, 3128 N. Hemlock, 92204.
E-mail: tlc@cet.com
For a complete listing, refer to the Special Care Facilities section.
Women's Drop In Center, 218 S. Howard, 92204-1419
For a complete listing, refer to the Special Care Facilities section.
CHEWELAH. *DominiCare*, 303 E. King St., P.O. Box 1070, 99109
For a complete listing, refer to the Special Care Facilities section.
CLARKSTON. *Lewis and Clark District Council of St. Vincent de Paul* Office:, 604 Second St., 99403. Tel: 509-758-7061; Fax: 509-758-9545.
For a complete listing, refer to the Special Care Facilities section.
COLVILLE. *The Rhodena, A Washington Non-profit Organization* Mailing Address: P.O. Box 1453 Spokane, 99210-1453.
For a complete listing, refer to the Special Care Facilities section.
DAYTON. *St. Vincent de Paul Store*, 257 E. Main St., 99328. Tel: 509-382-4146
For a complete listing, refer to the Special Care Facilities section.
MANITO STATION. *Spokane Boys' Ranch, Inc.*, P.O. Box 8087, 99203. Tel: 509-448-1411
For a complete listing, refer to the Special Care Facilities section.
PASCO. *St. Vincent de Paul Store*, 1120 W. Sylvester, 99301. Tel: 509-547-2341; Fax: 509-547-7804
For a complete listing, refer to the Special Care Facilities section.
WALLA WALLA. *Catholic Children and Family Service*, 5 W. Alder St., Ste. 333, 99362. Tel: 509-525-0572; Fax: 509-525-0576
For a complete listing, refer to the Special Care Facilities section.
St. Vincent de Paul Store, 308 W. Main St., 99362. Tel: 509-525-3903 (Store); 529-6778 (Office)
For a complete listing, refer to the Special Care Facilities section.

[I] SENIOR CITIZEN HOUSING

SPOKANE. *Cathedral Plaza Apartments*, W. 1120 Sprague Ave., 99204
For a complete listing, refer to the Special Care Facilities section.
The Delaney, W. 242 Riverside Ave., 99201
For a complete listing, refer to the Special Care Facilities section.
Fahy Garden Apartments, W. 1403 Dean Ave., 99201
For a complete listing, refer to the Special Care Facilities section.
Fahy West Apartments, W. 1523 Dean Ave., 99201
For a complete listing, refer to the Special Care Facilities section.
The O'Malley, E. 707 Mission Ave., 99202
For a complete listing, refer to the Special Care Facilities section.
Rockwood Lane / Court, E. 221 Rockwood Blvd., 99202
For a complete listing, refer to the Special Care Facilities section.
Senior Citizen Housing, W. 242 Riverside Ave., 99201. Tel: 509-624-6060
For a complete listing, refer to the Special Care Facilities section.
CLARKSTON. *Austen Manor*, 1222 Chestnut St., 99403
For a complete listing, refer to the Special Care Facilities section.
PULLMAN. *Pioneer Square*, S.E. 220 Kamiaken, 99163
For a complete listing, refer to the Special Care Facilities section.
WALLA WALLA. *Garden Court Apartments*, Sixth & Alder Sts., 99362
For a complete listing, refer to the Special Care Facilities section.
Mike Foye Apartments, Sixth & Alder Sts., 99362
For a complete listing, refer to the Special Care Facilities section.

[J] HOMES FOR AGED

SPOKANE. *St. Joseph Care Center*, W. 20 Ninth Ave., 99204. Tel: 509-838-6437
For a complete listing, refer to the Special Care Facilities section.
St. Joseph dba St. Brendan Continuing Care Center, E. 17 Eighth Ave., 99202. Tel: 509-624-1161
For a complete listing, refer to the Special Care Facilities section.

[K] MONASTERIES AND RESIDENCES OF PRIESTS AND BROTHERS

SPOKANE. *Regis Community*, N. 1107 Astor St., 99202. Tel: 509-328-4220; Fax: 509-484-2818. Most Rev. Robert L. Whelan, S.J. (Fairbanks), (Retired); Revs. Robert L. Fitts, S.J., Supr.; James P. Goodwin, S.J.; James P. Hurley, S.J.; Anton P. Jahner, S.J.; Leo B. Kaufmann, S.J.; Paul P. Luger, S.J.; James McCready, S.J.; James D. Nelson, S.J.; Joseph D. Ringwood, S.J.; Edmund J. Robinson, S.J.; Robert J. Schlim, S.J.; Michael T. Shannon, S.J.; Richard J. Sisk, S.J.; John R. Thatcher, S.J.; Bros. Stephen Karpinski, S.J.; James J. Lee, S.J.; Fenton J. Melia, S.J.; M. John Miller, S.J.; George A. McMonagle, S.J.

[L] CONVENTS AND RESIDENCES FOR SISTERS

SPOKANE. *Convent of the Holy Names,* 2911 W. Fort George Wright Dr., 99224. Tel: 509-328-4310; Fax: 509-328-9824.
E-mail: snjm@connectinc.com
Sisters of the Holy Names of Jesus and Mary. Sr. Shirley Roberg, S.N.J.M., Prov. Dir. Professed Sisters 209.

Dominican Center, Sinsinawa Dominican Sisters, 3102 W. Fort George Wright Dr., 99224-5297. Tel: 509-328-8033; Fax: 509-325-9877.
E-mail: dcentersp@aol.com
Sisters 20.

Dominican House, N. 5621 Lacey St., 99207. Tel: 509-489-9112. Dominican Sisters 2.

Dominican Sisters, E. 427 Augusta, 99207. Tel: 509-487-9280.

Holy Names Foundation, 2911 W. Fort George Wright Dr., 99224. Tel: 509-328-7470; Fax: 509-328-9824. Sr. Shirley Roberg, S.N.J.M., Prov. Dir. Support for educational activities of Sisters of the Holy Names of Jesus and Mary.

Holy Spirit Community, 2416 E. 46th Ave., 99223-6412. Tel: 509-448-6224. Elisabeth M. Pfeiffer, Pres.

Mary of the Angels Convent, E. 4624 Jamieson Rd., 99223-2028. Tel: 509-448-0674; Fax: 509-448-5192.
E-mail: keatjll@ieway.com
Western Regional Admin. of Franciscan Sisters of Perpetual Adoration. Sr. Patricia Gordon, F.S.P.A., Reg. Admin. Sisters 4; Professed Sisters in Region 63.

Monastery of St. Clare, 4419 N. Hawthorne St., 99205-1399. Tel: 509-327-4479. Sr. Mary Rita Dolan, O.S.C., Abbess. Poor Clare Nuns, Solemn Vows.
Papal Enclosure Novitiate. Professed Cloistered Nuns 9.

Mount St. Joseph. Retirement residence and community. 12 W. Ninth Ave., 99204-2394. Tel: 509-838-2594; Fax: 509-838-3220. Sisters of Providence, St. Ignatius Province. Bob Vail, Gen. Mgr.; Sr. Ida Mae Marceau, Supr. Sisters 63.

Sisters of Providence, St. Ignatius Province, 9 E. Ninth Ave., 99202-1295. Tel: 509-455-4884; Fax: 509-455-4882. Sr. Eileen Croghan, S.P., Prov. Supr. Sisters of Providence, St. Ignatius Province (a Washington non-profit corporation), Sisters of Providence of Montana, Sisters of Providence Institutions, Members of Providence Services (a Washington non-profit corporation). Sisters 5.

NEWPORT. *Carmelite Sisters of Mary,* 2892 State Rd. 211, 99156. Sr. Leslie L. Lund, Prioress. Sisters 2; Hermitages 4.

[M] RETREAT HOUSES

SPOKANE. *Immaculate Heart Retreat Center,* 6910 S. Ben Burr Rd., 99223. Tel: 509-448-1224; Fax: 509-448-1623. Sr. K.C. Young, O.P., Dir.; Rev. Msgr. William Van Ommeren.

KAIROS House of Prayer, 1714 W. Stearns Rd., 99208. Tel: 509-466-2187. Sr. M. Florence Leone, Poch, O.S.F., Coord. Provides a place called to a prayerful, reflective environment. Spiritual direction is available.

TUM TUM. *House of the Lord Retreat Center, Inc.,* P.O. Box 1034, 99034. Tel: 509-276-2219. Ramona Salvatore, Dir.

[N] NEWMAN CENTERS

CHENEY. *Catholic Newman Center at Eastern Washington University,* 837 Elm St., 99004. Tel: 509-235-8402. Rev. James Severyn Westbrook, Chap. Campus Ministry: Jolie Hagan-Monasterio; Kevin Hagan.

PULLMAN. *Washington State University - St. Thomas More Catholic Newman Center,* N.E. 820 B St., P.O. Box 2070, College Station, 99165. Tel: 509-332-6311. Rev. Michael Krieg, Chap.; Sr. Rosalie Locati, S.P., Campus Min.

[O] MISCELLANEOUS

SPOKANE. *The Catholic Foundation of the Spokane Diocese,* W. 1023 Riverside Ave., P.O. Box 1453, 99210-1453. Tel: 509-358-4280; Fax: 509-358-7302. Steven C. Kocharhook, Ph.D., Exec. Dir.

Dominican Health Services, N. 5633 Lidgerwood, 99207. Tel: 509-482-2576. Ronald J. Schurra, Pres.; Mr. Ronald DeArth, Vice Pres. Finance; Ms. Barbara Savage, Vice Pres. Mission Svcs. Serves as a multi-hospital system which includes Holy Family Hospital in Spokane, Mount Carmel Hospital in Colville, and St. Joseph's Hospital of Chewelah in Chewelah.

Dominican Network, N. 5633 Lidgerwood St., 99207. Tel: 509-482-2576. Ronald J. Schurra, Pres.; Ronald DeArth, Vice Pres. Finance; Bob Wellmon, Treas.; Earl Davenport, Sec. Serves as a member of Dominican Health Services, a multi-health care system which includes Dominican Health Services, Holy Family Hospital, Spokane; Mount Carmel Hospital, Colville; St. Joseph's Hospital of Chewelah, Chewelah; and Holy Family Hospital Adult Day Health, Spokane; Deer Park Health Center & Hospital, Deer Park; Domini Care, Chewelah.

Dominican Outreach Foundation, c/o Dominican Center, W. 3102 Fort George Wright Dr., 99224. Tel: 509-328-8033. James G. Falkner, Pres. Supports the Sisters educational, religious, and charitable ministries.

Holy Names Music Center, 3910 W. Custer Dr., 99224. Dr. Judith L. Myers, Exec. Dir. Sisters 5; Lay Teachers 31; Students 560.
Sponsored by Sisters of the Holy Names, Washington Province.

Immaculate Heart Retreat Center Foundation, S. 6910 Ben Burr Rd., 99223-1819.

Kateri Northwest Ministry Institute, 330 E. Boone, 99202-1778. Tel: 509-324-6305.
E-mail: dzpe38a@prodegy.com
Directors: Rev. Richard R. Mercy, S.J.; Mr. Paul Q. Kane. Purpose: Evangelization and training of Native Americans in the four Northwestern states and one Canadian province for all ministries in the Catholic Church and service in the native community, with attention to recovery ministries from Alcoholism and Dysfunctional Families. Goal: The development of fully indigenous Catholic churches in Urban centers and on Reservations.

Providence Services, 9 E. Ninth Ave., 99202-1295. Tel: 509-455-4884.
E-mail: dominicare@diix.com

Serra Club of Spokane, P.O. Box 414, 99220-0414.

Sisters of Providence, St. Ignatius Province Reserve Fund Trust, 9 E. Ninth Ave., 99202-1295. Tel: 509-455-4884; Fax: 509-455-4882.

SPOKANE CATHOLIC INVESTMENT TRUST, P.O. Box 1453, 99210-1453. Most Rev. William S. Skylstad, Pres. A Washington Non-Profit Corporation established to invest funds on behalf of the charitable organizations organized within the Catholic Diocese of Spokane.

Transitional Program for Women, W. 3102 Fort George Wright Dr., 99224. Tel: 509-328-6702.
E-mail: transprog@aol.com
Monica Walters, Pres.
Transitions.
Miryam's House of Transition.
Transitional Living Center.
Women's Drop In Center.

DAYTON. *Project Timothy: Christian Service Center,* P.O. Box 3, 99328. Tel: 509-382-2943. Mailing Address: 112 S. First St., 99328-1307.
Sponsored by St. Joseph's & St. Mark's Churches. Sophie J. Arebalos, Dir. Total Assisted 4,500.

PASCO. *Tri-Cities Preparatory School.* (A Development Committee), c/o Gerald F. Roach, 428 W. Shoshone, 99301. A proposed high school located in the Diocese of Spokane.

RELIGIOUS INSTITUTES OF MEN REPRESENTED IN THE DIOCESE

For further details refer to the corresponding bracketed number in the Religious Institutes of Men or Women section.

[0520]—*Franciscan Friars.* (Santa Barbara Prov.).—O.F.M.

[0690]—*Jesuit Fathers and Brothers.*—S.J.

RELIGIOUS INSTITUTES OF WOMEN REPRESENTED IN THE DIOCESE

[1780]—*Congregation of the Sisters of the Third Order of St. Francis of Perpetual Adoration.*—F.S.P.A.

[1070-03]—*Dominican Sisters.*—O.P.

[3760]—*Order of St. Clare.*—O.S.C.

[2970]—*School Sisters of Notre Dame.*—S.S.N.D.

[3350]—*Sisters of Providence.*—S.P.

[1650]—*The Sisters of St. Francis of Philadelphia.*—O.S.F.

[3840]—*Sisters of St. Joseph of Carondelet.*—C.S.J.

[1990]—*Sisters of the Holy Names of Jesus and Mary.*—S.N.J.M.

DIOCESAN CEMETERIES

SPOKANE. *Catholic Cemeteries of Spokane,* 7200 N. Wall St., 99208. Dennis Fairbank, Dir.

Holy Cross, 7200 N. Wall St., 99208. Tel: 509-328-1070.

St. Joseph, 17825 Trent, 99216. Tel: 509-891-6240.

NECROLOGY

(No Deaths)

Diocese of Springfield-Cape Girardeau

(Dioecesis Campifontis-Capitis Girardeauensis)

Most Reverend

JOHN J. LEIBRECHT, D.D., PH.D.

Bishop of Springfield-Cape Girardeau; ordained March 17, 1956; appointed October 23, 1984; consecrated December 12, 1984. *Office: The Catholic Center, 601 S. Jefferson Ave., Springfield, MO, 65806-3143.*

Chancery Office: The Catholic Center, 601 S. Jefferson Ave., Springfield, MO, 65806-3143. Tel.: 417-866-0841; Fax: 417-866-1140.

ESTABLISHED AUGUST 24, 1956.

Square Miles 25,719.

Comprises the following Counties in the State of Missouri: Barry, Barton, Bollinger, Butler, Cape Girardeau, Carter, Cedar, Christian, Dade, Dallas, Dent, Douglas, Dunklin, Greene, Howell, Iron, Jasper, Laclede, Lawrence, McDonald, Madison, Mississippi, New Madrid, Newton, Oregon, Ozark, Pemiscot, Polk, Reynolds, Ripley, Scott, Shannon, Stoddard, Stone, Taney, Texas, Wayne, Webster and Wright.

For legal titles of parishes and diocesan institutions, consult The Catholic Center.

STATISTICAL OVERVIEW

Personnel	
Bishop	1
Abbots	1
Retired Abbots	2
Priests: Diocesan Active in Diocese	57
Priests: Active Outside Diocese	5
Priests: Retired, Sick or Absent	14
Number of Diocesan Priests	76
Religious Priests in Diocese	67
Extern Priests in Diocese	4
Ordinations:	
Religious Priests	2
Permanent Deacons in Diocese	5
Total Brothers	83
Total Sisters	133
Parishes	
Parishes	68
With Resident Pastor:	
Resident Diocesan Priests	51
Resident Religious Priests	13
Without Resident Pastor:	
Administered by Priests	4
Missions	21
Professional Ministry Personnel:	
Brothers	1
Sisters	9
Lay Ministers	16
Welfare	
Catholic Hospitals	5
Total Assisted	278,162
Homes for the Aged	2
Total Assisted	356
Day Care and Extended Day Care Centers	1
Total Assisted	50
Special Centers for Social Services	1
Total Assisted	1,833
Other Institutions	1
Total Assisted	30,912
Educational	
Diocesan Students in Other Seminaries	4
Seminaries, Religious	2
Students Religious	26
Total Seminarians	30
High Schools, Diocesan and Parish	3
Total Students	815
Elementary Schools, Diocesan and Parish	23
Total Students	3,862
Catechesis/Religious Education:	
High School Students	1,571
Elementary Students	3,836
Total Students Under Catholic Instruction	10,114
Teachers in the Diocese:	
Priests	1
Sisters	13
Lay Teachers	239
Vital Statistics	
Receptions into the Church:	
Infant Baptism Totals	694
Adult Baptism Totals	443
Received into Full Communion	232
First Communions	1,231
Confirmations	956
Marriages:	
Catholic	159
Interfaith	241
Total Marriages	400
Deaths	551
Total Catholic Population	56,968
Total Population	1,050,206

Former Bishops—Most Rev. CHARLES H. HELMSING, D.D., cons. as Titular Bishop of Axomis and Auxiliary Bishop of Archdiocese of St. Louis, April 19, 1949; appt. Bishop of Springfield-Cape Girardeau, Aug. 24, 1956; transferred to Diocese of Kansas City-St. Joseph, Jan. 27, 1962; died Dec. 20, 1993.—Most Rev. IGNATIUS J. STRECKER, D.D., appt. April 7, 1962; cons. June 20, 1962; transferred to Archdiocese of Kansas City in Kansas, Sept. 10, 1969.—His Eminence WILLIAM CARDINAL BAUM, S.T.D., appt. Feb. 18, 1970; cons. April 6, 1970; transferred to Archdiocese of Washington, May 9, 1973; elevated to Cardinal, May 24, 1976 appointed to the Prefect of the Sacred Congregation Seminaries and Catholic Institutes, Jan. 15, 1980.—His Eminence BERNARD CARDINAL LAW, D.D., ord. May 21, 1961; appt. Bishop of Springfield-Cape Girardeau, Oct. 22, 1973; cons. Dec. 5, 1973; appt. Archbishop of Boston, Jan. 23, 1984; elevated to Cardinal, May 25, 1985.

Vicars General—Rev. Msgr. PHILIP A. BUCHER, V.G.; Rev. Msgr. THOMAS E. REIDY, V.G.; Rev. Msgr. RICHARD C. ROLWING, V.G.

Chancery Office—The Catholic Center, 601 S. Jefferson Ave., Springfield, 65806-3143. Tel: 417-866-0841; Fax: 417-866-1140.

Chancellor—Rev. Msgr. THOMAS E. REIDY, V.G.

Vice Chancellor—Rev. THOMAS P. KIEFER, J.C.L.

Regional Priest Moderators—Region I: Rev. THOMAS E. ALLEN, Region II: Rev. JOHN S. BRAUN, Region III: Rev. GREGORY E.J. ZATINA, Region IV: Rev. MARK C. ERNSTMANN, Region V: Rev. SHERMAN B. WALL, O.M.I., Region VI: Rev. JAMES J. UNTERREINER, Region VII (A): Rev. J. FRIEDEL,Region VII (B): Rev. FREDERICK J. LUTZ, Region VIII: Rev. Msgr. WILLIAM J. STANTON, Region IX: Rev. JOHN SHELEY.

Office of Administration

Catholic Foundation Of The Diocese Of Springfield-Cape Girardeau—Most Rev. JOHN J. LEIBRECHT, D.D., Ph.D., Pres.; Rev. Msgr. THOMAS E. REIDY, V.G., Vice Pres.; Mrs. JANET L. SMITH, Sec. Treas.

Development and Properties—Mr. THOMAS B. WALMSLEY.

Diocesan Development Fund—Mr. THOMAS B. WALMSLEY, Dir. Development and Properties; Mr. RICHARD G. BATH; Rev. MARK J. BINDER; Rev. LEONARD J. CHAMBERS; Mrs. JEANETTE A. CURTISS.

Finance—Mrs. JANET L. SMITH.

Financial Council—Mrs. JANET L. SMITH, Director of Finance; Mr. THOMAS B. WALMSLEY, Diocesan Dir. of Devel. & Properties; Mrs. PATRICIA HOPKINS; Mr. GEORGE MARINO; Mr. JAMES MOORE; Mr. PETER RAMSOUR; Mr. JAMES P. REINAGEL; Mr. O. J. TAYLOR; Mrs. KAY A. VAN PELT.

Office Of Education

Catholic Schools—Sr. JANE HOSCH, O.S.F. Ph.D., Supt. of Schools.

Communications (Public Relations)—Mrs. MARILYN VYDRA, Dir.

Ecumenism—Rev. JOHN F. GAGNEPAIN, C.M.

Media Library—Mrs. MARILYN VYDRA, Supvr.

"The Mirror", Newspaper, Diocese of Springfield-Cape Girardeau—Rev. MARK G. BOYER, M.A., M.Div., Editor; Mrs. MARILYN VYDRA, Staff Asst.; Mrs. KARLA ESSNER, Staff Asst.

Religious Education—Sr. ROSALIE DIGENAN, D.C., M.Ed., Dir.

Office Of Ministry

Campus Ministries—Rev. EDDIE DELEON, C.M.F., Southwest Missouri State Univ. Campus Min. Tel: 417-865-0802. Rev. J. FRIEDEL, Southeast Missouri State Univ. Campus Min. Tel: 573-335-3899.

Diocesan Spiritual Director—Rev. JOHN F. GAGNEPAIN, C.M. Tel: 573-547-7276.

Family Ministries—Mr. TROY CASTEEL, M.S., Dir.

Diocesan Council on Family Ministry—Region I, JIM NEWTON; MARGE NEWTON, Region II, DIANE WHITNEY; Rev. DANIEL HIRTZ, Region III and IV, MARGARET SCHATZ; SHIRLEY WIRTH; Rev. PATRICK TETER,Region V, Rev. ERNEST J. MARQUART, Region VI, Rev. JAMES J. UNTERREINER, Region VII, Rev. J. PATRICK WISSMAN; TERESA LEGRAND, Region VIII, Rev. MARK J. BINDER; JACK JACKOVIC; PAT JACKOVIC, Region IX, MAGGIE SANDERS; Rev. MICHAEL V. MCDEVITT; Sr. SANDY COMPASS, O.S.U.

Natural Family Planning—Mr. TROY CASTEEL, M.S., L.P.C., Dir.

Rite Of Christian Initiation Of Adults—Rev. PAUL J. MCLOUGHLIN, Co-Dir.; Sr. ROSALIE DIGENAN, D.C., M.Ed., Co-Dir.

Hispanic Ministries—Sr. SANDRA STRAUB, Dir.

Social Ministry-Resettlement—Sr. FRAN STEIN, R.S.M., Dir.; Sr. PATRICIA SULLIVAN, D.C., Volunteer.

Regional Catholic Leadership—Rev. DAVID F. HULSHOF, Dir.

Regional Leaders—Region I, Sr. MARY NORBERT FLESCH, R.S.M.; Mr. RICHARD SNOWBERGER, Region

II, Mr. MICHAEL HAMMOND; Mr. KENT BOURSHESKI; Mrs. STACIE DURKIN, Region III-A, Mr. GENE CONFALONE; Mrs. PHYLLIS CONFALONE, Region III-B, Mrs. DOROTHY MEZZACAPPA; Mrs. CARYN WULLNER, Region IV-A, Mrs. MARGARET BISHOP; Mrs. KAY CHARLES, Region V-A, Mr. HARRY CLARK; Mrs. CONNIE CLARK; Ms. BERNICE GIBSON, Region V-B, Mr. PATRICK STEPHENS; Mrs. LYNN LEWIS; Mr. ED PRATT, Region V-C, Rev. CHARLES COSTELLO; Mrs. JEAN HORST, Region VI, Dr. RAYMOND DRONEY; Rev. JAMES UNTERREINER, Region VII-A, Vacant Region VII-B, Mrs. PAT MOORE, Region VIII, Rev. ROGER LEVEILLEE; Mrs. KATHY MITCHELL; Ms. JAN STEPHENS, Region IX, Ms. BARBARA BATH; Mr. ROBERT SMITH.

Tribunal—

Judicial Vicar—Rev. Msgr. THOMAS E. REIDY, V.G.

Adjutant Judicial Vicar—Rev. THOMAS P. KIEFER, J.C.L.

Judge—Rev. Msgr. MICHAEL F. SWALINA, S.T.D.; Rev. VINCENT BERTRAND, J.C.L.

Auditor—Sr. INEZ HALLINAN, C.S.J.

Promoter of Justice—Rev. Msgr. PHILIP A. BUCHER, V.G.

Advocate—Rev. Msgr. EDWARD M. EFTINK, Ph.D.; Revs. MICHAEL V. McDEVITT, M.A.; DAVID F. HULSHOF.

Defenders of the Bond—Rev. Msgr. PHILIP A. BUCHER, V.G.; Rev. MARK E. ERNSTMANN, M.A.

Notary—Mrs. LINDA MURPHY; Mrs. MARIE MEYER.

Vicars For The Religious—Rev. Msgr. THOMAS E. REIDY, V.G.; Rev. ROBERT A. SCHUMACHER.

Vocations-Seminarians—Rev. DAVID F. HULSHOF, Dir.

Associate Director of Vocations/Seminarians—Rev. THOMAS P. KIEFER, J.C.L.; Sr. BERTHA FRANCO, C.C.V.I.

Youth Ministry—Ms. LEIGH STERTEN, Dir.

Catholic Scouting—Rev. DAVID COON, Diocesan Chap. Tel: 417-887-0600. Rev. RANDY TOCHTROP, Assoc. Diocesan Chap. Tel: 573-335-9347.

Camp Re-NEW-All—Miss VIRGINIA SANDER, Camp Dir.; Miss VALERIE ZIMMER, Camp Dir.; Ms. MARY KELSO, Sec.

Office Of Worship

Office of Worship—Rev. PAUL J. McLOUGHLIN, Dir. & Coord.

Liturgical Commission—Ms. MARY BETH WITTRY. Tel: 417-883-0837. Rev. PAUL J. McLOUGHLIN, Exec. Sec.

Priests's Eucharistic League Confraternity Of The Most Blessed Sacrament—Rev. MICHAEL V. McDEVITT, Dir.

Officials And Committees

Catholic Relief Services—Rev. Msgr. THOMAS E. REIDY, V.G.

Cemeteries—Rev. Msgr. THOMAS E. REIDY, V.G.

Censor Of Books—Rev. MARK C. ERNSTMANN, S.T.L., M.Ed. Tel: 417-546-5208.

Health Affairs—Mr. TROY CASTEEL, M.S., L.P.C., Dir.

Holy Childhood Association—Rev. Msgr. MICHAEL F. SWALINA, S.T.D. Tel: 573-748-5183.

Missionary Apostolate—Society for the Propagation of the Faith, Rev. Msgr. MICHAEL F. SWALINA, S.T.D. Tel: 573-748-5183.

Mission of the Laity—Apostleship of Prayer, Rev. Msgr. MICHAEL F. SWALINA, S.T.D. Tel: 573-748-5183.

National Shrine Of The Immaculate Conception—Rev. Msgr. THOMAS E. REIDY, Dir.

Priests' Mutual Benefit Society—Rev. LEONARD CHAMBERS, Pres.; Rev. STEPHEN SCHNEIDER, Vice Pres.; Rev. Msgr. THOMAS E. REIDY, V.G., Exec. Sec.; Rev. Msgr. JOHN J. RYNISH; Revs. JOHN A. BRATH; RALPH J. DUFFNER; NORMAND G. VARONE.

Priests' Purgatorial Society—Revs. MARK C. ERNSTMANN, S.T.L., M.Ed., Dir. Tel: 417-546-5208. BENEDICT W. HARTER, Sec.

Pro-Life Director—Sr. FRAN STEIN R.S.M., Dir.

Rural Life Movement—Rev. SYLVESTER W. BAUER. Tel: 573-744-5913.

Diocesan Consultative Groups

Diocesan Consultors—Rev. JOHN A. BRATH; Rev. Msgr. PHILIP A. BUCHER, V.G.; Revs. THOMAS P. KIEFER, J.C.L.; ERNEST J. MARQUART; Rev. Msgr. THOMAS E. REIDY, V.G.; Rev. JAMES L. REYNOLDS; Rev. Msgr. WILLIAM J. STANTON; Rev. Msgr. JOHN H. WESTHUES, Pres. of the Presbyteral Council (Ex Officio).

Presbyteral Council—Revs. JUSTIN D. MONAGHAN, Pres. JOHN M. HARTH, Vice Pres. JAMES J. UNTERREINER, Sec. JOHN S. BRAUN; FRANCIS BRENNAN, S.J.; JOEL DERKS, O.S.B.; JOHN J. FRIEDEL; THOMAS P. KIEFER; Rev. Msgr. MICHAEL F. SWALINA. Appointed Members: Rev. Msgr. PHILIP A. BUCHER, V.G.; Rev. Msgr. RICHARD C. ROLWING; Rev. Msgr. THOMAS E. REIDY, V.G.

Diocesan Pastoral Council—Rev. LEONARD CHAMBERS, Exec. Sec.

Diocesan School Board—Sr. JANE HOSCH, O.S.F., Ph.D., Supt.

Diocesan Communications Advisory Board—Rev. MARK BOYER, Co-Chm.; Mrs. MARILYN VYDRA, Co-Chm.

Diocesan Lay Endowment Board—Rev. DAVID F. HULSHOF, Chm.

Catholic Organizations And Movements

Cursillo Movement—

Secretariat for Cursillo—Rev. ROGER L. LEVEILLEE, Diocesan Chap.; Rev. WILLIAM M. HODGSON, Asst. Diocesan Chap.

Daughters of St. Francis de Sales—Rev. Msgr. JOSEPH E. GOSCHE, Diocesan Chap., Rev. THOMAS P. KIEFER, J.C.L., Chap.

Diocesan Council Of Catholic Women (DCCW)—Revs. JAMES J. UNTERREINER, Diocesan Spiritual Moderator; DAVID F. HULSHOF, Assoc. Spiritual Moderator; BENGIE GRAY, Pres. Tel: 417-887-5977.

Charismatic Prayer Groups—Mr. KLAUS TAMME. Tel: 417-887-8070. Rev. ROGER L. LEVEILLEE. Tel: 573-379-3401.

St. Vincent De Paul Society—Rev. Msgr. THOMAS E. REIDY, V.G., Diocesan Chap.

Apostolates And Commissions

Apostolate to the Deaf—Rev. DAVID L. MILLER, Dir. Tel: 417-476-2463.

Diocesan Peace and Justice Commission—Sr. FRAN STEIN, R.S.M.; Mr. MICK GILLIAM, Chm. Tel: 417-469-3747. Rev. SYLVESTER BAUER. Tel: 573-744-5913.

State Office

Diocesan Delegates To The Missouri Catholic Conference—

Public Policy Committee—Sr. ROSALIE DIGENAN, D.C., M.Ed.; Mr. MICK GILLIAM.

CLERGY, PARISHES, MISSIONS AND PAROCHIAL SCHOOLS

CITY OF SPRINGFIELD
(Greene County)

1—CATHEDRAL OF ST. AGNES (1908), Rev. Thomas P. Kiefer; Deacon Clarence (Bud) McKay. In res., Rev. David F. Hulshof.
Res., 533 S. Jefferson Ave., 65806. Tel: 417-831-3565; Fax: 417-865-0367. [CEM][JC]
School—531 S. Jefferson Ave., 65806. Tel: 417-866-5038; Fax: 417-866-2906. Ms. Jeanne Skahan, Prin.
Lay Teachers 11; Students 234.
Catechesis/Religious Programs—Students 106.

2—HOLY TRINITY (1966), Rev. Msgr. Thomas E. Reidy, V.G. In res., Revs. Frank C. Palermo; Antonio Riganon.
Res., 2818 E. Bennett, 65804. Tel: 417-883-3440. [JC]
Catechesis/Religious Programs—Students 157.

3—IMMACULATE CONCEPTION (1868), Revs. Stephen A. Schneider; David N. Coon; Deacon William McNamee.
Res., 3535 S. Fremont, 65804. Tel: 417-887-9769. [JC]
Church—3555 S. Fremont, 65804. Tel: 417-887-0600; Fax: 417-881-7087.
School—3555A S. Fremont, 65804. Tel: 417-881-7000. Mrs. Ann Meese, Prin.
Lay Teachers 25; Students 605.
Catechesis/Religious Programs—Mrs. Kathy Lukavich, D.R.E.
Students 210.

4—SACRED HEART (1882), Rev. Joseph Peplansky, C.M.F. Mailing Address: 1609 N. Summit Ave., 65803. Tel: 417-869-3646.
Res., Villa Claret, 1530 N. Summit, 65803. Tel: 417-869-0075. [JC]
Catechesis/Religious Programs—Students 93.

5—ST. ELIZABETH ANN SETON (1981), Revs. Fergus Monaghan; Patrick A. Teter; Sr. Barbara Geers, S.S.N.D.
Church—2200 W. Republic Rd., 65807. Tel: 417-887-6472; Fax: 417-887-7027. [CEM]
Catechesis/Religious Programs—Tel: 417-887-6088. Sr. Helen Therese Nienhaus, D.R.E.
Students 355.

6—ST. JOSEPH'S (1892), Revs. Joel Derks, O.S.B.; Anthony Shidler, O.S.B., Chap., St. John's Medical Center.
Res., 1115 N. Campbell Ave., 65802. Tel: 417-865-1112. [JC]
School—515 W. Scott, 65802. Tel: 417-866-0667; Fax: 417-866-2862. Leon Witt, Prin.
Lay Teachers 8; Students 145.
Catechesis/Religious Programs—Students 86.

CITY OF CAPE GIRARDEAU
(Cape Girardeau County)

1—CATHEDRAL OF ST. MARY (1868), Rev. Msgr. Richard C. Rolwing, V.G.; Rev. Randolph Tochtrop.
Res., 629 William St., 63703. Tel: 573-335-9347; Fax: 573-334-8939. [CEM][JC]
School—210 S. Sprigg, 63703. Tel: 573-335-3840.
Lay Teachers 13; Students 205.
Catechesis/Religious Programs—Students 25.
Old St. Vincent's—(Chapel of Ease).

2—ST. VINCENT DE PAUL (1838), Revs. Milton Fleming Ryan, C.M.; Joseph Williams, C.M.; Bro. Kenneth J. Lund. In res., Rev. Anthony J. Palanga, C.M.
Res., 741 Forest, 63701. Tel: 573-335-7667; Fax: 573-335-0034.
School—1919 Ritter Dr., 63701. Tel: 573-334-9594.
Lay Teachers 21; Students 480.
Catechesis/Religious Programs—Students 167.

OUTSIDE THE CITIES OF SPRINGFIELD AND CAPE GIRARDEAU

Advance, Stoddard Co., St. Joseph (1905), Rev. Frederick J. Lutz.
Res., P.O. Box 640, 63730. Tel: 573-722-3504. [CEM]
Catechesis/Religious Programs—Students 94.
Mission—Glennon, Bollinger Co., St. Anthony. [CEM]

Aurora, Lawrence Co., Holy Trinity (1906), Rev. Peter J. Morciniec.
Res., Hwy. 60 & Carnation Rd., P.O. Box 533, 65605. Tel: 417-678-2403. [CEM]
Catechesis/Religious Programs—Students 80.

Benton, Scott Co., St. Denis (1840), Rev. Normand G. Varone.
Res., P.O. Box 127, 63736. Tel: 573-545-3864; Fax: 573-545-3017. [CEM]
School—P.O. Box 189, 63736. Tel: 573-545-3017. Mrs. Deborah McCann, Prin.
Lay Teachers 6; Students 82.
Catechesis/Religious Programs—Students 70.

Billings, Christian Co., St. Joseph (1879), Rev. James L. Reynolds.
Res., P.O. Box 100, 65610. Tel: 417-744-2112. [CEM]
Catechesis/Religious Programs—Students 106.

Bolivar, Polk Co., Sacred Heart (1946), Rev. Gregory E.J. Zatina.
Res., 1405 W. Fair Play St., P.O. Box 146, 65613. Tel: 417-326-5596. [CEM]
Catechesis/Religious Programs—Students 103.
Mission—Humansville, Polk Co., St. Catherine, P.O. Box 42, Humansville, 65674. Tel: 417-754-8825.

Branson, Taney Co., Our Lady of the Lake (1951), Rev. Msgr. Philip A. Bucher, V.G.
Res., 202 Vaughn Dr., 65616. Tel: 417-334-2928; Fax: 417-334-6883.
Catechesis/Religious Programs—Mrs. Shirley Wirth, D.R.E.
Students 164.

Buffalo, Dallas Co., St. William (1946), Rev. Bruce Swift, O.S.B.
Res., c/o Sacred Heart Parish, P.O. Box 8, Conway, 65632. Tel: 417-589-6782.

Carthage, Jasper Co., St. Ann (1872), Rev. Timothy Mai Vinh Loc, C.M.C.
Res., 908 S. Clinton St., 64836. Tel: 417-358-1841.
School—1156 Grand, 64836. Tel: 417-358-2674; Fax: 417-358-4902.
Lay Teachers 5; Students 95.
Catechesis/Religious Programs—Students 92.

Caruthersville, Pemiscot Co., Sacred Heart (1900), Rev. Joseph Campbell.
Res., 605 Ward Ave., 63830. Tel: 573-333-4301.
Catechesis/Religious Programs—Students 41.

Chaffee, Scott Co., St. Ambrose (1907), Rev. Allan L. Saunders.
Res., 419 S. Third St., 63740. Tel: 573-887-3953. [CEM]
School—Tel: 573-887-6711. Sr. Jacklyn Pritchard, C.D.P., Prin.
Sisters 1; Lay Teachers 8; Students 108.
Catechesis/Religious Programs—Students 53.

Charleston, Mississippi Co., St. Henry (1874), Rev. Richard Lause, C.M.
Res., 304 Court St., 63834. Tel: 573-683-4737; Fax: 573-683-4737.

School—306 Court St., 63834. Tel: 573-683-6218. Mrs. Kay Glastetter, Prin.
Lay Teachers 7; Students 80.
Catechesis/Religious Programs—Students 25.

Conway, Laclede Co., Sacred Heart (1908), Rev. Bruce Swift.
Res., Box 8, 65632. Tel: 417-589-6782. [CEM]

Dexter, Stoddard Co., Sacred Heart (1889), Rev. John Sheley.
Res., 103 E. Market St., 63841. Tel: 573-624-8888.
Church—102 E. Castor, 63841. Tel: 573-624-7333.
Catechesis/Religious Programs—Students 109.
Convent—115 E. Market St., 63841. Tel: 573-624-3306.

Doniphan, Ripley Co., St. Benedict (1859), Rev. David J. Dohogne.
Res., 306 Kegler, 63935. Tel: 573-996-3301. [CEM]
Mission—Grandin, Carter Co., St. Anne.

El Dorado Springs, Cedar Co., St. Elizabeth (1946), Rev. William C. Krudwig.
Res., 609 S. Main, 64744. Tel: 417-876-3216. [CEM]
Catechesis/Religious Programs—Students 50.
Mission—Stockton, Cedar Co., St. Peter the Apostle, 308 E. Oak St., P.O. Box 583, Stockton, 65785. Tel: 417-276-5588.

Forsyth, Taney Co., Our Lady of the Ozarks (1980), Rev. Mark C. Ernstmann.
Res., 355 Shadowrock Dr., P.O. Box 639, 65653. Tel: 417-546-5208.

Fredericktown, Madison Co., St. Michael (1827), Rev. Amel Shibley, Admin.
Res., 304 W. Main St., P.O. Box 618, 63645. Tel: 573-783-2182; Fax: 573-783-5230. [CEM]
Catechesis/Religious Programs—Students 63.

Glennonville, Dunklin Co., St. Teresa 1905, Rev. Glenn A. Eftink; Deacon Fred Hirtz.
Res., Rte. No. 1, Box 371, Campbell, 63933. Tel: 573-328-4544. [CEM]
School—Rte. No. 1, Box 369, Campbell, 63933. Tel: 573-328-4197. Janet Kuper, Prin.
Sisters 1; Lay Teachers 6; Students 99.

Houston, Texas Co., St. Mark (1975), Rev. Mark Binder.
Res., 117 S. Oak Crest, 65483. Tel: 417-967-3589.
Missions—Roby, Texas Co., St. Vincent de Paul; Licking, Texas Co., St. John The Baptist.

Ironton, Iron Co., Ste. Marie Du Lac (1878), Rev. James J. Unterreiner. In res., Rev. Anthony M. Gaydos, O.S.M., Senior Priest.
Res., 350 S. Main St., 63650. Tel: 573-546-2611. [CEM]
Catechesis/Religious Programs—Students 91.
Missions—Lesterville, Reynolds Co., Our Lady of Sorrows; Viburnum, Iron Co., St. Philip Benizi.
Chapel—Pilot Knob, Arcadia Valley Hospital.

Jackson, Cape Girardeau Co., Immaculate Conception (1874), Rev. Msgr. Edward M. Eftink.
Res., 208 S. Hope St., Ste. 101, 63755. Tel: 573-243-3182; Fax: 573-243-6833. [CEM]
School—308 S. Hope St., 63755. Tel: 573-243-5013. Tracy Holland, M.A., Prin.
Sisters 1; Lay Teachers 11; Students 246.
Catechesis/Religious Programs—Students 224.

Joplin, Jasper Co., St. Mary (1938), Rev. Raymond W. Kunkel.
Res., 2415 Moffet Ave., 64804. Tel: 417-623-3333; Fax: 417-623-4015. [JC]
School—505 W. 25th St., 64804. Tel: 417-623-1465. Mrs. Tracey Welch, Prin.
Lay Teachers 13; Students 270.
Catechesis/Religious Programs—Students 93.

St. Peter (1877), Rev. Leonard R. Chambers; Deacon Edward V. Ellman.
Res., 812 Pearl Ave., 64801-4396. Tel: 417-623-8643; Fax: 417-623-0866. [JC]
School—802 Byers, 64801-4396. Tel: 417-624-5605. Mr. Clay Kubicek, Prin.
Lay Teachers 8; Students 99.
Catechesis/Religious Programs—Students 93.

Kelso, Scott Co., St. Augustine (1878), Rev. M. Oliver Clavin.
Res., 201 S. Messmer, Box 26, 63758. Tel: 573-264-4724.
School—230 S. Messmer, P.O. Box 97, 63758-0097. Tel: 573-264-4644; Fax: 573-264-1475. Mr. Thomas Howard, Prin.
Lay Teachers 8; Students 140.
Catechesis/Religious Programs—Students 54.

Kennett, Dunklin Co., St. Cecilia (1923), Rev. Francis Brennan, S.J.
Res., College & North Bypass, P.O. Box 306, 63857. Tel: 573-888-2412; Fax: 573-888-0613.

Kimberling City, Stone Co., Our Lady of the Cove (1979), Rev. John A. Brath.
Res., Lake Rd. 13-50, Box 548, 65686. Tel: 417-739-4700.
Catechesis/Religious Programs—Students 147.

Lamar, Barton Co., St. Mary (1904), Rev. Thomas E. Allen.
Res., 200 E. 17th St., 64759. Tel: 417-682-2492. [CEM]
Catechesis/Religious Programs—Students 63.
Mission—Golden City, Barton Co., St. Joseph.

Lebanon, Laclede Co., St. Francis De Sales (1870), Rev. Msgr. Raymond V. Orf.
Res., 345 Grand St., 65536. Tel: 417-532-4811; Fax: 417-532-8847. [CEM]
Catechesis/Religious Programs—Students 160.
Chapel—Bennett Springs, Sportman's Chapel.

Leopold, Bollinger Co., St. John (1856), Rev. Williams A. Huggins.
Res., P.O. Box 83, 63760. Tel: 573-238-3300. [CEM]
Catechesis/Religious Programs—Students 174.

Malden, Dunklin Co., St. Ann (1890), Rev. Glenn A. Eftink; Deacon Fred Hirtz.
Mailing Address: c/o St. Teresa Parish, Rt. 1, Box 371, Campbell, 63933.
Church—304 N. Douglas St., 63863.

Mansfield, Wright Co., Immaculate Heart of Mary (1943), Revs. Leonard M. Baldus, O.M.I.; Robert J. Olson, O.M.I.
Res., Rte. 6, Box 6700, Ava, 65608. Tel: 417-924-3779; 683-5249.
Catechesis/Religious Programs—Students 119.
Missions—Ava, Douglas Co., St. Leo the Great, Rte. 6, Box 6700, Ava, 65608. Tel: 417-683-5249; Gainesville, Ozark Co., St. William, P.O. Box 367, Gainesville, 65655. Tel: 417-679-4804. Rev. Gerald Fuller, O.M.I.

Marshfield, Webster Co., Holy Trinity (1892), Rev. Vincent E. Bertrand.
515 E. Washington, 65706-1865. Tel: 417-468-2228.
Res., 125 N. Locust, 65706.
Catechesis/Religious Programs—Students 73.

Monett, Barry Co., St. Lawrence (1891), Rev. John S. Braun.
Res., 405 Seventh St., 65708. Tel: 417-235-3286; Fax: 417-235-3721. [CEM]
School—407 Seventh St., 65708. Tel: 417-235-3721. Sr. Dominic Rechtorik, V.S.C., Prin.
Sisters 1; Lay Teachers 3; Students 89.
Catechesis/Religious Programs—Students 115.

Mountain Grove, Wright Co., Sacred Heart (1893), Rev. Justin Huelsing, O.M.I.
Res., 302 E. State St., 65711. Tel: 417-926-3803.
Mission—Cabool, Texas Co., St. Michael.

Mountain View, Howell Co., St. John Vianney (1951), Rev. Ernest J. Marquart; Deacon Charles Costello.
Res., 808 State Rd. Y, P.O. Box 38, 65548. Tel: 417-934-2649.
Mission—Eminence, Shannon Co., St. Sylvester.

Mount Vernon, Lawrence Co., St. Susanne (1939), Rev. Msgr. John H. Westhues.
Res., P.O. Box 126, 65712. Tel: 417-466-4190.
Catechesis/Religious Programs—Students 85.
Mission—Greenfield, Dade Co., St. Patrick.

Neosho, Newton Co., St. Canera (1871), Revs. John M. Harth; Joseph Tran Van Liem, C.M.C.
Res., 504 S. Washington St., 64850. Tel: 417-451-3411. [JC]
Catechesis/Religious Programs—Students 151.
Mission—Noel, McDonald Co., Nativity of Our Lord, P.O. Box 555, Noel, 64854.

New Hamburg, Scott Co., St. Lawrence (1847), Rev. Ralph J. Duffner.
Res., R.R. 1 (New Hamburg), Box 540, Benton, 63736. Tel: 573-545-3317. [CEM]
Catechesis/Religious Programs—Students 112.

New Madrid, New Madrid Co., Immaculate Conception (1789), Rev. Msgr. Michael F. Swalina.
Res., 605 Davis St., 63869. Tel: 573-748-5183.
School—560 Powell, 63839. Tel: 314-748-5123. Ms. Agnes J. Harrington, Prin.
Lay Teachers 5; Students 51.
Catechesis/Religious Programs—Students 50.

Oran, Scott Co., Guardian Angel (1892), Rev. Lewis E. Hejna.
Res., P.O. Box 158, 63771. Tel: 573-262-3210. [CEM 2]
School—610 Church St., 63771. Tel: 573-262-3583. Mrs. Barbara Tyler, Prin.
Sisters 2; Lay Teachers 5; Students 90.
Catechesis/Religious Programs—Students 54.

Ozark, Christian Co., St. Joseph the Worker (1961), Rev. Paul J. McLoughlin.
Res., 1796 N. State Hwy. NN, 65721. Tel: 417-581-6328; Fax: 417-581-4957.
Catechesis/Religious Programs—Students 220.

Piedmont, Wayne Co., St. Catherine of Siena (1873), Rev. Matthew J. Rehrauer.
Res., 109 Piedmont Ave., 63957. Tel: 573-223-4924.
Catechesis/Religious Programs—Students 60.
Missions—Van Buren, Carter Co., St. George, Tel: 573-323-8576; Williamsville, Wayne Co., Our Lady of Sorrows.

Pierce City, Lawrence Co., St. Mary (1883), Rev. Daniel J. Hirtz.
Res., 200 Front St., 65723. Tel: 417-476-2827; Fax: 417-476-3025. [CEM 2]
School—202 Front St., 65723. Tel: 417-476-2824. Mr. Jay Bierorette, Prin.
Lay Teachers 7; Students 100.
Catechesis/Religious Programs—Students 61.

Poplar Bluff, Butler Co., Sacred Heart (1891), Rev. Michael V. McDevitt.
Res., 123 N. Eighth St., 63901. Tel: 573-785-9635; Fax: 573-785-8397. [CEM]
School—Eighth Ave. & Vine, 63901-5034. Sr. Patricia Rhoten, O.S.V., Prin.
Lay Teachers 9; Students 151.
Catechesis/Religious Programs—Students 126.
Station—Poplar Bluff, V.A. Hospital.

Portageville, New Madrid Co., St. Eustachius (1902), Rev. Roger L. Leveille.
Res., 200 W. Fourth St., 63873. Tel: 573-379-3401.
School—214 W. Fourth St., 63873. Tel: 573-379-3525; Fax: 573-379-3843. Mrs. Sue Ellen Flynn, Prin.
Sisters 1; Lay Teachers 5; Students 87.

Pulaskifield, Barry Co., SS. Peter and Paul (1892), Rev. David L. Miller.
Res., P.O. Drawer L, Pierce City, 65723. Tel: 417-476-2463. [CEM]
Catechesis/Religious Programs—Students 112.
Mission—Cassville, Barry Co., St. Edward, 107 W. 17th St., Box 492, Cassville, 65625. Tel: 417-847-3569.

Salem, Dent Co., Sacred Heart (1880), Rev. Robert A. Landewe.
Res., 602 W. Butler, 65560. Tel: 573-729-4291.
Catechesis/Religious Programs—Mr. Patrick J. Keefe, D.R.E.
Students 68.
Mission—Bunker, Reynolds Co., Christ the King, P.O. Box 177, Bunker, 63629.
Chapel—Montauk, St. Jude.

Sarcoxie, Newton Co., St. Agnes (1870), Rev. Jacob S. Biernacki.
Res., 26952 Cherry Rd., 64862. Tel: 417-548-3540; Fax: 417-548-3540. [CEM]

Scott City, Scott Co., St. Joseph (1911), Rev. J. Patrick Wissman.
Res., 604 Sycamore, 63780. Tel: 573-264-4500; Fax: 573-264-1325. [CEM]
School—606 Sycamore, 63780. Tel: 573-264-2600. Mrs. Darlene Leonard, Prin.
Lay Teachers 6; Students 82.

Seneca, Newton Co., St. Mary (1884), Revs. John M. Harth; Joseph Than Van Liem, C.M.C.
Res., P.O. Drawer N, 64865. Tel: 417-776-3786. [CEM]

Shell Knob, Barry Co., Holy Family (1978), Rev. Thomas Thro, S.J.
Res., Lake Rd. 39-30, P.O. Box 229, 65747. Tel: 417-858-3678.

Sikeston, Scott Co., St. Francis Xavier's (1893), Rev. Msgr. William J. Stanton; Rev. Robert A. Schumacher.
Res., 217 W. Center St., 63801. Tel: 573-471-2447.
School—106 N. Stoddard, 63801. Tel: 573-471-0841. Sr. Agnes Therese Aydt, S.S.N.D., Prin.
Sisters 3; Lay Teachers 6; Students 159.
Catechesis/Religious Programs—Students 96.

Verona, Lawrence Co., Sacred Heart (1874), Rev. Peter J. Morciniec.
Res., P.O. Box 37, 65769. Tel: 417-498-6754. [CEM]
Catechesis/Religious Programs—Students 55.

Webb City, Jasper Co., Sacred Heart (1908), Rev. Rick L. Jones.
Res., 909 N. Madison, 64870. Tel: 417-673-4249; Fax: 417-673-1944.
Catechesis/Religious Programs—Students 115.

West Plains, Howell Co., St. Mary (1902), Rev. Justin Monaghan.
Res., 965 S. Thayer Ave., 65775. Tel: 417-256-2556; Fax: 417-256-9251.
School—957 S. Thayer Ave., 65775. Tel: 417-256-8634.
Sisters 3; Lay Teachers 4; Students 90.
Catechesis/Religious Programs—Students 113.
Mission—Thayer, Oregon Co., Sacred Heart.

Willow Springs, Howell Co., Sacred Heart (1897), Rev. Sherman B. Wall, O.M.I.
Church—1050 W. Bus Hwy. 60-63, 65793. Tel: 417-469-2447. [CEM]
Mission—White Church, Howell Co., St. Joseph, Rte. 1, Pamona, 65789.

Chaplains of Public Institutions

SPRINGFIELD. *Diocesan Hospital Ministry* 2818 E. Bennett, 65804. Tel: 417-883-3440. Rev. Frank C. Palermo.

U.S. Medical Center 1900 W. Sunshine, 65802. Tel: 417-862-7041, Ext. 255. Rev. Antonio R. Rigonan, Chap.; Sr. Pauline Grady, A.S.C.

FORDLAND. *Ozark Correctional Center* Rte. 1, P.O.Box 1-P, 65652. Tel: 417-767-4491. Reverend Father Bruce Swift, O.S.B.

JOPLIN. *Joplin Hospital Ministry* 1102 W. 32nd St., 64801. Tel: 417-781-2727. Rev. Benedict W. Harter.

POPLAR BLUFF. *Poplar Bluff Hospital Ministry.* Revs. David Dohogne; Michael McDevitt Tel: 573-785-9635.

Special Assignment:
Reverend Fathers—
Boyer, Mark G., Editor of "The Mirror", 1703 S. National, Springfield, MO 65804-1123. Tel: 417-887-4811
Friedel, John (J.) F., Chap., Southeast Missouri State University, 512 N. Pacific, Cape Girardeau, MO 63701. Tel: 573-335-3899
Hodgson, William M., Hispanic Ministry, P.O. Box 1006, Aurora, MO 65605. Tel: 417-840-2761
Hulshof, David F., Vocation Dir., Dir. Regional Catholic Leadership, 533 S. Jefferson Ave., Springfield, MO 65806. Tel: 417-863-9211
Morey, Charles W., P.O. Box 11172, Springfield, MO 65708. Tel: 417-887-8245
Palermo, Frank C., Hospital Ministry, 2818 E. Bennett, Springfield, MO 65804. Tel: 417-883-3440

On Duty Outside the Diocese:
Reverend Fathers—
Carr, Gary M., Prin., Holy Name School, 433 Jackson St., Ketchikan, AK 99901. Tel: 907-225-2570
Drewelow, David C., 5308 W. 99th Ter., Overland Park, KS 66207
Nichols, Edward, Church of the Nativity Parish, 705 E. Brandon Blvd., Brandon, FL 33511. Tel: 813-684-5320

Military Chaplains:
Reverend Fathers—
Wilk, Mitchell S., Chap., U.S.A., Offices of the Chaplain, HH, 2D, FSB 2D LD, Unit #15057, APO, AP 96224-0318

Leave of Absence:
Reverend Fathers—
Casteel, Michael J., 3840 S. Virginia Pl., Springfield, MO 65807. Tel: 417-887-5287
Gregovich, Lawrence B., P.O. Box 2374, St. Peters, MO 63376

Retired:
Reverend Monsignors—
Gosche, Joseph E., P.O. Box 207, 308 Albert St., Cape Girardeau, MO 63702-0207. Tel: 573-651-8645
McGrane, Walter J., 420 Moffet Ave., Apt. 4, Joplin, MO 64801. Tel: 417-781-6388
Rynish, John F., 620 W. Scott, Springfield, MO 65802
Reverend Fathers—
Baker, John W., Franciscan Villa, 620 W. Scott, Springfield, MO 65802
Bauer, Sylvester W., Rte. 1, P.O. Box 24B, Freeburg, MO 65035
Boeding, Damian, 725 Ohio Ave., Joplin, MO 64801-4925
Brownfield, Frowin, 526 S. Jefferson #2, Springfield, MO 65806. Tel: 417-865-6761
Edwards, Byron H., 35 Air Rd., P.O. Box 422, Higden, AR 72067
Eschbacher, Jerome J., 620 W. Scott, Springfield, MO 65802
Harter, Benedict W., St. John's Medical Center, 2727 McClelland Blvd., Joplin, MO 64804. Tel: 417-781-2727
Holterman, Herbert J., Green Meadow Retirement Home, Room 113, Linn, MO 65051
Ilmberger, Clement F., 3601 W. Silver Springs Rd., Ocala, FL 34475
Seyer, James A., 150 S. Silver Springs Rd., #4, Cape Girardeau, MO 63701. Tel: 573-651-3939
Shibley, Amel A., 371 Etherton Dr., Cape Girardeau, MO 63701. Tel: 573-335-0221

INSTITUTIONS LOCATED IN THE DIOCESE

[A] SEMINARIES, RELIGIOUS, OR SCHOLASTICATES

AVA. *Assumption Novitiate (Trappists)*, Mailing Address: Rte. 5, Box 1056, 65608. Tel: 417-683-5110; Fax: 417-683-5658. Rt. Rev. James Conner, O.C.S.O., Abbot; Rev. Cyprian Harrison, O.C.S.O., Novice Master.

CARTHAGE. *Congregation of the Mother Co-Redemptrix*, 1900 Grand Ave., 64836. Tel: 417-358-7787; Fax: 417-358-9508. Very Rev. Joseph M. Tran Ngoc Diep, C.M.C., Prov.

[B] HIGH SCHOOLS, DIOCESAN

SPRINGFIELD. *Springfield Catholic High School.* Coed. 2340 S. Eastgate, 65804-2832. Tel: 417-887-8817; Fax: 417-885-1165. Mr. Dean O. Crayton, Prin.; Mr. Christopher Stecklein, Asst. Prin. Lay Teachers 33; Students 317.

Springfield Catholic School System, 1763 E. Elm, 65802-3227. Tel: 417-865-5567; Fax: 417-865-5278.

CAPE GIRARDEAU. *Notre Dame Regional High School*, 1912 Ritter Dr., 63701. Tel: 314-335-6772; Fax: 573-335-3458.
Co-Instructional Regional High School. School Sisters of Notre Dame. Sr. Mary Ann Fischer, S.S.N.D., Prin. Priests 1; Sisters 3; Lay Teachers 26; Students 375.

JOPLIN. *McAuley Regional High School*, 930 Pearl Ave., 64801. Tel: 417-624-9320; Fax: 417-626-8334. Jeanette Stengel, Prin. Lay Teachers 15; Students 142.

St. Mary. (Grades PreK-5), 505 W. 25th St., 64804. Tel: 417-623-1465. Mrs. Tracey Welch, Prin. Lay Teachers 13; Students 270.

St. Peter's Junior High School. (Grades 6-8), 802 Byers, 64801. Tel: 417-624-5605. Mr. Clay Kubicek, Prin. Lay Teachers 8; Students 99.

[C] GENERAL HOSPITALS

*CAPE GIRARDEAU. *St. Francis' Medical Center*, 211 St. Francis Dr., 63703. Tel: 573-335-1251
For a complete listing, refer to the Hospitals section.

JOPLIN. *St. John's Regional Health Center, Mercy LifeCare Systems, Inc.*, 2727 McClelland Blvd. J, 64804. Tel: 417-885-2000; Fax: 417-888-8730
For a complete listing, refer to the Hospitals section.

St. John's Regional Medical Center; Mercy Lifecare Systems, Inc., 2727 McClelland Blvd., 64804. Tel: 417-781-2727; Fax: 417-625-2910
For a complete listing, refer to the Hospitals section.

MOUNTAIN VIEW. *St. Francis Hospital*, P.O. Box 82, 65548. Tel: 417-934-2246; Fax: 417-934-6024
For a complete listing, refer to the Hospitals section.

PILOT KNOB. *Arcadia Valley Hospital*, P.O. Box 548, 63663. Tel: 573-546-3924; Fax: 573-546-2918
For a complete listing, refer to the Hospitals section.

[D] SPECIAL HOSPITALS

SPRINGFIELD. *St. John's Mercy Villa*, 1100 E. Montclair, 65807. Tel: 417-888-8500; Fax: 417-888-8532
For a complete listing, refer to the Special Care Facilities section.

[E] MONASTERIES AND RESIDENCES OF PRIESTS AND BROTHERS

SPRINGFIELD. *Claretians Missionaries' Residence-Villa Claret*, 1530 N. Summit, 65803. Tel: 417-869-0075. Revs. Wayne J. Barron, C.M.F.; Eddie DeLeon, C.M.F.; Joseph Peplansky; Bro. Thomas Haerle, C.M.F.

Congregation of Mother Co-Redemptrix, Our Lady of the Rosary House, 418 S. Kimbrough, 65806. Tel: 417-869-3822. Rev. Francis M. Luong Mihn Tuat, C.M.C., Dir. Priests 1; Brothers 10.

AVA. *Assumption Abbey (Trappist)*, Rte. 5, Box 1056, 65608. Tel: 417-683-5110; Fax: 417-683-5658. Rt. Revs. James Conner, O.C.S.O., Abbot; Robert Matter, Abbot Emeritus; Cyprian Harrison, O.C.S.O., Abbot Emeritus; Revs. David Blackburn, O.C.S.O., (Mercy Villa); Leon Brockman, O.C.S.O.; Richard Fox, O.C.S.O.; Donald Joseph Hamilton, O.C.S.O.; Theodore Koster, O.C.S.O.; Anthony Menz, O.C.S.O., (Manhattan, KS). Priests 6; Brothers 10.

CARTHAGE. *Congregation of the Mother Co-Redemptrix, United States Assumption Province*, 1900 Grand Ave., 64836. Tel: 417-358-7787; Fax: 417-358-9508. Very Rev. Joseph M. Tran Ngoc Diep, C.M.C., Prov.; Revs. Francis Xavier M. Do Cao Tung, C.M.C., Asst. I; Anselm M. Dinh Vuong Can, C.M.C., Asst. II; John D.M. Ngo Duc Vuong, C.M.C., Treas.; Athanasius M. Nguyen Linh Uy, C.M.C.; Paul M. Nguyen Mang Cach, C.M.C.; Joseph M. Cao Xuan Canh, C.M.C.; Michael M. Do Quang Chinh, C.M.C.; Pius M. Nguyen Quang Dan, C.M.C.; Raymond M. Nguyen Chau Dien, C.M.C.; John Bosco M. Pham Tien Duc, C.M.C.; John Eudes M. Vu Quang Huy, C.M.C.; Leo M. Vu Dinh Huyen, C.M.C.; Barnabas M. Nguyen Duc Kien, C.M.C.; Felix M. Dinh Viet Luan, C.M.C.; Peter M. Ngo Chau Minh, C.M.C.; Bartholomew M. Pham An Su, C.M.C.; Cyril M. Vu Thanh Thien, C.M.C.; John Bosco M. Pham Trung Thuc, C.M.C.; Bartholomew Pham Minh Van, C.M.C.; Aloysius M. Tran Thanh Liem, C.M.C.; John Eudes M. Tran Dinh Diem, C.M.C.; James M. Pham Ngoc Bich, C.M.C.; Bernard M. Nguyen Trong Thuong, C.M.C.; Bros. Maximilien Kolbe M. Bui Khoa Dang, C.M.C.; John Vianney M. Do Thanh Nhan, C.M.C.; Benedict M. Duong Tri Le, C.M.C.; John M. Hoang Hiep Nghia, C.M.C.; Philip M. Lam Ba Trong, C.M.C.; Stephen M. Lam Tuan Vu, C.M.C.; Dominic M. Le Thanh Thai, C.M.C.; Philip M. Le Hai Tin, C.M.C.; Anselm M. Le Hoang Lan, C.M.C.; John M. Nguyen Tuan Bang, C.M.C.; Francis M. Nguyen Hung Cuong, C.M.C.; Henry M. Nguyen Minh Han, C.M.C.; John Bosco M. Nguyen Khanh Hung, C.M.C.; Anthony M. Nguyen Gia Huu, C.M.C.; Aloysius M. Nguyen An Khang, C.M.C.; Pius V M. Nguyen Trung Thu, C.M.C.; Thomas More M. Nguyen Long Truong, C.M.C.; Bede M. Nguyen Quang Tuyen, C.M.C.; Alphonsus Pham Cao Khiet, C.M.C.; Mathew M. Pham Ngoc Thach, C.M.C.; Joseph C.M. Pham Cong Tho, C.M.C.; Stephen Tran Minh Giac, C.M.C.; Patrick M. Tran The Mac, C.M.C.; Bernardine M. Tran Hien Si, C.M.C.; John Tran Trung Thanh, C.M.C.; Philip Neri M. Tran Chinh Trung, C.M.C.; Paul M. Tran Quyen Vuong, C.M.C.; Thomas M. Trinh Van Chi, C.M.C.; Paul Miki M. Vu Phung Hiep, C.M.C.; Anthony M. Vu Dinh Huan, C.M.C.; John M. Vu Toan Khoa, C.M.C.; Matthew Vu Duc Kim, C.M.C.; Bernard-Due M. Vu Hien Ton, C.M.C.; Alphonsus M. Vu Toan Tri, C.M.C.; Dominic M. Nguyen Trung Chanh, C.M.C.; John M. Nguyen Duc Hien, C.M.C.; Cyprian M. Nguyen Van Hien, C.M.C.; George M. Ngo Trung Hau, C.M.C.; Gregory M. Tran Vi, C.M.C.; Joachim M. Nguyen Khoa Cu, C.M.C.; Justine M. Nguyen Tri Ky, C.M.C.; Philip Neri M. Pham Tien Duy, C.M.C.; Lawrence M. Nguyen Chau Hy, C.M.C.; Barnabas M. Nguyen Minh Triet, C.M.C.; Raymond M. Tran Huu Thao, C.M.C.; Francis M. Vu Huu Muc, C.M.C., Sec.; Phillip M. Tran Binh Kha, C.M.C.; Martin M. Le Dinh Lam, C.M.C.; John B.M. Nguyen Duc Hien, C.M.C.; Dominic H.M. Nguyen Trung Chanh, C.M.C.; Francis S.M. Nguyen Phu Tuc, C.M.C.; Beda M. Nguyen Tam Nang, C.M.C.; Phillip Neri M. Do Thanh Cao, C.M.C.; Ephrem M. Tran Huy Phat, C.M.C.; Benedict M. Duong Toan Phuong, C.M.C.; Mark M. Le Tien Hoa, C.M.C.; Cyrill M. Vu Van Hao, C.M.C.; Vincent M. Tran Quoc An, C.M.C.; Polycarp M. Nguyen Long Toan, C.M.C.; Timothy M. Tran Viet Thang, C.M.C.; Anthony Padua M. Nguyen Huan Du, C.M.C.; Philip M. Dinh Cuong Linh, C.M.C.; Anthony M. Le Dat Chuan, C.M.C.; John M. Nguyen Hung Dao, C.M.C.; Ephrem M. Ran Thong Tue, C.M.C.; James M. Do Long Van, C.M.C.; Bernard M. Hoang Thy Pham, C.M.C.; Bonaventure M. Mai An Sung, C.M.C.; Simon M. Nguyen Hieu Tu, C.M.C.; Hilary M. Tran Ha Nhuan, C.M.C. Priests 23; Brothers 70; Novices 10; Postulants 18; Candidates 29. Mater Dei Building. (Home for retired priests). In res., (Not members of the Congregation of the Mother Co-Redemptrix). Revs. Peter Tran Dien; Joseph Dinh Tuan Ngan; Joseph Cao Phuong Ky, S.S.; John M. Phan Cong Binh; Simon Huynh Tan Cong; James Do Ba Cong; Dominic Mai Minh Luan.

MARIONVILLE. *The Society of Our Mother of Peace, Sons of Our Mother of Peace*, Queen of Heaven Solitude, Rte. 1, Box 107A, 65705. Tel: 417-744-2011. Revs. Placid Guste, S.M.P., Supr.; John R. Hansen, S.M.P. Legal Title: *The Society of Our Mother of Peace, Sons of Our Mother of Peace - Queen of Heaven Solitude.*

[F] CONVENTS AND RESIDENCES FOR SISTERS

SPRINGFIELD. *Congregation of Mary Queen*, 625 S. Jefferson Ave., 65806. Tel: 417-869-9842. Sisters 6.

St. Anne Monastery, 424 E. Monastery St., 65807-6099. Tel: 417-881-2115. Mother Mary Charles Nelson, O.C.D., Prioress. Discalced Carmelite Nuns 5.

Sisters of Mercy of the Americas. (St. Louis), 1260 E. Sunshine, 65804. Tel: 417-882-1297. Sisters 11.

AVA. *Nazareth Hermitage*, Rte. 5, Box 1122, 65608. Sisters 6.

MARIONVILLE. *The Society of Our Mother of Peace, Daughters of Our Mothers of Peace*, Rte. 1, Box 107A, 65705. Tel: 417-744-2011. Legal Title: *The Society of Our Mother of Peace, Daughters of Our Mother of Peace, Queen of Heaven Solitude.* Sisters 5.

PILOT KNOB. *Our Lady of the Valley*, Box 548, 63663. Tel: 573-546-2590. Franciscan Sisters of Mary 4.

REPUBLIC. *Little Portion Franciscans*, 645 Assisi Way, 65738. Tel: 417-732-6684; Fax: 417-732-6684. Sisters 5.

[G] RETREAT HOUSES

AVA. *Assumption Abbey*. (Trappist), Rte. 5, Box 1056, 65608. Tel: 417-683-5110; Fax: 417-683-5658. Rt. Rev. James Connor, O.C.S.O., Abbot.

MARIONVILLE. *The Society of Our Mother of Peace, Daughters of Our Mother of Peace*, Rte. 1, Box 107A, 65705. Tel: 417-744-2011. Legal Title: *The Society of Our Mother of Peace, Daughters of Our Mother of Peace, Queen of Heaven Solitude*.

REPUBLIC. *Cordis House*, 648 S. Assisi Way, 65738. Tel: 417-732-8602. Rev. Eric Kahn, O.F.M.; Sr. Coletta Wrasman, P.H.J.C.

Little Portion Retreat Center, 645 S. Assisi Way, 65738. Tel: 417-732-6684. Sr. Roberta Cusack, O.S.F., Co-ord.

[H] SHRINES

CARTHAGE. *Shrine of Immaculate Heart of Mary*, 1900 Grand Ave., 64836. Tel: 417-358-8580; Fax: 417-358-9508. Rt. Rev. Joseph Calasanz Tran Ngoc Diep, C.M.C., Prov.

[I] NEWMAN CENTERS

SPRINGFIELD. *The Nancy McGregor House, Southwest MO State University, Drury College, Ozarks Technical Community College*, Catholic Campus Ministry, 847 S. Holland, 65806. Tel: 417-865-0802. Rev. Eddie DeLeon, C.M.F., Dir.

CAPE GIRARDEAU. *Southeast Missouri State University, Newman Center*, 512 N. Pacific, 63701. Tel: 573-335-3899; Fax: 573-334-0088. Rev. John J. Freidel, Chap.

BRANSON. *Catholic Christian Newman Association*. (College of the Ozarks), 202 Vaughn, 65616. Tel: 417-334-5549. Sr. Cynthia Hruby, N.D., Campus Min.

WEBB CITY. *Newman Club, Missouri Southern College*, 909 N. Madison, 64870. Rev. Rick L. Jones, Chap., Newman Club, Missouri Southern State College, Joplin. Tel: 417-673-2044.

[J] MISCELLANEOUS

SPRINGFIELD. *Franciscan Villa*, 620 W. Scott, 65802. Tel: 417-869-5417. Gene Vestal, Admin.

The Kitchen, 1630 N. Jefferson, 65803. Tel: 417-831-6452. Sr. Lorraine Biebel, O.S.F., Coord.

Queen of Angels DayCare Center, 625 S. Jefferson, 65806. Tel: 417-869-9842; Fax: 417-832-0852.

**St. John's Health System, Inc.*, 1235 E. Cherokee, 65804. Tel: 417-885-2000.

CARTHAGE. *Office of the Immaculate Heart of Mary Shrine*, 1749 Grand Ave., 64836. Tel: 417-358-8580; Fax: 417-358-3954.

ELLINGTON. *Casa Guadalupe, Family Growth Center*, P.O. Box 417, 63638. Tel: 573-663-2720; 663-7322.

RELIGIOUS INSTITUTES OF MEN REPRESENTED IN THE DIOCESE

For further details refer to the corresponding bracketed number in the Religious Institutes of Men or Women section.

[1330]—*Congregation of the Missions (Vincentians)*.—C.M.

[]—*Congregation of the Mother Coredemptrix*.—C.M.C.

[0520]—*Franciscan Friars*.—O.F.M.

[0360]—*Missionary Sons of the Immaculate Heart of Mary (Claretians)*.—C.M.F.

[0910]—*Oblates of Mary Immaculate (Oblates)*. (Central Prov.).—O.M.I.

[0350]—*Order of Cistercians of the Strict Observance (Trappist)*.—O.C.S.O.

[0200]—*Order of St. Benedict (Benedictines)*.—O.S.B.

[1240]—*Order of the Servants of Mary (Servites)*. (Chicago Prov.).—O.S.M.

[1030]—*Paulist Fathers*.—C.S.P.

[0690]—*Society of Jesus (Jesuits)*. (Missouri Prov.).—S.J.

[]—*The Society of Our Mother of Peace*.—S.M.P.

RELIGIOUS INSTITUTES OF WOMEN REPRESENTED IN THE DIOCESE

[0100]—*Adorers of the Blood of Christ*. (Ruma).—A.S.C.

[0230]—*Benedictine Sisters of the Pontifical Jurisdiction*. (Columbia).—O.S.B.

[0230]—*Benedictine Sisters of the Pontifical Jurisdiction*. (Eau Claire, WI).—O.S.B.

[]—*Congregation of Mary, Queen*.—C.M.R.

[0460]—*Congregation of the Sisters of Charity of the Incarnate Word*. (San Antonio).—C.C.V.I.

[0760]—*Daughters of Charity of St. Vincent de Paul*. (St. Louis).—D.C.

[0920]—*Daughters of St. Francis of Assisi*. (Lacon, Illinois).—D.S.F.

[0420]—*Discalced Carmelite Nuns*.—O.C.D.

[1415]—*Franciscan Sisters of Mary*.—F.S.M.

[1780]—*Franciscan Sisters of Perpetual Adoration*.—F.S.P.A.

[1240]—*Franciscan Sisters, Daughters of the Sacred Hearts of Jesus and Mary*. (Wheaton).—O.S.F.

[]—*Little Portion Franciscans*.—O.S.F.

[]—*Nazareth Hermitage*.

[2960]—*Notre Dame Sisters*. (Omaha).—N.D.

[3230]—*Poor Handmaids of Jesus Christ*. (Donaldson, IN).—P.H.J.C.

[2970]—*School Sisters of Notre Dame*. (St. Louis).—S.S.N.D.

[2970]—*School Sisters of Notre Dame*. (Dallas).—S.S.N.D.

[0430]—*Sisters of Charity of the Blessed Virgin Mary*. (Dubuque).—B.V.M.

[0990]—*Sisters of Divine Providence*. (St. Louis Prov.).—C.D.P.

[1010]—*Sisters of Divine Providence of San Antonio, TX*.—C.D.P.

[2575]—*Sisters of Mercy of the Americas*. (Cedar Rapids, IA Region).—R.S.M.

[2575]—*Sisters of Mercy of the Americas*. (Dallas, PA Region).—R.S.M.

[2575]—*Sisters of Mercy of the Americas*. (St. Louis, MO Region).—R.S.M.

[2575]—*Sisters of Mercy of the Americas*. (Omaha, NE Region).—R.S.M.

[2990]—*Sisters of Notre Dame*. (Chardon, OH).—S.N.D.

[1530]—*Sisters of St. Francis*. (Sylvania, OH).—O.S.F.

[1570]—*Sisters of St. Francis of the Holy Family*. (Dubuque).—O.S.F.

[3840]—*Sisters of St. Joseph of Carondelet*. (St. Louis).—C.S.J.

[3830]—*Sisters of St. Joseph of LaGrange, IL*.—C.S.J.

[3270]—*Sisters of the Most Precious Blood*. (O'Fallon, MO).—C.PP.S.

[3320]—*Sisters of the Presentation of the B.V.M.* (Fargo).—P.B.V.M.

[1720]—*Sisters of the Third Order Regular of St. Francis of Our Lady of Lourdes*. (Rochester, MN).—O.S.F.

[]—*The Society of Our Mother of Peace*.—S.M.P.

[4110]—*Ursuline Nuns (Roman Union)*. (Crystal City, MO).—O.S.U.

[4120]—*Ursuline Nuns of the Congregation of Paris*. (Maple Mount, Kentucky).—O.S.U.

[4160]—*Vincentian Sisters of Charity*. (Pittsburg, PA).—V.S.C.

NECROLOGY

(No Deaths)

Diocese of Springfield in Illinois

(Dioecesis Campifontis in Illinois)

Most Reverend

DANIEL L. RYAN, D.D., J.C.L.

Bishop of Springfield in Illinois; ordained May 3, 1956; ordained Titular Bishop of Surista in Mauritania and auxiliary to the Bishop of Joliet in Illinois September 30, 1981; appointed Bishop of Springfield in Illinois November 22, 1983; installed January 18, 1984. *Res., P.O. Box 1667, Springfield, IL, 62705-1667. Office: Catholic Pastoral Center, 1615 W. Washington St., P.O. Box 3187, Springfield, IL, 62708-3187.* Tel.: 217-698-8500; Fax: 217-698-0802.

FORMERLY DIOCESE OF QUINCY.

ERECTED JULY 29, 1853.

SEE TRANSFERRED TO ALTON, JANUARY 9, 1857. TO SPRINGFIELD, OCTOBER 26, 1923.

Square Miles 15,139.

Comprises the following Counties of Illinois: Adams, Bond, Brown, Calhoun, Cass, Christian, Clark, Coles, Crawford, Cumberland, Douglas, Edgar, Effingham, Fayette, Greene, Jasper, Jersey, Macon, Macoupin, Madison, Menard, Montgomery, Morgan, Moultrie, Pike, Sangamon, Scott and Shelby.

For legal titles of parishes and diocesan institutions, consult the Chancery Office.

Catholic Pastoral Center: 1615 W. Washington St., P.O. Box 3187, Springfield, IL, 62708-3187. Tel.: 217-698-8500; Fax: 217-698-8602.

STATISTICAL OVERVIEW

Personnel	
Bishop	1
Priests: Diocesan Active in Diocese	98
Priests: Active Outside Diocese	8
Priests: Diocesan in Foreign Missions	1
Priests: Retired, Sick or Absent	39
Number of Diocesan Priests	146
Religious Priests in Diocese	65
Extern Priests in Diocese	6
Ordinations:	
Diocesan Priests	3
Transitional Deacons	2
Permanent Deacons in Diocese	2
Total Brothers	19
Total Sisters	707
Parishes	
Parishes	166
With Resident Pastor:	
Resident Diocesan Priests	79
Resident Religious Priests	19
Without Resident Pastor:	
Administered by Priests	62
Administered by Women Religious	6
Professional Ministry Personnel:	
Brothers	4
Sisters	30
Lay Ministers	39
Welfare	
Catholic Hospitals	8
Total Assisted	901,359
Homes for the Aged	3
Total Assisted	400
Residential Care of Children	1
Total Assisted	130
Day Care and Extended Day Care Centers	1
Total Assisted	12
Specialized Homes	1
Total Assisted	49
Residential Care of Disabled	1
Total Assisted	93
Educational	
Diocesan Students in Other Seminaries	11
Seminaries, Religious	1
Students Religious	10
Total Seminarians	21
Colleges and Universities	2
Total Students	1,672
High Schools, Diocesan and Parish	4
Total Students	1,033
High Schools, Private	3
Total Students	1,655
Elementary Schools, Diocesan and Parish	54
Total Students	12,791
Catechesis/Religious Education:	
High School Students	3,221
Elementary Students	10,864
Total Students Under Catholic Instruction	31,257
Teachers in the Diocese:	
Priests	4
Brothers	1
Sisters	46
Lay Teachers	846
Vital Statistics	
Receptions into the Church:	
Infant Baptism Totals	2,481
Adult Baptism Totals	322
Received into Full Communion	524
First Communions	2,847
Confirmations	3,052
Marriages:	
Catholic	558
Interfaith	560
Total Marriages	1,118
Deaths	1,757
Total Catholic Population	168,967
Total Population	1,106,124

Former Bishops—Rt. Rev. HENRY DAMIAN JUNCKER, D.D., cons. April 28, 1857; died Oct. 2, 1868.—Rt. Rev. PETER JOSEPH BALTES, D.D., cons. Jan. 23, 1870; died Feb. 15, 1886.—Rt. Rev. JAMES RYAN, D.D., cons. May 1, 1888; died July 2, 1923.—Most Rev. JAMES A. GRIFFIN, D.D., cons. Feb. 25, 1924; died Aug. 5, 1948.—Most Rev. WILLIAM A. O'CONNOR, D.D., cons. March 7, 1949; installed March 17, 1949; retired July 22, 1975; died Nov. 14, 1983.—Most Rev. JOSEPH A. MCNICHOLAS, D.D., cons. March 25, 1969; installed Sept. 3, 1975; died April 17, 1983.

Vicars General—Very Rev. THOMAS P. HOLINGA, V.G., Dir. Clergy Personnel; Very Rev. JOHN A. RENKEN, V.G., Moderator of the Curia.

Deans—

Alton Deanery—Very Rev. VIRGIL W. MANK, V.F.

Decatur Deanery—Very Rev. KEVIN W. VANN, V.F.

Effingham Deanery—Very Rev. LEO J. ENLOW, V.F.

Jacksonville Deanery—Very Rev. JOHN W. SPREEN, V.F.

Litchfield Deanery—Very Rev. LAWRENCE AUDA, V.F.

Quincy Deanery—Very Rev. JOHN P. BEVERIDGE, V.F.

Springfield Deanery—Very Rev. PATRICK J. WRIGHT, V.F.

Chancellor—Very Rev. EUGENE E. COSTA.

Tribunal Personnel—Very Rev. JOHN A. RENKEN, Judicial Vicar; Very Rev. KENNETH C. STEFFEN, Adjutant Judicial Vicar; Sr. ESTHER REDMANN, O.S.U., Diocesan Judge; Bro. PATRICK SHEA, O.F.M., Defender of the Bond; BARBARA BETTWY, Advocate/Auditor.

Diocesan Finance Officer—Mr. JOHN J. MAXWELL, C.P.A.

Diocesan Curia—

All diocesan agencies and councils are located at the Catholic Pastoral Center, unless the contrary is indicated., *Catholic Pastoral Center, 1615 W. Washington St., P.O. Box 3187, Springfield, 62708-3187.* Tel: 217-698-8500; Fax: 217-698-0802.

Office of the Bishop—Most Rev. DANIEL L. RYAN, D.D., J.C.L.; Very Rev. EUGENE E. COSTA, S.T.L., Exec. Asst.

Office for Campus Ministry—Mr. ROY LANHAM, Dir., *909 E. Lincoln Ave., Charleston, 61920.* Tel: 217-348-0188.

Office for Catholic Charities (Central Administration)—Mr. LAWRENCE DRURY, Exec. Dir., *800 S. Fifth St., Springfield, 62703.* Tel: 217-523-9201; Fax: 217-523-5624.

Office for Catholic Education—Sr. MARILYN JEAN RUNKEL, O.P., Dir.; Mrs. ROSE MERSINGER, Assoc. Dir., Elementary Education; Mrs. CHRIS MALMEVICK, Assoc. Dir., Adult Education/Catechist Formation; Ms. BARB BURRIS, Assoc. Dir., Planning; Mrs. JO BUCKLEY, Exec. Sec.; Mrs. JACQUELINE ARMSTRONG, Elementary & Secondary School/School Planning & Devel. Sec.; Mrs. ANTOINETTE COLCLASURE, Adult Educ. & Catechist Formation Sec.; Ms. SUSAN DONNELLY, Statistics/Data Specialist.

Board of Catholic Education—Mr. BOB BERGMAN; Sr. JUDITH HILBING, O.P.; Ms. HELEN KLOSTERMANN; Rev. DANIEL LACOUNT; Rev. DAVID S. LANTZ; Bro. JAMES LEWNARD, C.S.V.; Mr. RICHARD LUCIDO; Mr. EDWARD MCCARTHY; Mr. LEE W. MARTEN; Sr. THERESE MACKINNON, D.C.; Mrs. JAN MULROONEY-KUHN; Rev. DAVID PETERS; Ms. GINA S. PINTO; Mr. PETER SIMONCINI; Mr. PETER MICHAEL VOELZ; Sr. JOANN VOLK, S.S.N.D.

Media Resource Center (Library)—Sr. MATTHIAS CLARKE, O.P., Contact; Mrs. JOAN REED, Sec.

Office for Catholic Times—Mr. DAVID BAKKE, Dir. & Editor; Mrs. LAURIE WEAKLEY, Office Mgr.; Mr. KEVIN HECKER, Layout & Design Coord.; Mrs. CATHERINE LOCHER, Reporter; Mrs. DIANE SCHLINDWEIN, Reporter; Mrs. BELINDA MULSHINE, Advertising; Mrs. MARIAN GREENAN, Comptroller; Mrs. BARBARA DAVIS, Sec. & Receptionist . Fax: 217-698-0619.

Office for Chancellor/Planning Coordinator—Very Rev. EUGENE E. COSTA, S.T.L.; Miss PATRICIA BOLT, Sec.

Office for Communications—Ms. KATHIE SASS, Dir. Tel: 217-467-5535 (Pager); Fax: 217-698-0619.

Office for Family and Youth Ministry—Mrs. DONNA DAUSMAN, Dir.; Mr. TIM PFAU, Assoc. Dir. for Youth Ministry; Mrs. JANA DOTY, Assoc. Dir. for Family Enrichment; Mrs. LANA BASDEN, Sec.

Office for Finances—Mr. JOHN J. MAXWELL, Dir.; Mr. TOM REISER, Assoc. Dir. Property, Buildings and Cemeteries; Mrs. EDNA MAE BROWN, Assoc. Dir. Insurance-Fire, Extended Coverage, Vandalism, Multi-Peril Liability, Workers Compensation, Boiler, Unemployment, Lay Employee Pension Plan, Priests' Personal Property, Seminarians' Medical Care and Coordinator for Lay Employee Health Insurance; Mr. DAN GAUWITZ, Programmer & Analyst; Mr. TIM BARNHART, Accounting Mgr. Accountants: Miss LAURA BURDZILAUSKAS; Mrs. CHRISTINA

DAVIS; Mrs. CHERYL KANNALL, Coord., Annual Catholic Svcs. Appeal; Mrs. KAREN REGAN, Clerk, Annual Catholic Svcs. Appeal; Miss BARBARA OZANIC, Sec.

Diocesan Health Insurance Plan Committee—Rev. GERALD BUNSE; Mrs. EDNA MAE BROWN; Ms. BARB BURRIS; Ms. JUDY KOHLRUS; Mr. LEO LENN; Very Rev. VIRGIL MANK; Mr. JOHN MAXWELL; Mrs. JOAN MCKINNEY; Mr. HENRY PETRILLI; Mr. THOMAS REISER; Very Rev. JOHN RENKEN, V.G.; Ms. SUSAN VASQUEZ.

Lay Employees' Pension Plan Administrative Committee—Mrs. EDNA MAE BROWN; Mr. LEO LENN; Mr. JOHN MAXWELL; Mrs. ROSE MERSINGER; Mr. HENRY PETRILLI; Very Rev. JOHN RENKEN, V.G.; Mr. THOMAS REISER; Bro. PATRICK SHEA, O.F.M.; Rev. Msgr. PAUL SHERIDAN; Mr. GARY STREMSTERFER; Rev.

Commission for Buildings and Property—Rev. DANIEL BERGBOWER; Mr. H. F. BOYLE; Mr. ROBERT BUDNIK, Chm.; Sr. CHAMINADE KELLY, O.S.F.; Very Rev. VIRGIL MANK; Mr. JOHN MAXWELL; Rev. DAVID PETERS; Very Rev. JOHN RENKEN, V.G.; Mr. THOMAS REISER, Consultant.

Office for Lay Ministry—Rev. DAVID LANTZ, Dir.; Mrs. JOAN REED, Sec.

Advisory Board—Sr. JANE BOOS, S.S.N.D.; Sr. KATHLEEN COUR, O.P.; Mrs. DONNA DAUSMAN; Mrs. MARY HANDLEY; Mr. ELIOT KAPITAN; Mrs. SUE MORRIS; Mr. TIM PFAU; Very Rev. JOHN A. RENKEN, V.G.; Sr. MARILYN JEAN RUNKEL, O.P.; Sr. SUZANNE SIMS, O.S.U.; Very Rev. KENNETH STEFFEN.

Track "A" (Area Specialization) Coordinators—Catechetical Leadership Ministry, Mrs. CHRIS MALMEVICK, *Catholic School Leadership Ministry,* Sr. MARILYN JEAN RUNKEL, O.P., *Clinical Pastoral Care Ministry,* Mrs. MARY HANDLEY, *Family Life Ministry,* Very Rev. KENNETH STEFFEN; Mrs. DONNA DAUSMAN,*Liturgical Ministry: Christian Initiation of Adult Leadership Skills;* Mr. ELIOT KAPITAN,*Liturgical Ministry: Liturgical Leadership Skills,* Sr. KATHLEEN COUR, O.P., *Social Concerns Ministry,* Sr. JANE BOOS, S.S.N.D., *Tribunal Advocacy Ministry,* Very Rev. JOHN A. RENKEN, V.G., *Youth Ministry,* Mr. TIM PFAU.

Track "B" (Parish Life Ministry) Coordinator—Very Rev. JOHN A. RENKEN, V.G.

Office for Lay Organizations—Rev. JOHN R. OSSOLA, Dir.; Miss SHARON MASTERSON, Sec.

Office for Ministry to Priests—Rev. HENRY SCHMIDT, Dir., *800 Stevenson Dr., Springfield, 62703.* Tel: 217-529-1606.

Office for the Missions—Rev. JOHN BURNETT, Dir.; Mrs. RITA GREENWALD, Prog. Coord.; Mr. BRUCE COMPTON, Admin. Asst., *P.O. Box 7025, Springfield, 62791-7025.*

Office for Rural Life—Mr. JOSEPH BERGSCHNEIDER, Dir.; Mrs. MAYME BERGSCHNEIDER, Assoc. Dir., *31 Westfair Dr., Jacksonville, 62650.* Tel: 217-243-2832.

Office for Social Concerns—Sr. JANE BOOS, S.S.N.D., Dir.; Mrs. SUE MORRIS, Assoc. Dir.; Mrs. NANCY HARPER, Assoc. Dir. Deaf Ministry. Tel: 217-245-4299 (v/tty).; Mrs. ELAINE VONDERHEIDE, Assoc. Dir. Special Needs. Tel: 217-342-2718. Mrs. MARTHA MAYFIELD, Assoc. Dir. Oper. Tel: 217-698-9581 (tty).

Diocesan Task Force Against Racial Injustice—RENEE SAUNCHES, Co-Chm. Tel: 217-875-7251. MARY CLUNEY JOHN, Co-Chm. Tel: 217-429-1452.

Campaign for Human Development Advisory Board and Allocation Committee—Sr. JANE BOOS, S.S.N.D., Dir.; Mr. LARRY DRURY. Deanery Representatives: Mr. HERB REISINGER, Alton Deanery; Mr. WILLIAM JOYNER, Decatur Deanery; Mr. KEN HANDLEY, Decatur Deanery; Mr. FRED FASIG, Effingham Deanery; Ms. RUTH ANN STEWART, Jacksonville Deanery; Mrs. MARGUERITE SCHNEIDER, Quincy Deanery; Mrs. NICOLE WELCH, Quincy Deanery; Mr. LLOYD MOSLEY, Springfield Deanery; Mr. LEROY JORDAN, Springfield Deanery. Members At Large: Mr. KEN STEINER.

Elizabeth Ann Seton Parish Program Board—Sr. JANE BOOS, S.S.N.D., Pres.; Bro. PATRICK SHEA, O.F.M., Vice-Pres. CAROLYN BODEWES, Exec. Dir. FRITZIE BELZ, Sec. & Treas. ANDREW BODEWES, Youth Advisor; ANNE HESSLAN DONDAVILLE; LARRY DRURY; MARY FITZGERALD; ALLISON LAABS; Very Rev. VIRGIL MANK, V.F.; LAURA PHIPPS; RUTH ANN STAAB; MARY DELLERT, Program Sec.

Hispanic Sacramental Ministry—Sr. RENE LAWLESS, O.P. Tel: 217-243-2815.

Office for Stewardship and Development—Mrs. MARLENE MULFORD, Acting Dir.; Mrs. CATHY FURKIN, Sec.

Steering Committee—Ms. BARBARA BURRIS; Rev. THOMAS DENNIS; Mrs. CATHY FURKIN; Mrs. CHERYL KANNALL; Mr. JOHN J. MAXWELL; Mrs. MARLENE MULFORD; Mr. HENRY PETRILLI; Very Rev. JOHN A. RENKEN, V.G.; Ms. KATHIE SASS; Very Rev. KENNETH STEFFEN.

Office for the Tribunal—Very Rev. JOHN A. RENKEN, S.T.D., J.C.D., M.A. (Civil Law), Judicial Vicar (Dir.); Very Rev. KENNETH C. STEFFEN, J.C.L., M.A., D.Min., Adjutant Judicial Vicar (Assoc. Dir.); Sr. ESTHER REDMANN, O.S.U., J.C.L., (Judge); Bro. PATRICK SHEA, O.F.M., J.C.D., J.D., (Defender of the Bond); Miss BARBARA BETTWY, (Advocate/Auditor); Mrs. JEAN KIRK, (Office Mgr./Notary); Mrs. LANA BASDEN, (Sec./Notary).

Office of the Vicar General / Director of Clergy Personnel—Very Rev. THOMAS P. HOLINGA, V.G., *711 S. Sixth St., P.O. Box 234, Petersburg, 62675-0234.* Tel: 217-632-2561(Rectory); 632-7118(Office); Fax: 217-632-7154.

Commission for the Care of Infirm and Retired Priests—Revs. GERALD BUNSE; T. J. DAVENPORT; THOMAS P. HOLINGA; MICHAEL KUSE; VIRGIL MANK; CHARLES MULCRONE; MARTIN O'HARA; JOHN RENKEN; TERENCE TRACEY.

Office of the Vicar General / Moderator of the Curia—Very Rev. JOHN A. RENKEN, V.G., S.T.D., J.C.D., M.A.(Civil Law). Tel: 217-629-9109 (Evenings & Weekends). Bro. PATRICK SHEA, O.F.M., J.C.D., J.D., Exec. Asst. to the Vicar General & Legal Counsel; Mrs. DORIS RAY, Assoc. to the Vicar General-Records Mgmt. Office Mgr. & Notary; Mrs. CAROL MULLER, Exec. Sec. & Notary; Mrs. JOAN REED, Special Projects Coord. & Notary; Mrs. NANCY GILLITUK, Receptionist for Catholic Pastoral Center.

Office for Vocations—Rev. MICHAEL KUSE, Dir., *1119 S. 7th St., Quincy, 62301.* Tel: 217-222-2759; Fax: 217-222-6463.

Office for Worship—Sr. KATHLEEN COUR, O.P., Dir.; Mr. ELIOT KAPITAN, Assoc. Dir., RCIA; Mrs. JAN GRIGGS, Sec.

Commission for the Liturgy—Mr. JERRY BAUMAN; Mr. RICH BYERS; Sr. KATHLEEN COUR, O.P.; Mrs. SHARRY GOETZ; Revs. BARRY HARMON; ROBERT JALLAS; Mr. PAUL JOHNSON; Mr. ELIOT KAPITAN; Mrs. MARY KELDERMANS; Rev. JOSEPH RING, Chm.; Mrs. CAROL SEIFERT.

Councils

Diocesan Finance Council—Sr. CHRISTINE BRAMLET, O.S.U.; Sr. LINDA HAYES, O.P.; Mr. WILFRED KALTENBACH; Mr. WILLIAM KESSLER; Mr. LEO LENN, Chm.; Dr. ROBERT MANDEVILLE; Rev. JAMES NEUMAN. Consultants: Very Rev. JOHN RENKEN, V.G.; Mr. JOHN J. MAXWELL; Mr. THOMAS REISER.

Presbyteral Council—Most Rev. DANIEL L. RYAN, Pres.; Revs. MICHAEL BARRETT, O.F.M.; GERALD BUNSE; EUGENE E. COSTA; JEFFREY GOECKNER; JEFFREY GRANT; THOMAS HENSELER; THOMAS HOLINGA; ROBERT JALLAS; CARL KEMME; MICHAEL KUSE; DANIEL LACOUNT, Vice Chm. KEVIN LAUGHERY; LAMBERT LEYKAM, O.F.M.; VIRGIL MANK; WILLIAM MAUL, Chm. CHARLES NELSON; JOHN A. RENKEN, V.G., Sec. & Treas. KENNETH STEFFEN; JOHN TITUS; EUGENE WEITZEL, C.S.V.

Catholic Charities Institutions

Area Offices—

Alton. Catholic Charities of Alton and Wood River—RICK FACCIN, Area Dir., *735 Park Dr., Alton, 62002.* Tel: 618-462-0634; Fax: 618-462-3209.

Carlinville. Catholic Charities—PATRICIA A. POPE, Area Dir., *525 W. Second South St., Carlinville, 62626.* Tel: 217-854-4511; Fax: 217-854-8049.

Decatur. Catholic Charities—MARIE RADEMACHER, Area Dir., *247 W. Prairie, Decatur, 62523.* Tel: 217-428-3458.

Effingham. Catholic Charities—Sr. BETH MARIE RUDER, D.C., Area Dir., *601 W. Fayette, Effingham, 62401.* Tel: 217-342-9800; Fax: 217-342-3873.

Granite City. Catholic Charities—DAVE DALY, Area Dir., *2105 State St., Granite City, 62040.* Tel: 618-877-1184; Fax: 618-877-1890.

Quincy. Catholic Social Services—Sr. MARY SHAW, A.S.C., Area Dir., *926 State St., Quincy, 62301.* Tel: 217-222-0958; Fax: 217-222-8737.

Springfield. Catholic Charities—MARY STONE, Area Dir., *120 S. 11th St., Springfield, 62703.* Tel: 217-525-0500; Fax: 217-525-0554.

Institutions—

Alton. Catholic Children's Home—Mr. LAWRENCE DRURY, Dir. STEVEN ROACH, Admin., *1400 State St., Alton, 62002.* Tel: 618-465-3594; Fax: 618-465-4023.

Springfield. St. Monica's Center—Mr. LAWRENCE DRURY, Dir. JUDITH A. COMERIO, Admin., *109 E. Lawrence Ave., Springfield, 62704.* Tel: 217-523-7922; Fax: 217-525-8241.

Springfield. St. John's Breadline—430 N. Fifth St., Springfield, 62701. Tel: 217-528-6098.

CLERGY, PARISHES, MISSIONS AND PAROCHIAL SCHOOLS

CITY OF SPRINGFIELD
(Sangamon County)

1—CATHEDRAL OF THE IMMACULATE CONCEPTION (1928), Revs. John R. Ossola; Thomas J. Dennis.
Res., 524 E. Lawrence Ave., P.O. Box 1667, 62705. Tel: 217-522-3342; Fax: 217-522-1151. [JC]
School—Tel: 217-523-2652; Fax: 217-523-2750.
Springfield Dominican Sisters 4; Lay Teachers 20; Students 218; Preschool 22.

2—BLESSED SACRAMENT (1924), Revs. John C. Burnett; Christopher Comerford.
Res., 1725 S. Walnut Ave., 62704. Tel: 217-528-7521; Fax: 217-528-3137.
School—Tel: 217-522-7534; Fax: 217-522-7542.
Lay Teachers 28; Students 479.
Catechesis / Religious Programs—Students 75.

3—CHRIST THE KING (1963), Revs. David S. Lantz; David Zimmerman.
Res., 1930 Barberry Dr., 62704. Tel: 217-546-3527; Fax: 217-793-6393.
School—Tel: 217-546-2159; Fax: 217-546-0291.
Lay Teachers 23; Students 504.
Catechesis / Religious Programs—Elementary, 1920 Barberry Dr., 62704.
Students 78.

4—LITTLE FLOWER (1947), Revs. Henry C. Schmidt; Allen Kemme.
800 Stevenson Dr., 62703. Tel: 217-529-1606; Fax: 217-529-1649. [JC]
School—Tel: 217-529-4511; Fax: 217-529-3622.
Sisters 2; Lay Teachers 30; Students 401.
Catechesis / Religious Programs—Students 108.

5—ST. AGNES (1889), Very Rev. Patrick J. Wright, V.F.; Revs. Mark A. Schulte; Robert T. Becker.
Res., 245 N. Amos Ave., 62702. Tel: 217-793-1330; Fax: 217-793-3212.
School—Tel: 217-793-1370; Fax: 217-793-1238.
Lay Teachers 23; Students 520.
Catechesis / Religious Programs—Students 210.

6—ST. ALOYSIUS (1928), Revs. John Titus; Donald Meehling; Rodney Schwartz.
Res., 2119 N. 20th St., 62702. Tel: 217-544-4554.
School—Tel: 217-544-4553.
Lay Teachers 23; Students 431.
Catechesis / Religious Programs—Students 431.

7—ST. FRANCES CABRINI (1948), Revs. John M. Titus, Admin.; Rodney A. Schwartz.
Res., 1020 N. Milton Ave., 62702. Tel: 217-522-8555; Fax: 217-522-8555.
School—Tel: 217-528-8302.
Lay Teachers 12; Students 101.

8—ST. JOSEPH (1875), Rev. Patrick W. Render, C.S.V.
Res., 1345 N. Sixth St., 62702. Tel: 217-544-7426; Fax: 217-544-7467.
School—Tel: 217-523-6597.
Ursuline Sisters 1; Lay Teachers 14; Students 203.
Catechesis / Religious Programs—Students 63.

9—ST. PATRICK, Rev. John E. Eck, C.S.V.
Res., 1720 S. Grand Ave., E., P.O. Box 4302, 62708. Tel: 217-528-0436. [JC]
School—Tel: 217-523-7670.
Springfield Dominican Sisters 1; Lay Teachers 12; Students 92.

10—SS. PETER AND PAUL (1859) (German), Rev. Frank J. O'Hara.
Res., 426 N. Sixth St., 62702. Tel: 217-523-3681. [JC]

11—SACRED HEART OF JESUS (1884) (German), Rev. John E. Eck, C.S.V. In res., Rev. Eugene Cieslik (Poland).
Res., 725 S. 12th St., 62703. Tel: 217-523-1861. [JC]

OUTSIDE THE CITY OF SPRINGFIELD

Alexander, Morgan Co., Visitation B.V.M., Rev. Joseph P. Kerber.
Mailing Address: P.O. Box 20, New Berlin, 62670. Tel: 217-488-2410; Fax: 217-488-2410.
Church—Old U.S. 36, 62601.

Altamont, Effingham Co., St. Clare (1874), Revs. Angel Sierra, Admin.; John M. Savoree.
Res., 216 N. Ninth St., 62411. Tel: 618-483-5346. [CEM]
Catechesis / Religious Programs—Students 160.

Alton, Madison Co.,

1—SS. PETER AND PAUL, (1855), Revs. Thomas G. Meyer, O.M.I.; Gerard Sniechota, O.M.I.; Bro. Herb Beimert, O.M.I.
Res., 717 State St., 62002. Tel: 618-465-4221; Fax: 618-465-0346. [JC]
School—Tel: 618-465-8711.
Lay Teachers 9; Students 200.

2—IMMACULATE CONCEPTION-ST. MARY'S, (1858), Revs. John Paul Klein, O.M.V.; Daniel Barron, O.M.V.; Craig MacMahon, O.M.V.; William Mullen, O.M.V.; Deacon John Wykes.

Res., 525 E. Fourth St., 62002. Tel: 618-465-4284; Fax: 618-463-4637. [CEM]
School—Tel: 618-465-8523.
Sisters of St. Francis of the Martyr of St. George 4; Lay Teachers 10; Students 222.
Catechesis/Religious Programs—Students 289.

3—St. Patrick, (1883), Revs. Daniel Barron, O.M.V.; Craig MacMahon, O.M.V.; John Paul Klein, O.M.V.; William Mullen, O.M.V.; Deacon John Wykes.
Res., 525 E. Fourth St., 62002. Tel: 618-465-4284.
Church—918 E. Fifth St., 62002. Fax: 618-463-4637. [JC]

4—St. Matthew, (1947), Rev. Robert J. Jallas.
Res., 1015 Milton Rd., 62002-3167. Tel: 618-465-8582; Fax: 618-465-5994.
School—Tel: 618-462-6032.
Lay Teachers 10; Students 157.

Arcola, Douglas Co., St. John the Baptist (1865), Rev. Michael D. Mullink; Sr. Phyllis Schenk, O.P.
Res., 205 S. Locus St., Box 133, 61910. Tel: 217-268-3545;268-3766. [JC]
Catechesis/Religious Programs—210 S. Pine St., 61910.
Students 131.

Arenzville, Cass Co., St. Fidelis (1859) (German), Rev. Eugene J. Weitzel, C.S.V.
Res., 215 W. Fifth St., Beardstown, 62618. Tel: 217-323-4345. [JC]

Ashland, Cass Co., St. Augustine (1875), Rev. John W. Spreen.
Res., 320 N. Saratoga, P.O. Box 438, 62612. Tel: 217-476-8856. [CEM]
Catechesis/Religious Programs—Students 56.

Assumption, Christian Co., Assumption B.V.M. (1870), Rev. Alan Hunter.
Res., 301 St. Peter St., 62510. Tel: 217-226-3536; Fax: 217-226-3538. [CEM]
Catechesis/Religious Programs—Tel: 217-226-3205.
Students 58.

Athens, Menard Co., Holy Family (1903), Rev. Eugene E. Costa.
Res., 129 Stardust Dr., Sherman, 62684. Tel: 217-523-3816; Fax: 217-523-3954.
Church—Springfield Rd., 62613. Tel: 217-636-8238.
Catechesis/Religious Programs—Students 87.

Auburn, Sangamon Co., St. Benedict (1903), Rev. Daniel E. LaCount.
Res., 126 E. Washington St., P.O. Box 168, 62615. Tel: 217-438-6222. [JC]
Catechesis/Religious Programs—Students 151.

Barry, Pike Co., Holy Redeemer (1954), Rev. Donald F. Sederwall.
Res., 226 E. Adams, Pittsfield, 62363. Tel: 217-285-4321; Fax: 217-285-9400. [JC]

Batchtown, Calhoun Co., St. Barbara (1910), Rev. John Sullivan, O.F.M.
Office: P.O. Box 38, Brussels, 62013. Tel: 618-883-2400; Fax: 618-883-2511.
Res., Meppen Ln., Meppen, 62013. Tel: 618-883-2309. [CEM]

Beardstown, Cass Co., St. Alexius (1838), Rev. Eugene J. Weitzel, C.S.V.
Res., 215 W. 5th St., 62618. Tel: 217-323-4345. [CEM]
Catechesis/Religious Programs—Tel: 217-323-1888.
Students 76.
Mission—Arenzville, Cass Co., St. Fidelis, 100 E.N., 62711.

Belleview, Calhoun Co., St. Agnes (1900) (German), Rev. Sylvano Pera, O.F.M.
Res., 404 Main St., P.O. Box C, Hardin, 62047. Tel: 618-576-2517. [CEM]

Beltrees, Jersey Co., St. Michael (1877), Rev. Charles F. Hurkes, O.M.I.
Res., 11 N. Evans St., P.O. Box 218, Grafton, 62037. Tel: 618-786-3512. [CEM]
Church—Beltrees Rd., 62022.

Benld, Macoupin Co., St. Joseph (1915), Rev. Lawrence Auda.
Res., 304 N. Macoupin, Gillespie, 62033. Tel: 217-839-3456.
Church—310 W. Central Ave., 62009. Tel: 217-835-4701.

Bethalto, Madison Co., Our Lady Queen of Peace (1945), Rev. Kevin B. Sullivan.
Res., 132 Butcher St., P.O. Box 100, 62010. Tel: 618-377-6519; Fax: 618-377-6519.
School—Tel: 618-377-6401; Fax: 618-377-6146.
Lay Teachers 12; Students 173.
Catechesis/Religious Programs—Students 67.

Bethany, Moultrie Co., St. Isidore (1865), Rev. James D. O'Shea.
Res., 400 Woodland Ln., Mount Zion, 62549. Tel: 217-864-3467; Fax: 217-864-3091. [CEM]

Bishop Creek, Effingham Co., St. Aloysius (1865), Rev. Edwin O. Albers, O.F.M.
Res., R.R. 2, Box 125, Dieterich, 62424. Tel: 217-925-5579. [CEM]
Catechesis/Religious Programs—Students 243.

Black Jack, Madison Co., St. John the Baptist. Closed. For inquiries for parish records contact the Chancery.

Bluffs, Scott Co., St. Patrick (1871), Rev. Charles T. Nelson.
Res., 108 Pearl St., Winchester, 62694. Tel: 217-742-5224.

Brighton, Macoupin Co., St. Alphonsus (1868) (German), Rev. Raphael Paul.
Res., 918 N. Main St., 62012. Tel: 618-372-3352; Fax: 618-372-8133.
Catechesis/Religious Programs—Students 75.

Brocton, Edgar Co., St. Thomas Aquinas (1899). Closed. For inquiries for parish records contact the Chancery.

Brussels, Calhoun Co., St. Mary (1851), Rev. John Sullivan, O.F.M.
Office: P.O. Box 38, 62013. Tel: 618-883-2400; Fax: 618-883-2511.
Res., Meppen Ln., Meppen, 62013. Tel: 618-883-2309. [CEM]
School—Tel: 618-883-2124. Mrs. Jo Ann Nolte, Prin.
Lay Teachers 6; Students 96.

Buffalo, Sangamon Co., St. Joseph (1882), Sr. Lois Kikkert, O.P., Parish Life Coord.
Res., 410 Anne St., P.O. Box 47, Illiopolis, 62539. Tel: 217-486-3851.
Church—302 W.S. St.
Catechesis/Religious Programs—Students 28.

Bunker Hill, Macoupin Co., St. Mary (1926), Rev. Robert N. Porter.
Res., 300 S. Putnam, P.O. Box A-H, 62014-9512. Tel: 618-585-4700; Fax: 618-585-3449. [CEM]
Catechesis/Religious Programs—Students 62.

Camp Point, Adams Co., St. Thomas (1860), Rev. Anthony J. Thieman.
Res., #6 Paradise Ave., P.O. Box 228, Liberty, 62347-0228. Tel: 217-645-3444.
Church—Spring St. & Ohio St., 62320.
Parish Hall: Tel: 217-593-6685.
Catechesis/Religious Programs—Sr. Joan Schnorbus, C.PP.S., D.R.E.
Students 66.

Carlinville, Macoupin Co., St. Mary's of the Immaculate Conception. Closed. For inquiries for parish records contact St. Joseph.

SS. Mary & Joseph. SS. Mary & Joseph was formed by the merger of St. Mary's of the Immaculate Conception & St. Joseph. Rev. R. Dean Probst.
Res., 1011 Ravine, P.O. Box 647, 62626-0647. Tel: 217-854-8034; Fax: 217-854-9118. [JC]
Church—State Rte. 108 E., P.O. Box 647, 62626. Tel: 217-854-7151; Fax: 217-854-9228.
Catechesis/Religious Programs—Holy Family School of Religion, Tel: 217-854-9220.
Students 270.

Carrollton, Greene Co., St. John the Evangelist (1858), Rev. Barry J. Harmon.
Res., 414 Third St., 62016-1319. Tel: 217-942-3551; Fax: 217-942-6767. [CEM]
School—426 Third St., 62016-1319. Tel: 217-942-6814. Mr. Gary E. Miller, Prin.
Lay Teachers 9; Students 153.
Catechesis/Religious Programs—Students 50.

Casey, Clark Co., St. Charles Borromeo (1878), Rev. Jeffery A. Grant.
Church—300 E. Jefferson, P.O. Box 72, 62420.
Res., 110 Lincoln Dr., P.O. Box 156, Greenup, 62428. Tel: 217-923-3523.

Chandlerville, Cass Co., St. Basil. Merged with St. Luke, Virginia.

Charleston, Coles Co., St. Charles Borromeo (1873), Revs. Robert L. Meyer; Joseph G. Ring.
Res., 921 E. Madison St., 61920. Tel: 217-345-3332; Fax: 217-345-4252.
Catechesis/Religious Programs—Students 224.

Chatham, Sangamon Co., St. Joseph (1920), Rev. Robert B. Franzen.
Res., 700 E. Spruce, 62629. Tel: 217-483-3772; Fax: 217-483-4581.
Catechesis/Religious Programs—62629. Tel: 217-483-4514.
Students 520.

Coffeen, Montgomery Co., St. John the Baptist (1898), Rev. Carl Schmidt.
Res., 400 Jefferson, P.O. Box 278, 62017. Tel: 217-534-2220. [CEM][JC]

Collinsville, Madison Co., SS. Peter and Paul (1855) (Italian), Revs. Robert Morris; J. Michael Jenkins; Sr. Mary Magdelen Fearon, O.S.U., Pastoral Assoc.
Res., 207 Vandalia St., 62234. Tel: 618-345-4343. [CEM]
School—Tel: 618-344-5450; Fax: 618-344-5536.
Lay Teachers 24; Students 394.
Catechesis/Religious Programs—Students 116.

Dalton City, Moultrie Co., Sacred Heart (1891). Closed. For inquiries for parish records contact the Chancery.

Decatur, Macon Co.,

1—Holy Family, (1959), Rev. Carl A. Kemme; Sr. Marianne Nolan, O.P., Pastoral Assoc.
Res., 2400 S. Franklin St., 62521. Tel: 217-423-6223; Fax: 217-423-6237. [JC]
School—Tel: 217-423-7049.
Springfield Dominican Sisters 4; Lay Teachers 13; Students 269; Preschool 51.
Catechesis/Religious Programs—Students 76.

2—Our Lady of Lourdes, (1958), Revs. Kevin W. Vann; Jeffrey W. Goeckner.
Res., 3850 Lourdes Dr., 62526. Tel: 217-877-4404; Fax: 217-877-5257. [JC]
School—3950 Lourdes Dr., 62526-1799. Tel: 217-877-4408; Fax: 217-872-3655.
Springfield Dominican Sisters 1; Lay Teachers 15; Students 336.
Catechesis/Religious Programs—Students 171.

3—St. Patrick, (1853), Rev. Donald L. Wolford.
Res., 407 E. Eldorado St., 62523. Tel: 217-429-5363; Fax: 217-429-8206. [JC]
School—Tel: 217-423-4351.
Lay Teachers 11; Students 203.
Catechesis/Religious Programs—Students 68.

4—St. James, (1877), Sr. Glenda Bourgeois, Parish Life Coord.; Very Rev. Martin Mangan, V.F., Priest Mod.
Res., 742 E. Clay St., 62521. Tel: 217-428-7733; Fax: 217-428-7426. [JC]
School—Tel: 217-422-7031; Fax: 217-422-2121.
Lay Teachers 12; Students 112.
Catechesis/Religious Programs—Students 70.

5—St. Thomas the Apostle, (1925), Rev. Dennis D. Kollross.
Res., 2160 N. Edward St., P.O. Box 2697, 62524-2697. Tel: 217-877-4146; Fax: 217-877-4147.
Catechesis/Religious Programs—62524-2697.
Students 48.

Dieterich, Effingham Co., Immaculate Conception (1905), Rev. Edwin O. Albers, O.F.M.
Res., R.R. 2, P.O. Box 125, 62424. Tel: 217-925-5579. [CEM]
Catechesis/Religious Programs—Students 90.

Divernon, Sangamon Co., Sacred Heart (1905), Rev. Daniel E. LaCount, Admin.
Res., 125 E. Washington St., Auburn, 62530. Tel: 217-438-6222. [CEM]
Church—230 S. Lincoln, 62530. Tel: 217-628-3629.

East Alton, Madison Co., St. Kevin (1959), Rev. Delix Michel, Admin.
Res., 108 Airwood Dr., E., 62024. Tel: 618-259-3363; Fax: 618-259-3363.
School—Tel: 618-259-6040.
Lay Teachers 8; Students 113.
Catechesis/Religious Programs—Students 90.

Edgewood, Effingham Co., St. Anne (1865), Revs. Angel Sierra, Admin.; John M. Savoree.
Res., 216 N. Ninth, Altamont, 62411. Tel: 618-483-5346.

Edwardsville, Madison Co., St. Boniface (1869) (German), Rev. John Corredato, C.S.V. In res., Rev. Erwin M. Savela, C.S.V.
Res., 110 N. Buchanan St., P.O. Box 423, 62025. Tel: 618-656-6450; Fax: 618-656-7669. [CEM]
Preschool:—.
Students 66.
School—Tel: 618-656-6917.
Lay Teachers 12; Students 225; Preschool 66.
Catechesis/Religious Programs—Students 205.

St. Mary (1842), Revs. Gerald L. Bunse; D. Patrick Gibbons.
Res., 1802 Madison, 62025. Tel: 618-656-4857; Fax: 618-656-1715. [JC]
School—Tel: 618-656-1230.
Priests 2; Lay Teachers 16; Students 244.
Catechesis/Religious Programs—Students 155.

Effingham, Effingham Co., Sacred Heart (1892), Rev. Daniel J. Bergbower.
Res., 405 S. Henrietta, P.O. Box 870, 62401. Tel: 217-347-7177; Fax: 217-347-0728. [JC]
School—Tel: 217-342-4060; Fax: 217-342-9251.
Lay Teachers 14; Students 235.
Catechesis/Religious Programs—Students 145.

St. Anthony of Padua (1858), Very Rev. Leo J. Enlow; Revs. Christopher Brey; Angel Sierra.
Res., 417 N. Third, P.O. Box 764, 62401. Tel: 217-347-7129; Fax: 217-342-6980. [CEM]
School—Tel: 217-347-0419; Fax: 217-347-2749.
Sisters 4; Lay Teachers 26; Students 474.

High School—Tel: 217-342-6969; Fax: 217-342-6997.
Priests 3; Lay Teachers 17; Students 229.
Catechesis/Religious Programs—Fax: 217-347-6980.
Students 60.

Farmersville, Montgomery Co., St. Mary (1876), Rev. Kevin M. Laughery.
Res., 310 Nobbe St., P.O. Box 80, 62533-0080. Tel: 217-227-3349; Fax: 217-698-8620. [CEM][JC]
School—St. Isidore, Tel: 217-227-3359.
Lay Teachers 6; Students 67.

Fieldon, Jersey Co., St. Mary, Rev. William Hembrow.
Res., 306 N. Washington, Jerseyville, 62052. Tel: 618-498-3416. [CEM]

Franklin, Morgan Co., Sacred Heart of Jesus (1886), Rev. Joseph P. Kerber.
Mailing Address: P.O. Box 20, New Berlin, 62670. Tel: 217-488-2410; Fax: 217-488-2410. [CEM]
Office & Res.—P.O. Box 20, New Berlin, 62670.
Church—62638.
Parish Center—Tel: 217-675-2631.
Catechesis/Religious Programs—Students 65.

Gillespie, Macoupin Co., SS. Simon and Jude (1879), Rev. Lawrence Auda.
Res., 304 N. Macoupin St., 62033. Tel: 217-839-3456. [CEM]
School—Tel: 217-839-2888.
Lay Teachers 4; Students 45.
Catechesis/Religious Programs—Students 80.

Girard, Macoupin Co., St. Patrick (1887), Rev. Kevin M. Laughery.
Res., 310 Nobbe St., P.O. Box 80, Farmersville, 62533-0080. Tel: 217-227-3349; Fax: 217-698-8620.
Catechesis/Religious Programs—Tel: 217-627-3575.
Students 86.

Glen Carbon, Madison Co., St. Cecilia (1928), Rev. Stephen J. Pohlman.
Res., 155 N. Main St., 62034. Tel: 618-288-3200; Fax: 618-288-3292.
Catechesis/Religious Programs—St. Cecilia Family Life Center, Tel: 618-288-5523.
Students 147.

Godfrey, Madison Co., St. Ambrose (1947), Very Rev. Virgil Mank, V.F.; Mr. Les Himstedt, Pastoral Assoc.; Mr. Patrick Fitzgerald, Pastoral Min.
Church—820 W. Homer Adams Pkwy., 62035. Tel: 618-466-2921; Fax: 618-466-2959.
Res., 3307 Morkel Dr., 62035. Tel: 618-466-6408.
School—Tel: 618-466-4216. Mary Jo Jacobs, Prin.
Lay Teachers 24; Students 422.
Catechesis/Religious Programs—Students 143.

Grafton, Jersey Co., St. Patrick (1871), Rev. Charles F. Hurkes, O.M.I.
Res., 11 N. Evans, P.O. Box 218, 62037. Tel: 618-786-3512.

Granite City, Madison Co., Holy Family (1988), Revs. William P. Fisherkeller, C.S.V.; Thomas F. Wise, C.S.V.
Res., 2606 Washington Ave., 62040-4810. Tel: 618-877-7158; Fax: 618-877-7105. [JC]
School—Tel: 618-877-5500.
Springfield Dominican Sisters 2; Lay Teachers 16; Students 318.
Catechesis/Religious Programs—Tel: 618-452-8244.
Students 148.

St. Elizabeth (1871), Rev. Thomas Liebler. In res., Rev. Francis Tebangura (Uganda).
Res., 2301 Pontoon Rd., 62040. Tel: 618-931-2916; Fax: 618-931-2928. [JC]
School—Tel: 618-931-0125.
Lay Teachers 13; Students 211.
St. Elizabeth Preschool—2300 Pontoon Rd., 62040. Tel: 618-931-0127.
Catechesis/Religious Programs—Students 110.

Grantfork, Madison Co., St. Gertrude (1872), Rev. James A. Flach.
Res., 120 N. Windmill, P.O. Box 457, Marine, 62061. Tel: 618-887-4535. [CEM]
Catechesis/Religious Programs—12514 Frey Rd., Highland, 62249. Tel: 618-675-2883. Shirley Schwarz, D.R.E.
Students 72.

Green Creek, Effingham Co., St. Mary Help of Christians (1860) (German), Rev. Emil G. Helfrich, O.M.I.
Res., R.R. 3, Box 162, Effingham, 62401. Tel: 217-844-2062. [CEM]
Catechesis/Religious Programs—Tel: 217-895-2166.
Students 71.

Greenfield, Greene Co., St. Michael (1880), Rev. Edward Groesch.
Res., 411 Sheffield, 62044. Tel: 217-368-2176. [CEM]

Greenup, Cumberland Co., Christ the King (1937), Rev. Jeffery A. Grant.
Res., 110 Lincoln Dr., P.O. Box 156, 62428. Tel: 217-923-3523.
Catechesis/Religious Programs—Students 70.

Greenville, Bond Co., St. Lawrence (1868), Rev. Victor J. Kaltenbach.
Res., 512 S. Prairie St., 62246. Tel: 618-664-3169. [CEM]
Catechesis/Religious Programs—Tel: 618-664-0960.
Students 170.

Griggsville, Pike Co., Holy Family. Closed. For details for parish records see St. Mary, Pittsfield.

Hagaman, Macoupin Co., St. Catherine (1905), Rev. Edward Groesch.
Res., 411 Sheffield, Greenfield, 62044. Tel: 217-368-2176.

Hardin, Calhoun Co., St. Norbert (1872) (German), Rev. Sylvano Pera, O.F.M.
Res., 404 Main St., P.O. Box C, 62047. Tel: 618-576-2517. [CEM]
School—(Grades 1-5). Tel: 618-576-2514.
Lay Teachers 3; Students 58.
Catechesis/Religious Programs—Tel: 618-576-2628.
Students 80.

Highland, Madison Co., St. Paul (1846), Revs. David L. Peters; Robert W. Spriggs.
Res., 1412 Ninth St., 62249. Tel: 618-654-2339; Fax: 618-654-9980. [CEM]
School—(Grades PreK-8). Tel: 618-654-7525.
Sisters 1; Lay Teachers 25; Students 402.
Catechesis/Religious Programs—1420 Ninth St., 62249. Tel: 618-654-4313.
Students 375.

Hillsboro, Montgomery Co., St. Agnes (1840), Rev. George L. Morelock.
Res., 216 E. Tremont, P.O. Box 98, 62049. Tel: 217-532-5288. [CEM]
Catechesis/Religious Programs—Tel: 217-532-2631.
Students 166.

Hume, Edgar Co., St. Michael (1876), Rev. Paul H. Skelton.
Res., 208 N. Pine, Box 17, Villa Grove, 61956. Tel: 217-832-8352.

Illiopolis, Sangamon Co., Visitation B.V.M. (1866), Sr. Lois Kikkert, O.P., Parish Life Coord.
Res., 410 Anne St., P.O. Box 47, 62539. Tel: 217-486-3851. [CEM][JC]

Island Grove, Jasper Co., St. Joseph (1874), Rev. Edwin O. Albers, O.F.M.
Res., R.R. 2, Box 125, Dieterich, 62424. Tel: 217-925-5579. [CEM]
Catechesis/Religious Programs—Students 96.

Jacksonville, Morgan Co., Our Saviour (1851), Revs. Ken J. Venvertloh; Thomas Hagstrom.
Mailing Address: 453 E. State St., 62650. Tel: 217-245-6184; Fax: 217-245-6185. [CEM]
School—62650. Tel: 217-243-8621. Mrs. Peggy Goodwin, Prin.
Lay Teachers 21; Students 364.
High School—Routt Catholic High School, 500 E. College, 62650. Tel: 217-243-8563; Fax: 217-243-3138. Dr. Robert Clancy, Prin.
Lay Teachers 13; Students 146.
Catechesis/Religious Programs—Tel: 217-245-7633.
Students 149.

Jerseyville, Jersey Co., Holy Ghost (German), Rev. William Hembrow.
Res., 306 N. Washington St., 62052. Tel: 618-498-3416. [JC]
School—St. Francis/Holy Ghost School. See St. Francis. Tel: 618-498-4916.
Catechesis/Religious Programs—Students 195.

St. Francis Xavier (1857), Rev. William E. Kekeisen.
Res., 506 S. State St., P.O. Box 260, 62052-0260. Tel: 618-498-3518. [CEM][JC]
School—St. Francis/Holy Ghost School, Tel: 618-498-4823.
St. Francis: (Grades K & 5-8) 412 S. State St., 62052. Tel: 618-498-4823.; Holy Ghost: (Grades 1-4) 309 N. Washington St., 62052. Tel: 618-498-4910. Sr. Zita Telkamp, C.D.P., Prin.
Sisters 1; Lay Teachers 20; Students 358.
Catechesis/Religious Programs—Tel: 618-498-5497.
Students 38.

Kampsville, Calhoun Co., St. Anselm (1877) (German), Rev. Sylvano Pera, O.F.M.
Res., 404 Main St., P.O. Box C, Hardin, 62047. Tel: 618-576-2517. [CEM]

Kincaid, Christian Co., St. Rita (1920), Rev. Charles G. Dahlby.
Res., P.O. Box 439, 62540. Tel: 217-237-4339.
Catechesis/Religious Programs—Students 55.

Liberty, Adams Co., St. Brigid (1860), Rev. Anthony J. Thieman.
Church—P.O. Box 228, 62347. Tel: 217-645-3444. [CEM]
Res., #6 Paradise Ave., P.O. Box 228, 62347-0228.
Catechesis/Religious Programs—Sr. Joan Schorbus, C.PP.S., D.R.E.
Students 103.

Lillyville, Cumberland Co., Sacred Heart of Jesus (1877) (German), Rev. Emil G. Helfrich, O.M.I.
Mailing Address: 127 County Rd. 100 E., Sigel, 62462.
Res., R.R. 3, Box 162, Effingham, 62401. Tel: 217-844-2062. [CEM]
Catechesis/Religious Programs—Tel: 217-844-2221.
Students 67.

Litchfield, Montgomery Co., Holy Family (1988). Former St. Mary, founded in 1857. Rev. David L. Schmidt.
Res., 419 S. State St., 62056. Tel: 217-324-2776; Fax: 217-324-2868. [CEM]
Catechesis/Religious Programs—211 E. Columbia St., 62056. Tel: 217-324-5834.
Students 103.

Livingston, Madison Co., Sacred Heart (1913), Rev. George Radosevich Tel: 618-635-8490.
Res., 188 Livingston Ave., P.O. Box 458, 62058. Tel: 618-637-2211. [CEM]

Lovington, Moultrie Co., St. Mary. Closed. Sacramental records are located at Our Lady of the Holy Spirit.

Macon, Macon Co., St. Stanislaus (1866), Rev. Alan Hunter.
Res., 301 St. Peter St., Assumption, 62510. Tel: 217-226-3536; Fax: 217-226-3538. [JC]

Madison, Madison Co., Our Lady of Czestochowa (1912). (St. Mary). Rev. James Keefner, O.F.M., Admin.
Res., 1621 10th St., 62060. Tel: 618-452-5180. [JC]

Marine, Madison Co., St. Elizabeth (1856), Rev. James A. Flach.
Res., 120 N. Windmill St., P.O. Box 457, 62061. Tel: 618-887-4535. [CEM]
Catechesis/Religious Programs—4500 State Rte. 4, Alhambra, 62001. Tel: 618-887-4614. Evelyn Duffin, D.R.E.
Students 75.

Marshall, Clark Co., St. Mary (1847), Rev. Jeffery A. Grant, Admin.
Mailing Address: 414 S. Sixth St., 62441.
Res., 110 Lincoln Dr., P.O. Box 156, Greenup, 62428. Tel: 217-923-3523; 826-2845. [CEM]
Catechesis/Religious Programs—Students 115.

Maryville, Madison Co., Mother of Perpetual Help (1938), Rev. J. Michael Ewert, O.F.M.
Res., 200 N. Lange, 62062. Tel: 618-344-6464.
School—St. John Neumann School, Tel: 618-345-7230; Fax: 618-345-4350.
Springfield Dominican Sisters 1; Lay Teachers 16; Students 311.
Catechesis/Religious Programs—Tel: 618-344-9666.
Students 132.

Mattoon, Coles Co., Immaculate Conception (1856), Rev. Herman J. Niebrugge.
Res., 320 N. 21st St., P.O. Box 468, 61938-0468. Tel: 217-235-0539; Fax: 217-235-0593. [CEM]
School—Tel: 217-235-0431.
Lay Teachers 9; Students 169.
Catechesis/Religious Programs—Tel: 217-234-6648.
Students 103.

Medora, Macoupin Co., St. John the Evangelist (1914) (German), Rev. Raphael Paul, Admin.
Res., c/o St. Alphonsus Church, 918 N. Main St., Brighton, 62012. Tel: 217-372-3352; Fax: 618-372-8133.

Mendon, Adams Co., St. Edward (1890), Rev. Louis Schlangen.
Res., R.R. 1, Box 36, 62351. Tel: 217-936-2289. [CEM]
Catechesis/Religious Programs—Students 96.

Meppen, Calhoun Co., St. Joseph (1864), Rev. John Sullivan, O.F.M.
Office: P.O. Box 38, Brussels, 62013. Tel: 618-883-2400; Fax: 618-883-2511. [CEM]
Res., Meppen Ln., 62013. Tel: 618-883-2309.

Michael, Calhoun Co., St. Michael (1864) (German), Rev. Sylvano Pera, O.F.M.
Res., 404 Main St., P.O. Box C, Hardin, 62047. Tel: 618-576-2517. [CEM 2][JC]

Montrose, Effingham Co., St. Rose of Lima (1879), Revs. Lambert Leykem, O.F.M.; Patrick Curtis, O.F.M.
Mailing Address: P.O. Box 68, 62445. Tel: 217-924-4337. [CEM]
Catechesis/Religious Programs—Students 134.

Morrisonville, Christian Co., St. Maurice (1870), Rev. John T. Hannigan (CHI) Admin.
Res., 706 E. Fourth St., P.O. Box 45, 62546-0045. Tel: 217-526-3363; Fax: 217-526-3110. [CEM]

School—(Grades 1-8). Tel: 217-526-3534.
Lay Teachers 4; Students 51.
Catechesis/Religious Programs—Students 65.

Mount Olive, Macoupin Co., Ascension (1886) (Croatian), Rev. Larry Anschutz, Admin.
Res., 705 E. Main St., 62069. Tel: 217-999-4981. [CEM]
Catechesis/Religious Programs—Students 70.
Holy Trinity (1912) (Slovak), Rev. Larry Anschutz, Admin.
Res., 705 E. Main St., 62069. Tel: 217-999-4981. [CEM]

Mount Sterling, Brown Co., Holy Family (1864), Rev. Thomas Henseler.
Res., 401 W. North St., P.O. Box 252, 62353. Tel: 217-773-3233. [CEM]
School—Tel: 217-773-2825; Fax: 217-773-2825.
Lay Teachers 11; Students 122.
Catechesis/Religious Programs—Students 88.

Mt. Zion, Macon Co., Our Lady of the Holy Spirit (1976), Rev. James D. O'Shea.
Res., 400 Woodland, 62549. Tel: 217-864-3467; Fax: 217-864-3091.
Catechesis/Religious Programs—Tel: 217-864-4941.
Students 102.

Moweaqua, Shelby Co., St. Frances de Sales (1895), Rev. Alan Hunter.
Res., 301 St. Peter St., Assumption, 62510. Tel: 217-226-3536; Fax: 217-226-3538. [JC]

Murrayville, Morgan Co., St. Bartholomew (1883), Rev. Charles T. Nelson.
Res., P.O. Box 47, 62668. Tel: 217-882-3781. [CEM]

Neoga, Cumberland Co., St. Mary of the Assumption (1897), Rev. W. Jeffrey Holtman.
Res., Church St., P.O. Box 68, Sigel, 62462. Tel: 217-844-3371. [CEM]
Church—690 N. Walnut St., 62447. Tel: 217-895-2166.
Catechesis/Religious Programs—Students 96.

New Berlin, Sangamon Co., Sacred Heart of Mary (1858), Rev. Joseph P. Kerber.
Res., 404 E. Birch, P.O. Box 20, 62670. Tel: 217-488-2410; Fax: 217-488-2410. [CEM]
School—Tel: 217-488-3545.
Sisters of Notre Dame 1; Lay Teachers 6; Students 81.
Catechesis/Religious Programs—Students 85.

New Douglas, Madison Co., St. Ubaldus (1872), Rev. George Radosevich Tel: 618-635-8490.
Res., 322 E. Main St., Staunton, 62088. Tel: 618-635-8590. [CEM]

Newton, Jasper Co., St. Thomas (1873), Rev. Joseph Molloy.
Res., 402 W. Jourdan St., P.O. Box 225, 62448. Tel: 618-783-8741; Fax: 618-783-2224. [CEM 3]
School—Tel: 618-783-3517.
Lay Teachers 8; Students 126.
Catechesis/Religious Programs—Students 204.

Niantic, Macon Co., St. Ann (1889), Sr. Lois Kikkert, O.P., Parish Life Coord.
Mailing Address: P.O. Box 47, Illiopolis, 62539.
Res., 410 Anne St., Illiopolis, 62539. Tel: 217-486-3851. [JC]
Church—North St. & Macon St., 62551.

Nokomis, Montgomery Co., St. Louis (1870), Rev. Pat G. Jakel.
Res., 311 S. Elm St., 62075-1310. Tel: 217-563-7146; 563-7808 (Personal); Fax: 217-563-8671. [CEM]
School—509 E. Union, 62075. Tel: 217-563-7445.
Lay Teachers 7; Students 123.
Catechesis/Religious Programs—Students 68.

North Arm, Edgar Co., St. Aloysius (1817), Rev. William J. Overmann.
Res., P.O. Box 577, Paris, 61944. Tel: 217-466-3355; Fax: 217-463-3005. [CEM]

Oblong, Crawford Co., Our Lady of Lourdes (1954), Rev. Richard W. Weltin.
Res., 207 E. Walnut St., P.O. Box 428, Robinson, 62454. Tel: 618-544-7526.

Oconee, Shelby Co., Sacred Heart of Jesus (1872) (German), Rev. Don J. Roberts, Admin.
Res., P.O. Box 45, 62553. Tel: 217-539-4325. [CEM]

Palmyra, Macoupin Co., Holy Rosary (1954), Rev. August Sperl.
c/o Sacred Heart Church: 721 N. Springfield St., Virden, 62690. Tel: 217-965-4545.

Pana, Christian Co., St. Patrick (1858), Rev. Donald M. Cunningham, S.J.
Res., 6 E. Fifth St., P.O. Box 440, 62557. Tel: 217-562-5396; Fax: 217-562-2308. [CEM]
School—Sacred Heart, Tel: 217-562-2425. Mr. David L. Jones, Prin.
Lay Teachers 8; Students 164.
Catechesis/Religious Programs—Tel: 217-824-6120.
Students 54.

Panama, Bond Co., Sacred Heart (1916), Rev. Carl Schmidt.
Res., 400 Jefferson, P.O. Box 278, Coffeen, 62017. Tel: 217-534-2220. [JC]

Paris, Edgar Co., St. Mary (1849), Rev. William J. Overmann.
Res., P.O. Box 577, 528 N. Main St., 61944. Tel: 217-466-3355. [CEM]
School—Tel: 217-463-3005; Fax: 217-463-3005.
Lay Teachers 5; Students 84.
Catechesis/Religious Programs—Students 142.

Pawnee, Sangamon Co., St. Mary (1899) (Irish-German), Rev. Charles G. Dahlby.
Res., Tel: 217-237-4339. [CEM]
Catechesis/Religious Programs—Tel: 217-625-7540.
Students 87.

Petersburg, Menard Co., St. Peter (1868), Very Rev. Thomas P. Holinga, V.G.
Res., 711 S. Sixth St., 62675. Tel: 217-632-7118; Fax: 217-632-2561. [CEM]
Catechesis/Religious Programs—Students 226.

Pierron, Madison and Bond Cos., Immaculate Conception (1892), Rev. Msgr. Paul W. Sheridan.
Res., P.O. Box 25, 62273. Tel: 618-654-3604. [CEM]
Catechesis/Religious Programs—Students 102.

Pittsfield, Pike Co., Immaculate Conception (1870), Rev. Donald F. Sederwall.
Res., 226 E. Adams, 62363. Tel: 217-285-4321; Fax: 217-285-9400. [CEM][JC]
Catechesis/Religious Programs—Tel: 217-285-4774.
Students 83.

Pocahontas, Bond Co., St. Nicholas, Rev. Msgr. Paul W. Sheridan.
Res., P.O. Box 25, Pierron, 62273. Tel: 618-654-3604.

Quincy, Adams Co.,

1—St. Anthony of Padua, (1859), Revs. Richard Bendorf, O.F.M.; Irenaeus Kimminau, O.F.M.
Res., Quincy University, 1800 College Ave., 62301. Tel: 217-222-8020. [CEM]
Church—2223 St. Anthony Rd., 62301. Tel: 217-222-5996; Fax: 217-222-5996.
School—Tel: 217-224-6477.
Lay Teachers 5; Students 74.
Catechesis/Religious Programs—Students 104.

2—St. Boniface, (1837) (German), Rev. John Carberry.
Res., 117 N. Seventh St., 62301. Tel: 217-222-3000. [JC]
School—Tel: 217-223-6999.
Lay Teachers 6; Students 74.

3—St. Dominic, (1977), Rev. Donald Knuffman.
Res., 3800 Columbus Rd., P.O. Box 3364, 62301. Tel: 217-224-9102. [JC]
Church—4100 Columbus Rd., 62301.
School—Tel: 217-224-0041.
Lay Teachers 12; Students 215.

4—St. Francis Solanus, (1860), Revs. Austin Albers, O.F.M.; Eugene Middendorf, O.F.M.; Michael Barrett, O.F.M.
Res., 1721 College Ave., 62301. Tel: 217-222-2898; Fax: 217-222-2948. [JC]
School—Lay Teachers 11; Students 312.
Catechesis/Religious Programs—1721 College Ave., 62301. Tel: 217-222-4077.
Students 106.

5—St. John the Baptist, (1880) (German), Rev. John P. Beveridge.
Res., 1019 Cedar St., P.O. Box 3505, 62305-3505. Tel: 217-222-4622; Fax: 217-222-5554. [JC]
School—(Grades PreK-8). Tel: 217-228-1477.
Lay Teachers 9; Students 235.
Catechesis/Religious Programs—Students 10.

6—St. Joseph, (1868), Revs. Richard Bendorf, O.F.M.; Irenaeus Kimminau, O.F.M.
Res., Quincy University, 1800 College Ave., 62301. Tel: 217-228-5429.
Church—R.R. 1, 62301. Tel: 217-434-8442. [CEM]
Catechesis/Religious Programs—Students 134.

7—St. Mary, (1867). (Immaculate Conception). Rev. Michael Kuse.
Res., 1119 S. Seventh St., 62301. Tel: 217-222-2759; Fax: 217-222-6463. [JC]
School—Tel: 217-223-3388.
Lay Teachers 10; Students 213.
Catechesis/Religious Programs—Students 100.

8—St. Peter, (1839) (Irish), Rev. Roy R. Bauer.
Res., 2600 Maine St., 62301. Tel: 217-222-3155; Fax: 217-222-3584. [JC]
School—Tel: 217-223-1120.
Lay Teachers 26; Students 589.
Catechesis/Religious Programs—Students 112.

9—St. Rose of Lima, (1892) (Irish), Rev. Charles A. Edwards, Admin.
Res., P.O. Box 370, 62306-0370. Tel: 217-222-2511. [JC]

Ramsey, Fayette Co., St. Joseph (1870) (German-Irish), Rev. Don J. Roberts.
Res., 118 E. Main, P.O. Box 455, 62080. Tel: 618-423-2424. [CEM]
Catechesis/Religious Programs—Students 36.

Raymond, Montgomery Co., St Raymond (1881), Rev. William Maul.
Res., 306 S. McElroy, P.O. Box 349, 62560. Tel: 217-229-4435. [CEM]
Catechesis/Religious Programs—Students 88.

Riverton, Sangamon Co., St. James (1871), Co-Pastors: Very Revs. John A. Renken, V.G.; Kenneth C. Steffen.
Res., 112 N. Sixth St., P.O. Box 590, 62561-0590. Tel: 217-629-9109 (Rectory); 629-7717 (Office).
Catechesis/Religious Programs—Tel: 217-629-7717. Mrs. Karen Buckman, D.R.E.
Students 165.

Robinson, Crawford Co., St. Elizabeth (1908), Rev. Richard W. Weltin.
Res., 207 E. Walnut St., 62454. Tel: 618-544-7526.
Catechesis/Religious Programs—Tel: 618-544-9327.
Students 215.

Rochester, Sangamon Co., Church of St. Jude (1976), Rev. Patrick Cahill, C.S.V.
Res., 633 S. Walnut St., 62563. Tel: 217-498-9197; Fax: 217-498-7180.
Parish Center: 635 S. Walnut St., 62563. Tel: 217-498-9524.
Catechesis/Religious Programs—Students 220.

St. Elmo, Fayette Co., St. Bonaventure (1843), Revs. Angel Sierra, Admin.; John M. Savoree.
Res., 216 N. Ninth, Altamont, 62411. Tel: 618-483-5346. [CEM]
Catechesis/Religious Programs—Students 144.
St. Mary (1904), Revs. Angel Sierra, Admin.; John M. Savoree.
Res., 216 N. Ninth, Altamont, 62411. Tel: 618-483-6464.

St. Jacob, Madison Co., St. James (1894), Rev. James A. Flach.
Res., 120 N. Windmill St., Box 457, Marine, 62061. Tel: 618-887-4535.
Catechesis/Religious Programs—111 Bethel Mine Rd., Caseyville, 62232. Tel: 618-345-4779. Lori Nicholas, D.R.E.
Students 76.

Ste. Marie, Jasper Co., St. Mary of the Assumption (1837) (French-German), Sr. Ancilla Caulfield, O.P., Parish Life Coord.
Res., P.O. Box 68, 62459. Tel: 618-455-3155. [CEM]
Catechesis/Religious Programs—P.O. Box 68, 112 W. Embarras St., 62459.
Students 102.
Mission—Oblong, Crawford Co., St. Valentine's Chapel, Oblong, 62449.

Shelbyville, Shelby Co., Immaculate Conception (1879), Res., N. First at Washington St., P.O. Box 233, 62565. Tel: 217-774-3434.
Catechesis/Religious Programs—Students 85.

Sherman, Sangamon Co., St. John Vianney (1934), Rev. Eugene E. Costa.
Res., 129 Stardust Dr., P.O. Box 229, 62684. Tel: 217-523-3816; Fax: 217-523-3954.
Catechesis/Religious Programs—Students 97.

Shipman, Macoupin Co., St. Denis (1876), Rev. Robert N. Porter.
Res., P.O. Box A H, Bunker Hill, 62014-9512. Tel: 618-585-4700; Fax: 618-585-3449. [CEM]

Shumway, Effingham Co., Church of the Annunciation (1879), Rev. Alexis Pruemer, O.F.M.
Res., P.O. Box 96, 62461. Tel: 217-857-6404. [CEM]
Catechesis/Religious Programs—Students 85.

Sigel, Shelby Co., St. Michael the Archangel (1867), Rev. W. Jeffrey Holtman.
Res., Box 68, 62462. Tel: 217-844-3371. [CEM]
School—Tel: 217-844-2231.
Sisters 1; Lay Teachers 8; Students 167.
Catechesis/Religious Programs—Students 224.

Staunton, Macoupin Co., St. Michael (1875), Rev. George Radosevich.
Office: P.O. Box 240, 62088. Tel: 618-635-3140; Fax: 618-635-3140.
Res., 322 E. Main, 62088.
Tel: 618-635-8490. [JC 2]

School—419 E. Main, 62088. Tel: 618-635-3210. Religious 1; Lay Teachers 6; Students 86.
Catechesis/Religious Programs—Students 162.

Stonington, Christian Co., Holy Trinity (1879) (Irish-German), Rev. Martin O'Hara.
Mailing Address: P.O. Box 257, 62567. Tel: 217-325-3697.
Res., 108 N. Elm, P.O. Box 257, 62567.
Church—308 N. Elm St., 62567. Tel: 217-325-3691.
Catechesis/Religious Programs—Students 61.

Sullivan, Moultrie Co., St. Columcille (1905), Rev. John E. Sohm.
Res., 516 W. Jackson, P.O. Box 464, 61951. Tel: 217-728-4040.
Catechesis/Religious Programs—Students 73.

Taylorville, Christian Co., St. Mary (1845), Rev. John O'Connell.
Res., 116 W. Adams St., P.O. Box 470, 62568. Tel: 217-824-8178.
School—(Grades PreK-6). Tel: 217-824-6501.
Lay Teachers 11; Students 198.
Catechesis/Religious Programs—Students 181.

Teutopolis, Effingham Co., St. Francis of Assisi (1839), Very Rev. Lambert Leykam, O.F.M.; Revs. Vitus J. Duschinsky, O.F.M.; Patrick Curtis, O.F.M.; Bros. Paulinus Johnson, O.F.M.; James Lause, O.F.M.
Res., 203 E. Main St., P.O. Box 730, 62467. Tel: 217-857-6404; Fax: 217-857-1031. [CEM]
Catechesis/Religious Programs—Tel: 217-857-6477; 857-1500. D.R.E.: Sr. Ann Vincent Siemer, S.S.N.D., (Grade School); Mrs. Maureen Broeker, (High School).
Students 1,088.

Troy, Madison Co., St. Jerome (1881), Rev. Steven A. Janoski.
Res., 511 S. Main, P.O. Box 94, 62294. Tel: 618-667-3397; Fax: 618-667-2697. [CEM 2]
School—St. John Neumann, Maryville, Tel: 618-345-7200; Fax: 618-345-4350.
Catechesis/Religious Programs—107 Wayland, 62294. Tel: 618-667-6571; Fax: 618-667-2697. Judy Werp, D.R.E.
Students 350.

Tuscola, Douglas Co., Forty Martyrs (1865), Rev. Michael D. Mullink; Sr. Pyllis Schenk, O.P.
Res., 201 E. Van Allen St., P.O. Box 352, 61953. Tel: 217-253-4412; Fax: 217-253-5010.
Catechesis/Religious Programs—Students 206.

Vandalia, Fayette Co., Mother of Dolors (1850), Rev. Stephen T. Sotiroff.
Res., 322 N. Seventh St., P.O. Box 377, 62471. Tel: 618-283-0214; Fax: 618-283-0751. [CEM]
Catechesis/Religious Programs—Students 129.

Venice, Madison Co., St. Mark (1871), Rev. Delix Michel (Haiti).
Res., Sixth and Broadway, 62090. Tel: 618-451-1411. [JC]

Villa Grove, Douglas Co., Sacred Heart (1906), Rev. Paul H. Skelton.
Res., 208 N. Pine, Box 17, 61956. Tel: 217-832-8352.
Catechesis/Religious Programs—Students 83.
Mission—Hume, Edgar Co., St. Michael's, Center St., Hume, 61932. Tel: 217-887-2482.

Virden, Macoupin Co., Sacred Heart (1914) (Slovak). St. Catherine's (1866)- Merged in 1978. Rev. August J. Sperl.
Res., 721 N. Springfield, 62690. Tel: 217-965-4545.
Catechesis/Religious Programs—Students 108.

Virginia, Cass Co., St. Luke (1840), Rev. Ken J. Venvertloh.
Res., 240 E. Myrtle St., 62691. Tel: 217-452-7529.
Catechesis/Religious Programs—Students 58.

Waverly, Morgan Co., St. Sebastian (1856), Rev. Daniel E. LaCount.
Office and Residence: 125 E. Washington St., Auburn, 62615. Tel: 217-438-6222. [CEM]

White Hall, Greene Co., All Saints (1883), Rev. Barry J. Harmon.
Res., c/o St. John, 414 Third St., Carrollton, 62016. Tel: 217-942-3551; Fax: 217-942-6767.
Church—S. Main St., 62092.

Wilsonville, Macoupin Co., Holy Cross (1854), Rev. Robert N. Porter.
Res., 300 S. Putnam, P.O. Box A-H, Bunker Hill, 62014-9512. Tel: 618-585-4700; Fax: 618-585-3449.

Winchester, Scott Co., St. Mark (1860), Rev. Charles T. Nelson.
Res., 108 Pearl St., 62694. Tel: 217-742-5224. [CEM]

Witt, Montgomery Co., St. Barbara (1905), Rev. Pat G. Jakel.
Res., 311 S. Elm St., Nokomis, 62075-1310. Tel: 217-563-7146; 563-7808 (Personal); Fax: 217-563-8671. [CEM]

Wood River, Madison Co., St. Bernard (1919), Rev. James L. Neuman.
Res., 345 Acton Ave., 62095. Tel: 618-254-0679 (Office); Fax: 618-254-2690.
School—Tel: 618-254-2697.
Lay Teachers 10; Students 157.
Catechesis/Religious Programs—Students 68.

Chaplains of Public Institutions

ALTON. *Alton State Hospital*. Vacant. St. Matthew Parish, 1015 Milton Rd., 62002. Tel: 618-465-8582.

HILLSBORO. *Graham Correctional Center*. 306 S. McElroy, P.O. Box 349, Raymond, 62560. Tel: 217-229-4435. Rev. George L. Morelock, Chap.

JACKSONVILLE. *Illinois State Hospital*. Attended by Our Savior Parish. 462 E. State St., 62650. Tel: 217-245-6184.
School for the Blind. Attended by Our Savior Parish. 462 E. State St., 62650. Tel: 217-245-6184.
School for the Deaf. Attended by Our Savior Parish. 462 E. State St., 62650. Tel: 217-245-6184.

MOUNT STERLING. *Western Illinois Correctional Center*. Attended by Holy Family Parish. 401 W. North St., 62353. Tel: 217-773-3233.

QUINCY. *Illinois Veterans' Home* 1901 N. 18th, 62301. Tel: 217-224-0591. Rev. Richard M. Jeske, O.F.M.

TAYLORVILLE. *Taylorville Correctional Center*. Attended by St. Mary Parish. 116 W. Adams St., P.O. Box 248, 62658. Tel: 217-824-8178.

VANDALIA. *Vandalia Correctional Center*. Attended by Mother of Dolors Parish. 322 N. Seventh, 62471. Tel: 618-283-0214.

On Duty Outside the Diocese:
Reverend Fathers—
Chiola, Richard, St. John's University, Collegeville, MN 56821
Habing, Paul, Prelatura, Apt. 102, Ayaviri-Puno, Peru
Meyer, Bernard A., 2425 Sage Rd., Apt. 45, Houston, TX 77056. Tel: 713-629-4822
Porter, Robert G., St. Rose of Lima Church, 226 S. Atlantic St., Dillon, MN 59725. Tel: 406-683-4391
Trojcak, Ronald, 59 Orkney Crescent, London, Ontario N5X 3R7 Canada
Westhoff, Frank D., P.O. Box 715, Columbia, MO 65205. Tel: 314-445-5335

Military Chaplains:
Reverend Fathers—
Blickhan, Donald, Chap., U.S. Army.
Gallenbach, Thomas, Chap., U.S. Air Force
Nolan, John, Chap., U.S. Air Force

Special or Other Diocesan Assignment:
Kraft, Philip, 929 Rickard Rd. Ct., Box 7492, Springfield, IL 62791. Tel: 217-793-3218

Unassigned:
Simburger, R. Joseph

Absent on Leave:
Reverend Fathers—
Cernich, Joseph
DeGrand, Robert
Lichtenberger, Doug
Poterucha, Michael
Schaver, David
Schwellenbach, Aloysius

Retired:
Reverend Monsignors—
Bretz, John W., St. Joseph's Home, 3306 S. Sixth St., Springfield, IL 62703. Tel: 217-529-4883
Heinen, Paul, P.O. Box 363, Jerseyville, IL 62052. Tel: 618-498-2208
Plocki, Robert, 191 Steward Dr., Tiburnon, CA 94920. Tel: 415-435-2731
Toliusis, Casimir, 624 Sumner St., Carlinville, IL 62626. Tel: 217-854-7314
Will, Irvin R., 100 Marian Pkwy., Sherman, IL 62684
Reverend Fathers—
Campbell, John, 295 Mellody Rd., Lake Forest, IL 60045. Tel: 708-295-1875
Corrigan, F. J., 1625 W. Washington, Springfield, IL 62702. Tel: 217-793-0515
Damjanov, Zvonimir, c/o Olga Milicic, A.B. Simica 8, 21213 Kastel Gomilica, Croatia-Hruatiska. Tel: 011-385-21-220-239
Davenport, Thomas J., 1625 W. Washington, Springfield, IL 62702. Tel: 217-793-0515
Donohoe, Peter, 714 Douglas Pl., Alton, IL 62002. Tel: 618-463-0521
Gierut, Casimir, P.O. Box 156, Westmont, IL 60559
Heintz, Robert L., 422 Foulds Ave., Alton, IL 62002. Tel: 618-462-9747
Higgins, Patrick O., 76 Centre Dr., Manhasset, NY 11030
Houran, J. William, 3233 N.E. 32nd Ave., Apt. 902, Fort Lauderdale, FL 33308. Tel: 305-566-9802
Keane, Brendan, 9504 Windsor Club Cir., Fort Myers, FL 33903. Tel: 941-693-7172
Kennedy, John, 60 Spring Lake Estates, Quincy, IL 62301. Tel: 217-224-5288
Kondrath, James A., 9412 Francisco, Evergreen Park, IL 60642. Tel: 708-425-7164
Lee, Francis, 636 Hampshire St., Quincy, IL 62301. Tel: 217-223-1200
Mack, Henry J., 38742 N. Drexel Blvd., Antioch, IL 60002. Tel: 312-395-1949
Mascari, Peter, 115 Stardust Dr., Sherman, IL 62684. Tel: 217-789-0611
McCarthy, Joseph F., 130 Curtis Ave., Burlington, VT 05401
Miller, Joseph, 127 Stardust Dr., Sherman, IL 62684. Tel: 217-523-5803
Mulcrone, Charles, 1625 W. Washington, Springfield, IL 62702. Tel: 217-698-4857
O'Reilly, Joseph, 1319 Tendick St., #3, Jacksonville, IL 62650-3120
Quilligan, Maurice, 905 Andra Dr., Maryville, IL 62062. Tel: 618-344-5164
Rieck, Raymond, 632 Sheridan Dr., Venice, FL 34292
Schmidt, Anthony, 520 S. Second St., #906, Lincoln Tower Suites, Springfield, IL 62701
Sheahan, John F., Marian Heights Apartments, 20 Marian Hills Dr., Alton, IL 62002. Tel: 618-465-9209
Simpson, Roger, 271 E. Myrtle St., Virginia, IL 62691. Tel: 217-452-3168
Sullivan, James, 10311 Mason Ave., Oak Lawn, IL 60453-4335
Tamulis, Anthony J., 412 W. Fourth St., Mount Olive, IL 62069
Tracey, Terence, St. Francis Convent, Sangamon Ave., Springfield, IL 62794-9431

INSTITUTIONS LOCATED IN THE DIOCESE

[A] SEMINARIES, RELIGIOUS OR SCHOLASTICATES

GODFREY. *Immaculate Heart of Mary Novitiate*, 4563 Levis Ln., 62035. Tel: 618-466-2233; Fax: 618-466-2430. Revs. Lorne T. McDonald, O.M.I.; Stephen Conserva, O.M.I.; Darrell Rupiper, O.M.I. Priests 3; Clerical Novices 10.

[B] COLLEGES AND UNIVERSITIES

QUINCY. *Quincy University*, (1860) 1800 College Ave., 62301. Tel: 217-222-8020; 228-5318.
Web site: www.quincy.edu
For a complete listing, refer to the Colleges and Universities section.

[C] JUNIOR COLLEGES

SPRINGFIELD. *Springfield College in Illinois*, 1500 N. Fifth St., 62702. Tel: 217-525-1420
For a complete listing, refer to the Colleges and Universities section.

[D] HIGH SCHOOLS, PRIVATE

SPRINGFIELD. *Sacred Heart-Griffin*, 1200 W. Washington St., 62702. Tel: 217-787-1595; Fax: 217-787-9856.
Web site: www.shg.org
Springfield Dominican Sisters. Sr. Kathleen Anne Tait, O.P., Prin.; Sr. Margaret Joanne Grueter, Vice Prin. Priests 4; Brothers 1; Sisters 14; Lay Teachers 53; Students 883.
Ursuline Academy, 1400 N. Fifth St., 62702. Tel: 217-523-5169; Fax: 217-523-2131. Dr. Karen Hunter Anderson. Priests 1; Ursuline Sisters 1; Lay Teachers 21; Students 260.

ALTON. *Marquette Catholic High School*, 219 E. Fourth St., 62002. Tel: 618-463-0580. John L. Rogers, Prin. Brothers 1; Sisters 1; Lay Teachers 27; Students 349.

DECATUR. *St. Teresa High School*, 2710 N. Water St., 62526. Tel: 217-875-2431. Mr. Lowell Brosamer, Prin. Priests 1; Ursuline Sisters 1; Lay Teachers 24; Students 306.

EFFINGHAM. *St. Anthony High School*, 304 E. Roadway Ave., P.O. Box 545, 62401. Tel: 217-342-6969.
E-mail: sahs@stanthony.com
Web site: www.stanthony.com
Priests 1; Lay Teachers 15; Students 229.

JACKSONVILLE. *Routt Catholic High School*, 500 E. College, 62650. Tel: 217-243-8563. Lay Teachers 14; Students 146.

QUINCY. *Quincy Notre Dame High School*, 1400 S. 11th, 62301-7299. Tel: 217-223-2479; Fax: 217-223-0023. Ray E. Heilmann, Prin. School Sisters of Notre Dame 1; Lay Teachers 31; Students 522.

[E] HIGH SCHOOLS, PAROCHIAL

SPRINGFIELD. High Schools are maintained in the following parishes (for particulars refer to the individual parish listing): St. Anthony, Effingham; Our Saviour, Jacksonville.

[F] THE CATHOLIC CHARITIES OF THE DIOCESE OF SPRINGFIELD IN ILLINOIS

SPRINGFIELD. *Catholic Charities of Springfield*, 120 S. 11th St., 62703. Tel: 217-525-0500. Mary Stone, Area Dir. Total Assisted 12,065; Total Staff 58.
Community Services, 108 E. Cook St., 62704. Tel: 217-523-4551.
Clinic For Kids, 502 N. Sixth St., 62702. Tel: 217-523-1474.
St. John's Breadline, 430 N. Fifth St., 62702. Tel: 217-528-6048.
St. John's Breadline, 430 N. Fifth St., 62702. Tel: 217-528-6098. Meals Served Annually 160,000.
Society of St. Vincent de Paul (Diocesan Central Council), 800 S. Fifth St., 62703. Tel: 217-523-9201.

ALTON. *Alton Catholic Charities*, 735 Park Dr., 62002. Tel: 618-462-0634; Fax: 618-462-3209. Rick Faccin, Area Dir. Total Assisted 620; Total Staff 13.

CARLINVILLE. *Carlinville Catholic Charities*, 525 W. Second S., 62626. Tel: 217-854-4511; Fax: 217-854-8049. Ms. Patricia Pope, Area Dir. Total Assisted 265; Total Staff 12.

DECATUR. *Catholic Charities Community Services*, 401 N. Martin Luther King Jr. Dr., 62523. Tel: 217-428-5724. Judy Rogers, On Site Supvr.; Marie Rademacher, Area Dir. Total Assisted 11,838; Total Staff 1.
Decatur Catholic Charities, 247 W. Prairie Ave., 62523. Tel: 217-428-3458; Fax: 217-428-4415. Mrs. Marie Rademacher, Area Dir. Total Assisted 16,000; Total Staff 30.

EFFINGHAM. *Catholic Charities of Effingham*, 601 W. Fayette, 62401. Tel: 217-342-9800; Fax: 217-342-3873. Sr. Beth Marie Ruder, D.C., Area Dir. Total Assisted 1,536; Total Staff 12.

GRANITE CITY. *Quad-Cities Catholic Charities*, 2105 State St., 62040. Tel: 618-877-1184; Fax: 618-877-1890. Mr. David Daly, Area Dir. Total Assisted 4,226; Total Staff 13.

QUINCY. *Catholic Social Services*, 926 State St., 62301. Tel: 217-222-0958; Fax: 217-222-8737. Sr. Mary Shaw, A.S.C., Area Dir. Total Assisted 280; Total Staff 13.

[G] CHILDREN'S HOMES

ALTON. *Catholic Children's Home*, 1400 State St., 62002. Tel: 618-465-3594; Fax: 618-465-4023.
E-mail: cch1400@ezl.com
For a complete listing, refer to the Special Care Facilities section.

[H] GENERAL HOSPITALS

SPRINGFIELD. *St. John's Hospital*, 800 E. Carpenter St., 62769. Tel: 217-544-6464.
E-mail: alaabs@st-johns.org
For a complete listing, refer to the Hospitals section.

ALTON. *Saint Anthony's Health Center*, Saint Anthony's Way, P.O. Box 340, 62002-0340. Tel: 618-465-2571
For a complete listing, refer to the Hospitals section.

DECATUR. *St. Mary's Hospital*, 1800 E. Lake Shore Dr., 62521. Tel: 217-464-2966; Fax: 217-464-1616
For a complete listing, refer to the Hospitals section.

EFFINGHAM. *St. Anthony's Memorial Hospital*, 503 N. Maple St., 62401. Tel: 217-342-2121
For a complete listing, refer to the Hospitals section.

GRANITE CITY. *St. Elizabeth Medical Center*, 2100 Madison Ave., 62040. Tel: 618-798-3000; Fax: 618-798-3508
For a complete listing, refer to the Hospitals section.

HIGHLAND. *St. Joseph's Hospital*, 1515 Main St., 62249. Tel: 618-654-7421; Fax: 618-654-2012
For a complete listing, refer to the Hospitals section.

LITCHFIELD. *St. Francis Hospital*, 1215 Franciscan Dr., P.O. Box 1215, 62056. Tel: 217-324-2191
For a complete listing, refer to the Hospitals section.

TAYLORVILLE. *St. Vincent Memorial Hospital*, 201 E. Pleasant St., 62568. Tel: 217-824-3331; Fax: 217-824-2099
For a complete listing, refer to the Hospitals section.

[I] SPECIAL CARE INSTITUTIONS

SPRINGFIELD. *Brother James Court*, 2500 St. James Rd., 62707. Tel: 217-544-4876.
E-mail: bjcicfdd@aol.com
For a complete listing, refer to the Special Care Facilities section.
St. Monica's Center, 109 E. Lawrence Ave., 62704. Tel: 217-523-7922; Fax: 217-525-8241
For a complete listing, refer to the Special Care Facilities section.

[J] HOMES FOR AGED

SPRINGFIELD. *Pope John Paul Apartments*, 1 Pope John Paul Plaza, 62703. Tel: 217-528-1771; Fax: 217-528-5110
For a complete listing, refer to the Special Care Facilities section.
St. Joseph's Home, 3306 S. Sixth St. Rd., 62703. Tel: 217-529-5596
For a complete listing, refer to the Special Care Facilities section.

ALTON. *Marian Heights Apartments*, 20 Marian Heights Dr., 62002. Tel: 618-462-0363
For a complete listing, refer to the Special Care Facilities section.

[K] MONASTERIES AND RESIDENCES OF PRIESTS AND BROTHERS

SPRINGFIELD. *Franciscan Brothers of the Holy Cross*, 2500 St. James Rd., 62707. Tel: 217-544-4876.
E-mail: ffsc@aol.com
Bro. Raphael Kreikemeier, F.F.S.C., Supr.
Priests' Purgatorial Society, Catholic Pastoral Center, 1615 W. Washington, P.O. Box 3187, 62708-3187. Tel: 217-698-8500.
Priests' Retirement Facility, Catholic Pastoral Center, 1625 W. Washington, 62702. Tel: 217-793-0515. Revs. Thomas J. Davenport; Francis J. Corrigan; Charles P. Mulcrone. Priests 3.

QUINCY. *St. Francis Solanus Friary*, 1721 College Ave., 62301. Tel: 217-222-2898. Revs. Austin Albers, O.F.M., Pastor; Eugene Middendorf, O.F.M.; Michael Barrett, O.F.M., Guardian & Supr. Priests 3.

SHERMAN. *Our Lady of Angels Friary*, 59 Woodsmill Dr., 62684. Tel: 217-496-2803; 496-2066. Retirement Community of Our Lady of Friars Minor (Sacred Heart Province). Bro. Joseph Sandlin, Guardian; Revs. Ralph Zetzl, Vicar; Owen Blum, O.F.M.; William Barnickel, O.F.M.; Roger Niemeyer, O.F.M.; Laurin Buzynski, O.F.M.; Hugolinus Kiener, O.F.M.; Walfrid Boesche, O.F.M.; Fabiano Merz, O.F.M.; Ralph Scherrer, O.F.M.; Ianatius Eckelkamp, O.F.M.; Warren Peternel, O.F.M.; Apollinaris Wackenheim, O.F.M.; Donulus Wunderlich, O.F.M.; Cecil Koop, O.F.M.; John Ostdiek, O.F.M.; Humbert Korgie, O.F.M.; Ladislas Siekaniec, O.F.M.; Bros. Justin Deken, O.F.M.; Kevin O'Connell, O.F.M.; Patrick Shea, O.F.M.; Denis Snelling, O.F.M.; Francis Stein, O.F.M.; Joseph Weithman, O.F.M.

TEUTOPOLIS. *St. Francis Assisi Friary*, 203 E. Main St., P.O. Box 730, 62467-0730. Tel: 217-857-6404; Fax: 217-857-1031. Revs. Lambert Leykam, O.F.M.; Vitus J. Duschinsky, O.F.M.; Patrick Curtis, O.F.M.; Cal Giesen, O.F.M.; Alexis Pruemer, O.F.M.; Theodore Bracco, O.F.M.; Edwin O. Albers, O.F.M.; Bros. Paulinus Johnson, O.F.M.; James Lause, O.F.M., Theologian. Priests 6.

[L] CONVENTS AND RESIDENCES FOR SISTERS

SPRINGFIELD. *Convent of Our Lady of the Sacred Heart*, 1237 W. Monroe St., 62704. Tel: 217-787-0481. Legal Title: *Dominican Sisters of Springfield in Illinois*. Motherhouse of the Springfield Dominican Sisters. Motherhouse and Novitiate of the Dominican Sisters of Springfield in Illinois. Sr. Mary Jean Traeger, O.P., Prioress Gen.; Sr. Judith Hilbing, O.P., Vicaress Gen.; Sr. M. Regina Graham, O.P., Prioress; Rev. John H. Gerlach, O.P., Chap. Sisters in the Congregation 330; in Motherhouse 116; Novices 5.
Daughters of Divine Love Congregation, 2523 St. James Rd., 62707. Tel: 217-528-2418. Sr. Mary Henry, D.D.L. Sisters 4.
St. Francis Convent, 4849 LaVerna Rd., P.O. Box 19431, 62794-9431. Tel: 217-522-3386. Motherhouse of the Hospital Sisters of the Third Order of St. Francis. Mailing Address: P.O. Box 19431, 62794-9431. Sr. Bernadine Gutowski, O.S.F., Prov. Supr.; Sr. Mary Kelly, O.S.F., Religious Coord. Chaplains: Revs. Terence Tracey; John Ostdiek. Sisters 163. Other Locations: 2101 Shabbona, 62702. Tel: 217-789-4936. Sisters 3. 2405 Shabbona, 62702. Tel: 217-525-2137. Sisters 3. 2501 Sherborn Rd., 62702. Tel: 217-528-6492. Sisters 2. 4145 Sunderland Dr., Decatur, 62526. Tel: 217-877-2278. Sisters 4. 4309 Leslie Ln., Decatur, 62526. Tel: 217-875-2147. Sisters 3. 710 St. Anthony Ave., Effingham, 62401. Tel: 217-342-2873. Sisters 4. 1635 Main St., Highland, 62249. Tel: 618-654-9759. 52 Fairview, 62704. Tel: 217-529-3050. 75 Sunflower Dr., Highland, 62249. Tel: 618-654-9759. Sisters 3.
Ursuline Convent, 1400 N. Fifth St., 62702. Tel: 217-789-7910. Ursuline Nuns of the Roman Union in Community 35.

ALTON. *St. Francis Convent*, 2120 Central Ave., P.O. Box 9020, 62002-9020. Tel: 618-463-2750. Headquarters of the Province St. Elizabeth and Novitiate of the Sisters of St. Francis of the Martyr St. George. Mother M. Ingeborg, O.S.F., Prov. Final Professed 68 (in US + 36 in Brazil); Junior Professed 24 (in US + 8 in Brazil); Novices 10 (in US + 6 in Brazil); Postulants 5 (in US).
Ursuline Convent of the Holy Family of the Ursuline Nuns of the Roman Union, 845 Danforth St., 62002. Tel: 618-465-9112. Sr. Theresa Davey, O.S.U., Prioress. Sisters 24. Ursuline Infirmary, 845 Danforth St., 62002. Tel: 618-465-0791. Sr. Elizabeth Carpentier. Sisters 34.

[M] NEWMAN CENTERS

CARLINVILLE. *Blackburn College*, State Route 108 East, P.O. Box 647, 62626. Tel: 217-854-7151.

CHARLESTON. *Eastern Illinois University Newman Center*, 909 E. Lincoln Ave., 61920. Tel: 217-348-0188. Rev. Robert L. Meyer, Chap.; Mr. Roy Lanham, Dir.; Mrs. Holly Walters, Volunteer Coord.

DECATUR. *Millikin University Newman Catholic Community*, P.O. Box 2697, 62524-2697. Tel: 217-877-4146. Rev. Dennis D. Kollross, Chap.

EDWARDSVILLE. *Southern Illinois University Catholic Campus Ministry*, P.O. Box 1059, 62026-1059. Tel: 618-692-3246.
E-mail: catholic@siue.edu
Web site: www.siue.edu/STACTV/NEWMAN/nsu.html
Mr. Nassef Girgis, Dir. Total Staff 1.

GODFREY. *Lewis and Clark Junior College Newman Center*.
E-mail: catholic@siue.edu
P.O. Box 1059, Edwardsville, 62026-1059. Tel: 618-692-3246. Mr. Nassef Girgis, Dir.

JACKSONVILLE. *Illinois College Newman Center*, 462 E. State St., 62650. Tel: 217-245-6184. Rev. Thomas Hagstrom, Chap.
MacMurray College Newman Center, 462 E. State St., 62650. Tel: 217-245-6184. Rev. Thomas Hagstrom, Chap.

[N] MISCELLANEOUS LISTINGS

SPRINGFIELD. *Catholic Care Center, Inc.*, One Pope John Paul Plaza, 62703. Tel: 217-528-1771; Fax: 217-528-5110. Mr. Leo A. Lenn, Pres. Directors: John Maxwell, Treas.; Ramon Robertson, Vice Pres.; James Forstall, Sec.; Bob Budnik; Hugh Graham, III; Thomas Reiser, Exec. Sec.; Sr. Joan Winkler, D.S.F.; Mrs. Eugena Costa.
Diocesan Care Management, Inc., 1 Pope John Paul Plaza, 62703. Tel: 217-528-1771; Fax: 217-528-5110. Most Rev. Daniel L. Ryan, J.C.L., D.D., Pres.; Mr. Leo Lenn, Dir.
Foundation for the People of the Diocese of Springfield in Illinois, Catholic Pastoral Center, 1615 W. Washington, 62702. Legal Title: *The Foundation for the People of the Roman Catholic Diocese of Springfield in Illinois*.
Hospital Sisters Health System, 4936 LaVerna Rd., P.O. Box 19431, 62794-9431. Tel: 217-523-4747. Sr. Jomary Trstensky, O.S.F., Pres.
Hospital Sisters of St. Francis Foundation, Inc., 4936 LaVerna Rd., P.O. Box 19431, 62794-9431. Tel: 217-523-4747. Sr. Jomary Trstensky, O.S.F., Contact Person.
Hospital Sisters Services, Inc., 4936 LaVerna Rd., P.O. Box 19431, 62794-9431. Tel: 217-523-4747. Sr. Jomary Trstensky, O.S.F., Pres.
Hunger, Inc., 800 S. Fifth St., 62703. Tel: 217-253-9201. Most Rev. Daniel L. Ryan, Chm.
Leadership Conference of Women Religious Region 8, 1237 W. Monroe, 62704. Tel: 217-787-9914; Fax: 217-787-8106. Sr. Barbara Nelson, I.B.V.M., Chm.; Sr. Margaret Mary Kopish, A.S.C., Vice Chair; Sr. Mary Jean Traeger, O.P., Sec.; Sr. Karen Bland, O.S.B., Treas.
Sponsored Activity: Project IRENE. 1237 W. Monroe, 62704. Tel: 217-787-9914; Fax: 217-787-8106.
E-mail: irene@dio.org
Sr. Marcelline Koch, O.P., Project Dir.
Legion of Mary, 945 S. 4th St., 62702. Tel: 217-528-5268. Betty Pishlar, Comitium Pres.
**Springfield Developmental Center Ltd.*, 2500 St. James Rd., 62707. Tel: 217-525-8271.
E-mail: sdcstjames@aol.com
Developmental Training Program for Developmentally Disabled Adults. Cathy S. Barnett, Dir. Lay Staff 21; Clients 73.
Villa Maria - Catholic Life Center, 1903 E. Lake Dr., 62707. Tel: 217-529-2213. Mrs. Martina Kocher, Activities Coord.
Weber House - Weber Care Corporation, 2520 St. James Rd., 62707. Tel: 217-522-8406. Bro. Raphael Kreikemeier, Exec. Dir.; Denise Klaves, Dir. Bed capacity 6; Residence capacity 6.

ALTON. *Saint Anthony's Foundation, Inc.*, Saint Anthony's Way, P.O. Box 340, 62002-0340. Tel: 618-465-2571.
Affiliates: Saint Anthony's Health System and Saint Anthony's Health Center. William E. Kessler, Pres.

Saint Anthony's Health System, Inc., St. Anthony's Way, P.O. Box 340, 62002-0340. Tel: 618-465-2571. Affiliates: Saint Anthony's Health Center and Saint Anthony's Foundation, Inc. William E. Kessler, Pres.; Rev. Craig MacMahon, O.M.V., Chap. Sisters of St. Francis of the Martyr St. George 1.

Saint Clare's Hospital, 915 E. Fifth St., 62002. Tel: 618-463-5150.
A Division of Saint Anthony's Health Center. William E. Kessler, Pres.; Rev. Craig MacMahon, O.M.V., Chap. Sisters of St. Francis of the Martyr St. George 19.

St. Francis Day Care Center, 710 College Ave., P.O. Box 9020, 62002-9020. Kindergarten & Day Care Center. Sisters of St. Francis of the Martyr St. George 2.

RIVERTON. *Benincasa-Dominican Renewal Center*, 7th and Adams Sts., P.O. Box 679, 62561-0679. Tel: 217-629-8469. Sr. Melanie Roetker, O.P., Dir.

SULLIVAN. *Fields-Wright Medical Facility, Inc.*, 2 W. Adams, 61951. Tel: 217-728-8316. Sponsored by Hospital Sisters of St. Francis. Keith L. Callahan, Pres.; Sr. Jomary Trstensky, O.S.F., Contact Person.

RELIGIOUS INSTITUTES OF MEN REPRESENTED IN THE DIOCESE

For further details refer to the corresponding bracketed number in the Religious Institutes of Men or Women section.

[1320]—*Clerics of St. Viator.* (Chicago Prov.).—C.S.V.

[0510]—*Franciscan Brothers of the Holy Cross.*—F.F.S.C.

[0520]—*Franciscan Friars.* (Sacred Heart Province).—O.F.M.

[0690]—*Jesuit Fathers and Brothers.* (Missouri Province).—S.J.

[0910]—*Oblates of Mary Immaculate.* (Central Province).—O.M.I.

[0940]—*Oblates of the Virgin Mary.*—O.M.V.

[0430]—*Order of Preachers (Dominicans).*—O.P.

[]—*Society of Jesus.* (Missouri Prov.).—S.J.

RELIGIOUS INSTITUTES OF WOMEN REPRESENTED IN THE DIOCESE

[0100]—*Adorers of the Blood of Christ.* (Ruma, IL; Wichita, KS).—A.S.C.

[0230]—*Benedictine Sisters of Pontifical Jurisdiction.* (Nauvoo, IL).—O.S.B.

[2100]—*Congregation of the Humility of Mary.*—C.H.M.

[1710]—*Congregation of the Third Order of St. Francis of Mary Immaculate, Joliet, IL.*—O.S.F.

[0760]—*Daughters of Charity of St. Vincent De Paul.* (East Central Prov.).—D.C.

[1070-10]—*Dominican Sisters.*—O.P.

[1070-13]—*Dominican Sisters.*—O.P.

[1440]—*Franciscan Sisters of the Poor.*—S.F.P.

[1820]—*Hospital Sisters of Third Order of St. Francis.*—O.S.F.

[2575]—*Institute of the Sisters of Mercy of the Union of the Americas.* (Chicago, IL).—R.S.M.

[3230]—*Poor Handmaids of Jesus Christ.*—P.H.J.C.

[2970]—*School Sisters of Notre Dame.* (St. Louis, MO).—S.S.N.D.

[1680]—*School Sisters of St. Francis.*—O.S.F.

[3520]—*Servants of the Holy Heart of Mary.*—S.S.C.M.

[0430]—*Sisters of Charity of the Blessed Virgin Mary.*—B.V.M.

[0990]—*Sisters of Divine Providence.* (St. Louis Prov.).—C.D.P.

[3360]—*Sisters of Providence of Saint Mary-of-the-Woods, Indiana.*—S.P.

[1570]—*Sisters of St. Francis of the Holy Family.*—O.S.F.

[1580]—*Sisters of St. Francis of the Immaculate Conception.*—O.S.F.

[1600]—*Sisters of St. Francis of the Martyr St. George.*—O.S.F.

[]—*Sisters of St. Joseph.* (India).

[3270]—*Sisters of the Most Precious Blood (O'Fallon, MO).*—C.PP.S.

[4110]—*Ursuline Nuns (Roman Union).* (Central Prov.).—O.S.U.

DIOCESAN CEMETERIES

SPRINGFIELD. *Calvary Cemetery Association.*

CARLINVILLE. *Calvary Cemetery Association.*

DECATUR. *Calvary Cemetery Association.*

EDWARDSVILLE. *Calvary Cemetery Association.*

LITCHFIELD. *Holy Cross Cemetery Association.*

MOUNT STERLING. *Catholic Cemetery Association.*

QUINCY. *Catholic Cemetery Association.*

NECROLOGY

† Colavecchio, John A., (Retired). —Died March 26, 1997.

† Hughes, James, (Retired). —Died April 30, 1997.

† Suddes, Rev. Msgr. James A., (Retired). —Died Sept. 5, 1997.

† Worland, T. Vincent, Altamont, IL, St. Clare. —Died Aug. 3, 1997.

Diocese of Springfield in Massachusetts

(Dioecesis Campifontis)

Most Reverend

THOMAS LUDGER DUPRE, D.D., J.C.D.

Bishop of Springfield; ordained May 23, 1959; appointed Auxiliary Bishop of Springfield and Titular Bishop of Hodelm April 19, 1990; consecrated May 31, 1990; appointed Bishop of Springfield March 14, 1995; installed May 8, 1995. *Res., 68 Elliot St., Springfield, MA, 01101. Mailing Address: P.O. Box 1730, Springfield, MA, 01101.*

Most Reverend

JOSEPH F. MAGUIRE, D.D.

Retired Bishop of Springfield; ordained June 29, 1945; appointed Auxiliary Bishop of Boston and Titular Bishop of Mactaris December 1, 1971; consecrated February 2, 1972; appointed Coadjutor Bishop of Springfield with right of succession April 3, 1976; officially installed as Bishop of Springfield on November 4, 1977; resigned December 27, 1991. *Res., 76 Elliot St., P.O. Box 1730, Springfield, MA, 01101.*

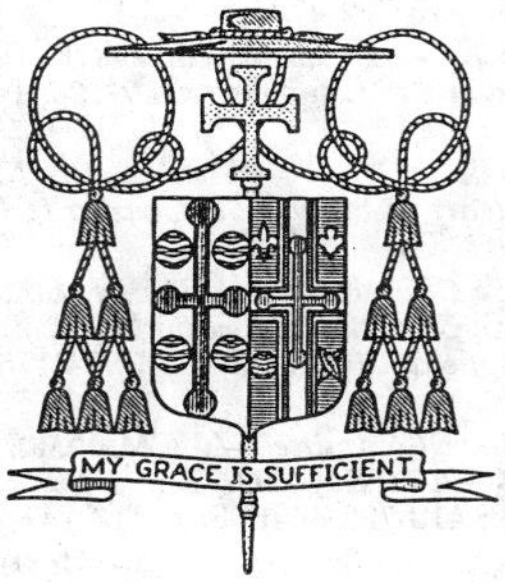

ESTABLISHED JUNE 14, 1870.

Square Miles 2,822.

Comprises the Counties of Berkshire, Franklin, Hampden and Hampshire in the State of Massachusetts.

For legal titles of parishes and diocesan institutions, consult the Chancery Office.

Chancery Office: P.O. Box 1730, Springfield, MA, 01101. Tel.: 413-732-3175; Fax: 413-737-2337.

STATISTICAL OVERVIEW

Personnel	
Bishop	1
Retired Bishops	2
Priests: Diocesan Active in Diocese	153
Priests: Active Outside Diocese	12
Priests: Retired, Sick or Absent	38
Number of Diocesan Priests	203
Religious Priests in Diocese	52
Ordinations:	
Permanent Deacons	8
Permanent Deacons in Diocese	51
Total Brothers	10
Total Sisters	650
Parishes	
Parishes	133
With Resident Pastor:	
Resident Diocesan Priests	109
Resident Religious Priests	13
Without Resident Pastor:	
Administered by Priests	10
Administered by Permanent Deacons	1
Missions	15
Pastoral Centers	1
Closed Parishes	3
Professional Ministry Personnel:	
Brothers	1
Sisters	44
Lay Ministers	52
Welfare	
Catholic Hospitals	1
Total Assisted	129,000
Health Care Centers	1
Total Assisted	140
Homes for the Aged	6
Total Assisted	931
Residential Care of Children	1
Total Assisted	125
Day Care and Extended Day Care Centers	1
Total Assisted	102
Specialized Homes	1
Total Assisted	200
Special Centers for Social Services	2
Total Assisted	3,720
Residential Care of Disabled	1
Total Assisted	5,000
Educational	
Diocesan Students in Other Seminaries	11
Seminaries, Religious	1
Total Seminarians	11
Colleges and Universities	1
Total Students	1,187
High Schools, Diocesan and Parish	4
Total Students	1,798
Elementary Schools, Diocesan and Parish	34
Total Students	7,254
Non-residential Schools for the Disabled	1
Total Students	1,200
Catechesis/Religious Education:	
High School Students	6,348
Elementary Students	25,164
Total Students Under Catholic Instruction	42,962
Teachers in the Diocese:	
Sisters	47
Lay Teachers	503
Vital Statistics	
Receptions into the Church:	
Infant Baptism Totals	4,286
Adult Baptism Totals	153
Received into Full Communion	233
First Communions	4,176
Confirmations	3,038
Marriages:	
Catholic	1,162
Interfaith	302
Total Marriages	1,464
Deaths	4,078
Total Catholic Population	291,350
Total Population	800,600

Former Bishops—Most Rev. PATRICK THOMAS O'REILLY, D.D., cons. Sept. 25, 1870; died May 28, 1892.—Most Rev. THOMAS DANIEL BEAVEN, cons. Oct. 18, 1892; died Oct. 5, 1920.—Most Rev. THOMAS M. O'LEARY, D.D., cons. Sept. 8, 1921; died Oct. 10, 1949.—Most Rev. CHRISTOPHER J. WELDON, D.D., cons. March 24, 1950; retired Oct. 15, 1977; died March 19, 1982.—Most Rev. JOHN A. MARSHALL, D.D., cons. Bishop of Burlington, Jan. 25, 1972; installed Bishop of Springfield, Feb. 18, 1992; died July 3, 1994.—Most Rev. JOSEPH F. MAGUIRE, D.D., cons. Auxiliary Bishop of Boston, Feb. 2, 1972; installed Bishop of Springfield, Nov. 4, 1977; retired Dec. 27, 1991.

Vicar General—Rev. Msgr. RICHARD S. SNIEZYK, Vicar General and Moderator of the Curia, *65 Elliot St., P.O. Box 1730, Springfield, 01101.* Rev. Msgr. LEO A. LECLERC, *St. Rose de Lima Rectory, 600 Grattan St., Chicopee, 01020.*

Episcopal Vicars—Vicars for the Clergy: Revs. DAVID JOYCE; GEORGE FARLAND; Rev. KARL HULLER, Vicar for Finance; Sr. JUDITH O'CONNELL, S.S.J., Vicar for Religious, *65 Elliot St., P.O. Box 1730, Springfield, 01101.* Rev. JOHN J. VARLEY, Berkshire Vicariate; Vacant; Franklin-Hampshire Vicariate; Rev. HUGH CREAN, Hampden East Vicariate; Rev. HOWARD MCCORMICK, Hampden Central and Hampden West Vicariate.

Chancery Office—76 Elliot St., Springfield, 01105. Mailing Address: P.O. Box 1730, Springfield, 01101. Tel: 413-732-3175; Fax: 413-737-2337.

Chancellor—Rev. DANIEL P. LISTON, J.C.L.

Vice-Chancellors—Rev. ROBERT W. THRASHER, J.C.D.; Sr. CAROL CIFATTE, C.S.J., J.C.L.

Vicar for Canonical Affairs—Rev. DANIEL P. LISTON, J.C.L.

Secretary to the Bishop—Rev. WILLIAM J. HAMILTON.

Judicial Vicar—Rev. JOHN L. SULLIVAN, J.C.L.

Adjutant Judicial Vicars—Rev. Msgr. ROGER VIAU, J.C.D.; Rev. JOHN P. MCDONAGH, J.C.L.

Director of the Tribunal—Sr. CLAIRE LAPOINTE, S.A.S.V., J.C.L.

Judges—Rev. Msgr. JOHN F. HARRINGTON, P.A., J.C.L.; Rev. DANIEL R. FOLEY, J.C.D.; Rev. Msgr. JOSEPH I. JOHNSON, J.C.D.; Revs. HENRY KARWEL, O.F.M.Conv., J.C.L.; DANIEL P. LISTON, J.C.L.; JOHN J. SHEA, J.C.D.; ROBERT W. THRASHER, J.C.D.

Promotor of Justice—Rev. JOHN R. BOURQUE, J.C.D.

Defenders of the Bond—Sr. CAROL CIFATTE, C.S.J., J.C.L.; Sr. CLAIRE LAPOINTE, S.A.S.V., J.C.L.; Rev. JOHN P. MCDONAGH, J.C.L.

Tribunal Instructor—Rev. EDWARD KENNEDY, J.C.L.

Procurators-Advocate—Revs. JEDDIE P. BROOKS; JUAN GARCIA, C.R.I.C.; Rev. DANIEL B. BRUNTON.

Psychotherapeutic Counselor—Rev. J. DONALD R. LAPOINTE, L.I.C.S.W.

Psychological Experts—MARTIN J. MARKEY, Ph.D.; ROBERT SAISI, Ph.D., Ed.D.

Notaries—Mrs. CAROL MENDREK; Ms. MARGARET LARO; Mrs. ELLEN RIVERS; Ms. BARBARA OGONOSKI.

Diocesan Tribunal—65 Elliot St., P.O. Box 1730, Springfield, 01101. Tel: 413-452-0664; Fax: 413-747-8482.

Bishop's Commission for Clergy—Rev. Msgr. RICHARD S. SNIEZYK, Chm.; Revs. DAVID JOYCE; CHRISTOPHER CONNELLY; EUGENE HONAN; JAMES JOYCE; GERARD LAFLEUR; LEO A. LECLERC; HOWARD W. MCCORMICK; KENNETH J. TATRO.

Bishop's Cabinet—Rev. Msgr. RICHARD S. SNIEZYK; Rev. Msgr. LEO A. LECLERC; Rev. Msgr. THOMAS F. DEVINE; Revs. KARL HULLER; DANIEL P. LISTON; MICHAEL DOYLE; Sr. JUDITH O'CONNELL, S.S.J.; Sr. JUDITH SMELTZ, S.S.J.; Sr. BETTE GOULD, S.S.J.; Mr. MICHAEL GRAZIANO.

Diocesan Commission for Ecumenism—Rev. BRUCE N. TEAGUE, Chm., *76 Elliot St., P.O. Box 1730, Springfield, 01101.* Tel: 413-732-3175.

Diocesan Commission for the Liturgy—Rev. WILLIAM J. HAMILTON, Chm., *Christian Education Center, 625 Carew St., Springfield, 01104.* Tel: 413-732-3175.

Diocesan Director of Ceremonies—Rev. WILLIAM J. HAMILTON, *76 Elliot St., P.O. Box 1730, Springfield, 01101.* Tel: 413-732-3175; Fax: 413-737-2337.

Diocesan Consultors—Rev. Msgr. THOMAS F. DEVINE; Rev. Msgr. JOHN F. HARRINGTON, P.A., J.C.L.; Rev. Msgr. RICHARD S. SNIEZYK; Rev. Msgr. LEO A. LECLERC; Revs. HUGH F. CREAN; KARL HULLER; DAVID J. JOYCE; GERARD A. LAFLEUR; DANIEL P. LISTON, J.C.L.

Deans—Rev. TIMOTHY J. CAMPOLI, Franklin Deanery; Rev. ROLAND J. GALIPEAU, Greater Holyoke Deanery; Rev. THOMAS M. SHEA, Greater Springfield I Deanery; Rev. GEORGE A. FARLAND, Greater Springfield II Deanery; Rev. GERARD A. LAFLEUR, Hampden Central Deanery; CHARLES KUZMESKI, Hampden East Deanery; Rev. KENNETH J. TATRO, Hampden West Deanery; ROBERT J. COONAN, Hampshire Deanery; Vacant; Northern Berkshire Deanery; Rev. JOHN A. KOONZ, Southern Berkshire Deanery.

Presbyteral Council—Rev. Msgr. THOMAS F. DEVINE; Rev. Msgr. JOHN F. HARRINGTON, P.A., J.C.L.; Rev. Msgr. RICHARD SNIEZYK; Rev. Msgr. LEO LECLERC; Revs. HUGH F. CREAN; VERNON P. DECOTEAU; CHRISTOPHER CONNELLY; RICHARD SCIOLI, C.S.S.; KARL HULLER; DAVID J. JOYCE; GERARD A. LAFLEUR; DANIEL P. LISTON, J.C.L.; MICHAEL SHERSHANOVICH; PAUL E. MANSHIP; JAMES P. MENGE; CHRISTOPHER MALATESTA; FRANCIS MANNING.

Co-Vicars For Clergy—Revs. GEORGE FARLAND; DAVID JOYCE, *65 Elliot St., P.O. Box 1730, Springfield, 01101.* Tel: 413-732-3175.

Vicar for Finance—Rev. KARL HULLER, *65 Elliot St., P.O. Box 1730, Springfield, 01101.* Tel: 413-732-3175.

Assistant to the Vicar for Finance—Rev. JOHN P. MCDONAGH.

Vicar for Religious—Sr. JUDITH O'CONNELL, S.S.J., Vicar, *65 Elliot St., P.O. Box 1730, Springfield, 01101.* Tel: 413-452-0609.

Diocesan Offices and Directors

Apostolate to the Handicapped—Rev. ROBERT F. WAGNER, Dir., *Bureau for Exceptional Children and Adults, 537 Northampton St., P.O. Box 1039, Holyoke, 01041.* Tel: 413-538-7450 (voice and TTY); Fax: 413-536-5691.

Apostolate of the Suffering—ROBERT J. LETASZ, Dir., *P.O. Box 535, Chicopee, 01021.* Rev. ADRIEN T. REMY, Chap., *Mont Marie, Holyoke, 01040.*

Blue Army—Rev. ALBERT E. BRETON, *St. Theresa's Rectory, 74 Bridge St., Agawam, 01001.* Tel: 413-786-4451.

Building Commission—Rev. JAMES SCAHILL, Chm., *St. Mary Rectory, 840 Page Blvd., Springfield, 01104-2799.* Tel: 413-739-0456.

Building Consultant—Mr. FREDERICK R. PIQUETTE, *65 Elliot St., P.O. Box 1730, Springfield, 01101.* Tel: 413-452-0672; Fax: 413-785-5449.

Campaign for Human Development—Rev. MICHAEL J. DOYLE, Cabinet Sec.; Sr. ANNETTE M. MCDERMOTT, S.S.J., Dir., *65 Elliot St., P.O. Box 1730, Springfield, 01101.* Tel: 413-452-0697; Fax: 413-746-3421.

The Catholic Charismatic Renewal of Springfield, Inc.—Rev. GERALD BRADY, *Holy Trinity Rectory, Main St., Hatfield, 01038.* Tel: 413-247-3133. Sr. MARGARET WALSH, S.S.J., Coord., *P.O. Box 4668, Springfield, 01101-4668.* Tel: 413-247-9001; Fax: 413-247-5605.

Catholic Charities—Rev. MICHAEL J. DOYLE, M.S.W., *65 Elliot St., P.O. Box 1730, Springfield, 01103.* Tel: 413-452-0613.

Annual Catholic Appeal—Revs. KARL HULLER, Exec. Dir. MICHAEL J. DOYLE, Coord. of Allocations; PATRICIA EVANS, Coord. of Admin., *65 Elliot St., P.O. Box 1730, Springfield, 01101., Mailing Address: P.O. Box 1730, Springfield, 01101.* Tel: 413-452-0629; Fax: 413-732-4297.

Catholic Nurses Council—Rev. LAWRENCE J. BERNIER, Chap., St. Michael's Rectory, *128 Maple St., East Longmeadow, 01023.* Tel: 413-525-4253.

Catholic Relief Services—Rev. MICHAEL J. DOYLE, *65 Elliot St., P.O. Box 1730, Springfield, 01101.* Tel: 413-732-3175.

Cemeteries—Rev. FRANCIS P. LAVELLE, Diocesan Dir. of Cemeteries, *St. Michael's Cemetery, 1601 State St., Springfield, 01109.* Tel: 413-733-0659. Rev. DAVID FARLAND, Dir., *Saint Michael's Cemetery, 1601 State St., Springfield, 01109.* Tel: 413-733-0659., *Gate of Heaven Cemetery, 421 Tinkham Rd., Springfield, 01129.* Tel: 413-782-4731.

Censor of Books—Rev. Msgr. THOMAS F. DEVINE, *519 Longmeadow St., Longmeadow, 01106.* Tel: 413-567-3124.

Clergy Counseling Service—Rev. GEORGE A. FARLAND, *Sacred Heart Rectory, 395 Chestnut St., Springfield, 01104.* Tel: 413-732-3721.

Commission on Church Music—Rev. WILLIAM J. HAMILTON, Chm., *Christian Education Center, 625 Carew St., Springfield, 01104.* Tel: 413-732-3175; Fax: 413-732-1944.

Communications Committee—Mr. MICHAEL GRAZIANO, Chm., *65 Elliot St., P.O. Box 1730, Springfield, 01101.* Tel: 413-732-4546; Fax: 413-747-0273.

Chalice of Salvation (Televised Mass)—Br. TERRENCE A. SCANLON, C.P., Dir., *65 Elliot St., P.O. Box 1730, Springfield, 01101.* Tel: 413-732-3175.

Continuing Education for Priests—Rev. JOHN T. SMEGAL, *North American Martyrs Rectory, 17 Juleann Dr., R.R. 01, Box 37, Lanesboro, 01237-9518.* Tel: 413-442-2063.

Office of Religious Education-CCD—Sr. PAULA ROBILLARD, S.S.J., Dir. JOAN SMOLA, Consultant for R.C.I.A. VIRGINIA WEBB, Consultant, *Christian Education Center, 625 Carew St., Springfield, 01104.* Tel: 413-452-0807; Fax: 413-452-0817. THERESA O'KEEFE, Berkshire Consultant, *100 Briggs Ave., Pittsfield, 01201.* Tel: 413-443-3187.

Cursillo Movement—Deacon JOHN BLEDSOE, Dir. English-Speaking Cursillo Movement, *84 Bardwell St., South Hadley, 01075.* Tel: 413-532-6671. Rev. REGIS J. GIROUX, Dir. Spanish-Speaking Cursillo Movement, *445 Plainfield St., Springfield, 01107.* Tel: 413-736-0076.

Diocesan Board of Christian Education—Rev. Msgr. THOMAS F. DEVINE, Chm., *625 Carew St., Springfield, 01104.* Tel: 413-732-3175.

Diocesan Office of Black Catholic Ministry—Mr. MICHAEL JONES, Coord., *255 King St., P.O. Box 81036, Springfield, 01138.* Tel: 413-732-0772.

Diocesan Office for Communications—Mr. MICHAEL A. GRAZIANO, Coord., *65 Elliot St., P.O. Box 1730, Springfield, 01101.* Tel: 413-732-4546; Fax: 413-747-0273.

Director of Personnel—Sr. CAROL CIFATTE, C.S.J., J.C.L.

Education—Sr. BETTE GOULD, S.S.J., Supt. of Schools; Sr. JANICE CARMEN, S.N.D., Coord. Student Svcs.; Sr. MAUREEN TOOMEY, S.N.D., Dir. Personnel, *Christian Education Center, 625 Carew St., Springfield, 01104.* Tel: 413-452-0830; Fax: 413-452-0817.

Director of Pittsfield Catholic Schools—Priests Committee: Revs. JAMES JOYCE, Chm. HENRY DORSCH; GARY DAILEY; MICHAEL SHERSHANOVICH; JOHN VARLEY, *22 Maplewood Ave., Pittsfield, 01201.* Tel: 413-443-9686.

Family Life Bureau—625 Carew St., Springfield, 01104. Tel: 413-732-3175.

Fiscal Affairs—WILLIAM F. LABROAD, JR., Finance Officer; Miss JEANNE M. DESROSIERS, Controller, *65 Elliot St., P.O. Box 1730, Springfield, 01101.* Tel: 413-452-0696; Fax: 413-785-5449.

Holy Childhood Association—Rev. Msgr. JOHN F. HARRINGTON, P.A., J.C.L., Dir., *65 Elliot St., P.O. Box 1730, Springfield, 01101.* Tel: 413-732-3175.

Holy Family League of Charity—c/o Office of Catholic Charities, P.O. Box 1730, Springfield, 01101. Tel: 413-732-3175.

Marriage Counseling—Rev. JOHN J. JOHNSON, Dir. Counselors: Mr. ALFRED A. D'AMATO; Mrs. ROSEMARY CASTONGUAY, *65 Elliot St., P.O. Box 1730, Springfield, 01101.* Tel: 413-452-0621; Fax: 413-747-0273.

Massachusetts Catholic Conference—Rev. Msgr. LEO A. LECLERC, V.G., *65 Elliot St., P.O. Box 1730, Springfield, 01101.* Tel: 413-732-3175. Rev. MICHAEL J. DOYLE, *65 Elliot St., P.O. Box 1730, Springfield, 01101.* Tel: 413-732-3175. Rev. RICHARD S. SNIEZYK, *65 Elliot St., P.O. Box 1730, Springfield, 01101.* Tel: 413-732-3175.

Ministry to the Deaf—Sr. CAROL LAREAU, S.S.J., *34 Nye St., Springfield, 01104.* Tel: 413-736-0020.

Ministry to the Divorced and Separated—Pastoral Ministry Office, Christian Education Center, 625 Carew St., Springfield, 01104. Tel: 413-732-3175.

Ministry to Priests—Rev. JOHN T. SMEGAL, *North American Martyrs Rectory, 17 Juleann Dr., R.R. 01, Box 37, Lanesboro, 01237.* Tel: 413-442-2063.

Newman Apostolate and Campus Ministry—Rev. FRANCIS LAVELLE, *Newman Center, 472 N. Pleasant St., Amherst, 01002.* Tel: 413-549-0300.

Parish Councils— Vacant.

Pastoral Ministry—Sr. JUDITH SMELTZ, S.S.J., *Christian Education Center, 625 Carew St., Springfield, 01104.* Tel: 413-452-0824; Fax: 413-452-0817.

Permanent Diaconate—Rev. TIMOTHY J. MURPHY, Dir.; Deacon JOSEPH GARDE, Co-Dir., *65 Elliot St., P.O. Box 1730, Springfield, 01101.* Tel: 413-452-0674; Fax: 413-747-0273.

Planned Giving—Rev. GEORGE G. GREENWAY, Dir., *65 Elliot St., P.O. Box 1730, Springfield, 01101.* Tel: 413-732-3175.

Press—"The Catholic Observer"; Mrs. SHARON ROULIER, Editor, *65 Elliot St., P.O. Box 1730, Springfield, 01101.* Tel: 413-732-3175; Fax: 413-747-0273.

Priests' Retirement Program—Rev. RICHARD SNIEZYK, V.G., Chm., *65 Elliot St., P.O. Box 1730, Springfield, 01101.*

Pro-Life Commission—Rev. JOHN L. SULLIVAN, J.C.L., *65 Elliot St., P.O. Box 1730, Springfield, 01101-1730.* Tel: 413-732-3175.

Propagation of the Faith—Rev. Msgr. JOHN F. HARRINGTON, P.A., J.C.L., *65 Elliot St., P.O. Box 1730, Springfield, 01101.* Tel: 413-452-0675.

Radio and Television—MICHAEL GRAZIANO, Coord. of Communications; Bro. TERRENCE SCANLON, C.P., Dir., *Catholic Communications Office, 65 Elliot St., P.O. Box 1730, Springfield, 01101.* Tel: 413-732-3175; Fax: 413-747-0273.

Refugee Resettlement Program/Immigration Services—Rev. MICHAEL J. DOYLE, Dir.; TUNG T. PHAM; Ms. ANNA BARANOVSKI, *65 Elliot St., P.O. Box 1730, Springfield, 01101.* Tel: 413-632-3175.

Representative of the Bishop at—Mercy Hospital, Springfield: Dr. KEVIN SCHMIDT, Mont Marie Health Care Center: Rev. DANIEL P. LISTON, J.C.L., Providence Hospital, Holyoke: Rev. KARL HULLER, Sisters of Providence Care Centers, Inc.: Rev. JOHN L. SULLIVAN, J.C.L., Our Lady of Providence Children's Center, West Springfield: Rev. J. DONALD R. LAPOINTE, L.I.C.S.W., Sisters of Providence Health System: Mr. WILLIAM COLLINS.

Retired Priests' Service—Rev. EDWARD M. CALLAHAN, *Sacred Heart Rectory, 395 Chestnut St., Springfield, 01104.*

Southeast Asian Apostolate—Rev. QUYNH DINH TRAN, Dir., *Saint Thomas Aquinas Rectory, 35 Harriet St., Springfield, 01107.* Tel: 413-827-7525.

Spanish Apostolate—Revs. MICHAEL J. DOYLE, Dir., *Blessed Sacrament Rectory, 1777 Dwight St., Springfield, 01107.* Tel: 413-736-8208. FRANCIS E. REILLY, Dir., *Casa Maria, 51 Hamilton St., Holyoke, 01040.* Tel: 413-533-6016. PAUL E. MANSHIP, *Holy Family Rectory, P.O. Box 91333, Springfield, 01139-1333.* Tel: 413-732-1422.

Springfield Diocesan Council of Catholic Women—Mrs. KATHERINE KUBERA, Pres., *11 Orchard Rd., East Longmeadow, 01028.*

Vigilance, Council of—The Deans.

Vocations—Rev. CHRISTOPHER MALATESTA, *65 Elliot St., P.O. Box 1730, Springfield, 01101.* Tel: 413-452-0816; Fax: 413-452-0817.

Office of Youth Ministry—Vacant, *Christian Education Center, 625 Carew St., Springfield, 01104.* Tel: 413-732-3175; Fax: 413-732-1944.

CLERGY, PARISHES, MISSIONS AND PAROCHIAL SCHOOLS

CITY OF SPRINGFIELD
(Hampden County)

1—ST. MICHAEL'S CATHEDRAL (1847), Revs. Karl Huller, Rector; John P. McDonagh, Assoc. Rector.
Res., 260 State St., 01103. Tel: 413-781-3656.

2—ALL SOULS (1908) (Spanish), Revs. Michael Doyle, Admin.; Juan Garcia (Peru). In res., Rev. Steven McGuigan.
Res., 445 Plainfield St., 01107. Tel: 413-736-0076; Fax: 413-731-0962. [CEM]
Catechesis/Religious Programs—Students 58.

3—BLESSED SACRAMENT (1953) (Hispanic), Revs. Michael J. Doyle; Juan F. Garcia, C.R.I.C. (Peru); Sr. Jane Morrissey, S.S.J., Pastoral Min.; Deacon Genaro Medina.
Res., 1777 Dwight St., 01107. Tel: 413-736-8208; Fax: 413-731-0962.
Catechesis/Religious Programs—Sr. Mary Cronin, D.M., D.R.E.
Students 301.

4—HOLY CROSS (1949), Revs. Thomas M. Shea; Daniel S. Pacholec. In res., Rev. Msgr. Robert E. Foudy, Pastor Emeritus.

Res., 221 Plumtree Rd., 01118. Tel: 413-783-4111; Fax: 413-783-4112.
School—153 Eddywood St., 01118. Tel: 413-782-5246. Sr. Patricia Rumse, S.S.J., Prin.
Sisters of St. Joseph 2; Lay Teachers 25; Students 498.
Catechesis/Religious Programs—175 Eddywood St., 01118. Tel: 413-782-8284.
Students 223.

5—HOLY FAMILY (1901) (African American-Hispanic), Rev. Paul E. Manship, Admin.; Sr. Jeannette Pierre Louis; Deacon Raphael Velazquez.
Res., 235 Eastern Ave., 01109. Tel: 413-732-1422.
Catechesis/Religious Programs—Students 85.

6—HOLY NAME (1909), Revs. Hugh F. Crean, S.T.D.; Christopher D. Connelly; Donald L. Barron; Sr. Catherine Leary, S.S.J., Pastoral Min.
Res., 323 Dickinson St., 01108. Tel: 413-733-5823; Fax: 413-788-6481.
School—37 Alderman St., 01108. Tel: 413-736-4235. Martha Kelliher, Prin.
Sisters of St. Joseph 2; Lay Teachers 25; Students 445.
Catechesis/Religious Programs—Tel: 413-736-4145. Mrs. Elizabeth Sharon, D.R.E.
Students 300.
Center—57 Alderman St., 01108. Tel: 413-734-7113.

7—IMMACULATE CONCEPTION (1905) (Polish), Revs. Adrian J. Benoit; Stefan J. Niemczyk.
Res., 25 Parker St. (Indian Orchard), 01151. Tel: 413-543-3627; Fax: 413-543-4301.
School—34 Kopernick St., 01151. Tel: 413-543-2897.
Felician Sisters 2; Lay Teachers 8; Students 176.
Catechesis/Religious Programs—Mrs. Mary Arabik, D.R.E.
Students 101.

8—OUR LADY OF HOPE (1906), Revs. David J. Joyce; John V. Corbett, C.Ss.R. In res., Revs. Matthew J. O'Connor; George V. Joyce (WDC).
Res., 577 Carew St., 01104. Tel: 413-739-7369. [CEM]
School—474 Armory St., 01104. Tel: 413-734-4125.
Lay Teachers 25; Students 550.
Catechesis/Religious Programs—Students 156.

9—OUR LADY OF MT. CARMEL (1907) (Italian), Rev. Richard A. Scioli, C.S.S.; Sr. Elizabeth A. Matuszek, S.S.J., Pastoral Assoc.
Res., 123 William St., 01105. Tel: 413-734-5433; Fax: 413-731-0680.
School—36 Margaret St., 01105. Tel: 413-739-3616.
Daughters of Mercy 1; Lay Teachers 15; Students 150.
Catechesis/Religious Programs—Students 387.
Convent—56 Margaret St., 01105. Tel: 413-733-7410.
Mission—West Springfield, Hampden Co., St. Ann, 576 Memorial Ave., West Springfield, 01089. Tel: 413-736-3101. Revs. James E. Flanagan, C.S.S.; Joseph Massaro, C.S.S.

10—OUR LADY OF THE ROSARY (1917) (Polish), Revs. John P. Skowronski; Stanley Sokol; Deacon Rodney Szymczyk.
Res., 28 Underwood St., 01104. Tel: 413-733-0508.
Catechesis/Religious Programs—Tel: 413-739-2210.
Students 70.

11—OUR LADY OF THE SACRED HEART (1929), Rev. William Tourigny; Deacon Paul Wallen.
Office: 51 Rosewell Ave., 01109. Tel: 413-782-8041; Fax: 413-783-9150.
Res., 417 Boston Rd., 01109.
School—52 Rosewell Ave., 01109. Tel: 413-782-8021.
Sisters of St. Joseph 2; Lay Teachers 19; Students 394.
Catechesis/Religious Programs—Cindee Gagnon, D.R.E.
Students 140.

12—SACRED HEART (1872), Rev. George A. Farland. In res., Revs. Edward M. Callahan Tel: 413-772-3721; Mark S. Stelzer.
Res., 395 Chestnut St., 01104. Tel: 413-732-3721; Fax: 413-733-5731.
Catechesis/Religious Programs—Students 157.

13—ST. ALOYSIUS (1873) (French). Merged with St. Matthew, Springfield to form St. Jude, Indian Orchard.

14—ST. CATHERINE OF SIENA (1961), Revs. Charles F. Gonet; John G. Lessard-Thibodeau; Deacon Joseph Garde.
Res., 1023 Parker St., 01129. Tel: 413-783-8619; Fax: 413-783-2344.
Catechesis/Religious Programs—Tel: 413-783-8691.
Students 370.

15—ST. JOSEPH'S (1873) (French), Rev. George Greenway, Admin.
Res., 82 Howard St., 01105. Tel: 413-733-3527; 733-3745.

16—ST. MARY'S (1948), Rev. James J. Scahill. In res., Rev. Msgr. Richard S. Sniezyk.
Res., 840 Page Blvd., 01104. Tel: 413-739-0456.
Catechesis/Religious Programs—Tel: 413-736-1622.
Students 231.

17—ST. MATTHEW'S (1878). Merged with St. Aloysius, Springfield to form St. Jude, Indian Orchard.
School—90 Berkshire St., 01151. Tel: 413-543-1066.
Sisters of St. Joseph 1; Lay Teachers 18; Students 170.

18—ST. PATRICK'S (1961), Rev. Thomas M. Courtney; Deacon George Kozach.
Res., 1900 Allen St., 01118-1820. Tel: 413-783-6201; Fax: 413-783-7787.
Catechesis/Religious Programs—Alan E. O'Dell, D.R.E.
Students 270.

19—ST. PAUL (1960), Rev. Francis H. Crombie; Deacon Robert Morrissey.
Res., 51 Fenimore Blvd., 01108. Tel: 413-737-4422 (Rectory); 736-1539 (Church).
Catechesis/Religious Programs—Students 150.
Mission—East Longmeadow, Hampden Co., St. Joseph's, 146 Vineland Ave., East Longmeadow, 01028. Tel: 413-737-8650.

20—ST. THOMAS AQUINAS (1908) (French-Vietnamese), Rev. William A. Pomerleau. In res., Rev. Quynh Dinh Tran, Dir. Southeast Asian Apostolate.
Res., 35 Harriet St., 01107-1898. Tel: 413-732-7525.
Mission—Springfield, Center for South East Asian Apostolate, Tel: 413-827-7525. Rev. John Pham, Dir.

OUTSIDE THE CITY OF SPRINGFIELD

Adams, Berkshire Co., Notre Dame des Sept Douleurs (1882) (French), Rev. Daniel J. Boyle.
Res., 21 Maple St., P.O. Box 231, 01220-0231. Tel: 413-743-0577; Fax: 413-743-4665.
St. Stanislaus Kostka (1902) (Polish), Rev. John C. Chwalek.
Res., 25 Hoosac St., 01220. Tel: 413-743-0041. [CEM]
School—108 Summer St., 01220. Tel: 413-743-1091.
Felician Sisters 2; Lay Teachers 9; Students 190.
Catechesis/Religious Programs—Students 170.
Convent—23 Hoosac St., 01220. Tel: 413-743-1221.
St. Thomas Aquinas (1875), Rev. Daniel J. Boyle.
Res., 2 Columbia St., P.O. Box 231, 01220-0231. Tel: 413-743-0577; Fax: 413-743-4665.
Catechesis/Religious Programs—Students 619.

Agawam, Hampden Co., St. John the Evangelist (1946), Revs. Howard W. McCormick; William Lunney.
Res., 833 Main St., 01001. Tel: 413-786-8105; Fax: 413-789-6266.
Catechesis/Religious Programs—Students 513.
St. Theresa of the Child Jesus (1883), Rev. Albert E. Breton.
Res., 74 Bridge St., 01001. Tel: 413-786-4451.
Catechesis/Religious Programs—Students 163.
Mission—Agawam, Hampden Co., St. Anthony, 108 Bridge St., 01001. Tel: 413-786-3724. Rev. John L. Sullivan, Admin.

Amherst, Hampshire Co., St. Brigid's (1872), Rev. Bruce N. Teague Tel: 413-253-1828.
Res., 122 N. Pleasant St., P.O. Box 424, 01004. Tel: 413-253-2829; Fax: 413-256-6181. [CEM]
Catechesis/Religious Programs—Tel: 413-253-9873. D.R.E.: Jane Bacon; Mary Delabvueve.
Students 227.

Belchertown, Hampshire Co., St. Francis of Assisi (1926), Revs. Vernon Decoteau; Alfred Cournoyer.
Res., 10 Park St., 01007. Tel: 413-323-6272; Fax: 413-323-4307.
Catechesis/Religious Programs—D.R.E.: Mrs. Shelly Rose; Patrick Hegarty.
Students 737.

Bondsville, Hampden Co., St. Bartholomew's (1878), Rev. Eugene J. Plasse.
Res., 76 Thorndike St., Palmer, 01069. Tel: 413-283-5091; 283-8841 (Church). [JC]
Catechesis/Religious Programs—Students 71.
St. Adalbert's (1910), Rev. Normand F. Mailloux, M.S.
Res., 18 Depot St., P.O. Box 1083, 01009. Tel: 413-283-3000.

Brimfield, Hampden Co., St. Christopher's (1953), Rev. Walter A. Swift.
Church—20 Sturbridge Rd., Rte. 20, P.O. Box 387, 01010. Tel: 413-245-7274; Fax: 413-245-7274.
Rectory—16 Sturbridge Rd., Rte. 20, 01010.
Catechesis/Religious Programs—Students 245.
Mission—Wales, Hampden Co., St. Monica.
Station—Holland, St. Bernadette's.

Cheshire, Berkshire Co., St. Mary of the Assumption (1926), Rev. Thomas B. Begley.
Res., 159 Church St., 01225. Tel: 413-743-2110.
Catechesis/Religious Programs—Students 251.

Chicopee, Hampden Co.,

1—ASSUMPTION, (1885) (French), Rev. Gerard A. LaFleur, V.F. In res., Rev. Michael H. Devlin.
Res., 104 Springfield St., 01013. Tel: 413-592-1597.
Catechesis/Religious Programs—Tel: 413-592-9344.
Students 120.

2—HOLY NAME OF JESUS, (1838), Rev. James J. Flahive.
Res., 33 South St., 01013. Tel: 413-592-0122. [CEM]
School—63 South St., 01013. Tel: 413-592-6857.
Sisters of Notre Dame 3; Lay Teachers 11; Students 230.
Catechesis/Religious Programs—Tel: 413-592-7813.
Students 120.

3—NATIVITY OF THE BLESSED VIRGIN MARY, (1897) (French), Rev. Robert H. Riel.
Res., 780 Chicopee St., 01013-2747. Tel: 413-532-9421; Fax: 413-532-1410.
Catechesis/Religious Programs—Tel: 413-536-3310.
Students 105.

4—ST. ANNE'S, (1912), Rev. J. Victor Carrier; Deacons Edward J. Finnie, (Retired); Frederick J. Pelletier.
Res., 30 College St., 01020. Tel: 413-532-7503.
Catechesis/Religious Programs—Tel: 413-533-8038.
Students 366.

5—ST. ANTHONY'S, (1926) (Polish), Revs. Benedict Fagone, O.F.M.Conv.; Michael Slonecki, O.F.M.Conv.
Res., 56 St. Anthony St., 01013. Tel: 413-538-9475; Fax: 413-538-9859.
Catechesis/Religious Programs—Students 64.

6—ST. GEORGE'S, (1893) (French), Rev. Ronald P. Lussier.
Res., 202 E. Main St., 01020. Tel: 413-598-8622.
School—Consolidated to form St. Joan of Arc/St. George School. 587 Grattan St., 01020. Tel: 413-533-1475.
Catechesis/Religious Programs—Students 225.

7—ST. MARY'S, (1939), Rev. Francis M. Kennedy; Deacon Joseph A. Smith.
Res., 840 Chicopee St., 01013. Tel: 413-532-1854.
Catechesis/Religious Programs—Students 100.

8—ST. PATRICK'S, (1872) (Irish), Rev. J. Donald Lapointe. In res., Rev. John Betit.
Res., 319 Broadway, 01020. Tel: 413-592-4178. [CEM]
School—125 Montgomery St., 01020. Tel: 413-594-8166.
Sisters of Saint Joseph 3; Lay Teachers 11; Students 321.
Catechesis/Religious Programs—Tel: 413-592-4344.
Students 340.

9—ST. ROSE DE LIMA, (1909) (French), Revs. Leo A. Leclerc; Christopher Waitekus; Deacon Leon Mireault.
Res., 600 Grattan St., 01020. Tel: 413-536-4558; Fax: 413-536-4559. [CEM][JC]
School—St. Joan of Arc/St. George School, 587 Grattan St., 01020. Tel: 413-533-1475; Fax: 413-533-1418.
Sisters of the Presentation of Mary 5; Lay Teachers 15; Students 378.
Catechesis/Religious Programs—Tel: 413-536-6038.
Students 334.

10—ST. STANISLAUS BASILICA, (1891) (Polish), Revs. Michael Kolodziej, O.F.M.Conv.; Albert Scherer, O.F.M.Conv.; Anthony Francis Spilka, O.F.M.Conv.; Adalbert Piatkowski, O.F.M.Conv.; Bro. William Sudyka, O.F.M.Conv. In res., Revs. Placid Kaczorek, O.F.M.Conv.; Herbert Baloga, O.F.M.Conv.; Bro. Frank Grimaldi, O.F.M.Conv.
Res., 566 Front St., 01013. Tel: 413-594-6669; Fax: 413-594-5259. [CEM]
School—Tel: 413-592-5135. Sr. Deborah Ciolek, F.S.S.J., Prin.
Franciscan Sisters of St. Joseph 4; Lay Teachers 24; Students 452.
Catechesis/Religious Programs—Tel: 413-592-7955.
Students 225.

Dalton, Berkshire Co., St. Agnes (1907), Rev. John A. Koonz; Deacon Pasqual Baldasaro.
Res., 489 Main St., 01226. Tel: 413-684-0125.
School—30 Carson St., 01226. Tel: 413-684-3143.
Sisters of St. Joseph 2; Lay Teachers 16; Students 330.
Catechesis/Religious Programs—33 Apple Tree Ln., 01226. Tel: 413-684-1745.
Students 460.

Easthampton, Hampshire Co., Immaculate Conception (1871) (Irish), Revs. Richard M. Runte; John K. Sheaffer.
Res., 33 Adams St., 01027. Tel: 413-527-9778. [CEM]
School—Notre Dame-Immaculate Conception School, Tel: 413-527-6133. Miss Wendy E. Woods, Prin.
Lay Teachers 12; Students 252.
Catechesis/Religious Programs—11 Clifford St., 01027. Tel: 413-527-1588.
Students 650.

Our Lady of Good Counsel (1906) (French), Rev. Thomas R. Champigny.
Res., 35 Pleasant St., 01027. Tel: 413-527-9588.
School—Notre Dame-Immaculate Conception, Tel: 413-527-6133.
Lay Teachers 11; Students 249.
Catechesis/Religious Programs—Students 250.

Sacred Heart (1909) (Polish), Rev. Ronald F. Sadlowski.
Res., 33 Knipfer Ave., 01027. Tel: 413-527-9036; Fax: 413-527-9036. [CEM]
Catechesis/Religious Programs—Students 165.

East Longmeadow, Hampden Co., St. Michael's (1894), Rev. Lawrence J. Bernier, V.F.; Sr. Mary McGeer, S.S.J., Pastoral Assoc.
Res.& Mailing Address: 128 Maple St., 01028. Tel: 413-525-4253; Fax: 413-525-4254.
Catechesis/Religious Programs—Tel: 413-525-0371. Mrs. Shirley Skiffington, D.R.E.
Students 927.

Feeding Hills, Hampden Co., Sacred Heart (1946), Rev. Kenneth J. Tatro; Sr. Eileen Sullivan, S.S.J., Pastoral Min.; Deacon James Martone.
Res., 1103 Springfield St., 01030. Tel: 413-786-8200.
Catechesis/Religious Programs—Tel: 413-789-6705. Kathryn Patterson, D.R.E.
Students 1,714.

Granby, Hampshire Co., Immaculate Heart of Mary (1951), Rev. John J. Shea.
Res., 256 State St., 01033. Tel: 413-467-9821.
Catechesis/Religious Programs—Tel: 413-467-3566.
Students 486.

Great Barrington, Berkshire Co., St. Peter's (1864), Rev. William H. Wallis.
Res., 16 Russell St., 01230. Tel: 413-528-1157. [CEM]
Catechesis/Religious Programs—Students 220.

Greenfield, Franklin Co., Blessed Sacrament (1960), Rev. Timothy J. Campoli, V.F.
Res., 182 High St., 01301. Tel: 413-773-3311; Fax: 413-773-5785. [CEM]
School—Holy Trinity School, 10 Beacon St., 01301. Tel: 413-773-3831. Sr. Christine Lavoie, S.S.J., Prin.
Lay Teachers 16; Students 184.
Catechesis/Religious Programs—Tel: 413-774-2918.
Students 181.

Holy Trinity (1868), Rev. James Paul Menge; Deacon Donald Chabot.
Res., 133 Main St., P.O. Box 965, 01302-0965. Tel: 413-774-2884.
Catechesis/Religious Programs—Students 160.

Sacred Heart (1912) (Polish), Team Ministry: Rev. Stanley J. Aksamit; Deacon Albert Routhier.
Res., St. Mary's, 90 Seventh St., Turners Falls, 01376. Tel: 413-863-2585; 772-6377; Fax: 413-863-8978. [CEM]
Catechesis/Religious Programs—Students 71.

Hadley, Hampshire Co., Holy Rosary (1916) (Polish), Rev. William P. Murphy, Admin.
Res., 120 Russell St., P.O. Box 375, 01035. Tel: 413-584-1326; Fax: 413-587-0224. [CEM]
Catechesis/Religious Programs—Tel: 413-586-6209.
Students 230.

St. John's (1915), Rev. William P. Murphy, Admin.
Mailing Address: P.O. Box 597, 01035.
Res., 49 Middle St., 01035. Tel: 413-584-4185.
Catechesis/Religious Programs—Tel: 413-586-6209.
Students 230.

Hampden, Hampden Co., St. Mary's (1951), Rev. Timothy J. Murphy.
Res., 27 Somers Rd., 01036. Tel: 413-566-8843. [CEM]
Catechesis/Religious Programs—Students 340.

Hatfield, Hampshire Co., St. Joseph's (1899), Rev. Robert J. Coonan.
Mailing Address: P.O. Box 34, 01038.
Res., 11 School St., 01038. Tel: 413-247-9079.
Catechesis/Religious Programs—Students 177.

Holy Trinity (1916) (Polish), Rev. Gerald Brady.
Res., 73 Main St., P.O. Box 110, 01038. Tel: 413-247-3133. [CEM]

Haydenville, Hampshire Co., St. Mary's (1889), Rev. Ronald G. Yargeau.
Res., 173 Main St., P.O. Box 277, 01039-0277. Tel: 413-268-7212. [CEM]
Catechesis/Religious Programs—Students 139.

Hinsdale, Berkshire Co., St. Patrick's (1868), Rev. R. Joseph LeVay.
Res., 43 Church St., P.O. Box 428, 01235. Tel: 413-655-2208. [CEM]
Catechesis/Religious Programs—78 Washington St., Becket, 01223.
Students 96.
Mission—Becket, St. Matthew.

Holyoke, Hampden Co.,

1—Blessed Sacrament, (1913), Revs. Peter G. Loughran; C. Lee Gilbertson; Deacon Kenneth P. Gray. In res., Revs. James D. McKenna; Ronald Renaud.
Res., 1945 Northampton St., 01040. Tel: 413-532-0713.
School—21 Westfield Rd., 01040. Tel: 413-536-2236.
Sisters of St. Joseph 2; Lay Teachers 24; Students 394.
Catechesis/Religious Programs—15 Westfield Rd., 01040. Tel: 413-532-8647.
Students 306.
Mission—Holyoke, Hampden Co., Holyoke Soldier's Home Chapel, 110 Cherry St., 01040. Tel: 413-532-9475.

2—Holy Cross, (1905), Rev. Roland J. Galipeau. In res., Rev. William J. Hamilton; Rev. Msgr. John F. Harrington, P.A.
Res., 23 Sycamore St., 01040. Tel: 413-532-5661.
Catechesis/Religious Programs—Tel: 413-536-8832. Raymond Cournoyer, D.R.E.
Students 227.

3—Holy Family, (1949), Rev. Robert W. Thrasher; Deacon Joseph A. Badame. In res., Rev. Richard Bondi.
Res., 15 Holy Family Rd., 01040. Tel: 413-536-6777.
Catechesis/Religious Programs—Tel: 413-536-1665.
Students 133.

4—Immaculate Conception, (1905), Revs. William D. LaFosse, M.S.; Henri Durand, M.S.; Deacon Lincoln Rael. In res., Rev. William J. Doherty, M.S.
Res., 54 N. Summer St., 01040. Tel: 413-532-5784; Fax: 413-532-8852. [JC]
Catechesis/Religious Programs—Students 52.

5—Mater Dolorosa, (1896) (Polish), Revs. Raphael Zwolenkiewicz, O.F.M.Conv.; John Bambol, O.F.M.Conv.; Andrew Skiba, O.F.M.Conv.; Adam Ziolkowski, O.F.M.Conv.; Bro. Stephen Murphy, O.F.M.Conv., Pastoral Assoc.
Offices: Tel: 413-532-7889.
Res., 71 Maple St., 01040. Tel: 413-532-8272; Fax: 413-538-6754. [CEM]
School—25 Maple St., 01040. Tel: 413-532-2831.
Franciscan Sisters of St. Joseph 1; Lay Teachers 14; Students 297.
Catechesis/Religious Programs—Students 143.

6—Our Lady of Perpetual Help, (1890) (French-Canadian), Administrators: Revs. Regis Giroux; Francis E. Reilly.
Res., 271 Chestnut St., 01040. Tel: 413-534-4407; 532-9751; Fax: 413-552-3779. [CEM][JC 2]
School—Tel: 413-536-5703.
Lay Teachers 12; Students 157.

7—Our Lady of the Rosary, (1886). Closed. For inquiries for parish records contact the Chancery.

8—Precious Blood, (1869). Closed. Parish records at Our Lady of Perpetual Help.

9—Sacred Heart, (1876), Administrators: Revs. Regis Giroux; Francis E. Reilly.
Res., 435 Maple St., 01040. Tel: 413-532-4282. [JC]
Catechesis/Religious Programs—Tel: 413-532-0107.
Students 356.

10—St. Jerome's, (1856), Rev. Daniel R. Foley, V.F.
Res., 169 Hampden St., 01040. Tel: 413-532-6381. [CEM]

Housatonic, Berkshire Co., Corpus Christi (1899), Rev. Anthony J. Jutt.
Res., 520 Main St., Box 569, 01236. Tel: 413-274-3443. [CEM]
Catechesis/Religious Programs—Students 76.

All Saints (1913) (Polish), Rev. Anthony J. Jutt.
Res., 204 Highland St., 01236. Tel: 413-274-6517.
Catechesis/Religious Programs—Students 62.

Huntington, Hampshire Co., St. Thomas (1886), Rev. Donald A. Noiseux.
Res., 8 E. Main St., P.O. Box 547, 01050. Tel: 413-667-3350. [CEM]
Catechesis/Religious Programs—Students 110.
Mission—Chester, Hampden Co., St. John, Middlefield St., Chester, 01011.

Indian Creek, St. Jude, Rev. Mark Stelzer, Admin.
Res., 1326 Worcester St., Indian Orchard, 01151.
Chapel—Pinevale St., Indian Orchard.

Lanesboro, Berkshire Co., North American Martyrs (1969), Rev. John T. Smegal, Admin.; Deacon William C. Moesley.
Res., 17 Juleann Dr., 01237. Tel: 413-442-2063.
Catechesis/Religious Programs—Students 145.

Lee, Berkshire Co., St. Mary's (1857), Revs. Gary M. Dailey; Brian F. McGrath.
Res., 40 Academy St., 01238. Tel: 413-243-0275; Fax: 413-243-1926. [CEM]
School—115 Orchard St., 01238. Tel: 413-243-1079.
Sisters of St. Joseph 3; Lay Teachers 9; Students 221.
Catechesis/Religious Programs—Students 270.
Missions—Otis, Berkshire Co., St. Mary of the Lakes, Tel: 413-269-4200; South Lee, Berkshire Co., St. Francis of Assisi.

Leeds, Hampshire Co., St. Catherine's (1911), Rev. Vincent M. O'Connor.
Res., 195 Main St., 01053. Tel: 413-584-1726.
Catechesis/Religious Programs—Students 170.

Lenox, Berkshire Co., St. Ann's (1891), Rev. Daniel B. Brunton; Deacon George Keator.
Res., 134 Main St., 01240. Tel: 413-637-0157. [CEM]
Catechesis/Religious Programs—Tel: 413-637-4027. Mrs. Helen Stuart, D.R.E.
Students 292.

Lenox Dale, Berkshire Co., St. Vincent de Paul's (1904), Rev. Daniel B. Brunton. In res., Rev. John J. Bonzagni Tel: 413-637-1085.
Mailing Address: P.O. Box 259, 01242-0259.
Res., 29 Crystal St., 01242. Tel: 413-637-3525.
Catechesis/Religious Programs—Students 65.

Longmeadow, Hampden Co., St. Mary's (1936), Rev. Msgr. Thomas F. Devine; Rev. Dariusz P. Wudarski; Deacon Donald Higby.
Res., 519 Longmeadow St., 01106. Tel: 413-567-3124.
School—56 Hopkins Pl., 01106. Tel: 413-567-0907.
Sisters of St. Joseph 2; Lay Teachers 12; Students 245.
Catechesis/Religious Programs—Tel: 413-567-3420.
Students 890.

Ludlow, Hampden Co.,

1—Christ the King, (1948) (Polish), Rev. Raymond A. Soltys.
Res., 41 Warsaw Ave., 01056. Tel: 413-583-2630.
Catechesis/Religious Programs—Students 242.

2—Our Lady of Fatima, (1948) (Portugese), Rev. Vitor Oliveira, Admin.
Res., 438 Winsor St., 01056. Tel: 413-583-2312; Fax: 413-547-0207.
Catechesis/Religious Programs—Students 571.

3—St. John the Baptist, (1904) (French), Rev. Homer P. Gosselin; Deacon Edward Faber. In res., Rev. Lionel E. Bonneville.
Res., 181 Hubbard St., 01056. Tel: 413-583-3467; Fax: 413-583-2036.
School—217 Hubbard St., 01056. Tel: 413-583-8550.
Sisters of St. Ann 3; Lay Teachers 15; Students 275.
Catechesis/Religious Programs—Tel: 413-583-4258.
Students 271.

4—St. Mary, (1968), Rev. Francis J. Manning; Deacons Robert L. Duval; Louis Pancotti.
Res., 12 Cedar St., 01056. Tel: 413-583-2691.
Catechesis/Religious Programs—Students 411.

Millers Falls, Franklin Co., St. John's (1898), Rev. Dennis P. Bombardier.
Res., 5 Church St., 01349. Tel: 413-659-3435.
Mission—Erving, Franklin Co., St. Blanche, 16 East Prospect, Erving, 01344.

Monson, Hampden Co., St. Patrick's (1878), Rev. Jeddie P. Brooks; Deacon Bernard Pellissier.
Res., 22 Green St., P.O. Box 473, 01057. Tel: 413-267-3622. [CEM]
Catechesis/Religious Programs—Students 306.

North Adams, Berkshire Co.,

1—Holy Family, (1997). Merged with Our Lady of Incarnation, North Adams, to become Our Lady of Mercy, North Adams.

2—Notre Dame, (1875), Revs. Michael Twardzik; David Darcy; Deacon Robert R. Moulton.
Res., 228 E. Main St., 01247. Tel: 413-663-7131.
Catechesis/Religious Programs—Students 125.

3—Our Lady of the Incarnation, (1955). Merged with Holy Family, North Adams, to become Our Lady of Mercy, North Adams.

4—OUR LADY OF MERCY, Revs. Michael Twardzik; David Darcy; Deacon Robert Moulton.
Parish Center—635 State Rd., 01247. Tel: 413-663-3976.
Catechesis/Religious Programs—Tel: 413-662-2083. Jackie Gould, D.R.E.
Students 175.
Shrine—1288 Massachusetts Ave., 01247.

5—OUR LADY OF MERCY SHRINE, (1997). Consolidation of Holy Family, North Adams, and Our Lady of the Incarnation, North Adams. Revs. Michael Twardzik; David Darcy; Deacon Robert Moulton.
1288 Massachussetts Ave., 01247. Tel: 413-663-7131; Fax: 413-664-4940.
Catechesis/Religious Programs—Tel: 413-662-2038. Jackie Gould, D.R.E.
Students 94.

6—ST. ANTHONY OF PADUA, (1903) (Italian), Rev. Daniel J. O'Hear.
Res., 70 Marshall St., 01247. Tel: 413-663-3112.
Catechesis/Religious Programs—Tel: 413-663-7331.
Students 210.

7—ST. FRANCIS, (1863), Revs. Michael W.T. Twardzik; David M. Darcy.
Res., 12 Union St., 01247. Tel: 413-663-5316; Fax: 413-663-3938. [CEM]
Catechesis/Religious Programs—Tel: 413-662-2038.
Students 585.

Northampton, Hampshire Co.,

1—ANNUNCIATION, (1878), Revs. Roy H. Duquette; John S. Lis, Parochial Vicar.
Res., 42 Beacon St., P.O. Box 60055, Florence, 01062-0055. Tel: 413-584-1520.
Catechesis/Religious Programs—87 Beacon St., Florence, 01062-0055. Tel: 413-584-2041. Cindy Teynor, D.R.E.
Students 210.

2—BLESSED SACRAMENT, (1899) (Spanish), Rev. Daniel P. Liston; Deacon Francis J. McCarthy.
Res., 336 Elm St., 01060. Tel: 413-584-1280.
Catechesis/Religious Programs—Tel: 413-586-1111.
Students 225.

3—SACRED HEART, (1886) (French), Rev. Merle L. Lavoie.
Res., 101 King St., 01060. Tel: 413-584-7422.
Catechesis/Religious Programs—Tel: 413-584-4339. Mrs. Helen Lucey, D.R.E.
Students 65.

4—ST. JOHN CANTIUS, (1904) (Polish), Rev. Merle L. Lavoie.
Res., 10 Hawley St., 01060. Tel: 413-584-1510; Fax: 413-586-5776. [CEM]

5—ST. MARY OF THE ASSUMPTION, (1866) (Irish), Rev. Eugene D. Honan. In res., Rev. Leo James Hoar.
Res., 3 Elm St., P.O. Box 180, 01061. Tel: 413-584-7310; Fax: 413-584-4788. [CEM]
Catechesis/Religious Programs—Tel: 413-586-1111.
Students 150.

Northfield, Franklin Co., St. Patrick (1973), Rev. John J. Ayers; Deacon Arthur E. Ratte.
Res., 80 Main St., 01360-1022. Tel: 413-498-2728. [CEM]
Catechesis/Religious Programs—Students 150.

Orange, Franklin Co., St. Mary (1903), Rev. James E. Diemand; Deacons Joseph S. Bucci, Jr.; James F. Donelan.
Res., 19 Congress St., 01364. Tel: 978-544-2900.
Catechesis/Religious Programs—Tel: 978-544-8105.
Students 203.

Palmer, Hampden Co., St. Thomas the Apostle (1864), Rev. Eugene J. Plasse; Deacon Edward J. Tenczar.
Res., 76 Thorndike St., 01069. Tel: 413-283-5091. [CEM]
Catechesis/Religious Programs—Tel: 413-283-5651.
Students 365.

Pittsfield, Berkshire Co.,

1—HOLY FAMILY, (1912) (Polish), Revs. Alexander Szymborski, C.R.L., Admin.; Eugene A. Suszek.
Res., 133 Seymour St., 01201. Tel: 413-442-2036.
Catechesis/Religious Programs—21 Danforth St., 01201. Tel: 413-442-4065. John Arasimowiez, D.R.E.
Students 87.

2—NOTRE DAME, (1868) (French), Rev. Earl Hebert; Deacon Ralph R. Cyr.
Res., 50 Melville St., 01201. Tel: 413-499-2736.

3—OUR LADY OF MT. CARMEL, (1903) (Italian), Revs. Geoffrey J. Deeker, C.S.S.; Rinaldo A. Ribezzi, C.S.S.; Joseph H. Fellin, C.S.S.
Res., 359 Fenn St., 01201. Tel: 413-442-4458; Fax: 413-496-9607.
Catechesis/Religious Programs—Tel: 413-445-4856.
Students 125.
Mission—Pittsfield, Berkshire Co., All Souls, 51 Pembroke Ave., 01201. Tel: 413-442-5090.

4—SACRED HEART, (1919), Revs. James K. Joyce; Royal J. Gardner; Deacon James A. Hager. Pastoral Ministers: Sr. Barbara Burke; Sr. Kathryn Flanagan.
Res., 191 Elm St., 01201. Tel: 413-443-6960.
School—Regional School, (Grades K-5) One Meadow Lane, 01201. Tel: 413-443-6379.
Sisters of St. Joseph 1; Lay Teachers 19; Students 339.
Catechesis/Religious Programs—Tel: 413-442-5564. D.R.E.: Mr. Robert Esposito; Mrs. Margaret Dextradeur.
Students 679.

5—ST. CHARLES, (1893), Rev. Peter A. Gregory; Sr. Barbara C. Faille, S.S.J., Pastoral Assoc.; Deacon William G. Moesley.
Res., 89 Briggs Ave., 01201. Tel: 413-442-7470; Fax: 413-445-5267.
Catechesis/Religious Programs—100 Briggs Ave., 01201. Tel: 413-442-0591.
Students 274.

6—ST. FRANCIS, (1960), Rev. John J. Mara.
Res., 80 Morningview Dr., 01201. Tel: 413-499-1955.
Catechesis/Religious Programs—Tel: 413-448-2987.
Students 152.

7—ST. JOSEPH'S, (1849), Rev. Michael Shershanovich; Deacon Eugene C. Momnie.
Res., 414 North St., 01201. Tel: 413-445-5789. [CEM]

8—ST. MARK'S, (1913), Rev. Henry L. Dorsch. In res., Rev. Msgr. Joseph I. Johnson, P.A., V.F., Pastor Emeritus; Rev. William Eckert (CAM).
Res., 27 Onota St., 01201. Tel: 413-447-7510.
Catechesis/Religious Programs—400 Columbus Ave. Ext., 01201. Tel: 413-442-8444.
Students 363.

9—ST. MARY THE MORNING STAR, (1915), Rev. Ralph A. Pollone.
Res., 665 Tyler St., 01201. Tel: 413-445-5008.
Catechesis/Religious Programs—Students 150.
Convent—75 Plunkett St., 01201. Tel: 413-447-7533.

10—ST. TERESA, (1926), Rev. John J. Varley.
Res., 290 South St., 01201. Tel: 413-442-2202.
Catechesis/Religious Programs—Tel: 413-443-5366.
Students 184.

Russell, Hampden Co., Our Lady of the Rosary (1969), Rev. Armando C. Russo.
Res., Huntington Rd., 01071. Tel: 413-862-4418. [JC]
Catechesis/Religious Programs—Students 165.

Sheffield, Berkshire Co., Our Lady of the Valley (1901), Rev. Frederick L. Heberle; Deacon Herbert L. Cary.
Res., 99 Maple Ave., 01257. Tel: 413-229-3028. [CEM]
Catechesis/Religious Programs—Students 150.
Missions—Mill River, Berkshire Co., Immaculate Conception; Monterey, Berkshire Co., Our Lady of the Hills.

Shelburne Falls, Franklin Co., St. Joseph's (1883), Rev. John A. Roach.
Res., 34 Monroe Ave., 01370. Tel: 413-625-6405.
Catechesis/Religious Programs—Students 125.
Missions—Colrain, Franklin Co., St. John the Baptist, Church St., Colrain, 01346; Charlemont, Franklin Co., St. Christopher, Rte. 2, Charlemont, 01339.

South Deerfield, Franklin Co., St. James (1895), Rev. Julius A. Jutt.
Res., 85 Main St., 01373. Tel: 413-665-4535.
Catechesis/Religious Programs—Students 239.
Mission—Conway, Franklin Co., St. Mark.

St. Stanislaus B. and M. (1908) (Polish), Rev. Philippe Roux.
Mailing Address: 29 Sugarloaf St., 01373.
Res., 27 Sugarloaf St., 01373. Tel: 413-665-2417. [CEM]
Catechesis/Religious Programs—33 Sugarloaf St., 01373. Tel: 413-665-4656.
Students 180.

South Hadley, Hampshire Co., St. Theresa of the Infant Jesus (1946), Revs. Cyril J. Burns; Richard Riendeau; Deacon Thomas A. Callahan.
Res., 9E Parkview Dr., P.O. Box 159, 01075. Tel: 413-532-3228.
Catechesis/Religious Programs—Tel: 413-538-6276; 532-1905. Margaret Jodoin, D.R.E.
Students 1,197.

St. Patrick's (1877), Rev. Richard M. Turner; Deacon John Bledsoe. In res., Rev. David R. Raymond.
Res., 30 Main St., 01075. Tel: 413-532-2850. [CEM]
Catechesis/Religious Programs—Tel: 413-534-7080.
Students 539.

Southwick, Hampden Co., Our Lady of the Lake (1951), Rev. Timothy J. Hallahan.
Res., 224 Sheep Pasture Rd., P.O. Box 1148, 01077. Tel: 413-569-0161.
Catechesis/Religious Programs—Rose M. Salzer, D.R.E.
Students 361.

Stockbridge, Berkshire Co., St. Joseph's (1922), Rev. Leonard Perreault. In res., Most Rev. Thomas R. Manning, O.F.M. Tel: 413-298-3748.
Mailing Address: 11 Elm St., P.O. Box 434, 01262.
Res., 30 Albany Rd., West Stockbridge, 01266. Tel: 413-232-4427. [CEM]

Thorndike, Hampden Co., St. Mary's (1876), Deacon Edward J. Tenczar, Admin.
Mailing Address: 80 Main St., 01079. Tel: 413-283-3501.
Res., 25 Cheney St., Three Rivers, 01080. Tel: 413-283-5776.

Three Rivers, Hampden Co., St. Anne's (1882) (French), Rev. Sylvio E. Levesque.
Res., 2230 Main St., 01080. Tel: 413-283-5041; Fax: 413-863-8978. [CEM]
Catechesis/Religious Programs—Students 182.

SS. Peter and Paul (1903) (Polish), Rev. Robert J. Ceckowski.
Res., 2267 Main St., 01080. Tel: 413-283-6030. [CEM]
Catechesis/Religious Programs—Tel: 413-283-8814.
Students 238.
Convent—358 Main St., 01080. Tel: 413-283-7402.
The Sisters Minor of Mary Immaculate 4.

Turners Falls, Franklin Co., St. Mary's (1872), Rev. Stanley J. Aksamit; Deacon Albert Routhier.
Res., 90 Seventh St., 01376. Tel: 413-863-2585; Fax: 413-863-8978. [CEM]
Catechesis/Religious Programs—Students 182.

Our Lady of Czestochowa (1909) (Polish), Rev. Charles J. DiMascola.
Res., 84 K St., 01376. Tel: 413-863-4748. [CEM]
Catechesis/Religious Programs—Students 130.

St. Anne (1884) (French), Rev. Stanley J. Aksamit; Deacon Albert Routhier.
Mailing Address: 90 Seventh St., 01376. Tel: 413-863-2585. [CEM]
Church—J St., 01376. Fax: 413-863-4678.

Ware, Hampshire Co., All Saints (1860), Rev. Edward T. Fitzgerald.
Res., 17 North St., 01082. Tel: 413-967-4963. [CEM]
Catechesis/Religious Programs—Students 127.

Our Lady of Mt. Carmel (1871) (French), Rev. Paul A. Bombardier.
Res., 17 Convent Hill Rd., 01082. Tel: 413-967-5704. [CEM]
Catechesis/Religious Programs—Tel: 413-967-6101.
Students 127.

St. Mary's (1905) (Polish), Revs. Charles H. Kuzmeski; Henry Karwel, O.F.M.Conv.
Res., 60 South St., 01082. Tel: 413-967-5913; Fax: 413-967-4679. [CEM]
School—59 South St., 01082. Tel: 413-967-9936; Fax: 413-967-8217.
Sisters of Immaculate Conception 3; Lay Teachers 9; Students 245.
Catechesis/Religious Programs—Tel: 413-967-5914.
Students 244.

Westfield, Hampden Co.,

1—HOLY TRINITY, (1903) (Polish), Revs. Gerald R. Biron, M.S.; Rene J. Butler, M.S.
Res., 335 Elm St., 01085. Tel: 413-568-1506.
School—(Grades K-8) 331 Elm St., 01085. Tel: 413-568-4352. Mrs. Janet Snow, Prin.
Lay Teachers 13; Students 161.
Catechesis/Religious Programs—Students 231.

2—OUR LADY OF THE BLESSED SACRAMENT, (1910), Rev. Francis X. Sullivan.
Res., 6 Union St., 01085. Tel: 413-562-3450.
Catechesis/Religious Programs—Tel: 413-562-3615. D.R.E.: Sr. M. Barbara Ebbe; Mrs. Deborah Lanoue.
Students 540.

3—St. Casimir's, (1915) (Lithuanian), Rev. John J. Brennan. In res., Rev. Columkille O'Grady, C.P.; Bro. Terrence A. Scanlon, C.P.
Res., 22 State St., 01085. Tel: 413-568-5421; Fax: 413-562-3879.
Catechesis/Religious Programs—Tel: 413-568-6261.
Students 63.

4—St. Mary's, (1862), Revs. Anthony J. Creane; John C. Salatino; James A. Sipitkowski; Deacon Francis D. Rogers.
Res., 30 Bartlett St., 01085. Tel: 413-562-5477; Fax: 413-562-5478. [CEM]
School—Tel: 413-568-2388.
Sisters 4; Lay Teachers 14; Students 253.
High School—Tel: 413-568-5692.
Sisters 2; Lay Teachers 16; Students 145.
Catechesis/Religious Programs—Tel: 413-568-1127. D.R.E.: Mrs. Kay Mowatt, Elementary; Mrs. Dona Kane, Elementary; Mrs. Constance Patten, High School.
Students 645.
Convent—86 Mechanic St., 01085. Tel: 413-568-8077.
Sisters of St. Joseph 3.

5—St. Peter's, (1913) (Slovak), Rev. John J. Brennan; Sr. Ann Marie Yenca, O.S.F., Pastoral Min. In res., Rev. John T. Dean.
Res., 22 State St., 01085. Tel: 413-568-5421; Fax: 413-562-3879.
Catechesis/Religious Programs—32 State St., 01085. Tel: 413-568-6261. Sr. Marcella Meluch, O.S.F., D.R.E.
Students 215.
Convent—St. Peter's Convent, 33 State St., 01085.
Sisters 3.

West Springfield, Hampden Co., Immaculate Conception (1877), Rev. Michael J. Twohig. In res., Rev. John J. Johnson.
Res., 475 Main St., 01089-3998. Tel: 413-736-4071.
Catechesis/Religious Programs—Students 134.

St. Louis de France (1895) (French), Rev. Norman B. Bolton.
Res., 817 Main St., 01089. Tel: 413-733-8026.

St. Thomas the Apostle (1904) (Irish), Revs. John T. Cain; Steven Amo. In res., Rev. Herbert Schmidt (Italy).
Res., 47 Pine St., 01089. Tel: 413-739-4779; Fax: 413-739-1608. [CEM]
School—89 Pine St., 01089. Tel: 413-739-4131.
Sisters of St. Joseph 2; Lay Teachers 26; Students 488.
Catechesis/Religious Programs—75 Pine St., 01089. Tel: 413-737-8267; Fax: 413-739-1608. Mrs. Meagan Baillard, D.R.E.
Students 915.

West Stockbridge, Berkshire Co., St. Patrick's (1871), Rev. Leonard Perreault.
Res., Albany Rd., 01266. Tel: 413-232-4427. [CEM]

Wilbraham, Hampden Co., St. Cecilia's (1951), Rev. Joseph M. Soranno; Sr. Mary McCue, S.N.D., Pastoral Ministry.
Res., 7 Maple St., 01095. Tel: 413-596-4232; Fax: 413-596-9937.
Catechesis/Religious Programs—64 Main St., 01095. Tel: 413-596-9937. Sr. Mary Patrice Mahoney, S.N.D., D.R.E.
Students 1,100.

Williamstown, Berkshire Co., St. Patrick's (1887). Merged with St. Raphael, Williamstown, to form SS. Patrick and Raphael, Williamstown.

SS. Patrick and Raphael (1997), Rev. William F. Cyr.
Mailing Address: P.O. Box 616, 01267-2414.
Res., 54 Southworth St., 01267. Tel: 413-458-4946; Fax: 413-458-4954.
Catechesis/Religious Programs—53 Southworth St., 01267. Tel: 413-458-5443.
Students 238.

St. Raphael (1891). Merged with St. Patrick, Williamstown, to form SS. Patrick and Raphael, Williamstown.

Chaplains of Public Institutions

Springfield. *Baystate Medical Center, Springfield Hospital Unit.* Rev. Michael H. Devlin, Assumption Rectory, 104 Springfield St., Chicopee, 01013. Tel: 413-592-1597. Rev. Steven McGuigan, All Souls, 445 Plainfield, 01107. Tel: 413-736-0076.
Olympus Specialty Hospital Sacred Heart Rectory, 395 Chestnut St., 01104. Tel: 413-732-3721. Rev. Edward M. Callahan.
Wesson Memorial Hospital Unit Sacred Heart Rectory, 395 Chestnut St., 01104. Tel: 413-732-3721. Rev. Edward M. Callahan.
Wesson-Women's Hospital Unit Tel: 413-736-8773. Revs. Michael H. Devlin; Philip G. Gallerani.

Holyoke. *Soldiers' Home.* Served by Blessed Sacrament Parish. Tel: 413-532-0713.

Monson. *State Hospital.* Bureau for Exceptional Children and Adults. 537 Northampton St., Box 1039, Holyoke, 01041. Tel: 413-538-7450. Rev. Robert F. Wagner; Deacon Rodney Szymczk.

Northampton. *Veterans Administration Hospital* 421 N. Main St., 01060. Tel: 413-584-4040. Rev. Lionel Bonneville.

Pittsfield. *Berkshire Medical Center* Tel: 413-447-2000. Rev. Leroy Smith, One County Rte. 13, Chatham Center, N.Y 12184-9639. Tel: 413-392-4516.

Westfield. *Western Massachusetts Hospital.* Served by Our Lady of the Blessed Sacrament Parish. Tel: 413-562-3450.

On Duty Outside the Diocese:
Reverend Fathers—
Bermudez, Jose, Intercessors of the Lamb, 4014 N. Post Rd., Omaha, NE 68112
DesRosiers, Denis, 300 Vernon St., #2, Oakland, CA 94610
Devino, Terrence P., S.J., Arrupe House, 35 Creighton St., Jamaica Plain, MA 02130
Marchese, Joseph P., Chap., Boston College, Chestnut Hill, MA 02167
Pham, Pierre, Diocese of San Jose, Vietnamese Mission, 389 East Santa Clara St., San Jose, CA 95113
Potvin, Raymond H., Professor Emeritas, Catholic University, Box 1264, Washington, DC 20064
Tuohey, John F., Mercy Health Systems Oklahoma, 4300 West Memorial Rd., Oklahoma City, OK 73120-8362

Military Chaplains:
Reverend Fathers—
Walsh, Francis E., Office of the Chap., PSC 476, Box 61, FPO, AP 96322-1102

Graduate Studies:
Reverend Fathers—
Bonzagni, John, Catholic University, St. Joseph Seminary, 1200 Varnum St., N.E., Washington, DC 20017
Caron, David, Catholic Theological Union, 5401 S. Cornell, Chicago, ILL 60615
Schmitt, Thomas, Gregorian University, Rome, Italy

Absent on Leave:
Reverend Fathers—
Cuff, Thomas E.
DiFabio, Mark
Dube, Donald V.
Graves, Alfred C.
Lavigne, Richard R.
Meehan, Richard
Savage, Warren
Sousa, Kevin
Sullivan, Charles J.

Retired:
Reverend Monsignors—
Foudy, Robert E., Holy Cross Rectory, 221 Plumtree Rd., Springfield, MA 01118
Guerin, Eugene E., Mont Marie Health Care Center, Holyoke, MA 01040
Harrington, John F., Holy Cross Rectory, 23 Sycamore St., Holyoke, MA 01040
Johnson, Joseph I., St. Mark Rectory, 27 Onota St., Pittsfield, MA 01201
Montcalm, Rosario L.U., 47 Pine Grove Dr., South Hadley, MA 01075-2196
Viau, Roger, St. Michael's Residence, 86 Wendover Rd, Springfield, MA 01118
Reverend Fathers—
Allen, William F., 18 Casino Ave., Chicopee, MA 01013
Anoia, John, 820 Jasmine Way, Clearwater, FL 34616
Baranowski, Xavier S., 13 Griswold Rd., G.N.B., P.O. Box 322, Niantic, CT 06357
Bernard, Paul J., 56 Sutton Rd., Millbury, MA 01527
Bourque, John R., 79 Clover Ln., P.O. Box 561, Mashpee, MA 02649
Cronin, James E., 14 Fairlawn Dr., Worcester, MA 01602
Darling, Franklin, 10D Elm Terrace, Greenfield, MA 01301. Tel: 413-772-6187
Delehanty, Thomas F., 2C Stonypoint Dr., P.O. Box 425, Ware, MA 01082
Desilets, Donald A., 35 Raymond Rd., Guildrod, CT 06437
Fennessey, Luke T., St. Michael's Residence, 86 Wendover Rd., Springfield, MA 01118
Forand, Clarence W., #293, 281 Chauncey Walker St., Belchertown, MA 01007
Fournier, W. Donald, 474 Grattan St., Chicopee, MA 01020
Gallerini, Philip G., 630 Friar Rd., Winter Park, FL 32792
Gauvreau, Thomas H., 32 Richards St., North Adams, MA 01247
Greene, Thomas S., St. Michael's Residence, 86 Wendover Rd., Springfield, MA 01118
Lucey, John P., P.O. Box 636, Norwell, MA 02061
Lynes, Thomas E., P.O. Box 212, Old Saybrook, CT 06475
Malboeuf, Gerald L., 12 Cedar St., Ludlow, MA 01056
McCarthy, Thomas J., Holyoke Geriatric Center, 45 Lower Westfield Rd., Holyoke, MA 01040
McKenna, James, 1945 Northhampton St., Holyoke, MA 01040
Moreau, Ernest P., 4851 Gandy Blvd., 15-31, Tampa, FL 01104
O'Connor, Francis A., 22 Fiske St., Worcester, MA 01602
Ozimek, Eugene F., Mount St. Vincent Nursing Home, 35 Holy Family Rd., Holyoke, MA 01040
Pagano, Peter E., 1215 Massachusetts Ave., North Adams, MA 01247
Pham, John H., Willowood Nursing Home, Great Barrington, MA
Posco, Raphael A., Charlene Manor, 130 Colrain Rd., Greenfield, MA 01301
Quigley, J. Joseph, Newman Center, 472 N. Pleasant St., Amherst, MA 1002
Remy, Adrien T., Mont Marie Motherhouse, Holyoke, MA 01040
Riedl, Paul D., Mount St. Vincent Nursing Home, 35 Holy Family Rd., Holyoke, MA 01040
Rocha, Manuel, St. Michael's Residence, 86 Wendover Rd., Springfield, MA 01118
Sexton, John J., St. Michael's Residence, 86 Wendover Rd., Springfield, MA 01118
Sgueglia, Charles J.M., 44 Dexter St., Methuen, MA 01844
Sullivan, Francis J., St. Michael's Residence, 86 Wendover Rd., Springfield, MA 01118
Switalksi, Casimir S., Mount St. Vincent Nursing Home, 35 Holy Family Rd., Holyoke, MA 01040
Tokarz, John, St. Michael's Residence, 86 Wendover Rd., Springfield, MA 01118

Permanent Deacons:
Badame, Joseph, Holy Family, Holyoke
Baldasaro, Pasqual, St. Agnes, Dalton
Bledsoe, John, St. Patrick, South Hadley
Bucci, Joseph
Callahan, Thomas A., St. Theresa, South Hadley
Cary, Herbert L., Our Lady of the Valley, Sheffield
Chabot, Donald P., Holy Trinity, Greenfield
Chapdelaine, Roland G., Springfield Municipal Hospital
Cyr, Ralph R., Notre Dame, Pittsfield
Diaz, Celso B., On Duty Outside the Diocese
Donelan, James, St. Mary, Orange
Duval, Robert L., St. Mary of the Assumption, Ludlow
Faber, Edward H., St. John the Baptist, Ludlow
Finnie, Edward J., (Retired)
Fleury, Bernard J.
Garde, Joseph, St. Catherine, Springfield
Geary, Coleman P., On Duty Outside the Diocese
Gray, Kenneth, Blessed Sacrament, Holyoke
Hager, James A., Sacred Heart, Pittsfield
Herrick, Eugene, Burlington, VT
Higby, Donald, St. Mary, Longmeadow
Keator, George, St. Ann, Lenox
Kozach, George, St. Patrick Church, Chicopee
Martone, James A., Sacred Heart, Feeding Hills
McCarthy, Francis J., Blessed Sacrament, Northampton
Medina, Genaro, Sr., Spanish Apostolate at Blessed Sacrament, Springfield
Miller, Lucien M., Campus Ministry, Univ. of Massachusetts, Amherst
Mireault, Leon, St. Rose de Lima, Chicopee
Moesley, William C., St. Charles, Pittsfield
Momnie, Eugene C., St. Joseph, Pittsfield
Moore, Donald E., (Retired)
Morrissey, Robert J., St. Paul, Springfield
Moulton, Robert R., Notre Dame, Holy Family & Our Lady of Incarnation, North Adams
O'Brien, John P., On Duty Outside the Diocese
Pancotti, Louis, St. Mary, Ludlow
Pelletier, Frederick J., St. Ann, Chicopee
Pellissier, Bernard, St. Patrick, Monson
Rael, C. Lincoln, Immaculate Conception, Holyoke
Ratte, Arthur E., St. Patrick, Northfield
Rivera, Jose, On Duty Outside the Diocese
Rogers, Francis, St. Mary, Westfield
Szymzyk, Rodney J., Our Lady of the Rosary, Springfield
Tenczar, Edward J., St. Thomas the Apostle, Palmer
Velazquez, Raphael, Holy Family, Springfield
Wallen, Paul, Our Lady of the Sacred Heart, Springfield

INSTITUTIONS LOCATED IN THE DIOCESE

[A] SEMINARIES, RELIGIOUS, OR SCHOLASTICATES

GRANBY. *St. Hyacinth College and Seminary,* 01033. Friary. Tel: 413-467-7180. College: Tel: 413-467-7191. Order of Friars Minor Conventual; Liberal Arts and Sciences. Certificates in Lay Ministry, Biblical Studies, and Catholic Spirituality. Revs. Jude Surowiec, O.F.M.Conv., Chief Academic Officer (Pres.) and Registrar, Co-Dir. Lay Ministry Program; Claude Jarmak, O.F.M.Conv.; James E. McCurry, O.F.M.Conv., Guardian and Dir. of Militia Immaculata. Tel: 413-467-9190; Zeno Wierzbinski, O.F.M.Conv., (Retired); Jeremy Chodacki, O.F.M.Conv., (Retired); Cyprian Sondej, O.F.M.Conv., (Retired). Priests 6; Non-Resident Students 55.

[B] COLLEGES AND UNIVERSITIES

CHICOPEE. *College of Our Lady of the Elms,* 01013. Tel: 413-594-2761; Fax: 413-592-4871.
E-mail: keating@elms.edu
Web site: www.elms.edu
For a complete listing, refer to the Colleges and Universities section.

[C] HIGH SCHOOLS, DIOCESAN

SPRINGFIELD. *Cathedral High School,* 260 Surrey Rd., 01118. Tel: 413-782-5285. Sr. Denise Granger, S.S.J., Prin.; Rev. David R. Raymond, Spiritual Dir. Priests 1; Sisters 8; Lay Teachers 69; Students 984.

HOLYOKE. *Holyoke Catholic High School,* 91 Chestnut St., 01040. Tel: 413-533-0347. Sisters of St. Joseph. Rev. David R. Raymond, Spiritual Dir.; Mr. William Fitzgerald, Prin. Priests 2; Sisters 7; Lay Teachers 25; Students 382.

PITTSFIELD. *St. Joseph Central High School,* 22 Maplewood Ave., 01201. Tel: 413-447-9121; Fax: 413-443-7020. Sisters of St. Joseph. Margaret Downing, Prin. Sisters 1; Lay Teachers 27; Students 261.

[D] ELEMENTARY SCHOOLS, DIOCESAN

SPRINGFIELD. *Catholic Schools of Chicopee.* Diocesan School Department, Christian Education Center. 625 Carew St., 01104. Tel: 413-732-3175. Students 1,480; Total Staff 67.

Sacred Heart School, 370 Stafford St., 01104. Tel: 413-733-3630. Ms. Carol Brown, Prin. Sisters 2; Lay Teachers 11; Students 163.

[E] ORPHANAGES

WEST SPRINGFIELD. *The Brightside for Families & Children* 2112 Riverdale St. Springfield, 01089. Tel: 413-788-7366.
For a complete listing, refer to the Special Care Facilities section.

[F] GENERAL HOSPITALS

SPRINGFIELD. *CHE - Mercy Mass. Hosp. Corp.,* 271 Carew St., 01120. Tel: 413-748-9000
For a complete listing, refer to the Hospitals section.

Mercy Hospital, 271 Carew St., Box 9012, 01102-9012. Tel: 413-748-9000
For a complete listing, refer to the Hospitals section.

TURNERS FALLS. *Farren Care Center, Inc.,* 340 Montague City Rd., 01376. Tel: 413-774-3111
For a complete listing, refer to the Hospitals section.

[G] FAMILY SERVICES

SPRINGFIELD. *Marriage Counseling Service,* 65 Elliot St., P.O. Box 1730, 01101-1730. Tel: 413-732-3175; 732-2909; Fax: 413-747-0273. Rev. John J. Johnson, S.T.D., L.M.F.T., Dir. Counselors: Mr. Alfred A. D'Amato, Ed.D., L.M.F.T.; Mrs. Rosemary Castonguay, M.Ed., L.M.H.C. Total Staff 4; Total Assisted 623.

HOLYOKE. *Mont Marie Child Care Center, Inc.,* Mont Marie, 01040. Tel: 413-536-2964. Sr. Eleanor T. Harrington, S.S.J., Dir. Sisters of St. Joseph 1; Total Staff 19; Children 102.

Providence Ministries for the Needy, Inc., 476 Appleton St., P.O. Box 6269, 01041. Tel: 413-536-9109; Fax: 413-536-1137.
E-mail: PMN10@Juno.com
Sponsored by the Sisters of Providence of Holyoke, MA. Mr. Robin L. Goshea, Admin. Total Staff 18; Total Assisted 51,831.

Broderick House. An around-the-clock family shelter. 56 Cabot St., P.O. Box 6269, 01041. Tel: 413-534-7610. D. Jean Wright, Mgr. Capacity 35.

SRO. Single Room Occupancy for low income women without children. Capacity 5.

Margaret's Pantry. Provides emergency food to families and individuals.

St. Jude's Center. Distributes clothing, furniture, and household items to the poor.

St. Joseph of Arimathia Guild. Provides advocacy to assure a dignified funeral and burial of the dead poor.

Loreto House. An around-the-clock shelter for homeless men. 264 Elm St., P.O. Box 6269, 01041. Tel: 413-532-7859. Charles Carter, Mgr. Capacity 18.

Kate's Kitchen. A community kitchen which provides one meal daily to anyone in need - no questions asked. 264 Elm St., P.O. Box 6269, 01041. Tel: 413-532-0233. Capacity 99.

NORTHAMPTON. *Christian Life Center,* 95 King St., 01060. Tel: 413-584-7422.

PITTSFIELD. *Catholic Charities Counseling Office,* 467 North St., Rm. 15, P.O. Box 1372, 01202. Tel: 413-443-3169. Thomas A. Duane, L.I.C.S.W., Supr. Counselors: Robert T. Sykes; Janet M. O'Brien. Total Staff 3; Total Assisted 720.

TURNERS FALLS. *Montague Catholic Social Ministries, Inc.,* 25 Sixth St., 01376. Tel: 413-863-4805.
E-mail: kitlh@aol.com
Sr. Kathleen Hinga, S.S.J., Contact Person.
Purpose: To assist in providing information and referral, adult education, leadership and neighborhood development, partnership, coalition building and participation, facilitate parish concerns and social justice efforts. Total Staff 2; Total Assisted 3,000.

[H] HOMES FOR AGED

SPRINGFIELD. *St. Michael's Residence,* 86 Wendover Rd., 01118. Tel: 413-783-6773
For a complete listing, refer to the Special Care Facilities section.

HOLYOKE. *Mont Marie Health Care Center, Inc.,* 34 Lower Westfield Rd., 01040. Tel: 413-536-0853; Fax: 413-533-3275
For a complete listing, refer to the Special Care Facilities section.

Sisters of Providence Care Centers, Inc., 35 Holy Family Rd., 01040-2758
For a complete listing, refer to the Special Care Facilities section.

[I] MONASTERIES AND RESIDENCES OF PRIESTS AND BROTHERS

STOCKBRIDGE. *Congregation of Marians,* Eden Hill, 01262. Tel: 413-298-3931; Fax: 413-298-1146; 298-1211.
E-mail: wadziordz@aol.com
Web site: http://www.marian.org/
Province: Tel: 413-298-1101; Fax: 413-298-0207. Revs. Walter Dziordz, M.I.C., Prov. Supr.; Kazimierz Chwalek, M.I.C., Prov. Econome; Bro. Kenneth Galisa, M.I.C., Prov. Sec.
The National Shrine of Divine Mercy: Tel: 413-298-3931; Fax: 413-298-3910. Rev. Seraphim Michalenko, M.I.C., Shrine Rector.
Marian Helpers Center: Tel: 413-298-3691; Fax: 413-298-3583. Bro. Andrew R. Maczynski, M.I.C., Dir., Marian Helpers Center.
Divine Mercy International: Tel: 413-298-3931; Fax: 413-298-4559. Revs. Seraphim Michalenko, M.I.C., Dir.; George Kosicki, C.S.B., Asst. Dir.
John Paul II Institute of Divine Mercy: Revs. Seraphim Michalenko, M.I.C., Dir.; George Kosicki, C.S.B., Asst. Dir. In res. Revs. Kazimierz Chwalek, M.I.C., Local Supr.; Fidelis Grabowski, M.I.C.; Walter Dziordz, M.I.C.; Walter Pelczynski, M.I.C.; Seraphim Michalenko, M.I.C.; Bros. Walter Gurgul, M.I.C. (Our Lady of Mercy Province, England); Ireneus Chodakowski, M.I.C. (Our Lady of Mercy Province, England); John Bryda, M.I.C.; Alphie Gagne, M.I.C.; Fred Wells, M.I.C.; Ken Galisa, M.I.C.; Andrew Maczynski, M.I.C., House Econome; Andrew Kwasnica, M.I.C. (Divine Providence Province, Poland). Priests 14; Oblate Sisters of the Most Eucharist 7; Brothers 6.
On Duty Outside Of House: Revs. Bernard Backiel, M.I.C.; Richard J. Drabik, M.I.C.; John J. Gayton, M.I.C.; Francis Duda, M.I.C.; Martin Rzeszutek, M.I.C.
On Duty Outside the U.S.A.: Revs. Mark Garrow, M.I.C., Third Gen. Councillor, Gen. Dir. Formation; Casimir Krzyzanowski, M.I.C., Sec. Gen., Postulator Gen., Procurator Gen.

[J] CONVENTS AND RESIDENCES FOR SISTERS

SPRINGFIELD. *Convent of the Good Shepherd,* 280 Tinkham Rd., 01129. Tel: 413-783-1251. Sr. Clare Marie Klein. Contemplative Sisters of the Good Shepherd 16; Total Staff 2.

HOLYOKE. *Daughters of the Heart of Mary Provincial Residence,* 1339 Northampton St., 01040-1913. Tel: 413-532-7406; Fax: 413-533-4217. Sr. Miriam Najimy, D.H.M., Prov. Total in Residence 38; Total Staff 3.

Marian Residence, 1365 Northampton St., 01040. Tel: 413-534-4502; Fax: 413-534-7353. Sr. Margaret E. Linehan, D.H.M., Supr.

Marian Center, 1365 Northampton St., 01040. Tel: 413-534-4502. Sr. M. Jeannette Levangie, D.H.M., Supr. Daughters of the Heart of Mary 24. Daughters of the Heart of Mary 23.

Mont Marie, 01040. Tel: 413-536-0853. Motherhouse of the Sisters of St. Joseph of Springfield. Sr. Constance Quinlan, S.S.J., Pres.; Sr. Mary Quinn, S.S.J., Vice Pres.; Rev. Adrien T. Remy, Chap.

Mont Marie Child Care, Inc. Total Assisted 103; Total Staff 19.

Mont Marie Health Care Center, Inc. Total Assisted 72; Total Staff 80.

Mont Marie Conference Center. Total Staff 9. Sisters 400; Total Staff 48.

Provincial House and Formation House, 1039 Northampton St., 01040. Tel: 413-532-8156. Franciscan Missionary Sisters of Assisi. Sr. Norbert Petrucci, S.F.M.A., Vice Prov. Sisters 6.

Sisters of Providence Infirmary, 1223 Main St., 3rd Fl., 01040-5394. Tel: 413-493-2750; Fax: 413-493-2759.
E-mail: sisprov@javanet.com
Web site: http://www.sisofprov.org
Motherhouse of the Sisters of Providence. Sr. Ruth McGoldrick, S.P., Pres. of Congregation; Rev. Edward M. Kennedy, Chap. In Residence. Sisters 124.

Sisters of Providence Infirmary, 1233 Main St., 3rd Floor, 01040-5394. Tel: 413-493-2750; Fax: 413-493-2759.

Sisters of Providence Health System, Inc. Includes an array of Health and Social Service Institutions in the Diocese. 1233 Main St., 01040-4080. Sr. Kathleen Popko, S.P., Pres., CEO.

Providence Ministries for the Needy, Inc., P.O. Box 6269, 01041-6269. Tel: 413-536-9109.

Genesis Spiritual Life Center, 53 Mill St., Westfield, 01085-4253. Tel: 413-562-3627.

Queen of Peace Centennial House, 64 North St., Greenfield, 01301. Tel: 413-772-2000.

TYRINGHAM. *Order of the Visitation of Holy Mary,* Monastery of the Visitation, P.O. Box 432, 01264. Tel: 413-243-3995. Sr. Mary Francis Metz. Order of the Visitation of Holy Mary 16.

WEST SPRINGFIELD. *Cana,* 686 Elm St., 01089. Tel: 413-732-9311. Sisters of Providence 4.

Monastery of the Mother of God, Dominican Nuns (Contemplative), 1430 Riverdale St., 01089-4698. Tel: 413-736-3639; Fax: 413-736-0850. Perpetual Adoration of the Most Blessed Sacrament. Sr. Mary St. John, O.P., Prioress; Rev. John T. Carrigan, O.P., Chap. Solemnly Professed Nuns 22; Temporarily Professed 4.

[K] RETREAT HOUSES AND CHRISTIAN LIFE CENTERS

SPRINGFIELD. *Center for Spiritual Direction.* Memorial House, Mercy Hospital. P.O. Box 9012, 01102-9012. Tel: 413-734-8843; 788-0195. Sr. Mary Marrin, S.S.J., Coord. Sisters 4; Total Staff 5; Laystaff 1.

WESTFIELD. *Genesis Spiritual Life Center,* 53 Mill St., 01085. Tel: 413-562-3627; Fax: 413-572-1060. Sr. Elizabeth Oleksak, S.P., Admin.; Sr. Ann Horgan, S.P., Asst. Admin; Ms. Ann McGaharn, Program Coord.; Sr. Vivian Pyne, S.S.J., Registrar. Total Staff 10; Total in Residence 2.

WILLIAMSTOWN. *Mount Carmel Retreat Center,* Oblong Rd., P.O. Box 613, 01267. Tel: 413-458-3164; Fax: 413-458-9420. Revs. Richard Champigny, O.Carm.; Maurice Cummings, O.Carm. Priests 1.

[L] INFORMATION CENTERS

SPRINGFIELD. *St. Francis of Assisi Chapel and Catholic Information Center,* 254 Bridge St., 01103-1410. Tel: 413-733-3101, 733-9298; Fax: 413-731-0691.
E-mail: padrepio@wca.com
Revs. Terrence O. O'Toole, O.F.M.Cap., Rector & Guardian; Andrew Drew, O.F.M.Cap.; Zachary Grant, O.F.M.Cap., Vicar; Raymond Hand, O.F.M.Cap.; Walter O'Brien, O.F.M.Cap., (Retired); John Schug, O.F.M.Cap.; Dominic Silvestro; Bro. Andrew Duclos, O.F.M.Cap. Priests 7.

CHICOPEE. *Open Window Book and Gift Shop of the Diocese of Springfield, Inc.,* 12-14 Center St., 01013. Tel: 413-594-5111. Mrs. Ann M. Kotfila, Mgr.

[M] SPANISH APOSTOLATES

SPRINGFIELD. *Casa Cristo Rey,* 1777 Dwight St., 01107. Tel: 413-736-2167; Fax: 413-731-0962.
E-mail: mjdbs@aol.com
Revs. Michael J. Doyle; Juan F. Garcia, C.R.I.C. (Peru); Deacon Genaro Medina.

HOLYOKE. *Casa Maria,* 51 Hamilton St., 01040. Tel: 413-533-6016. Revs. Francis E. Reilly, Dir.; Regis Giroux. Pastoral Assocs.: Sr. Ninfa Arellano, S.P.; Sr. M. Immaculate Conception, S.P.

NORTHAMPTON. *Spanish Apostolate,* Blessed Sacrament Rectory, 336 Elm St., 01060. Tel: 413-584-1280. Rev. Daniel P. Liston.

[N] BUREAU FOR EXCEPTIONAL CHILDREN AND ADULTS

HOLYOKE. *Bureau for Exceptional Children and Adults Inc.*, 537 Northampton St., Box 1039, 01041. Tel: 413-538-7450; Fax: 413-536-5691. Rev. Robert F. Wagner, Dir.; Sr. Joan Magnani, S.S.J., Assoc. Dir. Sisters 2; Deacons 1; Lay Staff 3.

PITTSFIELD. *Bureau for Exceptional Children and Adults*, 414 North St., 01201. Tel: 413-538-7450; Fax: 413-536-5691. Rev. Robert F. Wagner; Sr. Joan Magnani, S.S.J., Assoc. Dir. Sisters 2; Deacons 1; Lay Staff 3.

[O] YOUTH SERVICES

GOSHEN. *Holy Cross Camp Grounds*, Cape St., P.O. Box 501, 01032-0501. Tel: 413-268-7819. Rev. Matthew J. O'Connor. Total Staff 3.

PITTSFIELD. *Catholic Youth Center*, 26 Melville St., 01201. Tel: 413-445-5496. Mr. Vincent P. Marinaro, Exec. Dir.

[P] NEWMAN APOSTOLATES AND CAMPUS MINISTRIES

AMHERST. *University of Massachusetts and Amherst College, Newman Center*, 472 N. Pleasant St., 01002-1739. Tel: 413-549-0300. Revs. Francis P. Lavelle; J. Joseph Quigley; Christopher Malatesta, In Residence; Sr. Kathleen Keough, S.S.J.; Sr. Connie Roy, S.S.J.; Deacon Lucien Miller.

College of Our Lady of the Elms College (Chicopee), 291 Springfield St., Chicopee, 01013. Tel: 413-594-2761.

Bay Path College (Longmeadow), St. Mary's Rectory, 519 Longmeadow St., Longmeadow, 01106-2299. Tel: 413-567-3124.

Berkshire Community College (Pittsfield), St. Mark's Rectory, 27 Onota St., Pittsfield, 01201-3194. Tel: 413-447-7510.

Served through the priests at St. Mark's Rectory, Pittsfield.

Massachusetts College of the Liberal Arts (North Adams). Revs. Michael Twardzik; David Darcy.

St. Francis of Assisi, 12 Union St., North Adams, 01247. Tel: 413-663-5316.

Smith College (Northampton), Helen Hills, Hills Chapel, Northampton, 01063. Tel: 413-585-2750; 585-2752. Elizabeth E. Carr, Ph.D., Chap.

Mount Holyoke College (South Hadley), Office of the Chaplains, Eliot House, South Hadley, 01075. Tel: 413-538-2054.

American International College; Springfield College; Springfield Tech Comm. College. (Springfield). Rev. Leo James Hoar, Campus Min.

St. Mary Rectory, 3 Elm St., P.O. Box 180, Northampton, 01061-0180. Tel: 413-748-3210.

Springfield College Campus Ministry Center, Beveridge Center, 263 Alden St., Springfield, 01109-3797. Tel: 413-748-3208; 3209.

Western New England College (Springfield), 1215 Wilbraham Rd., Springfield, 01119-2684. Tel: 413-782-1628; 549-0300.

Western New England Catholic. Rev. Norman Bolton, Chap.

Saint Louis de France Rectory, 817 Main St., West Springfield, 01089. Tel: 413-733-8026.

Westfield State College (Westfield). Rev. John T. Dean.

St. Peter's Rectory, 22 State St., Westfield, 01085-3814. Tel: 413-568-5421.

Williams College (Williamstown), Baxter Hall, 39 Chapin Hall Drive, Williamstown, 01267-2569. Tel: 413-597-2483.

Holyoke Community College (Holyoke), 303 Homestead Ave., Holyoke, 01040. Tel: 413-538-7000, Ext. 511. Rev. Lee Gilbertson, Chap.

[Q] MISCELLANEOUS

SPRINGFIELD. *Good Shepherd Association of Springfield Mass.*, 280 Tinkham Rd., 01129. Tel: 413-783-1251. Sisters 16; Total Staff 2.

GRANBY. *Knights of the Immaculata Movement (Militia Immaculatae, M.I.)*. (established 1931), St. Hyacinth College-Seminary, 66 School St., 01033. Tel: 413-467-9190. Rev. James E. McCurry, O.F.M.Conv., Dir.

HOLYOKE. *Mont Marie Conference Center*, 34 Lower Westfield Rd., 01040. Tel: 413-536-0853.
E-mail: ssj2@aol.com
Agnes Fleming, Dir.

SPHS Corporation, 1233 Main St., 01040. Tel: 413-539-2600; Fax: 413-539-2640. Sr. Ruth McGoldrick, S.P., Chair & Pres.

RELIGIOUS INSTITUTES OF MEN REPRESENTED IN THE DIOCESE

For further details refer to the corresponding bracketed number in the Religious Institutes of Men or Women section.

[]—*The Association of Marian Helpers of Stockbridge, MA.*

[0470]—*The Capuchin Fathers.* (St. Mary's Prov.).—O.F.M.Cap.

[0270]—*Carmelite Fathers and Brothers.* (St. Elias Prov.).—O.Carm.

[0740]—*Congregation of Marians of the Immaculate Conception.*—M.I.C.

[1000]—*Congregation of the Passion.* (West Hoboken, NJ).—C.P.

[0480]—*Conventual Franciscans.*—O.F.M.Conv.

[0720]—*The Missionaries of Our Lady of La Salette.*—M.S.

[1280]—*Stigmatine Fathers and Brothers.*—C.S.S.

RELIGIOUS INSTITUTES OF WOMEN REPRESENTED IN THE DIOCESE

[1830]—*Contemplative Sisters of the Good Shepherd.*—C.G.S.

[0860]—*Daughters of Mary of the Immaculate Conception.*—D.M.

[0890]—*Daughters of Our Lady of Mercy.*—D.M.

[0810]—*Daughters of the Heart of Mary.*—D.H.M.

[0820]—*Daughters of the Holy Spirit.*—D.H.S.

[1050]—*Dominican Contemplative Nuns.*—O.P.

[1170]—*Felician Sisters.*—C.S.S.F.

[1330]—*Franciscan Missionary Sisters of Assisi.*—S.F.M.A.

[1470]—*Franciscan Sisters of St. Joseph.*—F.S.S.J.

[1180]—*Franciscan Sisters of the Allegany, New York.*—O.S.F.

[]—*Schonestatt Sisters of Mary.*

[1700]—*School Sisters of St. Francis.*—O.S.F.

[]—*Sister of the Most Holy Soul of Christ.*—S.S.Ch.

[]—*Sisters Minor of Mary Immaculate.*—S.M.M.I.

[3000]—*Sisters of Notre Dame de Namur.*—S.N.D.deN.

[3340]—*Sisters of Providence.*—S.P.

[3718]—*Sisters of St. Ann.*—S.S.A.

[3750]—*Sisters of St. Chretienne.*—S.S.Ch.

[3830-16]—*Sisters of St. Joseph.*—S.S.J.

[3850]—*Sisters of St. Joseph of Chambery.*—C.S.J.

[0150]—*Sisters of the Assumption.*—S.A.S.V.

[3320]—*Sisters of the Presentation of the B.V.M.*—P.B.V.M.

[3310]—*Sisters of the Presentation of Mary.*—P.M.

[4190]—*Visitation Nuns.*—V.H.M.

DIOCESAN CEMETERIES

SPRINGFIELD. *Gate of Heaven*, 421 Tinkham Rd., 01129. Tel: 413-782-4731. Rev. David Farland, Dir. Cemeteries.

St. Michael's, 1601 State St., 01109. Tel: 413-733-0659. Rev. Francis Lavelle, Diocesan Dir. Cemeteries.

HOLYOKE. *Calvary*, Northampton St., 01040. Tel: 413-733-0659.

INDIAN ORCHARD. *St. Aloysius Cemetary*, Berkshire Ave., 01151.

NECROLOGY

† Fennessey, Luke Thomas, (Retired). —Died June 14, 1997.

† Graham, James M., (Retired). —Died July 3, 1997.

† Lapean, Gerald J., Springfield, MA, Our Lady of the Sacred Heart. —Died Jan. 21, 1997.

Diocese of Steubenville

(Dioecesis Steubenvicensis)

Most Reverend

GILBERT I. SHELDON, D.D., D.MIN.

Bishop of Steubenville; ordained February 28, 1953; appointed Auxiliary and Titular Bishop of Taparura April 20, 1976; consecrated June 11, 1976; appointed to Steubenville January 28, 1992; installed April 2, 1992. *Mailing Address: P.O. Box 969, Steubenville, OH, 43952-5969.*

Most Reverend

ALBERT H. OTTENWELLER, D.D., S.T.L.

Retired Bishop of Steubenville; ordained June 19, 1943; appointed Titular Bishop of Perdices and Auxiliary of Toledo April 17, 1974; consecrated May 29, 1974; appointed to Steubenville October 11, 1977; installed November 22, 1977; retired April 2, 1992. *Res., 609 N. Seventh St., Steubenville, OH, 43952.*

Chancery Office: 422 Washington St., P.O. Box 969, Steubenville, OH, 43952-5969. Tel.: 740-282-3631; Fax: 740-282-3327.

ESTABLISHED 1944.

Square Miles 5,913.

Comprises these thirteen Counties in the State of Ohio: Athens, Belmont, Carroll, Gallia, Guernsey, Harrison, Jefferson, Lawrence, Meigs, Morgan, Monroe, Noble and Washington.

For legal titles of parishes and diocesan institutions, consult the Chancery Office.

STATISTICAL OVERVIEW

Personnel	
Bishop	1
Retired Bishops	1
Priests: Diocesan Active in Diocese	65
Priests: Active Outside Diocese	13
Priests: Retired, Sick or Absent	45
Number of Diocesan Priests	123
Religious Priests in Diocese	26
Extern Priests in Diocese	5
Ordinations:	
Permanent Deacons	1
Permanent Deacons in Diocese	5
Total Brothers	8
Total Sisters	84
Parishes	
Parishes	75
With Resident Pastor:	
Resident Diocesan Priests	73
Resident Religious Priests	1
Without Resident Pastor:	
Administered by Priests	1
Missions	3
Professional Ministry Personnel:	
Brothers	2
Sisters	4
Lay Ministers	13
Welfare	
Catholic Hospitals	2
Total Assisted	232,712
Homes for the Aged	1
Total Assisted	87
Special Centers for Social Services	1
Total Assisted	5,800
Residential Care of Disabled	1
Total Assisted	50
Educational	
Diocesan Students in Other Seminaries	7
Total Seminarians	7
Colleges and Universities	1
Total Students	1,997
High Schools, Diocesan and Parish	3
Total Students	709
Elementary Schools, Diocesan and Parish	15
Total Students	2,823
Catechesis/Religious Education:	
High School Students	887
Elementary Students	2,906
Total Students Under Catholic Instruction	9,329
Teachers in the Diocese:	
Sisters	6
Lay Teachers	195
Vital Statistics	
Receptions into the Church:	
Infant Baptism Totals	681
Adult Baptism Totals	345
Received into Full Communion	1,026
First Communions	847
Confirmations	1,198
Marriages:	
Catholic	184
Interfaith	205
Total Marriages	389
Deaths	818
Total Catholic Population	47,122
Total Population	526,097

Former Bishops—Most Rev. JOHN KING MUSSIO, D.D., J.C.D., named First Bishop of Steubenville. Ordained for Diocese of Cincinnati Aug. 15, 1935; appt. First Bishop of Steubenville, March 16, 1945; cons. May 1, 1945; retired Oct. 11, 1977; died April 15, 1978.

Vicar General—Rev. Msgr. ROGER J. FOYS, V.G., *422 Washington St., P.O. Box 969, Steubenville, 43952-5969.* Tel: 740-282-3631.

Moderator of the Curia—Rev. Msgr. ROGER J. FOYS, V.G., *Res., 422 Washington St., P.O. Box 969, Steubenville, 43952-5969.* Tel: 740-282-3631.

Chancellor—Mrs. LINDA A. NICHOLS.

Chancery Office—422 Washington St., P.O. Box 969, Steubenville, 43952-5969. Tel: 740-282-3631; Fax: 740-282-3327.

Diocesan Finance Office—Rev. Msgr. ROGER J. FOYS, V.G., Dir.; Mr. DAVID FRANKLIN, Comptroller, *P.O. Box 969, Steubenville, 43952-5969.* Tel: 740-282-3631.

Diocesan/Parish Share Campaign—Rev Msgr. ROGER J. FOYS, V.G., Dir. MARTIN THOMPSON, Assoc. Dir. Tel: 740-282-3631.

Diocesan Tribunal—422 Washington St., P.O. Box 969, Steubenville, 43952-5969. Tel: 740-282-3631.

Judicial Vicar—Very Rev. KURT H. KEMO, J.C.L.

Adjutant Judicial Vicar—Rev. Msgr. ROGER J. FOYS, V.G.

Defender of the Bond—Rev. Msgr. GERALD E. CALOVINI.

Auditors/Defenders of the Bond—Revs. THOMAS A. CHILLOG; WILLIAM D. CROSS.

Secretary to the Tribunal & Notary—COLLEEN BAHEN.

Judges—Rev. Msgr. ROGER J. FOYS, V.G.; Rev. Msgr. MARK J. FROEHLICH; Rev. Msgr. ROBERT H. PUNKE, V.F.; Rev. Msgr. GENE W. MULLETT, V.F.; Revs. VINCENT J. HUBER; JAMES DUNFEE.

Diocesan Data Processing—Rev. Msgr. ROGER J. FOYS, V.G., Dir.; Mr. ANTHONY TARGOSS, Mgr.; MARTIN B. THOMPSON, Assoc. Manager, *422 Washington St., P.O. Box 969, Steubenville, 43952-5969.* Tel: 740-282-3631.

Office of the Permanent Diaconate—Most Rev. GILBERT I. SHELDON; Very Rev. KURT H. KEMO, J.C.L., Dir.; Rev. Msgr. ROGER J. FOYS; Rev. Msgr. ROBERT J. KAWA; Rev. Msgr. THOMAS C. PETRONEK; Revs. WILLIAM D. CROSS; JAMES M. DUNFEE, *P.O. Box 969, Steubenville, 43952-5969.* Tel: 740-282-3631; Fax: 740-282-3327.

Diocesan Deaneries and Deans

Deans—Rev. Msgr. GEORGE W. YONTZ, V.F., Annunciation Deanery; Rev. Msgr. GERALD E. CALOVINI, V.F., Immaculate Heart of Mary Deanery; Rev. Msgr. JOHN C. KOLESAR, V.F., Mother of God Deanery; Rev. Msgr. PATRICK GAUGHAN, V.F., Nativity of Mary Deanery; Rev. Msgr. ROBERT H. PUNKE, V.F., Presentation Deanery; Rev. Msgr. WILLIAM C. YONTZ, V.F., Visitation Deanery; Rev. Msgr. CHARLES HIGHLAND, V.F., Assumption Deanery; Rev. Msgr. J. MICHAEL CAMPBELL, V.F., Coronation Deanery; Rev. Msgr. WILLIAM MYERS, V.F., Immaculate Conception Deanery; Rev. Msgr. GENE W. MULLETT, V.F., Queen of Peace Deanery.

Continuing Education/Alliance of Priests—Rev. Msgr. ROGER J. FOYS, V.G., Dir.; Rev. Msgr. LEWIS F. GAETANO; Rev. Msgr. GERALD E. CALOVINI, V.F.; Very Rev. KURT H. KEMO, J.C.L.; Revs. WILLIAM D. CROSS; THOMAS A. CHILLOG.

Pastoral Staff—Most Rev. GILBERT I. SHELDON, D.D., D.Min.; Rev. Msgr. ROGER J. FOYS, V.G., Chm.; Rev. Msgr. JAMES A. BOEHM; Mrs. LINDA A. NICHOLS; Very Rev. KURT H. KEMO, J.C.L.; Rev. THOMAS A. CHILLOG; Rev. Msgr. GERALD E. CALOVINI, V.F.; Sr. ANNE FLYNN, S.C.; Sr. MARY ANN CORR, S.C.; Rev.

KEVIN L. GREENWOOD; Dr. PETER CHILA; Rev. WILLIAM D. CROSS; Mr. BRIAN HARVEY.

Presbyteral Council—Most Rev. GILBERT I. SHELDON, D.D., D.Min., Pres.; Rev. Msgr. GERALD E. CALOVINI, V.F.; Rev. Msgr. WILLIAM R. CORNELIUS; Revs. TIMOTHY MCGUIRE; VINCENT J. HUBER; Rev. Msgr. JOSEPH A. NEALON; Revs. THOMAS A. MAGARY; DAVID GAYDOSIK; THOMAS A. CHILLOG; WILLIAM D. CROSS, Exec. Sec. WALTER HEINZ; Very Rev. KURT H. KEMO, J.C.L., Vice Chm.; Revs. LEONARD T. CENCULA; THOMAS NAU; RICHARD DAVIS, T.O.R.; CHESTER PABIN; Rev. Msgr. ROGER J. FOYS, V.G., Chm.; Mrs. LINDA NICHOLS, Recording Sec.

College of Consultors—Rev. Msgr. GERALD D. CALOVINI, V.F.; Rev. Msgr. WILLIAM R. CORNELIUS; Rev. WALTER HEINZ; Very Rev. KURT H. KEMO, J.C.L.; Rev. RONALD MOHNICKEY, T.O.R.; Rev. Msgr. ROGER J. FOYS, V.G.

Priests Personnel Board—Rev. MARTIN HOLLER, Southern Area; Rev. Msgr. WILLIAM R. CORNELIUS, Senior Clergy; Rev. Msgr. PATRICK GAUGHAN, V.F., Middle Age Clergy; Rev. Msgr. ROBERT KAWA, Northern Area; Rev. Msgr. VICTOR CINSON, Younger Clergy; Rev. JAMES DUNFEE, Central Area; Rev. Msgr. ROGER J. FOYS, V.G., Ex Officio.

Diocesan Offices and Directors

Building Commission—Mr. BRIAN HARVEY, Chm., *P.O. Box 969, Steubenville, 43952-5969.* Tel: 740-282-3631; Fax: 740-282-3327.

Building & Property Director—Mr. BRIAN HARVEY, *P.O. Box 969, Steubenville, 43952-5969.* Tel: 740-282-3631; Fax: 740-282-3327.

Campus Ministry—Rev. MARTIN J. HOLLER, *75 Stewart St., Athens, 45701.* Tel: 740-592-2711.

Office of Christian Formation—Sr. MARY ANN CORR, S.C., Dir., *P.O. Box 969, Steubenville, 43952-5969.* Tel: 740-282-3631; Fax: 740-282-3327.

Diocesan Communications—Rev. Msgr. GERALD E. CALOVINI, V.F., *P.O. 969, Steubenville, 43952-5969.* Tel: 740-282-3631; Fax: 740-282-3327.

Continuing Education of Priests—Very Rev. KURT H. KEMO, J.C.L., Dir., *P.O. Box 969, Steubenville, 43952-5969.* Tel: 740-282-3631; Fax: 740-282-3327.

Diocesan Financial Advisory Committee—Rev. Msgr. ROGER J. FOYS, V.G., Chm., *422 Washington St., P.O. Box 969, Steubenville, 43952-5969.* Tel: 740-282-3631; Fax: 740-282-3327.

Diocesan Director of Cemeteries—Rev. Msgr. JOHN C. KOLESAR, V.F., *P.O. Box 597, Adena, 43901.* Tel: 740-546-3463.

Diocesan Director of Ecumenism—Rev. Msgr. DONAL O'CARROLL, *St. Mary Church, P.O. Box 188, Lafferty, 43951.* Tel: 740-968-3200.

Diocesan Office of Worship—Very Rev. KURT H. KEMO, J.C.L., Dir., *P.O. Box 969, Steubenville, 43952-5969.* Tel: 740-282-3631; Fax: 740-282-3327.

Education Board—Sr. MARY ANN CORR, S.C., Supt., Schools, *P.O. Box 969, Steubenville, 43952-5969.* Tel: 740-282-3631; Fax: 740-282-3327.

Health Panel of the Clergy—Rev. Msgr. DONAL O'CARROLL, Contact Person, *St. Mary Church, P.O. Box 188, Lafferty, 43951.* Tel: 740-968-3200.

Holy Childhood Association—Vacant.

Hospitals—Trinity Health System, *Trinity Medical Center, West, 4000 Johnson Rd., Steubenville, 43952.* Tel: 740-264-8000; Fax: 740-264-8620., *Trinity Medical Center, East, 380 Summit Ave., Steubenville, 43952.* Tel: 740-283-7000. FRED B. BROWER, Pres. Tel: 740-283-7390. Tel: 740-264-8303. Rev. JOHN MCCOY, Chap. Tel: 740-264-8133; 8000.

National Catholic Rural Life Conference—Rev. Msgr. CHARLES HIGHLAND, V.F., Dir., *Res., R.F.D. 2, Marietta, 45750.* Tel: 740-896-2060.

Central Office of Catholic Charities—Rev. Msgr. GERALD E. CALOVINI, V.F., Dir., *P.O. Box 969, Steubenville, 43952-5969.* Tel: 740-282-3631; 1-800-339-7890; Fax: 740-282-3327. Services: Campaign for Human Development; Respect Life; Child Welfare & Family Life; Information & Referral; Substance Abuse & AIDS Ministry, Jefferson County RSVP: Tel: 740-282-9232., St. Steubenville, Housing for Elderly: Tel: 740-282-9232., Samaritan House: Tel: 740-282-0563.

Priest Retirement Committee—Rev. Msgr. JAMES C. MARSHALL, *Holy Rosary Church, 200 Rosemont Ave., Steubenville, 43952.* Tel: 740-264-4880.

Propagation of the Faith—Rev. Msgr. THOMAS C. PETRONEK, *P.O. Box 969, Steubenville, 43952.* Tel: 740-282-3631.

Publication, "Steubenville Register"—Most Rev. GILBERT I. SHELDON, D.D., D.Min., Pres.; Rev. Msgr. JAMES A. BOEHM, Editor/Publisher, *422 Washington St., P.O. Box 160, Steubenville, 43952.* Tel: 740-282-3631; Fax: 740-282-3238., *Res., Blessed Sacrament, 852 Main St., Wintersville, 43953.* Tel: 740-264-0868.

RCIA—Very Rev. KURT H. KEMO, J.C.L., Dir., *P.O. Box 969, Steubenville, 43952-5969.* Tel: 740-282-3631; Fax: 740-282-3327.

St. Vincent de Paul Society—Rev. Msgr. GERALD E. CALOVINI, V.F., Dir., *422 Washington St., P.O. Box 969, Steubenville, 43952-5969.* Tel: 740-282-3631.

Schools—Sr. MARY ANN CORR, S.C., Supt., *P.O. Box 969, Steubenville, 43952-5969.* Tel: 740-282-3631; Fax: 740-282-3327.

Seminary Review Board—Rev. KEVIN L. GREENWOOD, Chm., *Pontifical College Josephinum, 7625 N. High St., Columbus, 43235-1498.* Tel: 614-885-5585.

Vicar for Religious—Rev. Msgr. J. MICHAEL CAMPBELL, V.F., *St. Gabriel, P.O. Box 275, Minerva, 44657.* Tel: 740-868-4498.

Vicar for Retired Priests—Rev. VINCENT J. HUBER, *1225 N. River Ave., Toronto, 43964.* Tel: 740-537-4433.

Vocations—Rev. KEVIN L. GREENWOOD, Dir., *Pontifical College Josephinum, 7625 N. High St., Columbus, 43235-1498.* Tel: 614-885-5585.

Woman's Club—Rev. Msgr. ROGER J. FOYS, V.G., Moderator; Mrs. JOANNE RAHA, Pres., *2133 Wilson Ave., Mingo Jct., 43938.* Tel: 740-282-1612.

CLERGY, PARISHES, MISSIONS AND PAROCHIAL SCHOOLS

CITY OF STEUBENVILLE
(Jefferson County)

1—HOLY NAME CATHEDRAL, Very Rev. Timothy Shannon, Rector; Rev. Frederick C. Kihm.
Rectory: 411 S. Fifth St., 43952. Tel: 740-282-7322. [JC]

2—HOLY FAMILY, Rev. Richard Tuttle; Deacon Dominic Cerrato, Pastoral Assoc.
Res., 2608 Hollywood Blvd., 43952. Tel: 740-264-2825. [JC]

3—HOLY ROSARY, Rev. Msgr. James C. Marshall; Rev. John McCoy.
Res., 200 Rosemont Ave., 43952. Tel: 740-264-4880. [JC]
School—Central Grade School.
Sisters of St. Dominic 1; Lay Teachers 22; Students 402.

4—IMMACULATE HEART OF MARY CHAPEL. Closed. For inquiries for parish records contact the Chancery.

5—OUR LADY OF NORTH AMERICA MARTYRS, Rev. John Galea.
Res., 1685 Township Rd. 378, 43952-6959. Tel: 740-283-2983; Fax: 740-283-2107. [JC]

6—ST. ANTHONY OF PADUA, Very Rev. Timothy Shannon; Rev. Frederick C. Kihm.
Res., 411 S. 5th St., 43952. Tel: 740-282-7322. [JC]
School—All Saints, Tel: 740-282-4201.

7—ST. PETER'S, Rev. Msgr. George W. Yontz; Rev. Richard Battocletti; Bro. Patrick Geary, I.H.M., Pastoral Assoc.
Res., 425 N. Fourth St., 43952. Tel: 740-282-7612; 282-9263. [JC]
School—All Saints Central School, Tel: 740-282-4201.
Lay Teachers 10; Students 150.

8—ST. PIUS X, Rev. Msgr. William R. Cornelius. In res., Rev. Msgr. Frederick A. Pasquinelli, (Retired).
Res., 700 Lovers Ln., 43952. Tel: 740-264-7681. [JC]
School—Aquinas Central, R.D. 3, Lovers Ln., 43952.
Lay Teachers 15; Students 277.

9—ST. STANISLAUS, Rev. Msgr. George W. Yontz; Rev. Richard Battocletti.
Mailing Address: 425 N. 4th St., 43952. Tel: 740-282-7612. [JC]

OUTSIDE THE CITY OF STEUBENVILLE

Adena, Jefferson Co., St. Casimir's, Rev. Msgr. John C. Kolesar.
Res., 221 Hanna Ave., 43901. Tel: 740-546-3463. [CEM]

Amsterdam, Jefferson Co., St. Joseph, Rev. Virgil Reischman.
Res., P.O. Box 35, 43903. Tel: 740-543-3652. [CEM]

Athens, Athens Co., Christ the King University Parish, Rev. Msgr. Donald E. Horak; Rev. Martin J. Holler, Dir. Campus Ministry.
Res., 75 Stewart St., 45701. Tel: 740-592-2711; Fax: 740-594-3314.
St. Paul's, Rev. Msgr. Patrick E. Gaughan, V.F.
Res., 38 N. College St., 45701. Tel: 740-593-7822. [CEM]
Chapel—Guysville, St. John.

Barnesville, Belmont Co., Assumption, Rev. Charles E. Mascolino.
Res., 306 W. Main St., 43713. Tel: 740-425-2181. [CEM]

Barton, Belmont Co., Our Lady of Angels, Rev. Michael Rotolo.
Res., P.O. Box 768, 43905. Tel: 740-695-3039.

Bellaire, Belmont Co., St. John, Rev. Msgr. Gene W. Mullett; Rev. Ralph Salciccia (Italy).
Res., 3745 Tallman Ave., 43906. Tel: 740-676-0051. [JC]
School—Central Grade School.
Lay Teachers 12; Students 226.
St. Michael's, Rev. Msgr. Gene W. Mullett.
Res., c/o St. John Church, 415 37th St., 43906. Tel: 740-676-0051. [CEM][JC]

Belle Valley, Noble Co., Corpus Christi, Rev. Dale F. Tornes.
Res., c/o St. Stephen Church, P.O. Box 186, Caldwell, 43724. Tel: 740-732-4129.
Church—Main St., 43717. Tel: 614-732-7202. [CEM]

Belpre, Washington Co., St. Ambrose, Rev. David L. Huffman.
Res., 120 Maple St., P.O. Box 426, 45714. Tel: 740-423-7422; Fax: 740-423-7422. [CEM]

Beverly, Washington Co., St. Bernard, Rev. Msgr. Robert J. Kawa.
Res., 307 Seventh St., 45715. Tel: 740-984-2555. [CEM]

Blaine, Belmont Co., All Saints, Rev. Michael Rotolo.
Res., 53839 National Rd., P.O. Box 337, 43909. Tel: 740-635-0642.

Bridgeport, Belmont Co., St. Anthony of Padua, Rev. Msgr. Francis Manieri.
Res., 630 Main St., 43912. Tel: 740-635-0283. [JC]
St. Joseph, Rev. Msgr. Mark J. Froehlich.
Res., 68210 Neola Ave., 43912. Tel: 740-635-0408; Fax: 740-635-1166. [JC]
School—Tel: 740-635-3313.
Lay Teachers 12; Students 203.

Brilliant, Jefferson Co., Our Lady of Fatima. Closed. Sacramental records are located at St. Agnes, Mingo Junction.

Buchtel, Athens Co., St. Patrick. Consolidated with St. Andrew to form St. Mary of the Hills, Nelsonville.

Burkhart, Monroe Co., St. Joseph's, Rev. Msgr. Thomas C. Petronek, Parochial Admin.; Rev. James M. Dunfee.
Mailing Address: c/o St. Sylvester Church, 330 S. Main St., Woodsfield, 43793. Tel: 740-472-0187; Fax: 740-472-1994.

Byesville, Guernsey Co., Holy Trinity, Rev. Msgr. William C. Yontz.
Res., 222 S. Fifth St., Box 26, 43723. Tel: 740-685-2184. [CEM]
School—Central Grade School, Tel: 740-685-2573.
Lay Teachers 6; Students 75.

Cadiz, Harrison Co., St. Teresa, Rev. Thomas A. Vennitti.
Res., 143 E. South St., 43907. Tel: 740-942-2211.

Caldwell, Noble Co., St. Stephen, Rev. Dale F. Tornes.
Res., 1036 Belford St., Box 186, 43724. Tel: 740-732-4129. [CEM]

Cambridge, Guernsey Co., St. Benedict, Rev. Robert D. Borer; Rev. Msgr. Thomas C. Petronek.
Res., 714 Gomber Ave., 43725. Tel: 740-432-7609.
School—Tel: 740-432-6751; Fax: 740-432-4961.
Franciscan Sisters of Christian Charity 5; Lay Teachers 9; Students 148.

Carlisle, Noble Co., St. Michael, Rev. Samuel Saprano.
Res., R.D. 1, Caldwell, 43724. Tel: 740-838-4842. [CEM]

Carrollton, Carroll Co., Our Lady of Mercy, Rev. David L. Gaydosik.
Res., 616 Roswell Rd., N.W., P.O. Box 155, 44615. Tel: 330-627-4664; Fax: 330-627-6341.

Chesapeake, Lawrence Co., St. Ann, Rev. James M. Bryant.
Res., 310 Third Ave., Box 428, 45619-0428. Tel: 740-867-4434.

Churchtown, Washington Co., St. John the Baptist, Rev. Msgr. Charles F. Highland, V.F.
Res., R.F.D. 2, Marietta, 45750. Tel: 740-896-2060. [CEM]
School—Central Grade School, Tel: 740-896-2697.
Lay Teachers 10; Students 119.

Colerain, Belmont Co., St. Frances Cabrini, Rev. Msgr. David E. Reasbeck.
Res., Rte. 250, Box 38, 43916. Tel: 740-635-9933.

Dillonvale, Jefferson Co., St. Adalbert, Rev. Leonard Cencula.
Res., P.O. Box 577, 43917. Tel: 740-769-2186. [CEM]

Fairpoint, Belmont Co., St. Joseph, Rev. Thomas J. Graven.
Mailing Address: 71793 Church St., P.O. Box 308, Maynard, 43937.
Church—46982 Columbia St., Box 98, 43927. Tel: 740-695-0840; 695-2618.

Flushing, Belmont Co., St. Paul's, Rev. Msgr. John A. Cymbor.
Res., 115 Morristown Rd., Box 45, 43977. Tel: 740-968-4159. [CEM]

Fulda, Noble Co., Immaculate Conception, Rev. Samuel Saprano.
Res., 43700 Fulda Rd., Caldwell, 43724. Tel: 740-732-4576. [CEM]

Gallipolis, Gallia Co., St. Louis, Rev. Msgr. William R. Myers, V.F.
Res., 85 State St., 45631. Tel: 740-446-0669; Fax: 740-446-9858. [CEM]

Glouster, Athens Co., Holy Cross, Rev. John Mucha.
Rectory: 31 Republic Ave., 45732. Tel: 740-767-3068.
Res., 110 E. Washington St., Nelsonville, 45764. Tel: 740-753-1770; Fax: 740-753-4199. [CEM]
Church—Corner of Madison & Republic Avenues, 45732.

Harriettsville, Noble Co., St. Henry, Rev. Victor Cinson, Jr., Admin.
Mailing Address: R.D. 1, Box 90-B, Lowell, 45744. Tel: 740-896-2207.
Church—Rte. 1, 34575 Church St., CR 47, Lower Salem, 45745. Tel: 740-585-2383. [CEM]

Hopedale, Harrison Co., Sacred Heart, Rev. Thomas A. Vennitti; Deacon Mark Miravalle.
Res., 205 Cross St., P.O. Box 445, 43976-0445. Tel: 740-937-2301. [JC]

Ironton, Lawrence Co., St. Joseph, Revs. Thomas R. Nau; Gary A. Zalenski.
Res., 905 S. Fifth St., P.O. Box 499, 45638. Tel: 740-532-0561; 532-0712. [JC]

St. Lawrence, Revs. Thomas R. Nau; Gary A. Zalenski.
Res., 905 S. Fifth St., P.O. Box 499, 45638-0499. Tel: 740-532-0561. [JC]
School—St. Lawrence Central Grade School, (Grades K-6). Tel: 740-532-5052.
Lay Teachers 10; Students 136.
High School—St. Joseph Central High School, (Grades 7-12). Tel: 740-532-0485.
Lay Teachers 12; Students 83.

Lafferty, Belmont Co., St. Mary, Rev. Msgr. Donal O'Carroll.
Res., P.O. Box 188, 43951. Tel: 740-968-3200. [CEM]

Lore City, Guernsey Co., SS. Peter and Paul, Rev. Thomas A. Chillog.
Res., P.O. Box 175, 43755. Tel: 740-685-5582. [CEM]

Lowell, Washington Co., Our Lady of Mercy, Rev. Victor Cinson, Jr.
Res., R.D. 1, Box 90-B, 45744. Tel: 740-896-2207. [CEM]

McConnelsville, Morgan Co., St. James, Rev. Paul Walker.
Res., 257 Bell Ave., P.O. Box 539, 43756. Tel: 740-962-2856.

Malvern, Carroll Co., St. Francis Xavier, Rev. Thomas Marut.
Res., 125 Carrollton St., P.O. Box 486, 44644. Tel: 330-863-0305. [CEM]

Marietta, Washington Co., St. Mary's, Rev. Msgr. Edward Kakascik; Rev. Chester Pabin.
Res., 506 Fourth St., 45750. Tel: 740-373-3643; Fax: 740-376-2956. [CEM]
School—320 Marion St., 45750. Tel: 740-374-8181; Fax: 740-374-8602.
Lay Teachers 12; Students 286.

Martins Ferry, Belmont Co., St. Mary, Revs. Thomas A. Magary; Norbert Connelly.
Res., 20 N. Fourth St., 43935. Tel: 740-633-1416. [CEM]
School—St. Mary Central, 24 N. Fourth St., 43935. Tel: 740-633-5424. Sr. Louise Smith, S.C.N., Prin.
Sisters 1; Lay Teachers 9; Students 241.

Maynard, Belmont Co., St. Stanislaus, Rev. Thomas J. Graven.
Res., 71793 Church St., P.O. Box 308, 43937. Tel: 740-695-2618.

Miltonsburg, Monroe Co., St. John the Baptist, Rev. Msgr. Thomas C. Petronek, Parochial Admin.; Rev. James M. Dunfee.
Church: 35560 Miltonsburg-Calais Rd., Woodsfield, 43793. Tel: 740-472-0187. [CEM]
Res., 330 S. Main St., Woodsfield, 43793.

Minerva, Stark Co., St. Gabriel the Archangel, Rev. Msgr. John Michael Campbell. In res., Rev. Msgr. Cronan T. Molloy, (Retired).
Res., 400 West High, P.O. Box 275, 44657. Tel: 330-868-4498.

Mingo Junction, Jefferson Co., Annunciation, Rev. Msgr. Lewis F. Gaetano; Sr. June Smith, O.S.F., Pastoral Assoc.
Church—110 Valley Rd., 43938. Tel: 740-535-1491; Fax: 740-535-0039.

St. Agnes, Rev. Msgr. Lewis F. Gaetano; Sr. June Smith, O.S.F., Pastoral Assoc.
Mailing Address: 204 St. Clair St., 43938. Tel: 740-535-1491; Fax: 740-535-0039. [CEM]
School—Central Grade School, Tel: 740-535-1012; Fax: 740-535-0039.
Franciscan Sisters of Christian Charity 3; Lay Teachers 11; Students 165.

St. Bernadette. Closed. Sacramental records are located at St. Agnes, Mingo Junction.

Morges, Carroll Co., St. Mary, Rev. David L. Gaydosik.
Res., 8012 Bachelor Rd. N.W., P.O. Box 690, Waynesburg, 44688. Tel: 330-866-2023; Fax: 330-627-6341. [CEM]

Neffs, Belmont Co., Sacred Heart, Rev. Timothy P. McGuire.
Res., 54038 St. Mary Ave., P.O. Box 425, 43940-0425. Tel: 740-676-3277; Fax: 740-676-3400.

Nelsonville, Athens Co., St. Mary of the Hills. Consolidated St. Andrew, Nelsonville consolidated with St. Patrick, Buchtel to form St. Mary of the Hills. Rev. John Mucha.
Res., 110 E. Washington St., 45764. Tel: 740-753-1770; Fax: 740-753-4199.

Pine Grove, Lawrence Co., St. Mary, Rev. Francis L. Kinney, C.PP.S.
Res., Box 639, Ironton, 45638. Tel: 740-532-2420. [CEM]

Piney Fork, Jefferson Co., St. Therese, Rev. A. Donald Mantica, Admin.
Res., Box 25, 43941. Tel: 740-733-7820; 733-7595.

Pomeroy, Meigs Co., Sacred Heart, Rev. Walter E. Heinz.
Res., 161 Mulberry Ave., P.O. Box 592, 45769. Tel: 740-992-5898. [CEM]

Powhatan Point, Belmont Co., St. John Vianney, Rev. Timothy P. McGuire.
Res., 54038 St. Mary Ave., P.O. Box 425, Neffs, 43940-0425.
Church: 295 Hwy. 7, N., 43942. Tel: 740-676-3277; Fax: 740-676-3400.

Richmond, Jefferson Co., St. John Fisher, Rev. Msgr. Kenneth Uram.
Res., R.D. 1, 43944. Tel: 740-765-4142.

St. Clairsville, Belmont Co., St. Mary's, Rev. Msgr. Robert H. Punke.
Res., 230 W. Main St., 43950. Tel: 740-695-9993.
School—Central Grade School, 226 W. Main St., 43950. Tel: 740-695-3189; Fax: 740-695-3851.
Lay Teachers 14; Students 240.

Shadyside, Belmont Co., St. Mary, Rev. Paul D. Welton. 350 E. 40th St., P.O. Box 68, 43947. Tel: 740-676-3282.

Smithfield, Jefferson Co., Our Lady, Queen of Peace, Rev. A. Donald Mantica.
Res., P.O. Box 453, 43948. Tel: 740-733-7595. [JC]

Temperanceville, Belmont Co., St. Mary's, Rev. Charles E. Mascolino.
Res., R.D. 1, Barnesville, 43713. Tel: 740-679-2912; 425-2181. [CEM]

Tiltonsville, Jefferson Co., St. Joseph, Rev. Msgr. George R. Coyne; Sr. Luke Boiarski, S.C.N., Pastoral Assoc.
Res., 204 Mound St., 43963. Tel: 740-859-4018; Fax: 740-859-6041.

Toronto, Jefferson Co., St. Francis of Assisi, Rev. Msgr. Roger J. Foys, V.G.; Very Rev. Kurt H. Kemo; Rev. Vincent J. Huber; Bro. Anthony Motto, I.H.M., Pastoral Assoc.
Res., 1225 N. River Ave., 43964. Tel: 740-537-4433; Fax: 740-537-9305. [JC]
School—Tel: 740-537-2151; Fax: 740-537-9380.
Vincentian Sisters of Charity 1; Lay Teachers 8; Students 121.

St. Joseph's, Rev. Msgr. Roger J. Foys, V.G.; Very Rev. Kurt H. Kemo; Rev. Vincent J. Huber; Bro. Anthony Motto, I.H.M., Pastoral Assoc.
Res., 1225 N. River Ave., 43964. Tel: 740-537-4433; Fax: 740-537-9305. [JC]

Vincent, Washington Co., St. Ambrose. Consolidated with St. Ambrose, Belpre.

Wintersville, Jefferson Co., Blessed Sacrament, Rev. Msgr. Gerald E. Calovini; Rev. William D. Cross. In res., Rev. Msgr. James A. Boehm.
Res., 852 Main St., 43953-3870. Tel: 740-264-0868; Fax: 740-264-5449. [JC]
School—Aquinas Elementary, (Grades K-8) R.D. No. 3, Lovers Ln., Steubenville, 43952. Tel: 740-264-3651.

Our Lady of Lourdes, Rev. Msgr. Gerald E. Calovini; Rev. William D. Cross.
Res., P.O. Box 2612, 43953. Tel: 740-264-2798; 282-3631 (Office); Fax: 740-264-5449.

Woodsfield, Monroe Co., St. Sylvester, Rev. Msgr. Thomas C. Petronek, Parochial Admin.; Rev. James M. Dunfee.
Res., 330 S. Main St., 43793. Tel: 740-472-0187; Fax: 740-472-1994. [CEM]
School—Central Grade School, Tel: 740-472-0321.
Franciscan Sisters of Christian Charity 4; Lay Teachers 6; Students 169.

Yorkville, Jefferson Co., St. Lucy's, Rev. Bernard Krajcovic.
Res., 107 St. Lucy Ave., 43971. Tel: 740-859-2274.

DIOCESAN MISSIONS

Bloomingdale, Jefferson Co., St. Thomas More Mission. Closed. Sacramental records are located at St. John Fisher, Richmond.

Chauncey, Athens Co., St. Jude Mission. Closed. Sacramental records are located at St. Paul Church, Athens.

Crescent, Belmont Co., St. Elizabeth Mission. Closed. Sacramental records are located at St. Stanislaus Church, Maynard.

Freeport, Harrison Co., St. Matthias Mission, Rev. William D. Cross.
Res., 852 Main St., Wintersville, 43953. Tel: 740-264-0868.
Church—Main St., Box 195, 43973. Tel: 740-658-3300; Fax: 740-264-5449.

Hammondsville, Jefferson Co., Nativity of Our Lord Mission. Closed. Sacramental records are located at St. Joseph Church, Toronto.

Jewett, Harrison Co., Our Lady of Perpetual Help Mission, Rev. John M. Galea.
Mailing Address: & Res.—1685 Twp. Rd. 378, Steubenville, 43952-6959. Tel: 740-946-2400; Fax: 740-283-2107.

Sardis, Monroe Co., St. John Bosco Mission, Revs. Thomas C. Petronek, Parochial Admin.; James M. Dunfee.
Res., c/o St. Sylvester Church, 330 S. Main St., Woodsfield, 43793. Tel: 740-472-0187; Fax: 740-472-1994.

Tappan Lake, Harrison Co., Christ the King Summer Mission. Closed. Sacramental records are located at: 143 E. South St., Cadiz 43907. Tel: 740-942-2211.

Toronto, Jefferson Co., Servants of Christ the King, Rev. Msgr. Roger J. Foys.
Res., 1225 N. River Ave., 43964. Tel: 740-537-4433; Fax: 740-537-9305.

Tupper Plains, Meigs Co., Our Lady of Loretto Church. Closed. Sacramental records are located at Sacred Heart Church, Pomeroy.

On Duty Outside the Diocese:
Reverend Monsignors—
Wippel, John, 10105 Portland Pl., Silver Springs, MD 20901. Tel: 301-593-9345; 816-942-8400
Reverend Fathers—
Calabrese, Charles L., TCU, Box 297310, Fort Worth, TX 76129-0001. Tel: 817-923-2176; 921-7830
Cronin, Frank C., Ohio University, Ellis Hall, Athens, OH 45701. Tel: 614-592-6147; 593-2812
Dinger, Clair M., Immaculate Conception Church, 420 North St., Milan, MI 48160. Tel: 313-439-2667
Direnzo, Michael J., Chap., 21 Titan Dr., San Pedro, CA 90732. Tel: 310-831-5857; 363-1956
Gallagher, Robert A., 5539 Lucky Ln., Wichita Falls, TX 76306. Tel: 817-885-3676
Goodbout, George E., Our Lady of the Lake Regional Medical Center, 5000 Hennessy Blvd., Baton Rouge, LA 70809. Tel: 504-765-8896
Greenwood, Kevin L., Pontifical College Josephinum, 7625 N. High St., Columbus, OH 43235-1498. Tel: 614-885-5585
Massucci, Joseph D., University of Dayton, 330 Chaminade Hall, Dayton, OH 45469-0510. Tel: 513-299-3730
McCarthy, John R., St. Philomena Church, 13824 Euclid Ave., Cleveland, OH 44114. Tel: 216-541-3540
Mellott, David, 5400 Roland Ave., Baltimore, MD 21210. Tel: 410-433-8622; 323-3200
Pliauplis, Christopher, St. Joseph Church, 45 Church St., Ronkonkoma, NY 11779. Tel: 516-223-0723
Safraniec, Joseph, Chap., Chaplain's Office (125), Dept. of VAMC, 1 Veteran's Dr., Minneapolis, MN 55417. Tel: 617-725-2027
Smith, Martin D., 231 W. Fourth St., Apt. 712-A, Cincinnati, OH 45202. Tel: 513-241-4504

Absent on Leave:
Reverend Monsignors—
Travis, Terrance A., 849 Pine Cone Oval, Sagamore Hills, OH 44067-2232
Reverend Fathers—
Bernas, Elwood S., 30675 Park St., #106, Lindstrom, MN 55045-9618. Tel: 612-257-5605
Bielanski, Joseph J., 246 Dorland #4, San Francisco, CA 94114
Gadzinski, Mark, 363 W. 2nd Ave., Columbus, OH 43201
Holmes, John, 464 S. Powell, Columbus, OH 43204. Tel: 614-276-5161
Huffman, Timothy J., Our Lady of Nazareth Church, 24411 Electric Rd., Roanoke, VA 24018. Tel: 540-774-0857
McLaughlin, Eugene
Moran, Charles

Retired:
Reverend Monsignors—
Adams, George J., 785 Broad St., Brockway, PA 15824. Tel: 814-265-8371
Cappelli, Angelo J., 19241 Edgefield, Apt. 101, Harperswoods, MI 48225. Tel: 313-882-6683
Giannamore, Anthony J., 8110 Clyo Rd., Centerville, OH 45458. Tel: 513-435-3626; 433-7224
Luciana, Lawrence J., c/o St. Joseph Church, 1304 Sixth Ave., P.O. Box 369, Huntington, WV 25708-0369. Tel: 304-525-5202
Maher, Patrick K., Corville, Roscrea Co., Tipperary, Ireland. Tel: 0505-22600
Metzger, Paul E., 428 Cambridge Dr., Middleton, OH 45042. Tel: 513-424-4576
Molloy, Cronan T., St. Gabriel Church, 400 W. High St., P.O. Box 275, Minerva, OH 44657. Tel: 330-868-4498
Nealon, Joseph A., P.O. Box 158, Carrollton, OH 44615-0158. Tel: 330-627-7083; 627-7647
Nugent, James B., 97D Georgetown Dr., Columbus, OH 43214. Tel: 614-431-5221
Pasquinelli, Frederick A., St. Pius X Church, 700 Lovers Ln., Steubenville, OH 43952. Tel: 740-264-7681
Pollack, Joseph, The Colony House, Apt. 124, 941 Pocahontas Dr., Fort Walton Beach, FL 32547. Tel: 904-863-9887
Wadowicz, Joseph M., 106 Via Estrada #A, Laguna Hills, CA 92653-4077. Tel: 714-770-6691
Zekas, Stanley, 4409 Country Club Dr., Apt. 46, Steubenville, OH 43952. Tel: 740-266-6947
Reverend Fathers—
Belfield, John, P.O. Box 119, Avon Park, FL 33825. Tel: 813-386-0631
Bober, Bernard, 1711 S. Jefferson, New Castle, PA 16102-1524. Tel: 412-652-4127
Borosh, Carl, Box 587, Barton, OH 43905. Tel: 740-695-0827
Connor, Francis J., 10248 Snead Circle N., Sun City, AZ 85351. Tel: 602-977-7141
Deasio, August J., 935 Yellow Mills Rd., Shortsville, NY 14548. Tel: 716-289-9406
Gallagher, Cornelius F., 10520 Oakmont Ave., Sun City, AZ 85351. Tel: 602-974-5902
Lyden, Dennis P., St. Joseph Church, P.O. Box 98, Fairpoint, OH 43927. Tel: 614-695-0840
Maciejewski, Richard J., 1497 Beckwith Ave., N.E., Grand Rapids, MI 49505-5811. Tel: 616-454-4565
Marr, James G., 7529 Walnut Ln., Philadelphia, PA 19138
Martinosky, Joseph A., 603 Franklin Ave., Apt. #1, Columbus, OH 43215. Tel: 614-258-3043
Mascolino, Robert A., P.O. Box 4032, Steubenville, OH 43952-8032. Tel: 740-282-7675
Nadzam, John B., 258 Schwab Ave., Munhall, PA 15120-2239. Tel: 412-461-0623
Pandolfo, Anthony, River Bridge-The Island, 1063 Island Manor Dr., West Palm Beach, FL 33413. Tel: 407-439-5685
Patala, William S., Lancia Country Club Manor, 575 Lovers Ln., Steubenville, OH 43952
Raab, Alexander, Caritas Altenh, St. Antonius Filchner Str. 42, 81476, Munich 7, Germany. Tel: 4989-759-4464
Reardon, John J., P.O. Box 68, Shadyside, OH 43947-0068
Rothbauer, Francis J., 3515 Steubenville Rd., S.E., Amsterdam, OH 43903. Tel: 330-739-4564
Salciccia, Ralph, Country Club Retirement Center, 55801 Connomara Dr., Bellaire, OH 43906
Sartori, Peter V., 416 Buena Vista, Columbus, OH 43228. Tel: 614-878-4066
Stromski, Adam F.X., 17530 S.W. 90th Ave., Miami, FL 33157. Tel: 305-251-9948
Voytko, Geo., 2341 Shelva Dr., Akron, OH 44321. Tel: 330-745-8424
Zahorchak, Michael, Holy Rosary Church, P.O. Box 151, Seeleyville, IN 47878. Tel: 812-877-1279

Permanent Deacons:
Cerrato, Dominic, 162 Twp. Hwy. 202, Bloomingdale, OH 43910. Tel: 740-944-1846
Helgeson, Ray (SAC), 1205 Maryland Ave., Steubenville, OH 43952. Tel: 740-282-7925
Hickey, Gerald, 1803 Williams Pl., Steubenville, OH 43952. Tel: 740-283-1585
Meagher, Lawrence, 4620 Lexington Dr., Steubenville, OH 43952. Tel: 614-264-3122
Miravalle, Mark, P.O. Box 338, Hopedale, OH 43976. Tel: 740-283-6433 Fax: 740-937-2555

INSTITUTIONS LOCATED IN THE DIOCESE

[A] COLLEGES AND UNIVERSITIES

STEUBENVILLE. *Franciscan University of Steubenville*, University Blvd., 43952. Tel: 740-283-3771.
E-mail: admissions@franuniv.edu
Web site: www.franuniv.edu
For a complete listing, refer to the Colleges and Universities section.

[B] HIGH SCHOOLS, CENTRAL

STEUBENVILLE. *Catholic Central High School*, 320 West View, 43952. Tel: 740-264-5538.
E-mail: SCCH_KV@omeresa.ohio.gov
Mr. Kenneth Voss, Prin.; Rev. Msgr. Roger J. Foys, Pastoral Admin. Lay Teachers 26; Students 403.

BELLAIRE. *St. John Central High School*, 3625 Guernsey St., 43906. Tel: 740-676-4932.
E-mail: BSJH_RM@omeresa.ohio.gov
Lay Teachers 19; Students 237.

[C] JUNIOR-SENIOR CENTRAL HIGH SCHOOLS

IRONTON. *St. Joseph Central*. (Grades 7-12), 45638. Tel: 740-532-0485.
E-mail: jmains@Scoca.ohio.gov
James J. Mains, Prin. Lay Teachers 12; Students 93.

[D] PRIVATE SCHOOLS

CARROLLTON. *St. John Villa*, P.O. Box 457, 44615. Tel: 330-627-9789; Fax: 330-627-4826. Residential facility for persons with developmental disabilities. Sr. Elaine Weber, O.S.F., Exec. Dir. Faculty Staff 72; Students 50.

[E] GENERAL HOSPITALS

STEUBENVILLE. *Trinity Health System*
For a complete listing, refer to the Hospitals section.

[F] MONASTERIES AND RESIDENCES OF PRIESTS AND BROTHERS

STEUBENVILLE. *Diocesan Brotherhood of Immaculate Heart of Mary*. Villa Maria Motherhouse. Villa Maria Motherhouse, 609 N. Seventh St., 43952. Tel: 740-283-2462. Bro. Dominic Carroll, I.H.M., Supr. Gen. Professed Brothers 4.

Holy Spirit Monastery, Franciscan Way, 43952. Tel: 614-283-3771. Revs. Thomas Bourque, T.O.R.; Brian Cavanaugh, T.O.R.; Richard Davis, T.O.R.; Jose Del Toro, T.O.R.; Robert Hilz, T.O.R.; Stanley Holland, T.O.R.; Joseph Lehman, T.O.R.; Ronald Mohnickey, T.O.R., Local Min.; Aidan Mullaney, T.O.R.; Daniel Pattee, T.O.R.; David Pivonka, T.O.R.; Michael Scanlan, T.O.R.; Dominic Scotto, T.O.R.; Daniel Sinisi, T.O.R.; Laurence Uhlman, T.O.R.; Bro. Joseph Johnsson, T.O.R. In res. Revs. Giles Dimock, O.P.; Conrad Harkins, O.F.M.; David Testa (ALB). Priests 18; Brothers 1.

BLOOMINGDALE. *Hermits of Mt. Carmel*, Rte. 2, Box 41A, 43910. Tel: 740-944-1048. Sisters 2.

Holy Family Hermitage, 1501 Fairplay Rd., 43910-7971. Tel: 740-765-4511. Revs. Basil Corriere, e.c., Prior; Paul Vankeirsbilck, e.c.; Mauro Ventura, Regular Oblate. Hermits 4; Priests 2; Regular Oblate Priest 1; Temporary Vows 1.

[G] CONVENTS AND RESIDENCES FOR SISTERS

STEUBENVILLE. *Sacred Heart Villa*, 36 Villa Dr., 43953-7129. Tel: 740-282-3801. Sr. Rosalba Putrino, Supr. Handmaids of Reparation of the Sacred Heart of Jesus, Motherhouse of America Foundation. Engaged in Kindergarten, Pre-Kindergarten and Parish work.

CARROLLTON. *Motherhouse and Novitiate of Sisters of Our Lady of Charity*, 44615-9399. Tel: 330-627-7647. Sr. Kevin Crain, Supr. Professed Sisters 13.

TORONTO. *Franciscan Sisters Third Order Regular of Penance of the Sorrowful Mother*, 170 Little Church Rd., 43964. Tel: 740-544-5542. Sr. Jean Daugherty, T.O.R., Supr. Sisters 13; Novices 4; Postulants 5.

[H] SHRINES

FATIMA. *Our Lady of Fatima Shrine*. Mailing Address: Parish Offices, P.O. Box 499, Ironton, 45638-0499. Old Rte. 52, Franklin Furnace, 45629. Mr. Lawrence Holtzapfel. Tel: 740-532-2696.

[I] NEWMAN CENTERS

STEUBENVILLE. *Jefferson County Technical Institute*, c/o Christ the King Chapel, Franciscan Univ. of Steubenville, Franciscan Way, 43952. Tel: 740-283-6277. Rev. Ronald H. Mohnickey, Contact Person.

ATHENS. *Christ the King University Parish - Ohio University*, 75 Stewart St., 45701. Tel: 740-592-2711. Rev. Msgr. Donald E. Horak; Rev. Martin J. Holler, Dir. Campus Ministry.

BEVERLY. *Washington Technical College*, R.F.D. #2, 45750. Tel: 740-896-2060. Rev. Msgr. Charles F. Highland.

MARIETTA. *Marietta College*, c/o St. Mary Church, 506 Fourth St., 45750. Tel: 740-373-3643. Rev. Msgr. Edward Kakascik, Dir.

NELSONVILLE. *Hocking Technical College*, 45764. Rev. John Mucha, Dir., Res., 110 E. Washington St., 45764. Tel: 740-753-1770.

RIO GRANDE. *Rio Grande University*, 91 State St., 45674. Tel: 740-446-0669. Rev. Msgr. William R. Myers, Contact Person.

ST. CLAIRSVILLE. *Ohio University - Eastern*, c/o St. Mary's Church, 230 W. Main St., 43950. Tel: 614-695-9993. Rev. Msgr. Robert H. Punke, Contact Person.

Ohio University - Ironton Branch, c/o St. Joseph Church, P.O. Box 112, Ironton, 45638. Tel: 740-532-0712. Rev. Thomas Nav, Contact Person.

[J] MISCELLANEOUS LISTINGS

STEUBENVILLE. *Campaign for Human Development*, P.O. Box 969, 43952. Tel: 740-282-3631; Fax: 740-282-3327. Rev. Msgr. Gerald E. Calovini, Diocesan Dir.

Catholic Community Center, P.O. Box 521, 148 S. Fourth St., 43952. Tel: 740-282-7566. Mr. Brian Harvey, Board Chm.; Mr. Michael J. Barber, Exec. Dir.; Mr. Raymond Saccoccia, Business Mgr.

**Catholics United for the Faith, Inc.*, 827 N. Fourth St., 43952. Tel: 740-28-FAITH; Fax: 740-283-4011.
E-mail: camarin1@aol
Curtis A. Martin, Pres.

Charismatic Renewal, P.O. Box 969, 43952-5969. Tel: 740-282-3631. Rev. Msgr. Roger J. Foys.

Diocesan Committee of Administrative Review, P.O. Box 969, 43952. Tel: 740-282-3631. Rev. Msgr. Roger J. Foys, V.G.

F.I.R.E., Franciscan University, University Blvd., 43952. Tel: 740-283-6318.
E-mail: jrook@franuniv.edu
Mr. Jack Rook, Admin. A Catholic Alliance for Faith, Intercession, Repentance, and Evangelism.

Holy Name Society. St. Joseph Church, 68210 Neola Ave., Bridgeport, 43912. Tel: 740-635-0408.
E-mail: 102372,1553compuserve
Rev. Msgr. Mark J. Froehlich, Dir.

Information & Referral, P.O. Box 969, 43952. Tel: 740-282-6880; 800-339-7890. Ms. Diana Jackson, Dir.

Lay Employees Pension Plan, P.O. Box 969, 43952. Tel: 740-282-3631. Rev. Msgr. Roger J. Foys.

Marian Manor, Inc., 180 N. Fourth St., 43952. Tel: 740-282-9232. Mr. Anthony Satkowski, A.H.M., Mgr.

Natural Family Planning, P.O. Box 969, 43952. Tel: 740-282-3631; 800-339-7890.

Ohio Conference Advisory Council, P.O. Box 969, 43952. Tel: 740-282-3631. Mrs. Eileen Carpino, Lay Women's Rep.; Rev. David L. Huffman, Priest Rep.; Mr. John Sissler, Laymen Rep.

RCIA, P.O. Box 969, 43952. Tel: 740-282-3631; Fax: 740-282-3327. Very Rev. Kurt H. Kemo, J.C.L., Dir.

Synod Committee, 422 Washington St., P.O. Box 969, 43952. Tel: 740-282-3631. Rev. Msgr. Roger J. Foys, V.G., Contact Person.

**The Fraternity of Priests, Inc.*, 100 Belleview Blvd., 43952. Tel: 740-283-4400. Revs. Forrest Rouelle, International Coord. & Chm., Board of Directors; Daniel Cook, Guest Master of Visitation House.

BELPRE. *Boy Scouts*, P.O. Box 426, 45714. Tel: 740-423-7422.
Web site: http://www.rc.net/steubenville/st_ambrose
Rev. David L. Huffman, Dir.

BEVERLY. *Marriage Encounter*. Mailing Address: St. Bernard Church, 307 Seventh St., 45715. Tel: 740-984-2555. Rev. Msgr. Robert J. Kawa, Dir.

BLOOMINGDALE. *Apostolate for Family Consecration*, John Paul II Holy Family Center, 3375 County Rd. 36, 43910-7903. Tel: 740-765-4301.
E-mail: info@familyland.org
Web site: www.familyland.org

BRIDGEPORT. *Cursillo Moderator*, St. Anthony Church, 630 Main St., 43912. Tel: 740-635-0283. Rev. Msgr. Francis Manieri; Mrs. Peggy Cotton, Lay Dir.

CAMBRIDGE. *Propagation of the Faith Holy Childhood Association*, St. Benedict Church, 714 Gomber Ave., 43725. Rev. Msgr. Thomas C. Petronek.

MARIETTA. *Search*, St. John's Church, Churchtown, R.D. 2, 45750. Tel: 740-896-2060. Rev. Msgr. Charles F. Highland, Diocesan Dir.

MARTINS FERRY. *Catholic Daughters of the America*, 626 Columbus Ave., 43935. Mrs. Elaine Kiss, State Regent & Contact Person.

WORTHINGTON. *Seminary Review Board Vocations*, P.O. Box 537, 43085. Tel: 614-885-5585; Fax: 614-781-8826. Rev. Kevin L. Greenwood.

RELIGIOUS INSTITUTES OF MEN REPRESENTED IN THE DIOCESE

For further details refer to the corresponding bracketed number in the Religious Institutes of Men or Women section.

[0680]—*Brothers of the Immaculate Heart of Mary.*—I.H.M.

[0230]—*Camaldolese Hermits of the Congregation of Monte Corona.*—Er.Cam.

[]—*Carmelite Missionaries of Mary Immaculate.*—C.M.M.I.

[0740]—*Marians of the Immaculate Conception (St. Stanislaus Kostka Province).*—M.I.C.

[0910]—*Oblates of Mary Immaculate (St. Paul's Province).*—O.M.I.

[0560]—*Third Order of Saint Francis. (Sacred Heart Prov.).*—T.O.R.

RELIGIOUS INSTITUTES OF WOMEN REPRESENTED IN THE DIOCESE

[]—*Carmelite Hermits of Reparation.*—E.C.R.

[0370]—*Carmelite Sisters of the Most Sacred Heart of Los Angeles.* (Alhambra, CA).—O.C.D.

[]—*Congregation of St. Joseph, Cleveland, OH.*—C.S.J.

[1070-02]—*Dominican Sisters, Columbus.*—O.P.

[1230]—*Franciscan Sisters of Christian Charity, Manitowac, WI.*—O.S.F.

[]—*Franciscan Third Order Regular Sisters of the Sorrowful Mother.*—T.O.R.

[1880]—*Handmaids of the Sacred Heart of Jesus for Reparation.*—A.R.

[2760]—*Missionary Sisters of the Immaculate Conception.* (Paterson, NJ).—S.M.I.C.

[0500]—*Sisters of Charity of Nazareth.*—S.C.N.

[0570]—*Sisters of Charity of Seton Hill, Greensburg, PA.*—S.C.

[]—*Sisters of Holy Family of Nazareth.*—C.S.F.N.

[]—*Sisters of Notre Dame de Namur, Cincinnati, OH.*

[3073]—*Sisters of Our Lady of Charity.*

[]—*Sisters of St. Francis of Assisi, Milwaukee, WI.*

[1530]—*Sisters of St. Francis of the Congregation of Our Lady of Lourdes, Sylvania, Ohio.*—O.S.F.

[3840]—*Sisters of St. Joseph of Carondelet.*—C.S.J.

[4160]—*Vincentian Sisters of Charity.*—V.S.C.

NECROLOGY

† Brown, Francis, (Retired). —Died Nov. 9, 1996.

† Marrer, Robert, (Retired). —Died Sept. 27, 1996.

† Truczynski, Richard, (Retired). —Died Oct. 25, 1996.

Diocese of Stockton

(Dioecesis Stocktoniensis)

Most Reverend

DONALD W. MONTROSE, D.D.

Bishop of Stockton; ordained May 7, 1949; appointed Titular Bishop of Vescovio and Auxiliary of Los Angeles on March 25, 1983; consecrated May 12, 1983; translated Bishop of Stockton December 19, 1985; installed February 20, 1986. *Office: 1105 N. Lincoln St., Stockton, CA, 95203. Mailing Address: P.O. Box 4237, Stockton, CA, 95204.* Tel.: 209-466-0636.

ESTABLISHED JANUARY 13, 1962.

Square Miles 10,023.

Legal Title: The Roman Catholic Bishop of Stockton, a Corporation Sole.

Comprises six Counties in the State of California-viz., Alpine, Calaveras, Mono, San Joaquin, Stanislaus and Tuolumne.

For legal titles of parishes and diocesan institutions, consult the Chancery Office.

Chancery Office: P.O. Box 4237, Stockton, CA, 95204-0237. Tel.: 209-466-0636; Fax: 209-941-9722.

STATISTICAL OVERVIEW

Personnel	
Bishop	1
Priests: Diocesan Active in Diocese	42
Priests: Active Outside Diocese	1
Priests: Retired, Sick or Absent	15
Number of Diocesan Priests	58
Religious Priests in Diocese	22
Extern Priests in Diocese	11
Ordinations:	
Diocesan Priests	1
Permanent Deacons in Diocese	26
Total Brothers	4
Parishes	
Parishes	32
With Resident Pastor:	
Resident Diocesan Priests	21
Resident Religious Priests	4
Without Resident Pastor:	
Administered by Priests	7
Missions	8
Pastoral Centers	2
Professional Ministry Personnel:	
Brothers	1
Sisters	19
Lay Ministers	47
Welfare	
Catholic Hospitals	3
Total Assisted	322,514
Homes for the Aged	2
Total Assisted	283
Special Centers for Social Services	1
Total Assisted	25,000
Educational	
Diocesan Students in Other Seminaries	10
Total Seminarians	10
High Schools, Diocesan and Parish	2
Total Students	1,354
Elementary Schools, Diocesan and Parish	12
Total Students	3,395
Catechesis/Religious Education:	
High School Students	927
Elementary Students	11,816
Total Students Under Catholic Instruction	17,502
Teachers in the Diocese:	
Priests	4
Brothers	2
Sisters	5
Lay Teachers	139
Vital Statistics	
Receptions into the Church:	
Infant Baptism Totals	4,303
Adult Baptism Totals	530
Received into Full Communion	538
First Communions	3,130
Confirmations	1,913
Marriages:	
Catholic	724
Interfaith	209
Total Marriages	933
Deaths	1,357
Total Catholic Population	180,678
Total Population	1,051,540

Former Bishops—Most Rev. HUGH A. DONOHOE, D.D., ord. June 14, 1930; appt. Titular Bishop of Taium and Auxiliary of San Francisco Aug. 2, 1947; cons. Oct. 7, 1947; appt. to Stockton Feb. 21, 1962; transferred to Fresno Aug. 27, 1969; died Oct. 26, 1987.—Most Rev. MERLIN J. GUILFOYLE, D.D., J.C.D., ord. June 10, 1933; appt. Titular Bishop of Bulla and Auxiliary of San Francisco Aug. 15, 1950; cons. Sept. 21, 1950; translated to Bishop of Stockton Nov. 19, 1969; retired Feb. 26, 1980; died Nov. 20, 1981.—Most Rev. ROGER M. MAHONY, D.D., ord. May 1, 1962; appt. Titular Bishop of Tamascani and Auxiliary of Fresno, Jan. 7, 1975; cons. March 19, 1975; translated Bishop of Stockton Feb. 26, 1980; elevated to Archbishop of Los Angeles July 16, 1985; elevated to Cardinal, June 28, 1991.

Chancery Office—1105 N. Lincoln St., Stockton, 95203., Mailing Address: P.O. Box 4237, Stockton, 95204-0237. Tel: 209-466-0636; Fax: 209-941-9722.

Vicar General—Rev. Msgr. JAMES E. CAIN.

Episcopal Vicar for Judicial Affairs—Rev. Msgr. RICHARD J. RYAN, J.C.D.

Episcopal Vicar for Religious Vocations—Rev. JOSEPH P. ILLO.

Chancellor—Rev. Msgr. RICHARD J. RYAN, J.C.D.

Business Manager—RICHARD CHAFFEY, Dir., Admin. & Fin. Svcs.

Special Assistant for Administrative Affairs—Rev. ROBERT J. PEREIRA.

Diocesan Tribunal—1105 N. Lincoln St., Stockton, 95203., Mailing Address: P.O. Box 4237, Stockton, 95204-0237. Tel: 209-466-0636; Fax: 209-941-9722.

Officialis—Rev. Msgr. RICHARD J. RYAN, J.C.D.

Vice-Officialis—Revs. GEORGE F. LACEY; JOHN J.M. FOSTER, J.C.L.

Judges—Revs. HARMON SKILLIN, J.C.D.; DAVID DEIBEL, J.C.L; Mrs. DEBORAH A. BARTON, J.C.L.

Tribunal Personnel—LENORE SYPNIESKI; Mrs. DIANE TARICCO, Notary.

Diocesan Consultors—Revs. CHARLES COUNTIE, O.Carm.; LARRY GUERRERO; EUGENE TRAINER; KHOI PHAM; ROBERT J. PEREIRA; LEO SUAREZ; ROBERT SILVA; LAWRENCE MCGOVERN, S.T.L. Ex Officio Members: Rev. Msgr. JAMES E. CAIN, V.G.; Rev. ARMANDO VERGARA; Rev. Msgr. RICHARD RYAN, J.C.D.; Rev. JOHN P. FALLON, O.S.F.S.

Deans—Rev. WILLIAM C. MOORE, Deanery I; Rev. JOHN ARMISTEAD, S.T.L., Deanery II; Rev. ALOYS CONRAD GRUBER, Deanery III; Rev. JOHN M. PRUETT, Deanery IV.

The Roman Catholic Welfare Corporation of Stockton—Mailing Address: P.O. Box 4237, Stockton, 95204. 1105 N. Lincoln St., Stockton, 95203-0237. Tel: 209-466-0636; Fax: 209-941-9722.

Diocesan Offices and Directors

Apostleship of Prayer—Rev. GEORGE LACEY, *P.O. Box 4237, Stockton, 95204-0237.* Tel: 209-466-0636.

Building Committee—Rev. Msgr. JAMES E. CAIN, V.G., Chm.; Rev. Msgr. RICHARD J. RYAN J.C.D.; Rev. FRANCIS PRENDERGAST, Sec. LEONARD M. ABBOTT.

Catholic Charities—MARGE VERNER, *1106 N. El Dorado, Stockton, 95202.* Tel: 209-948-1501.

Catholic Youth Organization—MICHAEL SCRIVEN, Sports Dir., *1618 W. Longview, Stockton, 95207.* Tel: 209-477-1107.

Cemeteries—Rev. Msgr. JAMES E. CAIN, V.G., Dir., *Mailing Address: P.O. Box 4237, Stockton, 95204-0237.* Tel: 209-466-0636. *1105 N. Lincoln St., Stockton, 95203.*

Censor Librorum—Vacant.

Centro Catolico de Pastoral Hispana—Mrs. DIGNA RAMIREZ-LOPEZ, Office: *1125 N. Lincoln St., Stockton, 95203.* Tel: 209-464-1976.

Communications Department—PATRICK JOYCE, Office: *1125 N. Lincoln St., P.O. Box 4237, Stockton, 95204-0237.* Tel: 209-466-5811.

Newspaper—"The Catholic Lantern".

Continuing Education of Clergy—Rev. EUGENE TRAINER, *505 West Granger Ave., Modesto, 95350-4299.* Tel: 209-524-7421.

Cursillo Movement-English and Spanish—Rev. ARMANDO VERGARA, Dir.

Stewardship Office—JOAN HART.

Development Department—GEORGE REINERT, Dir., *1125 N. Lincoln St., P.O. Box 4237, Stockton, 95204-0237.* Tel: 209-466-5812.

Diocesan Pastoral Council—Rev. HARMON D. SKILLIN, J.C.D., Chm., *P.O. Box 4237, Stockton, 95204-0237.* Tel: 209-948-3450.

Ecumenism—Rev. PATRICK WALKER, Dir., *650 Rose St., Turlock, 95380-4186.* Tel: 209-634-8578.

Education, Religious—Sr. DIANE SMITH, C.S.J., Dir. School of Ministry; Sr. GLORIA DEJESUS SANCHEZ, E.F.M.S., Diocesan Dir. of Religious Education, Central Office: *1125 N. Lincoln St., Stockton, 95203.* Tel: 209-466-6796. Contact this office for various CCD Centers.

Education, Special—YVONNE HARROLD, Dir., *1125 N. Lincoln St., Stockton, 95203.* Tel: 209-466-9374. Programs for physically & mentally impaired.

Engaged Encounter—CAROL HAGAN; LEE HAGAN, *P.O. Box 576107, Modesto, 95355.* Tel: 209-521-1252.

English Language School of Ministries Program—Sr. DIANE SMITH, *1105 N. Lincoln St., P.O. Box 4237, Stockton, 95204-0237.* Tel: 209-466-0636.

Spanish School of Ministries Program—JORGE ECHEVERRIA.

Episcopal Liaison of Catholic Charismatic Renewal—WILLIAM BRENNAN, Ph.D., *13 Pardee Ln., Stockton, 95207.* Tel: 209-474-0571.

Family Life Commission—Rev. MARK WAGNER, *2728 Topeka St., River Bank, 95367-2252.* Tel: 209-869-2996.

Liturgical Commission—Rev. JOHN J.M. FOSTER, J.C.L., Chm., *1105 N. Lincoln St., P.O. Box 4237, Stockton, 95204-0237.* Tel: 209-466-0636.

Newman Apostolate—The Newman House, Rev. DAVID FONTAINE, O.Carm., Dir., *4101 N. Manchester, Stockton, 95207.* Tel: 209-951-0881. Rev. LONACHAN W. AROUJE, *Catholic Campus Community, 1560 Geer Rd., Suite 1, Box 33, Turlock, 95380.* Tel: 209-632-2415.

Order of Christian Initiation of Adults—Rev. Msgr. RICHARD J. RYAN, J.C.D., *1105 North Lincoln St., Stockton, 95203.* Tel: 204-466-0636.

Permanent Diaconate Program—Deacon JOHN RYAN, Dir., *163 W. Eaton Ave., Tracy, 95376.* Tel: 209-835-4560.

Pontifical Association of Holy Childhood—Rev. ROBERT J. PEREIRA, *1105 N. Lincoln St., P.O. Box 4237, Stockton, 95204-0237.* Tel: 209-466-0636.

Priests, Health and Retirement Board—Rev. Msgr. JAMES E. CAIN, V.G.; Rev. Msgr. RICHARD RYAN, J.C.D.; Rev. Msgr. WILLIAM C. HUGHES; Revs. EDWARD DONOHOE; JOHN PRUETT, *1105 N. Lincoln St., P.O. Box 4237, Stockton, 95204-0237.* Tel: 209-466-0636.

Propagation of the Faith—Rev. ROBERT J. PEREIRA, Dir., *P.O. Box 4237, Stockton, 95204.* Tel: 209-466-0636.

Respect Life Office—Community of Caring Program & Natural Family Planning Program—1125 N. Lincoln St., Stockton, 95203. Tel: 209-463-1118.

Vicar for Religious Women—Sr. ANN VENITA BRITTO, F.C., *St. Joseph Convent, 1168 S. Country Club Dr., Stockon, 95204.*

Schools—Sr. MAUREEN O'BRIEN, F.C., Supt.; Rev. Msgr. JAMES E. CAIN, V.G., Fiscal Advisor, *P.O. Box 4237, Stockton, 95204-0237.* Tel: 209-464-3775.

Child Help - Our Investment - Catholic Education - Scholarship—(CHOICES) A division of the Roman Catholic Welfare Corporation of Stockton; Sr. MARY ANN BISAILLON, D.H.S., Coord., *Mailing Address: P.O. Box 4237, Stockton, 95204-0237.* Tel: 209-464-3775.

Vocations—Revs. JOSEPH P. ILLO, Dir., *Mailing Address: P.O. Box 4237, Stockton, 95204.* Tel: 209-835-4560.

Youth Ministry—CHRISTIANE ROCELI, English Dir. JOSE LOPEZ CEJA, Spanish Coord., *1125 N. Lincoln St., Stockton, 95203.* Tel: 209-463-1118.

Catholic Committee on Scouting—Mr. PAT DODD, Chm.; Rev. JOHN J.M. FOSTER, J.C.L., Chap., *1105 N. Lincoln St., P.O. Box 4237, Stockton, 95204-0237.* Tel: 209-466-0636.

CLERGY, PARISHES, MISSIONS AND PAROCHIAL SCHOOLS

CITY OF STOCKTON
(San Joaquin County)

1—CATHEDRAL OF THE ANNUNCIATION (1955), Revs. Robert J. Silva; Joseph P. Illo; John J.M. Foster, J.C.L.
Res., 425 W. Magnolia St., 95203-2412. Tel: 209-463-1305; Fax: 209-463-0807.
School—1110 N. Lincoln St., 95203. Tel: 209-465-0205; Fax: 209-465-1274. Mrs. Carla Donaldson, Prin.
Lay Teachers 14; Students 290.
Catechesis/Religious Programs—Students 292.

2—ST. BERNADETTE (1955), Rev. William C. Moore.
Res., 2544 Plymouth Rd., 95204. Tel: 209-465-3081; Fax: 209-547-1327.
Catechesis/Religious Programs—Tel: 209-465-9547.
Students 175.

3—ST. EDWARD (1967) (Hispanic),
Res., 731 S. Cardinal Ave., 95215. Tel: 209-466-3020.
Catechesis/Religious Programs—Tel: 209-466-0719.
Students 240.

4—ST. GEORGE (1951), Revs. John M. Armistead; Editho Mascardo; Peter Carota; Deacons Jim Janukites; Don Rodgers; Arturo Sanchez; Sr. Gladys Guenter, S.H.F., Pastoral Admin.; Sr. Ancila De La O, S.H.F., Pastoral Assoc.
Res., 120 W. Fifth St., 95206-2695. Tel: 209-463-3413.
School—144 W. Fifth St., 95206. Tel: 209-463-1540. Mr. Alan Cook, Prin.
Sisters 1; Lay Teachers 13; Students 261.
St. George REALMS Foundation—.
Catechesis/Religious Programs—Students 347.
Missions—French Camp, San Joaquin Co., Good Shepherd, P.O. Box 354, French Camp, 95231. Tel: 209-982-0578; Lathrop, San Joaquin Co., Our Lady of Guadalupe, 16019 Cambridge Dr., Lathrop, 95330. Tel: 209-858-4834.

5—ST. GERTRUDE (1913) (Mexican-American), Revs. Charles G. Countie, O.Carm.; Thomas J. Alkire, O.Carm.; Deacon Jorge Torres. In res., Rev. Jeffry L. Fairfield, O.Carm.
Res., 1663 E. Main St., 95205. Tel: 209-466-0278.
School—1701 E. Main St., 95205. Tel: 209-941-0301. Mrs. Olga Rodriguez, Prin.
Lay Teachers 9; Students 220.
Catechesis/Religious Programs—Tel: 209-941-0501.
Students 352.

6—ST. LINUS (1965), Rev. Lawrence M. Guerrero, Admin. In res., Rev. Jose Domingo Ruiz.
Res., 2620 S. B St., 95206. Tel: 209-465-1430; Fax: 209-465-0299.
Catechesis/Religious Programs—Students 625.
Convent—2600 S. B St., 95206. Tel: 209-465-0416.

7—ST. LUKE (1951) (Vietnamese), Revs. Harmon D. Skillin, J.C.D.; Dean McFalls; Tuan Nguyen, S.D.B. (Vietnam); Titian A. Miani, (Retired); George F. Lacey, (Retired); Deacon Joseph Artesi; Ms. Victoria Kimball, Parish Admin.
Res., 3847 N. Sutter St., 95204. Tel: 209-948-3450; Fax: 209-948-2841.
School—4005 N. Sutter St., 95204. Tel: 209-464-0801; Fax: 209-466-1150. Mr. Patrick O'Neill, Prin.
Lay Teachers 11; Students 375.
Catechesis/Religious Programs—Tel: 209-462-0410.
Students 125.
Convent—230 E. Atlee St., 95204. Tel: 209-463-6533.

8—ST. MARY OF THE ASSUMPTION (1851), Revs. Alvaro U. Araque; Jairo H. Ramirez; Deacon Julian Sepulveda.
Res., 203 E. Washington St., 95202. Tel: 209-948-0661; Fax: 209-948-0673.
Catechesis/Religious Programs—Tel: 209-946-9536.
Students 149.

9—ST. MICHAEL (1921) (Italian), Rev. J. Patrick Walker, Admin. In res., Rev. Msgr. Richard Ryan.
Res., 5882 N. Ashley Ln., 95215-9308. Tel: 209-931-0639; Fax: 209-931-3621.
Catechesis/Religious Programs—Tel: 209-931-2696.
Students 240.

10—PRESENTATION OF B.V.M. (1952), Revs. Michael E. Kelly; Hung Joseph Nguyen, S.D.B.
Res., 1521 McClellan Way, 95207. Tel: 209-472-2150; Fax: 209-472-0541.
Ministry Center—6715 Leesburg Pl., 95207.
School—1635 W. Benjamin Holt Dr., 95207. Tel: 209-472-2140. Mrs. Linda Boragno-Dopp, Prin.
Lay Teachers 14; Students 305.
Catechesis/Religious Programs—Students 730.

OUTSIDE CITY OF STOCKTON

Angels Camp, Calaveras Co., St. Patrick (1856) (Italian), Rev. Henry P. Johnston.
Res., P.O. Box 576, 95222. Tel: 209-736-4575; Fax: 209-736-2217. [CEM][JC]
Catechesis/Religious Programs—820 S. Main, 95222. Tel: 209-736-4458.
Students 135.
Missions—Murphys, Murphys Co., St. Patrick, 619 Sheepranch Rd., Murphys, 95247. Tel: 209-728-2854; Arnold, Arnold Co., Our Lady of the Sierra, 1301 Linebaugh Rd., Arnold, 95223. Tel: 209-795-7625.

Ceres, Stanislaus Co., St. Jude (1962) (Hispanic), Revs. Octavio Escobar; Francisco Naranjo.
Res., 3824 Mitchell Rd., 95307-9422. Tel: 209-537-0516; Fax: 209-537-3412. [CEM]

Escalon, San Joaquin Co., St. Patrick (1878), Rev. Mark Wagner, Admin.
Res., 19399 E St., Rte. 120 Hwy., Ripon, 95366. Tel: 209-838-2133.
Catechesis/Religious Programs—Tel: 209-838-3101.
Students 400.

Hughson, Stanislaus Co., St. Anthony (1921) (Hispanic), Revs. Ernesto Arbelaez, Admin.; Robert D. O'Neill; Deacon Raymond Flanders.
Mailing Address: P.O. Box 909, 95256. Tel: 209-883-4310; Fax: 209-883-2531.
Res., 2020 Euclid Rd., 95256.
Catechesis/Religious Programs—Tel: 209-883-2280.
Students 493.
Mission—La Grange, Stanislaus Co., St. Louis, Floto St., La Grange, 95329. [CEM]

Linden, San Joaquin Co., Holy Cross (1963), Rev. Armando Vergara.
Res., 18633 E. Front St., P.O. Box 52, 95236. Tel: 209-887-3341.
Catechesis/Religious Programs—Tel: 209-887-2263.
Students 250.

Lockeford, San Joaquin Co., St. Joachim (1997) (Hispanic), Rev. Enda J. Maguire.
Mailing Address: P.O. Box 232, 95237. Tel: 209-727-3912.
Catechesis/Religious Programs—Students 74.

Lodi, San Joaquin Co., St. Anne (1904), Revs. Thomas P. Hayes; Gustavo Quintero; Murty M. Fahy, O.S.F.S.; Peter Auer; Deacons Juan Mendez; Porfirio Cisneros; Don Bo.
Mailing Address: P.O. Box 480, 95241. Tel: 209-369-1907; Fax: 209-369-1971.
Office: 215 W. Walnut St., 95240.
Res., 150 S. Pleasant St., 95241. [CEM]
School—200 S. Pleasant St., 95241. Tel: 209-333-7580. Mr. Dennis Taricco, Prin.
Lay Teachers 12; Students 287.
Catechesis/Religious Programs—D.R.E.: Sr. Francine M. Zamaudio, E.F.M.S.; Sr. Isabel De La Eucarista, E.F.M.S.
Students 680.
St. Anne's Endowment—Tel: 209-334-1935; Fax: 209-334-0178.
Mission—Thornton, San Joaquin Co., Mater Ecclesiae, 26500 Sacramento Blvd., 95241.

Mammoth Lakes, Mono Co., St. Joseph (1939), Rev. Andrew C. Dachauer, S.J.; Bro. Daniel C. Corona, S.J.; Deacon Eliseo Gutierrez.
Res., P.O. Box 372, 93546. Tel: 760-934-6276; Fax: 760-934-6276.
Missions—Bridgeport, Mono Co., Infant of Prague, Hwy. 395, Bridgeport, 93517.; Lee Vining, Mono Co., Our Savior of the Mountains, 2nd & Mono, Lee Vining, 93541.; Walker, Mono Co., Our Lady of the Valley, Walker Community Center, Walker, 96107.
Catechesis/Religious Programs—Students 115.

Manteca, San Joaquin Co., St. Anthony (1917), Revs. Lawrence J. McGovern, V.F.; Alexandre Pacheco; Gilberto Arango; Deacon Alfredo Maestas. In res., Rev. Theodore Lambert.
Res., 525 E. North St., 95336. Tel: 209-823-7197; Fax: 209-823-5238.
School—Tel: 209-823-4513. Stephanie Papas, Prin.
Lay Teachers 9; Students 220.
Catechesis/Religious Programs—Tel: 209-239-4302.
Students 740.
St. Vincent de Paul Society—Tel: 209-823-8099.
St. Anthony School Educational Foundation—.

Modesto, Stanislaus Co., St. Joseph (1967), Revs. Joseph P. O'Hare; Neville Jansze.
Res., 1813 Oakdale Rd., 95355. Tel: 209-551-4973; Fax: 209-551-3213.
Catechesis/Religious Programs—Tel: 209-551-0593.
Students 680.
Our Lady of Fatima (1951), Rev. John M. Pruett; Rev. Msgr. William P. Kennedy, V.F., (Retired); Revs. Eugene Trainer; Khoi Pham; Deacon Stanley Gumerlock.
Res., 505 W. Granger Ave., 95350. Tel: 209-524-7421; Fax: 209-524-7713.
School—501 W. Granger Ave., 95350. Tel: 209-524-4170; Fax: 209-524-3960. Linda Partlow, Prin.
Lay Teachers 14; Students 305; Extended Day Care 100.
Catechesis/Religious Programs—Tel: 209-529-0843.
Students 943.
The Monsignor William P. Kennedy Education Foundation—.
St. Stanislaus (1881), Revs. Bill McDonald; Gilbert L. Arango (Colombia); George Nimal (Sri Lanka); Alvaro Lopez (Colombia); Primitivo Gonzalez (Mexico).
Res., 709 J St., P.O. Box 292, 95353. Tel: 209-524-4381; Fax: 209-524-1910.
School—1416 Maze Blvd., 95351. Tel: 209-524-9036; Fax: 209-524-4344. Mr. Paul Fogerty, Prin.
Sisters 1; Lay Teachers 12; Students 315.
Catechesis/Religious Programs—Tel: 209-522-6534.
Students 500.

Newman, Stanislaus Co., St. Joachim (1909), Revs. Louis L. Sweeny; Francisco Campechano.
Res., 1121 O St., 95360. Tel: 209-862-3528.
Catechesis/Religious Programs—Tel: 209-862-2878.
Students 220.

Oakdale, Stanislaus Co., St. Mary of the Annunciation (1902), Revs. Aloys Conrad Gruber, Pastor; Bernard J. Mannion, V.F., Pastor Emeritus; Louis Garcia; Deacon Roberto Magdaleno.
Res., 1225 Olive Ave., 95361. Tel: 209-847-2715; Fax: 209-847-7348.
Catechesis/Religious Programs—Tel: 209-847-3498.
Students 220.

Patterson, Stanislaus Co., Sacred Heart (1917), Revs. Andrew E. Bellisario, C.M.; James Osendorf, C.M.; Minh J. Pham, C.M.
Res., 529 I St., 95363. Tel: 209-892-9321; Fax: 209-892-2102.
School—505 M St., 95363. Tel: 209-892-3544. Marian De Groot, Prin.
Students 195.
Catechesis/Religious Programs—Tel: 209-892-6381.
Students 423.
Mission—Crows Landing, Stanislaus Co., Immaculate Heart of Mary, H St., Crows Landing, 95313.
Station—Westley, Guadalupe Center.

Riverbank, Stanislaus Co., St. Frances of Rome (1953), Revs. Thomas M. Rajanayagam (Sri Lanka); Juan de la Cruz Zape (Columbia); Deacon Felipe Vallejo.
Res., 2827 Topeka St., 95367. Tel: 209-869-2996.
Catechesis/Religious Programs—Tel: 209-869-5830.
Students 355.

San Andreas, Calaveras Co., St. Andrew (1963) (Caucasian), Revs. William L. Kraft; Martin Starc, Pastor Emeritus; George C. Campos.
Res., 162 Church Hill Rd., P.O. Box 550, 95249. Tel: 209-754-3815.
Catechesis/Religious Programs—Students 136.
Missions—Mokelumne Hill, Calaveras Co., St. Thomas Aquinas, 8398 Lafayette St., Mokelumne Hill, 95245.; West Point, Calaveras Co., Our Lady of Fatima, 22581 Hwy. 26, West Point, 95255.

Sonora, Tuolumne Co., St. Patrick (1851), Revs. William Kraft; John Foley, O.S.F.S.; Sr. Nancy P. O'Shea, S.N.D., Pastoral Assoc.
Res., 116 W. Bradford Ave., 95370. Tel: 209-532-7139; Fax: 209-532-4389. [CEM 5][JC]
Catechesis/Religious Programs—Students 250.
Missions—Big Oak Flat, Tuolumne Co., Our Lady of Mt. Carmel, Cemetery Rd., Big Oak Flat, 95321. Tel: 209-962-2156; Columbia, Tuolumne Co., St. Anne, 22518 Church Ln., Columbia, 95310.

Tracy, San Joaquin Co., St. Bernard's (1908), Revs. Ivo D. Rocha; Mario Castaneda; Matthew O'Donnell; Deacon John Ryan.
Res., 163 W. Eaton Ave., 95376. Tel: 209-835-4560, Ext. 110; Fax: 209-835-4588.
School—165 W. Eaton Ave., 95376. Tel: 209-835-4560, Ext. 130. Mrs. Diane Rothschild, Prin.
Sisters 1; Lay Teachers 13; Students 315.
Catechesis/Religious Programs—Tel: 209-835-4560, Ext. 116.
Students 780.
Convent—165 W. Eaton Ave., 95376. Tel: 209-835-7391. Daughters of the Cross.

Turlock, Stanislaus Co., Sacred Heart (1910), Revs. Francis Prendergast; John P. O'Neill, O.S.F.S.; Oscar A. Pelaez.
Res., 650 Rose St., 95380. Tel: 209-634-8578; 8579; Fax: 209-634-7124.
School—1225 Cooper Ave., 95380. Tel: 209-634-7787; Fax: 209-634-0156. Mrs. Donna Noceti, Prin.
Sisters 2; Lay Teachers 11; Students 300.
Preschool—Tel: 209-667-5512. Debra Cannella, Prin.
Lay Teachers 4; Students 72.
Catechesis/Religious Programs—Sacred Heart Religious Education, 1250 Cooper #1, 95380. Tel: 209-634-5111.
Students 652.
Convent—1301 Cooper Ave., 95380. Tel: 209-634-7708.
Our Lady of the Assumption of the Portuguese (1973), Rev. Manuel F. Sousa.
Mailing Address: P.O. Box 2030, 95381. Tel: 209-634-2222; 634-3140; Fax: 209-634-2366.
Res., 2602 S. Walnut Rd., 95380.
Catechesis/Religious Programs—Tel: 209-874-5739.
Students 254.

Twain Harte, Tuolumne Co., All Saints (1962), Rev. John Fitzgerald, Admin.; Deacon Edward Zoma.
Res., 18674 Cherokee Dr., P.O. Box 642, 95383. Tel: 209-586-3161. [JC]
Catechesis/Religious Programs—Students 90.
Mission—Tuolumne, Tuolumne Co., St. Joseph, Tuolumne, 95379.
Stations—Pinecrest. (Summer).; Strawberry. (Winter).

Chaplains of Public Institutions

STOCKTON. *DeWitt Nelson Training Center* 7650 Newcastle Rd., P.O. Box 213003, 95213-9003. Tel: 209-944-6187. Rev. William Linakis, S.A., Chap.
Karl Holton School 7650 Newcastle Rd., P.O. Box 213002, 95213-9002. Tel: 209-944-6364. Rev. Theodore Lambert, Chap.
Northern California Women's Facility 7150 Arch Rd., P.O. Box 213006, 95213-9006. Tel: 209-943-1600. Mr. Randy Rainwater, Chap.
O.H. Close School 7650 Newcastle Rd., P.O. Box 213001, 95213-9001. Tel: 209-944-6135; 944-6349. Rev. Pius Kurera, Chap.
Stockton Developmental Center. Vacant. 510 E. Magnolia St., 95202-3288. Tel: 209-948-7111.

FRENCH CAMP. *San Joaquin County Jail.* Vacant. 999 W. Matthews Rd., 95231. Tel: 209-468-4562.
San Joaquin General Hospital. Vacant. 500 W. Hospital Rd., 95231. Tel: 209-468-6000.

JAMESTOWN. *Sierra Conservation Center.* Mailing Address: P.O. Box 497, 95327-1213. Tel: 209-984-5291. Rev. Ray Abella, O.S.F.S., Chap.

TRACY. *Deuel Vocational Institution.* Mailing Address: P.O. Box 400, 95376-3593. Tel: 209-466-8055. Rev. Ron Rissling, O.M.I., Chap.

On Special or Other Diocesan Assignment:
Reverend Monsignors—
Cain, James E., Vicar Gen.
Reverend Fathers—
Pereira, Robert J., Special Asst. for Admin. Affairs

On Duty Outside the Diocese:
Reverend Fathers—
Sullivan, George D., 197 Collingwood, San Francisco, CA 94114

Absent on Leave:
Reverend Fathers—
Gabino, Pedro
Garcia, Louis
Myers, William S.

Retired:
Reverend Monsignors—
Doyle, Walter H., Pastor Emeritus, Mailing Address: P.O. Box 1618, Diamond Springs, CA 95619
Kennedy, William P., Pastor Emeritus, Our Lady of Fatima Church, 1635 Sherwood Ave., Modesto, CA 95350-4299
Reverend Fathers—
Coghlan, John A., Pastor Emeritus, 1152 De Haro, San Francisco, CA 94107
Donohoe, Edward, 5835 Cherokee Rd., #69, Stockton, CA 95215
Ford, William A., St. Mary Star of the Sea, 888 Blvd. of the Arts, #1508, Sarasota, FL 34236
Hughes, William C., Casa Manana, 3700 N. Sutter St., #272, Stockton, CA 95204
Lacey, George F., Pastor Emeritus, 3700 N. Sutter St., Stockton, CA 95204
McCaffrey, James Leo, 27 Miramonte Dr., Moraga, CA 94556
Miani, Titian A., Casa Manana, 3700 N. Sutter St., #207, Stockton, CA 95204

Permanent Deacons:
Artesi, Joseph, St. Luke's, Stockton
Brennan, William, Stockton
Broderick, Thomas, St. Anthony, Hughson
Cisneros, Porfirio, St. Anne, Lodi
Flanders, Raymond, St. Anthony, Hughson
Garza, Hector, St. George, Stockton
Griego, Nick, St. Patrick, Sonora
Gumerlock, Francis, Our Lady of Fatima, Modesto
Hernandez, Arnold, Sacred Heart, Patterson
Isobaker, Joseph, St. Joseph's Medical Center, Stockton
Janukites, James, St. George, Stockton
Maestas, Alfredo, St. Anthony, Manteca
Magdaleno, Roberto, St. Mary, Oakdale
Mendez, Juan, St. Anne, Lodi
Neumann, Stanley, St. Patrick, Sonora
Reyes, Domingo, St. Linus, Stockton
Rippey, William, Leave of Absence
Rodgers, Donald, St. George, Stockton
Ryan, John G., St. Bernard, Tracy
Sanchez, Arturo, St. Anthony, Manteca
Schepcoff, Jacques, Annunciation, Stockton
Sepulveda, Julian R., St. Mary of the Assumption, Stockton
Torres, Jorge, St. Gertrude, Stockton
Vallejo, Felipe, St. Frances of Rome, Riverbank
Vargo, John, St. Jude, Ceres
Warren, William E., St. Joachim, Lockeford
Zoma, Edward T., St. Patrick, Sonora

INSTITUTIONS LOCATED IN THE DIOCESE

[A] HIGH SCHOOLS, DIOCESAN

STOCKTON. *St. Mary's High School*, 5648 N. El Dorado St., P.O. Box 7247, 95267-0247. Tel: 209-957-3340; Fax: 209-957-0861.
E-mail: stmarysstock@connectinc.com
Non-resident students. Rev. John P. Fallon, O.S.F.S., Pres.; Mr. Peter Morelli, Prin.; Revs. John A. Lindsay, O.S.F.S.; Clark T. Kelley, O.S.F.S.; Bros. James Dorazio, O.S.F.S.; Neil McMenamin, O.S.F.S. Priests 3; Brothers 2; Sisters 1; Lay Teachers 58; Students 929.
St. Mary's High School Foundation.

MODESTO. *Central Catholic High School*, 200 S. Carpenter Rd., 95351. Tel: 209-524-9611; Fax: 209-524-4913. Non-resident students. Mr. Jim Pecchenino, Pres.; Dr. Rex Wetzel, Prin. Lay Teachers 26; Administrators 5; Students 425.
Central Catholic High School Foundation. Tel: 209-524-6818; 524-9611.

[B] CATHOLIC CHARITIES

STOCKTON. *The Catholic Charities of the Diocese of Stockton*, 1106 N. El Dorado St., 95202. Tel: 209-948-1501. Marge M. Verner, Exec. Dir.; Mr. Woody Bagley, Chm. Corp. Bd.
The following services and programs are listed according to counties:
SAN JOAQUIN COUNTY:
Homemaker-Companion Program, 1106 N. El Dorado, 95202. Julie Homan, Prog. Mgr. Homemakers 20; Clients Served 135. (See separate listing for Modesto).
Refugee Resettlement (U.S.C.C.), 1106 N. El Dorado, 95202. Tel: 209-948-2557. Mr. Kham O. Baccam, Resettlement Dir. Case Managers 1; Refugees Resettled 100.
Respite Care Program, 1106 N. El Dorado, 95202. Tel: 209-948-1582. Julie Homan, Prog. Mgr. Caretakers 15; Clients Served 50.
Making the Right Connections, 1106 N. El Dorado, 95202. Tel: 209-948-1501. Marge Verner, Dir. Students per year 800.
Senior Home Repair, 1106 N. El Dorado, 95202. Tel: 209-948-1582. Julie Homan, Prog. Mgr. Part-time Repairman; Seniors Served 162.
Transcultural Health Outreach, 1106 N. El Dorado, 95202. Co-Directors: Sr. Judy McDonnell; Lyn Kirkconnell. Total Staff 8; Clients Served 500.
Counseling Services, 1106 N. El Dorado, 95202. Tel: 209-948-1501. Marge M. Verner, Dir.
Emergency Food Distribution, 1106 N. El Dorado, 95202. Tel: 209-466-4210. Allen Nesset, Coord. Clients Served 700 per month.
STANISLAUS COUNTY: Homemaker Program (Modesto), 400 12th St., Modesto, 95354. Tel: 209-529-3784. Nancy Brookshער, Coord. Homemakers 11; Clients 207.
Long Term Care Ombudsman Program, 400 12th St., Ste. 4, Modesto, 95354. Tel: 209-529-3784. Jane Weinheimer, Prog. Mgr. Ombudsman 18; Facilities Monitored 257; Clients served 6,000.
Senior Transportation, 400 12th St., Ste. 4, Modesto, 95354. Tel: 209-529-3784. Collette Pepelis, Coord. Part-time Staff 1; Seniors Served 120.
Elder Abuse Program, 400 12th St., Ste. 4, Modesto, 95354. Tel: 209-529-3784. Jane Weinheimer, Prog. Mgr. Community-wide education.
Eldercare Management, 400 12th St., Ste. 4, Modesto, 95354. Tel: 209-529-3784. Nancy Brookshер, Coord. Part-time Staff 2; Seniors Served 125.
Laura's House, 400 12th St., Ste. 4, Modesto, 95354. Residential substance abuse program. Marge Verner, Prog. Mgr. Full-time Staff 3; Part-time Staff 5; Maximum Occupancy 45.
MOTHER LODE:
Long Term Care Ombudsman Program, 171 N. Washington St., Sonora, 95370. Tel: 209-532-6272. Tom McHenry, Coord. Ombudsmen 12; Facilities Monitored 14; Clients Served 650.
Elder Abuse Program, 171 N. Washington St., Sonora, 95370. Tel: 209-532-6272. Tom McHenry, Coord. Community-wide education.
Legal Advocacy Program, 171 N. Washington St., Sonora, 95370. Tel: 209-532-6262. Celia Gainer, Coord. Part-time Staff 1; Legal Advisor 1; Clients Served 100.

[C] GENERAL HOSPITALS

STOCKTON. *Catholic Healthcare West System San Joaquin-Sierra Region*, 1800 N. California St., P.O. Box 213008, 95213-9008. Tel: 209-943-2000
For a complete listing, refer to the Hospitals section.
St. Joseph's Behavioral Health Center, 2510 N. California St., 95204. Tel: 209-948-2100
For a complete listing, refer to the Hospitals section.

St. Joseph's Medical Center of Stockton, 1800 N. California St., P.O. Box 213008, 95213-9008. Tel: 209-943-2000
For a complete listing, refer to the Hospitals section.

MANTECA. *St. Dominic's Hospital,* 1777 W. Yosemite Ave., P.O. Box 1307, 95337. Tel: 209-825-3500
For a complete listing, refer to the Hospitals section.

[D] HOMES FOR AGED

STOCKTON. *Casa Manana Inn,* 3700 N. Sutter St., 95204. Tel: 209-466-4046
For a complete listing, refer to the Special Care Facilities section.

Garden Oaks, 3334 Wagner Heights Rd., 95209. Tel: 209-956-3401
For a complete listing, refer to the Special Care Facilities section.

St. Joseph's Regional Housing Corp., 1805 N. California St., Ste. 407, 95204. Tel: 209-467-6312
For a complete listing, refer to the Special Care Facilities section.

[E] CONVENTS AND RESIDENCES FOR SISTERS

STOCKTON. *Daughters of the Holy Spirit,* St. Gertrude Convent, 1655 E. Main St., 95205. Tel: 209-462-9445. Sisters 4.

Dominican Sisters of San Rafael, California, St. Joseph's Convent, 407 E. Walnut St., 95204. Tel: 209-462-8486. Sisters 9.

Eucharistic Franciscan Missionary Sisters, Blessed Sacrament Convent, 1205 N. San Joaquin St., 95202. Tel: 209-462-3906. Sisters 7.

Holy Cross Sisters, Casita Esperanza, P.O. Box 9, 95201. Tel: 209-467-8042.

Holy Family Sisters, 4900 N. Hwy. 99, #146, 95212. Tel: 209-931-2949. 16019 Cambridge Dr., Lathrop, 95330. Tel: 209-858-4834; Fax: 209-858-4834.

Maryknoll Sisters, 25 S. Commerce St., No. 237, 95202. Tel: 209-462-9394.

Sacro Costato Missionary Sisters, St. Luke's Convent, 230 E. Atlee St., 95204. Tel: 209-462-6533. Sisters 3.

Sisters of Charity of the Blessed Virgin Mary, Presentation Convent, 6830 Leesburg Pl., 95207. Tel: 209-951-5373. Sisters 3.

Sisters of St. Joseph of Carondelet, 1639 W. Swain, 95207. Tel: 209-957-7090.

MODESTO. *Sisters of the Cross of the Sacred Heart of Jesus,* Cloistered Convent, 1320 Maze Blvd., 95351. Tel: 209-526-3525. Sisters 8; Postulants 3; Novices 4.

Sisters of the Holy Cross, 601 W. Granger Ave., Apt. 116, 95350. Tel: 209-529-0401. Sr. Mary Mulvaney, C.S.C., (Retired).

PATTERSON. *Daughters of the Holy Spirit,* Sacred Heart Convent, 505 M St., 95363. Tel: 209-892-3410. Sisters 4.

SONORA. *Sisters of Notre Dame De Namur.*
E-mail: stpats@sonnet.com
Mailing Address: c/o St. Patrick Church, 116 W. Bradford Ave., 95370-4924.

TRACY. *The Daughters of the Cross,* St. Bernard Convent, 165 W. Eaton Ave., 95376. Tel: 209-835-7391. Sisters 6.

TURLOCK. *Sisters of the Sacred Hearts of Jesus and Mary,* Sacred Heart Convent, 1301 Cooper Ave., 95380. Tel: 209-634-7708. Sisters 3.

[F] RETREAT CENTERS

COPPEROPOLIS. *Madonna of Peace Renewal Center.* (Youth Facility), 2010 Hunt Rd., P.O. Box 71, 95228. Tel: 209-785-2157 (Office). Total in Residence 2; Total Staff 2.

[G] MISCELLANEOUS

STOCKTON. *The Bishop's Educational Foundation, Diocese of Stockton,* 1105 N. Lincoln St., 95203.

Instituto Fe y Vida, 1737 W. Benjamin Holt Dr., 95207.
E-mail: carmenc@inreach.com
Total Staff 3.

St. Mary's High School Foundation, Box 7247, 95267-0247. Tel: 209-957-3340.
E-mail: stmarysstock@connectinc.com

San Lorenzo Ruiz De Manila, 2079 Del Rio Dr., 95204.

LODI. *St. Anne's Endowment,* 215 W. Walnut St., 95240. Tel: 209-369-1907.

MANTECA. *St. Vincent de Paul Society,* 525 E. North St., 95336. Tel: 209-823-8099. Total Staff 25; Total Assisted 13,000.

MODESTO. *Central Catholic High School Foundation,* 200 Carpenter Rd., 95351. Tel: 209-524-6822. Volunteer Board Members 25.

Father John C. Silva Education Foundation, P.O. Box 292, 95353.

The Monsignor William P. Kennedy Education Foundation, 501 W. Granger Ave., 95350. Tel: 209-524-4170.

TURLOCK. *The McElligott Sacred Heart School Foundation,* 650 Rose St., 95380. Tel: 209-634-8578. Rev. Francis Prendergast, Dir. Total Staff 25; Total Students 300.

RELIGIOUS INSTITUTES OF MEN REPRESENTED IN THE DIOCESE

For further details refer to the corresponding bracketed number in the Religious Institutes of Men or Women section.

[0270]—*Carmelite Fathers and Brothers.*—O.Carm.
[0530]—*Franciscan Friars of the Atonement.*—S.A.
[0690]—*Jesuit Fathers and Brothers.* (California, Columbia Prov.).—S.J.
[0910]—*Oblates of Mary Immaculate.*—O.M.I.
[0920]—*Oblates of St. Francis De Sales.* (Toledo-Detroit Prov.).—O.S.F.S.
[1190]—*Salesians of St. John Bosco.*—S.D.B.
[]—*Vincentian Fathers.*

RELIGIOUS INSTITUTES OF WOMEN REPRESENTED IN THE DIOCESE

[1920]—*Congregation of the Sisters of the Holy Cross.* (Notre Dame, IN).—C.S.C.
[0780]—*Daughters of the Cross of Liege.*—F.C.
[0820]—*Daughters of the Holy Spirit.* (Putnam, CT).—D.H.S.
[1070-04]—*Dominican Sisters.* (San Rafael).—O.P.
[1150]—*Eucharistic Franciscan Missionary Sisters.*—E.F.M.S.
[2470]—*Maryknoll Sisters of St. Dominic.*—M.M.
[]—*Missionary Sisters of the Sacred Side of Jesus and the Sorrowful Mother.* (Italy).—M.S.C.
[2519]—*Religious Sisters of Mercy.*—R.S.M.
[0430]—*Sisters of Charity of the Blessed Virgin Mary.* (Dubuque, IA).—B.V.M.
[3000]—*Sisters of Notre Dame de Namur.*—S.N.D.deN.
[3840]—*Sisters of St. Joseph of Carondelet.*—C.S.J.
[]—*Sisters of the Cross of the Sacred Heart of Jesus.* (Tijuana, Mexico).—R.C.S.C.J.
[1960]—*Sisters of the Holy Family.* (San Francisco).—S.H.F.
[3320]—*Sisters of the Presentation of the B.V.M.* (San Francisco).—P.B.V.M.
[3680]—*Sisters of the Sacred Hearts of Jesus and Mary.*—S.H.J.M.

DIOCESAN CEMETERIES AND MAUSOLEUMS

STOCKTON. *San Joaquin Cemetery and Mausoleum.* Mr. Al Vigil, Supt.

ESCALON. *St. John Cemetery.* Cynthia A. Rodriguez, Office Mgr.

MODESTO. *St. Stanislaus Cemetery and Chapel Crypts.* Gretchen Storm, Office Mgr.

NECROLOGY

† Gleeson, John P., (Retired). —Died May 1, 1997.

Diocese of Superior

(Dioecesis Superiorensis)

Most Reverend

RAPHAEL M. FLISS, D.D.

Bishop of Superior; ordained May 26, 1956; appointed Coadjutor Bishop of Superior with right of succession November 6, 1979; ordained December 20, 1979; succeeded to See, June 27, 1985. *Res., Gitchinadji Dr., Superior, WI, 54880. Office: 1201 Hughitt Ave., Superior, WI, 54880. Mailing Address: Box 969, Superior, WI, 54880.*

ESTABLISHED MAY 3, 1905.

Square Miles 15,715.

Comprises the Counties of Ashland, Barron, Bayfield, Burnett, Douglas, Iron, Lincoln, Oneida, Polk, Price, Rusk, Sawyer, St. Croix, Taylor, Vilas and Washburn in the State of Wisconsin.

Incorporated under the laws of the State of Wisconsin as the *Diocese of Superior.*

For legal titles of parishes and diocesan institutions, consult the Chancery.

Chancery Office: 1201 Hughitt Ave., Box 969, Superior, WI, 54880. Tel.: 715-392-2937; Fax: 715-392-2015.

STATISTICAL OVERVIEW

Personnel	
Bishop	1
Priests: Diocesan Active in Diocese	50
Priests: Active Outside Diocese	4
Priests: Retired, Sick or Absent	26
Number of Diocesan Priests	80
Religious Priests in Diocese	14
Extern Priests in Diocese	1
Ordinations:	
Diocesan Priests	3
Permanent Deacons	1
Permanent Deacons in Diocese	40
Total Brothers	2
Total Sisters	125
Parishes	
Parishes	115
With Resident Pastor:	
Resident Diocesan Priests	48
Resident Religious Priests	9
Without Resident Pastor:	
Administered by Priests	50
Administered by Permanent Deacons	3
Administered by Women Religious	2
Administered by Lay People	3
Pastoral Centers	2
Professional Ministry Personnel:	
Sisters	9
Lay Ministers	13
Welfare	
Catholic Hospitals	5
Total Assisted	105,263
Homes for the Aged	2
Total Assisted	350
Day Care and Extended Day Care Centers	4
Total Assisted	200
Special Centers for Social Services	4
Total Assisted	4,300
Residential Care of Disabled	15
Total Assisted	2,450
Other Institutions	10
Total Assisted	2,500
Educational	
Diocesan Students in Other Seminaries	10
Total Seminarians	10
Elementary Schools, Diocesan and Parish	18
Total Students	3,082
Catechesis/Religious Education:	
High School Students	3,932
Elementary Students	8,874
Total Students Under Catholic Instruction	15,898
Teachers in the Diocese:	
Brothers	1
Sisters	13
Lay Teachers	194
Vital Statistics	
Receptions into the Church:	
Infant Baptism Totals	1,090
Adult Baptism Totals	229
Received into Full Communion	146
First Communions	1,483
Confirmations	1,116
Marriages:	
Catholic	302
Interfaith	233
Total Marriages	535
Deaths	1,266
Total Catholic Population	88,575
Total Population	387,290

Former Bishops—Rt. Rev. AUGUSTIN FRANCIS SCHINNER, D.D., ord. March 7, 1886; cons. July 25, 1905; resigned Jan. 15, 1913; appt. Bishop of Spokane, WA, March 18, 1914; died Feb. 7, 1937.—Rt. Rev. JOSEPH M. KOUDELKA, D.D., ord. Oct. 8, 1875; cons. Auxiliary Bishop of Cleveland and Titular Bishop of Germanicopolis, Feb. 25, 1908; transferred to Milwaukee as Auxiliary Bishop, Sept. 4, 1911; appt. to the See of Superior, Aug. 6, 1913; died June 24, 1921.—Rt. Rev. JOSEPH G. PINTEN, D.D., ord. Nov. 1, 1890 elected Dec. 3, 1921; cons. May 3, 1922; transferred to the See of Grand Rapids, June 25, 1926; retired Nov. 1, 1940; died Nov. 6, 1945.—Most Rev. THEODORE H. REVERMAN, D.D., ord. July 26, 1901; cons. Nov. 30, 1926; died July 18, 1941.—Most Rev. WILLIAM PATRICK O'CONNOR, D.D., Ph.D., ord. March 10, 1912; cons. March 7, 1942; transferred to the See of Madison, Jan. 15, 1946.—His Eminence ALBERT GREGORY MEYER, D.D., S.S.L., ord. July 11, 1926; appt. Feb. 18, 1946; cons. April 11, 1946; promoted to Archbishop of Milwaukee, July 21, 1953; transferred to Archbishop of Chicago, Sept. 19, 1958; created Cardinal, Dec. 14, 1959; died April 9, 1965.—Most Rev. JOSEPH JOHN ANNABRING, D.D., ord. May 3, 1927; appt. Jan. 27, 1954; cons. March 25, 1954; died Aug. 27, 1959.—Most Rev. GEORGE A. HAMMES, D.D., Bishop Emeritus of Superior; appt. March 28, 1960; cons. May 24, 1960; retired June 27, 1985; died April 11, 1993.

Chancery—1201 Hughitt Ave., Box 969, Superior, 54880. Tel: 715-392-2937; Fax: 715-392-2015.

Vicar General—Very Rev. EDWARD G. MEULEMANS, *Res., 1410 Baxter Ave., Superior, 54880.* Tel: 715-392-8511.

Moderator of the Curia—Very Rev. PHILIP J. HESLIN, Ph.D., *1201 Hughitt Ave., P.O. Box 969, Superior, 54880.* Tel: 715-392-2937.

Chancellor—Sr. EILEEN LANG, F.S.P.A., D.Min.

Secretary to Bishop—Mrs. SHERYL PETREY.

Diocesan Tribunal—1201 Hughitt Ave., Box 969, Superior, 54880. Tel: 715-392-2937.

Judicial Vicar—Very Rev. JAMES F. TOBOLSKI, J.C.L.

Promotor of Justice—Very Rev. EDWARD G. MEULEMANS.

Defender of the Bond—Rev. WILLIAM G. HORATH.

Advocate—Sr. RITA MARIE SCHNEIDER, S.S.N.D.

Notary—Mrs. PATTI J. HOLT.

Vicar for Canonical Affairs—Very Rev. JAMES F. TOBOLSKI, J.C.L.

Vicar for Religious—Sr. EILEEN LANG, F.S.P.A.

Diocesan Pastoral Council—Most Rev. RAPHAEL M. FLISS, D.D., Pres.; South Central Deanery: WARREN WAGNER; EVELYN LOMPA; JEROME THIER, Eastern Deanery: NANCY LEVANETZ; JOSEPH BENBENEK; ALAN ZYHOWSKI, Northwest Deanery: MARY GIESEN, Vice Chm. PETER MORAN; ROBERT ULBRICH, North Central Deanery: ROBERT BAKER; DAVID HNATH; MARY JO HOLZHAEUSER, Southwest Deanery: SAMUEL CARI; LARRY WOJCHIK, Chm. WILLIAM HANSEN. Ex Officio Members: Very Revs. EDWARD G. MEULEMANS; PHILIP J. HESLIN; Sr. MARY ANTHONY MENTING, S.C.S.C.; Sr. ANITA SWANSEN, O.S.M.; Sr. MICHON DESMOND, F.S.P.A.; Sr. EILEEN LANG, F.S.P.A., Liaison.

Deaneries and Deans—Northwest Deanery: Very Rev. JAMES F. TOBOLSKI, Southwest Deanery: Very Rev. PETER F. SZLESZINSKI, North Central Deanery: Very Rev. VERNON J. OLMER, O.F.M., South Central Deanery: Very Rev. DENNIS T. MEULEMANS, East Deanery: Very Rev. JAMES R. HORATH.

Pastoral Consultors—Revs. JOHN A. DRUMMY; GERALD P. HARRIS; DAVID P. OBERTS.

Presbyteral Council & Diocesan Consultors—Most Rev. RAPHAEL M. FLISS, Pres.; Very Rev. PHILIP J. HESLIN; Very Rev. EDWARD G. MEULEMANS; Very Rev. DENNIS T. MEULEMANS, Vice Chm.; Very Rev. PETER F. SZLESZINSKI; Very Rev. JAMES F. TOBOLSKI, Sec.; Revs. JOHN A. DRUMMY; ALOYS EBACH, C.PP.S., Chm. WILLIAM H. GREEN, Treas. GERALD A. HAGEN; BRENDAN J. KUNDA; BRENNAN SCHMIEG, O.F.M.

Personnel Placement Board—Very Rev. EDWARD MEULEMANS; Revs. DAVID P. OBERTS; ALBERT L. VERDEGAN; KEVIN GORDON, Sec. THOMAS E. THOMPSON; GREGORY HOPEFL; JAMES P. POWERS.

Conciliation and Arbitration Board—THOMAS DUFFY, Chm. REBECCA JEAN ECK; Rev. DAVID P. OBERTS; RAYMOND RYNDA; Sr. RITA MARIE SCHNEIDER, S.S.N.D., Sec.

Diocesan Offices and Directors

Apostleship of Prayer—Contact Chancery.

Apostolate of the Sea—Contact Chancery.

Bureau of Information—Mr. SAM LUCERO, Dir., *1512 N. 12th St., Superior, 54880.* Tel: 715-392-8268.

Catholic Charities Bureau—Mr. BRIAN SOLAND, M.A., Exec. Dir., Office: *1416 Cummings Ave., Box 219, Superior, 54880.* Tel: 715-394-6617; Fax: 715-394-5951.

Hudson District Office—Box 222, Hudson, 54016. Tel: 715-386-3701.

Rhinelander District Office—Box 566, Rhinelander, 54501. Tel: 715-362-3329.

Catholic Boy and Girl Scout—Rev. THOMAS E. THOMPSON, *P.O. Box 295, Rib Lake, 54470.* Tel: 715-427-5259.

Catholic Women, Council of—Rev. JAMES S. DABRUZZI, Chap., *206 Wisconsin St., N. #202, Hudson, 54016.* Tel: 715-381-2815. Mrs. HALCYON KASMAREK, Pres., *9248 Cty. Hwy. J, Minocqua, 54548.* Tel: 715-356-3994.

Censor Librorum—Appointed in each case by the Most Rev. Ordinary.

Charismatic Renewal Liaison—Rev. JAMES J. KRAKER; Sr. CASIMIRA BENBENEK, O.S.M., Assoc. Liaison.

Christian Formation—Sr. GENEVIEVE SCHILLO, C.S.J., Ph.D., *1201 Hughitt Ave., P.O. Box 969, Superior, 54880.* Tel: 715-392-1042., *Res., 404 24th Ave., E., Superior.* Tel: 715-398-3002.

Cursillo Movement—Rev. BRENNAN SCHMIEG, O.F.M., Spiritual Dir. Secretaries: Mrs. MARY JIRELE; Mr. AL JIRELE, *27607 Thompson Bay Rd., Webster, 54893.* Tel: 715-866-8732.

Diocesan Coordinator of Health Affairs—Rev. KEVIN GORDON, *111 West Marshall St., Rice Lake, 54868.* Tel: 715-234-2032.

Ecumenical Commission—Very Rev. JAMES F. TOBOLSKI, *P.O. Box 969, Superior, 54880.* Tel: 715-392-2937.

Evangelization, Office of—Sr. EILEEN LANG, F.S.P.A., *P.O. Box 969, Superior, 54880.* Tel: 715-392-2937.

Family Life Apostolate—Rev. WILLIAM H. GREEN, Dir., *417 Dakota Ave., P.O. Box 32, Hayward, 54893.* Tel: 715-634-2867.

Holy Childhood Association—Rev. JOHN J. SPANJERS, Dir., *P.O. Box 118, Turtle Lake, 54889.* Tel: 715-986-4651.

Liturgical Commission—Deacon ARTHUR E. GILDE LAMADRID, Chm., *P.O. Box 969, Superior, 54880.* Tel: 715-392-2937.

Newman Apostolate—Superior: Newman Student Center, University of Wisconsin, Mr. MATTHEW CETNAR, *P.O. Box 969, Superior, 54880.* Tel: 715-394-7710. River Falls: Newman Center—WSU, *423 E. Cascade, River Falls, 54022.* Rev. NORMAN VOLK, O.M.I., Chap., *Res., 423 E. Cascade, River Falls, 54022.* Tel: 715-425-7600.

Newspaper—"Catholic Herald", Superior Edition; Mr. SAM LUCERO, Editor, *1512 N. 12th St., P.O. Box 969, Superior, 54880.* Tel: 715-392-8268., *Res., 1413 E. 3rd St., Superior, 54880.* Tel: 715-398-5027. Rev. ROBERT M. URBAN, Contributing Editor, *Res., R.R. 2, Box 62A, Glenwood City, 54013.* Tel: 715-265-7133.

Permanent Diaconate Program—Deacon TIMOTHY J. KUEHN, Dir., *P.O. Box 969, Superior, 54880.* Tel: 715-392-2937. Rev. DENNIS M. MULLEN, Consultant-Instructor. Tel: 715-822-2948.

Respect Life Office—Mrs. ALICE MARTIN, *501 E. River Ave., Ladysmith, 54548-1526.* Tel: 715-532-6023.

Propagation of the Faith—Rev. JOHN J. SPANJERS, *St. Ann Church, P.O. Box 118, Turtle Lake, 54889.* Tel: 715-986-4651.

Radio and Television—Mr. SAM LUCERO, Dir., *1512 N. 12 St., Superior, 54880.* Tel: 715-392-8268., *Res.* Tel: 715-398-5027.

The Bishop George A. Hammes Center for Religious Education and Youth Ministry—Deacon ROGER CADOTTE, Dir., *315 W. Fifth St., P.O. Box 280, Haugen, 54841.* Tel: 715-234-5044; Fax: 715-234-5241.

Branch Office of Religious Education—1201 Hughitt Ave., P.O. Box 969, Superior, 54880. Tel: 715-392-1042.

Sisters Council—Sr. ROSINE KAMINSKI, O.S.F., *419 S. 3rd. St., Chetek, 54728.* Tel: 715-924-3514.

St. Pius Priest Fund—Bd. of Dirs.: Most Rev. RAPHAEL M. FLISS, Pres.; Very Revs. JAMES R. HORATH, Treas. PETER F. SZLESZINSKI; Revs. WILLIAM H. GREEN; WILLIAM G. HORATH; Very Rev. DENNIS MEULEMANS; Rev. DAVID P. OBERTS; Very Rev. JAMES F. TOBOLSKI, Sec.; Revs. DENNIS MULLEN, Vice Pres. JOHN J. SPANJERS; GEORGE L. VOTRUBA; JAMES P. POWERS.

St. Vincent De Paul Society—Very Rev. EDWARD G. MEULEMANS, Moderator; Mr. JAMES T. TRACY, Pres., *2409 Hammond Ave., Superior, 54880.* Tel: 715-394-3185. Deacon STAN MERCIER, *40 S. Main St., Rice Lake, 54868.* Tel: 715-234-2372., *2811 Pioneer Ave., Rice Lake, 54568.* Tel: 715-234-7003.

Superintendent of Schools—Vacant, Office: *1201 Hughitt Ave., Box 969, Superior, 54880.* Tel: 715-392-1042.

Vocation—Rev. KEVIN M. GORDON, Dir., *111 W. Marshall St., Rice Lake, 54868.* Tel: 715-234-2032. Asst. Dirs.: Sr. BONNIE ALHO, O.S.M.; Rev. JOHN R. GERRITTS.

Office of Worship—Vacant, *1201 Hughitt Ave., P.O. Box 969, Superior, 54880.* Tel: 715-392-2937.

CLERGY, PARISHES, MISSIONS AND PAROCHIAL SCHOOLS

CITY OF SUPERIOR
(Douglas County)

1—CATHEDRAL OF CHRIST THE KING (1886), Very Rev. Edward G. Meulemans, V.G., Rector; Rev. Andrew P. Ricci; Deacon Arthur Gil de Lamadrid.
Res., 1410 Baxter Ave., 54880. Tel: 715-392-8511. [CEM]
School—Cathedral School, 1419 Baxter Ave., 54880. Tel: 715-392-2976; Fax: 715-392-2977. Roy Hamlin, Prin.
Lay Teachers 28; Students 422.

2—ASSUMPTION OF THE B.V.M. (1891). Also serves St. William. Rev. George L. Votruba.
Res., 5617 Tower Ave., 54880. Tel: 715-394-4883.

3—ST. ANTHONY (1870). Also serves St. Anthony, Lake Nebagamon. Rev. Dean T. Buttrick; Deacon Timothy J. Kuehn.
Res., 4315 E. 3rd St., 54880. Tel: 715-398-3261.

4—SS. CYRIL AND METHODIUS (Slovak). Closed. For sacramental records contact Cathedral of Christ the King.

5—ST. FRANCIS XAVIER (1853), Very Rev. James F. Tobolski; Deacon Philip Martineau.
Res., 710 16th Ave., E., 54880. Tel: 715-398-3033; Fax: 715-398-3074. [CEM]
Church—2316 E. 4th St., 54880. Tel: 715-398-7174.

6—ST. LOUIS. Closed. For sacramental records contact Cathedral of Christ the King.

7—ST. PATRICK. Closed. For sacramental records contact Cathedral of Christ the King.

8—ST. STANISLAUS (Polish). Closed. For sacramental records contact Cathedral of Christ the King.

9—ST. WILLIAM (1908), Rev. George L. Votruba; Very Rev. Philip J. Heslin, Pastoral Supr.; Deacon Jack McKenna; Darlene Olson, Parish Dir.
Res., 3095 E. Country Rd. B, 54880. Tel: 715-399-2450. [CEM]

OUTSIDE THE CITY OF SUPERIOR

Almena, Barron Co., Sacred Heart of Jesus Church (1890), Rev. John J. Spanjers; Deacon Timothy J. Byrnes.
Res., Box 118, Turtle Lake, 54889-0118. Tel: 715-986-4651. [CEM]

Amery, Polk Co., St. Joseph (1890), Rev. John A. Drummy; Deacon Florian Heiser.
Res., 404 Wisconsin Ave., 54001. Tel: 715-268-7717; Fax: 715-268-9986.

Ashland, Ashland Co., Our Lady of the Lake Catholic Community (1872), Very Rev. Vernon J. Olmer, O.F.M.; Rev. Conan Mitchell, O.F.M.
Res., 106 2nd Ave. E., 54806. Tel: 715-682-7620. [CEM]
School—215 E. Lake Shore Dr., 54806. Tel: 715-682-7622. Bro. Joseph Rogenski, Prin.
Brothers 1; Franciscan Sisters of Perpetual Adoration 1; Lay Teachers 17; Students 165.
Holy Family (Polish). Closed. Inquiries should be directed to Our Lady of the Lake Parish.

Balsam Lake, Polk Co., Our Lady of the Pines (1875), Rev. Daniel J. Dahlberg; Deacon Fred E. Johnson.
Res., P.O. Box 399, Osceola, 54020-0399. Tel: 715-294-2243.

Barron, Barron Co., St. Joseph (1907). Also serves St. Peter, Cameron and St. Boniface, Chetek. Rev. Gerard I. Willger.
Res., 827 E. LaSalle Ave., 54812. Tel: 715-537-3255; Fax: 715-537-3252.

Bayfield, Bayfield Co., Holy Family (1878). Also serves St. Joseph, LaPointe, St. Ann, Cornucopia and St. Francis, Red Cliff. Rev. Glenn Phillips, O.F.M.
Res., P.O. Box 1290, 54814. Tel: 715-779-3316.
Church—P.O. Box 1290, 54814. Tel: 715-779-3316. [CEM 2]
School—Holy Family/St. Francis School, 233 N. 1st St., P.O. Box 1290, 54814. Tel: 715-779-3342. Sr. Phyllis Wilhelm, O.S.F., Prin.
Lay Teachers 5; Students 59.

Birchwood, Washburn Co., St. John Evangelist (1908), Rev. David P. Oberts; Deacons Stanley J. Mercier; Harvey G. Drost.
Res., 2411 W. 23rd St., Rice Lake, 54868. Tel: 715-234-2917.

Bloomville, Lincoln Co., St. John the Baptist (1908), Rev. Michael J. Tupa, Pastoral Supr.; Michele Rein, Parish Dir.; Deacons Bernard J. Lyngdal; Darrell P. Smerz; C. Dan Towle.
Res., N10090 County B., Tomahawk, 54487. Tel: 715-453-2561. [CEM]

Boulder Junction, Vilas Co., St. Anne (1938). Also serves St. Mary, Sayner, and St. Rita, Presque Isle. Rev. Brendan J. Kunda.
Res., P.O. Box 110, 54512. Tel: 715-385-2390. [CEM]

Bruce, Rusk Co., St. Mary (1893), Rev. John R. Long; Deacon James E. Roberge.
Res., P.O. Box 207, Weyerhaeuser, 54895. Tel: 715-353-2400. [CEM]

Butternut, Ashland Co., Immaculate Conception (1880), Rev. Linus Evers, C.PP.S.
113 N. 4th St., P.O. Box 6, 54514-0006.
Res., 256 E. 2nd St., P.O. Box 182, Glidden, 54537-0182. Tel: 715-264-3471. [CEM]

Cable, Bayfield Co., St. Ann (1902), Rev. William H. Green, Pastoral Supr.; Sr. Virginia Schwartz, O.S.M., Parish Dir.; Deacon Joseph E. Reuter.
P.O. Box 37, 54821-0037. Tel: 715-798-3855.
Res., 417 Dakota Ave., P.O. Box 32, Hayward, 54843. Tel: 715-634-2867.

Cameron, Barron Co., St. Peter (1908), Rev. Gerard I. Willger.
Res., 827 E. LaSalle Ave., Barron, 54812. Tel: 715-537-3255.
Church—9th & Arlington, 54822.

Catawba, Price Co., St. Paul the Apostle (1907). Also serves St. John the Baptist, Prentice. Rev. Dismas B. Kalcic, O.S.B.
Res., W9485 Hwy. 8, P.O. Box 137, 54515-0137. Tel: 715-474-2223. [CEM]

Centuria, Polk Co., St. Patrick (1856), Rev. Daniel J. Dahlberg; Deacon Fred E. Johnson.
Res., Hwy. 35 & Tenth Ave., Box 399, Osceola, 54020-0399. Tel: 715-294-2243. [CEM]

Chelsea, Taylor Co., Assumption of the Blessed Virgin Mary (1887), Rev. Thomas E. Thompson, Pastoral Supr.; Deacons Michael D. Cullen, Parish Dir.; Paul M. Ochodnicky.
Mailing Address: P.O. Box 186, Westboro, 54490. Tel: 715-427-5266.

Chetek, Barron Co., St. Boniface (1880), Rev. Gerard I. Willger, Pastoral Supr.; Sr. Rosine Kaminski, O.S.F., Parish Dir.
Res., 419 S. Third St., 54728. Tel: 715-924-3514. [CEM]

Clam Lake, Ashland Co., St. George (1890), Rev. Linus Evers, C.PP.S.
Res., P.O. Box 182, Glidden, 54527. Tel: 715-264-3471.

Clear Lake, Polk Co., St. John (1890). Also serves St. Bridget, Stanton. Rev. Joseph C. Trinka.
Res., Box 337, 54005. Tel: 715-263-2032.

Cornucopia, Bayfield Co., St. Ann (1914), Rev. Glenn Phillips, O.F.M.
Res., P.O. Box 1290, Bayfield, 54814. Tel: 715-779-3316.

Crescent Lake, Burnett Co., Sacred Hearts of Jesus and Mary (1857), Rev. William J. Murphy, Parochial Admin.
Res., P.O. Box 7, Webster, 54893. Tel: 715-866-7321. [CEM]

Cumberland, Barron Co., St. Anthony The Abbot (1893), Rev. Dennis M. Mullen.
Res., 900 Anthony St., 54829. Tel: 715-822-2948. [CEM 2]

Danbury, Burnett Co., Our Lady of Perpetual Help (1920), Rev. William J. Murphy, Parochial Admin.
Res., P.O. Box 7, Webster, 54893. Tel: 715-866-7321. [CEM]

Dauby, Bayfield Co., St. Peter (1918), Rev. Barry Schneider, O.F.M.
Res., P.O. Box 97, Iron River, 54847. Tel: 715-372-4756.

Dobie, Barron Co., Our Lady of Lourdes (1875). Also serves Holy Trinity, Haugen, and St. John the Evangelist, Birchwood. Rev. David P. Oberts; Deacons Stanley J. Mercier; Harvey Drost.
Res., 2411 W. 23rd St., Rice Lake, 54868. Tel: 715-234-2917. [CEM]

Eagle River, Vilas Co., St. Peter the Fisherman (1894), Rev. Robert J. Koszarek; Sr. Marla Clercx, O.S.M., Pastoral Assoc.; Deacons Albert A. Goodrich; John "Skip" McCaughn.
Res., 509 Wall St., Box 728, 54521. Tel: 715-479-8704; Fax: 715-477-2017. [CEM]
School—115 S. 3rd St., P.O. Box 729, 54521. Tel: 715-479-4332. Dr. Helene Machac, Prin.
Lay Teachers 7; Students 92.

Erin, St. Croix Co., St. Patrick (1857), Rev. James J. Kraker; Deacon Joseph F. Paron.
Res., P.O. Box 18, Hammond, 54015. Tel: 715-796-2244. [CEM]

Farmington, St. Croix Co., Assumption of the Blessed Virgin Mary (1869), Rev. James J. Brinkman; Deacon A. Maurice Baillargeon.
Res., 140 Church Hill, P.O. Box 9, Somerset, 54025. Tel: 715-247-3310. [CEM]

Fifield, Price Co., St. Francis of Assisi (1888), Rev. Aloys Ebach, C.PP.S.; Deacon Chester E. Ball, Jr.
Res., 276 S. 5th Ave., Park Falls, 54552. Tel: 715-762-4494.

Flambeau, Rusk Co., St. Francis of Assisi (1866), Rev. Philip J. Juza, Parochial Admin.
Res., N657 Co. Rd. VV, Sheldon, 54766. Tel: 715-868-3475. [CEM]

Frederic, Polk Co., St. Dominic (1904). Also serves Immaculate Conception, Grantsburg. Rev. David R. Lusson; Deacon Stanley Marczak; Joanie McKeown, Pastoral Assoc.
Res., 107 W. Birch St., Box 606, 54837. Tel: 715-327-8119. [CEM]

Georgetown, Polk Co., Our Lady of the Holy Rosary (1906), Rev. Daniel J. Dahlberg; Deacon Florian H. Heiser.
Res., P.O. Box 399, Osceola, 54020-0399. Tel: 715-294-2243. [CEM]

Gilman, Taylor Co., SS. Peter and Paul (1910). Also serves St. Stanislaus, Lublin. Rev. James P. Bartelme.
Res., Box 100, 54433. Tel: 715-447-8510. [CEM]

Glenwood City, St. Croix Co., St. John the Baptist (1886). Also serves St. Bridget, Wilson. Rev. James J. Kraker; Deacon Wesley G. Tuttle.
Res., P.O. Box 18, Hammond, 54015-0018. Tel: 715-796-2244. [CEM]

Glidden, Ashland Co., Most Precious Blood (1884). Also serves Immaculate Conception, Butternut and St. George, Clam Lake. Rev. Linus Evers, C.PP.S.
Res., Box 182, 54527. Tel: 715-264-3471. [CEM]

Gordon, Douglas Co., St. Anthony of Padua (1878), Rev. Vincent M. Bromley; Deacon Peter R. Huntowski.
Res., P.O. Box 303, Solon Springs, 54873. Tel: 715-378-4431.

Grantsburg, Burnett Co., Immaculate Conception (1909), Rev. David R. Lusson; Deacon Stanley J. Marczak; Joanie McKeown, Pastoral Assoc.
Res., 107 W. Birch St., P.O. Box 606, Frederic, 54837. Tel: 715-327-8119.

Hammond, St. Croix Co., Immaculate Conception (1877). Also serves St. Patrick, Erin, St. John the Baptist, Glenwood City & St. Brigit, Wilson. Rev. James J. Kraker; Deacon Joseph F. Paron.
Res., P.O. Box 18, 54015-0018. Tel: 715-796-2244. [CEM]

Harrison, Lincoln Co., St. Augustine (1905), Rev. Michael J. Tupa, Pastoral Supr.; Deacons Clarence D. Towle; Bernard J. Lyngdal; Darrell P. Smerz; Michele Rein, Dir.
Res., Tomahawk N10090 Hwy. B, Tomahawk, 54487. Tel: 715-453-2561. [CEM]

Haugen, Barron Co., Holy Trinity (1896), Rev. David P. Oberts; Deacons Harvey G. Drost; Stanley J. Mercier.
Res., 2411 W. 23rd St., Rice Lake, 54868. Tel: 715-234-2917. [CEM]

Hawkins, Rusk Co., St. Mary Czestowchowa (1913), Rev. John C. Anderson; Deacons Richard J. Brockbank; Jerome J. Drahos; Richard D. Leonhard.
Res., 611 S. 1st St., Ladysmith, 54848. Tel: 715-532-3051.

Hayward, Sawyer Co., St. Joseph's (1882). Also serves St. Ann, Cable. Rev. William H. Green.
Res., P.O. Box 32, 54843. Tel: 715-634-2867.

Highbridge, Ashland Co., St. Anthony (1880), Rev. Gerald Hagen.
Res., P.O. Box 17, Mellen, 54546. Tel: 715-274-3701.

Hudson, St. Croix Co., St. Patrick (1840), Very Rev. Peter F. Szleszinski; Rev. Lewis E. Burden; Deacons Peter Braum; Bernard Drevnick.
Res., 1500 Vine St., 54016. Tel: 715-381-5120.
School—403 St. Croix St., 54016. Tel: 715-386-3941. Rita Bibeau, Prin.
Lay Teachers 18; Students 339.

Hurley, Iron Co., St. Mary of the Seven Dolors (1885). Also serves Sacred Heart, Montreal; Holy Redeemer, Pence; and St. Ann, Saxon. Rev. Robert E. O'Connell; Deacon Russell J. Lundgren.
Res., 404 Iron St., 54534. Tel: 715-561-2606. [CEM]

Ino, Bayfield Co., St. Florian (1913), Rev. Gabriel C. Zepczyk, Admin.
Res., P.O. Box 97, Iron River, 54847. Tel: 715-372-4756. [CEM]

Iron River, Bayfield Co., St. Michael (1892). Also serves St. Peter, Dauby. Rev. Barry Schneider, O.F.M.
Res., P.O. Box 97, 54847. Tel: 715-372-4756. [CEM]

Jump River, Taylor Co., St. Michael (1915), Rev. Philip J. Juza, Parochial Admin.
Res., N657 Co. Rd. VV, Sheldon, 54766. Tel: 715-452-5374.

Lac du Flambeau, Vilas Co., St. Anthony Catholic Church (1862), Rev. John P. Stremski; Sr. Corinne Kabara, R.S.M., Pastoral Assoc.
Mailing Address: Box 38, 54538. Tel: 715-588-3148.
Res., 650 Old Abe Rd., 54538. [CEM]

Ladysmith, Rusk Co., Our Lady of Sorrows (1906). Also serves St. Mary, Hawkins, and St. Anthony, Tony. Rev. John C. Anderson; Deacons Richard J. Brockbank; Jerome J. Drahos.
Res., 611 S. 1st St., 54848. Tel: 715-532-3051.
School—105 E. Washington Ave., 54848. Tel: 715-532-3232. Tami Stewart, Prin.
Lay Teachers 10; Students 133.

Lake Nebagamon, Douglas Co., St. Anthony (1899), Rev. Dean T. Buttrick; Deacon Timothy J. Kuehn.
Res., 4315 E. 3rd St., Superior, 54880. Tel: 715-398-3261.

Lake Tomahawk, Oneida Co., St. John Vianney (1859), Rev. James A. Hoffman.
Res., P.O. Box 30, Woodruff, 54568. Tel: 715-356-6284.

Land-O'-Lakes, Vilas Co., St. Albert (1894). Also serves St. Mary, Phelps. Rev. William F. Speerstra.
Res., Box 237, 54540. Tel: 715-547-3558.

LaPointe, Bayfield Co., St. Joseph (1669), Rev. Glenn Phillips, O.F.M.
Res., Box 1290, Bayfield, 54814. Tel: 715-779-3316. [CEM]

Lublin, Taylor Co., St. Stanislaus (1907) (Polish), Rev. James P. Bartelme.
Res., P.O. Box 100, Gilman, 54433. Tel: 715-447-8510. [CEM]

Manitowish Waters, Vilas Co., Our Lady Queen of Peace (1858), Rev. Michael L. Crisp, Parochial Admin.
Res., 3136 Lakeview Ave., P.O. Box 575, Mercer, 54547. Tel: 715-476-2697.

Medford, Taylor Co., Our Lady of the Holy Rosary (1870), Very Rev. Dennis T. Meulemans; Sr. Shirley Wagner, F.S.P.A., Pastoral Assoc.
Res., 424 W. Cedar St., P.O. Box 503, 54451. Tel: 715-748-3288; Fax: 715-748-6643. [CEM]
School—215 S. Washington Ave., P.O. Box 503, 54451. Tel: 715-748-3336. Patricia Dougherty, Prin.
Sisters of Mary 1; Lay Teachers 11; Students 145.

Mellen, Ashland Co., Holy Rosary (1886). Also serves St. Anthony, Highbridge. Rev. Gerald Hagen.
Res., P.O. Box 17, 54546. Tel: 715-274-3701.

Mercer, Iron Co., St. Isaac Jogues and Companions (1912). Also serves Our Lady, Queen of Peace, Manitowish Waters. Rev. Michael L. Crisp, Parochial Admin.
Res., P.O. Box 575, 54547. Tel: 715-476-2697.

Merrill, Lincoln Co., St. Francis Xavier (1875), Very Rev. James R. Horath; Deacon Richard G. Heckman.
Res., 1708 E. 10th St., 54452. Tel: 715-536-2803; Fax: 715-536-7536. [CEM]
Schools—St. Francis Elementary, 1708 E. 10th St, 54452. Tel: 715-536-2803.; St. Francis Middle School, 500 W. 8th St., 54452. Tel: 715-536-4954. Karen Barrett-Evjue, Prin.
Lay Teachers 12; Students 169.

St. Robert Bellarmine (1886). Closed. For inquiries for parish records contact the Chancery.

Minocqua, Oneida Co., St. Patrick (1893), Rev. Joseph N. Miller.
Res., P.O. Box 107, 54548. Tel: 715-356-3440. [CEM]

Minong, Washburn Co., St. Mary (1904), Rev. Vincent M. Bromley; Deacon Peter R. Huntowski.
Res., P.O. Box 303, Solon Springs, 54873. Tel: 715-378-4431.

Montreal, Iron Co., Sacred Heart of Jesus (1904), Rev. Robert E. O'Connell; Deacon Russell J. Lundgren.
Res., 404 Iron St., Hurley, 54534. Tel: 715-561-2606.

Moquah, Bayfield Co., Ss. Peter and Paul (1912). Also serves St. Florian, Ino. Rev. Gabriel C. Zepczyk, Admin.
Res., P.O. Box 97, Iron River, 54847. Tel: 715-746-2549. [CEM 2]

New Post, Sawyer Co., St. Ignatius (1884), Rev. Gregory J. Hopefl.
Res., Rte. 2, Box 340, Stone Lake, 54876-9545. Tel: 715-865-3669.

New Richmond, St. Croix Co., Immaculate Conception (1884), Rev. Allan P. Bradley; Deacon Hugh C. Mayer.
Office: 151 S. Washington Ave., 54017-1523. Tel: 715-246-4652.
Res., 140 Pershing Ave., 54017-1518. Tel: 715-246-2294. [CEM]
School—257 S. Washington Ave., 54017. Tel: 715-246-2469. Mary Jensen, Prin.
Lay Teachers 9; Students 134.

Odanah, Ashland Co., St. Mary (1855), Rev. Michael Lange, O.F.M.
Res., Box 182, 54861. Tel: 715-682-8350.

Osceola, Polk Co., St. Joseph (1915). Also serves Our Lady of the Pines, Balsam Lake, St. Patrick, Centuria & Our Lady of the Holy Rosary, Georgetown. Rev. Daniel J. Dahlberg; Deacon Fred E. Johnson.
Res., Hwy. 35 & 10th Ave., Box 399, 54020. Tel: 715-294-2243; Fax: 715-294-2495.

Park Falls, Price Co., St. Anthony (1881). Also serves St. Francis of Assisi, Fifield. Rev. Aloys Ebach, C.PP.S.; Deacon Chester Ball.
Res., 276 S. 5th Ave., 54552. Tel: 715-762-4494.
School—200 S. 5th Ave., 54552. Tel: 715-762-4494. Beatrice Weiland, Prin.
Priests 1; Lay Teachers 12; Students 162.

Pelican Lake, Oneida Co., St. John (1905), Rev. Michael T. Hayden; Deacons Matthew C. Porten; Michael O. Harvey.
Res., 110 S. Conro St., Rhinelander, 54501. Tel: 715-362-4012. [CEM]

Pence, Iron Co., Holy Redeemer (1908), Rev. Robert E. O'Connell; Deacon Russell J. Lundgren.
Res., 404 Iron St., Hurley, 54534. Tel: 715-561-2606.

Phelps, Vilas Co., St. Mary (1908), Rev. William F. Speerstra.
Res., P.O. Box 237, Land O'Lakes, 54540. Tel: 715-547-3558.

Phillips, Price Co., Our Lady of the North (1876), Rev. Terence Fitzmaurice, O.S.B.
Res., 125 N. Argyle Ave., 54555. Tel: 715-339-2222. [CEM]

Pier-Willow, Oneida Co., St. Francis of Assisi (1887), Rev. Michael J. Tupa; Deacons Bernard J. Lyngdal; Darrell P. Smerz; C. Dan Towle.
Res., 320 E. Washington Ave., Tomahawk, 54487. Tel: 715-453-2878. [CEM]

Prentice, Price Co., St. John (1886), Rev. Dismas B. Kalcic, O.S.B.
Res., W9485 Hwy. 8, P.O. Box 137, Catawba, 54515-0137. Tel: 715-474-2223.

Presque Isle, Vilas Co., St. Rita (1950), Rev. Brendan J. Kunda.
Res., P.O. Box 110, Boulder Junction, 54512. Tel: 715-385-2390.

Radisson, Sawyer Co., Sacred Heart (1919), Rev. Albert L. Verdegan.
Res., P.O. Box 216, Winter, 54896. Tel: 715-266-3441.

Red Cliff, Bayfield Co., St. Francis (1861), Rev. Glenn Phillips, O.F.M.
Res., P.O. Box 1290, Bayfield, 54814. Tel: 715-779-3316. [CEM]

Reserve, Sawyer Co., St. Francis of Solanus (1889) (Indian). Also serves St. Ignatius, New Post, and St. Philip, Stone Lake. Rev. Gregory J. Hopefl.
Rte. 2, Box 340, Stone Lake, 54876-9545. Tel: 715-865-3669. [CEM]
School—St. Francis Solanus, P.O. Box 341, Stone Lake, 54876. Tel: 715-865-3662. Sr. M. Felissa Zander, S.S.S.F., Prin.
Sisters of St. Francis 2; Lay Teachers 3; Students 93.

Rhinelander, Oneida Co., Immaculate Conception (1883). Also serves St. John, Pelican Lake. Rev. Michael T. Hayden; Deacons Michael O. Harvey; Mathew C. Porten.
Res., 110 S. Conro St., 54501. Tel: 715-362-4012. [CEM]

St. Joseph's (1909), Rev. John R. Gerritts; Deacon Ronald J. Bosi.
Res., 1350 N. Stevens St., 54501. Tel: 715-362-3169. [CEM]
Schools—St. Joseph's, 1340 N. Stevens St., 54501. Tel: 715-362-5588. Yvonne VandenBerg, Prin.; St. Mary's, 103 E. King, 54501. Tel: 715-362-5588. Yvonne VandenBerg, Prin.; Rhinelander Catholic Central.
Franciscan Sisters of Christian Charity 2; Lay Teachers 10; Students 304.

Rib Lake, Taylor Co., St. John the Baptist (1896), Rev. Thomas E. Thompson; Deacon Paul M. Ochodnicky.
Res., P.O. Box 295, 54470. Tel: 715-427-5259. [CEM]

Rice Lake, Barron Co., St. Joseph (1878), Rev. Kevin M. Gordon; Sr. Bonnie Alho, O.S.M., Pastoral Assoc.
Res., 111 W. Marshall St., 54868. Tel: 715-234-2032; Fax: 715-234-7757. [CEM]
School—St. Joseph School, 128 Humbird St., 54868. Tel: 715-234-7721; Fax: 715-234-5062. Tamara Sharp, Prin.
Sisters of St. Joseph of the Third Order of St. Francis 1; Lay Teachers 11; Students 238.

River Falls, St. Croix Co., St. Bridget (1854), Rev. Gerald P. Harris; Deacon Lawrence P. Hennemann.
Res., 547 N. Dallas St., P.O. Box 86, 54022. Tel: 715-425-1870; Fax: 715-425-1871. [CEM]
School—135 E. Division St., 54022. Tel: 715-425-1872; Fax: 715-425-1873. Catherine Bunke, Prin.
Lay Teachers 14; Students 185.

Sanborn, Ashland Co., St. Anne (1895), Rev. Gerald A. Hagen.
Res., P.O. Box 17, Mellen, 54546. Tel: 715-274-3701.

Sarona, Washburn Co., St. Catherine (1917), Rev. James J. Jackson.
Res., 409 Summit St., Spooner, 54801. Tel: 715-635-3105.

Saxon, Iron Co., St. Ann's (1886), Rev. Robert O'Connell; Sr. Caroline Pfeiffer, C.S.J., Pastoral Assoc.; Deacon Russell J. Lundgren.
Res., 404 Iron St., Hurley, 54534. Tel: 715-561-2606. [CEM]

Sayner, Vilas Co., St. Mary (1912), Rev. Brendan J. Kunda.
Res., P.O. Box 110, Boulder Junction, 54512. Tel: 715-542-3480.

Sheldon, Rusk Co., St. John the Apostle (1955). Also serves St. Michael, Jump River, and St. Francis of Assisi, Flambeau. Rev. Philip J. Juza, Parochial Admin.
Res., N657 Co. Rd. VV, 54766. Tel: 715-452-5374.

Shell Lake, Washburn Co., St. Joseph (1880), Rev. James J. Jackson.
Res., 409 Summit St., Spooner, 54801. Tel: 715-635-3105. [CEM]

Solon Springs, Douglas Co., St. Pius X (1878). Also serves St. Anthony of Padua, Gordon; St. Mary, Minong. Rev. Vincent M. Bromley.
Res., Box 303, 54873. Tel: 715-378-4431. [CEM]

Somerset, St. Croix Co., St. Anne (1851). Also serves Assumption of the Blessed Virgin Mary, East Farmington. Rev. James J. Brinkman; Deacon A. Maurice Baillargeon.
Res., P.O. Box 9, 54025. Tel: 715-247-3310.
School—140 Church Hill Rd., 54025. Tel: 715-247-3762. Ann Mitchell, Prin.
Sisters of St. Joseph of Medaille, Crookston 1; Lay Teachers 6; Students 136.

Spooner, Washburn Co., St. Francis De Sales (1886). Also serves St. Joseph, Shell Lake & St. Catherine, Sarona. Rev. James J. Jackson.
Res., 409 Summit St., 54801. Tel: 715-635-3105. [CEM 2]
School—300 Oak St., 54801. Tel: 715-635-2774.
Lay Teachers 10; Students 104.

Stanton, St. Croix Co., St. Bridget (1875), Rev. Joseph C. Trinka.
Res., P.O. Box 337, Clear Lake, 54005. Tel: 715-263-2032. [CEM]

Stetsonville, Taylor Co., Sacred Heart of Jesus (1884), Rev. Frederick Brost.
Res., 322 W. CTH A, 54480. Tel: 715-678-2395. [CEM]

Stone Lake, Sawyer Co., St. Philip (1905), Rev. Gregory J. Hopefl.
Res., Rte. 2, Box 340, 54876. Tel: 715-865-3669.

Strickland, Rusk Co., Assumption of the Blessed Virgin Mary (1897), Rev. John R. Long; Deacon James E. Roberge.
Res., 251 1st St., P.O. Box 207, Weyerhaeuser, 54895. Tel: 715-353-2400. [CEM]

Sugar Camp, Oneida Co., St. Kunegunda (1892), Rev. Philip Dan Stack; Deacon Albert A. Goodrich.
Res., 6895 Hwy. 17 N., Rhinelander, 54501. Tel: 715-272-1191. [CEM]

Three Lakes, Oneida Co., St. Theresa (1892), Rev. William G. Horath.
Res., 1701 Superior St., P.O. Box 8, 54562. Tel: 715-546-2159.

Tomahawk, Lincoln Co., St. Mary (1887). Also serving: St. Francis of Assisi, Pier-Willow; St. Augustine, Harrison; St. John the Baptist, Bloomville. Rev. Michael J. Tupa; Deacons Bernard J. Lyngdal; Darryl P. Smerz; C. Dan Towle.
Res., 320 E. Washington Ave., 54487. Tel: 715-453-2878. [CEM]
School—110 N. 7th St., 54487. Tel: 715-453-3542. Mary A. Cherf, Prin.
Lay Teachers 9; Students 124.

Tony, Rusk Co., St. Anthony de Padua (1901), Rev. John C. Anderson; Deacons Jerome J. Drahos; Richard J. Brockbank; Richard D. Leonhard.
Res., 611 S. 1st St., Ladysmith, 54848. Tel: 715-532-3051. [CEM]

Turtle Lake, Barron Co., St. Ann (1882). Also serves Sacred Heart of Jesus, Almena. Rev. John J. Spanjers; Deacon Timothy Byrnes.
Res., P.O. Box 118, 54889. Tel: 715-986-4651. [CEM]

Washburn, Bayfield Co., St. Louis (1882), Rev. Brennan Schmieg, O.F.M.
Res., 217 W. 7th St., Box 070, 54891. Tel: 715-373-2132.
School—713 Washington Ave., P.O. Box 70, 54891. Tel: 715-373-5322. Loretta Bagby, Prin.
Lay Teachers 5; Students 78.

Webster, Burnett Co., St. John the Baptist (1880). Also serves Sacred Hearts of Jesus and Mary, Crescent Lake, and Our Lady of Perpetual Help, Danbury. Rev. William J. Murphy, Parochial Admin.; Deacon Ralph Heffner.
Res., 26455 S. Muskey Ave., Box 7, 54893. Tel: 715-866-7321. [CEM]

Westboro, Taylor Co., St. Theresa (1904). Also serves Our Lady of Perpetual Help, Whittlesey, and Assumption of B.V.M., Chelsea. Rev. Thomas E. Thompson, Pastoral Supr.; Deacons Paul Ochodnicky; Michael D. Cullen, Parish Dir.
Res., P.O. Box 186, 54490. Tel: 715-427-5266.

Weyerhaeuser, Rusk Co., SS. Peter and Paul (1891). Also serves Assumption B.V.M., Strickland, and St. Mary, Bruce. Rev. John R. Long.
Res., Box 207, 54895. Tel: 715-353-2400. [CEM 2]

Wilson, St. Croix Co., St. Bridget (1886), Rev. James J. Kraker; Deacon Wesley G. Tuttle.
Res., P.O. Box 18, Hammond, 54015-0018. Tel: 715-796-2244. [CEM]

Whittlesey, Our Lady of Perpetual Help (1891), Rev. Thomas E. Thompson, Pastoral Supr.; Deacons Paul M. Ochodnicky; Michael D. Cullen, Parish Dir.
Res., P.O. Box 186, Westboro, 54490. Tel: 715-427-5266. [CEM]

Winter, Sawyer Co., St. Peter (1908), Rev. Albert L. Verdegan.
Res., P.O. Box 216, 54896. Tel: 715-266-3441. [CEM]

Woodruff, Oneida Co., Our Lady Queen of the Universe (1955). Also serves St. John Vianney, Lake Tomahawk. Rev. James A. Hoffman.
Res., Box 30, 54568. Tel: 715-356-6284.

Chaplains of Public Institutions

SUPERIOR. *Middle River Center* 54880. Rev. Vincent M. Bromley.

On Special or Other (Arch)Diocesan Assignment:
Reverend Fathers—
Heslin, Philip J., Moderator of the Curia, Chancery, Box 969, Superior, WI 54880

On Duty Outside the Diocese:
Reverend Monsignors—
Durst, Gerald F., Pontificial College Josephinum, Worthington, OH
Reverend Fathers—
Briody, Hugh J., Emmanual House of Providence, Clonfert, Ballinasole, Co. Galway, Ireland

---

Military Chaplains:
Reverend Fathers—
Gonia, Raymond L.

Graduate Studies:
Reverend Fathers—
Powers, James P., Edifice Deschatets, 175 Main St., Ottawa K1S IC3 Canada

---

On Leave:
Reverend Fathers—
Beutner, Edward F.
Murphy, Charles J.

Retired:
Reverend Fathers—
Anctil, Leo, 645 Knotty Oak Rd., Coventry, RI 02816-8227. Tel: 401-821-8199
Canfield, Joseph, 163 Schoolcraft St., Lake Linden, MI 49945. Tel: 906-286-1068
Cary, William J., 113 Tilltag Dr., #64, Balsam Lake, WI 54810. Tel: 715-485-3305
Corrigan, Austin B., 1900 New York Ave., Room 203 S., Superior, WI 54550. Tel: 715-395-0941
Dabruzzi, James S., Lake Mallalieu Apartments, 206 Wisconsin St., N. #202, Hudson, WI 54016. Tel: 715-381-2815
Dluge, James A., 2929 E. 4th St., Superior, WI 54880. Tel: 715-398-0500
Fraher, Leonard W., 804 Woodland Ln., New Richmond, WI 54017. Tel: 715-246-7855
Haefner, Charles, 2525 E. First St., Apt. 408, Fort Meyers, FL 33901. Tel: 813-337-4472
Heinen, Virgil O., 206 Wisconsin St., N., Apt. 102, Hudson, WI 54016. Tel: 715-381-9778
Kelchak, Joseph M., 4165 Oakmont Ct., Crown Point, IN 46307. Tel: 219-663-6726
Kleinheinz, Joseph L., 1809 N. 11th Ave., Wausau, WI 54401. Tel: 715-675-5758
Kowalski, Wladyslaw J., St. John the Baptist Parish (Peplin), 3308 Hwy. 153, Mosinee, WI 54455. Tel: 715-693-3604
Krynski, Leo, 1240 Easthill Dr., Wausau, WI 54401
Meyett, Irving C., 2528 E. 3rd St., Superior, WI 54880. Tel: 715-398-7196
Nesbitt, James B., 3157 South 66th St., Milwaukee, WI 53219. Tel: 414-545-1651
Niggemann, Bernard, 991 25th St., Chetek, WI 54728-7915. Tel: 715-859-2867
Pakosta, Francis, 13207 Hwy. G, Caledonia, WI 53108. Tel: 414-835-9020
Powell, Edward F., W6771 Branch Rd., Tomahawk, WI 54487-9230. Tel: 715-453-1357
Regh, John, W4598 Emery/Hackett Rd., Phillips, WI 54555-8574. Tel: 715-428-2268
Senn, Edward R., 28312 McKenze Rd., Spooner, WI 54801. Tel: 715-635-3295
Slowey, John P., 184 N. Eyder Ave., Phillips, WI 54555. Tel: 715-339-4068
Reverend Fathers—
Urban, Robert M., 463 W. Spruce St., Chippewa Falls, WI 54729. Tel: 715-723-2092
Reverend Fathers—
Wenninger, William, 1918 N. 21st St., Apt. 7, Superior, WI 54880. Tel: 715-394-4508
West, Norbert, House of Loreto, 2812 Harvard Ave., N.W., Canton, OH 44709. Tel: 216-492-1240
Very Rev.—
Schoone, Raymond L., 1900 New York Ave., Apt. E410, Superior, WI 54880. Tel: 715-395-0178

Permanent Deacons:
Baillargeon, Maurice, St. Anne, Somerset
Ball, Chester, St. Anthony, Park Falls
Bosi, Ronald, St. Joseph, Rhinelander
Braam, Peter, St. Patrick, Hudson
Brockbank, Richard J., Our Lady of Sorrows, Ladysmith
Byrnes, Timothy J., St. Ann, Turtle Lake
Cadotte, Roger, Bishop Hammes Center, Haugen
Cullen, Michael D., St. Theresa, Westboro
Drahos, Jerome J., St. Anthony, Tony
Drevnick, Bernard, St. Patrick, Hudson
Drost, Harvey, Holy Trinity, Haugen
Gil de Lamadrid, Arthur, Cathedral of Christ the King, Superior
Goodrich, Albert A., St. Peter, Eagle River
Harvey, Michael O., Immaculate Conception, Rhinelander
Heckman, Richard G., St. Francis Xavier, Merrill
Heffner, Ralph W., St. Dominic, Frederic
Heiser, Florian H., St. Joseph, Amery
Hennemann, Lawrence P., St. Bridget, River Falls
Huntowski, Peter R., St. Mary, Minong
Johnson, Fred, St. Joseph, Osceola
Kuehn, Timothy J., St. Anthony, Superior
Leonhard, Richard D., St. Anthony, Tony
Lundgren, Russell J., St. Mary, Hurley
Lyngdal, Bernard J., St. Mary, Tomahawk
Maier, Louis A., St. Theresa, Three Lakes
Marczak, Stanley, Immaculate Conception, Grantsburg
Martineau, Philip, St. Francis Xavier, Superior
Mayer, Hugh C., Immaculate Conception, New Richmond
McCaughn, John "Skip", St. Peter the Fisherman, Eagle River
McKenna, Jack, St. William, Pattison Park
Mercier, Stanley J., Our Lady of Lourdes, Dobie
Ochodnicky, Paul, St. Theresa, Westboro
Paron, Joseph F., Immaculate Conception, Hammond
Porten, Matthew C., Immaculate Conception, Rhinelander
Reuter, Joseph, St. Joseph, Hayward
Roberge, James, Ss. Peter & Paul, Weyerhaeuser
Smerz, Darrell, St. Mary, Tomahawk
Stefancin, Joseph
Towle, C. Dan, St. Augustine, Harrison
Tuttle, Wesley G., St. John the Baptist, Glenwood City

INSTITUTIONS LOCATED IN THE DIOCESE

[A] GENERAL HOSPITALS

SUPERIOR. *St. Mary's Hospital of Superior*, 3500 Tower Ave., 54880. Tel: 715-392-8281.
E-mail: tjacobson@smdl.org
For a complete listing, refer to the Hospitals section.

MERRILL. *Good Samaritan Health Center of Merrill, Wisconsin, Inc.*, 601 S. Center Ave., 54452. Tel: 715-536-5511
For a complete listing, refer to the Hospitals section.

NEW RICHMOND. *Holy Family Hospital*, 535 Hospital Rd., 54017. Tel: 715-246-2101
For a complete listing, refer to the Hospitals section.

RHINELANDER. *Sacred Heart-St. Mary's Hospitals, Inc.*, 1044 Kabel Ave., 54501. Tel: 715-369-6600
For a complete listing, refer to the Hospitals section.

TOMAHAWK. *Sacred Heart-St. Mary's Hospitals, Inc.*, 216 N. 7th St., 54487. Tel: 715-453-7700
For a complete listing, refer to the Hospitals section.

[B] HOMES FOR AGED

SUPERIOR. *St. Francis Home, Inc.*, 1800 New York Ave., 54880. Tel: 715-394-5591
For a complete listing, refer to the Special Care Facilities section.

[C] MONASTERIES

FIFIELD. *King of Martyrs Priory*, 54524. Tel: 715-339-2447. Rev. Clement Sobr, O.S.B.

[D] CONVENTS AND RESIDENCES FOR SISTERS

ARBOR VITAE. *Marywood Eastern Region Center*, 3560 Hwy. 51 N., 54568-9540. Tel: 715-385-2732; 385-3243; Fax: 715-385-9118.
E-mail: fspaer@juno.com
Franciscan Sisters of Perpetual Adoration. Sr. Michon Desmond, F.S.P.A., Reg. Leader. Professed 280.

HUDSON. *Carmel of the Sacred Heart*, 430 Laurel Ave., 54016. Tel: 715-386-2156.
E-mail: carmelit@pressenter.com
Web site: http://www.pressenter.com/~carmelit/
Sr. Gemma Angelo, Prioress. Sisters 6.

LADYSMITH. *Servants of Mary*, 1000 College Ave., W., 54848. Tel: 715-532-3364; 532-3365. Sr. Anita Swansen, O.S.M., Pres. Tel: 612-778-9344. Sisters 89.

MERRILL. *Holy Cross Provincial Office*, 501 S. Center Ave., 54452-3402. Tel: 715-539-5000.
E-mail: hcross@pcpros.net
Sr. Mary Anthony Menting, Prov.

Bell Tower Residence, Inc., 1500 O'Day St., 54452. Tel: 715-536-5575. Residence for the Elderly. Sisters 11; Lay Residents 62.

[E] CATHOLIC CHARITIES BUREAU

SUPERIOR. *Catholic Charities Bureau, Inc.*, 1416 Cummings Ave., P.O. Box 219, 54880. Tel: 715-394-6617. Brian Soland, M.A., Exec. Dir.; William Anderson, Chief Finance Officer; Anthony Coletta, Dir. Housing and Community Svcs. for the Elderly; David Bilden, Assoc. Dir. Human Svcs.; Terry Hendrick, Dir. Resources & Planning; Kurt Graves, Assoc. Dir. Health Svcs.; Richard Klun, Dir. Facilities Devel.; Marilyn Christopherson, Coord. Diocesan Rels.; Jennifer LeMone, Admin. Coord.

Housing Counseling Program, 1416 Cumming Ave., 54880. Tel: 715-394-6617. Terry Hendrick, Dir.

W - 2T Employment Services, 1416 Cumming Ave., 54880. Tel: 715-394-6617. Terry Hendrick, Dir.

Harborview Group Home-Handicapped, 910 E. 5th St., 54880. Tel: 715-394-2771. Eugene Chuzles, Dir.

Cypress House, 1415 Cypress, 54880. Tel: 715-394-2771. Eugene Chuzles, Dir.

Elmwood Apartments, 1020 Weeks Ave., 54880. Tel: 715-394-3447. Housing for Handicapped. Bruce Todd, Mgr.

Foster Grandparent Program, 1100 Weeks Ave., Ste. C, 54880. Tel: 715-394-5384. Margaret Hogg, Dir.

North Country Independent Living, Inc., 2231 Catlin Ave., Box 1245, 54880. Tel: 715-392-9118. John Nousaine, Dir.

Phoenix Villa, 1100 Weeks Ave., 54880. Tel: 715-392-3447. Housing for the Elderly. Bruce Todd, Mgr.

Retired Senior Volunteer Program, 1100 Weeks Ave., Ste. A, 54880. Tel: 715-394-4425. Helen Mikrot-Mattila, Dir.

Royalton Manor, Inc., 1900 New York Ave., 54880. Tel: 715-392-1014. Housing for the Elderly. Gregg Arseneau, Dir.

St. Francis Home in the Park, 1800 New York Ave., 54880. Tel: 715-394-5591. Judy Kurki-Coleman, Admin.

St. Francis Home South, 1500 N. 34th St., 54880. Tel: 715-392-1177. Kurt Graves, Admin.

Woodview Group Home, 6001 E. Third St., 54880. Tel: 715-394-2771. Residence for the Handicapped. Eugene Chuzles, Dir.

Apple River, Inc. (Amery), Minneapolis & Broadway, Amery, 54001. Tel: 715-236-2366. Housing for Mentally Disabled. Robert Heinze, Mgr.

Evergreen Apartments (Chetek), 707 Tainter Ave., Chetek, 54728. Tel: 715-236-2366. Housing for Elderly. Robert Heinze, Mgr.

Acorn Apartments (Crandon), 508 W. Washington, Crandon, 54520. Tel: 715-369-2550. Housing for Elderly. Carol Pederson, Mgr.

Phoenix Villa North (Cumberland), 1490 Arcade, Cumberland, 54829. Tel: 715-236-2366. Housing for Mentally Ill. Robert Heinze, Mgr.

Phoenix Villa of Hayward (Hayward), Rte. 10, 436 Muriel St., Hayward, 54843. Tel: 715-236-2366. Robert Heinze, Mgr.

Hudson Day Care Center (Hudson), 816 Fourth St., Hudson, 54016. Tel: 715-386-5912. Linda Groom, Dir.

Phoenix Villa of Iron River (Iron River), Hwy. H, Iron River, 54847. Tel: 715-392-3447. Housing for Elderly. Bruce Todd, Mgr.

Phoenix Villa of Lake Nebagamon (Lake Nebagamon), Main St., Lake Nebagamon, 54849. Tel: 715-392-3447. Housing for the Elderly. Bruce Todd, Mgr.

Black River Industries, Inc. (Medford), 639 S. 2nd St., Medford, 54451. Tel: 715-748-2950. Rehabilitation Center for Disabled. Bill Hrabe, Dir.

Maywood Apartments, 521 Lemke Ave., Medford, 54451. Tel: 715-369-2550. Housing for Handicapped. Carol Pederson, Mgr.

Acorn Apartments (Minong), P.O. Box 438, Minong, 54859. Residence for Elderly. Robert Heinze, Mgr. Tel: 715-236-2366.

Maywood Apartments (Plover), 2601 Madison Ave., Plover, 54467. Tel: 715-369-2550. Housing for Elderly. Carol Pederson, Mgr.

Headwaters. Inc. (Rhinelander), 1441 E. Timber Dr., Box 618, Rhinelander, 54501. Tel: 715-369-1337. Rehabilitation Center for Disabled. Elio Pascutti, Dir.

Phoenix Villa of Rhinelander, 1011 Mason St., Rhinelander, 54501. Tel: 715-369-2550. Carol Pederson, Mgr. Housing for Elderly.

Retired Senior Volunteer Program, P.O. Box 284, Rhinelander, 54501. Tel: 715-369-1919. Lori Strode, Dir.

Timberlane Apartments, 880 E. Timber Dr., Rhinelander, 54501. Tel: 715-369-2550. Housing for Elderly. Carol Pederson, Mgr.

Blue Valley, Inc (Rice Lake), 301 N. Wisconsin Ave., Rice Lake, 54868. Tel: 715-236-2366. Housing for Mentally Disabled. Robert Heinze, Mgr.

Phoenix Villa North, 1305 N. Wisconsin St., Rice Lake, 54868. Tel: 715-236-2366. Housing for Mentally Ill. Robert Heinze, Mgr.

Kids N' Company Day Care Center (River Falls), 410 S. 3rd St., River Falls, 54022. Tel: 715-425-9512. Linda Groom, Dir.

Evergreen Apartments (Shell Lake), 801 N. Lake Dr., Shell Lake, 54871. Tel: 715-236-2366. Housing for Elderly. Robert Heinze, Mgr.

Birchview Group Home (Siren), 7754 Rasmussen St., Siren, 54872. Tel: 715-349-5724. Residence for Disabled. Jim Auchue, Dir.

Diversified Services, Inc., Box 501, Siren, 54872. Tel: 715-349-5724. Rehabilitation Center for Disabled. James Auchue, Dir.

Lakewoods Apartments, Fourth Ave., Siren, 54872. Tel: 715-236-2366. Housing for Handicapped. Robert Heinze, Mgr.

Oakwood Apartments (Superior), 1112 John Ave., 54880. Tel: 715-392-3447. Housing for Chronically Mentally Ill. Bruce Todd, Mgr.

Acorn Apartments (Wisconsin Rapids), 2721 Tenth St. S., Wisconsin Rapids, 54494. Tel: 715-369-2550. Housing for Handicapped. Carol Pederson, Mgr.

The Dove Agency, Inc., 1416 Cumming Ave., 54880. Tel: 715-392-3133. Beth Carlson, Dir.

The Dove, Inc., 1416 Cumming Ave., 54880. Tel: 715-394-6617. Beth Carlson, Dir.

United Day Care, Inc., 1416 Cumming Ave., 54880. Tel: 715-386-5912. Linda Groom, Dir.

Westbay, Inc. (Washburn), 1416 Cumming Ave., 54880. Tel: 715-394-6617. Housing for the Mentally Ill. Anthony Coletta, Mgr.

[F] RETREAT HOUSES

AMERY. *Mount Carmel Hermitage*, 897 U.S. Hwy. 8, 54001-2541. Tel: 715-268-9313. Sr. Kristine Haugen, H.M.C., Coord.

ARBOR VITAE. *Marywood Franciscan Spirituality Center*, 3560 Hwy. 51, N., 54568-9540. Tel: 715-385-3750.
E-mail: pwittry@juno.com
Web site: www.fspa.org
Congregation of the Sisters of the Third Order of St. Francis of Perpetual Adoration (Franciscan Sisters of Perpetual Adoration), F.S.P.A. Co-Directors: Sr. Pauline Wittry, F.S.P.A.; Sr. Ronalda Hophan, F.S.P.A.; Sr. Jolynn Brehm, F.S.P.A.

RICE LAKE. *St. Francis Center*, 1111 E. Orchard Beach Ln., 54868. Tel: 715-234-4811.
E-mail: cbalio@discover-net.net

[G] NEWMAN CENTERS

SUPERIOR. *University of Wisconsin, Superior, Newman Community*, 823 N. 16th Ave., 54880. Tel: 715-394-7710. Mr. Matthew Cetnar, Dir.

RIVER FALLS. *St. Thomas More Newman Center*, 423 E. Cascade, 54022. Rev. Norman Volk, O.M.I.

[H] ASSOCIATION OF THE FAITHFUL

AMERY. *Hermits of Mt. Carmel*, 897 Hwy. 8, 54001. Tel: 715-268-5111. Sr. Kristine Haugen, H.M.C., Coord.

[I] MISCELLANEOUS

MERRILL. *Good Samaritan Health Center Foundation of Merrill, Wisconsin, Inc.*, 601 S. Center Ave., 54452. Tel: 715-536-5511. Michael Hammer, Pres. A not for profit corporation for the purpose of soliciting and receiving contributions for the benefit of Good Samaritan Health Center of Merrill, WI, Inc.

Sisters of Mercy of the Holy Cross Community Support Charitable Trust, 501 S. Center Ave., 54452-3402. Tel: 715-539-5000.
E-mail: hcross@pcpros.net
Sr. Mary Anthony Menting, S.C.S.C., Pres.

NEW RICHMOND. *Holy Family Hospital Foundation, Inc.*, 535 Hospital Rd., 54017. Tel: 715-246-2101; Fax: 715-243-7222. Jean Needham, Pres.

WEBSTER. *Thomas More Center for Preaching and Prayer, Inc.*, 27781 Leef Rd., 54893. Tel: 715-866-7436; Fax: 715-866-4277. Revs. Michael A. Champlin, O.P., Pres.; Nicholas W. Punch, O.P.; Sr. Joan Bakrey, O.S.F., Vice Pres.

WINTER. *Camp We-Ha-Kee.* (Girls), N. 8104 Barker Lake Rd., 54896. Sr. Arturo Cranston, O.P., Dir.

RELIGIOUS INSTITUTES OF MEN REPRESENTED IN THE DIOCESE

For further details refer to the corresponding bracketed number in the Religious Institutes of Men or Women section.

[0200]—*Benedictine Monks.* (Lisle, IL).—O.S.B.

[0520]—*Franciscan Friars.* (Sacred Heart Province).—O.F.M.

[0910]—*Oblates of Mary Immaculate Central Province.* St. Paul, MN.—OMI.

[0430]—*Order of Preachers-Province of St. Albert the Great.* Chicago.—OP.

[1060]—*Society of the Precious Blood.* (Kansas City.—C.PP.S.

RELIGIOUS INSTITUTES OF WOMEN REPRESENTED IN THE DIOCESE

[0320]—*Carmelite Nuns of the Ancient Observance.*—O.Carm.

[3710]—*Congregation of the Sisters of Saint Agnes.*—C.S.A.

[1780]—*Congregation of the Sisters of the Third Order of St. Francis of Perpetual Adoration (Franciscan Sisters of Perpetual Adoration).*—F.S.P.A.

[1710]—*Congregation of the Third Order of St. Francis of Mary Immaculate.* (Joilet, IL).—O.S.F.

[1230]—*Franciscan Sisters of Christian Charity.*—O.S.F.

[2970]—*School Sisters of Notre Dame (Mankato/Milwaukee).*—S.S.N.D.

[1680]—*School Sisters of St. Francis.*—S.S.S.F.

[3590]—*Servants of Mary (Servite Sisters).*—O.S.M.

[1070-03]—*Sinsinawa Dominican Congregation of the Most Holy Rosary.*—O.P.

[2575]—*Sisters of Mercy of the Americas.*—R.S.M.

[2630]—*Sisters of Mercy of the Holy Cross.*—S.C.S.C.

[1705]—*Sisters of St. Francis of Assisi, Milawaukee.*—O.S.F.

[3840]—*Sisters of St. Joseph of Carondelet.* (Prov. of St. Paul).—C.S.J.

[3880]—*Sisters of St. Joseph of Medaille.*—C.S.J.

[3930]—*Sisters of St. Joseph of the Third Order of St. Francis.* (Prov. of Immaculate Conception; St. Joseph Prov.).—S.S.J.-T.O.S.F.

[4100]—*Sisters of the Sorrowful Mother.* (Third Order of St. Francis).—S.S.M.

[1720]—*Sisters of the Third Order Regular of St. Francis of the Congregation of Our Lady of Lourdes.*—O.S.F.

NECROLOGY

(No Deaths)

Diocese of Syracuse

(Dioecesis Syracusensis)

Most Reverend

JAMES M. MOYNIHAN, D.D.

Bishop of Syracuse; ordained December 15, 1957; appointed Bishop of Syracuse April 4, 1995; consecrated and installed in See of Syracuse May 29, 1995. *Office: 240 E. Onondaga St., P.O. Box 511, Syracuse, NY, 13201-0511. Res., Cathedral of the Immaculate Conception, 295 E. Onondaga St., Syracuse, NY, 13202.*

Most Reverend

FRANK J. HARRISON, D.D.

Retired Bishop of Syracuse; ordained June 4, 1937; appointed Titular Bishop of Aquae and Auxiliary Bishop of Syracuse March 1, 1971; consecrated April 22, 1971; appointed Bishop of Syracuse November 16, 1976; installed February 6, 1977; retired June 16, 1987. *Res., Bishop Grimes Faculty House, 6655 Kirkville Rd., East Syracuse, NY, 13057.*

Most Reverend

THOMAS J. COSTELLO, D.D., V.G.

Auxiliary Bishop of Syracuse and Titular Bishop of Perdices; ordained June 5, 1954; appointed January 10, 1978; consecrated March 13, 1978. *Res., 1515 Midland Ave., Syracuse, NY, 13205.*

ESTABLISHED NOVEMBER 26, 1886.

Square Miles 5,749.

Corporate Title: The Roman Catholic Diocese of Syracuse NY.

Comprises the Counties of Broome, Chenango, Cortland, Madison, Oneida, Onondaga and Oswego.

For legal titles of parishes and diocesan institutions, consult the Chancery Office.

Chancery Office: P.O. Box 511, Syracuse, NY, 13201. Tel.: 315-422-7203; Fax: 315-478-4619.

STATISTICAL OVERVIEW

Personnel	
Bishop	1
Auxiliary Bishops	1
Retired Bishops	1
Priests: Diocesan Active in Diocese	224
Priests: Active Outside Diocese	20
Priests: Retired, Sick or Absent	53
Number of Diocesan Priests	297
Religious Priests in Diocese	44
Ordinations:	
Diocesan Priests	1
Transitional Deacons	2
Permanent Deacons in Diocese	62
Total Brothers	18
Total Sisters	497
Parishes	
Parishes	175
With Resident Pastor:	
Resident Diocesan Priests	165
Resident Religious Priests	7
Without Resident Pastor:	
Administered by Priests	3
Missions	18
Professional Ministry Personnel:	
Brothers	18
Sisters	497
Welfare	
Catholic Hospitals	3
Total Assisted	650,000
Homes for the Aged	52
Day Care and Extended Day Care Centers	1
Total Assisted	99
Specialized Homes	7
Total Assisted	401
Special Centers for Social Services	8
Total Assisted	56,616
Residential Care of Disabled	16
Total Assisted	562
Other Institutions	2
Total Assisted	344
Educational	
Diocesan Students in Other Seminaries	19
Seminaries, Religious	1
Students Religious	13
Total Seminarians	32
Colleges and Universities	1
Total Students	2,915
High Schools, Diocesan and Parish	5
Total Students	2,113
High Schools, Private	1
Total Students	482
Elementary Schools, Diocesan and Parish	43
Total Students	10,554
Elementary Schools, Private	1
Total Students	244
Catechesis/Religious Education:	
High School Students	8,500
Elementary Students	39,500
Total Students Under Catholic Instruction	64,340
Teachers in the Diocese:	
Priests	4
Brothers	3
Sisters	86
Lay Teachers	900
Vital Statistics	
Receptions into the Church:	
Infant Baptism Totals	5,691
Adult Baptism Totals	309
Received into Full Communion	646
First Communions	5,514
Confirmations	4,081
Marriages:	
Catholic	1,561
Interfaith	702
Total Marriages	2,263
Deaths	4,282
Total Catholic Population	372,665
Total Population	1,223,591

Former Bishops—Rt. Rev. PATRICK ANTHONY LUDDEN, D.D., ord. June 21, 1864; cons. May 1, 1887; died Aug. 6, 1912.—Rt. Rev. JOHN GRIMES, D.D., ord. Feb. 19, 1882; cons. May 16, 1909; Coadjutor Bishop, 1909-1912; succeeded to the See, Aug. 6, 1912; died July 26, 1922.—Most Rev. DANIEL JOSEPH CURLEY, D.D., ord. May 19, 1894; cons. May 1, 1923; died Aug. 3, 1932.—Most Rev. JOHN ALOYSIUS DUFFY, D.D., ord. June 13, 1908; cons. June 29, 1933; installed July 11, 1933; appt. Bishop of Buffalo, Jan. 9, 1937; installed in See of Buffalo, April 14, 1937; died Sept. 27, 1944.—Most Rev. WALTER A. FOERY, D.D., Ph.D., ord. June 10, 1916; appt. May 26, 1937; cons. Aug. 18, 1937; appt. assistant at the Pontifical Throne, Dec. 11, 1961; retired and named Titular Bishop of Miseno-Cape, Aug. 4, 1970; died May 10, 1978.—Most Rev. DAVID F. CUNNINGHAM, D.D., ord. June 12, 1926; appt. Titular Bishop of Lampsacus and Auxiliary Bishop of Syracuse, April 5, 1950; cons. June 8, 1950; appt. Coadjutor Bishop "Cum jure successiones," June 19, 1967; succeeded to the See, Aug. 4, 1970; died Feb. 22, 1979.—Most Rev. FRANK J. HARRISON, D.D., ord. June 4, 1937; appt. Titular Bishop of Aquae and Auxiliary Bishop of Syracuse, March 1, 1971; cons. April 22, 1971; appt. Bishop of Syracuse, Nov. 16, 1976; retired June 16, 1987.—Most Rev. JOSEPH T. O'KEEFE, D.D., Bishop of Syracuse; ord. April 17, 1948; appt. Titular Bishop of Tre Taverne and Auxiliary Bishop of New York, July 3, 1982; cons. Sept. 8, 1982; appt. Bishop of Syracuse, June 16, 1987; installed in See of Syracuse, Aug. 3, 1987; retired April 4, 1995; died Sept. 2, 1997.

Vicar General/Vicar for Parishes—Most Rev. THOMAS J. COSTELLO, D.D., *1515 Midland Ave., Syracuse, 13205.*

Vicars Forane—Northern Area Vicar: Rev. JAMES C. FRITZEN, *469 Main St., Phoenix, 13135.* Southern Area Vicar: Rev. Msgr. PETER J. OWENS, *9 Leroy St., Binghamton, 13905.* Eastern Area Vicars: Rev. PHILIP A. HEARN, *105 E. Liberty St., Rome, 13440.* Rev. DONALD H. KARLEN, *2 Barton Ave., Utica, 13502.* Western Area Vicars: Rev. RICHARD M. KOPP, *47 Syracuse St., Baldwinsville, 13027.* Rev. GEORGE F. SHEEHAN, *6651 Kirkville Rd., East Syracuse, 13057.*

Chancery Office—240 E. Onondaga St., Syracuse, 13202. Mailing Address: P.O. Box 511, Syracuse, 13201. Tel: 315-422-7203; Fax: 315-478-4619. Office Hours: Mon.-Fri. 8:30-4:30 Send official mail, including marriage dispensations, to Chancery.

Chancellor—Rev. MICHAEL P. MINEHAN, *6104 Cherry Valley Rd., LaFayette, 13084.*

Assistant Chancellor/Secretary to Bishop Moynihan—Rev. JOSEPH S. ZARESKI, *3127 James St., Syracuse, 13206.*

Board of Diocesan Consultors—Most Rev. THOMAS J. COSTELLO, D.D.; Rev. Msgr. WILLIAM M. KELLY; Rev. Msgr. PETER J. OWENS; Revs. MICHAEL J. CARMOLA; ROBERT D. CHRYST; JAMES C. FRITZEN; PHILIP A. HEARN; DONALD H. KARLEN; RICHARD M. KOPP; JAMES P. LANG; GREGORY C. LESTRANGE; THOMAS J. MCGRATH; GEORGE F. SHEEHAN.

Management Team—Most Rev. JAMES M. MOYNIHAN; Most Rev. THOMAS J. COSTELLO, D.D.; Revs. TIMOTHY S. ELMER; MICHAEL P. MINEHAN; JOSEPH H. PHILLIPS; ROBERT P. STEPHENSON; J. ROBERT YEAZEL; JOSEPH S. ZARESKI; Sr. FRANCINE BAUSER, C.S.J.; Sr. LAURA BUFANO, C.S.J.; Sr. MARY ANNE HEENAN, C.S.J.; Sr. EILEEN MCCANN; Mrs. GERRIE KALUZNY; Ms. DANIELLE MOEN-CUMMINGS.

Pastoral Council—Most Rev. JAMES M. MOYNIHAN, Pres.; Ms. KATHLEEN M. DYER, Exec. Sec., *101 Ridge Rd., Fulton, 13069.* Tel: 315-592-5566.

Pastoral Examiners—Revs. JOHN P. FENLON; MORITZ FUCHS; THOMAS KEATING; JAMES KENNEDY; RICHARD V. O'NEILL; DANIEL G. MURPHY; JOHN F. ROSE; JOSEPH SALERNO; JOSEPH S. ZARESKI.

Presbyteral Council—Most Rev. JAMES M. MOYNIHAN, Pres.; Rev. GREGORY C. LESTRANGE, Chm. Ex Officio: Most Rev. THOMAS J. COSTELLO; Rev. Msgr. PETER J. OWENS; Revs. JAMES C. FRITZEN; PHILIP A. HEARN; DONALD H. KARLEN; RICHARD M. KOPP; GEORGE F. SHEEHAN. Appointed: Revs. LAURENCE J. LORD; MICHAEL P. MINEHAN. Elected: Rev. Msgr. PAUL A. BRIGANDI; Rev. Msgr. ROBERT B. DAVERN; Rev. Msgr. JOHN M. ZEDER; Revs. PAUL F. ANGELICCHIO; JUSTIN A. BIASI, O.F.M.Conv.; FRANCIS J. CASE; EDMUND J. DURR; JAMES E. GEHL; DONALD J. HEBERT; THOMAS F. HOBBES; DAVID J. JAMES; THOMAS P. KOBUSZEWSKI; JAMES P. LANG; THOMAS J. MCGRATH; JOHN J. MULRANEN; SEAN P. O'BRIEN; JAMES L. RILEY; JOHN C. SCHOPFER; JAMES F. SMITH, S.J.; ROBERT B. STEPHENSON; RICHARD R. THOMPSON; PETER A. WILLIAMS.

Diocesan Tribunal—

Judicial Vicar—Rev. TIMOTHY S. ELMER.

Judges—Revs. ROBERT P. HYDE, J.C.L.; LAURENCE W. KENNEDY.

Associate Judges—Revs. DAVID J. BAEHR; JOHN J. MULRANEN; DANIEL G. MURPHY; ROBERT G. TIERNEY; DONALD C. VANAMBURGH; LEO J. WIMETT.

Defender of the Bond—Rev. MICHAEL P. MINEHAN, J.C.L.

Promotor of Justice—Rev. Msgr. JAMES A. MCCLOSKEY.

Notary of the Tribunal—KATHLEEN CUSHING.

Advocates—Sr. ANNA WALTER MOSSDORF, O.S.F.; MARGARET EDGECOMB.

Auditors—Revs. JOHN P. DONOVAN; MARK J. GANTLEY.

Case Coordinators/Staff—MARY BEALL; KATHLEEN CUSHING.

Vicar for Administration—Rev. MICHAEL P. MINEHAN, *240 E. Onondaga St., P.O. Box 511, Syracuse, 13201.* Tel: 315-422-7203.

Vicar for Community Services—Rev. ROBERT S. STEPHENSON, *240 E. Onondaga St., P.O. Box 511, Syracuse, 13201.* Tel: 315-424-1830.

Vicar for Parishes—Most Rev. THOMAS J. COSTELLO, D.D., *240 E. Onondaga St., P.O. Box 511, Syracuse, 13201.* Tel: 315-422-7203.

Vicar for Priests—Rev. J. ROBERT YEAZEL, *240 E. Onondaga St., P.O. Box 511, Syracuse, 13201.* Tel: 315-470-1460.

Vicar for Religious—Sr. FRANCINE BAUSER, C.S.J., *240 E. Onondaga St., P.O. Box 511, Syracuse, 13201.* Tel: 315-422-7203; 470-1468.

Diocesan Offices

Accounting—Ms. DEBRA SOCHAN, CFO, *P.O. Box 511, Syracuse, 13201.* Tel: 315-470-9045; Fax: 315-422-9139.

Adminstration—Rev. MICHAEL P. MINEHAN, Vicar, *P.O. Box 511, Syracuse, 13201.* Tel: 315-422-7203.

Archives—Mr. CARL ROESCH, Archivist, *P.O. Box 511, Syracuse, 13201.* Tel: 315-470-1493.

Asian Apostolate—Rev. JOHN TINH TRAN, C.M.C.; Sr. JUDITH HOWLEY, C.S.J., *215 N. State St., Syracuse, 13203.* Tel: 315-472-7043.

Benefits—Ms. CAROLYN CAIN, Dir., *P.O. Box 511, Syracuse, 13201.* Tel: 315-422-9091.

Black Catholic Ministry—Vacant, *P.O. Box 511, Syracuse, 13201.* Tel: 315-470-1463.

Boy Scouts/Girl Scouts—Rev. JAMES P. LANG, Chap., *St. Thomas More Chapel, 110 Walnut Pl., Syracuse, 13210.* Tel: 315-478-5959.

Building Commission—Most Rev. JAMES M. MOYNIHAN; Most Rev. THOMAS J. COSTELLO, D.D.; Revs. MICHAEL P. MINEHAN; JOHN S. FINNEGAR; JOSEPH E. SCARDELLA; Sr. LAURA BUFANO; Mr. THOMAS V. DADEY, Esq.; Mr. EDWARD T. KING; Mr. J. DOUGLAS ROSS; WILLIAM DORAN; JAMES A. MURPHY; EDWARD SAMOLIS; Ms. DEBRA J. SOCHAN.

Catholic Cemeteries—Rev. JAMES C. FRITZEN, Dir.; Mr. MARK LAZAROSKI, Exec. Dir., *2315 South Ave., Syracuse, 13207.* Tel: 315-475-4639; Fax: 315-422-0363.

Catholic Charities—Rev. ROBERT B. STEPHENSON, *P.O. Box 511, Syracuse, 13202.* Tel: 315-424-1830; Fax: 315-478-4619.

Onondaga County Director—Mr. BRIAN WALTON, *1654 W. Onondaga St., Syracuse, 13204.* Tel: 315-424-1806.

Downtown Emergency Assistance Office—SANDY SMITH, *264 E. Onondaga St., Syracuse, 13202.* Tel: 315-424-1876.

Broome County Director—Mr. JOSEPH G. SLAVIK, *232 Main St., Binghamton, 13905.* Tel: 607-729-9166.

Chenango County Director—JANE CODDINGTON, Dir., *3 O'Hara Dr., Norwich, 13815.* Tel: 607-334-8244.

Cortland County Director—PAULA CURRIE, *33-35 Central Ave., Cortland, 13045.* Tel: 607-756-5992.

Oneida and Madison Counties Director—Mr. DENNIS MANNING, *1408 Genesee St., Utica, 13502.* Tel: 315-724-2150.

Oswego County Director—ANDREA MCCABE, *365 First St., Fulton, 13069.* Tel: 315-598-3980.

Catholic Deaf Community—Rev. PETER T. WILLIAMS, Dir., *1119 Elm St., Utica, 13501.* Tel: 315-735-8184 (TTY/Voice).

Catholic Relief Services—Rev. ROBERT B. STEPHENSON, Dir., *P.O. Box 511, Syracuse, 13201.* Tel: 315-424-1830.

Catholic Schools—Sr. MARY ANNE HEENAN, C.S.J., Supt., *P.O. Box 511, Syracuse, 13201.* Tel: 315-470-1450. Rev. CHARLES S. VAVONESE, Assoc. Supt.; Mrs. SHEILA LIEGEL, Dir. Curriculum.

Northern & Western Regions—Sr. SHIRLEY BROWN, Area Supt., *P.O. Box 511, Syracuse, 13201.* Tel: 315-470-1450; Fax: 315-478-4619.

Southern Region—Dr. JOHN J. COLLIGAN, Area Supt., *206 Madison Ave., P.O. Box 7158, Endicott, 13761.* Tel: 607-748-1541; Fax: 607-748-0083.

Eastern Region—Ms. KATHLEEN COYE, Area Supt., *17 Herkimer Rd., Utica, 13502.* Tel: 315-735-2111; Fax: 315-735-3603.

Catholic Sun—Rev. DONALD BOURGEOIS, Editor in Chief & Gen. Mgr., *421 S. Warren St., Syracuse, 13202.* Tel: 315-422-8153; 800-333-0571; Fax: 315-422-7549.

Catholic Television—Mr. JAMES FUNSON, Dir., *1342 Lancaster Ave., Syracuse, 13210.* Tel: 315-472-3584; Fax: 315-472-8409.

Christopher Community—Mr. PETER WHITE, Exec. Dir., *1654 W. Onondaga St., Syracuse, 13204.* Tel: 315-414-1821.

Clerical Fund Society of the Roman Catholic Diocese of Syracuse—Most Rev. JAMES M. MOYNIHAN, Pres.; Most Rev. THOMAS J. COSTELLO, D.D., Vice Pres.; Rev. MICHAEL P. MINEHAN, Sec. & Treas.

Office of Communications—Ms. DANIELLE CUMMINGS, Dir., *P.O. Box 511, Syracuse, 13201.* Tel: 315-471-1476; Fax: 315-478-4619.

Council of Religious—Sr. ROSE GARRAMONE, O.S.F., Pres., *P.O. Box 511, Syracuse, 13201.*

Development Office—Mr. JERRY FARNSWORTH, *1342 Lancaster Ave., Syracuse, 13210.* Tel: 315-472-0203; 472-7902; Fax: 315-472-8409.

Disabilities Office—Mr. THOMAS CUNNINGHAM, JR., Dir., *P.O. Box 511, Syracuse, 13201.* Tel: 315-424-1830; Fax: 315-478-4619.

Ecumenical Commission—Rev. Msgr. RONALD C. BILL, Dir., *8229 S. Main St., Cicero, 13039.* Tel: 315-699-2752.

Family Life Education—Rev. JOSEPH H. PHILLIPS, Dir., *1342 Lancaster Ave., Syracuse, 13210.* Tel: 315-472-6754; Fax: 315-472-8409.

Finance Committee—Most Rev. JAMES M. MOYNIHAN; Revs. MICHAEL P. MINEHAN; J. ROBERT YEAZEL; Mr. JOHN D. BURKE, SR.; Mr. JOHN KIRSCH; Mr. JOSEPH MCGLYNN; Mr. JAMES MURPHY; Ms. CAROL PIEKLIK; Mr. ROGER W. SHAVER; Ms. DOREEN SIMMONS, Esq.; Ms. DEBRA SOCHAN.

Formation for Ministry—Deacon JOSEPH DANISZEWSKI, Dir., *P.O. Box 511, Syracuse, 13202.* Tel: 315-470-1421; Fax: 315-478-4619.

Health Care—Rev. ROBERT B. STEPHENSON, Dir., *P.O. Box 511, Syracuse, 13201.* Tel: 315-424-1830; Fax: 315-478-4619.

HOPE Appeal—Ms. LOUANN CHRISTO, Assoc. Dir., *1342 Lancaster Ave., Syracuse, 13210.* Tel: 315-472-0203; 800-295-4776; Fax: 315-472-8409.

Human Life Office—Mrs. CINDY FALISE, Dir., *P.O. Box 511, Syracuse, 13201.* Tel: 315-424-1830; Fax: 315-478-4619.

Liturgy—Sr. LAURA BUFANO, C.S.J., Dir., *P.O. Box 511, Syracuse, 13201.* Tel: 315-470-1425.

Parish Services/Purchasing—Mr. ROBERT GILL, Dir., *P.O. Box 511, Syracuse, 13201.* Tel: 315-470-9101; Fax: 315-422-9139.

Permanent Diaconate—Deacon LESLIE F. DISTIN, Dir., *P.O. Box 511, Syracuse, 13201.* Tel: 315-470-1466.

Priest Personnel—Rev. J. ROBERT YEAZEL, Dir., *P.O. Box 511, Syracuse, 13201.* Tel: 315-470-1460; Fax: 315-478-4619.

Priests' Personnel Committee—Most Rev. JAMES M. MOYNIHAN; Most Rev. THOMAS J. COSTELLO, D.D.; Revs. DAVID J. BAEHR; GERALD J. BUCKLEY; MICHAEL J. CARMOLA; KEVIN J. CORCORAN; JOHN P. FLANAGAN; MICHAEL P. MINEHAN; JAMES T. O'BRIEN; DANIEL J. O'HARA; JAMES T. QUEEN; CLARENCE F. RUMBLE; J. ROBERT YEAZEL.

Project Rachel—Mrs. CINDY FALISE, Dir., *P.O. Box 511, Syracuse, 13201.* Tel: 315-424-3737.

Personal Resource Center—Rev. NEAL QUARTIER, Dir., *420 Montgomery St., Syracuse, 13202.* Tel: 315-470-1462.

Propagation of the Faith—Rev. JOSEPH H. PHILLIPS, Dir., *1342 Lancaster Ave., Syracuse, 13210.* Tel: 315-472-3442; Fax: 315-472-8409.

Religious Education—Mrs. GERRIE KALUZNY, Dir., *P.O. Box 511, Syracuse, 13202.* Tel: 315-470-1431; Fax: 315-478-4619.

Eastern Region—Sr. KATHLEEN EIFFE, Dir., *One Sherman St., New Hartford, 13413.* Tel: 315-797-4030.

Northern Region—Sr. GERMANE HILSTON, Dir., *108 E. 6th St., Oswego, 13126.* Tel: 315-343-5557.

Southern Region—Sr. BERNICE ANN CARROLL, Dir., *1031 Chenango St., Binghamton, 13901.* Tel: 607-772-0071.

South (Norwich)—ANGIE DIAMOND, *Resource Center, 20 Randall Ave., Norwich, 13815.* Tel: 607-334-2883.

Western Region—MARY STANLEY, Dir., *1342 Lancaster Ave., Syracuse, 13210.* Tel: 315-472-6751. JEAN LOVAS, Resource Center. Tel: 315-472-6752.

West (Cortland)—Vacant, *44 N. Main St., Cortland, 13045.* Tel: 607-756-2532.

Respect for Life—Mrs. CINDY FALISE, Dir., *P.O. Box 511, Syracuse, 13201.* Tel: 315-424-1859.

Laymen & Laywomen Retreat Movements—Rev. MICHAEL J. CARMOLA, Dir., *Christ the King Retreat House, 500 Brookford Rd., Syracuse, 13224.* Tel: 315-446-2680.

Spanish Apostolate—Rev. ROBERT D. CHRYST, Dir., *170 Seymour St., Syracuse, 13204.* Tel: 315-442-9390.

Syracuse Catholic Press Association, Inc.—"The Catholic Sun"; Rev. DONALD BOURGEOIS, Editor in Chief & Gen. Mgr.; Most Rev. JAMES M. MOYNIHAN, Pres., *421 S. Warren St., Syracuse, 13202.* Tel: 315-422-2153; 1-800-333-0571; Fax: 315-422-7549.

Vocation Formation—Rev. NEAL E. QUARTIER, Dir., *P.O. Box 511, Syracuse, 13201.* Tel: 315-470-1452; Fax: 315-478-4619.

Vocation Promotion—Rev. JAMES F. QUINN, Dir., *P.O. Box 511, Syracuse, 13201.* Tel: 800-471-1468; Fax: 315-478-4619.

Youth Ministry—Sr. EILEEN MCCANN, C.S.J., Dir., *P.O. Box 511, Syracuse, 13201.* Tel: 315-470-1419; Fax: 315-478-4619.

CLERGY, PARISHES, MISSIONS AND PAROCHIAL SCHOOLS

CITY OF SYRACUSE
(Onondaga County)

1—THE CATHEDRAL OF THE IMMACULATE CONCEPTION (1841), Rev. Msgr. Joseph M. Champlin, Rector; Most Rev. James M. Moynihan; Revs. John Putano; John C. Schopfer; Neal E. Quartier; Deacon Pio Peter Carranti.

Res., 259 E. Onondaga St., 13202. Tel: 315-422-4177; Fax: 315-478-4619.

School—420 Montgomery St., 13202. Tel: 315-422-7217. Sr. Mary Jane Wilcox, D.C., Prin.

Daughters of Charity of St. Vincent de Paul 3; Lay Teachers 8; Students 144.

Stations—Castle Rest Nursing Home, Tel: 315-478-1641; Clinton St. Plaza, Tel: 315-475-2141; McCarthy Manor, Tel: 315-475-6390; Nursing Home, Tel: 315-474-4431.

2—ASSUMPTION B.V.M. (1844) (German), Revs. Patrick Gallagher, O.F.M.Conv.; Robert Amrhein, O.F.M.Conv.; Bartholomew Gaske, O.F.M.Conv.; Charles Nelipowitz, O.F.M.Conv.; Herman Seibert, O.F.M.Conv.; Jeffrey Keefe, O.F.M.Conv., Ph.D., Prov. Psychologist, Franciscan Counseling; Regis Rodda, O.F.M.Conv.; Michael Taylor, O.F.M.Conv.; Bros. John Douglas McMillan, O.F.M.Conv.; Thomas Connelly, O.F.M.Conv.

Res., St. Francis Friary, 812 N. Salina St., 13208. Tel: 315-422-4833; Fax: 315-422-4363. [CEM]

Assumption Cemetery Corporation—2401 Court St., 13208.

3—BLESSED SACRAMENT (1921), Revs. James T. O'Brien; Kevin Corcoran. In res., Rev. Joseph S. Zareski.

Res., 3127 James St., 13206. Tel: 315-437-3394; Fax: 315-463-1628.

School—(Grades PreK-6) 3129 James St., 13206. Tel: 315-437-1261. Mrs. Andrea Polcaro, Prin.

Sisters of St. Joseph of Carondelet 1; Lay Teachers 11; Students 299.

4—HOLY TRINITY (1891) (German), Rev. Edmund J. Durr; Sr. Mary Margaret Singer, C.S.J., Pastoral Assoc.
Res., 501 Park St., 13203. Tel: 315-474-8681; Fax: 315-474-3154.

5—MOST HOLY ROSARY (1913), Rev. Peter M. Creed; Deacon Donald M. McCabe. In res., Rev. James F. Quinn.
Res., 111 Roberts Ave., 13207-1397. Tel: 315-478-5749; Fax: 315-478-8629.
School—1031 Bellevue Ave., 13207. Tel: 315-476-6035; Fax: 315-476-0219. Eamon O'Neill, I.H.M., Prin.
Sisters 3; Lay Teachers 16; Students 237.

6—OUR LADY OF LOURDES (1947), Rev. Thomas P. Fitzpatrick; Deacon Leo Needham.
Res., 300 Valley Dr., 13207. Tel: 315-476-9576.
School—301 Valley Dr., 13207. Tel: 315-476-2296. Ms. Joan T. Smith, Prin.
Lay Teachers 8; Students 114.

7—OUR LADY OF POMPEI (1924) (Italian), Rev. Joseph E. Scardella. In res., Revs. John T. McGraw; Frederick A. Pompei; John Tinh Tran; Deacon Kenneth Money.
Res., 301 Ash St., 13208. Tel: 315-422-7163; Fax: 315-422-7164.
School—(Grades PreK-6) 915-917 N. McBride St., 13208. Tel: 315-422-8548.
Lay Teachers 12; Students 167.
Convent—920 N. McBride St., 13208. Tel: 315-422-7922. Franciscan Missionary Sisters of the Immaculate Conception

8—OUR LADY OF SOLACE (1926), Rev. William R. Jones. In res., Rev. Alfred J. Bebel.
Res., 516 Salt Springs Rd., 13224. Tel: 315-446-2060.

9—SACRED HEART (1892) (Polish), Revs. Peter W. Gleba; Stanley Dudkiewicz (Poland); Stanley Matula (Poland); Deacons James L. Morse; Joseph Daniszewski.
Res., 927 Park Ave., 13204. Tel: 315-422-2343. [CEM 2]
School—1001 Park Ave., 13204. Tel: 315-422-7372; Fax: 315-471-0591. Sr. Melanie Jaworski, C.S.S.F., Supr. & Prin.
Felician Sisters 3; Lay Teachers 17; Students 170.

10—ST. ANDREW THE APOSTLE (1953), Rev. Edward J. Reimer; Sr. Patricia Bergan, O.S.F., Pastoral Assoc.
Res., 124 Alden St., 13210. Tel: 315-476-8656.

11—ST. ANN (1955), Rev. John L. Roark. In res., Rev. Joseph H. Phillips.
Res., 4461 Onondaga Blvd., 13219. Tel: 315-468-1803.
School—Tel: 315-468-6441. Mrs. Nancy Toscano, Prin.
Sisters 1; Lay Teachers 7; Students 130.

12—ST. ANTHONY OF PADUA (1891), Rev. Robert D. Chryst. In res., Most Rev. Thomas J. Costello; Rev. Raul Echeverri-Tobon (Colombia).
Res., 1515 Midland Ave., 13205. Tel: 315-475-4114.

13—ST. BRIGID AND ST. JOSEPH (1926 and 1869), Rev. Laurence W. Kennedy; Deacon Leonard S. Monnat.
Res., 318 Herkimer St., 13204. Tel: 315-488-7122.

14—ST. CHARLES (1929), Rev. James H. Carey; Deacon Peter Vanelli; Sr. Paula Jude Egan, C.S.J., Parish Min.
Res., 417 S. Orchard Rd., 13219. Tel: 315-468-4122.
School—200 W. High Ter., 13219. Tel: 315-488-7631; Fax: 315-488-0617. Sr. Donna Driscoll, Prin.
Sisters 3; Lay Teachers 15; Students 244.
Convent—401 E. Corey Rd., 13219. Tel: 315-468-6041. Missionary Franciscan Sisters of the Immaculate Conception

15—ST. DANIEL (1932), Rev. Msgr. Eugene M. Yennock; Rev. Mark J. Gantley.
Res., 3004 Court St., 13208. Tel: 315-454-4946; Fax: 315-454-0978.
School—Tel: 315-455-7021. Sr. Ancilla Yim, Prin.
Sisters of the Third Franciscan Order 3; Lay Teachers 12; Students (K-6) 178; Students (PreK-K) 29.

16—ST. JAMES (1925), Revs. Michael T. Meagher; Daniel J. O'Hara. In res., Rev. Leonard Kotzbauer.
Res., 4845 S. Salina St., 13205. Tel: 315-469-7789.
School—(Grades PreK-6) 4837 S. Salina St., 13205. Tel: 315-492-1054. Sr. David Agnes DeForrest, Prin.
Sisters 2; Lay Teachers 11; Students 190.
Convent—111 Munson Dr., 13205. Tel: 315-492-3654. Sisters of the Third Franciscan Order M.C.
Station—Brighton Towers.

17—ST. JOHN THE BAPTIST (1827), Rev. John R. DeLorenzo. In res., Rev. Robert E. Brennan.
Res., 406 Court St., 13208. Tel: 315-478-0916.
School—1406 Park St., 13208. Tel: 315-422-6982. Mrs. Sally Lisi, Prin.
Sisters of St. Joseph of Carondelet 2; Lay Teachers 12; Students 190.

18—ST. JOHN THE EVANGELIST (1851), Rev. Robert B. Stephenson; Deacon John H. Collins. In res., Rev. Daniel C. Muscalino.
Res., 214 N. State St., P.O. Box 6482, 13203. Tel: 315-422-0786; Fax: 315-474-1045.

19—ST. LUCY (1872), Rev. James D. Mathews. In res., Rev. Msgr. Charles J. Fahey.
Res., 432 Gifford St., 13204. Tel: 315-475-7273; Fax: 315-475-7273.
School—(Grades K-5) 422 Gifford St., 13204. Tel: 315-478-6312. Ms. Karen McCann, Prin.
Lay Teachers 6; Students 90.

20—ST. PATRICK (1870), Rev. E. Peter Reddick.
Res., 216 N. Lowell Ave., 13204. Tel: 315-475-2185.
School—(Grades PreK-6) 210 Schuyler St., 13204. Tel: 315-476-4076. Cheryl Canfield, Prin.
Sisters of St. Joseph of Carondelet 6; Lay Teachers 10; Students 155.

21—ST. PETER (1890) (Italian), Rev. Tarcisio Bagatin, C.S.
Res., 709 James St., 13203. Tel: 315-472-4451; Fax: 315-422-3441.

22—ST. STEPHEN (1915) (Slovak), Revs. Peter W. Gleba; Tadeusz Rudnik (Canada).
Res., 305 N. Geddes St., 13204. Tel: 315-422-5224.

23—ST. THERESE THE LITTLE FLOWER OF JESUS (1926), Rev. Edward J. Reimer.
Res., 112 Lancaster Pl., 13210. Tel: 315-472-9934.
Parish Helpers—1226 Lancaster Ave., 13210. Tel: 315-472-2685.
Sisters of St. Joseph of Carondelet 1.

24—ST. VINCENT DE PAUL (1893), Rev. Alfred E. Nortz. In res., Rev. Wilbur J. Votraw.
Res., 342 Vine St., 13203. Tel: 315-479-6689; Fax: 315-479-6689.
Convent—1101 Burnet Ave., 13203. Tel: 315-479-8012. Sisters of St. Joseph of Carondelet

25—TRANSFIGURATION (1911) (Polish), Rev. Stanley M. Szewczyk.
Res., 740 Teall Ave., 13206. Tel: 315-479-6129; Fax: 315-479-6336.

OUTSIDE THE CITY OF SYRACUSE

Bainbridge, Chenango Co., St. John the Evangelist (1914), Rev. Donald E. Bourgeois.
Res., 34 S. Main St., 13733. Tel: 607-967-4481.
Mission—Afton, St. Agnes, Tel: 607-639-1200.

Baldwinsville, Onondaga Co., St. Augustine (1966), Rev. John Rose.
Res., 7333 O'Brien Rd., 13027. Tel: 315-638-0585.
St. Elizabeth Ann Seton (1985), Rev. John P. Wagner; Deacon William A. Dotterer.
Res., 3494 NY State Rte. 31, 13027. Tel: 315-652-4300; Fax: 315-622-1761.
St. Mary (1852), Rev. Richard M. Kopp.
Res., 47 Syracuse St., 13027. Tel: 315-635-5762. [CEM]
School—49 Syracuse St., 13027. Tel: 315-635-3977. Sr. Rose Marie, Prin.
Sisters of the Third Franciscan Order M.C. 1; Lay Teachers 8; Students 200.

Binghamton, Broome Co.,

1—ST. ANDREW, (1955), Rev. Gerald J. Buckley.
Res., 356 Conklin Ave., 13903. Tel: 607-722-4049.
Parish Center—356 Conklin Ave., 13903.

2—ST. ANN, (1925) (Slovak), Revs. Paul J. Keebler; Kevin J. Bunger, Spanish Apostolate.
Res., 346 Prospect St., 13905. Tel: 607-797-1856.

3—ST. CATHERINE OF SIENA, (1929), Rev. Laurence J. Lord; Sr. Karen Gaube, C.S.J., Pastoral Assoc.; Deacon Raymond Goskowski.
Res., 1031 Chenango St., 13901. Tel: 607-722-4388; Fax: 607-722-1336.

4—ST. CHRISTOPHER, (1940), Rev. Edward J. Zandy.
Res., 103 Castle Creek Rd., 13901. Tel: 607-723-0677.

5—SS. CYRIL AND METHOD, (1904) (Slovak), Rev. George Sandor, O.F.M.Conv. In res., Revs. Kenan McGowan, O.F.M.Conv.; Hilary Miketinac.
Res., 148 Clinton St., 13905. Tel: 607-724-1372; Fax: 607-724-1468.

6—ST. JOHN THE EVANGELIST, (1907), Revs. Paul J. Alciati; C. Patrick Keating.
Res., 1263 Vestal Ave., 13903. Tel: 607-722-0493; Fax: 607-722-0493.

7—ST. JOSEPH, (1914) (Lithuanian), Rev. John E. Mikalajunas.
Res., One Judson Ave., 13905. Tel: 607-797-5264; Fax: 607-797-5264.

8—ST. MARY OF THE ASSUMPTION, (1887; 1913), Rev. Msgr. Paul A. Brigandi; Rev. Clarence J. Cerwonka; Sr. Linda Gaige, C.S.J.
Res., 37 Fayette St., 13901. Tel: 607-723-5383.

9—ST. PATRICK, (1838), Rev. Msgr. Peter J. Owens; Rev. Charles Opondo-Owora (Africa). In res., Rev. Christopher Boretto.
Res., 9 Leroy St., 13905. Tel: 607-722-1060; Fax: 607-724-1466.
Convent—46 Oak St., 13905. Tel: 607-722-4745. Sisters of St. Joseph of Carondelet

10—ST. PAUL, (1896), Rev. Corey S. Van Kuren.
Res., 15 Doubleday St., 13901. Tel: 607-722-6492.

11—ST. STANISLAUS KOSTKA, (1914) (Polish), Rev. John E. Mikalajunas.
Res., 368 Prospect St., 13905-1810. Tel: 607-797-3564.
School—(Grades PreK-3) 372 Prospect St., 13905. Tel: 607-797-3793. Sr. M. Virginia Tarnacki, C.S.S.F., Prin.
Felician Sisters 3; Lay Teachers 4; Students 17.
Convent—376 Prospect St., 13905.

12—ST. THOMAS AQUINAS, (1927), Rev. James D. Tormey. In res., Rev. Msgr. Lawrence E. Giblin.
Res., One Aquinas St., 13905. Tel: 607-797-4015.

Boonville, Oneida Co., St. Joseph (1875), Rev. David J. Orzel.
Res., 110 Charles St., 13309. Tel: 315-942-4618. [CEM]
Convent—108 Charles St., 13309. Tel: 315-942-2019.
Sisters 2.

Brewerton, Onondaga Co., St. Agnes (1958), Rev. William T. Guckert.
Res., 5472 Miller Rd., 13209. Tel: 315-676-7050.

Bridgeport, Onondaga Co., St. Francis of Assisi (1952), Rev. Ralph White, O.F.M.Conv.
Res., P.O. Box 550, 13030-0550. Tel: 315-633-2561.
Parish Center—13030-0550. Tel: 315-633-9682.

Camden, Oneida Co., St. John (1852), Rev. Joseph P. Kennedy.
Res., 22 Church St., 13316. Tel: 315-245-1603. [CEM]

Camillus, Onondaga Co., St. Joseph (1852), Revs. John S. Finnegan; Joseph Egbule.
Res., 5600 W. Genesee St., 13031. Tel: 315-488-8490; Fax: 315-488-4214.

Canastota, Madison Co., St. Agatha (1883), Rev. Anthony F. Tosti. Pastoral Ministers: Sr. Florence Joseph Flaherty, D.C.; Sr. Loretta Genter, D.C.; Sr. Ellen Hensberry, D.C.; Sr. Catherine Marie McGranary, D.C.
Res., 329 N. Peterboro St., 13032. Tel: 315-697-7104; Fax: 315-697-7108. [CEM]
Convent—406 Spencer St., 13032. Tel: 315-697-7210.

Cazenovia, Madison Co., St. James (1847), Rev. Henry J. Pedzich.
Res., 6 Green St., 13035. Tel: 315-655-3441; Fax: 315-655-3442. [CEM]

Central Square, Oswego Co., St. Michael (1928), Rev. John J. Smegelsky; Deacon Leo Matzke.
Res., 598 S. Main St., P.O. Box 514, 13036. Tel: 315-676-2898.

Chadwicks, Oneida Co., St. Anthony of Padua (1907), Rev. Edward J. Hayes.
Res., 3364 Oneida St., P.O. Box 310, 13319. Tel: 315-737-8066.

Chenango Forks, Broome Co., St. Rita (1946), Rev. Stanley J. Gerlock.
Res., 2530 NY State Rte. 12, 13746. Tel: 607-648-8816.

Chittenango, Madison Co., St. Patrick (1853), Rev. Timothy Elmer.
Res., 1341 Murray Dr., 13037. Tel: 315-687-6105; Fax: 315-687-0046. [CEM]

Cicero, Onondaga Co., Sacred Heart (1888), Rev. Msgr. Ronald Bill; Rev. David J. James.
Res., 8229 S. Main St., 13039. Tel: 315-699-2752; Fax: 315-699-3775.

Clark Mills, Oneida Co., Church of the Annunciation (1908), Rev. J. Michael Carney.
Mailing Address: 7616 E. South St., Clinton, 13323.
Res., 25 South St., 13321. Tel: 315-853-6138.

Clayville, Oneida Co., St. Patrick (1864), Rev. William S. Baker.
Res., 8 Church St., Box 285, 13322. Tel: 315-839-5483. [CEM]

Cleveland, Oswego Co., St. Mary of the Assumption (1854), Rev. William C. Esposito.
Res., 148 State Rte. 49, 13042. Tel: 315-675-3542. [CEM]
Mission—Constantia, Oswego Co., St. Bernadette, State Rte. 49, Constantia, 13044.

Clinton, Oneida Co., St. Mary (1850), Rev. John P. Croghan.
Res., 13 Marvin St., 13323. Tel: 315-853-2935; Fax: 315-853-1440. [CEM]
School—(Grades K-6) Prospect St., 13323. Tel: 315-853-6196. Mrs. Linda DePhillips, Prin.
Lay Teachers 12; Students 148.

Cortland, Cortland Co., St. Anthony (1917) (Italian), Rev. Jerome A. Katz.
Res., 45 Crandall St., 13045. Tel: 607-756-7533; Fax: 607-756-7697.
St. Mary (1855), Rev. John P. Fenlon; Deacon Richard J. Dwyer.
Res., 44 N. Main St., 13045. Tel: 607-756-9967; Fax: 607-756-9968.
School—61 N. Main St., 13045. Tel: 607-756-5614. Sr. Harriet Hamilton, O.S.F., Prin.
Franciscan Sisters of Allegany 1; Lay Teachers 22; Students 382.

Deposit, Broome Co., St. Joseph (1851), Rev. John A. Booth.
Res., 98 Second St., 13754. Tel: 607-467-2291. [CEM]
Parish Center—74 Second St., 13754. Tel: 607-467-2226.

Dewitt, Onondaga Co., Holy Cross (1943), Revs. James E. Gehl; Gary M. Fukes. In res., Rev. Msgr. Daniel B. O'Brien, (Retired).
Res., 4112 E. Genesee St., 13214. Tel: 315-446-0473; Fax: 315-446-7608.
School—Tel: 315-446-4890. Sr. Rose Alice Carbery, O.S.F., Prin.
Sisters of the Third Franciscan Order M.C. 1; Lay Teachers 13; Students 194.

Durhamville, Oneida Co., St. Francis (1860) (German), Rev. Joseph F. Kehoe.
Res., 5334 Foster St., 13054. Tel: 315-363-1572. [CEM]
Mission—Irish Ridge, Oneida Co., St. Mary. [CEM]

East Syracuse, Onondaga Co., St. Matthew (1880), Revs. Robert D. Dwyer; Leo J. Heizman. In res., Rev. Msgr. Robert F. Lavin.
Res., 229 W. Yates St., 13057. Tel: 315-437-8318; Fax: 315-463-6399.
School—214 Kinne St., 13057. Tel: 315-437-1339. Sr. Julienne Brandt, O.S.F., Prin.
Sisters of the Third Franciscan Order M.C. 4; Lay Teachers 16; Students 280.

Endicott, Broome Co.,

1—OUR LADY OF GOOD COUNSEL, (1941), Revs. Richard J. Giblin; Darr F. Schoenhofen; Deacon Thomas M. Harley. In res., Rev. Robert A. Ours.
Res., 701 W. Main St., 13760. Tel: 607-748-7417.

2—ST. AMBROSE, (1908), Rev. Robert G. Tierney. In res., Revs. James J. O'Hanlon; Joseph Mattath, C.M.I. (India).
Res., 203 Washington Ave., 13760. Tel: 607-754-2330; Fax: 607-785-6947.

3—ST. ANTHONY OF PADUA, (1917) (Italian), Rev. Clarence F. Rumble; Deacons Dominick Rossi; Frank Longo. In res., Rev. Salvatore D'Alessandro.
Res., 306 Odell Ave., 13760. Tel: 607-754-4333; Fax: 606-757-3221.
School—Consolidated. See separate listing under Institutions Located in the Diocese.

4—ST. CASIMIR, (1928) (Polish), Rev. Mark A. Pasik.
Res., 212 N. McKinley Ave., 13760. Tel: 607-785-3262.

5—ST. JOSEPH, (1923) (Slovak), Rev. James P. Serowik.
Res., 207 Hayes Ave., 13760. Tel: 607-748-0442; Fax: 607-748-7725.
School—210 N. Jackson Ave., 13760. Tel: 607-748-8631; Fax: 607-748-7745. Sr. Denise Marie, S.S.C.M., Prin.
Sisters 2; Lay Teachers 11; Students 205.

Endwell, Broome Co., Christ the King (1949), Rev. Thomas F. Hobbes.
Res., 1501 Davis Ave., 13760. Tel: 607-785-3180.
Our Lady of Angels (1964), Rev. John D. Roock; Deacon George Phillips.
Res., 3600 Phyllis St., 13760. Tel: 607-754-1266.

Fairmount, Onondaga Co., Holy Family (1935), Rev. Paul F. Angelicchio; Deacon John P. Brody.
Res., 119 Chapel Dr., Syracuse, 13219. Tel: 315-488-3139; Fax: 315-487-1112.
School—130 Chapel Dr., 13219. Tel: 315-487-8515; Fax: 315-487-8515. Linda Shulkin, Prin.

Fayetteville, Onondaga Co., Immaculate Conception (1869), Rev. Gregory C. LeStrange. Pastoral Ministers: Sr. Marcia Barry, O.S.F.; Sr. Monica Zmolek, O.S.F. In res., Rev. Msgr. Edward J. Ryan; Rev. Msgr. James A. McKloskey.
Res., 400 Salt Springs St., 13066. Tel: 315-637-9846. [CEM]
School—Tel: 315-637-3961. Sr. Elizabeth John, O.S.F., Prin.
Sisters of the Third Franciscan Order M.C. 2; Lay Teachers 20; Students 261.

Florence, Oneida Co., St. Mary (1845), Rev. James T. Queen.
Res., c/o 1807 Bedford St., Rome, 13440. Tel: 315-336-3082; Fax: 315-336-3083. [CEM]
Mission—Redfield, Oswego Co., St. Paul, Redfield, 13437.

Forestport, Oneida Co., St. Patrick (1848), Rev. John E. Phelan.
Mailing Address: P.O. Box 1, 13338. Tel: 315-392-2341; Fax: 315-392-2341. [CEM]
Mission—Otter Lake, St. Mary of the Snows.

Fulton, Oswego Co., Holy Family (1930), Rev. Richard R. Thompson. In res., Rev. John J. Daley. Pastoral Assocs.: Sr. Dorothy A. Bunal, C.S.J.; Sr. Eleanor Grace Spiridilozzi, O.S.F.
Res., 45 W. Fourth St., 13069. Tel: 315-592-4159.
Immaculate Conception (1854), Rev. Carlo Stirpe.
Res., 57 S. Third St., 13069. Tel: 315-598-2118. [CEM]
St. Michael (1924) (Polish), Rev. Edmund S. Pilat.
Res., 301 Beech St., 13069. Tel: 315-592-7632.

Greene, Chenango Co., Immaculate Conception (1889), Rev. Richard Dellos.
Res., 20 Coventry Rd., 13778. Tel: 607-656-9546; Fax: 607-656-9546.

Hamilton, Madison Co., St. Mary (1869), Rev. Msgr. John R. Madden.
Res., 16 Wylie St., 13346. Tel: 315-824-2164. [CEM]

Hannibal, Oswego Co., Our Lady of the Rosary (1954), Rev. Moritz A. Fuchs.
Office: 923 Cayuga St., P.O. Box 185, 13074-0185. Tel: 315-564-5201.
Mission—Southwest Oswego, St. Joseph.

Hinckley, Oneida Co., St. Ann (1895), Rev. Vincent P. Long.
Res., 13352. Tel: 315-896-2540. [CEM]

Holland Patent, Oneida Co., St. Leo (1882), Rev. Vincent P. Long; Deacon Donald E. Joslin.
Res., 7937 Elm St., P.O. Box 185, 13354. Tel: 315-865-5371.

Homer, Cortland Co., St. Margaret (1908), Rev. R. Daniel DeLorme.
Res., 14 Copeland Ave., P.O. Box 356, 13077. Tel: 607-749-2542.

Jamesville, Onondaga Co., St. Mary (1899), Rev. Raymond B. Wood.
Res., 6437 E. Seneca Tpke., P.O. Box 368, 13078-0368. Tel: 315-469-6949.

Johnson City, Broome Co., Blessed Sacrament (1945), Rev. Msgr. James D. Kane.
Res., Cenacle Plaza, 13790. Tel: 607-797-5151; Fax: 607-766-9875.
St. James (1900), Revs. Thomas J. Ryan; Daniel M. Caruso. Pastoral Assocs.: Sr. Rose Margaret Noonan, C.S.J.; Sr. Catherine Joseph McDonough, D.C.; Mr. William P. Gallagher. In res., Rev. James J. Fallon.
Res., 155 Main St., 13790. Tel: 607-729-6147; Fax: 607-797-5966.
Convent—147 Main St., 13790. Tel: 607-797-5181.

Jordan, Onondaga Co., St. Patrick (1858), Rev. Albert J. Proud.
Res., 28 N. Main St., 13080. Tel: 315-689-9051. [CEM]

Kirkwood, Broome Co., St. Mary (1888), Rev. Thomas F. Catucci.
Res., 975 NY Rte. 11, 13795. Tel: 607-775-0086.

Lacona, Oswego Co., St. Frances Xavier Cabrini (1946), Rev. John F. Hogan, Jr.
Mailing Address: 35 Salina St., 13083. Tel: 315-387-3016; Fax: 315-298-3749.

Lafayette, Onondaga Co., St. Joseph (1866), Rev. Michael P. Minehan.
Res., 6104 Cherry Valley Rd., Box 169, 13084. Tel: 315-677-3439.

Lakeland, Onondaga Co., Our Lady of Peace (1935), Rev. John E. Fetcho.
Res., 203 Halcomb St., Syracuse, 13209. Tel: 315-487-6832.

Lee Center, Oneida Co., St. Joseph (1923), Rev. R. Paul Mathis. In res., Rev. Msgr. Francis J. Culkin.
Res., 13363. Tel: 315-336-2661.
Parish Center—Tel: 315-339-1890.

Liverpool, Onondaga Co.,

1—CHRIST THE KING, (1964), Rev. Jon P. Werner.
Res., 21 Cherry Tree Cir., 13090. Tel: 315-652-3233; 315-652-9266 (Parish Center); Fax: 315-652-5680.

2—IMMACULATE HEART OF MARY, (1950), Revs. John V. Ahern; Thomas P. Kobuszewski.
Res., 425 Beechwood Ave., 13088. Tel: 315-457-8060.

3—ST. JOHN, (1971), Rev. Gaetano T. Baccaro; Deacons George Maynard; Kenneth Money.
Res., 8290 Soule Rd., 13090. Tel: 315-652-6591; Fax: 315-652-6631.

4—ST. JOSEPH THE WORKER, (1890), Rev. Charles M. Major.
Res., 1001 Tulip St., 13088. Tel: 315-457-6060; Fax: 315-457-4119.

Maine, Broome Co., Holy Rosary (1944), Rev. Thomas F. Keating.
Res., 2596 Main St., Box 248, 13802. Tel: 607-862-3216.

Manlius, Onondaga Co., St. Ann (1920), Rev. Msgr. Charles H. Eckermann; Rev. Thomas I. Ward; Deacons John R. Murray; Gerard T. Pittman.
Res., 104 Academy St., 13104. Tel: 315-682-5181; Fax: 315-682-5248.

Marathon, Cortland Co., St. Stephen (1870), Rev. Lester E. Smith.
Res., 12 Academy St., P.O. Box 475, 13803. Tel: 607-849-3480.
Mission—Cincinnatus, Our Lady of Perpetual Help.

Marcellus, Onondaga Co., St. Francis Xavier (1873), Rev. J. Michael Donovan.
Res., P.O. Box 177, 1 W. Main St., 13108. Tel: 315-673-2531. [CEM]

Mattydale, Onondaga Co., St. Margaret (1926), Revs. Kevin E. Hannon; Edward F. McNally. In res., Rev. George F. Hartnett; Deacon Donald R. Whiting.
Res., 203 Roxboro Rd., Syracuse, 13211. Tel: 315-455-5534; Fax: 315-454-4102.
School—Sr. Miriam Anthony, Prin. Sisters of the Third Franciscan Order M.C. 3; Lay Teachers 13; Students 373.

Mexico, Oswego Co., St. Mary, Star of the Sea (1914), Rev. Stephen E. Wirkes.
Res., 3352 Main St., P.O. Box 487, 13114. Tel: 315-963-7182.

Minetto, Oswego Co., Our Lady of Perpetual Help (1932), Rev. Joseph M. Larkin.
Res., West River Rd., P.O. Box 236, 13115. Tel: 315-343-7922.

Minoa, Onondaga Co., St. Mary (1838), Rev. Dominic E. McGee, O.F.M.Conv.
Res., 401 N. Main St., 13116. Tel: 315-656-2257; Fax: 315-633-0672. [CEM]
Office: Tel: 315-656-3441.

Morrisville, Madison Co., St. Joan of Arc (1931), Rev. Thomas P. Durant.
Parish Office: P.O. Box 1087, 13408. Tel: 315-684-9551.
Res., St. Therese Rectory, Main St., Munnsville, 13409. Tel: 315-495-2424.

Munnsville, Madison Co., St. Therese of the Infant Jesus (1926), Rev. Thomas P. Durant.
Res., St. Therese Rectory, Main St., 13409. Tel: 315-495-2424; 684-9551 (Office).

New Berlin, Chenango Co., St. Theresa of the Infant Jesus (1955), Rev. Francis J. Case, Admin.
Res., 24 N. Main St., P.O. Box 780, 13411-0780. Tel: 607-847-6851.
Mission—Leonardsville, Our Lady of the Valley.

New Hartford, Oneida Co., Our Lady of the Rosary (1949), Rev. James L. Riley.
Res., 1736 Burrstone Rd., 13413. Tel: 315-724-0402.
St. John the Evangelist (1883), Revs. Paul J. Drobin; Frederick R. Mannara; Sr. Rose Benedict Troy, C.S.J., Pastoral Assoc.; Sr. Martha Vincent Larkin, C.S.J., D.R.E. In res., Rev. Msgr. Thomas J. Hayes.
Res., 66 Oxford Rd., 13413. Tel: 315-732-8521; Fax: 315-735-1569.
St. Thomas (1957), Rev. Robert Conrad. In res., Rev. John M. Quinn.
Res., 150 Clinton Rd., 13413. Tel: 315-735-8381.

New London, Oneida Co., Holy Cross (1968), Rev. Joseph F. Kehoe.
Res., 5334 Foster St., Durhamville, 13054. Tel: 315-363-1572.

New York Mills, Oneida Co., St. Mary (1909), Rev. Valentine C. Krul.
Res., 201 Main St., 13417. Tel: 315-736-4432; Fax: 315-736-8079. [CEM]
School—Consolidated. See separate listing under Institutions Located in the Diocese.

North Bay, Oneida Co., St. John (1843), Rev. Leo J. Wimett.
Res., P.O. Box A, 13123. Tel: 315-245-0853; Fax: 315-675-3213. [CEM]
Mission—Verona Beach, Oneida Co., St. Mary, Verona Beach, 13162.

North Syracuse, Onondaga Co., St. Rose of Lima (1926), Revs. James M. Kennedy; Frank Young; Sr. Corinne Mullen, O.S.F., Pastoral Min.
Parish Office: 409 S. Main St., 13212. Tel: 315-458-0283.
Res., 407 S. Main St., 13212. Tel: 315-458-0283.
School—411 S. Main St., 13212. Tel: 315-458-6036. Sr. Catherine Laboure, Prin.
Sisters of the Third Franciscan Order M.C. 6; Lay Teachers 27; Students 651.

Norwich, Chenango Co., St. Bartholomew the Apostle (1919), Rev. John R. Cramer. Pastoral Ministers: Sr. Julie Eigo, C.S.J.; Helen M. Markham.
Office: 8 Silver St., 13815. Tel: 607-336-2222; Fax: 607-334-3421.
Convent—79 E. Main St., 13815. Tel: 607-334-2527.
St. Paul (1851), Rev. Douglas Cunningham.
Res., 30 Pleasant St., 13815. Tel: 607-334-4931; Fax: 607-334-6521. [CEM]

Oneida, Madison Co., St. Joseph (1893), Rev. William A. Lorenz; Rev. Msgr. Matthew C. Luczycki.
Res., 121 St. Joseph Pl., 13421. Tel: 315-363-3280.
Parish Center—111 St. Joseph Pl., 13421. Tel: 315-363-5061.

St. Patrick (1843), Rev. William A. Mesmer.
Res., 347 Main St., 13421. Tel: 315-363-7570. [CEM]
School—354 Elizabeth St., 13421. Tel: 315-363-3620.
Lay Teachers 10; Students 179.

Onondaga Hill, Onondaga Co., St. Michael (1874), Rev. Richard P. Morisette. In res., Rev. James C. Hayes.
Res., 4782 W. Seneca Tpke., Syracuse, 13215. Tel: 315-469-6995.
Mission—Split Rock, St. Peter, 13031.

Oriskany, Oneida Co., St. Stephen, Protomartyr (1929), Rev. Walter F. Cannan.
Res., 106 Dexter Ave., P.O. Box 780, 13424. Tel: 315-736-9033.

Oriskany Falls, Oneida Co., St. Joseph (1870), Rev. Vincent J. Kelly.
Res., 229 Main St., 13425. Tel: 315-821-6122. [CEM]

Oswego, Oswego Co.,

1—St. John the Evangelist, (1869), Rev. Chester A. Misercola; Deacon Peter F. Benz, Pastoral Assoc., Bus. Mgr.
Res., 38 Erie St., 13126. Tel: 315-343-4961.

2—St. Joseph, (1915) (Italian), Rev. James M. Cesta; Deacon Joseph Chillemi.
Res., 178 W. Second St., 13126. Tel: 315-343-2160; Fax: 315-343-2164.

3—St. Louis, (1870) (French), Rev. George E. Wurz, Admin.
Res., 81 E. Fourth St., 13126. Tel: 315-343-8912.

4—St. Mary, (1850), Rev. David J. Baehr.
Res., 103 W. Seventh St., P.O. Box 118, 13126. Tel: 315-343-3953.
School—76 W. Sixth St., 13126. Tel: 315-343-0700.
Lay Teachers 12; Students 190.

5—St. Paul, (1830) (Irish), Rev. Eric K. Harer.
Res., 50 E. Mohawk St., 13126. Tel: 315-343-2333; Fax: 315-343-2334.
Church—134 E. Fifth St., 13126. Tel: 315-343-9764.
School—115 E. Fifth St., 13126. Tel: 315-343-6700. Mrs. Baiba Pierce, Prin.
Lay Teachers 12; Students 235.

6—St. Peter, (1862) (German), Rev. George E. Wurz, Admin.
Res., 83 E. Albany St., 13126. Tel: 315-343-1352.
Mission—Scriba, Sacred Heart.

7—St. Stephen the King, (1908) (Polish), Rev. Edmund Wolak.
Res., 138 Niagara St., Box 417, 13126. Tel: 315-343-0350; Fax: 315-343-0350.

Oxford, Chenango Co., St. Joseph (1849), Rev. Donald D. Cunningham.
Res., 3 Scott St., 13830. Tel: 607-843-7021. [CEM]
Station—New York State Veterans' Home, 13830.

Parish, Oswego Co., St. Ann (1950), Rev. Anthony J. Keeffe.
Res., P.O. Box 27, 13131. Tel: 315-625-7093. [CEM]
Mailing Address: P.O. Box 33, Williamstown, 13493. Tel: 315-964-2400.
Mission—Williamstown, St. Patrick.

Phoenix, Oswego Co., St. Stephen (1880), Rev. James C. Fritzen; Deacon Frank Forish.
Res., 469 Main St., 13135. Tel: 315-695-4531; 695-4608.

Pompey, Onondaga Co., Immaculate Conception (1850), Rev. Paul V. Carey.
Res., 7386 Academy St., 13138. Tel: 315-677-3061. [CEM]
Mission—Fabius, Onondaga Co., St. Paul, Fabius, 13063.

Pulaski, Oswego Co., St. John the Evangelist (1888), Rev. John F. Hogan, Jr.
23 Niagara St., 13142-4425. Tel: 315-298-5350; Fax: 315-298-3749.
Res., 68 Park St., 13142. Tel: 315-298-3863.

Rome, Oneida Co.,

1—St. John the Baptist, (1909) (Italian), Revs. Joseph J. Clemente; John M. Wood.
Res., 210 E. Dominick St., 13440. Tel: 315-337-0990. [CEM]

2—St. Mary of the Assumption, (1848). Unassigned. In res., Rev. Robert C. Weber.
Res., 210 W. Liberty St., 13440. Tel: 315-336-4832. [CEM]
Station—Rome, Betsy Ross HRF.

3—St. Paul, (1954), Rev. James T. Queen; Deacon Nicholas A. Rosher. In res., Rev. Msgr. William M. Kelly.
Res., 1807 Bedford St., 13440-2199. Tel: 315-336-3082; Fax: 315-336-3083.

4—St. Peter, (1837), Rev. Philip A. Hearn. Pastoral Assocs.: Sr. Elizabeth Colby, C.S.J.; Sr. Mary Catherine Marrone, C.S.J.; Sr. Phyllis Wulforst, C.S.J. In res., Rev. James A. Culver.
Res., 105 E. Liberty St., 13440. Tel: 315-336-5072; 337-8307. [CEM]

5—Transfiguration, (1909) (Polish), Rev. Matthew S. Wieczorek. In res., Revs. William C. Cahill; Eugene Rosielski.
Res., 111 Ridge St., 13440. Tel: 315-336-1152; Fax: 315-339-5931.
School—(Grades K-6) 400 S. James St., 13440. Tel: 315-336-3430; Fax: 315-334-4650. Mrs. Elizabeth Warwick, Prin.
Lay Teachers 7; Students 113.

Sanitaria Springs, Broome Co., St. Joseph (1914), Rev. Kevin J. Bunger, Admin.
Res., 659 New York Rte. 7, P.O. Box 429, Port Crane, 13833. Tel: 607-648-5209; Fax: 607-648-3570.

Sherburne, Chenango Co., St. Malachy (1858), Rev. Edmund A. Castronovo.
Res., 31 E. State St., 13460. Tel: 607-674-2791. [CEM]

Sherrill, Oneida Co., St. Helena (1917), Rev. John J. Costello.
Res., 210 Primo Ave., 13461. Tel: 315-363-3882. [CEM]

Skaneateles, Onondaga Co., St. Mary of the Lake (1855), Rev. Thomas J. McGrath; Deacon Robert Borchert.
Res., 81 Jordan St., 13152. Tel: 315-685-5083; Fax: 315-685-6377. [CEM]

Solvay, Onondaga Co., St. Cecilia (1903), Revs. Angelo L. Morbito; Robert J. Birchmeyer; Deacon Julius Kulak.
Res., 1001 Woods Rd., 13209. Tel: 315-488-3221.
Convent—502 Gertrude Ave., 13209. Tel: 315-468-1273. Sr. Anne Rutledge, O.S.F., Supr.

South Onondaga, Onondaga Co., Corpus Christi (1938), Rev. Dennis J. Hayes.
Res., 4466 S. Onondaga Rd., Nedrow, 13120. Tel: 315-492-0814.
Church—3126 Cedarvale Rd., R.D. 1, Nedrow, 13120. Tel: 315-492-0814.
Apostolate—Onondaga Indian Reservation. [CEM]

Taberg, Oneida Co., St. Patrick (1876), Rev. Francis A. Wapen.
Res., 9168 Main St., 13471. Tel: 315-336-4079. [CEM]
Mission—Glenmore, St. Anne, (1846).

Truxton, Cortland Co., St. Patrick (1854), Rev. David J. Jutton.
Res., 3656 Rte. 13, Box 15, 13158. Tel: 607-842-6326. [CEM]
Mission—DeRuyter, St. Lawrence.

Tully, Onondaga Co., St. Leo (1891), Rev. Louis F. Aiello.
Res., 10 Onondaga St., 13159. Tel: 315-696-5092; Fax: 315-696-5092.
Mission—Otisco, St. Patrick, P.O. Box 574, 13159.

Utica, Oneida Co.,

1—Blessed Sacrament, (1924), Rev. Robert L. Kelly; Sr. Teresa Waldron, O.S.F., Pastoral Min.
Res., 1603 St. Agnes Ave., 13501. Tel: 315-724-8131.
School—Consolidated. See separate listing under Institutions Located in the Diocese.

2—Holy Trinity, (1896) (Polish), Revs. Arthur R. Hapanowicz; Richard J. Wilczynski (Poland); Deacon Wilbur H. Hazard.
Res., 1206 Lincoln Ave., 13502. Tel: 315-724-7238; Fax: 315-797-2130. [CEM]
School—(Grades PreK-6) 1214 Lincoln Ave., 13502. Tel: 315-724-0540. Sr. Mary Beatrice, C.S.F.N., Supr.; Mrs. Judith Haucle, Prin.
Religious 4; Lay Teachers 8; Students 172.
Convent—1218 Lincoln Ave., 13502. Tel: 315-733-5492; Fax: 315-733-5492.

3—Our Lady of Lourdes, (1919), Revs. Donald H. Karlen; Sean P. O'Brien; Patrick Kanja Wachira (Kenya); Deacon Paul M. Mullin; Sr. Julia Coyle, S.A.; Sr. Rosita Finnerty, C.S.J. In res., Revs. Jerome F. Weber; Donald J. Bauer.
Res., 2 Barton Ave., 13502. Tel: 315-724-3155; Fax: 315-732-3346.
School—Consolidated. See separate listing under Institutions Located in the Diocese.

4—Sacred Heart, (1926), Rev. John Flanagan; Sr. Joan Blanch, C.S.J., Pastoral Assoc. In res., Rev. Hyacinth Seremet.
Res., 2115 Caroline St., 13502. Tel: 315-735-6105; Fax: 315-735-0216.
School—(Grades PreK-6) 1109 Ney Ave., 13502. Tel: 315-724-3612. Sr. Roseann Klosterman, C.S.J., Prin.
Religious 3; Lay Teachers 9; Students 195.

5—St. Agnes, (1887), Rev. Msgr. Francis J. Willenburg.
Res., 700 Kossuth Ave., 13501. Tel: 315-735-5273; Fax: 315-735-5274.
Convent—783 Blandina St., 13501. Tel: 315-732-1078.

6—St. Anthony of Padua, (1911) (Italian), Revs. Felix R. Colosimo; Anthony LaFache; Deacon William Dischiavo.
Res., 422 Tilden Ave., 13501. Tel: 315-732-1177.

7—St. Francis de Sales, (1876), Rev. Frederick D. Daley.
Res., 1119 Elm St., 13501. Tel: 315-732-6171; Fax: 315-735-3503.

8—St. George, (1911) (Lithuanian), Rev. Donald J. Hebert.
Res., 702 Columbia St., 13502. Tel: 315-735-4429. [CEM]

9—St. John, (1819), Revs. John A. Buehler; Canice N. Osuji (Nigeria); Luis Olguin, Spanish Apostolate, Tel: 315-724-0389. Pastoral Assocs.: Sr. Catherine Joseph Croghan, C.S.J.; Sr. Mary Theresa Kobosinski, D.C.; Deacon William R. Dischiavo.
Res., 240 Bleecker St., 13501. Tel: 315-724-6159.
Parish Apostolate Center—520 John St., 13501. Tel: 315-732-2417. Sr. Mary Theresa Kobosinski, D.C.

10—St. Joseph and St. Patrick, (1841 and 1849), Rev. Donald J. Hebert. In res., Revs. Joseph E. Moskal; John S. Drozdzal; James Q. Quinn; Theodore Lash, O.F.M.Conv.
Res., 702 Columbia St., 13502. Tel: 315-735-4429; Fax: 315-735-1691.

11—St. Mark, (1963), Rev. Lucian Urbaniak.
Res., 440 Keyes Rd., 13502. Tel: 315-724-1645.

12—St. Mary, (1870), Rev. Richard V. O'Neill.
Res., 421 South St., 13501. Tel: 315-724-0083.

13—St. Mary of Mt. Carmel, (1896) (Italian), Revs. Joseph Salerno; Luis Olguin; Peter Williams; Deacon Robert Riggalls.
Res., 648 Jay St., 13501. Tel: 315-735-1482; Fax: 315-735-9806.

14—St. Peter, (1872), Revs. Robert J. Kloster; Edward Kwoka.
Res., 422 Coventry Ave., 13502. Tel: 315-724-6310; Fax: 315-724-4942. [CEM]
School—(Grades PreK-6) 19 Herkimer Rd., 13502. Tel: 315-724-4708. Mrs. Maria Pilla, Prin.
Religious 1; Lay Teachers 13; Students 219.

15—St. Stanislaus, (1911) (Polish), Rev. Casimir J. Krzysiak.
Res., 607 Nichols St., 13501. Tel: 315-732-5919. [CEM]

Vernon, Oneida Co., Holy Family (1926; 1976), Rev. Edwin T. Comeskey.
Res., 4343 Peterboro St., P.O. Box 988, 13476. Tel: 315-829-3295.

Verona, Oneida Co., Our Lady of Good Counsel (1913), Rev. Edmund J. Morelle.
Res., 5259 Beacon Rd., P.O. Box 135, 13478. Tel: 315-363-7696.

Vestal, Broome Co., Our Lady of Sorrows (1941), Revs. Donald C. VanAmburgh; Lawrence Mbogo (Africa). In res., Rev. Matthew F. Brown.
Res., 157 Clark St., P.O. Box 408, 13850. Tel: 607-748-8287; Fax: 607-748-8016.

St. Vincent de Paul (1965), Rev. C. Vincent Lane; Deacon James P. Crowley. In res., Rev. Richard Hunt, S.J.
Res., 165 Clifton Blvd., 13850. Tel: 607-722-3988.

Warners, Onondaga Co., Our Lady of Good Counsel (1913), Rev. James C. Hayes.
Res., Newport Rd., Box 67, 13164. Tel: 315-672-3725.
Parish Hall—Tel: 315-672-3750.

Waterville, Oneida Co., St. Bernard (1850), Rev. Richard J. Kapral.
Res., 199 Stafford Ave., 13480. Tel: 315-841-4481. [CEM]
Mission—North Brookfield, St. Mary.

Whitesboro, Oneida Co., St. Anne (1965), Rev. Frederick J. Prevost. In res., Rev. Msgr. Thomas M. Doran.
Res., 8539 Clark Mills Rd., 13492-2754. Tel: 315-736-7672.

St. Paul (1883), Rev. Abraham L. Esper.
Res., 16 Park Ave., 13492. Tel: 315-736-1124; Fax: 315-768-7915.

Whitney Point, Broome Co., St. Patrick (1869), Rev. Robert P. Hyde.
Res., Box 711, 13862. Tel: 607-692-3911. [CEM]

Windsor, Broome Co., Our Lady of Lourdes (1947), Rev. Daniel G. Murphy.
Res., P.O. Box 361, 13865. Tel: 607-655-2116; 655-8118 (Parish Office).

Chaplains of Public Institutions

Hospitals

SYRACUSE. *Community General Hospital* Broad Rd., 13215. Tel: 315-492-5011. Rev. James C. Hayes; Sr. Mary Ann Kane, O.S.F.

Crouse Irving Memorial Hospital 736 Irving Ave., 13210. Tel: 315-470-7615. Rev. George Hartnett; Sr. Carmel Rose Nicita; Sr. Antonella Giba, C.S.J.

James Square Nursing Home. Attended from Blessed Sacrament Parish.

Loretto Geriatric Center 700 E. Brighton Ave., 13205. Tel: 315-469-5570. Rev. Wilbur J. Votraw.

Plaza Extended Care Facility Tel: 315-474-4431. Sr. Monica Hogan, C.S.J.

St. Camillus Health & Rehab Center 813 Fay Rd., 13219. Tel: 315-488-2951. Ms. Mary Grace McGuire, Chap.

St. Joseph's Hospital Health Center 301 Prospect Ave., 13203. Tel: 315-448-5116. Revs. Robert Amrhein, O.F.M.Conv.; Firmin Finn, O.F.M.Conv.; Sr. Marie Therese Nicholson, O.S.F.; Sr. Patrice Ward, O.S.F.; Sr. Mary Louise Williams, O.S.F.; Sr. Jacqueline Spiridlozzi, Dir.; Sr. Frances Agnes Ryan; Sr. Mary Daniel Golmbieski.

University Hospital 750 E. Adams St., 13210. Tel: 315-464-5540. Rev. Alfred J. Bebel; Sr. Mary Francellette.

Van Duyn Home & Hospital Tel: 315-469-5511. Rev. Msgr. Robert B. Davern; Susan Marcoccia.

Veterans Administration Hospital Res: 800 Irving Ave., 13210. Tel: 315-476-7461. Rev. Wilfred F. Evans.

BINGHAMTON. *Binghamton General Hospital* Tel: 607-762-2200. Rev. John Mikalajunas; Sr. Joan Thomas Mcherney, C.S.J.

Binghamton Psychiatric Hospital. Revs. John Booth; Gerald J. Buckley.

Broome Developmental Center Tel: 607-770-0211. Rev. Paul J. Keebler.

Our Lady of Lourdes Memorial Hospital 179 Riverside Dr., 13905. Tel: 607-798-5111. Sr. Ann Molesevick, D.C., Dir.; Rev. Christopher Boretto; Bro. Daniel Gallucci; Sr. Mary Roark; Sr. Catherine Marie McGranary.

JOHNSON CITY. *Wilson Memorial Hospital* 33 Harrison St., 13790. Tel: 607-763-6000. Rev. Timothy J. Taugher.

LIVERPOOL. *Developmental Center* 36 Grampian Rd. #5, 13090. Rev. Charles A. Aho.

ROME. *Central New York Developmental Services Office*. Vacant. P.O. Box 550, Lower South James, 13442-0550. Tel: 315-336-2300, Ext. 251.

UTICA. *Faxton Hospital* 1676 Sunset Ave., 13502. Tel: 315-738-6545. Sr. Maureen Denn, C.S.J.

St. Elizabeth Hospital 2209 Genesee St., 13501. Tel: 315-798-8100. Rev. Matthew Thelly; Sr. Irene Zegarelli, O.S.F.; Sr. Mary Nicholas Amodio, O.S.F.; Sr. Margaret Woods, O.S.F.

St. Luke Champlin Ave., 13503. Tel: 315-798-6000. Sr. Genevieve Ciscek, C.S.J.; Sr. Susanne Bonville, C.S.J.; Rev. Donald J. Hebert.

VESTAL. *Binghamton Nursing Homes* Our Lady of Sorrows, 157 Clark St., 13850. Tel: 607-748-8287. Rev. Matthew F. Brown, Pastoral Care Chap.

Psychiatric Facilities

SYRACUSE. *Hutchings Psychiatric Center* 406 Court St., 13208. Tel: 315-473-4980. Rev. John T. McGraw.

BINGHAMTON. *Binghamton Psychiatric Hospital* Tel: 607-724-1391. Revs. John Booth; Gerald J. Buckley.

MARCY. *Central New York Psychiatric Center* Old River Rd., Box 330, 13403. Tel: 315-736-8271. Rev. Richard O'Neill.

UTICA. *Mohawk Valley Psychiatric Center* 1400 Noyes at York, 13502. Rev. Frederick Daley.

Jails

SYRACUSE. *Elmcrest Children's Center*. Vacant. Salt Springs Rd., 13224.

Hillbrook Detention Center 4949 Velasko Rd., 13215. Tel: 315-492-1721. Sr. Judith Falk.

Jail Ministry Office. Vacant. 208 Slocum Ave., 13204. Tel: 315-424-1877.

Public Safety Building 342 Vine St., 13203. Tel: 315-424-1877. William M. Cuddy.

BINGHAMTON. *Broome County Jail*. Rev. Stanley Gerlock.

CORTLAND. *Cortland County Jail*. Vacant.

GEORGETOWN. *Camp Georgetown* 31 E. State St., Sheburne, 13346. Tel: 315-837-4446. Rev. Edmund A. Castronovo.

JAMESVILLE. *Jamesville Penitentiary* P.O. Box 143, 13078. Tel: 315-469-5581. Rev. Edward J. Reimer; Sr. Maura Rhode.

MARCY. *Mid-State Correctional Facility* 210 W. Liberty St., 13403. Tel: 315-768-8581. Rev. Robert C. Weber.

MOHAWK. *Oneida Correctional Facility I* P.O. Box 8450, Rome, 13440. Tel: 315-339-6880. Rev. William C. Cahill.

Oneida Correctional Facility II 578 Main St., P.O. Box 8450, Oneida, 13421. Deacon James Chappell.

NORWICH. *Norwich County Jail*. Vacant.

ORISKANY. *Oneida County Jail* 120 Dexter Ave., 13424. Tel: 315-736-9033. Rev. Richard J. Stuczko.

OSWEGO. *Oswego County Jail* 178 W. Second St., 13126. Tel: 315-343-2160. Rev. Msgr. Francis J. Furfaro.

ROME. *Walsh Facility* Tel: 315-339-5232. Rev. Luis Olguin.

SOUTH PLYMOUTH. *Camp Pharsalia*. Rev. Edmund A. Castronovo.

UTICA. *Marcy Correctional Facility* 15-8 Rox Pl., 13502. Tel: 315-768-1400. Deacon William Hotaling.

Special Assignment:
Reverend Fathers—
Aho, Charles A.
Bebel, Alfred J.
Brown, Matthew F.
Cahill, William C.
Carmola, Michael J.
Catucci, Thomas F.
Chryst, Robert D.
Costello, Thomas J.
Croghan, John P.
Davern, Robert B.
Dietrich, Michael A.
Donovan, John P.
Evans, Wilfred F.
Hartnett, George F.
Hayes, James C.
Hebert, Donald J.
Kopp, Richard M.
Lang, James Paul
Lauducci, V. James
Mattice, George F.
Minehan, Michael P.
Moynihan, James M.
Muscalino, Daniel C.
O'Heron, Edward J.
Olguin, Luis
Ours, Robert A.
Philips, Joseph H.
Pompei, Frederick A.
Quartier, Neal E.
Quinn, James F.
Sambor, David R.
Schopfer, John C.
Seremet, Hyacinth
Slater, Dennis W.
Sullivan, Robert J.
Taugher, Timothy J.
Vavonese, Charles S.
Votraw, William J.
Weber, Jerome F.
Weber, Robert C.
Williams, Peter A.
Worn, G. Peter
Yeazel, J. Robert

On Duty Outside the Diocese:
Reverend Monsignors—
Fahey, Charles J., Fordham University, New York, NY
Sewall, Charles H.
Reverend Fathers—
Bassano, Michael
Cincotta, Anthony
Harrold, John
Heintz, Daniel W.
Keane, Philip S., S.S.
Nichols, Louis J.
Pelkey, Richard
Rossetti, Stephen
Schoenhofen, Darr, North American College, Rome, Italy
Sears, G. David, Staten Island, NY
Wagner, John P.
Wallace, Harry C.
Walsh, Vincent
Woolever, James

Military Chaplains:
Reverend Fathers—
Dunn, Richard, U.S. Air Force
Elkin, Fredic F., U.S. Navy
Gryga, Theodore, U.S. Navy
Madej, Paul D., U.S. Navy

Graduate Studies:
Reverend Fathers—
Baranski, Andrew, The Catholic University of America, Washington, D.C.

Absent on Leave:
Reverend Fathers—
Lupa, Gerard
O'Leary, Patrick C.
Pichette, David
Quinn, James A.

Absent on Sick Leave:
Reverend Fathers—
Fallon, James J.
Florczyk, Walter
Moskal, Joseph E.

Retired:
Reverend Monsignors—
Borgognoni, Charles L.
Casey, Robert A.
Culkin, Francis J.
Denti, Carl J.
Dillon, Robert E.
Doran, Thomas M.
Dwyer, M. Shields
Furfaro, Francis J.
Giblin, Lawrence E.
Hayes, Thomas J.
Kantor, Adolph A.
Lavin, Robert F.
Luczycki, Matthew C.
McCloskey, James A.
O'Brien, Daniel B.
Ryan, Edward J.
Sammons, Francis L.
Reverend Fathers—
Bauer, Donald J.
Brennan, Robert E.
Cummings, Frederick F.
D'Alessandro, Salvatore
Daley, John J.
Doran, Matthew J.
Dwyer, William M.
Guyder, Thomas F.
Hall, Robert E.
Hearn, Edward C.
Hill, John H.
Jakubik, Emil
Kent, Joseph E.
Kiernan, Thomas
Libera, Angelo
Majdanik, Albin J.
Manning, Thomas J.
McCabe, William J.
McKay, Robert J.
Mulranen, John J.
Neary, Thomas E.
Nold, Joseph K.
O'Hanlon, James J.
Pilla, P. Carl
Ploeckl, Joseph M.
Prozny, Leopold V.
Regan, William P.
Segrue, Joseph D.
Sizing, Theodore
Stuczko, Richard J.
Tucker, Richard
Walsh, Bernard
Wright, Robert

Permanent Deacons:
Altmeter, Robert (ROC), Norwich
Ashley, John, Binghamton
Benz, Peter F., Baldwinsville
Blaine, Edward, Endicott
Borchert, Robert, Skaneateles
Brody, John P., Camillus
Brush, Wesley J., Madison, WI, (On Leave)
Busch, Robert L., Syracuse
Carranti, Pio Peter, Syracuse
Castro, Joseph, North Syracuse
Chappell, James C., Oneida
Chiesa, Richard J., Camillus
Chillemi, Joseph, Oswego
Collins, John H., Pennellville
Cretaro, John T., Oswego
Crosby, James P., Syracuse (On Leave)
Crossett, Thomas F., Johnson City (On Leave)
Crowley, James, Vestal
Dischiavo, William R., Utica
Distin, Leslie, Johnson City
Dotterer, William A., Liverpool
Droz, John J., Sr., (Retired), New Hartford
Dwyer, Richard J., Cortland
Forish, Frank M., Baldwinsville
Gallagher, James T., Binghamton (On Leave)
Goskowski, Raymond, Binghamton
Hachey, Thomas, North Syracuse
Harley, Thomas, Sanitaria Springs
Hazard, Wilbur, Utica
Hotaling, William P., Utica
Joslin, Donald E., Holland Patent
Kopec, John

Kotch, Myron, (Eastern Rite), Syracuse
Kulak, Julius F., Solvay
Longo, Frank A., Endicott
Mailloux, William, Baldwinsville
Manzene, Stephen, Liverpool
Matzke, Leo P., Central Square
Maynard, George E., Clay
McGrath, Michael B., Syracuse
Money, Kenneth, Liverpool
Monnat, Leonard S., Syracuse
Morse, James L., Syracuse
Mulvey, John, Syracuse
Murray, John, Manlius
Needham, Leo I., Syracuse
Nelson, John J., Kirkville
O'Connor, Charles, Syracuse
Phillips, George, Endwell
Pittman, Gerard, Fayetteville
Powers, Paul F., Afton
Riggalls, Robert, Sr., Waterville
Rossi, Dominic L., Endicott
Sims, John E., Endwell (On Leave from Diocese)
Sweenie, David, Oswego
Trepa, John, Greene
Vanelli, Peter P., Syracuse
Vinciguerra, Ralph S., Syracuse
Warren, Franklin, Oswego
Whiting, Donald R., North Syracuse
Wilber, Richard, Chesire, CT, (On Leave)
Winslow, Frank L., Utica
Woeste, James (NOR), Syracuse

INSTITUTIONS LOCATED IN THE DIOCESE

[A] SEMINARIES, RELIGIOUS, OR SCHOLASTICATES

SYRACUSE. *Saint Andrew Hall*, 420 Demong Dr., 13214-1499. Tel: 315-446-0142. Novitiate for the New York and Maryland Provinces, Society of Jesus. Revs. Bruce A. Maivelett, S.J., Rector & Dir. Novices; Damien A. O'Connell, S.J., Assoc. Dir.; Francis M. O'Connor, S.J., Min. & Treas. Priests 3; Novices 13.

SKANEATELES. *Roosevelt Hall*, 1 Tallcot Ln., 13152. Tel: 315-685-6417. Novitiate for the United States/Toronto Brothers of the Christian Schools. Bro. Timothy Wentworth, F.S.C., Dir. Novices. Brothers 8.

[B] COLLEGES AND UNIVERSITIES

SYRACUSE. *Le Moyne College*, 13214
For a complete listing, refer to the Colleges and Universities section.

[C] HIGH SCHOOLS, DIOCESAN

SYRACUSE. *Bishop Ludden Junior/Senior High School*, 815 Fay Rd., 13219. Tel: 315-468-2591. Mr. Dennis J. Meehan, Prin. Priests 1; Sisters 5; Lay Teachers 42; Students 684.

BINGHAMTON. *Seton Catholic Central High School of Broome County*, 70 Seminary Ave., 13905. Tel: 607-723-5307; Fax: 607-723-4811. Ms. Kathleen M. Dwyer, Prin.; Mr. Max Deus, Asst. Prin.; Rev. Robert A. Ours. Priests 1; Sisters 3; Lay Teachers 42; Students 444.

EAST SYRACUSE. *Bishop Grimes Jr./Sr. High School*, 6653 Kirkville Rd., 13057. Tel: 315-437-0356. Rev. George F. Sheehan, Prin. Priests 3; Sisters 4; Lay Teachers 34; Students 480.

ROME. *Rome Catholic Junior-Senior High School*, 800 Cypress St., 13440. Tel: 315-336-6190. Sr. Nora Gatto, D.C., Prin.; Rev. James T. Queen. Priests 1; Sisters 2; Lay Teachers 23; Students 285.

UTICA. *Notre Dame Jr./Sr. High School*, 2 Notre Dame Lane, 13502. Tel: 315-724-5118. Mrs. Kathleen Donovan. Sisters 4; Lay Teachers 47; Students 597.

[D] HIGH SCHOOLS, PRIVATE

SYRACUSE. *Christian Brothers Academy*. (Grades 9-12), 6245 Randall Rd., 13214. Tel: 315-446-5960. Bro. Michael Shubnell, F.S.C., Prin. Brothers of the Christian Schools 3; Sisters 1; Lay Teachers 45; Students 482.

[E] JUNIOR HIGH SCHOOLS, DIOCESAN

SYRACUSE. *All Saints Junior High School*, 301 Valley Dr., 13207. Tel: 315-472-7488. Joan Theresa Smith, Prin. Lay Teachers 3; Students 34.

[F] JUNIOR HIGH SCHOOLS, PRIVATE

SYRACUSE. *Christian Brothers Academy*. (Grades 7-8), 6245 Randall Rd., 13214. Tel: 315-446-5960. Students 244.

[G] CONSOLIDATED SCHOOLS

BINGHAMTON. *St. Catherine*. (Grades PreK-3), 1051 Chenango St., 13901. Tel: 607-722-2028. Ms. Mary Ellen Meskell, Prin. Lay Teachers 9; Students 141.
St. John the Evangelist. (Grades K-8), 9 Livingston St., 13903. Tel: 607-723-0703. Sr. Albert J. Guzzi, Prin. Religious 10; Lay Teachers 18; Students 370.
St. Patrick Academy. (Grades 4-8), 58 Oak St., 13905. Tel: 607-723-4601. Mr. Walter E. Jenkins, Prin. Lay Teachers 9; Students 91.
St. Thomas Aquinas. (Grades PreK-3), 3 Aquinas St., 13905. Tel: 607-797-6528. Sr. Patricia Coyle, O.S.F., Prin. Religious 1; Lay Teachers 9; Students 157.

ENDICOTT. *St. Anthony*. (Grades Nursery-4), 906 Jenkins St., 13760. Tel: 607-754-0875. Sr. Paul Kathryn Barno, C.S.J., Prin. Religious 1; Lay Teachers 8; Students 237.
Seton Catholic Middle School. (Grades 5-8), 1112 Broad St., 13760. Tel: 607-748-7423.
E-mail: syrsetonmend@connectinc.com
Ms. Anne Cowling, Prin. Lay Teachers 7; Students 131.

FULTON. *Fulton Catholic*, 309 Buffalo St., 13069. Tel: 315-593-2049. Serves the parishes of Fulton, Phoenix, Mexico, Hannibal, Central Square & Red Creek. Margaret Donnelly, Prin. Lay Teachers 12; Students 112; Pre-K 29.

JOHNSON CITY. *Blessed Sacrament*. (Grades PreK-3), Cenacle Plaza, 13790. Tel: 607-729-3302. Mary Ellen Kelley, Prin. Lay Teachers 12; Students 226.
St. James Middle School, 143 Main St., 13790. Tel: 607-797-5444; Fax: 607-797-6794.
E-mail: syrstjamejoh@connect.com
Mrs. Maria Carucci, Prin. Sisters 2; Lay Teachers 18; Students 218.

NORWICH. *Holy Family School*. (Grades PreK-6), 17 Prospect St., 13815. Tel: 607-334-6934. Sr. Marie Denise Monser, C.S.J., Prin. Sisters 1; Lay Teachers 11; Students 120.

ROME. *St. Peter*. (Grades K-6), 400 Floyd Ave., 13440. Tel: 315-336-2360. Sr. Cheryl Canfield, C.S.S.F., Prin. Religious 1; Lay Teachers 12; Students 166.

UTICA. *Our Lady of Lourdes*. (Grades PreK-6), 11 Barton Ave., 13502. Tel: 315-732-4374. Mrs. Carol Polito, Prin. Lay Teachers 26; Students 493.

VESTAL. *Our Lady of Sorrows*. (Grades PreK-4), 801 Main St., 13850. Tel: 607-785-3214.
E-mail: syrolsves@connect.net
Barbara Vanston, Prin. Lay Teachers 5; Students 187.

[H] CATHOLIC CHARITIES OF SYRACUSE

SYRACUSE. *Bishop Joseph T. O'Keefe, Inc.*, c/o 240 E. Onondaga St., 13202. Tel: 315-424-1830; Fax: 315-478-4619. Most Rev. James M. Moynihan; Rev. Michael P. Minehan, Chancellor; Most Rev. Thomas J. Costello, Vicar General; Rev. Robert B. Stephenson, Vicar Community Svcs.
Catholic Charities of the Roman Catholic Diocese of Syracuse, 240 E. Onondaga St., 13202. Tel: 315-424-1830. Rev. Robert B. Stephenson, Exec. Vice Pres.; Mr. Brian Walton, Area Dir., 1654 W. Onondaga St., 13204. Tel: 315-424-1800. Mr. Paul Welch, Assoc. Dir., 1654 W. Onondaga St., 13204. Tel: 315-424-1800. Kevin Domanico, Chief Financial Officer, 1654 W. Onondaga St., 13204. Tel: 315-424-1800. Kay Muller, Dir. Human Resources; Patricia Walton, Exec. Dir., Toomey Residential Svcs.; Mark Clary, Assoc. Dir.; Joseph O'Hara, Dir. Devel.; Dorothy Condon, Assoc. Dir., Neighborhood & Family Div.
Jail Ministry, Slocum House, 208 Slocum Ave., 13204. Mary Czelusniak, Coordinator.
Keener Seniors, 1654 W. Onondaga St., 13204. Tel: 315-424-1804. Nutrition Program for the Elderly. Mr. Michael Gannon, Dir.

BINGHAMTON. *Associated Catholic Charities*, 232 Main St., 13905. Tel: 607-729-9166. Mr. Joseph G. Slavik, Exec. Admin.
Catholic Charities Adolescent Group Home, 57 Chestnut St., 13905. Tel: 607-723-6355. Ms. Karen Cerasaro, Dir.
The Catholic Foundation of Broome County, 232 Main St., 13905. Tel: 607-729-9166; Fax: 607-729-2062. Mr. Robert W. Aber, Pres. Legal Title: *The Bishops Catholic Education and Charities Foundation, Inc.*
Catholic Social Services of Broome County, 232 Main St., 13905. Tel: 607-729-9166. Mr. Daniel L. Yeager, M.A., Exec. Dir.; Grazia Tonelli, C.S.W., Supervisor of Clinical Services.

CORTLAND. *Catholic Charities of Cortland County*, 33-35 Central Ave., 13045. Tel: 607-756-5992. Paula Currie, Dir.
Case Management Services.
Residential Services. (Lawrence House Community Residence). Supported Housing; Supportive Apartments; Alcohol Halfway House & Recovery Apartments.
Food Pantry. Emergency Assistance Program.
Catholic Charities-STEPS-TASA, 33-35 Central Ave., 13045. Tel: 607-756-5992; Fax: 607-756-5999. (Supportive Teen Education-Parents Services), TASA; Case Management; Men's Support Group.

FULTON. *Catholic Charities of Oswego County*, 365 W. First St., 13069. Tel: 315-598-3980. 108 E. Sixth St., Oswego, 13126. Tel: 315-343-9540. Andrea McCabe, Area Dir.

NORWICH. *Chenango County Catholic Charities*, 3 O'Hara Dr., 13815. Tel: 607-334-8244.
The Counseling Program. See separate listing.
Chenango House, 49 Fair St., 13815. Tel: 607-336-8939. Supervised by Community Residence Program.
Intensive Supportive Apartment Program. 49 Fair St., 13815. Tel: 607-336-4359.
Supported Housing Program. 49 Fair St., 13815. Tel: 607-336-4492.
Crossbridge Adolescent Home. Granville Hill Rd., 13460. Tel: 607-674-9422.
Community Residence Program. Catholic Charities of Chenango County, 3 O'Hara Dr., 13815. Tel: 607-334-8244; Fax: 607-336-5779. Provides housing for mentally ill adults and adolescent boys.
The Counseling Program. Catholic Charities of Chenango County, 3 O'Hara Dr., 13815. Tel: 607-334-8244; Fax: 607-336-5779. Jane Coddington, Dir. Provides comprehensive counseling for children/adults and specialized counseling for abused children.
Crime Victims-Witness Assistance Program. Catholic Charities of Chenango County, 3 O'Hara Dr., 13815. Tel: 607-336-1528. Provides 24 hour Hotline at 607-336-1101, Crisis Intervention, Safe Dwelling, Safe Housing; Court accompaniment; filing affidavits and claims with Crime Victims Board; advocacy with law enforcement agencies; information and referrals.

ONEIDA. *Madison County Catholic Charities*, 119 E. Walnut St., 13421. Tel: 315-363-5274. Dennis Manning, Exec. Dir.; Sue Panetta, Assoc. Dir.

ROME. *Catholic Charities of Rome*, 212 W. Liberty St., 13440. Tel: 315-337-8600. Kathleen O. Mahoney, Dir.

UTICA. *Catholic Charities, Eastern Region*, 1408 Genesee St., 13502. Tel: 315-724-2158. Mr. Dennis Manning, Area Dir.; Kathleen C. Eichenlaub, Dir. of Admin.; Anthony J. Conestabile, Dir. of Finance; Nanette Conney, Dir. of Residential Support; Kathleen O. Mahoney, Dir. of Family & Community Support.
Catholic Social Services of Utica, 1408 Genesee St., 13502. Tel: 315-724-3167. Leslee Kovel, Assoc. Dir.

[I] OFFICES OF HUMAN DEVELOPMENT

SYRACUSE. *Bishop Foery Foundation*, 401 South Ave., 13204. Tel: 315-474-6823. Socio-Educational instruction center for racial minorities.
Childcare Center. Larry King, Dir.

BINGHAMTON. *Broome County Human Development*, 232 Main St., 13905. Tel: 607-729-9166; Fax: 607-729-2062. Ms. Amy Fleming, Dir.

[J] ST. VINCENT DE PAUL SOCIETY

SYRACUSE. *St. Vincent de Paul Furniture and Clothing Inc.*, 500 Seymour St., 13204. Tel: 315-476-4797. 755 N. Salina, 13208. Tel: 315-476-4659; 476-4686; 475-1717. 2849 S. Salina, 13205. Mr. John Graham, Dir.; Mr. David Suchewski, Mgr.
St. Vincent de Paul Society, 500 Seymour St., 13204. Tel: 315-476-4797. Mr. John Graham, Dir.

FULTON. *St. Vincent de Paul Thrift Shop*, 365 W. First St., 13069. Tel: 315-598-3980.

[K] CATHOLIC YOUTH ORGANIZATIONS

SYRACUSE. *Alliance Division, Catholic Charities*, 1654 W. Onondaga St., 13204. Tel: 315-424-1880; Fax: 315-424-6045. Mark Clary, Assoc. Dir.
Brighton Family Center, 100 Edmund Ave., 13205. Tel: 315-424-9378. Ms. Patricia Campany, Dir.
Catholic Charities, 1654 W. Onondaga St., 13204. Tel: 315-424-1800. Brian Walton, Area Dir.
Family Division, Catholic Charities, 1654 W. Onondaga St., 13204. Tel: 315-424-1840. Mr. Hugh Gratz, Assoc. Dir.
Hawley Youth Organization, 716 Hawley Ave., 13203. Tel: 315-472-6343. Dotti Barraco Hetnar, Dir.
Near East Side Adventures Program, 1085 E. Genesee St., 13210. Tel: 315-472-6362. Richard Kline, Dir.
Neighborhood Division, Catholic Charities, 1654 W. Onondaga St., 13204. Tel: 315-424-1804. Mr. Paul Welch, Assoc. Dir.
Northside CYO, 527 N. Salina St., 13208. Tel: 315-474-7428.
Salina Civic Center, 2826 Lemoyne Ave., Mattydale, 13211. Tel: 315-455-7096. Sandra Diefendorf, Dir.
Toomey Residential and Community Services Corp., 1654 W. Onondaga St., 13204. Tel: 315-424-1845; Fax: 315-424-7567. Patricia M. Walton, Exec. Dir.
Vincent House, 514 Seymour St., 13204. Tel: 315-475-9844. Mr. John Graham, Branch Dir.

BINGHAMTON. *Broome County CYO,* 232 Main St., 13905. Tel: 607-729-5190. Kevin McGoff, Exec. Dir.

FULTON. *CYO Fulton,* 365 W. First St., 13069. Tel: 315-598-3980. Mr. James Smiley, Dir.

UTICA. *Catholic Charities, Youth Services Division,* 1408 Genesee St., 13502. Tel: 315-724-6118. Mr. James T. Carroll, Dir.

[L] CHILDREN'S INSTITUTIONS AND DAY CARE CENTERS

SYRACUSE. *DePaul Day Care Corporation,* 1654 W. Onondaga St., 13204. Tel: 315-424-8129. Mrs. Sharon Coulter, Dir.

House of Providence, 1654 W. Onondaga St., 13204. Tel: 315-424-1800. Mr. Brian Walton. Records only.

Sister Patricia Ann's Preschool dba Gingerbread House Preschool, 2500 Grant Blvd., 13208. Tel: 315-471-4198.

Dorn Day Care Center (dba Gingerbread House Day Care Center), 2500 Grant Blvd., 13208. Tel: 315-471-4198. Sr. Suzanne Dunn, O.S.F., Dir.

[M] DIOCESAN SUMMER CAMPS

SYRACUSE. *Lourdes Camp,* Office: 1654 W. Onondaga St., 13204. Tel: 315-424-1812; 673-2888 (Summer). Camp Address: 10 Mile Point, Skaneateles, 13152. Michael Preston, Dir.

UTICA. *Camp Nazareth,* Office: 1408 Genesee St., 13502. Tel: 315-724-6118. 112 Long Lake Rd., Woodgate, 13494. Tel: 315-392-3791. James T. Carroll, Dir.

[N] FAMILY LIFE BUREAUS

SYRACUSE. *Eastern Region,* c/o 1342 Lancaster Ave., 13210. Tel: 315-472-6754. Sue & Ronald Kielar, Dir.

Family Life Education, 1342 Lancaster Ave., 13210. Tel: 315-472-6754. Rev. Joseph H. Phillips, Dir.; Margaret Dupee, Coord., Family & Marriage Enrichment; Mary Ann Davis, Sec.; Karen Bandoblu, Coord., Marriage Prep. & Speakers Bureau; Patricia Ennis, Coord., Separated/Divorced, The Third Option, and Parenting; Nancy Devine, Coord. Northern Region; Sue & Ronald Kielar, Coordinators Eastern Region; Kathy Colligan, Coord. Southern Region.

Northern Region, 108 E. Sixth St., Oswego, 13126. Tel: 315-342-1463. Nancy Devine, Regional Dir., Office of Family Life Education.

Northern Region Religious Education Office & Special Education for Catechetics, 108 E. Sixth St., Oswego, 13126. Tel: 315-343-5557. Sr. Germaine Hilston, C.S.J., Dir.; Mary Jackson, Resource Center Staff.

Southern Region Family Life Education, 400 Corey Ave., Endicott, 13760. Tel: 607-786-0828. Kathleen Colligan, Dir.

[O] GENERAL HOSPITALS

SYRACUSE. *St. Joseph's Hospital Health Center,* 301 Prospect Ave., 13203. Tel: 315-448-5111; Fax: 315-448-6161
For a complete listing, refer to the Hospitals section.

BINGHAMTON. *Our Lady of Lourdes Memorial Hospital,* 169 Riverside Dr., 13905. Tel: 607-798-5111
For a complete listing, refer to the Hospitals section.

UTICA. *St. Elizabeth Hospital,* 2209 Genesee St., 13501. Tel: 315-798-8100
For a complete listing, refer to the Hospitals section.

[P] FACILITIES FOR THE AGED

SYRACUSE. *Bernardine Apartments, Inc.,* 417 Churchill Ave., 13205. Tel: 315-469-7786
For a complete listing, refer to the Special Care Facilities section.

Loretto, 700 E. Brighton Ave., 13205. Tel: 315-469-5561
For a complete listing, refer to the Special Care Facilities section.

Loretto Geriatric Community Residences, Inc., 5018 S. Salina St., 13205. Tel: 315-492-0896
For a complete listing, refer to the Special Care Facilities section.

Loretto Rest, Inc., 750 E. Brighton Ave., 13205. Tel: 315-469-5061
For a complete listing, refer to the Special Care Facilities section.

St. Camillus Health & Rehabilitation Center, 813 Fay Rd., 13219. Tel: 315-488-2951
For a complete listing, refer to the Special Care Facilities section.

OSWEGO. *Saint Luke's Residential Health Care Facility Co., Inc.,* 299 E. First St., 13126. Tel: 315-342-3166
For a complete listing, refer to the Special Care Facilities section.

UTICA. *St. Joseph Nursing Home,* 2535 Genesee St., 13501. Tel: 315-797-1230
For a complete listing, refer to the Special Care Facilities section.

[Q] SPECIALTY HOUSING

SYRACUSE. *Christopher Community, Inc.,* 1654 W. Onondaga St., 13204. Tel: 315-424-1821
For a complete listing, refer to the Special Care Facilities section.

Churchill Manor, Inc., 750 E. Brighton Ave., 13205. Tel: 315-424-1821
For a complete listing, refer to the Special Care Facilities section.

Hawley Winton Housing Development Fund, Inc., Walter Ludovico Apts., 340 Winton St., 13203. Tel: 315-422-0475
For a complete listing, refer to the Special Care Facilities section.

Ludden Housing Development Fund Company, Inc., 1654 W. Onondaga St., 13204. Tel: 315-424-1821
For a complete listing, refer to the Special Care Facilities section.

Marcellus Apartments Housing Development Fund Company, Inc. Mailing Address: 1654 W. Onondaga St., 13204. Tel: 315-424-1821.
For a complete listing, refer to the Special Care Facilities section.

Miller Road Housing Development Co., Inc., (Brewerton) Mailing Address: 1654 W. Onondaga St., 13204. Tel: 315-424-1821.
For a complete listing, refer to the Special Care Facilities section.

Mother Marianne Cope Housing Development Fund Co., Inc., 1654 W. Onondaga St., 13204. Tel: 315-424-1821
For a complete listing, refer to the Special Care Facilities section.

Mount St. James Corporation, 1654 W. Onondaga St., 13204. Tel: 315-424-1821
For a complete listing, refer to the Special Care Facilities section.

Pompei Housing Development Fund Company, Inc. c/o Christopher Community, Inc., 1654 W. Onondaga St., 13204. Tel: 315-424-1821.
For a complete listing, refer to the Special Care Facilities section.

Pond St. Housing Development Fund Co., Inc., Bishop Harrison Apartments, Pond St., 13208
For a complete listing, refer to the Special Care Facilities section.

Providence House Apartments, 1700 W. Onondaga St., 13204. Tel: 315-471-8427
For a complete listing, refer to the Special Care Facilities section.

St. Peter's Italian Church Housing Development Fund Co., Inc. Villa Scalabrini Apts., 709 James St., 13203
For a complete listing, refer to the Special Care Facilities section.

Stoneleigh Housing Development Fund Co., Inc., Stoneleigh Apartments, 400 Lamb Ave., Canastota, 13032
For a complete listing, refer to the Special Care Facilities section.

Tyson Place Housing Development Fund Company, Inc. Mailing Address: Blessed Sacrament Apartments, 1654 W. Onondaga St., 13204. Tel: 315-424-1821.
For a complete listing, refer to the Special Care Facilities section.

AUBURN. *Mercy Housing Development Fund Co., Inc.,* Mercy Apartments, 1 Thornton Ave., 13021. Tel: 315-253-2015
For a complete listing, refer to the Special Care Facilities section.

BALDWINSVILLE. *Smokey Hollow Housing Development Fund Company, Inc.* Mailing Address: St. Mary's Apartments, Baldwinsville, 1654 W. Onondaga St. Syracuse, 13204. Tel: 315-424-1821.
For a complete listing, refer to the Special Care Facilities section.

BREWERTON. *Bartell Road Housing Development Fund Co., Inc.,* Bartell Rd., 13029
For a complete listing, refer to the Special Care Facilities section.

CICERO. *Cicero Housing Development Fund Company Inc.* Mailing Address: 1654 W. Onondaga St. Syracuse, 13204. Tel: 315-424-1821.
For a complete listing, refer to the Special Care Facilities section.

FAYETTEVILLE. *Redfield South Housing Development Fund Co., Inc.,* Redfield Village Apartments, 380 Salt Springs Rd., 13066. Tel: 315-637-8280
For a complete listing, refer to the Special Care Facilities section.

NORTH SYRACUSE. *Pitcher Hill-Christopher Housing Development Fund Co., Inc.,* 114 Elbow Rd., 13212
For a complete listing, refer to the Special Care Facilities section.

OSWEGO. *St. Luke's Housing Development Fund Co., Inc.,* St. Luke's Apartments, W. First St., 13126
For a complete listing, refer to the Special Care Facilities section.

ROME. *C.N.C. Inc.,* W. Thomas St., 13440. Tel: 315-735-7545
For a complete listing, refer to the Special Care Facilities section.

Rome Mall Housing Development Fund Company, Inc. Mailing Address: 1654 W. Onondaga St. Syracuse, 13204. Tel: 315-424-1821.
For a complete listing, refer to the Special Care Facilities section.

TOWN OF GATES. *Steger Housing Development Fund Co., Inc.,* 4100 Lyell Rd 1654 W. Onondaga St. Syracuse, 13204. Tel: 315-424-1821.
For a complete listing, refer to the Special Care Facilities section.

UTICA. *Catherine St. Housing Development Fund Company, Inc.* Mailing Address: Mt. Carmel Apartments, 1654 W. Onondaga St. Syracuse, 13201-0511. Tel: 315-424-1821.
For a complete listing, refer to the Special Care Facilities section.

[R] PROGRAMS FOR THE HANDICAPPED

SYRACUSE. *L'Arche,* Office: 1232 Teall Ave., 13206. Tel: 315-479-8088; 479-8118. Robert Sackel, Dir. A Christian Community concerned with life sharing between persons with a developmental disability and persons who assist them. Homes at 1701 James St., 1226 Butternut St., & 1240-42 Teall Ave., Syracuse & 197 Hathaway Rd., DeWitt.

UTICA. *St. John and St. Joseph Home, Inc.,* 1408 Genesee St., 13502. Tel: 315-724-2150. Mr. Dennis J. Manning, Exec. Dir.

YORKVILLE. *The Heenan Spiritual Program for the Handicapped, Inc.,* 17 Sixth St., 13495. Tel: 315-736-4858. Mr. Stanley Zima, Dir.

[S] MONASTERIES AND RESIDENCES OF PRIESTS AND BROTHERS

SYRACUSE. *Jesuits at LeMoyne, Inc.,* 1419 Salt Springs Rd., 13214.
E-mail: jesuit@maple.lemoyne.edu
Revs. John B. Breslin, S.J., Rector; James F. Smith, S.J., Min.; Thomas J. Kent, S.J., Treas.; Robert A. Mitchell, S.J., Pres.; William J. Bosch, S.J.; Raymond A. Bucko, S.J.; Paul B. Campbell, S.J. (Ireland); J. Donald Clark, S.J.; Theodore J. Clarkson, S.J.; William S. Dolan, S.J.; James J. Hennesey, S.J.; Vincent W. Hevern, S.J.; Donald J. Kirby, S.J.; William J. McBrearty, S.J.; Thomas R. Marciniak, S.J.; Paul S. Naumann, S.J.; Joseph B. Neville, S.J.; Edmund G. Ryan, S.J.; Vincent B. Ryan, S.J.; Robert E. Scully, S.J.; Andrew L. Szebenyi, S.J. (Hungary); M. Donald Zewe, S.J. Priests 22.

St. Pius X Home, Inc., 714 E. Brighton Ave., 13205. Tel: 315-492-1711. Diocesan home for priests. In res. Rev. Msgr. Robert B. Davern; Rev. Msgr. Robert E. Dillon; Rev. Msgr. John R. Duffy; Revs. Robert J. McKay; Thomas F. Guyder; Robert Barett; P. Carl Pilla; Robert P. Wright; Joseph F. Kane; Joseph McNamara (ROC); William J. Brown; Bernard F. Walsh.

EAST SYRACUSE. *Bishop Grimes Priests Residence,* 6655 Kirkville Rd., 13057. Tel: 315-437-8385. Most Rev. Frank J. Harrison; Rev. Msgr. Frank L. Sammons; Revs. John J. Heagerty; William P. Regan; David R. Sambor; Charles S. Vavonese, Vianney House, 6651 Kirkville Rd., 13057. Revs. George F. Sheehan; J. Robert Yeazel, St. Camillus Nursing Home, Syracuse, 13219. Rev. Msgr. A. Robert Casey.

UTICA. *St. Vincent's Mission House,* 10475 Cosby Manor Rd., 13502. Tel: 315-724-9237. Congregation of the Mission, Province of New England Vincentian Fathers. Bro. Richard Glinski, C.M., Dir.; Revs. Casimir Kiczuk, C.M.; Henry Czekala, C.M.; Edmund Kowalski, C.M., St. Joseph Nursing Home; Bros. Francis Andrzejewski, C.M., St. Joseph's Nursing Home, Utica; Richard Glinski, C.M.

[T] CONVENTS AND RESIDENCES FOR SISTERS

SYRACUSE. *Convent of St. Anthony and Motherhouse of the Third Franciscan Order,* 1024 Court St., 13208. Sr. Eloise Emm, Local Min., Generalate Offices, 2500 Grant Blvd., 13208. Sr. Grace Anne Dillenschneider, O.S.F., Gen. Supr. Total Sisters in Diocese 232; Total in Community 352.

Dominican Monastery of the Perpetual Rosary, 802 Court St., 13208. Tel: 315-471-6762. Sr. Mary Augustine, O.P., Prioress. Cloistered Nuns 10; Extern Sisters 1.

Franciscan Formation House, 112 Michaels Ave., 13208-1718. Tel: 315-471-7893. Sisters of the Third Franciscan Order. Sisters 4.

St. Clare Convent, 1001 Court St., 13208.

WINDSOR. *Transfiguration Monastery,* 701 NY Rte. 79, 13865-2700. Tel: 607-655-2366.
E-mail: fendon@depitds.net
Camaldolese Benedictine Nuns. Sisters 4.

[U] RETREAT HOUSES

SYRACUSE. *Christ the King Retreat House,* 500 Brookford Rd., 13224. Tel: 315-446-2680. Rev. Michael J. Carmola, Dir.; Sr. Rose Raymond Wagner, O.S.F., Asst. Dir.; Maureen A. Gallivan, Business Mgr. General retreat house for priests, nuns, laity, and youth of Upstate New York. Priests 1; Sisters 1.

SKANEATELES. *Stella Maris Retreat Center,* 13152. Tel: 315-685-6836; Fax: 315-685-6836. Sisters of the Third Franciscan Order, M.C. Sr. John Olivia, O.S.F., Admin. & Dir. Retreat Ministry. Team oriented center for renewal.

[V] NEWMAN CENTERS

SYRACUSE. *LeMoyne College Newman Center,* 13214. Tel: 315-445-4110.

Onondaga Community College Newman Center, c/o 204 Alton St., 13210. Tel: 315-476-5857. Deacon John Mulety, Chap.

Syracuse University, St. Thomas More Foundation, Inc., Alibrandi Catholic Center, 110 Walnut Pl., P.O. Box 0038, 13210-0038. Tel: 315-478-5959.
E-mail: jplang@col.com
Rev. James P. Lang, Chap.

BINGHAMTON. *Broome Community College Newman Center,* 157 Clark St., P.O. Box 408, 13850. Tel: 607-748-8287.

CAZENOVIA. *Cazenovia College Newman Center,* 10 Seminary St., 13035. Steven R. Young, Chap.

CLINTON. *Hamilton College Newman Center,* 13323. Tel: 315-859-4129. Rev. John P. Croghan, Chap.

CORTLAND. *Newman Foundation of Cortland, Inc. at the State University College of New York,* 8 Calvert St., 13045. Tel: 607-753-6737. Rev. Edward J. O'Heron, Chap.

HAMILTON. *Catholic Newman Community of Colgate University,* 13 Oak Dr., 13346. Tel: 315-824-7680.
E-mail: jDonavan@macl.colgate.edu
Web site: www.z.colgate.edu
Rev. John P. Donovan.

MORRISVILLE. *Newman Association at SUNY Morrisville,* 210 Lab Classroom, 13408.
E-mail: DonovaJP@morrisville.edu
Web site: www.morrisville.edu/pages/newman
Legal Title: *St. Joan of Arc Newman Association at the State University of New York (SUNY) Morrisville Agricultural and Technical College.*

OSWEGO. *Newman Foundation, Inc., State University of New York,* Hall Newman Center, New St., P.O. Box 207, 13126. Tel: 315-341-7562.
E-mail: worn@Oswego.Oswego.edu
Rev. G. Peter Worn.

UTICA. *Mohawk Valley Community College.* Newman Apostolate, 1204 Sherman Dr., 13501. Tel: 315-797-3419; Fax: 315-735-5545. Deacon William Hotaling.

SUNY Institute of Technology at Utica/Rome Newman Center, 1433 Burrstone Rd., 13502. Tel: 315-792-3284.
E-mail: VJL3@Juno.com
Rev. V. James Lauducci, Chap. Legal Title: *State University of New York (SUNY) Institute of Technology at Utica/Rome Newman Center.*

Utica College of Syracuse University Newman Center, 1433 Burrstone Rd., 13502. Tel: 315-792-3284.
E-mail: VJL3@Juno.com
Rev. V. James Lauducci, Chap., Res., 1433 Burrstone Rd., 13502. Tel: 315-792-3284.

VESTAL. *Binghamton University Newman Center,* 400 Murray Hill Rd., 13850. Tel: 607-798-7202.
E-mail: Frbob@binghamton.edu
Web site: www.sa binghamton.edu/newman/newman.htm
Rev. Robert J. Sullivan, Chap.

[W] MISCELLANEOUS LISTINGS

SYRACUSE.

**David W. Barry Foundation,* 240 E. Onondaga St., P.O. Box 511, 13201-0511. Tel: 315-422-7203; Fax: 315-478-4619. Most Revs. James M. Moynihan, Pres.; Thomas J. Costello, Vice Pres.; Rev. Michael P. Minehan, Sec. & Treas.

Grimes Foundation. (Incorporated by special act of the New York State Legislature, May 1, 1916), 240 E. Onondaga St., 13202. Corporation created to establish and maintain charitable, religious and educational facilities within the Roman Catholic Diocese of Syracuse, New York. Most Rev. James M. Moynihan, D.D., Pres. Ex-Officio.

Lasalle Syracuse, Inc., 6245 Randall Rd., 13214.

Loretto Apartments Housing Development Fund Co., Inc., 700 E. Brighton Ave., 13205.

ONE (Opportunity Network in Economics), 1101 Burnet Ave., 13203. Tel: 315-479-6301. Kenneth Leeb, Dir.

Onondaga County Catholic School Foundation (Western Region Catholic School Foundation), 240 E. Onondaga St., P.O. Box 511, 13201-0511. Tel: 315-470-1450; Fax: 315-478-4619. Sr. Shirley Anne Brown, Area Supt. Western Region Schools.

St. Francis Social Adult Day Service, 1108 Court St., 13208. Tel: 315-424-1003; 1004. Sr. Christopher Dixon, O.S.F., Admin. A non-residential adult day-service providing holistic care for the frail elderly. Operated by the Sisters of the Third Franciscan Order.

Saint Thomas Preparatory Seminary Fund, P.O. Box 511, 13201. Incorporated under the Laws of the State of New York, 1963, as a Membership Corporation to solicit funds for the construction of a diocesan seminary.

Sisters of the Third Franciscan Order-Retirement Trust Fund, 2500 Grant Blvd., 13208. Tel: 315-425-0132; Fax: 315-425-0610.
E-mail: osfsyr@oxess.net

Spiritual Renewal Center, 1118 Court St., 13208.
E-mail: srcsyracuse@Sprintmail.com

BINGHAMTON. *Ladies of Charity,* 232 Main St., 13905. Tel: 607-729-9166.

ENDICOTT. *Bishop Harrison Education Foundation.* Mailing Address: P.O. Box 7158, 13760.

MAINE. *Mount St. Francis Hermitage.* Mailing Address: P.O. Box 276, 13802. Tel: 607-754-9813.

UTICA. *The Good News Foundation of Central New York,* 2306 Genesee St., 13502. Tel: 315-735-9730. Katherine Poupart, Dir.

RELIGIOUS INSTITUTES OF MEN REPRESENTED IN THE DIOCESE

For further details refer to the corresponding bracketed number in the Religious Institutes of Men or Women section.

[1350]—*Brothers of St. Francis Xavier.* (St. Joseph Prov., Milton, MA).—C.F.X.

[0330]—*Brothers of the Christian Schools.* (New York Prov.).—F.S.C.

[1330]—*Congregation of the Mission (Vincentian Fathers).*—C.M.

[1210]—*Congregation of the Missionaries of St. Charles.* (St. Charles Borromeo Prov.).—C.S.

[0480]—*Conventual Franciscans.*—O.F.M.Conv.

[0690]—*Jesuit Fathers and Brothers.* (New York Prov.).—S.J.

RELIGIOUS INSTITUTES OF WOMEN REPRESENTED IN THE DIOCESE

[0230]—*Benedictine Sisters of Pontifical Jurisdiction.* (Erie, PA).—O.S.B.

[]—*Camaldolese Benedictine Sisters.*—O.S.B.Cam.

[0330]—*Carmelite Sisters for the Aged and Infirm.*—O.Carm.

[0760]—*Daughters of Charity of St. Vincent de Paul.*—D.C.

[1050]—*Dominican Contemplative Nuns.*—O.P.

[1070-01]—*Dominican Sisters.*—O.P.

[1170]—*Felician Sisters.*—C.S.S.F.

[1180]—*Franciscan Sisters of Allegany, New York.*—O.S.F.

[1410]—*Franciscan Sisters of St. Joseph (Mill Hill).*—F.M.S.J.

[2575]—*Institute of the Sisters of Mercy of the Americas.* (New York, NY; Omaha, NE).—R.S.M.

[1360]—*Missionary Franciscan Sisters of the Immaculate Conception.*—O.S.F.

[3160]—*Parish Visitors of Mary Immaculate.*—P.V.M.I.

[0590]—*Sisters of Charity of Saint Elizabeth, Convent Station.*—S.C.

[3340]—*Sisters of Providence (Holyoke).*—S.P.

[3950]—*Sisters of Saint Mary of Namur.*—S.S.M.N.

[3780]—*Sisters of Saints Cyril and Methodius.*—SS.C.M.

[1800]—*Sisters of St. Francis of the Third Order Regular.* (Williamsville, New York).—O.S.F.

[3830-14]—*Sisters of St. Joseph.* (Rochester, NY).—S.S.J.

[3840]—*Sisters of St. Joseph of Carondelet.*—C.S.J.

[1970]—*Sisters of the Holy Family of Nazareth.*—C.S.F.N.

[1490]—*Sisters of the Third Franciscan Order.*—O.S.F.

[2160]—*Sisters, Servants of the Immaculate Heart of Mary.*—I.H.M.

[4110]—*Ursuline Nuns (Roman Union).*—O.S.U.

DIOCESAN CEMETERIES

SYRACUSE. *St. Mary-St. Agnes,* 2315 South Ave., 13207. Tel: 315-475-4639. Rev. James C. Fritzen, Dir.; Richard Dadey, Supt.; Daniel Moorhead, Asst. Supt.

CORTLAND. *St. Mary,* 4101 West Road, 13045. Tel: 607-756-8838. Rev. John Fenlon, Dir.; Russell Teeter, Supt.

JOHNSON CITY. *Calvary-St. Patrick,* 501 Fairview St., 13790. Tel: 607-797-2906. Daniel Vuille, Supt.; Ann Tesar, Sec.

OSWEGO. *St. Peter & St. Paul,* R.R. 04 Box 4B, Rte. 481, E. River Rd., 13126. Tel: 315-343-5002. Rev. Msgr. Paul A. Brigandi, Dir.; John Taber, Supt.

UTICA. *Calvary,* 2407 Oneida St., 13501. Tel: 315-735-2727. Rev. Msgr. William Donovan, Dir.; Donald Deck, Supt.

Holy Trinity, Chaplain Ave., 13502. Tel: 315-724-0616. Rev. Arthur R. Hapanowicz, Dir.; Daniel Williams, Supt.

St. Agnes, 601 Arthur St., 13501. Tel: 315-732-8588. Lawrence F. Hagan, Coord.; John McCarthy, Supt.

St. Mary, Webster St., 13501. Tel: 315-735-2727. Donald Deck, Supt.

WHITESBORO. *Mount Olivet,* 70 Wood Rd., 13492. Tel: 315-736-4446. Rev. Donald H. Karlen, Dir.; Joseph Usyk, Supt.

NECROLOGY

✠ O'Keefe, Most Rev. Joseph T., Retired Bishop of the Diocese of Syracuse. —Died Sept. 2, 1997.

† Dietrich, Michael A., Chap., Syracuse, NY, Psychiatric Center. —Died Aug. 8, 1997.

† Majdanik, Albin J., Binghamton, NY, St. Stanislaus. —Died April 20, 1997.

† Pepel, Anthony, Oswego, NY, St. Stephen. —Died Aug. 7, 1997.

Diocese of Toledo

(Dioecesis Toletana in America)

Most Reverend

JAMES R. HOFFMAN, D.D., J.C.L.

Bishop of Toledo; ordained July 28, 1957; appointed Titular Bishop of Italica and Auxiliary Bishop of Toledo April 18, 1978; ordained Bishop June 23, 1978; appointed to Toledo December 16, 1980. *Res., 2544 Parkwood Ave., Toledo, OH, 43610.*

Most Reverend

ROBERT W. DONNELLY, D.D.

Auxiliary Bishop of Toledo; ordained May 25, 1957; appointed Titular Bishop of Garba and Auxiliary Bishop of Toledo March 20, 1984; ordained Bishop May 3, 1984. *Res., 2544 Parkwood Ave., Toledo, OH, 43610.*

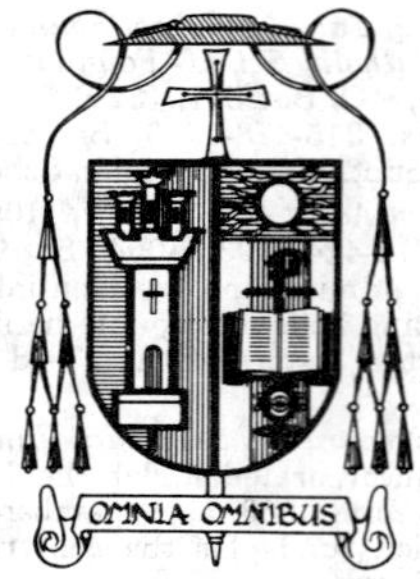

ESTABLISHED APRIL 15, 1910.

Square Miles 8,222.

Comprises the following Counties of northwest Ohio: Williams, Fulton, Lucas, Ottawa, Defiance, Henry, Wood, Sandusky, Erie, Paulding, Putnam, Hancock, Seneca, Huron, Van Wert, Allen, Wyandot, Crawford and Richland.

For legal titles of parishes and diocesan institutions, consult the Chancery.

Chancery: P.O. Box 985, Toledo, OH, 43697-0985. Tel.: 419-244-6711; Fax: 419-244-4791.

E-mail address: dheintschel@toledodiocese.org

STATISTICAL OVERVIEW

Personnel	
Bishop	1
Auxiliary Bishops	1
Retired Bishops	1
Priests: Diocesan Active in Diocese	147
Priests: Active Outside Diocese	9
Priests: Diocesan in Foreign Missions	2
Priests: Retired, Sick or Absent	60
Number of Diocesan Priests	218
Religious Priests in Diocese	57
Extern Priests in Diocese	6
Ordinations:	
Diocesan Priests	4
Transitional Deacons	1
Permanent Deacons	5
Permanent Deacons in Diocese	194
Total Brothers	9
Total Sisters	772
Parishes	
Parishes	163
With Resident Pastor:	
Resident Diocesan Priests	104
Resident Religious Priests	12
Without Resident Pastor:	
Administered by Priests	35
Administered by Permanent Deacons	4
Administered by Women Religious	8
Welfare	
Catholic Hospitals	8
Total Assisted	820,465
Health Care Centers	2
Total Assisted	424
Homes for the Aged	3
Total Assisted	459
Residential Care of Children	1
Total Assisted	75
Special Centers for Social Services	13
Total Assisted	8,200
Educational	
Diocesan Students in Other Seminaries	15
Total Seminarians	15
Colleges and Universities	2
Total Students	1,838
High Schools, Diocesan and Parish	10
Total Students	3,993
High Schools, Private	4
Total Students	2,884
Elementary Schools, Diocesan and Parish	84
Total Students	22,197
Elementary Schools, Private	3
Total Students	525
Catechesis/Religious Education:	
High School Students	3,032
Elementary Students	16,583
Total Students Under Catholic Instruction	51,067
Teachers in the Diocese:	
Priests	26
Sisters	107
Lay Teachers	1,582
Vital Statistics	
Receptions into the Church:	
Infant Baptism Totals	4,479
Received into Full Communion	702
First Communions	4,711
Confirmations	4,127
Marriages:	
Catholic	1,174
Interfaith	850
Total Marriages	2,024
Deaths	3,037
Total Catholic Population	327,921
Total Population	1,479,041

Former Bishops—Most Rev. JOSEPH SCHREMBS, D.D., appt. auxiliary of Grand Rapids, MI Jan. 8, 1911; cons. Feb. 22, 1911; transferred to Toledo, Aug. 11, 1911; transferred to Cleveland, OH, May 11, 1921; died Nov. 2, 1945.—His Eminence Cardinal SAMUEL A. STRITCH, D.D., cons. Bishop of Toledo, Nov. 30, 1921; appt. Archbishop of Milwaukee, Aug. 30, 1930; appt. Archbishop of Chicago, Dec. 27, 1939; created Cardinal, Feb. 18, 1946; named Pro-Prefect of the Sacred Congregation of the Propagation of the Faith, March 1, 1958; died in Rome, May 27, 1968.—Most Rev. KARL J. ALTER, D.D., LL.D., appt. Bishop of Toledo, April 17, 1931; cons. June 17, 1931; promoted to Archbishop of Cincinnati, June 14, 1950; died Aug. 23, 1977.—Most Rev. GEORGE REHRING, D.D., cons. Oct. 7, 1937; appt. Bishop of Toledo, July 18, 1950; retired Feb. 25, 1967; died Feb. 29, 1976.—Most Rev. JOHN A. DONOVAN, D.D., ord. Dec. 8, 1935; Titular Bishop of Rhasus and Auxiliary of Detroit, Sept. 6, 1954; ord. Bishop, Oct. 26, 1954; transferred Toledo, Feb. 25, 1967; retired July 29, 1980; died Sept. 18, 1991.

Chancery—Mailing Address: P.O. Box 985, Toledo, 43697-0985. 1933 Spielbusch, Toledo, 43624. Tel: 419-244-6711; Fax: 419-244-4791. Office Hours: Mon.-Fri. 8:30-5.

Vicar General—Most Rev. ROBERT W. DONNELLY, V.G., *1933 Spielbusch, Toledo, 43624., Mailing Address: P.O. Box 985, Toledo, 43697-0985.* Tel: 419-244-6711.

Cabinet—Most Rev. ROBERT W. DONNELLY, V.G., Sec. Personnel & Admin. Svcs. MICHAEL WASSERMAN, Secretariat of Ministeriel Leadership Formation; Sr. JANET DOYLE, O.P., Sec. of Catholic Youth & School Svcs.; Rev. Msgr. DONALD E. HEINTSHEL, Sec. Communications & Public Rels. DONALD L. WISLER, L.I.S.W., Sec. Catholic Charities; SALLY MALHOIT, Admin. Aide, *1933 Spielbusch, Toledo, 43624.* Tel: 419-244-6711.

Advisory To Bishop

All Diocesan Offices and Secretaries are located at 1933 Spielbusch, Toledo, OH 43624. Address all mail to: P.O. Box 985, Toledo, OH 43697-0985. Tel: 419-244-6711. unless otherwise indicated

Bishop's Education Council—JOHN STOEPLER, Pres.; Mrs. CAROL COLLINS, Vice Pres.; Dr. HARRY BASH; WILLIAM BOYLE; ROBERT DANIEL; DAVID WALROD; JOHN GILWEE; Mr. JAMES HAUDAN; Rev. JAMES HOLMER; Sr. MARY SUZANNE KENNEDY; Rev. KEITH J. MCCORMACK; JOHN C. MOORE; TOM NOE; DANIEL J. RING; Mrs. DEBRA SCHAEFER; Mrs. SALLY KOPPINGER; Mr. ROMAN ACE; Rev. ROBERT YEAGER.

Building Commission—Dr. GEORGE MURNEN, Chm.; Revs. GERALD J. CHMIEL; RICHARD T. WURZEL; Mr. DAVID BAGGETT; Mr. JAMES CIHAK; Dr. MARK PICKETT.

Consultors—Revs. MARVIN G. BORGER; GERALD L. CERANOWSKI; THOMAS LEYLAND; GREGORY L. PEATEE; J. MICHAEL RICKER; RICHARD WURZEL.

Deans—Defiance Deanery: Very Rev. EDWARD J. SCHLETER, V.F., Defiance, Henry and Paulding Counties; Fremont Deanery: Very Rev. RONALD LEJEUNE, V.F., Ottawa and Sandusky Counties; Lima Deanery: Very Rev. DAVID M. ROSS, V.F., S.T.L., J.C.D., Ph.D., Allen, Van Wert and Putnam Counties; Mansfield Deanery: Very Rev. HERBERT F. WEBER, V.F., Richland and Crawford Counties; Tiffin Deanery: Very

Rev. FRANCIS A. MURD, V.F., Seneca, Wyandot and Hancock Counties; Toledo Central: Very Rev. RONALD R. WARNIMONT, V.F., Toledo Northwest: Very Rev. ROBERT REINHART, Toledo Southwest: Very Rev. DENNIS METZGER, To-Lu-Wo Deanery: Very Rev. JOSEPH STEINBAUER, Acting Dean for East Lucas and Wood Counties; Sandusky Deanery: Very Rev. FRANKLIN P. KEHRES, V.F., Erie and Huron Counties; Will-Ful-L Deanery: Very Rev. FRED DUSCHL, Williams, Fulton and West Lucas Counties.

Diocesan Pastoral Council—CAROL HENS, Contact, *271 Chorus Ln., Toledo, 43615.*

Finance Committee—Most Rev. JAMES R. HOFFMAN; Most Rev. ROBERT W. DONNELLY, V.G.; Mr. RICHARD FAIST; Mr. ROBERT J. KIRK; Mr. THOMAS KRESS.

Priests' Council—Revs. THOMAS J. LEYLAND, Chm. Tel: 419-352-4195. RICHARD T. WURZEL, Vice Chm. Tel: 419-885-5791. GREGORY L. PEATEE, Sec. & Treas. Tel: 419-475-4348.

Sisters' Advisory Council—Sr. MARY SUE KENNEDY, O.P.A.D., *P.O. Box 985, Toledo, 43697-0985.* Tel: 419-244-6711.

Secretariat Of Administrative Services

Secretary-Vicar General—Most Rev. ROBERT W. DONNELLY, V.G., *P.O. Box 985, Toledo, 43697-0985.* Tel: 419-244-6711.

Diocesan Department Of Development—RICHARD WARING, Ph.D., Dir. DOROTHY LANGENDERFER, Assoc. Dir.

Financial Services—JOHN HEINZE, Dir.

Internal Auditor—Ms. SARA G. MARTIN, C.P.A.

Associate Auditor—Ms. SUZANNE STAPLETON.

MIS (Management Information Systems)—SHARON LANDIS, Coord.

Affiliated:

Cemeteries Office—JOHN E. CARPENTER, Dir., *5725 Hill Ave., Toledo, 43615-5852.* Tel: 419-531-5747; Fax: 419-531-0946.

Cemeteries—Calvary: *2424 Dorr St., Toledo, 43607.* Tel: 419-536-3751., Mount Carmel: *15 E. Manhattan Blvd., Toledo, 43608.* Tel: 419-536-3751., Resurrection: *5725 Hill Ave., Toledo, 43615.* Tel: 419-531-5747.

Catholic Office Building Services—Ms. PATRICIA STEIN, Mgr.

Court of Equity—Mrs. JUDITH GAJDOSTIK, Clerk; FRANK LINK, Presiding Judge, *3250 Hazelton Dr., Oregon, 43616.* Tel: 419-691-7436.

Judges—FRANCIS LANDRY; Sr. EMILY LECHLAK, O.S.F.S.; COLIN MCQUADE; PAULA MINZING; Rev. DANIEL RING; Sr. DOROTHY THUM, R.S.M.; HARRY WELSH; BRUCE WINTERS; Rev. RICHARD T. WURZEL.

Conciliators—JAMES CARUSO; RICHARD HANUSZ; JUDE SUTTER; JOHN F. WETLI.

Intake Officers—Mrs. JOHN HILLER; ROBERT J. SUTTER; CLARA WESOLEK; ELIZABETH ZEPF.

Synod Implementation Office—RITA BAUR, Coord. Sec.

DCCW (Diocesan Council of Catholic Women)—Mrs. CHRIS YOUNG, Pres., *1542 Ralston Cir., Ste. 207, Toledo, 43615.* Tel: 419-534-2252.

Secretariat Of Personnel

Secretary—Most Rev. ROBERT W. DONNELLY, V.G.

Vicar for Priests and Director of Ministry to Priests Program—Rev. RAYMOND C. SHEPERD, Vicar.

Vicar for Deacons—Rev. RAYMOND C. SHEPERD.

Vicar For Religious—Sr. MARY SUE KENNEDY, O.P., A.D.

Diocesan Case Manager—Mr. FRANK DILALLO.

Vicar for Seminarians—Rev. WILLIAM KUBACKI.

Priests' Personnel Board—Rev. KENNETH G. MORMAN, Chm. Members: Revs. FRANKLIN P. KEHRES, V.F.; KENNETH LILL; JOSEPH R. STEINBAUER; ROBERT J. WILHELM, V.F.; HERBERT J. WILLMAN, *2544 Parkwood Ave., Toledo, 43610-1317.* Tel: 419-255-1890; Fax: 419-244-0471.

Office of Personnel Services—Mr. JOHN LECHMAN, Dir.

Tribunal—

Director—Sr. MARCIA MARIE DESTATTE, S.N.D., J.C.L.

Judicial Vicar—Very Rev. JOHN A. MCCLURE, V.J., J.C.L., M.C.L.

Associate Judicial Vicar—Rev. JOHN C. REED, S.J.

Defenders of the Bond—Revs. THOMAS BEAUREGARD; STANLEY SZYBKA; Sr. MARCIA MARIE DESTATTE, S.N.D., J.C.L.; Rev. CHRISTOPHER VASKO, J.C.L.

Presiding Judges—Revs. JOSEPH O'BRIEN; JOHN THOMAS; JOHN C. REED; RONALD R. WARNIMONT, V.F.; JOHN A. MCCLURE, V.J., J.C.L., M.C.L.

Associate Judges—Revs. RAYMOND ETZEL; JAMES SAY; JAMES WALSH; Sr. MARCIA MARIE DESTATT, S.N.D., J.C.L.

Notaries—CHARLOTTE LAMMERS; ANGELA WALKER; Mrs. PAULA BUTLER.

Interdiocesan Appeals Court: Northwest Section—

Judicial Vicar—Very Rev. DAVID M. ROSS, V.F., S.T.L., J.C.D., Ph.D.

Defenders of the Bond—Revs. ROBERT TUCCERI; JOSEPH VAMOS.

Judges—Most Rev. JAMES R. HOFFMAN; Rev. Msgr. DONALD E. HEINTSCHEL; Revs. JAMES AUTH; JAMES CRYAN, O.S.F.S.; FREDERICK HUG; JOSEPH JAROS; WILLIAM PARKER; DENNIS SCHROEDER; JOHN A. THOMAS; RICHARD WURZEL.

Notary—Mrs. MARIAN KRASNIEWSKI,

Affiliated:

Retirement Plan for Lay Employees—Mrs. MARY C. DEPINET, Admin.

Employee Benefit Fund—Mrs. MARY C. DEPINET, Admin.

Secretariat of Ministerial Leadership Formation

Secretary—Mr. MICHAEL WASSERMAN.

Ministry and Adult Formation—Team Members: Sr. JOYCE MARIE BATES, S.N.D.; Mr. ALFREDO DIAZ; Mrs. JEANNINE BURCH; Sr. MARGARET MCGUINESS, O.P./A.D.; Mr. MICHAEL NACHMAN; Mr. LEO BISTAK; Sr. CATHERINE EDGAR, S.H.C.J.

Coordinator for Liturgy—Sr. GEORGETTE ZALEWSKA, R.S.M.,Affiliated Committees: RCIA Committee; Liturgical Commission.

Department of Global Concerns—Rev. BERNARD J. BOFF, Dir.

Mission of Accompaniment Pastoral Team—Rev. TIMOTHY M. KUMMERER, *All Souls Catholic Mission, Box 37, Binga, Zimbabwe, Africa.*

Ecumenical & Interreligious Affairs Commission—Rev. DAVID BRUNING, Chm., *6230 W. Tiffin St., Bascom, 44809.* Tel: 419-937-2715.

Shared Parish Ministry Group Co-Conveners—Sr. JOY BARKER, O.S.F.S.; Ms. PAMELA MESSEROLL.

Secretariat of Catholic Youth & School Services

Secretary—Sr. JANET DOYLE, O.P. Team Members: Sr. JULIA MARIE HUTCHISON, S.N.D.; Sr. MIRIAM EBLE, S.N.D.; Sr. MARY BURKE, S.N.J.M.; Ms. DONNA THERKELSEN; Sr. JOAN FRANCES FURLONG, S.N.D.; Sr. NADINE KASCHALK, C.P.P.S.; Mrs. SHARI BEIER; Sr. MARY JO SZPILA, S.N.D.; Mr. MICHAEL BEIER, Govt. Prog. Coord.

Catholic Club—PAUL SZYMANSKI, *1601 Jefferson Ave., Toledo.* Tel: 419-243-7255; Fax: 419-243-6337.

Chaplain for Youth—Rev. MELVIN VERHOFF.

Youth Ministry—Rev. MELVIN VERHOFF, Dir. JEFF MIELCAREK, CYO Dir. THOMAS MURNEN, Board Pres. Area Coordinators: SARAH NYE, Back to Earth, Mansfield Deanery. Tel: 419-492-2270. DIANE VERHOFF, Hearthstone, Lima Deanery. Tel: 419-523-5410. MARY KRYSTOWSKI, Heartland, Sandusky Deanery. Tel: 419-929-8722. CINDY MOLNAR, Prism, Toledo. Tel: 419-693-9293. MARY SLATTERY, Crossroads, Defiance & Will-Ful-L Deaneries. Tel: 419-542-7327. MARY ORTON, Two Rivers & Tiffin Deanery. Tel: 419-422-7774. LORI KAMELESKI, Beacon, Fremont Deanery. Tel: 419-542-7327. JOYCE MEYER, Kaleidoscope, Toledo. Tel: 419-478-5846. Affiliated Boards: Bishop's Education Council; Catholic Club; Mr. ERIC STOCKARD, Pres.

Resource Center—Sr. MARY SARTOR, S.N.D.

Campus Ministry—Rev. DANIEL ZAK, Dir., *333 Brookside Dr., Swanton, 43558-1097.*

Secretariat of Catholic Charities

Catholic Charities—Mr. DONALD L. WISLER, L.I.S.W., Sec. & Exec. Dir.

Direct Services Division:

Adoption Services—PEG GEHRING, Dir.

Counseling Department—ALAN WILLCOX, Dir. Serving Lucas, Wood, eastern Fulton & western Ottawa Counties.

Regional Offices:

Eastern—Mrs. NICOLE CUNNINGHAM, Dir., *249 W. Main St., Norwalk, 44857.* Tel: 419-668-3073; Fax: 419-663-5070. Serving Crawford, Erie, Huron, eastern Ottawa, Richland, Sandusky, Seneca and Wyandot Counties.

Western—SANDRA HERMAN, Dir., *1012 Ralston Ave., Defiance, 43512.* Tel: 419-782-4933; Fax: 419-784-4760. Serving Allen, Defiance, western Fulton, Hancock, Henry, Paulding, Van Wert and Williams Counties.

Social Ministry and Advocacy Division:

Parish and Community Outreach Department—LOUIS COCCHIARELLA, Dir. Tel: 419-244-6711.

English as a Second Language—Sr. MARCIA BUCHARD, F.M.I.

Hispanic Ministry—Sr. ESTELLA IBARRA, F.M.I.

Ministry to Aging—DONNA POSLUSZNY.

Parish Outreach/CCMT—MARGARET BOWMAN.

Project Mustard Seed—MSIMBI SHUMAN.

Social Action/Campaign for Human Development—Sr. JOAN MICHALIK, I.H.M., Dir.

Family Life/Respect Life—LUCY ABU-ABSI, Dir.

Rural Life Ministries—Sr. MARY CHRISTINE PRATT, O.S.U., Dir., *301 S. Main St., Fostoria, 44830.* Tel: 419-435-1543.

Ministry to Persons with Disabilities—JUDY DALTON; Dir., *Kateri Center, 443 Sixth St., Toledo, 43605.* Tel: 419-698-9696; 698-9914 (TTD).

Black Catholic Ministry—GAIL FRANKLIN, Dir.

Migrant Ministry—ALVINA COSTELLA. Tel: 419-244-6711.

Affiliated:

Mareda, Inc. (Vistula Management Co.)—JOHN KIELY, Dir., *P.O. Box 4719, Toledo, 43620.* Tel: 419-242-2300.

Madonna Homes—JEANETTE VANOVER, Mgr., *722 Huron St., Toledo, 43604.* Tel: 419-244-3758.

Regina Manor—JODY DOWNEY, Mgr., *3731 N. Erie St., Toledo, 43611.* Tel: 419-246-4731.

Delaware Acres—MELAINIE PARKS-BAYNARD, Mgr., *725 Buchanan, Fremont, 43420.* Tel: 419-334-9558.

Moody Manor—KATHY KEANE, Mgr., *2293-1/2 Kent St., Toledo, 43620.* Tel: 419-246-4737.

Hope Manor—CATHY CROSSEN, Mgr., *4702 Violet Rd., Toledo, 43623.* Tel: 419-246-4733.

Michaelmas Manor—HALLEY DOWNEY, Mgr., *3260 Schneider Rd., Toledo, 43614.* Tel: 419-246-4735.

St. Anthony Villa—GARY Q. TESTER, Dir., *2740 W. Central Ave., Toledo, 43606.* Tel: 419-473-1353.

St. Vincent De Paul Society—CHARLES NEUSER, Pres. SANDRA BLOOMQUIST, Vice Pres., *1001 Washington St., Toledo, 43624.* Tel: 419-243-6963.

Secretariat of Communications and Public Relations

Secretary—Rev. Msgr. DONALD E. HEINTSCHEL, *6832 Convent Blvd., Sylvania, 43560.* Tel: 419-882-1530.

Diocesan Archives—Rev. BRUCE FARMER, *c/o 2544 Parkwood Ave., Toledo, 43610.* Tel: 419-255-1890.

"Catholic Chronicle"—PATRICIA L. MORRISON, Mng. Editor, *2130 Madison Ave., P.O. Box 1866, Toledo, 43624.* Tel: 419-243-4178.

Affiliated:

Diocesan Directory—Mrs. RITA BAUR, Editor.

Other Organizations

CCMT (Central City Ministries of Toledo)—Co-chairpersons: Sr. VIRGINIA WELSH, O.S.F.T.; Ms. CANDICE RENNER; Miss SUZANNE STAPLETON; SHARON RAPPAPORT, Dir. Devel. & Public Rels. DENNIS PAKULSKI, Business Mgr., *1119 W. Bancroft St., Toledo, 43606.* Tel: 419-244-9516.

Corda Club—Co-Chm.: BECKY CRABTREE; MARY GUSTWILLER.

Cursillo Movement—Spiritual Directors: Rev. EDWARD J. LITTELMANN, *430 Main St., Huron, 44839.* Tel: 419-433-5725. Rev. JAMES E. BROWN, *821 N. Wheeling St., Toledo, 43605.* Tel: 419-693-2198. Deacon JOSE BAUTISTA, *10917 Nelson Rd., Bowling Green, 43402.* Tel: 419-352-6477. Sr. EDNA MICHEL, O.S.F.T., *200 St. Francis Ave., Tiffin, 44883.* Tel: 419-447-0435. Lay Directors: PAT MILLER; GUS MILLER, *4254 Co. Rd. 27, Helena, 43435.* Tel: 419-638-3790.

Diocesan Attorneys—JOHN HAYWARD; TOM PLETZ, *1000 Jackson St., Toledo, 43624.* Tel: 419-241-4201.

Diocesan Insurance Program—JOSEPH SPENTHOFF, Branch Mgr., *Gallagher-Bassett Insurance Services, 5640 Southwyck Blvd., Toledo, 43614.* Tel: 419-865-8821.

MCCR (Ministry To Catholic Charismatic Renewal)—Mr. ROY HANDY, *550 Clark St., Toledo, 43605-2296.*

Serra International—Mrs. JANET DELL, District Governor, *155 Gibson Ct., Tiffin, 44883.*

Lima Serra Club—Mr. EDWARD ODENWELLER, Pres., *11065 Dutch Rd., Delphos, 45833.*

Mansfield Serra Club—Mr. PAUL WEITZEL, Pres., *132 Betzstone Dr., Mansfield, 44907.*

Tiffin Serra Club—Mrs. JANET DELL, Pres., *95 Gibbon Ct., Tiffin, 44883.*

Toledo Serra Club—Mr. DAVID LINCOLN, *3310 Craigmoor Ave., Toledo, 43614.*

Secular Order of Discalced Carmelites—KENNETH KRASNIEWSKI, Contact Person, *Our Lady of the Holy Rosary Fraternity, 5631 304th St., Toledo, 43611.*

Secular Franciscans—(Formerly Third Order), Contact: Our Lady of Consolation Province Minister. Tel: 216-839-2023. Deacon JOHN KINDER, S.F.O.

St. Paschal Fraternity—1933 Spielbusch, Toledo, 43624. MARGARET L. SHANTEAU, *2929 131st St., Toledo, 43611.*

Worldwide Marriage Encounter—Registration Couple: JOE NOONAN; CHERYL NOONAN, *P.O. Box 871, Toledo, 44883.*

National Marriage Encounter, Northwest Ohio, Inc.—Registration Couple: DENNIS ALT; GAY ALT, *1448 State Rte. 4, Bellevue, 44811.* Tel: 419-483-5129.

Retrouvaille—Coordinating Couple: JEFF RUSSELL; TERRY RUSSELL. Tel: 419-868-6447. Registration Couple: STEVE KYLE; JANET KYLE. Tel: 419-882-2558.

Vision Time, Inc.—200 St. Francis Ave., Tiffin, 44883. Tel: 419-243-6723. Sr. NANCY WESTMEYER, O.S.F., Contact Person.

St. Francis de Sales High School Endowment Fund, Inc.—2323 W. Bancroft St., Toledo, 43607.

CLERGY, PARISHES, MISSIONS AND PAROCHIAL SCHOOLS

CITY OF TOLEDO
(Lucas County)

1—QUEEN OF THE MOST HOLY ROSARY CATHEDRAL (1915), Very Rev. Ronald R. Warnimont, Rector; Deacons Lawrence Adams; Hugh Murray; Jesus Villagomez. In res., Most Rev. James R. Hoffman; Most Rev. Robert W. Donnelly; Most Rev. Albert Ottenweller; Rev. Bernard J. Boff.
Office: 2535 Collingwood Blvd., 43610. Tel: 419-244-9575; Fax: 419-242-1901.
Res., 2544 Parkwood Ave., 43610-1300. Tel: 419-255-1890.
Church—2561 Collingwood Blvd. and Islington St., 43610. [JC]
School—Tel: 419-243-4396.
Sisters 2; Lay Teachers 12; Students 208.

2—BLESSED SACRAMENT (1924), Revs. Robert Reinhart; Joven Malanyaon (Philippines); Deacons Robert Gillen; Ronald Ludwikowski; Harold Welch. In res., Rev. Stephen Rogers.
Res., 4227 Bellevue Rd., 43613-3999. Tel: 419-472-2288. [JC]
School—2216 Castlewood Dr., 43613. Tel: 419-472-1121; Fax: 419-472-1679.
Catechesis/Religious Programs—Tel: 419-472-7526.
Students 580.

3—CHRIST THE KING (1953), Revs. Neil Lucas; Greg Peatee; Deacons Edward Frazier; Lawrence Trotter; Gerald Sortman; Rob Bezssek; Mrs. Suzanne Marciniak, Pastoral Assoc.
Res., 4100 Harvest Ln., 43623-4399. Tel: 419-475-4348; Fax: 419-475-4050. [JC]
School—Tel: 419-475-0909.
Sisters 1; Lay Teachers 20; Students 585.
Catechesis/Religious Programs—Students 300.

4—COMMUNITY OF THE RISEN CHRIST (1972), Rev. Michael G. Madden.
Res., P.O. Box 2751, 43606. Tel: 419-243-7255.

5—CORPUS CHRISTI, UNIVERSITY OF TOLEDO (1970), Rev. James J. Bacik; Deacon James Marcher; Ms. Pam Meseroll, Admin.; Thomas Puszczewicz, Pastoral Assoc. In res., Rev. Earl Loeffer.
Res., 2080 Brookdale Rd., 43606. Tel: 419-536-7796; 531-4992 (Office); Fax: 419-531-1775.

6—GESU (1920), Revs. Clement Metzger, S.J.; Paul A. Woefl, S.J.; Deacons Larry Petersen; Ed Kelley; Richard Warren.
Res., 2049 Parkside Blvd., 43607. Tel: 419-531-1421; Fax: 419-531-0270. [JC]
School—Tel: 419-536-5634; Fax: 419-531-8932.
Sisters of Notre Dame 1; Lay Teachers 25; Students 470.
Catechesis/Religious Programs—Students 97.

7—GOOD SHEPHERD (1873), Rev. Jerome Nowakowski; Deacon Leon Holmer. In res., Rev. Gerald E. Knueven.
Res., 550 Clark St., 43605. Tel: 419-691-5815. [JC]
Catechesis/Religious Programs—Students 50.

8—HOLY ROSARY (1906) (Slovak), Revs. Frank Eckart; Kenneth Morman; Deacon Richard Fazekas.
Res., 821 N. Wheeling St., 43605. Tel: 419-693-2198; Fax: 419-693-2198. [JC]
School—Tel: 419-691-1653.
Religious 1; Lay Teachers 9; Students 178.

9—IMMACULATE CONCEPTION (1868), Rev. Paul M. Kwiatkowski.
Res., 434 Western Ave., 43609. Tel: 419-243-1829.
School—Queen of Apostles Consolidated, 235 Courtland St., 43609. Tel: 419-241-7829; Fax: 419-241-4180. Sr. Brenda Haynes, S.N.D., Prin.
Students 142.
Catechesis/Religious Programs—Students 35.

10—LITTLE FLOWER OF JESUS (1928), Rev. Stephen P. Cairns.
Res., 5522 Dorr St., 43615. Tel: 419-537-6997; Fax: 419-537-1469. [JC]
School—Tel: 419-536-1194.
Lay Teachers 17; Students 368.
Catechesis/Religious Programs—Students 149.

11—OUR LADY OF LOURDES (1926) (Polish), Rev. Thomas Wehinger; Deacons Clifford Kujawa; Robert Pacholski; Steve Veselka.
Res., 6149 Hill Ave., 43615. Tel: 419-865-2345; Fax: 419-865-2545.
School—Tel: 419-866-0736.
Lay Teachers 9; Students 242.
Catechesis/Religious Programs—P.R.E.P. Sr. Dorothy Forman, O.S.F.S., Pastoral Assoc. & Christian Form. Dir.
Students 70.

12—OUR LADY OF PERPETUAL HELP (1918), Rev. Robert J. Wilhelm; Deacons Victor DeCrane; Daniel Quinn; Robert Lesinski; Michael Learned.
Res., 3464 Glynn Dr., 43614. Tel: 419-382-4992.
Church—2255 Central Grove, 43614. Tel: 419-382-5511; Fax: 419-382-7360. [JC]
School—(Grades PreK-8). Tel: 419-382-5696.
Lay Teachers 27; Students 556.
Catechesis/Religious Programs—Kathy Dusseau, D.R.E.
Students 98.

13—REGINA COELI (1954), Rev. James E. Auth; Deacons James Dudley; George Mitchell; Larry Schaupp; John Wiciak. In res., Rev. Raymond C. Sheperd.
Res., 530 Regina Pkwy., 43612. Tel: 419-476-0922 (Office); 476-2281 (Home).
School—Tel: 419-476-0920.
Lay Teachers 20; Students 367.
Catechesis/Religious Programs—Students 130.

14—SACRED HEART OF JESUS (1883) (German), Revs. Frank E. Eckart; Kenneth Morman; Deacon Howard Narges; Sr. Mary Maxine, S.N.D., Pastoral Assoc. In res., Revs. William J. Kubacki; Joel Buchman.
Res., 509 Oswald St., 43605. Tel: 419-698-1664. [JC]
School—Tel: 419-691-0869.
Sisters of Notre Dame 1; Lay Teachers 8; Students 229.
Catechesis/Religious Programs—Students 229.

15—ST. ADALBERT (1907) (Polish), Rev. Gerald R. Grupczynski, S.Ch.
Res., 3233 Lagrange St., 43608. Tel: 419-241-4179; Fax: 419-241-1136.
School—Tel: 419-243-5257; Fax: 419-243-6733.
Felician Sisters 3; Lay Teachers 9; Students 199.

16—ST. AGNES (1910), Revs. Richard G. Miller; Joseph L. Vamos; Deacons John C. Vogel; Clarence Fisher.
Res., 3854 Berkeley Dr., 43612. Tel: 419-478-2384; Fax: 419-478-6556. [JC]
School—Tel: 419-478-7778.
Franciscan Sisters 1; Lay Teachers 9; Students 191.
Catechesis/Religious Programs—Students 56.

17—ST. ANN. Consolidated with St. Teresa to form St. Martin de Porres. See separate listing.

18—ST. ANTHONY (1882) (Polish), Rev. Gerald E. Knueven, Admin.
Res., 1416 Nebraska Ave., 43607. Tel: 419-241-6465.

19—ST. CATHERINE OF SIENA (1930), Rev. Michael G. Hohenbrink; Sr. Nancy Ferguson, O.S.F., Pastoral Assoc. In res., Rev. Melvin Verhoff.
Res., 4555 N. Haven Ave., 43612. Tel: 419-478-9558; Fax: 419-478-9434.
School—1155 Corbin Rd., 43612. Tel: 419-478-9900.
Lay Teachers 21; Students 406.
Catechesis/Religious Programs—Students 70.

20—ST. CHARLES BORROMEO (1903), Rev. Thomas J. Extejt. In res., Rev. Bruce L. Farmer.
Res., 1842 Airport Hwy., 43609-2069. Tel: 419-385-7431; Fax: 419-385-9152. [JC]
School—Tel: 419-382-7271.
Lay Teachers 11; Students 205.
Catechesis/Religious Programs—Tel: 419-382-1643.
Students 70.

21—ST. CLEMENT (1947), Revs. Gary R. Miller; Raymond A. Fisher; Deacons Wilbur Moore; Ronald Peeps; Ray Burzynski.
Res., 3030 Tremainsville Rd., 43613. Tel: 419-472-2111; Fax: 419-479-3215. [JC]
School—Tel: 419-474-9657.
Lay Teachers 17; Students 372.
Catechesis/Religious Programs—Tel: 419-472-1259.
Students 375.

22—ST. FRANCIS DE SALES (1841), Sr. Kathleen Scott, L.C.M., Pastoral Admin.; Rev. Theodore Miller; Sr. Diane Marie Pfahler, S.N.D., Pastoral Assoc.
Office: 501 Cherry St., 43604. Tel: 419-243-4242.

23—ST. HEDWIG (1875) (Polish), Rev. Joseph J. Przybysz; Deacons Michael Pence; Thomas Bland.
Res., 2916 Lagrange St., 43608. Tel: 419-729-3148. [JC]
School—Tel: 419-729-3658.
Franciscan Sisters 2; Lay Teachers 13; Students 256.

24—ST. HYACINTH (1927) (Polish), Rev. Jonathan C. Wight; Deacon Irvin Gonsiorowski. In res., Rev. Thomas Beauregard.
Res., 719 Evesham Ave., 43607. Tel: 419-535-7077; Fax: 419-535-5915. [JC]
School—Tel: 419-535-7078.
Sisters of Notre Dame 1; Lay Teachers 8; Students 181.

25—ST. JAMES (1913), Rev. Paul M. Kwiatkowski; Deacon Bernabe Romo.
Res., 914 Colburn St., 43609. Tel: 419-243-2640.
School—Queen of Apostles, Tel: 419-241-7829; Fax: 419-241-4180.
Lay Teachers 11; Students 142.

26—ST. JOAN OF ARC (1978), Rev. Gerald L. Ceranowski; Deacons Stan Przybylek; Larry Lottier.
Res., 5856 Heatherdowns Blvd., 43614. Tel: 419-866-6181; Fax: 419-866-6142.
School—5850 Heatherdowns Blvd., 43614. Tel: 419-866-6177; Fax: 419-866-4107.
Lay Teachers 22; Students 599.
Catechesis/Religious Programs—Tel: 419-866-7177.
Students 138.

27—ST. JOHN THE BAPTIST (1918), Revs. Francis J. Speier; Richard Eberle, O.S.F.S.
Res., 5153 Summit St., 43611. Tel: 419-726-2034; Fax: 419-726-1447. [JC]
School—Tel: 419-726-7761; Fax: 419-726-1031.
Sisters 2; Lay Teachers 20; Students 495.
Catechesis/Religious Programs—Tel: 419-726-9141.
Students 133.

28—ST. JOSEPH (1854) (French), Rev. Stephen Majoros.
Mailing Address: P.O. Box 790, 43697. Tel: 419-248-4378.
Res., 626 Locust St., 43604.
Church—Erie & Locust Sts., 43604. [JC]

29—ST. JUDE (1955), Rev. Bernard A. Kokocinski. In res., Rev. Gerald J. Robinson.
Res., 3650 Victory Ave., 43607. Tel: 419-531-1294; Fax: 419-531-5812.
School—Tel: 419-531-4951.
Lay Teachers 10; Students 148.

30—ST. LOUIS (1872) (French), Revs. John R. Blaser; Jerome F. Nowakowski; Sr. Joy Barker, O.S.F., Pastoral Assoc.
Res., 459 6th St., 43605. Tel: 419-691-0422; Fax: 419-691-0422. [JC]
Outreach—Helping Hands Soup Kitchen, Tel: 419-691-0613. Sr. Barbara Vano, O.S.F., Program Dir.

31—ST. MARTIN DE PORRES (1990), Rev. P. Martin Donnelly; Deacon John Algee.
Res., 1119 W. Bancroft, 43606. Tel: 419-241-4544; Fax: 419-244-3676.
School—(Grades PreK-8). Tel: 419-241-2892. Mrs. Darlene Kelley, Prin.; Mrs. Clara Scialin, School Mgr.
Sisters of Notre Dame 1; Lay Teachers 11; Students 200.

32—ST. MARY OF THE ASSUMPTION (1854), Sr. Virgina Welsh, O.S.F., Pastoral Admin.; Rev. Theodore Miller, Chap.; Deacons Stanley Gogol; James Hendricks; Mark Bussemeier.
Res., 219 Page St., 43620. Tel: 419-243-9213; Fax: 419-243-5405. [JC]
School—Tel: 419-241-3361; Fax: 419-243-5405.
Sisters 2; Lay Teachers 10; Students 220.
Convent—217 Page St., 43620. Tel: 419-241-2349.

33—ST. MICHAEL (1900), Rev. Robert J. Fisher; Deacons John Grandowicz; Harry Yeackel.
Res., 420 Sandusky St., 43611. Tel: 419-726-1947.
School—St. Elizabeth Seton School, 1030 Clay St., 43608. Tel: 419-726-4471; Fax: 419-729-2481.
Sisters 2; Lay Teachers 7; Students 214.

34—ST. PATRICK (1863) (Irish), Rev. Michael Billian.
Res., 130 Avondale Ave., 43602. Tel: 419-243-6452; Fax: 419-243-7032.

35—ST. PATRICK OF HEATHERDOWNS (1956), Revs. Dennis M. Metzger; Keith A. Stripe; Mrs. Marla Overholt, Pastoral Assoc.; Deacons Carl Braham; Joe Kest; Albert Righi; Joe Windham. In res., Rev. Michael G. Madden.
Res., 4201 Heatherdowns Blvd., 43614. Tel: 419-381-1540; Fax: 419-381-2727. [JC]
School—Tel: 419-381-1775; Fax: 419-389-1161.
Sisters 5; Lay Teachers 34; Students 777.
Catechesis/Religious Programs—Tel: 419-381-0240. Ms. Kathy Juhasz, D.R.E.
Students 170.

36—SS. PETER AND PAUL (1866) (Hispanic), Rev. Richard E. Notter.
Office: 728 S. St. Clair St., 43609. Tel: 419-241-5822; Fax: 419-241-5822.
School—Queen of Apostles. (Also serves Immaculate Conception Parish and St. James Parish). 235 Courtland, 43609. Tel: 419-241-7829; Fax: 419-241-4140.
Lay Teachers 9; Students 141.
Catechesis/Religious Programs—Students 130.

37—ST. PIUS X (1953), Revs. Dennis J. Kelsch, O.S.F.S.; Thomas A. Landcraff, O.S.F.S. In res., Rev. John L. Graden, O.S.F.S.
Res., 2929 Ilger Ave., 43606. Tel: 419-535-7672; Fax: 419-535-7810.
School—Tel: 419-535-7688.
Lay Teachers 12; Students 248.

38—ST. STANISLAUS (1912) (Polish), Rev. Gerald E. Knueven.
Mailing Address: 1416 Nebraska Ave., 43607. Tel: 419-241-6465.
Church—421 N. Detroit Ave., 43607. Tel: 419-255-6245.

39—ST. STEPHEN (1898) (Hungarian), Revs. Frank Eckart; Kenneth Morman.
Res., 1880 Genesee St., 43605. Tel: 419-691-1673. [JC]
School—2018 Consaul, 43605. Tel: 419-691-8760.
Lay Teachers 13; Students 195.

40—ST. TERESA. Consolidated with St. Ann to form St. Martin de Porres. See separate listing.

41—ST. THOMAS AQUINAS (1915), Rev. John R. Blaser.
Res., 729 White St., 43605-2719. Tel: 419-698-1519; Fax: 419-698-5269.
School—Tel: 419-691-4328; Fax: 419-691-4365.
Lay Teachers 10; Students 240.
Catechesis/Religious Programs—Students 110.

42—ST. VINCENT DE PAUL (1928), Most Rev. James R. Hoffman, Admin.; Deacon Gerald Ignatowski.
Res., 1035 Woodward Ave., 43608. Tel: 419-726-1448. [JC]
School—St. Elizabeth Seton School, 1030 Clay St., 43608. Tel: 419-726-4471.
Sisters 3; Lay Teachers 7; Students 212.
Catechesis/Religious Programs—Students 212.

OUTSIDE THE CITY OF TOLEDO

Alvada, Seneca Co., St. Peter (1854), Rev. Leonard A. Kistler, C.PP.S.; Deacon Lewis E. Reinhart.
Mailing Address: 41 N. Perry St., P.O. Box 89, New Riegel, 44853. Tel: 419-595-2567. [CEM]
Catechesis/Religious Programs—Students 60.

Antwerp, Paulding Co., St. Mary (1868), Rev. Herman F. Scherger; Deacon Robert L. Nighswander, Admin.
Res., 303 S. Monroe St., P.O. Box G, 45813. Tel: 419-258-8335. [JC]
Catechesis/Religious Programs—Tel: 419-258-2651.
Students 129.

Archbold, Fulton Co., St. Peter (1846), Rev. Gary M. Ferguson.
Res., 614 N. Defiance St., 43502. Tel: 419-446-9288; Fax: 419-446-9288. [CEM]
Catechesis/Religious Programs—Tel: 419-446-2150.
Students 136.

Assumption, Fulton Co., St. Mary of Assumption (1877), Rev. Lawrence F. Varney; Deacon Joseph Repka.
Res. & Mailing Address: 2649 U.S. 20, Swanton, 43558. Tel: 419-644-4014. [CEM]
School—Holy Trinity, 2639 U.S. 20, Swanton, 43558. Tel: 419-644-3971; Fax: 419-644-5018.
Lay Teachers 9; Students 138; Preschool 10.
Catechesis/Religious Programs—12829 Brint Rd., Berkey, 43504. Tel: 419-829-3717. Rosemary Ott, D.R.E.
Students 65.

Attica, Seneca Co., SS. Peter and Paul (1882), Rev. Joseph P. Szybka.
Res., P.O. Box 461, 44807. Tel: 419-426-3043; Fax: 419-426-3043. [CEM]
Church—14204 E. County Rd. 56, 44807.
Catechesis/Religious Programs—Students 106.

Bascom, Seneca Co., St. Patrick (1864), Rev. David R. Bruning.
Res., 6230 W. Tiffin, Box 226, 44809. Tel: 419-937-2715. [CEM]
Parish Hall: Tel: 419-937-2713.
Catechesis/Religious Programs—Students 164.

Bellevue, Huron Co., Immaculate Conception (1859), Rev. Robert A. Tucceri; Deacons Robert Swartz; Frank Klein.
Res., 231 E. Center St., 44811. Tel: 419-483-3417; Fax: 419-483-2585. [CEM]
School—Immaculate Conception School, Tel: 419-483-6066; Fax: 419-483-5059.
Sisters 2; Lay Teachers 20; Students 341.
Catechesis/Religious Programs—Students 210.

Bethlehem, Richland Co., Sacred Heart of Jesus (1833), Rev. Gary R. Walters; Deacons Leo Hartings; Stephen R. Keller.
Office: 5746 State Rte. 61 S., Shelby, 44875. Tel: 419-342-2797. [CEM]
School—Tel: 419-683-1697.
Lay Teachers 6; Students 67.

Bismark, Huron Co., St. Sebastian (1846) (German), Rev. William Hoyng, C.PP.S.
Res., 16209 E. C. Rd. #46, Bellevue, 44811. Tel: 419-483-3231. [CEM]
Church—5582 Bismark Rd., Bellevue, 44811.
Catechesis/Religious Programs—Students 90.

Blakeslee, Williams Co., St. Joseph (1865) (German), Rev. Frederick J. Duschl.
Res., P.O. Box 196, 43505. Tel: 419-272-2214. [CEM]
School—Tel: 419-272-2914.
Lay Teachers 6; Students 66.
Catechesis/Religious Programs—Students 44.

Bluffton, Allen Co., St. Mary (1866), Sr. Yvonne Fischer, O.S.F., Pastoral Leader; Rev. David J. Beck, Chap.
Mailing Address: 160 N. Spring, P.O. Box 92, 45817. Tel: 419-358-8631.
Catechesis/Religious Programs—Students 204.

Bono, Lucas Co., Our Lady of Mt. Carmel (1917), Sr. Marilyn Gottemoeller, R.S.M., Pastoral Leader; Rev. Charles Denny, Chap.
Res., 1105 Elliston Rd., Martin, 43445. Tel: 419-836-7681; Fax: 419-836-7681.
Catechesis/Religious Programs—Students 45.

Bowling Green, Wood Co., St. Aloysius (1862), Rev. Thomas Leyland; Deacons Jose Bautista; Ramon Llanas.
Res., 150 S. Enterprise, P.O. Box 485, 43402. Tel: 419-352-4195; Fax: 419-352-4738.
School—Tel: 419-352-8614; Fax: 419-352-4178. Mrs. Mary K. Williams, Prin.
Lay Teachers 13; Students 279.
Catechesis/Religious Programs—Tel: 419-352-1139.
Students 270.

St. Thomas More University Parish (1967), Sr. Mary Kuhlman, O.S.F., Pastoral Leader; Rev. Richard J. Saelzler. In res., Revs. Paul Mueller; Joseph Weigman.
Res., 425 Thurstin, 43402. Tel: 419-352-7555; 255-3609; Fax: 419-352-7557.

Bryan, Williams Co., St. Patrick (1857), Rev. Charles F. Ritter; Deacons Dennis Jackson; Ignacio Garza; Tom Dominique.
Res., 704 S. Portland, 43506. Tel: 419-636-1044; Fax: 419-636-5054.
School—Tel: 419-636-3592.
Lay Teachers 12; Students 155.
Catechesis/Religious Programs—Tel: 419-636-8771.
Students 198.

Bucyrus, Crawford Co., Holy Trinity (1865) (German), Rev. Dennis A. Schroeder.
Res., 760 Tiffin Rd., 44820. Tel: 419-562-1346; Fax: 419-562-2784. [CEM]
School—Tel: 419-562-2741.
Lay Teachers 12; Students 213.
Catechesis/Religious Programs—Tel: 419-562-2645.
Students 170.

Carey, Wyandot Co., Our Lady of Consolation, Basilica-National Shrine (1867), Revs. Peter Damian Massengill, O.F.M.Conv.; Benjamin Knopp, O.F.M.Conv.; Alfred J. Sartor, O.F.M.Conv.; Bros. Andrew Bramanti, O.F.M.Conv.; Bryan Hoban, O.F.M.Conv.; Joseph Candel, O.F.M.Conv.; Deacons Arden Harold Nye; Jim Kitzler.
Res., 315 W. Clay St., 43316. Tel: 419-396-7107; Fax: 419-396-3355. [CEM]
School—Tel: 419-396-6166.
Lay Teachers 10; Students 173.
Catechesis/Religious Programs—Students 115.
Mission—Salem Township, Wyandot Co., St. Joseph. [CEM] Deacon Floyd Derr.

Cecil, Paulding Co., Immaculate Conception (1879), Rev. Herman F. Scherger; Deacon David Laker Tel: 419-899-2479.
Res., Rte. 2, 21706 State Rte. 114, Cloverdale, 45827. Tel: 419-488-3563. [CEM]
Church—Stratford St., 45821. Tel: 419-399-5644.

Cloverdale, Putnam Co., St. Barbara (1898) (German), Rev. Christopher P. Vasko, J.C.L.
Res., 160 Main St., P.O. Box 8, 45827. Tel: 419-488-2391; Fax: 419-488-2390. [CEM]

Clyde, Sandusky Co., St. Mary (1890), Rev. Peter V. Zafe; Deacon Tito Ollervides.
Res., 609 Vine St., 43410. Tel: 419-547-9610. [CEM]
School—615 Vine St., 43410. Tel: 419-547-9687. Sr. Rita Rogier, Prin.
Sisters 1; Lay Teachers 8; Students 147.
Catechesis/Religious Programs—Sr. Bonnie Smith, D.R.E.
Students 108.

Columbus Grove, Putnam Co., St. Anthony of Padua (1912) (German), Rev. Keith J. McCormack.
Res., 512 W. Sycamore St., 45830. Tel: 419-659-2263. [CEM]
School—Tel: 419-659-2103; Fax: 419-659-2974.
Sisters of the Most Precious Blood 3; Lay Teachers 12; Students 225.
Catechesis/Religious Programs—Students 148.

Continental, Putnam Co., St. John the Baptist (1907), Rev. Christopher P. Vasko, J.C.L., Admin.; Deacon Joseph Heeter.
203 E. Elm St., P.O. Box 368, 45831. Tel: 419-596-4319; Fax: 419-488-2390. [JC]

Crestline, Crawford Co., St. Joseph (1861) (German), Rev. Gary R. Walters; Deacons Joseph Burkhart; William Horning; William Rall.
Res., 331 N. Thoman St., 44827. Tel: 419-683-2015. [CEM]
School—333 N. Thoman St., 44827. Tel: 419-683-1284; Fax: 419-683-1284.
Lay Teachers 7; Students 130.
Catechesis/Religious Programs—Students 80.

Cuba, Putnam Co., St. Isidore (1917), Rev. John Hoying, C.PP.S.; Deacon Robert Klausing.
Res., 312 N. Broad St., Kalida, 45853. Tel: 419-532-3431; Fax: 419-532-3437. [CEM]

Custar, Wood Co., St. Louis (1864), Rev. Paul Fahrbach; Sr. Dionne Sartor, O.S.F., Pastoral Assoc., Tel: 419-669-3920.
Res., 22792 Defiance Pike, 43511. Tel: 419-669-2845. [CEM][JC]
School—22676 Defiance Pike, 43511-9716. Tel: 419-669-2878. Sue Hammer, Prin.
Sisters of St. Francis 1; Lay Teachers 5; Students 57.

Cygnet, Wood Co., Sacred Heart (1890), Sr. Betty Glemboski, O.S.F.S., Pastoral Leader.
Mailing Address: 115 E. Cherry St., North Baltimore, 45872-1134. Tel: 419-257-2319.
Church—Bradford St., 43413.

Defiance, Defiance Co., St. John the Evangelist (1850), Rev. George E. Wenzinger; Deacons Chris Mendez; Charles Baker; Randall Redington; Donald Meyer.
Res., 510 Jackson St., 43512. Tel: 419-782-7121. [CEM]
School—Tel: 419-782-2136; Fax: 419-784-5410.
Lay Teachers 15; Students 160.
Catechesis/Religious Programs—Students 335.

St. Mary (1873), Very Rev. Edward J. Schleter; Deacon George Newton, Pastoral Assoc.
Res., 707 Jefferson Ave., 43512. Tel: 419-782-2776.
School—(Grades PreK-6). Tel: 419-782-2751.
Lay Teachers 11; Students 218.
Catechesis/Religious Programs—Students 501.

Delphos, Allen Co., St. John the Evangelist (1844) (German), Revs. Thomas Gorman; Daniel Borgelt; Joyce Meyer, Pastoral Assoc.
Res., 331 E. Second St., 45833. Tel: 419-695-4050; Fax: 419-695-4060. [CEM]
School—Tel: 419-692-8561; Fax: 419-692-8561.
Sisters of Notre Dame 5; Lay Teachers 34; Students 722.
High School—Tel: 419-692-5371; Fax: 419-692-5371.
Sisters 2; Lay Teachers 20; Students 309.
Catechesis/Religious Programs—Tel: 419-692-1286.
Students 207.

Deshler, Henry Co., Immaculate Conception (1871), Rev. Paul Fahrbach; Sr. Dionne Sartor, O.S.F.T., Pastoral Assoc., Tel: 419-669-3920.
Mailing Address: 230 Allendale Ave., 43516. Tel: 419-278-3686.
Res., 22767 Defiance Pike, Custar, 43511. Tel: 419-669-3920.
Catechesis/Religious Programs—Students 70.

Edgerton, Williams Co., St. Mary (1865), Rev. Thomas E. Oedy; Deacon Roy Sanders.
Res., 133 Bement St., P.O. Box 355, 43517. Tel: 419-298-2932. [CEM]
School—Tel: 419-298-2531.
Sisters of St. Francis 1; Lay Teachers 6; Students 111.
Catechesis/Religious Programs—Tel: 419-298-3350.
Students 100.

Fayette, Fulton Co., Our Lady of Mercy (1943), Rev. James J. Holmer.
Res., Box 429, 43521. Tel: 419-237-2441.
Church—409 E. Main St., 43521.
Catechesis/Religious Programs—14691 E. Camden Rd., Waldron, MI 49288. Tel: 517-286-6496.
Students 84.

Findlay, Hancock Co., St. Michael (1834), Revs. Martin Nassr; Douglas Taylor; Ronald A. Schock; Deacons Robert Billmaier; Dorsey Hazelton; David Sadler; John Zoll.
Mailing Address: 422 Western Ave., 45840. Tel: 419-422-2646. [CEM]
School—Tel: 419-422-2512.
Lay Teachers 32; Students 583.
Catechesis/Religious Programs—Tel: 419-423-2123. Geri Leibfarth, D.R.E.
Students 425.

Fort Jennings, Putnam Co., St. Joseph (1848) (German), Rev. Michael Schelling.
Res., 135 Water St., P.O. Box 68, 45844-0068. Tel: 419-286-2132. [CEM]
Catechesis/Religious Programs—Tel: 419-286-2019.
Students 376.

Fostoria, Seneca Co., St. Wendelin (1858), Revs. Daniel J. Ring; Jose Corral; Kent Kaufman.
Res., 222 N. Wood St., P.O. Box 836, 44830. Tel: 419-435-1875; Fax: 419-435-7826. [CEM]
School—Tel: 419-435-1809.
Sisters of Notre Dame 1; Lay Teachers 22; Students 432.
High School—Tel: 419-435-8144; Fax: 419-436-4042.
Sisters 1; Lay Teachers 23; Students 234.
Catechesis/Religious Programs—Tel: 419-435-6681. Sr. Madeleva, O.S.F.S.
Students 242.

Fremont, Sandusky Co.,

1—Sacred Heart, (1956), Rev. Mark J. Herzog; Sr. M. Dean Pfahler, S.N.D., Pastoral Assoc.; Deacon Jose Sanchez.
Res., 550 Smith Rd., 43420. Tel: 419-332-7339; Fax: 419-332-9808. [JC]
School—(Grades K-8). Tel: 419-332-7102; Fax: 419-332-1542.
Sisters 3; Lay Teachers 18; Students 277.
Catechesis/Religious Programs—Students 117.

2—St. Ann, (1843), Rev. Gerald J. Chmiel; Deacons Alfredo Diaz; Norbert Wethington.
Res., 1021 W. State St., 43420. Tel: 419-332-7472; Fax: 419-332-2461. [JC]
School—Tel: 419-332-2461.
Lay Teachers 15; Students 185.
Catechesis/Religious Programs—Students 150.

3—St. Casimir, (1915) (Polish), Rev. Robert Weithman; Deacon Tom Ackerman.
Res., 537 Lime St., 43420. Tel: 419-332-1157. [JC]

4—St. Joseph, (1857) (German), Very Rev. Ronald J. LeJeune; Revs. Patrick Rohen; Dennis P. Hartigan; Deacons William Snyder; James Hammer.
Res., 709 Croghan St., 43420. Tel: 419-334-2638; Fax: 419-334-6929. [CEM][JC]
School—Tel: 419-332-5161; Fax: 419-332-7299.
Sisters 2; Lay Teachers 18; Students Grades (K-8) 336; Preschool 34.
Catechesis/Religious Programs—120 N. Clover St., 43420. Tel: 419-332-7367. Sr. Lucille Kime, S.N.D., D.R.E.
Students 190.

Frenchtown, Seneca Co., St. Nicholas (1857) (German-French), Rev. Alfred J. Sartor, O.F.M.Conv.
Res., 315 W. Clay St., Carey, 43316. Tel: 419-396-7107; Fax: 419-396-3355. [CEM]
Catechesis/Religious Programs—Students 151.

Galion, Crawford Co., St. Joseph (1853), Rev. Anthony A. Borgia; Deacons Kevin Wintersteller; Alfred Sisson; Gregory Kirk; Raymond Lyons, Jr.
Res., 135 N. Liberty St., 44833. Tel: 419-468-2884. [CEM]
School—(Grades PreK-8). Tel: 419-468-5436; Fax: 419-468-3611.
Sisters 3; Lay Teachers 9; Students 243.
Catechesis/Religious Programs—Students 155.

Genoa, Ottawa Co., Our Lady of Lourdes (1856), Rev. Thomas S. Quinn; Deacons William Perez; Phillip Dazley.
Church—204 Main St., 43430. Tel: 419-855-8501.
Catechesis/Religious Programs—Tel: 419-855-7181.
Students 305.

Gibsonburg, Sandusky Co., St. Michael Church (1892), Rev. Frederick J. Schill; Deacon Rene Gonzalez.
Res., 317 E. Madison St., 43431. Tel: 419-637-2255. [CEM]
Catechesis/Religious Programs—Students 223.

Glandorf, Putnam Co., St. John the Baptist (1834) (German), Rev. Harold C. Brown, C.PP.S.; Sr. Carol Pothast, Pastoral Assoc.; Deacon Robert M. Burwell.
Res., 109 Main St., Box 48, 45848. Tel: 419-538-6928; Fax: 419-538-6147. [CEM][JC]
Catechesis/Religious Programs—Tel: 419-538-6335.
Students 660.

Hamler, Henry Co., St. Paul (1886), Rev. Robert J. Kill; Deacon Donald Badenhop.
Res., 316 Chicago Ave., Holgate, 43527. Tel: 419-264-3321. [CEM]
Catechesis/Religious Programs—Students 66.

Hicksville, Defiance Co., St. Michael (1878). Attended by Edgerton. Rev. Thomas E. Oedy; Deacon Walter Conkle.
Mailing Address: P.O. Box 52, 43526. Tel: 419-542-8202.
Res., 133 W. Bement St., P.O. Box 355, Edgerton, 43517. Tel: 419-298-2932.
Catechesis/Religious Programs—Students 178.

Holgate, Henry Co., St. Mary (1886), Rev. Robert J. Kill; Deacon LaVon Mack.
Res., 316 Chicago Ave., 43527. Tel: 419-264-3321. [CEM]
Catechesis/Religious Programs—Students 66.

Huron, Erie Co., St. Peter (1888), Rev. Edward J. Littelmann; Deacons John Barrett; Jack Busam.
Res., 430 Main St., 44839. Tel: 419-433-5725; Fax: 419-433-7225. [JC]
School—Tel: 419-433-4640; Fax: 419-433-2118.
Lay Teachers 11; Students 155.
Catechesis/Religious Programs—Students 323.

Junction, Paulding Co., St. Mary (1846), Rev. David D. Tscherne; Deacon Richard Carnahan.
Mailing Address: 05480 Moser Rd., Rte. 3, Defiance, 43512. Tel: 419-393-2890.
Catechesis/Religious Programs—Tel: 419-594-2615.
Students 57.

Kalida, Putnam Co., St. Michael (1878), Rev. John Hoying, C.PP.S.; Deacon Robert Klausing.
Office: 312 N. Broad St., 45853. Tel: 419-532-3474; Fax: 419-532-3474.
Res., 206 N. Broad St., 45853. Tel: 419-532-3431; Fax: 419-532-3437. [CEM]
Catechesis/Religious Programs—Tel: 419-532-3494. Sr. Mary Louisa Heinl, S.N.D., D.R.E.
Students 610.
Mission—Cuba, Putnam Co., St. Isidore. [CEM]

Kansas, Seneca Co., St. James (1890), Rev. Omer Rethinger.
Res., c/o 875 State Rte. 635, Helena, 43435. Tel: 419-638-3041.
Parish Office—Tel: 419-638-3042.

Kelley's Island, Erie Co., St. Michael (1861), Rev. Nicholas J. Cunningham.
Mailing Address: P.O. Box 490, 43438-0490. Tel: 419-746-2481.

Kirby, Wyandot Co., St. Mary (1861), Rev. William D. Bodart; Sr. Barbara Jean Miller, Pastoral Assoc.
Res., 225 N. Eighth St., Upper Sandusky, 43351. Tel: 419-294-1268. [CEM]
Catechesis/Religious Programs—Students 101.

Landeck, Allen Co., St. John Baptist (1866), Rev. John W. Fleck.
Res., 14755 Landeck Rd., Rte. 1, Delphos, 45833. Tel: 419-692-0636. [CEM]
Catechesis/Religious Programs—Tel: 419-695-2141.
Students 129.
Mission—Spencerville, Allen Co., St. Patrick, 500 S. Canal, Spencerville, 45887. Tel: 419-695-4138.

Leipsic, Putnam Co., St. Mary (1873), Rev. John K. Joseph, C.M.I. (India).
Res., 318 State St., 45856. Tel: 419-943-2952. [CEM]
School—Tel: 419-943-2801.
Sisters of Notre Dame 3; Lay Teachers 8; Students 180.
Catechesis/Religious Programs—Students 272.

Lexington, Richland Co., Resurrection (1969), Rev. Stanley S. Szybka; Deacon James Hostutler.
Res., 2600 Lexington Ave., 44904. Tel: 419-884-0060; Fax: 419-884-0261.
Catechesis/Religious Programs—Students 336.

Liberty, Seneca Co., St. Andrew (1834), Rev. David R. Bruning.
Church—State Rte. 635 N., P.O. Box 226, Bascom, 44809. Tel: 419-937-2613.
Res., 6230 W. Tiffin St., Bascom, 44809. Tel: 419-937-2715. [CEM]
Catechesis/Religious Programs—Students 70.

Lima, Allen Co.,

1—St. Charles Borromeo, (1953), Very Rev. David M. Ross; Rev. Michael G. Dandurand.
Res., 2200 W. Elm, 45805. Tel: 419-228-7635; Fax: 419-229-2835. [JC]
School—Tel: 419-222-2536; Fax: 419-222-8720.
Lay Teachers 40; Students 717.
Catechesis/Religious Programs—Students 295.

2—St. Gerard, (1916), Very Rev. Denis J. Sweeney, C.SS.R.; Revs. Stephen S. Haynes, C.Ss.R.; Louis A. Olive, C.Ss.R.; Deacon Elias Pina. In res., Revs. Thomas J. Barrett, C.Ss.R.; Andrew Costello, C.Ss.R.
Res., 240 W. Robb Ave., 45801. Tel: 419-224-3080; Fax: 419-225-2231.
School—(Grades PreK-8). Tel: 419-222-0431; Fax: 419-224-6580.
Ursuline Sisters 1; Lay Teachers 19; Students 317.
Catechesis/Religious Programs—Students 275.
Stations—Allen Inn, Tel: 419-221-1346; Fax: 419-221-1125; Lima Manor, Tel: 419-227-2611; Fax: 419-224-4755; Allen Correctional Institute, Tel: 419-224-8000; Lima Correctional Institute, Tel: 419-225-8060; Oakwood Correctional Institute, Tel: 419-225-8052.

3—St. John the Evangelist, (1901), Rev. David J. Beck; Deacon Richard Gleason.
Res., 781 S. Main St., 45804. Tel: 419-223-4476. [JC]

4—St. Rose, (1856), Rev. J. Norbert Howe. In res., Rev. Todd Dominique.
Res., 479 N. West St., 45801-4294. Tel: 419-222-5521; Fax: 419-228-8439. [JC]
School—Tel: 419-223-6361; Fax: 419-222-2032. Mrs. Janet A. Swallow, Prin.
Sisters 1; Lay Teachers 10; Students 125.
Catechesis/Religious Programs—Students 75.

Lyons, Fulton Co., Our Lady of Fatima (1946), Rev. James J. Holmer; Deacon Gene Betz.
Mailing Address: & Church—P.O. Box 112, 43533. Tel: 419-923-3170.
Res., P.O. Box 429, Fayette, 43521. Tel: 419-237-2441. [CEM]
Catechesis/Religious Programs—1-8645-S, 43533. Helen Blanchong, D.R.E.
Students 112.

Mansfield, Richland Co., St. Mary (1949), Rev. Gregory R. Hite; Deacons Allan D. Kopp; Russell Shoemaker.
Res., 1630 Ashland Rd., 44905. Tel: 419-589-5464; Fax: 419-589-7085. [JC]
School—Tel: 419-589-2114; Fax: 419-589=2114.
Lay Teachers 9; Students 110.
Catechesis/Religious Programs—Students 91.

St. Peter (1844), Revs. Herbert F. Weber; James E. Halleron; Richard Kennedy.
Res., 54 S. Mulberry St., 44902. Tel: 419-524-2572; Fax: 419-522-2553. [CEM]
School—63 S. Mulberry St., 44902. Tel: 419-524-3351.
Sisters of St. Francis of Mary Immaculate (Joliet, IL) 1; Lay Teachers 23; Students 408.
High School—104 W. First St., 44903. Tel: 419-524-0979.
Sisters of St. Francis of Mary Immaculate (Joliet, IL) 1; Lay Teachers 26; Students 210.
Catechesis/Religious Programs—Students 182.

Marblehead, Ottawa Co., St. Joseph (1867) (Slovak), Rev. James E. Brown.
Res., 802 Barclay, 43440-2101. Tel: 419-798-4177; Fax: 419-798-4260. [CEM][JC]
Catechesis/Religious Programs—113 James St., 43440. Tel: 419-798-5543.
Students 115.

Marygrove, Lucas Co., Immaculate Conception (1840), Rev. Bruce Farmer, Chap.; Deacon David Vrooman, Pastoral Leader.
Res., 1750 Raab Rd., Swanton, 43558. Tel: 419-829-3451. [CEM]
Parish Office: 11383 Sylvania, Berkey, 43504. Tel: 419-829-5421.
Catechesis/Religious Programs—Holy Trinity School (Consolidated), 2639 U.S. Rte. 20, Swanton, 43558. Tel: 419-644-3971.
Students 250.

Marysdale, Defiance Co., Immaculate Conception (1873), Rev. William J. Martin.
Res., 16166 Speaker Rd., Sherwood, 43556. Tel: 419-899-2549. [CEM]
Catechesis/Religious Programs—Students 68.

Marywood, Seneca Co., St. Michael's (1839) (German), Rev. William Hoyng, C.PP.S.
Res., 16209 E.County Rd. 46, Bellevue, 44811. Tel: 419-483-3231. [CEM]
Catechesis/Religious Programs—Students 88.
Shrine—Sorrowful Mother. For further details see listing under Retreat Houses. Rev. Robert Kunisch, C.PP.S., Dir.

Maumee, Lucas Co., St. Joseph (1841), Revs. Jeffery P. Sikorski; Kenneth J. Lill; Deacons John Campbell; Kenneth Dickey; Richard Heban; Edward Irelan; Terry McCauley; Paul Morris; Sr. Adrian Walsh, O.S.F., Pastoral Assoc.
Res., 104 W. Broadway, 43537. Tel: 419-893-4848; Fax: 419-891-6968. [CEM]
School—Tel: 419-893-3304; Fax: 419-891-6969.
Lay Teachers 20; Students 351.
Catechesis/Religious Programs—Tel: 419-893-7025.
Students 415.

Milan, Erie Co., St. Anthony (1862), Rev. James A. Walsh.
Res., 145 Center St., P.O. Box 1200, 44846-1200. Tel: 419-499-4274. [CEM]

Catechesis/Religious Programs—Tel: 419-499-4300.
Students 170.

Miller City, Putnam Co., St. Nicholas (1888), Rev. A. Robert DeSloover.
Mailing Address: Box 36, 45864. Tel: 419-876-3481. [CEM]
Catechesis/Religious Programs—Kathy Degler, D.R.E.
Students 279.
Sister Parish—Holy Family, New Cleveland, Tel: 419-876-3155.

Millersville, Sandusky Co., St. Mary (1859), Rev. Omer Rethinger; Deacon George P. Miller.
Res., 875 State Rte. 635, Helena, 43435. Tel: 419-638-3041. [CEM]
Parish Office—Tel: 419-638-3042.
School—Tel: 419-638-3631.
Lay Teachers 6; Students 70.
Catechesis/Religious Programs—Students 65.
Mission—Kansas, Seneca Co., St. James, 875 SR635 Helena, 43435.

Monroeville, Huron Co., St. Joseph (1861), Rev. Lawrence C. Scharf.
Res., 66 Chapel St., P.O. Box 338, 44847. Tel: 419-465-4142; Fax: 419-465-2319. [CEM]
School—Tel: 419-465-2625.
Sisters of Notre Dame 3; Lay Teachers 10; Students 202.

Montpelier, Williams Co., Sacred Heart (1911), Rev. Frederick J. Duschl; Deacon Ralph Dominique.
Mailing Address: P.O. Box 196, Blakeslee, 43505. Tel: 419-485-5914.
Res., 220 S. East Ave., 43543.
Catechesis/Religious Programs—Students 120.

Napoleon, Henry Co., St. Augustine (1856), Rev. T. Patrick Scharf; Deacons Peter Calvillo; Louis Recker; Robert Bost; Bruce Buckmaster.
Office: 210 E. Clinton St., 43545. Tel: 419-592-7656; Fax: 419-592-6316. [CEM]
School—722 Monroe St., 43545. Tel: 419-592-3641.
Lay Teachers 10; Students 145.
Catechesis/Religious Programs—Students 194.

New Bavaria, Henry Co., Sacred Heart of Jesus (1893) (German), Rev. Stephen Stanbery; Deacon Kenneth Klear.
Res., 13-779 Road Y, Rte. 1, 43548. Tel: 419-653-4157. [CEM]
Catechesis/Religious Programs—Tel: 419-635-4121.
Students 137.
Mission—North Creek, Putnam Co., St. Joseph, 13-779 Rd. Y, Rte. 1, 43548.

New Cleveland, Putnam Co., Holy Family, Rev. A. Robert DeSloover.
Res., c/o Box 36, Miller City, 45864. Tel: 419-876-3481. [CEM]
Sister Parish—St. Nicholas, Miller City.
Catechesis/Religious Programs—Students 157.

New London, Huron Co., Our Lady of Lourdes (1853), Rev. Robert Haas.
Res., 18 Park Ave., 44851. Tel: 419-929-4401. [CEM]
Catechesis/Religious Programs—Students 137.

New Riegel, Seneca Co., St. Boniface (1834), Rev. Leonard A. Kistler, C.PP.S.; Deacon Lewis E. Reinhart.
Res., 41 N. Perry St., P.O. Box 89, 44853. Tel: 419-595-2567. [CEM]
Catechesis/Religious Programs—Students 236.

New Washington, Crawford Co., St. Bernard (1844), Rev. Robert L. Dendinger.
Res., 412 W. Mansfield, 44854. Tel: 419-492-2295. [CEM]
School—Tel: 419-492-2693.
Sisters 3; Lay Teachers 8; Students 171.
Catechesis/Religious Programs—Tel: 419-492-2973.
Students 87.

North Auburn, Crawford Co., Mother of Sorrows (1879), Rev. Robert L. Dendinger.
Mailing Address: 422 W. Mansfield, New Washington, 44854. Tel: 419-492-2295. [CEM]

North Baltimore, Wood Co., Our Lady of the Miraculous Medal (1891), Sr. Betty Glemboski, O.S.F.S., Pastoral Leader.
Res., 115 E. Cherry St., 45872-1134. Tel: 419-257-2319.
Catechesis/Religious Programs—Students 84.
Mission—Cygnet, Wood Co., Sacred Heart, Bradford St., Cygnet, 43413.

North Creek, Putnam Co., St. Joseph (1887) (German), Rev. Stephen Stanbery; Deacon Kenneth Klear.
Res., c/o 13-779 Road Y, Rte. 1, New Bavaria, 43548. Tel: 419-653-4157. [CEM]

Norwalk, Huron Co., St. Mary, Mother of the Redeemer (1860) (Irish), Rev. Nelson Beaver; Deacon Jack Bleile.
Res., 38 W. League St., 44857. Tel: 419-668-2005; Fax: 419-663-6234. [CEM]
School—Tel: 419-668-8780; Fax: 419-663-5770.
Sisters of Notre Dame 2; Lay Teachers 11; Students 276.
Catechesis/Religious Programs—77 State St., 44857. Tel: 419-668-8480; Fax: 419-668-3269.
Students 55.

St. Paul (1876) (German), Revs. Herbert Willman; Thomas McQuillen; Krzysztof Kardzis (Poland). In res., Rev. Harvey M. Keller, (Retired).
Res., 91 E. Main St., 44857. Tel: 419-668-6044; Fax: 419-663-5770. [CEM]
School—Tel: 419-668-6091.
Sisters of Notre Dame 1; Lay Teachers 21; Students 582.
High School—Tel: 419-668-3005; Fax: 419-668-6417.
Priests 1; Sisters 1; Lay Teachers 24; Students 290.
Catechesis/Religious Programs—Julie Wise, D.R.E. Students 107.

Oak Harbor, Ottawa Co., St. Boniface (1866), Rev. James E. Peiffer, Admin.
Res., 215 Church St., 43449. Tel: 419-898-1389; Fax: 419-898-2212.
School—Tel: 419-898-1340.
Lay Teachers 6; Students 70.
Catechesis/Religious Programs—Students 208.

Oregon, Lucas Co., St. Ignatius (1883) (Territorial), Rev. Albert B. Ceranowski.
Res., 212 N. Stadium Rd., 43616. Tel: 419-693-1150; Fax: 419-693-0063. [CEM]
Catechesis/Religious Programs—Tel: 419-693-7662.
Students 390.

Ottawa, Putnam Co., SS. Peter and Paul (1868), Revs. Thomas Hemm, C.PP.S.; Ralph Schneider, C.PP.S.; Deacon Jim Rump.
Res., 307 N. Locust St., 45875. Tel: 419-523-5216. [CEM]
School—Tel: 419-523-3697.
Lay Teachers 18; Students 350.
Catechesis/Religious Programs—320 N. Locust St., Tel: 419-523-5078.
Students 241.

Ottoville, Putnam Co., Immaculate Conception (1848), Rev. Sylvan W. Obergefell; Deacons Leon Turnwald; Jose Flores; Walter Miller. In res., Rev. Roger D. Bonifas.
Res., 189 Church St., Box 296, 45876. Tel: 419-453-3513; Fax: 419-453-3513. [CEM]
Catechesis/Religious Programs—Tel: 419-453-3702.
Students 535.

Paulding, Paulding Co., St. Joseph (1894), Rev. Cleo Schmenk; Deacon Francis Koenn.
Res., 314 N. Main St., 45879. Tel: 419-399-2576; Fax: 419-399-2577.
Catechesis/Religious Programs—Tel: 419-399-5668.
Students 179.

Payne, Paulding Co., St. John the Baptist (1892), Rev. Antony Cnackalackal; Deacons Donald Coughlin; David Jordan.
Res., P.O. Box 38, 203 W. Townline, 45880. Tel: 419-263-2469. [CEM]
School—Tel: 419-263-2114.
Sisters of St. Francis 2; Lay Teachers 4; Students 88.
Catechesis/Religious Programs—Students 75.

Perrysburg, Wood Co., St. Rose (1861), Revs. John A. Thomas; Charles E. Singler; Deacons Lawrence Tiefenbach; Ken Cappelletty; Ray Kemer.
Res., 215 E. Front St., 43551-2254. Tel: 419-874-2217; Fax: 419-874-7462. [CEM]
School—217 E. Front St., 43551-2254. Tel: 419-874-5631; Fax: 419-874-1002.
Lay Teachers 25; Students 447.
Catechesis/Religious Programs—Tel: 419-874-9474. Sr. Jeanne Marie Holtz, O.S.U, D.R.E.
Students 491.

Peru, Huron Co., St. Alphonsus Liguori (1828) (German), Rev. Nelson Beaver; Deacon George Stepanic.
Res., 38 W. League St., Norwalk, 44857. Tel: 419-668-2005; Fax: 419-663-6234. [CEM]
Catechesis/Religious Programs—1360 Settlement Dr., Norwalk, 44857. Tel: 419-668-5030; Fax: 419-663-5770.
Students 66.

Plymouth, Huron Co., St. Joseph (1864), Sr. Joann Brodman, O.S.F., Pastoral Leader; Rev. Paul E. Perry, Chap.
Res., 117 Sandusky St., 44865. Tel: 419-687-4611.

Port Clinton, Ottawa Co., Immaculate Conception (1861), Rev. Raymond Ensman; Sr. Mary Jane Fisher, R.S.M., Pastoral Assoc.
414 Madison St., 43452-1922. Tel: 419-734-4004; Fax: 419-734-3477.
School—109 W. Fourth St., 43452. Tel: 419-734-3315.
Sisters of Notre Dame 1; Lay Teachers 9; Students 160.
Catechesis/Religious Programs—Students 140.

Providence, Lucas Co., St. Patrick (1842) (Irish), Rev. F. Anthony Gallagher; Brenda Krukowski, Vol. Pastoral Min.
Mailing Address: 14010 U.S. 24, Grand Rapids, 43522-9678. Tel: 419-832-5215. [CEM]

Put-In-Bay, Ottawa Co., Mother of Sorrows, Rev. Nicholas J. Cunningham, Chap.
Mailing Address: Box 179, 43456. Tel: 419-285-2741.

Reed, Seneca Co., Assumption (1867) (German), Rev. William Hoyng, C.PP.S.
Res., 16209 E. County Rd. 46, Bellevue, 44811. Tel: 419-483-3231. [CEM]
Church—15030 E. Twp. Rd. 126, Bellevue, 44811.
Catechesis/Religious Programs—Students 68.

Republic, Seneca Co., St. Aloysius (1879), Rev. Joseph P. Szybka; Deacon Urban Arbogast.
Res., 211 East St., Box 250, 44867. Tel: 419-585-4411; Fax: 419-585-4411.
Catechesis/Religious Programs—Students 105.

Richfield Center, Lucas Co., St. Elizabeth of Hungary (1914), Rev. Bruce L. Farmer, Chap.; Deacon David S. Vrooman, Pastoral Leader.
Offices: 11383 Sylvania Ave., Berkey, 43504. Tel: 419-829-5421.
Res., 1750 N. Raab Rd., Swanton, 43558. Tel: 419-829-3451. [CEM]
Catechesis/Religious Programs—Holy Trinity School (Consolidated). See Immaculate Conception, Marygrove for details.

Rossford, Wood Co., All Saints (1990). Consolidated of SS. Cyril and Methodius and St. Mary Magdalene. Very Rev. Joseph Steinbauer; Deacons Jerry Nellett; Rick Vascik; Susan VanHersett, Pastoral Assoc.
Church—721 Dixie Hwy., 43460. Tel: 419-666-1393.
Res., 124 Maple St., 43460. Tel: 419-666-5633.
School—630 Lime City Rd., 43460. Tel: 419-661-2070; Fax: 419-661-2077.
Sisters 6; Lay Teachers 12; Students 281.
Catechesis/Religious Programs—Students 230.

St. Michael's Ridge, Defiance Co., St. Michael (1861), Rev. David D. Tscherne; Sr. Margie Verhoff, C.D.P., Pastoral Assoc. & D.R.E.
Res., 05480 Moser Rd., Rte. 3, Defiance, 43512. Tel: 419-497-2161. [CEM]
Catechesis/Religious Programs—Tel: 419-497-3122.
Students 153.

St. Stephen, Seneca Co., St. Stephen (1844), Rev. Joseph P. Szybka; Deacon Robert Felter.
Res., 12087 E. Township Rd. 44, Attica, 44807. Tel: 419-426-1145; Fax: 419-426-1145. [CEM]

Salem Twp., Wyandot Co., St. Joseph (1849) (English), Revs. Damian Massengill, O.F.M.Conv.; Benjamin Knopp, O.F.M.Conv.; Deacon Floyd Derr.
Res., 315 Clay St., Carey, 43316. Tel: 419-396-7107. [CEM]
Mission—Carey, Wyandot Co., O.L.C., Carey, 43316.

Sandusky, Erie Co., Holy Angels (1840), Rev. Nicholas Weibl; Sr. Mary de Porres Westrick, S.N.D., Pastoral Assoc. In res., Rev. William L. Richter, (Retired).
Res., 1605 W. Jefferson Ave., 44870. Tel: 419-625-3698; Fax: 419-625-5183. [JC]
School—Tel: 419-626-3075.
Lay Teachers 12; Students 166.
Catechesis/Religious Programs—Mary A. Zang, D.R.E.
Students 170.

St. Mary (1855) (German), Revs. Philip S. Feltman; Joseph T. Poggemeyer; Deacon Joseph A. Singler.
Res., 429 Central Ave., 44870. Tel: 419-625-7465; Fax: 419-626-2834. [CEM][JC 3]
School—530 Decatur St., 44870. Tel: 419-626-1648.
Sisters of Notre Dame 2; Lay Teachers 24; Students 450.
High School—410 W. Jefferson St., 44870. Tel: 419-626-1892; Fax: 419-621-2252.
Sisters of Notre Dame 2; Priests 4; Lay Teachers 25; Students 296.
Catechesis/Religious Programs—Tel: 419-626-0614.
Students 279.

SS. Peter and Paul (1866), Revs. Franklin P. Kehres; Mark E. Davis; Deacons Milton Opper; Raymond Middaugh; John Downey; Sr. Martha Bertke, C.PP.S., Pastoral Assoc.
Res., 510 Columbus Ave., 44870. Tel: 419-625-6655; Fax: 419-625-6576. [CEM][JC]
School—Tel: 419-625-1017.
Sisters of St. Francis of the Congregation of Our Lady of Lourdes 2; Lay Teachers 16; Students 287.
Catechesis/Religious Programs—J. Michael Tynan, D.R.E.
Students 240.

Shelby, Richland Co., Most Pure Heart of Mary (1866) (German), Rev. John C. Missler; Deacons Harry L. Turner; Dennis Burkett.
Res., 29 West St., 44875. Tel: 419-347-2381. [CEM]
School—Tel: 419-342-2626; Fax: 419-347-2072.
Sisters 1; Lay Teachers 11; Students 250.
Catechesis/Religious Programs—Sr. Karen Elliott, C.PP.S., D.R.E.
Students 250.

Spencerville, Allen Co., St. Patrick (1858), Rev. John Fleck.
Res., 14755 Landeck Rd., Rte. 1, Delphos, 45833. Tel: 419-692-0636. [JC]
Catechesis/Religious Programs—Students 127.

Stryker, William Co., St. John the Evangelist (1861) (German-Hispanic), Rev. Gary M. Ferguson.
Res., c/o 614 N. Defiance St., Archbold, 43502. Tel: 419-682-1372.

Swanton, Fulton Co., St. Richard (1893), Rev. Daniel J. Zak; Beverly Bingle, Pastoral Assoc.; Deacon Timothy Worline.
Res., 333 Brookside Dr., 43558. Tel: 419-826-2791; Fax: 419-826-7256. [CEM]
School—Tel: 419-826-5041. Kathleen Gallagher, Prin.
Lay Teachers 10; Students 175.
Catechesis/Religious Programs—Students 220.

Sycamore, Wyandot Co., St. Pius X (1951), Revs. Frank A. Murd; William J. Rose; Deacon John Daniel.
Res., 85 S. Sandusky St., Tiffin, 44883-3098. Tel: 419-447-2087; Fax: 419-447-9940.

Sylvania, Lucas Co., St. Joseph (1873), Revs. Richard T. Wurzel; Joseph P. Cardone; Sr. Patricia Gist, C.PP.S.; Deacons Robert Bodette; William Ulmer.
Res., 5373 S. Main St., 43560. Tel: 419-885-5791; Fax: 419-882-5235. [CEM]
School—5411 S. Main St., 43560. Tel: 419-882-6670; Fax: 415-885-1990.
Sisters 1; Lay Teachers 38; Students 783.
Catechesis/Religious Programs—Tel: 419-885-2181.
Students 920.

The Bend, Defiance Co., St. Stephen (1855), Rev. William J. Martin.
Res., 16166 Speaker Rd., Rte. 1, Sherwood, 43556. Tel: 419-899-2549. [CEM]
Catechesis/Religious Programs—Students 71.
Mission—Marysdale, Defiance Co., Immaculate Conception, 16166 Speaker Rd., 43556.

Tiffin, Seneca Co., St. Joseph (1845), Rev. James K. Say; Deacon Daniel Scherger. In res., Rev. Msgr. Edward C. Dunn.
Res., 36 Melmore St., 44883-3098. Tel: 419-447-5848; Fax: 419-447-7580. [CEM]
School—357 S. Washington St., 44883. Tel: 419-447-5790.
Sisters 1; Lay Teachers 17; Students 400.
Catechesis/Religious Programs—Students 235.

St. Mary (1831), Very Rev. Francis A. Murd; Rev. William J. Rose; Sr. Maryann Drians, O.S.F., Pastoral Assoc.; Deacons Walter Beat; Robert Hartzell; Donald Worland. In res., Rev. G. Allan Fillman.
Res., 85 S. Sandusky St., 44883. Tel: 419-447-2087; Fax: 419-447-9940. [CEM]
School—75 S. Sandusky St., 44883. Tel: 419-447-5202; Fax: 419-447-0142.
Lay Teachers 23; Students 309; Preschool 84.
Catechesis/Religious Programs—Tel: 419-448-9341.
Students 271.

Upper Sandusky, Wyandot Co., St. Peter (1857), Rev. William D. Bodart.
Res., 225 N. 8th St., 43351. Tel: 419-294-1268. [CEM][JC]
School—Tel: 419-294-1395.
Sisters of Mercy 2; Lay Teachers 5; Students 198.
Catechesis/Religious Programs—Students 80.

Van Wert, Van Wert Co., St. Mary (1876), Rev. Joseph M. Schmelzer; Deacons Norbert Reinhart; Andrew McMahon.
Res., 601 Jennings Rd., 45891. Tel: 419-238-3979.
School—Tel: 419-238-5186.
Lay Teachers 7; Students 120.
Catechesis/Religious Programs—611 Jennings Rd., 45891. Tel: 419-238-3079. Mrs. Cherie Freewalt, D.R.E.
Students 185.

Vermilion, Erie Co., St. Mary (1851), Rev. Stephen J. Blum; Deacon John Hartman; Sr. Eve Marie Korzym, O.S.F., Pastoral Assoc.
Res., 731 Exchange St., P.O. Box 397, 44089. Tel: 216-967-8711; Fax: 216-967-8712. [JC]
School—5450 Ohio St., 44089. Tel: 216-967-7911.
Sisters 1; Lay Teachers 8; Students 194.
Catechesis/Religious Programs—Students 345.

Wakeman, Huron Co., St. Mary (1852) (Irish), Deacon John M. Kinder, Pastoral Admin.
Mailing Address: P.O. Box 276, 44889. Tel: 216-839-2023. [CEM]
Church—46 E. Main St., 44889. Tel: 216-839-2023.

Walbridge, Wood Co., St. Jerome (1962), Rev. William C. Parker.
Res., 300 Warner St., 43465. Tel: 419-666-2857; Fax: 419-661-2281.
School—(Grades PreK-8). Tel: 419-666-2855.
Sisters of St. Francis 1; Lay Teachers 13; Students 319.
Catechesis/Religious Programs—Students 289.

Wauseon, Fulton Co., St. Caspar (1850), Rev. Robert A. Holden; Deacons Juan Rodriguez; James Dominique; James Schmidt.
Res., 1205 N. Shoop Ave., 43567. Tel: 419-335-3656; Fax: 419-337-2413. [CEM]
Catechesis/Religious Programs—Tel: 419-337-2322.
Students 340.

Willard, Huron Co., St. Francis Xavier (1875), Rev. Paul E. Perry; Deacons Vincent Foos; Russell Niedermeier; Paul Jones.
Res., 21 W. Perry St., 44890. Tel: 419-935-1149; Fax: 419-933-6000. [CEM]
School—Tel: 419-935-4744.
Lay Teachers 7; Students 165.
Catechesis/Religious Programs—Students 150.

Chaplains of Public Institutions

TOLEDO. *St. Vincent Medical Center* 2213 Cherry St., 43608-2691. Tel: 419-321-3232. Rev. Joel Buchman.

LIMA. *St. Rita Hospital and Medical Center* 730 W. Market St., 45801. Rev. Vincent Hoying, C.PP.S.

MANSFIELD. *Mercy Hospital*. Vacant.

OREGON. *St. Charles Mercy Hospital* 2600 Navarre, 43616. Rev. Charles Denny.

SANDUSKY. *Soldiers and Sailors Home*. Rev. Bertrand J. Shenk, Res., 11911 Thomas Rd., Monroeville, 44847. Tel: 419-499-4395.

Special Assignment:
Reverend Fathers—
Sheperd, Raymond C., Toledo Diocesan Vicar for Priests
Yeager, Robert J., Diocesan Finance Management Conference

On Duty Outside the Diocese:
Reverend Fathers—
Brickner, Ronald J.
Hiltz, John T., 19767 Yorba Linda Blvd., Yorba Linda, CA 92686
Kummerer, Timothy, All Souls Catholic Mission, P.O. Box 37, Binga, Zimbabwe, Africa
McCullen, John L., St. Ambrose Church, Box 999, Deerfield Beach, FL 33441
Thomas, Robert R., P.O. Box 483, Green Valley, AZ 85614

Military Chaplains:
Reverend Fathers—
Brown, Michael, Chap., U.S. Navy.
Kirk, David R., Chap., US Army
Nordhaus, Jeffrey J., Lt. Chap., U.S. Navy.

Awaiting Assignment:
Reverend Fathers—
Lautermilch, David J.

Retired:
Reverend Monsignors—
Dunn, Edward C., 36 Melmore St., Tiffin, OH 44883
Mossing, Lawrence A., 2-11676-L, Wauseon, OH 43567
Smith, Bernard E., 3837 Secor Rd., Toledo, OH 43623
Yates, Robert J., 19100 N. Miami Ave., Miami, FL 33169
Reverend Fathers—
Ankenbrandt, Thomas W., 75 Tomb St., Tiffin, OH 44883
Badger, Arthur, 3607 Naples Dr., Toledo, OH 43615
Beauregard, Thomas, 719 Evesham, Toledo, OH 43607
Bonifas, Roger D., P.O. Box 296, Ottoville, OH 45876
Caballero, Francisco, P.O. Box 985, Toledo, OH 43697-0985
Crowley, Charles, 4845 Lake-to-Lake Rd., Greenbush, MI 48738
Curtis, Robert J., 1220 Tiffin Ave., Fremont, OH 43420
Dorley, Paul D., 4811 Estero Pl., Toledo, OH 43623-3734
Downey, Timothy M., 1125 S. East St., Bucyrus, OH 44820
Dunn, Richard C., 190 St. Francis Ave., #207, Tiffin, OH 44883
Etzel, Raymond A., 5679 Monroe St., #1015, Sylvania, OH 43560
Gillig, Russell F., 182 St. Francis Ave., Apt. 110, Tiffin, OH 44883
Hanacsek, John, 13-799 Rd. Y, Rte. 1, New Bavaria, OH 43548
Hernady, Martin, H-1016, Budapest, Derek U, 4, Hungary
Hoshock, Richard, 26869 Ayersville Rd., Defiance, OH 43512
Hug, Frederick I., 4900 Navarre Ave., Oregon, OH 43616
Jaros, Joseph P., 29317 Bates Rd., Perrysburg, OH 43551
Keller, Harvey M., 91 E. Main St., Norwalk, OH 44857
Klaus, Donald R., 15537 S.W. 110 Ter., Miami, FL 33196
Koerber, George M., 2930 W. Lincolnshire, Toledo, OH 43606
Lamantia, A. Robert, 247 Meadowwood, Perrysburg, OH 42551
Lehmkuhl, John, 921 Mulberry, Fremont, OH 43420
Lester, John E., 1001 N. Byrne Rd., Apt. 321, Toledo, OH 43607
Loeffler, Earl A., 2086 Brookdale, Toledo, OH 43606-3344
Lovisa, Eugene L., P.O. Box 677, Sylvania, OH 43560
Miorin, Albert C., 3423 Blackstone Island, P.O. Box 414, Colon, MI 49040
Mueller, Paul, P.O. Box 677, Bowling Green, OH 43402-0677
Niedermier, Jerome G., 5341 Glendale Dr., Harrison, MI 48625
Nieset, Frank E., 1876 E. Lynwood Dr., Concord, CA 94519
Nietfeld, Fred J., 10852 N. Kendall Dr., Miami, FL 33176
O'Brien, Joseph L., 2596 Sun Valley #202, Port Clinton, OH 43452
O'Grady, James W., 4900 Navarre Ave., Oregon, OH 43616
Ollivier, John, 2585 Sand Rd., Port Clinton, OH 43452
Ott, Carlton A., 4496 Whittlesey, Norwark, OH 44857-9244
Pitula, Zygmunt J., ul. 22 Lipca 8, 86050 Solec Kujawski, woj. Bydgoszcz, Poland
Radecki, Albin A., 4312 Holland-Sylvania Rd., #323, Toledo, OH 43623
Reichert, Ralph, 3230 Centennial Rd. #31, Sylvania, OH 43560
Richter, William, 1605 W. Jefferson St., Sandusky, OH 44870
Ringholz, Benedict E., 117 Leisure Ln., Norwalk, OH 44857
Rinkowski, George M., 3409 W. Alexis, Toledo, OH 43623
Risacher, James E., 308 Knollwood Village, Southern Pines, NC 28387
Ruess, Charles W., 507 Park Ave., Defiance, OH 43512
Schreiner, John E., 6488 State Rd., B-14, Parma, OH 44134-4161
Shanahan, John, 130 S. Cole St., Lima, OH 45305
Shenk, Bertrand J., 59 Executive Dr., Norwalk, OH 44851
Sherbno, John, c/o R.J. Bradner, 2854 Sylvania Ave., Toledo, OH 43613
Siecker, James A., 513 S. Race St., Van Wert, OH 45891-2169
Steinle, James, 312 Greenfield St., Tiffin, OH 44883-2427

Permanent Deacons:
Ackerman, Tom
Adams, Lawrence
Algee, John
Andrzejewski, Walter
Arbogast, Urban
Badenhop, Donald
Barrett, John
Bautista, Jose
Beat, Walter
Betz, Eugene
Billmaier, Robert
Bistak, Leo T.
Bland, Thomas
Bleile, Jack
Bodette, Robert
Bost, Robert
Braham, Carl
Buckmaster, Bruce
Burkett, Dennis
Burkhart, Joseph
Burwell, Robert M.
Burzynski, Raymond
Busam, Jack
Bussemeier, Mark

Calvillo, Pedro
Cappelletty, Ken
Carnahan, Richard
Carone, Thomas
Conkle, Walter
Contreras, Ignacio
Coughlin, Donald
Cousino, Wesley
Daniel, John
Dazley, Phil
DeCrane, Victor
Derr, Floyd
Diaz, Alfredo
Dickey, Kenneth
Dominique, James
Dominique, Ralph
Dominique, Tom
Downey, John F.
Dudley, James
Dunn, James
Etue, Tim
Fazekas, Richard
Feick, Michael
Felter, Robert
Flores, Jose
Foos, Vincent
Fox, Edward
Frazier, Edward
Fritz, Julius
Garza, Ignacio
Gillen, Robert
Gleason, Richard
Gogol, Stanley
Gonsiorowski, Irvin
Gonzalez, Rene
Grandowicz, John
Gryczewski, Edward
Hammer, James
Hartings, Leo
Hartman, John
Hartzell, Robert
Hazelton, Dorsey
Heban, Richard
Heeter, Joseph
Hellrung, Edward
Hendricks, James
Holmer, Leon
Horning, William
Hostutler, James
Hulderman, Joseph
Ignatowski, Gerald
Irelan, Ed
Jackson, Dennis
Jones, Paul
Jordan, David
Karpanty, David
Keller, Steve
Kelley, Edward L.
Kemer, Ray
Kest, Joseph, Jr.
Kinder, John
Klausing, Robert R.
Klear, Kenneth
Klein, Frank
Koenn, Francis
Kopp, Allan D.
Kozek, Richard
Kujawa, Clifford
Laker, David
Lesinski, Robert
Lira, Rudy
Llanos, Ramon
Lochotzki, William
Lopez, Valentin
Lottier, Larry
Ludwikowski, Ronald
Mack, La Von
Marshall, James
Martinez, Rosalio
McCabe, Patrick
McCauley, Terry
McMahon, Andy
Mendez, Chris
Meyer, Donald
Middaugh, Raymond
Miller, George
Miller, Walter
Mitchell, George
Moncher, James
Moore, Wilbur
Morris, Paul
Mumford, Robert
Murray, Hugh
Narges, Howard
Nellett, Gerald
Newton, George
Niedermeier, Russell
Niese, Thomas
Nighswander, Robert
Nye, Harold
Ollervides, Tito
Opper, Milton
Pacholski, Robert
Peeps, Ronald
Pence, Michael
Perez, Diego
Perez, William
Petersen, Laurence
Philpott, Terry
Pina, Elias
Przybylek, Stanley
Quinn, Daniel
Rall, William
Recker, Louis
Redington, Randall
Reinhart, Lewis E.
Reinhart, Norbert
Repka, Joseph
Righi, Al
Rodriguez, Juan
Romo, Bernabe
Romo, Jose
Rump, James
Sadler, David
Sanchez, Jose
Sanchez, Salvador
Sanders, Roy
Scherger, Daniel
Schmidt, James
Segura, Alfredo
Selmek, Zenon
Shoemaker, Russell
Singler, Joseph
Sisson, Alfred
Skeldon, Philip
Snyder, William
Sortman, Jerry
Stahl, John
Stepanic, George C.
Swartz, Robert
Tiefenbach, Lawrence
Trotter, Lawrence
Turner, Harry
Turnwald, Leon
Ulmer, William
Vascik, Rick
Veselka, Stephen
Villagomez, Jesus
Vogel, Curt
Vrooman, David
Warren, Richard
Welch, Harold
Westrick, Eugene
Wethington, Norbert
Wiciak, John
Windham, Joe
Winterstellar, Kevin
Wolf, Rudolph
Worland, Donald
Worline, Timothy
Wurm, Eugene
Yakir, Michael
Yeackel, Harry
Young, James
Zalewski, Stan
Zoll, Jack

INSTITUTIONS LOCATED IN THE DIOCESE

[A] COLLEGES AND UNIVERSITIES

SYLVANIA. *Lourdes College*, 6832 Convent Blvd., 43560. Tel: 419-885-3211.
E-mail: rturek@lourdes.edu
Web site: www.lourdes.edu
For a complete listing, refer to the Colleges and Universities section.

[B] HIGH SCHOOLS, DIOCESAN

TOLEDO. *Central Catholic High School*, 2550 Cherry St., 43608. Tel: 419-255-2280; Fax: 419-259-2848. Conducted by Diocesan Priests and Sisters. Mr. Jack J. Altenburger, Prin.; Revs. Michael R. Billian, Pastor & Pres.; Stephen G. Rogers; Mr. William G. Axe, Asst. Prin. Priests 2; Teaching Sisters 3; Lay Teachers 85; Students 1,230.

FREMONT. *St. Joseph Central Catholic High School*. Consolidated from St. Joseph, Fremont, St. Ann, Fremont, Sacred Heart, Fremont, St. Casimir, Fremont, St. Mary, Clyde, St. Mary, Millersville, & Immaculate Conception, Bellevue. 702 Croghan St., 43420. Tel: 419-332-9947; Fax: 419-332-4945. Rev. Dennis P. Hartigan. Priests 1; Lay Teachers 23; Students 344.

LIMA. *Central Catholic High School*, 720 S. Cable Rd., 45805. Mr. Dan Rupert, Prin. Lay Teachers 29; Students 435.

OREGON. *Cardinal Stritch High School*, 3225 Pickle Rd., 43616. Tel: 419-693-0465; Fax: 419-693-0465.
E-mail: toledocstrit@connecting.com
Serves parishes in Greater Toledo, including Oregon, Rossford, Perrysburg, Bono, Walbridge and Genoa. Rev. John F. Stites, Pastor & Pres.; Mr. Timothy Mahoney, Prin. Priests 1; Sisters 2; Lay Teachers 22; Students 347.

TIFFIN. *Calvert High School*, 152 Madison St., 44883. Mr. James V. Wright, Prin.; Michael Kaucher, Asst. Prin.; Rev. G. Allan Fillman. Priests 1; Sisters 1; Lay Teachers 24; Students 308.

[C] HIGH SCHOOLS, PRIVATE

TOLEDO. *Notre Dame Academy*, 3535 Sylvania Ave., 43623. Tel: 419-475-9359; Fax: 419-475-2558.
E-mail: administrator@ndal.tld.pvt.K12.us.oh
School for girls. Sisters of Notre Dame. Sr. Mary Carol Gregory, S.N.D., Pres & Prin. Sisters 15; Lay Teachers 39; Students 743.

St. Francis de Sales High School, 2323 W. Bancroft St., 43607. Tel: 419-531-1618.
E-mail: mlukas@sfs.utoledo.edu
Web site: http://www.sfs.utoledo.edu
School for boys. Oblates of St. Francis de Sales. Revs. Ronald W. Olszewski, O.S.F.S., Pres.; Martin C. Lukas, O.S.F.S., Prin.; Daniel J. Earley, O.S.F.S., (Retired); John I. Extejt, O.S.F.S. Faculty: Revs. Thomas P. O'Neill, O.S.F.S.; James R. Sanford, O.S.F.S.; James H. Roth, O.S.F.S.; John Ebenhoeh, O.S.F.S.; Thomas L. McNamara, O.S.F.S., (Retired); Paul G. Gillespie, O.S.F.S., (Retired); Richard Morse, O.S.F.S., Prov. Govt.; Bro. Paul Spader, O.S.F.S., (Retired). Priests 8; Lay Teachers 47; Students 748; Total Staff 66.

St. John's Jesuit High School, 5901 Airport Hwy., 43615. Tel: 419-865-5743.
E-mail: cwagner@stjohns.toledo.oh.us
Web site: www.stjohns.toledo.oh.us
School for boys. Jesuits of the Detroit Province. Revs. Donald Vettese, S.J., Pres.; Thomas J. Pipp, S.J.; Charles J. Sweeney, S.J.; Francis E. Canfield, S.J., Rector; David Watson, S.J.; Bros. John Sebian, S.J.; John Moriconi, S.J. Priests 5; Brothers 2; Lay Teachers 56; Students 824; Total Staff 93.

St. Ursula Academy, 4025 Indian Rd., 43606. Tel: 419-531-1693.
E-mail: bjn_stursacd@mavca2.mavca.ohio.gov
Ursuline Sisters of the Sacred Heart. Sr. Kathleen Padden, O.S.U., Pres.; Mrs. Jane Charette, Prin. Lay Teachers 42; Students 570; Total Staff 43.

[D] CONSOLIDATED ELEMENTARY SCHOOLS

TOLEDO. *Queen of Apostles*. Consolidated from Immaculate Conception, St. James, and SS. Peter & Paul. 235 Courtland, 43609. Tel: 419-241-7829. Sr. Mary Brenda Haynes, Prin. Sisters 3; Lay Teachers 9; Total Staff 12; Students 150.

ROSSFORD. *All Saints Catholic School*, 630 Lime City Rd., 43460. Tel: 419-661-2070.
E-mail: toledoasross@connectinc.com
Sr. Diana Lynn Eckel, Prin. Sisters 6; Lay Teachers 11; Total Staff 34; Students 281.

SWANTON. *Holy Trinity*. Consolidated from St. Elizabeth & Immaculate Conception. 2639 U.S. 20, 43558. Tel: 419-644-3971. Chris Knight, Prin. Lay Teachers 9; Students 138.

[E] ELEMENTARY SCHOOLS, PRIVATE

TOLEDO. *Ladyfield School*, 3837 Secor Rd., 43623. Tel: 419-475-5451.
E-mail: toledoladyf3@connectinc.com
Sisters of Notre Dame. Sr. Mary Jo Szpila, S.N.D. Sisters 11; Lay Teachers 10; Students 275.

WHITEHOUSE. *Lial Elementary School*, 5700 Davis Rd., 43571. Tel: 419-877-5167.
E-mail: toledolialw@connectinc.com
Sisters of Notre Dame. Sr. Margaret Mary Faist, S.N.D., Prin. Sisters 3; Lay Teachers 14; Students 190.

[F] ELEMENTARY SCHOOLS

TOLEDO. *Mary Immaculate School*, 3837 Secor Rd., 43623. Tel: 419-474-1688.
E-mail: toledomaryim@connectinc.com
Day School for children with learning disabilities. Sr. Mary Alan Miller, S.N.D., Prin. Sisters of Notre Dame 22; Students 82; Lay Teachers 5; Total Staff 27.

SYLVANIA. *St. Francis Education Center*, 6832 Convent Blvd., 43560. Tel: 419-885-3273. Preschool & Elementary Extended Care. Sisters of St. Francis 2; Lay Teachers 26; Students 250.

[G] CHILD CARE INSTITUTIONS

TOLEDO. *St. Anthony Villa / Boysville of Michigan, Inc.*, 2740 W. Central Ave., 43606. Tel: 419-473-1353;

Fax: 419-473-2963.
E-mail: bv.mhs.compuserve.com
Web site: www.boysville.org
For a complete listing, refer to the Special Care Facilities section.

[H] GENERAL HOSPITALS

TOLEDO. *Mercy Hospital*, 2200 Jefferson Ave., 43624-9988. Tel: 419-259-1500
For a complete listing, refer to the Hospitals section.
Riverside Mercy Hospital, 1600 N. Superior St., 43604. Tel: 419-251-0713
For a complete listing, refer to the Hospitals section.
St. Vincent Medical Center, 2213 Cherry St., 43608. Tel: 419-321-3232; Fax: 419-321-3810
For a complete listing, refer to the Hospitals section.

LIMA. *St. Rita's Medical Center*, 730 W. Market St., 45801. Tel: 419-227-3361
For a complete listing, refer to the Hospitals section.

OREGON. *St. Charles Mercy Hospital*, 2600 Navarre Ave., 43616. Tel: 419-698-7200; Fax: 419-698-7328
For a complete listing, refer to the Hospitals section.

SANDUSKY. *Providence Hospital Inc.*, 1912 Hayes Ave., 44870. Tel: 419-621-7000
For a complete listing, refer to the Hospitals section.

TIFFIN. *Mercy Hospital*, Sr. Janet Hay, 44883. Tel: 419-447-3130
For a complete listing, refer to the Hospitals section.

WILLARD. *Mercy Hospital of Willard*, 110 E. Howard St., 44890. Tel: 419-933-2931
For a complete listing, refer to the Hospitals section.

[I] SPECIAL HOSPITALS AND SANITORIA FOR INVALIDS

GREEN SPRINGS. *St. Francis Health Care Center*, 401 N. Broadway St., 44836. Tel: 419-639-2626; Fax: 419-639-6225
For a complete listing, refer to the Special Care Facilities section.

[J] HOMES FOR AGED

GREEN SPRINGS. *St. Francis Health Care Centre (ICF & Skilled)*, 401 N. Broadway St., 44836. Tel: 419-639-2626; Fax: 419-639-3559
For a complete listing, refer to the Special Care Facilities section.

OREGON. *Sacred Heart Home*, 4900 Navarre Ave., 43616-3599. Tel: 419-698-4331; Fax: 419-698-1109
For a complete listing, refer to the Special Care Facilities section.

TIFFIN. *St. Francis Home Inc.*, 182 St. Francis Ave., 44883
For a complete listing, refer to the Special Care Facilities section.

[K] MONASTERIES AND RESIDENCES OF PRIESTS AND BROTHERS

TOLEDO. *Oblates of St. Francis de Sales.* Provincial Residence, 2056 Parkwood Ave., 43620-1616. Tel: 419-243-5105; Fax: 419-243-8827. Very Rev. James F. Cryan, O.S.F.S., Prov.; Revs. Martin C. Lukas, O.S.F.S., Prin., St. Francis de Sales H.S.; John I. Extejt, O.S.F.S.; James H. Roth, O.S.F.S., Teacher, St. Francis de Sales H.S.; James R. Sanford, O.S.F.S., Teacher, St. Francis de Sales H.S.
Priests serving elsewhere: Rev. Ray G. Abella, O.S.F.S., 12651 Yankee Hill Rd., P.O. Box 1315, Columbia, CA, 95310. Tel: 209-532-7423. Rev. Kenneth N. McKenna, O.S.F.S., Novice Dir., 1131 Ventura, Brooklyn, MI, 49230. Tel: 517-592-4558. Rev. Fernan J. Brennan, O.S.F.S., (Retired), Sacred Heart Home for Aged/Little Sisters of the Poor, 4900 Navarre Ave., Oregon, 43616. Rev. G. Wm. Fischer, O.S.F.S., 10018 Seeley St., Lake City, PA, 16423. Tel: 814-774-9655. Rev. John L. Graden, O.S.F.S., 2929 Ilger, 43606. Tel: 419-535-7672. Rev. David M. Whalen, O.S.F.S., 81 Regal Rd., Toronto, Ontario, M6H-2J6, Canada. Tel: 416-656-3160. Rev. Edward A. Kuefer, O.S.F.S., (Retired), Norman Towers, #509, 810 W. Elm Ave., Monroe, MI, 48162. Tel: 313-457-1989. Rev. Stewart M. Lindsay, O.S.F.S., 2671 Lower Mountain Rd., Ransomville, NY, 14131-9754. Tel: 716-731-9694. Rev. John J. Loughran, O.S.F.S., 36109 Martin, Livonia, MI, 48154. Tel: 313-953-8846. Rev. Thomas A. Ribits, O.S.F.S., 152 Plymouth Ave., Buffalo, NY, 14201. Tel: 716-886-6597. Rev. James J. Sottek, O.S.F.S., (Retired), Elizabeth Scott House, Apt. 101, 2720 Albon Rd., Maumee, 43537. Tel: 419-868-6107. Revs. Anthony R. Ceresko, O.S.F.S., Foreign Missions; William G. Auth, O.S.F.S., Mexican Missions; Charles A. LaPenta, O.S.F.S., (Retired), Assumption Rectory, 711 Hickory St., Duncan, OK, 73533. Tel: 405-255-0590. Rev. David A. Kenehan, O.S.F.S., 3812 Vermont Ct., Alexandria, VA, 22304. Tel: 703-370-2040.
St. Francis de Sales High School Faculty House. 2323 W. Bancroft, 43607. Tel: 419-531-1619. Revs. Ronald W. Olszewski, O.S.F.S., Pres.; Richard E. Morse, O.S.F.S.; Paul G. Gillespie, O.S.F.S., (Retired); Thomas L. McNamara, O.S.F.S., (Retired); Bro. Paul V. Spaeder, O.S.F.S., (Retired); Revs. Daniel J. Earley, O.S.F.S., (Retired); John O. Ebenhoeh; Thomas P. O'Neill, O.S.F.S.; Bro. Alfred D. Durant, O.S.F.S., 722 N. Huron St., 43604-1754.
St. Francis de Sale High School Endowment Fund, Inc. Rev. Ronald W. Olszewski, O.S.F.S., Pres. Priests 14; Brothers 2.
St. Mary's Jesuit Community, 56 Birckhead Pl., 43608-2321. Tel: 419-244-9817. Revs. J. Peter Deane, S.J.; Thomas J. Powers, S.J.; John C. Reed, S.J.

CAREY. *Franciscan Mission Association*, 322 West St., 43316. Tel: 419-396-6455; Fax: 419-396-6455.
E-mail: CarlosBH@aol.com
Bro. Bryan Hoban, O.F.M.Conv., Dir.

[L] CONVENTS AND RESIDENCES FOR SISTERS

TOLEDO. *Kateri Catholic Center*, 443 Sixth St., 43605. Judy Dalton, Dir.
Monastery of the Visitation. (Contemplative), 1745 Parkside Blvd., 43607-1599. Tel: 419-536-1343. Sr. Sharon Elizabeth Gworek, V.H.M., Supr. Legal Title: *The Contemplative Order of the Visitation of Toledo, Ohio.* Sisters 17; Perpetual Vows 14; In Formation 3.
Notre Dame Convent, 3535 Sylvania Ave., 43623. Sisters of Notre Dame. Sr. Mary Bonita Sniegowski, S.N.D., Supr. Sisters 35.
Notre Dame Provincialate, 3837 Secor Rd., 43623-4484. Tel: 419-474-5485; Fax: 419-474-1336. Sisters of Notre Dame. Sr. Constance Marie Suchala, S.N.D., Prov.; Sr. Christine Marie Foos, Local Supr.; Rev. Msgr. Bernard E. Smith, Chap. Sisters 303.
Ursuline Convent of the Sacred Heart.
E-mail: toledoosu@connectinc.com
Congregational Offices & Novitiate, 4045 Indian Rd., 43606. Tel: 419-536-9587. Sr. Nancy Mathias, O.S.U., Gen. Supr.; Rev. Bernard J. Boff, Chap. Professed Sisters 105; Associates 122.

CAREY. *Franciscan Renewal Center/Pilgrim House*, 321 Clay St., 43316. Tel: 419-396-7970. Diocese of Toledo, auspices of Shrine of Our Lady of Consolation, Carey, OH. Lucy Pahl, Admin.

FREMONT. *Our Lady of the Pines Convent*, 1250 Tiffin St., 43420. Tel: 419-332-6522. Sr. Pauline Marie Swint, R.S.M.
St. Bernardine Home, 1220 Tiffin St., 43420. Tel: 419-332-8208. Sisters of Mercy of the Americas, Cincinnati Regional Community. Sr. Joan Marie Warnement, R.S.M., Admin.; Sr. Rose Olivieri, R.S.M., Coord.; Mrs. Carolyn Sue Hartenstein, Health Coord. Sisters 30.

SYLVANIA. *Sisters of St. Francis of the Congregation of Our Lady of Lourdes*, 6832 Convent Blvd., 43560-2897. Tel: 419-882-2016; Fax: 419-885-8643.
E-mail: zielinski2@aol.com
Sr. Ruth Marie Kachelek, O.S.F., Min. Gen.; Rev. Msgr. Donald Heintschel; Very Rev. John A. McClure, Chap. Legal Title: *Sisters of St. Francis of the Congregation of Our Lady of Lourdes, Motherhouse and Novitiate.* Professed Sisters 297.

TIFFIN. *St. Francis Convent*, 200 St. Francis Ave., 44883. Motherhouse and Novitiate, Sisters of St. Francis of Tiffin. Sr. Jacquelyn Doepker, Community Min.; Rev. G. Allan Fillman, Chap. Sisters 149; Total Staff 25.

WHITEHOUSE. *Lial Residence, Sisters of Notre Dame*, 5900 Davis Rd., 43571. Tel: 419-877-0431. Sr. Mary Alma Rose Langenderfer, S.N.D., Supr. Sisters 40.

[M] RETREAT HOUSES AND CENTERS OF SPIRITUALITY

BELLEVUE. *Sorrowful Mother Shrine*, 4106 State Rte. 269, 44811. Tel: 419-483-3435. Revs. Robert Kunisch, C.PP.S., Dir.; Donald Shea, C.PP.S.; James F. McCabe, C.PP.S.; John Nagele, C.PP.S.; Rocco Consentine, C.PP.S.; Bro. Norbert Hoying, C.PP.S.

FREMONT. *Our Lady of the Pines Retreat Center*, 1250 Tiffin St., 43420. Tel: 419-332-6522. Sisters of Mercy. Sr. Marianne Longo, R.S.M., Dir. Total in Residence 4; Total Staff 12.

SYLVANIA. *Sophia Counseling Center, Inc.*, 6832 Convent Blvd., 43560. Tel: 419-882-4529. Counselors: Sr. Rachel Marie Nijakowski, O.S.F.S., Psychologist (Ohio 4699); Sr. Sharon Pollnow, C.S.A., M.Ed., M.S.W., L.S.W.; Bonnie Schrock, M.A., L.S.W. Licensed Message Therapist, Registered Polarity Practitioner: Sr. Mary Ann Szydlowski, O.S.F.S., R.N.

TIFFIN. *St. Joseph Renewal Center*, 200 St. Francis Ave., 44883. Tel: 419-447-0435; Fax: 419-447-1612. Sisters of St. Francis, Tiffin. Sr. Barbara Westrick, O.S.F., Dir.

[N] CAMPUS MINISTRY

TOLEDO. *University of Toledo Campus Ministry.* Attended by Corpus Christi Parish. 2086 Brookdale Rd., 43606. Tel: 419-531-4992. Rev. James J. Bacik.

BLUFFTON. *Bluffton College Campus Ministry*, College Ave., 45817. Tel: 419-358-3000. Deacon John Stahl, Campus Min.

BOWLING GREEN. *Bowling Green State University Campus Ministry.* Attended by St. Thomas More University Parish. 425 Thurstin Ave., 43402. Tel: 419-352-7555.
E-mail: mkuhlma@bgnet.bgsu.edu
Revs. Joseph Weigman; Richard Saelzler; Sr. Mary Kuhlman, O.S.F., Pastoral Leader. Total in Residence 47; Total Staff 6.

DEFIANCE. *Defiance College Newman Campus Ministry*, 701 N. Clinton, 43512. Tel: 419-784-4010, Ext. 444. Sr. Rita Marie Schroeder, Newman Minister.

FINDLAY. *University of Findlay Campus Ministry*, 422 Western Ave., 45840. Tel: 419-423-2123. Donna Brown, Campus Min.

TIFFIN. *Heidelberg College Campus Ministry*, 310 E. Market St., 44883. Tel: 419-448-2058. Sr. Margaret Slowick, O.S.F., Campus Min.

[O] MISCELLANEOUS LISTINGS

TOLEDO. *Catherine's Early Childhood Center*, 2211B Jefferson Ave., 43624. Patricia L. Majer, Dir. Sisters of Mercy of the Americas, Cincinnati Regional Community. Total Assisted 164; Total Staff 19.
Catholic Club, The, 1601 Jefferson Ave., 43624. Tel: 419-243-7255. Mr. Paul Szymanski, Dir.
Catholic Foundation of the Diocese of Toledo, P.O. Box 985, 43697-0985. Mr. John Heinze, Contact Person.
The Catholic Migrant Farmworker Network, P.O. Box 985, 43697-0985. Rev. Richard E. Notter, Agent.
Christ Child Society of Toledo, P.O. Box 23022, 43623. Tel: 419-535-6633. Sue Savage, Pres.; Kathryn Wetli, Vice Pres.; Karen Landes, Treas.; Sheila Johnson, Sec.
Farley Health Care Corp., 1001 Madison St., 43608. Sisters of Mercy. Affiliated with Mercy Health System. Mr. Steven L. Mickus, Pres. & CEO.
Hope Manor, 4702 Violet Rd., 43623. Cathy Crossen, Mgr.
Kateri Catholic Center, Ministry with Hearing-Vision Disabled Persons, 443 Sixth St., 43605. Tel: 419-698-9914 (TDD); 698-9696 (Voice). Judy Dalton, Dir.
Madonna Homes, Inc., 722 N. Huron St., 43604. Jeannette Vanover, Assoc. Mgr. Units 196.
Mareda, Inc., 1931 Scottwood Ave., Ste. 700, P.O. Box 4719, 43620. Tel: 419-242-2300; Fax: 419-246-4703. Housing Agency of the Diocese of Toledo. John Kiely, Dir.
Michaelmas Manor, Inc., 3250-3260 Schneider Rd., 46314. Ora B. Milton, Mgr. A corporation organized and operated for the purpose of providing housing facilities and services to elderly persons and handicapped persons. Units for the Elderly 70; Units for the Physically Handicapped 24.
Moody Manor, 2293 1/2 Kent St., 43620. Tel: 419-241-6985. Margaret Miracola, Mgr. Family & Elderly Units 119.
Oblate Residences. Mailing Address: c/o 2056 Parkwood Ave., 43620-1616. 1225 Flaire Dr., 43615. Apartments 100.
Office of Global Concerns, 1933 Spielbusch Ave., 43624. Tel: 419-244-6711; Fax: 419-244-4791. Rev. Bernard J. Boff, Dir. Society for the Propagation of the Faith; Holy Childhood Association; Catholic Relief Services; Mission of Accompaniment. Mission of Accompaniment Pastoral Team: Rev. Timothy Kummerer, All Souls Catholic Mission Africa, P.O. Box 37, Binga, Zimbabwe.
Regina Manor, Inc., 3731 N. Erie St., 43611. Jody Downey, Mgr. Family & Elderly Units 180.
St. Charles Mercy Health Foundation, 222 N. 23rd St., 43624. Robert Maxwell, Foundation Chm.; Cathleen Nelson, CEO & Pres. St. Charles Mercy Hospital.
Sisters of Mercy Health System, North, 222 N. 23rd St., 43624. Randall D. Kordash, Pres. Total Staff 41.
Toledo Catholic Charities Corporation, 1933 Spielbusch Ave., 43624. John F. Heinze, Dir., Financial Svcs. The Catholic Charities Corporation is the Diocesan vehicle to collect and distribute endowment funds and bequests for charitable purposes.
U.T. Newman Foundation for Student Education and Development, 2086 Brookdale Rd., 43606. Tel: 419-531-4992. Rev. James Bacik.

BELLEVUE.
**Mary Lay Center*, 4500 State Rte. 269, 44811. Tel: 419-483-0762. Residence for staff of Sorrowful Mother Shrine. Rev. Robert Kunisch, C.PP.S., Mgr.

DELPHOS. *St. John Parish Foundation, Inc.* St. John the Evangelist Church, 331 E. Second St., 45833. Tel: 419-695-4050.

FINDLAY. *St. Michael Schools Educational Foundation*, 422 Western Ave., 45840. Michael J. Langevin, Pres.

FREMONT. *Delaware Acres, Inc.*, 725 S. Buchanan St., 43420. Tel: 419-334-9558. Melanie Parks-Baynard, Mgr. Family Units 68.

GREEN SPRINGS. *St. Francis Hospital Foundation*, 401 N. Broadway, 44836. Tel: 419-639-2626. Sr. Barbara Mary Novak.

LIMA. *Lima Central Catholic Educational Foundation*, 720 S. Cable Rd., 45805. George T. Scheid, Jr., Chm.

S.R.H.C. Foundation, 730 W. Market St., 45801-4667; Fax: 419-226-9750. Mr. James P. Reber, Pres.; Mr. Kenneth G. Payne, Sec.-Treas.

MAUMEE. *Diocesan Fiscal Management Conference - National Office*, 1910 Indian Wood Cir., Ste. 111, 43537-4029. Tel: 419-897-7916; 800-505-3362; Fax: 419-897-0888. Rev. Robert J. Yeager, Exec. Dir.

OREGON. *RSM Creative Services, Inc.*, 2600 Navarre Ave., 43616. Tel: 419-698-7341. Randall Kordash, Pres.

SANDUSKY. *The Providence Fund*, 1912 Hayes Ave., 44870. Tel: 419-621-7234; Fax: 419-621-7077. E-mail: scairelli@compuserve.com Hospital Foundation. Sr. Nancy Linenkugel, O.S.F., Chm.; Sandra E. Cairelli, B.A., Dir.

SWANTON. *St. Richard's School Endowment Foundation*, 333 Brookside Dr., 43558-1097.

SYLVANIA. *Franciscan Center*, 6832 Convent Blvd., 43560. Tel: 419-885-1547. Sr. Sheila Shea, O.S.F., Exec. Dir. Total Staff 14.

Franciscan Properties, Inc., 6832 Convent Blvd., 43560. Sr. Jeanne Stack, O.S.F., Pres. Total in Residence 109; Total Staff 3; Apartments 98.

Franciscan Services Corporation, 6832 Convent Blvd., 43560; Fax: 419-882-7360. Mr. John W. O'Connell, Pres.

Franciscan Shelters-Bethany House, 6832 Convent Blvd., 43560. Tel: 419-729-2017. Michelle Karcher-Clark, Contact Person.

Lourdes College Foundation, 6832 Convent Blvd., 43560. Tel: 419-885-3211. G. Patrick Williams, M.S., A.C.F.R.E., Pres. & CEO.

TIFFIN. *Mercy Tiffin Health Foundation*, 485 W. Market St., P.O. Box 727, 44883. Tel: 419-447-3130. Sr. Marie Catherine Wise, R.S.M., Chm.

St. Francis Home Memorial Foundation, Inc., 182 St. Francis Ave., 44883. Tel: 419-447-2723. Sr. Jane Schimmoeller, O.S.F., Chm.

St. Francis Villas, Inc., 182 St. Francis Ave., 44883. Tel: 419-447-2723. Sr. Jacquelyn Doepker, O.S.F., Chm.

Tiffin Calvert Foundation, P.O. Box 45, 44883. Robert Warnement, Pres.

Vision Time, Inc., 200 St. Francis Ave., 44883. E-mail: nwestmeyer@juno.com Mailing Address: P.O. Box 4887, Toledo, 43620. Sr. Nancy Westmeyer, O.S.F.

VERMILION. *St. Mary's Church Education Endowment Foundation*, Box 397, 44089. E-mail: jlima@leeca8.leeca.ohio.gov Mr. David Nocjar, Pres.

RELIGIOUS INSTITUTES OF MEN REPRESENTED IN THE DIOCESE

For further details refer to the corresponding bracketed number in the Religious Institutes of Men or Women section.

[0275]—*Carmelites of Mary Immaculate.*—C.M.I.

[0480]—*Conventual Franciscans.* (Mt. St. Francis, IN).—O.F.M.Conv.

[0520]—*Franciscan Friars.*—O.F.M.

[0690]—*Jesuit Fathers and Brothers.*—S.J.

[1110]—*Missionaries of the Sacred Heart of Jesus.* (Geneva, IL).—M.S.C.

[]—*Missionary Society of St. Thomas the Apostle.*—S.S.T.

[0910]—*Oblates of St. Francis de Sales.*—O.S.F.S.

[1070]—*Redemptorist Fathers.* (Baltimore Prov.).—C.SS.R.

[1260]—*Society of Christ.*—S.Ch.

[0420]—*Society of Divine Word.*—S.V.D.

[1060]—*Society of the Precious Blood.* (Cincinnati Prov.).—C.PP.S.

RELIGIOUS INSTITUTES OF WOMEN REPRESENTED IN THE DIOCESE

[3710]—*Congregation of the Sisters of Saint Agnes.*—C.S.A.

[1710]—*Congregation of the Third Order of St. Francis of Mary Immaculate, Joliet, IL.*—O.S.F.

[0790]—*Daughters of Divine Charity.*—F.D.C.

[1070-13]—*Dominican Sisters.*—O.P.

[1070-14]—*Dominican Sisters.*—O.P.

[1070-28]—*Dominican Sisters.*—O.P.

[1170]—*Felician Sisters.*—C.S.S.F.

[1430]—*Franciscan Sisters of Our Lady of Perpetual Help.*—O.S.F.

[2575]—*Institute of the Sisters of Mercy of the Americas.* (Cincinnati, OH).—R.S.M.

[2340]—*Little Sisters of the Poor.* (Baltimore Prov.).—L.S.P.

[3040]—*Oblate Sisters of Providence.* (Baltimore, MD).—O.S.P.

[3560]—*Servants of Jesus.*—S.J.

[0440]—*Sisters of Charity of Cincinnati, Ohio.*—S.C.

[0490]—*Sisters of Charity of Montreal (Grey Nuns).*—S.G.M.

[0580]—*Sisters of Charity of St. Augustine.*—C.S.A.

[1000]—*Sisters of Divine Providence of Kentucky.*—C.D.P.

[]—*Sisters of Mercy.* (Brooklyn Regional Community).—R.S.M.

[2990]—*Sisters of Notre Dame.*—S.N.D.

[1530]—*Sisters of St. Francis of the Congregation of Our Lady of Lourdes, Sylvania, Ohio.*—O.S.F.

[3830-11]—*Sisters of St. Joseph.*—S.S.J.

[2270]—*Sisters of the Little Company of Mary.*—L.C.M.

[3260]—*Sisters of the Precious Blood.* (Dayton, OH).—C.PP.S.

[1760]—*Sisters of the Third Order of St. Francis of Penance and Charity.*—O.S.F.

[2150]—*Sisters, Servants of the Immaculate Heart of Mary.*—I.H.M.

[4120-03]—*Ursuline Nuns of the Congregation of Paris.*—O.S.U.

[4120-06]—*Ursuline Nuns of the Congregation of Paris.*—O.S.U.

[4120]—*Ursuline Sisters of the Congregation of Paris.*—O.S.U.-B.C.

[4190]—*Visitation Nuns.*—V.H.M.

DIOCESAN CEMETERIES

TOLEDO. *Calvary*, 2224 Dorr St., 43607. Tel: 419-536-3751. Mr. John O'Connell, Mgr.

Mount Carmel, 15 E. Manhattan Blvd., 43608. Tel: 419-241-2015.

Resurrection, 5725 Hill Ave., 43615.

FREMONT. *St. Joseph.*

LIMA. *Gethsemane.*

SANDUSKY. *Calvary.*

NECROLOGY

† Bodart, William D., Upper Sandusky, OH, St. Peter. —Died Oct. 5, 1997.

† Pfeifer, William A., (Retired). —Died Sept. 4, 1997.

† Przybyla, Raymond E., (Retired). —Died Jan. 8, 1997.

† Schmit, Rev. Msgr. Jerome E., (Retired). —Died April 10, 1997.

† Shenk, Joseph D., (Retired). —Died Jan. 14, 1997.

Diocese of Trenton

(Dioecesis Trentonensis)

Most Reverend

JOHN M. SMITH, J.C.D., D.D.

Bishop of Trenton; ordained May 27, 1961; appointed Titular Bishop of Tre Taverne and Auxiliary Bishop of Newark December 1, 1987; consecrated January 25, 1988; appointed Bishop of Pensacola-Tallahassee June 25, 1991; installed July 31, 1991; appointed Coadjutor Bishop of Trenton November 21, 1995; appointed Bishop of Trenton July 1, 1997. Res., 901 W. State St., Trenton, NJ, 08618.

Most Reverend

JOHN C. REISS, D.D., J.C.D.

Retired Bishop of Trenton; ordained May 31, 1947; appointed Titular Bishop of Simidicca and Auxiliary of Trenton October 21, 1967; consecrated December 12, 1967; appointed Bishop of Trenton March 4, 1980; installed April 22, 1980; resigned July 1, 1997. *Res., Villa Nianney, 2301 Lawrenceville Rd., Trenton, NJ, 08648.*

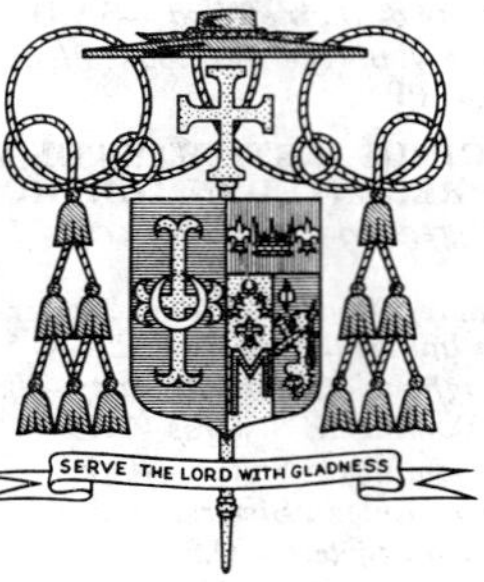

Chancery Office: 701 Lawrenceville Rd., P.O. Box 5147, Trenton, NJ, 08638. Tel.: 609-406-7400; Fax: 609-406-7412.

Legal Corporate Title: "The Diocese of Trenton."

ESTABLISHED AUGUST 11, 1881.

Square Miles 2,155.56.

Comprises four Counties in the State of New Jersey: Burlington, Mercer, Monmouth and Ocean.

For legal titles of parishes and diocesan institutions, consult the Chancery Office.

STATISTICAL OVERVIEW

Personnel	
Bishop	1
Retired Bishops	1
Priests: Diocesan Active in Diocese	163
Priests: Active Outside Diocese	15
Priests: Retired, Sick or Absent	57
Number of Diocesan Priests	235
Religious Priests in Diocese	72
Extern Priests in Diocese	48
Ordinations:	
Diocesan Priests	1
Transitional Deacons	1
Permanent Deacons	8
Permanent Deacons in Diocese	225
Total Brothers	61
Total Sisters	487
Parishes	
Parishes	128
With Resident Pastor:	
Resident Diocesan Priests	107
Resident Religious Priests	16
Without Resident Pastor:	
Administered by Priests	5
Missions	15
Welfare	
Catholic Hospitals	1
Total Assisted	143,858
Health Care Centers	1
Total Assisted	3,759
Homes for the Aged	1
Total Assisted	180
Residential Care of Children	9
Total Assisted	20
Day Care and Extended Day Care Centers	2
Total Assisted	246
Specialized Homes	13
Total Assisted	13,000
Special Centers for Social Services	13
Total Assisted	23,000
Other Institutions	1
Total Assisted	5,434
Educational	
Diocesan Students in Other Seminaries	18
Total Seminarians	18
Colleges and Universities	4
Total Students	2,422
High Schools, Diocesan and Parish	8
Total Students	6,363
High Schools, Private	3
Total Students	1,104
Elementary Schools, Diocesan and Parish	59
Total Students	21,126
Elementary Schools, Private	2
Total Students	462
Non-residential Schools for the Disabled	1
Total Students	20
Catechesis/Religious Education:	
High School Students	705
Elementary Students	58,584
Total Students Under Catholic Instruction	90,804
Vital Statistics	
Receptions into the Church:	
Infant Baptism Totals	10,719
Adult Baptism Totals	414
Received into Full Communion	931
First Communions	11,175
Confirmations	9,278
Marriages:	
Catholic	2,318
Interfaith	3,569
Total Marriages	5,887
Deaths	6,437
Total Catholic Population	701,557
Total Population	1,763,249

Former Bishops—Rt. Rev. MICHAEL J. O'FARRELL, D.D., cons. Nov. 1, 1881; died April 2, 1894.—Rt. Rev. JAMES A. MCFAUL, D.D., LL.D., cons. Oct. 18, 1894; died June 16, 1917.—Most Rev. THOMAS J. WALSH, S.T.D., J.C.D., cons. July 25, 1918; transferred to Newark, NJ, March 2, 1928.—Most Rev. JOHN J. MCMAHON, D.D., cons. April 26, 1928; died Dec. 31, 1932.—Most Rev. MOSES E. KILEY, S.T.D., cons. March 17, 1934; appt. Archbishop of Milwaukee, Jan. 1, 1940.—Most Rev. WILLIAM A. GRIFFIN, D.D., appt. Bishop of Trenton, May 22, 1940; cons. May 1, 1938; died Jan 1, 1950.—Most Rev. GEORGE W. AHR, S.T.D., appt. Bishop of Trenton, Jan. 28, 1950; cons. March 20, 1950; retired June 23, 1979; died May 5, 1993.—Most Rev. JOHN C. REISS, D.D., J.C.D., appt. Bishop of Trenton, March 4, 1980; installed April 22, 1980; retired July 1, 1997.

Vicar-General—Rev. Msgr. WILLIAM F. FITZGERALD, V.G., P.A., S.T.L., J.C.D., *701 Lawrenceville Rd., Trenton, 08648.*

Episcopal Vicars—Burlington County and Ocean County: Rev. Msgr. CASIMIR LADZINSKI, Monmouth and Mercer County: Rev. EUGENE M. REBECK.

Chancery Office—701 Lawrenceville Rd., P.O. Box 5147, Trenton, 08638. Tel: 609-406-7400; Fax: 609-406-7412.

Chancellor and Moderator of the Curia—Rev. GREGORY VAUGHAN.

Vice Chancellors—Rev. Msgr. EDWARD J. ARNISTER, J.C.L.; Sr. ANNE FULWILER, I.H.M., J.C.L.

Assistant Chancellors—Rev. Msgr. JOHN K. DERMOND, J.C.L.; Rev. Msgr. JAMES G. INNOCENZI.

Diocesan Tribunal—701 Lawrenceville Rd., Trenton, 08648. Tel: 609-406-7400; Fax: 609-406-7424.

Judicial Vicar—Rev. Msgr. JOHN K. DERMOND, J.C.L.

Associate Judicial Vicars—Rev. Msgr. JAMES G. INNOCENZI.

Defenders of the Bond—Rev. Msgr. ANTHONY L. CAPITANI, J.C.L.; Rev. CARLOS DAVANTES, J.C.L.; Sr. ANNE FULWILER, I.H.M., J.C.L.

Tribunal Judges—Rev. Msgr. EDWARD J. ARNISTER, J.C.L.; Rev. Msgr. SAMUEL CONSTANCE; Rev. Msgr. JOHN GIBBONS; Rev. Msgr. JOSEPH C. SHENROCK, S.T.L.; Rev. Msgr. WILLIAM E. MAGUIRE, S.T.D.; Rev. Msgr. WALTER E. NOLAN, M.Div., M.S.; Rev. Msgr. ARMAND A. PEDATA, J.C.D.; Rev. Msgr. ALFRED D. SMITH; Rev. Msgr. EDWARD D. STRANO; Rev. Msgr. LEONARD R. TOOMEY; Rev. Msgr. THADDEUS J. WOJCIEHOWSKI; Revs. RALPH W. STANSLEY, M.Div.; RONALD BECKER, M.Div.; THOMAS BRENNAN; EMMETT CARROLL, O.F.M.Conv.; LOUIS W. KRALOVICH, Th.M; EUGENE M. REBECK; JOHN SCULLY; CHARLES B. WEISER, Th.M.; Deacon JOSEPH HANNAWACKER.

Promotor of Justice—Rev. Msgr. LEONARD R. TOOMEY.

Notaries—PATRICIA ADAMO; JUDITH MCLAUGHLIN.

Diocesan Consultors—Rev. Msgr. CASIMIR H. LADZINSKI; Rev. Msgr. WILLIAM F. FITZGERALD, V.G., P.A., S.T.L., J.C.D.; Rev. Msgr. LEONARD R. TOOMEY; Rev. Msgr.

JOSEPH A. O'CONNOR; Rev. Msgr. THADDEUS J. WOJCIEHOWSKI; Rev. Msgr. ALFRED D. SMITH; Rev. Msgr. HUGH F. RONAN; Rev. Msgr. JAMES H. DUBELL.

Parish Priest Consultors—Rev. Msgr. CASIMIR H. LADZINSKI; Rev. Msgr. ALFRED D. SMITH; Rev. Msgr. SAMUEL C. CONSTANCE.

Diocesan Council of Priests—Most Rev. JOHN M. SMITH, Pres.; Revs. DANIEL GOWAN, Chm. BRIAN BUTCH, Vice Chm. EDWARD M. JAWIDZIK, Sec.; Rev. Msgr. JOHN K. DERMOND, J.C.L., Parliamentarian; Rev. Msgr. THOMAS LUEBKING, At-Large; Rev. JACK DWYER, At-Large.

Council of Deacons—Mr. BARRY TARZY, Pres.

County Representatives—Burlington Co.: Mr. RONALD KERR; Mr. BARRY TARZY, Mercer Co.: Mr. FRANK PRIHODA; JOSEPH HEPP, Monmouth Co.: Mr. RALPH IMHOLTE; Mr. MICHAEL AULETA, Ocean Co.: Mr. RICHARD HAUENSTEIN; Mr. JOHN GILCHRIST.

Diocesan Pastoral Council—Most Rev. JOHN M. SMITH, D.D., J.C.D.; GLORIA ANTRIM, Pres. JOANNE D'APOLITO, Vice Pres. HOWARD WHITE, Sec.

Finance Council—Rev. Msgr. WILLIAM F. FITZGERALD, V.G., P.A., S.T.L., J.C.D., Chm.; Mr. BERNARD MCGLONE; Hon. DANIEL O'DONNELL; Mr. EDWARD PIESLAK.

Censor Librorum—Rev. Msgr. WILLIAM E. MAGUIRE, S.T.D.

Synod Implementation Office—Rev. Msgr. EDWARD J. ARNISTER, J.C.L., Interim Contact.

Office of Planning and Development—Rev. Msgr. LEONARD F. TROIANO, *Chancery Office, 701 Lawrenceville Rd., P.O. Box 5147, Trenton, 08638.* Tel: 609-406-7400; Fax: 609-406-7414.

Vicariate For Organizational Services

Vicar—Rev. Msgr. WILLIAM F. FITZGERALD, V.G., P.A., S.T.L., J.C.D.

Chancery Office—701 Lawrenceville Rd., P.O. Box 5147, Trenton, 08638-0309. Tel: 609-406-7400; Fax: 609-406-7412.

Chancellor—Rev. GREGORY VAUGHAN.

Office of Finance—Rev. Msgr. WILLIAM F. FITZGERALD, V.G., P.A., S.T.L., J.C.D.

Finance Director—Ms. DARYL ROWE.

Building Commission—Rev. Msgr. FREDERICK A. VALENTINO, Chm.

Expansion and Development—Rev. Msgr. FREDERICK A. VALENTINO, Chm.

Budget Committee—Rev. Msgr. WILLIAM F. FITZGERALD, V.G., P.A., S.T.L., J.C.D., Chm.

Insurance and Pension—Rev. Msgr. WILLIAM F. FITZGERALD, V.G., P.A., S.T.L., J.C.D.

Office of Data Processing—Ms. KATHLEEN A. MOORE, Mgr., *701 Lawrenceville Rd., Trenton, 08648.* Tel: 609-406-7400; Fax: 609-406-7412.

Office of Human Resources—Mr. NORMAN E. LEAVER, Dir., *701 Lawrenceville Rd., P.O. Box 5147, Trenton, 08638-0309.* Tel: 609-406-7400; Fax: 609-406-7413.

Vicariate For Personnel Services

Vicar—Rev. Msgr. JOHN J. GIBBONS, *St. Dominic Church, 250 Old Squan Rd., Brick, 08724.* Tel: 732-840-1410; Fax: 732-840-0522.

Office of Priest Personnel—Rev. Msgr. WALTER E. NOLAN, M.Div., M.S., Dir., *701 Lawrenceville Rd., Trenton, 08648.* Tel: 609-406-7400.

Delegate for Religious—Sr. AGNES GUNN, I.H.M., Dir., *701 Lawrenceville Rd., Trenton, 08648.* Tel: 609-406-7400.

Office of Permanent Deacons—Rev. RALPH W. STANSLEY, Dir., *701 Lawrenceville Rd., Trenton, 08648.* Tel: 609-406-7417; Fax: 609-406-7411.

Vocations Office—Rev. ROBERT M. TYNSKI, Dir., Vocation, *701 Lawrenceville Rd., P.O. Box 5147, Trenton, 08638-0309.* Tel: 609-406-7400; Fax: 609-406-7413.

Vicariate For Social Services

Vicar—Rev. Msgr. JOSEPH C. SHENROCK, P.A., *St. Elizabeth Ann Seton, 30 Schoolhouse Rd., Whiting, 08759.* Tel: 732-350-5001; Fax: 732-350-4618.

Catholic Charities—Mr. FRANCIS E. DOLAN, Dir., *47 N. Clinton Ave., P.O. Box 1423, Trenton, 08607-1423.* Tel: 609-394-5181; Fax: 609-695-6978.

Peace and Justice—Rev. RONALD J. CIOFFI, Dir., *St. Joseph Church, 376 Maple Pl., Keyport, 07735.* Tel: 732-264-0322; Fax: 732-888-3280.

Catholic Relief Services and Campaign for Human Development—Rev. BRIAN T. BUTCH, *St. Paul's Church, 214 Nassau St., Princeton, 08540.* Tel: 609-924-1743.

Mount Carmel Guild—Sr. MARIAN IMMACULATE GILLEN, S.C., Exec. Sec., *73 N. Clinton Ave., Trenton, 08609.* Tel: 609-392-5159.

St. Vincent de Paul Society—Rev. ARTHUR F. CONLON, Dir., *St. Vincent de Paul Church, 555 Allentown Rd., Yardville, 08620.* Tel: 609-585-6470.

Health Care Facilities and Lay Ministry—Rev. Msgr. GEORGE A. ARDOS, *St. George Church, 1370 River Rd., Titusville, 08560.* Tel: 609-737-2015; Fax: 609-737-7863.

Holy Innocents Society—Mr. ANGELO ROMANELLO, Pres., *5 Shelburne Dr., Trenton, 08638.* Tel: 609-882-4567.

Office of Ecumenism—Rev. JEFFREY E. LEE, Dir., *St. Charles Borromeo, 2226 Riverton Rd., P.O. Box 2220, Cinnaminson, 08077.* Tel: 609-829-3322; Fax: 609-829-3411.

Cemeteries—Rev. Msgr. JAMES H. DUBELL, *St. Paul Church, 223 E. Union St., Burlington, 08016.* Tel: 609-386-0163; Fax: 609-386-1345.

Office of Catholic Persons with Disabilities—Sr. HELEN KLINE, S.S.J., Dir., *701 Lawrenceville Rd., Trenton, 08648.* Tel: 609-406-7400.

Vicariate For Catholic Education Services

Vicar—Rev. GREGORY VAUGHAN, *St. Raphael Church, 3500 S. Broad St., Trenton, 08610.* Tel: 609-585-7049; Fax: 609-585-5976.

Catholic Education Office—Dr. LARRY A. THOMPSON, Supt., *701 Lawrenceville Rd., Trenton, 08648.* Tel: 609-406-7400; Fax: 609-406-7429.

Elementary Education—Sr. MARY HELEN BEIRNE, S.S.J., Assoc. Supt. Tel: 609-406-7400.

Consultant for Curriculum and Special Program—Mrs. MARGARET BOLAND.

Office of Religious Education—Mrs. ROSEMARIE MCGINTY, M.A., Dir., *701 Lawrenceville Rd., Trenton, 08648.* Tel: 609-406-7400; Fax: 609-406-7418.

Elementary Religious Education—Sr. SHAUN KATHLEEN WILSON, C.S.B., M.A., Assoc. Dir.

Secondary Religious Education—Sr. SHAUN KATHLEEN WILSON, C.S.B., M.A., Assoc. Dir. Tel: 609-406-7400; Fax: 609-406-7418.

Office of Family Life—Rev. THOMAS N. GERVASIO, Dir., *701 Lawrenceville Rd., Trenton, 08648.* Tel: 609-406-7400; Fax: 609-406-7418.

Campus Ministry—Rev. GEORGE VAUGHAN, Dir., *St. Raphael Church, 3500 S. Broad St., Trenton, 08610.* Tel: 609-585-7049; Fax: 609-585-5976.

Office of Youth Ministry—Sr. DONNA D'ALIA, R.S.M., Dir., *701 Lawrenceville Rd., Trenton, 08648.* Tel: 609-406-7400; Fax: 609-406-7419.

Office of Adult Ministry—Sr. DONNA D'ALIA, R.S.M., Dir., *701 Lawrenceville Rd., Trenton, 08648.* Tel: 609-406-7400; Fax: 609-406-7419.

Catholic Youth Organization—Mr. THOMAS MLADENETZ, Exec. Dir., *920 S. Broad St., Trenton, 08611-2097.* Tel: 609-396-8383.

Monitor-Communications—Mr. JOSEPH M. DONADIEU, Editor-in-Chief, *701 Lawrenceville Rd., Trenton, 08648.* Tel: 609-406-7400.

"The Monitor" (Diocesan Newspaper)—Mr. JOSEPH M. DONADIEU, Exec. Dir. & Mng. Editor, *701 Lawrenceville Rd., Trenton, 08648.* Tel: 609-406-7400.

Vicariate For Christian Life Services

Vicar—Rev. Msgr. WILLIAM J. DAILEY, *St. Joseph Church, 540 N. Olden Ave., Trenton, 08638.* Tel: 609-394-5757; Fax: 609-599-4402.

Pontifical Mission Aid Societies—Rev. Msgr. RICHARD L. TOFANI, Dir., *701 Lawrenceville Rd., Trenton, 08648.* Tel: 609-406-7400.

Office of Parish Life and Evangelization—Sr. MARGARET MACKEY, O.S.F., Dir., *701 Lawrenceville Rd., Trenton, 08648.* Tel: 609-406-7400.

Diocesan Office of Worship—Rev. SAM A. SIRIANNI, Dir., *701 Lawrenceville Rd., Trenton, 08648.* Tel: 609-406-7400.

Cursillo—Rev. JOHN VINCENT BOWDEN, Spiritual Dir., *Church of Epiphany, 615 Thiele Rd., Brick, 08724.* Tel: 732-458-0220; Fax: 732-458-6921.

Legion of Mary—Rev. MICHAEL L. BURNS, Dir., *St. Mary's Church, 45 Crosswicks St., Bordentown, 08505.* Tel: 609-298-0261; Fax: 609-298-7178.

Martin House—Rev. BRIAN MCCORMICK, *Mailing Address: P.O. Box 1025, Trenton, 08606. 802 E. State St., Trenton, 08609.* Tel: 609-989-8143.

Migration and Refugee Services—Sr. JANET YURKANIN, I.H.M., Dir., *33 W. Front St., Trenton, 08608.* Tel: 609-394-8299.

Black Apostolate—Sr. M. LORETTO EVANS, O.S.B., *1 Center St., Trenton, 08611.* Tel: 609-695-8216.

Correctional Institutions—Rev. ROBERT SCHULZE, *701 Lawrenceville Rd., Trenton, 08648.* Tel: 609-406-7400.

Haitian Ministry—Sr. RUTH PODESTA, Dir., *33 Front St., Trenton, 08608.* Tel: 609-394-5693.

Hispanic Apostolate—Rev. Msgr. MANUEL FERNANDEZ, *St. John the Baptist Church, 272 Willow Ave., Long Branch, 07740.* Tel: 732-229-8527; Fax: 732-571-0280.

Korean Apostolate—Rev. MICHAEL LEE, *Immaculate Conception Church, 64 Broad St., Eatontown, 07724.* Tel: 732-389-3830.

Scouting—Rev. MICHAEL A. SANTANGELO,Catholic Committees on Scouting, *St. Joan of Arc, 100 Willowbend Rd., Marlton, 08053.*

Charismatic Renewal—Rev. H. BRENDAN WILLIAMS, *St. Veronica, 4215 Hwy. No. 9 N., Howell, 07731.* Tel: 732-363-4200; Fax: 732-370-3891.

Francis House of Prayer—Mailing Address: P.O. Box 392, Rancocas, 08073. Tel: 609-877-0509; Fax: 609-877-5810. Location: *39 Springside Rd., Mt. Holly, 08060.* Sr. MARCELLA SPRINGER, S.S.J.

Upper Room Spiritual Center—Sr. MAUREEN CONROY; Sr. MAUREEN CHRISTENSEN, *W. Bangs Ave. and Rte. 33, P.O. Box 1104, Neptune, 07753-1104.* Tel: 732-922-0550; Fax: 732-922-3904.

CLERGY, PARISHES, MISSIONS AND PAROCHIAL SCHOOLS

CITY OF TRENTON
(Mercer County)

1—ST. MARY CATHEDRAL (1868) (Hispanic), Revs. Raymond S. Bianchi, Rector; Roman A. Modino; Ridolfo Gonzalez; Deacons Emiliano Vazquez; Jose Beauchamps; Juan E. Valentin; Juan A. Rivera, Jr.
Res., 151 N. Warren St., 08608. Tel: 609-396-8447; Fax: 609-396-5624. [CEM]
Catechesis/Religious Programs—D.R.E.: Sr. Pilar Socorro Garcia; Sr. Susana Islas.
Students 265.
Convent—211 N. Warren St., 08608. Tel: 609-393-4356.
Sisters 2.

2—BLESSED SACRAMENT (1912), Rev. Msgr. Richard L. Tofani; Deacons Joseph A. Hannawacker; Louis F. Slee. In res., Rev. Rogatus L. Mpeka.
Res., 716 Bellevue Ave., 08618. Tel: 609-396-9231; Fax: 609-396-6432.
School—720 Bellevue Ave., 08618. Tel: 609-393-8036; Fax: 609-394-8757.
Lay Teachers 15; Students 167.
Station—Mercer Hospital, Tel: 609-394-4000.

3—HOLY ANGELS (1921), Revs. Sam A. Sirianni; Stanley W. Kryzston. In res., Rev. James P. McManimon; Deacons Robert Tharp; Daniel Chase; Salvatore Marcello; Dennis Slavin; Manuel Iglesias.
Res., 1733 S. Broad St., 08610. Tel: 609-396-8316; Fax: 609-393-3747.
School—10 New Cedar Ln., 08610. Tel: 609-396-8916.
Lay Teachers 12; Students 222.
Catechesis/Religious Programs—Sr. Jane Urban, R.S.M., D.R.E.
Students 206.
Convent—1701 S. Broad St., 08610. Tel: 609-393-2337.

4—HOLY CROSS (1891) (Polish), Rev. Msgr. Edward A. Arnister; Rev. Henry T. Krajewski, O.F.M.Cap.; Deacon John R. Grussler.
Res., 201 Adeline St., 08611. Tel: 609-393-4826; Fax: 609-278-1192. [CEM]
School—22 Grand St., 08611. Tel: 609-393-8407; Fax: 609-393-5313.
Lay Teachers 15; Students 255.
Convent—233 Adeline St., 08611. Tel: 609-392-3786.

5—IMMACULATE CONCEPTION (1874), Revs. Raynald Yudin, O.F.M.Conv.; Anthony Kall, O.F.M.Conv. In res., Rev. Paul Varga, O.F.M.Conv.; Bro. Robert Lynch, O.F.M.Conv.
Res., 540 Chestnut Ave., 08611. Tel: 609-392-5193; Fax: 609-989-1913.
School—Tel: 609-396-8347.
Sisters of St. Francis of Philadelphia 3; Lay Teachers 15; Students 250.
Catechesis/Religious Programs—Students 130.

6—INCARNATION (1947), Rev. Msgr. Hugh F. Ronan. In res., Rev. Msgr. Henry S. Bogdan.
Res., 1545 Pennington Rd., 08618. Tel: 609-882-2860; Fax: 609-637-0460.
School—1555 Pennington Rd., 08618. Tel: 609-882-3228.
Sisters, Servants of the Immaculate Heart of Mary (West Chester) 3; Lay Teachers 8; Students 265.
Catechesis/Religious Programs—Students 198.

7—OUR LADY OF THE DIVINE SHEPHERD (1941) (African American), Rev. Timothy M. Donnelly, S.V.D.
Res., 72 Pennington Ave., 08618. Tel: 609-393-4493; Fax: 609-989-7510.

8—OUR LADY OF GOOD COUNSEL (1942), Rev. Msgr. William F. Fitzgerald; Rev. Harry E. Cenefeldt; Deacon Robert Brady.
Res., 137 W. Upper Ferry Rd., 08628. Tel: 609-882-3277; Fax: 609-882-4375.
Catechesis/Religious Programs—Students 163.

9—OUR LADY OF MOUNT CARMEL. Closed. For Sacramental records please contact St. Mary Cathedral, Trenton.

10—OUR LADY OF SORROWS (1939), Revs. Paul S. Rimassa; Joseph Gnarackatt; Patrick J. McDonnell; Deacons Joseph Malloy; Anthony J. D'Agostino; Jeffery Pierfy.
Res., 3816 E. State St., 08619. Tel: 609-587-4372; Fax: 609-587-7998.
School—3800 E. State St. Ext., 08619. Tel: 609-587-4140; Fax: 609-584-8853.
Lay Teachers 27; Students 408.
Catechesis/Religious Programs—3800 E. State St. Ext., 08619. Tel: 609-587-2555. Mrs. Rita Lynn Everist, D.R.E.
Lay Teachers 65; Students 801.
Station—Mercer County Geriatric, Tel: 609-588-5859.

11—SACRED HEART (1814), Rev. Msgr. Leonard Troiand.
Res., 343 S. Broad St., 08608. Tel: 609-393-2801; Fax: 609-989-8997.
School—Tel: 609-396-7316; Fax: 609-396-4757.
Lay Teachers 9; Students 210.

12—ST. ANTHONY (1921), Rev. Msgr. Joseph L. Ferrante; Revs. Charles R. Kandula; Michael G. Lankford.
Res., 626 S. Olden Ave., 08629. Tel: 609-586-4181; Fax: 609-586-7206.
School—St. Anthony Grammar School, 530 S. Olden Ave., 08629. Tel: 609-586-5888; Fax: 609-631-9295.
Sisters 3; Lay Teachers 20; Students 417.
High School—McCorristin High School, 175 Leonard Ave., 08610. Tel: 609-586-3705; Fax: 609-586-6584.
Priests 2; Sisters 3; Lay Teachers 30; Students 574.
Catechesis/Religious Programs—530 South Olden Ave., 08629. Tel: 609-586-4330.
Students 242.

13—ST. FRANCIS OF ASSISIUM (1864) (German), Rev. Msgr. John K. Dermond; Rev. Castor G. Sanchez (Philippines). In res., Rev. Ronald Becker.
Res., 31 W. Front St., 08608. Tel: 609-393-4851; Fax: 609-393-4555. [CEM 2]

14—ST. GREGORY THE GREAT (1953), Revs. Richard D. LaVerghetta; Michael Manning, M.D.; Stephen Szmutko, S.V.D.; Deacons Richard D'Angelo; Joseph Glukowski; John Groffie; Allan Parr; Neil Pirozzi; William A. Wilson; Ralph LaMachia.
Res., 4620 Nottingham Way, 08690. Tel: 609-587-4877; Fax: 609-588-0192.
School—4680 Nottingham Way, 08690. Tel: 609-587-1131; Fax: 609-587-7704.
Sisters 1; Lay Teachers 49; Students 638.
Catechesis/Religious Programs—Sr. Alice Gallagher, S.S.J., D.R.E.
Students 1,160.
Convent—13 Stanley Dr., Robbinsville, 08691. Tel: 609-259-3384.

15—ST. HEDWIG (1904) (Polish), Revs. Henry F. Schabowski; Arcadius Klejnowski.
Res., 872 Brunswick Ave., 08638. Tel: 609-396-9068; Fax: 609-396-3171. [CEM 2]
School—641 Indiana Ave., 08638. Tel: 609-396-3960.
Felician Sisters 2; Lay Teachers 11; Students 200.
Catechesis/Religious Programs—Tel: 609-394-1534.
Students 163.

16—ST. JAMES (1919), Revs. Boniface Ruzich, O.SS.T.; Raphael Malcom-Hollis, O.SS.T.
Res., 29 E. Paul Ave., 08638. Tel: 609-393-4403; Fax: 609-393-6078.
Convent—1016 Princeton Ave., 08638. Tel: 609-695-4088.

17—ST. JOACHIM (1901) (Italian), Rev. Msgr. Thomas N. Gervasio; Rev. Charles B. Davantes; Deacon Guido Mattozzi.
Res., 19 Bayard St., 08611. Tel: 609-695-6089; Fax: 609-695-4376.
School—25 Bayard St., 08611. Tel: 609-394-1445.
Sisters 5; Lay Teachers 7; Students 187.
Catechesis/Religious Programs—Students 185.

18—ST. JOSEPH (1891), Rev. Msgr. William J. Dailey.
Res., 540 N. Olden Ave., 08638. Tel: 609-394-5757; Fax: 609-599-4402.
Catechesis/Religious Programs—Students 322.
Station—Helene Fuld Hospital, Tel: 609-394-6000.

19—ST. MICHAEL (1921) (Slovak), Rev. Msgr. James G. Innocenzi.
Res., 1130 Brunswick Ave., 08638. Tel: 609-393-4050; Fax: 609-393-7335.
Catechesis/Religious Programs—Students 67.

20—SS. PETER AND PAUL (1899) (Slovak), Rev. Francis Zalewski.
Res., 480 Centre St., 08611. Tel: 609-396-2214. [CEM]
Church—480 Second St., 08611.
Catechesis/Religious Programs—Students 50.

21—ST. RAPHAEL (1943) (White Horse), Revs. Gregory D. Vaughan; Michael P. Lang; James P. Quinn.
Res., 3500 S. Broad St., 08610. Tel: 609-585-7049; Fax: 609-585-5876.
School—151 Gropp Ave., 08610. Tel: 609-585-7733.
Sisters 6; Lay Teachers 14; Students 302.
Catechesis/Religious Programs—151 Gropp Ave., 08610. Tel: 609-585-3848.
Students 543.
Convents—3472 Broad St., 08610. Tel: 609-585-8203.
Contemplative Sisters of the Good Shepherd 12; 68 Lakeview Ct., 08620. Tel: 609-585-7041.
Sisters 4.
Station—Robert Wood Johnson University Hospital at Hamilton, Tel: 609-585-7900.

22—ST. STANISLAUS (1890) (Polish), Rev. Christian Wojciechowski, O.F.M.Conv.; Bro. Gerry Seipp, O.F.M.Conv.
Res., 60 Randall Ave., 08611. Tel: 609-396-9366; Fax: 609-396-3346. [CEM]
Catechesis/Religious Programs—Tel: 609-695-6424.
Students 10.

23—ST. STEPHEN (1903) (Hungarian), Rev. Francis Zalewski.
Mailing Address: P.O. Box 4563, 08611. Tel: 609-394-5965. [CEM]

24—ST. VINCENT DE PAUL (1954), Rev. Arthur F. Conlon.
Res., 555 Allentown Rd., Yardville, 08620. Tel: 609-585-6470; Fax: 609-585-0137.
Catechesis/Religious Programs—Students 53.

OUTSIDE THE CITY OF TRENTON

Allentown, Monmouth Co., St. John (1878), Rev. Joseph J. Procaccini; Cookie Angelina Maratea, Pastoral Assoc., Tel: 609-259-3586.
Res., 1282 Yardville-Allentown Rd., 08501. Tel: 609-259-3391; Fax: 609-259-3586. [CEM]
Catechesis/Religious Programs—Students 389.

Asbury Park, Monmouth Co., Holy Spirit (1879), Rev. Leonard P. Lang; Deacons Joseph D. Caroll; Edner Andre.
Res., 705 2nd Ave., Box 617, 07712. Tel: 732-775-0030; Fax: 732-775-7358. [CEM]
Mt. Calvary Cemetery—Rte. 66 and Neptune Blvd., Box 362, Neptune, 07754. Tel: 732-775-3320.
Our Lady of Mt. Carmel (1905) (Italian), Revs. Gerard F. Lynch, O.SS.T.; Joseph K. Mitko, O.SS.T.; Joseph J. Gross, O.SS.T.; Deacon Alfred E. Caponigro, Jr.
Res., 805 Pine St., 07712. Tel: 732-775-1056; Fax: 732-775-8767.
School—First Ave. & Pine St., 07712. Tel: 732-775-8989.
Sisters 3; Lay Teachers 15; Students 232.
St. Peter Claver (1943) (African American), Rev. Gerhard Vogel, S.V.D.; Deacon John Cook.
Res., 108 Ridge Ave., 07712. Tel: 732-775-4157; Fax: 732-774-4531.

Atlantic Highlands, Monmouth Co., St. Agnes (1890), Revs. Leon J Inverso; Bernardino C. Esguerra; Deacon James G. Crowley.
Res., 103 Center Ave., 07716. Tel: 732-291-0272; Fax: 732-291-4982.
School—Tel: 732-291-1050; Fax: 732-291-2035.
Lay Teachers 27; Students 390.
Catechesis/Religious Programs—Students 425.

Avon, Monmouth Co., St. Elizabeth (1907), Rev. Joseph A. Radomski. In res., Rev. Msgr. John J. Endebrock; Rev. Douglas V. Hermansen.
Res., 424 Lincoln Ave., 07717. Tel: 732-774-4089; Fax: 732-774-5848.
Catechesis/Religious Programs—Students 121.

Barnegat, Ocean Co., St. Mary (1942), Revs. Kenard J. Tuzeneu; Vincente Magdaraog.
Res., 747 West Bay Ave., P.O. Box 609, 08005. Tel: 609-698-5531; Fax: 609-698-6255. [CEM]
Catechesis/Religious Programs—Joan Haldenwang, D.R.E.
Students 1,330.

Bay Head, Ocean Co., Sacred Heart (1913), Revs. Thomas Brennan; Dominic A. Marchese, S.S.J.; Deacons John Czarnecki; James Tobin.
Res., 751 Main Ave., 08742. Tel: 732-899-1398; Fax: 732-899-2233.
Catechesis/Religious Programs—Students 72.

Bayville, Ocean Co., St. Barnabas (1966), Revs. Rocco A. Cuomo; Mark T. Devlin; Sr. Patricia McNiff, O.S.F., Pastoral Assoc.; Sr. Patricia Lally, O.P., Pastoral Assoc.; Deacons James H. Cummings; Peter M. Clausen; Michael A. Taylor.
Res., 33 Woodland Rd., Box I, 08721. Tel: 732-269-2208; Fax: 732-269-2557.
Catechesis/Religious Programs—Tel: 732-269-3590.
Students 1,282.

Belmar, Monmouth Co., St. Rose (1888), Rev. Msgr. Alfred D. Smith; Rev. Edward M. Jawidzik; Deacons Normand C. Bailey; Eugene G. Malhame.
Res., 603 Seventh Ave., 07719. Tel: 732-681-0512; Fax: 732-681-1693.
School—Tel: 732-681-5555; Fax: 732-681-5890.
Sisters 3; Lay Teachers 18; Students 574.
High School—Tel: 732-681-2858; Fax: 732-280-2745.
Sisters 5; Lay Teachers 41; Students 541.
Catechesis/Religious Programs—Tel: 732-681-6266.
Students 402.

Beverly, Burlington Co., St. Joseph (1864), Rev. G. William Evans; Deacons Herman J. Mosteller; Matthew J. Stap, (Retired); Ronald J. Ulmer; Charles A. Perkins.
Res., 524 Warren St., 08010. Tel: 609-387-0172; Fax: 609-386-8535.
School—805 Warren St., 08010. Tel: 609-387-0991.
Lay Teachers 15; Students 179.
Catechesis/Religious Programs—805 Warren St., 08010. Tel: 609-387-2928.
Students 138.

Bordentown, Burlington Co., St. Mary (1837), Rev. Michael J. Burns; Deacons Gary T. Richardson; David Harris; Harry Putnam. In res., Rev. Msgr. James S. Foley.
Res., 45 Crosswicks St., 08505. Tel: 609-298-0261; Fax: 609-298-7178. [CEM]
School—30 Elizabeth St., 08505. Tel: 609-298-1448. Sr. Joyce Marie Riley, Prin.
Sisters 2; Lay Teachers 10; Students 155.
Convent—49 Crosswicks St., 08505. Tel: 609-298-0220; Fax: 609-298-7178.
Catechesis/Religious Programs—Tel: 609-291-8281.
Students 425.

Bradley Beach, Monmouth Co., Ascension (1907), Rev. James J. Brady; Deacons John Gerard; James McNulty.
Res., 501 Brinley Ave., 07720. Tel: 732-774-0456; Fax: 732-775-9335.
Catechesis/Religious Programs—Students 151.

Brant Beach, Ocean Co., St. Francis of Assisi (1971), Revs. Andrew J. Reitz, O.F.M.; Raymond E. Hirt, O.F.M.; William Bried, O.F.M.; Francis DiSpigno, O.F.M.; Deacons Albert J. Schwind; James Dougherty.
Office: 4700 Long Beach Blvd., 08008. Tel: 609-494-8813; Fax: 609-494-1466.
Res., 100 3rd St., Beach Haven, 08008. Tel: 609-492-2893.
Catechesis/Religious Programs—Sr. Margaret Magee, O.S.F., D.R.E.
Students 541.
Missions—Beach Haven, Ocean Co., St. Thomas Aquinas, 2nd & Atlantic, 08008.; Loveladies, Ocean Co., St. Clare, 56th & Long Beach Blvd., 08008.; Surf City, Ocean Co., St. Thomas of Villanova, 13th & Long Beach Blvd., 08008.

Brick Town, Ocean Co., Epiphany (1973), Revs. John V. Bowden; David A. Hillier; Deacons Joseph McCormack; Ron Nowak; Michael Mullarkey; William Cortright.
Res., 615 Thiele Rd., 08724. Tel: 732-458-0220; Fax: 732-458-6921.
Catechesis/Religious Programs—Tel: 732-785-0576; 785-0872. Mrs. Janice Santanello, D.R.E.
Students 1,135.
Visitation (1942), Rev. William M. Dunlap; Deacon Edward Fischer, III. In res., Revs. Edito Amora (Philippines); Vincent Donadio; Deacons Salvadore Vicari; Leonard Kruk.
Res., 730 Lynnwood Ave., 08723-5302. Tel: 732-477-0028; Fax: 732-477-1274.
Catechesis/Religious Programs—Tel: 732-477-5217. Mrs. Nancy Grodberg, D.R.E.
Students 1,222.
St. Dominic (1962), Rev. Msgr. John J. Gibbons; Revs. Richard Basznianin; Genaro P. Daguplo (Philippines); Deacon Damian Ayers; Sr. Margaret Mary Foley, R.S.M., Pastoral Min.
Res., 250 Old Squan Rd., 08724. Tel: 732-840-1410; Fax: 732-840-0522.
School—Tel: 732-840-1412; Fax: 732-840-6457.
Sisters 6; Lay Teachers 26; Students 652.
Catechesis/Religious Programs—Tel: 732-840-1414. Mrs. Margaret Ferrara, D.R.E.
Students 670.

Browns Mills, Burlington Co., St. Ann (1906), Revs. Edwin J. Mathias; John F. Wake.
Church & Res.—22 Trenton Rd., 08015. Tel: 609-893-3246; Fax: 609-893-8056.
Catechesis/Religious Programs—Students 352.
Stations—Burlington Co. Minimum Security Jail.; Burlington Co. Juvenile Detention Center.; Deborah Heart & Lung Center.; Buttonwood Hall, Evergreen Park.

The Church of the Korean Martyrs (Korean), Rev. Matthias Ju Kob Seo, Admin.
Res., 3311 Town Court South, Lawrenceville, 08648. Tel: 609-716-9144; Fax: 609-899-9094.

Burlington, Burlington Co., St. Paul (1864), Rev. Msgr. James H. Dubell; Deacons George Carlin; Francis A. Jones.
Res., 223 E. Union St., 08016. Tel: 609-386-0163; Fax: 609-386-0085.
School—6th & James Sts., 08016. Tel: 609-386-1645; Fax: 609-386-1345.
Sisters of Mercy 1; Lay Teachers 21; Students 400.
Catechesis/Religious Programs—Students 280.

All Saints (1910) (Polish), Rev. Msgr. Martin M. Komosinski; Rev. Casimir Milewski.
Res., 502 High St., 08016. Tel: 609-386-0152.
School—510 High St., 08016. Tel: 609-387-9207; Fax: 609-387-1358.
Lay Teachers 14; Students 209.
Catechesis/Religious Programs—Students 38.

Cinnaminson, Burlington Co., St. Charles Borromeo (1961), Revs. Thomas J. Triggs; Jeffrey E. Lee; Sr. Jeanne Belli, S.S.J., Pastoral Assoc.; Deacons William S. Sepich; William Gallagher.
Res., 2226 Riverton Rd., P.O. Box 2220, 08077. Tel: 609-829-3322; Fax: 609-829-1852.
School—2500 Branch Pike, 08077. Tel: 609-829-2778; Fax: 609-829-3411.
Sisters of Mercy 1; Lay Teachers 24; Students 446.
Catechesis/Religious Programs—Tel: 609-829-9119. Mrs. Marie Serfling, D.R.E.
Students 787.

Colts Neck, Monmouth Co., St. Mary (1887), Rev. Edward J. Griswold.
Res., Hwy. 34 and Phalanx Rd., Box H, 07722. Tel: 732-780-2666; Fax: 732-780-0394.
Catechesis/Religious Programs—Tel: 732-294-8841.
Students 779.

Deal, Monmouth Co., St. Mary of the Assumption (1901), Revs. John G. DeSandre; Matthew Thelly; Deacons Kenneth M. McKenna; John McCabe.
Res., 46 Richmond Ave., 07723. Tel: 732-531-1409.
School—73 Wickapecko Dr., Ocean, 07712. Tel: 732-531-4433; Fax: 732-531-4054.
Lay Teachers 16; Students 257.
Catechesis/Religious Programs—Tel: 732-531-1889.
Students 254.

Delran, Burlington Co., Holy Name, Rev. Michael J. O'Connor; Mr. Jim Manaloris.
Res., 260 Conrow Rd., Box 1038, 08075. Tel: 609-461-6555; Fax: 609-461-1293.
Catechesis/Religious Programs—Students 390.

Eatontown, Monmouth Co., St. Dorothea (1905), Revs. Vincent E. Keane; Antonio G. Lanuza (Phillipines); Deacons Stephen W. Andrews; Edward R. Herr.
Res., 240 Broad St., 07724. Tel: 732-542-0148; Fax: 732-542-1531.
Catechesis/Religious Programs—Tel: 732-542-0303.
Students 532.

Immaculate Conception (1984) (Korean), Rev. Michael Lee.
Res., 64 Broad St., 07724. Tel: 732-389-3830; Fax: 732-389-2705.
Catechesis/Religious Programs—Students 60.

Englishtown, Monmouth Co., Our Lady of Mercy (1948), Rev. Charles R. Valentine.
Res., 58 Main St., 07726. Tel: 732-446-6324; Fax: 732-446-5179.
Catechesis/Religious Programs—Students 1,270.
Mission—Perrineville, Monmouth Co., St. Joseph, 58 Main St., 07726. Tel: 732-446-6324. [CEM]

Evesham Township, Burlington Co., St. Isaac Jogues (1996), Rev. Phillip C. Pfleger.
100 Green Brook Dr., Marlton, 08053. Tel: 609-797-0999; Fax: 609-797-0463.
Catechesis/Religious Programs—St. Joan of Arc Church, 100 WillowBend Rd., Marlton, 08053. Tel: 609-797-1811.
Students 988.

Fair Haven, Monmouth Co., Nativity (1954), Revs. Jerome M. Nolan; Richard R. Sweeny; Deacon John A. Cole.
Res., Ridge and Hance Rds., P.O. Box 66, 07704-0066. Tel: 732-741-1714; Fax: 732-741-6837.
Catechesis/Religious Programs—Tel: 732-741-4543. Mrs. Merrie Brambilla, D.R.E.
Students 700.

Farmingdale, Monmouth Co., St. Catherine of Siena (1912), Rev. Michael S. Vona; Deacon Michael J. Principato.
Res., 15 N. Main St., 07727. Tel: 732-938-5375; Fax: 732-938-3260.
Catechesis/Religious Programs—Tel: 732-938-4129.
Students 391.

Florence, Burlington Co., St. Clare (1874) (Irish/Italian), Rev. Felix F. Venza.
Res., 232 E. Front St., 08518. Tel: 609-499-0122. [CEM]
Catechesis/Religious Programs—Duffy House, 306 E. Front St., 08518.
Students 175.

Forked River, Ocean Co., St. Pius X (1961), Revs. George E. Deutsch; Robert T. Leahy; Deacons James Heller; Donald F. Kirkham; Sr. Theresa Gillespie, S.S.J., Pastoral Min.
Res., 203 W. Lacey Rd., 08731-3598. Tel: 609-693-5107; Fax: 609-693-6829.
Catechesis/Religious Programs—Tel: 609-693-2379.
Students 1,120.

Freehold, Monmouth Co., St. Rose of Lima (1871), Revs. Gerard J. McCarron; Miguel A. Virella, S.V.D.; Joseph N. Rosie. In res., Rev. William T. Schneider; Deacon John Wanat.
Res., 16 McLean St., 07728. Tel: 732-462-0859; Fax: 732-462-8173. [CEM]
School—51 Lincoln Pl., 07728. Tel: 732-462-2646; Fax: 732-462-0331.
Sisters 2; Lay Teachers 31; Students 643.
Catechesis/Religious Programs—Tel: 732-308-0215. Mrs. Michele Rizzo, D.R.E.
Students 830.

St. Robert Bellarmine (1971), Revs. Thomas J. O'Connor; Matthew Adackapara; Brendan Duggan, C.S.S.P.
61 Georgia Rd., 07728. Tel: 732-462-7429; Fax: 732-409-3496.
Catechesis/Religious Programs—Tel: 732-431-3404. Mrs. Margo Weber, D.R.E.
Students 1,195.

Hainesport, Burlington Co., Our Lady Queen of Peace (1944), Rev. Daniel Sullivan; Sr. Pat McGinley, S.S.J., Pastoral Assoc.; Sr. Grata Seidenburg, Parish Min.; Sr. Laurene Tracey, S.S.J, Pastoral Assoc.
Res., 1603 Marne Hwy., P.O. Box 188, 08036. Tel: 609-267-0230; Fax: 609-267-0372.
Catechesis/Religious Programs—Tel: 609-267-3641.
Students 386.

Highlands, Monmouth Co., Our Lady of Perpetual Help (1883), Rev. John M. Dobrosky.
Res., 141 Navesink Ave., 07732. Tel: 732-872-1290; Fax: 732-872-2796.
School—121 Miller St., 07732. Tel: 732-872-0281; Fax: 732-291-7907.
Franciscan Missionary Sisters of the Infant Jesus 3; Lay Teachers 7; Students 178.
Convent—159 Navesink Ave., 07732. Tel: 732-872-1420.
Sisters 3.

Hightstown, Mercer Co., St. Anthony of Padua (1885), Revs. Patrick J. Castles; Jacek Labinski; Deacons Thomas Garvey; Joseph Hepp; Frank Prihoda; Stephen Rasi; Patrick Kennedy.
Res., 251 Franklin St., 08520. Tel: 609-448-0141.
Catechesis/Religious Programs—Tel: 609-443-3318. Sr. Anne McCambley, S.S.J., D.R.E.
Students 788.

Holmdel, Monmouth Co., St. Benedict (1959), Revs. William C. Anderson; Daniel J. Ryan; Deacons Herbert J. Schwarz; Raymond R. Pelkowski.
Res., 165 Bethany Rd., 07733-1699. Tel: 732-264-4712; Fax: 732-264-9080.
School—Tel: 732-264-5578.
Lay Teachers 25; Students 458.
Catechesis/Religious Programs—Tel: 732-264-4714.
Students 757.

St. Catharine (1879), Rev. Eugene M. Rebeck; Deacons John P. Flanagan; James G. McGrath; Anthony Mustillo; Sr. Ann Murtha, O.P., Pastoral Assoc. In res., Rev. Joseph McGroarty, O.P.
Res., P.O. Box 655, 07733. Tel: 732-842-3963; Fax: 732-842-9283.
Catechesis/Religious Programs—Tel: 732-758-8568. Sr. Patricia Schladebeck, M.S.C., D.R.E.
Students 1,172.

Hopewell, Mercer Co., St. Alphonsus (1877), Rev. Ralph W. Stansley.
Res., 54 E. Prospect St., 08525. Tel: 609-466-0332; Fax: 609-466-2023. [CEM]
Catechesis/Religious Programs—Tel: 609-466-2694. Sr. Rosemary Hendry, O.S.F., D.R.E.
Students 234.

Howell Township, Monmouth Co., St. Veronica (1962), Revs. H. Brendan Williams; Norman St.John, S.V.D.; Donald J. O'Brien.
Res., 4215 Hwy. 9 N., Howell, 07731. Tel: 732-363-4200; Fax: 732-370-3891.
School—Tel: 732-364-4130; Fax: 732-363-4932.
Sisters 4; Lay Teachers 36; Students 709.
Catechesis/Religious Programs—Tel: 732-364-4137. Sr. Valerie Paccone, C.R., D.R.E.
Students 2,300.
Mission—Freewood Acres, Monmouth Co., St. Mary of the Assumption, Tel: 732-363-4200.

St. William the Abbot (1985), Rev. Msgr. Leo A. Kelty; Deacon Thomas Noone.
Mailing Address: P.O. Box 500, Allenwood, 08720. Tel: 732-840-3535; Fax: 732-840-3663.
Res., 2400 Lakewood-Allenwood Rd., Wall, 07719.
Catechesis/Religious Programs—Students 425.
Stations—Geraldine Thompson Nursing Home, Tel: 732-938-5250; Brisbane Child Treatment Center.

Jackson, Ocean Co., St. Aloysius Gonzaga (1964), Rev. Msgr. Casimir H. Ladzinski.
Res., 935 Bennetts Mills Rd., P.O. Box 1285, 08527. Tel: 732-370-0500; Fax: 732-370-3555.
School—Saint Aloysius Grammar School, Tel: 732-370-1515. Mrs. Julia Hungerford, Prin.
Catechesis/Religious Programs—Tel: 732-370-3123.
Students 830.

Keansburg, Monmouth Co., St. Ann (1924), Revs. Daniel Cahill; Pablo Gadenz; Deacons Edwin Cook; Robert Vlcej.
Res., 311 Carr Ave., 07734. Tel: 732-787-0315; Fax: 732-787-5254.
School—285 Carr Ave., 07734. Tel: 732-787-1027; Fax: 732-495-3338. Sr. Mary Dora McGrath, R.S.M., Prin.
Sisters 2; Lay Teachers 15; Students 310.
Catechesis/Religious Programs—Tel: 732-787-5744.
Students 600.
St. Ann Child Care Center—121 Main St., 07734. Tel: 732-787-7220.
Sisters 2; Students 80.
Bayshore Senior Day Center—100 Main St., 07734. Tel: 732-495-2454.
Sisters 1; Seniors Serviced 1,500.
Hansel and Gretel Preschool—267 Carr Ave., 07734. Tel: 732-787-9237.
Sisters 1; Children 95.
Project Paul—211 Carr Ave., 07734. Tel: 732-787-4887.

Keyport, Monmouth Co., St. Joseph (1854), Revs. Ronald J. Cioffi; James A. Conover; Ms. Jean Potter, Pastoral Assoc.; Deacon Christopher O'Brien. In res., Rev. Francis Tam.
Res., 376 Maple Pl., 07735. Tel: 732-264-0322; Fax: 732-888-3280. [CEM]
School—St. Joseph School, Maple Pl., 07735. Tel: 732-264-9459; Fax: 732-264-8696. Sr. Constance Gleason, R.S.M., D.R.E. & Prin.
Sisters 2; Lay Teachers 22; Students 481.
Catechesis/Religious Programs—Students 409.
Convent—301 Ryan St., 07747. Tel: 732-583-0578.

Jesus the Lord (1978), Rev. Jack Dwyer, Admin.
Res., 123 Broad St., 07735-0673. Tel: 732-739-0323; Fax: 732-264-8276.
Church—120 Broad St., 07735.
Catechesis/Religious Programs—Students 200.

Lakehurst, Ocean Co., St. John (1969), Rev. Ronald Bacovin; Deacons Gabriel Gregory; John Gilchrist; Anthony Tarala.
Res., 619 Chestnut St., 08733. Tel: 732-657-6347; Fax: 732-657-8690.
Catechesis/Religious Programs—Tel: 732-657-2348.
Students 465.

Lakewood, Ocean Co., St. Anthony Claret (1977). (Hispanic Parish for Ocean Co.). Revs. Pedro L. Bou, S.V.D.; Manuel Myvett, S.V.D.
Res., 780 Ocean Ave., 08701-3644. Tel: 732-367-8486; Fax: 732-367-0460.
Catechesis/Religious Programs—Sr. Mary Newett, D.R.E.
Students 180.

St. Mary of the Lake (1890), Rev. Msgr. Michael J. Walsh; Revs. Eugene Vavrick; Leon Buni; Deacons Thomas Cater; Silverius Galvan; John Cullinane; Anthony Martucci. Pastoral Ministers: Sr. Mary Franey, R.S.M.; Sr. Geraldine Contento, M.P.S.; Mrs. Terry Ginther, Pastoral Assoc.
Res., 43 Madison Ave., 08701. Tel: 732-363-0139; Fax: 732-905-1410. [CEM]
School—Holy Family School, E. County Line Rd., 08701. Tel: 732-363-4771; Fax: 732-363-2914. Sr. Laura M. Longo, M.P.S., Prin.; Sr. Gloria J. Barone, M.P.F., Asst. Prin.
Sisters 2; Lay Teachers 33; Students 843.
Catechesis/Religious Programs—Tel: 732-363-3043.
Students 590.
Mission—Lakewood, Ocean Co., Holy Family Church. Fax: 732-905-1410.

Lavallette, Ocean Co., St. Bonaventure (1921), Rev. Msgr. Frederick A. Valentino. In res., Rev. Eugene T. Keenan.
Res., 103 Washington Ave., 08735. Tel: 732-793-7291; Fax: 732-793-8204.

Lawrenceville, Mercer Co., St. Ann (1937), Revs. R. Vincent Gartland; Thomas Chester, J.C.L.; Deacon Gerald De Mauro.

Res., 1253 Lawrence Rd., 08648. Tel: 609-882-6491; Fax: 609-882-4366.
School—34 Rossa Ave., 08648. Tel: 609-882-8077; Fax: 609-882-0327. Mr. John McKenna, Prin.
Lay Teachers 22; Students 339.
Catechesis/Religious Programs—Tel: 609-882-1212.
Students 500.

Lincroft, Monmouth Co., St. Leo the Great (1958), Rev. James M. Clark; Deacon Robert R. Nimon. Pastoral Assocs.: Sr. Ann Barry, S.S.J.; Sr. Joan Dreisbach, O.S.F.
Res., 50 Hurley's Ln., 07738. Tel: 732-747-5466; Fax: 732-219-5181.
School—Tel: 732-741-3133; Fax: 732-741-2241.
Lay Teachers 29; Students 522.
Catechesis/Religious Programs—Tel: 732-530-0717.
Students 700.

Long Branch, Monmouth Co.,

1—Our Lady Star of the Sea, (1878), Rev. M. Joseph Mokrzycki; Deacon John G. Klincewicz; Sr. Diane Matera, R.S.M., Hospital Pastoral Min.
Res., 101 Chelsea Ave., 07740. Tel: 732-229-0526; Fax: 732-229-2886. [CEM]
Catechesis/Religious Programs—Students 87.
Station—Long Branch, Long Branch City.

2—Holy Trinity, (1906) (Italian), Rev. Albert Ricciardelli; Deacons Albert M. Pacitti; James A. Kelly; John A. Yaccarine.
Res., 408 Prospect St., 07740. Tel: 732-222-3216; Fax: 732-222-4313.
School—375 Exchange Pl., 07740. Tel: 732-222-8878; Fax: 732-222-8854.
Religious Teachers Filippni 3; Lay Teachers 11; Students 181.
Catechesis/Religious Programs—Tel: 732-870-1778.
Students 182.
Convent—380 Division St., 07740. Tel: 732-222-8535.

3—St. John the Baptist, (1984) (Spanish), Rev. Msgr. Manuel Fernandez.
Res., 272 Willow Ave., 07740. Tel: 732-229-8527; 229-8905; Fax: 732-571-0280.
Catechesis/Religious Programs—Tel: 732-571-1003.
Students 287.
Missions—Hightstown-Princeton, Mercer Co., Our Lady of Fatima; Freehold-Red Bank, Monmouth Co., Our Lady of Guadalupe.

4—St. Michael, (1885), Rev. Charles B. Weiser.
Res., 800 Ocean Ave., West End, 07740. Tel: 732-222-8080; Fax: 732-870-1174.
Catechesis/Religious Programs—Students 332.

Manalapan, Monmouth Co., St. Thomas More (1970), Revs. Paul A. Scaglione; John P. Bambrick; Deacons Keith J. Casey; James Mark Micali; John J. Zebrowski; John J. Walsh.
Res., 186 Gordon's Corner Rd., 07726. Tel: 732-446-6661; Fax: 732-446-6507.
Catechesis/Religious Programs—Tel: 732-446-3232.
Students 1,482.

Manasquan, Monmouth Co., St. Denis (1909), Revs. Robert J. Parenti; Dominic Dellaporte; Charles F.X. Dolan, S.J.
Res., 90 Union Ave., Box 340, 08736. Tel: 732-223-0287; Fax: 732-528-1901.
School—119 Virginia Ave., 08736. Tel: 732-223-4928.
Sisters 2; Lay Teachers 14; Students 301.
Catechesis/Religious Programs—Tel: 732-223-1161.
Students 609.
Chapel—Manasquan Beach, Our Lady Star of the Sea. (Summer).

Maple Shade, Burlington Co., Our Lady of Perpetual Help (1920), Revs. Bernard J. Keigher; Kenneth W. Ekdahl; Deacons Joseph McHugh; Ronald J. Kerr; Joseph A. Card; Michael P. Boehm; Lawrence W. Finn, Sr.; Joseph F. Seaman.
Res., 236 E. Main St., 08052. Tel: 609-667-8850; Fax: 609-667-3083.
School—Tel: 609-779-7526.
Sisters 5; Lay Teachers 14; Students 346.
Catechesis/Religious Programs—Students 366.

Marlboro, Monmouth Co., St. Gabriel (1885), Revs. Eugene J. Roberts; Michael J. Lynch; William Weider, T.O.R.; Deacons James C. Russo; James McKeon; Lester Owens.
Res., 100 N. Main St., 07746. Tel: 732-946-4487; Fax: 732-946-7276.
Catechesis/Religious Programs—Tel: 732-946-2696; Fax: 732-946-2080. Maureen P. Kelly, D.R.E.
Students 1,350.

Marlton, Burlington Co., St. Joan of Arc (1961), Rev. Msgr. Armand A. Pedata; Revs. Michael A. Santangelo; Adam Kearns; Deacon Barry Tarzy.
Church & Res.—100 Willow Bend Rd., 08053. Tel: 609-983-0077; Fax: 609-983-7716.
School—101 Evans Rd., 08053. Tel: 609-983-0774.
Sisters of St. Joseph 2; Lay Teachers 23; Students 497.
Catechesis/Religious Programs—Tel: 609-983-7575. Sr. Mary Elizabeth Maier, S.S.J., D.R.E.
Students 1,230.
Convent—99 Evans Rd., 08053. Tel: 609-983-0258.

Matawan, Monmouth Co., St. Clement (1965), Rev. John J. Scully; Deacon Donald C. Miller. In res., Rev. Thomas R. Rittenhouse.
Res., 172 Freneau Ave., 07747. Tel: 732-566-3616; Fax: 732-566-9275.
Catechesis/Religious Programs—Tel: 732-591-8090.
Students 843.

Medford, Burlington Co., St. Mary of the Lakes (1943), Revs. Joseph A. Tedesco; A. Edward Siecienski; Cesar R. Anson (Philippines); Deacons John M. Iadanza; Lawrence J. MacDonald, (Retired); Joseph R. Patton; W. Norman Talbot; Donald P. Doyle; Ronald Little.
Res., 40 Jackson Rd., 08055. Tel: 609-654-8208; Fax: 609-654-1734.
School—196 Rte. 70, 08055. Tel: 609-654-2546; Fax: 609-654-8125.
Sisters of St. Francis of Philadelphia 3; Sisters of St. Joseph 2; Lay Teachers 23; Students 478.
Catechesis/Religious Programs—196 Rte. 70, 08055. Tel: 609-654-8243.
Students 1,248.
Convents—27 Schoolhouse Dr., 08055. Tel: 609-654-5896. Sisters of St. Francis; 24 Summerhill Lane, 08055. Tel: 609-654-1941. Sisters of St. Joseph
St. Vincent DePaul Society-Medford: P.O. Box 1131, 08055. Tel: 609-953-0021; Fax: 609-953-2432. Mr. Paul V. Cannon, Treas.

Middletown, Monmouth Co., St. Catherine (1948), Rev. Daniel C. Hesko.
Res., 5 Shore Acres Ave., 07748. Tel: 732-787-1318; Fax: 732-787-6139.
Catechesis/Religious Programs—Tel: 732-495-7779.
Students 503.

Monmouth Beach, Monmouth Co., Church of the Precious Blood (1947), Rev. John T. Kielb; Deacon William Murray.
Res., 72 Riverdale Ave., 07750. Tel: 732-222-4756; Fax: 732-229-6448.
Catechesis/Religious Programs—Tel: 732-870-1293.
Students 238.

Moorestown, Burlington Co., Our Lady of Good Counsel (1879), Rev. Msgr. James J. McGovern; Rev. John J. Quinn; Deacons Frank Giglio; Francis P. McGann.
Res., 42 W. Main St., 08057. Tel: 609-235-0181; Fax: 609-235-4987. [CEM]
School—Tel: 609-235-7885; Fax: 609-235-2570. Sr. Michael Vincent Dailey, O.P., Prin.
Dominic Sisters of Hope 2; Lay Teachers 29; Students 497.
Catechesis/Religious Programs—Tel: 609-235-7136. Mrs. Linda M. Dix, D.R.E.
Students 744.

Mount Holly, Burlington Co., Sacred Heart (1848), Revs. Robert J.W. Schecker; David A. Adams.
Res., 260 High St., 08060-1404. Tel: 609-267-0209; Fax: 609-267-9293. [CEM]
School—250 High St., 08060. Tel: 609-267-1728; Fax: 609-267-1728.
Lay Teachers 24; Students 440.
Catechesis/Religious Programs—Students 550.
Mission—Jobstown, Burlington Co., St. Andrew, 2489 Monmouth Rd., Jobstown, 08041. Tel: 609-324-0806. Deacon John F. Hoefling.
Stations—County Jail, Tel: 609-267-3300; Burlington County Hospital Extended Care Center, Tel: 609-367-0700.

Christ the Redeemer (1976) (Hispanic), Rev. Victoriano F. Sandoval, O.S.A.
Res., 35 South Ave., 08060. Tel: 609-261-0181; Fax: 609-702-0017.
Catechesis/Religious Programs—250 High St., Mt. Holly, 08060. Tel: 609-267-1728.
Students 64.

Mount Laurel, Burlington Co., St. John Neumann (1978), Revs. Lino S. Parente, O.Cist. (Italy); Anselmo M. Florio, O.Cist. (Italy); Teclezghi Ucbaghiorghis, O.Cist.; Maurizio Nicoletti, O.Cist (Italy); Deacons John Hughes; Gene Hoch.
Res., 560 Walton Ave., 08054. Tel: 609-235-1330; Fax: 609-235-9632.
Catechesis/Religious Programs—Students 630.

Neptune, Monmouth Co., Holy Innocents (1959), Rev. G. Scott Shaffer; Deacon Michael Auleta. In res., Rev. Lawrence Kunnel.
Res., 3455 W. Bangs Ave., P.O. Box 806, 07753. Tel: 732-922-4242; Fax: 732-922-2848.
School—Tel: 732-922-3141; Fax: 732-922-6531.
Religious Teachers Filippini 2; Lay Teachers 14; Students 303.
Catechesis/Religious Programs—Students 245.
Stations—Convacenter Nursing Home.; Green Grove Nursing Home.; Heritage Hall Nursing Home.; Medicenter Nursing Home.; The Lodge, Kings Manor.

Our Lady of Providence (1981) (Spanish), Rev. James Vorwerk, S.V.D.; Sr. Grace Forker, S.S.J., Pastoral Assoc.; Deacon Victor L. Gomez. In res., Rev. Adam Midor, S.V.D.
Res., 1228 Fifth Ave., 07753. Tel: 732-776-7164; Fax: 732-776-7164.
Catechesis/Religious Programs—Students 142.

New Egypt, Ocean Co., Assumption (1853), Revs. Anthony M. Carotenuto; Robert R. Schulze; Deacons Martin Ervin; Raymond W. Staub, Jr.
Res., 76 Evergreen Rd., 08533. Tel: 609-758-2153; Fax: 609-758-6240. [CEM]
Catechesis/Religious Programs—Students 740.
Mission—Jackson, Ocean Co., Church of St. Monica, 679 W. Veteran's Hwy., Jackson, 08527. Tel: 732-928-0279; Fax: 732-928-1853.

New Monmouth, Monmouth Co., St. Mary (1878), Revs. Dennis A. Apoldite; Jeffrey J. Kegley; Gerald E. McBride; James D. Keating, O.P.; Sr. Laura Garges, O.S.F., Pastoral Assoc.; Deacon Henry Ernst.
Res., 26 Leonardville Rd., 07748. Tel: 732-671-0071; Fax: 732-671-6125.
School—538 Church St., 07748. Tel: 732-671-0129; Fax: 732-671-2653. Mrs. Victoria Quinn, Prin.
Sisters 4; Lay Teachers 34; Aides 12; Students 697.
High School—Mater Dei High School, Tel: 732-671-9100; Fax: 732-671-9214. Mr. Frank Poleski, Jr., Prin.; Mr. William V. Smith, Asst. Prin.
Lay Teachers 30; Students 417.
Catechesis/Religious Programs—Tel: 732-671-0124. Mrs. Alex Margaret Krasutsky, D.R.E.
Students 1,515.

Normandy Beach, Ocean Co., Our Lady of Peace (1979), Rev. Laszlo F. Rauch.
Residence and Mailing: P.O. Box 728, 7th Ave. & Rte. 35 S., 08739. Tel: 732-793-7803; Fax: 732-793-1808.
Catechesis/Religious Programs—Students 28.

Pennington, Mercer Co., St. James (1897), Revs. James J. McConnell; Thomas Confroy, O.S.B.; Deacons James W. Palsir; Samuel Sciarrotta.
Res., 115 E. Delaware Ave., 08534. Tel: 609-737-0122; Fax: 609-737-6912.
Catechesis/Religious Programs—Tel: 609-737-2717.
Students 772.

Point Pleasant, Ocean Co., St. Martha (1972), Revs. Patrick F. Magee; Dominick Dellaporte; Damian McElroy; Deacons Edward Maier; John Haney.
Res. & Mailing Address: 3800 Herbertsville Rd., 08742. Tel: 732-899-7269; 295-3630.
Catechesis/Religious Programs—Tel: 732-295-8252.
Students 617.

Point Pleasant Beach, Ocean Co., St. Peter (1882), Revs. Edward Costello, O.F.M.Conv.; Richard Rossell, O.F.M.Conv.; William D'Arcy, O.F.M.Conv.; Deacon Edwin H. Brookes, Jr.
Res., 406 Forman Ave., 08742. Tel: 732-892-0049; Fax: 732-295-9782.
School—Tel: 732-892-1260.
Sisters 4; Lay Teachers 12; Students 290.
Catechesis/Religious Programs—Tel: 732-899-4839.
Students 438.
Convent—401 Atlantic Ave., 08742. Tel: 732-899-2390.

Princeton, Mercer Co., St. Paul (1864), Rev. Msgr. Walter E. Nolan; Rev. Brian Butch; Deacons Maurice Benedetti; Paul LaChance; Michael Ross.
Res., 214 Nassau St., 08540. Tel: 609-924-1743; Fax: 609-924-7980. [CEM]
School—218 Nassau St., 08540. Tel: 609-921-7587; Fax: 609-921-0264.
Sisters 3; Lay Teachers 21; Students 390.
Catechesis/Religious Programs—Tel: 609-924-2681.
Students 395.

Red Bank, Monmouth Co., St. James (1864), Rev. Msgr. Philip A. Lowery; Rev. Alex Enriquez.
Res., 94 Broad St., 07701. Tel: 732-741-0500; Fax: 732-741-1489. [CEM]
(Grades Preschool).
Lay Teachers 2; Students 45.
School—St. James Grammar School, Tel: 732-741-3363; Fax: 732-933-4968.
Lay Teachers 27; Students 508.
High School—Red Bank Catholic High School, Tel: 732-747-1774; Fax: 732-747-1936.
Sisters 2; Lay Teachers 64; Students 790.
Station—Riverview Hospital, Tel: 732-530-2231; Fax: 732-530-2394.

St. Anthony (1920) (Italian), Rev. Joseph J. Miele.
Res., 121 Bridge Ave., 07701. Tel: 732-747-0813; Fax: 732-224-0059.
Catechesis/Religious Programs—16 Herbert St., 07701. Tel: 732-741-0261. Mrs. Patricia H. Foley, D.R.E.
Students 205.

Riverside, Burlington Co., St. Peter (1878), Revs. Julius Toth, O.F.M.Conv.; Evan Bucci, O.F.M.Conv., (Portuguese Apostolate); Deacon Joseph Fuoco. In res., Rev. Crispin Fuino, O.F.M.Conv.
Res., 102 Middleton St., Box 248, 08075. Tel: 609-461-0100; Fax: 609-764-6133.
School—St. Peter, Middleton and Hancock Sts., 08075. Tel: 609-461-1087.
Sisters 5; Lay Teachers 25; Students 409.
Catechesis/Religious Programs—Tel: 609-461-9343.
Students 295.

St. Casimir (1913) (Polish), Revs. Dennis Mason, O.F.M.Conv.; Stephen King, O.F.M.Conv. In res., Rev. Jude Michael Krill, O.F.M.Conv.
Res., 502 New Jersey Ave., 08075. Tel: 609-461-0532; Fax: 609-461-5781.
School & Preschool—500 New Jersey Ave., 08075. Tel: 609-461-7410; Fax: 609-461-2619.
Sisters 2; Lay Teachers 13; Students 213.
Catechesis/Religious Programs—Students 240.

Riverton, Burlington Co., Sacred Heart (1878), Rev. John P. Czahur; Deacons Joseph Knipp; Joseph Donadieu.
Res., 400 Thomas Ave., 08077. Tel: 609-829-0090; Fax: 609-829-2087.
Catechesis/Religious Programs—Tel: 609-829-1848.
Students 528.

Roebling, Burlington Co., Holy Assumption (1914), Rev. Francis Walter, O.F.M.; Deacon Robert D. Machion.
Res., 1290 Hornberger Ave., 08554. Tel: 609-499-0161; Fax: 609-499-3074.
School—Tel: 609-499-0045.
Lay Teachers 9; Students 212.
Catechesis/Religious Programs—Students 141.

Rumson, Monmouth Co., Holy Cross (1884), Rev. Joseph W. Hughes; Mr. Kevin Keelen, Pastoral Assoc.; Deacon Jay C. Harbeck.
Res., 30 Ward Ave., 07760. Tel: 732-842-0348; Fax: 732-842-3226.
School—(Grades PreK-8) 40 Rumson Rd., 07760. Tel: 732-842-0348.
Lay Teachers 25; Students 360.

Sea Girt, Monmouth Co., St. Mark (1953), Rev. Msgr. William J. Carton. In res., Rev. Msgr. Robert T. Bulman.
Res., 215 Crescent Pkwy., 08750. Tel: 732-449-6364; Fax: 732-449-1646.
Catechesis/Religious Programs—Tel: 732-449-8360.
Students 407.

Seaside Heights, Ocean Co., Our Lady of Perpetual Help (1946), Rev. Emmett Carroll, O.F.M. Conv.
Res., 100 Grant Ave., 08751. Tel: 732-793-6881; Fax: 732-793-7632.

Seaside Park, Ocean Co., St. Catharine of Siena (1906), Revs. Brennan Joseph Farleo, O.F.M.Conv., Supr. & Pastor; Timothy Lyons, O.F.M.Conv.; Armand Sorento, O.F.M.Conv.; Eugene Zwahl, O.F.M.Conv.; Eric Fenner, O.F.M.Conv.; Reginald Sweeney, O.F.M.Conv.
Res., 50 E. St., 08752. Tel: 732-793-0041; Fax: 732-793-5483.
Catechesis/Religious Programs—Students 326.

Spring Lake, Monmouth Co., St. Catharine (1901), Rev. Msgr. Thomas A. Luebking; Rev. K. Michael Lambeth; Deacons John P. O'Connor; David Fursman; Edward Jennings.
Res., 215 Essex Ave., 07762. Tel: 732-449-5765; Fax: 732-449-0916. [CEM 2]
School—Tel: 732-449-4424; Fax: 732-449-7876.
Sisters 3; Lay Teachers 38; Students 602.
Catechesis/Religious Programs—Students 595.
Convent—211 Essex Ave., 07762. Tel: 732-449-6199.
Mission—Spring Lake, Monmouth Co., St. Margaret.

Tabernacle, Burlington Co., Holy Eucharist (1982), Revs. Richard Milewski; Joseph Farrell; Deacons Joseph Lambarski; Stanley Orkis; John Zimmerle.
Office: 520 Medford Lakes Rd., 08088. Tel: 609-268-8383; Fax: 609-268-3294.
Catechesis/Religious Programs—Tel: 609-268-7742. Dolores Wright, D.R.E.
Students 715.
Stations—New Lisbon Developmental Center, Tel: 609-726-1000; Leisuretown Senior Citizen Community.

Toms River, Ocean Co.,

1—St. Joseph, (Dover Township) (1883), Rev. Msgr. Sean P. Flynn; Revs. William P. Gardner; Roberto Ignacio; Daniel F. Gowen; Deacons John E. Gormley; Francis J. Babuschak; Edwin L. Voll, Jr.; Frank J. McKenna.
Mailing Address: P.O. Box 387, 509 Hooper Ave., 08754. Tel: 732-349-0018; Fax: 732-286-7064. [CEM]
School—Tel: 732-349-2355; Fax: 732-349-1064.
Sisters 6; Lay Teachers 39; Students 921.
High School—Monsignor Donovan High School, Tel: 732-349-8801; Fax: 732-349-8956.
Sisters 7; Lay Teachers 73; Students 908.
Catechesis/Religious Programs—Tel: 732-914-2420.
Students 1,150.
Mission—Island Heights, Ocean Co., St. Gertrude, Ocean & Central Aves., 08732.

2—St. Justin, (Dover Township) (1972), Revs. William J. Nolan; Alejandro A. Gronifillo; Joseph Halpin; Deacons Gregory Wallack; Richard Hauenstein; David L. Shapiro; Brent McNally; Louis Cartnick; Michael Fullen.
Res., 975 Fischer Blvd., 08753. Tel: 732-270-3980; Fax: 732-929-9411.
Catechesis/Religious Programs—Tel: 732-270-3797. Mrs. Michele Williams, D.R.E.
Students 1,465.

3—St. Luke, (Dover Township) (1982), Rev. Louis W. Kralovich; Deacons Donald G. MacCarrick; Ronald R. Wicks; Stephen F. Delligatti.
Res., 1674 Old Freehold Rd., 08755. Tel: 732-286-2222; Fax: 732-914-1080.
Catechesis/Religious Programs—Tel: 732-505-0108. Mrs. Mary Goss, D.R.E.
Students 1,128.

4—St. Maximilian Kolbe, (Dover Township) (1985), Rev. Francis E. Santitoro.
Residence and Mailing Address: 130 Vare St., P.O. Box 4144, 08756. Tel: 732-914-0300; 914-8550 (Res.); Fax: 732-240-9517.

Tuckerton, Ocean Co., St. Teresa (1944), Revs. Terence O. McAlinden; Silvano Amora, Assoc.; Deacon James Petrauskas.
Res., 128 Cedar St., 08087. Tel: 609-296-2504; Fax: 609-296-4530.
Catechesis/Religious Programs—Tel: 609-296-1940. Miss Susan Eggert, D.R.E.
Students 725.
Mission—Little Egg Harbor, Ocean Co., St. Michael, 64 W. Calabreeze Way, 08087. Tel: 609-296-3105.

Union Beach, Monmouth Co., Holy Family (1942), Revs. Patrick G. Fitzpatrick; Stanislaus T. Polczyk; Francis Cheruparambil; Deacons George Hooker; John Clymore. Pastoral Ministers: Sr. Rose Mary Malague, R.S.M.; Sr. Gloria Jean Bateman.
Res., Hwy. 36, P.O. Box 56, Keyport, 07735. Tel: 732-264-1484; Fax: 732-264-8369.
School—Tel: 732-264-9549; Fax: 732-335-9605.
Sisters 2; Lay Teachers 20; Students 423.
Catechesis/Religious Programs—Tel: 732-264-7043. Sr. Denise O'Boyle, R.S.M., D.R.E.
Students 822.
Convents—440 Sullivan Pl., 07735. Tel: 732-739-3065. Mercy Convent; 41 Hemlock St., Hazlet, 07730. Tel: 732-264-5353. Holy Family Convent

Washington Crossing, Mercer Co., St. George (1924), Rev. Msgr. George A. Ardos; Most Rev. John C. Reiss; Revs. Ernest Siska; Robert Stefanotti; Sr. Dorothy Jancola, R.S.M., Pastoral Assoc.; Deacons James Toolan; Thomas Daily.
Res., 1370 River Rd., P.O. Box 324, Titusville, 08560. Tel: 609-737-2015; Fax: 609-737-7863.
Catechesis/Religious Programs—Tel: 609-730-1703.
Students 190.
Station—Mercer County Correction Center.

Wayside, Monmouth Co., St. Anselm (1972), Rev. Robert F. Kaeding.
Res., 1028 Wayside Rd., 07712. Tel: 732-493-4411; Fax: 732-493-4272.
Catechesis/Religious Programs—Students 767.

West Long Branch, Monmouth Co., St. Jerome (1956), Rev. Frederick W. Jackiewicz.
Res., 254 Wall St., 07764. Tel: 732-222-1424; Fax: 732-222-2291.
School—250 Wall St., 07764. Tel: 732-222-8686; Fax: 732-222-3064.
Sisters 3; Lay Teachers 14; Students 251.
Catechesis/Religious Programs—250 Wall St., 07764.
Students 159.
Convent—250A Wall St., 07764. Tel: 732-222-2016.

West Windsor, Mercer Co., Church of St. David the King (1988), Rev. Timothy J. Capewell; Deacons Thomas Baker; Roger Dinella.
Res., 517 W. Village Rd., Princeton Jct., 08550. Tel: 609-275-7111; Fax: 609-799-1984.
Church—One New Village Rd., Princeton Jct., 08550-2003.
Catechesis/Religious Programs—Students 780.

Whiting, Ocean Co., St. Elizabeth Ann Seton (1976), Rev. Msgr. Joseph C. Shenrock, P.A.; Rev. Antony P. Poovakulam; Deacons Kyron J. Purcell; Joseph Rider; Robert Wolfe; David McComb; Russell Alexander; Leo Montini; Ralph Cordasco; Thomas White.
Res., 30 Schoolhouse Rd., 08759. Tel: 732-350-5001; Fax: 732-350-0912.
Catechesis/Religious Programs—Tel: 732-350-7391.
Students 169.

Willingboro, Burlington Co., Corpus Christi (1959), Revs. Stanley P. Lukaszewski; Michael T. Babalya; Deacons James E. Ayrer; Stanley R. Olshevski; John F. Vassallo, Jr.; Joseph Billbrough. In res., Rev. Msgr. Richard C. Brietske.
Res., 63 Sylvan Ln., 08046. Tel: 609-877-5322; Fax: 609-877-1695.
School—Charleston & Sunset Rds., 08046. Tel: 609-877-2144; Fax: 609-877-3153.
Sisters 1; Lay Teachers 18; Students 365.
Catechesis/Religious Programs—Charleston & Sunset Rds., 08046. Tel: 609-871-4680.
Students 260.

Chaplains of Public Institutions

Trenton. *Catholic Persons with Disabilities, New Jersey School for Deaf.* Sr. Helen Kline, S.S.J.
Donnelly Memorial Hospital of City of Trenton. Rev. Paul S. Rimassa.
Helene Fuld Hospital St. Joseph Church, 08638. Rev. Msgr. William J. Dailey.
Mercer County Correction Center St. George Rectory, Titusville, 08560. Rev. Msgr. George A. Ardos.
New Jersey State Prison CN 861, 08629. Sr. Elizabeth Gnam.
St. Francis Medical Center. Revs. Joel F. Szydlowski, O.F.M.; Linus E. Kopczewski, O.F.M.; Rudolph Wieszczck, O.F.M.

Bordentown. *Bordentown Correction Center, Burlington County.* Vacant.
Edward R. Johnstone Training and Research Center. Attended from St. Mary's Church.

Burlington. *Burlington County Hospital & Extended Care Center.* 311 High St., Mount Holly, 08060. Rev. Robert J.W. Schecker.
Burlington County Jail. 260 High St., Mount Holly, 08060. Rev. Robert J.W. Schecker.

Marlboro. *New Jersey State Hospital* St. Rose of Lima, Freehold, 07728. Rev. William T. Schneider.

Monmouth. *Monmouth County Jail.* Rev. Robert F. Kaeding.

Neptune. *Jersey Shore Medical Center* Holy Innocents, 07753. Rev. Douglas U. Hermansen.

New Lisbon. *New Jersey State Colony* Holy Eucharist, Tabernacle, 08088. Tel: 609-726-1000. Rev. Richard Milewski.
Ocean County Jail. Attended by St. Joseph, Toms River.

Yardville. *Garden State Correctional Center.* Rev. Andrew Hadalski, S.V.D.

Military Installations

Colts Neck. *Naval Weapons Station Earle.* Rev. Robert Paner.

Fort Dix. *Fort Dix.* Rev. Raymond Steen.

Lakehurst. *U.S. Naval Air Warfare Center.* Rev. James F. Finley.

Little Silver. *Fort Monmouth.* Rev. Joseph D'Silva.

McGuire Air Force Base. *McGuire Air Force Base.* Rev. David Gaeta.

Sandy Hook. *Fort Hancock.* Vacant.

On Duty Outside the Diocese:
Reverend Monsignors—
Punderson, Joseph R., Villa Stritch, Via Della Nocetta 63, Rome, 00164 Italy
Reverend Fathers—
Barile, Ralph E.
Bicomong, Sergio, U.S. Penitentiary, Lewisburg, PA
Campoli, John F., His Love Ministry, P.O. Box 433, Allenhurst, NJ 07711
Fahey, Edward J., Wilmington, DE
Hendricks, John J., Society of St. James the Apostle, 24 Clark St., Boston, MA 02109
Krisak, Anthony F., S.S., 618 East St., NE, #B, Washington, DC 20002
Kselman, John J., S.S., Weston School of Theology, Three Phillips Pl., Cambridge, MA 02138
LaForge, Joseph M., Newark, DE
McKeone, William
Sauchelli, James J., Omaha, NE

Zec, John J., Mount St. Mary Seminary, Plangborn Hall 366, Emmitsburg, MD 21727

Military Chaplains:
Reverend Fathers—
Flood, Peter J., 2603 Dow Dr., Omaha, NE 68123-1736
Inghilterra, Vincent J., Office Post Chap., Fort Leonard Wood, MO 65473
Liguori, Henry A., 7216 Enterprise Dr., Las Vegas, NV 89117

Leave of Absence:
Reverend Fathers—
Brown, Gerard J.
Christian, John S.
Gallagher, Richard
Iazzetta, Frank J.
McGrath, Francis
McHugh, Joseph F.
McManimon, James P.
Pienciak, Daniel B.
Russo, John W.
Swift, Daniel
Valentino, Frederick

Retired:
Most Rev.—
Reiss, John C., Villa Vianney, 2301 Lawrenceville Rd., Lawrenceville, NJ 08648
Reverend Monsignors—
Bogdan, Henry S., Incarnation Church, 1545 Pennington Rd., Trenton, NJ 08618
Bradley, Paul F., 14 Mark Dr., Long Branch, NJ 07740
Bulman, Robert T., St. Mark's Church, 215 Crescent Pkwy., Sea Girt, NJ 08750
Capitani, Anthony L., 1305 Chambers St., Trenton, NJ 08610
Coffey, Thomas A., Villa Vianney, 2301 Lawrenceville Rd., Lawrenceville, NJ 08648
Constance, Samuel C., 521 Walden Cir., Robbinsville, NJ 08691
Endebrock, John J., St. Elizabeth's Church, 424 Lincoln Ave., Avon, NJ 07717
Foley, James S., St. Mary's Church, 45 Crosswicks St., Bordentown, NJ 08505
Henry, Edward C., 3 Colonial Club Dr., No. 305, Boynton Beach, FL 33435
Maguire, William E., 9-C Lafayette Dr., Whiting, NJ 08759
O'Connor, Joseph A., Villa Vianney, 2301 Lawrenceville Rd., Lawrenceville, NJ 08648
Strand, Edward, 431 S.E. 3rd St, Apt. 403, Dania, FL 33004
Toomey, Leonard R., Villa Vianney, 2301 Lawrenceville Rd., Lawrenceville, NJ 08648
Wilus, John M., 225 Walnut St., South Amboy, NJ 08879
Wojciehowski, Thaddeus J., Villa Vianney, 2301 Lawrenceville Rd., Lawrenceville, NJ 08648
Reverend Fathers—
Albano, George M., St. Maximillian Kolbe Church, P.O. Box 4144, Toms River, NJ 08756-4144
Atzert, Edward P., Morris Hall, 2361, Lawrenceville, NJ 08648
Bausch, William, Box 1068, Point Pleasant Beach, NJ 08742
Byrnes, John P., 339 Holiday Lake Dr., E., Holiday, FL 33589
Cammisa, James N., 15 Hastings Pl., Monmouth Beach, NJ 07750
Cervenak, Andrew, Janosikova 21, 08001 Presov, Slovak Republic
Clancy, Frederick J., 52 New Haven Way, Rossmoor, Jamesburg, NJ 08831
Coley, James E., Versaille Apt., 224 Sullivan Way, A5B, Trenton, NJ 08628
Cook, John B., 7777 46th Ave., N., Lot 12, St. Petersburg, FL 33709
Davis, Eugene V., Villa Vianney, 2301 Lawrenceville Rd., Lawrenceville, NJ 08648
Delzell, David G., Tower of David, P.O. Box 292, Uniondale, PA 18470
Dougherty, Edward J., Villa Vianney, 2301 Lawrenceville Rd., Lawrenceville, NJ 08648
Eelman, William C., 171 Lakeshore Dr., Southampton, NJ 08088
Farre, Raymond P., Spain
Gannon, Earl A., Morris Hall, 1 Bishop Dr., Lawrenceville, NJ 08648
Horvath, Stephen G., P.O. Box 112, Bushkill, PA 18324
Lloyd, Vincent A., 713 Egret Ct., Edgewater, FL 32032
Matera, Philip T., 750 Estates Blvd., Apt. 254, Mercerville, NJ 08619
Miller, Joseph B., Marcella Nursing & Rehab, 2305 Rancocas Rd., Burlington Twp., NJ 08916
Petri, John C., 259 Squirrel Ridge Rd., Leasburg, NC 27291
Porazzo, Francis J., 61 Foxglove Rd., Pleasant Plains, Toms River, NJ 08753
Rittenhouse, Thomas R., St. Clement's Church, 172 Freneau Ave., Matawan, NJ 07747
Rucinski, Joseph S., 181 N.E. 14th Ave., Hallandale, FL 33009
Siska, Ernest J., Villa Vianney, 2301 Lawrenceville Rd., Lawrenceville, NJ 08648
Slydan, Gerard S., 6216 41st Ave., Hyattsville, MD 27082
Sullivan, John E., Villa Vianney, 2301 Lawrenceville Rd., Lawrenceville, NJ 08648
Thompson, James A., 49A Cambridge Cir., Leisure Village West, Lakehurst, NJ 08733

Permanent Deacons:
Alexander, Russell, (Retired), St. Elizabeth Ann Seton, Whiting
Allen, John W., (Retired), St. George, Titusville
Amatelli, Nicholas W., St. Barnabas, Bayville
Andre, Edner, Holy Spirit, Asbury Park
Andrews, Stephen W., St. Dorothea, Eatontown
Armstrong, Robert B., St. Mary, Barnegat
Auleta, Michael A., Holy Innocents, Neptune
Ayers, Damian, St. Dominic's, Brick
Ayrer, James E., Corpus Christi, Willingboro
Babuschak, Francis J., St. Joseph, Toms River
Bailey, Normand C., St. Rose, Belmar
Baker, Thomas, St. David the King, Princeton Junction
Beauchamps, Jose, St. Mary Cathedral, Trenton
Benedetti, Maurice T., (Retired), St. Paul, Princeton
Billbrough, Joseph C., (Retired), Corpus Christi, Willingboro
Blackwell, M. Darrell, Sacred Heart, Mt. Holly
Boehm, Michael P., Our Lady of Perpetual Help, Maple Shade
Brady, Robert F., Our Lady of Good Council, West Trenton
Brookes, Edwin H., Jr., St. Peter, Point Pleasant
Caponigro, Alfred E., Our Lady of Mount Carmel, Asbury Park
Card, Joseph A., Our Lady of Perpetual Help, Maple Shade
Carlin, George M., St. Paul, Burlington
Carroll, Joseph D., Holy Spirit, Asbury Park
Cartnick, Louis C., St. Justin's, Toms River
Casa, James L., Sacred Heart, Mount Holly
Casey, Keith J., St. Thomas More, Manalapan
Cater, Thomas H., St. Mary of the Lake, Lakewood
Chase, Daniel A., Holy Angels, Trenton
Clausen, Peter M., St. Barnabas, Bayville
Clymore, John L., Holy Family, Union Beach
Cole, John A., (Retired), Nativity, Fair Haven
Cook, Edwin, St. Ann, Keansburg
Cook, John, Sr., St. Peter Claver, Asbury Park
Cordasco, Ralph J., St. Elizabeth Ann Seton, Whiting
Cortright, William L., Marlboro Psychiatric Hospital, Marlboro
Crowley, James, (Retired), St. Agnes Church, Atlantic Highlands
Cullinane, John F., St. Mary of the Lake, Lakewood
Cummings, James H., St. Barnabas, Bayville
Czarnecki, John W., Sacred Heart, Bay Head
D'Agostino, Anthony J., Our Lady of Sorrows, Mercerville
D'Angelo, Richard V., St. Gregory the Great, Trenton
Daily, Thomas P., St. George, Titusville
Delligatti, Stephen F., St. Luke, Toms River
DeLuca, Peter J., Our Lady of Good Counsel, Moorestown
DeMarco, Leonard F., Epiphany, Brick
DeMauro, Gerald E., St. Ann's, Trenton
Dinella, Roger P., St. David the King, Princeton Junction
Donadieu, Joseph M., Diocesan Office of Communications
Dougherty, James, St. Francis of Assisi, Brant Beach
Doyle, Donald P., St. Mary, Medford
Earley, Daniel C., St. Ann, Browns Mills
Eby, Richard, St. Veronica, Howell
Ernst, Henry J., St. Mary, New Monmouth
Ervin, Martin A., Assumption, New Egypt
Finn, Lawrence W., Our Lady of Perpetual Help, Maple Shade
Fischer, Edward, III, Visitation, Brick
Flanagan, John P., St. Catharine, Holmdel
Fullen, Michael P., Sr., St. Justin, Toms River
Fuoco, Joseph R., St. Peter, Riverside
Fursman, James David, St. Catherine, Spring Lake
Gallagher, Paul A., St. Dominic, Brick
Gallagher, William J., St. Charles Borromeo, Cinnaminson
Galvan, Silverius F., St. Mary of the Lake, Lakewood
Garvey, Thomas J., St. Anthony of Padua, Hightstown
Gerard, John J., (Retired), Ascension, Bradley Beach
Giglio, Frank E., Our Lady of Good Counsel, Moorestown
Gilchrist, John A., St. John Church, Lakehurst
Glukowsky, Joseph A., St. Gregory the Great, Trenton
Gomez, Victor L., Our Lady of Providence, Neptune
Gormley, John E., St. Joseph, Toms River
Gregory, Gabriel, St. John, Lakehurst
Gregory, Thomas J., St. Anthony of Padua, Hightstown
Groffie, John F., St. Gregory the Great, Trenton
Grussler, John R., Holy Cross, Trenton
Gularek, Theodore V., St. Veronica, Howell
Hambleton, Richard N., St. Mary, Barnegat
Haney, John J., St. Martha, Point Pleasant
Hannawacker, Joseph A., Blessed Sacrament, Trenton
Harbeck, Jay C., Holy Cross, Rumson
Harris, David M., St. Mary, Bordentown
Hauenstein, Richard A., St. Justin, Toms River
Heller, James T., (Retired), St. Pius X, Forked River
Henwood, Gerald V., Office of the Diaconate, Trenton
Hepp, Joseph L., St. Anthony of Padua, Hightstown
Herr, Edward R., St. Dorothea, Eatontown
Hoch, Eugene, St. John Neumann, Mount Laurel
Hoefling, John F., Sacred Heart, Mount Holly
Hooker, George C., Holy Family, Keyport
Huether, Vincent E., (Retired), Freehold
Hughes, John P., St. John Neumann, Mount Laurel
Iadanza, John M., St. Mary of the Lakes, Medford
Iglesias, Manuel F., Holy Angels, Trenton
Imholte, Ralph, St. Mary, Colts Neck
Jennings, Edward F., St. Catharine, Spring Lake
Johnson, James G., St. Mary, Barnegat
Jones, Francis A., St. Paul, Burlington
Katzer, Alfred W., St. Veronica, Howell
Kelly, James A., Holy Trinity, Long Branch
Kennedy, Patrick W., St. Anthony of Padua, Hightstown
Kerr, Ronald J., Sr., Our Lady of Perpetual Help, Maple Shade
Kirkham, Donald F., St. Pius X, Forked River
Klincewicz, John G., Our Lady, Star of the Sea, Long Branch
Knipp, Joseph P., Sacred Heart, Riverton
Kruk, Leonard B., Visitation, Brick
Lachance, Paul A., St. Paul, Princeton
LaManchia, Ralph A., St. Gregory the Great, Hamilton Square
Lambarski, Joseph A., Holy Eucharist, Vincentown
Little, Ronald J., St. Mary of the Lake, Medford
Littlefield, James J., St. Veronica, Howell
Lombardo, Earl H., St. Mary, Barnegat
MacCarrick, Donald G., St. Luke, Toms River
MacDonald, Lawrence, (Retired), St. Mary of the Lakes, Medford
Machion, Robert D., Holy Assumption, Roebling
Magee, James D., (Retired), St. Mary, Bordentown
Maier, Edward, (Retired), St. Martha, Point Pleasant
Malhame, Eugene G., Jr., St. Rose, Belmar
Malloy, Joseph J., Our Lady of Sorrows, Trenton
Manaloris, James A., Holy Name, Delran
Marcello, Salvatore, Holy Angels, Trenton
Martin, Patrick J., St. Mary, Barnegat
Martucci, Anthony R., St. Mary of the Lake, Lakewood
Mattozzi, Guido J., St. Joachim, Trenton
McCabe, John, St. Mary, Deal
McComb, David M., (Retired), St. Elizabeth Ann Seton, Whiting
McCormack, Joseph, Epiphany, Bricktown
McGann, Francis P., Jr., Our Lady of Good Counsel, Moorestown
McGrath, James, St. Catherine, Holmdel
McHugh, Joseph, Our Lady of Perpetual Help, Maple Shade
McKenna, Frank, St. Joseph, Toms River
McKenna, Kenneth M., St. Mary, Deal
McKeon, James, St. Gabriel, Marlboro
McNally, Brent G., St. Justin, Toms River
McNulty, James, (Retired), Ascension, Bradley Beach
Micali, James Mark, St. Thomas More, Manalapan
Miller, Donald C., St. Clement, Matawan
Moir, Gene F., St. Veronica, Howell
Mosteller, Herman, St. Joseph, Beverly
Mullarkey, Michael F., Epiphany, Brick
Murray, William, Precious Blood Church, Monmouth Beach
Mustillo, Anthony D., St. Catharine, Holmdel
Mylod, Philip J., (Retired), Jersey Shore Medical Center, Neptune
Nimon, Robert, St. Leo the Great, Lincroft
Noone, Thomas, St. William the Abbot, Allenwood
Nowak, Ronald, Epiphany, Bricktown
O'Brien, Christopher D., St. Joseph, Keyport
O'Brien, John, Office of Diaconate, Trenton

O'Connor, John P., (Retired), St. Catharine, Spring Lake
O'Donnell, John J., Our Lady Queen of Peace, Hainesport
Olshevski, Stanley R., Corpus Christi, Willingboro
Orkis, Stanley, Holy Eucharist, Vincentown
Owens, Lester J., St. Gabriel's, Marlboro
Pacitti, Albert, Holy Trinity, Long Branch
Palsir, James W., St. James, Pennington
Parr, Allan T., Sr., St. Gregory the Great, Trenton
Patton, Joseph R., St. Mary of the Lakes, Medford
Pelkowski, Raymond R., St. Benedict, Holmdel
Perkins, Charles A., St. Joseph, Beverly
Petrauskas, James J., St. Theresa's, Tuckerton
Pierfy, Jeffery, Our Lady of Sorrows, Mercerville
Pirozzi, Neil, St. Gregory the Great, Trenton
Price, Walter L., St. Ann, Browns Mills
Prihoda, Frank J., St. Anthony of Padua, Hightstown
Principato, Michael, St. Catherine, Farmingdale
Purcell, Kyron J., St. Elizabeth Ann Seton, Whiting
Putnam, Harry A., St. Mary, Bordentown
Rasi, Stephen P., St. Anthony, Hightstown
Restivo, Louis C., Sacred Heart, Mount Holly
Richardson, Gary T., St. Mary, Bordentown
Rider, Joseph H., St. Elizabeth Ann Seton, Whiting
Rivera, Juan A., St. Mary Cathedral, Trenton
Ross, Michael D., St. Paul's, Princeton
Rowley, William R., Sacred Heart, Mt. Holly
Russo, James C., St. Gabriel, Marlboro
Saake, Dennis J., St. Mark, Sea Girt
Schwarz, Herbert, St. Benedict, Holmdel
Schwind, Albert, St. Francis of Assisi, Brant Beach
Sciarrotta, Samuel P., St. James Church, Pennington
Seaman, Joseph F., Our Lady of Perpetual Help, Maple Shade
Seaton, George L., St. Theresa, Tuckerton
Sepich, William S., St. Charles Borromeo, Cinnaminson
Shapiro, David L., St. Justin, Toms River
Shea, Raymond A., St. Maximillian Kolbe, Toms River
Sherpensky, Frank, St. Ann, Browns Mills
Slavin, Dennis E., Office of Family Life, West Long Branch
Slee, Louis, Blessed Sacrament, Trenton
Sowa, Frank J., (Retired), St. Stanislaus, Trenton
Stap, Matthew J., (Retired), St. Joseph, Beverly
Staub, Raymond W., Jr., Assumption, New Egypt
Talbot, Norman, St. Mary of the Lakes, Medford
Tarala, Anthony M., (Retired), St. John's, Lakehurst
Tarzy, Barry R., St. Joan of Arc, Marlton
Taylor, Michael A., St. Barnabas, Bayville
Teran, Galo, St. Anthony Claret, Lakewood
Tharp, Robert, Holy Angels, Trenton
Tobin, James R., Sacred Heart, Bay Head
Toolan, James W., St. George, Titusville
Torres, Benito, S.S. Peter & Paul, Trenton
Ulmer, Ronald J., St. Joseph, Beverly
Valentin, Juan E., St. Mary Cathedral, Trenton
Vassallo, John F., Corpus Christi, Willingboro
Vazquez, Emiliano, St. Mary Cathedral, Trenton
Vicari, Salvatore J., Jr., Visitation, Brick Town
Vlcej, Robert J., St. Ann's, Keansburg
Vogel, Anthony D., St. Hedwig, Trenton
Voll, Edwin L., Jr., St. Joseph, Toms River
Wallack, Gregory B., St. Justin, Toms River
Walsh, James P., (Retired), Holy Innocent, Neptune
Walsh, John J., St. Thomas More, Manalapan
Wanat, John A., St. Rose of Lima, Freehold
White, Thomas, C. Wagner Youth Correctional Facility, Bordentown
Wicks, Ronald, St. Luke, Toms River
Wilson, William A., St. Gregory the Great, Hamilton Square
Wolfe, Robert A., (Retired), St. Elizabeth Ann Seton, Whiting
Yaccarine, John A., Holy Trinity, Long Branch
Young, Donald A., St. Mary, New Monmouth
Zadworny, Barry J., St. Hedwig, Trenton
Zebrowski, John J., St. Thomas More, Manalapan
Zimmerle, John O., Holy Eucharist, Vincentown

INSTITUTIONS LOCATED IN THE DIOCESE

[A] COLLEGES AND UNIVERSITIES

LAKEWOOD. *Georgian Court College*, 900 Lakewood Ave., 08701-2697. Tel: 732-364-2200; Fax: 732-367-3920
For a complete listing, refer to the Colleges and Universities section.

[B] HIGH SCHOOLS, DIOCESAN

TRENTON. *McCorristin High School*, 175 Leonard Ave., 08610. Tel: 609-586-3705; Fax: 609-586-6584. Mr. Joseph R. Lemme, Prin. Sisters 2; Lay Teachers 39; Students 515.

Notre Dame High School, 601 Lawrence Rd., 08648. Tel: 609-882-7900; Fax: 609-882-5723. Mr. Barry Edward Breen, Prin.; Mrs. Mary Liz Ivins, Asst. Prin.; Mr. David M. Milinowicz, Asst. Prin.; Rev. Michael E. Lang, Chap. Sisters of Mercy 1; Lay Teachers 69; Students 1,082.

BELMAR. *Saint Rose High School*, 605 Seventh Ave., 07719. Tel: 732-681-2858; Fax: 732-280-2745. Michele R. Campbell, Ph.D. Students 540; Sisters 6; Lay Teachers 45.

DELRAN. *Holy Cross High School*, 5035 Rte. 130 S., 08075. Tel: 609-461-5400; Fax: 609-764-0806. Sisters of I.H.M., Scranton, PA. Mr. Jerome T. McGowan, Prin.; Rev. Kenneth W. Ekdahl. Sisters 9; Lay Teachers 64; Students 1,118.

HOLMDEL. *St. John Vianney High School*, Line Rd., 07733. Tel: 732-739-0800; Fax: 732-739-0824. Mr. Joseph F. Deroba, Prin.; Rev. Jack Dover, Chap. Sisters 1; Lay Teachers 56; Students 935.

NEW MONMOUTH. *Mater Dei High School*, 538 Church St., 07748. Tel: 732-671-9100; Fax: 732-671-9214. Mr. Frank Poleski, Jr., Prin. Students 415; Lay Teachers 29.

RED BANK. *Red Bank Catholic High School*, 10 Peters Pl., 07701. Tel: 732-747-1774; Fax: 732-741-1936. Mr. Robert Abatemarco, Prin. Sisters 2; Lay Teachers 60; Students 793.

TOMS RIVER. *Monsignor Donovan High School*, 711 Hooper Ave., 08753. Tel: 732-349-8801; Fax: 732-286-7064. Mr. Edward Gere, Prin. Sisters 7; Lay Teachers 66; Students 914; Priests 1.

[C] HIGH SCHOOLS, PRIVATE

TRENTON. *Villa Victoria Academy*, 376 W. Upper Ferry Rd., 08628. Tel: 609-882-1700. Upper School, Grades 7-8 (Coed); Grades 9-12 (Girls). Sr. Mary Ann Gecina, M.P.F., Prin.; Sr. Lillian Harrington, M.P.F., Pres. Sisters 7; Lay Teachers 14; Students 126.

LINCROFT. *Christian Brothers Academy*, 07738. Tel: 732-747-1959; Fax: 732-747-1643. Bros. Andrew O'Gara, F.S.C.; Ralph Montedoro, F.S.C. Priests 1; Brothers 21; Lay Teachers 46; Students 900.

PRINCETON. *Stuart Country Day School of the Sacred Heart.* (Grades 9-12), 1200 Stuart Rd., 08540. Tel: 609-921-2330; Fax: 609-497-0784. Lay Teachers 24; Students 118.

[D] INTER-PARISH ELEMENTARY SCHOOLS

TRENTON. *Our Lady's Cathedral Academy.* (Grades PreK-8), 31 Chancery Ln., 08618. Tel: 609-394-5936; Fax: 609-394-7287. Sisters 1; Lay Teachers 18; Students 292.

MANAHAWKIN. *All Saints Regional Catholic School.* (Grades K-1), 179 S. Main St., 08050. Lay Teachers 2; Total Enrollment 24.

[E] ELEMENTARY SCHOOLS, PRIVATE

TRENTON. *Villa Victoria Academy.* (Grades PreK-6). (Coed), 376 W. Upper Ferry Rd., 08628. Tel: 609-883-5760; Fax: 609-882-8421. Lower School. Sr. Joan DiRienzo, M.P.F., Prin. Sisters 3; Lay Teachers 6; Students 130.

PRINCETON. *Stuart County Day School of the Sacred Heart.* (Grades PreK-8), 1200 Stuart Rd., 08540. Tel: 609-921-2330; Fax: 609-497-0784. Sisters 1; Lay Teachers 50; Students 392.

[F] CATHOLIC CHARITIES, DIOCESE OF TRENTON

TRENTON. *Catholic Charities*, 47 N. Clinton Ave., P.O. Box 1423, 08607. Tel: 609-394-5181; Fax: 609-695-6978. Mr. Francis E. Dolan, Exec. Dir.; George Bontcue, Assoc. Exec. Dir., Fiscal Affairs; Barry H. Cole, Ph.D., Assoc. Exec. Dir., Prog. Services; Michael R. Allen, Assoc. Exec. Dir., Community Affairs.

Burlington Behavioral Healthcare Division, 114 Delaware Ave., Burlington, 08016. Tel: 609-386-1746. Frank J. Helverson, Dir.

Mercer Behavioral Healthcare Division, 39 N. Clinton Ave., 08609. Tel: 609-394-9398. Jerome Lindauer, Dir.

Monmouth / Ocean Behavioral Healthcare Division, 36 W. Water St., Toms River, 08753. Tel: 908-505-3113. Robert G. Hodnett, Dir.

Emergency Services Division, P.O. Box 2387, Cinnaminson, 08077. Tel: 609-786-1868.

Family Growth Division, 39 N. Clinton Ave., 08609. Tel: 609-394-5157. Services for victims and perpetuators of family violence. Ronald C. Gering, Dir.

Providence House Division, P.O. Box 496, Willingboro, 08046. Services to women and children in danger of physical abuse. Jean Metz, Dir.

Our Lady of Light Chapel, 47 N. Clinton Ave., Box 1423, 08607-1423. Tel: 609-386-6221; Fax: 609-394-5181.

St. Michael Children's Home, c/o Diocese of Trenton, 701 Lawrenceville Rd., 08648.

[G] DAY CARE CENTERS

LONG BRANCH. *St. John the Baptist Family Center*, 272 Willow Ave., 07740. Tel: 732-229-8905; 229-8527; 571-1003; Fax: 732-571-0280. Day Care and Child Development Center. Children 210.

[H] CARE INSTITUTIONS FOR CHILDREN

TRENTON. *Sister Georgine School*, 544 Chestnut Ave., 08611. Tel: 609-396-5444
For a complete listing, refer to the Special Care Facilities section.

HOPEWELL. *St. Michael's Orphanage and Industrial School* Mailing Address: c/o the Diocese of Trenton, 701 Lawrenceville Rd. Trenton, 08648.
For a complete listing, refer to the Special Care Facilities section.

[I] GENERAL HOSPITALS

TRENTON. *St. Francis Medical Center*, 601 Hamilton Ave., 08629. Tel: 609-599-5000; Fax: 609-695-2744
For a complete listing, refer to the Hospitals section.

[J] SPECIAL HOSPITALS AND SANATORIA FOR INVALIDS

LAWRENCEVILLE. *Morris Hall / Saint Lawrence, Inc.*, 2381 Lawrenceville Rd., 08648. Tel: 609-896-9500
For a complete listing, refer to the Special Care Facilities section.

Morris Hall / Saint Lawrence, Inc., 1 Bishops' Dr., 08648-0498. Tel: 609-896-0006
For a complete listing, refer to the Special Care Facilities section.

[K] SPECIALIZED CHILD CARE AGENCIES

RED BANK. *Collier Group Home*, 180 Spring St., 07701. Tel: 732-842-8337
For a complete listing, refer to the Special Care Facilities section.

WICKATUNK. *Collier Services*, Collier High School, Conover Rd., 07765. Tel: 732-946-4771
For a complete listing, refer to the Special Care Facilities section.

[L] HOMES FOR AGED

TRENTON. *Cathedral Square Housing, Inc.*, 26 W. Hanover Pl., 08608. Tel: 609-392-1111
For a complete listing, refer to the Special Care Facilities section.

LAWRENCEVILLE. *Morris Hall-Saint Lawrence, Inc.*, 1 Bishops' Dr., P.O. Box 6498, 08648-0498. Tel: 609-896-0006
For a complete listing, refer to the Special Care Facilities section.

[M] MONASTERIES AND RESIDENCES FOR PRIESTS AND BROTHERS

TRENTON. *Villa Vianney* Lawrenceville, 2301 Lawrenceville Rd., P.O. Box 6589, 08648. Tel: 609-219-0177. In res. Most Rev. John C. Reiss; Rev. Msgr. Thomas A. Coffey; Rev. Msgr. Joseph A. O'Connor; Rev. Msgr. Leonard R. Toomey; Rev. Msgr. Thaddeus J. Wojciehowski; Revs. Eugene V. Davis; Edward Dougherty; Ernest Siska.

BORDENTOWN. *Society of the Divine Word*, 101 Park St., 08505. Tel: 609-298-0549; Fax: 609-298-6014. Very Rev. Martin Padovani, S.V.D., Rector; Revs. Patrick Connor, S.V.D.; Francis Mahon, S.V.D.; Norman R. St. John, S.V.D.; Patrick Wenrick, S.V.D.; Victor Butler, S.V.D.; Jacques Nyssen, S.V.D.; Joseph Gunning, S.V.D.; Stephen Szmutko, S.V.D.; James Artzer, S.V.D.; Jerome Brzakowski, S.V.D.; Charles Erb, S.V.D.; William Kelly, S.V.D.; Peter Silvester, S.V.D.; Vance Thorne, S.V.D.; Aloysius Turbek, S.V.D.; Paul McVinney, S.V.D.; Bros. Louis Gagnon, S.V.D.; Patrick Hegarty, S.V.D.; Thomas Granfield, S.V.D.; James Mullen, S.V.D.; Joseph Hornek, S.V.D.

LINCROFT. *Christian Brothers, St. La Salle Auxiliary*, 850 Newman Springs Rd., P.O. Box 238, 07738. Tel: 732-842-4359.

LaSalle Lincroft, Inc., 850 Newman Springs Rd., 07738. Tel: 732-842-7420. Bro. William Martin, Contact Person. Brothers 3.

De La Salle Hall, Inc., 810 Newman Springs Rd., 07738. Tel: 732-530-9470. Bro. Joseph Loewenstein, F.S.C., Dir. Brothers Retirement Home. Brothers 5; Lay Staff 35; Patients 23.

La Salle Provincialate Inc., 800 Newman Springs Rd., 07738. Tel: 732-842-7420; Fax: 732-530-3504. Brothers of the Christian Schools. Bro. Michael Corry, F.S.C., Prov.

The Vaugirard Religious & Charitable Trust, 800 Newman Springs Rd., 07738.

MOUNT LAUREL. *Cistercian Monastery of Our Lady of Fatima*, 564 Walton Ave., 08054-9582. Tel: 609-235-1330. Cistercian Fathers. Revs. Lino S. Parente, O.Cist., Prior, (Italy); Anselmo M. Florio, O.Cist.; Maurizio Nicoletti, O.Cist., (Italy); Teclezghi Ucbaghiorghis, O.Cist.

[N] CONVENTS AND RESIDENCES FOR SISTERS

TRENTON. Congregation of Marianites of Holy Cross. Sr. Vincent Dornbush, Admin.; Rev. James T. Burtchaell, C.S.C., Chap.

Notre Dame Diocesan Convent Lawrenceville. Intercongregational Living, 681 Lawrence Rd., 08648. Tel: 609-406-7433. Office for Religious. Tel: 609-406-7400; 800-552-5354. Sisters 21.

Sisters of St. Francis of Philadelphia, St. Clare Convent, 917 Melrose Ave., 08629. Tel: 609-695-7805. Sr. Albert Mary McSwiggen.

BORDENTOWN. *Franciscan Monastery of Saint Clare*, 201 Crosswicks St., 08505. Tel: 609-298-0016. Sr. Mary McCourt, O.S.C., Abbess.

HAMILTON SQUARE. *Sisters of St. Francis of Philadelphia*, Franciscan Convent, 24 Shelley Ln., 08690. Tel: 609-588-9076. Sr. Mary Rita Barbernitz.

HARVEY CEDARS. *Maris Stella Retreat House and Summer House*, 7201 Long Beach Blvd., 08008. Tel: 609-494-0499. Sisters of Charity of St. Elizabeth, Convent Station. Sr. Audrey Boettcher, Admin.

HAZLET. *St. Benedict's Convent*, 31 Cresci Blvd., 07730. Tel: 732-264-3553.

PRINCETON. *Our Lady of Princeton*, Great and Drakes Corner Rds., 08540. Tel: 609-924-1236. Sr. Vincent Dornbush, Admin.; Rev. James T. Burtchaell, C.S.C., Chap. Sisters 15.

WICKATUNK. *Convent of the Sisters of Good Shepherd*, 160 Conover Rd., 07765. Tel: 732-946-7877; 946-7886. Sisters of Good Shepherd of New Jersey. Virginia Daniels, Coord. Sisters 11.

[O] CHAPELS

TRENTON. *Our Lady of Light Chapel*, 47 N. Clinton Ave., Box 1423, 08607-1423. Tel: 609-386-6221; 394-5181.

LAWRENCEVILLE. *Our Lady of the Rosary Chapel*, 1 Bishop's Dr., Box 6498, 08648. Tel: 609-896-0006. Located in Morris Hall. Rev. Justin J. Herbst, Chap.

[P] HOUSES OF PRAYER

TRENTON. *Morning Star House of Prayer*, 312 W. Upper Ferry Rd., 08628. Tel: 609-882-2766. Sr. Geraldine Calabrese, M.P.F. Religious Teachers Filippini 2.

MOUNT HOLLY. *Francis House of Prayer*, 39 Springside Rd., 08060. Mailing Address: P.O. Box 392, Rancocas, 08073. Tel: 609-877-0509; Fax: 609-877-5810. Sr. Marcella Springer, S.S.J.

NEPTUNE. *The Upper Room Spiritual Center*, P.O. Box 1104, 07754-1104. Tel: 732-922-0550; Fax: 732-922-3904. Sr. Maureen Christensen, Co-Dir.; Sr. Maureen Conroy, Co-Dir.; Rev. Justin Capato, O.S.B.

[Q] RETREAT HOUSES

ELBERON. *Stella Maris Retreat House*, 981 Ocean Ave., 07740. Tel: 732-229-0602. Sr. Beatrice Ryan, C.S.J.P., Dir. Sisters of St. Joseph of Peace 3.

HARVEY CEDARS. *Maris Stella*, Sisters Retreat and Vacation Center, 7201 Long Beach Blvd., 08008. Tel: 609-494-0499. Sisters of Charity of St. Elizabeth. Sr. Audrey Boettcher, Admin.

LONG BRANCH. *San Alfonso Retreat House*, 755 Ocean Ave., P.O. Box 3098, 07740. Tel: 732-222-2731. Revs. John F. Murray, C.SS.R., Rector Dir.; Andrew Skeabeck, C.SS.R.; John Ruef, C.SS.R.; William Collins, C.SS.R.; Dennis Foley, C.SS.R.; John McGowan, C.SS.R.; Bros. Bernard Colleran, C.SS.R.; Thomas Rochacewicz; Sr. Miriam Carmelita Romanelli, S.S.J. Priests 6; Brothers 2; Sisters 1.

SOUTH MANTOLOKING. *St. Joseph by the Sea Retreat House*, 400 Rte. 35 N., 08738. Tel: 732-892-8494. Sr. Donna Gaglioti, M.P.F., Dir. Sisters 4.

[R] PERSONAL PRELATURES

PRINCETON. *Opus Dei*. (Prelature of the Holy Cross and Opus Dei), Mercer House, 34 Mercer St., 08540. Tel: 609-497-9448. Rev. C. John McCloskey.

[S] NEWMAN CENTERS

PRINCETON. *Campus Ministry for the Diocese of Trenton*, Aquinas Institute, Princeton University, 65 Stockton St., 08540. Tel: 609-924-1820. Rev. Thomas J. Mullelly, Dir. & Chap.

Emmaus House, Rider College, 2116 Lawrenceville Rd., Trenton, 08648. Tel: 609-896-0394.

Mercer County Community College, 1200 Old Trenton Rd., Hamilton Township, 08690. Tel: 609-896-0394.

Bede House, Trenton State College, 492 Ewingville Rd., Trenton, 08638. Tel: 609-771-9091. Rev. James Dever, O.F.S.F., Chap.

Georgian Court College, Lakewood Ave., Lakewood, 08701. Tel: 732-364-2200. Rev. Dennis Bajkowski, Campus Min.

Ocean County Community College. (Toms River). Rev. Louis W. Kralovich, Chap.

St. Luke Rectory, 1674 Old Freehold Rd., Toms River, 08753. Tel: 732-229-0403.

Monmouth University, Bethlehem House, 16 Beachwood Ave., West Long Branch, 07764. Tel: 732-229-0403. Rev. F. W. Jackiewicz, Chap.

[T] MISCELLANEOUS LISTINGS

TRENTON. *Martin House*, 802 E. State St., P.O. Box 1025, 08606. Tel: 609-989-1040. Revs. Brian McCormick; William J. McLaughlin.

Martin House Learning Center, 794 E. State St., P.O. Box 1025, 08606. Tel: 609-989-1040; Fax: 609-989-0933.

ASBURY PARK. *Mercy Center, Inc.*, 1106 Main St., 07712. Tel: 732-774-9397. Carol Ann Henry, R.S.M., Dir.

BRICK. *Mid-Life Directions*, 4 Palm Ave., 08723. Tel: 732-255-1239. Sr. Anne Brennan, C.S.J., Contact Person. Purpose: Ministry for personal and spiritual growth specifically for people in midlife and later years.

ELBERON. *Emmaus House*, 80 Norwood Ave., 07740. Tel: 732-229-5834. Sr. Patricia Mary Walsh, O.P., Admin.

LAKEWOOD. *Health and Retirement Planning: Intercommunity Project*, 900 Lakewood Dr., 08701-2697. Tel: 732-364-2200, Ext. 212. Sr. Jean Scharf, G.N.S.H. Purpose: to assist regional participating religious orders in meeting the health care and retirement needs of their members.

LAWRENCEVILLE. *Morris Hall / St. Lawrence, Inc.*, 2381 Lawrenceville Rd., 08648. Tel: 609-896-9500. Mr. Charles Brennan, Admin.; Rev. Justin J. Herbst, Chap.; Sr. Claire DeStefano, S.S.J., Dir. of Pastoral Care. Bed Capacity 116; Bed Licensure 116.

SWAINTON. *Holy Redeemer Visiting Nurse Agency, Inc.*, 1801 Rte. 9 N., 08210. Tel: 609-465-2082; 800-745-4693. Denise E. Collins, Pres. A subsidiary of Holy Redeemer Health System, Inc. Sponsor: Sisters of the Holy Redeemer, C.S.R. A Medicare Certified Home Health Agency serving patients in their own homes. A Medicare Certified Hospice Program providing services for terminally ill patients and their families. Outpatient Rehabiliation.

Atlantic County Office, 701 Rte. 50, Mays Landing, 08330. Tel: 609-625-2200; 800-788-3029.

Ocean County Office, 2214 Rte. 37 E., Toms River, 08753. Tel: 732-288-0868; 800-488-2669.

Holy Redeemer Rehabilitation Center, 1261 Rte. 9 S., Ste. 1, Cape May Court House, 08210. Tel: 609-465-3866.

RELIGIOUS INSTITUTES OF MEN REPRESENTED IN THE DIOCESE

For further details refer to the corresponding bracketed number in the Religious Institutes of Men or Women section.

[0200]—*Benedictine Monks*. (St. Mary's Abbey, Morristown, NJ).—O.S.B.
[0700]—*Saint Joseph's Society of the Sacred Heart*.—S.S.J.
[0030]—*Brothers of the Christian Schools*.—F.S.C.
[0270]—*Carmelite Fathers and Brothers*. (Prov. of the Most Pure Heart of Mary).—O.Carm.
[0340]—*Cistercian Fathers*.—O.Cist.
[0820]—*Congregation of the Fathers of Mercy*.—C.P.M.
[0390]—*Consolata Missionaries*.—I.M.C.
[0480]—*Conventual Franciscans*. (Provs. of the Immaculate Conception & St. Anthony of Padua).—O.F.M.Conv.
[0520]—*Franciscan Friars*. (Prov. of the Most Holy Name of Jesus).—O.F.M.
[0920]—*Oblates of Saint Francis de Sales*. (Wilmington-Philadelphia Prov.).—O.S.F.S.
[0430]—*Order of Preachers (Dominicans)*. (Prov. of St. Joseph).—O.P.
[1310]—*Order of the Holy Trinity*.—O.SS.T.
[1070]—*Redemptorist Fathers*. (Baltimore Prov.).—C.SS.R.
[0700]—*Saint Joseph's Society of the Sacred Heart (The Josephites)*.—S.S.J.
[0420]—*Society of the Divine Word*.—S.V.D.
[0560]—*Third Order Regular of Saint Francis*. (Prov. of the Most Sacred Heart of Jesus).—T.O.R.

RELIGIOUS INSTITUTES OF WOMEN REPRESENTED IN THE DIOCESE

[0233]—*Benedictine Sisters of Elizabeth, NJ*.—O.S.B.
[1810]—*Bernardine Sisters of Third Order of St. Francis*.—O.S.F.
[2410]—*Congregation of the Marianites of Holy Cross*.—M.S.C.
[1830]—*Contemplative Sisters of the Good Shepherd*.—R.G.S.
[1070-05]—*Dominican Sisters*. (Amityville, NY).—O.P.
[1070-15]—*Dominican Sisters*. (Blauvelt, NY).—O.P.
[1070-18]—*Dominican Sisters*. (Caldwell, NJ).—O.P.
[1070-06]—*Dominican Sisters*. (Newburgh, NY).—O.P.
[1070-11]—*Dominican Sisters*. (Sparkhill, NY).—O.P.
[1070-05]—*Dominican Sisters of Hope*. (Amityville, NY).—O.P.
[1170]—*Felician Sisters*.—C.S.S.F.
[1365]—*Franciscan Missionary Sisters of the Infant Jesus*.—F.M.I.J.
[1180]—*Franciscan Sisters of Allegany, NY*.—O.S.F.
[1425]—*Franciscan Sisters of Peace*.—F.S.P.
[1470]—*Franciscan Sisters of St. Joseph*.—F.S.S.J.
[1190]—*Franciscan Sisters of the Atonement (Graymoor)*.—S.A.
[]—*Franciscans Da Acao Pastoral of Sao Paolo, Brazil*.—F.A.P.
[1840]—*Grey Nuns of the Sacred Heart*.—G.N.S.H.
[2490]—*Medical Mission Sisters*.—S.C.M.M.
[2700]—*Missionary Catechists of the Sacred Hearts of Jesus & Mary*.—SS.CC.J.M.
[3040]—*Oblate Sisters of Providence*.—O.S.P.
[3760]—*Order of St. Clare*.—O.S.C.
[3465]—*Religious of the Sacred Heart of Mary*.—R.S.H.M.
[3430]—*Religious Teachers Filippini*.—M.P.F.
[2970]—*School Sisters of Notre Dame*.—S.S.N.D.
[]—*Sisters for Christian Community*.—S.F.C.C.
[0590]—*Sisters of Charity of Saint Elizabeth, Convent Station*.—S.C.
[0430]—*Sisters of Charity of the Blessed Virgin Mary*-(Dubuque, IA).—B.V.M.
[2575]—*Sisters of Mercy of the Americas*. (Dallas; Merion; New Jersey).—R.S.M.
[3000]—*Sisters of Notre Dame de Namur*. (Cincinnati).—S.N.D.deN.
[3730]—*Sisters of Order of St. Basil the Great*.—O.S.B.M.
[3360]—*Sisters of Providence of Saint Mary of the Woods, IN*.—S.P.
[3830]—*Sisters of Saint Joseph of Brentwood*. (New York).—C.S.J.
[]—*The Sisters of St. Francis of Baltimore*.
[1630]—*Sisters of St. Francis of Penance and Christian Charity*.—O.S.F.
[1650]—*The Sisters of St. Francis of Philadelphia*.—O.S.F.
[3840]—*Sisters of St. Joseph of Carondelet*.—C.S.J.
[3850]—*Sisters of St. Joseph of Chambery*.—C.S.J.
[3893]—*Sisters of St. Joseph of Chestnut Hill, Philadelphia*.—S.S.J.
[3890]—*Sisters of St. Joseph of Peace*.—C.S.J.P.
[1830]—*The Sisters of the Good Shepherd*.—R.G.S.
[1970]—*Sisters of the Holy Family of Nazareth*.—C.S.F.N.
[2110]—*Sisters of the Humility of Mary*.—H.M.
[3480]—*Sisters of the Resurrection*.—C.R.
[1490]—*Sisters of the Third Franciscan Order*. (Syracuse).—O.S.F.
[2170]—*Sisters, Servants of the Immaculate Heart of Mary*. (Philadelphia).—I.H.M.
[2160]—*Sisters, Servants of the Immaculate Heart of Mary*. (Scranton).—I.H.M.
[4060]—*Society of the Holy Child Jesus*.—S.H.C.J.
[4070]—*Society of the Sacred Heart*.—R.S.C.J.
[4120]—*The Ursuline Sisters of Brown County, OH*.—O.S.U.

NECROLOGY

† Campbell, William J., (Retired). —Died Oct. 7, 1997.

† DeMarcelli, Evasio, Princeton, NJ, St. Paul. —Died March 10, 1997.

† Frain, Rev. Msgr. Thomas J., (Retired). —Died Jan. 17, 1997.

† Getlik, Stephen B., (Retired). —Died July 20, 1997.

† Morello, Rev. Msgr. Amedeo L., (Retired). —Died Nov. 3, 1997.

† Murray, Robert P., (Retired). —Died Nov. 24, 1997.

† Ridge, Thomas P., (Retired). —Died Oct. 6, 1997.

Diocese of Tucson

(Dioecesis Tucsonensis)

Most Reverend

MANUEL D. MORENO, D.D.

Bishop of Tucson; ordained April 25, 1961; appointed Titular Bishop of Tanagra and Auxiliary of Los Angeles December 20, 1976; consecrated February 19, 1977; appointed Bishop of Tucson January 12, 1982. *Res., 192 S. Stone Ave., Box 31, Tucson, AZ, 85702.*

ESTABLISHED A VICARIATE-APOSTOLIC 1868.

ERECTED BY HIS HOLINESS POPE LEO XIII, MAY 8, 1897.

Square Miles 42,707.

Comprises the Counties of Cochise, Gila, Greenlee, Graham, La Paz, Pima, Pinal, Santa Cruz and Yuma in the State of Arizona.

For legal titles of parishes and diocesan institutions, consult the Chancery Office.

Chancery Office: 192 S. Stone Ave., Box 31, Tucson, AZ, 85702. Tel.: 520-792-3410.

Web site address: http://www.azstarnet.com/~rccdot

E-mail address: rccchan@azstarnet.com

E-mail address: rccdot@azstarnet.com

STATISTICAL OVERVIEW

Personnel	
Bishop	1
Priests: Diocesan Active in Diocese	83
Priests: Active Outside Diocese	9
Priests: Retired, Sick or Absent	21
Number of Diocesan Priests	113
Religious Priests in Diocese	73
Extern Priests in Diocese	26
Ordinations:	
Diocesan Priests	4
Permanent Deacons	1
Permanent Deacons in Diocese	127
Total Brothers	8
Total Sisters	331
Parishes	
Parishes	64
With Resident Pastor:	
Resident Diocesan Priests	52
Resident Religious Priests	12
Without Resident Pastor:	
Missions	31
Pastoral Centers	15
Professional Ministry Personnel:	
Brothers	8
Sisters	269
Welfare	
Catholic Hospitals	3
Total Assisted	299,790
Health Care Centers	1
Total Assisted	33,476
Special Centers for Social Services	1
Total Assisted	400,000
Other Institutions	1
Total Assisted	2,671
Educational	
Diocesan Students in Other Seminaries	8
Total Seminarians	8
High Schools, Diocesan and Parish	1
Total Students	1,412
High Schools, Private	2
Total Students	184
Elementary Schools, Diocesan and Parish	22
Total Students	5,128
Elementary Schools, Private	2
Total Students	312
Catechesis/Religious Education:	
High School Students	3,153
Elementary Students	14,550
Total Students Under Catholic Instruction	24,747
Teachers in the Diocese:	
Priests	5
Brothers	1
Sisters	43
Lay Teachers	273
Vital Statistics	
Receptions into the Church:	
Infant Baptism Totals	7,009
Adult Baptism Totals	367
Received into Full Communion	681
First Communions	5,529
Confirmations	3,281
Marriages:	
Catholic	1,046
Interfaith	245
Total Marriages	1,291
Deaths	2,314
Total Catholic Population	323,698
Total Population	1,277,646

Former Bishops—Most Rev. JOHN BAPTIST SALPOINTE, D.D., ord. December 21, 1851; appt. Vicar Apostolic of Arizona and Titular Bishop of Doryla Sept. 25, 1868; ord. June 20, 1869; appt. Coadjutor Archbishop of Santa Fe with right of succession April 12, 1884 and Titular Archbishop of Anazarba Oct. 3, 1884; succeeded to the See of Santa Fe July 18, 1885; resigned; appt. titular Archbishop of Tomi Jan. 27, 1894; died Tucson, July 15, 1898.—Most Rev. PETER BOURGADE, D.D., ord. Nov. 30, 1869; appt. Vicar Apostolic of Arizona Jan. 23, 1885 and Titular Bishop of Thaumacum Feb. 7, 1885 and; ord. May 1, 1885; appt. first Bishop of Tucson May 10, 1897; appt. fourth Archbishop of Santa Fe Jan. 7, 1899; died Chicago, May 17, 1908.—Most Rev. HENRY REGIS GRANJON, D.D., ord. Dec. 17, 1887; appt. second Bishop of Tucson April 19, 1900; ord. June 17, 1900; died Brignais, France, Nov. 9, 1922.—Most Rev. DANIEL JAMES GERCKE, D.D., ord. June 1, 1901; appt. third Bishop of Tucson June 21, 1923; ord. Nov. 6, 1923; resigned; appt. Titular Archbishop of Cotyaeum Oct. 26, 1960; died Tucson, March 19, 1964.—Most Rev. FRANCIS JOSEPH GREEN, D.D., ord. May 15, 1932; appt. Titular Bishop of Serra in Proconsulari and Auxiliary Bishop of Tucson May 29, 1953; cons. Sept. 17, 1953; appt. Coadjutor "cum jure successionis" May 11, 1960; succeeded to See to become fourth Bishop of Tucson Oct. 26, 1960; retired July 28, 1981; died May 11, 1995.

Vicar General—Rev. Msgr. ARSENIO S. CARRILLO, V.G.

Chancery Office—192 S. Stone Ave., P.O. Box 31, Tucson, 85702. Tel: 520-792-3410.

Secretary and Chancellor—Rev. JOHN P. LYONS, J.D., J.C.L., Office: *192 S. Stone Ave., Tucson, 85701.* Tel: 520-792-3410., *Res., 8840 E. 22nd St., Tucson;* Rev. ALBERT E. VERBRUGGHE, Vice Chancellor.

Fiscal Manager Office—Ms. DEBBIE BAHRYCHUK, CFO; Ms. TERESA POLASHEK, Asst. Mgr. DAVID KNIGHT, Finance & Systems, Senior Staff Acct. JENNIFER FLOYD, Account Oper., Senior Staff Acct., *P.O. Box 31, Tucson, 85702.* Tel: 520-792-3410.

Matrimonial Tribunal—Office: *192 S. Stone Ave., P.O. Box 31, Tucson, 85702.* Tel: 520-792-3410.

Judicial Vicar—Rev. ALBERT E. VERBRUGGHE, M.A., M.B.A., S.D.T., LL.D., J.C.D., Advocate of the Roman Rota.

Promoter of Justice—Rev. BRYAN SHERRY, J.C.L.

Judges—Rev. Msgr. THOMAS CAHALANE; Revs. JOHN BRENT BARDON; RONALD GAGNON; JOSEPH KRAUSE; JOHN P. LYONS, J.C.L.; TODD O'LEARY.

Defenders of the Bond—Revs. MICHAEL BUCCIARELLI; ROBERT FOSTER; CHARLES KNAPP; MICHAEL STALLINGS.

Advocates and Auditors—Revs. JOSEPH BAKER; CHARLES CLOUD; JAMES HOBERT; REVIN ARNOLD; CHARLES ASHLEY; DONALD DE GROOD; JOHN J. BRADY; RICHARD COSGROVE; THOMAS CURTI; MICHAEL DORAN; LUIS KAME; VINCENT LACSAMANA; JOHN E. LINDBERG; THOMAS MCHUGH; JAMES MCNULTY, SR.; MICHAEL J. MURRAY; GERALD SWEENEY.

Auditors, Notaries, Secretaries—CLARA MORENO; HELEN EVANS.

Professional Consultant—STEPHEN J. SCHILTZ, M.S.W.

Finance Council—Most Rev. MANUEL D. MORENO, D.D., Chm. Bd. DEBBIE BAHRYCHUK, Chief Financial Officer; MATT ELLIS, Cash & Investment; Rev. JOHN P. LYONS, Chancellor; ROBERT E. HESLINGA, Dir. Devel. Members: ALEX ACOSTA; JOHN T. GIRVIN; GARY GIESLER; HENRY AMADO; Mr. LAWRENCE MCDONOUGH; JOAN DONNELLY; Rev. FLOYD G. STROMBERG; Rev. Msgr. THOMAS P. CAHALANE; MARK MISTLER; HUMBERTO LOPEZ.

Investment Sub-Committee—HUMBERTO LOPEZ, Chm. DEBBIE BAHRYCHUK; CHARLES FOLEY; MATTHEW ELLIS; JOHN HALFEN; JOSEPH LADENBURG.

Audit Committee—JOHN GIRVIN, Chm. HENRY AMADO; Rev. Msgr. THOMAS P. CAHALANE; DEBBIE BAHRYCHUK; Rev. JOHN P. LYONS, J.D., J.C.L.

Catholic Foundation for the Diocese of Tucson—Most Rev. MANUEL D. MORENO, D.D., Chm. JOHN M. NEIS, Pres. RANDY T. CASTELLINI, Vice Pres.; Sr. BARBARA ANN STOWASSER, Treas. BERNARD J. SULLIVAN, M.D., Sec. PHILIP J. SILVERS, Ph.D., Past Pres. Members: Rev. GREGORY P. ADOLF; KATHLEEN B. COREY, ESQ.; ELENA D'AUTREMONT; FRED EMICH; DON EWING, M.D.; ANN B. FALLON; DENIS FITZGIBONS; FRANCEEN GREGOVICH; HUGH HEGARTY; MAURICE V. LATTARI; JULIETA B. PORTILLO; SONNY RODRIGUEZ; ROBERT HESLINGA, Exec. Dir. PAUL SCIONTI, Assoc. Dir. Honorary Members: ORA DECONCINI-MARTIN; REG T. MORRISON; JAMES M. MURPHY; JAMES

E. NEIHART; ALLAN NORVILLE; ELIZABETH ANN PARKMAN.

Catholic Relief Services—JACK COTTER, Diocesan Dir., *155 W. Helen, Tucson, 85705.* Tel: 520-623-0344.

Diocesan Consultors—Rev. Msgr. ARSENIO S. CARRILLO, V.G.; Rev. Msgr. RICHARD O'KEEFFE; Rev. Msgr. THOMAS CAHALANE; Revs. KEVIN CLINCH; STEVEN G. STENCIL; JOHN P. LYONS, J.D., J.C.L.

Council of Priests—Most Rev. MANUEL D. MORENO, D.D.; Rev. Msgr. ARSENIO S. CARRILLO, V.G.; Rev. Msgr. ROBERT D. FULLER; Rev. Msgr. RICHARD W. O'KEEFFE; Revs. RAYMOND RATZENBERGER; CHARLES MALONEY; ROBERT G. TAMMINGA; RAUL TREVIZO; DOMENICO C. PINTI; JOHN BRENT BARDON; MAXIMILIAN HOTLE, O.F.M.; MICHAEL R. BUCCIARELLI; MARCOS VELASQUEZ; PATRICK M. CRINO; EDWARD RYLE; JOHN P. LYONS, Chancellor; ALBERT E. VERBRUGGHE, Judicial Vicar & Vice Chancellor.

Vicar for Native Americans—Rev. MAXIMILIAN HOTTLE, O.F.M.

Clergy Health—Rev. EDWARD C. CARSCALLEN.

Ministry to Priests Program—Rev. EDWARD C. CARSCALLEN, Spiritual Dir., *221 C. Paseo Tierra, Green Valley, 85614.* Tel: 520-625-4330. Members: Revs. PAUL H. ROSALES; JAMES M. HOBERT; FLOYD STROMBERG; PAUL LAROCQUE; JEFFREY THUERAUF.

Vicar for Religious—Rev. CYPRIAN KILLACKEY, O.C.D., *Santa Cruz Parish, 1220 S. 6th Ave., P.O. Box 2830, Tucson, 85702.* Tel: 520-623-3833; Fax: 520-624-2833.

Vicar for Priests—Rev. JAMES M. HOBERT, *St. Bernard, P.O. Box 3101, Pirtleville, 85626.* Tel: 520-364-2762.

Vicars Forane—Rev. RAYMOND RATZENBERGER, Cochise Vicariate; Rev. MICHAEL R. BUCCIARELLI, Gila-Pinal East Vicariate; Rev. DOMENICO C. PINTI, Graham-Greenlee Vicariate; Rev. Msgr. ROBERT D. FULLER, Pima-Central Vicariate; Rev. ROBERT G. TAMMINGA, Pima-East Vicariate; Rev. RAUL TREVIZO, Pima-South Vicariate; Rev. JOHN BRENT BARDON, Pima-North Vicariate; Rev. MAXIMILIAN HOTTLE, O.F.M., Pima West Vicariate; Rev. CHARLES MALONEY, Pinal-West Vicariate; Rev. MARCOS VELASQUEZ, Santa Cruz Vicariate; Rev. Msgr. RICHARD W. O'KEEFFE, Yuma-La Paz Vicariate.

Diocesan Offices and Directors

Archives—DAN BROSNAN, Archivist, *8800 E. 22nd St., Tucson, 85710.* Tel: 520-886-5201, Ext. 42.

Board of Education—Ex Officio Members: Most Rev. MANUEL D. MORENO, D.D.; Sr. ROSA MARIA RUIZ, C.F.M.M., Supt. REGINA SASSEEN, Dir., Parish Life & Ministry; UDO COOK, Pres. JOHN GARY, Vice Pres. JEAN MCKENZIE, Sec.

Building and Real Estate Committee—Most Rev. MANUEL D. MORENO, D.D., Honorary Chm. JAMES RONSTADT, Chm. BRIAN MCCARTHY, Vice Chm. DEBBIE BAHRYCHUK, Fiscal; LIZ AGUALLO, Sec. LARRY MCGRATH, Property Mgr.; Rev. TODD O'LEARY; ANDREW B. MARUM; HECTOR MARTINEZ; BOB SUAREZ; CAROL E. SCHRADER; DANIEL ROEBACH; Rev. ROBERT THOMAS.

Cash and Investments—MATT F. ELLIS, Mgr., *P.O. Box 31, Tucson, 85702.*

Cemeteries—Tucson:; Vacant, *Holy Hope Cemetery, 3555 N. Oracle Rd., P.O. Box 5158, Tucson, 85703.* Tel: 520-888-0860.

Our Lady of the Desert Cemetery—2151 S. Avenida Los Reyes, Tucson, 85703. Tel: 520-885-9173.

Desert Vista Cemetery—2151 S. Avenida Los Reyes, Tucson, 85748. Tel: 520-885-9173.

Censor Librorum—Vacant.

Campaign For Human Development—JOANNE WELTER, Dir., *4725 E. Pima St., Tuscon, 85712.* Tel: 520-795-1633.

Charismatic Movement Liaison Team—Rev. FRANK G. CADY, Spiritual Dir. English Speaking Liaisons: HELEN FORTUNO, *Regina Cleri Center, 8800 E. 22nd St., Tucson, 85710.* Tel: 520-886-4645. Voz en el Dieserto, Hispanic Speaking Liaisons: SALVADOR GONZALES, *1748 S. 4th Ave., Tcson, 85713.* Tel: 520-628-1692.

Community Relations—FRED ALLISON, Dir., *P.O. Box 31, Tucson, 85702.* Tel: 520-792-3410.

Cursillo Movement—Deacon GUILLERMO LUGO, Spiritual Dir., *St. Patrick Parish, P.O. Box 611, Bisbee, 85603.* Tel: 520-432-5753.

Detention Ministry—BARBARA MATTUS, Coord., *192 S. Stone Ave., P.O. Box 31, Tucson, 85702.* Tel: 520-792-3410, Ext. 333; 326.

Development Services (Annual Appeal, Parish Stewardship)—ROBERT E. HESLINGA, Dir., *192 S. Stone Ave., P.O. Box 31, Tucson, 85702.* Tel: 520-792-3410.

Ecumenical Commission—Rev. Msgr. THOMAS F. CAHALANE, *1800 S. Kolb Rd., Tucson, 85710.* Tel: 520-747-1321.

Fiscal Manager—DEBBIE BAHRYCHUKA, *P.O. Box 31, Tucson, 85702.* Tel: 520-792-3410.

Holy Childhood Association—Rev. JOHN P. LYONS, Dir., *P.O. Box 31, Tucson, 85702.* Tel: 520-792-3410.

Interfaith Council—LAUVER EDIE. Tel: 520-745-9443.

Legion of Decency—Chancery Office, 192 S. Stone Ave., Tucson, 85702.

Diocesan Liturgical Commission—Chancery Office, 192 S. Stone Ave., Tucson, 85701. Tel: 520-792-3410.

Diocesan Parish Life and Ministry, Regina Cleri Center—REGINA SASSEEN, Dir. MICHAEL BERGER; RUBEN DAVALOS, Parish Svcs.; Sr. ROSA MARIA RUIZ, C.F.M.M., Supt., *Ministry of Catholic Schools, 8800 E. 22nd St., Tucson, 85710.* Tel: 520-886-5202.

Newspaper—"Catholic Vision", KATE CASSIDY, Mng. Editor, *P.O. Box 31, Tucson, 85702.* Tel: 520-792-3410.

Office of Due Process—Chancery Office, P.O. Box 31, Tucson, 85702. Tel: 520-792-3410.

Permanent Diaconate Program—Deacon LEON MAZZA, Dir., *P.O. Box 31, Tucson, 85702.* Tel: 520-792-3410; 745-1243.

Deacon Formation—Rev. DANIEL TAYLOR, Dir., *1815 S. 8th Ave., Yuma, 85364.* Tel: 520-782-1875.

Priests' Assurance Association—Most Rev. MANUEL D. MORENO, D.D., Pres. Ex Officio; Rev. JOHN P. LYONS, Sec. & Treas. Directors: Rev. Msgr. ROBERT D. FULLER; Revs. THOMAS MILLANE; DOMENICO C. PINTI; JOHN F. ALT.

Priests' Placement Advisory Board—All Vicars Forane: Rev. Msgr. ROBERT D. FULLER; Rev. Msgr. RICHARD W. O'KEEFFE; Revs. DOMENICO C. PINTI; MICHAEL R. BUCCIARELLI; RAYMOND RATZENBERGER; RAUL TREVIZO; ROBERT G. TAMMINGA; JOHN BRENT BARDON; MAXIMILIAN HOTTLE, O.F.M.; CHARLES MALONEY; MARCOS VELASQUEZ.

Chancellor—Revs. JOHN P. LYONS; ALBERT E. VERBRUGGHE, Vice-Chancellor; PATRICK M. CRINO, Vocations Dir.

Propagation of the Faith—Rev. Msgr. ARSENIO CARRILLO, Dir. Pro. Tem., *P.O. Box 31, Tucson, 85702.* Tel: 520-792-3410.

Property Manager—LARRY MCGRATH, Mgr., Office: *192 S. Stone Ave., P.O. Box 31, Tucson, 85702.* Tel: 520-792-3410.

Rural Life Bureau—Box 31, Tucson, 85702. Tel: 520-792-3410.

Tuscon Council of Religious—Sr. COLLEEN HARRIS, C.S.J., Leadership Team, *150 S. Irving Ave., Tucson, 85711.* Tel: 520-325-4580; 322-6601.

Vocations—Rev. PATRICK M. CRINO, Dir., *Mailing Address: P.O. Box 31, Tucson, 85701.* Tel: 520-792-3410; 623-6351.

[*]Catholic Commission—JIM DOBRY, Pres., *231 W. Smoot Dr., Tucson, 85705.* Tel: 520-887-6803.

Vietnamese Catholic Community of Tucson—Rev. JOHN TRAN BICH, C.S.S.C., *Regina Cleri Center, 8800 E. 22nd St., Tuscon, 85710.* Tel: 520-888-5223.

Encuentros de Promocion Juvenile—Rev. JAVIER PEREZ, Spiritual Dir., *P.O. Box 1053, Tucson, 85702-1053.* Tel: 520-624-7409.

CLERGY, PARISHES, MISSIONS AND PAROCHIAL SCHOOLS

CITY OF TUCSON
(Pima County)

1—ST. AUGUSTINE'S CATHEDRAL (1863), Rev. Msgr. Arsenio S. Carrillo, V.G., Rector Pro-Tem.; Rev. Gonzalo J. Villegas.
Res., 192 S. Stone Ave., 85701. Tel: 520-623-6351.
Catechesis/Religious Programs—Miss Barbara Valenzuela, D.R.E., Tel: 520-624-8627.
Students 528.

2—BLESSED KATERI TEKAKWITHA (1984) (Native American), Revs. Daniel P. McLaughlin, S.T.; Abram E. Dono, S.T.; Bro. David T. Sommer, S.T., Pastoral Assoc.
Res., 101 W. 31st St., 85713. Tel: 520-791-7774.
Catechesis/Religious Programs—Tel: 520-622-5363.
Students 425.
Missions—South Tucson, Pima Co., St. Nicholas Indian Center, 349 W. 31st St., 85713. Tel: 520-622-5363; Tuscon, Pima Co., San Martin, 418 W. 39th St., 85713.; Tucson, Pima Co., Santa Rosa, 2015 N. Calle Central, 85705. Tel: 520-622-3514; Cristo Rey; San Ignacio, 785 W. Shuoro, 85705.; Marana, San Juan.

3—HOLY FAMILY (1915), Rev. Joseph M. Baker; Deacon Carl Leinfelder. In res., Rev. John M. Fahey.
Res., 338 W. University Blvd., 85705. Tel: 520-623-6773; Fax: 520-623-3578.
Catechesis/Religious Programs—Students 189.
Mission—Tucson, Pima Co., Santa Rosa, 2015 N. Calle, 85705. Tel: 520-622-3514.

4—MISSION SAN XAVIER DEL BAC (1692) (Native American), Revs. Alberic Smith, O.F.M.; Kieran McCarty, O.F.M.; Peter Verheggen, O.F.M.; Bro. Michael Bearce, O.F.M.
Res., 1950 W. San Xavier Rd., 85746. Tel: 520-294-2624.
School—1980 W. San Xavier Rd., 85746. Tel: 520-294-0628. Sr. Jacqueline Koenig, O.F.M., Prin.
Sisters 6; Students 146.
Catechesis/Religious Programs—Tel: 520-294-0628.
Students 215.
Convent—1996 W. San Xavier Rd., 85746. Tel: 520-746-4779.

5—MOST HOLY TRINITY (1975), Rev. Ronald P. Gagnon.
Res., 1300 N. Greasewood, 85745. Tel: 520-622-1300.
Catechesis/Religious Programs—Tel: 520-884-9021.
Students 230.

6—OUR LADY OF FATIMA (1972), Rev. Peter M. McGloin; Deacons Frank S. Lundgren, Jr.; Robert Negrette.
Res., 5969 S. Sorrel Ln., 85746. Tel: 520-883-1717.
Catechesis/Religious Programs—Tel: 520-883-1717.
Students 255.
Mission—Tucson, St. Mary of the Desert.

7—OUR LADY, QUEEN OF ALL SAINTS (1987) (Hispanic), Rev. Floyd G. Stromberg; Deacons Oscar Magallanes; George Rodriguez.
Res., 2915 E. 36th St., 85713-4041. Tel: 520-622-8602; Fax: 520-622-4581.
Catechesis/Religious Programs—Maria Rodriguez, D.R.E.
Students 350.

8—OUR MOTHER OF SORROWS (1958), Rev. Msgr. Thomas P. Cahalane; Revs. Charles D. Knapp; Larry Kasper; Deacons Robert Speers; Thomas Tighe; Paul J. Welsh; Alfredo Silva.
Res., 1800 S. Kolb Rd., 85710. Tel: 520-747-1321; Fax: 520-790-3308.
School—Our Lady of Guadalupe Center for Children, 7041 E. Calle Denebola, 85710. Tel: 520-747-1027. Jean McKenzie, Ed.S., Prin.
Lay Teachers 27; Students 550.
Catechesis/Religious Programs—Linda Contreras, M.A., D.R.E.
Students 565.

9—SACRED HEART (1942), Revs. Joseph F. McGowan, O.Carm.; Anthony McNamara, O.Carm.; Deacon George Castelan.
Res., 601 E. Fort Lowell Rd., 85705. Tel: 520-888-1530; Fax: 520-888-1227.
Catechesis/Religious Programs—Tel: 520-888-3401.
Students 212.

10—ST. AMBROSE (1946), Revs. Francisco Maldonado; Dale Branson; Deacon Henry Gamboa.
Res., 300 S. Tucson Blvd., 85716. Tel: 520-622-6749; Fax: 520-622-6740.
School—Tel: 520-882-8678; Fax: 520-624-6853.
Lay Teachers 20; Students 360.
Catechesis/Religious Programs—Tel: 520-623-2925.
Students 350.

11—ST. CYRIL OF ALEXANDRIA (1948), Revs. William J. Dougherty, C.S.P.; Edward S. Pietrucha, C.S.P.; Robert J. Stulting, C.S.P., (Retired); Deacon Charles Pennington.
Res., 4725 E. Pima, 85712. Tel: 520-795-1633; Fax: 520-795-1639.
School—Tel: 520-881-4240; Fax: 520-795-0325. Mrs. JoAnn Sayre, Prin.
Lay Teachers 22; Students 398.
Catechesis/Religious Programs—Students 398.

12—ST. FRANCES CABRINI (1961), Rev. Msgr. Robert D. Fuller.
Res., 3201 E. Presidio Rd., 85716. Tel: 520-326-7670; Fax: 520-881-8480.
Catechesis/Religious Programs—Tel: 520-795-1110.
Students 151.

13—ST. FRANCIS DE SALES (1971), Revs. Robert G. Tamminga; Christopher Orndorff; Deacons Michael Ammerman; Frank J. Collura; Marvin Farmer; Charles Girard; Keith Pavlik; Dennis Scalpone; Leonard Fuller; Alvin Crockette; Hugh Montague; Robert Nevins; William Vigil.
Res., 1375 S. Camino Seco, 85710. Tel: 520-885-5908; Fax: 520-885-3109.
Catechesis/Religious Programs—Marian Gilbert, D.R.E.
Students 720.

14—ST. JOHN THE EVANGELIST (1934), Revs. Raul P. Trevizo; Juan Pablo Sanchez, O.S.B.; Liam Leahy; Deacons Ernesto Roche; Bernard Minetti; Jose Ojeda; Don Baker; Jose Duarte; Charles Gallegos, Jr.
Res., 602 W. Ajo Way, 85713. Tel: 520-624-7409; Fax: 520-740-1145.
School—Dr. Ernestina Fuentes, Prin. Lay Teachers 13; Students 250.
Catechesis/Religious Programs—Sr. Maria Emmanuel Martinez, D.R.E.
Students 835.

15—ST. JOSEPH (1953), Revs. John F. Allt; Frederic F. Curry, Pastor Emeritus; Sr. Marie Chapla, Pastoral Assoc.; Deacons George Herrick; Leon Mazza; Philip Garcia; Paul Converse; John Broussard. In res., Rev. James A. Freeman.
Res., 215 S. Craycroft Rd., 85711. Tel: 520-747-3100; Fax: 520-745-4606.
Parish Center—Tel: 520-747-3100.
School—Tel: 520-747-3060. Mrs. Ellen S. Kwader, Prin.
Lay Teachers 21; Students 506.
Catechesis/Religious Programs—Sharon Takerer, D.R.E.
Students 219.

16—ST. MARGARET'S (1951), Revs. Gilbert Levario, O.C.D.; Bernard Perkins, O.C.D.; Kevin McArdle, O.C.D.
Res., 801 N. Grande Ave., 85745. Tel: 520-622-0168; Fax: 520-882-8022. [CEM]
Catechesis/Religious Programs—Tel: 520-622-5982.
Students 405.

17—ST. MONICA (1964), Revs. Michael Martinez; Viliulfo Valderrama; Deacons John Garcia; Don Fisher; Tomas Morales; Eugene Fernandez.
Res., 212 W. Medina, 85706. Tel: 520-294-2694.
Catechesis/Religious Programs—Tel: 520-889-1944; Fax: 520-295-0335.
Students 1,120.

18—SAINT ODILIA (1965), Revs. John Brent Bardon; Richard E. Troutman; Deacon George Scherf.
Res. & Mailing Address—7570 Paseo del Norte, 85737-4499. Tel: 520-297-7271; 297-6361 (Office); Fax: 520-297-6361.
Catechesis/Religious Programs—Students 550.
Mission—Tucson, Pima Co., Santa Catalina, 14380 N. Oracle, 85739-9599. Tel: 520-825-9611; Fax: 520-825-9866. Sr. Carole Ruland, M.H.S.H., Admin.

19—ST. PIUS X (1969), Revs. Harry Ledwith; Richard Kingsley. In res., Rev. James G. Coleman.
Res., 1800 N. Camino Pio Decimo, 85715. Tel: 520-885-3573; Fax: 520-885-3573, Ext. 53.
Catechesis/Religious Programs—Karen Horton, D.R.E.
Students 655.

20—SAINTS PETER AND PAUL (1930), Revs. Van A. Wagner; Javier H. Perez; Donald J. Fiedler; Arthur Devine, (Retired). In res., Rev. Patrick M. Crino.
Res., 1946 E. Lee St., 85719. Tel: 520-327-6015.
School—Tel: 520-325-2431; Fax: 520-881-4690. Sr. Ann Patrick Adams, S.C., Prin.
Sisters of Charity from Seton Hall 4; Lay Teachers 25; Students 530.
Catechesis/Religious Programs—Tel: 520-327-1229.
Students 191.
Convent—1947 E. Adams St., 85719. Tel: 520-325-2234.

21—SANTA CRUZ (1919), Revs. Cyprian Killackey, O.C.D.; Richard Claassen, O.C.D.; Ignacio Bach, O.C.D.; Christopher LaRocca, O.C.D.
Res., P.O. Box 2830, 85702. Tel: 520-623-3833.
School—Tel: 520-624-2093; Fax: 520-624-2833.
Sisters 1; Lay Teachers 9; Students 210.
Catechesis/Religious Programs—Tel: 520-882-9687.
Students 523.
Missions—Tucson, Pima Co., Our Lady of Guadalupe, 401 E. 31st St., 85713.; Tucson, Pima Co., St. Anthony's Catholic Instruction Center and Capilla, 225 W. 34th St., 85713. Tel: 520-622-8972.

22—ST. ELIZABETH ANN SETON (1980), Revs. Thomas J. Millane; Remigio Tupaz Mariano, Jr.; Deacons James L. Burns; Leo Longoria; William Krueger.
Res., 8650 N. Shannon Rd., 85742. Tel: 520-297-7357; Fax: 520-797-8886.
Catechesis/Religious Programs—Tel: 520-297-8150. Roseanne Skapura, D.R.E.
Students 1,200.

23—ST. THOMAS THE APOSTLE (1984), Rev. Todd O'Leary (Ireland); Deacon Russell F. Kingery. In res., Rev. Timothy J. Howard, S.J.
Res., 5150 N. Valley View Rd., 85718. Tel: 520-577-8780; Fax: 520-577-0441.
Catechesis/Religious Programs—Tel: 520-577-8782; Fax: 520-577-0441.
Students 614.

OUTSIDE THE CITY OF TUCSON

Ajo, Pima Co., Immaculate Conception (1916), Rev. Richard J. Rego.
Office: 101 Rocalla, P.O. Drawer A F, 85321. Tel: 520-387-7049.
Catechesis/Religious Programs—Students 102.

Apache Junction, Pinal Co., St. George (1968), Rev. Charles F. Maloney; Deacon Bill Hughes. In res., Revs. Willard F. Wiesler; Robert Lindsay.
Res., 300 E. 16th Ave., 85219. Tel: 602-982-2929; Fax: 602-982-0036.
Catechesis/Religious Programs—Tel: 602-982-0036. Mrs. Stacy Filewicz-Ross, D.R.E.
Students 130.

Benson, Cochise Co., Our Lady of Lourdes (1895), Rev. Raymond Ratzenberger.
Mailing Address: 244 S. Gila, P.O. Box 2198, 85602. Tel: 520-586-3394; Fax: 520-686-3394.
Res., 210 Eighth St., 85602.
Catechesis/Religious Programs—Students 112.

Bisbee, Cochise Co., St. Patrick (1902), Rev. Stanley Nadolny; Deacons Guillermo Lugo; Robert Gonzales; Joseph L. Delgado.
Res., P.O. Box 164, 85603. Tel: 520-432-5753.
Catechesis/Religious Programs—Tel: 520-432-4012.
Students 299.
Mission—Naco, Cochise Co., St. Michael, 2090 W. Martinez, Naco, 85620.

Casa Grande, Pinal Co., St. Anthony (1932), Revs. Steven G. Stencil; David Reinders; Deacons Joseph McGeeney; Bill Kinney; Barnabas Radke; Anthony R. Miller; Patrick L. Dugan; Ramon G. Garcia.
Res., P.O. Drawer 12335, 85230-2335. Tel: 520-836-0601; Fax: 520-836-2985.
School—Tel: 520-836-7247. Mr. David Hernandez, III, Prin.
Lay Teachers 8; Students 160.
Catechesis/Religious Programs—Students 510.
Missions—Stanfield, Pinal Co., St. Mary, 85230-2335.; Maricopa, Pinal Co., St. Francis de Sales, P.O. Box 368, Maricopa, 85239-0368. Tel: 520-568-4605.

Clifton, Greenlee Co., Sacred Heart (1899), Rev. John F. Emanuel; Deacon Richard A. Gonzalez.
Mailing Address: P.O. Box 938, 85533.
Res., 329 Chase Creek, 85533. Tel: 520-865-2285; Fax: 520-865-3497.
Catechesis/Religious Programs—North Cornado Boulevard Parish Center.
Students 150.
Mission—Duncan, St. Mary, Third St., P.O. Box 554, 85534. Tel: 520-359-2343.
Convent—P.O. Box 554, Duncan, 85534.

Coolidge, Pinal Co., St. James (1947) (Hispanic), Rev. Jeffrey P. Thuerauf; Deacons Florentino Tarango; Viviano Leon.
Parish Center—401 W. Wilson Ave., 85228. Tel: 520-723-3063; Fax: 520-723-5580.
Res., 437 W. Wilson Ave., 85228. Tel: 520-723-4672.
Catechesis/Religious Programs—Tel: 520-723-5137.
Students 241.

Douglas, Cochise Co., Immaculate Conception (1907), Rev. Luis N. Chavez; Deacons Luciano Gonzales, Jr.; Jose S. Zapata.
Res., 928 C Ave., P.O. Box 1176, 85607. Tel: 520-364-8494.
School—Lestonnac Kindergarten and Day Care Center, Tel: 520-364-3956. Sr. Amparo Herrera, O.D.N., Prin.
Sisters of the Company of Mary 4; Lay Teachers 4; Students 84.
Catechesis/Religious Programs—Students 600.
Convent—Tel: 520-364-7658; Fax: 520-364-3645. Sisters of the Company of Mary

St. Luke (1950), Revs. James M. Hobert, Jr.; Robert E. Carney; Deacons Armando Moulinet; Gabe Saspe.
Res., 1211 15th St., 85607. Tel: 520-364-4411; Fax: 520-364-4412.
School—Loretto Central Catholic, 1200 14th St., 85607. Tel: 520-364-5754; Fax: 520-364-7844. Sr. Caridad Sandoval, O.C.D., Prin.
Sisters 6; Lay Teachers 6; Students 295.
Catechesis/Religious Programs—Tel: 520-364-7109.
Students 523.
Convent—Tel: 520-364-7658; Fax: 520-364-3645. Carmelite Sisters of the Most Sacred Heart of Los Angeles, Loretto Convent

Eloy, Pinal Co., St. Helen (1952) (Hispanic), Rev. Joseph G. Gorsuch.
Res., 205 W. 8th St., 85231. Tel: 520-466-7258.
Catechesis/Religious Programs—Tel: 520-466-7934. D.R.E.: Sr. Mary Eulema Lyvers, S.S.N.D.; Sr. Mary Elwyn Brink, S.S.N.D.
Students 830.

Florence, Pinal Co., Assumption of the Blessed Virgin Mary (1870), Rev. Charles W. Cloud.
Res., P.O. Box 2550, 85232. Tel: 520-868-5940.

Globe, Gila Co., Holy Angels (1905), Rev. Michael Bradly; Deacons Frank Castillo; Jim Gersitz; Richard Le Mieux.
Res., 201 S. Broad St., 85501. Tel: 520-425-3137; Fax: 520-425-3136.
School—1300 E. Cedar St., 85501. Tel: 520-425-5703; Fax: 520-425-5704. Sr. Leonie Bracken, Prin. & Admin.
Presentation Sisters 3; Lay Teachers 6; Students 195.
Catechesis/Religious Programs—Students 235.
Convent—Tel: 520-425-2034.

Green Valley, Pima Co., Our Lady of the Valley (1970), Revs. Joseph A. Lombardo; Robert Brazaskas; Deacons Francis E. Lambert; Pete Grimaldo; James Stotler.
Res., 505 N. La Canada Dr., 85614. Tel: 520-625-4536; Fax: 520-625-4536.
Catechesis/Religious Programs—Sahuarita, 85629. Tel: 520-625-4536.
Mission—Sahuarita, Pima Co., St. Martin de Porres, Sahuarita, 85629. Tel: 520-625-1154.

Hayden, Gila Co., St. Joseph's (1913), Rev. Kevin Clinch; Deacon Arnold Moreno.
Res., P.O. Drawer C, 85235. Tel: 520-356-7223.
Catechesis/Religious Programs—Tel: 520-356-6462.
Students 160.

Kearny, Pinal Co., Infant Jesus of Prague (1961), Rev. William A. Taft, Admin.
Res., 501 Victoria Cir., P.O. Box 459, 85237. Tel: 520-363-7205.
Catechesis/Religious Programs—Tel: 520-363-7428.
Students 80.

Mammoth, Pinal Co., Blessed Sacrament (1970) (Hispanic), Rev. Gilbert Padilla.
Res., 122 W. Church Dr., P.O. Box 20, 85618. Tel: 520-487-2451.
Catechesis/Religious Programs—Students 214.
Convent—Mammouth. Blessed Sacrament Convent

Marana, Pima Co., St. Christopher's (1954), Rev. L. Ignacio Gameros.
Res., 12101 Moore Rd., P.O. Box 188, 85653. Tel: 520-682-3375; Fax: 520-682-3928.
Education Center—Tel: 520-682-9011. Barbara Mattus, D.R.E.
Students 160.

Miami, Gila Co., Our Lady of the Blessed Sacrament (1915), Rev. Jay R. Luczak.
Res., P.O. Drawer E, 85539. Tel: 520-473-3568; Fax: 520-473-3338.
Catechesis/Religious Programs—Students 198.
Convent—Tel: 520-473-2010. Sacred Heart
Missions—Claypool, Gila Co., St. Joseph, 5678 Pineway St., Claypool, 85532.; Roosevelt Lake, Gila Co., St. Theresa.

Morenci, Greenlee Co., Holy Cross (1913), Rev. Raul H. Rosales.
Mailing Address: P.O. Box 216, 85540.
Res., 205 Fairbanks Rd., 85540. Tel: 520-865-3183; Fax: 520-865-3183.
Catechesis/Religious Programs—Tel: 520-865-5226.
Students 419.

Nogales, Santa Cruz Co., Sacred Heart (1897), Revs. Marcos C. Velasquez; Antonio Felipe Martinez; Robert A. Hyman.
Res., P.O. Box 968, 85628. Tel: 520-287-9221; Fax: 520-287-9224.
School—Sacred Heart, Tel: 520-287-5484; Fax: 520-287-6065. Sr. Esther Hugues, C.F.M.M., Supr. Minim Daughters of Mary Immaculate 3; Lay Teachers 12; Students 330.
Catechesis/Religious Programs—Tel: 520-397-0963.
Students 750.

San Felipe de Jesus (1987), Rev. Antonio A. Ruiz.
Mailing Address: P.O. Box 6600, 85628.
Res., 3272 Villa Hermosa, 85621. Tel: 520-761-3100; Fax: 520-281-4380.
Church—1901 Jose Gallego Ln., #1, 85621.
Catechesis/Religious Programs—Students 652.

Parker, La Paz Co., Sacred Heart (1950), Rev. Theodore Lobo; Deacon David Gonzales.
Res., 916 11th St., 85344. Tel: 520-669-2502.
Catechesis/Religious Programs—Students 150.
Missions—Poston, Kateri Tekawitha Indian Mission; Wenden, St. John the Baptist; Quartzsite, Queen of Peace.

Patagonia, Santa Cruz Co., St. Theresa (1955), Rev. Michael W. Stallings.
Res., Box 435, 85624. Tel: 520-394-2954; Fax: 520-394-2831.
Catechesis/Religious Programs—Students 93.
Mission—Sonoita, Santa Cruz Co., Our Lady of Angels, Fire Station, Sonoita, 85637.

Payson, Gila Co., Saint Philip the Apostle (1957), Rev. Joseph A. Krause; Sr. Marilita Michalski, O.S.F., Pastoral Min.
Res., 511 S. St. Philip, 85541-5144. Tel: 520-474-2392.
Catechesis/Religious Programs—Tel: 520-747-1269.
Students 104.

Pirtleville, Cochise Co., St. Bernard's (1914), Revs. James M. Hobert, Jr.; Robert E. Carney.
Res., P.O. Box 3101, 85626. Tel: 520-364-2762; Fax: 520-364-4412.
Catechesis/Religious Programs—Tel: 520-364-5994.
Students 123.
Chapels—Double Adobe, Our Lady of La Salette.; Douglas, Sacred Heart.

Rio Rico, Santa Cruz Co., Nativity of Our Lord Jesus Christ (1987), Rev. Frank G. Cady.
Mailing Address: P.O. Box 4024, 85648.
Res., 384 Cancun Corte, 85648. Tel: 520-281-8702; 281-7414.
Catechesis/Religious Programs—Students 253.

Safford, Graham Co., St. Rose of Lima (1937), In res., Revs. Domenico C. Pinti; Tadeusz Marek Sypko.
Res., 311 Central Ave., 85546. Tel: 520-428-4920.
Catechesis/Religious Programs—Tel: 520-428-4922.
Students 540.
Missions—Pima, Graham Co., Pima Mission, Pima, 85543.; Thatcher, Graham Co., Neuman Center, Thatcher, 85552.

San Carlos, Gila Co., San Carlos Catholic Mission (1918) (Apache), Rev. Gino L. Piccoli, O.F.M.
Res., P.O. Box 28, 85550. Tel: 520-475-2210; Fax: 520-475-2449.
School—Tel: 520-475-2449.
Sisters 5; Students 155.
Convent—P.O. Box 338, 85550. Tel: 520-475-2460; Fax: 520-475-2460. St. Charles
Mission—Bylas, Graham Co., Blessed Kateri Tekakwitha.

San Manuel, Pinal Co., St. Bartholomew (1954), Rev. Michael R. Bucciarelli.
Res., 609 Park Pl., Box 607, 85631. Tel: 520-385-4156.
Convent—313 Avenue A, P.O. Box 32, 85631. Tel: 520-385-4739. Sisters of Notre Dame de Namur
Mission—Oracle, Pinal Co., St. Helen, HCR 1, Box 2000, Oracle, 85623. Tel: 520-896-2708. Rev. Donald F. Jackson, Admin. In res., Rev. Paul J. Ranft, Pastor Emeritus.

Sierra Vista, Cochise Co., St. Andrew (1959), Revs. Gregory P. Adolf; Colman J. Nolan, S.T.
Res., 800 Taylor Dr., N.W., 85635. Tel: 520-458-2925; Fax: 520-452-0235.
Catechesis/Religious Programs—Tel: 520-458-4994.
Students 190.
Mission—Whetstone, Cochise Co., Good Shepherd.
Our Lady of the Mountains (1991), Rev. Robert R. Bryerton.
Res., 1425 Yaqui St., 85635. Tel: 520-378-2720; Fax: 520-378-6825.
Catechesis/Religious Programs—Tel: 520-378-7012.
Students 300.

Solomon, Graham Co., Our Lady of Guadalupe (1891), Rev. John J. Ancharski; Deacon Gilbert O. Martinez.
Res., P.O. Box 147, 85551. Tel: 520-428-0149.
Catechesis/Religious Programs—Students 63.
Mission—San Jose, Graham Co., San Jose.

Somerton, Yuma Co., Immaculate Heart of Mary (1954), Rev. Fernando L. Manzo.
Res., 310 W. Spring St., P.O. Box 597, 85350. Tel: 520-627-2918; Fax: 520-627-2918.
Catechesis/Religious Programs—Tel: 520-627-2244.
Students 660.
Mission—San Luis, Yuma Co., San Judas Tadeo, 22790 S. Hwy 95, P.O. Box 2888, San Luis, 85349. Tel: 520-627-8011; Fax: 520-627-3916. Rev. Julian Sanz.

Sunsites, Cochise Co., St. Jude Thaddius (1983), In res., Rev. Msgr. John A. Oliver.
Res., P.O. Box 328, Pearce, 85625. Tel: 520-826-3869.
Catechesis/Religious Programs—Students 55.
Mission—Elfrida, Cochise Co., St. Francis of Assisi, P.O. Box 587, Elfrida, 85610. Tel: 520-642-3879.

Superior, Pinal Co., St. Francis of Assisi Parish (1930), Rev. Augustine Kattady; Deacon Jesus Yanez.
Res., 11 Church Ave., 85273. Tel: 520-689-2250.
Catechesis/Religious Programs—St. Mary's Center, 100 Sunset Dr., 85273. Tel: 520-689-2116.
Students 185.

Tombstone, Cochise Co., Sacred Heart (1880), Rev. William J. Parenteau; Deacon Robert Sadorf.
Res., P.O. Box 547, 85638. Tel: 520-457-3364.
Catechesis/Religious Programs—Students 84.

Topawa, Pima Co., San Solano Missions - Tohono O'odham Indian Reservation (1908) (Native American). (For office and sacramental records pertaining to Tohono O'odham Indians and mission churches on the reservation, please refer to San Solano Missions at the P.O. Box 210, Topawa, AZ, 85639 address).
Mailing Address: P.O. Box 210, 85639. Tel: 520-383-2350. Revs. Maximilian Hottle, O.F.M., Admin.; Walter Holly, O.F.M.; Thomas Frost, O.F.M.

Tubac, Santa Cruz Co., St. Ann (1987), Rev. Clarke W. Moore.
Mailing Address: P.O. Box 2911, 85646-2911. Tel: 520-398-2646; Fax: 520-398-9711.
Missions—Amado, Santa Cruz Co., Assumption Chapel; Arivaca, Pima Co., St. Ferdinand.

Vail, Pima Co., Shrine of St. Rita in the Desert (1937), Rev. Robert Wicht, S.D.S. In res., Rev. Alan Wagner, S.D.S.
Res., P.O. Box 400, 85641. Tel: 520-762-5363.
Catechesis/Religious Programs—Students 74.

Willcox, Cochise Co., Sacred Heart (1936), Rev. Maurice O'Neil, S.S.
Res., P.O. Box 490, 85644. Tel: 520-384-3432.
Catechesis/Religious Programs—Students 120.
Missions—San Simon, Cochise Co., Our Lady of Perpetual Help, San Simon, 85605.; Bowie, Cochise Co., Our Lady of Guadalupe, Bowie, 85605.

Yuma, Yuma Co., Immaculate Conception (1866), Rev. Msgr. Richard W. O'Keeffe; Rev. Msgr. Gerald J. Brynda; Revs. Juan Guillen; Martin S. Martinez; Deacons Mark Nixen; Sampson; Fernando Mezquita.
Res., 509 Ave. B, 85364. Tel: 520-782-7516; Fax: 520-343-0172.
School—501 Ave. B, 85364. Tel: 520-783-5225. Sr. Theresa Feldkamp, O.S.F., Prin.
Franciscan Sisters of Christian Charity 4; Lay Teachers 13; Students 214.
Catechesis/Religious Programs—Tel: 520-783-1324. D.R.E.: Mark Nixen; Mary Tellez.
Students 934.
Missions—Yuma, Yuma Co., Our Lady of Guadalupe, 417 15th Ave., 85364.; Wellton, Yuma Co., St. Joseph the Worker, P.O. Box 357, Wellton, 85356. Tel: 520-785-4275. Rev. Msgr. Richard W. O'Keeffe, Admin.; Rev. Tomas G. Munoz.
Convent—500 24th Ave., 85364. Tel: 520-783-5224. Franciscan Sisters of Christian Charity 9.
St. Francis of Assisi (1948), Revs. Daniel Taylor; Perry McCoy, O.S.M.; Gilberto Malu Musumbu, M.S.P.; Deacons Paul Muthart; E. Joseph Pozzi; Carlo Duarte; Donald L. Larson; Gary Pasquinelli; Rick Hernandez; Bill McDonald; Rafael Vidal; Arnulfo Carbajal; Francisco Moreno.
Res., 1815 S. 8th Ave., 85364. Tel: 520-782-1875; Fax: 520-329-9479.
School—700 18th St., 85364. Tel: 520-782-1539. Veronica Lopez, Prin.
Franciscan Sisters of Christian Charity 2; Lay Teachers 12; Students 222.
Catechesis/Religious Programs—Tel: 520-783-7461. D.R.E.: Sherlyn Saladin, (English Apostolate); Lucy Quiroz, (Hispanic Apostolate).
Students 535.
St. John Neumann (1987), Rev. Damian M. Kobus, O.S.M.
Res., 11750 S. Mesa Dr., 85367. Tel: 520-342-3544.

Chaplains of Public Institutions

TUCSON. *Arizona Correctional Training Center*. Vacant. Santa Rita Unit, 10000 S. Wilmot Rd., 85777. Detention Ministry, P.O. Box 31, 85702. Tel: 520-792-3410, Ext. 326; 333.
Arizona Western College. Attended from St. John Newmann Parish, Yuma. 11750 S. Mesa Dr., 85365. Tel: 520-342-3544.
Christ the King Chapel 836 CSG/HC, Davis Monthan Air Force Base, 85707. Tel: 520-750-5411. Rev. Philip S. Llanos, Chap.
Kino Community Hospital. Attended from Santa Cruz, Tucson. 1220 S. Sixth, 85707. Tel: 520-623-3833. 2800 E. Ajo Way, 85713.
Metropolitan Correctional Complex 8901 S. Wilmont Rd., 85706. Tel: 520-741-3118. Rev. Patrick Dennis, Staff Chap., Detention Ministry, P.O. Box 31, 85702. Tel: 520-792-3410, Ext. 131. Barbara Mattus, Dir.
Tucson Medical Center 5301 E. Grant Rd., 85712. Rev. William Kohler, C.SS.R., Chap., Tel: 520-324-1290; Fax: 520-324-1702.
U.S. Veterans Hospital S. Sixth Ave., 85713. Tel: 520-792-1450. Chaplains: Revs. Roland Bedard, M.S.; Henry Dauphinais, M.S.
Villa Maria 4310 E. Grant Rd., 85712. Tel: 520-323-9351. Rev. Alexander Mills, Chap.

CATALINA. *Arizona Youth Center*. Attended from St. Odilia Parish. Santa Catalina Mission, Catalina Rural Branch, P.O. Box 8601, 85738. Tel: 520-825-9611.

FLORENCE. *Arizona State Prison* St. Dismas Chapel, P.O. Box 550, 85232. Tel: 520-868-5940. Rev. Lawrence Quilici, Chap.

FORT GRANT RURAL STATION. *Fort Grant Training Center* 85632. Revs. Maurice O'Neil, S.S.; John J. Ancharski.

FORT HUCHUCA. *Fort Huchuca Army Post* 85613. Rev. Arvids Bernans, Chap.

SAFFORD. *Conservation Center* Tel: 520-428-0149. Rev. John J. Ancharski.

SOLOMON. *Our Lady of Guadalupe* P.O. Box 147, 85551. Tel: 520-428-1049. Rev. John J. Ancharski.

WILLCOX. *Federal Prison Camp* 85546. Tel: 520-428-6600. Rev. Maurice O'Neil, S.S.

YUMA. *MCAS Chapel* Marine Corps Air Station, Davis Monthan Air Force Base, 85369. Tel: 520-341-2087. Rev. Ralph H. Sodano, Chap.
Yuma Regional Medical Center. Attended from St. Francis of Assisi. 1815 8th Ave., 85364. Tel: 520-782-1875.

Special Assignment:
Reverend Monsignors—
Carrillo, Arsenio S., Vicar General & Propagation of the Faith, Dir. Pro-Tem, P.O. Box 31, Tucson, AZ 85702. Tel: 520-792-3410
Reverend Fathers—
Carscallen, Edward C., Spiritual Dir. Ministry to Priests. Tel: 520-625-4330
Sherry, Bryan W., J.C.L., Canonical Consultant, 321 Washington Ave., Florence, AZ 85232. Tel: 520-886-3371

On Duty Outside the Diocese:
Reverend Fathers—
Bell, Brian T., U.S.A.F., 21-21st Space Wing/HQ, 455 Vincent St., Peterson AFB, CO 80914-1466
Gonzales, Robert A., Pontifical College Josephinum, 7625 N. High St., Columbus, OH 43085
McCarthy, Jeremiah J., Rector, St. John's Seminary, 5012 E. Seminary Rd., Camarillo, CA 93012
Ryle, Edward J., Exec. Dir., c/o Arizona Catholic Conference, 400 E. Monroe St., Phoenix, AZ 85004
Shuppert, William T.J., U.S.N. Dept. of Religious Ministries, P.O. Box 9023 NAS, Key West, FL 33040
Underwood, Gary E., U.S.A.F., 96 ABW/HC, 202 N. 8th St., Elgin AFB, FL 32542

Absent on Leave:
Reverend Monsignors—
Trupia, Robert C.
Reverend Fathers—
Cocio, Carlos
Garzon-Blanco, Armando
Noriega, Arnoldo
Rickson, Stephen E.
Rosensweig, Walter F.
Speers, David B.
Teta, Michael J.

Sabbatical Leave:
Reverend Fathers—
Thomas, Robert

Retired:
Reverend Monsignors—
Rosettie, Frederick D., 723 El Sol Cir., Benson, AZ 85602
Reverend Fathers—
Carscallen, Edward C., 221 S. Pas Tera C., Green Valley, AZ 85614
Connelly, George R., 826 N. Bellvedere, Tucson, AZ 85711
Costigan, Richard J., 3241 E. 23rd St., Tucson, AZ 85713
Cote, Gerald M., 5725 W. Box R St., Tucson, AZ 85713
Curry, Frederic F., 870 Natachee, Tucson, AZ 85710
Diehl, Michael C., 6333 Rancho Mission Rd., San Diego, CA 92109
Fahey, John M., P.O. Box 2911, Tubac, AZ 85646
Graff, Robert L., 5464 E. Boston St., Mesa, AZ 85205
LaRoque, Paul M., 392 W. Camino del Sonador, Green Valley, AZ 85614
McGrenra, Cornelius D., Laconnell, Aradra, Co. Donegal, Ireland
O'Flannigan, Thomas L., 409 W. Pontiac Dr. #6, Phoenix, AZ 85027
Ranft, Paul J., Box J, Oracle, AZ 85623
Rook, Paul, 3521 N. Flowing Wells Rd., Tucson, AZ 85705
Schlueter, Clemens M., P.O. Box 5886, Phoenix, AZ 85010

Whalen, Norman M., P.O. Box 911, San Marcos, TX 78666
Wiesler, Willard F., 300 E. 16th Ave., Apache Junction, AZ 85219

Permanent Deacons:
Ackerley, John K., St. Augustine Cathedral, Tucson
Adams, Thomas, Our Lady of Lourdes, Benson
Ammerman, Michael D., St. Francis de Sales, Tucson
Arbizo, Marcello A., St. Rose of Lima, Safford
Baker, Don, St. John the Evangelist, Tuscon
Bejarano, Thomas, St. Rose of Lima, Safford
Borquez, Henry S., St. Augustine Cathedral, Tucson
Broussard, John O., St. Joseph, Tucson
Bueno, Oscar L., St. Augustine's, Tucson
Burns, James, St. Elizabeth Ann Seton, Tucson
Carbajal, Arnulfo, St. Francis of Assisi, Yuma
Carmona, Salvador, St. Augustine Cathedral, Tuscon
Castelan, George P., Sacred Heart, Tucson
Castillo, Frank R., Holy Angels, Globe
Collura, Frank J., St. Francis de Sales, Tucson
Converse, Paul E., St. Joseph, Tucson
Crockette, Alvin, St. Francis de Sales, Tucson
Delgado, Joseph, St. Patrick, Tucson
Desmarais, Ronald, Our Lady of Lourdes, Benson
Duarte, Carlos V., St. Francis of Assisi, Yuma
Duarte, Jose, St. John the Evangelist, Tucson
Dugan, Patrick, St. Anthony of Padua, Casa Grande
Duran, Ralph, St. Rose of Lima, Safford
Farmer, Marvin F., (Retired), St. Francis de Sales, Tucson
Fernandez, Eugene, St. Monica, Tucson
Fisher, Donald, St. Monica, Tucson
Force, Richard C., Villa Maria de Guadalupe Geriatric Center, Tucson
Fullen, Samuel, Holy Cross, Morenci
Fuller, Leonard L., Development Office, Associate Director
Gallegos, Charles A., St. John the Evangelist, Tucson
Gamboa, Henry W.
Garcia, John A., St. Monica, Tucson
Garcia, Marcario, Immaculate Heart of Mary, Somerton
Garcia, Philip, St. Joseph, Tucson
Garcia, Ramon, St. Anthony of Padua, Casa Granade
Gaun, George, St. Andrew the Apostle, Sierra Vista
Gelabert, Carlos G., St. Margaret, Tucson
Gersitz, James M., Holy Angels, Globe
Girard, Charles, St. Francis de Sales, Tucson
Gonzales, David, Sacred Heart, Parker Dam, CA
Gonzales, Luciano, Jr., Immaculate Conception, Douglas
Gonzales, Richard A., Sacred Heart, Clifton
Gonzales, Robert J., St. Patrick, Bisbee & St. Michael Mission, Naco
Grijalva, Pilar, St. Anthony of Padua, Casa Grande
Grimaldo, Pedro, Our Lady of the Valley, Green Valley
Heames, Richard, Our Lady of the Mountains, Sierra Vista
Hernandez, Nieves, Office of Catholic Chaplain, Yuma
Hernandez, Richard R., St. Francis of Assisi, Yuma
Herrick, George R., St. Joseph's, Tucson
Hughes, William G., St. Anthony, Casa Grande
Kingery, Russell, St. Thomas the Apostle, Tucson
Kinney, William, St. Anthony of Padua, Casa Grande
Krueger, William, St. Elizabeth Ann Seton, Tucson
Lambert, Frank, Our Lady of the Valley, Green Valley
LaSalle, James F., St. Thomas More Newman Center, Tucson
Lee, Laurence, St. David
Leinfelder, Carl, Holy Family, Tucson
LeMieux, Richard, Holy Angels, Globe
Leon, Viviano, St. James, Coolidge
Longoria, Leopoldo "Leo", St. Elizabeth Ann Seton, Tucson
Lopez, Jose, St. Jude Thaddeus Mission, San Luis
Lugo, Guillermo A. (Bill), St. Patrick's, Bisbee
Lundgren, Frank S., Jr., Our Lady of Fatima, Tucson
Magallanes, Oscar, Our Lady, Queen of All Saints, Tucson
Marion, Kenneth, (Retired), Phoenix
Marshall, Russell L., Villa Maria Care Center, Tucson
Martinez, Carlos C., St. Augustine Cathedral, Tucson
Martinez, Frank B., St. Rose of Lima, Safford
Martinez, Gilbert O., Our Lady of Guadalupe, Solomon
Mazza, Leon S., St. Joseph, Tucson
McCandless, Charles, Our Lady of the Mountains, Sierra Vista
McDonald, William, St. Francis of Assisi, Yuma
McGeeney, Joseph, St. Francis de Sales Mission, Maricopa
Merritt, Willaim, Our Lady of the Mountains, Sierra Vista
Mezquita, Fernando, Immaculate Conception, Yuma
Milazzo, Mike, St. Andrew the Apostle, Sierra Vista
Miller, Anthony, St. Anthony of Padua, Casa Grande
Minetti, Bernard, St. John the Evangelist, Tucson
Montague, Hugh, St. Francis de Sales, Tucson
Morales, Tomas, St. Monica, Tucson
Moreno, Arnoldo L., St. Joseph, Hayden
Moreno, Francisco, St. Francis of Assisi, Yuma
Moulinet, Armando A., St. Luke's, Douglas
Murphy, J. James, Matrimonial Tribunal, Tucson
Muthart, Paul, St. Francis of Assisi, Yuma
Negrette, Robert, Our Lady of Fatima, Tucson
Nevins, Robert, St. Francis de Sales, Tucson
Nixen, Mark, Immaculate Conception, Yuma
Noriega, Rudy, Sacred Heart, Nogales
Ojeda, Jose, St. John the Evangelist, Tucson
Ornelas, Richard, Santa Cruz, Tucson
Pasquinelli, Gary, St. Francis of Assisi, Yuma
Paulus, Raymond V., Sacred Heart, Tucson
Pavlik, Keith F., St. Francis de Sales, Tucson
Pawloski, Chester E., Saints Peter and Paul, Tucson
Pennington, Charles H., St.Francis de Sales, Tucson
Pozzi, E. Joseph, St. Francis of Assisi, Yuma
Radke, Robert, St. Francis de Sales Mission, Maricopa
Roche, Ernest C., St. John the Evangelist, Tucson
Rodriguez, George M., Our Lady Queen of All Saints, Tucson
Rombach, Lionel E., St. Thomas More Chapel, Newman Center, Tucson
Sadorf, Robert G., Our Lady of the Mountains, Sierra Vista
Saladon, Jerry, St. Francis of Assisi, Yuma
Sampson, David, Immaculate Conception, Yuma
Sanchez, Falvio, St. Bartholomew, San Manuel
Saspe, Gabriel, St. Luke, Douglas
Scalpone, Dennis R., St. Francis de Sales, Tucson
Schaff, James, Our Lady of the Mountains, Sierra Vista
Scherf, George, St. Odilia, Tucson
Schneider, Paul L., Most Holy Trinity, Tucson
Silva, Alfredo A., Our Mother of Sorrows, Tucson
Speers, Robert M., Our Mother of Sorrows, Tucson
Stotler, Jim, Our Lady of the Valley, Green Valley
Tarango, Florentino, St. James, Coolidge
Tellez, Frank J., St. Rose of Lima, Safford
Terry, John, Holy Cross, Morenci
Tighe, Thomas P., Our Mother of Sorrows, Tucson
Valenzuela, Carlos, St. Augustine Cathedral, Tucson
Vega, Rodolfo, Sacred Heart, Nogales
Vidal, Rafael, St. Francis of Assisi, Yuma
Vigil, William, St. Francis de Sales, Tucson
Wagner, Thomas, St. Pius X, Tucson
Welsh, Paul J., Jr., Our Mother of Sorrows, Tucson
Williams, Miguel, Immaculate Conception, Yuma
Yanez, Jesus L. "Chuy", St. Francis of Assisi, Superior

INSTITUTIONS LOCATED IN THE DIOCESE

[A] HIGH SCHOOLS

TUCSON. *Salpointe Catholic High School*, 1545 E. Copper St., 85719. Tel: 520-327-6581; Fax: 520-327-8477. Priory, 1540 E. Glenn St., 85719. Tel: 520-325-1537. Carmelite Order. Revs. Simon Kenny, O.Carm., Prin.; Roy Conry, O.Carm., Prior; Foster Hanley, O.Carm.; Brian Henden, O.Carm.; John Malley, O.Carm. Brothers 1; Sisters 7; Lay Teachers 80; Students 1,412.

[B] HIGH SCHOOLS, PRIVATE

TUCSON. *Immaculate Heart High School*, 625 E. Magee Rd., 85704. Tel: 520-297-2851. Sr. Luisa Sanchez, I.H.M., Prin. Sisters of the Immaculate Heart of Mary 4; Lay Teachers 13; Students 108.

NOGALES. *Our Lady of Lourdes High School*, 555 Patagonia Rd., P.O. Box 1865, 85628. Tel: 520-287-5659; Fax: 520-287-2910. Sr. Barbara Monsequr, C.F.F.M., Prin.; Rev. Francis McCarthy, O.Carm., Chap. Priests 1; Minim Daughters of Mary Immaculate 5; Lay Teachers 12; Students 85.

[C] ELEMENTARY SCHOOLS, PRIVATE

TUCSON. *Immaculate Heart Academy*, 410 E. Magee Rd., 85704. Tel: 520-297-6672; Fax: 520-297-9152. Sr. M. Evelyn Soto, I.H.M., Prin. Sisters of the Immaculate Heart of Mary 3; Lay Teachers 19; Students 328.

[D] CATHOLIC COMMUNITY SERVICES

TUCSON. *Catholic Community Service of Southern Arizona, Inc.*, 155 S. Helen, 85703. Tel: 520-623-0344. E-mail: MARKCCCS@aol.com
Web site: www.ccs-soaz.org
Mailing Address: P.O. Box 5746, 85703. Ken Middleton, Corp. Board Pres.; Mr. John E. Cotter, M.S., CEO; John M. Schubert, Dir. Admin. Services.

Social Service Agencies: Pima County. (Including City of Tucson), 155 W. Helen St., Box 5746, 85703. Tel: 520-623-0344. Ronald A. Dankowski, Ph.D., Exec. Dir.

St. Nicholas of Myra Adoption Program, 899 N. Wilmot, No. C-4, 85711. Tel: 520-745-8791. Nancy Larison, C.I.S.W., Prog. Dir.

Catholic Community Services of Cochise County, 19 Howell Ave., Bisbee, 85603. Mr. Frank McDonough, M.S., Exec. Dir.

Migration and Refugee Services, 155 W. Helen, P.O. Box 5746, 85703. Tel: 520-623-0344. Loretta Tracy, M.S.W., Admin.

Santa Cruz Project, 2109 S. Sixth Ave., 85713. Tel: 520-623-0344. Sr. M. Teresa Apalategui, O.P., M.S.W., Admin.

Westside Nutrition Services, P.O. Box 5746, 85703. Tel: 520-623-0344. Ms. Linda Hutchings, M.S.R.D., Admin.

Merilac Lodge and Casa de Crianza, P.O. Box 5746, 85703. Tel: 520-623-0344. Sr. Mary Ann Bogosoff, C.S.A., Dir.

Immigration Counseling Service, 155 W. Helen St., 85703. Tel: 520-623-0344. Francisco Hoyos, Dir.

Field Offices:

Gila County Case Management, 175 E. Cedar St., Globe, 85501. Tel: 520-425-5130. Sherlyn Harris, M.A., C.O.G.

Catholic Community Services in Western Arizona, 690 E. 32nd St., Yuma, 85365. Tel: 520-341-9400. Patrick Fish, Exec. Dir.

Chaplaincy-Pastoral Ministry to Non-Denominational Nursing Homes, 155 W. Helen, 85703. Tel: 520-623-0344, Ext. 3058. Sr. Carolyn Nicolai, F.S.P., Coord.; Rev. Angelo Mastria, O.Carm., Chap.

Community Outreach Program for the Deaf, 268 W. Adams, 85705. Tel: 520-623-0344. Mrs. Marguerite Harmon, M.S.R., Exec. Dir.

Detention Ministry, 155 W. Helen, Box 5746, 85703-0746. Tel: 520-623-0344. Ms. Barbara Mattus, M.A., Dir.

St. Elizabeth of Hungary Out-Patient Clinic, 140 W. Speedway, 85705. Tel: 520-628-7871. Sr. Barbara Anne Stowasser, C.S.J., Exec. Dir.

Mobile Podiatry, Dentures and Eyeglasses Clinic, 140 W. Speedway Blvd., 85705. Tel: 520-628-7871.

Minority Liaison Agencies:

Pio Decimo Neighborhood Center, 848 S. 7th Ave., 85701. Tel: 520-622-2801. Margaret Kish, M.S.W., Exec. Dir.

Project Ayuda, 155 W. Helen, Box 5746, 85703. Robert Cowles, M.S.W., Pro. Dir.

Independent Allied Community Agencies Mobile Meals of Tucson, 155 W. Helen, P.O. Box 5746, 85703. Kay Nixon, Prog. Dir.

[E] GENERAL HOSPITALS

TUCSON. *Carondelet Health Network*, 1601 W. St. Mary's Rd., 85745-2682
For a complete listing, refer to the Hospitals section.

St. Elizabeth of Hungary Out-Patient Clinic, 140 W. Speedway Blvd., 85705. Tel: 520-628-7871.
E-mail: stelizccs@aol.com
For a complete listing, refer to the Hospitals section.

NOGALES. *Holy Cross Hospital, Inc.*, 1171 W. Target Range Rd., 85621. Tel: 520-287-2771; Fax: 520-287-7314; 287-8015
For a complete listing, refer to the Hospitals section.

[F] MONASTERIES AND RESIDENCES OF PRIESTS AND BROTHERS

TUCSON. *Carmelite Priory*, 1540 E. Glenn St., 85719. Tel: 520-325-1537. Very Revs. Ronald Oakham, O.Carm., Western Commissary Prov.; John Malley, O.Carm., Gen. Emeritus; Revs. Angelo Mastria, O. Carm., Prior; Simon Kenny, O.Carm., Prin.; Roy Conry, O.Carm.; Foster Hanley, O.Carm.; Vernon Malley, O.Carm.; Brian Henden, O. Carm.; Bros. Thomas Schrader, O.Carm.; Gerald Willick, O.Carm. Fathers and Brothers at Salpointe Catholic High School. Priests 7; Brothers 2.

Discalced Carmelite Fathers of St. Margaret's, 801 N. Grande Ave., 85745. Tel: 520-622-0168. Revs. Gilbert Levario, O.C.D.; Bernard Perkins, O.C.D.; Kevin McArdle, O.C.D.

Jesuit Community of the Vatican Observatory, 2017 E. Lee St., 85719. Tel: 520-795-9866. Jesuit Residence. Revs. Richard P. Boyle, S.J.; George V. Coyne, S.J., Dir. Vatican Observatory; Martin F. McCarthy, S.J.; Richard J. Murphy, S.J.; William R. Stoeger, S.J.; Andrew P. Whitman, S.J.; Bro. Guy Consolmagno, S.J.

**Vatican Observatory Foundation.*

Offices of The Vatican Observatory, Steward Observatory, The University of Arizona, 85721. Tel: 520-621-3225.

Kino House, 2844 E. 1st St., 85716. Tel: 520-327-7130. Jesuit Fathers residence. Rev. Charles W. Polzer, S.J., Supr., University of Arizona, Arizona State Museum, 85721. Tel: 520-621-6278. Rev. Christopher Corbally, S.J. (Vatican), Steward Observatory, University of Arizona. Tel: 520-621-3225.

Regina Cleri Center, 8800 E. 22nd St, 85710. Tel: 520-886-5223. Revs. Carlos Cocio; Armando Garzon-Blanco; John P. Lyons; James Modeen; Albert E. Verbrugghe; Rev. Msgr. Walter F. Rosensweig. In res. Most Rev. Francis A. Quinn, Bishop Emeritus of Sacramento, Domestic Department. Sisters of the Oblates of St. Martha 4.

Society of the Divine Word, 8 Tucson Ter., 85745. Tel: 520-791-2750.

CORTARO. *Desert House of Prayer*, 7350 W. Picture Rocks Rd., Box 570, 85652. Tel: 520-744-3825. Rev. John W. Kane, C.Ss.R.

ST. DAVID. *Holy Trinity Monastery*, P.O. Box 298, 85630. Tel: 520-720-4642; 720-4016. Benedictines. Revs. Louis B. Hasenfuss, O.S.B., Prior; Alcuin M. Almasy, O.S.B.; Lawrence M. Fedor, O.S.B.; Henri Capdeville, O.S.B.; Alexander Mills, O.S.B. Professed 13. Benedictine Sisters of Our Lady of Mount Olivet. Perpetually Professed 1.

SONOITA. *The Benedictine Monastery of Erlac in Sonoita*, P.O. Box 534, 85637. Tel: 520-394-2961. Rt. Rev. James R. Straif.

[G] CONVENTS AND RESIDENCES FOR SISTERS

TUCSON. *Benedictine Monastery*, 800 N. Country Club Rd., 85716. Tel: 520-325-6401. Sr. Dawn Annette Mills, O.S.B., Prioress. Sisters 22.

Carondelet Community, 6571 E. Carondelet Dr., 85710. Tel: 520-721-3832. Sisters 5.

Cathedral Convent, 435 S. 6th Ave., 85701. Sisters 3.

Guadalupe Community, 1833 W. St. Mary's Rd., 85745-2653. Tel: 520-620-4944. Sr. St. Charles Benton, C.S.J. Sisters 5.

Immaculate Heart Lodge Convent, 410 E. Magee Rd., 85704. Tel: 520-742-5896. Sr. Alice Marie Martinez, I.H.M., Prov. Supr.; Sr. Barbara Ann Gamboa, I.H.M., Supr. Sisters of the Immaculate Heart of Mary 6.

Masmitja Hall Community, 410 E. Magee Rd., 85704. Tel: 520-297-8961. Sr. Blanche M. Felix, Supr. Sisters of the Immaculate Heart of Mary 5.

Immaculate Heart Novititate, 4100 N. Sabino Canyon Rd., 85715. Tel: 520-885-4981. Sr. M. Dominic Pacheco, I.H.M., Novice Mistress. Sisters of the Immaculate Heart of Mary 1.

Immaculate Heart of Mary Provincial House, 4100 N. Sabino Canyon Rd., 85715. Tel: 520-886-4273. Sr. Alice Marie Martinez, I.H.M., Prov. Supr.; Sr. Evelyn Soto, I.H.M. Sisters of the Immaculate Heart of Mary 2.

Immaculate Heart Religious Center, 35 E. 15th St., 85701. Tel: 520-624-7221. Sr. Vivian Gallegos, I.H.M., Supr. Sisters of the Immaculate Heart of Mary 2.

Maria Community, 1835 W. St. Mary's Rd., 85745-2653. Tel: 520-620-4940. Sr. St. Joan Willert, C.S.J., Contact Person. Sisters 13.

Regina Cleri Convent, 8800 E. 22nd St., 85710. Tel: 520-296-9077. Sisters of the Oblates of St. Martha 4.

St. Ann Convent, 4100 Sabino Canyon Rd., 85715. Tel: 520-298-0064. Sr. M. Julian Valdez, Supr. Sisters of the Immaculate Heart of Mary 12.

St. Joseph Community, 6569 E. Carondelet Community, 85710. Tel: 520-721-3816.

Saints Peter and Paul Convent, 1947 E. Adams St., 85719. Tel: 520-325-2234.

San Xavier Mission, 1950 W. San Xavier Rd., 85746. Tel: 520-294-2624.

Sisters of the Holy Cross, 1947 E. Adams, 85719-4301. Tel: 520-622-7902.

Picture Rocks Retreat Center, P.O. Box 569, Cortaro, 85652. 355 San Carlos Ave., San Carlos, 85550.

DOUGLAS. *Loretto Convent*, 1200 - 14th St., 85607; Fax: 520-364-7844. Sr. Marina, O.C.D.

FLORENCE. *Chapel of the Gila*. (Historical Site), 255 E. 8th St., 85232. Mailing Address: P.O. Box 2550, 85232-0550.

GLOBE. *Holy Angels Convent*, 1300 E. Cedar, 85501. Tel: 520-425-2034. Union of the Sisters of the P.B.V.M.

NOGALES. *Our Lady of Lourdes Middle and High School*, P.O. Box 1865, 85628-1865; Fax: 520-287-2910. Minim Daughters of Mary Immaculate C.F.M.M. 11.

St. Joseph Convent, 405 N. Carondelet Dr., 85621-2454. Tel: 520-287-7139. Sr. Celia Ma. Ponce, C.F.M.M., Supr. Minim Daughters of Mary Immaculate C.F.M.M. 8.

SOMERTON. *Immaculate Heart of Mary Convent*, P.O. Box 2888, 85340.

SONOITA. *Santa Rita Abbey*, HC 1, Box 929, 85637-9705. Tel: 520-455-5595.
E-mail: BEVSRA@dakotacom.net
Cistercian Nuns of the Strict Observance, O.C.S.O. Mother M. Beverly Aitken, O.C.S.O., Prioress. Solemn Professed 10; Simple Professed 1; Novices 1; Postulants 1.

TOPAWA. *St. Catherine Convent*, P.O. Box 209, 85639.
E-mail: topsis@juno.com
Sr. Karen Krahenbuhl, O.S.F., Contact Person, Village Ministry Services. Sisters 4.

YUMA. *Immaculate Conception Convent*, 500 - 24th Ave., 85364. Tel: 520-783-5224. Sisters 9.

[H] RETREAT HOUSES

TUCSON. *Redemptorist Picture Rocks Retreat*, 7101 W. Picture Rocks Rd., 85743. Tel: 520-744-3400. Mailing Address: P.O. Box 569, Cortaro, 85652. Revs. Patrick O'Brien, C.SS.R.; Thomas Danielsen, C.SS.R.

[I] NEWMAN CENTERS

TUCSON. *University of Arizona*. St. Thomas More Newman Center, 1615 E. 22nd St., 85719. Tel: 520-327-6662; Fax: 520-327-6559. Revs. Albert Felice-Pace, O.P., Supr.; Fred Lucci, O.P.; Bro. Bryan Kromholtz, O.P.; Sr. Kathleen Rose, O.P. In res. Rev. Robert A. Burns, O.P.; Sr. Carol Monzon, O.P.; Sr. Patricia Walsh, O.P.

CASA GRANDE. *Central Arizona College, Holy Family Newman Center*, P.O. Box 12335, 85230-2335. Tel: 520-836-0601. Rev. Steven G. Stencil, Chap.

DOUGLAS. *Cochise Community College*, St. Luke, 1211 15th St., 85607. Rev. James M. Hobert, Jr.; Janet Fullen, Admin.; Ray Nadolny, Dir.

THATCHER. *Eastern Arizona Junior College*, 85552. Rev. Antony Navarria, St. Rose of Lima, 311 Central Ave., Tucson. Tel: 520-428-4920. Cecilia Roudeluesh, Pres., Newman Sustaining Board; Linda Hedges, Dir., Newman Assoc.

[J] MISCELLANEOUS LISTINGS

TUCSON. *Carondelet Foundation*, 350 N. Wilmot, 85710. Tel: 520-721-3853. Jannie Fernandez, Exec.Dir.

Casa de los Ninos Crisis Center, 1101 N. 4th Ave., 85705. Tel: 520-624-5600; Fax: 520-623-2443. Jeanne Landdeck-Sisco, Exec. Dir.; Sr. Kathleen Clark, C.S.J., Founding Dir. Emeritus.

Casa Maria, 401 E. 26th St., 85713. Tel: 520-624-0312. Mr. Brian Flagg, Contact Person.

Christ Child Society of Tucson, P.O. Box 36212, 85740-6212. Tel: 520-297-8437. Donna Landon, Pres.; Joan Nolan, Vice Pres.; Ann Marie Friend, Sec.; Carol Komarewich, Treas.

Diocese of Tucson Catholic Cemeteries. (Sole Corporation), 3555 N. Oracle Rd., 85705. Tel: 520-888-0860; Fax: 520-887-7360. Brian Molloy, Contact Person.

Integrated Auxiliaries The Friends of John Paul II Foundation. Dr. S.F. Poray-Tucholski, Pres., 10121 Prairie Hills Cir., Sun City, 85352. Dr. E.J. Bratkowsha-Kendall, Vice Pres./Treas., 5611 E. Rochridge Dr., Phoenix, 85018. Czeslaw A. Kozdroj, Esq., 10347 Campana Dr., Sun City, 85351. Mrs. Jacquelina M. Poray-Tucholski, 10121 Prairie Hills Cir., Sun City, 85351.

Knights of Columbus, 9019 E. Palms Park Dr., 85715. Tel: 520-886-7609. Mr. John H. Cardellina, Past State Deputy; Mr. John W. Tobin, State Deputy, 13621 N. 51st Pl., Scottsdale, 85254. Tel: 602-996-6192; 870-1600.

Magnificat - Tucson Chapter, 3560 N. Via San Juanito, 85749. Tel: 520-749-0633. Mrs. L. J. Elizabeth Celenza, Pres. A ministry to Catholic women.

Redemptorist Community Support Charity Trust. (Western Province), 7101 W. Picture Rocks Rd., 85743. Tel: 520-744-3400; Fax: 520-744-8021. Trustees: Revs. Patrick O'Brien, C.SS.R.; Stephen Meyer, C.SS.R.; Raymond Maiser, C.SS.R.

Retorno (Marriage Retorno), 4321 N. Ventana Dr., 85715. Tel: 520-792-2931; 744-3400; Fax: 520-744-8021. Contacts: Rev. Patrick O'Brien, C.SS.R. Tel: 520-744-3400; Kathy & Kevin Stogsdill.

St. Nicholas Indian Center, 349 W. 31st St., 85713. Tel: 520-622-5363; 792-0230. Revs. Daniel P. McLaughlin, S.T.; Abram E. Dono, S.T.; Bro. David T. Sommer, S.T.

Society of St. Vincent de Paul, 829 S. 6th Ave., 85701. Tel: 520-628-7837.

HEREFORD. *Our Lady of the Sierras Foundation*, 10310 Twin Oaks Dr., P.O. Box 269, 85615. Tel: 520-378-2950. Mr. Gerald A. Chouoinard, Pres.

ST. DAVID. *San Pedro Valley Center for the Arts*, Holy Trinity Monastery, Box 160, 85630. Tel: 520-720-4009. Patricia J. Don, Contact Person.

SONOITA. *Cistercian Studies Quarterly, Inc.*, Santa Rita Abbey, HC 1, Box 929, 85637-9705. Tel: 520-455-5595.
E-mail: hta@xmission.com
Web site: www.xmission.com/~hta/csq
Sr. Sheryl Chen, Contact.

[K] DIOCESAN CEMETERIES

TUCSON. *Holy Hope Cemetery and Mausoleum*, Office, 3555 N. Oracle Rd., P.O. Box 5158, 85703. Tel: 520-888-0860. Mr. Regis Flaherty, Admin.

Our Lady of the Desert Cemetery and Mausoleum, Office, 2151 S. Avenida Los Reyes, P.O. Box 5158, 85703. Tel: 520-885-9173.

RELIGIOUS INSTITUTES OF MEN REPRESENTED IN THE DIOCESE

For further details refer to the corresponding bracketed number in the Religious Institutes of Men or Women sections.

[0200]—*Benedictine Monks*.—O.S.B.
[0470]—*The Capuchin Friars*. (Prov. of St. Joseph).—O.F.M.Cap.
[0270]—*Carmelite Fathers and Brothers*. (Prov. of Most Pure Heart of Mary).—O.Carm.
[0360]—*Claretian Missionaries*.—C.M.F.
[1320]—*Clerics of St. Viator*.—C.S.V.
[1330]—*Congregation of the Mission*.—C.M.
[0260]—*Discalced Carmelites*. (Angol-Irish Prov.).—O.C.D.
[0520]—*Franciscan Friars*.—O.F.M.
[0650]—*Holy Ghost Fathers*. (Western Prov.).—C.S.Sp.
[0690]—*Jesuit Fathers and Brothers*. (Western Prov.).—S.J.
[0720]—*The Missionaries of Our Lady La Salette*. (Immaculate Heart of Mary Prov.).—M.S.
[0840]—*Missionary Servants of the Most Holy Trinity*.—S.T.
[0910]—*Oblates of Mary Immaculate*.—O.M.I.
[0430]—*Order of Preachers (Dominicans)*.—O.P.
[1030]—*Paulist Fathers*.—C.S.P.
[1070]—*Redemptorist Fathers*. (Oakland Prov.).—C.SS.R.
[1240]—*Servites*.—O.S.M.
[1200]—*Society of the Divine Savior*.—S.D.S.
[0420]—*Society of the Divine Word*.—S.V.D.
[1060]—*Society of the Precious Blood*.—C.PP.S.

RELIGIOUS INSTITUTES OF WOMEN REPRESENTED IN THE DIOCESE

[0100]—*Adorers of the Blood of Christ*.—A.S.C.
[0233]—*Benedictine Nuns*.—O.S.B.
[0230]—*Benedictine Sisters of Pontifical Jurisdiction*.—O.S.B.
[0370]—*Carmelite Sisters of the Most Sacred Heart of Los Angeles*.—O.C.D.
[0670]—*Cistercian Nuns of the Strict Observance*.—O.C.S.O.
[0700]—*Company of Mary*.—O.D.N.
[0220]—*Congregation of the Benedictine Sisters of Perpetual Adoration of Pontifical Jurisdiction*.—O.S.B.
[0460]—*Congregation of the Sisters of Charity of the Incarnate Word*.—C.C.V.I.
[3710]—*Congregation of the Sisters of St. Agnes*.—C.S.A.
[1920]—*Congregation of the Sisters of the Holy Cross*.—C.S.C.
[1780]—*Congregation of the Sisters of the Third Order of St. Francis of Perpetual Adoration*.—F.S.P.A.
[1710]—*Congregation of the Third Order of St. Francis of Mary Immaculate, Joliet, IL*.—O.S.F.
[1070-03]—*Dominican Sisters*.—O.P.
[1070-09]—*Dominican Sisters*.—O.P.
[1070-12]—*Dominican Sisters*.—O.P.
[1070-13]—*Dominican Sisters*.—O.P.
[1070-30]—*Dominican Sisters*.—O.P.
[1140]—*Eucharistic Missionaries of St. Dominic*.—O.P.
[1230]—*Franciscan Sisters of Christian Charity*.—O.S.F.
[1310]—*Franciscan Sisters of Little Falls, Minnesota*.—O.S.F.
[1425]—*Franciscan Sisters of Peace*.—F.S.P.
[2575]—*Institute of the Sisters of Mercy of the Americas*.—R.S.M.
[2490]—*Medical Mission Sisters*.—S.C.M.M.
[2675]—*Minim Daughters of Mary Immaculate*.—C.F.M.M.
[2720]—*Mission Helpers of the Sacred Heart*.—M.H.S.H.

[]—*Missionary Sisters of the Immaculate Conception.* (Montreal, Canada).—M.I.C.
[]—*Oblates of St. Martha.*—O.S.M.
[3130]—*Our Lady of Victory Missionary Sisters.*—O.L.V.M.
[3300]—*Presentation Sisters of the Blessed Virgin.*—P.B.V.M.
[]—*Religious of St. Joseph of Australia.*—R.S.J.
[2970]—*School Sisters of Notre Dame.*—S.S.N.D.
[1680]—*School Sisters of St. Francis.*—S.S.S.F.-O.S.F.
[3580]—*Servants of Mary.*—O.S.M.
[3590]—*Servants of Mary (Servite Sisters).*—O.S.M.
[3500]—*Servants of the Blessed Sacrament.*—S.S.S.
[]—*Seton Sisters of Our Lady of Guadalupe, Tucson.*—S.S.LOG.
[3620]—*Sister Servants of Mary Immaculate.*—S.S.M.I.
[0440]—*Sisters of Charity of Cincinnati, Ohio.*—S.C.
[480]—*Sisters of Charity of Leavenworth, Kansas.*—S.C.L.
[0570]—*Sisters of Charity of Seton Hill, Greensburg, Pennsylvania.*—S.C.
[3720]—*Sisters of Notre Dame de Namur.*—S.N.D.deN.
[3720]—*Sisters of St. Anne.*—S.S.A.
[1705]—*The Sisters of St. Francis of Assisi.*—O.S.F.
[1800]—*Sisters of St. Francis of the Third Order Regular (Williamsville, New York).*—O.S.F.
[3830-06]—*Sisters of St. Joseph.*—S.S.J.
[3830-13]—*Sisters of St. Joseph.*—C.S.J.
[3840]—*Sisters of St. Joseph of Carondelet.*—C.S.J.
[0260]—*The Sisters of the Blessed Sacrament for Indians and Colored People.*—S.B.S.
[1030]—*Sisters of the Divine Savior.*—S.D.S.
[1990]—*Sisters of the Holy Names of Jesus and Mary.*—S.N.J.M.
[2110]—*Sisters of the Humility of Mary.*—H.M.
[3270]—*Sisters of the Most Precious Blood.*—C.PP.S.
[3260]—*Sisters of the Precious Blood.* (Dayton, Ohio).—C.PP.S.
[3320]—*Sisters of the Presentation of the Blesssed Virgin Mary.*—P.B.V.M.
[1720]—*Sisters of the Third Order Regular of St. Francis of the Congregation of Our Lady of Lourdes.*—O.S.F.
[2090]—*Sisters, Home Visitors fo Mary.*—H.V.M.
[2150]—*Sisters, Servants of the Immaculate Heart of Mary.* (Monroe).—I.H.M.

NECROLOGY

† O'Dougherty, Rev. Msgr. Loyola, San Manuel, AZ, St. Bartholomew. —Died April 9, 1997.
† Phelan, Reginald L., (Retired). —Died Jan. 1, 1997.

Diocese of Tulsa

(Dioecesis Tulsensis)

Most Reverend

EDWARD J. SLATTERY

Bishop of Tulsa; ordained January 6, 1994 in Rome; installed January 12, 1994.

ESTABLISHED FEBRUARY 7, 1973.

Square Miles 26,417.

The Diocese of Tulsa comprises the following 31 Counties: Adair, Atoka, Bryan, Cherokee, Choctaw, Coal, Craig, Creek, Delaware, Haskell, Hughes, Latimer, LeFlore, McCurtain, McIntosh, Mayes, Muskogee, Nowata, Okfuskee, Okmulgee, Osage, Ottawa, Pawnee, Payne, Pittsburg, Pushmataha, Rogers, Sequoyah, Tulsa, Wagoner and Washington.

For legal titles of parishes and institutions, consult the Chancery Office.

Chancery Office: P.O. Box 2009, Tulsa, OK, 74101. Tel.: 918-587-3115; Fax: 918-587-6692.

Web site address: http:www.galstar.com / rctulsa / int /

E-mail address: chantul@aol.com

STATISTICAL OVERVIEW

Personnel	
Bishop	1
Priests: Diocesan Active in Diocese	55
Priests: Active Outside Diocese	3
Priests: Retired, Sick or Absent	19
Number of Diocesan Priests	77
Religious Priests in Diocese	20
Extern Priests in Diocese	6
Ordinations:	
Religious Priests	1
Permanent Deacons	5
Permanent Deacons in Diocese	47
Total Brothers	5
Total Sisters	123
Parishes	
Parishes	58
With Resident Pastor:	
Resident Diocesan Priests	43
Resident Religious Priests	5
Without Resident Pastor:	
Administered by Priests	9
Completely Vacant	1
Missions	23
Pastoral Centers	6
New Parishes Created	1
Professional Ministry Personnel:	
Sisters	14
Lay Ministers	34
Welfare	
Catholic Hospitals	2
Total Assisted	533,145
Homes for the Aged	1
Total Assisted	140
Specialized Homes	2
Total Assisted	89
Special Centers for Social Services	3
Total Assisted	57,604
Educational	
Diocesan Students in Other Seminaries	10
Total Seminarians	10
High Schools, Diocesan and Parish	1
Total Students	889
High Schools, Private	1
Total Students	363
Elementary Schools, Diocesan and Parish	9
Total Students	2,210
Elementary Schools, Private	2
Total Students	1,356
Catechesis/Religious Education:	
High School Students	1,776
Elementary Students	5,584
Total Students Under Catholic Instruction	12,188
Teachers in the Diocese:	
Priests	6
Brothers	4
Sisters	7
Lay Teachers	300
Vital Statistics	
Receptions into the Church:	
Infant Baptism Totals	1,038
Adult Baptism Totals	201
Received into Full Communion	321
First Communions	1,021
Confirmations	758
Marriages:	
Catholic	148
Interfaith	264
Total Marriages	412
Deaths	469
Total Catholic Population	54,206
Total Population	1,478,542

Former Bishops—Most Rev. BERNARD J. GANTER, D.D., ord. May 22, 1952; appt. Bishop of Tulsa, Dec. 19, 1972; ord. Feb. 7, 1973; transferred to Beaumont, Oct. 18, 1977.—Most Rev. EUSEBIUS J. BELTRAN, ord. May 14, 1960; appt. Bishop of Tulsa, Feb. 28, 1978; ord. April 20, 1978; transferred to Archdiocese of Oklahoma City, Nov. 24, 1992.

Vicar General—Rev. Msgr. DENNIS C. DORNEY.

Chancery Office—111 W. 5th, Ste. 400, Tulsa, 74103., Mailing Address: P.O. Box 2009, Tulsa, 74101. Tel: 918-587-3115; Fax: 918-587-6692. Office Hours: Mon.-Fri. 9-5.

Chancellor—Dr. EDWARD L. MAILLET, D.S.W.

Vice Chancellor—Rev. PATRICK J. GAALAAS.

Financial Administrator—Mr. PHILIP J. CREIDER, *P.O. Box 2009, Tulsa, 74101.* Tel: 918-587-3115.

Diocesan Senators—Most Rev. EDWARD J. SLATTERY; Rev. Msgr. DENNIS C. DORNEY, V.G.; Revs. J. RICHARD BRADLEY; PATRICK J. GAALAAS; CHRISTOPHER DAIGLE; J. PAUL DONOVAN; PAUL E. EICHHOFF; GREGORY A. GIER; WILLIAM HAMILL, O.S.A.; BERNARD C. JEWITT; MARTIN J. MORGAN; DANIEL H. MUEGGENBORG; TAM N. NGUYEN; MICHAEL R.K. ROONEY; JAMES D. WHITE.

Ex Officio—Rev. Msgr. DENNIS C. DORNEY.

Diocesan Consultors—Revs. J. RICHARD BRADLEY; PAUL E. EICHHOFF; PATRICK J. GAALAAS; BERNARD C. JEWITT; JAMES D. WHITE; Rev. Msgr. DENNIS C. DORNEY; Revs. DANIEL H. MUEGGENBORG; TAM N. NGUYEN.

Diocesan Marriage Tribunal—

Judicial Vicar—Rev. JOHN J. WADE.

Defenders of the Bond—Revs. KENNETH HARDER; MICHAEL J. KNIPE, J.C.L.; KHIET NGUYEN.

Judges—Deacons KASPER E. WEIGANT; GARY WALSH, P.P.

Accessory Auditor—Deacon GARY D. WALSH.

Interdiocesan Tribunal of Second Instance for Province of Oklahoma City—

Vice-Judicial Vicar—Rev. TAM N. NGUYEN, J.C.L.

Judges—Rev. Msgr. JAMES F. HALPINE; Rev. DANIEL A. PERLINSKI.

Defender of the Bond—Revs. THOMAS P. BILLER; WILLIAM J. SWIFT; JAMES D. WHITE.

Notary—Mrs. MARY JONES.

Priests' Personnel Committee—Rev. Msgr. DENNIS C. DORNEY, V.G.; Revs. J. RICHARD BRADLEY; STEPHEN A. MACAULAY; GARY D. SHERMAN; GREGORY A. GIER.

Seminary Board—Rev. Msgr. DENNIS C. DORNEY, V.G.; Mr. ROBERT J. LAFORTUNE; Revs. TIMOTHY L. DAVISON; DANIEL H. MUEGGENBORG; JOE C. TOWNSEND.

Federation of Religious of the Diocese of Tulsa—Leadership Team: Sr. MARILYN NORWOOD, O.S.B.; Sr. EUGENIA BROWN, O.S.B., *P.O. Box 3204, Tulsa, 74101.* Tel: 918-582-6247.

Diocesan Offices

Archivist—Mrs. MARY JONES, *P.O. Box 2009, Tulsa, 74101.* Tel: 918-587-3115.

Campaign for Human Development—Dr. EDWARD L. MAILLET, *P.O. Box 2009, Tulsa, 74101.* Tel: 918-587-3115.

Campus Ministry—Rev. JOHN JANGAM, Chap.; Mrs. JOANNE CRESCITELLI, Admin. Asst. PATRICK MARTIN, Campus Ministry, *The University of Tulsa, 440 S. Florence, Tulsa, 74104.* Tel: 918-599-0204. Rev. JOE C. TOWNSEND, *201 N. Knoblock St., Stillwater, 74074.* Tel: 405-372-6408., *Oklahoma State University, 201 N. Knoblock St., Stillwater, 74075.* Tel: 405-372-6408.

Catholic Charities of the Diocese of Tulsa—Mrs. HAZEL LEITCH, Dir., *739 N. Denver, Tulsa, 74106.* Tel: 918-585-8167.

Cemetery—Mr. JACK CHARON, Dir., *P.O. Box 2009, Tulsa, 74101.* Tel: 918-587-3115. Mr. JAMES LIICHOW, Supvr., *Calvary Cemetery, 91st and Harvard, Tulsa, 74136.* Tel: 918-299-7348.

Clergy Education—Rev. DANIEL MUEGGENBORG, *P.O. Box 2009, Tulsa, 74101.* Tel: 918-587-3115.

Diocesan Catholic Committee on Scouting—Mr. JOHN D. KNECHT, Dir., *18144 E. 95th St., North Owasso, 74055.* Tel: 918-272-5483.

Diocesan Council of Catholic Women—Rev. Msgr. JAMES F. HALPINE, *P.O. Box 3204, Tulsa, 74101.* Tel: 918-582-6274.

Ecumenism—Rev. BERNARD C. JEWITT, Dir., *4001 E. 101st St. S., Tulsa, 74137.*

Education—Rev. DANIEL H. MUEGGENBORG, Vicar of Religious Education, *P.O. Box 2009, Tulsa, 74101.* Tel: 918-587-3115.

Family Life Office—Mr. TIMOTHY J. SULLIVAN, Dir., *739 N. Denver, Tulsa, 74106.* Tel: 918-585-8167., *P.O. Box 6429, Tulsa, 74148.*

Parochial Schools—Mrs. ARDEN GLENN, Supt. Catholic Schools, *P.O. Box 2009, Tulsa, 74101.* Tel: 918-587-3115.

Health Affairs—Rev. KENNETH HEBERLEIN, Dir. Pastoral Care & Health Affairs, *1923 S. Utica, Tulsa, 74104.* Tel: 918-744-2689.

Prison and Social Ministry—Rev. DONALD W. BROOKS, *P.O. Box 2009, Tulsa, 74101.* Tel: 918-587-3115.

Hispanic Ministry—Revs. PATRICK BRANKIN, Dir. ROBERT M. DYE, Assoc. Dir., *1541 E. Newton Pl., Tulsa, 74106.* Tel: 918-584-2424.

Historian—Rev. JAMES D. WHITE, *P.O. Box 2009, Tulsa, 74101.*

Pastoral Studies Institute—Ms. MONICA SKRZYPCZAK, Coord., *P.O. Box 2009, Tulsa, 74101.* Tel: 918-587-3115.

Office of Divine Worship—Revs. JAMES D. WHITE, Dir. MATTHEW J. GERLACH, Assoc. Dir.

Newspaper "Eastern Oklahoma Catholic"—Mr. JAMES SELLARS, Editor, *P.O. Box 520, Tulsa, 74101.* Tel: 918-587-3115.

Office of Permanent Diaconate—Rev. J. RICHARD BRADLEY, Vicar of Deacons; Sr. MARIE AMANDA ALLARD, O.P., Dir. Formation, *P.O. Box 2009, Tulsa, 74101.* Tel: 918-587-3115.

Propagation of Faith—Rev. MATTHEW J. GERLACH, Coord., *P.O. Box 3204, Tulsa, 74101.* Tel: 918-582-6247.

Guatemala Mission—Mikatokla, Santiago Atitlan, Dept. Solola, Guatemala, Central America; Rev. TOM MC SHERRY.

Stewardship and Development—Mr. JON CALDER, Dir., *P.O. Box 2009, Tulsa, 74101.* Tel: 918-587-3115.

Vocations—Rev. TIMOTHY L. DAVIDSON, *440 S. Florence, Tulsa, 74104.* Tel: 918-599-0204.

Catholic Student Ministries—440 S. Florence, Tulsa, 74104. Tel: 918-599-0204.

Young Adult Ministry—Mr. CHARLES MICHIE, *P.O. Box 2009, Tulsa, 74101.* Tel: 918-587-3115.

Youth Ministry—Mr. CHARLES MICHIE, *P.O. Box 2009, Tulsa, 74101.* Tel: 918-587-3115.

CLERGY, PARISHES, MISSIONS AND PAROCHIAL SCHOOLS

CITY OF TULSA
(Tulsa County)

1—HOLY FAMILY CATHEDRAL (1899), Rev. Gregory A. Grier, Rector; Rev. Msgr. James F. Halpine, Rector Emeritus; Revs. Matthew J. Gerlach; Khiet Nguyen; Sr. Eugenia Brown, O.S.B., Pastoral Assoc. & D.R.E. In res., Revs. Donald W. Brooks; John Jangam.
Res., 122 W. 8th St., P.O. Box 3204, 74101. Tel: 918-582-6247; Fax: 918-599-8334. [JC]
School—820 S. Boulder St., 74119. Tel: 918-582-0422. Mrs. Patricia Mohatt Lewis, Prin.
Lay Teachers 9; Students 120.
Catechesis/Religious Programs—Fax: 918-599-8334.
Students 140.

2—COMMUNITY OF SAINT PETER, Revs. James W. Jackson, F.S.S.P., Chap.; George Gabet, F.S.S.P.
Mailing Address: 1720 E. Apache, 74110. Tel: 918-425-0486; Fax: 918-425-2077.
Res., 1728 E. Apache, 74110.

3—ST. AUGUSTINE'S (1955), Rev. Gary Sherman; Sr. Phyllis Vaske, O.S.F., Pastoral Asst.; Deacon Theodore Prudhomme.
Mailing Address: 633 E. Marshall Pl., 74106.
Church—1720 E. Apache.
Res., 1313 N. Xenophon, 74127. Tel: 918-587-2965.
Convent—Tel: 918-428-3280.

4—ST. BERNARD OF CLAIRVAUX (1978), Revs. Bernard C. Jewitt; Patrick W. Eastman; Deacons Richard Campbell; John Hancock; Alan Mikell.
Res., 4001 E. 101st St., 74137. Tel: 918-299-9406; Fax: 918-299-7796.
Catechesis/Religious Programs—Sharon Lechtenberg, D.R.E.
Students 756.

5—ST. CATHERINE (1925), Rev. Christopher P. Daigle; Deacons Bill Coburn; Sid Starr.
Res., 4532 S. 25th Ave., 74107. Tel: 918-446-8124; Fax: 918-446-4506. [JC]
School—2515 W. 46th St., 74107. Tel: 918-446-9756.
Sisters of St. Francis of the Martyr St. George 3; Lay Teachers 8; Students 152.
Catechesis/Religious Programs—Students 58.

6—CHRIST THE KING (1917), Revs. Martin Morgan; Ken Harder; Sr. Joan Duerst, O.P., Pastoral Asst.; Sr. Connie Lennartz, O.P.; Deacon Loren F. Luschen. In res., Rev. Robert M. Dye.
Office: 1520 S. Rockford Ave., 74120. Tel: 918-584-4788; 4789; Fax: 918-584-0055.
Res., 1530 S. Rockford Ave., 74120. Tel: 918-584-6693. [JC]
Christ the King Board of Education Endowment Trust—.
School—Marquette School, 1519 S. Quincy, 74120. Tel: 918-584-4631; Fax: 918-584-0055. James J. Pohlman, Prin.
Lay Teachers 26; Students 375.
Catechesis/Religious Programs—Students 85.

7—ST. FRANCIS XAVIER-OUR LADY OF GUADALUPE (1926 (Hispanic), Revs. Timothy L. Davison; Forrest O'Brien. In res., Rev. Tim Daley.
Res., 2515 E. 1st St., 74110. Tel: 918-592-6770. [JC]
Church—2510 E. Admiral Blvd., 74110.
Catechesis/Religious Programs—Teresa Sotelo, D.R.E.
Students 824.

8—IMMACULATE CONCEPTION (1923). Unassigned.
Mailing Address: P.O. Box 2009, 74101.

9—ST. JOSEPH CHURCH (1977) (Vietnamese), Rev. Hoang Viet Le.
Res., 14905 E. 21st St., 74134. Tel: 918-438-1380; 437-9481.
Catechesis/Religious Programs—Students 74.

10—CHURCH OF THE MADALENE (1946), Revs. Daniel H. Mueggenborg; Thomas P. Biller; Sr. Marie Pierre Fleming, O.S.B., Pastoral Assoc.; Deacon John Steward. In res., Rev. James D. White.
Res., 3188 E. 22nd St., 74114. Tel: 918-744-0023; Fax: 918-744-0024. [JC]
Catechesis/Religious Programs—Tel: 918-744-9417. Mrs. Kay Bashaw, D.R.E.
Students 72.

11—CHURCH OF ST. MARY (1954), Rev. Msgr. Dennis C. Dorney, V.G.; Revs. William J. Swift; Jack A. Gleason.
Office: 1347 E. 49th Pl., 74105. Tel: 918-749-1423; Fax: 918-747-9532. [JC]
School—1365 E. 49th Pl., 74105. Tel: 918-749-9361. Francis Smith, Prin.
Lay Teachers 23; Students 342.
Catechesis/Religious Programs—Sr. Colleen Nolan, O.P., D.R.E.
Students 289.

12—ST. MONICA'S (1926) (African American), Rev. Gary Sherman; Sr. Phyllis Vaske, O.S.F., Pastoral Asst.; Deacon Theodore Prudhomme.
Res., 1313 N. Xenophon, 74127. Tel: 918-587-2965 (Office); 585-8280 (Res.).

13—OUR LADY OF GUADALUPE. Closed. For sacramental records contact St. Francis Xavier-Our Lady of Guadalupe, Tulsa.

14—SS. PETER AND PAUL (1950), Rev. Tam N. Nguyen; Deacon Tommy Young.
Res., 1436 N. 67th E. Ave., 74115. Tel: 918-836-2596; Fax: 918-836-2597. [JC]
School—1428 N. 67th E. Ave., 74115. Tel: 918-836-2165; Fax: 918-836-2596. Bonnie Jones, Prin.
Lay Teachers 17; Students 185.
Catechesis/Religious Programs—Karen Campbell, D.R.E.
Students 78.

15—ST. PIUS X (1955), Rev. Thomas M. Hildebrand; Deacon Kasper Weigant.
Office: 1727 S. 75 E. Ave., 74112. Tel: 918-622-4488; Fax: 918-622-1239. [JC]
Res., 7628 E. 17th St., 74112. Tel: 918-664-9723.
School—1717 S. 75 E. Ave., 74112. Tel: 918-627-5367. Holly Goodwin, Prin.
Lay Teachers 25; Students 426.
Catechesis/Religious Programs—Eileen Dolan, D.R.E.
Students 195.

16—RESURRECTION (1968), Rev. Michael J. Knipe.
Office: P.O. Box 33169, 74153. Tel: 918-663-1907; Fax: 918-663-2533.
Res., 4612 S. Granite, 74135. Tel: 918-664-8319.
Church—4804 S. Fulton, 74135. Tel: 918-663-1907.
Catechesis/Religious Programs—Linda Nicholson, D.R.E.
Students 150.

17—ST. THOMAS MORE (1972), Rev. Gerald J. Coleman; Deacon Ned Doty.
Res., Tel: 918-663-9238.
Church—2720 S. 129 E. Ave., 74134. Tel: 918-437-0168.
Catechesis/Religious Programs—Aline Harbison, D.R.E.
Students 220.

OUTSIDE CITY OF TULSA

Antlers, Pushmataha Co., St. Agnes (1897), Rev. John J. Marquardt; Sr. Teresa Twomey, S.M.G., Pastoral Min.
Res., 402 N.E. 2nd, P.O. Box 206, 74523. Tel: 580-298-6113.
Mission—Clayton, Pushmataha Co., Holy Trinity, P.O. Box 747, 74523. Tel: 918-569-4767.
Station—Farris, McLeod Correctional Center, Tel: 405-889-6651; Fax: 405-889-2264.

Bartlesville, Washington Co., St. John's (1906), Rev. Stephen E. Austin; Deacons Joseph Richard; Dan Willis.
Res., 715 S. Johnstone Ave., 74003. Tel: 918-336-4353; Fax: 918-336-4354. [CEM]
School—Tel: 918-336-0603; Fax: 918-336-0603. Kurt Nelson, Prin.
Lay Teachers 15; Students 108.
Catechesis/Religious Programs—Tonja Senn, D.R.E.
Students 137.

The Community of St. James (1965), Rev. William K. Skeehan.
Res., 5500 Douglas Ln., 74006. Tel: 918-333-5307.
Catechesis/Religious Programs—Tel: 918-335-0844; Fax: 918-335-0856. Jeanette Pearson, D.R.E.
Students 220.
Mission—Nowata, Nowata Co., St. Catherine, 217 W. Modoc, Nowata, 74048. Tel: 918-273-0737.

Bixby, Tulsa Co., St. Clement's (1958), Rev. Thomas K. Melton.
Res., 21 W. Stadium, 74008. Tel: 918-366-3164.
Catechesis/Religious Programs—Tel: 918-366-3166.
Students 116.

Broken Arrow, Tulsa Co., St. Anne (1936), Rev. Dovan Nguyen; Deacons John Crescitelli; Gary Walsh.
Res., 301 S. 9th St., 74012. Tel: 918-251-4206; Fax: 918-251-8719. [JC]
Catechesis/Religious Programs—Tel: 918-251-5414. Christian Jones, D.R.E.
Students 200.

St. Benedict (1980), Revs. Patrick J. Gaalaas; Desmond Okpogba; Deacons John Donnelly; Lee Ellis.
Res., 2305 S. Chestnut, 74102. Tel: 918-455-7353.
Church—2200 W. Ithica St., 74012. Tel: 918-455-4451; Fax: 918-451-2199.
Catechesis/Religious Programs—Students 718.

Claremore, Roger Co., St. Cecilia (1911), Rev. Paul E. Eichhoff; Deacons Vincent Mrasek; Peter Schmidt.
Res., 1304 N. Dorothy, 74017. Tel: 918-341-2343.
Catechesis/Religious Programs—Tel: 918-341-4238.
Students 300.

Cleveland, Osage, St. Joseph (1905),
Mailing Address: 1314 Lynn Ave., Pawhuska, 74056. Tel: 918-287-1477.
Church—Osage and C Ave., 74020. Tel: 918-258-2333.
Mission—Hominy, Osage Co., 421 S. Petit, Hominy, 74035.

Coalgate, Coal Co., Blessed Sacrament (1889), Rev. George J. Pupius (OKL).
Res., 1300 E. Beverly, Ada, 74820. Tel: 405-332-2450; Fax: 405-436-1226. [JC]

Collinsville, Tulsa Co., St. Therese (1906), Rev. Patrick Brankin; Deacon Donel Tucker.
Res., 1007 N. 19th St., Box 297, 74021. Tel: 918-371-2704.
Catechesis/Religious Programs—Jane Webb, D.R.E.
Students 137.

Coweta, Wagoner Co., St. Vincent de Paul (1981), Rev. Patrick J. Gaalaas; Deacon James A. Pierret, Admin.
Res., 1100 S. G St., P.O. Box 771, 74429-0771. Tel: 918-486-4757.
Catechesis/Religious Programs—Students 35.

Cushing, Payne Co., SS. Peter and Paul (1894), Rev. M.E. Cashen; Deacons Jack Berry; Alfonso A. Cardenas.
Res., 214 N. Steele St., Box 828, 74023. Tel: 918-225-0644. [CEM]
Catechesis/Religious Programs—Students 78.
Mission—Drumright, Creek Co., St. Mary, Cimarron & Wood, Drumright, 74030.

Dewey, Washington Co., Our Lady of Guadalupe (1955), Rev. Stephen E. Austin; Deacon Richard Chamberlain, Dir. Parish Life.
Res., 400 W. Ninth St., 74029. Tel: 918-534-3420.
Catechesis/Religious Programs—Students 54.

Durant, Bryan Co., St. William, Rev. Norbert Karava; Deacon Albert Miller.
Res., 802 University Blvd., 74701. Tel: 405-924-1989.
Catechesis/Religious Programs—Students 63.
Mission—Atoka, St. Patrick Church.

Fairfax, Osage Co., Sacred Heart (Osage Indian), Rev. Kenneth W. Lewis.
Mailing Address: 1314 Lynn Ave., Pawhuska, 74056. Tel: 918-287-1477.

Grove, Delaware Co., St. Elizabeth (1949), Rev. Alex Kennedy. In res., Rev. Kenneth A. King.
Res., 1653 113th St. N.W., 74344. Tel: 918-786-9312 (Church).

Hartshorne, Pittsburg Co., Holy Rosary (1895), Rev. Robert K.C. Cain; Deacon Clement W. Bradley.
Res., 102 Center Point Rd., Wilburton, 74548. Tel: 918-465-3996. [CEM][JC]
Catechesis/Religious Programs—Students 38.
Missions—Talihina, Leflore Co., St. Catherine of Siena, Second & Gann Sts., Talihina, 74571. Tel: 918-567-2587; Wilburton, Latimer Co., Sacred Heart, 102 Center Point Rd., Wilburton, 74578.

Henryetta, Okmulgee Co., St. Michael (1912), Rev. Neal E. Brogan.
Res., 1004 W. Gentry St., P.O. Box 148, 74437. Tel: 918-652-3445. [JC]

Holdenville, Hughes Co., St. Stephen's (1905), Rev. Matthew J. Brown, O.S.B.
Res., 515 E. Highway, P.O. Box 935, 74848. Tel: 405-379-2512.
Mission—Okemah, Okfuska Co., St. Teresa, (1927) 8th and Broadway, Okemah, 74859.

Hugo, Choctaw Co., Immaculate Conception, Rev. Robert Bond, Glmy.
Res., HC69, Box 36-1, 74743. Tel: 580-326-7300.
Mission—Boswell, Choctaw Co., St. Jude, 511 11th St., Boswell, 74727.

Idabel, McCurtain Co., St. Francis De Sales (1945), Revs. John T. Brown, Glmy.; Joseph Dean, Glmy.
Res., 13 S.E. Jefferson, 74745. Tel: 580-286-3275.
Catechesis/Religious Programs—Students 60.
Mission—Valiant, McCurtain Co., Good Shepherd, P.O. Box 1016, Valiant, 74764. Tel: 580-933-4742. In res., Rev. John Buzga, Glmy.
Mission—Plunketville, McCurtain Co., St. Henry. [CEM]

Krebs, Pittsburg Co., St. Joseph's (1886), Rev. Chi Peter Phung; Deacon Bill Anderson.
Res., P.O. Box 621, 74554. Tel: 918-423-6695. [CEM]
Catechesis/Religious Programs—Tel: 918-423-7130. Sharon Dunbar, D.R.E.
Students 133.
Mission—Eufaula, McIntosh Co., St. Paul's, 6th & Forest, 74554. Tel: 918-689-7345.
Stations—Jackie Brannon Correctional Center, Tel: 918-426-4470; Fax: 918-426-0004; Oklahoma State Penitentiary, McAlester, Tel: 918-423-4700; Fax: 918-423-3862.

Langley, Mayes Co., St. Frances of Rome, Rev. Alex Kennedy, Admin.; Deacon Charles Toppins, Coord. Parish Life.
Res., Hwy. 28, P.O. Box 267, 74350-0267. Tel: 918-782-2248. [CEM][JC]

McAlester, Pittsburg Co., St. John (1895), Rev. Amalor Vima.
Res., 300 E. Washington Ave., Box 220, 74502. Tel: 918-423-0810; Fax: 918-423-8824. [CEM]
Catechesis/Religious Programs—Tel: 918-423-1458. D.R.E.: Cathy Swope; Kathy Black.
Students 145.
Mission—Pittsburg, Pittsburg Co., St. Edwards, 74502.

Miami, Ottawa Co., Sacred Heart (1900), Rev. Michael R. Rooney; Deacon Marvin Morris.
Res., 2515 N. Main, 74354. Tel: 918-542-5281; Fax: 918-542-1764.
Catechesis/Religious Programs—Tel: 918-542-5898. Karen Painter, D.R.E.
Students 120.
Mission—Welch, Craig Co., St. Ann, P.O. Box 25, Welch, 74369.

Muskogee, Muskogee Co., Assumption. Closed. For sacramental records contact Saint Joseph Church, Muskogee.
Sacred Heart. Closed. For sacramental records contact Saint Joseph Church, Muskogee.
Saint Joseph Church (1992), Rev. J. Richard Bradley; Deacon Edwin Falleur, Pastoral Assoc. In res., Herman J. Foken.
Mailing Address: P.O. Box 189, 74402. Tel: 918-687-1351; Fax: 918-687-5541.
Church—321 N. Virginia, 74402. [CEM]
Parish Office and Residence—2310 W. Broadway, 74402. Tel: 918-687-1351; 683-2098 (Rectory).
School—(Grades PreK-8) 323 N. Virginia, 74403. Tel: 918-683-1291; Fax: 918-682-5374. Sharon McKee, Prin.
Lay Teachers 10; Students 192.
Catechesis/Religious Programs—Carleen Falleur, D.R.E.
Students 250.
Chapel—Sacred Heart, 2300 W. Broadway, 74402.

Okmulgee, Okmulgee Co., St. Anthony's (1910), Rev. Bryan V. Brooks. Pastoral Assocs.: Sr. Mary Fox, O.P.; Sr. Loretta McIluenna, O.P.
Res., 515 S. Morton Ave., P.O. Box 698, 74447. Tel: 918-756-4385; Fax: 918-756-3719. [JC]
School—Marian Academy, (Grades PreK-5). Tel: 918-756-9042. Sr. Loretta McIluenna, O.P., Prin.
Catechesis/Religious Programs—Students 55.
Mission—Okmulgee, Okmulgee Co., Uganda Martyrs, 808 E. 3rd, 74447.

Owasso, Tulsa Co., St. Henry (1957), Rev. J. Paul Donovan; Deacon Vernon Foltz.
Mailing Address: P.O. Box 181, 74055-0181. Tel: 918-272-3710.
Res., 903 N. Elm, 74055. Tel: 918-272-7387.
Church—8500 Owasso Expy., 74055.
Catechesis/Religious Programs—Linda Hogan, D.R.E.
Students 286.

Pawhuska, Osage Co., Immaculate Conception (1887) (Osage Indian), Rev. Leonard H. Higgins.
Res., 1314 N. Lynn Ave., 74056. Tel: 918-287-1414. [JC]
Catechesis/Religious Programs—Students 45.
Missions—Barnsdall, Osage Co., St. Mary, 3rd and Chestnut, Barnsdall, 74002.; Shidler, Osage Co., St. Ann. Gypsy St. & Taylor St.

Pawnee, Pawnee Co., St. John (1907), Rev. Joe C. Townsend.
Mailing Address: 201 N. Knoblock, Stillwater, 74075. Tel: 405-372-6408.
Church—8th St. and Oak, 74058.

Poteau, Leflore Co., Immaculate Conception (1903), Rev. Khiet T. Nguyen.
Church—410 Bagwell St., 74953. Tel: 918-647-3475.
Res., 502 N. Bagwell St., 74953. Tel: 918-647-3475.
Station—Hodgens, Ouachita Correctional Training Center.
Missions—Stigler, Haskell Co., St. Joseph, 126 S. Broadway, 74462.; Spiro, Leflore Co., St. Elizabeth Seton, Hwy. 9, 74959.

Pryor, Mayes Co., St. Mark's (1942), Rev. Arthur T. O'Hara.
Res., 1507 S. Vann, P.O. Box 576, 74362. Tel: 918-782-2950.
Catechesis/Religious Programs—Tel: 918-825-4186. Phyllis Buffo, D.R.E.
Students 115.

Sallisaw, Sequoyah Co., St. Francis Xavier (1952), Rev. Jeffrey S. Polasek; Deacon Robert Barnes.
Church—2110 N. Dogwood, 74955. Tel: 918-775-6217; Fax: 918-775-6217.
Catechesis/Religious Programs—Students 52.
Missions—Cookson, Cherokee Co., St. John the Evangelist, P.O. Box 4, Cookson, 74427. Tel: 918-457-4427; Webbers Falls, Muskogee Co., St. Joseph, P.O. Box 53, Webber Falls, 74470. Tel: 918-464-2422; Roland, Sequoyah Co., Blessed Kateri Tekakwitha, P.O. Box 17, 918-427-3064 74954.

Sand Springs, Tulsa Co., St. Patrick's (1919), Rev. Kenneth S. Fulton; Deacons Bob Garrett; Noel Hollingshead.
Res., 204 E. Fourth, 74063. Tel: 918-245-5254. [JC]
Catechesis/Religious Programs—Students 144.
Mission—Mannford, Creek Co., Our Lady of the Lake.

Sapulpa, Creek Co., Sacred Heart (1907), Rev. Jake A. Males; Deacon Francis Decker.
Church—1777 E. Grayson Ave., 74066. Tel: 918-224-0944. [JC]
Catechesis/Religious Programs—Raelyn McDonald, D.R.E.
Students 100.

Skiatook, Osage Co., Sacred Heart (1921). (Formerly St. William). Rev. Peter F. Dally, Admin.; Deacon Millard Kizzia.
Office: 3504 E. Independance, Tulsa, 74115. Tel: 918-896-1176.
Res., 109 W. 5th St., 74070.
Catechesis/Religious Programs—Students 72.
St. Joseph's (1928). Closed. For inquiries for parish records contact the Chancery.

Stillwater, Payne Co., St. Francis Xavier (1895), Rev. Robert T. Schlitt; Deacon Paul Govek.
Res., 623 S. West St., Box 909, 74076. Tel: 405-372-6886. [JC]
Catechesis/Religious Programs—Tel: 405-372-7987. D.R.E.: Cecilia Crane; Bobbi Bryson; Bryan Beard.
Students 129.
St. John University Parish and Catholic Student Center (1965), Revs. Joe C. Townsend; Kenneth Iheanacho; Deacons Bill Moler; Tom Haan; Dick Berberet.
Res., 201 N. Knoblock, 74075. Tel: 405-372-6408; Fax: 405-372-6409.
Catechesis/Religious Programs—Tel: 405-372-7987. D.R.E.: CC Crane, (PreK-12); Bobbi Bryson, (Confirmation); Bryan Beard, (Grades 7-12).
Students 194.

Tahlequah, Cherokee Co., St. Brigid (1966), Rev. Charles J. Swett.
Res., 807 Crafton St., 74464. Tel: 918-456-8388.
Catechesis/Religious Programs—Tel: 918-456-4204. Donna Ballew, D.R.E.
Students 70.

Vinita, Craig Co., Holy Ghost (1892), Rev. Alex Kennedy.
Res., 120 W. Sequoyah Ave., 74301. Tel: 918-256-2281.
Catechesis/Religious Programs—Tel: 918-256-3118. Sr. Mary Grace Sieben, D.R.E.
Students 66.
Stations—Eastern State Hospital.; Vinita, Northeastern Correctional Facility.

Wagoner, Wagoner Co., Holy Cross (1895), Rev. Stephen A. MacAulay.
Res., P.O. Box 710, 74477. Tel: 918-485-5145.
Church—S.W. 15th & Pierce, 74477.
Catechesis/Religious Programs—Tel: 918-485-8228. Sherry Ruyle, D.R.E.
Students 43.

Special Assignment:
Reverend Fathers—
Brooks, Donald W., Prison Ministry, P.O. Box 2009, Tulsa, OK 74101
Daley, Timothy J.
White, James D., Historian and Dir. of Office of Divine Worship, P.O. Box 2009, Tulsa, OK 74101

On Duty Outside the Diocese:
Reverend Fathers—
McSherry, Tom
Minh, Vu Duc, U.S. Air Force
Wells, Peter B., Rome

Retired:
Reverend Monsignors—
Halpine, James F., P.O. Box 3204, Tulsa, OK 74101
Maszkiewicz, Mark, 1426 S. Columbia Ave., Tulsa, OK 74104
Reverend Fathers—
Bartnik, Harry S., Franciscan Villa Apt. 2, 17110 E. 51st St. S., Broken Arrow, OK 74012
Foken, Herman J., P.O. Box 189, Muskogee, OK 74402-0189
Keohane, Daniel C., Franciscan Villa, 17110 E. 51st. St. S., Broken Arrow, OK 74012
King, Kenneth A., 1653 113th St., N.W., Grove, OK 74344
Lange, Lawrence P., 13001 E. 40th St., No. 1011, Tulsa, OK 74134
Lundberg, John W., 43 California Ave., Middletown, NY 10940
Mazaika, Joseph J., 1710 Walnut, Grand Prairie, TX 75050
McCarthy, Jerry, Franciscan Villa, 17110 E. 51st St., S., Broken Arrow, OK 74012
McGlinchey, James J., 1767 S. Wheeling, Tulsa, OK 74104
O'Neil, Lee E., P.O. Box 515, Gulf Shores, AL 36542
Perlinski, Daniel A., 1748 S. Wheeling Ave., Tulsa, OK 74104
Pickett, Robert T., 1414 E. 49th St., Tulsa, OK 74105-4798
Richard, Edward, 4112 Blue Ridge St., North Port, FL 34287

Permanent Deacons:
Anderson, Bill, St. Joseph, Krebs
Barnes, Robert, Blessed Kateri Tekakwitha, Roland
Berberet, Richard, St. John University Parish, Stillwater
Berry, Jack L., Sts. Peter & Paul, Cushing
Bradley, Clement W., Sacred Heart, Wilburton
Breazille, James E., Stillwater
Campbell, Richard, St. Bernard, Tulsa
Cardenas, Alfonso, SS. Peter & Paul, Cushing
Chamberlain, Richard, Our Lady of Guadalupe, Dewey
Coburn, Wilfred C., St. Catherine, Tulsa
Crescitelli, John, St. Anne, Broken Arrow
Decker, Francis I., Sacred Heart, Sapulpa
DeLeon, Felix, St. Francis/OLOG, Tulsa
Donnelly, John E., St. Benedict, Broken Arrow
Doty, Edward, St. Thomas More, Tulsa

Elliott, Gregg, St. Francis Hospital, Tulsa
Ellis, Lee, St. Benedict, Broken Arrow
Falleur, Edwin E., St. Joseph, Muskogee
Foltz, Vernon, St. Henry, Owasso
Garrett, James R., St. Patrick, Sand Springs
Gerrior, Joseph A., On Medical Leave
Haan, Tom, St. John University Parish, Stillwater
Hancock, John, St. Bernard, Tulsa
Hollingshead, Noel, St. Patrick, Sand Springs
Kizzia, Millard H., Sacred Heart, Skiatook
Litwack, Stephen J., Unassigned
Loney, Tom, St. Joseph, Bristow
Luschen, Loren F., Christ the King, Tulsa
Mikell, Alan G., St. Bernard, Tulsa
Miller, Albert J., Unassigned
Miller, Bill, St. Joseph, Muskogee
Moler, William J., St. John University Parish, Stillwater
Morris, Marvin D., Sacred Heart, Miami
Mrasek, Vincent J., St. Cecilia, Claremore
Perez, Jose, St. Thomas More, Tulsa
Pierret, James A., St. Vincent de Paul, Coweta
Prudhomme, Theodore, St. Monica & St. Augustine, Tulsa
Richard, Joseph N., St. John, Bartlesville
Schmidt, Peter, St. Cecilia, Claremore
Starr, Sid, St. Catherine, Tulsa
Steward, John N., Church of the Madalene, Tulsa
Toppins, Charles A., St. Frances of Rome, Langley
Tucker, Donel, St. Theresa, Collinsville
Walsh, Gary D., Marriage Tribunal, Tulsa; St. Anne, Broken Arrow
Weigant, Kasper E., St. Pius X, Tulsa
Willis, Daniel H., St. John, Bartlesville
Young, Thomas, SS. Peter & Paul, Tulsa

INSTITUTIONS LOCATED IN THE DIOCESE

[A] HIGH SCHOOLS, DIOCESAN

TULSA. *Bishop Kelley High School*, 3905 S. Hudson, 74135-5699. Tel: 918-627-3390. Alan V. Weyland, Academic Prin.; Bro. David Poos, F.S.C., Dir. Prin.; Marianne Stich, Campus Min. Brothers 4; Sisters 3; Lay Teachers 72; Students 889.

[B] HIGH SCHOOLS, PRIVATE

TULSA. *Cascia Hall Preparatory School*. (Grades 6-12), Mailing Address: Box 52247, 74152. Tel: 918-742-7373. 2520 S. Yorktown Ave., 74114. Augustinians (Order of St. Augustine). Coed College Preparatory School. Revs. Bernard C. Scianna, O.S.A., Headmaster; James J. Sheridan, O.S.A.; John H. Gaffney, O.S.A.; Philip C. Cook, O.S.A.; Henry V. Spielmann, O.S.A.; Theodore E. Tack, O.S.A.; Michael Schweifler, O.S.A., Prior; William A. Perez, O.S.A.; Bro. John M. Hibbard, O.S.A., Dean of Students Campus Min. Priests 8; Brothers 1; Sisters 1; Lay Teachers 41; Students 567.

[C] ELEMENTARY SCHOOLS, DIOCESAN

BROKEN ARROW. *All Saints School*, 299 S. 9th St., 74012. Tel: 918-251-3000.
E-mail: allsaint@iamerica.net
Mrs. Fran Smith, Prin. Lay Teachers 14; Students 213.

[D] ELEMENTARY SCHOOLS, PRIVATE

TULSA. *Monte Cassino School*. (Grades PreK-8), 2206 S. Lewis, 74114. Tel: 918-743-4471. Sr. Mary Clare Buthod, O.S.B., Dir.-Prin. Sisters 5; Lay Teachers 73; Students 1,152.

[E] GENERAL HOSPITALS

TULSA. *Marian Health System, Inc.*, P.O. Box 4753, 74159-0753
For a complete listing, refer to the Hospitals section.

Saint Francis Hospital, Inc., 6161 S. Yale Ave., 74136. Tel: 918-494-2200
For a complete listing, refer to the Hospitals section.

St. John Health System, Inc., 1923 S. Utica, 74104 Fax: 918-744-2716
For a complete listing, refer to the Hospitals section.

St. John Medical Center, Inc., 1923 S. Utica Ave., 74104. Tel: 918-744-2345
For a complete listing, refer to the Hospitals section.

[F] HOMES FOR THE AGED

TULSA. *Frances Streitel Senior Care Corporation*, 1923 S. Utica Ave., 74104. Tel: 918-744-2471
For a complete listing, refer to the Special Care Facilities section.

St. John Villas, Inc., 1923 S. Utica, 74104. Tel: 918-744-2180; Fax: 918-744-2716
For a complete listing, refer to the Special Care Facilities section.

[G] CONVENTS AND RESIDENCES FOR SISTERS

TULSA. *St. Joseph Monastery*, 2200 S. Lewis, 74114-3100. Tel: 918-742-4989; Fax: 918-744-1374.
E-mail: stjoseph@juno.com
Motherhouse of Benedictine Sisters (Federation of St. Scholastica). Sr. Barbara Austin, O.S.B., Prioress. Sisters in Community 38.

Sisters of Saint Joseph, 3942 S. Trenton, 74105. Sisters in Community 2.

BROKEN ARROW. *St. Clare Convent*, 17600 E. 51st St., 74012. Tel: 918-355-2740. Sr. Ida Nieberle, Coord. Sisters in Community 16.

Sisters of the Sorrowful Mother - Our Lady of Sorrows Convent, 17600 E. 51st St., 74012. Tel: 918-355-5581. Sr. M. Gordiana, Coord. Sisters 26.

Sisters of the Sorrowful Mother - U.S./Caribbean Province, Inc., 17600 E. 51st St., 74012. Tel: 918-355-1148. Sr. Dorothy Ann M. Dirkx, U.S./Caribbean Prov. Sisters 218.

SAND SPRINGS. *Benedictine Sisters of Perpetual Adoration*, 18701 W. Monastery Rd., 74063. Tel: 918-245-2734. Osage Monastery, OM Forest of Peace Benedictine Convent of Perpetual Adoration in Oklahoma, Inc. Sr. M. Pascaline Coff, O.S.B., Supr. Sisters 5.

[H] NEWMAN CENTERS

TULSA. *University of Tulsa Newman Center*, 440 S. Florence, 74104. Tel: 918-599-0204. Rev. John Jangam, Chap.; Patrick Martin, Campus Min.; Joann Crescitelli, Admin. Asst.

MIAMI. *Northeastern Oklahoma A & M College Newman Center*.
E-mail: mrooney@galstar.com
Mailing Address: 2515 N. Main, 74354. 200 I N.E. St., 74354. Tel: 918-542-5281. Rev. Michael R. Rooney, Chap.

STILLWATER. *St. John's University Parish and Catholic Student Center*, 201 N. Knoblock, 74075. Tel: 405-372-6408. Revs. Kenneth Iheanacho; Joe C. Townsend; Sr. Sheila Carroll, Campus Min.; Deacons Bill Moler; Thomas Haan; Richard Berberet.

TAHLEQUAH. *Northeastern State University Catholic Student Organization*, 807 Crafton St., 74464. Tel: 918-456-8388. Rev. Charles J. Swett.

[I] MISCELLANEOUS

TULSA. *Bishop Kelley High School Endowment Trust*, P.O. Box 2009, 74101. Tel: 918-587-3115; Fax: 918-587-6692.

Catholic Foundation of Eastern Oklahoma, Inc., Mailing Address: P.O. Box 2009, 74101. 111 W. 5th, Ste. 400, 74103. Tel: 918-587-3115. Mr. Jon Calder, Dir. Stewardship & Devel.

St. John Medical Center Foundation, Inc., 1923 S. Utica, 74104. Tel: 918-749-3553.

St. Joseph Residence, Inc., P.O. Box 6429, 74148. Total Assisted 33; Total Staff 6.

CLAREMORE. *Apostolate for the Most Holy Rosary and the Brown Scapular Association*, 1300 S. Lone Elm Rd., 74017. Tel: 918-341-5612.
E-mail: Twohtsrsry@aol.com
Mr. Robert C. Tayrien, Pres. & Contact Person.

MUSKOGEE. *St. Joseph School Endowment Trust*, P.O. Box 189, 74402. Tel: 918-687-1351.

RELIGIOUS INSTITUTES OF MEN REPRESENTED IN THE DIOCESE

For further details refer to the corresponding bracketed number in the Religious Institutes of Men or Women section.

[0140]—*The Augustinians (Province of Our Mother of Good Counsel)*.—O.S.A.
[0330]—*Brothers of the Christian Schools*. (Province of St. Louis).—F.S.C.
[0570]—*Glenmary Home Missioners*.—Glmy.
[0690]—*Jesuit Fathers and Brothers*. (Province of St. Louis).—S.J.

RELIGIOUS INSTITUTES OF WOMEN REPRESENTED IN THE DIOCESE

[0230]—*Benedictine Sisters of Pontifical Jurisdiction*. (Atchison, KS).—O.S.B.
[1010]—*Congregation of Divine Providence of San Antonio, Texas*.—C.D.P.
[0220]—*Congregation of the Benedictine Sisters of Perpetual Adoration of Pontifical Jurisdiction*.—O.S.B.
[]—*Congregation of the Benedictine Sisters of the Sacred Hearts*.—O.S.B.
[0470]—*Congregation of the Sisters of Charity of the Incarnate Word, Houston, TX*.—C.C.V.I.
[1070-03]—*Dominican Sisters*.—O.P.
[]—*Franciscan Sisters of Chicago*. (Lemont, IL).—O.S.F.
[3640]—*Poor Servants of the Mother of God*.—S.M.G.
[2150]—*Servants of the Immaculate Heart of Mary, Southwest Province*.—I.H.M.
[]—*Sisters of St. Francis of Penance & Christian Charity*. (Denver, CO).—O.S.F.
[1570]—*Sisters of St. Francis of the Holy Family*.—O.S.F.
[1600]—*Sisters of St. Francis of the Martyr St. George*.—O.S.F.
[3830]—*Sisters of St. Joseph*.—S.S.J.
[4100]—*Sisters of the Sorrowful Mother (Third Order of St. Francis)*.—S.S.M.
[]—*Ursuline Nuns*. (Paola, KS).—O.S.U.

CEMETERIES

TULSA. *Calvary*, 9101 S. Harvard, 74136. Tel: 918-743-5571. Mailing Address: P.O. Box 2009, 74101. Tel: 918-587-3115. James S. Liichow, Suprv.; Mr. Jack Charon, Dir.

NECROLOGY

† Cefai, John M., (Retired). —Died June 28, 1997.
† Finn, Rev. Msgr. Cecil E., (Retired). —Died Oct. 31, 1996.
† O'Connell, Maurice J., Broken Arrow, OK, St. Anne. —Died Nov. 27, 1996.

Diocese of Tyler

(Dioecesis Tylerensis)

Most Reverend

EDMOND CARMODY, D.D.

Bishop of Tyler; ordained to the priesthood June 8, 1957; appointed Auxiliary Bishop of San Antonio November 8, 1988; consecrated December 15, 1988; appointed Bishop of the Diocese of Tyler March 24, 1992; installed May 25, 1992. *Mailing Address: 1015 E.S.E. Loop 323, Tyler, TX, 75701-9663.* Tel.: 903-534-1077; Fax: 903-534-1370.

ESTABLISHED DIOCESE OF TYLER ON DECEMBER 12, 1986.

Square Miles 22,971.

Comprises the following Counties in the State of Texas: Anderson, Angelina, Bowie, Camp, Cass, Cherokee, Delta, Franklin, Freestone, Gregg, Harrison, Henderson, Hopkins, Houston, Lamar, Leon, Marion, Morris, Nacogdoches, Panola, Rains, Red River, Rusk, Sabine, San Augustine, Shelby, Smith, Titus, Trinity, Upshur, Van Zandt, and Wood.

For legal titles of parishes and diocesan institutions, consult the Chancery Office.

Chancery: 1015 E.S.E. Loop 323, Tyler, TX, 75701-9663. Tel.: 903-534-1077; Fax: 903-534-1370.

E-mail address: BpCarmody@aol.com

STATISTICAL OVERVIEW

Personnel	
Bishop	1
Priests: Diocesan Active in Diocese	22
Priests: Active Outside Diocese	1
Priests: Retired, Sick or Absent	4
Number of Diocesan Priests	27
Religious Priests in Diocese	22
Extern Priests in Diocese	25
Ordinations:	
Diocesan Priests	2
Transitional Deacons	3
Permanent Deacons	4
Permanent Deacons in Diocese	34
Total Brothers	2
Total Sisters	65
Parishes	
Parishes	33
With Resident Pastor:	
Resident Diocesan Priests	24
Resident Religious Priests	9
Without Resident Pastor:	
Missions	25
Pastoral Centers	3
New Parishes Created	3
Professional Ministry Personnel:	
Brothers	1
Sisters	6
Lay Ministers	11
Welfare	
Catholic Hospitals	4
Total Assisted	195,697
Health Care Centers	7
Total Assisted	376,638
Special Centers for Social Services	1
Total Assisted	120
Educational	
Diocesan Students in Other Seminaries	11
Total Seminarians	11
High Schools, Diocesan and Parish	1
Total Students	121
Elementary Schools, Diocesan and Parish	4
Total Students	729
Catechesis/Religious Education:	
High School Students	1,320
Elementary Students	4,496
Total Students Under Catholic Instruction	6,677
Teachers in the Diocese:	
Brothers	1
Sisters	5
Lay Teachers	67
Vital Statistics	
Receptions into the Church:	
Infant Baptism Totals	1,433
Adult Baptism Totals	239
Received into Full Communion	271
First Communions	1,411
Confirmations	712
Marriages:	
Catholic	175
Interfaith	89
Total Marriages	264
Deaths	361
Total Catholic Population	49,326
Total Population	1,185,155

Former Bishop—Most Rev. CHARLES E. HERZIG, D.D., First Bishop of Tyler; ord. May 31, 1955; Bishop of Tyler; appt. Dec. 12, 1986; cons. Feb. 24, 1987; died Sept. 7, 1991.

Vicar General—Rev. JOHN A. BRENNAN, *Chancery, 1015 E.S.E. Loop 323, Tyler, 75701-9663.* Tel: 903-534-1077; Fax: 903-534-1370.

Chancery—1015 E.S.E. Loop 323, Tyler, 75701-9663. Tel: 903-534-1077; Fax: 903-534-1370. Office Hours: Mon.-Fri. 8:30a.m.-5p.m.

Chancellor—Rev. GAVIN N. VAVEREK, J.C.L., *1015 E.S.E. Loop 323, Tyler, 75701-9663.* Tel: 903-534-1077.

Archivist—Mrs. MARY SEDBERRY. Tel: 903-534-1077.

College of Consultors—Rev. Msgr. JOHN A. BRENNAN, V.G.; Rev. Msgr. SAMUEL S. METZGER; Rev. Msgr. GERALD A. PRIEST; Rev. Msgr. JAMES E. YOUNG; Revs. ALPHONSE ANTHONY; RONALD DIEGEL; HAROLD PAULSEN; BERNARD PUSTEJOVSKY; BENJAMIN SMYLIE; GAVIN N. VAVEREK.

Deans—Rev. RONALD DIEGEL, East Central Deanery; Rev. Msgr. GERALD PRIEST, Northeast Deanery; Rev. ALPHONSE ANTHONY, Northwest Deanery; Rev. Msgr. JAMES E. YOUNG, Southeast Deanery; Rev. HAROLD P. PAULSEN, Southwest Deanery; Rev. Msgr. SAMUEL S. METZGER, West Central Deanery.

Tribunal Office—1015 E.S.E. Loop 323, Tyler, 75701-9663. Tel: 903-534-1077; Fax: 903-534-1370.

Judicial Vicar—Rev. Msgr. JOSEPH E. STRICKLAND, J.C.L.

Defender of the Bond—Rev. GAVIN N. VAVEREK, J.C.L.

Administrator/Notary—Mrs. MARGARET OPPENHEIMER.

Notary—Mrs. MARY SEDBERRY. Tel: 903-534-1077.

DIOCESAN ADMINISTRATION

Finance Officer—Mr. JAMES R. SMITH, *1015 E.S.E. Loop 323, Tyler, 75701-9663.* Tel: 903-534-1077.

Diocesan Finance Council—Mr. BILL SULLIVAN, Chm.; Rev. Msgr. JOHN A. BRENNAN; Mr. JAMES CHIARIZIO; Mrs. JANET HUNT; Mr. JAMES KENNEDY; Mr. WESLEY RIVERS; JAMES R. SMITH; Mr. FRED WULF.

Diocesan Building Board—Mr. BILLY CORDOVA, Chm.; Rev. DAN DAUGHERTY; Mr. TOM DEIBEL; Mrs. CHERYL FLOOD; Mr. JAMES R. SMITH; Rev. GAVIN N. VAVEREK.

East Texas Catholic Foundation—JAMES R. SMITH, Dir., *1015 E.S.E. Loop 323, Tyler, 75701-9663.* Mr. DAVID CARLILE; Mrs. SUZIE HAIR; Mr. VINCE RICHBOURG; Mr. WALTER VOLZ; Mr. PAUL WALSH; Mr. TOM WOLF.

Priests' Pension Board—Rev. Msgr. JOHN A. BRENNAN, Chm.; Mr. JAMES R. SMITH, Treas.; Rev. Msgr. JAMES E. YOUNG; Revs. GAVIN N. VAVEREK; A. PETER WHITNEY.

Campaign for Human Development—Mrs. MARY SEDBERRY. Tel: 903-534-1077.

Catholic School Superintendent—Sr. JOSEPH MARIE KASEL, S.S.N.D., *1015 E.S.E. Loop 323, Tyler, 75701-9663.*

Diocesan School Board—Mr. PAUL WALKER, Chm.; Mrs. MARTHA ROBERTS, Sec.; Mr. WILLIAM BARTUSH; Mrs. BONNIE SHIVERS; Dr. JAMES STOCKS; Mrs. SUE PLATZER; Mr. GEORGE WING.

Director of Religious Education—Mrs. LINDA PORTER.

Pastoral Ministries—Rev. BERNARD PUSTEJOVSKY, Dir., *1015 E.S.E. Loop 323, Tyler, 75701-9663.* Tel: 903-534-1077.

Family Life/Youth Ministry—Mr. EDWARD RUESEWALD, Dir., *1015 E.S.E. Loop 323, Tyler, 75701-9663.* Tel: 903-534-1077.

Tyler Catholic Committee on Scouting—Rev. MICHAEL DOYLE, Chap., *1113 S. Main St., Lindale, 75771-1078.* Tel: 903-228-4079. Mr. JERRY STOCK, Chm., *905 Happiness St., Longview, 75601.* Tel: 903-757-7524.

Campus Ministries—Co-Directors: Rev. BERNARD PUSTEJOVSKY; Mr. EDWARD RUESEWALD.

Missions Office—Mrs. JOYCE CRAVENS. Tel: 903-534-1077.

Priests' Personnel Board—Rev. Msgr. JAMES E. YOUNG, Chm.; Rev. Msgr. SAMUEL S. METZGER; Rev. Msgr. GERALD A. PRIEST; Rev. Msgr. JOSEPH E. STRICKLAND; Revs. ALPHONSE ANTHONY; RONALD DIEGEL; RUBEN FIGUEROA; HAROLD P. PAULSEN; BERNARD PUSTEJOVSKY.

Presbyteral Council—Rev. BERNARD PUSTEJOVSKY, Chm.; Rev. Msgr. JOHN A. BRENNAN; Rev. Msgr. SAMUEL S. METZGER, Sec.; Rev. Msgr. GERALD PRIEST; Rev. Msgr. JAMES E. YOUNG; Revs. ALPHONSE ANTHONY; RONALD DIEGEL, Vice Chm. HAROLD PAULSEN; BENJAMIN SMYLIE; GAVIN N. VAVEREK.

Office of Clergy Development/Continuing Education—Rev. BERNARD PUSTEJOVSKY, *1015 ESE Loop 323, Tyler, 75701-9663.* Tel: 903-534-1077.

Permanent Diaconate Co-Directors—Rev. BENEDICT COMISKY, *201 N. Vale St., Jefferson, 75657-2143.* Tel: 903-665-2869. Deacon JOHN K. SHAFFER, *2508 Appleby Sand Rd., Nacogdoches, 75961-4524.* Tel: 409-569-8544.

Vocations Director—Rev. GAVIN N. VAVEREK, *1015 E.S.E. Loop 323, Tyler, 75701-9663.* Tel: 903-534-1077. Mr. JIM FINEGAN, Vocations Awareness Board Chm.; Rev. BERNARD PUSTEJOVSKY, Asst. Dir.

Communications Director—Mr. JAMES H. D'AVIGNON,

1015 E.S.E. Loop 323, Tyler, 75701-9663. Tel: 903-534-1077.

Bishop's Annual Appeal—Mrs. JUDY GREEN, Dir., *1015 E.S.E. Loop 323, Tyler, 75701-9663.* Tel: 903-534-1077.

Newspaper "Catholic East Texas"—Mr. JAMES H. D'AVIGNON, Editor. Reporters: Mrs. SUSAN DEMATTEO NECESSARY; Mrs. JOANNE FLORES EMBLETON, *1015 E.S.E. Loop 323, Tyler, 75701-9663.* Tel: 903-534-1077; Fax: 903-534-1370.

DIOCESAN OFFICES

Diocesan Council of Catholic Women—Ms. BARBARA GARDINER, Pres., *502 Lansdown, Marshall, 75670.* Tel: 903-938-1051. Rev. GAVIN N. VAVEREK, Moderator, *2108 Ridgewood, Longview, 75605-1999.* Tel: 903-757-5855.

Respect Life Program—Rev. GAVIN N. VAVEREK, *2108 Ridgewood, Longview, 75605-1999.* Tel: 903-757-5855. Co-Directors: JOE DUDAS; MARGE DUDAS, *1605 H. G. Mosley Blvd., Longview, 75604.* Tel: 903-295-8608.

Disaster Relief Director—Mr. ROY SHEAR, *621 Bentley Ct., Tyler, 75703.* Tel: 903-561-0425.

CLERGY, PARISHES, MISSIONS AND PAROCHIAL SCHOOLS

CITY OF TYLER
(Smith County)

1—CATHEDRAL OF THE IMMACULATE CONCEPTION (1987), Rev. Msgr. Joseph E. Strickland, J.C.L.; Revs. Mahendra Anandappa, S.S.S.; Mani T. Mathai (India); Augustine Tharappel (India); Anthony K.W. McLaughlin; Deacons Anthony George; Dwight Hall; Ramiro Martinez; Ramon Noriega; William O'Sullivan. Pastoral Associate Ministries: Sr. Susan Seitz, O.S.F. Social Services: Deacon Ramon Noriega Tel: 903-592-0027.
Office: 423 S. Broadway, 75702. Tel: 903-592-1617; Fax: 903-593-7326.
Res., 114 W. Front St., 75702. Tel: 903-592-5462.
Schools—St. Gregory School, 500 S. College St., 75702. Tel: 903-595-4109; Fax: 903-592-8626. Kathy Shieldes Harry, Prin.
Lay Teachers 27; Students 337; Bishop T. K. Gorman Middle School, 1405 E.S.E. Loop 323, 75701. Tel: 903-561-2424; Fax: 903-561-2645. Dr. Rosemary Henry, Prin.
Students 155.
Bishop Gorman High School—Tel: 903-561-2424. Priests 1; Lay Teachers 23; Students 146.
Catechesis/Religious Programs—Fax: 903-561-1645.
Lay Teachers 74; Students 620.
Missions—Lindale, Smith Co., Holy Family, P.O. Box 1071, Lindale, 75771-1078. Tel: 903-882-4079; Fax: 903-882-8382. Rev. Michael Doyle; Tyler, Smith Co., Our Lady of Guadalupe, 922 Old Omen Rd., 75701-3709. Tel: 903-593-2006. Rev. Said Duran.
Chapel—St. Paul, 1015 E.S.E. Loop 323, 75702.

OUTSIDE THE CITY OF TYLER

Athens, Henderson Co., St. Edward Church (1947), Rev. Msgr. Samuel S. Metzger; Deacon William Flores.
Res., 800 E. Tyler, 75751-2140. Tel: 903-675-2509.
Catechesis/Religious Programs—Dennis Womack, D.R.E., Tel: 903-425-4342.
Students 184.
Missions—Canton, Van Zandt Co., St. Theresa, Hwy. 859, R.R. 6, Box 138, Canton, 75103-9806. Tel: 903-567-4286. Rev. Mathew Edassery.; Chandler, Van Zandt Co., St. Boniface, (1997) P.O. Box 762, Chandler, 75758-0762. Rev. Susil Fernando.

Atlanta, Cass Co., St. Catherine of Siena Church (1965), Rev. Abraham Mathews (India). In res., Rev. Luka K. Ulahannan, M.S.F.S.
Res., 309 N. Louise St., P.O. Box 985, 75551. Tel: 903-796-4494; Fax: 903-796-9990.
Catechesis/Religious Programs—Tel: 903-796-8491. Roberta Boitnott, D.R.E.
Students 67.

Canton, Van Zandt Co., St. Theresa (1980), Rev. Mathew Edassery, Admin.; Deacon William Flores.
Mailing Address: R.R. 6, Box 138, 75103-9806. Tel: 903-567-4286.
Catechesis/Religious Programs—Students 95.
Mission—Wills Point, Van Zandt Co., St. Luke, 450 E. James St., Wills Point, 75169. Tel: 903-873-1238. Rev. Ouseph Thekumthala.

Carthage, Panola Co., St. William of Vercelli (1948), Rev. Benjamin Smylie.
Mailing Address: P.O. Drawer F, 75633. Tel: 903-693-3776.
Res., 202 W. Loop 436, 75633-0240. Tel: 903-693-3766; Fax: 903-693-9006.
Catechesis/Religious Programs—Donna Hanks, D.R.E.
Students 95.

Center, Shelby Co., St. Therese (1951), Rev. Arulappa Devaraj.
Res., Rte. 2, Box 1093, 75935-9269. Tel: 409-598-8458; Fax: 409-598-5599. [CEM 2]
Catechesis/Religious Programs—Students 53.
Mission—Timpson, Shelby Co., Epiphany. Rev. Devaraj Arulappa.

Clarksville, Red River Co., St. Joseph (1870), Rev. George Varakukala, H.G.N., (India) Admin.
Res., 500 E. Broadway, 75426-3110. Tel: 903-427-5044. [CEM]

Crockett, Houston Co., St. Francis of the Tejas (1931), Revs. Tej Lal, I.M.S. (India); Sales T. (Ranjan) Cletus, I.M.S. (India).
Res., 609 N. Fourth, 75835-4001. Tel: 409-544-5338; Fax: 409-544-7914.
Catechesis/Religious Programs—Kathy Price, D.R.E.
Students 125.
Mission—Centerville, Leon Co., St. Leo the Great, P.O. Box 356, Centerville, 75833-0356. Tel: 903-536-5012.

Daingerfield, Morris Co., Our Lady of Fatima (1951) (Hispanic), Rev. Leo Schloemer.
Mailing Address: Rte. 1, Box 4B, 75638-9704.
Res., Bert & Tiger Streets, 75638. Tel: 903-645-5637. [CEM]
Catechesis/Religious Programs—Students 59.

Diboll, Angelina Co., Our Lady of Guadalupe (1971) (Hispanic), Rev. Alirio Corrales.
Mailing Address: P.O. Box 310, 75941-0310. Tel: 409-829-3650; Fax: 409-829-3650. [CEM]
Res., 100 Maynard St., 75941. Tel: 409-829-2690.
Catechesis/Religious Programs—Tel: 409-829-2981. Mrs. Valerie Maynard, D.R.E.
Students 92.

Fairfield, Freestone Co., St. Bernard of Clairvaux (1976), Rev. A. Peter Whitney, Admin.
Res., 630 W. Main, 75840-1418. Tel: 903-389-4616.
Catechesis/Religious Programs—Tel: 903-389-2444.
Students 163.
Mission—Buffalo, Leon Co., Blessed Kateri Tekakwitha, (1979) 403 W. Commerce, P.O. Box 878, Buffalo, 75831-0878. Tel: 903-322-3705. Rev. Theodore Rydelek, Admin.
Catechesis/Religious Programs—Bonnie Romeo, D.R.E.
Students 92.
Mission—Teague, Freestone Co., St. Mary, 609 Cedar, 75840-1617. Tel: 254-739-3692. Rev. Jesus Suarez (Colombia).
Station—Hilltop Lakes, Leon Co.

Gun Barrel City, Henderson Co., St. Jude (1975), Revs. Andrew Melel, O.I.C., (India) Admin.; Joseph Kallookalam, C.M.I. (India); Deacons A. Howard Palms; Richard Sykora.
Res., 103 Luther Ln., 75147-9358. Tel: 903-887-1452 (Office); 887-5803 (Res.). [JC]
Catechesis/Religious Programs—Mrs. Edna Beltz, D.R.E.
Students 85.
Mission—Malakoff, Henderson Co., Mary Queen of Heaven, P.O. Box 508, 2269 CR 1703, Malakoff, 75148-4905. Tel: 903-489-2366.

Hemphill, Sabine Co., St. Pius I (1939), Rev. Basil P. Hoan.
Corner Hwy. 184 and Barber St., P.O. Box 1925, 75948-1925. Tel: 409-787-3287; 787-4189 (Res.). [CEM]
Mission—St. Augustine, San Augustine Co., San Augustine. Hwy. 21.

Henderson, Rusk Co., St. Jude (1934), Rev. Dariusz Pawlowski (Poland) Admin.
Res., 200 Morningside, P.O. Box 128, 75652. Tel: 903-657-4398; Fax: 903-657-4472.
Catechesis/Religious Programs—Tel: 903-657-4472. Gina Juarez, D.R.E.
Students 150.

Jacksonville, Cherokee Co., Our Lady of Sorrows (1954), Revs. Peter Revel (Sri Lanka) Admin.; Sebastian Kallarackal, C.M.I.; Mahendra Anandappa, S.S.S.
Res., 1023 Corinth Rd., 75766-9801. Tel: 903-586-4538; Fax: 903-586-4996.
Catechesis/Religious Programs—Fax: 903-586-1559. Grace Traylor, D.R.E.
Students 189.
Mission—Rusk, Cherokee Co., Sacred Heart, P.O. Box 947, Rusk, 75785. Tel: 903-683-2494.
Res., 351 E. 6th, Apt.7, Rusk, Tel: 903-683-2494.

Jefferson, Marion Co., Immaculate Conception (1867), Revs. Ben Comisky, O.S.B.; Joseph Kurian.
Res., 201 N. Vale St., 75657-2143. Tel: 903-665-2869; Fax: 903-665-8778. [CEM]
Catechesis/Religious Programs—Tel: 903-665-8805.
Students 31.
Mission—Waskom, Harrison Co., St. Lawrence Brindisi, P.O. Box 928, Waskom, 75292-0928. Tel: 903-687-2385.
Catechesis/Religious Programs—Tel: 903-687-3532.
Students 36.

Kilgore, Gregg Co., Christ the King (1936), Revs. Mark Kusmirek; Diego Alberto Ossa Mora (Colombia); John Whitsell; Deacons Dennis Gilchrist; William Holda.
Res., 1407 Broadway, 75662-3209. Tel: 903-984-3716; Fax: 903-984-1426.
Catechesis/Religious Programs—Liz Adams, D.R.E.
Students 228.
Mission—Overton, Rusk Co., Our Lady Queen of Angels, 221 State Hwy. East, P.O. Box 322, Overton, 75684. Tel: 903-984-0537.

Longview, Gregg Co., St. Anthony (1880), Revs. Thaddeus Majkut (Poland) Admin.; Henry Lorenc (Poland); Deacon Joseph Pipak.
Mailing Address: 400 N. 6th St., 75601.
Res., 908 E. Olive, 75601. Tel: 903-758-0116; Fax: 903-758-8603.
Church—506 N. 6th St., 75601.
Catechesis/Religious Programs—Students 214.

St. Mary (1982), Revs. Gavin Vaverek, J.C.L.; A. Maria Michael; Deacon John Borens.
Res., 2108 Ridgewood Dr., 75601-1999. Tel: 903-757-5855.
School—405 Hollybrook Dr., 75601-2464. Tel: 903-753-1657; Fax: 903-758-7347. Mrs. Janel Garner, Prin.
Lay Teachers 21; Students 264; Religious 3.
Catechesis/Religious Programs—Tel: 903-757-5891; Fax: 903-758-5074. Len Budai, D.R.E.
Students 353.
Mission—Hallsville, Harrison Co., Our Lady of Grace, P.O. Box 782, Hallsville, 75650. Rev. Jose Kannampuzha (India).

Lufkin, Angelina Co., St. Patrick (1928), Revs. Eduardo Nevares, M.S.; Ronald A. Beauchemin, M.S.; Thomas J. Huhn, M.S. In res., Bro. Fabian Fuemmeler, M.S.
Res., 2118 Lowry St., 75901-1316. Tel: 409-634-6833; Fax: 409-634-6891.
School—St. Patrick School, (Grades PreK-6). Tel: 409-634-6719. Larry Gaudet, Prin.
Religious 1; Lay Teachers 7; Students 51.
Catechesis/Religious Programs—Tel: 409-639-3676. D.R.E.: Martina Torres, (PreK-6); Barbara Klimpt, (7-12).
Students 350.

Marshall, Harrison Co., St. Joseph (1874), Rev. Ron Diegel; Deacon Adrian Roden.
Res., 410 N. Alamo Blvd., 75670-3450. Tel: 903-935-2536; Fax: 903-938-1591. [CEM]
School—St. Joseph School, (Grades PreK-6) 2307 S. Garrett, 75670. Tel: 903-935-5502. Dr. Doris Wong, Prin.
Lay Teachers 8; Students 78.
Catechesis/Religious Programs—Students 165.
Mission—Tatum, Panola Co., San Pedro the Fisherman. Hwy. 43.

Mineola, St. Peter the Apostle (1937), Rev. Bernard Boteju (Germany).
Res., Newsom and Meadowbrook, P.O. Box 1022, 75773-7022. Tel: 903-569-3665; Fax: 903-569-6961. [JC]
Catechesis/Religious Programs—Students 100.

Mount Pleasant, Titus Co., St. Michael (1917), Revs. Ruben Figueroa, O.F.M., Admin.; Stephen Joseph Duyka; Deacons Joe Ibarra Moreno; Barry Beckman.
1403 E. First St., 75455-4715. Tel: 903-572-5227; Fax: 903-572-9659.
Res., 310 Denman Dr., 75455-4157. Tel: 903-572-5611.
Catechesis/Religious Programs—Thelma Longoria, D.R.E.
Students 210.

Nacogdoches, Nacogdoches Co., Sacred Heart (1716), Rev. Msgr. James E. Young; Rev. Octavio Suarez; Deacon William Kennedy.
2508 Appleby Sand Rd., 75961-4524. Tel: 409-564-7807; Fax: 409-564-8777.
Res., 504 North St., 75961. Tel: 409-564-7134.
Catechesis/Religious Programs—Tel: 409-564-5321. Sr. Mary Ann Aman, C.H.M., D.R.E.
Students 251.
Missions—Chireno, Nacogdoches Co., Our Lady of Lourdes, 75961. Tel: 409-598-8458. [CEM][JC]
Rev. Devaraj Arulappa.
Moral, Nacogdoches Co., Immaculate Conception, Hwy. 7 West, 75961. Tel: 409-564-7807; Fax: 409-564-7807. [CEM]
Chapel—Nacogdoches, St. Mary's Chapel, Stephen

F. Austin State University, 211 E. College, 75961. Tel: 409-564-0661. Rev. John W. Logan, O.P.

New Boston, Bowie Co., St. Mary of the Cenacle (1918), Rev. James P. Korah, S.I.O.L. (India).
Mailing Address: P.O. Box 914, 75570-0914. Tel: 903-628-6186; Fax: 903-628-6186. [JC]
Res., 212 Magnolia St., 75570. Tel: 903-628-2323.
Catechesis/Religious Programs—Tel: 903-628-2323.
Students 52.
Mission—New Boston, Bowie Co., Hooks Catholic Community, 75570-0914.

Palestine, Anderson Co., Sacred Heart (1893), Revs. Harold P. Paulsen; Zacharias Kunnakkattuthara (India); Deacon Alex Kobar. Prison Chaplains: Deacons Bryan Carey; Eli Calonge.
Res., 503 N. Queen St., 75801-2718. Tel: 903-729-2463. [CEM]
Sacred Heart Preschool—503 N. Queen St., 75801-2718.
Catechesis/Religious Programs—Tel: 903-729-5375. David Bunch, D.R.E.
Students 258.
Mission—Frankston, Anderson Co., St. Charles Borromeo, 1101 Hwy. 155 N., Frankston, 75763. Rev. Zacharias S. Kunnakkattuthara.

Paris, Lamar Co., Our Lady of Victory (1880), Rev. Alphonse Anthony (India).
Res., 3300 Clarksville St., 75460. Tel: 903-784-1000; Fax: 903-784-3946.
Catechesis/Religious Programs—Helen Ressler, D.R.E.
Students 154.

Pittsburg, Camp Co., Holy Cross (1987), Rev. Robert Poandl, Glmy.
Mailing Address: P.O. Box 846, 75686-0846.
413 Hill Ave., Pittsburgh, 75686. Tel: 903-856-6944.
Res., 100 Arch Davis Rd., 75686. Tel: 903-856-7609.
Catechesis/Religious Programs—Students 140.

Sulphur Springs, Hopkins Co., St. James (1880), Rev. Christopher Shackelford, Admin.; Deacons Donald R. Brown; Jose Hernandez; William O'Brien; Loren Seely.
Mailing Address: P.O. Box 93, 75483-0093.
297 Texas St., 75483. Tel: 903-885-1222; Fax: 903-885-5855.
Res., 303 Texas St., 75483. Tel: 903-885-2873.
Catechesis/Religious Programs—Tel: 903-885-0157. Laura Deckard, D.R.E.
Students 288.
Missions—Emory, Rains Co., St. John the Evangelist, P.O. Box 93, 75482. Rev. Christopher Shackelford.; Gilmer, Upshur Co., St. Francis of Assisi, P.O. Box 704, Gilmer, 75644. Tel: 903-569-3665. Rev. Daniel Gonzalez.; Mt. Vernon, Franklin Co., Sacred Heart, P.O. Box 918, Mt. Vernon, 75457. Tel: 903-537-7489. Rev. John Barczyk.; Winnsboro, Wood Co., St. Ann, P.O. Box 733, Winnsboro, 75494-0733. Tel: 903-629-7884. Rev. Elangovan Anandan (India).

Texarkana, Bowie Co., Sacred Heart (1874), Rev. Msgr. Gerald Priest; Rev. Jerry Dobosz (Poland); Deacon Keith A. Woods.
Res., 4505 Elizabeth St., 75503-2998. Tel: 903-794-4444; Fax: 903-792-1529. [CEM 2]
Catechesis/Religious Programs—Tel: 903-792-6846.
Students 250.

Trinity, Trinity Co., Most Holy Trinity (1972), Rev. Felix Chirapurathel, O.Praem., (India) Admin.
Res., Rte. 1, Box 61-X, 75862-9801. Tel: 409-594-6664; Fax: 409-594-6664.

Union Grove-Gladewater, Upshur Co., St. Theresa of the Infant Jesus (1945), Rev. Henry J. Lenz, M.S.; Deacon Guy Blasingame.
Mailing Address: P.O. Box 967, Gladewater, 75647-0967.
Old Hwy. 271 & Point Pleasant Rd., Union Grove, Tel: 903-845-2306.
Catechesis/Religious Programs—Students 100.

Whitehouse, Smith Co., Prince of Peace (1996), Rev. Daniel L. Daugherty.
Mailing Address: P.O. Box 456, 75771-1078.
Res., 14588 Hwy. 110 S., 75791. Tel: 903-581-9600; Fax: 903-561-4946.
Catechesis/Religious Programs—Students 113.

Chaplains of Public Institutions

FAIRFIELD. *Boyd Unit, Texas Department of Criminal Justice.* Rev. A. Peter Whitney, Mailing Address: 630 W. Main, 75840-1418.

LOVELADY. *Eastham Unit, Texas Department of Corrections* Rte. 1, Box 93, 75851. Tel: 409-636-7147. Rev. Virginio Vazquez (CC) Chap., Mailing Address: P.O. Box 1974, Huntsville, 77342-1914.

NEW BOSTON. *Telford Unit.* Deacon Donald R. Brown Tel: 903-628-2706.

PALESTINE. *Beto I Unit and Louie C. Powledge Unit, Texas Department of Corrections.* Rev. Robert Herald, Chap., Mailing Address: Beto I Unit & Louie C. Powledge Unit, Texas Department of Corrections, Rte. 2, Box 2250, 75801-9612. Tel: 903-723-5074, Ext: 342 (Beto I Unit); 723-5074 (Louie C. Powledge Unit).

RUSK. *Jerry H. Hodge Unit, TDCC.* Deacon Bryan Carey, P.O. Box 999, 75785-0999. Tel: 903-683-5781.
Rusk State Hospital and Skyview Unit, Texas Dept. of Corrections. Rev. Sebastian Kallarackal, C.M.I., Chap., P.O. Box 947, 75785-0947. Tel: 903-683-2494.

TENNESSEE COLONY. *Michael Unit, Texas Department of Corrections.* Deacon Elie P. Calonge, Chap., Michael Unit, Box 4500, 75886-4500. Tel: 903-928-2311.

Special Assignment:
Reverend Monsignors—
Joseph, Milam, Pres., University of Dallas, 1845 E. Northgate, Irving, TX 75062. Tel: 214-721-4047

Retired:
Reverend Monsignors—
Szapka, Edward J., 123 S. Houston, Longview, TX 75602-1103
Reverend Fathers—
Knaresborough, Francis J., 1621 E. 42nd St., Rm. 404A, Texarkana, AR 75502
Weihrer, John A., Priest's Residence, 2407 E. Holcomb, Houston, TX 75773-0699

Absent on Sick Leave:
Reverend Fathers—
Zakshesky, Francis, c/o Mrs. Regina Zakshesky, 605 Miller St., Alpena, MI 49707

Permanent Deacons:
Beckman, Barry L., St. Michael, Mt. Pleasant
Blasingame, Guylan, St. Theresa, Union Grove
Borens, John, St. Mary, Longview
Bridwell, William H., Christ the King, Kilgore
Brown, Donald R., Telford Unit, New Boston
Calonge, Elie P., Michael Unit, Tennessee Colony, TDC
Carey, Thomas B., Michael Unit, TDC, Tennessee Colony
Flores, William, St. Theresa, Canton
George, Anthony, (Retired), Cathedral of the Immaculate Conception, Tyler
Germann, Joseph, St. Ann, Winnsboro
Gilchrist, Dennis S., Christ the King, Kilgore
Hall, Dwight S., (Inactive), Cathedral of the Immaculate Conception, Tyler
Hernandez, Jose, St. James, Sulphur Springs
Holda, William M., Christ the King, Kilgore
Kennedy, William C., III, Sacred Heart, Nacogdoches
Kobar, Alex, Sacred Heart, Palestine
Martinez, Ramiro, Cathedral of the Immaculate Conception, Tyler
Milton, John, Assignment Outside Diocese
Moreno, Joe Ibarra, St. Michael, Mt. Pleasant
Mullen, Sam, St. Ann, Winnsboro
Noriega, Ramon, Cathedral of the Immaculate Conception, Tyler
O'Brien, William E., St. James, Sulphur Springs
O'Sullivan, William H., (Retired), Cathedral of the Immaculate Conception, Tyler
Palms, Howard A., St. Jude, Gun Barrel City
Pipak, Joseph, St. Anthony, Longview
Reyes, Jesus, Our Lady of Guadalupe, Diboll
Roden, John Adrian, St. Joseph, Marshall
Rojas, Gonzalo
Seely, Loren G., St. James, Sulphur Springs
Shaffer, John K., Sacred Heart, Nacogdoches
Suarez, Santiago, St. Joseph, Marshall
Sykora, Richard L., St. Jude, Gun Barrel City
Villalobos, Manuel
Woods, Keith A., Sacred Heart, Texarkana

INSTITUTIONS LOCATED IN THE DIOCESE

[A] GENERAL HOSPITALS

TYLER. *Trinity Mother Frances Health System,* 800 E. Dawson St., 75701. Tel: 903-593-8441
For a complete listing, refer to the Hospitals section.

PARIS. *St. Joseph Hospital and Health Center,* 820 Clarksville St., P.O. Box 9070, 75461. Tel: 903-785-4521; Fax: 903-737-3848
For a complete listing, refer to the Hospitals section.

TEXARKANA. *St. Michael Health Care Center,* 2600 St. Michael Dr., 75503
For a complete listing, refer to the Hospitals section.
St. Michael Rehabilitation Hospital, 2400 St. Michael Dr., 75503.
E-mail: gormert@smh.sch.org
For a complete listing, refer to the Hospitals section.

[B] MONASTERIES AND RESIDENCES OF PRIESTS

PALESTINE. *Hermitage,* Rte. 3, Box 3575, 75801. Rev. Denis Walsh. Other Institutions: Houses of Religious Men 1; Total in Residence 1; Total Staff 1.
Prayer Mountain Hermitage, Rte. 3, Box 3574, 75801. Sr. Mary Vogel, H.S.S.R.

[C] CONVENTS AND RESIDENCES FOR SISTERS

LUFKIN. *Monastery of the Infant Jesus,* 1501 Lotus Ln., 75904-2699. Tel: 409-634-4233. Cloistered Dominican Nuns. Sr. Mary John, O.P., Prioress; Rev. Joseph H. Determan, O.P. Professed Sisters 22.

[D] CAMPUS MINISTRY

TYLER. *Tyler Junior College and The University of Texas at Tyler Newman Center,* 423 S. Broadway, 75702. Tel: 903-592-1617. Attended from the Cathedral of the Immaculate Conception. Rev. Michael Doyle. Tel: 903-592-1617.

KILGORE. *Kilgore Junior College Newman Center,* 1407 Broadway, 75662. Tel: 903-984-2501. Rev. Mark Kusmirek.

NACOGDOCHES. *Stephen F. Austin University Catholic Student Center,* P.O. Box 7051, SFASU, 75962. Tel: 409-564-0661. Rev. John D. Logan, O.P., Chap. Other Institutions: Newman Centers; Total in Residence 1; Total Staff 1.

[E] MISCELLANEOUS

TYLER.
**Tyler Catholic School Foundation,* 1015 E.S.E. Loop 323, 75701-9663. Tel: 903-534-8807; Fax: 903-534-8807. Mailing Address: P.O. Box 131175, 75713. O. V. Emery, Exec. Dir.

LONGVIEW.
**Longview Catholic School Endowment Fund,* 405 Hollybrook, 75605.

LUFKIN.
**Lufkin School Foundation,* 2118 Lowry, 75901.
**St. Patrick School Fund,* 2118 Lowry, 75901.

RELIGIOUS INSTITUTES OF MEN REPRESENTED IN THE DIOCESE

For further details refer to the corresponding bracketed number in the Religious Institutes of Men or Women section.

[0600]—*Brothers of the Congregation of the Holy Cross.*—C.S.C.
[]—*Carmelite of Mary Immaculate.*—C.M.I.
[0360]—*Claretian Missionaries.*—C.M.F.
[0220]—*Congregation of the Blessed Sacrament.*—S.S.S.
[0570]—*Glenmary Home Missioners.*—Glmy.
[]—*Heralds of Good News.*
[]—*Indian Missionary Society.*—I.M.S.
[0720]—*The Missionaries of Our Lady of La Salette.*—M.S.
[]—*Missionaries of St. Francis de Sales.*—M.S.F.S.
[0430]—*Order of Preachers - Dominicans.*—O.P.
[]—*Order of the Imitation of Christ.*—O.I.C.
[]—*Religious Congregation of the Little Flower.*—C.S.T.
[]—*Secular Institute of Our Lady.*—S.I.O.L.

RELIGIOUS INSTITUTES OF WOMEN REPRESENTED IN THE DIOCESE

[0230]—*Benedictine Sisters of Pontifical Jurisdiction.*—O.S.B.
[2100]—*Congregation of the Humility of Mary.*—C.H.M.
[]—*Congregation of the Mother of Carmel.*—C.M.C.
[0470]—*Congregation of the Sisters of Charity of the Incarnate Word, Houston, Texas.* (San Antonio, TX).—C.C.V.I.
[1050]—*Dominican Contemplative Nuns.*—O.P.
[1070-19]—*Dominican Sisters of Houston, Texas (Congregation of the Sacred Heart).*—O.P.
[1310]—*Franciscan Sisters of Little Falls, MN.*—O.S.F.
[]—*Hermit Sisters of St. Romuald.*—H.S.S.R.
[2970]—*School Sisters of Notre Dame.*—S.S.N.D.
[4090]—*Sisters of Social Service.*—S.S.S.
[1570]—*Sisters of St. Francis of the Holy Family.*—O.S.F.
[1970]—*Sisters of the Holy Family of Nazareth.*—C.S.F.N.

NECROLOGY

† Przydacz, John, Chap., Tyler, TX, Mother Francis Hospital. —Died Sept. 28, 1997.

Diocese of Venice

(Diocesis Venetiae in Florida)

Most Reverend

JOHN J. NEVINS, D.D.

Bishop of Venice; ordained June 6, 1959; appointed Titular Bishop of Rusticiana and Auxiliary of Miami February 6, 1979; consecrated March 24, 1979; appointed First Bishop of Venice July 17, 1984; installed October 25, 1984. *Res., P.O. Box 2006, Venice, FL, 34284.*

ESTABLISHED OCTOBER 25, 1984.

Square Miles 9,035.

Comprises the Counties of Charlotte, Collier, DeSoto, Glades, Hardee, Hendry, Highlands, Lee, Manatee and Sarasota in the State of Florida.

For legal titles of parishes and diocesan institutions, consult the Chancellor.

To Serve with Mercy

Catholic Center: P.O. Box 2006, Venice, FL, 34284. Tel.: 941-484-9543; Fax: 941-484-1121.

Web site address: dioceseofvenice.org

E-mail address: reception@diocese.venice.fl.us

STATISTICAL OVERVIEW

Personnel	
Bishop	1
Priests: Diocesan Active in Diocese	66
Priests: Active Outside Diocese	3
Priests: Retired, Sick or Absent	20
Number of Diocesan Priests	89
Religious Priests in Diocese	76
Extern Priests in Diocese	72
Ordinations:	
Diocesan Priests	4
Transitional Deacons	1
Permanent Deacons in Diocese	59
Total Brothers	20
Total Sisters	141
Parishes	
Parishes	50
With Resident Pastor:	
Resident Diocesan Priests	38
Resident Religious Priests	12
Without Resident Pastor:	
Missions	10
Professional Ministry Personnel:	
Brothers	3
Sisters	33
Lay Ministers	59
Welfare	
Catholic Hospitals	2
Total Assisted	197,439
Health Care Centers	8
Total Assisted	72,960
Homes for the Aged	5
Total Assisted	321
Specialized Homes	5
Total Assisted	200
Special Centers for Social Services	10
Total Assisted	29,809
Educational	
Diocesan Students in Other Seminaries	15
Total Seminarians	15
High Schools, Diocesan and Parish	3
Total Students	1,600
Elementary Schools, Diocesan and Parish	9
Total Students	3,483
Catechesis/Religious Education:	
High School Students	2,743
Elementary Students	9,512
Total Students Under Catholic Instruction	17,353
Teachers in the Diocese:	
Priests	5
Brothers	1
Sisters	20
Lay Teachers	295
Vital Statistics	
Receptions into the Church:	
Infant Baptism Totals	2,943
Adult Baptism Totals	254
Received into Full Communion	505
First Communions	2,733
Confirmations	2,193
Marriages:	
Catholic	511
Interfaith	369
Total Marriages	880
Deaths	2,116
Total Catholic Population	174,548
Total Population	1,385,308

Catholic Center—1000 Pinebrook Rd., Venice, 34292. Tel: 941-484-9543; Fax: 941-484-1121. *Mailing Address: P.O. Box 2006, Venice, 34284.*

Office of the Bishop—Sr. CARMELLA T. DECOSTY, S.N.J.M., Exec. Asst.; Ms. KATHRYN BLISS, Exec. Sec.

Vicar General—Very Rev. THOMAS G. ANGLIM, V.G.

Chancellor and Moderator of the Curia—Very Rev. JEROME A. CAROSELLA.

Administrative Assistant to the Chancellor/Notary—Miss JEANNE C. HICKEY.

College of Consultors—Rev. Msgr. ROBERT SCHIEFEN, J.C.D.; Very Revs. THOMAS G. ANGLIM, V.G.; JEROME A. CAROSELLA, Chancellor; EDWARD D. MORETTI, V.E.; NEIL FLEMMING, V.F.; ROBERT D. TABBERT, V.F.; ESTEBAN G. SOY, Treas.; Revs. GERARD FINEGAN; NICANOR LOBATO; VINCENT SHEEHY; JOSEPH STEARNS.

Episcopal Vicars and Deans—Very Rev. EDWARD D. MORETTI, V.E., Northern and Eastern Deaneries; Vacant, Southern and Central Deaneries; Very Rev. JOSE J. RUIZ, V.F., Eastern Deanery; Very Rev. NEIL FLEMMING, V.F., Central Deanery; Very Rev. ROBERT D. TABBERT, V.F., Southern Deanery; Very Rev. FAUSTO STAMPIGLIA, S.A.C., V.F., Northern Deanery.

Presbyteral Council—Very Rev. THOMAS G. ANGLIM, V.G.; Very Rev. ROBERT R. CANNON, J.C.L., Moderator; Very Rev. JEROME A. CAROSELLA, Chancellor; Very Rev. EDWARD D. MORETTI, V.E.; Very Rev. JOSE J. RUIZ, V.F.; Very Rev. NEIL FLEMMING, V.F.; Very Rev. ESTEBAN SOY; Very Rev. FAUSTO STAMPIGLIA, S.A.C., V.F.; Very Rev. ROBERT D. TABBERT, V.F.; Revs. NORMANDO FELIZ; GERALD P. GROGAN; JANUSZ JANCARZ; JEROME P. KAYWELL, Sec.; THADDEUS KLOC; NICANOR LOBATO; CHARLES MALLEN, C.SS.R.; STEPHEN E. MCNAMARA; JOSEPH E. STEARNS.

Theologian to the Bishop—Rev. FAUSTO STAMPIGLIA, S.A.C.

Censor Librorum—Rev. JOEL SCHEVERS, O.Carm., M.A., Th.M.

Vicar for Clergy—Very Rev. EDWARD D. MORETTI, V.E.

Vicar for Religious—Sr. CHRYSTA LERHINAN, I.H.M.

Priest Personnel Board—Rev. STEPHEN E. MCNAMARA, Chm.

Continuing Education of Clergy—Rev. MARK HEUBERGER.

Official Archivist—Very Rev. JEROME A. CAROSELLA.

Historical Archivist—Mrs. GAIL M. MCGRATH.

Delegate of the Bishop for Sexual Misconduct Cases—Dr. TERRY REILLY, D.Min., M.A., Case Mgr.

Diocesan Tribunal—All Pastoral Center searches for information prior to October 25, 1984, should be directed to the Diocese of St. Petersburg for Manatee, Hardee, Sarasota, DeSoto, Glades, Charlotte and Lee Counties; to the Diocese of Orlando for Highlands Co. and to the Archdiocese of Miami for Hendry and Collier Counties.

Judicial Vicar—Very Rev. ROBERT R. CANNON, M.Th., J.C.L.

Assessor/Auditor Administrator—Dr. TERRY H. REILLY, M.A., D.Min.

Defenders of the Bond—Revs. JOEL SCHEVERS, O.Carm., M.A., Th.M.; JOSEPH S. AMATO, J.C.L.

Promoter of Justice—Rev. Msgr. ROBERT SCHIEFEN, J.C.D.

Judges—Very Rev. ROBERT R. CANNON, M.Th., J.C.L.; Revs. JOSEPH S. AMATO, J.C.L.; DENNIS KLEMME, J.C.D.; JOHN V. DOLCIAMORE, S.T.L., J.C.L.; Rev. Msgr. JAMES MCGRATH, J.C.D.; Rev. Msgr. ELLSWORTH KNEAL, J.C.D.

Ecclesiastical Notaries—Mrs. JOHANNA MARONE; Miss JOANNE COYNE; Mrs. ANN MANRODT; Mrs. ZONIA HERRERA.

Vicar for Marriage Matters—Very Rev. ROBERT R. CANNON, M.Th., J.C.L.

Diocesan Offices

Building Department—Very Rev. ESTEBAN SOY, Dir.; Mr. RAYMOND HADDAD, Assoc. Dir.

Campaign for Human Development—Ms. MARIA TERESA GASTON, Dir.

Campus Ministry—Rev. JOHN H.R. ELLIS, D.Min., Dir., *The Newman House at the New College Campus, 528 58th St., Sarasota, 34243-2104.* Tel: 941-355-2099; 6415. *Mailing Address: Catholic Campus Ministries, 333 Somerset Ave., Sarasota, 34243-1926.*

Northern Deanery—Campus Ministers serving: New College, Manatee Community College (North Campus), Ringling School of Art & Design, University of South Florida (Manatee and Sarasota Counties): Miss ELEANOR CLUNE; Mrs. BURGESS ELLIS; Rev. JOHN H.R. ELLIS; Miss JENENE GARGUILO; Mrs. PAT GARGUILO; Mrs. TERRY MOSSLER; Ms. JUDY PARSONS; Mrs. SUE SOBZAK; Mrs. BABS WARREN; Mr. DENNIS WARREN, Campus Minister serving: Manatee Community College (South Campus); Vacant.

Eastern Deanery—Campus Ministers serving: South Florida Community College; Rev. GERALD P. GROGAN; Ms. PATRICIA A. WHITE. Tel: 941-453-4757.

Southern Deanery—Campus Minister serving: Florida Gulf Coast University, Edison Community College (Fort Myers and Naples), University of South Florida (Lee County); Rev. RICK WOJNICKI, O.S.F.S. Tel: 941-275-8783.

[*]Catholic Charities of the Diocese of Venice, Inc.—Mrs. ROSEMARY WINDER STRANGE, A.C.S.W., Exec. Dir.

Catholic Relief Services/Operation Rice Bowl—Ms. MARIA TERESA GASTON, Dir.

Communications Department—Mrs. GAIL M. MCGRATH, Dir.; Mrs. SARA BRINN, Exec. Sec.

The Florida Catholic, Venice Edition—Most Rev. JOHN J. NEVINS, D.D., Publisher; Miss JEAN A. PALOMBO, Editor/Reporter.

The Florida Catholic of Venice, Inc.—Very Rev. JEROME A. CAROSELLA, Pres. & Dir.; Mrs. GAIL M. MCGRATH, Sec. & Dir.; Mr. JOHN G. BAUER, Treas. & Dir.

Catholic Mass on Television—Mrs. GAIL M. MCGRATH, Exec. Producer; Mrs. SARA BRINN, Production Coord. & Leaflet Missals. Production Assistants: Mrs. CONSTANCE STENDARDO; Ms. KATHLEEN BRENDEL.

Community Information—Mrs. GAIL M. MCGRATH.

Media and Public Relations—Mrs. GAIL M. MCGRATH.

Venice Catholic Communications, Inc.—1000 Pinebrook Rd., Venice, 34292. Most Rev. JOHN J. NEVINS, D.D., Pres. & Dir.; Very Rev. JEROME A. CAROSELLA, Vice Pres. & Dir.; Mrs. GAIL M. MCGRATH, Sec. & Treas. & Dir.

Data Processing Office—Mr. WILLIAM TWOHIG, Mgr.; Ms. PAMELA BURKE, Asst. Dir.

Development Office/Annual Bishop's Appeal—Mr. WILLIAM MCCARTHY, Dir.; Mrs. MARIAN DODSON, Asst. Dir. Devel. Oper.

Diaconate—Co-Directors: Revs. THADDEUS KLOC; FAUSTO STAMPIGLIA, S.A.C.

Ecumenical and Interreligious Affairs—Revs. WILLIAM ADAMS; JOEL SCHEVERS, O.Carm.; Ms. JOANNE WEBER.

Education—Sr. ROBERTA SCHMIDT, C.S.J., Dir.; Sr. REGIS KRUSNIEWSKI, S.S.N.D., Dir., Catechetical Ministry; Mrs. ROSEMARY BRATTON, Supt. of Schools; Bros. PAUL HENNESSY, C.F.C., Pres., School for Pastoral Ministry; E. THOMAS HEWITT, C.F.C., Coord., Migrant Education Apostolate, Los Hermanos.

Finance Department—Very Rev. ESTEBAN SOY, Diocesan Treas.; Mr. JOHN BAUER, Dir.; Mrs. LEIGH MORROW, Controller.

Insurance—Mr. DAN DURKIN, Mgr.; Mrs. ZONIA HERRERA, Coord.

Legal—Mrs. VICTORIA H. PFLUG, Esq.; Mrs. LORRAINE CARRIERE, Legal Sec.

Ministry to Cultural Groups—

African Caribbean (Hatian) American Ministry (AFCAM)—Rev. JOHN RONALD JOSEPH, Dir.

Hispanic, Migrant and Spanish Speaking Apostolates/National Migration Week—Rev. NICANOR LOBATO, Dir.

Juventud Hispana (Hispanic Youth Ministry)—Rev. JOSE GONZALEZ, *The Guadalupe Center.*

Ministry to People with AIDS—Sr. FRANCES NEVOLO, O.L.C., Sarasota County; Sr. JUDY H. SIMONIS, C.S.J., Charlotte County; Sr. MARY JOHN FRANEY, O.L.C., Lee County.

Pastoral Ministries—Dr. MIMI REILLY, D.Min., Dir.

Bishop's Critical Concerns Committee—Mr. JAMES HANKS, Chm.

Charismatic Renewal—Very Rev. ROBERT R. CANNON, M.Th., J.C.L., Spiritual Dir.

Contemplative Prayer—Rev. ROBERT MATTINGLY, Spiritual Moderator.

Divorced and Separated Ministry—Rev. GERARD BENSON, O.Carm., Coord.

Family Life Office—(includes Parenting and all Marriage Enrichment and Marriage Preparation programs); Dr. MIMI REILLY, D.Min., Dir.; Mrs. PATRICIA HINES, Assoc. Dir.

Lay Ministry Office—Dr. MIMI REILLY, D.Min., Dir.

Renew—Evangelization—Mrs. PATRICIA HINES.

Older Catholics, Apostolate for—Dr. ANNE SWING, D.Min., Dir.

Parish Pastoral Ministers—Dr. MIMI REILLY, D.Min., Coord.

Peace and Social Justice—Mr. ROBERT HENNEMEYER.

Persons with Disabilities, Apostolate for—Mrs. OLIVIA BECKER, Dir.

Respect Life—Rev. NICHOLAS MCLOUGHLIN, Moderator; Very Rev. ROBERT R. CANNON, M.Th., J.C.L., Assoc. Moderator; Mrs. OLIVIA BECKER, Exec. Dir.

Project Rachel—Tel: 800-329-4787.

Youth Ministry Office—Mrs. LORRAINE SMITH, Exec. Dir.

Teens Encounter Christ—Rev. JOSEPH CLIFFORD, Spiritual Moderator.

Scouting—Rev. TIMOTHY NAVIN, Spiritual Dir.

Prison Ministry—Priests of the Diocese; Deacon EDWARD D. LUNDY.

Rural Life—Very Rev. JOSE J. RUIZ, V.F., Dir.

Vocations/Seminarian Formation—Revs. JOSEPH STEARNS, Dir. ROBB MONGIELLO, Assoc. Dir. CELESTINO GUTIERRES, Assoc. Dir. MARK HEUBERGER.

Other Offices

Propagation of the Faith/Mission Cooperative Program—Rev. EDWARD PICK, Dir.

Third Millenium—Sr. REGIS KRUSNIEWSKI, S.S.N.D.

Organizations

Cursillo Movement—Rev. CHARLES MALLEN, C.SS.R., Spiritual Dir.; Mrs. IRENE BAUER, Lay Dir.

Secretariado Hispano de Cursillos—Rev. AURELIANO SANTA OLAYA, Dir. Espiritual; Mr. CARMELO ORTEGA, Dir. Laico.

Holy Childhood Association—Rev. EUGENE MCCARTHY, Dir.

International Order of Alhambra, La Mancha Caravan 250—Mr. WILLIAM LEYDEN, Grand Commander.

Legion of Mary—Revs. VINCENT CLEMENTE, Manasota Curia: RAFAEL PADILLA, Southwest Florida Curia.

Serra International—Mr. FRANKLIN THEN.

St. Vincent DePaul Society—Mr. WILLIAM J. MARTYN, Diocesan Trustee.

Venice Diocesan Council of Catholic Women—Rev. CLAUDE BRUBAKER, Spiritual Dir.; Mrs. MARIAN VAN WINKLE, Pres.

Advisory Groups to the Bishop

Audit Committee—Mr. STEPHEN BUCKLEY, Esq., Chm.

Finance and Investment Committee—Mr. THOMAS OWENS, Chm.

Insurance Committee—Very Rev. THOMAS G. ANGLIM, V.G., Chm.

Liturgy Commission—Rev. EUGENE RYAN, Chm.

Pension Plan Board of Trustees (Archdiocese of Miami/Dioceses of St. Petersburg and Venice)—Very Rev. THOMAS G. ANGLIM, V.G., Co-Vice Chm.

Planning and Development Committee—Very Rev. THOMAS G. ANGLIM, V.G., Chm.

Priest Personnel Board—Rev. STEPHEN E. MCNAMARA, Chm.

Real Estate Board—Revs. JEROME A. CAROSELLA, Co-Chm. NEIL FLEMMING, Co-Chm.

Resource Team—Dr. TERRY REILLY, D.Min., Case Mgr.

CLERGY, PARISHES, MISSIONS AND PAROCHIAL SCHOOLS

CITY OF VENICE
(Sarasota County)

1—EPIPHANY CATHEDRAL (1958), Very Rev. Esteban G. Soy, Rector; Revs. Donald J. Koch; Chester Domaszewicz; Joel Schevers, O.Carm., (Retired); Peter F. Brudzynski, (Retired); Richard J. Mueller; Piotr Zawadzki; Deacons John L. Blackburn, (Retired); Richard Nowak; Coleman Geary; Robert Tomasso; Francis Cole.

Res., 310 Sarasota St., 34285. Tel: 941-484-3505; Fax: 941-488-9333.

School—316 Sarasota St., 34285. Tel: 941-488-2215; Fax: 941-488-2216. Dewayne Byrnes, Prin.

School Sisters of Notre Dame 1; Lay Teachers 21; Students 371.

Catechesis/Religious Programs—Tel: 941-485-2325. Sr. Frances Lalor, R.S.M., D.R.E. Students 377.

Convent—237 Nassau St., N., 34285. Tel: 941-484-4765.

2—OUR LADY OF LOURDES (1986), Revs. Vincent J. Sheehy; Jack A. Cosentino (FAR); Deacon James Cooper. In res., Rev. Robert R. Cannon.

Res., 1301 Center Rd., 34292. Tel: 941-497-2931; Fax: 941-497-5849.

Catechesis/Religious Programs—Students 110.

OUTSIDE THE CITY OF VENICE

Arcadia, De Soto Co., St. Paul (1885), Revs. William Adams, S.T.L.; Juan Pascual de Miguel.

Res., 1208 N.E. Oak St., 34266. Tel: 941-494-2611; Fax: 941-494-6385.

Catechesis/Religious Programs—Tel: 941-494-2835. Students 253.

Avon Park, Highlands Co., Our Lady of Grace (1956), Rev. Gerald P. Grogan.

Res., 595 E. Main St., 33825. Tel: 941-453-4757; Fax: 941-453-4757.

Catechesis/Religious Programs—Tel: 941-453-7537. Patricia A. White, D.R.E. Students 164.

Boca Grande, Lee Co., Our Lady of Mercy (1988), Very Rev. Jerome A. Carosella.

Res., P.O. Box 181, 33921. Tel: 941-964-2254; Fax: 941-964-1124.

Bokeelia, Lee Co., Our Lady of the Miraculous Medal (1965), Rev. J. Thomas Pohto, O.S.A.

Res., 12175 H. Stringfellow Rd., 33922. Tel: 941-283-0456; Fax: 941-283-1118.

Catechesis/Religious Programs—Students 50.

Bonita Springs, Lee Co., St. Leo (1962), Revs. Thaddeus Kloc; Sofonias Ortez.

Res., 28290 Beaumont Rd., 34134. Tel: 941-992-0901; Fax: 941-992-5282.

Catechesis/Religious Programs—Cynoi Rypl, D.R.E. Students 208.

Mission—Bonita Springs, Lee Co., Hispanic Mission, 33923.

Bradenton, Manatee Co., Sacred Heart (1969), Revs. Michael Mullen, I.C., Admin.; Michael O'Neill, I.C. In res., Rev. Daniel Sloan, I.C.

Res., 1220 15th St. W., 34205. Tel: 941-748-2221; Fax: 941-748-1744.

Catechesis/Religious Programs—Students 113.

St. Joseph (1927), Revs. Carmelo Cadarso (Spain); Edward F. Gibbons.

Res., 2704 33rd Ave., W., 34205. Tel: 941-756-3732; Fax: 941-758-1244.

School—Tel: 941-755-2611; Fax: 941-755-2611. Sr. Christine Patrick, S.P., Prin.

Sisters 2; Lay Teachers 26; Students 432.

Catechesis/Religious Programs—Tel: 941-755-4335. Sr. Carolyn Glynn, S.P., D.R.E. Students 280.

SS. Peter and Paul the Apostles (1987), Very Rev. Edward D. Moretti, V.E.; Revs. Dennis Cooney; Anthony Pastucci.

Office: 2850 75th St., W., 34209. Tel: 941-795-1228; Fax: 941-794-0127. [CEM]

Catechesis/Religious Programs—Tel: 941-798-9705; Fax: 941-794-3012. AnnaLuisa Huffman, D.R.E. Students 375.

Cape Coral, Lee Co., St. Andrew (1964), Very Rev. Neil Flemming; Revs. Arnold Zebrowski; Jerome P. Kaywell; Rafael Padilla; Deacons Dennis Hedge; Lowell O'Grady.

Res., 2628 Del Prado Blvd., P.O. Box 845, 33910-0845. Tel: 941-574-4545; Fax: 941-574-2450.

School—(Grades K-8). Tel: 941-772-3922; Fax: 941-772-7182. Sr. Elizabeth Dunn, O.P., Prin.

Sinsinawa Dominicans 5; Lay Teachers 24; Students 520.

Catechesis/Religious Programs—Tel: 941-574-2411. Mr. Carmine Macedonio, D.R.E. Students 910.

Blessed Katharine Drexel (1990), Revs. John F. Deary, O.S.A.; John J. Sheridan, O.S.A.

Office: 1922 S.W. 20th Ave., 33991. Tel: 941-283-9501; Fax: 941-283-9502.

Catechesis/Religious Programs—Theresa Idler, D.R.E. Students 300.

Clewiston, Hendry Co., St. Margaret (1932) (Spanish), Rev. Santo Cigolini, C.S. (Brazil).

Res., 208 N. Deane Duff Ave., 33440. Tel: 941-983-8585; Fax: 941-983-9673.

Catechesis/Religious Programs—Tel: 941-983-8844. Sr. Esther Gutierrez, D.R.E. Students 280.

Englewood, Sarasota Co., St. Raphael (1957), Rev. Thomas J. Walsh, O.Carm.; Rev. Msgr. Ferdinand A. Evans (CIN) (Retired); Rev. Stanley S. Kromer, O.Carm.

Res., 770 Kilbourne Ave., 34223. Tel: 941-474-9595; Fax: 941-475-5697.

Catechesis/Religious Programs—Tel: 941-473-2359. James & Eileen Beiersdorfer, D.R.E. Students 108.

Fort Myers, Lee Co.,

1—ST. VINCENT DE PAUL, (1986), Rev. David Arle; Deacon Joseph Jolin.

Church & Mailing Address—13031 State Rd. 80, 33905. Tel: 941-693-0818; Fax: 941-693-0818.

Catechesis/Religious Programs—Fax: 941-693-8459. Students 140.

2—CHURCH OF THE RESURRECTION OF OUR LORD, (1974), Revs. Stephen E. McNamara; Adelbert Buscher, O.S.B.; Oliver Toner, O.Carm.
Parish Center & Mailing Address: 8121 Cypress Lake Dr., 33919. Tel: 941-481-7172; Fax: 941-481-8007.
Church—8051 Cypress Lake Dr., 33919.
Catechesis/Religious Programs—Tel: 941-481-6863. Joan Kamm, D.R.E.
Students 276.

3—ST. CECILIA, (1965), Revs. Thomas E. Murphy, O.S.F.S.; David J. Devlin, O.S.F.S.; Bro. Harry F. McGovern, O.S.F.S., Pastoral Assoc. In res., Revs. Richard J. Wojnicki, O.S.F.S., Campus Min.; John T. Doyle, O.S.F.S., (Retired); Deacons Bill Brodeur; Lorin Fortier.
Res., 5632 Sunrise Dr., 33919. Tel: 941-936-3635; Fax: 941-936-2108.
Catechesis/Religious Programs—Jane Westerman, D.R.E.
Students 180.

4—ST. COLUMBKILLE, (1993), Revs. Charles K. Sullivan; Thomas J. Palko, O.S.F.S.
Church—12171 Iona Rd., 33908. Tel: 941-489-3973; Fax: 941-432-0066.

5—ST. FRANCIS XAVIER, (1910), Very Rev. Thomas M. Anglim; Revs. Stanislaus Pierog (Poland); Marian Konobrocki.
Res., P.O. Box 912, 2133 Heitman St., 33902. Tel: 941-334-2161; Fax: 941-332-4178.
School—Tel: 941-334-7707; Fax: 941-334-8605. Sr. Elaine Mahoney, O.S.F., Prin.
Franciscan Sisters of Allegany 2; Lay Teachers 27; Students 650.
Catechesis/Religious Programs—2048 Heitman St., 33902. Tel: 941-334-7636.
Students 167.
Missions—Fort Myers, Lee Co., Our Lady of Perpetual Help, 2063 Lafayette St., 33901. Tel: 941-334-2234; San Jose, Lee Co., Jesus the Worker, 4235 Figuera, 33905. Tel: 941-332-2829.

6—OUR LADY OF LIGHT, (1990), Revs. Angelo F. Maraldo, O.S.F.S.; Mark Wrightson, O.S.F.S.
Office: 19680 Cypress View Dr., 33912. Tel: 941-267-7088; Fax: 941-267-5481.
Res., 9404 Windlake Dr., 33912. Tel: 941-267-2228. [CEM]
Catechesis/Religious Programs—Tel: 941-267-7033.
Students 442.

7—HISPANIC MISSIONS OF FORT MYERS, (Hispanic), Rev. Aureliano Santa-Olaya.
Res., 472 Figuera Ave., 33905. Tel: 941-693-5330; Fax: 941-693-5243. [JC]
Churches—Jesus the Worker. (Jesus Obrero). 4235 Michigan Link, 33916. Tel: 941-332-2829; San Jose, 10750 Gladiolus Dr., 33908. Tel: 941-481-1143.
Catechesis/Religious Programs—Tel: 941-693-6448.
Students 270.

Fort Myers Beach, Lee Co., Ascension (1962), Rev. Thomas J. Goggin; Deacon Charles Kiesel.
Res., 6025 Estero Blvd., 33931. Tel: 941-463-6754; Fax: 941-765-1923.
Catechesis/Religious Programs—Students 22.

Golden Gate, Collier Co., St. Elizabeth Seton (1975), Revs. Joseph A. Spinelli, O.S.A.; James V. Vitali, O.S.A.
Res., 2760 52 Ter., S.W., 34116. Tel: 941-455-3900; Fax: 941-455-6895.
School—Tel: 941-455-2262; Fax: 941-455-0549. Mrs. Judy Mankowski, Prin.
Lay Teachers 13; Students 290.
Catechesis/Religious Programs—Tel: 941-455-9598. Cecelia Andretta, D.R.E.
Students 354.

Grove City, Charlotte Co., St. Francis of Assisi (1978), Revs. Bartholomew Larkin, O.Carm.; Morris Wells, O.Carm.
Res., 80 Oakland Hills Pl., Rotanda West, 33947. Tel: 941-697-4899; Fax: 941-697-0602.
Church—5265 Placida Rd., 34224. [CEM]
Catechesis/Religious Programs—Sr. Monica Hayes, D.R.E.
Students 120.

Holmes Beach, Manatee Co., St. Bernard's (1956), Revs. Patrick E. Farrell; Donald E. Baier.
Res., 248 S. Harbor Dr., 34217, P.O. Box 1036, 34218. Tel: 941-778-4769; Fax: 941-778-4644.
Catechesis/Religious Programs—Tel: 941-778-0277. Alice White, D.R.E.
Students 95.

Immokalee, Collier Co., Our Lady of Guadalupe (1957), Revs. Vilmar Orsolin, C.S.; Onorio Benacchio, C.S.; Jean Woady Louis.
Res., 207 S. 9th St., 34142. Tel: 941-657-2666; Fax: 941-657-3431.
Catechesis/Religious Programs—Mrs. Maria Marquez, D.R.E.
Students 185.

LaBelle, Hendry Co., Our Lady Queen of Heaven (1975), Revs. Normando Feliz; Origenes Noboa, Pastoral Assoc.; Deacon Vincent Walsh.
Res., 355 S. Bridge St., P.O. Box 357, 33935. Tel: 941-675-0030; Fax: 941-675-0756. [JC]
Catechesis/Religious Programs—Tel: 941-675-7447; 675-3724. Sr. Muriel Cameron, D.R.E.
Students 220.

Lake Placid, Highland Co., St. James, Revs. Vincent Llaria (Spain); Leo J. Culliton (BUF) (Retired); John J. Koros (OM) (Retired); Raymond Jones (DET) (Retired).
Mailing Address: 3380 Placid View Dr., 33852. Tel: 941-465-3215; Fax: 941-465-0649. [JC]
120 Citrus Rd., N.E., 33852. Rev. Raymond Jones (DET), (Retired), 779 Hawk Ave., 33852.
Catechesis/Religious Programs—Students 30.
Comunidad Catolica Hispana Santiago Apostol, Highlands, (1991) (Hispanic), Rev. Jose Gonzalez.
Mailing Address: P.O. Box 899, 33862. Tel: 941-385-6762; Fax: 941-385-3337.
Res., 685 CR 621 E., 33852. Tel: 941-465-1800.
Catechesis/Religious Programs—Students 50.

Lehigh Acres, Lee Co., St. Raphael (1962), Revs. James Flemming; Walter Swietek (Poland); Deacons James Jacob; Lambert Kuhr; Armindo Guzman.
Res., 2514 Lee Blvd., 33971. Tel: 941-369-1831; Fax: 941-369-1039. [JC]
Catechesis/Religious Programs—Tel: 941-369-6424. James C. Brantner, D.R.E.
Students 240.

Longboat Key, Manatee Co., St. Mary Star of the Sea (1973), Rev. Edward Pick.
Res., 4280 Gulf of Mexico Dr., Box 60, 34228. Tel: 941-383-1255; Fax: 941-383-8758.

Marco Island, Collier Co., San Marco (1971), Revs. Eugene J. McCarthy; Stanislaw J. Strycharz.
Res., 851 San Marco Rd., 33937. Tel: 941-394-5181; Fax: 941-394-1385.
Catechesis/Religious Programs—Tel: 941-394-4068. David Swierczek, D.R.E.
Students 264.
Mission—Everglades City, Collier Co., Holy Family, 200 Datura St., Everglades City, 33929.

Moore Haven, Glades Co., St. Joseph the Worker (1960) (Spanish), Rev. Emilian Swiatecki.
Res., Hwy. 27 and St. Rd. 78, P.O. Box 1109, 33471. Tel: 941-946-0696; Fax: 941-946-3444. [JC]
Mission—Buckhead Ridge, Glades Co., St. Theresa of the Child Jesus, Hwy. 78 & Chobee Loop, Box 1109, 33471. Tel: 941-946-0696.

Murdock, Charlotte Co., St. Maximilian Kolbe (1988), Rev. Robert Mattingly; Deacons Louis Cosentino; Edgar Cobett.
Office: 1441 Spear St., 33948. Tel: 941-743-6877; Fax: 941-743-9176.
Catechesis/Religious Programs—Barbara Sutton, Pastoral Assoc.
Students 45.

Naples, Collier Co.,

1—ST. ANN, (1935), Very Rev. Robert D. Tabbert, V.F.; Revs. George Ratzmann; Julius Lang.
Res., 407-439 Ninth Ave., S., 33940. Tel: 941-262-4256; Fax: 941-262-4296.
School—542 Eighth Ave., S., 33940. Tel: 941-262-4110; Fax: 941-262-3991. Sr. George Francis Riseling, S.N.J.M., Acting Prin.
Sisters 1; Lay Teachers 22; Students 302.
Catechesis/Religious Programs—Tel: 941-262-4785.
Students 246.

2—ST. JOHN THE EVANGELIST, (1988), Revs. Thomas J. Glackin; Donald H. Henry.
Res., 625 111th Ave., N., 34108. Tel: 941-566-8740; Fax: 941-566-9117. [CEM]
Catechesis/Religious Programs—Students 600.

3—ST. PETER THE APOSTLE, (1974), Revs. Timothy M. Navin, Admin.; Robert M. Murphy; Deacons David Nolan; John J. O'Neill; Robert L. Tetrault; Michael Salerno.
Res., 5130 Rattlesnake Hammock Rd., 34113. Tel: 941-774-3337; Fax: 941-774-3077.
Catechesis/Religious Programs—Students 299.
Mission—San Pedro, Collier Co., 5330 Caldwell St., 34113. Tel: 941-774-3111. Rev. Felix Alarcon (RVC).

4—ST. WILLIAM, (1973), Revs. Joseph E. Stearns; John F. Costello.
Res., 750 Seagate Dr., 34103-2886. Tel: 941-261-4883; Fax: 941-261-8729. [JC]
Catechesis/Religious Programs—Tel: 941-263-5429. Debra Mahr, D.R.E.
Students 285.

North Port, Sarasota Co., San Pedro (1964), Rev. Patrick C. Organ.
Res., 14380 Tamiami Tr., 34287. Tel: 941-426-2500; 426-6810; Fax: 941-423-8710.
Catechesis/Religious Programs—Tel: 941-426-2893.
Students 229.

Palmetto, Manatee Co., Holy Cross (1956), Revs. Nicanor Lobato; Robert J. Brague (SCR).
Res., 506-26th St. W., 34221. Tel: 941-729-3891. [JC]

Parrish, Manatee, St. Francis Xavier Cabrini (1992), Rev. Janusz Jancarz (Poland).
Res., 12001 69th St., P.O. Box 221, 34219. Tel: 941-776-9097; Fax: 941-776-1307.

Port Charlotte, Charlotte Co., St. Charles Borromeo (1959), Revs. Nicholas McLoughlin; William Penn; Thomas Wantland; John J. Mulvey; Vicente M. Martin.
Office and Church: 21505 Augusta Ave., Ste. 4, 33952. Tel: 941-625-4754; Fax: 941-625-0256. [JC]
School—Tel: 941-625-5533; Fax: 941-625-7359. Dr. Mary Santini, Prin.
Lay Teachers 14; Students 256.
Catechesis/Religious Programs—21505 Augusta Ave., Ste. 5, 33952. Tel: 941-625-5407. Mrs. Elizabeth Hinks, D.R.E.
Students 340.
San Antonio (1993), Rev. Thomas J. Zedar.
24445 Rampart Blvd., 33980. Tel: 941-624-3799; Fax: 941-624-6184.
Catechesis/Religious Programs—Students 212.

Punta Gorda, Charlotte Co., Sacred Heart (1954), Rev. Robert Mongiello; Deacons Edward D. Lundy; Anthony Zammett.
Res., 211 W. Charlotte Ave., 33950-5546. Tel: 941-639-3957; Fax: 941-639-2061.
Catechesis/Religious Programs—Tel: 941-639-9545. Sr. Josine Perez, D.R.E.
Students 140.

Sanibel, Lee Co., St. Isabel (1973), Rev. Msgr. Robert W. Schiefen; Rev. Carmen A. Caruso (JOL).
Res., 3559 Sanibel-Captiva Rd., 33957. Tel: 941-472-2763; Fax: 941-472-5351.
Catechesis/Religious Programs—Tel: 941-395-0070.
Students 107.

Sarasota, Sarasota Co.,

1—INCARNATION, (1958), Revs. Gerard Finegan; Joseph Clifford; John J. Ludden; Jeremiah Spillane; Deacon Joseph Cirieco.
Res., 2929 Bee Ridge Rd., P.O. Box 5516, 34277-5516. Tel: 941-921-6631; Fax: 941-927-2521.
School—Tel: 941-924-8588; Fax: 941-925-1248. Sr. Monica Paul Fraser, Prin.
Sisters 2; Lay Teachers 19; Students 305.
Catechesis/Religious Programs—Tel: 941-924-9566. John Garisto, D.R.E.
Students 611.

2—OUR LADY QUEEN OF MARTYRS, Manatee Co., (1959), Revs. Joseph Connolly, T.O.R.; Damian-Vincent Amantia, T.O.R.; Louis McIntyre, T.O.R.; Deacon Jesse E. Pipher. In res., Rev. Sean Sullivan, T.O.R., (Retired).
Res., 833 Magellan Dr., 34243. Tel: 941-755-1826; Fax: 941-753-1654. [CEM]
Catechesis/Religious Programs—34243. Tel: 941-755-3497. Nina Powell, D.R.E.
Students 360.

3—ST. MARTHA, (1912), Revs. Fausto Stampiglia, S.A.C.; Benedict Abraham, S.A.C.; Jose Poovakulath, S.A.C.; Vincent L. Clemente, Hospital Min.; Joseph S. Amato, J.C.L.; Celestino Gutierrez, Spanish Min.; Deacon John D. Wren, Jr.
Res., 235 Adelia St., P.O. Box 1706, 34230. Tel: 941-366-4210; Fax: 941-954-8434.
School—801 N. Orange Ave., 34236. Tel: 941-953-4181; Fax: 941-366-5580. Miss Carolyn Wheelock, Prin.
Lay Teachers 16; Students 321.
Catechesis/Religious Programs—Bro. R. Patrick Wilson, D.R.E.
Students 455.

4—ST. MICHAEL THE ARCHANGEL, (1958), Revs. Claude E. Brubaker; John C. Rourke.
Res., 5394 Midnight Pass Rd., 34242. Tel: 941-349-4174; Fax: 941-349-6388.
Catechesis/Religious Programs—Sr. Luke Crawford, S.P., D.R.E.
Students 87.

5—ST. PATRICK, (1988), Revs. Arthur W. Hannaway; George Brennan.
Res., 7900 Bee Ridge Rd., 34241. Tel: 941-378-1703; Fax: 941-378-2153.
Catechesis/Religious Programs—Tel: 941-378-1521.
Students 585.

6—ST. THOMAS MORE, (1979), Revs. Eugene D. Ryan; Jerome Callahan, O.Carm. Tel: 941-922-3273; Deacon Robert Horvath.
Mailing Address: 2506 Gulf Gate Dr., 34231. Tel: 941-923-1691; Fax: 941-923-1692.
Res., 2612 Regatta Dr., 34231. [CEM]

Catechesis/Religious Programs—Tel: 941-921-6334.

Students 17.

Sebring, Highlands Co., St. Catherine (1929), Very Rev. Jose H. Ruiz, V.F.; Rev. Robert E. Onze (BGP).

Res., 862 Bay St., P.O. Box 389, 33870. Tel: 941-385-0049; Fax: 941-385-5169. [CEM 2][JC]

Catechesis/Religious Programs—Tel: 941-385-3993. Sr. Joseph Louise Reichlin, O.S.F., D.R.E.

Students 106.

Wauchula, Hardee Co., St. Michael (1969) (Spanish-Creole), Revs. Michael Koncik, C.SS.R.; Edmund Regensburger, C.SS.R.; George H. Bridge, C.SS.R.; James J. Burke, C.SS.R.

Res., 408 Heard Bridge Rd., Rte. 2. Box 8A, 33873. Tel: 941-773-4089; Fax: 941-773-5641.

Catechesis/Religious Programs—Tel: 941-773-4215.

Students 400.

Convent—409 Alice St., 33873. Tel: 941-773-4215. Vincentian Sisters of Charity

Sisters 3.

Missions—Bowling Green, Hardee Co., Holy Child, Chester Ave., Bowling Green, 33834.; Zolfo Springs, Hardee Co., San Alfonso Catholic Center, Schoolhouse Rd., Zolfo Springs, 33890.

On Duty Outside the Diocese:
Reverend Fathers—
Heuberger, Mark, Treas., St. Vincent de Paul Regional Seminary, 10701 S. Military Tr., Boynton Beach, FL 33436 Italy

---

Military Chaplains:
Reverend Fathers—
Kowalik, Jacek, Lackland AFB, TX 78236-1038
McLaughlin, Paul E., U.S. Navy, U.S. Marine Corps Air Station, Beaufort, SC 29904-5001

Awaiting Assignment:
Reverend Fathers—
Sikorski, Leszek M.

Absent on Leave:
Reverend Fathers—
Cikovic, Charles
Espin, Orlando O.
McGraw, John
McLoughlin, Edward

Absent on Sick Leave:
Reverend Monsignors—
LaFemina, Anthony A.
Reverend Fathers—
Morillo, Jose

Priests Released from Diocesan Assignment:
Reverend Fathers—
O'Connell, William
Walk, Donald J.

Graduate Studies:
Reverend Fathers—
Menzies, Scott

Retired:
Reverend Monsignors—
Mouch, Frank M.
O'Dowd, John
Reverend Fathers—
Bentivoglio, Louis
Cronin, David
Dittman, Bernard F.
Duggan, Joseph P.
Gonzalez, Mario
Gorr, Benjamin
Loncar, Sebastian
Moran, Joseph P.
Romero, William

Permanent Deacons:
Attridge, James (NY)
Blackburn, John L.
Brodeur, Wilfred (CIN)
Cabrera, Crescencio (BO)
Camacho, Francis (FR)
Cirieco, Joseph
Cobett, Edgar
Cole, Francis (HRT)
Cook, James (TR)
Cooper, James
Cosentino, Louis A. (Y)
Crant, Ellis (PHX)
DiMeglio, Michael
DiSalvo, Aldo (HRT)
Dubay, Frank
Fathauer, Ronald (MIA)
Fortier, W. Lorin
Fox, Leonard (TOL)
Geary, Coleman (SFD)
Gilbert, John
Grant, Russ (WH)
Gratkowski, Daniel (PEO)
Groh, Al (TR)
Guzman, Armindo (MIL)
Harkin, John
Hedge, Dennis
Horvath, Robert (NY)
Jackson, Frank (TR)
Jacob, James (HRT)
Jolin, Joseph (NOR)
Kiesel, Charles
King, Lorin (WOR)
Kuhr, Lambert (SAG)
Loafman, Frank (DET)
Lundy, Edward
McGreen, Michael (RVC)
Nolan, David W.
Nowak, Richard (JOL)
O'Grady, Lowell
O'Neill, John
Pipher, Jessie (NY)
Rowland, James (TR)
Salerno, Michael (JOL)
Schaupp, Larry (TOL)
Tetrault, Robert (JOL)
Thoresen, Norman (MIL)
Tomasso, Robert (CHI)
Urrico, Francis (PRO)
Walsh, Vincent P. (FR)
Walton, Gilbert Jr. (HRT)
Wren, John, Jr.
Zammett, Antony (HRT)

INSTITUTIONS LOCATED IN THE DIOCESE

[A] HIGH SCHOOLS

FORT MYERS. *Bishop Verot High School*, 5598 Sunrise Dr., 33919. Tel: 941-936-6700; Fax: 941-936-1753. Oblates of St. Francis de Sales. Revs. Christopher J. Hudgin, O.S.F.S., Prin. & Supr.; Joseph A. Beattie, O.S.F.S.; John A. Beattie, O.S.F.S.; Hugh McGuigan, O.S.F.S.; Patrick O'Connor, O.S.F.S. Priests 5; Lay Teachers 48; Students 685; Total Staff 74.

NAPLES. *St. John Neumann High School*, 3000 53rd St., S.W., 34116. Tel: 941-455-3044; Fax: 941-455-2966. Congregation of Christian Brothers. Bros. F. Damian Ryan, C.F.C., Prin.; John C. O'Neill, C.F.C.; Edward Sheehan, C.F.C.; Spencer Tafuri, C.F.C. Brothers 4; Lay Teachers 19; Students 299.

SARASOTA. *Cardinal Mooney High School*, 4171 Fruitville Rd., 34232. Tel: 941-371-4917; Fax: 941-371-6924. Sisters of Notre Dame of Chardon, OH. Sr. Mary Lucia Haas, S.N.D., Pres.; Mr. Stephen J. Christie, Prin. Sisters 4; Lay Teachers 38; Students 625; Total Staff 65.

[B] SCHOOLS FOR THEOLOGICAL, SPIRITUAL, PASTORAL AND PERSONAL FORMATION

PORT CHARLOTTE. *Blessed Edmund Rice School for Pastoral Ministry*, 2200 Kings Hwy., Bldg. 3L, Ste. 65, 33980-5760. Tel: 941-624-6339; Fax: 941-629-8555. Bro. Paul K. Hennessy, C.F.C., Pres. Priests 1; Sisters 1; Brothers 1; Students 96; Total Staff 7.

[C] MIGRANT EDUCATION

BONITA SPRINGS. *Migrant Education Apostolate, Los Hermanos*, P.O. Box 716, 34133. Tel: 941-947-9098. Brothers 3.

[D] GENERAL HOSPITALS

VENICE. *Bon Secours-Venice Healthcare Corp.*, 540 The Rialto, 34285. Tel: 941-483-7664.
E-mail: roy_hess@BSHSI.com
Web site: www.bshsi-florida.com
For a complete listing, refer to the Hospitals section.

PORT CHARLOTTE. *Bon Secours-St. Joseph Hospital*, 2500 Harbor Blvd., 33952. Tel: 941-625-4122.
E-mail: jim_hoff@bshsi.com
For a complete listing, refer to the Hospitals section.

[E] NURSING AND CONVALESCENT HOMES

PORT CHARLOTTE. *Bon Secours-St. Joseph Nursing Care Center, Inc.*, 2370 Harbor Blvd., 33952. Tel: 941-624-5966; Fax: 941-624-3963
For a complete listing, refer to the Special Care Facilities section.

[F] RESIDENCES FOR THE AGED

FORT MYERS. *Villa Francisco*, 2140 Cottage St., 33901. Tel: 941-332-3229
For a complete listing, refer to the Special Care Facilities section.

PORT CHARLOTTE. *St. Charles Housing I, Inc.*, 2550 Easy St., 33952. Tel: 941-624-2266
For a complete listing, refer to the Special Care Facilities section.

St. Charles Housing II, Inc., 22250 Vick St., 33980. Tel: 941-624-4404; Fax: 941-624-5556
For a complete listing, refer to the Special Care Facilities section.

SARASOTA. *St. Martha's Housing II, Inc.*, 800 N. Lemon Ave., 34236. Tel: 941-365-7913; Fax: 941-365-8887
For a complete listing, refer to the Special Care Facilities section.

St. Martha's Housing, Inc., 1576 Eighth St., 34236. Tel: 941-366-4448
For a complete listing, refer to the Special Care Facilities section.

[G] MONASTERIES AND RESIDENCES OF PRIESTS AND BROTHERS

VENICE. *Carmel in Venice*, 244 Harbor Dr., S., 34285. Tel: 941-485-0606. Revs. Gerard Benson, O.Carm.; Joel Schevers, O.Carm. Priests 2.

St. Alphonsus Residence, 1230 Schooner Ln., 34292. Tel: 941-485-3673. Rev. Charles Mallen, C.SS.R., Supr.

Xavieran Brothers, 609 Cornwell on the Gulf, 34285. Tel: 941-484-9641. Brothers of St. Francis Xavier - Retired. Brothers 2.

ENGLEWOOD. *Society of St. Edmund Residence*, 611 W. Harvard St., 34223. Tel: 941-473-8214. Revs. Casimir Cichanowicz, S.S.E.; Gerard Grace, S.S.E.; Edward Leary, S.S.E.; Francis Moriarty, S.S.E.; Maurice F. Ouellet, S.S.E.; Thomas D. Sullivan, S.S.E., Facilitator; Bro. George Francis Huyer, S.S.E.

FORT MYERS. *Oblates of St. Francis de Sales*, 5598 Sunrise Dr., 33919. Tel: 941-939-5334. Priests 5.

NAPLES. *St. John Neumann High School Faculty Residence*, 3180 53rd St., S.W., 33999. Tel: 941-455-2255. Congregation of Christian Brothers. Brothers 4.

SARASOTA. *Congregation of the Holy Ghost*, 438-464 Golden Gate Pt., 34236. Tel: 941-955-1546; 941-957-3025; Fax: 941-953-4725. Revs. Raymond J. Kulwicki, C.S.Sp., Supr.; Stephen J. Lasko, C.S.Sp.; John R. Kanda, C.S.Sp.; Timothy T. McDonough, C.S.Sp.; William J. Jackson, C.S.Sp.; Henry C. Schoming, C.S.Sp.; Henry C. Lemmens, C.S.Sp.; David C. Marshall, C.S.Sp.; Cornelius Van Der Poel, C.S.Sp.; Anthony A. Bacher, C.S.Sp.; Louis F. Dolan, C.S.Sp.; W. Robert Graves, C.S.Sp. Total in Residence 12.

Holy Cross Florida Regional Center, 1635 4th St., 34236. Tel: 941-365-0722. Holy Cross Brothers Residence.

[H] CONVENTS AND RESIDENCES FOR SISTERS

FORT MYERS BEACH. *San Damiano Monastery of St. Clare.* (Solemn Vows, Papal Enclosure), 6029 Estero Blvd., 33931-4325. Tel: 941-463-5599; Fax: 941-463-4993. Poor Clares. Sr. Mary Emmanuel Kilkenny, O.S.C., Abbess. Cloistered Sisters 4.

[I] RETREAT CENTERS

VENICE. *Our Lady of Perpetual Help Retreat and Spirituality Center*, 3989 S. Moon Dr., 34292. Tel: 941-486-0233. Rev. Charles Mallen, C.SS.R., Dir.

ALVA. *Mother of God House of Prayer*, 17880 Cypress Creek Rd., 33920. Tel: 941-728-3614; Fax: 941-728-3760. Sr. Sallie Latkovich, C.S.J., Dir. Total in Residence 3; Total Staff 5.

BRADENTON. *Zacchaeus Retreat House*, St. Joseph Parish, 2704 33rd Ave., W., 34205. Tel: 941-755-5812; Fax: 941-753-4095.

[J] CATHOLIC CHARITIES

VENICE. *Catholic Charities of the Diocese of Venice, Inc.*, 1000 Pinebrook Rd., 34292. Rosemary Winder Strange, Exec. Dir.

Our Mother's House, 405 Manatee Ct., 34285. Tel: 941-485-6264.
Web site: www.ymnetwork.net/omh.
Catherine Christensen, Dir. Total Assisted 100; Total in Residence 10 women. Social housing program for single mothers offering free child care.

Adult residents must attend full-time educational or vocational training.

ARCADIA. *Catholic Charities of De Soto County*, 1210 E. Oak St., 34266. Tel: 941-494-1068; Fax: 941-494-1671.

Care-A-Van, 1210 E. Oak St., 34266. Tel: 941-494-1068. Total Assisted 3,872; Total Staff 5.

FORT MYERS. *Catholic Hispanic Social Services*, 4235 Michigan Ave. Link, P.O. Box 50301, 33994. Tel: 941-337-4193; Fax: 941-332-2799. A. Lissette, Dir. Total Assisted 3,772; Total Staff 7.

IMMOKALEE. *Guadalupe Social Services*, 211 S. Ninth St., P.O. Box 5034, 34143. Tel: 941-657-6242; Fax: 941-657-7761.
E-mail: brjim@juno.com
Total Assisted 4,052; Total Staff 5.

NAPLES. *Catholic Charities of Collier County*, Counseling Services, 2210 Santa Barbara Blvd., 34116. Tel: 941-455-2655; Fax: 941-455-7235.

Emergency Assistance, Family Resource Center, 2408 Linwood Ave., Ste. #1, 34112. Tel: 941-793-0059.

PALMETTO. *Palmetto Catholic Charities*, 506 26 St., W., 34221. Tel: 941-721-0924 (Housing); Fax: 941-722-1063. Total Assisted 1,900; Total Staff 3.

SARASOTA. *Catholic Charities District I*. Counseling Services. 1900 Main St., Ste. 204, 34236. Tel: 941-957-4496; Fax: 941-951-0223. Emergency Assistance. Tel: 941-955-6597.

Refugees Employed & Productive (REAP), 4029 N. Washington Blvd., Ste. K, 32434. Tel: 941-359-0352; Fax: 941-359-2244.

[K] FOUNDATIONS

VENICE. *Cardinal Mooney High School Foundation*, Catholic Center, 1000 Pinebrook Rd., 34292. Mailing Address: P.O. Box 2006, 34284. Tel: 941-484-9543.

Foundation for the Care of the Migrant Poor, 1000 Pinebrook Rd., 34292.

FORT MYERS. *The Bishop Verot High School Foundation*, 5598 Sunrise Dr., 33919. Tel: 941-936-6700. Rev. Christopher J. Hudgin, O.S.F.S.

St. Francis Xavier School Foundation, 2133 Heitman St., 33901. Tel: 941-334-2161; Fax: 941-332-4178. Very Rev. Thomas M. Anglim, V.G., Pres.; Dr. Michael Kyle, Chm.

NAPLES.

**St. Ann School Foundation, Inc.*, 407 Ninth Ave., S., 34102. Jean K. Clagett, Exec. Dir.

SARASOTA. *Incarnation School Foundation*, 2911 Bee Ridge Rd., 34239.

[L] MISCELLANEOUS LISTINGS

FORT MYERS. *Societies of St. Vincent de Paul*, 2200 First St., 33901. Tel: 941-334-2736. Mr. William J. Martyn, Diocesan Trustee.
District Council of Fort Myers, District Council of Manasota, District Council of Naples.

IMMOKALEE.

**The Guadalupe Center*, 211 S. Ninth St., P.O. Box 1053, 33934. Tel: 941-657-4361; Fax: 941-657-6816. Sr. Judith A. Dohner, H.M., Dir. Total Assisted 40,000; Total Staff 25.

LAKE PLACID. Mailing Address: P.O. Box 899, 33862. Tel: 941-385-6762. Rev. Jose Gonzalez, Priest-in-Charge of the Spanish speaking people of Highlands Co.

PORT CHARLOTTE. *Pregnancy Crisis Careline, Inc.*, 2500 Harbor Blvd., P.O. Box 3028, 33949-3028. 21234 Olean Blvd., Ste. 4, P.O. Box 3028, 33949-3028. Olivia S. Becker, Dir. & Pres. Total Assisted 3,435; Total Staff 60.

SARASOTA. *Bethesda House*. (AIDS Ministry), P.O. Box 1706, 34230. Tel: 941-366-1886. Sr. Frances Nevolo, O.L.C. Total Assisted 3,944; Total Staff 2.

RELIGIOUS INSTITUTES OF MEN REPRESENTED IN THE DIOCESE

For further details refer to the corresponding bracketed number in the Religious Institutes of Men or Women section.

[0140]—*The Augustinians*.—O.S.A.
[0200]—*Benedictine Monks*.—O.S.B.
[1350]—*Brothers of St. Francis Xavier (Sacred Heart Province, St. Joseph Province)*.—C.F.X.
[0600]—*Brothers of the Congregation of Holy Cross*.—C.S.C.
[0270]—*Carmelite Fathers & Brothers*.—O.Carm.
[0310]—*Congregation of Christian Brothers*.—C.F.C.
[0480]—*Conventual Franciscans*.—O.F.M.Conv.
[0430]—*Dominican Fathers*.—O.P.
[0650]—*Holy Ghost Fathers*.—C.S.Sp.
[0300]—*Institute of Charity (Rosminians)*.—I.C.
[1210]—*Missionaries of St. Charles Scalabrians*.—C.S.
[0590]—*Missionaries of the Holy Apostles*.—M.Ss.A.
[0920]—*Oblates of St. Francis de Sales*.—O.S.F.S.
[1000]—*Passionist Fathers*.—C.P.
[1070]—*Redemptorist Fathers*.—C.SS.R.
[0700]—*St. Joseph's Society of the Sacred Heart*.—S.S.J.
[0110]—*Society of African Missions*.—S.M.A.
[0440]—*Society of St. Edmund*.—S.S.E.
[0990]—*Society of the Catholic Apostolate*.—S.A.C.
[0560]—*Third Order Regular of St. Francis*.—T.O.R.

RELIGIOUS INSTITUTES OF WOMEN REPRESENTED IN THE DIOCESE

[0270]—*Congregation of Bon Secours*. (Marriotsville, MD).—C.B.S.
[1070-15]—*Congregation of St. Dominic (Sisters of St. Dominic of Blauvelt, NY)*.—O.P.
[1920]—*Congregation of the Sisters of the Holy Cross*.—C.S.C.
[1710]—*Congregation of the Third Order of St. Francis of Mary Immaculate*.—O.S.F.
[1070-06]—*Dominican Sisters of Hope*.—O.P.
[1070-02]—*Dominican Sisters of St. Mary of the Springs*.—O.P.
[1070-13]—*Dominican Sisters / Congregation of the Most Holy Rosary (Adrian Dominicans)*.—O.P.
[1070-03]—*Dominican Sisters / Sinsinawa Dominican Congregation of the Most Holy Rosary*.—O.P.
[1170]—*Felician Sisters*.—C.S.S.F.
[1180]—*Franciscan Sisters of Allegheny, NY*.—O.S.F.
[2420]—*Marist Missionary Sisters*.—S.M.S.M.
[1845]—*Missionares Guadalupanas del Espiritu Santo*.—M.G.Sp.S.
[]—*Missionaries Daughters of Our Blessed Lady of the Light, Yucatan, Mexico*.—M.H.M.L.
[1360]—*Missionary Franciscan Sisters of the Immaculate Conception*. (Newton, MA).—O.S.F.
[2800]—*Missionary Sisters of the Most Sacred Heart of Jesus of Hilltrup*.—M.S.C.
[3070]—*North American Union of Sisters of Our Lady of Charity*.—N.A.U.-O.L.C.
[3760]—*Order of St. Clare*.—O.S.C.
[3465]—*Religious of the Sacred Heart of Mary (Eastern North American Province)*.—R.S.H.M.
[2970]—*School Sisters of Notre Dame*. (Baltimore Prov.) and Northeastern Prov. (Wilton, CT).—S.S.N.D.
[1680]—*School Sisters of St. Francis*.—O.S.F.
[0590]—*Sisters of Charity of St. Elizabeth, Convent Station*.—S.C.
[0430]—*Sisters of Charity of the Blessed Virgin Mary*.—B.V.M.
[]—*Sisters of Mercy, Co. Longford, Ireland*.—R.S.M.
[2990]—*Sisters of Notre Dame*. (Chardon, OH).—S.N.D.
[3360]—*Sisters of Providence of St. Mary-of-the-Woods, IN*.—S.P.
[3720]—*Sisters of St. Ann*. (Marlboro, MA).—S.S.A.
[1630]—*Sisters of St. Francis of Pennance and Christian Charity*.—O.S.F.
[1650]—*Sisters of St. Francis of Philadelphia*.—O.S.F.
[3830-01]—*Sisters of St. Joseph of Boston*.—C.S.J.
[3840]—*Sisters of St. Joseph of Carondelet*.—C.S.J.
[3830-08]—*Sisters of St. Joseph of Cleveland*.—C.S.J.
[3830-14]—*Sisters of St. Joseph of Rochester*.—S.S.J.
[1990]—*Sisters of the Holy Name of Jesus and Mary*.—S.N.J.M.
[2110]—*Sisters of the Humility of Mary*.—H.M.
[2180]—*Sisters of the Immaculate Heart of Mary*. (Miami).—I.H.M.
[3730]—*Sisters of the Order of St. Basil the Great*.—O.S.B.M.
[1490]—*Sisters of the Third Franciscan Order*.—O.S.F.
[1710]—*Sisters of the Third Order of St. Francis*.—O.S.F.
[1760]—*Sisters of the Third Order of St. Francis of Penance and of Charity*. (Tiffin, OH).—O.S.F.
[2150]—*Sisters, Servants of the Immaculate Heart of Mary*. (Monroe, MI).—I.H.M.
[2160]—*Sisters, Servants of the Immaculate Heart of Mary*. (Scranton, PA).—I.H.M.
[4060]—*Society of the Holy Child Jesus*.—S.H.C.J.
[4070]—*Society of the Sacred Heart*.—R.S.C.J.
[4160]—*Vincentian Sisters of Charity*.—V.S.C.

NECROLOGY

† Beaumont, Joseph, (Retired). —Died June 22, 1997.

Diocese of Victoria in Texas

(Dioecesis Victoriensis in Texia)

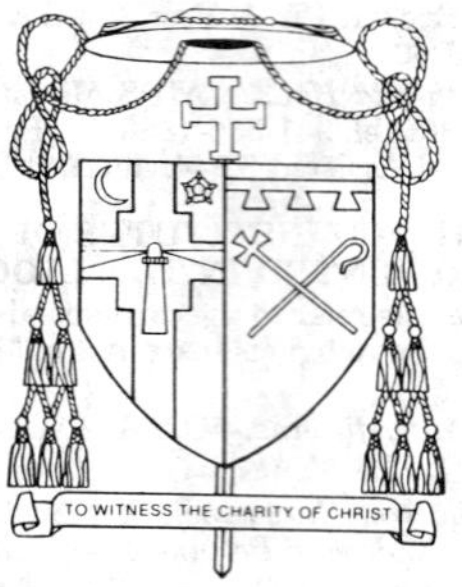

Most Reverend

DAVID E. FELLHAUER, PH.D., J.C.D.

Bishop of Victoria; ordained May 29, 1965; appointed Second Bishop of Victoria in Texas April 7, 1990; consecrated and installed May 28, 1990. *Res., 302 East Red River, Victoria, TX, 77901. Direct all official correspondence to: P.O. Box 4070, Victoria, TX, 77903.*

Legal Title: Diocese of Victoria in Texas.

ESTABLISHED AND CREATED A DIOCESE, MAY 29, 1982.

Square Miles Approximately 9,609.

Comprises the Counties of Calhoun, DeWitt, Goliad, Jackson, Lavaca, Matagorda, Victoria, Wharton and Colorado; also Fayette County west of the Colorado River in the State of Texas.

For legal titles of parishes and diocesan institutions, consult the Chancery Office.

Chancery Office: P.O. Box 4070, Victoria, TX, 77903. Tel.: 512-573-0828; Fax: 512-573-5725.

STATISTICAL OVERVIEW

Personnel	
Bishop	1
Priests: Diocesan Active in Diocese	44
Priests: Active Outside Diocese	3
Priests: Diocesan in Foreign Missions	1
Priests: Retired, Sick or Absent	8
Number of Diocesan Priests	56
Religious Priests in Diocese	10
Extern Priests in Diocese	10
Permanent Deacons in Diocese	21
Total Brothers	1
Total Sisters	131
Parishes	
Parishes	50
With Resident Pastor:	
Resident Diocesan Priests	40
Resident Religious Priests	5
Without Resident Pastor:	
Administered by Priests	5
Missions	21
Professional Ministry Personnel:	
Brothers	1
Sisters	21
Lay Ministers	15
Welfare	
Homes for the Aged	1
Total Assisted	59
Educational	
Diocesan Students in Other Seminaries	9
Students Religious	2
Total Seminarians	11
High Schools, Diocesan and Parish	2
Total Students	166
High Schools, Private	1
Total Students	425
Elementary Schools, Diocesan and Parish	12
Total Students	2,208
Elementary Schools, Private	1
Total Students	500
Catechesis/Religious Education:	
High School Students	2,991
Elementary Students	7,167
Total Students Under Catholic Instruction	13,468
Teachers in the Diocese:	
Sisters	23
Lay Teachers	213
Vital Statistics	
Receptions into the Church:	
Infant Baptism Totals	1,538
Adult Baptism Totals	80
Received into Full Communion	137
First Communions	1,619
Confirmations	1,253
Marriages:	
Catholic	351
Interfaith	145
Total Marriages	496
Deaths	964
Total Catholic Population	108,562
Total Population	255,276

Former Bishops—Most Rev. CHARLES V. GRAHMANN, D.D., ord. March 17, 1956; appt. Titular Bishop of Equilio and Auxiliary of San Antonio, June 30, 1981; cons. Aug. 29, 1981; appt. First Bishop of Victoria, April 14, 1982; installed May 29, 1982; appt. Coadjutor of Dallas, Dec. 18, 1989; succeeded to See, July 14, 1990.

Chancery Office—1505 E. Mesquite Ln., Victoria, 77901. Mailing Address: P.O. Box 4070, Victoria, 77903. Tel: 512-573-0828; Fax: 512-573-5725. Office Hours: Mon.-Fri. 8:30-4:30.

Vicars General—Rev. Msgr. THOMAS C. MCLAUGHLIN, *P.O. Box 4070, Victoria, 77903.* Rev. Msgr. JAMES C. BRUNNER, *2001 Katy St., Bay City, 77414.*

Chancellor—Rev. Msgr. THOMAS C. MCLAUGHLIN, V.G., *P.O. Box 4070, Victoria, 77903.* Vice-Chancellor, Rev. GARY W. JANAK, J.C.L., *St. Joseph Church, P.O. Box 734, Yoakum, 77995.* Tel: 512-293-3518.

Diocesan Consultors—Rev. Msgr. THOMAS C. MCLAUGHLIN, V.G.; Rev. Msgr. JAMES C. BRUNNER, V.G.; Revs. JOHN C. BILY; GARY W. JANAK; CASIMIR JARZOMBEK, V.F.; TIMOTHY KOSLER, V.F.; LAWRENCE MATULA, V.F.; JOHN C. PETERS, V.F.; DONALD R. RUPPERT.

Vicars Forane—Victoria Deanery: Rev. MICHAEL HARROLD, V.F., *Our Lady of Victory Cathedral, 1309 E. Mesquite Ln., Victoria, 77901.* Tel: 512-575-4741. Cuero Deanery: Rev. WILLIAM DORAN, V.F., *SS. Peter & Paul, HC-01, P.O. Box 49B, Meyersville, 77974.* Tel: 512-275-3868. Edna Deanery: Rev. CASIMIR JARZOMBEK, V.F., *St. Anthony Church, P.O. Box 900, Palacios, 77465.* Tel: 512-972-2446. El Campo Deanery: Rev. LAWRENCE MATULA, V.F., *St. Robert Bellarmine Church, 512 Tegner, El Campo, 77437.* Tel: 409-543-4298. Hallettsville Deanery: Rev. JOHN C. PETERS, V.F., *Sacred Heart Church, P.O. Box H, Hallettsville, 77964.* Tel: 512-798-5888. Schulenburg Deanery: Rev. TIMOTHY KOSLER, V.F., *St. Rose of Lima Church, 1010 Lyons Ave., Schulenburg, 78956.* Tel: 409-743-3117.

Presbyteral Council—Rev. Msgr. THOMAS C. MCLAUGHLIN, V.G.; Rev. Msgr. JAMES C. BRUNNER, V.G.; Revs. JOHN C. PETERS, V.F.; CASIMIR JARZOMBEK, V.F.; LAWRENCE MATULA, V.F.; WILLIAM DORAN, V.F.; DANIEL GIORGI, O.SS.T.; JOHN BILY; MICHAEL HARROLD, V.F.; TIMOTHY KOSLER, V.F.; GARY W. JANAK; CHARLES SONNIER; MICHAEL LYONS; VICTOR SCOCCO, O.SS.T.; GABRIEL MAISON; DAN MORALES; DONALD RUPPERT.

Diocesan Tribunal—1505 E. Mesquite Ln., Victoria, 77901. Tel: 512-573-0760.

Judicial Vicar—Rev. Msgr. THOMAS C. MCLAUGHLIN, V.G.

Judges—Revs. JOHN C. BILY; MICHAEL HARROLD, V.F.; GARY JANAK, J.C.L.; GABRIEL MAISON, J.C.D.; CELESTINO SAY.

Promoter of Justice—Appointed as needed.

Procurator Advocate—Revs. BENTON THURMOND; MICHAEL LYONS; CHARLES DWOMOH; MATTHEW HUEHLEFELD.

Defenders of the Bond—Revs. EUSTACE HERMES; DAN MORALES; TIMOTHY KOSLER, V.F.; DANIEL P. KAHLICH; THU VAN NGUYEN; FRANK LENZ; GREG KORENEK.

Notaries—Mrs. MINNIE BOCHAT; Mrs. MARY HAAS.

Priests' Personnel Board—Rev. Msgr. THOMAS C. MCLAUGHLIN, V.G., Chancellor; Rev. Msgr. JAMES C. BRUNNER, V.G.; Revs. JOHN C. PETERS, V.F.; MICHAEL HARROLD, V.F.; LAWRENCE MATULA, V.F.; TIMOTHY KOSLER, V.F.; WILLIAM DORAN, V.F.; CASIMIR JARZOMBEK, V.F.

Building Board—Deacon A. R. WEARDEN; Mr. AL HESSLER; Mr. HENRY SCHROEDER; Mr. CHARLES BLUNTZER; Mr. JAMES MIORI; Mr. ED MARTINKA.

Business Administration Office—Deacon A. R. WEARDEN, Mgr.; Mrs. JUNE OHRT; Mrs. SHARON JONES, *P.O. Box 4070, Victoria, 77903.* Tel: 512-573-0828.

Campaign For Human Development and Catholic Relief Services—Rev. GERARD CERNOCH, Dir., *SS. Cyril and Methodius Church, P.O. Box 66, Shiner, 77984.* Tel: 512-594-3836.

Catholic Youth and Family Life Ministry—Mrs. BERNADETTE MERTA, Dir., *1505 E. Mesquite Ln., P.O. Box 4070, Victoria, 77901.* Tel: 512-573-0828.

Charismatic Renewal Movement—Sr. PERPETUA HAWES, I.W.B.S., *808 E. Nueces, Victoria, 77902.* Tel: 512-578-8456.

Council of Catholic Women (DCCW)—Rev. MICHAEL O'SHAUGHNESSEY, V.F., Moderator, *506 N. Allen, Edna, 77957.* Tel: 512-782-3588. Mrs. LILLIE MAE SCHERER, Chm., *1907 Locust Ave., Victoria, 77901.* Tel: 512-573-9547.

Diocesan Cemeteries—Rev. EUSTACE HERMES, Dir., *2303 E. Locust, P.O. Box 3098, Victoria, 77903.* Tel: 512-575-7337.

Diocesan Finance Board—Deacon A. R. WEARDEN; Mrs. BEATRICE GONZALEZ; Mrs. DOROTHY JORDAN; Mr. OTTO KALISHKO; Mr. ROMAN SHIMEK; Mr. GLEN VILLAFRANCA; Mr. JOHN STEVENSON; Rev. DONALD RUPPERT; Rev. Msgr. THOMAS C. MCLAUGHLIN, V.G.; Rev. Msgr. JAMES C. BRUNNER, V.G.

Diocesan Services Appeal—Mrs. DOROTHY JORDAN, Dir., *1505 E. Mesquite Ln., P.O. Box 4070, Victoria, 77901.* Tel: 512-573-0828.

Diocesan Office of Spiritual Renewal Center—Rev. THEODORE HAAG, O.F.M., *718A Gussie Schmidt Rd., Victoria, 77905-4303.* Tel: 512-572-0836.

Ecumenical Commission—Rev. WAYNE FLAGG, *SS. Peter & Paul, Rte. 2, Box 26, New Ulm, 78950.* Tel: 409-732-3430.

Presidio of La Bahia—Mr. NEWTON WARZECHA, *P.O. Box 57, Goliad, 77963.* Tel: 512-645-3752.

Liturgical Commission—Rev. EDWARD J. WINKLER, *310 N. Stevenson, Eagle Lake, 77434.* Tel: 409-234-2842.

Office of Catholic Schools—Sr. GLORIA CAIN, S.N.N.D., Supt., *P.O. Box 4070, Victoria, 77903.*

Permanent Diaconate Program—Rev. GABRIEL MAISON, J.C.D., Dir., *1505 E. Mesquite Ln., P.O. Box 4070, Victoria, 77903., P.O. Box 399, Moulton, 77975.*

Propagation of the Faith, Holy Childhood Association—Rev. Msgr. THOMAS C. MCLAUGHLIN, V.G., Dir.

Mission Cooperative Plan—Rev. Msgr. THOMAS C. MCLAUGHLIN, V.G., Dir., *Chancery Office, P.O. Box 4070, Victoria, 77903.*

Religious Education—Sr. DIGNA VELA, I.W.B.S., Dir., *1505 E. Mesquite Ln., P.O. Box 4070, Victoria, 77903.* Tel: 512-573-0828.

Respect Life-Pro Life—Rev. Msgr. JAMES C. BRUNNER, V.G., *Holy Cross Church, 2001 Katy St., Bay City, 77414.* Tel: 409-245-6379.

Rural Life Conference—Vacant.

Scouting—Rev. THU VAN NGUYEN, *St. Philip the Apostle, 304 W. Church St., El Campo, 77437.* Tel: 409-543-3770.

"The Catholic Lighthouse", Diocesan Newspaper—Ms. JACQUELINE SROUJI, Editor, *P.O. Box 4070, Victoria, 77903.* Tel: 512-573-0828.

Vietnamese American Apostolic Center—Rev. JOSEPH PHAM DUC TRIN, *St. Anthony Church, P.O. Box 900, Palacios, 77465.* Tel: 512-972-2685.

Vocations—Rev. MICHAEL LYONS, *P.O. Box 4070, Victoria, 77903.* Tel: 512-573-0828.

Director of Seminarians—Rev. GARY W. JANAK, *St. Joseph Church, P.O. Box 734, Yoakum, TX. 77995.* Tel: 512-741-5302.

CLERGY, PARISHES, MISSIONS AND PAROCHIAL SCHOOLS

CITY OF VICTORIA
(Victoria County)

1—OUR LADY OF VICTORY CATHEDRAL, Revs. Michael Harrold; Charles Dwomoh.
Res., 1309 E. Mesquite Ln., 77901. Tel: 512-575-4741.
School—Tel: 512-575-5391; 578-5454. Sr. M. Leonita Barron, I.W.B.S., Prin.
Sisters 2; Lay Teachers 28; Students 518.
Catechesis/Religious Programs—Tel: 512-575-8132. Betty Mitchell, D.R.E.
Students 675.

2—HOLY FAMILY OF JOSEPH, MARY & JESUS, Revs. Gregory E. Korenek, Admin.; Peter Kaplinski; Deacon Steve Borowicz.
Office: 704 Mallette Dr., 77904. Tel: 512-573-5304.

3—OUR LADY OF LOURDES, Rev. Celestino Say, Admin.
Res., 105 N. William, 77901. Tel: 512-575-3813.

4—OUR LADY OF SORROWS, Revs. Raul P. Rendon, O.SS.T.; Wolfgang Mimms, O.SS.T.; Victor Scocco, O.SS.T.; Deacons Edward Molina; Jesus Perez.
Res., 208 W. River St., P.O. Box 2548, 77901. Tel: 512-575-2293. [JC]
Catechesis/Religious Programs—Sr. Anna M. Lozano, M.C., D.R.E.
Students 939.
Convent—209 W. Murray St., 77901. Tel: 512-575-7654. Missionary Catechists of the Sacred Hearts of Jesus and Mary (Violetas)
Sisters 4.
Mission—Victoria, Victoria Co., Holy Trinity, 2511 Ozark, 77901.

5—ST. MARY'S, Revs. Joseph Hybner; Dominic Antwi; Deacons Richard Wearden; James Koenig; Dudley Pagel.
Res., 402 S. Main, P.O. Box 2448, 77902. Tel: 512-573-4328. [JC]

OUTSIDE THE CITY OF VICTORIA

Ammannsville, Fayette Co., St. John The Baptist, Rev. Timothy Kosler, Admin. Pro-tem.
Mailing Address: 7745 Mensik Rd., Schulenburg, 78956. [CEM]
Mission—Holman, St. Wenceslaus. [CEM]

Bay City, Matagorda Co., Holy Cross, Rev. Msgr. James C. Brunner, V.G.
Res., 2001 Katy St., 77414. Tel: 409-245-6379. [CEM 2][JC]
School—Sr. M. Geraldine Pavlik, I.W.B.S., Prin.
Sisters 2; Lay Teachers 5; Students 176.
Convent—Tel: 409-245-3173.
Mission—Wadsworth, Sacred Heart.
Our Lady of Guadalupe, Rev. Edward Daniel Boren, O.F.M.; Bro. Camillus Smith, O.F.M.
Res., 1412 12th St., 77414. Tel: 409-245-2010.

Blessing, Matagorda Co., St. Peter's, Rev. Peter Higgins.
Res., Box 395, 77419. Tel: 512-588-6241. [CEM][JC]
Mission—Markham, St. Robert.

Bloomington, Victoria Co., St. Patrick, Rev. Jacinto Olguin; Deacon Fred Soto.
Res., P.O. Box 217, 77951. Tel: 512-897-1155.

Cistern, Fayette Co., SS. Cyril and Methodius, Rev. Msgr. Stanley J. Petru.
Res., Holy Rosary Church, Hostyn 936 FM 2436, LaGrange, 78945. Tel: 409-247-4441.
Church—113 Manchester St., Flatonia, 78941. Tel: 512-865-2222. [CEM 2]

Columbus, Colorado Co., St. Anthony's, Rev. Daniel P. Kahlich.
Res., P.O. Box 669, 78934. Tel: 409-732-2562. [CEM]
School—635 Bonham, 78934. Tel: 409-732-5505. Mrs. Charlyne Spanihel, Prin.
Lay Teachers 12; Students 137.

Cuero, Dewitt Co., Our Lady of Guadalupe, Rev. Daniel Giorgi, O.SS.T., Admin.; Deacon Robert Ruiz.
Res., 705 W. Broadway, P.O. Box 547, 77954. Tel: 512-275-3135.
St. Michael, Rev. Johnson Owusu-Boateng.
Res., 302 E. Church St., 77954. Tel: 512-275-3554.
School—208 N. McLeod, 77954. Tel: 512-277-3854.
Lay Teachers 9; Students 106.

Eagle Lake, Parish of the Nativity (1995), Rev. Edward J. Winkler.
Res., 310 N. Stevenson St., 77434. Tel: 409-234-2842.

East Bernard, Wharton Co., Holy Cross, Rev. Donald R. Ruppert.
Res., 839 Church St., P.O. Box 280, 77435. Tel: 409-335-7551. [CEM]
Convent—Tel: 409-335-4071.

Edna, Jackson Co., St. Agnes, Rev. Michael A. O'Shaughnessy; Deacon Manuel Hernandez.
Res., 506 N. Allen, 77957. Tel: 512-782-3588.

El Campo, Wharton Co., St. Philip the Apostle, Revs. Thu Van Nguyen; Michael Lyons; Deacon Jarrel Nohavitza.
Res., 304 W. Church St., 77437. Tel: 409-543-3770. [CEM]
School—Tel: 409-543-2901. Sr. Marjorie Vincik, S.S.C.J., Prin.
Lay Teachers 18; Students 250.
Catechesis/Religious Programs—D.R.E.: Mr. Steve Kroeger; Mrs. Maureen Kroeger.
Students 379.
St. Robert Bellarmine, Rev. Lawrence Matula, V.F.; Sr. Elizabeth Riebschlaeger, C.C.V.I., Pastoral Assoc.; Deacon Margarito Cervantez, Jr.
Res., 512 Tegner St., 77437. Tel: 409-543-4298.

Flatonia, Fayette Co., Sacred Heart, Rev. Charles B. Carolan.
Res., P.O. Box 186, 78941. Tel: 512-865-3568; Fax: 512-865-2518. [CEM]

Frelsburg, Colorado Co., SS. Peter and Paul (1836), Rev. Wayne N. Flagg; Deacon Charles Glynn.
Res., R.R. 2, Box 26, New Ulm, 78950. Tel: 409-732-3430. [CEM]

Ganado, Jackson Co., Assumption of the B.V.M., Rev. Arnold Anders.
Mailing Address: P.O. Box 369, 77962. Tel: 512-771-3425.
Res., 108 S. Sixth St., 77962. [CEM]

Goliad, Goliad Co., Immaculate Conception, Rev. Raphael Baidoo, O.SS.T.
Res., P.O. Box 49, 77963. Tel: 512-645-3095. [CEM 2]
Missions—Charco, Our Lady of Guadalupe; Fannin, Our Lady of Assumption; Berclair, Immaculate Heart of Mary.
Shrine—Our Lady of Loreto (Old Franciscan Mission).

Hallettsville, Lavaca Co., Sacred Heart, Rev. John C. Peters, V.F.; Deacons Joey Targac; W.S. (Sonny) Rogers.
Res., P.O. Box H, 77964. Tel: 512-798-5888. [CEM]
School—Tel: 512-798-4251. Mr. David Smolik, Prin. (Elementary & High School).
Sisters 2; Lay Teachers 15; Students 187.
High School—313 S. Texana, 77964.
Sisters 1; Lay Teachers 10; Students 110.
St. Mary, Rev. John C. Peters, Admin.
Church—Rte. 4, Box 369, 77964. Tel: 512-798-2128. [CEM 4]

High Hill, Fayette Co., Nativity of the Blessed Virgin Mary, Rev. Edward C. Bartsch, Admin.
Mailing Address: 2833 FM 2672, Schulenburg, 78956-5603. Tel: 409-561-8455. [CEM]
Res., 821 FM 1295, Flatonia, 78941. Tel: 512-865-3560.

Hillje, Wharton Co., St. Andrew, Rev. Clement Quainoo; Deacon Edward Wendel.
Mailing Address: Rte. 3, Box 39, El Campo, 77437. Tel: 409-648-2864. [CEM]
Mission—Louise, St. Procopius. [CEM]

Hostyn, Fayette Co., Holy Rosary, Rev. Msgr. Stanley J. Petru.
Res., 936 FM 2436, La Grange, 78945. Tel: 409-247-4441. [CEM]

Hungerford, Wharton Co., St. John the Baptist, Rev. Henry C. Rachunek.
Res., P.O. Box 121, 77448. Tel: 409-532-4747.

Inez, Victoria Co., St. Joseph's, Rev. Benton A. Thurmond.
Res., P.O. Box 337, 77968. Tel: 512-782-3181. [CEM]

Koerth, Lavaca Co., St. John the Baptist, Rev. Charles Sonnier.
Res., P.O. Box 201, Sweet Home, 77987. Tel: 512-741-3206. [CEM][JC]

Mentz, Colorado Co., St. Roch (1850), Rev. Wayne N. Flagg; Deacon Charles Glynn.
Mailing Address: Rte. 2, Box 191, Alleyton, 78935. Tel: 409-732-3460.

Meyersville, DeWitt Co., SS. Peter & Paul, Rev. William Doran.
Res., HC-01, Box 49B, 77974. Tel: 512-275-3868.
Mission—Westhoff, St. Aloysius.

Moulton, Lavaca Co., St. Joseph's, Rev. Gabriel Maison.
Res., P.O. Box 399, 77975. Tel: 512-596-4674; Fax: 512-596-4826. [CEM]

Nada, Colorado Co., Nativity of the Blessed Virgin Mary, Rev. Joseph A. Koebel.
Res., P.O. Box 97, 77460. Tel: 409-758-3218. [CEM]
School—St. Mary's, P.O. Box 128, 77460. Tel: 409-758-3267. Mr. Thomas Rohwer, Prin.
Lay Teachers 5; Students 52.

New Taiton, Wharton Co., St. John Nepomucene, Rev. Msgr. Julius A. Petru.
Res., Rte. 1, Box 250, El Campo, 77437. Tel: 409-543-6985. [CEM]

Palacios, Matagorda Co., St. Anthony's, Rev. Casey Jarzombek; Deacon Michael Vieira.
Res., 1004 Magnusson, Box 900, 77465. Tel: 512-972-2446.
Vietnamese Apostolate—100 Vietnam, 77465. Tel: 512-972-2685. Rev. Joseph Pham duc Trin.

Plum, Fayette Co., SS. Peter and Paul, Rev. Jerome J. Stryk.
Res., P.O. Box 97, 78952. Tel: 409-242-3600.

Port Lavaca, Calhoun Co., Our Lady of the Gulf, Revs. Dan Morales; Matthew Huehlefeld; Deacon Alonzo F. Calzada.
Res., 415 W. Austin St., P.O. Box 87, 77979. Tel: 512-552-6140.
School—Our Lady of the Gulf School, Tel: 512-552-2774. Sr. Mary Clare Jones, O.S.F., Prin.
Sisters 3; Lay Teachers 4; Students 60.
Catechesis/Religious Programs—Sr. M. Perpetua, I.W.B.S., D.R.E.
Students 600.
Missions—Point Comfort, St. Ann; Port O'Connor, St. Joseph; Seadrift, St. Patrick.

Praha, Fayette Co., St. Mary's, Rev. Edward C. Bartsch.
Res., 821 FM 1295, Flatonia, 78941. Tel: 512-865-3560. [CEM]

St. John, Fayette Co., St. John the Baptist, Rev. Brian Crookes.
Res., St. John Rd., Box 135, Schulenburg, 78956. Tel: 409-562-2222. [CEM]
Mission—Moravia, Lavaca Co., Ascension of Our Lord. [CEM]

Schulenburg, Fayette Co., St. Rose of Lima, Rev. Timothy Kosler, V.F.
Res., 1010 Lyons Ave., Box 310, 78956. Tel: 409-743-3117. [CEM]
School—400 Black, 78956. Tel: 409-743-3080. Mrs. Judy Roeder, Prin.
Sisters 1; Lay Teachers 11; Students 169.

Shiner, Lavaca Co., SS. Cyril and Methodius, Rev. Gerard Cernoch; Deacon Paul Patek. In res., Rev. Daniel O'Brien.
Res., Box 66, 77984. Tel: 512-594-3836. [CEM]
School—Mrs. Patricia Pesek, Prin. Sisters 1; Lay Teachers 10; Students 211.
High School—Mrs. Patricia Pesek, Prin. Sisters of the Incarnate Word and Blessed Sacrament 1; Lay Teachers 8; Students 56.

Sweet Home, Lavaca Co., Queen of Peace, Rev. Charles Sonnier.
Res., P.O. Box 201, 77987. Tel: 512-741-3206. [CEM][JC]

Vanderbilt, Jackson Co., St. John Bosco, Rev. James Deaconson.
Res., P.O. Box 337, 308 Garcitas St., 77991. Tel: 512-284-3361.
Mission—LaSalle, St. Theresa. [CEM]

Weimar, Colorado Co., St. Michael, Rev. John C. Bily.
Res., Box 36, 78962. Tel: 409-725-6714. [CEM]
School—Tel: 409-725-8461. Sr. M. Laura Toman, I.W.B.S., Prin.
Sisters of the Incarnate Word and Blessed Sacrament 2; Lay Teachers 7; Students 156.
Mission—Dubina, Fayette Co., SS. Cyril and Methodius.

Wharton, Wharton Co., Holy Family, Rev. Joseph L. Vrana; Deacon Alvin Matthys.
Res., 2011 Briar Ln., 77488. Tel: 409-532-3593.
Mission—Boling, St. Joseph.
Our Lady of Mt. Carmel, Revs. Raymond A. Jackson, C.S.B.; James Blocher, C.S.B.
Res., 506 S. East Ave., 77488. Tel: 409-532-3492.

Yoakum, Lavaca Co., St. Joseph, Revs. Gary W. Janak, J.C.L.; William Lambe. In res., Rev. Charles Kram.
Res., 210 Schrimscher St., Box 734, 77995. Tel: 512-293-3518. [CEM]
School—Sr. Isabel Estrada, I.W.B.S., Prin. Sisters of the Incarnate & Blessed Sacrament 2; Lay Teachers 13; Students 186.
Mission—Hochheim, St. Ann. [CEM]

Yorktown, Dewitt Co., Holy Cross, Rev. Frank B. Lenz.
Res., Rte. 2, Box 152, 78164. Tel: 512-564-2893. [CEM][JC 2]
Missions—Yorktown, San Luis; Nordheim, St. Ann's.

On Duty Outside the Diocese:
Reverend Fathers—
Euresti, Jesse, Austin, TX
Henninger, George, Indianapolis, IN
Mensah, Gabriel, Military Chap., U.S. Navy

Retired:
Reverend Monsignors—
Schmidtzinsky, Victor
Reverend Fathers—
Bernasconi, Gino
Caponi, Jerome
Halata, William
Hermes, Eustace A.
Janson, Eugene
O'Brien, Daniel
Quiroz, Guido M.

Permanent Deacons:
Borowicz, Stephen James Michael
Calzada, Alonzo Farias
Cervantez, Margarito Candelario, Jr.
Glynn, Charles Jacky
Harper, Linard
Hernandez, Manuel
Koenig, James Nicholas
Matthys, Alvin
Molina, Edwardo Pina
Nohavitza, Jarrel Joseph
Pagel, Dudley Meryl
Patek, Paul, Sr.
Perez, Jesus Castillo
Rogers, Walter Smith, Jr.
Ruiz, Robert
Soto, Fred
Targac, Joseph
Tran, Luan Van
Vieira, Michael
Wearden, Arthur R.
Wendel, Edward

INSTITUTIONS LOCATED IN THE DIOCESE

[A] HIGH SCHOOLS, PRIVATE

VICTORIA. *St. Joseph High School*, 110 E. Red River, 77901. Tel: 512-573-2446. Mr. William H. McArdle, Jr., Pres.; Sr. M. Emilie Eilers, I.W.B.S., Prin.; Sr. Michael Rose Stanzel, Vice Prin. Academics. Lay Teachers 35; Students 425.

[B] ELEMENTARY SCHOOLS, PRIVATE

VICTORIA. *Nazareth Academy*, 206 W. Convent, 77901. Tel: 512-573-6651. Sr. Kathleen Goike, I.W.B.S., Prin. Sisters of the Incarnate Word and Blessed Sacrament 6; Lay Teachers 23; Students 500. Attended from St. Mary's, Our Lady of Lourdes, Our Lady of Victory, Holy Family and Our Lady of Sorrows' Churches.

[C] HOMES FOR AGED

HILLJE. *Czech Catholic Home For The Aged* Rte. 3, Box 40 El Campo, 77437. Tel: 409-648-2628.
For a complete listing, refer to the Special Care Facilities section.

[D] PERSONAL PRELATURES

SCHULENBURG. *Opus Dei*. Featherock Conference Center, 934 Holub Rd., 78956-5324. Tel: 409-743-3071.

[E] CONVENTS AND RESIDENCES FOR SISTERS

VICTORIA. *Franciscan Monastery of St. Clare*, 107 N. Depot St., 77901. Tel: 512-576-6347. Sr. Gabriel Zwiener, O.S.C., Supr.
Incarnate Word Convent, 1101 N.E. Water St., 77901-9298. Tel: 512-575-2266; Fax: 512-575-2165. Sr. Stephana Marbach, I.W.B.S., Supr. Gen.; Sr. M. Mildred Truchard, Local Supr. Sisters 63.
Missionary Catechists of the Sacred Hearts of Jesus and Mary, 209 W. Murray St., 77901. Sr. Antonieta Salazar, M.C.SS.CC.J.M., Supr. Sisters 4.

[F] MONASTERIES & RESIDENCES OF PRIESTS & BROTHERS

VICTORIA. *Trinity House*. Novitiate Holy Trinity Fathers. 1511 E. Commercial St., 77901. Tel: 512-573-7059. Revs. Thomas Dymowski, O.SS.T.; Victor Scocco, O.SS.T.

[G] CAMPUS MINISTRY

VICTORIA. *Campus Ministry Center*, 2803 N. Ben Jordan, 77901. Tel: 512-578-1428.

WHARTON. *Wharton County Junior College Catholic Student Association*, 911 Boling Hwy., 77488.

[H] MISCELLANEOUS

VICTORIA. *Endowment Fund for the Catholic Diocese of Victoria in Texas*, P.O. Box 4070, 77903-4070. Mr. Arthur R. Wearden, Mailing Contact.
Jeanne Chezard De Matel Fund, 1101 N.E. Water St., 77901-9293.
Sisters of the Incarnate Word and Blessed Sacrament of Victoria, 1101 N.E. Water St., 77901-9298. Sr. Stephana Marbach, I.W.B.S., Supr. Gen. & Mailing Contact. Legal Title: *Sisters of the Incarnate Word and Blessed Sacrament of Victoria, Texas Medical and Retirement Trust.*

RELIGIOUS INSTITUTES OF WOMEN REPRESENTED IN THE DIOCESE

For further details refer to the corresponding bracketed number in the Religious Institutes of Women section.

[2200]—*Congregation of the Incarnate Word and Blessed Sacrament.*—I.W.B.S.
[2700]—*Missionary Catechists of the Sacred Hearts of Jesus and Mary.*—M.C.SS.CC.J.M.
[3760]—*Order of St. Clare.*—O.S.C.
[]—*School Sisters of Notre Dame.*
[]—*School Sisters of St. Francis.*—S.S.S.F.
[0460]—*Sisters of Charity of Incarnate Word.*—C.C.V.I.
[0570]—*Sisters of Charity of Seton Hill, Greensburg, Pennsylvania.*—S.C.
[3950]—*Sisters of St. Mary of Namur.*—S.S.M.N.
[1010]—*Sisters of the Divine Providence of San Antonio, Texas.*—C.D.P.
[]—*Sisters of the Sacred Heart of Jesus.*—S.S.H.J.

NECROLOGY

(No Deaths)

Archdiocese of Washington

(Archidioecesis Washingtonensis)

His Eminence

JAMES CARDINAL HICKEY, S.T.D., J.C.D.

Archbishop of Washington; ordained June 15, 1946; ordained Auxiliary Bishop of Saginaw April 14, 1967; appointed Bishop of Cleveland June 5, 1974; appointed Archbishop of Washington June 17, 1980; installed August 5, 1980; created Cardinal June 28, 1988. *Office. Archdiocesan Pastoral Center, 5001 Eastern Ave., P.O. Box 29260, Washington, DC, 20017.* Tel.: 301-853-4540; Fax: 301-853-5359.

Archdiocesan Pastoral Center: 5001 Eastern Ave., P.O. Box 29260, Washington, DC, 20017. Tel.: 301-853-4500; Fax: 301-853-5346.

Most Reverend

ALVARO CORRADA, S.J., D.D., V.G.

Auxiliary Bishop of Washington, Titular Bishop of Rusticiana; ordained July 6, 1974; consecrated August 4, 1985; on assignment, as Apostolic Administrator, Diocese of Caguas. *Mailing Address: Bishop's House, P.O. Box 8698, Caguas, PR, 00726.*

Most Reverend

LEONARD J. OLIVIER, S.V.D., D.D., V.G.

Auxiliary Bishop of Washington, Titular Bishop of Leges; ordained June 29, 1951; consecrated December 20, 1988. *Res., 3340 St. Peter's Church Rd., Waldorf, MD, 20601.* Tel.: 301-843-1388; Fax: 301-843-1041.

Most Reverend

WILLIAM E. LORI, S.T.D., V.G.

Auxiliary Bishop of Washington, Vicar General in Curia, Titular Bishop of Bulla; ordained May 14, 1977; consecrated April 20, 1995. *Res., 5001 Eastern Ave., P.O. Box 29260, Washington, DC, 20017.* Tel.: 301-853-4520; Fax: 301-853-5346.

ESTABLISHED ARCHDIOCESE JULY 22, 1939; SEPARATED FROM BALTIMORE NOVEMBER 15, 1947; BECAME A METROPOLITAN SEE OCTOBER 12, 1965.

Square Miles 2,104.

Comprises the District of Columbia and Montgomery, Prince George's, St. Mary's, Calvert and Charles Counties in Maryland.

The Province of Washington has as a Suffragan, the Diocese of St. Thomas in the Virgin Islands.

For legal titles of parishes and archdiocesan institutions, consult the Chancery Office.

STATISTICAL OVERVIEW

Personnel	
Cardinal	1
Archbishop	1
Auxiliary Bishops	3
Abbots	1
Retired Abbots	2
Priests: Diocesan Active in Diocese	236
Priests: Active Outside Diocese	23
Priests: Diocesan in Foreign Missions	1
Priests: Retired, Sick or Absent	76
Number of Diocesan Priests	336
Religious Priests in Diocese	565
Extern Priests in Diocese	131
Ordinations:	
Diocesan Priests	6
Religious Priests	5
Transitional Deacons	2
Permanent Deacons	11
Permanent Deacons in Diocese	242
Total Brothers	149
Total Sisters	829
Parishes	
Parishes	139
With Resident Pastor:	
Resident Diocesan Priests	123
Resident Religious Priests	16
Without Resident Pastor:	
Missions	8
Pastoral Centers	1
Professional Ministry Personnel:	
Brothers	3
Sisters	31
Lay Ministers	303
Welfare	
Catholic Hospitals	3
Total Assisted	461,970
Health Care Centers	5
Total Assisted	92,338
Homes for the Aged	10
Total Assisted	956
Residential Care of Children	1
Total Assisted	382
Day Care and Extended Day Care Centers	5
Total Assisted	770
Specialized Homes	8
Total Assisted	1,169
Special Centers for Social Services	68
Total Assisted	104,216
Residential Care of Disabled	44
Total Assisted	217
Other Institutions	10
Total Assisted	23,881
Educational	
Seminaries, Diocesan	1
Students from This Diocese	8
Students from Other Diocese	57
Diocesan Students in Other Seminaries	24
Seminaries, Religious	30
Students Religious	171
Total Seminarians	203
Colleges and Universities	3
Total Students	20,363
High Schools, Diocesan and Parish	1
Total Students	700
High Schools, Private	16
Total Students	7,755
Elementary Schools, Diocesan and Parish	78
Total Students	22,126
Elementary Schools, Private	9
Total Students	1,538
Non-residential Schools for the Disabled	1
Total Students	71
Catechesis/Religious Education:	
High School Students	3,064
Elementary Students	25,579
Total Students Under Catholic Instruction	81,399
Teachers in the Diocese:	
Priests	30
Scholastics	3
Brothers	16
Sisters	122
Lay Teachers	2,370
Vital Statistics	
Receptions into the Church:	
Infant Baptism Totals	7,011
Adult Baptism Totals	585
Received into Full Communion	693
First Communions	6,153
Confirmations	4,826
Marriages:	
Catholic	1,276
Interfaith	775
Total Marriages	2,051
Deaths	2,878
Total Catholic Population	495,321
Total Population	2,388,916

Former Bishops—Most Rev. MICHAEL J. CURLEY, D.D., cons. Bishop of St. Augustine, June 30, 1914; promoted to the See of Baltimore, Aug. 10, 1921; named Archbishop of Baltimore and Washington, July 22, 1939; died May 16, 1947.—His Eminence PATRICK CARDINAL O'BOYLE, cons. Jan. 14, 1948; retired March 3, 1973; died Aug. 10, 1987.—His Eminence WILLIAM CARDINAL BAUM, installed May 8, 1973; appt. Prefect, Sacred Congregation for Catholic Education in the Vatican, Jan. 15, 1980; Major Penitentiary; appt. April 6, 1990.

Regional Offices—Most Rev. ALVARO CORRADA, S.J., D.D., V.G., Auxiliary Bishop of Washington; Regional Bishop of Montgomery Co., Upper and Middle Prince George's Co., Office: *826 Wayne Ave., Silver Spring, MD, 20910.* Tel: 301-589-3261; Fax: 301-589-2550. Most Rev. LEONARD J. OLIVIER, S.V.D., D.D., V.G., Auxiliary Bishop of Washington; Regional Bishop for Northeast and Southeast Washington, Lower Prince George's Co., Charles, Calver and St. Mary Counties, Office: *3340 St. Peter's Church Rd., Waldorf, MD, 20601.* Tel: 301-843-1388; Fax: 301-843-1041. Most Rev. WILLIAM E. LORI, S.T.D., V.G., Auxiliary Bishop of Washington; Vicar General in Curia; Regional Bishop for Northwest East and Northwest West Washington, *Res., 5001 Eastern Ave., P.O. Box 29260, Washington, 20017.* Tel: 301-853-4520; Fax: 301-853-5346.

Unless otherwise indicated, all Archdiocesan Offices, including the Chancery and the Tribunal, are located in the Archdiocesan Pastoral Center, *5001 Eastern Ave., P.O. Box 29260, Washington, 20017.* Tel: 301-853-4500; Fax: 301-853-5346. Office Hours: Mon.-Fri. 8:30-5.

Vicars General—Most Rev. WILLIAM E. LORI, S.T.D.; Most Rev. LEONARD J. OLIVIER, S.V.D., D.D.; Rev. Msgr. WILLIAM J. KANE, Ph.D.

Episcopal Vicar for Hispanic Catholics—Rev. FRANCISCO GONZALEZ, S.F., *826 Wayne Ave., Silver Spring, MD, 20910.* Tel: 301-589-3261; Fax: 301-589-2550.

Moderator of the Curia—Most Rev. WILLIAM E. LORI, V.G., S.T.D. Tel: 301-853-4520; Fax: 301-853-5346.

Chancellor—Rev. Msgr. BERNARD C. GERHARDT, S.T.L., J.C.D. Tel: 301-853-4520; Fax: 301-853-5346.

Canonical Consultant to the Cardinal—Sr. ELIZABETH McDONOUGH, O.P., J.C.D.

Archivist—Deacon BERNARD A. BERNIER. Tel: 301-853-5316.

Secretary To The Archbishop—Rev. BARRY KNESTOUT. Tel: 301-853-4537; Fax: 301-853-5359.

Secretariats—Catholic Education: Mr. DANIEL CURTIN, Parish Life & Worship: Rev. ROBERT CARY HILL, Clergy: Rev. Msgr. WILLIAM ENGLISH, Women Religious: Sr. HELEN SCARRY, R.J.M., Finance & Management: Rev. Msgr. KEVIN FARRELL, Social Concerns: Rev. Msgr. RALPH KUEHNER, Communications: (See separate sections below).

Executive Directors—Office of Black Catholics: Mrs. JACQUELINE WILSON, Office of Hispanic Pastoral Affairs: Miss MARGARITA ROQUE, (See separate sections below).

The Tribunal

Judicial Vicar—Rev. Msgr. JOSEPH F. SADUSKY, M.Div., M.Ch.A., J.C.D. Tel: 301-853-4543; Fax: 301-853-7674.

Asst. Judicial Vicar—Rev. GODFREY T. MOSLEY, J.C.D.

Judges—Rev. Msgr. E. ROBERT ARTHUR, P.A., S.T.B., J.C.L.; Rev. Msgr. BERNARD C. GERHARDT, S.T.L., J.C.D.; Revs. G. PAUL HERBERT, J.C.L.; ROBERT J. BOZEK, J.C.L.; VINCENT J. RIGDON, M.A., J.C.L.; JAMES PROVOST, J.C.D.; GEORGE E. STUART, J.C.L.; BECHET SOULE, O.P., Ph.D., J.C.D.; Deacon JOSEPH B. McGRATH, J.C.L.; Sr. ELIZABETH McDONOUGH, O.P., J.C.D.

Promoter of Justice—Rev. DAVID F. O'CONNOR, S.T., J.C.D.

Defenders of the Bond—Revs. DAVID F. O'CONNOR, S.T., J.C.D.; KEVIN T. HART, J.C.D.; JOSEPH BUI TRANG NGHIEM, M.A., S.T.L., J.U.D.; MICHAEL J. KING, J.C.D.

Auditors—Rev. MICHAEL W. DOUGLAS; Deacons JOHN G. HAMILTON; ANTHONY J. McMAHON.

Advocates—Rev. Msgr. THOMAS M. WELLS, M.A.; Revs. GEORGE E. GOLDEN, M.Div.; ROBERT G. AMEY; DONALD BRICE; MARK E. BRENNAN; JOHN T. DAKES, S.T.L.; PAUL D. LEE, S.T.D.; MICHAEL W. DOUGLAS.

Notaries—Sr. M. PAUL, O.P.; Mrs. BARBARA McGUIRE; Ms. PATRICIA A. PERKINSON; Mrs. STEPHANIE POTTS; Mrs. DENISE SMITH.

Consultative Groups

Archdiocesan College of Consultors—Most Rev. LEONARD J. OLIVIER, S.V.D., D.D.; Most Rev. WILLIAM E. LORI, S.T.D.; Rev. Msgr. THOMAS M. DUFFY; Rev. Msgr. RAYMOND G. EAST; Rev. Msgr. JOHN J. ENZLER; Rev. Msgr. DONALD S. ESSEX; Rev. Msgr. BERNARD C. GERHARDT; Rev. Msgr. W. RONALD JAMESON; Rev. Msgr. WILLIAM J. KANE, Ph.D.; Rev. Msgr. THOMAS A. KANE; Rev. GODFREY T. MOSLEY.

Archdiocesan Pastoral Council—His Eminence JAMES CARDINAL HICKEY, Pres.; Mrs. HARRIET HAYES, Sec.; Most Rev. WILLIAM E. LORI; Rev. ROBERT CARY HILL; Mr. CARLOS AQUINO; Mrs. CONCHITA BROWN; Mr. RONAL CALDWELL; Mr. JOSEPH CAREY; Mr. JAMES CONNELL; Judge RICHARD A. COOPER; Ms. ALICE CULBRETH; Ms. LUISA DUARTE; Mrs. LAURENCE LONG; Mr. RANSFORD PALMER; Ms. ROSA MARIA SALAZAR; Ms. SUSAN OLDEN-STAHL; MICHAEL T. STEELE, Esq.; Ms. JANE TENNYSON; Ms. COLLEEN M. WALSH; Ms. MARY LOUISE WEBB.

Archdiocesan Finance Council—His Eminence JAMES CARDINAL HICKEY, Pres.; Rev. Msgr. DONALD ESSEX; Most Rev. WILLIAM E. LORI; Rev. Msgr. KEVIN FARRELL; W. SHEPHERDSON ABELL; FRED J. BRINKMAN; DANIEL CALLAHAN; JEREMIAH C. COLLINS; RICHARD GRAVES; PAUL INTERDONATO; EUGENE I. KANE; Sr. CAROL KEEHAN; ROBERT LIGHTHIZER; MICHAEL McGARRY; B. FRANCIS SAUL, II.

Deans—Rev. Msgr. RONALD JAMESON, Northwest West, D.C.; Rev. Msgr. PETER VAGHI, Northwest East, D.C.; Rev. RAYMOND J. WADAS, Southeast, D.C.; Rev. EDDIE TOLENTINO, Northeast, D.C.; Rev. MILTON JORDAN, Upper Montgomery County; THOMAS WELLS, Middle Montgomery County; Rev. Msgr. Rev. JOHN PENNINGTON, Lower Montgomery County; Rev. Msgr. WILLIAM F.X. BERRY, Upper Prince George's County; Rev. MICHAEL J. KING, Middle Prince George's County; Rev. MARK HUGHES, Lower Prince George's County; Rev. PAUL M. DUDZIAK, Calvert County; Rev. MATTHEW SIEKIERSKI, Charles County; Rev. JAMES P. MEYERS, St. Mary's County.

Council of Priests—His Eminence JAMES CARDINAL HICKEY, Pres.; Rev. Msgr. W. RONALD JAMESON, Moderator; Rev. Msgr. DONALD S. ESSEX, Vice Moderator; Rev. Msgr. PETER J. VAGHI, Treas.; Rev. ROBERT CARY HILL, Sec.

Sisters' Senate—Sr. PAULA GOETTELMANN, C.S.C., Pres.; Sr. MARY ANN PHELAN, S.P., Vice Pres.; Sr. ROSE ANN HITCHENS, D.C., Sec.

Secretariat For Education

Secretary for Catholic Education—Mr. DANIEL F. CURTIN, B.S., M.Ed., M.A. Tel: 301-853-4519; Fax: 301-853-7670.

Assistant Secretary for Education—Rev. CHARLES PARRY. Tel: 301-853-5358.

Superintendent of Schools—Mr. LAWRENCE CALLAHAN. Tel: 301-853-4518.

Assistant Superintendent for Secondary Schools—Bro. WILLIAM GRIFFIN, C.F.X. Tel: 301-853-4597.

Assistant Superintendent for Elementary Schools—Mrs. TRUDY SAMPUGNARO. Tel: 301-853-4553.

Director of Curriculum Services—Sr. EILEEN CLINTON, I.H.M. Tel: 301-853-5353.

Director of School Personnel—Ms. SUZETTE CHAGNON. Tel: 301-853-4549.

Director of Instructional Services—Mrs. NOEL GESSNER. Tel: 301-853-4590.

Director of Professional Development—Mrs. MARY STANTON. Tel: 301-853-4552.

Financial Officer—Mrs. KIMBERLY HOOD. Tel: 301-853-5356.

School Marketing—VINCENT P. CLARK. Tel: 301-853-4589. Executive Director, *Center City Consortium.* Tel: 202-234-4611.

Board of Education—Mr. CARL E. GIRTH, Pres.

Special Education Consultant—REBECCA S. SALON. Tel: 202-529-7600.

Office of Youth Ministry/CYO—Rev. LeROY FANGMEYER, Exec. Dir. Tel: 301-853-4591; Fax: 301-853-4501. Rev. Msgr. JOHN J. ENZLER, Coord., Devel. Tel: 301-365-1415. Rev. JOSEPH DEL VECCHIO, S.S.J., Assoc. Dir.

Our Lady of Mattaponi Retreat Center—Rev. ROBERT MORDINO, Dir., *301-952-9074.*

CYO Programs—THOMAS J. MANCO, Dir. Tel: 301-853-5382.

Ministry Development Coordinator Adult Training—BARBARA GAGLIOTTI. Tel: 301-853-5380.

Ministry Development Facilitator—LYDIA CHANDLEE, (Hispanic). Tel: 301-853-5377.

Ministry Development Facilitator—DARREN FOSTER, (African American). Tel: 301-853-5375.

Scouting—Rev. Msgr. JOHN BRADY, Chap. Coord. Tel: 301-769-3332. FRANK ROSSOMONDO, Arch. Lay Coord., Cath. Comm. Boy Scouts & Camp Fire. Tel: 301-770-7450. ROBERT KAMMER, Arch. Lay Chm., Cath. Comm. Boy Scouting. Tel: 301-942-0882. Arch. Co-Chm., Girl Scouts: BARBARA ANN FOSTER. Tel: 301-972-2067. JOAN TREACY. Tel: 301-924-0394.

Our Lady of Mattaponi Youth Retreat and Conference Center—Tel: 301-952-9074; Fax: 301-952-0609.

Office for Religious Education—Mr. LAWRENCE RILLA, S.T.L., Dir. Tel: 301-853-4506; Fax: 301-853-7687.

Coordinator for Catechist Formation—ELIZABETH SIEGEL. Tel: 301-853-5386.

Implementation Coordinator—JAMES PAULEY. Tel: 301-853-4531.

At-Large Field Representative—MICHAEL BERRY. Tel: 301-853-5385.

Hispanic Catholics Religious Education—Vacant.

Special Religious Education—DOLORES WILSON, Coord. Tel: 301-853-4560.

D.J. Corbett Media Center—Sr. GRACE MANLEY, R.J.M., Coord. Tel: 301-853-2200.

Campus Ministry, University of Maryland at College Park—Rev. ROBERT KEFFER, Dir. Tel: 301-864-6233; Fax: 301-864-8411.

Propagation of the Faith—Rev. VINCENT RIGDON, Archdiocesan Dir. Tel: 301-853-4527; Fax: 301-853-7670.

Mission Education Coordinator—Vacant.

Holy Childhood Association—Rev. VINCENT RIGDON, Dir. Tel: 301-853-4527.

Sacred Heart Basic Adult Education Center—Sr. MARIE LUCEK, O.P., Dir.; Sr. DELPHINE VASQUEZ, H.M., Asst. Dir. Tel: 202-462-6499.

Secretariat For Parish Life and Worship

Secretary for Parish Life and Worship—Rev. ROBERT CARY HILL. Tel: 301-853-4557; Fax: 301-853-7670. Mrs. VI COLLINS, Admin. Asst., Notary Public. Tel: 301-853-4558.

Office for Adult Religious Formation—Sr. BARBARA ANNE GOODING, R.S.M., Dir. Tel: 301-853-5331.

Office for Ecumenical and Interreligious Affairs—Rev. PAUL LEE, Dir. Tel: 301-853-5378.

Office for Evangelization—Ms. MARTHA FERNANDEZ-SARDINA, Dir. Tel: 301-853-4596.

Office for Hispanic Liturgical Ministry-RCIA—Vacant.

Office for Family Life Ministry—Mrs. JOAN O'BRIEN, Dir. Tel: 301-853-4546. Mrs. JEM SULLIVAN, Marriage Prep Coord. Tel: 301-853-4551.

Natural Family Planning—Mrs. ANNE LANCTOT, Dir. Tel: 301-853-4561.

Office for Persons with Disabilities—Ms. DOLORES WILSON, Dir. Tel: 301-853-4560.

Office of Worship—Rev. WALTER J. TAPPE, Dir. Tel: 301-853-4595. Sr. CONSTANCE WARD, S.S.J., Admin. Asst. Tel: 301-853-4594; Fax: 301-853-7684.

Alcoholism and Substance Abuse, Consultant on—Rev. JAMES J. POWDERLY, *520 Veirs Mill Rd., Rockville, MD, 20852.* Tel: 301-424-5550; Fax: 301-424-5579.

Charismatic Renewal Regional Service Committee—Rev. DONALD DeROZA; Mrs. DONALD DeROZA, *13103 Tamarack Rd., Silver Spring, MD, 20994.* Tel: 301-384-5568.

Cursillo Movement—Rev. PETER R. ALLIATA, Spiritual Dir., *St. James, 3628 Rhode Island Ave., Mt. Rainier, MD, 20712.* Tel: 301-927-0567. Lay Directors: LARRY JACKSON; SYLVIA JACKSON, *6002 40th Ave., Hyattsville, MD, 20782.* Tel: 301-864-9275.

St. Francis of Assisi Catholic Church and Center for the Deaf—Rev. EDWARD J. HELM, Dir., *7202 Buchanan St., Landover Hills, MD, 20784.* Tel: 301-459-7464; Fax: 301-459-8186.

Ministry for the Deaf—Rev. GERARD A. TRANCONE, *Gallaudet University, 800 Florida Ave., N.E., Washington, 20002.* Tel: 202-651-5102 (Voice & TDD).

Holy Name Society—Rev. Msgr. THOMAS A. KANE, *4101 Norbeck Rd., Rockville, MD, 20853.* Tel: 301-924-2284; Fax: 301-929-3017.

Ancient Order of Hibernians—Mr. JAMES CLARKE, *7108 Plantation Ln., Rockville, MD, 20852.* Tel: 301-881-4512.

Archdiocesan Council of Catholic Women—Rev. ROBERT G. AMEY, Spiritual Dir., *11801 Claridge Rd., Wheaton, MD, 20705.* Tel: 301-946-3636; Fax: 301-946-5061. Mrs. ANGELA WEEKS, Pres., *7501 Democracy Blvd., Bethesda, MD, 20817.* Tel: 301-365-1887.

Blue Army of our Lady of Fatima—Rev. Msgr. WILLIAM F. O'DONNELL, Spiritual Dir., *St. Thomas the Apostle, 2665 Woodley Rd. N.W., Washington, 20008-4199.* Tel: 202-234-1488. Mrs. ANNA ZACYNSKI, *14518 Perrywood Dr., Burtonsville, MD, 20866.* Tel: 301-236-4012.

Catholic Daughters of the Americas Court District of Columbia No. 212—Mrs. VIRGINIA BORKENHAGEN, Regent, *1805 19th St. N.W., Washington, 20009.* Tel: 202-667-1613.

Catholic Hospital Chaplains—Rev. JOSEPH O'BRIEN, *Cardinal O'Boyle Residence, 1150 Varnum St. N.E., Washington, 20017.* Tel: 202-219-7100.

Health Care Concerns Coordinator—Rev. J. WILFRED PARENT, *St. Peter's, 3320 St. Peter Dr., Waldorf, MD, 20602.* Tel: 301-843-8916; Fax: 301-843-3163.

Catholic Interracial Council of Washington, DC—Mrs. MADELINE FURTH, Pres., *3224 Northampton St. N.W., Washington, 20015.* Tel: 202-966-6794.

Catholic War Veterans of the United States—JOSEPH DE PASQALE, National Commander, *119 N. Lee St., Alexandria, VA, 22314.* Tel: 703-549-3622; Fax: 703-684-5196. Mrs. ADELAIDE KOWANSKY, Pres., *5900 Carlton Ln., Bethesda, MD, 20816.* Tel: 301-229-2420.

Society of St. Francis de Sales—Rev. LEWIS FIORELLI, O.S.F.S., *1621 Otis St., N.E., Washington, 20018.* Tel: 202-269-5677. Mrs. JOAN McDERMOTT, Eastern U.S.A. Regional Dir., *17 Lakeview Trail, Fairfield, PA, 17320.* Tel: 717-642-6647.

First Friday Club—Rev. Msgr. JOSEPH JOSHUA MUNDELL, Spiritual Dir., *4000 Harewood Rd. N.E., Washington, 20017.* Tel: 202-332-8888; Fax: 202-332-0173.

International Federation of Catholic Alumnae—*The Catholic University of America, 416 Administration Bldg., Washington, 20017.* Tel: 202-526-5916.

John Carroll Society—Rev. Msgr. PETER VAGHI, Chap., *619 10th St. N.W., Washington, 20001.* Tel: 202-347-2713. Mr. STEPHEN URBANCZYK, Pres., *4344 Forest Lane, N.W., Washington, D.C., 20007.* Tel: 202-364-8867.

Knights of Columbus—Most Rev. WILLIAM E. LORI, S.T.D., Chap., *P.O. Box 29260, Washington, 20017.* Tel: 202-526-8300.

Knights of St. Jerome—Mr. VINCENT BISBOE, *St. Peter Claver, St. Inigoes, MD.* Tel: 301-872-5377.

Knights of St. John—Most Rev. LEONARD OLIVIER, *St. Peter's, P.O. Box 2352, Waldorf, MD, 20601.* Tel: 301-843-1388; Fax: 301-843-1041.

Womens Retreat League—Sr. FRANCES FLYNN, S.A., Dir., *4000 Harewood Rd. N.E., Washington, 20017.* Tel: 202-529-1111; Fax: 202-529-2102.

Engaged Encounter—Contact the Office of Family Life. Tel: 301-853-4561.

Marriage Encounter-Worldwide—Contact the Office of Family Life. Tel: 301-853-4561.

Sodality Union—Rev. GREGORY C. BUTTA, *St. Augustine Parish, 1419 V St., N.W., Washington, 20009-5810.* Tel: 202-265-1470. Mrs. GRACIELA STEVENS, Pres., *13103 Clarion Ct., Ft. Washington, MD, 20744.* Tel: 301-292-1055.

Secretariat For Social Concerns

Secretary—Rev. Msgr. Ralph Kuehner. Tel: 301-853-4556; Fax: 301-853-7671.

Associated Catholic Charities—Edward J. Orzechowski, M.S.W., Pres., *1438 Rhode Island Ave. N.E., Washington, 20018.* Tel: 202-526-4100.

A.C.C. Housing & Initiative Corp.—1438 Rhode Island Ave. N.E., Washington, 20018. Tel: 202-526-4100.

A.C.C. Model Cities Corp.—1125 Neal St. N.E., Washington, 20002. Tel: 202-396-8100.

A.C.C. Otis Street Corp.—1438 Rhode Island Ave. N.E., Washington, 20018. Tel: 202-526-4100.

SHARE, DC, Inc.—5170 Lawrence Pl., P.O. Box 768, Bladensburg, MD, 20710. Tel: 301-864-3115.

Anchor Mental Health Association, Inc.—Rev. Msgr. John G. Kuhn, Dir., *1001 Lawrence St. N.E., P.O. Box 29058, Washington, 20017-0058.* Tel: 202-635-5900.

Pro-Life Office—Mr. Thomas Grenchik, Dir. Tel: 301-853-4555; Fax: 301-853-7671.

Birthing & Care Center—Ms. Vincenta Correa, *817 Varnum St., N.E., Washington, 20017.* Tel: 202-526-2229; Fax: 202-526-1226.

Campaign for Human Development—Ms. Sandy Mattingly-Paulen. Tel: 301-853-5340.

Office of Social Development—Rev. Msgr. Ralph Kuehner. Tel: 301-853-4556; Fax: 301-853-7671.

St. Vincent de Paul Society—Mr. Arthur M. McKnew, Pres. Tel: 301-864-2106.

Project Rachel—Ms. Ana Padilla, *817 Varnum St., N.E., Washington, 20017.* Tel: 202-269-4673; Fax: 202-526-1226.

Ladies of Charity—Mrs. Margaret Hedley, Pres., *1438 Rhode Island Ave. N.W., Washington, 20018.* Tel: 202-526-4100. Rev. Carl F. Dianda, Spiritual Dir., *St. Francis de Sales Parish, Washington, 20018.* Sr. Letitia, D.C., Moderator, *Providence Hospital, Washington, 20017.*

Lt. Joseph P. Kennedy Institute—Dr. Richard Birkel, Pres./CEO, *801 Buchanan St. N.E., Washington, 20017.* Tel: 202-529-7600.

St. Ann's Infant & Maternity Home—Sr. Josephine Murphy, D.C., Admin., *4901 Eastern Ave., Hyattsville, MD, 20782.* Tel: 301-559-5500.

Christ Child Society—Pat Scanlon, Pres.; Rev. Msgr. W. Louis Quinn, Spiritual Dir., *5101 Wisconsin Ave. N.W., Washington, 20016.* Tel: 202-966-9250.

Community Center of the Missionaries of Charity—Sr. Mary Elizabeth Seton, M.C., Supr., *3310 Wheeler Rd. S.E., Washington, 20032.* Tel: 202-562-6890.

Missionaries of Charity—Sr. Pietra, M.C., Supr., *Gift of Peace Home, 2800 Otis St. N.E., Washington, 20017.* Tel: 202-269-3313. Sr. M. Lizen, M.C., Supr., *Mother Teresa's Infant Home, 5649 Western Ave. N.W., Washington, 20015.* Tel: 202-237-6633.

Victory Housing, Inc.—Mr. James A. Brown, Jr., Exec. Dir., *1515-17 Dunster Rd., Rockville, MD, 20854.* Tel: 301-279-9200.

Byron House, Inc.—1515 Dunster Rd., Rockville, MD, 20854. Tel: 301-279-9200.

Raphael, Inc.—Mr. James A. Brown, Jr., Pres., *1515 Dunster Rd., Rockville, MD, 20854.* Tel: 301-279-9200.

Faith House—Sr. Josephine Murphy, D.C., Admin., *4903 Eastern Ave., Hyattsville, MD, 20782.* Tel: 301-559-5500.

Malta House, Inc.—Mr. James A. Brown, Jr., Pres., *1515 Dunster Rd., Rockville, MD, 20854.* Tel: 301-279-9200.

Bartholomew House, Inc.—Mr. James Brown, *1515 Dunster Rd., Rockville, MD, 20854.* Tel: 301-279-9200.

Avondale Park Apartments, Inc.—Mr. James Brown, Jr., *1515 Dunster Rd., Rockville, MD, 20854.* Tel: 301-279-9200.

Manor Apartments, Inc.—Mr. James A. Brown, Jr., Pres., *1515 Dunster Rd., Rockville, MD, 20854.* Tel: 301-279-9200.

District of Columbia Catholic Conference—Mr. Ronald Jackson. Tel: 301-853-5342; Fax: 301-853-7671.

Secretariat For The Clergy

Secretary for Services for Clergy, Religious Men and Secular Institutes—Rev. Msgr. William J. English. Tel: 301-853-4550; Fax: 301-853-7671.

Director of Priests Personnel—Rev. Msgr. William J. English. Tel: 301-853-4550.

Assistant to the Secretary for Clergy—Rev. Peter J. Reynierse. Tel: 301-853-4583.

Director, Vocations for Men—Rev. Mark Brennan. Tel: 301-853-4580.

Associate Director, Vocations for Men—Rev. James M. Stack. Tel: 202-362-3323.

Continuing Education for Clergy—Rev. Paul D. Lee. Tel: 301-853-5378.

St. John Vianney House—Rev. Msgr. William English, Dir., *4214 Saul Rd., Kensington, MD, 20895.* Tel: 301-942-1191.

Director, Permanent Diaconate—Deacon William T. Ditewig. Tel: 301-853-4582.

Associate Director, Permanent Diaconate—Rev. Peter J. Reynierse. Tel: 301-853-4583.

Priests Retirement Board—Rev. Kevin Hart, Chm. Tel: 202-966-6575.

Cardinal O'Boyle Residence for Priests—Rev. Joseph A. O'Brien, Rector, *P.O. Box 29206, Washington, 20017.* Tel: 202-269-7818.

Serra Club of Washington—Mrs. Lorraine Nosacek, *12306 Malin Ln., Bowie, MD, 20715.* Tel: 301-262-5755.

Serra Club of Downtown Washington—Mr. Herbert Harmon, *5029 Domain Pl., Alexandria, VA, 22311.* Tel: 703-379-2799.

Serra Club of Prince George's Co.—Mr. Robert Prangley, *6114 42nd Pl., Hyattsville, MD, 20781.* Tel: 301-927-8106.

Serra Club of Southern Maryland—Rev. Walter Rourke, Pres., *10548 Wicomico Ridge Rd., Charlotte Hall, MD, 20622.* Tel: 301-884-7464.

Liaison with Council of Priests—(see Consultative Bodies) Religious priests and brothers, Secular Institutes, Consultant on Alcoholism.

Secretary For Women Religious

Secretary for Services to Women Religious and Secular Institutes—Sr. Helen Scarry, R.J.M. Tel: 301-853-4576; Fax: 301-853-7671.

Liaison with Sisters' Senate—(see Consultative Bodies).

Secretariat For Finance and Management

Secretary For Finance and Management—Rev. Msgr. Kevin Farrell. Tel: 301-853-4523; Fax: 301-853-2787.

Accounting and Financial Management—Mr. Richard B. Graves, Controller. Tel: 301-853-4525.

Facilities Management—Mr. Richard de Stwolinski. Tel: 301-853-4572; Fax: 301-853-7679.

Materials and Pastoral Center Management—Ms. Alessandra Styles. Tel: 301-853-4532; Fax: 301-853-7673.

Personnel and Benefits—Dorothy Moore, Dir. Tel: 301-853-4513; Fax: 301-853-7680.

Archdiocesan Building Committee—Rev. Msgr. Joseph A. Ranieri, Chm.

Paul VI Institute for the Arts—Rev. Msgr. Michael Di Teccia Farina, Dir., *924 G St. N.W., Washington.* Tel: 202-347-1450.

Archdiocesan Finance Council—(see Consultative Bodies).

Carroll Publishing Company—(see Secretariat for Communications).

Archdiocesan Sacred Arts Committee—Rev. Msgr. W. Ronald Jameson, *1725 Rhode Island Ave. N.W., Washington, 20036.* Tel: 202-347-3215; Fax: 202-347-7184.

Cornerstone for Tomorrow, Inc.—Rev. Msgr. Kevin Farrell, *P.O. Box 29260, Washington, 20017.* Tel: 301-853-4523.

Priest Retirement Fund of the Archdiocese of Washington, Inc.—Rev. Msgr. Kevin Farrell, *P.O. Box 29260, Washington, 20017.* Tel: 301-853-4523.

Parish Accounting—Mr. Terrence Farrell.

Parish Audit Department—Ms. Heather Holland.

Development Office

Office of Development—Gregory F. Gannon, Dir. Tel: 301-853-4574; Fax: 301-853-7671.

Cardinal's Stewardship Appeal—Tel: 301-853-4575.

Office of Planned Giving—Vacant.

Office of Communications

Director—Mrs. Dawn Ceol. Tel: 301-853-4516 (Asst.). Tel: 301-853-4515; Fax: 301-853-7672.

Radio & TV Programming—Mr. John Capobianco. Tel: 301-853-4515.

Carroll Publishing Company—His Eminence James Cardinal Hickey, Publisher; Mr. Thomas Schmidt, Pres. Tel: 301-853-4562; Fax: 301-853-3349.

Newspaper—"The Catholic Standard", Mark Zimmerman, Editor. Tel: 301-853-4599; Fax: 301-853-3349., *"El Pregonero"*; Mr. Oscar Reyes, Editor. Tel: 301-853-4504; Fax: 301-853-3349.

Office Of Black Catholics

Executive Director—Mrs. Jacqueline E. Wilson. Tel: 301-853-4579; Fax: 301-853-7671. Coordinating Office for the Black Catholic History Center; Combating Racism; Black Catholic Congress; REJOICE! Conference on Black Catholic Liturgy; Archdiocesan Mass Choir; Other Programs & Resources for Leadership and Evangelization in the Black Community.

Council of Black Catholics—Mrs. Ruby Tynes, Contact Person.

Office Of Hispanic Pastoral Affairs

Executive Director—Ms. Margarita Roque. Tel: 301-853-4566; Fax: 301-853-7671.

Spanish Catholic Center—Rev. Mark Poletunow, O.F.M.Cap, Dir., *1618 Monroe St. N.W., Washington, 20010.* Tel: 202-483-5665; Fax: 202-234-7323.

CLERGY, PARISHES, MISSIONS AND PAROCHIAL SCHOOLS

DISTRICT OF COLUMBIA

1—St. Matthew Cathedral (1840), Rev. Msgr. W. Ronald Jameson; Revs. James D. Watkins; Jose Lobaton, O.F.M.; G. Paul Herbert; Deacons Ulysses Rice; Lawrence C. Gordon. In res., Rev. Msgr. Bernard C. Gerhardt.

Res., 1725 Rhode Island Ave., N.W., 20036. Tel: 202-347-3215; Fax: 202-347-7184.

2—St. Aloysius, Washington, (1859), Revs. R. Bruce Bavinger; John A. Conlin, S.J.; Joseph M. McCloskey, S.J.; Deacons Jesse Dudley; Willis Daniels.

Res., 19 Eye St., N.W., 20001. Tel: 202-336-7200; Fax: 202-898-1449.

Father McKenna Center—Tel: 202-842-1112. Paul J. Magno, Dir.

3—St. Ann, Washington, (1869), Rev. Msgr. William J. Awalt; Revs. David W. Beaubien; Joseph B. Pierce; Deacon Robert W. Whitaker.

Res., 4001 Yuma St., 20016. Tel: 202-966-6288; Fax: 202-966-7722.

School—(Grades PreK-8). Tel: 202-363-4460. Mrs. Barbara Kelly, Prin.

Catechesis / Religious Programs—Students 212.

4—Annunciation, Washington, (1948), Rev. Msgr. James F. Montgomery; Revs. James M. Stack; Donald Brice. In res., Rev. Brien R. McCarthy.

Res., 3125 39th St., N.W., 20016. Tel: 202-362-3323; Fax: 202-363-4057.

School—3825 Klingle Pl., 20016. Tel: 202-362-1408. Sr. Claire Smith, S.H.C.J., Prin.

Sisters of Holy Child Jesus 5; Lay Teachers 14; Students 201.

Catechesis / Religious Programs—Students 55.

Convent—3200 39th St., N.W., 20016. Tel: 202-362-1464.

5—St. Anthony, Washington, (1892), Rev. Msgr. Richard Burton; Rev. Berard L. Marthaler, O.F.M.Conv.; Deacon John Kelly. In res., Revs. Barthasar Kim; Victor Wong (Nanking); John Rodney, S.V.D.; Kesete Ghebreyohannes (Ethiopia); Joseph Njoroge Ngugi (Kenya).

Res., 1029 Monroe St., N.E., 20017. Tel: 202-526-8822; Fax: 202-526-1543.

School—Tel: 202-526-4657; Fax: 202-832-5567.

Lay Teachers 17; Students 264.

Catechesis / Religious Programs—Students 36.

6—Assumption, Washington, (1916), Revs. T. Ansgar Laczko; Everett Pearson.

Res., 3401 Martin Luther King Jr. Ave., S.E., 20032-1597. Tel: 202-561-4178; Fax: 202-561-0336.

School—Tel: 202-562-7070; Fax: 202-574-5829. Mr. Christopher Kelly, Prin.

Lay Teachers 10; Students 180.

7—St. Augustine, Washington, (1858) (African American), Rev. Msgr. Russell L. Dillard; Revs. George W. Wilson; John Payne, O.S.A.

Parish Office—1419 V St., N.W., 20009. Fax: 202-234-1787.

Res., 1425 V St., N.W., 20009. Tel: 202-265-1470.

School—1421 V St., N.W., 20009. Tel: 202-667-2608. Shelore C. Williams, Prin.

Oblate Sisters of Providence 2; Lay Teachers 13; Students 220.

Catechesis / Religious Programs—Students 180.

8—St. Benedict the Moor, Washington, (1946) (African American), Rev. Roderick J.D. Coates, S.S.J.

Res., 320 21st St., N.E., 20002. Tel: 202-397-3895; Fax: 202-398-3415.

School—Tel: 202-397-3897; Fax: 202-388-7874. Sr. Brenda Cherry, O.S.P., Prin.

Oblate Sisters of Providence 2; Lay Teachers 20; Students 245.

Convent—Tel: 202-398-7696.

9—St. Blaise. (Croation Pastoral Mission). Rev. Gabriel Badurina, T.O.R.
Res., St. Jerome House of Study, 1359 Monroe St., N.E., 20017. Tel: 202-832-6364.

10—Blessed Sacrament, Shrine of the Most, Washington, (1911), Rev. Msgr. Thomas M. Duffy; Revs. Philip A. O'Shea; Percival L. D'Silva; Raymond F. Schmidt; Deacons John M. Leonard; Joseph B. McGrath.
Res., 6001 Western Ave., N.W., 20015. Tel: 202-966-6575; Fax: 202-966-9255.
School—5841 Chevy Chase Pkwy., N.W., 20015. Tel: 202-966-6682; Fax: 202-966-4938. Mrs. Frances Scango, Prin.
Lay Teachers 30; Students 489.
Catechesis/Religious Programs—Tel: 202-363-8938. D.R.E.: Mrs. Kathleen Curtin; Mrs. Patricia Armelin, (Grades K-6); Ms. Susan Mitchell (Grades 7-12).
Students 375.

11—St. Dominic Church & Priory, Washington, (1852), Very Revs. Francis C. Duffy, O.P., Prior; William A. Newman, O.P., Subprior; Revs. Donald P. Thibault, O.P.; John A. McMahon, O.P.; Robert D. Riley, O.P.; Robert L. Walker, O.P.; Edmund J. Way, O.P.; Robert R. Haller, O.P.; Raymond Vandegrift, O.P.; Bro. Fabian Butler, O.P. In res., Revs. Cornelius T. Kane, O.P.; Guy B. Dupont, O.P; John J. Ryan, O.P.; Joseph J. Jurasko, O.P.; Joseph A. Cote, O.P.; Charles V. Lucier, O.P.; Alfred Gately, O.P.; J. Aumann, O.P.; W. Becket Soule, O.P.; Michael Novacki, O.P.; Thomas Collins, O.P.; Bros. Leon Mancinelli, O.P.; Fidelis Spalding, O.P.
Res., 630 E St., S.W., 20024. Tel: 202-554-7863; Fax: 202-554-0231.

12—Epiphany, Washington, (1925), Rev. Winthrop Brainerd.
Res., 2712 Dumbarton Ave., N.W., 20007. Tel: 202-965-1610; Fax: 202-337-8377.

13—St. Francis de Sales, Washington, Revs. Carl F. Dianda; Robert T. Guillen; Deacons Floyd H. Agostinelli; Harold Jackson. In res., Revs. John S. Wintermyer; Henry Slevin; Christian Nwaka Egbulem, O.P.
Res., 2021 Rhode Island Ave., N.E., 20018. Tel: 202-529-7451.
School—Sisters 2; Lay Teachers 9; Students 230.

14—St. Francis Xavier (1924), Rev. Michael A. Salah; Deacon Anthony Smith. In res., Rev. Msgr. John L. Bailey.
Res., 2800 Pennsylvania Ave., S.E., 20020. Tel: 202-582-5021; Fax: 202-581-7224.
School—Tel: 202-581-2010; Fax: 202-582-5244. Mrs. Kathleen Pardue, Prin.
Sisters 1; Lay Teachers 9; Students 140.
Catechesis/Religious Programs—Students 79.
Convent—2812 Pennsylvania Ave., S.E., 20020. Tel: 202-584-5621. Sisters of St. Joseph Sr. M. Brigid S.S.J., Supr.; Sr. Miriam Naughton.

15—St. Gabriel, Washington, (1920), Rev. Patrick J. McCaffrey; Deacon Robert L. Berry. In res., Rev. Tesfamariam Baraki.
Res., 26 Grant Cir., N.W., 20011. Tel: 202-726-9092; Fax: 202-291-0334.
School—Tel: 202-726-9212; Fax: 202-726-1881. Mrs. Mary Hawkins, Prin.
Lay Teachers 9; Students 250.

16—Holy Comforter—St. Cyprian, Washington, (1893) (African American), Revs. Eddie Tolentino; Charles Pope; Deacons Charles Edelin; Kevin Butler. In res., Rev. F. Michael Bryant.
Res., 1357 E. Capitol St., S.E., 20003. Tel: 202-546-1885; Fax: 202-544-1385.
School—Tel: 202-547-7556; Fax: 202-547-5686. Dr. Mary Leighton, Prin.
Oblate Sisters of Providence 3; Lay Teachers 9; Students 170.
Catechesis/Religious Programs—Tel: 202-547-2510. Mrs. Dolores Gorham, D.R.E.
Students 243.

17—Holy Name, Washington, (1892) (African American), Rev. David P. Russell; Deacons James Ford; William Thomas.
Res., 920 11th St., N.E., 20002. Tel: 202-397-2525.
School—Tel: 202-397-1614. Sr. Owen Patricia Bonner, S.S.J., Prin.
Sisters of St. Joseph 3; Lay Teachers 15; Students 230.

18—Holy Redeemer, Washington, (1922) (African American), Rev. David Bava.
Res., 206 New York Ave., N.W., 20001. Tel: 202-347-7510; Fax: 202-628-0401.
School—Holy Redeemer School, (Grades PreK-8) 1135 New Jersey Ave., N.W., 20001. Tel: 202-638-5789. Mrs. Mildred Tyler, Prin.
Priests 1; Sisters 3; Deacons 1; Lay Teachers 10; Students 250.
Catechesis/Religious Programs—Students 62.

19—Holy Rosary, Washington, (1913) (Italian), Rev. Charles Zanoni, C.S.
Res., 595 Third St., N.W., 20001-2703. Tel: 202-638-0165; Fax: 202-638-0793.

20—Holy Trinity, Washington, (1787), Revs. Lawrence J. Madden, S.J.; Richard P. McHugh, S.J.; Joseph P. Lacey, S.J.; Paul J. McCarren, S.J.; Gerard J. Campbell, S.J.; Douglas F. Peduti, S.J.
Church—36th St., N.W., between N and O Sts., 20007.
Parish Center Offices—3513 N St., N.W., 20007.
Res., 3514 O St., N.W., 20007. Tel: 202-337-2840; Fax: 202-337-9048.
School—Tel: 202-337-2339; Fax: 202-337-0368.
Sisters of St. Joseph (Chestnut Hill, PA) 2; Lay Teachers 33; Students 339.
Catechesis/Religious Programs—Students 660.

21—National Shrine Of The Immaculate Conception, Washington,

22—Immaculate Conception, Washington, (1864) (African American), Rev. Msgr. J. Joshua Mundell.
Res., 1315 8th St., N.W., 20001. Tel: 202-332-8888; Fax: 202-332-0173.
School—(Grades PreK-6) 711 N St., N.W., 20001. Tel: 202-234-1093. Sr. Carol Ann Knight, S.H.C.J., Prin.
Sisters 1; Lay Teachers 7; Students 133.

23—Incarnation, Washington, (1934) (African American), Rev. Joseph S. Macek, S.S.J.; Deacons Hiram Haywood; Harry Draper; Alfred Brokenborough; Thomas Forbes.
Res., 880 Eastern Ave., N.E., 20019. Tel: 202-396-0942; Fax: 202-396-6064.
Catechesis/Religious Programs—Students 60.

24—St. Joseph on Capitol Hill, Washington, (1869), Revs. Paul E. Lavin; Christopher T. Begg. In res., Rev. Eugene Henrick (JOL).
Res., 313 Second St., N.E., 20002. Tel: 202-547-1223; Fax: 202-547-4189.

25—Kidane-Mehret Ge'ez Rite Catholic Church, Washington, (1984) (Ethiopian-Eritrean), Rev. Tesfamariam Baraki.
Mailing Address: 1001 Lawrence St., N.E., P.O. Box 29616, 20017.
Res., 26 Grant Cir., N.W., 20011. Tel: 202-529-8420; Fax: 202-529-8523.
Catechesis/Religious Programs—Students 80.

26—Church of St. Louis, Washington. (Eglise St. Louis). Rev. Andre Millot.
Res., 4125 Garrison St., N.W., 20016. Tel: 202-537-0709; Fax: 202-244-9649.
Catechesis/Religious Programs—Students 187.

27—St. Luke, Washington, (1957), Revs. Stephen F. Brett, S.S.J., J.D., Ph.D.; Joseph N. Begay, S.S.J.; Deacons Earle W. Coleman; Joseph M. Conrad.
Res., 4925 E. Capitol St., 20019-5202. Tel: 202-584-8322; Fax: 202-584-3421.
Catechesis/Religious Programs—Students 61.

28—St. Martin of Tours, Washington, (1901), Rev. Michael J. Kelley.
Res., 1908 N. Capitol St., 20002. Tel: 202-232-1144; Fax: 202-832-6772.
Catechesis/Religious Programs—Students 60.

29—St. Mary, Mother of God, Washington, Rev. David Conway; Deacon Bernard Johnson.
Res., 727 Fifth St., N.W., 20001. Tel: 202-289-7771.

30—Nativity, Washington, (1901) (African American), Rev. Joseph R. Sileo.
Res., 6000 Georgia Ave., N.W., 20011. Tel: 202-726-6262.
School—Tel: 202-723-3322; Fax: 202-291-0219. Valerie Smith, Prin.
Sisters 8; Lay Teachers 15; Students 240.
Catechesis/Religious Programs—Tel: 202-829-4051. Sr. Stephanie Romiti, S.P.C., D.R.E.
Students 150.

31—Nigerian Catholic Community, Rev. Aloysius Achonwa.
Res., Nativity Parish, 6000 Georgia Ave., N.W., 20011. Tel: 202-726-8363.

32—Our Lady of Perpetual Help, Washington, (1920), Rev. Lowell D. Case, S.S.J.; Bro. Marx Tyree, S.S.J.; Deacons Ira Chase; Thomas Jones.
Res., 1600 Morris Rd., S.E., 20020. Tel: 202-678-4999; Fax: 202-610-3189.
School—Tel: 202-889-1662 (Grades PreK-4); 678-0211 (Grades 5-8). Principals: Sr. Mary Elizabeth Semmelmayer, S.S.N.D.; Mrs. Charlene Hursey.
Brothers 1; School Sisters of Notre Dame 1; Lay Teachers 13; Students 220.
Catechesis/Religious Programs—Students 89.

33—Our Lady Queen of the Americas, Washington, (1986) (Hispanic-Portuguese), Rev. Jose I. Somoza, O.F.M.; Deacons Bartolo Serafini; Jorge Vargas. In res., Rev. Ademir Guerini, C.S.
Church, Office and Residence—2200 California St., N.W., 20008. Tel: 202-332-8838; Fax: 202-332-2967.
Catechesis/Religious Programs—Sr. Felipa Blazquez, C.ach., D.R.E.
Students 236.

34—Our Lady Queen of Peace, Washington, (1948) (African American), Rev. George W. Wilson; Deacons Reginald Thomas; Alfred Miller. Pastoral Assocs.: Sr. Roberta Sobus, D.C.; Mr. Ernest Adams.
Res., 3800 Ely Pl., S.E., 20019. Tel: 202-582-8600; Fax: 202-575-3317.
School—Tel: 202-584-4278; Fax: 202-584-1922. Sr. Mary Patrick Costello, D.C., Prin.
Daughters of Charity of St. Vincent de Paul 5; Lay Teachers 13; Students 200.
Catechesis/Religious Programs—Tel: 202-581-4986.
Students 195.
Convent—3740 Ely Pl., S.E., 20019. Tel: 202-581-4963; Fax: 202-584-1922.

35—Our Lady of Victory, Washington, (1906), Rev. William E. Foley; Deacons Edward Redding; Leo Flynn. In res., Rev. Msgr. Harry A. Echle; Rev. Emanuel Magro.
Res., 4835 MacArthur Blvd., N.W., 20007. Tel: 202-337-4835; Fax: 202-338-4759.
School—4755 Whitehaven Pkwy., N.W., 20007. Tel: 202-337-1421; Fax: 202-338-4759. Susan Milloy, Prin.
Lay Teachers 17; Students 143.

36—St. Patrick, Washington, (1794), Rev. Msgr. Peter J. Vaghi; Revs. George Madathiparampil; Paul F. Liston, Senior Priest; Deacon John J. McGinness. In res., Rev. Msgr. Michael diTeccia Farina; Rev. Anthony Frontiero (MAN).
Res., 619 Tenth St., N.W., 20001-4587. Tel: 202-347-2713; Fax: 202-347-1401.

37—St. Peter, Washington, (1821), Rev. Michael J. O'Sullivan. In res., Rev. Msgr. Joseph F. Sadusky; Revs. Thomas J. Sheehan; Joseph R. Sileo.
Res., 313 Second St., S.E., 20003. Tel: 202-547-1430; Fax: 202-547-5732.
School—422 Third St., S.E., 20003. Tel: 202-544-1618; Fax: 202-547-5101. Mary M. Randolph, Prin.
Lay Teachers 22; Students 231.
Catechesis/Religious Programs—Tel: 202-544-1618.
Students 45.

38—Portuguese Catholic Community, Rev. Ademir Guerini, C.S.
Res., Our Lady Queen of the Americas, 2200 California St., N.W., 20008.

39—Shrine of the Sacred Heart, Washington, (1899), Revs. Francis X. Russo, O.F.M.Cap.; Stephen Carter, O.F.M.Cap.; Moises Villalta, O.F.M.Cap.; Paul Zaborowski, O.F.M.Cap.; Deacons Sylvester Brown; James Quander, (Retired). In res., Revs. Joseph Mindling, O.F.M.Cap.; Thomas Weinandy, O.F.M.Cap.
Res., 3211 Pine St., 20010. Tel: 202-234-8000 (Day); 234-8002 (Night); Fax: 202-234-9159.
School—1625 Park Rd., N.W., 20010. Tel: 202-265-4828; Fax: 202-265-0595. Juana Brown, Prin.
Lay Teachers 17; Students 217.
Catechesis/Religious Programs—Tel: 202-667-2446.
Students 370.

40—St. Stephen Martyr, Washington, (1867), Rev. Msgr. Kenneth W. Roeltgen; Revs. M. Valentine Keveny; Paul E. Murray. In res., Rev. Raymond B. Kemp.
Res., 2436 Pennsylvania Ave., N.W., 20037. Tel: 202-785-0982; Fax: 202-785-1574.

41—St. Teresa of Avila, Washington, (1879), Rev. Msgr. Raymond East; Deacons Ralph Cyrus; Lawrence Miles.
Res., 1430 Minnesota Ave., S.E., 20020. Tel: 202-678-3709; Fax: 202-678-3325.
Catechesis/Religious Programs—Students 63.

42—St. Thomas Apostle, Washington, (1909), Rev. Thomas G. Morrow; Rev. Msgr. Henry Otero; Rev. Harry W. Jacobs; Deacon William C. Boesman. In res., Rev. Msgr. William F. O'Donnell.
Res., 2665 Woodley Rd., N.W., 20008. Tel: 202-234-1488; Fax: 202-234-1480.
Catechesis/Religious Programs—Students 54.

43—St. Thomas More, Washington, Revs. Raymond J. Wadas; John P. Kinter; Deacon Nerus O. Martin, Jr.
Res., 4275 4th St., S.E., 20032. Tel: 202-562-0431.
School—Mrs. Wilma Durham, Prin. Lay Teachers 10; Students 250.

44—St. Vincent De Paul, Washington, (1903) (African American), Rev. Joseph F. Del Vecchio.
Res., 14 M St., S.E., 20003-3511. Tel: 202-488-1354; Fax: 202-488-7899.
Catechesis/Religious Programs—Students 62.

CHURCHES IN MARYLAND

Avenue, St. Mary's Co., Holy Angels (1906), Rev. Msgr. John B. Brady; Rev. Msgr. Aloysius E. O'Connor, Pastor Emeritus.
Res., 21340 Colton Point Rd., 20609-2422. Tel: 301-769-3332; Fax: 301-769-2541. [JC]
School—Holy Angels-Sacred Heart, Tel: 301-769-3389; Fax: 301-769-4948.
Priests 2; Lay Teachers 10; Students 174.
Catechesis/Religious Programs—Students 50.

Baden, Prince Georges Co., St. Michael (1957), Rev. Louis J. Faust; Deacon Harvey Ballard.
Res. and Mailing Address—17510 Horsehead Rd., Brandywine, 20613. Tel: 301-888-1498; Fax: 301-579-0019.
Catechesis/Religious Programs—Tel: 301-579-6409; Fax: 301-579-0019.
Students 132.
Mission—Baden, Prince Georges Co., St. Dominic's. [CEM]

Barnesville, Montgomery Co., St. Mary Church and Shrine of Our Lady of Fatima, Rev. George B. Reid.
Res., 18230 Barnsville Rd., P.O. Box 67, 20838. Tel: 301-972-8660. [CEM]

Beltsville, Prince Georges Co., St. Joseph (1963), Rev. Roderick D. McKee; Deacon Andrew J. Betz. In res., Revs. Robert Cary Hill; Albert H. Ledoux (ALT).
Res., 11007 Montgomery Rd., 20705. Tel: 301-937-7183; Fax: 301-937-7780.
School—Tel: 301-937-7154.
Lay Teachers 10; Students 262.
Catechesis/Religious Programs—Tel: 301-937-7419.
Students 205.

Benedict, Charles Co., St. Francis de Sales (1903), Rev. Saverio T. Vitturino.
Res., 7185 Benedict Ave., P.O. Box 306, 20612-0306. Tel: 301-274-3416; 870-4991; Fax: 301-274-0689.
Catechesis/Religious Programs—7209 Benedict Ave., 20612.
Students 66.

Bethesda, Montgomery Co.,

1—St. Bartholomew, (1960), Rev. Msgr. James T. Beattie; Revs. Mark Ervin; Luis G. Salcedo.
Res., 7212 Blacklock Rd., 20817. Tel: 301-229-7933; Fax: 301-229-7998.
School—6900 River Rd., 20817. Tel: 301-229-5586. Mrs. Kathleen Miller, Prin.
Sisters 1; Lay Teachers 17; Students 225.
Catechesis/Religious Programs—Tel: 301-229-3413; Fax: 301-229-7998.
Students 325.

2—St. Jane Frances de Chantal, (1950), Rev. Msgr. Donald S. Essex; Revs. Alan R. Helwig; Ronald A. Potts; Aaron Joseph, O.P.; Deacons A. David Allen; Grafton Kellor.
Res., 9701 Old Georgetown Rd., 20814. Tel: 301-530-1550; Fax: 301-493-8953.
School—9525 Old Georgetown Rd., 20814. Tel: 301-530-1221; Fax: 301-530-1688. Mrs. Betsy Hamilton, Prin.
Lay Teachers 25; Students 511.
Catechesis/Religious Programs—Tel: 301-530-1640.
Students 200.

3—Little Flower, Rev. Msgr. William J. Kane; Rev. Msgr. Joseph B. Coyne; Revs. Stephen F. Nash; George Stuart; Deacons Gary Davies; Richard Schopfer.
Res., 5607 Massachusetts Ave., 20816. Tel: 301-320-4538; Fax: 301-320-4541.
School—Tel: 301-320-3273; Fax: 301-320-2867.
Sisters of the Immaculate Heart of Mary 5; Lay Teachers 18; Students 258.
Catechesis/Religious Programs—Tel: 301-320-5233.
Students 210.

4—Our Lady of Lourdes, (1926) (Spanish), Rev. Msgr. Thomas M. Wells; Revs. William J. Silk, Senior Priest; Mario E. Dorsonville; Deacon John Shewmaker. In res., Rev. Msgr. W. Louis Quinn.
Res., 7500 Pearl St., 20814. Tel: 301-654-1287; Fax: 301-986-8716.
School—Tel: 301-654-5376. Patrick Serra, Prin.
Sisters 1; Lay Teachers 14; Students 183.
Catechesis/Religious Programs—Tel: 301-654-5954.
Students 130.

5—Our Lady of Vietnam, (1990) (Vietnamese), Revs. Peter Nguyen-Thanh-Long; Hilary Tran-Khac Hy, (Retired); Deacon John Huong Nguyen.
Res., 11812 New Hampshire Ave., Silver Spring, 20904. Tel: 301-622-4895; Fax: 301-625-9384.

Bowie, Prince Georges Co.,

1—Ascension, (1893), Revs. James S. Betz; Samuel L. Craig; Deacons Finis Thompson; Raymond Barrett; Thomas Elliott.
Mailing Address: P.O. Box 96, 20719. Tel: 301-262-2227; Fax: 301-805-5053. [CEM]
Catechesis/Religious Programs—Tel: 301-262-8604. Pamela Rozanski, D.R.E.
Students 274.

2—Sacred Heart, (1892), Rev. Msgr. John F. Hogan; Deacon H. Jeffrey Raffensperger.
Res., 16501 Annapolis Rd., 20715. Tel: 301-262-0704; Fax: 301-805-4686. [CEM]
Catechesis/Religious Programs—Tel: 301-262-1221. Sr. M. John Helene Meskill, O.S.F., D.R.E.
Students 230.

3—St. Edward, (1972), Rev. Thomas F. Kehoe; Rev. Msgr. Louis W. Albert; Deacons Kevin Barry; David Barnes; Joseph Welch.
Res., 16304 Pond Meadow Ln., 20716. Tel: 301-249-9199.
Catechesis/Religious Programs—Tel: 301-249-9599; Fax: 301-249-1303.
Students 300.

4—St. Pius X, (1962), Revs. W. Paul Hill; Raymond H. Moore; Deacons Robert J. Tracy; Eugene Mastrangelo; Andrew Nosacek.
Res., 3300 Moreland Pl., 20715. Tel: 301-262-2141.
Church—14720 Annapolis Rd., 20715. Fax: 301-262-2142.
School—Tel: 301-262-0203; Fax: 301-805-8875.
Sisters of St. Joseph 3; Lay Teachers 28; Students 595.
Catechesis/Religious Programs—Cathy Gallagher, D.R.E.
Students 473.

Bryantown, Charles Co., St. Mary (1793), Rev. Ralph C. Torsiello; Deacons Eugene Burroughs; Henry Middleton.
Res., 13715 Notre Dame Pl., 20617-2224. Tel: 301-870-2220; 274-3187; Fax: 301-274-0253. [CEM]
School—Tel: 301-932-6883.
School Sisters of Notre Dame 1; Lay Teachers 9; Students 232.
Catechesis/Religious Programs—Tel: 301-274-4357.
Students 310.

Burtonsville, Montgomery Co., Resurrection Parish (1981), Revs. John R. Pennington, III; Charles E. Brown; Sr. Mary Louise Full, C.S.C., Pastoral Assoc.; Deacon Donald DeRoze.
Res., 3315 Greencastle Rd., 20866. Tel: 301-236-5200; Fax: 301-236-5204.
Catechesis/Religious Programs—Tel: 301-236-5200.
Students 651.

Bushwood, St. Mary's Co., Sacred Heart (1755), Rev. Francis J. Early.
Res., 20618. Tel: 301-769-3100. [JC]
Catechesis/Religious Programs—See Holy Angels-Sacred Heart School, Avenue, MD, for details.
Students 57.

Camp Springs, Prince Georges Co., St. Philip the Apostle, Revs. Charles McCann; Bernard R. Ihrie, Jr., Senior Priest; Deacon Frank D. Clarke.
Res., 5416 Henderson Way, 20746. Tel: 301-423-4244.
School—Lay Teachers 10; Students 196.

Chapel Point, Charles Co., St. Ignatius (1641), Rev. Salvador Jordan, S.J.
Res., St. Thomas Manor, 8855 Chapel Point Rd., Port Tobacco, 20677. Tel: 301-934-8245. [CEM]
Catechesis/Religious Programs—Christine Mais, D.R.E.
Students 194.

Chaptico, St. Mary's Co., Our Lady of the Wayside (1938), Rev. John P. Stack.
Res., Rte. 238, P.O. Box 97, 20621. Tel: 301-884-2502; Fax: 301-884-0381.
School—Mother Catherine Spalding Tri Parish School, Tel: 301-884-3165.
Lay Teachers 14; Students 290.
Mailing Address: Rte. 238, Helen, 20638. Tel: 301-884-3165; Fax: 301-884-3165.
Catechesis/Religious Programs—Students 111.

Cheverly, Prince Georges Co., St. Ambrose (1886), Rev. G. William Finch; Deacon Edwin Beller. In res., Revs. Edward Evans; Francis Walsh.
Res., 3107 63rd Ave., 20785. Tel: 301-773-9300; Fax: 301-773-2611.
School—Tel: 301-773-0223; Fax: 301-773-9218. Mrs. Barbara Edmonson, Prin.
Lay Teachers 12; Students 265.
Catechesis/Religious Programs—Tel: 301-341-3284.
Students 50.

Chillum, Prince Georges Co., St. John Baptist de la Salle (1951), Revs. Robert C. Richardson; James Holloway.
Res., 5706 Sargent Rd., 20782. Tel: 301-559-3636; Fax: 301-559-3062.
Catechesis/Religious Programs—Students 73.

Clinton, Prince Georges Co., Church of St. John the Evangelist (1875), Revs. Thomas W. Pollard; Richard A. Scott; Robert P. Buchmeier; Deacons Anthony Moll; Carl Blaesing.
Res., 8908 Old Branch Ave., 20735. Tel: 301-868-1070; Fax: 301-868-7915. [CEM]
School—Tel: 301-868-2010; Fax: 301-856-8941. Sr. Jean Louise Bachetti, I.H.M., Prin.
Sisters of the Immaculate Heart of Mary 3; Lay Teachers 13; Students 262.
Catechesis/Religious Programs—Tel: 301-868-3026. Sr. Blanche Twigg, M.H.S.H., D.R.E.
Students 249.

College Park, Prince Georges Co., Holy Redeemer (1912), Revs. William F. Berry; Robert A. Finamore; Deacon Bartholomew Merella.
Res., 4902 Berwyn Rd., 20740. Tel: 301-474-3920; Fax: 301-441-4954.
School—Tel: 301-474-3993; Fax: 301-441-8137. Gregory E. Jones, Prin.
Religious 1; Lay Teachers 15; Students 270.
Catechesis/Religious Programs—Tel: 301-474-4299. Mrs. Sandra Tucker, D.R.E.
Students 153.

St. Andrew Kim (1974) (Korean), Revs. Jung Soon (Benedict) Shin; Jun Gui (Michael) Choi.
Res., 8108 54th Ave., 20740. Tel: 301-474-0186; Fax: 301-474-6785. [CEM][JC]

Damascus, Montgomery Co., St. Paul (1957), Revs. Peter J. Sweeney; Walter J. Norris, Pastor Emeritus; Deacons Vince Moskaitis; John Finerty; David Terrar; Charles Weschler.
Res., 9240 Damascus Rd., 20872. Tel: 301-253-2027; Fax: 301-391-6755.
Catechesis/Religious Programs—Tel: 301-253-5941; Fax: 301-391-9755.
Students 790.

Darnestown, Montgomery Co., Our Lady of the Visitation (1991), Rev. Raymond L. Fecteau; Deacon Paul DiDuca.
Res., 14200 Darnestown Rd., 20874-3008. Tel: 301-948-5536; Fax: 301-948-7452.
Catechesis/Religious Programs—Students 183.

Mary of Nazareth Roman Catholic Elementary School (1994), Sr. Francis Stavalo, Prin.
Res., 14131 Seneca Rd., 20874. Tel: 301-869-0940; Fax: 301-869-0942.
Catechesis/Religious Programs—Students 210.

Derwood, Montgomery Co., St. Francis of Assisi (1972), Revs. Donald P. Worch; Joseph Zalotay; Deacons Pascal Hong; Wilbur Pinder; Robert Whitfield.
Res., 6701 Muncaster Mill Rd., 20855. Tel: 301-840-1407; Fax: 301-258-5080.
Catechesis/Religious Programs—Tel: 301-258-9193.
Students 645.

Dunkirk, Calvert Co., Jesus the Good Shepherd (1985), Rev. Paul M. Dudziak.
Res., 1555 Mount Harmony Rd. W., Owings, 20736. Tel: 301-855-4400; Fax: 410-257-6334.
Catechesis/Religious Programs—Students 559.
School—Cardinal Hickey Academy, 1601 W. Mt. Harmony Rd., Owings, 20736. Tel: 410-286-0404; Fax: 410-257-6334. Ms. Lynn Leaf, Prin.

Forestville, Prince George Co., Church of the Holy Spirit (1966), Rev. Michael J. Murray.
Res., 1717 Ritchie Rd., 20747. Tel: 301-336-3707; Fax: 301-324-1649.
Catechesis/Religious Programs—Students 65.

Mt. Calvary (1942), Revs. George E. Golden; David Thompson; Mrs. Dawn Woods, Pastoral Assoc.
Res., 6700 Marlboro Pike, 20747. Tel: 301-735-5532; Fax: 301-735-2005. [CEM]
School—Tel: 301-735-5262; Fax: 301-736-5044.
Brothers 1; Sisters 1; Lay Teachers 28; Students 370.
Catechesis/Religious Programs—6704 Marlboro Pike, 20747. Tel: 301-420-4499.
Students 130.

Fort Washington, Prince Georges Co., St. Ignatius (1849), Revs. Mark F. Hughes; Robert P. Wummer. In res., Rev. Salvatore A. Criscuolo.
Res., 2315 Brinkley Rd., Oxon Hill, 20744. Tel: 301-567-4740. [CEM]
School—2317 Brinkley Rd., Oxon Hill, 20744. Tel: 301-567-4090. Mrs. Rosemarie Garten, Prin.
Lay Teachers 11; Students 220.

Gaithersburg, Montgomery Co., St. John Neumann (1978), Rev. John T. Dakes.
Church—9000 Warfield Rd., 20882. Tel: 301-977-5492; Fax: 301-977-3559.
Res., 8900 Lochaven Dr., 20882.
Catechesis/Religious Programs—Tel: 301-977-7990; Fax: 301-330-3235.
Students 503.

St. Martin (1920) (Spanish), Revs. Michael J. Mellone; Edward J. Filardi; William A. Ryan; Deacons Lawrence Bell; Eugene J. Cummins, Jr.; Stanley E. Weightman; Kenneth Barrett.
Res., 201 S. Frederick Ave., 20877. Tel: 301-840-1830; Fax: 301-990-7538.

School—Tel: 301-840-1748. Mrs. Shirley Wise, Prin.
Lay Teachers 16; Students 289.
Catechesis/Religious Programs—Tel: 301-840-1838. M. Patricia Dorney, D.R.E.
Students 1,095.

St. Rose of Lima (1972), Rev. Robert D. Duggan; Deacon James McCann.
Mailing Address: 11701 Clopper Rd., 20878-1024. Tel: 301-948-7545; Fax: 301-869-2170. [CEM]
Catechesis/Religious Programs—Mary Ann Deak, D.R.E.
Students 637.

Garrett Park, Montgomery Co., Holy Cross (1960), Rev. Msgr. Vincent S. Gatto; Revs. Leroy J. Fangmeyer; Thomas J. Nelson.
Res., 4900 Strathmore Ave., P.O. Box 249, 20896. Tel: 301-942-1020; Fax: 301-949-3543.
School—Tel: 301-949-0053; Fax: 301-949-5074. Sr. Miriam R. Brosnan, Prin.
Lay Teachers 25; Students 268.
Catechesis/Religious Programs—Tel: 301-942-8790.
Students 127.

Germantown, Montgomery Co., Mother Seton Parish (1974), Revs. Milton E. Jordan; Jeffrey M. Defayette; Deacons William Vita; Timothy Enright; Philip Cooper.
Res., 19951 Father Hurley Blvd., 20874. Tel: 301-924-3838; Fax: 301-428-4951.
Catechesis/Religious Programs—Students 606.

Great Mills, St. Mary's Co., Holy Face, Rev. John F. Myslinski.
Res., 20634. Tel: 301-994-0525; Fax: 301-994-1547. [CEM]
School—Little Flower, Tel: 301-994-0404.
Sisters 3; Lay Teachers 16; Students 300.
Catechesis/Religious Programs—Students 120.

Greenbelt, Prince Georges Co., St. Hugh (1947), Revs. Thomas F. Crowley; Walter J. Tappe.
Res., 135 Crescent Rd., 20770. Tel: 301-474-4322; Fax: 301-474-9263.
School—145 Crescent Rd., 20770. Tel: 301-474-4071; Fax: 301-474-3950. Mrs. Harriann Walker, Prin.
Lay Teachers 17; Students 270.
Catechesis/Religious Programs—Tel: 301-474-0239.
Students 80.

Hillcrest Heights, Prince Georges Co., Holy Family (1952), Rev. Michael W. Fisher.
Res., 2210 Callaway St., 20748. Tel: 301-894-2222; Fax: 301-894-2938.
School—2200 Callaway St., 20748. Tel: 301-894-2323.
Catechesis/Religious Programs—Students 235.

Hilltop, Charles Co., St. Ignatius Loyola (1851), Rev. Matthew E. Thompson; Deacon Frank L. Hopson.
Mailing Address: P.O. Box 278, Port Tobacco, 20677. Tel: 301-934-9630. [CEM]

Hollywood, St. Mary's Co., St. John (1690), Rev. Msgr. Martin P. Harris; Rev. Gary R. Studniewski.
Res., P.O. Box 69, 20636. Tel: 301-373-2281; Fax: 301-373-8984. [CEM]
School—Tel: 301-373-2142. Patricia T. Suit, Prin.
Students 261.
Catechesis/Religious Programs—Virginia Bauer, D.R.E.
Students 285.

Huntingtown, Calvert Co., Jesus the Divine Word Parish (1994), Rev. Roger A. Soley.
Res., 710 Joy Lee Ct., 20639-9239. Tel: 301-855-1825; Fax: 410-535-9057.
Catechesis/Religious Programs—Students 198.

Hyattsville, Prince Georges Co., St. Jerome (1886), Rev. Msgr. Joseph A. Ranieri; Rev. Msgr. Joseph L. Teletchea, Pastor Emeritus; Deacons Jerome Tintle; David Duggin. In res., Rev. Jerome Plotkowski (SFE).
Res., 5205 43rd Ave., 20781. Tel: 301-927-6684; Fax: 301-927-9167.
School—Tel: 301-277-4568; Fax: 301-927-6684. Dr. Joyce Volpini, S.N.D., Prin.
Sisters of Notre Dame de Namur 3; Lay Teachers 23; Students 561.
Convent—5300 43rd Ave., 20781. Tel: 301-864-2016.
Child Center—Tel: 301-699-1314.
Catechesis/Religious Programs—Students 36.

St. Mark (1958), Revs. Julio Alvarez; Timothy K. Baer; Deacons Antonio Chaves; Edward Holson; Philip Ricker; Nathaniel D. Cordova; Mark Gallagher. In res., Rev. Charles Parry.
Res., 7501 Adelphi Rd., 20783. Tel: 301-422-8300; Fax: 301-422-2313.
School—Tel: 301-422-7440; Fax: 301-422-7710.
Lay Teachers 26; Students 571.
Catechesis/Religious Programs—Tel: 301-422-7822.
Students 296.

Indian Head, Charles Co., St. Mary Star of the Sea (1918), Rev. William F. Goode; Deacon Thomas O. Hill.
Res., 30 Mattingly Ave., 20640. Tel: 301-753-9177; Fax: 301-753-6995. [CEM]
School—Tel: 301-283-6151.
Lay Teachers 14; Students 182.
Catechesis/Religious Programs—Tel: 301-375-9466.
Students 165.

Issue, Charles Co., Holy Ghost (1880), Rev. John D. Vail; Deacon Walter Rourke.
Res., 15848 Rock Point Rd., Newburg, 20664. Tel: 301-259-2515; Fax: 301-259-2289. [CEM]
Catechesis/Religious Programs—Tel: 301-259-0237.
Students 60.
Mission—Rock Point, Charles Co., St. Francis de Sales, 13675 Furbush Rd., Newburg, 20664. Tel: 301-259-0254.

Kensington, Montgomery Co., Holy Redeemer (1948), Revs. Walter L. Lawrence; Kevin C. Kennedy; Deacon Frank A. Robey. In res., Rev. Michael T. Jones.
Res., 9705 Summit Ave., 20895. Tel: 301-942-2333; Fax: 301-942-1041.
School—9715 Summit Ave., 20895. Tel: 301-942-3701; Fax: 301-942-4981. Trish Beeks, Prin.
Lay Teachers 34; Students 475.
Catechesis/Religious Programs—Tel: 301-942-3430. Miss Suzanne Shaffer, D.R.E.
Students 104.

Largo, Prince Georges Co., St. Joseph (1922) (African American), Rev. Michael J. King, J.C.D.; Deacon Leon Bechet.
Res., 2020 St. Joseph Dr., 20774. Tel: 301-773-4838; Fax: 301-773-6832.
Catechesis/Religious Programs—Tel: 301-773-2480.
Students 160.

Landover Hills, Prince Georges Co., St. Mary's Catholic Church (1948), Revs. Joseph P. Kennedy; Stephen M. Cocca; John E. Gorman, S.D.S.; Michael J. Blackwell, Senior Priest; Deacons B. Paul Blaine, (Retired); Michael J. Taylor; Stephen M. Robinson. In res., Rev. Thomas Poovannal.
Res., 7401 Buchanan St., 20784-2323. Tel: 301-577-8844; Fax: 301-306-5543.
School—7207 Annapolis Rd., 20784. Tel: 301-577-0031; Fax: 301-577-5485. Mrs. Mary Anne Patchan, Prin.
Lay Teachers 16; Students 323.
Catechesis/Religious Programs—Tel: 301-577-2478; Fax: 301-459-1355.
Students 134.

Syro-Malankara Mission, Rev. Thomas Poovannal.
Res., 7401 Buchanan St., 20784-9998. Tel: 301-577-8844; Fax: 202-399-7953.

Lanham, Prince Georges Co., St. Matthias (1960), Rev. Msgr. John J. Scanlan; Rev. Eamon McManus; Deacons John E. Connor; Ronald W. Schneider; Lawrence W. Murphy. In res., Rev. Paul Farren (Ireland).
Res., 9475 Annapolis Rd., 20706. Tel: 301-459-4814; Fax: 301-577-2259.
School—Tel: 301-577-9412. Mr. Robert E. Love, Prin.
Lay Teachers 16; Students 309.
Catechesis/Religious Programs—Tel: 301-577-6567.
Students 170.

La Plata, Charles Co., Sacred Heart (1901), Revs. Matthew J. Siekierski; Keith A. Woods; Bernard C. O'Leary, S.J.; Deacon George V. Foster.
Res., 201 St. Mary's Ave., P.O. Box Z, 20646. Tel: 301-934-2261; Fax: 301-934-5435. [CEM]
School—Archbishop Neale School, Tel: 301-934-9595; Fax: 301-753-1717. Sr. Helene Fee, Prin.
Sisters of the Immaculate Heart of Mary 2; Lay Teachers 36; Students 509.
Catechesis/Religious Programs—Tel: 301-934-3386. Barbara L. Perricone, D.R.E.
Students 320.

Laurel, Prince Georges Co., St. Mary (1843), Revs. V. James Lockman; Kevin P. O'Reilly; Robert L. Keesler, Pastor Emeritus; Joseph G. Stankavage; Deacons Donald Parker; Douglas Sinchak.
Res., 114 St. Mary's Pl., 20707. Tel: 301-725-3080; 953-3255; Fax: 301-725-2409. [CEM]
School—Tel: 301-498-1433. Alberta Martino, Prin.
Lay Teachers 27; Students 358.
Catechesis/Religious Programs—Tel: 301-490-8770. Sr. Loretta Primus, S.F.C.C., D.R.E.
Students 780.

St. Nicholas (1967), Rev. John M. Barry; Deacon Francis Hannagan.
Res., 8603 Contee Rd., 20708. Tel: 301-490-5116; 5117; Fax: 301-490-1527.

Catechesis/Religious Programs—Tel: 301-776-8303.
Students 245.

Leonardtown, St. Mary's Co., St. Aloysius (1710), Revs. James P. Meyers; Patrick E. Dempsey.
Res., 22800 Washington St., P.O. Box 310, 20650. Tel: 301-475-8064; Fax: 301-475-8762. [CEM]
School—The Father Andrew White, S.J., Tel: 301-475-9795; Fax: 301-475-3537.
Sisters 1; Lay Teachers 15; Students 282.
Catechesis/Religious Programs—Tel: 301-475-8680.
Students 135.

Lexington Park, St. Mary's Co., Immaculate Heart of Mary (1947), Rev. Thomas A. Gude.
Mailing Address: P.O. Box 6, 20653. Tel: 301-863-8144; Fax: 301-863-8180. [CEM]
Catechesis/Religious Programs—Tel: 301-863-8793. Patricia DeCarlo, D.R.E.
Students 224.

McConchie, Charles Co., St. Catherine of Alexandria (1911), Rev. Matthew E. Thompson; Deacon Frank L. Hopson.
Mailing Address: P.O. Box 278, Port Tobacco, 20677. Tel: 301-934-9630. [CEM]

Mechanicsville, St. Mary's Co., Immaculate Conception (1876), Rev. Msgr. Paul J. Gozaloff.
Mailing Address: P.O. Box 166, 20659. Tel: 301-884-3123; Fax: 301-884-7437.
Catechesis/Religious Programs—Tel: 301-884-3016.
Students 255.

Medley's Neck, St. Mary's Co., Our Lady's (1776), Rev. Robert J. Kosty; Deacon Thomas C. Spalding, Sr.
Mailing Address: P.O. Box 111, Leonardtown, 20650. Tel: 301-475-8403; Fax: 301-475-6632. [CEM]
Catechesis/Religious Programs—Students 65.

Mitchellville, Prince Georges Co., Holy Family (1938), Rev. Michael C. Kidd; Deacons Arturo Mallari; Matthew Reilly.
Mailing Address: P.O. Box 1599, 20717. Tel: 301-249-2266; Fax: 301-249-2524. [CEM]
Catechesis/Religious Programs—Tel: 301-249-1167.
Students 135.

Morganza, St. Mary's Co., St. Joseph, Rev. Neal A. Ward; Deacon James A. Somerville.
Res., 20660. Tel: 301-884-4229. [JC]

Mount Rainier, Prince Georges Co., St. James (1905) (Hispanic), Revs. Peter R. Alliata; Agustin Mateo Ayala; Deacons Rodney R. Forbes; John H. Turner. In res., Rev. Auxentius Panares.
Res., 3628 Rhode Island Ave., 20712. Tel: 301-927-0567; Fax: 301-927-5289.
Catechesis/Religious Programs—Tel: 301-922-0567.
Students 192.

Newport, Charles Co., St. Mary (1674), Rev. Frederick H. MacIntyre.
Res., 11555 St. Mary's Church Rd., Charlotte Hall, 20622. Tel: 301-934-8825; Fax: 301-934-0245. [CEM]
Catechesis/Religious Programs—Students 83.

Newtowne, St. Mary's Co., St. Francis Xavier (1640), Rev. John S. Mattingly.
Res., 21370 Newtowne Neck Rd., Leonardtown, 20650. Tel: 301-475-9885; Fax: 301-475-5662. [CEM]
Catechesis/Religious Programs—Students 108.

Norbeck, Montgomery Co., St. Patrick (1966), Rev. Msgr. Thomas A. Kane; Revs. Paul McKane, O.S.B.; Alfred J. Harris; Deacon Ronald Crowley.
Res., 4101 Norbeck Rd., Rockville, 20853. Tel: 301-924-2284; 2285; Fax: 301-929-3017.
Catechesis/Religious Programs—Tel: 301-929-9314.
Students 600.

North Beach, Calvert Co., St. Anthony (1905), Rev. Robert S. Grace; Deacons John F. Lynch; Michael L. Hoffman.
Res., 8960 Bay Ave., 20714. Tel: 410-257-2368; 301-855-7756 (Washington); Fax: 301-855-6839.
Catechesis/Religious Programs—Tel: 202-855-0897. Sr. Anne Parker, D.R.E.
Students 292.

Olney, Montgomery Co., St. Peter (1898), Revs. Thomas M. Kalita; Damian Shadwell; Robert Panke. In res., Rev. Canice Treacy.
Res., 2900 Sandy Spring Rd., 20832. Tel: 301-924-3774; Fax: 301-774-5259.
School—Tel: 301-774-9112. Mrs. Carol Mikoni, Prin.
Lay Teachers 22; Students 312.
Catechesis/Religious Programs—Tel: 301-570-4952. D.R.E.: Mrs. Gloria Zapiain, (Grades PreK-5); Mr. Robert Bellows, (Grades 6-8).
Students 982.

Oxon Hill, Prince Georges Co., St. Columba (1960), Revs. Godfrey Mosley; Seraphim Molina; Deacon Richard Fisher.
Res., 7804 Livingston Rd., 20745. Tel: 301-567-5506; Fax: 301-567-6546.

School—7800 Livingston Rd., 20745. Tel: 301-567-6212; Fax: 301-567-6907.
Lay Teachers 11; Students 269.
Catechesis/Religious Programs—Tel: 301-567-6113.
Students 161.

Piscataway, Prince Georges Co., St. Mary (1830), Revs. Kevin Hart; Mark W. Ervin; Daniel Paul Leary.
Res., 13401 Piscataway Rd., Clinton, 20735. Tel: 301-292-0527; Fax: 301-292-8786. [CEM]
School—Tel: 301-292-2522.
Lay Teachers 13; Students 261.
Catechesis/Religious Programs—Tel: 301-292-2486.
Students 123.

Pomfret, Charles Co., St. Joseph (1763), Rev. J. Michael Quill.
Mailing Address: P.O. Box 100, 20675. Tel: 301-870-3041; 609-4670; Fax: 301-609-7564. [CEM]
Catechesis/Religious Programs—Students 235.

Poolesville, Montgomery Co., Our Lady of the Presentation (1992), Rev. Y. David Brault.
Mailing Address: P.O. Box 428, 20837. Tel: 301-349-2045; 972-7504; Fax: 301-349-5423.
Catechesis/Religious Programs—Students 247.

Potomac, Montgomery Co., Our Lady of Mercy (1959) (Korean-Chinese), Rev. Msgr. John J. Enzler; Rev. William C. Metzdorf; Deacons F. Ian Ravenscroft; James Yun.
Res., 9200 Kentsdale Dr., 20854. Tel: 301-365-1415; Fax: 301-365-3104. [CEM]
School—9222 Kentsdale Dr., 20854. Tel: 301-365-4477; Fax: 301-365-3423. Sr. Virginia Pfau, I.H.M., Prin.
Sisters 1; Lay Teachers 24; Students 281.
Catechesis/Religious Programs—Tel: 301-365-1318.
Students 275.

Prince Frederick, Calvert Co., St. John Vianney (1965), Rev. Peter J. Daly.
Res., 105 Vianney Ln., 20678-4123. Tel: 410-535-0223; 301-855-1928; Fax: 410-535-4422. [CEM]
Catechesis/Religious Programs—Tel: 410-535-4395. Jeanette M. Pedone, D.R.E.
Students 290.

Ridge, St. Mary's Co., St. Michael (1824), Rev. Karl A. Chimiak.
Res., 20680. Tel: 301-872-4321. [CEM]
School—P.O. Box 429, 20680. Tel: 301-872-5454.
Sisters of St. Joseph of Chambery (Hartford, CT) 3; Lay Teachers 8; Students 220.
Catechesis/Religious Programs—Students 98.

Riverdale, Prince Georges Co., St. Bernard (1950), Revs. Maurice V. O'Connell; An Ngoc Vu; Deacons Ferd Meyer; John Waltz; Alfredo Hidalgo. In res., Rev. Hector Bruno de Jesus (Puerto Rico).
Res., 5700 St. Bernard Dr., 20737-2185. Tel: 301-277-1000; Fax: 301-277-3464.
School—Tel: 301-864-3801; Fax: 301-864-2912. Mrs. Barbara Etzel, Prin.
Lay Teachers 12; Students 259.
Catechesis/Religious Programs—Tel: 301-277-4220; Fax: 301-277-3464. Mrs. Carol Clement, D.R.E.
Students 125.

Rockville, Montgomery Co.,

1—St. Elizabeth, (1964), Rev. John F. MacFarlane.
Res., 917 Montrose Rd., 20852. Tel: 301-881-1380; Fax: 301-881-3068.
School—Tel: 301-881-1824; Fax: 301-881-6035.
Lay Teachers 22; Students 410.
Catechesis/Religious Programs—Students 180.

2—Shrine of St. Jude, (1956), Revs. Oliver McGready; William D. Byrne; G. Ralph Duffy; Timothy S. Galban; Deacon Nicholas E. Scholz. In res., Rev. Timothy J. O'Sullivan.
Res., 12701 Veirs Mill Rd., 20853. Tel: 301-946-8200; Fax: 301-946-4527.
School—Tel: 301-946-7888; Fax: 301-929-8927.
Lay Teachers 31; Students 541.
Catechesis/Religious Programs—Tel: 301-949-2336.
Students 224.

3—St. Mary, (1813), Rev. Msgr. Adam J. Kostick; Rev. L. James Downs; Deacon Daniel Kostka. In res., Rev. James J. Powderly.
Res., 520 Veirs Mill Rd., 20852. Tel: 301-424-5550; Fax: 301-424-5579. [CEM]
School—Tel: 301-762-4179; Fax: 301-762-8507.
Lay Teachers 15; Students 293.
Catechesis/Religious Programs—Tel: 301-762-8750.
Students 401.
Mission—Rockville, Montgomery Co., Our Lady of China, 1001 Grandin Ave., 20851. Tel: 301-294-3574. Rev. Paul Tsau.

4—St. Raphael, (1966), Revs. Michael Wilson; Miguel Umana, (Hispanic Ministry); John Ming Ruan; Deacons Daniel Thompson; Lawrence Gordon; John Pistone; Richard Mattocks; Frank Salatto.
Mailing Address: 1592 Kimblewick Rd., 20854.
Res., 1590 Kimblewick Rd., 20854. Tel: 301-762-2143; Fax: 301-762-0719.
Catechesis/Religious Programs—Students 880.

Rosaryville, Prince George's Co., Church of the Most Holy Rosary (1966), Rev. J. Isidore Dixon; Deacon Donald Carroll.
Res., 11704 Duley Station Rd., Upper Marlboro, 20772. Tel: 301-856-3880; 3881; Fax: 301-856-3944. [CEM]
Catechesis/Religious Programs—Tel: 301-868-5475. Mary Farrimond, D.R.E.
Students 130.

St. Inigoes, St. Mary's Co., St. Peter Claver, Rev. Patrick A. Smith.
Res., P.O. Box 240, 20684. Tel: 301-872-5460. [CEM]

St. Mary's City, St. Mary's Co., St. Cecilia (1974), Rev. Francis W. Krastel.
Res., 47950 Mattapany Rd., P.O. Box 67, 20686-0067. Tel: 301-862-4600; Fax: 301-863-7780. [JC]

Seat Pleasant, Prince Georges Co., St. Margaret (1908) (African American), Rev. Martin Gomes, SS.CC.; Deacons John Hill; Sam Minor.
Res., 408 Addison Rd., S., 20743. Tel: 301-336-3344; Fax: 301-336-5501.
School—410 Addison Rd., S., 20743. Tel: 301-336-3113.
Catechesis/Religious Programs—Students 205.
Mission—St. Matthias.

Silver Spring, Montgomery Co.,

1—St. Andrew Apostle, (1959), Rev. Msgr. Thomas P. Kelley; Rev. Charles V. Antonicelli. In res., Revs. Joseph J. Kleinstuber; Vincent J. Rigdon; Deacon Kevin M. Mukri.
Res., 11600 Kemp Mill Rd., 20902. Tel: 301-649-3700; Fax: 301-681-3527.
School—Tel: 301-649-3555; Fax: 301-649-2352. Mrs. Joan Hosmer, Prin.
Lay Teachers 26; Students 553.
Catechesis/Religious Programs—Tel: 301-649-4200.
Students 214.

2—St. Bernadette, (Four Corners), Rev. Samuel C. Giese; Deacons Bernard A. Bernier; Dennis J. O'Neill; Thomas E. Roszkowski.
Res., 70 University Blvd., E., 20901. Tel: 301-593-0357; Fax: 301-593-3088.
School—Tel: 301-593-5611; Fax: 301-593-9042.
Sisters 3; Lay Teachers 18; Students 450.
Catechesis/Religious Programs—Mrs. Jane Bailey, D.R.E.
Students 144.

3—St. Camillus, (1951), Revs. Michael Tyson, O.F.M.; Jud Weiksnar, O.F.M.; Bro. Henry Fulmer, O.F.M.; Deacon Peter Barbernitz. In res., Rev. Alban Maguire, O.F.M.
Res., 1600 St. Camillus Dr., 20903. Tel: 301-434-8400; Fax: 301-434-8041.
School—1500 St. Camillus Dr., 20903. Tel: 301-434-2344; Fax: 301-434-7726.
Sisters 1; Brothers 1; Lay Teachers 21; Students 323.
Catechesis/Religious Programs—Tel: 301-434-2111. Pauline Fournier, D.R.E.
Students 386.
Child Care—(Four Corners), Tel: 301-439-1640; Fax: 301-439-7078. Mary Beth Smedley, Dir.
Certified Child Care Workers 17.

4—St. Catherine Laboure, (Wheaton) (1951), Rev. Robert G. Amey; Rev. Msgr. W. Joyce Russell, Pastor Emeritus; Rev. Rory T. Conley; Deacons Carlos Contreras; Raymond L. Chaput. In res., Rev. Santos Rene Maldonado.
Res., 11801 Claridge Rd., 20902. Tel: 301-946-3636; Fax: 301-946-5064.
School—Tel: 301-946-1717; Fax: 301-946-9572.
Daughters of Charity 3; Lay Teachers 24; Students 511.
Catechesis/Religious Programs—Tel: 301-946-3010.
Students 851.

5—Christ the King, (Wheaton) (1961), Revs. Robert J. Bozek; Luis Antonio Marroquin.
Res., 2300 East-West Hwy., 2301 Colston Dr., 20910. Tel: 301-589-8616; Fax: 301-587-1929.
Catechesis/Religious Programs—Tel: 301-589-8620. Sr. Dorothy A. Owen, R.S.C.J., D.R.E.
Students 244.

6—St. John the Baptist, (Spring Brook) (1960), Rev. Francis G. Kazista; Rev. Msgr. E. Carl Lyon; Rev. John J. Hurley; Deacons Norman Keller; Jack Hamilton.
Res., 12319 New Hampshire Ave., 20904. Tel: 301-622-1122; Fax: 301-625-9266.
School—Tel: 301-622-3076. Marianne Moore, Prin.
Servants of the Holy Heart of Mary 1; Lay Teachers 15; Students 267.
Catechesis/Religious Programs—Tel: 301-622-3933. Patricia Roberts, D.R.E.
Students 420.

7—St. John the Evangelist, (Wheaton) (1774), Revs. Oliver Mahedy; Thomas A. Meighan; Joseph F. Perkins; Deacon Dan P. Stallings.
Res., 10103 Georgia Ave., 20902. Tel: 301-681-7663; Fax: 301-681-8793. [CEM]
School—Tel: 301-681-7656; Fax: 301-681-7656. Sr. Kathleen Lannak, I.H.M., Prin.
Sisters-Servants of Immaculate Heart of Mary 4; Lay Teachers 22; Students 345.
Catechesis/Religious Programs—Tel: 301-681-7634.
Students 187.

8—St. Michael, (Wheaton) (1930), Rev. Peter C. Cronin; Rev. Msgr. Joseph W. Hartman, Pastor Emeritus; Rev. John R. Clark; Deacons Tom C. Newman; John A. Marinari; Roberto Salgado. In res., Rev. Michael W. Douglas.
Res., 824 Pershing Dr., 20910. Tel: 301-589-1155; Fax: 301-589-3470.
School—824 Wayne Ave., 20910. Tel: 301-585-6873; Fax: 301-587-1142. Sr. Mary Raymond, Prin.
Lay Teachers 15; Students 276.
Catechesis/Religious Programs—Students 253.

9—Our Lady of Grace, (Leisure World) (1983), Rev. Msgr. John J. Madigan; Deacon Paul Pernecky, (Retired).
Res., 3134 Adderley Ct., 20906. Tel: 301-598-4233; Fax: 301-598-0843.

10—Our Lady Queen of Poland and Saint Maximilian Kolbe, (Leisure World) (1983) (Polish), Rev. Krzysztof Oska, S.Ch. (Poland).
Res., 9700 Rosensteel Ave., 20910. Tel: 301-589-1857.
Catechesis/Religious Programs—Students 50.

Solomons, Calvert Co., Our Lady Star of the Sea (1888), Rev. Richard E. Gardiner; Deacons John G. Etzel; Robert L. Connelly; Thomas B. Ricker.
Mailing Address: Box 560, 20688. Tel: 410-326-3535; Fax: 410-326-3679. [CEM]
School—Tel: 410-326-3171; Fax: 410-326-9478. Sr. Rosella Summe, C.D.P., Prin.
Sisters 2; Lay Teachers 9; Students 203.
Catechesis/Religious Programs—Jane Murphy, V.R.C., D.R.E.
Students 350.

Suitland, Prince George's Co., St. Bernardine (1966), Rev. Arnold W. DePorter.
Res., 2400 Brooks Dr., 20746-1144. Tel: 301-736-0707; Fax: 301-736-2984.

Takoma Park, Prince Georges Co., Our Lady of Sorrows (1932), Revs. James J. Suntum, S.F.; Jose Maria Conde, S.F.; Deacon James Wilson, Jr.
Res., 1006 Larch Ave., 20912. Tel: 301-891-3500; Fax: 301-891-1523.
School—1010 Larch Ave., 20912. Tel: 301-891-2555; Fax: 301-270-6919. Mrs. Gail Ruffin, Prin.
Lay Teachers 11; Students 281.
Catechesis/Religious Programs—Tel: 301-891-2033.
Students 105.

Upper Marlboro, Prince Georges Co., Saint Mary of the Assumption (1848), Rev. Msgr. Richard A. Hughes; Rev. Joseph A. Jenkins; Deacons Frank Klco; Anthony Barrasso.
Res., 14908 Main St., 20772. Tel: 301-627-3255; Fax: 301-627-5533. [CEM]
School—Tel: 301-627-4170; Fax: 301-627-6383. Mrs. Carol Marvin, Prin.
Sisters - Servants of the Immaculate Heart of Mary 4; Students 305.
Catechesis/Religious Programs—Tel: 301-627-4542. Mr. Charles Long, D.R.E.
Students 120.

Valley Lee, St. Mary's Co., St. George (1851), Rev. Robert B. Riedel; Deacon David R. Powell.
Mailing Address: P.O. Box 9, 20692. Tel: 301-994-0607; Fax: 301-994-1793. [CEM]
Chapel—St. George's Island, St. Francis Xavier.
Catechesis/Religious Programs—Tel: 301-994-0737.
Students 79.

Waldorf, Charles Co., St. Peter (1700), Rev. Msgr. Andrew J. Cassin; Revs. J. Wilfrid Parent; Prudencio Sanchez; Deacon Charles J. Wilson.
Res., 3320 St. Peter's Dr., 20601. Tel: 301-843-8916; Fax: 301-843-3163. [CEM]
School—Tel: 301-843-1955; Fax: 301-843-6371. Judith DeLucco, Prin.
Lay Teachers 29; Students 525.
Catechesis/Religious Programs—Tel: 301-843-9583. Sr. Mary Elizabeth Sakach, S.N.D., D.R.E.
Students 266.

Our Lady Help of Christians (1980), Rev. Eamon Dignan.
Mailing Address: 100 Village St., 20602-1837. Tel: 301-645-7112.

Res., 930 Barrington Dr., 20602-2838. Tel: 301-843-8823; Fax: 301-645-3635.
Catechesis/Religious Programs—Sr. Margery Rose, M.H.S.H., D.R.E.
Students 584.

Chaplains of Public Institutions

WASHINGTON. *General Hospital.* Rev. Thomas Poovannal, Chap.
St. Elizabeth's Hospital (Government Operated) National Rehabilitation Hospital and Children's Medical Center, 20032. Tel: 202-574-7018. Rev. Benedict Faneye, O.P., Chap.
Washington Hospital Center. Revs. John S. Wintermyer, Chap.; Auxentius Panares, Assoc. Chap.

BETHESDA, MD. *National Institutes of Health, Clinical Center.* Rev. Eugene J. Linehan, S.J.

LANHAM, MD. *P.G. Doctor's Hospital.* Vacant. St. Matthias Parish, 20706.

Special Ministries:
Reverend Monsignors—
McMain, Robert O., Special Delegate for the Preservation of Historic Documents & Artifacts
O'Donnell, William F., Dir., Catholic Cemeteries
Roensch, Roger C., Dir., Spiritual Programs and Pilgrimages, Basilica of the National Shrine of the Immaculate Conception
Reverend Fathers—
Adams, John E., Dir., S.O.M.E.
Begg, Christopher T., Catholic University of America
Bradley, Denis J.M., Georgetown University
Bryant, Michael, Chap., District of Columbia Jail
Criscuolo, Salvatore A., Chap., Police and Fire Dept.
Hargrove, Jerry E., Chap., Howard University
Helm, Edward J., Catholic Deaf Center
Jones, Michael T., Chap., Good Counsel High School
Keffer, Robert F., Newman Center, University of Maryland
Kemp, Raymond B., Fellow, Woodstock Theological Center, Georgetown University
Kleinstuber, Joseph J., Dir., Admissions, Public Rels. & Recruiting, St. John's College
Kuhn, John G., Dir., Anchor Mental Health Assoc.
McCarthy, Brien R., Chap., American University
Montgomery, William L., Teacher, Carroll High School
Mordino, Robert F., Dir., CYO Retreats
Mudd, John, Dir., Fundraising Carroll High School
O'Brien, Joseph A., Rector, Cardinal O'Boyle Residence
O'Brien, Raymond C., Asst. Dean, Catholic University
Powderly, James J., Substance Abuse Coord.
Rigdon, Vincent J., Dir., Propagation of the Faith
Stack, James M., Assoc. Dir., Office of Vocations for Men
Trancone, Gerard A., Center for the Deaf

Pastoral Center Special Ministries:
Most Rev.—
Lori, William E., Vicar General in Curia
Reverend Monsignors—
English, William J., Sec., Clergy
Farrell, Kevin J., Sec., Finance & Mgmt.
Gerhardt, Bernard C., Chancellor
Kane, William J., Vicar General
Sadusky, Joseph F., Judicial Vicar Tribunal
Reverend Fathers—
Bozek, Robert J., Tribunal
Brennan, Mark E., Dir., Vocations for Men
Douglas, Michael W., Tribunal
Fangmeyer, Leroy J., Exec. Dir., Office of Youth Ministry
Herbert, G. Paul, Tribunal
Hill, R. Cary, Sec., Parish Life & Worship
Knestout, Barry, Sec., Archbishop
Lee, Paul D., Dir., Continuing Educ. of Clergy & Dir., Office for Interreligious & Ecumenical Affairs.
Parry, Charles, Asst. Sec. Catholic Educ.
Reynierse, Peter J., Asst. to the Sec. for Clergy and Asst. Dir. of the Permanent Diaconate
Tappe, Walter J., Dir., Office of Worship

Hospital & Nursing Home Ministries:
Reverend Monsignors—
Hurley, Leonard F.
Reverend Fathers—
Kinter, John P.
McKay, John F.
Panares, Auxentius
Samaha, Jeffrey F.
Walsh, Francis M.
Wintermyer, John S.

On Duty Outside the Archdiocese:
Reverend Monsignors—
Albacete, Lorenzo, New York
Bazan, Joaquin, Albuquerque, NM
Gillen, James G., Vatican City State, Europe
Langsfeld, Paul J., Mount St. Mary Seminary, Emmitsburg, MD
Roensch, Roger, Vatican City State
Reverend Fathers—
Culkin, Michael, Lancaster, PA
Gancayco, Richard K., Bolivia
Holt, Paul-Stephen, New York
Izac, Andre C., North Carolina
Jacobs, Peter
Kuebler, A.M. Seamus, Massachusetts
Murphy, Francis J., Pastoral Center, Reno, NV
Oberle, James, California
Sanz, Jose, Antonio, TX
Slevin, Henry, Vietnam
Twohig, Christopher T., Ireland
Ulshafer, Thomas, S.S., Baltimore, MD

Military Chaplains:
Reverend Fathers—
Cunningham, Gerard M.
Cusick, Kevin M.
Fitz-Patrick, David M.
Hines, J. William
Lee, Matthew (J.T.)
Mudd, David A.
Saltysiak, Paul M.
Siriani, Klaus-Werner J.

Absent On Leave:
Reverend Fathers—
Burke, Herbert
Chimiak, Mark

Retired:
Reverend Monsignors—
Albert, Louis W., 1514 Perrel Ln., Bowie, MD 20716
Arthur, E. Robert, Jeanne Jugan Residence, 4200 Harewood Rd., N.E., Washington, DC 20017
Bailey, John L., St. Francis Xavier, Washington, DC
Benson, John D., Washington, DC
Coyne, Joseph B., Carroll Manor, 1150 Varnum St., N.E., Washington, DC 20017
DiNardo, Ramon A., The Westchester, 4000 Cathedral Ave., Apt. 854-B, Washington, DC 20016
Dooley, R. Joseph, (Outside the Diocese)
Echle, Harry A., Our Lady of Victory, Washington, DC 20007
Farina, Michael F., St. Patrick, Washington, DC
Grodavent, Thomas J., 7 Scott Rd., Colorado Springs, CO 80906
Hartman, Joseph W., Cardinal O'Boyle Residence, P.O. Box 29206, Washington, DC 20017
Jimenez, Armando, Cardinal O'Boyle Residence, P.O. Box 29206, Hyattsville, MD 20017
Lyon, E. Carl, St. John the Baptist, Silver Spring, MD
McMain, Robert O., St. Ann, Washington, DC
Mohan, Robert Paul
O'Connor, Aloysius E., Holy Angels, Avenue, MD
Quinn, W. Louis, Our Lady of Lourdes, Bethesda, MD
Russell, W. Joyce, Carroll Manor, 1150 Varnum St., N.E., Washington, DC 20017
Teletchea, Joseph L., St. Jerome, Hyattsville, MD
Reverend Fathers—
Barry, Paul, 5404 Bye St., Capitol Heights, MD 20743
Bender, Lawrence, S.S., St. Martin's Retirement & Nursing Home, 601 Maiden Choice Ln., Baltimore, MD 21228
Bloom, R. Frederick, 6304 Waverley Dr., Frederick, MD 21702
Bober, Francis J., 2475 Virginia Ave., N.W., #407, Washington, DC 20037
Bonfigilo, Anthony J., 12790 Griffing Blvd., North Miami, FL 33161
Branch, Leslie, Carroll Manor, 1150 Varnum St., N.E., Washington, DC 20017
Brogan, Hugh T., 678 Main St., Sugar Notch, PA 18706
Caimi, Luke A., Rte. 11, Box 312, Hendersonville, NC 28739
Casey, James E., 3507 Farragut Ave., Kensington, MD 20895
Connor, John V., 137 Bayshore Dr., South Bethany, DE
DiNorcia, Americo, Gaithersburg, MD
Duffy, G. Ralph, Shrine of St. Jude, Rockville, MD
Evans, Edward, St. Ambrose, Cheverly, MD 20785
Finan, James
Flaherty, Francis T., P.O. Box 321, Deal, NJ 07723
Gallagher, Roger P., Cardinal O'Boyle Residence, P.O. Box 29206, Washington, DC 20017
Hartel, Edward T., Washington, DC
Higgins, John J., 300 Ocean Ave., Seabright, NJ 07760
Holden, Paul, Lot 72A, Massey's Landing, Millsboro, DE 19966
Ihrie, Bernard R., 3637 Bay Dr., Edgewater, MD 21037
Januszkiewicz, Henry, 4281 Inca Dove Ct., Naples, FL 34119
Joy, James B., Jr.
Joyce, George V., 15 Orchard St., Holyoke, MA 01040
Keesler, Robert L., St. Mary, Laurel, MD
Kemp, Patrick W., 2900 Shipmaster Way, #301, Annapolis, MD 21401
Lubey, John A., Cardinal O'Boyle Residence, P.O. Box 29206, Washington, DC 20017
McCormack, Brendan, Bethesda, MD
McGuigan, Robert, Jeanne Jugan Residence, 4200 Harewood Rd., N.E., Washington, DC 20017
McMahon, John B., 575-B Turnberry Blvd., Newport News, VA 23602
Murphy, Desmond P., 6200 Westchester Park Dr., #705, College Park, MD 20740
Newman, Aloysius T., 6260 Crain Hwy., P.O. Box 2225, LaPlata, MD 20646
Norris, Walter J., St. Paul's, Damascus, MD
Norton, Joseph E., Jeanne Jugan Residence, 4200 Harewood Rd., N.E., Washington, DC 20017
O'Shea, Philip A., Blessed Sacrament, Washington, DC
Pagone, Joseph, Granada Nursing Home, 4107 Libert Hts., Baltimore, MD 21207
Petrella, Robert
Pritchard, Edward, Washington, DC
Quinones, Miguel P., Cardinal O'Boyle Residence, P.O. Box 29206, Washington, DC 20017
Roy, J. Jean, 15 Talmuth Ave., Haverhill, MA 01830
Salcedo, Luis G., St. Bartholomew, Bethesda, MD
Schaefer, Thomas, Washington, DC
Schellenberg, Milton A., 5914 Welborn Dr., Bethesda, MD 20816
Sheehan, Thomas J., St. Peter, Washington, DC
Smith, Alphonsus M., Washington, DC
Studney, J. Edward, Cardinal O'Boyle Residence, P.O. Box 29206, Washington, DC 20017
Tou, Louis, 510 Edmonston Dr., Rockville, MD 20851
Tran-Khac-Hy, Hilarius, Gaithersburg, MD
Trapold, John T., New Jersey
Treacy, Canice, St. Peter, Olney, MD
Twiddy, Paul, Charlotte Hall Veteran's Home, Rte. 5, Charlotte Hall, MD 20622
Wharton, Robert H., Cardinal O'Boyle Residence, P.O. Box 29206, Washington, DC 20017
Winnenberg, John O., San Diego, CA
Znotinas, John, 2712 Fairlawn St., Temple Hills, MD 20748

Permanent Deacons:
Abbate, Paul J., St. Joseph, Archdiocese of Agana
Agostinelli, Floyd D., St. Francis de Sales, Washington, DC
Allen, David A., St. Jane de Chantal, Bethesda, MD
Allen, Robert F., St. John Neumann, Gaithersburg, MD
Bailey, Aston A., Unassigned
Ballard, Harvey W., St. Michael, Baden, MD
Barnes, David J., St. Edward the Confessor, Bowie, MD
Barnes, John R., St. Joseph, Pomfret, MD
Barrasso, Anthony T., Mount Calvary, Forestville, MD
Barrett, Kenneth, St. Martin, Gaithersburg, MD
Barrett, Raymond J., Ascension, Bowie, MD
Barry, T. Kevin, St. Edward, Bowie, MD
Battaglia, Thomas D., Reedville, VA
Bechet, Leon J., St. Joseph, Landover, MD
Begg, George B., Jr., St. Jane de Chantal, Bethesda, MD
Bell, Lawrence G., St. Martin, Gaithersburg, MD
Beller, Edwin J., (Retired)
Bernier, Bernard A., Jr., St. Bernadette, Silver Spring, MD
Berry, Robert L., St. Gabriel, Washington, DC
Betz, Andrew J., St. Joseph, Beltsville, MD
Black, Joseph L., Santa Fe, NM
Blaesing, Carl F., St. John the Evangelist, Clinton, MD
Blaine, B. Paul, Jr., (Retired)
Bobbitt, John W., St. Stephen Martyr, Washington, DC
Boesman, William C., St. Thomas the Apostle, Washington, DC
Brink, Edward J., St. Mary, Upper Marlboro, MD
Briscoe, John A., Assumption, Washington, DC
Brokenborough, Alfred T., Incarnation, Washington, DC
Brown, James H., Holy Redeemer, Washington, DC
Brown, Sylvester, Sacred Heart, Washington, DC
Brown, William J., III, Peacham, VT
Burroughs, Eugene, St. Mary, Bryantown, MD
Butler, Kevin A., Sr., Holy Comforter/St. Cyprian, Washington, DC
Cahoon, David L., Jr., St. Mary, Barnesville, MD
Cain, Leonard F., Wyomissing, PA

Carr, James, Resurrection, Burtonsville, MD
Carroll, Donald T., Holy Rosary, Upper Marlboro, MD
Chaput, Raymond L., St. Catherine Laboure, Silver Spring, MD
Chase, Ira E., Our Lady of Perpetual Help, Washington, DC
Chaves, Antonio, St. Mark's, Hyattsville, MD
Coates, Vincent J., St. Joseph, Capitol Hill, DC
Coleman, Earle W., St. Luke, Washington, DC
Collins, Gerald A., Holy Family, Hillcrest Hts., MD
Connelly, Robert L., Our Lady Star of the Sea, Solomons, MD
Connor, James E., Salisbury, MD
Connors, John A., (Retired)
Conrad, Joseph M., St. Luke, Washington, DC
Contreras, Carlos E., St. Catherine La Boure, Silver Spring, MD
Cooper, Philip J., Mother Seton, Germantown, MD
Cordova-Ferrer, Nathaniel, St. Mark, Hyattsville, MD
Crowley, Ronald C., St. Patrick, Rockville, MD
Cummins, Don E., Tacoma, WA
Cummins, Eugene J., Jr., St. Martin, Gaithersburg, MD
Cyrus, Ralph W., St. Teresa of Avila, Washington, DC
Daniels, Willis, St. Aloysius, Washington, DC
Davies, Gary, Little Flower, Bethesda, MD
Davis, William E., Wilmington, NC
DeRoze, Donald G., Resurrection, Burtonsville, MD
DiDuca, Paul, Our Lady of the Visitation, Darnestown, MD
Ditewig, William, Holy Redeemer, Kensington, MD
Donlon, Jerome A., Holy Cross, Garrett Park, MD
Draper, Harry R., Incarnation, Washington, DC
Dudley, Jesse J., St. Aloysius, Washington, DC
Dunne, Joseph E., Durango, CO
Ealey, Ronald R., Wichita, KS
Edelin, Charles E., Jr., Holy Comforter-St. Cyprian, Washington, DC
Elliott, Thomas B., Ascension, Bowie, MD
Emley, William P., Jr., St. Ignatius, Chapel Point, MD
Enderle, Francis X., Military Services Archdiocese
Enright, Timothy D., Mother Seton, Germantown, MD
Etzel, John G., Our Lady Star of the Sea, Solomons, MD
Feneis, Albert G.
Finerty, John F., St. Paul, Damascus, MD
Fisher, Richard A., St. Columba, Oxon Hill, MD
Flanagan, Michael W., Our Lady Help of Christians, Waldorf, MD
Flynn, Leo, Our Lady of Victory, Washington, DC
Forbes, Rodney R., St. James, Mt. Rainier, MD
Forbes, Thomas S., Incarnation, Washington, DC
Ford, James A., Holy Name, Washington, DC
Fortney, Charles R., St. Joseph, Morganza, MD
Foster, George, Unassigned
Garcia, David F., New Mexico
Genis, Thomas P., Immaculate Conception, Washington, DC
Gignilliat, Robert L., St. Joseph, Pomfret, MD
Gordon, Lawrence C., St. Matthew's Cathedral, Washington, DC
Hamilton, John G., St. John Baptist, Silver Spring, MD
Hannagan, Francis L., St. Nicholas, Laurel, MD
Haywood, Hiram H., Jr., Basilica of the Shrine of the Immaculate Conception, Washington, DC
Hidalgo, Alfredo, St. Bernard, Riverdale, MD
Hill, Charles, S.O.M.E., Washington, DC
Hill, Thomas O., Sr., (Retired)
Hoffman, Michael R., St. Anthony, North Beach, MD
Holson, Edward, St. Mark, Hyattsville, MD
Hong, Pascal, St. Francis of Assisi, Derwood, MD
Hopson, Frank, St. Ignatius, Hilltop, MD
Hume, W. Michael, Duluth, MN
Interlandi, Joseph S., St. Peter, Olney, MD
Jackson, Harold I., St. Francis de Sales, Washington, DC
Jardeleza, Jack, (Retired)
Johnson, Bernard C., St. Mary Mother of God, Washington, DC
Johnson, Samuel A., Our Lady of Perpetual Help, Washington, DC
Jones, Thomas R., Our Lady of Perpetual Help, Washington, DC
Keller, Grafton T., St. George, Valley Lee, MD
Keller, Norman B., (Retired)
Kelly, John D., St. Anthony, Washington, DC
Klco, Frank, St. Mary, Upper Marlboro, MD
Kostka, Daniel S., St. Mary, Rockville, MD
Kraemer, Francis W., Sr., St. Peter, Washington, DC
Kronschnabel, Michael C., Archdiocese of Baltimore, MD
Kube, Carl B., Roseville, CA
Kunsemiller, John H., Archdiocese of Los Angeles, CA
L'Heureux, George G., Unassigned
Lacovaro, James G., Archbishop Carroll High School, Washington, DC
Lemon, John, St. Peter, Olney, MD
Lennon, Joseph M., (Retired)
Leonard, John M., (Retired)
Levy, Richard A., Jr., Archdiocese of San Francisco, CA
Locke, John W., Hedgesville, VA
Luetjen, Palmer, St. Jane de Chantal, Bethesda, MD
Lynch, John F., St. Anthony, North Beach, MD
Mallari, Arturo O., Holy Family, Mitchellville, MD
Mallon, Charles A., Orlando, FL
Mangold, Charles C., (Retired)
Marinari, A. John, St. Michael, Silver Spring, MD
Martin, E. Chad, Jesus the Good Shephard, Dunkirk, MD
Martin, J. Murry, St. Mary, Upper Marlboro, MD
Martin, Nerus O., Jr., St. Thomas More, Washington, DC
Mastrangelo, Eugene K., St. Pius X, Bowie, MD
Mattocks, Richard E., St. Raphael, Rockville, MD
McAskill, Donald K., Fredericksburg, VA
McCann, James C., St. Rose of Lima, Gaithersburg, MD
McGinness, John J., St. Patrick, Washington, DC
McGlade, H. Donald, National Naval Medical Center
McGrath, Joseph B., (Retired)
McMahon, Anthony, National Naval Medical Center
Merella, Bartholomew J., Holy Redeemer, College Park, MD
Meyer, Ferdinand, St. Bernard, Riverdale, MD
Middleton, Henry D., III, St. Mary, Bryantown, MD
Migliorini, Louis, Sr.,(Retired), Ocean City, MD
Miles, Lawrence A., St. Teresa of Avila, Washington, DC
Miller, Alfred A., Jr., Our Lady Queen of Peace, Washington, DC
Miller, Lawrence L., Archdiocese for Military Services, U.S.A.
Minor, Samuel L., Jr., St. Margaret, Seat Pleasant, MD
Moll, Anthony W., St. John, Clinton, MD
Moskaitis, J. Vincent, St. Paul, Damascus, MD
Mukri, Kevin, St. Andrew the Apostle, Silver Spring, MD
Murati, George, St. Augustine, FL
Newman, C. Thomas, St. Michael, Silver Spring, MD
Nguyen, John H., Our Lady of Vietnam, Silver Spring, MD
Nosacek, Andrew J., St. Pius X, Bowie, MD
O'Neill, Dennis J., St. Bernadette, Silver Spring, MD
Oettinger, Frank F., Diocese of Orlando
Olivares, Jose, St. Raphael, Rockville, MD
Om, Michael W., Our Lady of Mercy, Potomac, MD
Paolucci, Robert J., St. Ambrose, Cheverly, MD
Parker, Charles J., Leave of Absence
Parker, Donald A., St. Mary of the Mills, Laurel, MD
Pernecky, Paul, (Retired)
Picard, Adrien D., Columbia, MD
Pinder, Wilbur L., Jr., St. Francis of Assisi, Derwood, MD
Ponzette, John, St. Mary, Laurel, MD
Powell, David R., St. George, Valley Lee, MD
Price, Robert, St. Margaret of Scotland, Seat Pleasant, MD
Pyle, Jay Allen, St. Matthias, Lanham, MD
Quander, James W., (Retired)
Raffensperger, Jeffrey, Sacred Heart, Bowie, MD
Ravenscroft, F. Ian, Our Lady of Mercy, Potomac, MD
Redding, Edward R., Our Lady of Victory, Washington, DC
Reilly, Matthew B., Jr., Holy Family, Mitchellville, MD
Rice, Ulysses, St. Matthew Cathedral, Washington, DC
Ricker, Philip W., St. Mark, Hyattsville, MD
Ricker, Thomas B., Jr., Our Lady Star of the Sea, Solomons, MD
Robey, Frank A., Jr., Holy Redeemer, Kensington, MD
Robinson, Stephen M., St. Mary, Landover Hills, MD
Roszkowski, Thomas E., St. Bernadette, Silver Spring, MD
Rourke, Walter G., Holy Ghost, Issue, MD
Salgado, Roberto, Capilla Latina, Washington, DC
Scholz, Nicholas E., Shrine of St. Jude, Rockville, MD
Schopfer, Richard J., Little Flower, Bethesda, MD
Serafini, Bartolo, Capilla Latina, Washington, DC
Sferrella, Joseph J., York, PA
Shewmaker, John B., Our Lady of Lourdes, Bethesda, MD
Sinchak, J. Douglas, St. Mary of the Mills, Laurel, MD
Smith, Anthony S., St. Francis Xavier, Washington, DC
Somerville, James, St. Joseph, Morganza, MD
Somerville, John W., Bascilica of the Shrine of the Immaculate Conception, Washington, DC
Spalding, Thomas C., Our Lady's Church, Medley's Neck, MD
Springer, James R., El Paso, TX
Stackpole, Terrell U., Campus Ministry, Univ. of Maryland, College Park, MD
Stallings, Dan P., Sr., St. John Evangelist, Silver Spring, MD
Stewart, John P., St. Teresa of Avila, Washington, DC
Sweeney, Anthony J., III, Immaculate Heart of Mary, Lexington Park, MD
Taylor, Michael J., St. Mary, Landover Hills, MD
Terrar, David B., St. Paul, Damascus, MD
Testudine, Joseph, Airmen's & Soldier's Home, Washington, DC
Thomas, Reginald A., Our Lady Queen of Peace, Washington, DC
Thomas, William, Holy Name, Washington, DC
Thompson, Daniel R., St. Raphael, Rockville, MD
Thompson, Finis E., Ascension, Bowie, MD
Thurston, Reynaldo J., Leave of Absence
Tintle, Jerome A., St. Jerome, Hyattsville, MD
Treacy, Robert J., Diocese of Wilmington
Trichel, Allen J., Our Lady of Help of Christians, Waldorf, MD
Vargas, Jorge W., Our Lady Queen of the Americas, Washington, DC
Vergot, John J., (Retired)
Vita, William A., Jr., Mother Seton, Germantown, MD
Wakefield, Walter W., III, Diocese of Cincinnati, OH
Waltz, John F., St. Bernard, Riverdale, MD
Weightman, Stanley, St. Bernard, Riverdale, MD
Welch, Joseph, St. Edward, Bowie, MD
Weschler, Charles A., St. Paul, Damascus, MD
West, Richard A., (Retired)
Whitaker, Robert W., St. Ann, Washington, DC
White, Robert C., Sr., St. Augustine, Washington, DC
Whitfield, Robert J., St. Francis of Assisi, Derwood, MD
Wilbur, Carl, N.I.H., Bethesda, MD
Wilkinson, Lawrence A., St. Anthony, Washington, DC
Wilson, Charles J., St. Martin, Washington, DC
Wilson, James, Our Lady of Sorrows, Takoma Park, MD
Yates, Paul F., (Retired)
Yun, James, Our Lady of Mercy, Potomac, MD
Ziemianski, Lawrence L., Arlington, VA
Zuluaga, Gustavo, Hispanic Catholic Center, Washington, DC
Zusi, J. Michael, Archdiocese of Baltimore, MD

INSTITUTIONS LOCATED IN THE ARCHDIOCESE

[A] SEMINARIES, ARCHDIOCESAN

WASHINGTON. *Theological College of the Catholic University of America*, 401 Michigan Ave., N.E., 20017. Tel: 202-319-5900; Fax: 202-319-5909.
Web site: http://www.theologicalcollege.org
Sulpician Fathers. Legal Title: *The Sulpician Seminary of Washington.*
Faculty: Revs. Howard P. Bleichner, S.S., Ph.D., Rector; William J. Moorman, O.SS.T.; David D. Thayer, S.S., S.T.L., Ph.D.; Albert C. Giaquinto, S.S., M.A., S.T.L.; Thomas R. Hurst, S.S., S.T.L., Ph.D., Vice Rector; Bro. Donald Boccardi, S.M. Priests 5; Religious 1; Students 67.

[B] SEMINARIES, RELIGIOUS OR SCHOLASTICATES

WASHINGTON. *Atonement Seminary-Franciscan Friars of the Atonement*, 145 Taylor St., N.E., 20017. Tel: 202-529-1114. Rev. Patrick Cogan, S.A., Admin. In res. Revs. Paul Ojibway, S.A.; Carmen Giuliano, S.A.; Dennis Murphy, S.A., (Retired); Clement St. Jacques, S.A., (Retired). Priests 5; Brothers 1; Students 1.

Augustinian College, Order of St. Augustine, 3700 Oakview Ter., N.E., 20017-2521. Tel: 202-635-5299; Fax: 202-635-5296. Revs. Martin L. Smith, O.S.A., Prior & Treas.; Robert J. Guessetto, O.S.A., Dir., Professed Prog. & Prenovices. In res. Revs. Francis J. Horn, O.S.A.; Brian Frawley, O.S.A.; Francis J. Doyle, O.S.A. Priests 5; Students 7.

DeSales School of Theology, 721 Lawrence St., N.E., 20017. Tel: 202-269-9412; Fax: 202-526-2720. Rev.

John W. Crossin, O.S.F.S., Pres. Priests 8; Brothers 1; Sisters 1; Lay Teachers 2; Total Enrollment 60.

Deshairs Community-Oblates of St. Francis de Sales Residence, 1621 Otis St., N.E., 20018-2321. Tel: 202-526-7403. Revs. Lewis S. Fiorelli, O.S.F.S.; Donald J. Heet, O.S.F.S.; Bro. John M. Carroll, O.S.F.S. Priests 2; Brothers 1.

Diocesan Laborer Priests, House of Studies (1966), 3706 15th St., N.E., 20017. Tel: 202-832-4217; Fax: 202-526-5692. Revs. Rutilio J. del Riego, Dir.; Joseph M. Ambros; Thomas E. Murphy; Gabriel Calvo. Priests 4; Total Enrollment 3.

Dominican House of Studies, 487 Michigan Ave., N.E., 20017. Tel: 202-529-5300; Fax: 202-636-4460. Very Rev. John C. Vidmar, O.P., Prior; Revs. Brian J. Shanley, O.P., Subprior; Vincent Wiseman, O.P., Student Master; Very Rev. Thomas P. McCreesh, O.P., Pres., Pontifical Faculty; Bro. Martin Downey, O.P., Economic Admin.; Revs. John W. Burke, O.P., Dir. Word of God Institute; Joseph Augustine DiNoia, O.P., Exec. Dir. Secretariate - Doctrine/Pastoral Practices NCCB; Peter M. Batts, O.P.; Steven C. Boguslawski, O.P.; Michael Ciccone, O.P.; Pierre H. Conway, O.P.; William J. Conlan, O.P.; Lawrence J. Donohoo, O.P.; John Martin Egan, O.P.; Norman H. Fenton, O.P.; Kenneth Harkins, O.P.; Mark Heath, O.P.; William J. Hill, O.P.; John Frederick Hinnebusch, O.P.; John Patrick McGovern, O.P.; Kevin McGrath, O.P.; Gabriel Pivarnik, O.P.; Kurt Pritzl, O.P.; Matthew Rzeczkowski, O.P.; Albert Paretsky, O.P.; Joseph Tortorici, O.P. In res. Revs. Philip Pan, O.P.; Paul Pluth, O.S.B.; Liem Tran, O.P.; Mark Wenzinger, O.S.B. Priests 29; Brothers 1; Clerical Students 23; Seminarians 23.

Franciscan Fathers, T.O.R., Tau Fraternity, 1359 Monroe St., N.W., 20017. Tel: 202-526-6324. Candidates 6.

Franciscan Mission Service of North America, 401 Michigan Ave., N.E., 20017. Tel: 202-832-1762; Fax: 202-832-1778.
E-mail: jnangle@ico.apc.org
Sr. Jean Amore, S.M.I.C., Coord., Overseas Lay Ministry Prog.; Rev. Joseph Nangle, O.F.M., Exec. Dir. Priests 1; Sisters 1; Lay Staff 2.

Josephite Pastoral Center, 1200 Varnum St., N.E., 20017. Tel: 202-526-9270; 9271. Rev. John G. Harfmann, S.S.J., Dir.; Maria M. Lannon, Assoc. Dir. Priests 1; Brothers 2; Deacons 1; Lay Women 5.

Marian Fathers Scholasticate, 3885 Harewood Rd., N.E., 20017. Tel: 202-526-8884; Fax: 202-832-6551.
E-mail: dcmarion@aol.com
Web site: http://www.marion.org
Revs. Lawrence P. Dunn, M.I.C., Supr.; Joseph Roesch, M.I.C., Asst. Supr. & Formation Dir.; Dan Papineau, M.I.C., Seminarian, Second Counselor; David Briggs, M.I.C., Seminarian, Third Counselor; Revs. John Kobza, M.I.C.; Jaroslaw Gamrot, M.I.C. (Poland); Joseph Sielski, M.I.C. Tel: 410-778-7088. Priests 5; Students 8.

Marist College, The Scholasticate, 220 Taylor St., N.E., 20017-1095. Tel: 202-529-2821.
E-mail: marist@erols.com
Revs. Edwin L. Keel, S.M., Rector & Supr.; Joseph C. Hurtuk, S.M., Formation Team. Priests 2; Scholastics 5.

Maryknoll Fathers and Brothers, 4834 16th St., N.W., 20011. Tel: 202-726-4252; Fax: 202-726-0466. Revs. Francis Higdon, M.M., Dir.; Daniel Dolan, M.M.; Bros. John Blazo, M.M., Mission Educ. Dept.; Ronald Rinella, M.M.

Office of Justice and Peace, P.O. Box 29132, 20017. Tel: 202-832-1780; Fax: 202-832-5159.
E-mail: mknolldc@igc.org
Rev. Peter Ruggere, M.M.

Monastery of Our Lady of Mount Carmel, 2131 Lincoln Rd., N.E., 20002. Tel: 202-832-6622. Legal Title: *Monastery of Our Lady of Mount Carmel-House of Studies Order of Discalced Carmelite Friars*. Revs. Steven Payne, O.C.D., Prior; Valerian Noronha, O.C.D.; Theodore Centala, O.C.D.; Kieran Kavanaugh, O.C.D.; Francis Miller, O.C.D.; Joseph Koh, O.C.D.; Bros. Antonine DiSabella, O.C.D.; Bryan Paquette, O.C.D.; Edward O'Donnell, O.C.D.; Michael Stoegbauer, O.C.D.; Sebastian Reak, O.C.D. Priests 6; Brothers 5; Students 2.

Oblate College/Oblate Center for Mission Studies, 391 Michigan Ave., N.E., 20017-1586. Tel: 202-529-5244. Revs. Harry Winter, O.M.I., Ph.D.; Henry L. Lemoncelli, O.M.I., M.Ed., Supr.; Raymond Prybis, O.M.I., Ph.D. Ed., Treas.; David N. Power, O.M.I., S.T.D.; Matthew Casey, O.M.I.; Charles W. Gilles, O.M.I.; Donald Joyce, O.M.I., M.A.; John J. Leddy, O.M.I., M.A.; George F. McLean, O.M.I., Ph.D.; Calixtus Fernando; Seamus Finn, O.M.I., Ph.D.; Richard McAlear, O.M.I., S.T.L., Vocations; Gode Iwele, O.M.I., S.T.L.; Paul Costello, O.M.I.; J. William Sheehan, O.M.I., M.A., Prov.; Edmund Reginald, O.M.I.; James E. Sullivan, O.M.I.; William Antonio; Bros. Thomas Cruise, O.M.I.; Michael Holly, O.M.I. Priests 16; Brothers 2; Priests Foreign Countries 2.

Oblates of St. Francis de Sales, 721 Lawrence St., N.E., 20017. Tel: 202-269-9410; Fax: 202-526-4323. DeSales Hall Residence: Revs. James R. Yeakel, O.S.F.S., Supr. & Dir. Formation Office; James J. Greenfield, O.S.F.S., Postulant Dir.; Joseph P. Jocco, O.S.F.S., Vocation Dir.; William F. Davis, O.S.F.S.; Deacon Joseph T. Brennan; Bros. Michael O'Neill McGrath, O.S.F.S., Artist, Bee Still Studio; Robert M. Carter, O.S.F.S.; Patrick G. Press, O.S.F.S. Priests 4; Brothers 3; Scholastics 4; Postulants 7.

Vocation Office. Tel: 202-526-5651; Fax: 202-526-5653.
E-mail: jjocco@osfs.org

Bee Still Studio. Tel: 202-526-7074; Fax: 202-526-3969.

DeSales Center for Lay Spirituality. Tel: 202-526-5651; Fax: 202-526-5653.
E-mail: desales@osfs.org
Bro. Edward F. Ogden, O.S.F.S., Exec. Dir.

Formation Office. Tel: 202-269-9410; Fax: 202-526-4323.

Queen of Pious Schools House of Studies-Piarist Fathers, 1339 Monroe St., N.E., 20017-2510. Tel: 202-529-7734. Revs. Andrew C. Buechele, Sch.P., Ph.D., Rector & Master of Clerics; Theodore E. Podson, Sch.P., M.E., San Antonio/Amarillo, TX; Mario B. Vizcaino, Sch.P., M.A., S.T.L., Miami, FL; Washington, DC. Priests 3.

St. Bonaventure Friary, 3514 15th St., N.E., 20017. Tel: 202-529-5324; 832-0953; Fax: 202-635-4871. Revs. Adam E. Bunnell, O.F.M.Conv., Ph.D.; John D. Burkhard, O.F.M.Conv.; Berard L. Marthaler, O.F.M.Conv., S.T.D., Ph.D.; Henry Madigan, O.F.M.Conv.; Thomas Reist, O.F.M.Conv.; Marcelo DaLuz, O.F.M.Conv. In res. Bro. Philip Kelly, O.F.M.Conv. Priests 6; Students 10.

St. Francis Friary-Capuchin College, 4121 Harewood Rd., N.E., 20017-1593. Tel: 202-529-2188. Revs. John A. Pavlik, O.F.M.Cap., Supr., Formation Dir.; Francis Yacobi, O.F.M.Cap., Vicar; James Froehlich, O.F.M.Cap., Treas.; Christopher Rengers, O.F.M.Cap.; Thomas Russman, O.F.M.Cap.; Sebastian F. Miklas, O.F.M.Cap.; J. Daniel Mindling, O.F.M.Cap.; Titus Yoon, O.F.M.Conv. (Korea); Carroll L. Warner, O.F.M.Cap.; Mark Poletunow, O.F.M.Cap.; Emilio Ibeas (Spain); Vincent Fortunato, O.F.M.Cap.; Luis Pepeu, O.F.M.Cap. (Brazil); Alvadi Marmentini, O.F.M.Cap. (Brazil); Bros. Michael Letosak, O.F.M.Cap.; Alfred Vincent, O.F.M.Cap.; Charles McElroy, O.F.M.Cap.; Gerald Wentz, O.F.M.Cap. (DEN); Thomas Purcell, O.F.M.Conv. Priests 13; Scholastics 8; Brothers 5; Total Enrollment 9.

St. Joseph's Seminary, 1200 Varnum St., N.E., 20017. Tel: 202-526-4231; 526-4229 (Student). St. Joseph's Society of the Sacred Heart-Josephite Fathers & Brothers. Very Rev. John L.M. Filippelli, S.S.J., Rector; Revs. James A. Hayes, S.S.J., Vice Rector; John A. Carroll, S.S.J., Spiritual Dir.; John G. Harfmann, S.S.J., Dir. Josephite Pastoral Center; James E. McLinden, S.S.J., Vocation Dir.; Bros. Thomas Vincent, S.S.J.; Earl Kent, S.S.J. In res. Revs. Robert Kinel, S.S.J.; Howard Johnson; John Doerfler; J.T. Putnam; Rev. Msgr. Godwin Akpan, M.S.P. (Nigeria); Revs. Cosmas Nwosuh, M.S.P. (Nigeria); Stephen Achi, M.S.P. (Nigeria). Priests 12; Franciscan Sisters of St. Joseph 4.

St. Paul's College, 3015 Fourth St., N.E., 20017-1199. Tel: 202-832-6262; Fax: 202-269-2507. Paulist Fathers. Revs. Frank R. Desiderio, C.S.P., Supr. & Dir. Ministerial Formation; Ronald G. Roberson, C.S.P., S.E.O.D.; Paul D. Huesing, C.S.P., Ph.D., Assoc. Dir. of Formation & Treas.; Lawrence E. Boadt, C.S.P., S.S.D.; Kenneth G. Boyack, C.S.P., D.Min.; Thomas E. Comber, C.S.P.; John P. Donahue, C.S.P.; John J. Geaney, C.S.P.; John E. Lynch, C.S.P., Ph.D.; Neil J. McEleney, C.S.P., S.S.L.; Lawrence Rice, C.S.P.; Robert S. Rivers, C.S.P. Priests 12; Sisters 6; Laity 7; Students 13.

Washington Theological Union, 6896 Laurel St., N.W., 20012. Tel: 202-726-8800.
Web site: http://www.wtu.edu
Legal Title: *Washington Theological Union, Inc.* Established in 1968 as the Coalition of Religious Seminaries. The Union is a school of theology owned by seven religious communities: Carmelite Order, Provinces of the Most Pure Heart of Mary and St. Elias; Congregation of the Sacred Hearts of Jesus and Mary; Order of Friars Minor, Province of the Most Holy Name of Jesus; Order of Friars Minor Conventual; Province of Our Lady of Consolation; Order of St. Augustine, Province of St. Thomas; Redemptorist Fathers and Brothers. Revs. Vincent de P. Cushing, O.F.M., S.T.D., Pres.; Anthony De Conciliis, Academic Dean. Priests 21; Sisters 5; Lay Teachers 1; Students 263.

Whitefriars Hall, 1600 Webster St., N.E., 20017. Tel: 202-526-1221; Fax: 202-526-9217. Rev. Lukas Schmidt, O.Carm., Prior & Formation Dir.; Sr. Angele Sadlier, O.Carm., Assoc. Dir. of Formation; Revs. Gregory Houck, O.Carm., Assoc. Dir. of Formation; David Blanchard, O.Carm.; Quinn Conners, O.Carm.; Donald W. Buggert, O.Carm.; Patrick McMahon, O.Carm.; Roland Murphy, O.Carm.; George Kennedy, O.Carm.; Andrew Skotnicki, O.Carm.; John Welch, O.Carm.; Lambert Yore, O.Carm.; Raul Maravi, O.Carm.; Craig Morrison, O.Carm.; Bruce Taggart, O.Carm.; Bro. Raphael Sutherland, O.Carm. Friars in Solemn Profession 3; Sisters in Final Profession 1; Brothers in First Profession 5; Pre-Novitate Students 4.

The Carmelitana Library. Tel: 202-526-1221, Ext. 121. Rev. Patrick McMahon, O.Carm., Ph.D.

BELTSVILLE, MD. *The Saint LaSalle Auxiliary*, P.O. Box 1610-C, 20704-1610. Tel: 301-210-7444. Bro. Charles Lackes, F.S.C., Dir.
The Auxiliary is the Development Office for the Christian Brothers of the Baltimore Province. Brothers 2; Lay Staff 3.

BROOKEVILLE, MD. *Marian Novitiate*, 19101 Georgia Ave., Box 220, 20833. Tel: 301-774-2242.
Web site: http://www.marian.org
Bro. Leonard Konopka, M.I.C., Supr.; Rev. Shaun O'Connor, M.I.C.; Bro. Michael Opalacz, M.I.C. Priests 1; Brothers 2.

Marian Spiritual Center, 19101 Georgia Ave., Box 50, 20833. Tel: 301-774-5454. Bro. Leonard Konopka, M.I.C., Supr.; Rev. Shaun O'Connor, M.I.C.; Bro. Michael Opalacz, M.I.C. Priests 1; Brothers 2.

CHEVERLY, MD. *Damien House*, 6013 Inwood St., 20785. Tel: 301-386-4840.
E-mail: ssccdc@aol.com
Congregation of the Sacred Hearts. Rev. Ambrose R. Forgit, SS.CC. Priests 2; Brothers 1.

SILVER SPRING, MD. *Austin Friars Hall, Order of St. Augustine*, 2123 Edgewater Pkwy., 20903-1210. Tel: 301-445-2583. Revs. Joseph F. Wimmer, O.S.A., Prior & Treas.; Robert P. Hickey, O.S.A.; Cedric M. Wilson, O.S.A.; Maximo J. Ortiz, O.S.A. Priests 4.

Holy Family Seminary, 401 Randolph Rd., P.O. Box 4138, 20904. Tel: 301-622-3582. Very Rev. Luis Picazo, S.F., Vice Prov. Supr.; Revs. Joseph Cubells, S.F.; Francisco Gonzalez, S.F.; Jim Sunturn, S.F.; John A. Sierra, S.F.; Palmo Valente, S.F.; Marvin Archuleta, S.F.; Jose Ma. Conde, S.F.; Bro. Sebastian Lee, S.F. Priests 6; Brothers 1; Students 2.

Holy Name College, 1650 St. Camillus Dr., 20903. Tel: 301-434-3400. House of Studies for Holy Name Province of the Order of Friars Minor. Revs. Daniel McLellan, O.F.M., Ph.D., Supr. & Dir. Formation; James P. Scullion, O.F.M., Ph.D., Vicar & Asst. Dir. Formation; Daniel P. Grigassy, O.F.M., Ph.D.; Juniper Capece, O.F.M.; Nguyen Khoa, O.F.M.; Peter C. Sheridan, O.F.M. Solemnly Professed Friars 6; Simply Professed Friars 12.

Salvatorian Community, 14506 Dunsinane Ter., 20906. Tel: 301-598-1883.
E-mail: jgormandsds@raffle.org
Society of the Divine Savior/Salvatorians. Rev. John E. Gorman, S.D.S., Reg. Supr.; Bro. James Rieden, S.D.S., Vicar Supr.; Revs. Glen Willis, S.D.S.; Richard Maloney, S.D.S.; Eliot Nitz, S.D.S.; Roman Stadtmueller, S.D.S.; Robert Ross, S.D.S.; Philip Vogel, S.D.S.; William Remmel, S.D.S.; David Bergner, S.D.S.; Robert Nugent, S.D.S.; Donald Skwor, S.D.S.; Joseph Turner, S.D.S.; Kevin Cray, S.D.S.; Julian Guzman, S.D.S. Priests 14; Brothers 5; Lay Members 25.

WEST HYATTSVILLE, MD. *Pallottine Seminary at Green Hill*, 2009 Van Buren St., 20782. Tel: 301-422-3777. Society of the Catholic Apostolate. Rev. John G. Biermann, S.A.C., Rector, Dir. of Preparatory Formation. Priests 1.

WHEATON, MD. *Holy Ghost Fathers Development Office*, 11411 Amherst Ave., 20902. Tel: 301-933-6130. Rev. Thomas P. Tunney, C.S.Sp., Dir.

St. Thomas More Friary, Third Order Regular of St. Francis, 2303 Patternbond Dr., 20902. Tel: 301-649-9000. Bro. Didacus R. Wilson, T.O.R., Local Min. In res. Rev. Ambrose K. Phillips, T.O.R., Vicar. Priests 1; Solemnly Professed Brothers 1.

[C] COLLEGES AND UNIVERSITIES

WASHINGTON. *Catholic University of America, The*, (1887) Nugent Hall/Executive Offices, 20064. Tel: 202-319-5000.
E-mail: webmaster@cua.edu
For a complete listing, refer to the Colleges and Universities section.

**Georgetown University*, (1789) 37th and O Sts., N.W., 20057. Tel: 202-687-0100.
E-mail: umhoferm@gunet.georgetown.edu
Web site: http://www.georgetown.edu
For a complete listing, refer to the Colleges and Universities section.

Trinity College, Michigan Ave. and Franklin St., N.E., 20017. Tel: 202-939-5000
For a complete listing, refer to the Colleges and Universities section.

[D] HIGH SCHOOLS, ARCHDIOCESAN

WASHINGTON. *Archbishop Carroll High School.* (Coed), 4300 Harewood Rd., N.E., 20017. Tel: 202-529-0900; Fax: 202-529-5989. Mr. John T. Butler, Pres.; Revs. Leslie Branch; William L. Montgomery; John Mudd. Priests 3; Sisters 3; Lay Teachers 50; Students 710.

[E] HIGH SCHOOLS, PRIVATE

WASHINGTON. *Georgetown Visitation Preparatory School*, 1524 35th St., N.W., 20007. Tel: 202-337-3350.
E-mail: name@visi.org
Web site: http://www.ee.cua.edu/~georgvis
Sr. Mary Berchmans Hannan, V.H.M., Pres.; Mr. Dan Kerns, Headmaster. Sisters 3; Teachers 60; Students 425.

Gonzaga College High School, 19 Eye St., N.W., 20001. Tel: 202-336-7100.
Web site: http://achilles.gonzaga.pvt.k12.dc.us
Society of Jesus. Rev. Allen P. Novotny, S.J., Pres.; Dr. Joseph J. Ciancaglini, Headmaster; Revs. Daniel K. Lahart, S.J., Vice Pres., Finance & Admin.; Robert J. Rokusek (DET), Chap.; James R. Conroy, S.J., Rector. Jesuit Community. Revs. Lucien F. Longtin, S.J.; Eugene A. Nolan, S.J.; Thomas Clifford, S.J.; Kenneth E. Meehan, S.J.; Gerald V. O'Connor, S.J.; Bruce A. Steggert, S.J.; John B. Woodward, S.J. In res. Revs. Walter J. Burghardt, S.J.; David R. Brooks, S.J.; John A. Conlin, S.J.; Harry F. Geib, S.J.; Henry G. Heffernan, S.J.; Joseph M. McCloskey, S.J.; Anthony I. McHale, S.J.; Francis X. Moan, S.J.; Francis M. O'Connor, S.J.; William P. Sampson, S.J.; Bro. Donald Dixon, S.J.; Mr. James J. Kelly, S.J. Priests 20; Brothers 1; Lay Teachers 65; Scholastics 1; Students 810.

Oakcrest School. (Grades 7-12), 4101 Yuma St., N.W., 20016. Tel: 202-686-9736. College Preparatory for Girls. Ms. Barbara Falk, Dir. Priests 1; Lay Teachers 19; Students 150.

St. Anselm's Abbey School. (Grades 6-12), 4501 South Dakota Ave., N.E., 20017. Tel: 202-269-2350. Operated by the Benedictine Monks of St. Anselm's Abbey. Seven year college preparatory courses. Rev. Dom Peter Weigand, O.S.B., Headmaster. Priests 6; Brothers 3; Lay Teachers 41; Students 224.

St. John's College High School (1851). (Boys Grades 7-8, Coed Grades 9-12), 2607 Military Rd., N.W., 20015. Tel: 202-363-2316.
E-mail: sjchsmil@st-johns.pvt.k12.dc.us
Web site: http://www.st-johns.pvt.k12.dc.us
Brothers of the Christian Schools. Legal Title: *St. John's College.* College Preparatory, Elective Army Junior ROTC. Bro. Hal DeLuca, F.S.C., Prin. Priests 1; Brothers 13; Sisters 1; Lay Teachers 37; Students 575.

BETHESDA, MD. *Mater Dei School, Inc.*, 9600 Seven Locks Rd., 20817. Tel: 301-365-2700; 301-365-2701; Fax: 301-365-2710. Mr. Christopher S. Abell, Prin. Students 230.

Stone Ridge School of the Sacred Heart, 9101 Rockville Pike, 20814. Tel: 301-657-4322; Fax: 301-657-2381.
E-mail: adyer@stoneridge.org Religious of the Sacred Heart. Sr. Anne Dyer, Headmistress. Sisters 8; Lay Teachers 81; Students 735.

BLADENSBURG, MD. *Elizabeth Seton High School*, 5715 Emerson St., 20710-1844. Tel: 301-864-4532.
E-mail: admin@e-seton.pvt.k12.md.us
Web site: http://www.e-seton.pvt.k12.md.us
Sr. Vincentia Goeb, D.C., Pres.; Mrs. Geraldine Buckley, Prin. Daughters of Charity of St. Vincent de Paul 4; Lay Staff 73; Girls 549.

FORESTVILLE, MD. *Bishop McNamara High School.* (Coed), 6800 Marlboro Pike, 20747. Tel: 301-735-8401; Fax: 301-735-0934.
E-mail: bmhs@erols.com
Web site: http://www.dsport/mcnamara/McNamara.html
Holy Cross Brothers. Ms. Heather Gossart, Pres.; Mr. Marco Clark, Prin. Sisters 1; Brothers 8; Lay Teachers 62; Students 685.

GAITHERSBURG, MD. *Mother of God School*, P.O. Box 2418, 20886. Tel: 301-990-2088.
E-mail: mogsadmn@erols.com
Students 148.

HYATTSVILLE, MD. *De Matha Catholic High School*, 20781. Tel: 301-864-3666.
Web site: stag.demartha.pvt.k12.md.us
Conducted by the Trinitarian Fathers of the Province of the Immaculate Heart of Mary. Rev. William J. Sullivan, O.SS.T., Rector; Mr. John L. Moylan, Prin. Priests 3; Brothers 1; Lay Teachers 65; Students 941.

KENSINGTON, MD. *The Academy of the Holy Cross, Inc.*, 4920 Strathmore Ave., 20895. Tel: 301-942-2100; Fax: 301-929-6440. Legal Title: *The Academy of the Holy Cross, Inc.* Sr. Katherine Kase, C.S.C., Prin. Sisters 12; Lay Teachers 32; Students 425.

LAUREL, MD. *St. Vincent Pallotti High School*, 20707. Tel: 301-725-3228. Missionary Sisters of the Catholic Apostolate. Stephen J. Edmonds, Prin. Priests 1; Sisters 3; Lay Teachers 36; Students 450.

LEONARDTOWN, MD. *St. Mary's Ryken High School*, 22600 Camp Calvert Rd., 20650. Tel: 301-475-2814; 932-4422; Fax: 301-475-7972. Sponsored by the Xaverian Brothers. Mr. Harry L. Swaney, Pres.; Mr. Jonathan Grant, Prin. Brothers 1; Lay Teachers 41; Students 575.

NORTH BETHESDA, MD. *Georgetown Preparatory School*, 20852. Tel: 301-493-5000; Fax: 301-530-9531.
E-mail: jesuit@gprep.org
Web site: http://www.gprep.org
Jesuit Community. Society of Jesus. Dr. James P. Power, Headmaster; Revs. Henry B. Haske, S.J., Supr.; Thomas E. Roach, S.J., Pres.; Aloysius C. Galvin, S.J.; James A.P. Byrne, S.J.; William J. Elliott, S.J.; Raymond M. Lelii, S.J. Tel: 301-881-1380 Ext. 24; Eugene J. Linehan, S.J.; Vincent M. O'Brien, S.J.; Garrett D. Orr, S.J. Priests 9; Brothers 1; Scholastics 1; Lay Teachers 44; Students 432.

POTOMAC, MD. *Connelly School of the Holy Child.* (Grades 6-12), 9029 Bradley Blvd., 20854. Tel: 301-365-0955. Sisters of the Holy Child Jesus. College Preparatory for Girls. Maureen K. Appel, Headmistress. Sisters 1; Lay Teachers 45; Students 384.

The Heights School. (Grades 3-12), 10400 Seven Locks Rd., 20854. Tel: 301-365-4300. College Preparatory for Boys. Mr. Joseph W. McPherson, Headmaster. Priests 2; Lay Teachers 28; Students 270.

WHEATON, MD. *Good Counsel High School*, 11601 Georgia Ave., 20902. Tel: 301-942-1155; Fax: 301-942-3656. Xaverian Brothers. Mr. Michael E. Murphy, Pres.; Mr. Charles P. Dusterhoff, Prin.; Revs. Michael T. Jones, Chap.; Barry R. Gross (LFT), Diocesan. Priests 2; Brothers 1; Sisters 2; Lay Teachers 74; Students 1,012.

[F] ELEMENTARY SCHOOLS, PRIVATE

BETHESDA, MD. *The Woods Academy*, 6801 Greentree Rd., 20817. Tel: 301-365-3080. Mary Worch, Head of School. Students 216; Lay Teachers 25.

[G] SPECIAL SCHOOLS

WASHINGTON. *Lt. Joseph P. Kennedy, Jr., Institute*, 801 Buchanan St., N.E., 20017. Tel: 202-529-7600. Rev. Dr. Richard C. Birkel, Ph.D., Pres. & CEO. Nonprofit Organization Serving Children and Adults With Developmental Disabilities: Adult Learning & Employment Services. Staff 40; Participants 275. Family & Personal Support Services. Staff 18; Participants 47. Early Intervention & Preventive Services. Staff 29; Participants 45. Kennedy Education. (Includes Kennedy School, Outreach Program to Catholic Schools and Inclusion 2000). Staff 44; Students 85+. Residential Division. Staff 76; Residents 63. Administration Division. Staff 26. Community Living Partnership. Staff 3; Families 43. The Lt. Joseph P. Kennedy, Jr., Institute of the Archdiocese of Washington is a private, nonprofit organization providing education, training and employment, therapeutic and residential services to children and adults with developmental disabilities.

ROCKVILLE, MD. *The Frost Center*, Society of the Divine Savior, 4915 Aspen Hill Rd., 20853. Tel: 301-933-3451.
E-mail: seanmcl@frostcenter.com
Bro. Sean McLaughlin, S.D.S., Dir.; Rev. Glen Willis, S.D.S., Business Mgr.; Bros. Roger Nelson, S.D.S.; Peter Farnesi, S.D.S., Plant Mgr. A School and Therapy Program for Emotionally Disturbed Teens and Families. Priests 1; Brothers 3; Staff 25; Students 45.

[H] CATHOLIC CHARITIES OF THE ARCHDIOCESE

WASHINGTON. *Catholic Charities of the Archdiocese of Washington, Inc.*, 1438 Rhode Island Ave., N.E., 20018. Tel: 202-526-4100. Mr. Edward Orzechowski, M.S.W., Pres.

Montgomery County Regional Office, 1504 St. Camillus Dr., Silver Spring, MD, 20903. Tel: 301-434-2550.

Prince George's County Regional Office, 6706 Marlboro Pike, Forestville, MD, 20747. Tel: 301-568-9529.

Calvert County Office, P.O. Box 779, Prince Frederick, MD, 20678. Tel: 410-535-0865.

Southern Maryland Regional Office, The Charles Bldg., 513 E. Charles St., La Plata, MD, 20646. Tel: 301-934-2582. Total Assisted 80,000; Total Staff 230.

[I] ARCHDIOCESAN VOLUNTEER ORGANIZATIONS

WASHINGTON. *Archdiocesan Association of Ladies of Charity*, P.O. Box 10038, 20018. Mary L. Linstrom, Pres. Purpose: individual charity work, usually of emergency nature and support various other agencies, foodbanks, child care centers and pregnancy aid centers.

RIVERDALE, MD. *Society of St. Vincent de Paul*, Archdiocese of Washington, 6028 Mustang Dr., 20737.
Office of Archdiocesan Council. Tel: 301-864-2106.

[J] ORPHANAGES AND INFANT HOMES

HYATTSVILLE, MD. *St. Ann's Infant and Maternity Home*, 4901 Eastern Ave., 20782. Tel: 301-559-5500; Fax: 301-853-6985
For a complete listing, refer to the Special Care Facilities section.

[K] GENERAL HOSPITALS

WASHINGTON. *Center for Life of Providence Hospital*, 1150 Varnum St., N.E., 20017
For a complete listing, refer to the Hospitals section.

De Paul Foundation, Inc., 1150 Varnum St., N.E., 20017
For a complete listing, refer to the Hospitals section.

Georgetown University Hospital, 3800 Reservoir Rd., N.W., 20007. Tel: 202-784-3000
For a complete listing, refer to the Hospitals section.

Providence Health Services, Inc., 1150 Varnum St., N.E., 20017
For a complete listing, refer to the Hospitals section.

SILVER SPRING, MD. *Holy Cross Hospital of Silver Spring, Inc.*, 1500 Forest Glen Rd., 20910. Tel: 301-754-7000; Fax: 301-754-7012
For a complete listing, refer to the Hospitals section.

[L] HOMES FOR AGED

WASHINGTON. *Cardinal O'Boyle Residence for Priests*, 1150 Varnum St., N.E., 20017
For a complete listing, refer to the Special Care Facilities section.

Jeanne Jugan Residence-St. Joseph's Villa, 4200 Harewood Rd., N.E., 20017-1554. Tel: 202-269-1831
For a complete listing, refer to the Special Care Facilities section.

BELTSVILLE, MD. *Ammendale Normal Institute of Prince George's County-La Salle Hall*, (1880) 6001 Ammendale Rd., 20705. Tel: 301-210-7443
For a complete listing, refer to the Special Care Facilities section.

HYATTSVILLE, MD. *Sacred Heart Home Inc.*, 5805 Queens Chapel Rd., 20782. Tel: 301-277-6500
For a complete listing, refer to the Special Care Facilities section.

MITCHELLVILLE, MD. *Villa Rosa Nursing Home, Inc.*, 3800 Lottsford Vista Rd., 20721-4026. Tel: 301-459-4700; Fax: 301-459-0754
For a complete listing, refer to the Special Care Facilities section.

[M] MONASTERIES AND RESIDENCES OF PRIESTS AND BROTHERS

WASHINGTON. *Carmelite Community*, 1136 McKenna Walk, N.W., 20001. Tel: 630-971-0050. Revs. Andrew Skotnicki, O.Carm., Ph.D., Prior; David Blanchard, O.Carm., Ph.D.; Patrick Thomas McMahon, O.Carm., Ph.D.

Carroll House, 1225 Otis St., N.E., 20017. Tel: 202-529-1252. Jesuit House of Studies at the Catholic University. Revs. James P. Bradley, S.J., Supr.; Christopher M. Cullen, S.J.; Francis T. Gignac, S.J.; Jerome M. Hall, S.J.; Brian VanHove, S.J.; Gabriel Mmassi (East Africa). Priests 6; Total Staff 1.

Commissariat of the Holy Land, Franciscan Monastery - Mount St. Sepulchre, 1400 Quincy St., N.E., 20017. Tel: 202-526-6800.
E-mail: sebastian@pressroom.com
Web site: http://www.pressroom.com/franciscan/
Bro. Callistus Welch, O.F.M., Guardian, and Commissary of the Holy Land; Revs. Kevin Treston, O.F.M., Almanac Editor, Spiritual Asst. to Sec. Franciscan Order; James Brabandt, O.F.M., Dir. of Candidates; Patrick Flannigan, O.F.M.; Sabin Plechta, O.F.M.; Stephen F. Sabbagh, O.F.M.; Francis X. Sihuay, O.F.M. (Peru); Manuel Ybarra, O.F.M., Vicar & Vice Commissary, Procurator; Mark Hurst, O.F.M.; Brian McTommoney, O.F.M. Priests 9; Brothers 14; Solemnly Professed 25; Postulants 4; Novices 3; Missionaries in the Holy Land 24.

Divine Word College, 1025 Michigan Ave., N.E., 20017. Tel: 202-526-5047. Revs. Raymond T. Lennon, S.V.D., Rector; Henry Gaska, S.V.D. (Poland); John Rodney, S.V.D.; Raymond Sanders, S.V.D.; Peter De Ta Vo, S.V.D. (Vietnam); Robert Mertes, S.V.D.; Phelin Jordan (Ireland); Jun Inoue, S.V.D. (Japan); Anumu Quaye-Foli, S.V.D. (Togo); Darius Piwowarczyk, S.V.D. (Poland); Xavier Thirukudumbam, S.V.D. (India); Esteban DeLeon (Philippines); Omer Ngaway (Congo); John Szukalski; Bros. G. Raker,

S.V.D., Treas.; Bernard Spitzley, S.V.D., Formation Dir.; Julio Mothlelet Perez (Mexico); Tam Nguyen (Vietnam). Divine Word College has 40 Priests and Brothers in Residence. Seventeen of these are members of the S.V.D.; the other 23 are from other religious communities or dioceses in the U.S.A., and are studying at the Catholic University or the John Paul II Institute. We offer them our House for the duration of their studies. Residents 40.

Glenmary House of Studies, 1323 Quincy St., N.E., 20017. Tel: 202-635-0163; 526-1339. Rev. Chet Artysiewicz, Dir. Students in Residence 3; Total in Residence 6; Total Staff 1.

Holy Redeemer College (1930), 3112 Seventh St., N.E., 20017. Tel: 202-529-4410; 529-4484; Fax: 202-832-1321. Opened in 1930. Redemptorist Theology Residence Since 1985. Legal Title: *Holy Redeemer College*. Very Rev. Philip Dabney, C.SS.R., Rector & Dir. Formation; Revs. Kevin O'Neil, C.SS.R., Asst. Dir. Formation; James Wallace, C.SS.R., Vicar; James Dowds, C.SS.R., Vocation Dir.; Dennis Billy, C.SS.R.; Mark Tucker, C.SS.R.; Bro. Jeffrey Rolle, C.SS.R.; Revs. James Coen, C.SS.R.; Thomas Forrest, C.SS.R. Owned and Operated by the Redemptorists of the Baltimore Province for their Own Religious Candidates. Students Attend Washington Theological Union. Priests 8; Brothers 1; Religious Students 10.

The Jesuit Community at Georgetown University, 37th and O Sts., N.W., 20057. Tel: 202-687-1700; Fax: 202-687-7679.
E-mail: jbhgu@aol.com
Rev. William J. Byron, S.J., Rector; Bros. John B. Hollywood, S.J., Admin. & Treas.; Steven L. Alvey, S.J.; Revs. Francis Alves, S.J. (India); Edward W. Bodnar, S.J.; Thomas J. Buckley, S.J.; Timothy J. Cadigan, S.J.; Martin J. Calkins, S.J. (Detroit); Martin J. Casey, S.J.; Paul L. Cioffi, S.J.; T. Byron Collins, S.J.; Patrick J. Conroy, S.J. (Oregon); Walter A. Cook, S.J.; Robert F. Drinan, S.J. (New England); Robert J. Dullahan, S.J.; Joseph T. Durkin, S.J.; Stephen M. Fields, S.J.; Joseph A. Fitzmyer, S.J.; Gerald P. Fogarty, S.J.; James J. Fox, S.J. (NY); William L. George, S.J.; Julio Giulietti, S.J. (New England); Joseph A. Haller, S.J.; Patrick A. Heelan, S.J. (Ireland); Otto H. Hentz, S.J.; Brendan Hurley, S.J.; Edward J. Ingebretsen, S.J. (California); Josef Kadlec, S.J.; William J. Kaifer, S.J.; John R. Keating, S.J. (New York); John T. Kelly, S.J.; Gustaaf M. Keppens, S.J.; Thomas M. King, S.J.; John P. Langan, S.J. (DET); Robert B. Lawton, S.J.; John A. Lucal, S.J. (DET); James A. Martin, S.J.; John F. Martin, S.J.; Brian O. McDermott, S.J.; William C. McFadden, S.J.; Dennis L. McNamara, S.J. (Wisconsin); Paul D. McNelis, S.J.; Richard T. McSorley, S.J.; Ralph E. Metts, S.J.; William H. Millerd, S.J.; Joseph M. Moffitt, S.J.; Keith F. Muccino, S.J.; G. Ronald Murphy, S.J.; Daniel C. O'Connell, S.J. (Missouri); Joseph F. O'Connell, S.J.; Leo J. O'Donovan, S.J.; Ladislas Orsy, S.J. (Hungary); Scott R. Pilarz, S.J.; J. Eugene Poirier, S.J. (China); Kevin P. Quinn, S.J. (New York); Bro. George F. Reilly, S.J.; Revs. Alvaro Ribeiro, S.J. (China); Vincent S. Saldanha, S.J. (India); Solomon I. Sara, S.J. (New England); James V. Schall, S.J. (California); Francis Schemel, S.J.; James M. Shea, S.J.; John Songster, S.J.; Joseph F. Sweeney, S.J.; Terrence Toland, S.J.; Joseph N. Tylenda, S.J.; Jeffrey von Arx, S.J. (New York); James P.M. Walsh, S.J.; William Watson, S.J. (Oregon); Kevin W. Wildes, S.J.; John W. Witek, S.J. (Chicago). Priests 68; Brothers 3.

K Street Jesuit Community, 320 K St., N.E., 20002. Tel: 202-546-1958. Revs. James E. Hug, S.J., Supr.; Fred Kammer, S.J.; Joseph R. Hacala, S.J.; Vincent P. DeCola, S.J. Residents 4.

La Salette Community, 1243 Monroe St., N.E., 20017. Legal Title: *Missionaries of La Salette Corporation*. Rev. Joseph G. Bachand, M.S., Dir.

Leonard Neale House, 1726 New Hampshire Ave., N.W., 20009. Tel: 202-387-5375; 387-5376. Revs. Thomas F. Gleeson, S.J.; Charles L. Currie, S.J.; Daniel C. McDonald, S.J.; James F. LaFontaine, S.J.; George T. Dennis, S.J.; Richard C. Burbach, S.J.; Thomas M. Rockford, S.J.; Bradley M. Schaeffer, S.J.; Richard J. Ryscavage, S.J.; Andrew J. Christiansen, S.J.; Theodore F. Zuern, S.J. Priests 11; Total Staff 12.

Marist Provincial House, 815 Varnum St., N.E., 20017-2199. Tel: 202-529-4800.
E-mail: wrowland@aol.com
The Marists Provincial Headquarters of the Washington Province of the Society of Mary, Marist Fathers and Brothers. Very Rev. William F. Rowland, S.M., Prov.; Revs. Valentine A. Becker, S.M., Archivist; Thomas E. Dubay, S.M.; Joseph M. Fleury; Philip S. Gage, S.M.; Charles A. Girard; John H. Harhager, S.M.; Mark G. Kenney, S.M.; George M. Lepping, S.M.; Joseph J. McLaughlin, S.M.; Howard C. Smith, S.M.; Timothy F. Sugrue, S.M., Business Mgr.
Priests Not Listed Elsewhere: Rev. Charles J. Barrett, S.M., (Retired), 8617 Limestone Ave., Tampa, FL, 33615-1427. Rev. Charles F. Brogley, S.M., (Retired), Sacred Heart Manor, 6445 Germantown Ave., Philadelphia, PA, 19119. Rev. Thomas G. Carey, S.M., (Retired), Sts. Mary & Joseph Home, 4291 Richmond Rd., Cleveland, OH, 44122-6199. Rev. Edward C. Corrigan, S.M., (Retired), Sts. Mary & Joseph Home, 4291 Richmond Rd., Cleveland, OH, 44122-6199. Rev. Richmond J. Egan, S.M., 1661 York Ave., Apt. 4-A, New York, NY, 10128-6555. Rev. Joseph D. Fenton, S.M., St. Columban Church, 10801 Stanford Ave., Garden Grove, CA, 92640. Rev. Leo A. Foley, S.M., (Retired), Malta House, 4916 LaSalle Rd., Hyattsville, MD, 20782-3302. Rev. Edward F. Fuss, S.M., (Retired), 5118 Walsh Ave., East Chicago, IN, 46312. Rev. Thomas B. Hogan, S.M., (Retired), 8617 S. Komensky Ave., Chicago, IL, 60652. Rev. Stanley W. Hosie, S.M., 2440 Virginia Ave., N.W., D-1301, 20037-2601. Rev. Timothy G. Keating, S.M., 6200 Westchester Park Dr., Apt. 1113, College Park, MD, 20740-2840. Rev. Leonard P. Kellermann, S.M., (Retired), Mary Joseph Residence, 4201 Woodland Dr., New Orleans, LA, 70131-7398. Rev. Alatini Kolofo'ou, S.M., St. Nicholas Church, 8603 Contee Rd., Laurel, MD, 20708-1499. Rev. John J. Martell, S.M., (Retired), Mary Joseph Residence, 4201 Woodland Dr., New Orelans, LA, 70131-7398. Rev. George J. Meiluta, S.M., (Retired), St. Joseph Home for the Aged, 1182 Holland Rd., Holland, PA, 18966. Rev. John J. Moore, S.M., (Retired), Mary Joseph Residence, 4201 Woodland Dr., New Orleans, LA, 70131-7398. Rev. Leonard J. Moran, S.M., (Retired), 1516 Council Dr., Sun City Center, FL, 33573-5324. Rev. Edward J. Murray, S.M., (Retired), 11528 Sandy Hill Dr., Orlando, FL, 32821-7909. Rev. Vincent J. O'Connell, S.M., (Retired), Chateau de Notre Dame Nursing Home, 2832 Burdette St., New Orleans, LA, 70125-2596. Rev. Patrick D. Primeaux, S.M., 150 Burns St, #6-C, Forest Hills, NY, 11375-6111. Rev. John A. Richmond, S.M., (Retired), Jeanne Jugan Residence, 4200 Harewood Rd., N.E., 20017-1554. Rev. Robert J. Stahl, S.M., (Retired), Chateau de Notre Dame Nursing Home, 2820 Burdette St., Apt. 705, New Orleans, LA, 70125-2596. Rev. Edward J. Templeton, S.M., (Retired), Lafon Nursing Home, 6900 Chef Menteur Hwy., New Orleans, LA, 70126-5296. Rev. John J. White, S.M., (Retired), St. Gerald Church, 9349 S. Central Ave., Oak Lawn, IL, 60453-2386.

Missionaries of Africa, 1624 21st St., N.W., 20009. Tel: 202-232-5154. Provincial House. Revs. William F. Moroney, M.Afr., Asst. Prov.; David J. Goergen, M.Afr., Prov. Treas.; Roger Bisson, M.Afr.; Albert Jamme, M.Afr. (Belgium); Sjef Donders, M.Afr. (Holland); George Markwell, M.Afr.; Pierre Benson, M.Afr. (Canada), Community Coord.; Bro. Charles Feldmann, M.Afr. Priests 7; Brothers 1; Total Staff 6.

Missionaries of the Company of Mary-Montfort Missionaries, 1302 Quincy St., N.E., 20017. Tel: 202-832-8319. Rev. Donald G. LaSalle, S.M.M., Dir. Formation. Residents 1.

Missionary Oblates of Mary Immaculate, Provincial Office: 391 Michigan Ave., N.E., 20017. Tel: 202-529-5958. Very Rev. J. William Sheehan, O.M.I., Prov.; Rev. Henry Lemoncelli, O.M.I., Admin. Asst.

St. Anselm's Abbey, 4501 South Dakota Ave., N.E., 20017. Tel: 202-269-2300; Fax: 202-269-2312. Benedictine Foundation at Washington, DC, Order of St. Benedict. Rt. Revs. Aidan Shea, O.S.B., Abbot; Alban Boultwood, O.S.B.; Revs. James A. Wiseman, O.S.B., Prior; Urban Schnaus, O.S.B.; Hugh Monmonier, O.S.B.; Daniel Kirk, O.S.B.; Joseph Jensen, O.S.B.; John Farrelly, O.S.B.; David Granfield, O.S.B.; Patrick Granfield, O.S.B.; Hilary Hayden, O.S.B.; Thomas Fahy, O.S.B.; Edmund Henkels, O.S.B.; Michael Hall, O.S.B.; Christopher Wyvill, O.S.B.; Mark Sheridan, O.S.B.; Peter Weigand, O.S.B.; Giles LeVasseur, O.S.B.; Isaac Borocz, O.S.B.; Benet Hill, O.S.B.; Paul McKane, O.S.B.; Boniface von Nell, O.S.B. Priests 21; Brothers 5.

St. Louis Friary, 831 Varnum St., N.E., 20017. Tel: 202-529-0171. House of Post-Novitiate Formation for Franciscan Friars, T.O.R., Province of the Most Sacred Heart of Jesus. Revs. Peter Lyons, T.O.R.; John Carroll, T.O.R.; Samuel Vaccarella, T.O.R.; James Morman, T.O.R. Friars in Post-Novitiate Formation 8; Total in Residence 13.

Woodstock Jesuit Community, 1419 35 St., N.W., 20007. Tel: 202-337-7750. Revs. James Connor, S.J., Supr.; Thomas J. Reese, S.J.; J. Leon Hooper, S.J.; Gasper F. LoBiondo, S.J.; William J. Walsh, S.J.; Rev. Msgr. Richard M. Liddy. Priests 6.

ADELPHI, MD. *Father Thomas O'Keeffe Missionary Cenacle*, 2717 Curry Dr., 20783. Tel: 301-422-8039. Rev. Stephen Ernst, S.T., Dir.

Missionary Servants of the Most Holy Trinity, 1733 Metzerott Rd., 20783. Senior Ministry Residence. Revs. Gabriel Hannan, S.T.; Lambert Stack, S.T.; Gerald Swift, S.T.; Charles Tague, S.T.; Paul Keenan, S.T.; Denis Fitzgerald, S.T.; Shaun McCarty, S.T.; William Coombs, S.T., Asst. Dir.; Bros. Malachy Sofield, S.T.; Raymond Ise, S.T.; Robert Conway, S.T.; Jonathan Daneski, S.T.; Howard Piller, S.T., Dir.; David Koessler, S.T.; Daniel McCauley, S.T.; Loughlan Sofield, S.T.

HYATTSVILLE, MD. *St. John de Matha Monastery, Order of Most Holy Trinity*, 4310 Madison St., 20781. Tel: 301-927-6418; Fax: 301-927-0807. Revs. Thomas N. Cerulo, O.SS.T., Supr.; Albert M. Anuszewski, O.SS.T., Vicar; Thomas A. Morris, O.SS.T.; Bro. Patrick Wildgen, O.SS.T. Priests 3; Brothers 6; Scholastics 4; Affiliates 6; Total Staff 4.

POTOMAC, MD. *Legionaries of Christ*, 10211 Norton Rd., 20854. Tel: 301-299-0806; Fax: 301-299-0809. Revs. William Izquierdo, L.C., Supr.; Richard Gill, L.C.; Daniel Long, L.C.; James Swanson, L.C.; Bros. Robert Vandenberg, L.C.; Michael Sliney, L.C.; Robert deCesear, L.C.; Robert Presutti, L.C.

RIVERDALE, MD. *Holy Spirit Missionary Cenacle* 1996, 5809 Riverdale Rd., 20737. Tel: 301-277-7442; Fax: 301-209-0355. Rev. Austin Walsh, S.T., Dir. Tel: 301-277-7476. In res. Rev. Sidney H. Griffith, S.T., Semantics/Early Christian Studies, Faculty, Catholic University of America. Tel: 301-927-4919; Bro. Richard McCann, S.T., Asst. Mission Procurator, Trinity Missions, Silver Spring, MD. Tel: 301-209-9638. Theological Students 3; Novices 2.

SILVER SPRING, MD. *Gemelli House*. Franciscan Friars-Holy Name Province, 10400 Lorain Ave., 20901. Tel: 301-681-9478; Fax: 301-681-7170. Revs. Kenneth R. Himes, O.F.M., Guardian; Vincent de Paul Cushing, O.F.M.; Dominic V. Monti, O.F.M.; Bros. Thomas E. Conway, O.F.M.; Joseph LaGressa, O.F.M.; Stephen O'Kane, O.F.M.; Sean E. O'Brien, O.F.M.; Russel Murray, O.F.M.; Daniel P. Sulmasy, O.F.M.

TAKOMA PARK, MD. *Society of African Missions (S.M.A.)*, 256 N. Manor Cir., 20912-4561. Tel: 301-270-2008.
E-mail: smausa-v@ix.netcom.com
Web site: http://www.smafathers.org
Revs. Eugene Riordan, S.M.A., Supr.; M. Clark Yates, S.M.A., Asst. Supr., Formation Staff; Austin Charles Ochu, S.M.A., Dir. of Formation.

Lay Mission Program, 207 S. Manor Cir., 20912-4555. Tel: 301-891-2014 (Home); 301-891-2037 (Office). Theresa Hicks, Dir.

Vocations Office, 209 Lincoln Ave., 20912-5738. Tel: 301-270-8435. Rev. Brendan Darcy, S.M.A., Vocation Dir.

Justice, Peace & Environmental Care Office, 209 Lincoln Ave., 20912-5738. Tel: 301-270-4756. Dr. Stephen Price, Ph.D., Dir. Priests 4; Lay S.M.A. 1; Lay Candidates 6.

UNIVERSITY PARK, MD. *Holy Trinity Missionary Cenacle* (1995), 4001 Van Buren St., 20782. Tel: 301-779-0939; Fax: 301-699-1745. Bros. Jordan Baxter, S.T., Custodian; Alexis Norton, S.T. Tel: 301-699-1729; Revs. Leonard Bachmann, S.T. Tel: 301-277-2629; David O'Connor, S.T. Tel: 301-699-3508; Randall Woods, S.T. Tel: 301-277-1473.

[N] MINISTRY TO PRIESTS

KENSINGTON, MD. *St. John Vianney House*, 4214 Saul Rd., 20895. Tel: 301-942-1191. Rev. Msgr. William J. English.

[O] CONVENTS AND RESIDENCES FOR SISTERS

WASHINGTON. *Archivists for Congregations of Women Religious*, ACWR National Office, Trinity College, 125 Michigan Ave, N.E., 20017. Tel: 202-884-9441; Fax: 202-884-9229. Sr. Rosalie McQuaide, C.S.J.P., Contact Person. Purpose: Preservation of the archives of Roman Catholic women religious congregations and collaboration with historians in making known the lives and works of women religious.

Daughters of Wisdom, 914 Perry Pl., N.E., 20017. Tel: 202-529-3343. Sisters 2.

Franciscan Sisters of Atonement, 4000 Harewood Rd., N.E., 20017. Tel: 202-529-1111. Sisters 7; Total Staff 9.

Georgetown Visitation Convent, 1500 35th St., N.W., 20007. Tel: 202-337-0350. Mother Mary deSales McNabb, Supr. Professed Sisters 29.

Institute of Our Lady of Mount Carmel, 4415 Eighth St., N.E., 20017. Total Assisted 48; Total Staff 7.

Julie Billiart Residence, 1625 16th St., N.W., 20009. Tel: 202-232-3300.
E-mail: jbilliartr@aol.com
Inter-Community Residence for Sisters. Sisters 18.

Little Sisters of Jesus, 1740 Euclid St., N.W., Apt. 1, 20009. Sisters 3.

Little Sisters of the Poor, 4200 Harewood Rd., N.E., 20017. Tel: 202-269-1831. Sisters 21.

Missionaries of Charity, 3310 Wheeler Rd., S.E., 20032. Tel: 202-562-6890. Sisters 6; Total Assisted 16,181.

Missionaries of Charity, Gift of Peace Convent, 2800 Otis St., N.E., 20018. Tel: 202-269-3313. Sr. M. Manorama, M.C., Supr. Total Assisted 50; Total in Residence 45; Total Staff 25.

Oblates Sisters of the Most Holy Eucharist, 2907 Ellicott Ter., N.W., 20008. Tel: 202-244-7714. Sisters 8.

Poor Clares of Perpetual Adoration, 3900 13th St., N.E., 20017-2699. Tel: 202-526-6808. Cloistered Monastery of Perpetual Adoration. Cloistered Nuns 9.

Religious of the Sacred Heart, 821 Varnum St., N.E., 20017. Tel: 202-635-7987.
E-mail: kcollins@rscj.org
Sr. Catherine Collins, R.S.C.J., Dir. Center for Educational Design & Communication. Sisters 2.

Rosary House of Studies-Dominican Sisters of The Presentation, 1201 Monroe St., N.E., 20017. Tel: 202-529-1768. Sisters 5.

St. Dominic's Monastery, 4901 16th St., N.W., 20011. Tel: 202-726-2107. Dominican Nuns, a Contemplative Community with Solemn Vows and Papal Enclosure. Sr. Mary Dominic, O.P., Prioress. Sisters 10.

Sisters of St. Mary of Washington, 5001 Eastern Ave., 20017.

Sisters of the Holy Child Jesus, 1033 Newton St., N.E., 20017. Tel: 202-526-6832.
E-mail: kagosser@erols.com
Novitiate Community. Sisters 7.
Other Convents: 1244 Monroe St., N.E., 20017. Tel: 202-832-3237. Sisters 5.
Immaculate Conception School (1 Sister); St. Anthony's School (1 Sister).

Sisters of the Third Franciscan Order-Syracuse, NY, 1334 Perry St., N.E., 20017-2531. Tel: 202-526-8017. Sisters 3.

ANACOSTIA, WASHINGTON. *Missionaries of Charity (Contemplatives)*, 1244 V St., S.E., 20020-7016. Tel: 202-889-6100. Sr. M. Andrea, M.C., Supr.

BALTIMORE, MD. *Comtemplative Sisters of the Good Shepherd*, 4100 Maple Ave., 21227-4099.

CHEVY CHASE, MD. *Missionary Sisters of Our Lady of Africa*, 3715 Williams Ln., 20815. Tel: 301-654-2047.

FORT WASHINGTON, MD. *The Missionary Catechists of St. Therese of the Infant Jesus, Inc.*, 2400 Brinkley Rd., 20744. Tel: 301-839-7751. Sr. Marilou P. Paulo, M.C.S.T., Pres. Sisters 4.

HYATTSVILLE, MD. *DeMatha Convent*, 4310 Madison St., 20781. Oblates of St. Martha, Saltillo, Mexico. Sisters 3; Total Staff 3.

KENSINGTON, MD. *Sisters of the Holy Cross*, Saint Angela Hall, 5000 Strathmore Ave., 20895. Tel: 301-949-2244. Legal Title: *Sisters of the Holy Cross, Inc.* Retirement House for the Sisters of the Holy Cross. Sr. Marian Daniel, C.S.C., Supr. Sisters 27.

Academy of the Holy Cross Convent, 4920 Strathmore Ave., 20895. Tel: 301-942-2102. Sisters 14. Legal Title: *The Academy of the Holy Cross, Inc.*

Holy Cross Hospital Convent, 1523 Forest Glen Rd., 20910. Tel: 301-681-5596. Sisters 6.

Our Lady of the Woods, 9820 Dameron Dr., 20902. Tel: 301-681-5732.

Sisters of the Holy Cross, 4523 32nd St., Mount Rainier, 20712. Tel: 301-927-0712. Sisters 3. 12623 Laurie Dr., 20904. Tel: 301-236-4967. Sisters 3. Holy Cross Convent, 4900 Strathmore Ave., Garrett Park, 20896. Tel: 301-933-2213. Sisters 5.

Our Lady of Lourdes Convent, 4511 East-West Hwy., Bethesda, 20814. Tel: 301-986-5741. Sisters 3.

LANHAM-SEABROOK, MD. *Mission Helpers of the Sacred Heart*, 9471 Annapolis Rd., 20706. Tel: 301-459-8078. Sisters 6.

LAUREL, MD. *Pallotti Convent*, 404 Eighth St., 20707. Tel: 301-725-1717. Sr. M. Karen Lester, S.A.C., Local Supr. Professed Sisters 10; Total Assisted 124; Total Staff 3.

MOUNT RAINIER, MD. *Congregation of Jesus and Mary, Provincialate*, 3706 Rhode Island Ave., 20712. Tel: 301-277-3594; Fax: 301-277-8656. Sr. Rosemary Mangan, R.J.M., Prov. Administrative Team 3; Staff 2.
Other Residences: Religious of Jesus and Mary, 6709 41st Ave., University Park, 20782. Tel: 301-779-0662. Sisters 3. 6908 Wake Forest Dr., College Park, 20740. Tel: 301-699-3931. Sisters 3. 3521 13th St., N.W., Washington, DC, 20010. Tel: 202-265-8811. Sisters 3. Jesus Mary Provincialate, St. James Convent, 3706 Rhode Island Ave., 20712. Tel: 301-277-3334. Sisters 7.

PORT TOBACCO, MD. *Carmel of Port Tobacco*, 5678 Mount Carmel Rd., 20646-9611. Professed 11.

SILVER SPRING, MD. *Carmelite Sisters of Charity*, 701 Beacon Rd., 20903. Tel: 301-434-6344. Formation House. Sr. Maria-Pilar Chamorro, C.C.V., Reg. Supr.; Sr. Amaya Duralde, C.C.V., First Councilor & Formation Dir.; Sr. Maria Carmen De Juan, C.C.V., Second Councilor & Treas.

Good Shepherd Provincialate, 504 Hexton Hill Rd., 20904-3300. Tel: 301-384-1169; Fax: 301-384-8889.
E-mail: lawlorb@juno.com
Legal Title: *Sisters of the Good Shepherd of the City of Washington, DC.* Sr. M. Brigid Lawlor, R.G.S., Prov. Sisters 5.

Good Shepherd Corporation dba Shepherd's Dwelling. (Residence for women with AIDS), Washington, DC. Total Assisted 2; Total Staff 1.

Proyecto Nino. (Day Care program for children & parents). Total Staff 2.

Sister of Charity of St. Charles Borromeo, Inc., 11320 Classical Ln., 20901. Tel: 301-681-9665. Sr. Caecilia H. Hadiwijana, Pres.

Sisters of Mercy of the Americas Administrative Center, 8300 Colesville Rd., Ste. 300, 20910. Tel: 301-587-0423; Fax: 301-587-0533.
E-mail: srsofmercy@aol.com
Web site: http://www.sistersofmercy.org
Legal Holdings; Mercy Action, Inc.; McAuley Institute, Inc.; Mercy Corps., Inc. Sr. Doris Gottemoeller, R.S.M., Pres. Administrative Team 5.

Sisters of the Holy Names (S.N.J.M.), 715 Pershing Dr., 20910. Tel: 301-587-1717; Fax: 301-587-1717.
E-mail: snjm715@aol.com
Other Convents: 519 Varnum St., N.W., 20011. Tel: 202-829-8671. Sisters 3. 9212 Glenville Rd., 20901. Tel: 301-593-3385. 10705 Torrance Dr., 20902. Sisters 5.

[P] RETREAT HOUSES

WASHINGTON. *Washington Retreat House, Inc.* (1930), 4000 Harewood Rd., N.E., 20017. Tel: 202-529-1111. Franciscan Sisters of the Atonement. Sr. Frances B. Flynn, S.A., Dir. Sisters 7; Total in Residence 7; Total Staff 9.

FAULKNER, MD. *Loyola on the Potomac Retreat House*, P.O. Box 9, 20632. Tel: 301-934-8862; 870-3515; 870-3725. Rev. Stephen M. Garrity, S.J., Supr. & Dir. Associate Directors: Revs. Francis J. Miles, S.J.; Richard C. Schmidt, S.J.; Joseph A. Kemme, S.J.; Sr. Patricia McDermott, I.H.M. Total in Residence 4; Total Staff 5.

UPPER MARLBORO, MD. *Our Lady of Mattaponi Youth Retreat and Conference Center*, 11000 Mattaponi Rd., 20772. Tel: 301-952-9074; Fax: 301-952-0609. Rev. Robert F. Mordino. Total in Residence 1; Total Staff 3.

[Q] NATIONAL SHRINE

WASHINGTON. *Basilica of the National Shrine of the Immaculate Conception*, 400 Michigan Ave., N.E., 20017. Tel: 202-526-8300; Fax: 202-526-8313.
E-mail: shrine@cris.com
Web site: http://www.nationalshrine.com
Rev. Msgr. Michael J. Bransfield (PH), Rector; Revs. Daniel J. Maher (ARL), Assoc. Rector; Walter R. Rossi (SCR), Dir. Pilgrimages; John J. Leddy, O.M.I., Spiritual Counselor; Columba J. Enright, T.O.R., Spiritual Counselor.

[R] HOUSES OF PRAYER

WASHINGTON. *Madonna House*, 220 C St., N.E., 20002. Tel: 202-547-0177. Catherine A. Mitchell, Dir. Total in Residence 4; Total Staff 4.

[S] OFFICES OF CAMPUS MINISTRY

WASHINGTON. *Archdiocesan Campus Ministry.*

American University, Kay Spiritual Life Center, 4400 Massachusetts Ave., N.W., 20016-8010. Tel: 202-885-3327.
E-mail: bmccart@american.edu
Rev. Brien R. McCarthy; Dr. Karin Thornton, Assoc. Chap.

Gallaudet University Catholic Community, 20002. Rev. Gerard A. Trancone, 7202 Buchanan St., Landover Hills, MD, 20784. Tel: 202-651-5102.

George Washington Univ. Newman Center, 2210 F St., N.W., 20037. Tel: 202-676-6855. Rev. James J. Greenfield, O.S.F.S., Chap.

Howard Univ. Newman Center, 2417 First St. N.W., 20001. Tel: 202-529-0900. Rev. Gerard Hargrove, Chap.

Washington Hospital School of Nursing Newman Club. Rev. John S. Wintermeyer, Chap.

University of Maryland Catholic Student Center, 4141 Guilford Dr., College Park, MD, 20740. Tel: 301-864-6223; 6224. Rev. Robert F. Keffer, Chap. & Dir. of Campus Ministry for Archdiocese; Sr. Rita Ricker, R.J.M., Assoc.

St. Mary's College Campus Ministry, P.O. Box 67, St. Mary's City, MD, 20686. Tel: 301-862-4600. Rev. Francis W. Krastel.

[T] PERSONAL PRELATURES

WASHINGTON. *Opus Dei*, 2301 Wyoming Ave., N.W., 20008. Tel: 202-234-1567.
Web site: http://www.opusdei.org
Prelature of the Holy Cross and Opus Dei. Revs. Malcolm M. Kennedy; Deo G. Rosales; Lawrence A. Kutz.
Other Residence: 4300 Garrison St., N.W., 20016. Tel: 202-362-2419. Revs. William G. Shaughnessy; Ronald Gillis.

[U] SECULAR INSTITUTES

WASHINGTON. *Caritas Christi*, Bladensburg Rd., N.E., P.O. Box 41372, 20018. A Secular Institute of Pontifical Right. Sr. Helen St. Denis, C.C.

Community of Christ, 1003 Kearney St., N.E., 20017. Tel: 202-832-9710; 797-8806. Rev. John Adams (RIC), Moderator. A Private Association Community of Archdiocesan Right for Priest, Lay Men and Lay Women. The Community of Christ Purpose is Simple Lifestyle, Poverty Ministry, Spiritual Growth and Prayer of Community Members.

WEST BETHESDA, MD. *Missionaries of the Kingship of Christ*, P.O. Box 34513, 20827-0513. Rev. Dominic V. Monti, O.F.M.

[V] MISCELLANEOUS

WASHINGTON. *"The Americas"*, Catholic University of America, Gibbons Hall, Room B 17, 20064. Tel: 202-319-5890; Fax: 202-319-5569.

**Africa Faith & Justice Network*, P.O. Box 29378, 20017. Tel: 202-832-3412; Fax: 202-832-9051. Sr. Maura Browne, S.N.D., Exec. Dir.

American Catholic Philosophical Association, The Catholic University of America, 20064. Tel: 202-319-5518; Fax: 202-319-6408.
E-mail: cua-acpa@cua.edu
Web site: http://www.cus.edu/www/org/acpa
Dr. Therese-Anne Druart, Sec.

Archbishop Carroll High School, 4300 Harewood Rd., N.E., 20017. Tel: 202-529-0900; Fax: 202-529-5989. Records Center for the Archdiocese of Washington.

Alumni Office. John Badaczewski, Dir. Tel: 202-529-0900 Ext. 32.

Archdiocese of Cotabato, 391 Michigan Ave., N.E., 20017. Tel: 202-529-5244. Most Rev. Philip F. Smith, O.M.I., D.D.; Mrs. Anne Weeks, Sec. to the Archbishop.

Black Leadership and Christ's Kingdom Society, P.O. Box 4579, 20017. Tel: 202-529-4860; 301-888-2566. Rev. Robert S. Pittman, S.S.S., Dir. Total in Residence 8; Total Staff 14.

CARA, Center for Applied Research in the Apostolate, Georgetown University, 20057. Tel: 202-687-8080; Fax: 202-687-8083.
E-mail: froehle@guvax.georgetown.edu
Dr. Bryan T. Froehle, Exec. Dir.

Carmelite Institute, 1600 Webster St., N.E., 20017. Tel: 202-635-3534.
E-mail: mail@carmeliteinstitute.org
Web site: http://www.carmeliteinstitute.org
Rev. John Welch, O.Carm., Pres. Tel: 202-526-1221 Ext. 118.

Carroll Manor Nursing & Rehabilitation Center, 1150 Varnum St., N.E., 20017-2180. Tel: 202-269-7100; Fax: 202-269-7816. Rev. Msgr. Leonard F. Hurley, Chap.; Rev. Brian J. O'Connell, C.M.

Catholic Biblical Association, Catholic University of America, 296 Leahy Hall, 20064. Tel: 202-319-5519.
E-mail: cua-cathbib@cua.edu
Web site: http://www.cua.edu/www/org/cbib
Rev. Joseph Jensen, O.S.B., Exec. Sec.

Catholic Historical Society of Washington, 2665 Woodley Rd., N.W., 20008. Tel: 202-234-1488. Rev. Msgr. Robert O. McMain.

Catholic Information Center, 825 15th St., N.W., 20005. Tel: 202-783-2062.
E-mail: cath.info.dc@worldnet.att.com
Rev. L. Michael Curtin. Total Staff 18.

Center of Concern, 3700 13th St., N.E., 20017. Tel: 202-635-2757; Fax: 202-832-9494.
E-mail: coc@igc.apc.org
Web site: http://www.coc.org/coc
Rev. James E. Hug, S.J., Exec. Dir.

Centro Maria, 650 Jackson St., N.E., 20017. Tel: 202-635-1697; Fax: 202-635-7246.
E-mail: centroma@erols.com
Sr. Ma. Cristina Lopez, R.M.I., Dir.

Christ Child Society of Washington, DC, Inc., 5101 Wisconsin Ave., N.W., 20016. Tel: 202-966-9250. Alicia Caulfield Brown, Pres. A Non-Profit, Volunteer Organization with Membership of Approximately 1,000 Persons. Its Volunteers Actively Participate in the Operation of the Society's Programs Which are Directed by a Paid Staff Composed of Administrative Professionals and Clinical Social Workers. Total Assisted 13,999; Total staff 22.

The Christian Institute for the Study of Human Sexuality. 8901 New Hampshire Ave., Silver Spring, MD, 20903-3611. Tel: 301-422-5500; Fax: 301-422-5519.
E-mail: jesedcntr@aol.com
Rev. James J. Gill, S.J., M.D., Dir.

Christian Life Communities, Washington Area Promoters: 5040 Nebraska Ave., N.W., 20008-2938. Tel: 202-363-4593. Ms. Margaret Fox, 201 E. Wayne Ave., Silver Spring, MD, 20901-3808. Tel: 301-495-2969; Fax: 301-495-7318. Fred and Betty Leone.

Communio: International Catholic Review, 487 Michigan Ave., N.E., 20017.
E-mail: communio@aol.com
David L. Schindler, Contact Person.

The Community of St. John, 1215 Quincy St., N.E., 20017; Fax: 202-529-4253. David L. Schindler, Contact Person. Total in Residence 5.

Council for Research in Values and Philosophy, The Catholic University of America, 20064. Tel: 202-319-5636; Fax: 202-319-6089; 800-659-9962.
E-mail: gua-rup@cua.edu
Web site: http://www.cua.edu/~mclean
Rev. George F. McLean, O.M.I., Sec.

District of Columbia Detention Facility, Office of Chaplain, 1901 D St., S.E., 20003. Tel: 202-547-1715. Rev. F. Michael Bryant, Ph.D., Chap. Total in Residence 2,000; Total Staff 20.

Dorothy Day Catholic Worker, 503 Rock Creek Church Rd., N.W., 20010. Tel: 202-882-9649. Total Assisted 200; Total Staff 8.

**Education for Parish Service Programs*, Trinity College, 125 Michigan Ave., N.E., 20017-1094. Tel: 202-884-9020; Fax: 202-483-0253.
E-mail: epsdc@erols.com

Equestrian Order of the Holy Sepulchre of Jerusalem - Middle Atlantic Lieutenancy of the U.S., P.O. Box 9611, 20016-9611. Tel: 301-963-0459; Fax: 301-840-9880. Lt. Bernard J. Ficarra, M.D., K.G.C.H.S.

Ethiopian and Eritrean Catholic Mission, USA, 100 Lawrence St., N.E., 20017. Tel: 202-829-3934. Rev. Tesfamariam Baraki (Ethiopia), Dir.

Fellowship of Catholic Scholars, Catholic University, School of Philosophy, 20064. Tel: 203-319-5259. Dr. Jude P. Dougherty, Exec. Sec. Research and Scholarship.

The Franciscan Federation, Third Order Regular of the Sisters and Brothers of the United States, 817 Varnum St., N.E., P.O. Box 29080, 20017. Tel: 202-529-2334; Fax: 202-529-7016.

Holy Childhood Association, 1720 Massachusetts Ave., N.W., 20036. Tel: 202-775-8637; Fax: 202-429-2987. Rev. Francis W. Wright, C.S.Sp., National Dir.

**Institute for Pastoral Renewal, Inc.*, c/o Jesuit Community, Georgetown University, 20057. Tel: 202-687-4164; Fax: 202-687-2045.
E-mail: 103102.1417@compuserve.com
Rev. Paul L. Cioffi, S.J., Dir. 527 Priests attend retreats, workshops, and seminars on liturgical renewal. None in residence. Two part-time staff members.

Institute of Carmelite Studies and ICS Publications, 2131 Lincoln Rd., N.E., 20002. Tel: 800-832-8489; Fax: 202-832-8967.
E-mail: PayneOCD@erols.com
Revs. Regis Jordan, O.C.D., Chm.; Kieran Kavanaugh, O.C.D., Publisher; Steven Payne, O.C.D., Editor, ICS Publications; Bro. Bryan Paquette, O.C.D., Business Mgr. & Promotion Dir.

Jesuit Conference, Inc., 1616 P St., N.W., Ste. 400, 20036-1405. Tel: 202-462-0400; Fax: 202-328-9212. P.O. Box 34513, Bethesda, MD, 20827. Revs. Gregory F. Lucey, S.J., Pres.; Daniel C. McDonald, S.J., Exec. Sec.

The Jesuit Educational Center for Human Development. 8901 New Hampshire Ave., Silver Spring, MD, 20903-3611. Tel: 301-422-5500; Fax: 301-422-5519.
E-mail: jesedcntr@aol.com
Rev. James J. Gill, S.J., M.D., Dir.

Jesuit Missions, Inc., 1616 P St., N.W., #400, 20036. Tel: 202-462-0400; Fax: 202-328-9212.
E-mail: USAJRS@aol.com
Rev. Richard J. Ryscavage, S.J., Pres.

Jesuit Refugee Service, 1616 P St., N.W., #400, 20036-2286. Tel: 202-462-5200; Fax: 202-328-9212.
E-mail: USAJRS@aol.com
Rev. Richard J. Ryscavage, S.J., Natl. Coord.

Jesuit Secondary Education Association, 1616 P St., N.W., Ste. 400, 20036-1405. Tel: 202-667-3888.
E-mail: jsea@jsea.org
Revs. Joseph F. O'Connell, S.J., Pres.; Ralph E. Metts, S.J., Vice Pres.; James F. Fox, S.J., Vice Pres.; Shelly C. Frieden, Admin. Coord.; Silvia Bailey Gonzalez, Receptionist. Total Staff 6.

Jesuit Social Ministries-National Office, 1616 P St., N.W., Ste. 400, 20036-1405. Tel: 202-462-0400; Fax: 202-328-9212.
E-mail: britishr@aol.com
Ms. British Robinson, Acting Dir.

Jesuit Volunteers: International, P.O. Box 25478, 20007. Tel: 202-687-1132; Fax: 202-687-5082.
E-mail: jvi@gunet.georgetown.edu
Web site: http://guweb.georgetown.edu/jvc
Staff 4; Lay Volunteers/Foreign Missions 70.

The John Carroll Society, P.O. Box 29260, 20017. Jane Golden Belford, Pres.; Rev. Peter J. Vaghi.

McKenna House, 1501 Park Rd., N.W., 20010. Tel: 202-332-7333. Hagos Weldegiorgis, Prog. Mgr.

**Missionary Vehicle Association, Inc.* MIVA America. 1400 Michigan Ave., N.E., 20017. Tel: 202-635-3444.
E-mail: mivamerica@aol.com
Revs. Philip DeRea, M.S.C., National Dir.; Anthony F. Krisak, S.T.D.

The Morley Institute, 1814 1/2 N St., N.W., 20036. Tel: 202-861-7790; Fax: 202-861-7788.
E-mail: acrane@crisismagazine.com
Web site: http://www.crisismagazine.com

Mount Carmel House, 471 G Pl., N.W., 20001. Tel: 202-289-6315. Sr. Ann Forrest, O.S.F., Dir. Transitional Rehabilitative Housing for Women with 26 beds.

National Black Sisters' Conference, 3027 Fourth St., N.E., 20017. Tel: 202-529-9250; Fax: 202-529-9370.
E-mail: nbsc@igc.apc.org
Sr. Patricia J. Chappell, S.N.D.deN., Pres. Total Staff 2.

National Catholic Conference for Interracial Justice, 1200 Varnum St., N.E., 20017-2796. Tel: 202-529-6480; Fax: 202-526-1262. Deacon Joseph M. Conrad, Jr., Exec. Dir.

National Christ Child Society, Inc., 5101 Wisconsin Ave., N.W., Ste. 304, 20016. Tel: 202-363-9516; 800-814-2149; Fax: 202-966-2880.
E-mail: nccs@nationalchristchildsoc.org
Web site: http://www.nationalchristchildsoc.org
Mrs. Kathleen L. Gibbons, Pres., National Christ Child Society, Inc.

National Institute for the Family, Inc., 3019 Fourth St., N.E., 20017. Tel: 202-462-2591. Rev. Donald B. Conroy, S.T.L., Ph.D. (GBG), Exec. Dir.; Dr. Carolyn Gutowski, M.A.T., Ph.D., Research Dir. Research Program: Intergenerational Parish Ministry. Seminary and Lay Leadership Training in association with the Washington Theological Union.

Nativity of the Blessed Virgin (German Mission). Mailing Address: Archdiocese of Washington, P.O. Box 29260, 20017. Tel: 301-853-4520; Fax: 301-853-5346. Physical Location, 6330 Linway Ter., McLean, VA, 22101. Tel: 703-356-4473. Rev. Msgr. Bernd Kaut.

**Notre Dame Education Center*, 125 Michigan Ave., N.E., 20017.

Paul VI Institute for the Arts, 924 G St., N.W., 20001. Tel: 202-347-1450. Rev. Msgr. Michael diTeccia Farina.

Paulist Media Works, 3055 4th St., N.E., 20017-1102. Tel: 202-269-6064; Fax: 202-269-4304. Revs. John Geaney, C.S.P., Exec. Dir.; Lawrence Rice, C.S.P., Assoc. Dir.; Sue Donovan, Pres.

Paulist National Catholic Evangelization Assoc., 3031 Fourth St., N.E., 20017-1102. Tel: 202-832-5022; Fax: 202-269-0209. Rev. Kenneth G. Boyack, C.S.P., Dir.; Sr. Susan Wolf, S.N.D., Assoc. Dir.; Rev. Robert S. Rivers, C.S.P., Dir. of Parish & Diocesan Svcs.; Mr. Denny Marcotte, Gen. Business Mgr.; Mr. Edward Maurer, Dir. Financial Devel.; Ms. Maria Luisa Gaston, Dir., Hispanic Ministry; Rev. Thomas E. Comber, C.S.P., Dir., PNCEA/Prison Ministries.

S.M.A. Social Concerns Department, 1242 Newton St., N.E., 20017. Rev. Edward Galvin, S.M.A., Dir.

S.N.D.B.C. Charitable Trust, 3037 Fourth St., N.E., 20017. Tel: 202-832-8770.
E-mail: sndclaire@aol.com
Sr. Claire McCormick, S.N.D., Exec. Sec.

St. Vincent Pallotti Center for Apostolic Development, Inc., P.O. Box 893, Cardinal Sta., 20064. Tel: 202-529-3330; Fax: 202-529-0911.
E-mail: palotti01@aol.com
Web site: http://www.cua.edu/www/org/palloti
Dr. Andrew D. Thompson, Natl. Dir. Total Assisted 15,000; Total Staff 4.

Sisters of Notre Dame de Namur Base Communities, Inc., 3037 Fourth St., N.E., 20017.
E-mail: sndclaire@aol.com
Sisters 17.

Sovereign Military Order of Malta-Federal Association of the U.S.A., 1730 M St., N.W., Ste. 403, 20036. Tel: 202-331-2494; Fax: 202-331-1149.
E-mail: smomfausa@aol.com
Web site: http://www.smom.org
William J. Page, Pres.; Joseph J. Dempsey, Jr., Exec. Dir.

Spanish Catholic Center, P.O. Box 11450, 20008. Tel: 202-483-5665. 1618 Monroe St., N.W., 20010. Tel: 202-483-5665; 462-3482.

District of Columbia Health Center, 1618 Monroe St., N.W., 20010. Tel: 202-332-6664.

Spanish Catholic Center Langley Office, 1015 University Blvd. E., Silver Spring, MD, 20903. Tel: 301-431-3773.

Maryland Health Center, 1015 University Blvd. E., Second Floor, Silver Spring, MD, 20903. Tel: 301-434-3999.

Spanish Catholic Center Gaithersburg Office, 117 N. Frederick Ave., Gaithersburg, MD, 20877. Tel: 301-417-9113; 9114; 417-9588.

District of Columbia Social Services, 1618 Monroe St., N.W., 20010. Tel: 202-483-1520.

Spiritual Life, 2131 Lincoln Rd., N.E., 20002. Tel: 202-832-8489; Fax: 202-832-8967.
E-mail: edodonnell@aol.com
A Quarterly of Contemporary Spirituality. Bros. Bryan Paquette, O.C.D., Business Mgr.; Edward O'Donnell, O.C.D., Editor; Michael Stoegbauer, O.C.D., Promotion Mgr.

Theological Studies, Inc., Georgetown University, 37th and O St., N.W., 20057. Tel: 202-338-0754. Publisher of the Quarterly Theological Studies. Revs. Michael A. Fahey, S.J., Editor; John R. Keating, S.J., Mgr.

Woodstock Theological Center, Georgetown University, Box 571137, 20057-1137. Tel: 202-687-3532.
E-mail: woodstck@guvax.georgetown.edu
Web site: http://guweb.georgetown.edu/woodstock/
Revs. James L. Connor, S.J., Dir.; John P. Langan, S.J.; Walter J. Burghardt, S.J.; J. Leon Hooper, S.J.; Raymond B. Kemp; Gasper F. LoBiondo, S.J.; Thomas J. Reese, S.J.; Rev. Msgr. Richard M. Liddy; Revs. Joseph N. Tylenda, S.J.; William J. Walsh, S.J.

BETHESDA, MD. *Alpha Omega, Inc. The Legion of Christ Inc.*, Our Lady of Bethesda Retreat Center, 7007 Bradley Blvd., 20817. Tel: 301-365-0612; Fax: 301-469-7522. Rev. Richard Gill, L.C.

Center for International Resources, Inc. (CIRIMEX), 4603 Cheltenham Dr., 20814. Tel: 301-652-2463; Fax: 301-652-2473. Spanish language and Latin cultural training center. Sr. Kathryn A. Bissell, Chm., Exec. Dir., U.S.A.; Sr. Caridad Inda, Chm., Exec. Dir., Mexico.

Lay Women's Association, Villa Cortona, P.O. Box 34513, 20827. Tel: 301-469-7085. National Headquarters of the LWA.

Natural Family Planning Center of Washington, DC, Inc., P.O. Box 30239, 20824-0239.
E-mail: hklaus@dgsys.com
8514 Bradmoor Dr., 20817-3810. Tel: 301-897-9323; Fax: 301-571-5267. Teen STAR and Holistic Sexuality Programs. Total in Residence 2; Total Staff 3.

CAPITAL PLAZA, MD. *Archdiocese of Washington Division, The Blue Army*. World Apostolate of Fatima, P.O. Box 6702, 20789. Tel: 301-322-4978.
E-mail: bluearmy@ix.netcom.com
Web site: http://www.bluearmy.com
Patricia B. Whiteman, Pres.; Rev. Msgr. William F. O'Donnell, Spiritual Dir.

FRONT ROYAL, VA. *Human Life International*, 4 Family Life, 22630. Tel: 540-635-7884.
E-mail: frmarx@aol.com
Rev. Paul B. Marx, O.S.B.

GAITHERSBURG, MD. *Emmanuel, Inc.*, Mother of God School, P.O. Box 2418, 20886-2418. Tel: 301-990-2088. Students 127; Total Staff 17.

HYATTSVILLE, MD. *Faith House, Inc.*, 4901 Eastern Ave., 20782. Tel: 301-559-5500. Sr. Josephine Murphy, CEO. Total Assisted 8.

Prison Outreach Ministry, P.O. Box 2173, 20784. Tel: 310-773-1926. Rev. Michael Bryant, Chap. Total in Residence 1,800.

KENSINGTON, MD. *Inter Mirifica*, P.O. Box 241, 20895. Tel: 301-942-9577; Fax: 301-942-9572. Rev. John Hardon, S.J.; Dolores O'Connell, Contact Person. Religious publications.

LANDOVER HILLS, MD. *Catholic Deaf Center*, 7202 Buchanan, 20784. Tel: 301-459-7464 (TDD); 459-7465 (Voice); Fax: 301-459-8186.
E-mail: ehelm@aol.com
Rev. Edward J. Helm, Dir. In res. Rev. Gerard A. Trancone. Total in Residence 2; Total Staff 3.

POMFRET, MD. *Ministr-O-Media, Inc.*, St. Joseph Church, 20675. Tel: 301-870-3990. Rev. Msgr. John B. Brady, Pres.

POTOMAC, MD. *Youth for the Third Millennium*, P.O. Box 60001, 20859. Tel: 301-365-3205; Fax: 301-469-7522. Mr. Paul Bernetsky, Exec. Dir.

ROCKVILLE, MD. *Avondale Park Apartments, Inc.*, c/o Victory Housing, 1515 Dunster Rd., 20854. Tel: 301-279-9200.

SEAT PLEASANT, MD. *Osmund Program*, 6407 Rolling Ridge Dr., 20743. Tel: 301-350-0566. Francis W. Kraemer, Jr., Pres.

SILVER SPRING, MD. *All Hallows Mission Fund, Inc.*, P.O. Box 3691, 20918.

Apostleship of Prayer, League of the Sacred Heart, 8611 Cedar St., 20910-4324. Tel: 301-589-3894. Rev. Gerard P. Bell, S.J., Archdiocesan Dir.

Camp St. Charles, Inc., 104 Bishop Dr., 20905. Tel: 301-384-5432.
E-mail: gwillis@frostcenter.com
Web site: http://www.achiever.com/freehmpg/csc
Rev. Glen Willis, S.D.S. Total Assisted 600; Total Staff 35.

Catholics Committed to Support the Pope, 9402 Stateside Ct., 20903. Tel: 301-434-3245; 434-7763; Fax: 301-277-4047. George P. Morse, K.G.C.S.G., Pres. & Publisher. Councilors: His Eminence James Cardinal Hickey; His Eminence John Cardinal O'Connor; His Eminence Mario Luigi Cardinal

Ciappi; His Eminence Edouard Cardinal Gagnon; His Eminence Alfonso Cardinal Lopez Trujillo; Dr. William E. May. Theological Advisors: Most Rev. William E. Lori; Rev. Msgr. Peter J. Elliott. Prepares and Distributes World-Wide Eleven-Volume Series Precis of Official Catholic Teaching for Rectors, Seminarians, Nuncios, Bishops and Others with Particular Application to Seminaries and Teaching.

Friends of John Paul II Foundation, 9700 Rosensteel Ave., 20910. Tel: 301-589-1857. Rev. Stanislaw Hajkowski, S.Ch.

Leadership Conference of Women Religious in the U.S.A., 8808 Cameron St., 20910. Tel: 301-588-4955. Sr. Anne Munley, I.H.M., Pres.; Sr. Mary Waskowiak, R.S.M., Vice Pres.; Sr. Nancy Schreck, O.S.F., Past Pres.; Sr. Mary Ann Gschwind, F.S.P.A., Sec.; Sr. Judith Ann Karam, C.S.A.; Sr. Margaret Cafferty, P.B.V.M., Exec. Dir.

Lumen Catechetical Consultants, Inc., P.O. Box 1761, 20915. Tel: 301-593-1066; Fax: 301-593-1689. Mr. John M. Capobianco, Pres. Provides Consulting & Production Services to Catholic Organizations; Assist in Development and Production of Catechetical Materials in Various Media.

National Association for Treasurers of Religious Institutes, 8824 Cameron St., 20910-4113. Tel: 301-587-7776.
E-mail: natri@erols.com
Bro. Henry Sammon, F.M.S., Pres.; Sr. Carol Wester, O.P., Exec. Dir.

Oblate Conference, 8818 Cameron St., 20910. Tel: 301-565-0060; Fax: 301-589-2897.
E-mail: sfinn@igc.apc.org
Rev. Seamus Finn, O.M.I., National Coord.

Saint Luke Institute, Inc., 8901 New Hampshire Ave., 20903. Tel: 301-445-7970; Fax: 301-422-5400.
E-mail: stever@sli.org
Rev. Stephen J. Rossetti, Ph.D., D. Min., CEO. Total Assisted 65; Total Staff 75.

SOAR, 1400 Spring St., Ste. 3200, 20910-2735. Tel: 301-589-9811; Fax: 301-589-2482. Rita A. Hofbauer, Pres.

Spanish Catholic Center, Office of the, 1015 University Blvd., E., 20903. Tel: 301-431-3773; Fax: 301-431-0886. Sr. Carmen Banegas, C.A.Ch., Coord.

Washington Catholic Charismatic Service Committee, 13103 Tamarack Rd., 20904. Tel: 301-384-5568. Deacon Donald DeRoze.

TAKOMA PARK, MD. *Dominican Friar Residence - Southern Dominican Province*, 8019 Glenside Dr., 20912-7326. Tel: 301-439-4495. Total in Residence 2.

WALDORF, MD. *Body of Christ Farm Community, Inc.*, 3325 Martha Pl., 20601. Tel: 301-888-2566. Rev. Robert S. Pittman, S.S.S., Dir.

RELIGIOUS INSTITUTES OF MEN REPRESENTED IN THE ARCHDIOCESE

For further details refer to the corresponding bracketed number in the Religious Institutes for Men or Women section.

[0140]—*The Augustinians.*—O.S.A.
[0200]—*Benedictine Monks.*—O.S.B.
[1350]—*Brothers of St. Francis Xavier.*—C.F.X.
[0330]—*Brothers of the Christian Schools.* (Baltimore Prov.).—F.S.C.
[0600]—*Brothers of the Congregation of Holy Cross.*—C.S.C.
[0400]—*Canons Regular of the Order of the Holy Cross.*—O.S.C.
[0470]—*The Capuchin Friars.* (Prov. of St. Augustine).—O.F.M.Cap.
[0270]—*Carmelite Fathers & Brothers.*—O.Carm.
[1140]—*Congregation of the Sacred Hearts of Jesus and Mary.*—SS.CC.
[0480]—*Conventual Franciscans.*—O.F.M.Conv.
[0260]—*Discalced Carmelite Fathers (Prov. of the Most Pure Heart of Mary).*—O.C.D.
[0520]—*Franciscan Friars (Commissariat of the Holy Land).*—O.F.M.
[0530]—*Franciscan Friars of the Atonement.*—S.A.
[0650]—*Holy Ghost Fathers (Eastern Prov.).*—C.S.Sp.
[0690]—*Jesuit Fathers and Brothers (Prov. of Maryland).*—S.J.
[0730]—*Legionaries of Christ.*—L.C.
[0740]—*Marian Fathers.*—M.I.C.
[0770]—*The Marist Brothers.*—F.M.S.
[0780]—*Marist Fathers.*—S.M.
[0800]—*Maryknoll.*—M.M.
[0850]—*Missionaries of Africa.*—M.Afr.
[0720]—*The Missionaries of Our Lady of La Salette.*—M.S.
[1210]—*Missionaries of St. Charles (Scalabrinians).*—C.S.
[0590]—*Missionaries of the Holy Apostle.*—M.Ss.A.
[0840]—*Missionary Servants of the Most Holy Trinity.*—S.T.
[0870]—*Montfort Missionaries.*—S.M.M.
[0910]—*Oblates of Mary Immaculate (Eastern Prov.).*—O.M.I.
[0920]—*Oblates of St. Francis de Sales.*—O.S.F.S.
[0430]—*Order of Preachers (Dominican) (Prov. of St. Joseph).*—O.P.
[1310]—*Order of the Holy Trinity (American Prov.).*—O.SS.T.
[1030]—*Paulist Fathers.*—C.S.P.
[1040]—*Piarist Fathers.*—Sch.P.
[0610]—*Priests of the Congregation of Holy Cross.* (Indiana Prov.).—C.S.C.
[1070]—*Redemptorist Fathers.* (Baltimore Prov.).—C.Ss.R.
[0700]—*St. Joseph Society of the Sacred Heart.*—S.S.J.
[0110]—*Society of African Missions.*—S.M.A.
[1260]—*Society of Christ.*—S.Ch.
[0990]—*Society of the Catholic Apostolate (Immaculate Conception Prov.).*—S.A.C.
[1200]—*Society of the Divine Savior.* (Milwaukee, WI).—S.D.S.
[0420]—*Society of the Divine Word.*—S.V.D.
[1290]—*Society of the Priests of Saint Sulpice.*—S.S.
[0640]—*Sons of the Holy Family.*—S.F.
[0560]—*Third Order Regular of Saint Francis (Prov. of the Immaculate Conception).*—T.O.R.

RELIGIOUS INSTITUTES OF WOMEN REPRESENTED IN THE ARCHDIOCESE

[0230]—*Benedictine Sisters of Pontifical Jurisdiction.* (Elizabeth, NJ; Duluth, MN).—O.S.B.
[1810]—*Bernardine Sisters of the Third Order of St. Francis.*—O.S.F.
[0340]—*Carmelite Sisters of Charity.*—C.Ch.
[1920]—*Congregation of the Sisters of the Holy Cross.*—C.S.C.
[0760]—*Daughters of Charity of St. Vincent de Paul.*—D.C.
[0960]—*Daughters of Wisdom.*—D.W.
[0420]—*Discalced Carmelite Nuns.*—O.C.D.
[1050]—*Dominican Contemplative Nuns.*—O.P.
[1070-03]—*Dominican Sisters.*—O.P.
[1100]—*Dominican Sisters of Charity of the Presentation of the Blessed Virgin.*—O.P.
[1470]—*Franciscan Sisters of St. Joseph.*—H.F.S.J.
[1190]—*Franciscan Sisters of the Atonement.*—S.A.
[0410]—*Institute of the Sisters of Our Lady of Mt. Carmel.*—O.Carm.
[2330]—*Little Sisters of Jesus.*—L.S.J.
[2320]—*Little Sisters of the Holy Family.*—P.S.S.F.
[2340]—*Little Sisters of the Poor.*—L.S.P.
[2345]—*Little Workers of the Sacred Hearts of Jesus and Mary.*—P.O.S.C.
[2490]—*Medical Mission Sisters.*—S.C.M.M.
[2720]—*Mission Helpers of the Sacred Heart.*—M.H.S.H.
[2710]—*Missionaries of Charity.*—M.C.
[2820]—*Missionary Sisters of Our Lady of Africa.*—M.S.O.L.A.
[2900]—*Missionary Sisters of St. Charles Borromeo.*—M.S.S.C.B.
[2865]—*Missionary Sisters of the Sacred Heart of Our Lady of Guadalupe.*—M.S.C.Gpe.
[3530]—*Missionary Sisters, Servants of the Holy Spirit.*—S.Sp.S.
[3040]—*Oblate Sisters of Providence.*—O.S.P.
[]—*Oblate Sisters of the Most Holy Eucharist.*—O.S.S.E.
[3210]—*Poor Clares of Perpetual Adoration.*—P.C.P.A.
[3450]—*Religious of Jesus and Mary.*—R.J.M.
[2970]—*School Sisters of Notre Dame.*—S.S.N.D.
[3520]—*Servants of the Holy Heart of Mary.*—S.S.C.M.
[3620]—*Sister Servants of Mary Immaculate.*—S.S.M.I.
[0500]—*Sisters of Charity of Nazareth.*—S.C.N.
[0570]—*Sisters of Charity of Seton Hill, Greensburg, Pennsylvania.*—S.C.
[1000]—*Sisters of Divine Providence of Kentucky.*—C.D.P.
[2575]—*Sisters of Mercy of the Americas.*—R.S.M.
[3000]—*Sisters of Notre Dame de Namur.* (Maryland, Chesapeake & Base Communities Prov.).—S.N.D.deN.
[3360]—*Sisters of Providence of St. Mary-of-the-Woods, IN.*—S.P.
[3893]—*Sisters of Saint Joseph of Chestnut Hill, Philadelphia.*—S.S.J.
[3718]—*Sisters of St. Ann.*—S.S.A.
[3740]—*Sisters of St. Casimir.*—S.S.C.
[1650]—*Sisters of St. Francis of Philadelphia.*—O.S.F.
[3830-13]—*Sisters of St. Joseph.*—C.S.J.
[3850]—*Sisters of St. Joseph of Chambery.*—C.S.J.
[3890]—*Sisters of St. Joseph of Peace.*—C.S.J.P.
[3980]—*Sisters of St. Paul of Chartres.*—S.P.C.
[3140]—*Sisters of the Catholic Apostolate (Pallotine).*—S.A.C.
[1830]—*Sisters of the Good Shepherd.*—R.G.S.
[1950]—*Sisters of the Holy Family.*—S.S.F.
[1990]—*Sisters of the Holy Names of Jesus and Mary.*—S.N.J.M.
[2110]—*Sisters of the Humility of Mary.*—H.M.
[1720]—*Sisters of the Third Order Regular of St. Francis of the Congregation of Our Lady of Lourdes.*—O.S.F.
[2160]—*Sisters, Servants of the Immaculate Heart of Mary.*—I.H.M.
[4060]—*Society of the Holy Child Jesus.*—S.H.C.J.
[4070]—*Society of the Sacred Heart.*—R.S.C.J.
[4190]—*Visitation Nuns.*—V.H.M.

ARCHDIOCESAN CEMETERIES

WASHINGTON. *The Catholic Cemeteries of the Archdiocese of Washington, Inc.* 13801 Georgia Ave., Silver Spring, MD, 20906. Tel: 301-871-1300. All offices 9-4:30 P.M. Mr. Frank Markowski, Dir.; Rev. Msgr. William F O'Donnell, Dir.

Mount Olivet, 1300 Bladensburg Rd., N.E., 20002. Tel: 202-399-3000. Warren A. Meny.

St. Mary's, 2121 Lincoln Rd., N.E., 20002. Tel: 202-635-7444. Warren A. Meny.

CLINTON, MD, 8000 Woodyard Rd., 20735. Tel: 301-868-5141. Harry S. Lancaster, Jr.

LEONARDTOWN, MD, Box 379, 20650. Tel: 301-475-5005. Mr. John A. Spalding.

SILVER SPRING, MD. *Gate of Heaven*, 13801 Georgia Ave., 20906. Tel: 301-871-6500. Samuel E. French, Jr., Mgr.

St. John's Forest Glen, Rosensteel Ave., 20910. Tel: 301-871-6500. Samuel E. French, Jr.

NECROLOGY

† Byron, Joseph F., Potomac, MD, Our Lady of Mercy. —Died Sept. 29, 1997.
† Cole, J. Gerard, (Retried). —Died Oct. 6, 1997.
† Duffy, Gabriel F., Washington, DC, Epiphany. —Died May 20, 1997.
† Martin, Bernard E., Silver Spring, MD, St. Bernadette. —Died April 26, 1997.
† Murphy, Rev. Msgr. John J., (Retired). —Died Sept. 15, 1997.

Diocese of Wheeling-Charleston

(Dioecesis Vhelingensis carolopolitanus)

Most Reverend

BERNARD W. SCHMITT, D.D.

Bishop of Wheeling-Charleston; ordained May 28, 1955; appointed Titular Bishop of Walla Walla and Auxiliary Bishop of Wheeling-Charleston May 31, 1988; ordained to the Episcopacy August 1, 1988; appointed Seventh Bishop of Wheeling-Charleston March 30, 1989; installed May 17, 1989. *Address all correspondence to: 1300 Byron St., P.O. Box 230, Wheeling, WV, 26003.*

ESTABLISHED AS DIOCESE OF WHEELING JULY 19, 1850.; REDESIGNATED DIOCESE OF WHEELING-CHARLESTON OCTOBER 4, 1974

Square Miles 24,282.

Comprises the entire State of West Virginia.

For legal titles of parishes and diocesan institutions, consult the Chancery Office.

Chancery Office: 1300 Byron St., P.O. Box 230, Wheeling, WV, 26003. Tel.: 304-233-0880; Fax: 304-233-0890.

Web site address: www.dwc.org

STATISTICAL OVERVIEW

Personnel	
Bishop	1
Retired Bishops	1
Priests: Diocesan Active in Diocese	77
Priests: Active Outside Diocese	4
Priests: Retired, Sick or Absent	42
Number of Diocesan Priests	123
Religious Priests in Diocese	58
Extern Priests in Diocese	9
Ordinations:	
Diocesan Priests	1
Permanent Deacons in Diocese	29
Total Brothers	9
Total Sisters	309
Parishes	
Parishes	115
With Resident Pastor:	
Resident Diocesan Priests	71
Resident Religious Priests	26
Without Resident Pastor:	
Administered by Priests	18
Missions	29
Pastoral Centers	18
Professional Ministry Personnel:	
Brothers	4
Sisters	31
Lay Ministers	24
Welfare	
Catholic Hospitals	3
Total Assisted	293,161
Health Care Centers	2
Homes for the Aged	5
Residential Care of Children	1
Special Centers for Social Services	5
Educational	
Diocesan Students in Other Seminaries	13
Total Seminarians	13
Colleges and Universities	1
Total Students	1,556
High Schools, Diocesan and Parish	7
Total Students	1,718
High Schools, Private	1
Total Students	47
Elementary Schools, Diocesan and Parish	26
Total Students	5,248
Elementary Schools, Private	2
Total Students	235
Catechesis/Religious Education:	
High School Students	1,987
Elementary Students	6,649
Total Students Under Catholic Instruction	17,453
Teachers in the Diocese:	
Priests	4
Sisters	14
Lay Teachers	486
Vital Statistics	
Receptions into the Church:	
Infant Baptism Totals	1,283
Adult Baptism Totals	340
Received into Full Communion	294
First Communions	1,794
Confirmations	1,536
Marriages:	
Catholic	269
Interfaith	395
Total Marriages	664
Deaths	1,320
Total Catholic Population	103,069
Total Population	1,793,477

Former Bishops—Rt. Rev. RICHARD VINCENT WHELAN, D.D., cons. March 21, 1841; Bishop of Richmond; transferred to Wheeling in 1850; died July 7, 1874.—Rt. Rev. JOHN JOSEPH KAIN, D.D., cons. May 23, 1875; transferred June 15, 1893, to the Titular Archiepiscopal See of Oxyrynchia; appt. July 6, 1893; Coadjutor "cum jure successionis" to the Most Rev. Archbishop of St. Louis, MO; created Archbishop of St. Louis, May 21, 1895; died Oct. 13, 1903.—Rt. Rev. PATRICK JAMES DONAHUE, D.D., cons. April 8, 1894; died Oct. 4, 1922.—Most Rev. THOMAS J. MCDONNELL, D.D., LL.D., cons. Sept. 15, 1947; appt. Auxiliary Bishop of New York, June 21, 1947; appt. Coadjutor of Wheeling, March 7, 1951; died Feb. 25, 1961.—Most Rev. JOHN J. SWINT, D.D., LL.D., appt. Auxiliary Bishop of Wheeling Feb. 22, 1922; cons. May 11, 1922; appt. Bishop of Wheeling Dec. 11, 1922; promoted to rank of Archbishop "ad personam," March 12, 1954; died Nov. 23, 1962.—Most Rev. JOSEPH H. HODGES, D.D., ord. Dec. 8, 1935; appt. Titular Bishop of Rusadus and Auxiliary of Richmond Aug. 8, 1952; cons. Oct. 15, 1952; transferred to Wheeling See as Coadjutor, "cum jure successionis", May 24, 1961; succeeded to the See Nov. 23, 1962; died Jan. 27, 1985.—Most Rev. FRANCIS B. SCHULTE, D.D., ord. May 10, 1952; appt. Titular Bishop of Afufenia and Auxiliary Bishop of Philadelphia; cons. Bishop Aug. 12, 1981; transferred to Wheeling July 31, 1985; transferred to Archdiocese of New Orleans Feb. 14, 1989.

Vicar General—Rev. JOHN R. GALLAGHER, V.G., *1300 Byron St., P.O. Box 230, Wheeling, 26003.* Tel: 304-233-0880.

Chancery Office—1300 Byron St., P.O. Box 230, Wheeling, 26003. Office Hours: Mon.-Fri. 8:30-4:30. Tel: 304-233-0880; Fax: 304-233-0890.

Chancellor—Rev. JOHN R. GALLAGHER, V.G.

Diocesan Tribunal—All Rogatory Commissions should be addressed to the office of the Diocesan Tribunal, *P.O. Box 588, Wheeling, 26003.* Tel: 304-233-0880.

Judicial Vicar—Rev. RICHARD W. SHODA, J.C.L.

Associate Judicial Vicar—Rev. HILARION V. CANN, S.T.L., J.C.D.

Administrator of the Tribunal—Sr. MARY BYRON, S.S.J., J.C.L.

Promotor Justitiae—Rev. PATRICK A. CONDRON.

Defensores Vinculi—Revs. EUGENE S. OSTROWSKI; Sr. MARY BYRON, S.S.J., J.C.L.

Judices Pro-Synodales—Revs. HILARION V. CANN, S.T.L., J.C.D.; FREDERICK P. ANNIE; Sr. MARY BYRON, S.S.J., J.C.L.; EMIL J. DOBOSZ; JOHN S. LEDFORD; WILLIAM J. NOLTE; EUGENE S. OSTROWSKI; EUGENE J. WEBER.

Diocesan Consultors—Very Rev. F. LEON ALEXANDER, V.F.; Revs. JOSEPH L. PETERSON; FREDERICK P. ANNIE; Very Rev. EDWARD M. BELL, V.F.; JOHN R. GALLAGHER, V.G.; P. EDWARD SADIE.

Vicar for Religious—Vacant, *1300 Byron St., P.O. Box 230, Wheeling, 26003.* Tel: 304-233-0880.

Delegate for Clergy—Rev. ROBERT G. PARK, *7 13th St., P.O. Box 230, Wheeling, 26003.* Tel: 304-233-0880.

Office for Clergy Development—Rev. FREDERICK P. ANNIE, Dir., *P.O. Box 230, Wheeling, 26003.* Tel: 304-233-0880; Fax: 304-233-0890.

Vicars Forane—Very Rev. STEPHEN D. DUBE, V.F., Wheeling Vicariate; Very Rev. PATSY J. IAQUINTA, V.F., Beckley Vicariate; Very Rev. F. LEON ALEXANDER, V.F., Charleston Vicariate; Very Rev. JEROME MCKENNA, C.P., V.F., Clarksburg Vicariate; Very Rev. JOHN V. DIBACCO, JR., V.F., Martinsburg Vicariate; Very Rev. EDWARD M. BELL, V.F., Parkersburg Vicariate; Very Rev. WILLIAM A. ANDERSON, V.F., Weston Vicariate.

Finance Council—P.O. Box 230, Wheeling, 26003.

Finance Officer—Rev. JOHN R. GALLAGHER, V.G., *P.O. Box 230, Wheeling, 26003.* Tel: 304-233-0880.

Diocesan Seminary Committee—Rev. JOHN R. GALLAGHER, Exec. Sec.

Diocesan Offices and Directors

Adoration, Union of Daily—Vacant.

Apostleship of Prayer—Rev. JOHN ROCK S.J., *P.O. Box 230, Wheeling, 26003.*

Archivist—Rev. JOHN R. GALLAGHER, V.G., *P.O. Box 230, Wheeling, 26003.*

Behavioral Counseling and Ministry—Rev. ROBERT G. PARK, *7 13th St., P.O. Box 230, Wheeling, 26003.* Tel: 304-233-0880.

Blessed Sacrament, Confraternity of the—Vacant, *P.O. Box 230, Wheeling, 26003.*

Board of Education—Mr. JOHN ELCESSER, Pres., *P.O. Box 230, Wheeling, 26003.* Tel: 304-233-0880.

Building Committee—Mr. DONALD P. MORRIS, Building & Property Supvr., *P.O. Box 230, Wheeling, 26003.* Tel: 304-233-0880.

Catholic Community Services, Inc.—Mr. GEORGE E. SMOULDER, Exec. Dir., *7 13th St., P.O. Box 230, Wheeling, 26003-0030.* Tel: 304-233-0880. Northern Regional Office: *7 13th St., P.O. Box 230, Wheeling,*

26003-0030. Tel: 304-233-0880., *3101 Main St., Weirton, 26062-4711.* Tel: 304-748-1081. Western Regional Office: *8024 Court Ave., Hamlin, 25523.* Tel: 304-824-5069. Central Regional Office: *235 High St., Ste. 210, Morgantown, 26505.* Tel: 304-292-6597. Southern Regional Office: *P.O. Box 386, 865 Mercer St., Princeton, 24740-2909.* Tel: 304-425-4306. Eastern Regional Office: *20 S. Marsham St., Romney, 26757.* Tel: 304-822-5414.

Catholic University, Friends of—Rev. JOHN R. GALLAGHER, V.G., Dir., *P.O. Box 230, Wheeling, 26003.* Tel: 304-233-0880.

Cemeteries—Rev. CHARLES B. TEUFEL, Dir., *1300 Charles St., Wellsburg, 26070.* Tel: 304-737-0429.

Censor Librorum—Vacant.

West Virginia Council of Catholic Women—Sr. KATHLEEN DURKIN, S.S.J.,Diocesan: BETTY CHARLES, *203 East Dr., Princeton, 24720.* Tel: 304-425-8665.

Stewardship and Development, Office of—Mr. BRYAN MINOR, Dir., *P.O. Box 230, Wheeling, 26003.* Tel: 233-0880.

Diaconal Council—Mr. TRUMAN A. LIPSCOMB, Chm., *P.O. Box 1, Masontown, 26542.* Tel: 304-864-5512 (H); 329-1063(W).

Finance Office—Rev. JOHN R. GALLAGHER, V.G.; Mr. JOHN L. HOFFMAN, Business Mgr., *1300 Byron St., P.O. Box 230, Wheeling, 26003.* Tel: 304-233-0880.

Health Affairs, Coordinator of—Sr. DIANE BUSHEE, S.A.C., *St. Mary's Hospital, 2900 First Ave., Huntington, 25702.* Tel: 304-526-1234., *P.O. Box 230, Wheeling, 26003.* Tel: 304-233-0880.

Hispanic Affairs—Rev. EUGENE J. WEBER, Dir., *407 Jackson St., Fairmont, 26554-2998.* Tel: 304-366-0948.

Holy Childhood Association—Mr. VICTOR A. BOERIO, *11 13th St., P.O. Box 230, Wheeling.* Tel: 304-233-0880.

Holy Name Society—Vacant, *97 14th St., P.O. Box 230, Wheeling, 26003.* Tel: 304-233-0880.

Home and Foreign Missions, Society for the Propagation of the Faith and Catholic Students' Mission Crusade—Very Rev. A. JAMES MYLES, V.F., Diocesan Dir., *P.O. Box 230, Wheeling, 26003.*

Hospitals, Representative for Catholic—Sr. DIANE BUSHEE, S.A.C., *St. Mary's Hospital, 2900 First Ave., Huntington, 25702.* Tel: 304-526-1234.

Human Resources, Office of—Mr. MICHAEL NAU, Dir., *P.O. Box 230, Wheeling, 26003.* Tel: 304-233-0880.

Infirm Priests Association—Most Rev. BERNARD W. SCHMITT, D.D., Pres.; Rev. JOHN R. GALLAGHER, V.G., Sec. & Treas., *P.O. Box 230, Wheeling, 26003.* Tel: 304-233-0880.

Justice and Peace, Office of—Mr. GEORGE SMOULDER, Dir. Tel: 304-233-0880., *7 13th St., P.O. Box 230, Wheeling, 26003.*

Legion of Mary—Rev. RICHARD W. SHODA, J.C.L., Spiritual Dir., *201 Richardson St., P.O. Box W, Bethany, 26032.* Tel: 304-829-4622.

Migration and Refugee Services, Office of—Mrs. KIM KEENE, Dir., *1033 Quarrier St., Ste. 105, Charleston, 25301.* Tel: 304-343-1036.

Natural Family Planning—Ms. NANCY J. BOTKIN. Tel: 304-343-1036.

Pastoral Council—*P.O. Box 230, Wheeling, 26003.* Tel: 304-233-0880.

Pastoral Ministry for Religious—*1300 Byron St., P.O. Box 230, Wheeling, 26003.* Tel: 304-233-0880.

Pastoral Planning, Office of—Rev. EUGENE S. OSTROWSKI, Dir., *1300 Byron St., P.O. Box 230, Wheeling, 26003.* Tel: 304-233-0880.

Presbyteral Council—Rev. LARRY W. DORSCH, Chm., *1213 Byron St., P.O. Box 230, Wheeling, 26003.* Tel: 304-233-0880.

Priests Eucharistic League—Rev. THADDEUS J. GRONDALSKI, Dir., *1276 National Rd., Wheeling, 26003.*

Public Affairs Representative—G. NICHOLAS CASEY, JR., ESQ., *Ste. 700, One Valley Square, P.O. Box 1746, Charleston, 25326.* Tel: 304-345-2000.

Purchasing Agency, Diocesan—*1300 Byron St., P.O. Box 230, Wheeling, 26003.* Tel: 304-233-0880.

Religious Unity, Diocesan Commission for—Rev. JOHN H. MCDONNELL, Chm., *4807 Staunton Ave. S.E., Charleston, 25304-1951.* Tel: 304-925-2864.

Resettlement of Displaced Persons—Mr. GEORGE SMOULDER, Dir., *P.O. Box 230, Wheeling, 26003.* Tel: 304-233-0880.

Respect Life Office—Rev. D. BRIAN SHODA, *St. Leo Parish, Sulphur Spring Rd., P.O. Box 93, Inwood, 25428-0093.* Tel: 304-229-8945.

Rural Life Apostolate—Vacant.

Scholarship Association—Mr. JOHN ELCESSER, Sec. & Treas., *P.O. Box 230, Wheeling, 26003.* Tel: 304-233-0880.

Scouting—Rev. STEPHEN D. DUBE, *229 California Ave., Weirton, 26062-3729.* Tel: 304-723-2054.

Social Ministries, Department of—Mr. GEORGE SMOULDER, Dir., *7 13th St., P.O. Box 230, Wheeling, 26003.* Tel: 304-233-0880.

Vocations, Office of—Rev. JOHN R. GALLAGHER, Dir., *1300 Byron St., P.O. Box 230, Wheeling, 26003.* Tel: 304-233-0880.

West Virginia State Catholic Conference—Rev. JOHN R. GALLAGHER, Dir., *1300 Byron St., P.O. Box 230, Wheeling, 26003.* Tel: 304-233-0880.

Women's Affairs, Office of—Vacant, *1300 Byron St., P.O. Box 230, Wheeling, 26003.* Tel: 304-233-0880.

Women's Counseling and Referral Center—Sr. MARY LOUISE LISOWSKI, S.C., *7 13th St., Wheeling, 26003.* Tel: 304-233-0880.

Catholic Education and Formation

Catholic Education and Formation, Dept. of—Ms. MARY F. SAMSA, Dir., *11 13th St., P.O. Box 230, Wheeling, 26003-0030.* Tel: 304-233-0880.

Adult Formation—Mr. JAMES J. RUPP, Coord., *11 13th St., P.O. Box 230, Wheeling, 26003-0030.* Tel: 304-233-0880.

Catholic Charismatic Renewal—Very Rev. PATSY J. IAQUINTA, V.F., Liaison, *P.O. Box 608, Bluefield, 24701.* Tel: 304-327-5623.

Cursillo—Mr. EDWARD A. MARN, Lay Dir.

Communications—Rev. LARRY W. DORSCH, Dir. Communications, *1213 Byron St., P.O. Box 230, Wheeling, 26003-0030.* Tel: 304-233-0880.

Audio-Visuals—Mrs. CONNIE GORDER, *1213 Byron St., P.O. Box 230, Wheeling, 26003-0030.* Tel: 304-233-0880.

"Catholic Spirit, The"—Mr. SCOTT WEINBERG, Editor, *1213 Byron St., P.O. Box 230, Wheeling, 26003-0030.* Tel: 304-233-0880.

TV-Radio-Media Services—Mr. TED ROUSE, Exec. Producer, *1213 Byron St., P.O. Box 230, Wheeling, 26003-0030.* Tel: 304-233-0880.

Confraternity of Christian Doctrine—Mrs. ANNE COMEAUX, Coord., *11 13th St., P.O. Box 230, Wheeling, 26003-0030.* Tel: 304-233-0880.

Evangelization—Mr. BRYAN S. REISING, Coord., *1213 Byron St., P.O. Box 230, Wheeling, 26003-0030.* Tel: 304-233-0880.

Family Life—Vacant, *11 13th St., P.O. Box 230, Wheeling, 26003-0030.* Tel: 304-233-0880.

Christian Family Movement—

Marriage Preparation—

Phoenix Group—

Liturgical Practices—Vacant, *11 13th St., P.O. Box 230, Wheeling, 26003-0030.* Tel: 304-233-0880.

Liturgical Art and Architecture Commission—Very Rev. WILLIAM A. ANDERSON, V.F., Chm.

Liturgical Music—Vacant.

Schools, Superintendent of—Mr. JOHN F. ELCESSER, Supt.; Mr. VICTOR A. BOERIO, Asst. Supr. & Admin & Finance, *11 13th St., P.O. Box 230, Wheeling, 26003-0030.* Tel: 304-233-0880.

Curriculum—Sr. MARY LOU PALAS, S.C., Diocesan Coord.

Religious Education in Catholic Schools—Vacant, *11 13th St., P.O. Box 230, Wheeling, 26003-0030.* Tel: 304-233-0880.

Ministry with Persons who are Disabled—Ms. MICHELLE M. BOWE, *1213 Byron St., P.O. Box 230, Wheeling, 26003-0030.* Tel: 304-233-0880.

Youth Ministry—Mr. MICHAEL R. HALL, Diocesan Coord., *7 13th St., P.O. Box 230, Wheeling, 26003-0030.* Tel: 304-233-0880.

Campus Ministry—Mr. MICHAEL R. HALL, Diocesan Coord., *7 13th St., P.O. Box 230, Wheeling, 26003-0030.* Tel: 304-233-0880.

Teens Encounter Christ (TEC)—Mr. MICHAEL R. HALL.

Regional Coordinators for Catholic Education and Formation—

Region 1: Wheeling-Weirton—Mr. MARC LARRIVEE, Reg. Coord., *Paul VI Pastoral Center, 667 Stone and Shannon Rd., Wheeling, 26003.* Tel: 304-277-1897.

Region 2: Charleston-Huntington-Logan—Vacant.

Region 3: Beckley-Bluefield—Sr. MELISSA HESTER, I.H.M., Reg. Coord., *P.O. Box 7254, Sprague, 25926-0254.* Tel: 304-255-6531.

Region 4: Clarksburg-Fairmont-Parkersburg—Sr. MARIAN MILLS, C.S.J., Reg. Coord., *510 E. Pike St., Clarksburg, 26301.* Tel: 304-624-5701.

Region 5: Elkins-Weston—Mrs. CAROLYN SANTILLI, Reg. Coord., *P.O. Box 278, Buckhannon, 26201.* Tel: 304-472-5698.

Region 6: Keyser-Martinsburg—Sr. M. SHAWN SCANLAN, S.N.D.deN., Reg. Coord., *2 Lincoln St., P.O. Box 588, Fort Ashby, 26719-0588.* Tel: 304-298-4472.

CLERGY, PARISHES, MISSIONS AND PAROCHIAL SCHOOLS

CITY OF WHEELING
(Ohio County)

1—ST. JOSEPH'S CATHEDRAL (1828). Including former parishes: Blessed Trinity, St. Joan of Arc, and Sacred Heart. Rev. Larry W. Dorsch, Rector. In res., Revs. John R. Gallagher; Eugene S. Ostrowski; Robert G. Park; Frederick P. Annie.
Res., 14 13th St., 26003-0051. Tel: 304-233-4121; Fax: 304-233-4129.
School—Wheeling Catholic Elementary School, 26003. Tel: 304-233-1515.

2—BLESSED TRINITY (1931). Closed. Merged with St. Joseph's Cathedral.

3—CORPUS CHRISTI (1916), Rev. A. James Myles.
Res., 1516 Warwood Ave., 26003-7197. Tel: 304-277-2911.
School—Sr. Johnette Dzuba, V.S.C., Prin. Sisters of St. Joseph 2; Lay Teachers 10; Students 241.
Station—West Liberty.

4—IMMACULATE CONCEPTION (ST. MARY) (1873). Closed. Merged with St. Alphonsus.

5—OUR LADY OF PEACE (Mt. Olivet) (1962), Rev. Raymond D. Jablinske.
Res., 2 Allendale Rd., Mt. Olivet, 26003-4601. Tel: 304-242-6575.
School—Tel: 304-242-1383. Mrs. C'Ann Reilly, Prin. Lay Teachers 11; Students 222.

6—SACRED HEART (1903). Closed. Merged with St. Joseph's Cathedral.

7—ST. ALPHONSUS (1856). Including former parishes St. Mary and St. Ladislaus. Rev. Patrick A. Condron.
Church & Res.: 2111 Market St., 26003-3827. Tel: 304-232-4353.
School—Wheeling Catholic Elementary School, 26003.

8—ST. JOAN OF ARC (1923). Closed. Merged with St. Joseph's Cathedral.

9—ST. LADISLAUS (1902). Closed. Merged with St. Alphonsus.

10—ST. MICHAEL'S (1897), Revs. James M. Sobus; George J. Romage; Deacon Paul J. Smith.
Res., 1225 National Rd., 26003-5791. Tel: 304-242-1560; Fax: 304-243-5710.
School—1221 National Rd., 26003. Tel: 304-242-3966.
Lay Teachers 24; Students 521.

11—ST. VINCENT DE PAUL'S (1895), Revs. James LaCrosse, S.M.; H. Joseph Wilhelm, S.M.; Deacons Paul H. Bischof, Jr.; Ronald J. Wojcicki.
Res., 2244 Marshall Ave., 26003-7421. Tel: 304-242-0406; Fax: 304-243-0837.
School—Tel: 304-242-5844.
Sisters 2; Lay Teachers 18; Students 309.
Mission—Triadelphia, Ohio Co., Our Lady of Seven Dolors, Chapel Hill Rd., Triadelphia, 26059. Tel: 304-547-5342. [CEM]

CITY OF CHARLESTON
(Kanawha County)

1—SACRED HEART CO-CATHEDRAL (1866), Revs. P. Edward Sadie, Rector; John P. McDonough; Deacon John J. Lynch.
Res., 1032 Virginia St. E., 25301-2879. Tel: 304-342-8175; Fax: 304-344-3907. [CEM]
School—Tel: 304-346-5491. Mrs. Debra Sullivan, Prin.; Miss Lynn Nehoda, Asst. Prin.
Lay Teachers 27; Students 497.

2—ST. ANTHONY (1905), Rev. Richard J. Zelik, O.F.M.Cap.; Deacon David Wuletich. In res., Bro. Phillip Hainen, O.F.M.Cap.; Rev. Kieran Quinn, O.F.M.Cap.
Res., 1000 Sixth St., 25302. Tel: 304-342-2716.
School—Tel: 304-346-8441. Ms. Myrtolyn English.
Capuchin Brother 1; Sister of Divine Providence 1; Lay Teachers 13; Students 120.

3—ST. AGNES (1923), Rev. John H. McDonnell.
Res., 4807 Staunton Ave., S.E., 25304. Tel: 304-925-2836; Fax: 304-925-4423.
School—4801 Staunton Ave., S.E., 25304. Tel: 304-925-4341. Sr. Judith Ann Teufel, S.S.J., Prin.
Sisters of St. Joseph 1; Lay Teachers 14; Students 222.
Convent—300 49th St., S.E., 25304. Tel: 304-925-2480.

OUTSIDE THE CITIES OF WHEELING AND CHARLESTON

Beckley, Raleigh Co., St. Francis De Sales (1907), Revs. Samuel S. Sacus; William K. Matheny, Jr.; Deacons W. Donald Wise; John F. Ziolkowski.
Res., 614 S. Oakwood Ave., 25801. Tel: 304-253-3695; Fax: 304-253-3694. [CEM]
School—Tel: 304-252-4087.
Lay Teachers 10; Students 133.
Mission—Whitesville, Boone Co., St. Joseph the Worker, (1958) P.O. Box 444, Whitesville, 25209-0444. Tel: 304-854-2997; Fax: 304-854-2997. Sr. Ann Marie Liston, S.J.C., Pastoral Coord.

Beech Bottom, Brooke Co., Holy Family. Closed. See St. John, Wellsburg.

Belington, Barbour Co., Resurrection Mission (1978), Sr. Teresa Reddington, S.S.J., Dir.
Res., 701 Brown Ave., 26250. Tel: 304-823-1576.

Belle, Kanawha Co., St. John (1951), Rev. Albert Alexandrunas, O.F.M.Cap.
Res., 321 E. Tenth St., 25015. Tel: 304-949-3063.
Mission—Coalburg, Kanawha Co., Good Shepherd, Box 16, East Bank, 25067. Tel: 304-595-6002.

Benwood, Marshall Co., St. John's (1875), Rev. John C. Valentine.
Res., 622 Main St., 26031. Tel: 304-232-6455.
School—Sts. James and John Consolidated School, Tel: 304-232-1587. Mrs. Erin Beth Olexo, Prin.
Lay Teachers 7; Students 81.

Berkeley Springs, Morgan Co., St. Vincent de Paul (1931), Rev. John S. Ledford; Deacon John W. Locke.
Res., 116 S. Washington St., 25411-1577. Tel: 304-258-1311; Fax: 304-258-7559. [CEM]

Bluefield, Mercer Co., Sacred Heart (1895), Very Rev. Patsy Iaquinta, V.F.
Res., 1017 Wyoming St., P.O. Box 608, 24701. Tel: 304-327-5623; Fax: 304-327-7769.

Bridgeport, Harrison Co., All Saints (1946), Rev. Harry N. Cramer.
Res., 317 E. Main St., 26330-1750. Tel: 304-842-2283.
School—Harrison Co. Catholic School System, Tel: 304-624-5129.

Buckhannon, Upshur Co., Holy Rosary (1921), Rev. James B. McCafferty, S.M.
Res., 35 Franklin St., 26201. Tel: 304-472-3414; Fax: 304-472-3414.
Mission—Pickens, Randolph Co., Sacred Heart, Pickens, 26230. [CEM]

Camden, Lewis Co., St. Boniface (Leading Creek) (1875), Rev. Will Roger Malave.
Res., Rte. 2, Box 25, 26338-9737. Tel: 304-269-1767. [CEM]
Chapel—St. Clara, St. Clare. [CEM]

Cameron, Marshall Co., St. Martin (1871), Rev. Francis A. O'Kruta.
Res., 1 Fitzgerald Ave., 26033. Tel: 304-686-3551. [CEM]

Charles Town, Jefferson Co., St. James (1889). Includes St. Peter, Harper's Ferry. Rev. James J. Chetock.
Res., 311 S. George St., P.O. Box 370, 25414-0370. Tel: 304-725-5558; Fax: 304-725-1685. [CEM]

Cheat Lake, Monongalia Co., St. Luke (1980), Rev. Jeremiah F. McSweeney.
Res., Rte. 6, Box 145CC, Morgantown, 26505-9211. Tel: 304-594-2353; Fax: 304-594-2359.
School—St. Francis Central Catholic School, 375 Birch St., Morgantown, 26505. Tel: 304-598-0133; Fax: 304-598-2690.
Mission—Bruceton Mills, Preston Co., Mary Help of Christians, (1983) Bruceton Mills, 26525. Tel: 304-379-4220.

Chester, Hancock Co., Sacred Heart (1902), Rev. F. Rodger Hughes.
Res., 424 Fourth St., Box 313, 26034-0313. Tel: 304-387-0198.

Clarksburg, Harrison Co., Immaculate Conception (1864), Revs. Cesidio J. Federico; Peter A. Giannamore.
Res., 126 E. Pike St., 26301-2155. Tel: 304-622-8280. [CEM]
Parish Office: Tel: 304-622-8243.
St. James (1924), Rev. Robert A. Perriello; Deacons Anthony P. Santilli; Donald F. Molinari.
Res., 2107 Pride Ave., 26301-1819. Tel: 304-622-1668; Fax: 304-622-4618.
School—Harrison County Catholic School System, Tel: 304-623-1026; 622-9831; Fax: 304-623-1026.

Coalton, Randolph Co., St. Patrick Church (1918), Very Rev. William A. Anderson, V.F.
Res., 200 Church St., P.O. Box 99, 26257-0099. Tel: 304-636-5754. [CEM 4]

Dunbar, Kanawha Co., Christ the King, Rev. Dean G. Borgmeyer.
Res., 2219 22nd St., P.O. Box 339, Nitro, 25143. Tel: 304-755-0791.
Church—1508 Grosscup Ave., 25064-2925. Tel: 304-768-2527.

Elkins, Randolph Co., St. Brendan (1897), Very Rev. William A. Anderson, V.F.
Res., 1 Park St., P.O. Box 2205, 26241. Tel: 304-636-0467; 636-0546. [CEM]

Elkview, Kanawha Co., Our Lady of the Hills, Rev. John C. Reich.
Res., 4084 Indian Creek Rd., 25071-9328. Tel: 304-965-7670; Fax: 304-965-7670.
Mission—Clendenin, Kanawha Co., Catholic Community of Clendenin, 63 Elk River Rd., S., Clendenin, 25045. Tel: 304-548-7147. Co-Directors: Sr. Jacqueline Le Boeuf, S.S.A.; Sr. Marguerite St. Amand, S.S.A.

Fairmont, Marion Co.,

1—St. Peter's, (1873), Rev. Eugene J. Weber.
Res., 407 Jackson St., 26554-2998. Tel: 304-366-0948; Fax: 304-367-0739. [CEM]
School—Fairmont Catholic Grade School, Tel: 304-363-5313.

2—Immaculate Conception, (1960), Rev. Casey B. Mahone.
Res., 413 Maryland Ave., P.O. Box 1726-E, 26554. Tel: 304-363-1840.
School—Fairmont Catholic Grade School, Tel: 304-363-5313.

3—St. Anthony, (1964), Rev. Gary P. Naegele.
Res., 1660 Mary Lou Retton Dr., 26554-2099. Tel: 304-363-1328.
School—Fairmont Catholic Grade School, Tel: 304-363-5313.

4—St. Joseph's, (1909), Rev. S. Brian Owens.
Res., 219 Robinson St., 26554-3045. Tel: 304-366-1967. [CEM]
School—Fairmont Catholic Grade School, Tel: 304-363-5313.
Mission—Barrackville, Marion Co., All Saints, (1924).

Farmington, Marion Co., St. Peters (1921), Rev. Donald X. Higgs.
Res., 1304 Mill St., P.O. Box 150, 26571-0150. Tel: 304-825-6651.

Follansbee, Brooke Co., St. Anthony's (1906), Revs. Anthony Cincinnati; Anthony Thurston.
Res., 1017 Jefferson St., 26037-1334. Tel: 304-527-2286.

Fort Ashby, Mineral Co., Annunciation of the Lord, Rev. D. Kent Durig.
Res., P.O. Box 553, 26719-0553. Tel: 304-298-3392.

Franklin, Pendleton Co., St. Elizabeth Ann Seton, Rev. James J. Creedon, M.Ss.A. Co-Directors: Sr. Pauline Laurence, S.S.A.; Sr. Yvette Dargy, S.S.A.
Church & Res.—P.O. Box 890, 26807. Tel: 304-358-7012.

Gary, McDowell Co., Our Lady of Victory (1904), Rev. Nguyen Ngoc That Son; Sr. Mary Denise Thomas, I.H.M., Parochial Coord.
Church—P.O. Box 130, 24836. Tel: 304-448-2749.
Res., HC 76, P.O. Box 402, Powhatan, 24877-0167. Tel: 304-862-3494. [CEM]

Gassaway, Braxton Co., St. Thomas, Rev. Elmer Nadicksbernd, S.V.D.; Sr. Mary Weatherly, C.D.P., Pastoral Assoc.
Res., 624 Kanawha St., 26624-1208. Tel: 304-364-5895.

Glen Dale, Marshall Co., St. Jude (1968), Rev. William J. Stenger, Sr.
Res., 710 Jefferson Ave., P.O. Box 147, 26038-0147. Tel: 304-845-8165 (Rectory); 845-2646 (Office).

Glenville, Gilmer Co., Good Shepherd (1958), Rev. Edwin G. Daschbach, S.V.D.
Res., 701 Mineral Rd., 26351-1310. Tel: 304-462-7130; Fax: 304-462-7130.

Grafton, Taylor Co., St. Augustine (1852), Rev. Ronald G. Prechtl.
Res., 17 W. Washington St., 26354-1398. Tel: 304-265-1848; 265-3861 (Office). [CEM 2]

Grant Town, Marion Co., St. Anthony's (1907), Rev. James H.T. Brady, S.O.L.T.
Res., 102 Church St., P.O. Box 219, 26574-0219. Tel: 304-278-5371.
Mission—Rivesville, Marion Co., Our Lady of the Assumption, 207 Clayton St., Rivesville, 26588.

Harpers Ferry, Jefferson Co., St. Peter (1830). Closed. Merged with St. James, Charles Town.

Harrisville, Ritchie Co., Christ Our Hope (1980), Rev. Thomas Karachira; Sr. Kathryn Holohan, O.S.F., Pastoral Assoc.; Deacon John F. Maher.
Res., Rte. 1, Box 44A, 26362. Tel: 304-643-4261.
Chapel—Pennsboro, St. Joseph. [CEM]

Hinton, Summers Co., St. Patrick (1874), Rev. John N. Duhaime.
Res., 309 Second Ave., P.O. Box 8, 25951-0008. Tel: 304-466-3966. [CEM]
Mission—Alderson, Greenbrier Co., St. Mary of the Greenbrier, P.O. Box 441, Alderson, 24910. Tel: 304-445-7967.

Holden, Logan Co., St. Mary's (1961). Consolidated with Our Lady of Mount Carmel, Logan, to form St. Francis of Assisi, Logan.

Huntington, Cabell Co.,

1—St. Joseph's, (1872), Rev. Msgr. Lawrence J. Luciana; Rev. M. Julian Marneni.
Res., 1304 Sixth Ave., P.O. Box 369, 25708. Tel: 304-525-5202; Fax: 304-525-3972. [CEM]
School—520 Thirteenth St., 25701. Tel: 304-522-2644. Mrs. Georgeann Warfuel, Prin.
Lay Teachers 9; Students 135.

2—Our Lady of Fatima, (1952), Rev. Joseph L. Peterson; Sr. Mary Grace Wee Tom, R.S.M., Pastoral Assoc.
Res., 545 Norway Ave., 25705. Tel: 304-525-0866; Fax: 304-525-0390.
School—535 Norway Ave., 25705. Tel: 304-523-2861; 523-2863. Mrs. Marcia McDonald, Prin.
Sisters 1; Lay Teachers 16; Students 182.

3—Sacred Heart, (1934), Rev. Andrew G. Kranyc; Sr. Mary Terence Wall, S.A.C., Pastoral Assoc.
Res., 2015 Adams Ave., 25704-1419. Tel: 304-429-5234.

4—St. Peter Claver, (1937) (African-American), Rev. Andrew G. Kranyc; Sr. Patricia Burke, S.M.S.M., Parochial Coord.
Res., 828 Fifteenth St., 25701. Tel: 304-523-7311.

Hurricane, Putnam Co., Catholic Church of the Ascension (1980), Rev. Paul J. Wharton.
Res., 905 Hickory Mill Rd., 25526. Tel: 304-562-5816; Fax: 304-562-3589.

Huttonsville, Randolph Co., St. John Bosco (1948), Very Rev. William Anderson, V.F., Admin.; Deacon Louis J. Belldina.
Res., Rte. 1, Box 9D, 26273-9737. Tel: 304-335-2165; Fax: 304-335-2165.
Station—Huttonsville Correctional Center, Tel: 304-338-6323.

Inwood, Berkeley Co., St. Leo (1982), Rev. D. Brian Shoda.
Res., Sulphur Spring Rd., P.O. Box 93, 25428-0093. Tel: 304-229-8945; Fax: 304-229-9755.

Keyser, Mineral Co., Assumption (1874), Rev. Ivan M. Lebar, T.O.R.; Bro. Luke D. Stone, T.O.R., Pastoral Assoc.
Res., 34 James St., 26726-2721. Tel: 304-788-2488. [CEM]

Kingwood, Preston Co., St. Sebastian's (1914), Revs. Jerome McKenna, C.P.; William Davin, C.P.; Deacon Truman A. Lipscomb.
Res., P.O. Box 519, 26537. Tel: 304-329-1519; Fax: 304-329-2546. [CEM 3]
Church—322 E. Main St.
Mission—Terra Alta, Preston Co., St. Edward.

Logan, Logan Co., St. Francis of Assisi (1996), Rev. David J. Schmitt.
Res., 561 Main St., 25601-3899. Tel: 304-752-3017.

Lubeck, Wood Co., St. Monica's (1976), Rev. John H. Fahey.
Res., R.R. 1, Box 362, Washington, 26181-9615. Tel: 304-863-5580. [CEM]
Church—State Rte. 68.

Madison, Boone Co., St. Mary, Queen of Heaven (1957), Rev. James E. O'Connor.
Res., P.O. Box 467, 25130-0467. Tel: 304-369-4538; Fax: 304-369-6268.
Church—51 Madison Ave., 25130.
Mission—Chapmanville, Logan Co., St. Barbara, (1979) H.C. 74, Box 3018, Chapmanville, 25508-9522. Tel: 304-855-7962. Sr. Carol Symon, S.N.D., Parochial Coord.

Man, Logan Co., St. Edmund (1961), Rev. David J. Schmitt.
Mailing Address: 106 Bridge St., 25635.
Res., 561 Main St., Logan, 25601-3899. Tel: 304-752-3017.
Church—110 S. Bridge St., 25634-1002. Tel: 304-583-2476.

Mannington, Marion Co., St. Patrick's (1897), Rev. Donald X. Higgs.
Res., 204 Furbee Ave., 26582-1399. Tel: 304-986-2321.
Mission—Littleton, Wetzel Co., Assumption of the Blessed Virgin Mary, (1859) Littleton, 26581. [CEM]

Marlinton, Pocahontas Co., St. John Neumann (1977), Rev. George Manjadi; Deacon William B. Strange, Jr.
Res., 714 10th Ave., 24954-1314. Tel: 304-799-6778.
Mission—Bartow, Pocahontas Co., St. Mark the Evangelist, (1977) Bartow, 24920.

Martinsburg, Berkeley Co., St. Joseph's (1803), Very Rev. John V. DiBacco, Jr., V.F.
Res., 219 S. Queen St., 25401-3213. Tel: 304-264-8947; Fax: 304-263-7357. [CEM]
School—Tel: 304-267-6447; Fax: 304-267-7394.
Daughters of Charity of Vincent de Paul 1; Lay Teachers 16; Students 290.
Mission—Hedgesville, Berkeley Co., St. Bernadette, 205 W. Main St., P.O. Box 11, Hedgesville, 25427. Tel: 304-754-7830.

Masontown, Preston Co., St. Zita's (1962), Revs. Jerome McKenna, C.P.; William Davin, C.P.; Deacon Truman A. Lipscomb.
Res., P.O. Box 519, Kingwood, 26537-0519. Tel: 304-329-1519; Fax: 304-329-2546.
Church—Tel: 304-864-5512.

Maysel, Clay Co., Church of The Risen Lord (1972), Rev. Elmer Nadicksbernd, S.V.D.
Mailing Address: HC 60, Box 7, 25133. Tel: 304-587-4740.
Res., 624 Kanawha St., Gassaway, 26624.

McMechen, Marshall Co., St. James (1900), Rev. John C. Valentine.
Res., 326 Logan St., 26040-1096. Tel: 304-232-1227.
School—Sts. James and John Consolidated Schools, Tel: 304-232-1587.
Lay Teachers 7; Students 81.

Monongah, Marion Co., Holy Spirit (1982), Rev. James J. Neville, S.J.
Res., 687 Maple Ter., 26554-116. Tel: 304-534-3020. [CEM]

Montgomery, Fayette Co., Immaculate Conception (1888). Unassigned.
Res., P.O. Box 65, 25136. Tel: 304-442-2101.
Mission—Boomer, Fayette Co., St. Anthony Shrine, (1928).

Moorefield, Hardy Co., Epiphany of the Lord (1980), Rev. Gerard A. Petta, M.S.A. In res., Rev. Michael A. Nofi, M.S.A.
Res., Rte. 2, Box 400, 26836. Tel: 304-434-2547.
Church—Rte. 55.

Morgantown, Monongalia Co., St. Theresa's (1901), Rev. Mario R. Claro.
Res., 44 Beechurst Ave., 26505-4912. Tel: 304-296-5353.
School—St. Francis Central Catholic School, 375 Birch St., 26505. Tel: 304-598-0133.

St. John's University Parish, Newman Hall (1966), Revs. James A. Haley, C.S.P.; Michael E. Evernden, C.S.P.; Deacon Joseph Prentiss.
Res., 1481 University Ave., 26505-5598. Tel: 304-296-8231; Fax: 304-296-4650.
School—St. Francis Central Catholic School, 375 Birch St., 26505. Tel: 304-598-0133.

Moundsville, Marshall Co., St. Francis Xavier's (1857), Revs. Ronan J. Deegan, T.O.R.; Albert Driesch, T.O.R.
Res., 912 Seventh St., 26041. Tel: 304-845-1593.
School—(Grades K-8). Tel: 304-845-2562; Fax: 304-845-0016. Mr. Frank Giannamore.
Lay Teachers 11; Students 117; Preschool 16.
Station—Northern Regional Jail and Correctional Facility, Tel: 304-843-4067.

Mullens, Wyoming Co., St. John the Evangelist (1923), Rev. Pericles P. Malacaman; Sr. Katherine O'Neil, I.H.M., Pastoral Assoc.
Res., 13 Terry St., 25882-1624. Tel: 304-294-8128.
Mission—Pineville, Wyoming Co., Holy Cross, Rte. 10, P.O. Box 927, Pineville, 24874. Tel: 304-732-6199; 732-8302 (Rectory).

New Cumberland, Hancock Co., Immaculate Conception (1904), Rev. Ronald A. Getsinger.
Res., 1016 Ridge Ave., P.O. Box 666, 26047-0666. Tel: 304-564-5068.

New Martinsville, Wetzel Co., St. Vincent de Paul (1901), Rev. Charles J. Schneider, V.F.; Sr. Catherine Mullooly, S.S.J., Pastoral Assoc.
Res., 21 Rosary Rd., 26155-1602. Tel: 304-455-4615; Fax: 304-455-4617.

Nitro, Kanawha Co., Holy Trinity (1962), Rev. Dean G. Borgmeyer.
Res., 2219 22nd St., P.O. Box 339, 25143-0339. Tel: 304-755-0791; Fax: 304-755-3473.
Mission—Bancroft, Putnam Co., St. Patrick, 207 Jefferson St., P.O. Box 238, Bancroft, 25011. Tel: 304-586-3485; Fax: 304-586-3485.

Oak Hill, Fayette Co., SS. Peter and Paul (1906), Rev. Harold W. Moore.
Res., Oyler Ave., P.O. Box 1247, 25901-1247. Tel: 304-465-5445. [CEM]
School—Tel: 304-465-5045; Fax: 304-465-5045. Mrs. Karen Willson, Prin.
Lay Teachers 9; Students 131.

Ona, Cabell Co., St. Stephen (1980), Rev. Bert W. Valdes.
Res., 2491 James River Tpke., 25545-9722. Tel: 304-743-3234.

Paden City, Tyler and Wetzel Cos., Mater Dolorosa (1921), Rev. Joseph Ezharath (India).
Res., 302 E. Main St., 26159-1736. Tel: 304-337-9837.
Mission—Middlebourne, Tyler Co., St. Lawrence, Box 267, Middlebourne, 26149. Tel: 304-758-4649.

Parkersburg, Wood Co., St. Francis Xavier's (1853), Rev. Michael P. O'Reilly.
Res., 532 Market St., 26101-5144. Tel: 304-422-3145; Fax: 304-422-3142. [CEM 3]

St. Margaret Mary (1923), Rev. Edward M. Bell; Deacons Gerald B. Goetemann; George B. Showalter.
Res., 2500 Dudley Ave., 26101-2695. Tel: 304-428-1262; Fax: 304-422-4905.

Petersburg, Grant Co., St. Mary's, Rev. James J. Creedon, M.S.A.
Res., 5 Pierpont St., 26847-1633. Tel: 304-257-1057.
Church—4 Grant St., 26847.

Philippi, Barbour Co., St. Elizabeth Parish and Newman Center (1953), Rev. Damian P. Drass, T.O.R.
Res., College Hill, Rte. 3, Box 257, 26416-9581. Tel: 304-457-2641. Deacon A. Ray Shaw, III.; Res., Rte. 3, Box 38-I, 26416-9581. Tel: 304-457-1408.

Point Pleasant, Mason Co., Sacred Heart (1948), Rev. Regis Schlick, O.F.M.Cap.
Res., 2222 Jackson Ave., 25550-2004. Tel: 304-675-4602.
Mission—Mason, Mason Co., St. Joseph, (1856) 3rd St. & Pomeroy St., Mason, 25260. [CEM]

Powhatan, McDowell Co., Sacred Heart (1895), Rev. Nguyen Ngoc That Son.
Res., HC 76, Box 402, 24877-0167. Tel: 304-862-3494.

Princeton, Mercer Co., Sacred Heart (1915), Rev. Lawrence Wrenn; Sr. Theresa Metz, S.S.J., Pastoral Assoc.
Res., 507 Harrison St., 24740-3198. Tel: 304-425-3664.
Mission—Peterstown, Monroe Co., St. Peter, 203 Mill St., P.O. Box 644, Peterstown, 24963-0644. Tel: 304-753-4279. Sr. Molly Bauer, S.S.J., Parochial Coord.
Campus Ministry, Concord College—Athens, 24712. Tel: 304-384-9502.

Rainelle, Greenbrier Co., Sacred Heart, Rev. Harold F. Dunn, M.S.A.
Res., 401-13th St., 25962-1703. Tel: 304-438-8687.
Chapel—Springdale, Sacred Heart. (1876). [CEM]
Station—Rainelle, Alderson Federal Prison.

Ravenswood, Jackson Co., St. Matthew (1957), Rev. John H. Fahey; Sr. Rosanne Fogarty, O.S.M., Parochial Coord.
Res., 600 Crooks Ave., 26164-1312. Tel: 304-273-2175; Fax: 304-273-2175.

Richwood, Nicholas Co., Holy Family (1904), Revs. William F. Seli, S.M.; Jerome D. Rawa, S.M.; Bro. Richard McKenna, S.M.
Res., 4 Maple St., 26261-1318. Tel: 304-846-2873. [CEM]

Ridgeley, Mineral Co., St. Anthony (1916), Rev. D. Kent Durig.
Res., Box 553, Fort Ashby, 26719-0553. Tel: 304-298-3392.

Romney, Hampshire Co., Our Lady of Grace (1951), Rev. Joseph A. Salazar, M.S.A.
Res., 299 School St., P.O. Box 871, 26757-0871. Tel: 304-822-5561.

Ronceverte, Greenbrier Co., St. Catherine of Siena (1892), Rev. John C. McGinnity.
Res., 407 Walnut St., 24970-1233. Tel: 304-647-4515.
Missions—Lewisburg, Monroe Co., St. Louis, (1977) P.O. Box 1814, Lewisburg, 24901. Tel: 304-645-5208; Union, Monroe Co., St. Andrew, (1977) P.O. Box 347, Union, 24983-0347. Tel: 304-772-5849. Sr. Molly Bauer, S.S.J., Parochial Coord.
Station—Williamsburg, Mary Immaculate, (1879). [CEM]
Chaplaincy—WV School of Osteopathic Medicine.

St. Albans, Kanawha Co., St. Francis of Assisi, Rev. Patrick M. McDonough; Deacon Robert B. Lilly.
Res., 1023 Sixth Ave., P.O. Box 1406, 25177-1406. Tel: 304-727-3033.
School—Priests 1; Lay Teachers 11; Students 179.

St. Joseph Settlement, Marshall Co., St. Joseph's (1853), Rev. Frank A. O'Kruta.
Res., R.F.D. 1, Box 203, Proctor, 26055-9705. Tel: 304-455-4303; Fax: 304-455-2804. [CEM]

St. Marys, Pleasants Co., St. John (1913), Rev. Thomas Karachira (India); Deacon John F. Maher.
Mailing Address: P.O. Box 338, 26170-0338.
Res., 310 Washington St., 26170-1313. Tel: 304-684-7669.

Salem, Harrison Co., Sacred Heart (1915), Rev. Donald E. Hile.
Res., Rtes. 23 S. & 50, P.O. Box 248, 26426-0248. Tel: 304-782-2277. [CEM]

Shepherdstown, Jefferson Co., St. Agnes (1794), Rev. T. Matthew Rowgh.
Res., 108 S. Duke, P.O. Box 1603, 25443-1603. Tel: 304-876-6436.

Shinnston, Harrison Co., St. Ann's, Rev. Karl R. Wohinc.
Res., 610 Pike St., 26431-1451. Tel: 304-592-2733.
Mission—Spelter, Harrison Co., Holy Family, Spelter, 26438.

Sistersville, Tyler Co., Holy Rosary (1898), Rev. Joseph Ezharath (India).
Church—519 Main St., 26175-1405. Tel: 304-652-6381; 337-9837 (Rectory).

South Charleston, Kanawha Co., Blessed Sacrament (1941), Rev. F. Leon Alexander; Deacon John J. Hanna.
Res., 305 E St., 25303-1597. Tel: 304-744-5523; Fax: 304-744-5669.

Spencer, Roane Co., Holy Redeemer (1957), Rev. Don Tranel, Glmy.
Res., 424 Parkersburg Rd., 25276-1024. Tel: 304-927-2013.
Missions—Elizabeth, Wirt Co., St. Elizabeth of Hungary, (1977) Hwy. 14, P.O. Box 191, Elizabeth, 26143. Tel: 304-275-4226. Sr. Nancy Fortkort, O.S.F., Pastoral Assoc.; Grantsville, Calhoun Co., Jesus Christ, Prince of Peace, (1977) Hwy. 16, P.O. Box 416, Grantsville, 26147. Tel: 304-354-7824.

Star City, Monongalia Co., St. Mary's (1952), Rev. Carl E. Bauer; Deacon John Shultz; Jeanne Howell, Pastoral Assoc.; Angela Merlnar, Admin. Assoc.
Res., 3344 University Ave., P.O. Box 4204, 26504-4204. Tel: 304-599-3747; Fax: 304-599-3769.
School—St. Francis Central Catholic School, 375 Birch St., Morgantown, 26505. Tel: 304-598-0133; Fax: 304-598-2690.

Stonewood, Harrison Co., Our Lady of Perpetual Help (1955), Rev. Edward Sabo, T.O.R.
Res., 707 Third St., 26301-4896. Tel: 304-623-2334; Fax: 304-623-9988.

Summersville, Nicholas Co., St. John The Evangelist (1849), Revs. William F. Seli, S.M.; Jerome D. Rawa, S.M.
Res., 1704 Webster Rd., 26651-1049. Tel: 304-872-2554. [CEM]

Thomas, Tucker Co., St. Thomas Aquinas (1897), Rev. Lino P. Ebejer.
Res., P.O. Box 300, 26292-0300. Tel: 304-463-4488. [CEM]
Mission—Parsons, Tucker Co., Our Lady of Mercy, (1960) 221 Water St., P.O. Box 97, Parsons, 26287-0097. Tel: 304-478-4575. Sr. Patricia Marren, S.C., Parochial Coord.

Vienna, Wood Co., St. Michael's (1956), Rev. Anthony J. Conlon; Deacon James R. Kelly.
Res., 5501 Fourth Ave., 26105-2007. Tel: 304-295-6109.

War, McDowell Co., Christ the King (1942), Rev. Donald L. Meuret, Jr.
Res., P.O. Box 728, 24892-0728. Tel: 304-875-3827.

Wayne, Wayne Co., Nativity of Our Lord (1980), Rev. Leonard A. Smith, Admin.
Res., 110 W. 4th Ave., Williamson, 25661-3112. Tel: 304-235-2982.
Church—Rte. 2, Box 2502, 25570-9738. Tel: 304-272-6176.
Station—Genoa Christian Center, P.O. Box 67, Genoa, 25517. Tel: 304-385-4583; Fax: 304-385-4583. Sr. Monica Schieber, C.P.P.S., Dir.

Webster Springs, Webster Co., St. Anne's (1920), Rev. Xavier Cooney, S.V.D.
Res., 160 McGraw, 26288-1134. Tel: 304-847-5512.

Weirton, Brooke Co., St. Paul's (1910), Rev. Thomas E. Schiffer; Deacon Edwin T. Mullavey.
Res., 140 Walnut St., 26062-4521. Tel: 304-748-4118. [CEM]
School—Tel: 304-748-5225. Ms. Bette Burns, Prin.
Lay Teachers 11; Students 200.

Sacred Heart of Mary, Hancock Co., (1916) (Polish), Rev. J. Stephen Vallelonga; Deacon Richard W. Mankowski.
Res., 175 Stroud Ave., 26062-3995. Tel: 304-723-0703; Fax: 304-723-0729.
School—Tel: 304-723-1560.
Lay Teachers 14; Students 124.

St. Joseph the Worker, Hancock Co., (1957), Very Rev. Stephen D. Dube, V.F.; Rev. William Joseph Kuchinsky. In res., Rev. Franklin A. Neville.
Res., 229 California Ave., 26062-3729. Tel: 304-723-2054; 723-2057; Fax: 304-723-3961.
School—Tel: 304-723-1970. Mr. Albert Boniti, Prin.
Lay Teachers 13; Students 183.

Welch, McDowell Co., St. Peter, Rev. Donald L. Meuret, Jr.
Res., 111 Virginia Ave., 24801-2424. Tel: 304-436-2014.
Chapel—Kimball, Our Lady Queen of the Apostles. (1959).

Wellsburg, Brooke Co., St. John The Evangelist (1857), Rev. Charles B. Teufel.
Res., 1300 Charles St., 26070-1408. Tel: 304-737-0429. [CEM]
School—Tel: 304-737-0511. Mrs. Tonette Alward, Prin.
Lay Teachers 10; Students 140.
Mission—Beech Bottom, Brooke Co., Holy Family (Formerly Power), (1980) Box 7, Beech Bottom, 26030. Tel: 304-394-5929. Sr. Ellen Dunn, O.P., Parochial Coord.
Station—Bethany College Campus Ministry, 201 Richardson St., Bethany, 26032. Tel: 304-829-4622.

Weston, Lewis Co., St. Patrick's (1845), Rev. James J. Murphy.

Res., 222 Center Ave., 26452-2029. Tel: 304-269-3048.

School—Tel: 304-269-5547; Fax: 304-269-5547. Sr. Eileen Marie Sinnott, S.S.J., Prin.

Lay Teachers 7; Students 114.
Chapels—Sandfork, St. Bernard. [CEM]
Roanoke, St. Bridget. [CEM]

Chaplaincy—Weston State Hospital, Tel: 304-269-3048.

Westover, Monogalia Co., St. Elizabeth Ann Seton (1977), Rev. Stanley T. Tuchalski.

Res., 213 Parkview, P.O. Box 2010, 26502-2010. Tel: 304-292-3819; Fax: 304-292-6257.

School—St. Francis Central Catholic School, 375 Birch St., Morgantown, 26502-2010. Tel: 304-598-0133.

Mission—Pursglove, Monongalia Co., St. Ursula, (1933). Tel: 304-599-7780.

West Union, Doddridge Co., St. Patrick's (1856), Rev. Donald E. Hile; Sr. Mary Clark, S.S.J., Parochial Coord.

Res., 503 W. Main St., 26456-1129. Tel: 304-873-2547.

White Sulphur Springs, Greenbrier Co., St. Charles Borromeo (1903), Rev. Joseph F. O'Reilly.

Res., P.O. Box 598, 24986. Tel: 304-536-1813. [CEM]

Chapel—Sweet Springs, St. John The Evangelist. (1859). [CEM 2]

Whitesville, Boone Co., St. Joseph the Worker (1958). Closed. See St. Francis De Sales, Beckley.

Williamson, Mingo Co., Sacred Heart (1911), Rev. Leonard A. Smith.

Res., 110 W. Fourth Ave., 25661-3112. Tel: 304-235-2982.

School—126 W. Fourth Ave., 25661. Tel: 304-235-3027.

Sisters 1; Lay Teachers 4; Students 40.

On Duty Outside the Diocese:
Reverend Fathers—
Chalany, Robert, 17 Cedar Lake Rd., Chester, CT 06412
Cullinane, Jeremiah J., Neuhoff Catholic Center, Southern Methodist University, 3057 University Blvd., Dallas, TX 75205. Tel: 214-987-0044
Fryer, Patrick L., Exec. Asst., NIG 2000 NAVY, Pentagon, Washington, DC 20350-4725. Tel: 703-614-4326 (Office); 924-1068 (Residence)
Quirk, Kevin M., Casa Santa Maria, Via dell' Umilta, 30, Rome, 00187 Italy. Tel: 011-396-690-011

Absent on Sick Leave:
Reverend Fathers—
Cupp, Edwin
Finnell, John H.
Lee, Michael G.
McCallister, Charles E.
McCormick, Michael

Absent on Leave:
Reverend Fathers—
Wash, Pat J.

Retired:
Reverend Monsignors—
O'Reilly, John L., 102 Allison Ave., Bridgeport, WV 26330
Staud, Sylvester W., Welty Apartments #411, 1276 National Rd., Wheeling, WV 26003-5743
Wanstreet, Joseph W., Good Shepherd Nursing Home, 159 Edgington Ln., Wheeling, WV 26003
Reverend Fathers—
Arnold, Andrew L., Welty Apartments #402, 1276 National Rd., Wheeling, WV 26003
Bandiera, Colombo F., 442 Ash St., Morgantown, WV 26505-6668
Bell, Milford C., Rte. 1, Box 171, Kearneysville, WV 25430-9727
Beyer, Leroy O., 889 Wess Rd., Mineral Point, PA 15942
Briggs, Everett F., Maple Terrace, P.O. Box 9066, Monongah, WV 26555-9066
Brunner, Frank J., Welty Apartments #404, 1276 National Rd., Wheeling, WV 26003
Campi, Vincent L., P.O. Box 856, Frederick, MD 21701
Cann, Hilarion V., 103 Allison Ave., Bridgeport, WV 26330
DeMeester, Peter, 1100 Willard Dr., Blacksburg, VA 24060
Dene, Joseph, 6 Cool View Ln., Bridgeport, WV 26330
Dobosz, Emil J., Good Shepherd Nursing Home, 159 Edgington Ln., Wheeling, WV 26003
Gillooly, Patrick J., 517 S. Green St., Berkeley Springs, WV 25411
Gornick, Thomas, 331 Third St., Trafford, PA 15085
Grondalski, Thaddeus J., Welty Apartments #409, 1276 National Rd., Wheeling, WV 26003-5743
Jacobs, Eugene S., Box 54, Loretto, PA 15940
Lombard, Roy A., Welty Apartments #405, 1276 National Rd., Wheeling, WV 26003-5743
Lukas, Andrew F., P.O. Box 201, Fairmont, WV 26555-0201
Lydon, Leo B., 236 Parkway Dr., Clarksburg, WV 26301
Maguire, Seamus J., Church of Our Lady of Perpetual Help, Harris Promenade, San Fernando, Trinidad, W.I.
Martis, Albin A., 5639 Midland Dr., Charleston, WV 25306
Mascioli, Joseph M., P.O. Box 11, 55 Monongahela Ave., WO, Morgantown, WV 26507
Nash, Robert C., P.O. Box 793, Deltaville, VA 23043
Nolte, William J., Jr., P.O. Box 2568, Martinsburg, WV 25401-2568
O'Donovan, Donal, Westwood, Chapel St., Dummanway, County Cork, Ireland
O'Loughlin, Eugene P., 362 Redford Ct., Wicklow, Greystone Co., Ireland
Rafferty, Thomas A., Box 9066, Monongah, WV 26554
Ralph, John, 1757 State St., Biloxi, MS 39531
Savage, Charles H., 336 Maxwell Ave., Chester, WV 26034-1528
Schmitt, Eugene A., c/o Ray Schmitt, 43 Williamsburg Cir., Wheeling, WV 26003
Snincak, Stephen A., 2104 Hyde Park St., Sarasota, FL 33579
Werner, Leo E., 324 Kenna Dr., South Charleston, WV 25309
Wojtus, Anthony, P.O. Box 3803, Charleston, WV 24338-3803
Wolan, Stephen J., 1276 National Rd., Wheeling, WV 26003

Permanent Deacons:
Bartemes, David W., Christ the King, Dunbar
Belldina, Louis J., St. John Bosco, Huttonsville
Bischof, Paul H., Jr., St. Vincent de Paul, Wheeling
Goetemann, Gerald B., St. Margaret Mary, Parkersburg
Grant, Russell J.
Hanna, John J., Blessed Sacrament, South Charleston
Higgs, Henry F., On Leave
Hill, Russell
Iafrate, Albert L.
Kelly, James R., St. Michael, Vienna
Lilly, Robert B.
Lipscomb, Truman A., St. Sebastian, Kingwood
Locke, John W., St. Vincent de Paul, Berkeley Springs
Lynch, John J., Sacred Heart, Charleston
Maher, John F., Christ Our Hope, Harrisville; St. John, St. Marys
Mankowski, Richard W., Sacred Heart of Mary, Weirton
Molinari, Donald F., St. James, Clarksburg
Moses, John T., St. Joseph Cathedral, Wheeling
Mullavey, Edwin T., St. Paul, Weirton
Prentiss, Joseph J., St. John University, Morgantown
Santilli, Anthony P., St. James, Clarksburg
Shaw, A. Ray, St. Elizabeth, Phillipi
Showalter, George B., St. Margaret Mary, Parkersburg
Shultz, John A., St. Mary, Star City
Smith, Paul J., St. Michael, Wheeling
Strange, William B., Jr., St. John Neumann, Marlinto
Wise, W. Donald, St. Francis De Sales, Beckley
Wojeicke, Ronald J., St. Vincent de Paul, Wheeling
Wuletich, David E., St. Anthony, Charleston
Ziolkowski, John F., St. Francis de Sales, Beckley

INSTITUTIONS LOCATED IN THE DIOCESE

[A] COLLEGES AND UNIVERSITIES

WHEELING. *Wheeling Jesuit University*, 316 Washington Ave., 26003-6295
For a complete listing, refer to the Colleges and Universities section.

[B] HIGH SCHOOLS, CENTRAL

WHEELING. *Central Catholic High School*, 75-14th St., 26003. Tel: 304-233-1660; Fax: 304-233-3187. Dr. Joseph F. Viglietta, Ph.D., Prin. Sisters of St. Joseph 1; Lay Teachers 25; Students 351.

CHARLESTON. *Charleston Catholic High School*, 1032 Virginia St., E., 25301. Tel: 304-342-8415; Fax: 304-344-0870. Mrs. Debra K. Sullivan, Prin. Lay Teachers 33; Students 469.

CLARKSBURG. *Harrison Co. Catholic School System. Notre Dame High School*. (Grades 7-12), 127 E. Pike St., 26301. Tel: 304-623-1026; Fax: 304-623-1026. Mr. Louie D. LeRoy, Prin. Lay Teachers 16; Students 162.

HUNTINGTON. *St. Joseph Central Catholic High School*, 600 13th St., 25701. Tel: 304-525-5096; Fax: 304-525-5083. Mr. Tod Faller, Prin.; Rev. Msgr. Lawrence Luciana, Pastor. Lay Teachers 12; Students 200.

MCMECHEN. *Bishop Donahue Memorial High School*. (For Marshall Co.), 325 Logan St., 26040. Tel: 304-233-3850; Fax: 304-233-8677. Mr. Vincent Paoletti, Prin. Lay Teachers 15; Students 120.

PARKERSBURG. *Parkersburg Catholic Junior-Senior High School*, 3201 Fairview Ave., 26101. Tel: 304-485-6341. Mr. Michael R. Hattman, Prin. Lay Teachers 21; Students 249.

WEIRTON. *Madonna High School*, 150 Michael Way, 26062. Tel: 304-723-0545; Fax: 304-723-0564. Lay Teachers 11; Students 168.

[C] HIGH SCHOOLS, PRIVATE

WHEELING. *Mount de Chantal Visitation Academy, Inc.*, 410 Washington Ave., 26003. Tel: 304-233-3771; Fax: 304-233-8598.
E-mail: Mountdec@ovnet.com
Day School. (Girls Grades PreK-12, Boys Grades PreK-4). Visitation Nuns. Sisters 6; Lay Teachers 29; Students 180.

[D] ELEMENTARY SCHOOLS, CENTRAL

WHEELING. *Wheeling Catholic Elementary School*, 77-14th St., 26003. Tel: 304-233-1515. Consolidation of the following parishes: St. Alphonsus; St. Ladislaus; St. Mary; St. Joseph; Sacred Heart. Sr. Mary Palmer, S.S.J., Prin. Sisters 1; Lay Teachers 9; Students 83.

BENWOOD. *SS. James and John Elementary School*, 52 Seventh St., 26031. Tel: 304-232-1587. Consolidation of the following parishes: St. John, Benwood; St. James, McMechen. Lay Teachers 7; Students 81.

CLARKSBURG. *Harrison County Catholic School System. St. Mary's Central Grade School*. (Grades K-6), 107 E. Pike St., 26301. Tel: 304-622-9831; Fax: 304-623-1026. Consolidation of the following parishes: All Saints, Bridgeport; Immaculate Conception, Clarksburg; St. James, Clarksburg; Our Lady of Perpetual Help, Stonewood; St. Ann, Shinnston; Sacred Heart, Salem. Lay Teachers 15; Students 145.

FAIRMONT. *Fairmont Catholic Grade School*. (Grades K-8), 416-A Madison St., 26554. Tel: 304-363-5313. Consolidation of the following parishes: St. Peter; Immaculate Conception; St. Anthony; St. Joseph. Sr. Mary DiDomenico, S.S.J., Prin. Sisters 1; Lay Teachers 13; Students 210.

MORGANTOWN. *St. Francis de Sales Central Elementary School*, 375 Birch St., 26505. Tel: 304-598-0133; Fax: 304-598-2690.
E-mail: Ingle@accessMt.net
Sr. Patricia Ann Foley, C.S.J. Sisters 2; Lay Teachers 27; Students 410.

PARKERSBURG. *Parkersburg Catholic Elementary School*, 810 Juliana St., 26101. Tel: 304-422-6694; Fax: 304-422-2469. Mr. Kevin Simonton, Prin. Lay Teachers 10; Students 203.

[E] ELEMENTARY SCHOOLS, PRIVATE

MONONGAH. *SS. Peter and Paul Catholic School*, 689 Maple Ter., P.O. Box 9086, 26555-9086. Tel: 304-534-3189. Sisters Auxiliaries of the Apostolate. Mrs. Rachel A. Merrifield, Prin. Sisters 1; Lay Teachers 9; Students 109.

[F] PASTORAL CENTERS

WHEELING. *Paul VI Pastoral Center*, 667 Stone & Shannon Rd., 26003. Tel: 304-277-3300. Miss Antoinette Oliver, Dir. In res. Rev. John H. Finnell. Capacity 72.

CHARLESTON. *John XXIII Pastoral Center*, 100 Hodges Rd., 25314. Tel: 304-342-0507. Deacon John J. Lynch, Dir. Capacity 166.

HUTTONSVILLE. *Bishop Hodges Pastoral Center*, Rte. 1, Box 9D, 26273. Tel: 304-335-2165.
E-mail: bhpc@city-net.com
Deacon Louis J. Belldina, Dir. Capacity 72.

KEARNEYSVILLE. *Priest Field Pastoral Center*, State Rte. 51, Box 133, 25430. Tel: 304-725-1435. Rev. Theodore Midile, T.O.R., Dir. Capacity 110.

[G] ASSOCIATED SPIRITUAL AND PASTORAL LIFE CENTERS

WHEELING. *Maryhill Hermitage*, 2264 Marshall Ave., 26003.

St. Joseph Center-Mount St. Joseph, Pogue Run Rd., 26003. Tel: 304-232-8160.
E-mail: SSJWHG@aol.com
Sr. Teresa Fleckenstein, S.S.J., Dir. Overnight Capacity 8; Daytime Capacity 25.

St. Thomas More Center, Mailing Address: P.O. Box 230, 26003. 2264 Marshall Ave., 26003. Tel: 304-233-0880. Accommodations for youth retreats, cursillo and area retreats.

Sisters of the Visitation, 410 Washington Ave., 26003. Tel: 304-232-3771. Legal Title: *Sisters of the Visitation of Holy Mary of Mount de Chantal, Inc.*

CHARLESTON. *Cenacle Retreat House*, 1114 Virginia St., E., 25301. Tel: 304-345-0926; Fax: 304-345-8206. Conducted by the Congregation of Our Lady of the Retreat in the Cenacle. Sr. Mary Pellicane, Dir. Sisters 5; Overnight Capacity 28; Daytime Capacity 50.

MORGANTOWN. *Our Lady of Good Counsel Franciscan Friary*, 493 Tyrone Rd., 26505-9199. Tel: 304-594-1714; Fax: 304-594-9247. Rev. Jude J. Mili, O.F.M., S.T.D., Dir. In res. Rev. John Agapito, C.P.M.; Deacon George J. Doerr.

OLD FIELDS. *Holy Spirit Hermitage*, H.C. 66, Box 20, 26845-9201. Rev. Richard B. Hite, M.S.A. In res. Sr. Joan Sutherland.

[H] GENERAL HOSPITALS

WHEELING. *Bishop Joseph H. Hodges Continuous Care Center*, Medical Park, 26003. Tel: 304-243-3800
For a complete listing, refer to the Hospitals section.

Wheeling Hospital, Medical Park, 26003. Tel: 304-243-3000
For a complete listing, refer to the Hospitals section.

BUCKHANNON. *St. Joseph's Hospital of Buckhannon, Inc.*, 1 Amalia Dr., 26201. Tel: 304-473-2000
For a complete listing, refer to the Hospitals section.

HUNTINGTON. *St. Mary's Hospital of Huntington, Inc.*, 2900 First Ave., 25702. Tel: 304-526-1234
For a complete listing, refer to the Hospitals section.

[I] NURSING HOMES

WHEELING. *Good Shepherd Nursing Home*, 159 Edgington Ln., 26003. Tel: 304-242-1093
For a complete listing, refer to the Special Care Facilities section.

[J] HOMES FOR AGED

WHEELING. *Welty Home for the Aged, Inc.*, 21 Washington Ave., 26003-6261. Tel: 304-242-5233
For a complete listing, refer to the Special Care Facilities section.

[K] HEALTH SERVICES

WHEELING. *Children's Health Care, Inc.*, 1300 Byron St., 26003
For a complete listing, refer to the Hospitals section.

HUNTINGTON. *Pallottine Health Services, Inc.*, 2900 First Ave., 25702. Tel: 304-526-1028.
E-mail: bushee@citynet.net
Web site: http://www.ST.MARYS.org
For a complete listing, refer to the Hospitals section.

PINEVILLE. *Children's Health Care, Inc.*, Pineville Children's Clinic, Box 1419, 24874. Tel: 304-732-7069.
E-mail: ecatters@MARShall.EDU
For a complete listing, refer to the Hospitals section.

RHODELL. *Rhodell Health Clinic*, P.O. Box 158, 25915. Tel: 304-683-4318
For a complete listing, refer to the Hospitals section.

[L] SOCIAL SERVICE INSTITUTIONS

WHEELING. *Catholic Charities Neighborhood Center*, 125-18th St., P.O. Box 6176, 26003-0713. Tel: 304-232-7157. Directors: Sr. Constance Dodd, S.M.; Bro. David Cooney, F.M.S.

Sisters of St. Joseph House of Hospitality, Inc., 110-15th St., 26003.

Society of St. Vincent de Paul, Society of St. Vincent de Paul Store, 23rd & Main Sts., 26003. Tel: 304-232-4230.

GHENT. *Catholic Center*, 478 Odd Rd., 25843. Tel: 304-787-3523.

HUTTONSVILLE. *Camp Tygart*, Rte. 1, Box 9D, 26273. Tel: 304-335-2130 (In Season); 335-2165 (Out of Season).
E-mail: MHALL@DWC.ORG
Diocesan Children's Camp. Mr. Michael Hall, Admin.

NAUGATUCK. *A.B.L.E. Families, Inc.*, P.O. Box 272, 25685. Tel: 304-393-4987.

SALEM. *Nazareth Farm*, Rte. 2, Box 194-3, 26426. Tel: 304-782-2742.
E-mail: NAZFARM@NORTHNAP.CITYNET.NET

[M] HOMES FOR DEPENDENT CHILDREN

WHEELING. *St. John's Home for Children*, 141 Key Ave., 26003-7412. Tel: 304-242-5633
For a complete listing, refer to the Special Care Facilities section.

[N] MONASTERIES AND RESIDENCES OF PRIESTS AND BROTHERS

WHEELING. *Webb Farm Residence*, 667 Stone & Shannon Rd., 26003. Tel: 304-277-4670. Rev. Charles E. McCallister.

CHARLESTON. *Capuchins-St. Anthony Friary*, 1000 Sixth St., 25302. Tel: 304-342-2716.
E-mail: CONRADCAP@citynet.net
Revs. Richard J. Zelik, O.F.M.Cap., Guardian; Kieran Quinn, O.F.M.Cap., Vicar & Chap.; Albert Alexandrunas, O.F.M.Cap.; Regis Schlick, O.F.M.Cap.; Philip Hainen, O.F.M.Cap.

HINTON. *Monastery of Christ on the Mountain*, 25951-0429. Tel: 304-466-4782.
E-mail: Regisocd@citynet.Net
Discalced Carmelite Hermits. Revs. Bonaventure Lussier, O.C.D.; Regis Jordan, O.C.D.; Bro. Gilbert Tovares, O.C.D.

[O] CONVENTS AND RESIDENCES FOR SISTERS

WHEELING. *Mt. St. Joseph*, Pogue Run Rd., 26003. Tel: 304-232-8160; Fax: 304-232-1404.
E-mail: SSJWHG@aol.com
Motherhouse of the Sisters of St. Joseph. Sr. Marguerite O'Brien, S.S.J., Pres. Professed Sisters 106. Attended by Wheeling Jesuit University.

North America Union Sisters of Our Lady of Charity, Inc., 141 Edgington Ln., 26003. Tel: 304-242-7070. Legal Title: *North American Union Sisters of Our Lady of Charity, Inc.* Sr. Martha Teresa Gomez, Local Supr.; Sr. Ellen Patrick Stapleton, Business Mgr. Sisters 21.

Sisters of the Visitation, Mount de Chantal, 410 Washington Ave., 26003. Tel: 304-232-1283.
E-mail: Mountdec@ovnet.com
Legal Title: *Sisters of the Visitation of Holy Mary of Mount de Chantal, Inc.* Sr. Mary Grace Flynn, V.H.M., Supr. Professed Sisters 29.
Attended by Wheeling Jesuit College.

MONONGAH. *SS. Peter and Paul Convent*, 689 Maple Ter., P.O. Box 9086, 26555. Tel: 304-534-3081. General Motherhouse of the Sisters Auxiliaries of the Apostolate. Sr. Angela Marie Pastore, S.A.A., Supr. Professed Sisters 6.
Attended by Holy Spirit Church.

[P] FOUNDATIONS

WHEELING. *Central Catholic High School Educational Foundation, Inc.*, 75-14th St., 26003.

Common Fund for Schools, P.O. Box 230, 26003.

Medical Park Foundation, Inc., One Medical Park, 26003.

Sisters of St. Joseph of Wheeling Foundation, Inc., Pogue Run Rd., 26003; Fax: 304-232-1404.
E-mail: SSJWHG@aol.com
Sr. Jane Harrington, S.S.J., Exec. Dir.

West Virginia Catholic Foundation, P.O. Box 230, 26003. Tel: 304-233-0880; Fax: 304-233-0890. Mr. Brian Minor, Contact Person.

CLARKSBURG. *Harrison County Catholic Education Foundation, Inc.*, 126 E. Pike St., 26301-2720.

PARKERSBURG. *De Sales Heights Monastery of the Visitation.* c/o P.O. Box 230, Wheeling, 26003.

Parkersburg Catholic Schools Foundation, Inc., 3201 Fairview Ave., 26104-2111.

Sisters of St. Joseph Charitable Fund, Inc., 4420 Rosemar Rd., Ste. 204, P.O. Box 4440, 26104-4440. Tel: 304-424-6080; Fax: 304-424-6081. Sr. Jane Harrington, S.S.J., Exec. Dir.

WEIRTON. *Society of Friends of Madonna High School, Inc.*, Park Ave., 26062.

[Q] NEWMAN CENTERS

CHARLESTON. *University of Charleston Newman Center*, 25364.

ATHENS. *Concord College Newman Center*, 301 Vermillion, P.O. Box 447, 24712. Tel: 304-425-3664. Rev. Lawrence Wrenn.

BETHANY. *St. John Fisher Catholic Chapel*, 201 Richardson St., Box W, 26032. Tel: 304-829-4622. Rev. Richard W. Shoda.

BUCKHANNON. *West Virginia Wesleyan College Newman Center*, 35 Franklin St., Box 848, 26201-0848. Tel: 304-473-8000. Rev. James B. McCafferty, S.M.

FAIRMONT. *Fairmont State College Newman Center*, 1101 Locust Ave., 26554. Tel: 304-363-2300. Rev. Jude Molnar, T.O.R.

HUNTINGTON. *Marshall Newman Center*, 1609 Fifth Ave., 25703. Tel: 304-525-4618.
E-mail: Petro@MARShall.edu
Web site: http://webpages.MARShall.Edu/~Petro
Rev. William J. Petro.

PHILIPPI. *Alderson-Broaddus College Newman Center*, College Hill, Rte. 3, Box 257, 26416. Tel: 304-457-2641. Rev. Damian P. Drass, T.O.R.

WEST LIBERTY. *West Liberty State College, St. Thomas Aquinas Campus Ministry*, 134 Chatham St., 26074. Tel: 304-336-7476; 829-4622 (Bethany). Mailing Address: Box W, Bethany, 26032. Rev. Richard W. Shoda.

[R] MISCELLANEOUS

WHEELING. *Retirement Trust Agreement of the Infirm Priests' Association of the Diocese of Wheeling-Charleston*, 1300 Bryon St., 26003. Rev. John R. Gallagher, Trustee.

Saint Francis Health System, Inc., Mount Saint Joseph, Poque Run Rd., 26003.
E-mail: SSJWHG@aol.com
Sr. Marguerite O'Brien, S.S.J., Pres.

Saint Francis Hospital, Inc., Mount Saint Joseph, Poque Run Rd., 26003.
E-mail: SSJWHG@aol.com
Sr. Marguerite O'Brien, Pres.

St. Joseph's Hospital of Parkersburg, Inc., Mount St. Joseph, Pogue Run Rd., 26003. Tel: 304-232-8160. Sr. Marguerite O'Brien, S.S.J., Pres.

Sisters of St. Joseph Health System, Inc, Mount St. Joseph, Pogue Run Rd., 26003.
E-mail: SSJWHG@aol.com

Sisters of St. Joseph Ministries Support Fund, Inc., Mount St. Joseph, Pogue Run Rd., 26003.
E-mail: SSJWHG@aol.com
Sr. Marguerite O'Brien, S.S.J., Pres.

PRINCETON. *West Virginia Council of Catholic Women*, 203 East Dr., 24720. Sr. Kathleen Durkin, S.S.J., Diocesan Moderator; Mrs. Betty Charles.

WEBSTER SPRINGS. *The Catholic Committee of Appalachia*, P.O. Box 662, 26288. Tel: 304-847-7215.
E-mail: CCA.ppal@worldnet.att.net

[S] CHILD CARE CENTERS

WHEELING. *Holy Family Child Care Center, Inc.*, 161 Edgington Ln., 26003. Tel: 304-242-5222
For a complete listing, refer to the Special Care Facilities section.

CLARKSBURG. *Madonna Day Care Center*, 444 E. Pike St., 26031. Tel: 304-622-4453
For a complete listing, refer to the Special Care Facilities section.

RELIGIOUS INSTITUTES OF MEN REPRESENTED IN THE DIOCESE

For further details refer to the corresponding bracketed number in the Religious Institutes of Men or Women section.

[0470]—*The Capuchin Friars.*—O.F.M.Cap.
[1330]—*Congregation of the Mission.*—C.M.
[1000]—*Congregation of the Passion.*—C.P.
[0260]—*Discalced Carmelite Fathers.*—O.C.D.
[0820]—*Fathers of Mercy.*—C.P.M.
[0520]—*Franciscan Friars.*—O.F.M.
[0570]—*Glenmary Home Missioners.*—Glmy.
[]—*Heralds of Good News Missionary Society.* (Eluru, India).—H.G.N.
[0690]—*Jesuit Fathers and Brothers.*—S.J.
[0770]—*Marist Brothers.*—F.M.S.
[0780]—*Marist Fathers.*—S.M.
[0590]—*Missionaries of the Holy Apostles.*—M.Ss.A.
[1030]—*Paulist Fathers.*—C.S.P.
[0420]—*Society of the Divine Word.*—S.V.D.
[0560]—*Third Order Regular of St. Francis.*—T.O.R.

RELIGIOUS INSTITUTES OF WOMEN REPRESENTED IN THE DIOCESE

[2100]—*Congregation of Humility of Mary.*—C.H.M.
[3110]—*Congregation of Our Lady of the Retreat in the Cenacle (Eastern Province).*—R.C.
[1920]—*Congregation of the Sisters of the Holy Cross.*—C.S.C.
[1730]—*Congregation of the Sisters of the Third Order of St. Francis.*—O.S.F.
[0760]—*Daughters of the Charity of St. Vincent de Paul (Emmitsburg Province).*—D.C.
[0960]—*Daughters of Wisdom.*—D.W.

[1070-02]—*Dominican Sisters.*—O.P.
[1070-14]—*Dominican Sisters.*—O.P.
[1105]—*Dominican Sisters of Hope.*—O.P.
[1430]—*Franciscan Sisters of Our Lady of Perpetual Help.*—O.S.F.
[2420]—*Marist Missionary Sisters.*—S.M.S.M.
[2430]—*Marist Sisters.*—S.M.
[2800]—*Missionary Sisters of the Most Sacred Heart Of Jesus.*—M.S.C.
[3070]—*North American Union Sisters of Our Lady of Charity.*—N.A.U.-O.L.C.
[3150]—*Pallottine Missionary Sisters.*—S.A.C.
[2970]—*School Sisters of Notre Dame.*—S.S.N.D.
[1680]—*School Sisters of St. Francis.*—O.S.F.
[3590]—*Servants of Mary (Servite Sisters).*—O.S.M.
[3830-08]—*Sister of St. Joseph of Cleveland.*—C.S.J.
[0140]—*Sisters Auxiliaries of the Apostolate.*—S.A.A.
[0570]—*Sisters of Charity of Seton Hill, Greensburg, PA.*—S.C.
[0590]—*Sisters of Charity of St. Elizabeth, Convent Station.* (Southern Province).—S.C.
[0590]—*Sisters of Charity of St. Elizabeth, Convent Station.* (Western Province).—S.C.
[0990]—*Sisters of Divine Providence (St. Peter Province).*—C.D.P.
[1000]—*Sisters of Divine Providence, Melbourne, Kentucky.*—C.D.P.
[2360]—*Sisters of Loretto at the Foot of the Cross.*—S.L.
[2575]—*Sisters of Mercy of the Americas.*—R.S.M.
[3000]—*Sisters of Notre Dame de Namur (California Province).*—S.N.D.deN.
[3000]—*Sisters of Notre Dame de Namur (Chesapeake Province).*—S.N.D.deN.
[3360]—*Sisters of Providence of St. Mary of the Woods, Indiana.*—S.P.
[3720]—*Sisters of St. Anne.*—S.S.A.
[1630]—*Sisters of St. Francis of Penance and Christian Charity.*—O.S.F.
[1650]—*Sisters of St. Francis of Philadelphia.*—O.S.F.
[1530]—*Sisters of St. Francis of the Congregation of Our Lady of Lourdes.*—O.S.F.
[3860]—*Sisters of St. Joseph of Cluny.*—S.J.C.
[3830-13]—*Sisters of St. Joseph of Pittsburgh.*—C.S.J.
[3830-05]—*Sisters of St. Joseph of Rockville Centre.*—C.S.J.
[3830-17]—*Sisters of St. Joseph of Wheeling.*—S.S.J.
[2110]—*Sisters of the Humility of Mary.*—H.M.
[3270]—*Sisters of the Most Precious Blood, O'Fallon, MO.*—C.P.P.S.
[3220]—*Sisters of the Poor Child Jesus.*—P.C.J.
[1760]—*Sisters of the Third Order of St. Francis of Penance and Charity.*—O.S.F.
[2160]—*Sisters, Servants of the Immaculate Heart of Mary.* (Scranton).—I.H.M.
[4060]—*Society of the Holy Child Jesus.*—S.H.C.J.
[4120-03]—*Ursuline Nuns of the Congregation of Paris.*—O.S.U.
[4160]—*Vincentian Sisters of Charity.*—V.S.C.
[4190]—*Visitation Nuns.* (Wheeling, WV).—V.H.M.

DIOCESAN CEMETERIES

WHEELING. *Mount Calvary* (1872), 1685 National Rd., 26003-5599. Tel: 304-242-0460. Rev. Charles B. Teufel, Dir.

NECROLOGY

† Jamula, Joseph M., (Retired). —Died June 14, 1997.

Diocese of Wichita

(Dioecesis Wichitensis)

Most Reverend

EUGENE J. GERBER, D.D.

Bishop of Wichita; ordained May 19, 1959; appointed Bishop of Dodge City October 16, 1976; ordained December 14, 1976; installed December 15, 1976; appointed Bishop of Wichita November 23, 1982; installed February 9, 1983. *Res., 307 E. Central, Wichita, KS, 67202.*

ESTABLISHED AUGUST 2, 1887.

Square Miles 20,021.

New boundaries established by Apostolic Letters dated May 19, 1951. Bounded on the west by the west lines of Rice, Reno, Kingman and Harper counties, south by Oklahoma, east by Missouri, and north by the north lines of Bourbon, Allen, Woodson, Greenwood, Morris, Marion, McPherson and Rice Counties in Kansas.

For legal titles of parishes and diocesan institutions, consult the Chancery Office.

The Chancery: 424 N. Broadway, Wichita, KS, 67202. Tel.: 316-269-3900; Fax: 316-269-3936.

STATISTICAL OVERVIEW

Personnel	
Bishop	1
Priests: Diocesan Active in Diocese	84
Priests: Active Outside Diocese	10
Priests: Diocesan in Foreign Missions	1
Priests: Retired, Sick or Absent	31
Number of Diocesan Priests	126
Religious Priests in Diocese	9
Ordinations:	
Diocesan Priests	2
Transitional Deacons	3
Permanent Deacons in Diocese	2
Total Sisters	385
Parishes	
Parishes	93
With Resident Pastor:	
Resident Diocesan Priests	68
Resident Religious Priests	1
Without Resident Pastor:	
Administered by Priests	24
Professional Ministry Personnel:	
Sisters	15
Lay Ministers	13
Welfare	
Catholic Hospitals	5
Total Assisted	466,826
Health Care Centers	2
Total Assisted	22,670
Homes for the Aged	2
Total Assisted	244
Specialized Homes	1
Total Assisted	44
Special Centers for Social Services	1
Total Assisted	14,240
Residential Care of Disabled	1
Total Assisted	5
Other Institutions	1
Total Assisted	3,940
Educational	
Diocesan Students in Other Seminaries	25
Total Seminarians	25
Colleges and Universities	1
Total Students	1,857
High Schools, Diocesan and Parish	4
Total Students	1,950
Elementary Schools, Diocesan and Parish	32
Total Students	7,481
Catechesis/Religious Education:	
High School Students	3,087
Elementary Students	8,194
Total Students Under Catholic Instruction	22,594
Teachers in the Diocese:	
Sisters	32
Lay Teachers	499
Vital Statistics	
Receptions into the Church:	
Infant Baptism Totals	2,513
Adult Baptism Totals	334
Received into Full Communion	368
First Communions	2,344
Confirmations	1,694
Marriages:	
Catholic	505
Interfaith	370
Total Marriages	875
Deaths	809
Total Catholic Population	107,337
Total Population	911,091

Former Bishops—Most Rev. JAMES O'REILLY, D.D., Bishop-Elect; died July 26, 1887.—Most Rev. JOHN JOSEPH HENNESSY, D.D., cons. Nov. 30, 1888; died July 13, 1920.—Most Rev. AUGUSTUS JOHN SCHWERTNER D.D., ord. June 12, 1897; cons. June 8, 1921; installed June 22, 1921; died Oct. 2, 1939.—Most Rev. CHRISTIAN HERMAN WINKELMANN, S.T.D., ord. June 11, 1907; cons. Auxiliary Bishop of St. Louis, Nov. 30, 1933; installed March 5, 1940; died Nov. 18, 1946.—Most Rev. MARK K. CARROLL, S.T.D., ord. June 10, 1922; appt. Feb. 15, 1947; cons. April 23, 1947; installed May 6, 1947; resigned Sept. 27, 1967; died Jan. 12, 1985.—Most Rev. LEO C. BYRNE, D.D., ord. June 10, 1933; appt. Titular Bishop of Sabidia and Auxiliary of St. Louis, May 21, 1954; cons. June 29, 1954; transferred to Wichita, "cum jure successionis" 1961; appt. Apostolic Administrator, Feb. 25, 1963; transferred to St. Paul and Minneapolis, Sept. 27, 1967; died Oct. 21, 1974.—Most Rev. DAVID M. MALONEY, S.S., S.T.L., J.C.D., former Bishop of Wichita; ord. Dec. 8, 1936; appt. Titular Bishop of Ruspae Auxiliary of Denver, Nov. 9, 1960; cons. Jan. 4, 1961; transferred to Wichita, Dec. 6, 1967; resigned July 16, 1982; died Feb. 15, 1995.

Vicars General—Rev. RONALD M. GILMORE, S.T.L., V.G., *424 N. Broadway, Wichita, 67202.*

Chancery Office—424 N. Broadway, Wichita, 67202. Tel: 316-269-3900; Fax: 316-269-3936.

Vicar for Priests—Rev. JOHN P. GILSEMAN, J.C.L.

Vicar General & Moderator of Diocesan Curia, Vicar for Pastoral Planning & Services—Rev. RONALD M. GILMORE, S.T.L., V.G.

Chancellor—Rev. ROBERT E. HEMBERGER, J.C.L.

Vice Chancellor—Rev. JOHN P. LANZRATH, S.T.L.; Sr. JACINTA LANGLOIS, A.S.C.

College of Consultors—Revs. ROBERT HEMBERGER, J.C.L.; JOHN P. GILSENAN, J.C.L.; Rev. Msgr. CHARLES F. WALSH; Revs. SHERMAN ORR; DWIGHT BIRKET; Rev. Msgr. DENIS DOUGHERTY; Revs. TERRANCE MCCLOSKEY, C.SS.R.; RONALD M. GILMORE, S.T.L., V.G.; THOMAS MCGREAD; THOMAS SCALETTY; DANIEL SPEXARTH; PAUL COAKLEY.

Parish Priests Consultors—Rev. Msgr. CHARLES F. WALSH; Revs. JOHN P. GILSENAN; CHARLES W. REGAN.

Tribunal—424 N. Broadway, Wichita, 67202. Tel: 316-269-3960.

Officialis—Rev. ROBERT E. HEMBERGER, J.C.L.

Vice Officialis—Rev. RICHARD F. STUCHLIK, S.T.L.

Judges—Revs. STEPHEN R. BAXTER, J.C.L.; JOHN P. GILSENAN, J.C.L.; MICHAEL E. NOLAN, J.C.L.; ROBERT E. HEMBERGER, J.C.L.; JOHN HOTZE, J.C.L.

Defenders of the Bond—Revs. J. PATRICK MANNION, J.C.L.; DOUGLAS CAMPBELL, J.C.L.

Procurator-Advocates—Sr. JACINTA LANGLOIS, A.S.C.

Notaries—Sr. JANICE GROCHOWSKY, C.S.J.; Mrs. ROBERTA RAU; Mrs. CLAUDINE WALD.

Deans—Revs. WILLIAM M. CARR, North Wichita; ARTHUR A. BUSCH, South Wichita; JOHN J. O'SHEA, East Wichita; Rev. THOMAS S. MCGREAD, West Wichita; IVAN C. ECK, Hutchinson; Rev. Msgr. CHARLES F. WALSH, Newton; Revs. FRANCIS COX, Wellington; THOMAS J. STROOT, Pittsburg; JOHN S. ZICH, Chanute.

Continuing Education of the Clergy Committee—Revs. BRIAN EGAN; JOSEPH GILE; ROBERT E. HEMBERGER, J.C.L., Prog. Dir. TERRENCE MCCLOSKEY, C.SS.R.; KENNETH J. SCHUCKMAN; KENNETH VAN HAVERBEKE; THOMAS M. HOISINGTON.

Diocesan Offices and Directors

Catholic Diocese of Wichita—Most. Rev. EUGENE J. GERBER, D.D., Pres.

Apostleship of Prayer—6900 E. 45th St., N., Wichita, 67226.

Catholic Charities—Ms. JANET VALENTE PAPE, Dir., *437 N. Topeka, Wichita, 67202.* Tel: 316-264-8344.

Catholic Life Center—424 N. Broadway, Wichita, 67202. Tel: 316-269-3900.

Cemeteries—Mr. JEROME GERBER, *424 N. Broadway, Wichita, 67202.* Tel: 316-269-3900.

Commission for Communications—Rev. ARTHUR A. BUSCH, *3205 Grand Ave., Wichita, 67218.* Tel: 316-682-1415.

Cursillo—Rev. JEROME A. BEAT, *2007 Arkansas, Wichita, 67203.* Tel: 316-262-4683.

Diocesan Apostolate for Previously Married Catholics—Rev. GERARD PECHT, C.SS.R., *Spiritual Life Center, 7100 E. 45th St., N., Wichita, 67226.* Tel: 316-744-0167.

Wichita Diocesan Charismatic Services—Rev. LEON J. KERSCHEN, Moderator, *314 S. Jefferson, Iola, 66749.* Tel: 316-365-3454. Rev. JAMES S. MAINZER, Assoc. Moderator, *St. James Church, 813 State St., Augusta, 67010.* Tel: 316-775-2155.

Diocesan Apostolate to Engaged Encounter—Rev. MICHAEL SCHEMM, *1807 Stevens, Parsons, 67357.*

Catholic Marriage Preparation-Evenings for Engaged—Rev. H. PATRICK MALONE, *1425 N. Chautauqua, Wichita, 67214.* Tel: 316-682-8712.

Diocesan Apostolate to Marriage Encounter—Rev. DANIEL J. SPEXARTH, *335 N. Annie St., R.R. #9, Wichita, 66861.* Tel: 316-522-4728.

Diocesan Apostolate to Widowed Catholics—Rev. GERALD PECHT, C.SS.R.

Diocesan Building Commission—Revs. DWIGHT BIRKET; PAUL COAKLEY; KENT HEMBERGER; ROBERT HEMBERGER; THOMAS SCALETTY; Mr. WILMER FREUND; Mr. RAWN HARBOR; Mr. FRED HERMES; Mr. DANIEL LOUGHMAN; Mrs. LINDA SNOOK; Mrs. THERESA WHITE.

Diocesan Commission on Christian Unity—Vacant.

Diocesan Council of Catholic Women—Rev. REINHARD C. ECK, Moderator, *424 N. Broadway, Wichita, 67202.*

Diocesan Director of Stewardship and Finance—Mr. DANIEL L. LOUGHMAN, *424 N. Broadway, Wichita, 67202.* Tel: 316-269-3900.

Diocesan Finance Committee—Most. Rev. EUGENE J. GERBER, D.D.; RONALD M. GILMORE, S.T.L., V.G.; Mr. DANIEL CARNEY; Mr. JOE DELLASEGA; Mr. RICHARD KERSCHEN; Mr. DANIEL L. LOUGHMAN; Mr. PATRICK E. O'SHAUGNESSY; Ms. MARILYN PAULY; Mr. DALE WIGGINS; Mr. PERRY WINTER.

Diocesan Liaison for Health Affairs—Rev. ROBERT E. HEMBERGER, J.C.L., *424 N. Broadway, Wichita, 67202.* Tel: 316-269-3962.

Diocesan Office for Ministry with Persons with Disabilities—Sr. M. VERONICE BORN, C.S.J., Dir., *Holy Family Center, 619 S. Maize Rd., Wichita, 67209.* Tel: 316-722-8159.

Education—Mr. ROBERT VOBORIL, Supt., *424 N. Broadway, Wichita, 67202.* Tel: 316-269-3950.

Office of Religious Education, C.C.D.—Ms. PATRICIA A. YATES, Dir., *424 N. Broadway, Wichita, 67202.* Tel: 316-269-3940.

Special C.C.D. Services—Vacant. Tel: 316-686-7171.

Latin America Missions and Volunteer Services—Sr. ANACLETA SCHUETTE, A.S.C., Dir., *424 N. Broadway, Wichita, 67202.* Tel: 316-269-3946.

Legion of Mary—Rev. JOHN C. REINKEMEYER, *638 Ave. D. W., Kingman, 67068.* Tel: 316-532-5440.

Liaison to Interfaith Rural Life Committee—Vacant.

Marriage and Family Life Services—Coordinated by Spiritual Life Center.

Natural Family Planning Office—Ms. MONIKA KING, Dir., *1148 S. Hillside, Ste. 10, Wichita, 67211.* Tel: 316-685-6776; Fax: 316-685-7540.

Newspaper: "The Catholic Advance" Diocesan Weekly—Mr. CHRISTOPHER M. RIGGS, Editor; Mr. DANIEL LOUGHMAN, Business Mgr., *424 N. Broadway, Wichita, 67202.* Tel: 316-269-3965.

Office of Development and Planned Giving—Vacant.

Office of Pastoral Life and Ministry—*424 N. Broadway, Wichita, 67202.* Tel: 316-269-3947.

Office of Worship—RAWN HARBOR, Dir., *424 N. Broadway, Wichita, 67202.* Tel: 316-269-3945.

Presbyteral Council—Rev. Msgr. CHARLES F. WALSH, Chm.; Revs. ROBERT E. HEMBERGER, J.C.L., Vice Chm. SHERMAN ORR; DWIGHT BIRKET; DANIEL SPEXARTH; PAUL COAKLEY, Sec. THOMAS SCALETTY; JOHN P. GILSENAN, J.C.L.; RONALD M. GILMORE, S.T.L., V.G.; JOHN P. LANZRATH; THOMAS MCGREAD; DENIS DOUGHERTY; TERRENCE MCCLOSKEY, C.SS.R.

Propagation of the Faith and Holy Childhood Assn.—Sr. ANACLETA SCHUETTE, A.S.C., Dir., *424 N. Broadway, Wichita, 67202.* Tel: 316-269-3946.

Respect Life Office—Vacant, *424 N. Broadway, Wichita, 67202.* Tel: 316-269-3948.

Retreats—Rev. TERRENCE MCCLOSKEY, C.SS.R., Dir., *Spiritual Life Center, 7100 E. 45th St. N., Wichita, 67226.* Tel: 316-744-0167.

Rural Life Conference—Vacant.

Social Service—Ms. JANET VALENTE PAPE, *437 N. Topeka, Wichita, 67202.* Tel: 316-264-8344.

Society of St. Vincent de Paul—Rev. KENT HEMBERGER.

Vocations—Rev. MATTHEW C. MCGINNESS, Dir., *424 N. Broadway, Wichita, 67202.*

Wichita Diocesan Hispanic Council—Vacant, *424 N. Broadway, Wichita, 67202.* Tel: 316-269-3900.

Youth and Young Adult Ministry—Mrs. CHRISTINE OSTROSKI, Dir., *424 N. Broadway, Wichita, 67202.* Tel: 316-269-3930.

CLERGY, PARISHES, MISSIONS AND PAROCHIAL SCHOOLS

CITY OF WICHITA
(Sedgwick County)

1—CATHEDRAL OF THE IMMACULATE CONCEPTION (1887), Revs. William M. Carr, Rector; Harold W. McCormick; Sr. Renee Kirmer, A.S.C., Pastoral Assoc. & D.R.E. In res., Revs. Joseph M. Gile; Bernard X. Gorges.
Res., 307 E. Central Ave., 67202. Tel: 316-263-6574. [JC]
Catechesis/Religious Programs—Students 120.

2—ALL SAINTS (1946), Rev. Arthur A. Busch.
Res., 3205 Grand St., 67218. Tel: 316-682-1415. [JC]
School—Tel: 316-682-6021; Fax: 316-682-8734. Dr. John Gahagan, Prin.
Lay Teachers 19; Students 333.
Catechesis/Religious Programs—Tel: 316-686-9736. Sr. Lorene Orth, A.S.C., D.R.E.
Students 147.

3—BLESSED SACRAMENT (1927), Revs. John P. Gilsenan; Jeffery A. Fasching. In res., Rev. James Wilkinson.
Res., 124 N. Roosevelt Ave., 67208. Tel: 316-682-4557. [JC]
School—Tel: 316-684-3752; Fax: 316-687-1082. Jim Grogan, Prin.
Sisters of St. Joseph 5; Lay Teachers 25; Students 434.
Catechesis/Religious Programs—Cindy Honton, D.R.E.
Students 50.
Convent—138 N. Roosevelt, 67208. Tel: 316-684-3977.

4—CHRIST THE KING (1950), Rev. Robert B. Wachter. In res., Rev. Sherman A. Orr.
Res., 4411 Maple Ave., 67209. Tel: 316-943-4353. [JC]
School—4501 Maple Ave., 67209. Tel: 316-943-4353. Richard Sleefe, Prin.
Sisters, Adorers of the Blood of Christ 2; Lay Teachers 13; Students 242.
Catechesis/Religious Programs—Students 75.

5—CHURCH OF THE MAGDALEN (1950), Revs. Kenneth S. VanHaverbeke; Cuong Scott Nguyen; Sr. Connie Beiriger, C.S.J., Pastoral Assoc.
Res., 457 S. Woodlawn St., 67218. Tel: 316-683-6516; Fax: 316-683-8407.
School—Tel: 316-683-5181; Fax: 316-683-9245. Eva Williams, Prin.
Lay Teachers 22; Students 514.
Catechesis/Religious Programs—Students 127.

6—CHURCH OF THE RESURRECTION (1965), Rev. Paul S. Coakley. In res., Rev. Joseph Gile.
Res., 4910 N. Woodlawn, 67220. Tel: 316-744-2776; Fax: 316-744-3027.
School—(Grades Prek-7). Tel: 316-744-3576; Fax: 316-744-3027. Sr. Marietta Conrardy, C.S.J., Prin.
Lay Teachers 12; Students 207.
Catechesis/Religious Programs—Debra Helberg, D.R.E.
Students 95.

7—HOLY SAVIOR (1948) (African American), Rev. H. Patrick Malone; Deacon Ronald Ealey, Pastoral Admin.
Res., 1425 N. Chautauqua, 67214. Tel: 316-682-8712; Fax: 316-682-4797.
School—Tel: 316-684-2141; Fax: 316-682-4797. Beverly Gutierrez, Prin.
Lay Teachers 12; Students 130.
Catechesis/Religious Programs—Students 85.

8—OUR LADY OF GUADALUPE. Closed. For sacramental records contact St. Margaret Mary, Wichita.

9—OUR LADY OF PERPETUAL HELP (1927), Rev. Floyd McKinney. Pastoral Assocs.: Sr. Clotilde Orduna; Sr. Virginia Alfaro; Sr. Guadalupe de la Rosa.
Res., 2351 N. Market St., 67219. Tel: 316-838-8373. [JC]
Catechesis/Religious Programs—Tel: 316-832-1670. D.R.E.: Johnny & Becky Palacioz.
Students 176.
Convent—2354 N. Market St., 67219. Tel: 316-838-3190.
Congregation of the Daughters of the Passion of Our Lord Jesus Christ and the Sorrows of Mary 3.
Parish Center—2409 N. Market St., 67219. Tel: 316-838-5750.

10—ST. ANNE (1955), Rev. Kent A. Hemberger; Mary Beth Steiner, Pastoral Assoc.
Office: 2801 S. Seneca, 67217-2399. Tel: 316-522-2383; Fax: 316-524-2370.
School—(Grades K-8). Tel: 316-522-6131.
Sisters 3; Lay Teachers 12; Students 248.
Catechesis/Religious Programs—Kevin Swinicki, D.R.E.
Students 195.

11—ST. ANTHONY (1887) (German), Rev. Hung Q. Pham.
Residence and Mailing: 325 Ohio, 67214. Tel: 316-269-4641.

12—ST. ELIZABETH ANN SETON (1982), Revs. James J. Billinger; Stuart M. Smeltzer.
Res., 645 N. 119th St. W., 67235. Tel: 316-721-1686; Fax: 316-721-1723. [CEM]
School—Tel: 316-721-5693. Mrs. Janet Eaton, Prin.
Lay Teachers 29; Students 578.
Catechesis/Religious Programs—Tel: 316-721-1686.
Students 415.

13—ST. FRANCIS OF ASSISI (1959), Revs. Thomas McGread, V.F.; Thomas Hoisington; Daryl Befort.
Res., 861 N. Socora, 67212. Tel: 316-722-4404; Fax: 316-722-4738.
School—Tel: 316-722-5171; Fax: 316-722-0492. Mr. Larry Conrardy, Prin.
Adorers of the Blood of Christ 4; Lay Teachers 34; Students 787.
Catechesis/Religious Programs—Richard George, D.R.E.
Students 541.

14—ST. JOSEPH (1886), Revs. Daniel H. Andree, C.SS.R.; Arthur W. Frost, C.SS.R.; Walter C. Karrer, C.SS.R.; Edward T. Morgan, C.SS.R.
Res., 145 S. Millwood Ave., 67213. Tel: 316-262-1877; Fax: 316-262-5250. [JC]
School—Tel: 316-265-7962; Fax: 316-265-7963. Mrs. Sheila Shaw, Prin.
Sisters 1; Lay Teachers 13; Students 196.
Catechesis/Religious Programs—Mrs. Pat Pilens, D.R.E.
Students 140.
Convent—St. Anne's, 128 S. Vine Ave., 67213. Tel: 316-262-4419. Dominican Sisters

15—ST. JUDE (1958), Rev. Thomas F. Scaletty; Sr. Mary Francis Morriss, Pastoral Assoc.
Res., 3130 Amidon Ave., 67204. Tel: 316-838-1963.
School—Tel: 316-838-0800; Fax: 316-838-0866. Mrs. Candace Buser, Prin.
Lay Teachers 13; Students 234.
Catechesis/Religious Programs—Debby Dean, D.R.E.
Students 216.

16—ST. MARGARET MARY (1954), Rev. Dwight Birket.
Res., 2701 Pattie, 67216. Tel: 316-262-1821; Fax: 316-267-1707.
School—(Grades Pre K-8). Tel: 316-267-4911; Fax: 316-267-1707. Mary Samms, Prin.
Lay Teachers 12; Students 205.
Catechesis/Religious Programs—Tel: 316-267-0120. Anne Schock, D.R.E.
Students 86.

17—ST. PATRICK (1895), Rev. Jerome A. Beat.
Res., 2007 Arkansas Ave., 67203. Tel: 316-262-4683; Fax: 316-262-6217. [JC]
School—2023 Arkansas Ave., 67203. Tel: 316-262-4071. Mr. Donald C. Wilson, Prin.
Sisters of St. Joseph 1; Lay Teachers 13; Students 232.
Catechesis/Religious Programs—Linda F. Gosche, D.R.E.
Students 95.
Convent—2045 Arkansas Ave., 67203. Tel: 316-267-0021.

18—ST. PAUL PARISH (1970), Rev. Matthew C. McGinness.
Res., 1810 N. Roosevelt, 67208. Tel: 316-684-6896; Fax: 316-684-2679.

19—ST. THOMAS AQUINAS (1957), Revs. John J. O'Shea; John Sherlock; Ned Blick; Sr. Donna Schauf, B.V.M., Pastoral Assoc. & D.R.E.
Res., 1321 Stratford Ln., 67206. Tel: 316-683-6569; Fax: 316-683-1028.
School—Tel: 316-684-9201; Fax: 316-684-7421. Miss Mary Sweet, Prin.
Lay Teachers 34; Students 635.
Catechesis/Religious Programs—Students 93.

20—ST. VINCENT DE PAUL (1955), Rev. Michael E. Baldwin.
Res., 123 N. Andover Rd., Andover, 67002. Tel: 316-733-1423; Fax: 316-733-1687.
Catechesis/Religious Programs—Tel: 316-729-7980. Ann Hughes, D.R.E.
Students 702.

OUTSIDE THE CITY OF WICHITA

Aleppo, Sedgwick Co., Immaculate Conception (1900), Revs. Philip J. Allen; John J. Curran.
Church—25741 W. 13th St., N., Garden Plain, 67050. Tel: 316-535-2210; Fax: 316-531-8820. [CEM]

Andale, Sedgwick Co., St. Joseph (1890) (German), Rev. Reinhard C. Eck.
Res., 318 Rush Ave., Box 8, 67001. Tel: 316-444-2196. [CEM]
Catechesis/Religious Programs—Mary Jo Hieger, D.R.E.
Students 290.

Anthony, Harper Co., Sacred Heart (1934). Closed. For inquiries for parish records contact the Chancery.

Arkansas City, Cowley Co., Sacred Heart (1886), Rev. Francis Cox.
Res., 325 S. C St., P.O. Box 895, 67005. Tel: 316-442-0566; Fax: 316-442-0566.

School—308 S. B St., Tel: 316-442-6550. Mr. Dean McGrath, Prin.
Sisters of the Adorers of the Blood of Christ 1; Lay Teachers 5; Students 87.
Catechesis/Religious Programs—Becky Hewitt, D.R.E.
Students 98.

Arma, Crawford Co., St. Joseph (1934), Rev. Donald R. Thissen.
Res., 310 W. South St., P.O. Box 948, 66712. Tel: 316-347-4525.

Augusta, Butler Co., St. James (1879), Rev. James S. Mainzer.
Res., 813 State St., 67010. Tel: 316-775-2155. [CEM]
School—Tel: 316-775-5721. Kathleen Patterson, Prin.
Sisters 1; Lay Teachers 5; Students 112.
Catechesis/Religious Programs—Tel: 316-733-5247. Bonnie Toombs, D.R.E.
Students 178.

Baxter Springs, Cherokee Co., St. Joseph (1868), Rev. Charles Middleton.
Res., 307 Galena, P.O. Box 296, Galena, 66739. Tel: 316-783-1693.

Burns, Marion Co., Immaculate Conception. Closed. For sacramental records contact Holy Family, Marion.

Bushton, Rice Co., Holy Name of Jesus (1878), Rev. James J. Roth.
Res., 67427. Tel: 316-562-3427. [CEM]
Catechesis/Religious Programs—Students 57.

Caldwell, Sumner Co., St. Martin of Tours (1888), Rev. Patrick Larkin.
Res., 428 N. Main, 67022. Tel: 316-845-6763. [JC]

Caney, Montgomery Co., Sacred Heart (1914), Rev. Edward J. Steinberger.
Res., P.O. Box 276, Moline, 67353-0276. Tel: 316-647-3577.

Capaldo, Crawford Co., St. Alice. Closed. For sacramental records contact Sacred Heart, Frontenac.

Castleton, Reno Co., St. Agnes (1872), Rev. Gerald F. Rowan.
Res., 211 E. Fifth, Hutchinson, 67501. Tel: 316-665-0475.

Cedar Vale, Chautauqua Co., St. Joseph. Closed. For inquiries for parish records contact the Chancery.

Chanute, Neosho Co., St. Patrick (1873), Rev. Michael J. Maybrier; Sr. Connie Haug, O.P., Pastoral Min. & D.R.E.
Res., 424 S. Central, 66720. Tel: 316-431-3165. [CEM]
School—(Grades PreK-5). Tel: 316-431-4020. Sr. Sylvana Schulte, Prin.
Sisters 2; Lay Teachers 6; Students 97.
Catechesis/Religious Programs—Tel: 316-431-3165.
Students 170.

Chase, Rice Co., St. Mary (1888) (German), Rev. Joseph P. Slomski, Admin.
Res., P.O. Box 306, 67524. Tel: 316-938-2382. [CEM][JC]

Cherokee, Crawford Co., St. Anastasia. Closed. For sacramental records contact Our Lady of Lourdes, Pittsburg.

Cherryvale, Montgomery Co., St. Francis Xavier's (1871), Revs. Stephen M. Thapwa (Burma); Kevin Trayers, (Retired).
Res., 202 S. Liberty St., 67335. Tel: 316-336-2337. [CEM]

Chetopa, Labette Co., Sacred Heart (1873), Rev. Larry Parker.
Res., 1112 W. Third., Oswego, 67356. Tel: 316-795-2262. [CEM]

Chicopee, Crawford Co., St. Barbara. Closed. For sacramental records contact Our Lady of Lourdes, Pittsburg.

Clonmel, Sedgwick Co., St. John (1879), Rev. Leroy Linnebur.
Res., 18630 W. 71st St., Viola, 67149. Tel: 316-545-7171; 794-2784; Fax: 316-794-2784. [CEM]
Parish Hall: Tel: 316-545-7211.
Catechesis/Religious Programs—D.R.E.: Sylvia Kerschen; Art Gentry.
Students 80.

Coffeyville, Montgomery Co., Holy Name (1869), Rev. Leo A. Kerschen.
Res., 408 Willow St., 67337. Tel: 316-251-0475. [CEM]
School—409 Willow St., 67337. Tel: 316-251-0480. Sr. Janice Roberts, Prin.
Sisters of St. Joseph 2; Lay Teachers 7; Students 157.
Catechesis/Religious Programs—Evelyn Goad, D.R.E.
Students 87.

Columbus, Cherokee Co., St. Rose (1887), Rev. Chrysostom Ah Maung (Burma).
Res., 115 W. Walnut St., 66725. Tel: 316-429-2639.
Catechesis/Religious Programs—Tel: 316-674-8587.
Students 51.

Colwich, Sedgwick Co., Sacred Heart (1901), Rev. Msgr. Denis R. Dougherty.
Res., 310 S. Fifth St., P.O. Box 578, 67030. Tel: 316-796-1224. [CEM]
Catechesis/Religious Programs—Students 337.

Conway Springs, Sumner Co., St. Joseph (1886), Rev. David W. Linnebur.
Res., 217 N. Sixth St., Box 157, 67031. Tel: 316-456-2276; Fax: 316-456-3317. [CEM]
School—Tel: 316-456-2270; Fax: 316-456-2272. Ms. Michaelita J. Wasinger, Prin.
Lay Teachers 8; Students 175.
Catechesis/Religious Programs—D.R.E.: Mike Ternes; Lillian Palsmeier.
Students 203.

Council Grove, Morris Co., St. Rose (1883), Rev. Paul J. Oborny.
Res., 316 Spencer St., 66846. Tel: 316-767-6412. [CEM]
Catechesis/Religious Programs—Tel: 785-499-5272. Deb Mayer, D.R.E.
Students 150.

Cunningham, Kingman Co., Sacred Heart (1908) (German), Rev. John Miller.
Res., P.O. Box 216, 67035. Tel: 316-298-2601; Fax: 316-298-2926. [CEM]
Catechesis/Religious Programs—Tel: 316-298-4038. Linda Kerschen, D.R.E.
Students 82.

Danville, Harper Co., Immaculate Conception (1883). Closed. For inquiries for parish records contact the Chancery.

Derby, Sedgwick Co., St. Mary's (1954), Rev. H. Jay Setter.
Res., P.O. Box 325, 722 N. Derby, 67037. Tel: 316-788-5525; Fax: 316-788-1577.
School—700 N. Derby, 67037. Tel: 316-788-3151. Mr. Charles Monckton, Prin.
Sisters of St. Joseph 2; Lay Teachers 13; Students 230.
Catechesis/Religious Programs—Tel: 316-788-1253.
Students 336.

El Dorado, Butler Co., St. John (1915), Rev. Msgr. Charles F. Walsh, V.F.
Res., 302 N. Denver Ave., 67042. Tel: 316-321-4796.
Catechesis/Religious Programs—Tel: 316-321-4933. Karen May, D.R.E.
Students 269.

Erie, Neosho Co., St. Ambrose (1915), Rev. John S. Zich.
Res., 519 N. Main, 66733. Tel: 316-244-3216.

Eureka, Greenwood Co., Sacred Heart (1881) (German), Rev. H. Michael Peltzer.
Res., 514 N. Elm St., 67045. Tel: 316-583-7100.
Catechesis/Religious Programs—Students 54.
Missions—Hamilton, Greenwood Co., St. John, Hamilton, 66853.; Madison, Greenwood Co., St. Teresa Of Avila, Madison, 66860. Tel: 316-437-2504.

Florence, Marion Co., St. Patrick. Closed. Merged with St. Mark, Marion; St. John Nepomucene, Pilsen; and Holy Redeemer, Tampa to form Holy Family, Marion.

Fort Scott, Bourbon Co., Mary Queen of Angels (1860), Rev. Brian Bebak.
Res., 716 S. Eddy St., P.O. Box 271, 66701. Tel: 316-223-4340. [CEM]
School—(Grades K-5). Tel: 316-223-6060. Thomas M. Gorman, Prin.
Lay Teachers 7; Students 73.
Catechesis/Religious Programs—Tel: 316-547-2519. Debbie Martin, D.R.E.
Students 78.

Fredonia, Wilson Co., Sacred Heart (1906), Rev. Stephen R. Baxter.
Res., 428 N. 12th St., 66736. Tel: 316-378-2694. [CEM]
Catechesis/Religious Programs—Tel: 316-378-3565. Judy Puckett, D.R.E.
Students 70.

Frontenac, Crawford Co., Sacred Heart (1891) (Italian), Rev. Patrick G. York.
Res., 100 S. Cherokee St., 66763. Tel: 316-231-7747.
Parish Hall: 102 S. Cherokee St., 66763. Tel: 316-232-2354. [CEM]
Catechesis/Religious Programs—Students 99.

Fulton, Bourbon Co., St. Patrick. Closed. For sacramental records contact Mary Queen of Angels, Fort Scott.

Galena, Cherokee Co., St. Patrick (1879), Rev. Charles Middleton.
Res., 307 Galena, P.O. Box 296, 66739. Tel: 316-783-1693.

Garden Plain, Sedgwick Co., St. Anthony (1901) (German), Revs. Philip J. Allen; John J. Curran.
Res., 615 N. Main, 67050. Tel: 316-535-2247; Fax: 316-531-8820. [CEM]
Catechesis/Religious Programs—Tel: 316-535-2593.
Students 364.

Girard, Crawford Co., St. Michael (1925), Rev. Donald R. Thissen.
Res., 106 N. Western, 66743. Tel: 316-724-8717.
Catechesis/Religious Programs—Joan Davied, D.R.E.
Students 126.

Greenbush, Crawford Co., St. Aloysius. Closed. For sacramental Records contact St. Michael, Girard.

Halstead, Harvey Co., Sacred Heart of Jesus (1874), Rev. James R. O'Shea.
Res., 419 Poplar, 67056. Tel: 316-835-2173. [JC]
Catechesis/Religious Programs—Box 307, Sedgwick, 67135. Tel: 316-772-5841. Louise Weber, D.R.E.
Students 151.

Hamilton, Greenwood Co., St. John (1888) (German), Rev. H. Michael Peltzer.
Res., 514 N. Elm St., Eureka, 67045. Tel: 316-583-7100.

Harper, Harper Co., Immaculate Conception. Closed. For inquiries for parish records contact the Chancery.

St. Joan of Arc (1997), Rev. Robert J. Hartmann.
Res., 1023 W. Main, P.O. Box 218, 67058. Tel: 316-896-7886; Fax: 316-896-1886; 888-896-1886.
Catechesis/Religious Programs—Karen Dunkelberger, D.R.E.
Students 90.
Missions—Danville, Anthony.

St. Patrick (1882). Closed. For inquiries for parish records contact the Chancery.

Haysville, Sedgwick Co., St. Cecilia (1959), Rev. Andy Kuykendall.
Res., 1802 W. Grand, 67060. Tel: 316-524-7801; Fax: 316-524-6183.
School—(Grades K-6) 1912 W. Grand, 67060. Tel: 316-522-0461; Fax: 316-524-6183. Sr. Eloise Hertel, O.P., Prin.
Sisters 3; Lay Teachers 6; Students 159.
Catechesis/Religious Programs—D.R.E.: JoAnne Audley; Marsha Miller.
Students 140.

Humboldt, Allen Co., St. Joseph (1867), Rev. Michael J. Maybrier; Sr. Cecilia Leiker, A.S.C., Pastoral Min. & D.R.E.
Church—514 Central St., 66748. Tel: 316-473-2129. [CEM]
Res., 424 S. Central Ave., Chanute, 66720. Tel: 316-431-3165.
Catechesis/Religious Programs—Tel: 316-473-2739.
Students 88.

Hutchinson, Reno Co., Holy Cross (1957), Rev. Brian J. Egan.
Res., 2631 Independence Rd., 67502. Tel: 316-665-5163. [JC]
School—2633 Independence Rd., 67502. Tel: 316-665-6168. Mr. Harry Heppler, Prin.
Lay Teachers 7; Students 202.
Catechesis/Religious Programs—Students 262.

Our Lady of Guadalupe (1927), Rev. Colin J. Boor.
Res., 612 S. Maple, South Hutchinson, 67505-2099. Tel: 316-662-6443.
Catechesis/Religious Programs—Mr. & Mrs. Martin Vieyra, D.R.E.
Students 100.

St. Teresa (1897), Rev. Richard Stuchlik, S.T.L. In res., Rev. Gerald F. Rowan.
Res., 211 E. Fifth St., 67501. Tel: 316-662-7812. [CEM]
School—215 E. Fifth St., 67501. Tel: 316-662-5601. Ms. Ellen Albert, Prin.
Lay Teachers 8; Students 193.
Catechesis/Religious Programs—Students 128.

Independence, Montgomery Co., St. Andrew (1869), Rev. Stephen M. Thapwa (Burma).
Res., 210 N. Fourth St., 67301. Tel: 316-331-1789. [CEM]
School—Tel: 316-331-2870. Kristie Blaes, Prin.
Lay Teachers 8; Students 113.
Catechesis/Religious Programs—Students 88.

Iola, Allen Co., St. John (1897), Rev. Leon J. Kerschen.
Res., 310 S. Jefferson Ave., 66749. Tel: 316-365-3454. [CEM][JC]
Catechesis/Religious Programs—Tel: 316-365-6041. Mrs. Charles A. Heffern (Bernita), D.R.E.
Students 178.

Kingman, Kingman Co., St. Patrick (1885) (Irish), Rev. John C. Reinkemeyer.
Res., 638 Ave. D W., 67068. Tel: 316-532-5440. [JC]
School—Tel: 316-532-5338. Mr. James Gales, Prin. Lay Teachers 9; Students 165.
Catechesis/Religious Programs—Tel: 316-532-5245. Helena Arnold, D.R.E.
Students 240.

Liberty, Montgomery Co., All Saints. Closed. For inquiries for parish records contact the Chancery.

Lindsborg, McPherson Co., St. Bridget of Sweden, Rev. Douglas Campbell.
Church—206 W. Swensson, P.O. Box 268, 67456. Tel: 913-227-3588.
Res., 520 E. Northview, McPherson, 67460. Tel: 316-241-0821; Fax: 316-241-8497.
Catechesis/Religious Programs—Mary Patrick, D.R.E.
Students 36.

Little River, Rice Co., Holy Trinity (1885), Rev. James N. Hoagland.
Res., 415 St. Francis St., Lyons, 67554. Tel: 316-257-3503.
Catechesis/Religious Programs—Tel: 316-489-6436. Mary Konen, D.R.E.
Students 46.

Lyons, Rice Co., St. Paul (1927), Rev. James N. Hoagland.
Res., 415 St. Francis St., 67554. Tel: 316-257-3503.
Catechesis/Religious Programs—Tel: 316-257-3314. Cheryl Steinert, D.R.E.
Students 123.

Madison, Greenwood Co., St. Teresa of Avila (1954) (German), Rev. H. Michael Peltzer.
Res., 514 N. Elm St., Eureka, 67045. Tel: 316-583-7100; 437-2504 (Church).

Marion, Marion Co., Holy Family 1992. Parish formed from merger of St. Mark, Marion; St. John Nepomucene, Pilsen; St. Patrick, Florence; and Holy Redeemer, Tampa. Rev. Stephen Gronert.
Residence and Mailing: 415 N. Cedar St., Box 97, 66861. Tel: 316-382-3422. [CEM 4]
Catechesis/Religious Programs—Tel: 316-382-3369. Rose Davidson, D.R.E.
Students 219.
Mission—Tampa, Marion Co., Holy Redeemer, 66861.

McPherson, McPherson Co., St. Joseph (1880), Rev. Douglas Campbell.
Res., 520 E. Northview, 67460. Tel: 316-241-0821; Fax: 316-241-8497.
School—Tel: 316-241-3913. Dr. Tamara Arnott, Prin.
Lay Teachers 6; Students 91.
Catechesis/Religious Programs—Krista Arrojo, D.R.E.
Students 179.
Mission—Lindsborg, St. Bridget of Sweden, 67456.

Moline, Elk Co., St. Mary's (1899), Rev. Edward J. Steinberger.
Res., Box 276, 67353-0276. Tel: 316-647-3577. [CEM]

Mount Vernon, Kingman Co., St. Rose (1911) (German-Irish), Rev. Ivan C. Eck.
Res., 13015 E. Maple Grove Rd., Mount Hope, 67108. Tel: 316-444-2210. [CEM]
Catechesis/Religious Programs—Tel: 316-542-3990.
Students 77.

Mulberry, Crawford Co., St. Gabriel. Closed. For sacramental records contact Sacred Heart, Frontenac.

Mulvane, Sumner Co., St. Michael the Archangel (1948), Rev. John P. Lanzrath.
Res., 545 E. Main, 67110. Tel: 316-777-4221; Fax: 316-777-1454.
Catechesis/Religious Programs—Tel: 316-777-0444. Karen Oblinger, D.R.E.
Students 222.

Neodesha, Wilson Co., St. Ignatius (1873), Rev. Stephen R. Baxter.
Res., P.O. Box 186, 66757. Tel: 316-378-2694. [CEM]
Catechesis/Religious Programs—Tel: 316-325-3244.
Students 40.

Newton, Harvey Co., St. Mary (1872), Rev. Kenneth J. Schuckman.
Res., 106 E. Eighth St., 67114. Tel: 316-282-0459. [CEM]
School—Tel: 316-282-1974. Mr. Richard Guy, Prin.
Sisters of St. Joseph 3; Lay Teachers 7; Students 199.
Catechesis/Religious Programs—Tel: 316-283-4991. Mrs. Marie Morford, D.R.E.
Students 158.

Our Lady of Guadalupe (1919) (Hispanic), Rev. John V. Hotze.
Res., 415 S. Ash St., 67114. Tel: 316-283-3499. [JC]
Catechesis/Religious Programs—Students 140.

Ost, Reno Co., St. Joseph (1880) (German), Rev. Ivan C. Eck.
Res., 13015 E. Maple Grove Rd., Mount Hope, 67108. Tel: 316-444-2210. [CEM]
Catechesis/Religious Programs—Tel: 316-444-2637.
Students 90.

Oswego, Labette Co., Mother of God (1878), Rev. Larry Parker.
Res., 1112 W. Third., Box 193, 67356. Tel: 316-795-2262. [JC]
Catechesis/Religious Programs—Students 56.

Oxford, Sumner Co., St. Mary (1872) (French), Rev. Michael E. Nolan.
Res., 412 E. Eighth St., Winfield, 67156. Tel: 316-221-3610. [JC]
Catechesis/Religious Programs—Myra Jacobs, D.R.E.
Students 30.

Parsons, Labette Co., Mary Queen of Peace (1909). Closed. For inquiries for parish records contact St. Patrick, Parsons.

St. Patrick (1872), Rev. Michael J. Schemm.
Res., 1807 Stevens Ave., 67357. Tel: 316-421-6762. [CEM 2][JC]
School—1831 Stevens Ave., 67357. Tel: 316-421-0710. Sr. Jacklyn Duncan, Prin.
Sisters of St. Joseph 2; Lay Teachers 8; Students 127.
Catechesis/Religious Programs—Students 320.

Pilsen, Marion Co., St. John Nepomucene. Closed. Merged with St. Mark, Marion; St. Patrick, Florence; and Holy Redeemer, Tampa to form Holy Family, Marion.

Piqua, Woodson Co., St. Martin (1884) (German), Rev. Ser Khu Wilson.
Res., 1368 Xylan Rd., 66761. Tel: 316-468-7441. [CEM]

Pittsburg, Crawford Co., Our Lady of Lourdes (1881), Revs. Thomas J. Stroot; Robert W. McElwee; Samuel J. Pinkerton.
Res., 916 N. Locust St., P.O. Box 214, 66762. Tel: 316-231-2135; Fax: 316-231-4804. [CEM]
School—St. Mary's Elementary, 213 E. Ninth, 66762. Tel: 316-231-6941. Mr. Frank Crespino, Prin.
Sisters of St. Joseph 1; Lay Teachers 22; Students 390.
High School—St. Mary-Colgan High School, 212 E. 9th, P.O. Box 266, Pittsburgh, 66762. Tel: 316-231-4690.
Sisters of St. Joseph 1; Priests 1; Lay Teachers 14; Students 156.
Catechesis/Religious Programs—Denise Loy, D.R.E.
Students 128.
Convent—821 N. Locust St., 66762. Tel: 316-231-6014.

St. Leo, Kingman Co., St. Leo the Great (1902) (German), Rev. John Miller.
Res., 8035 S.W. 160 Ave., Nashville, 67112. Tel: 316-246-5370. [CEM]
Catechesis/Religious Programs—P.O. Box 216, Cunningham, 67035. Tel: 316-298-2601.
Students 59.

St. Mark's, Sedgwick Co., St. Mark (1876) (German), Rev. John Patrick Mannion.
Res., R.F.D. 1, Colwich, 67030. Tel: 316-796-1604. [CEM]
Catechesis/Religious Programs—Mary Ann Hensley, D.R.E.
Students 180.

St. Paul, Neosho Co., St. Francis (1847), Rev. John Zich.
Res., 208 Washington St., P.O. Box 216, 66771-0216. Tel: 316-449-2224; Fax: 316-449-2224. [CEM 2]
Catechesis/Religious Programs—Tel: 316-449-2672. Mary Frances Casey, D.R.E.
Students 182.

Scammon, Cherokee Co., St. Bridget's (1868), Rev. Chrysostom Ah Maung.
Res., 155 W. Walnut, Columbus, 66725. Tel: 316-429-2639. [CEM]
Catechesis/Religious Programs—Tel: 316-479-2236.
Students 50.

Schulte, Sedgwick Co., St. Peter's (1905), Rev. Daniel J. Spexarth.
Res., 335 N. Annie St., R.R. 24, Wichita, 67215. Tel: 316-522-4728. [CEM]
School—Tel: 316-524-6585. Sr. Mary Rose Engel, Prin.
Sisters of St. Dominic 1; Lay Teachers 17; Students 284.
Catechesis/Religious Programs—Helen Ruth Welsby, D.R.E.
Students 169.
Convent—134 W. Peter St., R.R. 24, Wichita, 67215. Tel: 316-524-4259.

Sedan, Chautauqua Co., St. Robert Bellarmine (1962), Rev. Edward J. Steinberger.
Res., P.O. Box 276, Moline, 67353-0276. Tel: 316-647-3577.

Strong City, Chase Co., St. Anthony of Padua (1880), Rev. Paul J. Oborny.
Res., 316 Spencer, Council Grove, 66846. Tel: 316-767-6412. [CEM]
Catechesis/Religious Programs—Tel: 316-273-8617. Jeanette Black, D.R.E.
Students 50.

Tampa, Marion Co., Holy Redeemer. Now an oratory of Holy Family, Marion.

Walnut, Crawford Co., St. Patrick. Closed. For sacramental records contact St. Francis Church, St. Paul.

Waterloo, Kingman Co., St. Louis (1881) (German-Irish), Rev. Ivan C. Eck.
Res., 13015 E. Maple Grove Rd., Mt. Hope, 67108. Tel: 316-444-2210. [CEM]

Weir, Cherokee Co., Sacred Heart. Closed. For sacramental records contact St. Rose of Lima, Columbus.

Wellington, Sumner Co., St. Anthony (1884). All information is for both St. Anthony and St. Rose. Rev. Andrew J. Seiler.
Mailing Address: 210 North B St., 67152. Tel: 316-326-2522; Fax: 316-326-2527.
Catechesis/Religious Programs—Tel: 316-326-3480. Pam Montenegro, D.R.E.
Students 306.

St. Rose of Lima (1949) (Hispanic), Rev. Andrew J. Seiler; Sr. Connie Beiriger, C.S.J., Pastoral Assoc. & D.R.E.
Mailing Address: 210 N. B St., Wellingon, 67152. Tel: 316-326-2522.
Church—1205 E. Harvey, 67152. Tel: 316-326-3572.
Catechesis/Religious Programs—Tel: 316-326-3480.
Students 341.

West Mineral, Cherokee Co., Immaculate Conception. Closed. For sacramental records contact St. Rose of Lima, Columbus.

Willowdale, Kingman Co., St. Peter's (1884) (German), Rev. John P. Miller.
Res., P.O. Box 86, Zenda, 67159. Tel: 316-243-5451. [CEM]

Winfield, Cowley Co., Holy Name (1878), Rev. Michael E. Nolan.
Res., 412 E. Eighth St., 67156. Tel: 316-221-3610. [JC]
School—Tel: 316-221-0230. Mrs. Linda Gross, Prin.
Lay Teachers 6; Students 81.
Catechesis/Religious Programs—Tel: 316-221-4053. Fran Parks, D.R.E.
Students 100.

Yates Center, Woodson Co., St. Joseph (1957), Rev. Ser Khu Wilson.
Res., 107 E. Bell St., 66783. Tel: 316-625-2103.
Catechesis/Religious Programs—Tel: 316-625-2672.
Students 53.

Zenda, Kingman Co., St. John (1908) (German), Rev. John P. Miller.
Res., P.O. Box 86, 67159. Tel: 316-243-5451. [CEM]
Catechesis/Religious Programs—Linda Kerschen, D.R.E.
Students 63.

Chaplains of Public Institutions

WICHITA. *Sedgwick County Adult Local Detention Facility*. Rev. Daniel J. Spexarth.
Veterans Administration Hospital. Vacant.

HUTCHINSON. *Kansas State Industrial Reformatory*. 612 S. Maple, South Hutchinson, 67505. Tel: 316-662-6443. Rev. Colin J. Boor.

On Duty Outside the Diocese:
Reverend Fathers—
Conley, James, Ministry in Rome, Italy
Jackson, James
Joyce, Raymond
Machado, Jose, Apartado 407, Barquisimeto, Venezuela

McKnight, W. Shawn, Studies in Rome, Italy
Nolan, Joseph T
O'Connor, Charles
Quach, Binh The

Military Chaplains:
Reverend Fathers—
Schmid, Wayne L., 1436 Graham Ave., St. Louis, MO 63139

Retired:
Reverend Monsignors—
Gerstenkorn, Joseph J., 629 S. Vassar, Wichita, KS 67218
Hertel, Herbert N., 3214 Zimmerly, Wichita, KS 67218
Hogan, Vincent, 424 S. Central, Chanute, KS 66720
Lampe, Irvin F., 13014 La Terraza Dr., Sun City West, AZ 85375
Malone, Quintin J., 6900 E. 45th St., N., Wichita, KS 67226
Schmidt, George N., 6900 E. 45th St., N., Wichita, KS 67226
Smith, Charles A., 914 Torrey Pines Dr., Pasa Robles, CA 93446
Tonne, Arthur, 520 N. Freeborn, Marion, KS 66861. Tel: 316-382-3166
Reverend Fathers—
Bieberle, Victor, 29 Tiburon Way, Hot Springs, AR 71909
Dinan, John, 1915 N. Porter, Apt. A-78, Wichita, KS 67203
Finnegan, Peter J., 6900 E. 45th St., N., Wichita, KS 67226
Freed, Robert, 3330 E. Bellaire St., Wichita, KS 67218
Garrahy, Michael, 6900 E. 45th St., N., Wichita, KS 67226
Harvey, Charles K., 6900 E. 45th St., N., Wichita, KS 67226
Hay, Francis J., 6900 E. 45th St., N., Wichita, KS 67226
Kocour, Robert F., Apartado 407, Barquisimeto Lara, 3001-A Venezuela
Metcko, Leo E., 6900 E. 45th St., N., Wichita, KS 67226
Mullen, John, P.O. Box 246, Halstead, KS 67056
Mulvihill, Daniel R., RR 10, Box 14, Apt. 4, Joplin, MO 64804
O'Hare, Donald J., 950 82nd Ave., Vero Beach, FL 32996
O'Leary, David A., 6900 E. 45th St., N., Wichita, KS 67226
O'Malley, Michael W.
Pepe, Robert F., 4 Circle Dr., Port Duncan, Afton, OK 74331
Regan, Charles, 6900 E. 45th St. N., Apt. E 2, Wichita, KS 67226
Rusteika, John B., 5 Carballo Pl., Hot Springs Village, AR 71909
Spexarth, James, R.R. 1, P.O. Box 30, Marion, KS 66861
Stremel, Adolph, c/o P.A. Sullivan, 801 Main St., Victoria, KS 67671
Trayers, Kevin, 202 S. Liberty, Cherryvale, KS 67335
Walsh, Ulich
York, Edward, 46 Leicester Dr., Bella Vista, AR 72714

INSTITUTIONS LOCATED IN THE DIOCESE

[A] COLLEGES AND UNIVERSITIES

WICHITA. *Kansas Newman College*, 3100 McCormick Ave., 67213. Tel: 316-942-4291; Fax: 316-942-4483.
E-mail: thompsong@ksnewman.edu
Web site: www.ksnewman.edu
For a complete listing, refer to the Colleges and Universities section.

[B] HIGH SCHOOLS, DIOCESAN

WICHITA. *Bishop Mark K. Carroll High School*, 8101 W. Central, 67212. Tel: 316-722-2390; Fax: 316-722-6670.
E-mail: BCAROL1@feist.com
Web site: http://www.feist.com/~bcarol1;
Leticia C. Nielsen, Prin.; Rev. Sherman A. Orr. Tel: 316-943-4353. Priests 1; Sisters 5; Lay Teachers 43; Students 799.

Kapaun Mt. Carmel High School, 8506 E. Central, 67206. Tel: 316-634-0315.
E-mail: kapaun@feist.com
Web site: http://www.feist.com/-kapaun
Sr. Claire Faltus, O.S.F., Prin.; Rev. John Sherlock, Chap. Sisters 1; Priests 2; Lay Teachers 55; Students 796.

HUTCHINSON. *Trinity High School*, 1400 E. 17th, 67501. Tel: 316-662-5800. Dr. Richard Robl, Pres. of Hutchinson Catholic Schools; Mr. Brian Cordel, Prin.; Rev. Richard Stuchlik, Chap. Sisters 2; Lay Teachers 15; Students 199.

The Trinity High School Education Endowment Fund, 1400 E. 17th, 67501. c/o Eugene J. Gerber, 424 N. Broadway, Wichita, 67202.

PITTSBURG. *St. Mary-Colgan High School*, 212 E. 9th St., 66762. Tel: 316-231-4690. Rev. Thomas J. Stroot, Admin.; Mr. Patrick Forbes, Prin. Sisters of St. Joseph 1; Lay Teachers 14; Students 156.

[C] ELEMENTARY SCHOOLS, INTERPAROCHIAL

PARSONS. *St. Patrick School*, 1831 Stevens, 67357. Sr. Jacklyn Duncan, Prin. Consolidated from St. Mary's School and St. Patrick's School, Parsons. Sisters of St. Joseph 2; Lay Teachers 8; Students 127.

[D] SPECIAL EDUCATION

WICHITA. *Art of Learning Center*, 201 S. Millwood, 67213. Tel: 316-265-6853. Sr. Sibyllina Mueller, O.P., Dir. Speech, Language, Reading Therapy. Total Assisted 2,260; Total Staff 3.

[E] GENERAL HOSPITALS

WICHITA. *Via Christi Regional Medical Center, Inc.*
Web site: www.Via-Christi.org
St. Francis Campus, 929 N. St. Francis, 67124. Tel: 316-268-5000.
For a complete listing, refer to the Hospitals section.

Via Christi Rehabilitation Center, Inc., Our Lady of Lourdes Campus, 1151 N. Rock Rd., 67208. Tel: 316-634-3400
For a complete listing, refer to the Hospitals section.

FORT SCOTT. *Mercy Health System of Kansas, Inc.*, 821 Burke St., 66701. Tel: 316-223-7057; Fax: 316-223-5327
For a complete listing, refer to the Hospitals section.

INDEPENDENCE. *Mercy Health Systems of Kansas, Inc.-Independence*, 800 W. Myrtle St., 67301. Tel: 316-331-2200.
E-mail: abrau@mhsk.smhs.com
Web site: terraworld.net/mercy/
For a complete listing, refer to the Hospitals section.

PITTSBURG. *Mount Carmel Medical Center; Mount Carmel Foundation*, 1102 E. Centennial, 66762. Tel: 316-231-6100
For a complete listing, refer to the Hospitals section.

[F] HOMES FOR AGED

WICHITA. *Catholic Care Center, Inc.*, 6700 E. 45th St., N., 67226. Tel: 316-744-2020
For a complete listing, refer to the Special Care Facilities section.

Georgetown Village, Inc., 1655 Georgetown St., 67218. Tel: 316-685-0400; Fax: 316-685-0174
For a complete listing, refer to the Special Care Facilities section.

MULVANE. *Villa Maria*, 116 S. Central, 67110. Tel: 316-777-1129; Fax: 316-777-4406
For a complete listing, refer to the Special Care Facilities section.

[G] MONASTERIES AND RESIDENCES FOR PRIESTS AND BROTHERS

WICHITA. *Priests Retirement Center*, 6900 E. 45th St., N., 67226. Tel: 316-744-2020. Fred Hermes, CEO. Residents 16.

Redemptorist Community, 7100 E. 45th St., N., 67226. Tel: 316-744-0167; Fax: 316-744-8072.
E-mail: spiritlife@feist.com
Web site: http://www.feist.com/~spiritlife/index.html
Revs. J. Terrence McCloskey, C.SS.R., Supr.; Gerard J. Pecht, C.SS.R.; Frederick Arpin, C.SS.R. In res., Rev. Richard Boever, C.SS.R. Residents 4; Staff 3.

Redemptorist Mission House, 145 S. Millwood Ave., 67213. Tel: 316-262-1877.
E-mail: DANHA@aol.com
Revs. Daniel Andree, C.SS.R., Supr.; Walter Karrer, C.SS.R.; Edward Morgan, C.SS.R.; Arthur Frost, C.SS.R. Residents 4; Staff 4.

[H] CONVENTS AND RESIDENCES FOR SISTERS

WICHITA. *Blessed Sacrament Sisters of Charity*, 6547 St. James Pl., 67226. Tel: 316-744-8768; Fax: 316-744-3447. Sr. Michaela Park. Sisters 4.

Dominican House of Studies, 201 S. Millwood, 67213. Tel: 316-267-4551. Sisters of the Third Order of St. Dominic (Congregation of the Immaculate Conception, Great Bend, KS). Residents 9.

Medical Sisters of St. Joseph-United States Foundation, 3435 E. Funston, 67218. Tel: 316-686-4746. Sr. Audrey, Supr. Professed Sisters 3.

Mt. St. Mary Convent, Motherhouse and Novitiate of the Sisters of St. Joseph, 3700 E. Lincoln, 67218-2099. Tel: 316-686-7171; Fax: 316-689-4056.
E-mail: wichitasjc@feist.com
Web site: www.feist.com/~wichitacsj/
Sr. Veronice Born, C.S.J., Pres.; Rev. Robert E. Hemberger, Chap. Professed Sisters 202; Sisters in Temporary Profession 2.
Other Residences: 1103 S. Yale, 67218. 1124 S. Yale, 67218. 1144 S. Yale, 67218. 3427 E. Funston, 67218. 3333 Bellaire Ct., 67218-4807. 619 S. Maize Rd., 67209-1399. 7627 E. 37th N. #3701, 67226. 3427 E. Funston, 67218. KS, 1144 S. Yale. 1206 Regal, 67217. 1103 S. Yale, 67218-3013. 2045 Arkansas, 67203-2568. 138 N. Roosevelt, 67208-3717. 7036 E. Kellogg, Apt. F, 67207. 855 S. Sheridan, 67213.

Provincialate of the Sisters Adorers of the Blood of Christ, 1400 S. Sheridan, 67213. Tel: 316-943-1203; Fax: 316-943-1427. Sr. Charlotte Rohrbach, A.S.C., Supr.; Rev. Thomas Welk, C.PP.S., Chap. Professed Sisters 232; Postulants 1; Novices 1.

Sisters of the Immaculate Heart of Mary of Wichita, Inc. (I.H.M.), 605 N. Woodchuck, 67212. Tel: 316-722-9316. Sr. Giovanni Oliveri, I.H.M., Supr. Professed Sisters 9; Novices 3.

[I] RETREAT HOUSES

WICHITA. *Spiritual Life Center*, 7100 E. 45th St., N., 67226. Tel: 316-744-0167; Fax: 314-744-8072.
E-mail: spiritlife@feist.com
Web site: http://www.feist.com/~spiritlife/index.html
Revs. J. Terrence McCloskey, C.SS.R., Dir.; Joseph M. Gile, Assoc. Dir. Ministry Staff: Revs. Gerard J. Pecht, C.SS.R.; Frederick L. Arpin, C.SS.R.; Rhonda Lohkamp, R.C.I.A.; Linda Sargent, Prog. Dir. Residents 4; Staff 21.

[J] COMMUNITY CENTERS

WICHITA. *Catholic Charities*, 437 N. Topeka, 67202. Tel: 316-264-8344; Fax: 316-264-4442. Total Agency Staff 78; Total Individuals Assisted 8,684.

Counseling Services, 425 N. Topeka, 67202. Tel: 316-263-6941. Counseling 2,813 Individuals Served; Adoptions Completed 13; Individuals Served 297.

Harvest House, 437 N. Topeka, 67202. Tel: 316-264-8344. Staff 2; Centers 25; Members Assisted 1,600.

Anthony Family Shelter (and Emergency Services), 256 N. Ohio, 67214. Tel: 316-264-7233. Staff 15; Individuals Assisted 6,183.

Southeast Kansas Counseling, Pius X Catholic Center, 201 E. Cleveland, Pittsburgh, 66762. Tel: 316-231-3638. Staff 2; Clients Assisted 191.

Adult Day Services, 1209 Indiana, 67214. Tel: 316-264-9723. 13; Total Assisted 99.

St. Dismas Missioners, 437 N. Topeka, 67202. Tel: 316-264-8344. Volunteers visit jails and prisons.

Harbor House, P.O. Box 3759, 67201. Staff 13; Women & Children Assisted 455; Victims Advocate Program 2,046.

**Center of Hope*, 400 N. Emporia, 67202-2514. Sponsored by Adorers of the Blood of Christ. Sr. Stella Rosenhamer, A.S.C., Dir. Tel: 316-267-0222; Fax: 316-267-7778. Staff 2; Total Assisted 3,940.

Foster Grandparent Program, 437 N. Topeka, 67202. Tel: 316-264-8344. Ms. Janet Valente-Pape, Exec. Dir. Provides 75,424 hours of service. Staff 1; Assisted: 386 Children, 97 Foster Grandparents.

Guadalupe Clinic, 940 S. St. Francis, 67211. Tel: 316-264-8974. Ms. Patricia Kastens, Dir. Staff 6; Total Assisted 21,575.

Refugee Services, 437 N. Topeka, 67202. Tel: 316-264-0197. Ms. Janet Valente-Pape, Exec. Dir. Staff 2; Total Assisted 1,701.

[K] NEWMAN CENTERS

WICHITA. *Wichita State University*, 1810 N. Roosevelt, 67208. Tel: 316-684-6896; Fax: 316-684-2679. Rev. Matthew C. McGinness, Chap.

PITTSBURG. *St. Pius X Center (Pittsburg State University)*, 301A E. Cleveland, 66762. Tel: 316-235-1138.
E-mail: PSUNeuman@aol.com
Rev. Patrick G. York, Chap.

[L] CATHOLIC CHARITIES

WICHITA. *Catholic Charities, Inc.*, 437 N. Topeka, 67202. Tel: 316-264-8344; Fax: 316-264-4442.

Southeast Kansas Counseling, Piux X Catholic Center, 201 E. Cleveland, Pittsburg, 66762. Tel: 316-231-3638.

Adult Day Services, 1209 Indiana, 67214. Tel: 316-264-9723.

Anthony Family Shelter (and Emergency Services), 256 N. Ohio, 67214. Tel: 316-264-7233.

Harbor House, P.O. Box 3759, 67201.

[M] MISCELLANEOUS

WICHITA. *Christina House*, 856 N. Socora, 67212. Tel: 316-721-8159.

Diocesan Office, Ministry with Persons with Disabilities, 619 S. Maize Rd., 67209. Tel: 316-722-5381.

Gerard House, Inc., 3144 N. Hood, 67204. Tel: 316-832-0777; Fax: 316-832-1327. Lisa Egan, Dir. Shelter for Needy Pregnant Women.

Leaven International Corporation, 1400 S. Sheridan, 67213; Fax: 316-943-1427. Sr. Charlotte Rohrbach, Pres. A charitable organization of the Adorers of the Blood of Christ.

The Mary Magdalen Foundation, 457 S. Woodlawn, 67218. Tel: 316-683-6516.

Serra Club of Wichita - Downtown, 424 N. Broadway, 67202. Tel: 316-269-3900. Rev. Kenneth J. Schuckman, Chap.

Serra Club of Wichita - Metro, 424 N. Broadway, 67202. Tel: 316-269-3900. Rev. Thomas McGread, Chap.

Totus Tuus, Inc., 542 N. Oliver, 67218. Tel: 316-685-2069. Wayne Rziha, Contact.

Via Christi Foundation, Inc., 959 N. Emporia, Ste. 402, 67214. Tel: 316-268-5100; Fax: 316-291-7859. Mr. Robert Giroux, Pres. Owned by Congregation of the Sisters of St. Joseph of Wichita and the Sisters of Sorrowful Mother, sponsoring organization for 10 hospitals and long-term care facilities and their affiliated organization located in 3 states. Staff 8.

Via Christi Health Partners, Inc., 959 N. St. Francis, Ste. 302, 67214.
Web site: http://www.Via-Christi.org

Via Christi Health System, Inc., 929 N. St. Francis, 67214. Tel: 316-268-5000.
Web site: www.Via-Christi.org
Mr. LeRoy Rheault, Pres. & CEO. Owned by the Congregations of the Sisters of St. Joseph of Wichita and the Sisters of the Sorrowful Mother. Sponsoring organization for 8 hospitals and long-term care facilities and their affiliated organizations located in two states.

Via Christi Property Services, Inc., 959 N. St. Francis, Ste. 302, 67214.
Web site: http.www.Via-Christi.org

Via Christi Senior Services, Inc., 3720 E. Bayley, 67218. Tel: 316-689-4000.

RELIGIOUS INSTITUTES OF MEN REPRESENTED IN THE DIOCESE

For further details refer to the corresponding bracketed number in the Religious Institutes of Men or Women section.

[1070]—*Redemptorist Fathers.* (Province of St. Louis).—C.SS.R.

[1060]—*Society of the Precious Blood.* (Kansas City Prov.).—C.SS.R.

RELIGIOUS INSTITUTES OF WOMEN REPRESENTED IN THE DIOCESE

[0100]—*Adorers of the Blood of Christ.*—A.S.C.

[]—*Carmelite Sisters of St. Teresa.*—C.S.S.T.

[]—*Charity Sisters of the Blessed Sacrament.* (Korean Foundation).

[]—*Congregation of the Daughters of the Passion of Our Lord Jesus Christ and the Sorrows of Mary.*—C.F.P.

[1070-24]—*Dominican Sisters.*—O.P.

[1430]—*Franciscan Sisters of Our Lady of Perpetual Help.*—O.S.F.

[2575]—*Institute of the Sisters of Mercy of the Americas.*—R.S.M.

[2500]—*Medical Sisters of St. Joseph.*—M.S.J.

[0440]—*Sisters of Charity of Cincinnati, Ohio.*—S.C.

[0430]—*Sisters of Charity of the Blessed Virgin Mary.*—B.V.M.

[3830-18]—*Sisters of St. Joseph.*—C.S.J.

[2185]—*Sisters of the Immaculate Heart of Mary of Wichita.*—I.H.M.

[4100]—*Sisters of the Sorrowful Mother (Third Order of St. Francis).*—S.S.M.

[2150]—*Sisters, Servants of the Immaculate Heart of Mary.*—I.H.M.

NECROLOGY

† Colbert, C. Francis, (Retired). —Died April 7, 1997.

† Downs, Leroy J., (Retired). —Died Aug. 17, 1997.

Diocese of Wilmington

(Dioecesis Wilmingtoniensis)

Most Reverend

MICHAEL A. SALTARELLI, D.D.

Bishop of Wilmington; ordained May 28, 1960; appointed Titular Bishop of Mesarfelta and Auxiliary Bishop of Newark, June 12, 1990; episcopal ordination July 30, 1990;; appointed Eighth Bishop of Wilmington November 21, 1995; installed January 23, 1996.

Established March 3, 1868.

Square Miles Delaware 1,932; Maryland 3,375; Total 5,307.

Comprises the State of Delaware and the Counties of Caroline, Cecil, Dorchester, Kent, Queen Anne's, Somerset, Talbot, Wicomico and Worcester in Maryland.

For legal titles of parishes and diocesan institutions, consult the Chancery Office.

Chancery Office: 1925 Delaware Ave., Ste. 1A, Wilmington, DE. Tel.: 302-573-3100; Fax: 302-573-3128.

STATISTICAL OVERVIEW

Personnel	
Bishop	1
Priests: Diocesan Active in Diocese	88
Priests: Active Outside Diocese	12
Priests: Retired, Sick or Absent	28
Number of Diocesan Priests	128
Religious Priests in Diocese	91
Extern Priests in Diocese	16
Ordinations:	
Religious Priests	4
Permanent Deacons	1
Permanent Deacons in Diocese	46
Total Brothers	33
Total Sisters	287
Parishes	
Parishes	55
With Resident Pastor:	
Resident Diocesan Priests	49
Resident Religious Priests	3
Without Resident Pastor:	
Administered by Priests	1
Administered by Pastoral Teams, etc.	2
Missions	21
Pastoral Centers	10
Professional Ministry Personnel:	
Sisters	34
Lay Ministers	71
Welfare	
Catholic Hospitals	1
Total Assisted	311,000
Health Care Centers	2
Total Assisted	200
Homes for the Aged	4
Total Assisted	355
Residential Care of Children	4
Total Assisted	127
Day Care and Extended Day Care Centers	1
Total Assisted	161
Specialized Homes	1
Total Assisted	400
Special Centers for Social Services	18
Total Assisted	323,768
Residential Care of Disabled	1
Total Assisted	140
Educational	
Diocesan Students in Other Seminaries	6
Total Seminarians	6
High Schools, Diocesan and Parish	4
Total Students	2,858
High Schools, Private	3
Total Students	1,695
Elementary Schools, Diocesan and Parish	25
Total Students	9,783
Elementary Schools, Private	4
Total Students	1,018
Non-residential Schools for the Disabled	1
Total Students	77
Catechesis/Religious Education:	
High School Students	1,171
Elementary Students	8,853
Total Students Under Catholic Instruction	25,461
Teachers in the Diocese:	
Priests	21
Brothers	8
Sisters	63
Lay Teachers	943
Vital Statistics	
Receptions into the Church:	
Infant Baptism Totals	3,051
Adult Baptism Totals	201
Received into Full Communion	320
First Communions	2,685
Confirmations	2,055
Marriages:	
Catholic	562
Interfaith	463
Total Marriages	1,025
Deaths	1,428
Total Catholic Population	166,059
Total Population	1,089,820

Former Bishops—Rt. Rev. Thomas A. Becker, D.D., cons. Aug. 16, 1868; transferred to Savannah, 1886; died July 29, 1899.—Rt. Rev. Alfred A. Curtis, D.D., cons. Nov. 14, 1886; resigned 1896; named Titular Bishop of Echinus; died July 11, 1908.—Most Rev. John J. Monaghan, D.D., cons. May 9, 1897; resigned and named Titular Bishop of Lydda, July 10, 1925; died Jan. 7, 1935.—Most Rev. Edmond John FitzMaurice, D.D., cons. Nov. 30, 1925; resigned March 2, 1960 and named Titular Archbishop of Tomi; died July 25, 1962.—Most Rev. Hubert J. Cartwright, D.D., cons. Coadjutor "with right of succession," Oct. 24, 1956; died March 6, 1958.—Most Rev. Michael W. Hyle, D.D., cons. Sept. 24, 1958 as Titular Bishop of Christopolis and Coadjutor with right of succession; succeeded to See, March 2, 1960; died Dec. 26, 1967.—Most Rev. Thomas J. Mardaga, D.D., cons. Jan. 25, 1967; named Titular Bishop of Mutugenna; appt. Bishop of Wilmington, March 13, 1968; installed April 6, 1968; died May 28, 1984.—Most Rev. James C. Burke, O.P., cons. May 25, 1967; named Titular Bishop of Lamiggiga; Vicar Apostolic of Chimbote, Peru, 1962-1978 Served in Diocese of Wilmington, 1978-1994; died May 28, 1994.—Most Rev. Robert E. Mulvee, D.D., J.C.D., ord. June 30, 1957; Auxiliary Bishop of Manchester and Titular Bishop of Summa, Feb. 15, 1977; cons. April 14, 1977; appt. Bishop of Wilmington, Feb. 19, 1985; installed April 11, 1985; appt. to Diocese of Providence as Coadjutor Bishop of Providence, Feb. 7, 1995; installed March 27, 1995; succeeded to See, June 11, 1997.

Vicar General for Administration and Moderator of the Curia—Rev. Msgr. J. Thomas Cini, V.G., M.A., *1925 Delaware Ave., Ste. 2A, P.O. Box 2030, Wilmington, 19899.* Tel: 302-573-3118; Fax: 302-573-3128.

Vicar General for Pastoral Concerns and Chancellor—Rev. Msgr. Joseph F. Rebman, V.G., S.T.L., J.C.L., *1925 Delaware Ave., Ste. 1A, P.O. Box 2030, Wilmington, 19899.* Tel: 302-573-3100; Fax: 302-573-3128.

Episcopal Vicar for Clergy—Rev. Msgr. Clement P. Lemon, E.V.C., *1925 Delaware Ave., Ste. 3A, P.O. Box 2030, Wilmington, 19899.* Tel: 302-573-3144; Fax: 302-573-3128.

Pastoral Concerns Department

Secretary, Pastoral Concerns Department—Rev. Msgr. Joseph F. Rebman, V.G., S.T.L., J.C.L.

Chancery Office—Rev. Msgr. Joseph F. Rebman, V.G., S.T.L., J.C.L., Chancellor, *Mailing Address: P.O. Box 2030, Wilmington, 19899.* Office: *1925 Delaware Ave., Ste. 1A, Wilmington,* Office Hours: Mon.-Fri. 8:30-4:30. Tel: 302-573-3100; Fax: 302-573-3128. Send all marriage dispensation requests to Chancery Office.

Archives—Mr. Donn Devine, Archivist, *P.O. Box 4019, Greenville, 19807.* Tel: 302-655-0597.

Master of Ceremonies—Rev. Msgr. Joseph F. Rebman, V.G., S.T.L., J.C.L., *P.O. Box 2030, Wilmington, 19899.* Tel: 302-573-3100; Fax: 302-573-3128.

Censor of Books—Rev. Msgr. John H. Dewson, S.T.L., *Immaculate Heart of Mary, Wilmington, 19803.* Tel: 302-764-0357.

Ecumenical and Interreligious Affairs—Rev. Msgr. Joseph F. Rebman, V.G., S.T.L., J.C.L., Chancellor.

Diocesan Tribunal—*Mailing Address: P.O. Box 2030, Wilmington, 19899. 1925 Delaware Ave., Ste. 2B, Wilmington.* Tel: 302-573-3107; Fax: 302-573-3128.

Judicial Vicar—Very Rev. Theodore E. Olson, J.C.L.

Office Supervisor—Mrs. JoAnn Kubasko.

Court of First Instance Judges—Revs. George J. Brubaker, J.C.L.; Stanley R. Drupieski, O.S.F.S.; Sr. Mary Kathleen Kuenstler, P.H.J.C., J.C.D.; Mr. Albert R. Lanphear.

Auditors—Revs. Barry Langley, O.F.M.; James Nash; Deacon Francis Staab.

Defenders of the Bond—Jack D. Anderson, J.C.D.; Rev. Cyprian Rosen, O.F.M.Cap., J.C.L.

Secretaries/Notaries—Mrs. Marie Bradley; Mrs. Gail Esposito; Mrs. Patricia Killen.

Catholic Cemeteries—Rev. Msgr. Joseph F. Rebman, V.G., S.T.L., J.C.L., Dir.; Mr. Mark A. Christian, Exec. Dir., *Mailing Address: P.O. Box 2506, Wilmington, 19805.* Tel: 302-656-3323; Fax: 302-656-1069.

Supervisor of Institutional Chaplains—Rev. Msgr. Clement P. Lemon, E.V.C., *1925 Delaware Ave., Ste. 3A, P.O. Box 2030, Wilmington, 19899.* Tel: 302-573-3144; Fax: 302-573-3128.

Vocation Office—Rev. James Nash, Dir., *1925 Delaware Ave., Ste. 3A, P.O. Box 2030, Wilmington, 19899.* Tel: 302-573-3113; Fax: 302-573-3128.

Office for Deacons—Co-Directors: Rev. PAUL G. MAST; Deacon F. EDMUND LYNCH, *1925 Delaware Ave., Ste. 3A, P.O. Box 2030, Wilmington, 19899.* Tel: 302-573-2390; Fax: 302-573-3128.

Office for Clergy—Rev. Msgr. CLEMENT P. LEMON, E.V.C., Dir., *1925 Delaware Ave., Ste. 3A, P.O. Box 2030, Wilmington, 19899.* Tel: 302-573-3144; Fax: 302-573-3128.

Office for Parish Renewal & Evangelization—Rev. WILLIAM J. LAWLER, Dir., *303 Chesterfield Ave., Centreville, MD, 21617.* Tel: 410-758-0140; Fax: 410-758-4083.

Office for Religious—Sr. ELIZABETH A. SWEENEY, S.S.J., Dir., *Ste. 3A, 1925 Delaware Ave., P.O. Box 2030, Wilmington, 19899.* Tel: 302-573-3124; Fax: 302-573-3128.

Mission Office—Propagation of the Faith and Holy Childhood Association, Rev. JOHN P. KLEVENCE, Dir., *1626 N. Union St., P.O. Box 2030, Wilmington, 19899.* Tel: 302-573-3104; Fax: 302-573-2393.

Marian Devotions Office—Rev. Msgr. JOSEPH F. REBMAN, V.G., S.T.L., J.C.L., Dir. Assoc. Directors: Rev. JOSEPH J. PIEKARSKI; Deacon EDWARD A. DUNNING, *1925 Delaware Ave., P.O. Box 2030, Wilmington, 19899.* Tel: 302-573-3100; Fax: 302-573-3128.

Latino and Migrant Ministry—Rev. RUBEN A. SOTO, F.M.M., *135 Fourth St., Seaford, 19973.* Tel: 302-629-5705; Fax: 302-629-7403.

Hispanic Ministry Office—Mr. IGNACIO FRANCO, *2503 Centerville Rd., Wilmington, 19808.* Tel: 302-999-7930; Fax: 302-633-4960.

Christian Formation Department

Secretary, Christian Formation Department—Mr. EDMUND F. GORDON.

Catholic Schools—Sr. MARIE LOURDES VANSTON, I.H.M., Supt. Asst. Supts.: Sr. KATHLEEN CALLAGHAN, S.S.J.; Sr. PATRICIA CLUNE, C.S.J., *1626 N. Union St., Wilmington, 19806.* Tel: 302-573-3133; Fax: 302-573-3143.

Religious Education—Mr. EDMUND F. GORDON, Diocesan Dir. GLORIA REINHARDT, Asst. Dir., *1626 N. Union St., Wilmington, 19806.* Tel: 302-573-3130; Fax: 302-573-2393.

Ministry for Special Needs—Mrs. JO ANN DORA, Coord. Special Religious Education; Mrs. MARGARET WYNN, Coord. Hearing Impaired; Mr. BOB CICHOCKI, Vol. Liaison to the Physically Disabled, *1626 N. Union St., Wilmington, 19806.* Tel: 302-573-3130.

Office of Worship—Rev. KENNETH J. MARTIN, Dir., *1626 N. Union St., Wilmington, 19806.* Tel: 302-573-3137; Fax: 302-573-2393.

Educational Resource Center—Vacant, *1626 N. Union St., Wilmington, 19806.* Tel: 302-573-3136.

Catholic Youth Organization—Rev. JOHN P. HOPKINS, Dir.; Mr. BRIAN M.P. MCGLINCHEY, Assoc. Dir., *803 N. Broom St., Wilmington, 19805.* Tel: 302-658-3800; 3801; Fax: 302-658-7617.

Newman Apostolate—Very Rev. MICHAEL F. SZUPPER, Ph.D., Dir.; Rev. DAVID F. KELLEY, Assoc. Dir., *University of Delaware, 45 Lovett Ave., Newark, 19711.* Tel: 302-368-4728.

Youth Ministry—Rev. JOHN P. HOPKINS, Dir., *803 N. Broom St., Wilmington, 19806.* Tel: 302-658-3800.

Catholic Scouting—

Boy Scouts—Vacant, *1626 N. Union St., Wilmington, 19806.* Tel: 302-573-3130.

Girl Scouts—Rev. JOHN P. HOPKINS, Chap., *803 N. Broom St., Wilmington, 19806.* Tel: 302-658-3800; Fax: 302-658-7617.

Communication Department

Secretary, Communication Department—Mr. F. EUGENE DONNELLY.

Office of Public Relations, Radio and T.V.—Mr. F. EUGENE DONNELLY, Dir., *1626 N. Union St., Wilmington, 19899.* Tel: 302-573-3116; Fax: 302-573-2393.

"The Dialog"—(Weekly Diocesan Newspaper), Most Rev. MICHAEL A. SALTARELLI, Publisher; Mr. GARY MORTON, Editor, *P.O. Box 2208, Wilmington, 19899.* Editorial Offices: *1925 Delaware Ave., Ste. 3B, Wilmington, 19806.* Tel: 302-573-3109; 573-3112 (Advertising Dept.); Fax: 302-573-3128.

Finance Department

Financial Officer and Secretary, Finance Department—Mr. JOSEPH P. CORSINI, *Mailing Address: P.O. Box 2030, Wilmington, 19899. 1925 Delaware Ave., Ste. 1B, Wilmington, 19806.* Tel: 302-573-3105; Fax: 302-573-3128.

Development Office—Mrs. DEBORAH FOLS, Dir., *Mailing Address: 1925 Delaware Ave., Ste. 2A, Wilmington, 19899.* Tel: 302-573-3120; Fax: 302-573-3128.

Annual Catholic Appeal—Mrs. DEBORAH FOLS, Dir., *Mailing Address: 1925 Delaware Ave., Ste. 2A, Wilmington, 19899.* Tel: 302-573-3120; Fax: 302-573-3128.

Catholic Charities Department

Catholic Charities—Mr. ALLAN J. DAUL, A.C.S.W., Diocesan Sec. & Exec. Dir., *Fourth St. and Greenhill Ave., P.O. Box 2610, Wilmington, 19805.* Tel: 302-655-9624; Fax: 302-655-9753. (Refer to separate listings in the Institutions for detailed information on Catholic Charities and related organizations.).

Advisory Groups to the Bishop

College of Consultors—Rev. Msgr. JOSEPH F. REBMAN, V.G., Sec.; Rev. Msgr. J. THOMAS CINI, V.G.; Rev. Msgr. PAUL J. TAGGART; Rev. Msgr. CLEMENT P. LEMON; Revs. MICHAEL A. ANGELONI; JOHN O. BARRES; JOHN P. HOPKINS; WILLIAM F. GRANEY, *P.O. Box 2030, Wilmington, 19899.*

Priests' Council—Rev. MICHAEL A. ANGELONI, Exec. Officer; Rev. Msgr. JOSEPH F. REBMAN, V.G., Sec., *P.O. Box 2030, Wilmington, 19899.* Tel: 302-573-3100.

Deans—Very Rev. JOSEPH R. MCMAHON, V.F.; Very Rev. MICHAEL F. SZUPPER, V.F.; Very Rev. CHARLES L. BROWN, III, V.F.; Very Rev. JOHN MASTERSON, V.F.; Very Rev. STEPHEN J. CONNELL, V.F.; Very Rev. THOMAS J. PETERMAN, V.F.; Very Rev. CLEMENS D. MANISTA, V.F.; Very Rev. JOHN J. KAVANAUGH, V.F.

Finance Council—Rev. Msgr. J. THOMAS CINI, V.G., Chm., *P.O. Box 2030, Wilmington, 19899.* Tel: 302-573-3118.

Parish Priest Consultors—Revs. RALPH L. MARTIN; RICHARD A. REISSMANN; RAYMOND L. FORESTER; DANIEL W. GERRES.

Clergy Personnel Committee—Rev. Msgr. CLEMENT P. LEMON, E.V.C., Chm., *P.O. Box 2030, Wilmington, 19899.* Tel: 302-573-3144; Fax: 302-573-3128.

Priests' Continuing Formation Committee—Rev. JOHN P. HOPKINS, Chm., *P.O. Box 2030, Wilmington, 19899.* Tel: 302-658-3801; Fax: 302-658-7617.

Council of Religious—Mailing Address: P.O. Box 2030, Wilmington, 19899. Tel: 302-573-3124; Fax: 302-573-3128.

Diocesan Board of Catholic Education—Mr. EDMUND F. GORDON, Sec., *Mailing Address: 1626 N. Union St., Wilmington, 19806.* Tel: 302-573-3130; Fax: 302-573-2393.

Building Committee—Mr. PAUL S. ADAMS, JR., Chm., Diocese of Wilmington; Rev. Msgr. J. THOMAS CINI, V.G., Episcopal Liaison, *P.O. Box 2030, Wilmington, 19899.* Tel: 302-573-3118; Fax: 302-573-3128.

Liturgical Commission—Very Rev. CHARLES L. BROWN, III, V.F., Chm., *1626 N. Union St., Wilmington, 19806.* Tel: 302-573-3137; Fax: 302-573-2393.

Office for Pro Life Activities—Mr. THOMAS JEWETT, Chm., *P.O. Box 2610, Wilmington, 19805.* Tel: 302-655-9624; Fax: 302-655-9753.

Pastoral Council—Mr. ANTHONY G. FLYNN, Exec. Officer;Rev. Msgr. JOSEPH F. REBMAN, V.G., Sec., *Mailing Address: P.O. Box 2030, Wilmington, 19899.* Tel: 302-573-3100; Fax: 302-573-3128.

Public Affairs Advisory Committee—Co-Chairs: Rev. Msgr. J. THOMAS CINI, V.G.; Rev. THOMAS E. HANLEY, *P.O. Box 2030, Wilmington, 19899.* Tel: 302-573-3118; Fax: 302-573-3128.

Real Estate Committee—Rev. Msgr. JOSEPH F. REBMAN, V.G., Chm., *P.O. Box 2030, Wilmington, 19899.* Tel: 302-573-3100; Fax: 302-573-3128.

Parish Social Ministry—Mrs. PEGGY HEINS, Dir., *Fourth St. & Greenville Ave., P.O. Box 2610, Wilmington, 19805.* Tel: 302-655-9624; Fax: 302-655-9753.

Respect Life Committee—Mr. THOMAS JEWETT, Chm., *Fourth St. & Greenhill Ave., Wilmington, 19805.* Tel: 302-655-9624; Fax: 302-655-9753.

Due Process Commission—Contact: Very Rev. THEODORE E. OLSON, Clerk, *P.O. Box 2030, Wilmington, 19899.* Tel: 302-573-3107; Fax: 302-573-3128.

Diocesan Corporations

Catholic Cemeteries, Inc.—Rev. Msgr. JOSEPH F. REBMAN, V.G., Treas., *P.O. Box 2506, Wilmington, 19805.* Tel: 302-737-2524.

Catholic Diocese of Wilmington, Inc.—A corporation sole under the laws of the State of Delaware. Rev. Msgr. J. THOMAS CINI, V.G., Sec. & Treas., *Mailing Address: P.O. Box 2030, Wilmington, 19899.* Tel: 302-573-3118. Office: *1925 Delaware Ave., Wilmington, 19899.*

Catholic Diocese Foundation—Rev. Msgr. J. THOMAS CINI, V.G., Treas., *P.O. Box 2030, Wilmington, 19899.* Tel: 302-573-3118.

Catholic Ministry to the Elderly, Inc.—Rev. Msgr. J. THOMAS CINI, V.G., Treas., *P.O. Box 2030, Wilmington, 19899.* Tel: 302-573-3118.

Catholic Press of Wilmington, Inc.—Rev. Msgr. J. THOMAS CINI, V.G., Vice Pres. & Treas., *P.O. Box 2208, Wilmington, 19899.* Tel: 302-573-3118.

Catholic Charities, Inc.—Mr. ALLAN J. DAUL, A.C.S.W., Sec., *Fourth St. & Greenhill Ave., P.O. Box 2610, Wilmington, 19806.* Tel: 302-655-9624.

Catholic Youth Organization, Inc.—Rev. JOHN P. HOPKINS, Sec., *Mailing Address: P.O. Box 2030, Wilmington, 19899.* Tel: 302-658-3801.

Children's Home, Inc.—Mr. ALLAN J. DAUL, A.C.S.W., Sec., *Fourth St. & Greenhill Ave., P.O. Box 2610, Wilmington, 19806.* Tel: 302-655-9624.

Diocese of Wilmington Schools, Inc.—Rev. Msgr. J. THOMAS CINI, V.G., Sec. & Treas., *1626 N. Union St., Wilmington, 19806.* Tel: 302-573-3118.

Seton Villa, Inc.—Mr. ALLAN J. DAUL, A.C.S.W., Sec., *Fourth St. & Greenhill Ave., P.O. Box 2610, Wilmington, 19806.* Tel: 302-655-9624.

Siena Hall, Inc.—Mr. ALLAN J. DAUL, A.C.S.W., Sec., *Fourth St. & Greenhill Ave., P.O. Box 2610, Wilmington, 19806.* Tel: 302-655-9624.

Activities

Apostleship of Prayer—Very Rev. JOSEPH R. MCMAHON, V.F., *P.O. Box 2030, Wilmington, 19899.* Tel: 302-654-5519.

Campaign for Human Development—Mr. ALLAN J. DAUL, A.C.S.W., Diocesan Dir., *Fourth St. & Greenhill Ave., P.O. Box 2610, Wilmington, 19806.* Tel: 302-655-9624.

Catholic Charismatic Renewal—Rev. STANLEY A. IANIERI, Chap., *St. John the Beloved, 907 Milltown Rd., Wilmington, 19808.* Tel: 302-999-0211.

Catholic Relief Services Inc.—Rev. Msgr. JOSEPH F. REBMAN, V.G., Temp. Dir., *P.O. Box 2030, Wilmington, 19899.* Tel: 302-573-3107.

Commission for the Catholic Missions Among the Colored People and the Indians—Rev. Msgr. JOSEPH F. REBMAN, V.G., Diocesan Dir., *P.O. Box 2030, Wilmington, 19899.* Tel: 302-573-3100; Fax: 302-573-3128.

Cursillo Movement—Deacons F. EDMUND LYNCH, *2008 N. Bancroft Pkwy., Wilmington, 19806.* Tel: 302-654-7471. ROBERT H. NORMOYLE, *7 Whaler Ln., 2726 Ocean Pines, Berlin, MD, 21811.* Tel: 410-641-7438. JANE H. LEITNER, Lay Dir., *1 Windflower Rd., Newark, 19711.*

Delmarva Catholic Network, Inc.—Mr. F. EUGENE DONNELLY, Contact Person, *P.O. Box 2030, Wilmington, 19899.* Tel: 302-573-3116.

Diocesan Healing Ministry—JEANNE CASEY, Lay Dir., *533 Waterford Dr., Hockessin, 19707.* Tel: 302-239-5982.

KAIROS Ministries, Inc.—Rev. GREGORY CORRIGAN, Contact Person, *P.O. Box 269, Claymont, 19703.* Tel: 302-798-2904.

Korean Catholic Community, Inc.—Rev. MICHAEL DONG HOON KIM, Chap. DANIEL YOON, Contact Person, *c/o Immaculate Heart of Mary Church, 4701 Weldin Rd., Wilmington, 19803.* Tel: 302-764-0357.

St. Thomas More Society—Rev. Msgr. PAUL J. TAGGART, Diocesan Liaison, *Mailing Address: P.O. Box 2030, Wilmington, 19899.* Tel: 302-655-3130.

St. Vincent dePaul Society—Mr. FRANK A. BUSH, Pres., *18 Vassar Ave., New Castle, 19720.* Tel: 302-328-9592.

Organizations With Which Diocese Has Liaison

**Birthright of Delaware, Inc.*—Mrs. MARY JO FROHLICH, Dir., *1311 N. Scott St., Wilmington, 19806.* Tel: 302-656-7080.

The Christian Council of DE & MD's Eastern Shore—Rev. PATRICIA MCCLURG, Pres., *E-62 Omega Dr., Newark, 19713.* Tel: 302-366-0595.

**Delaware Citizens for Life*—Mr. THOMAS JEWETT, Chm., *Fourth St. & Greenhill Ave., P.O. Box 2610, Wilmington, 19806.* Tel: 302-655-9624.

Delawareans United for Education—Rev. Msgr. J. THOMAS CINI, V.G., *P.O. Box 2030, Wilmington, 19899.* Tel: 302-573-3100.

**Jesus House*—Mr. CHRISTIAN MALMGREM, Dir. ANGELA MALMGREM, Assoc. Dir.; Deacon JOSEPH CONTE, Chap., *2500 Milltown Rd., Wilmington, 19808.* Tel: 302-995-6859.

Maryland Catholic Conference—(An agency of the Archdiocese of Baltimore, Washington and the Diocese of Wilmington); Mr. RICHARD J. DOWLING, Exec.

Dir., *309 Cathedral St., Baltimore, MD, 21201.* Tel: 301-322-0901. Rev. Msgr. PAUL J. TAGGART, Diocesan Liaison, *P.O. Box 2030, Wilmington, 19899.* Tel: 302-655-3130.

National Catholic Ministry to the Bereaved—Sr. PATRICIA HAMILL, S.S.J., Contact Person, *P.O. Box 2030, Wilmington, 19899.* Tel: 302-762-1229.

National Conference of Christians and Jews—Very Rev. CLEMENS D. MANISTA, V.F., *345 Bear-Christiana Rd., Bear, 19701.* Tel: 302-322-6430.

Operation Help, Inc.—Rev. PATRICK SHAULES, S.J., Pres. MARCINDA HAEDGE, Sec. & Treas., *P.O. Box 134, Hartly, 19953.* Tel: 302-492-8985; Fax: 302-492-8360.

Regina Coeli Society—Rev. JOHN F. HECKLE, O.S.F.S., Chap., *1801 N. Broom St., Wilmington, 19802.* Tel: 302-655-1592.

World Wide Marriage Encounter—Contact Persons: Rev. CHRIS LABARGE, *Immaculate Conception, Marydel, MD, 21649.* Tel: 410-482-8939. MIKE CAMPBELL; NANCY CAMPBELL, *218 S. Third St., Denton, MD, 21629.* Tel: 410-479-0154. MIKE GRANEY; MARIE GRANEY, *2305 Inwood Rd., Wilmington, 19810.* Tel: 302-475-0925.

CLERGY, PARISHES, MISSIONS AND PAROCHIAL SCHOOLS

DELAWARE, CITY OF WILMINGTON
(New Castle County)

1—CATHEDRAL OF ST. PETER, Rev. William B. Kauffman, Rector; Deacon George M. Taylor, Jr. In res., Rev. Msgr. Joseph F. Rebman, V.G.; Rev. Carlos R. Vazquez.
Res., 500 West St., 19801. Tel: 302-654-5920; Fax: 302-654-6850.
School—310 W. 6th St., 19801. Tel: 302-656-5234. Daughters of Charity of St. Vincent de Paul 3; Lay Teachers 13; Students 205.

2—ST. ANN, Very Rev. Joseph R. McMahon, V.F.; Rev. William D. Melnick; Deacon James J. Lafferty, Jr. Pastoral Assts: Sr. John Regina Lang, M.S.B.T.; Sr. Marie Bernadette Lang, M.S.B.T.
Res., 2013 Gilpin Ave., 19806. Tel: 302-654-5519; 652-0152; Fax: 302-654-5527.
School—Tel: 302-652-6567; Fax: 302-652-4156. Mr. Ronald Bogia, Prin.
Lay Teachers 10; Students 268.
Catechesis/Religious Programs—Tel: 302-654-8504. Kathy Hockmuth, D.R.E.
Students 141.

3—ST. ANTHONY OF PADUA (Italian), Revs. Mark A. Hushen, O.S.F.S.; Paul J. Campbell, O.S.F.S.; Charles C. Garst, O.S.F.S.; Bro. Michael J. Rosenello, O.S.F.S. In res., Revs. Roberto Balducelli, O.S.F.S.; Mario Bugliosi, O.S.F.S.
Res., 901 N. DuPont St., 19805. Tel: 302-421-3700; Fax: 302-421-3709.
School—9th & Scott Sts., 19805. Tel: 302-421-3743; Fax: 302-421-3796. Mr. Bernard J. Fisher, Prin.
Sisters of St. Francis of Philadelphia 2; Lay Teachers 21; Students 515.
High School—Padua Academy, 905 N. Broom St., 19805. Tel: 302-421-3739; Fax: 302-421-3748. Sr. Ann Michele Zwosta, O.S.F., Prin.
Sisters 3; Lay Teachers 47; Brothers 1; Students 601.
Convents—1710 W. 9th St., 19805. Tel: 302-421-3754.
Sisters 2; 1401 W. 10th St., 19806. Tel: 302-421-3739.
Sisters 6.
St. Anthony's Education Fund, Inc.—901 N. DuPont St., 19805. Tel: 302-421-3700.

4—CHRIST OUR KING, Rev. Leonard J. Kempski; Deacon William J. Maloney, Jr. Pastoral Assocs.: Mrs. Jane Bradley; Mrs. Mary Patricia Phelan.
Res., 2810 N. Monroe St., 19802. Tel: 302-762-4140; Fax: 302-762-8414.
School—28th & Madison Streets, 19802. Tel: 302-762-4031.
Sisters of St. Joseph 2; Sisters of St. Francis 5; Lay Teachers 9; Students 148.

5—ST. ELIZABETH, Revs. Charles C. Dillingham; Edward J. Fahey, Jr.; Andrew Molewski. In res., Revs. Howard T. Clark; James Nash.
Res., 809 S. Broom St., 19805-4296. Tel: 302-652-3626; Fax: 302-658-5957.
School—1500 Cedar St., 19805-4249. Tel: 302-655-8208; Fax: 302-655-5457. Sr. M. Gerard, O.S.B., Prin.
Sisters of St. Benedict 3; Lay Teachers 24; Students 576.
High School—Tel: 302-656-3369; Fax: 302-656-7513. Sr. Mary Ellen, O.S.B., Prin.
Sisters 5; Lay Teachers 29; Students 448.

6—ST. HEDWIG (Polish), Revs. Joseph J. Piekarski; Joseph E. Wharton.
Res., 408 S. Harrison St., 19805. Tel: 302-594-1400.
School—Linden & Harrison Sts., 19805. Tel: 302-594-1402; Fax: 302-594-1407.
Felician Sisters 1; Lay Teachers 14; Students 290.

7—ST. JOSEPH'S R.C. CHURCH OF WILMINGTON, INC., Franciscan Pastoral Team: Rev. Barry J. Langley, O.F.M.; Bro. David W. Schlatter, O.F.M., Pastoral Mod.
Church—1012 French St., 19801. Tel: 302-658-4535.
Res., 1010 W. 4th St., 19805.

8—ST. MARY OF THE IMMACULATE CONCEPTION, Rev. James F. Trainor.
Res., 1414 King St., 19801. Tel: 302-652-0743.
Church—6th & Pine Sts., 19801.

9—ST. PATRICK, Rev. James F. Trainor.
Res., 1414 King St., 19801. Tel: 302-652-0743.

10—ST. PAUL'S, Franciscan Pastoral Team: Revs. Lawrence J. Hayes, O.F.M.; William McIntyre, O.F.M., Pastoral Mod. In res., Rev. Barry Langley, O.F.M.; Bro. David Schlatter, O.F.M.
Res., 1010 W. 4th St., 19805. Tel: 302-655-6596; Fax: 302-655-7684.
School—3rd & Van Buren Sts., 19805. Tel: 302-656-1372. Mr. Richard Adamo, Prin.
Lay Teachers 12; Students 215.

11—SACRED HEART. Closed. For inquiries for sacramental records contact Cathedral of St. Peter. Tel: 302-654-5920; Fax: 302-654-6850.

12—ST. STANISLAUS KOSTKA (Polish), Rev. Edward J. Kaczorowski.
Mailing Address: P.O. Box 30110, 19805-7110.
Res., 901 E. 7th St., 19801. Tel: 302-571-0622; Fax: 302-571-1508.

13—ST. THOMAS, Rev. John L. Taggart.
Res., 301 N. Bancroft Pkwy., 19805. Tel: 302-658-5131.
School—201 Bayard Ave., 19805. Tel: 302-654-0746; Fax: 302-426-1738.
Lay Teachers 18; Students 264.

DELAWARE
OUTSIDE THE CITY OF WILMINGTON

Bear, New Castle Co., St. Elizabeth Ann Seton, Very Rev. Clemens D. Manista, V.F.; Rev. Joseph V. Bozzelli.
Res., 345 Bear-Christiana Rd., 19701. Tel: 302-322-6430.
Catechesis/Religious Programs—Tel: 302-322-8194. Sr. Paula Marie, O.S.F., D.R.E.
Students 450.

Bellefonte, New Castle Co., St. Helena (Wilmington P.O.), Revs. Stanley J. Russell; John A. Sarro; Deacon Edward A. Dunning.
Res., 602 Philadelphia Pike, Wilmington, 19809. Tel: 302-764-0325.
School—210 Bellefonte Ave., Willmington, 19809. Tel: 302-762-5595; Fax: 302-762-6329.
Sisters of St. Joseph 4; Lay Teachers 8; Students 211; Assistants 3.
Catechesis/Religious Programs—Tel: 302-762-4280. Sr. Mary Goodbody, S.S.J., D.R.E.
Students 131.
Convent—610 Philadelphia Pike, Willmington, 19809. Tel: 302-764-3427.

Bethany Beach, Sussex Co., St. Ann, Very Rev. John J. Masterson; Deacons Edward Brink; Robert Tracy.
Res., 691 Garfield Ave., P.O. Box 149, 19930. Tel: 302-539-6449; Fax: 302-539-0657.
Catechesis/Religious Programs—Students 332.

Brandywood, New Castle Co., Church of the Holy Child (Wilmington P.O.), Revs. James T. Kirk, Jr.; Francis P. Kenney; Deacon Samuel Torres. In res., Rev. Oscar H. Frundt.
Res., 2500 Naamans Rd., Wilmington, 19810. Tel: 302-475-6486; Fax: 302-475-3458.
Catechesis/Religious Programs—Tel: 302-475-5477. Marguerite Gomes, D.R.E.
Students 222.

Claymont, New Castle Co., Holy Rosary, Rev. David F. Murphy; Deacons Richard J. Maichle; Allen Wolf. In res., Revs. Joseph Narimattam (India); Gregory M. Corrigan.
Res., 3200 Philadelphia Pike, 19703. Tel: 302-798-2904; 798-2987; Fax: 302-798-3609.
School—3110 Philadelphia Pike, 19703. Tel: 302-798-5584.
Sisters of St. Joseph 4; Lay Teachers 22; Students 445.
Catechesis/Religious Programs—Tel: 302-798-0123. Sr. Ann Hughes, S.S.J., D.R.E.
Students 210.

Delaware City, New Castle Co., St. Paul, Rev. Philip L. Siry.
Res., 209 Washington St., 19706. Tel: 302-834-4321; Fax: 302-834-1757.

Dover, Kent Co., Holy Cross, Revs. Thomas E. Hanley; Ralph T. Castelow; Roger DiBuo; Deacon Anthony Vinciguerra.
Res., 631 S. State St., 19901. Tel: 302-674-5780; Fax: 302-674-5783. [CEM]
School—Tel: 302-674-5784. Ms. Marcia Bertino, Prin.
Lay Teachers 32; Students 584.
Catechesis/Religious Programs—Carmella Jones, D.R.E.
Students 750.

Elsmere, New Castle Co., Corpus Christi (Wilmington P.O.), Revs. Francis J. Rogers; Steven B. Giuliano; Deacon John G. Parisi. In res., Very Rev. Theodore E. Olson, J.V.
Res., 901 New Rd., Elsmere, Wilmington, 19805. Tel: 302-994-2922; Fax: 302-892-3315.
School—907 New Rd., Elsmere, Wilmington, 19805. Tel: 302-995-2231. Sr. Donna Desien, O.S.F., Prin.
Sisters 4; Lay Teachers 23; Students 576.
Catechesis/Religious Programs—Tel: 302-998-2864. Sr. Maryanne Bemiller, S.S.J., D.R.E.
Students 91.
Convent—912 New Rd., Elsmere, Wilmington, 19805. Tel: 302-994-5641.

Fairfax, New Castle Co., St. Mary Magdalen (Wilmington P.O.), Very Rev. John F. O'Brien; Revs. Stephen C. Lonek; Mark A. Kelleher; Deacons Richard Recce; Tony Catka.
Res., 7 Sharpley Rd., P.O. Box 7085, Wilmington, 19803. Tel: 302-652-6800; Fax: 302-652-6806.
School—9 Sharpley Rd., Wilmington, 19803. Tel: 302-656-2745. Barbara Wanner, Prin.
Lay Teachers 34; Students 522.
Catechesis/Religious Programs—Tel: 302-652-7141. Sheila Meara, D.R.E.
Students 203.

Garfield Park, New Castle Co., Holy Spirit (New Castle P.O.), Rev. Charles W. Wiggins.
Res., 12 Winder Rd., Garfield Park, New Castle, 19720. Tel: 302-658-1069.
School—Church Dr., New Castle, 19720. Tel: 302-658-5345.
Sisters 4; Lay Teachers 10; Students 254.

Georgetown, Sussex Co., St. Michael the Archangel, Rev. William F. Graney; Deacon Joseph Baker.
Res., 202 Edward St., 19947. Tel: 302-856-6451; Fax: 302-855-0671.
Mission—Millsboro, Sussex Co., Mary Mother of Peace, Rte. 24, 19966.

Greenville, New Castle Co., St. Joseph on the Brandywine, Very Rev. Stephen J. Connell; Rev. William P. Mathesius, D.Min.; Deacon F. Edmund Lynch.
Res., 10 Old Church Rd., Wilmington, 19807. Tel: 302-658-7017; Fax: 302-428-0639. [CEM]
Catechesis/Religious Programs—Tel: 302-656-7185. Joan Kornacki, D.R.E.
Students 190.

Hockessin, New Castle Co., St. Mary of the Assumption, Revs. Roy F. Pollard; Paul Calamari; Deacon John W. Freebery, Jr. In res., Rev. Msgr. Clement P. Lemon; Rev. Paul G. Mast.
Res., 7200 Lancaster Pike, P.O. Box 1240, 19707. Tel: 302-239-7100; Fax: 302-239-8219. [CEM]
Catechesis/Religious Programs—Tel: 302-239-3199. Mr. John D. Ryan, D.R.E.
Students 634.

Liftwood, New Castle Co., Immaculate Heart of Mary (Wilmington P.O.), Revs. Daniel W. Gerres; Norman P. Carroll; Sr. Brigid Clarahan, Pastoral Min. In res., Rev. Msgr. J. Thomas Cini; Rev. Msgr. John H. Dewson.
Res., 4701 Weldin Rd., Liftwood, Wilmington, 19803. Tel: 302-764-0357; Fax: 302-762-1510.
School—1000 Shipley Rd., Liftwood, Wilmington, 19803. Tel: 302-764-0977; Fax: 302-764-0375. Karen Himelreich, Prin.
Lay Teachers 29; Students 524.
Catechesis/Religious Programs—Tel: 302-762-5550. Sr. Natalie Dombrowski, D.R.E.
Students 294.

Middletown, New Castle Co., St. Joseph, Revs. Thomas A. Flowers; Joseph M.P.R. Cocucci.
Res., 115 Cleaver Farm Rd., Box 196, 19709. Tel: 302-378-5800; Fax: 302-378-5808. [CEM]
Catechesis/Religious Programs—Tel: 302-378-5802. Susan L. Long, D.R.E.
Students 700.
Mission—Chesapeake City, Cecil Co., St. Rose of Lima, Lock St., 21915. Tel: 410-885-5533.
Shrine—Warwick, St. Francis Xavier-Old Bohemia.

Milford, Kent and Sussex Cos., St. John the Apostle, Revs. Michael A. Angeloni; Christopher A. Kopec;

Deacons James D. Malloy; Anthony Bianco.
Res., 506 Seabury Ave., 19963-2217. Tel: 302-422-5123; Fax: 302-422-5720.
Catechesis/Religious Programs—Students 285.
Mission—Harrington, Kent Co., St. Bernadette, 109 Dixon, Harrington, 19952. Tel: 302-398-8269.

New Castle, New Castle Co., St. Peter, Revs. Arthur B. Fiore; James D. Hreha; Deacon James Handler.
Res., 35 E. 5th St., 19720. Tel: 302-328-2335; Fax: 302-328-0519. [CEM]
School—6th & Harmony Sts., 19720.
Lay Teachers 17; Students 286.
Catechesis/Religious Programs—Sr. Joan Lewis, S.S.J., D.R.E.
Students 105.

Newark, Newcastle Co., Parish of the Resurrection, Rev. Joseph J. Drobinski; Deacons Joseph J. Conte; Francis J. Huhn; Al Rose, Sr. Office: 3000 Videre Dr., Skyline Ridge, Wilmington, 19808. Tel: 302-368-0146; Fax: 302-368-3536.
Res., 119 Larkspur Rd., 19711. Tel: 302-737-3066.
Catechesis/Religious Programs—Jo Singer, D.R.E.
Students 296.

St. John the Baptist-Holy Angels, New Castle Co., Revs. Richard A. Reissmann; David A. Baumgartel; John A. Grasing; Deacon Hugh J. McCann.
Res., 82 Possum Park Rd., 19711. Tel: 302-731-2200; Fax: 302-731-2434. [CEM]
School—Tel: 302-731-2210.
Lay Teachers 25; Students 557.
Catechesis/Religious Programs—Tel: 302-731-2209.
Students 428.

St. Thomas More Oratory, New Castle Co. (Personal Parish for Students & Faculty of University of Delaware). Very Rev. Michael F. Szupper, V.F.; Rev. David F. Kelley.
Res., 155 Haines St., 19711. Tel: 302-368-5020; Fax: 302-368-2548.
Church—45 Lovett Ave., 19711. Tel: 302-368-4728.

Ogletown, New Castle Co., Holy Family (Newark P.O.), Revs. William E. Irwin; Joseph M. Laforge; Deacons William Murrian; John L. Seador. In res., Rev. Kenneth J. Martin.
Res., 15 Gender Rd., P.O. Box 8093, Newark, 19714. Tel: 302-368-4665; Fax: 302-368-4667.
Catechesis/Religious Programs—Tel: 302-368-8976. Melody Duffy, D.R.E.
Students 860.

Wilmington, New Castle Co., St. Catherine of Siena (Wilmington P.O.), Rev. John M. Hynes; Deacons John J. Falkowski, Jr.; Francis J. Staab.
Res., 2503 Centerville Rd., 19808. Tel: 302-633-4900; Fax: 302-633-4960.
School—Tel: 302-633-4902.
Lay Teachers 16; Students 300.
Catechesis/Religious Programs—2503 Centerville Rd., Tel: 302-633-4903. Sr. Theresa Cappelli, D.R.E.
Students 175.

Rehoboth, Sussex Co., St. Edmond, Rev. Philip P. Sheekey. In res., Rev. Patrick A. Brady; Deacon John A. Smith.
Office: 409 King Charles St., P.O. Box 646, Rehoboth Beach, 19971. Tel: 302-227-4550; Fax: 302-227-4557.
Res., 402 King Charles St., P.O. Box 646, Rehoboth Beach, 19771.
Catechesis/Religious Programs—Tel: 302-227-4553. Sr. Eileen Lally, M.H.S.H., D.R.E.
Students 257.
Mission—Lewes, Sussex Co., Shrine of St. Jude.

Seaford, Sussex Co., Our Lady of Lourdes, Revs. Patrick W. Gaffney, C.SS.R.; Pasquale Tremonte, C.SS.R.
Res., 528 Stein Hwy., P.O. Box 719, 19973. Tel: 302-629-3591. [CEM]
Catechesis/Religious Programs—Mrs. Debra Depta, D.R.E.
Students 322.

Sherwood Park, New Castle Co., St. John the Beloved, Very Rev. John J. Kavanaugh, V.F.; Revs. Stanley A. Ianieri; Frederick Kochan; Deacon James Haley.
Res., 907 Milltown Rd., Wilmington, 19808. Tel: 302-999-0211; Fax: 302-999-9184.
School—903 Milltown Rd., Wilmington, 19808. Tel: 302-998-5525.
Sisters of St. Francis of Philadelphia 2; Lay Teachers 30; Students 617.
Catechesis/Religious Programs—Tel: 302-994-7757. Pauline Berlingieri, D.R.E.
Students 425.

Smyrna, Kent Co., St. Polycarp, Rev. Ralph L. Martin.
Res., 135 Ransom Ln., 19977. Tel: 302-653-8279; Fax: 302-653-3509.
Catechesis/Religious Programs—Tel: 302-653-4101. Sr. Ellen Gerlach, D.R.E.
Students 195.

Wilmington Manor, New Castle Co., Our Lady of Fatima (New Castle P.O.), Revs. John J. Mink; Thomas J. Protack, S.T.L.; Deacon Joseph C. Romans.
Res., 801 Dupont Blvd., New Castle, 19720. Tel: 302-328-3431; 328-5773; Fax: 302-328-6318.
School—Tel: 302-328-2803; Fax: 302-328-5427.
Lay Teachers 29; Students 585.
Catechesis/Religious Programs—Tel: 302-328-0307. D.R.E.: Nancy-Jo Stryker; Patricia Walker.
Teachers 23; Students 261.

Woodcrest, New Castle Co., St. Matthew, Revs. Michael J. Cook; William M. Hazzard; William J. Klapps, (Retired U.S.N.); Deacon Harold Chalfant.
Res., 3 Curtis Ave., Wilmington, 19804. Tel: 302-633-5850; Fax: 302-633-6022.
School—One Fallon Ave., 19804. Tel: 302-633-5860. Sisters Servants of the Immaculate Heart of Mary 3; Lay Teachers 25; Students 525.

MARYLAND

Cambridge, Dorchester Co., St. Mary Refuge of Sinners, Rev. Bruce Byrolly.
Res., 1515 Glasgow St., Box 218, 21613. Tel: 410-228-4770. [CEM]
Catechesis/Religious Programs—Sr. Kathleen Winkleman, O.S.F., D.R.E.
Students 70.
Mission—Meekin's Neck, Dorchester Co., St. Mary, Star of the Sea. [CEM]

Centreville, Queen Anne Co., Mother of Sorrows, Rev. William J. Lawler.
Res., 303 Chesterfield Ave., 21617. Tel: 410-758-0140; Fax: 410-758-4083.
Catechesis/Religious Programs—Sr. Juliana Dischler, O.P., D.R.E.
Students 167.
Mission—Queenstown, Queen Anne Co., St. Peter, 5329 Ocean, Gateway, 21658.

Chester, Kent Island, Queen Anne Co., St. Christopher, Revs. Theodore Heyburn, C.SS.R.; Brendan Greany, C.SS.R.
Res., Box 660, Harbor Dr., Chester, 21619. Tel: 410-643-6220; Fax: 410-643-4055.
Catechesis/Religious Programs—Students 476.

Chestertown, Kent Co., Sacred Heart, Rev. Leonard J. Blakely.
Res., 508 High St., 21620. Tel: 410-778-3160; Fax: 410-810-0427. [CEM]
Catechesis/Religious Programs—Sr. Constance Davis, D.R.E.
Students 180.
Missions—Rock Hall, W. Main St., Kent Co., St. John; Betterton, Most Precious Blood. 1910 Main St.

Easton, Talbot Co., SS. Peter and Paul, Revs. Paul F. Jennings, Jr.; Edmund T. Coppinger.
Res., 215 Goldsborough St., 21601. Tel: 410-822-2344.
School—900 High St., 21601. Tel: 410-822-2275; Fax: 410-820-0136.
Lay Teachers 28; Students 506.
High School—Lay Teachers 19; Students 252.
Catechesis/Religious Programs—Students 265.
Missions—Cordova, Talbot Co., St. Joseph; St. Michaels, St. Michael, Lincoln Ave., 21663.

Elkton, Cecil Co., Immaculate Conception, Revs. Daniel J. McGlynn; Michael J. Carrier.
Res., 300 Maryland Ave., P.O. Box 345, 21922. Tel: 410-398-1100; Fax: 410-398-1175. [CEM]
School—455 Bow St., 21921. Tel: 410-398-2636; 398-4161.
Sisters of St. Francis of Philadelphia 2; Lay Teachers 17; Students 271.
Catechesis/Religious Programs—Tel: 410-392-3551. Sr. Grace Andrew, D.R.E.
Students 524.
Mission—North East, Cecil Co., St. Jude. 928 Turkey Point.

Galena, Kent Co., St. Dennis, Very Rev. Thomas J. Peterman, V.F.
Mailing Address: P.O. Box 249, 21635. Tel: 410-648-5145; Fax: 410-648-5767. [CEM]

Marydel, Caroline Co., Immaculate Conception, Rev. Christopher LaBarge.
Res., 522 Main St., Box 399, 21649. Tel: 410-482-7687; Fax: 410-482-7253.
Catechesis/Religious Programs—Tel: 410-482-8939.
Students 128.

Ocean City, Worcester Co., St. Mary, Star of the Sea, Revs. John P. Klevence; Bert Akers, S.J.; Deacons Robert Normoyle; Richard McCarthy.
Res., 208 S. Baltimore Ave., 21842. Tel: 410-289-9419.
Catechesis/Religious Programs—Tel: 410-289-7038; Fax: 410-289-4385. Mary Lou Jones, D.R.E.
Students 193.
Mission—Ocean City, Worcester Co., Holy Saviour, Philadelphia Ave. & 17th St., Ocean City, 21842. Tel: 410-289-3463.

St. Luke and St. Andrew, Revs. William J. Porter; Patrick J. O'Neil; Deacon Jack H. Campbell.
Office: 144th St. & Lighthouse Ave., P.O. Box 2117, 21842. Tel: 410-250-0300; 0301; Fax: 410-250-0417.
Res., 403 141st St., P.O. Box 2117, 21842. Tel: 410-250-0399; Fax: 410-250-0417.
Catechesis/Religious Programs—Tel: 410-250-0342. Mrs. Mary Anne Blatzheim, D.R.E.
Students 160.
Mission—Ocean Pines, St. John Neumann.

Perryville, Cecil Co., Church of the Good Shepherd, Rev. Raymond L. Forester.
Res., 828 Aiken Ave., 21903. Tel: 410-642-6534; Fax: 410-642-2234.
School—810 Aiken Ave., 21903. Tel: 410-642-6265; Fax: 410-642-6522.
Sisters 1; Lay Teachers 10; Students 187.
Missions—Port Deposit, Cecil Co., St. Teresa; Rising Sun, Cecil Co., St. Agnes.

Pocomoke City, Worcester Co., Holy Name of Jesus, Rev. Raymond F. Weisman; Deacon John Costello.
Res., 1913 Old Virginia Rd., P.O. Box 179, 21851. Tel: 410-957-1215; Fax: 410-957-1214.
Catechesis/Religious Programs—Patrick Russo, D.R.E.
Students 115.
Mission—Westover, Somerset Co., St. Elizabeth.

Ridgely, Caroline Co., St. Benedict, Rev. Robert E. Coine; Deacon Harold D. Jopp, Jr.
Res., 408 Central Ave., P.O. Box 459, 21660. Tel: 410-634-2253; Fax: 410-634-1997.
Catechesis/Religious Programs—Tel: 410-634-1921.
Students 194.
Mission—Denton, Caroline Co., St. Elizabeth, First St. & Franklin St. [CEM]

Salisbury, Wicomico Co., St. Francis De Sales, Very Rev. Charles L. Brown, III, V.F.; Revs. James B. Smith; Joseph Kandathiparampil; Deacons Carl R. Beers; J. David Shearer; Ron R. Siers; James Conner; David L. Rodgers.
Res., 514 Camden Ave., 21801. Tel: 410-742-6443; Fax: 410-742-9410.
School—500 Camden Ave., 21801. Tel: 410-749-6662; Fax: 410-749-6924. Sr. Betty Pflieger, R.S.M., Prin.
Lay Teachers 19; Students 289.
Catechesis/Religious Programs—Tel: 410-546-2908. Mrs. Michele Harris, D.R.E.
Students 474.
Convent—417 Wicomico St., 21801. Tel: 410-742-9343.
Mission—Delmar, Holy Redeemer, Bi-State Blvd. & Chestnut St., 21875.

Secretary, Dorchester Co., Our Lady of Good Counsel, Rev. Anthony F. Greco.
Res., 109 Willow Street, P.O. Box 278, 21664. Tel: 410-943-4300; Fax: 410-943-1357. [CEM]
Catechesis/Religious Programs—Sr. Juliana Dischler, O.P., D.R.E.
Students 87.
Mission—Bethlehem, Caroline Co., Holy Child, P.O. Box 278, Bethlehem, 21664.

Chaplains of Public Institutions

National Guard

WILMINGTON. *Delaware Air National Guard* 901 New Rd., 19805. Tel: 302-994-2922. Rev. Francis J. Rogers, Chap.
Delaware Army National Guard 4701 Weldin Rd., 19803. Chaplains: Revs. Daniel W. Gerres; John J. Mink; David F. Murphy.

Health Care

WILMINGTON. *A.I. du Pont Institute*. Rev. David A. Baumgartel, Chap., Tel: 302-764-0357.
St. Francis Hospital 7th St. & Clayton St., 19805. Tel: 302-421-4577. Revs. Joseph Narimattam; Jeremiah Brady, S.S.J.

DELAWARE CITY. *Governor Bacon Health Center*. Rev. Philip L. Siry, Chap., Tel: 302-834-4321.

ELSMERE. *Veteran's Hospital* 1601 Kirkwood Hwy., Tel: 302-994-2511. Chaplains: Revs. John P. Connery, O.S.F.S.; William J. Dougherty, O.S.F.S., Asst. Chap.

NEW CASTLE. *Delaware State Hospital*. Rev. Carlos R. Vazquez, Chap.

NEWARK. *Christiana Care Health System* 4755 Ogleton-Stanton Rds., Tel: 302-733-1900; 733-1280. Chaplains: Revs. John Finn, O.S.F.S.; Mark Kopacz; Joseph J. McKenna, O.S.F.S.; Edward Glapiak.

PERRY POINT, MD. *Veterans Admin*. Revs. John J. Abraham Tel: 410-642-2411; Stephen E. Jeselnick; Jeffrie S. Reynolds.

SMYRNA, MD. *Delaware Home & Hospital for the Chronically Ill*. Rev. Ralph L. Martin, Chap., Tel: 302-653-8279.

Correctional Facilities

WILMINGTON. *Ferris School and Bridge House.* Deacon George M. Taylor, Jr., Chap., Tel: 302-995-2350.
Gander Hill Correctional Center. Rev. Daniel W. Gerres, Chap., Tel: 302-764-0357.

SMYRNA, MD. *Delaware Correctional Center.* Deacon George Taylor, Chap., Tel: 302-653-9261 Ext. 487.

WESTOVER, MD. *Eastern Correctional Institution.* Rev. Edward M. Aigner, Jr., Chap., Tel: 410-651-9000; 651-2054 (Res.).

Campus Ministry

CHESTERTOWN, MD. *Washington College* Sacred Heart, 508 High St., 21620. Tel: 410-778-3160. Rev. Leonard J. Blakely, Chap.

DOVER. *Wesley College.* Very Rev. Michael F. Szupper, Chap., Tel: 302-368-4728.

NEWARK. *University of Delaware* St. Thomas More Oratory, 45 Lovett Ave., 19711. Tel: 302-368-4728. Chaplains: Very Rev. Michael F. Szupper, Ph.D., Dir. Campus Ministry; Rev. David F. Kelley, Assoc. Dir.

PRINCESS ANNE, MD. *University of Maryland, Eastern Shore* P.O. Box 490, 21853. Tel: 410-651-2054. Rev. Edward M. Aigner, Chap.

SALISBURY, MD. *Salisbury State College.* Vacant. St. Francis de Sales, 514 Camden Ave., 21801. Tel: 410-742-6443.

Apostleship of the Sea:
Reverend Fathers—
Kauffman, William B., Chap., Cathedral of St. Peter, 500 West St., Wilmington, De 19801. Tel: 302-654-5920

Nursing Homes:
Reverend Fathers—
Storck, Edward J., Chap., Victorian Sq., 1504-2 N. Broom St., #17, Wilmington, DE 19806-3048. Tel: 302-428-1415

Special or Other Diocesan Assignment:
Reverend Monsignors—
Schierse, Paul J., 5029 Sylvia Rd., Drexel Hill, PA 19026
Reverend Fathers—
Clark, Howard T., 809 S. Broom St., Wilmington, DE 19805
Glapiak, Edward, 3 Towne Estates, Apt. G3, Wilmington, DE 19805
Hopkins, John P., Dir. Catholic Youth Organizations & Youth Ministry, 803 N. Broom St., Wilmington, DE 19805. Tel: 302-658-3800
Kopacz, Mark W., P.O. Box 7173, Newark, DE 19704
McDermott, Michael J., 2200 Limestone Rd., Wilmington, DE 19808
Richardson, James E., 2001 Eden Rd., Wilmington, DE 19810. Tel: 302-529-7280

On Duty Outside the Diocese:
Reverend Monsignors—
Koper, Francis B., SS. Cyril and Methodius Seminary, Orchard Lake, MI 48033
Reverend Fathers—
Barres, John O., Casa Santa Maria, Via Dell'Umilta, 30, Rome, 00187 Italy
Brubaker, George J., Catholic Relief Services, 209 W. Fayette St., Baltimore, MD 21201-3403
Delaney, James T., Mt. St. Mary's College, Emmitsburg, MD 21727
Gallagher, Michael J., Trinity College, Theology Dept., 125 Michigan Ave., Washington, DC 20017
McMahon, Kevin T., St. Charles Borromeo Seminary, 1000 E. Wynnewood Rd. Overbrook, Philadelphia, PA 19096
Pagano, Bernard T., St. Mary of Mt. Virgin, 190 Sanford St., New Brunswick, NJ 08901
Turley, Sean F., SS. Michael and James, Haunton near Tamworth, Staffordshire, B799HL (1848), Great Britain

---

Military Chaplains:
Reverend Fathers—
Mullen, Owen J., 637 Canby Rd., Wahiawa, HI 96786
Papp, Christopher, Chap., USAF, 11707 Andriana Maria, San Antonio, TX 78253
Volmi, Dennis G., 3197A Minuteman St., Hill AFB, UT 84056

Absent on Sick Leave:
Reverend Fathers—
Casari, Michael T., P.O. Box 2030, Wilmington, DE 19899
Jackson, James M., P.O. Box 2030, Wilmington, DE 19899
McCloskey, Daniel J., 294 Merrifield Ave., Oceanside, NY 11572

Retired:
Reverend Monsignors—
Dewson, John H., Immaculate Heart of Mary, 4701 Weldin Rd., Wilmington, DE 19803
Taggart, Paul J., 1401 Pennsylvania Ave., #1411, Wilmington, DE 19806
Reverend Fathers—
Brady, Patrick A., St. Edmond, P.O. Box 646, Rehoboth Beach, DE 19971
Breen, Stephen B., Vianney House, 905 Milltown Rd., Wilmington, DE 19808
Carley, Edward B., 302 Condo Park Blvd., Laurel St., Santurce, PR 00913
Clarahan, Eugene F., Vianney House, 905 Milltown Rd., Wilmington, DE 19808
DeLuca, Francis G., Fahey Court, 100 Pastime Dr., Apt. 307, Syracuse, NY 13208
Dempster, Douglas W., P.O. Box 370, Marydel, MD 21649
Eckrich, James P., 773 Paper Mill Rd., Newark, DE 19711
Frundt, Oscar H., Church of the Holy Child, 2500 Naamans Rd., Wilmington, DE 19810
Gardocki, Thomas F., 4620 Sylvanus Dr., Wilmington, DE 19803
Gomolski, Joseph T., 241 Balboa Dr., Poinciana, FL 34758
Gorski, Alex F., 1401 Pennsylvania Ave., Apt. 1205, Wilmington, DE 19806
Harney, Peter, Manor Care Nursing Home, 5651 Limestone Rd., Wilmington, DE 19808
Horgan, Joseph C., Vianney House, 905 Milltown Rd., Wilmington, DE 19808
Jennings, William E., 2303 Inglewood Dr., Wilmington, DE 19803
Klapps, William J., Caravel Farms, 260 Benjamin Blvd., Bear, DE 19701
McGann, L. Philip, 5541 Bay Ave., Ocean City, NJ 08226
Paris, Charles W., Box 752, Toms River, NJ 08754
Perkins, Russell H., P.O. Box 2437, Manteo, NC 27954
Plokhooy, Christopher H., Vianney House, 905 Milltown Rd., Wilmington, DE 19808
Power, Walter D., Golden Legend Senior Residence, 24 Misty Meadow Ln., Port Deposit, MD 21904
Rhodes, George V., P.O. Box 5964, Wilmington, DE 19808

Permanent Deacons:
Baker, Joseph G., St. Michael the Archangel, Georgetown, DE
Becker, John J., (Retired)
Beers, Carl (NYC), St. Francis de Sales, Salisbury, MD
Bianco, Anthony A., St. John the Apostle, Milford, DE
Brink, Edward J., St. Ann, Bethany Beach, DE
Campbell, Jack H., (Retired)
Catka, Tony E., St. Mary Magdalen and Family Life Bureau, Wilmington, DE
Chalfant, Harold F., St. Matthew, Wilmington, DE
Conner, James, St. Frances de Sales, Salisbury, MD
Conte, Joseph J., Parish of the Resurrection, Newark, DE
Costello, John L., Holy Name of Jesus, Pocomoke City, MD
Dunning, Edward A., St. Helena and Marian Devotions, Wilmington, DE
Falkowski, John J., Jr., St. Catherine of Siena, Wilmington, DE
Freebery, John W., Jr., St. Mary of the Assumption, Hockessin, DE
Haley, James J., St. John the Beloved, Wilmington, DE
Handlir, James, St. Peter, New Castle, DE
Huhn, Francis J., Parish of the Resurrection, Newark, DE
Jopp, Harold D., Jr., St. Benedict's, Ridgely, MD
Lafferty, James J., Jr., St. Ann's, Wilmington, DE
Lynch, Edmund F., St. Joseph on the Brandywine, Greenville, DE
Maichle, Richard J., Sr., Holy Rosary, Claymont, DE
Malloy, James D., St. John the Apostle, Milford, DE
Maloney, William J., Jr., Christ Our King, Wilmington, DE
McCann, Hugh J., (Retired)
McCarthy, Richard, St. Mary Star of the Sea, Ocean City, MD
Murrian, William J., Holy Family, Ogletown, DE
Normoyle, Robert H., St. Mary Star of the Sea, Ocean City, MD
O'Connor, Howard J., Holy Family, Newark, DE
Parisi, John G., Corpus Christi, Wilmington, DE
Passwaters, Arcy A., Our Lady of Lourdes, Seaford, DE
Recce, Richard L., St. Mary Magdalen, Wilmington, DE
Rodgers, David F., St. Francis de Sales, Salisbury, MD
Romans, Joseph C., Our Lady of Fatima, New Castle and Christiana Div., Christiana Care Health System, Newark, DE
Rose, Albert F., Parish of the Resurrection, Seton Villa, Siena Hall, Newark, DE
Seador, John L., Holy Family, Newark, DE
Shearer, John David, St. Francis de Sales, Popular Hill Correctional Center, Salisbury, MD
Siers, Ronald (L), St. Francis de Sales, Salisbury, MD
Smith, John A., St. Edmund, Rehoboth Beach, DE
Snow, Austin M., Jr., Immaculate Heart of Mary, Wilmington, DE; Chap., Seton Villa & Siena Hall, Wilmington, DE
Staab, Francis J., St. Catherine of Siena, Wilmington, DE
Taylor, George M., Jr., Cathedral of St. Peter & Ferris School, Wilmington, DE
Torres, Samuel, Church of the Holy Child, Wilmington, DE
Tracy, Robert, St. Ann, Bethany Beach, DE
VanBourgondien, Cornelius J., SS Peter and Paul, Easton, MD
Vinciguerra, Anthony P., Holy Cross, Dover, DE
Wolf, Allen S., Claymont, DE, Holy Rosary; Christiana Div., Christiana Care Health System, Newark, DE

INSTITUTIONS LOCATED IN THE DIOCESE

[A] HIGH SCHOOLS, DIOCESAN

WILMINGTON. *St. Mark's High School,* Pike Creek Rd., 19808. Tel: 302-738-3300. Dr. John C. Monnig, Prin.; Rev. Gregory M. Corrigan. Priests 1; Sisters 5; Lay Teachers 101; Students 1,563.

WYOMING. *St. Thomas More Academy,* P.O. Box 521, 19934. Tel: 302-736-3560; Fax: 302-736-3561. Dr. Ralph A. Leitner, Prin.

[B] HIGH SCHOOLS, PRIVATE

WILMINGTON. *Salesianum School,* 1801 N. Broom St., 19802. Tel: 302-654-2495; 655-1592; Fax: 302-654-7767. Revs. Thomas J. McGee, O.S.F.S., Prin.; John J. Fisher, O.S.F.S., Asst. Prin & Supr.; Robert D. Kenney, O.S.F.S.; Thomas B. Curran, Pres.; Charles M. Chamberlain, O.S.F.S.; Kevin M. Nadolski; Stephen E. Shott, O.S.F.S.; R. Douglas Smith, O.S.F.S.; Thomas J. Tucker, O.S.F.S.; J. Christian Beretta; Paul E. Burke, O.S.F.S.; John P. Connery, O.S.F.S.; John A. Kowalewski; Stanley R. Drupieski, O.S.F.S.; John F. Heckel, O.S.F.S.; Joseph J. McKenna, O.S.F.S.; John P. Spellman, O.S.F.S.; Vincent de Paul Burke, O.S.F.S.; John M. Mokluk, O.S.F.S.; Bro. Joseph G. Schodowski, O.S.F.S. Priests 13; Brothers 1; Lay Teachers 61; Boys 1006.

Ursuline Academy of Wilmington, DE, Inc., 1106 Pennsylvania Ave., 19806. Tel: 302-658-7158; Fax: 302-658-4297.
Web site: www.ursuline.org
(Coed Grades Early Childhood-3, All Girls Grades 4-12). Ms. Angela M. Boyle, Pres. Lay Faculty 72; Ursuline Nuns 1; Students 675.

CLAYMONT. *Archmere Academy,* 3600 Philadelphia Pike, 19703. Tel: 302-798-6632; Fax: 302-798-7290.
E-mail: generale-mailbox@archmere.claymont.de.us
Web site: www.archmere.claymont.de.us
Coed College Prepatory High School. Rt. Rev. Robert F. Kelly, O.Praem., Prior; Revs. Timothy F. Mullen, O.Praem., Headmaster; James D. Bagnato, O.Praem.; Jeffrey T. Cesarone, O.Praem.; Michael T. Collins, O.Praem.; Paul J. DeAntoniis, O.Praem.; Blaise P. Krautsack, O.Praem.; Brian A. Zielinski, O.Praem.; Paul R. Fisher, O.Praem. Priests 8; Lay Teachers 47; Students 487.

RIDGELY, MD. *The Benedictine School Habilitation Center,* 21660. Tel: 410-634-2115. Dixie Hughlett, Coord. Sisters 3; Lay Personnel 32; Students 42. Open Community Program MD/DE. Ages 21 and older. Tel: 410-634-1990. Eleanor Sweeney, Coord. Students 62; Lay Teachers 17.

[C] ELEMENTARY SCHOOLS, PRIVATE

WILMINGTON. *Saint Edmond's Academy.* (Grades 4-8), 2120 Veale Rd., 19810. Tel: 302-475-5370; Fax: 302-475-2256.
E-mail: academy@magpage
Web site: www.magpage.com/~academy
Bros. Michael A. Smith, C.S.C., Headmaster; Joseph Ash, C.S.C.; Edward Quintal, C.S.C.; James DeTemple, C.S.C.; David Parrish, C.S.C.; Thomas

Meany, C.S.C.; Thomas Durney, C.S.C.; Stanislao Esposito, C.S.C. Brothers of Holy Cross 8; Lay Teachers 18; Boys 261.

CHILDS, MD. *Mount Aviat Academy*. (Grades 1-8), 21916. Oblate Sisters of St. Francis de Sales. Sr. John Marie, O.S.F.S., Prin. Sisters 7; Lay Teachers 11; Students 210.

Oblate Sisters' Kindergarten and Nursery, Villa Aviat, 399 Childs Rd., 21916-0085. Tel: 410-398-3699. Oblate Sisters of St. Francis de Sales 2; Lay Teachers 2; Students 50.

RIDGELY, MD. *The Benedictine School for Exceptional Children*, 14299 Benedictine Ln., 21660. Tel: 410-634-2112. Sisters of St. Benedict. Sr. Jeanette Murray, O.S.B., Dir.; Rev. Francis J. Rinaldi, O.S.F.S., Chap. Sisters 9; Lay Personnel 10; Students 117.

Benedictine School for Exceptional Children Foundation, Inc., 14299 Benedictine Ln., 21660. Sr. Jeannette Murray, O.S.B., Dir. Sisters 1; Lay Staff 3.

[D] DIOCESAN CATHOLIC CHARITIES PROGRAM

WILMINGTON. *Catholic Charities, Inc.*, 2601 W. 4th St., P.O. Box 2610, 19805-0610. Tel: 302-655-9624; Fax: 302-655-9753. Mr. Allan J. Daul, A.C.S.W., Diocesan Sec. & Exec. Dir.; Ms. Barbara Grieco, M.C., M.B.A., Deputy Dir. & Dir. Children's Services; Katrina Furlong, B.A., Div. Dir.; Mr. Albert F. Rose, Jr., M.B.A., Dir. Finance; Ms. Donna Connor, B.A., Dir. Devel. Staff 180; Individuals Served 57,333; Fuel Program 31,333. New Castle. Tel: 302-654-6474. Sussex. Tel: 302-856-6200. Kent. Tel: 302-674-1782.

Social Service Counseling Centers. 4th St. & Greenhill Ave., P.O. Box 2610, 19805-0610. Tel: 302-655-9624.

Dover Office. 442 S. New St., Dover, 19904. Tel: 302-674-1600.

Georgetown Office. 600 N. Dupont Hwy., Georgetown, 19947. Tel: 302-856-9578.

Salisbury Office. 1405 Wesley Dr., Salisbury, MD, 21801. Tel: 410-749-1121.

Children's Services (adoption and foster care). 4th St. & Greenhill Ave., P.O. Box 2610, 19805-0610. Tel: 302-655-9624. Ms. Neomi Litonjua, L.C.S.W., Supvr.

Family & Individual Services (including Family Life Bureau). 4th St. & Greenhill Ave., P.O. Box 2610, 19805-0610. Tel: 302-655-9624. Mr. Thomas R. Jewett, M.C., Admin.

Community and Family Support Services.

Crisis Alleviation. 4th St. & Greenhill Ave., P.O. Box 2610, 19805-0610. Tel: 302-654-6473. Sharon Truitt, Contact Person, 121 W. Loockerman St., Dover, 19904. Tel: 302-674-4016; Fax: 302-674-4018. Betty Fean, Contact Person; Katrina Furlong, Div. Dir., New Castle Co. Tel: 302-654-6474. Kent Co. Tel: 302-674-1782. Sussex Co. Tel: 302-856-6200.

Energy Assistance. New Castle Co. Tel: 302-654-9295. Kent Co. Tel: 302-674-1782. Sussex Co. Tel: 302-856-6310.

Immigration & Refugee Program. 4th St. and Greenhill Ave., P.O. Box 2610, 19805-0610. Tel: 302-654-6460. Mabel N. Sturgeon, Contact Person.

Catholic Charities Thrift Shop. 1320 E. 23rd St., 19802. Tel: 302-764-2717. Diane Kelly, Mgr.

Catholic Charities Thrift Shop. 2000 W. 4th St. (4th St. & Union Sts.), 19805. Tel: 302-655-9300. Lorraine Shannon, Mgr.

Child & Adult Care Food Program. 442 S. New St., P.O. Box 495, Dover, 19904. Tel: 302-674-1600; 1-800-239-2839. Donna Costilow, Contact Person, New Castle Co. Tel: 302-366-0392. Hanne Dawson-Holt, Contact Person, Sussex Co. Tel: 302-856-9578. Pat Miller, Contact Person.

Addiction Services.

Center for Pastoral Care. Fifth St. & Greenhill Ave., P.O. Box 2610, 19805-0610. Tel: 302-656-0651. Eugene Dyszlewski, M.Ed., M.Div., Dir.

Residential Services. 2307 Kentmere Pkwy., 19806. Tel: 302-656-2183. Barbara Grieco, M.C., M.B.A., Deputy Dir. & Dir. of Children's Services.

Siena Hall, Inc. 2307 Kentmere Pkwy., 19806. Tel: 302-656-2183. Barbara Grieco, M.C., M.B.A., Deputy Dir. & Dir. of Children's Services.

Seton Villa, Inc. 800 Bellevue Rd., 19809. Tel: 302-762-2982. Barbara Grieco, M.C., M.B.A., Deputy Dir. & Dir. of Children's Services.

Children's Home. 2901 Green St., Claymont, 19703. Tel: 302-798-0601. Barbara Grieco, M.C., M.B.A., Deputy Dir. & Dir. of Children's Services.

Casa San Francisco. 127 Broad St., P.O. Box 38, Milton, 19968. Tel: 302-684-8694; Fax: 302-684-2808. Ms. Marion Bau, M.A., Mgr.; Pat Saez, Contact Person.

Delaware Day Treatment Center. 1156 W. Walker Rd., Dover, 19904. Tel: 302-674-8211. Valleree R. Roach, M.S.W., Program Dir., Georgetown Office, 231 S. Race St., Georgetown, 19947. Tel: 302-855-9520. Valleree R. Roach, M.S.W., Prog. Dir.

Seton Center. 30632 Hampden Ave., P.O. Box 401, Princess Anne, MD, 21853. Tel: 410-651-9608.

Office for Parish Social Ministry. 4th St. & Greenhill Ave., P.O. Box 2610, 19805-0610. Tel: 302-655-9624. Margaret P. Heins, Dir.

[E] RESIDENCES FOR CHILDREN

WILMINGTON. *Seton Villa, Inc.*, 800 Bellevue Rd., 19809. Tel: 302-762-2982
For a complete listing, refer to the Special Care Facilities section.

Siena Hall, Inc., 2307 Kentmere Pkwy., 19806. Tel: 302-656-2183
For a complete listing, refer to the Special Care Facilities section.

CLAYMONT. *Children's Home, Inc.*, 2901 Green St., 19702. Tel: 302-798-0601
For a complete listing, refer to the Special Care Facilities section.

[F] OTHER WELFARE AGENCIES

(Not under jurisdiction of Department of Social Concerns)

WILMINGTON. *Home of Divine Providence, Inc.-Bayard House*, 300 Bayard Ave., 19805. Tel: 302-654-1184
For a complete listing, refer to the Special Care Facilities section.

Ministry of Caring, Inc., 506 N. Church St., 19801-4812. Tel: 302-652-5523; Fax: 302-652-1919
For a complete listing, refer to the Special Care Facilities section.

NEWARK. *Our Lady of Grace Home for Children, Inc.*, 487 E. Chestnut Hill Rd., 19713. Tel: 302-738-4658; 737-6650
For a complete listing, refer to the Special Care Facilities section.

RIDGELY, MD. *St. Martin's Ministries*, 14259 Benedictine Ln., 21660. Tel: 410-634-2497
For a complete listing, refer to the Special Care Facilities section.

[G] HOMES FOR AGED

WILMINGTON. *The Antonian*, 1701 W. 10th St., 19805. Tel: 302-421-3758
For a complete listing, refer to the Special Care Facilities section.

Franciscan Health System / Care at Wilmington, 801 N. Broom St., 19806. Tel: 302-652-3861
For a complete listing, refer to the Special Care Facilities section.

St. Patrick's House, Inc., 115 E. 14th St., 19801. Tel: 302-654-6908
For a complete listing, refer to the Special Care Facilities section.

Vianney House, 905 Milltown Rd., 19808. Tel: 302-636-0200
For a complete listing, refer to the Special Care Facilities section.

HOCKESSIN. *Franciscan Health System / Care at Brackenville*, 100 St. Clare Dr., 19707. Tel: 302-234-5420
For a complete listing, refer to the Special Care Facilities section.

NEWARK. *Jeanne Jugan Residence*, 185 Salem Church Rd., 19713
For a complete listing, refer to the Special Care Facilities section.

Marydale Retirement Village, 135 Jeandell Dr., 19713. Tel: 302-368-2784
For a complete listing, refer to the Special Care Facilities section.

[H] GENERAL HOSPITALS

WILMINGTON. *St. Francis Hospital, Inc.*, 7th and Clayton Sts., P.O. Box 2500, 19805-0500. Tel: 302-575-8300
For a complete listing, refer to the Hospitals section.

[I] MONASTERIES AND RESIDENCES OF PRIESTS AND BROTHERS

WILMINGTON. *Brothers of Holy Cross, St. Edmond's Academy*, 2120 Veale Rd., 19810. Bro. Joseph W. Ash, C.S.C., Dir. Religious. Brothers 8.

Capuchin Franciscan Friars, St. Francis Renewal Center, 1901 Prior Rd., 19809. Tel: 302-798-1454; Fax: 302-798-3360. Revs. Cyprian Rosen, O.F.M.Cap., Guardian, Dir.; Thomas Pietrantonio, O.F.M.Cap., Vicar; Bro. Nicholas Mormando, O.F.M.Cap.

DeSales House, 1600 Brinckle Ave., 19806. Tel: 302-656-4342. Revs. William R. Gore, O.S.F.S., Supr.; John A. Finn, O.S.F.S.; William J. Dougherty, O.S.F.S.; John J. Hurley, O.S.F.S.; William H. Juergens, O.S.F.S.; Joseph D. Bowler, O.S.F.S.; William J. Keech, O.S.F.S.; Richard D. Leone, O.S.F.S. Priests 8.

Oblates of St. Francis De Sales. Residence of the Provincial, 2200 Kentmere Pkwy., P.O. Box 1452, 19899. Tel: 302-656-8529. Very Rev. Joseph G. Morrissey, O.S.F.S., Prov.; Revs. Edward T. Fitzpatrick, O.S.F.S., Dir. Personnel; Richard R. De Lillio, O.S.F.S., Dir. Devel.; Joseph P. Jocco, O.S.F.S., Dir. Vocations; Francis J. Hanlon, O.S.F.S., Dir. Senior Oblates; Robert A. Mancini, O.S.F.S., Treas.; Walter R. Dean, O.S.F.S.; Anthony J. Pinizzotto, O.S.F.S.; George S. Salzmann, O.S.F.S.; William J. Hultberg, O.S.F.S. Military Chaplains: Revs. John F. Friel, O.S.F.S.; James J. MacNew, O.S.F.S.; Stanley J. Dombrowski, O.S.F.S. Priests 13.

St. Felix Friary, 119 N. Jackson St., 19805-3670. Tel: 302-652-7010; Fax: 302-652-8943. Rev. Ronald Giannone, O.F.M.Cap., Guardian; Bro. Kevin O'Loughlin, O.F.M.Cap., Vicar. Brothers 4.

CHILDS, MD. *Oblates of St. Francis De Sales*. Retirement and Retreat Center, 1120 Blue Ball Rd., 21916. Tel: 410-398-3040; Fax: 410-398-0116. Rev. John W. Brennan, O.S.F.S., Supr. In res. Rev. Joseph A. Baird, O.S.F.S.; Rev. John J. Bradunas, O.S.F.S.; Revs. George J. Brownholtz, O.S.F.S.; Francis T. Christof, O.S.F.S.; Edward J. Friel, O.S.F.S.; George W. Martyn, O.S.F.S.; John J. Conmy, O.S.F.S.; Hugh E. Duffy, O.S.F.S.; Joseph T. Dunn, O.S.F.S.; James E. Cassidy, O.S.F.S.; James V. O'Neill, O.S.F.S.; Thomas F. Malloy, O.S.F.S.; Vincent J. Kowalewski, O.S.F.S.; Louis R. McCartney, O.S.F.S.; James J. McGuire, O.S.F.S.; Michael B. Donovan, O.S.F.S.; Hugh J. McKenna, O.S.F.S.; Anthony T. Schelich, O.S.F.S.; Joseph E. Stafford, O.S.F.S.; Joseph E. Woods, O.S.F.S. Brothers 8.

CLAYMONT. *Immaculate Conception Priory of the Canons Regular of Premontre*, 3600 Philadelphia Pike, 19703-0103. Tel: 302-792-2791. Rt. Rev. Robert F. Kelly, O.Praem., Prior; Revs. Timothy F. Mullen, O.Praem, Headmaster; James D. Bagnato, O.Praem.; Walter J. Burke, O.Praem.; Jeffrey T. Cesarone, O.Praem.; Francis J. Ciliberti, O.Praem.; Michael T. Collins, O.Praem.; Paul J. DeAntoniis, O.Praem., Sub Prior; John A. D'Antonio, O.Praem.; Mark D. Falcone, O.Praem., Vocation Dir.; Paul R. Fisher, O.Praem.; Martin A. Frigo, O.Praem.; Blaise P. Krautsack, O.Praem.; Edward J. Smith, O.Praem., Treas.; Brian A. Zielinski, O.Praem. Priests 15.

Norbertine Fathers of Delaware, Inc., 2600 Philadelphia Pike, 19703-0130. Tel: 302-792-2791. Rt. Rev. Robert F. Kelly, O.Praem., Prior; Rev. Edward J. Smith, O.Praem, Canonry Treas.

SEAFORD. *Missionary Fraternity of Mary, USA, Ltd.*, 340 Pine St., 19973. Tel: 302-629-5705; Fax: 302-629-7403. Revs. Ruben Albano Soto, F.M.M.; Juan Vincente Hidalgo, F.M.M.

[J] CONVENTS AND RESIDENCES FOR SISTERS

WILMINGTON. *Casa de San Jose - Franciscan Sisters of Our Lady of the Sacred Heart*, 601 N. Jackson St., 19805. Tel: 302-654-8200. Sr. Ann Marie Gonzales, O.S.F., Supr. Sisters 3.

Monastery of St. Veronica Giuliani. (Strict Enclosure), 816 Jefferson St., 19801. Tel: 302-654-8727; Fax: 302-652-1919. Capuchin Poor Clare Nuns of Delaware. Mother Maria del Carmen Quiroz, O.S-.C.Cap., Abbess; Rev. Ronald Giannone, O.F.M.Cap., Chap. Sisters 13; Postulants 2; Novices 1.

Our Lady of Peace Convent, 1801 W. 8th St., 19805. Tel: 302-426-1809. The Sisters of St. Francis of Philadelphia 3.

St. Benedict, 113 Canterbury Dr., 19803. Tel: 302-478-3754. Sisters of St. Benedict 4.

St. Francis Convent, 701 N. Rodney St., 19805. Tel: 302-652-8489. The Sisters of St. Francis of Philadelphia 11.

St. Mark's Faculty Residence, 2503 Pike Creek Rd., 19808-3615. Tel: 302-738-5440. Intercommunity Sisters 18.

Ursuline Academy Inc., The, 1104 Pennsylvania Ave., 19806. Tel: 302-656-5890. Sr. Julia Dennehy, O.S.U., Supr. Sisters 15.

CHILDS, MD. *Villa Aviat Convent*, 399 Childs Rd., 21916. Tel: 410-398-3699. Oblate Sisters of St. Francis de Sales. Sr. Anne Elizabeth, O.S.F.S., Supr. Sisters 14.

EASTON, MD. *Eastern Shore Co-op*, 304 Prospect Ave., 21601. Tel: 410-820-7437. Sisters 3.

NEW CASTLE. *Our Lady of Fatima Convent*, 100 W. Grant Ave., 19720. Tel: 302-328-2752. Sr. Anna May Coll, Supr. The Sisters of St. Francis of Philadelphia (Semi-retired) 10.

PRINCESS ANNE, MD. *Seton Center, Sisters of Charity*. (Convent Station), P.O. Box 401, 21853. Tel: 410-651-9608. Sisters 4; Assisted 15,277.

RIDGELY, MD. *St. Gertrude's Monastery, Motherhouse and Novitiate of the Sisters of St. Benedict*, 14259 Benedictine Ln., 21660. Tel: 410-634-2497; Fax: 410-634-1410. Sr. Mary Paul McLaughlin, O.S.B., Prioress. In res. Rev. Francis J. Rinaldi, O.S.F.S., Chap. Sisters 42.

SALISBURY, MD. *Joseph House, Little Sisters of Jesus & Mary.*, P.O. Box 1755, 21802. Tel: 410-543-1645. Sr. Mary Elizabeth Gintling, Dir. Sisters 6; Postulants 1.

[K] SECULAR INSTITUTES

WILMINGTON. *St. Francis De Sales Secular Institute*, 3127 Charing Cross, 19808. Tel: 302-234-8616. Mary H. Robinson, Formation Dir. U.S.A. & Contact; Joan Bereswill, Dir. U.S.A. Tel: 703-591-5196.

Secular Franciscan Order. (San Damiano Fraternity), P.O. Box 234m, 19732. Tel: 302-762-3713. Mr. Andrew Zampini, S.F.O., Min.

Secular Franciscan Order. (St. Patrick's Fraternity), 1901 Prior Rd., 19809. Tel: 302-328-2350. Loretta Juras, S.F.O., Local Min.; Bro. Nicholas Mormando, O.F.M.Cap., Spiritual Asst.

CHESTERTOWN, MD. *Secular Order of Discalced Carmelites.* (Annunciation Community), 201 N. Queen St., 21620. Tel: 410-778-0557. Mrs. Bernadette M. Stenger, Pres.; Bro. Bryan Paquette, O.C.D., Spiritual Asst.

DOVER. *Secular Institute of the Two Hearts*, P.O. Box 1719, 19901. Tel: 302-678-3246. Agnes Frias, Supr.

SALISBURY, MD. *Secular Order of Discalced Carmelites.* (Mary, Mother of Life Community), 631 Ridge Rd., 21811. Tel: 410-742-1777. Mrs. Marianne Chapin; Bro. Bryan Paquette, O.C.D., Spiritual Asst.

[L] RETREAT HOUSES, GENERAL

WILMINGTON. *St. Francis Renewal Center*, 1901 Prior Rd., 19809. Tel: 302-798-1454; Fax: 302-798-3360. Revs. Cyprian Rosen, O.F.M.Cap., Guardian, Dir.; Thomas Pietrantonio, O.F.M.Cap., Vicar; Bro. Nicholas Mormando, O.F.M.Cap. Priests 2; Brothers 1.

CHILDS, MD. *De Sales Centre*, 1120 Blue Ball Rd., 21916. Tel: 410-398-3383. Rev. Michael B. Donovan, O.S.F.S., Dir.

[M] RETREAT HOUSES, WOMEN

CHILDS, MD. *Oblate Sisters of St. Francis de Sales*, Villa Aviat, 21916. Tel: 410-398-3699.

RIDGELY, MD. *Berg Retreat Center*, St. Gertrude's Monastery, 14259 Benedictine Ln., 21660. Tel: 410-634-2497. Benedictine Sisters.

[N] INFORMATION CENTERS

WILMINGTON. *The Franciscan Center*, 833 N. Market St., 19801-3078. Tel: 302-656-0711. Bro. David W. Schlatter, O.F.M., Dir.; Rev. Barry J. Langley, O.F.M., Asst. Dir.

[O] NEWMAN CENTERS

CHESTERTOWN, MD. *Washington College Newman Center*, Sacred Heart, 508 High St., 21620. Tel: 410-778-3160. Rev. Leonard J. Blakely, Chap.

NEWARK. *Univ. of Delaware Newman Center*, St. Thomas More Oratory, 45 Lovett Ave., 19711. Tel: 302-368-4728.
E-mail: szuptmo@udel.edu
Very Rev. Michael F. Szupper, Ph.D., Chap. & Diocesan Dir. Campus Ministry; Rev. David F. Kelly, M.Div.

Delmar Organization of Catholic Students - DOCS. Kimberly S. Zitzner, B.A., Dir.

Salisbury State College, St. Francis de Sales, 514 Camden Ave., Salisbury, MD, 21801. Tel: 410-742-6443. University of Maryland Eastern Shore, P.O. Box 490, Princess Anne, MD, 21853. Tel: 410-651-2054. Rev. Edward M. Aigner, Chap.

Wesley College. Tel: 302-368-4728. Very Rev. Michael F. Szupper, Chap.

Washington College, 508 High St., Chestertown, MD, 21260. Tel: 410-778-3160. Rev. Leonard J. Blakely, Chap.

Wesley College Newman Center, St. Thomas More Oratory, 45 Lovett Ave., 19711. Tel: 302-368-4728.
E-mail: szuptmo@udel.edu

RELIGIOUS INSTITUTES OF MEN REPRESENTED IN THE DIOCESE

For further details refer to the corresponding bracketed number in the Religious Institutes of Men or Women section.

[0600]—*Brothers of the Congregation of Holy Cross.* (Eastern Province).—C.S.C.

[0900]—*Canons Regular of Premontre.*—O.Praem.

[0470]—*The Capuchin Friars.* (Prov. of the Stigmata).—O.F.M.Cap.

[0740]—*Congregation of Marian of the Immaculate Conception.*—M.I.C.

[0520]—*Franciscan Friars.* (Holy Name Prov.).—O.F.M.

[0690]—*Jesuit Fathers and Brothers.*—S.J.

[0855]—*Missionary Fraternity of Mary.*—F.M.M.

[0853]—*Missionary Servants of Christ.*—M.S.C.

[]—*Oblate Apostles of the Two Hearts.*—O.A.T.H.

[0920]—*Oblates of St. Francis de Sales.*—O.S.F.S.

[1070]—*Redemptorist Fathers.* (Baltimore, MD).—C.SS.R.

[0700]—*St. Joseph's Society of the Sacred Heart.* (Baltimore, MD).—S.S.J.

[1240]—*Servites.*—O.S.M.

[0560]—*Third Order Regular of Saint Francis.*—T.O.R.

RELIGIOUS INSTITUTES OF WOMEN REPRESENTED IN THE DIOCESE

[0100]—*Adorers of the Blood of Christ.*—A.S.C.

[0230]—*Benedictine Sisters of Pontifical Jurisdiction.*—O.S.B.

[3765]—*Capuchin Poor Clare Sisters.*—O.S.C.Cap.

[]—*Carmelite Sisters of Charity of Vedruna.*—C.C.V.

[0760]—*Daughters of the Charity of St. Vincent de Paul.*—D.C.

[1070-09]—*Dominican Sisters.*—O.P.

[1070-11]—*Dominican Sisters.*—O.P.

[1170]—*Felician Sisters.*—C.S.S.F.

[1180]—*Franciscan Sisters of Allegheny, New York.*—O.S.F.

[]—*Franciscan Sisters of Our Lady of the Sacred Heart.*—O.S.F.

[2331]—*Little Sisters of Jesus and Mary.*—L.S.J.M.

[2340]—*Little Sisters of the Poor.*—L.S.P.

[2720]—*Mission Helpers of the Sacred Heart.* (Prov. of Baltimore).—M.H.S.H.

[2790]—*Missionary Servants of the Most Blessed Trinity.*—M.S.B.T.

[3060]—*Oblates Sisters of St. Francis de Sales.*—O.S.F.S.

[3230]—*Poor Handmaids of Jesus Christ.*—P.H.J.C.

[2575]—*Religious Sisters of Mercy of the Americas.* (Baltimore, MD; Merion, PA).—R.S.M.

[2970]—*School Sisters of Notre Dame.*—S.S.N.D.

[0590]—*Sisters of Charity of Saint Elizabeth, Convent Station.* (Southern, Western Provs.).—S.C.

[0990]—*Sisters of Divine Providence.* (St. Peter Prov.).—C.D.P.

[2990]—*Sisters of Notre Dame.*—S.N.D.

[3780]—*Sisters of Saints Cyril and Methodius.*—SS.C.M.

[1650]—*Sisters of St. Francis of Philadelphia.*—O.S.F.

[3840]—*Sisters of St. Joseph of Carondelet.* (Prov. of St. Louis).—C.S.J.

[3893]—*Sisters of St. Joseph of Chestnut Hill, Philadelphia.*—S.S.J.

[3890]—*Sisters of St. Joseph of Peace.*—C.S.J.P.

[3730]—*Sisters of the Order of St. Basil the Great.*—O.S.B.M.

[2160]—*Sisters, Servants of Immaculate Heart of Mary.*—I.H.M.

[4060]—*Society of the Holy Child Jesus.*—S.H.C.J.

[4110]—*Ursuline Nuns (Roman Union).* (Eastern Prov.).—O.S.U.

DIOCESAN CEMETERIES

WILMINGTON. *All Saints*, Box 2506, 19805. Tel: 302-737-2524; Fax: 302-737-4091. Office, Kirkwood Hwy., 19805. Mark A. Christian, Exec. Dir.; Thomas J. Kane, Supt.

Cathedral, Box 2506, 19805. Tel: 302-656-3323; Fax: 302-656-1069. Office, 2400 Lancaster Ave., 19805. Mark A. Christian, Exec. Dir. & Supt.

NECROLOGY

† Iocco, Vincent V., New Castle, DE, St. Peter the Apostle. —Died July 11, 1997.

Diocese of Winona

(Dioecesis Winonensis)

Most Reverend

LORAS J. WATTERS, D.D.

Retired Bishop of Winona; ordained June 7, 1941; appointed Titular Bishop of Fidoloma and Auxiliary Bishop of Dubuque June 23, 1965; consecrated August 26, 1965; transferred to Winona January 8, 1969; retired October 14, 1986; appointed Apostolic Administrator October 14, 1986. *Res., 618 Forest, Apt. D, Pacific Grove, CA, 93950.* Tel.: 408-373-3715.

Pastoral Center: 55 W. Sanborn St., P.O. Box 588, Winona, MN, 55987. Tel.: 507-454-4643; Fax: 507-454-8106.

ESTABLISHED NOVEMBER 26, 1889.

Square Miles 12,282.

Comprises the Counties of Winona, Wabasha, Olmsted, Dodge, Steele, Waseca, Blue Earth, Watonwan, Cottonwood, Murray, Pipestone, Rock, Nobles, Jackson, Faribault, Martin, Freeborn, Mower, Fillmore and Houston in the State of Minnesota.

For legal titles of parishes and diocesan institutions, consult the Pastoral Center.

STATISTICAL OVERVIEW

Personnel	
Retired Bishops	1
Priests: Diocesan Active in Diocese	72
Priests: Active Outside Diocese	7
Priests: Retired, Sick or Absent	50
Number of Diocesan Priests	129
Religious Priests in Diocese	13
Extern Priests in Diocese	4
Ordinations:	
Diocesan Priests	1
Permanent Deacons in Diocese	3
Total Brothers	22
Total Sisters	496
Parishes	
Parishes	118
With Resident Pastor:	
Resident Diocesan Priests	63
Resident Religious Priests	3
Without Resident Pastor:	
Administered by Priests	47
Administered by Women Religious	5
Missions	1
Pastoral Centers	2
Closed Parishes	4
Professional Ministry Personnel:	
Sisters	15
Lay Ministers	50
Welfare	
Catholic Hospitals	2
Total Assisted	62,617
Health Care Centers	1
Total Assisted	4,622
Homes for the Aged	7
Total Assisted	771
Day Care and Extended Day Care Centers	3
Total Assisted	7,845
Specialized Homes	3
Total Assisted	145
Special Centers for Social Services	5
Total Assisted	10,283
Residential Care of Disabled	1
Total Assisted	35
Other Institutions	1
Total Assisted	93
Educational	
Seminaries, Diocesan	1
Students from This Diocese	3
Students from Other Diocese	29
Diocesan Students in Other Seminaries	6
Total Seminarians	9
Colleges and Universities	1
Total Students	1,462
High Schools, Diocesan and Parish	4
Total Students	1,195
Elementary Schools, Diocesan and Parish	28
Total Students	5,429
Catechesis/Religious Education:	
High School Students	5,339
Elementary Students	12,209
Total Students Under Catholic Instruction	25,643
Teachers in the Diocese:	
Priests	11
Sisters	22
Lay Teachers	322
Vital Statistics	
Receptions into the Church:	
Infant Baptism Totals	1,890
Adult Baptism Totals	83
Received into Full Communion	254
First Communions	2,189
Confirmations	2,029
Marriages:	
Catholic	445
Interfaith	371
Total Marriages	816
Deaths	1,129
Total Catholic Population	148,445
Total Population	528,303

Former Bishops—Rt. Rev. JOSEPH B. COTTER, D.D., cons. Dec. 27, 1889; died June 28, 1909.—Rt. Rev. PATRICK R. HEFFRON, D.D., cons. May 19, 1910; died Nov. 23, 1927.—Most Rev. FRANCIS M. KELLY, D.D., cons. June 9, 1926; transferred to Diocese of Winona, Feb. 10, 1928; transferred to Titular See of Nasal, Oct. 17, 1949; died June 24, 1950.—Most Rev. EDWARD A. FITZGERALD, D.D., cons. Sept. 12, 1946; Auxiliary Bishop of Dubuque; transferred to Winona, Oct. 20, 1949; retired and transferred to the Titular See of Zerta, Jan. 8, 1969; died March 30, 1972.—Most Rev. LORAS J. WATTERS, D.D., ord. June 7, 1941; appt. Titular Bishop of Fidoloma and Auxiliary Bishop of Dubuque, June 23, 1965; cons. Aug. 26, 1965; transferred to Winona, Jan. 8, 1969; retired Oct. 14, 1986; appt. Apostolic Administrator, Oct. 14, 1986.—Most Rev. JOHN G. VLAZNY, D.D., ord. Dec. 20, 1961; appt. Auxiliary Bishop of Chicago and Titular Bishop of Stagno, Oct. 31, 1983; cons. Dec. 13, 1983; appt. Bishop of Winona, May 19, 1987; installed July 29, 1987; appt. Archbishop of Portland, Oct. 28, 1997.

Vicar General—VACANT.

Chancellor—Mr. JOHN M. VITEK, *55 W. Sanborn St., P.O. Box 588, Winona, 55987.* Tel: 507-454-4643; Fax: 507-454-8106.

Notary—Rev. WILLIAM M. BECKER, *IHM Seminary, 700 Terrace Heights, Winona, 55987.* Tel: 507-457-7373.

Deans—Rev. EDWARD F. MCGRATH, Winona; Rev. DALE E. TUPPER, Rochester; Rev. THOMAS J. JENNINGS, Austin-Albert Lea; Rev. JOHN M. KUNZ, Mankato; Rev. GERALD C. KOSSE, Worthington.

Diocesan Consultors—Rev. Msgr. ROY E. LITERSKI; Rev. Msgr. J. RICHARD FEITEN; Revs. DONALD W. GRUBISCH; MICHAEL J. HOEPPNER; THOMAS J. JENNINGS; JOSEPH L. KEEFE; JOHN M. KUNZ; GERALD A. MAHON; JAMES A. MCCAULEY; DONALD P. SCHMITZ.

Finance Council—Rev. MICHAEL J. HOEPPNER; Mr. JOHN M. VITEK, Chancellor; Mr. ROBERT HOODECHECK; Mrs. SHARON WAGNER; Mr. JOHN BROADWATER, Finance Officer; Rev. ROBERT G. MEYER; Mrs. KATE KELLY; Mr. ROCKY SIELER; Sr. JOAN BLANK, O.S.F.

Diocesan Board of Administration—(Civil Corporation): Rev. MICHAEL J. HOEPPNER; Mr. JOHN M. VITEK, Sec.; Mr. ROBERT HOODECHEK; Mrs. SHARON WAGNER.

Judicial Officers—Censors of Books and Periodicals: Revs. WILLIAM M. BECKER; PATRICK J. RUGEN; JACK L. KROUGHDue Process Panel: Dr. MATT VETTER, *Saint Mary's University of MN, Winona, 55987.*

Marriage Tribunal—55 W. Sanborn St., P.O. Box 588, Winona, 55987. Tel: 507-454-4643.

Vicar Judicial—Rev. EDWARD F. MCGRATH, J.C.L.

Adjutant Vicar Judicial—Vacant.

Regional Tribunal Judge—Rev. Msgr. FRANK W. KLEIN, J.C.L.

Regional Tribunal Defender of the Bond—Rev. DONALD P. SCHMITZ, M.A.

Defenders of the Bond—Revs. DONALD J. SCHMITZ; JACK KROUGH; WILLIAM J. KULAS, J.C.L.

Advocates—Revs. DONALD F. CONNELLY; GERALD C. KOSSE; PAUL HEITING; Mr. THOMAS HEALY.

Promoter of Justice—Rev. DONALD P. SCHMITZ.

Notaries—Ms. KAREN EICH; Mrs. CAROL NEPPL.

Diocesan Offices and Directors

All Diocesan Offices and Directors are located at the Pastoral Center (unless otherwise indicated), 55 W. Sanborn St., P.O. Box 588, Winona, 55987. Tel: 507-454-4643; Fax: 507-454-8106. Please send all matrimonial dispensations and permissions to the Tribunal office.

Curia—

Chancellor and Pastoral Planning—Mr. JOHN M. VITEK.

Finances—Mr. JOHN BROADWATER.

Catholic Charities—Mr. LLOYD W. LENARZ, *111 Market St., P.O. Box 379, Winona, 55987.* Tel: 507-454-2270; Fax: 507-457-3027.

Social Action—Mr. TODD GRAFF.

Communications - "The Courier"—Mr. IVAN KUBISTA.

Office of RCIA, Liturgy and Evangelization—Sr. JEAN ERSFELD, S.S.N.D.

Education, Human Resources and Schools—Mrs. P. J. THOMPSON.

Education, Religious Education—Sr. JOANNE LOECHER, O.S.F.

Youth and Family Life—Mrs. ALMA RICHARD.

Ministry Formation—Mr. BRADLEY HARMON.

Additional Ministries—

Annual Diocesan Appeal—Mrs. DIANE M. ZITTEL, Dir.

Director of Clergy Education—Rev. MICHAEL J. HOEPPNER.

Ecumenism—Rev. WILLIAM M. BECKER, *IHM Seminary, 700 Terrace Heights, Winona, 55987.* Tel: 507-457-7373.

Propagation of the Faith—Rev. DONALD P. SCHMITZ, *Church of the Resurrection, 1600 11th Ave. S.E.,*

Rochester, 55904-5499. Tel: 507-288-5528; Fax: 507-252-0763.

Vicar for Hispanic Ministry—Rev. HILARY R. BRIXIUS, *Church of St. James, 623 4th St., St. James, 56081.* Tel: 507-375-3542.

Coordinator of Diocesan Health Ministry—Rev. JAMES F. BURYSKA, Diocesan Dir. of Hospitals, *St. Mary's Hospital, 1216 2nd St. S.W., Rochester, 55902.* Tel: 507-255-5551; Fax: 507-255-3125.

Advisory Bodies—

Presbyteral Council—

Bishop—VACANT.

Ex Officio—Rev. MICHAEL J. HOEPPNER.

Deans—Rev. EDWARD F. MCGRATH, Winona; Rev. DALE E. TUPPER, Rochester; Rev. THOMAS J. JENNINGS, Austin-Albert Lea; Rev. JOHN M. KUNZ, Mankato; Rev. GERALD C. KOSSE, Worthington.

Elected Members—Revs. RICHARD M. COLLETTI; GERALD W. CONWAY; JOHN W. OZBUN; CHARLES I. COLLINS; DONALD W. ZENK; DONALD J. SCHMITZ; THEODORE J. HOTTINGER, S.J.; MARK C. MCNEA; GREGORY P. LEIF; ANDREW J. BEERMAN.

Executive Committee of the Presbyteral Council—Revs. DALE E. TUPPER, Vice Pres. RICHARD M. COLLETTI, Sec./Treas. WILLIAM M. BECKER.

Appointed Members—Rev. Msgr. ROY E. LITERSKI; Revs. DONALD P. SCHMITZ; JOSEPH P. PETE; DONALD W. GRUBISCH; WILLIAM M. BECKER.

Priestly Assignments Committee—Revs. MICHAEL J. HOEPPNER; RICHARD M. COLLETTI; DONALD P. SCHMITZ.

Diocesan Pastoral Council—Rev. MICHAEL J. HOEPPNER; Mr. JOHN M. VITEK, Chancellor/Dir., Pastoral Planning; Sr. JANET WERMERSKIRCHEN, S.S.N.D.; Mrs. MAUREEN ANDERSON; Mr. DANIEL BRODERICK; Mr. DAVE DUNN; Mrs. NANCY MCLOONE; Mrs. PATRICIA MCCORMICK; Sr. SHIRLEY SCHMITZ, O.S.F.; Bro. JOSEPH MARTIN; Mr. LARRY DOSE; Rev. JOSEPH P. PETE; Miss FRANCES JANOUS; Mrs. DEANN KAPLAN; Ms. SYDELLE MCCABE; Mrs. FRANCES GREBIN; Mr. ANTONIO CASILLAS; Ms. ROBIN HART.

Priests' Pension Board— Rev. Msgr. ROY E. LITERSKI; Revs. GERALD W. CONWAY; PAUL E. NELSON; Bro. LOUIS DETHOMASIS; Mr. TIMOTHY GEISLER; Mr. JOHN BROADWATER, Treas.; Mr. THOMAS CROWLEY.

Commission on Sacred Liturgy—Rev. JOHN M. SAUER, Exec. Chm.; Sr. JEAN ERSFELD, S.S.N.D., Dir. (Ex Officio); Mr. RICHARD BREITER; Rev. RICHARD M. COLLETTI; Sr. ROSEMARIE WHITEHEAD, O.S.F.; Rev. GERALD C. KOSSE; Mrs. SUSAN SHEPHARD; Mr. MARK KIEFFER; Mr. JAMES STOLPA; Ms. BETSY DIERCHS; Ms. JACKIE OLSON.

Vocations Council—Revs. JAMES P. STEFFES, Dir. JAMES C. BERNING; MARTIN T. SCHAEFER; RUSSELL G. SCEPANIAK; THOMAS A. LOOMIS; Sr. JUDI ANGST, O.S.F.; Sr. DIANE PERRY, S.S.N.D.; Mrs. PAMELA J. THOMPSON; DICK BREITER; THERESE BREITER.

Winona Diocesan Organizations-Agencies-Programs

Archives—Mr. JOHN M. VITEK, *Pastoral Center, 55 W. Sanborn St., P.O. Box 588, Winona, 55987.* Tel: 507-454-4643; Fax: 507-454-8106.

Boy Scouts—Mrs. ALMA RICHARD, Coord.

Chaplain—Rev. JAMES C. BERNING. Tel: 507-836-8030.

Chairman-Catholic Committee on Scouting, Diocese of Winona—Mr. WILLIAM SMALL, *118 Main St., Fairmont, 56031.* Tel: 507-235-3874.

Catholic Charities—Mr. LLOYD W. LENARZ, Dir., *111 Market St., P.O. Box 379, Winona, 55987.* Tel: 507-454-2270; Fax: 507-457-3027.

Catholic Charities Board—Mrs. ANN MERCHLEWITZ, Chm.

Regional Offices—

Albert Lea—315 E. Clark St., Box 890, Albert Lea, 56007. Tel: 507-377-3664.

Austin—2001 2nd Ave. N.W., Austin, 55912. Tel: 507-433-3062.

Mankato—423 W. 7th St., Mankato, 56001. Tel: 507-387-5586.

Owatonna—512 S. Elm St., Owatonna, 55060. Tel: 507-455-2008.

Rochester—117 E. Center St., Ste. B, Rochester, 55904. Tel: 507-287-2047; Fax: 507-287-2050.

Winona—111 Market St., P.O. Box 379, Winona, 55987. Tel: 507-454-2270; Fax: 507-457-3027.

Worthington—1118 Oxford St., Worthington, 56187. Tel: 507-376-9757.

Social Action Office—TODD GRAFF, *111 Market St., P.O. Box 379, Winona, 55987.* Tel: 507-454-2270; Fax: 507-457-3027.

Parish Social Ministry—TODD GRAFF.

Rural Life Ministry—TODD GRAFF.

Campaign for Human Development—TODD GRAFF.

Catholic Relief Services—TODD GRAFF.

Developmentally Challenged—TODD GRAFF.

HIV-AIDS Ministry—TODD GRAFF.

Disaster Relief Services—TODD GRAFF.

Hispanic Ministry—Sr. ROSE ANN FICKER, S.S.N.D., *1051 Linn Ave., Owatonna, 55060.* Tel: 507-451-0516.

Refugee Resettlement—117 E. Center St., Ste. B, Rochester, 55904. Tel: 507-287-2047; Fax: 507-287-2050.

Cemeteries—Mr. JOHN M. VITEK.

Charismatic Renewal—Sr. MARY ANN SCHAENZER, S.S.N.D., *R.R. 1 Box 339, Mankato, 56001-9752.* Tel: 507-345-2989 (Office); 507-345-5880 (Home).

Council of Catholic Women—Mrs. ELIZABETH BOLER, Pres., *308 10th Ave., S.E., Rochester, 55904.* Tel: 507-289-0656. Rev. THOMAS J. HARGESHEIMER, Diocesan Moderator. Tel: 507-451-4854.

Diocesan Self-Insurance Plan—Gallagher-Bassett Insurance Service, 111 Riverfront, P.O. Box 30127, Winona, 55987. Tel: 507-454-6452.

Hospitals—Rev. JAMES F. BURYSKA, *St. Mary's Hospital, Rochester, 55901.* Tel: 507-282-4425.

Girl Scouts—Mrs. ALMA RICHARD, Coord., *55 W. Sanborn St., P.O. Box 588, Winona, 55987.* Tel: 507-454-4643; Fax: 507-454-8106.

Marriage Preparation/Enrichment—Mrs. ALMA RICHARD, *55 W. Sanborn St., P.O. Box 588, Winona, 55987.* Tel: 507-454-4643; Fax: 507-454-8106.

Respect Life—Mrs. ALMA RICHARD, *55 W. Sanborn St., P.O. Box 588, Winona, 55987.* Tel: 507-454-4643; Fax: 507-454-8106.

Sexual Misconduct Policy Issues—Mr. JOHN M. VITEK, *Pastoral Center, 55 W. Sanborn St., P.O. Box 588, Winona, 55987.* Tel: 507-454-4643; Fax: 507-454-8106.

CLERGY, PARISHES, MISSIONS AND PAROCHIAL SCHOOLS

CITY OF WINONA
(Winona County)

1—CATHEDRAL OF THE SACRED HEART (1950), Revs. John M. Sauer, Rector; Michael C. Ruthenberg, O.P. In res., Rev. Cyril Fabian, O.P.
Res., 360 Main St., 55987-3299. Tel: 507-452-4770; Fax: 507-454-1974. [JC]
School—See listings under Centralized Catholic Schools.
Catechesis/Religious Programs—Students 186.

2—ST. CASIMIR'S (1906), Rev. James W. Hennessy.
Res., 624 W. Broadway, 55987-2721. Tel: 507-452-3434. [JC]
Catechesis/Religious Programs—Tel: 507-454-7311.
Students 116.

3—ST. JOHN NEPOMUCENE (1888) (Bohemian). Attended by St. Stanislaus, Winona.
625 E. Fourth St., 55987-4297. Tel: 507-452-5430.
Catechesis/Religious Programs—602 E. Fifth St., 55987.
Students 46.

4—ST. MARY'S (1911), Rev. Joseph L. Keefe.
Res., 1303 W. Broadway, 55987-2395. Tel: 507-452-5656. [JC]
School—See listings under Centralized Catholic Schools.
Catechesis/Religious Programs—Tel: 507-452-4585.
Students 187.

5—ST. STANISLAUS (1871) (Polish), Rev. Robert G. Meyer.
Res., 625 E. Fourth St., 55987-4297. Tel: 507-452-5430.
School—See listings under Centralized Catholic Schools.
Catechesis/Religious Programs—602 E. Fifth St., 55987. Tel: 507-452-3766.
Students 152.

OUTSIDE THE CITY OF WINONA

Adams, Mower Co., Sacred Heart (1886) (German), Rev. Gregory P. Leif.
Res., 412 Main St., P.O. Box 352, 55909-9998. Tel: 507-582-3321. [CEM]
School—(Grades 1-8). Tel: 507-582-3120. Sr. Yvonne Elskamp, Prin.
Sisters 1; Lay Teachers 7; Students 130.
Catechesis/Religious Programs—Tel: 507-582-3321.
Students 43.
Convent—Tel: 507-582-3304.

Adrian, Nobles Co., St. Adrian (1877), Rev. Gerald C. Kosse.
Res., 512 Maine Ave., P.O. Box 475, 56110-0475. Tel: 507-483-2317. [CEM]
Catechesis/Religious Programs—108 E. Sixth St., 56110. Tel: 507-483-2480.
Students 231.

Albert Lea, Freeborn Co., St. Theodore's (1882), Rev. Robert J. Schneider.
Res., 315 E. Clark St., Box 890, 56007. Tel: 507-373-0603. [CEM]
School—See listings under Centralized Catholic Schools. Patricia Lindeman, Prin.
Parish Center—323 E. Clark St., 56007. Tel: 507-373-9657; Fax: 507-373-9657.
Catechesis/Religious Programs—Tel: 507-373-2987; Fax: 507-373-9657.
Students 498.

Altura, Winona Co., St. Anthony's (1919). Attended by St. Rose of Lima.
180 S. Fremont, P.O. Box 727, Lewiston, 55952-0727. Tel: 507-523-2428. [JC]
Catechesis/Religious Programs—Students 85.

Austin, Mower Co., St. Augustine's (1857), Rev. Paul E. Nelson.
Res., 405 Fourth St., N.W., 55912-3091. Tel: 507-437-4537. [JC]
School—See listings under Centralized Catholic Schools.
Catechesis/Religious Programs—Students 194.

St. Edward's (1960), Rev. Paul E. Nelson, Admin.
Res., 2000 Oakland Ave., W., 55912-1599. Tel: 507-433-1841; Fax: 507-433-9680. [JC]
School—See listings under Centralized Catholic Schools.
Catechesis/Religious Programs—Students 92.

Queen of Angels (1936), Rev. Virgil S. Duellman.
Res., 1001 Oakland Ave., E., 55912. Tel: 507-433-1888. [JC]
School—See listings under Centralized Catholic Schools. Tel: 507-433-8745.
Catechesis/Religious Programs—912 First Ave., N.E., 55912. Tel: 507-433-8474.
Students 167.
Convent/Retreat House—1009 E. Oakland Ave., 55912. Tel: 507-437-4015; 437-6921 (Sisters' Res.).

Blooming Prairie, Steele Co., St. Columbanus (1878), Rev. Richard J. Dernek.
Res., 114 E. Main, 55917-1427. Tel: 507-583-2529; 583-2784. [CEM]
Catechesis/Religious Programs—Tel: 507-583-2784.
Students 211.

Mission—Hayfield, Dodge Co., Sacred Heart, P.O. Box 27, Hayfield, 55940-0027. Tel: 507-477-2256.

Blue Earth, Faribault Co., SS. Peter and Paul's (1866), Rev. John W. Ozbun.
Res., 214 S. Holland, 56013. Tel: 507-526-5626. [CEM]
Catechesis/Religious Programs—Tel: 507-526-2816.
Students 225.

Brewster, Nobles Co., Sacred Heart (1901) (German). Attended by St. Francis Xaiver, Windom.
548 17th St., Windom, 56101-1217. Tel: 507-831-3300. [CEM]
Catechesis/Religious Programs—P.O. Box 187, 56119. Tel: 507-842-5584. Loretta Smith, D.R.E.
Students 80.

Brownsdale, Mower Co., Our Lady of Loretto (1946). Attended by St. Edward, Austin. Rev. Jack Krough.
2000 Oakland Ave., W., Austin, 55912-1599. Tel: 507-433-1841.
Catechesis/Religious Programs—Tel: 507-584-6476.
Students 36.

Brownsville, Houston Co., St. Patrick's (1871) (Irish). Attended by St. Peter.
P.O. Box 355, Hokah, 55941-0355. Tel: 507-894-4242. [CEM][JC 2]
Catechesis/Religious Programs—P.O. Box 155, 55919. Tel: 507-482-6769.
Students 45.

Byron, Olmsted Co., Christ the King (1965), Rev. Charles I. Collins.
Res., 202 Fourth St., N.W., P.O. Box 1000, 55920-1000. Tel: 507-775-6455; Fax: 507-775-0501.
Catechesis/Religious Programs—Tel: 507-775-0501.
Students 249.

Caledonia, Houston Co., St. Mary (1975), Rev. Donald J. Schmitz.
Res., 513 S. Pine St., P.O. Box 406, 55921-0406. Tel: 507-724-3804; Fax: 507-724-2001. [CEM]
School—(Grades K-8). Tel: 507-724-3355. Sr. Cheryl Marie Wagner, S.S.N.D., Prin.
Priests 1; Sisters 2; Lay Teachers 13; Students 206.
Catechesis/Religious Programs—Students 196.
Convent—308 E. South, 55921. Tel: 507-724-2069.

Canton, Fillmore Co., The Assumption (1891). Attended by Nativity of B.V.M.
640 First Ave., S.W., P.O. Box 596, Harmony, 55939-0596. Tel: 507-886-2393; Fax: 507-886-2393. [CEM][JC]

Chatfield, Fillmore Co., St. Mary's (1866), Rev. Daniel R. Dernek.
Office: 405 S.W. Bench St., 55923. Tel: 507-867-3922; Fax: 507-867-3922. [CEM 2][JC]
Catechesis/Religious Programs—405 Bench St., S.W., 55923. Tel: 507-867-3138.
Students 195.

Claremont, Dodge Co., St. Francis de Sales (1869). Attended by St. John Baptist de La Salle, Dodge Center.
20 Second St., N.E., P.O. Box 310, Dodge Center, 55927-0310. Tel: 507-374-6830. [CEM][JC]
Catechesis/Religious Programs—Students 32.

Currie, Murray Co., Immaculate Heart of Mary (1883), Rev. Paul C. Evers.
Res., 501 Mill St., P.O. Box 174, 56123-0174. Tel: 507-763-3145.
Catechesis/Religious Programs—Students 107.

Dakota, Winona Co., Holy Cross (1890), Rev. Joseph C. Frisch.
Res., Box 387, 55925. Tel: 507-643-6163.
Catechesis/Religious Programs—Students 34.

Deerfield, Steele Co., Corpus Christi (1869). Attended by Christ the King, Medford.
205 N.W. Second Ave., P.O. Box 120, Medford, 55049-9508. Tel: 507-451-6353.

Delavan, Faribault Co., Mater Dolorosa (1889). Attended by St. Mary, Winnebago.
P.O. Box 308, Winnebago, 56098-0308. Tel: 507-893-4242. [CEM]

Dodge Center, Dodge Co., St. John Baptist de La Salle (1945), Rev. Milo L. Ernster.
Res., 20 Second St. N.E., P.O. Box 310, 55927. Tel: 507-374-6830.
Catechesis/Religious Programs—Tel: 507-374-6765.
Students 72.

Dundee, Nobles Co., St. Mary. Closed. For inquiries about sacramental records contact St. Gabriel, Fulda.

East Chain, Martin Co., Holy Family (1925) (Polish). Attended by St. John Vianney, Fairmont.
Res., 901 S. Prairie Ave., Fairmont, 56031-3098. Tel: 507-235-5535. [CEM]

Easton, Faribault Co., Our Lady of Mount Carmel (1866), Rev. John P. Wilmot, M.H.M., Admin.
Res., 27 Main St., P.O. Box 8, 56025-0008. Tel: 507-787-2303. [CEM]
School—(Grades K-8). Tel: 507-787-2233.
Priests 1; Lay Teachers 9; Students 61.
Catechesis/Religious Programs—Students 71.

Elba, Winona Co., St. Aloysius (1877) (German-Luxembourg). Attended by St. Charles Borromeo, St. Charles.
736 Church Ave., St. Charles, 55972-1426. Tel: 507-932-3294. [CEM]

Ellendale, Freeborn Co., St. Aidan (1857). Attended by St. Joseph, Owatonna.
512 S. Elm St., Owatonna, 55060-3399. Tel: 507-451-4854. [CEM]
Catechesis/Religious Programs—Students 82.

Ellsworth, Nobles Co., St. Mary's (1885). Attended by St. Catherine, Luverne.
203 E. Brown St., Luverne, 56156-1599. Tel: 507-283-8502. [CEM]
Catechesis/Religious Programs—Tel: 712-479-2444.
Students 46.

Eyota, Olmsted Co., Holy Redeemer (1891). Attended by St. Mary, Chatfield.
405 S.W. Bench St., Chatfield, 55923-1352. Tel: 507-867-3922; Fax: 507-867-3922.
Catechesis/Religious Programs—Students 207.

Fairmont, Martin Co., St. John Vianney (1952) (Hispanic), Revs. Joseph B. Fogal; Richard P. Loomis.
Parish Office: 901 S. Prairie Ave., 56031-3098. Tel: 507-235-5535. [CEM]
School—(Grades PreK-7) 911 S. Prairie Ave., 56031. Tel: 507-235-5304. Bruce Tepfer, Prin.
Priests 2; Lay Teachers 11; Students 176.
Catechesis/Religious Programs—Tel: 507-235-5903.
Students 367.

Fountain, Fillmore Co., St. Lawrence O'Toole (1872) (Irish). Attended by St. Columban, Preston.
408 N.W. Preston St., Preston, 55965. Tel: 507-765-3886. [JC]

Fulda, Murray Co., St. Gabriel's (1882) (German), Rev. Eugene E. Egan.
Res., 307 W. Lake Ave., 56131-9402. Tel: 507-425-2595. [CEM]
Catechesis/Religious Programs—Tel: 507-425-2369.
Students 182.

Geneva, St. Mary (1867) (Irish). Attended by All Saints, New Richland. Rev. Thien Nguyen.
307 1st St. S.W., P.O. Box 185, New Richland, 56072-0185. Tel: 507-465-8217; 465-8381. [CEM]
Catechesis/Religious Programs—Tel: 507-583-7530.
Students 43.

Good Thunder, Blue Earth Co., St. Joseph (1879). Attended by St. Teresa, Mapleton.
104 Silver St., W., P.O. Box 305, Mapleton, 56065. Tel: 507-524-3127. [CEM]
Catechesis/Religious Programs—Tel: 507-278-3444.
Students 77.

Grand Meadow, Mower Co., St. Finbarr's (1878). Attended by St. Ignatius, Spring Valley.
213 W. Franklin St., Spring Valley, 55975-1312. Tel: 507-346-7565. [CEM]
Church—504 1st St. S.W., P.O. Box 326, 55951. Tel: 507-754-5190.
Catechesis/Religious Programs—Students 141.

Guckeen, Faribault Co., Our Lady of Mercy (1903). Attended by Sts. Peter and Paul, Blue Earth.
214 S. Holland, Blue Earth, 56013. Tel: 507-526-5626.

Hammond, Wabasha Co., St. Clement's. Closed. For inquires for parish records contact SS. Peter and Paul, Mazeppa.

Harmony, Fillmore Co., The Nativity of the Blessed Virgin (1906), Rev. Stephen J. Peterson.
Res., 640 First Ave., S.W., P.O. Box 596, 55939-0596. Tel: 507-886-2393.
Catechesis/Religious Programs—Students 82.

Hayfield, Dodge Co., Sacred Heart (1935). Attended by St. Columbanus, Blooming Prairie. Rev. Richard Dernek.
114 E. Main St., Blooming Prairie, 55917-1427. Tel: 507-583-2529.
Catechesis/Religious Programs—Tel: 507-477-2297.
Students 115.

Heron Lake, Jackson Co., Sacred Heart (1884) (German). Attended by St. Francis Xavier, Windom.
548 17th St., Windom, 56101-1217. Tel: 507-831-3300. [CEM]
Catechesis/Religious Programs—Students 131.

Hokah, Houston Co., St. Peter's (1876) (German), Rev. Paul J. Breza.
Res., P.O. Box 355, 55941-0355. Tel: 507-894-4242. [CEM][JC 2]
School—(Grades K-8). Tel: 507-894-4375; 894-4944. Norman Valiska, Prin.
Lay Teachers 8; Students 104.

Houston, Houston Co., St. Mary's (1873). Attended by St. Joseph, Rushford.
101 Rushford Ave., W., P.O. Box 577, Rushford, 55971-0557. Tel: 507-864-2257. [CEM]

Iona, Murray Co., St. Columba's (1891) (Irish). Attended by St. Gabriel, Fulda.
307 W. Lake Ave., Fulda, 56131-9402. Tel: 507-425-2595. [CEM]
Catechesis/Religious Programs—Students 37.

Jackson, Jackson Co., Good Shepherd (1891) (Czech-Bohemian), Rev. Charles J. Quinn. In res., Revs. Urban Neudecker Tel: 507-764-5374; Jerome Verdick Tel: 507-847-2939.
Res., 311 N. Sverdrup Ave., P.O. Box 65, 56143-1329. Tel: 507-847-2504; Fax: 507-847-5322. [CEM]
Catechesis/Religious Programs—Tel: 507-847-2719.
Students 176.

Janesville, Waseca Co., St. Ann's (1876), Rev. Sylvester F. Brown.
307 W. Second St., P.O. Box 218, 56048-0218. Tel: 507-234-6244. [CEM]
Catechesis/Religious Programs—Tel: 507-234-5753.
Students 195.

Jasper, Pipestone Co., St. Joseph's (1890). Attended by St. Leo's, Pipestone.
106 4th St., S.E., P.O. Box 0036, Pipestone, 56154-0036. Tel: 507-825-3152; Fax: 507-825-4492. [CEM]
Catechesis/Religious Programs—Students 45.

Jeffers, Cottonwood Co., St. Augustine's (1912). Closed. For inquiries about sacramental records contact St. Francis Xavier, Windom.

Johnsburg, Mower Co., St. John's (1859) (German). Attended by Sacred Heart, Adams.
412 Main St., P.O. Box 352, Adams, 55909-9998. Tel: 507-582-3321. [CEM]

Kasson, Dodge Co., Holy Family (1976). Attended by Christ the King, Byron. Rev. Charles I. Collins.
202 Fourth St., N.W., P.O. Box 1000, Byron, 55920-1000. Tel: 507-775-6455; Fax: 507-775-0501. [CEM]
Catechesis/Religious Programs—Tel: 507-634-7520.
Students 274.

Kellogg, Wabasha Co., St. Agnes (1900), Rev. Harold E. Gavin.
Res., P.O. Box 8, 55945-0008. Tel: 507-767-4965.
Catechesis/Religious Programs—Students 78.

Immaculate Conception (1881). Attended by St. Agnes, Kellogg.
P.O. Box 8, Kellog, 55945-0008. Tel: 507-767-4965.
Catechesis/Religious Programs—Students 78.

La Crescent, Houston Co., The Crucifixion (1856), Rev. Donald W. Grubisch.
Res., 407 S. Second St., 55947-1326. Tel: 507-895-4720. [CEM 2]
School—(Grades K-6) 420 S. Second St., 55947. Tel: 507-895-4402. Robert Adams, Prin.
Lay Teachers 10; Students 159.
Catechesis/Religious Programs—1380 Lancer Blvd., 55947. Tel: 507-895-2700.
Students 333.
Convent—423 S. Second St., 55947. Tel: 507-895-6867.

Lake City, Wabasha Co., St. Mary's of the Lake (1877), Rev. James S. McCauley.
Res., 419 Lyon Ave., 55041-1649. Tel: 612-345-4134.
Catechesis/Religious Programs—Students 285.

Lake Crystal, Blue Earth Co., Holy Family (1900). Attended by St. Joseph the Worker, Mankato. Rev. Joseph P. Pete.
Res., 816 Hubbell Ave., Mankato, 56001-2197. Tel: 507-388-3766; Fax: 507-388-3766. [CEM]
Catechesis/Religious Programs—Tel: 507-726-2725.
Students 124.

Lakefield, Jackson Co., St. Joseph (1897). Attended by Good Shepherd, Jackson.
311 N. Sverdrup Ave., P.O. Box 65, Jackson, 56143-1329. Tel: 507-847-2504. [CEM]
Catechesis/Religious Programs—410 Broadway Ave., Box 517, 56150. Tel: 507-662-5819.
Students 119.

Lake Wilson, Murray Co., St. Mary (1916). Attended by St. Ann, Slayton.
2747 29th St., Slayton, 56172-9998. Tel: 507-836-8030. [JC]
Catechesis/Religious Programs—Students 52.

Lamoille, Winona Co., Precious Blood (1900). Closed. For inquiries about sacramental records contact Holy Cross, Dakota.

Lanesboro, Fillmore Co., St. Patrick (1871) (Irish). Attended by St. Columban, Preston.
408 N.W. Preston St., R.R. 2, Box 11, Preston, 55965. Tel: 507-765-3886. [JC]
Catechesis/Religious Programs—Students 50.

Le Roy, Mower Co., St. Patrick's (1878). Attended by St. Ignatius, Spring Valley. Rev. Russell G. Scepaniak.
213 W. Franklin St., Spring Valley, 55975-1312. Tel: 507-346-7565. [CEM]
Catechesis/Religious Programs—Tel: 507-324-5032.
Students 122.

Lewiston, Winona Co., St. Rose of Lima (1876), Rev. Michael J. Hoeppner.
Res., 180 S. Fremont, P.O. Box 727, 55952. Tel: 507-523-2428. [CEM]
Catechesis/Religious Programs—Students 187.

Lismore, Nobles Co., St. Anthony's (1887) (German-Irish), Rev. Gerald C. Kosse; Sr. Brenda Penning, S.S.N.D., Parish Dir.
Mailing Address: 310 Third Ave., S., P.O. Box 158, 56155-0158. Tel: 507-472-8262. [CEM]
Catechesis/Religious Programs—Tel: 507-472-8262.
Students 51.

Litomysl, Holy Trinity (1877) (Czech). Attended by St. Joseph, Owatonna.
512 S. Elm St., Owatonna, 55060-3399. Tel: 507-451-4845.
Mailing Address: 9946 S.E. 24th Ave., Owatonna, 55060. Tel: 507-451-3482. [CEM]
School—St. Isidore, (Grades K-8). Tel: 507-451-5876. Stacy Wobschall, Prin.
Priests 2; Lay Teachers 3; Students 32.

Luverne, Rock Co., St. Catherine's (1881), Rev. Paul Heiting.
203 E. Brown, 56156-1599. Tel: 507-283-8502. [CEM]
Catechesis/Religious Programs—Tel: 507-283-8071.
Students 239.

Lyle, Mower Co., Queen of Peace (1946) (German). Attended by St. Peter, Rose Creek.
R.R. 1, Box 1E, Rose Creek, 55970-9701. Tel: 507-433-1532.
Catechesis/Religious Programs—Tel: 507-325-4677.
Students 60.

Mabel, Fillmore Co., St. Olaf (1954). Attended by Nativity of B.V.M., Harmony.
640 First Ave. S.W., P.O. Box 596, Harmony, 55939-0596. Tel: 507-886-2393; Fax: 507-886-2393. [JC]

Catechesis/Religious Programs—Students 106.

Madelia, Watonwan Co., St. Mary (1872), Rev. Peter J. Klein.
Res., 212 First St., N.E., 56062-1701. Tel: 507-642-8305.
School—(Grades PreK-6). Tel: 507-642-3324. Mrs. Robin Osland, Prin.
Priests 1; Lay Teachers 8; Students 120.
Convent—13 Crosby Ave., N.E., 56062. Tel: 507-642-3323.
Catechesis/Religious Programs—Students 86.

Madison Lake, Blue Earth Co., All Saints (1894), Rev. James D. Russell.
Parish Endowment Fund, Inc. of All Saints Church: P.O. Box 217, 56063-0217. Tel: 507-243-3319. [CEM]
School—(Grades PreK-6) P.O. Box 158, 56053-0158. Tel: 507-243-3819. Sr. Mary Kay Ash, S.S.N.D., Prin.
Priests 1; Sisters 3; Lay Teachers 3; Students 64; Preschool 18.
Catechesis/Religious Programs—Students 151.
Convent—Tel: 507-243-3010.

Mankato, Blue Earth Co.,

1—SS. PETER AND PAUL'S, (1858) (German), Revs. Karl Voelker, S.J.; Ervin J. Czarnecki, S.J.; Theodore Hottinger, S.J.; Charles L. Kerr, S.J.; Bro. James Becwar, S.J.
Res., 105 N. Fifth St., 56001-4442. Tel: 507-388-2995.
School—See listings under Centralized Catholic Schools. Tel: 507-387-3316.
Pastoral Center—512 Mulberry St., 56001-4442. Tel: 507-388-1664.
Catechesis/Religious Programs—Tel: 507-387-6228; Fax: 507-388-7628.
Students 327.
Mission—Mankato, Blue Earth Co., St. Francis Xaiver.

2—ST. FRANCIS XAVIER MISSION CHAPEL. Attended by SS. Peter and Paul, Mankato.
105 N. Fifth St., 56001. Tel: 507-388-2995.
Church—Fourth Ave., 56001.
Catechesis/Religious Programs—Students 144.

3—ST. JOHN THE BAPTIST'S, (1884), Rev. Richard M. Colletti.
Res., 632 S. Broad St., 56001-3890. Tel: 507-625-3131; Fax: 507-625-3270. [JC]
School—See listings under Centralized Catholic Schools.
Catechesis/Religious Programs—Tel: 507-625-3389.
Students 470.

4—ST. JOSEPH THE WORKER, (1957), Revs. Joseph P. Pete; James J. Seitz.
Res., 816 Hubbell Ave., 56001. Tel: 507-388-3766; Fax: 507-388-3766. [JC]
School—See listings under Centralized Catholic Schools.
Catechesis/Religious Programs—423 W. 7th St., 56001. Tel: 507-625-3450.
Students 208.
Convent—Tel: 507-388-2515.

Mapleton, Blue Earth Co., St. Teresa's (1876), Rev. Joseph W. Mountain; Sr. Lalande Hennen, S.S.N.D., Dir.
Res., 104 Silver St., P.O. Box 305, 56065. Tel: 507-524-3127. [CEM]
Catechesis/Religious Programs—Tel: 507-524-4606.
Students 195.

Mazeppa, Wabasha Co., SS. Peter and Paul (1860), Rev. Richard J. Engels, Admin.
Res., 1st St. S., P.O. Box 224, 55956-0224. Tel: 507-843-3885.
Catechesis/Religious Programs—Students 138.

Medford, Steele Co., Christ the King (1943), Rev. Robert D. Herman.
Res., 205 N.W. Second Ave., P.O. Box 120, 55049-9508. Tel: 507-451-6353.
Catechesis/Religious Programs—Students 132.

Minneiska, Wabasha Co., St. Mary's (1867). Attended by Holy Trinity, Rollingstone.
83 Main St., Rollingstone, 55969-9759. Tel: 507-689-2351.

Minnesota City, Winona Co., St. Paul's (1924), Rev. Edward Cunningham, O.M.I.
Res., P.O. Box 26, 55959-0026. Tel: 507-689-2485. [CEM]
Catechesis/Religious Programs—Students 20.

Minnesota Lake, Faribault Co., St. John the Baptist (1865). Attended by Our Lady of Mount Carmel, Easton. Rev. John P. Wilmot, M.H.M.
Mailing Address: P.O. Box 8, Easton, 56025-0008. Tel: 507-787-2303.
Church—P.O. Box 158, 56068. Tel: 507-462-3636. [CEM]
Catechesis/Religious Programs—Tel: 507-462-3791.
Students 118.

New Richland, Waseca Co., All Saints (1879), Rev. Thien Van Nguyen.
Res., P.O. Box 185, 56072-0185. Tel: 507-465-8217. [CEM]
Catechesis/Religious Programs—Students 104.

Oak Ridge, Winona Co., Immaculate Conception (1875). Closed. For inquiries about sacramental records contact Holy Trinity, Rollingstone.

Owatonna, Steele Co., St. Joseph's (1891), Revs. Thomas J. Hargesheimer; Hubert Boschert, S.J.; Deacon Paul Hillyer.
Res., 512 S. Elm St., 55060-3399. Tel: 507-451-4845.
School—See listings under Centralized Catholic Schools.
Catechesis/Religious Programs—Students 411.
Sacred Heart (1866) (Czech), Rev. Thomas J. Jennings; Deacon George Anderberg.
Res., 810 S. Cedar Ave., 55060-3297. Tel: 507-451-1588. [JC]
School—See listings under Centralized Catholic Schools. Tel: 507-451-2694; Fax: 507-451-9554.
Catechesis/Religious Programs—Marian Dr., 55060. Tel: 507-451-2699.
Students 381.

Pipestone, Pipestone Co., St. Leo's (1887), Rev. Martin T. Schaefer.
Res., 106 Fourth St. S.E., P.O. Box 36, 56164-0036. Tel: 507-825-3152; Fax: 507-825-4492. [CEM]
Catechesis/Religious Programs—Students 252.

Plainview, Wabasha Co., St. Joachim's (1858) (German-Irish), Rev. Donald F. Connelly.
Res., 900 W. Broadway, 55964-1039. Tel: 507-534-3321. [CEM]
Catechesis/Religious Programs—Tel: 507-534-2887.
Students 446.

Preston, Fillmore Co., St. Columban (1869) (Irish), Rev. Thomas A. Loomis.
Res., 408 N.W. Preston St., 55965. Tel: 507-765-3886. [JC]
Catechesis/Religious Programs—Students 50.

Rochester, Olmsted Co.,

1—HOLY SPIRIT, (1990), Rev. Dale E. Tupper.
Office: 5455 50th Ave., N.W., 55901. Tel: 507-280-0638; Fax: 507-288-5155.
Res., Tel: 507-281-8323. [JC]
School—See listings under Centralized Catholic Schools.
Catechesis/Religious Programs—Students 179.

2—PAX CHRISTI, (1973), Revs. LaVern E. Trocinski; James F. Callahan, S.M.A.
Res., 4135-18th Ave., N.W., 55901-0460. Tel: 507-282-8542; Fax: 507-289-8741. [JC]
School—See listings under Centralized Catholic Schools.
Catechesis/Religious Programs—Tel: 507-282-8938; Fax: 507-289-8741.
Students 726.

3—RESURRECTION, (1967), Rev. Donald P. Schmitz.
Res., 1600-11th Ave., S.E., 55904-5499. Tel: 507-288-5528; Fax: 507-252-0763. [JC]
School—See listings under Centralized Catholic Schools.
Catechesis/Religious Programs—Students 622.

4—ST. BRIDGET'S, (1857). Attended by St. Bernard, Stewartville. Rev. Gregory Havel.
116 4th Ave. S.E., Stewartville, 55976. Tel: 507-533-8257. [CEM]
Catechesis/Religious Programs—Students 75.

5—ST. FRANCIS OF ASSISI, (1937) (German-Irish), Rev. Donald J. Lovas.
Res., 338 11th Ave., S.E., 55904. Tel: 507-288-7313; Fax: 507-281-5997. [JC]
School—See listings under Centralized Catholic Schools. Tel: 507-288-4816; Fax: 507-288-4815.
Catechesis/Religious Programs—Tel: 507-289-2427.
Students 133.

6—ST. JOHN'S, (1863), Revs. Gerald A. Mahon; Andrew J. Berman; Deacon Gumisindo Gonzales. In res., Revs. Jose Perumpuzha (India); Juan Randell Badillo (Mexico).
Res., 11 4th Ave., S.W., 55902-3098. Tel: 507-288-7372; Fax: 507-288-7373. [JC]
School—See listings under Centralized Catholic Schools. Tel: 507-282-5248.
Catechesis/Religious Programs—Students 200.

7—ST. PIUS X, (1954), Revs. Paul W. Surprenant; Michael J. Cronin.
Res., 1315-12th Ave., N.W., 55901-1744. Tel: 507-288-8238. [JC]
School—See listings under Centralized Catholic Schools. Tel: 507-282-5161; Fax: 507-282-5107.
Catechesis/Religious Programs—Tel: 507-289-6317; Fax: 507-286-8769.
Students 290.
Convent—1203 N.W. 13th Ave., 55901. Tel: 507-282-9200.

Rollingstone, Winona Co., Holy Trinity (1862), Rev. Edward F. McGrath.
Res., 83 Main St., 55969-9759. Tel: 507-689-2351; Fax: 507-689-2251. [CEM]

Rose Creek, Mower Co., St. Peter's (1885), Rev. Ruben C. Spinler.
Res., R.R. 1, Box 1E, 55970. Tel: 507-433-1532. [CEM]
Catechesis/Religious Programs—Students 83.

Rushford, Fillmore Co., St. Joseph's (1868), Rev. William J. Kulas.
Res., 101 Rushford Ave., W., P.O. Box 577, 55971-0577. Tel: 507-864-2257. [CEM]
Catechesis/Religious Programs—Students 93.

St. Charles, Winona Co., St. Charles Borromeo (1867) (Irish-German), Rev. Louis G. Cook.
Res., 736 Church Ave., 55972-1426. Tel: 507-932-3294. [CEM]
Catechesis/Religious Programs—Tel: 507-932-3303.
Students 257.

St. Clair, Blue Earth Co., Immaculate Conception (1874), Rev. Matthew Vanissery.
Res., 120 Church St., P.O. Box 100, 56080-0100. Tel: 507-245-3448. [CEM]
Catechesis/Religious Programs—Students 218.

St. James, Watonwan Co., St. James (1873), Rev. Hilary R. Brixius.
Res., 623 Fourth St., 56081-1824. Tel: 507-375-3542. [CEM]
Catechesis/Religious Programs—Marcia Hurley, D.R.E.
Students 208.

St. Kilian, Nobles Co., St. Kilian (1903) (German-Irish). Attended by St. Anthony, Lismore.
Mailing Address: 310 Third Ave., S., P.O. Box 158, Lismore, 56155-0158. Tel: 507-472-8262. [CEM]
Catechesis/Religious Programs—Students 21.

Sherburn, Martin Co., St. Luke's (1888). Attended by Good Shepherd, Jackson.
Res., 311 N. Sverdrup Ave., P.O. Box 65, Jackson, 56143-1329. Tel: 507-847-2504; Fax: 507-847-5322. [CEM]
Catechesis/Religious Programs—Tel: 507-764-5029.
Students 134.

Slayton, Murray Co., St. Ann's (1897), Rev. James C. Berning.
Res., 2747 29th St., 56172. Tel: 507-836-8030. [CEM]
Catechesis/Religious Programs—Tel: 507-836-6261.
Students 122.

Spring Valley, Fillmore Co., St. Ignatius (1878), Rev. Russell G. Scepaniak.
Res., 213 Franklin St., 55975-1312. Tel: 507-346-7565. [CEM]
Catechesis/Religious Programs—Students 119.

Stewartville, Olmsted Co., St. Bernard's (1894), Rev. Gregory G. Havel.
Res., 116 Fourth Ave. S.E., 55976. Tel: 507-533-8257. [CEM]
Catechesis/Religious Programs—Tel: 507-533-8192.
Students 315.

Theilman, Wabasha Co., St. Joseph's (1903). Attended by St. Mary of the Lake, Lake City.
419 Lyon Ave., Lake City, 55041. Tel: 612-345-4134. [CEM]

Trimont, Martin Co., St. Joseph. Closed. For inquiries for parish records see Good Shepherd, Jackson.

Truman, Martin Co., St. Katherine (1954). Attended by St. Mary, Madelia.
212 First St., N.E., Madelia, 56062-1702. Tel: 507-642-8305.
Catechesis/Religious Programs—Students 67.

Twin Lakes, Freeborn Co., St. James (1876), Rev. Donald W. Zenk, Admin.
Res., 602 31st St., N.W., Austin, 55912. Tel: 507-437-3579.

Vernon Center, Blue Earth Co., St. Matthew (1911). Attended by St. Teresa, Mapleton.
Mailing Address: 104 Silver St., W., P.O. Box 305, Mapleton, 56065. Tel: 507-524-3127. [CEM]
Catechesis/Religious Programs—Students 80.

Wabasha, Wabasha Co., St. Felix (1858), Rev. Gerald W. Conway.
Res., 117 W. Third St., 55981-1201. Tel: 612-565-3931. [CEM]

School—(Grades K-6) 130 Third St., E., 55981. Tel: 612-564-4446. Sr. M. Joann McMahon, S.S.N.D., Prin.
Priests 1; Sisters 2; Lay Teachers 6; Students 168.
Catechesis/Religious Programs—Tel: 612-565-3718.
Students 170.
Convent—36 Bailey Ave., 55981. Tel: 612-565-4578.

Waldorf, Waseca Co., St. Joseph's (1878). Attended by Immaculate Conception, St. Clair.
P.O. Box 100, St. Clair, 56080-0100. Tel: 507-245-3448. [CEM]
Catechesis/Religious Programs—Students 64.

Waseca, Waseca Co., Sacred Heart (1869), Rev. John M. Kunz.
Res., 111 Fourth St., N.W., 56093-2413. Tel: 507-835-1222. [CEM][JC 2]
School—(Grades PreK-4) 308 W. Elm Ave., 56093. Tel: 507-835-2780. Sandra Allaire, Prin.
Priests 1; Lay Teachers 11; Students 158.
Catechesis/Religious Programs—Tel: 507-835-1500.
Students 514.
Convent—400 Second Ave., N.W., 56093. Tel: 507-835-4867.

Wells, Faribault Co., St. Casimir's (1880) (Polish), Rev. Eugene F. Stenzel.
Res., 320 Second Ave., 56097-1399. Tel: 507-553-5391. [CEM]
School—(Grades K-8) 330 Second Ave., S.W., 56097. Tel: 507-553-5822. Katy Schmitz, Prin.
Lay Teachers 10; Students 121.
Catechesis/Religious Programs—Students 262.

West Albany, Wabasha Co., St. Patrick's of West Albany (1865). Attended by SS. Peter and Paul.
1st St. S., P.O. Box 224, Mazeppa, 55956-0224. Tel: 507-843-3885. [CEM]
Catechesis/Religious Programs—Students 55.

Westbrook, Cottonwood Co., St. Anthony's (1909). Attended by Immaculate Heart of Mary, Currie.
501 Mill St., P.O. Box 174, Currie, 56123-0174. Tel: 507-763-3145. [CEM]

West Concord, Dodge Co., St. Vincent de Paul (1945) (German). Attended by St. John Baptist de La Salle, Dodge Center.
20 Second St., N.E., Box 310, Dodge Center, 55927-0310. Tel: 507-374-6830. [CEM]
Catechesis/Religious Programs—P.O. Box 117, 55985. Tel: 507-527-2384.
Students 84.

Wilmont, Nobles Co., Our Lady of Good Counsel (1903). Attended by St. Adrian, Adrian.
605 4th Ave., c/o St. Adrian Parish, P.O. Box 475, Adrian, 56110-0475. Tel: 507-483-2317. [CEM]
Catechesis/Religious Programs—Tel: 507-926-5305.
Students 82.

Wilson, Winona Co., Immaculate Conception (1874). Attended by Cathedral of the Sacred Heart.
360 Main St., Winona, 55987-3299. Tel: 507-452-4770.

Windom, Cottonwood Co., St. Francis Xavier's (1898), Rev. Andrew D. Olsem.
Res., 548 17th St., 56101-1217. Tel: 507-831-3300.
Catechesis/Religious Programs—532 17th St., 56101. Tel: 507-831-1985.
Students 226.

Winnebago, Faribault Co., St. Mary's (1893), Rev. John F. Traufler.
Res., P.O. Box 308, 56098-0308. Tel: 507-893-4242. [CEM]
Catechesis/Religious Programs—Students 120.

Woodstock, Pipestone Co., St. Martin's (1882). Attended by St. Leo, Pipestone.
Mailing Address: 106 Fourth St., S.E., P.O. Box 36, Pipestone, 56164-0036. Tel: 507-825-3152; Fax: 507-825-4492. [CEM]

Worthington, Nobles Co., St. Mary's (1886), Revs. Kevin Connolly; Peter L. Schuster.
Res., 1215 Seventh Ave., 56187-2297. Tel: 507-376-6005; Fax: 507-376-9167. [CEM]
School—(Grades K-6) Twelfth St. & Eighth Ave., 56187. Tel: 507-376-5236. Matthew Schoen, Prin.
Sisters 1; Lay Teachers 6; Students 160.
Catechesis/Religious Programs—1206 Eighth Ave., 56187. Tel: 507-372-2090.
Students 410.
Convent—1221 Seventh Ave., 56187. Tel: 507-376-4035.

Wykoff, Fillmore Co., St. Kilian's (1887). Closed. For inquiries about sacramental records contact St. Ignatius, Spring Valley.

Chaplains of Public Institutions

ROCHESTER. *Federal Medical Center* Bureau of Prisons, 2110 Center St. E., 55904. Sr. Emile Bormann, Chap.

WASECA. *Federal Correctional Institution.* 920 St. Andrews Pl., Owatonna, 55060. Deacon George T. Anderberg.

On Duty Outside the Diocese:
Reverend Fathers—
Brandenhoff, Peter B., 8859 Spring Lane, Woodbury, MN 55125
Maher, Robert G., 591 Bandera Dr., Camarillo, CA 93010
Murtagh, Lawrence, Box 66, Stockholm, SD 57264
Reker, Timothy T., NCCB, 3211 4th St. NE, Washington, DC 20017-1194

Military Chaplains:
Reverend Fathers—
Arnoldt, David M., 207 Whitworth Dr., Martinez, GA 30907

Graduate Studies:
Reverend Fathers—
Cook, Thomas E., North American College, Vatican City State, Rome 00120 Italy

---

Absent on Leave:
Reverend Fathers—
Cashman, Joseph C.
Gallagher, Chester G.
Hodapp, Timothy L.
Moore, Jon H.
Taylor, Robert H.
Verdick, Jerome F.

Retired:
Reverend Monsignors—
Dittman, Harold J., 1920 S. First St., #203, Minneapolis, MN 55454
Gallas, Francis A., 500 Preston St. N.W., Preston, MN 55965
Habiger, James D., 2115 Summit Ave., Box 4174, St. Paul, MN 55105
Klein, Edward, St. Elizabeth Hospital, 1200 W. 5th Grant Blvd., Wabasha, MN 55981-1098
Klein, Frank W., 1855 Waas Valley Rd., Dresbach, MN 55947
Literski, Roy E., 1328 D. McNally Dr., Winona, MN 55987
McGinnis, Joseph R., St. Elizabeth Hospital, 1200 W. 5th Grant Blvd., Wabasha, MN 55981-1098
Ploof, Thomas M., 220 S. Broadway, 1122 Center Plaza, Rochester, MN 55904
Speltz, Richard, 604 S. Third St., La Crescent, MN 55947-1234
Tighe, Emmett F., Madonna Towers #800/802, 4001 19th Ave. N.W., Rochester, MN 55901
Reverend Fathers—
Clinton, Kenneth J., 117 E. Paquin St., Apt. 102, Waterville, MN 56096
Cody, John F., 2485 Canabury Dr., Apt. 105, St. Paul, MN 55117
Curtis, William D., St. Elizabeth Hospital, 1200 W. 5th Grant Blvd., Wabasha, MN 55981-1098
Dandelet, James D., P.O. Box 46, Easton, MN 56025
Eikens, Leroy F., 728 First Ave., S.W. #403, Rochester, MN 55902-3307
Enright, Frank E., Sacred Heart Hospice, 1200 12th St., S.W., Austin, MN 55912-2699
Ginther, Lawrence P., 5125 W. Seventh St., Apt. 8, Winona, MN 55987-5616
Gits, Douglas J., 1420 4th St. S.E., Rochester, MN 55904-4716
Glynn, Francis M., St. Elizabeth Hospital, 1200 W. 5th Grant Blvd., Wabasha, MN 55981-1098
Haberman, Clayton J., 5371 Elkton Tr., Faribault, MN 55021-8453
Halloran, Jerome D., 5653 B Lake Murray Blvd., La Mesa, CA 92041
Halloran, Paul F., R.R. 2, Box 69A, Akeley, MN 56433-9507
Jewison, Harry P., 1024 Ninth St., N.E., Rochester, MN 55906
Kellen, Elmer W., 104 Park St., Box 171, Minnesota Lake, MN 56068
Kerrigan, Bernard, 300 Bridge St., P.O. Box 37, Millville, MN 55957
Kulas, Robert A., 7510 Cahill Rd., #201B, Edina, MN 55439
Kunz, Francis P., 240 Hudson Ave., E., Mankato, MN 56001
LaPlante, Joseph A., 31 Robinson Dr., Wabasha, MN 55981-3016
Leary, Donald G., #1504, 220 S. Broadway, Rochester, MN 55902
Loosbrock, Donald L., 149 Pioneer Dr., Wabasha, MN 55981
Mountain, Edward C., 420 11th St., S.E., Owatonna, MN 55060
Mountain, Harold B., 50 Teton Ln., #124, Mankato, MN 56001
Mountain, Joseph W., 5371 Elkton Tr., Faribault, MN 55021-8453
Neudecker, Urban C., P.O. Box 904, Sherburn, MN 56171
Peterson, Cyril P., c/o Jack Peterson, Box 238, Missouri Valley, IA 51555
Riordan, Richard J., 920 S. 10th St., St. James, MN 56081
Schaefer, Edgar J., 409 3rd St. N.W., Rochester, MN 55901
Schaefer, Vernon J., 825 Essex Pkwy. N.W., #247, Rochester, MN 55901
Schiltz, Roger J., 1532 Glenrosa Dr., N. Las Vegas, NV 89031-5548
Smith, Leland J., 468 Center St., Winona, MN 55987
Speck, James A., 528 Maceman St., Apt. 108, Winona, MN 55987-2486
Sullivan, Wilfred, Parker Oaks, 211 6th St. N.W., Winnebago, MN 56098
Vincent, John F., 513 S. Seventh St., Apt. C, LaCrescent, MN 55947-1275
Zenk, Donald W., St. James Church, c/o 602 31st St., N.W., Austin, MN 55912

INSTITUTIONS LOCATED IN THE DIOCESE

[A] SEMINARIES, DIOCESAN

WINONA. *Immaculate Heart of Mary Seminary*, 700 Terrace Hts. #43, 55987-1399. Tel: 507-457-7373; Fax: 507-457-8601.
E-mail: ihms@smumn.edu
Affiliated with Saint Mary's University of MN. Revs. William M. Becker, Rector; James P. Steffes, Dir. Spiritual Formation & Spiritual Dir.; Joseph A. LaPlante, Extern Spiritual Dir.; David C. Kunz, Dean Student Life & Spiritual Dir. Priests 3; Lay Staff 3; Students 32.

[B] COLLEGES AND UNIVERSITIES

WINONA. *Saint Mary's University of Minnesota*, 700 Terrace Hts., 55987-1399. Tel: 507-452-4430; 800-635-5987; Fax: 507-457-1633.
E-mail: admissions@smumn.edu
Web site: http://www.smumn.edu
For a complete listing, refer to the Colleges and Universities section.

[C] CENTRALIZED CATHOLIC SCHOOLS

WINONA. *Cotter High School.* (Grades 9-12), 1115 W. Broadway, 55987. Tel: 507-453-5002; Fax: 507-453-5006.
E-mail: jeanne-marie.faller@mps.org
Dr. Jeanne-Marie Faller, Prin., CEO; William Crozier, Campus Min. Priests 1; Lay Teachers 32; Students 392.

Winona Area Catholic Schools, 352 Center St., 55987. Co-Administrators: Mrs. Carol Wilant; Dr. Donna E. Harris.

St. Mary's Primary School. (Grades PreK-1), 1315 W. Broadway, 55987. Tel: 507-452-2890. Mrs. Carol Wilant, Co-Admin.

Cathedral Elementary School. (Grades 2-4), 352 Center St., 55987. Tel: 507-452-4936; Fax: 507-454-1473. Mrs. Carol Wilant, Co-Admin. Students 235.

St. Stanislaus Middle School. (Grades 5-8), 602 E. Fifth St., 55987. Tel: 507-452-3766. Dr. Donna E. Harris, Co-Admin. Students 374.

Winona Area Catholic Schools Foundation, 360 Main St., 55987.

ALBERT LEA. *St. Theodore School.* (Grades K-5), 323 E. Clark St., 56007. Tel: 507-373-9657; Fax: 507-373-9657. Patricia Lindeman, Prin. Lay Teachers 5; Students 70.

AUSTIN. *Austin Area Catholic Schools*, 511 N.W. Fourth Ave., 55912. Tel: 507-433-6630.

St. Augustine's - St. Edward. (Grades PreK-4), 511 N.W. Fourth Ave., 55912. Tel: 507-433-8859. Richard J. Cook, Prin. Lay Teachers 6; Students 127.

Queen of Angels. (Grades 5-8), 912 First Ave., N.E., 55912. Tel: 507-433-8745. Richard J. Cook, Prin. Lay Teachers 10; Students 126.

Pacelli Senior High School. (Grades 9-12), 311 Fourth St., N.W., 55912. Tel: 507-437-3278; Fax: 507-433-5693. Gregory J. Hereford, Prin.; Alice Duffy-Meyer, Campus Min. Lay Teachers 11; Students 95.

United Catholic Schools Foundation of Austin, MN, Inc., 511 N.W. Fourth Ave., 55912. Tel: 507-433-6630. Mrs. Alice Snater, Financial Sec.

MANKATO. *Mankato Area Catholic Schools*, 145 Good Counsel Dr., 56001-3146; Fax: 507-388-3081.
E-mail: jimr@mail.macs.mankato.mn.us
Mr. James Rouse, Supt.

St. Joseph - St. John School. (Grades K-3), 820 Hubbell, 56001-2100. Tel: 507-388-2536; Fax: 507-388-3766. Ms. Nancy Hackenmiller, Prin. Lay Teachers 4; Students 61.

SS. Peter and Paul School. (Grades K-3), 110 N. Sixth St., 56001. Tel: 507-387-3316; Fax: 507-388-2750. Ms. Nancy Hackenmiller, Prin. Lay Teachers 9; Students 174.

Fitzgerald Middle School. (Grades 6-8), 110 N. Fifth St., 56001-4499. Tel: 507-388-9344; Fax: 507-388-2750.
E-mail: rsa@macs.mankato.mn.us
Sr. Mary Donald Miller, S.S.N.D., Prin. Sisters 2; Lay Teachers 11; Students 164.

Loyola High School. (Grades 9-12), 145 Good Counsel Dr., 56001-3146. Tel: 507-388-2997; Fax: 507-388-3081.
E-mail: jimr@macs.mankato.mn.us
Mr. James Rouse, Prin.; Rev. James J. Seitz, Campus Min. Priests 1; Lay Teachers 17; Students 217.

Holy Rosary School. (Grades 4-5), 546 Grant Ave., 56003. Tel: 507-345-6765; Fax: 507-388-2017. Sr. Mary Donald Miller, S.S.N.D., Prin. Lay Teachers 4; Students 102.

OWATONNA. *St. Mary's School.* (Grades PreK-8), Marian Dr., 55060. Tel: 507-451-2694; Fax: 507-451-9554. Mr. Gerald Kent, Prin. Sisters 1; Lay Teachers 24; Students 350.

ROCHESTER. *Rochester Catholic Schools*, 621 W. Center St., 55902. Tel: 507-280-0349. Norm Glismann, Supt.

St. Francis School. (Grades PreK-8), 318 11th Ave., S.E., 55904. Tel: 507-288-4816; Fax: 507-288-4815. Mrs. Diane Schwinghammer, Prin. Priests 4; Lay Teachers 25; Students 545.

St. John School. (Grades 1-8), 424 W. Center St., 55902. Tel: 507-282-5248; Fax: 507-282-1343. Mr. Ronald Gaines, Prin. Priests 2; Sisters 1; Lay Teachers 25; Students 286.

St. Pius X School. (Grades K-8), 1205 12th Ave., 55901. Tel: 507-282-5161; Fax: 507-282-5107. Sr. Patricia Gehling, S.S.N.D., Prin. Priests 5; Sisters 2; Lay Teachers 32; Students 580.

Lourdes High School of Rochester, Inc. (Grades 9-12), 621 W. Center St., 55902. Tel: 507-289-3991; Fax: 507-289-4008. Mr. Dennis Nigon, Prin.; Sherri Broadhead, Campus Min. Priests 1; Sisters 2; Lay Teachers 35; Students 491.

Holy Spirit School. (Grades K-5), 5455 50th Ave., N.W., 55901. Tel: 507-288-8818. Ronald Gaines, Prin. Lay Teachers 11; Students 263.

[D] GENERAL HOSPITALS

ROCHESTER. *Poverello Foundation*, St. Marys Hospital, 1216 S.W. Second St., 55902. Tel: 507-255-5158
For a complete listing, refer to the Hospitals section.

**Saint Marys Hospital*, 55902-1970. Tel: 507-255-5123; Fax: 507-255-3125
For a complete listing, refer to the Hospitals section.

WABASHA. *St. Elizabeth's Hospital*, 1200 5th Grant Blvd., W., 55981. Tel: 612-565-4531
For a complete listing, refer to the Hospitals section.

[E] SPECIAL HOSPITALS AND REHABILITATION FACILITIES

WINONA. *St. Francis Community Programs of Minnesota, Inc.*, 725 W. Broadway, 55987. Tel: 507-454-7711
For a complete listing, refer to the Special Care Facilities section.

ROCHESTER. *Guest House*, 4800 48th St., N.E., P.O. Box 954, 55903. Tel: 800-634-4155; 507-288-4693.
E-mail: ghousemn@infonet.isl.net
Web site: http://ic.net/~ghouse/ghouse.html
For a complete listing, refer to the Special Care Facilities section.

[F] HOMES FOR AGED

WINONA. *St. Anne Hospice, Inc.*, 1347 W. Broadway, 55987. Tel: 507-454-3621
For a complete listing, refer to the Special Care Facilities section.

AUSTIN. *Sacred Heart Hospice, Inc.*, 1200 Twelfth St., S.W., 55912. Tel: 507-433-1808
For a complete listing, refer to the Special Care Facilities section.

ROCHESTER. *Madonna Towers of Rochester, Inc.*, 4001 19th Ave., N.W., 55901. Tel: 507-288-3911; Fax: 507-288-0393
For a complete listing, refer to the Special Care Facilities section.

WABASHA. *St. Elizabeth's Health Care Center*, 626 Shields Ave., 55981. Tel: 612-565-4581
For a complete listing, refer to the Special Care Facilities section.

[G] CONVENTS AND RESIDENCES FOR SISTERS

HOUSTON. *Hermits of St. Mary of Carmel, H.S.M.C.*, R.R. 1, Box 143, 55943-9737. Sr. Rosemary Quinn, H.S.M.C., Supr.; Rev. David Wechter, O.C.S.O. (DUB). Sisters 6.

JACKSON. *Convent of Religious Sisters of Mercy*, R.R. 3, Box 79, 56143. Tel: 507-847-5498; Fax: 507-847-5689. Sr. Marie Paul Lockerd, R.S.M., Local Supr. Sisters 5.

MANKATO. *Provincial House of the School Sisters of Notre Dame*, Convent of Our Lady of Good Counsel, 170 Good Counsel Dr., 56001-3138. Tel: 507-389-4200.
E-mail: kduvalssnd@juno.com
Web site: www.ssnd.org/test/
Religious in Province 486; Sisters in Motherhouse 160; Novices 4; Lay Staff 150.
School Sisters of Notre Dame at Mankato, MN, Inc.
School Sisters of Notre Dame at Mankato, MN, Inc. Charitable Trust.
School Sisters of Notre Dame Cooperative Investment Fund.

ROCHESTER. *Congregational Center of the Sisters of the Third Order Regular of St. Francis of the Congregation of Our Lady of Lourdes*, Assisi Heights, Box 4900, 55903. Tel: 507-282-7441; Fax: 507-282-7762.
E-mail: risa@aol.com
Sr. Valerie Usher, O.S.F., Pres. & Community Min.; Revs. James Buryska; James Kunz. Legal Title: *Academy of Our Lady of Lourdes.* Sisters 403.

[H] RETREAT HOUSES AND CENTERS OF SPIRITUALITY

WINONA. *Tau Center*, 511 Hilbert St., 55987. Tel: 507-454-2993.
E-mail: taucentr@luminet.net
Web site: www.winonanet.com/orgs/taucenter
Sr. Joan Blank, O.S.F., Facility Dir. Total in Residence 12; Total Staff 22.

AUSTIN. *Queen of Angels Center*, 1009 Oakland Ave., E., 55912. Tel: 507-437-4015. Kathleen Finnegan, Dir. Volunteers 25.

MANKATO. *Good Counsel Education Center*, 151 Good Counsel Dr., P.O. Box 8968, 56002. Tel: 507-389-4287. Susan J. Ward, Dir.

ROCHESTER. *Assisi Community Center*, Assisi Hts., Box 4900, 55903. Tel: 507-280-2180; Fax: 507-280-2190. Joan Elkins, Dir.

[I] NEWMAN CENTERS

WINONA. *St. Thomas Aquinas Newman Center*, 475 Huff St., 55987. Tel: 507-452-2781. Mr. Thomas Parlin, Dir.

MANKATO. *Newman Center*, 1331 Warren St., 56001. Tel: 507-387-4154. Ms. Sydelle McCabe, Dir.; Rev. Richard M. Colletti, Chap.

[J] MISCELLANEOUS LISTINGS

WINONA.

**Diocese of Winona Deposit & Loan*, 55 W. Sanborn St., Box 588, 55987. Tel: 507-454-4643; Fax: 507-454-8106.

Diocese of Winona Foundation, 55 W. Sanborn St., Box 588, 55987. Tel: 507-454-4643; Fax: 507-454-8106.

St. Mary's Parish of Winona Endowment Fund, Inc., 1303 W. Broadway, 55987. Tel: 507-452-5656. Rev. Joseph L. Keefe, Contact.

Saint Mary's Press, Christian Brothers Publications, 702 Terrace Hts., 55987. Tel: 507-457-7900.
E-mail: smpress@smp.org
Web site: http://www.smp.org
Rev. Robert P. Stamschror; Bro. Damian Steger, F.S.C., Pres.

Third Order Regular Common Franciscan Novitiate, Inc., Tau Center, 511 Hilbert St., 55987. Tel: 507-454-0184.
E-mail: skberger@juno.com

ALBERT LEA. *St. Theodore Catholic School Endowment*, 315 E. Clark St., Box 890, 56007-0890. Tel: 507-373-0603. Rev. Robert J. Schneider, Contact.

JACKSON. *Sacred Heart Mercy Health Care Center*, 803 Fourth St., 56143. Tel: 507-847-3571. Sr. Patricia Glowski, R.S.M., Admin. Patients assisted annually 4,622; Total Staff 5.

RELIGIOUS INSTITUTES OF MEN REPRESENTED IN THE DIOCESE

For further details refer to the corresponding bracketed number in the Religious Institutes of Men or Women section.

[0330]—*Brothers of the Christian Schools.*—F.S.C.

[0240]—*Camillian Fathers and Brothers.* (North American Province).—O.S.Cam.

[0400]—*Canons Regular of the Order of the Holy Cross.* (Province of St. Odilla).—O.S.C.

[0340]—*Cistercian Fathers.* (Abbey of Our Lady of New Malleray).—O.Cist.

[0350]—*Cistercians Order of the Strict Observance, (Trappists).*—O.C.S.O.

[0690]—*Jesuit Fathers and Brothers.* (Wisconsin Province).—S.J.

[0830]—*Mill Hill Missionaries.*—M.H.M.

[0910]—*Oblates of Mary Immaculate.* (Central Province).—O.M.I.

[0430]—*Order of Preachers (Dominicans).* (Chicago Province).—O.P.

[0110]—*Society of African Missions.*—S.M.A.

[0370]—*Society of St. Columban.*—S.S.C.

RELIGIOUS INSTITUTES OF WOMEN REPRESENTED IN THE DIOCESE

[0230]—*Benedictine Sisters of Pontifical Jurisdiction.*—O.S.B.

[1780]—*Congregation of the Sisters of the Third Order of St. Francis of Perpetual Adoration.* (Eastern, Central Regions).—F.S.P.A.

[1070-13]—*Dominican Sisters.*—O.P.

[1070-14]—*Dominican Sisters.*—O.P.

[1310]—*Franciscan Sisters of Little Falls.*—O.S.F.

[]—*Hermits of Mount Carmel (Contemplative Community).*—H.M.C.

[2470]—*Maryknoll Sisters of St. Dominic.*—M.M.

[2519]—*Religious Sisters of Mercy of Alma, Michigan.*—R.S.M.

[2970]—*School Sisters of Notre Dame.*—S.S.N.D.

[1680]—*School Sisters of St. Francis.*—O.S.F.

[0430]—*Sisters of Charity of the Blessed Virgin Mary.*—B.V.M.

[1705]—*The Sisters of St. Francis of Assisi.*—O.S.F.

[1570]—*Sisters of St. Francis of the Holy Family.*—O.S.F.

[3320]—*Sisters of the Presentation of the B.V.M.*—P.B.V.M.

[4100]—*Sisters of the Sorrowful Mother (Third Order of St. Francis).*—S.S.M.

[1720]—*Sisters of the Third Order Regular of St. Francis of the Congregation of Our Lady of Lourdes.*—O.S.F.

[4110]—*Ursuline Nuns (Roman Union)* (Central Prov.).—O.S.U.

DIOCESAN CEMETERIES

WINONA. *Catholic Cemeteries of Winona*, 55 W. Sanborn St., P.O. Box 588, 55987. Mr. John M. Vitek.

NECROLOGY

† Clasen, Leonard A., (Retired). —Died Nov. 22, 1996.

Diocese of Worcester

(Dioecesis Wigorniensis)

Most Reverend

DANIEL P. REILLY, D.D.

Bishop of Worcester; ordained May 30, 1953; appointed Bishop of Norwich June 17, 1975; consecrated August 6, 1975; appointed Bishop of Worcester October 27, 1994; installed December 8, 1994. *Res., 2 High Ridge Rd., Worcester, MA, 01602.*

Most Reverend

GEORGE E. RUEGER, D.D., V.G.

Auxiliary Bishop of Worcester; ordained January 6, 1958; appointed Auxiliary Bishop of Worcester and Titular Bishop of Maronana January 19, 1987; consecrated February 25, 1987. *Res., 2 High Ridge Rd., Worcester, MA, 01602.*

Chancery Office: 49 Elm St., Worcester, MA, 01609. Tel.: 508-791-7171; Fax: 508-753-7180.

ESTABLISHED JANUARY 14, 1950.

Square Miles 1,532.

Comprises the County of Worcester in the State of Massachusetts.

For legal titles of parishes and diocesan institutions, consult the Chancery Office.

STATISTICAL OVERVIEW

Personnel	
Bishop	1
Auxiliary Bishops	1
Abbots	3
Priests: Diocesan Active in Diocese	174
Priests: Active Outside Diocese	20
Priests: Retired, Sick or Absent	60
Number of Diocesan Priests	254
Religious Priests in Diocese	116
Ordinations:	
Religious Priests	1
Permanent Deacons in Diocese	67
Total Brothers	78
Total Sisters	550
Parishes	
Parishes	125
With Resident Pastor:	
Resident Diocesan Priests	122
Resident Religious Priests	3
Without Resident Pastor:	
Missions	3
Professional Ministry Personnel:	
Brothers	2
Sisters	37
Lay Ministers	73
Welfare	
Catholic Hospitals	1
Total Assisted	174,000
Homes for the Aged	7
Total Assisted	25,000
Residential Care of Children	1
Total Assisted	18
Day Care and Extended Day Care Centers	6
Total Assisted	450
Specialized Homes	2
Total Assisted	280
Special Centers for Social Services	10
Total Assisted	31,000
Other Institutions	1
Total Assisted	177
Educational	
Seminaries, Diocesan	1
Students from This Diocese	5
Diocesan Students in Other Seminaries	13
Total Seminarians	18
Colleges and Universities	3
Total Students	5,537
High Schools, Diocesan and Parish	4
Total Students	2,695
High Schools, Private	4
Total Students	1,260
Elementary Schools, Diocesan and Parish	21
Total Students	5,707
Elementary Schools, Private	2
Total Students	593
Non-residential Schools for the Disabled	1
Total Students	67
Catechesis/Religious Education:	
High School Students	7,400
Elementary Students	21,398
Total Students Under Catholic Instruction	44,675
Teachers in the Diocese:	
Priests	5
Brothers	13
Sisters	37
Lay Teachers	493
Vital Statistics	
Receptions into the Church:	
Infant Baptism Totals	4,786
Adult Baptism Totals	174
Received into Full Communion	253
First Communions	4,764
Confirmations	2,870
Marriages:	
Catholic	1,134
Interfaith	277
Total Marriages	1,411
Deaths	3,836
Total Catholic Population	301,660
Total Population	790,700

Former Bishops—His Eminence JOHN CARDINAL WRIGHT, D.D., ord. Dec. 8, 1935; appt. Titular Bishop of Aegea and Auxiliary Bishop of Boston, May 10, 1947; cons. June 30, 1947; transferred to new See of Worcester, Jan. 28, 1950 enthroned March 7, 1950; appt. Bishop of Pittsburgh, Jan. 28, 1959; created Cardinal, April 28, 1969; transferred to the Roman Curia Prefect, Sacred Congregation for the Clergy; died Aug. 10, 1979.—Most Rev. BERNARD J. FLANAGAN, D.D., J.C.D., resigned March 31, 1983; died Jan. 28, 1997.—Most Rev. TIMOTHY J. HARRINGTON, D.D., retired Oct. 27, 1994; died March 23, 1997.

Vicars General—Most Rev. GEORGE E. RUEGER, D.D., V.G., *2 High Ridge Rd., Worcester, 01602.* Tel: 508-755-3165.

Chancery Office—49 Elm St., Worcester, 01609. Tel: 508-791-7171; Fax: 508-753-7180.

Diocesan Director of Educational Services—Most Rev. GEORGE E. RUEGER, D.D., V.G., *49 Elm St., Worcester, 01608.* Tel: 508-791-7171.

Diocesan Director of Fiscal Affairs—Rev. Msgr. EDMOND T. TINSLEY, V.G., *49 Elm St., Worcester, 01609.* Tel: 508-791-7171.

Diocesan Director for Human Services (and Catholic Relief Services)—Rev. Msgr. EDMOND T. TINSLEY, V.G., *Res., 77 Mulberry St., Leicester, 01524.* Tel: 508-892-4886.

Diocesan Expansion Fund—Most Rev. GEORGE E. RUEGER, D.D.; Mr. KEVIN CONDRON, Chm., *49 Elm St., Worcester, 01609.* Tel: 508-791-7171.

Diocesan Finance Committee—JOSEPH GIOVINO, Chm., *49 Elm St., Worcester, 01609.*

Diocesan Tribunal—Address all communications to: *49 Elm St., Worcester, 01609.* Tel: 508-791-7171.

Vicar for Canonical Affairs and Judicial Vicar—Rev. F. STEPHEN PEDONE, J.C.L., *49 Elm St., Worcester, 01609.*

Associate Judicial Vicars—Rev. PAUL T. O'CONNELL, J.C.D., Assoc. Judicial Vicar.

Judges—Rev. HENRY G. BOWEN, J.C.D.; Rev. Msgr. JOHN J. KELLIHER; Revs. ROBERT J. KASLYN, S.J., J.C.D.; PAUL T. O'CONNELL, J.C.D.; F. STEPHEN PEDONE, J.C.L.

Promotor of Justice—Vacant.

Psychologist—Sr. MARY DANIEL MALLOY, R.S.M.

Secretary and Defender of the Bond—Deacon GEORGE L. O'TOOLE.

Advocates—Revs. ROLAND L. GAMACHE; THOMAS E. MAHONEY; LEO BARRY; JAMES P. KERRIGAN.

Notary—JUDITH M. GAUTHIER.

Diocesan Consultors—Most Rev. GEORGE E. RUEGER, D.D., V.G.; Rev. Msgr. RICHARD J. CARELLI; Revs. CHARLES DUMPHY; ROLAND GAMACHE; JOSEPH NALLY; ARTHUR OUILLETTE; F. STEPHEN PEDONE; ROCCO M. PICCOLOMINI; Rev. Msgr. FRANCIS J. SCOLLEN; Rev. JOSEPH SZWACH; Rev. Msgr. EDMOND T. TINSLEY.

Deans—Rev. CHARLES F. MONROE, Area I; Rev. MICHAEL BAFARO, Area II; Rev. JAMES B. O'SHEA, Area III; Rev. MARTIN P. DONAHUE, Area IV; Rev. JOHN E. HORGAN, Area V; Rev. PAUL J. TOUGAS, Area VI; Rev. MAURICE GILBERT, Area VII; Rev. DANIEL R. MULCAHY, Area VIII; Rev. CHESTER J. MISIEWICZ, Area IX; Rev. FRANCIS T. GOGUEN, Area X; Rev.

FRANK J. LIISTRO, Area XI; Rev. ROLAND J. GAMACHE, Area XII; Rev. JAMES J. CLIFFORD, Area XIII; (Retired).

Vicar for Clergy—Rev. ROCCO M. PICCOLOMINI, *Res., Our Lady of Mt. Carmel-St. Ann, 53 E. Central St., Worcester, 01605.*

Vicar for Religious—Sr. PAULA KELLEHER, *49 Elm St., Worcester, 01609.* Tel: 508-791-7171.

Diocesan Offices and Directors

The Adopt-a-Student Endowment Trust—MICHAEL J. COOGAN, Dir., *49 Elm St., Worcester, 01609.* Tel: 508-791-7171.

Apostleship of Prayer and Eucharistic Crusade—Rev. THADDEUS X. STACHURA, *Our Lady of Czestochowa, 34 Ward St., Worcester, 01610.* Tel: 508-755-5959.

Apostolate Office of Divine Mercy and Healing—Rev. RALPH A. DIORIO, Dir., *P.O. Box 668, Worcester, 01613-0668.* Tel: 508-791-0427.

Archivist—Most Rev. GEORGE E. RUEGER, *49 Elm St., Worcester, 01609.* Tel: 508-791-7171.

Brazilian Pastoral Ministry—Sr. BARBARA CICCOLINI, *49 Elm St., Worcester, 01609.* Tel: 508-791-7171, Ext. 153; Fax: 508-753-7180.

Bishop's Fund—OWEN C. COOGAN, Dir., *49 Elm St., Worcester, 01609.* Tel: 508-791-7171.

Building Commission Members—Rev. Msgr. GEORGE E. DENOMME; Most Rev. GEORGE E. RUEGER, D.D., V.G.; Rev. Msgr. EDMUND G. HADDAD; Rev. Msgr. EDMOND T. TINSLEY; Revs. LEE BARTLETT, Chm. JOHN FOLEY; ROBERT JOHNSON; THADDEUS STACHURA; JOHN THOMAS; Mr. HENRY MILLER; Mrs. MARY SLOCUM, *49 Elm St., Worcester, 01609.* Tel: 508-791-7171.

Campus Ministry—Rev. PETER J. SCANLON, Vicar for College Communities, *Diocesan Office, P.O. Box 903, Worcester, 01613., Res., The Center, 19 Schussler Rd., Worcester, 01609.* Tel: 508-757-6097., Newman Center: *281 Highland Ave., Fitchburg, 01420.* Tel: 508-345-2688.

Catholic Charities—CATHERINE LOEFFLER, Dir., *10 Hammond St., Worcester, 01610-1513.* Tel: 508-798-0191. (Refer to separate listings for detailed information on Catholic Charities and related organizations).

Cemeteries—Mr. FRANCIS F. ELLIOTT, Dir.; Rev. JOHN CAHILL, Priest liaison, *260 Cambridge St., Worcester, 01610.* Tel: 508-757-7415.

Charismatic Renewal, Office of—Mr. MICHAEL FREEL, Liaison, *St. Joseph, West St., P.O. Box 284, Berlin, 01503.* Tel: 508-365-6492.

Clergy Benefit Plan—Rev. JOHN J. FOLEY, *1052 Pleasant St., Worcester, 01602.*

Collaborative for Education and Ministry: Institute for Academic and Pastoral Development—Most Rev. GEORGE E. RUEGER, Chancellor.

Communication Office—RAYMOND L. DELISLE, Dir., *49 Elm St., Worcester, 01609.* Tel: 508-791-5357.

Continuing Education of the Clergy—Rev. MICHAEL ROSE, Dir., *89 Main St., S. Grafton, 01560.* Tel: 508-839-5354.

Cursillo—Rev. ROBERT A. GRATTAROTI, Dir., *37 Worcester Rd., Charlton City, 01508.* Tel: 508-248-7862.

Development Office—Bishop's Fund, Good Sheperd Endowment Fund, Adopt-A-Student, Annual Catholic School Appeal, Project Share for Christ, The Adopt-A-Student Endowment Trust. Mr. OWEN C. COOGAN, Dir., *49 Elm St., Worcester, 01609.* Tel: 508-754-0574; Fax: 508-754-2768.

Diocesan Expansion Fund—Mr. KEVIN CONDRON, Chm. Members: JANET S. SIMONDS; Revs. PATRICK HAWTHORNE; FRANK J. LIISTRO; RICHARD REIDY; Most Rev. GEORGE E. RUEGER; Rev. Msgr. EDMOND T. TINSLEY; Mrs. PATRICIA JONES; Mrs. JOAN HOULE.

Diocesan Scouts—Boy Scout Office: *120 Hill St., Whitinsville, 01588.* Tel: 508-234-0346., Girl Scout Office:*120 Hill St., Whitinsville, 01588.* Tel: 508-234-0346. Rev. RICHARD REIDY, *19 Chatham St., Worchester, 01609.*

Ecumenical and Interreligious Affairs, Diocesan Office for—Sr. THERESE DION, S.S.A., *49 Elm St., Worchester, 01609.*

Elderly, Ministry to—Rev. THOMAS M. BARRY, *48 Vernon St., Worcester, 01610.*

Evangelization, Office of—Rev. LAWRENCE J. ESPOSITO, Chm., *49 Elm St., Worcester, 01609.*

Family Life Ministry—Co-Directors: Mr. RONALD V. ARCIERI; Mrs. JANET M. ARCIERI, *49 Elm St., Worcester, 01609.* Tel: 508-791-7171.

Finance Office—Rev. Msgr. EDMOND T. TINSLEY, V.G., Fiscal Affairs; JEROME D. JUSSAUME, Mgr., Finance, *49 Elm St., Worcester, 01609.* Tel: 508-791-7171. Rev. DENNIS J. O'BRIEN, Dir.; Rev. JAMES FITTON, House of Priestly Formation, *761 Main St., Leicester, 01524.*

Haitian Ministries Coalition of the Diocese of Worcester—Deacon PETER R. FAFORD, Co-Chm. LINDA M. FAFORD, Co-Chm. & Treas.; Mrs. CONNIE BARNA, Sec.; Rev. WILLIAM KONICKI, Project Coord.; Dr. SITA RAM UPADHYAY; Rev. BRIAN O'TOOLE; Mrs. LOIS KOLOSKY, Adopt-A-Student; Rev. OLIVER BLANCHETTE, Advisory Board; Sr. ALICE RICHARDS, Advisory Board; ROBERT LANGLOIS, Micro Loan Project, *Office for Youth Ministry, 120 Hill St., Whitinsville, 01588.* Tel: 508-234-0346; Fax: 508-234-0348.

Holy Childhood Association—Rev. Msgr. THOMAS J. NEEDHAM, Dir., *353 Grove St., Worcester, 01605.* Tel: 508-754-8419.

Meet-the-Father Ministry, Inc.—Mrs. EILEEN GEORGE, Contact Person, *363 Greenwood St., Millbury, 01527.*

Newspaper—*"The Catholic Free Press"*, GERARD E. GOGGINS, Exec. Editor, *51 Elm St., Worcester, 01609.* Tel: 508-757-6387.

Office for Worship—Rev. ROBERT JOHNSON, Dir., *19 Chatham St., Worcester, 01609.* Tel: 508-798-0417.

Pastoral Associate Ministry Consultative Board—Sr. PAULA KELLEHER, S.S.J., Chm., *49 Elm St., Worcester, 01609.* Tel: 508-791-7171.

Permanent Diaconate—Co-Directors: Revs. ROCCO M. PICCOLOMINI; JAMES AQUINO, *49 Elm St., Worcester, 01609.*

Presbyteral Council—Most Rev. DANIEL P. REILLY, Pres.; Most Rev. GEORGE E. RUEGER; Revs. F. STEPHEN PEDONE; JAMES J. AQUINO; Rev. Msgr. RICHARD J. CARELLI; Revs. JOSEPH M. NALLY, Chm. ROCCO PICCOLOMINI; JOSEPH F. SZWACH; Rev. Msgr. EDMOND T. TINSLEY, Sec.; Revs. PAUL J. TOUGAS, Treas. CHARLES F. MONROE, Vice Chm., *Chancery Bldg., 49 Elm St., Worcester, 01609.* Tel: 508-791-7171.

Priests' Personnel Board—Rev. ROCCO M. PICCOLOMINI, *Our Lady of Mt. Carmel-St. Ann, 53 E. Central St., Worcester, 01605.* Tel: 508-792-4574.

Priests' Retirement Residence—Rev. JOHN F. CAHILL, Admin., *222 June St., Worcester, 01602.* Tel: 508-791-0311.

Pro-Life—Rev. CHESTER J. DEVLIN, Dir./Educational Coord., *49 Elm St., Worcester, 01609.*

Propagation of the Faith—Rev. Msgr. THOMAS J. NEEDHAM, Dir., *353 Grove St., Worcester, 01605.* Tel: 508-754-8419.

Religious Education Office—Rev. Msgr. LOUIS R. PIERMARINI, Dir., *49 Elm St., Worcester, 01609.* Tel: 508-791-7171., *Res., St. Roch, 334 Main St., Oxford, 01540.*

North County Office Fitchburg—Mrs. MARY G. HOVENESIAN, Assoc. Dir./North Country Coord., *89 Sheridan St., Fitchburg, 01420.* Tel: 508-345-6636.

School Department—Mr. CHARLES E. MCMANUS, Supt. PATRICIA M. HALPIN; Mr. TIMOTHY RIOUX, Assoc. Supt., Schools, *49 Elm St., Worcester, 01609.* Tel: 508-791-7171.

Social Justice, Peace and Integrity of Creation, Office of—RACHELLE COMTOIS, Chm., *49 Elm St., Worcester, 01609.* Tel: 508-791-7171.

Spanish Apostolate—Rev. JOSE A. RODRIGUEZ, Bishop's Liaison, *429 Main St., Worcester, 01610., 49 Elm St., Worchester, 01609.* Tel: 508-791-7171.

St. Vincent dePaul Society—*Central and Greater Worcester District Council*—FRANCES PIKE, Pres.; Rev. Msgr. EDMOND T. TINSLEY, Spiritual Dir., *Res., 77 Mulberry St., Leicester, 01524.* Tel: 508-892-4886.

Northern Worcester County District Council—JOHN YOVINO, Pres.; Rev. Msgr. LEO J. BATTISTA, Chap.

Southern Worcester County District Council—ALFRED E. BALLARD, Pres.; Rev. J. NORMAND TREMBLAY, Chap.

Tri-Conference Retirement Fund for Religious—Sr. PAULA KELLEHER, S.S.J., Diocesan Coord., *49 Elm St., Worcester, 01609.* Tel: 508-791-7171.

Vicar for Priests—Rev. ROCCO M. PICCOLOMINI, *53 E. Central St., Worcester, 01605.*

Vicar for Religious—Sr. PAULA KELLEHER, S.S.J., *49 Elm St., Worcester, 01609.* Tel: 508-791-7171.

Vietnamese Apostolate—Rev. PHUONG VAN NGUYEN, *1052 Pleasant St., Worcester, 01602., 44 Temple St., Worcester, 01605.* Tel: 508-756-7165.

Vocation Office—Rev. THOMAS SULLIVAN, Dir., *49 Elm St., Worcester, 01609.* Tel: 508-756-7165.

Worcester Diocesan Commission for Women—Mrs. MARY DONOVAN, Chm., *49 Elm St., Worcester, 01609.* Tel: 508-791-7171.

Youth Ministry—LISA KELLY, Interim Dir., Office: *Oakhurst, 120 Hill St., Whitinsville, 01588.* Tel: 508-234-0346.

CLERGY, PARISHES, MISSIONS AND PAROCHIAL SCHOOLS

CITY OF WORCESTER
(Worcester County)

1—ST. PAUL'S CATHEDRAL (1866), Revs. Richard F. Reidy, Rector; Joseph P. Mahoney; Daniel Becker; Deacons James P. Quinlivan, Sr.; Francisco Escobar. In res., Revs. David E. Doiron; Robert K. Johnson.
Res., 38 High St., 01609. Tel: 508-799-4193; Fax: 508-752-6308.
Catechesis/Religious Programs—Tel: 508-755-1414.
Students 209.

2—ASCENSION (1911), Rev. Joseph A. Adamo.
Res., 48 Vernon St., 01610. Tel: 508-752-4459; Fax: 508-752-8821.

3—BLESSED SACRAMENT (1912), Rev. Charles J. Dumphy. In res., Rev. Thomas Landry.
Res., 551 Pleasant St., 01602. Tel: 508-755-5291; Fax: 508-755-6891.
Catechesis/Religious Programs—Epiphany House, Tel: 508-752-4368. Sr. Mary M. Duffy, S.S.J., D.R.E.
Students 145.

4—CHRIST THE KING (1936), Revs. John J. Foley; Phuong Van Nguyen; Sr. Bernadette Lavoie, S.S.A., Pastoral Assoc.; Deacon Joseph M. Banieukiewicz.
Res., 1052 Pleasant St., 01602. Tel: 508-754-5361; Fax: 508-753-0448.
Catechesis/Religious Programs—Tel: 508-752-5514. Susan J. Wenc, D.R.E.
Students 833.

5—HOLY NAME OF JESUS (1893) (French), Rev. Msgr. Joseph V. Sirois. In res., Rev. Gerard L. Bertin.
Res., 51 Illinois St., 01610. Tel: 508-799-2792; Fax: 508-799-2368.
Catechesis/Religious Programs—Tel: 508-756-6370.
Students 133.

6—IMMACULATE CONCEPTION (1873), Rev. Msgr. Thomas J. Needham.
Res., 353 Grove St., 01605. Tel: 508-754-8419; Fax: 508-756-2192.
Catechesis/Religious Programs—Father Connor Center, Tel: 508-791-5887; Fax: 508-754-8508.
Students 171.

7—NOTRE DAME DES CANADIENS - ST. JOSEPH (1869) (French), Revs. Richard G. Roger; Thomas B. Fleming; Mary G. Guerin, Pastoral Assoc.
Res., 5 Whitman Rd., 01609. Tel: 508-754-6722; Fax: 508-797-1191. [CEM]
Catechesis/Religious Programs—Students 58.

8—OUR LADY OF THE ANGELS (1916), Revs. Charles F. Monroe; William E. Champlin. Pastoral Assocs.: Sr. Barbara Collins, S.N.D.; Deacon Alphonse Desautels.
Res., 1222 Main St., 01603. Tel: 508-791-0951; Fax: 508-753-9531.
School—1220 Main St., Rear, 01603. Tel: 508-752-5609; Fax: 508-798-9634. John F. Hanson, Prin.
Lay Teachers 17; Students 320.
Catechesis/Religious Programs—Tel: 508-754-4165.
Students 549.

9—OUR LADY OF CZESTOCHOWA (1903) (Polish), Revs. Thaddeus X. Stachura; Anthony S. Kazarnowicz.
Res., 34 Ward St., 01610. Tel: 508-755-5959; Fax: 508-767-1644.
School—St. Mary's, (Grades K-6) 50 Richland St., Tel: 508-753-0484. Sr. M. Dorothea Prin. & D.R.E.
Sisters of the Holy Family of Nazareth 3; Lay Teachers 9; Students 178.
St. Mary's Jr. & Sr. High School—Tel: 508-753-1170; Fax: 508-795-0560. Mark Manzello, Prin.
Sisters 2; Lay Teachers 16; Students 176.
Catechesis/Religious Programs—Students 220.

10—OUR LADY OF FATIMA (1952), Rev. Louis J. Gould; Sr. Emanuela Bacci, X.M.M., Spanish Apostolate; Deacon Vincent Librandi. In res., Rev. Edward M. Ryan.
Res., 7 Auburn St., 01605. Tel: 508-755-3820; Fax: 508-755-7196.
Catechesis/Religious Programs—Students 127.

11—OUR LADY OF LORETO (1966) (Italian), Rev. James J. Aquino; Deacon Nicholas CaraDonna.
Res., 33 Massasoit Rd., 01604. Tel: 508-753-5001; Fax: 508-754-1537.
Catechesis/Religious Programs—37 Massasoit Rd., 01604. Tel: 508-799-2445.
Students 151.

12—OUR LADY OF LOURDES (1949), Rev. James B. O'Shea. In res., Rev. Bernard J. Conlin, (Retired).
Res., 1290 Grafton St., 01604. Tel: 508-757-0789; Fax: 508-757-0048.
Catechesis/Religious Programs—Tel: 508-753-5773. Jo-Ann Bafaro, D.R.E.
Students 180.

13—OUR LADY OF MT. CARMEL AND ST. ANN (1872) (Italian), Rev. Michael P. Bafaro. In res., Rev. Rocco Piccolomini.
Res., 53 E. Central St., 01605. Tel: 508-752-2964; Fax: 508-755-3506.

Catechesis/Religious Programs—Tel: 508-791-6139. Joan D'Argenis, D.R.E.
Students 282.

14—OUR LADY OF THE ROSARY (1911), Rev. Msgr. John J. Kelliher; Rev. James M. Shea.
Res., 23 Fales St., 01606. Tel: 508-853-1640; Fax: 508-853-2426.
Catechesis/Religious Programs—Father Riley Center, 9 Emerson Rd., 01604. Tel: 508-852-5474. Sr. Irene Moran, M.P.V., D.R.E.
Students 530.

15—OUR LADY OF VILNA (1925) (Lithuanian), Rev. Alphonse A. Volungis.
Res., 153 Sterling St., 01610. Tel: 508-752-1825.

16—SACRED HEART (1880), Rev. Lee F. Bartlett. In res., Rev. Peter J. Scanlon.
Res., 596 Cambridge St., 01610. Tel: 508-752-1608; Fax: 508-757-2462.
Catechesis/Religious Programs—Students 124.

17—ST. ANDREW THE APOSTLE (1954), Rev. James F. Carmody; Sr. Therese Gosselin, S.S.A., Pastoral Assoc.
Res., 16 Vineyard St., 01603. Tel: 508-754-6057; Fax: 508-754-0830.
Catechesis/Religious Programs—Tel: 508-752-4701.
Students 127.

18—ST. BERNARD (1916), Rev. Edmund F. Falvey.
Res., 236 Lincoln St., 01605. Tel: 508-791-3104; Fax: 508-791-7124.
Catechesis/Religious Programs—One Harlow St., 01605.
Students 60.

19—ST. CASIMIR'S (1894) (Lithuanian), Rev. Anthony N. Nockunas, M.I.C., Temporary Admin. In res., Rev. John C. Petruaskas, M.I.C.
Res., 41 Providence St., 01604. Tel: 508-754-5142; Fax: 508-770-8060.

20—ST. CATHERINE OF SWEDEN (1952), Rev. George J. Ridick; Sr. Kathleen McGurk, Pastoral Assoc.; Deacon Thomas Wagner.
Res., 3 Wiser Ave., 01607. Tel: 508-752-1624; Fax: 508-797-1196.
Catechesis/Religious Programs—Tel: 508-793-2187.
Students 105.

21—ST. CHARLES BORROMEO (1954), Revs. Henry G. Bowen; Quynh Dinh Tran; Deacon Peter R. Faford.
Res., 341 June St., 01602. Tel: 508-799-4031; Fax: 508-792-6675.
Catechesis/Religious Programs—Sr. Elaine Potvin, S.S.A., D.R.E.
Students 212.

22—ST. CHRISTOPHER (1956), Rev. Martin P. Donahue; Deacon Henry Morrissey.
Res., 950 W. Boylston St., 01606. Tel: 508-853-1492; Fax: 508-853-4338.
Catechesis/Religious Programs—Tel: 508-853-3302.
Students 215.

23—ST. GEORGE (1951), Revs. Henry A. Donoghue; Stephen G. Copper. In res., Rev. F. Stephen Pedone.
Res., 40 Brattle St., 01606. Tel: 508-853-0183; Fax: 508-854-0864.
Catechesis/Religious Programs—Tel: 508-852-1784. Miss Diane Fitch, D.R.E.
Students 732.

24—ST. JOAN OF ARC (1950), Revs. Joseph M. Nally; Emerito Ortiz; Sr. Soledad Chacon, R.O.D.A., Pastoral Assoc.
Res., 570 Lincoln St., 01605. Tel: 508-852-3232; Fax: 508-852-3223.
Catechesis/Religious Programs—Students 450.

25—ST. JOHN'S (1834), Rev. Joseph A. Coonan. In res., Rev. Joseph P. Mahoney.
Res., 44 Temple St., 01604. Tel: 508-756-7165; Fax: 508-754-5153.
Catechesis/Religious Programs—Mrs. Donna Mastrovito, D.R.E.
Students 134.

26—ST. MARGARET MARY (1922), Rev. Patrick J. Hawthorne; Deacon Bruce Vidito.
Res., 77 Alvarado Ave., 01604. Tel: 508-753-5788; Fax: 508-797-1644.
Catechesis/Religious Programs—Students 95.

27—ST. PETER (1884), Rev. Msgr. Francis J. Scollen; Rev. Jose Andres Rodriguez. In res., Rev. John F. Madden.
Res., 929 Main St., 01610. Tel: 508-752-4674.
Catechesis/Religious Programs—Tel: 508-752-0797; Fax: 508-767-1511.
Students 282.

28—ST. STEPHEN'S (1887), Rev. William F. Sanders; Deacon James F. DiPadua, Jr. In res., Rev. Thomas M. Barry, D.
Res., 16 Hamilton St., 01604. Tel: 508-755-3165; Fax: 508-755-0937.
School—355 Grafton St., Tel: 508-755-3209. Sr. Constance Gosselin, S.S.A., Prin.
Sisters 6; Lay Teachers 13; Students 292.
Catechesis/Religious Programs—Ramona Kneeland, D.R.E.
Students 240.

OUTSIDE THE CITY OF WORCESTER
(In the County of Worcester)

Ashburnham, St. Denis (1951), Rev. Joseph J. Jurgelonis; Deacons Michael P. Connor; Richard Desjardins.
Res., 85 Main St., P.O. Box 418, 01430. Tel: 978-827-5806; Fax: 978-827-1191. [CEM]
Catechesis/Religious Programs—Tel: 978-827-4892.
Students 386.

Athol, Our Lady Immaculate (1882), Rev. Stephen D. Johnson; Deacons James L. Linderman; Robert Dio.
Res., 192 School St., 01331-2399. Tel: 978-249-2738; Fax: 978-249-0447. [CEM 2]
Catechesis/Religious Programs—Tel: 978-249-7690. Sharon Maher, D.R.E.
Students 340.
Mission—South Royalston, Worcester Co., Our Lady Queen of Heaven, Rte. 68, South Royalston, 01368. Tel: 978-249-4103.

St. Francis (1912), Rev. Raymond P. Messier.
Res., 105 Main St., 01331. Tel: 508-249-3361.

Auburn, St. Joseph's (1907), Revs. Richard F. Trainor; Dennis O. O'Malley.
Res., 194 Oxford St., 01501. Tel: 508-832-2074; Fax: 508-832-8894.
Catechesis/Religious Programs—Tel: 508-832-5975. Ms. Susan Landry, D.R.E.
Students 773.

North American Martyrs (1952), Rev. John F. Gee.
Res., 8 Wyoma Dr., 01501. Tel: 508-798-8779; Fax: 508-791-6614.
Catechesis/Religious Programs—Tel: 508-798-0612. Priscilla Underwood, D.R.E.
Students 130.

Baldwinville, St. Vincent De Paul (1955), Rev. John E. Kelley.
Res., 18 Pleasant St., 01436. Tel: 978-939-8851; Fax: 978-939-2120.
Catechesis/Religious Programs—Tel: 978-939-8290.
Students 151.

Barre, St. Joseph's (1896), Rev. Thomas H. Hultquist; Deacon Walter Doyle.
Res., 90 Common St., 01005. Tel: 978-355-4463; Fax: 978-355-0136.
Catechesis/Religious Programs—Tel: 978-355-6402.
Students 222.
Mission—Wheelwright, Hardwick Co., St. Augustine, 98 Church Ln., Wheelwright, 01094. Tel: 978-355-4463.

Berlin, St. Joseph the Good Provider (1973), Rev. Lawrence J. Esposito.
Res., 52 West St., Box 284, 01503-0284. Tel: 978-365-6492; 838-2915 (Office); Fax: 978-365-9133.
Catechesis/Religious Programs—Students 120.

Blackstone, St. Paul's (1850), Rev. James D. Champion.
Res., 48 St. Paul St., 01504. Tel: 508-883-6726; Fax: 508-883-2079. [CEM]
Catechesis/Religious Programs—Tel: 508-883-3542; Fax: 508-883-2079.
Students 374.

St. Theresa (1929) (French), Rev. Richard H. Labonte.
Res., 630 Rathbun St., 01504. Tel: 508-883-7206; Fax: 508-883-5250.
Catechesis/Religious Programs—Tel: 508-883-7527.
Students 160.

Bolton, St. Francis Xavier (1953), Rev. Robert L. Killion.
Res., 808 Main St., 01740. Tel: 508-779-2750; Fax: 508-779-0337.
Catechesis/Religious Programs—Students 115.

Boylston, St. Mary of the Hills (1952), Rev. Paul J. Tougas; Deacon Raymond H. Bolduc.
Res., 630 Cross St., 01505. Tel: 508-869-6771; Fax: 508-869-3465.
Catechesis/Religious Programs—Tel: 508-869-6776; Fax: 508-869-0418.
Students 205.

Brookfield, St. Mary's (1885), Rev. Eugene F. Berthiaume.
Res., 4 Howard St., 01506. Tel: 508-867-3188; Fax: 508-867-4313.
Catechesis/Religious Programs—Students 75.

Charlton City, St. Joseph's (1900), Revs. Robert A. Grattaroti; J. Normand Tremblay; Deacons Lawrence F. Miskell; William S. Miller.
Res., Box 338, 01508. Tel: 508-248-7862; Fax: 508-248-5832.
Catechesis/Religious Programs—Tel: 508-248-7986. Gerrie Nowicki, D.R.E.
Students 773.

Clinton, St. John the Evangelist (1849), Revs. Thomas V. Walsh; Robert D. Bruso. Pastoral Assocs.: Sr. Theresa Sullivan, P.B.V.M.; Sr. Sheila Finnegan, S.N.D.
Res., 149 Chestnut St., 01510. Tel: 508-368-0366; Fax: 508-368-4359. [CEM]
Catechesis/Religious Programs—Tel: 508-368-0052.
Students 625.

Our Lady of Jasna Gora (1913) (Polish), Rev. Richard T. Zuscak.
Res., 128 Franklin St., 01510. Tel: 508-365-2724; Fax: 508-365-5705.
School—St.Mary's, R128 Franklin St., 01510. Tel: 508-365-3137. Dale Gorski, Prin.
Lay Teachers 8; Students 170.

Our Lady of the Rosary (1909), Rev. J. Brendan Nally.
Res., One Cross St., 01510. Tel: 508-365-3621; Fax: 508-368-3082.
Catechesis/Religious Programs—Students 90.

Dudley, St. Andrew Bobola (1963) (Polish), Revs. Joseph F. Szwach; Joseph Bielonko.
Res., 54 W. Main St., P.O. Box 98, 01571. Tel: 508-943-5633; Fax: 508-949-6701. [JC]
Catechesis/Religious Programs—Students 97.

St. Anthony's (1969), Rev. Paul F. Campbell.
Res., 22 Dudley Hill Rd., Box 277, 01571-0277. Tel: 508-943-0470. [CEM]
Catechesis/Religious Programs—Tel: 508-949-0335; Fax: 508-943-5663.
Students 327.

East Brookfield, St. John the Baptist (1952), Rev. Joseph G. Loiselle.
Res., 121 Blaine Ave., 01515. Tel: 508-867-3738; Fax: 508-867-3301.
Catechesis/Religious Programs—Tel: 508-885-4506.
Students 96.

East Douglas, St. Denis (1870), Rev. William N. Cormier.
Res., 23 Manchaug Rd., 01516. Tel: 508-476-2002; Fax: 508-476-2022. [CEM]
Catechesis/Religious Programs—Students 374.

East Templeton, Holy Cross (1952), Rev. George L. O'Brien.
Res., 25 Lake Ave., P.O. Box 418, 01438. Tel: 978-632-2121; Fax: 978-630-3890.
Catechesis/Religious Programs—Tel: 978-632-2194.
Students 202.

Fiskdale, St. Anne's and St. Patrick's (1886), Revs. Donald B. Espinosa, A.A.; Paul Vandreuil, A.A.; Aidan M. Furlong, A.A.; Oliver R. Blanchette, A.A.; Deacon Clarence H. Martel.
Res., 16 Church St., 01518. Tel: 508-347-7338; Fax: 508-347-2982. [CEM]
Catechesis/Religious Programs—Tel: 508-347-9353.
Students 467.

Fitchburg

1—ST. ANTHONY OF PADUA (1908), Rev. John M. Siciliano, Temp. Admin.; Deacon John B. LeBlanc.
Res., 2 Beekman St., 01420. Tel: 978-342-4706; Fax: 978-342-8160.
School—(Grades PreK-8). Tel: 978-345-7785; Fax: 978-342-5110. Margaret Haneisen.
Sisters 1; Lay Teachers 11; Students 243.
Catechesis/Religious Programs—Tel: 978-342-2491.
Students 108.

2—ST. BERNARD'S (1847) (Irish), Rev. H. Edward Chalmers. In res., Revs. Thomas M. Tierney; Theodore R. Laperle.
Res., 240 Water St., 01420. Tel: 978-343-7459; Fax: 978-343-0193. [CEM]
School—254 Summer St., 01420. Tel: 978-342-1948; Fax: 978-342-1153.
Sisters of the Presentation of the Blessed Virgin Mary 2; Lay Teachers 10; Students 250.
Catechesis/Religious Programs—Students 185.

3—ST. CAMILLUS DE LELLIS (1953), Rev. Richard P. Lewandowski; Deacon Benjamin A. Nogueira.
Res., 333 Mechanic St., 01420. Tel: 508-342-7921; Fax: 508-345-2688.
Catechesis/Religious Programs—Students 178.

4—ST. FRANCIS OF ASSISI (1903), Rev. Gerald A. Dorais; Deacon William Colon, Spanish Ministry. In res., Rev. Angel Matos, Spanish Ministry.
Res., 63 Sheridan, 01420. Tel: 508-342-9651; Fax: 508-342-7936.
Catechesis/Religious Programs—Tel: 508-342-3521. Susan Hanno, D.R.E.
Students 125.

5—IMMACULATE CONCEPTION (1886) (French), Rev. Msgr. Richard E. Collette; Deacons Norman Prince; Raymond P. Dauphinais; John Aliskevicz.

Res., 59 Walnut St., 01420. Tel: 508-342-5851; Fax: 508-345-2491.
Catechesis/Religious Programs—Students 56.

6—St. Joseph's (1890), Rev. John R. Dolan, M.S.; Deacons Andre W. Croteau; David R. Isabelle. In res., Revs. John J. Nally, M.S.; John Hughes, M.S.; James Weeks.
Res., 49 Woodland St., 01420. Tel: 508-345-7997; Fax: 508-345-7678. [CEM]
School—35 Columbus St., 01420. Tel: 508-343-3630. Karen Croteau, Prin.
Lay Teachers 10; Students 221.
Catechesis/Religious Programs—Tel: 508-345-7997. Bette Gilman, D.R.E.
Students 120.

7—Madonna of the Holy Rosary (1955), Rev. Frank J. Liistro.
Res., 118 Theresa St., 01420. Tel: 978-342-1290; Fax: 978-345-3032.
Catechesis/Religious Programs—Tel: 978-345-4906. Judy A. Alario, D.R.E.
Students 210.

8—Sacred Heart of Jesus (1867) (Irish), Rev. John A. Dwyer; Deacon Edgar B. Blackwelder.
Res., 22 Cottage St., 01420. Tel: 508-342-9606.
Catechesis/Religious Programs—Students 72.

Gardner

1—Holy Spirit (1955), Revs. Andre M. Gariepy; Angel Matos, Spanish Ministry.
Res., 45 Metcalf St., 01440. Tel: 978-632-3333; Fax: 978-632-3630.
Catechesis/Religious Programs—Students 215.

2—St. Joseph's (1908) (Polish), Rev. Thomas M. Tokarz.
Res., 358 Pleasant St., 01440. Tel: 978-632-0375; Fax: 978-632-1282. [CEM]

3—Our Lady of the Holy Rosary (1884) (French), Revs. J. Andre Guenette; Laurie Leger, M.S.; Deacon Arthur Giard.
Res., 135 Nichols St., 01440. Tel: 508-632-0253; Fax: 508-630-1773. [CEM]
School—99 Nichols St., 01440. Tel: 508-632-8656; Fax: 508-630-1433.
Sisters of the Presentation of Mary 6; Lay Teachers 16; Students 378.
Catechesis/Religious Programs—Students 172.

4—Sacred Heart of Jesus (1874), Rev. Donald H. Baker; Deacon Paul J. Carrier.
Res., 166 Cross St., 01440. Tel: 508-632-0237; Fax: 508-630-2459. [CEM]
Parish Center: 100 Central St., 01440. Tel: 508-632-0217 (Deacon's Office).
School—Sacred Heart Elementary, Lynde St., 01440. Tel: 508-632-0950. Frank Peterlin, Prin.
Lay Teachers 9; Students 183.
Catechesis/Religious Programs—Tel: 508-632-0218.
Students 334.
Day Care—Tel: 508-632-5745. Mrs. Jane Pineo, Dir.

Gilbertville, St. Aloysius (1894), Rev. Chester J. Misiewicz.
Res., 58 Church St., P.O. Box 542, 01031-0542. Tel: 413-477-6493; Fax: 413-477-6493. [CEM]
Catechesis/Religious Programs—Students 94.

Grafton, St. Philip's (1869), Rev. Anthony T. Marteka.
Res., 12 West St., 01519. Tel: 508-839-3325; Fax: 508-839-1310. [CEM]
Catechesis/Religious Programs—Tel: 508-839-9130.
Students 210.

Harvard, St. Theresa's (1950), Rev. Normand R. Gaumond; Deacon John W. Lee.
Res., 15 Still River Rd., P.O. Box P, 01451. Tel: 508-456-3563; Fax: 508-456-8352.
Catechesis/Religious Programs—Tel: 508-456-8807. Lorretta DiPietro, D.R.E.
Students 253.

Hopedale, Sacred Heart of Jesus (1935), Rev. Raymond M. Goodwin, Jr.; Deacon Joseph Manella.
Res., 187 Hopedale St., Box 16, 01747. Tel: 508-473-1900; Fax: 508-473-1745.
Catechesis/Religious Programs—Tel: 508-473-1701. Carol Pellegrino, D.R.E.
Students 553.

Jefferson, St. Mary's (1884), Rev. Andre N. Remillard; Maureen Smith, Pastoral Assoc.
Res., 114 Princeton St., 01522. Tel: 508-829-4508; Fax: 508-829-0429. [CEM]
Catechesis/Religious Programs—Tel: 508-829-6758. Charlene Dahlin, D.R.E.
Students 566.

Lancaster, Immaculate Conception (1915), Rev. Edward P. Lettic.
Res., 28 Packard St., P.O. Box 95, 01523. Tel: 508-365-6582; Fax: 508-365-3097.
Catechesis/Religious Programs—Students 280.

Leicester, St. Joseph's (1851), Rev. Michael A. DiGeronimo; Carol Cornacchioli, Pastoral Assoc.
Res., 759 Main St., 01524. Tel: 508-892-7407; Fax: 508-892-4753. [CEM]
Catechesis/Religious Programs—Tel: 508-892-9081. Colleen A. Bernard, D.R.E.
Students 326.
Day Care, Caring Place—Tel: 508-892-3168.
Students 54.

St. Pius X (1956), Rev. Michael A. DiGeronimo; Carol A. Cornacchioli, Pastoral Assoc.
Mailing Address: 759 Main St., 01524. Tel: 508-892-7407; Fax: 508-892-4753.
Church—1161 Main St., 01524.
Catechesis/Religious Programs—Tel: 508-892-9081.
Students 326.

Leominster

1—St. Anna's (1937), Rev. Ronald G. Falco.
Res., 199 Lancaster St., 01453. Tel: 508-537-5293; Fax: 508-537-2950.
School—Tel: 508-534-4770. Rita Bernard, Prin.
Priests 1; Sisters 1; Lay Teachers 12; Students 205.
Catechesis/Religious Programs—Students 335.

2—Holy Family of Nazareth (1963), Rev. Thomas F. Egan.
Res., 800 Union St., 01453. Tel: 978-537-3016; Fax: 978-534-1119.
Catechesis/Religious Programs—Tel: 978-537-5660. Sr. Patricia Roddy, P.B.V.M., D.R.E.
Students 261.

3—St. Cecilia's (1900) (French), Rev. Francis T. Goguen; Rev. Msgr. George E. Denomme; Rev. John G. Hillier; Deacon Ronald J. Aubuchon.
Res., 170 Mechanic St., 01453. Tel: 978-537-6541; Fax: 978-840-1965. [CEM]
Catechesis/Religious Programs—Tel: 978-534-6907. Sr. Anne Arpin, D.H.S., D.R.E.
Students 302.
Convent—190 Mechanic St., 01453.
Daughters of the Holy Spirit 3.

4—St. Leo's (1872), Revs. John E. Doran; Joseph M. Dolan. In res., Rev. Leo J. O'Neil.
Res., 108 Main St., 01453. Tel: 508-537-7257; Fax: 508-840-6182. [CEM]
School—120 Main St., 01453. Tel: 508-537-1007. Sr. Brian Elizabeth Barnicle, Prin.
Sisters of the Presentation of the Blessed Virgin Mary 6; Lay Teachers 18; Students 310.
Catechesis/Religious Programs—Tel: 508-537-1194.
Students 440.

5—Our Lady of the Lake (1952), Rev. Timothy M. Brewer; Deacon Fred A. Harkins.
Res., 1400 Main St., 01453. Tel: 978-342-2978; Fax: 978-342-8738.
Catechesis/Religious Programs—Tel: 978-345-7469. Sr. Rosemary Fay, S.N.D., D.R.E.
Students 470.

Linwood, Good Shepherd (1904), Rev. Daniel R. Mulcahy, Jr.; Deborah R. Blicharz, Pastoral Assoc., D.R.E.
Res., 121 Linwood St., P.O. Box 517, 01525. Tel: 508-234-7726; Fax: 508-234-0964.
Catechesis/Religious Programs—Tel: 508-234-5340.
Students 250.

Lunenburg, St. Boniface (1950), Rev. Edward D. Niccolls; Sr. Mary E. LeBlanc, P.B.V.M., Pastoral Assoc.; Deacon Joseph M. Cieri. In res., Rev. Donald C. Ouellette.
Res., 817 Massachusetts Ave., 01462. Tel: 978-582-4008; Fax: 978-582-9302.
Catechesis/Religious Programs—Tel: 978-582-6650; Fax: 978-582-9355. Mr. Thomas J. Griffin, D.R.E.
Students 480.

Manchaug, St. Anne's (1900), Rev. Stanley F. Krutcik.
Res., 31 Main St., Box 311, 01526. Tel: 508-476-2405; Fax: 508-476-4443.
Catechesis/Religious Programs—Students 51.

Mendon, St. Michael's (1952), Rev. Thomas E. Mahoney; Deacon Ernest E. Desmarais.
Res., 29 North Ave., P.O. Box 33, 01756. Tel: 508-478-4456; Fax: 508-634-2665.
Catechesis/Religious Programs—Students 282.

Milford, St. Mary of the Assumption (1848), Revs. Michael G. Foley; David B. Galonek; Eusiquio Munoz; Sr. Theresa Lucier, S.P., Pastoral Assoc.
Res., 27 Pearl St., 01757. Tel: 508-473-2000; Fax: 508-473-6907. [CEM]
School—Tel: 508-473-7303.
Sisters 1; Lay Teachers 14; Students 274.
Catechesis/Religious Programs—St. Mary's Parish Center, 17 Winter St., 01757. Tel: 508-478-7440. Martha LaFreniere Harris, D.R.E.
Students 817.

Sacred Heart (1905), Rev. Paul D. Burns, C.S.S. Pastoral Ministers: Sr. Claire Belforti, S.S.J.; Sr. Estelle Santarpia, S.S.J.
Res., 5 E. Main St., 01757. Tel: 508-473-0331; Fax: 508-478-4993. [CEM]
Catechesis/Religious Programs—Tel: 508-473-1036. Sr. Catherine Walsh, R.S.M., D.R.E.
Students 587.

Millbury, Assumption (1884) (French), Rev. Richard A. Fortin.
Res., 16 Waters St., 01527. Tel: 508-865-2657; Fax: 508-865-4866.
School—21 Grove St., 01527. Tel: 508-865-5404; Fax: 508-865-5404. Sr. Rita St. Onge, S.A.S.V., Prin.
Lay Teachers 11; Students 248.
Assumption Preschool—Tel: 508-865-6872.
Catechesis/Religious Programs—Students 62.

St. Brigid (1849), Revs. Thomas J. Markey; Robert E. Kelley.
Res., 59 Main St., 01527. Tel: 508-865-6624; Fax: 508-865-3101. [CEM]
Catechesis/Religious Programs—Tel: 508-865-2752. Mrs. Gloria Schimke, D.R.E.
Students 483.

Millville, St. Augustine's (1884), Rev. Jean Paul Gagnon; Deacon William Lucier.
Res., 17 Lincoln St., 01529. Tel: 508-883-6678; Fax: 508-883-5878.
Catechesis/Religious Programs—15 Lincoln St., 01529. Tel: 508-883-8794.
Students 206.

Northboro, St. Bernadette (1959), Rev. Chester J. Devlin.
Res., 266 Main St., P.O. Box 743, 01532. Tel: 508-393-2838; Fax: 508-393-2718.
School—(Grades PreK-3) 266 Main St., 01532. Tel: 508-351-9905. Marcella A. Wilson, Prin.
Lay Teachers 4; Students 80.
Catechesis/Religious Programs—Tel: 508-393-7445. Judi Winning, Pastoral Assoc.& D.R.E.
Students 176.

St. Rose of Lima (1883), Rev. James A. Houston; Sr. M. Cathleen Toomey, R.S.M.
Res., 244 W. Main St., P.O. Box 685, 01532. Tel: 508-393-2413; Fax: 508-393-4922.
Catechesis/Religious Programs—P.O. Box 387, Tel: 508-393-6444. Mrs. Laverne Bertin, D.R.E.
Students 675.

Northbridge, St. Peter (1903), Rev. John F. Connell.
Res., 39 Church Ave., 01534. Tel: 508-234-2156; Fax: 508-234-5123.
Catechesis/Religious Programs—Tel: 508-234-6355. Barbara Ramian, D.R.E.
Students 159.

North Brookfield, St. Joseph's (1867), Rev. Richard T. Carey.
Res., 28 Mt. Pleasant St., 01535. Tel: 508-867-6811; Fax: 508-867-7756. [CEM]
Catechesis/Religious Programs—27 Mt. Pleasant St., 01535. Tel: 508-867-9302.
Students 342.

North Grafton, St. Mary's (1952), Rev. John J. Bagley; Sr. Beatrice Monette, S.A.S.V., Pastoral Assoc.
Res., 17 Waterville St., 01536. Tel: 508-839-3993; Fax: 508-839-1330.
Catechesis/Religious Programs—Tel: 508-839-4236. Patricia Verderese, D.R.E.
Students 400.

North Oxford, St. Ann's (1906), Rev. James M. Steuterman; Sr. Jeanne Rouillard, S.A.S.V., Pastoral Assoc.
Res., 652 Main St., P.O. Box 488, 01537. Tel: 508-987-8892; Fax: 508-987-1598.
Catechesis/Religious Programs—P.O. Box 488, N. Oxford, 01537. Tel: 508-987-1869.
Students 217.

Otter River, St. Martin's (1864), Revs. Cornelius F. O'Leary; William G. O'Brien, Temp. Admin.
Res., 248 State Rd., 01436. Tel: 508-939-5588; Fax: 508-939-2305.
Church—247 State Rd., 01436.
Catechesis/Religious Programs—Students 67.

Oxford, St. Roch's (1886), Rev. Gerard P. Walsh. In res., Rev. Msgr. Louis R. Piermarini.
Res., 334 Main St., 01540. Tel: 508-987-8987; Fax: 508-987-0107. [CEM]
Catechesis/Religious Programs—Tel: 508-987-2382.
Students 353.

Paxton, St. Columba's (1951), Rev. John D. Thomas.
Res., 10 Richards Ave., 01612. Tel: 508-755-0408; Fax: 508-767-0759.
Catechesis/Religious Programs—Tel: 508-753-4126. Sr. Catherine Guild, R.S.M., D.R.E.
Students 286.

Petersham, St. Peter (1968), Rev. Raymond P. Messier.
Mailing Address: Main St., 01366. Tel: 508-249-3361.
Res., St. Francis, 105 Main St., Athol, 01331.

Princeton, Prince of Peace (1967), Rev. James J. Caldarella; Sr. Teresa Rose Carchidi, Pastoral Assoc.

Res., 5 Worcester Rd., P.O. Box 305, 01541. Tel: 508-464-2871; Fax: 508-464-0449.
Catechesis/Religious Programs—Students 219.

Rochdale, St. Aloysius-St. Jude (1904), Rev. Peter H. White.
Res., 2 Church Pl., P.O. Box 296, 01542-0296. Tel: 508-892-8296; Fax: 508-892-8296.
Catechesis/Religious Programs—Mrs. Terri Smith, D.R.E.
Students 220.

Rutland, St. Patrick's (1938), Rev. James P. Kerrigan; Deacon William J. Vigliotti.
Res., 290 Main St., Box 163, 01543. Tel: 508-886-4309; Fax: 508-886-2897.
Church—258 Main St., 01543. Tel: 508-886-6131.
Catechesis/Religious Programs—Tel: 508-886-4984. Michele Curtis, D.R.E.
Students 430.

Shrewsbury, St. Anne's (1950), Revs. Edward J. Moran; Robert Spellman; Sr. Charlene O'Leary, P.B.V.M., Pastoral Assoc. In res., Rev. Nelson Grandi (Brazil).
Res., 130 Boston Tpke., 01545. Tel: 508-757-5154; Fax: 508-797-9520. [CEM]
Catechesis/Religious Programs—Tel: 508-752-5040. Karen Weigold, D.R.E.
Students 585.

St. Mary's (1922), Revs. Paul T. O'Connell; Brian O'Toole; Leo Lancaster.
Res., 18 Summer St., 01545. Tel: 508-845-0161; Fax: 508-842-9132.
School—Tel: 508-842-1601; Fax: 508-845-1535. Jeanne Marie Gocha, Prin.
Sisters 1; Lay Teachers 13; Students 229.
Catechesis/Religious Programs—Tel: 508-845-1154. Mary Jane Person, D.R.E.
Students 902.

South Ashburnham, St. Anne (1895), Rev. Joseph J. Jurgelonis; Deacons Michael P. Connor; Richard Desjardins.
Pastoral Office: 85 Main St., P.O. Box 418, Ashburnham, 01430-0418. Tel: 978-827-5806; Fax: 978-827-1191.

South Barre, St. Thomas-A-Becket (1923), Rev. Mark M. Szymcik.
Res., P.O. Box 186, Vernon Ave., 01074. Tel: 508-355-2228; Fax: 508-355-0042.
Catechesis/Religious Programs—Fax: 508-355-2228.
Students 96.

Southborough, St. Anne (1886), Rev. Thirburse F. Millott.
Res., 20 Boston Rd., P.O. Box 403, 01772. Tel: 508-485-0141; Fax: 508-481-9374.
Catechesis/Religious Programs—Tel: 508-481-3159. Teresa F. Katuska, D.R.E.
Students 361.

St. Matthew (1956), Rev. James B. Flynn.
Res., 105 Southville Rd., 01772. Tel: 508-485-2285; Fax: 508-485-4437. [JC]
Catechesis/Religious Programs—Tel: 508-229-2429.
Students 218.

Southbridge

1—St. Hedwig's (1916) (Polish), Rev. Joseph J. Pijunowski.
Res., 29 Summer St., 01550. Tel: 508-764-6947; Fax: 508-764-7707. [CEM]

2—Notre Dame (1869), Revs. Maurice L. Gilbert; Edward J. Hanlon; Deacon Michael J. Corby.
Res., 61 Marcy St., 01550. Tel: 508-765-0601; Fax: 508-764-4148. [CEM 3]
Catechesis/Religious Programs—Religious Education Center, 20 Marcy St., 01550. Tel: 508-764-8018.
Students 267.

3—Sacred Heart (1908) (French), Rev. Charles R. Armey; Deacon Thomas Skonieczny.
Res., 40 Charlton St., 01550. Tel: 508-764-6964; Fax: 508-764-3320.
Catechesis/Religious Programs—Tel: 508-765-5597.
Students 85.

4—St. Mary's (1861), Revs. Peter J. Joyce; Paul W. Lemire; Deacon Richard Olson.
Res., 263 Hamilton St., 01550. Tel: 508-764-3226; Fax: 508-764-3209. [CEM]
Catechesis/Religious Programs—Saint Peter's Center, 297 Hamilton St., 01550. Tel: 508-765-0245. D.R.E.: Sr. Ines Calvo, R.O.D.A., Pastoral Asst.; Mrs. Beth Tobin, Pastoral Asst.
Students 467.

South Grafton, St. James (1887), Rev. Michael F. Rose; Deacon Edward Richards.
Res., 89 Main St., 01560. Tel: 508-839-5354; Fax: 508-839-5430.
Catechesis/Religious Programs—Tel: 508-839-6800.
Students 341.

Spencer, Mary, Queen of the Rosary (1994). Merged Merger of St. Mary and Our Lady of the Rosary. Revs. James F. Hoey; Bartholomew Salter, C.S.C.; Deacon Harry M. Sweet.
Office: 60 Maple St., 01562. Tel: 508-885-3111; Fax: 508-885-4905.
Res., 46 Maple St., 01562. Tel: 508-885-3806. [CEM]
Catechesis/Religious Programs—Tel: 508-885-3332. Mrs. Carol St.John, D.R.E.
Students 542.

Our Lady of the Rosary (1854). Merged with St. Mary's to form Mary, Queen of the Rosary.

Sterling, St. Richard of Chichester (1953), Rev. Thomas B. Garlick; Sr. Anne Marie Wildenhain, S.S.J., Pastoral Assoc.
Res., 4 Bridge St., P.O. Box 657, 01564. Tel: 508-422-8881; Fax: 508-422-0291.
Catechesis/Religious Programs—Patricia Cole, D.R.E.
Students 303.

Sutton, St. Mark (1966), Revs. John E. Horgan; Joseph W. McKiernan.
Res., 356 Boston Rd., 01590. Tel: 508-865-3860; Fax: 508-865-5095.
Catechesis/Religious Programs—Anne Licopoli, D.R.E.
Students 642.

Upton, Holy Angels (1874), Rev. Laurence V. Brault.
Res., 2 Nelson St., 01568. Tel: 508-529-6981; Fax: 508-529-6317.
Catechesis/Religious Programs—Tel: 508-529-3109. Simone Caron, D.R.E.
Students 301.

Uxbridge, St. Mary's (1853), Rev. Ernest P. Allega.
Res., 77 Mendon St., 01569. Tel: 508-278-2226; Fax: 508-278-7949. [CEM]
Catechesis/Religious Programs—Tel: 508-278-3777. Evelyn LaDuke, D.R.E.
Students 408.

Warren, St. Paul's (1872), Rev. Roland L. Lajoie.
Res., 1082 Main St., 01083-1027. Tel: 413-436-7327; Fax: 413-436-7324. [CEM]
Catechesis/Religious Programs—Combined with St. Thomas Aquinas, Warren.
Students 121.

Webster, St. Joseph's (1887) (Polish), Rev. Anthony Czarnecki.
Res., 53 Whitcomb St., 01570. Tel: 508-943-0467; Fax: 508-943-0808. [CEM]
School—Tel: 508-943-0378; Fax: 508-949-0581. Sr. Mary Angelia Rzasa, Prin.
Felician Sisters 4; Lay Teachers 11; Students 308.
Catechesis/Religious Programs—Students 60.

Sacred Heart of Jesus (1870), Rev. Michael J. Roy; Deacons Roland R. Michaud; Laurent Mongeau.
Res., 18 E. Main St., 01570. Tel: 508-943-3140; Fax: 508-943-2213. [CEM]
School—Tel: 508-943-2735. Sr. Constance Bayeur, S.S.A., Prin.
Sisters of St. Anne 2; Lay Teachers 11; Students 265.
Catechesis/Religious Programs—Tel: 508-943-0113.
Students 151.

St. Louis (1853), Revs. Joseph A. Marcotte; Bernard Davenport.
Res., 15 Lake St., 01570. Tel: 508-943-0240; Fax: 508-943-0801. [CEM]
School—Tel: 508-943-0257; Fax: 508-943-0257. Sr. Gertrude Lanouette, Prin.
Sisters 2; Lay Teachers 9; Students 250.
Catechesis/Religious Programs—Tel: 508-943-0817.
Students 401.

Westborough, St. Luke the Evangelist (1870), Revs. George O. Lange; Steven M. LaBaire; Sr. Mary Martina Lively, Pastoral Assoc.
Res., 70 W. Main St., 01581. Tel: 508-366-5502; Fax: 508-366-6049. [CEM]
Catechesis/Religious Programs—One Ruggles St., 01581. Tel: 508-366-8509. Patricia Najarian, D.R.E.
Students 800.

West Boylston, Our Lady of Good Counsel (1869), Rev. John F. Burke. In res., Rev. Francis Roberge.
Res., 111 Worcester St., 01583. Tel: 508-835-3606; Fax: 508-835-5456. [CEM]
Catechesis/Religious Programs—Tel: 508-835-6336. Thomas Faucher, D.R.E.
Students 490.

West Brookfield, Sacred Heart of Jesus (1950), Rev. Peter D. Shea.
Res., 10 Milk St., 01585-0563. Tel: 508-867-6469; Fax: 508-867-3670. [CEM]
Parish Center: Tel: 508-867-4460.
Catechesis/Religious Programs—Students 100.

Westminster, St. Edward the Confessor (1951), Rev. George A. Charland.
Res., 10 Church St., 01473. Tel: 508-874-2362; Fax: 508-840-1024.
Catechesis/Religious Programs—Students 280.

West Warren, St. Stanislaus (1913) (Polish), Rev. Charles E.J. Borowski.
Res., 2270 Main St., P.O. Box 723, 01092-0503. Tel: 413-436-5110; Fax: 413-436-0556.

St. Thomas Aquinas (1893), Rev. Roland L. Lajoie.
Res., St. Paul's Rectory, 1082 Main St., P.O. Box 1027, Warren, 01083. Tel: 413-436-7327; Fax: 413-436-7324.
Catechesis/Religious Programs—Combined with St. Paul, Warren.

Whitinsville, St. Patrick's (1889), Revs. Michael Broderick; Paul Doherty; Deacon Anthony R. Surozenski.
Res., 7 East St., P.O. Box 60, 01588. Tel: 508-234-5656; Fax: 508-234-6845. [CEM]
Catechesis/Religious Programs—Tel: 508-234-6826. MaryAnn DiGregorio, D.R.E.
Students 563.

Winchendon, Immaculate Heart of Mary (1870), Rev. Roland L. Gamache. Pastoral Assistants: Sr. Anne O'Shea, P.M.; Mr. Mark J. Carrier.
Res., 52 Spruce St., 01475. Tel: 508-297-0280; Fax: 508-297-3577. [CEM]
Catechesis/Religious Programs—Tel: 508-297-2699. Sr. Pauline Grenier, P.M., D.R.E.
Students 240.
Convent—Our Lady of Sorrows, Tel: 508-297-0275. Sisters of the Presentation of Mary 2.

Chaplains of Public Institutions

Worcester. *ADCARE Hospital of Worcester*. Vacant.
Air National Guard. Serviced by Catholic Charities priests.
Hahnemann Hospital. Serviced by Priests of St. Bernard, St. Joan of Arc, Immaculate Conception, Our Lady of the Rosary Churches.
Memorial Hospital. Catholic Pastoral Ministry: Rev. Thomas Landry.
University of Mass Medical Center. Rev. Edward M. Ryan.
Worcester Belmont House. Serviced by St. Margaret Mary Church.
Worcester Detention Center. Serviced by Urban Ministry.
Worcester State Hospital. Rev. Francis J. Roach, Chap.

Boylston. *Worcester County Jail and House of Correction*. Rev. Leo J. O'Neil, Chap.
Worcester County Sanitarium. Rev. Leo J. O'Neil, Chap.

Gardner. *Massachusetts Correctional Institution*. Rev. Thomas M. Tierney, Chap.

Lancaster. *Massachusetts Correctional Institution*. Vacant.

Otter River. *Walter E. Fernald State School*. Rev. John E. Kelley.

On Special or Other (Arch)Diocesan Assignment:
Reverend Fathers—
Banach, Michael, Vatican Diplomatic Corp.
Beaulieu, Peter R., Worcester Memorial Hospital
Ciambelli, Blase A., Westboro State Hospital
DiOrio, Ralph A., Apostolate of Healing
Doiron, David E., Pastoral Counseling
Gothing, Donald B., Admin., Capilia de la Santisima Trinidad, 69 Lincoln Ter., Leominster, MA 01453. Tel: 508-534-5258
Kilcoyne, Terence T., On Sabbatical

On Duty Outside the Diocese:
Reverend Monsignors—
Banach, Michael, Nunciatura Apostolica, Avenida Arce 2990, Casilla Postal 136, La Paz, Bolivia
Kelly, Francis D., Rector, Pope John XXIII Seminary
Mongelluzzo, James A., P.O. Box 2545, Worcester, MA 01613
Reverend Fathers—
Carr, David W., 740 Palm Trail, Delray Beach, FL 33447
Dunkley, George
Gerardo, John A., 532 Lamont Ave., Staten Island, NY 10312
Hill, George H., Abbey of the Genesee, Piffard, NY 14533
Hokanson, Richard P., 1524 E. Moorehead St., Charlotte, NC 28203
Imse, James L., 425 Cedar St., Medford, WI 54451
Kelly, David F., Duquesne Univ., Theology Dept., Pittsburgh, PA 15219
Roy, F. Gilles, Apartado 46, Sicuani (Via Cuzco), Peru

Military Chaplains:
Reverend Fathers—
Bomba, Paul M.
Boucher, Roger R.
Grochowski, Bernard J.
Rocheford, Dennis J.

Absent on Leave:
Reverend Fathers—
Bernard, Andre, Diocese of Santa Rosa
Blizard, David
Branconnier, Gerard
Damian, Ronald
Gelineau, H. Raymond
Kane, Thomas
Kardas, Thaddeus
Kelly, Robert
Nicewicz, Edward
Ritacco, Richard
Szantyr, John
Teczar, Thomas
Wondolowski, Robert

Retired:
Reverend Monsignors—
Battista, Leo
Carelli, Richard J., 30 Julio Dr., Shrewsbury, MA 01545
Daley, Thomas J., Vianney House, 222 June St., Worcester, MA 01602
Haddad, Edmond G., Vianney House, 222 June St., Worcester, MA 01602
Hannigan, Richard F., Vianney House, 222 June St., Worcester, MA 01602
Lenk, Charles, Southgate, 30 Julia Dr., Shrewsbury, MA 01545
Martin, John P., 37 Ridgeway Cir., Springfield, MA 01118
O'Brien, John J., 264 Springfield St., Springfield, MA 01107
Page, Raymond J., Southgate of Shrewsbury, 30 Julio Dr., Apt. 612, Shrewsbury, MA 01545
Reverend Fathers—
Anger, Raymond G., 30 Julio Dr., Apt. 317, Shrewsbury, MA 01545
Archey, Eugene C., P.O. Box 2025, Central Berkshire Blvd., Pittsfield, MA 01202
Ash, Joseph H., 49 Elm St., Worcester, MA 01690
Banach, Henry S., 64 Oakwood Ln., Worcester, MA 01604
Barrett, John W., 49 Elm St., Worcester, MA 01609
Barry, Leo, 15 Sandro Cir., Warwick, RI 02886
Bedard, J. Raymond, Hilltop Condo #23, Shawne Rd., Sandwich, MA
Carberry, Francis J., 7 Causeway St., Fitchburg, MA 01420
Clifford, James J., 35 Julio Dr., Shrewsbury, MA 01545
Conlin, Bernard J., Our Lady of Lourdes Rectory, 1290 Grafton St., Worcester, MA 01604
Debitetto, Ronald E., 66 Stetson St., Hyannis, MA 02601
Devaney, Roy J., 532 Grove St., Worcester, MA 01605
DiPucchio, Anthony F.X., 151 Loring Ave., Box 1024, West Dennis, MA 02670
Dutram, Charles J., 880 School St., Webster, MA 01570
Dyer, Edward J., 30 Apricot St., Worcester, MA 01603
Foley, Paul T., Shrewsbury Nursing Home, 66 S. Shrewsbury, Shrewsbury, MA 01545
Fontaine, John-Paul, 68 Natal Ave., East Falmouth, MA 02536
Gallagher, William J., P.O. Box 351, Woodstock, VA 22664
Gariepy, Robert E., 320 Sprice Dr., Ashburnham, MA 01453
Gilgun, Bernard E.
Gionet, Urbain J., Southgate of Shrewsbury, 30 Julio Dr., Apt. 112, Shrewsbury, MA 01545
Harrity, Francis P., 115 Prescott St., Clinton, MA 01510
Hebert, Raymond L., P.O. Box 2835, St. Petersburg, FL 33731-2835
Hebert, Roland G., Southgate of Shrewsbury, 30 Julio Dr., Apt. 109, Shrewsbury, MA 01545
Holland, George G., Box 488, North Oxford, MA 01537
Kurzawski, Casimir J., 220 Lakeview Ave., Syracuse, NY 13204
Lamothe, C. Romero, 51 Chapel St., Chicopee, MA 01020
Lange, Raymond L., Southgate of Shrewsbury, 30 Julio Dr., Apt. 219, Shrewsbury, MA 01545
Laperle, Theodore R., St. Bernard Rectory, 240 Water St., Fitchburg, MA 01420
LeBeau, Cyril A., Vianney House, 222 June St., Worcester, MA 01602
Manahan, Martin J., 865 Grove St., Worcester, MA 01605
Mattimore, William F.
McGovern, William W., Vianney House, 222 June St., Worcester, MA 01602
McKenna, John J., 88 Melba Ave., Springfield, MA 01104
McNamara, Philip D., 30 Julio Dr., Shrewsbury, MA 01545
Moynahan, Joseph A., Southgate of Shrewsbury, 30 Julio Dr., Apt. 338, Shrewsbury, MA 01545
O'Brien, Thomas F., 7 Woodland Dr., Paxton, MA 01612
O'Brien, William G.
O'Donoghue, Brendon W., 30 Julio Dr., Apt. 246, Shrewsbury, MA 01545
Ouillette, Arthur A., 165 Sunset Dr., P.O. Box 1285, Charlton City, MA 01508
Pelletier, Edgar A., 9504 Via Segovia, New Port Richey, FL 33552
Porrello, Joseph J., Southgate of Shrewsbury, 30 Julio Dr., Apt. 508, Shrewsbury, MA 01545
Poulin, Robert P., 153 Crown Dr., Naples, FL 33942
Prunier, Arthur J., 22 Thorne St., Worcester, MA 01604
Raftery, William J., Tara Knoll, Box 307, Manomet, MA 02345
Sullivan, Andrew J., 20 Birmingham Rd., Worcester, MA 01606
Yankauskas, Albin J., Shrewsbury Nursing Home, 66 South St., Shrewsbury, MA 01545

Permanent Deacons:
Aiken, Raymond E., (Retired)
Aliskevicz, John J., Burbank Hospital, Fitchburg
Arsenault, Roger D., Holy Rosary, Gardner
Aubuchon, Ronald J., St. Cecilia, Leominster
Baniukiewicz, Joseph M., Christ the King, Worcester
Benvenuti, Clement E., (Retired)
Blackwelder, Edgar B., Sacred Heart of Jesus, Fitchburg
Bolduc, Raymond H., (Retired)
Bosse, Raymond J., (Retired)
Brown, Paul E., Deaf Ministry Catholic Charities, Worcester, St. Mary, Uxbridge
Burns, Robert J., St. John, Worcester
CaraDonna, Nicholas M., Jr., Our Lady of Loreto, Worcester
Carbone, Francis A., (Retired)
Carrier, Paul J., Sacred Heart of Jesus, Gardner
Cieri, Joseph M., St. Boniface, Lunenburg
Colon, William B., Hispanic Community, St. Francis, Fitchburg
Connor, Michael P., St. Dennis, Ashburnham; St. Ann, South Ashburnham
Corby, Michael P., Notre Dame, Southbridge
Croteau, Andre W., St. Joseph, Fitchburg
Daluga, Richard B., St. Mary, Milford
Dauphinais, Raymond P., Worcester County House of Correction, West Boylston
Desautels, Alphonse T., Our Lady of the Angels, Worcester
Desjardin, Richard C., St. Dennis/St. Ann, Ashburnham
Desmarais, Ernest E.
Devine, Philip E., St. Mary, Shrewsbury
DeVito, Frederick A., (Retired)
Dio, Robert F., Our Lady of the Holy Rosary, Gardner
DiPadua, James F., Jr., St. Stephen, Worcester
Doyle, Walter F., Refugee Apostolate, Worcester; St. Joseph, Barre; St. Augustine, Wheelright
Dunphy, Melvin A., On Duty Outside of Diocese
DuVarney, Joseph T.
Escobar, Francisco, St. Paul Cathedral, Worcester
Faford, Peter R., St. Charles Borromeo Haitian Ministry Coalition, Whitinsville
Fenner, Harry, (Retired)
Foster, Deane C., (Retired)
Giard, Arthur J., Jr., Our Lady of the Holy Rosary, Gardner
Gilholly, Philip E., St. Francis of Asissi, Athol; St. Peter, Petersham
Green, Amos H., Sr., (Retired)
Harkins, Frederick A., Our Lady of the Lake, Leominster
Ladroga, William J.
LeBlanc, John B., St. Anthony of Padua, Fitchburg
Lee, John W., (Retired)
Librandi, Vincent A., Our Lady of Fatima, Worcester
Linderman, James L., Our Lady Immaculate, Athol
Lucier, William J., St. Augustine, Millville
Manella, Joseph R., Sacred Heart, Hopedale
Martel, Clarence H., St. Anne's/St. Patrick, Sturbridge
McCaffrey, Joseph A., St. Anne, Southboro
Michaud, Roland R., Sacred Heart, Webster
Miller, William S., St. Joseph, Charlton
Miskell, Lawrence F., St. Joseph, Charlton
Mongeau, Laurent M., Sacred Heart, Webster
Montiverdi, Gerald M., University of Massachusetts Medical Center, Worcester
Morrissey, Henry F., (Retired)
Neal, Edmond
Nogueira, Benjamin A., Campus Ministry, Fitchburg State College, Fitchburg
O'Connor, Richard J., (Retired)
O'Toole, George L., Diocesan Tribunal, Diocese of Worcester
Olson, Richard V., St. Mary, Southbridge
Pagano, Matteo A., (Retired), 25 Lebeaux Dr., Shrewsbury, MA 01545
Prince, Norman A., Immaculate Conception, Fitchburg
Quinlivan, James P., Sr., St. Paul, Worcester
Richards, Edward J., St. James, South Grafton
Showalter, John A.
Skonieczny, Thomas A., Sacred Heart, Southbridge
Starr, Peter J.
Surozenski, Anthony R., St. Patrick, Whitinsville
Sweet, Harry M., Mary Queen of the Rosary, Spencer
Tatro, Leo J., (Retired)
Vidito, Bruce R., St. Margaret Mary, Worcester
Vigliotti, William J., St. Patrick, Rutland
Wagner, Thomas A., St. Catherine of Sweden, Worcester

INSTITUTIONS LOCATED IN THE DIOCESE

[A] SEMINARIES, RELIGIOUS, OR SCHOLASTICATES

SPENCER. *St. Joseph's Abbey School of Theology and Institute of Monastic Studies*, 01562. Tel: 508-885-8700; Fax: 508-885-8701.
E-mail: Frplacid@aol.com
Web site: www.spencerabbey.com
Rt. Rev. Damian Carr, Abbot & Rector; Revs. Joseph Chu Cong, Prior; Dominic Whedbee, O.C.S.O., Novice Master; Edward John Mullaney, O.C.S.O., Vocation Dir.; Luke Truhan, O.C.S.O., Dean of Studies; Bros. Robert Robinson O.C.S.O., Subprior; Aelred Marrah, O.C.S.O., Dean of Juniors. Professors 6; Students 3.

[B] COLLEGES AND UNIVERSITIES

WORCESTER. *Assumption College*, 500 Salisbury St., 01615-0005. Tel: 508-767-7000; Fax: 508-756-1780.
E-mail: info@ave.assumption.edu
Web site: http://www.assumption.edu
For a complete listing, refer to the Colleges and Universities section.
College of the Holy Cross, Inc., 01610. Tel: 508-793-2011
For a complete listing, refer to the Colleges and Universities section.

PAXTON. *Anna Maria College*, 01612. Tel: 508-849-3300; Fax: 508-849-3334.
E-mail: rzukowsk@anna-maria
Web site: http://www.anna-maria.edu
For a complete listing, refer to the Colleges and Universities section.

[C] HIGH SCHOOLS, CENTRAL

WORCESTER. *Holy Name Central Catholic Junior/Senior High School*, 144 Granite St., 01604. Tel: 508-753-6371; Fax: 508-831-1287. Rev. John F. Madden, Headmaster; Mrs. Mary E. Riordan, Prin.; Rev. James B. Flynn. Priests 2; Sisters 2; Lay Teachers 56; Students 850.
St. Peter-Marian Central Catholic Junior/Senior High School, 781 Grove St., 01605-3196. Tel: 508-852-5555. Mr. Matthew R. Sturgis, Headmaster; Miss Patricia Aubertine, Prin.; Mrs. Joanne Ethier, Asst. Prin.; Rev. Gerard Bertin. Priests 1; Sisters 3; Lay Teachers 56; Students 1,048.

FITCHBURG. *St. Bernard's Central Catholic High School*, 45 Harvard St., 01420. Tel: 978-342-3212. Mr. John A. Bierden, Headmaster; Mr. Patrick O'Shea, Prin. In res. Rev. Donald C. Ouellette. Priests 1; Sisters 4; Lay Teachers 30; Students 475.

SOUTHBRIDGE. *Trinity Catholic Academy*, 11 Pine St., 01550. Tel: 508-765-5991; Fax: 508-765-0237.
E-mail: worcsch16@connect.com
Mrs. Madeleine Brouillard, Prin. Lay Teachers 12; Students 207.

[D] HIGH SCHOOLS, PAROCHIAL

WORCESTER. *St. Mary's Junior/Senior High School*, 50 Richland St., 01610. Tel: 508-753-1170. Congregation of the Sisters of the Holy Family of Nazareth. Mark F. Manzello, Prin. Sisters 2; Lay Teachers 17; Students 174.

[E] HIGH SCHOOLS, PRIVATE

WORCESTER. *Notre Dame Academy*, 425 Salisbury St., 01609. Tel: 508-757-6200; Fax: 508-757-7200. A Private Day School for Girls. Sr. Ann Morrison, S.N.D., Prin. Sisters of Notre Dame de Namur 4; Other Religious Orders 2; Lay Teachers 29; Girls 318.

FITCHBURG. *Notre Dame Preparatory School*. (Grades

7-12), 171 South St., 01420. Tel: 978-343-7635. Mr. Jeff Hammond, Headmaster. Lay Teachers 10; Students 65.

SHREWSBURY. *St. John's High School*, 378 Main St., 01545. Tel: 508-842-8934; Fax: 508-842-3670. Xaverian Brothers. Bro. J. Conal Owens, C.F.X., Headmaster. Brothers 12; Lay Teachers 53; Boys 1,009.

STILL RIVER. *St. Benedict High School*, 254 Still River Rd., P.O. Box 22, 01467. Tel: 978-456-8017. Sr. Ann Mary, M.I.C.M., Prin. Sisters 2; Students 1.

[F] ELEMENTARY SCHOOLS, CENTRAL

WORCESTER. *St. Peter's Central Catholic Elementary School*, 865 Main St., 01610. Tel: 508-791-6496. Sisters of St. Joseph. Mrs. Maryann Pour Previti, Head of School; Josephine Dansereau, Teaching Prin. Lay Teachers 24; Students 346; Preschool Students 32; Total Enrollment 378.

MILFORD. *Milford Catholic Elementary School*, 11 E. Main St., 01757. Tel: 508-473-7303. Sr. Patricia Murphy, S.S.J., Prin. Sisters of St. Joseph 1; Lay Teachers 14; Students 274.

UXBRIDGE. *Our Lady of Valley Regional Elementary School*, 75 Mendon St., 01569. Tel: 508-278-5851. Sr. Kathleen Duffy, S.S.J., Prin. Sisters 1; Lay Teachers 8; Students 191; Part-Time Teachers 3.

[G] ELEMENTARY SCHOOLS, PRIVATE

WORCESTER. *Venerini Academy*, 27 Edward St., 01605. Tel: 508-753-3210; Fax: 508-754-6050. Mrs. Patricia Marmen, Prin. Sisters 5; Lay Teachers 21; Students 322.

LEOMINSTER. *Julie Country Day School*, 365 Lindell Ave., 01453. Tel: 508-537-4939. Sr. Marguerite Timothy, S.N.D., Prin. Sisters 10; Lay Teachers 28; Students 264.

[H] CATHOLIC CHARITIES

WORCESTER. *Catholic Charities*, 10 Hammond St., 01610-1513. Tel: 508-798-0191; Fax: 508-797-5659. Catherine Loeffler, Diocesan Dir.; Gerard E. LaFleche, Dir., Financial Mgmt.

Northern Worcester Co., 53 Highland Ave., Fitchburg, 01420. Tel: 978-343-4879; Fax: 978-345-4161. Jacqueline Hager, Area Admin.

Athol Office, 12 Riverbend St., Athol, 01331. Tel: 978-249-4563; Fax: 978-249-2545. Jacqueline Hager, Area Admin.

Southbridge Office, 79 Elm St., Southbridge, 01550-2601. Tel: 508-765-5936; Fax: 508-764-4153. Eldelmira A. Spence, Area Admin.

Blackstone Valley/Greater Milford Area Office, 9 Spring St., Whitinsville, 01588. Tel: 508-234-3800; Fax: 508-234-2321. Noreen Landry, Area Admin.

Clinton Office, 208 Church St., Clinton, 01510-2502. Tel: 978-365-7391. Jacqueline Hager, Area Admin.

Life-Line, 126 Main St., Room 6, Milford, 01715. Tel: 508-478-9632.

Senior Employment Service, 10 Hammond St., 01610-1513. Tel: 508-798-0191; Fax: 508-797-5659. Edward P. Binnall, Admin.

Refugee Resettlement, 10 Hammond St., 01610-1513. Tel: 508-798-0191; Fax: 508-797-5659. Sr. Theresa Khen Doan, Admin.

Family & Community Services, 10 Hammond St., 01610-1513. Tel: 508-798-0191; Fax: 508-797-5659. Sara Glenn, Admin.

Home Care Services, 10 Hammond St., 01610-1513. Tel: 508-798-0191; Fax: 508-797-5659. Rachel T. Renaud, Admin.

Literacy Volunteers, 10 Hammond St., 01610-1513. Tel: 508-798-0191; Fax: 508-797-5659. Madelyn Morales, Admin.

Crozier House, 10 Hammond St., 01610-1513. Tel: 508-798-0191; Fax: 508-797-5659. A Half-Way House for Substance Abusing Men. J. David Mulrooney, Admin.

Mercy Centre (Developmental Disabilities). Special Education Day Program and Sheltered Workshop for Developmentally Disabled Youngsters and Adults, 25 W. Chester St., 01605-1136. Tel: 508-852-7165; Fax: 508-856-9755. Heather McDonald, Admin.

Youville House Shelter for Homeless Families, 133 Granite St., 01604-4500. Tel: 508-753-3084; Fax: 508-754-0139. Sara Glenn, Admin. Total Assisted 29,000; Total Staff 340.

[I] CHILD CARE AGENCIES

WORCESTER. *Guild of St. Agnes*, 133 Granite St., 01604. Tel: 508-756-8371. Mr. Edward Madaus, Dir. Day Care Centers for Infants, Toddlers, Preschoolers & School-age Children. Children aged 8 weeks-9 years. Children 211. Family Day Care Program ages 2 months-5 years. Children 160. For all: Total Staff 135.

FITCHBURG. *Guild of St. Agnes*, 62 Dover St., 01420. Tel: 508-343-3042. Total Assisted 120; Total Staff 12.

LEICESTER. *McAuley Nazareth Home for Boys*, 01524. Tel: 508-892-4886. Sisters of Mercy. Sr. Mary T. Barry, R.S.M., Exec. Dir.; Rev. Msgr. Edmond T. Tinsley, Chap. Sisters 5; Boys 18; (Residents); Special Education School: Boys 18; Lay Teachers 4.

[J] GENERAL HOSPITALS

WORCESTER. *Saint Vincent Hospital, Inc.*, 25 Winthrop St., 01604. Tel: 508-798-1234; Fax: 508-798-1240
For a complete listing, refer to the Hospitals section.

[K] SPECIAL HOSPITALS AND SANATORIA

WORCESTER. *Notre Dame Long Term Care Center*, 559 Plantation St., 01605. Tel: 508-852-3011; Fax: 508-852-0397
For a complete listing, refer to the Special Care Facilities section.

Providence Extended Care Center, 119 Providence St., 01604. Tel: 508-860-5000
For a complete listing, refer to the Special Care Facilities section.

MILLBURY. *Providence House Nursing Home of Millbury*, 29 Main St., 01527. Tel: 508-865-6106
For a complete listing, refer to the Special Care Facilities section.

SOUTHBRIDGE. *Providence House Nursing Home of Southbridge*, 84 Chapin St., 01550. Tel: 508-765-9133
For a complete listing, refer to the Special Care Facilities section.

WHITINSVILLE. *St. Camillus Hospice, Inc.*, 447 Hill St., 01588. Tel: 508-234-7306; Fax: 508-234-7597
For a complete listing, refer to the Special Care Facilities section.

St. Camillus Nursing Home Inc., 447 Hill St., 01588. Tel: 508-234-7306
For a complete listing, refer to the Special Care Facilities section.

[L] HEALTH SERVICES

WORCESTER. *Our Lady of Mercy Health Care Center, Inc.*, 101 Barry Rd., 01609. Tel: 508-798-3727
For a complete listing, refer to the Hospitals section.

Pernet Family Health Service, 237 Millbury St., 01610. Tel: 508-755-1228
For a complete listing, refer to the Hospitals section.

[M] HOMES FOR AGED

WORCESTER. *Vianney House*, 222 June St., 01602. Tel: 508-791-0311
For a complete listing, refer to the Special Care Facilities section.

LEOMINSTER. *Presentation Health Care Center*, 99 Church St., 01453-3147. Tel: 978-537-7856
For a complete listing, refer to the Special Care Facilities section.

[N] MONASTERIES AND RESIDENCES OF PRIESTS AND BROTHERS

WORCESTER. *Assumptionists (Augustinians of the Assumption)*, 50 Old English Rd., 01609. Tel: 508-754-6276. Revs. Alexis A. Babineau, A.A.; Andre E. Dargis, A.A.; Louis F. Dion, A.A.; Roland O. Guilmain, A.A.; Leonard LaRocque, A.A.; Bros. Paul Maurice Gosselin, A.A., Treas.; Omer Gemme, A.A.; Armand Lemaire, A.A.; John-Thomas McHugh, A.A.; Odoric Roy, A.A. Priests 5; Brothers 5; Total Staff 2.

Assumptionists of Assumption College, Emmanuel House, 512 Salisbury St., 01609-1326. Tel: 508-767-7523; Fax: 508-793-9701.
Web site: http://www.assumption.edu
Revs. Roger R. Corriveau, A.A., Supr.; Donat R. Lamothe, A.A., Treas.; Barry Bercier, A.A.; Wilfrid J. Dufault, A.A.; David M. Gallo, A.A.; Richard L. Lamoureaux, A.A.; Bro. Robert Francis Beaulac, A.A. Total in Residence 7; Total Staff 1.

Jesuits of Holy Cross College, Inc., 01610. Tel: 508-793-2011.
E-mail: JHiggins@Holycross.edu
Web site: Holy Cross
Revs. John J. Higgins, S.J., Rector; John E. Brooks, S.J.; Richard P. Burke, S.J.; Edmund K. Cheney, S.J.; Terrence W. Curry, S.J.; Alfred R. Desautels, S.J.; James J. Drohan, S.J.; Charles J. Dunn, S.J.; William H. Fitzgerald, S.J.; Michael F. Ford, S.J.; J. Thomas Hamel, S.J.; James M. Hayes, S.J.; Lionel P. Honore, S.J.; Anthony J. Kuzniewski, S.J.; Joseph J. LaBran, S.J.; Vincent A. Lapomarda, S.J.; Brian F. Linnane, S.J.; John J. MacDonnell, S.J.; Earle L. Markey, S.J.; Charles R. McKenney, S.J.; Francis X. Miller, S.J.; James J. Miracky, S.J.; Paul J. Nelligan, S.J.; William J. O'Halloran, S.J.; Joseph B. Pomeroy, S.J.; John P. Reboli, S.J.; Gerard C. Reedy, S.J.; William E. Reiser, S.J.; Philip C. Rule, S.J.; Joseph S. Scannell, S.J.; William E. Stempsey, S.J.; Edward J. Vodoklys, S.J.; Thomas W. Worcester, S.J. Priests 33. Casa Santa Maria del Camino, Inc., 6 Claremont St., 01610. Tel: 508-798-0104. Rev. William E. Reiser, S.J., Pres.

LEICESTER. *Father James Fitton House of Priestly Formation*, 761 Main St., 01524. Tel: 508-892-8439; Fax: 508-892-4539. Rev. Dennis J. O'Brien, Dir.

PETERSHAM. *St. Mary's Monastery*, N. Main St., P.O. Box 345, 01366. Tel: 508-724-3350.
E-mail: franselm@one800.net
Rev. Anselm Atkinson, O.S.B., Supr. Priests-Monks 2; Monks 3; Novices 1; Postulants 1.

SHREWSBURY. *Passionist Fathers of Shrewsbury, Inc., Calvary Retreat Center*, 59 South St., P.O. Box 219, 01545-0219. Tel: 508-842-8821. Very Rev. Francis Landry, C.P., Rector; Revs. Joseph Sedley, C.P., Dir. Novices; Christopher Cleary, C.P.; Edward Wolanski, C.P.; Xavier Hayes, C.P., Vice Rector; Vincent Segotta, C.P.; Bro. August Parlavechio, C.P., Econome; Patrick Daugherty, (Novice); William Maguire, (Novice). Priests 6; Brothers 1; Novices 2.

Xaverian Brothers, 378 Main St., 01545. Tel: 508-845-1878; Fax: 508-842-3670. Bro. Stephen Comeau, C.F.X., Dir. Brothers 10.

SPENCER. *St. Joseph's Abbey*, 01562-1233. Tel: 508-885-8700.
E-mail: sjaspencer@aol.com
Web site: www.SpencerAbbey.org
The Cistercian Order of the Strict Observance (Trappists). Legal Title: *The Cistercian Abbey of Spencer, Inc.* Rt. Revs. Damian Carr, O.C.S.O.; Paschal Skutecky, O.C.S.O., Retired Abbot; Very Rev. Joseph Chu Cong, O.C.S.O., Prior; Revs. George Calhoun, O.C.S.O.; Laurence Bourget, O.C.S.O.; Peter Zemanick, O.C.S.O., (On Leave); Adrian Proback, O.C.S.O.; Raphael Simon, O.C.S.O.; Pius Rivera-Martinez, O.S.C.O.; Basil Byrne, O.C.S.O.; Eugene Lacasse, O.C.S.O.; Simon Sansone, O.C.S.O.; Edward Steriti, O.C.S.O.; M. Basil Pennington, O.C.S.O.; Matthew Flynn, O.C.S.O.; Gabriel Bertoniere, O.C.S.O., (in service outside the community); Patrick Brown, O.C.S.O.; Kevin Hunt, O.C.S.O.; Placid McSweeney, O.S.C.O.; Robert Morhous, O.C.S.O.; Vincent Dwyer, O.C.S.O.; Henry Scarborough, O.C.S.O.; Gerald Sears, O.C.S.O.; Edward John Mullaney, O.C.S.O.; Kizito Thompson, O.C.S.O., (On Leave); Marius Granato, O.C.S.O.; Aquinas Keane, O.C.S.O.; Luke Truhan, O.C.S.O.; Aidan Logan, O.C.S.O., (on leave to Military Ordinariate); Francis Rodriguez, O.C.S.O., (in service outside the community); Andrew Johnson, O.C.S.O., (On Leave); Isaac Keeley, O.C.S.O., (in service outside the community); Dominic Whedbee, O.C.S.O.; David Lavitch, O.C.S.O., (in service outside the community); James Palmigiano, O.C.S.O. Solemnly Professed 79; Simply Professed 3; Novices 2; Total Priests in Community 36; Total in Community 84.

STILL RIVER. *Benedictine Monks, St. Benedict Abbey* (Harvard), 252 Still River Rd., P.O. Box 67, 01467. Tel: 978-456-3221. Rt. Rev. Gabriel Gibbs, O.S.B., Abbot; Very Rev. Xavier Connelly, O.S.B., Prior; Revs. Basil Rechenburg, O.S.B.; Peter Connelly, O.S.B.; Anthony Kloss, O.S.B.; Marc Crilly, O.S.B.; Andrew Koch, O.S.B. In res. Rev. Francis Xavier (Sri Lanka). Priests 7; Brothers 12; Oblates 1.

WHITINSVILLE. *St. Camillus Community*, 497 Hill St., 01588. Tel: 617-234-3648; Fax: 508-234-7597. Bros. Thomas Farrell, O.S.Cam., Supr.; John Wiejkus, O.S.Cam.; Rev. John Gallagher, O.S.Cam. Priests 1; Brothers 2.

[O] CONVENTS AND RESIDENCES FOR SISTERS

WORCESTER. *Carmelite Sisters of the Eucharist, Inc.*, 8 Berwick St., 01602. Tel: 508-799-2092. Sisters 5.

Convent of Notre Dame, 555 Plantation St., 01605. Sisters of Notre Dame de Namur. Sr. Catherine T. Connolly, S.N.D., 555 Plantation St. Sr. Mary Anderson; Sr. Catherine Louise Beauregard; Sr. Adelaide Bisol; Sr. Mathilde Callahan; Sr. Kathleen Therese Cassidy; Sr. Frances St. Mary Congdon; Sr. Catherine Thomas Connolly; Sr. Irene Cotreau; Sr. Mary Perpetua Daly; Sr. Claire Aloyse Doherty; Sr. Mary Raphael Doody; Sr. Ellen Christine Doran; Sr. Agnes Marie Dwyer; Sr. Constance Marie Ecker; Sr. Bernadette Joseph Flood; Sr. Charlotte Flynn; Sr. Margaret St. Joseph Flynn; Sr. Rosina Gallahue; Sr. Mary Estelle Gaudet; Sr. Dorothy Ann Gill; Sr. Eleanor Harkins; Sr. Alice Roberta Kelleher; Sr. Ellen Marie Kennedy; Sr. Margaret Teresa Kirk; Sr. Marie Gabriel Mahoney; Sr. Mary McCarthy; Sr. Patrice McCarthy; Sr. Helen McEleney; Sr. Margaret Middleton; Sr. Rose Elizabeth Monahan; Sr. Irene Frances Mullin; Sr. Marie Murphy; Sr. Sandra Maria Napier; Sr. Catherine Neylon; Sr. Ursula Marie O'Brien; Sr. Catherine Aloyse O'Donnell; Sr. Mary Ellen O'Donnell; Sr. Patricia O'Donnell; Sr. Julie Patricia O'Neill; Sr. Aloyse Otis; Sr. Caroline Marie Smith; Sr. Barbara Winn. Sisters of Notre Dame 45.

Harper Residence, Res., 11 Beechmont St., 01609. Tel: 508-792-1619. Sisters 7.

Little Franciscans of Mary, 2 Dupont St., 01604-3706. Tel: 508-755-0878. Sr. Rena Mae Gagnon, P.F.M., Reg. Supr. Tel: 508-755-0878. Sisters 2.

Little Franciscans of Mary, 101 Plantation St., 01604. Tel: 508-755-8605. Sr. Jacquelyn Alix, P.F.M., Supr. Sisters 21.

Little Sisters of the Assumption, Pernet Family Health Service, Inc., 237 Millbury St., 01610. Tel: 508-755-1228. Family Health Agency. Nursing and Family Development Services-Home Based.
Religious Venerini Sisters Provincial Office, 23 Edward St., 01605. Sr. Hilda Ponte, M.P.V., Prov. Coord. Sisters 34; Total in Residence 26.
St. Joseph's Home (Residence for Women), 52 High St., 01609. Tel: 508-755-7707. Sr. Leona Donahue, R.S.M., Dir. Sisters of Mercy 1; Women 62; Total Staff 6.
Sisters of Mercy, 101 Barry Rd., 01609. Tel: 508-798-3727. Sisters 21.
Sisters of St. Anne, Esther House, 1015 Pleasant St., 01602. Tel: 508-757-6053. Sisters 8; Total in Residence 5; Total Staff 8.
Sisters of St. Joseph, S.S.J., 783 Grove St., 01605. Tel: 508-852-1659. Sisters 3.
Sisters of the Assumption of the Blessed Virgin, 316 Lincoln St., 01605. Tel: 508-856-9383; Fax: 508-853-0881. Estelle Dube, S.A.S.V. Tel: 978-724-3468; Sr. Lorraine Normand, S.A.S.V., Treas. Tel: 508-856-9450.
Sisters of the Holy Family of Nazareth, 119 Endicott St., 01610. Tel: 508-753-3835. Sr. M. Roberta, C.S.F.N., Supr. Sisters 5.
Xaverian Missionary Society of Mary, Headquarters: 242 Salisbury St., 01609-1639. Tel: 508-757-0514. Sr. Rita Davoli, X.M.M., Supr. Sisters 4.

LEOMINSTER. *Sacred Heart Convent*, 318 Lindell Ave., 01453. Sisters of Notre Dame de Namur 2.
St. Cecilia's Convent, 196 Mechanic St., 01453. Tel: 508-534-6907. Daughters of the Holy Spirit 4.
St. Julie Convent, 342 Lindell Ave., 01453. Sr. Marguerite Timothy, S.N.D., Prin. Sisters of Notre Dame de Namur 3.
The Sisters of the Presentation of the Blessed Virgin Mary, New Windsor, NY, 99 Church St., 01453. Tel: 978-537-7108; Fax: 978-840-1564. Mt. St. Joseph, 880 Jackson Ave., New Windsor, NY, 12553. Tel: 914-564-6620; 564-0513 (Admin. Office); Fax: 914-567-0219 (Admin. Office). Ministries are in the areas of education in parochial elementary and high schools; pastoral services; health care; social services. Sr. Catherine Cleary, Pres.; Sr. Eileen Shea, House Coord. Professed Sisters 200.

PETERSHAM. *Assumption Residence of the Sisters of the Assumption of the Blessed Virgin*, 211 N. Main St., Box 128, 01366. Tel: 508-724-3468. Co-Administrators: Sr. Estelle Dube, S.A.S.V.; Sr. Lucille Pleau, S.A.S.V. Professed Sisters 62.
St. Scholastica Priory, 271 N. Main St., Box 606, 01366. Tel: 508-724-3213; Fax: 508-724-3574. Benedictine Nuns (Cloistered). Very Rev. Mary Clare Vincent, O.S.B., Prioress; Sr. Mary Frances Wynn, O.S.B., Sub Prioress. Nuns in Solemn Vows 10; in Simple Vows 1; Claustral Oblates 1; Novices 1.

STILL RIVER. *Sisters of Saint Benedict Center, Slaves of the Immaculate Heart of Mary Inc.*, St. Ann House, 254 Still River Rd., P.O. Box 22, 01467. Tel: 508-456-8017.
E-mail: micm@bicnet.net
Mother Teresa Beneway, M.I.C.M. Professed Sisters 17; Novices 3; Postulants 1; Live-In Oblates 2.

WEBSTER. *St. Joseph Convent*, 5 Maynard St., 01570. Tel: 508-943-2228. Sr. Mary Angelia Rzasa, C.S.S.F., Supr. Felician Sisters 4.

[P] RETREAT HOUSES AND HOUSE OF PRAYER

WORCESTER. *Community of Teresian Carmelites* (1971), 30 Chrome St., P.O. Box 826, 01613-0826. Tel: 508-752-5734; 756-1086 (24-hour prayer line). Bro. Paul-Joseph Richard, C.T.C., Supr. Gen.; Sr. Debra-Therese Carroll, C.T.C., Prioress; Bro. Dennis-Anthony Wyrzykowski, C.T.C., Vicar; Sr. Donna-Bernadette Allen, C.T.C., Chapter Councilor. Dir. Vocations: Bro. Daniel-Francis Charpentier, C.T.C., Dir., Vocations for Men; Sr. Susan-Elizabeth Terkanian, C.T.C., Dir., Vocations for Women; Ms. Loretta M. Carroll, C.T.C.S., Community Sec.; Ms. Christine M. Chabot, C.T.C.S., Community Treas.; Rev. Francis A. Roberge, Chap. Solemly Professed Sisters 3; Solemnly Professed Brothers 3; Novices 1.

SHREWSBURY. *Calvary Retreat Center, Passionist Community*. (See separate listing under Monasteries and Residences for Men.), 59 South St., P.O. Box 219, 01545-0219. Tel: 508-842-8821. Very Rev. Francis Landry, C.P., Rector & Retreat Dir.; Revs. Joseph Sedley, C.P., Dir. Novices; Edward Wolanski, C.P.; Christopher Cleary, C.P.; Xavier Hayes, C.P., Vice Rector; Vincent Segotta, C.P.; Bro. August Parlavechio, C.P., Econome; Patrick Daugherty, (Novice); William Maguire, (Novice). Total in Residence 9; Total Staff 40.

SPENCER. *Mary House, Inc.*, 186 N. Spencer Rd. (Rte. 31), P.O. Box 20, 01562. Tel: 508-885-5450. House of Prayer and Contemplation. Ms. Joyce Thomasmeyer, Pres.
St. Joseph Abbey, N. Spencer Rd., 01562. Tel: 508-885-8710.
Web site: www.spencerabbey.org
Guest house and Retreat house. Revs. Gerald Sears, O.C.S.O., Guestmaster; Placid McSweeney, O.C.S.O., Asst. Guestmaster.

STILL RIVER. *Benedictine Monks, St. Benedict Abbey* (Harvard). (See separate listing under Monasteries and Residences for Men.), 252 Still River Rd., P.O. Box 67, 01467. Tel: 978-456-3221. Rt. Rev. Gabriel Gibbs, O.S.B., Abbot.

[Q] NEWMAN CHAPLAINS AND CENTERS

WORCESTER. *Campus Ministry*, P.O. Box 903, 01613.
E-mail: priest@WPI.edu
Web site: http://www.wpi.edu/~newman
Rev. Peter J. Scanlon, S.T.L., Vicar. Total Staff 23.
Assumption College, 500 Salisbury St., 01609. Rev. Roland O. Guilmain, A.A.; Mr. Peter Hart; Mr. John Fleming; Sr. Cecilia Hervas, R.A.; Frank Corbin, Ph.D.
Becker College, 19 Schussler Rd., 01609. Tel: 508-757-6097. Rev. Peter J. Scanlon, S.T.L., Chap., Religious Center.
Clark University, Box A-62, 01610. Tel: 508-793-7737. Beth Duffy Schaper, M.Ed.
Holy Cross College, The Office of the College Chaplain. Ms. Katherine McElaney, Dir.; Revs. Joseph J. LaBran, S.J.; James M. Hayes, S.J.; Michael F. Ford, S.J.; Paul Covino; Marybeth Cearns-Barrett; Andrea Goodrich; Sr. Lucille Cormier, S.A.S.V.
Becker College at Leicester. Refer to Diocesan Office.
Quinsigamond Community College, 670 W. Boylston St., 01606. Tel: 508-853-2300, Ext. 300. Sr. Helen Egan, S.S.J.
University of Massachusetts Medical School. Refer to Diocesan Office.
Worcester State College, Campus Ministry Center, 486 Chandler St., 01602. Tel: 508-793-8017. Rev. Francis A. Roberge, M.A., M.Div.
Worcester Polytechnic Institute, Religious Center at WPI, 19 Schussler Rd., 01609. Tel: 508-757-6097. Rev. Peter J. Scanlon, S.T.L.
Collegiate Religious Center, 19 Schussler Rd., 01609. Tel: 508-757-6097. Rev. Peter J. Scanlon, S.T.L.
Nichols College (Dudley), 01570. Tel: 508-943-1560. Rev. Conrad S. Pecevich, D.Min.
Fitchburg State College (Fitchburg), Newman Center, 281 Highland Ave., 01420. Tel: 508-345-2688. Rev. Richard P. Lewandowski, M.A., M.Div.; Deacon Benjamin A. Nogueira; Lois I. Nogueira, Chap.; Roger Racene, Dir., Development & Progress.
Mt. Wachusett Community College (Gardner), Campus Ministry at MW CC, 419 Green St., Gardner, 01440. Tel: 508-632-6600, Ext. 193. Ms. Elaine Stickney, M.S., M.Ed.; Ms. Maureen Andrews, M.Ed.

PAXTON. *Anna Maria College*, Office of Campus Ministry, 01612-1198. Tel: 508-849-3398; 3399.
E-mail: @anna-maria.edu
Web site: http://www.anna-maria.edu
Sr. Sarah Landis, I.H.M. Total Staff 1.

[R] MISCELLANEOUS

WORCESTER. *Casa Santa Maria del Camino, Inc.*, 6 Claremont Sq., 01610. Tel: 508-798-0104. Rev. William E. Reiser, S.J., Pres. Total in Residence 4; Total Staff 1. Pastoral Outreach Center for the Hispanic Community.
The Charlton Charitable Corporation, Inc. Diocese of Worcester. 49 Elm St., 01609.
The Guild of Our Lady of Providence. Mailing Address: Chancery Office of the Diocese of Worcester, 49 Elm St., 01609. Tel: 508-791-5357; Fax: 508-753-7180.
Monsignor Thomas Griffin Foundation, 49 Elm St., 01609. Tel: 508-791-7171. Rev. Msgr. Edmond T. Tinsley, Contact Person.
PACE - Parents Alliance for Catholic Education, 781 Grove St., 01605. Tel: 508-852-2200; Fax: 508-856-0792.
E-mail: paceinc@connectinc.com
Stephen A. Perla, Exec. Dir.
St. Peter-Marian Endowment Trust, c/o St. Peter-Marian Central Catholic Junior/Senior High School, 781 Grove St., 01605. Tel: 508-852-5555.

GARDNER. *House of Peace & Education, Inc.*, 20 Barthel Ave., 01440. Tel: 978-630-4752. Maxyene D. Schneider, S.S.J., Exec. Dir. Purpose: Neighborhood educational center for disadvantaged women and children.

PETERSHAM. *St. Bede's Publications*, 271 N. Main St., P.O. Box 545, 01366. Tel: 508-724-3407; Fax: 508-724-3574.
E-mail: info@stbedes.org
Web site: http://www.stbedes.org
Mother Mary Clare Vincent, O.S.B.
St. Mary and St. Scholastica Church, Inc., 271 N. Main St., Box 606, 01366.

SPENCER. *Cistercian Publications, Inc.*, St. Joseph's Abbey, 01562. Tel: 508-885-8730.
Web site: www.wreich.edu/cistern/
Dr. Ernst Breisach, Pres.; Dr. E. Rozanne Elder, Exec. Vice Pres. & Mng. Editor; Rev. M. Basil Pennington, O.C.S.O., Sec.

WHITINSVILLE. *St. Camillus Institute, Inc.*, 447 Hill St., 01588. Tel: 617-234-7306. Very Rev. William F. Cronin, O.S.Cam., Pres. Order of the Servants of the Sick (St. Camillus).

RELIGIOUS INSTITUTES OF MEN REPRESENTED IN THE DIOCESE

For further details refer to the corresponding bracketed number in the Religious Institutes of Men or Women section.

[0130]—*Assumptionists*.—A.A.
[0200]—*Benedictine Monks*. (Petersham; Still River).—O.S.B.
[1350]—*Brothers of St. Francis Xavier*.—C.F.X.
[0350]—*Cistercians Order of the Strict Observance (Trappists)*.—O.C.S.O.
[0790]—*Congregation of Maronite Monks*.—O.Mar.
[1000]—*Congregation of the Passion*.—C.P.
[0690]—*Jesuit Fathers and Brothers*.—S.J.
[0740]—*Marian Fathers*.—M.I.C.
[0720]—*Missionaries of Our Lady of LaSalette*. (Seven Dolors Prov.).—M.S.
[0240]—*Order of St. Camilus - Camillian Fathers and Brothers*.—O.S.Cam.
[1280]—*Stigmatine Fathers and Brothers*.—C.S.S.

RELIGIOUS INSTITUTES OF WOMEN REPRESENTED IN THE DIOCESE

[0230]—*Benedictine Sisters of Pontifical Jurisdiction*. (Petersham; Rutland; Eau Clare, WI).—O.S.B.
[0192]—*Carmelite Sisters of the Eucharist, Inc*.—C.S.E.
[0820]—*Daughters of the Holy Spirit*.—D.H.S.
[1070-06]—*Dominican Sisters*. (Newburgh, NY).—O.P.
[1170]—*Felician Sisters*.—C.S.S.F.
[2575]—*Institute of the Sisters of Mercy of the Americas*. (New York, NY).—R.S.M.
[2280]—*Little Franciscans of Mary*.—P.F.M.
[2310]—*Little Sisters of the Assumption*.—L.S.A.
[2790]—*Missionary Servants of the Most Blessed Trinity*.—M.S.B.T.
[2420]—*Missionary Sisters of the Society of Mary (Marist)*.—S.M.S.M.
[3390]—*Religious of the Assumption*.—R.A.
[2070]—*Religious of the Holy Union of the Sacred Hearts*.—S.U.S.C.
[4180]—*Religious Venerini Sisters*.—M.P.V.
[]—*Sisters Oblates to Divine Love*.—R.O.D.A.
[3000]—*Sisters of Notre Dame de Namur*. (Boston, Ipswich, Japan and Connecticut Provs.).—S.N.D.deN.
[3340]—*Sisters of Providence*.—S.P.
[3720]—*Sisters of Saint Anne*.—S.S.A.
[1650]—*The Sisters of St. Francis of Philadelphia*.—O.S.F.
[3830-01]—*Sisters of St. Joseph*. (Boston, Brighton).—C.S.J.
[3830-16]—*Sisters of St. Joseph*.—S.S.J.
[3815]—*Sisters of Ste. Jeanne D'Arc*.—S.J.A.
[0150]—*Sisters of the Assumption*.—S.A.S.V.
[1970]—*Sisters of the Holy Family of Nazareth*.—C.S.F.N.
[3310]—*Sisters of the Presentation of Mary*.—P.M.
[3320]—*Sisters of the Presentation of the B.V.M.*—P.B.V.M.
[4230]—*Xaverian Missionary Society of Mary, Inc*.—X.M.M.

DIOCESAN CEMETERIES

WORCESTER. *St. John's*.

NECROLOGY

✠ Flanagan, Most Rev. Bernard J., Retired Bishop of the Diocese of Worcester. —Died Jan. 28, 1997.
✠ Harrington, Most Rev. Timothy J., Retired Bishop of the Diocese of Worcester, Worcester, MA, St. John. —Died March 23, 1997.
† Capuano, John J., Worcester, MA, Our Lady of Mount Carmel - St. Ann. —Died Feb. 7, 1997.
† Choquette, Paul A., Fitchburg, MA, Immaculate Conception. —Died Nov. 20, 1996.
† Dion, Gerald C., Oxford, MA, St. Roach. —Died Jan. 10, 1997.
† Janczukowicz, Rev. Msgr. Chester J., Worcester, MA, Our Lady of Czestochowa. —Died May 20, 1997.
† O'Flaherty, John P., North Grafton, MA, St. Mary's. —Died Nov. 21, 1996.

Diocese of Yakima

(Dioecesis Yakimensis)

Most Reverend

CARLOS A. SEVILLA, S.J., D.D.

Bishop of Yakima; ordained June 3, 1966; appointed Auxiliary Bishop of San Francisco December 6, 1988; Episcopal ordination January 25, 1989; appointed Bishop of Yakima December 31, 1996; installed February 17, 1997. *Address all correspondence to: 5301-A Tieton Dr., Yakima, WA, 98908.*

ESTABLISHED JUNE 23, 1951.

Square Miles 17,787.

Legal Title: Corporation of the Catholic Bishop of Yakima.

Comprises the following Counties in the State of Washington: Benton, Chelan, Douglas, Grant, Kittitas, Klickitat and Yakima.

For legal titles of parishes and diocesan institutions, consult the Pastoral Office.

Pastoral Office (Chancery): 5301-A Tieton Dr., Yakima, WA, 98908. Tel.: 509-965-7117; Fax: 509-966-8334.

E-mail address: dioyak@televar.com

STATISTICAL OVERVIEW

Personnel	
Bishop	1
Priests: Diocesan Active in Diocese	40
Priests: Active Outside Diocese	7
Priests: Retired, Sick or Absent	12
Number of Diocesan Priests	59
Religious Priests in Diocese	11
Extern Priests in Diocese	6
Ordinations:	
Diocesan Priests	4
Transitional Deacons	2
Permanent Deacons	1
Permanent Deacons in Diocese	25
Total Brothers	3
Total Sisters	53
Parishes	
Parishes	41
With Resident Pastor:	
Resident Diocesan Priests	32
Resident Religious Priests	3
Without Resident Pastor:	
Administered by Priests	6
Missions	4
Pastoral Centers	2
Professional Ministry Personnel:	
Sisters	18
Lay Ministers	20
Welfare	
Catholic Hospitals	3
Total Assisted	315,869
Day Care and Extended Day Care Centers	2
Total Assisted	230
Special Centers for Social Services	6
Total Assisted	32,376
Educational	
Diocesan Students in Other Seminaries	19
Total Seminarians	19
Elementary Schools, Diocesan and Parish	7
Total Students	1,950
Catechesis/Religious Education:	
High School Students	1,802
Elementary Students	4,607
Total Students Under Catholic Instruction	8,378
Teachers in the Diocese:	
Sisters	10
Lay Teachers	100
Vital Statistics	
Receptions into the Church:	
Infant Baptism Totals	2,963
Adult Baptism Totals	119
Received into Full Communion	156
First Communions	1,683
Confirmations	694
Marriages:	
Catholic	359
Interfaith	143
Total Marriages	502
Deaths	474
Total Catholic Population	67,336
Total Population	461,000

Former Bishops—Most Rev. JOSEPH P. DOUGHERTY, D.D., First Bishop of Yakima; ord. June 14, 1930; appt. July 9, 1951; cons. Sept. 26, 1951; resigned Feb. 5, 1969; died July 10, 1970.—Most Rev. CORNELIUS M. POWER, D.D., Second Bishop of Yakima; ord. June 3, 1939; appt. Feb. 5, 1969; cons. May 1, 1969; elevated to Metropolitan See of Portland in Oregon, Jan. 24, 1974; died May 22, 1997.—Most Rev. NICOLAS E. WALSH, D.D., Third Bishop of Yakima; ord. June 6, 1942; appt. Sept. 5, 1974; cons. Oct. 28, 1974; installed Oct. 30, 1974; transferred to Archdiocese of Seattle as Auxiliary Bishop, Aug. 10, 1976; resigned Sept. 6, 1983; died April 22, 1997.—Most Rev. WILLIAM S. SKYLSTAD, D.D., Fourth Bishop of Yakima; cons. May 12, 1977; transferred to Spokane as Bishop of Spokane, April 17, 1990.—Most Rev. FRANCIS E. GEORGE, O.M.I., Ph.D., S.T.D., Fifth Bishop of Yakima; appt. July 10, 1990; cons. Sept. 21, 1990; appt. Metropolitan See of Portland in Oregon, April 30, 1996; appt. Metropolitan See of Chicago, April 8, 1997.

Pastoral Office (Chancery)—5301-A Tieton Dr., Yakima, 98908. Tel: 509-965-7117; Fax: 509-966-8334.

Vicar General—Rev. Msgr. PERRON J. AUVE, *5301-A Tieton Dr., Yakima, 98908-3493.*

Vicar for Priests—Rev. JOHN J. MCDONNELL.

Chancellor and Moderator of the Curia—Very Rev. RONALD W. METHA.

Vice-Chancellor—Mrs. GAYLE MILLER.

Diocesan Tribunal—*5301-D Tieton Dr., Yakima, 98908.* Tel: 509-965-7123.

Judicial Vicar—Very Rev. MICHAEL J. IBACH, J.C.L.

Adjutant Judicial Vicar—Very Rev. Sir JOHN F. HENEGHAN, J.C.L.

Administrator—Vacant.

Judges—Very Rev. MICHAEL J. IBACH, J.C.L.; Very Rev. Sir JOHN F. HENEGHAN, J.C.L.

Defenders of the Bond—Rev. Msgr. PERRON J. AUVE; Rev. Msgr. JOHN A. ECKER; Revs. THOMAS C. CHAMPOUX; RICHARD A. WUERTZ; Mrs. MATILDA M. SMITH.

Advocates—Clergy and pastoral ministers by appointment.

Notaries—Mrs. ANGELITA T. SALDIVAR; Mrs. EILEEN WALKER.

Diocesan Consultors—Rev. Msgr. PERRON J. AUVE; Rev. THOMAS C. CHAMPOUX; Rev. Msgr. JOHN A. ECKER; Revs. JOHN J. MURTAGH; ARGEMIRO OROZCO; JOSE DE JESUS RAMIREZ; LAWRENCE T. REILLY; RICHARD D. SEDLACEK; RICHARD A. WUERTZ.

Diocesan Offices, Commissions, Committees

Campaign for Human Development—Mrs. VIRGINIA SANTILLANES, *5301-B Tieton Dr., Yakima, 98908.* Tel: 509-965-7110.

Catholic Charities—Mr. JOHN L. YOUNG, Exec. Dir., Office: *5301-C Tieton Dr., Yakima, 98908.* Tel: 509-965-7100.

Catholic Women, Council of—Rev. JOHN M. SHAW, *213 N. Beech, Toppenish, 98948.*

Charismatic Renewal—Rev. Msgr. PERRON J. AUVE, Liaison, *5301-A Tieton Dr., Yakima, 98908.* Tel: 509-965-7117.

Conciliation Board—Rev. THOMAS C. CHAMPOUX; Mr. PAT COCKRILL; Mrs. MARY KOWALSKI; Mrs. TRUDY LEDWICH; Mrs. SANDY SEWARD, *5301-C Tieton Dr., Yakima, 98908.* Tel: 509-965-7100.

Cursillo, English—Rev. JOHN G. O'SHEA, *7409 W. Clearwater, Kennewick, 99336.* Tel: 509-735-8558.

Spanish—Mr. RAMON MATA, *1706 S. Vancouver, Kennewick, 99336.* Tel: 509-586-9995.

Development Office/Catholic Foundation—Mr. DONALD M. KLIPPSTEIN, Dir., *5301-A Tieton Dr., Yakima, 98908.* Tel: 509-965-7117.

Diocesan Coordinator for Health Affairs—Rev. THOMAS C. CHAMPOUX, *5301-C Tieton Dr., Yakima, 98908.* Tel: 509-965-7100.

Diocesan Commission for the Catechumenate—Mr. PETE BRAUN, Chm.; Mrs. LUCY GARCIA; Mrs. MARY HAMELIN; Sr. MARY ANN HERRES, S.N.J.M.; Rev. THOMAS KUYKENDALL; Mrs. JACQUE LOYND; Deacon ROBERT SCHROM.

Diocesan Commission on Public Worship—Rev. THOMAS S. KUYKENDALL, Chm.; Mrs. NANCY BARTLETT; Mrs. CHERIE HANSES; Mr. FELIP HOLBROOK; Deacon RAY MILLER; Rev. ARGEMIRO OROZCO; Sr. MARIA DE JESUS YBARRA, O.P.

Diocesan Pastoral Council—Most Rev. CARLOS A. SEVILLA, S.J.; Rev. RICHARD KEOLKER; Sr. MARGARET BALL; Deacon LEROI RICE; MARY ACKERMAN; CAROL GRAVA; COURTNEY GUDERAIN; ESPERANZA HERNANDEZ; VIOLA MATA; MARY SUE MCMAHON; EDWARD PEREZ; KARL REUSS; SANDY SEWARD; JOHNETTE SULLIVAN; KEN WISE.

Diocesan Millenium Planning Committee—Rev. Msgr. PERRON J. AUVE, Chm.; Rev. OSMAR AGUIRRE; Mrs. SYLVIA BRULE; Mrs. SUE CONNOLLY; Mr. MARK EVEVARD; Mr. ROBERT FONTANA; Mr. JOHN HANSON; Rev. RICHARD KEOLKER; Rev. KEVIN MINDER; Mr. RICHARD SEVIGNY; Mrs. SHANNON SEVIGNY; Mr. MARIO VILLANUEVA; Mrs. JANE VILLANUEVA.

Ecumenical Liaison—Rev. Msgr. JOHN A. ECKER, *15 S. 12th Ave., Yakima, 98902.* Tel: 509-575-3713.

Engaged Encounter—Mr. RON MELTON; Mrs. CAROL GEIER, *2344 Benton, Richland, 99352.* Tel: 509-375-3023.

Engaged Encounter, Spanish—Sr. MARIA DE JESUS YBARRA, O.P., *5301-B Tieton Dr., Yakima, 98908.* Tel: 509-965-7110.

Diocesan Finance Council—Rev. Msgr. PERRON J. AUVE, *Pastoral Center, 5301-A Tieton Dr., Yakima, 98908.* Very Rev. RONALD W. METHA, *5301-A Tieton Dr., Yakima, 98908.* Dr. ROBERT CASH; Mr. RICHARD GASSELING; Mr. DONALD M. KLIPPSTEIN; Mr. BILL MCCURLEY; Mrs. PAT MYERS; Mrs. PEGGY ROY; Mr. JIM TUTTLE; Mr. LARRY WRIGHT; Rev. RICHARD A. WUERTZ.

Marriage Encounter, English—Mr. RICH BRESHEARS; Mrs. MARY ANN BRESHEARS, *1840 W. 23rd, Kennewick, 99337.* Tel: 509-582-4804.

Spanish—Rev. JOSE DE JESUS RAMIREZ, *P.O. Box 308, Granger, 98932.*

Ministry & Education Center—Mrs. CATHY COLVER, Admin. & Supt. of Schools, *5301-B Tieton Dr., Yakima, 98908.* Tel: 509-965-7110.

Hispanic Religious Education and Ministry Formation—Sr. MARIA DE JESUS YBARRA, O.P., Dir.

Evangelization and Lay Formation—Mr. ROBERT FONTANA, Dir.

Missionary Formation of Lay Evangelizers—Sr. SUSANNE THIBAULT, M.S.B.T.; Sr. PATRICIA WINDER, M.S.B.T., *15880 Summitview Rd., Cowiche, 98923.* Tel: 509-678-5535.

Religious Education—Ms. REE KEARNS, Dir.

Youth/Young Adult Director—Mr. PATRICK FLYNN.

Youth/Young Adult Hispanic Ministry—Mr. CARLOS CARRILLO.

Deacon Director—Deacon JOHN CORNELL, *2504 W. Chestnut, Yakima, 98902.*

Northwest Regional Office for Hispanic Affairs—Rev. HELIODORO LUCATERO, Dir., *5301-F Tieton Dr., Yakima, 98908.* Tel: 509-488-5653.

Personnel Board—Rev. THOMAS C. CHAMPOUX; Rev. ARGEMIRO OROZCO; Rev. Msgr. MARTIN O. SKEHAN; Rev. RICHARD D. SEDLACEK; Very Rev. RONALD W. METHA, Ex Officio; Rev. Msgr. PERRON J. AUVE; Rev. Msgr. JOHN J. MCDONNELL.

Press (Central Washington Catholic)—Very Rev. RONALD W. METHA, Editor, *5301-A Tieton Dr., Yakima, 98908.* Tel: 509-965-7117.

Presbyteral Council Executive Committee—Rev. Msgr. PERRON J. AUVE; Rev. Msgr. JOHN A. ECKER, Chm.; Rev. Msgr. JOHN MARASCIULO; Very Rev. RONALD W. METHA; Revs. DONAL P. KENNEDY; KEVIN MINDER; ARGEMIRO OROZCO; JOHN G. O'SHEA; RONALD J. PATNODE; JOSE DE JESUS RAMIREZ.

Native American Ministries—Sr. MARGARET BALL, S.N.J.M., *109 N. E St., Toppenish, 98948.* Tel: 509-877-2751.

Natural Family Planning—Mrs. DOLORES LACOURSIERE, *422 S. 15th Ave., Yakima, 98902.* Tel: 509-452-9960.

Prison Ministry—Rev. GEORGE PURDY, S.J., *P.O. Box 128, Naches, 98937.* Tel: 509-653-2534.

Retreat Center—

St. Peter Retreat Center—Rev. FRANCISCO HERNANDEZ, Dir., *15880 Summitview Rd., Cowiche, 98923.* Tel: 509-678-4935.

Respect Life Committee—Mr. RUBEN BEEDLE; Rev. THOMAS C. CHAMPOUX; Mr. BILL FROMHERZ; Mr. CHUCK GONSALEZ; Mrs. DEE GONSALEZ; Mrs. JAN JOHNSON; Dr. GEORGE HOTCHKO; Dr. ANNE NEALEN; Mrs. SUSAN SCHWAEGLER; Mrs. DEE SCHWAB; Mrs. CHERI VAUSE; Sr. MARIA DE JESUS YBARRA, O.P., *5301-B Tieton Dr., Yakima, 98908.* Tel: 509-965-7110.

Scouting—Rev. WILLIAM E. SHAW, Chap., *P.O. Box 567, Zillah, 98953.* Tel: 509-829-5433. Deacon BILL DRONEN, Chm.; Mr. CARLOS CARRILLO; Mr. MARC DESGROSEILLIER; Mrs. CINDY DESGROSEILLIER; Mrs. CHARLENE DRONEN; Mr. PATRICK FLYNN; Mrs. ILIANA GARZA; Mr. JOHN WARREN.

Social Justice Commission—Revs. OSMAR AGUIRRE; THOMAS C. CHAMPOUX; Mrs. LINDA CONROY; Mr. CHRIS CASSIDY; Mrs. TERRI AGUILERA-FLEMMING; Ms. ROSALINDA GUILLEN; Mrs. PATTY HOUTS-HUSSEY; Mr. TOM MARAVILLA; Mr. FRANK MCGREE; Rev. KEVIN MINDER; Mr. VIC ROHRET; Sr. GRACIELA ROSAS; Mrs. YVONNE SMITH, *5301-B Tieton Dr., Yakima, 98908.* Tel: 509-965-7110.

Hispanic Ministries—Rev. ARGEMIRO OROZCO, Dir., *210 N. Beech, Toppenish, 98948.* Tel: 509-865-4040.

St. Vincent de Paul Society—Rev. THOMAS C. CHAMPOUX, Spirtual Dir., Office: *5301-C Tieton Dr., Yakima, 98908.* Tel: 509-965-7100.

Vocations—Rev. Msgr. JOHN A. ECKER, Dir., *15 S. 12th Ave., Yakima, 98902.* Tel: 509-575-3713.

CLERGY, PARISHES, MISSIONS AND PAROCHIAL SCHOOLS

CITY OF YAKIMA
(Yakima County)

1—ST. PAUL CATHEDRAL (1924), Rev. Msgr. John A. Ecker; Rev. Emmett W. Sarsfield; Deacon Ray Miller; Alma Ahlbrecht, Pastoral Assoc.
Res., 15 S. 12th Ave., 98902. Tel: 509-575-3713; Fax: 509-453-7497. [CEM 2][JC]
School—(Grades K-8) 1214 W. Chestnut Ave., 98902. Tel: 509-575-5604.
Lay Teachers 18; Students 310.
Catechesis/Religious Programs—Students 230.

2—HOLY FAMILY, Rev. John J. Murtagh; Rev. Msgr. John J. McDonnell; Deacons John Cornell; Jim Kramper.
Res., 5315 Tieton Dr., 98908. Tel: 509-966-0830.
Catechesis/Religious Programs—Tel: 509-966-0788.
Students 600.
Mission—Ahtanum, Yakima Co., Holy Cross, Tel: 509-966-0865.

3—HOLY REDEEMER (1962), Revs. Thomas S. Kuykendall; Roberto B. Saenz, S.J., Admin.; Sr. Judeen Seeberger, O.S.B., Pastoral Assoc.; Deacon Duane Berger.
Res., 1609 Landon Ave., 98902. Tel: 509-248-2241. [JC]
Catechesis/Religious Programs—Tel: 509-457-3435.
Students 136.

4—ST. JOSEPH'S, Revs. Patrick A. Carroll, S.J.; Thomas R. Royce, S.J.; William Vogel, S.J.; Mary E. Bischoff, Admin. In res., Revs. Neill R. Meany, S.J.; John T. Rashford, S.J., Chap., Providence Yakima Medical Center; Charles Schmitz, S.J.
212 N. 4th St., 98901-2499. Tel: 509-248-1911; Fax: 509-248-2604.
School—St. Joseph/Marquette, Tel: 509-575-5555; Fax: 509-457-5621.
Sisters of Providence 2; Lay Teachers 20; Students 404.
Catechesis/Religious Programs—Students 270.

OUTSIDE THE CITY OF YAKIMA

Benton City, Benton Co., St. Frances Xavier Cabrini (1963), Rev. Richard D. Sedlacek.
Church—Horn Rd., 99320. Tel: 509-786-1783.

Bridgeport, Douglas Co., St. Anne's (1964), Revs. Richard Wuertz; Arturo Rodriguez (Mexico).
215 W. Allen Ave., P.O. Box 1089, Chelan, 98816. Tel: 509-682-2433.
Catechesis/Religious Programs—Students 47.
Mission—Mansfield, Douglas Co., St. Mary, (1909).

Cashmere, Chelan Co., St. Francis Xavier (1915), Rev. Maurice F. Peterson; Deacon Bill Dronen.
Res., 307 Angier, 98815. Tel: 509-782-2643.
Catechesis/Religious Programs—Students 60.

Chelan, Chelan Co., St. Francis de Sales (1904), Revs. Richard A. Wuertz Tel: 509-682-2433; Arturo Rodriquez (Mexico) Hispanic Ministry, Tel: 509-682-2702.
215 W. Allen Ave., P.O. Box 1089, 98816. Tel: 509-682-2433; 682-2702.
Catechesis/Religious Programs—Students 166.

Cle Elum, Kittitas Co., St. John the Baptist (1913), Rev. Msgr. John Marasciulo.
Res., 303 W. 2nd St., 98922. Tel: 509-674-2531.
Catechesis/Religious Programs—Lissa Ballard, D.R.E.
Students 44.

Cowiche, Yakima Co., St. Peter's (1959) (Spanish), Rev. Francisco J. Hernandez; Deacon Walter A. Burnham.
Res., 15880 Summitview Rd., 98923. Tel: 509-678-4164; Fax: 509-678-4936.
Catechesis/Religious Programs—Tel: 509-678-5335; Fax: 509-678-4164.
Students 75.

East Wenatchee, Douglas Co., Holy Apostles (1962), Revs. Seamus Kerr; Alvaro Diez; Deacon Bill Loranger.
Res., P.O. Box 7279, 98802. Tel: 509-884-5444.
Catechesis/Religious Programs—1315 N.E. 8th St., 98801. Tel: 509-884-5444. D.R.E.: Debbie Patterson; Kristie Tuttle.
Students 223.

Ellensburg, Kittitas Co., St. Andrew's (1884), Rev. Msgr. Perron Joseph Auve; Deacon Jack Spence.
Res., 401 S. Willow St., 98926. Tel: 509-962-9819; Fax: 509-962-9846. [CEM]
Catechesis/Religious Programs—Students 216.

Ephrata, Grant Co., St. Rose of Lima, Rev. Richard Mel House.
Parish Office: 323 D St., S.W., 98823. Tel: 509-754-3640; Fax: 509-754-4064. [CEM]
School—(Grades PreK-8) 520 S.E. Blvd., 98823. Tel: 509-754-4901.
Lay Teachers 9; Students 110.
Catechesis/Religious Programs—Tel: 509-754-1296. Angela Stacy, D.R.E.
Students 130.

Goldendale, Klickitat Co., Holy Trinity (1884), Rev. Thomas V. Lane.
Res., 210 S. Schuster St., P.O. Box 186, 98620. Tel: 509-773-4516. [CEM]
Catechesis/Religious Programs—Lynette Anderson, D.R.E.
Students 75.

Grand Coulee, Grant Co., St. Henry's, Rev. Lawrence T. Reilly; Deacon Dan Farrell.
Res., 590 Grand Coulee Ave., W., P.O. Box P, 99133. Tel: 509-633-1180.
Catechesis/Religious Programs—Students 54.

Grandview, Yakima Co., Blessed Sacrament (1954), Revs. Robert P. Himes; Mario A. Salazar.
Res., 1201 Missouri, 98930. Tel: 509-882-1657; Fax: 509-882-1107.
Catechesis/Religious Programs—Students 238.

Granger, Yakima Co., Our Lady of Guadalupe (1966) (Hispanic), Rev. J. Jesus Ramirez; Deacon Al Rizzo.
Res., 608 Ave., E., P.O. Box 308, 98932. Tel: 509-854-1558.
Catechesis/Religious Programs—Tel: 509-854-2511.
Students 54.

Hartline, Grant Co., St. Patrick's (1955). Served from Grand Coulee. Rev. Lawrence T. Reilly.
P.O. Box 925, Coulee City, 99115. Tel: 509-633-1180.
Mission—Coulee City, Grant Co., Holy Angels, Grand Coulee, 99133.

Kennewick, Benton Co., Holy Spirit (1980), Rev. John G. O'Shea; Deacon John E. Powers.
Office: 7409 W. Clearwater, 99336. Tel: 509-735-8558.
Catechesis/Religious Programs—Tel: 509-735-8558. D.R.E.: Lori Casey; Lynne Frantz.
Students 263.

St. Joseph's (1911), Revs. Richard D. Sedlacek; Daniel G. Dufner; Sr. Robert Joseph, C.S.J., Pastoral Assoc.; Deacons William Mich; Gilberto Garcia. In res., Rev. Msgr. Desmond P. Dillon.
Res., 520 S. Garfield, 99336. Tel: 509-586-3820; Fax: 509-586-3558.
School—901 W. 4th Ave., 99336. Tel: 509-586-0481.
Sisters of St. Joseph of Carondelet 6; Lay Teachers 16; Students 418.
Catechesis/Religious Programs—Tel: 509-582-8460. Robert L. Fitzsimmons, D.R.E.
Students 280.

Leavenworth, Chelan Co., Our Lady of the Snows (1912), Rev. Maurice F. Peterson; Deacon Don Griek.
Res., 145 Wheeler St., 98826. Tel: 509-548-5119.
Catechesis/Religious Programs—Tel: 509-548-7234.
Students 72.

Mabton, Yakima Co., Immaculate Conception (1910), Res., 1201 Missouri, Grandview, 98930. Tel: 509-882-1657; Fax: 509-882-1107.
Mailing Address: P.O. Box 275, 98935. Tel: 509-882-1657; Fax: 509-882-1107.
Catechesis/Religious Programs—Students 70.

Mattawa, Grant Co., Our Lady of the Desert, Rev. Solomon P. Covarrubias.
Mailing Address: P.O. Box 1717, 99349. Tel: 509-932-5424.
Catechesis/Religious Programs—Students 112.

Moses Lake, Grant Co., Our Lady of Fatima (1955), Revs. John Morse, S.J.; Felix M. Rodriguez; Deacon Robert Schrom. In res., Rev. Msgr. Martin O. Skehan, (Retired).
Res., 318 W. Northshore Dr., 98837. Tel: 509-765-6729; Fax: 509-765-0114.
Parish Center—300 N. White Dr., 98837.
Catechesis/Religious Programs—Cheryl Coulter, D.R.E.
Students 353.

Moxee City, Yakima Co., Holy Rosary (1900) (French-Canadian), Rev. Msgr. William M. Gallagher, Admin. In res., Rev. Msgr. Edmund G. McGrath, (Retired).
Res., 201 N. Iler., P.O. Box 279, Moxee, 98936. Tel: 509-453-4061; Fax: 509-573-3699. [CEM]
Catechesis/Religious Programs—Tel: 509-453-6754. Patricia Verhey, D.R.E.
Students 288.
Convent—Tel: 509-248-6723.

Naches, Yakima Co., St. John's (1959), Rev. George Purdy, S.J.
Res., 211 Moxee Ave., P.O. Box 128, 98937. Tel: 509-653-2534.

Prosser, Benton Co., Sacred Heart (1901), Revs. Donal P. Kennedy; Bulmaro Alvarado Martinez.
Res., 1905 Highland Dr., 99350. Tel: 509-786-1783.
Catechesis/Religious Programs—Tel: 509-973-2265. Cynthia O'Brien, D.R.E.
Students 126.

Quincy, Grant Co., St. Pius X (1955), Revs. Kenneth M. Kron; Mario P. Salazar.
Res., 805 N. Central Ave., P.O. Box 308, 98848. Tel: 509-787-2622; 787-3116.
Catechesis/Religious Programs—Kathleen Horning, D.R.E.
Students 325.

Richland, Benton Co., Christ the King (1946), Revs. Thomas C. Champoux; Gary Norman; Deacons Robert DaValle; LeRoi Rice; Alfred Rizzo.
Office: 1126 Long Ave., 99352. Tel: 509-946-1675; Fax: 509-946-9940.
School—1122 Long Ave., 99352. Tel: 509-946-6158.
Lay Teachers 19; Students 383.
Catechesis/Religious Programs—Tel: 509-946-1675. LeRoi Rice, D.R.E.
Students 462.

Roslyn, Kittitas Co., Immaculate Conception, Rev. William Byron.
Mailing Address: Idaho B, Box 611, 98941. Tel: 509-674-2531.

Royal City, Grant Co., St. Michael the Archangel, Rev. Salomon P. Covarrubias; Deacon Francisco Martinez.
Res., P.O. Box 340, 99357. Tel: 509-346-2730.
Catechesis/Religious Programs—Students 130.

Selah, Yakima Co., Our Lady of Lourdes (1975), Very Rev. Michael J. Ibach.
Res., 1112 W. Fremont, 98942. Tel: 509-697-4633.
Catechesis/Religious Programs—Sandra Seward, D.R.E.
Students 165.

Sunnyside, Yakima Co., St. Joseph's (1936), Revs. Osmar Aguirre; Antonio Castaneda-Cerna; James Spezzano.
Res., 920 S. 6th St., 98944. Tel: 509-837-2243; Fax: 509-837-7063.
School—(Grades K-8). Tel: 509-839-2241.
Missionary Daughters of the Most Pure Virgin Mary 2; Lay Teachers 9; Students 160.
Catechesis/Religious Programs—Tel: 509-839-4758.
Students 400.
Convent—Tel: 509-837-2242.
Missionary Daughters of the Most Pure Virgin Mary 6.

Toppenish, Yakima Co., St. Aloysius (1908), Revs. Argemiro Orozco, Hispanic Ministry; Robert Sewvello; Jose de Loza, S.S.P.
Religious Education Center—214 N. Beech St., 98948. Tel: 509-865-2565; 865-4725; 865-2380; Fax: 509-865-7882.
St. Vincent De Paul Center—11 S. B, 98948. Tel: 509-865-5311.
Catechesis/Religious Programs—Darlene Riojas, D.R.E.
Students 253.

Wapato, Yakima Co., St. Peter Claver (1908), Rev. Kevin W. Minder; Deacons John Kassinger; Antonio Osorio.
Res., 509 S. Satus Ave., 98951. Tel: 509-877-2813; Fax: 509-877-6207.
Catechesis/Religious Programs—Tel: 509-877-4881.
Students 348.

Warden, Grant Co., Queen of All Saints (1966), Revs. John Morse, S.J.; Felix M. Rodriguez.
318 W. Northshore Dr., Moses Lake, 98837. Tel: 509-765-6729; Fax: 509-765-0114.
Catechesis/Religious Programs—Tel: 509-349-0403.
Students 140.

Waterville, Douglas Co., St. Joseph's (1892), Rev. Bonifacio Salvana.
Res., Poplar St., P.O. Box 519, 98858. Tel: 509-745-8205. [CEM]
Catechesis/Religious Programs—Noreen Daling, D.R.E.
Students 62.

Wenatchee, Chelan Co., St. Joseph's (1903), Revs. Ronald J. Patnode; David Jimenez; Deacon Bill Osborn.
Res., 504 S. Chelan, P.O. Box 2138, 98807. Tel: 509-662-4569; Fax: 509-663-8437.
School—(Grades PreK-5). Tel: 509-663-2644; Fax: 509-663-8474.
Lay Teachers 9; Students 165.

White Salmon, Klickitat Co., St. Joseph (1912) (Spanish), Rev. Thomas S. Dahlquist.
Res., 240 N.W. Washington., P.O. Box 2049, 98672. Tel: 509-493-2828.
Catechesis/Religious Programs—Tel: 509-493-2961.
Students 60.

White Swan, Yakima Co., St. Mary's (1847) (Native American-Hispanic), Rev. John Shaw.
Res., P.O. Box 417, 98952. Tel: 509-874-2436. [CEM]
Catechesis/Religious Programs—Anita Griffin, D.R.E.
Students 35.

Zillah, Yakima Co., Resurrection (1963), Revs. William E. Shaw; Enrique L. Camacho.
Mailing Address: P.O. Box 567, 98953-0567. Tel: 509-829-5433.
Catechesis/Religious Programs—Tel: 509-829-6244. Betty Collins, D.R.E.
Students 105.

Special Assignment:
Reverend Fathers—
Bunnell, Thomas J., S.J., 1510 N. Edison St., Kennewick, WA 99336
Diaz, Francisco G., E. 429 Sharp, Spokane, WA 99202

On Duty Outside the Diocese:
Reverend Fathers—
Cerezo, Alberto F., 11637 100th Ave., N.E., #C2W, Kirkland, WA 98034
Dorian, Brendan, 330 West Coral Gables Dr., Phoenix, AZ 85023
Gallagher, Brian T., P.O. Box 443, Wassaic, NV 12592
Kenna, Joseph J., 929 Lakefront Dr., Bowie, MD 20721
Keolker, Richard F., Mount Angel Seminary, 119 Anselm, St. Benedict, OR 97373
Moore, Michael, 218 Ackerman, Clifton, NJ 07011

Military Chaplains:
Reverend Fathers—
Greene, Daniel P., V.A. Admin. Med. Ctr., Chaplain Serv., Bay Pines, FL 33744

Retired:
Reverend Monsignors—
Dillon, Desmond P., St. Joseph Parish, 520 S. Garfield, Kennewick, WA 99336
McGrath, Edmond G., P.O. Box 279, Moxee City, WA 98936-0279
Skehan, Martin O., W. 318 Northshore Dr., Moses Lake, WA 98837
Reverend Fathers—
Byron, Patrick J., Our Lady's House, Pallashill, Pallasgreane, Limerick, Ireland
Camacho, Enrique, Apartado Postal 7 Cocula, Jalisco, CP 48500 Mexico
Hannick, Anthony S., 1600 Roosmoor Pkwy., Walnut Creek, CA 94553
Heneghan, John F., Waverly Collacoon, Mayo, Ireland
King, Anthony S., 4602 Tieton Dr., Yakima, WA 98908
Schindler, John H., P.O. Box 356, Chelan, WA 98816
Shields, Robert J., 4602 Tieton Dr., Yakima, WA 98908
Tholen, John, 5301-A Tieton Dr., Yakima, WA 98908
Wawrzynski, Edward A., U.S.A.F.R., 5856 106th Ter., N., Pinellas Park, FL 34666

Permanent Deacons:
Alvarado, Berney, 91 York Ln., Zillah, WA 98953
Berger, Duane, 1706 Lower Ahtanum, Yakima, WA 98903
Burnham, Walter, 300 S. 76th Ave., #67, Yakima, WA 98908
Chavez, Nestor, 706 S. 8th St., Yakima, WA 98901
Cornell, John, 2504 W. Chestnut, Yakima, WA 98902
DaValle, Robert, 1837 Marshall Ave., Richland, WA 99352
Dronen, Bill, 306 Railroad Ave., Cashmere, 98815
Gilberto, Garcia, 18 N. Mayfield, Kennewick, WA 99336
Griek, Don, P.O. Box 1023, Leavenworth, WA 98826
Henn, Thomas W., 455 Carner Ct. W., Richland, WA 99352
Kassinger, John, 1314 N. Ave., #4, Sunnyside, WA 98944
Kramper, James, 111 N. 26th Ave., Yakima, WA 98902
Loranger, Bill, 1104 10th St., N.E., East Wenatchee, WA 98801
Martinez, Frank, 3790 Rd. 10.4 S.W., Royal City, WA 99357
Mich, William, 601 N. Reed, Kennewick, WA 99336
Miller, Ray, 2412 W. Chestnut, Yakima, WA 98902
Osborn, Bill, 410 Cottage Ave., Cashmere, WA 98815
Osorio, Antonio, 14 S. I St., Toppenish, WA 98948
Powers, John, 3103 S. Dayton, Kennewick, WA 98837
Reyna, Lupe, 1130 S. Grand, Moses Lake, WA 98837
Rice, LeRoi, 1845 Mahan Ave., Richland, WA 99352
Rizzo, Al, 135 MacArthur St., Richland, WA 99352
Schrom, Robert, 7240 Rd. 17, S.W., Royal City, WA 99357
Spence, Jack, 351 Hanson Rd., Ellensburg, WA 98926

INSTITUTIONS LOCATED IN THE DIOCESE

[A] COLLEGES AND UNIVERSITIES

*TOPPENISH. *Heritage College*, 3240 Fort Rd., 98948. Tel: 509-865-2244.
Web site: www.heritage.edu
For a complete listing, refer to the Colleges and Universities section.

[B] HOSPITALS

YAKIMA. *Providence Yakima Medical Center*, 110 S. 9th Ave., 98902. Tel: 509-575-5000
For a complete listing, refer to the Hospitals section.

RICHLAND. *Carondelet Behavioral Health Center*, 1175 Carondelet Dr., 99352. Tel: 509-943-9104
For a complete listing, refer to the Hospitals section.

TOPPENISH. *Providence Hospital*, 504 W. 4th Ave., P.O. Box 672, 98948. Tel: 509-865-3105
For a complete listing, refer to the Hospitals section.

[C] CATHOLIC SOCIAL SERVICE CATHOLIC CHARITIES

YAKIMA. *Carroll Children's Center*, 5301 Tieton Dr., Ste. H, 98908. Tel: 509-965-7104. Maureen Mould, Dir. Capacity 115; Total Assisted 320; Total Staff 22.

Catholic Charities of the Diocese of Yakima, 5301-C Tieton Dr., 98908. Tel: 509-965-7100. Mr. John L. Young, Exec. Dir.

Catholic Family and Child Service, 5301 Tieton Dr., Ste. C, 98908. Tel: 509-965-7100. Mrs. Darlene Darnell, M.S.W., Agency Dir. Total Assisted 23,320; Total Staff 65.

Day Care Nutrition, 5301-C Tieton Dr., 98908. Tel: 509-965-7107.

St. Vincent de Paul Store, 2629 S. First St., 98903. Tel: 509-457-5111. Mr. Frank McGree, Mgr. (Of All Stores in Diocese). Total Staff 14.

CHELAN. *St. Vincent de Paul Store*, 404 E. Woodin, P.O. Box 2387, 98816. Tel: 509-682-3655.

ELLENSBURG. *St. Vincent de Paul Store*, 1200 Canyon St., 98926. Tel: 509-925-2167. Total Staff 12.

EPHRATA. *Catholic Family and Child Service*, P.O. Box 191, 98823. Tel: 509-754-2211.

GRANDVIEW. *Catholic Family and Child Service*, 322 Division, P.O. Box 22, 98930. Tel: 509-882-3050. Kathryn J. Wilson, Branch Mgr. Total Assisted 1,206; Total Staff 5.

KENNEWICK. *St. Vincent de Paul Store*, 1401 W. Kennewick Ave., 99336. Tel: 509-586-1053.

MOSES LAKE. *Catholic Family and Child Service of Moses Lake-Ephrata*, 414 Burress St., P.O. Box 672, 98837. Tel: 509-765-1875; Fax: 509-766-1836. Mr. James Anglin, Branch Mgr. Total Assisted 859; Total Staff 6.

RICHLAND. *Catholic Family and Child Service*, 2139 Van Giesen, P.O. Box 1504, 99352. Tel: 509-946-4645.
E-mail: uolchore@inkport
Judith Dirks, Branch Dir. Total Assisted 2,250; Total Staff 28.

SUNNYSIDE. *St. Vincent de Paul Store*, 305 North Ave., 98944. Tel: 509-837-2055. Total Staff 13.

WENATCHEE. *Catholic Family and Child Service*, Morris Bldg., No. 320, 23 S. Wenatchee Ave., 98801. Tel: 509-662-6761.
E-mail: rkennedy@cfcs.net
Ray Kennedy, Branch Dir. Total Assisted 5,920; Total Staff 38.

St. Vincent de Paul Store, 330 S. Wenatchee Ave., 98801. Tel: 509-662-6010. Total Staff 8.

[D] RETIREMENT HOMES

YAKIMA.

**The Gamelin Association-Providence House*, 314 N. 4th St., 98901-2459. Tel: 509-452-5017. Sr. Shaughn Gorman, Dir. Low income housing for elderly.

[E] VOLUNTEER SERVICES

YAKIMA. *Holy Family Parish Conference*, 5315 Tieton Dr., 98908. Tel: 509-966-0830.

Holy Redeemer Parish Conference, 1609 Landon Ave., 98902. Tel: 509-248-2241. Raymond Faith, Pres.

St. Joseph's Parish Conference, 212 N. 4th St., 98901. Tel: 509-248-1911. Mrs. O. Gress, Pres.

St. Paul's Parish Conference, 15 S. 12th Ave., 98902. Tel: 509-575-3713; Fax: 509-453-7497.
E-mail: stpaul@wolfenet.com
Dave Uhlman, Pres.; Phil Salatino, Vice Pres.; Fred Schilling, Treas.

Society of St. Vincent de Paul, Particular Council of Yakima, 2629 S. First St., 98903. Tom Crehlen, Pres. Total Staff 13.

EAST WENATCHEE. *Holy Apostles Parish Conference*, P.O. Box 7279, 98801. Tel: 509-884-5444. Paul White, Pres.

KENNEWICK. *St. Joseph Parish Conference*, 520 S. Garfield, 99336. Tel: 509-586-7569; Fax: 509-586-3558. Total Staff 10.

MOSES LAKE. *Our Lady of Fatima Parish Conference*, W. 318 Northshore Dr., 98837. Tel: 509-765-6729.
E-mail: jmorse@qwksilver.com
Wayne Vadnais, Pres.

RICHLAND. *Christ the King Parish Conference*, 1126 Long Ave., 99352. Tel: 509-946-1675. Bob Morford, Pres.

TOPPENISH. *St. Aloysius Parish Conference*, 213 N. Beech St., 98948. Tel: 509-865-4725.

St. Vincent de Paul Center, 213 N. Beech St., 98948. 11 S. B St., 98948. Tel: 509-865-5311. Adriana Hede, Dir. Total Assisted 5,771; Total Staff 1.

WENATCHEE. *St. Joseph Parish Conference, St Vincent de Paul*, 1125 Idaho St., 98801. Tel: 509-662-4569. V. E. Houck, Pres.

WHITE SALMON. *St. Joseph Parish Conference*, P.O. Box 1161, 98672. Tel: 509-493-1980. Leo Gauvin, Pres.

[F] RETREAT HOUSES

COWICHE. *St. Peter the Apostle Retreat Center*, 15880 Summitview Rd., 98923. Tel: 509-678-4164.
E-mail: mhenyan111@aol.com
Rev. Francisco Hernandez. Total in Residence 3; Total Staff 7.

[G] CAMPUS MINISTRY

ELLENSBURG. *Catholic Campus Ministry at Central Washington University*, 706 N. Sprague, 98926. Tel: 509-925-3043.
E-mail: ccm-cwu@televar.com
Mr. Joseph Kiesel-Nield, Dir. & Campus Min. Total in Residence 4; Total Staff 1.

[H] MISCELLANEOUS LISTINGS

YAKIMA. *La Salle High School, Yakima, Inc.*, 402 E. Yakima Ave., Ste. 730, 98901-2760. Tel: 509-248-7886; Fax: 509-248-2641. Bro. Daniel Morgan, CEO & Prin.

Reach Youth Ministry, Christ the King Center, 1704 Grant, 98902. Tel: 509-575-8754; Fax: 509-575-0940.
E-mail: reachym@prodigy.net
Mark Evevard, Dir. Total Assisted 8,000; Total Staff 6.

SUNNYSIDE. *Ministerio Nueva Vida*, P.O. Box 911, 98944. Tel: 509-839-4331.

TOPPENISH. *Association of Catholic Sisters for Educational Opportunities for the Poor*, 3240 Fort Rd., 98948. Sr. Kathleen Ross, S.N.J.M., Pres.

RELIGIOUS INSTITUTES OF MEN REPRESENTED IN THE DIOCESE

For further details refer to the corresponding bracketed number in the Religious Institutes of Men or Women section.

[0200]—*Benedictine Monks (American Cassinese Congregation)*.—O.S.B.

[0330]—*Brothers of the Christian Schools*. (Prov. of San Francisco).—F.S.C.

[0690]—*Jesuit Fathers and Brothers (Oregon Providence)*.—S.J.

RELIGIOUS INSTITUTES OF WOMEN REPRESENTED IN THE DIOCESE

[0230]—*Benedictine Sisters of Pontifical Jurisdiction*.—O.S.B.

[1070-20]—*Dominican Sisters*.—O.P.

[]—*Missionary Daughters of the Most Pure Virgin Mary*.

[2790]—*Missionary Servants of the Most Blessed Trinity*.—M.S.B.T.

[3350]—*Sisters of Providence (Prov. of Sacred Heart)*.—S.P.

[3840]—*Sisters of St. Joseph of Carondelet*.—C.S.J.

[1990]—*Sisters of the Holy Names of Jesus and Mary*.—S.N.J.M.

[2160]—*Sisters, Servants of the Immaculate Heart of Mary*.—I.H.M.

NECROLOGY

(No Deaths)

Diocese of Youngstown

(Dioecesis Youngstoniensis)

Most Reverend

THOMAS J. TOBIN, D.D.

Bishop of Youngstown; ordained July 21, 1973; appointed Titular Bishop of Novica and Auxiliary Bishop of Pittsburgh, November 3, 1992; appointed Fourth Bishop of Youngstown; installed February 2, 1996

Chancery Office: 144 W. Wood St., Youngstown, OH, 44503. Tel.: 330-744-8451; Fax: 330-742-6448; 744-2848.

Web site address: www.doy.org

E-mail address: siffrin@connectinc.com

Most Reverend

BENEDICT C. FRANZETTA, D.D.

Retired Auxiliary Bishop of Youngstown; ordained April 29, 1950; appointed Titular Bishop of Oderzo and Auxiliary July 29, 1980; consecrated September 4, 1980; retired September 4, 1996. *Res., St. Columba Rectory, 159 W. Rayen Ave., Youngstown, OH, 44503.*

Most Reverend

JAMES W. MALONE, D.D.

Retired Bishop of Youngstown; ordained May 26, 1945; appointed Titular Bishop of Alabanda and Auxiliary January 2, 1960; consecrated March 24, 1960; appointed Apostolic Administrator January 22, 1966; succeeded to the See May 2, 1968; retired December 4, 1995. *Res., 6796 Tanglewood Dr., Youngstown, OH, 44512.*

ESTABLISHED MAY 15, 1943.

CANONICALLY ERECTED JULY 22, 1943.

Square Miles 3,404.

Comprises six Counties in the northeastern part of the State of Ohio, namely, Ashtabula, Columbiana, Mahoning, Portage, Stark and Trumbull Counties.

For legal titles of parishes and diocesan institutions, consult the Chancery Office.

STATISTICAL OVERVIEW

Personnel	
Bishop	1
Retired Bishops	2
Priests: Diocesan Active in Diocese	120
Priests: Active Outside Diocese	9
Priests: Diocesan in Foreign Missions	1
Priests: Retired, Sick or Absent	70
Number of Diocesan Priests	200
Religious Priests in Diocese	31
Extern Priests in Diocese	1
Ordinations:	
Diocesan Priests	1
Permanent Deacons	2
Permanent Deacons in Diocese	56
Total Brothers	23
Total Sisters	273
Parishes	
Parishes	106
With Resident Pastor:	
Resident Diocesan Priests	95
Resident Religious Priests	7
Without Resident Pastor:	
Administered by Priests	2
Administered by Women Religious	2
Missions	2
New Parishes Created	1
Professional Ministry Personnel:	
Sisters	23
Lay Ministers	52
Welfare	
Catholic Hospitals	2
Total Assisted	384,873
Health Care Centers	4
Total Assisted	90,623
Homes for the Aged	5
Total Assisted	418
Day Care and Extended Day Care Centers	3
Total Assisted	199
Specialized Homes	7
Total Assisted	662
Special Centers for Social Services	7
Total Assisted	81,229
Other Institutions	2
Total Assisted	28
Educational	
Diocesan Students in Other Seminaries	9
Total Seminarians	9
Colleges and Universities	1
Total Students	1,241
High Schools, Diocesan and Parish	6
Total Students	2,849
Elementary Schools, Diocesan and Parish	45
Total Students	12,374
Catechesis/Religious Education:	
High School Students	3,925
Elementary Students	14,339
Total Students Under Catholic Instruction	34,737
Teachers in the Diocese:	
Priests	5
Sisters	49
Lay Teachers	862
Vital Statistics	
Receptions into the Church:	
Infant Baptism Totals	3,523
Adult Baptism Totals	369
Received into Full Communion	795
First Communions	3,723
Confirmations	2,881
Marriages:	
Catholic	805
Interfaith	585
Total Marriages	1,390
Deaths	2,996
Total Catholic Population	257,200
Total Population	1,224,766

Former Bishops—Most Rev. JAMES A. MCFADDEN, S.T.D., LL.D., appt. Titular Bishop of Bida and Auxiliary of Cleveland, May 13, 1932; cons. Sept. 8, 1932; appt. Bishop of Youngstown, June 2, 1943; died Nov. 16, 1952.—Most Rev. EMMET M. WALSH, D.D., ord. Jan. 15, 1916; appt. Bishop of Charleston, June 20, 1927; appt. Titular Bishop of Rhaedestus and Coadjutor, Sept. 8, 1949; succeeded to See, Nov. 16, 1952; died March 16, 1968.—Most Rev. JAMES W. MALONE, D.D., ord. May 26, 1945; appt. Titular Bishop of Alabanda and Auxiliary, Jan. 2, 1960; appt. Apostolic Administrator, Jan. 22, 1966; succeeded to See, May 2, 1968; retired Dec. 4, 1995.—

All Diocesan offices and personnel can be reached at 144 W. Wood St., Youngstown, OH, 44503, Tel: 330-744-8451, Fax: 330-742-6448; 744-2848 unless otherwise indicated.

Chancery Office

Vicar General and Moderator of the Curia—Rev. ROBERT J. SIFFRIN.

Chancellor—Mrs. NANCY YUHASZ.

"The Catholic Exponent", Diocesan Newspaper—Most Rev. THOMAS J. TOBIN, Publisher; Mr. LOUIS JACQUET, Editor & Gen. Mgr. Tel: 330-744-5251.

Catholic Women, Diocesan Council of—Rev. JAMES A. CLARKE, Moderator, *157 Ohio Ave., Salem, 44460.* Tel: 330-332-0336.

College of Consultors—Rev. Msgr. MICHAEL CARIGLIO; Rev. GERALD DELUCIA; Rev. Msgr. JOHN DEMARINIS; Rev. Msgr. JOHN FINNIGAN; Revs. TERRENCE HAZEL; JAMES MCKARNS; JOHN MULQUEEN; Rev. Msgr. ROBERT SIFFRIN; Rev. DANIEL VENGLARIK.

Communications—

Catholic Television Network of Youngstown (CTNY)—Rev. GERALD DELUCIA, Pastoral Dir., *P.O. Box 430, Canfield, 44406-0430.* Tel: 330-533-2243.

Public-Media Relations—NANCY YUHASZ.

Development / Stewardship—Mr. PAT PALOMBO, Dir., The Foundation of the Roman Catholic Diocese of Youngstown.

Ecumenism—Rev. JOSEPH WITMER, Dir., Ecumenical Commission, *342 S. Chillicothe, Aurora, 44202.* Tel: 330-562-8519.

Office of Missions / Evangelization—Rev. PAUL HILL, M.S.C., Dir.

Scouting, Diocesan Office—Rev. LEO WEHRLIN, Dir., *409 W. Main St., Ravenna, 44266.* Tel: 330-296-6434.

Department of Canonical Services; Rev. Msgr. WILLIAM J. CONNELL, J.C.L., Exec. Dir., *141 W. Rayen Ave., Youngstown, 44503.* Tel: 330-744-8451

Office of Conciliation—

Matrimonial Dispensations—

Tribunal—
Judicial Vicar—Rev. Msgr. WILLIAM J. CONNELL, J.C.L.
Adjutant Judicial Vicar—Rev. Msgr. MICHAEL J. CARIGLIO, J.C.L.
Judges—Rev. Msgr. PETER M. POLANDO, J.C.L.; Revs. LAWRENCE C. FYE; ROBERT A. SABATINO, Ph.D.
Defenders of the Bond—Rev. Msgr. MARTIN SUSKO, J.C.L.; Revs. FREDERICK LUKEHART; RICHARD REIS.
Advocates—Revs. BERNARD N. GAETA; J. PATRICK MANNING; BRIAN MULCAHY, O.P.; KEVIN PETERS; JOHN A. ZURAW; Sr. PAULINE DALPE, O.S.U.
Promoter of Justice—Rev. MARTIN SUSKO, J.C.L.
Notaries—BARBARA ROGICH; JULIE TABAKA; COLLEEN HARRIS.

Department of Catholic Charities Services

Sr. CONSOLATA KLINE, H.M., Exec. Dir
Office of Social Action—Mr. BRIAN CORBIN, Dir., Environment, Hunger & Rural Life Committee; Housing & Community Devel. Committee; Minorities Commission; Respect Life Committee; Diocesan Commission on the Role of Women in the Church and in Society.
Office of Social Services—Mrs. MARY ELLEN ANDERSON, Dir., Health & Human Svcs. Commission, Antonine Sisters Adult Day Care Center; Sr. CONSOLATA KLINE, H.M., Liaison to St. Vincent DePaul Society.
St. Vincent DePaul Society—Mr. PETER ANANIA, Pres., *235 Wick Ave., Youngstown, 44503.* Tel: 330-746-5222.

Department of Clergy and Religious Services

Rev. Msgr. JOHN ZURAW, Exec. Dir
Office of Vocations—Rev. Msgr. JOHN ZURAW, Dir.
Serra International, Serra Club of Youngstown—Rev. FREDERICK LUKEHART, Chap., *4545 New Road, Austintown, 44515.* Tel: 216-792-1919.
Office for Clergy Services—Rev. Msgr. JOHN ZURAW, Dir.
Priests' Council—Rev. JAMES KORDA, Chm., *811 Oak St., Youngstown, 44506.* Tel: 330-747-3533.
Office of Continuing Education—Rev. STEPHEN POPOVICH, Dir., *4490 Norquest Blvd., Youngstown, 44515.* Tel: 330-793-9988.
Office of Priests' Personnel Advisor—Rev. THOMAS EISWEIRTH, *400 Lincoln Park Dr., Youngstown, 44506.* Tel: 330-747-6080.
Office of Permanent Diaconate—Rev. ROBERT SABATINO, Dir.
Office of Religious—Sr. ROSEMARY MURRAY, H.M., Dir.
Diocesan Conference of Religious—Sr. ROSEMARY MURRAY, H.M., Dir.

Department of Financial Services

Rev. JOHN H. DEMARINIS, Treasurer & Econome; Mr. ROBERT A. HOFFMAN, Exec. Dir., Finance & Oper
Office of Finance—Mr. JOHN DIDEK, JR., Dir., Finance; Mrs. MARGARET FISHER, Dir., Finance; Sr. M. GERTRUDE PARIS, O.S.U, Dir. Admin. Svcs.
Office of Cemeteries—Rev. Msgr. FRANK A. CARFAGNA, Dir.
Office of Data Processing—Mr. LOUIS ORBIN, Dir.

Department of Pastoral and Educational Services

Rev. Msgr. KENNETH E. MILLER, Exec. Dir
Office of Catholic Schools—Dr. NICHOLAS WOLSONOVICH, Supt.; Sr. MARY BRENDON ZAJACK, S.N.D., Asst. Supt. Curriculum; Mr. THOMAS WELCSH, Dir. Certificated Personnel; Mr. WALLACE DUNNE, Dir. Gov't Programs & Resource Devel.
Board of Education—Sr. JACQUELYN HERPY, O.S.U., Pres. LINDA BURKEY, Vice Pres.
The Catholic Diocese of Youngstown Educational Fund, Inc.
Office of Religious Education—BARBARA WALKO, Diocesan Dir., *225 Elm St., Youngstown, 44503.* Tel: 330-744-8451. THOMAS SAULINE, Consultant; CARLETTE CHORDAS, Media Resources.
Board of Religious Education—MARGARET MCCARTHY, Pres. RALPH BARONE, Vice Pres.
Office of Youth Ministry—Sr. DIANNE LIVINGSTONE, M.H.S.H., Dir.; Mr. JAMES MERHAUT, Assoc. Dir.
Office of Campus Ministry—Sr. PATRICIA SLATER, S.N.D., Diocesan Dir., *254 Madison Ave., Youngstown, 44503.* Tel: 330-747-9202.
Hiram College—Rev. RICHARD J. PENTELLO, *St. Ambrose Parish, 10692 Freedom St., Garrettsville, 44231.* Tel: 330-527-4105.
Immaculate Heart of Mary University Parish (Kent State Newman Center)—Rev. JOHN JEREK, Pastor; MARCIE BIRCHER, Campus Min., *1424 Horning Rd., Kent, 44240.* Tel: 330-678-0240.
Stark State College of Technology-Kent State Stark—Sr. VIRGINIA COLDREN, C.S.J., *Interfaith Campus Ministry, 6200 Frank Ave. N.W., Canton, 44720.* Tel: 330-489-1000 ext. 1992; 494-6170 ext. 264.
Walsh University—Rev. DON MILLER, O.F.M.; Sr. CAROL HEBERT, S.S.J., *2020 Easton St., N.W., North Canton, 44720.* Tel: 330-490-7342; 490-7341.
Youngstown State University—Sr. PATRICIA SLATER, S.N.D., *254 Madison Ave., Youngstown, 44504.* Tel: 330-747-9202.
Office of Worship—FRAN AMER, Dir.
Office of Lay Ministry Formation—EILEEN NOVOTNY, Dir.
Office of Marriage & Family Life—Mr. GREGORY JACKSON, Dir.

Other Ministries

Catholic Alumni Club of Youngstown, Inc.—Rev. ANDREW TORMA, M.S.C., Chap., *3128 Logan Ave., Youngstown, 44505.* Tel: 330-759-9539.
Charismatic Prayer Group—Rev. ROBERT EDWARDS, Dir., *271 Chestnut St., Lisbon, 44432.* Tel: 330-424-7648.
Disabled Services—
Physically and Developmentally—Rev. TERRENCE HAZEL, Chap., *281 Glenview Dr., Canfield, 44406.* Tel: 330-533-6839.
Deaf and Hearing Impaired—Rev. ROBERT SIFFRIN, Chap., *144 W. Wood St., Youngstown, 44503.* Tel: 330-744-8451.
Spanish Speaking—Rev. THOMAS CARNEY, M.S.C., *50 Struthers-Coitsville Rd., Youngstown, 44505.* Tel: 330-755-3633.

CLERGY, PARISHES, MISSIONS AND PAROCHIAL SCHOOLS

CITY OF YOUNGSTOWN
(Mahoning County)

1—CATHEDRAL OF ST. COLUMBA (1847), Rev. Lawrence C. Fye, M.Ed., V.F.; Rev. Msgr. William J. Connell, J.C.L., Vice Rector. In res., Most Rev. Benedict C. Franzetta, D.D., V.G., (Retired).
Res., 159 W. Rayen Ave., 44503. Tel: 330-744-5233. [JC]
Catechesis/Religious Programs—Students 50.

2—HOLY NAME (1916) (Slovak), Rev. Michael E. Ronik.
Res., 613 N. Lakeview Ave., 44509. Tel: 330-799-8873.

3—IMMACULATE CONCEPTION (1882), Rev. J. James Korda; Sr. Mary Lee Nalley, O.S.U., Pastoral Min.
Res., 811 Oak St., 44506. Tel: 330-747-3533; Fax: 330-747-3533.
School—810 Oak St., 44506. Tel: 330-747-9471; Fax: 330-747-5022. Mrs. Pat Yacucci, Prin.
Lay Teachers 9; Students 216.
Catechesis/Religious Programs—Students 76.

4—IMMACULATE HEART OF MARY, Mahoning Co., (1954), Rev. Stephen Popovich. In res., Rev. William Yurko.
Res., 4490 Norquest Blvd., 44515. Tel: 330-793-9988.
School—Tel: 330-799-1944; Fax: 330-799-0151.
Sisters 3; Lay Teachers 9; Students 253.
Catechesis/Religious Programs—Tel: 330-799-4202.
Students 200.

5—OUR LADY OF HUNGARY (1929) (Hungarian), Rev. John E. Reiss, O.F.M.
Res., 545 N. Belle Vista, 44509. Tel: 330-799-6829 (Office).

6—OUR LADY OF MT. CARMEL (1908) (Italian), Rev. Msgr. Michael J. Cariglio, J.C.L.; Deacon Joseph Nohra.
Res., 343 Via Mt. Carmel, 44505. Tel: 330-743-4144; Fax: 330-743-1035.
Catechesis/Religious Programs—Tel: 216-743-3508.
Students 180.

7—SACRED HEART OF JESUS (1888), Rev. Thomas Eisweirth; Deacon Joseph Zamary.
Res., 400 Lincoln Park Dr., 44506. Tel: 330-747-6080; Fax: 330-747-7003.
School—Combined with Immaculate Conception. Tel: 330-747-9471.
Catechesis/Religious Programs—Students 62.

8—ST. ANTHONY'S (1898) (Italian), Rev. Msgr. John H. DeMarinis.
Res., 1125 Turin Ave., 44510. Tel: 330-744-5091.

9—ST. BRENDAN'S (1923), Rev. Richard A. Brobst. In res., Rev. Robert Siffrin.
Res., 2800 Oakwood Ave., 44509. Tel: 330-792-3875; 792-3876; Fax: 330-792-9080.
School—144 N. Schenley Ave., 44509. Tel: 330-799-9741.
Catechesis/Religious Programs—Students 203.

10—ST. CASIMIR'S (1903), Rev. Sy Kaminski.
Office: 149 Jefferson St., 44510. Tel: 330-743-3951.
Res., 1115 Eveningstar Dr., Rome, 44085-9763. Tel: 440-563-5316.

11—ST. CHRISTINE'S (1953), Revs. David W. Rhodes; Patrick B. Ferraro.
Res., 3165 S. Schenley Ave., 44511. Tel: 330-792-3829; Fax: 330-792-3820. [CEM]
School—3125 S. Schenley Ave., 44511. Tel: 330-792-4545; Fax: 330-792-6888.
Lay Teachers 20; Students 538.
Catechesis/Religious Programs—Tel: 216-793-0544.
Students 926.

12—SS. CYRIL AND METHODIUS, Mahoning Co., (1896) (Slovak). Unassigned.
Res., 252 E. Wood St., 44503. Tel: 330-743-5291.
Catechesis/Religious Programs—Students 54.

13—ST. DOMINIC'S (1923), Revs. Joseph P. Allen, O.P.; William J. Rock, O.P.; Ernest Kelly, O.P., Chap. South Side; Matthew Erickson, O.P.; Robert R. Heuschkel; Andre-Joseph Lacasse, O.P.
Res., 77 E. Lucius Ave., 44507. Tel: 216-783-1900; Fax: 216-783-2396.
School—3403 Southern Blvd., 44507. Tel: 330-782-1123; Fax: 330-782-4616. John R. Rozzo, Prin.
Lay Teachers 13; Students 204.
Catechesis/Religious Programs—Students 190.

14—ST. EDWARD'S (1917), Rev. Frank M. Lehnerd.
Res., 240 Tod Ln., 44504. Tel: 330-743-2308; Fax: 330-743-8321.
School—(Grades K-8). Tel: 330-746-0576; Fax: 330-744-7042.
Lay Teachers 15; Students 229.
Catechesis/Religious Programs—Students 40.

15—ST. ELIZABETH'S (1922) (Slovak), Rev. George M. Duritsa, Admin.
Res., 124 Keystone St., Campbell, 44405. Tel: 330-747-4085; Fax: 330-747-8647.

16—ST. JOSEPH (1966), Revs. Frederick Lukehart; Edward Brienz; Deacon Michael Robert.
Res., 4545 New Rd., Austintown, 44515. Tel: 330-792-1919; Fax: 330-792-5233.
School—Tel: 330-793-1250.
Lay Teachers 12; Students 230.
Catechesis/Religious Programs—Tel: 216-792-1934. Mrs. Lori Pugh, D.R.E.
Students 851.

17—ST. MATTHIAS (1914) (Slovak), Rev. Msgr. Peter M. Polando, J.C.L.; Deacon Salvatore DiFrancesco.
Res., 915 Cornell St., 44502-2765. Tel: 330-788-5082; Fax: 330-788-2383.
School—2800 Shady Run Rd., 44502-2700. Tel: 330-788-0241.
Vincentian Sisters of Charity 3; Lay Teachers 10; Students 179.
Convent—937 Cornell St., 44502-2765. Tel: 330-788-5732.
Catechesis/Religious Programs—Students 165.

18—ST. PATRICK'S (1911), Rev. Edward P. Noga.
Res., 1420 Oak Hill Ave., 44507. Tel: 330-743-1109; Fax: 330-743-8810.
Catechesis/Religious Programs—Combined with St. Stanislaus. 430 Williamson, 44507. Tel: 330-747-3015.
Students 59.

19—SS. PETER AND PAUL'S, Mahoning Co., (1911) (Croatian), Rev. Branimir Radetic.
Res., 421 Covington St., 44510. Tel: 330-747-6762.
Catechesis/Religious Programs—Students 56.

20—ST. ROSE OF LIMA (1961) (Hispanic), Rev. Thomas A. Carney, M.S.C.; Deacon Felipe Colon.
Res., 50 Struthers-Coitsville Rd., 44505. Tel: 330-755-3633.
Catechesis/Religious Programs—Students 111.

21—ST. STANISLAUS KOSTKA'S (1902) (Polish), Rev. Edward J. Neroda; Deacon Michael Schlais.
Res., 430 Williamson Ave., 44507. Tel: 330-747-8503.
Catechesis/Religious Programs—Tel: 330-747-3015.
Students 36.

22—ST. STEPHEN OF HUNGARY (1905) (Magyar), Rev. Melvin E. Rusnak.
Church—854 Wilson Ave., 44506. Tel: 330-743-1905.

OUTSIDE THE CITY OF YOUNGSTOWN

Alliance, Stark Co., St. Joseph's (1859), Rev. Donald L. Feicht.
Res., 427 E. Broadway, 44601. Tel: 330-821-5760; Fax: 330-821-5783. [CEM][JC]
Catechesis/Religious Programs—Students 140.
Regina Coeli (1958), Rev. Frank D. Mintjal; Sr. Yvonne Horning, O.P., Pastoral Assoc.
Res., 663 Fernwood Blvd., 44601-2796. Tel: 330-821-5880; Fax: 330-821-5880.

School—733 Fernwood Blvd., 44601-2796. Tel: 330-829-9239; Fax: 330-829-9239.
Lay Teachers 11; Students 200.
Catechesis/Religious Programs—Yvonne Welch, D.R.E.
Students 130.

Andover, Ashtabula Co., Our Lady of Victory (1949), Rev. Lawrence Frient.
Res., 481 S. Main St., P.O. Box 669, 44003-9778. Tel: 216-293-6218.
Catechesis/Religious Programs—Students 52.

Ashtabula, Ashtabula Co., Mother of Sorrows (1890), Rev. Bernard N. Gaeta.
Res., 1514 W. 6th St., 44004. Tel: 440-964-3922.
Catechesis/Religious Programs—Tel: 440-964-8802.
Students 108.

Our Lady of Mt. Carmel (1902) (Italian), Rev. Michael D. Balash.
Res., 1200 E. 21st St., 44004. Tel: 440-998-4111; Fax: 440-998-7829.
Catechesis/Religious Programs—Students 225.

St. Joseph's (1862), Rev. Philip Miller; Deacons Richard Johnson; Alan Prasek.
Res., 3330 Lake Ave., 44004. Tel: 440-992-0330; Fax: 440-993-3579. [CEM]
Mission—Ashtabula, Ashtabula Co., Our Lady of Miracles (St. Joseph Mission), 4317 West Ave., 44004. Tel: 440-997-7121.
Catechesis/Religious Programs—Students 210.

Aurora, Portage Co., Our Lady of Perpetual Help (1955), Rev. Joseph W. Witmer; Sr. Lu Haidnick, C.D.P., Pastoral Assoc.
Res., 342 S. Chillicothe Rd., 44202-7814. Tel: 330-562-8519; Fax: 330-562-2529.
Catechesis/Religious Programs—Ms. Beth Frank, D.R.E.
Students 555.

Boardman, Mahoning Co., St. Charles Borromeo's (1926), Revs. Daniel M. Venglarik; Thomas J. Crum; Deacons Michael A. Kocjancic; Thomas Soich; Peter Gross, Business Mgr.
Res., 7345 Westview Dr., Youngstown, 44512. Tel: 330-758-2325; Fax: 330-758-2004.
School—7325 Westview Dr., Youngstown, 44512. Tel: 330-758-6689; Fax: 330-758-7404.
Sisters 1; Lay Teachers 30; Students 671.
Catechesis/Religious Programs—Tel: 216-758-8063. Mrs. Judy Magielski, D.R.E.
Students 943.
Convent—7515 Oregon Tr., Youngstown, 44512. Tel: 330-758-2396.

St. Luke (1962), Rev. Joseph A. Fata; Deacon Richard Milanek. In res., Revs. Gregory Fedor; Kenneth Miller.
Res., 5235 South Ave., 44512. Tel: 330-782-9783; Fax: 330-782-1574.
School—Tel: 330-782-4060; Fax: 330-782-4842.
Lay Teachers 12; Students 250.
Catechesis/Religious Programs—Students 500.

Brewster, Stark Co., St. Therese (1928). Unassigned.
Res., 456 Wabash Ave., S., 44613. Tel: 330-767-3622. [JC]

Campbell, Mahoning Co., St. John the Baptist (1919) (Slovak), Rev. John S. Trimbur; Deacon Ronald J. Bunofsky.
Res., 159 Reed Ave., 44405. Tel: 330-755-4141; Fax: 330-755-1022. [CEM]
Catechesis/Religious Programs—Tel: 330-755-5251.
Students 58.

St. Joseph the Provider (1919) (Polish), Rev. Leo J. Pleban.
Res., 633 Porter Ave., 44405. Tel: 330-755-0266.
School—Tel: 330-755-4747; Fax: 330-755-4749.
Lay Teachers 9; Students 203.

St. Lucy's (1937) (Italian), Rev. Msgr. John P. Ashton, Ph.D.
Res., 394 Tenney Ave., 44407-1695. Tel: 330-755-4132.
Catechesis/Religious Programs—Tel: 330-755-1367.
Students 89.

Canal Fulton, Stark Co., SS. Philip and James (1845), Rev. John R. Lody.
Res., 412 High St., 44614. Tel: 216-854-2332. [CEM]
School—Tel: 330-854-2823; Fax: 330-854-1109. Ms. Mary Fiala, Prin.
Lay Teachers 14; Students 217.
Catechesis/Religious Programs—Students 136.

Canfield, Mahoning Co., St. Michael's (1963), Rev. Terrence J. Hazel; Sr. ZoeAnn Reiter, H.M., Pastoral Min.
Res., 281 Glenview Dr., 44406. Tel: 330-533-6839; Fax: 330-533-6839.
Catechesis/Religious Programs—Tel: 330-533-5275. Dottie Miller, D.R.E.
Students 703.

Canton, Stark Co.,

1—All Saints, (1920) (Polish), Rev. Msgr. John C. Finnigan.
Res., 1386 Henry Ave., S.W., 44706. Tel: 330-453-6429.

2—Our Lady of Peace, (1952), Revs. John Nentwick; John E. Zuzik.
Res., 833 39th St., N.W., 44709. Tel: 330-492-0757; Fax: 330-492-1214.
School—1001 39th St., N.W., 44709. Tel: 330-492-0622; Fax: 330-492-0959.
Sisters 1; Lay Teachers 22; Students 437.
Catechesis/Religious Programs—Tel: 330-492-0929.
Students 175.

3—Sacred Heart, (1922) (Slovak), Rev. William Shipe; Deacon Edward Briestensky.
Res., 1620 Clark Ave., S.W., 44706. Tel: 330-453-1028.

4—St. Anthony's, (1908) (Italian), Rev. Thomas G. Bishop.
Res., 1530 11th St., S.E., 44707. Tel: 330-452-9539; Fax: 330-452-4870.
Catechesis/Religious Programs—Students 150.

5—St. Benedict, (1923), Rev. Carl J. Forgach.
Res., 2207 Third St., S.E., 44707. Tel: 330-452-0751.
Benedict Center: Tel: 330-453-3642.
Church—E. Tuscarawas St. & Girard Ave., S.E., 44707.
Catechesis/Religious Programs—Students 67.

6—St. Joan of Arc, (1944), Revs. Thomas P. Dyer; Kevin Peters; Deacon David Conversino. In res., Rev. John J. Daum.
Res., 4940 Tuscarawas St., W., 44708-5012. Tel: 330-477-6796; 6797; Fax: 330-477-0594.
School—120 Bordner Ave., S.W., 44710. Tel: 330-477-2972; Fax: 330-478-2606.
Lay Teachers 15; Students 450.
Catechesis/Religious Programs—166 Bordner Ave., S.W., 44710. G. David Weikart, D.R.E.
Students 461.

7—St. John the Baptist, (1823), Rev. Ronald M. Klingler; Deacon Carl Burkhardt.
Res., 627 McKinley Ave., N.W., 44703. Tel: 330-454-8044. [CEM]

8—St. Joseph's, (1902), Revs. Frank A. Carfagna; James Zanni; Deacon Wilbur J. Bagley.
Res., 2427 W. Tuscarawas St., 44708. Tel: 330-453-2526.
School—126 Columbus Ave., N.W., 44708. Tel: 330-454-9787.
Lay Teachers 13; Students 274.
Catechesis/Religious Programs—Tel: 330-454-2144.
Students 295.

9—St. Mary, (1899), Rev. Gerald J. Sommer, M.S.C.; Deacon Frederick C. Scarletto.
Res., 1602 Market Ave., S., 44707. Tel: 330-453-2110.
Catechesis/Religious Programs—Students 103.

10—St. Michael the Archangel, (1952), Revs. Bradford N. Helman; Charles T. Poore; Sr. Mary Cunningham, H.M., Pastoral Assoc.
Res., 3430 St. Michael's Blvd., N.W., 44718. Tel: 330-492-3119; Fax: 330-492-0339.
School—3505 St. Michael's Blvd., N.W., 44718. Tel: 330-492-2657. Mrs. Patricia Gembar, Prin.
Sisters 2; Lay Teachers 17; Students 526.
Catechesis/Religious Programs—Mr. Michael Ress, D.R.E.
Students 620.

11—St. Paul's, (1907), Rev. Joseph P. Martin; Mrs. Sally Dick, Pastoral Assoc.
Res., 1459 Superior Ave., N.E., 44705. Tel: 330-456-7555. [JC]
Catechesis/Religious Programs—Students 130.

12—St. Peter's, (1845), Rev. Msgr. John C. Finnigan. In res., Rev. Robert Bruce.
Res., 726 Cleveland Ave., N.W., 44702. Tel: 330-453-8493; Fax: 330-453-8083. [CEM]
School—702 Cleveland Ave., N.W., 44702. Tel: 330-452-0125.
Sisters of Notre Dame 3; Lay Teachers 9; Students 211.
Catechesis/Religious Programs—Students 143.

Champion, Trumbull Co., St. William (1963), Rev. Michael J. Smar; Sr. Mary Cora Skrivan, S.N.D., D.R.E.
Res., 5411 Mahoning Ave., N.W., Warren, 44483. Tel: 330-847-8677.
Catechesis/Religious Programs—Tel: 330-847-7026.
Students 224.

Columbiana, Columbiana Co., St. Jude (1966), Rev. Thomas G. Ziegler.
Res., 180 7th St., 44408. Tel: 330-482-2351.
Catechesis/Religious Programs—Tel: 330-482-2888. Ms. Mary Glasser, D.R.E.
Students 295.

Conneaut, Ashtabula Co., St. Mary's (1888), Rev. Nathan S. Willis.
Res., 480 State St., 44030. Tel: 216-599-8855. [CEM][JC]
Catechesis/Religious Programs—Students 250.

St. Frances Cabrini (1954), Rev. Andrew Edward Gretchko.
Res., 744 Mill St., 44030. Tel: 216-599-8570; Fax: 216-593-6772.
School—Tel: 440-593-1677; Fax: 440-593-6772.
Oblate Sisters of the Sacred Heart 1; Lay Teachers 8; Students 160.
Catechesis/Religious Programs—Students 105.

Cortland, Trumbull Co., St. Robert Bellarmine Parish (1952), Rev. Carl Kish.
Res., 4659 Niles-Cortland Rd., N.E., 44410. Tel: 330-637-4886; Fax: 330-637-0608. [CEM]
Catechesis/Religious Programs—Students 553.

Dungannon, Columbiana Co., St. Philip Neri (1817), Rev. Paul L. Gubser.
Res., Hanoverton P.O., 44423. Tel: 330-223-1973. [CEM]

East Liverpool, Columbiana Co., St. Aloysius (1838) (Irish), Rev. John D. MulQueen.
Res., 235 W. 5th St., 43920. Tel: 330-385-7131. [CEM]
School—335 W. 5th St., 43920. Tel: 330-385-5963.
Lay Teachers 8; Students 220.
Catechesis/Religious Programs—Students 57.

St. Ann's (1915), Rev. George J. Balasko.
Res., 1506 Pennsylvania Ave., 43920. Tel: 330-385-5582.

East Palestine, Columbiana Co., Our Lady of Lourdes (1880), Revs. Daniel Cipar, M.S.C.; Delso Torok, Pastor Emeritus.
Res., 200 E. Main St., 44413. Tel: 330-426-9346; Fax: 330-426-9346. [CEM]
Catechesis/Religious Programs—20 N. James St., 44413. Tel: 330-426-2254.
Students 155.

Garrettsville, Portage Co., St. Ambrose (1944), Rev. Richard J. Pentello; Deacon Robert Rapp.
Res., 10692 Freedom St., 44231. Tel: 330-527-4105; Fax: 330-527-2500.

Geneva, Ashtabula Co., Assumption B.V.M. (1915), Rev. Paul R. Tobin.
Res., 594 W. Main St., 44041. Tel: 216-466-3427.
School—Tel: 216-466-2104. Sr. Mary Gloria Auer, R.S.M., Prin.
Lay Teachers 12; Students 155.
Catechesis/Religious Programs—Students 161.

Girard, Trumbull Co., St. Rose (1892), Rev. Msgr. Martin S. Susko, V.F.; Revs. Frank Zanni; Richard M. Reis; Tony Augustine, Pastoral Min.; Sr. Lucille Conley, H.M., Pastoral Ministry; Deacons Kevin Lamar; Paul Milligan. In res., Rev. Msgr. John Andrew Zuraw.
Res., 48 E. Main St., 44420. Tel: 330-545-4351; Fax: 330-545-0119.
School—65 E. Main St., 44420. Tel: 330-545-1163. Sr. Carole Suhar, O.S.U., Prin.
Sisters 2; Lay Teachers 17; Students 346.
Catechesis/Religious Programs—Tel: 216-545-1216. Marjorie O'Malley, D.R.E.
Students 708.

Hubbard, Trumbull Co., St. Patrick's (1869), Revs. Timothy H. O'Neill; James R. Johnson, S.P.; John A. Murray, (Retired); Deacon Robert Friedman.
Res., 315 N. Main St., 44425. Tel: 330-534-1928; Fax: 330-534-0820. [CEM]
School—38 E. Water St., 44425. Tel: 330-534-2509; Fax: 330-534-0305.
Lay Teachers 14; Students 232.
Catechesis/Religious Programs—225 N. Main St., 44425. Tel: 330-534-8304; 534-4111. Sr. Darla J. Vogelsang, O.S.U., D.R.E.
Students 601.

Jefferson, Ashtabula Co., St. Joseph Calasanctius (1858), Rev. Stephen M. Wassie.
Res., 32 E. Jefferson St., 44047. Tel: 216-576-3651.
Catechesis/Religious Programs—Tel: 216-576-3339.
Students 150.

Kent, Portage Co., St. Patrick's (1864), Revs. Timothy Kenney; Joseph Ruggieri.
Res., 313 N. Depeyster St., 44240. Tel: 330-673-5849; Fax: 330-673-5849. [CEM]
School—127 Portage St., 44240. Tel: 330-673-7232; Fax: 330-678-6612.
Lay Teachers 19; Students 336.
Catechesis/Religious Programs—Tel: 330-677-4433.
Students 399.

Immaculate Heart of Mary (1953), Rev. John M. Jerek.
Res., 1424 Horning Rd., 44240. Tel: 330-678-0240; Fax: 330-678-7780.
Catechesis/Religious Programs—Students 130.

Kingsville, Ashtabula Co., St. Andrew (1936), Rev. Nathan S. Willis.
Res., 3700 Rte. 193, 44048. Tel: 216-599-8855; 440-224-0987 (Church). [CEM]

Kinsman, Trumbull Co., St. Patrick (1957). Attended by Our Lady of Victory, Andover.
481 S. Main St., P.O. Box 669, Andover, 44003-9778. Tel: 216-293-6218.
Catechesis/Religious Programs—6397 State Rte. 87 N.E.
Students 71.

Lake Milton, Mahoning Co., St. Catherine (1956), Rev. David W. Merzweiler.
Res., 1254 Grandview Rd., 44429-9542. Tel: 330-654-4001.
Catechesis/Religious Programs—Students 71.

Leetonia, Columbiana Co., St. Patrick's (1861), Rev. Thomas J. Ungashick.
Res., 167 Main St., P.O. Box 67, 44431. Tel: 330-427-6577. [CEM]
Catechesis/Religious Programs—Students 132.

Lisbon, Columbiana Co., St. George (1820), Rev. Robert Edwards; Deacon David H. Arend.
Res., 271 W. Chestnut St., 44432. Tel: 330-424-7648.
Catechesis/Religious Programs—Tel: 330-424-0109.
Students 94.
Mission—West Point, Columbiana Co., St. Agatha, P.O. Box 462, West Point, 44492. Tel: 330-424-0155.

Louisville, Stark Co., St. Louis (1838) (French-German), Revs. Frederick Slaven; Homer G. Oliver.
Res., 300 N. Chapel St., 44641. Tel: 330-875-1658. [CEM]
School—Tel: 330-875-1467; Fax: 330-875-2511.
Lay Teachers 12; Students 233.
Catechesis/Religious Programs—Tel: 330-875-3777.
Students 290.

Sacred Heart of Mary (1833), Rev. William B. Kraynak.
Res., 8277 Nickelplate Ave., N.E., 44641. Tel: 330-875-2827; Fax: 330-875-2410. [CEM]
School—8267 Nickelplate Ave., N.E., 44641. Tel: 330-875-5167. Donna Shadle, Prin.
Lay Teachers 9; Students 95.
Catechesis/Religious Programs—Students 130.

Lowellville, Mahoning Co., Our Lady of the Holy Rosary (1867), Rev. Gerald M. DeLucia.
Res., 131 E. Wood St., 44436. Tel: 330-536-6436; Fax: 330-536-9188. [CEM]
Catechesis/Religious Programs—Students 195.

McDonald, Trumbull Co., Our Lady of Perpetual Help (1943), Rev. Daniel J. Kulesa.
Res., 618 Ohio Ave., 44437. Tel: 330-530-6929.
Catechesis/Religious Programs—601 Indiana Ave., 44437. Tel: 330-530-1111.
Students 197.

Mantua, Portage Co., St. Joseph's (1923), Rev. Thomas J. McCarthy.
Res., 11045 St. Joseph Blvd., 44255. Tel: 330-274-2114; Fax: 330-274-2412.
Parish Center—Tel: 330-274-2253.
School—Tel: 330-274-2268.
Lay Teachers 12; Students 210.
Catechesis/Religious Programs—Students 208.

Massillon, Stark Co.,

1—St. Barbara's, (1867) (German), Rev. Thomas Cebula; Mrs. Pauline Brady, Pastoral Assoc.
Res., 2813 Lincoln Way, N.W., 44647. Tel: 330-833-6898; Fax: 330-833-5164. [CEM]
School—2825 Lincoln Way, N.W., 44647. Tel: 330-833-9510; Fax: 330-833-3297.
Sisters 1; Lay Teachers 9; Students 255; Preschool Children 33.
Catechesis/Religious Programs—Students 122.

2—National Shrine of St. Dymphna, (1938). Located on grounds of Massilon Psychiatric Center. Rev. Matthew M. Herttna, Chap. & Dir.
Church—3000 Erie St., S., P.O. Box 4, 44648-0004. Tel: 330-833-8478.

3—St. Joseph's, (1863), Rev. Raymond L. Paul.
Res., 322 Third St., S.E., 44646. Tel: 330-833-2607. [CEM]
Parish Center and Office—330 Fourth St., S.E., 44646. Tel: 330-833-4907; 833-6088; Fax: 330-833-3907.
Catechesis/Religious Programs—Students 155.

4—St. Mary's, (1839), Revs. James R. Kolp; John P. Tully; Robert E. Brengartner; Deacons Edwards Kurkas; Joseph Fries.
Res., 206 Cherry Rd., N.E., 44646. Tel: 330-833-8501; Fax: 330-833-3359. [CEM]
School—640 First St., N.E., 44646. Tel: 330-832-9355; Fax: 330-832-9030.
Sisters 4; Lay Teachers 18; Students 473.
Catechesis/Religious Programs—Tel: 216-832-5719.
Students 472.

Masury, Trumbull Co., St. Bernadette (1940), Rev. Robert J. Hannon.
Res., 7800 Locust St., 44438. Tel: 330-448-8015; Fax: 330-448-0432.
Catechesis/Religious Programs—Brookfield Junior High, Brookfield, Tel: 330-448-3003.
Students 160.

Maximo, Stark Co., St. Joseph (1850), Rev. William E. Bantz.
Res., 12055 Easton St., N.E., P.O. Box 219, 44650. Tel: 330-823-7809. [CEM]
Catechesis/Religious Programs—Students 147.

Middlebranch, Stark Co., St. Therese Little Flower (1929), Revs. Kevin L. Fete; Edward F. Varble, Pastor Emeritus.
Res., 2040 Diamond St., N.E., North Canton, 44720. Tel: 330-494-2759; Fax: 330-494-2536.
Catechesis/Religious Programs—Students 285.

Mineral Ridge, Trumbull Co., St. Mary's (1870), Rev. Richard Murphy.
Res., 3504 Main St., 44440. Tel: 330-652-7761; Fax: 330-652-7765.
Catechesis/Religious Programs—Students 106.

Navarre, Stark Co., St. Clement's (1830), Rev. Robert G. Gibas.
Res., 216 Wooster St., E., 44662. Tel: 330-879-5900; Fax: 330-879-5138. [CEM]
School—Tel: 330-879-2645.
Lay Teachers 9; Students 186.
Catechesis/Religious Programs—Students 175.

New Middletown, Mahoning Co., St. Paul the Apostle (1952), Rev. Nicholas R. Shori.
Res., 10143 Main St., P.O. Box 515, 44442. Tel: 330-542-3466. [JC]
Catechesis/Religious Programs—Tel: 330-542-3824.
Students 378.

Newton Falls, Trumbull Co., St. Joseph (1846), Rev. John P. Madden.
Res., 131 W. Quarry St., 44444-1560. Tel: 330-872-5742; Fax: 330-872-5744. [JC]
School—Tel: 330-872-7676; Fax: 330-872-1013.
Students 165.
Catechesis/Religious Programs—Tel: 330-872-9947.
Students 174.

St. Mary (1928), Rev. John P. Madden.
Res., 131 West Quarry St., 44444. Tel: 330-872-5742; Fax: 330-872-5744. [CEM][JC]

Niles, Trumbull Co., Our Lady of Mt. Carmel (1907) (Italian), Revs. Peter Chiodo, C.PP.S.; Albert DePascale, C.PP.S.; Gus Constantinides, C.PP.S.
Res., 381 Robbins Ave., 44446. Tel: 330-652-5825; Fax: 330-544-1872.
School—Tel: 330-652-5547; Fax: 330-652-9646.
Sisters 2; Lay Teachers 18; Students 320.
Catechesis/Religious Programs—Students 222.

St. Stephen's (1853), Rev. John H. Gubser.
Res., 129 W. Park Ave., 44446. Tel: 330-652-4396; Fax: 330-652-4396. [CEM]
School—(Grades PreK-8) 45 S. Chestnut, 44446. Tel: 330-652-5511; Fax: 330-652-4264.
Lay Teachers 10; Students 220; Preschool 56.
Catechesis/Religious Programs—Students 160.

North Canton, Stark Co., St. Paul's (1845), Revs. James E. McKarns; John Warner.
Res., 241 S. Main St., 44720. Tel: 330-499-2201; Fax: 330-499-8106. [CEM]
School—303 S. Main St., 44720. Tel: 330-494-0223; Fax: 330-494-3226. Jackie Zufall, Prin.
Lay Teachers 21; Students 460.
Catechesis/Religious Programs—Tel: 330-494-4036.
Students 775.

North Jackson, Mahoning Co., St. James Parish Family (1945), Rev. David W. Merzweiler.
Office Address: 50 Rosemont Rd., 44451.
Res., 1254 Grandview Rd., Lake Milton, 44429. Tel: 330-654-4001.
Catechesis/Religious Programs—Tel: 330-538-2602.
Students 112.

Orwell, Ashtabula Co., St. Mary (1922) (Polish), Rev. Raymond J. Thomas.
Res., 103 N. Maple, Box 217, 44076. Tel: 440-437-6262. [CEM]
Catechesis/Religious Programs—Tel: 440-437-8216.
Students 95.

Poland, Mahoning Co., Holy Family (1956), Revs. Philip P. Conley; Michael Swierz.
Res., 2729 Center Rd., 44514. Tel: 330-757-1545; Fax: 330-757-4443.
School—Tel: 330-757-3753; Fax: 330-757-7648.
Sisters 2; Lay Teachers 24; Students 390.
Catechesis/Religious Programs—Students 854.

Randolph Township, Portage Co., St. Joseph (1831), Rev. Edward R. Wieczorek.
Res., 2643 Waterloo Rd., Mogadore, 44260. Tel: 330-628-9941; Fax: 330-628-9942. [CEM]
School—Tel: 330-628-9555.
Sisters of Notre Dame 2; Lay Teachers 12; Students 238.
Catechesis/Religious Programs—Tel: 330-628-4844.
Students 348.

Ravenna, Portage Co., Immaculate Conception (1854), Revs. Robert A. Sabatino; Leo J. Wehrlin; Deacon Russell J. Brode.
Res., 409 W. Main St., 44266. Tel: 330-296-6434. [CEM]
School—225 S. Sycamore St., 44266. Tel: 330-296-4817; Fax: 330-296-2925.
Lay Teachers 9; Students 198.
Catechesis/Religious Programs—Tel: 330-296-4549.
Students 401.

Rock Creek, Ashtabula Co., Sacred Heart (1956), Rev. Edward Kowaleski; Deacon John D. Pallo.
Res., 3409 N. Main St., P.O. Box 305, 44084. Tel: 216-563-3010. [JC]
Catechesis/Religious Programs—Students 88.

Rootstown, Portage Co., St. Peter of the Fields (1868), Sr. Regina Zeleznik, S.N.D., Parish Coord.; Deacon Thomas Shay.
Res., 3487 Old Forge Rd., 44272. Tel: 330-325-7543. [CEM]
Catechesis/Religious Programs—Students 120.

Salem, Columbiana Co., St. Paul's (1881), Rev. Msgr. James A. Clarke. Pastoral Assocs.: Donna Lynn; Amanda Raymond. In res., Rev. David Schilder, (COL).
Res., 157 Ohio Ave., 44460. Tel: 330-332-0336; Fax: 330-332-0337.
School—925 E. State St., 44460. Tel: 330-337-3451; Fax: 330-337-3452.
Lay Teachers 10; Students 171.
Catechesis/Religious Programs—Tel: 330-332-4373. D.R.E.: Richard Mattiussi; Donna Dermotta.
Students 428.

Salineville, Columbiana Co., St. Patrick's (1873), Rev. Paul L. Gubser.
Res., P.O. Box 66, Summitville, 43962. Tel: 330-679-2511.
Church—611 Jefferson St., 43945. Tel: 216-223-1871. [CEM]

Sebring, Mahoning Co., St. Ann (1908), Sr. Maureen Smith, H.M.
Res., 323 S. 15th St., 44672. Tel: 330-938-2033; Fax: 330-938-2033.
Catechesis/Religious Programs—Students 90.

Streetsboro, Portage Co., St. Joan of Arc (1965), Revs. Robert V. Flynn; James F. Stenson, Pastor Emeritus.
Res., 8894 State Rte. 14, 44241. Tel: 330-626-3424; Fax: 330-626-3422.
Catechesis/Religious Programs—Tel: 330-626-2050.
Students 265.

Struthers, Mahoning Co., Holy Trinity (1907) (Slovak), Rev. Stephen C. Karas.
Res., 250 N. Bridge St., 44471. Tel: 330-755-2115; Fax: 330-750-9431.

St. Nicholas (1865), Revs. Philip E. Rogers; Thomas J. Kraszewski; Deacon John Terranova; Mrs. Rita DeFrance, Pastoral Assoc.
Res., 775 5th St., 44471-1795. Tel: 330-750-2555.
Parish Office—764 5th St., 44471-1704. Tel: 330-755-9819; Fax: 330-755-9949.
School—762 5th St., 44471-1704. Tel: 330-755-2128.
Lay Teachers 11; Students 240.
Catechesis/Religious Programs—Tel: 330-755-6245. Miss Stephanie Tarajack, D.R.E.
Students 440.

Summitville, Columbiana Co., St. John's (1852), Rev. Paul L. Gubser.
Res., 16017 Smith Rd., 43962. Tel: 216-223-1871. [CEM]

Uniontown, Stark Co., Holy Spirit (1979), Rev. John Zapp.
Res., 2952 Edison St., N.W., 44685. Tel: 330-699-4500; 877-1695.
Catechesis/Religious Programs—Students 363.

Vienna, Trumbull Co., Queen of the Holy Rosary, Rev. Gary Dilley, F.S.S.P.
Res., 291 Scoville Rd., P.O. Box 276, 44473. Tel: 330-856-4204.

St. Vincent de Paul (1934), Rev. Thomas F. Murphy.
Res., 4453 Warren-Sharon Rd., 44473. Tel: 330-394-2461; 1-800-645-6684.
Catechesis/Religious Programs—Tel: 330-394-2361.
Students 144.

Warren, Trumbull Co.,

1—BLESSED SACRAMENT, (1959), Rev. Donald E. King.
Res., 3020 Reeves Rd., N.E., 44483. Tel: 330-372-2215; Fax: 330-372-6380.
Schools—Queen of Angels Building, (Grades K-4).; St. Mary Middle School, (Grades 5-8) 3000 Reeves Rd., N.E., 44483. Tel: 330-372-2375; Fax: 330-372-2375. Mrs. Helen Erickson, Prin.
Sisters of Divine Providence 1; Lay Teachers 14; Students 232.
Catechesis/Religious Programs—Tel: 330-372-6930.
Students 548.

2—CHRIST OUR KING, (1951), Rev. Thomas M. Spisak.
Res., 1000 Tod Ave., S.W., 44485. Tel: 330-395-3747.

3—SS. CYRIL AND METHODIUS, (1928) (Slovak), Rev. Thomas M. Spisak.
Res., 185 Laird Ave., N.E., 44483. Tel: 330-393-9766.
Catechesis/Religious Programs—Students 91.

4—ST. JAMES, (1947), Revs. Charles W. Crumbley Tel: 330-369-3518; James Walker; Sr. Marie Clarice Bates, S.N.D., Pastoral Assoc.
Res., 2533 Burton St., S.E., 44484. Tel: 330-369-3888; Fax: 330-369-2761.
Schools—Queen of Angels Building, (Grades K-4) 44484. Tel: 330-369-4218.
Lay Teachers 10; Students 130; St. Mary Middle School, (Grades 5-8) 261 Elm Rd., 44483. Tel: 216-399-5154. Sr. Mary Judith Anne Sabau, S.N.D., Prin.
Catechesis/Religious Programs—2106 Arbor St., S.E., 44484. Sr. Mary Ann McFadden, S.N.D., D.R.E.
Students 87.

5—ST. JOSEPH, (1928) (Polish), Rev. John P. Turk. In res., Rev. George Popovich.
Res., 1346 Vernon St., N.W., 44483. Tel: 330-393-0226. [CEM]

6—ST. MARY'S, (1835), Rev. Bernard R. Schmalzried.
Res., 232 Seneca St., N.E., 44481. Tel: 330-393-8721; 394-3426. [CEM]
Catechesis/Religious Programs—Students 55.

7—ST. PIUS X, (1959), Rev. William J. Loveless.
Res., 1401 Moncrest Ave., N.W., 44485. Tel: 330-399-8881; 399-8882.
Schools—Queen of Apostles Building, (Grades K-4).; St. Mary Middle School, (Grades 5-8). Tel: 216-399-5411. Sr. Theresa Dolan-Dixon, Prin.
Lay Teachers 6; Students 135.
Catechesis/Religious Programs—Students 53.

Waynesburg, Stark Co., St. James (1928), Rev. Michael D. Seifert.
Res., 400 W. Lisbon St., 44688. Tel: 330-866-9449.
School—Tel: 330-866-9556.
Lay Teachers 7; Students 98.
Catechesis/Religious Programs—Students 89.

Wellsville, Columbiana Co., Immaculate Conception (1842), Rev. George J. Balasko.
Res., 1021 Riverside Ave., 43968. Tel: 330-532-3445. [CEM]
Catechesis/Religious Programs—Tel: 330-532-2382. Mr. Robert Barto, D.R.E.
Students 102.

Windham, Portage Co., St. Michael's (1943), Rev. James Paul Lang.
Res., 9736 E. Center St., 44288. Tel: 330-326-3531.

On Duty Outside the Diocese:
Reverend Monsignors—
Reidy, Robert, Jerusalem
Reverend Fathers—
Bonnot, Bernard R., New York, NY
Dailey, John, El Salvador, Central America
Daprile, James, Cincinnati, OH
Deffenbaugh, Joseph T., Pensacola, FL
Nuzzi, Ronald

Military Chaplains:
Reverend Fathers—
Garvey, Michael, U.S. Navy
Mikstay, Michael, U.S. Marines

Sabbatical:
Reverend Fathers—
Manning, J. Patrick, St. Mary Seminary, Wickliffe, OH

Absent on Leave:
Reverend Fathers—
Fondriest, James
Grabowski, Dennis
James, Joseph
McCarragher, Timothy
O'Brien, James
Ryan, John
Santucci, Louis
Strader, Kenneth
Trucksis, Frederick
Vazquez, Jose
Ziemba, Howard

Retired:
Reverend Monsignors—
Adamko, Cyril A.
Fannon, Robert C.
Gutman, Gordon G.
Kelly, Thomas F.
Krispinsky, Joseph A.
Oliver, Homer G.
Reagan, Donald
Reverend Fathers—
Bakos, Stephen
Barrett, Robert P.
Beller, Joseph
Brengartner, Robert E.
Bruce, Robert J.
Cavanaugh, James K.
Chamberlain, Robert
Chonko, Michael J.
Curran, Gerald X.
Czaja, Joseph S.
Daum, John J.
Dobosiewciz, Leon W.
Duritsa, George M.
Esposito, Anthony
Fabrizio, Henry E.
Fasline, Anthony
Franko, George M.
Friedrich, Ralph
Herttna, Matthew M.
Hill, Robert
Horvath, Stephen
Hughes, Francis J.
Klein, Albert J.
Lettau, David
Lyons, John F.
Malik, Joseph
Marrokal, Donald
Matulik, Martin
McNally, Thomas C.
Murray, John
Nachtigal, Fred
Nist, Arthur
O'Leary, Patrick D.
Oser, Donald
Pierce, Blaine F.
Platt, Stewart
Rath, John G.
Rich, Orlando S.
Sargent, John
Schmidt, John W.
Slipski, William P.
Snock, Francis
Spitale, John
Stenson, James F.
Summers, John
Tamburrini, Joseph
Torok, Dezso
Vacca, Bernard
Varble, Edward F.
Welsch, John
Winca, George F.
Witt, William
Yablonsky, Gabriel
Yurko, William

Permanent Deacons:
Arend, David H., St. George, Lisbon
Bagley, Wilbur J., St. Joseph, Canton
Basile, Eugene, St. Jude, Columniana
Beil, David C., St. Christine, Youngstown
Brechbill, Kenneth W., St. Joseph, Massillon
Briestensky, Edward L., Sacred Heart, Canton
Brode, Russell J., Immaculate Conception, Ravenna
Brown, James, St. Christine, Youngstown
Bunofsky, Ronald J., St. John, Campbell
Burkhardt, Carl R., St. John the Baptist, Canton
Colon, Felipe, St. Rose of Lima, Youngstown
Conversino, David, St. Joan of Arc, Canton
Cosentino, Louis A., St. Jude, Columbia
Cuttica, Robert J., St. Christine, Youngstown
DiFrancesco, Salvatore, St. Matthias, Youngstown
Friedman, Robert J., St. Patrick, Hubbard
Fries, Joseph K., St. Mary, Massillon
Harvey, James G., St. William, Warren
Hatala, Ray H., Office of Permanent Diaconate
Hawkins, Edward, Holy Family, Poland
Ivan, Ellis C., Holy Spirit, Uniontown
Jaskiewicz, Albert F., St. Pius X, Warren
Johnson, Richard M., St. Joseph, Ashtabula
Klein, Robert E., St. Peter, Canton
Kocjancic, Michael A., St. Charles, Boardman
Krause, Harold R., SS. Philip & James, Canal Fulton
Kurkas, Edward G., St. Mary, Massillon
Lamar, Kevin T., St. Rose, Girard
Lambert, William H., St. Paul, North Canton
Layko, Ronald J., St. Christine, Youngstown
Medvez, Alvin A., St. Stephen, Youngstown; C.T.N.Y.
Milanek, Richard, St. Luke, Boardman
Milligan, Paul, St. Rose, Girard
Nohra, Joseph S., St. Maron & Mt. Carmel, Youngstown
Pallo, John D., Sacred Heart, Rock Creek
Pohl, Peter P., SS. Philip & James, Canal Fulton
Prasek, Alan, St. Joseph, Ashtabula
Rapp, Robert, St. Ambrose, Garrettsville
Roberts, Michael R., Jr., St. Joseph, Austintown
Rohr, Thomas J., SS. Philip & James, Canal Fulton
Scarletto, Frederick C., St. Mary, Canton
Schlais, Michael, St. Stanislaus, Youngstown
Shay, Thomas R., Sr., St. Peter of the Fields, Rootstown
Sherwood, Ronald D., Columbia-Mercy Medical Center, Canton
Soich, Thomas G., St. Charles, Boardman
Terranova, John, St. Nicholas, Struthers
Toth, Joseph P., Blessed Sacrament, Warren
Vaughan, John H., (Retired)
White, James A., St. Joseph, Randolph
Wyles, Steve, St. Joseph, Massillon
Zamary, Joseph J., Sacred Heart, Youngstown

INSTITUTIONS LOCATED IN THE DIOCESE

[A] SEMINARIES, RELIGIOUS, OR SCHOLASTICATES

YOUNGSTOWN. *Sacred Heart Retreat House & Renewal Center*, 3128 Logan Ave., P.O. Box 6074, 44501. Tel: 330-759-9539; Fax: 330-759-8235.
E-mail: sacredheartctr@worldnet.att.net
Very Rev. Walter J. Downs, M.S.C., Supr.; Revs. Paul J. Hill, M.S.C., Dir. Novices; Donovan Mulert, M.S.C.; Andrew Torma, M.S.C.; Gerald R.J. Sommer, M.S.C.; Daniel Cipar; Earl Henley, M.S.C.; Thomas Carney, M.S.C., St. Rose of Lima, 50 Struthers-Coitsville Rd., 44505. Tel: 330-755-3633. Applications for missions, retreats, recollection days, novenas and Forty Hours to be made to the Rev. Father Superior. Priests 7; Brothers 4.

CANFIELD. *Society of St. Paul*, P.O. Box 595, 44406. Tel: 330-533-5503; 533-1076. Bro. Aloysius Milella, S.S.P., Supr.; Revs. Jeffrey Mickler, S.S.P.; Thomas Fogarty, S.S.P.; Francis J. Parella, S.S.P.; Anthony L. Chenevey, S.S.P.; Bros. Dismas Beique, S.S.P.; Peter Scalise, S.S.P.; John Joachim Naranjo, S.S.P.; Richard Brunner, S.S.P.; Timothy Cicconi, S.S.P.; Luke Bedard, S.S.P.; Arthur McClelland, S.S.P.; David Griffin, S.S.P. Priests 4; Brothers 9; Novices 2.

[B] COLLEGES AND UNIVERSITIES

NORTH CANTON. *Walsh University*, 2020 Easton St., N.W., 44720-3396. Tel: 330-499-7090.
Web site: http://www.walsh.edu
For a complete listing, refer to the Colleges and Universities section.

[C] HIGH SCHOOLS, DIOCESAN

YOUNGSTOWN. *Cardinal Mooney High School*, 2545 Erie St., 44507. Tel: 330-788-5007; Fax: 330-788-4511. Sr. Jane Marie Kudlacz, H.M., Prin.; Rev. Gregory Fedor, Assoc. Prin. Priests 1; Sisters 1; Lay Teachers 43; Students 650.

Ursuline High School, 750 Wick Ave., 44505. Tel: 216-744-4563.
E-mail: ygnursuline@connect.com
Web site: www.ursuline.com
Rev. Richard Murphy, Assoc. Prin. Priests 1; Sisters 5; Lay Teachers 36; Students 600.

ASHTABULA. *SS. John & Paul School*. (Grades 7-12). St. John High School Building, 3320 Station Ave., 44004. Tel: 440-997-5531. Miss Albina Larson, Prin. Lay Teachers 9; Students 70.

CANTON. *Central Catholic High*, 4824 Tuscarawas St., W., 44708-5198. Tel: 330-478-2131; Fax: 330-478-6086. Rev. Robert W. Kaylor, Prin.; Mr. John Korecki, Asst. Prin.; Mr. Leo DeMatteis, Dean of Students; Mr. James Naegeli, Campus Ministry

Dir. Priests 1; Lay Teachers 47; Students 703; Total Staff 53.

LOUISVILLE. *St. Thomas Aquinas High School*, 2121 Reno Dr., N.E., 44641. Tel: 330-875-1631; Fax: 330-875-8469. Mr. Joseph Meranto, Prin.; Mr. Alan Digianantonio, Asst. Prin.; Miss Cindi Eby, Dean. Lay Teachers 42; Total Staff 45; Students 528.

WARREN. *John F. Kennedy High School*, 2550 Central Pkwy., S.E., 44484. Tel: 330-369-1804; Fax: 330-369-1125. Girard-Niles-Youngtown. Tel: 330-539-5242. Rev. William Petrunak, Chap.; Mr. James N. Ruffing,Prin.; Mr. James Boyle, Asst. Prin. Lay Teachers 24; Students 365.

[D] ELEMETARY SCHOOLS, DIOCESAN

ASHTABULA. *SS. John & Paul School*. (Grades K-6). Our Lady of Mt. Carmel Building, 2150 Columbus Ave., 44004. Tel: 440-997-5821. Mrs. Donna Timonere, Vice Prin. Lay Teachers 9; Students 273.

[E] MIDDLE SCHOOLS, DIOCESAN

WARREN. *Notre Dame School*, Queen of Peace Building, 261 Elm Rd., N.E., 44483. Tel: 330-399-5154. Mrs. Kathleen Mocker, Prin. Sisters 2; Lay Teachers 20; Students 305.

[F] PRIVATE SCHOOLS

CANFIELD. *Ursuline Preschool & Kindergarten*, 4300 Shields Rd., 44406. Tel: 330-792-4150. Sr. Jacquelyn Herpy, O.S.U., Dir.; Sr. Jan Gier, O.S.U., Asst. Dir. Ursuline Sisters 4; Lay Teachers 5; Students 230.

[G] GENERAL HOSPITALS

YOUNGSTOWN. *HM Health Services*, 4964 Belmont Ave., 44505-1046. Tel: 330-759-7484
For a complete listing, refer to the Hospitals section.
HM Health Services, St. Elizabeth Health Center, 1044 Belmont Ave., Box 1790, 44501. Tel: 330-480-3570
For a complete listing, refer to the Hospitals section.
St. Elizabeth Health Resources, Inc., P.O. Box 207, 44501
For a complete listing, refer to the Hospitals section.

WARREN. *St. Joseph Health Center*, 667 Eastland Ave., S.E., 44484. Tel: 330-841-4000; Fax: 330-841-4019
For a complete listing, refer to the Hospitals section.

[H] SPECIAL CARE FACILITIES

NORTH LIMA. *The Assumption Village*, 9800 Market St., 44452. Tel: 330-549-0740; Fax: 330-549-0701
For a complete listing, refer to the Special Care Facilities section.

[I] HOMES FOR AGED

CANTON. *House of Loreto*, 2812 Harvard Ave., N.W., 44709. Tel: 330-453-8137; Fax: 330-453-8140
For a complete listing, refer to the Special Care Facilities section.

HUBBARD. *Villa Maria Teresa*, 50 Warner Rd., 44425. Tel: 330-759-9329 (Villa); 875-4635 (Emmaus House)
For a complete listing, refer to the Special Care Facilities section.

LOUISVILLE. *Emmaus House*, 1515 California Ave., 44641. Tel: 330-875-4635
For a complete listing, refer to the Special Care Facilities section.
St. Joseph Care Center, 2308 Reno Dr., 44641. Tel: 330-875-5562; Fax: 330-875-8947
For a complete listing, refer to the Special Care Facilities section.

NORTH LIMA. *The Assumption Village*, 9800 Market St., 44452. Tel: 330-549-0740; Fax: 330-549-0701
For a complete listing, refer to the Special Care Facilities section.

[J] MONASTERIES AND RESIDENCES OF PRIESTS AND BROTHERS

YOUNGSTOWN. *Mt. Alverna Friary*, 517. S. Belle Vista Ave., 44509. Tel: 330-799-1888. Franciscan Fathers. Revs. Matthew J. Kiss, O.F.M., Guardian; Nicholas Dengl, O.F.M.; John Reis, O.F.M., Vicar, Pastor of Our Lady of Hungary; Sandor Krupa, O.F.M.; Deacon Kenneth Ghastin, O.F.M.; Bros. Reginald Antal, O.F.M.; Emery Kish, O.F.M. Total in Residence 7; Total Staff 6.

[K] CONVENTS AND RESIDENCES FOR SISTERS

CANFIELD. *Motherhouse and Educational Center of the Ursuline Sisters*, 4250 Shields Rd., 44406. Tel: 330-792-7636. Sr. Nancy Dawson, O.S.U., Gen. Supr. Total in Community 80; Total in Residence 51; Total Staff 5.
Ursuline Center, 4250 Shields Rd., 44406.

CANTON. *Sancta Clara Monastery*, 4200 N. Market Ave., 44714. Tel: 330-492-1171. Rev. Kieran M. Kay, O.F.M., Chap. Poor Clares of Perpetual Adoration. Cloistered Professed Nuns 14.

HUBBARD. *Villa Maria Teresa*, 50 Warner Rd., 44425. Tel: 330-759-9329. Sr. Joyce Candidi, O.S.H.J., Regl. Supr.; Sr. Augustina Cagnazzo, O.S.H.J., Convent Supr. Novitiate and American Headquarters of Oblate Sisters of the Sacred Heart of Jesus. Sisters 22; Total Staff 8.

[L] CATHOLIC CHARITIES SOCIAL SERVICE AGENCIES

ASHTABULA. *Catholic Service League*, 4200 Park Ave., 44004. Tel: 216-992-2121.
E-mail: ccashtabula@connectinc.com
Danita M. Eartly, Exec. Dir. Total Assisted 4,000; Total Staff 12.

CANTON. *Catholic Community Services of Stark County, Inc.*, 625 Cleveland Ave., N.W., 44702. Tel: 330-455-0374.
E-mail: ccstark@connectinc.com
876 Amherst Rd., N.E., Massillon, 44646. Tel: 330-833-8516. Professional Counseling and Licensed Adoption Social Service Agency. Mr. Daniel J. Fuline, A.C.S.W., L.I.S.W., CEO. Patients assisted annually 22,233; Total Staff 60.

KENT. *Family and Community Services of Catholic Charities*, 302 N. DePeyster St., 44240. Tel: 330-678-3911; Fax: 330-678-1264.
E-mail: ccportage@connectinc.com
Rev. Thomas McCarthy, Priests' Representative. Total Assisted 7,896; Total Staff 52.

WARREN. *Catholic Community Services, Inc. of Trumbull County*, 175 Laird Ave., N.E., 3rd Floor, 44483. Tel: 216-393-4254. Ms. Kathleen McCulloh, M.A., L.S.W., Exec. Dir. Family and Child Welfare Work in Trumbull Co. Total Staff 2.

[M] HOMES FOR WOMEN

YOUNGSTOWN. *Beatitude House*, 1515 Fifth Ave., 44504. Transitional Housing, Job Preparation, Job Training, and Case Management for Economically Disadvantaged Women. Sr. Margaret Scheetz, O.S.U., Dir. Total Assisted 44; Total Staff 9.

[N] RETREAT HOUSES

YOUNGSTOWN. *Sacred Heart Retreat and Renewal Center*, 3128 Logan Way, Box 6074, 44501. Tel: 330-759-9539; Fax: 330-759-8235. Society of the Missionaries of the Sacred Heart. Revs. Walter J. Downs, M.S.C., Dir.; Andrew Torma, M.S.C., Program Dir.; Bro. John Peralta, M.S.C., House Mgr. Residents 3; Total Staff 3.

[O] NEWMAN CENTERS

YOUNGSTOWN. *Newman Center at Youngstown State University*, 254 Madison Ave., 44504-1627. Tel: 330-747-9202.
E-mail: bb703@yfn.ysu.edu
Total Staff 4.

KENT. *Kent State University Newman Center*, 1424 Horning Rd., 44240. Rev. John M. Jerek; Ms. Barbara Kaluczky; Ms. Marcie Bircher; Ms. Andrea Warner; Mrs. Barbara DeGrand. Total in Residence 1; Total Staff 5.

[P] MISCELLANEOUS LISTINGS

YOUNGSTOWN. *Caritas Communities*, 225 Elm St., 44503. Tel: 330-744-8451; 384-1555; Fax: 330-742-6447.
E-mail: ay787@yfn.ysu.edu
Web site: www.rc.net/youngstown/catholic_charities
Sr. Denise Maher, H.M., Pres. & CEO; Brian Corbin, Chm.
As a member of Corporation of Catholic Charities Housing Opportunities and the Humility of Mary Housing Program, Caritas Communities will serve as Property Management Corporation for low income and special needs housing.
Catholic Charities Housing Opportunities Corporation, 225 Elm St., 44503. Tel: 330-744-8452, Ext. 275; Fax: 330-744-8447.
E-mail: doyccsocact@connectinc.com
Web site: www.rc.net/youngstown/catholic_charities
Mr. Brian Corbin, Pres. & CEO. Purpose: Provides coordination, integration and leadership in the provision of housing services which promote affordable housing in the community. Total Families Assisted 375; Total Staff 2.
Declaration of Trust of Trumbull, Department of Education, 225 Elm St., 44503. County Catholic School Endowment Fund.
Humility of Mary Information Systems, Inc., 1343 Belmont Ave., 44504.
St. Elizabeth Development Foundation, 1044 Belmont Ave., P.O. Box 1790, 44501-1790. Tel: 330-480-3349. Edward R. Toth, Jr., Pres. & CEO. Total Staff 2.

CANFIELD. *The Ursuline Center*, 4280 Shields Rd., 44406. Tel: 216-799-4941.

LOUISVILLE. *St. Thomas Aquinas High School Endowment Fund*, 2121 Reno Drive, N.E., 44641. Tel: 330-875-1631. Joseph Meranto, Pres.; Vickie Fonte, Sec.

WARREN. *St. Joseph Development Foundation*, 667 Eastland Ave., S.E., 44484. Edward R. Toth, Jr., Pres. & CEO.

[Q] DIOCESAN CEMETERIES

YOUNGSTOWN. *Calvary*, 248 S. Belle Vista Ave., 44509.
Resurrection, 300 N. Racoon Rd., 44515. Tel: 216-799-1900.

MASSILLON. *Calvary*, 3469 Lincoln Way, E., 44647.

WARREN. *All Souls*, Rte. 3, Box 500, 44483.

RELIGIOUS INSTITUTES OF MEN REPRESENTED IN THE DIOCESE

For further details refer to the corresponding bracketed number in the Religious Institutes of Men or Women section.

[0320]—*Brothers of Christian Instruction.*—F.I.C.

[]—*Congregation of the Apostles of Jesus.*—A.J.

[0480]—*Conventual Franciscans.*—O.F.M.Conv.

[0520]—*Franciscan Friars.* (Immaculate Conception Prov. of New York).—O.F.M.

[]—*Franciscans-Province of St. John the Baptist.*—O.F.M.

[1110]—*Missionaries of the Sacred Heart.*—M.S.C.

[]—*Order of Franciscans Minor.* (Holy Name Prov.).—O.F.M.

[0430]—*Order of Preachers (Dominicans).* (Prov. of St. Joseph).—O.P.

[1020]—*Pauline Fathers and Brothers.*—S.S.P.

[]—*Priestly Fraternity of St. Peter.*—F.S.S.P.

[1230]—*Servants of the Paraclete.*—s.P.

[1060]—*Society of the Precious Blood.* (Cincinnati Prov. & Italian).—C.PP.S.

RELIGIOUS INSTITUTES OF WOMEN REPRESENTED IN THE DIOCESE

[0100]—*Adorers of the Blood of Christ.*—A.S.C.

[]—*Antonine Sisters.*—A.S.

[]—*Benediction Sisters (Byzantine Sisters).*—O.S.B.

[1040]—*Congregation of the Divine Spirit.*—C.D.S.

[1710]—*Congregation of the Third Order of St. Francis of Mary Immaculate, Joliet, IL.*—O.S.F.

[1070-28]—*Dominican Sisters.*—O.P.

[]—*Mission Helpers of the Sacred Heart.*—M.H.S.H.

[3050]—*Oblate Sisters of the Sacred Heart of Jesus.*—O.S.H.J.

[3210]—*Poor Clares of Perpetual Adoration.*—P.C.P.A.

[0580]—*Sisters of Charity of St. Augustine.*—C.S.A.

[0990]—*Sisters of Divine Providence.*—C.D.P.

[2575]—*Sisters of Mercy of the Americas.*—R.S.M.

[2990]—*Sisters of Notre Dame.*—S.N.D.

[]—*Sisters of Our Lady of Kilimanjaro.*—C.D.N.K.

[3830-08]—*Sisters of St. Joseph.*—C.S.J.

[]—*Sisters of St. Joseph of Springfield.*—S.S.J.

[3910]—*Sisters of St. Joseph of St. Mark.*—S.J.S.M.

[3930]—*Sisters of St. Joseph of the Third Order of St. Francis.*—S.S.J.-T.O.S.F.

[2110]—*Sisters of the Humility of Mary.*—H.M.

[3730]—*Sisters of the Order of St. Basil the Great.*—O.S.B.M.

[4120-07]—*Ursuline Nuns of the Congregation of Paris.*—O.S.U.

[4160]—*Vincentian Sisters of Charity.*—V.S.C.

NECROLOGY

† Barrette, Rev. Msgr. Dacian, Brewster, OH, St. Therese. —Died Oct. 4, 1997.

† Braun, Warren, (Retired). —Died Jan. 14, 1997.

† Dempster, A. Patrick, (Retired). —Died Dec. 7, 1997.

† O'Neil, William J., (Retired). —Died Jan. 16, 1997.

† Tecca, Felix R., (Absent on Sick Leave). —Died Aug. 22, 1997.

Apostolate to Hungarians

Most Reverend

ATTILA MIKLOSHAZY, S.J., S.T.D.

Titular Bishop of Castel Minore and Bishop for the spiritual assistance to the Hungarian emigrant people; ordained June 18, 1961; appointed August 12, 1989; consecrated November 4, 1989. *Res., St. Augustine's Seminary, 2661 Kingston Rd., Scarborough, Ontario, Canada, M1M 1M3.* Tel.: 416-261-7207; Fax: 416-261-2529.

ESTABLISHED MAY 20, 1983.

The Apostolate of the Bishop of Hungarians living outside of Hungary extends territorially to all the Hungarian communities existing outside of Hungary. The main purpose of the Apostolate is to give spiritual assistance to them through and in cooperation with the local ordinary and pastors.

Former Bishop—Most Rev. LADISLAUS A. IRANYI, Sch.P., ord. March 13, 1938; appt. May 20, 1983; cons. July 27, 1983; died March 6, 1987.

Bishop's Office—2661 Kingston Rd., Scarborough, Ontario, Canada, M1M 1M3. Tel: 416-261-7202; Fax: 416-261-2529.

Delegate of the Bishop in Europe—Rev. Dr. FERENC CSERHATI, *Ung.Kath.Mission, Oberfohringerstr.40, D-81925, Munchen, Germany.* Tel: 49-89-982-637; Fax: 49-89-985-419.

Delegate of the Bishop in the U.S.A.—Rev. STEPHEN N. MUSTOS, Sch.P., *223 Third St., Passaic, NJ, 07055.* Tel: 201-779-0332; Fax: 201-778-4263.

American Hungarian Catholic Priests' Association—East Coast Division: Rev. STEPHEN MUSTOS, Sch.P., *223 Third St., Passaic, NJ, 07055.* Tel: 201-779-0332; Fax: 201-778-4263.

Hungarian Catholic League of America, Inc.—Rev. Msgr. WILLIAM I. VARSANYI, P.A., Chm., *One Cathedral Sq., Providence, RI, 02903.* Tel: 401-278-4515; Fax: 401-831-1947.

Hungarian Priests' Association in Canada—Rev. ALEXANDER EROS, S.J., *337 Hellems Ave., Welland, Ontario, Canada, L3B 3C2.* Tel: 905-734-3772.

Newspapers & Magazines—"Eletunk", (Our Life); Rev. OTTO FEJOS, Editor, *Landwehrstrasse 66, D-80336, Munchen 2, Germany.* Tel: 89-532-8288; Fax: 89-532-8245.

"HIS- Press Service"—published by the Hungarian Institute for Sociology of Religion. Rev. EMERIC ANDRAS, S.J., Editor, *Gerlgasse 10/3, A-1030, Wien, Austria.* Tel: 43-222-80-233; Fax: 1-78-41-91.

"Tavlatok"—(Perspectives), Quarterly on Worldview, Spirituality and Culture, ed. by the Unio Cleri Hungarici. Revs. FERENC SZABO, S.J.; FERENC NAGY, S.J., *Sodras u. 13, H-1026, Budapest, Hungary.* Tel: 1-176-7062.

"A Sziv"—(Sacred Heart Messenger), monthly, published by the Hungarian Jesuit Fathers. Rev. NEMESHEGYI PETER, S.J., Editor, *Pf. 586, H-1398, Budapest, Hungary.* Tel: 1-176-7062; Fax: 1-275-0269., Address in Canada:: *432 Sheppard Ave. E., Willowdale, Ontario, Canada, M2N 3B7.*

STATISTICS

Most personnel and institutions are under the jurisdiction of their local ordinaries.

NECROLOGY

Incorporated in diocesan and archdiocesan listings.

Lithuanian Apostolate For Lithuanian Catholics

Living Outside Lithuania

Most Reverend

PAUL A. BALTAKIS, O.F.M.

Titular Bishop of Egara and Bishop for Spiritual Assistance of Lithuanian Catholics Living Outside Lithuania; ordained August 24, 1952; appointed June 1, 1984; consecrated September 14, 1984. *Res., 361 Highland Blvd., Brooklyn, NY, 11207.* Tel.: 718-827-7932; Fax: 718-827-6696.

IN CARITATE SERVIAMUS DEO

ESTABLISHED JUNE 1, 1984.

The Apostolate of the Bishop for Lithuanian Catholics extends worldwide to all Lithuanian communities existing outside Lithuania, 75 percent of them in the U.S.A. The purpose of the apostolate is to give spiritual assistance to them, in cooperation with the local ordinaries and pastors. Specific faculties enabling the implementation of the Bishop's responsibilities were granted by the Holy See on July 21, 1986.

E-mail address: lcra@earthlink.net:

Former Lithuanian Bishops—Most Rev. VINCENTAS BRIZGYS, Ph.D., J.C.D., cons. May 19, 1940; Titular Bishop of Bosana; Auxiliary Bishop of Kaunas, Lithuania (Impeditus); died April 23, 1992.—Most Rev. ANTANAS DEKSNYS, Ph.D., cons. Jan. 15, 1969; Titular Bishop of Lavello, *Res., Villa Lithuania, Piazza Asti, 00182. Rome, Italy.*

Bishop's Office—361 Highland Blvd., Brooklyn, NY, 11207. Tel: 718-827-7932; Fax: 718-827-6696.

Secretary to the Bishop—Rev. EDMUNDAS PUTRIMAS.

"Bishop's Brief"—Quarterly information bulletin.

Bishop's Pastoral Council—Rev. ANTANAS SAULAITIS, S.J., Vice Pres.; Sr. IGNE MARIJOSIUS, Prog. Dir.; Mr. ALGIS SILBAJORIS, Information.

Lithuanian R. Catholic Religious Aid—Mrs. VIDA JANKAUSKAS, Exec. Dir., *351 Highland Blvd., Brooklyn, NY, 11207.* Tel: 718-647-2434; Fax: 718-827-6696.

Pontifical Lithuanian College of St. Casimir—Rev. Msgr. ALGIMANTAS BARTKUS, J.C.L., Rector, *via Casalmonferrato 20, 00182. Rome, Italy.* Tel: 06-70-24-908; Fax: 06-70-11-659.

Vocations and Public Relations Director—Rev. EDMUNDAS PUTRIMAS, *1011 College St., Toronto, Ontario, Canada, M6H-1A8.* Tel: 416-533-0621.

Publications—The Observer, Darbininkas, Draugas, Garsas, Journeys, Laiskai Lietuviams, Laivas, Moteru Dirva, Vytis, Musu Zinios, I Laisve.

World Lithuanian R. Catholic Priests' League—Rev. AGUSTINAS SIMANAVICIUS, O.F.M., Pres., *1011 College St., Toronto, Ontario, Canada, MGH 1A8.* Tel: 416-533-0621; Fax: 416-532-4816.

Lithuanian R. Catholic Priests' League of America—Rev. ALBERT CONTONS, Pres., *50 Orton-Marotta Way, Boston, MA, 02127.* Tel: 617-218-0353.

Lithuanian Franciscan Vice Province of St. Casimir—Very Rev. PLACIDAS BARIUS, O.F.M., Prov., *Kennebunkport, ME, 04046.* Tel: 207-967-2031; Fax: 207-967-5721.

Lithuanian Jesuit Province—Very Rev. ANTANAS SAULAITIS, S.J., Prov., *2345 W. 56th St., Chicago, IL, 60636.* Tel: 312-737-8400.

Lithuanian Marian Province of St. Casimir—Very Rev. DONALD PETRAITIS, M.I.C., Prov., *6336 Kilbourn Ave., Chicago, IL, 60636.* Tel: 312-582-1666.

Sisters of the Immaculate Conception of the Blessed Virgin Mary—Sr. PAULE SAVICKAITE, Prov., *Rte. 21, R.D. 2, Putnam, CT, 06260.* Tel: 203-928-7955; Fax: 203-928-1930.

Poor Sisters of Jesus Crucified and the Sorrowful Mother—Sr. MARY J. VALLERE, Supr. Gen., *261 Thatcher St., Brockton, MA, 02402.* Tel: 617-588-5070.

Sisters of St. Casimir—Sr. MARILYN KUZMICKUS, Gen. Supr., *2601 W. Marquette Rd., Chicago, IL, 60609.* Tel: 312-776-1324.

Benedictine Sisters—Sr. RAPHAELA, Supr., *333 Wallace Rd., Bedford, NH, 03102.* Tel: 603-472-3339.

Sisters of St. Francis—Sr. JOAN BRAZINSKI, Dir., *3603 McRoberts Rd., Pittsburgh, PA, 15234.* Tel: 412-882-9911.

INSTITUTIONS LOCATED IN THE DIOCESE

[A] SCHOOLS

CHICAGO, IL. *Maria High School.*
THOMPSON, CT. *Marionapolis Prep School.*

[B] HOSPITALS

CHICAGO, IL. *Holy Cross Hospital.*

[C] NURSING HOMES AND HOMES FOR THE AGED

BROCKTON, MA. *St. Joseph Manor Nursing Home.*
ELMHURST, PA. *St. Mary's Villa.*
HOLLAND, PA. *St. Joseph Nursing Home.*
LEMONT, IL. *Holy Family Villa.*
PUTNAM, CT. *Maulaitis Nursing Home.*

[D] MISCELLANEOUS

BROOKLYN, NY. *Franciscan Cultural Center.*
CHICAGO, IL. *Catholic Action Fund.*
Jesuit Lithuanian Center.
Lithuanian Cultural Institution.
Matulaitis Institute.
MANCHESTER, MI. *Dainava Conference Center and Camp.*
PUTNAM, IL. *American Lithuanian Catholic Archives.*
WEST BRATTLEBORO, VT. *Camp Neringa.*

[E] CEMETERIES

CHICAGO, IL. *St. Casimir Lithuanian.*

RELIGIOUS INSTITUTES OF MEN REPRESENTED IN THE DIOCESE

For further details refer to the corresponding bracketed number in the Religious Institutes of Men or Women section.

[]—*Congregation of the Marians Province of St. Casimir.* (Chicago, IL).
[]—*Franciscan Fathers of the Lithuanian Vicariate of St. Casimir.* (Kennebunkport, ME).
[]—*Jesuit Fathers of Della Strada.* (Chicago, IL).

RELIGIOUS INSTITUTES OF WOMEN REPRESENTED IN THE DIOCESE

[0200]—*Benedictine Sisters.* (Bedford, NH).—O.S.B.
[3240]—*Poor Sisters of Jesus Crucified and the Sorrowful Mother.* (Brockton, MA).—C.J.C.
[2140]—*Sisters of Immaculate Conception of the Blessed Virgin Mary.* (Putnam, CT).
[3740]—*Sisters of St. Casimir.* (Chicago, IL).—S.S.C.
[1690]—*Sisters of St. Francis.* (Pittsburgh, PA).—O.S.F.

STATISTICS

Most personnel and institutions are under the jurisdiction of their local ordinaries.

NECROLOGY

(No Deaths)

Personal Prelatures

Personal Prelatures

Personal prelatures are jurisdictional structures of a secular type which are established by the Holy See as an instrument within the hierarchical pastoral work of the Church to carry out special pastoral or missionary tasks. Personal prelatures are based on the principle of insertion into the local Church. In this they differ essentially from the personal dioceses, such as those constituted for the faithful of a particular rite, which are based on the principle of independence or autonomy in regard to local Churches.

Vatican II provided for setting up personal prelatures (see Decree, *Presbyterorum ordinis*, no. 10). Additional norms were established in subsequent pontifical legislation (see Motu proprio *Ecclesiae Sanctae* no. 1, no. 4, August 6, 1966 and the Apostolic Constitution *Regimini Ecclesiae Universae*, no. 49, no. 1, Aug. 15, 1967). General legislation concerning personal prelatures is contained in canons 294 to 297 of the 1983 Code of Canon Law.

Personal prelatures are to be established by the Holy See after hearing the views of the respective Episcopal Conferences (can. 294). They are governed by a Prelate according to statutes given by the Holy See. The Prelate is their proper Ordinary, who may incardinate priests and must look after their spiritual and temporal welfare (can. 295). Lay people can dedicate themselves by means of a contractural agreement, to the apostolic activities of the prelature (can. 296). And the statutes are to determine the relations of the prelature with the Ordinaries of the places in which the prelature works, with the prior consent of the Ordinaries (can. 297).

OPUS DEI

(Praelatura Sanctae Crucis et Operis Dei)

Reverend Monsignor

JAVIER ECHEVARRIA, J.D., J.C.D.

Prelate of the Prelature of the Holy Cross and Opus Dei; ordained August 7, 1955; appointed April 20, 1994; episcopal ordination January 6, 1995. *Curia of the Prelature, Viale Bruno Buozzi 73, 00197, Rome, Italy. Tel: 6-808-961.*

Erected by the Apostolic Constitution, "Ut sit," on November 28, 1982 by Pope John Paul II.

Opus Dei was founded on October 2, 1928 by Blessed Josemaria Escriva, to spread in all sectors of society a profound awareness of the universal call to sanctity in ordinary life and, more specifically, in the exercise of one's work.

Curia of the Prelature—Viale Bruno Buozzi, 73, 00197. Rome, Italy. Tel: 6-808-961.

Vicar General—Rev. Msgr. Fernando Ocariz, Ph.D., S.T.D., *Viale Bruno Buozzi 73, 00197. Rome, Italy.* Rev. Frederick Dolan, residing at the Curia of the Prelature.

Regional Vicar for the United States—Rev. Msgr. James A. Kelly, Ph.D., *99 Overlook Circle, New Rochelle, NY 10804.* Tel: 914-235-1201.

Delegate Vicar for the Midwest—Very Rev. William H. Stetson, J.D., J.C.D., *5800 N. Keating Ave., Chicago, IL 60646.* Tel: 312-283-5800.

Delegate Vicar for California—Very Rev. George M. Rossman, Ph.D., *765 14th Ave., San Francisco, CA 94118.* Tel: 415-386-0431.

Delegate Vicar for Texas—Very Rev. Michael J. Barrett, S.T.D., *5505 Chaucer Dr., Houston, TX 77005.* Tel: 715-523-4351.

Represented in the Archdioceses of Boston, Chicago, Los Angeles, Milwaukee, Newark, New York, St. Louis, San Antonio, San Francisco, Washington and in the Dioceses of Burlington, Dallas, Fort Wayne-South Bend, Galveston-Houston, Gary, Oakland, Palm Beach, Peoria, Pittsburgh, Providence, Trenton and Victoria.

REGIONAL VICARIATE FOR THE UNITED STATES

State of New York

New Rochelle—Rev. Msgr. James A. Kelly, Ph.D. Reg. Vicar; Revs. Robert Brisson; Edward Maristany. *99 Overlook Cir., New Rochelle, NY 10804.* Tel: 914-235-0198. Revs. Bradley K. Arturi; Orestes Gonzalez. *117 Overlook Cir., New Rochelle, NY 10804.* Tel: 914-235-6128.

New York—Revs. Robert A. Connor; Martin J. Miller. *330 Riverside Dr., New York, NY 10025.* Tel: 212-222-3285.

District of Columbia

Washington—Revs. Malcolm M. Kennedy; Deo G. Rosales; Lawrence A. Kutz. *2301 Wyoming Ave. N.W., Washington, DC 20008.* Tel: 202-234-1567; Revs. Ronald S. Gillis; William G. Shaughnessy. *4300 Garrison St. N.W., Washington, DC 20016.* Tel: 202-362-2419; Rev. L. Michael Curtin, *4955 Linnean Ave., N.W., Washington, DC 20008.* Tel: 202-237-6894.

State of Massachusetts

Cambridge—Revs. Salvador M. Ferigle; John C. Agnew. *25 Follen St., Cambridge, MA 02138.* Tel: 617-354-3204.

Chestnut Hill—Revs. Raphael F. Caamano; Richard W. Rieman; Alvaro Silva; Timothy H. Uhen; David J. Cavanagh. *481 Hammond St., Chestnust Hill, MA 02167.* Tel: 617-738-7348.

State of New Jersey

Princeton—Rev. C. John McCloskey. *34 Mercer St., Princeton, NJ 08540.* Tel: 609-497-9448.

South Orange—Revs. James W. Albrecht; Thomas J. Lamb. *170 Montrose Ave., South Orange, NJ 07079.* Tel: 201-763-8397.

State of Pennsylvania

Pittsburgh—Revs. Frank Hoffman; Joseph P. Landauer. *5090 Warwick Ter., Pittsburgh, PA 15213.* Tel: 412-683-8448.

State of Florida

Delray Beach—Revs. Christopher Schmitt; John J. Alvarez. *4409 Frances Dr., Delray Beach, FL 33445.* Tel: 305-498-1249.

State of Rhode Island

Providence—Rev. Michael J. Manz. *224 Bowen St., Providence, RI 02906.* Tel: 401-272-7834.

DELEGATE VICARIATE FOR THE MIDWEST

State of Illinois

Chicago—Very Rev. William H. Stetson, J.C.D. Delegate Vicar; Revs. Peter V. Armenio; John Meyer; Fred Piegl. *5800 N. Keating Ave., Chicago, IL 60646.* Tel: 312-283-5800; Rev. Claudio Urbano. *7225 N. Greenview Ave., Chicago, IL 60646.* Tel: 312-465-3468; Revs. John Debicki; Hilary Mahaney; Charles Ferrer; James Socias. *1825 N. Wood St., Chicago, IL 60622.* Tel: 312-278-2644.

Oak Park—Revs. Richard Schendt; Barry Cole. *829 S. Euclid, Oak Park, IL 60304.* Tel: 708-383-0928.

Urbana—Rev. Jerome L. Jung. , *715 W. Michigan, Urbana, IL 61801.* Tel: 217-367-6650.

State of Indiana

South Bend—Rev. Gerald Kolf, *1121 N. Notre Dame Ave., South Bend, IN 46617.* Tel: 219-232-0550.

State of Missouri

Kirkwood—Revs. Michael E. Giesler; Mark Mannion. *100 E. Essex Ave., Kirkwood, MO 63122.* Tel: 314-821-1608.

State of Wisconsin

Brookfield—Revs. Robert Bucciarelli; John Kubeck. *12900 W. North Ave., Brookfield, WI 53005.* Tel: 414-784-1523.

DELEGATE VICARIATE FOR THE STATE OF CALIFORNIA

San Francisco—Very Rev. George M. Rossman, Ph.D., Delegate Vicar; Revs. Torlach C. Delargy; Arne J. Panula. *765 14th Ave., San Francisco, CA 94118.* Tel: 415-386-0431.

Menlo Park—Rev. Salvador V. Serrano, *1835 Bay Laurel Dr., Menlo Park, CA 94025.* Tel: 415-327-1675.

Mill Valley—Rev. Jose P. Ruisanchez. *108 Kipling Dr., Mill Valley, CA 94941.* Tel: 415-388-4531.

Los Angeles—Revs. Rene J. Schatteman; John R. Waiss. *655 Levering Ave., Los Angeles, CA 90024.* Tel: 213-208-0941.

Berkeley—Rev. Paul A. Donlan. *2710 College Ave., Berkeley, CA 94705.* Tel: 510-548-2819.

DELEGATE VICARIATE FOR THE STATE OF TEXAS

Houston—Very Rev. Michael J. Barrett. S.T.D., Delegate Vicar; Revs. Jose Gomez; George W. Crafts. *5505 Chaucer Dr., Houston, TX 77005.* Tel: 713-523-4351.

Irving—Rev. John E. Solarski. *3610 Wingren, Irving, TX 75062.* Tel: 214-650-0064.

Eastern Church

Eastern Catholic Association (ECA)

The Eastern Catholic Associates is the association of all Eastern Catholic Bishops in the United States. All Eastern Catholic Bishops, diocesan bishops (and their equivalent in law) and auxiliaries are members. The Association represents the Armenian, Chaldean, Maronite Melkite, Romanian, Ruthenian and Ukrainian Churches. The Syriac, Syro-Malabar and Russian churches are also represented but without a bishop member since they presently have no established hierarchy in the United States. Officers of the Association are—*President:* Most Rev. NICHOLAS J. SAMRA, D.D., V.G., Auxiliary Bishop of Newton, 8525 Cole, Warren MI 48093-5239. Tel: 810-558-0143; Fax: 810-558-0144. *Vice President:* Most Rev. ROBERT M. MOSKAL, D.D., Bishop of the Ukrainian Diocese of St. Josaphat in Parma, 5720 State Rd., Parma, OH 44134-7180. Tel: 216-888-1522; Fax: 216-888-3477. *Secretary:* Most Rev. JOHN BOTEAN, Bishop of Romanian Catholic Diocese of St. George, Canton, 1121 44th St., N.E., Canton, OH 44714-1297. Tel: 330-492-4086; Fax: 330-493-1416.

Religious Education Department

The ECA has established the ECDD - The Eastern Catholic Conference of Diocesan Directors of Religious Education which oversees, through "God With Us Publications", all publications of catechetical materials published by it and used in Eastern Catholic Churches, mainly of Byzantine tradition. Rev. John S. Kachuba, M.A., Chm.-ECDD & Dir.-Religious Education, Eparchy of Parma, 532 Lloyd R., Euclid, OH 44132. Tel: 216-732-7292; Fax: 216-732-9434. Rev. Fred Saato, Asst. Chm./Dir.-Publications & Dir.-Education Services, Eparchy of Newton, 27 Lake Ave., Yonkers, NY 10703. Tel: 914-968-2428; Fax: 914-423-9239. Sr. Ann Laszok, O.S.B.M., Treas. & Bus. Mgr.-ECDD, 204 Olivia St., McKeesrocks, PA 15136. Tel: 412-481-9778; Fax: 412-331-8140. "God With Us Publications", P.O. Box 99203, Pittsburgh, PA 15233. Tel: 412-771-9119; Fax: 412-766-8244.

In addition to the Eastern Churches listed below there are other Eastern Churches in communion with Rome which do not have Ordinaries of their own in the United States. Consequently they are under the jurisdiction of the local Ordinary and the various parishes and institutions are incorporated in the Archdiocesan and Diocesan listings. Please consult these pages for full information regarding churches, personnel and statistics. For convenience, however, listed below are the Russian Eastern Churches and the cities in which they are located.

RUSSIAN

California

El Segundo (LA), St. Andrew

San Francisco (SFR), Our Lady of Fatima Center

New York

New York (NY), St. Michael Chapel (St. Patrick's Old Cathedral)

Armenian Catholic Exarchate of U.S.A. and Canada

Most Reverend

HOVHANNES TERTZAKIAN, O.M.VEN.

Apostolic Exarch for Armenian Catholics in the United States and Canada; ordained September 8, 1948; appointed Titular Bishop of Trebisonda and Apostolic Exarch for Armenian Catholics in the United States and Canada January 6, 1995; ordained April 29, 1995; installed May 7, 1995. *Office: 110 E. 12th, New York, NY, 10003-5395.*

Chancery & Vicar General Office: 110 E. 12th St., New York, NY, 10003-5395. Tel.: 212-477-2030; Fax: 212-477-2185.

Most Reverend

NERSES MIKAEL SETIAN, D.D., J.C.D.

Former Apostolic Exarch for the Armenian Catholics in the U.S.A. and Canada; born October 18, 1918; appointed Titular Bishop of Ancera and Apostolic Exarch for the Armenian Catholics in the U.S.A. and Canada July 3, 1981; ordained December 5, 1981; installed December 27, 1981; retired. *Res., c/o Our Lady Queen of Martyrs Church, 1327 Pleasant Ave., Los Angeles, CA, 90033.*

Legal Title: Apostolic Exarchate For Armenian Catholics In The United States of America.

STATISTICAL OVERVIEW

Personnel	
Bishop	1
Retired Bishops	1
Priests: Diocesan Active in Diocese	4
Number of Diocesan Priests	4
Religious Priests in Diocese	8
Total Sisters	14
Parishes	
Parishes	6
With Resident Pastor:	
Resident Diocesan Priests	4
Resident Religious Priests	2
Educational	
Elementary Schools, Diocesan and Parish	4
Total Students	1,006
Catechesis/Religious Education:	
Elementary Students	116
Total Students Under Catholic Instruction	1,122
Teachers in the Diocese:	
Priests	2
Sisters	12
Lay Teachers	90
Vital Statistics	
Receptions into the Church:	
Infant Baptism Totals	60
First Communions	36
Confirmations	60
Marriages:	
Catholic	14
Interfaith	11
Total Marriages	25
Deaths	36
Total Catholic Population	26,000

Chancery & Vicar General Office—*110 E. 12th St., New York, NY, 10003-5395.* Tel: 212-477-2030; Fax: 212-477-2185.

Vicar General—Rev. Msgr. SARKIS GABADIAN. Tel: 215-896-7789.

Chancellor—Rev. RAPHAEL ANDONIAN, O.M. Ven. Tel: 212-477-2030.

Newspaper Diocesan Bulletin—"The Eternal Flame", Office: *110 E. 12th St., New York, NY, 10003.* Tel: 212-477-2030.

Newspaper Diocesan Bulletin "VERELK"—Office: *1327 Pleasant Ave., Los Angeles, CA, 90033.* Tel: 213-267-1740.

Armenian Sacred Music—Rev. Msgr. JOSEPH KALAYJIAN.

CLERGY, PARISHES, MISSIONS AND PAROCHIAL SCHOOLS

STATE OF NEW YORK

Brooklyn, Kings Co., Visitation. Closed. For inquiries for parish records contact the Chancery.

New York, New York Co., St. Ann's Cathedral, Most Rev. Hovhannes Tertzakian, O.M.Ven.
Res., 110 E. 12th St., 10003. Tel: 212-477-2030; Fax: 212-477-2185.

STATE OF CALIFORNIA

Los Angeles, Los Angeles Co., Our Lady Queen of Martyrs, Revs. Raphael Minassian; Basil Ferhatian, C.M.Vd.
Res., 1327 Pleasant Ave., 90033. Tel: 213-261-9898; Fax: 213-261-0522.

STATE OF MASSACHUSETTS

Boston, Middlesex Co., Holy Cross, Rev. Raphael Andonian, O.M.Ven.
Res., 200 Lexington St., Belmont, 02178. Tel: 617-489-2280.

STATE OF MICHIGAN

Detroit, Wayne Co., St. Vartan's, Rev. Msgr. Joseph Kalajian, Ph.D.
Res., 8541 Greenfield Rd., 48228. Tel: 313-584-3345.

STATE OF NEW JERSEY

Paterson, Passaic Co., Sacred Heart (1927), Rev. Georges Kalousieh.
Res., 155 Long Hill Rd., Little Falls, 07424-2374. Tel: 201-890-0447; Fax: 201-890-0292.

STATE OF PENNSYLVANIA

Philadelphia, Philadelphia Co., St. Mark's Armenian Catholic (1924), Rev. Msgr. Sarkis Gabadian.
Res., 400 Haverford Rd., Wynnewood, 19096-2699. Tel: 610-896-7789; Fax: 610-896-0915.

INSTITUTIONS LOCATED IN THE DIOCESE

[A] SCHOOLS

STATE OF CALIFORNIA

LA CRESCENTA. *Mekhitarist School*, 4900 Maryland Ave., 91214. Tel: 818-249-6121; 6122; 6123; 6124; Fax: 818-249-0350. Revs. Augustin Szekula, Prin.; Mikael Akian.

MONTROSE. *Armenian Sisters of the Immaculate Conception*, 2361 Florencita Dr., 91020. Tel: 818-249-8783. Sr. Alphonsa Bedrossian, Supr. & Prin.

STATE OF MASSACHUSETTS

LEXINGTON. *Armenian Sisters Academy*, 6 Eliot Rd., 02173. Tel: 617-863-5962. Sr. Veronique Achikian, Supr. & Prin.

STATE OF PENNSYLVANIA

RADNOR. *Armenian Sisters Academy*, 440 Upper Gulph Rd., 19087. Tel: 215-687-4100; Fax: 610-687-2430. Sr. Louisa Kassarjian, Prin.

[B] RELIGIOUS INSTITUTES AND CONVENTS FOR WOMEN

STATE OF CALIFORNIA

MONTROSE. *Armenian Sisters of the Immaculate Conception*, 2361 Florencita Dr., 91020. Tel: 818-249-8783. Sr. Alphonsa Bedrossian, Supr. & Prin.

STATE OF MASSACHUSETTS

LEXINGTON. *Armenian Sisters of the Immaculate Conception*, 6 Eliot Rd., 02173. Tel: 617-863-5962. Sr. Veronique Achikian, Supr. & Prin.

STATE OF PENNSYLVANIA

RADNOR. *Armenian Sisters of the Immaculate Conception*, 440 Upper Gulph Rd., 19087. Tel: 215-688-9360; Fax: 610-687-2430. Sr. Louisa Kassarjian, Prin.

[C] EDUCATIONAL FOUNDATIONS

STATE OF CALIFORNIA

GLENDALE.

**Mekhitarian Educational Foundation*, 702 E. Glenoaks Blvd., 91207. Tel: 818-546-1967; Fax: 818-548-1166. Revs. Dadjad Yardemian, Exec. Dir.; Mesrop Sulahian.

NECROLOGY

(No Deaths)

Diocese of Newton (Melkite-Greek Catholic)

Most Reverend

JOHN A. ELYA, B.S.O., D.D.

Eparch of Newton; ordained February 17, 1952; appointed Auxiliary Bishop of Newton April 2, 1986; appointed Eparch of Newton November 25, 1993; installed January 25, 1994. *Res., 19 Dartmouth St., West Newton, MA, 02165.* Tel.: 617-969-8957; Fax: 617-969-4115.

Most Reverend

JOSEPH E. TAWIL, D.D., LL.D.

Eparch Emeritus of Newton; ordained July 20, 1936; consecrated January 1, 1960; appointed Apostolic Exarch October 29, 1969; appointed Eparch July 15, 1976; became emeritus December 12, 1989. *Res., 19 Dartmouth St., West Newton, MA, 02165.*

Most Reverend

NICHOLAS J. SAMRA, D.D.

Auxiliary Bishop of Newton and Protosyncellus; ordained May 10, 1970; appointed Auxiliary Bishop of Newton June 29, 1989. *Res., 8525 Cole St., Warren, MI, 48093.* Tel.: 810-558-0143; Fax: 810-558-0144.

THAT ALL MAY BE ONE

ESTABLISHED AS AN APOSTOLIC EXARCHATE JANUARY 10, 1966.

ELEVATED TO EPARCHY, JULY 15, 1976; EMBRACES ALL MEMBERS OF THE MELKITE GREEK CATHOLIC CHURCH IN THE UNITED STATES.

For legal titles of parishes and institutions, consult the Chancery Office.

The Chancery: 19 Dartmouth St., West Newton, MA, 02165. Tel.: 617-969-8957; Fax: 617-969-4115.

Web site address: http://www.dsha.k12.wi.us/Melkite/EPARCHY.htm

E-mail address: Deakandy@aol.com

E-mail address: abunaandre@prodigy.net

STATISTICAL OVERVIEW

Personnel	
Retired Archbishops	1
Bishop	1
Auxiliary Bishops	1
Priests: Diocesan Active in Diocese	32
Priests: Active Outside Diocese	3
Priests: Retired, Sick or Absent	8
Number of Diocesan Priests	43
Religious Priests in Diocese	19
Extern Priests in Diocese	4
Ordinations:	
Diocesan Priests	1
Permanent Deacons	3
Permanent Deacons in Diocese	27
Total Brothers	1
Total Sisters	3
Parishes	
Parishes	35
With Resident Pastor:	
Resident Diocesan Priests	26
Resident Religious Priests	9
Without Resident Pastor:	
Missions	6
Welfare	
Specialized Homes	2
Total Assisted	5,500
Special Centers for Social Services	1
Total Assisted	5,300
Educational	
Seminaries, Diocesan	1
Students from This Diocese	1
Seminaries, Religious	1
Students Religious	2
Total Seminarians	3
Catechesis/Religious Education:	
High School Students	262
Elementary Students	1,194
Total Students Under Catholic Instruction	1,459
Vital Statistics	
Receptions into the Church:	
Infant Baptism Totals	456
Adult Baptism Totals	22
Received into Full Communion	9
First Communions	499
Confirmations	566
Marriages:	
Catholic	114
Interfaith	26
Total Marriages	140
Deaths	172
Total Catholic Population	27,800

Former Bishops—Most Rev. JUSTIN A. NAJMY, B.A.O., D.D., born April 23, 1898; ord. Dec. 25, 1926; cons. May 29, 1966; installed June 4, 1966; died June 11, 1968.—Most Rev. JOSEPH E. TAWIL, D.D., LL.D., ord. July 20, 1936; cons. Jan. 1, 1960; appt. Apostolic Exarch, Oct. 29, 1969; appt. Eparch, July 15, 1976 became emeritus Dec. 12, 1989.—Most Rev. IGNATIUS GHATTAS, B.S.O., D.D., born Dec. 25, 1920; ord. July 7, 1946; appt. Dec. 12, 1989; cons. Feb. 23, 1990; died Oct. 11, 1992.

Diocesan Administration

Chancery Office—19 Dartmouth St., W. Newton, MA, 02165. Tel: 617-969-8957; Fax: 617-969-4115. Office Hours: Mon.-Fri. 9-5.

Protosyncellus—Most Rev. NICHOLAS J. SAMRA, D.D.

Chancellor—Deacon PAUL F. LAWLER, *19 Dartmouth St., W. Newton, MA, 02165.* Tel: 617-969-8957; Fax: 617-969-4115.

Diocesan Tribunal—18 New Dunstable Rd., Nashua, NH, 03060. Tel: 603-595-9815; Fax: 603-595-3452.

Judicial Vicar—Rt. Rev. GERASIMOS MURPHY, B.S.O., D.Min., J.C.D., *18 New Dunstable Rd., Nashua, NH, 03060.* Tel: 603-595-9815; Fax: 603-595-2389.

Defender of the Bond and Promoter of Justice—Rt. Rev. JOSEPH S. HAGGAR, M.A., J.C.L.; LOUISE TESSIER, J.C.L.

Judges—Revs. JOSEPH KOURY, J.C.D.; JOHN FARAJ, J.C.D.; HERBERT MAY, J.C.L.

Notaries—Deacons GEORGE YANY; PAUL LAWLER; LUCILLE LAROCHE.

Economos—Rev. ANDRE ST. GERMAIN.

Protopresbyters—Rt. Rev. JOSEPH HAGGAR, New England; Rt. Rev. PHILIP RACZKA, Mid-Atlantic; Rev. FRANK MILIENEWICZ, Southeast; Revs. IBRAHIM IBRAHIM, Mid-West; JAMES BABCOCK, West.

Consultative Bodies

College of Eparchial Consultors—Most Rev. NICHOLAS J. SAMRA; Rt. Rev. RONALD GOLINI, M.A., S.T.L.; Rt. Rev. WILLIAM HADDAD; Rt. Rev. JOSEPH S. HAGGAR, J.C.L.; Rt. Rev. GERASIMOS MURPHY, B.S.O., D.Min., J.C.D.; Rt. Rev. PHILIP RACZKA; Rt. Rev. ROMANOS V. RUSSO; Revs. FRANK J. MILIENEWICZ; IBRAHIM IBRAHIM; ANDRE ST. GERMAIN.

Presbyteral Council—Most Rev. JOHN A. ELYA, Pres.; Most Rev. NICHOLAS J. SAMRA; Rt. Rev. PHILIP RACZKA, Sec.; Rt. Rev. JOSEPH S. HAGGAR; Rt. Rev. EDWARD KAKATY; Revs. JOHN AZAR; JAMES BABCOCK; DAMON GEIGER, O.SS.T.; MARTIN HYATT, B.S.O.; FRANK MILIENEWICZ; JUSTIN ROSE; ANDRE ST. GERMAIN; BASIL SAMRA; ALEXEI SMITH; YOUSSEF A. YOUSSEF.

Diocese of Newton for the Melkites in the USA, Inc., a Massachusetts Corporation—Most Rev. JOHN A. ELYA; Most Rev. NICHOLAS J. SAMRA; Rt. Revs. JOSEPH S. HAGGAR; GERASIMOS MURPHY, B.S.O.; PHILIP RACZKA; ROMANOS RUSSO; Rev. ANDRE ST. GERMAIN; Deacon PAUL F. LAWLER.

Finance Council—Rev. ANDRE ST. GERMAIN, Economos; Mr. JOSEPH GHOLL; Mr. STANLEY SABA; Mrs. KATHLEEN SABA RICHARDS; Dr. JOHN NAZARIAN; Deacon ROBERT SHALHOUB; GILBERT SHASHA; RAYMOND KAYAL; EDMUND NAHOM.

Priest's Sickness & Disability, and Retirement Plans—Most Rev. NICHOLAS J. SAMRA; Rt. Rev. JOSEPH FRANCAVILLA; Rt. Rev. JOSEPH S. HAGGAR; Rt. Rev. PHILIP RACZKA; Revs. JOHN FARAJ; FRANK MILIENEWICZ; ALEXEI SMITH; ANDRE ST. GERMAIN.

Canonical Consultant—Rt. Rev. Archimandrite VICTOR J. POSPISHIL, J.C.D.; Rev. JOHN FARAJ, B.S.O., J.C.D; Rt. Rev. JOHN D. FARIS, J.C.O.D.; Rev. GEORGE D. GALLARO, J.C.O.D.

Legal Consultant—CAMILLE F. SARROUF, ESQ., *95 Commercial Wharf, Boston, MA, 02110.* Tel: 617-227-5800.

Liturgical Consultants—Rev. ROBERT TAFT, S.J.; Archimandrite EUTHIMIOS SKAFF, B.S.O.

Pastoral Offices and Commissions

Continuing Education of Clergy Office—Revs. DAMON GEIGER, Coord. PAUL FRECHETTE; GABRIEL GHANOUM; IGNATIUS HARRINGTON; FRED SAATO; ALEXEI SMITH.

National Association of Melkite Youth—Rev. SAMI BAROODY, *802 Rifle Camp Rd., W. Paterson, NJ, 07424.* Tel: 201-785-4144.

MAYA (Melkite Assoc. of Young Adults)—Rev. JUSTIN ROSE, *P.O. Box 245, Fullerton, CA, 92836.* Tel: 714-992-0652.

Ambassadors—Rev. GABRIEL GHANOUM, B.S.O., *126 S.E. 15 Rd., Miami, FL, 33129.* Tel: 305-856-8666.

National Association of Melkite Women—Rev. EDWARD KAKATY, *7 V.F.W. Pkwy., Boston, MA, 02131.* Tel: 617-323-5242.

Liturgical Commission—Most Rev. NICHOLAS SAMRA, Chm.; Rt. Rev. JOSEPH HAGGAR; Rt. Rev. VICTOR SAMAHA; Rt. Rev. EDWARD KAKATY; Rt. Rev. ROMANOS RUSSO; Revs. DAMON GEIGER, O.SS.T.; MARK MELONE.

Educational Services—Rev. FRED SAATO, M.A., *27 Lake Ave., Yonkers, NY, 10703.* Tel: 914-968-2428.

Vocations Office—Rt. Rev. PHILIP RACZKA, Coord., *233 Grant Ave., Newton Centre, MA, 02179.* Tel: 617-965-9862. Rt. Rev. EDWARD KAKATY; Revs. SAMI BAROODY; IGNATIUS HARRINGTON; FRANK MILIENEWICZ; ALEXEI SMITH.

"Sophia" (A Journal)—Rev. JOHN T. AZAR, JR., *11245 Rye St., N. Hollywood, CA, 91602.*

Ecumenical & Interreligious Commission—Rev. IBRAHIM IBRAHIM, B.S.O., *8023 Memphis Ave., Brooklyn, OH, 44144.* Rt. Rev. EDWARD G. KAKATY.

Order of St. Nicholas—Most Rev. NICHOLAS J. SAMRA, Grand Advisor; RAYMOND KAYAL, National Chm.; Revs. Chaplains: GABRIEL GHANOUM, B.S.O.; JOHN AZAR; IBRAHIM IBRAHIM, B.S.O., *Mailing Address: 19 Dartmouth St., W. Newton, MA, 02165.*

Associated Melkite Charities—Rev. PHILARET LITTLEFIELD, *1617 W. State St., Milwaukee, WI, 53233.* Tel: 414-342-1543.

CLERGY, PARISHES, MISSIONS AND PAROCHIAL SCHOOLS

STATE OF MASSACHUSETTS

Boston, Suffolk Co., Annunciation Cathedral, Rt. Rev. Edward G. Kakaty; Rev. John Ghaby; Deacon Paul Lawler.
Res., 7 V.F.W. Pkwy., 02131. Tel: 617-323-5242; Fax: 617-325-2662.

Lawrence, Essex Co., St. Joseph, Rev. Youssef A. Youssef, B.S.O.; Deacons Bryan McNeil; John MacMillan.
Res., 241 Hampshire St., 01841. Tel: 978-682-8152.

Worcester, Worcester Co., Our Lady of Perpetual Help, Rev. Paul G. Frechette.
Res., 256 Hamilton St., 01604. Tel: 508-752-4174.

STATE OF ALABAMA

Birmingham, Jefferson Co., St. George, Rev. Frank J. Milienewicz; Deacon Seraphim Ritchey.
Res., 425-Sixteenth Ave. S., 35205. Tel: 205-252-5788; Fax: 205-252-1085.

STATE OF ARIZONA

Phoenix, Maricopa Co., St. John of the Desert, Rev. Basil Samra.
Res., 2525 E. Osborn, 85016. Tel: 602-954-7258.

STATE OF CALIFORNIA

El Segundo, Los Angeles Co., St. Paul, Rev. Alexei R. Smith, Admin.
Res., 538 Concord, 90245. Tel: 310-322-1892; Fax: 310-322-1919.

Fremont, Alameda Co., St. Elias, Rev. James K. Graham.
Res., 45180 S. Grimmer Blvd., 94539. Tel: 510-656-5949.

Fullerton, Orange Co., Holy Cross, Revs. James K. Babcock; Justin Rose; Deacon Luigi Merandi.
Res., 706 S. Lemon St., 92632. Tel: 714-992-0652; Fax: 714-992-6505.

North Hollywood, Los Angeles Co., St. Anne, Revs. John T. Azar, Jr.; George Said Bisharat; Deacons George Sayegh; Marion Rimmer; George Karout.
Res., 11245 Rye St., 91602. Tel: 818-761-2034; Fax: 818-761-2922.

Oakland, Alameda Co., St. John The Theologian, Revs. Owen Carroll; Eugene M. Ludwig, O.F.M.Cap.
Res., 5 Gleneden Ave., 94611. Tel: 510-428-2234.

Sacramento, Sacramento Co., St. George, Rev. Mark E. Melone.
Church—1620 Bell St., 95825. Tel: 916-920-2900.

San Bernardino, San Bernardino Co., St. Philip. Attended by Fullerton. Revs. James K. Babcock, Admin.; Justin Rose.
Mailing Address: 706 S. Lemon St., Fullerton, 92632. Tel: 714-992-0652; Fax: 714-992-6505.

San Diego, San Diego Co., St. Jacob Mission. Services at Holy Angels Byzantine Catholic Church, 2235 Galahad Rd., San Diego. Rt. Rev. Nassir Matta, Admin.; Deacon Edward Bagdasar.
Mailing Address: 41770 Margarita Rd., Apt. #2109, Temecula, 92591. Tel: 909-308-1060.

Temecula, Riverside Co., Virgin Mary Mission, Rt. Rev. Nassir Matta, Admin.
Mailing Address: 41770 Margarita Rd., #2109, 92591. Tel: 909-308-1060.
Church—Churchill Plaza, Front St., San Diego.

STATE OF CONNECTICUT

Danbury, Fairfield Co., St. Ann, Rev. Basil R. Parent.
Mailing Address: 181 Clapboard Ridge Rd., 06811. Tel: 203-743-5119.

Waterford, New London Co., St. Ann, Rev. Athanase Hassey.
Res., 41 Cross Rd., 06385. Tel: 860-442-2211.

STATE OF FLORIDA

Miami, Dade Co., St. Jude, Rt. Rev. John W. Haddad, B.S.O.; Rev. Gabriel Ghanoum, B.S.O.
Res., 126 S.E. 15 Rd., 33129. Tel: 305-856-1500; Fax: 305-859-7982.

Delray Beach, Palm Beach Co., St. Nicholas. Served by Miami. Rev. Gabriel Ghanoum, B.S.O.
Res., 126 S.E. 15 Rd., Miami, 33129. Tel: 305-856-8666.

STATE OF GEORGIA

Atlanta, Fulton Co., St. John, Rt. Rev. William F. Haddad, B.S.O.
Res., 1428 Ponce de Leon Ave., N.E., 30307. Tel: 404-373-9522; Fax: 404-373-9522.

Augusta, Richmond Co., St. Ignatios of Antioch, Rev. Daniel Munn; Deacon Kent Plowman.
Church—1003 Merry St., 30914. Tel: 706-738-9388.
Mailing Address: P.O. Box 3351, 30904.
Res., 967 Meigs St., 30904. Tel: 706-738-5623.

STATE OF ILLINOIS

Northlake, Cook Co., St. John the Baptist, Rev. Albert Wehby, B.A.O.; Deacon Elias Sahyouni.
Res., 200 E. North Ave., 60164. Tel: 708-865-7050.

STATE OF INDIANA

Hammond, Lake Co., St. Michael the Archangel, Rev. Robert Rabbat, Admin.
Mailing Address: 7113 Columbia Ave., 46324. Tel: 219-844-9027.
Church—713 Columbia Ave., 46320.

South Bend, St. Joseph Co., St. John of Damascus, Rev. Robert L. Kerby; Deacon Lawrence Farhat.
Church—839 Woodcliff Dr., 46615.
Res., 918 Simon Ct., 46615. Tel: 219-233-5338.

STATE OF MICHIGAN

Lansing, Ingham Co., St. Joseph, Rt. Rev. Victor M. Samaha, B.C.O.
Res., 1913 S. Rundel Ave., 48910. Tel: 517-485-4053.

Plymouth, Wayne Co., St. Michael, Rev. Edmond J. Ghazal, B.C.O., Admin.
Church—585 N. Mill St., 48170. Tel: 313-414-6110.
Res., 8525 Cole St., Warren, 48093. Tel: 810-751-6017; 558-0027.

Warren, Macomb Co., Our Lady of Redemption, Most Rev. Nicholas J. Samra; Revs. George D. Gallaro; Edmond J. Ghazal, B.C.O.; Deacons Joseph Daratony; James Soloman.
Res., 8525 Cole St., 48093. Tel: 810-751-6017.

STATE OF NEW HAMPSHIRE

Manchester, Hillsborough Co., Our Lady of the Cedars, Rev. Eugene Mitchell, B.S.O.; Deacon Thomas P. Steinmetz.
Res., 161 S. Beech St., 03103. Tel: 603-623-8944.

STATE OF NEW JERSEY

Cliffside Park, Bergen Co., St. Demetrius, Rt. Rev. Philip G. Raczka, Admin.
Res., 802 Rifle Camp Rd., West Paterson, 07424. Tel: 201-890-4140.
Church—184 Cliff St., 07010.

West Paterson, Passaic Co., St. Ann's, Revs. Sami W. Baroody; Damon Geiger, O.SS.T.; Deacons Michael Jolly; Edward Bsarany; Roland Basinski; Robert Shalhoub.
Res., 802 Rifle Camp Rd., 07424. Tel: 201-785-4144; Fax: 201-890-9599.

STATE OF NEW YORK

Brooklyn, Kings Co., Church of the Virgin Mary, Rev. John Faraj, B.S.O.
Res., 216 Eighth Ave., 11215. Tel: 718-788-5454; Fax: 718-499-7702.

Rochester, Monroe Co., St. Nicholas, Rev. Kenneth Sherman; Deacon Edmond Elhilow.
Res., 1492 Spencerport Rd., 14606. Tel: 716-426-4218.

Utica, Oneida Co., St. Basil, Rt. Rev. Julien A. Eliane; Deacon Daniel Klockowski.
Res., 901 Sherman Dr., 13501. Tel: 315-732-4662.

Yonkers, Westchester Co., Christ the Savior Church, Rev. Fred Saato.
Res., 27 Lake Ave., 10703. Tel: 914-968-2428; Fax: 914-423-9239.

STATE OF OHIO

Akron, Summit Co., St. Joseph, Rev. Joseph Thomas, B.S.O.
Res., 600 W. Exchange St., 44302. Tel: 330-535-7364; Fax: 330-535-8037.

Brooklyn, Cuyahoga Co., St. Elias, Rev. Ibrahim Ibrahim, B.S.O.
Res., 8023 Memphis Ave., 44144. Tel: 216-661-1155; Fax: 216-661-3838.

Columbus, Franklin Co., Holy Resurrection, Rev. Ignatius Harrington.
Res., 363 W. Second Ave., 43201. Tel: 614-421-1325.

Zanesville, Muskingum Co., Holy Trinity, Rev. Ignatius Harrington.
Res., 363 W. Second Ave., Columbus, 43201. Tel: 614-421-1325.
Church—130 N. Fifth St., P.O. Box 2714, 43701.

STATE OF PENNSYLVANIA

Scranton, Lackawanna Co., St. Joseph, Rev. Philip Azoon.
Res., 130 N. Cabrini Ave., 18504. Tel: 717-343-6092.

STATE OF RHODE ISLAND

Central Falls, Providence Co., St. Basil the Great, Rt. Rev. Joseph S. Haggar; Archdeacon George M. Yany.
Church—445 Broad St., 02863.
Res., 111 Cross St., 02863. Tel: 401-722-1345; Fax: 401-722-2436.

Woonsocket, Providence Co., St. Elias, Rt. Rev. Joseph S. Haggar.
Church—80 Hamilton St., 02895.
Res., 111 Cross St., Central Falls, 02863. Tel: 401-722-1345.

STATE OF VIRGINIA

McLean, Fairfax Co., Holy Transfiguration, Rt. Rev. Joseph F. Francavilla; Deacon Paul Weyrich.
Res., 8501 Lewinsville Rd., 22102. Tel: 703-734-9198; Fax: 703-893-7248.

STATE OF WISCONSIN

Milwaukee, Milwaukee Co., St. George, Rev. Philaret Littlefield.
Res., 1617 W. State St., 53233. Tel: 414-342-1543.

On Special Projects:
Reverend Fathers—
Kirk, David, P.O. Box 1177, New York, NY 10035. Tel: 212-410-6006
McCarthy, Charles, 49 Burkeside Ave., Brockton, MA 02401. Tel: 508-588-1008
St. Germain, Andre, Economos, 19 Dartmouth St., West Newton, MA 02165

Military Chaplains:
Reverend Fathers—
Brown, Shaun
Gosselin, Lawrence

On Duty Outside the Eparchy:
Reverend Fathers—
Koury, James

Leave of Absence:
Reverend Fathers—
Adcock, Basil W.
Golini, Ronald
Moloney, Patrick W.

Retired:
Reverend Fathers—
Hassey, Athanase
King, James E.
Rt. Rev. Archimandri—
Aboody, Charles
Badaoui, Adib, B.S.O.
Chalhoub, Maximos
Dagher, George, B.S.O.
Hage, Simon
Jadaa, John
Mardelli, Maximos
Skaff, Elias B.

Deacons:
Bagdasar, Edward, San Diego, CA
Basinski, Roland, West Paterson, NJ
Bsarany, Edward, West Paterson, NJ
Daratony, Joseph, Warren, MI
Elhilow, Edmond, Rochester, NY
Farhat, Lawrence, Southbend, IN
Jolly, Michael, Paterson, NJ
Karout, George, North Hollywood, CA
Klockowski, Daniel, Utica, NY
Lawler, Paul, Boston, MA
MacMillan, John, Lawrence, MA
McNeil, Bryan, Lawrence, MA
Merandi, Luigi, Fullerton, CA
Plowman, Kent, Augusta, GA
Rimmer, Marion, North Hollywood, CA
Ritchey, Seraphim, Birmingham, AL
Sahyouni, Elias, Northlake, IL
Sayegh, George, N. Hollywood, CA
Shalhoub, Robert, West Paterson, NJ
Soloman, James, Warren, MI
Steinmetz, Thomas, Manchester, NH
Weyrich, Paul, McLean, VA
Whelan, James, B.S.O., Methuen, MA
Yany, George, Central Falls, RI

Deacons Serving Outside the Eparchy:
Boutros, Peter
Haddad, Gregory
Nasser, Andre P.
Richardson, David W.
Versage, Joseph V.

INSTITUTIONS LOCATED IN THE DIOCESE

[A] SEMINARIES

STATE OF MASSACHUSETTS

NEWTON. *Seminary of St. Gregory the Theologian*, 233 Grant Ave., 02159-2013. Tel: 617-965-9862. Rev. Emmanuel Charles McCarthy. Priests 1; Students 1.

METHUEN. *Seminary of St. Basil the Great*, 30 East St., 01844. Tel: 508-683-2471. Rt. Rev. Gerasimos Murphy, B.S.O., J.C.D., Dean. Priests 2; Seminarians 2.

[B] MONASTERIES AND RESIDENCES FOR PRIESTS AND BROTHERS

STATE OF MASSACHUSETTS

METHUEN. *Basilian Salvatorian Order*, 30 East St., 01844. Tel: 508-683-2471; Fax: 508-794-3452. Rt. Rev. Gerasimos Murphy, B.S.O., J.C.D., Reg. Supr.; Revs. Eugene Mitchell, B.S.O., General Economos; Fouad Nasre, B.S.O., Local Supr.; J.P. Martin A. Hyatt, B.S.O., Novice Master; Rt. Revs. George Dagher, B.S.O.; Simon Hage, B.S.O., (Retired); Antoine Nachef, B.S.O.; Lawrence Tumminelli, B.S.O.

[C] CONVENTS AND RESIDENCES FOR SISTERS

STATE OF CONNECTICUT

DANBURY. *Community of the Mother of God of Tenderness*, 79 Golden Hill Rd., 06811-4631. Tel: 203-794-1486. Sr. Mary Ann Socha, C.M.G.T., Pres. Sisters 3.

[D] SOCIAL MINISTRY

STATE OF NEW YORK

NEW YORK. *Emmaus East Harlem*, 2027 Lexington Ave., 10035. Tel: 212-410-6006. Healing community for 60 homeless persons.

Emmaus House/Harlem, 2027 Lexington, P.O. Box 1177, 10035. Tel: 212-410-6006. Rev. David Kirk, Pres. & Founder; Most Rev. John A. Elya, Chm. Community of homeless; men and women's shelter; community kitchen, and outreach.

Emmaus Inns, AIDS Ministry, 2027 Lexington, P.O. Box 1177, 10035. Tel: 212-410-6006. Homeless people with AIDS. Apartments 60.

[E] MISCELLANEOUS

STATE OF ALABAMA

BIRMINGHAM. *National Shrine of St. George*, 425 16th Ave., S., 35205. Tel: 205-252-5788. Rev. Frank J. Milienewicz.

STATE OF MASSACHUSETTS

LAWRENCE. *St. Joseph's Plains Community Center*, 245 Hampshire St., 01841. Tel: 508-685-6001. Rev. Youssef A. Youssef, B.S.O.

METHUEN. *St. Basil's Salvatorian Center*, 30 East St., 01844. Tel: 508-683-2959. Deacon Allan Ramey, Dir.

STATE OF NEW YORK

YONKERS. *The Friends of the Holy Land, Inc.*, 347 Mile Square Rd., 10701. Tel: 914-969-0887; 949-2106. Ernest F. Russo, Governor Gen., Patriarchal Order of the Holy Cross of Jerusalem.

STATE OF VIRGINIA

ALEXANDRIA. *The Galilee Fund*, 6908 Columbia Drive, 22307. Tel: 703-765-7836; Fax: 703-765-7834. Saba L. Shami, Pres.

RELIGIOUS INSTITUTES OF MEN REPRESENTED IN THE EPARCHY

For further details refer to the corresponding bracketed number in the Religious Institutes of Men or Women section.

[]—*Basilian Aleppian Order*. (Deir-es-Chir, Lebanon).—B.A.O.

[]—*Basilian Chouerite Order*. (St. John Monastery, Khonchara, Lebanon).—B.C.O.

[0190]—*Basilian Salvatorian Order*. (Holy Saviour Monastery, Sidon, Lebanon).—B.S.O.

NECROLOGY

(No Deaths)

Our Lady of Deliverance Syriac Catholic Diocese

in the United States and Canada

Most Reverend

JOSEPH YOUNAN, D.D.

Bishop of Our Lady of Deliverance; ordained September 12, 1971; ordained Bishop January 7, 1996; installed February 10, 1996. *Chancery Office: 502 Palisade Ave., Union City, NJ, 07087-5213.*

Chancery Office: 502 Palisade Ave., Union City, NJ, 07087-5213. Mailing Address: P.O. Box 8366, Union City, NJ, 07087-8262.

DIOCESE ESTABLISHED NOVEMBER 18, 1996.

STATISTICAL OVERVIEW

Personnel	
Bishop	1
Priests: Diocesan Active in Diocese	9
Priests: Active Outside Diocese	1
Number of Diocesan Priests	10
Religious Priests in Diocese	1
Ordinations:	
Diocesan Priests	2
Permanent Deacons in Diocese	4
Parishes	
Parishes	6
With Resident Pastor:	
Resident Diocesan Priests	5
Without Resident Pastor:	
Administered by Permanent Deacons	1
Missions	3
Educational	
Catechesis/Religious Education:	
High School Students	150
Elementary Students	250
Total Students Under Catholic Instruction	400
Vital Statistics	
Receptions into the Church:	
Infant Baptism Totals	60
Adult Baptism Totals	4
Received into Full Communion	48
First Communions	64
Confirmations	64
Marriages:	
Catholic	12
Interfaith	5
Total Marriages	17
Deaths	19
Total Catholic Population	12,070

Chancery—*502 Palisade Ave., Union City, NJ, 07087-5213.* Tel: 201-583-1067; Fax: 201-583-0212., *P.O. Box 8366, Union City, NJ, 07087-8262.*

Vicar General—Chorbishop PIERRE MELKI.

Chancellor—Rev. ST SUTTON. Tel: 201-583-1067.

Secretary—Rev. ST SUTTON. Tel: 201-583-1067.

CLERGY, PARISHES, MISSIONS AND PAROCHIAL SCHOOLS

STATE OF NEW JERSEY

1—OUR LADY OF DELIVERANCE (1986), Rev. Yousif Abdulmasih.

Res., 502 Palisade Ave., Union City, 07087-5213. Tel: 201-583-9590; Fax: 201-583-9639.

STATE OF CALIFORNIA

North Hollywood, Los Angeles Co., Sacred Heart Syriac. Served by Chancery personnel. Deacons Elia Azouz; George Qatto; Faisal Karesh.

Res., 10837 Collins St., 91601-2009. Tel: 818-766-7001; Fax: 818-766-7254.

San Diego, San Diego Co., Our Mother of Perpetual Help Mission, Deacon Emad Hanna Al-Shaikh, Pastoral Assoc.

Mailing Address: P.O. Box 152229, 92295. Tel: 619-660-1492.

STATE OF FLORIDA

Jacksonville, Duval Co., St. Ephrem. Served by Chancery personnel.

Res., 14608 Stacey Rd., 32250. Tel: 904-992-0025.

STATE OF ILLINOIS

Northbrook, Saint Mary Virgin Immaculate Syriac Catholic Mission. Administered by the Chancery Office.

Res., 425 N. Hillside, Hillside, IL 60162. Tel: 708-449-7947; Fax: 708-449-9813.

STATE OF MICHIGAN

Farmington Hills, Oakland Co., St. Toma, Rev. Toma B. Azizo.

Res., 20465 Farmington Rd., 48334-1940. Tel: 248-788-3437; Fax: 248-642-0645.

CANADA

Toronto, St. Joseph, Rev. Yousif Mansour, Admin.

Res., 222 Ridley Blvd., ON M5M 3M6. Tel: 416-485-7781; Fax: 416-489-4183.

Laval, St. Ephrem, Chorbishop Pierre Melki. Pastoral Assocs.: Rev. Bernard Antoun.

Res., 3000 Edouard Monpetit, PQ H7T 2T5. Tel: 514-682-7546; Fax: 514-682-7603.

Eparchy of Our Lady of Lebanon of Los Angeles

Most Reverend

JOHN GEORGE CHEDID, D.D.

Bishop of the Eparchy of Our Lady of Lebanon of Los Angeles; ordained December 21, 1951; appointed Titular Bishop of Callinicum and Auxiliary Bishop of St. Maron of Brooklyn October 28, 1980; consecrated January 25, 1981. *Res., Our Lady of Mt. Lebanon, 333 S. San Vicente Blvd., Los Angeles, CA, 90048.* Tel.: 310-247-8322.

Chancery Office: P.O. Box 16397, Beverly Hills, CA, 90209. Mailing Address: 331 S. San Vicente Blvd., Los Angeles, CA, 90048. Tel.: 310-247-8322; Fax: 310-247-9297.

Web site address: www.eparchyla.org

E-mail address: eparchyla@eparchyla.org

Comprises the States of Ohio, West Virginia, Illinois, Alabama, Michigan, Minnesota, Missouri, Texas, Utah, Arizona, Nevada, Oregon, California, Alaska, Hawaii, Indiana, Kentucky, Tennessee, Mississippi, Wisconsin, Iowa, Arkansas, Louisiana, North Dakota, South Dakota, Kansas, Oklahoma, Nebraska, Montana, Wyoming, Colorado, New Mexico, Idaho and Washington.

STATISTICAL OVERVIEW

Personnel	
Bishop	1
Priests: Diocesan Active in Diocese	26
Priests: Retired, Sick or Absent	2
Number of Diocesan Priests	28
Religious Priests in Diocese	7
Ordinations:	
Diocesan Priests	1
Transitional Deacons	1
Permanent Deacons	7
Total Brothers	8
Parishes	
Parishes	29
With Resident Pastor:	
Resident Diocesan Priests	22
Resident Religious Priests	4
Without Resident Pastor:	
Administered by Priests	3
New Parishes Created	1
Welfare	
Day Care and Extended Day Care Centers	1
Total Assisted	55
Educational	
Diocesan Students in Other Seminaries	4
Total Seminarians	4
Catechesis/Religious Education:	
Total Students Under Catholic Instruction	4
Teachers in the Diocese:	
Priests	1
Vital Statistics	
Receptions into the Church:	
Infant Baptism Totals	363
Adult Baptism Totals	22
Received into Full Communion	41
First Communions	195
Confirmations	241
Marriages:	
Catholic	109
Interfaith	34
Total Marriages	143
Deaths	170
Total Catholic Population	23,711

Chancery—Chorbishop GREGORY J. MANSOUR, Protosyncellus and Chancellor *331 S. San Vicente Blvd., Los Angeles, CA, 90048.* Tel: 310-247-8322; Fax: 310-247-9297., *P.O. Box 16397, Beverly Hills, CA, 90209.*

Advisor for Priests—Chorbishop ROBERT SHAHEEN.

College of Consultors—Chorbishop ROBERT SHAHEEN; Rev. Msgr. MICHAEL KAIL; Revs. ABDALLAH ZAIDAN, M.L.M.; DONALD SAWYER; FAOUZI ELIA; Chorbishop BERNARD KHACHAN; Chorbishop GREGORY J. MANSOUR.

Commission for Lebanon—Rev. ABDALLAH ZAIDAN, M.L.M.

Tribunal—

Defender of the Bond—Rev. ROBERT BISHOP, C.F.M.

Judicial Vicar—Chorbishop WILLIAM LESER, S.T.B.

Moderator of the Tribunal—Bishop JOHN CHEDID, J.C.D., S.T.L.

Procurator/Advocate—Rev. ABDALLAH E. ZAIDAN, M.L.M.; Chorbishop GERGORY J. MANSOUR, S.T.L.

Promoter of Justice—Rev. ROBERT BISHOP, C.F.M.

Notary—Miss SIUIN MORRISSY.

Eparchial Newsletter—*"Maronites Today"*; Rev. DONALD J. SAWYER, Editor, *P.O. Box 1891, Austin, TX, 78767.*

Office for Immigration—Rev. FAOUZI ELIA.

Office for Missions—Revs. DONALD J. SAWYER; ANTHONY SPINOSA.

Office for Pastoral Leadership and Stewardship—Rev. Msgr. MICHAEL KAIL.

Office of Communications—Rev. Msgr. RICHARD SAAD.

Office of Inter-faith/Ecumenical Affairs—Rev. ANTHONY SPINOSA, Dir.

Office of Liturgy—Vacant.

Office of Ministries—Rev. Msgr. RICHARD SAAD.

Office of Priestly Vocations—Rev. SHARBEL MAROUN.

Office of Religious Education—Rev. ANTHONY SALIM.

Office of Youth Ministries—Rev. SHARBEL MAROUN.

Presbyteral Council—Rev. Msgr. MICHAEL KAIL, Exec. Dir.; Chorbishop ROBERT SHAHEEN; Revs. ABDALLAH ZAIDAN, M.L.M.; DONALD SAWYER; Rev. Msgr. WILLIAM BONCZWESKI; Rev. Msgr. RICHARD SAAD; Revs. FAOUZI ELIA; GHATTAS KHOURY; Chorbishop BERNARD KHACHAN; Chorbishop GREGORY J. MANSOUR, Ex Officio.

Pro-Life Office—Rev. Msgr. WILLIAM BONCZWESKI; Rev. ANTOINE BAKH.

Family Life Office—Chorbishop ROBERT SHAHEEN, Dir.

Office for the Third Millenium—Rev. ANTHONY SPINOSA, Dir.

Eparchial Webmaster—Rev. JEAN AL NAHAL, M.L.M.

Properties Owned—

St. Maron Office Building—Detroit, MI.

Father Toubia Retirement Home—North Jackson, OH.

Bishop's Residence—Bel Air, CA.

Priest's Retirement Home—El Monte, CA.

Protopresbyters—Chorbishop ROBERT SHAHEEN, Mid-America Region; Rev. Msgr. MICHAEL KAIL, Midwest Region; Revs. ABDALLAH ZAIDAN, M.L.M., Southwest Region; DONALD SAWYER, Southern Region.

Spiritual Director for the National Apostolate of Maronites—Rev. Msgr. MICHAEL KAIL.

Order of St. Sharbel—BEVERLY KIMES, Pres. NINA BEJANY, Vice Pres., *Eparchy of Our Lady of Lebanon of Los Angeles, P.O. Box 16397, Beverly Hills, CA, 90209.* Chorbishop ROBERT SHAHEEN, Spiritual Dir.

CLERGY, PARISHES, MISSIONS AND PAROCHIAL SCHOOLS

STATE OF CALIFORNIA

Los Angeles, Los Angeles Co., Our Lady of Mt. Lebanon-St. Peter Cathedral (1923), Most Rev. John Chedid, D.D., S.T.L., J.C.D.; Rev. Abdallah E. Zaidan, M.L.M., Rector; Chorbishop Gregory J. Mansour, S.T.L., Chancellor.

Res., 333 S. San Vicente Blvd., 90048. Tel: 310-275-6634; Fax: 310-858-0856.

Anaheim, Orange Co., St. John Maron Mission (1988), Rev. Antoine Bakh; Subdeacon Alfred Harb.

Mailing Address: & Church: 1546 E. La Palma Ave., 92805. Tel: 714-520-5303; Fax: 714-520-4273.

Res., 601 N. Woods Ave., Fullerton, 92632. Tel: 714-525-4216.

Millbrae, San Mateo Co., Our Lady of Lebanon (1979) (Lebanese), Rev. Toufic Nasr, Admin.

Res., 600 El Camino Real N.W., P.O. Box 896, 94030. Tel: 415-589-9653; Fax: 415-866-3091.

San Diego, San Diego Co., Saint Ephrem Mission (1989), Rev. Nabil Mouannes, Admin.

Res., P.O. Box 130, Del Mar, 92014-0130. Tel: 619-285-9818; Fax: 619-285-9818.

Stockton, San Joaquin Co., Maronite Catholic Community, Rev. Toufic Nasr.

STATE OF ALABAMA

Birmingham, Jefferson Co., St. Elias (1910), Rev. Msgr. Richard D. Saad; Subdeacons Joseph Stephens; Samuel Wehby.

Res., 836 Eighth St. S., 35205-4567. Tel: 205-251-5057; 252-3867; Fax: 205-251-5028.

Catechesis/Religious Programs—Students 110.

STATE OF ARIZONA

Phoenix, Maricopa Co., Maronite Catholic Community, Rev. Nabil Mouannes, Admin.

STATE OF COLORADO

Denver, Denver Co., Maronite Catholic Community, Rev. Abdallah E. Zaidan, M.L.M., Protopresbyter & Admin.

STATE OF ILLINOIS

Hillside, Cook Co., Our Lady of Lebanon Church (1952)

(Lebanese), Rev. Victor Kayrouz. In res., Rev. Msgr. John Naffah, (Retired); Rev. Mansour Mattosha, Syriac Catholic Mission.
Res., 425 N. Hillside Ave., 60162. Tel: 708-449-5558; Fax: 708-449-9813.
Mission—Michigan City, La Porte Co., Maronite Catholic Community, Sacred Heart Church, Eighth St., Michigan City, IN 46360. Tel: 219-874-3491. Rev. Victor Kayrouz.

Peoria, Peoria Co., St. Sharbel (1973), Rev. Faouzi Y. Elia; Deacon James Siedlecki.
Res., 2914 W. Scenic Dr., 61615. Tel: 309-688-5555; Fax: 309-688-0431. [JC]

STATE OF KENTUCKY

Louisville, Jefferson Co., Maronite Catholic Community (1953), Rev. Victor Kayrouz.
Mailing Address: 425 N. Hillside Ave., Hillside, IL 60162. Tel: 708-449-5558; Fax: 708-449-9813.

STATE OF LOUISIANA

Baton Rouge, East Baton Rouge Parish, Maronite Catholic Community, Rev. Don Sawyer, Admin.
Tel: 512-458-3693; Fax: 512-451-9554.

Lafayette, Lafayette Parish, Maronite Catholic Community, Rev. Kenneth Morvant, Admin.

Lake Charles, Calcasieu Parish, Maronite Catholic Community, Rev. Don Sawyer, Admin.
Tel: 512-458-3693; Fax: 512-451-9554.

New Orleans, Orleans Civil Parish, Maronite Catholic Community, Rev. Msgr. Richard Saad, Admin.
Tel: 205-251-5057; Fax: 305-251-5028.

STATE OF MICHIGAN

Detroit, Wayne Co., St. Maron/St. Sharbel (1909), Rev. Louis Baz, St. Maron; Rev. Msgr. Kenneth A. Michael, St. Sharbel; Chorbishop Joseph C. Feghali, Pastor Emeritus.
Res., 11466 Kercheval, 48215. Tel: 313-824-0196; Fax: 313-824-0276. [CEM]
Res., 31601 Schoenherr Rd., Warren, 48093. Tel: 810-826-9688; Fax: 810-826-3521.
Catechesis/Religious Programs—Students 135.

Flint, Genesee Co., Our Lady of Lebanon (1973), Rev. Anthony S. Spinosa; Subdeacons Earl Matte; Charles Rossie; Martin Rachid.
Res., 4133 Calkins Rd., 48532. Tel: 810-733-1259; Fax: 810-732-2760.
Catechesis/Religious Programs—Students 65.

STATE OF MINNESOTA

Minneapolis, Hennepin Co., St. Maron (1948), Rev. Sharbel G. Maroun.
Res., 219 Sixth Ave. N.E., 55413. Tel: 612-379-2758; Fax: 612-379-7647.
Catechesis/Religious Programs—Tel: 612-631-2182.
Students 80.

St. Paul, Ramsey Co., Holy Family Church (1918), Rev. Bakhos Chidiac.
Res., 203 E. Robie St., 55107. Tel: 612-291-1116; Fax: 612-291-7009.

STATE OF MISSOURI

Columbia, Boone Co., Maronite Catholic Community, Chorbishop Robert Shaheen, Admin.
Tel: 314-621-0056; Fax: 314-231-9057.

St. Louis, St. Louis City Co., St. Raymond (1913), Chorbishop Robert J. Shaheen; Subdeacons Louis Peters; George Simon.
Res., 931 Lebanon Dr., 63104. Tel: 314-621-0056; Fax: 314-231-9057.
Catechesis/Religious Programs—Students 90.

STATE OF NEVADA

Las Vegas, Clark Co., St. Sharbel Mission, Rev. Jean Pierre Barakat, Admin.

STATE OF OKLAHOMA

Tulsa, Tulsa Co., Maronite Catholic Community, Rev. Don Sawyer, Admin.
Tel: 512-458-3693; Fax: 512-451-9554.

STATE OF OHIO

Cincinnati, Hamilton Co., St. Anthony of Padua (1910), Rev. Ghattas Khoury; Subdeacons Joseph Mousie; Arthur Evans.
Res., 2530 Victory Pkwy., 45206. Tel: 513-961-0120; Fax: 513-961-6058.

Cleveland, Cuyahoga Co., St. Maron (1915), Chorbishop Bernard C. Khachan; Deacon George M. Khoury; Subdeacon James Peters.
Res., 1245 Carnegie Ave., 44115. Tel: 216-781-6161; Fax: 216-781-6162. [JC]
Catechesis/Religious Programs—Students 84.

Columbus, Franklin Co., Maronite Catholic Community, Rev. Msgr. Michael J. Kail, Protopresbyter & Admin.

Dayton, Montgomery Co., Saint Ignatius Mission (1993) (Lebanese), Rev. Alfred Al-Badwi, Admin.
Mailing Address: 727 Beckman St., 45410. Tel: 937-253-2525.

Fairlawn, Summit Co., Our Lady of the Cedars of Mt. Lebanon (1937), Rev. Msgr. Michael J. Kail; Deacons Robert Foster; Fred Browne.
Res., 507 S. Cleveland-Massillon Rd., 44333-3019. Tel: 330-666-3598; Fax: 330-666-3897.
Catechesis/Religious Programs—Students 47.

Youngstown, Mahoning Co., St. Maron (1902) (Lebanese), Rev. Anthony J. Salim; Deacon Joseph Nohra; Subdeacon Thomas Craven.
Res., 1555 S. Meridian Rd., 44511-1199. Tel: 330-792-2371; 792-7671 (Center); Fax: 330-792-3026.
Catechesis/Religious Programs—Tel: 330-538-2567; Fax: 330-538-9820.
Students 148.

STATE OF OREGON

Portland, Multnomah Co., Saint Sharbel (1970), Rev. William Jonathan Decker.
Res., 1804 S.E. 16th Ave., 97214. Tel: 503-231-3853.
Mission—Seattle, Maronite Catholic Community, 97214. Rev. William Jonathan Decker, Admin.

STATE OF TEXAS

Austin, Travis Co., Our Lady's Maronite Parish (1982), Rev. Donald Sawyer, D.Min.; Deacon Joseph Crowley.
Mailing Address: (Church) 1320 E. 51st St., 78723. Tel: 512-458-3693; Fax: 512-451-9554.
Res., 5010 Caswell Ave., 78751. Tel: 512-454-6342.

El Paso, El Paso Co., St. Anthony of the Desert Mission, Rev. Georges Bou-Mssalem, Admin.
Res., 3617 Breckenridge St., 79935. Tel: 915-593-3121; Fax: 915-594-8515.

Houston, Harris Co., Our Lady of the Cedars Mission (1990), Rev. Milad T. Yaghi, M.L.M. In res., Rev. Ghassan Matar, M.L.M.
Mailing Address: P.O. Box 573002, 77257. [JC]
Res., 11935 Belfort Village, 77031. Tel: 713-568-6800; Fax: 713-564-6961.

Lewisville, Denton Co., Our Lady of Lebanon Mission (1990), Rev. Andre S. Estephan, M.L.M.
Res., 719 University Pl., 75067. Tel: 972-436-7617; Fax: 972-221-3430.
Catechesis/Religious Programs—Students 60.

San Antonio, Bexar Co., St. George Maronite (1925), Rev. Jean Al-Nahal, M.L.M., Admin.; Subdeacon Raymond E. Casillas. In res., Rev. Assaad El-Bacha, M.L.M. (Lebanon).
Res., 6070 Babcock Rd., 78240. Tel: 210-690-9569; Fax: 210-690-5093. [JC]
Catechesis/Religious Programs—Students 50.

STATE OF UTAH

Murray, Salt Lake Co., Saint Jude Church (1975), Rev. Gebran Bou-Merhi; Subdeacon Roger Dannels.
Res., 4893 Wasatch St., 84107. Tel: 801-268-2820.
Church—4900 Wasatch St., 84107. Tel: 801-265-2195; Fax: 801-268-2820.

STATE OF WEST VIRGINIA

Wheeling, Ohio Co., Our Lady of Lebanon (1906), Rev. Georges Chaanine.
Res., 2216 Eoff St., 26003. Tel: 304-233-1688; Fax: 304-232-8303. [JC]

Special Assignment:
Reverend Fathers—
Fisher, David, Adjunct Prof. of Theology, Marianist University of Dayton

---

Leave of Absence:
Reverend Fathers—
Coover, Thomas
Karem, Peter

Retired:
Chorbishop—
Trad, John
Reverend Monsignors—
Naffah, John
Reverend Fathers—
Hitti, Michael
Saad, Antoun

INSTITUTIONS LOCATED IN THE DIOCESE

[A] MONASTERIES AND RESIDENCES OF PRIESTS AND BROTHERS

SAN ANTONIO, TX. *The Congregation of Maronite Lebanese Missionaries*, Saint George Maronite Church, 6070 Babcock Rd., 78240. Tel: 210-690-9569; Fax: 210-690-5093.
E-mail: st.georgesa@stgeorgesa.org
Web site: (URL):www.stgeorgesa.org
Revs. Abdallah E. Zaidan, M.L.M., Supr.; Milad T. Yaghi, M.L.M.; Andre S. Estephan, M.L.M.; John Al-Nahal, M.L.M.; Assaad El-Bacha, M.L.M.; Ghassan Matar, M.L.M.; George Bou Sallem, M.L.M.

[B] CONVENTS AND RESIDENCES FOR SISTERS

NORTH JACKSON, OH. *Antonine Maronite Sisters of Youngstown, Inc.*, 2691 N. Lipkey Rd., 44451. Tel: 330-538-2567. Sisters 6. Antonine Sisters Adult Day Care, Inc., 2675 N. Lipkey Rd., 44451. Tel: 330-538-9822; Fax: 330-538-9820. Total Staff 11; Total Assisted 55.

[C] NATIONAL SHRINES

NORTH JACKSON, OH. *National Shrine of Our Lady of Lebanon*, 2759 N. Lipkey Rd., 44451. Tel: 330-538-3351.
E-mail: nsh@cisnet.com
Web site: www.nationalshrine.org
Rev. Msgr. William D. Bonczewski.

[D] RELIGIOUS COMMUNITIES OF MEN

PHILIPPI, WV. *Our Lady of Solitude Hermitage*, 334 S. Main St., 26416. Tel: 304-457-3330. Rev. Bernard Grunewald, ER. O.L.S., Supr.

[E] RESIDENCES FOR CLERGY

NORTH JACKSON, OH. *Father Toubia Retirement Home*, 2759 N. Lipkey Rd., 44451. Tel: 330-538-3351.
E-mail: nshrine@valunet.com
Web site: www.nationalshrine.org

[F] MISCELLANEOUS

LOS ANGELES. *Priest's Retirement Fund*, 333 S. San Vicente Blvd., 90048. Tel: 310-247-8322; Fax: 310-247-9297.

EL MONTE. *Priest's Retirement Home*. 333 S. San Vincente Blvd., Los Angeles, 90048.

RELIGIOUS INSTITUTES OF MEN REPRESENTED IN THE DIOCESE

For further details refer to the corresponding bracketed number in the Religious Institutes of Men section.

[0785]—*The Congregation of Maronite Lebanese Missionaries*. (San Antonio, TX).—M.L.M.

NECROLOGY

† Kleem, Ferris, Detroit, MI, St. Maron Church. —Died Sept. 23, 1997.

Byzantine Eparchy of Parma

Most Reverend

BASIL M. SCHOTT, O.F.M. D.D.

Bishop of Parma; ordained August 29, 1965; consecrated and installed July 11, 1996.

ESTABLISHED FEBRUARY 21, 1969.

Embraces all Byzantine Ruthenian Rite Catholics in the States of Illinois, Indiana, Iowa, Kansas, Michigan, Minnesota, Missouri, Nebraska, North Dakota, South Dakota and Wisconsin. Also the entire State of Ohio excluding the Counties of Ashtabula, Trumbull, Mahoning, Columbiana, Carroll, Harrison, Guernsey, Noble, Morgan, Athens, Meigs, Gallia and Lawrence.

For legal titles of parishes and diocesan institutions, consult the Chancery Office.

Chancery Office: 1900 Carlton Rd., Parma, OH, 44134. Tel.: 216-741-8773; Fax: 216-741-9356.

Web site address: http://www.parma.org

STATISTICAL OVERVIEW

Personnel	
Bishop	1
Priests: Diocesan Active in Diocese	29
Priests: Active Outside Diocese	1
Priests: Retired, Sick or Absent	9
Number of Diocesan Priests	39
Religious Priests in Diocese	2
Extern Priests in Diocese	1
Permanent Deacons in Diocese	3
Total Sisters	14
Parishes	
Parishes	38
With Resident Pastor:	
Resident Diocesan Priests	27
Resident Religious Priests	1
Without Resident Pastor:	
Administered by Priests	10
Missions	2
Closed Parishes	1
Professional Ministry Personnel:	
Sisters	14
Welfare	
Day Care and Extended Day Care Centers	1
Total Assisted	101
Special Centers for Social Services	1
Total Assisted	7,000
Educational	
Diocesan Students in Other Seminaries	3
Total Seminarians	3
Elementary Schools, Diocesan and Parish	2
Total Students	349
Catechesis/Religious Education:	
High School Students	176
Elementary Students	825
Total Students Under Catholic Instruction	1,353
Teachers in the Diocese:	
Sisters	5
Lay Teachers	18
Vital Statistics	
Receptions into the Church:	
Infant Baptism Totals	145
Adult Baptism Totals	13
Received into Full Communion	34
First Communions	155
Confirmations	133
Marriages:	
Catholic	39
Interfaith	23
Total Marriages	62
Deaths	190
Total Catholic Population	12,716

Former Bishops—Most Rev. EMIL J. MIHALIK, D.D., ord. Sept. 21, 1945; appt. first Bishop of the Ruthenian Eparchy of Parma, March 22, 1969; installed June 12, 1969; died Jan. 27, 1984.—Most Rev. ANDREW PATAKI, D.D., appt. Titular Bishop of Tellmisus and Auxiliary of Passaic, NJ, May 30, 1983; installed Aug. 23, 1983; succeeded to See, June 19, 1984; transferred Parma See, Aug 16, 1984; transferred Byzantine Eparchy of Passaic, Nov. 21, 1995.

Chancery Office—1900 Carlton Rd., Parma, OH, 44134. Tel: 216-741-8773; Fax: 216-741-9356.

Chancellor—Rev. MICHAEL J. HUSZTI, J.C.L.

Presbyteral Council—Rev. Msgr. ROBERT YARNOVITZ; Very Rev. MICHAEL EVANICK; Revs. DAVID HANNES, J.C.L.; EDWARD ZAVELL; JOHN KACHUBU; THOMAS LOYA; BASIL HUTSKO; DENNIS HRUBIAK; MICHAEL HUSZTI, J.C.L.; DAVID PETRAS, S.E.O.D.; BRUCE RIEBE.

Eparchial Treasurer—Rev. EDWARD ZAVELL,Eparchial Finance Council: JERRY LUCAS; EDWARD MAHER; THOMAS PERCIAK; HELEN IRION, Sec.

Eparchial Consultors—Rev. Msgr. ROBERT V. YARNOVITZ; Revs. EDWARD ZAVELL; MICHAEL EVANICK; DAVID PETRAS, S.E.O.D.; DENNIS HRUBIAK; DAVID HANNES, J.C.L.; EMIL MASICH; MICHAEL HUSZTI.

Protopresbyters—Ohio: Revs. EDWARD ZAVELL,Midwest: Rev. Msgr. FRANK KORBA,Great Lakes: Rev. JAMES KUBAJAK, M.Div.

Vicar Judicialis—Rev. DAVID HANNES, J.C.L.

Vicar Adjutant—Rev. MICHAEL J. HUSZTI, J.C.L.
Judge—Rev. NICHOLAS R.A. RACHFORD, J.C.L.
Secretary—Rev. NICHOLAS R.A. RACHFORD, J.C.L.
Defender of the Bond—Rev. JAMES KUBAJAK, M.Div.
Promoter of Justice—Rev. JAMES KUBAJAK, M.Div.
Notaries—Rev. JAMES BATCHA; HELEN IRION.

Eparchial Censors—Revs. DAVID PETRAS, S.E.O.D.; JOHN KACHUBA, M.A.

Eparchial Commissions

Sacred Liturgy—Rev. DAVID PETRAS, S.E.O.D., Chm.; Rev. Msgr. ROBERT V. YARNOVITZ; Revs. ROBERT BARTER; MICHAEL HAYDUK; VLADIMIR VANCIK, S.T.D.

Apostolate of St. Nicholas—Eparchial Director Cleveland West, Ohio: DAVID BASALLA, Spiritual Dir.; Rev. JAMES BATCHA, Chm. LORETTA NEMETH, Dir. Cleveland East: Rev. BRYAN R. EYMAN, (Chap.) Spiritual Dir. BRUCE ROYKO, Dir. Midwest: Chapter Dirs.: PAUL HOHRAN, St. Michael, Merrillville, IN; ANN MARIE ZIMA, St. Nicholas, Munster, IN; DON GRISHAM, St. Mary, Joliet, IL; HELEN TIMURA, St. Nicholas, Barberton, OH Great Lakes: Vacant.

Building Commission—Rev. Msgr. ROBERT V. YARNOVITZ, V.G., Chm.; Revs. DAVID PETRAS, S.E.O.D.; BRYAN EYMAN; CHARLES LIZANICH.

Cantors' Institute—NICOLETTE BOROS, Dir. Cantors' Institute Faculty: Revs. DAVID PETRAS, S.E.O.D.; DENNIS HRUBIAK; MICHAEL HAYDUK; MICHAEL J. HUSZTI, J.C.L.; JAMES BATCHA; NICHOLAS RACHFORD, J.C.L.,Cantors' Institute Advisory Board: EDWARD MAHER; VICTORIA BOROS; JERRY LUCAS; Revs. EDWARD ZAVELL; NICHOLAS RACHFORD.

Office of Religious Education—JOHN KACHUBA, M.A., Dir. Tel: 216-741-4102. Rev. BASIL HUTSKO, Great Lakes; Rev. Msgr. FRANK KORBA, Midwest.

Catechetical Board—Rev. Msgr. FRANK KORBA; Rev. JOHN KEBLESH; Sr. ELIZABETH JANETEPLEY, O.S.B.M.; BETTY BARANKO; MELVIN CANNON; RENA FULKA; Deacon RICHARD GUIDEN; TIMOTHY LOYA; LISA STANICH.

Associate Religious Education Directors—Midwest: Rev. Msgr. FRANK KORBA, Great Lakes:; Vacant.

Office of Youth Ministry—Revs. BRUCE RIEBE, Dir. BASIL HUTSKO, Great Lakes; JOHN KEBLESH, Ohio; Mr. THOMAS LOYA, Midwest.

Young Singles—Vacant.

Office of Family Life—FLORENCE BUKOVECKY, Dir.

Office of Lay Apostolate—ROBERT SHIRILLA, Dir.

Office of Evangelization and Missionary Activity—Rev. JAMES BATCHA, Dir.

Office of the Diaconate—Rev. DENNIS HRUBIAK, Dir.

Office of Vocations—Rev. DENNIS HRUBIAK, Dir.

Seminary Education and Priestly Formation Board—Rev. DAVID PETRAS, S.E.O.D., Chm.; Rev. Msgr. ROBERT V. YARNOVITZ; Revs. MICHAEL HAYDUK; DENNIS HRUBIAK; JOHN KACHUBA, M.A.; NICHOLAS RACHFORD, J.C.L.; EDWARD ZAVELL.

Clergy Life Commission—Rev. DENNIS HRUBIAK, Chm.; Rev. Msgr. BASIL SMOCHKO; Rev. Msgr. ROBERT V. YARNOVITZ; Revs. MICHAEL EVANICK; DAVID HANNES, J.C.L.; MICHAEL J. HUSZTI, J.C.L.; JAMES KUBAJAK, M.Div.; DAVID PETRAS, S.E.O.D.; NICHOLAS RACHFORD, J.C.L.; EDWARD ZAVELL.

Office of Communication—Rev. NICHOLAS RACHFORD, J.C.L., Dir. Eparchial Newspaper, "Horizons". Tel: 216-741-3312; Fax: 216-741-9356.

Vicar for Religious—Vacant.

Delegates for Priests—Rev. Msgr. ROBERT V. YARNOVITZ, Chm.; Rev. MICHAEL EVANICK; Rev. DENNIS HRUBIAK.

Priest's Pension Board—Rev. Msgr. FRANK KORBA, Chm.; Rev. Msgr. ROBERT V. YARNOVITZ; Revs. ROBERT BARTER; JAMES BATCHA; BASIL HUTSKO; JOSEPH POHORLAK; JOSEPH RADVANSKY; EDWARD ZAVELL.

Office of Ecumenical Activity—Rev. DAVID PETRAS, S.E.O.D., Dir.

History and Research—Rev. MICHAEL J. HUSZTI, J.C.L., Dir.

Stewardship Office—MARY S. LIZANICH.

Scouting Office—Rev. NICHOLAS RACHFORD, J.C.L., Dir. & Chap., Boy Scouts.

Eparchial Shrine of the Weeping Madonna of Mariapoch—(Burton, OH): President, The Most Rev. Ordinary of the Parma Eparchy; Revs. MICHAEL J. HUSZTI, J.C.L., Dir. & Admin. JOHN KOVACH, Parochial Vicar. Tel: 216-834-8807. Assisted by the Social Mission Sisters. Sr. M. FLORA, S.M.S., Supr. Tel: 216-834-4078.

Respect Life Office—PATRICK PEROTTI.

Pre-Cana Office—Rev. MICHAEL HAYDUK.

CLERGY, PARISHES, MISSIONS AND PAROCHIAL SCHOOLS

STATE OF OHIO

Parma, Cuyahoga Co., Saint John the Baptist, Cathedral, Rev. Msgr. Robert Yarnovitz. In res., Rev. Edmund Jadwisiak.
Church—1900 Carlton Rd., 44134-3129. Tel: 216-661-8658; Fax: 216-741-9356.
Res., 1703 Carlton Rd., 44134.
Holy Spirit, Rev. Dennis M. Hrubiak.
Res., 5500 W. 54th St., 44129-2274. Tel: 216-884-8452; Fax: 216-884-8453.

Akron, Summit Co., St. Michael the Archangel, Rev. Bernard Danber, O.S.A.
Res., 847 Crouse St., 44306-1125. Tel: 330-376-6633; Fax: 330-376-4149.

Barberton, Summit Co., St. Nicholas, Rev. Bernard Dunber, O.S.A., Admin.
Res., 1051 E. Robinson St., 44203-3852. Tel: 216-753-0018.

Bedford, Cuyahoga Co., St. Eugene, Rev. Joseph Repko.
Res., 264 Warrensville-Center Rd., 44146-2741. Tel: 216-232-7302.

Brecksville, Cuyahoga Co., St. Joseph, Rev. Bruce Riebe.
Res., 8111 Brecksville, 44141-1204. Tel: 216-526-1818; Fax: 216-526-0016.

Brunswick, Medina Co., St. Emilian, Rev. John W. Keblesh.
Res., 1231 Substation Rd., 44212-1911. Tel: 330-225-9857.

Burton, Geauga Co., Church of Weeping Madonna, Revs. Michael J. Huszti, Shrine Dir.; John Kovach.
Res., 17486 Mumford Rd., 44021-9640. Tel: 216-834-8807.
Shrine—Shrine of the Weeping Madonna of Mariapoch.
Social Mission Sisters of Hungary 2.

Cleveland, Cuyahoga Co., Holy Ghost, Rev. Quentin S. Koplinka, O.S.B.
Res., 2420 W. 14th St., 44113-4406. Tel: 216-861-2177.
St. Mary, Rev. Ronald K. Timock, Admin.
Res., 4600 State Rd., 44109-5243. Tel: 216-741-7979; Fax: 216-749-7981.
School—Tel: 216-749-7980. Sr. Joanne Lickvar, Prin.
Sisters of St. Basil the Great 3; Lay Teachers 10; Students 229.
St. Nicholas (Croatian), Rev. Quentin S. Koplinka, O.S.B.
Res., 3431 Superior Ave., 44114-4160. Tel: 216-361-5069; Fax: 216-361-5069.

Columbus, Franklin Co., St. John Chrysostom, Rev. Eugene R. Linowski.
Res., 5858 Cleveland Ave., 43231-2862. Tel: 614-882-7578; Fax: 614-890-6048.

Dayton, Montgomery Co., St. Barbara, Revs. Eugene R. Linowski, Admin.; Waldemar J. Kuchta.
Res., 5915 Springboro Pk., 45449-3249. Tel: 513-434-2051; Fax: 513-385-8559.

Euclid, Cuyahoga Co., St. Stephen, Rev. John S. Kachuba, M.A.
Res., 532 Lloyd Rd., 44132-1721. Tel: 216-732-7292; Fax: 216-732-9434.

Fairport Harbor, Lake Co., St. Michael, Rev. Bryan R. Eyman.
Res., 630 Plum St., 44077-5660. Tel: 216-357-7896.

Fairview Park, Cuyahoga Co., St. Mary Magdalene, Rev. Edward Zavell, V.F.
Res., 5390 W. 220th St., 44126-2968. Tel: 216-734-4644; Fax: 216-741-9365.

Lakewood, Cuyahoga Co., St. Gregory the Theologian, Rev. Msgr. Basil Smochko.
Res., 2035 Quail Ave., 44107-5217. Tel: 216-521-1081; Fax: 216-521-1081.

Lorain, Lorain Co., St. Michael, Rev. James Batcha.
Res., 3056 Reeves Ave., 44052-4274. Tel: 216-282-3808.
St. Nicholas, Rev. James Batcha.
Res., 2711 W. 40th St., 44053-2252. Tel: 216-282-7525; Fax: 216-282-9185.
School—2707 W. 40th St., 44053-2252. Tel: 216-282-3289. Sr. Elizabeth Jane Templey, Prin.
Sisters of Saint Basil the Great 2; Lay Teachers 7; Students 120.

Marblehead, Ottawa Co., St. Mary, Rev. Joseph R. Radvansky.
Res., 506 E. Main St., 43440-2232. Tel: 419-798-4283.

Mentor-on-the-Lake, Lake Co., St. Andrew the Apostle, Rev. Bryan R. Eyman.
Res., 5768 Andrews Rd., 44060-2608. Tel: 216-257-3620; Fax: 216-257-3620.

Northwood, Lucas Co., St. Michael the Archangel, Rev. James Kubajak, V.F.
Res., 2526 Skagway Dr., 43619. Tel: 419-691-5656; Fax: 419-691-7669.
Church—4001 Navarre Ave., Oregon, 43616.

Solon, Cuyahoga Co., St. John the Baptist, Rev. Michael J. Huszti.
Res., 36125 Aurora Rd., 44139-3841. Tel: 216-248-0417.

STATE OF ILLINOIS

Chicago, Cook Co., St. Mary, Rev. Thomas Loya, Admin. 60 W. 90th St., Oak Lawn, 60453. Tel: 815-726-6308.

Joliet, Will Co., St. Mary Assumption, Rev. Thomas Loya.
Res., 1004 Hacker Ave., 60432-1229. Tel: 815-726-6308.

STATE OF INDIANA

East Chicago, Lake Co., St. Basil's. Closed. For inquiries for parish records contact the Chancery.

Indiana Harbor Co., Holy Ghost. Closed. For inquiries for parish records contact the Chancery.

Indianapolis, Marion Co., St. Athanasius Church. Unassigned.
Res., 1117 Blaine Ave., 46221-1110. Tel: 317-632-4157.

Merrillville, Lake Co., St. Michael, Very Rev. Michael Evanick.
Res., 557 W. 57th Ave., 46410-2540. Tel: 219-980-0600.

Munster, Lake Co., Saint Nicholas, Rev. Msgr. Frank Korba, V.F.
Res., 8103 Columbia Ave., 46321-1802. Tel: 219-838-9380.

Whiting, Lake Co., Assumption of the Blessed Virgin, Rev. Joseph Pohorlak.
Res., 2011 Clark St., 46394-2023. Tel: 219-659-0277.

STATE OF MICHIGAN

Allen Park, Wayne Co., St. Stephen, Rev. Cyril Attak. In res., Rev. Msgr. John Kurty.
Res., 4141 Laurence Ave., 48101-3049. Tel: 313-382-5901.

Bay City, Bay Co., Saint George, Rev. Robert Stash.
Res., 204 N. Van Buren St., 48706-6519. Tel: 517-892-0763.

Detroit, Wayne Co., St. Nicholas, Rev. Robert J. Barter.
Church—19130 Beaconsfield St., 48224-1177. Tel: 313-521-6827.
St. John the Baptist. Closed. For inquiries for parish records contact the Chancery.

Flushing, Genesee Co., St. Michael, Rev. David A. Hannes.
Res., 2333 N. Elms Rd., 48433-9426. Tel: 810-659-4887; Fax: 810-659-8363.

Livonia, Wayne Co., Sacred Heart, Rev. Nicholas Ivan.
Res., 29125 W. Six-Mile Rd., 48152-3661. Tel: 313-522-3166.

Omer, Arenac Co., St. John, Rev. Robert Stash.
Mailing Address: P.O. Box 236, 48749-0236. Tel: 517-892-0763.
Res., 204 N. Van Buren St., Bay City, 48708-6519.

Sterling Heights, Macomb Co., St. Basil, Rev. Basil J. Hutsko.
Res., 4700 Metropolitan Pkwy., 48310-3905. Tel: 810-268-1082.

Taylor, Wayne Co., Christ the King. Closed. For inquiries for parish records contact the Chancery.

STATE OF MINNESOTA

Minneapolis, Hennepin Co., St. John the Baptist, Rev. Edward C. Wojciechowski.
Res., 2215 Third St., N.E., 55418-3422. Tel: 612-789-6252.

STATE OF MISSOURI

St. Louis, St. Louis Co., St. Louis Mission, Revs. Eugene Selzer; Paul Niemann; Joseph A. Weber.
Res., 9311 Stansberry Ave., 63134-3635. Tel: 314-428-7371; Fax: 314-428-1158.

Sugar Creek, Jackson Co., St. Luke, Byzantine Catholic Parish, Rev. Francis McGlynn.
Mailing Address: 700 E. 8th St., #910, Kansas City, 64106-1635.
Church—11411 Chicago, 64054. Tel: 816-842-3454; Fax: 816-842-3454.

STATE OF WISCONSIN

Bristol, Kenosha Co., St. Irene. Closed. For information regarding the Byzantine Catholic Community contact Rev. Gerald P. Schmitz, 4804 Seventh Ave., Kenosha, 53140-3397. Tel: 414-657-6875.

On Special or Other Diocesan Assignment:
Reverend Fathers—
Hayduk, Michael, Chap., Byzantine Nuns of St. Clare, 3600 Biddulph Ave., Cleveland, OH 44109
Rachford, Nicholas, 1703 Carlton Rd., Apt. A, Parma, OH 44134-3126

On Duty Outside the Diocese:
Reverend Fathers—
Petras, David M., Byzantine Catholic Seminary, Pittsburgh

Absent on Leave:
Reverend Fathers—
Chelena, Thomas
Francisko, Gary
Rebovich, John
Ruglovsky, Robert
St. Germain, Brian

Retired:
Reverend Monsignors—
Kurty, John
Reverend Fathers—
Jadwisiak, Edmund, 3964 E. State Rd., Port Clinton, OH 43452
Masich, Emil G., 3600 Biddulph Ave., Cleveland, OH 44109
Vancik, Vladimir, 18 Station St., Carnegie, PA 15106. Tel: 412-276-4093

Permanent Deacons:
Guiden, Richard
Hendricks, Lawrence
Kenes, Michael

INSTITUTIONS LOCATED IN THE DIOCESE

[A] CONVENTS AND RESIDENCES FOR SISTERS

North Royalton. *Motherhouse and Novitiate*, 6688 Cady Rd., 44133. Tel: 216-237-6800. Byzantine Nuns of St. Clare. Sisters, Parma Eparchy, Byzantine Ruthenian Province, Monastery of the Holy Protection of the Mother of God. Sr. Mary Philomena Horkavi, B.N.S.C., Supr.; Rev. Michael Hayduk, Chap.

[B] RELIGIOUS SHRINES

Burton. *Shrine of the Weeping Madonna of Mariapoch*, 17486 Mumford Rd., 44021. Tel: 216-834-8807. Revs. Michael J. Huszti, J.C.L., Shrine Dir.; John Kovach, Parochial Vicar; Sr. Flora, Supr. Tel: Convent Tel.: 216-834-4078.

[C] MISCELLANEOUS

Cleveland. *St. Mary Hospitality House*, 4600 State Rd., 44109. Tel: 216-749-7288. Dorothy Papke, Dir.

RELIGIOUS INSTITUTES OF WOMEN REPRESENTED IN THE DIOCESE

For further details refer to the corresponding bracketed number in the Religious Institutes of Women section.

[]—*Byzantine Nuns of St. Clare*. (Parma Eparchy).—B.N.S.C.

[3730]—*Sisters of the Order of St. Basil the Great*.—O.S.B.M.

[]—*Social Mission Sisters of Mariapoch*.—S.M.S.

NECROLOGY

† Felock, Michael, Barberton, OH, St. Nicholas. —Died May 12, 1997.

† McElaney, Robert, Indianapolis, IN, St. Athanasius. —Died Oct. 8, 1997.

Byzantine Catholic Diocese of Passaic

Most Reverend

ANDREW PATAKI, J.C.L., D.D.

Bishop of Passaic; appointed Titular Bishop of Tellmisus and Auxiliary Bishop of Passaic, May 30, 1983; consecrated August 23, 1983; appointed Bishop June 19, 1984; transferred to Parma See August 16, 1984; transferred to Passaic November 21, 1995.

Most Reverend

MICHAEL J. DUDICK, D.D.

Retired Bishop of Passaic; ordained November 13, 1945; appointed Bishop August 21, 1968; consecrated and installed October 24, 1968; retired November 21, 1995. *Res., 445 Lackawanna Ave., West Paterson, NJ, 07424.*

ESTABLISHED JULY 31, 1963.

Embraces all Catholics of the Byzantine-Ruthenian Rite in the States of New Jersey, Connecticut, Delaware, District of Columbia, Florida, Georgia, Maine, Maryland, Massachusetts, New Hampshire, New York, North Carolina, Rhode Island, South Carolina, Vermont, Virginia and all Eastern Pennsylvania within the western boundaries of the Counties of Franklin, Juniata, Lycoming, Mifflin, Union and Tioga.

For legal titles of parishes and diocesan institutions, consult the Chancery Office.

Chancery Office: 445 Lackawanna Ave., West Paterson, NJ, 07424. Tel.: 973-890-7777; Fax: 973-890-7175.

STATISTICAL OVERVIEW

Personnel	
Bishop	1
Retired Bishops	1
Priests: Diocesan Active in Diocese	74
Priests: Active Outside Diocese	4
Priests: Retired, Sick or Absent	16
Number of Diocesan Priests	94
Religious Priests in Diocese	7
Extern Priests in Diocese	5
Ordinations:	
Diocesan Priests	1
Transitional Deacons	1
Permanent Deacons in Diocese	17
Total Brothers	4
Total Sisters	21
Parishes	
Parishes	98
With Resident Pastor:	
Resident Diocesan Priests	71
Resident Religious Priests	2
Without Resident Pastor:	
Administered by Priests	25
Missions	7
Pastoral Centers	5
Educational	
Diocesan Students in Other Seminaries	8
Total Seminarians	8
Elementary Schools, Diocesan and Parish	1
Total Students	490
Catechesis/Religious Education:	
High School Students	365
Elementary Students	1,965
Total Students Under Catholic Instruction	2,828
Teachers in the Diocese:	
Sisters	8
Lay Teachers	20
Vital Statistics	
Receptions into the Church:	
Infant Baptism Totals	351
Adult Baptism Totals	16
Received into Full Communion	79
First Communions	398
Confirmations	333
Marriages:	
Catholic	103
Interfaith	45
Total Marriages	148
Deaths	580
Total Catholic Population	59,733

Former Bishops—Most Rev. STEPHEN J. KOCISKO, D.D., ord. March 30, 1941; appt. Titular Bishop of Theveste and Auxiliary of Exarchate of Pittsburgh, July 20, 1956; appt. First Eparch of Passaic, July 31, 1963; appt. Eparch of Pittsburgh, Dec. 21, 1967; installed March 5, 1968; elevated to Metropolitan Archbishop of Pittsburgh, Feb. 21, 1969; retired June 12, 1991; died March 7, 1995.—Most Rev. MICHAEL J. DUDICK, D.D., ord. Nov. 13, 1945; appt. Bishop of Passaic, Aug. 21, 1968; installed Oct. 24, 1968; retired Nov. 21, 1995.

Vicar General—Very Rev. GERALD DINO, O.E.S.L.

Syncelli-Episcopal Vicars of the Eparchy—

Susquehanna—Very Rev. JOHN CIGAN, *Holy Spirit Church, 360 Clinton St., Binghamton, NY, 13905.* Tel: 607-797-2122.

Central PA—Very Rev. LEONARD M. HOLLICK, *Saint Michael Church, 17 E. Blaine St., McAdoo, PA, 18237.* Tel: 717-929-1062.

New Jersey—Very Rev. BASIL RAKACZKY, O.S.B.M., *Saint Michael Church, 401 Hall Ave., Perth Amboy, NJ, 08861.* Tel: 732-826-0792.

New York-New England—Rev. Msgr. ROBERT SENETSKY, J.C.D., *Saints Peter and Paul Church, 705 Shenandoah Ave., Peekskill, NY, 10566.* Tel: 914-737-8249.

Middle States—Very Rev. JOHN BASARAB, *Epiphany of Our Lord Church, 3410 Woodburn Rd., Annandale, VA, 22003.* Tel: 703-573-3986.

Southern States—Very Rev. PETER LICKMAN, *Saint Basil Church, 1475 N.E. 199th Street, Miami, FL, 33179.* Tel: 305-651-0991.

Chancery Office—Eparchial Center, 445 Lackawanna Ave., W. Paterson, NJ, 07424. Tel: 973-890-7777; Fax: 973-890-7175. Office Hours: Mon.-Fri. 9-12 & 1-4.

Chancellor—Very Rev. ROBERT J. HOSPODAR, J.C.L.

Eparchial Finance Council—Very Rev. GERALD N. DINO, O.E.S.L.; Mr. FRANK FERRANTE, Attorney; Mr. RAYMOND DONOVAN; Mr. BERT REIMAN; Mr. JERRY LUCAS; Ms. VICKI WINDSOR; Mr. DOMINIC TANGREDI.

Canonical Consultant to the Bishop—Rev. BENEDICT A. DESOCIO, J.C.L.

Eparchial College of Consultors—Very Rev. GERALD DINO, O.E.S.L.; Very Rev. JOHN CIGAN; Very Rev. LEONARD M. HOLLICK; Very Rev. BASIL RAKACZKY, O.S.B.M.; Rev. Msgr. ROBERT SENETSKY, J.C.D.; Very Rev. JOHN BASARAB; Very Rev. PETER LICKMAN; Very Rev. ROBERT J. HOSPODAR, J.C.L.

Presbyteral Council—Ex Officio Members: Very Rev. GERALD DINO, O.E.S.L.; Very Rev. JOHN CIGAN; Very Rev. LEONARD M. HOLLICK; Very Rev. BASIL RAKACZKY, O.S.B.M.; Rev. Msgr. ROBERT SENETSKY, J.C.D.; Very Rev. JOHN BASARAB; Very Rev. PETER LICKMAN; Rev. Msgr. RAYMOND M. MISULICH, J.C.L. Elected Members: Very Rev. EDWARD G. CIMBALA; Revs. NICHOLAS DEPROSPERO; JOHN ZEYACK; Very Rev. CONAN TIMONEY; Revs. BASIL KRAYNYAK; ANDOR RAKACZKI. Appointed Members:: Rev. Msgr. ALAN BORSUK; Very Rev. ROBERT J. HOSPODAR, J.C.L.

Protopresbyters - Deans—Northern PA - Northern NY: Very Rev. EDWARD CIMBALA, Mid-PA: Very Rev. MICHAEL MONDIK, South PA: Very Rev. GREGORY J. NOGA, Northern NJ: Rev. Msgr. ROBERT G. MONETA, Central NJ: Very Rev. ROBERT RADVANSKY, New York - New England: Very Rev. ROBERT J. HOSPODAR, J.C.L., Middle States: Very Rev. CONAN TIMONEY, Southern States: Very Rev. ROBERT EVANCHO.

Eparchial Tribunal—445 Lackawanna Ave., West Paterson, NJ, 07424. Tel: 973-890-7777.

Judicial Vicar—Rev. Msgr. JOHN T. SEKELLICK, J.C.L.

Moderator of the Tribunal / Adjutant Judicial Vicar—Rev. BENEDICT A. DESOCIO, J.C.L.

Auditor—Rev. ROBERT J. WOYTEK, J.C.L.

Defender of the Bond—Rev. ROBERT J. HOSPODAR, J.C.L.

Promotor of Justice—Rev. ROBERT J. HOSPODAR, J.C.L.

Notaries—M. E. GAFFNEY.

Commissions, Departments and Institutions

Altar Boys Retreat Camp—Rev. JAMES HAYER.

Boy Scouts—Vacant.

Building and Properties Commission—Rev. Msgr. RAYMOND M. MISULICH, J.C.L., Chm.

Cemeteries Commission—Rev. Msgr. RAYMOND M. MISULICH, J.C.L., Chm.

Clergy Continued Education—Rev. JOHN ZEYACK, S.T.L., Dir.

Commission for Ecumenism—Rev. Msgr. ALAN BORSUK, Chm.

Communications and Telecommunications—Rev. JAMES HAYEN.

Evangelization—Rev. EDWARD G. CIMBALA, Chm.

Respect Life—Very Rev. ROBERT J. HOSPODAR, J.C.L., Chm.

Family Life—Rev. Msgr. JOHN T. SEKELLICK, J.C.L., Chm.

Eparchial Historian—Very Rev. ROBERT J. HOSPODAR, J.C.L.
Holy Name Society—Rev. Msgr. ROBERT G. MONETA, Chm.
Eparchial Liturgy and Art Commission—Rev. Msgr. ALAN BORSUK, Chm.
Eparchial Music Commission—Rev. ROBERT G. MONETA, Chm.
Eparchial Newspaper—The Eastern Catholic Life; Rev. JAMES HAYER, Editor; Rev. MATTHEW BUTRIE, Business Mgr./Assoc. Editor; Rev. GLENN DAVIDOWICH, Assoc. Editor. Tel: 973-890-7794.
Office of Religious Education—Dr. RICHARD NOVAK, Dir.
Retirement Plan Board—Under Review for Revision.
Saint Nicholas Shrine - Carpathian Village—Rev. MICHAEL SALNICKY, Dir., *P.O. Box 616, Canadensis, PA, 18325.* Tel: 717-595-3265.
Vocations—Revs. EDWARD G. CIMBALA, Chm.
Priesthood & Diaconate Formation Programs—Rev. EDWARD G. CIMBALA, Dir.
Vicar for Clergy—Vacant.
Vicar for Religious—Vacant.
Eastern Catholic Associates—Publication: God With Us; *445 Lackawanna Ave., West Paterson, NJ, 07424.*

CLERGY, PARISHES, MISSIONS AND PAROCHIAL SCHOOLS

STATE OF NEW JERSEY

Passaic, Passaic Co., St. Michael Cathedral, Rev. Marcel Szabo.
Res., 96 First St., 07055. Tel: 973-777-2553. [CEM]
Chapel—415 Lackawanna Ave., West Paterson, 07424. Tel: 973-256-0134.

Bayonne, Hudson Co., St. John the Baptist, Rev. Michael Yurista.
Res., 15 E. 26th St., 07002. Tel: 201-339-1840; Fax: 201-339-2640.

Carteret, Middlesex Co., St. Elias, Rev. Edward Semko.
Res., 42 Cooke Ave., 07008. Tel: 732-541-5213.

Dunellen, Middlesex Co., St. Nicholas, Rev. Leonard Kuberski.
Res., 121 Madison Ave., 08812. Tel: 732-968-3337.

East Brunswick, Middlesex Co., Nativity of Our Lord, Rev. James Hayer.
Res., 700 Old Bridge Tpke., 08816. Tel: 732-238-0865; Fax: 732-238-2950.

Edison, Middlesex Co., St. Nicholas, Very Rev. Robert J. Radvansky, Admin.; Rev. J. Michael Venditti.
Res., 215 May St., 08837. Tel: 732-661-1160.

Hillsborough Township, Somerset Co., St. Mary's, Rev. Msgr. Alan J. Borsuk.
Res., 1900 Brook Blvd., 08876. Tel: 908-725-0615.

Elizabeth, Union Co., SS. Peter and Paul, Rev. Michael Chubirko, S.D.B.
Res., 316 First Ave., 07206. Tel: 908-353-7246.

Flanders, Morris Co., Holy Wisdom, Rev. Daniel Staniskis.
Res., 197 Emmans Rd., 07836. Tel: 973-584-0414.

Jersey City, Hudson Co., St. Mary's, Rev. Robert J. Skurla.
Res., 231 Pacific Ave., 07304. Tel: 201-333-2975.

Linden, Union Co., St. George's, Very Rev. Gerald Dino, O.E.S.L.; Deacon William Tizio.
Res., 417 McCandless St., 07036. Tel: 908-486-6500; Fax: 908-486-6523.

Mahwah, Bergen Co., Holy Spirit, Rev. Marcel Szabo, Admin.
Res., Island Rd. at Church St., P.O. Box 825, 07430. Tel: 973-529-3269.

Newark, Essex Co., St. George, Rev. Msgr. Robert G. Moneta.
Res., 214 Warwick St., 07105. Tel: 973-589-7202.

New Brunswick, Middlesex Co., St. Joseph, Rev. Joseph Homa.
Res., 30 High St., 08901. Tel: 732-545-1686.

Perth Amboy, Middlesex Co., St. Nicholas, Very Rev. Robert J. Radvansky.
Res., 320 Washington St., 08861. Tel: 732-442-0418; Fax: 732-442-9120. [CEM]
St. Michael, Very Rev. Basil M. Rakaczky, O.S.B.M.
Res., 401 Hall Ave., 08861. Tel: 732-826-0792; Fax: 732-826-7993.

Phillipsburg, Warren Co., SS. Peter and Paul, Rev. Stephen Safko.
Res., 723 S. Main St., 08865. Tel: 908-454-5482.

Rahway, Union Co., St. Thomas the Apostle, Rev. John Zeyack, S.T.L.
Res., 1410 Church St., 07065. Tel: 732-382-5300.

Roebling, Burlington Co., St. Nicholas, Rev. Lawrence Wolf, O.S.B.M., Admin.
Res., 191 Norman Ave., 08554. Tel: 609-499-0058. [CEM]
Mission—South Hampton Twp., Vincentown Co., St. Jude, 50 Burrs Mill Rd., South Hampton Twp., 08088.

Somerset, Somerset Co., SS. Peter and Paul, Rev. Matthew Peter Butrie.
Res., 285 Hamilton St., 08873. Tel: 732-545-5500.

Toms River, Ocean Co., Our Lady of Perpetual Help, Rev. Charles Yastishock.
Res., 1937 Church Rd., 08753. Tel: 732-255-6272.

Trenton, Mercer Co., St. Mary of the Assumption, Rev. Msgr. Nicholas I. Puhak, V.F.; Deacon Thomas L. Vanisko.
Res., 411 Adeline St., 08611. Tel: 609-394-5004. [CEM]
School—Joyce Olshansky, Prin. Sisters of St. Basil the Great 2; Lay Teachers 7; Students 177.
Chapel—Hamilton Township, St. Mary Chapel.
St. Nicholas, Rev. Stephen J. Skinta, O.S.B.M.
Church—111 Adeline St., 08611. Tel: 609-695-5962. [CEM]
Res., 360 Monastery Ln., Matawan, 07747. Tel: 908-566-8445.

STATE OF CONNECTICUT

Bridgeport, Fairfield Co., Holy Trinity, Rev. Andor Rakaczki, S.T.D.
Res., 155 Scofield Ave., 06605. Tel: 203-334-7089; Fax: 203-334-5226.

Danbury, Fairfield Co., St. Nicholas, Rev. Michael George Popson.
Res., 13 Pembroke Rd., 06811. Tel: 203-743-1106; Fax: 203-743-5326.

Meriden, New Haven Co., St. Nicholas of Myra. Attended by Danbury.
Mailing Address: c/o 13 Pembroke Rd., Danbury, 06810.
Church—89 Summer St., 06450.

New Britain, Hartford Co., Holy Trinity, Rev. Alan Kapron.
Res., 121 Beaver St., 06051. Tel: 860-229-2531. [CEM]

Trumbull, Fairfield Co., St. John the Baptist, Rev. Glenn M. Davidowich, Admin.; Deacon William Sedlock.
Res., 100 St. John's Dr., 06611. Tel: 203-377-5967; Fax: 203-377-5968.

STATE OF FLORIDA

Coconut Creek, Broward Co., Our Lady of the Sign, Rev. Michael N. Kane.
Res., 7311 Lyons Rd., 33073. Tel: 954-429-0056.

Fort Pierce, Port St. Lucie Co., SS. Cyril and Methodius, Rev. Nicholas Kusevich.
Church—1002 Bahama Ave., P.O. Box 13015, 34979. Tel: 561-595-1021; Fax: 561-968-2021.

Jacksonville, Duval Co., Protection of the Mother of God. Closed. For inquiries for parish records, contact Holy Dormition, Ormond Beach, FL.

Lake Worth, Duval Co., Holy Apostles, Rev. Nicholas Kusevich.
Res., 4788 Clock Rd., 33463. Tel: 561-968-8500; Fax: 561-968-2021.

Miami, Dade Co., St. Basil's, Very Rev. Peter Lickman; Deacon Ford Slagle.
Res., 1475 N.E. 199 St., 33179. Tel: 305-651-0991; Fax: 305-651-4902.

New Port Richey, Pasco Co., St. Anne's, Rev. Basil William Kraynyak; Deacon John Buga.
Church and Res.: 7120 Massachusetts Ave., 34653. Tel: 813-849-1190.

North Fort Myers, Lee Co., All Saints Byzantine Catholic, Rev. James Mitchko.
Res., 10291 Bayshore Rd., 33917. Tel: 941-543-6363.
Mission—Naples.

Orlando, Orange Co., St. Nicholas of Myra, Rev. Salvatore A. Pignato; Deacon Robert Thanski.
Res., 5135 Sand Lake Rd., 32819. Tel: 407-351-0133.
Mission—Melbourne.

Ormond Beach, Volusia Co., Holy Dormition, Rev. Francis Gera.
Res., 17 Buckskin Ln., 32174. Tel: 904-677-8704.
Mission—St. Augustine, Protection of the Mother of God.

St. Petersburg, Pinellas Co., St. Therese, Very Rev. Robert Evancho; Deacon Joseph Ciarciaglino.
Res., 4226 33rd Ave., N., 33713. Tel: 813-323-4022; Fax: 813-323-8351.
Convent—1200 37th St., N., 33713. Tel: 813-322-0003.

STATE OF GEORGIA

Roswell, Fulton Co., Epiphany Byzantine Church, Rev. Philip P. Scott; Deacon Charles Appel.
Res., 2030 Old Alabama Rd., 30076. Tel: 770-993-0973.

STATE OF MARYLAND

Baltimore, Baltimore Co., Patronage of the Mother of God, Very Rev. Conan H. Timoney, C.P.
Church—1260 Stevens Ave., 21227. Tel: 410-247-4936.
Missions—Abingdon, St. Francis; Hagerstown, St. Ann's.

Beltsville, Prince George's Co., St. Gregory of Nyssa, Rev. Michael Kerestes.
Res., 12420 Old Gunpowder Rd., 20705. Tel: 301-953-9323; Fax: 301-953-1529.

STATE OF MASSACHUSETTS

South Hadley, Hampshire Co., St. Michael's. Attended by Holy Trinity, New Britain, CT.
Mailing Address: c/o 121 Beaver St., New Britain, CT 06051. Tel: 860-229-2531.
Church—15 Lincoln Ave., 01075.

STATE OF NEW YORK

Amherst, Erie Co., St. Stephen's, Rev. Joseph Bertha; Deacon Chester Fortuna, M.D.
Res., 620 Ayer Rd., Williamsville, 14221. Tel: 716-688-9290.

Binghamton, Broome Co., Holy Spirit, Very Rev. John J. Cigan.
Res., 360 Clinton St., 13905. Tel: 607-797-2122; Fax: 607-797-2167. [CEM]

Brooklyn, Kings Co., St. Elias. Administered from St. Mary's, New York.
Church—143 Kent St., 11232.
Saint Mary's Chapel. Attended by St. Mary's, New York.
Mailing Address: c/o St. Mary's: 246 E. 15th St., New York, 10003.
Church—197 34th St., 11232.

Endicott, Broome Co., SS. Peter and Paul's. Administered from Binghamton, NY. In res., Rev. Vincent M. Brady.
Res., 106 N. Rogers Ave., 13760. Tel: 607-785-3132. [CEM]

Granville, Washington Co., SS. Peter and Paul, Rev. Harold Stockert.
Res., 2 Park Ave., 12832. Tel: 518-642-2884; Fax: 518-642-1556. [CEM]

New York, New York Co., Exaltation of Holy Cross. Administered from St. Nicholas of Myra, White Plains, NY. Tel: 914-681-0659.
Church—323 E. 82nd St., 10028.
St. Mary's, Rev. Msgr. Raymond M. Misulich, J.C.L.; Rev. George Michael Malitz.
Res., 246 E. 15th St., 10003. Tel: 212-677-0516; Fax: 212-260-6071.

Olean, Cattaragus Co., St. Mary's. Administered from Amherst.

Peekskill, Westchester Co., SS. Peter and Paul, Rev. Msgr. Robert Senetsky, J.C.D.
Res., 705 Shenandoah Ave., 10566. Tel: 914-737-8249; Fax: 914-737-8438.

Smithtown, Suffolk Co., Resurrection, Rev. Daniel J. Bitsko.
Res., 37 Juniper Ave., 11787. Tel: 516-724-4979.

Westbury, Nassau Co., St. Andrew the Apostle, Rev. Daniel J. Bitsko, Admin.; Deacon Nicholas Daddona.
Church—275 Ellison Ave., 11590. Tel: 516-333-3266; 724-4979 (Office).

White Plains, Westchester Co., St. Nicholas of Myra, Very Rev. Robert J. Hospodar, J.C.L.
Res., 768 North St., 10605. Tel: 914-681-0659; Fax: 914-681-0238.

Yonkers, Westchester Co., St. Nicholas of Myra. Attended by St. Nicholas of Myra, White Plains. Rev. Robert J. Hospodar.
Mailing Address: c/o St. Nicholas of Myra, 768 North St., White Plains, 10605. Tel: 914-681-0659.

STATE OF NORTH CAROLINA

Cary, Wake Co., SS. Cyril & Methodius Byzantine Catholic, Rev. Richard Rohrer.
Res., 2510 Piney Plains Rd., 27511. Tel: 919-851-9266; Fax: 919-233-3997.

STATE OF PENNSYLVANIA

Allentown, Lehigh Co., St. Andrew the Apostle. Unassigned. Attended by St. Michael, Allentown.
Church—518 N. Second St., 18102. Tel: 610-432-6773.
St. Michael, Rev. Peter J. Hosak.
Res., 156 Green St., 18102. Tel: 610-432-6773.

Beaver Meadows, Carbon Co., SS. Peter and Paul, Rev. Peter Donish; Deacon Michael Pataki.
Res., P.O. Box 206, 18216. Tel: 717-455-1442; Fax:

717-455-7144. [CEM]

Bethlehem, Northampton Co., SS. Peter and Paul, Rev. Robert Slesinski, Ph.D.
Res., 1140 Johnston Dr., 18017. Tel: 610-867-2322; Fax: 610-867-7274.

Brockton, Schuylkill Co., St. Mary's. Attended by St. Clair.
131 S. Morris St., St. Clair, 17970. Tel: 717-429-0520.

Clarks Summit, Lackawanna Co., Transfiguration. Attended by St. Mary, Scranton.
Res., 1105 Gravel Pond Rd., 18411. Tel: 717-586-0100.

Coaldale, Schuylkill Co., St. John's. Attended by Lansford.
116 E. Bertsch St., Lansford, 18232. Tel: 717-645-2640.

Coatesville, Chester Co., St. Mary's, Very Rev. Gregory J. Noga, Admin.
Mailing Address: c/o St. Michael's, 203 Jacob St., Mont Clare, 19453. Tel: 610-933-2819; Fax: 610-935-9460.

Doylestown, Bucks Co., Christ the Saviour Byzantine Catholic Church at Our Lady of Czestochawa Shrine, Rev. Robert Lucas.
Res., 310 Aquetong Rd., New Hope, 18938. Tel: 215-862-9227.
Church—Ferry Rd., 18901.

Dunmore, Lackawanna Co., St. Michael, Rev. Theodore Rudy.
Res., 511 E. Drinker St., 18512. Tel: 717-344-2521. [CEM]

Forest City, Susquehanna Co., St. John the Baptist, Rev. Edward Stanko.
Res., 306 Susquehanna St., 18421. Tel: 717-785-5296. [CEM]

Freeland, Luzerne Co., St. Mary's, Rev. James Demko.
Res., 643 Fern St., 18224. Tel: 717-636-0700. [CEM]

Harrisburg, Dauphin Co., St. Ann, Rev. Michael P. Shear; Deacon George Kashi.
4709 Rockledge Dr., 17110. Tel: 717-236-2053.
Res., 5408 Locust Lane, 17109. Tel: 717-652-1415; Fax: 717-652-5471.

Hazleton, Luzerne Co., St. John the Baptist Church, Rev. Msgr. John Opalenick.
Res., 5 E. 20th St., 18201. Tel: 717-454-1142; Fax: 717-454-6120. [CEM 2]
School—201 N. Wyoming St., 18201. Tel: 717-454-5812. Sr. M. Leonora, O.S.B.M., Prin.
Sisters of St. Basil the Great 3; Students 95.
St. Mary's, Rev. Ronald Barusefski.
Res., 227 E. Beech St., 18201. Tel: 717-455-3232. [CEM]

Jessup, Lackawanna Co., Holy Ghost, Very Rev. Edward G. Cimbala.
Res., 313 First St., 18434. Tel: 717-489-2353; Fax: 717-489-7049. [CEM]
School—LaSalle Academy, Tel: 717-489-2010. Sr. M. Christopher Godlewski, S.S.C.M., Prin.
Sisters 4; Lay Teachers 22; Students 580.

Kingston, Luzerne Co., St. Mary's, Rev. Theodore Krepp.
Res., 321 Chestnut Ave., 18704. Tel: 717-287-0282; Fax: 717-283-0464. [CEM]

Lansford, Carbon Co., St. John the Baptist, Rev. Michael Krulak.
Res., 116 E. Bertsch St., 18232. Tel: 717-645-2640. [CEM]

Levittown, Bucks Co., Our Lady of Perpetual Help, Rev. Myron M. Badnerosky.
Res., 1787 Woodburne Rd., 19056. Tel: 215-945-5122.

Lopez, Sullivan Co., SS. Peter and Paul, Rev. Michael Mokris, Admin.
472 Church St., Swoyersville, 18704. Tel: 717-287-2306.

McAdoo, Schuylkill Co., St. Michael, Very Rev. Leonard Hollick.
Res., 17 E. Blaine St., 18237. Tel: 717-929-1062; Fax: 717-929-3239. [CEM]

Mahanoy City, Schuylkill Co., St. Mary's, Rev. Edward J. Higgins.
Res., 621 W. Mahanoy Ave., 17948. Tel: 717-773-2631. [CEM]

Minersville, Schuylkill Co., SS. Peter and Paul, Very Rev. Michael Mondik.
Res., 107 S. Fourth St., 17954. Tel: 717-544-2074; Fax: 717-544-2074. [CEM]

Mont Clare, Montgomery Co., St. Michael, Very Rev. Gregory J. Noga.
Res., 203 Jacob St., 19453. Tel: 610-933-2819; Fax: 610-935-9460.

Nanticoke, Luzerne Co., St. Mary's (Hanover). Attended by St. John's.
526 Church St., Wilkes-Barre, 18702.

Nesquehoning, Carbon Co., St. Mary's, Rev. George A. Bujnak.
Res., 141 W. High St., 18240. Tel: 717-669-6533. [CEM]

Old Forge, Lackawanna Co., St. Nicholas, Revs. Michael J. Salnicky, Admin.; Nicholas Kraynak.
Res., 140 Church St., 18518. Tel: 717-457-3042; Fax: 717-457-1906. [CEM]
Chapels—St. Nicholas, (1973), Rte. 940, Mount Pocono, 18344.; Saint Mary's, (1907), 700 Oak St., Taylor, 18517. [CEM]

Palmerton, Carbon Co., SS. Peter and Paul. Attended by St. Michael's, Allentown.
156 Green St., Allentown, 18102. Tel: 610-432-6773.

Philadelphia, Philadelphia Co., Holy Ghost, Rev. Eugene M. Hutter.
Res., 2310 S. 24th St., 19145. Tel: 215-334-5129.
Holy Trinity. Attended by Holy Ghost, Philadelphia. In res., Rev. Austin Mohrbacher.
Res., 6801 N. 10th St., 19126. Tel: 215-548-2837.

Pittston, Luzerne Co., St. Michael, Rev. Robert Kemeter.
Res., 205 N. Main St., 18640. Tel: 717-654-4564. [CEM]

Pottstown, Montgomery Co., St. John the Baptist, Rev. Nicholas DeProspero; Deacon Michael Erdek.
Res., 301 Cherry St., 19464. Tel: 610-326-1877; Fax: 610-326-1890. [CEM]

St. Clair, Schuylkill Co., St. Mary's, Rev. Christopher Petruska.
Res., 131 S. Morris St., 17970. Tel: 717-429-0520. [CEM]

Scranton, Lackawanna Co., St. John the Baptist, Rev. Robert W. Lozinski, C.S.C.
Res., 310 Broadway, 18505. Tel: 717-342-8930. [CEM]
St. Mary's Byzantine Catholic Church, Rev. Francis M. Twardzik, S.D.B.
Res., 310 Mifflin Ave., 18503. Tel: 717-342-8429. [CEM]

Sheppton, Schuylkill Co., St. Mary's. Attended by SS. Peter and Paul.
P.O. Box 206, Beaver Meadows, 18216. [CEM]

Swoyersville, Luzerne Co., St. Nicholas, Rev. Robert Woytek, J.C.L.
Res., 271 Tripp St., 18704. Tel: 717-287-4418. [CEM]

Taylor, Lackawanna Co., St. Mary's. Attended by Old Forge.
Res., 700 Oak St., 18517. Tel: 717-457-3042. [CEM]

Wilkes-Barre, Luzerne Co., St. Mary's, Rev. Msgr. John T. Sekellick, J.C.L.; Rev. Jody Baran.
Res., 695 N. Main St., 18705. Tel: 717-822-6028; Fax: 717-823-5423. [CEM]
School—522 Madison St., 18705. Tel: 717-823-8003; Fax: 717-823-8003. Sr. Janet Decker, O.S.B.M., Prin.
Sisters of St. Basil the Great 3; Students 191.
Mission—Glen Lyon, Luzerne Co., St. Michael.
St. John's, Rev. John Balog.
Res., 526 Church St., 18702. Tel: 717-825-4338; Fax: 717-825-0786.

Williamstown, Dauphin Co., Holy Spirit. Attended by Minersville.
107 S. Fourth St., Minersville, 17954. Tel: 717-544-2074. [CEM]

STATE OF VIRGINIA

Annandale, Fairfax Co., Epiphany of Our Lord, Very Rev. John G. Basarab; Deacons Gerald McDonnell; Vincent Obsitnik.
Res., 3410 Woodburn Rd., 22003. Tel: 703-573-3986; Fax: 703-573-0344.

Williamsburg, York Co., Ascension of Our Lord, Rev. Ronald Hatton.
Church—114 Palace Ln., 23185. Tel: 757-220-8098.
Res., 4528 Wimbledon Way, 23188. Tel: 757-253-5641; Fax: 757-253-9423.
Mission—Virginia Beach, Virginia Beach Co., Our Lady of Perpetual Help, 216 S. Parliament Dr., Virginia Beach, 23462. Tel: 757-456-0809.

Special or Other Diocesan Assignment:
Reverend Fathers—
DeSocio, Benedict, J.C.L., Chancery Office, 445 Lackawanna Ave., West Paterson, NJ 07424

On Duty Outside Diocese:
Reverend Fathers—
Custer, John S., SS. Cyril & Methodius Seminary, 3605 Perrysville Ave., Pittsburgh, PA 15214. Tel: 412-321-8383; 321-9936 (Fax)
DeFronzo, Anthony R., 767 Elm St., Rocky Hill, CT 06064
Fulton, Eugene, Larchmont Trinity Retreat, One Pryer Manor Rd., Larchmont, NY 10538. Tel: 914-632-3743
Hamperzonian, Jerry, Chap., VA Medical Center, 3350 La Jolla Village Dr., San Diego, CA 92161

Leave of Absence:
Reverend Fathers—
Drucker, James
Matrishion, Joseph
Paulshock, Emil
Siroki, David
Sopoliga, Michael

Absent on Sick Leave:
Reverend Fathers—
Czachor, Christopher
Kanar, Richard

Retired:
Reverend Monsignors—
Jackanich, Joseph, 4036 Lockwood Blvd., Youngstown, OH 44511. Tel: 216-505-0302
Reverend Fathers—
Billy, George, 404 McCandless St., Linden, NJ 07036. Tel: 908-925-5211
Brown, Charles, M.D., 432 N. Rose Ln., Haverford, PA 19126
Danilak, John, c/o 15 Sara Ln., Limerick, PA 19468-1049
Eles, Joseph, 150 Horizons E., Apt. 305, Boynton Beach, FL 33435. Tel: 407-731-2682
Luzetsky, Stephen, Juniper Manor, 70 W. Juniper St., Hazleton, PA 18201
Musko, Andrew, Holy Family Manor, 1200 Spring St., Bethlehem, PA 18018. Tel: 610-865-5595
Onesko, John, 440 Seaview Ave., Abscon, NJ 08902
Tigyer, Paul, P.O. Box 658, Hamlin, PA 18427. Tel: 717-689-2153

Permanent Deacons:
Appel, Charles M.
Buga, John
Ciarciaglino, Joseph M.
Daddona, Nicholas
Erdek, Michael A.
Fortuna, Chester
Guze, John G.
Kashi, George
Kuntz, Edward E.
McDonnell, Gerald E.
Obsitnik, Vincent
Pataki, Michael
Sedlock, William
Slagle, Ford
Thanski, Robert
Tizio, William
Vanisko, Thomas L.

INSTITUTIONS LOCATED IN THE DIOCESE

[A] MONASTERIES

MATAWAN. *Basilian Fathers of Mariapoch*, 360 Monastery Ln., 07747. Tel: 732-566-8445. Very Rev. Joseph J. Erdei, O.S.B.M., Supr.; Revs. Basil M. Rakaczky, O.S.B.M.; Stephen J. Skinta, O.S.B.M.; Lawrence Robert Wolf, O.S.B.M.

SYBERTSVILLE, PA. *Holy Dormition Monastery*, P.O. Box 270, 18251. Tel: 717-788-1212; Fax: 717-788-1212. Very Rev. James Carroll, O.F.M., Protohegumen; Revs. Paul Guthrie, O.F.M.; John Kapitan, O.F.M.; Marion Kawola, O.F.M.; Anthony Skurla, O.F.M.; Bros. William Benjamin, O.F.M.; Augustine Paulik, O.F.M.; Andrew Martino, O.F.M.; Douglas Shannon, O.F.M., Franciscan Friary, 50 Friars Ln., P.O. Box 4815, Stamford, CT, 06907. Tel: 203-322-0570.

[B] CONVENTS AND RESIDENCES FOR SISTERS

SUGARLOAF, PA. *Holy Annunciation Monastery*, R.R. 1, Box 1336, 18249. Tel: 717-788-1205. Discalced Byzantine Carmelite Nuns. Mother Marija of the Holy Spirit, O.C.D., Prioress. Nuns with Solemn Vows 8; Nuns with Temporary Vows 3; Novices 1.

[C] MISCELLANEOUS

PASSAIC. *Eastern Catholic Associates*, 96 First St., 07055. God with Us Publications, 445 Lackawanna Ave., West Paterson, 07424. Most Revs. Nicholas Samra, Pres.; Robert Moskal, Vice Pres.; Rt. Rev. John M. Boean, Sec.; Most Rev. Andrew Pataki, J.C.L., Registered Agent.

MIAMI, FL.
**Holy Cross Community*, 1245 Sunset Dr., 33183. Tel: 305-598-0009; Fax: 305-598-8455. Rev. Archimandrite Frank (Gregory) Wendt; Rev. Damian Gibault.

RELIGIOUS INSTITUTES OF MEN REPRESENTED IN THE DIOCESE

For further details refer to the corresponding bracketed number in the Religious Institutes of Men or Women section.

[0520]—*Franciscan Friars.*—O.F.M.

[0180]—*Order of St. Basil the Great.*—O.S.B.M.

RELIGIOUS INSTITUTES OF WOMEN REPRESENTED IN THE DIOCESE

[0420]—*Discalced Carmelite Nuns (Byzantine Rite).*—O.C.D.

[3730]—*Sisters of the Order of St. Basil the Great.*—O.S.B.M.

NECROLOGY

† Bovankovich, John, (Retired). —Died Nov. 11, 1997.

† Boysak, Basil, (Retired). —Died Aug. 20, 1997.

† Moskva, Emil, (Retired). —Died Jan. 26, 1997.

† Zajac, Rev. Msgr. Stephen, Old Forge, PA, St. Nicholas of Myra. —Died Oct. 10, 1997.

Metropolitan Archdiocese of Philadelphia Ukrainian

Most Reverend

STEPHEN SULYK, D.D.

Archbishop of Archdiocese of Philadelphia for Ukrainians; appointed Archbishop of Philadelphia for Ukrainians and Metropolitan of the Ukrainian Catholic Church in the USA on December 29, 1980. *Res., 827 N. Franklin St., Philadelphia, PA, 19123.*

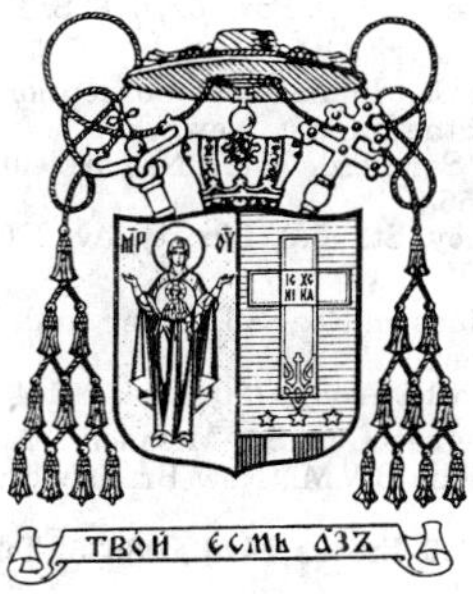

Chancery Office: 827 N. Franklin St., Philadelphia, PA, 19123. Tel.: 215-627-0143; Fax: 215-627-0377.

Most Reverend

WALTER PASKA

Auxiliary Bishop of Philadelphia Ukrainian; appointed February 4, 1992.

ESTABLISHED MAY 28, 1913.

The jurisdiction of the Metropolitan Archdiocese of Philadelphia includes the District of Columbia, the States of Virginia, Maryland, Delaware, New Jersey and eastern Pennsylvania to the eastern boundaries of the following Counties: Potter, Clinton, Center, Mifflin, Huntington and Fulton. With regard to persons, his subjects are all Catholics of the Byzantine Rite: 1. Who immigrated to this country from Galicia, Bucovina and other Ukrainian provinces; 2. Who descend from such persons (can. 755); 3. Women married to men referable to 1. and 2. if they comply with can. 98, n. 4; 4. Who in accordance with can. 98, n. 3 changed their Rite; 5. Converts to the Catholic Church of the Byzantine Rite; 6. And in fact all other Catholics of the Byzantine Rite who are attached to parishes subject to the jurisdiction of the Archbishop.

For legal titles of parishes and archdiocesan institutions, consult the Chancery Office.

STATISTICAL OVERVIEW

Personnel	
Archbishop	1
Auxiliary Bishops	1
Priests: Diocesan Active in Diocese	43
Priests: Active Outside Diocese	1
Priests: Retired, Sick or Absent	13
Number of Diocesan Priests	57
Religious Priests in Diocese	5
Extern Priests in Diocese	9
Permanent Deacons in Diocese	5
Total Brothers	3
Total Sisters	85
Parishes	
Parishes	77
With Resident Pastor:	
Resident Diocesan Priests	44
Resident Religious Priests	2
Without Resident Pastor:	
Administered by Priests	31
Professional Ministry Personnel:	
Brothers	3
Sisters	3
Welfare	
Homes for the Aged	1
Total Assisted	55
Day Care and Extended Day Care Centers	2
Total Assisted	40
Educational	
Seminaries, Diocesan	1
Students from This Diocese	18
Total Seminarians	18
Colleges and Universities	1
Total Students	693
High Schools, Private	1
Total Students	371
Elementary Schools, Diocesan and Parish	7
Total Students	1,704
Catechesis/Religious Education:	
High School Students	426
Elementary Students	2,610
Total Students Under Catholic Instruction	5,822
Teachers in the Diocese:	
Priests	2
Sisters	25
Lay Teachers	300
Vital Statistics	
Receptions into the Church:	
Infant Baptism Totals	315
Adult Baptism Totals	38
Received into Full Communion	6
First Communions	367
Confirmations	353
Marriages:	
Catholic	123
Interfaith	22
Total Marriages	145
Deaths	528
Total Catholic Population	68,024

Former Bishops—Most Rev. STEPHEN SOTER ORTYNSKY, O.S.B.M., D.D.,First Ukrainian Catholic Bishop of the United States; ord. July 18, 1891; cons. May 12, 1907; died March 24, 1916.—Most Rev. CONSTANTINE BOHACHEVSKY, D.D., S.T.D., appt. Bishop in the United States, May 20, 1924; appt. Metropolitan Archbishop of the Philadelphia Archeparchy, Byzantine Rite, Aug. 6, 1958; cons. June 15, 1924; died Jan. 6, 1961.—Most Rev. JOSEPH M. SCHMONDIUK, D.D., appt. Titular Bishop of Zeugma and Auxiliary of the Archeparchy of Philadelphia, July 20, 1956; transferred to the Diocese of Stamford See, Nov. 9, 1961; appt. Metropolitan Archbishop of Philadelphia, Oct. 1, 1977.—Most Rev. JOHN STOCK, D.D., appt. Titular Bishop of Pergamum and Auxiliary Bishop to the Archeparchy, Feb. 22, 1971; cons. May 25, 1971; died June 29, 1972.—Most Rev. AMBROSE SENYSHYN, O.S.B.M., D.D., appt. Auxiliary Bishop to the Philadelphia Bishop, July 6, 1942; appt. Exarch of Stamford, July 20, 1956; appt. Eparch of Stamford, Nov. 1, 1958; appt. Metropolitan Archbishop of Philadelphia, Aug. 14, 1961; died Sept. 11, 1976.—Most Rev. JOSEPH M. SCHMONDIUK, D.D., cons. Nov. 8, 1956; Archbishop of Archeparchy, Oct. 1, 1977; died Dec. 25, 1978.—His Eminence MYROSLAV CARDINAL LUBACHIVSKY, D.D., cons. Nov. 12, 1979; named Co-adjutor Major Archbishop of Lviw, March 24, 1980; transferred to Rome Assumed position of Major Archbishop of Lviw, Sept. 7, 1984. Created Cardinal, June 28, 1991.

Protosycellus—Most Rev. WALTER PASKA, J.C.D.

Chancellor—Sr. THOMAS HRYNEWICH, S.S.M.I. Tel: 215-627-0143.

Chancery Office—827 N. Franklin St., Philadelphia, PA, 19123-2097. Tel: 215-627-0143; Fax: 215-627-0377.

College of Archeparchial Counsultors—Most Rev. STEPHEN SULYK, D.D.; Most Rev. WALTER PASKA, J.C.D.; Rev. Msgr. JOHN BURA; Rev. Msgr. JOSEPH FEDOREK; Revs. ROMAN DUBITSKY; MARION KAWOLA, O.F.M.; Rev. Msgr. JAMES MELNIC.

Presbyteral Council—Most Rev. STEPHEN SULYK, D.D.; Most Rev. WALTER PASKA, J.C.D.; Rev. Msgr. JOHN BURA; Rev. ROMAN DUBITSKY; Rev. Msgr. MICHAEL FEDOROWICH; Rev. JOHN FIELDS; Rev. Archpriest MICHAEL HUTSKO; Revs. MARIAN KAWOLA, O.F.M.; NICK KOSTIUK; PAUL LABINSKY; Rev. Msgr. JAMES MELNIC; Rev. Msgr. RAYMOND REVAK; Rev. JOHN SENIW.

Archeparchial Corporation—Most Rev. STEPHEN SULYK, D.D., Pres.; Most Rev. WALTER PASKA, J.C.D., Vice Pres.; Rev. Msgr. JAMES MELNIC, Sec.; Revs. ROMAN DUBITSKY; JOHN FIELDS.

Archdiocesan Tribunal—827 N. Franklin St., Philadelphia, PA, 19123. Tel: 215-627-0143.

Judicial Vicar—Most Rev. WALTER PASKA, J.C.D.

Synodal Judges—Rev. Msgr. STEPHEN HRYNUCK, Ph.D.; Rev. Msgr. JOHN BILANYCH, J.U.D.; Rev. JAMES GRANT.

Defender of the Bond—Rev. DANIEL GUROVICH.

Promotor of Justice—Rev. Msgr. RONALD POPIVCHAK, Ph.D.

Notary—Sr. THOMAS HYRNEWICH, S.S.M.I.

Archeparchial Council for Economic Affairs—Most Rev. STEPHEN SULYK, D.D.; Rev. Archpriest MICHAEL HUTSKO; Revs. JOHN FIELDS; ANDREW FYLYPOWYCH; RICHARD HANUSEY; JOSEPH REH; IHOR SHUST; MICHAEL SMYLIE.

Archeparchial Econom—Rev. Archpriest MICHAEL HUTSKO; JOSEPH REH, Asst.

Protopresbyters (Deans)—Rev. Msgr. RONALD POPIVCHAK, Reading; Rev. Msgr. JAMES MELNIC, Philadelphia; Rev. Mitred Msgr. STEPHEN CHOMKO, Scranton; Rev. Msgr. JOSEPH FEDOREK; Rev. Archpriest MICHAEL HUTSKO, Shamokin.

Diocesan Offices and Directors

Acolyte Confraternity—Rev. Archpriest MICHAEL HUTSKO.

Apostleship of Prayer—Rev. JOHN SENIW.

Apostolate—Most Rev. STEPHEN SULYK, D.D.; Rev Archpriest MICHAEL HUTSKO; Rev. JOHN FIELDS.

Cemeteries—Sr. THOMAS HRYNEWICH, S.S.M.I.

Censors—Rev. Msgr. Dr. RONALD POPIVCHAK; Rev. Msgr. JOHN BURA.

Holy Name Society—Rev. JOHN CIURPITA.

Insurance Commission—Rev. Archpriest MICHAEL HUTSKO; JOSEPH REH.

League of Ukrainian Catholics—Sr. THOMAS HRYNEWICH, Archdiocesan Dir.

Press, The Way—Rev. JOHN M. FIELDS, English Editor; IVAN SKOCZYLAS, Ukrainian Editor.

Archdiocesan Bulletin—Office: *827 N. Franklin St., Philaldephia, PA, 19123.*

Priests Beneficial Fund—Most Rev. STEPHEN SULYK, D.D., Pres.; Rev. DANIEL GUROVICH, Sec. & Treas. Board Members: Rev. Archpriest MICHAEL HUTSKO; Rev. ROMAN DUBITSKY; Rev. Msgr. RAYMOND REVAK; Rev. Msgr. MICHAEL FEDOROWICH; Revs. JOHN SENIW; ANTHONY RADCHUK.

Office of Vocations—Rev. Msgr. RONALD POPIVCHAK.

Archdiocesan Radio Programs—"Christ Among Us", aired Sundays 9-9:30 am WTEL, 860 AM (Phila.); Rev. Msgr. JAMES MELNIC; Rev. JOHN SENIW.

Archieparchial Seminary Advisory and Admissions Board—Most Rev. STEPHEN SULYK, D.D.; Most Rev. WALTER PASKA, J.C.D.; Rev. Archpriest DAVID CLOONEY, Rector; Rev. Msgr. RONALD POPIVCHAK, Vocations Dir.; Rev. Msgr. JAMES MELNIC; Rev. Archpriest MICHAEL HUTSKO; Rev. JOHN FIELDS.

CLERGY, PARISHES, MISSIONS AND PAROCHIAL SCHOOLS

CITY OF PHILADELPHIA
(Philadelphia County)

1—IMMACULATE CONCEPTION OF BLESSED VIRGIN MARY, CATHEDRAL, Most Rev. Walter Paska, J.C.D.; Rev. Nestor Iwasiw.
Res., 833 N. Franklin St., 19123. Tel: 215-922-2845. [CEM]
Chapels—Immaculate Conception Cathedral Convent.; Missionary Sisters of Mother God Convent.; Chapel of St. Joseph of Arimathea and the Holy Myrrh-Bearing Women.

2—PROTECTION OF BLESSED VIRGIN MARY, Rev. T. Frank Patrylak.
Res., 100 S. Penn St., Clifton Heights, 19018. Tel: 610-626-9495.

3—ST. ANDREW. Attended by Cathedral of the Immaculate Conception, Philadelphia. In res., Rev. Ostap Oryshkewych.
427 Pine St., 19106. Tel: 215-925-7024.

4—ANNUNCIATION OF THE B.V.M., Rev. Msgr. James Melnic.
Res., 1204 Valley Rd., Melrose Park, 19127-3035. Tel: 215-635-1627.
Church—1206 Valley Rd., Melrose Park, 19127-3035.

5—ST. NICHOLAS, Revs. Evhen Moniuk (Ukraine); Wasyl Sivinsky (Ukraine).
Res., 871 N. 24th St., 19130-1988.
Church—24th & Poplar Sts., 19130-1988.

6—ST. JOSAPHAT'S, Rev. Msgr. James Melnic; Rev. Roman Pankiw (Ukraine).
Res., 2236 Orthodox St., 19137. Tel: 215-533-7968.
School—4521 Longshore Ave., 19135. Tel: 215-332-8008. Sr. Theodosia O.S.B.M., Prin.
Sisters 2; Lay Teachers 12; Students 404.
Convent—6932 Ditman St., 19135. Tel: 215-332-8488. Sisters of St. Basil the Great

7—SACRED HEART. Closed. For inquiries for parish records contact the Chancery.

8—CHRIST THE KING, Rev. Msgr. John Bilanych.
Res., 1629 W. Cayuga St., 19140. Tel: 215-455-2416.
Catechesis/Religious Programs—Students 77.

STATE OF DELAWARE

Wilmington, New Castle Co., St. Nicholas, Rev. William R. Gore, O.S.F.S.
Res., 801 Lea Blvd., 19802. Tel: 302-762-5511.

STATE OF MARYLAND

Baltimore, Baltimore Co., St. Michael's, Rev. Michael Michlik (Slovakia).
Res., 2401 Eastern Ave., 21224. Tel: 410-675-7557. [CEM]

Curtis Bay, Baltimore Co., SS. Peter and Paul. Attended by St. Michael's, Baltimore.
Church—1506 Church St., 21226-1440.

Chesapeake City, Cecil Co., St. Basil the Great. Attended by St. Nicholas, Wilmington.
Mailing Address: 801 Lea Blvd., Wilmington, DE 19802.
Catechesis/Religious Programs—Susan Hanchok, D.R.E.
Students 67.
Chapel—Chesapeake City, Sisters of St. Basil the Great.

Silver Spring, Montgomery Co., Holy Trinity, Rev. Taras R. Lonchyna, Admin.
Res., 16631 New Hampshire Ave., 20905-3919. Tel: 301-890-7730.

STATE OF NEW JERSEY

Bayonne, Hudson Co., Assumption B.V.M. Attended by SS. Peter and Paul, Jersey City.
Res., c/o SS. Peter and Paul, 30 Bentley Ave., Jersey City, 07304. Tel: 201-432-3122.
Church—30 E. 25th St., Box 260, 07002.

Carteret, Middlesex Co., St. Mary's, Rev. Anthony Radchuk.
Res., 719 Roosevelt Ave., 07008. Tel: 908-541-7678.

Cherry Hill, Camden Co., St. Michael's, Rev. John Ciurpita.
Res., 675 Cooperlanding Rd., 08002. Tel: 609-482-0938.

Elizabeth, Union Co., St. Vladimir's, Rev. Msgr. Joseph J. Fedorek; Rev. Petro Semanych (Ukraine); Deacon Arthur Dochych.
Res., 309 Grier Ave., 07202-3310. Tel: 201-352-8823. [CEM]
Catechesis/Religious Programs—Students 75.

Great Meadows, Warren Co., St. Nicholas. Attended by Holy Ghost, West Easton, PA. Rev. Bohdan Kin.
Mailing Address: c/o 315 Fourth St., West Easton, PA 18042.
Church—Rte. 46, P.O. Box 162, 07838. Tel: 908-637-4306.

Hillside, Union Co., Immaculate Conception. Attended by St. John the Baptist, Newark.
Res., 719 Sandford Ave., Newark, 07106. Tel: 201-371-1356.
Church—Bloy St. and Liberty Ave., 07205. Tel: 201-354-0472.

Jersey City, Hudson Co., SS. Peter and Paul, Rev. Marian Struc.
Res., 30 Bentley Ave., 07304. Tel: 201-432-3122.

Manville, Somerset Co., St. Michael's. Attended by Nativity of the B.V.M., New Brunswick. Rev. Paul Labinsky.
Church—1700 Brooks Blvd., 08835. Tel: 908-526-9195.

Marlboro, Monmouth Co., St. Volodymyr's. Attended by St. Mary's, Carteret.
Mailing Address: c/o 684 Alta Vista Pl., Perth Amboy, 08861. Tel: 908-826-0767.
Church—Rte. 520, 07746.
Catechesis/Religious Programs—Students 65.

Millville, Cumberland Co., St. Nicholas, Most Rev. Walter Paska; Rev. Viktor Bek (Ukraine).
Res., 373 Carmel Rd., 08332. Tel: 609-825-4826. [CEM]

Newark, Essex Co., St. John the Baptist, Revs. Frank Szadiak, C.SS.R.; John Stuchlak, C.SS.R.; Volodymyr Baran, C.SS.R.; Leonid Malkov, C.SS.R.; Bro. John Kanski, C.SS.R.
Res., 719 Sandford Ave., 07106. Tel: 201-371-1356.
School—Tel: 201-373-9359. Sr. Chrysostom Lukiw, O.S.B.M., Prin.
Sisters of St. Basil the Great 2; Lay Teachers 15; Students 118.
Catechesis/Religious Programs—Students 26.

New Brunswick, Middlesex Co., Nativity of B.V.M., Rev. Paul Labinsky.
Res., 86 Livingston Ave., 08901. Tel: 908-246-8385.

Passaic, Passaic Co., St. Nicholas, Revs. Joseph Szupa; Vasyl Bunyk (Ukraine).
Res., 216 President St., 07055. Tel: 201-777-0230.
School—Tel: 201-779-0249. Sr. Albina S.S.M.I., Prin.
Sisters 3; Lay Teachers 7; Students 122.

Perth Amboy, Middlesex Co., Assumption of B.V.M., Revs. Roman Dubitsky; Augustine Molodowitz; Deacon Paul Makar.
Res., 684 Alta Vista Pl., 08861. Tel: 908-826-0767.
School—Tel: 908-826-8721. Sr. Vladymira M.S.M.G., Prin.
Missionary Sisters of Mother of God 2; Lay Teachers 11; Students 240.

Ramsey, Bergen Co., St. Paul. Attended by St. John the Baptist, Whippany.
Res., 7 S. Jefferson Rd., Whippany, 07981. Tel: 201-887-3616.

Rutherford, Bergen Co., Annunciation B.V.M. Attended by St. Nicholas, Passaic.
Res., c/o St. Nicholas, 216 President St., Passaic, 07055. Tel: 201-777-0230.
Church—70 Home Ave., 07070.

Toms River, Ocean Co., St. Stephen's. Attended by Assumption of B.V.M., Perth Amboy. Rev. Roman Dubitsky; Deacon Paul Makar.
Res., c/o Assumption of B.V.M., 684 Alta Vista Pl., Perth Amboy, 08861. Tel: 908-826-0767.
Church—1344 White Oak Bottom Rd., 08755. Tel: 908-505-6293.

Trenton, Mercer Co., St. Josaphat's. Attended by St. Mary's, Bristol, PA.

Whippany, Morris Co., St. John the Baptist, Rev. Archpriest Uriy Markewuch.
Res., 7 S. Jefferson Rd., 07981. Tel: 201-887-3616.
Church—Rte. 10, 07981.

Williamstown, Gloucester Co., SS. Peter and Paul. Attended by St. Michael's, Cherry Hill.
Mailing Address: 675 Cooperlanding Rd., Cherry Hill, 08002. Tel: 609-482-0938. [CEM]

Woodbine, Cape May Co., St. Nicholas. Attended by Millville.
Mailing Address: 801 Carmel Rd., Millville, 08332.
Church—Lincoln Ave., 08270.

STATE OF PENNSYLVANIA

Alden Station, Luzerne Co., St. Vladimir. Attended by St. Nicholas, Glen Lyon. Rev. Msgr. Bohdan Olesh.
Res., c/o St. Nicholas, 194 E. Main St., Glen Lyon, 18617. Tel: 717-736-6382. [CEM]

Allentown, Lehigh Co., Immaculate Conception of B.V.M. Attended by St. Josaphat, Bethlehem.
Res., 1826 Kenmore Ave., Bethlehem, 18018.

Berwick, Columbia Co., SS. Cyril and Methodius, Rt. Rev. Mitred Msgr Stephen Chomko.
Res., 706 Warren St., 18603. Tel: 717-752-3172. [CEM]
Catechesis/Religious Programs—Students 66.

Bethlehem, Lehigh Co., St. Josaphat's, Rev. Daniel Gurovich.
Res., 1826 Kenmore Ave., 18018. Tel: 610-865-2521. [CEM]
Catechesis/Religious Programs—Students 169.

Bridgeport, Montgomery Co., SS. Peter and Paul, Rev. Msgr. Ronald P. Popivchak.
Res., 519 Union Ave., P.O. Box 126, 19405. Tel: 610-272-7035. [CEM]
Catechesis/Religious Programs—George Maxim, D.R.E.
Students 145.

Bristol, Bucks Co., St. Mary's, Rev. Msgr. Myron Grabowsky.
Res., 2026 Bath Rd., 19007. Tel: 215-788-7117.

Centralia, Columbia Co., Assumption of B.V.M. Attended by Mount Carmel. Rev. Daniel Troyan.
Res., 131 N. Beech St., Mount Carmel, 17851. Tel: 717-339-0650. [CEM]

Chester, Delaware Co., Holy Ghost, Rev. Msgr. John Bura.
Res., 3015 W. Third St., 19013. Tel: 610-494-7899; Fax: 610-494-2350.

Clifton Heights, Delaware Co., SS. Peter and Paul, Rev. T. Frank Patrylak.
Res., 104 S. Penn St., 19108.
Church—100 S. Penn St., 19018. Tel: 610-626-9495.

Edwardsville, Luzerne Co., St. Vladimir's, Rev. Alex Burak.
Res., 87 Zerbey Ave., 18704. Tel: 717-287-8471. [CEM]
Catechesis/Religious Programs—Tel: 717-822-1589. Mary Ann Mudrak, D.R.E.
Students 144.

Frackville, Schuylkill Co., St. Michael's, Rev. John Seniw.
Res., 45 S. Second St., 17931. Tel: 717-874-1101.
Catechesis/Religious Programs—Tel: 717-874-1101.
Students 50.

Glen Lyon, Luzerne Co., St. Nicholas, Rev. Msgr. Bohdan Olesh.
Res., 194 E. Main St., 18617. Tel: 717-736-6382.
Church—153 Main St., 18617.

Hazleton, Luzerne Co., St. Michael's. Attended by Protection B.V.M., McAdoo. Rev. Gregory Maslak.
Res., 74 N. Laurel St., 18201.

Lansdale, Montgomery Co., Presentation of Our Lord. Attended by St. Anne, Warrington. Rev. John Fields.
Mailing Address: 1545 Easton Rd., P.O. Box 417, Warrington, 18976.
Church—1564 Allentown Rd., 19446. Tel: 215-368-3993.

McAdoo, Schuylkill Co., St. Mary's, Rev. Gregory Maslak.
Church—210 W. Blaine St., 18237. Tel: 717-929-2804; Fax: 717-462-0517.

Mahanoy City, Schuylkill Co., St. Nicholas. Attended by St. Michael, Shenandoah.
Mailing Address: 114 Chestnut St., Shenandoah, 17976. [CEM]

Maizeville, Schuylkill Co., St. John the Baptist. Attended by St. Michael, Frackville.
Mailing Address: 45 S. Second St., Frackville, 17931. Tel: 717-874-1821. [CEM]
Church—Main St., 17934.

Marion Heights, Northumberland Co., Patronage of the Mother of God. Attended by SS. Peter & Paul, Mount Carmel.

Middleport, Schuylkill Co., Nativity of B.V.M., Rev. Michael Hutsko.
Res., 415 N. Front St., Minersville, 17954. Tel: 717-544-4581. [CEM]
Church—Kaska St., 17953.

Minersville, Schuylkill Co., St. Nicholas, Rev. Michael Hutsko.
Res., 415 Front St., 17954. Tel: 717-544-4581; Fax: 717-544-9653. [CEM]
School—Tel: 717-544-2800.
Sisters 4; Lay Teachers 8; Students 150.
Catechesis/Religious Programs—Students 105.

Moscow, Lackawanna Co., Holy Ghost. Attended by St. Vladimir's, Scranton.
Church—Aberdeen Rd., 18444.

Mount Carmel, Northumberland Co., SS. Peter and Paul, Rev. Daniel Troyan.
Res., 131 N. Beech St., 17851. Tel: 717-339-0650; Fax: 717-339-2715. [CEM]

Nanticoke, Luzerne Co., St. Nicholas, Rev. Jeffrey Paulish (SCR).
Res., 706 Warren St., Berwick, 18603. Tel: 717-752-3172.
Church—111 Green St., 18634.
Transfiguration of Our Lord, Rev. Nick Kostiuk.
Res., 240 Center St., 18634. Tel: 717-735-2262.

Northampton, Northampton Co., St. John the Baptist, Rev. Leonard Sinatra.
Res., 1343 Newport Ave., 18067. Tel: 610-262-4104. [CEM]
School—Tel: 610-262-2231. John Barner, Prin.
Lay Teachers 9; Students 130.

Olyphant, Lackawanna Co., SS. Cyril and Methodius, Very Rev. Msgr. Stephen Hrynuck.
Res., 135 River St., 18447. Tel: 717-489-2271. [CEM]
Catechesis/Religious Programs—Students 77.

Palmerton, Carbon Co., St. Vladimir's, Rev. Edward Levandusky.
Res., 101 Lehigh Ave., 18071. Tel: 610-826-2359.

Phoenixville, Chester Co., SS. Peter and Paul. Attended by SS. Peter and Paul, Bridgeport. Rev. Msgr. Ronald P. Popivchak.
Mailing Address: 519 Union Ave., P.O. Box 126, Bridgeport, 19405. Tel: 610-272-7035.

Plymouth, Luzerne Co., SS. Peter and Paul. Attended by Transfiguration of Our Lord, Nanticoke. Rev. Nick Kostiuk, Admin.
Mailing Address: 240 Center St., Nanticoke, 18634. Tel: 717-735-2262.

Pottstown, Montgomery Co., St. Michael's. Attended by Nativity B.V.M., Reading. Rev. Joseph Martyniuk.
Res., 1814 Philadelphia Ave., Reading, 19607. Tel: 610-376-0586. [CEM]

Reading, Berks Co., Nativity of Blessed Virgin Mary, Rev. Joseph Martyniuk.
Res., 1814 Philadelphia Ave., 19607. Tel: 610-376-0586. [CEM]

St. Clair, Schuylkill Co., St. Nicholas. Attended by Holy Trinity, St. Clair. Rev. John Wysochansky.
Res., c/o Holy Trinity, 254 N. Mill St., 17970. Tel: 717-429-2212. [CEM]
Church—N. Morris St., 17970.
Holy Trinity, Rev. John Wysochansky.
Res., 254 N. Mill St., 17970. Tel: 717-429-2212. [CEM]

Sayre, Bradford Co., Ascension of Our Lord. Attended by Elmira Heights, NY.
Res., 110 N. Higgins Ave., 18840. Tel: 717-888-2207. [CEM]

Scranton, Lackawanna Co., St. Vladimir's, Rev. Msgr. Raymond Revak.
Res., 430 N. Seventh St., 18503. Tel: 717-342-7023. [CEM]

Shamokin, Northumberland Co., Transfiguration of Our Lord, Rev. Msgr. Michael Fedorowich.
Res., 303 N. Shamokin St., 17872-5460. Tel: 717-648-5932. [CEM]
School—Tel: 717-648-6435. Sr. Anne Roman, S.S.M.I., Prin.
Sisters Servants of Mary Immaculate 2; Lay Teachers 9; Students 185.
Catechesis/Religious Programs—Students 100.

Shenandoah, Schuylkill Co., St. Michael's, Rev. Robert Hitchens.
Res., 114 S. Chestnut St., 17976. Tel: 717-462-0809; Fax: 717-462-0517. [CEM]

Simpson, Lackawanna Co., SS. Peter and Paul, Rev. Theodore Boholnick.
Res., 43 Rittenhouse St., 18407. Tel: 717-282-0331. [CEM]

Warrington, Bucks Co., St. Anne's, Rev. John Fields.
Res., 1545 Easton Rd., Box 417, 18976. Tel: 215-343-0779; Fax: 215-343-8060.
Catechesis/Religious Programs—Students 58.

West Easton, Northampton Co., Holy Ghost, Rev. Bohdan Kin.
Res., 315 Fourth St., 18042. Tel: 610-252-4266; Fax: 610-252-8533. [CEM]

Wilkes-Barre, Luzerne Co., SS. Peter and Paul. Attended by St. Vladimir's, Edwardsville. Rev. Alex Burak, Admin.
Church—635 N. River St., 18701. Tel: 717-823-1821. [CEM]
Catechesis/Religious Programs—Mary Ann Mudrak, D.R.E.
Students 49.

STATE OF VIRGINIA

Manassas, Prince William Co., Annunciation of the Blessed Virgin Mary. Attended by Holy Trinity, Silver Spring, MD. Rev. Taras R. Lonchyna, Admin.
Mailing Address: P.O. Box 2735, 22111.
Res., 16631 New Hampshire Ave., Silver Spring, MD 20905-3919. Tel: 301-890-7730. [CEM]
Church—6719 Hoadly Rd., 22111. Tel: 703-791-6635.

Richmond, Henrico Co., St. John the Baptist. Attended by Holy Trinity, Silver Spring, MD. Rev. Taras R. Lonchyna, Admin.
Res., 16631 New Hampshire Ave., Silver Spring, MD 20905-3919. Tel: 301-890-7730.
Chapel—Sisters of Verona Chapel, Tel: 804-359-4934.

DISTRICT OF COLUMBIA

Washington, District of Columbia, Ukrainian Catholic National Shrine of the Holy Family, Rev. Vasyl Kharuk (Ukraine) Admin. of Spiritualities; Deacon Theophil Staruch, Admin. of Temporalities.
Res., 4250 Harewood Rd., N.E., 20017. Tel: 202-526-3737; Fax: 202-526-1327.
Catechesis/Religious Programs—Students 152.

Absent on Leave:
Reverend Monsignors—
Canavan, Martin
Reverend Fathers—
Batcho, Michael
Korinchock, Joseph
Worschak, George D.

Retired:
Reverend Monsignors—
Pospishil, Victor J., 6 Michigan Dr., Matawan, NJ 07747
Stefaniuk, Dmytro, 911 N. Franklin St., #203, Philadelphia, PA 19123
Reverend Fathers—
Horoshko, Michael
Levytsky, Bohdan, R.D. No. 2, Box 431, Leighton, PA 18235
Oryshkewych, Ostap, 427 Pine St., Philadelphia, PA 19105

Permanent Deacons:
Dochych, Arthur J., Elizabeth, NJ
Latrick, Donald, Holy Family Ukrainian Catholic National Shrine, Washington, DC
Makar, Paul, Perth Amboy, NJ
Staruch, Theophil, Holy Family Ukrainian Catholic National Shrine, Washington, DC
Waak, Michael P., Perth Amboy, NJ

INSTITUTIONS LOCATED IN THE ARCHDIOCESE

[A] SEMINARIES, ARCHEPARCHY

WASHINGTON, DC. *St. Josaphat Seminary*, 201 Taylor St., N.E., 20017. Tel: 202-529-1177. Rev. Archpriest David Clooney, Rector; Rev. Taras Lonchyna, Spiritual Dir. Pro Tem.

[B] COLLEGES AND UNIVERSITIES

JENKINTOWN. *Manor Junior College*, 700 Fox Chase Rd., 19046. Tel: 215-885-2360; Fax: 215-576-6564
For a complete listing, refer to the Colleges and Universities section.

[C] HIGH SCHOOLS, PRIVATE

FOX CHASE MANOR. *St. Basil Academy*, 711 Fox Chase Rd., 19046. Tel: 215-745-5550; Fax: 215-885-4025. Sr. Carla Hernandez, O.S.B.M., Prin. Sisters 7; Lay Teachers 32; Students 350.

[D] HOMES FOR SENIOR CITIZENS

PHILADELPHIA. *Ascension Manor, Inc.*, 911 N. Franklin St., 19123. Tel: 215-922-1116
For a complete listing, refer to the Special Care Facilities section.

Home of Divine Providence, 209 W. Chestnut Hill Ave., 19118. Tel: 215-247-7107
For a complete listing, refer to the Special Care Facilities section.

[E] MONASTERIES AND RESIDENCES OF PRIESTS AND BROTHERS

SYBERTSVILLE. *Holy Dormition Monastery.* (Byzantine Slavonic Rite), P.O. Box 270, 18251. Tel: 717-788-1212. Very Rev. James Carroll, O.F.M., Protohegumen.

[F] CONVENTS AND RESIDENCES FOR SISTERS

PHILADELPHIA. *Motherhouse of the Missionary Sisters of Mother of God*, 711 N. Franklin St., 19123. Sr. Josepha Kruchinsky, M.S.M.G., Supr. Gen.
Nursery School. Students 35. Professed Nuns 11.
Sisters Servants of Mary Immaculate, Home of Divine Providence, 209 W. Chestnut Hill Ave., 19118-3703. Sr. Bernardine Symionow, S.S.M.I. Sisters 10.

CHESAPEAKE CITY, MD. *St. Basil's Convent*, 415 Lock St., 21915. Sisters O.S.B.M. Sr. M. Augustine, Supr.

FOX CHASE MANOR. *Provincial Motherhouse of the Sisters of St. Basil the Great*, 710 Fox Chase Rd., 19046. Tel: 215-663-9153; Fax: 215-728-6129. Sr. Dorothy Ann Busowski, O.S.B.M., Prov. Supr.; Sr. Elizabeth Bertoldi, O.S.B.M., Asst. Prov.; Rev. Vasyl Sivinsky (Ukraine), Chap. Tel: 215-379-4553. Councilors: Sr. Laura Palka, O.S.B.M.; Sr. Marie Francis Wolchansky, O.S.B.M.; Sr. Paula Jacynyk, O.S.B.M. Professed Sisters 71.

[G] MISCELLANEOUS

JENKINTOWN. *The Basileiad Library*, 700 Fox Chase Rd., 19046. Sisters of St. Basil the Great. Sr. Mary Anne Gorniowsky, O.S.B.M., Librarian.

RELIGIOUS INSTITUTES OF MEN REPRESENTED IN THE ARCHEPARCHY

For further details refer to the corresponding bracketed number in the Religious Institutes of Men or Women section.

[0520]—*Franciscan Friars.* (Slav-Byzantine Commissariat).—O.F.M.

[1070]—*Redemptorist Fathers.*—C.SS.R.

RELIGIOUS INSTITUTES OF WOMEN REPRESENTED IN THE ARCHEPARCHY

[2810]—*Missionary Sisters of Mother of God.*—M.S.M.G.

[3730]—*Sisters of the Order of St. Basil the Great.*—O.S.B.M.

[3610]—*Sisters Servants of Mary Immaculate.*—S.S.M.I.

ARCHDIOCESAN CEMETERIES

LANGHORNE. *Mother of Sorrows*, Langhorne & Yardley Rd., 19047. Tel: 215-627-0143.

NECROLOGY

† Batza, Rev. Msgr. Joseph, (Retired). —Died March 2, 1997.

† Borsa, Rev. Msgr. Anthony, Marlboro, NJ, St. Wolodymyr. —Died March 12, 1997.

Metropolitan Archdiocese of Pittsburgh, Byzantine

Most Reverend

JUDSON M. PROCYK, D.D.

Metropolitan Archbishop of Pittsburgh Byzantine; ordained May 19, 1957; appointed Archbishop of Pittsburgh Byzantine November 15, 1994; installed February 7, 1995. *Office: 66 Riverview Ave., Pittsburgh, PA, 15214. Res., 50 Riverview Ave., Pittsburgh, PA, 15214.*

Chancery Office: 66 Riverview Ave., Pittsburgh, PA, 15214. Tel.: 412-231-4000; Fax: 412-231-1697.

ESTABLISHED FEBRUARY 25, 1924.

RAISED TO ARCHEPARCHY FEBRUARY 21, 1969.

Embraces all Byzantine Ruthenian Rite Catholics in that part of the State of Pennsylvania west of the western boundaries of the Counties of Tioga, Lycoming, Union, Mifflin, Juniata and Franklin. In the State of Ohio, the Counties of Ashtabula, Athens, Belmont, Carroll, Columbiana, Gallia, Guernsey, Harrison, Jefferson, Lawrence, Mahoning, Meigs, Morrow, Morgan, Noble, Trumbull and Washington and also the States of Alabama, Arkansas, Kentucky, Louisiana, Mississippi, Oklahoma, Tennessee, Texas and West Virginia.

For legal titles of parishes and diocesan institutions, consult the Chancery Office.

STATISTICAL OVERVIEW

Personnel	
Archbishop	1
Abbots	1
Priests: Diocesan Active in Diocese	61
Priests: Retired, Sick or Absent	4
Number of Diocesan Priests	65
Religious Priests in Diocese	8
Ordinations:	
Diocesan Priests	2
Transitional Deacons	1
Total Brothers	4
Total Sisters	108
Parishes	
Parishes	85
With Resident Pastor:	
Resident Diocesan Priests	53
Resident Religious Priests	4
Without Resident Pastor:	
Administered by Priests	28
Missions	3
Closed Parishes	2
Professional Ministry Personnel:	
Sisters	4
Welfare	
Homes for the Aged	3
Total Assisted	295
Day Care and Extended Day Care Centers	3
Total Assisted	83
Educational	
Seminaries, Diocesan	1
Students from This Diocese	3
Students from Other Diocese	12
Total Seminarians	3
Elementary Schools, Diocesan and Parish	3
Total Students	551
Catechesis/Religious Education:	
High School Students	586
Elementary Students	2,484
Total Students Under Catholic Instruction	3,624
Teachers in the Diocese:	
Sisters	9
Lay Teachers	34
Vital Statistics	
Receptions into the Church:	
Infant Baptism Totals	301
Adult Baptism Totals	38
Received into Full Communion	73
First Communions	356
Confirmations	339
Marriages:	
Catholic	102
Interfaith	41
Total Marriages	143
Deaths	903
Total Catholic Population	81,129

Former Bishops—Most Rev. BASIL TAKACH, ord. Dec. 12, 1902; appt. May 20, 1924; cons. June 15, 1924; died May 13, 1948.—Most Rev. DANIEL IVANCHO, D.D., Titular Bishop of Europus; ord. Sept. 30, 1934; appt. Coadjutor Bishop, August 29, 1946; cons. Nov. 5, 1946; succeeded to May 13, 1948; retired Dec. 2, 1954; died Aug. 2, 1972.—Most Rev. NICHOLAS T. ELKO, D.D., cons. March 6, 1955; transferred to Rome, Dec. 22, 1967; died May 18, 1991.—Most Rev. STEPHEN J. KOCISCKO, D.D., cons. July 20, 1956; retired June 12, 1991; died March 7, 1995.—Most Rev. THOMAS V. DOLINAY, ord. May 16, 1948; appt. Titular Bishop of Thyatira and Auxiliary of Passaic, Sept. 23, 1976; cons. Nov. 23, 1976; appt. First Ordinary of the Byzantine Catholic Diocese of Van Nuys; installed March 1982; appt. Coadjutor Archbishop of Pittsburgh, March 13, 1990; installed May 29, 1990; succeeded to June 12, 1991; died April 13, 1993.—Most Rev. JOHN M. BILOCK, ord. Feb. 3, 1946; appt. Titular Bishop of Pergamo and Auxiliary Bishop to the Metropolitan Archbishop of Pittsburgh; installed March 1, 1973; cons. May 15, 1973; appt. Archdiocesan Administrator, April 20, 1993; died Sept. 8, 1994.

Chancery Office—66 Riverview Ave., Pittsburgh, 15214. Office Hours: Mon.-Fri. 9:30-12 and 12:30-4. Tel: 412-231-4000; Fax: 412-231-1697.

Vicar General—Rev. Msgr. RUSSELL A. DUKER, S.E.O.D.

Chancellor—Rev. Msgr. RUSSELL A. DUKER, S.E.O.D.

Vice-Chancellor—Rev. JOHN KUDRICK.

Treasurer—GREGORY S. POPIVCHAK, C.P.A.

Vicar for Clergy—Very Rev. JOHN G. PETRO, V.C.

Vicar for Religious—Rev. JAMES A. SPONTAK, V.R.

Vocations Director—Rev. DENNIS M. BOGDA.

Archdiocesan Tribunal—66 Riverview Ave., Pittsburgh, 15214.

Judicial Vicar—Very Rev. RICHARD J. WHETSTONE, J.C.O.L.

Pro-Synodal Judges—Revs. MICHAEL JUDE WYTISH, J.C.B.; ANSELM ORLOSKY, O.S.B.

Defender of the Bond—Rev. JOHN MIHALCO, S.E.O.L.

Promoter of Justice—Rev. Msgr. ALEXIS MIHALIK.

Notaries—Rev. GREGORY MICHALISIN; DONNA OBSINCS.

Secretary to the Tribunal—Sr. ELAINE KISINKO, O.S.B.M.

Archdiocesan Consultors—Rev. Msgr. RUSSELL A. DUKER, Vicar General; Revs. JOSEPH J. BORODACH; JOSEPH JUGAN; ROBERT J. KARL; Rev. Msgr. ANDREW D. PARVENSKY; Revs. JOHN G. PETRO; JOHN D. YCOBAK.

Deans—Rev. Msgr. WILLIAM G. LEVKULIC, Clairton Deanery; Rev. Msgr. RAYMOND A. BALTA, Johnstown Deanery; Very Rev. JOHN SALKO, Mon-Valley Deanery; Rev. Msgr. NICHOLAS X. SMICIKLAS, Greater Pittsburgh Deanery; Very Rev. SIMEON B. SIBENIK, North Central Deanery; Very Rev. JOSEPH JUGAN, Tri-State Deanery; Rev. Msgr. SYLVESTER HLADKY, Youngstown; Very Rev. RONALD LARKO, Southwest.

Presbyteral Council—Most Rev. JUDSON M. PROCYK, D.D., Pres. Ex-Officio Members: Rev. Msgr. RUSSELL A. DUKER, Vicar General; Very Rev. JOHN G. PETRO, Exec. Dir. Elected Members: Revs. DENNIS BOGDA; JOSEPH J. BORODACH; JOHN KUDRICK; JAMES SPONTAK; MICHAEL J. WYTISH, Sec. EUGENE YACKANICH; JOHN YCOBAK; Very Rev. RICHARD J. WHETSTONE.

Finance Council—Most Rev. JUDSON M. PROCYK, Metropolitan Archbishop; GREGORY S. POPIVCHAK, C.P.A., Archdiocesan Treas.; Rev. JOHN BORODACH; ANGELO F. MONACO; MICHAEL I. ROMAN.

Personnel Board—Most Rev. JUDSON M. PROCYK; Rev. Msgr. RUSSELL A. DUKER; Rev. JOHN M. KUDRICK; Very Rev. JOHN G. PETRO; Very Rev. ROBERT J. KARL; Rev. JOHN J. BORODACH, V.F.

Archdiocesan Offices and Directors

Priests' Pension Board—Ex-Officio Members: Most Rev. JUDSON M. PROCYK, Metropolitan Archbishop/ Chm.; Rev.Msgr. RUSSELL A. DUKER, Vicar General; GREGORY S. POPIVCHAK, Archdiocesan Treas.

Elected Deanery Representatives—Rev. Msgr. WILLIAM LEVKULIC, Sec., Clairton; Rev. DANIEL LOYA, Johnstown Deanery; Rev. JOHN LOUIS MINA, Mon-Valley Deanery; Rev. GEORGE EVANCHO, Greater Pittsburgh Deanery; Rev. SIMEON SIBENIK, North Central Deanery; Rev. ROBERT HALUS, Tri-State Deanery; Rev. FRANK FIRKO, Youngstown Deanery.

Newspaper—The Byzantine Catholic World, Official Publication of the Archeparchy. Most Rev. JUDSON M. PROCYK, D.D., Pres.; Rev. MICHAEL J. WYTISH, Editor.

Office of Religious Education—Sr. MORION DOBOS, O.S.B., Communications, *3605 Perrysville Ave., Pittsburgh, 15214.* Tel: 412-322-8773.

Byzantine Catholic Seminary Press—Rev. JOHN OPALENICK, Business Mgr., *3605 Perrysville Ave., Pittsburgh, 15214.* Tel: 412-322-8307.

Archdiocesan Archivist—Rev. JOHN L. MINA.

Assistant Archivists—Rev. ROBERT F. ORAVETZ; Sr. ELAINE KISINKO, O.S.B.M.

CLERGY, PARISHES, MISSIONS AND PAROCHIAL SCHOOLS

STATE OF PENNSYLVANIA

Munhall, Allegheny Co., St. John the Baptist Cathedral, Very Rev. Robert J. Karl, Rector; Rev. Andrew J. Deskevich.

Res., 210 Greentree Rd., 15120. Tel: 412-461-0944; Fax: 412-462-3495. [CEM]

St. Elias (Magyar), Rev. Eugene P. Yackanich.

Res., 4200 Homestead, Duquesne Rd., 15120. Tel: 412-461-1712. [CEM]

Aliquippa, Beaver Co., St. George. Unassigned.

Res., 1001 Clinton St., 15001. Tel: 412-375-2742.

Ambridge, Beaver Co., St. Mary's, Rev. Msgr. Edward V. Rosack.

Res., 624 Park Rd., 15003. Tel: 412-266-2030; Fax: 412-266-0799.

Arcadia, Indiana Co., Ascension. Attended by Barnesboro.

719 Chestnut Ave., Barnesboro, 15714. Tel: 814-948-8242. [CEM]

Avella, Washington Co., St. John the Baptist. Attended by Weirton, WV.
Res., P.O. Box 565, 15312. Tel: 412-587-5819. [CEM]

Barnesboro, Cambria Co., St. John the Baptist, Rev. Donald Valasek.
Res., 719 Chestnut Ave., 15714. Tel: 814-948-8242; Fax: 814-948-8252. [CEM]

Beaver, Beaver Co., Saint Nicholas Chapel, Very Rev. John G. Petro, Admin.
Res., 5400 Tuscarawas Rd., 15009-9513. Tel: 412-495-3400.

Beaverdale, Cambria Co., St. Mary's, Rev. Stephen Kolcun.
Res., P.O. Box 610, 15921. Tel: 814-487-7458; Fax: 814-487-4830. [CEM]

Braddock, Allegheny Co., SS. Peter and Paul, Rev. Blaise Kovach.
Res., 431 George St., 15104. Tel: 412-271-1297; Fax: 412-351-4015.

Bradenville, Westmoreland Co., St. Mary's, Rev. Joseph Borodach.
Res., R.R. #1, Box 75, 15620-9711. Tel: 412-537-5839; Fax: 412-532-1499. [CEM]

Brownsville, Fayette Co., St. Nicholas, Rev. Jerome Botsko.
Res., 302 Third Ave., 15417. Tel: 412-785-7573. [CEM]

Canonsburg, Washington Co., St. Michael, Very Rev. Joseph Jugan.
Res., 166 E. College St., 15317. Tel: 412-745-7117; Fax: 412-745-3097.

Charleroi, Washington Co., Holy Ghost, Rev. Wesley M. Mash.
Res., 828 Meadow Ave., 15022. Tel: 412-483-8622; Fax: 412-483-0696.

Clairton, Allegheny Co., Ascension of Our Lord, Rev. John L. Mina.
Res., 318 Park Ave., 15025. Tel: 412-233-7422. [CEM]

Clarence, Centre Co., St. Mary's. Attended by St. John the Baptist Church, Hawk Run. Rev. Donald J. Voss.
c/o St. John the Baptist Church, Hawk Run, 16840. Tel: 814-342-4315. [CEM]

Clymer, Indiana Co., St. Anne. Attended by Ernest.
P.O. Box 130, Ernest, 15739. Tel: 814-674-5552.

Coal Run, Indiana Co., Holy Cross. Attended by Homer City.
279 Yellow Creek St., Homer City, 15748. Tel: 412-479-2206.

Conemaugh, Cambria Co., Holy Trinity, Rev. Ronald W. Borsuk.
Res., 217 Fourth St., 15909. Tel: 814-535-5231; Fax: 814-535-2417.

Donora, Washington Co., St. Michael, Rev. John J. Borodach.
Res., 511 Murray Ave., 15033. Tel: 412-379-9751; Fax: 412-379-9752. [CEM]

Du Bois, Clearfield Co., Nativity of the Mother of God. Attended by Sykesville. Very Rev. Simeon B. Sibenik.
Res., 200 McCullough St., 15801. Tel: 814-371-4911.

Dunlo, Cambria Co., SS. Peter and Paul. Attended by Beaverdale.
P.O. Box 610, Beaverdale, 15921. Tel: 814-487-7458. [CEM]

Duquesne, Allegheny Co., SS. Peter and Paul, Rev. Msgr. William Levkulic.
Res., 701 Foster Ave., 15110. Tel: 412-466-3578. [CEM]

St. Mary's. Attended by St. Elias, Munhall.
Res., 1209 Kennedy Ave., 15110. Tel: 412-466-1914.

East Pittsburgh, Allegheny Co., St. Mary's, Rev. George Evancho.
Res., 317 Howard St., 15112. Tel: 412-824-1622.

Erie, Erie Co., SS. Peter and Paul, Rev. Julius Kubinyi.
Res., 3415 Wallace St., 16504. Tel: 814-825-8140.

Ernest, Indiana Co., St. Jude Thaddeus, Rev. Edward Pyo.
Res., Box 130, 15739. Tel: 412-463-3397.

Girard, Erie Co., SS. Cyril and Methodius, Rev. Dennis Logue, S.V.D.
Res., 1022 Tilden Ave., 16417. Tel: 814-774-3281; Fax: 814-774-5405.

Greensburg, Westmoreland Co., St. Nicholas of Myra, Rev. Regis Dusecina.
Res., 622 E. Pittsburgh St., 15601. Tel: 412-837-0295.

Hannastown, Westmoreland Co., St. Mary's. Attended by Greensburg.
622 E. Pittsburgh St., Greensburg, 15601. Tel: 412-837-0295.

Hawk Run, Clearfield Co., St. John the Baptist, Rev. Donald J. Voss.
Mailing Address: P.O. Box 2, 16840. Tel: 814-342-4315.

Herminie, Westmoreland Co., St. Mary's. Attended by North Huntington.
Res., 7 Second St., 15637. Tel: 412-446-5570.

Hermitage, Mercer Co., St. Michael, Rev. Frank A. Firko, S.T.L.
Res., 2230 Highland Rd., 16148. Tel: 412-981-6680; Fax: 412-981-7422. [CEM]

Homer City, Indiana Co., Holy Protection of Mary, The Mother of God, Rev. John Cuccaro.
Res., 279 Yellow Creek St., 15748. Tel: 412-479-2206.

Jerome, Somerset Co., SS. Peter and Paul. Attended by Windber.
803 Somerset Ave., Windber, 15963. Tel: 814-467-8044; Fax: 814-467-8044. [CEM]

Johnstown, Cambria Co., St. Mary's, Rev. Msgr. Raymond A. Balta.
Res., 411 Power St., 15906. Tel: 814-535-4132; Fax: 814-536-9017. [CEM]

Leisenring, Fayette Co., St. Stephen, Rev. Joseph Kapusnak.
Res., P.O. Box 128, 15455. Tel: 412-628-6611; Fax: 412-628-5009. [CEM]

Lyndora, Butler Co., St. John the Baptist, Rev. Dennis M. Bogda.
Res., 105 Kohler Ave., 16045. Tel: 412-287-5000; Fax: 412-287-6769. [CEM]

McKeesport, Allegheny Co., St. Nicholas, Rev. Stephen Veselenak, O.S.B.
Res., 410 Sixth Ave., 15132. Tel: 412-664-9131; Fax: 412-664-0854. [CEM]

Transfiguration of Our Lord. Attended by St. Nicholas, McKeesport.
Res., 121 Sixth Ave., 15132. Tel: 412-672-0728.

McKees Rocks, Allegheny Co., Holy Ghost, Rev. John Kudrick.
Res., 225 Olivia St., 15136. Tel: 412-771-3324; Fax: 412-331-1870.

Monessen, Westmoreland Co., Assumption of the Blessed Virgin, Rev. Msgr. Andrew D. Parvensky.
Res., 125 McKee Ave., 15062. Tel: 412-684-5662; Fax: 412-684-3301. [CEM]

Monongahela, Washington Co., St. Macrina. Attended by Charleroi.
Church—515 W. Main St., 15063.

Monroeville, Allegheny Co., Church of the Resurrection. Unassigned.
Res., 455 Center Rd., 15146. Tel: 412-372-8650; Fax: 412-372-1442.

Nanty-Glo, Cambria Co., St. Nicholas. Attended by Conemaugh.
Res., 1191 Second St., 15943. Tel: 814-749-0421.

New Salem, Fayette Co., St. Mary's, Rev. Joseph Chornyak.
Res., P.O. Box 487, 15468. Tel: 412-245-7188. [CEM]

North Hills-Gibsonia, Allegheny Co., St. Andrew the Apostle, Rev. David M. Misbrener, Admin.
Res., 235 Logan Rd., 15044. Tel: 412-625-1160; Fax: 412-625-1085.

North Huntingdon, Westmoreland Co., St. Stephen's, Rev. Gregory Michalisin.
Res., 90 Bethel Rd., 15642. Tel: 412-863-6776; Fax: 412-864-9685.

Patton, Cambria Co., SS. Peter and Paul, Rev. Donald Valasek.
Res., 516 Palmer Ave., 16668. Tel: 814-674-5552. [CEM]

Perryopolis, Fayette Co., St. Nicholas, Rev. Joseph Kapusnak.
Res., R.D. No. 1, Box 88, 15473. Tel: 412-736-4344; Fax: 412-736-4642. [CEM]

Pittsburgh, Allegheny Co.,

1—Holy Spirit, Rev. Msgr. Russell A. Duker, S.E.O.D.
Res., 4815 Fifth Ave., 15213. Tel: 412-687-1220; Fax: 412-687-1520.

2—Holy Ghost, Rev. Msgr. Peter Tay.
Res., 1437 Superior Ave., 15212. Tel: 412-321-5072; Fax: 412-321-0260.

3—St. John the Baptist. Attended by St. Pius X. In res., Rev. Michael Jude Wytish.
Res., 1720 Jane St., 15203. Tel: 412-431-1090. [CEM]

4—St. John Chrysostom, Rev. Richard Lambert.
Res., 506 Saline St., 15207. Tel: 412-421-0243; Fax: 412-422-3624.

5—Nativity of B.V.M.. Attended by St. John Chrysostom, Pittsburgh.
Res., 4027 Beechwood Blvd., 15217. Tel: 412-421-5231.

6—St. Pius X, Rev. Msgr. Nicholas X. Smiciklas.
Res., 2336 Brownsville Rd., 15210. Tel: 412-881-8344.

Portage, Cambria Co., SS. Peter and Paul, Rev. Myron E. Kochaba, O.S.B.
Res., 605 Prospect St., 15946. Tel: 814-736-9780; Fax: 814-736-8701. [CEM]

Punxsutawney, Jefferson Co., SS. Peter and Paul, Rev. Theodore J. Seginak, O.S.B.
Res., 714 Second Ave., 15767. Tel: 814-938-6564; Fax: 814-938-6551. [CEM 2]

Rankin, Allegheny Co., St. John's. Attended by East Pittsburgh. Rev. George Evancho.
317 Howard St., East Pittsburgh, 15112. Tel: 412-824-1622.
Church—44 Miller Ave., 15104.

Sagamore, Armstrong Co., St. Mary's. Attended by Ernest.
Box 130, Ernest, 15739. Tel: 412-463-3397. [CEM]

Scottdale, Westmoreland Co., St. John the Baptist, Very Rev. John H. Salko.
Res., 525 Porter Ave., 15683. Tel: 412-887-5072; Fax: 412-887-3365. [CEM]

Sheffield, Warren Co., St. Michael, Rev. David A. Bosnich.
Res., 407 School St., 16347. Tel: 814-968-5478; Fax: 814-968-4445. [CEM]

South Fork, Cambria Co., St. Michael's. Attended by SS. Peter and Paul Church, Portage. Rev. Myron E. Kochaba, O.S.B., Admin.
605 Prospect St., Portage, 15946. Tel: 814-736-9780; Fax: 814-736-8701. [CEM]

Sykesville, Jefferson Co., Holy Trinity, Very Rev. Simeon B. Sibenik.
Res., 104 Shaffer St., 15865. Tel: 814-894-5440; Fax: 814-894-2412. [CEM]

Tarentum, Allegheny Co., Sts. Peter and Paul, Rev. Gregory C. Mullaney.
Res., 339 E. 10th Ave., 15084. Tel: 412-224-3026; Fax: 412-224-5242.

Trauger, Westmoreland Co., St. Mary's, Rev. Christopher R. Burke.
Res., R.D. 3, Box 373-C, Latrobe, 15650. Tel: 412-423-3673; Fax: 412-423-1808. [CEM]

Uniontown, Fayette Co., St. John the Baptist, Very Rev. Richard J. Whetstone, J.C.O.L.
Res., 185 E. Main St., 15401. Tel: 412-438-6027; Fax: 412-438-1382. [CEM]
School—Tel: 412-439-2479; Fax: 412-438-2595. Sr. Regina Adams, O.S.B.M., Prin.
Sisters of St. Basil the Great 3; Lay Teachers 6; Students 90.

Upper St. Clair, Allegheny Co., St. Gregory Nazianzus, Rev. Bruno Asturi.
Res., 2005 Mohawk Rd., 15241. Tel: 412-835-7800.

Wall, Allegheny Co., Holy Trinity, Rev. Anselm Orlosky, O.S.B.
Res., 470 Wall Ave., 15148. Tel: 412-824-9803.

Windber, Somerset Co., St. Mary (Dormition) Church, Rev. Daniel Loya.
Res., 803 Somerset St., 15963. Tel: 814-467-8044; Fax: 814-467-8044. [CEM]

STATE OF OHIO

Ashtabula, Ashtabula Co., St. Nicholas, Rev. A. Edward Gretchko.
Res., 630 Plum St., 44004. Tel: 440-599-8570; Fax: 440-593-6772.

Boardman, Mahoning Co., Infant Jesus of Prague, Rev. Msgr. Alexis E. Mihalik.
Res., 7754 S. Ave. Extension, P.O. Box 7006, 44512. Tel: 330-758-6019; Fax: 330-758-6776.

Campbell, Mahoning Co., St. Michael, Rev. Msgr. Victor G. Romza.
Res., 463 Robinson Rd., Box 426, 44405. Tel: 330-755-4831. [CEM]

Mingo Junction, Jefferson Co., St. John the Baptist. Attended by St. Joseph, Toronto.
Church—207 Standard St., 43938. Tel: 614-535-0271.

Newton Falls, Trumbull Co., St. Michael, Rev. John Kasarda.
Res., 737 Ridge Rd., 44444. Tel: 330-872-5216. [CEM]

Pleasant City, Guernsey Co., St. Michael, Rev. Robert Halus.
Res., P.O. Box 226, 43772. Tel: 614-685-3292; Fax: 614-685-1015. [CEM]

Toronto, Jefferson Co., St. Joseph, Rev. Andrew Chura.
Res., 814 N. Fifth St., 43964. Tel: 614-537-1026.

Warren, Trumbull Co., SS. Peter and Paul's, Rt. Rev. Msgr. Sylvester Hladky; Rev. John J. Koza, III.
Res., 180 Belvedere Ave., N.E., 44483. Tel: 330-372-1875; Fax: 330-372-5965. [CEM]
School—195 Belvedere Ave., N.E., 44483. Tel: 330-372-1312; Fax: 330-372-9565. Sr. Margaret Mary, O.S.B., Ph.D., Prin.
Sisters of the Order of St. Benedict 3; Lay Teachers 17; Students 238.

Youngstown, Mahoning Co.,

1—Assumption of the Blessed Virgin, Rev. John D. Ycoback.
Res., 356 S. Belle Vista, 44509. Tel: 330-799-8163; Fax: 330-793-5360. [CEM]

2—St. Nicholas, Rev. David J. Shortt.
Res., 1898 Wilson Ave., 44506. Tel: 330-743-0419; Fax: 330-743-6888. [CEM]
School—Byzantine Catholic Central, 5512 Youngstown-Poland Rd., 44514. Tel: 330-757-9185; Fax: 330-757-8150.
Sisters 3; Lay Teachers 11; Students 223.

3—St. George. Attended by St. Nicholas, Youngstown. 1726 Canfield Rd., 44511. Tel: 330-782-2865.

4—St. John the Baptist. Closed. For inquiries for parish records contact the Chancery.

STATE OF TEXAS

Houston, Harris Co., St. John Chrysostom, Rev. John J. Mihalco.
Res., 5402 Acorn St., 77092-4255. Tel: 713-681-3580; Fax: 713-681-3466.
Mission—San Antonio, Bexar Co., Byzantine Catholic Mission.

Irving, Dallas Co., St. Basil the Great, Very Rev. Ronald Larko.
Res., 1118 E. Union Bower Rd., 75061. Tel: 972-438-5644.

San Antonio, Bexar Co., Byzantine Catholic Mission. Attended by St. John Chrysostom, Houston. Rev. John J. Mihalco.
5402 Acorn St., Houston, 77092-4255. Tel: 713-681-3580; Fax: 713-681-3466.

STATE OF WEST VIRGINIA

Morgantown, Monongalia Co., St. Mary's Holy Protection, Rev. James Spontak.
2115 Listravia Ave., P.O. Box 3698, 26503-3698. Tel: 412-439-4475; Fax: 412-438-8660.
Church—Tel: 304-296-2455.

Weirton, Hancock Co., St. Mary's, Rev. Edward Lucas.
Res., 3116 Elm St., 26062. Tel: 304-748-2087.

Awaiting Assignment:
Reverend Fathers—
Oravetz, Robert Franklin

Retired:
Reverend Monsignors—
Macko, John, P.O. Box 306, Lyndora, PA 16045
Reverend Fathers—
Gnall, Julian M., O.S.B., Chap., U.S. Navy, San Diego, CA
Gran, Thomas, 401 Cambria Ave., Windber, PA 15963
Mokris, Michael, 472 Church St., Swoyersville, PA 18704
Popovich, Josaphat, 5061 Stetson Dr., Prescott Valley, AZ 86314

INSTITUTIONS LOCATED IN THE ARCHDIOCESE

[A] SEMINARIES, ARCHDIOCESAN

Pittsburgh. *Byzantine Catholic Seminary of SS. Cyril and Methodius*, 3605 Perrysville Ave., 15214. Tel: 412-321-8383; Fax: 412-321-9936. Very Rev. John G. Petro, Rector. Tel: 412-321-7550; Revs. David M. Petras, Spiritual Dir. Tel: 412-321-5133; John S. Custer, Dean. Tel: 412-321-5993. Students for Priesthood 15.

[B] HOMES FOR AGED

Uniontown. *Mount Macrina Manor*, 520 W. Main St., 15401. Tel: 412-437-1400; Fax: 412-430-1095
For a complete listing, refer to the Special Care Facilities section.
St. Basil's Home, 530 W. Main St., Box 878, 15401. Tel: 412-437-7480; 437-5826
For a complete listing, refer to the Special Care Facilities section.

Warren, OH. *Infant of Prague Manor*, 169 Kenmore, N.E., 44483. Tel: 330-372-4700
For a complete listing, refer to the Special Care Facilities section.

[C] CHILD CARE CENTERS

Warren, OH. *Benedictine Early Learning Center*, 8628 Squires Ln., N.E., 44484. Tel: 330-856-5315. Mrs. Michelle Balzer, Admin. Early learning child care center/after school care and preschool. Sisters 1; Lay Teachers 1; Students 23.

[D] MONASTERIES AND RESIDENCES OF PRIESTS AND BROTHERS

Butler. *Holy Trinity Monastery*, P.O. Box 990, 16003. Rt. Rev. Leo R. Schlosser, O.S.B., Abbot/Hegumen; Very Rev. Anselm Orlosky, O.S.B., Prior; Bro. Michael Zetzer, O.S.B., Procurator. Priests 7; Brothers 4.

[E] CONVENTS AND RESIDENCES FOR SISTERS

Mount St. Macrina. *Motherhouse and Novitiate of the Sisters of St. Basil the Great.* Mailing Address: 500 W. Main St., P.O. Box 878, Uniontown, 15401. Sr. Ruth Plante, O.S.B.M., Prov. Supr.; Very Rev. James Spontak, S.T.L., Chap. Professed Sisters 96.

Warren, OH. *Queen of Heaven Monastery*, 8640 Squires Ln., N.E., 44484. Sr. Margaret Mary Schima, O.S.B., Prioress. Benedictine Sisters of the Byzantine Rite 12.

Youngstown, OH. *Byzantine Convent*, 5512 Youngstown-Poland Rd., 44514. Sisters of St. Basil the Great 4.

RELIGIOUS INSTITUTES OF MEN REPRESENTED IN THE ARCHDIOCESE

For further details refer to the corresponding bracketed number in the Religious Institutes of Men or Women section.

[0200]—*Benedictine Monks.*—O.S.B.

RELIGIOUS INSTITUTES OF WOMEN REPRESENTED IN THE ARCHDIOCESE

[]—*Benedictine Sisters of the Byzantine Rite.*—O.S.B.

[3730]—*Sisters of the Order of St. Basil the Great.*—O.S.B.M.

NECROLOGY

† Pohorlak, John Gregory, Newton Falls, OH, St. Michael. —Died Dec. 21, 1996.

† Simodejka, Rev. Msgr. Michael Andrew, Aliquippa, PA, St. George. —Died Oct. 2, 1997.

Romanian Catholic Diocese of Saint George's in Canton

Most Reverend

JOHN MICHAEL BOTEAN, D.D.

Bishop for the Romanian Byzantine Faithful of the United States; ordained May 18, 1986; appointed July 15, 1993; Episcopal Ordination August 24, 1996. *Res., 1121 44th St., N.E., Canton, OH, 44714-1297.* Tel.: 330-492-4086 (Office); Fax: 330-493-1416.

Most Reverend

LOUIS PUSCAS, D.D.

Bishop Emeritus for the Romanian Byzantine Faithful of the United States; ordained May 14, 1942; appointed Exarch December 4, 1982; Episcopal ordination June 26, 1983;; installed August 28, 1983; promoted first Eparch April 16, 1987; retired July 15, 1993. *Res., 609 N. Lincoln, Aurora, IL, 60505-2112.* Tel.: 630-897-8115.

ESTABLISHED DECEMBER 4, 1982.

ELEVATED FROM APOSTOLIC EXARCHATE FOR ROMANIAN BYZANTINE TO THE RANK OF AN EPARCHY (DIOCESE) MARCH 26, 1987.

Legal Title: The Romanian Catholic Diocese of St. George in Canton.

The Jurisdiction of the Romanian Catholic Diocese of Canton extends territorially to all of the United States.

Diocesan Offices: 1121 44th St., N.E., Canton, OH, 44714-1297. Tel.: 330-492-4086; Fax: 330-493-1416.

E-mail address: Romanian_Catholic@csi.com

STATISTICAL OVERVIEW

Personnel	
Bishop	1
Retired Bishops	1
Priests: Diocesan Active in Diocese	8
Priests: Active Outside Diocese	5
Priests: Retired, Sick or Absent	4
Number of Diocesan Priests	17
Religious Priests in Diocese	1
Extern Priests in Diocese	2
Permanent Deacons in Diocese	2
Parishes	
Parishes	15
With Resident Pastor:	
Resident Diocesan Priests	9
Resident Religious Priests	1
Without Resident Pastor:	
Administered by Priests	4
Completely Vacant	1
Missions	3
Educational	
Diocesan Students in Other Seminaries	1
Total Seminarians	1
Catechesis/Religious Education:	
High School Students	10
Elementary Students	50
Total Students Under Catholic Instruction	61
Teachers in the Diocese:	
Vital Statistics	
Receptions into the Church:	
Infant Baptism Totals	29
Adult Baptism Totals	2
Received into Full Communion	5
First Communions	19
Confirmations	31
Marriages:	
Catholic	6
Interfaith	2
Total Marriages	8
Deaths	37
Total Catholic Population	5,300

Former Bishop—Most Rev. LOUIS PUSCAS, ord. May 14, 1942; appt. Exarch, Dec. 4, 1982 Episcopal ordination, June 26, 1983; installed Aug. 28, 1983; promoted to first Eparch, April 16, 1987; retired July 15, 1993.

Chancellor—Rev. Deacon JOHN J. SKALA.

Vice Chancellor—Vacant.

Finance Officer—Mr. JAMES P. DERSHAW, C.P.A.

Board of Consultors—Very Rev. GEORGE DAVID, V.G.; Very Rev. GREGORY DUMA; Revs. MICHAEL MOISIN; MICHAEL KIRILA; GEORGE GAGE; ANDRE MATTHEWS.

Vicar General—Very Rev. GEORGE DAVID, V.G.

Vicar for Theological Affairs—Sr. THERESA KOERNKE, I.H.M., Ph.D.

Director of Religious Education—Rev. ANDRE MATTHEWS.

Pro-Life Commission—Mrs. ELIZABETH KIRILA, Chm.

Vicar Refugee/Migration Svcs.—Very Rev. GREGORY DUMA.

Director of Scouting Svcs.—Rev. Deacon GARY A. BOYCE, Dir.

Formation Council—Rev. RICHARD J. MUCOWSKI, O.F.M., Ph.D.; Sr. THERESA KOERNKE, I.H.M., Ph.D.; Rev. AUGUST J. DEASIO, M.A.; Very Rev. GREGORY DUMA.

CLERGY, PARISHES, MISSIONS AND PAROCHIAL SCHOOLS

STATE OF CALIFORNIA

Mission Hills, Los Angeles Co., St. Mary Romanian Catholic Mission. Closed. For inquiries for parish records contact the Chancery.

STATE OF ILLINOIS

Aurora, Du Page Co., St. George, Rev. Frederick Peterson, O.S.B.
Res., 850 Butterfield Rd., 60504-8609. Tel: 630-897-7215, Ext. 346; Fax: 630-897-0393.
Church—720 Rural St., 60505-2551. Tel: 630-851-4002; Fax: 630-851-4002.

St. Michael, Most Rev. Louis Puscas, D.D.
Res. & Church—609 N. Lincoln Ave., 60505-2112. Tel: 630-897-8115; Fax: 630-897-5923.

Chicago, Cook Co., Ss. Peter and Paul Mission, Rev. Aurel Pater.
Res., 4309 Olcott Ave., East Chicago, IN 46312-2649. Tel: 219-398-3760; Fax: 219-398-3760.
Mission—Chicago, 3107 Fullerton Ave., 60647.

STATE OF INDIANA

East Chicago, Lake Co., St. Nicholas, Rev. Aurel Pater. Church & Res.: 4309 Olcott Ave., 46312-2649. Tel: 219-398-3760; Fax: 219-398-3760.

STATE OF MICHIGAN

Dearborn, Wayne Co., St. Mary, Rev. Emmanuel G. Samayoa, Admin. Pro-Tem.
Church—823 S. Military, 48124-2109. Tel: 313-274-2347.
Res., 364 W. Saratoga, Ferndale, 48220-3335.

Detroit, Wayne Co., St. John the Baptist, Rev. Michael Kirila.
Res., 2371 Woodstock Dr., 48203-1060. Tel: 313-386-1046; Fax: 313-368-5358.

STATE OF NEW JERSEY

Roebling, Burlington Co., St. Mary, Very Rev. George David, V.G.
Church—181 Norman Ave., 08554-1125. Tel: 609-695-6093.

Trenton, Mercer Co., St. Basil, Very Rev. George David, V.G.
Res., 238 Adeline St., 08611-2420. Tel: 609-695-6093.

STATE OF NEW YORK

Astoria, Queens Co., St. Mary Romanian Catholic Mission, Rev. Alois Isvanca.
Res., 104-05 49th Ave., Corona, 11368-2808. Tel: 718-592-3860; Fax: 718-271-6726.
Church—104-05 49th Ave., Corona, 11368-2808.

STATE OF OHIO

Canton, Stark Co., St. Theodore, Very Rev. Gregory Duma.
Res., 1101 44th St. N.E., 44714-1297. Tel: 330-492-8413; Fax: 330-493-1416.

St. George Cathedral, Very Rev. Gregory Duma.
Res., 1101 44th St. N.E., 44714-1297. Tel: 330-492-8413; Fax: 330-493-1416. Most Rev. John Michael Botean, D.D.
Bishop's Residence: 1121 44th St. N.E., 44714-1297. Tel: 330-492-4086 (Chancery Office).

Chesterland, Geauga Co., Most Holy Trinity, Rev. Andre Matthews.
Res., St. Helena, 1367 W. 65th St., Cleveland, 44102-2109. Tel: 216-651-0965; Fax: 216-631-3853.
Church—8549 Mayfield Rd., 44026-2625. Tel: 216-729-7636.

Cleveland, Cuyahoga Co., St. Helena, Rev. Andre Matthews.

Res., 1367 W. 65th St., 44102-2109. Tel: 216-651-0965; Fax: 216-631-3853.

Lorain, Lorain Co., St. Basil, Rev. Andre Matthews. Res., St. Helena, 1367 W. 65th St., Cleveland, 44102-2109. Tel: 216-651-0965; Fax: 216-631-3853. *Church*—2305 E. 31st St., 44052-2015. Tel: 216-277-5646.

Youngstown, Mahoning Co., St. Mary, Rev. George D. Gage. Res., 7782 Glenwood Ave., Boardman, 44512-5823. Tel: 330-726-8573; Fax: 330-726-4102.

STATE OF PENNSYLVANIA

McKeesport, Allegheny Co., St. Mary, Rev. John M. Elanjileth. Res., 318 26th St., 15132-7014. Tel: 412-673-5552. Rev. James E. Reiter.; Res., 1105 10th Ave., Irwin, 15642-3827. Tel: 412-863-6837; Fax: 412-863-6997.

Sharon, Mercer Co., St. John, Rev. George D. Gage. Res., 7782 Glenwood Ave., Boardman, OH 44512-5823. Tel: 330-726-8573; Fax: 330-726-4102. *Church*—3056 Morefield Rd., Hermitage, 16148.

Special Assignment:
Reverend Fathers—
Kusevich, Nicholas
Moisin, Michael
Yossa, Kenneth F.

Leave of Absence:
Reverend Fathers—
Brown, Konstantin K.
Opris, Gheorghe

Retired:
Reverend Fathers—
Ciungu, John
Clinet, Mircea
Filip, John T.
Streza, Charles V.

Permanent Deacons:
Buga, John
Skala, John

NECROLOGY

† Mihai, Eugen, Astoria, NY, St. Mary Mission. —Died Oct. 2, 1997.

Ukrainian Catholic Diocese of St. Josaphat in Parma

Most Reverend

ROBERT M. MOSKAL, D.D.

Bishop of St. Josaphat in Parma; ordained March 25, 1963; appointed Titular Bishop of Agathopolis and Auxiliary Bishop of the Archeparchy of Philadelphia August 3, 1981; consecrated October 13, 1981; appointed First Bishop of St. Josaphat in Parma December 5, 1983. *Res., 5720 State Rd., P.O. Box 347180, Parma, OH, 44134.*

Chancery: 5720 State Rd., P.O. Box 347180, Parma, OH, 44134-7180. Tel.: 440-888-1522; Fax: 440-888-3477.

E-mail address: 110330.137@compuserve.com

ESTABLISHED DECEMBER 3, 1983.

The jurisdiction of the Bishop of St. Josaphat in Parma extends territorially through all the States of Ohio, Mississippi, West Virginia, Kentucky, Tennessee, Alabama, Georgia, North Carolina, South Carolina, Florida and western Pennsylvania. With regards to persons, his subjects are Catholics of the Byzantine Ukrainian Rite: 1. Who immigrated to this country from Galicia, Bucovina and other Ukrainian provinces; 2. Who descend from such persons (Can. 755); 3. Women married to men referable to 1 and 2, if they comply with (Can. 98, n.4); 4. Who in accordance with (Can. 98, n.3) changed their Rite; 5. Converts to the Catholic Church of the Byzantine Ukrainian Rite; 6. And in fact, all other Catholics of the Byzantine Ukrainian Rite who are attached to parishes subject to the jurisdiction of the Bishop of St. Josaphat in Parma.

For legal titles of parishes and diocesan institutions, consult the Chancery.

STATISTICAL OVERVIEW

Personnel	
Bishop	1
Priests: Diocesan Active in Diocese	33
Priests: Active Outside Diocese	1
Priests: Retired, Sick or Absent	8
Number of Diocesan Priests	42
Religious Priests in Diocese	1
Extern Priests in Diocese	3
Permanent Deacons in Diocese	9
Total Brothers	10
Total Sisters	10
Parishes	
Parishes	37
With Resident Pastor:	
Resident Diocesan Priests	28
Resident Religious Priests	1
Without Resident Pastor:	
Administered by Priests	8
Missions	3
Professional Ministry Personnel:	
Sisters	4
Welfare	
Homes for the Aged	2
Total Assisted	156
Educational	
Diocesan Students in Other Seminaries	3
Total Seminarians	3
Elementary Schools, Diocesan and Parish	2
Total Students	274
Catechesis/Religious Education:	
High School Students	68
Elementary Students	194
Total Students Under Catholic Instruction	539
Teachers in the Diocese:	
Sisters	3
Lay Teachers	27
Vital Statistics	
Receptions into the Church:	
Infant Baptism Totals	137
Adult Baptism Totals	2
First Communions	71
Marriages:	
Catholic	80
Interfaith	12
Total Marriages	92
Deaths	246
Total Catholic Population	11,566

Vicar General—Rev. Msgr. Mitrat LEO ADAMIAK.

Vicar General in Curia—Rev. Msgr. Mitrat THOMAS A. SAYUK.

Chancellor—Rev. Msgr. Mitrat THOMAS A. SAYUK.

Vice Chancellor—Rev. PETER WASLO.

Diocesan Treasurer—Rev. Msgr. Mitrat THOMAS A. SAYUK.

Chancery—5720 State Rd., P.O. Box 347180, Parma, OH, 44134-7180. Tel: 440-888-1522; Fax: 440-888-3477. Office Hours: Mon.-Fri. 10-12 & 2-4.

Secretary—Sr. LAURENCE M. LALIK, O.S.B.M.

Diocesan Consultors—Rev. Msgr. Mitrat LEO ADAMIAK; Rev. Msgr. Mitrat MICHAEL POLOWAY; Rev. Msgr. Mitrat MICHAEL REWTIUK; Rev. Msgr. GEORGE APPLEYARD; Rev. Msgr. RICHARD SEMINACK; Rev. Msgr. Mitrat THOMAS A. SAYUK; Very Rev. JAROSLAW MYCHASLENKO; Very Rev. Canon ROBERT HNATYSHYN; Very Rev. Canon WALTER WYSOCHANSKY.

Diocesan Corporation—Most Rev. ROBERT M. MOSKAL, Pres.; Rev. Msgr. LEO TYMKIW, Vice Pres.; Rev. Msgr. Mitrat THOMAS A. SAYUK, Sec. & Treas.

Diocesan Administrative Council—Most Rev. ROBERT M. MOSKAL; Rev. Msgr. LEO TYMKIW; Rev. Msgr. Mitrat LEO ADAMIAK; Rev. PETER WASLO; Rev. Msgr. Mitrat THOMAS SAYUK.

Protopresbyters-Deans—Western Deanery; Very Rev. JAROSLAW MYCHAJLENKO, Dean; Central Deanery: Rev. Msgr. Mitrat MICHAEL POLOWAY, Dean; Rev. Msgr. GEORGE APPLEYARD, Vice Dean; Eastern Deanery: Very Rev. JAMES POORMAN, Dean; Southern Deanery: Rev. Archpriest Mitrat MATTHEW BERKO, Dean; Rev. Msgr. JOHN STEVENSKY, Vice Dean.

Diocesan Offices and Directors

Acolyte Confraternity—Rev. STEVEN ZARICHNY.

Apostleship of Prayer—Rev. Msgr. LEO TYMKIW.

Catechetical Planning Committee—Sr. ANN LASZOK, O.S.B.M., Chm.; Rev. Msgr. RICHARD SEMINACK, D.R.E.; Rev. Msgr. GEORGE APPLEYARD; Sr. OLGA MARIE FARYNA, O.S.B.M.; Very Rev. JAROSLAW MYCHAJLENKO; Revs. XAVIER ELAMBASSERY; ANTHONY BALISTRERI; PETER WASLO.

Clergy Examiners—Rev. Msgr. Mitrat LEO ADAMIAK; Rev. Dr. Mitrat IVAN TYLAWSKYJ; Rev. Msgr. RICHARD SEMINACK; Very Rev. Canon WALTER WYSOCHANSKY.

Department of Religious Education—Rev. Msgr. RICHARD SEMINACK, Dir.; Sr. ANN LASZOK, O.S.B.M., Asst. Dir., *726 Washington Ave., Carnegie, PA, 15106.* Tel: 412-279-4652.

Diocesan Ecumenical Office—Rev. Msgr. GEORGE APPLEYARD, Dir.

Diocesan Promoter for the Cause of Metropolitan Andrew Sheptytsky—MICHAEL BILON; ESTHER BILON; Rev. Msgr. Mitrat THOMAS A. SAYUK.

Diocesan Resource Committee—Rev. Msgr. GEORGE APPLEYARD, Spiritual Dir. NICKOLAUS KOTOW, Chm. DAVID HODOWANETZ, Vice Chm. LILLIAN MISKO COURY, Sec. PETER HLUTKOWSKY, Treas.

Director of Liturgical Chant—STEPHEN ZINSKI; LILLIAN MISKO COURY; BRUCE SCILENY.

Director of Youth Ministries—Rev. ANTHONY BALISTRERI.

Lay Ministries—Sr. ANN LASZOK, O.S.B.M.; Sr. OLGA MARIE FARYNA, O.S.B.M.

League of Ukrainian Catholics (LUC)—Revs. STEVEN ZARICHNY, Spiritual Dir. of Ohio Council; MICHAEL POLOSKY, Spiritual Dir. of Western PA Council; Rev. Msgr. JOHN STEVENSKY, Organizer of Southern Deanery LUC.

League of Ukrainian Catholic Youth (LUCY)—Rev. ANTHONY BALISTRERI, Spiritual Dir.

Lector Training Team—Sr. ANN LASZOK, O.S.B.M., Dir.; Very Rev. JAROSLAW MYCHAJLENKO; JOHN KOWICK; JOANNE KOWICK.

Marian Sodalities—Sr. LAURENCE M. LALIK, O.S.B.M.

Obnova—Rev. WOLODYMYR WOLOSZCZUK, Dir.

Office for Evangelization—Rev. MICHAEL POLOSKY, Liaison.

Pastoral Ministry Office—Sr. ANN LASZOK, O.S.B.M., Coord.; Sr. MARINA BOCHNEWICH, O.S.B.M., Adult Spiritual Formation; KATHY KRUTYHOLOWA, Adult Spiritual Formation. Adult Religious Education: Dr. VERA KROKONKO; Deacon JEFFREY SMOLILO, *727 E. Carson St., Pittsburgh, PA, 15203.* Tel: 412-481-9778.

Permanent Diaconate Program—Rev. Msgr. Mitrat MICHAEL POLOWAY; Rev. Msgr. GEORGE APPLEYARD; Rev. Msgr. RICHARD SEMINACK; Rev. PETER WASLO, Dir.

Prayer League for Canonization of Metropolitan Andrew Sheptytsky—Rev. Msgr. Mitrat THOMAS SAYUK.

Presbyteral Council—Rev. Msgr. Mitrat LEO ADAMIAK; Rev. Msgr. Mitrat THOMAS A. SAYUK; Rev. Msgr. Mitrat MICHAEL POLOWAY; Rev. Msgr. Mitrat MICHAEL PEWTIUK; Rev. Msgr. RICHARD SEMINACK; Very Rev. JAMES POORMAN; Very Rev. Canon WALTER WYSOCHANSKY; Rev. Msgr. GEORGE APPLEYARD; Very Rev. JAROSLAW MYCHAJLENKO; Revs. XAVIER ELAMBASSERY; PETER WASLO; STEVEN ZARICHNY; STEVEN PALIWODA; ANTHONY BALISTRERI; JOHN CHIROVSKY; MICHAEL POLOSKY.

Priests' Continuing Education—Rev. PETER WASLO.

Vocation Director—Revs. STEVEN PALIWODA; MICHAEL POLOSKY.

Diocesan Committee for "Jubilee 2000"—Rev. MICHAEL BLISZCZ, Liaison.

Diocesan Personnel Board—Rev. Msgr. RICHARD SEMINACK; Very Rev. Canon WALTER WYSOCHANSKY; Rev. PETER WASLO; Rev. Dr. JOHN ROPKE.

CLERGY, PARISHES, MISSIONS AND PAROCHIAL SCHOOLS

STATE OF OHIO

1—ST. JOSAPHAT CATHEDRAL, Rev. Msgr. Mitred Michael Rewtiuk; Rev. Andrew Hanowsky.
Res., 5720 State Rd., 44134-2536. Tel: 440-886-2108.
School—Tel: 440-884-1812; Fax: 440-884-3435.
Sisters of St. Basil the Great 3; Lay Teachers 13; Students 159.

2—ST. ANDREW, Rev. Msgr. Leo Tymkiw; Rev. Peter Waslo.
Res., 7700 Hoertz Rd., 44134-6404. Tel: 440-843-9149.

3—POKROVA UKRAINIAN CATHOLIC PARISH, Rev. John M. Freishyn-Chirovsky.
Office: 6812 Broadview Rd., 44134. Tel: 440-524-0918; Fax: 440-524-0919. [CEM]
Res., 6790 Broadview Rd., 44134-4804. Tel: 440-524-2505.

4—HOLY GHOST, Rev. Michael Krupka.
Res., 1859 Carter Ave., 44301. Tel: 330-724-8277.

5—ST. ANNE, Very Rev. Canon Walter J. Wysochansky.
Res., 3055 S. Raccoon Rd., 44515-5351. Tel: 330-793-5436; 792-8555.
Church—4310 Kirk Rd., 44511-1899.
School—Tel: 330-792-9806; Fax: 330-792-3995.
Lay Teachers 14; Students 115.

6—ST. NICHOLAS. Attended by Akron.
Church—1020 Lippert Rd., 44704.

7—SS. PETER AND PAUL, Rev. Steven Zarichny.
Res., 2280 W. 7th St., 44113. Tel: 216-861-2176. [CEM]

8—ST. JOHN THE BAPTIST, Rev. Steven Paliwoda, Admin.
Res., 3038 Charleston Ave., 44055-2121. Tel: 440-277-7114.
Church—2445 E. 31st St., 44055.
Mission—Media.

9—ST. MICHAEL, Rev. Anthony Balistreri, Admin.
Res., 133 Walnut St., 43460-1248. Tel: 419-666-5627.

10—PROTECTION B.V.M., Very Rev. Jaroslaw Mychajlenko.
Res., 27275 Aurora Rd., 44139-1804. Tel: 440-248-4549.

11—HOLY TRINITY, Rev. Msgr. Mitred Leo Adamiak, V.G.
Res., 526 W. Rayen Ave., 44502-1124. Tel: 330-744-5820.

STATE OF FLORIDA

Apopka, Orange Co., St. Mary's, Mitred Archpriest Matthew Berko; Rev. Myroslaw Cisdyn.
Res., 20 E. Nightingale St., 32712. Tel: 407-880-1640.

Miami, Dade Co., Assumption of B.V.M., Rev. Msgr. John Stevensky.
Res., 39 N.W. 57th Ct., 33126. Tel: 305-262-4192; Fax: 305-261-9759.

North Port, Sarasota Co., Entrance of B.V.M. into the Temple, Mitred Archpriest Ivan Tylawskyj.
Res., 1078 N. Biscayne Dr., 34286. Tel: 813-426-7931.

St. Petersburg, Pinellas Co., Epiphany of Our Lord, Mitred Archpriest Matthew Berko; Rev. Myroslaw Cisdyn.
Res., 434 90th Ave., N., 33702. Tel: 813-576-1001.

Spring Hill, Hernando Co., St. Andrew. Served from St. Petersburg, FL. Mitred Archpriest Matthew Berko; Rev. Myroslaw Cisdyn.
Mailing Address: P.O. Box 5902, 34606. Tel: 813-577-0385.

STATE OF PENNSYLVANIA

Aliquippa, Beaver Co., Ss. Peter and Paul, Rev. Michael Derbish, O.F.M.
Res., 2001 Main St., 15001. Tel: 412-375-7016.

Altoona, Blair Co., Immaculate Conception. Attended by Barnesboro. Rev. Emanuel Rathapilly.
Res., 2020 20th St., 16601. Tel: 814-943-4553. [CEM]

Ambridge, Beaver Co., Ss. Peter and Paul, Revs. Michael Polosky; F. Alexander Ganzy.
Res., 404 6th St., 15003. Tel: 412-266-2262.

Barnesboro, Cambria Co., Immaculate Conception, Rev. Emanuel Rathapilly.
Res., 300 Campbell Ave., 15714. Tel: 814-948-9193.

Carnegie, Allegheny Co., Holy Trinity, Rev. Msgr. Richard Seminack; Rev. Michael Bliszcz.
Res., 730 Washington Ave., 15106. Tel: 412-279-4652. [CEM]

Ford City, Armstrong Co., St. Mary, Rev. Michael Sopp, Admin.
Res., 514 Ninth St., 16226. Tel: 412-763-1203. [CEM]

Jeannette, Westmoreland Co., St. Demetrius, Rev. Michael C. Kabel.
Res., 1013 Gaskill Ave., 15644-3307. Tel: 412-523-9389.

Johnstown, Cambria Co., St. John the Baptist, Rev. Anthony Kubacki, Admin.
Res., 606 Maple Ave., 15901. Tel: 814-535-2634. [CEM]

Latrobe, Westmoreland Co., Assumption of B.V.M., Rev. Xavier Elambassery.
Res., 526 Hillview Ave., 15650. Tel: 412-537-6450.

Lyndora, Butler Co., St. Michael, Rev. Douglas Lorance.
Res., 25 Hansen Ave., 16045-1325. Tel: 412-283-6230; Fax: 412-283-0363.

McKeesport, Allegheny Co., St. John the Baptist, Very Rev. Canon Robert Hnatyshyn.
Res., 1907 Eden Park Blvd., 15132. Tel: 412-672-0923.

McKees Rocks, Allegheny Co., St. John the Baptist. Attended by St. George, Pittsburgh. Rev. Msgr. George Appleyard.
Res., 3455 California Ave., Pittsburgh, 15212. Tel: 412-766-8801.
Church—204 Olivia St., 15136. Tel: 412-331-5605.

New Alexandria, Westmoreland Co., Nativity B.V.M. Attended by Latrobe.
526 Hillview Ave., Latrobe, 15650. Tel: 412-537-6450.
Church—Shersburg Rd., 15670. [CEM]

New Kensington, Westmoreland Co., St. Vladimir, Rev. Dr. John Ropke.
Res., 1601 Kenneth Ave., 15068. Tel: 412-339-9622.

Pittsburgh, Allegheny Co., St. George, Rev. Msgr. George Appleyard; Rev. Robert Masters.
Res., 3455 California Ave., 15212. Tel: 412-766-8801; Fax: 412-766-8244.

St. John the Baptist, Rev. Msgr. Mitred Michael Poloway.
Res., 109 S. Seventh St., 15203. Tel: 412-431-2531; Fax: 412-431-0727. [CEM]

Ramey, Clearfield Co., Annunciation B.V.M., Very Rev. James E. Poorman.
Res., P.O. Box 205, 16671. Tel: 814-378-7688. [CEM]

Revloc, Cambria Co., Protection Blessed Virgin Mary. Attended by Johnstown.
606 Maple Ave., Johnstown, 15901. Tel: 814-535-2634.
Church—560 Cambria Ave., P.O. Box 194, 15948-0914.

West Leechburg, Armstrong Co., St. Michael. Attended by Ford City, PA.
Mailing Address: 514 Ninth St., Ford City, 16226. Tel: 412-763-1203.
Church—Main St., 15656.

Wilmerding, Allegheny Co., Ss. Peter and Paul. Attended by Jeannette, PA.
Mailing Address: 1013 Gaskill Ave., Jeannette, 15644. Tel: 412-523-9389.
Church—163 State St., 15148-1323. Tel: 412-829-1833.

STATE OF WEST VIRGINIA

Wheeling, Ohio Co., St. Mary, Very Rev. Archpriest Philip Bumbar.
Res., 4136 Jacob St., 26003. Tel: 304-232-2168.

Absent on Leave:
Reverend Fathers—
Gribik, John

Graduate Studies:
Reverend Fathers—
Morozowich, Mark

Retired:
Reverend Monsignors—
Fedyk, Jaroslaw, Hollywood Trailer Park, 7230 4th St., N., Lot 1102, St. Petersburg, FL 33702
Kachmar, Walter, R.D. No. 5, Box 54, Blairsville, PA 15717-9139
Nestor, Michael, 867 N. Concord St., Gilbert, AZ 85234
Reverend Fathers—
Adamiak, Stephen, 5825 59th Way, N., St. Petersburg, FL 33709
Balaban, Oryst, 1532 Fourth Ave., Arnold, PA 15068-4402
Griffiths, James, 111 S. Cliff St., Apt. 6B6, Butler, PA 16001-6045
Woloszczuk, Wolodymyr, 4240 Timberline Blvd., Venice, FL 34293

Permanent Deacons:
Billy, Donald, 2515 McCollum Rd., Youngstown, OH 44509
Boyce, Gary, 240 Lindsey Rd., Munroe Falls, OH 44262
Dobosh, Michael, 7935 Carlyle Ave., Apt. 10, Miami Beach, FL 33141
Dukeley, Boris, 15008 S.W. 35th Cir., Ocala, FL 34473
Harwas, Roman, 300 S.W. 21st St., Okeechobee, FL 34974
Levy, Joseph M., 5216 Kerrington Dr., Gibsonia, PA 15044
Marko, Andrew, 33225 Electric Blvd., Avon Lake, OH 44012
Poklemba, Joseph, 1266 Signature Dr., Austintown, OH 44515
Smolilo, Jeffery, 7626 Keywest Dr., Parma, OH 44134

INSTITUTIONS LOCATED IN THE DIOCESE

[A] CONVENTS

PARMA. *St. Josaphat Convent*, 5720 State Rd., 44134-2536. Tel: 216-885-1245. Sisters of St. Basil the Great.

[B] HOMES FOR THE AGED

PARMA. *Shevchenko Manor*, 5620 W. 24th St., 44134-2751. Tel: 440-459-1440; Fax: 440-459-1442. Jennie Bochar, Mgr.

PITTSBURGH, PA. *Sheptytsky Arms*, 3505 Mexico St., 15212. Tel: 412-766-8802; Fax: 412-766-0938. Sr. Dennys Polovischak, S.S.M.I., Mgr.; Sr. Consolata Trudik, S.S.M.I., Sec.

NECROLOGY

† Nesevitch, Joseph, (Retired). —Died Oct. 4, 1997.

Eparchy of St. Maron of Brooklyn

Most Reverend

STEPHEN HECTOR DOUEIHI, S.T.D.

Bishop, Eparchy of Saint Maron of Brooklyn; born June 25, 1927; ordained August 14, 1955; appointed Second Eparchial Bishop of the Eparchy of Saint Maron of Brooklyn November 23, 1996; consecrated January 11, 1997; enthroned February 5, 1997. *Res., 8070 Harbor View Terrace, Brooklyn, New York, 11209.*

Most Reverend

FRANCIS M. ZAYEK, D.D., S.T.D., J.C.D.

Retired Bishop, Eparchy of St. Maron of Brooklyn; born October 18, 1920; ordained March 17, 1946; appointed Titular Bishop of Callinicum May 30, 1962; consecrated August 5, 1962; appointed Eparch of the Diocese of Saint Maron November 11, 1971; installed June 4, 1972; elevated to Archbishop December 22, 1982. *Res., 8070 Harbor View Terrace, Brooklyn, New York, 11209.*

ESTABLISHED AS AN APOSTOLIC EXARCHATE JANUARY 10, 1966; ELEVATED TO A DIOCESE NOVEMBER 11, 1971.

The jurisdiction of the Diocese extends to all the Maronite Catholics in New York, New Jersey, Pennsylvania, Florida, Georgia, North Carolina, South Carolina, Delaware, Virginia, District of Columbia, Maine, New Hampshire, Vermont, Massachusetts, Rhode Island, Connecticut and Maryland.

For legal titles of parishes and diocesan institutions, consult the Chancery Office.

Chancery Office: The Pastoral Center, 294 Howard Ave., Staten Island, NY, 10301-4409. Tel.: 718-815-0436; Fax: 718-815-0536.

STATISTICAL OVERVIEW

Personnel	
Retired Archbishops	1
Bishop	1
Abbots	1
Priests: Diocesan Active in Diocese	39
Priests: Active Outside Diocese	4
Priests: Retired, Sick or Absent	13
Number of Diocesan Priests	56
Religious Priests in Diocese	10
Ordinations:	
Transitional Deacons	1
Permanent Deacons	1
Permanent Deacons in Diocese	12
Total Sisters	8

Parishes	
Parishes	33
With Resident Pastor:	
Resident Diocesan Priests	33
Without Resident Pastor:	
Missions	3
Educational	
Seminaries, Diocesan	1
Catechesis/Religious Education:	
High School Students	356
Elementary Students	1,197
Total Students Under Catholic Instruction	1,553

Vital Statistics	
Receptions into the Church:	
Infant Baptism Totals	439
Adult Baptism Totals	11
Received into Full Communion	40
First Communions	318
Confirmations	330
Marriages:	
Catholic	113
Interfaith	28
Total Marriages	141
Deaths	229
Total Catholic Population	29,206

Protosyncellus (Vicar General)—Rev. Msgr. JOSEPH F. KADDO.

Chancellor—Rev. Msgr. JOSEPH F. KADDO.

Vicar for Canonical Services/Administration—Rev. FRANCIS J. MARINI, J.C.O.D.

Pastoral Center—294 Howard Ave., Staten Island, NY, 10301. Tel: 718-815-0436; Fax: 718-815-0536. Office Hours: Mon.-Fri. 9-12 & 1:30-4. Closed on Maronite holy days and national holidays.

Tribunal of the Eparchy of Saint Maron of Brooklyn—

Episcopal Moderator—Most Rev. STEPHEN HECTOR DOVEIHI, S.T.D.

Judicial Vicar—Rev. MICHAEL G. THOMAS, J.C.D.

Defender of the Bond—Rev. CARL MORRISON, J.C.L.

Promotor of Justice—Very Rev. THOMAS M. MARIN, J.C.L.

Advocates—Rev. KENNETH D. WHITAKER, J.C.L.; Ms. RITA FERKO JOYCE, J.D., J.C.L.

Presbyteral Council-Ex Officio Members—Most Rev. STEPHEN HECTOR DOVEIHI; Chorbishop SEELY BEGGIANI; Chorbishop JOSEPH LAHOUD, Northern District; Rev. Msgr. JOSEPH F. KADDO; Rev. Msgr. IGNACE SADAK; Rev. FAHED AZAR, Central District; Rev. GEORGE SEBAALI, Southern District.

Elected Members—Chorbishop JOSEPH LAHOUD; Rev. FRANCIS J. MARINI; Rev. Msgr. DAVID M. GEORGE.

Appointed Members—Rev. Msgr. NORMAN FERRIS; Rev. EDWARD T. WEDDER.

Protopresbyters—(I); Chorbishop JOSEPH LAHOUD,(Northern); Rev. FAHED AZAR,(Central); Rev. GEORGE SEBAALI,(Southern).

Lebanon Commission—Chorbishop SEELY BEGGIANI, Chm., *7164 Alaska Ave., N.W., Washington, DC, 20012.* Tel: 202-723-8831.

National Apostolate of Maronites National Office—Mr. JOHN ACERRA, Pres. ED SHINER, Exec. Sec., *P.O. 126, Dyker Heights Stn., Brooklyn, NY, 11228.* Tel: 718-232-7292.

Diocesan Offices and Directors

Communications—Rev. GEORGE SEBAALI, *4611 Sadler Rd., Glen Allen, VA, 23060.*

(Diocesan Newspaper) "The Maronite Voice"—Rev. GEORGE SEBAALI, Editor, *4611 Sadler Rd., Glen Allen, VA, 23060.* Tel: 804-270-7234; Fax: 804-273-9914.

Finance Council—Most Rev. STEPHEN HECTOR DOVEIHI, Chm.

Liturgy—Chorbishop HECTOR DOUEIHI, *294 Howard Ave., Staten Island, NY, 10301.* Tel: 718-815-0436.

Ministries (Permanent Deacons and Subdeacons)—Rev. EDWARD NEDDER, *375 Island Pond Rd., Springfield, MA, 01118.* Tel: 413-732-0589.

Order of Saint Sharbel—Mrs. BEVERLY KIMES, *National Office, 294 Howard Ave., Staten Island, NY, 10301.*

Pro-Life Director—Rev. KEVIN BEATON.

Religious Education—Chorbishop DOMINIC ASHKAR, *7164 Alaska Ave., N.W., Washington, DC, 20012.* Tel: 202-826-5554.

Vocations—Rev. Msgr. DAVID GEORGE, *P.O. Box 2567, Brockton, MA, 02405-2567.* Tel: 508-586-1428.

Youth Ministry Office—Rev. JOHN MORRISON, *182 4th St., Troy, NY, 12180.* Tel: 518-272-6073.

CLERGY, PARISHES, MISSIONS AND PAROCHIAL SCHOOLS

STATE OF NEW YORK

Brooklyn, Kings Co., Cathedral of Our Lady of Lebanon, Rev. Msgr. Ignace Sadek, Rector.
Res., 113 Remsen St., 11201. Tel: 718-624-7228; Fax: 718-624-8034.

Olean, Cattaraugus Co., St. Joseph, Rev. Donald N. Thomas.
Res., 331 N. Fourth St., 14760. Tel: 716-372-4311.

Troy, Rensselaer Co., St. Ann, Rev. John A. Morrison.
Res., 182 Fourth St., 12180. Tel: 518-272-6073.

Utica, Oneida Co., St. Louis Gonzaga, Rev. Bassam Saade.
Res., 520 Rutger St., 13501. Tel: 315-732-6019.

Williamsville, Erie Co., St. John Maron, Rev. Georges El-Khalli.

Res., 2040 Wehrle Dr., 14221-7041. Tel: 716-634-0669.

STATE OF CONNECTICUT

Danbury, Fairfield Co., St. Anthony, Rev. Moussa Joseph.
Res., 17 Granville Ave., 06810. Tel: 203-744-3372; Fax: 203-794-0949.

Torrington, Litchfield Co., St. Maron, Rev. Lawrence P. Michael.
Res., 613 Main St., 06790. Tel: 203-489-9015; Fax: 203-482-1614.

Waterbury, New Haven Co., Our Lady of Lebanon, Rev. Msgr. David M. Geokge.
Res., 8 E. Mountain Rd., 06706. Tel: 203-753-6633; 753-9428.

STATE OF FLORIDA

Miami, Dade Co., Our Lady of Lebanon, Rev. Michael G. Thomas.
Church—2055 Coral Way, 33145. Tel: 305-856-7449.
Res., 420 Como Ave., Coral Gables, 33146. Tel: 305-663-1438.

Orlando, Orange Co., St. Jude Mission, Revs. George Zina; Joseph Akiki.
Res., 6282 Sandcrest Cir., 32819. Tel: 407-363-7405.

West Palm Beach, Palm Beach Co., Mary Mother of Light Maronite Mission, Rev. Leonard Basinow.
Res., 2800 N. Ocean Dr. A22D, Singer Island, 33404. Tel: 407-881-5583.

Jacksonville, Duval Co., St. Maron Maronite, Rev. George Zina.
Res., P.O. Box 350148, 32235-0148. Tel: 904-721-3334.

STATE OF GEORGIA

Atlanta, Fulton Co., St. Joseph's Maronite Church, Rev. Peter Boulos.
Res., 502 Seminole Ave., N.E., 30307. Tel: 404-525-2504.

STATE OF MAINE

Waterville, Kennebec Co., St. Joseph, Rev. Samuel A. Najjar.
Res., 3 Appleton St., 04901. Tel: 207-872-8515.

STATE OF MASSACHUSETTS

Brockton, Plymouth Co., St. Theresa, Rev. Anthony Weiler.
Mailing Address: P.O. Box 2567, 02405. Fax: 508-587-8139.
Res., 10 Lebanon St., 02401. Tel: 508-586-1428.

Fall River, Bristol Co., St. Anthony of the Desert, Rev. Msgr. Norman J. Ferris.
Res., 300 N. Eastern Ave., 02723. Tel: 617-672-7653.

Jamaica Plain, Suffolk Co., Our Lady of the Cedars of Lebanon, Rev. Msgr. Joseph F. Lahoud.
Res., 61 Rockwood St., 02130. Tel: 617-522-0225; Fax: 617-522-0194.

Lawrence, Essex Co., St. Anthony, Rev. Msgr. James T. Khoury.
Res., 145 Amesbury St., 01841. Tel: 617-685-7233. [CEM]

New Bedford, Bristol Co., Our Lady of Purgatory, Rev. Charbel T. Semaan.
Res., 11 Franklin St., 02740. Tel: 508-996-8934; Fax: 508-996-2744.

Springfield, Hampden Co., St. Anthony, Rev. Edward T. Nedder; Deacon Terrence O'Connell.
Res., 419 Island Pond Rd., 01118-1002. Tel: 413-732-0589.
Church—375 Island Pond Rd., 01118-1002.

Worcester, Worcester Co., Our Lady of Mercy, Rev. David F. Michael.
Res., 70 Mulberry St., 01605. Tel: 617-752-4287.

STATE OF NEW HAMPSHIRE

Dover, Strafford Co., St. George, Rev. H. Paul Boackle.
Res., 66 Portland Ave., 03820. Tel: 603-742-1149.

STATE OF NEW JERSEY

Somerset, Somerset Co., St. Sharbel, Rev. Maroun Asmar.
Res., 12 Reeve St., 08873. Tel: 908-828-2055; Fax: 908-828-5488.

STATE OF NORTH CAROLINA

Fayetteville, Cumberland Co., Archangel Michael, Rev. Larry Jensen.
Res., 806 Arsenal Ave., 28305. Tel: 919-484-1531.

STATE OF PENNSYLVANIA

Easton, Northampton Co., Our Lady of Lebanon, Rev. Msgr. Sami Hayek.
Res., 54 S. Fourth St., 18042. Tel: 215-252-5275.

New Castle, Lawrence Co., St. John the Baptist, Rev. Joseph David.
Res., 2 W. Reynolds St., 16101. Tel: 412-658-0787.

Newtown Square, Delaware Co., St. Sharbel Mission, Rev. Paul Mooradd.
Res., 201 S. Newtown Square Rd., Newton Square, 19073. Tel: 610-353-5952.

Philadelphia, Philadelphia Co., St. Maron, Rev. Msgr. Sharbel Lischaa; Deacon Joseph Regan.
Res., 1010 Ellsworth St., 19147. Tel: 215-389-1300.

Pittsburgh, Allegheny Co., Our Lady of Victory, Rev. James A. Root.
Res., 1000 Lindsay Rd., Carnegie, 15106. Tel: 412-278-0841; Fax: 412-278-0846.

Scranton, Lackawanna Co., St. Ann, Rev. Kevin J. Beaton.
Res., 1320 Price St., 18504-3336. Tel: 717-344-2129.

Uniontown, Fayette Co., St. George, Rev. Christopher J. Henderson.
Res., Lebanon Ter., 15401. Tel: 412-437-5589.

Wilkes-Barre, Luzerne Co., St. George, Rev. Fahed Azar.
Res., 79 Loomis St., 18702. Tel: 717-824-3599.
St. Anthony, Rev. Fahed Azar.
Res., 253 Dana St., 18702. Tel: 717-824-4448.

STATE OF RHODE ISLAND

Pawtucket, Providence Co., Holy Trinity-St. George, Rev. Paul Mouawad.
Res., 50 Main St., 02860. Tel: 401-723-8444.

STATE OF VIRGINIA

Richmond, Richmond City Co., St. Anthony, Rev. George M. Sebaali.
Res., 4611 Sadler Rd., Glen Allen, 23060. Tel: 804-270-7234; Fax: 804-273-9914.

Roanoke, Roanoke City Co., St. Elias, Rev. Rodolph Wakim.
Res., P.O. Box 822, 24004. Tel: 703-342-9872; 344-9493.

DISTRICT OF COLUMBIA

Washington, District of Columbia, Our Lady of Lebanon Church, Chorbishop Dominic F. Ashkar.
Res., 7164 Alaska Ave., N.W., 20012. Tel: 202-829-5554.

On Duty Outside the Diocese:
Chorbishop—
Faris, John D.
Reverend Monsignors—
Beshara, Ronald M.
Reverend Fathers—
Amar, Joseph P.
Bartoul, William

Unassigned:
Reverend Monsignors—
Awad, Assad
Reverend Fathers—
Abi-Sarkis, Elias
Shaheen, Joseph

Retired:
Chorbishop—
Abi-Nader, Joseph
Saidi, Joseph
Trad, John
Most Rev.—
Zayek, Francis M.
Reverend Monsignors—
Antoun, Elie
Bistany, Joseph
Joseph, Joseph D.
Naffah, John
Reverend Fathers—
Akekee, Wlademer
Andary, John S.
El-Hayek, Nehmatallah
Hitti, Michael
Mahfoud, Peter
Saad, Antoun
Zogheib, Hares

Permanent Deacons:
Calabrese, Robert, Danbury, CT
Caporiccio, Richard, Arlington, VA
Joseph, Peter, Waterville, ME
Koury, Anthony, Easton, PA
Massoud, Donald, Fall River, MA
Mattar, Jean E., New Bedford, MA
Nashawaty, Nicholas, MA
Nasser, Andre, Fall River, MA
O'Connell, Terrence J., Springfield, MA
Ramey, Al, Lawrence, MA
Regan, Joseph W., Sewell, NJ
Salamy, Paul A., Utica, NY
Stowe, Richard, New Castle, PA

INSTITUTIONS LOCATED IN THE DIOCESE

[A] SEMINARIES, DIOCESAN

WASHINGTON, DC. *Our Lady of Lebanon Maronite Seminary*, 7164 Alaska Ave., N.W., 20012. Tel: 202-723-8831. Chorbishop Seely Beggiani, S.T.D., Rector.

[B] CONVENTS AND RESIDENCES FOR SISTERS

NORTH BROOKFIELD, MA. *Hermits of Jesus The Eternal Priest*, P.O. Box 421, 01535. Tel: 508-867-0134. Mother Elias, Supr.

RUTLAND, MA. *Mother of Light Community, Our Lady of Guadalupe Convent*, 374 Main St., P.O. Box 335, 01543-0335. Tel: 508-886-6745. Marionite Benedictine Sisters. Sr. Helen LaBud, O.S.B., Supr. Professed Sisters 5.

[C] RELIGIOUS COMMUNITIES OF MEN

BETHLEHEM, SD. *Holy Nativity Monastery*, 57708. Tel: 605-787-4606. Rev. Louis Marie Dauphinais, O.Mar., Supr. Priests 5.

PETERSHAM, MA. *Most Holy Trinity Monastery*, Dugway Rd., P.O. Box 605, 01366. Tel: 508-724-3347. Revs. William J. Driscoll, O.Mar., Abbot; Giles R. Goyette, O.Mar., Vicar; Michael Cernak, O.Mar.; Gean Marie Choiniere, O.Mar.; Louis Marie Dauphinais, O.Mar.; Elias Havel, O.Mar.; Francis DeGuzman, O.Mar.; Maron Morgan, O.Mar.; Martin Ferland, O.Mar.; Anthony Kramer, O.Mar. Priests 10; Brothers 4.

[D] RESIDENCES FOR CLERGY

BROOKLYN. *Bishop's Residence*, 8070 Harbor View Ter., 11209. Rev. Msgr. Joseph F. Kaddo.

STATEN ISLAND. *Pastoral Center*, 294 Howard Ave., 10301. Rev. Francis J. Marini, J.C.O.D.

[E] MISCELLANEOUS

NEW BEDFORD, MA. *Cedar Holdings, Inc.*, P.O. Box 51021, 02745-0035. Tel: 508-996-8934; Fax: 508-996-2744.

STATEN ISLAND. *Bishops Retirement Trust Fund*, 294 Howard Ave., 10301.
Order of St. Sharbel Trust Fund, 294 Howard Ave., 10301.
Priest Retirement Trust Fund, 294 Howard Ave., 10301.

WILLISTON, VT. *Blessed Rafka Retreat Center*, c/o Emmaus House, R.D. 2, Box 305A, 05495. Tel: 802-660-2528. Rev. Joseph Akiki.

NECROLOGY

† Abi-Nader, Maroun, (Retired). —Died Dec. 29, 1996.
† Kleem, Ferris, (Retired). —Died Sept. 23, 1997.

Diocese of St. Nicholas in Chicago for Ukrainians

Most Reverend

MICHAEL WIWCHAR, C.SS.R., D.D.

Bishop of Chicago; ordained June 28, 1959; appointed Third Bishop of the St. Nicholas Diocese; installed September 28, 1993. *Mailing Address: 2245 W. Rice St., Chicago, IL, 60622.*

Most Reverend

INNOCENT LOTOCKY, O.S.B.M., D.D., PH.D.

Retired Bishop of Chicago; ordained November 24, 1940; appointed Second Bishop of Chicago, January 29, 1981; consecrated March 1, 1981; installed April 2, 1981; retired September 28, 1993. *Mailing Address: 2245 W. Rice St., Chicago, IL, 60622.* Tel.: 773-276-8981.

Comprises all of the United States west of the western borders of Ohio, Kentucky, Tennessee and Mississippi.

For legal titles of parishes and diocesan institutions, consult the Chancery Office.

Chancery Office: 2245 W. Rice St., Chicago, IL, 60622. Tel.: 773-276-5080; 276-4537; Fax: 773-276-6799.

STATISTICAL OVERVIEW

Personnel	
Bishop	1
Retired Bishops	1
Abbots	1
Priests: Diocesan Active in Diocese	18
Priests: Active Outside Diocese	1
Priests: Retired, Sick or Absent	12
Number of Diocesan Priests	31
Religious Priests in Diocese	13
Extern Priests in Diocese	14
Ordinations:	
Diocesan Priests	1
Permanent Deacons	2
Permanent Deacons in Diocese	13
Total Brothers	10
Total Sisters	4
Parishes	
Parishes	35
With Resident Pastor:	
Resident Diocesan Priests	26
Resident Religious Priests	4
Without Resident Pastor:	
Administered by Priests	4
Administered by Permanent Deacons	1
Professional Ministry Personnel:	
Sisters	4
Educational	
High Schools, Diocesan and Parish	1
Total Students	90
Elementary Schools, Diocesan and Parish	2
Total Students	433
Catechesis/Religious Education:	
High School Students	20
Elementary Students	150
Total Students Under Catholic Instruction	693
Teachers in the Diocese:	
Sisters	4
Lay Teachers	50
Vital Statistics	
Receptions into the Church:	
Infant Baptism Totals	101
Adult Baptism Totals	5
First Communions	101
Confirmations	117
Marriages:	
Catholic	43
Interfaith	20
Total Marriages	63
Deaths	160
Total Catholic Population	10,186

Former Bishops—Most Rev. JAROSLAV GABRO, D.D., appt. First Bishop of Chicago, July 12, 1961; cons. Oct. 26, 1961; died March 28, 1980.—Most Rev. INNOCENT LOTOCKY, O.S.B.M., D.D., Ph.D., ord. Nov. 24, 1940; appt. Second Bishop of Chicago, Jan. 29, 1981; cons. March 1, 1981; installed April 2, 1981; retired Sept. 28, 1993.

Syncellus—Rev. Msgr. Canon WILLIAM M. BILINSKY.

Econome—Rev. ABRAHAM MILLER.

Chancery Office—2245 W. Rice St., Chicago, IL, 60622. Tel: 773-276-5080. If no answer. Tel: 773-276-4537; Fax: 773-276-6799. Office Hours: Mon.-Fri. 9-4.

Diocesan Consultors—Rt. Rev. Mitred Archpriest JOHN LAZAR; Very Rev. Canon WAYNE RUCHGY; Very Rev. Canon MICHAEL STELMACH; Revs. MYRON PANCHUK; RICHARD JANOWICZ.

Presbyteral Council—Rt. Rev. Mitred Archpriest JOHN LAZAR; Very Rev. Canon Msgr. WILLIAM M. BILINSKY; Very Rev. Canon IVAN KROTEC; Very Rev. Canon WAYNE RUCHGY; Very Rev. Canon MICHAEL STELMACH; Revs. MYKHAILO KUZMA; MYRON PANCHUK; PAVLO HAYDA.

Personnel Board—Revs. RICHARD JANOWICZ; MYRON PANCHUK; Very Rev. Canon WAYNE RUCHGY.

Tribunal—Through Special Permission of the Holy See, Local Latin Rite Tribunals Handle the Cases Within the Diocese.

Protopresbyters (Deans)—Rt. Rev. Mitred Archpriest JOHN LAZAR, Detroit Protopresbytery; Very Rev. Canon IVAN KROTEC, Chicago Protopresbytery; Very Rev. Canon MICHAEL STELMACH, Minneapolis Protopresbytery; Rev. RICHARD JANOWICZ, South-West Protopresbytery.

Eparchial Censor—Rev. SEBASTIAN SABOL, O.S.B.M.

Eparchial Catechetical Office—Rev. RICHARD L. KIROUAC, Dir.

Eparchial Bi-Monthly—"The New Star", IWANNA GORCHYNSKA, Editor, *2208 W. Chicago Ave., Chicago, IL, 60622.* Tel: 773-772-1919.

CLERGY, PARISHES, MISSIONS AND PAROCHIAL SCHOOLS

STATE OF ILLINOIS

1—ST. NICHOLAS UKRAINIAN CATHOLIC CATHEDRAL (1906), Most Rev. Michael Wiwchar, C.SS.R., Bishop; Revs. Myron Mykyta, Vicar; William MacKinnon, S.O.L.T.; Deacon Mychajlo Horodysky. In res., Rt. Rev. Mitred Arch Andrew Mykyta, (Retired); Rev. Richard Kirouac.

Res., 2238 W. Rice St., 60622. Tel: 773-276-4537; Fax: 773-276-5558. [CEM]

School—2200 W. Rice St., 60622. Tel: 773-384-7243; Fax: 773-384-7283. Sr. Irenea Hankewych, O.S.B.M., Supr. & Prin.

Sisters 2; Lay Teachers 14; Students 191.

Convent—2230 W. Rice St., 60622. Tel: 773-486-6820. Sisters of St. Basil the Great [JC]

2—ST. JOSEPH (N.W. Chicago) (1956) (Ukrainian), Revs. Pavlo Hayda; Thomas L. Glynn.

Res., 5000 N. Cumberland Ave., 60656. Tel: 773-625-4833; 625-4805 (Office).

Catechesis/Religious Programs—Students 60.

3—SS. VOLODYMYR AND OLHA (1968), Very Rev. Canon Ivan Krotec Tel: 312-455-0178; Rev. Myron Panchuk Tel: 773-666-6051; Deacon Michael Szyjan.

Parish Office: 2245 W. Superior St., 60612. Tel: 773-829-5209. [JC]

4—ST. MICHAEL'S, Very Rev. Canon John Kmech.

Res., 12211 S. Parnell Ave., 60628. Tel: 312-785-7443. [JC]

5—ST. MARY'S, Madison Co., Rev. Robert Piorkowski.

Res., 1312 Iowa St., 62060. Tel: 616-452-9118.

6—IMMACULATE CONCEPTION (1963) (Ukrainian), Very Rev. Mykhailo Kuzma.

Res., 745 S. Benton, 60067. Tel: 847-991-0820; Fax: 847-991-7873.

7—NATIVITY OF B. V. M., Cook Co., (1911) (Ukrainian), Revs. Walter Rybicky, O.S.B.M.; Demetrius Wysochansky, O.S.B.M.

Res., 8530 W. 131 St., 60464. Tel: 708-361-8876; 361-8820; Fax: 1-708-361-8820.

STATE OF ARIZONA

Phoenix, Maricopa Co., Assumption of B.V.M. (1959), Rev. Hugo Soutus.

Church—3720 W. Maryland Ave., 85019.

Res., 3650 W. Maryland Ave., 85019. Tel: 602-973-3667.

Tucson, Pima Co., St. Michael (1978). Attended by Phoenix. Rev. Yaroslaw Dowbush.
Res., 1557 N. Brown Way, 85732. Tel: 520-298-4967.

STATE OF CALIFORNIA

Los Angeles, Los Angeles Co., Nativity of B.V.M. (1947) (Ukrainian), Rev. Oleh Romanenko.
Res., 5154 De Longpre Ave., Hollywood, 90027. Tel: 213-663-6307; Fax: 213-663-0369.

Sacramento, St. Andrew the Apostle, Rev. John Lucas; Deacon Theodore Wroblicky, Admin.
Res., 1324 La Sierra Dr., 95864. Tel: 916-489-6373.

San Diego, San Diego Co., Our Lady of Perpetual Help (1960) (Ukrainian), Rev. David Fitzhugh; Very Rev. Canon Michael Kurylo, Pastor Emeritus.
Res., 4061 Winona Ave., 92105. Tel: 619-282-9538.

San Francisco, San Francisco Co., Immaculate Conception (1957) Ukrainian), Rev. Alexander Avramenko, Admin.
Res., 215 Silliman, 94134. Tel: 415-468-2601; Fax: 415-715-0291.

Santa Clara, Santa Clara Co., St. Vladimir. Attended by San Francisco. Rev. Alexander Avramenko.

STATE OF COLORADO

Denver, Denver Co., Transfiguration of Our Lord (1954), Rev. Wasyl Prokopiw.
Res., 4118 Shoshone St., 80211. Tel: 303-433-2347.

STATE OF INDIANA

Mishawaka, St. Joseph Co., St. Michael (1962), Rev. Richard L. Kirouac.
Res., 712 E. Lawrence St., 46544. Tel: 219-259-7173.

Munster, Lake Co., St. Josaphat (1958) (Ukrainian), Rev. John Hritzko.
Res., 8624 White Oak Ave., 46321. Tel: 219-923-0984; Fax: 219-923-0984.

STATE OF MICHIGAN

Dearborn, Wayne Co., St. Michael's (1962), Very Rev. Canon Wayne J. Ruchgy.
Res., 6340 Chase Rd., 48126. Tel: 313-582-1424; Fax: 313-582-8157.

Dearborn Heights, Wayne Co., Our Lady of Perpetual Help (1963), Very Rev. Archpriest John Lazar, Dean.
Res., 26606 Ann Arbor Trail, 48127. Tel: 313-278-0470.

Detroit, Wayne Co., St. John the Baptist (1918) (Ukrainian), Rev. Mario Daceehen, O.S.B.M.
Res., 3877 Clippert Ave., 48210. Tel: 313-897-7300; Fax: 313-897-7304. [JC]

Hamtramck, Wayne Co., Immaculate Conception of B.V.M. (1914) (Ukrainian), Very Rev. Tarcisio Lucavei, O.S.B.M., Pastor & Supr.; Revs. Constantine Wysochansky, O.S.B.M.; Sergio Saplak, O.S.B.M.; Hilarion Opaski.
Res., 11700 McDougall St., 48212. Tel: 313-893-1710; Fax: 313-893-0770.
School—29500 Westbrook, Warren, 48093. Tel: 810-574-2480. Doris Jurek, Prin.
Priests 1; Sisters 2; Lay Teachers 18; Students 242.
High School—29400 Westbrook, Warren, 48092. Tel: 810-574-2723; Fax: 810-574-0510. Michalene Weigle, Prin.
Priests 1; Sisters 1; Lay Teachers 18; Students 90.
Catechesis/Religious Programs—Students 342.
Convent—11745 Gallagher, 48212. Tel: 313-366-2061. Sisters of St. Basil the Great Sr. Frances O.S.B.M., Supr.
Sisters 2.

Flint, Genesee Co., St. Vladimir's (1950), Rt. Rev. Mitred Arch John Lazar, Admin., Dearborn Heights, MI.
Res., 3464 W. Pasadena Ave., 48504.

Grand Rapids, Kent Co., St. Michael's (1949) (Ukrainian), Deacon Jaroslau Bohatch, Admin.
Mailing Address: 4390 Woodside Oaks Dr., S.E., 49546-6216. Tel: 616-949-9593. [JC]

Warren, Macomb Co., St. Josaphat (1961) (Ukrainian), Revs. Basil Salkovski, O.S.B.M.; Sebastian Sabol, O.S.B.M.; Roman Hykawy, O.S.B.M.
Res., 26401 St. Josaphat Dr., 48091. Tel: 810-755-1740; Fax: 810-755-1399. [CEM]

STATE OF MINNESOTA

Minneapolis, Hennepin Co., St. Constantine (1913) (Ukrainian), Rev. Michael Stelmach.
Res., 515 University Ave., N.E., 55413-1944. Tel: 612-379-2394; Fax: 612-379-2470.

St. Paul, Ramsey Co., St. Stephen (1951) (Ukrainian). Attended by St. Constantine Church, Minneapolis.
Church—1260 Greenbrier St., 55106. Tel: 612-379-2394; Fax: 612-379-2470.

STATE OF MISSOURI

St. Joseph, Buchanan Co., St. Joseph's. Attended by Omaha, NE. Rev. Basil Buchek, Admin.
Church—526 Virginia, 64504. Tel: 816-238-1187.

St. Louis, St. Louis Co., Assumption B.V.M. (1894) (Ukrainian), Rev. Robert Piorkowski, Admin.
Church—11363 Oak Branch Dr., 63129.

STATE OF NEBRASKA

Lincoln, Lancaster Co., St. George's (1950), Rev. Basil Buchek, Admin.
Church—3330 N. 13th St., 68521. Tel: 402-435-5882; 345-1552.
Res., 1513 Martha St., Omaha, 68108.

Omaha, Douglas Co., Assumption of B.V.M. (1950), Rev. Basil Buchek, Admin.
Res., 1513 Martha St., 68108. Tel: 402-345-1552.

STATE OF NORTH DAKOTA

Belfield, Stark Co., St. John the Baptist (1946) (Ukrainian), Rev. Bohdan Nalysnyk, Admin.
Res., P.O. Box 428, 58622-0428. Tel: 701-575-4281. [CEM]

Fairfield, Billings Co., St. Demetrius (1905) (Ukrainian), Rev. Bohdan Nalysnyk, Admin.
Res., P.O. Box 428, Belfield, 58622-0428. Tel: 701-575-4281. [CEM]

Wilton, McLean Co., SS. Peter and Paul (1890) (Ukrainian), Rev. George L. Pruys, Admin.
Res., 106 N. 7th St., P.O. Box 275, 58579. Tel: 701-734-6464. [CEM]
Missions—Minot,; Mobridge.

STATE OF OREGON

Springfield, Lane Co., Nativity of the Mother of God (1981) (Ukrainian), Rev. Richard Janowicz.
Res., 704 Aspen St., 97477. Tel: 541-726-7309; Fax: 541-726-7309.

STATE OF TEXAS

Houston, Harris Co., Protection of the Mother of God (1957) (Ukrainian), Rev. Andrij Taras Dwulit, Admin.
Res., 9102 Meadowshire St., 77037. Tel: 713-447-2749. [JC]

STATE OF WISCONSIN

Milwaukee, Milwaukee Co., St. Michaels (1950) (Ukrainian), Rev. Volodymyr Zaiats.
Res., 1025 S. 11th St., P.O. Box 64012, 53204. Tel: 414-672-5616.

Chaplains of Public Institutions

Hospitals

CHICAGO, IL. *Resurrection and Our Lady of Resurrection.* Rev. Msgr. Canon William M. Bilinsky, Chap.
St. Mary of Nazareth Hospital Center. Rev. Abraham Miller, Chap.

On Duty Outside the Diocese:
Reverend Fathers—
Harmon, Philip Gregory, Admin., Byzantine Missions, 86-660 Lua Lualei Homestead Rd., Waianae, HI 96792. Tel: 808-696-2655; Fax: 808-696-2030
Marick, Thomas D., Byzantine Missions, Res., 1121 Ala Napunani, 704, Honolulu, HI 96818. Tel: 808-833-2472
Rt. Rev. Mitred Arch—
Riotte, Jules, Byzantine Missions, 86-660 Lua Lualei Homestead Rd., Waianae, HI 96792. Tel: 808-696-2655; Fax: 808-696-2030

Absent on Sick Leave:
Reverend Fathers—
Pedelesky, Nestor
Prodywus, Alexander

Retired:
Reverend Fathers—
Skaskiw, Bohdan, 3805 Dora Dr., Warren, MI 48091
Rt. Rev. Mitred Arch—
Mykyta, Andrew, 2238 W. Rice St., Chicago, IL 60622. Tel: 773-486-9247
Oleshko, Myroslaw, 10398 Deanne Dr., Sun City, AZ 85351. Tel: 602-974-3089
Rt. Rev. Mitred Msgr—
Knapp, Stephen V., 1675 Kilburn, Rochester Hills, MI 48306-3031. Tel: 810-652-4630
Leskiw, Peter, 1221 S. Sunflower Cir., Palm Springs, CA 92262. Tel: 619-322-2416
Very Rev. Canon—
Bobersky, Michael, 6209 E. McKellips, Mesa, AZ 85205. Tel: 602-985-7620
Kurylo, Michael, 3821-49th St., San Diego, CA 92105. Tel: 619-282-7958

Permanent Deacons:
Bohatch, Jaroslav, St. Michael, Grand Rapids, MI
Bozio, Michael, Transfiguration of Our Lord, Denver, CO
Horodysky, Mychajlo, St. Nicholas Cathedral, Chicago, IL
Hrycyniak, Stephen, St. Michael, Milwaukee, WI
Kordonowy, Leonard, St. John the Baptist, Belfield, ND; St. Demetrius, Fairfield, ND
May, Andrew, Downers Grove, IL
Plishka, Andrew, St. Joseph, Chicago, IL
Shyan, Michael, Ss. Volodymyr & Olha, Chicago, IL
Wasylyna, E., Phoenix, AZ
Wroblicky, Theodore Peter, Sacramento, CA
Zientek, Theodore, Holy Transfiguration Monastery, Redwood Valley, CA

INSTITUTIONS LOCATED IN THE DIOCESE

[A] MONASTERIES

REDWOOD VALLEY, CA. *Holy Transfiguration Monastery,* 17001 Tomki Rd., P.O. Box 217, 95470. Tel: 707-485-8959; Fax: 707-485-1122. Monks of Mount Tabor. Rt. Rev. Archimandri Boniface Luykx. Priests 4; Deacons 1; Novices 5; Professed Monks 12; Aggregates 12; Postulants 3.

RELIGIOUS INSTITUTES OF MEN REPRESENTED IN THE DIOCESE

For further details refer to the corresponding bracketed number in the Religious Institutes of Men or Women section.

[]—*Monks of Mt. Tabor.*

[0180]—*Order of St. Basil the Great.*—O.S.B.M.

[]—*Skete of Mt. Tabor.*

RELIGIOUS INSTITUTES OF WOMEN REPRESENTED IN THE DIOCESE

[3730]—*Sisters of the Order of St. Basil the Great.*—O.S.B.M.

NECROLOGY

† Bilos, Rt. Rev. Mitred Arch Leo, Palatine, IL, Immaculate Conception. —Died July 31, 1997.

Eparchy of Saint Thomas the Apostle

Most Reverend

IBRAHIM N. IBRAHIM, D.D.

First Bishop-Eparch of the Eparchy of Saint Thomas the Apostle-Chaldean Catholic Diocese of America; ordained December 30, 1962; appointed Chaldean Apostolic Exarch and Titular Bishop of Anbar, January 26, 1982; consecrated Bishop, March 7, 1982, in Baghdad, Iraq; installed April 18, 1982, in Detroit; appointed First Bishop Eparch to the Eparchy of Saint Thomas the Apostle-Chaldean Catholic Diocese of America, September 14, 1985. *Res., Chaldean Catholic Diocese of U.S.A., 25603 Berg Rd., Southfield, MI, 48034.*

Chancery Office: 25603 Berg Rd., Southfield, MI, 48034. Tel.: 248-351-0440; Fax: 248-351-0443.

EXARCHATE ERECTED JANUARY 26, 1982. ELEVATED TO THE RANK OF EPARCHY SEPTEMBER 14, 1985.

The Jurisdiction of the Eparchy extends territorially to all of the United States of America inclusive. With regard to persons, its subjects are all Catholics of the Chaldean or Assyrian-Chaldean Church: (1) Who immigrated to this country from the Middle East, especially from Iraq and Iran; (2) Who descends from such persons (can. 755); (3) Women married to men referable to (1) & (2) if they comply with can. 98, n. 4; (4) Who in accordance with can. 98, n. 3., changed their Rite; (5) Converts to the Catholic Church of the Chaldean Rite; (6) And in fact, all other Catholics of the Chaldean Rite who are attached to the parishes subject to the jurisdiction of the Eparch.

For legal titles of parishes and diocesan institutions, consult the Chancery Office.

STATISTICAL OVERVIEW

Personnel	
Bishop	1
Priests: Diocesan Active in Diocese	15
Priests: Active Outside Diocese	2
Priests: Retired, Sick or Absent	2
Number of Diocesan Priests	19
Ordinations:	
Parishes	
Parishes	12
With Resident Pastor:	
Resident Diocesan Priests	11
Without Resident Pastor:	
Administered by Priests	1

Welfare	
Homes for the Aged	1
Day Care and Extended Day Care Centers	1
Educational	
Students from This Diocese	3
Diocesan Students in Other Seminaries	3
Total Seminarians	6
Catechesis/Religious Education:	
Total Students Under Catholic Instruction	6

Vital Statistics	
Receptions into the Church:	
Infant Baptism Totals	989
Adult Baptism Totals	17
First Communions	851
Confirmations	1,006
Marriages:	
Catholic	368
Interfaith	22
Total Marriages	390
Deaths	156
Total Catholic Population	65,000

Chancery Office—25603 Berg Rd., Southfield, MI, 48034. Tel: 248-351-0440; Fax: 248-351-0443.

Vicar General—Rt. Rev. SARHAD Y. JAMMO, *2442 E. Big Beaver Rd., Troy, MI, 48083.* Tel: 248-528-3676; Fax: 248-524-1957.

College of Consultors—Rt. Rev. SARHAD Y. JAMMO, Vicar General; Revs. MANUEL BOJI; STEPHEN KALLABAT; HANNA CHEIKHO; JACOB YASSO; MICHAEL BAZZI; KAMAL BIDAWID; YOSHIA SANA; EMANUEL ISHO; NOEL GORGIS; EMANUEL RAYES; FRANK KALABAT.

Diocesan Corporation-The Chaldean Catholic Church of U.S.A.—Most Rev. IBRAHIM IBRAHIM, Pres.; Revs. MANUEL Y. BOJI, Sec. SARHAD Y. JAMMO, Treas.

Diocesan Bulletin—"The Star of Chaldeans", 25603 Berg Rd., Southfield, MI, 48034. Tel: 248-351-0440.

Eparchial Tribunal—Rev. STEPHEN H. KALLABAT, *Court of the First Instance, Chancery Office, 25603 Berg Rd., Southfield, MI, 48034.*

CLERGY, PARISHES, MISSIONS AND PAROCHIAL SCHOOLS

STATE OF MICHIGAN

Detroit, Wayne Co., Sacred Heart Chaldean Parish (1973), Rev. Jacob O. Yasso.
Res., 310 W. Seven Mile Rd., 48203. Tel: 313-368-6214 (Church); Fax: 313-891-0132.
Catechesis/Religious Programs—Students 200.
Convent—19138 Danbury, 48203. Tel: 313-368-7999. Chaldean Sisters

Oak Park, Oakland Co., Mar Addai Chaldean Parish (1979) (Chaldean), Revs. Stephen Kallabat; Suleiman Denha.
Res., 24010 Coolidge Hwy., 48237. Tel: 810-547-4648; Fax: 248-399-9089.
Catechesis/Religious Programs—Students 206.

Southfield, Oakland Co., Our Lady of Chaldeans Cathedral, Mother of God Chaldean Parish, Most Rev. Ibrahim Ibrahim; Revs. Manuel Y. Boji, Rector; Thomas Simon Nofaley; Frank Y. Kalabat; Sabri Iskander.
Res., 25585 Berg Rd., 48034. Tel: 248-356-0565; 356-0569; 356-9809 (Hall); Fax: 248-356-5235.
Catechesis/Religious Programs—Ann Antoon, D.R.E.
Students 420.
Convent—23754 Clarkson, 48034. Tel: 810-355-1318. Chaldean Sisters

Troy, Oakland Co., St. Joseph Chaldean Parish (1981), Rt. Rev. Sarhad Jammo; Revs. Emanuel Rayes; Jirjis Hanna.
Res., 2442 E. Big Beaver Rd., 48083. Tel: 248-528-3676; 524-1144 (Church); Fax: 248-524-1957.
Catechesis/Religious Programs—Students 420.
Convent—2554 Parasol, 48083. Tel: 248-740-2741. Chaldean Sisters
Mission—Flint, Genesee Co., (1993).

West Bloomfield, Oakland Co., St. Thomas Chaldean Catholic Parish (1992) (Chaldean), Rev. John Hanna Cheikho.
Mailing Address: 6900 Maple Rd., 48322. Tel: 248-788-2460; Fax: 248-788-2153.
Res., 3535 Indian Tr., Orchard Lake, 48324. Tel: 810-683-0333. [JC]
Catechesis/Religious Programs—Students 240.

STATE OF ILLINOIS

Chicago, Cook Co., St. Ephrem's Church (1904) (Chaldean-Assyrian), Rev. Msgr. Edward J. Bikoma.
Res., 2537 W. Bryn Mawr Ave., 60659. Tel: 773-271-8899. [JC]
Catechesis/Religious Programs—Students 100.
Mart Mariam Parish (1986) (Chaldean-Assyrian), Rev. Msgr. Edward J. Bikoma.
Mailing Address: 2537 W. Bryn Mawr, 60659.
Res., 2847 W. Chase Ave., 60645. Tel: 773-761-9401. [JC]

STATE OF CALIFORNIA

El Cajon, San Diego Co., St. Peter Chaldean Parish (1973) (Chaldean), Rev. Michael J. Bazzi; Faik Tominna, Parish Council Pres.
Res., 1627 Jamacha Way, 92019. Tel: 619-579-7913; 588-9921; Fax: 619-588-8281.
Catechesis/Religious Programs—Tel: 619-447-8876. Khelood Allos, D.R.E.
Students 650.
Convent—Tel: 619-588-6391. Chaldean Sisters

North Hollywood, Los Angeles Co., St. Paul Assyrian-Chaldean Catholic Parish (1980), Rev. Emanuel Hana Isho.
Res., 13050 Vanowen St., 91605. Tel: 818-765-3665; Fax: 818-765-0493.
Mission—Fullerton, Orange Co., St. George, 706 S. Lemon St., Fullerton, 92632.

San Jose, Santa Clara Co., St. Mary Assyrian-Caldean Parish (1987), Rev. Yoshia Sana.
Rectory: 6348 Mayo Dr., 95123. Tel: 408-378-6212. [JC]
Church—109 First St., Campbell, 95008. Tel: 408-378-6212.
Catechesis/Religious Programs—Students 65.

Turlock, Stanislaus Co., St. Thomas Assyrian-Chaldean Parish, Rev. Kamal Warda Bidawid.
Res., 2901 N. Berkeley Ave., 95380. Tel: 209-668-4500; Fax: 209-668-2762.
Convent—2937 N. Berkeley Ave., 95380. Tel: 209-634-2043. Chaldean Sisters
St. Thomas Retirement Center—Tel: 209-634-7252.

STATE OF ARIZONA

Scottsdale, Maricopa Co., Mar Auraha Chaldean Catholic Parish, Rev. Noel Gorgis, Admin.
Res., 6816 E. Cactus Rd., 85254. Tel: 602-596-6798; Fax: 602-596-9067.

On Assignment Outside the Diocese:
Reverend Fathers—
Buffington, Jon
Yadegar, Benn Beth

Leave of Absence:
Reverend Fathers—
Nofaley, Thomas Simon

Retired:
Reverend Fathers—
Ablahad, Najor, 28454 Red Leaf, Southfield, MI 48076. Tel: 248-569-5736

Ukrainian Catholic Diocese of Stamford

Most Reverend

BASIL H. LOSTEN, D.D., S.T.L., LL.D. (HON.)

Bishop of Stamford; ordained June 10, 1957; appointed Titular Bishop of Arcadiopolis and Auxiliary of Ukrainian Catholic Archeparchy of Philadelphia, March 15, 1971; consecrated May 25, 1971; appointed Apostolic Administrator of Archeparchy of Philadelphia, June 8, 1976; transferred to the Stamford See, September 20, 1977. *Res., 161 Glenbrook Rd., Stamford, CT, 06902.*

ESTABLISHED AUGUST 8, 1956.

The jurisdiction of the Bishop of Stamford extends territorially throughout all of New York State and the New England States. With regard to persons, his subjects are all members of the Ukrainian Catholic Church (Byzantine Rite), irrespective of where they received Baptism.

For legal titles of parishes and diocesan institutions, consult the Chancery Office.

Chancery Office: 14 Peveril Rd., Stamford, CT, 06902-3019. Tel.: 203-324-7698; Fax: 203-967-9948.

E-mail address: BASILEOS@aol.com

STATISTICAL OVERVIEW

Personnel	
Bishop	1
Priests: Diocesan Active in Diocese	24
Priests: Retired, Sick or Absent	11
Number of Diocesan Priests	35
Religious Priests in Diocese	17
Extern Priests in Diocese	28
Ordinations:	
Transitional Deacons	2
Permanent Deacons in Diocese	4
Total Brothers	5
Total Sisters	42
Parishes	
Parishes	49
With Resident Pastor:	
Resident Diocesan Priests	40
Resident Religious Priests	5
Without Resident Pastor:	
Administered by Priests	4
Missions	4
Pastoral Centers	2
Welfare	
Homes for the Aged	1
Total Assisted	28
Day Care and Extended Day Care Centers	1
Total Assisted	44
Special Centers for Social Services	1
Total Assisted	45
Educational	
Seminaries, Diocesan	1
Students from Other Diocese	59
Diocesan Students in Other Seminaries	1
Total Seminarians	1
High Schools, Diocesan and Parish	1
Total Students	140
Elementary Schools, Diocesan and Parish	4
Total Students	364
Catechesis/Religious Education:	
High School Students	19
Elementary Students	720
Total Students Under Catholic Instruction	1,244
Teachers in the Diocese:	
Sisters	7
Lay Teachers	28
Vital Statistics	
Receptions into the Church:	
Infant Baptism Totals	181
Adult Baptism Totals	9
Received into Full Communion	3
First Communions	158
Confirmations	171
Marriages:	
Catholic	78
Interfaith	22
Total Marriages	100
Deaths	385
Total Catholic Population	16,399

Former Bishops—Most Rev. AMBROSE SENYSHYN, O.S.B.M., D.D., installed as first Bishop of Stamford, Dec. 15, 1956; transferred to the Archeparchy of Philadelphia, Oct. 26, 1961; died Sept. 11, 1976.—Most Rev. JOSEPH M. SCHMONDIUK, D.D., Bishop of Stamford, Nov. 9, 1961; transferred to the Archeparchy of Philadelphia, Sept. 20, 1977; died Dec. 25, 1978.

Chancery Office—14 Peveril Rd., Stamford, CT, 06902-3019. Tel: 203-324-7698; Fax: 203-967-9948. Office Hours: 9-5.

Vicar General—Very Rev. PATRICK PASCHAK, O.S.B.M., V.G.

Econome—Rt. Rev. Mitred Msgr. JOHN TERLECKY.

Chancellor & Archivist—Rev. Msgr. LEON A. MOSKO.

Secretary—OKSANA DRAGAN.

Notary Public—OLGA KROHLEY.

Diocesan Consultors—Very Rev. PATRICK PASCHAK, O.S.B.M., V.G.; Rt. Rev. Mitred Msgr. JOHN TERLECKY; Rev. Msgr. LEON MOSKO; Rev. JAROSLAW NALYSNYK; Rev. VLADIMIR MARUSCEAC; Rev. IHOR MIDZAK.

Diocesan Tribunal—14 Peveril Rd., Stamford, CT, 06902-3019. Tel: 203-324-7698.

Vicar Judicial—Rt. Rev. Archimandrite Msgr. VICTOR POSPISHIL, J.C.D., S.E.O.D.

Judges—Rev. Msgr. GEORGE BINKOWSKI, B.S., M.S., B.D.

Defender of the Bond—"Ad Hoc" Appointment.

Notaries—Rev. MIROSLAV TROJANOWSKI; Rev. Deacon MARK HIRNIAK.

Diocesan Protopresbyters (Deans)—Albany: Rev. VLADIMIR MARUSCEAC, Acting Dean; Boston: Rev. JAROSLAW NALYSNYK, Acting Dean; Brooklyn: Rev. Msgr. GEORGE BINKOWSKI, B.S., M.S., B.D., Buffalo: Very Rev. MARIJAN PROCYK, Hartford: Rev. IHOR MIDZAK, Acting Dean; New York: Rev. MIROSLAW TROJANOWSKI, Acting Dean; Syracuse: Very Rev. JEFFREY A.G. RODEGHERO, Dean.

Presbyteral Council—Most Rev. BASIL LOSTEN; Very Rev. PATRICK PASCHAK, O.S.B.M., V.G.; Rev. Msgr. LEON MOSKO; Very Rev. MARIJAN PROCYK; Rev. MICHAEL BUNDZ; Rev. IVAN KASZCZAK; Very Revs. EDWARD YOUNG, B.A., S.T.B.; PETER OHIRKO, B.A.; Rev. IVAN MAZURYK; Rev. Canon LUBOMYR MUDRY; Rt. Rev. Mitred Msgr. JOHN TERLECKY, B.A., M.A., M.L.S.

Diocesan Offices and Directors

All offices are located at the following address unless otherwise noted: *14 Peveril Rd., Stamford, CT, 06902-3019.* Tel: 203-325-2116; Fax: 203-967-9948.

Administrative Council—Most Rev. BASIL H. LOSTEN; Very Rev. PATRICK PASCHAK, O.S.B.M., V.G.; Rev. Msgr. LEON MOSKO; Rt. Rev. Mitred Msgr. JOHN TERLECKY; Revs. IVAN KASZCZAK; ZBIGNIEW BREZIZCKI; IHOR MIDZAK.

Apostolate—Vacant.

Apostleship of Prayer—Rev. MARIJAN PROCYK.

Catechetics (Heritage Schools)—Rev. IHOR MIDZAK, S.T.B.

Cemeteries—Directors: Most Rev. BASIL H. LOSTEN, Pres. & Chm.; Rev. ZBIGNIEW BRZEZICKI, Exec. Dir.; Rev. Msgr. LEON MOSKO, Sec.; Very Rev. PATRICK PASCHAK, O.S.B.M., V.G.; Rt. Rev. Mitred Msgr. JOHN TERLECKY; Mr. LOUIS NIGRO; Mr. JOHN SENKO, *Holy Spirit Ukrainian Catholic Cemetery, 141 Sarah Wells Trail, Campbell Hall, NY, 10916.* Tel: 914-496-5506.

Censors—Very Rev. Archpriest EDWARD YOUNG; Rev. JONATHAN MORSE, Ph.D.; Very Rev. Archpriest CHARLES MEZZOMO.

Communications—Rev. Msgr. LEON MOSKO.

Development Office—Ms. MARION HRUBEC.

Diaconate, Permanent—Deacon WILLIS HOMICK.

Diocesan Charities and Missions—Most Rev. BASIL H. LOSTEN.

Ecumenical Commission—Most Rev. BASIL H. LOSTEN; Rev. IVAN KASZCZAK; Very Rev. Archpriest CHARLES MEZZOMO; Very Rev. EDWARD YOUNG.

Educational Institutions—Most Rev. BASIL H. LOSTEN; Rev. JAMES MORRIS; Rev. JEFFREY A.G. RODEGHERO; Sr. MICHELE YAKYMOVITCH, S.S.M.I.; Rev. Msgr. GEORGE BINKOWSKI, B.S., B.D., M.S., Supt. of Diocesan Schools.

Family Life—Rev. JONATHAN MORSE.

Holy Name Societies—Rev. PHILIP WEINER.

League of Ukrainian Catholics—Rev. ROBERT BATCHO, Spiritual Dir. (New England); Very Rev. MARIJAN PROCYK, Spiritual Dir. (New York).

Liturgical Commission—Rev. Msgr. LEON MOSKO; Rev. Msgr. PETER SKRINCOSKY; Rev. PHILIP WEINER; Very Rev. Archpriest CHARLES MEZZOMO; Very Rev. Archpriest EDWARD YOUNG; Very Rev. MARIJAN PROCYK; Revs. OLEKSA CHOUTER; IHOR MIDZAK.

Missionaries, Diocesan—Revs. PHILIP SANDRICK, O.S.B.M.; BERNARD PANCZUK, O.S.B.M.

Ukrainian Diocesan Museum—WASYL LENCYK, Ph.D., Dir. LUBOW WOLYNETZ, Curator.

Ukrinian Diocesan Library and Research Center—Rt. Rev. Mitred Msgr. JOHN TERLECKY, Dir.; Mrs. LUBOW WOLYNETZ, Librarian Archivist.

Press, Diocesan: "The Sower"—Rev. Msgr. LEON MOSKO, English Editor; Mr. OSYP ROSZKA, Ukrainian Editor; Rev. Deacon MARK HIRNIAK; WASYL LENCYK, Ph.D., Contributing Editor.

Priests' Benevolent Association—Rt. Rev. Mitred Msgr. JOHN TERLECKY.

Religious Communities, Vicar—Very Rev. PATRICK PASCHAK, O.S.B.M., V.G.

Religious Education—Rev. JONATHAN MORSE.

Sodalities, B.V.M.—Rev. GEORGE LUKACZYK.

Ukrainian Catholic Relief, Inc.—Rev. JONATHAN MORSE.

Ukrainian Library & Research Center—Mrs. LUBOW WOLYNEC, Dir., *39 Clovelly Rd., Stamford, CT, 06902.* Tel: 203-324-7698; Fax: 203-967-9948.

Vocations—Rev. IVAN KASZCZAK.

Youth Apostolate—Rev. JONATHAN MORSE.

Youth-For-Christ Association—Vacant.

CLERGY, PARISHES, MISSIONS AND PAROCHIAL SCHOOLS

STATE OF CONNECTICUT

1—ST. VLADIMIR CATHEDRAL, Fairfield Co., (1916) (Ukrainian), Rt. Rev. Mitred Msgr John Terlecky.
Res., 24 Wenzel Ter., 06902. Tel: 203-324-0242; Fax: 203-316-8284.
Catechesis/Religious Programs—Priests 1; Sisters 2; Lay Teachers 3; Students 22.

2—SS. PETER AND PAUL, New Haven Co., (1897) (Ukrainian), Rev. Robert J. Batcho.
Res., 105 Clifton Ave., 06401. Tel: 203-734-3895; Fax: 203-732-3191. [CEM]

3—PROTECTION OF B.V.M., Fairfield Co., (1950) (Ukrainian), Rev. Stepan Yanovski.
Church—Holy Protection of B.V.M. Ukrainian Catholic Church, 457 Noble Ave., 06608. Tel: 203-367-5054.
Res., 255 Barnum Ave., 06608. Tel: 203-367-5054.

4—ST. MARY DORMITION, New London Co., (1948) (Ukrainian), Rev. Christopher Rogalski.
Res., 178 Linwood Ave., 06415. Tel: 860-537-2069. [CEM]

5—ST. JOHN THE BAPTIST, Hartford Co., (1925) (Ukrainian). Attended by St. Michael's Ukrainian Church, Hartford. Rev. Ihor Midzak, Admin.
Church—26 New London Tpke., 06033.
Res., 135 Wethersfield Ave., Hartford, 06114. Tel: 860-525-7823; Fax: 860-727-8402.

6—ST. MICHAEL, Hartford Co., (1907) (Ukrainian), Rev. Ihor Midzak.
Church—125 Wethersfield Ave., 06114.
Res., 135 Wethersfield Ave., 06114. Tel: 860-525-7823; Fax: 860-727-8402. [CEM]
Saturday Ukrainian School—Tel: 860-728-8792.
Priests 2; Lay Teachers 11; Students 120.
Mission—Glastonbury, Hartford Co., St. John's, London Turnpike, 06114.

7—ST. JOSAPHAT, Hartford Co., (1951) (Ukrainian), Rev. Stepan Bereza.
Res., 303 Eddy Glover Blvd., 06053. Tel: 860-225-7340.
Catechesis/Religious Programs—Priests 1; Lay Teachers 3; Students 25.

8—ST. MICHAEL (1909) (Ukrainian), Rev. Paul Luniw.
Res., 569 George St., 06511. Tel: 203-865-0388; Fax: 203-752-0327.
St. Michaels Ukrainian Heritage School—(Saturdays).
Saturday Nursery School—Myron Melnyk, Prin.
Priests 1; Lay Teachers 5; Students 25.

9—ST. MICHAEL, Litchfield Co., (1910) (Ukrainian), Rev. George Lukaczyk; Deacon Paul Arena.
Res., 35 Allen St., 06786. Tel: 860-583-7588; Fax: 860-582-8064. [CEM]
Catechesis/Religious Programs—Tel: 860-582-1850. Donna Tuttle, D.R.E.
Priests 1; Lay Teachers 4; Students 25.

10—PROTECTION OF B.V.M., Windham Co., (1950) (Ukrainian), Rev. Pawlo Martyniuk, Admin.
Res., 69 Oak St., 06226. Tel: 860-423-5031; Fax: 860-423-5031.

STATE OF MASSACHUSETTS

Boston, Suffolk Co., Christ the King (1968), Rev. Jaroslaw Nalysnyk, Admin.
Res., 146 Forest Hills St., Jamaica Plain, 02130. Tel: 617-522-9720; Fax: 617-983-0309. [CEM]
Saturday Ukrainian School—.
Priests 1; Lay Teachers 3; Students 20.
Catechesis/Religious Programs—Priests 1; Lay Teachers 2; Students 20.

Fall River, Bristol Co., St. John-the-Baptist (1913). Attended by Woonsocket, RI. Rev. Msgr. Roman Golemba.
Church—339 Center St., 02724. Tel: 508-673-2353; Fax: 401-762-2733.
Res., 394 Blackstone St., Woonsocket, RI 02895. Tel: 401-762-2733. [JC]

Ludlow, Hampden Co., SS. Peter and Paul (1912)(1924) (Ukrainian), Rev. Kiril Angelov.
Res., 45 Newbury St., 01056. Tel: 413-583-2140.
Catechesis/Religious Programs—Priests 1; Students 14.

Pittsfield, Berkshire Co., St. John the Baptist (1921) (Ukrainian), Rev. Ivan Mazuryk.
Res., 18 Watson St., 01201. Tel: 413-443-6798.

Salem, Essex Co., St. John the Baptist (1918) (Ukrainian), Rev. James Morris, Admin.
Mailing Address: P.O. Box 206, 01970-0206. Tel: 508-745-3151.
Church—124 Bridge St., 01970.
Catechesis/Religious Programs—Tel: 617-599-8138.
Students 12.

South Deerfield, Franklin Co., Holy Ghost (1920) (Ukrainian), Rev. Kiril Angelov.
Res., 44 Sugarloaf St., 01373. Tel: 413-665-3880.
Catechesis/Religious Programs—Priests 1; Lay Teachers 2; Students 15.

STATE OF NEW HAMPSHIRE

Manchester, Hillsboro Co., Protection of B.V.M. (1908) (Ukrainian), Rev. Joseph Lazor.
Church—54 Walnut St., 03104. Tel: 603-622-0034; Fax: 603-642-8961.
Res., 2 Partridge Ln., East Kingston, 03827. Tel: 603-642-5865.
Catechesis/Religious Programs—Sarah B. Lazor, D.R.E.
Priests 1; Lay Teachers 3; Students 24.

STATE OF NEW YORK

Amsterdam, Montgomery Co., St. Nicholas (1909) (Ukrainian), Rev. Marian Kostyk.
Res., 24 Pulaski St., 12010. Tel: 518-842-8731; Fax: 518-842-1384. [CEM]

Auburn, Cayuga Co., SS. Peter and Paul (1901) (Ukrainian), Rev. Mihail Dubovici, Admin.
Res., 132 Washington St., 13021. Tel: 315-252-5573; Fax: 315-252-7469.
School—(Grades K-8). Tel: 315-252-5567. Sr. M. Boniface, O.S.B.M., Prin.
Sisters of St. Basil the Great 2; Lay Teachers 7; Students 138.
Catechesis/Religious Programs—Sisters 1; Lay Teachers 3; Students 30.

Bath, Steuben Co., Christ the King. Closed. For inquiries for parish records contact the Chancery.

Bronx, Bronx Co., St. Mary Protectress (1943) (Ukrainian), Rev. Mauricio Popadiuk, O.S.B.M.
Church—1745 Washington Ave., 10457. Tel: 718-731-9392.
Res., East Beach Dr., Glen Cove, 11542. Tel: 516-671-0545; Fax: 516-676-7465. [JC]

Brooklyn, Kings Co., Holy Ghost (1913) (Ukrainian), Rev. Paul Wolensky.
Church—160 N. 5th St., 11211. Tel: 718-782-9592; Fax: 718-599-2905.
Mailing Address: 161 N. Fifth St., 11211.
School—Tel: 718-782-0664. Lynda Larsen, Prin.
Priests 1; Lay Teachers 7; Students 91.

St. Nicholas (1916) (Ukrainian), Rev. Bohdan Karas, Admin.
256 19th St., 11215. Tel: 718-389-8744.

Buffalo, Erie Co., St. Nicholas (1894) (Ukrainian), Very Rev. Marijan Procyk.
Res., 308 Fillmore Ave., 14206. Tel: 716-852-7566; Fax: 716-855-1319.
Catechesis/Religious Programs—Elaine P. Nowadly, D.R.E.
Priests 1; Students 28.

Cohoes, Albany Co., SS. Peter and Paul (1907) (Ukrainian), Rev. Vladimir Marusceac.
Res., 198 Ontario St., 12047. Tel: 518-237-0535; Fax: 518-237-2397.

Elmira Heights, Chemung Co., St. Nicholas (1895) (Ukrainian), Rev. Philip Weiner.
Res., 410 E. McCanns Blvd., 14903. Tel: 607-734-1221; Fax: 607-737-7569.
Catechesis/Religious Programs—Irene Moffe, D.R.E.
Priests 1; Lay Teachers 6; Students 39.

Fresh Meadows, Queens Co., Annunciation of the B.V.M. (1957) (Ukrainian), Rev. Msgr. George Binkowski.
Res., 48-26 171st St., 11365. Tel: 718-939-4116; Fax: 718-939-3696.

Glen Spey, Sullivan Co., St. Volodymyr (1961) (Ukrainian), Rev. Peter Gronski.
Res., 2105 Rte. 41, 12737-5618. Tel: 914-856-5500. [JC]

Hamptonburgh, Orange Co., St. Andrew's (1983) (Ukrainian), Rev. Zbigniew Brzezicki.
Res., 141 Sarah Wells Tr., Campbell Hall, 10916. Tel: 914-496-5506.
Catechesis/Religious Programs—Priests 1; Lay Teachers 1; Students 14.

Hempstead, Nassau Co., St. Vladimir (1944) (Ukrainian), Very Rev. Archpriest Charles Mezzomo, Admin.
Res., 709 Front St., 11550. Tel: 516-481-7717; Fax: 516-481-3435.
Parish Center: 226 Uniondale Ave., Uniondale, 11553. Tel: 516-485-0775.
Saturday Ukrainian School—.
Priests 1; Lay Teachers 8; Students 36.
Catechesis/Religious Programs—Priests 1; Lay Teachers 7; Students 38.

Hudson, Columbia Co., St. Nicholas (1923) (Ukrainian), Rev. Ivan Mazuyk.
Res., 29 S. Second St., 12534. Tel: 518-828-5226; Fax: 518-828-6749.

Hunter, Greene Co., St. John the Baptist (1962) (Ukrainian). Administered from Holy Trinity Parish, R.R. 1, Box 129 Foordmore Rd., Kerhonkson, NY 12446, 914-626-2864.

Johnson City, Broome Co., Sacred Heart Ukrainian Catholic Church (1944) (Ukrainian), Rev. Ihor Stets.
Res., 230 Ukrainian Hill Rd., 13790. Tel: 607-797-6293; Fax: 607-797-6293. [CEM]
Saturday Ukrainian School—Tel: 607-798-9148.
Lay Teachers 3; Students 25.
Catechesis/Religious Programs—Tel: 607-723-7660. Christina Litwak, D.R.E.
Lay Teachers 5; Students 49.

Kenmore, Erie Co., St. John the Baptist (1904) (Ukrainian), Rev. Maxim Kobasuk, O.S.B.M.
Res., 3275 Elmwood Ave., 14217. Tel: 716-873-5011; Fax: 716-871-8804.

Kerhonkson, Ulster Co., Holy Trinity (1965) (Ukrainian), Rev. Oleksa Chouter.
Mailing Address: 211 Foordmore Rd., 12446.
Church—R.R. I-129, 12446. Tel: 914-626-2864.
Saturday Ukrainian School—.
Priests 1; Lay Teachers 2; Students 12.

Lackawanna, Erie Co., Our Lady of Perpetual Help (1925) (Ukrainian), Rev. Wasyl Hrynkiw.
Res., 1182 Ridge Rd., 14218. Tel: 716-823-6182; Fax: 716-823-6550.
Catechesis/Religious Programs—D.R.E.: Annette M. Nayda; Maria Slabyk.
Priests 1; Lay Teachers 2; Students 8.

Lancaster, Erie Co., St. Basil (1921) (Ukrainian), Rev. Robert Moreno.
Res., 12 Embry Pl., 14086. Tel: 716-683-0313; Fax: 716-651-9873.
Church—3657 Walden Ave., 14086.

Little Falls, Herkimer Co., St. Nicholas (1912). Attended by Amsterdam. Rev. Marian Kostyk.
Res., 150 Furnace St., 13365. Tel: 315-823-4474.

Long Island City, Queens Co., Holy Cross (1944) (Ukrainian), Revs. Philip Sandrick, O.S.B.M.; Gregory Chmylar, O.S.B.M.; Cyril Iszczuk, O.S.B.M. In res., Very Rev. Chistopher Woytyna, O.S.B.M., Prov.
Res., 31-12 30th St., 11106. Tel: 718-932-4060.
Catechesis/Religious Programs—Priests 2; Religious 1; Lay Teachers 2; Students 25.

New York, New York Co., St. George (1905) (Ukrainian), Very Rev. Patrick Paschak, O.S.B.M.; Revs. Lawrence Lawryniuk, O.S.B.M.; Taras Prokopiw, O.S.B.M.; Bernard Panczuk.
Res., 30 E. Seventh St., 10003. Tel: 212-674-1615; Fax: 212-475-7017.
School—215 E. Sixth St., 10003. Tel: 212-473-3130. Sr. Gabriel O.S.B.M., Prin.
Sisters of St. Basil the Great 1; Lay Teachers 8; Students 100.
High School—Tel: 212-473-3323.
Sisters 1; Lay Teachers 10; Students 140.

Niagara Falls, Niagara Co., Protection of B.V.M. (1920) (Ukrainian), Rev. Demetrius Laptuta, C.SS.R.
Res., 2713 Ferry Ave., 14301. Tel: 716-284-7066; Fax: 716-282-6902.

Ozone Park, Queens Co., St. Mary Protectress (Ukrainian), Very Rev. Peter Ohirko.
Res., 97-06 87th St., NY 11416. Tel: 718-845-5366.
Saturday Ukrainian School—.
Priests 1; Lay Teachers 2; Students 12.

Riverhead, Suffolk Co., St. John the Baptist (1924) (Ukrainian), Rev. Ihor Tarasiw.
Res., 820 Pond View Rd., 11901. Tel: 516-727-2766; Fax: 516-727-2766. [CEM]
Church—Franklin St., 11901.

Rochester, Monroe Co., St. Josaphat (1909) (Ukrainian), Rev. Msgr. John Squiller; Rev. Janus Jedrychowski.
Res., 940 Ridge Road E., 14621. Tel: 716-467-6457; Fax: 716-467-7296.
School—95 Stanton Ln., 14621. Tel: 716-266-8700. Sr. Bernitta Dub, S.S.M.I., Prin.
Priests 2; Sisters Servants of Mary Immaculate 2; Lay Teachers 11; Students 126.
Catechesis/Religious Programs—Lay Teachers 6; Students 148.
Convent—910 Ridge Rd., E., 14621. Tel: 716-266-1540.

Epiphany of Our Lord (1958) (Ukrainian), Rev. Vasile Godenciuc.
Res., 202 Carter St., 14621. Tel: 716-266-4036; Fax: 716-323-9691. [JC]

Rome, Oneida Co., St. Michael (1914) (Ukrainian). Attended by St. Vladimir, Utica. Rev. Michael Bundz.

Res., 296 Genessee St., Utica, 13502. Tel: 315-735-5138; Fax: 315-735-0443.
Church—133 River St., 13440. [CEM]

Spring Valley, Rockland Co., SS. Peter and Paul (1913) (Ukrainian), Rev. Ivan Tykhovytch.
Res., 41 Collins Ave., 10977. Tel: 914-356-1634; Fax: 914-425-2749.
Catechesis/Religious Programs—Tel: 201-529-4208. Irene Gojdycz, D.R.E.
Lay Teachers 4; Students 20.

Staten Island, Richmond Co., Holy Trinity (1949) (Ukrainian), Very Rev. Canon Lubomyr Mudry.
Res., 288 Vanderbilt Ave., 10304. Tel: 718-442-2555.

Syracuse, Onondaga Co., St. John the Baptist (1900), Very Rev. Jeffrey A.G. Roderhero; Rev. Stepan Kuklich; Deacons Myron Kotch; Volodymyr Kucaj.
Res., 207 Tompkins St., 13204. Tel: 315-478-5109; Fax: 315-471-9867.
Catechesis/Religious Programs—Priests 2; Lay Teachers 5; Students 40.

Troy, Rensselaer Co., Protection of B.V.M. (1952) (Ukrainian). Attended by SS. Peter and Paul, Cohoes. Rev. Vladimir Marusceac.
Res., 198 Ontario St., Cohoes, 12047. Tel: 518-237-0535; Fax: 518-237-2397. [JC]
Church—459 Second St., 12180. Tel: 518-274-5318.

Utica, Oneida Co., St. Volodymyr the Great (1950) (Ukrainian), Rev. Michael Bundz, Admin.
Res., 296 Genessee St., 13502. Tel: 315-735-5138; Fax: 315-735-0443. [CEM]
Saturday Ukrainian School—.
Priests 1; Lay Teachers 1; Students 15.

Watervliet, Albany Co., St. Nicholas (1905) (Ukrainian), Rev. Mikhail Myshchuk.
Res., 2410-4th Ave., 12189. Tel: 518-273-6752; Fax: 518-273-4456. [CEM][JC]
Saturday Ukrainian School & C.C.D.—.
Lay Teachers 6; Students 30.

West Islip, Suffolk Co., Holy Family (1924) (Ukrainian), Rev. Miroslaw Jatsiv.
Res., 471 Montauk Hwy., 11795-4475. Tel: 516-661-0031; Fax: 516-321-4368.

Yonkers, Westchester Co., St. Michael (1899) (Ukrainian), Rev. Miroslaw Trojanowski.
Res., 21 Shonnard Pl., 10703. Tel: 914-963-0209; Fax: 914-969-6269.
Catechesis/Religious Programs—Priests 1; Students 93.

STATE OF RHODE ISLAND

Woonsocket, Providence Co., St. Michael (1908), Rev. Msgr. Roman Golemba.
Res., 394 Blackstone St., 02895. Tel: 401-762-2733; Fax: 401-762-2733. [CEM][JC]
Church—396 Blackstone St., 02895.

Special Assignment:
Reverend Monsignors—
Mosko, Leon A., Chancellor
Reverend Fathers—
Morse, Jonathan, Ukrainian Catholic Relief, Inc.
Shubiak, Stephen, U.S. Chap. Corps

Retired:
Mitred Archpriest—
Andrushkiw, Vladimir, 195 Glenbrook Rd., Stamford, CT 06902
Rev. Archpriest—
Pelensky, Ihor, P.O. Box 533, Westmoreland, NY 13490
Reverend Monsignors—
Chrepta, Stephen J., 16134 Veronica St., East Detroit, MI 48021
Feddish, Basil, 83 Sylvester Ave., Hawthorne, NJ 07506
Reverend Canons—
Sharanevych, Emile, 332 Foordmore Rd., Kerhonkson, NY 12446. Tel: 914-626-4947
Shust, Yaroslav, Shevchenko Manor, 5620 W. 24th St., Parma, OH 44134. Tel: 216-459-1440
Reverend Fathers—
Graskow, Paul, 3415 La Fayette Ave., S., Seattle, WA 98144
Humanitzki, Theodore, 11416 Pine Forest Dr., New Port Richey, FL 34654. Tel: 813-856-4432
Rt. Rev. Mitred Msgr—
Chomko, Stephen, 706 Warren St., Berwick, PA 18603
Very Rev.—
Figol, Volodymyr, St. Basil Seminary, 195 Glenbrook Rd., Stanford, CT 06902

Permanent Deacons:
Cybulski, Marius, Christ the King, Boston, MA
Hirniak, Mark, St. Vladimir, Stamford, CT
Homick, Willis, SS. Peter & Paul, Auburn, NY
Kotch, Myron, St. John the Baptist, Syracuse, NY
Malachowsky, Yourij, Holy Cross, Long Island City, NY

INSTITUTIONS LOCATED IN THE DIOCESE

[A] SEMINARIES, DIOCESAN

STAMFORD. *St. Basil College*, 195 Glenbrook Rd., 06902-3099. Tel: 203-324-4578; Fax: 203-357-7681. Most Rev. Basil H. Losten, D.D., S.T.L., LL.D., Chm., Board of Directors; Revs. Edward Young, B.A., S.T.B., Rector; Ivan Kaszczak, B.A., M.A., M.Ed., Vice Rector & Dean of Men; Rev. Msgr. Peter Skrincosky, B.A., M.S., S.E.O.D., Dir. of Spiritual Formation; Rt. Rev. Mitred Msgr John Terlecky, B.A., M.A., M.L.S., Bursar; Revs. Robert Smolley, B.S., M.Div., Prefect for Students; Bohdan Danylo, B.S., S.T.B., Prefect & Procurator; Edward Bordeau, Ph.D., Dean and Registrar; Ms. Lubow Wolynetz, B.A., M.L.S., Librarian. Household Dept. in charge of the Institute of Catechists of the Heart of Jesus.

[B] SEMINARIES, RELIGIOUS

GLEN COVE, NY. *Basilian Fathers Novitiate of the Order of St. Basil the Great*, E. Beach Dr., 11542. Tel: 516-671-0545; Fax: 516-676-7465.
E-mail: mpopadiuk@aol.com
Very Rev. Mauricio Popadiuk, O.S.B.M., Supr. & Master of Novices; Revs. Theodosius Ilicki, O.S.B.M., Asst. Master of Novices; Julian Katrij, O.S.B.M.; Hilarion Benedik, O.S.B.M.; Athanasius B. Pekar, O.S.B.M. Priests 5; Brothers 2; Novices 2; Scholastics 5.

[C] NURSERY SCHOOLS

STAMFORD. *St. Ann's Nursery School*, 111 W. North St., 06902. Tel: 203-323-1237; 348-5675. Missionary Sisters of Mother of God 6; Nursery 44; Staff 3.

[D] ADULT FACILITIES

SLOATSBURG, NY. *St. Joseph's Home*, 125 Sisters Servants Ln., Box 25, 10974-0025. Tel: 914-753-2555
For a complete listing, refer to the Special Care Facilities section.

[E] MONASTERIES AND RESIDENCES OF PRIESTS AND BROTHERS

NEW YORK, NY. *Provincialate of Basilian Fathers*. Res., 31-12 30th St., Long Island City, 11106. Tel: 718-278-6622. Very Rev. Chistopher Woytyna, O.S.B.M., Protohegumen. Priests 24; Scholastics 8; Brothers 3; Novices 2.

WEST BURKE, VT. *Mary Theotokos Centre*, P.O. Box 88, 05871-0088. Tel: 802-467-1132.
E-mail: stefan@sovernet
Rev. Stephen C. von Fauer, Supr.

[F] MONASTERIES OF NUNS

STAMFORD. *Missionary Sisters of Mother of God*, 111 W. North St., 06902. Tel: 203-323-1237. Sr. Josepha Kruchinsky, M.S.M.G., Supr.; Rev. Jonathan Morse, Chap.

MIDDLETOWN, NY. *Nuns of St. Basil the Great*, Sacred Heart Monastery, 209 Keasel Rd., 10940-9624. Tel: 914-343-1308. Mother M. Georgianna Snihur, O.S.B.M., Supr. Sisters 6.

SLOATSBURG, NY. *Immaculate Conception Provincialate*, Sisters Servants Ln., 9 Emmanuel Dr., P.O. Box 6, 10974-0006. Tel: 914-753-2840. Sisters Servants of Mary Immaculate Conception Province. Sr. Michele Yakymovitch, S.S.M.I., Prov. Supr. Sisters 19.

[G] MISCELLANEOUS

STAMFORD. *Institute of Catechists of the Heart of Jesus*, 161 Glenbrook Rd., 06902. Tel: 203-327-6374. Cecilia Daciuk, Supr. Total Members 7.

**Ukrainian Catholic Relief, Inc.*, 14 Peveril Rd., 06902.
E-mail: morseucrstamford@worldnet.att.net

SLOATSBURG, NY. *St. Mary's Villa Spiritual, Cultural & Educational Center*, 150 Sisters Servants Ln., P.O. Box 6, 10974-0006. Tel: 914-753-5100. Sr. Jonathan Duchensky, S.S.M.I., Coord.

RELIGIOUS INSTITUTES OF MEN REPRESENTED IN THE DIOCESE

For further details refer to the corresponding bracketed number in the Religious Institutes of Men or Women section.
[0180]—*Order of St. Basil the Great.*—O.S.B.M.
[1070]—*Redemptorists.*—C.Ss.R.

RELIGIOUS INSTITUTES OF WOMEN REPRESENTED IN THE DIOCESE

[]—*Institute of Catechists of the Heart of Jesus.*
[2810]—*Missionary Sisters of Mother of God.*—M.S.M.G.
[3730]—*Sisters of the Order of St. Basil the Great.*—O.S.B.M.
[3610]—*Sisters Servants of Mary Immaculate.*—S.S.M.I.

NECROLOGY

(No Deaths)

Byzantine Eparchy of Van Nuys

Most Reverend

GEORGE M. KUZMA, D.D.

Bishop of Van Nuys; ordained May 29, 1955; appointed Auxiliary Bishop of the Byzantine Eparchy of Passaic, November 11, 1986; consecrated February 4, 1987; appointed Bishop of Eparchy of Van Nuys, October 23, 1990; installed as Second Bishop of Van Nuys, January 15, 1991. *Res., 8141 N. 16 St., Phoenix, AZ, 85020.*

ESTABLISHED DECEMBER 3, 1981.

Embraces all Catholics of the Byzantine-Ruthenian Church in the States of California, Oregon, Washington, Idaho, Nevada, Arizona, Utah, Wyoming, Montana, Colorado, New Mexico, Alaska and Hawaii.

For legal titles of parishes and diocesan institutions, consult the Chancery Office.

Legal Title: The Byzantine Catholic Bishop of Van Nuys, a Corporation Sole.

Principal Patron-Patronage of the Mother of God (Pokrov).

Chancery Office: 8131 N. 16 St., Phoenix, AZ, 85020. Tel.: 602-861-9778; Fax: 602-861-9796.

E-mail address: EVNizer@aol.com

STATISTICAL OVERVIEW

Personnel	
Bishop	1
Priests: Diocesan Active in Diocese	13
Priests: Active Outside Diocese	2
Priests: Diocesan in Foreign Missions	1
Priests: Retired, Sick or Absent	3
Number of Diocesan Priests	19
Religious Priests in Diocese	4
Ordinations:	
Diocesan Priests	1
Permanent Deacons	1
Permanent Deacons in Diocese	5
Total Brothers	4
Total Sisters	5
Parishes	
Parishes	16
With Resident Pastor:	
Resident Diocesan Priests	14
Resident Religious Priests	2
Without Resident Pastor:	
Missions	2
Pastoral Centers	2
Professional Ministry Personnel:	
Sisters	2
Welfare	
Other Institutions	1
Total Assisted	27
Educational	
Diocesan Students in Other Seminaries	4
Total Seminarians	4
Catechesis/Religious Education:	
High School Students	101
Elementary Students	378
Total Students Under Catholic Instruction	483
Vital Statistics	
Receptions into the Church:	
Infant Baptism Totals	84
Adult Baptism Totals	11
Received into Full Communion	21
First Communions	112
Confirmations	134
Marriages:	
Catholic	11
Interfaith	4
Total Marriages	15
Deaths	25
Total Catholic Population	2,905

Former Bishop—Most Rev. THOMAS V. DOLINAY, D.D., ord. May 16, 1948; cons. Nov. 23, 1976; appt. Tutular Bishop of Thyatira and Auxiliary of Passiac, Sept. 23, 1976; appt. First Ordinary of the Byzantine Catholic Diocese of Van Nuys, CA; installed March 9, 1982; appt. Coadjutor Archbishop of Pittsburgh Byzantine Rite, March 13, 1990; succeeded to June 12, 1991; died April 13, 1993.

Chancery Office—Byzantine Catholic Eparchy of Van Nuys, Pastoral Center, 8131 N. 16th St., Phoenix, AZ, 85020. Tel: 602-861-9778; Fax: 602-861-9796. Office Hours: Mon.-Thurs. 10-3; Fri. 10-1.

Protosyncellus and Chancellor—Rt. Rev. WESLEY IZER, S.D.B.

Syncelli—Northwest Vicariate: Very Rev. STEPHEN GRESKOWIAK, Italo-Greeks Vicariate: Rt. Rev. FRANCIS M. VIVONA, S.T.M., J.C.L., Southwest Vicariate: Very Rev. STEPHEN WASHKO.

Treasurer—Sr. CELESTINE PETRUSKA, O.S.B.M.

Eparchial Consultors - Presbyteral Council—Very Rev. STEPHEN GRESKOWIAK; Rt. Rev. WESLEY IZER, S.D.B.; Rt. Rev. JOSEPH STANICHAR, V.F.; Very Rev. STEPHEN WASHKO; Rt. Rev. FRANCIS M. VIVONA, S.T.M., J.C.L.

Diocesan Matrimonial Tribunal—Office of the Tribunal Eparcy of Van Nuys, 336 E. Desert Inn Rd., P.O. Box 18316, Las Vegas, NV, 89114-8316. Tel: 702-735-1210; Fax: 702-735-5146.

Judicial Vicar—Rt. Rev. FRANCIS M. VIVONA, S.T.M., J.C.L.

Promoter of Justice—Very Rev. Archpriest MICHAEL MORAN, J.C.D.

Secretary—Ms. SIDNEY MARSH.

Defender—Rev. PHILIP ACQUARO, C.S.B., J.C.D.

Judge—Very Rev. STEPHEN WASHKO.

Notary—Ms. SIDNEY MARSH.

Building Commission—Most Rev. GEORGE M. KUZMA; Rt. Rev. WESLEY IZER, S.D.B.; Deacon RICHARD WORTMAN.

Director of Religious Education and Evangelization—Sr. BARBARA SWINDELLS, O.S.B.M.

Eparchial Finance Commission—Most Rev. GEORGE M. KUZMA, Chm.; Rt. Rev. WESLEY IZER, S.D.B.; Sr. CELESTINE PETRUSKA, O.S.B.M.; Mrs. JOSEFINA DANOVICH; Mr. WILLIAM GOMBAR.

Vocation Director—Rev. ROBERT M. PIPTA.

Ecclesiatical Notary—Rev. ROBERT M. PIPTA.

Liturgy & Music Commission—Very Rev. STEPHEN WASHKO, Chm.; Revs. JOSEPH HUTSKO; ROBERT M. PIPTA; Sr. CHRISTOPHER MALCOVSKY, O.S.B.M.; Mr. BASIL RABAYDA, JR.

"Eparchial Newsletter"—Rt. Rev. WESLEY IZER, S.D.B., Editor.

Director of Development & Stewardship—Sr. CHRISTOPHER MALCOVSKY, O.S.B.M.

CLERGY, PARISHES, MISSIONS AND PAROCHIAL SCHOOLS

STATE OF ARIZONA

Gilbert, Maricopa Co., St. Thomas the Apostle, Rev. Philip A. Acquaro, C.S.B., Admin.; Deacon John Miller.
Mailing Address: P.O. Box 667, 85299-0667.
19 W. Bruce Ave., 85233. Tel: 602-497-5799.

Phoenix, Maricopa Co., St. Stephen. (Byzantine Catholic Pro-Cathedral). Very Rev. Stephen G. Washko, Rector; Sr. Christopher Malcovsky, O.S.B.M., Pastoral Assoc.
Res., 8141 N. 16th St., 85020-3999. Tel: 602-943-5379.
Convent—St. Stephen Convent, 8141 N. 16th St. #27, 85020. Tel: 602-944-5121; Fax: 602-861-9796. Sisters 3.

Tucson, Pima Co., St. Melany, Rev. William Skurla.
Church—1212 N. Sahuara, 85712-5018. Tel: 520-886-4225; Fax: 520-751-4574.

STATE OF ALASKA

Anchorage, Anchorage Co., Saint Nicholas of Myra, Rev. Stephen Greskowiak.
Res., 2200 Arctic Blvd., 99503-1909. Tel: 907-277-6731; Fax: 907-277-6731.

STATE OF CALIFORNIA

Van Nuys, Los Angeles Co., Cathedral of St. Mary, Very Rev. Archpriest Michael Moran, Rector; Sr. Barbara Swindells, O.S.B.M., Pastoral Assoc.; Deacon Michael Hladky, (Retired).
Res., 5329 Sepulveda Blvd., 91411-3441. Tel: 818-907-5511.
Convent—5335 Sepulveda Blvd., 91411-3441. Tel: 818-907-1261.

Anaheim, Orange Co., Annunciation, Rev. Msgr. George N. Vida (PBR).
Res., 319 N. Harbor Blvd., 92805-2599. Tel: 714-533-6292.

Fontana, San Bernardino Co., St. Nicholas, Rev. Kurt Burnette, Admin.
Res., 9112 Oleander Ave., 92335-5599. Tel: 909-822-9917.

Fresno, Fresno Co., Byzantine Catholic Community of Fresno, CA. Closed. For inquiries for parish records contact the Chancery.

Los Gatos, Santa Clara Co., St. Basil the Great, Rev. William O'Brien, Admin.
Res., 14263 Mulberry Ave., 95030. Tel: 408-871-0911; Fax: 408-871-0919.

Palm Springs, Riverside Co., Byzantine Catholic Community of Palm Springs, CA. Closed. For inquiries for parish records contact the Chancery.

Sacramento, Sacramento Co., St. Philip the Apostle, Rev. John Kapitan, O.F.M., Admin.; Deacon Richard Wortman.
Mailing Address: 7001 Florin Rd., 95828-3015. Tel: 916-383-1552; Fax: 916-386-0256.

San Diego, San Diego Co., Holy Angels, Rev. Melvin Rybarczyk, C.R., Admin.
Mailing Address: 2235 Galahad Rd., 92123-3931. Tel: 619-277-2511; Fax: 619-277-5792.

San Luis Obispo, San Luis Obispo Co., Saint Anne, Rev. Edmund M. Idranyi, Admin.; Mr. Julius Dicky,

Financial Admin.

Mailing Address: 222 Foothill Blvd., 93405-1540. Tel: 805-543-8883.

San Mateo, San Mateo Co., St. Macrina. Closed. All records at the Chancery Office.

Stockton, San Joaquin Co., Byzantine Catholic Community of Stockton. Closed. For inquiries for parish records contact the Chancery.

STATE OF COLORADO

Colorado Springs, El Paso Co., Byzantine Catholic Mission. Attended by Holy Protection of the Mother of God, Denver.

1201 S. Elizabeth St., Denver, 80210. Tel: 303-778-8283.

Denver, Denver Co., Holy Protection of the Mother of God, Rev. Joseph Hutsko.

Res., 1074 S. Cook St., 80209-4923.

Church—1201 S. Elizabeth St., 80210. Tel: 303-778-8283.

STATE OF NEVADA

Las Vegas, Clark Co., Our Lady of Wisdom Italo-Greek Mission.

P.O. Box 18316, 89114-8316. Tel: 602-735-1210; Fax: 702-735-5146. Rt. Rev. Archimandri Francis Vivona, Syncellus; Deacon Joshua Alves.

St. Gabriel the Archangel, Rev. Robert M. Pipta, Admin.

Church—2250 E. Maule Ave., 89119-4607. Tel: 702-361-2431; Fax: 702-361-2431#1.

STATE OF NEW MEXICO

Albuquerque, Bernalillo Co., Our Lady of Perpetual Help, Rev. Christopher L. Zugger.

Res., 1840 Palomas Dr. N.E., 87110-5113. Tel: 505-256-1787.

Church—1837 Alvarado N.E., 87110. Tel: 505-256-1539; Fax: 505-256-1278.

Las Cruces, Dona Ana Co., Byzantine Catholic Mission. Closed. Records are located at Albuquerque Parish.

STATE OF OREGON

Portland, Multnomah Co., Byzantine Catholic Community of Portland, OR. Attended by St. George, Olympia, WA. Rev. Michael Durka.

Mailing Address: 9730 Yelm Hwy., Olympia, WA 98513. Tel: 360-413-5651.

Chapel—8261 S.E. Clatsop, 97266.

STATE OF UTAH

Salt Lake City, Salt Lake Co., Byzantine Catholic Mission. Closed. For inquiries for parish records contact the Chancery.

STATE OF WASHINGTON

Olympia, Thurston Co., St. George Byzantine, Rev. Michael Durka, Admin.

Res., 9730 Yelm Hwy, 98513. Tel: 360-413-5651.

Seattle, King Co., St. John Chrysostom, Rt. Rev. Joseph Stanichar, Pastor.

Res., S. 1305 Lander St., 98144-5038. Tel: 206-329-9219; Fax: 206-322-6930.

Spokane, Spokane Co., SS. Cyril & Methodius, Rev. David Logan, Admin.

Res., N. 4315 Evergreen Rd., 99216-1298. Tel: 509-922-4527.

Walla Walla, Walla Walla Co., Byzantine Catholic Mission. Closed. For inquiries for parish records contact the Spokane parish.

On Special Assignment:

Reverend Fathers—

Kovach, John, Shrine of the Weeping Madonna, 17486 Mumford Rd., Burton, OH 44021-9640

Michalenko, Alexei, Chap., Georgetown Law Center, 600 New Jersey Ave., N.W., Washington, DC 20001

On Leave:

Reverend Fathers—

Barrand, James

Retired:

Reverend Fathers—

Dorich, John, 8141 N. 16th St., Phoenix, AZ 85020-3999

Ridella, Joseph, 66295 Hacienda Ave., Desert Hot Springs, CA 92240

Rt. Rev. Mitred Arch—

Artim, Michael, 13211 Venus Way, Anchorage, AK 99515-3915

Permanent Deacons:

Alves, Joshua (CHI), Las Vegas, NV

Hladky, Michael, Van Nuys, CA

Miller, John (PHX), Gilber, AZ

Wortman, Richard, Sacramento, CA

INSTITUTIONS LOCATED IN THE DIOCESE

[A] RELIGIOUS COMMUNITIES

PHOENIX. *Congregation of Saint Basil*, 8141 N. 16th St., #22, 85020-3901. Tel: 602-395-0457. Rev. Philip A. Acquaro, C.S.B.

St. Stephen Convent, 8141 N. 16th St. #27, 85020. Tel: 602-944-5121; Fax: 602-861-9796. Sr. Christopher, O.S.B.M.; Sr. Celestine, O.S.B.M.; Sr. Madeline, O.S.B.M.

Salesians of Don Bosco, 8141 N. 16th St., #19, 85020-3999. Tel: 602-943-5379. Rt. Rev. Wesley W. Izer, S.D.B.

NEWBERRY SPRINGS, CA. *Holy Resurrection Monastery*. (Monastic Community of Men est. Aug. 4, 1995), 45704 Valley Center Rd., P.O. Box 130, 92365. Tel: 760-257-4008; Fax: 760-257-3362. Rev. Nicholas Zachariadis, Hegumen; Bros. Maximos Davies, Protos; Basil Doty.

REDLANDS, CA. *Byzantine Brothers of St. Francis*, 9458 Buckeye St., 92374. Tel: 909-793-1127.

E-mail: brmike@aol.com

Bros. Michael Sullivan, B.B.S.F., Supr.; John Gray, B.B.S.F., Treas.

VAN NUYS, CA. *Saint Mary Convent*, 5335 Sepulveda Blvd., 91411-3441. Tel: 818-907-1261. Order of Sisters of St. Basil the Great. Sr. Barbara Swindells, O.S.B.M.; Sr. Fabiola Boruta, O.S.B.M.

RELIGIOUS INSTITUTES OF MEN REPRESENTED IN THE DIOCESE

For further details refer to the corresponding bracketed number in the Religious Institutes of Men or Women section.

[0170]—*Basilian Fathers.*—C.S.B.

[]—*Byzantine Brothers of St. Francis.*—B.B.S.F.

[0520]—*Franciscan Friars.*—O.F.M.

[1190]—*Salesians of Don Bosco.*—S.D.B.

RELIGIOUS INSTITUTES OF WOMEN REPRESENTED IN THE DIOCESE

[3730]—*Sisters of the Order of St. Basil the Great.*—O.S.B.M.

NECROLOGY

(No Deaths)

U.S. TERRITORIAL SEES

Archdiocese of Agana

Most Reverend

ANTHONY SABLAN APURON, O.F.M.CAP., D.D.

Archbishop of Agana; ordained August 26, 1972; appointed Auxiliary Bishop December 8, 1983; ordained Titular Bishop of Muzuca February 19, 1984; appointed Apostolic Administrator to the Archdiocese October 27, 1985; succeeded to Metropolitan See May 11, 1986. *Res., Archbishop's Residence, 196-B Cuesta San Ramon, Agana, GU, 96910.* Tel.: 671-472-6116; 472-6573; Fax: 671-477-3519.

ERECTED BY POPE PIUS X, MARCH 1, 1911 AND COMMITTED TO THE ORDER OF FRIARS MINOR CAPUCHIN. EXTENDED TO ALL THE MARIANAS ISLANDS, JULY 4, 1946, WAKE ISLAND, JUNE 14, 1948. ELEVATED TO A DIOCESE, OCTOBER 14, 1965, AS A SUFFRAGAN OF SAN FRANCISCO. ELEVATED TO METROPOLITAN ARCHDIOCESE, MAY 20, 1984 WITH A SUFFRAGAN SEE, DIOCESE OF CAROLINE-MARSHALLS AND DIOCESE OF CHALAN KANOA (SUBSEQUENTLY ADDED JANUARY 13, 1985). MEMBER OF CEPAC CONFERENCE. MEMBER OF FEDERATION OF CATHOLIC BISHOPS CONFERENCE OF OCEANIA. OBSERVER TO NCCB-USCC CONFERENCE.

GUAM IS A TERRITORY OF THE U.S.A. BY ACT OF THE U.S. CONGRESS JULY 21, 1949.

Legal Title: *Archbishop of Agana, a Corporation Sole.*

STATISTICAL OVERVIEW

Personnel	
Archbishop	1
Priests: Diocesan Active in Diocese	23
Priests: Active Outside Diocese	2
Priests: Retired, Sick or Absent	2
Number of Diocesan Priests	27
Religious Priests in Diocese	19
Ordinations:	
Diocesan Priests	1
Permanent Deacons in Diocese	10
Total Brothers	1
Total Sisters	120
Parishes	
Parishes	24
With Resident Pastor:	
Resident Diocesan Priests	13
Resident Religious Priests	11
Without Resident Pastor:	
Professional Ministry Personnel:	
Lay Ministers	1
Welfare	
Homes for the Aged	1
Total Assisted	59
Day Care and Extended Day Care Centers	4
Total Assisted	459
Specialized Homes	4
Total Assisted	1,194
Special Centers for Social Services	1
Total Assisted	5,345
Residential Care of Disabled	1
Total Assisted	78
Educational	
Diocesan Students in Other Seminaries	3
Students Religious	2
Total Seminarians	5
High Schools, Diocesan and Parish	2
Total Students	817
High Schools, Private	1
Total Students	245
Elementary Schools, Diocesan and Parish	7
Total Students	2,557
Catechesis/Religious Education:	
High School Students	1,680
Elementary Students	6,620
Total Students Under Catholic Instruction	11,924
Teachers in the Diocese:	
Priests	1
Sisters	45
Lay Teachers	253
Vital Statistics	
Receptions into the Church:	
Infant Baptism Totals	2,730
Adult Baptism Totals	30
Received into Full Communion	26
First Communions	1,502
Confirmations	747
Marriages:	
Catholic	213
Interfaith	7
Total Marriages	220
Deaths	434
Total Catholic Population	115,080
Total Population	136,421

Former Vicars-Apostolic—Most Rev. FRANCIS X. VILLA Y MATEU, O.F.M.Cap., D.D., cons. Titular Bishop of Adraha, Oct. 1, 1911; died at Agana, Jan. 1, 1913.—Most Rev. AUGUSTIN BERNAUS Y SERRA, O.F.M.Cap., D.D., cons. Titular Bishop of Milopotamo, May 9, 1913; transferred to Vicariate-Apostolic of Bluefields, Nicaragua, 1914.—Most Rev. JOAQUIN FELIPE OLAIZ Y ZABALZA, O.F.M.Cap., D.D., cons. Titular Bishop of Docimeo, Nov. 30, 1914; died at Pamplona, Spain, Dec. 8, 1945.—Most Rev. MIGUEL ANGEL OLAND Y URTEAGA, O.F.M.Cap., D.D., cons. Titular Bishop of Lagina, May 5, 1935; resigned and made Asst. at Pontifical Throne Aug. 20, 1945; died at Agana, Guam May 21, 1970.—Most Rev. APOLLINARIS W. BAUMGARTNER, O.F.M.Cap., D.D., cons. Sept. 18, 1945; appt. First Bishop of Agana, Oct. 14, 1965; died at Agana, Guam Dec. 18, 1970.—Most Rev. FELIXBERTO CAMACHO FLORES, ord. April 30, 1949; appt. Apostolic Admin., Diocese of Agana, May 2, 1969; appt. Titular Bishop of Stonj, March 19, 1970; cons. May 17, 1970; succeeded to See, May 15, 1971; died Oct. 25, 1985.

Archdiocesan College of Consultors—Revs. DAVID C. QUITUGUA; ADRIAN CRISTOBAL; AGUSTIN GUMATAOTAO, O.F.M.Cap.; JOSE ANTONIO ABAD; JUAN CAMACHO; JAMES BENAVENTE; KENNETH HEZEL, S.J.; JOSE VILLAGOMEZ, O.F.M.Cap.

Vicar General and Moderator of the Curia—Rev. DAVID C. QUITUGUA.

Chancellor—Rev. ADRIAN CRISTOBAL.

Chancery Office—

Finance Officer and Business Mgr.—Mr. DOMINIC KIM. Assistants: Mrs. MARIA GUIAO; Mrs. ANITA DIZON.

Records Office—Mrs. JUNE UNGACTA.

Computers—Mr. MANNY CRUZ.

Receptionist—Mrs. DAWN DOYLE, Chancery Office: *196-B Cuesta San Ramon, Agana, 96910.* Tel: 671-472-6116; 472-8024; 472-6573; Fax: 671-477-3519. Office Hours: Mon.-Fri. 8-12 & 1-4.

Finance Council—Rev. JUAN CAMACHO. Tel: 671-646-5649; 472-6116. Sr. MARY STEPHEN TORRES, R.S.M. Tel: 671-646-7246. Mr. T. ROY SULLIVAN. Tel: 617-472-8891.

Archdiocesan Offices and Directors

Alee Shelter Program for Spousal Abuse—Sr. EILEEN MEARNS, R.G.S., Dir., *c/o Catholic Social Services, P.O. Box EJ, Agana, 96910.* Tel: 671-646-1924.

Campaign For Human Development—Sr. MARIA THECLA CAMACHO, R.S.M., Dir., *P.O. Box 17211, Inarajan, 96916.* Tel: 671-828-8285.

Campus Ministry—Rev. KENNETH HEZEL, S.J., Dir. Tel: 671-734-3507; Fax: 671-734-2943.

Catholic Charismatic Movement—Vacant.

Catholic Charities-Guam—Rev. ADRIAN CRISTOBAL, Chm., *196-B Cuesta San Ramon, Agana, 96910.* Tel: 671-472-6116.

Catholic Daughters of the Americas—Mrs. JOSEPHINE MCDONALD, Regent; Rev. DAVID I.A. QUITUGUA, Chap. Tel: 671-477-5632.

Catholic Education Office—Rev. JOSE ANTONIO ABAD, Vicar Catholic Educ.; Dr. KENNETH CARRIVEAU, Supt. Catholic Schools; Sr. JEAN ANN CRISOSTOMO, S.S.N.D., Associate Supt.; Mrs. BERNADETTE LOU O. SABLAN, Development/Mktg. Dir. of the Catholic Schools Office. Tel: 671-472-6116; Fax: 671-477-3519.

Catholic Educational Radio—Mr. JOHN DUNGCA, Program Mgr., *P.O. Box DZ, Agana, 96910.* Tel: 671-477-1875; Fax: 671-477-5656.

Catholic Social Services - Guam—Mrs. CERILA RAPADAS, Dir., *P.O. Box EJ, Agana, 96910.* Tel: 671-649-5717; Fax: 671-649-9224.

Cemetery Council—Rev. Msgr. ZOILO L.G. CAMACHO, Pres.

Chaplains—See separate listing.

Communications—Rev. BRIGIDO ARROYO, Dir., *P.O. Box 2553, Agana, 96910.* Tel: 671-472-6427.

Confraternity of Christian Mothers—Rev. ADRIAN CRISTOBAL, Spiritual Dir.; Mrs. PATRICIA GUERRERO, Pres.

Cursillo in Christianity Movement—Rev. JOEL DE LOS REYES, Spiritual Dir. Tel: 671-472-6116.

Office of Family and Youth Ministry—Coordinators: Mr. JOSE CALUAG; Mrs. JOSIE CALUAG, *196-B Cuesta San Ramon, Agana, 96910.* Tel: 671-472-6116; Fax: 671-472-4406.

Interfaith Volunteer Caregivers, Inc.—Mr. JESUS BAZA, Dir. Tel: 671-472-2944; Fax: 671-477-2273.

Guma San Francisco—Mr. JOHN LIZAMA, *P.O. Box 306, Agana, 96910.* Tel: 671-472-6068.

Knights of Columbus—Hon. VIC CHIONG, District Deputy; Rev. BRIGIDO ARROYO, Chap. Knights of Columbus No. 5666, *P.O. Box BP, Agana, 96910.* Pale San Vitores Council, JOSE M. QUICHOCHO, Grand Knight Archbishop Felixberto Flores Council, Mr. EDWIN CARBONEL, Grand Knight, *P.O. Box 1252, Tamuning, 96911.*

Knights of Saint Sylvester—Knight Sir CRISTOBAL DUENAS. Tel: 671-472-6201.

Korean Catholic Community—Rev. PETER KANG, *P.O. Box 155, Agana, 96910.* Tel: 671-472-3330; Fax: 671-472-3340.

Legion of Mary—Mrs. JUANITA ULLOA, Pres.

Liturgical Commission—Rev. PATRICK GARCIA, Chm., *Cuesta San Ramon, Agana, 96910.*

Marriage Preparation Programs—

Evenings for the Engaged—Contact Couple: FRANCIS GUERRERO; CONNIE GUERRERO, *c/o Barrigada Church, 229 San Roke St., Barrigada, 96913.*

Catholic Engaged Encounter—Rev. JOSE ANTONIO ABAD; Vicar Catholic Educ. Tel: 671-472-6116.

Marriage Encounter—Vacant.

Ministry with Persons with Disabilities—Ms. CATHERINE LEON GUERRERO, Dir. Tel: 671-472-3141.

Office of Religious Education—Rev. EFREN ADVERSARIO, Assoc. Dir.; Mrs. HELEN A.Q. FLORES, Sec. Tel: 671-472-6116; Fax: 671-472-3519.

Pontifical Holy Childhood Association & Pontifical Society for the Propagation of the Faith—Rev. Msgr. ZOILO L.G. CAMACHO. Tel: 671-632-5659.

Secular Franciscans—Rev. DANIEL CRISTOBAL, O.F.M.Cap., Spiritual Dir.

Tribunal—

Judicial Vicar—Rev. DAVID C. QUITUGUA, J.C.D.

Promoter of Justice—Rev. JOSE VILLAGOMEZ, O.F.M.Cap.

Defender of the Bond—Rev. ADRIAN CRISTOBAL.

Associate Judges—Rev. Msgr. ZOILO CAMACHO; Sr. MARIA ANA LEE, O.P., J.C.L.; Rev. RAYMOND CEPEDA.

Advocates—Revs. EFREN ADVERSARIO; JAMES BENAVENTE.

Notary—Rev. FELIXBERTO LEON GUERRERO, O.F.M.Cap.

Office of Vocations—Revs. ADRIAN CRISTOBAL, Co-Dir. JAMES BENAVENTE, Co-Dir., *196-B Cuesta San Ramon, Agana, 96910.* Tel: 671-472-6116; 472-8024; 472-6201; Fax: 671-472-3519; 472-1729.

CLERGY, PARISHES, MISSIONS AND PAROCHIAL SCHOOLS

CITY OF AGANA
ISLAND OF GUAM

1—DULCE NOMBRE DE MARIA CATHEDRAL - BASILICA (1669), Most Rev. Anthony Sablan Apuron, O.F.M.Cap., D.D.; Revs. James L.G. Benavente; David C. Quitugua; Deacon John Dierking.
Res., 207 Archbishop Felixberto C. Flores St., 96910. Tel: 671-472-6201; 477-1842; Fax: 671-472-1729.
Catechesis/Religious Programs—Students 110.

OUTSIDE THE CITY OF AGANA

Agana Heights, Our Lady of the Blessed Sacrament (1948), Rev. George E.D. Maddock, O.F.M.Cap.
Res., 135 Gunut Cir., 96919. Tel: 671-472-6246; Fax: 671-472-3335.
Catechesis/Religious Programs—Eleanor Cruz, D.R.E.
Students 250.

Agat, Our Lady of Mount Carmel (1957), Rev. Jose Villagomez, O.F.M.Cap.; Deacon Frank Tenorio.
Res., 135 Gunut Cir., Agana Heights, 96919. Tel: 671-565-2136; Fax: 671-565-9678. [CEM]
Catechesis/Religious Programs—Tel: 671-565-9676.
Students 293.

Asan, Holy Family, Nino Perdido, Rev. Rodolfo Arejola.
Res., P.O. Box 45, Agana, 96910. Tel: 671-477-2211.

Barrigada, San Vicente Ferrer (1947), Revs. Adrian F. Cristobal; Joel de los Reyes; Deacons Pedro S. Guerrero; Jeffrey San Nicolas.
Res., 229 San Roke St., 96913. Tel: 671-734-4573; 734-4586; Fax: 671-734-5858.
Catechesis/Religious Programs—Tel: 671-734-4586. Mr. Vincent Reyes Untalan, D.R.E.
Students 336.

Chalan Pago, Nuestra Senora de la Paz y Buen Viaje, Rev. Daniel Cristobal, O.F.M.Cap.
Res., 135 Gunut Cir., Agana Heights, 96919. Tel: 671-734-3723; Fax: 671-472-8431.
Catechesis/Religious Programs—Tel: 671-734-4223.
Students 380.

Dededo, Santa Barbara (1947), Rev. Msgr. Zoilo L.G. Camacho; Revs. Tomasito Tibudan; James McDonough; Manuel Jerus; Deacon Ramon Diaz.
Res., 315 W. Sta., Barbara Ave., 96912. Tel: 671-632-5659; 632-9534.
Catechesis/Religious Programs—D.R.E.: Ann Tydingco; Virginia Avaricio; Cristeta Deliquina; Terry Cruz; Alvin Alvarez.
Students 1,250.

Inarajan, St. Joseph (1680), Rev. Efren F. Adversario.
Res., P.O. Box 170022, 96917. Tel: 671-828-8102; Fax: 671-477-3519. [CEM]
Catechesis/Religious Programs—Students 172.

Maina, Our Lady of the Purification (1949), Rev. Simeon Balmeo.
Res., P.O. Box 4477, Agana, 96910. Tel: 671-477-7256.
Catechesis/Religious Programs—Students 68.

Malojlo, San Isidro (1977), Rev. Manuel Trenchera.
Res., HCR Box 17083, Inarajan, 96917. Tel: 671-828-8454; Fax: 671-828-0001. [JC]
Catechesis/Religious Programs—Students 174.

Mangilao, Santa Teresita (1951), Rev. Joseph English, O.F.M.Cap.
Res., 192 Rte. 10, P.O. Box 306, Agana, 96910. Tel: 671-734-2100; Fax: 671-734-2171.
Catechesis/Religious Programs—Students 386.

Merizo, San Dimas and Our Lady of the Rosary (1680), Rev. Eric Forbes, O.F.M.Cap.
Res., P.O. Box 6099, 96916. Tel: 671-828-8056; Fax: 671-828-3100. [CEM]
Catechesis/Religious Programs—Students 444.

Mongmong, Nuestra Senora de Las Aquas (1969), Rev. Patrick Kenny Q. Garcia.
Res., P.O. Box 163, Agana, 96910. Tel: 671-477-6754; Fax: 671-477-1510.
Catechesis/Religious Programs—Tel: 671-477-3563. Mrs. Therese Mallari, D.R.E.
Students 150.

Ordot, San Juan Bautista (1947), Rev. David I.A. Quitugua.
Res., P.O. Box 49, Agana, 96910. Tel: 671-472-8341; Fax: 671-472-2324.
Catechesis/Religious Programs—Students 110.

Piti, Assumption of Our Lady (1930), Rev. Wilfredo Lorilla.
Mailing Address: 314 Assumption Dr., 96925.
Res., 96910. Tel: 671-472-2272; Fax: 671-477-1955.
Catechesis/Religious Programs—Students 167.

Santa Rita, Our Lady of Guadalupe (1944), Rev. Jack Niland, O.F.M.Cap.
Res., P.O. Box 4632, Agana, 96910. Tel: 671-565-2160; Fax: 671-565-7078.
Catechesis/Religious Programs—Mrs. Cecilia Cruz, D.R.E.
Students 405.

Sinajana, Saint Jude Thaddeus (1962), Rev. Felixberto Leon Guerrero, O.F.M.Cap.; Deacon Anthony C. Leon Guerrero.
Church & St. Jude Rectory—122 Avenida Bien Venida, 96926. Tel: 671-475-6530; 6531; Fax: 671-477-5353.
Catechesis/Religious Programs—Sr. Gloria Aquon, F.S.P.A., D.R.E.
Students 383.

Talofofo, San Miguel (1945), Rev. Agustin Gumataotao, O.F.M.Cap.
Res., 71 San Miguel St., 96930. Tel: 671-789-1069; Fax: 671-789-7665.
Catechesis/Religious Programs—Tel: 671-789-0130. Marie E. Meno, D.R.E.
Students 292.

Tamuning, St. Anthony and St. Victor (1946), Revs. Brigido U. Arroyo; James Ch'e; Jose Antonio P. Abad; Deacon Mario L. Celis. In res., Revs. Manuel Ombao; Hermogenes Quiambo.
Res., P.O. Box 7707, 96931. Tel: 671-646-7181; 646-8044; Fax: 671-646-1039.

Toto, Immaculate Heart of Mary (1948), Rev. Alfonso Asis; Deacon Jose Santos.
Res., P.O. Box 2552, Agana, 96910. Tel: 671-477-9118.
Catechesis/Religious Programs—Students 136.

Tumon Bay, Blessed Diego Luis de San Vitores Church (1970), Rev. Juan L.G. Camacho.
Res., P.O. Box 24363, GMF, 96921. Tel: 671-646-5649; Fax: 671-649-6887.
Catechesis/Religious Programs—Students 63.

Umatac, San Dionisio (1680), Rev. Eric Forbes, O.F.M.Cap.
Res., P.O. Box 6099, Merizo, 96916. Tel: 671-828-8056; Fax: 671-828-3100. [CEM]
Catechesis/Religious Programs—Students 60.

Yigo, Our Lady of Lourdes (1947), Revs. Vito B. San Andres; Michael C. Crisostomo; Deacon Fred Otte.
Res., P.O. Box 11001, 96929. Tel: 671-653-2584; Fax: 671-653-4746.
Catechesis/Religious Programs—Tel: 671-653-1102. D.R.E.: Femy Castro; Trinie Cruz; Elaine Gogue; Thelma Lumbre.
Students 681.

Yona, San Francisco d'Assisi (1954), Rev. Patrick Castro, O.F.M.Cap.
Res., San Fidelis Friary, 135 Gunut Cir., Agana Heights, 96919. Tel: 671-789-1491; Fax: 671-789-2845. [CEM]
Catechesis/Religious Programs—Josephine Santos, D.R.E.
Students 258.

On Duty Outside the Archdiocese:
Reverend Fathers—
Cepeda, Ray, St. Paul Univ., Quebec
D'Arcy, William, Armed Forces
Perez, Antonio, St. Mary's Seminary, Baltimore, MD

Retired:
Reverend Monsignors—
Calvo, Oscar, P.O. Box 518, Agana, GU 96910. Tel: 671-477-8544
Reverend Fathers—
Brouillard, Louis A., 525 9th St., Pine City, MN 55063

INSTITUTIONS LOCATED IN THE ARCHDIOCESE

[A] HIGH SCHOOLS

AGANA. *Academy of Our Lady of Guam*, 233 W. Archbishop Felixberto C. Flores St., 96910. Tel: 671-477-8203; Fax: 671-477-8555.
E-mail: acad@aolg.aolg.edu.gu
Web site: http://www.aolg.edu.gu
Sisters of Mercy. Sr. Francis Jerome Cruz, R.S.M., Prin. Sisters 6; Lay Teachers 26; Staff 11; Students 425.

The Father Duenas Memorial School, P.O. Box FD, 96932. Tel: 671-734-2261; 734-2263; Fax: 671-734-5738.
E-mail: fdms2@ite.net
Mr. William Roth, Prin. Priests 3; Sisters 3; Lay Teachers 25; Students 392.

TALOFOFO. *Notre Dame High School*, 480 San Miguel St., 96930. Tel: 671-789-1745; 789-1675; Fax: 671-789-4847.
E-mail: notredame@kuentos.guam.net
Sr. Regina Paulino, S.S.N.D., Prin. Sisters 5; Lay Teachers 22; Students 245.

[B] ELEMENTARY AND JUNIOR HIGH SCHOOLS

AGAT. *Our Lady of Mt. Carmel School*, P.O. Box 7830, 96928. Tel: 671-565-5128; Fax: 671-565-3539. Sr. Bernadette Quintanilla, S.S.N.D., Prin. Sisters 3; Lay Teachers 17; Students 170.

DEDEDO. *Santa Barbara School*, 274-A W. Santa Barbara Ave., 96912. Tel: 671-632-5578; 632-2789; Fax: 671-632-1414. Mailing Address: 274-B W. Santa Barbara Ave., 96912. Sr. Bernadette Marie Leon Guerrero, R.S.M., Prin. Sisters 4; Lay Teachers 27; Students 441.

GMF. *St. Francis School*, P.O. Box 22199, 96921. Tel: 671-789-1270; 789-3900; Fax: 671-789-5052. Sr. Vincent Marie Balajadia, S.S.N.D., Prin.; Sr. Lourdes Pangelinan, S.S.N.D. Sisters 3; Lay Teachers 17; Students 302.

San Vicente School. 196 Bejong St., Barrigada, 96913. Tel: 671-735-4240; Fax: 671-734-8718. Sr. Mary Juan Camacho, S.S.N.D., Prin. Sisters 1; Lay Teachers 26; Students 386.

SINAJANA. *Bishop Baumgartner Memorial School*, 281 Calle Angel Flores St., 96926. Tel: 671-472-6670. Sr. Mary Charles Cameron, R.S.M., Pres. Cathedral Grade School merged with Bishop Baumgartner Middle School to form Bishop Baumgartner Memorial School. Sisters 4; Lay Teachers 35; Students 547.

TAMUNING. *Saint Anthony School*, 529 Chalan San Antonio, 96911. Tel: 671-647-1140; Fax: 671-649-7130.
E-mail: sasdev@ite.net
Sr. Doris San Agustin, R.S.M., Prin. Sisters 4; Lay Teachers 37; Students 568.

YIGO. *Dominican School*, 114 Chalan Pale Roman - Lagu, Rte. 1, 96929. Tel: 671-653-3021; Fax: 671-653-3090. Sr. Zenaida Ancheta, O.P., Prin. Sisters 4; Lay Teachers 11; Students 125.

[C] KINDERGARTEN AND NURSERY SCHOOLS

AGANA HEIGHTS. *Maria Artero Nursery*, 161 A Sunset Dr., 96919. Tel: 671-472-8777. Sr. Jacintha Marsil, M.M.B., Prin. Sisters 3; Lay Teachers 3; Students 60.

ORDOT. *Dominican Child Development Center*. P.O. Box 10342, Sinajana, 96926. Tel: 671-477-7228; Fax: 671-472-4282. Sr. Loreto Galang, O.P., Prin. Sisters 5; Lay Teachers 4; Aides 5; Students 130.

PEREZVILLE-TAMUNING. *Mercy Heights Nursery and Kindergarten, Inc.*, 211 San Vitores St., 96911. Tel: 671-646-1185. Sr. Mary Roberta Taitano, R.S.M., Admin. Students 179.

TAI. *Infant of Prague Nursery and Kindergarten, Inc.* P.O. Box 22865, GMF, 96921. Tel: 671-734-2785. Sisters of Mercy. Sr. Seville Cabuhat, R.S.M., Admin. Students 150.

[D] CATHOLIC CHARITIES

AGANA. *Catholic Social Services of Guam*, P.O. Box EJ, 96910. Tel: 671-649-5717; 646-1924; 646-4974; Fax:

671-649-9224. Mrs. Cerila Rapadas, Exec. Dir.; Sr. Callista Camacho, R.S.M., Deputy Dir. Total Assisted 5,345; Total Staff 262.

Alee Shelter Program for Spouse Abuse, P.O. Box EJ, 96910. Tel: 472-6729; 472-6709. Sr. Eileen Mearns, R.G.S., Dir.

[E] MONASTERIES AND RESIDENCES OF PRIESTS

AGANA HEIGHTS. *St. Fidelis Friary*. Mailing Address: 135 Gunut Cir., 96919. Tel: 671-472-6339; Fax: 671-472-3335. Headquarters of Capuchin Friars (Vice Province, Star of the Sea). Very Rev. Agustin Gumataotao, O.F.M.Cap., Vice Prov.; Revs. Felix Leon Guerrero, O.F.M.Cap., Novice Master & Postulant Dir.; Paulo Kosaka, O.F.M.Cap.; Bros. Brian Champoux, O.F.M.Cap., Post-Noviate Formation Dir.; Maurice Moreau, O.F.M.Cap.
In Formation: Bros. Bryant Bamba; Robert Wolford; Hamilton Nukuto; Revs. Michael Cruz, O.F.M.Cap., Hawaii; Soke Maluafiti, O.F.M.Cap., Hawaii; Andre Eduvala, O.F.M.Cap.; Douglas Antipas, O.F.M.Cap.
Priests Retired: Revs. Eymard McKinnon, O.F.M.Cap.; Randolph Nowak, O.F.M.Cap., Hawaii.
Priests Abroad: Revs. Paul Minchak, O.F.M.Cap., Hawaii; Gordon Combs, O.F.M.Cap., Hawaii; Robert Phelps, O.F.M.Cap., Hawaii; Andrew Mannetta, O.F.M.Cap., Hawaii; Michel W. Dalton, O.F.M.Cap., Hawaii.

[F] CONVENTS AND RESIDENCES FOR SISTERS

AGANA. *Cathedral Mercy Convent*, P.O. Box 3070, 96932. Tel: 671-477-9291. Sisters of Mercy 7.

AGANA HEIGHTS. *Mercedarian Missionaries of Berriz*, 161 A Sunset Dr., 96932. Mailing Address: P.O. Box 3487, Agana, 96910. Tel: 671-477-8303; Fax: 671-472-2326. Sr. Isabel Seman, M.M.B., Regl. Coord. Sisters 9.

AGAT. *Mt. Carmel Community*, P.O. Box 7705, 96928. Tel: 671-565-2369. Sr. Carmen Francis Siguenza, S.S.N.D.; Sr. Bernadette Quintanilla, S.S.N.D.; Sr. Clare Marie Quichocho, S.S.N.D.; Sr. Rose Marie Manibusan, S.S.N.D. Sisters 4. Sisters teach at Mt. Carmel Elementary & Jr. High.

BARRIGADA. *San Vicente Community*, 201 Bejong St., 96913. Tel: 671-734-3010. Mailing Address: c/o Notre Dame Regional Center, 480 San Miguel St., Talofofo, 96930. Tel: 671-734-3010. Sisters 3. Sisters teach at San Vicente Elementary & Jr. High.

DEDEDO. *Santa Barbara Convent*, 274 B. W. Santa Barbara St., 96912. Tel: 671-632-2384; Fax: 671-632-1414. Institute of the Sisters of Mercy of the Americas, North Carolina Region. Sisters 4.

INARAJAN. *Convent of Mercy Sisters*, P.O. Box 17211, 96916. Tel: 671-828-8285. Institute of Sisters of Mercy of the Americas, North Carolina Region 2.

MALOJLO. *Discalced Order Of Carmelites Monastery*. P.O. Box 17084, Inarajan, 96917. Tel: 671-828-8280; Fax: 671-828-0001. Order of Discalced Carmelites. Mother Conception de Carlos, O.C.D., Prioress. Sisters 13.

ORDOT. *Religious Missionaries of St. Dominic*, P.O. Box 10342, 96926. Tel: 671-477-7228; 472-1524. Total in Residence 6; Total Staff 6.

Sisters of the Good Shepherd Convent. P.O. Box 3596, Agana, 96932. Tel: 671-472-3393; Fax: 671-472-8486. Sr. Helena Cusack, R.G.S., Supr.; Sr. Eileen Mearns, R.G.S.; Sr. Carol McClenon, R.G.S.; Sr. Stella Mangona, R.G.S. Total Assisted 376; Total Staff 16. Sisters work at abuse shelters under Catholic Social Services and Campus Ministry.

PEREZVILLE-TAMUNING. *Mercy Heights Convent*, 211 San Vitores St., 96911. Tel: 671-646-7246; Fax: 671-649-1822.
E-mail: guamrsm@iftech.net
Sr. Mary Angela Perez, R.S.M., Guam Region Pres. Administrative Residence and Offices of the Institute of the Sisters of Mercy of the Americas, North Carolina Region. Sisters in residence teaching and working in Tamuning and Agana. Sisters 16.

SINAJANA. *St. Jude Thaddeus Convent*. P.O. Box 394, Agana, 96910. Tel: 671-472-6041. Franciscan Sisters of Perpetual Adoration.

TAI. *Mercy Convent and Formation House*. P.O. Box 22865, Barrigada, 96921. Tel: 671-734-3312. Institute of the Sisters of Mercy of the Americas, North Carolina Region. Professed Sisters in various Apostolates and Sisters in basic formation. Sisters 12.

TALOFOFO. *Notre Dame Community*, 480 San Miguel St., 96930. Tel: 671-789-1629; Fax: 671-789-3810.

S.S.N.D. Regional House, 480 San Miguel St., 96930. Tel: 671-789-7763; 789-0501; Fax: 671-789-3810.
E-mail: francine@kuentos.guam.net
St. Augustine Community. Tel: 671-789-5965.
Mother Theresa. Tel: 671-789-0501.
Notre Dame Community. Tel: 671-789-1629.
Mother Caroline Community. Tel: 671-789-5189. Regional Councilors: Sr. M. Francine Perez, S.S.N.D., Regl. Leader; Sr. Joseph Ann Quinene, S.S.N.D.; Sr. Tarcisia Sablan, S.S.N.D. Sisters 28.

[G] MISCELLANEOUS LISTINGS

AGANA. *Our Lady of the Waters House of Prayer*. (Retreat Center), P.O. Box 163, 96932. Tel: 671-477-3422; Fax: 671-477-3766.

Saint Vincent de Paul Society, c/o Santa Teresita Parish, P.O. Box 306, 96910. Tel: 671-734-2100. Mr. John Lizama, Pres. Tel: 671-472-6068.

Secular Franciscans, P.O. Box CF, 96910. Tel: 671-472-6023; 472-6339. Rev. Daniel Cristobal, O.F.M.Cap., Spiritual Dir.; Mrs. Carmen Manibusan, Pres.

BARRIGADA. *Saint Dominic's Senior Care Home*. 350 N. Sabana Barrigada Dr., Barrigada Heights, 96913. Tel: 671-632-9370; 632-9378; 9379; Fax: 671-637-1679. Sr. Fe Dural, O.P., Admin. Total in Residence 59; Total Staff 70.

MANGILAO. *Campus Ministry, Newman Center, University of Guam*. Box 23142, Barrigada, 96921. Tel: 671-734-3507; Fax: 671-734-2943.
E-mail: khezel@ite.net
Rev. Kenneth J. Hezel, S.J.; Sr. Stella Mangona, R.G.S. Total in Residence 1; Total Staff 3.

RELIGIOUS INSTITUTES OF MEN REPRESENTED IN THE ARCHDIOCESE

For further details refer to the corresponding bracketed number in the Religious Institutes of Men or Women section.

[0470]—*The Capuchin Friars*. (Vice Prov. of Mary, Star of the Sea).—O.F.M.Cap.

[0690]—*Jesuit Fathers and Brothers*. (N.Y. Prov.).—S.J.

RELIGIOUS INSTITUTES OF WOMEN REPRESENTED IN THE ARCHDIOCESE

[1780]—*Congregation of the Sisters of the Third Order of St. Francis of Perpetual Adoration*. (La Crosse, WI).—F.S.P.A.

[0420]—*Discalced Carmelite Nuns*.—O.C.D.

[2510]—*Mercedarian Missionaries of Berriz*.—M.M.B.

[]—*Order of Saint Benedict*.—O.S.B.

[]—*Religious Missionaries of St. Dominic*.—O.P.

[2970]—*School Sisters of Notre Dame*. (Mequon, WI).—S.S.N.D.

[2575]—*Sisters of Mercy of the Americas*. (Belmont, NC).—R.S.M.

[1830]—*Sisters of the Good Shepherd*.—R.G.S.

NECROLOGY

(No Deaths)

Diocese of Arecibo, Puerto Rico

(Dioecesis Arecibensis)

Most Reverend

INAKI MALLONA TXERTUDI, C.P.

Bishop of Arecibo; ordained March 27, 1956; appointed December 14, 1991; consecrated January 6, 1992; installed January 25, 1992. *Res., 206 Dr. Salas St., P.O. Box 616, Arecibo, PR, 00613-0616.*

Most Reverend

MIGUEL RODRIGUEZ, C.SS.R., D.D.

Retired Bishop of Arecibo; ordained June 22, 1958; appointed January 21, 1974; consecrated March 23, 1974; retired March 1990. *Res., Apartado 238, Aguadilla, PR, 00605-0238.*

ESTABLISHED APRIL 30, 1960.

Square Miles 833.08.

Comprises the mid-northern part of the Island.

The Chancery: 206 Dr. Salas St., P.O. Box 616, Arecibo, PR, 00613. Tel.: 787-878-3180; Fax: 787-880-2661.

STATISTICAL OVERVIEW

Personnel	
Bishop	1
Retired Bishops	1
Priests: Diocesan Active in Diocese	56
Priests: Active Outside Diocese	22
Priests: Retired, Sick or Absent	6
Number of Diocesan Priests	84
Religious Priests in Diocese	43
Ordinations:	
Diocesan Priests	4
Permanent Deacons in Diocese	6
Total Brothers	7
Total Sisters	147
Parishes	
Parishes	59
With Resident Pastor:	
Resident Diocesan Priests	43
Resident Religious Priests	16
Without Resident Pastor:	
Missions	228
Pastoral Centers	1
Welfare	
Homes for the Aged	4
Total Assisted	428
Residential Care of Children	2
Total Assisted	48
Specialized Homes	1
Total Assisted	412
Special Centers for Social Services	1
Total Assisted	1,411
Educational	
Seminaries, Diocesan	1
Students from This Diocese	2
Diocesan Students in Other Seminaries	8
Total Seminarians	10
Colleges and Universities	1
Total Students	707
High Schools, Diocesan and Parish	14
Total Students	2,699
Elementary Schools, Diocesan and Parish	14
Total Students	4,209
Catechesis/Religious Education:	
High School Students	2,375
Elementary Students	14,010
Total Students Under Catholic Instruction	24,010
Teachers in the Diocese:	
Priests	13
Brothers	5
Sisters	43
Lay Teachers	386
Vital Statistics	
Receptions into the Church:	
Infant Baptism Totals	3,427
Adult Baptism Totals	202
Received into Full Communion	23
First Communions	2,805
Confirmations	2,587
Marriages:	
Catholic	655
Interfaith	46
Total Marriages	701
Deaths	959
Total Catholic Population	383,018
Total Population	550,678

Former Bishops—Most. Rev. ALFRED F. MENDEZ, C.S.C., ord. 1935; cons. Oct. 28, 1960; retired Jan., 1974; died Jan. 28, 1995.—Most. Rev. MIGUEL RODRIQUEZ, C.S.S.R., D.D., ord. June 22, 1958; appt. Jan. 21, 1974; cons. March 23, 1974; retired March, 1990.

Secretary to the Bishop—SOR MARIA J. FONTANEZ, O.P.

Chancery Office—206 Dr. Salas St., P.O. Box 616, Arecibo, 00613. Tel: 787-878-3180; Fax: 787-880-2661.

Vicar General—Rev. SERAPIO FERNANDEZ, P.H., *P.O. Box 616, Arecibo, 00613.* Tel: 787-878-3180; 878-3110.

Chancellor—Rev. JOSEPH D. SCHRECK, O.F.M.Cap., *P.O. Box 616, Arecibo, 00613.* Tel: 787-878-3180.

Vice Chancellor—Miss SYLVIA VARGAS.

Secretary—Miss SYLVIA VARGAS.

Vicar of Diocesan Pastor Affairs—Rev. MIGUEL MERCADO.

Diocesan Consultors—Rev. Msgr. BUENAVENTURA BALLESTER, P.H.; Revs. SERAPIO FERNANDEZ; MIGUEL MERCADO; JOSEPH SCHRECK, O.F.M.Cap.; ELIAS FERNANDEZ, O.SS.T.; CARMELO URARTE; FRANCISCO CONCEPCION.

Diocesan Pastoral Council—Revs. SERAPIO FERNANDEZ; MIGUEL MERCADO; ELIAS FERNANDEZ; BENJAMIN QUINONES; MELQUIADES ROJAS; SOR ROSA DE FATIMA.

Dean of Arecibo Zone—Rev. Msgr. BUENAVENTURA BALLESTER, P.H., *P.O. Box 140637, Arecibo, 00614-0637.* Tel: 787-878-4910.

Dean of El Calvario Zone—Rev. ELIAS FERNANDEZ, O.SS.T., *P.O. Box 525, Isabela, 00662.* Tel: 787-872-2563.

Dean of Vega Baja Zone—Rev. FRANCISCO CONCEPCION, *P.O. Box 775, Vega Alta, 00692.* Tel: 787-883-4875.

Diocesan Offices and Directors

Confraternity of Christian Doctrine—Sr. ROSA DE FATIMA, O.P., *Calle Mariano Abril, Box 1151, Arecibo, 00612.* Tel: 787-878-8401.

Cursillos de Cristiandad—Rev. VICTOR ROJAS, *P.O. Box 1826, Arecibo, 00613.* Tel: 787-872-2563.

Diocesan Council of Catholic Women—Vacant.

Propagation of Faith—Rev. MANUEL P. CARDENAS, M.N.M.

Holy Childhood—Rev. MANUEL P. CARDENAS, M.N.M.

Director of Youth—Rev. CARLOS E. GRANADOS, *Box 2164, Arecibo, 00613.* Tel: 787-878-1528.

Legion of Mary—Vacant.

Movimiento Familiar Cristiano (CFM)—Vacant.

Prison Services—Vacant, *Box 673, Arecibo, 00613.* Tel: 787-878-4910.

Seminario Jesus Maestro College Seminary—Rev. VICTOR ROJAS, Dir., *Box 2164, Arecibo, 00613.* Tel: 787-878-1528.

Seminary Board—Rev. VICTOR ROJAS.

Pastoral Vocational Program—Revs. MIGUEL MERCADO; VICTOR ROJAS; ROBERTO VEGA.

Superintendent of Schools—Miss LYDIA HERNANDEZ, *P.O. Box 1683, Arecibo, 00613.* Tel: 787-878-1095; Fax: 787-878-1095.

Catholic Charities—Sr. ROBERTA GRZELAK, *Box 616, Arecibo, 00613.* Tel: 787-878-6580.

Retreat House, Centro Diocesano Mons. Mendez—Vacant, *Apdo. 2164, Arecibo, 00613.* Tel: 787-878-4796.

Boy Scouts—Vacant.

Hospital Chaplains—

Regional—Miss ESTHER COSTA.

Municipal—Sr. MARIA ESTELA RESTREPO, C.B.P. Tel: 787-878-7272.

Buen Pastor—Vacant.

Cathedral of San Felipe Apostol Priests—Revs. ROBERTO VEGA; CESAR RAMIREZ.

Susoni—Vacant.

Vocations—Rev. VICTOR ROJAS, *Apdo. 2164, Arecibo, 00613.* Tel: 787-878-1528.
Police Chaplain—Rev. FRANCISCO CONCEPCION.

Promotion and Human Development Office—Sr. ROBERTA GZELACK, C.D.P., *P.O. Box 616, Arecibo, 00613.* Tel: 787-878-6580.

Sociedad San Vincente de Paul (Vincentinos)—Mr. ANGEL GINES, Pres. Consejo Diocesano. Tel: 787-884-5087; 854-2562.

CLERGY, PARISHES, MISSIONS AND PAROCHIAL SCHOOLS

CITY OF ARECIBO

1—CATHEDRAL OF SAN FELIPE APOSTOL (1616), Revs. Roberto Vega, Rector; Cesar Ramirez.
Res., De Diego St., Box 577, 00613. Tel: 809-878-1149.
Convent—251 Magallanes St., 00613. Tel: 787-878-7179.
Dominican Sisters of Fatima 5.
Chapels—Islote II, Sagrada Familia.; Islote III (Sector Vibora), San Juan Evangelista.; Sector Boam, Maria Reina.; Islote I (Vigia), N.S. del Carmen.

2—CHURCH OF SAGRADO CORAZON DE JESUS (1961), Rev. Msgr. Buenaventura Ballester, P.H.; Rev. Elvin Irizarry.
Res., Box 140637, 00614. Tel: 787-878-4910; Fax: 787-879-2124. [JC]
School—Colegio San Felipe, Box 673, 00613. Tel: 809-878-3532. Judith Colon, Prin. (Elem./High).
Lay Teachers 37; Students 383.
Catechesis/Religious Programs—Students 150.

3—NUESTRA SENORA DEL CARMEN (1961), Revs. Alberto Diaz; Delfin Rodriguez.
Res., Bo. Cotto No. 985, P.O. Box 9949, Cotto Sta., 00613. Tel: 787-878-1268. [JC]
School—Hogar-Colegio La Milagrosa, Ave., Cotto, 00613. Tel: 809-878-0341.
Sisters of Charity 7; Lay Teachers 26; Students 467.
Catechesis/Religious Programs—Students 268.
Chapels—Abra S. Francisco, San Antonio.; Rodriguez Olmo, San Francisco.

4—SANTA ANA (1961), Rev. Luis Rios Cappiello.
Res., Bo. Santana, Box 318, 00613. Tel: 787-881-6005. [JC]
Catechesis/Religious Programs—Students 333.
Chapels—Factor II, N.S. del Carmen.; Santuario Cristo de los Milagros.

5—CHURCH OF CHRIST THE KING (1967), Rev. Serapio Fernandez.
Res., Box 1932, 00613. Tel: 809-878-9214.
Catechesis/Religious Programs—Students 155.
Chapel—Bo. Hato Arriba, Maria Auxiliadora.

6—OUR LADY OF HOPE (1986), Rev. Enrique A. Perez.
Res., Box 489, 00613. Tel: 787-880-1943. [JC]
Catechesis/Religious Programs—Students 37.
Chapels—Cantagallo, Sgdo. Corazon de Jesus.; Plan Bonito, San Rafael.

7—NUESTRA SENORA DE FATIMA (1967), Revs. Ignacio Pili, C.M.; Gilberto Da Silva, C.M.
Res., Box 667, Sabana Hoyos, 00688. Tel: 787-881-8274. [JC]
Catechesis/Religious Programs—Students 145.
Chapels—Garrochales, S. Fco. de Asis.; Ballaja, N.S. del Carmen.; Garrochales, La Milagrosa, San Luis.; Espino, Immaculada Concepcion.

8—INMACULADO CORAZON DE MARIA (1987), Rev. Juan B. Franco.
Res., Box 1282, Sabana Hoyos, 00688. [JC]
Chapels—Bo. Asomante, San Isidro.; Bo. Carolina, Sagrado Corazon de Jesus.; Bo. Arrozal, San Jose.; Los Muertos, San Francisco.

9—LA MILAGROSA (1973), Rev. Angel M. Santos.
Res., Box 204, Bajadero, 00616. Tel: 787-881-0295. [JC]
Catechesis/Religious Programs—Students 227.
Chapels—Bajadero, Immaculada Concepcion.; Domingo Ruiz, N.S. La Providencia.; Carreras, San Judas.; Biafara, N.S. La Virgen del Carmen.

10—SAN JUAN BOSCO (1971), Rev. Melquiades Rojas.
Res., Urb. Jardines de Arecibo, Calle R-Y-26, 00613. Tel: 787-879-1070.
School—Tel: 809-879-2069.
Lay Teachers 15; Students 327.
Catechesis/Religious Programs—Students 140.
Chapel—Las Canelas, N.S. La Dolorosa, San Daniel.
Sisters of Mercy 3.

11—CHURCH OF SAN MARTIN DE PORRES (1973), Revs. Edwin Mercado; Antonio Laglera.
Res., Calle 6 F-12, Box 14-2142, Urb. Univ. Gardens, 00613. Tel: 787-878-1822.
Catechesis/Religious Programs—Students 300.
Chapels—Victor Rojas II, San Jose Obrero.; Bo. Obrero, Immaculada Concepcion.

12—CHURCH OF SANTA TERESITA (1980), Rev. Gabriel Maduro.
Res., Road 492, KM 1.9, P.O. Box 9242, Cotto Station, 00613. Tel: 787-878-7015. [JC]
Catechesis/Religious Programs—Students 50.
Chapels—Hato Arriba, N.S. La Providencia.; Barrancas, La Milagrosa.

13—CHURCH OF SANTA CECILIA (1981), Rev. Jose M. Casco.
Res., HC-02 Box 13674, 00612. Tel: 787-879-3364. [JC]
Catechesis/Religious Programs—Students 120.
Chapels—Calichosa, San Jose.; Los Canos, San Martin de Porres.; La Guinea, La Milagrosa.

14—SANTISIMO SACRAMENTO (1990), Rev. Miguel Mercado.
Res., Ste. 109, P.O. Box 4015, 00613. Tel: 787-880-6513. [JC]
Catechesis/Religious Programs—Students 65.
Chapels—Del Valle, La Milagrosa.; Jobos, San Pascual.

OUTSIDE OF ARECIBO

Barceloneta, Church of Our Lady of Mt. Carmel (1882), Revs. Thomas Sharkey, C.S.Sp., Pastor; Gerard Siegfried, C.S.Sp.; Felix Rivera.
Res., P.O. Box 187, 00617. Tel: 809-846-5625. [JC]
Catechesis/Religious Programs—Students 148.
Chapels—Garrochales I, N.S. de Fatima.; Palmas Altas, San Antonio.; Punta Palma, N.S. del Mar.

Our Lady of Victory (1963), Rev. Leon Perez, Admin.
Res., Ste. 125, Call Box 2020, 00617. Tel: 809-846-6120.
Catechesis/Religious Programs—Students 85.
Chapels—Parcelas Imberry, San Jose Obrero.; Quebrada, Immaculate Heart of Mary.; Tiburones, N.S. de Fatima.

Camuy

1—ST. JOSEPH (1827), Revs. Adrian Jimenez; David Rivas.
Res., P.O. Box 414, 00627. Tel: 809-898-3620. [JC]
Catechesis/Religious Programs—Students 377.
Convent—.San Jose Hermanas Terciarias Capuchinas 4.
Chapels—Membrillo, N.S. La Monserrate.; Puente (Zarzas), Sagrado Corazon.; Puente (Zarza Parcelas), N.S. La Milagrosa.; Puente (Sector Pica), N.S. del Rosario.; Abra Honda, Espiritu Santo.; Zanjas, Immaculada Concepcion.

2—OUR LADY OF THE MIRACULOUS MEDAL (1962). (El Calvario). Revs. Zenaido Martin; Manuel M. Flores.
Res., HC-01 Buzon 5240, 00627. Tel: 787-898-5825. [JC]
Catechesis/Religious Programs—Students 322.
Chapels—Planas II, Santiago Apostol.; Puertos, Sagrado Corazon.; Cienaga, Cristo Rey.; Camuy Arriba, N.S. del Carmen.; Sector Riego, Santa Clara.; Sector Mani, Sagrado Corazon.

3—OUR LADY OF ASUMPTION (1984), Rev. Antonio Caraballo.
Res., HC-02 Box 8047, 00627. Tel: 787-898-8038. [JC]
Catechesis/Religious Programs—Students 372.
Chapels—Cibao Ocasio, N.S. del Perpetuo Socorro.; Callejones, Sagrado Corazon.; Callejones II, San Pablo de la Cruz.; Cibao Lugo, Maria Auxiliadora.

4—OUR LADY OF MONSERRATE (1961), Rev. Antonio J. Vazquez.
Res., HC-03 Box 16512, Quebradillas, 00678-9820. Tel: 787-898-6784. [JC]
Catechesis/Religious Programs—Students 200.
Convent—Tel: 787-896-6176.
Hermanes Angeles Custodios 2.
Chapels—Piletas (Lares), N.S. del Carmen.; Guajataca (Queb.), N.S. de Fatima.; Aibonito Beltran, San Antonio.; Cibao (S. Sebastian), Santa Ana.; Planas I (Isabela), Santa Cruz.; Planas II, N.S. del Rosario.

Ciales, Holy Rosary (1820), Revs. Salvador Rodrigo, O.Carm.; Elias Pascual; Luis Miranda, O.Carm.; Gabriel M. Torres.
Res., P.O. Box 26, 00638. Tel: 787-871-2205; 871-3485. [JC]
School—P.O. Box 1334, 00638. Tel: 787-871-1318. Mrs. Juanita Natal, Prin.
Lay Teachers 21; Students 374.
Catechesis/Religious Programs—Students 739.
Chapels—Pozas, San Elias.; Cialitos, Buen Pastor.; Hato Viejo, Corazon de Jesus.; Hato Viejo, San Antonio.; Jaguas, Santa Clara.; Pesa, San Ignacio.; Cialitos-Cruces, Corazon de Maria.; Toro Negro, N.S.; Bo. Marias, Maternidad de la Virgen.

N.S. Madre del Redentor (1988), Rev. Wiktor Tarnawski.
Res., P.O. Box 1181, 00638. Tel: 787-871-2404. [JC]
Catechesis/Religious Programs—Students 200.
Chapels—Yunes, San Jose.; Fronton (Sabana), Perpetuo Socorro.; Cordillera 5, N.S. La Providencia.; Limon, Smo. Rosario.; Cordillera 7, Sagrada Familia.

Corozal, Holy Family (1804), Revs. Eugenio Gayarre; Ramon Olivencia.
Res., P.O. Box 474, 00783. Tel: 787-859-2595. [JC]
School—Tel: 787-859-2420.
Sisters of St. Joseph 9; Lay Teachers 35; Students 971.
Catechesis/Religious Programs—Students 926.
Chapels—Guarico Palmarejo I, San Judas Tadeo.; Palmarejo II, San Vicente.; Palmarejo II, San Francisco de Asis.; Dos Bocas II, Santa Teresita.; Cibuco, N.S. del Carmen.; Abras, San Jose.; Urb. Sylvia, Perpetuo Socorro.

Corozal-Padilla, Our Lady of the Seven Sorrows (1984), Revs. Luis A. Vazquez, Admin.; Miguel Rivera.
Res., P.O. Box 740, 00783. Tel: 787-859-1900.
Catechesis/Religious Programs—Students 700.
Chapels—Padilla Hermita, San Rafael.; Padilla Hormiga, San Martin.; Cieneguita (V.A.), N.S. del Perpetuo Socorro.

Corozal-Palmarito, La Milagrosa, Revs. Benjamin Quinones, C.R.L., Pastor; Rafael J. Gonzalez, C.R.L.
Res., HC-03 Box 13976, 00783. Tel: 787-859-5306.
Catechesis/Religious Programs—Students 514.
Convent—HC-03 Box 14048, 00783. Tel: 787-859-8151.
Hnas. de San Francisco (Secular Institute) 3.
Chapels—Maguelles, Cristo Rey.; Mana, N.S. de Fatima.; Radio Oro, Nuestra Senora del Carmen.

Corozal-Palos Blancos, Christ the King (1968), Rev. Francisco J. Anduaga, C.R.L., Admin.
Res., P.O. Box 1091, Corozal, 00783. Tel: 787-859-7313. [JC]
Catechesis/Religious Programs—Students 725.
Chapels—Cuchillas, N.S. del Perpetuo Socorro.; Negros, N.S. del Rosario.; Palos Blancos, Santa Teresita.; Palos Blancos, San Antonio.

Florida, Our Lady of Mercy (1887), Rev. Casimiro Domeck.
Res., P.O. Box 437, 00650. Tel: 787-822-2670. [JC]
Catechesis/Religious Programs—Students 120.
Chapels—Monte Bello, N.S. del Carmen.; Pajornal (Bta.), Santa Rosa de Lima.

Hatillo, Our Lady of Mt. Carmel (1830), Revs. Fernando Morell, Pastor; Jorge Virella.
Res., P.O. Box 2, 00659. Tel: 809-898-5300. [JC]
School—Tel: 787-898-2800.
Sisters de la Caridad del Cardenal Sancha 6; Lay Teachers 51; Students 844.
Catechesis/Religious Programs—Students 610.
Chapels—Carrizales, Sagrado Corazon.; Corcovados, Immaculada Concepcion.; Capaez, N.S. Perpetuo Socorro.; Carrizales, San Jose.; Santa Rosa, Santa Rosa de Lima.; Lechuga: San Pio X.; Palma Gordo: Sagrada Familia.

Our Lady of Guadalupe (1961), Revs. Victor R. Borrero, S.E.M.V., Prior; Luis Maria de la Cruz, S.E.M.V.; Rene A. Maria del Nino Jesus, S.E.M.V.; Anibal Jesus Hostia de la Purisima, S.E.M.V.; David A. Maria Alabanza de la Trin, S.E.M.V.; Alberto Jesus Gloria de la Inmaculada, S.E.M.V.; Sr. Teresa Maria V. de la Eucaristia.
Res., Carr. Ins. 129, Arecibo to Lares, P.O. Box 1131, Arecibo, 00613. Tel: 787-898-8035.
Catechesis/Religious Programs—Students 348.
Chapels—Pajuil, Santa Rosa de Lima.; Buena Vista, Inmaculada Concepcion.; Bda Colon, N.S. La Providencia.; Sector Naranjito, San Jose.

Perpetual Help (1961), Rev. Jose Estensoro.
Res., Ste. 113, P.O. Box 59003, 00659. Tel: 787-898-7771. [JC]
Catechesis/Religious Programs—Students 291.
Chapels—Aibonito, Cristo Rey.; Berrocal, Sagrado Corazon de Jesus.; Sonadora, La Milagrosa.; Mariposa, N.S. del Carmen.; Cantera, Ntra. Sra. de la Paz.

Isabela, St. Anthony (1835), Revs. Pedro Bustinza, O.SS.T.; Wilfredo Echevarria, O.SS.T.; Jorge I. Mantilla, O.SS.T.
Res., Box 525, 00662. Tel: 787-872-2563. [JC]
School—Sisters of St. Dominic 5; Lay Teachers 31; Students 530.
Catechesis/Religious Programs—Students 792.
Chapels—Medina, Sma. Trinidad.; Curva, Santa Rosa de Lima.; Cotto, San Martin de Porres.; Arenales Bajo, N.S. La Monserrate.; Vendrel, N.S. La Providencia.; Jobos, Buen Pastor.; Guayabos, Espiritu Santo.; Arenales A., El Salvador.; Arenales Alto, Sagrado Corazon, Tel: 787-872-0015.
Sister of Trinity (Valencia) 4.; Hogar Infantil/Jesus Nazareno, Isabella.

Our Lady of Mount Carmel (1983), Rev. Elias Fernandez, C.SS.T.
Res., Box 1555, 00662. Tel: 787-872-5550. [JC]
Catechesis/Religious Programs—Students 300.
Chapels—Poncito, Santos Inocentes.; Planas, La Encarnacion.; La Tuna, San Juan de Mata.; Galateo Bajo, La Milagrosa.

Lares, St. Joseph (1827), Revs. Esteban Barruetabena; Ignacio Goiburu, C.P.; Mariano Arrien, C.P.
Res., P.O. Box 103, 00669. Tel: 787-897-2067. [JC]
School—Tel: 809-897-2640.
Hermanas Pasionistas 4; Lay Teachers 14; Students 259.
Catechesis/Religious Programs—Students 640.
Chapels—Piletas II, San Carlos.; Sebruguillo, La Resurreccion.; Piletas Arece, La Milagrosa.; Tabonuco, La Providencia.
Hermanas Josefinas de Mexico 6.

St. Judas Tadeos (1986), Rev. Angel R. Diaz, Admin.
Res., P.O. Box 1109, 00669. Tel: 809-897-3540. [JC]
Catechesis/Religious Programs—Students 225.
Chapels—Palmar Llano, Perpetuo Socorro.; Vega de los Acevedo, La Dolorosa.; Buenos Aires, Sgda. Familia de Nazaret.; Matilde, San Antonio.

Manati

1—La Candelaria (1738), Revs. Emilio Tovar, C.M.; Santiago Arribas, C.M.
Res., Calle Padial #2, 00674. Tel: 787-854-2013. [JC]
School—Sisters of Charity 10; Lay Teachers 35; Students 863.
Catechesis/Religious Programs—Students 30.
Chapels—Pugnado, N.S. del Perpetuo Socorro.; Villa Amalia, La Milagrosa.; Cortes, Sagrado Corazon.; Polvorin, La Monserrate.; Ceiba, Espiritu Santo.

2—Our Savior, Rev. Angel Pagan.
Res., P.O. Box 465, 00674. Tel: 787-884-3664.
School—Colegio Marista, P.O. Box 462, 00764. Tel: 787-854-1075.
Marist Brothers 5; Lay Teachers 25; Students 513.
Catechesis/Religious Programs—Students 100.
Chapels—San Jose, San Jose.; Lagunas Tierra Nueva, N.S. de Lourdes.; Guayaney, San Martin de Porres.

3—Sagrada Familia (1972), Revs. Francisco J. Marredan, C.M.; Ramon O. Tirado, C.M.
Res., P.O. Box 704, 00674. Tel: 787-854-2858. [JC]
Catechesis/Religious Programs—Students 216.
Chapels—Parcelas Marquez, San Judas Tadeo.; Palo Alto, N.S. La Monserrate.; Polvorin, La Milagrosa.

4—Nuestra Senora del Mar (1978), Rev. Jesus A. Rodriguez.
Res., Apdo. 1183, 00674. Tel: 787-854-5388. [JC]
Catechesis/Religious Programs—Students 200.
Chapels—Tierras Nuevas, Santa Rosa de Lima.; Sector Cantito, La Milagrosa.; Boquillas, Nuestra Senora del Carmen.

Morovis, Nuestra Senora del Carmen (1820), Revs. Antonio Rodriguez, O.Carm.; Jose Oliveras, O.Carm.; Jesus Monreal, O.Carm.
Res., Box 428, 00687. Tel: 787-862-2620. [JC]
Catechesis/Religious Programs—Students 2,169.
Chapels—San Lorenzo, N.S. del Rosario.; Perchas, N.S. del Carmen.; Pastos, N.S. del Carmen.; Rio Grande, La Milagrosa.; Morovis Sur, San Jose.; Unibon, San Miguel.; Vaga III, La Milagrosa.; MPatron I, Sagrada Familia.; Cuchillas, Segrado Corazon.; Morovis Sur, Inmaculada Concepcion.

St. Paul Apostle (1985), Rev. Tomas Pagan.
Res., P.O. Box 537, 00687. Tel: 787-862-4684. [JC]
Catechesis/Religious Programs—Students 690.
Chapels—Franquez, Nino de Praga.; Franquez Carretera, La Providencia.; Torrecillas, Senor de los Milagros.

Orocovis, San Juan Bautista (1838), Revs. Jose L. Gomez, S.D.B.; Julian San Nicasio, S.D.B.; Francisco Juan, S.D.B.; Santos A. Cepeda, S.D.B.
Res., P.O. Box 2114, 00720. Tel: 787-867-2210. [JC]
School—Tel: 787-867-2295.
Salesians Sisters 6; Lay Teachers 15; Students 224.
Catechesis/Religious Programs—Students 1,350.
Chapels—Sabana, Angeles Custodios.; Botijas I, Cristo Resucitado.; Botijas II, Santa Clara.; El Puente, San Pablo.; Mata de Cana, Sagrado Corazon.; Damian Arriba, Espiritu Santo.; Montebello, N.S. del Carmen.; Guadalupe, N.S. La Guadalupe.; Gato Bajura, N.S. La Providencia.; Gato, San Judas Tadeo.

Our Lady of Fatima (1975), Rev. Tosello Giangiacomo, C.S.Sp.
Res., Box 2118, 00720. Tel: 787-867-3277. [JC]
Catechesis/Religious Programs—Students 383.
Chapels—Bermejales, Cristo de la Salud.; Bauta, N.S. La Dolorosa.; Damian Arriba, N.S. del Perpetuo Socorro.; Pellejas I, Espiritu Santo.; Miraflores, San Martin.

Quebradillas, San Raphael (1828), Revs. Victor Sanchez, Admin.; Tomas Santos. In res., Rev. Msgr. Ernesto Munoz.
Res., Box 57, 00678. Tel: 787-895-2035. [JC]
School—Tel: 809-895-2280.
Sisters 4; Lay Teachers 13; Students 311.
Catechesis/Religious Programs—Students 450.
Chapels—San Jose, San Jose.; Quebrada, N.S. del Carmen.; Chivos, Santa Cruz.; Cacao, La Milagrosa.; Parcelas San Antonio, N.S. La Monserrate.; San Antonio, San Antonio.; Charcas, N.S. del Perpetuo Socorro.; Las Talas, La Guadalupe.
Hermanes Dominicas Presentacion 5.

Sacred Heart (1977), Rev. Carmelo Urarte.
Res., Box 1569, 00678. Tel: 787-895-3033. [JC]
Catechesis/Religious Programs—Students 245.
Chapels—San Antonio, San Miguel.; Yeguada, N.S. del Perpetuo Socorro.; El Verde, Madre Dolorosa.

Utuado

1—San Miquel (1746), Revs. Roy Martinez, O.F.M.Cap.; Jose A. Carrion, O.F.M.Cap.; Alberto Figueroa, O.F.M.,Cap.; Joseph Schreck, O.F.M.Cap.; Jose McCarthy, O.F.M.Cap. In res., Bros. Bernardo Ayala, O.F.M.Cap.; Jose E. Sanchez, O.F.M.Cap.
Res., 8 Barcelo St., P.O. Box 10, 00641. Tel: 787-894-2696. [JC]
Schools—Elementary School, Progreso St., Box 10, 00641. Mrs. Nereida Huertas, Prin.
Lay Teachers 22; Students 134; Intermediate and High School, San Miguel Ave., Box 10, 00641. Tel: 809-894-9386. Mrs. Maria F. Pagan, Prin.
Lay Teachers 22; Students 114.
Catechesis/Religious Programs—Students 536.
Chapels—Puente Blanco, San Fidel.; Arenas, San Martin.; Sabana Grande, N.S. del Perpetuo Socorro.

2—San Pedro y San Pablo (1988), Rev. Rafael Nuno.
Res., Box 679, 00641. Tel: 787-894-0696. [JC]
Catechesis/Religious Programs—Students 146.
Chapels—Las Palmas, San Francisco.; Vivi Arriba, Immalculada Concepcion.; La Pica, La Milagrosa.; Consejo, San Jose.; Vivi Abajo, Nuestra Senora de la Divina Providencia.
Monastery Mother of God Cloistered 30.

3—Our Lady of Angels (1967), Rev. Hector Zayas.
Res., Box 98, Angeles, 00611. Tel: 809-894-7722. [JC]
Catechesis/Religious Programs—Students 134.
Chapels—Corcho, San Jose.; Santa Isabela, N.S. La Monserrate.; Las Vegas, Sagrada Familia.

4—Nuestra Senora del Monte Carmelo (1981), Rev. Pedro Hernandez.
Res., P.O. Box 299, Caonillas-Utuado, 00641. Tel: 787-894-7340. [JC]
Catechesis/Religious Programs—Students 35.
Chapels—Mameyes, San Antonio.; Tetuan III, Sagrado Corazon.; Tetuan II, Cristo Salvador.; Don Alonso, La Milagrosa.

5—Our Lady of Sorrows (1983), Rev. Jesus Sendra.
Res., Box 161, Angeles, 00611. Tel: 787-894-7144. [JC]
Catechesis/Religious Programs—Students 54.
Chapels—Roncador, San Martin de Porres.; Cayuco, Cristo Rey.; Jacanas, N.S. la Monserrate.

Vega-Alta, Immaculate Conception of Blessed Virgin Mary (1805), Revs. Francisco Concepcion; Cesar Santos.
Res., P.O. Box 775, 00692. Tel: 787-883-4875.
Catechetical Center—Calle Colon 17, 00692.
Sisters of Charity 4; Students 464.
Chapels—Maricao IV, Sagrado Corazon.; Bajura II, San Vicente.; Bajura I, Santa Ana.; Candelaria, Inmaculado Corazon de Maria.; Maricao II, N.S. La Guadalupe.

Santa Ana (1967), Rev. Jesus Diaz.
Res., Urb. Santa Ana, Apartado 2105, Calle 3H9, 00692. Tel: 787-883-2502.
Catechesis/Religious Programs—Students 146.
Chapel—Espinosa, N.S. del Carmen.

Perpetuo Socorro (1975), Rev. Francisco Jimenez, Admin.
Res., Box 9018, Sabana Branch, Vega-Baja, 00694. Tel: 787-883-5776. [JC]
Catechesis/Religious Programs—Students 85.
Chapels—Sabana (V.B.), San Vicente.; Cerro Gordo, N.S. del Carmen.

Vega-Baja

1—Holy Rosary (1794), Revs. Jose A. Rodriguez, Admin.; Edgardo Nunez.
Res., P.O. Box 1388, 00694. Tel: 787-858-2969. [JC]
School—Sisters 2; Lay Teachers 41; Students 595.
Catechesis/Religious Programs—Students 415.
Chapels—Arenales, San Jose.; Almirante, N.S. de Fatima.; Alto de Cuba, La Santa Cruz.

2—N.S. de la Providencia (1970), Rev. Angel Diaz.
Res., Guarico Rd. 14 Urb. Box 4056, Jardines de Vega Baja, 00694. Tel: 809-858-2171. [JC]
Catechesis/Religious Programs—Students 300.
Chapels—Brisas de Tortuguero, San Jose.; Vega Baja Lakes, San Pedro.

3—The Blessed Trinity (1971), Rev. Ricardo Majan, Admin.
Res., P.O. Box 58, Almirante Sur Station, 00694. Tel: 809-858-8743.
Catechesis/Religious Programs—Students 310.
Chapels—Almirante Norte, Sagrada Familia.; Patron II, N.S. La Providencia.

4—Our Lady of Carmen-Playa (1976), Rev. Bertulfo Acevedo, Admin.
Res., Apdo. 4095, 00694. Tel: 809-858-4275. [JC]
Catechesis/Religious Programs—Students 40.
Chapels—Naranjos, San Judas Tadeo.; San Demetrio, Divino Nino Jesus.

5—Parroquia de San Martin de Porres (1967), Rev. Efrain Montesino.
Res., P.O. Box 254, Vega Baja, 00694. Tel: 809-858-1485. [JC]
Catechesis/Religious Programs—Students 229.
Chapels—Panaini, Del Carmen.; Pugnado Adentro, San Jose.; Vila Colombo, St. Anthony.

6—Our Lady of Lourdes (1984), Rev. Msgr. Victorino Cobeaga.
Res., P.O. Box 4414, 00694. Tel: 809-855-4942. [JC]
Catechesis/Religious Programs—Students 515.
Convent—Tel: 809-855-0341.
Hermanas Terciarias Capuchinas 3.
Chapels—Rio Abajo, Santa Rosa de Lima.; Quebrada Arenas, San Juan Bautista.; Las Granjas, S. Francisco de Asis.

7—Our Lady of Mt. Carmel (1968), Rev. Luis Velazquez.
Res., P.O. Box 1417, 00694. Tel: 809-855-0159. [JC]
Catechesis/Religious Programs—Students 490.
Chapels—Pueblo Nuevo, La Milagrosa.; Sabana Hoyos, San Judas.; Santa Rosa, La Guadalupe.

Special Assignment:
Reverend Fathers—
Guzman, Alfredo S.J. (Colombia), Pontifical Catholic University of Puerto Rico
Mercado, Edwin, Interdiocesan Tribunal of Ponce, Judicial Ministry of Arecibo
Portalatin, Antonio, Vice Rector, Seminario Sta. Maria de los Angeles, San Juan, PR
Rojas, Victor, Jesus Maestro Seminary, Arecibo
Soberal, Jose, Dimas Catholic Education for Universitues Svcs., Bayamon

---

On Duty Outside the Diocese:
Reverend Fathers—
Alvarez, Antonio, Estados Unidos
Ariza, Campo E., Diocese of Caguas
Davila, Andres, Estados Unidos
Fernandez, Daniel, Studying in Rome
Flores, Jose A., Diocese of Caguas
Garcia, Jose L., Spain
Gomez, Walter, Estados Unidos
Granados, Carlos E., Studying in Colombia, S.A.
Guerrero, Jose Ma., Espana
Hernandez, Jimmy, Urb. Santa Marina, 24 St. Mary's St., Quebradillas, PR 00687. Tel: 895-2898
Irizarry, Alan
Irizarry, Rafael, Diocese of Ponce
Jiminez, P. Victorino, Espana
Leiva, Emilio
Lopez, Juan J.
Morales, Angel, Archdiocese of San Juan
Morales, Salomon, Archdiocese of San Juan
Nunez, Philip, Miami, FL
Rodriguez, Salvador, Diocese of Caguas
Rojas, Victor, Seminario Jesus Maestro, P.O. Box 2164, Arecibo, PR 00613. Tel: 878-1598
Santiago, Angelo, Leave of Absence

Retired:
Reverend Fathers—
Betti, Jose, Spain
Lizarraga, Joaquin, Spain
Martinez, Francisco, Spain
San Llorente, Faustino, P.O. Box 4196, Vega Baja, PR 00694
San Llorente, Ricardo, Spain

INSTITUTIONS LOCATED IN THE DIOCESE

[A] EDUCATIONAL

ARECIBO. *Pontificia Universidad Catholica de Puerto Rico, Recinto de Arecibo*, Mailing Address: P.O. Box 4045, 00613. Tel: 809-881-1212. Rev. Alfredo Guzman, S.J., Chap. Priests 3; Lay Teachers 44; Students 707.

Seminario de Jesus Maestro, Mailing Address: P.O. Box 2164, 00613. Tel: 787-878-1528. Rev. Victor Rojas. Total Enrollment 10.

[B] HOMES FOR AGED AND ORPHANS

ARECIBO. *Hogar de Ancianos San Vicente* Mailing Address: P.O. Box 4196 Vega Baja, 00694.
For a complete listing, refer to the Special Care Facilities section.

Hogar Sta. Maria Eufrasia, Calle Andres Garcia, No. 10, 00612. Tel: 878-5166
For a complete listing, refer to the Special Care Facilities section.

La Milagrosa Home for Orphan Girls, Cotto Ave., No. 987, 00612. Tel: 809-878-6231
For a complete listing, refer to the Special Care Facilities section.

San Rafael Home for Aged, 00612
For a complete listing, refer to the Special Care Facilities section.

ISABELA. *Hogar Infantil Jesus Nazareno, Inc.*, P.O. Box 1671, 00662
For a complete listing, refer to the Special Care Facilities section.

LARES. *Fundacion Irma Fe*, Calle Comerio No. 52, 00669. Tel: 787-897-6090
For a complete listing, refer to the Special Care Facilities section.

VEGA ALTA. *Mision Juan XXIII*, 00692
For a complete listing, refer to the Special Care Facilities section.

RELIGIOUS INSTITUTES OF MEN REPRESENTED IN THE DIOCESE

For further details refer to the corresponding bracketed number in the Religious Institutes of Men or Women section.

[]—*Canonigos Regulares Lateranenses de San Agustin*. (Bronx, NY).—C.R.L.
[0470]—*Capuchin Friars*. (Province of Pittsburgh).—O.F.M.Cap.
[0270]—*Carmelite Fathers and Brothers*. (Province de Aragon, Valencia, Espana).—O.Carm.
[1330]—*Congregation of the Mission*. (Vice-Province of Puerto Rico).—C.M.
[1000]—*Congregation of the Passion*. (Bilbao, Spain).—C.P.
[]—*Esclavos de la Eucaristia y Maria Virgen*.—E.E.M.V.
[0650]—*Holy Ghost Fathers*. (Eastern Province).—C.S.Sp.
[0770]—*Marist Brothers*.—F.M.S.
[]—*Misioneros Natividad de Maria*.—M.N.M.
[1310]—*Order of the Holy Trinity*. (Viscaya, Spain Province).—O.SS.T.
[1190]—*Salesians of Don Bosco*. (Province of Madrid).—S.D.B.

RELIGIOUS INSTITUTES OF WOMEN REPRESENTED IN THE DIOCESE

[]—*Congregation of Sisters of Passion*. (Mexico).
[0760]—*Daughters of Charity of St. Vincent de Paul*.—D.C.
[1070-05]—*Dominican Sisters*.—O.P.
[1100]—*Dominican Sisters of Charity of the Presentation of the Blessed Virgin*.—O.P.
[]—*Dominican Sisters of Fatima*. (Yauco PR).
[]—*Hermanas de San Jose de Corozal*. (Corozal).
[]—*Hermanas del Buen Pastor*.
[]—*Hermanas Esclaves del Santisimo y la Inmaculada*.
[]—*Hermanas Josefinas*. (Mexico).
[]—*Hermanas San Francisco*. (Instituto Religioso).
[]—*Misioneras de la Sagrada Familia*. (Instituto Secular).
[]—*Misioneras Sagrado Corazon*. (Santo Domingo).
[]—*Monasterio Madre de Dios - Cloistered Dominican Nuns*.
[]—*Salesian Sisters*. (Cuba).
[]—*Siervas de Maria*.
[]—*Sisters of Charity of Cardinal Sancha*. (Santo Domingo).
[0990]—*Sisters of Divine Providence*. (Pittsburgh).—C.D.P.
[]—*Sisters of Mercy*. (Spain).
[3930]—*Sisters of St. Joseph of the Third Order of St. Francis*. (South Bend, IN).—S.S.J.-T.O.S.F.
[2460]—*Sisters of Virgin Mary of Mount Carmel, Carmelite Nuns*.

NECROLOGY

(No Deaths)

Diocese of Caguas, Puerto Rico

(Dioecesis Caguana)

Most Reverend

ENRIQUE HERNANDEZ RIVERA D.D.

Bishop of Caguas; ordained June 8, 1968; appointed Titular Bishop of Vanalla, North Africa and Auxiliary Bishop of San Juan June 11, 1979; consecrated August 17, 1979; appointed Bishop of Caguas February 13, 1981; officially installed March 8, 1981. *Res., Bishop's House, Box 8698, Caguas, PR, 00726.* Tel.: 787-747-5885; 747-5787; Fax: 787-747-5616; 747-5767.

Most Reverend

ALVARO CORRADA DEL RIO, S.J., D.D., V.G.

Apostolic Administrator of Caguas; ordained July 6, 1974; appointed Titular Bishop of Rusticiana; Auxiliary Bishop of Washington, D.C.; consecrated August 4, 1985; appointed Apostolic Administrator "sede plena et ad nutum sanctae" July 4, 1997. *Res., Bishop's House, P.O. Box 8698, Caguas, PR, 00726.* Tel.: 787-747-5885; 747-5787; Fax: 787-747-5616.

ESTABLISHED NOVEMBER 1964.

Square Miles 737.

Comprises east and southeast portion of Puerto Rico and the Islands of Culebra and Vieques.

Patroness of the Diocese: Maria, Madre de la Iglesia - November 12, 1988.

Web site address: home.coqui.net./obicag:

E-mail address: obicag@coqui.net

STATISTICAL OVERVIEW

Personnel	
Bishop	1
Abbots	1
Priests: Diocesan Active in Diocese	65
Priests: Retired, Sick or Absent	2
Number of Diocesan Priests	67
Religious Priests in Diocese	53
Extern Priests in Diocese	1
Ordinations:	
Diocesan Priests	3
Transitional Deacons	6
Permanent Deacons	57
Permanent Deacons in Diocese	63
Total Brothers	1
Total Sisters	130
Parishes	
Parishes	43
With Resident Pastor:	
Resident Diocesan Priests	34
Resident Religious Priests	9
Without Resident Pastor:	
Welfare	
Health Care Centers	1
Total Assisted	100
Educational	
Seminaries, Diocesan	1
Students from This Diocese	20
High Schools, Diocesan and Parish	1
Total Students	110
High Schools, Private	6
Total Students	2,851
Elementary Schools, Diocesan and Parish	4
Total Students	650
Elementary Schools, Private	13
Total Students	4,248
Catechesis/Religious Education:	
High School Students	4,794
Elementary Students	7,288
Total Students Under Catholic Instruction	12,082
Teachers in the Diocese:	
Priests	19
Scholastics	4
Brothers	4
Sisters	17
Lay Teachers	365
Vital Statistics	
Receptions into the Church:	
Infant Baptism Totals	7,670
Adult Baptism Totals	490
Received into Full Communion	8,160
First Communions	5,630
Confirmations	3,350
Marriages:	
Catholic	1,180
Interfaith	24
Total Marriages	1,204
Deaths	1,680
Total Catholic Population	515,000
Total Population	653,012

Former Bishop—Most Rev. RAFAEL GROVAS, D.D., S.T.D., Ph.D., J.C.L., Retired Bishop of Caguas; retired Feb. 13, 1981; appt. Jan. 19, 1965; ord. April 7, 1928; cons. March 28, 1965; died Sept. 9, 1991.

Vicar General—Rev. EDWARD SANTANA.

Sec. Chancellor—Rev. DANIEL P. CRONIN.

Sec. Vice Chancellor—Sr. CARMEN GONZALEZ, C.D.P.

Diocesan Consultors—Rev. Msgr. MIGUEL A. MENDOZA; Revs. ANTONIO MATA; HIPOLITO RIVERA; AURELIO ADAN; JOSE M. CALVO; EUSEBIO RAMOS; EDWARD SANTANA.

Diocesan Tribunal of Caguas—Rev. EDWARD SANTANA, J.C.D., Judicial Vicar, *P.O. Box 9779, Caguas, 00726.* Tel: 787-286-8595; Fax: 787-286-8620.

Board of Diocesan Government—Revs. AURELIO ADAN; FELIX OLIVERAS VILLANUEVA; Deacon JOSE RODRIGUEZ.

Priests Senate—Rev. Msgr. MIGUEL A. MENDOZA; Revs. ANTONIO MATA; HIPOLITO RIVERA; JOSE M. CALVO; KHARLOSG LOPEZ; BALTAZAR NUNEZ; ORLANDO DE JESUS; JAVIER HERNANDEZ; AURELIO ADAN; EDWARD SANTANA; ANTONIO CARTAGENA; ANGEL CUADRADO, O.deM.; FELICIANO RODRIGUEZ.

Diocesan Offices and Directors

Economic Administrator—Rev. FELIX OLIVERAS VILLANUEVA, *Box 8698, Caguas, 00726.* Tel: 787-747-5885; 747-5787.

Planning Vicar—Vacant, *Box 8698, Caguas, 00726.* Tel: 787-747-5885; 747-5787.

Cursillos de Cristiandad—Vacant.

Catholic Youth—Rev. JOHN ALICEA, *Box 8698, Caguas, 00726.* Tel: 787-744-6738.

Catholic Social Action—Rev. OSCAR RIVERA, *Caguas, 00726.* Tel: 787-747-5885; 747-5787.

Catholic School Consultors—DOMICIANO GARCIA, *Box 8699, Caguas, 00726.* Tel: 787-743-1171.

Catechetical Delegate—Deacon JOSE RODRIGUEZ, *Box 8698, Caguas, 00726.* Tel: 787-747-5885.

Building Commission—Revs. AURELIO ADAN; D. JOSE RODRIGUEZ, *Box 8698, Caguas, 00726.* Tel: 787-747-5885; 747-5787.

Liturgical Consultor—Rev. DANIEL CRONIN, *Box 8698, Caguas, 00626.* Tel: 787-747-5885.

Communication Office—Rev. PEDRO ORTIZ, *Box 8698, Caguas, 00726.* Tel: 809-746-3783.

Guerra Contra el Hambre (War on Hunger)—Rev. ROBERTO SOTO, *Box 8698, Caguas, 00726.* Tel: 787-747-5767.

Vincentian Society—Sr. SADOT SANTANA, *Box 8698, Caguas, 00726.*

Consejo de Laicos—JOSE RODRIGUEZ, *Parr. San Pedro Hotel, Calle 1. A. 11, Caguas, 00725.*

Hospitals—Revs. ANTONIO CHOCARRO; JOSE FLORES, *Box 8698, 00726.*

Legion of Mary—Rev. CLEMENTE CAHILL, *Box 967, Caguas, 00726.* PETRA FLORES, *Box 5215, Caguas, 00726.*

Master of Ceremonies—Rev. DANIEL CRONIN, *Box 8698, Caguas, 00726.* Tel: 809-747-5885. Rev. JOSE ANTONIO ORTIZ, *Parr. San Jose, Box 2038, Aibonito, 00705.*

Pastoral Vicar—Rev. FELICIANO RODRIGUEZ, *Box 8698, Caguas, 00726.* Tel: 787-286-0075.

Schools—*Box 8699, Caguas, 00726.* Tel: 787-743-1171. *School Superintendent*—Mr. DOMICIANO GARCIA.

Vocations—Rev. JORGE CARDONA, *P.O. Box 8698, Caguas, 00726.* Tel: 787-747-5885; Fax: 787-857-3585.

CLERGY, PARISHES, MISSIONS AND PAROCHIAL SCHOOLS

CITY OF CAGUAS

1—CATHEDRAL DULCE NOMBRE DE JESUS (1730). Redemptorist Fathers. Revs. Gerardo Campbell, C.SS.R., Rector; Clemente Cahill, C.SS.R.; Juan Ramon Hernandez, C.SS.R.; Jose Orlando Serrano; Bro. Pedro Hernandez. In res., Rev. Damian Wall.
Res., 3 Corchado St., Box 967, 00726. Tel: 787-743-4311; 2927; Fax: 787-743-7567.
School—Colegio Catolico de Caguas, Acosta St., Box 967, 00726. Tel: 787-743-2385. School Sisters of Notre Dame. Sr. Bernardine Marie, S.S.N.D.
Sisters 2; Lay Teachers 43; Students 1,031; Aids 10.
High School—Notre Dame, Urb. Borinquen, Box 541, 00726. Tel: 787-743-3693; 5501; Fax: 787-258-9648. School Sisters of Notre Dame. Mr. Jose G. Grillo.
Priests 2; Sisters 4; Lay Teachers 68; Students 1,200.
Chapels—Nuestra S. Perpetuo Socorro, (1929), 24 Aguayo St., 00726.; San Gerardo, (1940), 221 B St., B-14, Jardines de Caguas, 00726.; San Vicente de Paul, 221 B St., Brooklyn.; La Sagrada Familia, (1978), 1004 P St., Bda. Morales.

2—SAN JOSE (1960). (Discalced Carmelites from Spain). Revs. Antonio Mata, O.C.D., Rector; Jesus H. Barrientos, O.C.D.; Alejandro Moral, O.C.D.; Luis Cestero.
Res., Coral St., Villa Blanca, Box 1101, 00726. Tel: 787-743-2032.
School—(Spanish Discalced Carmelite Sisters) Box 806, 00625. Tel: 787-743-2037; Fax: 787-258-0683. Sr. Soledad Diaz, C.M., Prin.
Priests 2; Sisters 5; Lay Teachers 28; Students 609.
High School—Tel: 787-744-8993; Fax: 787-744-4111. Mrs. Brenda Figueroa de Soler, Prin.
Priests 1; Lay Teachers 22; Students 442.
Chapel—Bairoa, Nuestra Senora del Rosario, (1981), Tel: 787-743-5889.

3—SAGRADO CORAZON DE JESUS (1963), Rev. Felix Oliveras Villanueva.
Res., HC 04, Box 45078, Bo. Beatriz, 00726. Tel: 787-747-5170.
Chapels—Bo. Beatriz, Cristo Rey, (1960).; San Martin, (1994).

4—NUESTRA SENORA DE LA PROVIDENCIA (1967), Rev. Hilario Rivera.
Res., Urb. Villa del Carmen, Box 6318, 00626. Tel: 787-743-8200.
Stations—Urb. Mariolga.; Caserio Publico.; Los Flamboyanes.; Rio Verde.

5—SANTISIMO SACRAMENTO (1967). Blessed Sacrament Fathers. Revs. Jose' Martin Eguiguren; Jesus Maria Maiza, S.S.S.; Adrian Alicea, S.S.S.; Domingo Gayarre, S.S.S.
Res., Calle Caney A-11, Caguax, 00725. Tel: 787-743-8444; Fax: 787-743-8444.
Chapels—Urb. Caguas Norte, San Antonio de Padua.; Nuestra S. de Guadalupe, 5th St., Urb. Jose Delgado.

6—NUESTRA SENORA DEL PERPETUO SOCORRO (1968), Revs. Oscar Rivera; Angel Molina.
Res., Calle 2, A-13, Villa Nueva, 00725. Tel: 787-744-1420.
Stations—Bo. Canaboncito, San Patricio, (1926).; Villa Esperanza, San Judas Tadeo, (1960).; Bo. Canaboncito (Las Parcelas), Sagrado Corazon.; Urb. Turabo Gardens, Nuestra S. del Carmen, (1988).

7—EL SALVADOR (1970), Rev. Orlando De Jesus Gomez.
Res., Parcelas Bo. Boringuen, HC 03, Buzon 38888, 00625-9723. Tel: 787-747-0091; Fax: 787-747-0091.
Catechesis/Religious Programs—Students 300.
Chapels—Bo. San Salvador, Cristo Rey, (1922).; Sector Anon, San Alfonso, (1929).; Bo. San Salvador, Sector Hato, Nuestra S. del Carmen, (1911).

8—INMACULADO CORAZON DE MARIA (1971), Revs. Vincente Penalba, C.M.F.; Severiano Garcia, C.M.F.; Humberto Evangelista, C.M.F.
Mailing Address: HC 05, Box 57564, Caguas, 00725-9233. Tel: 787-747-6336.
Catechesis/Religious Programs—Students 230.
Chapels—Bo. La Barra, Cristo Rey, (1971).; San Antonio, (1950).; Bo. La Mesa, N.S. Providencia, (1982).; Bo. La Mesa, Nuestra S. del Carmen.; Bo. Quebrada Arenas, San Felipe.; Guasabara, Sta. Teresa del Nino Jesus, (1995).

9—SAN PABLO APOSTOL (1982), Rev. Roberto Solivan Gonzales.
Res., Kennedy U-32 Urb. Jose Mercado, Caguas, 00625. Tel: 787-743-3546.
Chapels—Bo. Tomas de Castro I, Nuestra S. de Guadalupe, (1928).; Bo. Tomas de Castro II, Santa Rose de Lima.; Sector Ramal, San Martin, (1969).

10—SAN PEDRO APOSTOL (1982), Rev. Antonio Munoz.
Res., Urb. Bonneville, Box 7112, Caguas, 00726. Tel: 787-746-0031.

11—SAN JUAN APOSTOL Y EVANGELISTA (1982), Rev. Antonio Cartagena.
Res., Urb. Residencial Bairoa, Calle 27, Cagey, 00633-9522. Tel: 787-744-6359; Fax: 787-743-8266.
Catechesis/Religious Programs—Students 200.

12—SANTISIMA TRINIDAD (1986), Rev. Efrain Zabala.
Res., Bo. Hormigas, Box 9630, Caguas, 00725. Tel: 787-747-6967.

13—MARIA MADRE DE LA IGLESIA, Rev. Hermenegildo Alayon.
Calle #3, Esq. 6, Urb Valle Tolima, Caguas, 00726. Tel: 787-258-4481.

14—DIVINO NINO (1995), Rev. Campo Emilio Ariza.
Mailing Address: P.O. Box 9416, 00726. Tel: 787-746-1450; Fax: 787-746-1450.
Catechesis/Religious Programs—Students 160.

OUTSIDE THE CITY OF CAGUAS FROM LAS AMERICAS EXPRESS WAY TOWARD THE WEST

Aibonito, Aibonito Co., Church of St. Joseph (1897), Revs. Jose Antonio Ortiz; Angel Luis Cintron; Deacons Antonio Torres; Modesto Reyes; Ezequiel Collazo; Cristobal Rolon; Otilio Rivera.
Res., Box 2038, 00705. Tel: 787-735-3741; Fax: 787-735-4436.
Catechesis/Religious Programs—Students 1,900.
Chapels—Bo. Asomante (Cuadritos), Nuestra S. del Carmen, (1959).; Bo. Asomante (Abejas), Inmaculada Concepcion (1965).; Bo. Pasto, Nuestra S. de Guadalupe, (1970).; Nuestra S. de la Providencia, (1982), Palestina St.; Bo. Rabanal (Parcelas), Nuestra S. de Fatima, (1972).; Ext. San Luis, Nuestra S. del Carmen, (1986).; La Plata, La Milagrosa, (1986).
Mission—Llanos, Sector El Juicio.

Aguas Buenas, Aguas Buenas Co., Church of Tres Santos Reyes (1838). Redemptorist Fathers. Revs. Andres Spacht, C.Ss.R.; John V. Caskey, C.Ss.R.; Carlos Corbett, C.Ss.R.; Carlos Valles, C.Ss.R.
Res., 5 Munoz Rivera St., Box 1, 00703. Tel: 787-732-2741.
School—Academia San Alfonso, Tel: 787-732-8288. Sr. Myrtha E. Arroyo de Lopez, Prin.
Lay Teachers 15; Students 249.
Chapels—Bo. Sumidero, Nuestra S. del Perpetuo Socorro, (1933).; Sector Corujas del Barrio Sumidero, Sta. Juliana, (1984).; Bo. Sonadora, Sagrado Corazon, (1937).; Bo. Jagueyes Abajo, San Jose, (1939).; Bo. Jagueyes Quinta, Divino Redentor, (1947).; Bo. Caguitas, Madre del Perpetuo Socorro, (1941).; Bo. Caguitas, Sector La Brusca.; Parcelas Santa Clara, Santa Clara, (1974).

Espiritu Santo, Rev. Encarnacion Nieves.
Res., Box 1250, 00703. Tel: 787-732-1270.
Chapels—Carr. 156, Santa Teresita, (1929).; Bo. Mulitas Alvelo, De Todos los Santos, (1974).; Bo. Mulitas Tiza, San Gerardo Mayela, (1974).

Barranquitas, Barranquitas Co., Church of St. Anthony of Padua (1808; 1988), Rev. Msgr. Miguel A. Mendoza; Revs. Jorge Cardona; Luis Ruiz.
Res., Box 1099, 00794. Tel: 787-857-3585.
Catechesis/Religious Programs—Students 1,800.
Chapels—San Francisco de Asis, (1960).; Bo. Mana, Virgen del Carmen, (1963).; Bo. Canabon, Virgen de la Providencia, (1968).; Bo. Helechal, San Jose Obrero, (1968).; Bo. Quebrada Grande, Nuestra Sra. de la Monserrate, (1968).; Bo. Palo Hincado, Virgen del Perpetuo Socorro, (1975).; Bo. Lajitas, Nuestra S. del Pilar, (1970).; Sector La Torre, Santa Cruz, (1975).; Bo. Helechal, San Martin de Porres, (1950).

San Andres Apostol (1986), Revs. Victor Raul Ortiz, Ph.D.; Raul Santos; Israel Berrios; Deacons Joaquin Ortiz; Optaciano Rivera; Angel Mercado.
Res., Bo. Quebradillas, Box 490, 00794. Tel: 787-875-5424; Fax: 787-875-5424.
Catechesis/Religious Programs—Students 241.
Chapels—Bo. Palomas, Comerio, San Jose, (1925).; Bo. Quebradillas, Barranquitas, Corazon de Jesus, (1940; 1987).; Bo. Cedro Arriba, Naranjito, San Antonio de Padua, (1864).; Bo. Quebradillas, Barranquitas, Inmaculada Concepcion y Santa Cruz, (1957).; Bo. Cedro Arriba, Naranjito, Santuario Maria Auxiliadora, (1992).

Cayey, Cayey Co., Nuestra Senora de la Asuncion (1787). Mercedarian Fathers. Revs. Fidel Fernandez, O.M., Supr.; Pedro J. Silva Bisbal, O.M.; Jose L. Garcia, O.M.; Pedro Ruiz Valero, O.M.
Res., Casa Parroquial, P.O. Box 37 2887, 00737-2887. Tel: 787-738-2763.
Catechesis/Religious Programs—Students 1,069.
Chapels—Bo. Jajome, Sagrado Corazon de Jesus, (1935).; Bo. Pasto Viejo, Nuestra S. del Carmen, (1937; 1988).; Bo. Toita, Nuestra S. de la Merced, (1946).; Res. Brisas de Cayey, San Ramon Nonato, (1978).; Bo. Maton Arriba, Santa Teresita del Nino Jesus, (1987).

Nuestra Senora de la Merced (1968), Revs. Angel Cuadrado, O.de.M.; Jesus Saez Castrillo, O.de.M.; Elias Lorenzana, O.de.M.; Gregorio Dafonte.
Res., Reparto Montellano, Box 1840, 00737. Tel: 787-738-3872.
Chapels—Bo. Vegas, San Ramon Nonato, (1961).; Bo. Culebras, Nuestra S. del Carmen, (1973).; Bo. Farallon, San Pedro Nolasco, (1980).; San Pedro Armengol (La Plata), (1994).

San Esteban Protomartir (1985), Rev. Rafael A. Rodriguez; Deacons Anibal Gonzalez; Felix Montanez; Silvestre Rodriguez.
Res., Bo. Guavate, 22601 Sector Nieves, 00736-9522. Tel: 787-747-4555.
Chapels—Bo. Borinquen Pradera, Nuestr Senora del Carmen, (1910).; Bo. Guavate, San Jose de la Montana, (1951; 1990).

Cidra, Cidra Co., Nuestra Senora del Carmen (1818), Revs. Baltazar Nunez Henandez; Edwin Rafael Hernandez Ortiz; Miguel Gil Diaz; Deacons Diego Reyes; Alfonso Delgado; Carlos A. Sola.
Res., Centro Plaza Municipal, Box 359, 00739. Tel: 787-739-2406; Fax: 787-739-4991.
Chapels—Bo. Rio Abajo, Madre del Salvador.; Urb. Treasure Valley, La Milagrosa.; Bo. Bayamon-Centenejas I, La Inmaculada.; Bo. Montellano, Santa Teresa del Nino Jesus.; Bo. Bayamon-Certenejas II, Perpetuo Socorro.; Bo. Bayamon-Juan del Valle, Nuestra Senora del Rosario.; Bo. Arena-Santa Clara, San Joaquin.; Bo. Ceiba-Hevia, Nuestra Senora del Rosario.; Bo. Arenas, Nuestra Senora de la Providencia.; Bo. Ceiba, Cristo Rey.; Bo. Bayamon-San Jose, San Jose.; Bo. Rincon, San Francisco de Asis.; Bo. Sud, La Milagrosa.; Bo. Sud, San Pablo.

Nuestra Senora de Fatima (1963), Rev. Isidro Nazabal.
Res., Bo. Rabanal, Box 214, 00739. Tel: 787-739-0633.
Catechesis/Religious Programs—Students 596.
Chapels—Bo. Toita, Sagrado Corazon de Jesus, (1960).; Bo. Salto, San Vicente, (1965).; Bo. Honduras, Perpetuo Socorro, (1970).; Bo. Rabanal, Bo. Salvador, (1970).; Bo. Parcelas, La Milagrosa, (1978).; Bo. Salto, Nuestra Senora de la Providencia.; Bo. Salto, Santa Teresita, (1982).; Santo Cristo de Los Milagros, (1987).

Comerio, Comerio Co., Santo Cristo de la Salud (1832), Revs. Raul Morales Berrios-Parroco; Roberto Angel Soto.
Box 1139, 00762. Tel: 787-875-4525.
Res., Calle Santiago R Palmer #12, 00782.
Chapels—Bo. Sabana, Nuestra Senora del Santisimo Rosario, (1966).; Bo. Rio Hondo, Nuestra Senora de Fatima, (1953).; Bo. Palomas, Santa Ceceilia, (1954).; Bo. Cedrito, Virgen de la Providencia, (1958).; Bo. Rio Hondo-Sector Las Parcelas, San Pablo, (1965).; Bo. Pinas Arriba, Nuestra Senora del Carmen, (1973).; Bo. Naranjo-Sector Las Parcelas, San Antonio de Padua, (1977).; Bo. Vega Redonda, San Francisco de Asis, (1977).; Bo. Cejas, Santa Rose de Lima, (1980).; Bo. Dona Elena, San Martin de Porres, (1950).; Rio Hondo II, Maria Madre de la Iglesia.

Naranjito, Naranjito Co., San Miguel Arcangel (1831), Revs. Hipolito Torres; Juan B. Medina; Enrique Gomez.
Res., Centro Parroquial, Box 68, 00719. Tel: 787-869-2840; Fax: 787-869-3050.
Chapels—Bo. Nuevo, Santa Rosa de Lima, (1953).; Bo. Lomas Centro, Virgen del Carmen, (1954).; Bo. Anones, La Milagrosa, (1962).; Bo. Lomas Valles, San Judas Tadeo, (1963).; Bo. Guadiana, La Monserrate, (1967).; Bo. Achiote, Sagrado Corazon, (1978).; Bo. Nuevo Parcelas, San Vicente de Paul, (1981).; Bo. Cedro Abajo, San Jose, (1981).

OUTSIDE THE CITY OF CAGUAS FROM LAS AMERICAS EXPRESS WAY TOWARD THE EAST COAST

Ceiba, Ceiba Co., San Antonio de Padua (1840), Rev. Carlos N. Cotto.
Res., Plaza St., Box 77, 00735. Tel: 787-885-2530.
Missions—Ceiba, Sagrado Corazon de Jesus, Bo. Saco, 00735.; Ceiba, Ceiba Co., N.S. del Carmen, Parcelas de Aguas Claras, 00735.; Bo. Rio Abajo, Ceiba Co., N.S. del Perpetuo Socorro Bo. Rio Abajo, Ceiba, 00735.
Chapel—Bo. Daguao, Nuestra Senora de Fatima, (1968).
Catechesis/Religious Programs—Students 110.

Fajardo, Fajardo Co., Santiago Apostol (1766). Redemptorist Fathers. Revs. Alfonso Amador, C.Ss.R.; Hector Garcia, C.Ss.R.; Julio Delgado, C.Ss.R.
Res., 16 Garrido Morales St., Box 806, 00738. Tel: 787-863-2365.
Chapels—Bo. Florencio, Santa Elena, (1962).; Bo. Quebrada Vueltas, Perpetuo Socorro, (1965).; La Milagrosa, (1978).; Santa Isidra, Santiago Apostol.

Santisimo Redentor (1993), Rev. Kharlosg Lopez.
Res., Urb. Monte Brisas, Calle C-V-19, 00738. Tel: 787-863-5227; Fax: 787-860-0560.
Catechesis/Religious Programs—Students 140.

Gurabo, Gurabo Co., San Jose (1822), Revs. Efrain Lopez; Alberto Martinez; Deacon Clemente Guzman Cardona.
Res., 7 Santiago Iglesias St., Box 733, 00778. Tel: 787-737-2656.
Chapels—Bo. Jagual, Sagrado Corazon de Jesus, (1951).; Bo. Jaguas Llano, Virgen del Carmen, (1967).; Bo. Navarro, San Francisco Javier, (1968).; Bo. Santa Rita, Santa Rita, (1968).; La Milagrosa, (1973), Bo. Hato Nuevo.; Bo. Celada, Santa Francisca Javier Cabrini, (1967).; Bo. Santa Barbara, Santa Maria del Camino, (1987).; Bo. Hato Nuevo, La Milagrosa, (1982).; Bo. Jaguas Loma, San Miguel, (1989).; Bo. Mamey II, Ntra. Sra. del Carmen.
Catechesis/Religious Programs—Students 315.

Humacao, Humacao Co., Dulce Nombre de Jesus (Pueblo) (1763), Revs. Eusebio Ramos Morales; Luis Antonio Alicea; David Diaz Matos; Deacon Angel Cruz Cruz.
Res., 3 Font Martelo St., Box 546, 00791. Tel: 787-852-0868; Fax: 787-850-6448. [JC]
Chapels—San Agustin, (1955), Parcela No. 44.; Nuestra Senora de la Candelaria, (1956), Parcela No. 30, Candelero Arriba.; Candelero Arriba San Jose, (1957), Carr. 922 Cotto Mabu.; Bo. Junquito, Nuestra Senora de Fatima, (1962).; Bo. Candelero Abajo, Santa Teresita, (1965).; Caserio Roig, San Pedro y San Pablo, (1986).; Bo. Parcelas Catano, Nuestra Senora de la Providencia.; Bo. Buena Vista, Perpetuo Socorro, (1944).
Centers—Centro Comunal Palmas del Mar; Urbanizacion Villa Humacao.

Maria Reina de la Paz (Pueblo) (1989), Revs. Rafael Perez, O.S.B.; Eric R. Buermann, O.S.B.; Mauro Simpson, O.S.B.; Ignacio Aguirre, O.S.B.; Deacon Rafael Ulfret.
Mailing Address: Villa Universitaria, Box 10160 CUH Sta., 00792.
Res., Villa Universitaria, Calle 4 A20, 00792. Tel: 787-850-3081; Fax: 787-850-3080.
Catechesis/Religious Programs—Students 120.
Chapels—Sagrado Corazon de Jesus, (1940).; San Martin de Porres, (1962).; Bo. Mariana IV.; Buen Pastor, (1970).; Bo. Tejas, Cristo Rey, (1976).; Bo. Mariana II, Santa Rosa de Lima, (1978).; Comunidad Vista Hermosa.

Humacao Playa, Humacao Co., Nuestra Senora del Carmen (Punta Santiago) (1970), Rev. Pedro Oyarbide.
Res., Box 91, Punta Santiago, 00741. Tel: 787-850-2125; Fax: 787-850-2125.
Catechesis/Religious Programs—Calle 5 #103 Verde Mar, P.O. Box 91, Punta Santiago, 00741. Students 215.
Chapel—Bo. Pasto Viejo, Sector El batey, Nuestra Senora del Perpetuo Socorro, (1937; 1986).

Juncos, Juncos Co., Inmaculada Concepcion (1797), Revs. Jose M. Calvo Muniain; Miguel Arregui Moso.
Res., Almodovar St. #18, Box 1728, 00777. Tel: 787-724-2431; Fax: 787-734-0350.
Catechesis/Religious Programs—Students 81.
Chapels—Bo. Canta Gallo, Cristo Redentor, (1975).; Bo. Ceiba Sur, Sagrado Corazon, (1976).; Bo. Valenciano Sector Amigo, Espiritu Santo, (1976).; Bo. Ceiba Norte, Cristo Rey, (1978).; Bo. Valenciano Arriba, San Juan Bautista, (1979).; Bo. Ceiba Norte Sector Chinos, Buen Pastor, (1979).; Bo. Pinas, Santa Cruz, (1981).; Bo. Lirios, San Jose, (1978).; Bo. Canta Gallo Secto Reparto Valenciano, Maria Reina De La Paz, (1993).
Mission—Bo. Placita.

Las Piedras, Las Piedras Co., Inmaculada Concepcion (1801), Revs. Jose A. De Leon; Heriberto Mejias Castrillon.
Res., Box 324, 00771. Tel: 787-733-2381.
Catechesis/Religious Programs—Tel: 787-733-8325. Hna. Monica Mantilla, D.R.E. Students 186.
Chapels—Bo. Montones I, Perpetuo Socorro, (1935).; Bo. Tejas Asomonte, Nuestra Senora de la Providencia, (1955).; Bo. La Fermina, Jesus de Nazaret, (1979).; Bo. Montones IV, Santa Teresa del Nino Jesus, (1980).; Bo. Montones II, San Juan Bautista, (1982).
Mission—Salon Usos Multiples-April Gardens, Las Piedras.

San Juan Bautista (Bo. Pueblito del Rio) (1971), Rev. Tomas Galarza.
Res., Bo. Pueblito del Rio, HC 02, Buzon 4467, 00771. Tel: 787-733-6444.
Chapels—Finca Roig, San Juan Bautista, (1911; 1940).; Bo. Boqueron, La Sagrada Familia, (1957).; Bo. Pena Pobre, Santo Tomas de Aquino, (1964).; Bo. Rio Blanco, La Milagrosa, (1972).; Bo. Mango, San Francisco Javier.; Bo. Pasto Seco, El Buen Pastor.

Maunabo, Maunabo Co., San Isidor Labrador (1799), Revs. Boris Espinosa; Franklin Rodriguez Cotton.
Res., Box 248, 00707. Tel: 787-861-2595.
Chapels—Nuestra Senora del Carmen, (1962).; Bo. La Playa, Nuestra Senora de la Providencia, (1971).; Bo. Mattuyas, Nuestra Senora de la Candelaria, (1974).; Bo. Palo Seco, San Judas Tadeo, (1975).; Bo. Emajaguas, San Antonio de Padua, (1977).
Missions—Bo. Quebrada Arenas,; Bo. Lizas,; Bo. Talante,; Bo. Tumbao,; Bo. La Pica,; Bo. California.

Naguabo, Naguabo Co., Nuestra Senora del Rosario (1794), Revs. P. Jose A. Rivera Maldonado; Juan Jose Colon.
Res., Box 665, 00718. Tel: 787-874-2235; Fax: 787-874-0150. [JC]
Chapels—Nuestra Senora del Perpetuo Socorro, (1946).; Bo. Maizales, Nuestra Senora de la Altagracia, (1963).; Bo. Duque, Nuestra Senora de Fatima, (1965).; Bo. Florida, Nuestra Senora del Perpetuo Socorro, (1942).; Nuestra Senora del Carmen Playa Hucares, (1920).; Bo. Mariana, Nuestra Senora de la Providencia, (1965).; Bo. Santiago y Lima (Botija), Santa Rosa de Lima, (1975).
Missions—Barrio Rio, Sector Brazo Seco,; Barrio Cecilia, Sector La Fe.

San Lorenzo, San Lorenzo Co., Nuestra Senora de la Mercedes (1810), Revs. Samuel Santiago, C.Ss.R.; Federico J. Consla, C.Ss.R.; Dennis Demko, C.Ss.R.; Santiago Mallen, C.Ss.R.; Juan McKenna, C.Ss.R.
Res., Munoz Rivera 55, Apartado 1280, 00754-1280. Tel: 787-736-2571; Fax: 787-736-1213.
Chapels—Bo. Quebrada Honda, Santa Teresita de Jesus, (1948).; Bo. Jagual, Nuestra Senora del Carmen, (1952).; Bo. Quemados, Nuestra Senora del Perpetuo Socorro, (1957).; Bo. Cerro Gordo Abajo, Santisimo Redentor, (1965).; Bo. Quebrada, Jesus Maestro.; Bo. Florida, Santa Monica.; Bda. Roosevelt, Nuestra Senora del Carmen, (1968).; Bo. Hato Km. 6, Nuestra Senora del Perpetuo Socorro, (1968).; Bo. Cayaguas, San Alfonso Maria de Ligorio, (1972).; Bo. Cerro Gordo Arriba, Nuestra Senora del Perpetuo Socorro, (1977).; Bo. Lorenzo del Valle, Inmaculado Corazon de Maria, (1978).; Bo. Santa Clara, San Gerardo, (1986).; Urb. Los Flamboyanes, Bo. Florida, Nuestra Senora de Lourdes, (1988).
Catechesis/Religious Programs—Students 708.

Sagrado Corazon de Jesus y 12 Apostoles (Bo. Espino) (1986), Rev. Luis Antonio Rivera.
Res., Bo. Espino, HC 30, Box 32716, 00754. Tel: 787-736-9090; Fax: 787-736-9090.
Chapels—San Francisco de Asis, (1988), Carr. 181.; Santa Rosa de Lima, (1989), Carr. 181.; San Jose, (1959), Carr. 181.

Yabucoa, Yabucoa Co., Santos Angeles Cutodios (1793), Revs. Javier Hernandez; P. Rafael Mateo, C.Ss.R.; Ramon Santana; Deacons Rafael Medina; Juan Ramon Delgado.
Res., Box 7, 00767. Tel: 787-893-2250 (Res.); 893-3347 (Office); Fax: 787-266-0841.
Catechesis/Religious Programs—Students 335.
Chapels—Bo. Rosa Sanchez, Santa Rosa de Lima.; Bo. Pueblo, Parroquia Santos Angeles Custodios.; Bo. Jacanas Granjas, San Juan Evangelista.; Bo. Jac. Piedra Blanca, Sagrado Corazon, (1976).; Bo. Tejas Piedra Azul, Sta. Maria Reina Paz.; Bo. Martorell, Santa Teresita del Nino Jesus.; Bo. Tejas, Ntra. Sra. de la Divina Providencia.; Bo. Playita Cuesta, San Bernardo.; Bo. Playita Arriba, S. Antonio de Padua, (1947).; Bo. Playita Parcelas, Virgen Milagrosa.; Bo. Quebradillas, Ntra. Sra. del Carmen.; Bo. Guayabota, La Sagrada Familia, (1948).; Bo. Calabazas Arriba, San Jose, (1942).; Bo. Quebrada Grande, San Benito.; Bo. Playa Guayanes, Ntra. Sra. del Carmen.; Bo. Aguacate, Ntra. Sra. del Perpetuo Socorro, (1937).; Bo. Jagueyes, Inmaculada Concepcion, (1910).; Bo. Ingenio, Santisima Trinidad.; Bo. Camino Nuevo, San Jeronimo.

OUTSIDE THE MAIN ISLAND OF PUERTO RICO, THE SMALL ISLANDS

Culebra, Culebra Co., Nuestra Senora del Carmen (1889; 1990), Rev. Renelmo Ramirez.
Mailing Address: P.O. Box 236, 00775. Tel: 787-742-0133.

Vieques, Vieques Co., Inmaculada Concepcion (1840), Revs. Nelson Lopez Aponte; Jhon Jaime Florez Gallo; Deacons Justino Lopez Ortiz; Pedro Ramos.
Res., 442 Lebruon St., 00765. Tel: 787-741-2241.
Chapels—Bo. Puerto Real, Sagrado Corazon de Jesus, (1949).; Bo. Esperanza, San Gerardo, (1952).; Bo. Monte Santo, Nuestra Senora del Perpetuo Socorro, (1945).; Bo. Santa Maria, Virgen del Carmen, (1942).; Bo. Destino, Nuestra Senora de Fatima, (1950).

Chaplains of Public Institutions

CAGUAS. *Government Regional Hospital*. Rev. Antonio Chocarro,.
Hospital Hima. Rev. Jose Flores.

Retired:
Reverend Fathers—
Gutierrez, Julio
Martinez, Alfredo

INSTITUTIONS LOCATED IN THE DIOCESE

[A] PAROCHIAL SCHOOLS

CAGUAS. *Academia Cristo de los Milagros*, Box 7618, 00726-7618. Tel: 787-743-4855; 743-3131; 743-4242; Fax: 787-746-1428. Students 1,424; Priests 2; Lay Teachers 56.

Colegio Catolico Notre Dame Elemental, Box 967, 00726. Tel: 787-743-2385; 743-2524; Fax: 787-743-7567. Students 1,031; Priests 4; Brothers 1; Sisters 2; Lay Teachers 43; Aids 10.

Colegio Catolico Notre Dame Superior, Box 541, 00726. Tel: 787-743-3693; 743-5501; Fax: 787-258-9648. E-mail: josegrillo@hotmail.com
Students 1,221; Priests 2; Sisters 4; Lay Teachers 71.

Colegio San Jose Elemental, Box 806, 00726. Tel: 787-743-2032; Fax: 787-258-0683. Students 609; Priests 2; Sisters 5.

Colegio San Jose Superior, Box 1101, Y/O 1749, 00726. Tel: 787-744-8993; Fax: 787-744-4111. Priests 1; Lay Teachers 21; Students 421.

Colegio San Juan Apostol y Evangelista, P.O. Box 459, 00726-0459; Fax: 787-743-8266. Students 358.

Escuela Nuestra Sra. de la Providencia, P.O. Box 1723, 00726. Tel: 787-747-8866. Students 55.

AGUAS BUENAS. *Academia San Alfonso*. (Grades PreK-9), Pio Rechani St., Box 1, 00703. Tel: 787-732-8288. Students 249; Lay Teachers 15.

AIBONITO. *Colegio Parroquial San Jose*, Box 812, 00705. Tel: 787-735-7235. Students 107; Priests 1; Lay Teachers 12.

BARRANQUITAS. *Colegio San Francisco de Asis Elemental y Superior*, Box 789, 00794. Tel: 787-857-2123. Brothers 2; Sisters 3; Students 280.

CAYEY. *Colegio Nuestra Senora de la Merced*, Lucia Vazquez St., 00736. Tel: 787-738-3438; Fax: 787-263-5837. (Nuestra Senora de la Asuncion Parish). Students 470.

FAJARDO. *Colegio Santiago Apostol*. (Grades K-12), Box 907, 00738. Tel: 787-863-0524; 863-0445; Fax: 787-860-6655. Students 655; Priests 2; Sisters 1; Lay Teachers 33.

GURABO. *Colegio Ntra. Sra. De Pilar*, P.O. Box 733, 00778. Tel: 787-737-1400. Mrs. Awilda Velazquez Cotto. Students 132.

HUMACAO. *Colegio Nuestra Senora del Perpetuo Socorro de Humacao, Inc.*, P.O. Box 910, 00792. Tel: 787-852-0845; 850-0025; Fax: 787-852-8706. Students 444.

Colegio San Antonio Abad. (Benedictines), Box 729, 00792. Tel: 787-852-1616. Sra. Zenaida Aponte, Prin. Students 437; Priests 1; Lay Teachers 28.

Colegio San Benito, Box 728, 00792. Tel: 787-852-1365; 850-7075. Students 746; Sisters 1; Lay Teachers 40.

JUNCOS. *Colegio Corazon de Maria*. (Grades PreK-9), Box 1776, Calle Fraternidad Esq. Escute, 00777-1776. Tel: 787-734-5551; 734-5565; Fax: 787-734-2724. Priests 1; Sisters 2; Lay Teachers 12; Students 143.

NARANJITO. *Academia Santa Teresita*, Box 244, 00719. Tel: 787-869-5101; 869-6054. Students 556.

[B] RETREAT HOUSES

AGUAS BUENAS. *Casa Cristo Redentor* (1967), Box 8, 00703-0008. Tel: 787-732-5161; Fax: 787-732-1115. Revs. Marcos Wise, C.SS.R.; Terry Tull, C.SS.R.; Bro. Mateo Perez, C.SS.R.

AIBONITO. *Casa Manresa*, Box 1319, 00705. Tel: 787-735-8016; 8017; Fax: 787-735-2421. Revs. Aurelio Adan, Dir.; German Vargas Agudelo.

JUNCOS. *Casa Cursillos de Cristiandad of Caguas*. (Lay Corp. of Cursillistas), Salida de Juncos Carretera 919, 00666. Tel: 787-734-7068.

SAN LORENZO. *Casa Charlie Rodriguez*, P.O. Box 1190, 00754. Tel: 787-736-5750. Rev. Edward Santana, J.C.D.

[C] MONASTERIES AND RESIDENCES OF PRIESTS

CAGUAS. *Misioneros Hijos del Inmaculado Corazon de Maria (Claretianos)*, Bo. Rio Canas HC-05 Box 57564, 00725-9233.

AIBONITO. *Casa Salesiana de Retiros*, P.O. Box 2019, 00705. Tel: 787-735-2486. Revs. Antonio Robles; Luis Dalbon; Isidro Fernandez; Bros. Santiago Arroyo; Jose Artigas.

HUMACAO. *San Antonio Abad Abbey of the Order of St. Benedict*, Box 729, 00792. Tel: 787-852-1616; Fax: 787-852-1920.
E-mail: santabad@coqui.net
Rt. Rev. Oscar Rivera, O.S.B., Abbot; Very Rev. Eduardo Torrelas, Prior; Revs. Jaime Reyes, O.S.B.; Bernardo Watrin, O.S.B.; Julian Simon, O.S.B.; Bros. Aristedes Pacheco, Sub Prior; Felix Neussendorfer; Tarcisio Medina; Gregorio Valentin; Randolph Perkins; Roberto Rossi. Brothers 6; Novices 2.

[D] CLOISTER SISTERS

AGUAS BUENAS. *Reina de la Paz Convent*, Box 1183, 00703. Tel: 787-732-5339.

NARANJITO. *Visitation Nuns*, Box 302, 00719. Tel: 787-869-0861.

[E] SHRINES

SAN LORENZO. *Diocesan Shrine Our Lady of Mount Carmel*, P.O. Box 1190, 00754. Tel: 787-736-5750. Rev. Edward Santana, J.C.D., Rector.

[F] MISCELLANEOUS

CAGUAS. *Diocesan Tribunal of Caguas*, P.O. Box 9779, 00726. Tel: 787-286-8595; Fax: 787-286-8620. Rev. Edward Santana, J.C.D., Judicial Vicar.

Instituto Secular de Ntra. Sra. de la Altagracia, Calle 13, L23. Urb. Delgado, 00725. Tel: 787-744-3628. Isabel Vazquez Rivera; Casilda Noboa Noboa; Maria Melendez Rivera; Ramonita Lopez Diaz; Zoraida Santos; Judith Colon; Olga Rodriguez Bennios; Maria Isabel Colon; Prixda Santos Agosto; Doris Roque Julia; Natividad Ramos Ramos; Evelyn Rosado.

Movimiento Juan XXIII, P.O. Box 7229, 00726. Tel: 787-747-3748. Rev. Jose Flores.

Voluntarios en Accion, Contra el Sida, P.O. Box 656, 00726.

RELIGIOUS INSTITUTES OF MEN REPRESENTED IN THE DIOCESE

For further details refer to the corresponding bracketed number in the Religious Institutes of Men or Women section.

[0200]—*Benedictine Monks.* (Collegeville, MN).—O.S.B.

[]—*Claretian Fathers.*—C.M.F.

[0220]—*Congregation of the Blessed Sacrament.* (N. Spain Prov.).—S.S.S.

[0650]—*Holy Ghost Fathers.* (Eastern Prov.).—C.S.Sp.

[0690]—*Jesuit Fathers and Brothers.* (New York Prov.).—S.J.

[]—*Mercedarian Fathers.* (Spain).

[0840]—*Missionary Servants of the Most Holy Trinity.*—S.T.

[0910]—*Oblates of Mary Immaculate.* (Eastern Prov.).—O.M.I.

[1070]—*Redemptorist Fathers.* (San Juan Prov.).—C.SS.R.

[1190]—*Salesians of Don Bosco.* (Cuba).—S.D.B.

RELIGIOUS INSTITUTES OF WOMEN REPRESENTED IN THE DIOCESE

[0230]—*Benedictine Sisters of Pontifical Jurisdiction.* (St. Joseph, MN).—O.S.B.

[0420]—*Discalced Carmelite Nuns.* (Spain).—O.C.C.

[]—*Franciscan Nuns (Cloistered).*

[2790]—*Missionary Servants of the Most Holy Trinity.* (Spain).—M.S.B.T.

[3760]—*Order of St. Clare.*—P.C.C.

[]—*Sacred Heart Sisters.*

[]—*Salesian Sisters.*

[2970]—*School Sisters of Notre Dame.* (Wilton, CT).—S.S.N.D.

[]—*Siervas de Maria.* (Spain).

[0640]—*Sisters of Charity of St. Vincent de Paul.* (Puerto Rico Prov.).—S.C.

[]—*Sisters of Fatima.* (Diocesan).

[1650]—*The Sisters of St. Francis of Philadelphia.*—O.S.F.

[2150]—*Sisters Servants of the Immaculate Heart of Mary.*—I.H.M.

[4190]—*Visitation Nuns.* (Cloistered).—V.H.M.

NECROLOGY

† Alonso Ordonez, Juan Nicasio, Caguas, PR, Sagrado Corazon de Jesus. —Died Sept. 20, 1997.

Diocese of The Caroline Islands

Most Reverend

MARTIN J. NEYLON, S.J., D.D.

Retired Bishop of the Caroline Islands; ordained June 18, 1950; appointed Titular Bishop of Libertina October 2, 1969, *"cum jure successionis"*; consecrated February 2, 1970; succeeded as Vicar Apostolic September 20, 1971; appointed First Bishop of Carolines-Marshalls May 3, 1979; installed February 3, 1980; retired June 6, 1995. *Res., Vicariate Residence, P.O. Box 250, Chuuk, Caroline Islands, FM, 96942.* Tel.: 691-330-2313; Fax: 691-330-4394.

Most Reverend

AMANDO SAMO, D.D.

Bishop of the Caroline Islands; ordained Priest December 10, 1977; appointed Titular Bishop of Libertina and Auxiliary Bishop of the Caroline and Marshalls May 10, 1987; ordained Bishop August 15, 1987; named Coadjutor February 3, 1994; named Bishop of the Diocese March 25, 1995; installed June 6, 1995. *Res., P.O. Box 939, Chuuk, Caroline Islands, FM, 96942.* Tel.: 691-330-2399; Fax: 691-330-4585.

Square Miles Ocean 1,800,000.

Total Population of 127,855.

Vicariate of the Caroline Islands erected December 10, 1905 and committed to the Order of Friars Minor Capuchin, extended to the Mariana Islands March 1, 1911.

Vicariate of the Marianas and Caroline and Marshall Islands erected May 4, 1923 and committed to the Society of Jesus. Marianas Islands separated July 4, 1946. Diocese of the Caroline-Marshalls created February 3, 1980. The Marshalls made a separate Prefecture Apostolic August 15, 1993, and the Diocese renamed "Diocese of the Caroline Islands."

Civilly it includes the four Federated States of Micronesia (Chuuk, Kosrae, Pohnpei and Yap) and the Republic of Palau.

E-mail address: Diocese@mail.fm:

STATISTICAL OVERVIEW

Personnel	
Bishop	1
Retired Bishops	1
Priests: Diocesan Active in Diocese	12
Priests: Active Outside Diocese	1
Number of Diocesan Priests	13
Religious Priests in Diocese	14
Ordinations:	
Diocesan Priests	1
Permanent Deacons in Diocese	39
Total Brothers	2
Total Sisters	38
Parishes	
Parishes	21
With Resident Pastor:	
Resident Diocesan Priests	9
Resident Religious Priests	2
Without Resident Pastor:	
Administered by Permanent Deacons	8
Administered by Lay People	2
Missions	2
Professional Ministry Personnel:	
Brothers	1
Sisters	8
Lay Ministers	4
Educational	
Diocesan Students in Other Seminaries	10
Students Religious	5
Total Seminarians	15
High Schools, Diocesan and Parish	3
Total Students	456
High Schools, Private	2
Total Students	341
Elementary Schools, Diocesan and Parish	4
Total Students	1,632
Elementary Schools, Private	1
Total Students	229
Catechesis/Religious Education:	
High School Students	250
Elementary Students	3,350
Total Students Under Catholic Instruction	6,273
Teachers in the Diocese:	
Priests	6
Scholastics	5
Brothers	1
Sisters	24
Lay Teachers	111
Vital Statistics	
Receptions into the Church:	
Infant Baptism Totals	1,522
Adult Baptism Totals	205
Received into Full Communion	22
First Communions	854
Confirmations	860
Marriages:	
Catholic	222
Interfaith	29
Total Marriages	251
Deaths	276
Total Catholic Population	64,881
Total Population	127,855

Former Bishops—Most Rev. SALVADOR WALLAESER, O.F.M.Cap., cons. Titular Bishop of Tanagra, Aug. 21, 1912; resigned June 23, 1919; died Jan. 1, 1946; Most Rev. SANTIAGO LOPEZ DE REGO, S.J., Titular Bishop of Dionisiopolis; cons. Aug. 26, 1923; resigned June 2, 1939; died Aug. 5, 1940; Most Rev. THOMAS J. FEENEY, S.J., cons. Titular Bishop of Agno, Sept. 8, 1951; died Sept. 9, 1955; Most Rev. VINCENT I. KENNALLY, S.J., cons. Titular Bishop of Sassura, March 25, 1957; resigned Sept. 20, 1971; died April 12, 1977; Most Rev. MARTIN J. NEYLON, S.J., ord. Bishop, Feb. 2, 1970; succeeded to as Vicar Apostolic, Sept. 20, 1970; named to be Bishop of the new diocese, May 3, 1979; installed as first Bishop of the Diocese of the Carolines-Marshalls, Feb. 3, 1980; retired June 6, 1995.

Chancery Office—Neepwukos, Chuuk: P.O. Box 939, Chuuk, FM, 96942. Tel: 691-330-2399; Fax: 691-330-4585.

Vicar General and Chancellor—Rev. JOHN F. CURRAN, S.J., J.C.L.

Diocesan Consultors—Revs. JULIO ANGKEL; JOHN F. CURRAN, S.J.; WILLIAM J. MCGARRY, S.J.; APOLLINARIS THALL, S.J.; FELIX YAOCH, S.J.

Finance Committee—Rev. JOHN F. CURRAN, S.J.; Mr. SANTI ASANUMA; Mr. ERHARD ATEN; Mr. TONY GANNGIYAN; Mr. WILLIAM IRIARTE; Mr. T. ROY SULLIVAN.

Episcopal Vicars—

Chuuk—Rev. JULIO ANGKEL, *P.O. Box 337, Chuuk, FM, 96942.* Tel: 691-330-2672; Fax: 691-330-4394.

Palau—Rev. FELIX YAOCH, S.J., *P.O. Box 128, Palau, PW, 96940.* Tel: 680-488-2226; Fax: 680-488-1819.

Pohnpei-Kosrae—Rev. WILLIAM J. MCGARRY, S.J., *P.O. Box 160, Pohnpei, FM, 96941.* Tel: 691-320-4661; Fax: 691-320-5876.

Yap—Rev. APOLLINARIS THALL, S.J., *P.O. Box "A", Yap, FM, 96943.* Tel: 691-350-2265/2547; Fax: 691-350-4746.

Diocesan Tribunal—

Judical Vicar—Rev. WILLIAM J. RAKOWICZ, S.J.

Defenders of the Bond—Most Rev. MARTIN J. NEYLON, S.J., D.D.; Revs. FLORENTINUS AKKIN; NEIL POULIN, S.J.; RUSK SABURO.

Notaries—Rev. PATRICK J. SULLIVAN, S.J.; Miss ELSA VELOSO.

Director, Pontifical Missions Societies—Rev. JOHN F. CURRAN, S.J.

Director, Apostleship of Prayer—Rev. KENNETH J. HEZEL, S.J.

Vocations—Most Rev. AMANDO SAMO.

CLERGY, PARISHES, MISSIONS AND PAROCHIAL SCHOOLS

CHUUK (TRUK) STATE, CAROLINE ISLANDS

Mailing Address: for Chuuk State: P.O. Box 250, Chuuk, Caroline Islands, FM 96942 unless otherwise noted.

Moen, Immaculate Heart of Mary Cathedral (Weeno) (Tunnuk), Rev. David Lewis; Deacons Edwin Shuru; Chitaro William; Yostaro Noporu.

School—St. Cecilia's. Mr. Mariano Marcus, Prin.

Mercedarian Missionaries of Berriz 4; Lay Teachers 31; Students 735.

Mission—Noomwunwiito Islands.

Holy Family Church (Weeno) (Nepukos), Rev. Kirino B. Halley; Deacons Eliot Cholymay; Bername Itiraw.

Fefan, Sacred Heart, Rev. Julio Angkel.

Missions—Parem; Tsis; Hall Islands; Magur, Marie

Chapel; Ono, Sacred Heart; Onari, St. Cecilia; Pisarach, St. Catherine of Siena.

Ulul, Sacred Heart. Closed. For inquiries for parish records contact the Chancery.

Udot, St. Francis Assisi, Rev. Cuthbert Yiftheg; Deacons John Fritz; Eichy Karsom.
Mission—Romanum, St. Joseph.

Tol, Assumption of the Blessed Virgin Mary, Rev. Edmond Ludwick; Deacons Angken Rapun; Roke Rokop; Kintin Rawit; Itoi Ruta; Oiken Victus; Misa Sewen; Francisco Ykuta; Lukas Paulus.
School—St. Julia. Sr. Yolanda Delgadillo, M.M.B., Prin.
Mercedarian Missionaries of Berriz 4; Lay Teachers 8; Students 131.
Missions—Puluwat; Santiago; Pulusuk, Our Lady of Fatima; Tamatam, Maria Lourdes; Punlap, Sacred Heart.

Puluwat, Santiago Church, Rev. Basilio Dilipy.
Missions—Pulusuk, Our Lady of Fatima; Tamatam, Maria Lourdes; Punlop, Sacred Heart.

Dublon, St. Anthony's (Toloas), Rev. Florentinus Akkin; Deacon Tobias Soram.

Lukunor, Sacred Heart, Rev. Julio Angkel.
Missions—Satowan; Kuttu; Moch; Ettal; Namoluk; Oneop; Ta; Nama; Piis; Losap.

POHNPEI STATE, CAROLINE ISLANDS

Mailing Address: for Pohnpei State: P.O. Box 160, Pohnpei, Caroline Islands, FM 96941 Tel: 691-320-2557, unless otherwise noted.

Kolonia, Our Lady of Mercy, Deacons Martiniano Rodriguez, Admin.; Geronimo Victor.
Tel: 691-320-2557.
School—Pohnpei Catholic School.
Sisters 4; Lay Teachers 17; Students 229.
Missions—Kapingmarangi; Sapwuahfik; Kosrae.

Awak, St. Joseph, Deacons Adelino Lorens, Admin.; Manuel Amor.
Tel: 691-320-4363.

Ipwutek, St. Augustine, Deacon Alius Dorres, Admin.
Tel: 691-320-3970.

Palikir, St. Paul, Deacon Salus Olbet, Admin.
Tel: 691-320-5822.

Porrassapw, Christ the King, Deacons Koropin Kermen, Admin.; Thomas Santos.
Tel: 691-320-3744; 320-4986.

Seinwar, Most Pure Heart of Mary, Rev. Rex Edwin.
Tel: 691-320-3573.

Sokehs, St. Peter's, Rev. Etwel Pelep.
Tel: 691-320-3038.

Tamoroi, Sacred Heart, Deacon Peter Silbanuz, Admin.
Tel: 691-320-4363.
Mission—Metip.

YAP STATE, CAROLINE ISLANDS

Mailing Address: for Yap State: P.O. Box A, Yap, Caroline Islands, FM 96943 Tel: 691-350-2265; 350-2547; Fax: 691-350-2784.

Nemar, St. Mary, Rev. Apollinaris I. Thall, S.J.
School—St. Mary's. Sr. Walter Marie Ray, S.S.N.D., Prin.
Sisters 2; Lay Teachers 14; Students 308.

Gagil, St. Joseph, Rev. Neil C. Poulin, S.J.
Tel: 691-350-2598.

Tomil, St. Peter Chanel, Rev. Neil C. Poulin, S.J.

Ulithi and Neighboring Islands, Queen of Heaven, Rev. Nicholas Rahoy; Deacon John Rulmal.
Mission—Ngulu.

Woleai and Neighboring Islands, St. Ignatius, Rev. Nicholas Rahoy.

REPUBLIC OF PALAU, CAROLINE ISLANDS

Mailing Address: for Palau: P.O. Box 128, Koror, Palau PW 96940. Tel: 680-488-2226; Fax: 680-488-1819

Koror, Sacred Heart, Revs. Rusk R. Saburo; Felix K. Yaoch, S.J., Vicar; John Paul Ililau.
School—Maris Stella. Mr. Felix Okabe, Prin.
Brothers 1; Mercedarian Missionaries of Berriz 4; Lay Teachers 19; Students 358.
Missions—Ngcheangl,; Sonsorol.
Convent— Our Lady of Lourdes
Mercedarian Missionaries of Berriz 7.
Manresa Jesuit Novitiate—Rev. Daniel J. Mulhauser, S.J., Dir.

Angaur, Holy Rosary, Rev. Juan Bizkarra, S.J.

Babeldaob, Catholic Churches, Revs. Rusk R. Saburo; John Paul Ililau.

Permanent Deacons:
Albert, Joseph, Uman, Chuuk
Amor, Manuel, Awak, Pohnpei
Cholymay, Eliot, Moen, Chuuk
Dorres, Aluis, Enimwahn, Pohnpei
Else, Pelsiano, Sapwuahfik, Pohnpei
Elukan, Augustine, Gagil-Tomil, Yap
Felichoo, Francisco, Gagil-Tomil, Yap
Fichibman, Donald, Gagil-Tomil, Yap
Fritz, John, Udot, Chuuk
Itiraw, Bername, Moen, Chuuk
John, Sandy, Romanum, Chuuk
Karsom, Eichy, Udot, Chuuk
Kermen, Koropin, Kiti, Pohnpei
Lawrence, Adelino, Uh, Pohnpei
Lorens, Adelino, Uh, Pohnpei
Mailos, Salvador, Uman, Chuuk
Meisa, Akiuo, Uman, Chuuk
Nimas, Andreas, Uman, Chuuk
Noporu, Yostaro, Fono, Chuuk
Olbet, Saulus, Palikir, Pohnpei
Oneitam, Nory, Uman, Chuuk
Paulus, Lucas, Fanapanges, Chuuk
Pelep, Etwel, Kolonia, Pohnpei
Pelep, Misael, (Retired), Kolonia, Pohnpei
Rapun, Angken, Tol, Chuuk
Rawit, Kintin, Wonei, Chuuk
Rodriguez, Martiniano, Kolonia, Pohupei
Rokop, Roke, Tol, Chuuk
Rulmal, John B., Ulithi, Yap
Ruta, Itol, Tol, Chuuk
Sam, Karlos, Uman, Chuuk
Santos, Thomas, Wene, Pohnpei
Sewell, Misa, Tol, Chuuk
Shuru, Edwin, Moen, Chuuk
Silbanuz, Peter, Tamworoi, Pohnpei
Soram, Tobias, Tolowas, Chuuk
Sos, Iakim, Uman, Chuuk
Victor, Geronimo, Kolonia, Pohnpei
Victus, Oiken, Pwene, Chuuk
William, Chitaro, Moen, Chuuk
Ykuta, Francisco, Pwene, Chuuk

INSTITUTIONS LOCATED IN THE DIOCESE

[A] PASTORAL RESEARCH INSTITUTE

POHNPEI. *Micronesia Seminar*, P.O. Box 160, 96941. Tel: 691-320-4067; Fax: 691-320-5876. Revs. Francis X. Hezel, S.J., Dir.; Gregory F. Muckenhaupt, S.J., Asst. Dir. & Dir. Lay Assistants 1.

[B] HIGH SCHOOLS

CHUUK. *Saramen Chuuk Academy*, P.O. Box 662, 96942. Tel: 691-330-4442; Fax: 691-330-4452. Mr. Patrick Blank, Prin.; Deacon Eliot Cholymay. Sisters 3; Lay Teachers 14; Students 237.

Xavier High School, P.O. Box 220, 96942. Tel: 691-330-4266; Fax: 691-330-4753. Rev. Patrick J. Sullivan, S.J., Dir.; Mrs. Lynn Polloi, Prin. Priests 2; Lay Teachers 12; Scholastics 5; Students 172.

PALAU, PW. *Mindszenty High School*, P.O. Box 69, 96940. Tel: 680-488-2437. Ms. Justa Polloi, Prin. Priests 1; Mercedarian Sisters 1; Lay Teachers 14; Students 169.

POHNPEI. *Our Lady of Mercy Vocational Training School*, P.O. Box 73, 96941. Tel: 691-320-3168. Sr. Maria Perez-Caballero, M.M.S., Prin. Mercedarian Sisters 2; Lay Teachers 5; Students 50.

PATS (Pohnpei Agriculture and Trade School), P.O. Box 39, 96941. Tel: 691-320-2991; Fax: 691-320-6046. Revs. Joseph E. Billotti, S.J., Dir.; Paul L. Horgan, S.J., Chap.; Edward A. Soucie, S.J., Asst. Dir.; Bro. Terence N. Todd, S.J., Asst. Dir. Priests 3; Brother Teaching 1; Lay Teachers 36; Students 172.

[C] RESIDENCES OF PRIESTS AND BROTHERS

KOLONIA, POHNPEI. *Jesuit House*, P.O. Box 160, 96941. Tel: 691-320-2317; Fax: 691-320-5876. In res. Very Rev. Francis X. Hezel, S.J., Regional Supr.; Revs. Gregory F. Muckenhaupt, S.J., Supr.; William J. McGarry, Vicar.

KOROR, PALAU, PW. *Manresa Jesuit House*, P.O. Box 128, 96940. Tel: 680-488-2226; Fax: 680-488-1819; 488-1725. Revs. Felix K. Yaoch, S.J., Supr.; Daniel J. Mulhauser, S.J., Master of Novices. Priests 2.

TUNNUK, CHUUK. *Vicariate Residence*, P.O. Box 250, 96942. Tel: 691-330-2313; Fax: 691-330-4394. In res. Most Rev. Martin J. Neylon, S.J., D.D.; Revs. Kirino B. Halley; David Lewis. Priests 2.

[D] RESIDENCES OF SISTERS

AWAK, POHNPEI. *Sisters of Marie Auxiliatrice*, P.O. Box 1375, 96942. Tel: 691-320-2626. Sr. Hikari Saito, M.A., Supr. Sisters 6; Novices 2; Postulants 1.

COLONIA, YAP. *Maryknoll Sisters*, P.O. Box 26, 96943. Tel: 691-350-2148 (Colonia). Sr. Joanne McMahon, M.M., Contact Person. Sisters 3.

School Sisters of Notre Dame, P.O. Box 111, 96943. Tel: 691-350-2345. Sr. Walter Marie Ray, S.S.N.D., Contact Person. Sisters 2.

KOLONIA, POHNPEI. *Mercedarian Missionaries of Berriz*, P.O. Box 73, 96941. Tel: 691-320-2558. Sr. Maria Perez-Caballero, M.M.B., Coord. Sisters 5.

KOROR, PALAU, PW. *Mercedarian Missionaries of Berriz*, P.O. Box 56, 96940. Tel: 680-488-2272. Sr. Sabina Basilius, M.M.B., Coord. Sisters 7.

NEEPWUKOS, CHUUK. *Religious Sisters of Mercy*, 96942. Sr. Cabrini Taitano, R.S.M., Coord. Sisters 2.

School Sisters of Notre Dame, P.O. Box 824, 96942. Tel: 691-330-2900. Sr. Bernard Umpingco, S.S.N.D., Coord. Sisters 2.

TOL, CHUUK. *Mercedarian Missionaries of Berriz*, P.O. Box 190, 96942. Sr. Yolanda Delgadillo, M.M.B., Coord. Sisters 6.

WEENO, CHUUK. *Mercedarian Missionaries of Berriz*, P.O. Box 67, 96942. Tel: 691-330-4587. Sr. Faustina Nedelec, M.M.B., Coord. Sisters 5.

RELIGIOUS INSTITUTES OF MEN REPRESENTED IN THE DIOCESE

For further details refer to the corresponding bracketed number in the Religious Institutes of Men or Women section.

[0690]—*Jesuit Fathers and Brothers*. (New York Prov.)—S.J.

RELIGIOUS INSTITUTES OF WOMEN REPRESENTED IN THE DIOCESE

[2470]—*Maryknoll Sisters of St. Dominic*.—M.M.
[2510]—*Mercedarian Missionaries of Berriz*.—M.M.B.
[2970]—*School Sisters of Notre Dame*.—S.S.N.D.
[2575]—*Sisters of Mercy of the Americas*.—R.S.M.
[]—*Sisters of Marie Auxiliatrice*.—M.A.

NECROLOGY

(No Deaths)

Diocese of Chalan Kanoa

(Dioecesis Vialembensis)

Most Reverend

TOMAS A. CAMACHO, D.D.

Bishop of Chalan Kanoa; ordained June 14, 1961; appointed Prelate of Honor by Pope Paul VI in 1974; appointed Bishop of Chalan Kanoa November 8, 1984; consecrated and installed January 13, 1985. *Res., Mount Carmel Rectory, P.O. Box 745, Saipan, MP, 96950.* Tel.: 670-234-3000.

ESTABLISHED NOVEMBER 8, 1984.

Square Miles 183.61.

Corporate Title: "Bishop of Chalan Kanoa, a Corporation Sole."

Comprises the Mariana Island chain except for Guam, known legally as the Commonwealth of the Northern Mariana Islands.

For legal titles of parishes and diocesan institutions, consult the Chancery Office.

Web site address: www.mtccnmi.com/community/diocese:

E-mail address: diocese@mtccnmi.com

STATISTICAL OVERVIEW

Personnel	
Bishop	1
Priests: Diocesan Active in Diocese	5
Priests: Active Outside Diocese	1
Number of Diocesan Priests	6
Religious Priests in Diocese	1
Extern Priests in Diocese	5
Permanent Deacons in Diocese	3
Total Sisters	35
Parishes	
Parishes	9
With Resident Pastor:	
Resident Diocesan Priests	6
Resident Religious Priests	1
Without Resident Pastor:	
Administered by Priests	2
Missions	2
New Parishes Created	1
Professional Ministry Personnel:	
Lay Ministers	99
Welfare	
Special Centers for Social Services	1
Total Assisted	664
Educational	
High Schools, Diocesan and Parish	1
Total Students	721
Elementary Schools, Diocesan and Parish	2
Total Students	292
Catechesis/Religious Education:	
High School Students	583
Elementary Students	1,583
Total Students Under Catholic Instruction	3,179
Teachers in the Diocese:	
Priests	2
Sisters	5
Lay Teachers	42
Vital Statistics	
Receptions into the Church:	
Infant Baptism Totals	586
First Communions	83
Confirmations	37
Marriages:	
Catholic	32
Interfaith	1
Total Marriages	33
Deaths	139
Total Catholic Population	47,322
Total Population	56,189

Chancery Office—P.O. Box 745, Saipan, MP, 96950. Tel: 670-234-3000; Fax: 670-235-3002.

Vicar General—Rev. GARY BRADLEY, S.J.

Diocesan Consultors—Revs. MANUEL CORCUERA; SALVADOR DUMAS; ROGER P.T. TENORIO; GARY BRADLEY, S.J.; MICHAEL MARTIN.

Chancellor—Rev. ROGER P.T. TENORIO.

Diocesan Business Office—Mrs. LOLITA MAFNAS BABAUTA, Exec. Sec.; Sr. ASCENSION ZAMBRA, O.P., Archivist and Librarian, *Address all communications to: Chancery Office,, P.O.Box 745, Saipan, MP, 96950.* Tel: 670-234-3000.

Diocesan Services and Associations

Superintendent of Catholic Schools—Rev. ROGER P.T. TENORIO, *P.O. Box 745, Saipan, MP, 96950.* Tel: 670-234-3000; 234-8888.

Office of Religious Education—Sr. BRIGID PEREZ, R.S.M., Dir., *P.O. Box 745, Saipan, MP, 96950.* Tel: 670-234-3000.

Catholic Daughters of America—Mrs. FELICIDAD OGUMORO, Regent.

Karidat—Ms. LORI OGUMORO, Chm.; Ms. ANGIE GUERRERO, Exec. Dir.

Catholic Cemetery—Mr. MARLON CARLOS; CRIS SABLAN, Consultant.

Catholic Charismatic Renewal—Sr. ANTONIETA ADA, M.M.B.

Christian Mothers Association—Mrs. RITA C. GUERRERO, Island Board Pres. Vacant; Vice Pres. Vacant; Sec. & Treas.

Oran Katolico (Catholic T.V. Hour)—Rev. ISAAC AYUYU.

Diocesan Publications Office—Rev. ISAAC AYUYU, Dir.; Mr. RUY V. POLISTICO, Editor *"North Star"(Diocesan Newspaper)* "Umanidat" (A Journal) and Chamorro Language Devotional Materials.

Diocesan Tribunal—Rev. ROGER P.T. TENORIO, Judge & Instructor; Mrs. DEBORAH BARTON, J.C.L., Defender of the Bond, *P.O.Box 745, Saipan, MP, 96950.*

Eucharistic Adoration Society—Most Rev. TOMAS A. CAMACHO; ELIZABETH CHO; FRANCISCO PALACIOS.

Holy Name Society—Vacant.

Hospital Chaplain—Rev. ISIDRO OGUMORO, *Commonwealth Health Center, Navy Hill, Saipan.*

Korean Catholic Community—Rev. MYUNG KIM SUNG, Spiritual Dir., *P.O. Box 693, Saipan, MP, 96950.* Tel: 670-234-7878; 234-7177.

Commission for Worship—Mrs. MARGARITA OLOPAI-TAITANO, Chm.

Saipan Marriage Preparation—Rev. ISAAC AYUYU, Co-ord.

Vocations—Vacant.

Office for Worship—Rev. ISAAC AYUYU.

Youth Ministry—Rev. ROGER P.T. TENORIO, Dir.

Commission on Justice and Development—Ms. MARGARITA OLOPAI-TAITANO, Chm.; Mr. RICHARD SEMAN; Mr. JOHN GONZALEZ; Mr. ERIC GREGOIRE, Staff.

Diocesan Human Rights Advocate—Mr. ERIC GREGORIE.

Mount Carmel School, Inc.—Mr. DANIEL NIELSEN, Chm.; Sr. KATHLEEN SARMIENTO, R.S.M., Pres.

San Francisco de Borja School, Inc.—Ms. BENITA MANGLONA, Pres.; Sr. BENEDICT SAN NICOLAS, R.S.M., Pres.

Prison Chaplain—Rev. JOSE DAVID.

Police and Fire Chaplain—Vacant.

CLERGY, PARISHES, MISSIONS AND PAROCHIAL SCHOOLS

ISLAND OF SAIPAN

Chalan Kanoa Village, Cathedral of Our Lady of Mt. Carmel, Most Rev. Tomas A. Camacho; Rev. Isaac Ayuyu; Deacon Richard D. Shewman.

P.O. Box 745, Saipan, 96950. Tel: 670-234-3000.

School—Mt. Carmel Elementary and High School, P.O. Box 8, 96950. Tel: 670-234-6184; 234-7188. Sr. Kathleen Sarmiento, R.S.M., Pres.

Shrines—Chalan Kanoa, Sacred Heart, District 1.; Chalan Kanoa, Our Lady of Fatima, District 3.

Oratory—Mercedarian Missionary Sisters of Berriz. Formation House and Little House.

Garapan Village, District 11, Kristo Rai Parish, Rev. Gary Bradley, S.J.

Oratories—Maturana House of Prayer; Navy Hill, Commonwealth Health Center Chapel.

San Antonio Village, District 6, San Antonio De Padua Parish, Rev. J. Rudolpho Colendrino.

Res., Mt. Carmel Rectory, P.O. Box 745, Saipan, 96950. Tel: 670-234-3000.

San Jose Village, District 7, San Jose Parish, Rev. Matthew Blockley.

Res., P.O. Box 745, Saipan, 96950. Tel: 670-234-3000.

Church—Tel: 670-234-6991.

Shrine—Chalan Laulau, Immaculate Heart of Mary.

Tanapag Village, District 8, Santa Remedios, Rev. Rolando Petronio.

Res., Cathedral Rectory, P.O. Box 745, Saipan, 96950. Tel: 670-234-6960.

San Roque Village, District 9, San Roque Parish, Rev. Rolando Petronio.

Res., Cathedral Rectory, P.O. Box 745, Saipan, 96950. Tel: 670-234-6960.

San Vicente Village, District 10, San Vicente Ferrer Parish, Rev. Roger P.T. Tenorio.

Res., Mt. Carmel Rectory, P.O. Box 745, Saipan, 96950. Tel: 670-234-3000.

Mission—Saipan, Santa Soledad Mission, (1995). Rev. Roger P.T. Tenorio.

Shrine—As Teo, Our Lady of Lourdes.

Saipan, San Jude Parish, Rev. Jose David.

Mailing Address: P.O. Box 745, 96950. Tel: 670-234-3000; Fax: 670-235-3002.

ISLAND OF ROTA

Songsong Village, San Francisco de Borja Parish, Rev. Manuel R. Corcuera (Philippines).

Res., Catholic Rectory, Songsong Village, P.O. Box 542, Rota, 96951. Tel: 670-532-3000.

School—San Francisco de Borja School, Inc., Tel: 670-532-5000. Sr. Benedict San Nicolas, R.S.M., Admin.

Shrines—Teneto, Our Lady of Fatima; New Village, Liyo, San Jude Tadeo; Patten Gogue, Santa Lourdes; District #1, Sacred Heart; Our Lady of Perpetual Help.

San Isidro Mission Parish (Sinapalo), Rev. Msgr. Louis Antonelli.

Res., Songsong Village, P.O. Box 542, Rota, 96951. Tel: 670-532-3000.

ISLAND OF TINIAN

San Jose Village, San Jose, Rev. Salvador Dumas (Philippines); Deacon Segundo Castro.

Res., Catholic Rectory, San Jose Village, Tinian, 96952. Tel: 670-433-3000.

Shrine—San Isidro.

DIOCESAN MISSIONS

1—San Jose Chapel,

2—Santa Cruz Chapel. (Alamagan).

3—San Ignacio Chapel. (Pagan).

4—Santa Cruz Chapel. (Agrihan).

INSTITUTIONS LOCATED IN THE DIOCESE

[A] RESIDENCES OF SISTERS

Saipan. *Formation House*, P.O. Box 136, 96950. Tel: 670-234-6127. Sr. Martha Ramarui, M.M.B., Local Coord. Sisters 3; Novices 4; Postulants 4.

Little House, P.O. Box 245, 96950. Tel: 670-234-6127. Sr. Antonieta Ada, M.M.B., Local Coord. Sisters 6.

Maturana House of Prayer, P.O. Box 1178, 96950. Tel: 670-322-9713; 322-6373. Sr. Mary Ann Hartman, M.M.B., Local Coord. Mercedarian Missionaries of Berriz 3.

San Antonio Parish Convent, P.O. Box 745, 96950. Tel: 670-234-1752. Sisters 4.

Rota. *Rota Mercy Convent*, P.O. Box 542, 96951. Tel: 670-532-3522. Sr. Benedict San Nicolas, R.S.M., Local Supr. Religious Sisters of Mercy 3.

RELIGIOUS INSTITUTES OF MEN REPRESENTED IN THE DIOCESE

For further details refer to the corresponding bracketed number in the Religious Institutes of Men or Women section.

[0690]—*The Society of Jesus.*—S.J.

[0420]—*Society of the Divine Word.*—S.V.D.

RELIGIOUS INSTITUTES OF WOMEN REPRESENTED IN THE DIOCESE

[]—*Dominican Sisters of the Holy Rosary.*—O.P.

[2510]—*Mercedarian Missionaries of Berriz.*—M.M.B.

[2519]—*Sisters of Mercy, Religious.*—R.S.M.

NECROLOGY

(No Deaths)

Prefecture Apostolic of the Marshall Islands

Very Reverend

JAMES C. GOULD, S.J.

First Prefect Apostolic of the Marshall Islands; appointed First Prefect Apostolic of the Marshall Islands April 23, 1993; installed August 15, 1993. *Res., Cathedral of the Assumption, P.O. Box 8, Majuro, MH, 96960.* Tel.: 011-692-625-6657; Fax: 011-692-625-5520.

Square Miles 500,000.

Total Population (est.) 50,000.

Prefecture Apostolic of the Marshall Islands divided from the Diocese of the Carolines-Marshalls and erected on August 15, 1993 and committed to the Society of Jesus, New York Province. Area is that of the Republic of the Marshall Islands which is civilly under a Compact of Free Association with the United States.

P.O. Box 8:, Majuro, MH, 96960. Tel.: 011-692-625-6657; Fax: 011-692-625-5520.

E-mail address: jgould@ntamar.com

STATISTICAL OVERVIEW

Personnel	
Priests: Active Outside Diocese	1
Number of Diocesan Priests	1
Religious Priests in Diocese	5
Permanent Deacons in Diocese	2
Total Brothers	2
Total Sisters	16
Parishes	
Parishes	4
With Resident Pastor:	
Resident Religious Priests	2
Without Resident Pastor:	
Administered by Priests	2
Missions	7
Pastoral Centers	1
Professional Ministry Personnel:	
Brothers	2
Sisters	16
Educational	
Diocesan Students in Other Seminaries	1
Total Seminarians	1
High Schools, Diocesan and Parish	2
Total Students	299
Elementary Schools, Diocesan and Parish	6
Total Students	1,223
Catechesis/Religious Education:	
High School Students	57
Elementary Students	335
Total Students Under Catholic Instruction	1,915
Teachers in the Diocese:	
Priests	1
Brothers	1
Sisters	8
Lay Teachers	81
Vital Statistics	
Receptions into the Church:	
Infant Baptism Totals	152
Adult Baptism Totals	4
Received into Full Communion	30
First Communions	165
Confirmations	32
Marriages:	
Catholic	15
Interfaith	4
Total Marriages	19
Deaths	16
Total Catholic Population	4,000
Total Population	50,000

Prefecture Consultors—Rev. R. RICHARD MCAULIFF, S.J.; Sr. JOAN CREVCOURE, M.M.; Mrs. NEIMAT REIMERS; Mr. OSCAR DE BRUM.

Finance Committee—Mr. ALEX BING; Mr. ALAN FOWLER.

Judicial Vicar—Rev. WILLIAM J. RAKOWICZ, S.J., *P.O. Box 250, Chuuk, FM, 96942.*

Defenders of the Bond—Most Rev. MARTIN J. NEYLON, S.J.; Rev. R. RICHARD MCAULIFF, S.J.

Notary—Mrs. VERONICA KILUWE.

Vocations—Rev. Msgr. JAMES C. GOULD, S.J., *P.O. Box 8, Majuro, MH, 96960.*

CLERGY, PARISHES, MISSIONS AND PAROCHIAL SCHOOLS

MARSHALL ISLANDS

Mailing Address: for the Marshalls: P.O. Box 8, Majuro, MH 96960. Tel: (011) 692-625-6675; Fax: (011) 692-625-5520, unless otherwise noted.

Majuro, Cathedral of the Assumption, Rev. Msgr. James C. Gould, S.J.; Revs. R. Richard McAuliff, S.J.; Leonard G. Hacker, S.J.; Deacon Alfred Capelle.
Tel: 692-625-8307; Fax: 692-625-6507.
School—Sisters 2; Lay Teachers 22; Students 343.
High School—Sisters 2; Lay Teachers 9; Students 110.
Mission—Majuro Atoll, Laura.

Ebeye, Queen of Peace, Rev. Msgr. James C. Gould, S.J.; Revs. James P. Croghan, S.J.; Joseph Kanono, M.S.C.
Mailing Address: P.O. Box 5065, Marshall Islands, 96960. Tel: 692-329-3400; Fax: 692-625-3689.
School—School Sisters of Notre Dame 2; Lay Teachers 24; Students 510.
High School—Missionaries of the Sacred Heart (Brothers) 2; Lay Teachers 8; Students 189.
Mission—Kwajalein, Santo.

Kwajalein, Blessed Sacrament, Rev. William Sullivan, S.J.
Mailing Address: P.O. Box 1711, APO AP, 96555.
Tel: 805-355-2116;355-4535; Fax: 805-355-1787.

Outer Island Parish, Rev. Msgr. James C. Gould, S.J.
Schools—Arno.
Lay Teachers 5; Students 81; Jaluit.
Lay Teachers 5; Students 90; Wotje.
Lay Teachers 4; Students 79.
Missions—Arno; Ailinglaplap; Jaluit; Likiep; Namorik; Wotje.

Special Assignment:
Reverend Fathers—
Young, David, Military Chap.

INSTITUTIONS LOCATED IN THE DIOCESE

[A] MISCELLANEOUS

MAJURO. *Catholic Apostolic Center: Ajeltake*, P.O. Box 8, 96960. Tel: 011-692-247-7797; Fax: 011-692-625-5520. Sr. Damiana Kauea, O.L.S.H.

NECROLOGY

(No Deaths)

Diocese of Mayaguez, Puerto Rico

(Dioecesis Maiaguezensis)

Most Reverend

ULISES AURELIO CASIANO VARGAS, D.D.

Bishop of Mayaguez; ordained May 30, 1967; appointed Bishop March 4, 1976; ordained April 30, 1976. *Res., P.O. Box 2272, Mayaguez, PR, 00709.* Tel.: 809-833-2475; 833-5411 (Office).

Erected by the Bull *"Qui arcano Dei"* on March 1, 1976, by Pope Paul VI.

Comprises a portion of the southwest of the Island.

STATISTICAL OVERVIEW

Personnel	
Bishop	1
Retired Bishops	1
Priests: Diocesan Active in Diocese	34
Priests: Active Outside Diocese	1
Priests: Retired, Sick or Absent	6
Number of Diocesan Priests	41
Religious Priests in Diocese	35
Extern Priests in Diocese	2
Ordinations:	
Diocesan Priests	4
Religious Priests	2
Transitional Deacons	1
Permanent Deacons in Diocese	3
Total Brothers	5
Total Sisters	151
Parishes	
Parishes	29
With Resident Pastor:	
Resident Diocesan Priests	20
Resident Religious Priests	9
Without Resident Pastor:	
Pastoral Centers	154
Professional Ministry Personnel:	
Sisters	17
Lay Ministers	500
Welfare	
Catholic Hospitals	1
Total Assisted	113,023
Homes for the Aged	1
Total Assisted	150
Special Centers for Social Services	1
Total Assisted	1,450
Educational	
Diocesan Students in Other Seminaries	6
Total Seminarians	6
Colleges and Universities	1
Total Students	1,800
High Schools, Diocesan and Parish	3
Total Students	760
High Schools, Private	4
Total Students	1,170
Elementary Schools, Diocesan and Parish	3
Total Students	982
Elementary Schools, Private	7
Total Students	2,380
Catechesis/Religious Education:	
High School Students	1,288
Elementary Students	10,347
Total Students Under Catholic Instruction	18,733
Teachers in the Diocese:	
Priests	5
Brothers	3
Sisters	6
Lay Teachers	310
Vital Statistics	
Receptions into the Church:	
Infant Baptism Totals	5,063
Adult Baptism Totals	259
Received into Full Communion	134
First Communions	3,051
Confirmations	3,217
Marriages:	
Catholic	1,031
Interfaith	42
Total Marriages	1,073
Deaths	2,511
Total Catholic Population	360,000
Total Population	491,518

Vicar General—Rev. Msgr. Gonzalo Diaz.

Episcopal Vicars—
For Pastoral—Rev. Rogelio Mur, O.Carm.
For Diocesan Administration—Rev. Msgr. Gonzalo Diaz.

Chancery Office—P.O. Box 2272, Mayaguez, 00681. Tel: 787-833-5411.

Chancellor—Rev. Msgr. Gonzalo Diaz.

Diocesan Consultors—Rev. Msgr. Francis R. Lopez; Rev. Msgr. Romualdo M. Ortiz; Rev. Msgr. Gonzalo Diaz; Rev. Rafael Sastre.

Diocesan Board of Administration—Rev. Msgr. Francis R. Lopez; Rev. Msgr. Hector Ortiz.

Administrator—Mr. Efrain Motta Ferrer.

Censor Librorum—Rev. Jose Moreno.

Diocesan Offices and Directors

Youth Apostolate—Rev. Rafael Mendez.

Communications Media—Rev. Nomar J. Calero; Sr. Maria Socorro Bonilla, O.P.

Cursillos de Cristiandad—Rev. Msgr. Gonzalo Diaz.

Holy Childhood—Most Rev. Hermin Negron.

Legion of Mary—Rev. Msgr. Angel Latre.

Supt. of Schools—Sr. Vivina Gracia, C.S.J.

Religious Consultor—Jose Moreno.

Catechetics—Sr. Carleta Munoz, C.S.J.

Christian Family Movement—Rev. Roberto Soler.

Religious Coordinators—Vacant.

Development and Planification—Vacant.

Vocations—Rev. Nomar J. Calero.

Lay Pastoral Development—Rev. Msgr. Francis R. Lopez, Rector, *Instituto de la Fe, Box 2272, Mayaguez, 00709.*

Catholic Social Services—Sr. Silvia Arias, M.S.B.T., Dir., *Ramos Antonini No. 25 Oeste, Box 2272, Mayaguez, 00681.*

CLERGY, PARISHES, MISSIONS AND PAROCHIAL SCHOOLS

CITY OF MAYAGUEZ

1—Cathedral of Our Lady of Purification (1763), Revs. Angel Leonides Soto, Admin.; Nomar J. Calero; Edward Acevedo Lugo.
Res., P.O. Box 220, Mayaguez, 00681-0220. Tel: 787-831-2444.
Schools—Academy of the Immaculate Conception, Tel: 809-265-7860. Mr. Monico Sanabria, Elementary Prin.; Mr. Donny Ramos, High School Prin.
Lay Teachers 48; Students: Elementary 479; High School 484; Colegio La Milagrosa, Tel: 809-834-0350. Sr. Trinidad Irizarry, Prin.
Sisters of Charity 5; Lay Teachers 28; Students: Elementary 205; High School 150.
Missions—Mayaguez, Maria Socorro de los Cristianos Barrio Leguisamo; Mayaguez, Santa Ana. Quebrada Grande.

2—Our Lady of Mt. Carmel, Revs. Felix E. Catala, C.SS.R.; Sergio Del Carmen Espinosa, C.SS.R.; Sr. Elisa Doherty, O.P., Pastoral Min.
Res., Box 3166, Mayaguez, 00681. Tel: 787-831-6544; 832-2036 (Office).
Missions—Mani, Infant of Prague; Mani, Capilla de la Mora.
School—Mrs. Ester Rivera Santaliz, Prin. Sisters 1; Lay Teachers 19; Students 288.
Catechesis/Religious Programs—Students 347.

3—Ascension (1968), Rev. Jose Fco. Baez Camacho.
Res., Box 4361, Salud Sta., Mayaguez, PR 00681-4361. Tel: 787-832-0766.
Missions—Bo. Limon, St. Teresita; Bo. Las Vegas, Our Lady of Perpetual Help; Bo. El Porvenir, Ntra. Sra. de la Providencia (Rep. Masias).
Catechesis/Religious Programs—Students 130.

4—Church De El Buen Pastor (1986), Rev. Thomas R. Mitchell.
Res., San Gerardo St., No. A-1-A, Mayaguez Ter., Mayaguez, 00680. Tel: 809-833-8800.
Catechesis/Religious Programs—Students 137.
Missions—Alturas de Mayaguez, El Senor de Los Milagros, Tel: 809-265-5936; Parcelas Soledad, Sta. Teresita.

5—Nuestra Senora De Fatima (1986), Rev. Edwin Lugo Silva, Admin.
Res., Parcelas Castillo C-2, Mayaguez, 00680. Tel: 787-833-0794. [JC]
Catechesis/Religious Programs—Students 110.
Missions—Mayaguez, Cristo Rey, Andalucia St., Sultana, 00680; Mayaguez, Espiritu Santo, Sagitario St., Villa del Oeste, Sabalos, 00680; Mayaguez, Corpus Christi, Urb. Vista Verde, 00680.

6—Sacred Heart (1959), Revs. Toribio Pascual Diez, O.S.B.; Paulino Mazuelas, O.S.B.; Antonio M. Galban, O.S.B.; Gerardo Ibarra Rodriguez, O.S.B.; Frank Perez Martinez, O.S.B.
Res., R.F.D. 348 Buzon 400, Mayaguez, 00680. Tel: 787-832-1464.

School—St. Benedict College. (for boys), Tel: 809-832-9626. Rev. Paulino Mazuelas, O.S.B., Prin.
Lay Teachers 30; Students: Elementary 424; High School 148.
Missions—Rosario, San Jose; Rio Hondo, San Carlos y San Antonio; Bo. Malezas, La Milagrosa.

7—Santa Teresita (1970), Rev. Fernando Palacio.
Res., Principe St., 203 Bo. Colombia, Mayaguez, 00680. Tel: 787-832-2872.

8—San Vicente (1965), Revs. Juan Lamela, C.M.; Manuel Araujo, C.M.; Tomas de la Puebla, C.M.
Res., Ave. Guanajibo, No. 401, Mayaguez, 00680. Tel: 787-832-8874. [JC]
Catechesis/Religious Programs—Students 100.

9—Church of the Resurrection (1988), Rev. Angel Mendez.
Res., Balboa 285, Mayaguez, 00680. Tel: 787-831-6180.
Catechesis/Religious Programs—Students 165.
Chapels—Consumo, Jesus Redentor.; Rio Canas, Nuestra Senora del Perpetuo Socorro.; Barrio Quemado, Nuestra Senor del Carmen.

OUTSIDE THE CITY OF MAYAGUEZ

Aguada, St. Francis of Assisi (1692), Revs. Jose Luis Diez Gabela, O.S.A. (Spain); Lesmes Bernabe Lazaro, O.S.A. (Spain); German Lombo, O.S.A. (Spain); Isaias Revilla, O.S.A. (Spain); Edwin Cruz, O.S.A.
Res., P.O. Box 608, 00602. Tel: 787-868-2630.
Missions—Sabana, San Jose; Laguna, Santa Rita; Cruces, Santa Monica; Galicia-Columbani, Santo Tomas de Villanueva; Jaguey Chiquito, San Agustin; Rio Grande, Perpetuo Socorro; Naranjo Militar, Ntra. Sra. de Monserrate; Atalaya, Ntra. Sra. de Altagracia; Naranjo-Guanabanas, San Pablo; Marias, Asuncion de Maria; Cerro Gordo, Buen Consejo; Mamey, Perpetuo Socorro; Guaniquilla, Ntra. Sra. del Carmen; Carrizales, Ntra. Sra. de las Mercedes; Malpaso-Cesar Ruiz, Immaculada Concepcion; Bajio, Sagrada Familia; Quebrada Larga, Sgdo. Corazon de Jesus; Rio Grande-Playa, Ntra. Sra. del Carmen; Guayabo, El Buen Pastor; Piedras Blancas, Ntra. Sra. Reina de la Paz.
Convent—Calle Jose Hernandez, Box 1136, 00602. Hermanas de la Caridad del Cardenal Sancha

Santuario Protomartires de la Concepcion (1524), Rev. Roberto Soler.
Res., Bo. Espinar, Buzon 1162, 00602. Tel: 787-891-2889.
Chapels—Bo. Palmar, El Buen Pastor; Bo. Tablonar, El Nino Jesus.

Aguadilla, St. Charles Borromeo, Revs. Felipe Santiago, C.SS.R.; Cesar Jaramillo, C.SS.R.; Angelo G. Sanchez, C.SS.R.; Juan Edgardo Rosario, C.SS.R.; James Mc Swigan, C.SS.R.
Res., P.O. Box 238, 00605. Tel: 809-891-0575. [CEM]
School—Tel: 787-891-1445; Fax: 787-882-3270. Mrs. Nydia E. Ugarte, Prin.
Lay Teachers 46; Students: Elementary 405; High School 335.
Convents—Tel: 787-882-3629. Sr. Nilsa Gonzalez, Supr.
Salesian Sisters 4; Tel: 787-891-7496. Sr. Violeta Meduvely, M.C., Supr.
Missionaries of Charity 4.
Chapels—Bo. Corrales, Our Lady of Perpetual Help.; Caimital Alto, St. John Baptist; Victoria-Nuestra, Senora de la Victoria; Esteves, N. S. del Rosario; Bda. Caban, Ntra. Sra. de la Sagrada Familia.

La Milagrosa (1920), Rev. Ramon E. Albino.
Res., Urb. Marbella, Calle 1 Num. 379, 00605. Tel: 809-891-7014.
Missions—Borinquen, Our Lady of Victory; Camaseyes, Our Lady of Fatima; San Judas Tadeo, Playuelas.

San Jose Obrero (1975), Revs. Franklin Santana, M.C.; Hiran Santiago; Mario Borgonovo.
Res., Poblado San Antonio, Box 425, San Antonio, 00690. Tel: 787-890-2449; Fax: 787-826-2494.
Missions—Bo. Guerrero, La Providencia; Ramey-Maleza, Los Santos Reyes.

Anasco, St. Anthony Abbot (1730), Revs. Rogelio Mur Aguilar, O.Carm.; Juan Maria Amoros, O.Carm.; Jorge Rivera Maldonado, O.Carm.
Res., Box 392, 00610. Tel: 809-826-2215.
Missions—Miraflores, Chapel of Our Lady of Perpetual Help; La Playa, Our Lady of Carmel; Bo. Espino, St. Lawrence Martyr; Bo. Pinales, La Immaculade; Bo. Carreras, La Providencia; Bo. Cerro Gordo, Our Lady of Monserrat; Bo. Marias, St. Rita; Bo. Oveja, Cristo Redentor; Bo. Pozo Hondo, Santa Rosa de Lima.
Jesus Maestro Casa de Formaction—.

Cabo Rojo, St. Michael (1783), Revs. Jose A. Acaba; Angel Ortiz; Jose R. Linares.
Res., Box 625, 00623. Tel: 787-851-1283; Fax: 787-255-2757.
School—Miss Elba I. Santana Colon, Prin. Sisters 1; Lay Teachers 44; Students: High School 317; Elementary 382.
Missions—Puerto Real, Our Lady of Mt. Carmel; Joyuda, St. John the Baptist; Boqueron, St. Joseph; Llanos Tunas, Our Lady of Good Counsel; Las Palmas, St. Rita; Monte Grande, St. Jude Thaddeus; El Corozo, Cristo Rey; Betances, Our Lady of Fatima; Conde Avila, St. Martin de Porres; Bo. Miradero, Ntro. Sra. de la Providencia.

Hormigueros, Shrine of Our Lady of Monserrate (1874), Rev. Msgr. Gonzalo Diaz Hernandez; Rev. Angel Roman Ramos.
Res., Box 24, 00660. Tel: 787-849-2260.
Convent—Box 185, 00660. Tel: 787-849-2055. Sr. Maria Encarnacion, O.P., Supr.
Sisters of Fatima for Social Work 4.
Missions—Bo. Lavadero, Sagrado Corazon de Jesus; Bo. Jaquitas, Ntra. Sra. de la Paz; Bo. Carretera Nueva, La Asuncion; Bo. Guanajibo, San Martin de Porres; Bo. El Hoyo, Santa Rosa de Lima.

El Salvador (1969), Rev. Raphael Sastre.
Res., Box 567, 00660. Tel: 787-834-1993.
Chapels—Valle Hermoso Arriba, San Judas Tadeo; Parcelas S. Romualdo, Sta. Teresita.

Lajas, Our Lady of the Purification (1883), Revs. Rafael Mendez, Admin.; Rene Javier Hernandez.
Res., Box 425, 00667. Tel: 809-899-1911.
School—St. Louis Academy Sisters of St. Joseph. (Brooklyn). Tel: 787-899-4080. Sr. Teresita Alicea, C.S.J., Prin.
Sisters 2; Lay Teachers 24; Students: Elementary 140; High School 152.
Catechesis/Religious Programs—Students 110.
Convent— La Providencia
Missions—Bo. La Plata, Sagrado Corazon de Jesus, Parcelas #201, 00667; Bo. Lajas Arriba (La Tea), Ntra. Sra. del Perpetuo Socorro, Carretera 118 Km 0, 00667; Bo. Lajas Arriba (Parcelas), San Pablo, Parcelas #48, 00667; Bo. Parcelas Santa Rosa, Santa Rosa de Lima, Comunidad Sta. Rosa #35, 00667; Bo. Parcelas Palmarejo, San Judas Tadeo, Parcelas #172, 00667; Bo. Palmarejo II, San Juan Bautista, Parcela #80, 00667.

De la Merced Parish (1971), Rev. Jorge Caro; Deacon Ramon Cardona.
Res., P.O. Box 1023, 00667-1063. Tel: 787-899-1910.
Missions—Bo. Maguayo, Ntra. Sra. de la Monserrate, Carr. 101 Ramal 303 K.2.4, Bo. Maguayo, 00667.; Bo. Parguera, San Pedro, Carr. 304 Calle Principal, Bo. Parguera, 00667.; Bo. Cuesta Blanca, Ntra. Sra. de Monserrate, Carr. 116 Parcellas Cuesta Blanca #264, Bo. Cuesta Blanca, 00667.; Bo. Salinas, Ntra. Sra. del Carmen, Carr. 324 K. 5.6, Bo. Salinas, 00667.; Bo. Paris, Ntra Sra. del Perpetuo Socorro, Carr. 306, Bo. Paris, 00667.

Las Marias, Immaculate Heart of Mary (1868), Rev. Delroy Thomas Scott.
Res., Box 126, 00670. Tel: 787-827-3300.
Missions—Anones, San Jose, Carr. 406, Km. 3.9, 00607; Buena Vista, La Milagrosa, Carr. 124, R. 370, Km. 6.8 Int Buena Vista, 00670; Palma Escrita, N.S. de Fatima.

Maricao, St. John the Baptist (1864), Rev. Angel L. Rios, M.C.
Res., Box 453, 00606. Tel: 787-838-2014.
Missions—Bucarabones, Sagrado Corazon; Indiera Fria, Santa Rosa.
Chapel—Montoso, Immaculado Corazon de Maria, Tel: 787-838-2272. Sr. Inocencia Olmeda, O.P., Supr.
Dominican Sisters of Our Lady of Fatima 6.

Moca, Our Lady of Monserrate (1772), Revs. Santiago Rivera Allende; David Perez Mendez; Orlando Rosas Muniz; Juan Bautista Morales; Rev. Msgr. Hector Ortiz.
Res., P.O. Box 435, 00716. Tel: 787-877-2765.
Catechesis/Religious Programs—Lydia Soto, D.R.E. Students 1,914.
Missions—Bo. Cerro Gordo, San Judas; Bo. Voladoras Lomas, Espiritu Santo; Bo. Voladoras Parcelas, Sagrada Familia; Bo. Naranjo, Corazon de Jesus; Bo. Cuchillas La Salle, Santos Guillermo y Mateo; Bo. Chucillas Sabana, Corazon de Jesus; Bo. Limon, Virgen del Rosario; Bo. Cuchillas Loperena, Virgen del Carmen; Bo. Cordero, Virgen Monserrate; Bo. Rocha Magueyes, La Providencia; Bo. Punta Brava, San Pedro; Bo. Capa Barreto, Virgen del Rosario; Bo. Capa Bosque, Cristo Salvador; Bo. Cerro Gordo, La Inmaculada; Bo. Aceituna, San Martin de Porres.

Rincon, St. Rose of Lima (1789), Revs. Edgardo Acosta; Edgardo Lopez Hernandez; Deacon Fausto Duran.
Res., Box 128, 00677. Tel: 787-823-2650.
Missions—Bo. Calvache, Santa Rosa; Bo. Atalaya, El Cristo de la Reconciliacion; Bo. Corcega, La Milagrosa; Bo. Cruces, Sagrado Corazon de Jesus; Bo. Puntas, Nuestra Senora del Carmen; Bo. Jaguey, San Jose.

Rosario, Rosary, Rev. Vicente Perez Roig.
Res., Box 692, 00636. Tel: 787-832-3533.
Missions—Rosario, Nuestra Senora del Rosario; Bo. Rosario Penon, La Monserrate, Bo. Rosario Penon, 00680.

Sabana Grande, Church of San Isidro (1813), Revs. Hector E. Rivera; Harry Lopez Vazquez.
Res., Box 817, 00637. Tel: 787-873-4475.
Convent—Tel: 809-873-2750. Sr. Barbara Duran, O.P., Supr.
Sisters 4.
Missions—El Papayo, Cristo Rey, Carr.368 R.367 KM.2.0, 00637.; Susua, La Resurreccion, Carr.121 Calle Azucena, 00637. Tel: 809-873-0382; Bo. Maginas, Sagrado Corazon de Jesus, Calle Rable #44-Carr.121 K. 5.0, 00637. Tel: 809-873-1368; Bo. La Pica, San Jose, Carr. 121 Km. 4.1, 00637. Tel: 809-873-4231; Bo. Cerro Gordo, San Francisco de Asis, Carr.369 Km.1.4, 00637. Tel: 809-873-8048; Bo. Molinas, Ntra. Sra. de Monserrate, Carr.2 R.365 Km.2.8 Int., 00637. Tel: 809-873-2656; Bo. Guaras, Ntra. Sra. de Fatima, Carr.328 Km.3.6, 00637. Tel: 809-873-0886; Bo. La Torre, Santa Catalina de Siena, Carr.388 Km.5.9 Int., 00637. Tel: 809-873-7591; Bo. La Maquina, Santa Ana, Carr.114 R.363 Km.2.4, 00637.; Bo. Santana Pichel, Ntra. Sra. del Rosario, Carr.120 Km.6, 00637. Tel: 809-873-3707; Bo. El Hoyo, La Virgen Milagrosa, Carr.364 Km.7 Interior, 00637.; Bo. Rayo Plata, San Judas Tadeo, Carr.117 Km.10.7, 00637.; Bo. Sta. Ana Moreno, Sta Lucia, Carr.120 Km.3.1, 00637. Tel: 809-873-7962.

San German, San German de Auxerre, Revs. Humberto Lopez; Marcelino Arocho; Rev. Msgr. Francis R. Lopez; Rev. Edgar Antonio Carlo Rodriguez.
Res., Box 305, 00683. Tel: 787-892-1027.
School—Tel: 809-892-1009. Sr. Maria Ines Martin, C.S.J., Prin.
Sisters of St. Joseph (Brooklyn) 2; Lay Teachers 39; Students: Elementary 537; High School 204.
Catechesis/Religious Programs—Students 250.
Missions—Duey, Chapel of St. Augustin; Hoconuco, Chapel of St. Joseph; Maresua, Gruta de Lourdes; Cotuy, Our Lady of Fatima; Sabana Eneas, San Judas Tadeo.

St. Rose of Lima (1967), Revs. Urbano Saenz, O.S.A.; Roberto Garcia, O.S.A.; Francisco Larran, O.S.A.
Res., Box 364, 00683. Tel: 787-892-1276.
Missions—Bo. Guama, N. Sra. de la Consolacion; Bo. Minillas Carretera, Perpetuo Socorro; Bo. Retiro Tea, Santa Rita; Bo. Minillas Valle, Santa Monica; Bo. Cain, St. Martin de Porres.

San Sebastian, San Sebastian Martir (1752), Revs. Miguel Angel San Martin, C.P.; Jose J. Almendariz; Bernardo Onaindia, C.P.; Lino Muzquiz, C.P.
Res., P.O. Box 801, 00685. Tel: 787-896-1028.
School—Tel: 809-896-5728. Julio Arocho, Prin.
Lay Teachers 26; Students 362.
Catechesis/Religious Programs—Students 1,010.
Missions—Bo. Perchas 1, Cristo Rey; Bo. Perchas 11, La Pasion; Bo. Calabazas, San Gabriel de la Dolorosa; Bo. La Lechuza, La Asuncion; Bo. Juncal, Santa Teresita; Bo. Aibonito Guerrero, Ntra. Sra. del Carmen; Bo. Saltos, San Judas Tadeo; Bo. Hato Arriba, San Patricio; Bo. Hato Arriba (Parcelas), San Pablo de la Cruz; Bo. Altozano, Ntra. Sra. de Fatima; Bo. Robles, Sagrado Corazon; Bo. Hoyamala, San Jose Obrero; Bo. Parcelas Guacio (Parcelas), Santa Cruz.

On Special Assignment:
Reverend Fathers—
Diaz, Gonzalo, Chancellor, Box 24, Hormingueros, PR

INSTITUTIONS LOCATED IN THE DIOCESE

[A] HOSPITALS

San German. *Hospital of the Immaculate Conception*, Box 285, 00683
For a complete listing, refer to the Hospitals section.

[B] INSTITUTIONS

Mayaguez. *Asylum for the Poor and Aged*, Calle Post 62, 00680. Sisters of Charity (Spanish). Sr. Cruz M. Fontan, Supr. Sisters 6; Beds 113; Residents 102.

Convent of the Servants of Mary, Hostos Ave. 401, 00708. Tel: 787-832-0391. Sisters care for the sick in their homes and hospital. Sr. Prudencia Lopez de Arroyave, Supr. Sisters 17.

HORMIGUEROS. *Residence for the Aged, San Jose*, Valle Hermoso, 00660. Tel: 787-832-4243. Sr. Celsa Vazquez, Supr. Sisters 13; Residents 150.

[C] PERSONAL PRELATURES

MAYAGUEZ. *Opus Dei (Prelature of the Holy Cross and Opus Dei)*, 69 Orquideas St., Ensanche Martinez, 00680. Tel: 787-833-6461. Rev. Jose Francisco Tejeda.

RELIGIOUS INSTITUTES OF MEN REPRESENTED IN THE DIOCESE

For further details refer to the corresponding bracketed number in the Religious Institutes of Men or Women section.

[]—*Acies Christi*. (Spain).

[0140]—*Augustinians*.—O.S.A.

[0200]—*Benedictine Monks*. Spain.—O.S.B.

[0270]—*Carmelite Fathers and Brothers*. (Spain).—O.Carm.

[1330]—*Congregation of the Mission*. (Vice Province of Puerto Rico).—C.M.

[1000]—*Congregation of the Passion*.—C.P.

[1070]—*Redemptorist Fathers*.—C.SS.R.

[]—*Salesian Fathers*.

RELIGIOUS INSTITUTES OF WOMEN REPRESENTED IN THE DIOCESE

[]—*Acies Christi*. (Spain).

[]—*Carmelitas de Clausura*. (Spain).

[1070-13]—*Dominican Sisters*.—O.P.

[]—*Hermanas de la Caridad*.

[]—*Hermanas MM. del Buen Pastor*. (Puerto Rico).

[]—*Hermanas Salesianas*. (Spain).

[]—*Hermanas Teatinas*. (Spain).

[2340]—*Little Sisters of the Poor*.—L.S.P.

[]—*Madames of the Sacred Heart*.

[2790]—*Missionary Servants of the Most Blessed Trinity*.—M.S.B.T.

[]—*Monasterio Santa Maria del Monte Carmelo*.

[3580]—*Servants of Mary*. (Spain).—O.S.M.

[0650]—*Sisters of Charity of St. Vincent de Paul*. (Spanish).—S.C.

[]—*Sisters of Fatima*. (Puerto Rico).

[]—*Sisters of Schoenstatt*. (Germany).

[]—*Sisters of St. Joseph*. (Brooklyn).

NECROLOGY

(No Deaths)

Diocese of Ponce, Puerto Rico

(Dioecesis Poncensis)

Most Reverend

JUAN FREMIOT TORRES, D.D.

Bishop of Ponce; ordained April 10, 1950; appointed Bishop November 4, 1964; consecrated December 21, 1964. *Res., Bishop's House, P.O. Box 205, Sta. 6, CUPR, Ponce, PR, 00732.* Tel.: 809-848-5265; Fax: 809-841-1778.

Most Reverend

RICARDO SURINACH CARRERAS, D.D.

Titular Bishop of Aquae Albae in Mauretania and Auxiliary Bishop of Ponce; ordained April 13, 1957; appointed May 26, 1975; consecrated July 25, 1975. *Res., P.O. Box 205, Sta. 6, Ponce, PR, 00732.* Tel.: 809-848-5265; Fax: 809-841-1778.

ESTABLISHED NOVEMBER 21, 1924.

Square Miles 830.

Comprises the south portion of the Island of Puerto Rico and is in the Ecclesiastical Province of Puerto Rico.

STATISTICAL OVERVIEW

Personnel	
Bishop	1
Auxiliary Bishops	1
Priests: Diocesan Active in Diocese	42
Priests: Active Outside Diocese	32
Priests: Retired, Sick or Absent	8
Number of Diocesan Priests	82
Religious Priests in Diocese	56
Extern Priests in Diocese	13
Ordinations:	
Diocesan Priests	3
Permanent Deacons in Diocese	56
Total Brothers	1
Total Sisters	225
Parishes	
Parishes	40
With Resident Pastor:	
Resident Diocesan Priests	27
Resident Religious Priests	13
Without Resident Pastor:	
Missions	2
Pastoral Centers	229
Welfare	
Homes for the Aged	2
Total Assisted	289
Specialized Homes	1
Total Assisted	40
Special Centers for Social Services	1
Total Assisted	3,540
Other Institutions	1
Total Assisted	1,575
Educational	
Seminaries, Diocesan	1
Students from This Diocese	7
Students from Other Diocese	4
Diocesan Students in Other Seminaries	3
Seminaries, Religious	2
Students Religious	9
Total Seminarians	19
Colleges and Universities	1
Total Students	10,801
High Schools, Diocesan and Parish	20
Total Students	3,393
Elementary Schools, Diocesan and Parish	22
Total Students	6,244
Catechesis/Religious Education:	
Total Students Under Catholic Instruction	20,457
Teachers in the Diocese:	
Priests	14
Sisters	50
Lay Teachers	1,040
Vital Statistics	
Receptions into the Church:	
Infant Baptism Totals	5,282
Adult Baptism Totals	3,146
Received into Full Communion	616
First Communions	5,516
Confirmations	5,151
Marriages:	
Catholic	1,505
Interfaith	35
Total Marriages	1,540
Total Catholic Population	442,000
Total Population	551,525

Former Bishops—Most Rev. EDWIN V. BYRNE, D.D., cons. in Philadelphia, Nov. 30, 1925; transferred to San Juan, PR; promoted to Archbishop of Santa Fe, NM, June 15, 1943; died July 25, 1963.—Most Rev. ALOYSIUS J. WILLINGER, C.Ss.R., D.D., ord. July 2, 1911; appt. Bishop of Ponce March 8, 1929; cons. Oct. 28, 1929; appt. Titular Bishop of Bida and Coadjuctor of Monterey-Fresno (cum jure successionis), Dec. 12, 1946; installed Bishop of Monterey-Fresno, Jan. 3, 1953; resigned Oct. 25, 1967; died July 25, 1973.—Most Rev. JAMES E. MCMANUS, C.SS.R., D.D., J.C.D., transferred to the Archdiocese of New York, Nov. 27, 1963.—His Eminence LUIS CARDINAL APONTE, D.D., ord. April 10, 1950; appt. Titular Bishop of Lares and Auxiliary of Ponce, July 23, 1960; cons. Oct. 12, 1960; appt. Coadjuctor Bishop of Ponce, April 16, 1963; appt. Bishop of Ponce, Nov. 18, 1963; installed Feb. 20, 1964; promoted to Archbishop of San Juan, Nov. 4, 1964; installed Jan. 15, 1965; created Cardinal, March 5, 1973.

Vicar General—Most Rev. RICARDO SURINACH, D.D.

Pro-Vicar General—Rev. Msgr. PEDRO J. BALLESTER.

Chancellor—Rev. Msgr. HERMINIO DE JESUS.

Vice Chancellor—Rev. Msgr. JUAN ESPONA.

Bishop's Secretary—Rev. Msgr. JUAN ESPONA.

Episcopal Vicar for Diocesan Administration—Rev. Msgr. HERMINIO DE JESUS.

Episcopal Vicar for Pastoral Coordination—Rev. Msgr. ANDRES GUERRERO.

Episcopal Vicar for Clergy Affairs—Rev. Msgr. ROBERTO GARCIA-BLAY.

Tribunal Interdiocesano de Puerto Rico—Most Rev. JUAN FREMIOT TORRES, D.D., Moderator, *P.O. Box 229, Station 6, Calle Isabel No. 31, Ponce, 00732.* Tel: 787-843-4902; Fax: 787-841-7483. First instance for the Dioceses of Mayaguez and Ponce. Second Instance for the Archdiocese of San Juan.

Judicial Vicar—Rev. ELIAS MORALES.

Associate Judicial Vicars—Revs. MANUEL SANTIAGO; CARLOS ROMAN.

Judges—Mayaguez: Rev. Msgr. GONZALO DIAZ, Ponce: Rev. ISIDRO GONZALEZ; Mr. ABRAHAM MORALES.

Diocesan Consultors—Most Rev. RICARDO SURINACH, D.D.; Rev. Msgr. PEDRO J. BALLESTER; Rev. Msgr. HERMINIO DE JESUS; Rev. Msgr. MARCOS A. PANCORBO; Rev. Msgr. FRANCISCO VELEZ; Rev. Msgr. RAFAEL SANTIAGO; Rev Msgr. JUAN ESPONA; Rev. JOSE LOZANO.

Diocesan Board of Administration—Most Rev. RICARDO SURINACH, D.D.; Rev. Msgr. MARCOS PANCORBO; Rev. Msgr. PEDRO J. BALLESTER; Mr. FERNANDO ROSADO; Deacon ALBERTO CASTRO; Mr. SANTIAGO RAMOS.

Parish Priests Consultors—Rev. Msgr. MARCOS PANCORBO; Rev. Msgr. ANDRES GUERRERO; Rev. Msgr. HERMINIO DE JESUS.

Notaries—Rev. Msgr. JUAN ESPONA; Mrs. CONCEPCION MORA; Mrs. LUZ DELIA MEDINA; Mrs. MARIA V. RODRIGUEZ; Mrs. IRIS YOLANDA PAGAN, M.J.

Censores Librorum—Revs. PERFECTO ALVAREZ, O.S.A.; FELIX LAZARO, Sch.P.; BRIAN HARRISON, O.S.

Administrator—Rev. Msgr. JUAN ESPONA.

Diocesan Offices and Directors

Catechesis—Sr. FATIMA RIVERA, O.P., *P.O. Box 1064, Ponce, 00733.* Tel: 787-842-9178; Fax: 787-259-1718.

Catholic Youth Organization—Vacant.

Children of Mary—Rev. Msgr. ANDRES GUERRERO.

Committee for Community Planning—Rev. Msgr. HERMINIO DE JESUS.

Communications—Sr. LOURDES MERCADO, O.P., *P.O. Box 986, Ponce, 00733.* Tel: 809-843-1548.

Cursillos de Cristiandad—Mr. BENJAMIN PAGAN, *Marvesa, La Rambla, Ponce, 00731.*

Ecumenism—Rev. Msgr. ANDRES GUERRERO, *Box 205, Sta. 6, Ponce, 00732.*

Legion of Mary—Rev. Msgr. ANDRES GUERRERO, *P.O. Box 205, Sta 6, Ponce, 00732.*

Liturgical Commission—Most Rev. RICARDO SURINACH, D.D.; Rev. Msgr. JUAN ESPONA, *P.O. Box 205, Sta. 6, Ponce, 00732.*

Sacred Music Commission—Rev. ABEL DI MARCO.
St. Vincent de Paul Conferences—Dr. RAFAEL BLASINI, *Cristo Rey Parish, 7W Ext. La Rambla, Ponce, 00731.*
Superintendent of Schools—Sr. MARIA UNA, R.A.D., *Sta. 6, P.O. Box 557, Ponce, 00732.* Tel: 787-848-4020; Fax: 787-844-5987.
Vigilance for the Faith—Most Rev. RICARDO SURINACH, D.D.
Vocations—Rev Msgr. JESUS R. DIEZ ANTONANZAS; Rev. ALFREDO ALVAREZ LACRUZ, *P.O. Box 110, Sta. 6, Ponce, 00732.* Tel: 787-848-5265.
Institute of Family Orientation—Deacon JESUS M. PAGAN, *Sta. 6, Ponce, 00732.* Tel: 787-840-6018.

CLERGY, PARISHES, MISSIONS AND PAROCHIAL SCHOOLS

CITY OF PONCE

1—CATHEDRAL OF OUR LADY OF GUADALUPE (1692), Rev. Msgr. Marcos A. Pancorbo; Rev. Carlos Roman; Deacon Jose Mercado.
Res., 28 Cristina St., Box 210 Sta. 6, 00732. Tel: 787-842-0134; Fax: 787-848-9104.

2—CHRIST THE KING (1964), Rev. Juan Rodriguez Orengo; Deacon Anibal Rosario.
Res., 7 W. Ext., La Rambla, 00731. Tel: 809-843-3028; Fax: 809-840-7398.
School—Tel: 787-843-0766; Fax: 787-843-6443. Mr. Jorge Almodovar Lucena, Prin.
Students 284.
Missions—Urb. Santa Teresita, Ponce Co., Santa Teresita Calle 33, Parque Central,; Rio Chiquito, Ponce Co., Nino Jesus de Praga Bo. Los Claves,; Ponce, La Dolorosa. Villa Ponce - Rambla #4st.

3—CHURCH OF THE RESURRECTION (1967), Rev. Msgr. Roberto Garcia Blay; Rev. Esteban Santaella; Deacon Rafael Castro.
Res., Glenview Gardens, A-Q 8 W. 22nd St., 00731. Tel: 787-842-7167.
Missions—Bo. La Yuca, Ponce Co., Immaculate Heart of Mary; Bo. Collado, Ponce Co., Our Lady of Monserrate; Bo. Las Vallas, Ponce Co., San Lucas; Ponce, Saint Joseph Bo. La Yuca,; Ponce, Our Lady of Carmel. Bo. Carmelita.

4—OUR LADY OF MT. CARMEL (1883), Revs. Miguel Alvarez, Sch.P.; Jose Mateo, Sch.P.; Agustin Lopez, Sch.P.
Res., P.O. Box 118, Playa de Ponce, 00734. Tel: 787-842-1333; Fax: 787-841-6861.
School—Tel: 787-842-5018. Mrs. Paquita Alvarado, Prin.
Students 201.
Missions—Villa del Carmen, Ponce Co., San Martin de Porres, Constancia Ave., 00734. Tel: 809-848-4355; Bo. Salistral, Ponce Co., Santa Marta.

5—SANTA TERESITA (1930), Revs. Edward Maldonado, O.F.M.Cap.; Roberto Martinez, O.F.M.Cap.; Francisco Garcia, O.F.M.Cap.; Deacons Casildo Rodriquez; Juan Rios.
Res., Box 7244, 342 Victoria St., 00732. Tel: 787-842-3137; 842-5055 (Friary); Fax: 787-844-7267.
School—342 Victoria St., 00732. Tel: 787-842-4110. Mrs. Mildred Reyes, Prin.
Students 300.
Catechesis/Religious Programs—Students 300.

6—SAN CONRADO (1948), Rev. Msgr. Pedro J. Ballester; Rev. Msgr. Rafael Santiago; Deacon Emerito Lopez.
Res., Box 7362, 00732. Tel: 809-843-0560.
School—P.O.Box 7111, 00732. Tel: 787-843-1405; 842-2293; Fax: 787-841-7303. Sr. Nildred Rodriguez, C.S.J., Prin.
Students 817.
Catechesis/Religious Programs—Students 817.

7—SANTA MARIA (1952), Revs. Thomas Cahill, M.J.; Christopher Foeckler, M.J.; Michael J. Diemer, M.J.
Res., Box 101, Sta. 6, 00732. Tel: 787-848-5370; Fax: 787-848-3313.
School—Tel: 787-842-1164. Mrs. Lydia Otero, Prin.
Students 934.

8—LA MILAGROSA (1928), Revs. Ignacio Alonso, C.M.; Javier Inigo, C.M.; Juan M. Zurutuza, C.M.; Deacons Ramon L. Vazquez; Carlos Burgos.
Res., Guadalupe No. 2, 00731. Tel: 787-842-3188; Fax: 787-284-1100. [CEM]
School—Tel: 787-842-1164. Mrs. Carmen Pasarell, Prin.
Students 566.
Catechesis/Religious Programs—Students 566.

9—LA MERCED (1928), Revs. Modesto Vaca, O.de.M.; Antonio Garcia, O.deM.; Jose Luis Iturraran, O.de.M.; Deacons Carlos M. Rodriguez-Guilbe; Jose D. Ruiz.
Res., Luna St., No. 9, 00731. Tel: 787-842-0069; Fax: 787-842-0603.

10—LA SANTISIMA TRINIDAD (1971), Revs. Alejandro Nistal, O.SS.T.; Jose Luis Fernandez, O.SS.T.; Alfonso Rementeria, O.SS.T.; Deacon Francisco Lugo.
Res., Las Delicias, Box 8226, 00732. Tel: 787-842-6073; Fax: 787-842-6073.
Missions—Bo. Magueyes, Ponce Co., San Juan de Mata, Box 8226, 00732.; Bo. Guaragoa, Ponce Co., San Andres, 00732.; Bo. Guaragoa, Arriba, Ponce Co., Santa Ana, 00732.; Bo. Marueno, Arriba, Ponce Co., N.S. Fatima, 00732.; Parcelas de Marueno, Ponce Co., San Antonio de Padua, 00732.; Bo. Madrigal, Ponce Co., N.S. del Rosario, 00732.; Bo. Pastillo, Ponce Co., Inmaculada, 00732.; Bo. Corral Viejo, Ponce Co., Cristo Rey, 00732.; Bo. Santas Pascuas, Ponce Co., Resurreccion, 00732.

11—SAN JOSE OBRERO (1979), Revs. Brian Harrison, O.S.; Anthony Tyrrell, O.S.; Christopher de Herrera, O.S.; Deacon Nestor Rentas.
Res., El Tuque, Calle 1 No. 3, Box 8027, 00732. Tel: 787-843-9072.
Mission—Punto Oro, Ponce Co., Ntra. Sra. del Pilar.

12—SAN JOSE (1965), Revs. Santiago Soria, O.C.D.; Mariano Fraile, O.C.D.; Alexio de Armas, O.C.D.; Bro. Fray Jorge Llorentes, O.C.D.; Deacon David Rodriguez.
Res., Urb. San Jose, Calle 6, Box 8414, 00732. Tel: 787-843-3910; Fax: 787-843-1994.

13—SANTUARIO SAN JUDAS TADEO (1964), Revs. Benigno Lopez, O.de. M.; Ramon Conde Ocampo, O.de.M.; Pedro Ruiz, O.de.M.; Javier Errecalde, O.de.M.; Vicente Salas Avello, O.de.M.; William Rabelo, O. de M.
Res., P.O. Box 7046, 00732. Tel: 787-843-0572.
School—Oblates to the Divine Love, Tel: 787-844-2610. Mrs. Zaida Toro, Prin.
Students 612.
Kindergarten—Urb. Constancia H-467, 00731. Tel: 787-843-5378; Fax: 787-842-5079.
Students 271. Sisters of the Love of God (Spain). Sr. Paz Martinez, R.A.D., Prin.
Mission—Bo. Cuatro Calles, Ponce Co., St. Anthony.

14—SAN VICENTE-CANTERA, Revs. Jose Cummings, C.M.; Eugenio Villafranca, C.M.; Luis Brioso, C.M.
Res., Mayor Cantera No. 67, 00731. Tel: 809-843-1976.
Mission—Rio Chiquito, Ponce Co., San Vicente.

15—CHURCH OF THE SACRED HEART (1969), Revs. Jose M. Galan; Perfecto Alvarez, O.S.A.; Deacon Reinaldo Rivera.
Res., Alta Vista C 21-S-6, 00731. Tel: 787-843-4891.
Mission—Bo. La Cuarta, Ponce Co., San Pedro Nolasco.

16—CHURCH OF THE GOOD SHEPHERD (1968), Rev. Jose Lozano; Deacons David Ramos; Rafael D. Ruiz; Andres Maldonado.
Res., Calle 35, H.H. 14, Jardines del Caribe, 00731. Tel: 787-843-6202.
Mission—Bo. Quebrado del Agua, Ponce Co., La Milagrosa, 00731.

17—OUR LADY OF MT. CARMEL (1973), Revs. Antonio Ferre; Jose Antonio Lopez Vega; Deacons Ladislao Laboy; Jose M. Vazquez.
Res., Box 187, Coto Laurel, 00780. Tel: 787-848-2030.
Missions—Bo. Hoyos, Ponce Co., Santa Maria Virgen, 00780.; Bo. Las Raices, Ponce Co., Sagrado Corazon de Jesus, Carr. 511 K. 15, 00780.; Bo. Real Anon Abajo, Ponce Co., San Mateo, 00780.; Bo. Real Anon Arriba, Ponce Co., San Martin de Porres, 00780.

18—CHURCH SANTISIMO SACRAMENTO (1984), Revs. Wilberto Reyes, L.D.; Angel Oscar Alvez, L.D.; Jordi Roca, L.D.
P.O. Box 212, Sta. 6, 00732.
Res., Urb. Lirios del Sur, Calle 15-I #1, 00731. Tel: 787-843-0245.

Parishes in Formation

1—CHURCH OUR LADY OF MIRACULOUS MEDAL, Rev. Msgr. Marcos A. Pancorbo, Admin.
Res., P.O. Box 210, Sta. 6, 00732. Tel: 787-842-0134.

2—CHURCH SAN PATRICIO, Rev. Felix Emilio Alvarado, Admin.
Res., La Pica, Cr. Buzon 234-B, 00730. Tel: 787-828-6350.

OUTSIDE THE CITY OF PONCE

Adjuntas, Adjuntas Co., St. Joachim (1815), Revs. Alfonso Amezcua, O.R.C.; Manuel C. Martinez, O.R.C.; Deacons Samuel Sepulveda; Radames Marcucci.
Res., 14 Rius Rivera St., 00601. Tel: 787-829-3145; Fax: 787-829-3145.
School—San Joaquin Elementary and Intermediate, 12 Primo Delgado St., 00601. Tel: 787-829-3040. Ms. Carmen Bauza, Prin.
Students 147.
Missions—Garzas, San Francisco; Vegas Arriba, Sta. Ana; Tres de Jayuya, Santa Teresita; Pellejas, Santa Rosa; Yahuecas, Virgen del Carmen; Tanama, Sagrado Corazon; Guilarte, San Antonio; Vegas Abajo, La Milagrosa; Limani, Inm. Corazon de Maria.

Aguirre, Guayama Co., Sacred Heart (1946), Rev. Jose Carlos Vargas.
Res., Box 260, Aguirre, 00704. Tel: 787-853-3620.
School—Perpetuo Socorro, Barrio/Coqui, 00704. Tel: 787-853-2270. Sr. Isabel Cruz, R.A., Prin.
Students 614.
Missions—Las Mareas, St. Judas; Coqui, Our Lady of Perpetual Help; San Felipe, St. Martin de Porres; Aguirre, La Milagrosa.

Arroyo, Arroyo Co., Our Lady of Mt. Carmel (1855), Revs. Eduardo Garcia; Eliud Aponte.
Res., Box 388, 00714. Tel: 787-839-3465.
Catechesis/Religious Programs—P.O. Box 25, 00714. Students 170.
Missions—Bo. Pitahaya, Ntra Sra. del Carmen; Bda. Marin, La Milagrosa; Bo. Yaurel Palmarejo, San Jose; Bo. Palmas, Ntra Sra. de Fatima; Bo. Yaurel Santa Clara, San Martin.

Castaner, Our Lady of the Miraculous Medal (1969), Rev. Miguel A. Dimas, O.R.C.; Deacon William Ramos.
Res., Box 1006, 00631. Tel: 787-897-5843.
Missions—Bartolo, Immaculate Conception; Mirasol, La Virgen; Rio Prieto, Milagrosa.

Coamo, Coamo Co., St. Blase (1616), Rev. Msgr. Andres Guerrero; Revs. Pedro Faustino Echeverria; Cristobal Reilly, S.T.; Deacon Angel A. Negron.
Res., Box 196, 00769. Tel: 787-825-1122.
School—Ntra. Sra. de Valvanera, Box 1903, 00769. Tel: 787-825-1145. Mrs. Maria Rivera Cansobre, Prin.
Students 432.
Catechesis/Religious Programs—Students 432.
Missions—Coamo Arriba, Coamo Co., Sacred Heart, Box 196, 00769.; Los Llanos, Coamo Co., St. Anthony, 00769.; Palmarejo, Coamo Co., Sacred Heart of Mary, 00769.; Pulguillas, Coamo Co., Christ the King, 00769.; Hayales, Coamo Co., Our Lady of Mt. Carmel, 00769.; Santa Catalina, Coamo Co., Miraculous Virgin, 00769.; Santa Catalina, Coama Co., Sacred Heart Sector Descalabrado,; Coamo, Coamo Co., Saint James Sector Cilantro,; Pedro Garcia, Coamo Co., Miraculous Virgin, 00769.; Santa Ana, Coamo Co., Santa Ana, 00769.; Rio Jueyes, Coamo Co., Our Lady of Lourdes, 00769.; San Diego, Coamo Co., San Diego, 00769.; Emanueli, Coamo Co., Holy Family, 00769.; Las Flores, Coamo Co., San Martin, 00769.; Melendez, Coamo Co., Our Lady of Fatima, 00769.

Ensenada, Sacred Heart (1963), Revs. Gerardo Ramirez; Elias Morales; Deacon Wallis S. Sanchez.
Res., Box 179, 00647. Tel: 787-821-2857.
Missions—Salinas-Providencia, Divina Providencia; Bo. Fuig., Monserrate.

Guanica, Guanica Co., St. Anthony Abbot (1888), Revs. Gerardo Ramirez; Elias Morales; Deacon Reinaldo Galarza.
Res., Box 804, 00653. Tel: 787-821-2147.
School—Blessed Imelda, Dr. Veve Str. 26, 00653. Tel: 787-821-2714; Fax: 787-821-2714. Mrs. Lissette M. Ortiz, Prin.
Students 178.
Missions—Bo. Belgica, Guanica Co., Cristo Rey; Bo. Santa Juanita, Guanica Co., N. Sra. Rosario; Bo. Luna, Guanica Co., San Judas; Bo. La Luna, Guanica Co., N. Sra Fatima; Bda. Esperanza, Guanica co., La Providencia.

Guayama, Guayama Co., St. Anthony of Padua (1736), Revs. Antonio Hernandez, C.Ss.R.; Thomas J. Gavigan, C.Ss.R.; Vicente Dionne, C.Ss.R.; Hector Colon, C.Ss.R.; Jorge Colon, C.Ss.R.; Deacon Alberto Montanez.
Res., Box 2820, 00785. Tel: 787-864-4100; Fax: 787-864-5494.
School—St. Anthony, Box 777, 00785. Tel: 787-864-2062; Fax: 787-864-1450.
Students 571. Principals: Mr. Pedro J. Rivera; Mrs. Evelyn Adams.
School—St. Alphonse Liguori, Box 777, 00785. Mr. Pedro J. Rivera, Prin.
Students 99.
Missions—Caimital, Our Lady of Perpetual Help; Bo. Puente Jobos, SS. Peter and Paul; Palmas, St. Gerard; Carmen, Our Lady of Mt. Carmel; Bo. Olimpo, Cristo Rey; Bo. Corazon, La Candelaria; Colonia Villodos, Perpetuo Socorro; Bo. Puerto Jobos, San Francisco de Asis; Bo. Guamani, Sgdo.

Corazon; Bo. Carite, San Martin; Bo. Barrancas, La Monserrate.

Guayanilla, Guayanilla Co., Immaculate Conception (1841), Revs. Raymond L. Rivera; Orlando Rivera; Deacons Miguel Sepulveda; Jesus Rodriguez.
Res., P.O. Box 560383, 00656-0383. Tel: 787-835-3035.
School—Immaculate Conception, P.O. Box 560573, 00656-0573. Tel: 787-835-2230; Fax: 787-835-3035. Sr. Alejandrina Torres, H.C.C.S., Prin.
Students 250.
Missions—Barrio Sierra Baja, Our Lady of Mt. Carmel; Magas Arriba, Perpetuo Socorro; Quebradas, San Francisco de Asis; Barrio Indios, San Juan Bosco; Consejo Alto, La Monserrate; Macana Rio, Virgen de Fatima; Quebrada Honda, Nuestra Senora; Macana Parcelas, San Martin de Porres.

Jayuya, Jayuya Co., Our Lady of Monserrate (1883), Revs. Felix Emilio Alvarado; Manuel Santiago; Jose Luis Larreategui, Sch.P.; Felix Lazaro, Sch.P.; Esteban Santaella; Deacons Luis Rosario; Carlos Orama; Jose A. Perez.
Res., Calle Figueras 13, 00664. Tel: 787-828-6350; Fax: 787-828-5062.
Missions—Collares, Jayuya Co., Cristo Rey, Figueras #13, 00664.; Coabbey, Jayuya Co., San Jorge, 00664.; Canalizo, Jayuya Co., La Milagrosa, 00664.; Gripinas, Jayuya Co., Buen Pastor, 00664.; Zama, Jayuya Co., Santa Cecila, 00664.; Hoyo Planas, Jayuya Co., Esp. Santo, 00664.; Mameyes, Jayuya Co., S. Antonio, 00664.; Salto, Jayuya Co., Santos Reyes, 00664.; Saliente, Jayuya Co., San Francisco, 00664.; Puerto Plata, Jayuya Co., San Juan, 00664.; La Pica, San Patricio Co.,; Hogares Seguros, San Antonio Co.

Juana Diaz, Juana Diaz Co., St. Raymond Nonato (1798), Rev. Msgr. Francisco Velez; Rev. Msgr. Joaquin Alicea; Rev. Santiago Solla; Deacons Hector L. Santiago; Narciso Ortiz.
Res., Box 1426, 00795. Tel: 787-837-2390.
Missions—Pastillo, Cotopaso Co., Santiago Apostol; Rio Canas, Rio Canas Abajo, San Judas; Jacaquas, Bo. Jacaguas, N.S. de Fatima; Collores, Bo. Jacaguas, La Milagrosa; Las Margaritas, Bo. Collores Arriba, Santiago, Ap.; Corral, P. Socorro; Guayabal, Bo. Guayabal, Our Lady of the Rosary; Callabo, Bo. Callabo, San Ramon; Bo. Rio Cana Arriba, La Merced.

Santa Teresita (Arus) (1984), Rev. Adalin Rivera; Deacons Pedro Garcia-Malavet; Secundino Torres.
Res., P.O. Box 131, Sta. 6, Ponce, 00732. Tel: 787-844-6670.
Missions—San Martin de Porres. (Singapur); Divine Mercy. (Piedra Aguza); Pastillito, Manzanilla, Our Lady of Carmel. (Galicia).

Nuestra Senora de Lourdes (Aguilita) (1984), Rev. Msgr. Herminio de Jesus; Deacons Jose Mendez; Cirilo Carmona; Ruperto Reyes; Jaime Velez; Fernando Perez.
Res., P.O. Box 1824, 00795. Tel: 787-837-1097.
Catechesis/Religious Programs—P.O. Box 1824, 00795. Tel: 787-260-2144.
Students 232.

Patillas, Inmaculado Corazon de Maria (1811), Revs. Alberto Muniz; Rafael Alvarado de Jesus; Deacon Francisco Vega.
Res., Box 635, 00723. Tel: 787-839-5333.
Missions—Bo. Marin Alto, Pastillas, Pastillas Co., Perpetuo Socorro; Bo. Guarderraya, Pastillas, Pastillas Co., Madre Cabrini; Bo. Recio, Pastillas, Pastillas Co., Sto. Cristo de Los Milagros; Bo. Jacaboa, Pastillas, Pastillas Co., Carmen; Bo. El Bajo, Pastillas, Pastillas Co., Cristo Rey; Bo. Providencia, Pastillas, Pastillas Co., Providencia; Bo. Los Pollos, Pastillas, Pastillas Co., Santa Rosa de Lima; Bo. Los Barros, Pastillas, Pastillas Co., S. Juan Evangelista; Bo. El Real, Pastillas, Pastillas Co., San Guillermo; Bo. Jagual, Pastillas, Pastillas Co., Carmen.

Penuelas, Penuelas Co., St. Joseph (1793), Revs. Segismundo Cintron; Francisco Sirvent-Dominguez; Deacons Carmelo Vazquez; Jose E. Gelpi; Glidden R. Perez; Joaquin Masoller.
Res., Box 25, 00624. Tel: 787-836-1038.
Missions—El Rucio, Penuelas Co., La Milagrosa, Carr. #391, 00624.; El Alto, San Antonio Carr. #132,; Macana, Fatima Carr. #131,; Tallaboa Alta, Santa Ana St. Domingo, Carmen Carr. #132,; Bo Barreal, Cristo de la Salud Carr. #386,; Quebrada Ceiba, Milagrosa Carr. #387,; Corozal, San Antonio. Carr. #387.

Sacred Heart (Tallaboa) (1928), Rev. Agustin Grinena.
Res., HC 01, Box 13063, 00624. Tel: 787-836-1164.
Mission—Bo. Buena Vista, Holy Family.

Salinas, Our Lady of Monserrat (1854), Revs. Angel Sanchez; Edwin Vazquez-Vega; Deacon Pablo F. Miranti.
Res., Box 1172, 00751. Tel: 787-824-2215.
Missions—Plena, San Jose; Coco, Santa Ana; Parcelas Vazquez, Esp. Santo; Bo. Las Palmas, Virg. del Carmen; Naranjo, Santa Marta; Las Ochenta, Inmaculada Concepcion; Bo. Playita, Virgen Milagrosa; Bo. Playa, Carmen; Sabana Llana, Perpetuo Socorro.

Santa Isabel, St. James (1854), Revs. Ismael Larena; Moises Navascues, Sch.P.; Deacon Jaime Martinez.
Res., Box 137, 00757. Tel: 809-845-2450; Fax: 809-845-2485.
Catechesis/Religious Programs—Students 300.
Missions—Playita Cortada, San Patricio; Bo. Penuelas, Virgen del Rosario; Bo. Paso Secos, Virgen del Rosario; Bo. Ollas, Monserrate; Jauca, San Ignacio de Loyola.

Villalba, Our Lady of Mt. Carmel (1917), Revs. Jose Diego Rodriguez; Emiliano Alamo; Fausto Ramos; Deacons Javier Gonzalez; Ramon A. Resto.
Res., Box 432, 00766. Tel: 787-847-0695.
School—Box 1033, 00766. Tel: 787-847-2875. Sr. Ana M. Santamarta, R.A.D., Prin.
Students 321.
Convent—Tel: 809-847-2874; 847-2391. Sisters of the Love of God
Missions—Romero, Sagrado Corazon, HC01 Box 5081, 00766. Tel: 787-847-1591; Bo. Vista Alegre, Jesus Crucificado, 00766.; Bo. Mogote, Santisima Tinidad, 00766.; Bo. Cerro Gordo, Espiritu Santo, 00766.; Bo. Jagueyes Arriba, La Milagrosa, 00766.; Bo. Corillo, San Pedro, 00766.; Bo. Palmarejo, San Jose, 00766.; Bo. Higuero, Santisimo Sacramento, 00766.; Bo. Camarones, Jesus Crucificado, 00766.; Bo. Canonilla Abajo, Maria Madre de la Iglesia, 00766.; Bo. Sierrita Caonillas, Cristo de la Salud, 00766.; Barrio Jaguey, Madre Cabrini, 00766.; Barrio Semil, Santa Cecilia, 00766.; Barrio Apeadero, San Alfonso, 00766.; Barrio Hatillo, Sagrada Familia, 00766.; Bo. Camarones-Los Robles, San Antonio, 00766.; Bo. Hatillo Viejo, La Milagrosa, 00766.; Bo. Cuchilla del Limon, La Asuncion, 00766.; Bo. Limon, Virgen de la Amargura, 00766.; Bo. Dajas, N.S. del Carmen, 00766.

Our Lady Mother of Divine Providence (Mission Noell) (1962), Revs. Raymond D. Middendorf, S.M.; James A. Imhof, S.M., Pastoral Assoc.
Res., Box 1556, 00766. Tel: 787-867-2052.
Missions—Bo. Alturita, Cacao Co., Our Lady of Mt. Carmel; Bo. Cacao, Cacao Co., Imm. Concepcion; Bo. El Frio, Ala de La Piedra Co., Nino de Praga; Bo. Guineo, Ala de La Piedra Co., Santa Ana; Bo. Bauta, Bauta Abajo Co., N.S. del Rosario; Bo. Damian Abajo, Damian Abajo Co., N.S. del Pilar; Bo. Pozas, Damian Abajo Co., N.S. Monserrate; La Piedra, Ala de La Piedra Co., O.L. of Perp. Help; Matrullas, Cacao Co., Sacred Heart of Jesus; Ortiga, Bauta Abajo Co., San Mateo.

Yauco, Holy Rossary (1756), Revs. Jose Martin, O.P.; Jose Luis Alonso, O.P.; Alfredo Vallina, O.P.; Fortunato Bodero, O.P.; Felix Martinez del Cura, O.P.; Jose Fernandez, O.P.; Isidoro Crespo, O.P.
Res., Box 46, 00698. Tel: 809-856-1222; Fax: 809-856-6845.
School—Box 26, 00698. Tel: 787-856-1001; Fax: 787-267-1238. Mrs. Judith Negron, Prin.
Students 658.
Convent—Tel: 787-856-1573. Sisters Of Fatima for Social Work Sr. Luisa Caraballo, O.P., Supr.
Sisters 16.
Missions—Collores, Sacred Heart; Duey, Virgin of Mt. Carmel; Barinas, St. James; Las Vegas, Sta. Teresita; Lluberas, St. Joseph; Cambalaches, Our Lady of Perpetual Help; Carrizales, Our Lady of Montserrat; Algarrobos, Our Lady of Fatima; Sierra Alta, St. Lucy; Almacigo Bajo, St. Martin de Porres; Naranjo, St. Anthony; Diego Hdez, St. Anthony; Quebradas, Sacred Heart; Aguas, St. Martin; Almacigo Alto, S. Juan Macias.

St. Martin de Porres (1969), Rev. Juan J. Saliva; Deacon Saba Gonzalez.
Res., Las Palomas, Box 2005, 00698. Tel: 787-856-3617.
Convent—Box 62, Santa Rita, 00698. Tel: 787-856-1476. Sisters of Fatima-Motherhouse Sr. Virgenmina Morell, O.P., Mother Gen.
Sisters 100; Novices 4.
Missions—Bo. Susa, Guanica Co., Santa Rita; Bo. Susa, Guanica Co., N.S. de La Providencia; Bo. Arenas de Guancia, Guancia Co., S. Martin de Porres; Bo. Susa, Yauco Co., S. Francisco de Asis; Bo. Susa, Yauco Co., N.S. de La Monserrate.

Special Assignment:
Reverend Monsignors—
Bellester, Pedro J., Pro-Vicar Gen.
Espona, Juan, Admin. & Vice Chancellor

On Duty Outside the Diocese:
Reverend Monsignors—
Abad, Federico, Paseo de los Cubos 1, Burgos, 09003 Spain
Reverend Fathers—
Alvarez, Pablo D., 110 W. 35th St., Apt. 3, Hialeah, FL 33012
Arguinzoniz, Francisco, Apartado 70, Durango, Vizcaya, Spain
Barrett, Kevin S., Chap., Apostolate of Family Consecration, P.O. Box 151, Bloomingdale, OH 43910-0151
Colon, Jose E., Colinas Montecarlo, Bldg. D-35, San Juan, PR 00927
DuChez, Daniel B., O.S., Carmel of the Holy Family, P.O. Box 1720, Georgetown, CA 95634
Duran, Alfonso M., M.J., Via Lorenzo il Magnifico 47, Int 7, Rome, 00162 Italy
Ewald, Daniel M.J., P.O. Box 348097, Chicago, IL 60634
Fernandez Cartagena, Elias, Jard. Arroyo, Calle D-D-13, Arroyo, PR 00714
Fletcher, Patrick, CMR 402 Box 1104, APO, AE 09180
Garcia, E. Roberto, B. Real Abajo KM 4, Ponce, PR 00731
Garcia, Salvador, Villafruela, Burgos, Spain
Gelis, Mark, M.J., Via Lorenzo il Magnifico 47, Int 7, Rome, 00162 Italy
Gusiora, Alphonsus, P.O. Box 61, Enugwu-Ukwu (Anambra State), Nigeria
Kelty, Edward, O.S., Via Concordia 1, Rome, 00183 Italy
Kuffel, Thomas P., O.S., Via Concordia 1, Rome, 00183 Italy
MacIssac, Charles S., O.S., 8828 Murphy Gulch Rd., Littleton, CO 80127
Malachowski, Christopher, O.S., Corpus Christi Institute, 703 Pinon Dr., Santa Fe, NM 87501
Margola, Joseph F., 1831 N. Cambridge Ave., Milwaukee, WI 53202-1001
Medina, George, P.O. Box 286, East Boston, MA 02128
Mezquida, Ramon, San Jose 4, Alqueria Condesa 46715, Valencia, Spain
Munoz, Rafael, P.O. Box 187, Barceloneta, PR 00657
Nicoletti, Robert, M.J., Via Lorenzo il Magnifico 47, Int 7, Rome, 00162 Italy
Nischan, James R., 1625 Mayo Ave., Owensboro, KY 42301
Porada, Casey, O.S., St. Mary's Rectory, 580 I St., David City, NE 68632
Quinones, Leoncio, Urb. Apolo, Guaynabo, PR 00657
Rodriguez, Plinio, Apartado 1918, Santo Domingo, Dominican Rep.
Sancho Piquer, Enrique, Calvario 49, 2, 4, Pafelbunoli, Valencia, Spain
Serrano, Dionisio, Maestro Ripoll 14, 28006 Madrid, Spain
Vota, Paul, M.J., P.O. Box 256528, Chicago, IL 60625
Weslin, Norman U., O.S., 151 Harvard St., Colorado Springs, CO 80911
Zayas, Antonio, Naranjito, PR 00767

Retired:
Reverend Monsignors—
Colon, Jose, Box 242, Merceditas, PR 00715
Irizarry, Raul, Marginal 11 Urb. Mercedita, Ponce, PR 00731
Reverend Fathers—
Cano, Emilio, Box 21012, Rio Piedras, PR 00928
Oria, Manuel, Box 242, Merceditas, 00715 PR
Pacho, Jesus, 2065 Ave. Las Americas, Apt. 207, Ponce, PR 00731-9427
Ramos, Fausto, Box 5081 HC-01, Villalba, PR 00766

INSTITUTIONS LOCATED IN THE DIOCESE

[A] SEMINARIES

PONCE. *Diocesan Seminary.* (Major Interdiocesan), Sta. 6, P.O. Box 110, 00732-2110. Tel: 787-848-4380; Fax: 787-848-4380. Rev. Msgr. Jesus R. Diez Antonanzas, Rector; Rev. Alfredo Alvarez Lacruz, Spiritual Dir. Priests 2; Lay Staff 2; Seminarians 11.

[B] COLLEGES & UNIVERSITIES

PONCE. *The Pontifical Catholic University of Puerto Rico,* 2250 Avenida de las Americas, 00731-6382. Tel: 787-841-2000
For a complete listing, refer to the Colleges and Universities section.

[C] SCHOOLS - INSTITUTES OF EDUCATION

PONCE. *Centro San Francisco.* Mailing Address: Box 10479, 00732. Tel: 787-844-2434; Fax: 787-842-2776. Sisters of St. Joseph. Sr. Anita Moseley, C.S.J., Prin. Sisters 3; Lay Teachers 22; Librarians 2; Social Workers 2; Counselor 1; Students 312.

Colegio El Ave Maria, Dr. Luis Bartolomei 6, Rep. Valle Alegre, 00731. Tel: 787-284-2453. Operarias del Divino Maestro. Sr. Milagros Pizarro, O.D.M., Prin. Sisters 4; Lay Teachers 9; Students 316.

Colegio Sagrado Corazon, Calle Obispado Final, 00731. Tel: 787-842-0339; Fax: 787-843-0250. Religious of the Sacred Heart. Mrs. Maria Serrano, Prin. Sisters 1; Lay Teachers 44; Students 645.

Holy Family School, Avenida Hostos 7, 00731. Tel: 787-842-3208; Fax: 787-844-6773. Sisters of Charity. Sr. Ediltrudis Acevedo, H.C., Prin. Sisters 5; Lay Teachers 20; Students 419.

COTO LAUREL. *Colegio Ponceno*. (Day School). Mailing Address: Colegio Ponceno, HC 06, Box 4701, 00780-9508. Tel: 787-848-2525; Fax: 787-259-4282. Piarists Fathers. Revs. Julio Torralba, Sch.P.; Juan L. Cabrerizo, Sch.P.; Benito Forcano, Sch.P.; Fernado Torres, Sch.P. Priests 4; Lay Teachers 64; Students 1,094.

PLAYA PONCE. *Centros Sor Isolina Ferre, Inc.*, P.O. Box 213, 00734. Tel: 787-843-1910. Missionary Servants of the Most Blessed Trinity. Sr. M. Isolina Ferre, M.S.B.T., CEO; Sr. Rosita M. Bauza, M.S.B.T., Exec. Dir. Center for social services, health and technical education, artistic, cultural, economic, domestic and spiritual formation. Priests 1; Sisters 5; Lay Teachers 40; Councilors 8; Coordinators 26; Community Lay Leaders 128; Students 3,040.

[D] HOMES FOR THE AGED

PONCE. *Home for Aged and Infirm*, Barrio Sabenetas, P.O. Box 2127, 00731. Tel: 787-840-7575
For a complete listing, refer to the Special Care Facilities section.

[E] MONASTERIES AND RESIDENCES OF PRIESTS AND BROTHERS

PONCE. *Residencia Asis*. (Postulantado), 342 Victoria St., Box 7244, 00732. Tel: 787-842-5055; Fax: 787-844-7267. Revs. Edward Maldonado, O.F.M.Cap., Guardian & Postulant Dir.; Roberto Martinez, O.F.M.Cap.; Francisco Garcia, O.F.M.Cap. Postulants 4.

[F] CONVENTS & RESIDENCES OF SISTERS

PONCE. *Convent Apostolate*. Mailing Address: Box 8300, 00732. Tel: 787-842-4340. Mother Rufina Nagore, R.A., Supr. Sisters Apostolate of the Sacred Heart of Jesus 17.

Convent of Servants of Mary, Ext. La Rambla, Calle Siervas de Maria 500, 00731. Tel: 787-842-2336. Mother Ana Gil, S.M., Supr. Religious 24; Postulants 3; Novices 10; Administered in the home 950.

PLAYA DE PONCE. *Blessed Trinity Missionary Cenacle*, Box 213, 00734. Tel: 787-844-1627. Sr. Isolina Ferre, M.S.B.T., Custodian; Sr. Rosita Maria Bauza, M.S.B.T., Coord. Sisters 5.

[G] PERSONAL PRELATURES

ALHAMBRA, PONCE. *Prelature of the Holy Cross and Opus Dei*, 8 Alcazar, 00731. Tel: 787-844-2661. Revs. Luis F. Montoya; Andres Eiroa.

[H] MISCELLANEOUS

PONCE. *Albergue La Providencia, Inc.*, P.O. Box 10142, 00732. Tel: 787-841-2119. Rev. Francisco Garcia, O.F.M.Cap., Dir. Refuge Center for AIDS patients. Total Assisted 40; Total Staff 30.

Apostolate for Family Consecration. Mailing Address: International Spanish Center, Box 205, Sta. 6, 00732. Tel: 787-848-5265.

Institucion Magdalena Aulina - Operarias Parroquiales. (Secular Institute), Simon de la Torre 43, 00731. Tel: 787-842-7209.

Miles Jesu, Ladies House, P.O. Box 165, Station 6, 00732. Tel: 787-840-9436. Men's House, Parroquia Santa Maria Reina, P.O. Box 166, Sta. 6, 00732. Tel: 787-848-5370.

Oblates of Wisdom. Mailing Address: Box 205, Sta. 6, 00732. Rev. Brian W. Harrison, O.S., Reg. Dir.

Pastoral Care of the Sick. Mailing Address: P.O. Box 205 Sta. 6, 00732. Tel: 787-844-2080 Ext. 1208, 787-848-7157. Sr. Teresa Jensen, C.S.J., Dir.

Shelter for the Homeless. Mailing Address: Misioneras De La Caridad, P.O. Box 177 Sta. 6, 00732. Tel: 787-841-5443. Sr. Mary Selma Thomas, M.C., Supr. Missionaries of Charity (Mother Theresa of Calcutta). Sisters 6; Residents 50; Total Assisted 80.

PENUELAS. *Training School for the Lay Apostolate (Hermanos Cheos)*. Mailing Address: P.O. Box 118, 00624. Rev. Msgr. Marcos A. Pancorbo, Dir.; Bro. William Perez Ramos, Pres. Brothers 97.

RELIGIOUS INSTITUTES OF MEN REPRESENTED IN THE DIOCESE

For further details refer to the corresponding bracketed number in the Religious Institutes of Men or Women section.

[0140]—*The Augustinians*.—O.S.A.
[0470]—*The Capuchin Friars (Vice Province of Puerto Rico)*.—O.F.M.Cap.
[0270]—*Carmelite Fathers & Brothers*.—O.Carm.
[1330]—*Congregation of the Mission*.—C.M.
[]—*Esclavos de la Eucaristia y Maria Virgen*.—S.E.M.V.
[0650]—*Holy Ghost Fathers*. (Eastern Prov.).—C.S.Sp.
[]—*Lumen Dei*.—L.D.
[]—*Operarios Del Reino De Cristo*.—O.R.C.
[0430]—*Order of Preachers-Dominicans*. (Holland Prov.).—O.P.
[1310]—*Order of the Holy Trinity*. (Spain).—O.SS.T.
[1040]—*Piarist Fathers*. (Spain).—Sch.P.
[1070]—*Redemptorist Fathers*. (San Juan Prov.).—C.SS.R.

RELIGIOUS INSTITUTES OF WOMEN REPRESENTED IN THE DIOCESE

[0130]—*Apostles of the Sacred Heart of Jesus*.—A.S.C.J.
[0340]—*Carmelite Sisters of Charity*.—C.a.Ch.
[]—*Congregacion Hermanas de N.S. del Perpetuo Socorro*.—N.S.P.S.
[1070-05]—*Dominican Sisters*.—O.P.
[]—*Hermanas Del-Amor De Dios*.
[]—*Hermanas Dominicas de Fatima*.—O.P.
[]—*Hermanas Terciarias Capuchinas de la Sagrada Familia (Coamo, Ponce)*.—T.C.
[]—*Hijas de la Caridad del Card. Sancha*.—H.C.C.S.
[2340]—*Little Sisters of the Poor*.—L.S.P.
[2710]—*Missionaries of Charity*.—M.C.
[2790]—*Missionary Servants of the Most Blessed Trinity*.—M.S.B.T.
[]—*Religious de los Santos Angeles Custodios (Adjuntas, Ponce)*.—R.A.C.
[3580]—*Servants of Mary*.—O.S.M.
[]—*Sisters of Charity of St. Vincent de Paul*.—H.C.
[]—*Sisters of St. Joseph*.—S.S.J.
[2150]—*Sisters, Servants of the Immaculate Heart of Mary*.—I.H.M.

NECROLOGY

† Vazquez, Elion, (Retired). —Died Aug. 19, 1997.

Diocese of Samoa-Pago Pago

Most Reverend

JOHN QUINN WEITZEL, M.M.

Bishop of Samoa-Pago Pago; ordained June 11, 1955; appointed First Bishop of Samoa-Pago Pago October 29, 1986. *Fatuoaiga: P.O. Box 596, Pago Pago, American Samoa, 96799.* Tel.: 684-699-1402; Fax: 684-699-1459.

E-mail address: QUINN@samoatelco.com

CREATED A DIOCESE NOVEMBER, 1982.

The Diocese of Samoa-Pago Pago includes the islands of Tutuila; Swains; Manu'a Is., Ofu, Olosega & Ta'u; Aunu'u and Rose Island.

STATISTICAL OVERVIEW

Personnel	
Bishop	1
Priests: Diocesan Active in Diocese	9
Number of Diocesan Priests	9
Religious Priests in Diocese	1
Permanent Deacons in Diocese	19
Total Sisters	13
Parishes	
Parishes	9
With Resident Pastor:	
Resident Diocesan Priests	8
Without Resident Pastor:	
Administered by Lay People	1
Missions	1
New Parishes Created	1
Professional Ministry Personnel:	
Sisters	13
Lay Ministers	23
Welfare	
Homes for the Aged	1
Total Assisted	26
Day Care and Extended Day Care Centers	1
Total Assisted	105
Special Centers for Social Services	1
Total Assisted	560

Educational	
Diocesan Students in Other Seminaries	11
Total Seminarians	11
High Schools, Diocesan and Parish	2
Total Students	305
Elementary Schools, Diocesan and Parish	2
Total Students	433
Catechesis/Religious Education:	
High School Students	250
Elementary Students	1,826
Total Students Under Catholic Instruction	2,825
Teachers in the Diocese:	
Sisters	5
Lay Teachers	42

Vital Statistics	
Receptions into the Church:	
Infant Baptism Totals	302
Adult Baptism Totals	62
Received into Full Communion	62
First Communions	34
Confirmations	6
Marriages:	
Catholic	43
Interfaith	2
Total Marriages	45
Deaths	55
Total Catholic Population	11,405
Total Population	58,070

Vicar General of Diocese—Rev. MIKAELE FALANIKO.

Chancellor—IVONA T. MAUGA.

Diocesan Consultors—Revs. VAN CAMP TAVAI; MASELINO PAULO; MIKAELE FALANIKO.

Bishop's Pastoral Council—Rev. MIKAELE FALANIKO, Chm.; Mrs. MARILYN ANESI, Sec.

Fatu-O-Aiga Multipurpose Cultural and Pastoral Center—Pastoral Team: Rev. VAN CAMP TAVAI, Dir. Rev. EMANI TEVAGA, Faculty Member.

Sagata Ana Society—Mrs. ISAPELA IESE.

Sacred Heart Society—AGNES GABBARD.

Vicar for Youth—TAGATAESE MAUGAOTEGA, F.K., Dir. of Youth.

Director of Vocations—Rev. VIANE ETUALE.

Port Chaplain—Deacon NIKOLAO PULA.

Hospital Chaplain—Deacon CATECHIST LAFAELE AUNOA, F.K.

Prison Chaplain—Deacon TOETOFI TAVALE, F.K.

Director of Propagation of the Faith—Rev. PETELO SILIAKO.

CLERGY, PARISHES, MISSIONS AND PAROCHIAL SCHOOLS

SAMOA-PAGO PAGO

1—CATHEDRAL OF THE HOLY FAMILY (1986), Most Rev. John Quinn Weitzel, M.M.; Rev. Viane Etuale; Deacons Anetele'a Puletasi; Lito Roque; Francis Leasiolagi; Toetofi Tavale; Edward Simon. In res., Rev. James Lenihan, M.M.
Mailing Address: Fatuoaiga, P.O. Box 3594, 96799-3594. Tel: 684-699-1446; Fax: 684-699-1459.
Catechesis/Religious Programs—Tel: 684-699-2209; Fax: 684-699-1459. D.R.E.: Deacons Lito Roque; Toetofi Tavale; Mrs. Iacinta Muliagatele. Students 530.
Mission—Manu'a Island, Mary, Star of the Sea, Tel: 684-677-3103.

2—CO-CATHEDRAL OF ST. JOSEPH THE WORKER (Fagatogo) (1974), Rev. Emani Tevaga, Admin.; Deacons Lutia Timoteo; Nikolao Pula; Tavita Pereira.
Mailing Address: Fagatogo, P.O. Box AA, 96799. Tel: 684-633-1548.
Catechesis/Religious Programs—Students 235.
Missions—Utulei; Fagasa, Tel: 684-633-1352; Pago Pago, Tel: 684-633-4035; Faga'alu, Tel: 684-633-2560.

3—CHRIST THE KING (Malaeloa) (1983), Paselio Lemalu, F.K., Admin. & Catechist; Deacon Aukuso Gabriel.
Mailing Address: P.O. Box 596, 96799. Tel: 684-699-1402; Fax: 684-699-1459.
Catechesis/Religious Programs—Deacon Tagataese Maugaotega, D.R.E. Students 195.

4—CHURCH OF ST. PAUL (Ili'ili) (1974), Rev. Van Camp Tavai. Pastoral Assocs.: Deacons Sagapolutele Malaeola; Naisina Ma'ileoli.
Mailing Address: Ili'ili, P.O. Box 2004, 96799. Tel: 684-688-7671; Fax: 684-699-1459.
Office: Fatuoaiga—P.O. Box 596, 96799. Tel: 684-699-5710.
Catechesis/Religious Programs—Deacon Naisina Ma'ileoi, D.R.E. Students 315.
Missions—Faleniu,; Futiga, Tel: 684-688-7765; Pava'ia'i, Tel: 684-688-7653; Aasu/Aoloau, Tel: 684-688-9766.

5—CHURCH OF ST. PETER AND PAUL (Lauli'i) (1969), Rev. Msgr. Etuale Lealofi; Deacons Setefano Lesa; Fred Pele.
Mailing Address: P.O. Box 985, 96799. Tel: 684-644-5581; Fax: 684-644-2582.
Catechesis/Religious Programs—Tel: 684-644-4697. D.R.E.: Lafaele Mageo; Teofilo Laulu; Vitaliano Iosefo. Students 158.
Missions—Masefau, Tel: 684-622-7131; Faga'itua, Tel: 684-622-7130; Sa'ilele.

6—CHURCH OF THE HOLY CROSS (Leone) (1861), Revs. Mikaele Falaniko; Falniko Atonio.
Mailing Address: Leone, P.O. Box 1206, 96799. Tel: 684-688-7663; Fax: 684-699-1459.
Mission—Amaluia.
Catechesis/Religious Programs—D.R.E.: Asalemo Taulamano; Iolesio Iosefo. Students 510.

7—CHURCH OF THE IMMACULATE CONCEPTION (Lepua) (1867), Rev. Sebastian Chacko, Admin.
Mailing Address: Lepua, P.O. Box 398, 96799. Tel: 684-644-5512; Fax: 684-644-2427. [CEM]
Catechesis/Religious Programs—Tel: 684-644-2411. D.R.E.: Paulo Luamanu; Timoteo Tatino; Fili Afoa. Students 250.
Missions—Afono, Tel: 684-644-4797; Aua, Tel: 684-644-5826.

8—CHURCH OF SACRED HEART (Alao) (1989), Rev. Petelo Siliako; Deacon Sogimaletavai Leo.
Mailing Address: Alao, P.O. Box 4175, 96799. Tel: 684-622-7029; Fax: 684-699-1459.
Catechesis/Religious Programs—Students 21.
Missions—Aoa, Tel: 684-622-7416; Amouli, Tel: 684-622-7613.

Permanent Deacons:
Auelua, Ukirifi
Aunoa, Lafaele
Folau, Kalini
Gabriel, August
Lafaele, Setefano
Leasiolagi, Francis
Leo, Herman Sogimaletavai
Ma'ileoi, Naisina
Maugaotega, Tagataese
Pele, Tupuaga Fred
Pereira, Tavita
Pula, Taafulisia Nikolao
Puletasi, Niuatoa Andy

Roque, Rolito
Sagapolutele, Anthony Malaeola
Simon, Edward
Tavale, Toetofi
Timoteo, Lutia Laupapa
Toilolo, Felise

INSTITUTIONS LOCATED IN THE DIOCESE

[A] PRESCHOOLS

PAGO PAGO. *Mary The Mother Montessori Pre-School*, c/o Diocese of Samoa-Pago Pago, Fatuoaiga-P.O. Box 596, 96799. Tel: 684-699-1402; Fax: 684-699-1459. Sisters 1; Lay Teachers 6; Students 80.

[B] ELEMENTARY SCHOOLS, PAROCHIAL

LEONE. *St. Theresa*, P.O. Box 883, 96799-0596; Fax: 684-688-1114. Missionary Sisters of the Society of Mary. Sr. Palepa Ioane, S.M.S.M., Prin. & Supr. Sisters 3; Lay Teachers 10; Students 258.

LEPUA. *St. Francis/Marist*, Fatuoaiga, P.O. Box 429, 96799-0429; Fax: 684-699-1459. Missionary Sisters of the Society of Mary. Sr. Mary de Paul, S.M.S.M., Prin. & Supr. Sisters 1; Lay Teachers 11; Students 175.

[C] HIGH SCHOOLS, PAROCHIAL

LEPUAPUA. *Fa'asao High School*, P.O. Box 729, 96799; Fax: 684-688-2055.
E-mail: fa'asao@samoatelco.com
Mrs. Veronika Mortenson Mata'utia, Prin.; Catherine Satele, Co-Admin. Sisters 2; Lay Teachers 10; Volunteer Lay Missionaries 1; Students 184.

MALAELOA. *Marist High School*, Fatuoaiga, P.O. Box K, 96799; Fax: 684-688-2336. Mrs. Lina Galea'i-Scanlan, Prin.; Paselino Lemalu, Vice Prin. Lay Teachers 6; Students 130.

[D] HOMES FOR AGED & SPECIAL CARE FOR CHILDREN

PAGO PAGO. *Nazareth House*, P.O. Box 1510, 96799. Tel: 684-699-2101; Fax: 684-699-1459
For a complete listing, refer to the Special Care Facilities section.

[E] MISCELLANEOUS

PAGO PAGO. *Catholic Social Services, Inc.*, P.O. Box 596, 96799. Tel: 684-699-5683; Fax: 684-699-1459.
E-mail: quinn@samoatelco.com
Ms. Theresa Griffith, M.S.W., Dir. Total Assisted 560; Total Staff 3.

RELIGIOUS INSTITUTES OF MEN REPRESENTED IN THE DIOCESE

For further details refer to the corresponding bracketed number in the Religious Institutes of Men or Women section.

[0800]—*Maryknoll.*—M.M.

RELIGIOUS INSTITUTES OF WOMEN REPRESENTED IN THE DIOCESE

[2420]—*Marist Missionary Sisters, Inc. (Missionary Sisters of the Society of Mary).*—S.M.S.M.
[2470]—*Maryknoll Sisters of St. Dominic.*—M.M.
[3242]—*Poor Sisters of Nazareth.*—P.S.O.N.
[]—*Religious Sisters of the Virgin Mary.*—R.V.M.

NECROLOGY

(No Deaths)

Archdiocese of San Juan, Puerto Rico

(Sancti Joannis Portoricensis)

His Eminence

LUIS CARDINAL APONTE MARTINEZ, D.D.

Archbishop of San Juan; ordained April 10, 1950; appointed Titular Bishop of Lares and Auxiliary of Ponce July 23, 1960; consecrated October 12, 1960; appointed Coadjutor Bishop of Ponce April 16, 1963; appointed Bishop of Ponce November 18, 1963; installed February 20, 1964; promoted to Archbishop of San Juan November 4, 1964; installed January 15, 1965; Created Cardinal March 5, 1973. *Res., 50 Cristo St., P.O. Box S-1967, San Juan, PR, 00903.* Tel.: 809-725-4975; 727-7373 (Office).

Most Reverend

FRANCOIS BACQUE

Apostolic Delegate for Puerto Rico. *Office: Ponce de Leon Ave. #256, San Juan, PR, 00907. Mailing Address: P.O. Box 191771, San Juan, PR, 00919-1771.* Tel.: 809-723-1280; Fax: 809-723-1280.

Most Reverend

HECTOR M. RIVERA, D.D.

Titular Bishop of Tubune in Numidia and Auxiliary Bishop of San Juan, PR; ordained June 12, 1966; appointed June 11, 1979; consecrated August 17, 1979. *Res., Lomas de Carolina, Calle Yunquecito UU #18, Carolina, PR, 00987.* Tel.: 727-7373. *Mailing Address: P.O. Box 1967, San Juan, PR, 00902-1967.*

Most Reverend

HERMIN NEGRON SANTANA, D.D.

Titular Bishop of Gegi, North Africa and Auxiliary Bishop of San Juan, PR; ordained May 30, 1969; appointed June 30, 1981; consecrated September 7, 1981. *Res., Calle 6, D-9 Urb. Royal Town, Bayamon, PR, 00956.* Tel.: 809-730-4310. *Archbishop's Office: San Jorge St., No. 201, Santurce, P.P. Mailing Address: P.O. Box S-1967, San Juan, PR, 00903.* Tel.: 809-727-7373.

ERECTED AUGUST 8, 1511.

ERECTED AN ARCHDIOCESE APRIL 30, 1960.

Square Miles 353.

Comprises the northeast portion of the Island of Puerto Rico, with a Total Population of 1,260,000.

Chancery Office: P.O. Box S-1967, San Juan, PR, 00902.

STATISTICAL OVERVIEW

Personnel	
Cardinal	1
Archbishop	1
Auxiliary Bishops	2
Priests: Diocesan Active in Diocese	142
Priests: Active Outside Diocese	1
Priests: Retired, Sick or Absent	11
Number of Diocesan Priests	154
Religious Priests in Diocese	145
Ordinations:	
Religious Priests	2
Transitional Deacons	1
Permanent Deacons	16
Permanent Deacons in Diocese	260
Total Brothers	36
Total Sisters	433
Parishes	
Parishes	152
With Resident Pastor:	
Resident Diocesan Priests	102
Resident Religious Priests	50
Without Resident Pastor:	
Pastoral Centers	150
Welfare	
Catholic Hospitals	2
Total Assisted	19,325
Health Care Centers	2
Total Assisted	381
Homes for the Aged	5
Total Assisted	954
Residential Care of Children	3
Total Assisted	110
Day Care and Extended Day Care Centers	37
Total Assisted	1,295
Specialized Homes	2
Total Assisted	60
Educational	
Seminaries, Diocesan	2
Students from This Diocese	25
Diocesan Students in Other Seminaries	9
Seminaries, Religious	6
Students Religious	22
Total Seminarians	56
Colleges and Universities	2
Total Students	9,620
High Schools, Diocesan and Parish	20
Total Students	5,411
High Schools, Private	30
Total Students	6,780
Elementary Schools, Diocesan and Parish	27
Total Students	10,806
Elementary Schools, Private	42
Total Students	14,136
Catechesis/Religious Education:	
High School Students	4,902
Elementary Students	19,711
Total Students Under Catholic Instruction	71,422
Teachers in the Diocese:	
Priests	34
Scholastics	2
Brothers	20
Sisters	130
Lay Teachers	2,210
Vital Statistics	
Receptions into the Church:	
Infant Baptism Totals	12,642
Adult Baptism Totals	1,172
First Communions	7,716
Confirmations	5,557
Marriages:	
Catholic	2,404
Interfaith	142
Total Marriages	2,546
Total Catholic Population	886,994
Total Population	1,233,743

Former Bishops—Rev. ALONSO MANSO, D.D., appt. May 1513.—Most Rev. JAMES H. BLENK, S.M.D.D., appt. Bishop of Puerto Rico, June 12, 1899; died April 20, 1917.—Most Rev. WILLIAM A. JONES, O.S.A., cons. Feb. 24, 1907; died Jan. 1921.—Most Rev. GEORGE J. CARUANA, D.D., promoted to the Apostolic Delegation of Mexico, 1925; promoted to Nunciature Apostolic of Cuba, 1927.—Most Rev. EDWIN VINCENT BRYNE, D.D., former Bishop of Ponce, Puerto Rico; cons. Nov. 30, 1925; appt. March 1929; promoted to Archdiocese of Santa Fe, June 15, 1943; died July 25, 1963.—Most Rev. JAMES PETER DAVIS, cons. Oct. 9, 1943; transferred to Archdiocese of Santa Fe, June, 1943; installed Feb. 25, 1964; retired Oct. 1974.

Vicars General—Most Rev. HECTOR RIVERA, D.D.; Most Rev. HERMIN NEGRON SANTANA, D.D.; Rev. Msgr. CELESTINO LINERA.

Episcopal Vicars—

for Administration of Temporalities—Rev. Msgr. BAUDILIO MERINO.

for Religious Women for Education—Rev. Msgr. BAUDILIO MERINO.

for Pastoral Affairs—Most Rev. HECTOR RIVERA.

for Geographic-Pastoral Zones—San Juan-Santurce: Rev. JUAN MARTINEZ, S.D.B., Bayamon: Rev. DANIEL TRUJILLO, Carolina: Rev. JOAQUIN RIVERA, Rio Piedras: Rev. REINALDO SAGARDIA, Rio Grande: Rev. EMILIO TORO FRANCO, Guaynabo-Puerto Nuevo: Rev. MARIO A. GUIJARRO.

Chancery Office—P.O. Box S-1967, San Juan, 00902.

Chancery Affairs—Rev. Msgr. C. LINERA.

Metropolitan Tribunal—

Moderator—His Eminence LUIS CARDINAL APONTE.

Judicial Vicar—Rev. Msgr. JAIME CAPO.

Adjunt Judicial Vicars—Revs. REINALDO SAGARDIA; SALVADOR RODRIGO, O.C.

Judges—Revs. LUIS O. CAPACETTI; REINALDO SAGARDIA; Rev. Msgr. FERNANDO FELICES.

Defenders of the Bond—Rev. FLORENTINO SANZ.

Instructors—Vacant.

Diocesan Consultors—Most Rev. HERMIN NEGRON SANTANA, D.D.; Most Rev. HECTOR RIVERA; Rev. Msgr. CELESTINO LINERA; Rev. Msgr. RAFAEL FONTANEZ; Rev. Msgr. JAMIE CAPO; Rev. Msgr. BAUDILIO MERINO; Rev. Msgr. FERNANDO FELICES.

Censor Librorum—Vacant.

Examinatores Cleri—Vacant.

Pro-Synodal Examiner—Vacant.

Archdiocesan Offices and Directors

Boy Scouts—Rev. LORENZO RUIZ, S.D.B., *Calle Lutz 370, Santurce.*

Catechetics—Most Rev. HECTOR RIVERA, Archdiocesan Coord., *Calle San Jorge 201, Santurce, 00914.*

Catechetics Center—San Juan-Santurce: Sr. ROSA MA. REYES; Sr. MARTA TOBON, Bayamon: Sr. IMELDA

MORALES, Rio Piedras: Sr. AILEEN BARDEN, Guaynabo-Ptonuevo: Sr. ROSE MORALES, Rio Grande: Sr. MARTHA L. GIL, Carolina: Sr. MARIA EUGENIA MORENO.

Catholic Social Action—Sr. CLOTILDE ARCE, H.C., Dir.

Children of Mary—Vacant.

Christian Family Movement—Rev. DAMIAN ARTIAGA, Dir., *Pastoral Office, Ave. Americo Miranda No. 1161, Reparto Metropolitano, Rio Piedras, 00921.* Tel: 809-783-4952.

Commission for Commun—Vacant.

"El Visitante"—Weekly Catholic Paper for All Dioceses (Interdiocesan). Published By The P.R., Episcopal Conference. Most Rev. INAKI MALLONA, C.P., Pres.; Rev. EFRAIN ZABALA, Editor; Dr. ANIBAL COLON ROSADO, Dir., *Mailing Address: P.O. Box 41305, Minillas Sta., Santurce, 00940-1305.* Tel: 809-728-3710; 728-3656. Offices: *Pumarada St. 1704, Santurce, 00914.*

Radio Stations—WORO and WKVM, *c/o Box 1967, San Juan, 00903.*

Television Station—WPRV-TV CHANNEL 13, *Carolina.*

Commission for Sacred Art—Dr. ARTURO DAVILA, *Univ. of Puerto Rico, Rio Piedras, 00921.*

Commission for Sacred Liturgy—Vacant.

Commission for Sacred Music—Rev. Msgr. FRANCISCO ARENAS, Chm., *Calle Encarnacion, No. 1564, Caparra Heights, 00920.*

Clergy Social Security (Prevision Social del Clero)—Revs. ARMANDO ALVAREZ, Pres. VIRGILIO MARTINEZ, Treas. PEDRO CAMPANA, Sec., *San Jose, Bloque ZM-215, Urb. Villa Caparra, Guaynabo, 00657.*

Cursillos De Cristiandad—Rev. Msgr. JAIME CAPO; Rev. VINCENTE FERNANDEZ-MARINO, *G.P.O. Box 1809, San Juan, 00936.*

Emigrant Aid—Sr. CLOTILDE ARCE, H.C.

Holy Childhood Association—Rev. PRISCILO MANUEL CARDENAS, D.D., *106 Ruiz Belvis St.66, Floral Park, P.O. Box 1882, Hato Rey, 00917.* Tel: 809-754-0995.

Holy Name Society—Rev. TEODORO VEERKAMP, O.P., *P.O. Box 1968, Bayamon, 00619.*

Hospitals—925 Isaura Arnau St., Country Club, Rio Piedras, 00924.

Istepa—Instituto Superior de Teologia y Pastoral, Apartado 11, 714 Caparra Heights Sta., Rio Piedras, 00920. Tel: 809-792-5320; 792-5324.

Labor Relations—Vacant.

Legion of Mary—Deacon JOSE LUIS PORRATA, *P.O. Box 5037, Puerta de Tierra Sta., San Juan, 00906.*

Marriage Encounter—1161 Americo Miranda Ave., Rio Piedras, 00921. Tel: 809-752-3163.

Master of Ceremonies to the Cardinal—Deacon PEDRO AREVALO.

Movimiento "Por Un Mundo Mejor"—Rev. JUAN J. GENOVARD, M.SS.CC., *Calle Duke 211, University Gardens, Rio Piedras, 00927.* Tel: 809-765-2255; 765-8042.

Nocturnal Adoration—Vacant.

Operation Head Start—862 Carmen Hernandez St., El Comandante, Rio Piedras, 00924. Tel: 809-752-5762; 752-3040.

Head Start-Municipality of San Juan—Rev. FRANCISCO RUBALCABA, Dir., *900 Eider St., Country Club, Rio Piedras, 00924.* Tel: 809-768-0580; 757-1913.

Our Lady of Providence Association—Vacant.

Perpetual Adoration—Rev. FRANCISCO QUINONES, Dir.; Mrs. VIRGINIA ALVAREZ, Asst., *Mailing Address: Box S-763, San Juan, 00902.* Tel: 809-725-7734.

Pius Union of the Clergy—Rev. Msgr. CELESTINO LINERA, *Mailing Address: P.O. Box 1967, San Juan, 00903.*

Propagation of the Faith—Rev. PRISCILO MANUEL CARDENAS, *100 Ruiz Belvis St., Floral Park, P.O. Box 1882, Hato Rey, 00917.*

Santa Maria de los Angeles Seminary—Rev. Msgr. FERNANDO FELICES, Rector & Promoter of Vocations; Rev. IVAN HUERTAS COLON, *Mailing Address: P.O. Box 11, 714, Caparra Heights Sta., Rio Piedras, 00922.* Tel: 809-781-6166; 783-1919. *Ave. De Diego 930, Urb. La Riviera, Rio Piedras, 00921.*

San Jose Minor Seminary—Rev. FREDDY ALECIO, Rector, *Demetrio O'Dally St. 1000, Country Club, Rio Piedras, 00924.* Tel: 809-768-3157.

Serra Clubs—Calle Encarnacion 1564, Caparra Heights, Rio Piedras, 00922., Mailing Address: P.O. Box 11, 238 Caparra Heights, Sta., Rio Piedras, 00920. Tel: 809-783-1919.

Society For The Protection of Children—His Eminence LUIS CARDINAL APONTE MARTINEZ, Dir. Admin., *Mailing Address: P.O. Box S-1967, San Juan, 00903.* Tel: 809-727-7373.

Superintendent of Schools—Mr. RAFAEL MORALES, Supt.; Mrs. BLANCA MARQUEZ, Asst.; Rev. EDDIE RIVERA, Religion Program Dir., Mailing Address: *Pumarada 1708, Santurce, 00912.* Tel: 809-268-6700; 268-6980.

War Against Hunger—Mrs. BERTA ALVIRA DE RODRIQUEZ, *San Jorge St., No. 201, Santurce, 00914., Mailing Address: P.O. Box 8812, Santurce, 00910.* Tel: 809-767-3348; 727-7373.

Young Catholic Action—Vacant, *c/o P.O. Box S-1967, San Juan, 00903.*

Young Christian Students—Bro. BENJAMIN, F.S.C., *40 Betances St., Bayamon, 00619.*

Young Catholic University Students—Rev. BAUDILIO GUZMAN, S.J., *Mariana Bracetti 10, Rio Piedras, 00925.* Tel: 809-767-3348.

Young Christian Workers—Vacant.

CLERGY, PARISHES, MISSIONS AND PAROCHIAL SCHOOLS

CITY OF SAN JUAN

1—CATEDRAL DE SAN JUAN BAUTISTA (1522). (Nuestra Sra. de los Remedios). Rev. Raul Saez Munoz, Rector.
Res., 151 Cristo St., Box S-2145, 00903. Tel: 809-722-0861.
Chapels—Santo Cristo.; Santa Ana.

2—SAN AGUSTIN (1889), Revs. Tomas J. Travers, C.SS.R.; Robert Gaugler, C.SS.R.; James McSwigan, C.SS.R.; Miguel A. Garcia, C.SS.R. In res., Revs. Jose Rached, C.SS.R., Prov. Supr.; Juan A. Gaucci, C.SS.R.
Res., 265 Ponce de Leon Ave., Pta. de Tierra, 00902. Tel: 787-722-4289; Fax: 787-725-7737.
School—Colegio San Agustin, P.O. Box 9066557, 00906.
225 Ponce de Leon Ave., Box 5007, 00902. Tel: 809-722-4544. Marie Benitez Alonso, Prin.
Lay Teachers 15; Students 313.

3—NUESTRA SENORA DE LA ALTAGRACIA (1968), Rev. Franco Gutierrez (Spain); Deacon Ildefonso Lugo.
Mailing Address: Apartado 29493, 65 Inf. Sta., Rio Piedras, 00924-9493.
Res., Calle Felipe Gutierrez 672, Urb. Villa Prades, Rio Piedras, 00924. Tel: 809-765-0281.
School—Tel: 809-763-7755; Fax: 809-756-5195. Mrs. Zaida Silva, Prin.
Priests 1; Sisters 2; Lay Teachers 3; Students 433.

4—SAN ANTONIO (1908), Revs. Juan Benarick, Vice Prov.; Jose Antonio Cruz; Ramon H. Negron.
Res., Calle Arzuaga #218, Esq. Frailes Capuchinos, Apartado 21350, 00928. Tel: 787-765-0606; 765-1180; Fax: 787-764-4070.
School—Tel: 787-764-0090. Principals: Jeannette Freeman, Preschool; Fe Villafane, Elementary; Miguel Rosa, Intermediate & High School.
Priests 2; Sisters 2; Lay Teachers 77; Students 1,365.
Mission—Nuestra Senora del Buen Consejo.

5—ASUNCION DE LA VIRGEN (1972), Rev. P. Juan Santa.
Res., Calle Calve No., Urb. Antonsanti, Rio Piedras, 00928. Tel: 787-250-6771.

6—NUESTRA SENORA DE BELEN (1960), Rev. Joaquin Mansilla.
Mailing Address: P.O. Box 10,845, Caparra Heights, 00922. Tel: 809-792-3014; 792-3115; 793-2485.
Res., Ave., San Patricio Calle 6 (Final), Guaynabo.
School—Principals: Lilia Rivera; Rosa B. Pintor.
Priests 1; Lay Teachers 73; Students 1,128.

7—NTR. SRA. DE LA CARIDAD DEL COBRE (1969), Rev. Pablo Hughes, O.M.I.; Bro. Val LeClerc, O.M.I.
Mailing Address: Box 4023, 00936-4023.
Res., Urb. Buena Vista, Calle 5, No. 124, Hato Rey, 00917. Tel: 787-753-0108.
Mission—Hato Rey, Sma. Trinidad, Calle Buenos Aires, No. 25, Parada 27, Hato Rey 00919.

8—NUESTRA SENORA DEL CARMEN (1923), Rev. P. William Torres Pagan.
Mailing Address: P.O. Box 7275, Bo. Obrero Sta., Santurce, 00916-7275. Tel: 787-727-0737.
Res., Ave., Borinquen, Esq., Calle 8, Num. 609, Barrio Obrero, Santurce, 00916.
School—Father Berrios, Tel: 787-726-4851; Fax: 787-728-4860. Sr. Carmen Herrera Acevedo, H.C.C.S., Prin.
Sisters 3; Lay Teachers 9; Students 241.
Mission—San Martin de Porres.

9—SANTA CATALINA LABOURE (1977), Rev. Hilario Rivera Gonzalez.
Mailing Address: Ruta RFD 6, Box 9972, Rio Piedras, 00928. Tel: 809-720-0303.
Res., Barrio Caimito, Rio Piedras, 00928.
Missions—Medalla Milagrosa; San Pablo.

10—SANTA CECILIA (1969), Rev. Jose Ma. Lopez Mairal; Deacon Victor Merced de la Paz.
Mailing Address: P.O. Box 415, El Senorial Sta., 00926-0415.
Res., Carr Cupey Km. 3 Hm. 8, Rio Piedras, 00926. Tel: 787-755-8670; 761-5461 (Parish House).
Chapels—Asilo Santa Teresa Jornet, Tel: 787-761-5805; Fax: 787-755-5575; Capilla San Augustin.

11—CORPUS CHRISTI, Rev. Pablo Valenzuela; Deacons Francisco Gierbolini; Miguel Mendez; Luis R. Perez; Juan Figueroa; Rene Morales; Reinaldo Del Valle; Jose Perez.
Res., Calle Jose Abad, 1224 Urb. Club Manor, Rio Piedras, 00924. Tel: 809-757-5821.
Mission—Santo Domingo.

12—CRISTO REDENTOR, Rev. Damian Carvajal.
Res., Calle Ganges 140, Urb. El Paraiso, Rio Piedras, 00926. Tel: 809-764-1583.

13—CRISTO REY (1965), Rev. Msgr. Antonio Gomez; Deacon Victor Reyes.
Mailing Address: P.O. Box 29695, 65 Inf., Rio Piedras, 00929-0695.
Res., Calle Jaime Drew, No. 789, Urb. Los Maestros, Rio Piedras, 00929. Tel: 809-767-3289.
School—Tel: 809-767-0922. Sr. Jacinta Gutierrez, H.T.F., Prin.
Sisters 2; Lay Teachers 15.

14—NUESTRA SENORA DE LA ESPERANZA (1962), Rev. Carlos Dionisio Cruz.
Res., Calle Republica No. 864, Urb. Hipodromo, Parada 20, Box, Santurce, 00910. Tel: 809-723-5998.
Mission—Ntra. Sra. de la Providencia.
Chapel—Doctors Hospital.

15—ESPIRITU SANTO (1941), Rev. Valeriano Miguelez.
Res., 74 Ruiz Belvis St., Floral Park, Box 259, Hato Rey, 00919. Tel: 809-754-0570.
School—75 Ruiz Belvis Ave., Box 1715, Tel: 809-754-0490; 754-0555. Sr. Enedina Santos, Prin.
Priests 1; Lay Teachers 36; Students 713.
Chapel—Hospital Ntra. Sra. de Guadalupe.

16—NTRA. SRA. DE FATIMA (1967), Revs. Julio Fernandez Dominguez, O.M.; Martin Garamendi, O.M.; Jose M. Gallego, O.M.; Javier Gutierrez, O.M.
Mailing Address: P.O. Box 190396, 00919-0396.
Res., 608 Munoz Rivera Ave., Stop 34, Urb. Baldrich. Hato Rey, Box 396, Hato Rey, 00919.
School—La Merced, (1949), Box 606, 00919. Tel: 809-765-2388; 765-7342; 754-1162. Mrs. Rita Saveedra de Bravo, Prin., Tel: 809-766-3181.
Lay Teachers 36; Students 754.
Mission—Egida del Maestro.

17—FRANCISCA JAVIERA CABRINI (1967). (Santa Madre Cabrini). Rev. Msgr. Francisco Arenas; Rev. Rogelio Carod; Deacon Francisco Huertas.
Res., 1564 Encarnacion St., Caparra Heights, 00920. Tel: 809-783-7447; 782-0517 (College).
School—Colegio Madre Cabrini, Tel: 809-792-6180; 792-8745. Sr. M. Sacred Heart, O.S.F., Prin. Elementary. High School Principals: Sr. Ann Marie Gavin; Mrs. Mayra Mendez.
Sisters 3; Lay Teachers 36; Students 411.

18—SAN FRANCISCO DE ASIS (1858), Rev. Ramon Jaime Casellas, O.F.M.Cap.
Res., 301 San Francisco St., Box 9024231, 00902. Tel: 787-724-1131; Fax: 787-721-4616.
Mission—San Juan, Capilla San Conrado, Bo. La Perla, 00902.

19—SAN FRANCISCO DE MONTE ALVERNIA, Rev. David Arrieta.
Res., Calle 10 #15 Ext. San Augustin, Rio Piedras, 00926. Tel: 809-765-8824.

20—SAN FRANCISCO JAVIER, Rev. Perfecto Fondevila; Deacons Elidio Aldarondo; Abel De Varona; Jose Hernandez.
Res., Calle 19, G46. Urb. Fair View, Barrio Cupey Bajo, Rio Piedras, 00926. Tel: 809-761-2115.

21—NUESTRA SRA. DE GUADALUPE (1951), Rev. Juan Miranda; Deacon Andres Figueroa.
Mailing Address: G.P.O. Box 4125, 00936. Tel: 809-782-0016.
Res., 19th St., N.E. No. 1, Puerto Nuevo, 00920.
School—Tel: 809-782-0330; Fax: 809-781-3139. Mrs. Teresita Hernandez, Prin.
Lay Teachers 35; Students 860.

22—SAN IGNACIO DE LOYOLA (1958), Revs. Fabian Rodriguez, S.J.; Jorge Ferrer, S.J.; Jorge Ambert, S.J.; Guillermo Arias, S.J.
Res., Calle Narciso 1904, Rio Piedras, 00927-6706. Tel: 809-751-7680.
Jesuit Community—Revs. Juan J. Santiago, S.J.; Carlos J. Lavergne, S.J.; William J. Hendricks, S.J.; Juan Lopez Pedraz, S.J.; Francisco Marrero, S.J.; Jose Angel Borges, S.J.; Francisco Santiago, S.J.; Arthur A. Clarke, S.J.; Alberto Villaverde, S.J.; Baudilio Guzman, S.J.; Frank Golden, S.J.; Donald Vega, S.J.; Alfredo Guzman, S.J.; Walter Janer, S.J.; Bro. Jose Feliz, S.J.
Res., Calle Sauco 1940, Rio Piedras, 00927-6728. Tel: 809-765-3814.
School—Tel: 809-765-8190. Rev. Juan J. Santiago, S.J., Prin.
Sisters 2; Lay Teachers 18; Students 862.
Chapel—Hospital Psiquiatria.

23—INMACULADO CORAZON DE MARIA (1961), Rev. Msgr. Rafael Matienzo; Deacon Benjamin Totti.
Mailing Address: P.O. Box 10932, San Juan., 00922. Tel: 787-782-0245.
Res., Ferrer y Ferrer St., Urb. Santiago Iglesias, 00922. Tel: 787-782-4176; Fax: 787-782-4176.
School—Priests 2; Sisters 2; Lay Teachers 18; Students 296.
Missions—Monacillos, San Fernando; San Fernando.
Chapels—Colegio Ntra. Sra. de la Providencia.; Metropolitan Hospital.

24—JESUS MAESTRO (1968), Revs. Julian Martinez, C.M.; P. Bernardo Hernandez, C.M.; Deacons Miguel De la Sota; William Gomez; Rafael Velazquez.
Res., Segre, 1725 Urb. San Fernando, Rio Piedras, 00926. Tel: 787-763-8291.
Mission—Jesus de Nazaret.

25—SAN JORGE (1965), Revs. Jesus Santoalla; Luis Ricardo Gerena; Deacon Enrique Alvarez.
Res., Calle San Jorge 157, Box 6427, Santurce, 00914-0427. Tel: 809-724-7780.
School—1701-03 Colon St., 00911. Tel: 809-722-3182; 723-5182. Mrs. Maria T. Ambrusso, Prin.
Brothers 1; Lay Teachers 70; Students 812.

26—SAN JOSE (Villa Caparra), Rev. Msgr. Rafael Fontanez; Rev. James Tirado; Deacons Luis Colon; Carlos Ralat; Ramon Rodriguez.
Res., 1948 Urb. Villa Caparra, Bloque ZM 215, Guaynabo, 00966. Tel: 809-781-1155.
School—Calle A. 32, (Villa Caparra), Tel: 809-783-1995; 792-7538. Sr. Catherine Ortiz, O.P., Prin.; Sr. John Christian, Supr.
Priests 4; Sisters 5; Lay Teachers 76; Students 1,286.

27—SAN JOSE OBRERO (1956), Revs. Ruben Gonzalez, C.M.F.; Humberto Evangelista, C.M.F.; Jose Munoz, C.M.; Bro. Zacarias Pichardo, C.M.F.; Deacon Eugenio Rivera.
Mailing Address: Box 3753, San Jose Branch, Rio Piedras, 00930. Tel: 809-767-1448.
Res., Urb. San Jose, Calle 11 17, Urb. San Jose, Rio Piedras, 00923.
Missions—Bo. Plebiscito, San Antonio Ma. Claret; San Martin de Porres-Sierra Maestra.

28—SAN JUAN BOSCO (1945), Revs. Juan Martinez, S.D.B.; Antonio Polo, S.D.B., Supr.; Enrique Mendez, S.D.B.; Lorenzo Ruiz; Bros. Victorino Cayado, S.D.B.; Jose Artiagas, S.D.B.
Res., 370 Lutz St., P.O. Box 14, 125 Barrio Obrero Sta., Santurce, 00916. Tel: 809-726-1420; 726-0232.
Missions—La Milagrosa; Ntra. Sra. del Rosario; San Martin de Porres.

29—SAN JUAN DE LA CRUZ, Rev. Mario Mesa, O.F.M.Cap.; Deacon Martin Nieves.
Res., Ste. 216 Ave. Emiliano Pol 497 Urb. La Cumbre, Rio Piedras, 00926. Tel: 809-731-2016.

30—SAN JUAN EVANGELISTA (1962), Rev. Nicanor Valdes; Deacon Miguel De la Sota.
Res., Calle Church Hill, J-5, Urb. Torrimar, Guaynabo, 00922-0151. Tel: 809-783-3522.
Preescolar "LAURA"—Tel: 809-781-5325. Rev. Nicanor Valdes, Dir.
Priests 1; Sisters 1; Lay Teachers 13; Students 85.
Mission—San Francisco de Asis.

31—NUESTRA SENORA DE LOURDES (1969), Rev. Msgr. Efranin Rodriguez; Deacons Dionilo Torres; Enemias Garcia.
Res., Puerto Rico Ave., Cr. of Colton St., P.O. Box 14452, Bo. Obrero Sta., Santurce, 00916. Tel: 809-726-4643.

32—SAN LUCAS, Rev. Reinaldo Sagardia; Deacons Jose Rodriguez; Miguel Colon; Hactor Cruz D'Choudens.
Res., Pio Baroja St., No. 380, Urb. El Senorial, Rio Piedras, 00926. Tel: 809-761-5476.

33—SANTA LUISA DE MARILLAC (1962), Rev. Victoriano Ramos; Deacon Jose Lopez.
Res., Ave. Emiliano Pol, Urb. La Cumbre, Rio Piedras, 00926. Tel: 809-720-3150.
School—Nuestra Senora del Pilar.
R.R. #3, Box 3120, Rio Piedras, 00928.; Carretera #839, Km. 4 Hm. 4, Rio Piedras, 00928. Tel: 809-767-6962. Jose Marlasca, Prin.
Priests 1; Sisters 5; Lay Teachers 21; Students 591.

34—SAN LUIS GONZAGA (1965), Rev. Jose Antonio Landrau; Deacon Silverio Rubio.
Res., Calle Ronda A-17, Urb. Villa Andalucia, Rio Piedras, 00926. Tel: 809-761-9438.

35—SAN LUIS REY (1967), Rev. Virgilio Martinez; Deacon Vicente Ruiz.
Res., Calle 43 S.E. Final Urb. Reparto Metropolitano, Rio Piedras, 00921. Tel: 809-767-6235.
School—Calle 43 S.E. #469, Reparto Metropolitano, Rio Piedras, 00921. Tel: 809-767-4006. Mrs. Laura Genero, Prin.
Sisters 1; Lay Teachers 10; Students 209.

36—MARIA MADRE DE LA IGLESIA (1967), Rev. Gregorio Bravo; Deacons George Gonzalez; Eugenio Torres.
Res., 1123 Calle 3, Urb. Villa Nevarez, Rio Piedras, 00927. Tel: 809-765-0600.

37—MARIA AUXILIADORA (1962), Revs. Nicolas Navarro; Miguel A. Rivera; Adan L. Marrero; Nicanor Sta. Maria, S.D.B., (Apostolate of the Sea); Rogelio Barrango, S.D.B.; Andres Rivera, S.D.B.; Antonio Polo, S.D.B.; Bro. Jose Cabo.
Res., Carpenter Rd., Box 14367, Bo. Oberero Sta., Santurce, 00916. Tel: 787-726-1995; 727-5346; Fax: 787-268-1869.
School—Colegio San Juan Bosco, 00916.
Priests 2; Religious 15; Lay Teachers 12; Students 284.
Catechesis/Religious Programs—Students 300.
Missions—Sagrado Corazon; Nra. Sra. del Altagracia; Ntra. Sra. de Fatima; Santisima Trinidad.

38—SANTA MARIA DE LOS ANGELES (1954), Rev. Leonardo Rodriguez Jimenez.
Mailing Address: Box 10716, 00922-0716. Tel: 787-792-2640.
Res., De Diego Ave., No. 930, Urb. La Rivera, Rio Piedras.
Mission—Ntra. Senora de la Caridad del Cobre, Calle 35.0.1027, 00921. Tel: 787-792-6613.

39—SAN MATEO (1773), Rev. Msgr. Manuel Rivera.
Res., Calle San Mateo, Esq. San Jorge, Stop 25, Santurce, 00912. Tel: 809-722-4158.

40—NUESTRA SENORA DE LA MERCED (1940), Revs. Jose Maria Reyes, O.de.M.; Fidel Fernandez, O.de.M.; Manuel Cid, O.de.M.
Res., Calle Antolinin, Corner to Espada St., Urb. Roosevelt, G.P.O. Box 4133, Hato Rey, 00936. Tel: 809-763-3657.

41—NTRA. SRA. DE LA MEDALLA MILAGROSA (1957), Rev. Ovidio Ortega Lemus.
Res., 209 Mayaguez St., Hato Rey, 00919. Tel: 809-751-2335.

42—NTRA. SRA. DE LA MONSERRATE (1913), Revs. Vidal Ortega, O.S.A.; Herber Nazario, O.S.A.; Urbano Saenz, O.S.A.; Felipe Fernandez, O.S.A.; Isaias Gonzalez, O.S.A.; Felix Moratiel, O.S.A.
Res., 1058 Fernandez Juncos Ave., Box 13, 726, Santurce, 00908. Tel: 787-722-3134; Fax: 787-722-3134.
School—Santa Monica, Tel: 809-723-2573; 723-3845. Ms. Eva Luz Torres Perez, Prin. Elementary.
Sisters 1; Lay Teachers 42; Students 670.
Mission—Santa Ana.

43—SAN PABLO (1965), Rev. Jose Guillermo Hernandez; Deacons Jose Alicea; Tomas Ramirez; Orlando Sanchez.
Res., Duero St., No. 370, Urb. Villa Borinquen, Puerto Nuevo, 00920. Tel: 809-783-1790.
Mission—Ntra. Sra. de la Caridad.

44—SANTOS PEDRO Y PABLO LOS APOSTOLES, Rev. James Marin.
Res., Jardines Berwind, 65 de Inf., Rio Piedras, P.O. Box 29231, 00929. Tel: 809-750-2715.

45—NTRA. SRA. DEL PERPETUO SOCORRO (1941), Revs. Armando Alvarez; Jesus Gomez Hernandez; Deacons Latino Merino; Jose L. Porrata.
Res., 656 Union St., Miramar, Santurce, 00907. Tel: 809-721-1015; 721-1016.
School—Marti St., 00903. Tel: 809-724-1447; 721-4540. Principals: Mrs. Laura F. de Vega; Sr. Armand Marie, S.S.N.D.
Priests 1; Lay Teachers 102; Students 1,305.

46—NUESTRA SENORA DE LA PIEDAD (1956), Revs. Inmanol Alberdi, C.P.; Juan Bautista Benguria; Esteban Barruetabena, C.P., Supr.; Bro. Juan Landia, C.P.
Res., 13 Marginal St., Urb. Extension, Villamar, Isla Verde, Box 6277, Loiza Sta., Santurce, 00914. Tel: 809-726-2880.
School—Tel: 809-727-7585. Principals: Sr. Shelia O'Brien, S.S.J.; Dr. Juan B. Benguria.
Priests 1; Sisters 4; Lay Teachers 77; Students 829.

47—NUESTRA SENORA DEL PILAR (1714), Revs. Teodoro Calzada, C.M.; Higinio Madrazo, C.M.; Maximiano Santos, C.M.; Pascual Sota, C.M.; Deacons Cesar Guiven; Jose Luis Velazquez.
Res., Plaza de Recreo, Rio Piedras, Box 21134, 00928-1134. Tel: 809-764-5088.
Mission—Rio Piedras, Santa Teresita de Nino Jesus, 00925.
Chapels—Colegio La Milagrosa, De Diego St., Rio Piedras, Tel: 809-765-6114; San Jose, Hogar, Lasalle, Rio Piedras, Tel: 809-763-1730.

48—SAN PIO X (1970), Rev. Manuel Otero; Deacons Julio Sanchez; Juan B. Perez.
Res., Carretera 848, K-1.2, P.O. Box 631, Urb. St. Just, Trujillo Alto, 00978. Tel: 787-761-5040. [CEM]

49—NUESTRA SENORA DE LA PROVIDENCIA (1959), Rev. Msgr. Baudilio Merino; Deacons Nelson Figueroa; Pedro Rivera; Luis Vazquez.
Res., Santa Agueda St., No. 1731, Urb. Sagrado Corazon, Rio Piedras, 00927. Tel: 809-765-6240.
School—Carretera #176, Km. 2.7-C/Sta. Agueda 1733-Urb. San Gerardo, Rio Piedras, 00926. Tel: 809-767-6552; 767-6755. Maria M. Lee de Cobo, Prin.
Lay Teachers 63; Students 891.

50—NUESTRA SENORA DE LA PROVIDENCIA (1973), Rev. Eddie Rivera.
Res., 219 Aponte St., Santurce, 00912. Tel: 809-727-1878.

51—MARIA REINA DEL MUNDO (1971), Rev. Felix Varas.
Mailing Address: G.P.O. Box 3828, 00936-3828. Tel: 809-767-1372.
Res., Caserio Nemesio Canales, Roosevelt Ave. Puerto Nuevo, Rio Piedras.

52—RESURRECCION DEL SENOR (1968), Revs. Cruz Ajuria, O.F.M.; Luis Zabala, O.F.M.; Victorio Beain, O.F.M.; Tomas Gondra.
Res., Calle 31, S.O. 797, Urb. Las Lomas, Rio Piedras, 00921. Tel: 809-792-1416; 792-5939.

53—SANTA ROSA DE LIMA (1971), Rev. Jose D'Artiaga; Deacons Pedro Costa; Vicente Rio.
Res., Calle Lesbos No. 1765, Urb. Venus Gardens, Rio Piedras, 00926. Tel: 809-761-6586.

54—SAGRADA FAMILIA (1971), Rev. Msgr. Tomas Su; Deacon Vivente Colon.
Res., Ave. 65 de Inf., Esquina Calle 7, No. 112, Hills Brothers, Sabana Llana, P.O. Box 29, 311, 65 Infantry Sta., Rio Piedras, 00929. Tel: 787-767-1723.

55—SAGRADO CORAZON DE JESUS (1971), Revs. Basilio Roldan; Pablo Torres, C.M.; Jose Yanez, C.M.
Res., Calle Oxford 251, Esq. Howard Urb. University Gardens, Rio Piedras, 00927. Tel: 809-765-4798; 765-5267.
School—Iteramericana y Palma Real: Urb. University Gardens, Rio Piedras, 00927. Tel: 809-765-9430. Sr. Rose Colette, O.S.F., Prin. Sup.; Sr. Maria Kivick, O.S.F., Prin. Elm.

56—SAGRADO CORAZON DE JESUS (1909), Rev. Rafael Candelas.
Res., Ponce de Leon Ave., 1308, Stop 19, Box 8312, F.J. Sta., Santurce, 00910. Tel: 809-722-0235.

57—SANTISMO SACRAMENTO (1967), Rev. Jose Francisco Quiceno.
Res., 500 Jerusalem St., Urb. Matienzo Cintron, Rio Piedras, 00923. Tel: 809-764-3448.
Chapel—Hnas. Santos Angeles Custodios.

58—SANTISIMO SALVADOR (1965), Revs. Angel Millan Lazaro, Sch.P. (Spain); Leopoldo Laredo, Sch.P.; Javier Goicoechea, Sch.P. (Spain); Francisco Javier Lopez, Sch.P.; Jose Andres Basols, Sch.P., Supr.; Cecilio Lacruz, Sch.P.; Rafael Capo Iriarte, Sch.P.; Deacons Julio Alvarez; Luis O. del Rio.
Res., Niza St., 575, Urb. Villa Capri, Rio Piedras, 00924. Tel: 787-761-3314; Fax: 787-755-1595. [JC]
School—Calasanz, (1968), Ave. Montecarlo, P.O. Box 29067, 65 Inf. Sta., Rio Piedras, 00929. Tel: 787-750-2500; Fax: 787-257-0450. Jose Besosa, Prin.
Priests 6; Lay Teachers 42; Students 514.
Missions—Rio Piedras, N. Sra. de la Paz, C/1 Esq. C/8 Urb. Berwid States, 00924.; Rio Piedras, San Jose de Calasanz, Calle #23 408 Parc. Hills Brothers, 00924.

59—STELLA MARIS (1965), Rev. Eral Jose Rivas-Campiz.
Res., 69 Cervantes St., Condado, Santurce, 00907. Tel: 809-723-2240; Fax: 809-722-3200.

60—SANTA TERESA JORNET, Rev. German Vargas; Deacon Vicente Lasanta.
Res., Carr. 176 Camino el Mundo, Km. 5.3 Cupey Alto Aptdo. 415, El Senorial Sta., Rio Piedras, 00926. Tel: 809-748-0185.
Missions—Cupey, San Martin de Porres Carrt. 176 H. 10.0,; Cupey, Virgen de la Salud. Camino Los Guayabos Carr. 176.

61—SANTA TERESITA DEL NINO JESUS (1930), Revs. Tomas Ciscar, O.C., Sup. Regional; Franco Barreneche, O.C.; Tarcisio Gotay, O.C.; Francisco Armell, O.C.; Enrique Oria, O.C.
Res., 2059 Loiza St., Santurce, 00911. Tel: 809-727-0181; 727-0030; Fax: 809-728-0056.
Schools—Tel: 809-727-4260; 727-4317; 727-4358. Flor M. Caraballo, Prin.
Priests 1; Sisters 1; Lay Teachers 47; Students 577; Colegio Sagrada Familia, Urb. Llorens Torres, Santurce, Tel: 809-726-0570. Ana Rita Castro, Prin. Lay Teachers 6; Students 178.
Mission—Sagrada Familia, Tel: 809-726-0570.

62—SAN VICENTE DE PAUL (1940), Revs. Pascual Sota, C.M., Prov. Supr.; Evaristo Oliveras, C.M.; Bernardo Hernandez; Eugenio Sadaba, C.M.; Victor Santos; Bro. Wilfredo Acevedo, C.M.
Res., 1651 Los Angeles, Corner to Fernandez Juncos Ave., 19118, Fernandez Juncos Sta., Santurce, 00910. Tel: 809-727-3963.
School—709 Bolivar St., Box 8699, Tel: 809-727-4273; Fax: 809-728-2263. Mrs. Isabel Casana, Prin.
Sisters 3; Lay Teachers 17; Students 386.
Missions—Santa Catalina; San Jose; La Inmaculada.

OUTSIDE THE CITY OF SAN JUAN

Bayamon

1—San Agustin (1964), Revs. Benigno Palomo Casares, O.S.A.; Eliseo Garcia, O.S.A.; Gonzalo Gonzalez, O.S.A.; Deacons Ignacio Perez; Cristobal Rivera; Pedro Miranda.
Res., Lomas Verdes Calle Duende 2E-21, Box 4263, Urb. Bayamon Gardens Branch, 00956. Tel: 809-785-8611.
School—(1964), Tel: 809-786-8055. Mr. Catalino Munoz Flores, Prin.
Sisters 3; Lay Teachers 23; Students 769.
Missions—Bayamon, San Martin de Porres, c/1 Barrio Juan Sanchez, 00959.; Bayamon, Casa San Agustin; Bayamon, Villas de San Agustin.

2—San Antonio Maria Claret (1966), Revs. Jose Felix Nunez, C.M.F.; Marcelino Romero, C.M.F.; Deacon Jose Dolores Rivera.
Res., D-24 Castiglioni Ave., Box 3292, Urb. Bayamon Gardens, 00957. Tel: 809-797-3337.

3—Catalina de Siena, Revs. Marcos Luis Espinel, O.P.; Francisco Garcia, O.P.; Roberto Arzela, O.P.; Deacons Francisco Cruz; Victor Lopez; Antonio Santiago; Nicomedes Cosmo; Jose Rios; Agapito Diaz.
Res., Santa, Urb. Hermanas Davila, Calle 10, Q-3, P.O. Box 4188, 00959-4188. Tel: 787-785-2381; Fax: 787-269-5065.

4—Cristo Salvador, Rev. Enrique Vazquez (Spain).
Mailing Address: P.O. Box 459, 00960-0459.
Church—Carr. 177, Los Filtros; Casa Linda del Sur #N-205, 00959. Tel: 809-720-2348.

5—Nuestra Sra. de los Dolores (1976), Rev. Raul Quesada Gil; Deacons Francisco Hernandez; Noel A. Vazquez.
Res., Bloque DD-25, 18th St., Urb. Alturas de Flamboyan, 00959. Tel: 787-786-7494.

6—Santo Domingo de Guzman (1976), Rev. Juan Burgos, O.P.; Deacons Angel Davila; Louis J. Marin; Hector Negron; Jose A. Rodriguez; William Rodriguez.
Res., Ext. La Milagrosa Calle 2, P.O. Box 1968, 00960. Tel: 809-786-8592; 785-6542.

7—Santa Elena, Rev. Daniel Trujillo.
Res., Calle 6, H-14, P.O. Box 366, Gardens Sta., 00960. Tel: 787-785-6604.

8—Invencion de la Santa Cruz (1750), Revs. Natividad Acevedo, O.P.; Beltran Idsert; Victor Aviles; Deacon Jose A. Bermudez.
Res., 12 Degetau St., 00619. Tel: 809-785-2134.

9—San Jose (1964), Revs. Jose Nieto, C.M.F.; Hector Cuadrado, C.M.F.; Jose Antonio Munoz, C.M.F.; Deacons Jose Rosado; Jose Torres.
Res., Dakar, F-169, Forest View, 00956. Tel: 787-785-6675; Fax: 787-785-0670.
School—Academia Claret, Tel: 787-785-6685. Sr. Maria Huertas, Prin.
Priests 1; Lay Teachers 22; Students 440.

10—San Juan Bautista de la Salle (1979), Revs. Jose M. Garcia Bazton, M.SS.CC.; Manuel Soler Pala, M.SS.CC.; Deacons Francisco Ortiz; Jose Vega; Jorge Rivera.
Res., 19 Rio Cialitos St., 1ra. Secc. Estancias Rio Hondo, 00961. Tel: 809-787-9567.

11—San Miguel Arcangel (1962), Rev. Francisco Medina; Deacons Jose Pena; Santiago Latorre.
Mailing Address: G.P.O. Box 1714, San Juan, 00936-1714. Tel: 787-787-4459; Fax: 787-787-4459.
Res., Urban. Jardines de Caparra, Calle 12A-AB., No. 32, 00619.

12—Nuestra Senora de la Milagrosa (1968), Rev. Hernan Adarve; Deacon Angel Rondon.
Res., Carr. 864, No. 82, Bo. Hato Tejas, P.O Box 2104, 00960. Tel: 809-785-6620.

13—Ascension Del Senor (1984), Revs. Epifanio Fernandez, O.SS.T.; Javier Elorriaga, O.SS.T.; Deacons Aureliz Garcia; Juan Perez del Valle. In res., Rev. Pedro Gorena.
Mailing Address: P.O. Box 3367, 00958-3367. Tel: 809-799-6120.
Res., Calle 34, BI No. 18, Urb. Rexville, 00958.

14—Espiritu Santo. (Parish in Formation). Rev. Pedro Corena, O.SS.T.
Mailing Address: Box 3367, 00958-3367. Tel: 809-799-6120.
Res., Calle 1, E #18, Bella Vista Gardens, 00957. Tel: 809-799-8604.

15—Ntra. Sra. de la Monserrate (1985), Revs. Isaias Alvarez, O.S.A.; Domingo Aller, O.S.A.; Deacons Luis A. Rodriguez; Jesus Lopez.
Res., Carr. 167, Km. 5.6, Bo. Santa Olaya, P.O. Box 3948, Bayamon Gardens, 00958. Tel: 809-797-0708; 799-7340; Fax: 809-797-9953.
Missions—Cristo Rey; Bayamon, Ntra. Sra. de la Esperanza; Bayamon, Santa Monica.

16—Nuestra Senora del Perpetuo Socorro (1976), Rev. Victor Perez, O.P.; Deacons Felix Calderon; Anastacio Del Rio; Ramon L. Roman; Miguel Velez.
Res., Comerio St. No. 192, 00956. Tel: 809-785-0381; 780-4367.
Convent—Tel: 809-785-6542.

17—La Resurreccion del Senor (1987), Most Rev. Hermin Negron, D.D.; Deacons Angel Luis Oyola; Feliciano Ortiz.
Res., Calle 12 F-1, Urb. Royal Town, 00956. Tel: 787-730-4310.

18—Santa Rita de Casia (1967), Revs. Mario Gonzalez, O.S.A., Supr.; Felix Moratiel, O.S.A.; Bro. Agustin Sanchez, O.S.A; Deacons Jose Perez; Eliezer Toro; Gregorio Velez (MIA); Ramon Luis Rivera (PCE).
Res., Ave. Hostos NS-8, Urb. Santa Juanita, 00956. Tel: 809-786-3971.
Retired House—Ntra. Sra. del Buen Consejo.
Missions—Bayamon, San Jose; Bayamon, Sagrado Corazon de Jesus; Bayamon, Ntra. Sra. del Carmen.

19—Santa Rosa de Lima (1978), Rev. Pedro Campana; Deacons Fernando Baez; Ricardo D'Auria; Ricardo Longueira; Juan R. Santos.
Res., Calle 12, Bloque No. 28; Casa No. 9, Urb. Santa Rosa, 00959. Tel: 787-798-2300; 787-1676; 798-2829; Fax: 787-780-3680.
School—Calle Main. Sr. Doris M. Lopez, O.P., Prin.
Sisters 8; Lay Teachers 40; Students 930.
Catechesis/Religious Programs—Students 930.

20—Nuestra Senora del Rosario (1971), Rev. Jaime Vazquez Rojas; Deacons Luis Echegaray; Luis A. Navedo.
Res., Calle Zaragoza, Bloque, B No. 35, Esq. Calle Vizcaya, Urb. Villa Espana, 00961. Tel: 809-787-0418.

21—Nuestra Sra. del Rosario (1993), Rev. Dario Martinez.
Mailing Address: Box 3917, 00958.
Res., Carr. 816 Km. 2.2, Barrio Nuevo, Tel: 809-730-6000.

22—Sagrada Familia (1976), Rev. Alvaro Silva (Colombia); Deacons Americo Arroyo; Gumercindo Colon; Ramon L. Ortiz.
Res., Calle Caracas and Valparaiso, Urb. Ext. Forest Hills, P.O. Box 8478, 00960. Tel: 787-798-2010.
School—Tel: 787-785-2792; Fax: 787-787-7700. Mrs. Carmen Mendez Bosque, Prin.
Lay Teachers 14; Students 299.
Catechesis/Religious Programs—Students 160.

23—Santa Maria (1984), Revs. Tomas Cabello; Francisco Gomez; Camilo Riono; Bro. Zacarias Richardo; Deacons Jose Ramon Cruz; Rafael Araya.
Res., Calle 24, II No. 21, Carr 167, Res. Cana, 00957. Tel: 809-797-7248; 797-8230.
Missions—San Gerardo de Mayella; Sagrado Corazon.

24—Santa Teresa de Avila (1983), Rev. Juan Curran, O.M.I.
Res., Calle Repto. Teresita, P.O. Box 9404, 00960. Tel: 809-787-8758; Fax: 809-780-3680.
Mission—San Martin de Porres.

25—Santiago Apostol (1966), Revs. Antonio Picornell, M.SS.CC.; Pedro Arturo Rondon, M.SS.C.; Deacons Luis F. Cordero; Felix Lopez; Juan Melendez; Angel Pabon.
Res., Urb. Sierra Bayamon, Calle 23, Bloque 23, Num. 17, 00961. Tel: 809-786-9179; Fax: 809-269-3965.
School—Mrs. Zoraida N. de Alonso, Prin. Priests 1; Lay Teachers 11; Students 284.

26—Santo Domingo De Guzman (1984), Rev. Nestor Yulfo; Deacons Virgilio Andino; Ramon Ramos.
Res., Parcelas Van Scoy-Bella Vista, Calle Principal Esq., Calle, 00958. Tel: 809-797-5510; 799-0148.

Canovanas

1—Nuestra Senora del Pilar (1937), Rev. Carmelo Soto; Deacon Jose Rivera.
Res., 77 Luis Hernaiz St., P.O. Box 1615, 00729. Tel: 809-876-2655.
School—3 Luis Hernaiz St., 00729. Tel: 809-876-3020. Mr. Samuel Rey Saldana, Dir.
Sisters 5; Lay Teachers 19; Students 563.
Mission—San Francisco Javier.

2—Resurreccion del Senior, Revs. Raymond Riding, S.T.; Francis Conkle; Martin Van Trieste, S.T.; Deacon Pedro Florez.
Res., La, Parcelas de San Isidro, Carret. Bo. Mediania a Loiza, P.O. Box 896, 00729. Tel: 787-876-3917; Fax: 787-256-4836.
Mission—Ntra. Sra. de la Providencia.

3—Sagrado Corazon de Jesus, Rev. Orlando Londono, Admin.; Deacon Julio Ortiz.
Mailing Address: P.O. Box 1637, 00679-1637. Tel: 809-876-1355.

4—Santa Maria Madre de Dios (1971), Rev. Vicente Pasqualetto, S.T.
Res., E-189 Girasol St., Loiza Valley, 00729. Tel: 787-876-0827; Fax: 787-876-0827.
Mission—Capilla Cristo Salvador. Sector Pueblo Indio.

5—San Jose, Rev. Francisco Quintero; Deacon Raul Figueroa.
Res., Bo. Campo Rico Box 807, 00729. Tel: 809-876-4941.
Missions—Palma Sola, Ntra. Sra. de la Asuncion Carrt. 957 Km. 6.8,; Alturas de Campo Rico., Ntra. Sra. Del Carmen. Carrt. 185 Km. 5.3.

Carolina

1—San Andres (1982), Rev. Raul A. Quesada; Deacons Marino Hernandez; Gilberto Mejias.
Res., Calle 401, Esq. Calle 482, Cuarta Extension, Urb. Country Club, Rio Piedras, 00982. Tel: 809-769-7076.

2—Santa Bernardita Soubirous (1982), Rev. Wilfredo Pena Moredo; Deacons Ismael Colon; Eladio Figueroa; Angel Rivera; Rafael Zanabria; Ramon Santiago.
Mailing Address: P.O. Box 29826, Rio Piedras, 00929-0826. Tel: 809-762-0375.
Res., Calle Espioncela, Esquina Calle Torcaza, Country Club, Rio Piedras, 00982. Tel: 809-762-5740; 257-7643.

3—Santa Clara de Asis (1966), Revs. Fernando Hortiguela, O.F.M.; Leandro Abarrategui, O.F.M.; Jose Francisco Labaka, O.F.M.; Deacons Luis Del Rio Pitre; Jose A. Morales; Luis Montes; Juan Ubarri.
Res., Via 14-2JL No. 456 Urb. Villa Fontana, 00983. Tel: 809-768-1708; Fax: 809-757-5044.
School—(1968), Tel: 809-768-7110. Mrs. Elsie Mujica, Prin.; Rev. Leanardo Abarratelegui, Dir.
Lay Teachers 21; Students 403.
Missions—San Francisco de Asis; Carolina, Parque Bolivariano 5-JL. Villa Fonta Park.

4—Santo Cristo de la Agonia, Rev. Jorge J. Castillejo-Llusia; Deacon Ernesto Rivera.
Res., Santo, Calle Robles 39, Urb. Eduardo J. Saldana, P.O. Box 5108, 00984-5108. Tel: 787-768-0374.

5—Santo Cristo de los Milagros (1971), Rev. Celso Martinez.
Res., Ave. Sanchez Castano, Urb. Villa Carolina, P.O. Box 834, 00985. Tel: 809-768-3810.
School—Colegio Maria Auxiliadora, Box 797, Tel: 809-762-0350; 768-6924. Lelis R. Iglesias, Prin.
Sisters 5; Lay Teachers 23; Students 1,639.

6—Epifania Del Senor, Rev. Msgr. Hernan A. Piedrahita-Tamayo; Deacons Roberto Mendia; Ibrahim Mestre.
Res., Calle Calais 425, Ext. El Comandante, 00982-3601. Tel: 787-752-1149.

7—San Felipe Apostol (1971), Rev. Rafael Suazo; Deacons Eugenio Balasguide; Jose Vazquez.
Res., Calle 419, Bloque 165, No. 3, Ext. Villa Carolina, P.O. Box 1494, 00964. Tel: 809-762-6520.

8—San Fernando (1851), Rev. Joaquin Rivera; Deacons Jose Birriel; Enrique Colon; Santiago Diaz Rosa; Presbitero Rivera; Jose Torres.
Res., Calle Munoz Rivera, No. 65, P.O. Box 128, 00986. Tel: 809-769-0170.

9—Santa Gema Galgani (1971), Revs. Atanasio Amundarain, C.P.; Anselmo Andicoechea, C.P.; Felix Barruetabena, C.P.
Res., Marina Ave. No. 1454, Urb. Bahia Vistamar, P.O. Box 2789, 00984. Tel: 809-769-5663.
School—Mrs. Lilia Luna de Anaya, Prin. Sisters 1; Lay Teachers 26; Students 579.

10—Inmaculata Concepcion (1966), Rev. Hernan Berdugo.
Mailing Address: Apartado 3562, 00984-3562.
Res., Urb. Valle Arriba Heights, Calle 145-C-D-Num. 10, 00984. Tel: 787-276-1527; Fax: 787-272-1527.

11—Jesus Mediador, Rev. Freddy Alecio (Guatemala); Deacons Candido Martinez; Edwin Rivera.
Res., Calle Demetrio O'Dally 1000, Country Club, Rio Piedras, 00982. Tel: 809-768-3157.

12—San Juan de Dios (1971), Rev. Silverio Rueda; Deacon Luis R. O'Neill.
Res., R-19-A Canaria St., Jardines de Borinquen, P.O. Box 3179, 00984. Tel: 809-757-5060.
Mission—La Sagrada Familia.

13—Nuestra Senora de Lourdes (1956), Rev. Francisco Rubalcaba; Deacons Emilio Caceres; Alejandro Hernandez; Edwin Perez; Nelson Soto.
Mailing Address: P.O. Box 29793, Rio Piedras, 00929-0793.
Res., Calle Antonio Luciano, Esq. Calle Cruzado, Ext. El Comandante, 00630. Tel: 809-769-5740; 752-3716.

14—NTRA. SRA. DEL CARMEN (1984), Rev. Antonio Garcia (Spain); Deacons Ernie Diaz; Cesar Avila; Martin Morales.
Res., K-8 Monte Membrillo St., Lomas-Mansiones Carolina, P.O. Box 299, 00984-0299. Tel: 787-757-4454; Fax: 787-757-4454.
School—Sr. Mary Ellen, C.S.F.N., Prin. Priests 1; Sisters 2; Lay Teachers 23; Students 331.

15—NTRA. SRA. REINA DE LA PAZ (1969), Rev. Miguel Ferrer; Deacons Euripidez Lugo; Miguel Marrero; Manuel Reyes; Efigenio Rivera.
Res., Calle 6, Final, Urb. Sabana Gardens, P.O. Box 3688, 00983. Tel: 809-752-5607.

16—NTRA. SRA. REINA DE LOS ANGELES (1971), Rev. Miguel A. Ferrer; Deacon Ildefonso Berrios.
Res., N-17 Calle A, Urb. Los Angeles, 00979-1162. Tel: 809-791-2594.

17—SANTISIMA TRINIDAD (1982), Rev. Luis Angel Torres; Deacons Luis Colon; Esteban Valle; Bienvenido Domenech.
Res., Ave. Campo Rico PA-16, Tercera Extension, Urb. Country Club, Rio Piedras, 00982. Tel: 809-769-5665.

18—CRISTO REY (1971), Rev. Eduardo Toscano; Deacon Pedro E. Velez.
Res., Barrio Canovanillas, Carret. No. 857, K-2, 00987. Tel: 809-757-8712.
Missions—Parque Encuestra, S. Francisco de Asis Calle 23 N-25 Urb.; Bo. Canovanas, Maria Auxiliadora Carrt. 857 Km. 3.6; Bo. Cambute, Santa Cruz. Urb. Los Caobos Park.

19—NTRA. SRA. DE FATIMA. (Parish in Formation). Rev. Eduardo Gallego; Deacon Domingo Ocasio.
Res., Bo. Cedros, Carr 853, Km 13, P.O. Box 12076 Bo. Cedras, 00985. Tel: 809-750-8562.

20—SAN VALENTIN (1971), Rev. Francisco Jose Quiceno; Deacons Miguel Diaz; Antonio Quintana; Jose A. Pappeterra.
Res., Calle San Luis 128, Urb. Rolling Hills, P.O. Box 9382, 00988-9382. Tel: 787-750-5277.
Missions—Santa Rosa; San Antonio.

21—SAN FRANCISCO DE ASIS (1988), Rev. Frank de la Rosa Peguero (Dominican Republic); Deacon Justo Montanez.
Res., Calle 22 #0-31 A, Urb. Metropolis, 00987. Tel: 809-768-8860.

Catano, San Francisco de Sales (1969), Revs. Demetrio Coello, S.D.B.; Abraham Cepeda, S.D.B.; Homero Berancourt, S.D.B.
Res., Ave., Flor del Valle Bloque BB-No. 108, Urb. Las Vegas, P.O. Box 567, 00963. Tel: 809-788-5036; Fax: 809-788-8163.
Missions—Santo Domingo; Maria Auxiliadora; San Judas Tadeo (Santuario).

Santa Rosa de Lima (1973), Rev. Julio Victor Garcia Padron (Cuba); Deacon Filiberty De Jesus.
Res., 16 Parque St., Barrio Amelia, Guaynabo, 00965. Tel: 809-781-5855; 783-9731.
Mission—Barriada Vietnam, La Milagrosa.

Nuestra Senora del Carmen (1893), Revs. Alberto Pagan, O.P.; Felix Struik, O.P.; Deacons Pedro Flores; Angel Oquendo; Enrique Rivera. In res., Rev. Malaky Clune, O.P.
Res., Calle Tren Num. 42, P.O. Box 427, 00963. Tel: 809-788-1098; Fax: 809-788-5905.
Missions—San Martin de Porres; San Jose Obrero.

Dorado, San Antonio de Padua (1842), Revs. Carlos Jimenez Van Derdys; Luis Eduardo Villada; Deacons Benito Lugo; Jose Marrero; Bernardino Medina; Arcadio Nunez; Luis Marcial Rivera; Romulo Rodriguez.
Res., P.O. Box 602, 00646. Tel: 809-796-1143.

Ntra. Sra. de La Salud (1982), Rev. Manuel Garcia; Deacons Hilario De Leon; Cresencio Rosario.
Res., Parcela 202, Buzon 210, Urb. San Antonio, Bo. Higuillar, P.O. Box 470, 00646. Tel: 809-796-3418.

Guaynabo

1—CORAZON DE JESUS (1992), Rev. Jesus Vieites, SS.CC.; Deacon Jacinto Ortiz.
Mailing Address: Carr. 834 Km. 2.2, Bo. Sonadora, Apartado 225, 00970-0225. Tel: 809-789-2014.

2—EL BUEN PASTOR (1970), Rev. Francisco Jimenez; Deacon Manuel Andino.
Res., Avenida Apolo, Urb. Apolo, Box 1848, 00970-1848. Tel: 809-789-2653.
Chapel—Colegio El Buen Pastor.

3—MARIA MADRE DE MI SENOR, Rev. Alberto Lopez; Deacon Julio H. Ortiz.
Res., P.O. Box 2150, 00970-2150. Tel: 809-789-1837.
Mission—Guaynabo, Ntra. Sra. del Carmen. Bo. Frailes Llanos Sector Los Baez.

4—SAN JUAN M. VIANNEY (1972). (Santo Cura de Ars). Rev. Florentino Sanz.
Res., Calle-2-F-14, Urb. Hillside, Rio Piedras, 00926. Tel: 809-790-2014.
Missions—La Milagrosa; Cristo del Perdon; Dulce Nombre de Maria; Ntra. Sra. del Carmen.

5—MARIA MADRE DE LA MISERICORDIA (1995), Rev. Msgr. Jaime Capo'; Revs. Luis O. Capacetti; Vicente Fernandez; Carlos Ortiz.
Mailing Address: 274 Ave. Santa Ana, Plaza Alta Mall Suite 136, 00969-3304.
Res., Avenue Santa Ana Km. 13.2, La Villa de Torrimar, 00969-3304. Tel: 787-789-0090; Fax: 787-790-7596.

6—SAN PEDRO MARTIR DE VERONA (1769), Rev. Mario A. Guijarro de Corzo; Deacons Carlos Rivera Martinez; Gumersindo Negron Morales; Humberto Reyes Anciano; Angel Loyola Zayas.
Res., Calle Tapia No. 5, P.O. Box 32, 00970. Tel: 809-720-2361; Fax: 809-272-8770.
School—Alpierre St., Urb. Colimar, P.O. Box 2560, 00970. Sr. Alicia Velazquez, R.A., Prin.
Priests 2; Sisters 9; Lay Teachers 45; Students 740.

7—DIVINO NINO JESUS (1992), Rev. Rodolfo Lamas (Cuba); Deacon Gerardo Comulada.
Res., PBM 143, HC-01, Box 29030, Caguas, 00725-8900. Tel: 787-720-0203; Fax: 787-720-0203.
Missions—San Rafael Arcangel; Jesus Nazareno; El Buen Pastor.

8—NUESTRA SENORA DE LA PAZ (1992), Revs. Javier Esparza, SS.CC.; Esteban Beltran, SS.CC.; Francisco Martinez, SS.CC.
Bo. Guaraguao, Apartado 225, 00970-0225. Tel: 809-789-2014.

9—SAGRADOS CORAZONES (1968), Revs. Mateo Mateo, SS.CC.; Jose Ma. Garcia, SS.CC.; Deacons Ivan E. Dominguez; Ulpiano H. Rivera; Israel Suarez.
Res., Urb. Ponce de Leon, 208 Ave. Esmeralda, 00969. Tel: 809-720-6151; Fax: 809-720-6151.
School—Avenue A., Tel: 809-720-2585; Fax: 809-720-6035. Fybi Crespo, Prin.
Sisters 3; Lay Teachers 35; Students 830.
Mission—Virgen de la Paz.

Loiza, San Patricio (1719), Rev. Marco Antonio Sanchez, S.T. (Mexico); Deacons Santiago Acosta; Marcos Penaloza; Pastor Perez; Angel Pizarro.
Res., Calle Espiritu Santo #10, Box 504, 00772-0504. Tel: 787-876-2229; Fax: 787-876-2229.
Missions—Santa Rosa; Ntra. Sra. del Perpetuo Socorro; Santisima Trinidad; San Antonio; Ntra. Sra. de Fatima; San Rafael-Villa Nevarez.

Santiago Apostol, El Mayor (1971), Revs. Manuel Prado, C.M.; Luis Renier Brioso, C.M.
Res., Apdo. 118, Barrio Mediania, 00772-0118. Tel: 809-876-1879.
Missions—Ntra. Sra. Perpetuo Socorro; La Milagrosa; La Providencia; Nino de Praga.

Luquillo, Madre del Redentor (1993), Rev. Carlos Alfredo Rivero-Perez.
Church—Barrio Pitaya, Sector Casablanca, Carr. 983, Km. 1.5, 00773.
Res., Apartado 591, 00773—0591. Tel: 787-889-0733; Fax: 787-889-0733.

San Jose (1797), Rev. Emilio Toro; Deacons Raul Figueroa; Felipe Rivera.
Res., Calle Soledad No. 15, P.O. Box 493, 00773-0493. Tel: 809-889-2590; Fax: 809-889-6180.
Missions—San Judas; Ntra. Sra. del Cobre.

Palmer, Cristo Rey (1970), Rev. Calixto Soto.
Res., Calle Principal, P.O. Box 382, 00721-0382. Tel: 809-887-3552.
Missions—La Milagrosa; Ntra. Sra. de la Providencia.

Rio Grande, Nuestra Senora del Carmen (1840), Revs. Jesus M. Ciriza; Antonio Romero, M.SS.CC.; Juan Pocovi, M.SS.CC.
Res., No. 9 del Carmen St., Box 845, 00745-0845. Tel: 809-887-2365.
School—Calle 14 Urb. Alturas de Rio Grande, P.O. Box 818, 00745. Mrs. Elsa Quinones Santiago, Prin.
Missions—Rio Grande, Nuestra Senora de Fatima Bo. El Verde,; Jardines de Rio Grande, Ntra. Sra. de Guadalupe; Rio Grande, San Pedro Bo. Bartolo,; Alturas de Rio Grande, La Milagrosa. Calle 14.

San Francisco de Asis, Rev. Hernan Berdugo; Deacon Manuel Llanos.
Res., Barrio Malpica, P.O. Box 1449, 00745. Tel: 809-888-5302.

Toa Alta

1—SAN ESTEBAN, PROTOMARTIR (1985), Rev. Jose Antonio Carrion-Parroco (Cuba).
Res., Urb. La Providencia, Calle 7 1L-8, 00953. Tel: 787-799-2925; Fax: 787-799-2925.
Convent—Santa Cruz Convent, Barrio Pajaros, Sector Los Frailes, 00953. Dominican Sisters of the Holy Cross of Amityville
Mailing Address: RR-5, Box 4103, Bayamon, 00956. Tel: 787-799-7950.
Chapel—Capilla Cristo Rey, Sector La Cuerda, Barrio Bucarabones, 00953.

2—SAN FERNANDO (1751), Revs. Angel Figueroa; Jesus Alberto Garcia; Deacons Jose Diaz; Jose Narvaez; Felipe Collazo; Luis Rivera.
Res., P.O. Box 63, Calle Jose de Diego, 00954. Tel: 809-870-2585.
Missions—San Antonio; San Judas Tadeo.

3—SAN JOSE, Rev. Jairo Salazar (Colombia); Deacons Francisco Villamil; Pablo Irene; Enrique Laureano.
Mailing Address: P.O. Box 777, 00954-0777.
Church—Barrio Rio Lajas, 00953.
Res., R.R. 2 Buzon 5929, 00953-0063. Tel: 809-870-6415.
Missions—Ntra. Sra. del Camino; Virgen del Carmen; Cristo de los Milagros; Santa Teresita; Sagrada Familia; Sagrado Corazon.

4—NUESTRA SENORA DE LA MEDALLA MILAGROSA, Rev. Luis Alberto Sierra; Deacons German Hernandez; Santos Nieves.
Res., Bo. Quebrada Cruz, P.O. Box 335, 00954-0335. Tel: 809-870-4090.
Missions—Nuestra Senora del Carmen; Sagrado Corazon de Jesus; Santa Teresa.

5—N. SRA. DE LA PROVIDENCIA, Rev. Carlos Verdia, C.M.F.; Deacons Gregorio Cuevas; Jose C. Pacheco.
Res., P.O. Box 3836, Bayamon Gardens Sta. Bo. Pinas, Bayamon, 00958. Tel: 787-797-1618.
Missions—N. Sra. de Fatima; La Resurreccion.

Toa Baja

1—NUESTRA SENORA DE COVADONGA, Rev. Francisco Arana; Deacon Efrain Narvaez.
Mailing Address: Box 9076, Bayamon, 00960-9076. Tel: 809-251-6466.
Res., Calle 13 Esq. Calle 14, Urb. Covadonga, 00940.
Missions—Ntra. Sra. de Lourdes; San Martin de Porres.

2—NTRA. SRA. DE LA CANDELARIA, Rev. Heriberto Londono; Deacons Anselmo Miranda; Roberto Ortiz; Camildo Ortiz.
Res., Carret. No. 863, Km. 0.6, P.O. Box 892, 00951-0892. Tel: 809-251-0503.
Missions—Cristo Rey; Santa Maria; Santisima Trinidad.

3—ESPIRITU SANTO (1965), Revs. Luis Gonzalez-Chao; Roberto Garcia; Deacons Pablo Maldonado; Jose Miranda; Miguel Torres; Guillermo Vaello.
Res., Paseo Damisela No. 1453, Urb. Levittown, P.O. Box 50272, Levittown Sta., 00950. Tel: 809-784-4805.
School—Paseo Damiseala 1453, 00632. Tel: 809-784-0905. Rosa I. Perez, Prin.
Lay Teachers 16; Students 793.
Mission—Toa Baja, N. Sra. del Carmen, Calle Carmen, Bo. Palo Seco, 00759.

4—JOSE OBRERO, Revs. Luis Lizarralde, O.F.M.; Dario Carrero, O.F.M., Supr.; Alfonso Guzman, O.F.M.
Res., San, Barrio Sabana Seca, Box 173, 00952-0173. Tel: 809-784-1400.
Missions—Ntra. Sra. del Carmen; San Martin de Porres.

5—SAN PEDRO APOSTOL (1745), Rev. Juan Patron (Peru); Deacon Gerardo Trujillo.
Res., 47, Las Flores St., P.O. Box 513, 00951. Tel: 809-794-1327.
School—Calle Basilio Milan #13, Apartado 513, 00759.
Catechesis/Religious Programs—Students 260.
Chapels—St. Teresita; Ntra. Sra. de Guadalupe; San Jose; San Pablo.

6—SANTISIMA TRINIDAD (1978), Rev. Juan M. Beristain; Deacons Eusebio Jaca; Justo Ortiz.
Mailing Address: Apartado 50378, Levittown, 00950-0378. Tel: 809-784-2889.
Res., Calle 500 Levittown, 00950. Tel: 809-261-2716; 784-2889.

Trujillo Alto

1—SAN BARTOLOME (1985), Revs. Jose M. Alcocer, M.SS.CC.; Leoncio Mejia, M.SS.CC.; Deacons Alberto Gomez; Pablo Torres.
Res., X-1 Calle 16, Urb. Ciudad Universitaria, 00976. Tel: 787-755-0120.

2—SANTA CRUZ (1801), Rev. Edgar Pinto (Peru); Deacons Alfredo Aponte; Domingo Vargas.
Res., J. Diaz St., Box 1808, 00977. Tel: 809-761-0507.
School—Dr. Fernandez St., 00977. Tel: 809-761-1100. Sr. Maria Ramon Santiago, O.S.F., Dir.; Mrs. Ana L. Monzon de Matos, Prin.
Sisters 3; Lay Teachers 25; Students 452.

3—SAN FRANCISCO DE ASIS (1992), Rev. Isidro Giber Valero; Deacon Hector Rivera.
Res., Bo. Quebrada Grande, Cdad. Colon P.O. Box 1316, 00977-1316. Tel: 809-748-5584.
Missions—La Milagrosa; San Jose de la Montana; La Inmaculada Concepcion.

4—BIENVENTURADA VIRGEN MARIA DE LOURDES, Rev. Pedro Luis Reyes Lebron; Deacon Oscar Sanchez.
Res., Santuario, Gruta de Lourdes, Barrio. Cuevas, P.O. 1081, 00977. Tel: 809-761-0571. [JC]

5—San Judas Tadeo (1980), Rev. Miguel Pons; Deacon Jose Baez.
Mailing Address: Apartado 1535, 00977-1535.
Res., Calle 7, Urbanizacion El Conquistador, 00977-1535. Tel: 809-755-5993.
Missions—El Divino Pastor; Ntra. Sra. del Carmen.

Resident Chaplains:
Reverend Monsignors—
Valdes, Angel, Hospital del Maestro, Hato Rey
Reverend Fathers—
Mairal, Jose Ma. Lopez, Hogar de Sta. Teresa Jornet, Bo. Cupey, Rio Piedras, Trujillo Alto, PR
Ortega, Ovidio, Hogar de Ntra. Sra. de la Providencia, Ave. Ponce de Leon, Puerta de Tierra, Trujillo Alto, PR

On Duty Outside the Archdiocese:
Reverend Fathers—
Del Valle, Tomas
Esteve, Alfonso
Parello, Joseph J., St. Patrick Church, Smithtown, NY
Roldan, Juan
Sutil, Florencio
Torres, Ivan
Vicente, Julian

Graduate Studies:
Reverend Fathers—
Reyes, Pedro Luis, Rome

Retired:
Reverend Monsignors—
Cruz, Remberto
Oya, Eufrasio
Reverend Fathers—
Cruz, Gilbert J. (Spain)
Diaz, Alvaro
Egurrola, Vicente

Permanent Deacons:
Acosta, Santiago
Aldarondo, Elidio
Alicea, Angel L.
Alicea, Jose
Almodovar, Cesar
Alvarez, Enrique
Alvarez, Julio
Andino, Manuel
Andino, Virgilio
Aponte, Alfredo
Araya, Antonio
Araya, Rafael
Arevalo, Pedro Nel
Arroyo, Americo
Avila, Cesar
Ayala, Gregorio
Baez, Fernando
Baez, Jose
Balasquide, Eugenio
Bermudez, Jose A.
Berrios, Ildefonso
Birriel, Jose
Caban, Manuel
Caceres, Emilio
Calderon, Felix
Camacho, Manuel
Carmona, Eduardo
Carrasquillo, Jose
Casanova, Jorge
Castillo, Jose M.
Claudio, Pedro
Collazo, Felipe
Colon, Enrique
Colon, Francisco
Colon, Gumesindo
Colon, Ismael
Colon, Luis
Colon, Miguel
Colon, Rafael
Colon, Vicente
Comulada, Gerardo
Cordero, Luis
Cosme, Nicomedes
Costa, Pedro
Cotto, Bartolome
Cotto, Felix
Cruz, Francisco
Cruz, Hector
Cruz, Jose
Cuevas, Alfonso
Cuevas, Gregorio
D'Auria, Ricardo
Davila, Angel
De Jesus, Filiberty
De Jesus, Jose
De La Sota, Miguel
De Leon, Hilario
De Verona, Abel
Del Rio, Anastacio
Del Rio, Luis O.
Del Rio Pitre, Luis
Del Valle, Reinaldo
Delgado, Alfonso
Diaz, Agapito
Diaz, Ernie P.
Diaz, Jose
Diaz, Miguel
Diaz, Santiago
Diaz, Vidal
Domenech, Bienvenido
Dominguez, Ivan
Echegaray, Luis
Estrada, Martin
Falcon, Jose E.
Figueroa, Andres
Figueroa, Eladio
Figueroa, Juan
Figueroa, Nelson
Figueroa, Raul
Flores, Pedro
Franco, Porfirio
Garcia, Aureliz
Garcia, Enemias
Gierbolini, Francisco
Gomez, Alberto
Gomez, William
Gonzalez, Antonio
Gonzalez, Eduardo
Gonzalez, George
Gonzalez, Luis A.
Gonzalez, Pablo
Gonzalez, Pedro
Guiven, Cesar H.
Hernandez, Alejandro
Hernandez, Francisco
Hernandez, German
Hernandez, Jose
Hernandez, Marino
Huertas, Francisco
Irene, Pablo
Jaca, Eusebio
Lasanta, Vicente
Latorre, Santiago
Laureano, Enrique
Laureano, Juan
Llanos, Manuel
Longueira, Ricardo
Lopez, Felix
Lopez, Jesus
Lopez, Jose E.
Lopez, Victor
Loyola, Angel
Lugo, Benito
Lugo, Casiano
Lugo, Euripides
Lugo, Ildefonso
Maldonado, Eliezer
Maldonado, Pablo J.
Marin, Louis J.
Marini, Edwin
Marrero, Jose M.
Marrero, Miguel A.
Martinez, Candido
Martinez, Francisco
Martinez, Ricardo
Medina, Bernardino
Mejias, Gilberto
Melendez, Juan
Mendez, Miguel
Mendia, Roberto
Merced de la Paz, Victor
Merino, Latino
Mestre, Ibrahim
Miranda, Anselmo
Miranda, Jose
Miranda, Pedro
Montanez, Justo
Montes, Luis J.
Morales, Angel A.
Morales, Carlos R.
Morales, Jose
Morales, Martin
Morales, Rene
Narvaez, Efraim
Narvaez, Jose
Navedo, Luis A.
Negron, Gumersindo
Negron, Hector
Nerys, Jose A.
Nieves, Martin
Nieves, Santos
Nunez, Pedro
O'Neill, Luis R.
Ocasio, Domingo
Oliveras, Jose
Oquendo, Angel
Ortiz, Camildo
Ortiz, Enrique
Ortiz, Feliciano
Ortiz, Francisco
Ortiz, Jacinto
Ortiz, Julio
Ortiz, Julio H.
Ortiz, Justo
Ortiz, Pedro
Ortiz, Rafael
Ortiz, Ramon L.
Ortiz, Roberto
Oyola, Angel L.
Pabon, Angel
Pabon, Angel A.
Pacheco, Jose C.
Padilla, Isaias
Pappeterra, Jose
Pena, Jose
Penaloza, Marcos
Perez, Edwin
Perez, Ignacio
Perez, Jose
Perez, Jose R.
Perez, Juan
Perez, Juan B.
Perez, Luis R.
Perez, Pastor
Pineiro, Carlos
Pizarro, Angel M.
Porrata, Jose L.
Quintana, Antonio
Ralat, Carlos
Ramirez, Ferdinand
Ramirez, Tomas
Ramon, Ramon L.
Ramos, Ramon
Reyes, Humberto
Reyes, Manuel
Reyes, Rafael
Reyes, Victor
Rios, Jose M.
Rios, Vicente
Rios, William
Rivera, Angel
Rivera, Carlos
Rivera, Cristobal
Rivera, Edwin
Rivera, Efigenio
Rivera, Enrique
Rivera, Ernesto
Rivera, Eugenio
Rivera, Felipe
Rivera, Hector
Rivera, Jorge L.
Rivera, Jose
Rivera, Jose R.
Rivera, Jose A.
Rivera, Luis
Rivera, Luis Marcial
Rivera, Pedro
Rivera, Presbitero
Rivera, Prudencio
Rivera, Ramon L.
Rivera, Ulpiano
Robles, Jose L.
Rodriguez, Jose
Rodriguez, Jose A.
Rodriguez, Jose R.
Rodriguez, Juan
Rodriguez, Luis A.
Rodriguez, Orlando
Rodriguez, Ramon
Rodriguez, Romulo
Rodriguez, William
Rondon, Angel L.
Rosado, Jose
Rosario, Crescencio
Rubio, Silverio
Ruiz, Vicente
Sanabria, Rafael
Sanchez, Alejandro
Sanchez, Julio
Sanchez, Orlando
Sanchez, Oscar
Santiago, Antonio
Santiago, Ramon
Santiago, Vitelio
Santos, Juan Ramon
Santos, Marcos
Soto, Nelson
Suarez, Israel
Toro, Eliezer
Torres, Dionilo
Torres, Eugenio
Torres, Jose
Torres, Jose A.
Torres, Miguel A.
Torres, Pablo
Totti, Benjamin
Trujillo, Gerardo
Ubarri, Juan

Vaello, Guillermo
Valle, Esteban
Vargas, Domingo
Vazquez, Jose R.
Vazquez, Luis A.
Vazquez, Noel A.
Vega, Jose P.
Velazquez, Rafael
Velez, Gregorio
Velez, Miguel
Velez, Pedro
Villamil, Francisco

INSTITUTIONS LOCATED IN THE ARCHDIOCESE

[A] COLLEGES & UNIVERSITIES

BAYAMON. *Bayamon Central University*, Avenida Zaya Verde, Bo. Hato Tejas, P.O. Box 1725, 00960-1725. Tel: 787-786-3030. The University is composed of the following: Department of the Humanities; Department of Business Administration; Department of Natural Sciences; Department of Education; Division of Graduate Studies; Adult Education Program; Student Support Services Program.
Governing Board: Rev. Felix A.P. Struik, O.P., Pres. Council of Founders; Mr. Raymond L. Martinez, Pres. Bd. of Trustees.
Administration: Dr. Maria de los A. Ortiz, Pres.; Dr. Gabriel Ramos, Dean Academic Affairs; Mr. Antonio Rosario, Dean Admin. & Finances; Mr. Arcadio Figueroa, Dean Students; Ibis Rodriguez, Prof. & Dir. Humanities; Nelida Melendez, Prof. & Dir. Education; Lydia Villamil, Prof. & Dir. Natural Sciences; Mr. Angel Berrios, Dir. Institutional Devel.; Mr. Enrique Arias, Esq., Dir. Human Resources; Mr. Victor Colon, Registrar; Mrs. Christine Hernandez, Dir. Admissions; Mr. Henry Miranda, Dir. Student Financial Aid; Mr. Carlos Altamirano, Dir. Academic Resource Ctr.
Faculty: Revs. Felix A.P. Struik, O.P.; Luis Espinel, O.P.; Enrique Oria, O.Carm.; Angel Diaz Caceres; Mario Rodriguez Leon, O.P.; Angel Dario Carrero; Teodoro Veerkamp, O.P.; Marcelino Romero, C.M.F.; Domingo Aller, O.S.A.; Jorge Macias, C.S.S.R.; Jose Diman Soberal; Manuel Soler Pala. Lay Teachers 143; Total Enrollment 3,300.

[B] ELEMENTARY & HIGH SCHOOLS

SAN JUAN. *Colegio Parvulos Inmaculada Corazon de Maria*, 263 San Sebastian St., 00901. Tel: 809-722-1334. Sr. Ana I. Alvarado, Prin. Sisters 4; Lay Teachers 6; Students 158.

BAYAMON. *Colegio Ntra. Sra. del Rosario*, Calle 5, AA-7, Repto. Valencia, 00619. Tel: 809-798-5100. Sr. Ma. Ana Jimenez Maldonado, O.P., Prin. Students 338.
Colegio Santa Rosa, Calle Marti 15, P.O. Box 6032, 00619. Tel: 809-785-1195. Mrs. Esther Lopez, Prin. Lay Teachers 15.
Escuela Superior Catolica de Bayamon, Jazmin Esq. Millones, 2na. Ext. Lomas Verdes, P.O. Box 4225, 00956. Tel: 787-798-1548; 798-2329; 798-2747; Fax: 787-798-2620. Mrs. Maria C. de Marxuach, Dir. & Prin. Students 675.
Santo Domingo, 191 Comerio St., 00619. Tel: 809-785-0381. Ms. Carmen Ma. Ocasio Correa, Prin. Lay Teachers 12; Students 293.
Santo Tomas de Aquino. Affiliated with the Central University of Bayamon. Mailing Address: P.O. Box 1557, 00960-1557. Tel: 787-785-2530 (High School); 785-3838 (Elementary); Fax: 787-786-5015 (H.S.); 798-0180 (Elem.). Mrs. Carmen J. Acosta, Elem. Prin.; Mrs. Micaela Hurtado, H.S. Prin. Lay Teachers 48; Students 1,183.

GUAYNABO. *Colegio Marista*, Alturas de Torrimar, 00969. Tel: 787-789-2186; 789-2187; Fax: 787-720-7020. E-mail: marista1@icepr.com
Bro. Felipe Vegas, Prin. Priests 1; Brothers 9; Lay Teachers 80; Students 1,330.
Colegio Ntra. Sra. De La Caridad, Carretera Estatal #19, X-19, Villa Caparra., 00966. Tel: 787-781-8835. St. Joseph of the Mountain Sisters. Mother Josefina Jimenez, S.J., Prin. Sisters 9; Lay Teachers 14; Students 222.

HATO REY. *Colegio Lourdes*, 87 Mayaguez St., 00917. Tel: 787-767-6106; 756-5436; Fax: 787-767-5282. Mailing Address: P.O. Box 190847, San Juan, 00919-0847. Sr. Maria Paz Asiain, O.P., Dir. Sisters 4; Lay Teachers 30; Students 555.

RIO PIEDRAS. *Colegio La Milagrosa*, 107 De Diego Ave., 00925. Tel: 809-765-6114. Sr. Maria Flores., H.C., Prin. Sisters 8; Lay Teachers 15; Students 557.
Colegio Nuestra Senora De La Providencia. (Girls), Ave. San Ignacio #1358, Urb. Altamesa, 00921. Tel: 809-781-7506. Spanish Mercedarian Sisters. Sr. Dolores Sanchez, Prin. Sisters 7; Lay Teachers 46; Students 978.
Colegio Nuestra Senora Del Carmen, R.R. 2, Box 15, 00928. Tel: 809-761-8010. Mr. Angel M. Castillo, Prin.; Mrs. Maria L. Defillo de Bernardo, Prin. Sisters 7; Lay Teachers 41; Students 780.
Colegio San Jose. Mailing Address: Box 21300, 00928. Bro. Joaquin Suarez, S.M., Prin. Brothers 8; Lay Teachers 35; Students 578.

SANTURCE. *Academia Sagrado Corazon*. Mailing Address: Box 11368, Fernandez Juncos Sta., 00910. Tel: 809-721-3300. Rev. Francisco Quinones, Spiritual Dir.; Mrs. Alma de la Vega, Prin. Lay Teachers 37; Students 564.
Colegio La Inmaculada, Stop 26, Ave. Ponce De Leon #1711, 00909. Tel: 809-727-6673. Sr. Mary Zuluaga, F.M., Prin. Sisters 10; Lay Teachers 24; Students 558.
Colegio Maria Auxiliadora, 2273 Eduardo Conde, 00915. Tel: 809-726-8288. Sr. Elia M. Rioseco, F.M.A., Prin. Sisters 16; Lay Teachers 15; Students 481.

[C] SPECIAL SCHOOLS AND SEMINARIES

SAN JUAN. *Instituto Psicopedagogico De P.R.*, Km. 8, Hm. 5, Carretera Bayamon Box 3949, 00904. Tel: 809-782-4680. Jesus Nazarene Sisters. Mother Avelina, Supr. Beds 64; Sisters 9; Patients assisted annually 122.
Seminario Mayor Regional San Juan Bautista, Ave. De Diego No. 930, Urb. La Riviera, P.O. Box 11714, 00922-1714. Tel: 809-783-0645; 273-8090. Revs. Fernando Felices, Rector; Antonio Portalatin, Vice Rector.

BAYAMON. *Seminario Misionero del Espiritu Santo*, Calle Zaya Verde #44, Bo. Hato Tejas, 00959. Tel: 809-786-8231; 780-1201. Rev. Cornelius T. McQuillan, C.S.Sp., M.Div., Prin. Supr.
Teologado Padre Liberman, Calle C#D 19, Urb. La Milagrosa, 00619-4892. Tel: 809-787-2398. Rev. Felix Abreu Montilla, C.S.Sp., Dir.

RIO PIEDRAS. *Fraternidad Santa Maria de Los Angeles*, Expreso Trujillo Alto, Km. 1 Hm. 1. Tel: 809-761-8060. Revs. John Bednarik, O.F.M.Cap., Dir. Novices; Ramon J. Cosellas; Mario Mastrangelo, O.F.M.Cap., Mailing Address: Aptdo. 1864, 00760.
Jesuit Novitiate, Calle Jose Fidalgo Diaz, 2106, Barrio Caimito Abajo, R.F.D. 3, Buzon 5348, 00928. Tel: 809-790-3557. Revs. Orlando Torres, S.J., Master of Novices & Supr.; John Talbot, S.J. Seminarians 24.
Seminario Menor San Jose, Demetrio O'Dally St. 1000 Country Club, 00924. Tel: 809-768-3157. Rev. Freddy Alecio, Rector.

TOA ALTA. *Santo Domingo de Guzman Priory*, Ruta #2, Buzon 5905, Barrio Rio Lajas, 00953. Tel: 809-870-4540. Rev. Natividad Acevedo Fizcaya, O.P., Dir.

[D] SPECIAL CENTERS

SAN JUAN. *Santa Ana Chapel*. Perpetual Adoration, Calle Tetuan 203, Box 763, 00902. Tel: 809-725-7734. Rev. Raul Saez, Rector.

HATO REY. *Renovacion Conyugal*, Calle Sargento Medina 363, 00918. Tel: 787-751-6011; 766-1363. Rev. Jorge Ambert, S.J., Dir.

RIO PIEDRAS. *Centro Capuchino*, Expreso Trujillo Alto, Km. 1 Hm. 1. Tel: 787-761-8410. Mailing Address: Apto. 1865, 00977-1865. Rev. Jaime Perez Munoz, O.F.M.Cap., Dir.
Centro Universitario Catolico, 10 Mariana Bracetti St., Box 22862, U.P.R. Sta., 00931. Tel: 809-767-3348. Revs. Baudilio Guzman, S.J., Dir.; Juan Lopez Pedraz, S.J., Coop.

[E] CLINICS, HEALTH CENTERS

SAN JUAN. *Centro Medico de P.R.*, Calle 10 #1030, Puerto Nuevo, 00920. Apdo. 347, 00936. Tel: 809-763-7272
For a complete listing, refer to the Hospitals section.
Our Lady of Providence Mailing Address: P.O. Box 9020614, 00902-0614. Tel: 787-725-5358.
For a complete listing, refer to the Hospitals section.
VA Medical Center, One Veterans Plaza, 00927-5800. Tel: 809-758-7575, Ext. 3324
For a complete listing, refer to the Hospitals section.

RIO PIEDRAS. *Hospital del Maestro*, Calle Flamboyanes #218, Hyde Park, 00929. Tel: 809-763-8383
For a complete listing, refer to the Hospitals section.

SANTURCE. *Hospital de Diego*, Ave. de Diego #310, Pda. 22, 00908. Tel: 809-724-1700
For a complete listing, refer to the Hospitals section.

[F] HOMES AND RESIDENCES

DORADO. *Santuario del Espiritu Santo*, Box 187, 00646-0187. Tel: 809-796-2798
For a complete listing, refer to the Special Care Facilities section.

HATO REY. *Jesuit Community - Casa Claver*, 398 Francisca Sein, 00917
For a complete listing, refer to the Special Care Facilities section.

PUERTA DE TIERRA. *Asylum For The Aged and Infirm*, Hogar de la Providencia, Stop 5, 00906. Tel: 809-722-1331
For a complete listing, refer to the Special Care Facilities section.

RIO PIEDRAS. *Asylum For Orphan Girls*, 107 Jose de Diego St. S., 00925. Tel: 809-765-6114
For a complete listing, refer to the Special Care Facilities section.
Centro N. Sra. de la Providencia, R.F.D. #2, Box 16T, 00928. Tel: 809-761-0273
For a complete listing, refer to the Special Care Facilities section.
Hogar Carmelitano, Urb. San Martin, 00924. Tel: 809-769-6510
For a complete listing, refer to the Special Care Facilities section.
Hogar Santa Teresa Jornet for the Aged, Cupey Alto, Km. 3, Hm. 8, Box 21012, 00928. Tel: 787-761-5805
For a complete listing, refer to the Special Care Facilities section.

[G] PERSONAL PRELATURES

GUAYNABO. *Opus Dei*. (Prelature of the Holy Cross and Opus Dei), Region of Puerto Rico of the Prelature, A-35, Villa Caparra, 00966. Tel: 787-783-6206. Very Rev. Vicente Ariza, Reg. Vicar; Revs. Alfredo Gastalver; Gonzalo Diaz; Martin Llambias; Javier Bernaola; Jaime Guixa.

[H] MONASTERIES AND RESIDENCES FOR PRIESTS AND BROTHERS

SAN JUAN, PUERTO RICO. *The Capuchin Formation Trust of Puerto Rico*.

RIO PIEDRAS. *The Viceprovince of Saint John the Baptist, Puerto Rico, of the Order Friars Minor Capuchins*, Calle Arzuaga, 218, Apartado Postal 21350, 00928-1350. Tel: 787-764-3090; Fax: 787-764-4070. E-mail: pochi@coqui.net
Rev. John Bednarik, O.F.M.Cap., Vice Prov. Min.

[I] MISCELLANEOUS

MEDIANIA ALTA WARD, LOIZA. *Centro Esperanza, Inc.*, 1st St., Parcelas Vieques Development, 00772. Tel: 787-876-1545; Fax: 787-876-1545. Mailing Address: P.O. Box 482, Loiza, 00772-0482. Tel: 787-876-1545. Sr. Carmen Gloria Alayon, H.C., Dir. & Contact Person. Sponsored by: Sisters of Charity, Saint Vincent de Paul.

RELIGIOUS INSTITUTES OF MEN REPRESENTED IN THE ARCHDIOCESE

For further details refer to the corresponding bracketed number in the Religious Institutes of Men or Women section.

[0470]—*The Capuchin Friars*. (Vice Prov. of Puerto Rico).—O.F.M.Cap.
[0270]—*Carmelite Fathers & Brothers*. (Prov. of Arago, Valentina, Spain).—O.Carm.
[0360]—*Claretian Missionaries*. (Spain).—C.M.F.
[0310]—*Congregation of Christian Brothers*. (Antilles Prov.).—C.F.C.
[0820]—*Congregation of the Fathers of Mercy*. (Madrid, Spain).—C.P.M.
[1330]—*Congregation of the Mission*. (Prov. of Puerto Rico).—C.M.
[1000]—*Congregation of the Passion*. (Bibao).—C.P.
[]—*Congregation of the Terciarios Capuchinos Ntra. Sra. de los Dolores*. (Spain).—T.C.
[0520]—*Franciscan Friars*. (Spain).—O.F.M.
[0650]—*Holy Ghost Fathers*. (American Prov.).—C.S.Sp.
[0690]—*Jesuit Fathers and Brothers*. (New York Prov.).—S.J.
[0740]—*Marian Fathers*.—M.I.C.
[0770]—*The Marist Brothers*.—F.M.S.
[1120]—*Missionaries of the Sacred Hearts of Jesus and Mary*. (Spain).—M.SS.CC.
[0840]—*Missionary Servants of the Most Holy Trinity*.—S.T.
[0430]—*Order of Preachers-Dominicans*. (Hollan Prov.).—O.P.
[1310]—*Order of the Holy Trinity*. (Spain).—O.SS.T.
[1040]—*Piarist Fathers*. (Spain).—Sch.P.
[1070]—*Redemptorist Fathers*. (San Juan Prov.).—C.SS.R.
[1190]—*Salesians of Don Bosco*. (Antilles Prov.).—S.D.B.
[0760]—*Society of Mary*. (New York Prov.).—S.M.

RELIGIOUS INSTITUTES OF WOMEN REPRESENTED IN THE ARCHDIOCESE

[0100]—*Adorers of the Blood of Christ*. (Red Bud, IL; San Juan).—A.S.C.
[]—*Apostolado del Sagrado Corazon de Jesus*. (Madrid, Spain).
[1810]—*Bernardine Sisters of the Third Order of St. Francis*. (Villanova, PA).—O.S.F.
[]—*Carmelitas Misioneras*. (Barcelona, Spain).

[]—*Compania de las Hijas de la Caridad de San Vicente de Paul.* (Paris, France).
[1070-02]—*Dominican Sisters.*—O.P.
[1070-05]—*Dominican Sisters.*—O.P.
[1070-06]—*Dominican Sisters.*—O.P.
[1070-13]—*Dominican Sisters.*—O.P.
[]—*Dominicanas Terciarieas del Santisimo Sacramento.* (Cadiz, Spain).
[]—*Hermanas Carmelitas de la Caridad.* (Barcelona, Spain).
[]—*Hermanas Carmelitas de Madre Candelaria (Venezuela).*
[]—*Hermanas Carmelitas Teresas de San Jose (Barcelona, Spain).*
[]—*Hermanas de la Amistad Misionera en Cristo Obrero.* (Spain).
[]—*Hermanas de la B.V. Maria del Monte Carmleo.* (Orihuela, Spain).
[]—*Hermanas de la Caridad del Cardenal Sancha.*
[]—*Hermanas de la Compania del Salvador.* (Spain).
[]—*Hermanas de Santos Angeles Custodios.* (Bilbao, Spain).
[]—*Hermanas Dominicas de la Presentacion.* (Tours, France; Colombia).
[]—*Hermanas Dominicas de Nuestra Senora de Fatima.* (Yauco).
[]—*Hermanas Dominicas de Nuestra Senora del Rosario de Fatima.*
[]—*Hermanas Hospitalarias de Jesus Nazareno.* (Cordoba, Spain).
[]—*Hermanas Mercedarias de la Caridad.* (Madrid, Spain).
[]—*Hermanas Misioneras de los Sagrados Corazones.* (Palma de Mallorca, Spain).
[]—*Hermanitas de los Ancianos Desamparados.* (Valencia, Spain).
[]—*Hijas de Maria Auxiliadora.* (Torino, Italy).
[]—*Instituto Misionero Hijas de San Pablo.* (Rome, Italy).
[]—*Instituto Santa Mariana de Jesus (Hermanas Marianitas).* (Ecuador).—R.M.
[]—*Madres de Desamparados y San Jose de la Montana.* (Valencia, Spain).
[]—*Madres Escolapis.* (Rome).
[]—*Misioneras de Cristo Salvador.*
[]—*Misioneras del Buen Pastor.* (Caguas).
[]—*Misioneras del Santisimo Sacramento y Maria Inmaculada.* (Spain).
[]—*Misioneras Dominicas del Santisimo Rosario.* (Madrid, Spain).
[]—*Misioneras Guadalupanas del Espiritu Santo.* (Morelia, Mexico).
[2720]—*Mission Helpers of the Sacred Heart.*—M.H.S.H.
[2790]—*Missionary Servants of the Most Blessed Trinity.* (Philadelphia, PA).—M.S.B.T.
[]—*Monjas de la Orden de la Bienventurada Virgen Maria de Monte Carmelo.*
[]—*Oblates del Santisimo Redentor.* (Madrid, Spain).
[]—*Religiosas del Amor de Dios.* (Spain).
[]—*Religiosas del Sagrado Corazon.* (Rome, Italy).
[]—*Religiosas Oblates del Divino Amor.*
[]—*Religiosas Teatinas de la Inmaculada Concepcion.* (Rome).
[]—*Religiosas Terciarias de San Francisco de Asis y de la Inmaculada Concepcion.* (Valencia, Spain).
[2970]—*School Sisters of Notre Dame.* (Wilton, CT).—S.S.N.D.
[]—*Siervas de Maria y Ministras de los Enfermos.* (Rome, Italy).
[2570]—*Sisters of Mercy.* (Pittsburgh, PA).—R.S.M.
[1620]—*Sisters of Saint Francis of Millvale, Pennsylvania.*—O.S.F.
[1650]—*Sisters of St. Francis of Philadelphia.*—O.S.F.
[1800]—*Sisters of St. Francis of the Third Order Regular.* (Williamsville, New York).—O.S.F.
[3830]—*Sisters of St. Joseph.* (Brentwood).—C.S.J.
[3930]—*Sisters of St. Joseph of the Third Order of St. Francis.*—S.S.J.-T.O.S.F.
[1970]—*Sisters of the Holy Family of Nazareth.*—C.S.F.N.
[1490]—*Sisters of the Third Franciscan Order.*—O.S.F.
[2150]—*Sisters, Servants of the Immaculate Heart of Mary.*—I.H.M.
[]—*Terciarias Franciscanas de la Purisima.* (Murcia, Spain).

NECROLOGY

(No Deaths)

Diocese of St. Thomas in the Virgin Islands

Most Reverend

ELLIOTT G. THOMAS, D.D.

Bishop of St. Thomas in the Virgin Islands; ordained June 6, 1986; consecrated and installed as Bishop December 12, 1993.

ESTABLISHED AS PRELATURE OF VI, JULY 23, 1960.

ESTABLISHED AS DIOCESE OF ST. THOMAS IN THE VIRGIN ISLANDS APRIL 20, 1977

Comprises the Islands of St. Thomas, St. Croix and St. John.

Chancery Office: P.O. Box 301825, Charlotte Amalie, VI, 00803. Tel.: 340-774-3166; 776-1865; Fax: 340-774-5816.

E-mail address: af574@virgin.usvi.net

STATISTICAL OVERVIEW

Personnel	
Bishop	1
Priests: Diocesan Active in Diocese	7
Priests: Active Outside Diocese	3
Priests: Retired, Sick or Absent	1
Number of Diocesan Priests	11
Religious Priests in Diocese	6
Extern Priests in Diocese	3
Permanent Deacons in Diocese	22
Total Brothers	2
Total Sisters	14
Parishes	
Parishes	8
With Resident Pastor:	
Resident Diocesan Priests	5
Resident Religious Priests	2
Without Resident Pastor:	
Administered by Priests	1
Missions	2
Welfare	
Day Care and Extended Day Care Centers	4
Total Assisted	91
Special Centers for Social Services	6
Total Assisted	754
Educational	
Diocesan Students in Other Seminaries	3
Total Seminarians	3
High Schools, Diocesan and Parish	2
Total Students	282
Elementary Schools, Diocesan and Parish	3
Total Students	584
Catechesis/Religious Education:	
High School Students	226
Elementary Students	993
Total Students Under Catholic Instruction	2,088
Teachers in the Diocese:	
Priests	2
Brothers	1
Sisters	2
Lay Teachers	58
Vital Statistics	
Receptions into the Church:	
Infant Baptism Totals	412
Adult Baptism Totals	25
Received into Full Communion	22
First Communions	295
Confirmations	194
Marriages:	
Catholic	79
Interfaith	37
Total Marriages	116
Deaths	164
Total Catholic Population	30,000
Total Population	110,000

Former Bishops—Most Rev. EDWARD J. HARPER, C.SS.R., D.D., ord. June 18, 1939; appt. July 23, 1960; cons. Oct. 6, 1960; named first residential bishop of Diocese of St. Thomas in the Virgin Islands, April 20, 1977; retired Oct. 15, 1985; died Dec. 2, 1990.—Most Rev. SEAN P. O'MALLEY, O.F.M.Cap., ord. Aug. 29, 1970; named coadjutor, May 30, 1984; ord. Bishop, Aug. 2, 1984; installed Oct. 16, 1985; transferred Fall River Aug. 11, 1992.

Chancery Office—P.O. Box 301825, Charlotte Amalie, 00803. Tel: 340-774-3166; 776-1865; Fax: 340-774-5816.

Acting Chancellor—Deacon FRANK VERAART. Tel: 340-774-3166.

Fiscal Officer—CARL PENN.

Diocesan Consultors—Revs. GEORGE FRANKLIN; ALFRED BRADLEY, C.SS.R.; Rev. Msgr. MICHAEL KOSAK.

Religious Education Office—Vacant.

Youth Coordinator—Rev. KENNETH GADDY, *P.O. Box 547, Frederiksted, St. Croix, 00841.* Tel: 340-772-0138.

Hispanic Ministry—Revs. ALEJANDRO SANCHEZ; GERVASIO MALAVE, C.SS.R.; SERAPIO LOPEZ, O.F.M.

Historian—Rev. GEORGE FRANKLIN. Tel: 340-775-1650.

Catholic Charities of the Virgin Islands, Inc.—Sr. LOUIS MARIE BRYAN, S.C., Exec. Dir., *P.O. Box 10736, Charlotte Amalie, 00801.* Tel: 340-777-8518; Fax: 340-777-4875.

Family Education Program—ALVIN HENLEY, *Charlotte Amalie.* Tel: 340-777-4981; 777-4991.

Projects for Assistance in the Transition from Homelessness (PATH)—Ms. AVILDA MATTHIAS, *P.O. Box 10736, Charlotte Amalie, 00801.* Tel: 340-777-8518.

Catholic Schools Office—Mrs. DIANA PARKER, Dir., *P.O. Box 301825, Charlotte Amalie, 00803.* Tel: 340-777-5583; Fax: 340-774-5816.

Vocations—Rev. JEROME FEUDJIO, Dir., *P.O. Box 301767, St. Thomas, 00803.* Tel: 340-774-0201.

Charismatic Movement—Deacon HYACINTHE GEORGE, St. Croix: Rev. Msgr. MICHAEL KOSAK, St. Croix:

Diocesan Television Network—Mr. BERNARD GIBS, Dir. of Operations, *P.O. Box 301825, VDS, Charlotte Amalie, 00803.* Tel: 340-777-4828.

Caribbean Catholic Network—Channel 7, *P.O. Box 1160, Kingshill, St. Croix, 00851.* Tel: 340-779-3000.

Catholic Television Network (CTN)—Channel 16, *Charlotte Amalie, 00803.*

Diocesan Newspaper—"The Catholic Islander"; Ms. MARY CONWAY, Editor, *P.O. Box 301825, Charlotte Amalie, 00803.* Tel: 340-777-5583; Fax: 340-774-5816.

Communications Coordinator—Rev. Msgr. MICHAEL KOSAK.

Prison Ministry—Deacon ARNOLD HELENESE, St. Croix: Rev. JEROME FEUDJIO, St. Thomas:

Natural Family Planning Coordinator—Sr. LOUIS MARIE BRYAN, S.C. Tel: 340-777-8518.

Permanent Diaconate—Rev. ANTHONY FARRELL, Dir. Tel: 340-774-0201.

Shelters for the Homeless—Sr. LOUIS MARIE BRYAN, S.C., Exec. Dir., *Bethlehem House, P.O. Box 10736, Charlotte Amalie, 00801.* Tel: 340-774-4663., St. Croix: Tel: 340-778-1227., Administration: Tel: 340-777-8518; Fax: 340-777-4475.

ANSWER (Teenage Pregnancy Program)—12C Bjerge Gade, P.O. Box 10736, Charlotte Amalie, 00801. Tel: 340-774-6418., St. Croix: *P.O. Box 246, Christiansted, St. Croix, 00821.* Tel: 340-773-0132; Fax: 340-773-0302.

CLERGY, PARISHES, MISSIONS AND PAROCHIAL SCHOOLS

ISLAND OF ST. THOMAS
(Catholic Population, 12,500)

1—CATHEDRAL OF STS. PETER AND PAUL (1773) (West Indian), Revs. Gervasio Malave, C.SS.R.; Alejandro Sanchez; Jerome Feudjio, Admin.; Deacons William Summer; Jose Vasquez; Frank Veraart; Arturo Watlington. In res., Revs. Cecil Corneille; Anthony Farrell.

Mailing Address: P.O. Box 301767, Charlotte Amalie, 00803. Tel: 340-774-0201; Fax: 340-776-9586.

Res., 22A Kronprindsens Gade (Main St.), Charlotte Amalie, 00803.

Schools—Sts. Peter and Paul School, (Grades Jr.K-12) P.O. Box 301706, 00803. Tel: 340-774-5662; Fax: 340-777-5355. Mrs. Barbara Kenny, Asst. Prin.

Sisters 1; Lay Teachers 13; Grades Jr.K-6 Students 166; Tel: 340-774-2199. Mrs. Sara Connell, Prin.

Priests 2; Lay Teachers 15; Grades 7-12 Students 182.

Catechesis/Religious Programs—Students 111.

Convent—31 A Prindcesse Gade, P.O. Box 303785, Charlotte Amalie, 00803. Tel: 340-774-0248; Fax: 340-774-5816. Sisters of Charity of St. Elizabeth

Mission—Carenage, Chapel of St. Anne, P.O. Box 301767, 00803. Tel: 340-714-1101; Fax: 340-776-9586. Rev. Jerome Feudjio; Deacon Alberto Olive.

2—OUR LADY OF PERPETUAL HELP (1926), Rev. Cecil Corneille, Admin.; Deacon William Kenny.

Mailing Address: P.O. Box 304983, Charlotte Amalie, 00803. Tel: 340-774-0885; Fax: 340-774-0885. [CEM]
Catechesis/Religious Programs—Students 65.

3—Holy Family Parish (1969), Rev. Msgr. Prosper Askew; Deacons Leonard Monsanto; Austin Medina.
Res., Cassi Hill, P.O. Box 502218, St. Thomas, 00805. Tel: 340-775-1650; Fax: 340-775-1750.
Catechesis/Religious Programs—Gloria Etienne, D.R.E.
Students 100.

ISLAND OF ST. JOHN
(Catholic Population 300)

1—Our Lady of Mt. Carmel Parish (1962), Rev. Neil Scantlebury.
Res., P.O. Box 241, St. John, 00831. Tel: 340-776-6339 (Res. & Office); Fax: 340-693-7685.

ISLAND OF ST. CROIX
(Catholic Population, approx. 17,200)

1—Church St. Ann (1823), Rev. Msgr. Michael F. Kosak; Revs. Simon Peter O'Pira; Bernard Campbell; Deacons Arnold Helenese; Joseph Mark; Ed Cave; Norbert Xavier; Neville Charles; Hyacinthe George, Pastoral Assoc.
Mailing Address: 42 Barrenspot Hill, Box 1160, Kingshill, St. Croix, 00851-1160. Tel: 340-778-0484; Fax: 340-779-3151.
Catechesis/Religious Programs—Students 228.
Chaplaincy—Herbert Grigg Home for the Aged, Tel: 340-778-0708.

2—Church of the Holy Cross (1755), Revs. Alfred Bradley, C.SS.R.; James R. Cascione, C.SS.R.; Robert Lennon, C.SS.R.; Bro. Leonard Samuel, C.SS.R.; Deacons Ulric Benjamin; Carlos Calderon; Angel Tito Maldonado; James Matthews.
Res., Box 1069, Christiansted, St. Croix, 00821-1069. Tel: 340-773-7564; Fax: 340-713-9149.
School—St. Mary's, P.O. Box 4090, Christiansted, St. Croix, 00822. Tel: 340-773-0117; Fax: 340-773-1166. Susan Diverio, Prin.
Lay Teachers 14; Students 158.
Catechesis/Religious Programs—Tel: 340-773-7564; Fax: 340-713-9149. D.R.E.: Rev. James Cascione, C.Ss.R; Mrs. Christina James.
Students 255.
Mission—LBJ Village, U.S.V.I., Sacred Heart Chapel, P.O. Box 1069, Christiansted, 00821.
Blessed Peter Donder's Formation Residence—P.O. Box 24839-Gallows Bay, Christiansted, St. Croix, 00824-0839. Tel: 340-692-9999; Fax: 340-692-9997. Bro. Leonard Samuel, C.Ss.R., Dir.
Res., 20 Prince St., Christiansted, St. Croix, 00820. Tel: 340-692-9999; Fax: 340-692-9997.
Convent—P.O. Box 3058, Christiansted, St. Croix, VI 00821. Tel: 340-773-1950. Missionaries of Charity

3—Church of St. Patrick (1765) (African-Caribbean), Revs. Michael Hopkins, C.SS.R.; Kenneth Gaddy, C.SS.R.; Deacons Felix Francis; Emith Fludd; Angel Maldonado.
Mailing Address: Box 547, Frederiksted, St. Croix, 00841. Tel: 340-772-0138; Fax: 340-772-0142.
School—P.O. Box 988, Frederiksted, St. Croix, 00841. Tel: 340-772-0138; Fax: 340-772-4488. Mary McIntosh, Prin.
Lay Teachers 19; Students 260.
Catechesis/Religious Programs—Students 135.
Convent—Caribbean Center, P.O. Box 95, Frederiksted, St. Croix, 00841. Tel: 340-772-0341. Missionary Sisters of the Immaculate Heart of Mary
DeMeester Residence: P.O. Box 52, St. Croix, 00841. Tel: 340-772-0132.
Light of Christ Retreat Center—New St., P.O. Box 547, St. Croix, 00841. Tel: 340-772-4782; Fax: 340-772-0142.

4—Church of St. Joseph (1947), Rev. Serapio Lopez; Deacons James Verhoff; Conrad Williams.
Mailing Address: P.O. Box 2150, Kingshill, St. Croix, 00851-2150. Tel: 340-692-2005; Fax: 340-692-2748. [JC]
Res., Mt. Pleasant, Frederiksted, St. Croix, 00841.
Catechesis/Religious Programs—Students 300.
Convent—P.O. Box 1847, Kingshill, St. Croix, 00851. Tel: 340-778-5773; Fax: 340-778-5773. West Indian Franciscans

Chaplaincies

These chaplaincies only pertain to the Island of St. Thomas.

St. Thomas. *Lucinda Millin Home for the Aged.*
Queen Louise Home for the Aged.
St. Thomas Hospital and Community Health Center.

Permanent Deacons:
Benjamin, Ulric
Calderon, Carlos
Cave, Edward
Charles, Neville
Fludd, Emith
Francis, Felix
George, Hyacinthe
Helenese, Arnold
Kenny, William
Maldonado, Angel
Mark, Joseph T.
Matthew, James
Medina, Austin
Monsanto, Leonard
Olive, Alberto
Summer, William
Vazquez, Jose
Veraart, Frank
Verhoff, James
Watlington, Arturo
Williams, Conrad
Xavier, Norbert

INSTITUTIONS LOCATED IN THE DIOCESE

[A] INTERPAROCHIAL HIGH SCHOOLS

St. Croix. *St. Joseph High School*, 3 Mt. Pleasant, Rte. 2, Frederiksted, 00840. Tel: 340-692-2455; Fax: 340-692-2458. Gloria H.C. Waterman, Prin. Brothers 1; Sisters 1; Lay Teachers 10; Students 100.

[B] ORGANIZATIONS IN THE DIOCESE

St. Thomas. *Miscellaneous Organizations.* (For further information contact the Chancery Office.). Box 301825, Charlotte Amalie, 00803. Tel: 340-774-3166; Fax: 340-774-5816.
E-mail: af574@virgin.usvi.net
Catholic Daughters of the Americas. Mrs. Angelita Jennings, Regent. Tel: 340-774-7943.
COR (Christ in Others Retreat). Rev. Kenneth Gaddy, C.SS.R. Tel: 340-772-0138.
Cursillo Movement, St. Croix. Rev. James R. Cascione, C.SS.R. Tel: 809-773-7564.
Knights of Columbus, St. Croix. Bertil MacGregor, Deputy. Tel: 340-773-7135; John Maduro. Tel: 340-774-6488.
Legion of Mary. Rev. James R. Cascione, C.SS.R. Tel: 340-773-7564.
Lumen 2000/Caribbean Region. Rev. Msgr. Michael F. Kosak. Tel: 340-778-0484.
Propagation of the Faith. Rev. Simon Peter Opira, Dir. Tel: 340-778-0484.
Secular Franciscans. Sr. Patricia Alexander, W.I.F., Spiritual Asst. Tel: 340-778-5773.
Fraternity Our Lady of the Angels. Deacon Conrad Williams, Min. Tel: 340-778-1733; Mrs. Cleo Hobson, Min. Tel: 340-775-0666.
St. Vincent de Paul Society. Christian Begraff. Tel: 340-773-0176.
Catholic Charities of the Virgin Islands. Sr. Louis Marie Bryan, S.C., Exec. Dir. Tel: 340-777-8518.
Disciples of the Holy Spirit, Inc., P.O. Box 1160, Kingshill, St. Croix, 00851. Rev. Msgr. Michael F. Kosak, Dir. For all: Total Assisted 754; Total Staff 30.

RELIGIOUS INSTITUTES OF MEN REPRESENTED IN THE DIOCESE

For further details refer to the corresponding bracketed number in the Religious Institutes of Men or Women section.

[0920]—*Oblates of St. Francis De Sales.*—O.S.F.S.
[1070]—*Redemptorist Fathers.*—C.SS.R.

RELIGIOUS INSTITUTES OF WOMEN REPRESENTED IN THE DIOCESE

[]—*Association of West Indian Franciscans.*—W.I.F.
[2710]—*Missionaries of Charity.*—M.C.
[2750]—*Missionary Sisters of the Immaculate Heart of Mary.*—I.C.M.
[0590]—*Sisters of Charity of Saint Elizabeth (Convent Station).*—S.C.

NECROLOGY

(No Deaths)

PART III
Canada and Mexico

APOSTOLIC NUNCIATURE

(For Canada)

Apostolic Pro-Nuncio:
Most Reverend Carlo Curis, Titular Archbishop of Medeli.
Counsellor—Rev. Msgr. Vito Rallo
Res., 724 Manor Ave., Rockcliffe Park, Ottawa, Ont., Canada, K1M OE3
Tel: 613-746-4914; Fax: 613-746-4786.

PROVINCE OF EDMONTON

Archdiocese of Edmonton; Dioceses of Calgary, and St. Paul.

PROVINCE OF GATINEAU-HULL

Archdiocese of Gatineau-Hull, Dioceses of Amos, Mont-Laurier and Rouyn-Noranda.

PROVINCE OF HALIFAX

Archdiocese of Halifax; Dioceses of Antigonish, Charlottetown, and Yarmouth.

PROVINCE OF KINGSTON

Archdiocese of Kingston; Dioceses of Alexandria-Cornwall, Peterborough, and Sault Ste. Marie.

PROVINCE OF MONTREAL

Archdiocese of Montreal; Dioceses of Joliette, Saint-Jean-Longueuil, St. Jerome, and Valleyfield.

PROVINCE OF MONCTON

Archdiocese of Moncton; Dioceses of Edmundston, Bathurst, and St. John.

PROVINCE OF OTTAWA

Archdiocese of Ottawa; Dioceses of Hearst, Pembroke, and Timmins.

PROVINCE OF QUEBEC

Archdiocese of Quebec; Dioceses of Chicoutimi, Ste. Anne-de-la-Pocatiere, and Trois-Rivieres.

PROVINCE OF RIMOUSKI

Archdiocese of Rimouski; Dioceses of Gaspe, and Baie Comeau.

PROVINCE OF REGINA

Archdiocese of Regina; Dioceses of Prince Albert, Gravelbourg, Saskatoon, and Muenster.

PROVINCE OF SHERBROOKE

Archdiocese of Sherbrooke; Dioceses of St. Hyacinthe, and Nicolet.

PROVINCE OF ST. BONIFACE

Archdiocese of St. Boniface.

PROVINCE OF ST. JOHN'S

Archdiocese of St. John's; Dioceses of Grand Falls, and St. George's.

PROVINCE OF TORONTO

Archdiocese of Toronto; Dioceses of Hamilton, London, St. Catharines, and Thunder Bay.

PROVINCE OF VANCOUVER

Archdiocese of Vancouver; Dioceses of Kamloops, Nelson, and Victoria.

PROVINCE OF KEEWATIN-LE PAS

Archdiocese of Keewatin-Le Pas; Dioceses of Churchill-Baie D'Hudson, Moosonee, and Labrador City-Schefferville.

PROVINCE OF GROUARD-MCLENNAN

Archdiocese of Grouard-McLennan; Dioceses of Mackenzie-Fort Smith, Prince George, and Whitehorse.

ARCHDIOCESE OF WINNIPEG

(Immediately subject to the Holy See)

PROVINCE OF UKRAINIAN BYZANTINE RITE

Metropolitan See of Winnipeg; Ukrainian Eparchates of Edmonton, New Westminster, Saskatoon, and Toronto.

MILITARY ORDINARIATE

CANADIAN CONFERENCE OF CATHOLIC BISHOPS

SECRETARIAT OF THE CANADIAN HIERARCHY
(Established October 12, 1943)

Address: 90 Parent Ave., Ottawa, Ont. K1N 7B1. Tel: 613-241-9461.

Rev. M. Emilius Goulet, P.S.S., General Secretary, (French Sector).
Vacant-General Secretary, (English Sector).
Mr. Gerald Baril, Asst. General Secretary, (French).
Mr. Bede M. Hubbard, Asst. General Secretary, (English).

MEMBERS AND OFFICERS C.C.C.B. PERMANENT COUNCIL

Executive Committee and Permanent Council: President: His Eminence Cardinal Jean-Claude Turcotte (Montreal). Vice-President: Most Rev. Gerald Wiesner (Prince George).

Co-Treasurers: Most Rev. Anthony F. Tonnos (Hamilton); Rev. Msgr. Henri Goudreault, O.M.I. (Grouard-McLennan)

Programmes and Priorities Committee Representatives: Rev. Msgr. Andre Gaumond (Sherbrooke); Most Rev. Brendan O'Brien (Pembroke).

Representants Des Regions-Regional Representatives: Atlantic - Most Rev. James H. MacDonald (St. John's); Ontario - Rev. Msgr. Andre Vallee, P.M.E. (Hearst); Quebec - Rev. Msgr. Martin Veillte (Trois-Rivieres); West - Rev. Msgr. Henri Goureault, C.M. (Grouard-McLennan)

Representants Des Secteurs-Sector Representatives: Most Rev. Jacques Berthelet (Saint-Jean-Longueuil); Most Rev. Blaise E. Morand (Prince Albert); Most Rev. Anthony F. Tonnos (Hamilton); Most Rev. James Weisgerber (Saskatoon).

Membres De Droit-Ex Officio Members: His Eminence Cardinal Jean-Claude Turcotte (Montreal); Most Rev. Maurice Couture (Quebec); Most Rev. Aloysius Ambrozic (Toronto); Most Rev. Michael Bzdel, C.Ss.R., (Metropolitan, Winnipeg). Most Rev. Francis J. Spence (Kingston).

Programmes and Priorities Committee: Most Rev. Gerald Wiesner, C.M.I., (Prince George); Rev. Msgr. Andre Gaumond (Sherbrooke); Most Rev. Henri Goudreault, O.M.I., (Grouard-McLennan); Most Rev. Francis J. Spence (Kingston); Most Rev. Terrance Prendergast, S.J., (Toronto); Most Rev. Brendan O'Brien (Pembroke); Most Rev. Francois Thibodeau (Edmundston).

EPISCOPAL COMMISSIONS

The CCCB's nine episcopal Commissions are appointed by the Permanent Council to undertake study and projects in specific areas of pastoral work. Six Commissions serve nationally and three Commissions relate to the French and English Sectors.

National Level

Social Affairs

Most Revs. Francois Thibodeau, Chm.; Bertrand Blanchet; Marcel A.J. Gervais; Nicola De Angelis; Pierre Morissette; Peter Sutton.

Canon Law - Inter Rite

Most Revs. Jean-Guy Couture, Chm.; Thomas B. Fulton; James M. Wingle; Severian Yakymyshyn.

Commission for Relations with Associations of Priests, Religious, and Laity

Most Revs. James H. MacDonald, Chm.; Jean-Guy Hamelin; Terrence Prendergast; Raymond Dumais.

Missions

Most Revs. J. Faber MacDonald, Chm.; Thomas J. Lobsinger; Andre Vallee; **Andre Gaumond**

Ecumenism

Most Revs. Brendan O'Brien, Chm.; Vincent Cadieux; Vital Masse; Gilles Ouellet; Denis Croteau; Cornelius Pasichny

Theology

Most Revs. Henri Goudreault, Chm.; Gerard Drainville; Adam Exner; Aloysius Ambrozic; Laurent Noel; Gerald Wiesner.

Sector Level

English Sector

Social Communications

Most Revs. Fred Colli, Chm.; Michael Bzdel, C.Ss.R.; Vernon Fougere; John Sherlock.

Christian Education

Most Revs. Anthony F. Tonnos, Chm.; Raymond J. Lahey; Peter Mallon; John M. O'Mara.

Liturgy

Most Revs. John S. Knight, Chm.; James M. Hayes; Peter Novecosky; Blaise Morand.

French Sector

Social Communications

Most Revs. Roger Ebacher, Chm.; Robert Lebel; Jean-Louis Plouffe; Andre Richard.

Christian Education

Most Revs. Gilles Cazabon, Chm.; Gerard Dionne; Gilles Lussier; Raymond Roussin.

Liturgy

Most Revs. Antoine Hacault, Chm.; Jacques Berthelet; Clement Fecteau; Jude Saint-Antoine.

ARCHDIOCESES

Edmonton. *Archbishop*—Most Rev. Joseph Neil MacNeil, D.D.; *Chancellor*—Rev. C. Michael McCaffery; *Archdiocesan Office*—8421 101 Ave., Edmonton, Alberta T6A 0L1. Tel: 403-469-1010; Fax: 403-465-3003.

Gatineau-Hull. *Archeveque*—Most Rev. Roger Ebacher; *Chancellor*—Mrs. Lucy Gorman McCoy; *Chancery Office*—180, boulevard Mont-Bleu, Hull, P.Q., J8Z 3J5. Tel: 819-771-8391; Fax: 819-778-8969.

Grouard-McLennan. *Archeveque*—Most Rev. Henri Goudreault, O.M.I., D.D.; *Chancellor*—Rev. Charles Lavoi, O.M.I.; *Chancery Office*—Archbishop's Residence, P.O. Box 388, McLennan, Alberta T0H 2L0. Tel: 403-324-3002; Fax: 403-324-3952.

Halifax. *Archbishop*—Most Rev. Austin-E. Burke; *Chancellor*—Rev. Msgr. Martin Curie; *Vice Chancellor*—Deacon John Mac Neil; *Chancery Office*—P.O. Box 1527, Halifax, N.S. B3J 2Y3. Tel: 902-429-9800; Fax: 902-423-5201.

Keewatin-Le Pas. *Archbishop*—Most Rev. Peter-Alfred Sutton, O.M.I., D.D.; *Chancellor*—Rev. Wojciech Kowal, O.M.I.; *Chancery Office*—Archbishop's Residence, 108-1st St. West, P.O. Box 270, Le Pas, Manitoba, R9A 1K4. Tel: 204-623-2503; Fax: 204-623-6121.

Kingston. *Archbishop*—Most Rev. Francis Spence, D.D.; *Vicar General*—Rev. T. J. Raby; *Chancellor*—Rev. M.J. Lynch; *Chancery Office*—390 Palace Rd., Kingston, Ont., K7L 4T3. Tel: 613-548-4461; Fax: 613-548-4744.

Moncton. *Archeveque*—Most Rev. Ernest Leger; *Chancellor*—Bro. F. Merville Gagnon, I.C.; *Chancery Office*—452, rue Amirault, Dieppe, N.B., E1A 1G3. Tel: 506-857-9531; Fax: 506-857-9533.

Montreal. *Archeveque*—His Eminence Cardinal Jean-Claude Turcotte; *Auxiliary Bishops*—Most Revs. Andre Cimichella; Jude Saint-Antoine; Andre Rivest; Neil E. Willard. *Vicars General*—Rev. Msgr. Robert Beaupre, C.S.S.; Most Rev. Neil E. Willard; *Chancellor*—Rev. Michel Parent, C.S.S., V.E., Chancery Office—2000 Sherbrooke St. W., Montreal, Quebec, H3H 1G4. Tel: 514-931-7311; Fax: 514-931-3432.

Montreal. *Archeparch*—Rev. Msgr. Michel Hakim; *Chancellor*—Rev. Msgr. Georges Coriaty, B.S. *Chancery Office*—34, Maplewood, Montreal, Quebec H2V 2M1. Tel: 514-272-6430; Fax: 514-272-2341.

Montreal. *Eparch*—Most Rev. Joseph Khoury, 12475 Grenet, Montreal, Quebec H4J 2K4. Tel: 514-331-2807; Fax: 514-334-5723.

Ottawa. *Archbishop*—Most Rev. Marcel A.J. Gervais; *Auxiliary Bishops*—Most Revs. Paul Marchand;

Fred Colli.*Vicar General*—Most Rev. Fred Colli; *Chancellor*—Rev. Msgr. Roger Morin, P.A., V.E.; *Chancery Office*—1247 Kilborn Place, Ottawa, Ont., K1H 6K9. Tel: 613-738-5025; Fax: 613-738-0130.

Quebec. *Archeveque*—Most Rev. Maurice Couture, Primate of Canada; *Auxiliary Bishops*—Most Revs. Jean-Pierre Blais; Marc Leclerc; Eugene Tremblay. *Vicar General* — Most Rev. Marc Leclerc;*Chancellor*—Sr. Lucienne Boisvert, S.C.S.L.; *Chancery Office*—1073, boul. Rene Levesque Ouest, Quebec G1S 4R5. Tel: 418-688-1211; Fax: 418-688-1399. Residence: Archeveche de Quebec—2, Port Dauphin, C.P. 459, Haute-Ville, Quebec G1R 4R6. Tel: 1-418-692-3935; Fax: 418-692-5272.

Regina. *Archbishop*—Most Rev. Peter Mallon, D.D.; *Chancellor*—Rev. J. Balzer. *Chancery Office*—445 Broad St. N., Regina, Sask. S4R 2X8. Tel: 306-352-1651; Fax: 306-545-0510.

Rimouski. *Archeveque*—Most Rev. Bertrand Blanchet, P.M.E. *Chancellor*—Rev. Yves-Marie Melanqon; *Chancery Office*—34 Rue de L'Eveche Ouest, P.O. Box 730, Rimouski, P.Q. G5L 7C7. Tel: 418-723-3320; Fax: 418-722-8978.

St. Boniface. *Archeveque*—Most Rev. Antoine Hacault, D.D.; *Vicar GenerealRev.* Msgr. Henri Perron, P.H.; —*Chancellor*—Rev. Msgr. Roland Belanger. *Chancery Office*—151, Ave. de la Cathedrale, Saint-Boniface, Man., R2H 0H6. Tel: 204-237-9851; Fax: 204-231-2652.

St. John's, Nfld. *Archbishop*—Most Rev. James H. MacDonald, D.D.; *Chancellor*—Rev. Douglas Stamp; *Chancery Office*—Pastoral Center, P.O. Box 37, St. John's, Nfld. A1C 5N5. Tel: 709-726-3660; Fax: 709-753-5600.

Sherbrooke. *Archeveque*—Most Rev. Andre Gaumond; *Chancellor*—Sr. Cecile Grenier, P.M.; *Archdiocesan Office*—130 rue de la Cathedrale, C.P. 430, Sherbrooke, Quebec, J1H 5K1. Tel: 819-563-9934; Fax: 819-562-0125.

Toronto. *Archbishop*—Most Rev. Aloysius M. Ambrozic; *Auxiliary Bishops & Vicars General*—Most Revs. John Knight; Nicolas De Angelis; Terrence Prendergast; Anthony G. Meagher. *Chancellor*—Rev. John K. Murphy. *Chancery Office*—1155 Yonge, Toronto, Ontario, M4T 1W2. Tel: 416-934-0606; Fax: 416-934-3433.

Vancouver. *Archbishop*—Most Rev. Adam Exner; *Vicar General*—Rev. Msgr. David Monroe. *Chancellor*—Rt. Rev. Gregory N. Smith; *Chancery Office*—150 Robson St., Vancouver, B.C., V6B 2A7. Tel: 604-683-0281; Fax: 604-683-4288.

Winnipeg. *Archbishop*—Leonard J. Wall; *Chancellor and Episcopal Vicar General*—Rev. D. Ward Jamieson.*Chancellor*—Rev. W. Richard Arsenault, J.C.L., V.E. *Chancery Office*—1495 Pembina Hwy., Winnipeg, Manitoba, R3T 2C6. Tel: 204-452-2227; Fax: 204-475-4409.

DIOCESES

Alexandria-Cornwall. *Eveque*—Most Rev. Eugene-P. LaRocque, D.D.; *Chancellor*—Rev. Denis Vaillancourt; 220, Chemin Montreal, P.O. Box 1388, Cornwall, Ontario, K6H 5V4. Tel: 613-933-1138; Fax: 613-937-4931.

Amos. *Eveque*—Most Rev. Gerard Drainville; *Chancellor*—Sr. Rejeanne Veillette. *Chancery Office*—450 nord, rue Principale, Amos, P.Q., J9T 2M1. Tel: 819-732-6515; Fax: 819-732-7994.

Antigonish. *Bishop*—Most Rev. Colin Campbell, D.D.; *Chancellor*—Sr. Florence Steele, C.S.M. *Chancery Office*—P.O. Box 1330, 155 Main St., Antigonish, Nova Scotia, B2G 2L7. Tel: 902-863-3335; Fax: 902-863-0037.

Baie-Comeau. *Eveque*—Most Rev. Pierre Morissette; *Vicar General*— Rev. Germain Gagnon; *Chancellor*—Sr. Jeanne-Mance Caron, S.C.I.M.; *Chancery Office*—639 rue de Bretagne, Baie-Comeau, Quebec, G5C 1X2. Tel: 418-589-5744; Fax: 418-295-3145.

Bathurst. *Eveque*—Most Rev. Andre Richard, C.S.C.; *Vicar General*—Rev. Zoel Saulnier; *Chancellor*—Rev. Lionel Comeau; *Chancery Office*—Bishop's Res., 645 Ave. Murray, P.O. Box 460, Bathurst, New Brunswick. E2A 3Z4. Tel: 506-546-1420; Fax: 506-546-1423.

Calgary. *Bishop*—Most Rev. Paul O'Byrne; *Chancellor & Vicar for Matrimonial Affairs*—Sr. Rose-Anne Engel, O.S.U.; Bishop's Office, Catholic Pastoral Centre, Room 290, 120, 17 Avenue, S.W., Calgary, Alberta, T2S 2T2. Tel: 403-218-5524; Fax: 403-264-0272.

Charlottetown. *Bishop*—Most Rev. J. Vernon Fougere; *Vicar General*—Rev. Arthur O'Shea; *Chancellor*—Rev. Lydon Hogan, J.C.L.; *Chancery Office*—P.O. Box 907 - 350 North River Rd., Charlottetown, Prince Edward Island, CIA 7L9. Tel: 902-368-8005; Fax: 902-368-1644.

Chicoutimi. *Eveque*—Most Rev. Jean-Guy Couture, D.D.; *Auxiliary Bishop*—Most Rev. Roch Pedneault, D.D., V.G.; *Vicars Generals*—Most Rev. Roch Pedneault; Rev. Yvan Tremblay; *Chancellor*—Msgr. Jean-Roch Gaudin, C.S.S.; *Chancery Office*—602 rue Racine Est. Chicoutimi, P.Q., G7H 6J6. Tel: 418-543-0783; Fax: 418-543-2141.

Churchill-Hudson Bay. *Eveque*—Mgr. Reynald Rouleau, O.M.I.; *Vicar Gen.*—R.P. Robert Lechat, O.M.I.; *Chancery Office*—P.O. Box 10, Churchill, Manitoba, R0B 0E0. Tel: 204-675-2541; Fax: 204-675-2140.

Edmundston. *Eveque*—Most Rev. Francois Thibodeau, C.J.M.; *Chancellor*—Sr. Ronilla Sirois, R.H.S.J.; *Chancery Office*—Centre diocesan, Edmundston, New Brunswick, E3V 3K1. Tel: 506-735-5578; Fax: 506-735-4271.

Gaspe. *Eveque*—Most Rev. Raymond Dumais; *Chancellor*—Sr. Marie-Paule Couturier, F.M.A.; *Chancery Office*—P.O. Box 440, 172, rue Jacques-Cartier, Gaspe, Quebec, G0C 1R0. Tel: 418-368-2274; Fax: 418-368-3772.

Grand Falls. *Bishop*—Most Rev. Joseph Faber MacDonald, D.D.; *Vicar General*—Rt. Rev. E.T. Bromley; *Vice Chancellor*—Sr. Sarah Moore, P.B.V.M.; *Chancellor*—Rev. Brain Dunn, J.C.D.; *Chancery Office*—8A Church Rd. - P.O. Box 771, Grand Falls, Windsor, Nfld., A2A 2M4. Tel: 709-489-4019. Fax: 709-489-6393.

Gravelbourg. *Eveque*—Most Rev. Raymond Roussin, S.M.; *Vicar General*—Lucien Rodrigue. *Chancery Office*—Bishop's Residence, P.O. Box 690, Gravelbourg, Sask., SOH IXO. Tel: 306-648-2615; Fax: 306-648-2477.

Hamilton. *Bishop*—Most Rev. Anthony Tonnos; *Auxiliary Bishop*—Most Rev. Matthew Ustrzycki; *Vicar General*—Rev. Msgr. John Newstead. *Chancellor*—Rev. Gerard P. Bergie; *Chancery Office*—700 King St., W. Hamilton, Ont., L8P 1C7. Tel: 905-528-7988; Fax: 905-528-1088.

Hearst. *Eveque*—Most Rev. Andre Vallee; *Chancellor*—Rev. Rene Grandmont; *Chancery Office*—P.O. Box 1330, 76-7th St., Hearst, Ont., P0L IN0. Tel: 705-362-4903; Fax: 705-362-4421.

Joliette. *Eveque*—Most Rev. Gilles Lussier; *Chancellor*—Sr. Jacynthe Ricard; *Chancery Office*—2, rue Saint-Charles-Borromee nord, C.P. 470, Joliette, P.Q., J6E 6H6. Tel: 514-753-7596; Fax: 514-759-0929.

Kamloops. *Bishop*—Most Rev. Lawrence Sabatini, D.D.; *Vicar General*—Rt. Rev. John MacIntyre; *Chancellor*—Sr. Marie R. MacDonald, C.S.M.; *Chancery Office*—635A Tranquille Rd., Kamloops, B.C., V2B 3H5. Tel: 250-376-3351; Fax: 250-376-3363.

Labrador City-Schefferville. *Bishop*—Most Rev. Douglas Crosby, O.M.I.; *Vicar General*—Rev. Joseph Baril, O.M.I.; *Chancellor*—Sr. Ann Adams, R.S.R.; *Chancery*—318 Ave. Elizabeth, C.P. 545, Labrador City, Labrador (NSLd.) A2V 2K7. Tel: 709-944-2046; Fax: 709-944-5798.

London. *Bishop*—Most Rev. John M. Sherlock, D.D.; *Auxiliary Bishop*—Most Rev. Richard Grecco, T.H.D.; *Vicar General*—Rev. R. Anthony Daniels; *Chancellor*—Rev. J. Richard Boll; *Chancery Office*—1070 Waterloo St., London, Ont., N6A 3Y2. Tel: 519-433-0658; Fax: 519-433-0011.

Mackenzie-Fort Smith. *Bishop*—Most Rev. Denis Croteau, O.M.I. *Chancery Office*—5117, 52nd. St., Yellowknife, N. W. T., X1A 1T7. Tel: 867-920-2129; Fax: 867-873-9021.

Mont-Laurier. *Eveque*—Most Rev. Jean Gratton, D.D.; *Vicar General*—Rev. Msgr. Jean Levert; *Chancellor*—Sr. Denise Savard, S.C.O.; *Chancery Office*—Bishop's House, 435, rue de la Madone, Mont-Laurier, P.Q., J9L 1S1. Tel: 819-623-5530; Fax: 819-623-9523.

Moosonee. *Eveque*—Most Rev. Vincent Cadieux, O.M.I.; *Vicar General*—Rev. Rodrigue Vezina, O.M.I.; *Chancellor*—Sr. Marie-Berthe Demers, O.S.U. *Chancery Office*—P.O. Box 40, Moosonee, Ont., PL0 IY0. Tel: 705-336-2908; Fax: 705-336-2759.

Nelson. *Bishop*—Most Rev. Eugene J. Conney; *Judicial Vicar*—Rev. Wayne Phliger; *Vicar General*—Rev. Charles Mulvihill;*Chancellor*—Rev. Michael E. Bannon. *Chancery Office*—813 Ward St., Nelson, B.C., V1L 1T4. Tel: 250-354-4740; Fax: 250-352-1737.

Nicolet. *Eveque*—Most Rev. Raymond Saint-Gelais, D.D.; *Vicar General*—Rev. Andre Genest; *Chancellor*—Rev. Msgr. Simon Heroux; *Chancery Office*—Bishop's House, 49 rue Mgr. Bruneault, Nicolet, P.Q., J3T 1X7. Tel: 819-293-4696; Fax: 819-293-4653.

Pembroke. *Bishop*—Most Rev. Brendan M. O'Brien, S.T.D., D.D.; *Vicar General*—Rev. Msgr. Michael J. Barry, P.A.; Mgr. Douglas N. Bridge, P.h.; *Chancellor*—Rev. Msgr. Robert L. Borne, P.H., J.C.D.; *Chancery Office*—188 Renfrew St., P.O. Box 7, Pembroke, Ont., K8A 6X1. Tel: 613-735-7652. Bishop's Fax: 613-732-1714.

Peterborough. *Bishop*—Most Rev. James L. Doyle; *Vicar General*—Rev. Msgr. Clayton O'Donoghue, P.A.; *Chancellor*—Sr. Gaudentia; *Chancery Office*—350 Hunter St. W., Box 175, Peterborough, Ont., K9J 6Y8. Tel: 705-745-5123; Fax: 705-745-2555.

Prince Albert. *Bishop*—Most Rev. Blaise Morand, D.D.; *Chancellor*—Rev. Chislain Gaudet; *Chancery Office*—1415-4 Ave. W., Prince Albert, Sask., S6V 5H1. Tel: 306-922-4747; Fax: 306-922-4754

Prince George. *Bishop*—Gerald Wiesner, O.M.I., D.D.; *Vicar General*—Rev. Msgr. Yvan McCormack, O.M.I.; *Chancellor*—Rev. James E. Larkin, O.M.I.; *Chancery Office*—P.O. Box 7000, 2935 Highway 16 West, Prince George, B.C., V2N 3Z2. Tel: 250-964-4424; Fax: 250-964-2101.

Rouyn-Noranda. *Eveque*—Most Rev. Jean-Guy Hamelin, D.D.; *Vicar General*—Rev. Robert Charron; *Chancellor*—Sr. Rosia Douaire, N.D.A.; *Chancery Office*—515 Cuddihy Ave., Rouyn-Noranda, Quebec, J9X 4C5. Tel: 819-764-4660; Fax: 819-764-3972.

St. Catharines. *Bishop*—Most Rev. John A. O'Mara, D.D.; *Chancellor*—Rev. Wayne Kirkpatrick, J.C.L.; *Chancery Office*—122 Riverdale Ave., St. Catharines, Ont., L2R 4C2. Tel: 905-684-0154; Fax: 905-684-2185.

St. George's. *Bishop*—Most Rev. Raymond J. Lahey; *Vicar General*—Rev. John Collins, P.P.; *Chancellor*—Rev. Msgr. William J. Boone, P.H.; *Chancery Office*—16 Hammond Dr., Corner Brook, Newfoundland, A2H 2W2. Tel: 709-635-5444; Fax: 709-639-8662.

St. Hyacinthe. *Eveque*—Most Rev. Louis-de-Gonzague Langevin, M.Afr.; *Vicar General*—Rev. Andre Vincent; *Chancellor*—Mgr. Jean-Roch Choiniere, P.H.; *Chancery Office*—C.P. 190, 1900 Ouest, Girouard, St. Hyacinthe, P.Q., J2S 7B4. Tel: 514-773-8581; Fax: 514-774-1895.

Saint-Jean-Longueuil. *Eveque*—*Bishop*—Most Rev. Jacques Berthelet, C.S.V.; *Vicar General*—Rev. Msgr. Roland Roch Martin; *Chancellor*—M. l'Abbe Jacques Leboeuf; *Chancery Office*—740 boul. Ste. Foy, Box 40, Longueuil, P.Q., J4K 4X8. Tel: 514-679-1100; Fax: 514-679-1102.

St. Jerome. *Eveque*—Oilles Cazabon, O.M.I.; *Auxiliary Bishop*—Most Rev. Vidal Masse; *Vicar General*—Rev. Msgr. Lue Cyr, P.H.; *Chancellor*—M. L'Abbe Claude Massicotte, V.E.; *Chancery Office*—355 St. George St., C.P. 580, Saint. Jerome, P.Q., J7Z 5V3. Tel: 514-432-9742; Fax: 514-432-8155.

Saint John, N.B. *Vacant*—Most Rev. J. Edward Troy, D.D.; *Vicar General*—Rev. Msgr. Geroge W. Martin; *Chancellor*—Rev. John W. Keoughan; *Chancery Office*—1 Bayard Dr., St. John, N.B., E2L 3L5. Tel: 506-653-6800; Fax: 506-653-6812.

St. Paul in Alberta. *Eveque*—Most Rev. Thomas Collins; *Vicar General & Chancellor*—Rev. Msgr. Jean-Luc Pigeon, P.H., V.E., V.G.; *Chancery Office*—4410, 51st Ave. Saint. Paul, Alberta, T0A 3A2. Tel: 403-645-3277; Fax: 403-645-6099.

Sainte-Anne-de-la-Pocatiere. *Bishop*—Most Rev. Clement Fecteau; *Chancellor*—Rev. Roland Picard, V.G.; *Chancery Office*—1200 4e Ave., C.P. 430, La Pocatiere, P.Q., G0R 1Z0. Tel: 418-856-1811; Fax: 418-856-5513.

Saskatoon. *Bishop*—Most Rev. V. James Weisgerber; *Vicar General*—Very Rev. Ronald Beechinor; *Chancellor*—Very Rev. Paul Donlevy. *Chancery Office*—100 5th Ave. N. Saskatoon, Saskatchewan, S7K 2N7. Tel: 306-242-1500; Fax: 306-244-6010.

Sault Ste. Marie. *Bishop*—Most Rev. Jean-Louis Plouffe; *Auxiliary Bishops*—Most Rev. Bernard F. Pappin; Most Rev. Paul-Andre Durocher *Vicar General & Chancellor*—Rev. Msgr. N. F. Clement; *Chancery Office*—387 Algonquin, P.O. Box 510, North Bay, Ont., P1B 8J1. Tel: 705-476-1300; Fax: 705-476-9087; *Sudbury Office*—435 Ave. Notre Dame, Sudbury, Ont., P3C 5K6. Tel: 705-673-4566; Fax: 705-675-7593.

Thunder Bay. *Vacant*—*Chancellor*—Sr. S. Grexton, C.S.J.; *Chancery Office*—P.O. Box 756, Thunder Bay, Ont., P7C 4W6. Tel: 807-343-9313; Fax: 807-343-9114.

Timmins. *Eveque*—Most Rev. Gilles Cazabon, O.M.I.; *Vicar General*—Rev. Maurice Magnan; *Chancellor*—Sr. Gisele Roy, C.N.D.; *Chancery Office*—65 E. Jubilee Ave., Timmins, Ont., P4N 5W4. Tel: 705-267-6224; Fax: 705-267-6226.

Trois-Rivieres. *Eveque*—Most Rev. Martin Veillette; *Vicar General*—Rev. Yvon Leclerc; *Chancellor*—Rev. Guy Panneton; *Chancery Office*—362, rue Bonaventure, C.P. 879, Trois-Rivieres, P.Q., G9A 5J9. Tel: 819-374-9847; 374-9847; Fax: 819-375-6382.

Valleyfield. *Eveque*—Most Rev. Robert Lebel, D.D.; *Vicar General*—Rev. Gilles Bergeron; *Chancellor*—Mme. Monique Boisvert, i.j.r.; *Chancery Office*—11, rue de l'Eglise, Valleyfield, QC., J6T 1J5. Tel: 514-373-8122; Fax: 514-371-0000.

Victoria. *Bishop*—Most Rev. Remi J. De Roo, S.T.D.; *Vicar General*—Rev. Sigismono Lajoie, O.F.M.; *Chancellor*—Rt. Rev. Michael Lapierre; *Chancery Office*—1-4044 Nelthorpe St., Victoria, B.C., V8X 2A1. Tel: 250-479-1331; Fax: 250-479-5423.

Whitehorse. *Bishop*—Most Rev. Thomas Lobsinger, O.M.I., *Chancellor*—Sr. Margaret Coyle, S.C.I.C.; *Chancery*—406 Steele St., Whitehorse, Yukon Y1A 2C8. Tel: 867-668-3826; Fax: 867-667-4713.

Yarmouth. *Bishop*—James M. Wingle; *Vicar General*—Rev. Gerald LeBlanc; *Chancellor*—Sr. Jeanne Cottreau, S.C.; *Chancery Office*—P.O. Box 278, 53 Park St., Yarmouth, Nova Scotia, B5A 4B2. Tel: 902-742-7163; Fax: 902-742-2465.

ABBEY

Abbey Nullius of St. Peter. *Abbot-Ordinary*—Rt. Rev. Peter Novecosky, O.S.B.; *Vicar General*—Rev. Leo Hinz, O.S.B.; *Chancellor*—Rev. Roman Schneider, O.S.B.; *Chancery Office*—St. Peter's Abbey, Muenster, Saskatchewan, SOK 2YO. Tel: 306-682-1788; Fax: 306-682-1766.

UKRAINIAN CATHOLIC PROVINCE

Archeparchy and Metropolitan See of Winnipeg. *Archeparch Metropolitan*—Most Rev. Michael Bzdel, C.Ss.R., D.D.; *Chancellor*—Rev. Stephen Soroka; *Chancery Office—233 Scotia St., Winnipeg, Man., R2V 1V7. Tel: 204-338-7801; Fax: 204-339-4006.*

Eparchy of Toronto. *Eparch*—Most Rev. Isidore Borecky, D.D.; *Apostolic Administrator*—Most Rev. Roman Danylak, J.U.D.; *Chancery Office*—143 Franklin Ave., Toronto, Ont., M6P 3Y9. Tel: 416-538-1436. Fax: 416-962-7725.

Eparchy For Slovaks. *Vacant*—*Apostolic Administrator*—Rev. John Fetsco, C.Ss.R.; *Chancery Office*—223 Carlton Rd., Unionville, Ont., L3R 3M2. Tel: 905-477-4867; Fax: 905-887-1032.

Eparchy of Edmonton. *Eparch*—Most Rev. Lawrence Huculak; *Chancellor*—Rev. Joseph Royer; *Chancery Office*—9645-108 Ave., Edmonton, Alta, T5H 1A3. Tel: 403-424-5496; Fax: 403-425-2330.

Eparchy of Saskatoon. *Eparch*—Most Rev. Cornelius Ivan Pasichny, O.S.B.M.; *Vicar General*—Rt. Rev. Msgr. Rudolph Luzney; *Chancellor*—Rt. Rev. V. Mudri; *Chancery Office*—866 Saskatchewan Crescent E., Saskatoon, Sask., S7N 0L4. Tel: 306-653-0138; Fax: 306-653-0138.

Eparchy of New Westminster. *Eparch*—Most Rev. Severian Yakymyshyn, O.S.B.M., D.D.; *Eparch's Residence*—502-5th Ave., New Westminster, B.C., V3L 1S2. Tel: 604-524-8824; 524-4158; Fax: 604-521-8015.

Information for the Apostolic Exarchate for Catholic Armenians for Canada and the United States; Our Lady of Deliverance for Syriac Catholics in the United States and Canada; and the Hungarian Emigrants can be found by referring to the table of contents found at the beginning of the Directory.

MILITARY ORDINARIATE OF CANADA

Military Ordinary—Vacant.*Chaplain General*—Brigadier General Rev. Jean Pelletier - Tel: 613-992-6021; *Dir. of Chaplaincy Administration*—Colonel Rev. Murray Farwell - Tel: 613-996-5444; *Dir. of Pastoral Services*—Commander Richard Marchand - Tel: 613-992-1399; *Chancellor*—Major Rev. Sylvain Maurais; *Curia Address*—Chaplain General (RC), National Defence Hq., Ottawa, Ont., Canada, K1A 0K2. Tel: 613-992-1400; Fax: 613-992-6025.

United States of Mexico

UNITED STATES OF MEXICO

The United States of Mexico (Estados Unidos Mexicanos) are ecclesiastically divided into 14 Provinces (14 Archdioceses, 56 Dioceses, 7 Prelacies, and 1 Vicariate Apostolic).

Apostolic Nuncio—Most Rev. Justo Mullor Garcia, D.D., Res. Juan Pablo II No. 118, Col. Guadalupe Inn, Deleg. Alvaro Obregon, 01020 Mexico, D.F. (Apartado Postal 19-106, 03910 Mexico, D.F.) Tel: 525-663-3999; 663-4115; 663-4168; Fax: 525-663-5308.

Secretaries—Rt. Rev. Msgr. Jose Spiteri.

PROVINCE OF ACAPULCO

ARCHDIOCESE OF ACAPULCO. Established March 18, 1958. Elevated to an archdiocese on February 10, 1983.
Archbishop—Most Rev. Rafael Bello Ruiz, D.D.; Apartado Postal 201, 39300 Acapulco, Guerrero. Tel: 5274-82-07-63; Fax: 5274-82-07-63.

DIOCESE OF CIUDAD LAZARO CARDENAS. Established in 1985.
Bishop—Most Rev. Salvador Flores Huerta, D.D.
Bishop Emeritus—Most Rev. Jesus Sahagun de la Parra, D.D.; Apartado Postal 500, 60950 Cd. Lazaro Cardenas, Michoacan. Tel: 52753-2-34-88; Fax: 52753-2-29-84.

DIOCESE OF CHILPANCINGO-CHILAPA. Established March 16, 1863. Chilapensis.
Bishop—Most Rev. Efren Ramos Salazar; Apartado Postal 185; 39000 Chilpancingo, Guerrero. Tel: 52747-1-05-92; 1-06-12; Fax: 52747-2-01-13.

DIOCESE OF CIUDAD ALTAMIRANO. Established October 27, 1964. Civitatis Altamirensis.
Bishop—Most Rev. Carlos Garfias Merlos, D.D (Archbishop of Acapulco); Apartado Postal 17, 40660 Ciudad Altamirano, Guerrero. Tel: 52-767-2-00-37; 2-17-74; Fax: 52767-2-19-12.

DIOCESE OF TLAPA. Established 1994.
Bishop—Most Rev. Alejo Zavala Castro, D.D.; Anexo Catedral, Centro, 41300 Tlapa de Comonfort, Guerrero. Tel: 52-747-6-08-35; 6-09-02.

PROVINCE OF CHIHUAHUA

ARCHDIOCESE OF CHIHUAHUA. Established June 23, 1891. Created Archbishopric November 22, 1958. Chihuahuensis.
Archbishop—Most Rev. Jose Fernandez Arteaga, D.D.; *Archbishop Emeritus*—Most Rev. Adalberto Almeida Merino, D.D.; Apartado Postal 7, 31000 Chihuahua, Chihuahua. Tel: 52-14-10-32-02; 10-32-03; Fax: 5214-10-56-21.

DIOCESE OF CIUDAD JUAREZ. Established April 10, 1957. Civitatis Juarezensis.
Bishop—Most Rev. Renato Ascencio Leon, D.D.; *Bishop Emeritus*—Most Rev. Manuel Talamas Camandari, D.D.; Apartado Postal 188, 32000 Cd. Juarez, Chihuahua. Tel: 52-16-15-09-92; 15-09-82; Fax: 5216-15-00-24.

DIOCESE OF CUAUHTEMOC-MADERA. Established April 25, 1966. Civitatis Materiensis.
Bishop—Most. Rev. Juan Guillermo Lopez, S.,D.D. Apartado Postal 209; 31500 Cuauhtemoc, Chihuahua. Tel & Fax: 52-5-157-2-11-97.

PRELACY OF NUEVO CASAS GRANDES. Established April 13, 1977. Neograndicasensis.
Prelate—Most Rev. Hilario Chavez Joya, M.N.M., D.D., Bishop-Prelate of Nuevo Casas Grandes; Apartado Postal 198, 31700 Nuevo Casas Grandes, Chihuahua. Tel: 52-169-4-05-20; Fax: 52-169-4-36-15.

DIOCESE OF PARRAL.
Bishop—Most Rev. Jose Andres Corral Arredondo, D.D.; Apartado Postal 313, 33800 H. del Parral, Chihuahua. Tel: 52-152-2-03-71; Fax: 52-152-2-03-71.

DIOCESE OF TARAHUMARA.
Bishop—Most Rev. Jose Luis Dibildox Martinez, D.D.; Apartado Postal 11, 33190 Guachochi, Chihuahua. Tel: 52-154-3-02-07; Fax: 52-154-3-07-04.

PROVINCE OF DURANGO

ARCHDIOCESE OF DURANGO. Established September 17, 1620. Created Archbishopric June 23, 1891. Durangensis.
Archbishop—Most Rev. Jose Trinidad Medel Perez, D.D.; *Auxiliary Bishop*—Most Rev. Juan de Dios Caballero Reyes, D.D.; *Archbishop Emeritus*—Most Rev. Antonio Lopez Avina, D.D.; Apartado Postal 116, 34000 Durango, Durango. Tel: 52-18-11-42-42; 11-98-44; Fax: 52-18-12-88-81.

DIOCESE OF CULIACAN. Established May 24, 1883. Formerly Sinaloensis, as of February 16, 1959 became Culiacanensis.
Bishop—Most Rev. Benjamin Jimenez Hernandez, D.D.; *Bishop Emeritus*—Most Rev. Luis Rojas Mena, D.D.; Apartado Postal 666, 80220 Culiacan, Sinaloa. Tel: 52-67-12-32-72; 12-14-97; Fax: 52-67-12-14-97.

DIOCESE OF MAZATLAN. Established November 22, 1958. Mazatlanensis.
Bishop—Most Rev. Rafael Barraza Sanchez, D.D.; Apartado Postal 1, 82000 Mazatlan, Sinaloa. Tel: 52-69-81-33-52; Fax: 52-69-81-04-28.

DIOCESE OF TORREON. Established June 9, 1957. Torreonensis.
Bishop—Most Rev. Luis Morales Reyes, D.D.; *Bishop Emeritus*—Most Rev. Fernando Romo Gutierrez, D.D.; Apartado Postal 430, 27000 Torreon, Coahuila. Tel: 52-17-12-30-43; Fax: 52-17-12-57-81.

PRELACY OF EL SALTO. Established June 12, 1968. Saltensis in Mexico.
Bishop—Most Rev. Manuel Mireles Vaquera, D.D., Bishop-Prelate of El Salto; Apartado Postal 58, 34950, El Salto, Durango. Tel: 52-187-6-00-70 (Phone & Fax).

PROVINCE OF GUADALAJARA

ARCHDIOCESE OF GUADALAJARA. Established July 13, 1548. Created Archbishopric March 19,

1863. Formerly Compostellana now Guadalajarensis.
Archbishop—His Eminence Juan Cardinal Sandoval Iniguez, D.D.; *Auxiliary Bishops*—Most Rev. Ramon Godinez Flores; Most Rev. Javier Navarro Rodriguez, D.D.; Most Rev. J. Luis Chavez Botello, D.D.; Most Rev. Jose Trinidad Gonzalez r., D.D.; *Bishop Emeritus*—Most Rev. Antonio Sahagun Lopez; *Bishop Auxiliary Emeritus*—Most Rev. Adolfo Hernandez Hurtado, D.D.; Apartado Postal 1-331, 44100 Guadalajara, Jalisco. Tel: 52-3-614-55-04; Fax: 52-3-658-23-00.

DIOCESE OF AGUASCALIENTES. Established August 27, 1899. De Aguas Calientes.
Bishop—Most Rev. Rafael Munoz Nunez, D.D.; Apartado Postal 628, 20000 Aguascalientes, Aguascalientes. Tel: 52-49-15-32-61; Fax: 52-49-16-33-12.

DIOCESE OF AUTLAN. Established January 28, 1961. Rivoriensis.
Bishop—Most Rev. Lazaro Perez Jimenez, D.D. Apartado Postal 8, 48900 Autlan, Jalisco. Tel: 52-338-2-12-28 (Phone & Fax).

DIOCESE OF COLIMA. Established December 11, 1881. Colimensis.
Bishop—Most Rev. Gilberto Valbuena Sanchez, D.D.; *Bishop Emeritus*—Most Rev. Rogelio Sanchez Gonzalez, D.D.; Apartado Postal 1, 28000 Colima, Colima. Tel: 52-331-2-02-62; Fax: 52-331-2-43-44.

DIOCESE OF TEPIC. Established June 22, 1891. Tepicensis.
Bishop—Most Rev. Alfonso Humberto Robles Cota, D.D., Apartado Postal 15, 63137 Tepic, Nayarit. Tel: 52-321-4-46-45;4-46-47; Fax: 52-321-3-20-23.

DIOCESE OF ZACATECAS. Established January 26, 1863. Zacatecensis.
Diocesan Administrator—Very Rev. Fernando Chavez Ruvalcaba; *Bishop Emeritus*—Most Rev. Jose Pablo Rovalo Azcue, D.D.,
Apartado Postal 1, 98000 Zacatecas, Zacatecas. Tel: 52-492-2-65-37; 2-12-74; Fax: 52-492-2-23-42. *Archbishop Emeritus—Most Rev. Javier Lozano Barragan, D.D., Pres.-Pontifical College for Health Agents, Via della Conciliazione 3, 00193 Rome, Italia. Tel: 39-6-698-3138; Fax: 39-698-3139.*

PRELATURE OF JESUS MARIA OF NAYAR. Established May 24, 1962. Nayariana de Jesu et Maria.
Bishop—Most Rev. Antonio Perez Sanchez, O.F.M., D.D., Bishop-Prelate of Jesus Maria of Nayar; *Bishop Emeritus*—Most Rev. Manuel Romero Arvizu, D.D.; Apartado Postal 33-B, 63150 Tepic, Nayarit. Tel: 52-321-3-38-80; 2-14-21.

DIOCESE OF SAN JUAN DE LOS LAGOS. Established March 25, 1972. Sancti Ioannis a Lacubus.
Bishop—Most Rev. Jose Trinidad Sepulveda Ruiz-Velasco, D.D.; Apartado Postal 1, 47000 San Juan de los Lagos, Jalisco. Tel: 52-378-5-05-70; 5-06-57; 5-09-26; Fax: 52-378-5-29-71.

DIOCESE OF CIUDAD GUZMAN. Established March 25, 1972. Civitatis Gusmanopolitana.
Bishop—Most Rev. Serafin Vasquez Elizalde, D.D.; Apartado Postal 86, 49000 Cd. Guzman, Jalisco. Tel: 52-341-2-19-94; 2-05-28. Fax: 52-341-2-15-44.

PROVINCE OF HERMOSILLO

ARCHDIOCESE OF HERMOSILLO. Established May 7, 1779. Created Archbishopric September 4, 1963. Hermosillensis, formerly Sonorensis.
Archbishop—Most Rev. Jose Ulises Macias Salcedo, D.D.; *Archbishop Emeritus*—Most Rev. Carlos Quintero Arce, D.D.; Apartado Postal 1, 83260 Hermosillo, Sonora. Tel: 52-62-13-21-38; Fax: 52-62-13-13-27.

DIOCESE OF CIUDAD OBREGON. Established June 20, 1959. Civitatis Obregonensis.
Bishop—Most Rev. Vicente Garcia Bernal, D.D.; Apartado Postal 402, 85000 Cd. Obregon, Sonora. Tel: 52-641-3-20-98; Fax: 52-641-4-99-94.

DIOCESE OF LA PAZ. Established March 30, 1988. Paciensis in California Inferiori Meridionali.
Bishop—Most Rev. Braulio Rafael Leon Villegas, D.D.; Apartado Postal 25, 23000 La Paz, Baja California Sur. Tel: 52-112-2-25-96; 2-02-08; Fax: 52-112-2-82-72.

DIOCESE OF MEXICALI. Established April 12, 1966. Mexicalensis.
Bishop—Most Rev. Jose Isidro Guerrero G., D.D.; Apartado 3-547, 21100 Mexicali, Baja California Norte. Tel: 52-65-52-40-09; Fax: 52-65-52-45-96.

DIOCESE OF TIJUANA. Established June 13, 1963. Tigiuanaensis, formerly Vicariate Apostolic of Tijuana (July 13, 1957), formerly Californiae Inferioris (January 20, 1874).
Bishop—Most Rev. Rafael Romo Munoz; Apartado Postal 226, 22000 Tijuana, Baja California Norte. Tel: 52-66-84-84-11; 84-84-12; Fax: 52-66-84-76-83.

PROVINCE OF MEXICO

ARCHDIOCESE OF MEXICO. Established Sept. 2, 1530. Created Archbishopric February 12, 1546. Mexicana.
Archbishop Primate—His Eminence Most Rev. Norberto Cardinal Rivera Carrera, D.D.; *Auxiliary Bishops*—Most Rev. Luis Mena Arroyo, D.D.; Most Rev. Abelardo Alvarado Alcantara; Most Rev. Jose de Jesus Martinez Z., D.D.; *Archbishop Primate Emeritus*—His Eminence Most Rev. Ernesto Cardinal Corripio Ahumada, D.D.;*Bishop Auxiliary Emeritus*—Most Rev. Francisco Maria Aguilera Gonzalez, D.D.; Apartado Postal 24-433, 06700 Mexico, D.F. Tel: 52-5-525-1110; 208-3200; Fax: 52-5-208-5350.

DIOCESE OF ATLACOMULCO. Established December 27, 1984.
Diocesan Administrator—Very Rev. Rodrigo Guadarrama Rosas; Apartado Postal 22, 50450 Atlacomulco, Edo. de Mexico. Tel. & Fax: 52-712-2-05-53.

DIOCESE OF CUERNAVACA. Established June 23, 1891. Cuernavacensis.
Bishop—Most Rev. Luis Reynoso Cervantes, D.D.; Apartado Postal 13, 62000 Cuernavaca, Morelos. Tel: 52-73-18-45-90; 18-96-46; Fax: 52-73-18-63-18.

DIOCESE OF TOLUCA. Established June 4, 1950. Tolucensis.
Bishop—Most Rev. Francisco Robles Ortega, D.D.; Apartado Postal 82, 50000 Toluca, Edo. de Mexico. Tel: 52-72-15-25-35; 15-39-59; Fax: 52-72-14-69-55.

DIOCESE OF TULA. Established February 27, 1961. Tullanensis.
Bishop—Most Rev. Octavia Villegas Aguilar, D.D.; Apartado Postal 31, 42800 Tula de Allende, Hidalgo. Tel: 52-773-2-02-75 (Phone & Fax).

DIOCESE OF TULANCINGO. Established January 22, 1862. Tulancingensis.
Bishop—Most Rev. Pedro Aranda-Diaz Munoz, D.D.; Apartado Postal 14, 43600 Tulancingo, Hidalgo. Tel: 52-775-3-10-10 (Phone & Fax).

PROVINCE OF TLALNEPANTLA

ARCHDIOCESE OF TLALNEPANTLA. Established March 31, 1964. Tlalnepantlana. Established as Archdiocese June 28, 1989.
Archbishop—Most Rev. Ricardo Guizar Diaz, D.D.; Apartado Postal 268 y 270, 54000 Tlalnepantla, Edo. de Mexico. Tel: 52-5-565-39-44; 565-39-56; 565-82-90; Fax: 52-5-565-27-51.

DIOCESE OF TEXCOCO. Established April 30, 1960. Texcocensis.
Bishop—Most Rev. Carlos Aguiar Retes, D.D.; *Bishop Emeritus*—Most Rev. Magin C. Torreblanca Reyes, D.D.; Apartado 35, 56100 Texcoco, Edo. de Mexico. Tel: 52-595-4-02-82; 4-35-63. Fax: 52-595-4-08-69.

DIOCESE OF CUAUTITLAN. Established February 5, 1979.
Bishop—Most Rev. Manuel Samaniego Barriga, D.D.; Apartado Postal 14-21, 54800 Cuautitlan, Edo. de Mexico. Tel: 52-5-872-19-96; Fax: 52-5-872-3004.

DIOCESE OF NETZAHUALCOYOTL. Established May 1, 1979.
Bishop—Most Rev. Jose Maria Hernandez Gonzalez, D.D.; *Bishop Emeritus*—Most Rev. Jose Melgoza Osorio, D.D.; Apartado Postal 89, 57700 Cd. Netzahualcoyotl, Edo. de Mexico. Tel: 52-5-797-6132; 797-8301; Fax: 52-5-765-9804.

DIOCESE OF ECATEPEC.
Bishop—Most Rev. Onesimo Cepeda Silva, D.D.; Apartado Postal 95, 55000 Ecatepec de Morelos, Edo de Mexico. Tel: 52-5-116-0976; Fax: 52-5-882-4019.

PROVINCE OF MONTERREY

ARCHDIOCESE OF MONTERREY. Established December 15, 1777. Created Archbishopric June 28, 1898. Monterreyensis formerly Linarensis.
Archbishop—His Eminence Most Rev. Adolfo Antonio Cardinal Suarez Rivera, D.D.; *Auxiliary Bishops*—Most Rev. Jose Lizares Estrada, D.D.; Most Rev. Alfonso Hinojosa Berrones, D.D.; *Chancery*—Apartado Postal 7, 64000 Monterrey, Nuevo Leon. Tel: 52-83-45-24-66; 45-24-18; Fax: 52-83-45-35-57.

DIOCESE OF CIUDAD VALLES. Established November 27, 1960. Vallipolitana.
Bishop—Most Rev. Jose Guadalupe Galvan Galindo, D.D.; *Chancery*—Apartado Postal 170, 79000 Ciudad Valles, San Luis Potosi. Tel: 52-138-2-25-97; Fax: 52-138-2-47-96.

DIOCESE OF CIUDAD VICTORIA. Established December 21, 1964. Civitatis Victoriensis.
Bishop—Most Rev. Antonio Gonzalez Sanchez, D.D.; *Chancery*—Apartado Postal 335, 87000 Ciudad Victoria, Tamaulipas. Tel: 52-131-2-80-83; Fax: 52-131-6-48-11. *Bishop Emeritus*—Most Rev. Raimundo Lopez Mateos, D.D., Res., Roger Bacon College - Franciscan Friars, 2400 Marr St., El Pasto, TX 79903.

DIOCESE OF LINARES. Established April 30, 1962. Linarina.
Bishop—Most Rev. Ramon Calderon Batres, D.D.; Apartado Postal 70, 67700 Linares, Nuevo Leon. Tel: 52-821-2-00-54; Fax: 52-821-2-07-50.

DIOCESE OF MATAMOROS. Established February 16, 1958. Matamorensis.
Bishop—Most Rev. Francisco Javier Chavolla Ramos, D.D.; Apartado Postal 70, 87351 H. Matamoros, Tamaulipas. Tel: 52-88-13-36-58; Fax: 52-88-16-06-08.

DIOCESE OF NUEVO LAREDO. Established January 10, 1990. Nuevo Laredensis.
Bishop—Most Rev. Ricardo Watty Urquidi, M.Sp.S., D.D.; Apartado Postal 20-B, 88280 Nuevo Laredo, Tamaulipas. Tel: 52-871-5-29-28; 5-83-95; Fax: 52-871-5-57-99.

DIOCESE OF SALTILLO. Established June 23, 1891. Saltillensis.
Bishop—Most Rev. Francisco Raul Villalobos Padilla, D.D.; Apartado Postal 25, 25000 Saltillo, Coahuila. Tel: 52-84-12-37-84; Fax: 52-84-14-92-67.

DIOCESE OF TAMPICO. Established March 6, 1870. Tampicensis formerly Civitatis Victoriae or Tamaulipana.
Bishop—Most Rev. Rafael Gallardo Garcia, O.S.A., D.D.; Apartado Postal 545, 89000 Tampico, Tamaulipas. Tel: 52-12-12-28-10; 12-28-02; Fax: 52-12-12-67-81.

PROVINCE OF MORELIA

ARCHDIOCESE OF MORELIA. Established August 11, 1536. Created Archbishopric March 19, 1863. Moreliensis.
Archbishop—Most Rev. Alberto Suarez Inda, D.D.;
Bishop Emeritus—Most Rev. Estanislao Alcaraz, F., D.D.;
Chancery—Apartado Postal 17, 58000 Morelia, Michoacan. Tel: 52-43-12-05-23; 12-37-38; Fax: 52-43-12-37-44.

DIOCESE OF APATZINGAN. Established April 30, 1962. Apatzinganiensis.
Bishop—Most Rev. Miguel Patino Velazquez, M.S.F., D.D., Calle Esteban Vaca Calderon 100, 60600 Apatzingan, Michoacan. Tel: 52-453-4-17-87; Fax: 52-453-4-22-26.

DIOCESE OF TACAMBARO. Established July 26, 1913. Tacambarensis.
Bishop—Most Rev. Rogelio Cabrera Lopez, D.D. Apartado Postal 4, 61650 Tacambaro, Michoacan. Tel: 52-454-6-00-44; Fax: 52-454-6-07-30.

DIOCESE OF ZAMORA. Established January 26, 1862. Zamorensis.
Bishop—Most Rev. Carlos Suarez Cazarez, D.D.; *Chancery*—Apartado Postal 18, 59600 Zamora, Michoacan. Tel: 52-351-2-12-08; 2-04-82; Fax: 52-351-5-40-20.

PROVINCE OF OAXACA

ARCHDIOCESE OF OAXACA. Established 1535. Created Archbishopric June 23, 1981.
Archbishop—Most Rev. Hector Gonzalez Martinez, D.D.; *Auxiliary Bishop*—Most Rev. Miguel Angel Alba Diaz, D.D.; *Archbishop Emeritus*—Most Rev. Bartolome Carrasco Briseno, D.D.; Apartado Postal 31, 68000 Oaxaca, Oaxaca. Tel: 52-951-6-48-22; Fax: 52-951-4-13-48.

DIOCESE OF SAN CRISTOBAL DE LAS CASAS. Established March 19, 1539. S. Christophori de las Casas.
Bishop—Most Rev. Samuel Ruiz Garcia, D.D; *Bishop Coadjutor*—Most Rev. Raul Vera Lopez, O.P., D.D; *Chancery*—Av. 20 de Noviembre 1, Centro, 29200 San Cristobal de las Casas, Chiapas. Tel: 52-967-8-00-53; Fax: 52-967-8-31-36.

DIOCESE OF TAPACHULA. Established June 19, 1957. Tapacolensis.
Bishop—Most Rev. Felipe Arizmendi Esquivel, D.D.; Apartado Postal 70, 30700 Tapachula, Chiapas. Tel: 52-962-6-15-03; Fax: 52-962-6-50-24.

DIOCESE OF TEHUANTEPEC. Established June 23, 1891, in San Andres Tuxtla, State of Veracruz. Transferred May 23, 1959 to Tehuantepec, State of Oaxaca, Tehuantepecensis.
Bishop—Most Rev. Arturo Lona Reyes, D.D.; *Bishop Coadjutor*—Most Rev. Felipe Padilla Cardona, D.D.; Apartado Postal 93, 70760 Tehuantepec, Oaxaca. Tel: 52-971-5-00-60; Fax: 52-971-5-14-42.

DIOCESE OF TUXTLA GUTIERREZ. Established October 27, 1964. Tuxtlensis.
Bishop—Most Rev. Felipe Aguirre Franco, D.D.; *Chancery*—Anexo a St. Domingo, 1a Poniente Norte 232, 29000 Tuxtla Gutierrez, Chiapas. Tel: 52-961-2-21-54; Fax: 52-961-1-35-67.

DIOCESE OF TUXTEPEC. Established January 8, 1979.

Bishop—Most Rev. Jose de Jesus Castillo Renteria, M.N.M., D.D.; Apartado Postal 9, 68300 Tuxtepec, Oaxaca. Tel: 52-287-5-00-42.

PRELACY OF MIXES. Decreed on December 21, 1964. Mixepolitana.
Bishop-Prelate—Most Rev. Braulio Sanchez Fuentes, S.D.B., D.D., Bishop-Prelate of Mixes; Res., Ayutla-Mixes, Oaxaca; Mailing Address: Av. H. Colegio Militar No. 721, Colonia Reforma, 70283 Ayutla-Mixes, Oaxaca. Tel: 52-951-5-25-56 (Phone & Fax).

PRELACY OF HUAUTLA. Decreed October 7, 1972. Huautlensis.
Bishop-Prelate—Most Rev. Hermenegildo Ramirez Sanchez, M.J., D.D.; Apartado Postal 2, 68500 Huautla de Jimenez, Oaxaca. Tel: 52-237-8-00-19 (Phone & Fax).

PROVINCE OF SAN LUIS POTOSI

ARCHDIOCESE OF SAN LUIS POTOSI. Established August 31, 1854. S. Ludovici Potesiensis.
Archbishop—Most Rev. Arturo Antonio Szymanski Ramirez, D.D.; Apartado Postal 1, 78000 San Luis Potosi, S.L.P. Tel: 52-48-12-45-55; 12-22-50; Fax: 52-48-12-79-79.

DIOCESE OF CELAYA. Established October 13, 1973. Celayensis.
Bishop—Most Rev. Jesus Humberto Velazquez Garay, D.D.; Apartado Postal 207, 38000 Celaya, Guanajuato. Tel: 52-461-2-43-98 (Phone & Fax).

DIOCESE OF LEON. Established January 26, 1863. Leonensis.
Bishop—Most Rev. Jose Guadalupe Martin Rabago, D.D.; *Bishop Emeritus*—Most Rev. Anselmo Zarza Bernal, D.D.; *Chancery*—Pedro Moreno 312, 37000 Leon, Guanajuato. Tel: 52-47-13-27-47; Fax: 52-47-13-08-15.

DIOCESE OF QUERETARO. Established January 26, 1882. Queretarensis.
Bishop—Most Rev. Mario de Gasperin Gasperin, D.D.; Apartado Postal 49, 76000 Queretaro, Queretaro. Tel: 52-42-12-10-33; Fax: 52-42-12-18-45.

DIOCESE OF MATEHUALA.
Bishop—Most Rev. Rodrigo Aguilar M., D.D. Apartado Postal 140, 78700 Matehuala, San Luis Potosi. Tel: 52-488-2-35-05; Fax: 52-488-2-08-42.

PROVINCE OF PUEBLA DE LOS ANGELES

ARCHDIOCESE OF PUEBLA DE LOS ANGELES. Established October 13, 1525. Created Archbishopric August 11, 1903. Angelorum formerly Tlascalensis.
Archbishop—Most Rev. Rosendo Huesca Pacheco, D.D.; Apartado Postal 235, 72000 Puebla, Puebla. Tel: 52-22-32-62-12; Fax: 52-22-46-22-77.

DIOCESE OF HUAJUAPAN DE LEON. Established November 13, 1903. Huajuapanensis.
Diocesan Administrator—Most Rev. Felipe Padilla Cardona, D.D.; *Bishop Emeritus*—Most Rev. Jose De Jesus Aguilera Rodriguez, D.D.; Apartado Postal 43, 69000 Huajuapan de Leon, Oaxaca. Tel: 52-953-2-07-97; Fax: 52-953-2-06-36.

DIOCESE OF HUEJUTLA. Established November 24, 1922. Huejutlensis.
Bishop—Most Rev. Salvador Martinez Perez, D.D.; *Chancery*—Apartado Postal 8, 43000 Huejutla, Hidalgo. Tel: 52-129-6-01-85 (Phone & Fax).

DIOCESE OF TEHUACAN. Established January 13, 1962. Tehuacaniensis.
Bishop—Most Rev. Mario Espinosa Contreras, D.D. Apartado Postal 137, 75700 Tehuacan, Puebla. Tel: 52-238-3-20-00; Fax: 52-238-3-14-68.

DIOCESE OF TLAXCALA. Established May 23, 1959. Tlaxcalensis.
Bishop—Most Rev. Luis Munive Escobar, D.D.; *Coadjutor Bishop*—Most Rev. Jacinto Guerrero Torres, D.D.; Apartado Postal 84, 90000 Tlaxcala, Tlaxcala. Tel: 52-246-2-07-23; Fax: 52-246-2-0739.

PROVINCE OF XALAPA

ARCHDIOCESE OF XALAPA. Established March 19, 1863. Created Archbishopric June 29, 1951. Jalapensis, formerly Verae Crucis.
Archbishop—Most Rev. Sergio Obeso Rivera, D.D.; Apartado Postal 359, 91000 Xalapa, Veracruz. Tel: 52-28-17-29-35; 52-28-17-55-78.

DIOCESE OF PAPANTLA. Established November 24, 1922. Papantlensis.
Bishop—Most Rev. Lorenzo Cardenas Aregullin, D.D.; *Bishop Emeritus*—Most Rev. Genaro Alamilla Arteaga, D.D.; *Chancery*—Apartado Postal 27, 73800 Teziutlan, Puebla. Tel: 52-231-2-01-69.

DIOCESE OF SAN ANDRES TUXTLA. Established May 23, 1959. On March 14, 1984, the Diocese of San Andres Tuxtla was divided into two jurisdictions: San Andres Tuxtla and the New Diocese of Coatzacoalcos, as a suffragan diocese of Jalapa.
Bishop—Most Rev. Guillermo Ranzahuer Gonzalez, D.D.; Constitucion y Morelos s/n, 95700 San Andres Tuxtla, Veracruz. Tel: 52-294-2-12-45; Fax: 52-294-2-03-74.

DIOCESE OF COATZACOALCOS. Established March 14, 1984. Coatzacoalsensis.
Bishop—Most Rev. Carlos Talavera Ramirez, D.D.; Apartado Postal 513, 96400 Coatzacoalcos, Veracruz. Tel: 52-921-2-59-03; Fax: 52-921-2-73-23.

DIOCESE OF TUXPAN. Established June 9, 1962. Tuxpaniensis.
Bishop—Most Rev. Luis Gabriel Cuara Mendez, D.D. Juarez 30, Col. Centro, 92800 Tuxpan, Veracruz. Tel: 52-783-4-00-28 (Phone & Fax).

DIOCESE OF VERACRUZ. Established January 19, 1963. Verae Crucis.
Bishop—Most Rev. Jose Guadalupe Padilla Lozano, D.D.; Insurgentes Veracruzanos 470, Paseo del Malecon, 91700 Veracruz, Veracruz. Tel: 52-29-32-20-26; 52-29-31-24-13.

PROVINCE OF YUCATAN

ARCHDIOCESE OF YUCATANENSIS. Established December 16, 1561. Created Archbishopric November 11, 1906.
Archbishop—Most Rev. Emilio Carlos Berlie Belaunzaran, D.D.; *Archbishop Emeritus*—Most Rev. Manuel Castro Ruiz, D.D.; Calle 58, 501 Centro, 97000 Merida, Yucatan. Tel: 52-99-28-62-14.

DIOCESE OF CAMPECHE. Established July 25, 1845. Campecorensis.
Bishop—Most Rev. Jose Luis Amezcua, D.D.; *Bishop Emeritus*—Most Rev. Jesus Garcia Ayala, D.D.; Apartado Postal 127, 24000 Campeche, Campeche. Tel: 52-981-6-26-05; Fax: 52-981-6-03-39.

DIOCESE OF TABASCO. Established May 25, 1880. Tabasquensis.
Bishop—Most Rev. Florencio Olvera Ochoa, D.D.; Apartado Postal 97, 86000 Villahermosa, Tabasco. Tel: 52-93-12-13-97; Fax: 52-93-12--19-05.

PRELACY OF CANCUN-CHETUMAL. Established November 21, 1970. Chetumaliensis.
Bishop-Prelate—Most Rev. Jorge Bernal Vargas, L.C., D.D.; Apartado Postal 165, 77000 Chetumal, Quintana Roo. Tel: 52-983-2-06-38; Fax: 52-983-2-25-70.

EPARCHY OF NUESTRA SENORA DEL PARAISO (Melquite Greek Rite). *Bishop*—Most Rev. Antonio Mouhanna, D.D.; Iglesia de Porta Coeli, Venustiano Carranza 107, 06060 Mexico, D.F. Tel: 52-5-542-0225; Fax: 52-5-575-1687.

MEXICAN BISHOPS' CONFERENCE—Most Rev. Luis Morales Reyes, Bishop of Torreon, Pres.; Most Rev. Jose Guadalupe Martin Rabago, Bishop of Leon, Vice Pres.; Most Rev. Abelardo Alvarado Alcantara, Auxiliary Bishop of Mexico, Sec. Gral.; Most Rev. Gilberto Valbuena Sanchez, Bishop of Colima, Treas.; Most Rev. Jose Guadalupe Martin, Auxiliary Bishop of Guadalajara, First Vocal; Most Rev. Mario de Gasperin Gasperin, Second Vocal; Rev. Luis Guillermo Herrera Herrera, Exec. Sec.; Prolongacion Misterios 24-B, Col. Tepeyac Insurgentes, 07020 Mexico, D.F. Tel: 52-5-781-84-62; 577-54-01; 577-54-31. Fax: 52-5-577-5489.

SHRINE OF OUR LADY OF GUADALUPE. Abbot Rt. Rev. Msgr. Guillermo Schulenburg; Very Rev. Carlos Warnholtz Bustillos; Basilica de N.S. de Guadalupe, Apartado 14-120, 07050 Mexico, D.F. Tel: 52-5-577-6022; 577-6088; Fax: 52-5-577-5038.

CONFERENCIA DE INSTITUTOS RELIGIOSOS DE MEXICO. Rev. Jose Morales Orozco, S.J., Pres.; Rev. Ruben Cabello Ramos, S.J., Sec. Gral.; Sr. Mariela Pena Kipper, R.S.C.J., Vice Pres.; Bro. Joaquin Flores Segura, S.M.S., Vice Pres.; Vocals: Sr. Constanza Aguilar Abril; Sr. Maria Luisa Chapa Urquidi, M.E.S.S.T.; Sr. Raquel Hernandez Garcia, H.J.; Sr. Delia Esther Peruyera Cruz, O.D.N.; Sr. Elena Andrade Moreno, F.M.M.; Rev. Jorge Ortiz Gonzalez, M.Sp.S.; Rev. Joaquin Azcona M., S.V.D.; Rev. Roberto Balmori Cinta, M.J.; Rev. Aaron J. Cahuantzi Bello, S.CH.P.; Rev. Miguel Conca Malo, O.P.; Av. Amores 1318, Col. del Valle, 03100 Mexico, D.F. Tel: 52-5-604-5414; Fax: 52-5-604-9555.

American Foreign Missions

Augustinian Missions (O.S.A.)

Foreign Missions of the American Provinces of the Order of St. Augustine (O.S.A.)

Foreign Missions

Provincial Headquarters

Province of Our Mother of Good Counsel (Midwestern): *Tolentine Center,* 20300 Governors Highway, Olympia Fields, IL 60461-1081. Tel: 708-748-5435; Fax: 708-481-2090. Very Rev. David L. Brecht, O.S.A. Ord: '65, Prov.; Bro. John J. Stobba, O.S.A., Mission Procurator.

Midwestern Augustinian Religious serving in foreign missions: Most Rev. John C. McNabb, O.S.A., D.D., ord. 52, *Peru;* Most Rev. Daniel T. Turley, O.S.A., ord. 68, *Peru;* Revs. Alfred M. Burke, O.S.A. Ord: '57, *Japan;* Charles J. Bodden, O.S.A. Ord: '78, *Peru;* Richard Palmer, O.S.A. Ord: '87, *Peru;* Robert F. Prevost, O.S.A. Ord: '82, *Peru;* John P. Tasto, O.S.A. Ord: '82, *Mexico;* John A. Tyma, O.S.A. Ord: '59, *Peru;* Bro. David L. Sharp, O.S.A., *Peru.*

Augustinian Religious from other Provinces serving in our foreign missions: Revs. Joseph F. Girone, O.S.A. Ord: '81, *Peru (Villanova);* Robert P. Terranova, O.S.A. Ord: '73, *Peru (Villanova);* Aquilino D. Gonzalez, O.S.A. Ord: '72, *Peru (Villanova);* Richard Mullen, O.S.A. Ord: '81, *Peru (Villanova);* John J. Lydon, O.S.A. Ord: '84, *Peru (Villanova);* Jesus Gusman Zavala, O.S.A. Ord: '60, *Peru (Michoacan);* Jose L. Hernan Dez Plata, O.S.A. Ord: '74, *Peru (Mexico);* Juan M. Zanabria Vergara, O.S.A. Ord: '85, *Peru (Mexico);* Sebastian Ortega Rodriguez, O.S.A. Ord: '93, *Peru (Michoacan).*

Province of St. Thomas of Villanova (Eastern): P.O. Box 338, Villanova, PA 19085-0338. Tel: 610-525-3330; Fax: 610-520-0618. Very Rev. John E. Deegan, O.S.A. Ord: '61, Prior Prov. Tel: 610-525-9962. Revs. Richard D. Appicci, O.S.A. Ord: '60, Dir. Missions; Anthony P. Burrascano, O.S.A. Ord: '79, Mission Procurator.

U.S. Religious serving in foreign missions: Revs. John J. Lydon, O.S.A. Ord: '84; Joseph F. Girone, O.S.A. Ord: '81, *Peru;* Patrick B. McStravog, O.S.A. Ord: '89, *Japan;* Richard G. Mullen, O.S.A. Ord: '81; Maurice J. Mahoney, O.S.A. Ord: '60; Thomas P. Dwyer, O.S.A. Ord: '53; Aquilino D. Gonzalez, O.S.A. Ord: '72; Robert P. Terranova, O.S.A. Ord: '73; Michael J. Hilden, O.S.A. Ord: '73; Michael H. Stanley, O.S.A. Ord: '81; Edward V. Hattrick, O.S.A. Ord: '56; Thomas P. Purcell, O.S.A. Ord: '43.

American Benedictine Foreign Missions (O.S.B.)

American - Cassinese Congregation Foreign Missions

St. Vincent Archabbey: 300 Fraser Purchase Rd., Latrobe, PA 15650-2686. Tel: 412-532-6600. Rt. Rev. Douglas R. Nowicki, O.S.B., Ord. 72, Archabbot; Rev. Noel H. Rothrauff, O.S.B. Ord: '54, Mission Dir.

U.S. Religious serving Abroad: Bros. Anthony Kirsch, O.S.B., Subprior, *Brazil;* Nicholas Koss, O.S.B., Prior, *Taiwan;* Revs. Leo P. Rothrauff, O.S.B. Ord: '56, *Brazil;* Job J. Foote, O.S.B. Ord: '89, *Honduras.*

St. John's Abbey: Box 2015, Collegeville, MN 56321-2015; Fax: 612-363-3082.

U.S. Religious serving Abroad: Very Rev. Kieran Nolan, O.S.B. Ord: '59, Prior, *Japan;* Revs. Neal Henry Lawrence, O.S.B. Ord: '60, *Japan;* Very Rev. Daniel Ward, O.S.B. Ord: '71, Prior, *Nassau;* Revs. Fintan Bromenshenkel, O.S.B. Ord: '45, *Nassau;* Francisco Schulte, O.S.B. Ord: '79, *Nassau;* George Wolf, O.S.B. Ord: '44, *Nassau;* Anthony Hellenberg, O.S.B. Ord: '66, *Nassau;* Thomas Wahl, O.S.B. Ord: '58, *Japan;* Cyprian Weaver, O.S.B. Ord: '72, *Taiwan;* William Skudlarek, O.S.B. Ord: '64, *Japan.*

St. Benedict's Abbey: Atchison, KS 66002. Tel: 913-367-5341; Fax: 913-367-6230. Rt. Rev. Barnabas Senecal, O.S.B., Abbot.

U.S. Religious serving in Brazil: Most Rev. Herbert Hermes; Very Rev. Kieran McInerey, O.S.B. Ord: '52; Rev. Duane Roy, O.S.B. Ord: '67.

St. Procopius Abbey: 5601 College Rd., Lisle, IL 60532. Tel: 630-969-6410; Fax: 630-969-6426.

U.S. Religious serving in China: Very Rev. Alban Hrebic, O.S.B. Ord: '52, Prior.

Assumption Abbey: P.O. Box A, Richardton, ND 58652. Tel: 701-974-3315.

U.S. Religious serving in South America: Very Rev. Philip Vanderlin, O.S.B. Ord: '80, Prior; Revs. Efraim Villegas, O.S.B. Ord: '88, Subprior; Sebastian Schmidt, O.S.B. Ord: '60; Carlos Suarez, O.S.B. Ord: '86; Francis Wehri, O.S.B. Ord: '61; Gonzalo Blanco, O.S.B. Ord: '92; Nicolas Cano Ord: '97; Milton Martinez Ord: '97; Bros. Fabio Mejia; Manuel Cely.

Mount Angel Abbey: St. Benedict, OR 97373. Tel: 503-845-3030; Fax: 503-845-3594. Monks of Mount Angel Abbey (Benedictines).

U.S. Religious serving in Mexico: Very Rev Konrad Shaefer, O.S.B. Ord: '80; Revs. Louis Charvet, O.S.B. Ord: '45; Michael Mee, O.S.B. Ord: '78.

Marmion Abbey: 850 Butterfield Rd., Aurora, IL 60504.

U.S. Religious serving in Central America: Very Rev. John Brahill, O.S.B. Ord: '82, Prior; Revs. Matthias Zinkan, O.S.B. Ord: '40; Gerald Benkert, O.S.B. Ord: '34; Carlos Quintana, O.S.B. Ord: '49.

St. Benedict's Abbey: Benet Lake, WI 53102.

U.S. Religious serving in Mexico: Rt. Rev. Robert Schoofs, O.S.B. Ord: '58; Bro. George Koenigs, O.S.B.

Blue Cloud Abbey: Marvin, SD 57251. Tel: 605-432-5528; Fax: 605-432-4754. Rt. Rev. Thomas Hillenbrand Ord: '65, Supr. & Mission Dir.

U.S. Religious serving in Guatemala: Revs. Basil Dilger, O.S.B. Ord: '61; Cletus Miller, O.S.B. Ord: '44; Bernardine Ness, O.S.B. Ord: '64.

New Subiaco Abbey: Subiaco, AR 72865; Fax: 501-934-4328. Rt. Rev. Jerome Kodell, O.S.B., Supr.

U.S. Religious serving in Central America: Revs. Richard Walz, O.S.B. Ord: '67, Prior; Bruno Fuhrmann, O.S.B. Ord: '54; Bros. Benedict Silva, O.S.B.; Omar Castillo, O.S.B.; Maurus Glenn, O.S.B.; Sergio Coc, O.S.B.

St. Paul's Abbey: Newton, NJ 07860. Tel: 973-383-2470; Fax: 973-383-5782.

U.S. Religious serving Abroad: Revs. Damian Milliken, O.S.B. Ord: '58, *Tanzania;* Peter W. Blue, O.S.B. Ord: '70, *South Africa.*

American Capuchin Missions (O.F.M.Cap.)

Missions of the American Provinces of the Order of Friars Minor Capuchin (The Capuchin Friars) in the United States and other countries

General Headquarters: Via Piemonte, 70, 00187, Rome, Italy; Most Rev. John Corriveau, O.F.M.Cap., Gen. Min.; Rev. Linus Faeh, O.F.M.Cap., Sec. Gen. for the Missions.

Provincial Headquarters

Capuchin Foreign Missions

Province of St. Joseph: 1740 Mt. Elliott Ave., Detroit, MI 48207; Fax: 313-922-0404. Revs. Daniel Fox, O.F.M.Cap. Ord: '75, Prov. Minister; James Zelinski, O.F.M.Cap. Ord: '61, Mission Sec.

U.S. Religious serving Abroad: Revs. Charles Bantle, O.F.M.Cap. Ord: '48, *Japan;* Evarist Bertrand, O.F.M.Cap. Ord: '63, *Nicaragua;* Paul Craig, O.F.M.Cap. Ord: '66, *Middle East;* Camillus Doerfler, O.F.M.Cap. Ord: '45, *Nicaragua;* Francis Solanus Fary, O.F.M.Cap. Ord: '67, *Nicaragua;* Ralph Fellenz, O.F.M.Cap. Ord: '68, *Middle East;* Carmel Flora, O.F.M.Cap. Ord: '53, *Australia;* Bro. Patrick Forton, O.F.M.Cap., *Nicaragua;* Revs. Glenn Gessner, O.F.M.Cap. Ord: '60, *Nicaragua;* Kevin Heagerty, O.F.M.Cap. Ord: '61, *Panama;* Walter Kasuboski, O.F.M.Cap. Ord: '74, *Panama;* Wilbert Lanser, O.F.M.Cap. Ord: '59, *Nicaragua;* Benjamin Markwell, O.F.M.Cap. Ord: '66, *Middle East;* Theodore Niehaus, O.F.M.Cap. Ord: '65, *Nicaragua;* John Francis Samsa, O.F.M.Cap. Ord: '61, *Honduras;* Most Rev. Paul Schmitz, O.F.M.Cap., Bishop-Vicar Apostolic of Bluefields; Revs. August Seubert, O.F.M.Cap. Ord: '57, *Nicaragua;* Wendelin Shafer, O.F.M.Cap. Ord: '46, *Nicaragua;* Gregory Smutko, O.F.M.Cap. Ord: '58, *Costa Rica;* Bernard Wagner, O.F.M.Cap. Ord: '63, *Nicaragua;* Lawrence Webber, O.F.M.Cap. Ord: '80, *Costa Rica;* Andre Weller, O.F.M.Cap. Ord: '63, *Panama;* Nicholas Widhammer, O.F.M.Cap. Ord: '63, *Middle East;* Joseph Wolf, O.F.M.Cap. Ord: '64, *Nicaragua.*

Province of St. Augustine: 220 37th St., Pittsburgh, PA 15201. Tel: 412-682-6011; Fax: 412-682-0506. Very Rev. Philip Fink, O.F.M.Cap. Ord: '77, Prov. Min.; Rev. Francis Fugini, O.F.M.Cap. Ord: '54, Coord. of Missions.

U.S. Religious serving in Puerto Rico (St. John the Baptist Vice Province): Revs. John Bednarik, O.F.M.Cap. Ord: '68, Vice-Prov.; Mario Mastrangelo, O.F.M.Cap. Ord: '58; Leo Morgan, O.F.M.Cap. Ord: '44; Joel Ostrowski, O.F.M.Cap. Ord: '51; Regis Schlick, O.F.M.Cap. Ord: '65.

U.S. Religious serving in Papua New Guinea (St. Michael the: Archangel Vice Province of Papua New Guinea and the Solomon Islands); Revs. Allan Wasiecko, O.F.M.Cap. Ord: '68, Vice-Prov.; Emilio Biosco, O.F.M.Cap. Ord: '94; Samuel Driscoll, O.F.M.Cap. Ord: '59; William Fey, O.F.M.Cap. Ord: '68; Dunstan Jones, O.F.M.Cap. Ord: '61; Benjamin Madden, O.F.M.Cap. Ord: '58; Brian Newman, O.F.M.Cap. Ord: '61; Cyril Repko, O.F.M.Cap. Ord: '62; Bro. Raymond Ronan, O.F.M.Cap.; Revs. Colman Studeny, O.F.M.Cap. Ord: '61; Roger White, O.F.M.Cap. Ord: '65; Jonathan Williams, O.F.M.Cap. Ord: '71.

Province of St. Mary: 30 Gedney Park Dr., White Plains, NY 10605. Tel: 914-761-3008. Very Rev. Bernard Smith, O.F.M.Cap. Ord: '64, Prov.; Rev. Peter Kaseta, O.F.M.Cap. Ord: '67, Mission Sec.

U.S. Religious serving Abroad: Most Rev.; Anthony Apuron, O.F.M.Cap., Archbishop of Agana; Revs. Wayne Berndt, O.F.M.Cap. Ord: '83, *Japan;* Roderick Brennan, O.F.M.Cap. Ord: '45, *Nicaragua;* Jeremiah Cassidy, O.F.M.Cap. Ord: '56, *Japan;* Patrick Castro, O.F.M.Cap. Ord: '87, *Guam;* Louis Chiusano, O.F.M.Cap. Ord: '57, *Japan;* Gordon Combs, O.F.M.Cap. Ord: '64, *Guam;* Daniel Cristobal, O.F.M.Cap. Ord: '59, *Guam;* Roland Daigle, O.F.M.Cap. Ord: '84, *Japan;* Michel Dalton, O.F.M.Cap. Ord: '78, *Guam;* Peter Danaher, O.F.M.Cap. Ord: '84, *Costa Rica;* Joseph English, O.F.M.Cap. Ord: '90, *Guam;* Eric Forbes, O.F.M.Cap. Ord: '90, *Guam;* Lee G. Friel, O.F.M.Cap. Ord: '56, *Guam;* Earl Gallagher, O.F.M.Cap. Ord: '71, *Honduras;* Agustin Gumataotao, O.F.M.Cap. Ord: '73, *Guam;* Most Rev. Peter B. Ishigami, O.F.M.Cap., Retired Bishop of Naha, *Japan;* Revs Paul Kosaka, O.F.M.Cap. Ord: '84, *Guam;* Felixberto Leon-Guerrero, O.F.M.Cap. Ord: '86, *Guam;* Robert L. Maher, O.F.M.Cap. Ord: '74, *Guam;* Andrew Mannetta, O.F.M.Cap. Ord: '83, *Guam;* Jose McCarthy, O.F.M.Cap. Ord: '60, *Puerto Rico;* Eymard McKinnon, O.F.M.Cap. Ord: '54, *Guam;* George Maddock, O.F.M.Cap. Ord: '64, *Guam;* Paul Minchak, O.F.M.Cap. Ord: '69, *Guam;* Bartholomew Minson, O.F.M.Cap. Ord: '64, *Japan;* John Niland, O.F.M.Cap. Ord: '76, *Guam;* Randolph Nowak, O.F.M.Cap. Ord: '52, *Guam;* LaSalle Parsons, O.F.M.Cap. Ord: '57, *Japan;* Robert Phelps, O.F.M.Cap. Ord: '66, *Guam;* Raymond Richard, O.F.M.Cap. Ord: '72, *Honduras;* Patrick Sullivan, O.F.M.Cap. Ord: '71, *Cuba;* Jose Villagomez, O.F.M.Cap. Ord: '74, *Guam;* Peter Von Essen, O.F.M.Cap. Ord: '56, *Japan;* John Szamreta, O.F.M.Cap. Ord: '81, *Japan.*

The Seraphic Mass Association-Capuchin Mission Association , St. Mary's Province, 210 West 31st St., New York, NY 10001-2876.

This Association supports the Capuchin Foreign Mission

Province of the Stigmata: St. Francis Center, 67 Lawrence Rd., Lafayette, NJ 07848. Tel: 973-383-6465. Brian Tomlinson, O.F.M.Cap. Ord: '65, Local Min.; Bro. Julius Tkaczyk, O.F.M.Cap., Assoc.

U.S. Religious serving in Zambia: Revs. Daniel Gomez, O.F.M.Cap. Ord: '61; Charles Hanley, O.F.M.Cap. Ord: '80; Bros. Rudolph Pieretti, O.F.M.Cap.; Crispin Valeri, O.F.M.Cap.

American Carmelite Missions (O.Carm)

Carmelite Foreign Missions

Foreign Missions of the American Province of the Most Pure Heart of Mary

Provincial Headquarters: Carmelite Provincial Office, 1317 Frontage Rd., Darien, IL 60561; Fax: 630-971-0195. Very Rev. Leo McCarthy, O.Carm. Ord: '62, Prov.

Mission Office: Carmelite Missions, Darien, IL 60561. Rev. John Malley, O.Carm. Ord: '56, Mission Dir.

U.S. Religious serving in Peru: Revs. Herbert Jones, O.Carm. Ord: '60; Gerald Payea, O.Carm. Ord: '70, Formation Dir.; Joseph Lucchesi, O.Carm. Ord: '84; Michael Sgarioto, O.Carm. Ord: '85, Pastor; Kevin Lafey, O.Carm. Ord: '72; Rev. Msgr. Alban Quinn, O.Carm. Ord: '49; Revs. Joseph Cilia, O.Carm. Ord: '68; Salvador Bartolo, O.Carm. Ord: '52; Michael LaFay, O.Carm. Ord: '60; Ferdinand Lansang, O.Carm. Ord: '96; James Geaney, O.Carm. Ord: '59.

U.S. Religious serving in Mexico: Revs. John Hertel, O.Carm. Ord: '53; Thomas Jordan, O.Carm. Ord: '70; Joel Moelter, O.Carm. Ord: '51; William Smith, O.Carm. Ord: '54; Frank Sanchez, O.Carm. Ord: '; Paul Hensen, O.Carm., Ord.

Comboni Missionaries (Verona Fathers) (M.C.C.J.)

Comboni Foreign Missions

Legal Title: *Comboni Missionaries of the Heart of Jesus, Inc.*

U.S. Headquarters: Comboni Mission Center, 8108 Beechmont Ave., Cincinnati, OH 45255-3194. Tel: 513-474-4997; Fax: 513-474-0382. Revs. John Converset, M.C.C.J. Ord: '71, Prov. Supr.; Joseph Bragotti, M.C.C.J. Ord: '62, Mission Dir. & Vice Prov.

U.S. Religious serving Abroad: Revs. Albert Anichini, M.C.C.J. Ord: '62, *Uganda;* Manuel Baeza, M.C.C.J. Ord: '96, *South Africa;* David Baltz, M.C.C.J. Ord: '67, *Uganda;* Michael Barton, M.C.C.J. Ord: '75, *Kenya;* David Bohnsack, M.C.C.J. Ord: '94, *Kenya;* Angel Camorlinga, M.C.C.J. Ord: '96, *Ecuador;* Dennis Conway, M.C.C.J. Ord: '68, *Italy;* James Francez, M.C.C.J. Ord: '57, *Mexico;* Louis Gasparini, M.C.C.J. Ord: '65, *Peru;* William Jansen, M.C.C.J. Ord: '66, *Guatemala;* Luis Monzon-Tapia, M.C.C.J. Ord: '95, *Zambia;* Paul O'Donnell, M.C.C.J. Ord: '93, *Philippines;* Raymond Pax, M.C.C.J. Ord: '65, *Kenya;* Brian Quigley, M.C.C.J. Ord: '77, *Malawi.*

American Conventual Franciscan Missions (O.F.M.Conv.)

Conventual Franciscan Foreign Missions

General Headquarters: Convento SS. XII Apostoli Piazza SS. Apostoli, 51, 00187, Roma, Italia. Most Rev. Enrique Montero, O.F.M.Conv., Sec. Gen. for the Missions.

Provincial Headquarters

Province of the Immaculate Conception: P.O. Box 629, 517 Washington Ave., Rensselaer, NY 12144. Very Rev. Canice Connors, O.F.M.Conv. Ord: '61, Prov. & Mission Dir. Tel: 518-472-1000.

U.S. Religious serving Abroad: Revs. Bertrand Hodes, O.F.M.Conv. Ord: '39; Maury Marhafer, O.F.M.Conv. Ord: '54; Martin de Porres Ward, O.F.M.Conv. Ord: '55, Spiritual Dir. (Seminary); Most Rev. Elias Manning, O.F.M.Conv., Bishop of Valenca, Brazil.

Province of Saint Anthony of Padua: Provincial House & Office of Mission Procurator, 12300 Folly Quarter Rd., Ellicott City, MD 21042-1419. Tel: 410-531-9200; Fax: 410-531-4881. Very Rev. Mark L. Curesky, O.F.M.Conv. Ord: '75, Minister Prov.; Rev. Martin Kobos, O.F.M.Conv. Ord: '76, Mission Procurator.

Franciscan Mission Association 66 School St., Granby, MA 01033. Tel: 413-467-9196. Rev. Placid Kaczorek, O.F.M.Conv. Ord: '64, Mission Dir.

U.S. Religious serving Abroad: Revs. Vincent Lachendro, O.F.M.Conv. Ord: '63, *Philippines;* Jerome Lukaszewski, O.F.M.Conv. Ord: '48, *Japan;* Paul Marut, O.F.M.Conv. Ord: '72, *Ghana;* Ron Roll, O.F.M.Conv. Ord: '80, *Honduras;* Bro. Mitchell Sawicki, O.F.M.Conv., *Ghana;* Revs. Dominic Slemba, O.F.M.Conv. Ord: '51, *Ghana;* Nicholas Swiatek, O.F.M.Conv. Ord: '68, *Japan;* Giles Zakowicz, O.F.M.Conv. Ord: '75, *Ghana.*

Province of Our Lady of Consolation: Provincial Office, Mt. St. Francis, IN 47146. Rev. Kent Biergans, O.F.M.Conv., Min. Prov.

Religious serving Abroad: Revs. Gerard Scioscia, O.F.M.Conv., Pastor; Juniper Cummings, O.F.M. Conv., Custos; Bros. Aloysius Wagener, O.F.M. Conv.; Bryan Hoban, O.F.M.Conv.; Kamil Wenzel, O.F.M.Conv., Pastor & Guardian; John Doyle, O.F.M.Conv.; Aloysius Jacoby, O.F.M.Conv., Guardian and Pastor; Gerhard Wenzel, O.F.M. Conv.; Efisio Steri, O.F.M.Conv., Guardian; Joseph Scoma, O.F.M.Conv.; Werner Iten, O.F.M.Conv., Pastor; Joseph Weissling, O.F.M. Conv., Guardian; Hugo Lamm, O.F.M.Conv., *Kitwe, Zambia;* Revs. Lawrence Mattingly, O.F.M.Conv., *Costa Rica;* Emil Cook, O.F.M.Conv., *Honduras;* Ronald Roll, O.F.M.Conv., *Honduras;* Ivan Rohloff, O.F.M. Conv., *Honduras;* Pius Uitendaal, O.F.M.Conv., Pastor, Zambia; Terence Tobin, O.F.M.Conv., Guardian, Zambia; Jude Rochford, O.F.M.Conv., Zambia; Mark Weaver, O.F.M.Conv., Custos, *Honduras;* Bro. Anthony Droll, O.F.M.Conv., *Zambia;* Revs. Thomas Merrill, O.F.M.Conv., *Costa Rica;* Raymond Mallett, O.F.M.Conv., *Costa Rica;* Fritz O'Kelly, O.F.M.Conv.

Province of Saint Bonaventure: Provincial Office, 6107 N. Kenmore Ave., Chicago, IL 60660-2797. Tel: 773-274-7681; Fax: 773-274-9751. Very Rev. Anthony Labedis, O.F.M.Conv. Ord: '60, Minister Prov.; Rev. Michael Suszynski, O.F.M.Conv. Ord: '86, Mission Dir.

U.S. Religious serving Abroad: Rev. John Calgaro, O.F.M.Conv. Ord: '74, *Mexico;* Bros. Paschal Metzger, O.F.M.Conv., *Mexico;* Stanislaus Zabkiewicz, O.F.M.Conv., Zambia.

Crosier Fathers Missions (O.S.C.)

Crosier Foreign Missions

Crosier Fathers and Brothers (Canons Regular of the Order of the Holy Cross)

U.S. Address: Crosier Missions-Province of St. Odilia, 3510 Vivian Ave., Shoreview, MN 55126-3852. Tel: 612-486-7456; Fax: 612-486-7589. Very Rev. John Neville, O.S.C. Ord: '61, Prov.; Rev. David E. Gallus, O.S.C. Ord: '66, Mission Dir.

U.S. Religious serving Abroad: Very Rev. Glen Lewandowski, O.S.C. Ord: '74, *Indonesia;* Rev. Ernest Martello, O.S.C. Ord: '70, *Zaire;* Bro. Clarence Neuner, O.S.C., *Indonesia;* Rev. Virgil Petermeier, O.S.C. Ord: '77, *Indonesia;* Robert Rossi, O.S.C Ord: '70, *Zaire;* Bro. James Scher, O.S.C., *Indonesia;* Most Rev. Alphonse Sowada, O.S.C., *Indonesia;* Rev. Gregory Poser, O.S.C. Ord: '75, *Indonesia.*

American Divine Word Missionaries (S.V.D.)

Society of the Divine Word Foreign Missions

Missions of the American Provinces of the Society of the Divine Word (S.V.D.) commonly known as Divine Word Missionaries

Latin: Societas Verbi Divini.

Provincial Headquarters in the U.S.A.

Chicago Province: Society of the Divine Word-Province of Blessed Joseph Freinademetz, S.V.D., 1985 Waukegan Rd., P.O. Box 6038, Techny, IL 60082-6038. Tel: 847-272-2700; Fax: 847-272-2517. Very Rev. Stanley Uroda, S.V.D. Ord: '74, Prov. Supr.; Rev. Thomas A. Krosnicki, S.V.D. Ord: '66, Mission Dir. for all three Provinces.

Publication: *Divine Word Missionaries.*

Southern Province: Society of the Divine Word-Province of St. Augustine, 201 Ruella Ave., Bay St. Louis, MS 39520-4638. Tel: 228-467-4322. Very Rev. Clifton Labbe, S.V.D. Ord: '69, Prov. Supr.

Western Province: Society of the Divine Word, P.O. Box 77-F, Los Angeles, CA 90007. Tel: 213-483-3013. Very Rev. Eamonn Donnelly, S.V.D. Ord: '70, Prov. Supr.

American Divine Word Missionaries in Overseas Missions: Most Rev. Leo Arkfeld, S.V.D., *Papua New Guinea;* Revs. Thomas Ascheman, S.V.D. Ord: '82, *Italy;* Daniel Bauer, S.V.D. Ord: '74, *Taiwan;* Francis Beemsterboer, S.V.D. Ord: '51, *Ghana;* Andrew Biller, S.V.D. Ord: '61, *Philippines;* Joseph Bisson, S.V.D. Ord: '63, *Papua New Guinea;* Michael Blume, S.V.D. Ord: '72, *Rome;* Bro. William Brennan, S.V.D., *Vietnam;* Revs. Francis Budenholzer, S.V.D. Ord: '72, *Taiwan;* Joseph Bugner, S.V.D. Ord: '63, *Papua New Guinea;* Most Rev. John Bukovsky, S.V.D., *Russia;* Revs. Francis Bures, S.V.D. Ord: '53, *Japan;* Vincent Burke, S.V.D. Ord: '61, *Ghana;* Dennis Callan, S.V.D. Ord: '87, *Taiwan;* Thomas Cassidy, S.V.D. Ord: '45, *Philippines;* Emil Cernaj, S.V.D. Ord: '51, *Australia;* David Cornett, S.V.D. Ord: '87, *Congo;* Richard Daschbach, S.V.D. Ord: '64, *Indonesia;* Anthony Dugay, S.V.D. Ord: '62, *Ghana;* Felix Eckerman, S.V.D. Ord: '47, *India;* Elmer Elsbernd, S.V.D. Ord: '65, *Papua New Guinea;* Bro. Xavier Eshman, S.V.D., *Paraguay;* Revs. Kenneth Feehan, S.V.D. Ord: '59, *Papua New Guinea;* Lloyd Fiedler, S.V.D. Ord: '70, *Philippines;* Patrick Fincutter, S.V.D. Ord: '55, *Papua New Guinea;* Frederick Fox, S.V.D. Ord: '50, *England;* Bro. Ronald Fratzke, S.V.D., *Australia;* Revs. Paul Gootee, S.V.D. Ord: '55, *Indonesia;* Robert Grochowski, S.V.D. Ord: '96, *Japan;* Lawrence Hambach, S.V.D. Ord: '61, *Indonesia;* John Healy, S.V.D. Ord: '43, *Philippines;* Bro. John Heckel, S.V.D., *Ghana;* Revs. James Heisig, S.V.D. Ord: '69, *Japan;* Edward Herberger, S.V.D. Ord: '60, *Jamaica;* Raymond Hober, S.V.D. Ord: '60, *Philippines;* Bros. Patrick Hogan, S.V.D., *Taiwan;* Andre Hotchkiss, S.V.D., *Kenya;* Revs. Clement Hotze, S.V.D. Ord: '47, *Ghana;* Alan Jenkins, S.V.D. Ord: '73, *Mexico;* Robert Johnson, S.V.D. Ord: '92, *Montserrat (Caribbean;* Most Rev. Raymond Kalisz, S.V.D., *Papua New Guinea;* Bros. Stephen Kerekes, S.V.D., *Papua New Guinea;* Lawrence Kieffer, S.V.D., *Papua New Guinea;* Revs. Jon Kirby, S.V.D. Ord: '71, *Ghana;* Robert Kisala, S.V.D. Ord: '85, *Japan;* Richard Kraft, S.V.D. Ord: '55, *Philippines;* Albert Kretschmer, S.V.D. Ord: '47, *Ghana;* Ronald Lange, S.V.D. Ord: '71, *Ghana;* Paul LaForge, S.V.D. Ord: '58, *Japan;* Lawrence LaPlante, S.V.D. Ord: '67, *Philippines;* William Liebert, S.V.D. Ord: '57, *Papua New Guinea;* James Liebner, S.V.D. Ord: '85, *Taiwan;* Michael Lindstrom, S.V.D. Ord: '82, *Japan;* Bro. Damien Lunders, S.V.D., *Papua New Guinea;* Revs. Matthew Lunzer, S.V.D. Ord: '45, *Papua New Guinea;* John Khien Luu, S.V.D. Ord: '92, *Australia;* David Mayer, S.V.D. Ord: '66, *Japan;* Dennis McKillip, S.V.D. Ord: '47, *Philippines;* John McSherry, S.V.D. Ord: '61, *Philippines;* Peter Michael, S.V.D. Ord: '40, *Philippines;* Francis Mihalic, S.V.D. Ord: '44, *Papua New Guinea;* Bro. Henry Miller, S.V.D., *Antigua/Caribbean;* Revs. Theodore Murnane, S.V.D. Ord: '59, *Philippines;* John Musinsky, S.V.D. Ord: '44, *Rome;* Paul Nadolny, S.V.D. Ord: '89, *Mexico;* Lawrence Nemer, S.V.D. Ord: '60, *Australia;* Joseph Trong Nguyen, S.V.D. Ord: '91, *Philippines;* Peter Sam Cao Nguyen, S.V.D. Ord: '86, *Korea;* Joseph Nguyen Minh Vu, S.V.D. Ord: '96, *Australia;* Donald O'Connor, S.V.D. Ord: '64, *Papua New Guinea;* Vincent Ohlinger, S.V.D. Ord: '68, *Papua New Guinea;* Anthony Patik, S.V.D. Ord: '42, *Papua New Guinea;* Stanley Plutz, S.V.D. Ord: '53, *Philippines;* Jefferson Pool, S.V.D. Ord: '92, *Philippines;* William Popp, S.V.D. Ord: '49, *Indonesia;* Thomas Potts, S.V.D. Ord: '61, *Ghana;* Robert Pung, S.V.D. Ord: '44, *Rome;* Bro. Mark Rastall, S.V.D., *Australia;* Revs. Andrew Rentko, S.V.D. Ord: '49, *Mexico;* Robert Riemer, S.V.D. Ord: '60, *Japan;* Roger Risse, S.V.D. Ord: '54, *Indonesia;* James Risse, S.V.D. Ord: '61, *Philippines;* Eugene Rochford, S.V.D. Ord: '74, *Rome;* Charles Scanlon, S.V.D. Ord: '54, *Philippines;* Bartley Schmitz, S.V.D. Ord: '44, *Taiwan;* Eugene Schmitz, S.V.D. Ord: '67, *Indonesia;* Charles Schneider, S.V.D. Ord: '46, *Ghana;* William Seifert, S.V.D. Ord: '67, *Papua New Guinea;* John Seland, S.V.D. Ord: '68, *Japan;* Werner Shadeg, S.V.D. Ord: '45, *Papua New Guinea;* Norbert Shadeg, S.V.D. Ord: '49, *Indonesia;* Otto Shelly, S.V.D. Ord: '42, *Australia;* Arnold Steffen, S.V.D. Ord: '57, *Papua New Guinea;* Victor Stevko, S.V.D. Ord: '57, *Australia;* Nicholas Strawn, S.V.D. Ord: '62, *Indonesia;* David Streit, S.V.D. Ord: '69, *Rome;* Richard Szippl,

S.V.D. Ord: '81, *Japan;* Gerald Theis, S.V.D. Ord: '80, *Papua New Guinea;* Richard Thibeau, S.V.D. Ord: '57, *Mexico;* Bro. Wayne Till, S.V.D., *Papua New Guinea;* Revs. Frederick Timp, S.V.D. Ord: '71, *Ghana;* Joseph Huynh Tran, S.V.D. Ord: '93, *Taiwan;* Thomas Umbras, S.V.D. Ord: '81, *Mexico;* Edward Vargo, S.V.D. Ord: '63, *Thailand;* Joseph Vu Dao, S.V.D. Ord: '88, *Philippines;* Lawrence Wagner, S.V.D. Ord: '44, *Mexico;* Wilbert Wagner, S.V.D. Ord: '40, *Mexico;* John Wald, S.V.D. Ord: '43, *Papua New Guinea;* Bro. Daniel Yunck, S.V.D., *Paraguay;* Rev. Jerome Ziliak, S.V.D. Ord: '47, *India.*

American Dominican Missions (O.P.)

Dominican - Order of Preachers Foreign Missions

Foreign Missions of the American Provinces of the Order of Preachers

Provincial Headquarters

Province of St. Joseph (Eastern): 141 E. 65th St., New York, NY 10021. Tel: 212-734-4784. Very Rev. Norman Alfred Haddid, O.P. Ord: '61, Prov.; Bro. Thomas-Aquinas Dolan, O.P., Mission Dir.

U.S. Religious serving in Pakistan: Revs. J. M. Connors, O.P. Ord: '51; J. F. Arnold, O.P. Ord: '56; T. C. McVey, O.P. Ord: '60; J. A. Breen, O.P. Ord: '63; J. Nuttall, O.P. Ord: '69; L. L. Turon, O.P. Ord: '55; G. L. Sukovaty, O.P. Ord: '51.

Priests 7.

U.S. Religious serving in Peru: Revs. J. L. Dolan, O.P. Ord: '60; Thomas K. Kraft, O.P. Ord: '86.

U.S. Religious serving in Kenya: Very Rev. W. T. Sinkele, O.P. Ord: '73, Vicar Prov. & Supr.; Revs. M. B. Schepers, O.P. Ord: '56; L. M. Shea, O.P. Ord: '52; Edward Gorman, O.P. Ord: '92; T. R. Heath, O.P. Ord: '50; David D. Izzo, O.P. Ord: '94; Kieran J. Healy, O.P. Ord: '61; John P. Gerhard, O.P. Ord: '53; Bertrand E. Ebben, O.P. Ord: '59.

U.S. Religious serving elsewhere: Revs. D. G. Doherty, O.P. Ord: '57, *Philippines;* Frank I.Sutman, O.P. Ord: '85, *Russia;* Christopher Cardone, O.P. Ord: '86, *Solomon Islands;* Stanley Azaro, O.P. Ord: '75, *Lithuania.*

Province of St. Albert the Great (Central): 1909 S. Ashland Ave., Chicago, IL 60608-2994; Fax: 312-829-8471. Very Rev. Edward M. Ruane, O.P. Ord: '69, Prov.; Rev. Bede Jagde, O.P. Ord: '60, Dir., - *St. Dominic Mission Society.*

U.S. Religious serving in Bolivia: Revs. Patrick Reardon, O.P. Ord: '60; Thomas Lynch, O.P. Ord: '86; Chrysostom Geraets, O.P. Ord: '56; Mark Paraday, O.P. Ord: '83; Daniel Roach, O.P. Ord: '56; James Spahn, O.P. Ord: '81.

U.S. Religious serving in Honduras: Rev. James Q. Barnett, O.P. Ord: '65.

U.S. Religious serving in Kenya: Rev. Lewis M. Shea, O.P. Ord: '52.

U.S. Religious serving in Nigeria: Revs. Peter Otillio, O.P. Ord: '57; Joseph H. Kenny, O.P. Ord: '50; Thomas K. McDermott, O.P. Ord: '83; Justus Pokrzewinski, O.P. Ord: '60; Edward H. Riley, O.P. Ord: '60; Gilbert Thesing, O.P. Ord: '75; Ambrose Windbacher, O.P. Ord: '54; Bro. Stephen Lucas, O.P.

Province Of The Holy Name: (Western Dominican Province), 5877 Birch Court, Oakland, CA 94618. Very Rev. Daniel Syverstad, O.P. Ord: '82, Prov., (Please refer to the section of Religious Institutes for Men for further details.).

Southern Dominican Province: Province of St. Martin de Porres, 1421 N. Causeway Blvd.-Ste. 200, Metairie, LA 70001-4144. Tel: 504-837-2129; Fax: 504-837-6604. Very Rev. Alberto Rodriguez, O.P. Ord: '71, Prov.; Rev. John Raymond Corr, O.P. Ord: '56, Dir. Southern Dominican Global Missions.

U.S. Religious serving abroad: Revs. James L. Dolan, O.P. Ord: '60, *Peru;* Carmen Mele, O.P. Ord: '80, *Costa Rica;* Jesus Guerra, O.P. Ord: '57, *Venezuela;* Vincent Huu Du Nguyen, O.P. Ord: '46, *Calgary, Alberta, Canada;* Bertrand Ebben, O.P. Ord: '59, *Arusha Tanzania.*

American Franciscan Missions (O.F.M.)

Franciscan Foreign Missions

Missions of the American Provinces of the Order of Friars Minor (Franciscans) in the United States and other countries

Holy Name Province: 135 W. 31st St., New York, NY 10001-3439. Bro. Gordon Clark, O.F.M., Prov. Promoter of the Missions, Sec. Missionary Evangelization.

U.S. Religious serving in Japan: Revs. Jerome A. Donnelly, O.F.M. Ord: '39; Bede Fitzpatrick, O.F.M. Ord: '55; Campion Lally, O.F.M. Ord: '53; Bartholomew McMahon, O.F.M. Ord: '62; Lucian A. Mulhern, O.F.M. Ord: '62; Donnan P. Murray, O.F.M. Ord: '56; Callistus Sweeney, O.F.M. Ord: '; Stanislaus Widomski Ord: '62.

U.S. Religious serving Brazil: Most Revs. John Burke O.F.M.; Benedict D. Coscia, O.F.M.; Capistran F. Heim, O.F.M.; Revs. David J. Babcock, O.F.M. Ord: '53; Donald J. Chin, O.F.M. Ord: '67; Alexander F. Eustace, O.F.M. Ord: '50; Thomas J. Fox, O.F.M. Ord: '46; Berard J. Hanlon, O.F.M. Ord: '63; John J. Janson, O.F.M. Ord: '41; Juvenal F. Leahy, O.F.M. Ord: '58; Ignatius J. McGeady, O.F.M. Ord: '48; Aloysius Siracuse, O.F.M. Ord: '47; Joseph Sullivan, O.F.M. Ord: '55.

U.S. Religious serving in Peru: Revs. Mariano Gagnon, O.F.M. Ord: '58; Mariano Guzman, O.F.M. Ord: '57; Christopher J. Dunn, O.F.M. Ord: '82; Bros. Declan McCabe, O.F.M.; Carlos Sarmiento, O.F.M.; Rev. Anthony Wilson, O.F.M. Ord: '87.

U.S. Religious serving in Taiwan: Rev. Pius Lui, O.F.M. Ord: '53.

U.S. Religious serving in Bolivia: Most Rev. Thomas R. Manning, O.F.M., ord. 47; Revs. Clement J. Comesky, O.F.M. Ord: '55; Gavin P. Hanlon, O.F.M. Ord: '56; Ignatius Harding, O.F.M. Ord: '65; William R. Keenan, O.F.M. Ord: '56; Thomas J. Kornacki, O.F.M. Ord: '88; Conor Mullaly, O.F.M. Ord: '51; Bernardine Ward, O.F.M. Ord: '42.

U.S. Religious serving in Israel: Revs. William DeBiase, O.F.M. Ord: '65; Edward J. Dillon, O.F.M. Ord: '55.

U.S. Religious serving in Africa: Revs. Roy Corrigan, O.F.M. Ord: '55; Joseph B. Ehrhardt, O.F.M. Ord: '76; Michael S. Joyce, O.F.M. Ord: '76; Finian A. Riley, O.F.M. Ord: '55; Charles A. Steen, O.F.M. Ord: '64; Bro. Paschal Gallagher, O.F.M.

U.S. Religious serving in Puerto Rico: Rev. Alfonso D. Guzman, O.F.M. Ord: '71.

Franciscan Province of the Immaculate Conception: 125 Thompson St., New York, NY 10012. Rev. Alban V. Montella, O.F.M. Ord: '55, Sec./Missionary Evangelization & Franciscan Missionary Union.

Province-affiliated Religious serving in Honduras: Revs. Peter Paul Meilak, O.F.M. Ord: '49; Albert Gauci, O.F.M. Ord: '71; Bro. Guillermo Salgado, O.F.M.; Rev. Ubladimiro Rivera, O.F.M. Ord: '75; Most Revs. Maurice Muldoon, O.F.M.; Gerald Scarpone, O.F.M.; Revs. Roberto Camilleri, O.F.M. Ord: '75; Angelo Falzon, O.F.M. Ord: '84; Joseph Bonello, O.F.M. Ord: '85; Donald Salazar, O.F.M. Ord: '67.

Province-affiliated Religious serving in Guatemala: Revs. Athanasius Iazzetta, O.F.M. Ord: '54; Miguel Blanco Guevera, O.F.M. Ord: '37; Rocco Famiglietti, O.F.M. Ord: '47; Ottaviano Battolini, O.F.M. Ord: '43; Robert Siguere, O.F.M. Ord: '73.

Province-affiliated Religious serving in El Salvador: Revs Flavian Mucci, O.F.M. Ord: '63; Guy Vellardita, O.F.M. Ord: '58, *San Pedro;* Rafael Fernandez, O.F.M. Ord: '87.

Sacred Heart Province: 3140 Meramec St., St. Louis, MO 63118. Tel: 314-353-3421. Revs. Kurt Hartrich, O.F.M. Ord: '66, Prov.; Thomas Gardner, O.F.M. Ord: '79, Promoter of the Missions, *Franciscan Missionary Union.* Tel: 314-353-7729.

U.S. Religious serving in Brazil: Revs. Michael Grawe, O.F.M. Ord: '70; Gregory Kemner, O.F.M. Ord: '55; Nestor Windolph, O.F.M. Ord: '55.

U.S. Religious serving in Alaska: Revs. William E. Cardy, O.F.M. Ord: '72; Joseph Hemmer, O.F.M. Ord: '59; Bro. Robert Ruzicka, O.F.M.

U.S. Religious serving Elsewhere: Rev. Louis B. Antl, O.F.M. Ord: '48, *Italy;* Bro. Jeffrey Haller, O.F.M., *Taiwan;* Revs. Albert Haase, O.F.M. Ord: '83, *Taiwan;* James Perluzzi, O.F.M. Ord: '65, *Italy;* Michael Perry, O.F.M. Ord: '84, *England;* Basil Tsung, O.F.M. Ord: '53, *Taiwan.*

St. Barbara Province: 1500 34th Ave., Oakland, CA 94601; Fax: 510-536-3970.

U.S. Religious serving Overseas: Bro. Norbert Binder, O.F.M., *Philippines;* Revs. Melvin Stanley, O.F.M. Ord: '52, *Philippines;* Martin Gates, O.F.M. Ord: '63, *Mexico;* Camillus Cavagnaro, O.F.M. Ord: '46, *Mexico;* Elias Galvez, O.F.M. Ord: '56, *Mexico;* John Peterson Ord: '63, *Mexico;* Bros. Miguel Lozano, O.F.M., *Mexico;* Ivo Toneck, O.F.M., *Mexico;* Leo Gonzalez, O.F.M., *Israel;* Gerard Saunders, O.F.M., *Peru;* Rev. Oscar Mendez, O.F.M. Ord: '89, *El Salvador;* Bros. Elmer Yung. O.F.M., *Guatemala;* John Summers, O.F.M., *Thailand.*

Assumption B.V.M. Province: Pulaski, WI 54162. Tel: 920-822-5422; Fax: 920-822-5423. Revs. Paul Reczek, O.F.M. Ord: '72, Minister Prov.; Hugh Zurat, O.F.M. Ord: '62, *Franciscan Evangelization Center - Assumption Province,* Milwaukee, WI 53215. Tel: 414-383-7934; Fax: 414-349-0119.

Publication: *Mission Newsletter.*

U.S. Religious serving Abroad: Revs. Laurian Wegner, O.F.M. Ord: '78, *Japan;* Bro. Augustine Fraszczak, O.F.M., *Philippines;* Revs. Lyle Chrobak, O.F.M. Ord: '62, *Mexico;* Henry Howaniec, O.F.M. Ord: '56, *Kazakhstan;* Blase Karas, O.F.M. Ord: '59, *Russia.*

Province of St. John the Baptist: 1615 Vine St., Cincinnati, OH 45210-1222. Tel: 513-721-4700; Fax: 513-421-9672. Bro. Scott Obrecht, O.F.M., Dir.-Secretariat for Missionary Evangelization & Franciscan Missionary Union.

Publications: *Monthly newsletter, Friarworks.*

U.S. Religious serving Abroad: Revs. Malachy Brogan, O.F.M. Ord: '57, *Holy Land;* Harold Geers, O.F.M. Ord: '60, *Philippines;* Bede Clancy, O.F.M. Ord: '44, *Philippines;* Carl Kemphues, O.F.M. Ord: '56, *Philippines;* Elgar Nadon, O.F.M. Ord: '59, *Philippines;* Joseph Hund, O.F.M. Ord: '89, *Philippines;* Bro. Philip Wilhelm, O.F.M., *Philippines;* Revs. Bernardin Schneider, O.F.M. Ord: '44, *Japan;* David Turnbull, O.F.M. Ord: '57, *Phillipines;* Bertram Tiemeyer, O.F.M. Ord: '47, *Philippines;* Max Langenderfer, O.F.M. Ord: '73, *Kenya;* James Fehrenbach, O.F.M. Ord: '71, *Germany;* Bro. Ambrose Beam, O.F.M., *Holy Land;* Revs. Gil Wohler, O.F.M. Ord: '62, *South Africa;* Lawrence Landini, O.F.M. Ord: '61, *South Africa;* Bro. Roger Covero, O.F.M., *Philippines;* Revs. Daniel Kroger, O.F.M. Ord: '73, *Philippines;* John Quigley, O.F.M. Ord: '72, *Rome;* Howard Hudepohl, O.F.M. Ord: '54, *South Africa.*

VI Slav-Byzantine Missions, U.S.A.

Custody of St. Mary of the Angels. Byzantine-Slavonic Rite (New Canaan, CT)

Established by decree of the Most Rev. Minister General of the Order of Friars Minor on November 7, 1947, with the approbation of the Sacred Congregation for the Oriental Church on October 28, 1947, among the peoples of the Byzantine Rite

Commissariats of the Holy Land: 1400 Quincy St. N.E., Washington, DC 20017. Tel: 202-526-6800; Fax: 202-529-9889. Bros. Callistus Welch, O.F.M., Commissary; David Wathen, O.F.M.; James Paul Brabandt, O.F.M.; Revs. Pio Jackson, O.F.M. Ord: '91; Joshua Doyle, O.F.M., Brian McTommoney, O.F.M. Ord: '53.

St. Anthony Friary: 3140 Meramec St., St. Louis, MO 63118. Rev. Thomas Gardner, O.F.M. Ord: '79, Commissary.

St. Joseph's Friary: 218 East 12th St., Los Angeles, CA 90015. Rev. Martial Luebke, O.F.M. Ord: '39, Commissary.

Custody of the Holy Land: Jordan, Israel, Lebanon, Syria, Cyprus, Egypt and Rhodes.

U.S. Religious serving Abroad: Bro. Aloysius Florio, O.F.M., *Rome, Italy;* Rev. Xavier Geiser, O.F.M. Ord: '55, *Jerusalem, Israel;* Bros. Roger Petras, O.F.M., *Nicosia, Cyprus;* Michael Raum, O.F.M., *Jerusalem, Israel;* Ambrose Beam, O.F.M., *Rhodes;* Thomas Courtney, O.F.M., *Syria;* Revs. Peter Vasko, O.F.M. Ord: '87, *Jerusalem, Israel;* Raphael Bonanno, O.F.M., Rome; George Lewett, O.F.M. Ord: '88, *Bethlehem, Isreal;* Athanasius Macora, O.F.M. Ord: '92, *Jerusalem, Israel;* Matthias Rendon, O.F.M. Ord: '92, *Jerusalem, Israel;* Danielmose Shroeder, O.F.M. Ord: '91, *Jerusalem, Israel;* Guillermo Jaramillo, O.F.M. Ord: '94, *Jerusalem, Israel;* Bros. Leo Gonzales, O.F.M., *Mt. Tabor, Israel;* Angel Beda Ison, O.F.M., *Jerusalem, Israel.*

Franciscan Friars Of The Atonement (S.A.)

General Headquarters: St. James Friary, P.O. Box 5, Garrison, NY 10524. Tel: 914-424-3038; Fax: 914-424-3978. Rev. Thomas Orians, S.A. Ord: '92, Mission Coord., Office, P.O. Box 300, Graymoor, Garrison, NY 10524-0300. Tel: 914-424-3671, Ext. 3412.

For detailed information on the U.S. Religious working in foreign: missions, please refer to the listings; under the Archdiocese of New York section entitled; "Monasteries and Residences of Priests and Brothers", Graymoor, Garrison, NY.

Holy Cross Mission Center (C.S.C.)

U.S. Headquarters and Procure: Holy Cross Mission Center for Cross-Cultural Ministries, P.O. Box 543, Notre Dame, IN 46556. Tel: 219-631-5477; Fax: 219-631-6813. Rev. James T. Rahilly, C.S.C. Ord: '64, Dir.

Legal Title: *Holy Cross Foreign Mission Society, Inc.*

Holy Cross Foreign Missions

Indiana Province: Congregation of Holy Cross, 1304 East Jefferson, South Bend, IN 46617.

Midwest Province: Congregation of Holy Cross, Box 460, Notre Dame, IN 46556.

Eastern Province: Congregation of Holy Cross, 835 Clinton Ave., Bridgeport, CT 06604-2393.

South-West Province: Congregation of Holy Cross, 3001 S. Congress Ave., #1046, Austin, TX 78704-6489.

Eastern Province of Brothers: Congregation of Holy Cross, 85 Overlook Cir., New Rochelle, NY 10804-4501.

Southern Province of Priests: Congregation of Holy Cross, 2111 Brackenridge St., Austin, TX 78704-4322.

U.S. Religious serving in foreign missions: Revs. Robert R. Baker, C.S.C. Ord: '70, *Peru;* Duane Balcerski, C.S.C. Ord: '71; James T. Banas, C.S.C. Ord: '57, *Bangladesh;* Bro. Kevin Barey, C.S.C., *Brazil;* Rev. Gerald R. Barmasse, C.S.C. Ord: '76, *Chile;* Bro. Donald Becker, C.S.C., *Bangladesh;* Rev. Thomas V. Bednar, C.S.C. Ord: '85, *Chile;* Bros. Thomas More Beere, C.S.C., *Bangladesh;* John Benesh, C.S.C., *Peru;* Rev. F. Frederick Bergmann, C.S.C. Ord: '39, *Bangladesh;* Bro. Richard Burgie, C.S.C., *Brazil;* Revs. Arthur J. Colgan, C.S.C. Ord: '73, *Peru;* Charles A. Delaney, C.S.C. Ord: '49, *Chile;* Philip T. Devlin, C.S.C. Ord: '56, *Peru;* Joseph M. Doherty, C.S.C. Ord: '41, *Chile;* Joseph A. Dorsey, C.S.C. Ord: '57, *Chile;* Bro. Ronald Drahozal, C.S.C., *Bangladesh;* Rev. David E. Farrell, C.S.C. Ord: ', *Peru;* Bros. John Flood, C.S.C., *Uganda;* Frederick Cosgrove, C.S.C., *Uganda;* William Gates, C.S.C., *Ghana;* Revs. Robert Gilbo, C.S.C. Ord: '67, *Chile;* Robert G. Gilmour, C.S.C. Ord: '68, *Ghana;* Bros. Vincent Gross, C.S.C., *Ghana;* Thomas Giumenta, C.S.C., *Chile;* Alan Gugel, C.S.C., *Uganda;* Alan Harrod, C.S.C., *Uganda;* John Harris, C.S.C., *Nepal;* Ronald Hein, C.S.C., *Brazil;* Alberic Houle, C.S.C., *Bangladesh;* Revs. Robert T. Hesse, C.S.C. Ord: '58, *Uganda;* Eugene E. Homrich, C.S.C. Ord: '55, *Bangladesh;* Charles Houser, C.S.C. Ord: '46, *Bangladesh;* James W. Irwin, C.S.C. Ord: ', *Mexico;* Malcolm D. Johnson, C.S.C. Ord: '59, *Chile;* Bros. Richard F. Johnson, C.S.C., *Ghana;* Thomas Keefe, C.S.C., *Uganda;* Rev. Bros. Joseph Kinsman, C.S.C., *Brazil;* Bernard Klim, *Uganda;* Revs. Paul Kollman, C.S.C. Ord: ', *Uganda;* T. Daniel Kennerk, C.S.C. Ord: '53, *Bangladesh;* Bros. Jerome F. Kreotsch, C.S.C., *Ghana;* Donald Kuchenmeister, C.S.C., *Chile;* Alfred Ledet, C.S.C., *Brazil;* Dismas Lenzi, C.S.C., *Brazil;* Rev. Joseph Lehane, C.S.C. Ord: '57, *Bangladesh;* Bro. Norbert Lengerich, C.S.C., *Brazil;* Revs. L. Peter Logsdon, C.S.C. Ord: '68, *Mexico;* George Lucas, C.S.C. Ord: '72, *Uganda;* Bros. Robert Ludwig, C.S.C., *Israel;* Peter Celestine Maranto, C.S.C., *Brazil;* Revs. H. Thomas McDermott, C.S.C. Ord: '79, *Uganda;* Russell McDougall, C.S.C. Ord: '91, *Italy;* Bro. Frederick McGlynn, C.S.C., *Ghana;* Most Rev. Mark G. McGrath, C.S.C., *Panama;* Rev. Joseph Moyer, C.S.C. Ord: '94, *Mexico;* Bros. Harold Naudet, C.S.C., *Brazil;* James Nichols, C.S.C., *Uganda;* Revs. Bertram A. Nelson, C.S.C. Ord: ', *Bangladesh;* Daniel A. Panchot, C.S.C. Ord: '65, *Mexico;* Gerald T. Papen, C.S.C. Ord: '63, *Chile;* Leonard D. Paul, C.S.C. Ord: ', *Kenya;* Joseph S. Peixotto, C.S.C. Ord: '61, *Bangladesh;* William Persia, C.S.C. Ord: '62, *Peru;* James Phalen, C.S.C. Ord: ', *Peru;* George F. Pope, C.S.C. Ord: '58, *Bangladesh;* Richard L. Potthast, C.S.C. Ord: '67, *Uganda;* Francis Quinlivan, C.S.C. Ord: '70, *Bangladesh;* Bros. Leonard Reeson, C.S.C., *Brazil;* Frank Robinson, C.S.C., *Brazil;* Rev. Cornelius J. Ryan, C.S.C. Ord: '66, *Uganda;* Paul Schaefer, C.S.C., *Brazil;* Most Rev. Charles A. Schleck, C.S.C., ord. 51, *Italy;* Revs. Thomas Shea, C.S.C. Ord: '67, *Peru;* Robert G. Simon, C.S.C. Ord: '61, *Chile;* Thomas W. Smith, C.S.C. Ord: '72, *Kenya;* Bro. William St. Romain, C.S.C., *Brazil;* Rev. Frederick A. Schmidt, C.S.C. Ord: '37, *Mexico;* Bro. Sergio Stolf, C.S.C., *Brazil;* Rev. Richard E. Stout, C.S.C. Ord: '71, *Kenya;* Bros. J. Rodney Struble, C.S.C., *Bangladesh;* Nicholas Thielman, C.S.C., *Bangladesh;* Revs. Richard W. Timm, C.S.C. Ord: '49, *Bangladesh;* Robert Plasker, C.S.C. Ord: '57, *Chile;* Donald Fetters, C.S.C. Ord: '76, *Chile;* James J. Ferguson, C.S.C. Ord: '65, *Uganda;* Bros. Ernest Turk, C.S.C., *Brazil;* Robert Weinmann, C.S.C., *Brazil;* Matthew Lyons, C.S.C., *Chile;* Robert Nebus, C.S.C., *Uganda;* John Paige, C.S.C., *Uganda;* Joseph Walsh, C.S.C., *Kenya;* Thomas Dillman, C.S.C., *Ghana;* Revs. Gerald J. Whelan, C.S.C. Ord: '55, *Chile;* Richard J. Wunsch, C.S.C. Ord: '66, *Uganda.*

Priests 55; Brothers 43.

Holy Ghost Fathers (C.S.Sp.)

Holy Ghost Foreign Missions

U.S.A. - East Province: Holy Ghost Fathers, 6230 Brush Run Rd., Bethel Park, PA 15102; Fax: 412-831-0970. Rev. Christopher P. Promis, C.S.Sp. Ord: '72, Prov.

U.S. Religious serving Abroad: Revs. Remo J. Bonifazi, C.S.Sp. Ord: '45, *Republic of South Africa;* William H. Christy, C.S.Sp. Ord: '92, *Arusha, Tanzania;* Charles S. Giambrone, C.S.Sp. Ord: '60, *Arusha, Tanzania;* Francis A. Greff, C.S.Sp. Ord: '47, *Arusha, Tanzania;* Joseph M. Herzstein, C.S.Sp. Ord: '63, *Kilimanjaro;* Mortimer F. Kane, C.S.Sp. Ord: '56, *Arusha, Tanzania;* Joseph L. Kelly, C.S.Sp. Ord: '50, *Arusha;* Richard J. LeClair, C.S.Sp. Ord: '51, *Arusha, Tanzania;* Edward T. Marchessault, C.S.Sp. Ord: '64, *Arusha, Tanzania;* Josaphat Msongore, C.S.Sp. Ord: '63, *Arusha, Tanzania;* Patrick A. Patten, C.S.Sp. Ord: '78, *Arusha, Tanzania;* Edward J. Raszewski, C.S.Sp. Ord: '47, *Arusha, Tanzania;* Bro. Francis Sullivan, C.S.Sp., *Arusha, Tanzania;* Rev. Vincent G. Stegman, C.S.Sp. Ord: '62, *Ethiopia.*

Jesuit Volunteers: International (S.J.)

U.S. Headquarters: Jesuit International Volunteers, P.O. Box 25478, Washington, DC 20007. Tel: 202-687-1132; Fax: 202-687-5082. Rev. Vincent De-Cola, S.J., Dir.

A Christian service organization offering young College educated lay men and women an opportunity to volunteer in a developing country in collaboration with Jesuits. Volunteers serve for two years without returning to the U.S.

Jesuit Missions (S.J.)

Jesuit Foreign Missions

Jesuit Mission Inc. An official missionary organization of the Provinces of the United States Assistancy of the Society of Jesus.

National Headquarters: Jesuit Missions, 1616 P St., N.W., #400, Washington, DC 20036. Tel: 202-462-0400; Fax: 202-328-9212. Revs. Richard J. Ryscavage, S.J. Ord: '77, Pres.; J. P. Horrigan, S.J. Ord: '69, Vice Pres.; Daniel C. McDonald, S.J. Ord: '81, Sec.-Treas.; Exec. Committee; Revs. William T. Wood, S.J. Ord: '48; Theodore T. Taheny, S.J. Ord: '56.

Provinces

Society of Jesus: California Province, 284 Stanyan St., San Francisco, CA 94118. Tel: 415-221-1588.

Legal Title: *California Jesuit Missionaries;* Revs. John A. Privett, S.J. Ord: '72, Prov.; Theodore T. Taheny, S.J. Ord: '56, Mission Dir.

U.S. Religious serving in foreign missions: Revs. Louis G. Aldrich, S.J. Ord: '86, *Republic of China;* William A. Ameche, S.J. Ord: '81, *Mexico;* Ferdinand T. Azevedo, S.J. Ord: '70, *Brazil;* Robert Becka, S.J. Ord: '60, *Japan;* Walter Brennan, S.J. Ord: '60, *Japan;* James Chevedden, S.J. Ord: '78, *Republic of China;* Robert Chiesa, S.J. Ord: '68, *Japan;* Robert Cunningham, S.J. Ord: '55, *Philippines;* Bro. Richard Devine, S.J., *Japan;* Revs. John R. Donahue, S.J. Ord: '79, *Honduras;* John Donald, S.J. Ord: '72, *Honduras;* Rev. Msgr. Kevin D. Ballard, S.J. Ord: '85, *Nepal;* Revs. Gustavo Fernandez, S.J. Ord: '67, *Honduras;* Thomas W. Franxman, S.J. Ord: '64, *Philippines;* Thomas E. Splain, S.J. Ord: '71, *Fiji Islands;* Fred Green, S.J. Ord: '58, *Peru;* Bro. Robert Griffin, S.J., *Philippines;* Revs. Robert B. Grimaldi, S.J. Ord: '68, *Honduras;* John R. LeVecke, S.J. Ord: '84, *Chile;* Kieth Barry Martinson, S.J. Ord: '75, *Republic of China;* George G. Martinson, S.J. Ord: '73, *Republic of China;* Edward Murphy, S.J. Ord: '43, *Republic of China;* Paul O'Brien, S.J. Ord: '38, *Thailand;* John B. Palm, S.J. Ord: '41, *Republic of China;* Paul Pollock, S.J. Ord: '73, *Thailand;* Bro. Donald Poetzl, S.J., *Mexico;* Revs. David Reed, S.J. Ord: '64, *Republic of China;* Robert Ronald, S.J. Ord: '65, *Republic of China;* Daniel Ross, S.J. Ord: '66, *Republic of China;* Richard Schneck, S.J. Ord: '72, *Ecuador;* Revs. Glen E. Smith, S.J. Ord: '63, *Japan;* Norman Walling, S.J. Ord: '61, *Hong Kong;* Charles Welsh, S.J. Ord: '72, *Republic of China.*

Priests 34; Brothers 3; Scholastics 2.

Society of Jesus: Chicago Province, 2059 N. Sedgwick St., Chicago, IL 60614. Tel: 312-975-8181.

Legal title: Jesuit International Missions,, (Formerly, Jesuits in Peru, Chicago Province, and Patna Jesuit Mission Society; Revs. Bradley M. Schaeffer, S.J. Ord: '77, Prov.; Gerald P. Grace, S.J. Ord: '54, Prov. Asst. Intl. Ministries.

U.S. Religious serving in foreign missions: Revs. Robert E. Beckman, S.J. Ord: '56, *Peru;* Fred F. Bergewisch, S.J. Ord: '55, *Peru;* Theodore B. Bowling, S.J. Ord: '53, *India;* Lawrence V. Brooks, S.J. Ord: '74, *Nepal;* Patrick M. Casey, S.J. Ord: '72, *Peru;* Francis M. Chamberlain, S.J. Ord: '68, *Peru;* Terrence P. Charlton, S.J. Ord: '76, *Kenya;* Martin P. Coyne, S.J. Ord: '66, *Nepal;* Cornelius L. Curtin, S.J. Ord: '56, *Nepal;* Edwin J. Daly, S.J. Ord: '59, *India;* Robert M. Deiters, S.J. Ord: '58, *Japan;* Robert L. Dolan, S.J. Ord: '73, *Peru;* James J. Donnelly, S.J. Ord: '59, *Nepal;* Jerome F. Durack, S.J. Ord: '60, *India;* William J. Everett, S.J. Ord: '53, *Japan;* Kevin H. Flaherty, S.J. Ord: '83, *Peru;* Charles J. Fox, S.J. Ord: '44, *India;* Kevin E. Gallagher, S.J. Ord: '61, *Peru;* Anthony J. Grollig, S.J. Ord: '55, *India;* John J. Kenealy, S.J. Ord: '58, *India;* Jeffrey L. Klaiber, S.J. Ord: '74, *Peru;* Richard T. Lambert, S.J. Ord: '67, *India;* Charles A. Law, S.J. Ord: '64, *Nepal;* Roman B. Lewicki, S.J. Ord: '65, *India;* John K. Locke, S.J. Ord: '64, *Nepal;* Benjamin R. Morin, S.J. Ord: '56, *Peru;* Charles L. Murtaugh, S.J. Ord: '69, *Peru;* James M. O'Leary, S.J. Ord: '91, *Peru;* John L. O'Malley, S.J. Ord: '63, *Japan;* Edward Schmidt, S.J. Ord: '71, *Peru;* John Sima, S.J. Ord: '76, *Peru;* Ludwig F. Stiller, S.J. Ord: '62, *Nepal;* Eugene L. Watrin, S.J. Ord: '52, *Nepal;* Joseph F. Willmes, S.J. Ord: '48, *India.*

Priests 44.

Detroit Province: 7303 West Seven Mile Rd., Detroit, MI 48221-2198. Tel: 313-861-7500.

Legal Title: *Jesuit International Missions,, (Formerly, Patna Jesuit Mission Society;* Revs. John F. Libens, S.J. Ord: '70, Prov.; Richard H. Twohig, S.J. Ord: '65, Mission Dir.

U.S. Religious serving in foreign missions: Revs. Paul H. Besanceney, S.J. Ord: '56, *Sudan;* Leo P. Cachat, S.J. Ord: '66, *Nepal;* Martin L. Chase, S.J. Ord: '91, *Denmark;* Richard W. Cherry, S.J. Ord: '69, *Tanzania;* Bro. Richard L. Cure, S.J., *Japan;* Revs. Gerald A. Drinane, S.J. Ord: '62, *India;* James W. Cox, S.J. Ord: '51, *India;* Thomas E. Gafney, S.J. Ord: '65, *Nepal;* William G. Goudreau, S.J. Ord: '52, *India;* Eugene F. Hattie, S.J. Ord: '53, *Uganda;* Paul S. Kehres, S.J. Ord: '51, *India;* James J. Kenney, S.J. Ord: '57, *India;* Joseph Knecht, S.J. Ord: '60, *India;* Kenneth M. Kunert, S.J. Ord: '57, *Uganda;* Bro. Joseph A. LaMielle, S.J., *India;* Revs. Norman Langenderfer, S.J. Ord: '54, *India;* Robert J. Mayer, S.J. Ord: '57, *India;* Casper J. Miller, S.J. Ord: '64, *Nepal;* Joseph E.

Mulligan, S.J. Ord: '73, *Nicaragua;* James J. Regan, S.J. Ord: '67, *Peru;* Robert H. Schmidt, S.J. Ord: '69, *India;* William A. Schock, S.J. Ord: '62, *Philippines;* John D. Smith, S.J. Ord: '59, *India;* Thomas F. Tobin, S.J. Ord: '65, *India;* Michael J. Vjecha, S.J. Ord: '87, *Rwanda;* Theodore W. Walters, S.J. Ord: '56, *Tanzania;* George M. Ziebert, S.J. Ord: '41, *India.*

Priests 25; Brothers 2.

Society of Jesus: Maryland Province, 5704 Roland Ave., Baltimore, MD 21210. Tel: 410-532-1400; Fax: 410-532-1419. Rev. James R. Stormes, S.J. Ord: '79, Prov. & Mission Dir.

Legal Title: *Jesuit Mission Bureau, Maryland Province, Inc., Jesuit Jamshedpur Mission Society, Inc.*

U.S. Religious serving in foreign missions: Revs. Eugene J. Barber, S.J. Ord: '63, *Chile;* Gerard S. Barry, S.J. Ord: '63, *Japan;* John K. Bingham, S.J. Ord: '58, *India;* Joseph H. Bittner, S.J. Ord: '39, *Philippines;* Bernard J. Boyle, S.J. Ord: '65, *Chile;* Edward J. Brady, S.J. Ord: '59, *Sudan;* Robert F. Currie, S.J. Ord: '71, *Nicaragua;* William J. Currie, S.J. Ord: '67, *Japan;* Angelo D'Agostino, S.J. Ord: '66, *Kenya;* Edgar J. Debany, S.J. Ord: '84, *Ghana;* John J. Deeney, S.J. Ord: '52, *India;* James M. Desjardins, S.J. Ord: '77, *Russia;* Carl L. Dincher, S.J. Ord: '57, *India;* Edward C.A. Dougherty, S.J. Ord: '72, *South Africa;* Thomas M. Gavin, S.J. Ord: '75, *Chile;* John F. Guidera, S.J. Ord: '56, *India;* Robert E. Hamm, S.J. Ord: '68, *Nigeria;* John F. Henry, S.J. Ord: '55, *Chile;* George A. Hess, S.J. Ord: '50, *India;* F. Scott Howell, S.J. Ord: '77, *Japan;* Richard A. Kenna, S.J. Ord: '57, *India;* Sigmund J. Laschenski, S.J. Ord: '55, *Thailand;* Michael J. Lynch, S.J. Ord: '93, *Hong Kong;* John J. Mawhinney, S.J. Ord: '65, *El Salvador;* Edward H. McGrath, S.J. Ord: '53, *India;* Edward H. Nash, S.J. Ord: '46, *India;* John J. Nissel, S.J. Ord: '56, *Japan;* George W. Quickley, S.J. Ord: '80, *Nigeria;* James D. Redington, S.J. Ord: '78, *Zimbabwe;* Eugene M. Rooney, S.J. Ord: '57, *Chile;* John W. Swope, S.J. Ord: '86, *Chile;* Dominic J. Totaro, S.J. Ord: '67, *Nigeria;* David L. Ungerleider, S.J. Ord: '77, *Mexico;* Eugene A. Welch, S.J. Ord: '60, *India;* Charles E. Wolf, S.J. Ord: '49, *Philippines.*

Priests 35; Scholastics 1.

Society of Jesus: Missouri Province, 4511 W. Pine Blvd., St. Louis, MO 63108. Tel: 314-361-7765; Fax: 314-758-7164.

Legal Title: *The Jesuits of the Missouri Province;* Revs. Frank Reale, S.J. Ord: '81, Prov.; John A. Apel, S.J. Ord: '69, Mission Dir.

U.S. Religious serving in foreign missions: Rev. Robert T. Costello, S.J. Ord: '63, *Canada;* Bro. Clyde C. Croy, S.J., *Belize;* Rev. Kevin L. Cullen, S.J. Ord: '86, *Uganda;* Bro. Gerardino Diaz, S.J., *Honduras;* Revs. Leonard E. Dieckman, S.J. Ord: '62, *Belize;* Mauricio Gaborit, S.J. Ord: '78, *El Salvador;* Vernon R. Heinsz, S.J. Ord: '73, *Zimbabwe;* Carl J. Heumann, S.J. Ord: '72, *Belize;* Charles T. Hunter, S.J. Ord: '45, *Belize;* John M. Hunthausen, S.J. Ord: '70, *Italy;* John L. Maher, S.J. Ord: '74, *Belize;* Donald J. Murphy, S.J. Ord: '61, *Nicaragua;* Joseph A. Murphy, S.J. Ord: '73, *South Africa;* Maurice M. Murray, S.J. Ord: '66, *Belize;* Bro. James O. O'Leary, S.J., *Honduras;* Rev. Robert F. O'Toole, S.J. Ord: '67, *Italy;* Raymond A. Pease, S.J. Ord: '68, *Honduras;* Richard D. Perl, S.J. Ord: '78, *Belize;* Robert P. Raskowski, S.J. Ord: '46, *Belize;* Francis J. Ring, S.J. Ord: '47, *Belize;* Jesus R. Riveroll, S.J. Ord: '88, *England;* Frank J. Schmitt, S.J. Ord: '83, *Belize;* James M. Short, S.J. Ord: '61, *Belize;* Robert A. Simms, S.J. Ord: '46, *Belize;* Carl F. Starkloff, S.J. Ord: '65, *Canada;* Ricardo Steinmetz, S.J. Ord: '55, *Mexico;* John J. Stochl, S.J. Ord: '54, *Belize;* Raymond L. Sullivant, S.J. Ord: '66, *Spain;* James H. Swetnam, S.J. Ord: '58, *Italy;* Bro. Karl D. Swift, S.J., *Belize;* Harold A. Teel, S.J., *Belize;* Revs. J. Timothy Thompson, S.J. Ord: '70, *Belize;* Jorge R. Toruno, S.J. Ord: '44, *Guatemala;* Thomas M. Valiquette, S.J. Ord: '64, *South Africa;* Bro. N. Aloysius Vogt, S.J., *Belize;* Revs. Robert D. Voss, S.J. Ord: '72, *Honduras;* Jarrell D. Wade, S.J. Ord: '65, *Honduras;* Francis K. Wallace, S.J. Ord: '46, *Panama;* John B. Warner, S.J. Ord: '74, *Honduras;* Leo F. Weber, S.J. Ord: '56, *Belize;* John J. Welch, S.J. Ord: '55, *Italy;* Robert A. White, S.J. Ord: '62, *Italy;* Thomas G. Williams, S.J. Ord: '60, *Belize;* John H. Willmering, S.J. Ord: '68, *Honduras.*

Priests 38; Brothers 6.

Society of Jesus: New England Province, 771 Harrison Ave., Boston, MA 02118. Tel: 617-266-7233; Fax: 617-536-8074.

Legal Title: *The Society of Jesus of New England;* Revs. Robert J. Levens, S.J. Ord: '81, Prov.; Thomas H. Schneider, S.J. Ord: '79, Mission Liaison.

U.S. Religious serving in foreign missions: Most Revs. Lawrence J. Burke, S.J., *Bahamas;* Samuel E. Carter, S.J., *Jamaica;* Revs. Dudley R.C. Adams, S.J. Ord: '92, *Jamaica;* Harry W. Ball, S.J. Ord: '42, *Jamaica;* John P. Banks, S.J. Ord: '51, *Jamaica;* Joseph F. Brennan, S.J. Ord: '56, *Jamaica;* Thomas J. Brodley, S.J. Ord: '72, *Jamaica;* John J. Bresnahan, S.J. Ord: '58, *Jamaica;* Clarence J. Burby, S.J. Ord: '67, *Jordan;* Robert B. Campbell, S.J. Ord: '57, *Lebanon;* John A. Carty, S.J. Ord: '59, *Egypt;* William A. Clark, S.J. Ord: '93, *Jamaica;* Bro. Calvin A. Clarke, S.J., *Jamaica;* Revs. Vincent F. Connolly, S.J. Ord: '70, *Jamaica;* William A. Connolly, S.J. Ord: '46, *Jamaica;* Richard A. Deshaies, S.J. Ord: '92, *Jamaica;* John J. Donohue, S.J. Ord: '59, *Lebanon;* Thomas J. Fitzpatrick, S.J. Ord: '68, *Jordan;* Louis L. Grenier, S.J. Ord: '49, *Jamaica;* Richard P. Guerrera, S.J. Ord: '73, *Mozambique;* Alwyn C. Harry, S.J. Ord: '54, *Jamaica;* Paul R. Hayes, S.J. Ord: '62, *Bahamas;* Donald L. Larkin, S.J. Ord: '66, *Jamaica;* Michael D. Linden, S.J. Ord: '80, *Jamaica;* Joseph A. MacWade, S.J. Ord: '61, *Jamaica;* Martin F. McDermott, S.J. Ord: '64, *Lebanon;* Gerard R. McKeon, S.J. Ord: '86, *Jamaica;* Gerald L. McLaughlin, S.J. Ord: '59, *Jamaica;* Oliver E. Nickerson, S.J. Ord: '54, *Jamaica;* Kevin G. O'Connell, S.J. Ord: '69, *Jordan;* Joseph V. Owens, S.J. Ord: '71, *Honduras;* Normand A. Pepin, S.J. Ord: '63, *Alaska;* Leo F. Quinlan, S.J. Ord: '45, *Jamaica;* Francis J. Ryan, S.J. Ord: '56, *Jamaica;* Martin J. Schade, S.J. Ord: '88, *Jamaica;* Thomas H. Schneider, S.J. Ord: '79, *Jamaica;* Paul A. Schweitzer, S.J. Ord: '70, *Brazil;* James F. Sheehan, S.J. Ord: '61, *Bahamas;* Lester O. Shields, S.J. Ord: '94, *Jamaica;* David A. Skelskey, S.J. Ord: '80, *Ethiopia;* John J. Sullivan, S.J. Ord: '44, *Jamaica;* Thomas Vallamattam, S.J. Ord: '64, *Jamaica;* Maurice B. Walsh, S.J. Ord: '46, *Jamaica.*

Bishop 2; Priests 39; Brothers 1.

Society of Jesus: New Orleans Province, 211 Pere Marquette Bldg., New Orleans, LA 70112. Tel: 504-525-4043.

Legal Title: *Jesuit Mission Bureau;* Rev. Edward B. Arroyo, S.J. Ord: '75, Prov.

U.S. Religious serving in foreign missions: Revs. Donald G. Bahlinger, S.J. Ord: '59, *Paraguay;* Edward G. Benya, S.J. Ord: '84, *Brazil;* David C. Borbridge, S.J. Ord: '63, *Brazil;* Bro. Anthony S. Coco, S.J., *Brazil;* Revs. Fred Cooley, S.J. Ord: '54, *Sri Lanka;* Claude Daly, S.J. Ord: '43, *Sri Lanka;* Carlos E. de la Cruz, S.J. Ord: '75, *Paraguay;* Alfonso Del Marmol, S.J. Ord: '51, *Sri Lanka;* Edward J. Dougherty, S.J. Ord: '70, *Brazil;* A. Gerard Fineran, S.J. Ord: '50, *Brazil;* Bro. Robert E. Hollingsworth, S.J., *Brazil;* Revs. O. Kenneth Johnson Ord: '92, *Zambia;* Leo V. Leise, S.J. Ord: '94, *Paraguay;* Roland J. Lesseps, S.J. Ord: '65, *Zambia;* Lloyd Lorio, S.J. Ord: '56, *Sri Lanka;* Patrick S. Madigan, S.J. Ord: '83, *Zimbabwe;* Francis X. Mayer, S.J. Ord: '50, *Sri Lanka;* Joseph H. Meyer, S.J. Ord: '46, *Sri Lanka;* Harry Miller, S.J. Ord: '54, *Sri Lanka;* Harold J. Rahm, S.J. Ord: '50, *Brazil;* David H. Romero, S.J. Ord: '91, *Brazil;* Stephen C. Rowntree, S.J. Ord: '75, *Kenya;* John F. Schroder, S.J. Ord: '53, *Belize;* John Stacer, S.J. Ord: '63, *Zimbabwe;* Charles B. Thibodeaux, S.J. Ord: '59, *Paraguay;* Bro. Terence N. Todd, S.J., *Micronesia;* Rev. Harold J. Weber, S.J. Ord: '44, *Sri Lanka.*

Priests 27; Brothers 3; Scholastics 1.

Society of Jesus: New York Province, 39 E. 83rd St., New York, NY 10028. Tel: 212-774-5500. Revs. Kenneth J. Gavin, S.J. Ord: '75, Prov.; William T. Wood, S.J. Ord: '48, Asst. Prov.-International Apostolates.

U.S. Religious serving in foreign missions: Revs. Gerald W. Aman, S.J. Ord: '73, *Nigeria;* Charles J. Beirne, S.J. Ord: '69, *Guatemala;* Henry J. Bertels, S.J. Ord: '62, *Rome;* Joseph E. Billotti, S.J. Ord: '63, *Micronesia;* Joseph H. Bittner, S.J. Ord: '39, *Philippines;* Kenneth C. Bogart, S.J. Ord: '56, *Philippines;* Robert A. Bomeisl, S.J. Ord: '52, *Philippines;* James J. Bowes, S.J. Ord: '66, *Rome;* J. Dean Brackley, S.J. Ord: '76, *El Salvador;* Gary J. Bradley, S.J. Ord: '75, *Micronesia;* Philip J. Calderone, S.J. Ord: '56, *Philippines;* John J. Carroll, S.J. Ord: '55, *Philippines;* Joseph A. Cavanagh, S.J. Ord: '62, *Micronesia;* John E. Chambers, S.J. Ord: '64, *Philippines;* Arthur A. Clarke, S.J. Ord: '47, *Puerto Rico;* Francis X. Clark, S.J. Ord: '43, *Philippines;* James P. Croghan, S.J. Ord: '85, *Micronesia;* John J. Curran, S.J. Ord: '59, *Micronesia;* Francis J. Cusimano, S.J. Ord: '68, *Nigeria;* Theodore E. Daigler, S.J. Ord: '36, *Philippines;* Vincent P. DeCola, S.J. Ord: '88, *Micronesia;* Thomas F. Denny, S.J. Ord: '60, *Philippines;* Francis C. Dolan, S.J. Ord: '60, *Philippines;* James F. Donelan, S.J. Ord: '53, *Philippines;* Martin Doyle, S.J. Ord: '91, *Micronesia;* Gaston Duchesneau, S.J. Ord: '44, *Philippines;* James P. Dunne, S.J., *Philippines;* Paul V. Finster, S.J. Ord: '45, *Philippines;* Robert J. Flynn, S.J. Ord: '50, *Japan;* Matthew N. Fullam, S.J. Ord: '42, *Philippines;* Joseph A. Galdon, S.J. Ord: '59, *Philippines;* Pasquale T. Giordano, S.J. Ord: '72, *Philippines;* Francis N. Glover, S.J. Ord: '58, *Philippines;* Very Rev. James C. Gould, S.J. Ord: '74, *Micronesia, Pref. Apostolic, Marshall Islands;* Revs. George R. Graziano, S.J. Ord: '59, *Japan;* Thomas H. Green, S.J. Ord: '63, *Philippines;* Leonard G. Hacker, S.J. Ord: '47, *Micronesia;* John J. Halligan, S.J. Ord: '61, *Ecuador;* Robert E. Hamm, S.J. Ord: '68, *Nigeria;* William L. Hayes, S.J. Ord: '44, *Philippines;* Gerald W. Healy, S.J. Ord: '46, *Philippines;* Victor J. Helly, S.J. Ord: '54, *Philippines;* William J. Hendricks, S.J. Ord: '64, *Puerto Rico;* Very Rev. Francis X. Hezel, S.J. Ord: '66, *Micronesia;* Revs. Kenneth J. Hezel, S.J. Ord: '66, *Guam;* Michael P. Hilbert, S.J. Ord: '83, *Rome;* Donald J. Hinfey, S.J. Ord: '63, *Ghana;* Robert C. Hogan, S.J. Ord: '64, *Philippines;* Raymond T. Holscher, S.J. Ord: '72, *Philippines;* Paul J. Horgan, S.J. Ord: '68, *Micronesia;* Joseph A. Johnston, S.J. Ord: '52, *Australia;* William P. Klintworth, S.J. Ord: '61, *Philippines;* John G. Krebs, S.J. Ord: '65, *Philippines;* William H. Kreutz, S.J. Ord: '69, *Philippines;* Bartholomew P. Lahiff, S.J. Ord: '55, *Philippines;* Dennis M. Leder, S.J. Ord: '76, *Guatemala;* Francis C. Madigan, S.J. Ord: '49, *Philippines;* Paul J. Maher, S.J. Ord: '64, *Nigeria;* Donald C. Maldari, S.J. Ord: '85, *Haiti;* William J. Malley, S.J. Ord: '64, *Philippines;* John J. Madden, S.J. Ord: '69, *Nigeria;* Richard R. McAuliff, S.J. Ord: '92, *Micronesia;* Daniel F. McCoy, S.J. Ord: '45, *Japan;* James A. McDonough, S.J. Ord: '41, *Guam;* Francis X. McFarland, S.J. Ord: '50, *Ghana;* William J. McGarry, S.J. Ord: '58, *Micronesia;* Thomas B. McGrath, S.J. Ord: '64, *Micronesia;* Gerald J. McIntyre, S.J. Ord: '74, *Zimbabwe;* James A. McKeough, S.J. Ord: '54, *Philippines;* Daniel J. McNamara, S.J. Ord: '80, *Philippines;* James T. Meehan, S.J. Ord: '63, *Philippines;* Michael D. Moga, S.J. Ord: '64, *Philippines;* John F. Moran, S.J. Ord: '57, *Philippines;* Gregory F. Muckenhaupt, S.J. Ord: '88, *Micronesia;* Daniel J. Mulhauser, S.J. Ord: '60, *Micronesia;* Ugo R. Nacciarone, S.J. Ord: '64, *Zambia;* Most Rev. Martin J. Neylon, S.J., *Micronesia;* Revs. James J. O'Brien, S.J. Ord: '59, *Philippines;* Joseph F. O'Brien, S.J. Ord: '44, *Philippines;* James O'Donnell, S.J. Ord: '61, *Philippines;* Thomas H. O'Gorman, S.J. Ord: '63, *Philippines;* Thomas J. O'Shaughnessy, S.J. Ord: '44, *Philippines;* John J. Phelan, S.J. Ord: '58, *Philippines;* Calvin H. Poulin, S.J. Ord: '62, *Nigeria;* Neil C. Poulin, S.J. Ord: '66, *Micronesia;* George W. Quickley, S.J. Ord: '80, *Nigeria;* William J. Rakowicz, S.J. Ord: '80, *Micronesia;* Francis E. Reilly, S.J. Ord: '53, *Philippines;* James B. Reuter, S.J. Ord: '46, *Philippines;* Robert A. Rice, S.J. Ord: '53, *Philippines;* Joseph L. Roche, S.J. Ord: '58, *Philippines;* Michael F. Rooney, S.J. Ord: '72, *Philippines;* Robert T. Rush, S.J. Ord: '59, *Japan;* Patrick J. Ryan, S.J. Ord: '68, *Ghana;* Ramon A. Salomone, S.J. Ord: '65, *Nigeria;* Ronald W. Sams, S.J. Ord: '59, *Micronesia;* William J. Schmitt, S.J. Ord: '58, *Philippines;* Peter Schineller, S.J. Ord: '70, Supr., *Nigeria-Ghana Region;* Herbert Schneider, S.J. Ord: '70, *Philippines;* John N. Schumacher, S.J. Ord: '57, *Philippines;* Arthur F. Shea, S.J. Ord: '38, *Philippines;* John R. Sheehan, S.J. Ord: '92, *Nigeria;* Paul M. Sheehan, S.J. Ord: '52, *Philippines;* Joseph J. Smith, S.J. Ord: '57, *Philippines;* Thomas B. Steinbugler, S.J. Ord: '61, *Philippines;* John A. St. George, S.J. Ord: '52, *Rome;* Robert J. Suchan, S.J. Ord: '56, *Philippines;* William T. Suchan, S.J. Ord: '58, *Micronesia;* Patrick J. Sullivan Ord: '71, *Micronesia;* William M. Sullivan, S.J. Ord: '66, *Micronesia;* John F. Talbot, S.J. Ord: '59, *Puerto Rico;* Terence N. Todd, S.J., *Micronesia;* Dominic J. Totaro, S.J. Ord: '67, *Nigeria;* Donald M. Vega, S.J. Ord: '65, *Puerto Rico;* Juan C. Villegas, S.J. Ord: '75, *Colombia;* Robert P. Walsh, S.J. Ord: '60, *Philippines;* Charles E. Wolf, S.J. Ord: '46, *Philippines;* John H. Zupez, S.J. Ord: '67, *Philippines.*

Priests 91; Brothers 2; Scholastics 1.

Society of Jesus: Oregon Province, 2222 N.W. Hoyt, Portland, OR 97210. Tel: 503-227-1174.

Legal Title: *American Jesuits in Africa;* Revs. Robert B. Grimm, S.J. Ord: '76, Prov.; Charles E. Schmitz, S.J. Ord: '72, Mission Dir.

U.S. Religious serving in foreign missions: Revs. Arnold R. Beezer, S.J. Ord: '64, *Honduras;* Thomas J. Bunnell, S.J. Ord: '74, *Peru;* Joseph B. Danel, S.J. Ord: '52, *Zambia;* John V. Hennessy, S.J. Ord: '72, *China;* Peter J. Henriot, S.J. Ord: '70, *Zambia;* Ronald E. Hidaka, S.J. Ord: '74, *Zambia;* William J. Loyens, S.J. Ord: '58, *Malawi;* James P. McGloin, S.J. Ord: '74, *Zambia;* Howard L. Morrison, S.J. Ord: '58, *Zambia;* Bartholomew J. Murphy, S.J. Ord: '72, *Kenya;* John J. O'Leary, S.J. Ord: '60, *Zambia;* Michael J. Schultheis, S.J. Ord: '65, *Brazil;* Joseph H. Small, S.J. Ord: '60, *Kenya;* Roy W. Thaden, S.J. Ord: '73, *Zambia;* Peter R. Titland, S.J. Ord: '70, *Zambia.*

Priests 15.

Society of Jesus: Wisconsin Province, 3400 W. Wisconsin Ave., P.O. Box 08277, Milwaukee, WI 53208. Tel: 414-937-6949; Fax: 414-937-6950.

Legal Title: *Jesuit Mission Service, Inc.;* Revs. D. Edward Mathie, S.J. Ord: '68, Prov.; James E. Grummer, S.J. Ord: '82, Mission Dir.

U.S. Religious serving in foreign missions: Revs. Francis X. Buchmeier, S.J. Ord: '73, *Korea;* William J. Callahan, S.J. Ord: '72, *Uganda;* John V. Daly, S.J. Ord: '66, *Korea;* Emil J. Denemark, S.J. Ord: '81, *Korea;* Robert W. Dundon, S.J. Ord: '69, *Zimbabwe;* Jonathan Haschka, S.J. Ord: '75, *Kenya;* Francis E. Hogan, S.J. Ord: '47, *Honduras;* Daniel J. Kenney, S.J. Ord: '63, *Kenya;* Robert J. Kelly, S.J. Ord: '52, *Korea;* Eugene C. Kollasch, S.J. Ord: '59, *Korea;* John D. Mace, S.J. Ord: '68, *Philippines;* Peter E. Marchetti, S.J. Ord: '77, *Nicaragua;* Francis H. Mathy, S.J. Ord: '58, *Japan;* Robert K. McIntosh, S.J. Ord: '72, *Korea;* Charles C. Murphy, S.J. Ord: '62, *Kenya;* Philip E. Pick, S.J. Ord: '50, *Honduras;* Basil M. Price, S.J. Ord: '54, *Korea;* Robert P. Raszkowski, S.J. Ord: '46, *Belize;* Francis J. Ring, S.J. Ord: '47, *Belize;* John R. Schak, S.J. Ord: '61, *Argentina;* Nicholas E. Schiel, S.J. Ord: '55, *Honduras;* Christopher A. Spalatin, S.J. Ord: '71, *Korea;* Norbert J. Tracy, S.J. Ord: '55, *Korea;* Anthony J. Wach, S.J. Ord: '72, *Uganda.*

Priests 23.

Maryknoll (M.M.)

A community of American secular priests and brothers. Established in 1911 by action of the United States Hierarchy. Authorized by Pope Pius X, with later approvals by Pope Benedict XV and Pope Pius XI

U.S. Foundation: Maryknoll Society Center & Administrative Offices, Catholic Foreign Mission Society of America, P.O. Box 303, Maryknoll, NY 10545-0303. Tel: 914-941-7590; Fax: 914-762-0316. Revs. Raymond J. Finch, M.M. Ord: '76, Supr. Gen. & Pres.; Jeremiah R. Burr, M.M. Ord: '67, Vicar Gen. & Vice Pres.; Thomas P. Henehan, M.M. Ord: '65, Asst. Gen.; Michael J. Snyder, M.M. Ord: '78, Asst. Gen.; Bro. Wayne J. Fitzpatrick, M.M., Asst. Gen.

The Society is incorporated in New York, under the legal title; *Catholic Foreign Mission Society of America, Incorporated.* It is also incorporated in California, Hawaii, Illinois, Massachusetts, Minnesota, Missouri, and New Jersey.

For detailed information regarding statistics, activities in the Archdioceses and Dioceses in the United States, Properties owned or sponsored and Houses in the United States, and the placement of the Maryknollers in the various Archdioceses and Dioceses, please refer to the sections for Religious Institutes of Men and the designated Archdioceses and Dioceses.

Maryknoll Foreign Missions

Maryknollers serving overseas:.

Religious serving in Tanzania: Revs. John C. Sivalon, M.M. Ord: '75, Regional Supr.; J. Ernest Brunelle, M.M. Ord: '59; James A. Conard, M.M. Ord: '56; William F. Daley, M.M. Ord: '56; John W. Eybel, M.M. Ord: '70; Paul E. Fagan, M.M. Ord: '60; J. Francis Flynn, M.M. Ord: '52; Herbert T. Gappa, M.M. Ord: '68; Joseph G. Healey, M.M. Ord: '66; Richard A. Hochwalt, M.M. Ord: '51; Robert A. Jalbert, M.M. Ord: '79; Leo R. Kennedy, M.M. Ord: '59; Ramon J. McCabe, M.M. Ord: '56; Howard E. O'Brien, M.M. Ord: '55; Daniel F. Ohmann, M.M. Ord: '55; Edward J. Quinn, M.M. Ord: '51; Joseph A. Reinhart, M.M. Ord: '50; David J. Schwinghamer M.M. Ord: '73; Thomas J. Shea, M.M. Ord: '67; David A. Smith, M.M. Ord: '85; William S. Stanley, M.M. Ord: '92; Kenneth J. Sullivan, M.M. Ord: '57; Donald F. Sybertz, M.M. Ord: '55; Thomas A. Tiscornia, M.M. Ord: '73; John W. Waldrep, M.M. Ord: '90; Richard W. Bauer, M.M. Ord: '85; Jose Padin, M.M. Ord: '97; Kenneth F. Thesing, M.M. Ord: '69; William A. Vos, M.M. Ord: '64.

Priests 29; Brothers 4.

Religious serving in Bangladesh: Revs. Robert T. McCahill, M.M. Ord: '64, Unit Coord.; William J. McIntire, M.M. Ord: '67; Douglas F. Venne, M.M. Ord: '59.

Priests 3.

Religious serving in Bolivia: Revs. Thomas A. McBride, M.M. Ord: '57; Denis P. Browne, M.M. Ord: '47; William J. Coy, M.M. Ord: '55; James W. Fitzgerald, M.M. Ord: '50; Bernard R. Garrity, M.M. Ord: '47; John F. Gorski, M.M. Ord: '63; Michael A. Gould, M.M. Ord: '54; Sigmund S. Jamroz, M.M. Ord: '66; Francis T. McGourn, M.M. Ord: '64, Regional Supr.; Paul A. O'Brien, M.M. Ord: '59; John J. Ogurchock, M.M. Ord: '54; Arthur J. Prall, M.M. Ord: '52; William Senger, M.M. Ord: '73.

Priests 13; Brothers 3.

Religious serving in Brazil: Revs. Daniel F. McLaughlin Ord: '61; William F. Marley, M.M. Ord: '52; James L. Hilgeman, M.M., M.D. Ord: '65; Gerald M. Wickenhauser, M.M. Ord: '62, Unit Coord.

Priests 4.

Religious serving in Chile: Revs. Dale F. Barron, M.M. Ord: '65; Paul M. Sykora, M.M. Ord: '76; Donald J. Blesnuk, M.M. Ord: '85; Richard L. Brooker, M.M. Ord: '55; Joseph H. Cappel, M.M. Ord: '35; John J. Gallahue, M.M. Ord: '62; Thomas P. Golden, M.M. Ord: '51; Frederick J. Hegarty, M.M. Ord: '53; John A. Jensen, M.M. Ord: '44; Ernest C. Lukaschek, M.M. Ord: '64; Elmer J. Meyer, M.M. Ord: '54; George F. Painter, M.M. Ord: '44; Richard J. Sammon, M.M. Ord: '56; J. Lawrence Schanberger, M.M. Ord: '49; Eugene W. Toland, M.M. Ord: '64; James R. Weckesser, M.M. Ord: '55.

Priests 16; Brothers 1.

Religious serving in El Salvador: Revs. Thomas R. Amarillas, M.M. Ord: '68; William M. Boteler, M.M. Ord: '68; David C. Kelly, M.M. Ord: '57.

Priests 3.

Religious serving in Guatemala: Revs. Gerald J. Persha, M.M. Ord: '70; William F. Mullan, M.M. Ord: '62; Robert F. Crohan, M.M. Ord: '62; Thomas P. Fox, M.M. Ord: '56; Joseph W. Halpin, M.M. Ord: '52; Ronald W. Hennessey, M.M. Ord: '64, Reg. Supr.; James P. LaCoste, M.M. Ord: '56; Kevin A. Lynch, M.M. Ord: '61; John J. McGovern, M.M. Ord: '54; Joseph C. Nerino, M.M. Ord: '50; William J. Price, M.M. Ord: '56; John J. Ruessmann, M.M. Ord: '79.

Priests 11; Brothers 2.

Religious serving in Honduras: Revs. John M. Breen, M.M. Ord: '51; Robert F. Coyne, M.M. Ord: '83; Richard C. Frank, M.M. Ord: '53; Paul D. Belliveau, M.M. Ord: '69; David E. LaBuda, M.M. Ord: '71; Charles T. Huegelmeyer, M.M. Ord: '51; Ronald J. Potter, M.M. Ord: '61.

Priests 7.

Religious serving in Hong Kong: Revs. John F. Ahearn, M.M. Ord: '73; Robert F. Astorino, M.M. Ord: '70; Peter J. Barry, M.M. Ord: '65; Robert C. Bayne, M.M. Ord: '63; Anthony V. Brennan, M.M. Ord: '61; Sean P. Burke, M.M. Ord: '78; John J. Casey, M.M. Ord: '56; John A. Cioppa, M.M. Ord: '59; Vincent F. Corbelli, M.M. Ord: '60; John P. Cuff, M.M. Ord: '69; Thomas E. Danaher, M.M. Ord: '62; Charles R. Dittmeier, M.M. Ord: '70; Scott T. Harris, M.M. Ord: '78; Laurence A. Dugas, M.M. Ord: '54; Stephen B. Edmonds, M.M. Ord: '40; Lawrence W. Flynn, M.M. Ord: '87; John E. Geitner, M.M. Ord: '53; John P. Grady, M.M. Ord: '55; William J. Grimm, M.M. Ord: '77; Thomas F. Goekler, M.M. Ord: '67; Adam B. Gudalefsky, M.M. Ord: '59; Denis J. Hanly, M.M. Ord: '59; Matthew H. Kelleher, M.M. Ord: '67; Timothy Kilkelly, M.M. Ord: '90; Michael J. McKeirnan, M.M. Ord: '41; Edward F. Malone, M.M. Ord: '52; Thomas A. Peyton, M.M. Ord: '58, Reg. Supr.; Ronald R. Saucci, M.M. Ord: '65; Michael J. Sloboda, M.M. Ord: '85; Leo B. Shea, M.M. Ord: '66; Eugene A. Thalman, M.M. Ord: '60; John C. Tynan, M.M. Ord: '62; John G. Sullivan, M.M. Ord: '60; John G. Sullivan, M.M. Ord: '60; C. Thomas Wilcox, M.M. Ord: '51; Elmer P. Wurth, M.M. Ord: '56.

Priests 35; Brothers 2.

Religious serving in Indonesia: Revs. Robert F. Baudhuin, M.M. Ord: '54; Vincent P. Cole, M.M. Ord: '71.

Priests 2.

Religious serving in Japan: Revs. Patrick F. O'Donoghue, M.M. Ord: '50, Reg. Supr.; Roy C. Assenheimer, M.M. Ord: '65; Richard A. Aylward, M.M. Ord: '53; Gerald L. Beausoleil, M.M. Ord: '52; Anthony B. Brodniak, M.M. Ord: '54; Alfonso Kim, M.M. Ord: '97; Richard Czajkcwski, M.M. Ord: '61; Regis B. Ging, M.M. Ord: '66; James H. Gorman, M.M. Ord: '52; Kevin J. Hanlon, M.M. Ord: '89; Joseph H. Hermes, M.M. Ord: '62; James R. Jackson, M.M. Ord: '58; Walter T. Kelleher, M.M. Ord: '56; Joseph V. Maynard, M.M. Ord: '48; James J. Mylet, M.M. Ord: '75; Robert V. Nehrig, M.M. Ord: '54; Bryce T. Nishimura, M.M. Ord: '56; James K. Nishimuta, M.M. Ord: '54; James W. O'Neill, M.M. Ord: '55; Francis A. Riha, M.M. Ord: '68; Kenneth C. Sleyman, M.M. Ord: '90; Donald J. Vittengl, M.M. Ord: '56; Clarence J. Witte, M.M. Ord: '35; Louis J. Wolken, M.M. Ord: '46; Robert R. Zahn, M.M. Ord: '55.

Priests 25; Brothers 1; Seminarians 1.

Religious serving in Kenya: Revs. Richard M. Baker, M.M. Ord: '71; Edward M. Dougherty, M.M. Ord: '79; Francis J. Breen, M.M. Ord: '70; Thomas J. Burke, M.M. Ord: '55; Donald F. Donovan, M.M. Ord: '55; David A. Lemkuhl Ord: '79; William Fryda, M.M. Ord: '88; Carroll B. Houle, M.M. Ord: '62, Reg. Supr.; William T. Knipe, M.M. Ord: '58; Michael C. Kirwen, M.M. Ord: '63; James J. Kuhn, M.M. Ord: '51; John J. Lange, M.M. Ord: '58; Edwin Metzer Ord: '55; Edward J. Phillips, M.M. Ord: '74; Richard J. Quinn, M.M. Ord: '54; James R. Roy, M.M. Ord: '61; Richard P. Smith, M.M. Ord: '76; Robert W. Vujs, M.M. Ord: '61; Maurice J. Zerr, M.M. Ord: '51.

Priests 18; Brothers 5.

Religious serving in Korea: Most Rev. William J. McNaughton, M.M., D.D., Bishop of Inchon; Revs. Roman G. Theisen, M.M. Ord: '54, Reg. Supr.; Richard Agustin, M.M. Ord: '85; Francis H. Beninati, M.M. Ord: '55; Carl A. Costa, M.M. Ord: '71; Thomas R. Egan, M.M. Ord: '64; Gerald J. Farrell, M.M. Ord: '57; Russell J. Feldmeier, M.M. Ord: '80; Alfred J. Fleming, M.M. Ord: '60; James M. Gilligan, M.M. Ord: '55; Gerard E. Hammond, M.M. Ord: '60; Robert M. Lilly, M.M. Ord: '60; John P. Meehan, M.M. Ord: '59; James J. Najmowski, M.M. Ord: '76; Gerald P. O'Connor, M.M. Ord: '69; Fernand Paquet, M.M. Ord: '56; Robert R. Pellini, M.M. Ord: '59; David L. Pfeiffer, M.M. Ord: '66; Richard S. Rolewicz, M.M. Ord: '65; James P. Sinnott, M.M. Ord: '60; Joseph A. Slaby, M.M. Ord: '66; John F. Soltis, M.M. Ord: '62; Edward J. Whelan, M.M. Ord: '61; Michael O. Zunno, M.M. Ord: '53.

Priests 23; Bishops 1.

Religious serving in Mexico: Revs. Richard L. Clifford, M.M. Ord: '53; Francis W. Collins, M.M. Ord: '49; Roman A. Kasprzak, M.M. Ord: '51; Martin P. Keegan, M.M. Ord: '65; Thomas E. Lavelle, M.M. Ord: '55, Reg. Supr.; John P. Lomasney, M.M. Ord: '43; John P. Martin, M.M. Ord: '66, Reg. Supr.; John R. McGuire, M.M. Ord: '43; Charles A. Murray, M.M. Ord: '51; Peter J. Petrucci, M.M. Ord: '49; Thomas C. Saunders, M.M. Ord: '65; Eugene A. Theisen, M.M. Ord: '53; Robert E. Tobin, M.M. Ord: '57.

Priests 13; Brothers 1.

Religious serving in the Middle East Unit: Revs. John F. Felago, M.M. Ord: '68, Unit Coord.; Lance P. Nadeau, M.M. Ord: '90.

Priests 2; Brothers 3.

Religious serving in Nepal: Rev. Robert J. Lloyd, M.M. Ord: '62.

Priests 1.

Religious serving in Peru: Revs. Michael J. Briggs, M.M. Ord: '76; Thomas J. Burns, M.M. Ord: '69; Bernard P. Byrne, M.M. Ord: '56, Reg. Supr.; Charles H. Cappel, M.M. Ord: '44; Edmund L. Cookson, M.M. Ord: '65; Joseph J. Donovan, M.M. Ord: '79; Joseph Fedora, M.M. Ord: '84; Stephen P. Judd, M.M. Ord: '78; James J. Madden, M.M. Ord: '; Patrick J. Donovan, M.M. Ord: '57; Philip N. Erbland, M.M. Ord: '66; Joseph A. Farrell, M.M. Ord: '59; Thomas F. Garrity, M.M. Ord: '46; Joseph L. Hamel, M.M. Ord: '85; Robert E. Hoffman, M.M. Ord: '60; Robert A. Hurteau, M.M. Ord: '89; Joseph A. Kowalczyk, M.M. Ord: '61; Richard G. Laszewski, M.M. Ord: '51; James Lynch, M.M. Ord: '74; Gerard T. McCrane, M.M. Ord: '59; Martin F. Murphy, M.M. Ord: '51; James M. O'Brien, M.M. Ord: '49; James V. Roth, M.M. Ord: '54; James J. Stefaniak, M.M. Ord: '50.

Priests 21; Brothers 1; Seminarians 1.

Religious serving in the Philippine Islands: Revs. James H. Kroeger, M.M. Ord: '67; Herman W. Cisek, M.M. Ord: '65; John F. Coholan, M.M. Ord: '46; Robert L. Depinet, M.M. Ord: '61; Francis J. Felter, M.M. Ord: '69; James T. Ferry, M.M. Ord: '56; William P. Heffernan, M.M. Ord: '55; James C. Kalchthaler, M.M. Ord: '56; Ralph S. Kroes, M.M. Ord: '58; William J. LaRousse, M.M. Ord: '80; James D. McAuley, M.M. Ord: '80; Donald P. McQuade, M.M. Ord: '65; Walter J. Maxcy, M.M. Ord: '47; John B. Northrop, M.M. Ord: '74; Clyde Philipps, M.M. Ord: '78, Reg. Supr.; Edward D. Shellito, M.M. Ord: '80; J. David Sullivan, M.M. Ord: '60; John D. Walsh, M.M. Ord: '56.

Priests 18; Brothers 2.

Religious serving in Taiwan: Revs. Alan T. Doyle, M.M. Ord: '64; Kurt J. Anderson, M.M. Ord: '72, Reg. Supr.; James V. Buttino, M.M. Ord: '47; Michael G. Collins, M.M. Ord: '59; James A. Collignon, M.M. Ord: '53; Robert F. Crawford, M.M. Ord: '61; Richard M. Devoe, M.M. Ord: '56; Richard E. Downey, M.M. Ord: '44; Alan T. Doyle, M.M. Ord: '64; Clarence A. Engler, M.M. Ord: '59; Edward J. Flanigan, M.M. Ord: '56; Albert V. Fedders, M.M. Ord: '37; Donald F. Glover, M.M. Ord: '70; Delos A. Humphrey, M.M. Ord: '54; John B. Keaney, M.M. Ord: '55; Raymond H. Kelley, M.M.

Ord: '58; John F. Kennedy, M.M. Ord: '55; Lawrence F. McCulloch, M.M. Ord: '70; J. Donald McGinnis, M.M. Ord: '53; John P. McKernan, M.M. Ord: '52; James T. Manning, M.M. Ord: '48; Leonard J. Marron, M.M. Ord: '57; John J. Moran, M.M. Ord: '66; Eugene M. Murray, M.M. Ord: '58; Nhuan D. Nguyen, M.M. Ord: '93; Brendan M. O'Connell, M.M. Ord: '63; Francis T. O'Donnell, M.M. Ord: '55; Norbert A. Pacheco, M.M. Ord: '79; Anthony V. Polyak, M.M. Ord: '62; Carroll I. Quinn, M.M. Ord: '45; Francis Rebol, M.M. Ord: '53; Louis B. Rost, M.M. Ord: '55; Francis F. Schexnayder, M.M. Ord: '64; R. Russell Sprinkle, M.M. Ord: '35; Peter A. Wu, M.M. Ord: '61; Richard E. Zeimet, M.M. Ord: '64.

Priests 34.

Religious serving in Thailand: Revs. John C. Barth, M.M. Ord: '91; Daniel A. Boyd, M.M. Ord: '82; Thomas J. Dunleavy, M.M. Ord: '75; Roberto T. Fuentes, M.M. Ord: '92; James W. Kofski, M.M. Ord: '91; James P. Noonan, M.M. Ord: '60, Unit Co-ord.; Thomas J. O'Brien, M.M. Ord: '74; William T. O'Leary, M.M. Ord: '61; Thomas E. Pesaresi, M.M. Ord: '85; Lawrence D. Radice, M.M. Ord: '85; Charles P. Robak, M.M. Ord: '70.

Priests 11; Brothers 1.

Religious serving in Samoa: Most Rev. J. Quinn Weitzel, M.M.

Priests 1; Brothers 2.

Religious serving in Venezuela: Revs. Thomas Ahearn, M.M. Ord: '68, Unit Coord.; Joseph A. Heim, M.M. Ord: '61; Donald P. McNamara Ord: '61.

Priests 3; Priests Associates 1.

Religious serving in Italy: Revs. Joseph V. McCabe, M.M. Ord: '77; Edward A. Hayes, M.M. Ord: '59, Procurator, *Collegio Maryknoll*, Via Sardegna 83, Rome, Italy, 00187.

Priests 2.

Missionaries of Africa (M.Afr.)

Missionaries of Africa Foreign Missions

U.S. Headquarters: Province of North America, 1624-21 St. N.W., Washington, DC 20009-1055. Tel: 202-232-5154; Fax: 202-332-8640. Rev. William Moroney, M.Afr. Ord: '61, Asst. Prov.

U.S. Religious serving in Africa: Revs. Richard Archambault, M.Afr. Ord: '73; John J. Braun, M.Afr. Ord: '57; William Curran, M.Afr. Ord: '66; Rene Dionne, M.Afr. (Spain) Ord: '61; J. Philip Reed, M.Afr.; William Dyer, M.Afr.; Roger A. LaBonte, M.Afr. Ord: '62; Michel J. Lavoie, M.Afr. Ord: '70; John Lynch, M.Afr. Ord: '62; J. Philip Reed, M.Afr. Ord: '88; Thomas Reilly, M.Afr. Ord: '78; Richard Roy, M.Afr. Ord: '71; Bros. Vernon Zachman, M.Afr.; Martin Chapper, M.Afr.; James Heintz, M.Afr.

Missionaries of the Sacred Heart (M.S.C.)

Missionaries of the Sacred Heart Foreign Missions

Missionaries of the Sacred Heart: P.O. Box 270, 305 S. Lake St., Aurora, IL 60507. Tel: 630-892-2371; 892-8400 (Prov. Supr.); Fax: 630-892-1678. Very Rev. David Foxen, M.S.C. Ord: '67, Prov. Supr.; Revs. Thomas Cain, M.S.C. Ord: '65, Treas.; Raymond Diesbourg, M.S.C. Ord: '74, Sec. & Editor, *M.S.C. Spotlite*.

Publication: *M.S.C. Spotlite.*

Religious serving in Papua New Guinea: Revs. Steve Boland, M.S.C. Ord: '86; David DeLuca, M.S.C. Ord: '66; Henry Einhaus, M.S.C. Ord: '60; Hilary Fischer, M.S.C. Ord: '57; Bro. Anton Freitas, M.S.C.; Revs. Anthony Gendusa, M.S.C. Ord: '40; Joseph Gleixner, M.S.C. Ord: '65, Regional Supr.; Bernard Miller, M.S.C. Ord: '59; Bros. James Miller, M.S.C.; Patrick O'Hara, M.S.C.; Daniel Rakow, M.S.C.; Joseph Tesar, M.S.C.; Rev. Leon Weisenberger, M.S.C. Ord: '59.

Religious serving in Colombia, South America: Very Rev. Howard Fath, M.S.C. Ord: '61, Section Supr.; Rev. Wilson Tascon, M.S.C. Ord: '90; Michael Miller, M.S.C. Ord: '85; German Barona Monsalve, M.S.C. Ord: '86; Tito Medina Mora, M.S.C. Ord: '92; Javier Bautista Pinillos, M.S.C. Ord: '95.

Religious serving in Namibia, Africa: Rev. Francis Westhoff, M.S.C. Ord: '35.

Missionhurst (C.I.C.M.)

Missionhurst Foreign Missions

American Headquarters (1946): Congregation of the Immaculate Heart of Mary, 4651 N. 25th St., Arlington, VA 22207. Tel: 703-528-3800; Fax: 703-528-5355. Rev. Joseph Lapauw, C.I.C.M. Ord: '73, Prov. Supr.

Publication: *Missionhurst.*

U.S. Religious serving Abroad: Revs. Vidal Ludan, C.I.C.M. Ord: '76, Prov. Supr., *Brazil;* Albert De-Crits, C.I.C.M. Ord: '40, *Belgium;* Albert Verbeke, C.I.C.M. Ord: '46, *Belgium;* Jos Cobbe, C.I.C.M. Ord: '67, Prov. Supr., *Indonesia;* Jean Marie Kayranga, C.I.C.M. Ord: '53, Prov. Supr., *Cameronn;* Leonard Kasanda, C.I.C.M. Ord: '64, Prov. Supr., *Kasayi;* Ven de la Cruz, C.I.C.M. Ord: '94, *Guatemala;* Roy Shea, C.I.C.M. Ord: '86, *Brazil;* Bro. Robert Dixon, C.I.C.M., *Brazil;* Revs. Paul Bouchaert, C.I.C.M. Ord: '68, Prov. Supr., *Haiti;* Tim Atkins, C.I.C.M. Ord: '74, *Haiti;* Revs. Joseph R. Guerrero, C.I.C.M. Ord: '85, Prov. Supr., *Guatemala;* Alphonse Rigouts, C.I.C.M. Ord: '48, *Guatemala;* Ramon Caluza, C.I.C.M. Ord: '79, Prov. Supr., *Dominican Republic;* Stan Szarwark, C.I.C.M. Ord: '64, *Dominican Republic;* Paul Delaere, C.I.C.M. Ord: '43, *Dominican Republic;* Camilo Boesmans, C.I.C.M. Ord: '47, *Dominican Republic;* Gerard Rogmans, C.I.C.M. Ord: '55, *Dominican Republic;* Bro. Leon Delanoy, C.I.C.M., *Dominican Republic;* Revs. Herman Louwagie, C.I.C.M. Ord: '58, Supr., *Mexico;* Thomas Matondo, C.I.C.M. Ord: '82, Prov. Supr., *Kinshasa, Congo;* Bro. Jerry Galloway, C.I.C.M., *Kinshasa, Zaire;* Revs. Ward Van Haegenborgh, C.I.C.M. Ord: '55, Prov. Supr., *North Belgium;* Jules Spriet, C.I.C.M. Ord: '44, *Belgium;* Albert Weyts, C.I.C.M. Ord: '44, *Belgium;* Paul Van Houtteghem, C.I.C.M. Ord: '48, *Belgium;* Paul VanMalderen, C.I.C.M. Ord: '40, *Belgium;* Joseph Verswyvel, C.I.C.M. Ord: '52, *Belgium;* Vincent VandeWeyer, C.I.C.M. Ord: '48, *Belgium;* Paul Serruys, C.I.C.M. Ord: '36; Victor De Clercq, .C.I.C.M. Ord: '37, *Belgium;* Marcel Josson, C.I.C.M. Ord: '36, *Belgium;* William Missinne, C.I.C.M. Ord: '54, *Belgium;* Angel Luciano, C.I.C.M. Ord: '72, Prov. Supr., *Philippines;* Luke Moortgat, C.I.C.M. Ord: '65, *Philippines;* Ludo Goossens, C.I.C.M. Ord: '69, Prov. Supr., *Japan;* John Raymaker, C.I.C.M. Ord: '64, *Japan;* Michael Hann, C.I.C.M. Ord: '73, *Rome, Italy;* John B. Peters, C.I.C.M. Ord: '53, *Rome, Italy.*

American Oblate Missions (O.M.I.)

Home and Foreign Missions of the American Provinces of the Missionary Oblates of Mary Immaculate (Oblate Fathers).

Oblate Conference of the U.S., 8818 Cameron St., Silver Spring, MD 20910. Tel: 301-565-0060; Fax: 301-589-2897. Rev. Seamus Finn, O.M.I. Ord: '76, National Coord.

Oblates Foreign Missions

Eastern Province: 391 Michigan Ave., N.E., P.O. Box 29152, Washington, DC 20017. Tel: 202-529-5958; Fax: 202-636-9444. Very Rev. William Sheehan, O.M.I. Ord: '58, Prov.

Publication: *The Oblate World.*

Southern Province: 7711 Madonna Dr., San Antonio, TX 78216. Tel: 210-349-1475; Fax: 210-349-7411. Very Rev. Eugene Canas, O.M.I. Ord: '64, Prov.

Publication: *Province Newsletter.*

Northern U.S. Province: 61 Burns Hill Rd., Hudson, NH 03051. Tel: 603-883-3233; Fax: 603-883-6089. Very Rev. Arthur Obin, O.M.I. Ord: '64, Prov.; Rev. Charles Breault, O.M.I. Ord: '59, Treas.

Publication: *Oblate World, Oblate Foreign Missions,* 46 Mt. Washington St., Lowell, MA 01854-3498. Tel: 978-458-4380; Fax: 978-454-5308. Bro. Augustin Cote, O.M.I., Dir.; Revs. Bernard Belley, O.M.I. Ord: '54; Real Bourque, O.M.I. Ord: '54; Francis Dolan, O.M.I. Ord: '73, Treas.; Raymond Lacasse, O.M.I. Ord: '58.

Central Province: 267 E. 8th, St. Paul, MN 55101. Tel: 612-292-8622; Fax: 612-292-8769. Very Rev. David Kalert, O.M.I. Ord: '64, Prov.

Publications: *Oblates,* 15 S. 59th St., Belleville, IL 62222.

Western Province: 14065 Nordhoff St.., Arleta, CA 91331. Tel: 818-891-0579; Fax: 818-893-9819. Very Rev. David Ullrich, O.M.I. Ord: '71, Prov.; Rev. Edward J. Collins, O.M.I. Ord: '46, Mission Procurator, 1109 Coronel St., San Fernando, CA 91340.

U.S. Religious serving in the Philippines Islands: Most Rev. Philip Smith, O.M.I., Archbishop of Cotabato; Most Rev. George Dion, O.M.I., Bishop of Jolo (Retired); Revs. Armand Carignan, O.M.I. Ord: '53; Maurice Hemann, O.M.I. Ord: '50; Richard Pommier, O.M.I. Ord: '66; Charles Prass, O.M.I. Ord: '45; Robert Sullivan, O.M.I. Ord: '41; Cletus Ternes, O.M.I. Ord: '61; Richard Weixelman, O.M.I. Ord: '65.

U.S. Religious serving in Haiti: Revs. Richard Bolduc, O.M.I. Ord: '64; Alfred Charpentier, O.M.I. Ord: '71; Real Corriveau, O.M.I. Ord: '61; Omer Duplessis, O.M.I. Ord: '43; Roger Hallee, O.M.I. Ord: '63, Prov.; John Henault, O.M.I. Ord: '63; Roland Gagnon, O.M.I. Ord: '51; Charles Heon, O.M.I. Ord: '64; Leroy Landry, O.M.I. Ord: '61; Albert Lirette, O.M.I. Ord: '45; Raymond Marquis, O.M.I. Ord: '74; Francis Mitchell, O.M.I. Ord: '44; Roger Paradis, O.M.I. Ord: '48; Mauril Rancourt, O.M.I. Ord: '60; John St. Cyr, O.M.I. Ord: '61; Andre Tanguay, O.M.I. Ord: '53; Joseph Vaillancourt, O.M.I. Ord: '46; Marc Boisvert, O.M.I. Ord: '84.

U.S. Religious serving in Tahiti: Rev. Roger Roy, O.M.I. Ord: '49.

U.S. Religious serving in Indonesia: Rev. Lucien Bouchard, O.M.I. Ord: '55.

U.S. Religious serving in Brazil: Very Rev. James Gibbons, O.M.I. Ord: '69, Prov.; Revs. Roger Bergkamp, O.M.I. Ord: '64; Thomas Brown, O.M.I. Ord: '55; Peter Curran, O.M.I. Ord: '71; Thomas Delaney, O.M.I. Ord: '60; John Drexel, O.M.I. Ord: '62; Edward Figueroa, O.M.I. Ord: '60; Robert Fitzpatrick, O.M.I. Ord: '71; Bro. Daniel Hayes, O.M.I.; Very Rev. Bruce Heit, O.M.I. Ord: '64, Vicar Prov.; Revs. James Kohmetscher, O.M.I. Ord: '55; Edmund Leising, O.M.I. Ord: '46; William Lindkugel, O.M.I. Ord: '45; Louis Lougen, O.M.I. Ord: '79; Gerald McGovern, O.M.I. Ord: '57; Paul Medeiros, O.M.I. Ord: '64; Robert Mayer, O.M.I. Ord: '67; Daniel Meehan, O.M.I. Ord: '61; David O'Brien, O.M.I. Ord: '59; Thomas O'Brien, O.M.I. Ord: '55; Robert Reardon, O.M.I. Ord: '68; William Reinhard, O.M.I. Ord: '61; Anthony Rendon, O.M.I. Ord: '67; William Sheehan, O.M.I. Ord: '42; James Sullivan, O.M.I. Ord: '53; Charles Tierney, O.M.I. Ord: '73.

U.S. Religious serving in Canada: Revs. Richard G. Cote, O.M.I. Ord: '60; Normand Bonneau, O.M.I. Ord: '76.

U.S. Religious serving in Japan: Very Rev. John Mahoney, O.M.I. Ord: '54, Prov.; Revs. Raymond Bourgoin, O.M.I. Ord: '66; John Deely, O.M.I. Ord: '70; Francis Hahn, O.M.I. Ord: '72; Richard Harr, O.M.I. Ord: '52; Ronald Laframboise, O.M.I. Ord: '67; Thomas Maher, O.M.I. Ord: '57; William Maher, O.M.I. Ord: '66; Jerome Novotney, O.M.I. Ord: '68; Angelo Siani, O.M.I. Ord: '65, Prov.; Bertram Silver, O.M.I. Ord: '54; Edward Williams, O.M.I. Ord: '57.

U.S. Religious serving in Mexico: Revs. Carlos DeAnta, O.M.I. Ord: '50; Philip Ehrhardt, O.M.I. Ord: '27; Daniel Gagnon, O.M.I. Ord: '87; Robert Hickl, O.M.I. Ord: '79; Richard Junius, O.M.I. Ord: '56; Edwin Krzewinski, O.M.I. Ord: '52; Ernest Liekens, O.M.I. Ord: '61; Vincent Louwagie, O.M.I. Ord: '68; James Lyons, O.M.I. Ord: '; Curtis Moffat, O.M.I. Ord: '; Augustine Petru, O.M.I. Ord: '53; Francis Pfeifer, O.M.I. Ord: '; Gilberto Pinon, O.M.I. Ord: '71; Gregorio Ramos, O.M.I. Ord: '50; Raymond Schoenstein, O.M.I. Ord: '; John Schwider, O.M.I. Ord: '40; Jose Torres, O.M.I. Ord: '74; Robert Ward, O.M.I. Ord: '61; George Protopapas, O.M.I. Ord: '43; Gerald Kapustka, O.M.I. Ord: '65, *Guatemala.*

Religious in Scandinavian Missions: Bros. Olof Asblom, O.M.I.; Daniel Bozek, O.M.I.; Revs. Michael Bradley, O.M.I. Ord: '66; Allen Courteau, O.M.I. Ord: '76; Urban Figge, O.M.I. Ord: '67; Franz Hoyos, O.M.I. Ord: '86; Frank Jobst, O.M.I. Ord: '72; Leo Kertz, O.M.I. Ord: '63; Thomas M. Killeen, O.M.I. Ord: '58; Lon Konold, O.M.I. Ord: '77; Alex Kons, O.M.I. Ord: '55; Paul Marx, O.M.I. Ord: '65; Carroll Parker, O.M.I. Ord: '61; Clyde Rausch, O.M.I. Ord: '68; John Schoeberle, O.M.I. Ord: '61;

Karl Smeenk, O.M.I. Ord: '50; Per Waago, O.M.I. Ord: '; Eric Westerberg, O.M.I. Ord: '86; Gerald Orsino, O.M.I. Ord: '66, *Bangkok, Thailand.*

U.S. Religious serving in Zambia: Revs. Paul Duffy, O.M.I. Ord: '62; Patrick Gitzen, O.M.I. Ord: '75; Jack Joyce, O.M.I. Ord: '61; Edward R. Matthews, O.M.I. Ord: '84; John Staak, O.M.I. Ord: '95; Brian Walker, O.M.I. Ord: '; Ronald Walker, O.M.I. Ord: '61.

Oblates of St. Francis de Sales Missions (O.S.F.S.)

Oblates of St. Francis de Sales Foreign Missions

U.S. Mission Headquarters: Office of the Mission Procurator Oblates of St. Francis de Sales, 1801 N. Broom St., Wilmington, DE 19802. Revs. Francis D. Dougherty, O.S.F.S. Ord: '38, Procurator. Tel: 302-652-3202. John J. Hurley, O.S.F.S. Ord: '68, Procurator. Tel: 302-654-2238. Francis J. Gross, O.S.F.S., Mission Procurator, Toledo-Detroit Prov., 69 O'Hara Rd., Tonawanda, NY 14150. Tel: 716-694-4950.

U.S. Religious serving in Africa & South America: Revs. Leon V. Bonikowski, O.S.F.S. Ord: '65; George J. Brownholtz, O.S.F.S. Ord: '69; Edward P. Canavan, O.S.F.S., John J. Coyne, O.S.F.S. Ord: '71; Walter DeSa, O.S.F.S.; Walter J. Hartlove, O.S.F.S. Ord: '48; Peter J. Harvey, O.S.F.S. Ord: '60; Robert J. Hindley, O.S.F.S. Ord: '58; Most Rev. John B. Minder, O.S.F.S., D.D.; Revs. Michael Moore, O.S.F.S.; Edmund F. O'Rourke, O.S.F.S.; Harry J. Schlight, O.S.F.S. Ord: '44; Most Rev. Edward J. Schlotterback, O.S.F.S., D.D.; Revs. Alfred J. Smuda, O.S.F.S. Ord: '66; Joseph A. Travers, O.S.F.S.

American Passionist Missions (C.P.)

Passionist Foreign Missions

Home and Foreign Missions of the American Provinces of the Congregation of the Passion

General Motherhouse: SS. Giovanni e Paolo 13, Rome, 00184. Italy. Most Rev. Jose Augustin Orbegozo, C.P., Supr. Gen.

Provincial Headquarters U.S.A.

St. Paul of the Cross Province: Province Pastoral Center, 80 David St., South River, NJ 08882. Tel: 908-257-7177. Very Rev. Robert Joerger, C.P. Ord: '77, Prov. Supr.; Very Rev. Lucian Clark, C.P. Ord: '65, Dir. of Ministries; Very Rev. Paul Ruttle, C.P. Ord: '80, Sec.

U.S. Religious Serving Abroad: Rev. Richard Award, C.P. Ord: '81, *West Indies;* Bro. Louis Bouchard, C.P., *Philippines;* Revs. Thomas Brislin, C.P. Ord: '68, *Bahamas;* Herbert Eberly, C.P. Ord: '58, *Philippines;* Henry Free, C.P. Ord: '58, *Philippines;* Aelred Lacomara, C.P. Ord: '57, *Africa;* Richard Leary, C.P. Ord: '46, *West Indies;* Bernard McEachern, C.P. Ord: '64, *Philippines;* Bro. Robert McKenna, C.P., *Philippines;* Revs. Bonaventure Moccia, C.P. Ord: '52, *Rome;* Peter O'Rourke, C.P. Ord: '64, *New Guinea;* David Roberts, C.P. Ord: '52, *Bahamas;* Bro. Michael Stomber, C.P., *West Indies;* Revs. Martin J. Tooker, C.P. Ord: '46, *West Indies;* Hilarion Walters, C.P. Ord: '47, *Philippines.*

Priests 14; Brothers 3.

Mission Procurators

Eastern: Revs. Lucian Clark, C.P. Ord: '65, Dir., 80 David St., South River, NJ 08882; Sebastian Kolinovsky, C.P. Ord: '51, Passionist Missionaries, Monastery Pl., Union City, NJ 07087. Bro. Leo Di-Fiore, C.P., Passionist Overseas Missions, 148 Monastery Ave., Pittsburgh, PA 15203.

Canada: 2102 Kipling Ave., Rexdale, ON M9W 4K5.

Philippines: Rev. Bernard McEachern, C.P. Ord: '64, Procurator, P.O. Box 1290 MCCPO, Metro Manila 1252, Makati.

China: Passionist Mission Procurator, Maryknoll House, Stanley, Hong Kong.

Holy Cross Province (Western): Immaculate Conception Monastery, 5700 N. Harlem Ave., Chicago, IL 60631. Tel: 773-631-6336; Fax: 773-631-8059. Very Rev. Michael Joseph Stengel, C.P. Ord: '57, Prov.; Rev. Luke Connolly, C.P. Ord: '52, Mission Appeals.

Mission Procurators

Western: Mr. Edward Scholl, Dir.; Rev. Luke Connolly, C.P. Ord: '52, Mission Appeals, *Passionist Missions, Inc.,* 5700 N. Harlem Ave., Chicago, IL 60631. Tel: 773-631-1686; *Procuration Office of Holy Cross Province-Passionist, Missions, Inc.*

Japan: Rev. Francis Horack, C.P. Ord: '42, *Japan Passionist Missions,* Passionist Community 10-1, Yamate-cho, Mefu Takarazuka-shi,, Hyogo Prefecture 665. Japan. Tel: 0797 84-3111.

Korea: Rev. Richard Thomson, C.P. Ord: '69, Passionist Vice Provincialate, Tobong P.O. Box 57, Seoul, 132-600. Korea.

India: Rev. Walter Kaelin, C.P. Ord: '42, 1924 Newburg Rd., Louisville, KY 40205.

U.S. Religious serving in Japan: Revs. Ward Biddle, C.P. Ord: '51; Gabriel Brecheteau, C.P. Ord: '48; Francis Horack, C.P. Ord: '42; Leonard Kosatka, C.P. Ord: '59; Denis McGowan, C.P. Ord: '55; Ronan Newbold, C.P. Ord: '69; Clement Paynter, C.P. Ord: '52; Matthew Vetter, C.P. Ord: '38.

Also serving in Japan are the: Cloistered Passionist Nuns; Mother Marie Paul, C.P.; Supr.

Sisters 15.

U.S. Religious serving Elsewhere: Revs. Justin Bartoszek, C.P. Ord: '64, *Korea;* Richard Thomson, C.P. Ord: '69, *Korea;* Bro. Laurence Finn, C.P., *Korea;* Revs. Joseph Moons, C.P. Ord: '77, *India;* Joseph Vanleuwen, C.P. Ord: '64, *India;* Warren Womack, C.P. Ord: '49, *Sweden.*

American Redemptorist Fathers (C.Ss.R.)

Mission of the Provinces and Vice-Provinces in the United States and other countries and lands

Redemptorist Foreign Missions

Baltimore Province: Redemptorist Fathers of New York, 7509 Shore Rd., Brooklyn, NY 11209; Fax: 718-630-5666. Very Rev. George J. Keaveney, C.Ss.R. Ord: '66, Prov.

Publication: *Perpetual Help World,* 294 E. 150th St., New York, NY 10051.

U.S. Religious serving in Paraguay: Revs. Antonio Cannoles, C.Ss.R. Ord: '69; Robert Hopwood, C.Ss.R. Ord: '52.

U.S. Religious serving in St. Lucia, W.I.: Revs. John M. Hamrogue, C.Ss.R. Ord: '63; John J. O'Toole, C.Ss.R. Ord: '53; Joseph E. Bertrand, C.Ss.R. Ord: '55; John P. Gallagher, C.Ss.R. Ord: '95; Rodney J. Olive, C.Ss.R. Ord: '86; Henrique Schulterbrandt, C.Ss.R. Ord: '94.

U.S. Religious serving in Dominica, W.I.: Revs. Jerome Moody, C.Ss.R. Ord: '73; Joseph F. Krastel, C.Ss.R. Ord: '64; John F. Murray, C.Ss.R. Ord: '94.

Denver Province: P.O. Box 300399, Denver, CO 80203-0399. Tel: 303-370-0036; Fax: 303-370-0036. Very Rev. Richard Thibodeau, C.Ss.R. Ord: '76, Prov.; Rev. Wilfred Lowery, C.Ss.R. Ord: '49, Dir.-Foreign Missions, P.O. Box 6, Glenview, IL 60025. Tel: 847-724-0425; Fax: 847-724-8953.

U.S. Religious serving in Brazil: Revs. Vince Aggeler, C.Ss.R. Ord: '58; Joseph Butz, C.Ss.R. Ord: '70; Willliam Fitzgerald, C.Ss.R. Ord: '43; John Gouger, C.Ss.R. Ord: '65; Donnell Kirchner, C.Ss.R. Ord: '66; Patrick Keyes, C.Ss.R. Ord: '89; Patrick McBride, C.Ss.R. Ord: '85; John McCarthy, C.Ss.R. Ord: '62; Thomas McIntosh, C.Ss.R. Ord: '66; Most Rev. Alfred Novak, C.Ss.R., Bishop of Paranagua, Brazil; Most Rev. Gutemberg Regis, C.Ss.R., Bishop of Coari, Brazil; Bro. Leo Patin, C.Ss.R.; Revs. William Steiner, C.Ss.R. Ord: '54; Joseph Stenger, C.Ss.R. Ord: '57; Andrew Thompson, C.Ss.R. Ord: '81; Edward Vella, C.Ss.R. Ord: '85; Ronald Weninger, C.Ss.R. Ord: '49.

U.S. Religious serving in Thailand: Revs. Charles Beierwaltes, C.Ss.R. Ord: '67; Raymond Brennan, C.Ss.R. Ord: '59; Charles Cotant, C.Ss.R. Ord: '41; Most Rev. Clarence Duhart, C.Ss.R., Retired Bishop; Revs. Francis Gautreaux, C.Ss.R. Ord: '50; Joseph Maier, C.Ss.R. Ord: '65; Robert Martin, C.Ss.R. Ord: '50; Patrick Morrissy, C.Ss.R. Ord: '55; Lawrence Patin, C.Ss.R. Ord: '63; Most Rev. George Phimphisan, C.Ss.R., Bishop of Udon Thani; Revs. Michael Shea, C.Ss.R. Ord: '64; Harold J. Thiel, C.Ss.R. Ord: '56; Leo Travis, C.Ss.R. Ord: '54; William Wright, C.Ss.R. Ord: '60.

U.S. Religious serving in Nigeria: Revs. William M. Cleary, C.Ss.R. Ord: '62; William A. Peterson, C.Ss.R. Ord: '67; Richard Thiele, C.Ss.R. Ord: '54; John Willett, C.Ss.R. Ord: '61; Robert Wirth, C.Ss.R. Ord: '64.

St. Columban's Foreign Mission Society (S.S.C.)

THE COLUMBAN FATHERS

Founded in 1918 with the approval of Pope Benedict XV. Placed under the patronage of St. Columban and made a Pontifical Society by Pope Pius XI.

Generalate: St. Columban's, Grange Rd., Donaghmede Dublin 13, Ireland. Very Rev. Nicholas Murray, S.S.C. Ord: '62, Supr. Gen.

U.S. Foundation & Administration: Columban Fathers, St. Columbans, NE 68056. Tel: 402-291-1920. Very Rev. Brendan O'Sullivan, S.S.C. Ord: '70, Dir.; Rev. James J. Hastings, S.S.C. Ord: '72, Vice Dir.

Publication: *Columban Mission.*

Legal Title: St. Columban's Foreign Mission Society. The Society is incorporated in California, Illinois, Massachusetts, Nebraska, New York, Rhode Island, and Registered in Pennsylvania.

St. Columban's Foreign Mission

House of Post-Graduate Studies: Collegio Colombano, Corso Trieste, 57, Roma, 00198. Italy. Very Rev. Padhraic O'Loughlin, S.S.C. Ord: '57, Procurator Gen.

U.S. Religious serving Overseas: Revs. Edward A. Allen, S.S.C. Ord: '30, *Philippines;* Clarence Beckley, S.S.C. Ord: '66, *Brazil;* William D. Bourke, S.S.C. Ord: '54, *Philippines;* Thomas Browning, S.S.C. Ord: '90, *Taiwan;* John A. Buckley, S.S.C. Ord: '68, *Brazil;* John Burger, S.S.C. Ord: '73, *Japan;* Vincent J. Busch, S.S.C. Ord: '74, *Philippines;* Richard W. Cannon, S.S.C. Ord: '54, *Philippines;* Salvatore S. Caputo, S.S.C. Ord: '76, *Korea;* Francis P. Carroll, S.S.C. Ord: '62, *Japan;* David J. Clay, S.S.C. Ord: '62, *Philippines;* John Comiskey, S.S.C. Ord: '68, *Philippines;* Neil Boyle, S.S.C. Ord: '43, *Ireland;* Edward T. McKenna, S.S.C. Ord: '49, *Great Britain;* Charles Duster, S.S.C. Ord: '61, *Fiji;* William Hennessey, S.S.C. Ord: '35, *Philippines;* Michael Hoban, S.S.C. Ord: '70, *Chile;* Quentin F. Kalick, S.S.C. Ord: '42, *Philippines;* David Padrnos, S.S.C. Ord: '71, *Japan;* Ronald Kelso, S.S.C. Ord: '73, *Japan;* Donald Kill, S.S.C. Ord: '72, *Philippines;* Charles Lintz, S.S.C. Ord: '70, *Korea;* John Marley, S.S.C. Ord: '50, *Ireland;* Vincent McCarthy, S.S.C. Ord: '64, *Brazil;* James J. McCaslin, S.S.C. Ord: '54, *Hong Kong;* Joseph McSweeny, S.S.C. Ord: '90, *Taiwan;* John P. Moran, S.S.C. Ord: '50, *Philippines;* Robert E. Mosher, S.S.C. Ord: '82, *Chile;* Richard L. Pankratz, S.S.C. Ord: '74, *Philippines;* Desmond Quinn, S.S.C. Ord: '54, *Philippines;* Edward I. Quinn, S.S.C. Ord: '55, *Fiji;* Francis A. Regan, S.S.C. Ord: '66, *Britain;* Paul Richardson, S.S.C. Ord: '54, *Philippines;* Michael O'Loughlin, S.S.C. Ord: '60, *Ireland;* Thomas Shaughnessy, S.S.C. Ord: '66, *Philippines;* David M. Sheehan, S.S.C. Ord: '53, *Korea;* Robert P. Sweeney, S.S.C. Ord: '59, *Korea;* Albert Utzig, S.S.C. Ord: '83, *Korea;* Thomas Walsh, S.S.C. Ord: '57, *Chile;* Vincent J. Youngkamp, S.S.C. Ord: '59, *Japan.*

Priests 40.

Brothers of the Sacred Heart (S.C.)

Brothers of the Sacred Heart Foreign Missions

Provincial House: 685 Steere Farm Rd., Pascoag, RI 02859. Tel: 401-568-3361; Fax: 401-568-9810. Bros. Robert F. Breault, S.C., Prov. Supr.; Paul Hebert S.C., Mission Procurator. The Brothers of the Sacred Heart have mission schools and stations in Lesotho, Uganda, Zambia, and Zimbabwe.

Brothers 96; Brothers in Africa 48.

Salesians of Don Bosco (S.D.B.)

Salesians of Don Bosco Foreign Missions

Salesian Provincial House: 148 Main St.-Box 639, New Rochelle, NY 10802-0639. Tel: 914-636-4225. Very Rev. Patrick Angelucci, S.D.B. Ord: '76, Prov.; Rev. James Marra, S.D.B. Ord: '83, Procurator.

U.S. Religious serving Abroad: Revs. Henry Bonetti, S.D.B. Ord: '73, *China;* Dominic DeBlase, S.D.B. Ord: '61, *Sierra Leone;* Robert Falk, S.D.B. Ord: '63, *Korea;* Lawrence Gilmore, S.D.B. Ord: '84, *Liberia;* Edward Liptak, S.D.B. Ord: '59, *Tanzania;* Harry Peterson, S.D.B. Ord: '61, *Chile;* John Thompson, S.D.B. Ord: '79, *Sierra Leone;* John Trisolini, S.D.B. Ord: '67, *Korea;* Bros. George Marquis, S.D.B., *Sierra Leone;* John Cosgrove, S.D.B., *Sierra Leone.*

Salesian Provincial House: 1100 Franklin St., San Francisco, CA 94109. Tel: 415-441-7144; Fax: 415-441-7155. Very Rev. Nicholas J. Reina, S.D.B. Ord: '78, Prov.

U.S. Religious serving Abroad: Revs. Albert Mengon, S.D.B. Ord: '66, *Sierra Leone;* Christian Kot, S.D.B. Ord: '94, *Sierra Leone;* Bros. Joseph Reza, S.D.B., *Ethiopia.*

Salvatorian Missions (S.D.S.)

Salvatorian Foreign Missions

U.S.A. Provincial Headquarters: Salvatorian Provincial Residence, 1735 Hi-Mount Blvd., Milwaukee, WI 53208-1720. Tel: 414-258-1735. Very Rev. Dennis D. Thiessen, S.D.S. Ord: '78, Prov.

U.S.A. Procurator: 1735 Hi-Mount Blvd., Milwaukee, WI 53208-1720. Tel: 414-258-1735. Rev. Eric Middlecamp, S.D.S. Ord: '52, Mission Dir.

Publication: *The Salvatorian Newsletter.*

U.S. Religious serving in Tanzania: Revs. Carl Gleason, S.D.S. Ord: '56; James Weyker, S.D.S. Ord: '69; Bro. Donald Maurer, S.D.S.; Rev. David Brusky, S.D.S. Ord: '52.

Society of African Missions (S.M.A.)

Society of African Missions

U.S. Provincial Headquarters: Society of African Missions, 23 Bliss Ave., Tenafly, NJ 07670. Tel: 201-567-0450; 567-9085; Fax: 201-567-7156; 541-1280. Rev. Douglas B. Gilbert, S.M.A. Ord: '83, Prov. Supr.

U.S. Religious serving Abroad: Revs. Terrance Doherty, S.M.A. Ord: '70, *Liberia;* James Gessler, S.M.A. Ord: '63, *Liberia;* James Hayes, S.M.A. Ord: '55, *Cote d'Ivoire;* James C. Hickey, S.M.A. Ord: '46, *Liberia;* Michael Moran, S.M.A. Ord: '81, *Liberia;* Austin Charles Ochu, S.M.A. Ord: '92, *Ghana.*

Society of St. Edmund (S.S.E.)

Edmundite Foreign Missions

U.S. Foundation: Edmundite Generalate, 270 Winooski Park, Colchester, VT 05439. Tel: 802-654-3400; Fax: 802-654-3409. Very Rev. Joseph L. Hart, S.S.E. Ord: '55, Supr. Gen.

U.S. Religious serving Abroad: Revs. Edward J. Dubriske, S.S.E. Ord: '64, *Venezuela;* Howard J. Muehlberger, S.S.E. Ord: '71, *Venezuela;* Philippe Simonnet, S.S.E. Ord: '52, *France.*

The Society of Mary (S.M.)

MARIST FATHERS

Marist Foreign Missions

General Motherhouse: Via Alesandro Poerio, 63, 00152, Rome, Italy. Very Revs. Joaquin Fernandez, S.M. Ord: '68, Supr. Gen.; Friedrich Arnold, S.M. Ord: '70, Vicar Gen.

U.S. Mission Promoter: Marist Missions, 29 Isabella St., Boston, MA 02116-5216. Tel: 617-482-0832; Fax: 617-482-1570. Rev. J. Armand Robichaud, S.M. Ord: '50, Dir.

Missions in Brazil, Burundi, Fiji, Japan, New Caledonia, Norway, Papua New Guinea, Peru, Philippine Islands, Samoa, Senegal, Solomon Islands, Tonga, Vanuatu, Venezuela, Wallis & Futuna, Republic of Cameroon.

U.S. Religious serving Abroad: Revs. John P. Bolduc, S.M. Ord: '70, *Senegal;* Raymond Coolong, S.M. Ord: '71, *Peru;* Paul Frechette, S.M. Ord: '76, *Peru;* John Galvin, S.M. Ord: '63, *Solomon Islands;* Carlton Grenier, S.M. Ord: '54, *Papua New Guinea;* John Keady, S.M. Ord: '47, *Papua New Guinea;* Nicholas Kutulas, S.M. Ord: '55, *Papua New Guinea;* Louis Morosini, S.M. Ord: '56, *Solomon Islands;* Joseph Pusateri, S.M. Ord: '65, *Samoa;* Bertrand Soucy, S.M. Ord: '53, *Vanuatu;* Neil Soucy, S.M. Ord: '62, *New Caledonia.*

Society of St. James the Apostle

Society of St. James the Apostle, Inc.: 24 Clark St., Boston, MA 02109. Tel: 617-742-4715; Fax: 617-723-7389. Revs. Gabriel Troy (BO) Ord: '66, Dir.; Milton Eggerling (OAK) Ord: '54.

Founded by His Eminence Richard Cardinal Cushing, in 1958 to recruit Diocesan Priest volunteers for South America.

Serving in Peru: Revs. John E. Davis (FAR) Ord: '69; Frank Fairbairn (BO) Ord: '69; George Flynn (BO) Ord: '56; Donald Gorski (CHR) Ord: '59; Eugene K. Kirke (BO) Ord: '62; Paul Madden (JKS) Ord: '70; Joseph I. Martin (BO) Ord: '56; Rudolph Masciarelli (BO) Ord: '49; J. Joseph McCarthy (BO) Ord: '66; Philip McKenna (MOB); John O'Leary (MIA) Ord: '67; Gerard O'Meara (BO) Ord: '76; Hugh Joseph Shields (PH) Ord: '72; Raymond O'Sullivan (BO) Ord: '68; John J. Pashby (BO) Ord: '60; William Pearsall (BO) Ord: '53; Jules Roos (PIT) Ord: '56; Desmond Tynan (BO) Ord: '67.

Serving in Bolivia: Revs. William Baker (ALT) Ord: '82; Donald J. Bowen (FR) Ord: '64; James Coleman (P) Ord: '73; Raymond Cowell (CHI) Ord: '56; Thomas Domurat (BO) Ord: '79; Paul M. Koch (DM) Ord: '61; Charles Stanley (BO) Ord: '71; John L. Sullivan (BO) Ord: '52; Thomas Oates (BO) Ord: '63; John Michael Ricker (TOL) Ord: '55.

Serving in Ecuador: Revs. James Cribbin (SD) Ord: '85; John Hendricks (TR) Ord: '52; John Gordon (MET) Ord: '85; John Grimes (BO) Ord: '71; Cornelius Kiely (BAK) Ord: '67; Cornelois B. Lynch (PRO) Ord: '54; John J. Moriarty (JOL) Ord: '62; Robert Thomas (BO) Ord: '61.

Third Order Regular Missions (T.O.R.)

Third Order Regular of St. Francis

T.O.R. Foreign Missions

Provincial Residence: Province of the Most Sacred Heart of Jesus, 215 57th St., Pittsburgh, PA 15201. Tel: 412-781-8333. Very Rev. Edmund F. Carroll, T.O.R. Ord: '57, Minister Prov.; Bro. Mark McBride, T.O.R., Prov. Dir. of Foreign Missions.

U.S. Religious serving Abroad: Revs. Gerald J. King, T.O.R. Ord: '71, *Brazil;* Joseph A. Markalonis, T.O.R. Ord: '66, *Brazil;* Most Rev. Urban E. McGarry, T.O.R., D.D., (Retired), *India;* Rev. Paul R. Pavlik, T.O.R. Ord: '59, *Brazil;* Most Rev. Adrian J. Veigle, T.O.R., D.D., (Retired), *Brazil.*

Province of the Immaculate Conception: Provincial Residence, P.O. Box 29655, Brookland Station, Washington, DC 20017. Tel: 202-526-3332. Very Rev. Robert J. D'Aversa, T.O.R., Minister Prov.

U.S. Religious serving in Europe: Very Rev. Seraphin Conley, T.O.R., General Counselor Rome.

Missionary Servants of the Most Holy Trinity (S.T.)

Trinity Missions

International Headquarters

Generalate: 1215 N. Scott St., Arlington, VA 22209-3097. Tel: 703-276-8646; Fax: 703-522-2656. Rev. Domingo Rodriguez, S.T. Ord: '67, Supr. Gen.; Bro. Hilary Mettes, S.T., Sec. Gen.

U.S. Religious serving abroad: Revs. Rudy Breunig, S.T. Ord: '65, *Costa Rica;* Francisco Gomez, S.T. Ord: '83, *Mexico;* Charles Gordon, S.T. Ord: '67, *Costa Rica;* Antonio Hernandez Velez, S.T. Ord: '57, *Columbia;* Louis E. Murphy, S.T. Ord: '60, *Columbia;* Eugene Mueller, S.T. Ord: '55, *Costa Rica;* Kevin Nugent, S.T. Ord: '51, *Costa Rica;* Victor Santiago Mateo, S.T. Ord: '82, *Mexico;* Harold Stone, S.T. Ord: '59, *Mexico;* Bruce Ward, S.T. Ord: '60, *Mexico;* Guy Wilson, S.T. Ord: '78, *Costa Rica.*

American Vincentian Missions (C.M.)

Vincentian Foreign Missions

Provincial Headquarters

Eastern Province: St. Vincent's Seminary, 500 East Chelten Ave., Philadelphia, PA 19144. Tel: 215-848-1985; Fax: 215-844-2085. Very Rev. Joseph L. Levesque, C.M. Ord: '67, Prov.

U.S. Religious serving abroad: Revs. Elmer Bauer, III, C.M. Ord: '93, *Concepcion, Panama;* John J. Buckley, C.M. Ord: '57, *Addis Ababa, Ethiopia;* Thomas M. Byrnes, C.M. Ord: '50, *Balboa, Panama;* John J. Carney, C.M. Ord: '82, *Puerto Armuelles, Panama;* Juan Chavarria, C.M. Ord: '95, *Balboa, Panama;* Joseph V. Cummins, C.M. Ord: '72, *Puerto Armuelles, Panama;* Robert P. Crawford, C.M. Ord: '47, *Philippines;* Edison Famania, C.M. Ord: '94, *Balboa, Panama;* Patrick J. Griffin, C.M. Ord: '79, *Rome;* Alcibiades Guerra, C.M. Ord: '90, *Volcan, Panama;* Thomas Hynes, C.M. Ord: '59, *Solomon Islands;* Jose Pio Jimenez, C.M. Ord: '68, *Balboa, Panama;* Teodoro Justavino, C.M. Ord: '90, *Panama City, Panama;* John E. Kane, C.M. Ord: '70, *Balboa, Panama;* Arthur J. Kolinsky, C.M. Ord: '71, *Puerto Armuelles, Panama;* Alan J. McLellan, C.M. Ord: '65, *Colon, Panama;* John J. MacGillivray, C.M. Ord: '76, *Colon, Panama;* Robert P.

Maloney, C.M. Ord: '66, *Rome;* Francis Maguire, C.M. Ord: '51, *Addis Ababa, Ethiopia;* Jose Angel Medina, C.M. Ord: '88, *Concepcion, Panama;* Emmet J. Nolan, C.M. Ord: '92, *Concepcion, Panama;* John P. Prager, C.M. Ord: '82, *Volcan, Panama;* Teodoro A. Rios, C.M. Ord: '76, *Concepcion, Panama;* John D. Rutledge, C.M. Ord: '51, *Balboa, Panama;* Francisco Samudio, C.M. Ord: '92, *Panama City, Panama;* Charles G. Schuster, C.M. Ord: '55, *Soloy, Panama;* Thomas A. Sendlein, C.M. Ord: '72, *Taiwan;* Harold G. Skidmore, C.M. Ord: '50, *Balboa, Panama;* Juan Wardrope, C.M. Ord: '89, *Panama City, Panama.*

Midwest Province: Vincentian Fathers and Brothers, 13663 Rider Trail N., Earth City, MO 63045-1512. Tel: 314-344-1184; Fax: 314-344-2989. Very Rev. William E. Hartenbach, C.M. Ord: '64, Prov.

U.S. Religious serving in foreign missions: Revs. Gerald Brown, C.M. Ord: '57; Stephen Gallegos, C.M. Ord: '88; Very Rev. Robert Wood, C.M. Ord: '56, Supr.; Revs. Francis A. Gaydos, C.M. Ord: '47; W. Barry Moriarty, C.M. Ord: '67; Thomas G. O'Hern, C.M. Ord: '77; John T. Richardson, C.M. Ord: '49; Very Rev. Hugh F. O'Donnell, C.M. Ord: '61, Prov.; Revs. Edward Gallagher, C.M. Ord: '78; Jacob Johnson, C.M. Ord: '47; Robert W. Chap, C.M. Ord: '66; Richard Preuss, C.M. Ord: '73.

Southern Province: Congregation of the Mission, 3826 Gilbert Ave., Dallas, TX 75219-4346. Tel: 214-526-0234 or 526-2421; Fax: 214-526-3477. Very Rev. George J. Weber, C.M. Ord: '54, Prov.

Xaverian Missionary Fathers (S.X.)

Xaverian Foreign Missions

U.S. Foundation: Xaverian Missionary Fathers, 12 Helene Ct., Wayne, NJ 07470. Tel: 201-942-2975; Fax: 201-942-5012. Revs. Francis Signorelli, S.X. Ord: '59, Prov.; Herondi Fernandes, S.X. Ord: '76, Local Supr.; Frank B. Grappoli, S.X. Ord: '63, Treas. & Mission Dir.; Dario Maso, S.X. Ord: '82, Vocation Ministry.

Religious Serving Abroad: Most Rev. George Biguzzi, S.X., *Sierra Leone;* Revs. Danilo Boschetto, S.X. Ord: '70, *Mexico;* Carl Chudy, S.X. Ord: '86, *Philippines;* Oscar De LaTorre, S.X. Ord: '87, *Bangladesh;* Revs. Gerard Furlan, S.X. Ord: '58, *Sierra Leone;* Francis Gugliotta, S.X. Ord: '52, *Brazil;* Greg Holm, S.X. Ord: '87, *Japan;* Danilo Lago, S.X. Ord: '77, *Brazil;* Rene Lovat, S.X. Ord: '57, *Cameroun;* Mark Marangone, S.X. Ord: '84, *Colombia;* Joseph Matteucig, S.X. Ord: '84, *Taiwan;* Adolph Menendez, S.X. Ord: '68, *Mexico;* Victor Mosele, S.X. Ord: '60, *Sierra Leone;* Gino Nasini, S.X. Ord: '65, *Brazil;* Bruno Orru, S.X. Ord: '63, *Indonesia;* Julian Perozzi Ord: '82, *Taiwan;* Luciano Peterlini, S.X. Ord: '63, *Sierra Leone;* Mario Pezzotti, S.X. Ord: '59, *Brazil;* Franco Qualizza, S.X. Ord: '71, *Indonesia;* Noel Tomasi, S.X. Ord: '60, *Congo;* James Tully, S.X. Ord: '75, *Sierra Leone.*

Missionary Activities

RELIGIOUS SOCIETIES ENGAGED IN MISSIONARY WORK

Augustinian Recollect Fathers: *Province of St. Nicholas of Tolentine U.S. Delegation,* 2800 Scurz Ave., Bronx, NY 10465. Tel: 718-823-0460. Rev. Jose Luis Duenas, O.A.R., Supr. Delegate.

Engaged in missionary work among Spanish-speaking people. Sustains mission personnel in the Archdiocese of New York, Newark and in the Dioceses of Las Cruces and El Paso.

Augustinian Recollect Fathers and Brothers (1944): *Province of St. Augustine,* 29 Ridgeway Ave., West Orange, NJ 07052. Very Rev. Francis E. Peluso, O.A.R., Prov. Supr.

Missionary work among Spanish-speaking people established in colonies throughout a notable part of the U.S. and active in cursillo and retreat work in the Archdiocese of New York.

Blessed Sacrament Fathers And Brothers: *Province of St. Ann,* 5384 Wilson Mills Rd., Cleveland, OH 44143.

Brothers of the Christian Schools: *U.S.A. & Toronto Regional Office of the De La Salle Christian Brothers Conference,* 4351 Garden City Dr., Ste. 200, Landover, MD 20785. Tel: 301-459-9410; Fax: 301-459-8056.

The missionary activities administered by The Christian Brothers Conference include Bethlehem University, West Bank; East Africa; Eritrea/Ethiopia & St. Vincent Island, West Indies. Individual Province Mission responsibilities include San Francisco: Mexico, Tijuana; Toronto: The Grenadines & Nigeria. Christian Brothers also serve as missionaries in the Philippines & Central America.

*** Christian Foundation for Children and Aging:** One Elmwood Ave., Kansas City, KS 66103. Tel: 913-384-6500; 800-875-6564. Robert K. Hentzen, Pres.; Most Rev. Raymond A. Lucker, Member of the Board; Louis Finocchario, Contact Person.

Christian Foundation for Children and Aging (CFCA) is an international Catholic mission organization dedicated to raising mission consciousness here at home and helping the poor at Catholic mission sites abroad. Founded by Catholic lay people in 1981, CFCA's develops support through "sponsorship" — linking a child or aging friend in need with a sponsor in a mutually beneficial relationship. Sponsor assistance helps provide food, medical care, opportunity for education while at the same time permitting the sponsor to get to know the culture and life of their sponsored friend. CFCA currently works with over 40 missionary orders and the local church in 23 developing countries and also sponsors an extensive lay volunteer program.

Claretian Missionaries: *Headquarters of Western Province,* 1119 Westchester Pl., Los Angeles, CA 90019. Very Rev. Ralph Berg C.M.F., Prov. Tel: 213-734-1824; Fax: 213-737-0301.

Headquarters of Eastern Province, 400 N. Euclid Ave., Oak Park, IL 60302. Tel: 708-848-2076. Very Rev. Theodore Cirone, C.M.F., Prov.

Please refer to the Religious Institutes of Men section for activities and representation in the United States.

Publications: monthly magazine, *U.S. Catholic;* extensive line of Pamphlets and Paperback Books;, bimonthly, *Newsletter; Fides-Claretian.*

Claret Center, 5536 S. Everett Ave., Chicago, IL Resources for Counseling and Spiritual Directions. Chicago, IL.

Missions outside the United States entrusted to the Claretians: Guatemala, Cameroons.

Columban Sisters (1922 Ireland): 73 Mapleton St., Brighton, MA 02135. Tel: 617-782-5683; Fax: 617-789-3569. Sr. Ruth Duckert, S.S.C., Reg. Coord., The Missionary Sisters of Saint Columban are also known as the Columban Sisters.

The Columban Sisters are religious women called to bring the good news of Christ to all in need, particularly the poor and the oppressed and those who have not yet had the Gospel proclaimed to them. The congregation strives to respond to the needs of the people by dedication to the work of evangelization through pastoral, educational, medical, and social ministries, and supporting the efforts of the local church where its members are sent. The congregation also endeavors, through programs of mission education and animation, to deepen an awareness of global vision and world justice.

Active in the U.S. in the Archdioceses of Boston, Chicago and Los Angeles, and in the Diocese of Buffalo.

Active outside the U.S. in Ireland, England, Scotland, Hong Kong, Korea, Philippines, Peru, Chile and Pakistan.

Comboni Missionaries of the Heart of Jesus, Inc. (Verona Fathers) Provincial Headquarters: *Comboni Mission Center,* 8108 Beechmont Ave., Cincinnati, OH 45255-3194. Tel: 513-474-4997. Revs. John Converset, M.C.C.J., Prov.; Joseph Bragotti M.C.C.J., Mission Dir., Foreign mission society, both priests and brothers, founded by Bishop Daniel Comboni, Vicar Apostolic of Central Africa.

Active in the Archdioceses of Chicago, Cincinnati, Los Angeles and Newark.

Comboni Missionaries work with local churches in: Africa—Benin, Central African Republic, Egypt, Eritrea, Ethiopia, Ghana, Kenya, Malawi, Mozambique, South Africa, Sudan, Chad, Togo, Uganda, Zambia and Zaire; Asia—Philippines, Macau; Latin America—Brazil, Chile, Colombia, Costa Rica, Ecuador, El Salvador, Guatemala, Mexico and Peru; North America—Canada and the United States.

Training Centers: Africa—Ethiopia, Kenya, Malawi, Mozambique, South Africa, Togo, Egypt, Sudan, Uganda, Zaire; Asia—Philippines; Europe— Austria, England, France, Germany, Italy, Poland, Portugal and Spain; Latin America—Brazil, Colombia, Costa Rica, Ecuador, Mexico and Peru; North America—United States.

Publications: *Comboni Press Network Newsletter; Comboni Press Feature Service;, Comboni Mission Newsletter.*

Comboni Missionary Sisters: *American Headquarters,* 1307 Lakeside Ave., Richmond, VA 23228. Tel: 804-262-8827; Fax: 804-264-2906. Sr. Ruth Ann Bryden, Prov. Supr.

An international congregation of 1,890 sisters founded by Bishop Daniel Comboni in 1872 in Verona, Italy. Engaged in pastoral and catechetical work; education; social services; health services; building Christian communities; training of local church leaders in Africa, Latin America and Middle East.

The American Province recruits and trains sisters for the foreign mission, mission education, fundraising for missions, pastoral ministry among the poor, and day care centers.

Congregation of Alexian Brothers: *Immaculate Conception Province, U.S. Provincial Headquarters,* 600 Alexian Way, Elk Grove Village, IL 60007. Bro. Edward Walsh, Provincial.

Missionary healthcare work in Davao City, Philippines directed by four Alexian Brothers. Please refer to the Religious Institutes of Men section for activities and representation in the United States.

Congregation of Christian Brothers: *Eastern American Province, United States Headquarters,* 21 Pryer Terr., New Rochelle, NY 10804. Bro. J. B. Moffett, C.F.C., Prov.; Bro. C. F. Miller, C.F.C., Mission Dir.

Missionary and educational work in China, Italy, Peru, Sudan, West Indies.

Congregation of the Holy Ghost and of the Immaculate Heart of Mary (1872): 6230 Brush Run Rd., Bethel Park, PA 15102. Tel: 412-831-0302; Fax: 412-831-0970; *Holy Ghost Fathers and Brothers (C.S.Sp.), Eastern Province;* Very Rev. Christopher P. Promis, C.S.Sp., Prov., *Western Province,* (1963), 1700 W. Alabama St., Houston, TX 77098-2808. Tel: 713-522-2882; 713-522-2667; Fax: 713-522-8063. Very Rev. Donald S. Nesti, C.S.Sp., Prov.

Missionary work among the abandoned, including first evangelization, teaching, care of homeless children, and pastoral ministry.

Missionaries serve in 17 (arch)dioceses in the United States; the Archdiocese of San Juan and the Dioceses of Arecibo in Puerto Rico; the Diocese of Ciudad Valles and the Archdiocese of San Luis Potosi in Mexico; and the Diocese of Arusha, Mbulu and Zanzibar in Tanzania. Nairobi in Kenya; Bethlehem in South Africa; and Awasa in Ethiopia. Other establishments in North and South America, Europe, Africa and Australia.

Missionaries of Our Lady of La Salette: *Province of Our Lady of Seven Dolors,* 915 Maple Ave., Hartford, CT 06114-2330. Tel: 860-956-8870. Very Rev. James H. Kuczynski, M.S., Prov. Supr.; Rev. John R. Nuelle, M.S., Procurator, 85 New Park Ave., Hartford, CT 06106-2184.

Active in Archdiocese of Buenos Aires, Dioceses of Santiago del Estero and Cordoba, Argentina; Cochabamba, Bolivia.

Please refer to the Religious Institutes of Men section for activities and representation in the United States.

Congregation of the Missionaries of Our Lady of La Salette: 947 Park St., P.O. Box 2965, Attleboro, MA 02703-0965. Tel: 508-222-7171; Fax: 508-222-6178; *Immaculate Heart of Mary Province La Salette Provincial House;* Very Rev. Dennis Loomis, M.S., Prov. Supr.; Rev. William Slight, M.S., Procurator. Tel: 508-226-7747.

The southern portion of Isabela, Diocese of Ilagan is entrusted to the care of the Province Ina ng Pagasa, originating from the Immaculate Heart of Mary Province of the La Salette Missionaries. The La Salette Mission Seminary was established in 1962 in Santiago, Isabela, Philippines.

Please refer to the Religious Institutes of Men section for representation and statistics in the United States. Also active in the Archdiocese of Montreal and the Dioceses of London, Ontario and Gatineau-Hull, Quebec, Canada; Manila, Imus and Ilagan, Philippines; Bangalore, Trivandrum and Irinjalakuda, Kerala, S. India.

Congregation of the Priests of the Sacred Heart, The: *U.S. Provincialate Offices,* P.O. Box 289, Hales Corners, WI 53130-0289. Tel: 414-425-6910. Very Rev. John Czyzynski, S.C.J., Prov. Supr.

Please refer to the Religious Institutes of Men section for other activities and representation in the United States.

Missionary work in the home and foreign missions; educational activities; welfare work, especially in industrial centers. Home Missions: Lower Brule and Cheyenne Indian Reservations, South Dakota; Black Missions, Diocese of Jackson, Mississippi; Spanish-speaking Apostolate, Dioceses of Brownsville, Galveston-Houston, and Archdiocese of San Antonio.

Foreign Missions: Zaire, Cameroon, Mozambique, South Africa, Brazil, Argentina, Uruguay, Chile, Venezuela, Indonesia and Finland.

Congregation of the Resurrection: *Resurrection Catholic Missions of the South, Inc.,* 2815 Forbes Dr., Montgomery, AL 36110. Tel: 334-263-4221; Fax: 334-263-4999.

The Resurrection Catholic Missions is a seven-building complex that includes a home for handicapped and severely mentally retarded children, an early childhood development facility for preschoolers, a church and elementary school, as well as an outreach program to homebound elders and an addictions counseling/prevention program; *Resurrection Catholic Nursing Home,* Marbury, AL 36051.

Please refer to the Religious Institutes of Men section for activities and representation in the United States. Active also in Australia, Brazil, Bolivia, Bulgaria, Canada, Germany, Jamaica, Mexico and Poland.

Consolata Missionaries (1901): *Provincial Headquarters,* 2301 Hwy. 27, P.O. Box 5550, Somerset, NJ 08875. Tel: 908-297-9191; Fax: 908-940-3121. Rev. Anthony Bellagamba, I.M.C., Reg. Supr.

Legal Title: *Consolata Society for Foreign Missions.*

Serving in 20 countries around the world and in the United States.

Publication: *Consolata Missionaries.*

Consolata Missionary Sisters (1910): 6801 Belmont Ave., N.E., P.O. Box 371, Belmont, MI 49306. Tel: 616-361-2072; Fax: 616-361-2049. Sr. Cecilia Clara Zamboni, M.C., Supr.

The congregation is committed to all types of missionary apostolate, primarily in African and South American countries.

Corpus Christi Carmelites: 516 Broadway, Newport, RI 02840. Sr. Teresa Winefride, O.Carm., Supr.

Sisters work as catechists and social workers in America and abroad; own and/or operate homes for the aged, girls, and sick children; hostels; day nurseries; do ministry work in prisons and hospitals and educational work in kindergartens, primary and secondary schools.

Crosier Fathers and Brothers: *Crosier Missions,* 3510 Vivian Ave., Shoreview, MN 55126-3852. Tel: 612-486-7456; Fax: 612-486-7589. Rev. David E. Gallus, O.S.C., Mission Dir.

Legal Title: *Canons Regular of the Order of the Holy Cross.*

Missionary work among the Asmat tribes of Irian Jaya Indonesia, since 1958.
Publications: quarterly by province, *Crossview*, irregular schedule anthropological study, *An Asmat Sketch Book*.

Daughters of Mary Help of Christians: *St. Philip Apostle Province,* 655 Belmont Ave., Haledon, NJ 07508. Mother Theresa Kelly, F.M.A., Prov.
Legal Title: *Missionary Society of the Salesian Sisters, Inc.*
Missionary work in home and foreign countries; catechetical, educational and training centers; social services; hostels, hospitals, clinics and dispensaries; mission centers, leper colonies and youth centers.
Active in U.S. within the Archdioceses of Newark and New York and in the Dioceses of Miami, Paterson, St. Petersburg, and Birmingham, Alabama.

Eucharistic Missionaries of St. Dominic: 3801 Canal Street, Suite 400, New Orleans, LA 70119. Tel: 504-486-1133; Fax: 504-486-6547. Sr. Dorothy Trosclair, O.P., Pres.
Missionary work and ministry in religious education; diocesan offices; pastoral associates; social service; parish administrators; spirituality- retreat center; home & clinic nursing; hospital chaplaincy; counseling; pastoral care of the sick in homes; literacy ministry to Mayan immigrants.

Franciscan Friars Of The Atonement-Generalate: *St. James Friary,* P.O. Box 5, Garrison, NY 10524-0005. Tel: 914-424-3038; Fax: 914-424-3978.
Mission activities outside of the U.S.: Japan. Also staff parishes in Western Canada, Ontario, England and the United States.

Franciscan Missionaries of Mary, The: *U.S. Provincial House,* 3305 Wallace Ave., Bronx, NY 10467; Fax: 718-547-4607. Sr. Mary Petrosky, Prov.
Founded in India in 1877, for the work of evangelization and development in non-Christian and de-Christianized countries. Active mission apostolate is centered in daily adoration of the Blessed Sacrament exposed.
This international congregation serves 856 missions in 56 provinces.
Missionary work of evangelization and development, catechetics, social work, nursing, community development programs, educational and public health programs, pastoral activity and various forms of ministry and service.

Franciscan Missionary Sisters for Africa: *American Headquarters Center for Promotion and Formation,* 172 Foster St., Box 35095, Brighton, MA 02135. Sr. Mary Jordan, O.S.F., Supr. Gen.
Missions in Ethiopia, Kenya, Uganda, South Africa, Zambia and Zimbabwe.
Publication: *The Daystar.*

Franciscan Mission Association: *Franciscan Mission House,* Washington Ave., Rensselaer, NY 12144. Tel: 518-465-0062; Fax: 518-465-3673. Bro. James Amrhein, O.F.M.Conv., Dir.
The American branch of the Franciscan Mission Crusade founded in 1924, approved by Pope Pius XI to further the work of the Conventual Franciscan Missionary Apostolate. The purpose is to aid the Mission of the Order in every possible way. The revenues of the Association accrue from the annual and perpetual enrollments in the Association, bequests, other free-will offerings and donations, membership in monthly mission club appeal.

Franciscan Mission Association (1953): *Province of Our Lady of Consolation, Franciscan Missions,* 322 West St., Carey, OH 43316. Tel: 419-396-6455. Bro. Bryan Hoban O.F.M.Conv., Dir.
The purpose of the association is to give financial and other material aid to the missionaries of Africa: the Dioceses of Ndola and Solwezi, Zambia; missionaries in the dioceses of Olancho, Tegucigalpa and Comayagua in Honduras and San Jose in Costa Rica; and missionaries of the Southwestern United States. Both living and deceased may be enrolled as members. Members of the laity have an active part in promoting the growth of the association as outlined in Vatican II.

Franciscan Mission Association, Inc.: *Province of St. Anthony of Padua,* 66 School St., Granby, MA 01033. Tel: 413-467-9196; Fax: 413-467-7944. Rev. Placid Kaczorek, O.F.M.Conv., Dir.
Founded to support the domestic and foreign missions of the Conventual Franciscans of St. Anthony Province.

Franciscan Sisters of Allegany: *St. Elizabeth Motherhouse,* Allegany, NY 14706. Sr. Margaret Mary Kimmins, O.S.F., Gen. Minister; Sr. Marie Dolores Gionta, O.S.F., Mission Society Dir.
Sisters serve in areas of education; health-care; pastoral ministry; migrant ministry in the U.S; missionary work in the archdiocese of Kingston and dioceses of Montego Bay, Mandeville, Jamaica; the archdioceses of Brazilia and Goiania, and LaPaz; dioceses of Anapolis, Ipameri, Jatai, Ruy Barbosa, Goias, Cristalandia, Brazil and Pando, Bolivia.
Congregation 446; foreign missions 97.
Publication: *Zeal.*

Franciscan Sisters, Daughters of the Sacred Hearts of Jesus and Mary: *Province of St. Clara,* P.O. Box 667, Wheaton, IL 60189-0667. Tel: 630-462-7422; Fax: 630-462-7148. Sr. Mary Ellen McAleese, O.S.F., Prov. Dir.
Active in U.S.-institutional and home health care; housing; education; pastoral ministry; care of elderly; wellness; long-term care; social services; spiritual direction and retreats in archdioceses of Milwaukee, St. Louis, Dubuque, Denver and Chicago; in dioceses of Joliet, Green Bay, LaCrosse, Springfield-Cape Girardeau and Gary. Outside the U.S.: Brazil, Nigeria.

Franciscan Sisters of Little Falls, MN: *Motherhouse,* Little Falls, MN 56345. Tel: 320-632-2981. Sr. Rose Margaret Schneider, Pres.
Serving in Catholic and non-sectarian hospitals; Catholic and non- sectarian nursing homes; group homes; apartments for the elderly; home health nursing; public health nursing; Catholic high schools; Catholic elementary schools; special education; Spirituality Farm, Native Americans; community colleges; state colleges and universities; religious education; parish ministry; liturgical music ministry; music center; holistic growth center; health and recreation center; retreat ministry; counseling/spiritual direction; social service; ministry to the poor; ministry to the migrants; clinics; consultant for healthcare & related organizations; art therapist, computer programmer; Pastoral ministry; Ministry to Native Americans; Education, health, social services in the Dioceses of Same, Tanzania, Africa; Kumbo, Cameroon, Africa; Quito, and Ecuador, S.A.

Franciscan Sisters of the Poor: *Congregational Office,* 133 Remsen St., Brooklyn, NY 11201. Tel: 718-643-1919; Fax: 718-643-9710. Sr. Jeanne M. Glisky, S.F.P., Pres.
Sisters serve in healing ministry; health care; social welfare; pastoral ministry in the U.S.; pastoral ministry and health care in the Dioceses of Rome, Padua and Messina in Italy. Mission ministry is represented in the Archdiocese of Goiania and in the Dioceses of Jatai and Ipameri in Brazil and in Kaolack and Dakar in Senegal, West Africa.
Number in Congregation 197; Mission ministry 20.

Glenmary Home Missioners, The (1939): *National Headquarters,* P.O. Box 465618, Cincinnati, OH 45246-5618. Rev. Jerry Dorn, Pres.
Glenmary is a society of secular priests and lay brothers, and the only home mission society dedicated exclusively to establishing the Catholic Church in small towns and rural areas of the United States. Statistics show that there are more than 180 counties that do not have a resident priest. The Glenmary society employs every available technique in organizing viable and effective Catholic parishes in these areas. Priests, Brothers and Lay associates are engaged in radio and television work, youth programs, systematic home visits, and a wide variety of projects designed to achieve better social conditions. When it is practical, these programs are conducted ecumenically; *Glenmary Research Center,* 235 E. Ponce de Leon Ave., Decatur, GA 30030. Sr. Mary Priniski, O.P., Dir., *Glenmary Religious Education Center,* 1312 Fifth Ave., N., Nashville, TN 37208. Rev. Dennis Holly, Dir.
Please refer to the Religious Institutes of Men section for activities and representation in the United States.
Publication: *The Glenmary Challenge.*

Glenmary Home Mission Sisters of America (1941): *Glenmary Sisters,* P.O. Box 22264, Owensboro, KY 42302-2264; Fax: 502-686-8759. Sr. Christine Beckett, Pres.
Glenmary is a community of women religious of diocesan right and the only home mission community dedicated to bringing mission presence and activity to the rural, small town areas of the United States. The sisters live and work among the poor, the sick, the oppressed and unchurched in Appalachia and the South in areas where less than 5% of the total population is Catholic. When possible the Sisters work in collaboration with the Glenmary Priests and Brothers and the Glenmary Co-Missioners. The Glenmary Sisters believe in a holistic approach to mission - the caring of the whole person - through their ministries of co-creating with local people a Catholic Christian faith community, ecumenism, evangelization, radio programs, pastoral outreach, religious education, home health, home visitations, and a wide variety of social services for the very poor.
Please refer to the Religious Institutes of Women section for activities in the United States.
Publication: *Kinship.*

Institute of Charity (Rosminian Fathers): *Rosmini House,* 2327 W. Heading Ave., Peoria, IL 61604.
Active in the Dioceses of Peoria, St. Petersburg and Venice.
Missions and missionary work in Tanga, Tanzania; New Zealand; Venezuela; and Kerela, India.

Jesuit Volunteers: International: P.O. Box 25478, Washington, DC 20007. Tel: 202-687-1132; Fax: 202-687-5082. Rev. Vincent DeCola, S.J., Dir.
A Christian service organization offering young college educated lay men and women an opportunity to volunteer in a developing country in collaboration with Jesuits. Volunteers serve for two years without returning to the U.S.

Mariannhill, Congregation of Missionaries of (1882): 23715 Ann Arbor Tr., Dearborn Hts., MI 48127. Rev. Aloysius Blonigen, C.M.M., Provincial Supr.
The American-Canadian province recruits and trains young men as priests and lay brothers for foreign missions, secures funds for the foreign missions, and does a limited amount of pastoral work at home.
Active in the Archdiocese of Detroit.
Outside the U.S.: South Africa, Zimbabwe, Papua New Guinea, Zambia, Brazil, Germany, Switzerland, Spain, Austria, Netherlands and Poland.
Publication: *Leaves.*
Worldwide membership:: Bishops 2; Priests 200; Brothers 111; Students Professed 57; Total Members 370.

Marist Missionary Sisters: *North American Provincial Office,* 349 Grove St., Waltham, MA 02154. Tel: 781-893-0149; Fax: 781-894-7610. Sr. Rosalie Warpeha, S.M.S.M., Prov.; Sr. Jeanette Misuira, S.M.S.M., Mission Promotor; Sr. Claire Rheaume, S.M.S.M., Vocation Directress.
We were founded in France in 1845 for mission in the South Pacific. Today, we are an International Missionary Congregation of 650 sisters (in seven provinces), serving the people of God in 28 countries around the world. The American Province has 126 sisters working in Massachusetts, Tennessee, Illinois, Iowa, Texas, Florida, Alaska, Arkansas, California, West Virginia, Louisiana, New York and Jamaica, W.I. Our mission is to bring the good news of God's love through spiritual and corporal works of mercy; catechetical, medical, educational and social services; pastoral ministry; formation of laity for leadership and a great concern for the poorest and most neglected. We work by preference among people of different cultures and languages, to bring about greater understanding, dignity and mutual respect.
Our formation is international with a French-speaking novitiate in New Caledonia, an English-speaking novitiate in New Zealand and a Spanish- speaking novitiate in Peru.
Province headquarters are in the United States, Italy, Australia, New Zealand, Peru, France and New Caledonia.
Legal Title: *Missionary Sisters of the Society of Mary, Inc.*
Please refer to the Religious Institutes of Women section for activities and representation in the United States.

Maryknoll Sisters of St. Dominic, Inc.: Maryknoll, NY 10545-0311. Sr. Helen O'Sullivan, M.M., Community Pres.; Sr. Joan Mury, M.M., Gen. Sec.
A Pontifical Institute under the jurisdiction of the Congregation for the Institutes of Consecrated Life. The purpose of the Maryknoll Sisters Congregation is to participate in the mission presence and activity of the universal Church so that God's reign of peace, justice and love may be proclaimed and witnessed to throughout the world. The Maryknoll Sisters embrace a plurality of ministries while giving a clear sign of Christian community; faith-sharing; self-gift in service through pastoral and catechetical work; basic ecclesial communities; education; social services; medical and health promotion work; services through hostels; services to refugees; and ministries that promote human rights, social justice and the dignity and equality of women.
Please refer to the Religious Institutes of Women section for activities in the United States.
Active in Bangladesh, Bolivia, Brazil, Cambodia, Central Pacific, Chile, Ecuador, El Salvador, Guatemala, Hong Kong, Indonesia, Japan, Kenya, Korea, Macau, Mexico, Nepal, Namibia, Nicaragua, Panama, Peru, Philippines, Sudan, Taiwan, Tanzania, Thailand, USA and Zimbabwe.

Medical Missionaries of Mary: *MMM Regional Center,* 563 Minneford Ave., City Island, NY 10464-1118. Tel: 718-885-0945; Fax: 718-885-0010. Sr. Philomena Sheerin, M.M.M., Supr. Gen.; Sr. Joanne Bierl, M.M.M., Regional Supr.
Missionary work in hospitals, clinics and leprosy treatment; public health and pastoral ministry centers in Africa, South America and Clinchco, VA.

Please refer to the Religious Institutes of Women section for activities and representation in the United States. Active also in Angola, Nigeria, Uganda, Tanzania, Liberia, Kenya, Malawi, Ethiopia, England, Ireland and Brazil.
Publication: quarterly, *The Mini MMM.*

Medical Mission Sisters: *North American Headquarters,* 8400 Pine Rd., Philadelphia, PA 19111; Fax: 215-342-3948. Sr. Elizabeth Koonthanam, M.M.S., Society Coord.; Sr. Maria Horning, M.M.S., North American Sector Coord.; Monica M. McGinley, Pub. Rels. Dir.
Legal Title: *Society of Catholic Medical Missionaries, Inc., Society of Catholic Medical Missionaries Generalate, Inc.,* (effective 1991).
Medical Mission Sisters have the special call in the Church of "being a healing presence at the heart of a wounded world." Members commit themselves "to promote healing and wholeness in all aspects of life" in the spirit of Jesus. They share life with those who are sick and have been made poor, trying to help them to live fully as human beings. Medical Mission Sisters' healing presence today involves a full range of preventitive, curative and promotive health services; health training programs; and development and social justice activities in Ghana, Uganda, Kenya, Ethiopia, Malawi, Congo, Pakistan, India, Belgium, Venezuela, Brazil, Peru, Indonesia, Philippines, Italy, Holland, Germany, England, and Mexico.
Medical Mission Houses in the United States are listed under the Religious Institutes of Women section.
Publication: *Medical Mission Sisters News.*

Mill Hill Missionaries: *St. Joseph's Missionary Society,* 222 W. Hartsdale Ave., Hartsdale, NY 10530. Tel: 914-682-0645; Fax: 914-682-0862. Very Rev. Terence J. Lee, M.H.M., Reg. Rep.; Very Rev. Theo M. Feldbrugge, M.H.M., Admin. & Reg. Bursar, Los Angeles.
An international society of priests and brothers, founded in 1866, devoted entirely to the missionary needs of the Church.
Active in the U.S., in the Archdioceses of New York, Los Angeles, and Chicago, and the Dioceses of Fall River, Metuchen, Scranton and Winona.
Active outside the United States. Canada: Diocese of Kingston, ONT. Cameroon: the Archdiocese of Bamenda and the Dioceses of Buea, Kumbo and Ngoundere. Congo: Diocese of Basankusu. Egypt: Diocese of Iskanderiya. Kenya: Archdioceses of Kisumu and Nairobi, and the Dioceses of Bungoma, Garissa, Homa-Bay, Kakamega, Kericho, Kisii, Nakuru, and Ngong. Sudan: Archdiocese of Khartoum, and the Dioceses of Malakal and Tombura-Yambio. Uganda: Archdiocese of Kampala, and the Dioceses of Jinja, Soroti, and Tororo. Zaire: Diocese of Basankusu. South Africa: Diocese of Port Elizabeth. China: Diocese of Hong Kong. India: Archdioceses of Hyderabad, Bangalore, and the Dioceses of Jamma-Srinagar and Varanasi. Indonesia: Diocese of Irian Jaya. Pakistan: Dioceses of Islamabad-Rawalpindi and Hyderabad. Malaysia: Archdiocese of Kuching, and the Dioceses of Keningau, Kota Kinabalu, Miri, and Sibu. Philippines: Archdioceses of Manila and Jaro, and the Dioceses of San Jose and Infanta. Australia: Diocese of Geraldton. New Zealand: Dioceses of Auckland and Hamilton. Bolivia: Archdiocese of Cochabamba. Brazil: Dioceses of Governador Valadares and Itaquai. Ecuador: Archdiocese of of Guayaquil. Netherlands Antilles: Diocese of Willemstad. Peru: Diocese of Chimbote.

Mission Helpers of the Sacred Heart: 1001 W. Joppa Rd., Baltimore, MD 21204-3787. Tel: 410-823-8585; Fax: 410-825-6355. Sr. Catharine Dagas, M.H.S.H., Pres.
A Pontifical, missionary congregation with principal work of evangelization and catechesis; adult religious education; instruction of youth and children; D.R.E. programs; pastoral ministers; pastoral associates; pastoral social ministers; special ministers of the Eucharist; ministry in homes and institutions; ministry to the elderly and infirm; catechesis of blind, deaf, retarded; campus ministry; hospital ministry; Hispanic pastoral ministry to adults and youth; spiritual direction and retreat work.
Please refer to the Religious Institutes of Women for activities and representation in the United States. Activities also in the Archdioceses of Caracas, Venezuela, and San Juan.
Publication: quarterly magazine, *The Mission Helper.*

Mission International, Inc.: 2301 Hwy. 27, Somerset, NJ 08873. Tel: 732-297-9191; Fax: 732-940-3121. Rev. Anthony Bellagamba, Chm.

Missionaries of Africa M.Afr.: *U.S. Province of North America Headquarters,* 1624 21st St., N.W., Washington, DC 20009-1055; Fax: 202-332-8640. Rev. William Moroney, M.Afr., Asst. Prov.
International and interracial missionary society of priests and brothers working in teams almost exclusively in Africa.
Active in the Archdioceses of Chicago and Washington and the Diocese of St. Petersburg.
Training centers and mission promotion centers in Brazil, Canada, Belgium, France, Germany, Great Britain, Holland, India, Ireland, Italy, Mexico, Philippines, Poland, Spain and Switzerland.
Missionary work in Algeria, Burundi, Chad, Ethiopia, Ghana, Kenya, Malawi, Mali, Mozambique, Nigeria, Rwanda, Senegal, Sudan, Tanzania, Tunisia, Uganda, Burkina Faso, Zaire, Zambia, South Africa, Ivory Coast, and Niger. Totaling 99 dioceses and archdioceses in Africa; Jerusalem.
Publication: newsletter, *Missionaries of Africa Report.*

Missionaries of the Holy Apostles: 24 Prospect Hill Rd., Cromwell, CT 06416. Tel: 860-632-3039; Fax: 860-632-3035. Very Rev. Benedict Klucinec, M.S.A., Prov. Animator; Rev. Martin Rooney, M.S.A., Sec. to the Prov.
Apostolic works consist in the promotion and training of adults for Christian leadership and for the diocesan or religious priesthood.
Please refer to the Religious Institutes of Men section for activities and representation in the United States. Activites also in Brazil, Venezuela, Colombia, Canada, and Peru.

Missionary Benedictine Sisters: *Provincial Motherhouse & Novitiate-Immaculata Convent,* 300 N. 18th St., Norfolk, NE 68701. Tel: 402-371-3438; Fax: 402-379-2877. Sr. M. Agnes Salber, O.S.B., Prioress.
Missionary work in elementary schools; catechetical programs; pastoral ministry; nursing homes; hospitals in the Archdiocese of Omaha and Diocese of New Ulm, Minnesota; Indian Mission, Northeast Nebraska; Hispanic ministry.
Missionary work outside the U.S. the Philippine Islands, Korea, Brazil, Argentina, Australia, China, India, Tanzania, Namibia, Kenya, Angola, South Africa, Portugal, Germany, Italy, Spain, Switzerland, Bulgaria and Uganda.

Missionary Servants of the Most Blessed Trinity: *Motherhouse, Novitiate and Generalate,* 3501 Solly Ave., Philadelphia, PA 19136; Fax: 215-335-7559. Sr. Siena Marie Wahl, M.S.B.T., Gen. Custodian.
The congregation's mission is the preservation of the faith. This involves nourishing the faithlife of those of the Roman Catholic tradition, cooperating in ecumenical endeavors, strengthening life-giving faith among all people, evangelization, actively promoting human development and social justice. The special apostolic intent is to advance and support the ministry of the laity in the mission of the Church, accomplished through the ministries of education, social work and health care on parish and diocesan levels.
Please refer to the Religious Institutes of Women section for activities and representation in the United States. Active also in the Archdiocese of San Juan and the Dioceses of Ponce, Caguas and Mayaguez in Puerto Rico as well as the Dioceses of Apatzingan and Texcoco in Mexico.

Missionary Servants of the Most Holy Trinity (Trinity Missions): 1215 N. Scott St., Arlington, VA 22209-3097. Tel: 703-276-8646; Fax: 703-522-2656. Rev. Domingo Rodriguez, S.T., Gen. Custodian; Bro. Hilary Mettes, S.T., Sec. Gen.; Rev. Randall Woods, S.T., Mission Procurator, P.O. Box 7130, Silver Spring, MD 20907-7130.
A clerical congregation of Pontifical Right founded for the preservation of the faith and missionary work wherever the Church directs. The major fields are the missionary areas of the southern United States and the Spanish-speaking people in the United States, Puerto Rico, Costa Rica and Mexico. The principal work is the development of Catholic lay leaders. There is also training for the missionary priesthood and brotherhood of the congregation.
Archdioceses of Boston, Milwaukee, Indianapolis, Los Angeles, Military Services-USA, Mobile, Newark, New Orleans, Philadelphia, St. Paul-Minneapolis, Washington DC, and San Juan and the Dioceses of Arlington, Biloxi, Boise, Birmingham, Cleveland, Jackson, Norwich, Ponce, PR, Orange, Paterson, San Bernardino, San Diego, Savannah, and Tucson. Also in Mexico, Columbia, and Costa Rica.
Publication: *Trinity Missions.*

Missionary Sisters of Our Lady of Africa: *American Headquarters,* 47 W. Spring St., Winooski, VT 05404. Sr. Nora Indelicato, Supr.
Missionary activities in Africa and Yemen: catechetical, pastoral ministry, social work, education and health programs, and the founding and forming of African Religious Congregations.

Missionary Sisters of St. Columban are also know as the Columban Sisters - please see entry under Columban Sisters for details.

Missionary Sisters of St. Peter Claver (1894): *American Headquarters,* P.O. Box 401, 667 Woods Mill Rd., S. Chesterfield, MO 63006. Tel: 314-434-8084. Sr. Mary Irene Brahmakulath.
The congregation is of Pontifical Jurisdiction, fostering interest in and obtaining funds and requisites for the missions. Apostolate of the press in Africa.
Legal Title: *The Sodality of St. Peter Claver for the African Missions.*
Publications: monthly magazine, *Echo from Africa,* annual, *Claver Almanac.*

Missionary Sisters of Our Lady of the Holy Rosary: *American Regional House and Novitiate,* 205 Cricket Ave., Ardmore, PA 19003. Tel: 610-896-1786. Sr. Monica Devine, Supr. Gen.; Sr. Paula Molloy, M.S.H.R., American Reg. Rep.
Founded for the evangelization of people in Africa and Latin America through educational, medical, social, pastoral and catechetical work.
Active in the U.S. in the Archdiocese of Philadelphia.
Active outside the U.S. in England, Ireland, Scotland, Nigeria, Sierra Leone, Cameroon, Ethiopia, Kenya, South Africa, Zambia, Ghana, Mexico and Brazil.

Missionary Sisters of the Immaculate Conception of the Mother of God: *Generalate,* 48 Garden Ave., West Paterson, NJ 07424; Fax: 973-279-2991. Sr. Luci Cesar Fontenele, S.M.I.C., Coord. Gen.
Missionary work in homes for the aged, catechetical and social service centers, schools, dispensaries and hospitals.
Active in the U.S. in the Archdiocese of Newark and the Dioceses of Austin, Galveston-Houston, Paterson, Portland, San Antonio and San Bernardino.
Active outside the U.S. in Brazil, Germany, Namibia, Philippines and Taiwan.

Missionary Sisters of the Immaculate Heart of Mary (1919): 238 E. 15th St., New York, NY 10003. Tel: 212-677-2959. Sr. Alene Grothues, Dist. Supr.
Please refer to the Religious Institutes of Women section for further details.

Missionary Sisters Servants of the Holy Spirit (1901): Techny, IL 60082-6026; Fax: 847-272-0113. Sr. Priscilla Burke, Prov. Supr.; Sr. Dolores Marie Kuhl, Supr.
Home and foreign missions including teaching, nursing and social work.
Please refer to the Religious Institutes of Women section for activities and representation in the United States. Also active in the Philippine Islands, New Guinea, China, Indonesia, Japan, India, Africa, Australia, Europe, South America, Taiwan, Mexico, Cuba and Korea.
Publication: *SSpS Mission.*

OPAM-America (1984): *National Office,* 2301 Hwy. 27, P.O. Box 5657, Somerset, NJ 08875-5657. Tel: 908-297-9090; Fax: 908-297-6799. Rev. John Bertello, I.M.C., Natl. Dir.
Charitable and educational organization established for the promotion of world literacy. It seeks to increase public awareness of the problem of illiteracy and its consequences, and encourage the American people to help eliminate it. The focus of the missionary and educational version of OPAM is to promote community development.

Operation Help, Inc.: P.O. Box 134, Hartly, DE 19953. Tel: 302-492-8985; Fax: 302-492-8360. Rev. Patrick Shaules, S.J., Pres.; Marcinda Haedge, Admin., For Contributions: P.O. Box 566, Wilmington, DE 19899.
Operation Help, Inc., is an independently incorporated non-profit organization dedicated to helping Catholic priests and sisters bring spiritual and material salvation to the destitute poor. It offers advice and funding and places a special emphasis on Asian and African mission areas.

Our Lady of Victory Missionary Sisters: Victory-Noll, Box 109, Huntington, IN 46750. Tel: 219-356-0628. Sr. Lucy Regalado, O.L.V.M., Pres.; Sr. Marjorie Curran, O.L.V.M., Gen. Sec.
Legal Title: *Our Lady of Victory Missionary Sisters, Inc.*
A Marian congregation proclaiming the Gospel in a personal, non-institutional way through pastoral ministry, religious education, social service and health- care programs in favor of the poor and oppressed.
Please refer to the Religious Institutes of Women section for activities and representation in the United States. Active also in foreign missions in Oruro, Bolivia.

Parish Visitors of Mary Immaculate: *Motherhouse Generalate and Novitiate-Marycrest,* P.O. Box 658, Monroe, NY 10950-0658. Tel: 914-783-2251. Sr. Carole Marie Troskowski, Gen. Supr.; Sr. Frances Walter, Gen. Sec.
Founded for the missionary visitation of families and individuals in the parish and for religious instruction of children and adults; assists parish priests in their ministry of evangelization, catechetical programs, spiritual surveys, census, informal visitation, follow-up religious counseling, religious social services, training laity.

Please refer to the Religious Institutes of Women section for activities and representation in the United States and overseas.
Publication: *The Parish Visitor.*

Passionist Sisters (1924): *Sisters of the Cross and Passion American Provincialate,* Holy Family Convent, One Wright Lane, North Kingstown, RI 02852. Sr. Ellen Downes, C.P., Prov. Supr.
Diversified apostolic works according to the needs of the Church; catechetical, pastoral and social work; educational functions; retreats; missionary in the United States and foreign countries Active also in Africa, Botswana, Europe, England, Ireland and Scotland, Latin America, Argentina, Chile, Peru, West Indies, Jamica and Papua New Guinea.
Please refer to the Religious Institutes of Women section for activities and representation in the United States.

Pontifical Institute for Foreign Missions, P.I.M.E., Inc.: *U.S. Region,* 17330 Quincy Ave., Detroit, MI 48221. Tel: 313-342-4066; Fax: 313-342-6816. Very Rev. Bruno Piccolo P.I.M.E., Prov. Supr.
Legal Title: *Pontifical Institute for Foreign Missions (P.I.M.E.), Inc.*
American Province recruits and trains priests and brothers for foreign missionary work; secures funds for foreign mission work and mission education activities.
Active in the Archdioceses of Detroit and the Dioceses of Columbus, Paterson and Palm Beach.
Outside the U.S. Brazil, Burma, Hong Kong, India, Japan, Bangladesh, Guinea-Bissau, Cameroon, Canada, Ivory Coast, Mexico, Papua New Guinea, Taiwan, Philippines, and Thailand.
Publication: national magazine, *PIME World.*

St. Joseph's Society of the Sacred Heart (Josephites): *Headquarters,* 1130 North Calvert St., Baltimore, MD 21202. Tel: 410-727-3386; Fax: 410-385-2231. Very Rev. Robert M. Kearns, S.S.J., Supr. Gen.. An organization of priests and brothers doing missionary work in the African American community of the United States.
Publication: *The Josephite Harvest.*

St. Patrick's Missionary Society: 70 Edgewater Rd., Cliffside Park, NJ 07010; Fax: 201-943-2946. Rev. James Barry, U.S. Supr.; Rev. Karl Langsdorf, Supr., Chicago, IL; Rev. Jeremiah Kiely, Supr., Saratoga, CA; Rev. James Barry, Supr., Cliffside Park, NJ.
A society of secular priests devoted entirely to the missionary needs of the Church.
Activities in the Archdioceses of Newark, Chicago, New Orleans, San Francisco and the Dioceses of San Jose, Paterson and Palm Beach. Outside the U.S. in Nigeria— Archdiocese of Lagos, Dioceses of Abakaliki, Calabar, Abuja, Minna, Ogoja, Warri, Port Harcourt and Missio Sui Juris Bomadi. Kenya— Archdiocese of Nairobi, Dioceses of Eldoret, Kitui, Lodwar and Nakuru. Sudan— Diocese of Torit. Malawi—Dioceses of Lilongwe, Chikwawa, Zomba and Mzuzu. Zambia—Archdiocese of Lusaka, Diocese of Chipata. Brazil—Archdioceses of Sao Paulo, Dioceses of Campo Limpo, Osasco, Santo Amaro, Sao Miguel Paulista and Campina Grande. Grenada—Diocese of St. George's. South Africa—Dioceses of Tzaneen and Witbank. Zimbabwe—Archdiocese of Harare and Diocese of Mutare. Cameroon—Archdiocese of Bamenda.
Publication: *Africa, St. Patrick's Mission.*

Salesian Missions: 2 Lefevre Ln., New Rochelle, NY 10801. Tel: 914-633-8344.
The Salesians were founded to help bring the Faith to all people, and contribute to their social and economic development through education, especially in trade and agricultural schools. The purpose of the society is the recruitment and preparation of vocations for the missions and the education of the American public on the needs of other people through lectures, mass media, direct mail and the magazine, *Salesian.* It is also the purpose of the society to educate the American public on the unique system of education developed by the society's founder, St. John Bosco, as well as to spread knowledge of his life and accomplishments. Funds are raised to implement the religious, educational and technical assistance projects of the society.
Please refer to the Religious Institutes of Men section for activities and representation in the United States. Represented in 120 countries throughout the world.
Publication: *Salesian.*

School Sisters of Notre Dame: *Milwaukee Province,* 13105 Watertown Plank Rd., Elm Grove, WI 53122-2291; Fax: 414-782-9850; Fax: 414-782-5725. Sr. Marilyn Kesler, Prov. Leader.
Please refer to the Religious Institutes of Women section I.D.# [2970] for provinces, activities and representations in the United States and overseas.

Sisters of the Blessed Sacrament for Indians and Colored People (1891): *St. Mary Generalate,* Bensalem, PA 19020-8502; Fax: 215-344-8174. Sr. Monica Loughlin, Pres.
Missionary work in the educational, catechetical and social services among Black and Native Americans as well as Haitians in the U.S. and Haiti.
Please refer to the Religious Institutes of Women section for activities and representation in the United States.
Publications: *Mission; The Peacemaker.*

Society of African Missions: *American Province,* 23 Bliss Ave., Tenafly, NJ 07670. Tel: 201-567-0450; Fax: 201-541-1280. Very Rev. Douglas B. Gilbert S.M.A., Prov.
Please refer to the Religious Institutes of Men section for activities and representation in the United States.
Active also in West Africa: Liberia—Diocese of Cape Palmas, Archdiocese of Monrovia, Diocese of Gbarnga; Ivory Coast—Archdiocese of Abidjan; Dioceses of Abengourou, Bondoukou, Bouake, Daloa, Gagnoa, Katiola, Grand-Bassam, Korhogo, Man, San Pedro and Yopougon; Ghana—Archdiocese of Cape Coast; Dioceses of Accra, Obvasi, Keta-Ho, Kumasi, Sekondi-Takoradi and Sunyani; Togo—Archdiocese of Lome; Dioceses of Atakpame and Sokode; Benin—Archdiocese of Cotonou; Dioceses of Abomey, Natitingou, Parakou and Porto-Novo; Nigeria—Archdioceses of Kaduna and Lagos; Dioceses of Benin City, Ibadan, Ijebu-Ode, Ilorin, Jos, Makurdi, Ondo and Warri; Niger—Diocese of Niamey; Cameroon—Archdiocese of Yaounde; Central African Republic—Archdiocese of Bangui; Dioceses of Bambari and Berberati. Central Africa: Zaire—Diocese of Kikwit. East Africa: Zambia—Diocese of Ndola. Egypt—Vicarate Apostolic of Alexandria. Tanzania—Dioceses of Geita and Shinyanga. Kenya—Archdiocese of Nairobi. Argentina—Archdiocese of Cordoba. Australia—Archdiocese of Perth. South Africa—Diocese of Rustenburg. Philippines—Archdiocese of Manila. South India: Tamil-Nadu. Poland—Warsaw.

Society of Mary: *Cincinnati Province, Marianist Provincialate,* 4435 E. Patterson Rd., Dayton, OH 45430-1095. Tel: 937-429-0794; Fax: 937-429-3195. Bro. Joseph H. Kamis, S.M., Prov.
Missionary work in the following territories: Archdiocese of Nairobi, Kenya and the Dioceses of Mzuzu, Malawi, Lusaka, Zambia, Africa; Diocese of Yokohama, Japan.

Society of Mary: *St. Louis Province,* P.O. Box 23130, St. Louis, MO 63156. Tel: 314-367-0390; Fax: 314-361-3131. Rev. Timothy Dwyer S.M., Prov.
Educational, parish and development work in the following territories: Archdioceses of Arequipa and Trujillo, Peru; Archdiocese of Ranchi, Bangalore in India; Diocese of Muzaffarpur, India; Dioceses of Coatzacoalcos and Queretaro, Mexico; Diocese of Dhaka, Bangladesh.

Society of Mary: *Province of the Pacific (Marianists),* P.O. Box 1775, Cupertino, CA 95015-1775; Fax: 408-253-5280. Very Rev. Timothy Eden, S.M., Prov.
Educational, social and parish work in the following mission territories: Mokpo, Inchon, and Seoul, South Korea; Archdioceses of Seoul and Kwangju, South Korea; Dioceses of Inchon and Suwon, South Korea.

Society of Mary: *New York Province,* 4301 Roland Ave., Baltimore, MD 21210-2793. Bro. Stephen Glodek, S.M., Prov.
Educational, social and parish work in the following mission territories: Archdiocese of San Juan and Diocese of Ponce, Puerto Rico. Also in Africa in Karonga, Malawi; Mzuzu, Malawi; Mombasa, Kenya; Nairobi, Kenya; and Lusaka, Zambia.

Society of St. Edmund: *Edmundite Generalate,* 270 Winooski Park, Colchester, VT 05439. Tel: 802-654-3400; Fax: 802-654-3409. Very Rev. Joseph L. Hart, S.S.E., Supr. Gen.
Legal Title: *Society of St. Edmund, Inc.*
Major missionary endeavors in the United States are in Selma, Alabama and surrounding areas, and in the inner city of New Orleans (LA).
See the Foreign Mission section for the list of priests serving abroad.
Publications: *Edmundite Missions.*

Society of the Precious Blood: *Cincinnati Province,* 431 E. Second St., Dayton, OH 45402; Fax: 513-228-6878. Very Rev. Kenneth F. Pleiman, C.PP.S., Prov. Dir.; Rev. James F. McCabe, C.PP.S., Prov. Sec.; Bro. Joseph J. Fisher, C.PP.S., Mission Procurator.
Mission activities outside the U.S. in Chile, Peru, South America, Guatemala, Central America; missions in La Tinta, Tucuru, Santiago, Purranque, Valdivia, LaOroya, Lima, Guatemala City.
Priests and brothers in foreign missions 38.
Publication: *C.PP.S. Today,* c/o Sorrowful Mother Shrine, 4106 St. Rt. 269, Bellevue, OH 44811. Rev. James F. McCabe, C.PP.S., Editor.

Sons of Mary Missionary Society (1954): 567 Salem End Rd., Framingham, MA 01702. Bro. Kevin Courtney, Major Coord.; Revs. John Coss, Financial Coord.; Henry Cicale, Councilor.
Dedicated to the ministry of healing: medical, catechetical and social apostolates in the home and foreign missions.
Legal Title: *Sons of Mary, Health of the Sick, Inc.*

Third Order Regular of St. Francis: *Province of the Most Sacred Heart of Jesus, Franciscan T.O.R. Missions,* P.O. Box 188, Loretto, PA 15940. Tel: 814-472-3348. Bro. Mark McBride, T.O.R., Prov. Dir. of Foreign Missions; Very Rev. Edmund Carroll, T.O.R., Minister Prov. Tel: 412-781-1232.
Secures missionaries and material aid to missions.
Active in the Archdioceses of Manaus and Sao Paulo; the Prelacy of Borba, Brazil; the Diocese of Bhagalpur, Bihar, India; and Diocese of Vice Province of Saint Joseph, Republic of South Africa.

Xaverian Missionary Fathers: *Provincial Headquarters,* 12 Helene Ct., Wayne, NJ 07470-2813. Tel: 973-942-2975; Fax: 973-942-5012. Very Rev. Francis Signorelli, S.X.
A religious society of priests and brothers dedicated exclusively to foreign mission work and the training of candidates for missionary life Active in Brazil, Zaire, Burundi, Chad, Cameroon, Bangladesh, Indonesia, Japan, Mexico, Sierra Leone, Colombia, Philippines, Taiwan, Italy, Spain and Great Britain.
Please refer to the Religious Institutes of Men section for activities and representation in the United States.
Publication: *Xaverian Missions Newsletter.*

Pontifical Missionary Societies.

A. The Pontifical Society for the Propagation of the Faith (1822): *National Office,* 366 Fifth Ave., New York, NY 10001. Tel: 212-563-8700; Fax: 212-563-8725. Most Rev. William J. McCormack, National Dir.; Rev. Msgr. James A. Moloney, Vice Pres.; Rev. Msgr. Bernard H. Sandheinrich, Treas.; Rev. Msgr. Andrew F. Connell, Asst. Treas.; Mr. James R. Borut, Asst. Sec.
International Officers Jozef Cardinal Tomko, Prefect of the Congregation for Evangelization of Peoples; Most Rev. Charles A. Schleck, C.S.C., Pres.; Rev. Msgr. Bernard A. Prince, Sec. Gen., Vatican City.
The Propagation of the Faith, under the direction of the Congregation for the Evangelization of Peoples, is established in every country where the Church is free to operate; it has a two-fold goal of promoting a universal missionary spirit and encouraging prayer and financial support for the local churches of the missions.
Each diocese in the United States has a director appointed by the Ordinary to promote the work of the Society through programs such as World Mission Sunday (the next-to-last Sunday in October) and Membership, presentations in seminaries, lesson plans and materials for mission animation in schools (grades 7-12) and parishes, news media and personal contact with parishes and diocesan organizations.
Offerings received by the Propagation of the Faith in the United States are joined with offerings from all other countries and distributed annually to more than 1,000 mission dioceses and vicariates.
Publication: quarterly, *Mission;* Most Rev. William J. McCormack, Publisher.

B. The Society of St. Peter Apostle (1889): *National Office,* 366 Fifth Ave., New York, NY 10001. Tel: 212-563-8700. Most Rev. William J. McCormack, National Dir.
International Officers Jozef Cardinal Tomko, Prefect of the Congregation for Evangelization of Peoples; Most Rev. Charles A. Schleck, C.S.C., Pres.; Rev. Msgr. Bernard A. Prince, Sec.-Gen., Vatican City.
The Society of St. Peter Apostle, under the direction of the Congregation for the Evangelization of Peoples, is established for the support of seminarians and novices in the missions. During 1995, there were 26,414 major seminarians, 54,089 minor seminarians and 9,608 novices receiving assistance from the Society of St. Peter Apostle. The Society also helps support local religious communities and retired native clergy. Each diocese in the United States has a local director who is also the Director of the Propagation of the Faith.

C. The Pontifical Missionary Union (1916): *National Office,* 366 Fifth Ave., New York, NY 10001. Tel: 212-563-8700. Most Rev. William J. McCormack, National Dir.; Rev. Eugene LaVerdiere, S.S.S., National Sec.
International Officers Jozef Cardinal Tomko, Prefect of the Congregation for Evangelization of Peoples; Most Rev. Charles A. Schleck, C.S.I., Pres.; Most Rev. Alessandro Staccioli, O.M.I., Intl. Sec.
The Missionary Union, under the direction of the Congregation for the Evangelization of Peoples, is established to inspire, deepen and sustain a mission spirit among priests, deacons, religious, seminari-

ans, candidates for the religious life and others in the pastoral ministry of the Church. The director in each diocese is also the Director of the Propagation of the Faith.

D. **Holy Childhood Association—(HCA Young Catholics In Mission):** *National Office,* 1720 Massachusetts Ave. N.W., Washington, DC 20036. Tel: 202-775-8637; Fax: 202-429-2987. Very Rev. Francis W. Wright, C.S.Sp., Natl. Dir., His Holiness Pope John Paul II, Supreme Head & Protector; Most Rev. Charles A. Schleck, C.S.C., Pres.; Rev. Msgr. Julio D. Botia Aponte, Sec. Gen., Vatican City.

Founded in 1843 by Bishop Charles de Forbin Janson. It is the official agency of the Church by which Catholic children of the world contribute through their prayers and sacrifices to the welfare of other children in more than 100 mission countries. Since its beginning, it has become the personal favorite of every Pope. In 1926, Pope Pius XI elevated the society to Pontifical rank. Holy Childhood endeavors to attain its ends through the united efforts of all Catholic children who are taught to recognize that sensitivity to others is an essential dimension of Christianity. Funds raised through children's efforts are directed to the Association's two-fold mandate, the majority being distributed annually to every part of the mission world by a Ponitifical Commission and a portion being directed to education of children in the United States.

The Education and Promotion Fund solicits adult donations for the purpose of underwriting HCA educational efforts so that a greater portion of children's donations reach children in need.

All allocations sent to the missions through the agency of the Holy Childhood are used solely in the interests of the children of these missions. The Association is officially established in all archdioceses and dioceses of the United States.

Missionary Societies, Mission Boards and their Diocesan Branches.

Committee on the Home Missions: 3211 Fourth St. N.E., Washington, DC 20017. Tel: 202-541-3010; Fax: 202-541-3322. Most Rev. Edward J. Slattery, Chm.; Dr. David M. Byers, Exec. Dir.

A committee of the National Conference of Catholic Bishops dedicated to support of the home missions. The CHM makes grants to extend the Church's presence as a means of salvation where it is not now present and to strengthen the Church's presence where it is weak. Grantees include dioceses, religious institutes and national, regional and interdiocesan Catholic organizations in the United States and its dependencies. The CHM funds a wide range of mission and evangelization activities; examples include parish support, seminary formation, lay ministry training, religious education, and Hispanic and Black ministry. Application materials are available September 1 of each year; the deadline for submission of completed applications is November 1. The CHM makes grant decisions once a year in March, and grants are disbursed in quarterly payments July through June. The CHM's funds come from two sources: a percentage of the receipts of the annual Mission Sunday Collection and a percentage of ordinary memberships in the Society for the Propagation of the Faith.

American Conventual Franciscan Missions: Refer to the American Foreign Mission section of the Directory and the Religious Institutes of Men section I.D. #[0480] for detailed information on provinces and activies.

Bureau of Catholic Indian Missions (1874): 2021 H St., N.W., Washington, DC 20006. Tel: 202-331-8542; Fax: 202-331-8544. His Eminence John Cardinal O'Connor, Pres.; His Eminence Anthony Cardinal Bevilacqua; His Eminence William Cardinal Keeler; Rev. Msgr. Paul A. Lenz, Exec. Dir.; Rev. Ted Zuern, S.J., Assoc. Dir.; Patricia L. O'Rourke, Asst. Sec. & Treas.

Collecting and distribution of funds for the support of American Indian missions. The Bureau represents the missions in Government relations, specifically in Washington, DC. Active throughout the United States, where American Indian, Eskimo and Aleute missions are present.

Publication: monthly newsletter, *The Bureau of Catholic Indian Missions.*

Catholic Church Extension Society of the United States of America, The (1905): 35 East Wacker Dr., Rm. 400, Chicago, IL 60601-2105. Tel: 312-236-7240. His Eminence Joseph Cardinal Bernardin, D.D., Chancellor; Most Rev. Oscar H. Lipscomb, Vice Chancellor; Rev. Msgr. Kenneth Velo, Pres.; Richard A. Ritter, Vice Pres. & Treas.; James L. Stott, Dir. Devel.

The Extension Society is a Papal fund-raiser that helps to support the Church in rural, remote and poor areas of the United States and its protectorates. The Society raises money through freewill donations, charitable gift annuities, trusts and will bequests.

Requests for funds are submitted by bishops in designated home mission dioceses. Funding is for religious purposes: construction of chapels and other home mission buildings; living expenses of priests, religious and lay people working for home missions; seminarian education; campus ministry; scholarships in religious education at Fordham University to those working in home mission catechetical programs; chapel furnishings; evangelization; religious education, including sponsorship of American Catholic radio show, parish calendars, videotapes on mission work in the U.S., and evangelization booklets.

Publications: *EXTENSION Magazine; Extension Parish Calendars.*

Catholic Medical Mission Board, Inc. (1928): 10 W. 17th St., New York, NY 10011-5765. Members of the Board: His Eminence John Cardinal O'Connor; Revs. Ferdinando D. Berardi; Vincent M. Cook, S.J.; John A. Donnelly; Dr. Theodore J. Dubuque, Jr., M.D.; Rev. Robert J. Fuhrman; Mr. Vincent J. Lewis; Dr. Andrew J. McGowan, Jr., M.D.; Thomas P. Melady; Thomas F. Murphy; Revs. William T. Wood, S.J.

The Catholic Medical Mission Board, Inc. (CMMB) provides pharmaceuticals and health care supplies for clinical facilities which treat victims of poverty in developing and transitional countires. Funds are used to buy medications in USA and in foreign markets which offer easier access to cost-efficient, quality purchases. In addition to its schedule of shipments, CMMB responds to health care emergencies. For the past 68 years, over $350 million in medicines and related supplies have been shipped to 2,000 clinical facilites in 30 countries. Financial aid is also granted to students matriculated in accredited health care education programs. CMMB's placement program assists health providers interested in volunteering for short-term and long-term tours of service at selected clinical sites around the world. Over 1,600 volunteer personnel have been recruited since CMMB's founding. Catholic Medical Mission Board, Inc. publishes Medical Mission News, a quarterly magazine which offers information on its programs. Recipients of shipments and health care placement opportunities are featured.

Catholic Missionary Union: 86-11 Midland Pkwy., Jamaica Estates, NY 11432. Tel: 718-291-5995. His Eminence John Cardinal O'Connor, Pres.; Rev. Edward Whitley, C.S.P., Sec. & Treas.

The corporation subsidizes missions to non-Catholics. Activities are in outlying districts of the South, particularly in those sections where there are few Catholics and facilities for practicing religion.

Catholic Near East Welfare Association (1926): 1011 First Ave., New York, NY 10022. His Eminence John Cardinal O'Connor, Pres. & Treas.; Most Rev. William H. Keeler, Vice Pres.; Rev. Msgr. Robert L. Stern, Sec. Gen.; Rev. Msgr. James M. Moynihan, Assoc. Sec. Gen.

A papal agency for humanitarian and pastoral support established by Pope Pius XI in 1926. It promotes awareness of the condition and the needs of the churches, institutions and persons under the jurisdiction of the Congregation for the Eastern Churches and the Permanent Interdiscasterial Commission for the Church on Eastern Europe. It raises and distributes funds to help meet the material and spiritual needs of the people it serves.

The Association works for people in those lands in which from ancient times the majority of Christians have been members of the various eastern churches. Its mandate extends to the churches and peoples of the Middle East, Northeast Africa, India and Eastern Europe. It encourages and provides assistance to projects and programs of pastoral support, humanitarian assistance, interfaith communication and public awareness.

Publication: bimonthly magazine, *Catholic Near East.*

Catholic Negro-American Mission Board (1907): 2021 H St., N.W., Washington, DC 20006. Tel: 202-331-8542. His Eminence John Cardinal O'Connor, Pres.; His Eminence Anthony Cardinal Bevilacqua; His Eminence William Cardinal Keeler; Rev. Msgr. Paul A. Lenz, Exec. Dir.; Patricia L. O'Rourke, Asst. Sec. & Treas.

Engaged in the support of priests and sisters throughout the states below Mason and Dixon Line, especially monthly support of sisters and lay teachers in poor black schools.

Active in the United States, particularly all states in the South.

Commissariat of the Holy Land: *Franciscan Monastery,* 14th and Quincy Sts., N.E., Washington, DC 20017. Tel: 202-526-6800; Fax: 202-529-9889. Bro. Callistus Welch, O.F.M.

Collecting funds for support of the sacred places, educational and charitable institutions in the Holy Land through the Good Friday collection, and educating young men for the Missions of the Custody of the Holy Land in Syria, Jordan, Lebanon, Cyprus, Rhodes, Israel and Egypt.

Commissariat of the Holy Land: 3140 Meramec St., St. Louis, MO 63118-4339. Tel: 314-353-7729; Fax: 314-353-2790. Rev. Thomas Gardner, O.F.M., Commissary.

Established for collecting and distributing funds for the support of the sacred places in the Holy Land. Regional Commissariat for the Ecclesiastical Provinces of Chicago, Cincinnati, Detroit, Dubuque, Indianapolis, Kansas City, Louisville, Milwaukee, Mobile, New Orleans, Oklahoma City, Omaha, St. Louis, St. Paul-Minneapolis and San Antonio.

Commissariat of the Holy Land: 218 E. 12th St., Los Angeles, CA 90015. Tel: 213-748-5394. Rev. Martial Luebke, O.F.M., Commissary; Rev. Warren Rouse, O.F.M., Vice Commissary.

Established to collect and distribute funds for support of the Sacred Shrines and educational and charitable institutions in the Holy Land. Assigned Territory: Ecclesiastical Provinces of Denver, Los Angeles, Portland (OR), San Francisco, Santa Fe and Seattle.

Commission for Catholic Missions Among the Colored People and the Indians (Black and Indian Mission Office) (1884): 2021 H St., N.W., Washington, DC 20006. Tel: 202-331-8542; Fax: 202-331-8544. Board of Directors: His Eminence John Cardinal O'Connor, Pres.; His Eminence Anthony Cardinal Bevilacqua; His Eminence William Cardinal Keeler; Rev. Msgr. Paul A. Lenz, Exec. Dir.; Patricia L. O'Rourke, Dir. Collection & Asst. Sec./Treas.

Organized by the Third Plenary Council as trustee of the funds collected in the churches for support of the Black and Indian mission work in the United States.

Publication: annual, *Annual Report.*

Dominican Mission Secretariate: 141 E. 65th St., New York, NY 10021-6607. Tel: 212-861-3776; Fax: 212-639-9823. Bro. Thomas Aquinas Dolan, O.P., Dir.

Founded by the Order of Preachers (Dominican Friars), Province of St. Joseph for the purpose of promoting American Dominican activity in the foreign missions throughout the world. Presently the Secretariate aids and supports work in the Archdioceses of Karachi and Lahore, the dioceses of Multan, Faisalabad and Islamabad-Rawalpindi in Pakistan. The Archdioceses of Lima and the diocese of Chimbote in Peru. Nairobi and Kisumu in Kenya. St. Petersburg, Russia; Vilnius, Lithuania; Calayan Island, Philippines, and the Solomon Islands.

Legal Title: *St. Jude Dominican Foreign Missions, Inc.* (formerly Rosary, Foreign Mission Society, Inc.); Special funds under the auspices of the Dominican Foreign Missions: *Handicapped Children Funds, Peru.*

Franciscan Custody of St. Mary of the Angels: *Holy Dormition Monastery,* P.O. Box 270, Sybertsville, PA 18251; Fax: 717-788-2431. Very Rev. James Carroll, O.F.M., Protohegumen.

Preparing missionaries to work among the people of Slav origin in the Byzantine Church.

General Secretariat of the Franciscan Missions, Inc.: P.O. Box 130, Waterford, WI 53185. Tel: 414-534-5470. Revs. Sereno Baiardi, O.F.M., Dir.; Sante de Angelis, O.F.M., Assoc. Dir.

General American office for assistance to Franciscan Missions under the auspices of the General Minister of the Order of Friars Minor.

Catholic Network Of Volunteer Service: 4121 Harewood Rd., N.E., Washington, DC 20017. Tel: 202-529-1100; 800-543-5046; Fax: 202-526-1094. James G. Lindsay, Exec. Dir.

National Office Team: Theresa Deere; Mary Ellen Moore; Jean Newell; Linda Iekel; Jennifer L. Schumacher; Margaret Weeks.

The Catholic Network of Volunteer Service promotes, recruits and refers volunteers to missions in the United States and overseas. We represent nearly 180 faith-based volunteer programs worldwide and work with the U.S. dioceses, religious communities and the private sector to determine their needs for help. The Catholic Network of Volunteer Service (CNVS) is committed to the goal that every Catholic man and woman be invited to consider a period of service in the missions, as a vital and important manifestation of the baptismal call of all Catholic people. Currently, 5,500 men and women are serving in CNVS member mission programs offering their gifts and abilities in full-time service to people in need. These volunteers are serving domestically for a summer, six months, a year or more, and they are serving internationally for two or more years at a time. They are single and married, recent college graduates and early retirees, doctors and teachers, parish ministers and social workers, community organizers, computer operators, legal aides and more. Gatherings: Annual Conference; Formation Workshops, Training Seminars.

Publications: annual, *Response*, biweekly, *How Can I Help?*, quarterly, *Lay Mission Handbook, Awards: The Father George Mader Award, given annually during the Fall meeting of the NCCB to honor organizations and individuals who promote the value of lay mission service.*

Missionary Association of Catholic Women (1916): *National Office*, 3501 S. Lake Dr., Milwaukee, WI 53235. Tel: 414-769-3406. Sr. Frances P. Cunningham, O.S.F., Contact Person.

Pontifical Association providing material and financial aid to home and foreign missions.

Miva-America Missionary Vehicle Association Inc.: *National Office*, 1400 Michigan Ave., N.E., Washington, DC 20017. Tel: 202-526-3444; Fax: 202-526-0830. Revs. Philip DeRea, M.S.C., Natl. Dir.; Anthony F. Krisak, Exec. Dir.; Sr. Patricia Bennett, S.N.D.de Namur, Mission Appeal Coord.

The Missionary Vehicle Association raises funds to provide vehicles (cars, trucks, jeeps, boats) to American Missionaries in developing and undeveloped countries, whose work depends on safe, adequate transportation to provide health care and education and preaching the Gospel.

Oblates of St. Francis de Sales (O.S.F.S.) (1906): *Wilmington-Philadelphia Province*, 2200 Kentmere Pkwy., Box 1452, Wilmington, DE 19899. Tel: 302-656-8529; Fax: 302-658-8052. Very Rev. Joseph G. Morrissey, O.S.F.S., Prov.

Toledo-Detroit Province, (1966), 2056 Parkwood Ave., Toledo, OH 43620. Tel: 419-243-5105. Very Rev. James F. Cryan, O.S.F.S., Prov.

American Mission Directors; Rev. John J. Hurley, O.S.F.S., 1600 Brinckle Ave., Wilmington, DE 19806. Rev. Francis J. Gross, O.S.F.S., 2056 Parkwood Ave., Toledo, OH 43620. Tel: 419-243-5105.

Missionary work in Republic of South Africa, Diocese of Keimeos; Nambia, Diocese of Keetmamshoop; South America—Uruguay, Archdiocese of Montevideo; Brazil, Archdioceses of Rio de Janeiro and Porto Alegre (Rio Grande de Sol), Dioceses of Bage (RGS), Cruz Alta (RGS), Frederico Westphalen (RGS), and Senhor do Bofim (Bahia); India, Archdiocese of Bangalore (province of Kerala); Haiti—Diocese of Les Gonaives; Mexico—Archdiocese of Merida.

Please refer to the Religious Institutes of Men section for activities and representation in the United States.

Provinces outside the United States: France, Germany, Austria, Switzerland, Italy, and Holland.

Pontifical Mission for Palestine (1949): 1011 First Ave., New York, NY 10022. Tel: 212-826-1480. Rev. Msgr. Robert L. Stern, Pres.; Rev. Denis Madden, Vice Pres.; Rev. Msgr. John F. McCarthy, Dir.-Vatican Office; Mr. Issam Bishara, Dir.-Beirut Office; Rev. Robert Reidy, Dir.-Jerusalem Office.

A papal agency for humanitarian and charitable assistance established by Pope Pius XII in 1949. Its mission is to assist, without regard to nationality or religion, all who suffer as a result of the repeated conflicts which have devastated Palestine and neighboring regions of the Middle East.

It encourages and supports projects and programs of relief, rehabilitation, development; collaboration with other agencies; and education.

St. Paul's Guild, Inc.: 1011 First Ave., Rm. 1940, New York, NY 10022. Rev. Msgr. Jeremiah Monahan, Chancellor.

Formerly National Catholic Converts' League, now interested in assisting former Protestant clergymen and former Protestant religious.

Tekakwitha Conference National Center, The (1939): 1800 9th Ave., South No. 20, Great Falls, MT 59405. P.O. Box 6768, Great Falls, MT 59406. Tel: 406-727-0147; Fax: 406-452-9845.

Non-profit organization established for evangelization within the Catholic Church with American Indians, Eskimos and missionaries working together at the national level to develop a Native American voice and presence in the Catholic Church. Catechesis, liturgy, youth ministry, Incultration and related areas within the Catholic Church are goals of the Conference.

Publication: quarterly newsletter, Cross & Feather News.

United States Conference of Secular Institutes

U.S.C.S.I.: P.O. Box 4556, 12th St. N.E., Washington, DC 20017.

Members of the U.S.C.S.I. are Secular Institutes of Diocesan or Pontifical right, canonically erected since 1947, following the promulgation of the Apostolic Constitution, "Provida Mater Ecclesia," by Pope Pius XII. The Institutes are listed on this page by the Congregation for the Institutes of Consecrated Life and for the Societies of Apostolic Life. The purpose of the U.S.C.S.I., canonically erected by the Congregation as of its 1976 statutes, is to offer the Institutes an opportunity to exchange experiences, conduct research, and promote ways to make the vocation and Institutes known. The executive council includes: Carol Winkler, Shoenstatt, President; Rev. Frank Mawn, Institute of the Heart of Jesus, Secretary; Anita Plourde, Oblate Missionary of Mary Immaculate, Treasurer; Dr. Helen St. Denis, Caritas Christi, Past President.

Caritas Christi: P.O. Box 5162, River Forest, IL 60305. Julia A. Lane, Natl. Sponsor. Forms and gives to the Church laywomen who according to their callings, talents and professional skills seek to respond to the love of Christ in their providential environment by following the demands of the Gospel.

Company of St. Paul: 52 Davis Ave., White Plains, NY 10605. Rev. Stuart Sandberg, Contact Person, (Lay People and Priests).

Founded in Milan, Italy November 17, 1920, under the auspices of Cardinal Andrew Ferrari; approved as a Secular Institute of Pontifical Right on June 30, 1950. Aim: The practice of evangelical counsels is the expression of consecration to God. Professional work becomes the main means of the apostolate.

Diocesan Laborer Priests: 3706 15th St. N.E., Washington, DC 20017. Tel: 202-832-4217; Fax: 202-526-5692. Rev. Rutilio J. del Riego, Delegate. A Secular Institute of Pontifical Right founded in Spain in 1886. The aim of the Institute is the promotion, sustenance and cultivation of apostolic, religious and priestly vocations.

St. Francis de Sales Secular Institute: 3503 Jean St., Fairfax, VA 22030. Tel: 703-591-5196. Joan Bereswill, Dir., (Laywomen).

Founded in Vienna, Austria; Pontifical Right 1964. Aim: Personal sanctification of its members living in the world according to the spirituality of St. Francis de Sales. Open to women: single, widowed and divorced who wish to embrace the consecrated life by the profession of vows.

Don Bosco Volunteers: P.O. Box 588, Hawthorne, NJ 07507-0588. Cathy Sylvester, Contact Person.

Founded as a Secular Institute for Women by Blessed Philip Rinaldi, S.D.B., in Turin, Italy in 1917. Approved as an Institute of Pontifical Right in 1978. Existing in 35 countries, with over 1,200 members. Aim: To live in the spirit of St. John Bosco, in a wide variety of apostolates in one's own environment, and in the service of the local church, particularly on behalf of youth An Institute for Men was founded in Rome in November, 1994. For information, see address above.

Handmaids of Divine Mercy: 2410 Hughes Ave., Bronx, NY 10458.

A Secular Institute for women who, through the practice of the evangelical, counsel in a faithful imitation of Jesus Christ. The members commit themselves to the service of the Church by a parish- or diocesan- oriented apostolate under the leadership of and in collaboration with the clergy

Institute of Secular Missionaries: 2710 Ruberg, Cincinnati, OH 45211. Evelyn Dilger, Contact Person, (Women).

Founded in Vitoria, Spain in 1939, approved as Secular Institute in 1955. Working for the integral good of humankind, specifically for the poor who need and claim most of the Church's support at this time. This endeavor is taken within the spirit of the Beatitudes and in communion with the Church.

Missionaries of the Kingship of Christ: P.O. Box 34513, Bethesda, MD 20827. Under this title are included three distinct and juridically separate institutes following the spirituality of St. Francis of Assisi.

Women Missionaries of the Kingship of Christ.

Founded in Italy in 1919 and approved as an Institute of Papal Right in 1953. Existing in twenty-six countries, the American branch began in 1950 and has spread to 25 states. Through a consecrated life in the world they work individually in professions and apostolates for the reign of Christ in the world; Rev. Dominic Monti, O.F.M., Ecclesiastical Asst., Gemelli House, 10400 Lorain Ave., Silver Spring, MD 20901. Tel: 301-593-4479.

Men Missionaries of the Kingship of Christ.

Founded in Italy in 1928 as an institute of diocesan law and established in the United States in 1962. Their purpose is spreading the social reign of Christ through individual professions and occupations; Rev. Thomas Hartle, O.F.M., Ecclesiastical Asst., St. Mary Church, 17 Pompton Ave., Pompton Lakes, NJ 07442-1890. Tel: 201-831-6382.

Priest Missionaries of the Kingship of Christ.

Approved as an Institute of Pontifical Right, July 15, 1978; established in the United States, 1954.

Members are diocesan priests serving in the active ministry of their dioceses while promoting the social reign of Jesus Christ

Oblate Missionaries of Mary Immaculate: P.O. Box 303, Manville, RI 02838. P.O. Box 764, Lowell, MA 01853.

Founded in Canada on July 2, 1952. Approved of Pontifical Right March 24, 1984.

International Membership. The members profess the evangelical counsels. Unique spirituality based on five attitudes of life: presence of God, absence of criticism and complaints, service and peacemaking. Aim: Building and strengthening of the Kingdom of Christ in cooperation with the Church by bearing witness to the charity of Christ in the very midst of society

Opus Spiritus Sancti: 21 S.W. 3rd St., Pocahontas, IA 50574. Tel: 712-335-3242. Rev. Merle Kollasch, Regional Coord.

Pius X: Lynchville Park, Goffstown, NH 03045. Tel: 603-669-8614. (Men).

Founded in New Hampshire in 1940. Approved as a Secular Institute of Pontifical Right on Dec. 8, 1959. Aim: The general end is the perfection of its members. The members strive to achieve this aim through the effective practice in the world of the three evangelical counsels of perfection, and by making the promise to dedicate themselves totally to the particular apostolate of the Institute. The Institute also admits married or unmarried men as associate members.

Secular Institute of Schoenstatt Fathers: W. 284 N. 746 Cherry Ln., Waukesha, WI 53188. (Priests). Rev. Hector R. Vega, Supr.

Founded by Father Joseph Kentenich in 1965, approved as a Secular Institute of Pontifical Right, June 24, 1988. Aim: To aid the moral and religious renewal of society and the realization of the post-Vatican II mission of the Church, especially through priestly service to the International Schoenstatt Movement. About 200 ordained members in 20 nations worldwide.

Secular Institute of Schoenstatt Sisters of Mary: HC 04, Box 100, Rockport, TX 78382-9606. (Women).

Founded in Germany in 1926 by Father Joseph Kentenich; approved as a Secular Institute of Pontifical Right in 1948. Aim: The moral and religious renewal of society. The members practice a Marian lay asceticism as a means of growing in love for God, and consecrating the world to Him. They are active within the Schoenstatt Movement and in a wide variety of professional spheres.

Servitum Christi (Women): Mailing Address, 1209 Greenwood Ave., Pueblo, CO 81003. 184 East 76th St., New York, NY 10021. Ms. Elaine Kozlowski, Contact Person.

Origin inspired by St. Peter Julian Eymard (1868), founder of the Congregation of the Blessed Sacrament. Founded in Holland, 1952; approved as a Secular Institute of Diocesan Right May 8, 1963. Aim: To live the mystery of the Eucharist fully as consecrated lay persons and to make known its meaning so that the reign of Christ may come and the glory of God be revealed to the world.

Society of Our Lady of the Way: 2339 N. Catalina St., Los Angeles, CA 90027. Additional Members in Cleveland, OH; San Francisco, CA; Stamford, CT; New Orleans, LA; and Casper, WY (Women).

Founded in Vienna, Austria in 1936; approved as a Secular Institute of Pontifical Right in 1953. To Christianize the secular order, members are consecrated to God through the vows of chastity, obedience and poverty. They pursue individual apostolates, seeking to manifest Christ in all the circumstances of their life and work. Spirituality is Marian and Ignatian.

Voluntas Dei Institute (1958): 4557 Fairway Ct., Waterford, MI 48328. Rev. George F. Hazler, Contact Person.

Approved as a Secular Institute of Pontifical Right in 1987.

The Institute unites in a common ideal—priests, laymen and married couples as associate members. Aim: To discover the will of God, adhere to, love and carry it out in the world. The Voluntas from the same region meet regularly to pray, celebrate, and share the Word of God. They enrich each other with their human, Christian and apostolic experiences. Through this team, life and personal spiritual attitudes including the evangelical counsels are prolonged. The members seek to bear witness in their milieu, where they work, or with their families

Alphabetical Listing of Mission Churches in the United States

A

Aasu/Aoloau, AS, c/o [4] Pago Pago, AS, Church of St. Paul Church. (SPP)
Abernathy, TX, Hale Co., St. Isidore, c/o Petersburg, TX, Sacred Heart Church. (LUB)
Abeytas, NM, Socorro Co., San Antonio, c/o La Joya, NM, Our Lady of Sorrows Church. (SFE)
Abie, NE, Butler Co., SS. Peter and Paul, c/o Bruno, NE, St. Anthony Church. (LIN)
Abingdon, MD, St. Francis, c/o Baltimore, MD, Patronage of the Mother of God Church. (PSC)
Abo, NM, Torrance Co., c/o Mountainair, NM, St. Alice Church. (SFE)
Abram, TX, St. Mary Magdalene, c/o La Joya, TX, Our Lady, Queen of Angels Church. (BWN)
Absarokee, MT, St. Michael, c/o Columbus, MT, St. Mary's Church. (GF)
Acomita, NM, Cibola Co., St. Anne, c/o Acoma, NM, San Esteban, Acoma Catholic Indian Mission Church. (GLP)
Ada, MN, Norman Co., St. Joseph, c/o [1] Crookston, MN, Cathedral of the Immaculate Conception Church. (CR)
Adel, GA, Cook Co., St. Margaret Mary, c/o Lakeland, GA, Queen of Peace Church. (SAV)
Adel, OR, St. Richard, c/o Lakeview, OR, St. Patrick's Church. (BAK)
Adona, AR, Conway Co., St. Elizabeth's, c/o Bigelow, AR, St. Boniface's Church. (LR)
Adrian, OR, Our Lady of Guadalupe, c/o Nyssa, OR, St. Bridget of Kildare Church. (BAK)
Afono, AS, c/o [7] Pago Pago, AS, Church of the Immaculate Conception Church. (SPP)
Afton, NY, St. Agnes, c/o Bainbridge, NY, St. John the Evangelist Church. (SY)
Afton, WY, Lincoln Co., Holy Family, c/o Jackson, WY, Our Lady of the Mountains Church. (CHY)
Agawam, MA, Hampden Co., St. Anthony, c/o Agawam, MA, St. Theresa of the Child Jesus Church. (SPR)
Aguas, PR, St. Martin, c/o Yauco, PR, Holy Rossary Church. (PCE)
Aguila, AZ, Our Lady of Guadalupe, c/o Wickenburg, AZ, St. Anthony of Padua Church. (PHX)
Aguirre, PR, La Milagrosa, c/o Aguirre, PR, Sacred Heart Church. (PCE)
Ahtanum, WA, Yakima Co., Holy Cross, c/o [2] Yakima, WA, Holy Family Church. (YAK)
Ak Chin, AZ, St. Francis, c/o Bapchule, AZ, St. Peter's Church. (PHX)
Alameda, NM, Bernalillo Co., Our Lady of Mount Carmel, c/o Alameda, NM, Nativity of the Blessed Virgin Mary Church. (SFE)
Alamillo, NM, Socorro Co., c/o Socorro, NM, San Miguel Church. (SFE)
Alapaha, GA, Berrien Co., St. Ann, c/o Tifton, GA, Our Divine Saviour Church. (SAV)
Albany, IL, Whiteside Co., St. Patrick, c/o Fulton, IL, Immaculate Conception Church. (RCK)
Albany, NY, Albany Co., Albany Medical Center, c/o [16] Albany, NY, St. Teresa of Avila Church. (ALB)
Albany, NY, Albany Co., Child's Hospital & Eden Park Nursing Home, c/o [8] Albany, NY, St. James Church. (ALB)
Albany, WI, St. Patrick's, c/o Brodhead, WI, St. Rose Church. (MAD)
Alberton, MT, Mineral Co., St. Albert the Great, c/o Frenchtown, MT, St. John the Baptist Church. (HEL)
Albin, WY, Laramie Co., St. Joseph, c/o Pine Bluffs, WY, St. Paul's Church. (CHY)
Albuquerque, NM, Bernalillo Co., Prince of Peace, c/o [3] Albuquerque, NM, Community of the Risen Saviour Church. (SFE)
Albuquerque, NM, Bernalillo Co., San Jose de los Duranes, c/o [16] Albuquerque, NM, San Felipe de Neri Church. (SFE)
Alcalde, NM, Rio Arriba Co., c/o San Juan Pueblo, NM, St. John the Baptist Church. (SFE)
Alderson, WV, Greenbrier Co., St. Mary of the Greenbrier, c/o Hinton, WV, St. Patrick Church. (WH)
Alexander, ND, McKenzie Co., Our Lady of Consolation, c/o Watford City, ND, Epiphany Church. (BIS)
Alexandria, NE, Thayer Co., St. Mary's, c/o Fairbury, NE, St. Michael's Church. (LIN)
Algarrobos, PR, Our Lady of Fatima, c/o Yauco, PR, Holy Rossary Church. (PCE)
Algodones, NM, Sandoval Co., c/o Bernalillo, NM, Our Lady of Sorrows Church. (SFE)
Alice, ND, St. Henry, c/o Enderlin, ND, St. Patrick's Church. (FAR)
Alice, TX, Jim Wells Co., Sacred Heart, c/o Alice, TX, St. Joseph Church. (CC)
Alice, TX, Jim Wells Co., Santo Nino De Atocha, c/o Alice, TX, Our Lady of Guadalupe Church. (CC)
Allaben, NY, Ulster Co., Our Lady of Lourdes, c/o Phoenicia, NY, St. Francis de Sales Church. (NY)
Allagash Plantation, ME, St. Paul, c/o St. Francis, ME, St. Charles Church. (PRT)
Allen, SD, Bennett Co., St. John of the Cross, c/o Kyle, SD, Our Lady of Sorrows Church. (RC)
Allendale, SC, Barnwell Co., St. Mary, c/o Orangeburg, SC, Holy Trinity Church. (CHR)
Alma, GA, Bacon Co., St. Raymond, c/o Waycross, GA, St. Joseph's Church. (SAV)
Alma, MN, c/o Argyle, MN, St. Rose Church. (CR)
Almacigo Alto, PR, S. Juan Macias, c/o Yauco, PR, Holy Rossary Church. (PCE)
Almacigo Bajo, PR, St. Martin de Porres, c/o Yauco, PR, Holy Rossary Church. (PCE)
Almont, ND, Morton Co., St. Mary, Queen of Peace, c/o New Salem, ND, St. Pius V Church. (BIS)
Alpine, CA, Viejas, c/o Lakeside, CA, Blessed Kateri Tekakwitha Church. (SD)
Alto, TN, Franklin Co., St. Margaret Mary, c/o Decherd, TN, Good Shepherd Church. (NSH)
Altona, NY, Jericho, St. Alexis, c/o Altona, NY, Holy Angels Church. (OG)
Alturas de Campo Rico., PR, Ntra. Sra. Del Carmen, c/o [5] Canovanas, PR, San Jose Church. (SJN)
Alturas de Mayaguez, PR, El Senor de Los Milagros, c/o [4] Mayaquez, PR, Church De El Buen Pastor Church. (MGZ)
Alturas de Rio Grande, PR, La Milagrosa, c/o Rio Grande, PR, Nuestra Senora del Carmen Church. (SJN)
Alvord, IA, Lyon Co., Sacred Heart, c/o Rock Valley, IA, St. Mary's Church. (SC)
Alzada, MT, c/o Broadus, MT, St. David's Church. (GF)
Amado, AZ, Santa Cruz Co., Assumption Chapel, c/o Tubac, AZ, St. Ann Church. (TUC)
Amagansett, NY, Suffolk Co., St. Peter the Apostle, c/o East Hampton, NY, Most Holy Trinity Church. (RVC)
Amalia, NM, Taos Co., c/o Questa, NM, St. Anthony Church. (SFE)
Amaluia, AS, c/o [6] Pago Pago, AS, Church of the Holy Cross Church. (SPP)
Amarillo, TX, Potter Co., Laotian Catholic Community, c/o [11] Amarillo, TX, St. Thomas the Apostle Church. (AMA)
Amelia, NE, Holt Co., St. Joseph, c/o O'Neill, NE, St. Patrick Church. (OM)
Amelia, VA, Good Samaritan, c/o [2] Richmond, VA, Church of the Epiphany Church. (RIC)
American Fork, UT, Utah Co., St. Peter's, c/o Provo, UT, St. Francis of Assisi Church. (SLC)
Amherst, NE, Buffalo Co., St. John Capistran, c/o Elm Creek, NE, Immaculate Conception Church. (GI)
Amherst, VA, Amherst Co., Catholic Community of Amherst, c/o Scottsville, VA, St. George Church. (RIC)
Amouli, AS, c/o [8] Pago Pago, AS, Church of Sacred Heart Church. (SPP)
Anaheim, CA, Sacred Heart, c/o [3] Anaheim, CA, St. Justin Martyr Church. (ORG)
Andes, NY, St. Ann, c/o Margaretville, NY, Sacred Heart Church. (ALB)
Andice, TX, Santa Rosa, c/o Georgetown, TX, St. Helen's Church. (AUS)
Andrews, SC, Georgetown Co., St. Leo the Great, c/o Georgetown, SC, St. Mary's Church. (CHR)
Andrus Cove, LA, Jefferson Davis Parish, St. Gertrude Chapel, c/o Lake Arthur, LA, Our Lady of the Lake Church. (LKC)
Aneta, ND, Nelson Co., Sacred Heart, c/o Cooperstown, ND, St. George's Church. (FAR)
Angoon, AK, c/o Sitka, AK, St. Gregory of Nazianzen Church. (JUN)
Anguilla, MS, Our Mother of Mercy, c/o Belzoni, MS, All Saints Church. (JKS)
Anones, PR, San Jose, c/o Las Marias, PR, Immaculate Heart of Mary Church. (MGZ)
Ansley, NE, Custer Co., Sacred Heart, c/o Broken Bow, NE, St. Joseph's Church. (GI)
Antelope, OR, St. Mary's, c/o Wasco, OR, St. Mary's Church. (BAK)
Anthony, KS, c/o Harper, KS, St. Joan of Arc Church. (WCH)
Anton, TX, Hockley Co., St. Anthony, c/o Shallowater, TX, St. Phillip Benizi Church. (LUB)
Antonito, CO, Conejos Co., St. Augustine, c/o Conejos, CO, Our Lady of Guadalupe Church. (PBL)
Anza, CA, Cahuilla Indian Reservation, c/o Anza, CA, Sacred Heart Church. (SB)
Anza, CA, Riverside Co., Our Lady of the Snows, c/o Anza, CA, Sacred Heart Church. (SB)
Anza, CA, Riverside Co., Santa Rosa Indian Mission, c/o Anza, CA, Sacred Heart Church. (SB)
Anza, CA, Santa Rosa Reservation, c/o Anza, CA, Sacred Heart Church. (SB)
Aoa, AS, c/o [8] Pago Pago, AS, Church of Sacred Heart Church. (SPP)
Apache, OK, Caddo Co., Mother of Sorrows, c/o Elgin, OK, St. Ann Church. (OKL)
Arago, NE, Richardson Co., St. Mary's, c/o Rulo, NE, Immaculate Conception Church. (LIN)
Arapahoe, NE, Furnas Co., St. Germanus, c/o Cambridge, NE, St. John's Church. (LIN)
Arboles, CO, Archuleta Co., SS. Peter & Rose, c/o Ignacio, CO, St. Ignatius Parish Church. (PBL)
Arbuckle, CA, Colusa Co., Holy Cross, c/o Maxwell, CA, Sacred Heart Church. (SAC)
Ardmore, SD, St. Aloysius, c/o Edgemont, SD, St. James Church. (RC)
Ardmore, SD, Fall River Co., St. Aloysius, c/o Hot Springs, SD, St. Anthony's Church. (RC)
Ardoch, ND, Walsh Co., St. John the Baptist, c/o Minto, ND, Sacred Heart Church. (FAR)
Arenzville, IL, Cass Co., St. Fidelis, c/o Beardstown, IL, St. Alexius Church. (SFD)
Argusville, ND, St. William, c/o [1] Fargo, ND, St. Mary's Cathedral Church. (FAR)
Arivaca, AZ, Pima Co., St. Ferdinand, c/o Tubac, AZ, St. Ann Church. (TUC)
Arkadelphia, AR, Clark Co., St. Mary's, c/o Malvern, AR, St. John the Baptist Church. (LR)
Arlee, MT, Lake Co., Sacred Heart, c/o St. Ignatius, MT, St. Ignatius Church. (HEL)
Armagh, MO, Franklin Co., St. Patrick, c/o Catawissa, MO, St. James Church. (STL)
Arnold, CA, Arnold Co., Our Lady of the Sierra, c/o Angels Camp, CA, St. Patrick Church. (STO)
Arnold, NE, St. Agnes, c/o Stapleton, NE, St. John the Evangelist Church. (GI)
Arnot, PA, Tioga Co., St. Stanislaus Kostka, c/o Blossburg, PA, St. Mary's Church. (SCR)
Arock, OR, Holy Family, c/o Jordan Valley, OR, St. Bernard's Church. (BAK)
Arroyo Hondo, NM, Taos Co., c/o Arroyo Seco, NM, Holy Trinity Church. (SFE)
Ashdown, AR, Little River Co., St. Elizabeth Ann Seton, c/o De Queen, AR, St. Barbara's Church. (LR)
Ashfork, AZ, St. Anne, c/o Seligman, AZ, St. Francis Church. (PHX)
Ashland, NY, St. Joseph's Chapel, c/o Windham, NY, St. Theresa of Child Jesus Church. (ALB)
Ashley, ND, McIntosh Co., St. David, c/o Zeeland, ND, St. Andrew's Church. (FAR)
Ashtabula, OH, Ashtabula Co., Our Lady of Miracles (St. Joseph Mission), c/o Ashtabula, OH, St. Joseph's Church. (Y)
Ashton, NE, Sherman Co., St. Francis, c/o Farwell, NE, St. Anthony of Padua Church. (GI)
Ashuelot, NH, St. Michael, c/o Winchester, NH, St. Stanislaus Church. (MAN)
Aspen, CO, Snowmass in Snowmass Village, c/o Aspen, CO, St. Mary Church. (DEN)
Aspermont, TX, Stonewall Co., St. Mary, c/o Rotan, TX, St. Joseph Church. (LUB)
Asti, CA, Our Lady of Mt. Carmel, c/o Cloverdale, CA, St. Peter's Church. (SR)
Astor, FL, Lake Co., St. Hubert of the Forest, c/o [2] Ocala, FL, Our Lady of the Springs Church. (ORL)
Atalaya, PR, Ntra. Sra. de Altagracia, c/o Aguada, PR, St. Francis of Assisi Church. (MGZ)
Athena, OR, Sacred Heart, c/o Milton Freewater, OR, St. Francis of Assisi Church. (BAK)
Atlanta, GA, Fulton Co., San Felipe de Jesus Catholic

Mission, c/o [12] Atlanta, GA, Shrine of the Immaculate Conception Church. (ATL)
Atlanta, IL, Logan Co., St. Mary, c/o Lincoln, IL, Holy Family Church. (PEO)
Atlantic Mine, MI, Houghton Co., St. Mary, c/o Houghton, MI, St. Ignatius Loyola Church. (MAR)
Atoka, OK, St. Patrick Church, c/o Durant, OK, St. William Church. (TLS)
Atwood, CA, Orange Co., St. Theresa Chapel, c/o Placentia, CA, St. Joseph Church. (ORG)
Aua, AS, c/o [7] Pago Pago, AS, Church of the Immaculate Conception Church. (SPP)
Auburn, CA, Placer Co., St. Teresa of Avila, c/o Auburn, CA, St. Joseph Church. (SAC)
Auburn, PA, Susquehanna Co., St. Bonaventure, c/o Meshoppen, PA, St. Joachim's Church. (SCR)
Augusta, MT, Lewis and Clark Co., St. Matthias, c/o Fairfield, MT, St. John Church. (HEL)
Ault, CO, Weld Co., St. Mary, c/o Greeley, CO, Our Lady of Peace Church. (DEN)
Aurora, NM, San Miguel Co., c/o Villanueva, NM, Our Lady of Guadalupe Church. (SFE)
Austin, NV, St. Augustine, c/o Battle Mountain, NV, St. John Bosco Church. (RNO)
Austin, PA, Potter Co., St. Augustine, c/o Coudersport, PA, St. Eulalia Church. (E)
Austwell, TX, Refugio Co., St. Anthony of Padua, c/o Tivoli, TX, Our Lady of Guadalupe Church. (CC)
Autrain, MI, Alger Co., St. Therese, c/o Trenary, MI, St. Rita Church. (MAR)
Ava, MO, Douglas Co., St. Leo the Great, c/o Mansfield, MO, Immaculate Heart of Mary Church. (SPC)
Avoca, NE, Cass Co., Holy Trinity, c/o Syracuse, NE, St. Paulinus Church. (LIN)
Avoca, WI, St. Joseph, c/o Muscoda, WI, St. John the Baptist Church. (MAD)
Avon, MT, Powell Co., St. Theodore, c/o Deer Lodge, MT, Immaculate Conception Church. (HEL)
Avondale, LA, Jefferson Civil Parish, Assumption of Mary, c/o [2] Marrero, LA, St. Agnes Le Thi Thanh Church. (NO)
Avondale, PA, Chester Co., Santa Maria, Madra de Dios, c/o West Grove, PA, Assumption B.V.M. Church. (PH)
Ayrshire, IA, Palo Alto Co., Sacred Heart, c/o Ruthven, IA, Sacred Heart Church. (SC)
Azle, TX, Tarrant Co., Holy Trinity, c/o [16] Fort Worth, TX, St. Thomas Church. (FWT)

B

Babb, MT, St. Mary, Queen of the World, c/o Browning, MT, Church of the Little Flower Church. (HEL)
Baden, MD, Prince Georges Co., St. Dominic's, c/o Baden, MD, St. Michael Church. (WDC)
Badger, MN, Roseau Co., St. Mary's, c/o Roseau, MN, Sacred Heart Church. (CR)
Baggs, WY, Carbon Co., Our Lady of the Sage, c/o Rawlins, WY, St. Joseph's Church. (CHY)
Bagley, MN, Clearwater Co., St. Joseph, c/o Bemidji, MN, St. Philip's Church. (CR)
Bahner, MO, Pettis Co., St. John, c/o Sedalia, MO, Sacred Heart Church. (JC)
Bailey Island, ME, Precious Blood, c/o Brunswick, ME, St. Charles Church. (PRT)
Bainville, MT, Sacred Heart, c/o Culbertson, MT, St. Anthony's Church. (GF)
Bajio, PR, Sagrada Familia, c/o Aguada, PR, St. Francis of Assisi Church. (MGZ)
Baker, CA, San Bernardino Co., Our Lady of the Desert, c/o Barstow, CA, St. Joseph Church. (SB)
Bakersfield, CA, Kern Co., Holy Spirit, c/o [1] Bakersfield, CA, Our Lady of Guadalupe Church. (FRS)
Bakersfield, CA, Kern Co., San Clemente, c/o [2] Bakersfield, CA, Our Lady of Perpetual Help Church. (FRS)
Bakersfield, CA, Kern Co., St. Jude, c/o [1] Bakersfield, CA, Our Lady of Guadalupe Church. (FRS)
Bakersville, FL, St. Johns Co., Our Lady of Good Counsel, c/o Elkton, FL, St. Ambrose Church. (STA)
Bald Knob, AR, White Co., St. Richard, c/o Searcy, AR, St. James Church. (LR)
Baldwin, IA, Holy Trinity, c/o Maquoketa, IA, Sacred Heart Church. (DUB)
Ball Club, MN, Itasca Co., St. Joseph's, c/o Duluth, MN, Indian Missions Church. (DUL)
Ballantine, MT, Sts. Cyril & Methodius, c/o [4] Billings, MT, St. Bernard's Church. (GF)
Ballardville, MA, St. Joseph's, c/o Andover, MA, St. Augustine Church. (BO)
Baltimore, MD, Baltimore Co., Holy Redeemer Chapel, c/o [87] Baltimore, MD, Sacred Heart of Jesus Church. (BAL)
Baltimore, MD, Baltimore Co., St. Gerard's Chapel, c/o [87] Baltimore, MD, Sacred Heart of Jesus Church. (BAL)
Bancroft, WV, Putnam Co., St. Patrick, c/o Nitro, WV, Holy Trinity Church. (WH)
Banning, CA, Riverside Co., St. Mary, c/o Banning, CA, Precious Blood Church. (SB)
Banquete, TX, Nueces Co., St. Michael, c/o Agua Dulce, TX, St. Frances of Rome Church. (CC)
Barbeau, MI, Holy Family, c/o Rudyard, MI, St. Joseph Church. (MAR)
Barberville, FL, Volusia Co., San Jose Mission, c/o De Land, FL, St. Peter's Church. (ORL)
Bardstown, KY, Nelson Co., St. Mark, c/o Culvertown, KY, Immaculate Conception Church. (L)
Barinas, PR, St. James, c/o Yauco, PR, Holy Rossary Church. (PCE)
Barneston, NE, Gage Co., St. Joseph's, c/o Wymore, NE, St. Mary's Church. (LIN)
Barnesville, GA, Lamar Co., St. Ann, c/o Griffin, GA, Sacred Heart Church. (ATL)
Barneveld, WI, Immaculate Conception, c/o Ridgeway, WI, St. Bridget Church. (MAD)
Barnsdall, OK, Osage Co., St. Mary, c/o Pawhuska, OK, Immaculate Conception Church. (TLS)
Barnwell, SC, Barnwell Co., St. Andrew the Apostle, c/o Orangeburg, SC, Holy Trinity Church. (CHR)
Barrackville, WV, Marion Co., All Saints, c/o [4] Fairmont, WV, St. Joseph's Church. (WH)
Barriada Vietnam, Guaynabo, La Milagrosa, c/o Catano, PR, Santa Rosa de Lima Church. (SJN)
Barrineau Park, FL, Escambia Co., St. Elizabeth of Hungary, c/o Cantonment, FL, St. Jude Thaddeus Church. (PT)
Barrington, NH, Chapel of the Nativity, c/o Dover, NH, St. Joseph Church. (MAN)
Barrio Apeadero, PR, San Alfonso, c/o Villalba, PR, Our Lady of Mt. Carmel Church. (PCE)
Barrio Cecilia, Sector La Fe, PR, c/o Naguabo, PR, Nuestra Senora del Rosario Church. (CGS)
Barrio Hatillo, PR, Sagrada Familia, c/o Villalba, PR, Our Lady of Mt. Carmel Church. (PCE)
Barrio Indios, PR, San Juan Bosco, c/o Guayanilla, PR, Immaculate Conception Church. (PCE)
Barrio Jaguey, PR, Madre Cabrini, c/o Villalba, PR, Our Lady of Mt. Carmel Church. (PCE)
Barrio Rio, Sector Brazo Seco, PR, c/o Naguabo, PR, Nuestra Senora del Rosario Church. (CGS)
Barrio Semil, PR, Santa Cecilia, c/o Villalba, PR, Our Lady of Mt. Carmel Church. (PCE)
Barrio Sierra Baja, PR, Our Lady of Mt. Carmel, c/o Guayanilla, PR, Immaculate Conception Church. (PCE)
Barstow, TX, Our Lady of Refuge, c/o Pecos, TX, Santa Rosa Church Church. (ELP)
Bartlett, NH, Carroll, St. Joseph, c/o North Conway, NH, Our Lady of the Mountains Church. (MAN)
Bartolo, PR, Immaculate Conception, c/o Castaner, PR, Our Lady of the Miraculous Medal Church. (PCE)
Barton, MD, St. Gabriel, c/o Westernport, MD, St. Peter Church. (BAL)
Bartow, WV, Pocahontas Co., St. Mark the Evangelist, c/o Marlinton, WV, St. John Neumann Church. (WH)
Basile, LA, Assumption, c/o Basile, LA, St. Augustine Church. (LAF)
Basin, WY, Big Horn Co., St. Philip, c/o Greybull, WY, Sacred Heart Church. (CHY)
Bassett, NE, Rock Co., Holy Cross, c/o Ainsworth, NE, St. Pius X Church. (GI)
Basye, VA, Shenandoah Co., Our Lady of the Shenandoah, c/o Woodstock, VA, St. John Bosco Church. (ARL)
Batavia, NY, St. Pius X, c/o [3] Batavia, NY, St. Mary Church. (BUF)
Batesville, TX, Zavalaco Co., St. Patrick, c/o La Pryor, TX, St. Joseph Church. (SAT)
Bathgate, ND, Pembina Co., St. Anthony, c/o Walhalla, ND, St. Boniface's Church. (FAR)
Baxley, GA, Appling Co., St. Rose of Lima, c/o Hazlehurst, GA, Good Shepherd Church. (SAV)
Bay Mills, MI, Chippewa Co., Blessed Kateri Tekakwitha, c/o Brimley, MI, St. Francis Xavier Church. (MAR)
Bayamon, PR, Casa San Agustin, c/o [1] Bayamon, PR, San Agustin Church. (SJN)
Bayamon, PR, Cristo Rey, c/o [15] Bayamon, PR, Ntra. Sra. de la Monserrate Church. (SJN)
Bayamon, PR, Ntra. Sra. de la Esperanza, c/o [15] Bayamon, PR, Ntra. Sra. de la Monserrate Church. (SJN)
Bayamon, PR, Ntra. Sra. del Carmen, c/o [18] Bayamon, PR, Santa Rita de Casia Church. (SJN)
Bayamon, PR, Sagrado Corazon, c/o [23] Bayamon, PR, Santa Maria Church. (SJN)
Bayamon, PR, Sagrado Corazon de Jesus, c/o [18] Bayamon, PR, Santa Rita de Casia Church. (SJN)
Bayamon, PR, San Gerardo de Mayella, c/o [23] Bayamon, PR, Santa Maria Church. (SJN)
Bayamon, PR, San Jose, c/o [18] Bayamon, PR, Santa Rita de Casia Church. (SJN)
Bayamon, PR, San Martin de Porres, c/o [1] Bayamon, PR, San Agustin Church. (SJN)
Bayamon, PR, San Martin de Porres, c/o [24] Bayamon, PR, Santa Teresa de Avila Church. (SJN)
Bayamon, PR, Santa Monica, c/o [15] Bayamon, PR, Ntra. Sra. de la Monserrate Church. (SJN)
Bayamon, PR, Villas de San Agustin, c/o [1] Bayamon, PR, San Agustin Church. (SJN)
Bayard, NE, Morrill Co., Sacred Heart, c/o Bridgeport, NE, All Souls Church. (GI)
Bayfield, CO, La Plata Co., St. Bartholemew, c/o Ignacio, CO, St. Ignatius Parish Church. (PBL)
Bayside, TX, Refugio Co., St. Mary, c/o Woodsboro, TX, St. Therese, The Little Flower Church. (CC)
Bda. Esperanza, PR, Guanica co., La Providencia, c/o Guanica, PR, St. Anthony Abbot Church. (PCE)
Bda. Marin, PR, La Milagrosa, c/o Arroyo, PR, Our Lady of Mt. Carmel Church. (PCE)
Beach Haven, NJ, Ocean Co., St. Thomas Aquinas, c/o Brant Beach, NJ, St. Francis of Assisi Church. (TR)
Beach Lake, PA, Wayne Co., St. Bernard, c/o White Mills, PA, St. Joseph's Church. (SCR)
Bear Creek Township, PA, Luzerne Co., St. Christopher, c/o [8] Wilkes-Barre, PA, Holy Saviour Church. (SCR)
Beardsley, KS, Rawlins Co., St. John's, c/o St. Francis, KS, St. Francis Church. (SAL)
Beaulieu, MN, Mahnomen Co., St. Joseph, c/o Mahnomen, MN, St. Michael's Church. (CR)
Beaver, OK, Beaver Co., St. Frances Cabrini, c/o Woodward, OK, St. Peter's Church. (OKL)
Beaver Creek, CO, Eagle Co., Beaver Creek Chapel, c/o Edwards, CO, St. Clare of Assisi Church. (DEN)
Bechyne, ND, Walsh Co., SS. Peter & Paul, c/o Michigan, ND, St. Lawrence O'Toole Church. (FAR)
Becket, MA, St. Matthew, c/o Hinsdale, MA, St. Patrick's Church. (SPR)
Bedford, KY, Trimble Co., St. Matthew, c/o LaGrange, KY, Immaculate Conception Church. (L)
Bedford Hills, NY, Westchester Co., St. Matthias, c/o Katonah, NY, St. Mary of the Assumption Church. (NY)
Bee, NE, Seward Co., St. Wenceslaus, c/o Dwight, NE, Assumption Church. (LIN)
Beech Bottom, WV, Brooke Co., Holy Family (Formerly Power), c/o Wellsburg, WV, St. John The Evangelist Church. (WH)
Bel Air, MD, St. Mary Magdalen, c/o Bel Air, MD, St. Margaret Church. (BAL)
Belaire Cove, LA, Sacred Heart, c/o Ville Platte, LA, Sacred Heart of Jesus Church. (LAF)
Belcourt, ND, St. Ann, c/o Turtle Mountain Reservation, ND, (Chippewa Indians) Church. (FAR)
Belcourt, ND, Rolette Co., St. Anthony Indian Mission, c/o Belcourt, ND, St. Ann Church. (FAR)
Belcourt, ND, Rolette Co., St. Benedict, c/o St. John, ND, St. John the Baptist Church. (FAR)
Belfair, WA, Kitsap Co., Prince of Peace, c/o Port Orchard, WA, St. Gabriel's Church. (SEA)
Belgrade, MT, Valley of Flowers, c/o Three Forks, MT, Holy Family Church. (HEL)
Belgrade Lakes, ME, St. Helena, c/o Oakland, ME, St. Theresa Church. (PRT)
Bellevue, LA, Christ the King, c/o Grand Coteau, LA, St. Charles Borromeo Church. (LAF)
Bellflower, IL, Mclean Co., St. John, c/o Farmer City, IL, Sacred Heart Church. (PEO)
Bellwood, NE, Butler Co., St. Joseph's, c/o Bellwood, NE, St. Peter's Church. (LIN)
Bemidji, MN, Beltrami Co., Newman Center, c/o Bemidji, MN, St. Philip's Church. (CR)
Ben Bolt, TX, Jim Wells Co., St. Peter's Church, c/o Alice, TX, St. Elizabeth Church. (CC)
Bena, MN, St. Anne's, c/o Ball Club, MN, St. Joseph's Church. (DUL)
Bennettsville, SC, Marlboro Co., St. Denis, c/o Cheraw, SC, St. Peter's Church. (CHR)
Bent, NM, Our Lady of Guadalupe, c/o Mescalero, NM, St. Joseph Church. (LSC)
Benton, LA, Mary, Queen of Heaven, c/o Bossier City, LA, St. Jude Church. (SHP)
Benton, PA, Columbia Co., Christ the King, c/o Bloomsburg, PA, St. Columba Church. (HBG)
Benwood, MN, Roseau Co., St. Joseph, The Worker, c/o Roseau, MN, Sacred Heart Church. (CR)
Berclair, TX, Immaculate Heart of Mary, c/o Goliad, TX, Immaculate Conception Church. (VIC)
Bergland, MI, Ontonagon Co., St. Ann, c/o White Pine, MI, St. Jude Church. (MAR)
Berino, NM, Immaculate Conception, c/o Anthony, NM, St. Anthony's Church. (LSC)
Bermuda, LA, St. Charles, c/o Isle Brevelle, LA, St. Augustine's Church. (ALX)
Berne, NY, Albany Co., St. Bernadette, c/o Altamont, NY, St. Lucy Church. (ALB)
Berrien Springs, MI, St. Gabriel, c/o Buchanan, MI, St. Anthony Church. (KAL)
Berryville, AR, Carroll Co., St. Anne's, c/o Eureka Springs, AR, St. Elizabeth's Church. (LR)
Berryville, VA, Clark Co., c/o Winchester, VA, Sacred Heart of Jesus Church. (ARL)
Berthold, ND, Ward Co., St. Ann, c/o Foxholm, ND, St. Mary Church. (BIS)
Bertram, TX, Burnet Co., Holy Cross, c/o Burnet, TX, Our Mother of Sorrows Church. (AUS)
Betances, PR, Our Lady of Fatima, c/o Cabo Rojo, PR, St. Michael Church. (MGZ)
Bethel, ME, Oxford Co., Our Lady of the Snows, c/o Norway, ME, St. Catherine of Sienna Church. (PRT)

Bethlehem, MD, Caroline Co., Holy Child, c/o Secretary, MD, Our Lady of Good Counsel Church. (WIL)
Bethlehem, NH, Grafton Co., Christ the King, c/o Littleton, NH, St. Rose of Lima Church. (MAN)
Betterton, MD, Most Precious Blood, c/o Chestertown, MD, Sacred Heart Church. (WIL)
Beulah, CO, Pueblo Co., Our Lady of Lourdes, c/o [11] Pueblo, CO, St. Francis Xavier Church. (PBL)
Bevier, MO, Sacred Heart, c/o Macon, MO, Immaculate Conception Church. (JC)
Bibo, NM, Our Lady of Loretto, c/o Seboyeta, NM, Our Lady of Sorrows Church. (GLP)
Biddeford Pool, ME, York Co., St. Brendan, c/o Biddeford, ME, St. Mary's Church. (PRT)
Bieber, CA, Lassen Co., St. Stephen, c/o Burney, CA, St. Francis of Assisi Church. (SAC)
Big Bay, MI, Marquette Co., St. Mary, c/o [5] Marquette, MI, St. Michael Church. (MAR)
Big Elbow Lake, MN, Becker Co., St. Francis Cabrini, c/o Waubun, MN, St. Ann Church. (CR)
Big Lake, AK, Our Lady of the Lake, c/o Wasilla, AK, Sacred Heart Church. (ANC)
Big Oak Flat, CA, Tuolumne Co., Our Lady of Mt. Carmel, c/o Sonora, CA, St. Patrick Church. (STO)
Big Pine, CA, Inyo Co., St. Stephen, c/o Bishop, CA, Our Lady of Perpetual Help Church. (FRS)
Big Piney, WY, Sublette Co., St. Anne, c/o Pinedale, WY, Our Lady of Peace Church. (CHY)
Big Sky, MT, c/o Bozeman, MT, Resurrection Church. (HEL)
Big Sur, CA, Monterey Co., St. Francis of the Redwoods, c/o Carmel, CA, San Carlos Borromeo Basilica Church. (MRY)
Big Wells, TX, Dimmit Co., St. Michael, c/o Asherton, TX, Immaculate Conception Church. (SAT)
Bigfoot, TX, Frio Co., Our Lady of Mt. Carmel, c/o Von Ormy, TX, St. Peter the Fisherman Church. (SAT)
Billings, OK, Noble Co., Sacred Heart, c/o Perry, OK, St. Rose of Lima Church. (OKL)
Binger, OK, Binger Co., Our Lady of the Most Holy Rosary, c/o Anadarko, OK, St. Patrick's Church. (OKL)
Bird City, KS, Cheyenne Co., St. Joseph's, c/o St. Francis, KS, St. Francis Church. (SAL)
Bisbee, ND, Towner Co., c/o Rolette, ND, Sacred Heart Church. (FAR)
Biscoe, NC, Montgomery Co., Our Lady of the Americas, c/o Albemarle, NC, Our Lady of the Annunciation Church. (CHL)
Bismarck, MO, St. Francois Co., St. John, c/o Park Hills, MO, Immaculate Conception Church. (STL)
Black Canyon City, AZ, Yavapai Co., St. Philip Benizi, c/o Camp Verde, AZ, St. Frances Cabrini Church. (PHX)
Black Horse, PA, Montgomery Co., Our Lady of Mount Carmel, c/o [3] Norristown, PA, Holy Saviour Church. (PH)
Black Lake, LA, Our Lady of the Holy Rosary, c/o Campti, LA, Nativity of The Blessed Virgin Mary Church. (ALX)
Black Lake, NM, Colfax Co., St. Anthony, c/o Cimarron, NM, Immaculate Conception Church Church. (SFE)
Black Pipe-Corn Creek, SD, St. Joseph Hall, c/o Parmelee, SD, St. Agnes Church. (RC)
Blackville, SC, Barnwell Co., Sacred Heart, c/o Orangeburg, SC, Holy Trinity Church. (CHR)
Blackwater, AZ, Holy Family, c/o Bapchule, AZ, St. Peter's Church. (PHX)
Blackwell's Corner, CA, Kern Co., Nuestra Senora de la Paz, c/o Wasco, CA, St. John the Evangelist Church. (FRS)
Blaine, WA, Whatcom Co., St. Anne, c/o Ferndale, WA, St. Joseph Church. (SEA)
Blanca, CO, Costilla Co., St. James, c/o San Luis, CO, Sangre de Cristo Church. (PBL)
Blanchardville, WI, Immaculate Conception, c/o Hollandale, WI, St. Patrick Church. (MAD)
Blanconia, TX, Bee Co., St. Catherine, c/o Refugio, TX, Our Lady of Refuge Church. (CC)
Blencoe, IA, Monona Co., St. Bernard's, c/o Onawa, IA, St. John's Church. (SC)
Blooming Grove, PA, Good Shepherd, c/o Lords Valley, PA, St. John Neumann Church. (SCR)
Bloomingburgh, NY, Sullivan Co., Our Lady of the Assumption, c/o Middletown, NY, Our Lady of Mt. Carmel Church. (NY)
Bloomington, NE, Franklin Co., Sacred Heart, c/o Alma, NE, St. Joseph's Church. (LIN)
Blossburg, PA, Tioga Co., St. Andrew, c/o Blossburg, PA, St. Mary's Church. (SCR)
Blowing Rock, NC, Epiphany, c/o Boone, NC, St. Elizabeth Church. (CHL)
Blue Hill, NE, Webster Co., Holy Trinity, c/o Campbell, NE, St. Ann's Church. (LIN)
Blue Lake, CA, St. Joseph, c/o Arcata, CA, St. Mary's Church. (SR)
Blue Mountain Lake, NY, Hamilton Co., St. Paul, c/o Indian Lake, NY, St. Mary's Church. (OG)
Bluetown, TX, Cristo Rey, c/o Progreso, TX, Holy Spirit Church. (BWN)
Bluewater, NM, McKinley Co., Risen Savior, c/o [4] Gallup, NM, St. John Vianney Church. (GLP)
Bly, OR, St. James the Apostle, c/o Chiloquin, OR, Our Lady of Mt. Carmel Church. (BAK)
Bo Barreal, PR, Cristo de la Salud, c/o Penuelas, PR, St. Joseph Church. (PCE)
Bo. Aceituna, PR, San Martin de Porres, c/o Moca, PR, Our Lady of Monserrate Church. (MGZ)
Bo. Aibonito Guerrero, PR, Ntra. Sra. del Carmen, c/o San Sebastian, PR, San Sebastian Martir Church. (MGZ)
Bo. Altozano, PR, Ntra. Sra. de Fatima, c/o San Sebastian, PR, San Sebastian Martir Church. (MGZ)
Bo. Alturita, PR, Cacao Co., Our Lady of Mt. Carmel, c/o Villalba, PR, Our Lady Mother of Divine Providence Church. (PCE)
Bo. Arenas de Guancia, PR, Guancia Co., S. Martin de Porres, c/o Yauco, PR, St. Martin de Porres Church. (PCE)
Bo. Atalaya, PR, El Cristo de la Reconciliacion, c/o Rincon, PR, St. Rose of Lima Church. (MGZ)
Bo. Barrancas, PR, La Monserrate, c/o Guayama, PR, St. Anthony of Padua Church. (PCE)
Bo. Bauta, PR, Bauta Abajo Co., N.S. del Rosario, c/o Villalba, PR, Our Lady Mother of Divine Providence Church. (PCE)
Bo. Belgica, PR, Guanica Co., Cristo Rey, c/o Guanica, PR, St. Anthony Abbot Church. (PCE)
Bo. Buena Vista, PR, Holy Family, c/o Penuelas, PR, Sacred Heart Church. (PCE)
Bo. Cacao, PR, Cacao Co., Imm. Concepcion, c/o Villalba, PR, Our Lady Mother of Divine Providence Church. (PCE)
Bo. Cain, PR, St. Martin de Porres, c/o San German, PR, St. Rose of Lima Church. (MGZ)
Bo. Calabazas, PR, San Gabriel de la Dolorosa, c/o San Sebastian, PR, San Sebastian Martir Church. (MGZ)
Bo. California, PR, c/o Maunabo, PR, San Isidor Labrador Church. (CGS)
Bo. Calvache, PR, Santa Rosa, c/o Rincon, PR, St. Rose of Lima Church. (MGZ)
Bo. Camarones, PR, Jesus Crucificado, c/o Villalba, PR, Our Lady of Mt. Carmel Church. (PCE)
Bo. Camarones-Los Robles, PR, San Antonio, c/o Villalba, PR, Our Lady of Mt. Carmel Church. (PCE)
Bo. Cambute, PR, Santa Cruz, c/o [18] Carolina, PR, Cristo Rey Church. (SJN)
Bo. Canonilla Abajo, PR, Maria Madre de la Iglesia, c/o Villalba, PR, Our Lady of Mt. Carmel Church. (PCE)
Bo. Canovanas, PR, Maria Auxiliadora, c/o [18] Carolina, PR, Cristo Rey Church. (SJN)
Bo. Capa Barreto, PR, Virgen del Rosario, c/o Moca, PR, Our Lady of Monserrate Church. (MGZ)
Bo. Capa Bosque, PR, Cristo Salvador, c/o Moca, PR, Our Lady of Monserrate Church. (MGZ)
Bo. Carreras, PR, La Providencia, c/o Anasco, PR, St. Anthony Abbot Church. (MGZ)
Bo. Carretera Nueva, PR, La Asuncion, c/o Hormigueros, PR, Shrine of Our Lady of Monserrate Church. (MGZ)
Bo. Cerro Gordo, PR, Espiritu Santo, c/o Villalba, PR, Our Lady of Mt. Carmel Church. (PCE)
Bo. Cerro Gordo, PR, La Inmaculada, c/o Moca, PR, Our Lady of Monserrate Church. (MGZ)
Bo. Cerro Gordo, PR, Our Lady of Monserrat, c/o Anasco, PR, St. Anthony Abbot Church. (MGZ)
Bo. Cerro Gordo, PR, San Francisco de Asis, c/o Sabana Grande, PR, Church of San Isidro Church. (MGZ)
Bo. Cerro Gordo, PR, San Judas, c/o Moca, PR, Our Lady of Monserrate Church. (MGZ)
Bo. Chucillas Sabana, PR, Corazon de Jesus, c/o Moca, PR, Our Lady of Monserrate Church. (MGZ)
Bo. Collado, PR, Ponce Co., Our Lady of Monserrate, c/o [3] Ponce, PR, Church of the Resurrection Church. (PCE)
Bo. Corazon, PR, La Candelaria, c/o Guayama, PR, St. Anthony of Padua Church. (PCE)
Bo. Corcega, PR, La Milagrosa, c/o Rincon, PR, St. Rose of Lima Church. (MGZ)
Bo. Cordero, PR, Virgen Monserrate, c/o Moca, PR, Our Lady of Monserrate Church. (MGZ)
Bo. Corillo, PR, San Pedro, c/o Villalba, PR, Our Lady of Mt. Carmel Church. (PCE)
Bo. Corral Viejo, PR, Ponce Co., Cristo Rey, c/o [10] Ponce, PR, La Santisima Trinidad Church. (PCE)
Bo. Cruces, PR, Sagrado Corazon de Jesus, c/o Rincon, PR, St. Rose of Lima Church. (MGZ)
Bo. Cuatro Calles, PR, Ponce Co., St. Anthony, c/o [13] Ponce, PR, Santuario San Judas Tadeo Church. (PCE)
Bo. Cuchilla del Limon, PR, La Asuncion, c/o Villalba, PR, Our Lady of Mt. Carmel Church. (PCE)
Bo. Cuchillas La Salle, PR, Santos Guillermo y Mateo, c/o Moca, PR, Our Lady of Monserrate Church. (MGZ)
Bo. Cuchillas Loperena, PR, Virgen del Carmen, c/o Moca, PR, Our Lady of Monserrate Church. (MGZ)
Bo. Cuesta Blanca, PR, Ntra. Sra. de Monserrate, c/o Lajas, PR, De la Merced Parish Church. (MGZ)
Bo. Dajas, PR, N.S. del Carmen, c/o Villalba, PR, Our Lady of Mt. Carmel Church. (PCE)
Bo. Damian Abajo, PR, Damian Abajo Co., N.S. del Pilar, c/o Villalba, PR, Our Lady Mother of Divine Providence Church. (PCE)
Bo. El Bajo, Pastillas, PR, Pastillas Co., Cristo Rey, c/o Patillas, PR, Inmaculado Corazon de Maria Church. (PCE)
Bo. El Frio, PR, Ala de La Piedra Co., Nino de Praga, c/o Villalba, PR, Our Lady Mother of Divine Providence Church. (PCE)
Bo. El Hoyo, PR, La Virgen Milagrosa, c/o Sabana Grande, PR, Church of San Isidro Church. (MGZ)
Bo. El Hoyo, PR, Santa Rosa de Lima, c/o Hormigueros, PR, Shrine of Our Lady of Monserrate Church. (MGZ)
Bo. El Porvenir, PR, Ntra. Sra. de la Providencia (Rep. Masias), c/o [3] Mayaquez, Mayaguez, Ascension Church. (MGZ)
Bo. El Real, Pastillas, PR, Pastillas Co., San Guillermo, c/o Patillas, PR, Inmaculado Corazon de Maria Church. (PCE)
Bo. Espino, PR, St. Lawrence Martyr, c/o Anasco, PR, St. Anthony Abbot Church. (MGZ)
Bo. Fuig., PR, Monserrate, c/o Ensenada, PR, Sacred Heart Church. (PCE)
Bo. Guama, PR, N. Sra. de la Consolacion, c/o San German, PR, St. Rose of Lima Church. (MGZ)
Bo. Guamani, PR, Sgdo. Corazon, c/o Guayama, PR, St. Anthony of Padua Church. (PCE)
Bo. Guanajibo, PR, San Martin de Porres, c/o Hormigueros, PR, Shrine of Our Lady of Monserrate Church. (MGZ)
Bo. Guaragoa, PR, Ponce Co., San Andres, c/o [10] Ponce, PR, La Santisima Trinidad Church. (PCE)
Bo. Guaragoa, Arriba, PR, Ponce Co., Santa Ana, c/o [10] Ponce, PR, La Santisima Trinidad Church. (PCE)
Bo. Guaras, PR, Ntra. Sra. de Fatima, c/o Sabana Grande, PR, Church of San Isidro Church. (MGZ)
Bo. Guarderraya, Pastillas, PR, Pastillas Co., Madre Cabrini, c/o Patillas, PR, Inmaculado Corazon de Maria Church. (PCE)
Bo. Guerrero, PR, La Providencia, c/o Aguadilla, PR, San Jose Obrero Church. (MGZ)
Bo. Guineo, PR, Ala de La Piedra Co., Santa Ana, c/o Villalba, PR, Our Lady Mother of Divine Providence Church. (PCE)
Bo. Hatillo Viejo, PR, La Milagrosa, c/o Villalba, PR, Our Lady of Mt. Carmel Church. (PCE)
Bo. Hato Arriba, PR, San Patricio, c/o San Sebastian, PR, San Sebastian Martir Church. (MGZ)
Bo. Hato Arriba (Parcelas), PR, San Pablo de la Cruz, c/o San Sebastian, PR, San Sebastian Martir Church. (MGZ)
Bo. Higuero, PR, Santisimo Sacramento, c/o Villalba, PR, Our Lady of Mt. Carmel Church. (PCE)
Bo. Hoyamala, PR, San Jose Obrero, c/o San Sebastian, PR, San Sebastian Martir Church. (MGZ)
Bo. Hoyos, PR, Ponce Co., Santa Maria Virgen, c/o [17] Ponce, PR, Our Lady of Mt. Carmel Church. (PCE)
Bo. Jacaboa, Pastillas, PR, Pastillas Co., Carmen, c/o Patillas, PR, Inmaculado Corazon de Maria Church. (PCE)
Bo. Jagual, Pastillas, PR, Pastillas Co., Carmen, c/o Patillas, PR, Inmaculado Corazon de Maria Church. (PCE)
Bo. Jaguey, PR, San Jose, c/o Rincon, PR, St. Rose of Lima Church. (MGZ)
Bo. Jagueyes Arriba, PR, La Milagrosa, c/o Villalba, PR, Our Lady of Mt. Carmel Church. (PCE)
Bo. Jaquitas, PR, Ntra. Sra. de la Paz, c/o Hormigueros, PR, Shrine of Our Lady of Monserrate Church. (MGZ)
Bo. Juncal, PR, Santa Teresita, c/o San Sebastian, PR, San Sebastian Martir Church. (MGZ)
Bo. La Cuarta, PR, Ponce Co., San Pedro Nolasco, c/o [15] Ponce, PR, Church of the Sacred Heart Church. (PCE)
Bo. La Lechuza, PR, La Asuncion, c/o San Sebastian, PR, San Sebastian Martir Church. (MGZ)
Bo. La Luna, PR, Guanica Co., N. Sra Fatima, c/o Guanica, PR, St. Anthony Abbot Church. (PCE)
Bo. La Maquina, PR, Santa Ana, c/o Sabana Grande, PR, Church of San Isidro Church. (MGZ)
Bo. La Pica, PR, c/o Maunabo, PR, San Isidor Labrador Church. (CGS)
Bo. La Pica, PR, San Jose, c/o Sabana Grande, PR, Church of San Isidro Church. (MGZ)
Bo. La Plata, PR, Sagrado Corazon de Jesus, c/o Lajas, PR, Our Lady of the Purification Church. (MGZ)
Bo. La Torre, PR, Santa Catalina de Siena, c/o Sabana Grande, PR, Church of San Isidro Church. (MGZ)
Bo. La Yuca, PR, Ponce Co., Immaculate Heart of Mary, c/o [3] Ponce, PR, Church of the Resurrection Church. (PCE)
Bo. Lajas Arriba (La Tea), PR, Ntra. Sra. del Perpetuo Socorro, c/o Lajas, PR, Our Lady of the Purification Church. (MGZ)
Bo. Lajas Arriba (Parcelas), PR, San Pablo, c/o Lajas,

PR, Our Lady of the Purification Church. (MGZ)
Bo. Las Palmas, PR, Virg. del Carmen, c/o Salinas, PR, Our Lady of Monserrat Church. (PCE)
Bo. Las Raices, PR, Ponce Co., Sagrado Corazon de Jesus, c/o [17] Ponce, PR, Our Lady of Mt. Carmel Church. (PCE)
Bo. Las Vallas, PR, Ponce Co., San Lucas, c/o [3] Ponce, PR, Church of the Resurrection Church. (PCE)
Bo. Las Vegas, PR, Our Lady of Perpetual Help, c/o [3] Mayaquez, Mayaguez, Ascension Church. (MGZ)
Bo. Lavadero, PR, Sagrado Corazon de Jesus, c/o Hormigueros, PR, Shrine of Our Lady of Monserrate Church. (MGZ)
Bo. Limon, PR, St. Teresita, c/o [3] Mayaquez, Mayaguez, Ascension Church. (MGZ)
Bo. Limon, PR, Virgen de la Amargura, c/o Villalba, PR, Our Lady of Mt. Carmel Church. (PCE)
Bo. Limon, PR, Virgen del Rosario, c/o Moca, PR, Our Lady of Monserrate Church. (MGZ)
Bo. Lizas, PR, c/o Maunabo, PR, San Isidor Labrador Church. (CGS)
Bo. Los Barros, Pastillas, PR, Pastillas Co., S. Juan Evangelista, c/o Patillas, PR, Inmaculado Corazon de Maria Church. (PCE)
Bo. Los Pollos, Pastillas, PR, Pastillas Co., Santa Rosa de Lima, c/o Patillas, PR, Inmaculado Corazon de Maria Church. (PCE)
Bo. Luna, PR, Guanica Co., San Judas, c/o Guanica, PR, St. Anthony Abbot Church. (PCE)
Bo. Madrigal, PR, Ponce Co., N.S. del Rosario, c/o [10] Ponce, PR, La Santisima Trinidad Church. (PCE)
Bo. Maginas, PR, Sagrado Corazon de Jesus, c/o Sabana Grande, PR, Church of San Isidro Church. (MGZ)
Bo. Maguayo, PR, Ntra. Sra. de la Monserrate, c/o Lajas, PR, De la Merced Parish Church. (MGZ)
Bo. Magueyes, PR, Ponce Co., San Juan de Mata, c/o [10] Ponce, PR, La Santisima Trinidad Church. (PCE)
Bo. Malezas, PR, La Milagrosa, c/o [6] Mayaquez, PR, Sacred Heart Church. (MGZ)
Bo. Marias, PR, St. Rita, c/o Anasco, PR, St. Anthony Abbot Church. (MGZ)
Bo. Marin Alto, Pastillas, PR, Pastillas Co., Perpetuo Socorro, c/o Patillas, PR, Inmaculado Corazon de Maria Church. (PCE)
Bo. Marueno, Arriba, PR, Ponce Co., N.S. Fatima, c/o [10] Ponce, PR, La Santisima Trinidad Church. (PCE)
Bo. Minillas Carretera, PR, Perpetuo Socorro, c/o San German, PR, St. Rose of Lima Church. (MGZ)
Bo. Minillas Valle, PR, Santa Monica, c/o San German, PR, St. Rose of Lima Church. (MGZ)
Bo. Miradero, PR, Ntro. Sra. de la Providencia, c/o Cabo Rojo, PR, St. Michael Church. (MGZ)
Bo. Mogote, PR, Santisima Tinidad, c/o Villalba, PR, Our Lady of Mt. Carmel Church. (PCE)
Bo. Molinas, PR, Ntra. Sra. de Monserrate, c/o Sabana Grande, PR, Church of San Isidro Church. (MGZ)
Bo. Naranjo, PR, Corazon de Jesus, c/o Moca, PR, Our Lady of Monserrate Church. (MGZ)
Bo. Olimpo, PR, Cristo Rey, c/o Guayama, PR, St. Anthony of Padua Church. (PCE)
Bo. Ollas, PR, Monserrate, c/o Santa Isabel, PR, St. James Church. (PCE)
Bo. Oveja, PR, Cristo Redentor, c/o Anasco, PR, St. Anthony Abbot Church. (MGZ)
Bo. Palmarejo, PR, San Jose, c/o Villalba, PR, Our Lady of Mt. Carmel Church. (PCE)
Bo. Palmarejo II, PR, San Juan Bautista, c/o Lajas, PR, Our Lady of the Purification Church. (MGZ)
Bo. Palmas, PR, Ntra Sra. de Fatima, c/o Arroyo, PR, Our Lady of Mt. Carmel Church. (PCE)
Bo. Parcelas Guacio (Parcelas), PR, Santa Cruz, c/o San Sebastian, PR, San Sebastian Martir Church. (MGZ)
Bo. Parcelas Palmarejo, PR, San Judas Tadeo, c/o Lajas, PR, Our Lady of the Purification Church. (MGZ)
Bo. Parcelas Santa Rosa, PR, Santa Rosa de Lima, c/o Lajas, PR, Our Lady of the Purification Church. (MGZ)
Bo. Parguera, PR, San Pedro, c/o Lajas, PR, De la Merced Parish Church. (MGZ)
Bo. Paris, PR, Ntra Sra. del Perpetuo Socorro, c/o Lajas, PR, De la Merced Parish Church. (MGZ)
Bo. Paso Secos, PR, Virgen del Rosario, c/o Santa Isabel, PR, St. James Church. (PCE)
Bo. Pastillo, PR, Ponce Co., Inmaculada, c/o [10] Ponce, PR, La Santisima Trinidad Church. (PCE)
Bo. Penuelas, PR, Virgen del Rosario, c/o Santa Isabel, PR, St. James Church. (PCE)
Bo. Perchas 1, PR, Cristo Rey, c/o San Sebastian, PR, San Sebastian Martir Church. (MGZ)
Bo. Perchas 11, PR, La Pasion, c/o San Sebastian, PR, San Sebastian Martir Church. (MGZ)
Bo. Pinales, PR, La Immaculade, c/o Anasco, PR, St. Anthony Abbot Church. (MGZ)
Bo. Pitahaya, PR, Ntra Sra. del Carmen, c/o Arroyo, PR, Our Lady of Mt. Carmel Church. (PCE)
Bo. Placita, PR, c/o Juncos, PR, Inmaculada Concepcion Church. (CGS)
Bo. Playa, PR, Carmen, c/o Salinas, PR, Our Lady of Monserrat Church. (PCE)
Bo. Playita, PR, Virgen Milagrosa, c/o Salinas, PR, Our Lady of Monserrat Church. (PCE)
Bo. Plebiscito, PR, San Antonio Ma. Claret, c/o [27] San Juan, PR, San Jose Obrero Church. (SJN)
Bo. Pozas, PR, Damian Abajo Co., N.S. Monserrate, c/o Villalba, PR, Our Lady Mother of Divine Providence Church. (PCE)
Bo. Pozo Hondo, PR, Santa Rosa de Lima, c/o Anasco, PR, St. Anthony Abbot Church. (MGZ)
Bo. Providencia, Pastillas, PR, Pastillas Co., Providencia, c/o Patillas, PR, Inmaculado Corazon de Maria Church. (PCE)
Bo. Puente Jobos, PR, SS. Peter and Paul, c/o Guayama, PR, St. Anthony of Padua Church. (PCE)
Bo. Puerto Jobos, PR, San Francisco de Asis, c/o Guayama, PR, St. Anthony of Padua Church. (PCE)
Bo. Punta Brava, PR, San Pedro, c/o Moca, PR, Our Lady of Monserrate Church. (MGZ)
Bo. Puntas, PR, Nuestra Senora del Carmen, c/o Rincon, PR, St. Rose of Lima Church. (MGZ)
Bo. Quebrada Arenas, PR, c/o Maunabo, PR, San Isidor Labrador Church. (CGS)
Bo. Quebrado del Agua, PR, Ponce Co., La Milagrosa, c/o [16] Ponce, PR, Church of the Good Shepherd Church. (PCE)
Bo. Rayo Plata, PR, San Judas Tadeo, c/o Sabana Grande, PR, Church of San Isidro Church. (MGZ)
Bo. Real Anon Abajo, PR, Ponce Co., San Mateo, c/o [17] Ponce, PR, Our Lady of Mt. Carmel Church. (PCE)
Bo. Real Anon Arriba, PR, Ponce Co., San Martin de Porres, c/o [17] Ponce, PR, Our Lady of Mt. Carmel Church. (PCE)
Bo. Recio, Pastillas, PR, Pastillas Co., Sto. Cristo de Los Milagros, c/o Patillas, PR, Inmaculado Corazon de Maria Church. (PCE)
Bo. Retiro Tea, PR, Santa Rita, c/o San German, PR, St. Rose of Lima Church. (MGZ)
Bo. Rio Abajo, PR, Ceiba Co., N.S. del Perpetuo Socorro Bo. Rio Abajo, c/o Ceiba, PR, San Antonio de Padua Church. (CGS)
Bo. Robles, PR, Sagrado Corazon, c/o San Sebastian, PR, San Sebastian Martir Church. (MGZ)
Bo. Rocha Magueyes, PR, La Providencia, c/o Moca, PR, Our Lady of Monserrate Church. (MGZ)
Bo. Rosario Penon, PR, La Monserrate, c/o Rosario, PR, Rosary Church. (MGZ)
Bo. Salinas, PR, Ntra. Sra. del Carmen, c/o Lajas, PR, De la Merced Parish Church. (MGZ)
Bo. Salistral, PR, Ponce Co., Santa Marta, c/o [4] Ponce, PR, Our Lady of Mt. Carmel Church. (PCE)
Bo. Saltos, PR, San Judas Tadeo, c/o San Sebastian, PR, San Sebastian Martir Church. (MGZ)
Bo. Santa Juanita, PR, Guanica Co., N. Sra. Rosario, c/o Guanica, PR, St. Anthony Abbot Church. (PCE)
Bo. Santana Pichel, PR, Ntra. Sra. del Rosario, c/o Sabana Grande, PR, Church of San Isidro Church. (MGZ)
Bo. Santas Pascuas, PR, Ponce Co., Resurreccion, c/o [10] Ponce, PR, La Santisima Trinidad Church. (PCE)
Bo. Sierrita Caonillas, PR, Cristo de la Salud, c/o Villalba, PR, Our Lady of Mt. Carmel Church. (PCE)
Bo. Sta. Ana Moreno, PR, Sta Lucia, c/o Sabana Grande, PR, Church of San Isidro Church. (MGZ)
Bo. Susa, PR, Yauco Co., N.S. de La Monserrate, c/o Yauco, PR, St. Martin de Porres Church. (PCE)
Bo. Susa, PR, Guanica Co., N.S. de La Providencia, c/o Yauco, PR, St. Martin de Porres Church. (PCE)
Bo. Susa, PR, Yauco Co., S. Francisco de Asis, c/o Yauco, PR, St. Martin de Porres Church. (PCE)
Bo. Susa, PR, Guanica Co., Santa Rita, c/o Yauco, PR, St. Martin de Porres Church. (PCE)
Bo. Talante, PR, c/o Maunabo, PR, San Isidor Labrador Church. (CGS)
Bo. Tumbao, PR, c/o Maunabo, PR, San Isidor Labrador Church. (CGS)
Bo. Vista Alegre, PR, Jesus Crucificado, c/o Villalba, PR, Our Lady of Mt. Carmel Church. (PCE)
Bo. Voladoras Lomas, PR, Espiritu Santo, c/o Moca, PR, Our Lady of Monserrate Church. (MGZ)
Bo. Voladoras Parcelas, PR, Sagrada Familia, c/o Moca, PR, Our Lady of Monserrate Church. (MGZ)
Bo. Yaurel Palmarejo, PR, San Jose, c/o Arroyo, PR, Our Lady of Mt. Carmel Church. (PCE)
Bo. Yaurel Santa Clara, PR, San Martin, c/o Arroyo, PR, Our Lady of Mt. Carmel Church. (PCE)
Boardman, OR, Our Lady of Guadalupe, c/o Hermiston, OR, Our Lady of Angels Church. (BAK)
Bobtown, PA, Greene Co., Holy Family, c/o Bobtown, PA, St. Ignatius of Antioch Church. (PIT)
Bodega, CA, St. Teresa, c/o Occidental, CA, St. Philip Church. (SR)
Boiceville, NY, Ulster Co., Our Lady of La Salette, c/o Phoenicia, NY, St. Francis de Sales Church. (NY)
Boise City, OK, Cimarron Co., Good Shepherd, c/o Guymon, OK, St. Peter's Church. (OKL)
Boles Acres, NM, Our Lady of the Desert, c/o Alamogordo, NM, Immaculate Conception Church. (LSC)
Bolinas, CA, St. Mary Magdalen, c/o Olema, CA, Sacred Heart Church. (SFR)
Boling, TX, St. Joseph, c/o Wharton, TX, Holy Family Church. (VIC)
Bon Secour, AL, Baldwin Co., Our Lady of Bon Secour, c/o Magnolia Springs, AL, St. John the Baptist Church. (MOB)
Bonanza, OR, St. Frances Cabrini, c/o Merrill, OR, St. Augustine Church. (BAK)
Bongard, IL, Champaign Co., Immaculate Conception, c/o Philo, IL, St. Thomas Church. (PEO)
Bonhamtown, NJ, Middlesex Co., St. Margaret Mary Alacoque, c/o Edison, NJ, Guardian Angels Church. (MET)
Bonita Springs, FL, Lee Co., Hispanic Mission, c/o Bonita Springs, FL, St. Leo Church. (VEN)
Bonneau, SC, Berkeley Co., Our Lady of Peace, c/o Moncks Corner, SC, St. Philip Benizi Church. (CHR)
Booker, TX, St. Peter, c/o Perryton, TX, Immaculate Conception Church. (AMA)
Boomer, WV, Fayette Co., St. Anthony Shrine, c/o Montgomery, WV, Immaculate Conception Church. (WH)
Boone, CO, Pueblo Co., St. William, c/o Avondale, CO, Sacred Heart Church. (PBL)
Booneville, KY, Owsley Co., Booneville Catholic Church of the Holy Family, c/o Beattyville, KY, Queen of All Saints Church. (LEX)
Boonsboro, MD, Washington Co., St. James, c/o Hagerstown, MD, St. Mary Church. (BAL)
Boqueron, PR, St. Joseph, c/o Cabo Rojo, PR, St. Michael Church. (MGZ)
Borica, NM, Guadalupe Co., c/o Santa Rosa, NM, St. Rose of Lima Church. (SFE)
Borinquen, PR, Our Lady of Victory, c/o Aguadilla, PR, La Milagrosa Church. (MGZ)
Bosque, NM, Valencia Co., c/o Belen, NM, Our Lady of Belen Church. (SFE)
Boswell, OK, Choctaw Co., St. Jude, c/o Hugo, OK, Immaculate Conception Church. (TLS)
Boulder Valley, MT, Jefferson Co., St. John the Evangelist, c/o Boulder, MT, St. Catherine Church. (HEL)
Bowie, AZ, Cochise Co., Our Lady of Guadalupe, c/o Willcox, AZ, Sacred Heart Church. (TUC)
Bowling Green, FL, Hardee Co., Holy Child, c/o Wauchula, FL, St. Michael Church. (VEN)
Box Elder, MT, St. Anthony, c/o Big Sandy, MT, St. Margaret Mary Church. (GF)
Braddock, ND, Emmons Co., St. Katherine, c/o Hazelton, ND, St. Paul Church. (BIS)
Bradley, CA, Monterey Co., Our Lady of Guadalupe, c/o San Miguel, CA, San Miguel Church. (MRY)
Brainardsville, NY, Franklin Co., St. Jude, c/o Chateaugay, NY, St. Patrick Church. (OG)
Braithwaite, LA, Plaquemines Parish, Assumption of the Blessed Virgin, c/o Pointe a la Hache, LA, St. Thomas Church. (NO)
Branch, LA, St. Edmund, c/o Robert's Cove, LA, St. Leo IV Church. (LAF)
Branson, CO, Las Animas Co., Blessed Sacrament, c/o Trinidad, CO, Most Holy Trinity, Trinidad Area Catholic Community (Trinidad Cluster) Church. (PBL)
Brant Lake, NY, Warren Co., St. Teresa of Avila, c/o Hague, NY, Blessed Sacrament Church. (ALB)
Bremen, ND, Wells Co., St. Joseph, c/o Fessenden, ND, St. Augustine's Church. (FAR)
Bridgeport, CA, Mono Co., Infant of Prague, c/o Mammoth Lakes, CA, St. Joseph Church. (STO)
Bridger, SD, Ziebach Co., Immaculate Conception, c/o Eagle Butte, SD, All Saints Church. (RC)
Bridger, SD, Ziebach Co., Immaculate Conception, c/o Eagle Butte, SD, Cheyenne River Reservation Church. (RC)
Bridport, VT, Addison Co., St. Bernadette, c/o Middlebury, VT, Assumption of the Blessed Virgin Mary Church. (BUR)
Brier Hill, NY, St. Lawrence Co., Our Lady of Grace, c/o Morristown, NY, St. John the Evangelist Church. (OG)
Brisbane, CA, Our Lady of Guadalupe, c/o [54] San Francisco, CA, Visitacion, Church of the Church. (SFR)
Bristol, CO, Prowers Co., St. Mary, c/o Holly, CO, St. Frances of Rome Church. (PBL)
Bristol, IL, Kendall Co., St. Patrick, c/o Plano, IL, St. Mary Church. (JOL)
Broadview, MT, Little Flower, c/o Roundup, MT, St. Benedict's Church. (GF)
Brocket, ND, Ramsey Co., St. Joseph, c/o Lakota, ND, St. Mary's Church. (FAR)
Brockton, MT, Roosevelt Co., St. Anthony, c/o Poplar, MT, Our Lady of Lourdes Church. (GF)
Brockton, MT, St. Thomas, c/o Poplar, MT, Our Lady of Lourdes Church. (GF)
Bromley, AL, St. John, c/o Daphne, AL, Shrine of the Holy Cross Church. (MOB)

Bronte, TX, Coke Co., St. James, c/o Ballinger, TX, St. Mary Star of the Sea Church. (SAN)
Brookline, NH, Hillsborough Co., Infant Jesus, c/o Milford, NH, St. Patrick Church. (MAN)
Brooklyn, NY, Queens Co., Our Lady of Mount Carmel, c/o [190] Queens, NY, St. Leo Church. (BRK)
Brooklyn, NY, Regina Pacis Votive Shrine, c/o [126] Brooklyn, NY, St. Rosalia-Regina Pacis Church. (BRK)
Brown City, MI, Sanilac Co., Sacred Heart, c/o North Branch, MI, St. Mary's Burnside Church. (DET)
Brownlee, NE, Cherry Co., St. Joan of Arc, c/o Mullen, NE, St. Mary's Church. (GI)
Brownstown, IN, Jackson Co., Our Lady of Providence, c/o Seymour, IN, St. Ambrose Church. (IND)
Brownsville, OR, Linn Co., Holy Trinity, c/o Sweet Home, OR, St. Helen Church. (P)
Brownsville, TN, Haywood Co., c/o Jackson, TN, St. Mary's Church. (MEM)
Brownsville, TX, Cameron Co., Blessed Juan Diego de Guadalupe, c/o [2] Brownsville, TX, Christ the King Church. (BWN)
Brownsville, TX, Cameron Co., Sacred Heart, c/o [1] Brownsville, TX, Immaculate Conception Cathedral Church. (BWN)
Brownsville, TX, Cameron Co., St. Thomas, c/o [1] Brownsville, TX, Immaculate Conception Cathedral Church. (BWN)
Bruceton Mills, WV, Preston Co., Mary Help of Christians, c/o Cheat Lake, WV, St. Luke Church. (WH)
Bruni, TX, Webb Co., Sacred Heart, c/o Hebbronville, TX, Our Lady of Guadalupe Church. (CC)
Bruno, MN, Sacred Heart, c/o Sandstone, MN, St. Luke's Church. (DUL)
Brunswick, NE, Antelope Co., St. Ignatius, c/o Plainview, NE, St. Paul Church. (OM)
Bryce Canyon, UT, Garfield Co., St. Dominic, c/o Cedar City, UT, Christ the King Church. (SLC)
Bucarabones, PR, Sagrado Corazon, c/o Maricao, PR, St. John the Baptist Church. (MGZ)
Buchanan, ND, St. Margaret, c/o Jamestown, ND, The Basilica of St. James Church. (FAR)
Buckhead Ridge, FL, Glades Co., St. Theresa of the Child Jesus, c/o Moore Haven, FL, St. Joseph the Worker Church. (VEN)
Buckhorn, CA, Amador Co., Our Lady of the Pines, c/o Jackson, CA, St. Patrick's Church. (SAC)
Buena Vista, GA, Marion Co., St. Mary Magdalen, c/o Americus, GA, St. Mary Church. (SAV)
Buena Vista, PR, La Milagrosa, c/o Las Marias, PR, Immaculate Heart of Mary Church. (MGZ)
Buenavista, NM, Mora Co., c/o Mora, NM, St. Gertrude Church. (SFE)
Bueyeros, NM, Harding Co., c/o Roy, NM, Holy Family-St. Joseph Church. (SFE)
Buffalo, ND, St. Thomas, c/o Casselton, ND, St. Leo Church. (FAR)
Buffalo, OK, Harper Co., St. Joseph, c/o Woodward, OK, St. Peter's Church. (OKL)
Buffalo, TX, Leon Co., Blessed Kateri Tekakwitha, c/o Fairfield, TX, St. Bernard of Clairvaux Church. (TYL)
Buffalo, WI, St. Andrew, c/o Pardeeville, WI, St. Mary Church. (MAD)
Buffalo Creek, CO, Jefferson Co., St. Elizabeth, c/o Conifer, CO, Our Lady of The Pines Church. (DEN)
Buhach, CA, Merced Co., Immaculate Conception, c/o Atwater, CA, St. Anthony Church. (FRS)
Buhl, MN, Our Lady of the Sacred Heart, c/o Chisholm, MN, St. Joseph's Church. (DUL)
Bullhead, SD, Corson Co., St. Aloysius, c/o McLaughlin, SD, St. Bernard Church. (RC)
Bullhead, SD, Corson Co., St. Aloysius, c/o Standing Rock, SD, Standing Rock Reservation Church. (RC)
Bullville, NY, Orange Co., St. Paul, c/o Middletown, NY, Our Lady of Mt. Carmel Church. (NY)
Bunker, MO, Reynolds Co., Christ the King, c/o Salem, MO, Sacred Heart Church. (SPC)
Bunkerville, NV, Clark Co., La Virgen de Guadalupe, c/o Overton, NV, St. John, the Evangelist Church. (LAV)
Burchard, NE, Pawnee Co., Sacred Heart, c/o Steinauer, NE, St. Anthony Church. (LIN)
Bureau, IL, Bureau Co., St. Francis Xavier, c/o Granville, IL, Sacred Heart Of Jesus Church. (PEO)
Bureau, IL, Bureau Co., St. Francis Xavier, c/o Tiskilwa, IL, St. Mary's Church. (PEO)
Burkesville, KY, Cumberland Co., Holy Cross Catholic, c/o Albany, KY, Emmanuel Catholic Church. (L)
Burlington, TX, Milam Co., St. Michael's, c/o Rosebud, TX, St. Ann's Church. (AUS)
Burlington Junction, MO, Nodaway Co., St. Benedict Catholic Church, c/o Tarkio, MO, St. Paul the Apostle Church. (KC)
Burnham, PA, Mifflin Co., Mary Queen of All Saints, c/o Lewistown, PA, Sacred Heart of Jesus Church. (HBG)
Burnstad, ND, Logan Co., St. Clara, c/o Napoleon, ND, St. Philip Neri Church. (FAR)
Burnsville, NC, Yancey Co., Sacred Heart, c/o Mars Hill, NC, St. Andrew the Apostle Church. (CHL)
Busby, MT, Christ the King, c/o Lame Deer, MT, Blessed Sacrament Church. (GF)
Bush, LA, St. Tammany Civil Parish, St. Michael the Archangel, c/o Abita Springs, LA, St. Jane de Chantal Church. (NO)
Butner, NC, St. Bernadette, c/o Roxboro, NC, SS. Mary and Edward Church. (R)
Butte La Rose, LA, Sacred Heart, c/o Henderson, LA, Our Lady of Mercy Church. (LAF)
Buxton, NC, Our Lady of the Seas, c/o Kill Devil Hills, NC, Holy Redeemer Church. (R)
Bylas, AZ, Graham Co., Blessed Kateri Tekakwitha, c/o San Carlos, AZ, San Carlos Catholic Mission Church. (TUC)

C

Cabezon, NM, San Jose, c/o Cuba, NM, Immaculate Conception Church. (GLP)
Cabool, MO, Texas Co., St. Michael, c/o Mountain Grove, MO, Sacred Heart Church. (SPC)
Cactus, TX, Our Lady of Guadalupe, c/o Dumas, TX, SS. Peter and Paul Church. (AMA)
Cade, LA, St. Anthony, c/o Broussard, LA, St. Joseph Church. (LAF)
Caimital, PR, Our Lady of Perpetual Help, c/o Guayama, PR, St. Anthony of Padua Church. (PCE)
Cainsville, MO, Harrison Co., St. Mary's, c/o Bethany, MO, Blessed Sacrament Church. (KC)
Cairo, GA, Grady Co., St. Elizabeth Ann Seton, c/o Thomasville, GA, St. Augustine's Church. (SAV)
Calamine, WI, St. Michael, c/o Belmont, WI, St. Philomena Church. (MAD)
Caldwell, TX, San Salvador, c/o Bryan, TX, St. Anthony's Church. (AUS)
Calhoun, LA, St. Francis of Assisi, c/o West Monroe, LA, St. Paschal Church. (SHP)
Callabo, PR, Bo. Callabo, San Ramon, c/o Juana Diaz, PR, St. Raymond Nonato Church. (PCE)
Callaway, MN, Becker Co., Assumption, c/o Lake Eunice Township, MN, St. Mary of the Lakes Church. (CR)
Callaway, NE, St. Boniface, c/o Stapleton, NE, St. John the Evangelist Church. (GI)
Calvert, TX, Robertson Co., St. Mary, c/o Hearne, TX, St. Mary's Church. (AUS)
Camarillo, CA, Ventura Co., Cabrillo Chapel, c/o Ventura, CA, Sacred Heart Church. (LA)
Camaseyes, PR, Our Lady of Fatima, c/o Aguadilla, PR, La Milagrosa Church. (MGZ)
Cambalaches, PR, Our Lady of Perpetual Help, c/o Yauco, PR, Holy Rossary Church. (PCE)
Cambridge, IL, Henry Co., St. John Vianney, c/o Kewanee, IL, St. Francis of Assisi Church. (PEO)
Camden, AL, Wilcox Co., St. Joseph, c/o Orrville, AL, Immaculate Conception Church. (MOB)
Cameron, LA, Cameron Parish, St. Rose of Lima, c/o Creole, LA, Sacred Heart of Jesus Church. (LKC)
Cameron Corner, CA, St. Adelaide, c/o Jacumba, CA, St. Mary Magdalene Church. (SD)
Camilla, GA, Mitchell Co., St. John Vianney, c/o Moultrie, GA, Immaculate Conception Church. (SAV)
Camp Sacramento, CA, El Dorado Co., Our Lady of the Sierras, c/o South Lake Tahoe, CA, St. Theresa Church. (SAC)
Camp Summit, NY, N.Y.S. Correctional Facility, c/o Summit, NY, St. Anna Church. (ALB)
Camp Summit, NY, S.U.N.Y. Cobleskill College, c/o Summit, NY, St. Anna Church. (ALB)
Camp Wood, TX, Real Co., St. Mary Magdalen, c/o Rocksprings, TX, Sacred Heart of Mary Church. (SAT)
Campbell, NY, Steuben Co., St. Joseph, c/o Bradford, NY, St. Stanislaus Church. (ROC)
Campbellton, TX, Atascosa Co., Sacred Heart, c/o Pleasanton, TX, St. Andrew Church. (SAT)
Campo Indian Reservation, CA, Our Lady of Mount Carmel, c/o Jacumba, CA, St. Mary Magdalene Church. (SD)
Campobello, ME, St. Timothy's, c/o Lubec, ME, Sacred Heart Church. (PRT)
Campton, KY, Wolfe Co., Catholic Church of the Good Shepherd, c/o Beattyville, KY, Queen of All Saints Church. (LEX)
Canaan, NH, Grafton Co., St. Mary, c/o Enfield, NH, St. Helena Church. (MAN)
Canaan, PA, Wayne Co., St. Patrick, c/o Waymart, PA, St. Mary's Church. (SCR)
Canada de Los Alamos, NM, Santa Fe Co., Our Lady of Guadalupe, c/o [3] Santa Fe, NM, Cristo Rey Church. (SFE)
Canadohta Lake, PA, Crawford Co., Our Lady of Fatima, c/o Union City, PA, St. Teresa of Avila Church. (E)
Canalizo, PR, Jayuya Co., La Milagrosa, c/o Jayuya, PR, Our Lady of Monserrate Church. (PCE)
Candelaria, TX, Our Lady of Peace, c/o Presidio, TX, Santa Teresa de Jesus Church. (ELP)
Canjilon, NM, St. Juan Nepumoceno, c/o Chama, NM, St. Patrick Church. (SFE)
Cannon Ball, ND, Sioux Co., St. Elizabeth, c/o Fort Yates, ND, St. Peter - Catholic Indian Mission Church. (BIS)
Canon de Vallecitos, NM, Rio Arriba Co., c/o El Rito, NM, San Juan Nepomuceno Church. (SFE)
Canoncito, NM, Santa Fe Co., c/o Pecos, NM, St. Anthony Church. (SFE)
Canoncito, NM, San Lorenzo, c/o Tijeras, NM, Holy Child Church. (SFE)
Canones, NM, Rio Arriba Co., c/o Abiquiu, NM, St. Thomas Apostle Church. (SFE)
Canovanas, PR, Capilla Cristo Salvador, c/o [4] Canovanas, PR, Santa Maria Madre de Dios Church. (SJN)
Canovanas, PR, Ntra. Sra. de la Providencia, c/o [2] Canovanas, PR, Resurreccion del Senior Church. (SJN)
Canovanas, PR, San Francisco Javier, c/o [1] Canovanas, PR, Nuestra Senora del Pilar Church. (SJN)
Canton, NC, Haywood Co., Immaculate Conception, c/o Waynesville, NC, St. John the Evangelist Church. (CHL)
Canton, TX, Van Zandt Co., St. Theresa, c/o Athens, TX, St. Edward Church Church. (TYL)
Cantwell, AK, Denali National Park, c/o Healy, AK, Holy Mary of Guadalupe Church. (FBK)
Canyon, NM, Sandoval Co., c/o Jemez Pueblo, NM, San Diego Indian Missions Church. (SFE)
Canyon Ferry, MT, Our Lady of the Lake, c/o East Helena, MT, SS. Cyril and Methodius Church. (HEL)
Capitan, NM, Sacred Heart, c/o Carrizozo, NM, St. Rita Church. (LSC)
Caplis, LA, Bossier Parish, Mary, Queen of Peace, c/o Bossier City, LA, Christ the King Church. (SHP)
Capulin, NM, Rio Arriba Co., c/o Abiquiu, NM, St. Thomas Apostle Church. (SFE)
Carbondale, CO, Garfield Co., St. Mary of the Crown, c/o Basalt, CO, St. Vincent Church. (DEN)
Carenage, VI, Chapel of St. Anne, c/o [1] St. Thomas, VI, Cathedral of Sts. Peter and Paul Church. (STV)
Carey, OH, Wyandot Co., O.L.C., c/o Salem Twp., OH, St. Joseph Church. (TOL)
Carmen, PR, Our Lady of Mt. Carmel, c/o Guayama, PR, St. Anthony of Padua Church. (PCE)
Carnation, WA, King Co., St. Anthony, c/o Snoqualmie, WA, Our Lady of Sorrows Church. (SEA)
Carnegie, OK, Caddo Co., St. Richard, c/o Anadarko, OK, St. Patrick's Church. (OKL)
Carnuel, NM, Bernalillo Co., Holy Child, c/o Tijeras, NM, Holy Child Church. (SFE)
Caroga Lake, NY, St. Barbara, c/o Gloversville, NY, St. Mary of Mt. Carmel Church. (ALB)
Carolina, PR, La Sagrada Familia, c/o [12] Carolina, PR, San Juan de Dios Church. (SJN)
Carolina, PR, Parque Bolivariano 5-JL, c/o [3] Carolina, PR, Santa Clara de Asis Church. (SJN)
Carolina, PR, San Antonio, c/o [20] Carolina, PR, San Valentin Church. (SJN)
Carolina, PR, San Francisco de Asis, c/o [3] Carolina, PR, Santa Clara de Asis Church. (SJN)
Carolina, PR, Santa Rosa, c/o [20] Carolina, PR, San Valentin Church. (SJN)
Carpenter, WY, Laramie Co., St. Peter, c/o Pine Bluffs, WY, St. Paul's Church. (CHY)
Carrissa Plains, CA, San Luis Obispo Co., St. James Mission, c/o Santa Margarita, CA, Santa Margarita de Cortona Church. (MRY)
Carrizales, PR, Ntra. Sra. de las Mercedes, c/o Aguada, PR, St. Francis of Assisi Church. (MGZ)
Carrizales, PR, Our Lady of Montserrat, c/o Yauco, PR, Holy Rossary Church. (PCE)
Carroll, NH, St. Patrick, c/o Whitefield, NH, St. Matthew Church. (MAN)
Carroll Township, IA, St. Wenceslaus, c/o Clutier, IA, Immaculate Conception Church. (DUB)
Carson, MS, Jefferson Davis Co., St. Elizabeth, c/o Bassfield, MS, St. Peter Church. (BLX)
Cartersville, IA, St. John, c/o Rockwell, IA, Sacred Heart Church. (DUB)
Cartersville, VA, St. Catherine, c/o Powhatan, VA, St. John Neumann Church. (RIC)
Caruthers, CA, Fresno Co., Our Lady of the Assumption, c/o Riverdale, CA, St. Ann Church. (FRS)
Casa Colorada, NM, Valencia Co., c/o Tome, NM, Immaculate Conception Church. (SFE)
Cascade, CO, El Paso Co., Holy Rosary, c/o [10] Colorado Springs, CO, Sacred Heart Church. (COS)
Cascade, MT, Sacred Heart, c/o Fort Shaw, MT, St. Ann Church. (GF)
Cascade, PA, Lycoming Co., Assumption of the B.V.M., c/o [6] Williamsport, PA, St. Ann's Church. (SCR)
Cassville, MO, Barry Co., St. Edward, c/o Pulaskifield, MO, SS. Peter and Paul Church. (SPC)
Castine, ME, Hancock Co, Our Lady of Holy Hope, c/o Stonington, ME, St. Mary Star of the Sea Church. (PRT)
Castle Rock, WI, St. John Nepomucene, c/o Montfort, WI, St. Thomas Church. (MAD)
Catano, PR, Maria Auxiliadora, c/o Catano, PR, San Francisco de Sales Church. (SJN)

Catano, PR, San Jose Obrero, c/o Catano, PR, Nuestra Senora del Carmen Church. (SJN)
Catano, PR, San Judas Tadeo (Santuario), c/o Catano, PR, San Francisco de Sales Church. (SJN)
Catano, PR, San Martin de Porres, c/o Catano, PR, Nuestra Senora del Carmen Church. (SJN)
Catano, PR, Santo Domingo, c/o Catano, PR, San Francisco de Sales Church. (SJN)
Catarina, TX, Dimmit Co., St. Henry, c/o Asherton, TX, Immaculate Conception Church. (SAT)
Catatonk, NY, Tioga Co., St. Francis of Assisi, c/o Newark Valley, NY, St. John the Evangelist Church. (ROC)
Cathlamet, WA, Wahkiakum Co., St. Catherine, c/o Longview, WA, St. Rose de Viterbo Church. (SEA)
Cave Junction, OR, Josephine Co., St. Patrick, c/o Grants Pass, OR, St. Anne Church. (P)
Cayuga, ND, Sts. Peter & Paul, c/o Forman, ND, St. Mary's Church. (FAR)
Cazadero, CA, St. Colman, c/o Guerneville, CA, St. Elizabeth Church. (SR)
Cebolla, NM, Santo Nino, c/o Chama, NM, St. Patrick Church. (SFE)
Cedar Bluffs, NE, Saunders Co., St. Mary, c/o Colon, NE, St. Joseph's Church. (LIN)
Cedar Brook, NJ, Camden, Sacred Heart, c/o Blue Anchor, NJ, St. Lucy's Church. (CAM)
Cedar Creek, AZ, St. Anthony, c/o Cibecue, AZ, St. Catherine Church. (GLP)
Cedar Hill, NE, Saunders Co., Sacred Heart, c/o Morse Bluff, NE, St. George Church. (LIN)
Cedar Hill, TN, Robertson Co., St. Michael, c/o Springfield, TN, Our Lady of Lourdes Church. (NSH)
Cedaredge, CO, Delta Co., St. Philip Benizi, c/o Delta, CO, St. Michael Church. (PBL)
Cedarville, CA, Modoc Co., St. James, c/o Alturas, CA, Sacred Heart Church. (SAC)
Ceiba, PR, Sagrado Corazon de Jesus, Bo. Saco, c/o Ceiba, PR, San Antonio de Padua Church. (CGS)
Ceiba, PR, Ceiba Co., N.S. del Carmen, c/o Ceiba, PR, San Antonio de Padua Church. (CGS)
Celina, TN, Clay Co., Divine Savior, c/o Cookeville, TN, St. Thomas Aquinas Church. (NSH)
Center, MO, Ralls Co., St. Paul (Historic Church), c/o Perry, MO, St. William Church. (JC)
Center Barnstead, NH, Belknap Co., St. Paul, c/o Alton, NH, St. Joan of Arc Church. (MAN)
Center Harbor, NH, Belknap Co., Our Lady of Victory, c/o Meredith, NH, St. Charles Church. (MAN)
Centermoreland, PA, Luzerne Co., Blessed Sacrament, c/o Carverton, PA, St. Frances Cabrini Church. (SCR)
Centerville, TX, Leon Co., St. Leo the Great, c/o Crockett, TX, St. Francis of the Tejas Church. (TYL)
Central City, CO, Gilpin Co., St. Mary of the Assumption, c/o Idaho Springs, CO, St. Paul's Church. (DEN)
Centreville, MI, St. Clare, c/o Three Rivers, MI, Immaculate Conception Church. (KAL)
Cerrito, NM, San Miguel Co., c/o Villanueva, NM, Our Lady of Guadalupe Church. (SFE)
Cerro, NM, Taos Co., c/o Questa, NM, St. Anthony Church. (SFE)
Cerro Gordo, PR, Buen Consejo, c/o Aguada, PR, St. Francis of Assisi Church. (MGZ)
Chacon, NM, Mora Co., c/o Mora, NM, St. Gertrude Church. (SFE)
Chalan Kanoa Village, MP, Mercedarian Missionary Sisters of Berriz, c/o Chalan Kanoa Village, MP, Cathedral of Our Lady of Mt. Carmel Church. (CHK)
Challenge, CA, Yuba Co., St. Anthony, c/o Downieville, CA, Immaculate Conception Church. (SAC)
Chama, CO, Costilla Co., Immaculate Conception, c/o San Luis, CO, Sangre de Cristo Church. (PBL)
Chama, CO, Huerfano Co., Our Lady of Guadalupe, c/o Walsenburg, CO, St. Mary Church. (PBL)
Chamisal, NM, Taos Co., Santa Cruz Mission, c/o Penasco, NM, San Antonio de Padua Church. (SFE)
Chamita, NM, Rio Arriba Co., c/o San Juan Pueblo, NM, St. John the Baptist Church. (SFE)
Chandler, TX, Van Zandt Co., St. Boniface, c/o Athens, TX, St. Edward Church Church. (TYL)
Chaparral, NM, St. Thomas More, c/o Anthony, NM, St. Anthony's Church. (LSC)
Chapmanville, WV, Logan Co., St. Barbara, c/o Madison, WV, St. Mary, Queen of Heaven Church. (WH)
Charco, TX, Our Lady of Guadalupe, c/o Goliad, TX, Immaculate Conception Church. (VIC)
Charlemont, MA, Franklin Co., St. Christopher, c/o Shelburne Falls, MA, St. Joseph's Church. (SPR)
Charlestown, RI, Washington Co., St. James, c/o Charlestown, RI, St. Mary Church. (PRO)
Charley Creek, MT, St. Bernard's, c/o Sidney, MT, St. Matthew Church. (GF)
Charlo, MT, Mount Lake Co., St. Joseph's, c/o Ronan, MT, Sacred Heart Church. (HEL)
Chatom, AL, Washington Co., St. Paul, c/o Butler, AL, St. John Church. (MOB)
Cherokee, NC, Our Lady of Gaudalupe, c/o Maggie Valley, NC, St. Margaret Church. (CHL)
Cherokee, NC, Our Lady of Guadalupe, c/o Bryson City, NC, St. Joseph Church. (CHL)
Cherry Creek, SD, Ziebach Co., St. Joseph, c/o Eagle Butte, SD, All Saints Church. (RC)
Cherry Creek, SD, Ziebach Co., St. Joseph, c/o Eagle Butte, SD, Cheyenne River Reservation Church. (RC)
Cherryfield, ME, St. Michael's, c/o Machias, ME, Holy Name of Jesus Church. (PRT)
Chesapeake City, MD, Cecil Co., St. Rose of Lima, c/o Middletown, DE, St. Joseph Church. (WIL)
Chester, CA, Plumas Co., Christ the King, c/o Westwood, CA, Our Lady of the Snows Church. (SAC)
Chester, MA, Hampden Co., St. John, c/o Huntington, MA, St. Thomas Church. (SPR)
Chester, PA, Delaware Co., Blessed Katharine Drexel Center for Evangelization, c/o [2] Chester, PA, Blessed Katharine Drexel Church. (PH)
Chester, PA, Delaware Co., St. Hedwig Chapel, c/o Clifton Heights, PA, Sacred Heart Church. (PH)
Chesterfield, NH, Cheshire, Our Lady of the Lake, c/o Hinsdale, NH, St. Joseph Church. (MAN)
Chicago, IL, c/o Chicago, IL, Ss. Peter and Paul Mission Church. (ROM)
Chicago, IL, Cook Co., Sacred Heart, c/o [83] Chicago, IL, Holy Name of Mary Church. (CHI)
Childersburg, AL, Holy Name of Jesus, c/o Sylacauga, AL, St. Jude Church. (BIR)
Chili, NM, Rio Arriba Co., c/o Espanola, NM, Sacred Heart Church. (SFE)
Chilili, NM, Bernalillo Co., San Juan de Nepumoceno, c/o Tijeras, NM, Holy Child Church. (SFE)
China Lake, ME, St. Peter, c/o North Vassalboro, ME, St. Bridget's Church. (PRT)
Chino Valley, AZ, Yavapai Co., St. Catherine Laboure, c/o Prescott, AZ, Sacred Heart Church. (PHX)
Chippewa Lake, OH, Jesus Divine Redeemer, c/o Litchfield, OH, Our Lady Help of Christians Parish Church. (CLV)
Chireno, TX, Nacogdoches Co., Our Lady of Lourdes, c/o Nacogdoches, TX, Sacred Heart Church. (TYL)
Chocorua, NH, Carroll Co., Our Lady of Perpetual Help, c/o Center Ossipee, NH, St. Joseph Church. (MAN)
Choctaw, LA, St. James, c/o Kraemer, LA, St. Lawrence the Martyr Church. (HT)
Christine, TX, Ataseosa Co., St. Ignatius, c/o Jourdanton, TX, St. Matthew's Church. (SAT)
Christmas Valley, OR, Holy Family, c/o La Pine, OR, Holy Redeemer Church. (BAK)
Chugwater, WY, Platte Co., St. Theresa, c/o Wheatland, WY, St. Patrick's Church. (CHY)
Cincinnatus, NY, Our Lady of Perpetual Help, c/o Marathon, NY, St. Stephen Church. (SY)
Citra, FL, Marion Co., Christ the King, c/o [1] Ocala, FL, Blessed Trinity Church. (ORL)
Clallam Bay, WA, Clallam Co., St. Thomas the Apostle, c/o Forks, WA, St. Anne Parish Church. (SEA)
Clancy, MT, St. John's, c/o East Helena, MT, SS. Cyril and Methodius Church. (HEL)
Clanton, AL, Chilton Co., Church of the Resurrection, c/o Montevallo, AL, St. Thomas the Apostle Church. (BIR)
Claremont, VA, St. Anne, c/o Hopewell, VA, St. James Church Church. (RIC)
Clark, WY, Park Co., Our Lady of the Valley, c/o Powell, WY, St. Barbara Church. (CHY)
Clarkdale, AZ, Yavapai Co., St. Cecilia, c/o Cottonwood, AZ, Immaculate Conception Church. (PHX)
Clarksville, MO, Pike Co., Mary Queen of Peace, c/o Louisiana, MO, St. Joseph Church. (JC)
Clatskanie, OR, Columbia Co., St. John the Baptist, c/o Rainier, OR, Nativity B.V.M. Church. (P)
Claudell, KS, Phillips Co., St. Francis, c/o Phillipsburg, KS, SS. Philip and James Church. (SAL)
Claybanks, MI, St. John, c/o Montague, MI, St. James Church. (GR)
Claypool, AZ, Gila Co., St. Joseph, c/o Miami, AZ, Our Lady of the Blessed Sacrament Church. (TUC)
Clayton, AL, Barbour Co., Ventress Correctional Facility, c/o Eufaula, AL, Holy Redeemer Church. (MOB)
Clayton, GA, Rabun Co., St. Helena's, c/o Clarkesville, GA, St. Mark's Church. (ATL)
Clayton, NM, St. Francis Xavier, c/o Roy, NM, Holy Family-St. Joseph Church. (SFE)
Clayton, OK, Pushmataha Co., Holy Trinity, c/o Antlers, OK, St. Agnes Church. (TLS)
Clear Lake, IN, Steuben Co., St. Paul Chapel, c/o Angola, IN, St. Anthony Church. (FTW)
Clear Spring, MD, Washington Co., St. Michael, c/o Williamsport, MD, St. Augustine Church. (BAL)
Clearmont, WY, Johnson Co., St. Mary, c/o Buffalo, WY, St. John the Baptist Church. (CHY)
Clendenin, WV, Kanawha Co., Catholic Community of Clendenin, c/o Elkview, WV, Our Lady of the Hills Church. (WH)
Cleveland, GA, White Co., St. Paul the Apostle, c/o Blairsville, GA, St. Francis of Assisi Church. (ATL)
Cleveland, NM, Mora Co., c/o Mora, NM, St. Gertrude Church. (SFE)
Cleveland, OH, c/o [56] Cleveland, OH, Our Lady of Mount Carmel Church. (CLV)
Clifford, MI, St. Patrick's, c/o North Branch, MI, SS. Peter and Paul Church. (DET)
Climax Springs, MO, Our Lady of the Snows, c/o Hermitage, MO, St. Bernadette Church. (JC)
Clinton, AR, Van Buren Co., St. Jude, c/o St. Vincent, AR, St. Mary Church. (LR)
Clinton Corners, NY, Dutchess Co., St. Joseph, c/o Bangall, NY, Immaculate Conception Church. (NY)
Clintonville, NY, St. Catherine of Sienna, c/o Keeseville, NY, Church of the Immaculate Conception Church. (OG)
Cloquet, MN, Carlton Co., Holy Family Church, c/o Duluth, MN, Indian Missions Church. (DUL)
Cloudcroft, NM, Sacred Heart, c/o Alamogordo, NM, Immaculate Conception Church. (LSC)
Cloverdale, OR, Tillamook Co., St. Joseph, c/o Tillamook, OR, Sacred Heart Church. (P)
Clyde, TX, Callahan Co., Sts. Joachim and Ann, c/o [1] Abilene, TX, Sacred Heart Church. (SAN)
Clyde Park, MT, St. Margaret, c/o Livingston, MT, St. Mary's Church. (GF)
Coabbey, PR, Jayuya Co., San Jorge, c/o Jayuya, PR, Our Lady of Monserrate Church. (PCE)
Coahoma, TX, St. Joseph, c/o Big Spring, TX, Immaculate Heart of Mary Church. (SAN)
Coal Mine, TX, Atascosa Co., Immaculate Conception, c/o Lytle, TX, St. Andrew Church. (SAT)
Coalburg, WV, Kanawha Co., Good Shepherd, c/o Belle, WV, St. John Church. (WH)
Coaldale, PA, Schuylkill Co., St. Patrick (Seek), c/o Tamaqua, PA, St. Jerome Church. (ALN)
Coamo, PR, Coamo Co., Saint James, c/o Coamo, PR, St. Blase Church. (PCE)
Coamo Arriba, PR, Coamo Co., Sacred Heart, c/o Coamo, PR, St. Blase Church. (PCE)
Cochiti, NM, Sandoval Co., Indian Pueblo, c/o Pena Blanca, NM, Nuestra Senora De Guadalupe Church. (SFE)
Cochranton, PA, Crawford Co., Our Lady of Lourdes, c/o Frenchtown, PA, St. Hippolyte Church. (E)
Coco, PR, Santa Ana, c/o Salinas, PR, Our Lady of Monserrat Church. (PCE)
Cocodrie, LA, Our Lady of the Gulf, c/o Chauvin, LA, St. Joseph Church. (HT)
Coeburn, VA, St. Mary, c/o Norton, VA, St. Anthony Church. (RIC)
Cogswell, ND, Our Lady of Mercy, c/o Forman, ND, St. Mary's Church. (FAR)
Cohasset, MN, St. Augustine's, c/o Grand Rapids, MN, St. Joseph's Church. (DUL)
Cohoes, NY, Sacred Heart of Jesus, c/o [6] Cohoes, NY, St. Rita-Sacred Heart Church. (ALB)
Cokedale, CO, Las Animas Co., Sacred Hearts of Jesus and Mary, c/o Trinidad, CO, Our Lady of Mt. Carmel, Trinidad Area Catholic Community (Trinidad Cluster) Church. (PBL)
Cokeville, WY, Lincoln Co., St. Dominic, c/o Kemmerer, WY, St. Patrick's Church. (CHY)
Cole Camp, MO, Benton Co., SS. Peter & Paul, c/o Warsaw, MO, St. Ann Church. (JC)
Collares, PR, Jayuya Co., Cristo Rey, c/o Jayuya, PR, Our Lady of Monserrate Church. (PCE)
Collegeville, AL, Jefferson Co., Sacred Heart, c/o [18] Birmingham, AL, Our Lady Queen of the Universe Church. (BIR)
Collores, PR, Bo. Jacaguas, La Milagrosa, c/o Juana Diaz, PR, St. Raymond Nonato Church. (PCE)
Collores, PR, Sacred Heart, c/o Yauco, PR, Holy Rossary Church. (PCE)
Colon, MI, St. Barbara, c/o Bronson, MI, St. Mary's Church. (KAL)
Colonia Nueva, TX, Christ the King, c/o Donna, TX, St. Joseph Church. (BWN)
Colonia Villodos, PR, Perpetuo Socorro, c/o Guayama, PR, St. Anthony of Padua Church. (PCE)
Colonias, NM, Guadalupe Co., c/o Santa Rosa, NM, St. Rose of Lima Church. (SFE)
Colrain, MA, Franklin Co., St. John the Baptist, c/o Shelburne Falls, MA, St. Joseph's Church. (SPR)
Columbia, AL, Houston Co., Good Shepherd, c/o Dothan, AL, St. Columba Church. (MOB)
Columbia, CA, Tuolumne Co., St. Anne, c/o Sonora, CA, St. Patrick Church. (STO)
Columbia, KY, Adair Co., Good Shepherd, c/o Jamestown, KY, Holy Spirit Church. (L)
Columbia, LA, St. John, c/o Winnsboro, LA, St. Mary Church. (ALX)
Columbia, NC, All Souls, c/o Edenton, NC, St. Anne Church. (R)
Columbus, NM, Holy Family, c/o Deming, NM, St. Ann's Church. (LSC)
Comal, TX, Comal Co., St. Joseph, c/o New Braunfels, TX, SS. Peter and Paul Church. (SAT)
Commerce, GA, Jackson Co., St. Catherine Laboure, c/o Toccoa, GA, St. Mary's Church. (ATL)
Comstock, TX, Valverde Co., Mary, Queen of the Universe, c/o Del Rio, TX, St. Joseph's Church. (SAT)

Concepcion, TX, Duval Co., Immaculate Conception, c/o Premont, TX, St. Theresa of the Infant Jesus Church. (CC)
Concrete, WA, Skagit Co., St. Catherine, c/o Sedro Woolley, WA, Immaculate Heart of Mary Church. (SEA)
Conde Avila, PR, St. Martin de Porres, c/o Cabo Rojo, PR, St. Michael Church. (MGZ)
Conehatta, MS, St. Catherine, c/o Philadelphia, MS, Holy Rosary Church. (JKS)
Conesus, NY, Livingston Co., St. William, c/o Livonia, NY, St. Joseph Church. (ROC)
Congress Junction, AZ, Yavapai Co., Good Shepherd of the Desert, c/o Prescott, AZ, Sacred Heart Church. (PHX)
Consejo Alto, PR, La Monserrate, c/o Guayanilla, PR, Immaculate Conception Church. (PCE)
Constantia, NY, Oswego Co., St. Bernadette, c/o Cleveland, NY, St. Mary of the Assumption Church. (SY)
Contoocook, NH, Merrimack, St. Mary, c/o Henniker, NH, St. Theresa Church. (MAN)
Contreras, NM, Socorro Co., San Jose, c/o La Joya, NM, Our Lady of Sorrows Church. (SFE)
Conway, MA, Franklin Co., St. Mark, c/o South Deerfield, MA, St. James Church. (SPR)
Conway, ND, Walsh Co., St. Marks, c/o Pisek, ND, St. John Nepomucene Church. (FAR)
Cookson, OK, Cherokee Co., St. John the Evangelist, c/o Sallisaw, OK, St. Francis Xavier Church. (TLS)
Cooper Landing, AK, St. John Neumann Church, c/o Seward, AK, Sacred Heart Church. (ANC)
Copper Harbor, MI, Our Lady of the Pines, c/o Ahmeek, MI, Our Lady of Peace Church. (MAR)
Coqui, PR, Our Lady of Perpetual Help, c/o Aguirre, PR, Sacred Heart Church. (PCE)
Coral, MI, St. Clara, c/o Sand Lake, MI, Mary Queen of Apostles Church. (GR)
Cordell, OK, Washita Co., St. Anne, c/o Clinton, OK, St. Mary's Church. (OKL)
Cordova, MD, Talbot Co., St. Joseph, c/o Easton, MD, SS. Peter and Paul Church. (WIL)
Cordova, NM, Rio Arriba Co., San Antonio, c/o Chimayo, NM, Holy Family Church. (SFE)
Corning, AR, Clay Co., St. Joseph, c/o Engelberg, AR, St. John the Baptist Church. (LR)
Corona, NM, St. Therese of the Little Flower, c/o Carrizozo, NM, St. Rita Church. (LSC)
Corozal, PR, San Antonio, c/o Penuelas, PR, St. Joseph Church. (PCE)
Corpus Christi, TX, Nueces Co., Mary, Mother of the Church, c/o [4] Corpus Christi, TX, Holy Family Church. (CC)
Corpus Christi, TX, Nueces Co., Our Lady of Mount Carmel, c/o [7] Corpus Christi, TX, Our Lady of the Rosary Church. (CC)
Corpus Christi, TX, Nueces Co., St. Mary, c/o [19] Corpus Christi, TX, St. Peter Prince of Apostles Church. (CC)
Corral, PR, P. Socorro, c/o Juana Diaz, PR, St. Raymond Nonato Church. (PCE)
Corsica, PA, Jefferson Co., St. Ann, c/o Brookville, PA, Immaculate Conception Church. (E)
Cossayuna Lake, NY, c/o Salem, NY, Holy Cross Church. (ALB)
Costilla, NM, Taos Co., c/o Questa, NM, St. Anthony Church. (SFE)
Cotton City, NM, St. Jude, c/o Lordsburg, NM, St. Joseph Church. (LSC)
Cottonwood, CA, Shasta Co., St. Anne, c/o Anderson, CA, Sacred Heart Church. (SAC)
Cottonwood, MT, St. John, c/o Havre, MT, St. Jude Thaddeus Church. (GF)
Cotuy, PR, Our Lady of Fatima, c/o San German, PR, San German de Auxerre Church. (MGZ)
Coulee City, WA, Grant Co., Holy Angels, c/o Hartline, WA, St. Patrick's Church. (YAK)
Coupeville, WA, Island Co., St. Mary, c/o Oak Harbor, WA, St. Augustine Church. (SEA)
Courtenay, ND, Stustman Co., c/o Sanborn, ND, Sacred Heart Church. (FAR)
Coushatta, LA, Red River Parish, St. George, c/o Mansfield, LA, St. Joseph Church. (SHP)
Covelo, CA, Queen of Peace, c/o Willits, CA, St. Anthony Church. (SR)
Cox, SD, Harding Co., St. Agnes, c/o Buffalo, SD, St. Anthony Church. (RC)
Coyanosa, TX, Pecos Co., St. Isidore, c/o Fort Stockton, TX, St. Agnes Church. (SAN)
Coyote, NM, Rio Arriba Co., c/o Abiquiu, NM, St. Thomas Apostle Church. (SFE)
Craftsbury, VT, Orleans Co., Our Lady of Fatima, c/o Greensboro Bend, VT, St. Michael Church. (BUR)
Crane, OR, St. Thomas, c/o Burns, OR, Holy Family Church. (BAK)
Cranfield, MS, St. John the Baptist, c/o Natchez, MS, Holy Family Church. (JKS)
Crates, PA, Clarion Co., St. Nicholas, c/o New Bethlehem, PA, St. Charles Church. (E)
Crawfordsville, AR, Crittenden Co., Sacred Heart, c/o West Memphis, AR, St. Michael's Church. (LR)
Creede, CO, Mineral Co., Immaculate Conception, c/o Del Norte, CO, Holy Name of Mary Church. (PBL)
Crescent, OK, Logan Co., St. Margaret Mary, c/o Guthrie, OK, St. Mary's Church. (OKL)
Crescent City, IL, St. Joseph, c/o Watseka, IL, St. Edmund Church. (JOL)
Creswell, OR, Lane Co., St. Philip Benizi, c/o Cottage Grove, OR, Our Lady of Perpetual Help Church. (P)
Cripple Creek, CO, Teller Co., St. Peter's, c/o Woodland Park, CO, Our Lady of the Woods Church. (COS)
Cristo Rey, TX, La Victoria, c/o Grulla, TX, Holy Family Church. (BWN)
Crittenden, NY, St. Patrick, c/o Corfu, NY, St. Francis of Assisi Church. (BUF)
Crockett, CA, Contra Costa Co., St. Patrick, c/o Crockett, CA, St. Rose of Lima Church. (OAK)
Crockett Co., TN, c/o Humboldt, TN, Sacred Heart Church. (MEM)
Croghan, NY, Belfort, St. Vincent de Paul, c/o Croghan, NY, St. Stephen Church. (OG)
Croghan, NY, New Bremen, St. Peter, c/o Croghan, NY, St. Stephen Church. (OG)
Cromwell-Wright, MN, Immaculate Conception, c/o Carlton, MN, St. Francis Church. (DUL)
Crook, CO, Logan Co., St. Peters, c/o Julesburg, CO, St. Anthony Church. (DEN)
Crosbyton, TX, Crosby Co., St. Joseph, c/o Ralls, TX, St. Michael Church. (LUB)
Cross City, FL, Dixie Co., Holy Cross, c/o Chiefland, FL, St. John the Evangelist Church. (STA)
Crosstown, MO, Perry Co., St. James, c/o Perryville, MO, St. Vincent De Paul Church. (STL)
Crows Landing, CA, Stanislaus Co., Immaculate Heart of Mary, c/o Patterson, CA, Sacred Heart Church. (STO)
Cruces, PR, Santa Monica, c/o Aguada, PR, St. Francis of Assisi Church. (MGZ)
Crystal, ND, Pembina Co., St. Patrick, c/o Park River, ND, St. Mary's Church. (FAR)
Crystal Beach, TX, Galveston Co., St. Therese of Lisieux, c/o Port Bolivar, TX, Our Mother of Mercy Church. (GAL)
Crystal Lake, NY, c/o Greenville, NY, St. John the Baptist Church. (ALB)
Cuadrilla, TX, San Jose, c/o Fabens, TX, Our Lady of Guadalupe Church. (ELP)
Cuarteles, NM, c/o Santa Cruz, NM, Holy Cross Church. (SFE)
Cuba, OH, Putnam Co., St. Isidore, c/o Kalida, OH, St. Michael Church. (TOL)
Cubero, NM, Our Lady of Light, c/o San Fidel, NM, St. Joseph Church. (GLP)
Cuchillo, NM, St. Joseph, c/o Truth or Consequences, NM, Our Lady of Perpetual Help Church. (LSC)
Cuervo, NM, Guadalupe Co., c/o Santa Rosa, NM, St. Rose of Lima Church. (SFE)
Cummiskey, PA, Sullivan Co., St. Francis of Assisi, c/o Dushore, PA, St. Basil's Church. (SCR)
Cundiyo, NM, Rio Arriba Co., Santo Domingo, c/o Chimayo, NM, Holy Family Church. (SFE)
Cuny Table, SD, Shannon Co., St. Joseph, c/o Pine Ridge, SD, Holy Rosary Church. (RC)
Cupey, PR, San Martin de Porres, c/o [60] San Juan, PR, Santa Teresa Jornet Church. (SJN)
Cupey, PR, Virgen de la Salud, c/o [60] San Juan, PR, Santa Teresa Jornet Church. (SJN)
Curtis, MI, Mackinac Co., St. Timothy, c/o Grand Marais, MI, Holy Rosary Church Church. (MAR)
Custer, MT, St. Mary, c/o Hardin, MT, St. Joseph's Church. (GF)
Cuthbert, GA, Randolph Co., St. Luke, c/o Blakely, GA, Holy Family Church. (SAV)
Cygnet, OH, Wood Co., Sacred Heart, c/o North Baltimore, OH, Our Lady of the Miraculous Medal Church. (TOL)
Cypremort Point, LA, St. Francis, (Independent Mission), c/o Four Corners, LA, St. Peter the Apostle Church. (LAF)

D

Dahlia, NM, Guadalupe Co., c/o Anton Chico, NM, San Jose Church. (SFE)
Dallas, GA, Paulding Co., St. Vincent de Paul, c/o Lithia Springs, GA, St. John Vianney Church. (ATL)
Dallas City, IL, Hancock Co., Sacred Heart, c/o Nauvoo, IL, SS. Peter and Paul's Church. (PEO)
Dalton, NE, Cheyenne Co., St. Mary, c/o Bridgeport, NE, All Souls Church. (GI)
Danby, VT, Rutland Co., Holy Trinity, c/o East Dorset, VT, St. Jerome Church. (BUR)
Danforth, ME, St. Ann, c/o Lincoln, ME, St. Mary Church. (PRT)
Danville, KS, c/o Harper, KS, St. Joan of Arc Church. (WCH)
Danville, VT, Caledonia Co., Our Lady Queen of Peace, c/o Lyndonville, VT, St. Elizabeth Church. (BUR)
Darby, MT, Ravalli Co., St. Philip Benizi, c/o Hamilton, MT, St. Francis Church. (HEL)
Dardanelle, AR, Yell Co., St. Augustine's, c/o Russellville, AR, St. John's Church. (LR)
Darien, GA, McIntosh Co., Nativity of Our Lady, c/o Brunswick, GA, St. Francis Xavier Church. (SAV)
Darlington, SC, Darlington Co., St. Joseph the Worker, c/o Hartsville, SC, St. Mary the Virgin Mother Church. (CHR)
Darrington, WA, Snohomish Co., St. John Mary Vianney, c/o Arlington, WA, Immaculate Conception Church. (SEA)
Datil, NM, Nativity of the Blessed Virgin Mary, c/o Quemado, NM, Sacred Heart Church. (GLP)
Davenport Center, NY, Delaware Co., Chapel of St. Theresa the Little Flower, c/o South Kortright, NY, Church of the Most Precious Blood of Jesus Church. (ALB)
David City, NE, Butler Co., Assumption, c/o David City, NE, St. Mary's Church. (LIN)
Dawsonville, GA, Dawson Co., Christ Redeemer, c/o Dahlonega, GA, St. Luke Catholic Church. (ATL)
Dayton, IA, Christ the King, c/o Ogden, IA, St. John's Church. (SC)
Dayton, OR, Yamhill Co., St. Martin de Porres, c/o McMinnville, OR, St. James Church. (P)
Dayton, WI, St. James, c/o Belleville, WI, St. Mary of Lourdes Church. (MAD)
Dazey, ND, Barnes Co., St. Mary, c/o Sanborn, ND, Sacred Heart Church. (FAR)
De Bruce, NY, Sullivan Co., Sacred Heart, c/o Livingston Manor, NY, St. Aloysius Church. (NY)
De Ridder, LA, Beauregard Parish, St. Jude, c/o De Ridder, LA, St. Joseph's Church. (LKC)
Decatur, NE, Burt Co., Holy Family, c/o Tekamah, NE, St. Patrick Church. (OM)
Deerfield, KS, Kearny Co., Christ the King, c/o Garden City, KS, St. Mary Church. (DOD)
Deerwood, MN, St. Joseph, c/o Crosby, MN, St. Joseph's Church. (DUL)
Del City, KS, Korean Roman Catholic Community, c/o [9] Oklahoma City, OK, St. Paul, Apostle Church. (OKL)
Del Rey, CA, St. Katherine's, c/o Sanger, CA, St. Mary Church. (FRS)
Delhi, LA, Richland Parish, St. Theresa, c/o Rayville, LA, Sacred Heart Church. (SHP)
Dell City, TX, San Isidro, c/o Van Horn, TX, Our Lady of Fatima Church. (ELP)
Delmar, MD, Holy Redeemer, c/o Salisbury, MD, St. Francis De Sales Church. (WIL)
Delmas Dedeaux, MS, Harrison Co., Our Lady of Chartres, c/o [1] Gulfport, MS, St. Ann Church. (BLX)
Delta, UT, Millard Co., St. John Bosco, c/o Milford, UT, St. Bridget Church. (SLC)
Demarest, NJ, Bergen Co., St. Joseph Korean Catholic Community, c/o Demarest, NJ, St. Joseph's Church. (NEW)
Deming, WA, Whatcom Co., St. Peter, c/o Lynden, WA, St. Joseph's Church. (SEA)
Denmark, WI, All Saints, c/o New Denmark, WI, Holy Trinity Church. (GB)
Denmark, WI, New Denmark, Holy Trinity, c/o Denmark, WI, All Saints Church. (GB)
Dennis Port, MA, Barnstable Co., Our Lady of the Annunciation, c/o West Harwich, MA, Holy Trinity Church. (FR)
Denton, MD, Caroline Co., St. Elizabeth, c/o Ridgely, MD, St. Benedict Church. (WIL)
Denton, MT, St. Anthony, c/o Stanford, MT, St. Rose of Lima Church. (GF)
Denver, CO, Denver Co., St. Elizabeth of Hungary, c/o [12] Denver, CO, Holy Ghost Church. (DEN)
Denver, CO, St. Patrick, c/o [3] Denver, CO, Annunciation Church. (DEN)
Denver, NC, Lincoln Co., Holy Spirit, c/o Mooresville, NC, St. Therese Church. (CHL)
Dermott, AR, Chicot Co., Nativity of the Blessed Virgin Mary, c/o McGehee, AR, St. Mary Church. (LR)
DeRuyter, NY, St. Lawrence, c/o Truxton, NY, St. Patrick Church. (SY)
Des Moines, IA, Polk Co., Our Lady of Guadalupe, c/o [13] Des Moines, IA, Visitation Church. (DM)
Des Moines, NM, Union Co., Our Lady of Guadalupe, c/o Clayton, NM, St. Francis Xavier Church. (SFE)
Descanso, CA, San Diego Co., Our Lady of the Pines, c/o Descanso, CA, Our Lady of Light Church. (SD)
Detroit, OR, Marion Co., St. Christopher, c/o Sublimity, OR, St. Boniface Church. (P)
Deweese, NE, Clay Co., Assumption, c/o Lawrence, NE, Sacred Heart Church. (LIN)
Dexter, NY, Jefferson Co., St. Elizabeth Seton, c/o Brownville, NY, Immaculate Conception of the B.V.M. Church. (OG)
Dexter, OR, Lane Co., St. Henry, c/o Oakridge, OR, St. Michael Church. (P)
Dickey, ND, LaMoure Co., Assumption, c/o La Moure, ND, Holy Rosary Church. (FAR)
Dickson City, PA, Lackawanna Co., St. Thomas Apostle, c/o Dickson City, PA, Visitation of the Blessed Virgin Mary Church. (SCR)
Diego Hdez, PR, St. Anthony, c/o Yauco, PR, Holy Rossary Church. (PCE)
Diener Ranch At Five Points, CA, Fresno Co., Holy

Family Chapel, c/o Riverdale, CA, St. Ann Church. (FRS)

Dilia, NM, Guadalupe Co., c/o Anton Chico, NM, San Jose Church. (SFE)

Dilley, TX, Frio Co., St. Mary, c/o Dilley, TX, St. Joseph's Church. (SAT)

Dillon Valley, CO, Summit Co., Our Lady of Peace, c/o Breckenridge, CO, St. Mary Church. (DEN)

Dimmick Township, IL, Sacred Heart, c/o [3] La Salle, IL, Resurrection Church. (PEO)

Diomede, AK, St. Jude, c/o Nome, AK, St. Joseph Church. (FBK)

Dividing Ridge, KY, Pendleton Co., St. John's, c/o Williamstown, KY, St. William Church. (COV)

Dixfield, ME, St. Joseph, c/o Mexico, ME, St. Theresa Church. (PRT)

Dixon, NE, Dixon Co., St. Anne, c/o Laurel, NE, St. Mary Church. (OM)

Dobbins, CA, Yuba Co., Sacred Heart Church, c/o Marysville, CA, St. Joseph Church. (SAC)

Dobson, NC, Sacred Heart, c/o Mt. Airy, NC, Holy Angels Church. (CHL)

Dockton, WA, King Co., St. Patrick, c/o Vashon, WA, St. John Vianney Church. (SEA)

Dodge, NE, St. Wenceslaus, c/o Olean, NE, Sacred Heart Church. (OM)

Dodson, MT, Sacred Heart, c/o Malta, MT, St. Mary's Church. (GF)

Dodson, MT, St. Thomas, c/o Hays, MT, St. Paul's Indian Mission Church. (GF)

Doe Run, PA, Chester Co., St. Malachy, c/o Parkesburg, PA, Our Lady of Consolation Church. (PH)

Dolan Springs, AZ, Mohave Co., Our Lady of the Desert, c/o Kingman, AZ, St. Mary's Church. (PHX)

Dollar Bay, MI, Houghton Co., St. Francis of Assisi, c/o Hancock, MI, Resurrection Church. (MAR)

Dolores, CO, Montezuma Co., Our Lady of Victory Church, c/o Mancos, CO, St. Rita Church. (PBL)

Donalsonville, GA, Seminole Co., Church of the Incarnation, c/o Bainbridge, GA, St. Joseph's Church. (SAV)

Donken, MI, Houghton Co., Immaculate Heart of Mary, c/o Chassell, MI, St. Anne Church. (MAR)

Donnybrook, ND, Ward Co., St. Anthony, c/o Kenmare, ND, St. Agnes Church. (BIS)

Doraville, GA, Dekalb Co., Our Lady of the Americas, c/o [4] Atlanta, GA, Immaculate Heart of Mary Church. (ATL)

Dorothy, MN, Red Lake Co., St. Dorothy, c/o Red Lake Falls, MN, St. Joseph's Church. (CR)

Dorothy, NJ, Atlantic Co., St. Bernard, c/o Mays Landing, NJ, St. Vincent de Paul Church. (CAM)

Dorrance, KS, Russell Co., St. Joseph, c/o Wilson, KS, St. Wenceslaus Church. (SAL)

Dorris, CA, Siskiyou Co., Our Lady of Good Counsel, c/o Tulelake, CA, Holy Cross Church. (SAC)

Douglas, NE, Otoe Co., St. Martin's, c/o Palmyra, NE, St. Leo's Church. (LIN)

Dove Creek, CO, Dolores Co., St. Jude, c/o Cortez, CO, St. Margaret Mary Church. (PBL)

Downey, CA, Los Angeles Co., Los Padrinos Juvenile Hall, c/o Downey, CA, St. Raymond Church. (LA)

Downey, CA, Los Angeles Co., Rancho Los Amigos Hospital, c/o Downey, CA, St. Raymond Church. (LA)

Downs, KS, Osborne Co., St. Mary's, c/o Osborne, KS, St. Aloysius Church. (SAL)

Downsville, NY, Delaware Co., Holy Family, c/o Walton, NY, St. John the Baptist Church. (ALB)

Doylesburg, PA, Franklin Co., Our Lady of Refuge, c/o Chambersburg, PA, Corpus Christi Church. (HBG)

Doyline, LA, Webster Parish, Mary, Queen of the Holy Rosary, c/o Bossier City, LA, Christ the King Church. (SHP)

Drain, OR, Douglas Co., St. John the Apostle, c/o Sutherlin, OR, St. Francis Xavier Church. (P)

Drake, ND, McHenry Co., St. Margaret Mary, c/o Anamoose, ND, St. Francis Xavier Church. (FAR)

Draper, SD, Jones Co., St. Anthony of Padua, c/o Presho, SD, Christ the King Church. (RC)

Draper, UT, Salt Lake Co., St. John the Baptist, c/o [6] Sandy, UT, Blessed Sacrament Church. (SLC)

Drew, SD, Perkins Co., St. James, c/o Bison, SD, Blessed Sacrament Church. (RC)

Drewsey, OR, Our Lady of Loretto, c/o Burns, OR, Holy Family Church. (BAK)

Drifting, PA, Clearfield Co., St. Severin, c/o Frenchville, PA, St. Mary of the Assumption Church. (E)

Driftwood, PA, Cameron Co., St. James, c/o Emporium, PA, St. Mark Church. (E)

Driscoll, ND, Burleigh Co., St. Anthony, c/o Menoken, ND, St. Hildegard Church. (BIS)

Driscoll, TX, Nueces Co., St. James, c/o Bishop, TX, St. James Church. (CC)

Drummond Island, MI, Chippewa Co., St. Florence, c/o DeTour, MI, Sacred Heart Church. (MAR)

Drumright, OK, Creek Co., St. Mary, c/o Cushing, OK, SS. Peter and Paul Church. (TLS)

Dubina, TX, Fayette Co., SS. Cyril and Methodius, c/o Weimar, TX, St. Michael Church. (VIC)

Dublin, NH, Our Lady of the Snows, c/o Harrisville, NH, St. Denis Church. (MAN)

Dubois, WY, Fremont Co., Our Lady of the Woods, c/o Riverton, WY, St. Margaret's Church. (CHY)

Dubuisson, MS, Harrison Co., St. Ann, c/o DeLisle, MS, The Catholic Church in DeLisle Church. (BLX)

Duchesne, UT, Duchesne Co., Holy Spirit, c/o Roosevelt, UT, St. Helen's Church. (SLC)

Duey, PR, Chapel of St. Augustin, c/o San German, PR, San German de Auxerre Church. (MGZ)

Duey, PR, Virgin of Mt. Carmel, c/o Yauco, PR, Holy Rossary Church. (PCE)

Dulce, NM, St. Anthony, c/o Lumberton, NM, St. Francis of Assisi Church. (GLP)

Duluth, GA, Gwinnett Co., St. Monica, c/o Duluth, GA, St. Benedict Church. (ATL)

Dumas, AR, Desha Co., Holy Child Church, c/o McGehee, AR, St. Mary Church. (LR)

Duncan, AZ, St. Mary, c/o Clifton, AZ, Sacred Heart Church. (TUC)

Duncannon, PA, Perry Co., St. Bernadette, c/o Marysville, PA, Our Lady of Good Counsel Church. (HBG)

Dundee, NY, Yates Co., St. Andrew, c/o Penn Yan, NY, St. Michael Church. (ROC)

Dungannon, VA, St. Patrick, c/o Gate City, VA, St. Bernard Church. (RIC)

Dunmore, PA, Lackawanna Co., St. Casimir, c/o [5] Dunmore, PA, St. Mary of Mount Carmel Church. (SCR)

Dupree, SD, Ziebach Co., Sacred Heart, c/o Eagle Butte, SD, All Saints Church. (RC)

Dupree, SD, Ziebach Co., Sacred Heart, c/o Eagle Butte, SD, Cheyenne River Reservation Church. (RC)

Dupuyer, MT, Pondera Co., Holy Cross, c/o Valier, MT, St. Francis Church. (HEL)

Duran, NM, Torrance Co., c/o Vaughn, NM, St. Mary Church. (SFE)

Durham, CA, Butte Co., St. James, c/o Chico, CA, St. John the Baptist Church. (SAC)

Duryea, PA, Luzerne Co., St. Joseph's, c/o Duryea, PA, Sacred Heart of Jesus Church. (SCR)

Duvall, WA, King Co., Holy Innocents, c/o Snoqualmie, WA, Our Lady of Sorrows Church. (SEA)

E

Eagle, CO, Eagle Co., St. Mary, c/o Edwards, CO, St. Clare of Assisi Church. (DEN)

Eagle Harbor, MI, Holy Redeemer, c/o Ahmeek, MI, Our Lady of Peace Church. (MAR)

Eagle Nest, NM, Colfax Co., St. Mel, c/o Cimarron, NM, Immaculate Conception Church Church. (SFE)

Eagles Mere, PA, Sullivan Co., St. Francis of Assisi, c/o Dushore, PA, St. Basil's Church. (SCR)

Eagles Mere, PA, Sullivan Co., St. Francis of Assisi, c/o Mildred, PA, St. Francis of Assisi Church. (SCR)

Eagleville, CT, Tolland Co., St. Joseph, c/o Coventry, CT, St. Mary Church. (NOR)

Earth, TX, Lamb Co., St. Mary Magdalen, c/o Muleshoe, TX, Immaculate Conception Church. (LUB)

Easley, SC, Anderson Co., St. Luke, c/o Pickens, SC, Holy Cross Church. (CHR)

East Albany, VT, Orleans Co., St. John of the Cross, c/o Barton, VT, Conversion of St. Paul Church. (BUR)

East Barre, VT, Orange Co., Mother Cabrini, c/o Washington, VT, St. Cecilia Church. (BUR)

East Berkshire, VT, Franklin Co., Our Lady of Lourdes, c/o Richford, VT, All Saints Church. (BUR)

East Brewster, MA, Barnstable Co., Immaculate Conception, c/o Brewster, MA, Our Lady of the Cape Church. (FR)

East Durham, NY, Greene Co., Our Lady of Knock Shrine, c/o Cairo, NY, Sacred Heart Church. (ALB)

East Durham, NY, St. Mary, c/o Cairo, NY, Sacred Heart Church. (ALB)

East Fairfield, VT, Franklin Co., St. Anthony-St. George, c/o Fairfield, VT, St. Patrick Church. (BUR)

East Glacier, MT, Church of the Ascension, c/o Browning, MT, Church of the Little Flower Church. (HEL)

East Highlands, CA, San Bernardino Co., St. John Bosco, c/o Highland, CA, St. Adelaide Church. (SB)

East Killingly, CT, Windham Co., Our Lady of Peace, c/o Danielson, CT, St. James Church. (NOR)

East Longmeadow, MA, Hampden Co., St. Joseph's, c/o [19] Springfield, MA, St. Paul Church. (SPR)

East Quogue, NY, Suffolk Co., c/o Hampton Bays, NY, St. Rosalie's Church. (RVC)

East Raymond, ME, St. Raymond, c/o Windham, ME, Our Lady of Perpetual Help Church. (PRT)

East Sebago, ME, Our Lady of Sebago, c/o Gorham, ME, St. Anne Church. (PRT)

Eastman, GA, Dodge Co., St. Mark, c/o McRae, GA, Holy Redeemer Church. (SAV)

Eaton, CO, Weld Co., St. Michael, c/o Greeley, CO, Our Lady of Peace Church. (DEN)

Eatonville, WA, Pierce Co., Our Lady of Good Counsel, c/o Puyallup, WA, Holy Disciples Church. (SEA)

Eddyville, NE, Custer Co., St. Patrick, c/o Elm Creek, NE, Immaculate Conception Church. (GI)

Eden, VT, Lamoille Co., St. Gabriel, c/o Hyde Park, VT, St. Teresa Church. (BUR)

Eden, WY, Sweetwater Co., St. Christopher, c/o Pinedale, WY, Our Lady of Peace Church. (CHY)

Edenville, MI, Gladwin Co., St. Anne, c/o Coleman, MI, St. Philip Neri Church. (SAG)

Edgemont, SD, Fall River Co., St. James, c/o Hot Springs, SD, St. Anthony's Church. (RC)

Edgerly, LA, St. John Evangelist, c/o Vinton, LA, St. Joseph Church. (LKC)

Edgewater, FL, Volusia Co., St. Gerard, c/o New Smyrna Beach, FL, Sacred Heart Church. (ORL)

Edgewood, NM, Santa Fe Co., c/o Moriarty, NM, Estancia Valley Catholic Parish Church. (SFE)

Edison, NJ, Middlesex Co., St. Therese of the Infant Jesus, c/o [7] New Brunswick, NJ, St. Mary of Mount Virgin Church. (MET)

Edisto Island, SC, Charleston Co., SS. Frederick & Stephen, c/o Yonges Island, SC, St. Mary Church. (CHR)

Edmeston, NY, Nativity of B.V.M., c/o Morris, NY, Holy Cross Church. (ALB)

Edroy, TX, San Patricio Co., Our Lady of Guadalupe, c/o Odem, TX, Sacred Heart Church. (CC)

Edwardsville, PA, Luzerne Co., SS. Cyril and Methodius, c/o Larksville, PA, St. Anthony of Padua Church. (SCR)

Effie, LA, St. Winifred, c/o Deville, LA, St. John the Baptist Church. (ALX)

Egan, LA, Acadia Parish, St. Michael, c/o Iota, LA, St. Joseph Church. (LAF)

Ekalaka, MT, St. Joan of Arc, c/o Baker, MT, St. John the Evangelist Church. (GF)

El Alto, PR, San Antonio, c/o Penuelas, PR, St. Joseph Church. (PCE)

El Cajon, CA, Sycuan, c/o Lakeside, CA, Blessed Kateri Tekakwitha Church. (SD)

El Carmen, NM, Mora Co., c/o Mora, NM, St. Gertrude Church. (SFE)

El Corozo, PR, Cristo Rey, c/o Cabo Rojo, PR, St. Michael Church. (MGZ)

El Duende, NM, Rio Arriba Co., c/o Espanola, NM, Sacred Heart Church. (SFE)

El Guache, NM, Rio Arriba Co., c/o Espanola, NM, Sacred Heart Church. (SFE)

El Guique, NM, Rio Arriba Co., c/o San Juan Pueblo, NM, St. John the Baptist Church. (SFE)

El Indio, TX, Maverick Co., Our Lady of San Juan, c/o Eagle Pass, TX, Sacred Heart Church. (SAT)

El Macho, NM, San Miguel Co., c/o Pecos, NM, St. Anthony Church. (SFE)

El Papayo, PR, Cristo Rey, c/o Sabana Grande, PR, Church of San Isidro Church. (MGZ)

El Paso, TX, El Paso Co., Santa Teresita, c/o [38] El Paso, TX, San Judas Tadeo Church. (ELP)

El Pueblo, NM, San Miguel Co., San Antonio de Padua, c/o Ribera, NM, San Miguel Del Vado Church. (SFE)

El Rancho, NM, Santa Fe Co., c/o Pojoaque, NM, N.S. de Guadalupe del Valle de Pojoaque Church. (SFE)

El Rio, CA, Ventura Co., Santa Clara Chapel, c/o [2] Oxnard, CA, Santa Clara Church. (LA)

El Rucio, PR, Penuelas Co., La Milagrosa, c/o Penuelas, PR, St. Joseph Church. (PCE)

El Santuario, NM, Santa Fe Co., El Santuario Shrine, c/o Chimayo, NM, Holy Family Church. (SFE)

El Sauz, TX, Our Lady of Guadalupe, c/o Escobares, TX, Sacred Heart Church. (BWN)

El Valle, NM, Taos Co., San Miguel Archangel, c/o Chimayo, NM, Holy Family Church. (SFE)

Elba, NE, Howard Co., St. Joseph, c/o Farwell, NE, St. Anthony of Padua Church. (GI)

Elberton, GA, Elbert Co., St. Mary's, c/o Washington, GA, St. Joseph's Church. (ATL)

Elbridge, MI, St. Joseph Church, c/o Hart, MI, St. Gregory's Church. (GR)

Eleele, HI, Sacred Heart, c/o Kalaheo, HI, Holy Cross Church. (HON)

Elfrida, AZ, Cochise Co., St. Francis of Assisi, c/o Sunsites, AZ, St. Jude Thaddius Church. (TUC)

Elizabeth, CO, Our Lady of the Visitation, c/o Parker, CO, Ave Maria Church. (COS)

Elizabeth, IN, Harrison Co., St. Peter, c/o Corydon, IN, St. Joseph Church. (IND)

Elizabeth, LA, Allen Parish, St. Frances, c/o Oakdale, LA, Sacred Heart Church. (LKC)

Elizabeth, WV, Wirt Co., St. Elizabeth of Hungary, c/o Spencer, WV, Holy Redeemer Church. (WH)

Elk, CA, Blessed Sacrament, c/o Point Arena, CA, St. Aloysius Church. (SR)

Elk, TX, McLennon Co., St. Joseph, c/o Tours, TX, St. Martin Church. (AUS)

Elk Grove, WI, St. Peter, c/o Seymour, WI, Our Lady of Hope Church. (MAD)

Elka Park, NY, Greene Co., St. Francis de Sales, c/o Haines Falls, NY, Immaculate Conception Church. (ALB)

Elkhorn City, KY, Pike Co., St. Joseph the Worker, c/o Pikeville, KY, St. Francis of Assisi Church. (LEX)

Elkin, NC, Surry Co., St. Stephen, c/o North Wilkesboro, NC, St. John Baptist de LaSalle Church. (CHL)

Ellendale, IA, Plymouth Co., St. Joseph's, c/o Merrill,

IA, Assumption Church Church. (SC)
Ellijay, GA, Gilmer Co., Good Samaritan Mission, c/o Blue Ridge, GA, St. Anthony's Church. (ATL)
Elmer, LA, St. Peter, c/o Glenmora, LA, St. Louis Church. (ALX)
Elmwood, NE, Cass Co., St. Mary's, c/o Manley, NE, St. Patrick's Church. (LIN)
Elsie, NE, Perkins Co., Resurrection of Our Lord, c/o Wallace, NE, St. Mary's Church. (LIN)
Emanueli, PR, Coamo Co., Holy Family, c/o Coamo, PR, St. Blase Church. (PCE)
Eminence, KY, Henry Co., St. John Chrysostom, c/o Shelbyville, KY, Annunciation of the Blessed Virgin Mary Church. (L)
Eminence, MO, Shannon Co., St. Sylvester, c/o Mountain View, MO, St. John Vianney Church. (SPC)
Emmanuel, LA, Holy Rosary, c/o Cloutierville, LA, St. John the Baptist Church. (ALX)
Emory, TX, Rains Co., St. John the Evangelist, c/o Sulphur Springs, TX, St. James Church. (TYL)
Empire, LA, Plaquemines Parish, St. Ann, c/o Buras, LA, Our Lady of Good Harbor Church. (NO)
Empire, NV, St. Joseph the Worker, c/o Fernley, NV, St. Robert Bellarmine Church. (RNO)
Encinal, NM, Nativity of the Blessed Virgin Mary, c/o Laguna, NM, St. Joseph Church. (GLP)
Encino, NM, Torrance Co., c/o Vaughn, NM, St. Mary Church. (SFE)
Encino, TX, Brooks Co., St. Ann, c/o Falfurrias, TX, Sacred Heart Church. (CC)
England, AR, Lonoke Co., Holy Trinity, c/o [7] Little Rock, AR, Immaculate Conception Church. (LR)
Ensenada, NM, Rio Arriba Co., c/o Los Ojos, NM, San Jose Church. (SFE)
Eola, TX, Concho Co., St. Philip, c/o Eden, TX, St. Charles Church. (SAN)
Ephraim, UT, Sanpete Co., St. Jude, c/o Richfield, UT, St. Elizabeth's Church. (SLC)
Ericson, NE, Wheeler Co., St. Theresa of the Child Jesus, c/o Burwell, NE, Sacred Heart Church. (GI)
Erie, IL, Whiteside Co., St. Ambrose, c/o Prophetstown, IL, St. Catherine Church. (RCK)
Errol, NH, Coos Co., St. Pius X, c/o Colebrook, NH, St. Brendan Church. (MAN)
Erving, MA, Franklin Co., St. Blanche, c/o Millers Falls, MA, St. John's Church. (SPR)
Escobosa, NM, Bernalillo Co., San Isidro, c/o Tijeras, NM, Holy Child Church. (SFE)
Esmond, ND, Benson Co., St. Boniface, c/o Anamoose, ND, St. Francis Xavier Church. (FAR)
Esopus, NY, Ulster Co., Sacred Heart, c/o Port Ewen, NY, Presentation of the Virgin Mary Church. (NY)
Esparto, CA, Yolo Co., St. Martin, c/o Winters, CA, St. Anthony Church. (SAC)
Essex, IL, Kankakee Co., St. Lawrence O'Toole, c/o South Wilmington, IL, St. Lawrence Church. (JOL)
Estaca, NM, Rio Arriba Co., c/o San Juan Pueblo, NM, St. John the Baptist Church. (SFE)
Estancia, NM, Torrance Co., c/o Moriarty, NM, Estancia Valley Catholic Parish Church. (SFE)
Esther, LA, St. James, c/o Henry, LA, St. John Church. (LAF)
Estherwood, LA, St. Margaret, c/o Mermentau, LA, St. John the Evangelist Church. (LAF)
Ethete, WY, Fremont Co., St. Joseph, c/o St. Stephens, WY, St. Stephen's Church. (CHY)
Etna, CA, Siskiyou Co., St. Mary, c/o Fort Jones, CA, Sacred Heart Church. (SAC)
Ettal, FM, c/o Lukunor, FM, Sacred Heart Church. (CI)
Euclid, MN, Polk Co., St. Mary, c/o [1] Crookston, MN, Cathedral of the Immaculate Conception Church. (CR)
Eufaula, OK, McIntosh Co., St. Paul's, c/o Krebs, OK, St. Joseph's Church. (TLS)
Eunice, NM, St. Clare, c/o Jal, NM, St. Cecilia Church. (LSC)
Eureka, CA, St. Joseph, c/o Eureka, CA, St. Bernard Church. (SR)
Eureka, UT, Utah Co., St. Patrick Parish, c/o Payson, UT, San Andres Church. (SLC)
Europa, MS, Webster Co., St. John, c/o West Point, MS, Immaculate Conception Church. (JKS)
Everglades City, FL, Collier Co., Holy Family, c/o Marco Island, FL, San Marco Church. (VEN)
Everly, IA, Clay Co., St. Mary's, c/o Royal, IA, St. Louis Church. (SC)
Exeter, RI, Washington Co., Blessed Kateri Tekakwitha, c/o North Kingstown, RI, St. Bernard Church. (PRO)
Expressway Heights, TX, Nuestra Senora de Guadalupe, c/o Weslaco, TX, San Martin de Porres Church. (BWN)
Eynon, PA, Lackawanna Co., St. Mary of Vilna, c/o Eynon, PA, St. Mary's Czestochowa Church. (SCR)

F

Fabius, NY, Onondaga Co., St. Paul, c/o Pompey, NY, Immaculate Conception Church. (SY)
Faga'alu, AS, c/o [2] Pago Pago, AS, Co-Cathedral of St. Joseph the Worker Church. (SPP)
Faga'itua, AS, c/o [5] Pago Pago, AS, Church of St. Peter and Paul Church. (SPP)
Fagasa, AS, c/o [2] Pago Pago, AS, Co-Cathedral of St. Joseph the Worker Church. (SPP)
Fair Haven, NY, Cayuga Co., St. Jude Chapel, c/o Wolcott, NY, St. Thomas the Apostle Church. (ROC)
Fairfield, AL, Jefferson Co., St. Mary's, c/o [7] Birmingham, AL, Holy Family Church. (BIR)
Fairford, AL, Washington Co., Our Lady of Sorrows, c/o Chastang, AL, St. Peter the Apostle Church. (MOB)
Fairmount Springs, PA, Luzerne Co., St. Martha's, c/o Lake Silkworth, PA, Our Lady of Mount Carmel Church. (SCR)
Fairplay, CO, Park Co., St. Joseph, c/o Buena Vista, CO, St. Rose of Lima Church. (COS)
Fairview, MT, St. Catherine, c/o Sidney, MT, St. Matthew Church. (GF)
Fairview, OK, Major Co., St. Ann, c/o Bison, OK, St. Joseph's Church. (OKL)
Falcon, TX, Zapata Co., Santa Ana, c/o Zapata, TX, Our Lady of Lourdes Church. (CC)
Falcon Heights, TX, Holy Trinity, c/o Roma, TX, Our Lady of Refuge Church. (BWN)
Faleniu, AS, c/o [4] Pago Pago, AS, Church of St. Paul Church. (SPP)
Fall River Mills, CA, Shasta Co., Our Lady of the Valley, c/o Burney, CA, St. Francis of Assisi Church. (SAC)
Falls Village, CT, Litchfield Co., St. Patrick, c/o Canaan, CT, St. Joseph's Church. (HRT)
Falun, MN, Roseau Co., St. Philip, c/o Warroad, MN, St. Mary's Church. (CR)
Fannin, TX, Our Lady of Assumption, c/o Goliad, TX, Immaculate Conception Church. (VIC)
Farmersville, CA, Tulare Co., St. Anthony of Egypt, c/o Exeter, CA, Sacred Heart Church. (FRS)
Farmerville, LA, Our Lady of Perpetual Help, c/o West Monroe, LA, St. Paschal Church. (SHP)
Farnam, NE, Dawson Co., St. Joseph's, c/o Curtis, NE, St. James Church. (LIN)
Farrell, PA, Mercer Co., St. Paul, c/o [2] Farrell, PA, Our Lady of Fatima Church. (E)
Fashing, TX, Atascosa Co., St. Elizabeth, c/o Karnes City, TX, St. Cornelius Church. (SAT)
Fayette, AL, Fayette Co., Holy Family, c/o Winfield, AL, Holy Spirit Church. (BIR)
Faysville, TX, St. Theresa, c/o San Carlos, TX, St. Joseph the Worker Church. (BWN)
Faywood, NM, San Jose, c/o Hurley, NM, Infant Jesus Church. (LSC)
Federal Dam, MN, Sacred Heart, c/o Ball Club, MN, St. Joseph's Church. (DUL)
Federal Dam, MN, Sacred Heart, c/o Duluth, MN, Indian Missions Church. (DUL)
Fellsmere, FL, Indian River Co., c/o Fellsmere, FL, Our Lady of Guadalupe Mission Church. (PMB)
Fence Lake, NM, El Morro, c/o Tinaja, NM, San Lorenzo Church. (GLP)
Fierro, NM, St. Anthony, c/o Bayard, NM, Our Lady of Fatima Church. (LSC)
Fillmore, UT, Millard Co., Holy Family, c/o Milford, UT, St. Bridget Church. (SLC)
Fine, NY, St. Lawrence Co., St. Michael, c/o Star Lake, NY, St. Hubert Church. (OG)
Fingal, ND, Barnes Co., Holy Trinity, c/o Oriska, ND, St. Bernard's Church. (FAR)
Finlayson, MN, St. Joseph's, c/o Sandstone, MN, St. Luke's Church. (DUL)
Finley, ND, Steele Co., St. Olaf, c/o Hope, ND, St. Agatha's Church. (FAR)
Fish Creek, NY, SS. Peter & Paul, c/o West Leyden, NY, St. Mary's Nativity Church. (OG)
Fisher, MN, Polk Co., St. Francis, c/o East Grand Forks, MN, Sacred Heart Church. (CR)
Fishville, LA, St. Edward, c/o Jena, LA, St. Mary Church. (ALX)
Fitchville, CT, New London Co., St. John, c/o [2] Norwich, CT, Sacred Heart Church. (NOR)
Fitzgerald, GA, Ben Hill Co., St. William, c/o Douglas, GA, St. Paul's Church. (SAV)
Fitzwilliam, NH, St. Joseph, c/o Troy, NH, Immaculate Conception Church. (MAN)
Flagler, CO, Kit Carson Co., St. Mary, c/o Limon, CO, Our Lady of Victory(1925) Church. (COS)
Flanagan, IL, Livingston Co., St. Joseph, c/o Minonk, IL, St. Patrick's Church. (PEO)
Flatwoods, LA, St. Cyril, c/o Boyce, LA, St. Margaret Church. (ALX)
Flaxville, MT, St. Louis, c/o Scobey, MT, St. Philip Bonitus Church. (GF)
Fleming, CO, Logan Co., St. Peter the Apostle, c/o Holyoke, CO, St. Patrick Church. (DEN)
Flint, MI, Genesee Co., c/o Troy, MI, St. Joseph Chaldean Parish Church. (EST)
Florence, MT, Ravalli Co., St. Joseph, c/o Stevensville, MT, St. Mary Church. (HEL)
Florian, MN, Marshall Co., Assumption, c/o Greenbush, MN, Blessed Sacrament Church. (CR)
Florida, NY, Orange Co., St. Edward, c/o Warwick, NY, St. Stephen Church. (NY)
Floyd, VA, Floyd Co., Church of All Saints, c/o Woodlawn, VA, St. Joseph's Church. (RIC)
Folkston, GA, Charlton Co., St. Francis of Assisi, c/o St. Marys, GA, Our Lady Star of the Sea Church. (SAV)
Folly Beach, SC, Charleston Co., Our Lady of Good Counsel, c/o [11] Charleston, SC, Church of the Nativity Church. (CHR)
Folsom, NM, Union Co., St. Joseph, c/o Clayton, NM, St. Francis Xavier Church. (SFE)
Ford City, MO, Gentry Co., St. Patrick's, c/o Stanberry, MO, St. Peter's Church. (KC)
Foreman, AR, Little River Co., Sacred Heart, c/o De Queen, AR, St. Barbara's Church. (LR)
Forest City, MO, Holt Co., St. Patrick, c/o Savannah, MO, St. Rose of Lima Church. (KC)
Forest City, PA, Susquehanna Co., St. Agnes, c/o Forest City, PA, Sacred Heart of Jesus Church. (SCR)
Forest City, PA, Susquehanna Co., St. Anthony, c/o Forest City, PA, Sacred Heart of Jesus Church. (SCR)
Forest City, PA, Susquehanna Co., St. Michael, c/o Forest City, PA, Sacred Heart of Jesus Church. (SCR)
Forestville, MI, Sanilac Co., St. John Chrysostom, c/o Port Sanilac, MI, St. Mary Church. (SAG)
Forestville, PA, Butler Co., St. Anthony, c/o Slippery Rock, PA, St. Peter Church. (PIT)
Forked Island, LA, Immaculate Conception, c/o Cow Island, LA, St. Anne Church. (LAF)
Forrest, IL, Livingston Co., St. James, c/o Fairbury, IL, St. John the Baptist Church. (PEO)
Fort Adams, MS, St. Patrick, c/o Woodville, MS, St. Joseph Church. (JKS)
Fort Belknap Agency, MT, Sacred Heart, c/o Hays, MT, St. Paul's Indian Mission Church. (GF)
Fort Bridger, WY, Uinta Co., St. Helen, c/o Evanston, WY, St. Mary Magdalen Church. (CHY)
Fort Duchesne, UT, Uintah Co., Blessed Kateri Tekakwitha, c/o Roosevelt, UT, St. Helen's Church. (SLC)
Fort Garland, CO, Costilla Co., Holy Family, c/o San Luis, CO, Sangre de Cristo Church. (PBL)
Fort Lauderdale, FL, Broward Co., Divine Mercy, c/o [10] Miami, FL, Notre Dame d'Haiti Church. (MIA)
Fort Meade, FL, Polk Co., St. Elizabeth Ann Seton, c/o Bartow, FL, St. Thomas Aquinas Church. (ORL)
Fort Mill, SC, York Co., St. Philip Neri, c/o Rock Hill, SC, St. Anne's Church. (CHR)
Fort Myers, FL, Lee Co., Our Lady of Perpetual Help, c/o [5] Fort Myers, FL, St. Francis Xavier Church. (VEN)
Fort Payne, AL, DeKalb Co., Our Lady of the Valley, c/o Gadsden, AL, St. James Church. (BIR)
Fort Peck, MT, Our Lady of the Lake, c/o Glasgow, MT, St. Raphael's Church. (GF)
Fort Stanton, NM, Sacred Heart, c/o Ruidoso, NM, St. Eleanor Church. (LSC)
Fort Totten Reservation, ND, Benson Co., Seven Dolors Indian Mission, c/o Fort Totten Reservation, ND, (Sioux Indians) Church. (FAR)
Fort Valley, GA, Peach Co., St. Juliana, c/o Perry, GA, St. Patrick Church. (SAV)
Fort Washakie, WY, Fremont Co., Blessed Sacrament, c/o St. Stephens, WY, St. Stephen's Church. (CHY)
Fossil, OR, St. Catherine, c/o Condon, OR, St. John's Church. (BAK)
Foster City, MI, Dickinson Co., St. Joseph, c/o Channing, MI, St. Rose Church. (MAR)
Fountain, FL, Bay Co., Our Lady Queen of Peace, c/o Bayou George, FL, Our Lady of the Rosary Church. (PT)
Fowler, CO, Otero Co., Mary Queen of Heaven, c/o Rocky Ford, CO, St. Peter Church. (PBL)
Frances, CO, St. Francis, c/o Pagosa Springs, CO, Immaculate Heart of Mary Church. (PBL)
Frances, WA, Pacific Co., Holy Family, c/o Pe Ell, WA, St. Joseph's Church. (SEA)
Franconia, MN, Chisago Co., St. Francis Xavier, c/o Taylors Falls, MN, St. Joseph's Church. (STP)
Franconia, NH, Grafton, Our Lady of the Snows, c/o Littleton, NH, St. Rose of Lima Church. (MAN)
Franklin, NY, Delaware Co., St. Paul, c/o Sidney, NY, Sacred Heart Church. (ALB)
Franklin, VT, Franklin Co., St. Mary, c/o Sheldon Springs, VT, St. Anthony Church. (BUR)
Frankston, TX, Anderson Co., St. Charles Borromeo, c/o Palestine, TX, Sacred Heart Church. (TYL)
Frazer, MT, St. Joseph, c/o Wolf Point, MT, Immaculate Conception Church. (GF)
Fredericksburg, TX, Gillespie Co., Our Lady of Guadalupe, c/o Fredericksburg, TX, St. Mary's Church. (SAT)
Freehold-Red Bank, NJ, Monmouth Co., Our Lady of Guadalupe, c/o [3] Long Branch, NJ, St. John the Baptist Church. (TR)
Freeland, PA, Luzerne Co., St. Anthony's, c/o [1] Freeland, PA, St. Ann's Church. (SCR)
Freeland, PA, Luzerne Co., St. Casimir's, c/o [1] Freeland, PA, St. Ann's Church. (SCR)
Freeland, PA, Luzerne Co., St. John Nepomucene, c/o [1] Freeland, PA, St. Ann's Church. (SCR)

Freeport, FL, Walton Co., Christ the King, c/o De Funiak Springs, FL, St. Margaret Church. (PT)
Freeport, ME, St. Jude's, c/o Yarmouth, ME, Sacred Heart Church. (PRT)
Freewood Acres, NJ, Monmouth Co., St. Mary of the Assumption, c/o Howell Township, NJ, St. Veronica Church. (TR)
Freiburg, MI, Sanilac Co., St. Ignatius, c/o Argyle, MI, St. Joseph Church. (SAG)
French Camp, CA, San Joaquin Co., Good Shepherd, c/o [4] Stockton, CA, St. George Church. (STO)
French Village, MO, St. Francois Co., St. Anne, c/o Bonne Terre, MO, St. Joseph's Church. (STL)
Frenchtown, IN, Crawford Co., St. Joseph, c/o Frenchtown, IN, St. Bernard Church. (IND)
Frenstat, TX, Burleson Co., Holy Rosary, c/o Somerville, TX, St. Ann's Church. (AUS)
Fresno, CA, St. Francis, c/o [1] Fresno, CA, St. John Cathedral Church. (FRS)
Fried, ND, Sacred Heart, c/o Jamestown, ND, The Basilica of St. James Church. (FAR)
Friendship, NY, Sacred Heart, c/o Cuba, NY, Our Lady of Angels Church. (BUF)
Frilot Cove, LA, St. Ann, c/o Plaisance, LA, St. Joseph Church. (LAF)
Froid, MT, Immaculate Conception, c/o Culbertson, MT, St. Anthony's Church. (GF)
Fromberg, MT, St. Joseph, c/o Bridger, MT, Sacred Heart Church. (GF)
Fronton, TX, Lamb of God, c/o Roma, TX, Our Lady of Refuge Church. (BWN)
Fryeburg, ME, Oxford Co., St. Elizabeth Ann Seton, c/o Bridgton, ME, St. Joseph Church. (PRT)
Fulda, ND, McHenry Co., St. Anselm, c/o Balta, ND, Our Lady of Mount Carmel Church. (FAR)
Fullerton, CA, Orange Co., St. George, c/o [5] North Hollywood, CA, St. Paul Assyrian-Chaldean Church. (LA)
Fullerton, CA, Orange Co., St. George, c/o North Hollywood, CA, St. Paul Assyrian-Chaldean Catholic Parish Church. (EST)
Fullerton, ND, Dickey Co., St. Patrick, c/o Ellendale, ND, St. Helena's Church. (FAR)
Fulton, MS, Itawamba Co., Christ the King, c/o Amory, MS, St. Helen Church. (JKS)
Futiga, AS, c/o [4] Pago Pago, AS, Church of St. Paul Church. (SPP)

G

Gabbs, NV, St. Michael, c/o Hawthorne, NV, Our Lady of Perpetual Help Church. (RNO)
Gabriels, NY, Franklin Co., Assumption of the B.V.M., c/o Bloomingdale, NY, St. Paul Church. (OG)
Gackle, ND, Logan Co., St. Anne, c/o Windsor, ND, St. Mathias Church. (FAR)
Gainesville, MO, Ozark Co., St. William, c/o Mansfield, MO, Immaculate Heart of Mary Church. (SPC)
Galicia-Columbani, PR, Santo Tomas de Villanueva, c/o Aguada, PR, St. Francis of Assisi Church. (MGZ)
Galisteo, NM, Santa Fe Co., c/o Cerrillos, NM, St. Joseph Church. (SFE)
Gallatin, MO, Daviess Co., Mary Immaculate, c/o Hamilton, MO, Sacred Heart Church. (KC)
Gallegos, NM, Harding Co., c/o Roy, NM, Holy Family-St. Joseph Church. (SFE)
Gallina, NM, Rio Arriba Co., c/o Abiquiu, NM, St. Thomas Apostle Church. (SFE)
Gallinas, NM, San Miguel Co., Santo Nino, c/o Las Vegas, NM, Our Lady of Sorrows Church Church. (SFE)
Galveston, TX, Galveston Co., Queen of Peace Mission, c/o [4] Galveston, TX, St. Patrick Church. (GAL)
Galway, NY, St. Mary, c/o Broadalbin, NY, St. Joseph Church. (ALB)
Gamerco, NM, St. Joseph the Worker, c/o [2] Gallup, NM, St. Francis of Assisi Church. (GLP)
Garapan Village, District 11, MP, Maturana House of Prayer, c/o Garapan Village, District 11, MP, Kristo Rai Parish Church. (CHK)
Garapan Village, District 11, MP, Navy Hill, Commonwealth Health Center Chapel, c/o Garapan Village, District 11, MP, Kristo Rai Parish Church. (CHK)
Garcia, CO, Costilla Co., Sacred Heart of Jesus, c/o San Luis, CO, Sangre de Cristo Church. (PBL)
Gardiner, MT, St. William, c/o Livingston, MT, St. Mary's Church. (GF)
Gardner, CO, Huerfano Co., Sacred Heart, c/o Walsenburg, CO, St. Mary Church. (PBL)
Garrison, NY, Putnam Co., St. Joseph, c/o Cold Spring-on-Hudson, NY, Our Lady of Loretto Church. (NY)
Garzas, PR, San Francisco, c/o Adjuntas, PR, St. Joachim Church. (PCE)
Genesee, PA, Potter Co., Sacred Heart, c/o Galeton, PA, St. Bibiana Church. (E)
Geneseo, ND, Sargent Co., St. Martin, c/o Lidgerwood, ND, St. Boniface's Church. (FAR)
Geneva, AL, Geneva Co., St. Mary, c/o Enterprise, AL, St. John Church. (MOB)
Gentilly, MN, Polk Co., St. Peter, c/o [1] Crookston, MN, Cathedral of the Immaculate Conception Church. (CR)
George West, TX, Live Oak Co., c/o George West, TX, St. George Church. (CC)
Georgetown, CA, El Dorado Co., St. James, c/o Placerville, CA, St. Patrick's Church. (SAC)
Georgetown, CO, Clear Creek Co., Our Lady of Lourdes, c/o Idaho Springs, CO, St. Paul's Church. (DEN)
Georgetown, MN, Clay Co., St. John, c/o Dilworth, MN, St. Elizabeth Church. (CR)
Georgia, VT, Franklin Co., Ascension, c/o Fairfax, VT, St. Luke Church. (BUR)
Gerald, MO, Franklin Co., St. Gerald, c/o Port Hudson, MO, Holy Family Church. (STL)
Geraldine, MT, St. Margaret, c/o Fort Benton, MT, Immaculate Conception Church. (GF)
Geranium, NE, Valley Co., St. Wenceslaus, c/o Farwell, NE, St. Anthony of Padua Church. (GI)
Germfask, MI, Schoolcraft Co., St. Therese, c/o Grand Marais, MI, Holy Rosary Church Church. (MAR)
Geyser, MT, St. Cyril, c/o Stanford, MT, St. Rose of Lima Church. (GF)
Gila, NM, St. Isidore, c/o Silver City, NM, St. Vincent de Paul Church. (LSC)
Gilbert, IL, Kane Co., St. Mary, c/o Dundee, IL, St. Catherine of Siena Church. (RCK)
Gilchrist, OR, Our Lady of the Snows, c/o La Pine, OR, Holy Redeemer Church. (BAK)
Gilcrest, CO, Weld Co., Sacred Heart, c/o Greeley, CO, Our Lady of Peace Church. (DEN)
Gillett, AR, Arkansas Co., St. Henry's, c/o Stuttgart, AR, Holy Rosary Church. (LR)
Gilmer, TX, Upshur Co., St. Francis of Assisi, c/o Sulphur Springs, TX, St. James Church. (TYL)
Giltner, NE, Hamilton Co., St. Joseph's, c/o Aurora, NE, St. Mary's Church. (LIN)
Gladstone, ND, Dunn Co., St. Philip, c/o New Hradec, ND, SS. Peter and Paul Church. (BIS)
Gladstone, ND, Stark Co., St. Thomas the Apostle, c/o Lefor, ND, St. Elizabeth Church. (BIS)
Glasgo, CT, New London Co., St. Ann, c/o Voluntown, CT, St. Thomas Apostle Church. (NOR)
Glastonbury, CT, Hartford Co., St. John's, c/o [6] Hartford, CT, St. Michael Church. (STF)
Glen Haven, WI, St. Mary Help of Christians, c/o Cassville, WI, St. Charles Borromeo Church. (MAD)
Glen Lyon, PA, Luzerne Co., St. Denis, c/o Glen Lyon, PA, St. Adalbert's Church. (SCR)
Glen Lyon, PA, Luzerne Co., St. Michael, c/o Wilkes-Barre, PA, St. Mary's Church. (PSC)
Glen Lyon, PA, Luzerne Co., St. Michael's, c/o Glen Lyon, PA, St. Adalbert's Church. (SCR)
Glen Ullin, ND, Grant Co., St. Joseph, c/o Glen Ullin, ND, Sacred Heart of Jesus Church. (BIS)
Glencoe, LA, St. Joan of Arc, c/o Four Corners, LA, St. Peter the Apostle Church. (LAF)
Glendale, OR, Douglas Co., Holy Family, c/o Myrtle Creek, OR, All Souls Church. (P)
Glendale, RI, St. Louis Chapel, c/o Burrillville, RI, St. Patrick Church. (PRO)
Glendo, WY, Platte Co., Our Lady of Lourdes, c/o Douglas, WY, St. James Church. (CHY)
Glenmont, OH, Holmes Co., SS. Peter and Paul, c/o Millersburg, OH, St. Peter Church. (COL)
Glenmore, NY, St. Anne, c/o Taberg, NY, St. Patrick Church. (SY)
Glennon, MO, Bollinger Co., St. Anthony, c/o Advance, MO, St. Joseph Church. (SPC)
Glennville, GA, Tattnall Co., St. Jude, c/o Claxton, GA, St. Christopher Church. (SAV)
Glentana, MT, Holy Family, c/o Scobey, MT, St. Philip Bonitus Church. (GF)
Glenwood, NM, Catron Co., Santo Nino, c/o Alpine, AZ, St. Helena Church. (GLP)
Glorieta, NM, Santa Fe Co., c/o Pecos, NM, St. Anthony Church. (SFE)
Gloster, MS, Amite Co., Holy Family, c/o Woodville, MS, St. Joseph Church. (JKS)
Gluckstadt, MS, St. Joseph, c/o Madison, MS, St. Francis of Assisi Church. (JKS)
Gnesen, MN, St. Joseph, c/o [9] Duluth, MN, St. John's Church. (DUL)
Gold Beach, OR, Curry Co., St. Charles Borromeo, c/o Brookings, OR, Star of the Sea Church. (P)
Goldcreek, MT, Powell Co., St. Mary, c/o Drummond, MT, St. Michael Church. (HEL)
Golden, NM, Santa Fe Co., c/o Cerrillos, NM, St. Joseph Church. (SFE)
Golden City, MO, Barton Co., St. Joseph, c/o Lamar, MO, St. Mary Church. (SPC)
Golden Meadow, LA, Our Lady of La Salette, c/o Golden Meadow, LA, Our Lady of Prompt Succor Church. (HT)
Goldens Bridge, NY, Westchester Co., St. Michael, c/o Croton Falls, NY, St. Joseph Church. (NY)
Golondrinas, NM, Mora Co., c/o Mora, NM, St. Gertrude Church. (SFE)
Goltry, OK, Alfalfa Co., St. Michael, c/o Enid, OK, St. Gregory the Great Church. (OKL)
Golva, ND, Golden Valley Co., St. Mary, c/o Beach, ND, St. John the Baptist Church. (BIS)
Gonzales, TX, Gonzales Co., Sacred Heart, c/o Gonzales, TX, St. James Church. (SAT)
Gonzales Ranch, NM, San Miguel Co., c/o Villanueva, NM, Our Lady of Guadalupe Church. (SFE)
Goodhue, MN, Goodhue Co., Holy Trinity, c/o Belle Creek, MN, St. Columbkill Church. (STP)
Goodridge, MN, Pennington Co., St. Ann, c/o Thief River Falls, MN, St. Bernards Church. (CR)
Gorum, LA, St. Margaret Mary, c/o Boyce, LA, St. Margaret Church. (ALX)
Goshen, NJ, Cape May Co., St. Elizabeth, c/o Woodbine, NJ, St. Casimir's Church. (CAM)
Gothenburg, NE, Dawson Co., Our Lady of Good Counsel, c/o Cozad, NE, Christ the King Church. (GI)
Goudeau, LA, St. Charles, c/o Evergreen, LA, Little Flower Church. (ALX)
Grady, AR, Lincoln Co., Blessed Sacrament, c/o Star City, AR, St. Justin's Church. (LR)
Grafton, NY, Rensselaer Co., St. John Francis Regis, c/o Pittstown, NY, St. George Church. (ALB)
Granby, CO, Grand Co., Our Lady of the Snow, c/o Grand Lake, CO, St. Anne Church. (DEN)
Grand Chenier, LA, Cameron Parish, Immaculate Conception, c/o Grand Chenier, LA, St. Eugene Church. (LKC)
Grand Gorge, NY, Delaware Co., St. Philip Neri, c/o Stamford, NY, Sacred Heart Church. (ALB)
Grand Isle, VT, Grand Isle Co., St. Joseph, c/o South Hero, VT, St. Rose of Lima Church. (BUR)
Grand Portage, MN, Holy Rosary, c/o Grand Marais, MN, St. John's Church. (DUL)
Grand Portage, MN, Cook Co., Holy Rosary, c/o Duluth, MN, Indian Missions Church. (DUL)
Grand Ridge, IL, LaSalle Co., St. Mary, c/o Ransom, IL, St. Patrick's Church. (PEO)
Grandfalls, TX, Ward Co., St. Gertrude, c/o Monahans, TX, St. John the Apostle and Evangelist Church. (ELP)
Grandfield, OK, Tillman Co., Our Lady of Perpetual Help, c/o Walters, OK, St. Patrick Church. (OKL)
Grandin, MO, Carter Co., St. Anne, c/o Doniphan, MO, St. Benedict Church. (SPC)
Granite Falls, WA, Snohomish Co., Holy Cross, c/o Snohomish, WA, St. Michael's Church. (SEA)
Granjeno, TX, Our Lady of Fatima, c/o [2] Mission, TX, Our Lady of the Holy Rosary Church. (BWN)
Grant, MI, Our Lady of Guadalupe Church, c/o Newaygo, MI, St. Bartholomew's Church. (GR)
Grantsville, WV, Calhoun Co., Jesus Christ, Prince of Peace, c/o Spencer, WV, Holy Redeemer Church. (WH)
Granville, ND, McHenry Co., Our Lady of Perpetual Help, c/o Towner, ND, St. Cecilia's Church. (FAR)
Grass Flats, PA, Clearfield Co., SS. Peter & Paul, c/o Frenchville, PA, St. Mary of the Assumption Church. (E)
Grass Valley, OR, St. John the Baptist, c/o Wasco, OR, St. Mary's Church. (BAK)
Grassy Butte, ND, McKenzie Co., St. Peter Canisius, c/o Watford City, ND, Epiphany Church. (BIS)
Greasewood, AZ, Our Lady of the Rosary, c/o Ganado, AZ, All Saints Church. (GLP)
Great Falls, SC, Chester Co., St. Michael, c/o Lancaster, SC, St. Catherine's Church. (CHR)
Greeley, PA, Pike Co., Sacred Heart, c/o Shohola, PA, St. Ann's Church. (SCR)
Green Lake, ME, Our Lady of the Lake, c/o Ellsworth, ME, St. Joseph's Church. (PRT)
Green River, UT, Emery Co., St. Michael, c/o East Carbon, UT, Good Shepherd Church. (SLC)
Greene, ME, St. Francis, c/o Sabattus, ME, Our Lady of the Rosary Church. (PRT)
Greenfield, MO, Dade Co., St. Patrick, c/o Mount Vernon, MO, St. Susanne Church. (SPC)
Greensboro, AL, Hale Co., Our Lady of Lourdes, c/o Demopolis, AL, St. Leo Church. (BIR)
Greensboro, FL, Gadsden Co., Casa Guadalupana, Catholic Center for Evangelization, c/o Quincy, FL, St. Thomas the Apostle Church. (PT)
Greenup, KY, St. Lawrence, c/o Ashland, KY, Holy Family Church. (LEX)
Greenville, CA, Plumas Co., St. Anthony, c/o Quincy, CA, St. John Church. (SAC)
Greenwich, CT, Fairfield Co., St. Timothy's, c/o [2] Greenwich, CT, St. Michael the Archangel Church. (BGP)
Greenwood, NE, Cass Co., St. Joseph's, c/o Ashland, NE, St. Mary's Church. (LIN)
Greig, NY, Lewis Co., St. Thomas, c/o Glenfield, NY, St. Mary Church. (OG)
Gripinas, PR, Jayuya Co., Buen Pastor, c/o Jayuya, PR, Our Lady of Monserrate Church. (PCE)
Grundy, SD, St. Joseph, c/o Richlands, VA, St. Mary Church. (RIC)
Gruver, TX, Iglesia Castro Redentor, c/o Spearman, TX, Sacred Heart Church. (AMA)
Grygla, MN, Marshall Co., St. Clement, c/o Thief River Falls, MN, St. Bernards Church. (CR)
Guachupanque, NM, Rio Arriba Co., c/o Espanola, NM,

Sacred Heart Church. (SFE)

Guadalupe, NM, Sacred Heart of Mary, c/o Cuba, NM, Immaculate Conception Church. (GLP)

Guadalupita, NM, Mora Co., c/o Mora, NM, St. Gertrude Church. (SFE)

Gualala, CA, Mary, Star of the Sea, c/o Point Arena, CA, St. Aloysius Church. (SR)

Guaniquilla, PR, Ntra. Sra. del Carmen, c/o Aguada, PR, St. Francis of Assisi Church. (MGZ)

Guayabal, PR, Bo. Guayabal, Our Lady of the Rosary, c/o Juana Diaz, PR, St. Raymond Nonato Church. (PCE)

Guayabo, PR, El Buen Pastor, c/o Aguada, PR, St. Francis of Assisi Church. (MGZ)

Guayama, PR, Bo. Carite, San Martin, c/o Guayama, PR, St. Anthony of Padua Church. (PCE)

Guaynabo, PR, Cristo del Perdon, c/o [4] Guaynabo, PR, San Juan M. Vianney Church. (SJN)

Guaynabo, PR, Dulce Nombre de Maria, c/o [4] Guaynabo, PR, San Juan M. Vianney Church. (SJN)

Guaynabo, PR, El Buen Pastor, c/o [7] Guaynabo, PR, Divino Nino Jesus Church. (SJN)

Guaynabo, PR, Jesus Nazareno, c/o [7] Guaynabo, PR, Divino Nino Jesus Church. (SJN)

Guaynabo, PR, La Milagrosa, c/o [4] Guaynabo, PR, San Juan M. Vianney Church. (SJN)

Guaynabo, PR, Ntra. Sra. del Carmen, c/o [3] Guaynabo, PR, Maria Madre de Mi Senor Church. (SJN)

Guaynabo, PR, Ntra. Sra. del Carmen, c/o [4] Guaynabo, PR, San Juan M. Vianney Church. (SJN)

Guaynabo, PR, San Rafael Arcangel, c/o [7] Guaynabo, PR, Divino Nino Jesus Church. (SJN)

Guaynabo, PR, Virgen de la Paz, c/o [9] Guaynabo, PR, Sagrados Corazones Church. (SJN)

Guilarte, PR, San Antonio, c/o Adjuntas, PR, St. Joachim Church. (PCE)

Gulf Breeze, FL, Santa Rosa Co., Our Lady of the Assumption, c/o Gulf Breeze, FL, St. Ann Church. (PT)

Gulliver, MI, Schoolcraft Co., Divine Infant of Prague, c/o Engadine, MI, Our Lady of Lourdes Church. (MAR)

Gulnare, CO, Las Animas Co., San Jose, c/o Aguilar, CO, St. Anthony Church. (PBL)

Gussetville, TX, St. Joseph, c/o George West, TX, St. George Church. (CC)

Gwinner, ND, Sargent Co., St. Vincent, c/o Lisbon, ND, St. Aloysius Church. (FAR)

H

Hachita, NM, St. Catherine, c/o Lordsburg, NM, St. Joseph Church. (LSC)

Hackensack, MN, Sacred Heart, c/o Walker, MN, St. Agnes Church. (DUL)

Hagerman, NM, St. Catherine, c/o Dexter, NM, Immaculate Conception Church. (LSC)

Hagerstown, MD, St. Ann's, c/o Baltimore, MD, Patronage of the Mother of God Church. (PSC)

Hague, VA, Westmoreland Co., St.Paul, c/o Kilmarnock, VA, St. Francis de Sales Church. (ARL)

Haines Falls, NY, Greene Co., Wayside Shrine, c/o Haines Falls, NY, Immaculate Conception Church. (ALB)

Halaula, HI, Our Lady of Grace, c/o Hawi, HI, Sacred Heart Church. (HON)

Haleyville, AL, Winston Co., Our Lady of Guadalupe, c/o Jasper, AL, St. Cecilia Church. (BIR)

Halfway, OR, St. Therese, c/o [1] Baker, OR, Cathedral of St. Francis De Sales Church. (BAK)

Hall Islands, FM, c/o Fefan, FM, Sacred Heart Church. (CI)

Hallsville, TX, Harrison Co., Our Lady of Grace, c/o Longview, TX, St. Mary Church. (TYL)

Halstad, MN, Norman Co., Holy Family, c/o [1] Crookston, MN, Cathedral of the Immaculate Conception Church. (CR)

Halstad, MN, Norman Co., Holy Family, c/o Ada, MN, St. Joseph's Church. (CR)

Hamburg, AR, Ashley Co., c/o Crossett, AR, Holy Cross Church. (LR)

Hamilton, IL, Hancock Co., St. Mary, c/o Warsaw, IL, Sacred Heart Church. (PEO)

Hamilton, KS, Greenwood Co., St. John, c/o Eureka, KS, Sacred Heart Church. (WCH)

Hamilton City, CA, Glenn Co., St. Mary, c/o Orland, CA, St. Dominic Church. (SAC)

Hamlin, TX, Jones Co., Holy Trinity, c/o Anson, TX, St. Michael's Church. (LUB)

Hammond, OR, Clatsop Co., St. Francis de Sales, c/o Astoria, OR, St. Mary, Star of the Sea Church. (P)

Hampton, CT, Windham Co., Our Lady of Lourdes, c/o Brooklyn, CT, Our Lady of La Salette Church. (NOR)

Hampton, IL, Rock Island Co., St. Mary, c/o Rapids City, IL, St. John the Baptist Church. (PEO)

Hampton, SC, Hampton Co., St. Mary, c/o Ridgeland, SC, St. Anthony's Church. (CHR)

Hanalei, HI, St. William, c/o Kapaa, HI, St. Catherine Church. (HON)

Hanceville, AL, Cullman Co., St. Boniface, c/o Cullman, AL, Sacred Heart Church. (BIR)

Hanna, WY, Carbon Co., St. Joseph, c/o Saratoga, WY, St. Ann's Church. (CHY)

Hanover, NM, Holy Family, c/o Bayard, NM, Our Lady of Fatima Church. (LSC)

Happy Camp, CA, Siskiyou Co., All Saints, c/o Fort Jones, CA, Sacred Heart Church. (SAC)

Hardeeville, SC, Jasper Co., St. Anthony's, c/o Bluffton, SC, St. Andrew's Church. (CHR)

Hargill, TX, St. Frances Xavier Cabrini, c/o Raymondville, TX, Our Lady of Guadalupe Church. (BWN)

Harlem, MT, St. Thomas the Apostle, c/o Chinook, MT, St. Gabriel's Church. (GF)

Harlingen, TX, Le Moyne Chapel, c/o [4] Harlingen, TX, St. Anthony Church. (BWN)

Harmon, NY, Westchester Co., Church of the Good Shepherd, c/o Croton-on-Hudson, NY, Holy Name of Mary Church. (NY)

Harmony, WA, Lewis Co., St. Yves, c/o Morton, WA, Sacred Heart Church. (SEA)

Harquahala Valley, AZ, San Isidoro Labrador, c/o Buckeye, AZ, Saint Henry Church. (PHX)

Harrington, DE, Kent Co., St. Bernadette, c/o Milford, DE, St. John the Apostle Church. (WIL)

Harrison, NE, Sioux Co., Church of the Nativity of the Blessed Virgin Mary, c/o Crawford, NE, St. John the Baptist Church. (GI)

Hart, TX, St. John's, c/o Nazareth, TX, Holy Family Church. (AMA)

Hartley, IA, O'Brien Co., St. Joseph's, c/o Sanborn, IA, St. Cecilia's Church. (SC)

Hartselle, AL, Morgan Co., Holy Family, c/o Decatur, AL, St. Ann's Church. (BIR)

Harvard, MI, Kent Co., St. Margaret, c/o Greenville, MI, St. Charles Church. (GR)

Harwood, PA, Luzerne Co., St. Michael, c/o West Hazleton, PA, St. Francis of Assisi Church. (SCR)

Haskell, TX, Haskell Co., St. George, c/o Stamford, TX, St. Ann Church. (LUB)

Hastings-on-Hudson, NY, Westchester Co., Andras Nursing Home, c/o Hastings-on-Hudson, NY, St. Matthew Church. (NY)

Hato Rey, PR, Sma. Trinidad, c/o [7] San Juan, PR, Ntr. Sra. de la Caridad del Cobre Church. (SJN)

Hawk Run, PA, Clearfield Co., SS. Peter & Paul, c/o Morrisdale, PA, St. Agnes Church. (E)

Hawkinsville, CA, Siskiyou Co., Immaculate Conception, c/o Yreka, CA, St. Joseph Church. (SAC)

Hawley, MN, Clay Co., St. Andrew, c/o Lake Park, MN, St. Francis Xavier's Church. (CR)

Hawthorne, FL, Alachua Co., St. Philip Neri, c/o [1] Gainesville, FL, St. Patrick's Church. (STA)

Haxtun, CO, Phillips Co., Christ the King, c/o Holyoke, CO, St. Patrick Church. (DEN)

Hay Springs, NE, Sacred Heart, c/o Hemingford, NE, St. Bridget Church. (GI)

Hay Springs, NE, Sheridan Co., St. Columbkille, c/o Gordon, NE, St. Leo's Church. (GI)

Hayales, PR, Coamo Co., Our Lady of Mt. Carmel, c/o Coamo, PR, St. Blase Church. (PCE)

Hayden, NM, Quay Co., Holy Trinity, c/o Clayton, NM, St. Francis Xavier Church. (SFE)

Hayes, LA, Calcasieu Parish, St. Daniel Chapel, c/o Bell City, LA, St. John Vianney Church. (LKC)

Hayesville, NC, Clay Co., Immaculate Heart of Mary, c/o Murphy, NC, St. William Church. (CHL)

Hayfield, MN, Dodge Co., Sacred Heart, c/o Blooming Prairie, MN, St. Columbanus Church. (WIN)

Hayfork, CA, Trinity Co., Holy Trinity, c/o Weaverville, CA, St. Patrick Church. (SAC)

Haymarsh, ND, Morton Co., St. Clement, c/o Hebron, ND, St. Ann Church. (BIS)

Hazard, NE, Sherman Co., St. Gabriel, c/o Pleasanton, NE, St. Mary's Church. (GI)

Hazlehurst, MS, St. Martin, c/o Crystal Springs, MS, St. John Church. (JKS)

Hazleton, PA, Luzerne Co., Our Lady of Mount Carmel, c/o [4] Hazleton, PA, Holy Trinity Church. (SCR)

Hazleton, PA, Luzerne Co., SS. Peter and Paul, c/o West Hazleton, PA, Transfiguration Church. (SCR)

Hazleton, PA, Luzerne Co., St. Ladislaus, c/o [6] Hazleton, PA, St. Joseph's Church. (SCR)

He Dog, SD, St. Patrick Hall, c/o Parmelee, SD, St. Agnes Church. (RC)

Healdton, OK, Carter Co., St. Cecilia, c/o Ardmore, OK, St. Mary Church. (OKL)

Heart Butte, MT, Glacier Co., Holy Family Mission, c/o Heart Butte, MT, St. Anne Church. (HEL)

Heartwell, NE, Kearney Co., Holy Family, c/o Minden, NE, St. John's Church. (LIN)

Hebbronville, TX, Jim Hogg Co., Immaculate Conception, c/o Hebbronville, TX, Our Lady of Guadalupe Church. (CC)

Heber, CA, Sacred Heart, c/o Imperial, CA, St. Anthony of Padua Church. (SD)

Heber City, UT, Wasatch Co., St. Lawrence, c/o Park City, UT, St. Mary of the Assumption Church. (SLC)

Heber Springs, AR, Cleburne Co., St. Albert, c/o Searcy, AR, St. James Church. (LR)

Hedgesville, WV, Berkeley Co., St. Bernadette, c/o Martinsburg, WV, St. Joseph's Church. (WH)

Heidelberg, KY, Lee Co., St. Therese, c/o Beattyville, KY, Queen of All Saints Church. (LEX)

Helena, TX, Karnes Co., St. Helena, c/o Panna Maria, TX, Immaculate Conception of the Blessed Virgin Mary Church. (SAT)

Henderson, NY, Jefferson Co., Queen of Heaven, c/o Sackets Harbor, NY, St. Andrew Church. (OG)

Henryville, IN, Clark Co., St. Francis Xavier, c/o Charlestown, IN, St. Michael Church. (IND)

Hermeleigh, TX, Scurry Co., St. John, c/o Snyder, TX, St. Elizabeth's Church. (LUB)

Hermosa, SD, St. Michael's, c/o [1] Rapid City, SD, Cathedral of Our Lady of Perpetual Help Church. (RC)

Hernandez, NM, Rio Arriba Co., c/o Espanola, NM, Sacred Heart Church. (SFE)

Hershey, NE, Lincoln Co., Our Lady of Guadalupe, c/o Sutherland, NE, Sacred Heart Church. (GI)

Hesperia, MI, Christ the King, c/o Brunswick, MI, St. Michael's Church. (GR)

Hessel, MI, Mackinac Co., Our Lady of the Snows, c/o Goetzville, MI, St. Stanislaus Kostka Church. (MAR)

Hickory Hill, LA, St. Richard, c/o Marksville, LA, Holy Ghost Church. (ALX)

High Falls, NY, Ulster Co., Our Lady Help of Christians, c/o Rosendale, NY, St. Peter Church. (NY)

Highland, MO, Perry Co., St. Joseph, c/o Perryville, MO, St. Vincent De Paul Church. (STL)

Highlands, NC, Macon Co., Our Lady of the Mountains, c/o Franklin, NC, St. Francis of Assisi Church. (CHL)

Hightstown-Princeton, NJ, Mercer Co., Our Lady of Fatima, c/o [3] Long Branch, NJ, St. John the Baptist Church. (TR)

Highwood, MT, St. Jane Frances, c/o Belt, MT, St. Mark the Evangelist Church. (GF)

Hill Top, PA, Wayne Co., St. Cecilia, c/o Pleasant Mount, PA, St. James Church. (SCR)

Hillsboro, NM, Our Lady of Guadalupe, c/o Garfield, NM, San Isidro Church. (LSC)

Hingham, MT, Our Lady of Ransom, c/o Chester, MT, St. Mary's Church. (GF)

Hinsdale, MT, St. Albert, c/o Glasgow, MT, St. Raphael's Church. (GF)

Hinton, OK, Caddo Co., Sacred Heart, c/o Weatherford, OK, St. Eugene's Church. (OKL)

Hobart, OK, Kiowa Co., Sts. Peter & Paul, c/o Mangum, OK, Sacred Heart Church. (OKL)

Hobson, MT, Sacred Heart, c/o Stanford, MT, St. Rose of Lima Church. (GF)

Hochheim, TX, St. Ann, c/o Yoakum, TX, St. Joseph Church. (VIC)

Hoconuco, PR, Chapel of St. Joseph, c/o San German, PR, San German de Auxerre Church. (MGZ)

Hode, KY, Martin Co., St. John Neumann, c/o Louisa, KY, St. Jude Church. (LEX)

Hoehne, CO, Las Animas Co., St. John Baptist, c/o Trinidad, CO, Most Holy Trinity, Trinidad Area Catholic Community (Trinidad Cluster) Church. (PBL)

Hogares Seguros, PR, San Antonio Co., c/o Jayuya, PR, Our Lady of Monserrate Church. (PCE)

Hogeland, MT, St. Thomas Aquinas, c/o Chinook, MT, St. Gabriel's Church. (GF)

Hollandale, MS, Immaculate Conception, c/o Leland, MS, St. James Church. (JKS)

Hollis, OK, Harmon Co., Our Lady of Guadalupe, c/o Altus, OK, Prince of Peace Church. (OKL)

Holly Beach, LA, Holy Trinity, c/o Hackberry, LA, St. Peter Apostle Church. (LKC)

Holly Hill, SC, Orangeburg Co., St. Ann, c/o Summerton, SC, St. Mary's Church. (CHR)

Holman, NM, Mora Co., c/o Mora, NM, St. Gertrude Church. (SFE) Church. (SFE)

Holman, TX, St. Wenceslaus, c/o Ammannsville, TX, St. John The Baptist Church. (VIC)

Holualoa, HI, Immaculate Conception, c/o Holualoa, HI, St. Michael The Archangel Church. (HON)

Holyoke, MA, Hampden Co., Holyoke Soldier's Home Chapel, c/o [1] Holyoke, MA, Blessed Sacrament Church. (SPR)

Homer, IL, Champaign Co., St. Charles Borromeo, c/o Tolono, IL, St. Patrick's Church. (PEO)

Homer, LA, Claiborne Parish, St. Margaret, c/o Minden, LA, St. Paul Church. (SHP)

Homer, NE, Dakota Co., St. Cornelius, c/o South Sioux City, NE, St. Michael Church. (OM)

Hominy, OK, Osage Co., c/o Cleveland, OK, St. Joseph Church. (TLS)

Honokahua (Kapalua), HI, Sacred Hearts of Jesus and Mary, c/o Lahaina, HI, Maria Lanakila Church. (HON)

Honolulu, HI, The Oratory in Hawaii, c/o [8] Honolulu, HI, Holy Trinity Church. (HON)

Honomu, HI, Good Shepherd, c/o Papaikou, HI, Immaculate Heart of Mary Church. (HON)

Hooker, OK, Texas Co., Sacred Heart, c/o Guymon, OK, St. Peter's Church. (OKL)

Hopedale, IL, Tazewell Co., St. Joseph's, c/o Delavan, IL, St. Mary's Church. (PEO)

Hopeton, CA, St. John the Baptist, c/o Merced, CA, Our Lady of Mercy/St. Patricks Church. (FRS)
Hopland, CA, St. Francis, c/o Ukiah, CA, St. Mary of the Angels Church. (SR)
Hornitos, CA, Mariposa Co., St. Catherine of Sienna, c/o Mariposa, CA, St. Joseph Church. (FRS)
Horse Cave, KY, Hart Co., Our Lady of the Caves Church, c/o Glasgow, KY, St. Helen Church. (L)
Horse Springs, NM, St. Anne, c/o Aragon, NM, Santo Nino Church. (GLP)
Horseshoe Lake, AR, Crittenden Co., St. Mary's of the Lake, c/o West Memphis, AR, St. Michael's Church. (LR)
Hostyn Hill, TX, Fayette Co., St. Mary's, c/o Fayetteville, TX, St. John's Church. (AUS)
Hot Springs, MT, Sacred Heart, c/o Plains, MT, St. James Church. (HEL)
Hot Springs, NC, Madison Co., Chapel of the Redeemer, c/o Mars Hill, NC, St. Andrew the Apostle Church. (CHL)
Hotchkiss, CO, Delta Co., St. Margaret Mary, c/o Paonia, CO, Sacred Heart Church. (PBL)
Houston, MS, Chickasaw Co., Immaculate Heart of Mary, c/o Aberdeen, MS, St. Francis of Assisi Church. (JKS)
Hoyo Planas, PR, Jayuya Co., Esp. Santo, c/o Jayuya, PR, Our Lady of Monserrate Church. (PCE)
Hubbard, NE, Dakota Co., St. Mary, c/o Jackson, NE, St. Patrick Church. (OM)
Hubbard, OR, Marion Co., St. Agnes, c/o Woodburn, OR, St. Luke Church. (P)
Hudson, WY, Freemont Co., Ascension, c/o Lander, WY, Holy Rosary Church. (CHY)
Huff, ND, Morton Co., St. Martin, c/o St. Anthony, ND, St. Anthony Church. (BIS)
Hugo, CO, Lincoln Co., St. Anthony of Padua, c/o Limon, CO, Our Lady of Victory(1925) Church. (COS)
Hulberton, NY, Orleans Co., St. Rocco, c/o Holley, NY, St. Mary Church. (BUF)
Hulett, WY, Crook Co., St. Matthew's, c/o Newcastle, WY, Corpus Christi Church. (CHY)
Humansville, MO, Polk Co., St. Catherine, c/o Bolivar, MO, Sacred Heart Church. (SPC)
Humarock, MA, St. Theresa's, c/o Marshfield, MA, St. Christine Church. (BO)
Humboldt, AZ, St. Lawrence, c/o Prescott Valley, AZ, St. Germaine Church. (PHX)
Hume, IL, Edgar Co., St. Michael's, c/o Villa Grove, IL, Sacred Heart Church. (SFD)
Hunter, ND, Cass Co., St. Agnes, c/o Mayville, ND, Our Lady of Peace Church. (FAR)
Hunter, NY, Greene Co., St. Mary of the Mountains, c/o Haines Falls, NY, Immaculate Conception Church. (ALB)
Hunter, TX, Comal Co., St. John, c/o New Braunfels, TX, Our Lady of Perpetual Help Church. (SAT)
Huntingdon, TN, Carroll Co., Holy Family Church, c/o Camden, TN, St. Mary Church Church. (MEM)
Huntington, OR, St. Joachim, c/o Ontario, OR, Blessed Sacrament Church. (BAK)
Huntington, UT, Emery Co., San Rafael, c/o Price, UT, Notre Dame de Lourdes Church. (SLC)
Huntsville, UT, Weber Co., St. Florence, c/o [3] Ogden, UT, St. Joseph's Church. (SLC)
Hurdsfield, ND, Wells Co., St. Patrick, c/o Sykeston, ND, St. Elizabeth's Church. (FAR)
Hurley, MS, Jackson Co., St. Ann, c/o Moss Point, MS, St. Joseph Church. (BLX)
Hurricane Branch, MO, Chariton Co., St. Joseph, c/o Marceline, MO, St. Bonaventure Church. (JC)
Hyannis, NE, Grant Co., All Saint's, c/o Mullen, NE, St. Mary's Church. (GI)
Hysham, MT, St. Joseph, c/o Forsyth, MT, Immaculate Conception Church. (GF)

I

Imperial, TX, Pecos Co., Our Lady of Lourdes, c/o Fort Stockton, TX, St. Agnes Church. (SAN)
Independence, CA, Inyo Co., St. Vivian, c/o Lone Pine, CA, Santa Rosa Church. (FRS)
Indian Township, ME, St. Theresa's Chapel, c/o Indian Township, ME, St. Ann Church. (PRT)
Indian Village, LA, Sacred Heart Parish, Sacred Heart, c/o Kinder, LA, St. Philip Neri Church. (LKC)
Indiera Fria, PR, Santa Rosa, c/o Maricao, PR, St. John the Baptist Church. (MGZ)
Industry, TX, Austin Co., Immaculate Conception, c/o Bellville, TX, SS. Peter & Paul Church. (GAL)
Inglis, FL, Levy Co., St. Anthony the Abbot, c/o Williston, FL, Holy Family Church. (STA)
Interior, SD, Jackson Co., Holy Rosary, c/o Wall, SD, St. Patrick's Church. (RC)
Inverness, MT, Sacred Heart, c/o Chester, MT, St. Mary's Church. (GF)
Ione, CA, Amador Co., Mule Creek State Prison, c/o Ione, CA, Sacred Heart Church. (SAC)
Ione, CA, Amador Co., Preston School of Industry, California Youth Authority, c/o Ione, CA, Sacred Heart Church. (SAC)
Iowa, LA, Calcasieu Parish, St. Peter Claver, c/o Welsh, LA, St. Joseph Church. (LKC)
Iraan, TX, Pecos Co., St. Francis of Assisi, c/o McCamey, TX, Sacred Heart Church. (SAN)
Irasburg, VT, Orleans Co., St. John Vianney, c/o Orleans, VT, St. Theresa of Child Jesus Church. (BUR)
Irish Grove Rd., IL, Stephenson Co., St. Patrick, c/o Durand, IL, St. Mary Church. (RCK)
Irish Ridge, NY, Oneida Co., St. Mary, c/o Durhamville, NY, St. Francis Church. (SY)
Irishtown, MI, Gratiot Co., St. Patrick, c/o St. Louis, MI, St. Joseph Church. (SAG)
Isabel, SD, Dewey Co., St. Mary, c/o Timber Lake, SD, Holy Cross Church. (RC)
Island Heights, NJ, Ocean Co., St. Gertrude, c/o [1] Toms River, NJ, St. Joseph Church. (TR)
Isle LaMotte, VT, Grand Isle Co., St. Joseph, c/o Alburg, VT, St. Amadeus Church. (BUR)
Isle of Hope, GA, Our Lady of Good Hope, c/o [8] Savannah, GA, St. James Church. (SAV)
Isleboro, ME, St. Mary of the Isles, c/o Belfast, ME, St. Francis of Assisi Church. (PRT)
Islesford, ME, Our Lady Star of the Sea, c/o Northeast Harbor, ME, St. Ignatius Church. (PRT)
Italy, TX, Ellis Co., Epiphany, c/o Waxahachie, TX, St. Joseph Church. (DAL)
Iuka, MS, Tishomingo Co., St. Mary, c/o Booneville, MS, St. Francis of Assisi Church. (JKS)

J

Jacaquas, PR, Bo. Jacaguas, N.S. de Fatima, c/o Juana Diaz, PR, St. Raymond Nonato Church. (PCE)
Jackpot, NV, Elko Co., Blessed Miguel Pro, c/o Elko, NV, St. Joseph's Church. (RNO)
Jackson, AL, Clarke Co., Visitation, c/o Grove Hill, AL, Sacred Heart Church. (MOB)
Jackson, GA, Butts Co., St. Mary's, c/o McDonough, GA, St. James The Apostle Church. (ATL)
Jackson, NJ, Ocean Co., Church of St. Monica, c/o New Egypt, NJ, Assumption Church. (TR)
Jacksonville, OR, Jackson Co., St. Joseph, c/o Medford, OR, Sacred Heart of Jesus Church. (P)
Jaguey Chiquito, PR, San Augustin, c/o Aguada, PR, St. Francis of Assisi Church. (MGZ)
Jamaica Beach, TX, Galveston Co., Mary, Star of the Sea, c/o [5] Galveston, TX, St. Peter the Apostle Church. (GAL)
Jamestown, PA, Mercer Co., St. Margaret, c/o Greenville, PA, St. Michael Church. (E)
Jamestown, TN, Fentress Co., Fentress County Catholic Community, c/o Fairfield Glade, TN, St. Francis of Assisi Church. (KNX)
Jarales, NM, Valencia Co., c/o Belen, NM, Our Lady of Belen Church. (SFE)
Jardines de Rio Grande, PR, Ntra. Sra. de Guadalupe, c/o Rio Grande, PR, Nuestra Senora del Carmen Church. (SJN)
Jasper, FL, Hamilton Co., St. Therese of Lisieux, c/o Live Oak, FL, St. Francis Xavier Church. (STA)
Jasper, GA, Pickens Co., Our Lady of the Mountains, c/o Canton, GA, Our Lady of LaSalette Church. (ATL)
Jauca, PR, San Ignacio de Loyola, c/o Santa Isabel, PR, St. James Church. (PCE)
Jayton, TX, Kent Co., Epiphany, c/o Spur, TX, St. Mary Church. (LUB)
Jefferson, NH, Coos, St. Agnes, c/o Lancaster, NH, All Saints Church. (MAN)
Jefferson, OR, Marion Co., St. Thomas, c/o Scio, OR, St. Bernard Church. (P)
Jeffrey City, WY, Freemont Co., St. Brendan, c/o Lander, WY, Holy Rosary Church. (CHY)
Jenny Lind, AR, Sebastian Co., Sts. Sabina and Mary's Church, c/o Van Buren, AR, St. Michael's Church. (LR)
Jessenland, MN, St. Thomas, c/o Henderson, MN, St. Joseph Church. (NU)
Jessie, ND, Griggs Co., St. Lawrence, c/o Cooperstown, ND, St. George's Church. (FAR)
Jessup, PA, Lackawanna Co., St. Michael, c/o Jessup, PA, St. James Church. (SCR)
Jessup, PA, Lackawanna Co., St. Stanislaus, c/o Jessup, PA, St. James Church. (SCR)
Jobstown, NJ, Burlington Co., St. Andrew, c/o Mount Holly, NJ, Sacred Heart Church. (TR)
Jocko, MT, Lake Co., St. John Berchman's, c/o St. Ignatius, MT, St. Ignatius Church. (HEL)
Johnson, VT, Lamoille Co., St. John the Apostle, c/o Cambridge, VT, St. Mary Church. (BUR)
Johnson Bayou, LA, Our Lady of the Assumption, c/o Hackberry, LA, St. Peter Apostle Church. (LKC)
Johnson City, TX, Blanco Co., Good Shepherd, c/o Blanco, TX, St. Ferdinand's Church. (AUS)
Johnson Creek, WI, St. Mary Magdalene, c/o Lake Mills, WI, St. Francis Xavier Church. (MAD)
Johnsonville, SC, Florence Co., St. Patrick, c/o Lake City, SC, St. Philip's Church. (CHR)
Johnston City, IL, c/o Johnston City, IL, St. Paul Church. (BEL)
Joliet, MT, St. John, c/o Bridger, MT, Sacred Heart Church. (GF)
Jolon, CA, Monterey Co., South Shore of Lake San Antonio, c/o Jolon, CA, San Antonio Mission Church. (MRY)
Jonestown, PA, Lebanon Co., Our Lady of Fatima, c/o [1] Lebanon, PA, Assumption of the Blessed Virgin Mary Church. (HBG)
Jonesville, LA, St. Gerard, c/o Ferriday, LA, St. Patrick Church. (ALX)
Jordan, MT, St. John the Baptist, c/o Circle, MT, St. Francis Xavier Church. (GF)
Joyuda, PR, St. John the Baptist, c/o Cabo Rojo, PR, St. Michael Church. (MGZ)
Juana Diaz, PR, Divine Mercy, c/o Juana Diaz, PR, Santa Teresita Church. (PCE)
Juana Diaz, PR, Bo. Rio Cana Arriba, La Merced, c/o Juana Diaz, PR, St. Raymond Nonato Church. (PCE)
Juana Diaz, PR, San Martin de Porres, c/o Juana Diaz, PR, Santa Teresita Church. (PCE)
Judith Gap, MT, Wheatland Co., Immaculate Conception, c/o Harlowton, MT, St. Joseph Church. (HEL)
Julian, NE, Nemaha Co., St. Bernard's, c/o Paul, NE, St. Joseph's Church. (LIN)
Junction City, KY, Boyle Co., St. Patrick, c/o Danville, KY, SS. Peter & Paul Church. (LEX)
Juniata, NE, Adams Co., Assumption, c/o Roseland, NE, Sacred Heart Church. (LIN)
Juntura, OR, St. Charles, c/o Vale, OR, St. Patrick's Church. (BAK)

K

Kahakuloa, HI, St. Francis Xavier, c/o Waihee, HI, St. Ann Church. (HON)
Kahaluu, HI, St. Peter, c/o Holualoa, HI, St. Michael The Archangel Church. (HON)
Kake, AK, c/o Petersburg, AK, St. Catherine of Siena Church. (JUN)
Kalama, WA, Cowlitz Co., St. Joseph, c/o Woodland, WA, St. Philip's Church. (SEA)
Kalaoa, HI, Holy Rosary, c/o Holualoa, HI, St. Michael The Archangel Church. (HON)
Kalawao, HI, St. Philomena, c/o Kalaupapa, HI, St. Francis Church. (HON)
Kalikonani, HI, Church of the Ascension, Puako, c/o Kamuela, HI, Church of the Annunciation Church. (HON)
Kalskag, AK, c/o Aniak, AK, St. Theresa Church. (FBK)
Kannapolis, NC, St. Joseph, c/o Concord, NC, St. James Church. (CHL)
Kansas, OH, Seneca Co., St. James, c/o Millersville, OH, St. Mary Church. (TOL)
Kapingmarangi, FM, c/o Kolonia, FM, Our Lady of Mercy Church. (CI)
Kaplan, LA, Vermilion Parish, St. Frances Xavier Cabrini, c/o Kaplan, LA, Our Lady of the Holy Rosary Church. (LAF)
Karlsruhe, ND, McHenry Co., Sts. Peter & Paul, c/o Velva, ND, St. Cecilia's Church. (FAR)
Karthaus, PA, Clearfield Co., SS. John & Paul, c/o Frenchville, PA, St. Mary of the Assumption Church. (E)
Kaumakani, HI, St. Joseph, c/o Kekaha, HI, St. Theresa Church. (HON)
Kaupo, HI, St. Joseph, c/o Hana, HI, St. Mary Church. (HON)
Kawanui, HI, St. Paul, c/o Holualoa, HI, St. Michael The Archangel Church. (HON)
Kaycee, WY, Johnson Co., St. Hubert, c/o Buffalo, WY, St. John the Baptist Church. (CHY)
Keaau, HI, Holy Rosary, c/o Mountain View, HI, St. Theresa Church. (HON)
Kealakekua, HI, c/o Honaunau, HI, St. Benedict Church. (HON)
Keanae, HI, St. Gabriel, c/o Haiku, HI, St. Rita Church. (HON)
Keenesburg, CO, Weld Co., Holy Family, c/o Roggen, CO, Sacred Heart Church. (DEN)
Keithsburg, IL, Mercer Co., St. Mary's, c/o Aledo, IL, St. Catherine's Church Church. (PEO)
Kelliher, MN, Beltrami Co., St. Patrick, c/o Blackduck, MN, St. Ann's Church. (CR)
Kelly, NM, Socorro Co., c/o Socorro, NM, San Miguel Church. (SFE)
Kelseyville, CA, St. Peter, c/o Lakeport, CA, St. Mary Church. (SR)
Kenel, SD, Corson Co., Assumption of the Blessed Virgin Mary Church, c/o Standing Rock, SD, Standing Rock Reservation Church. (RC)
Kenel, SD, Corson Co., Our Lady of the Assumption Parish, c/o McLaughlin, SD, St. Bernard Church. (RC)
Kennebunk, ME, St. Monica's, c/o Kennebunk, ME, St. Martha's Church. (PRT)
Kensal, ND, Stutsman Co., c/o Carrington, ND, Sacred Heart Church. (FAR)
Kenyon, MN, Goodhue Co., St. Michael, c/o Pine Island, MN, St. Michael Church. (STP)

Kerhonkson, NY, Ulster Co., Our Lady of Lourdes, c/o Ellenville, NY, St. Mary and St. Andrew Church. (NY)

Keshena, WI, Menominee Co., St. Joseph of the Lake, South Branch, c/o Keshena, WI, St. Michael Church. (GB)

Kettleman City, CA, St. Cecilia, c/o Avenal, CA, St. Joseph Church. (FRS)

Kewanna, IN, Fulton Co., St. Ann, c/o Rochester, IN, St. Joseph Church. (LFT)

Keyapaha, SD, Tripp Co., St. Ann, c/o Winner, SD, Immaculate Conception Church. (RC)

Keystone, SD, Our Lady of Mount Carmel, c/o [1] Rapid City, SD, Cathedral of Our Lady of Perpetual Help Church. (RC)

Kilauea, HI, St. Sylvester, c/o Kapaa, HI, St. Catherine Church. (HON)

Kindred, ND, St. Maurice, c/o [5] Fargo, ND, St. Anthony of Padua Church. (FAR)

King, NC, Stokes Co., Good Shepherd, c/o Winston-Salem, NC, St. Benedict the Moor Church. (CHL)

King George, VA, King George Co., St. Anthony's, c/o Colonial Beach, VA, St. Elizabeth Church. (ARL)

Kingman, ME, St. James, c/o Lincoln, ME, St. Mary Church. (PRT)

Kings Beach, CA, Placer Co., Our Lady of the Lake, c/o Truckee, CA, Assumption of the Blessed Virgin Mary Church. (SAC)

Kings Mountain, NC, Cleveland Co., Christ the King, c/o Shelby, NC, St. Mary's Church. (CHL)

Kingston, NH, Rockingham Co., St. Frederick, c/o Newton, NH, Mary, Mother of the Church Church. (MAN)

Kingston, WI, St. Mary, c/o Markesan, WI, St. Joseph Church. (MAD)

Kinnear, WY, Fremont Co., St. Edward, c/o Riverton, WY, St. Margaret's Church. (CHY)

Kipahulu, HI, St. Paul, c/o Hana, HI, St. Mary Church. (HON)

Kirtland, NM, San Juan Catholic Center Ojo Amarillo Mission, c/o Waterflow, NM, Sacred Heart Church. (GLP)

Kissimmee, FL, Osceola Co., St. Catherine of Siena, c/o Kissimmee, FL, Holy Redeemer Church. (ORL)

Kit Carson, CO, Cheyenne Co., St. Augustine, c/o Cheyenne Wells, CO, Sacred Heart Church. (COS)

Kitzmiller, MD, Garrett Co., Immaculate Conception, c/o Oakland, MD, St. Peter the Apostle Church. (BAL)

Klagetoh, AZ, St. Anne, c/o Ganado, AZ, All Saints Church. (GLP)

Klamath, CA, St. Robert and Ann, c/o Crescent City, CA, St. Joseph Church. (SR)

Knickerbocker, TX, Tom Green Co., Immaculate Conception, c/o Eldorado, TX, Our Lady of Guadalupe Church. (SAN)

Knippa, TX, Uvalde Co., St. Joseph, c/o Sabinal, TX, St. Patrick's Church. (SAT)

Knox, ND, Benson Co., St. Mary, c/o Leeds, ND, St. Vincent de Paul Church. (FAR)

Koeltztown, MO, St. Boniface, c/o Argyle, MO, St. Aloysius Church. (JC)

Kolin, LA, Sts. Francis and Anne, c/o Deville, LA, St. John the Baptist Church. (ALX)

Koontz Lake, IN, Starke Co., St. Dominic, c/o Hamlet, IN, Holy Cross Church. (GRY)

Kosrae, FM, c/o Kolonia, FM, Our Lady of Mercy Church. (CI)

Kress, TX, Swisher Co., St. Paul's, c/o Tulia, TX, Church of the Holy Spirit Church. (AMA)

Kuttu, FM, c/o Lukunor, FM, Sacred Heart Church. (CI)

Kwajalein, MH, Santo, c/o Ebeye, MH, Queen of Peace Church. (MI)

L

L'Erable, IL, Iroquois Co., St. John the Baptist, c/o Ashkum, IL, Assumption of the Blessed Virgin Mary Church. (JOL)

La Bajada, NM, Sandoval Co., c/o Pena Blanca, NM, Nuestra Senora De Guadalupe Church. (SFE)

La Barge, WY, Lincoln Co., La Barge Catholic Community Center, c/o Kemmerer, WY, St. Patrick's Church. (CHY)

La Cienega, NM, Santa Fe Co., c/o [6] Santa Fe, NM, San Isidro Church. (SFE)

La Cueva, NM, Mora Co., c/o Mora, NM, St. Gertrude Church. (SFE)

La Grange, CA, Stanislaus Co., St. Louis, c/o Hughson, CA, St. Anthony Church. (STO)

La Grange, MO, Lewis Co., Notre Dame, c/o Canton, MO, St. Joseph Church. (JC)

La Honda, CA, San Mateo Co., Our Lady of Refuge, c/o Half Moon Bay, CA, Our Lady of the Pillar Church. (SFR)

La Isla, TX, San Luis, c/o Fabens, TX, Our Lady of Guadalupe Church. (ELP)

La Jara, CO, Conejos Co., Our Lady of the Valley, c/o Capulin, CO, St. Joseph Church. (PBL)

La Jara, NM, Santo Nino, c/o Cuba, NM, Immaculate Conception Church. (GLP)

La Lagunita, NM, San Miguel Co., c/o Ribera, NM, San Miguel Del Vado Church. (SFE)

La Luz, NM, Our Lady of the Light, c/o Alamogordo, NM, Immaculate Conception Church. (LSC)

La Madera, NM, Rio Arriba Co., c/o El Rito, NM, San Juan Nepomuceno Church. (SFE)

La Mesilla, NM, c/o Santa Cruz, NM, Holy Cross Church. (SFE)

La Paloma, TX, Our Lady of Lourdes, c/o Ranchito, TX, St. Ignatius Church. (BWN)

La Pica, PR, San Patricio Co., c/o Jayuya, PR, Our Lady of Monserrate Church. (PCE)

La Piedra, PR, Ala de La Piedra Co., O.L. of Perp. Help, c/o Villalba, PR, Our Lady Mother of Divine Providence Church. (PCE)

La Playa, PR, Our Lady of Carmel, c/o Anasco, PR, St. Anthony Abbot Church. (MGZ)

La Puebla, NM, c/o Santa Cruz, NM, Holy Cross Church. (SFE)

La Puente, NM, Rio Arriba Co., c/o Los Ojos, NM, San Jose Church. (SFE)

La Puerta, TX, St. Paul, c/o Rio Grande City, TX, Immaculate Conception Church. (BWN)

La Sara, TX, St. Patrick, c/o Raymondville, TX, Our Lady of Guadalupe Church. (BWN)

La Union, NM, Our Lady of Refuge, c/o Anthony, NM, St. Anthony's Church. (LSC)

La Valle, WI, Holy Family, c/o Lime Ridge, WI, St. Boniface Church. (MAD)

La Veta, CO, Huerfano Co., Christ the King, c/o Walsenburg, CO, St. Mary Church. (PBL)

La Villa, TX, Our Lady of Guadalupe, c/o Edcouch, TX, St. Theresa of the Infant Jesus Church. (BWN)

Lacassine, LA, Jefferson Davis Parish, St. John the Evangelist, c/o Iowa, LA, St. Raphael Church. (LKC)

Lacey, MI, Our Lady of Great Oak, c/o Delton, MI, St. Ambrose Church. (KAL)

Lackawaxen, PA, Pike Co., St. Mary, c/o Shohola, PA, St. Ann's Church. (SCR)

LaCrosse, IN, LaPorte Co., St. Martin, c/o Wanatah, IN, Sacred Heart Church. (GRY)

Laddonia, MO, Audrain Co., St. John, c/o Vandalia, MO, Sacred Heart Church. (JC)

Lafayette, LA, Gift of Mary Chapel, c/o [11] Lafayette, LA, St. Genevieve Church. (LAF)

Lafayette, LA, Our Lady of Good Hope, c/o [2] Lafayette, LA, St. Paul The Apostle Church. (LAF)

Laguna, PR, Santa Rita, c/o Aguada, PR, St. Francis of Assisi Church. (MGZ)

Lajitas, TX, Lajitas Mission, c/o Presidio, TX, Santa Teresa de Jesus Church. (ELP)

Lake Arthur, NM, Our Lady of Guadalupe, c/o Dexter, NM, Immaculate Conception Church. (LSC)

Lake Bonaparte, NY, St. Rita, c/o Harrisville, NY, St. Francis Solanus Church. (OG)

Lake Carmel, NY, Putnam Co., Our Lady of the Lake, c/o Carmel, NY, St. James the Apostle Church. (NY)

Lake Charles, LA, Calcasieu Parish, Christ the King, c/o [8] Lake Charles, LA, Our Lady Queen of Heaven Church. (LKC)

Lake Charles, LA, Calcasieu Parish, Our Lady of Fatima Chapel, c/o [2] Lake Charles, LA, Immaculate Heart of Mary Church. (LKC)

Lake Charles, LA, Calcasieu Parish, St. Martin de Porres, c/o [8] Lake Charles, LA, Our Lady Queen of Heaven Church. (LKC)

Lake City, CO, Hinsdale Co., St. Rose of Lima, c/o Gunnison, CO, St. Peter Church. (PBL)

Lake Como, PA, Wayne Co., Assumption of the B.V.M., c/o Pleasant Mount, PA, St. James Church. (SCR)

Lake Huntington, NY, Sullivan Co., Our Lady of the Lake, c/o Narrowsburg, NY, St. Francis Xavier Church. (NY)

Lake Peekskill, NY, Putnam Co., North American Martyrs, c/o Cortlandt Manor, NY, St. Columbanus Church. (NY)

Lake Titus, NY, Franklin Co., St. Mary, c/o Chasm Falls, NY, St. Helen Church. (OG)

Lake Wallenpaupack, PA, Pike Co., St. Veronica, c/o Hawley, PA, Blessed Virgin Mary, Queen of Peace Church. (SCR)

Lake Williams, ND, Kidder Co., Our Lady of the Lake, c/o Tappen, ND, St. Paul's Church. (FAR)

Lake Wylie, SC, York Co., All Saints, c/o York, SC, Divine Saviour Church. (CHR)

Lakeshore, MS, Hancock Co., St. John, c/o Clermont Harbor, MS, St. Ann Church. (BLX)

Lakeside, CA, Barona, c/o Lakeside, CA, Blessed Kateri Tekakwitha Church. (SD)

Lakeside, SD, Meade Co., St. Margaret, c/o New Underwood, SD, St. John the Evangelist Church. (RC)

Lakeview, NY, Nassau Co., Chapel, c/o West Hempstead, NY, St. Thomas, the Apostle Church. (RVC)

Lakewood, NJ, Ocean Co., Holy Family Church, c/o Lakewood, NJ, St. Mary of the Lake Church. (TR)

Lambert, MT, St. Theresa, c/o Sidney, MT, St. Matthew Church. (GF)

Lamesa, TX, Dawson Co., Our Lady of Guadalupe, c/o Lamesa, TX, St. Margaret Mary Church. (LUB)

Lancaster, MN, Kittson Co., Holy Rosary, c/o Hallock, MN, St. Patrick's Church. (CR)

Lankin, ND, Walsh Co., St. Joseph, c/o Pisek, ND, St. John Nepomucene Church. (FAR)

Lansford, ND, Bottineau Co., St. John, c/o Glenburn, ND, St. Philomena Church. (BIS)

Laona, WI, St. Leonard, c/o Newald, WI, St. Hubert Church. (GB)

Laporte, MN, Hubbard Co., St. Theodore, c/o Akeley, MN, St. John's Church. (CR)

Laporte, PA, Sullivan Co., Sacred Heart, c/o Dushore, PA, St. Basil's Church. (SCR)

Laporte, PA, Sullivan Co., Sacred Heart, c/o Mildred, PA, St. Francis of Assisi Church. (SCR)

Laredo, TX, Webb Co., San Francisco Javier, c/o [6] Laredo, TX, San Augustin Church. (CC)

Laredo, TX, Webb Co., Santa Cruz, c/o [4] Laredo, TX, Holy Redeemer Church. (CC)

Laredo, TX, Webb Co., Santo Nino Mission, c/o [6] Laredo, TX, San Augustin Church. (CC)

Las Colonias, NM, Taos Co., c/o Arroyo Seco, NM, Holy Trinity Church. (SFE)

Las Colonias, NM, San Miguel Co., c/o Pecos, NM, St. Anthony Church. (SFE)

Las Flores, PR, Coamo Co., San Martin, c/o Coamo, PR, St. Blase Church. (PCE)

Las Mareas, PR, St. Judas, c/o Aguirre, PR, Sacred Heart Church. (PCE)

Las Margaritas, PR, Bo. Collores Arriba, Santiago, Ap., c/o Juana Diaz, PR, St. Raymond Nonato Church. (PCE)

Las Milpas, TX, Nuestro Senor del Sagrado Corazon, c/o Pharr, TX, St. Jude Thaddeus Church. (BWN)

Las Nutrias, NM, Socorro Co., San Isidro, c/o La Joya, NM, Our Lady of Sorrows Church. (SFE)

Las Ochenta, PR, Inmaculada Concepcion, c/o Salinas, PR, Our Lady of Monserrat Church. (PCE)

Las Palmas, PR, St. Rita, c/o Cabo Rojo, PR, St. Michael Church. (MGZ)

Las Palomas, NM, San Ysidro, c/o Truth or Consequences, NM, Our Lady of Perpetual Help Church. (LSC)

Las Rucias, TX, Sacred Heart, c/o Ranchito, TX, St. Ignatius Church. (BWN)

Las Tablas, NM, Taos Co., c/o El Rito, NM, San Juan Nepomuceno Church. (SFE)

Las Vegas, PR, Sta. Teresita, c/o Yauco, PR, Holy Rossary Church. (PCE)

LaSal, UT, Grand Co., Sacred Heart, c/o Moab, UT, St. Pius X Church. (SLC)

LaSalle, TX, St. Theresa, c/o Vanderbilt, TX, St. John Bosco Church. (VIC)

Lathrop, CA, San Joaquin Co., Our Lady of Guadalupe, c/o [4] Stockton, CA, St. George Church. (STO)

Latimer, MS, Jackson Co., Christ the King, c/o Vancleave, MS, Catholic Church of the Holy Spirit Church. (BLX)

Lattimer Mines, PA, Luzerne Co., St. Mary, c/o Pardeesville, PA, St. Nazarius Church. (SCR)

Lattnerville, IA, Annunciation, c/o Peosta, IA, St. John the Baptist Church. (DUB)

Laurens, SC, Laurens Co., Holy Spirit, c/o Union, SC, St. Augustine's Church. (CHR)

Lavelle, PA, Schuylkill Co., St. Elizabeth, c/o Ashland, PA, St. Mauritius Church. (ALN)

Lawrence, NE, Nuckolls Co., St. Stephen's, c/o Lawrence, NE, Sacred Heart Church. (LIN)

Lawrenceville, VA, St. Bernard, c/o Emporia, VA, St. Richard Church. (RIC)

LBJ Village, VI, U.S.V.I., Sacred Heart Chapel, c/o [2] Christiansted, VI, Church of the Holy Cross Church. (STV)

Le Bleu Settlement, LA, Calcasieu Parish, St. Joseph, c/o Iowa, LA, St. Raphael Church. (LKC)

Le Doux, NM, Mora Co., c/o Mora, NM, St. Gertrude Church. (SFE)

Le Grand, CA, Merced Co., Our Lady of Lourdes, c/o Planada, CA, Sacred Heart Church. (FRS)

Leakesville, MS, Holy Trinity, c/o Waynesboro, MS, St. Bernadette Church. (BLX)

Leakey, TX, Real Co., St. Raymond of Pennafort, c/o Rocksprings, TX, Sacred Heart of Mary Church. (SAT)

Leaton, MI, Isabella Co., St. Charles, c/o Rosebush, MI, St. Henry Church. (SAG)

Lebanon Junction, KY, St. Clare, c/o Lebanon Junction, KY, St. Benedict Church. (L)

Ledgedale, PA, Wayne Co., St. Mary, c/o Lake Ariel, PA, St. Thomas More Church. (SCR)

Lee Vining, CA, Mono Co., Our Savior of the Mountains, c/o Mammoth Lakes, CA, St. Joseph Church. (STO)

Leeds, NY, St. Bridget, c/o Catskill, NY, St. Patrick Church. (ALB)

Leggett, CA, St. Cecilia, c/o Garberville, CA, Our Lady of the Redwoods Church. (SR)

Lehi, AZ, St. Paschal Baylon, c/o [4] Tempe, AZ, St. Margaret Church. (PHX)

Leicester, VT, Addison Co., St. Agnes, c/o Brandon, VT, St. Mary's Church. (BUR)

Leming, TX, Atascosa Co., Our Lady of Guadalupe, c/o Pleasanton, TX, St. Luke-Loire Church. (SAT)
Lemitar, NM, Socorro Co., c/o Socorro, NM, San Miguel Church. (SFE)
Lenorah, TX, Martin Co., St. Isidore, c/o Stanton, TX, St. Joseph's Church. (SAN)
Leo, MN, Roseau Co., St. Aloysius, c/o Greenbush, MN, Blessed Sacrament Church. (CR)
Leonardsville, NY, Our Lady of the Valley, c/o New Berlin, NY, St. Theresa of the Infant Jesus Church. (SY)
Leroy, ND, Pembina Co., St. Joseph, c/o Walhalla, ND, St. Boniface's Church. (FAR)
Lesterville, MO, Reynolds Co., Our Lady of Sorrows, c/o Ironton, MO, Ste. Marie Du Lac Church. (SPC)
Lewes, DE, Sussex Co., Shrine of St. Jude, c/o Rehoboth, DE, St. Edmond Church. (WIL)
Lewisburg, WV, Monroe Co., St. Louis, c/o Ronceverte, WV, St. Catherine of Siena Church. (WH)
Lewiston, CA, Trinity Co., St. Gilbert, c/o Weaverville, CA, St. Patrick Church. (SAC)
Lexington, IL, McLean Co., St. Mary, c/o Chenoa, IL, St. Joseph's Church. (PEO)
Lexington, NY, St. Francis de Sales, c/o Haines Falls, NY, Immaculate Conception Church. (ALB)
Lexington, OK, Cleveland Co., St. John the Baptist, c/o Purcell, OK, Our Lady of Victory Church. (OKL)
Lexington, TX, Lee Co., Holy Family, c/o Dime Box, TX, St. Joseph's Church. (AUS)
Leyba, NM, San Miguel Co., c/o Villanueva, NM, Our Lady of Guadalupe Church. (SFE)
Liberty, KY, Casey Co., Sacred Heart, c/o Clementsville, KY, St. Bernard Church. (L)
Licking, MO, Texas Co., St. John The Baptist, c/o Houston, MO, St. Mark Church. (SPC)
Lilburn, GA, Gwinnet Co., St. Stephen the Martyr, c/o Lilburn, GA, St. John Neumann Church. (ATL)
Limani, PR, Inm. Corazon de Maria, c/o Adjuntas, PR, St. Joachim Church. (PCE)
Lime Rock, NY, Genesee Co., St. Anthony, c/o Le Roy, NY, St. Peter Church. (BUF)
Lincoln, MT, Lewis and Clark Co., St. Jude's, c/o Helmville, MT, St. Thomas Church. (HEL)
Lincoln, NM, San Juan, c/o Ruidoso, NM, St. Eleanor Church. (LSC)
Lindale, TX, Smith Co., Holy Family, c/o [1] Tyler, TX, Cathedral of the Immaculate Conception Church. (TYL)
Lindsay, OK, Garvin Co., St. Peter's, c/o Pauls Valley, OK, St. Catherine of Siena Church. (OKL)
Lindsborg, KS, St. Bridget of Sweden, c/o McPherson, KS, St. Joseph Church. (WCH)
Linlithgo, NY, Nativity of Our Lord, c/o Germantown, NY, Resurrection Church. (ALB)
Linville, NC, Avery Co., St. Bernadette, c/o Spruce Pine, NC, St. Lucien Church. (CHL)
Lisco, NE, Garden Co., St. Gall, c/o Chappell, NE, St. Joseph's Church. (GI)
Litchfield, ME, Kennebec Co., St. Leo, c/o Richmond, ME, St. Ambrose Church. (PRT)
Litchfield, OH, Jesus the Christ Child, c/o Litchfield, OH, Our Lady Help of Christians Parish Church. (CLV)
Little Egg Harbor, NJ, Ocean Co., St. Michael, c/o Tuckerton, NJ, St. Teresa Church. (TR)
Little Italy, AR, Pulaski Co., St. Francis, c/o Bigelow, AR, St. Boniface's Church. (LR)
Little Meadows, PA, Susquehanna Co., St. Thomas the Apostle, c/o Friendsville, PA, St. Francis Xavier's Church. (SCR)
Little Orleans, MD, Allegany Co., St. Patrick's, c/o Hancock, MD, St. Peter's Church. (BAL)
Littleton, WV, Wetzel Co., Assumption of the Blessed Virgin Mary, c/o Mannington, WV, St. Patrick's Church. (WH)
Live Oak, CA, Sutter Co., Our Lady of Guadalupe, c/o Gridley, CA, Sacred Heart Church. (SAC)
Llano, TX, Holy Trinity Church, c/o Mason, TX, St. Joseph's Church. (AUS)
Llano Largo, NM, Taos Co., San Acacio Mission, c/o Penasco, NM, San Antonio de Padua Church. (SFE)
Llano Quemado, NM, Taos Co., N.S. del Carmel, c/o Ranchos De Taos, NM, San Francisco de Asis Church. (SFE)
Llano San Juan, NM, Taos Co., San Juan Nepomuceno Mission, c/o Penasco, NM, San Antonio de Padua Church. (SFE)
Llanos, PR, Sector El Juicio, c/o Aibonito, PR, Church of St. Joseph Church. (CGS)
Llanos Tunas, PR, Our Lady of Good Counsel, c/o Cabo Rojo, PR, St. Michael Church. (MGZ)
Lluberas, PR, St. Joseph, c/o Yauco, PR, Holy Rossary Church. (PCE)
Lobatos, CO, Sagrada Familia, c/o Conejos, CO, Our Lady of Guadalupe Church. (PBL)
Loch Lomond, CA, Our Lady of the Lake, c/o Middletown, CA, St. Joseph Church. (SR)
Lockney, TX, Floyd Co., San Jose, c/o Plainview, TX, St. Alice Church. (LUB)
Loda, IL, Iroquois Co., St. Joseph, c/o Paxton, IL, St. Mary Church. (JOL)
Lodgepole, NE, Cheyenne Co., Sacred Heart, c/o Chappell, NE, St. Joseph's Church. (GI)
Lodi, OH, Jesus Our Teacher, c/o Litchfield, OH, Our Lady Help of Christians Parish Church. (CLV)
Logan, NM, Quay Co., San Antonio, c/o Tucumcari, NM, St. Anne Church. (SFE)
Loiza, PR, La Milagrosa, c/o Loiza, PR, Santiago Apostol, El Mayor Church. (SJN)
Loiza, PR, La Providencia, c/o Loiza, PR, Santiago Apostol, El Mayor Church. (SJN)
Loiza, PR, Nino de Praga, c/o Loiza, PR, Santiago Apostol, El Mayor Church. (SJN)
Loiza, PR, Ntra. Sra. de Fatima, c/o Loiza, PR, San Patricio Church. (SJN)
Loiza, PR, Ntra. Sra. del Perpetuo Socorro, c/o Loiza, PR, San Patricio Church. (SJN)
Loiza, PR, Ntra. Sra. Perpetuo Socorro, c/o Loiza, PR, Santiago Apostol, El Mayor Church. (SJN)
Loiza, PR, San Antonio, c/o Loiza, PR, San Patricio Church. (SJN)
Loiza, PR, San Rafael-Villa Nevarez, c/o Loiza, PR, San Patricio Church. (SJN)
Loiza, PR, Santa Rosa, c/o Loiza, PR, San Patricio Church. (SJN)
Loiza, PR, Santisima Trinidad, c/o Loiza, PR, San Patricio Church. (SJN)
Loleta, CA, St. Patrick, c/o Fortuna, CA, St. Joseph Church. (SR)
Lolo, MT, Missoula Co., Spirit of Christ, c/o [2] Missoula, MT, Holy Family Church. (HEL)
Lometa, TX, Lampasas Co., Good Shepherd Catholic Church, c/o Lampasas, TX, St. Mary's Church. (AUS)
Lomice, ND, Walsh Co., St. Catherine, c/o Michigan, ND, St. Lawrence O'Toole Church. (FAR)
London, CA, Tulare Co., Santa Cruz, c/o Kingsburg, CA, Holy Family Church. (FRS)
Long Beach, CA, Los Angeles Co., Our Lady of Mt. Carmel, c/o [1] Long Beach, CA, St. Anthony Church. (LA)
Long Eddy, NY, Sullivan Co., St. Patrick, c/o Callicoon, NY, Holy Cross Church. (NY)
Long Island, ME, Great Diamond Island, c/o [8] Portland, ME, St. Christopher's Church. (PRT)
Longcreek, OR, St. Katherine, c/o John Day, OR, St. Elizabeth's Church. (BAK)
Lopeno, TX, Zapata Co., San Pedro, c/o Zapata, TX, Our Lady of Lourdes Church. (CC)
Lopezville, TX, Immaculate Conception, c/o San Juan, TX, St. John the Baptist Church. (BWN)
Loraine, TX, Mitchell Co., San Jose, c/o Colorado City, TX, St. Ann's Church. (SAN)
Lorenzo, TX, San Lorenzo, c/o Idalou, TX, St. Philip Benizi Church. (LUB)
Loreto, WI, St. Patrick, c/o Plain, WI, St. Luke Church. (MAD)
Loris, SC, Horry Co., Church of the Resurrection, c/o Conway, SC, St. James Church. (CHR)
Los Alamos, CA, Santa Barbara Co., St. Anthony's Church, c/o Santa Maria, CA, St. Louis de Montfort Church. (LA)
Los Angeles, CA, Assumption, c/o [5] Los Angeles, CA, Assumption Church. (LA)
Los Angeles, CA, Los Angeles Co., La Purisima Chapel, c/o [29] Los Angeles, CA, Our Lady of the Rosary of Talpa Church. (LA)
Los Angeles, CA, Los Angeles Co., San Felipe, c/o [23] Los Angeles, CA, Our Lady of Guadalupe Church. (LA)
Los Angeles, CA, Santo Nino, c/o [95] Los Angeles, CA, St. Vincent De Paul Church. (LA)
Los Angeles, CA, Los Angeles Co., St. John Bosco, c/o [83] Los Angeles, CA, St. Odilia Church. (LA)
Los Angeles, CA, St. Turibius, c/o [72] Los Angeles, CA, St. Joseph Church. (LA)
Los Chavez, NM, Valencia Co., c/o Belen, NM, Our Lady of Belen Church. (SFE)
Los Cordovas, NM, Taos Co., San Isidro, c/o Ranchos De Taos, NM, San Francisco de Asis Church. (SFE)
Los Coyotes Reservation, CA, San Diego Co., St. Isadore, c/o Santa Ysabel, CA, Santa Ysabel Indian Mission Church. (SD)
Los Ebanos, TX, St. Michael, c/o La Joya, TX, Our Lady, Queen of Angels Church. (BWN)
Los Garcias Ranch, TX, Sacred Heart, c/o Rio Grande City, TX, Immaculate Conception Church. (BWN)
Los Hueros, NM, Mora Co., c/o Wagon Mound, NM, Santa Clara Church. (SFE)
Los Le Febres, NM, Mora Co., c/o Wagon Mound, NM, Santa Clara Church. (SFE)
Los Lentes, NM, Valencia Co., c/o Los Lunas, NM, St. Clement Church. (SFE)
Los Llanos, PR, Coamo Co., St. Anthony, c/o Coamo, PR, St. Blase Church. (PCE)
Los Martinez, NM, Our Lady of Guadalupe, c/o Blanco, NM, St. Rose Church. (GLP)
Los Saenz, TX, Holy Family, c/o Roma, TX, Our Lady of Refuge Church. (BWN)
Los Sauces, CO, St. Anthony, c/o Capulin, CO, St. Joseph Church. (PBL)
Los Valdeses, CO, St. Francis of Assisi, c/o Del Norte, CO, Holy Name of Mary Church. (PBL)
Losap, FM, c/o Lukunor, FM, Sacred Heart Church. (CI)
Lott, TX, Falls Co., Sacred Heart, c/o Marlin, TX, St. Joseph's Church. (AUS)
Louise, TX, St. Procopius, c/o Hillje, TX, St. Andrew Church. (VIC)
Louisville, GA, Jefferson Co., St. Joan of Arc, c/o Waynesboro, GA, Sacred Heart Church. (SAV)
Loveladies, NJ, Ocean Co., St. Clare, c/o Brant Beach, NJ, St. Francis of Assisi Church. (TR)
Lovingston, VA, St. Mary, c/o Scottsville, VA, St. George Church. (RIC)
Lowell, VT, Orleans Co., St. Ignatius Loyola, c/o Troy, VT, Sacred Heart of Jesus Church. (BUR)
Lower San Francisco, NM, San Isidro, c/o Aragon, NM, Santo Nino Church. (GLP)
Loyalton, CA, Sierra Co., Holy Rosary, c/o Portola, CA, Holy Family Church. (SAC)
Lozano, TX, St. Vincent de Paul, c/o Rio Hondo, TX, St. Helen Church. (BWN)
Lucedale, MS, George Co., St. Lucy, c/o Wiggins, MS, St. Francis Xavier Church. (BLX)
Lucerne, CA, Queen of the Rosary, c/o Lakeport, CA, St. Mary Church. (SR)
Lucero, NM, Mora Co., c/o Mora, NM, St. Gertrude Church. (SFE)
Ludlow, IL, Champaign Co., Sacred Heart, c/o Thomasboro, IL, St. Elizabeth's Church. (PEO)
Luis Lopez, NM, Socorro Co., c/o Socorro, NM, San Miguel Church. (SFE)
Lull, TX, Capilla de San Jose, c/o Edinburg, TX, Sacred Heart Church. (BWN)
Lummi, WA, Whatcom Co., St. Joachim (Indian Reservation), c/o Ferndale, WA, St. Joseph Church. (SEA)
Lunenburg, VT, Essex Co., St. Leo, c/o Gilman, VT, St. Theresa Church. (BUR)
Luquillo, PR, Ntra. Sra. del Cobre, c/o Luquillo, PR, San Jose Church. (SJN)
Luquillo, PR, San Judas, c/o Luquillo, PR, San Jose Church. (SJN)
Luther, MI, St. Ignatius, c/o Baldwin, MI, St. Ann's Church. (GR)
Luther, OK, Oklahoma Co., Saint Theresa of the Infant Jesus, c/o Jones, OK, St. Robert Bellarmine Church. (OKL)
Lyden, NM, Rio Arriba Co., San Jose, c/o Dixon, NM, St. Anthony Church. (SFE)
Lyman, NE, Scotts Bluff Co., Sacred Heart, c/o Mitchell, NE, St. Theresa's Church. (GI)
Lyons, OR, Linn Co., St. Patrick, c/o Jordan, OR, Our Lady of Lourdes Church. (P)
Lyons, WI, St. Kilian's, c/o Lyons, WI, St. Joseph Church. (MIL)
Lyons Falls, NY, Lewis Co., St. John, c/o Port Leyden, NY, St. Martin Church. (OG)

M

Macana, PR, Fatima, c/o Penuelas, PR, St. Joseph Church. (PCE)
Macana Parcelas, PR, San Martin de Porres, c/o Guayanilla, PR, Immaculate Conception Church. (PCE)
Macana Rio, PR, Virgen de Fatima, c/o Guayanilla, PR, Immaculate Conception Church. (PCE)
MacDonaldton, PA, Somerset Co., St. Gregory, c/o Meyersdale, PA, SS. Philip and James Church. (ALT)
Macon, MS, Corpus Christi, c/o Starkville, MS, St. Joseph Church. (JKS)
Macy, NE, Thurston Co., Our Lady of Fatima, c/o Winnebago, NE, St. Augustine's Church. (OM)
Madawaska, ME, Aroostook Co., St. Michael's Chapel, c/o St. Agatha, ME, St. Agatha's Church. (PRT)
Maddock, ND, Benson Co., St. William, c/o Fessenden, ND, St. Augustine's Church. (FAR)
Madera, CA, Madera Co., St. Agnes, c/o Madera, CA, St. Joachim Church. (FRS)
Madera, PA, Clearfield Co., Immaculate Conception, c/o Houtzdale, PA, Christ the King Church. (E)
Madero, TX, Our Lady of Lourdes, c/o [2] Mission, TX, Our Lady of the Holy Rosary Church. (BWN)
Madill, OK, Marshall Co., Holy Cross, c/o Sulphur, OK, St. Francis Xavier Church. (OKL)
Madison, GA, Morgan Co., St. James, c/o Covington, GA, St. Augustine Church Church. (ATL)
Madison, KS, Greenwood Co., St. Teresa Of Avila, c/o Eureka, KS, Sacred Heart Church. (WCH)
Magas Arriba, PR, Perpetuo Socorro, c/o Guayanilla, PR, Immaculate Conception Church. (PCE)
Magdalena, NM, Socorro Co., c/o Socorro, NM, San Miguel Church. (SFE)
Mageetown, PA, Crawford Co., Immaculate Conception, c/o Titusville, PA, St. Titus Church. (E)
Magnolia, AR, Columbia Co., Immaculate Heart of Mary, c/o Camden, AR, St. Louis Church. (LR)
Magnolia, ID, St. Joseph's Chapel, c/o [1] Gloucester, MA, St. Ann Church. (BO)
Magnolia, MS, St. James, c/o Chatawa, MS, St. Teresa Church. (JKS)

Magur, FM, Marie Chapel, c/o Fefan, FM, Sacred Heart Church. (CI)
Majuro Atoll, MH, Laura, c/o Majuro, MH, Cathedral of the Assumption Church. (MI)
Makoti, ND, Ward Co., St. Elizabeth, c/o Parshall, ND, St. Bridget Church. (BIS)
Malaga, CA, Fresno, Christ the King, c/o [8] Fresno, CA, St. Anthony Claret Church. (FRS)
Malaga, NM, Cristo Rey, c/o Loving, NM, Our Lady of Grace Church. (LSC)
Malakoff, TX, Henderson Co., Mary Queen of Heaven, c/o Gun Barrel City, TX, St. Jude Church. (TYL)
Malpaso-Cesar Ruiz, PR, Immaculada Concepcion, c/o Aguada, PR, St. Francis of Assisi Church. (MGZ)
Mamey, PR, Perpetuo Socorro, c/o Aguada, PR, St. Francis of Assisi Church. (MGZ)
Mameyes, PR, Jayuya Co., S. Antonio, c/o Jayuya, PR, Our Lady of Monserrate Church. (PCE)
Manassa, CO, Conejos Co., St. Therese of the Child Jesus, c/o Capulin, CO, St. Joseph Church. (PBL)
Manderson, SD, Shannon Co., St. Agnes, c/o Porcupine, SD, Church of Christ the King Church. (RC)
Manderson, SD, Shannon Co., St. Peter's, c/o Porcupine, SD, Church of Christ the King Church. (RC)
Mani, PR, Capilla de la Mora, c/o [2] Mayaquez, PR, Our Lady of Mt. Carmel Church. (MGZ)
Mani, PR, Infant of Prague, c/o [2] Mayaquez, PR, Our Lady of Mt. Carmel Church. (MGZ)
Manito, IL, Mason Co., Immaculate Conception, c/o Havana, IL, St. Patrick's Church. (PEO)
Manitou Springs, CO, El Paso Co., Our Lady of Perpetual Help, c/o [10] Colorado Springs, CO, Sacred Heart Church. (COS)
Mankato, MN, Blue Earth Co., St. Francis Xaiver, c/o [1] Mankato, MN, SS. Peter and Paul's Church. (WIN)
Mannford, OK, Creek Co., Our Lady of the Lake, c/o Sand Springs, OK, St. Patrick's Church. (TLS)
Manset, ME, St. Peter's, c/o Northeast Harbor, ME, St. Ignatius Church. (PRT)
Mansfield, WA, Douglas Co., St. Mary, c/o Bridgeport, WA, St. Anne's Church. (YAK)
Mantador, ND, Richland Co., Sts. Peter & Paul, c/o Mooreton, ND, St. Anthony's Church. (FAR)
Manton, KY, Washington Co., Holy Rosary, c/o [3] Springfield, KY, Holy Trinity Church. (L)
Manu'a Island, AS, Mary, Star of the Sea, c/o [1] Pago Pago, AS, Cathedral of the Holy Family Church. (SPP)
Many, LA, Sabine Parish, St. Terence, c/o Many, LA, St. John the Baptist Church. (SHP)
Many Farms, AZ, St. Anthony, c/o Chinle, AZ, Our Lady of Fatima, Indian Mission Church. (GLP)
Manzano, NM, Torrance Co., c/o Mountainair, NM, St. Alice Church. (SFE)
Manzanola, CO, Otero Co., St. Joseph the Worker, c/o Rocky Ford, CO, St. Peter Church. (PBL)
Marak, TX, Milam Co., Ss. Cyril & Methodius, c/o Cyclone, TX, St. Joseph's Church. (AUS)
Marana, AZ, San Juan, c/o [2] Tucson, AZ, Blessed Kateri Tekakwitha Church. (TUC)
Marcellus, MI, Cass Co., St. Margaret Mary, c/o Mattawan, MI, St. John Bosco Church. (KAL)
Marenisco, MI, Gogebic Co., St. Catherine, c/o Wakefield, MI, Immaculate Conception of the Blessed Virgin Mary Church. (MAR)
Maresua, PR, Gruta de Lourdes, c/o San German, PR, San German de Auxerre Church. (MGZ)
Marian, TN, Marian Co., Virgin of the Poor Shrine, c/o South Pittsburg, TN, Our Lady of Lourdes Church. (KNX)
Marias, PR, Asuncion de Maria, c/o Aguada, PR, St. Francis of Assisi Church. (MGZ)
Maricopa, AZ, Pinal Co., St. Francis de Sales, c/o Casa Grande, AZ, St. Anthony Church. (TUC)
Marienville, PA, Forest Co., St. Anne, c/o Crown, PA, St. Mary Church. (E)
Marietta, OK, Love Co., Good Shepherd, c/o Ardmore, OK, St. Mary Church. (OKL)
Marion, NC, McDowell Co, Our Lady of the Angels, c/o Morganton, NC, St. Charles Borromeo Church. (CHL)
Marion, ND, LaMoure Co., St. Francis, c/o La Moure, ND, Holy Rosary Church. (FAR)
Marion, SC, Marion Co., Infant Jesus, c/o Dillon, SC, St. Louis Church. (CHR)
Marion, TX, Guadalupe Co., Immaculate Conception, c/o Schertz, TX, Church of the Good Shepherd Church. (SAT)
Marked Tree, AR, Poinsett Co., St. Norbert's, c/o Weiner, AR, St. Anthony's Church. (LR)
Markham, TX, St. Robert, c/o Blessing, TX, St. Peter's Church. (VIC)
Marlow, OK, Stephens Co., Immaculate Conception, c/o Duncan, OK, Assumption Church. (OKL)
Marmarth, ND, Slope Co., Immaculate Heart of Mary, c/o Bowman, ND, St. Charles Church. (BIS)
Marshall, AK, Our Lady of Guadalupe Russian Mission, c/o Marshall, AK, Immaculate Heart of Mary Church. (FBK)
Marshall, CA, Marin Co., St. Helen, c/o Tomales, CA, Church of the Assumption Church. (SFR)
Marshall, OK, Logan Co., St. Camillus, c/o Hennessey, OK, St. Joseph's Church. (OKL)
Marshfield, VT, Washington Co., North American Martyrs, c/o Montpelier, VT, St. Augustine Church. (BUR)
Martindale, TX, Caldwell Co., Immaculate Heart of Mary, c/o San Marcos, TX, St. John the Evangelist Church. (AUS)
Marysdale, OH, Defiance Co., Immaculate Conception, c/o The Bend, OH, St. Stephen Church. (TOL)
Marysville, MT, Lewis and Clark Co., Our Lady of Lourdes, c/o [3] Helena, MT, Our Lady of the Valley Church. (HEL)
Masefau, AS, c/o [5] Pago Pago, AS, Church of St. Peter and Paul Church. (SPP)
Mason, TX, c/o Llano, TX, Holy Trinity Church. (AUS)
Mason, WV, Mason Co., St. Joseph, c/o Point Pleasant, WV, Sacred Heart Church. (WH)
Mason City, IL, Mason Co., St. Columba, c/o Lincoln, IL, Holy Family Church. (PEO)
Mason City, NE, Custer Co., St. Thomas, c/o Broken Bow, NE, St. Joseph's Church. (GI)
Matador, TX, Motley Co., Our Lady of Guadalupe, c/o Floydada, TX, St. Mary Magdalen Church. (LUB)
Matrullas, PR, Cacao Co., Sacred Heart of Jesus, c/o Villalba, PR, Our Lady Mother of Divine Providence Church. (PCE)
Mattingly Settlement, OH, Muskingum Co., St. Mary, c/o Dresden, OH, St. Ann's Church. (COL)
Mattituck, NY, Suffolk Co., Our Lady of Good Counsel, c/o Cutchogue, NY, Sacred Heart Church. (RVC)
Matunuck, RI, Washington, St. Romuald, c/o South Kingstown, RI, St. Francis of Assisi Church. (PRO)
Maud, OK, Seminole Co., St. Cecelia, c/o Seminole, OK, Immaculate Conception Church. (OKL)
Maupin, OR, St. Mary's, c/o Dufur, OR, St. Alphonsus Church. (BAK)
Max, ND, McClean Co., Immaculate Conception, c/o Garrison, ND, St. Nicholas Church. (BIS)
Maxwell, NM, Colfax Co., c/o Springer, NM, St. Joseph Church. (SFE)
Mayaguez, PR, Corpus Christi, c/o [5] Mayaquez, PR, Nuestra Senora De Fatima Church. (MGZ)
Mayaguez, PR, Cristo Rey, c/o [5] Mayaquez, PR, Nuestra Senora De Fatima Church. (MGZ)
Mayaguez, PR, Espiritu Santo, c/o [5] Mayaquez, PR, Nuestra Senora De Fatima Church. (MGZ)
Mayaguez, PR, Maria Socorro de los Cristianos, c/o [1] Mayaquez, PR, Cathedral of Our Lady of Purification Church. (MGZ)
Mayaguez, PR, Santa Ana, c/o [1] Mayaquez, PR, Cathedral of Our Lady of Purification Church. (MGZ)
Mayer, AZ, St. Joseph, c/o Prescott Valley, AZ, St. Germaine Church. (PHX)
Maysville, MO, DeKalb Co., St. Aloysius, c/o Cameron, MO, St. Munchin Church. (KC)
Mayville, ND, State University Newman Club, c/o Mayville, ND, Our Lady of Peace Church. (FAR)
McCartys, NM, Cibola Co., Santa Maria de Acoma, c/o Acoma, NM, San Esteban, Acoma Catholic Indian Mission Church. (GLP)
McClellanville, SC, Charleston Co., McClellanville Mission, c/o Georgetown, SC, St. Mary's Church. (CHR)
McClusky, ND, Sheridan Co., Holy Family, c/o Sykeston, ND, St. Elizabeth's Church. (FAR)
McCook, NE, Red Willow Co., Sacred Heart, c/o McCook, NE, St. Patrick Church. (LIN)
McCook, NE, Red Willow Co., St. Ann's, c/o McCook, NE, St. Patrick Church. (LIN)
McCormick, SC, McCormick Co., Good Shepherd, c/o Abbeville, SC, Sacred Heart Church. (CHR)
McCrory, AR, Woodruff Co., St. Mary's, c/o Wynne, AR, St. Peter's Church. (LR)
McDermitt, NV, Humboldt Co., Sacred Heart, c/o Winnemucca, NV, St. Paul Church. (RNO)
McGill, NV, St. Michael's, c/o Ely, NV, Sacred Heart Church. (LAV)
McHenry, ND, Foster Co., SS. Peter & Paul, c/o New Rockford, ND, St. John's Church. (FAR)
McIntosh, SD, Corson Co., St. Bonaventure, c/o McLaughlin, SD, St. Bernard Church. (RC)
McKee, KY, Jackson Co., St. Paul, c/o Berea, KY, St. Clare Church. (LEX)
McRoberts, KY, Letcher Co., Holy Angels, c/o Jenkins, KY, St. George Church. (LEX)
Mead, CO, Weld Co., Guardian Angels, c/o Frederick, CO, St. Theresa Church. (DEN)
Meadowlands, MN, St. Mary's, c/o Floodwood, MN, St. Louis Church. (DUL)
Meadville, MS, St. Ann, c/o Natchez, MS, Assumption of the B.V.M. Church. (JKS)
Mechanic Falls, ME, Oxford Co., St. Mary, c/o Mechanic Falls, ME, Our Lady of Ransom Church. (PRT)
Mechanicsville, CT, Windham Co., Sacred Heart, c/o North Grosvenordale, CT, St. Joseph Church. (NOR)
Medanales, NM, Rio Arriba Co., c/o Abiquiu, NM, St. Thomas Apostle Church. (SFE)
Media, OH, c/o [8] Lorain, OH, St. John the Baptist Church. (SJP)
Medicine Bow, WY, Carbon Co., St. Malachy, c/o Saratoga, WY, St. Ann's Church. (CHY)
Medicine Lake, MT, St. Patrick, c/o Culbertson, MT, St. Anthony's Church. (GF)
Medicine Root, SD, Shannon, St. Stephens, c/o Kyle, SD, Our Lady of Sorrows Church. (RC)
Medina, ND, Stutsman Co., St. Mary, c/o Windsor, ND, St. Mathias Church. (FAR)
Medina Lake, TX, Bandera Co., St. Victor's Chapel, c/o Bandera, TX, St. Stanislaus Church. (SAT)
Medora, ND, Billings Co., St. Mary, c/o Belfield, ND, St. Bernard Church. (BIS)
Meeker, OK, Lincoln Co., St.Michael, c/o Prague, OK, St. Wenceslaus, National Shrine of the Infant Jesus of Prague Church. (OKL)
Meekin's Neck, MD, Dorchester Co., St. Mary, Star of the Sea, c/o Cambridge, MD, St. Mary Refuge of Sinners Church. (WIL)
Meeteetsee, WY, Park Co., St. Theresa, c/o Cody, WY, St. Anthony Church. (CHY)
Meherrin, VA, Sacred Heart, c/o Crewe, VA, St. John the Baptist Church. (RIC)
Melbourne, FL, c/o Orlando, FL, St. Nicholas of Myra Church. (PSC)
Melendez, PR, Coamo Co., Our Lady of Fatima, c/o Coamo, PR, St. Blase Church. (PCE)
Melrose, MT, Silver Bow Co., St. John The Apostle, c/o Dillon, MT, St. Rose of Lima Church. (HEL)
Melrose, NM, Curry Co., c/o Clovis, NM, Sacred Heart Church. (SFE)
Melstone, MT, Our Lady of Mercy, c/o Roundup, MT, St. Benedict's Church. (GF)
Melvin, IL, St. George, c/o Gibson City, IL, Our Lady of Lourdes Church. (JOL)
Melvin, TX, McCullogh Co., St. Francis Xavier, c/o Brady, TX, St. Patrick's Church. (SAN)
Melvindale, MI, St. Thomas Indian Catholic Mission, c/o Melvindale, MI, St. Mary Magdalen Church. (DET)
Merced, CA, Merced Co., El Nido, c/o Merced, CA, Sacred Heart Church. (FRS)
Merced, CA, Merced Co., St. George, c/o Merced, CA, Sacred Heart Church. (FRS)
Mercersburg, PA, Franklin Co., St. Luke the Evangelist, c/o Greencastle, PA, St. Mark the Evangelist Church. (HBG)
Mereta, TX, Tom Green Co., Holy Family, c/o Wall, TX, St. Ambrose Church. (SAN)
Merkel, TX, Taylor Co., Our Mother of Mercy, c/o Sweetwater, TX, Holy Family Church. (SAN)
Merna, NE, Custer Co., St. Paul, c/o Anselmo, NE, St. Anselm's Church. (GI)
Merrimac, WI, Sauk Co., St. Mary, Health of the Sick, c/o Durward's Glen, WI, St. Camillus Church. (MAD)
Merryville, LA, Beauregard Parish, St. Bridget, c/o De Ridder, LA, St. Joseph's Church. (LKC)
Mertzon, TX, Irion Co., St. Peter's, c/o Eldorado, TX, Our Lady of Guadalupe Church. (SAN)
Mesa de Poleo, NM, Rio Arriba Co., c/o Abiquiu, NM, St. Thomas Apostle Church. (SFE)
Mesita, NM, Sacred Heart, c/o Laguna, NM, St. Joseph Church. (GLP)
Mesquite, NM, Our Lady of Perpetual Help, c/o San Miguel, NM, San Miguel Church. (LSC)
Metip, FM, c/o Tamoroi, FM, Sacred Heart Church. (CI)
Metlakatla, AK, Holy Family, c/o Ketchikan, AK, Holy Name Church. (JUN)
Metter, GA, Candler Co., Holy Family, c/o Swainsboro, GA, Holy Trinity Church. (SAV)
Mexico Beach, FL, Bay Co., Our Lady of Guadalupe, c/o Panama City, FL, St. Dominic Church. (PT)
Miami, FL, La Milagrosa, c/o [3] Miami, FL, Corpus Christi Church. (MIA)
Miami, FL, La Purisima, c/o [25] Miami, FL, St. Kieran Church. (MIA)
Miami, FL, Nuestra Senora de Altagracia, c/o [3] Miami, FL, Corpus Christi Church. (MIA)
Miami, FL, San Francisco y Santa Clara, c/o [3] Miami, FL, Corpus Christi Church. (MIA)
Miami, FL, San Juan Bautista, c/o [3] Miami, FL, Corpus Christi Church. (MIA)
Michigamme, MI, Marquette Co., St. Agnes, c/o Champion, MI, Sacred Heart Church. (MAR)
Michigan City, IN, La Porte Co., Maronite Catholic Community, c/o Hillside, IL, Our Lady of Lebanon Church Church. (OLL)
Mico, TX, Medina Co., St. Francis of Assisi (Medina Lake Chapel), c/o Castroville, TX, St. Louis Church. (SAT)
Middle River, MN, Marshall Co., St. Joseph, c/o Greenbush, MN, Blessed Sacrament Church. (CR)
Middlebourne, WV, Tyler Co., St. Lawrence, c/o Paden City, WV, Mater Dolorosa Church. (WH)
Middleport, PA, Immaculate Heart of Mary Chapel, c/o New Philadelphia, PA, Sacred Heart Church. (ALN)
Middletown, IL, Logan Co., St. John the Baptist, c/o Elkhart, IL, St. Patrick Church. (PEO)
Middletown, PA, Susquehanna Co., St. Patrick, c/o Friendsville, PA, St. Francis Xavier's Church. (SCR)

Middleville, NY, St. Mary of the Assumption, c/o Newport, NY, St. John the Baptist Church. (ALB)
Midkiff, TX, Upton Co., St. Thomas, c/o St. Lawrence, TX, St. Lawrence Church. (SAN)
Midland, LA, St. Aloysius, c/o Morse, LA, Immaculate Conception Church. (LAF)
Midland, SD, Haakon Co., St. William, c/o Philip, SD, Sacred Heart Church. (RC)
Midwest, WY, Natrona Co., St. Francis Mission, c/o Casper, WY, St. Anthony of Padua Church. (CHY)
Milagro, NM, Guadalupe Co., c/o Santa Rosa, NM, St. Rose of Lima Church. (SFE)
Mildred, PA, Sullivan Co., St. Francis of Assisi, c/o Dushore, PA, St. Basil's Church. (SCR)
Milesville, SD, Haakon Co., St. Mary, c/o Philip, SD, Sacred Heart Church. (RC)
Milford Center, OH, Union Co., Sacred Heart, c/o Plain City, OH, St. Joseph Church. (COL)
Mill City, OR, Marion Co., St. Catherine of Siena, c/o Sublimity, OR, St. Boniface Church. (P)
Mill Creek, WI, St. John the Baptist, c/o Mazomanie, WI, St. Barnabas Church. (MAD)
Mill Rift, PA, Pike Co., Holy Family, c/o Matamoras, PA, St. Joseph's Church. (SCR)
Mill River, MA, Berkshire Co., Immaculate Conception, c/o Sheffield, MA, Our Lady of the Valley Church. (SPR)
Millen, GA, Jenkins Co., St. Bernadette, c/o Sylvania, GA, Our Lady of the Assumption Church. (SAV)
Millersview, TX, Concho Co., Our Lady of Guadalupe, c/o Eden, TX, St. Charles Church. (SAN)
Millerton, NY, Dutchess Co., St. Patrick, c/o Amenia, NY, Immaculate Conception Church. (NY)
Milligan, NE, Fillmore Co., St. Wenceslaus, c/o Friend, NE, St. Joseph's Church. (LIN)
Millington, MI, Tuscola Co., St. Bernard, c/o Vassar, MI, St. Frances Xavier Cabrini Church. (SAG)
Millsboro, DE, Sussex Co., Mary Mother of Peace, c/o Georgetown, DE, St. Michael the Archangel Church. (WIL)
Millwood, NY, Westchester Co., Our Lady of the Wayside, c/o Briarcliff Manor, NY, St. Theresa Church. (NY)
Milnor, ND, Sargent Co., St. Arnold, c/o Forman, ND, St. Mary's Church. (FAR)
Milo, ME, St. Paul, c/o Brownville Junction, ME, St. Francis Xavier Church. (PRT)
Milolii, HI, c/o Honaunau, HI, St. Benedict Church. (HON)
Milton, ND, Cavalier Co., St. Clothilde, c/o Wales, ND, St. Michael's Church. (FAR)
Milton, NH, Strafford Co., Sacred Heart, c/o Sanbornville, NH, St. Anthony Church. (MAN)
Minerva, KY, Mason Co., St. James, c/o Brooksville, KY, St. James Church. (COV)
Minnewauken, ND, Benson Co., St. James, c/o Leeds, ND, St. Vincent de Paul Church. (FAR)
Minot, ND, c/o Wilton, ND, SS. Peter and Paul Church. (STN)
Miraflores, PR, Chapel of Our Lady of Perpetual Help, c/o Anasco, PR, St. Anthony Abbot Church. (MGZ)
Mirando City, TX, Webb Co., St. Agnes, c/o Hebbronville, TX, Our Lady of Guadalupe Church. (CC)
Mirasol, PR, La Virgen, c/o Castaner, PR, Our Lady of the Miraculous Medal Church. (PCE)
Mission, SD, Todd Co., St. Thomas, c/o St. Francis, SD, Rosebud Reservation Church. (RC)
Mobridge, SD, c/o Wilton, ND, SS. Peter and Paul Church. (STN)
Mocanaqua, PA, Luzerne Co., Ascension, c/o Mocanaqua, PA, St. Mary, Our Lady of Perpetual Help Church. (SCR)
Moch, FM, c/o Lukunor, FM, Sacred Heart Church. (CI)
Mogollon, AZ, Our Lady, c/o Alpine, AZ, St. Helena Church. (GLP)
Mojave, CA, St. Francis, c/o Mojave, CA, St. Mary's Church. (FRS)
Mokelumne Hill, CA, Calaveras Co., St. Thomas Aquinas, c/o San Andreas, CA, St. Andrew Church. (STO)
Monacillos, PR, San Fernando, c/o [23] San Juan, PR, Inmaculado Corazon de Maria Church. (SJN)
Monarch, MT, St. Clement, c/o Belt, MT, St. Mark the Evangelist Church. (GF)
Moncla, LA, St. John the Baptist, c/o Fifth Ward, LA, Our Lady of Lourdes Church. (ALX)
Monet Ferry, LA, Holy Family, c/o Cloutierville, LA, St. John the Baptist Church. (ALX)
Mongaup Valley, NY, Sullivan Co., St. Joseph, c/o Monticello, NY, St. Peter Church. (NY)
Monmouth, ME, Kennebec Co., St. Stanislaus, c/o Winthrop, ME, St. Francis Xavier Church. (PRT)
Monte Alto, TX, Hidalgo Co., Christ the King, Holy Cross Catechetical Center, c/o Elsa, TX, Sacred Heart Church. (BWN)
Monte Aplanado, NM, Mora Co., c/o Mora, NM, St. Gertrude Church. (SFE)
Monte Grande, PR, St. Jude Thaddeus, c/o Cabo Rojo, PR, St. Michael Church. (MGZ)
Monte Rio, CA, St. Catherine, c/o Guerneville, CA, St. Elizabeth Church. (SR)
Montecello, NM, St. Ignatius, c/o Truth or Consequences, NM, Our Lady of Perpetual Help Church. (LSC)
Monterey, MA, Berkshire Co., Our Lady of the Hills, c/o Sheffield, MA, Our Lady of the Valley Church. (SPR)
Montesano, WA, Grays Harbor Co., St. John, c/o Elma, WA, St. Joseph's Church. (SEA)
Montezuma, GA, Macon Co., St. Michael, c/o Americus, GA, St. Mary Church. (SAV)
Montezuma, IN, Parke Co., Immaculate Conception, c/o Rockville, IN, St. Joseph Church. (IND)
Montgomery, AL, Montgomery Co., Resurrection Catholic Mission, c/o [8] Montgomery, AL, Resurrection Catholic Church Church. (MOB)
Montgomery, LA, St. Patrick, c/o Colfax, LA, St. Joseph Church. (ALX)
Monument, OR, St. Ann, c/o John Day, OR, St. Elizabeth's Church. (BAK)
Moody, TX, McLennan Co., Our Lady of San Juan, c/o McGregor, TX, St. Eugene Church. (AUS)
Moorcroft, WY, Crook Co., St. Patrick, c/o Gillette, WY, St. Matthew's Church. (CHY)
Moore, MT, St. Mathias, c/o Stanford, MT, St. Rose of Lima Church. (GF)
Moore, TX, Frio Co., St. Augustine, c/o Von Ormy, TX, St. Peter the Fisherman Church. (SAT)
Mooreland, OK, Woodward Co., Sacred Heart, c/o Woodward, OK, St. Peter's Church. (OKL)
Moorhead, MN, Clay Co., St. Thomas Newman Center, c/o Moorhead, MN, St. Joseph's Church. (CR)
Moquino, NM, Santa Rosalia, c/o Seboyeta, NM, Our Lady of Sorrows Church. (GLP)
Moral, TX, Nacogdoches Co., Immaculate Conception, c/o Nacogdoches, TX, Sacred Heart Church. (TYL)
Moravia, TX, Lavaca Co., Ascension of Our Lord, c/o St. John, TX, St. John the Baptist Church. (VIC)
Moretown, VT, Washington Co., St. Patrick, c/o Waitsfield, VT, Our Lady of the Snows Church. (BUR)
Morgan City, LA, St. Martin Parish, St. Rosalie, c/o Morgan City, LA, Holy Cross Church. (HT)
Morning View, KY, Kenton Co., Assumption of the Blessed Virgin, c/o Kenton, KY, St. Matthew Church. (COV)
Morongo Reservation, CA, Riverside Co., Indian Mission, c/o Banning, CA, Precious Blood Church. (SB)
Morrill, NE, Scotts Bluff Co., St. Ann, c/o Mitchell, NE, St. Theresa's Church. (GI)
Morris, CT, Litchfield Co., Our Lady of Hope, c/o Bantam, CT, Our Lady of Grace Church. (HRT)
Morris, PA, Tioga Co., Sacred Heart, c/o Wellsboro, PA, St. Peter's Church. (SCR)
Morris Run, PA, Tioga Co., St. Joseph, c/o Blossburg, PA, St. Mary's Church. (SCR)
Morristown, SD, Corson Co., Sacred Heart, c/o Lemmon, SD, St. Mary's Church. (RC)
Moses, NM, Union Co., Sacred Heart, c/o Clayton, NM, St. Francis Xavier Church. (SFE)
Mosquero, NM, Harding Co., c/o Roy, NM, Holy Family-St. Joseph Church. (SFE)
Mount Carmel, ND, Cavalier Co., Our Lady of Mount Carmel, c/o Wales, ND, St. Michael's Church. (FAR)
Mount Holly, VT, Rutland Co., St. Mary, c/o Wallingford, VT, St. Patrick Church. (BUR)
Mount Hope, WI, St. Lawrence O'Toole, c/o Fennimore, WI, St. Mary Church. (MAD)
Mount Ida, AR, Montgomery Co., All Saints, c/o Mena, AR, St. Agnes Church. (LR)
Mount Olive, NC, Duplin Co., Posada Guadalupana, c/o Clinton, NC, Immaculate Conception Church. (R)
Mount Olive, NC, Wayne Co., St. Mary, c/o Clinton, NC, Immaculate Conception Church. (R)
Mount Palatine, IL, Putnam Co., Immaculate Conception, c/o Hennepin, IL, St. Patrick's Church. (PEO)
Mount Pulaski, IL, Logan Co., St. Thomas Aquinas, c/o Elkhart, IL, St. Patrick Church. (PEO)
Mt. Vernon, TX, Franklin Co., Sacred Heart, c/o Sulphur Springs, TX, St. James Church. (TYL)
Mountain Iron, MN, Sacred Heart, c/o Virginia, MN, Sacred Heart Church. (DUL)
Mountain View, AR, Stone Co., St. Mary Mission, c/o Batesville, AR, St. Mary's Church. (LR)
Moxham, PA, Cambria Co., St. Anne's, c/o [18] Johnstown, PA, St. Therese of the Child Jesus Church. (ALT)
Mud Butte, SD, St. Joseph, c/o Belle Fourche, SD, St. Paul Church. (RC)
Mud Butte, SD, Meade Co., St. Joseph's Catholic Church, c/o Newell, SD, St. Mary Star of the Sea Church. (RC)
Mukilteo, WA, Snohomish Co., St. John Evangelist, c/o Everett, WA, St. Mary Magdalen Church. (SEA)
Mulvey, LA, St. David, c/o Gueydan, LA, St. Peter Church. (LAF)
Mumford, NY, Monroe Co., St. Patrick, c/o Caledonia, NY, St. Columba Church. (ROC)
Murdo, SD, Jones Co., St. Martin of Tours, c/o Presho, SD, Christ the King Church. (RC)
Murphys, CA, Murphys Co., St. Patrick, c/o Angels Camp, CA, St. Patrick Church. (STO)
Musselshell, MT, St. Honorata, c/o Roundup, MT, St. Benedict's Church. (GF)
Myrtle Point, OR, Coos Co., Sts. Ann and Michael, c/o Coquille, OR, Holy Name Church. (P)

N

Naco, AZ, Cochise Co., St. Michael, c/o Bisbee, AZ, St. Patrick Church. (TUC)
Nags Head, NC, Dare Co., Holy Trinity, c/o Kill Devil Hills, NC, Holy Redeemer Church. (R)
Naknek, AK, St. Theresa, c/o Dillingham, AK, Holy Rosary Church. (ANC)
Nama, FM, c/o Lukunor, FM, Sacred Heart Church. (CI)
Nambe, NM, Santa Fe Co., Nambe Indian Pueblo, c/o Pojoaque, NM, N.S. de Guadalupe del Valle de Pojoaque Church. (SFE)
Namoluk, FM, c/o Lukunor, FM, Sacred Heart Church. (CI)
Nanticoke, PA, Luzerne Co., Holy Child, c/o [2] Nanticoke, PA, Holy Trinity Church. (SCR)
Nanticoke, PA, Luzerne Co., St. Joseph, c/o Wanamie, PA, St. Mary's Church. (SCR)
Naper, NE, Boyd Co., Sacred Heart, c/o Butte, NE, SS. Peter and Paul Church. (OM)
Naples, FL, c/o North Fort Myers, FL, All Saints Byzantine Catholic Church. (PSC)
Naponee, NE, Franklin Co., St. Mary, c/o Alma, NE, St. Joseph's Church. (LIN)
Nara Visa, NM, Quay Co., Sacred Heart, c/o Tucumcari, NM, St. Anne Church. (SFE)
Naranjo, PR, Santa Marta, c/o Salinas, PR, Our Lady of Monserrat Church. (PCE)
Naranjo, PR, St. Anthony, c/o Yauco, PR, Holy Rossary Church. (PCE)
Naranjo Militar, PR, Ntra. Sra. de Monserrate, c/o Aguada, PR, St. Francis of Assisi Church. (MGZ)
Naranjo-Guanabanas, PR, San Pablo, c/o Aguada, PR, St. Francis of Assisi Church. (MGZ)
Naschitti, NM, St. Anthony, c/o Tohatchi, NM, St. Mary Church Church. (GLP)
Nashua, MT, Queen of the Angels, c/o Glasgow, MT, St. Raphael's Church. (GF)
Nashville, AR, Howard Co., St. Martin, c/o Hope, AR, Our Lady of Good Hope Church. (LR)
Nashville, GA, Berrien Co., St. Mary, c/o Lakeland, GA, Queen of Peace Church. (SAV)
Nashville, MI, St. Cyril, c/o Hastings, MI, St. Rose of Lima Church. (KAL)
Natalia, TX, Medina Co., St. John Bosco, c/o Lytle, TX, St. Andrew Church. (SAT)
Natural Bridge, NY, Jefferson Co., St. Henry, c/o Carthage, NY, St. James Minor Church. (OG)
Naubinway, MI, Mackinac Co., St. Stephen, c/o Engadine, MI, Our Lady of Lourdes Church. (MAR)
Naytahwaush, MN, Mahnomen Co., St. Anne, c/o Waubun, MN, St. Ann Church. (CR)
Near Hamlin, TX, Fisher Co., Sacred Heart, c/o Rotan, TX, St. Joseph Church. (LUB)
Nebish, MN, Beltrami Co., St. John, c/o Red Lake, MN, St. Mary's Mission Church Church. (CR)
Neche, ND, Pembina Co., SS. Nereus and Achilleus, c/o Cavalier, ND, St. Bridget's Church. (FAR)
Nederland, CO, Boulder Co., St. Rita, c/o [1] Boulder, CO, Sacred Heart of Jesus Church. (DEN)
Nekoma, ND, Cavalier Co., St. Edwards, c/o Langdon, ND, St. Alphonsus Church. (FAR)
Neligh, NE, Antelope Co., St. Theresa, c/o Neligh, NE, St. Francis Church. (OM)
Nelson, NE, Nuckolls Co., Sacred Heart, c/o Superior, NE, St. Joseph's Church. (LIN)
Nenzel, NE, Cherry Co., St. Mary, c/o Valentine, NE, St. Nicholas Church. (GI)
Nephi, UT, Utah Co., Our Lady of Victory Mission, c/o Payson, UT, San Andres Church. (SLC)
Nett Lake, MN, St. Louis Co., Immaculate Conception, c/o Duluth, MN, Indian Missions Church. (DUL)
Nevis, MN, Hubbard Co., Immaculate Conception, c/o Akeley, MN, St. John's Church. (CR)
New Almelo, KS, Norton Co., St. Joseph's Church, c/o Norton, KS, St. Francis of Assisi Church. (SAL)
New Boston, IL, Mercer Co., St. Theresa of the Little Flower, c/o Aledo, IL, St. Catherine's Church Church. (PEO)
New Boston, NY, Lewis Co., SS. Peter and Paul, c/o Copenhagen, NY, St. Mary Church. (OG)
New Boston, TX, Bowie Co., Hooks Catholic Community, c/o New Boston, TX, St. Mary of the Cenacle Church. (TYL)
New Deal, TX, Lubbock Co., Our Lady Queen of Apostles, c/o [7] Lubbock, TX, St. Patrick Church. (LUB)
New Dorp Beach, NY, Richmond Co., Our Lady of Lourdes, c/o [219] Staten Island, NY, Our Lady, Queen of Peace Church. (NY)
New Galilee, PA, Beaver Co., St. Ann, c/o Darlington, PA, St. Rose of Lima Church. (PIT)
New Germany, PA, Cambria Co., Immaculate Conception, c/o Summerhill, PA, St. John Church. (ALT)
New Leipzig, ND, Grant Co., St. John the Baptist, c/o

Mott, ND, St. Vincent de Paul Church. (BIS)
New Marion, IN, Ripley Co., St. Mary Magdalen, c/o Osgood, IN, St. John Church. (IND)
New Middletown, IN, Harrison Co., Most Precious Blood, c/o Corydon, IN, St. Joseph Church. (IND)
New Milford, PA, Susquehanna Co., St. John, c/o Great Bend, PA, St. Lawrence's Church. (SCR)
New Orleans, LA, Orleans Civil Parish, Our Lady of Guadalupe, c/o [1] New Orleans, LA, St. Louis Cathedral Church. (NO)
New Orleans, LA, Orleans Civil Parish, Our Lady of La Vang, c/o [14] New Orleans, LA, Mary, Queen of Vietnam Church. (NO)
New Orleans, LA, Jefferson Civil Parish, St. Joseph, c/o [2] Marrero, LA, St. Agnes Le Thi Thanh Church. (NO)
New River, AZ, Maricopa Co., Good Shepherd Mission, c/o [16] Phoenix, AZ, St. Luke Church. (PHX)
New Village, NJ, Warren Co., St. Christopher, c/o Phillipsburg, NJ, SS. Philip and James Church. (MET)
New York, NY, Richmond Co., Christ the King, c/o [214] Staten Island, NY, St. Mary of the Assumption Church. (NY)
New York, NY, New York Co., Gift of Love, c/o [120] New York, NY, St. Veronica Church. (NY)
Newald, WI, Argonne Co., St. Hubert, c/o Laona, WI, St. Leonard Church. (GB)
Newell, SD, St. Mary, Star of the Sea, c/o Belle Fourche, SD, St. Paul Church. (RC)
Newfields, NH, Rockingham Co., Sacred Heart, c/o Newmarket, NH, St. Mary Church. (MAN)
Newfound Lake, NH, Grafton Co., Our Lady of Grace, c/o Bristol, NH, St. Timothy Church. (MAN)
Newfoundland, PA, Wayne Co., St. Anthony of Padua, c/o Gouldsboro, PA, St. Rita Church. (SCR)
Newkirk, NM, Guadalupe Co., c/o Santa Rosa, NM, St. Rose of Lima Church. (SFE)
Newport, AR, Jackson Co., St. Cecilia, c/o Batesville, AR, St. Mary's Church. (LR)
Newport, KY, Campbell Co., Corpus Christi, c/o [1] Newport, KY, Holy Spirit Church. (COV)
Newport, KY, Campbell Co., St. Francis de Sales, c/o [1] Newport, KY, Holy Spirit Church. (COV)
Newport, KY, Campbell Co., St. Stephen, c/o [1] Newport, KY, Holy Spirit Church. (COV)
Newport, KY, Campbell Co., St. Vincent de Paul, c/o [1] Newport, KY, Holy Spirit Church. (COV)
Newton, MS, St. Anne, c/o Forest, MS, St. Michael Church. (JKS)
Newton, PA, Lackawanna Co., St. Benedict, c/o Clarks Summit, PA, Our Lady of the Snows Church. (SCR)
Newton Falls, NY, St. Lawrence Co., St. Anthony of Padua, c/o Star Lake, NY, St. Hubert Church. (OG)
Ngcheangl, FM, c/o Koror, FM, Sacred Heart Church. (CI)
Ngulu, FM, c/o Ulithi and Neighboring Islands, FM, Queen of Heaven Church. (CI)
Nicasio, CA, St. Mary, c/o Lagunitas, CA, St. Cecilia Church. (SFR)
Nicolaus, CA, Sutter Co., St. Boniface, c/o Lincoln, CA, St. Joseph Church. (SAC)
Niland, CA, Imperial Co., Immaculate Heart of Mary, c/o Calipatria, CA, St. Patrick Church. (SD)
Ninilchik, AK, St. Peter, c/o Homer, AK, St. John the Baptist Church. (ANC)
Nisswa, MN, St. Christopher's, c/o Pequot Lakes, MN, St. Alice's Church. (DUL)
No Water, SD, Shannon Co., Our Lady of Good Counsel, c/o Pine Ridge, SD, Holy Rosary Church. (RC)
Noble, LA, Sabine Parish, St. Catherine, c/o Noble, LA, St. Ann Church. (SHP)
Noel, MO, McDonald Co., Nativity of Our Lord, c/o Neosho, MO, St. Canera Church. (SPC)
Noomwunwiito Islands, FM, c/o Moen, FM, Immaculate Heart of Mary Cathedral Church. (CI)
Noonan, ND, Divide Co., St. Luke, c/o Crosby, ND, St. Patrick Church. (BIS)
Norbone, MO, Carroll Co., Sacred Heart, c/o Richmond, MO, Immaculate Conception Church. (KC)
Norcross, GA, Gwinnett Co., Mary, Our Queen, c/o Dunwoody, GA, All Saints Catholic Church. (ATL)
Nordheim, TX, St. Ann's, c/o Yorktown, TX, Holy Cross Church. (VIC)
Norias Ranch, TX, Santa Elena, c/o Sarita, TX, Our Lady of Guadalupe Church. (CC)
Norris, SD, Mellette Co., Sacred Heart, c/o St. Francis, SD, Rosebud Reservation Church. (RC)
North Brookfield, NY, St. Mary, c/o Waterville, NY, St. Bernard Church. (SY)
North Conway, NH, Carroll Co., St. Charles Borromeo, c/o North Conway, NH, Our Lady of the Mountains Church. (MAN)
North Creek, OH, Putnam Co., St. Joseph, c/o New Bavaria, OH, Sacred Heart of Jesus Church. (TOL)
North East, MD, Cecil Co., St. Jude, c/o Elkton, MD, Immaculate Conception Church. (WIL)
North Eastham, MA, Barnstable Co., Church of the Visitation, c/o Orleans, MA, St. Joan of Arc Church. (FR)
North Fork, CA, Madera Co., St. Joseph the Worker, c/o Bass Lake, CA, St. Dominic Savio Church. (FRS)
North Greenbush, NY, Rensselaer Co., Van Rensselaer Manor, County Welfare Home, c/o [8] Troy, NY, St. Michael the Archangel Church. (ALB)
North Haven, ME, Our Lady of Peace, c/o Camden, ME, Our Lady of Good Hope Church. (PRT)
North Hero, VT, Grand Isle Co., St. Benedict Joseph Labre, c/o South Hero, VT, St. Rose of Lima Church. (BUR)
North Hollywood, CA, Los Angeles Co., Our Lady of Zapopan, c/o Sun Valley, CA, Our Lady of the Holy Rosary Church. (LA)
North Platte, NE, Lincoln Co., St. Elizabeth Ann Seton, c/o Curtis, NE, St. James Church. (LIN)
North Powder, OR, St. Anthony, c/o [1] Baker, OR, Cathedral of St. Francis De Sales Church. (BAK)
North Pownal, VT, Our Lady of Lourdes, c/o Bennington, VT, Sacred Heart/St. Francis de Sales Church. (BUR)
North Salem, NY, Westchester Co., St. John, c/o Croton Falls, NY, St. Joseph Church. (NY)
North San Juan, CA, Nevada Co., St. John, c/o Downieville, CA, Immaculate Conception Church. (SAC)
North Swanzey, NH, St. Stephen, c/o West Swanzey, NH, St. Anthony Church. (MAN)
North Truro, MA, Barnstable Co., Our Lady of Perpetual Help, c/o Wellfleet, MA, Our Lady of Lourdes Church. (FR)
Northland, MI, Marquette Co., St. Joseph, c/o Gwinn, MI, St. Anthony Church. (MAR)
Northome, MN, Koochiching Co., St. Michael, c/o Blackduck, MN, St. Ann's Church. (CR)
Northwood, NH, Rockingham Co., St. Joseph, c/o Pittsfield, NH, Our Lady of Lourdes Church. (MAN)
Norton, VT, Essex Co., St. Bernard, c/o Island Pond, VT, St. James the Greater Church. (BUR)
Nortonville, ND, LaMoure Co., Holy Spirit, c/o Edgeley, ND, Transfiguration Church. (FAR)
Norwich, VT, Windsor Co., St. Francis of Assisi, c/o Bradford, VT, Our Lady of Perpetual Help Church. (BUR)
Nova-Savannah, OH, Jesus the Good Shepherd, c/o Litchfield, OH, Our Lady Help of Christians Parish Church. (CLV)
Novinger, MO, Adair Co., St. Rose of Lima, c/o Kirksville, MO, Mary Immaculate Church. (JC)
Nowata, OK, Nowata Co., St. Catherine, c/o Bartlesville, OK, The Community of St. James Church. (TLS)
Noxon, MT, c/o Thompson Falls, MT, St. William Church. (HEL)
Nuangola, PA, Luzerne Co., St. Ann, c/o Mountaintop, PA, St. Jude's Church. (SCR)
Nucla, CO, Montrose Co., Our Lady of Sorrows, c/o Telluride, CO, St. Patrick Church. (PBL)
Nuremberg, PA, Luzerne Co., St. Joseph, c/o Weston, PA, Sacred Heart Church. (SCR)

O

O'Connor, NE, Greeley Co., Our Lady of the Visitation, c/o Greeley, NE, Sacred Heart Church. (GI)
O'Connor Ranch, TX, Refugio Co., St. Dennis, c/o Tivoli, TX, Our Lady of Guadalupe Church. (CC)
Oak Beach, NY, Suffolk Co., c/o Babylon, NY, St. Joseph's Church. (RVC)
Oak Creek, CO, Routt Co., St. Martin Church of Tours, c/o Steamboat Springs, CO, Holy Name Church. (DEN)
Oak Forest, IN, Franklin Co., St. Cecilia of Rome, c/o St. Mary-of-the-Rock, IN, St. Mary-of-the-Rock Church. (IND)
Oak Grove, MO, Jackson Co., St. Jude the Apostle, c/o Odessa, MO, St. George Church. (KC)
Oakland, CA, Alameda Co., Mary Help of Christians, c/o [9] Oakland, CA, St. Elizabeth's Church. (OAK)
Oblong, IL, Crawford Co., St. Valentine's Chapel, c/o Ste. Marie, IL, St. Mary of the Assumption Church. (SFD)
Ocala National Forest, FL, Marion Co., St. Joseph of the Forest, c/o [2] Ocala, FL, Our Lady of the Springs Church. (ORL)
Ocate, NM, Mora Co., c/o Wagon Mound, NM, Santa Clara Church. (SFE)
Ocean City, MD, Worcester Co., Holy Saviour, c/o Ocean City, MD, St. Mary, Star of the Sea Church. (WIL)
Ocean Pines, MD, St. John Neumann, c/o Ocean City, MD, St. Luke and St. Andrew Church. (WIL)
Oceano, CA, San Luis Obispo Co., St. Francis of Assisi, c/o Arroyo Grande, CA, St. Patrick Church. (MRY)
Oconto, NE, St. Mary, c/o Stapleton, NE, St. John the Evangelist Church. (GI)
Odell, NE, Gage Co., St. Mary's, c/o Wymore, NE, St. Mary's Church. (LIN)
Odessa, TX, Ector Co., Our Lady of San Juan, c/o [3] Odessa, TX, St. Elizabeth Ann Seton Church. (SAN)
Odessa, TX, Ector Co., St. Martin de Porres, c/o [4] Odessa, TX, St. Joseph Church. (SAN)
Oelrichs, SD, Fall River Co., St. Martin, c/o Hot Springs, SD, St. Anthony's Church. (RC)
Ogema, MN, Becker Co., Most Holy Redeemer, c/o White Earth, MN, St. Benedict Church. (CR)
Ogilvie, MN, Kanabec Co., St. Kathryn, c/o Mora, MN, St. Mary's Church. (SCL)
Oglala, SD, Shannon Co., Our Lady of Sioux, c/o Pine Ridge, SD, Holy Rosary Church. (RC)
Ogunquit, ME, All Saints, c/o Wells, ME, St. Mary Church. (PRT)
Oilton, TX, Webb Co., St. Bridget, c/o Hebbronville, TX, Our Lady of Guadalupe Church. (CC)
Ojo Caliente, NM, Rio Arriba Co., c/o El Rito, NM, San Juan Nepomuceno Church. (SFE)
Ojo Feliz, NM, Mora Co., c/o Mora, NM, St. Gertrude Church. (SFE)
Ojo Sarco, NM, Rio Arriba Co., Santo Tomas, c/o Chimayo, NM, Holy Family Church. (SFE)
Okemah, OK, Okfuska Co., St. Teresa, c/o Holdenville, OK, St. Stephen's Church. (TLS)
Okmulgee, OK, Okmulgee Co., Uganda Martyrs, c/o Okmulgee, OK, St. Anthony's Church. (TLS)
Okolona, MS, Chickasaw Co., St. Theresa, c/o Aberdeen, MS, St. Francis of Assisi Church. (JKS)
Okreek, SD, Todd Co., St. Peter, c/o St. Francis, SD, Rosebud Reservation Church. (RC)
Okreek, SD, Todd Co., St. Peter's, c/o Mission, SD, St. Thomas the Apostle Church. (RC)
Olathe, CO, Montrose Co., Our Lady of Fatima, c/o Montrose, CO, St. Mary Church. (PBL)
Old River, LA, St. Anne, c/o Isle Brevelle, LA, St. Augustine's Church. (ALX)
Old Washington, TX, Washington Co., Blessed Virgin Mary, c/o Brenham, TX, St. Mary of the Immaculate Conception Church. (AUS)
Olga, ND, Cavalier Co., Our Lady of the Sacred Heart, c/o Walhalla, ND, St. Boniface's Church. (FAR)
Olivier, LA, St. Jude, c/o [4] New Iberia, LA, St. Edward Church. (LAF)
Olla, LA, St. William, c/o Winnfield, LA, Our Lady of Lourdes Church. (ALX)
Olmito, TX, Our Heavenly Father, c/o Los Fresnos, TX, St. Cecilia Church. (BWN)
Olton, TX, Lamb Co., St. Peter Apostle, c/o Hale Center, TX, St. Theresa's Church. (LUB)
Olympic Valley, CA, Placer Co., Queen of the Snows, c/o Tahoe City, CA, Corpus Christi Church. (SAC)
On the Creek, SD, Shannon Co., St. Paul, c/o Porcupine, SD, Church of Christ the King Church. (RC)
Onarga, IL, Iroquois Co., Our Lady of Guadalupe, c/o Gilman, IL, Immaculate Conception Church. (JOL)
Onari, FM, St. Cecilia, c/o Fefan, FM, Sacred Heart Church. (CI)
Oneida, PA, Schuykill Co., St. John the Baptist, c/o Sheppton, PA, St. Joseph Church. (ALN)
Oneop, FM, c/o Lukunor, FM, Sacred Heart Church. (CI)
Ono, FM, Sacred Heart, c/o Fefan, FM, Sacred Heart Church. (CI)
Onset, MA, St. Mary Star of the Sea, c/o Buzzards Bay, MA, St. Margaret Church. (FR)
Ookala, HI, St. James, c/o Papaaloa, HI, St. Anthony Church. (HON)
Oquawka, IL, Henderson Co., St. Andrew, c/o Monmouth, IL, Immaculate Conception Church. (PEO)
Oracle, AZ, Pinal Co., St. Helen, c/o San Manuel, AZ, St. Bartholomew Church. (TUC)
Orange Lake, NY, Orange Co., Our Lady of the Lake, c/o [1] Newburgh, NY, St. Patrick Church. (NY)
Orange Park, FL, Clay Co., Moosehaven Chapel, c/o Orange Park, FL, St. Catherine's Church. (STA)
Ordway, CO, Crowley Co., St. Peter Church, c/o Rocky Ford, CO, St. Peter Church. (PBL)
Orick, CA, St. Thomas, c/o McKinleyville, CA, Christ the King Church. (SR)
Orlando, FL, Orange Co., St. Ignatius Kim Korean Mission, c/o [1] Orlando, FL, St. James Cathedral Church. (ORL)
Orrin, ND, Pierce Co., Sacred Heart, c/o Balta, ND, Our Lady of Mount Carmel Church. (FAR)
Orrville, AL, Dallas Co., Mission of Immaculate Conception, c/o Camden, AL, St. Joseph Church. (MOB)
Ortiga, PR, Bauta Abajo Co., San Mateo, c/o Villalba, PR, Our Lady Mother of Divine Providence Church. (PCE)
Orting, WA, Pierce Co., SS. Cosmas and Damian, c/o Sumner, WA, St. Andrew Church. (SEA)
Ortiz, CO, San Juan Nepomuceno y San Cayetano, c/o Conejos, CO, Our Lady of Guadalupe Church. (PBL)
Osceola, MO, St. Clair Co., St. Catherine's, c/o Clinton, MO, Holy Rosary Church. (KC)
Osceola, NE, Polk Co., St. Mary's, c/o Osceola, NE, St. Vincent's Church. (LIN)
Oshkosh, NE, Garden Co., St. Elizabeth, c/o Chappell, NE, St. Joseph's Church. (GI)
Oslo, MN, Marshall Co., St. Joseph, c/o Warren, MN, SS. Peter and Paul Church. (CR)
Osnabrock, ND, Cavalier Co., St. Joseph, c/o Wales, ND, St. Michael's Church. (FAR)
Otis, MA, Berkshire Co., St. Mary of the Lakes, c/o Lee, MA, St. Mary's Church. (SPR)
Otisco, NY, St. Patrick, c/o Tully, NY, St. Leo Church. (SY)

Oto, IA, Woodbury Co., St. Mary's, c/o Mapleton, IA, St. Mary's Church. (SC)
Otter Lake, NY, St. Mary of the Snows, c/o Forestport, NY, St. Patrick Church. (SY)
Outlook, MT, St. Boniface, c/o Plentywood, MT, St. Joseph's Church. (GF)
Overton, NE, Dawson Co., Holy Rosary, c/o Elm Creek, NE, Immaculate Conception Church. (GI)
Overton, PA, Sullivan Co., St. Francis Xavier, c/o Dushore, PA, St. Basil's Church. (SCR)
Overton, TX, Rusk Co., Our Lady Queen of Angels, c/o Kilgore, TX, Christ the King Church. (TYL)
Owasco, NY, Cayuga Co., St. Ann, c/o [2] Auburn, NY, Sacred Heart Church. (ROC)
Owenton, KY, Owen Co., St. Edward, c/o Warsaw, KY, St. Joseph Church. (COV)
Owingsville, KY, Bath Co., St. Julie Billiart, c/o West Liberty, KY, Prince of Peace Church. (LEX)
Owl's Head, NY, Franklin Co., St. Joseph, c/o Chasm Falls, NY, St. Helen Church. (OG)
Oxford, NE, Furnas Co., St. Michael's, c/o Orleans, NE, St. Mary's Church. (LIN)
Oxnard, CA, Ventura Co., Christ the King, c/o [3] Oxnard, CA, Our Lady of Guadalupe Parish Church. (LA)

P

Paauilo, HI, St. Joseph, c/o Honokaa, HI, Our Lady of Lourdes Church. (HON)
Packing Town, OK, Oklahoma Co., Our Lady of Guadalupe, c/o [14] Oklahoma City, OK, Our Lady of Mount Carmel and St. Therese Little Flower Church. (OKL)
Paducah, TX, Cottle Co., St. Elizabeth, c/o Floydada, TX, St. Mary Magdalen Church. (LUB)
Page, ND, Cass Co., St. James, c/o Hope, ND, St. Agatha's Church. (FAR)
Pageland, SC, Chesterfield Co., St. Ernest, c/o Cheraw, SC, St. Peter's Church. (CHR)
Pago Pago, AS, c/o [2] Pago Pago, AS, Co-Cathedral of St. Joseph the Worker Church. (SPP)
Pagosa Junction, CO, Archuleta Co., St. John Baptist, c/o Pagosa Springs, CO, Immaculate Heart of Mary Church. (PBL)
Paguate, NM, St. Elizabeth, c/o Laguna, NM, St. Joseph Church. (GLP)
Pahrump, NV, Christ of the Desert, c/o Pahrump, NV, Our Lady of the Valley Church. (LAV)
Painesdale, MI, Houghton Co., Sacred Heart, c/o Chassell, MI, St. Anne Church. (MAR)
Paisley, OR, St. John the Apostle, c/o Lakeview, OR, St. Patrick's Church. (BAK)
Palisade, CO, Mesa Co., St. Ann, c/o Grand Junction, CO, Immaculate Heart of Mary Church. (PBL)
Palisade, NE, Hitchcock Co., Holy Family, c/o Trenton, NE, St. James Church. (LIN)
Palito Blanco, TX, Jim Wells Co., St. Joseph, c/o San Diego, TX, St. Francis de Paula Church. (CC)
Palma Escrita, PR, N.S. de Fatima, c/o Las Marias, PR, Immaculate Heart of Mary Church. (MGZ)
Palma Sola, PR, Ntra. Sra. de la Asuncion, c/o [5] Canovanas, PR, San Jose Church. (SJN)
Palmarejo, PR, Coamo Co., Sacred Heart of Mary, c/o Coamo, PR, St. Blase Church. (PCE)
Palmas, PR, St. Gerard, c/o Guayama, PR, St. Anthony of Padua Church. (PCE)
Palmer, IA, Pocahontas Co., St. Joseph's, c/o Pomeroy, IA, St. Mary's Church. (SC)
Palmer, MI, Marquette Co., Our Lady Perpetual Help, c/o Negaunee, MI, St. Paul Church. (MAR)
Palmer, PR, La Milagrosa, c/o Palmer, PR, Cristo Rey Church. (SJN)
Palmer, PR, Ntra. Sra. de la Providencia, c/o Palmer, PR, Cristo Rey Church. (SJN)
Palmetto, LA, St. Thomas, c/o Melville, LA, St. John the Evangelist Church. (LAF)
Palo Blanco, NM, Colfax Co., c/o Springer, NM, St. Joseph Church. (SFE)
Palolo, HI, Honolulu Co., St. James, c/o [11] Honolulu, HI, St. Patrick Church. (HON)
Panama, NY, Our Lady of the Snows, c/o French Creek, NY, St. Matthias Church. (BUF)
Panguitch, UT, Garfield Co., St. Gertrude, c/o Cedar City, UT, Christ the King Church. (SLC)
Paoli, IN, Orange Co., Our Lord Jesus Christ the King, c/o French Lick, IN, Our Lady of the Springs Church. (IND)
Paoli, WI, St. William, c/o Verona, WI, St. Andrew Church. (MAD)
Paplin, NE, Howard Co., Our Lady of Mount Carmel, c/o Farwell, NE, St. Anthony of Padua Church. (GI)
Paplin, NE, Howard Co., Our Lady of Mt. Carmel, c/o Ashton, NE, St. Francis Church. (GI)
Parachute, CO, Garfield Co., St. Brendan, c/o Rifle, CO, St. Mary's Church. (DEN)
Paradise, MI, Chippewa Co., Our Lady of Victory, c/o Newberry, MI, St. Gregory Church. (MAR)
Paradise Valley, NV, Humboldt Co., St. Alphonsus, c/o Winnemucca, NV, St. Paul Church. (RNO)
Paraje, NM, St. Mary Margaret, c/o Laguna, NM, St. Joseph Church. (GLP)
Paramount, CA, Catholic Korean Community of St. Raphael (Downey & Alondra), c/o Paramount, CA, Our Lady of the Rosary Church. (LA)
Parcelas de Marueno, PR, Ponce Co., San Antonio de Padua, c/o [10] Ponce, PR, La Santisima Trinidad Church. (PCE)
Parcelas Soledad, PR, Sta. Teresita, c/o [4] Mayaquez, PR, Church De El Buen Pastor Church. (MGZ)
Parcelas Vazquez, PR, Esp. Santo, c/o Salinas, PR, Our Lady of Monserrat Church. (PCE)
Parem, FM, c/o Fefan, FM, Sacred Heart Church. (CI)
Paris, MI, Mecosta Co., St. Anne, c/o Reed City, MI, St. Philip Neri Church. (GR)
Parishville, NY, St. Lawrence Co., St. Michael, c/o Colton, NY, St. Patrick Church. (OG)
Parks, LA, St. Louis, c/o Parks, LA, St. Joseph Church. (LAF)
Parmelee, SD, Todd Co., St. Agnes, c/o St. Francis, SD, Rosebud Reservation Church. (RC)
Parque Encuestra, PR, S. Francisco de Asis, c/o [18] Carolina, PR, Cristo Rey Church. (SJN)
Parsons, TN, Decatur Co., St. Regina, c/o Lexington, TN, St. Andrew Church. (MEM)
Parsons, WV, Tucker Co., Our Lady of Mercy, c/o Thomas, WV, St. Thomas Aquinas Church. (WH)
Pastillito, Manzanilla, PR, Our Lady of Carmel, c/o Juana Diaz, PR, Santa Teresita Church. (PCE)
Pastillo, PR, Cotopaso Co., Santiago Apostol, c/o Juana Diaz, PR, St. Raymond Nonato Church. (PCE)
Pastura, NM, Guadalupe Co., c/o Vaughn, NM, St. Mary Church. (SFE)
Patch Grove, WI, St. John, c/o Bloomington, WI, St. Mary Church. (MAD)
Patrick Springs, VA, Church of the Risen Lord, c/o Woodlawn, VA, St. Joseph's Church. (RIC)
Patten, ME, St. Paul, c/o Island Falls, ME, St. Agnes Church. (PRT)
Paul Smiths, NY, Franklin Co., St. Gabriel, c/o Lake Clear, NY, St. John in the Wilderness Church. (OG)
Pava'ia'i, AS, c/o [4] Pago Pago, AS, Church of St. Paul Church. (SPP)
Pawnee, TX, Bee Co., Our Lady of Guadalupe, c/o Three Rivers, TX, Sacred Heart Church. (CC)
Paxton, NE, Keith Co., St. Patrick, c/o Sutherland, NE, Sacred Heart Church. (GI)
Peapack, NJ, Somerset Co., St. Brigid, c/o Far Hills, NJ, St. Elizabeth Church. (MET)
Pecan Island, LA, Sacred Heart, c/o Cow Island, LA, St. Anne Church. (LAF)
Peck, MI, Sanilac Co., St. John, c/o Croswell, MI, St. Patrick Church. (SAG)
Pedro Garcia, PR, Coamo Co., Miraculous Virgin, c/o Coamo, PR, St. Blase Church. (PCE)
Peerless, MT, St. Ann, c/o Scobey, MT, St. Philip Bonitus Church. (GF)
Pejepscot, ME, Topsham Co., St. Andrew, c/o Brunswick, ME, St. John the Baptist Church. (PRT)
Pelican, AK, c/o [1] Juneau, AK, Cathedral of the Nativity of The Blessed Virgin Mary Church. (JUN)
Pellejas, PR, Santa Rosa, c/o Adjuntas, PR, St. Joachim Church. (PCE)
Pellets Island (New Hampton), NY, Orange Co., St. Andrew Bobola, c/o Florida, NY, St. Joseph Church. (NY)
Pembroke, GA, Bryan Co., Holy Cross, c/o Claxton, GA, St. Christopher Church. (SAV)
Pembroke, ME, St. John the Evangelist, c/o Eastport, ME, St. Joseph Church. (PRT)
Pengilly, MN, St. Kevin, c/o Nashwauk, MN, St. Cecilia's Church. (DUL)
Penitas, TX, St. Anthony, c/o La Joya, TX, Our Lady, Queen of Angels Church. (BWN)
Pennington, MN, St. Charles, c/o Cass Lake, MN, St. Charles Church. (DUL)
Pensacola, FL, Escambia Co., Church of Our Savior, c/o [13] Pensacola, FL, St. Paul Church. (PT)
Pentwater, MI, St. Vincent, c/o Weare Twp., MI, St. Joseph's Church. (GR)
Pep, TX, Hockley Co., St. Philip Neri, c/o Morton, TX, St. Ann Church. (LUB)
Perkinsville, NY, Steuben Co., Sacred Heart of Jesus, c/o Cohocton, NY, St. Pius V Church. (ROC)
Perrineville, NJ, Monmouth Co., St. Joseph, c/o Englishtown, NJ, Our Lady of Mercy Church. (TR)
Perrinton, MI, Gratiot Co., St. Martin De Porres, c/o Ithaca, MI, St. Paul the Apostle Church. (SAG)
Perry, MO, Monroe Co., St. Frances Cabrini, c/o Perry, MO, St. William Church. (JC)
Perry, WI, Holy Redeemer, c/o Mount Horeb, WI, St. Ignatius Church. (MAD)
Perry Park, KY, Owen Co., Transfiguration, c/o Carrollton, KY, St. John the Evangelist Church. (COV)
Perryville, KY, Boyle Co., St. Mary, c/o Harrodsburg, KY, St. Andrew Church. (LEX)
Peru, NE, St. Clara, c/o Auburn, NE, St. Joseph's Church. (LIN)
Pescadero, CA, San Mateo Co., St. Anthony, c/o Half Moon Bay, CA, Our Lady of the Pillar Church. (SFR)
Petaca, NM, Taos Co., c/o El Rito, NM, San Juan Nepomuceno Church. (SFE)
Peterstown, WV, Monroe Co., St. Peter, c/o Princeton, WV, Sacred Heart Church. (WH)
Petersville, MD, Frederick Co., St. Mary's, c/o Brunswick, MD, St. Francis of Assisi Church. (BAL)
Petit Mamou, LA, St. Jules, c/o Evangeline, LA, St. Joseph Church. (LAF)
Petrolia, CA, St. Patrick, c/o Ferndale, CA, Church of the Assumption Church. (SR)
Petronila, TX, Nueces Co., St. Vivian, c/o [7] Corpus Christi, TX, Our Lady of the Rosary Church. (CC)
Pettus, TX, Sacred Heart, c/o [1] Beeville, TX, Our Lady of Victory Church. (CC)
Phelps, KY, Pike Co., Jesus of the Mountains Catholic Church, c/o Pikeville, KY, St. Francis of Assisi Church. (LEX)
Philadelphia, MS, St. Theresa, c/o Philadelphia, MS, Holy Rosary Church. (JKS)
Philadelphia, NY, Jefferson Co., St. Joseph, c/o Antwerp, NY, St. Michael Church. (OG)
Philadelphia, PA, c/o [47] Philadelphia, PA, St. Francis Xavier Church. (PH)
Philadelphia, PA, Philadelphia Co., Holy Redeemer Chinese Church, c/o [79] Philadelphia, PA, St. John the Evangelist Church. (PH)
Philadelphia, PA, Philadelphia Co., St. Roch Chapel, c/o [109] Philadelphia, PA, Mother of Divine Grace Church. (PH)
Phillipsburg, KY, Marion Co., Our Lady of Fatima, c/o Calvary, KY, Holy Name of Mary Church. (L)
Philmont, NY, Pine Haven Home, c/o Philmont, NY, Sacred Heart Church. (ALB)
Philo, OH, Muskingum Co., St. Ann, c/o Zanesville, OH, St. Thomas Aquinas Church. (COL)
Phoenix, AZ, Maricopa Co., Our Lady of Fatima, c/o [7] Phoenix, AZ, SS. Anthony and Pius X Church. (PHX)
Phoenix, AZ, Maricopa Co., Santa Rosa Chapel, c/o [1] Phoenix, AZ, SS. Simon and Jude Cathedral Church. (PHX)
Phoenix, AZ, Maricopa Co., St. Philip the Deacon Catholic Center, c/o [17] Phoenix, AZ, St. Mark Church. (PHX)
Phoenix, AZ, Maricopa Co., St. Pius X, c/o [7] Phoenix, AZ, SS. Anthony and Pius X Church. (PHX)
Picacho, NM, St. Joseph, c/o Ruidoso, NM, St. Eleanor Church. (LSC)
Pickens, WV, Randolph Co., Sacred Heart, c/o Buckhannon, WV, Holy Rosary Church. (WH)
Pickerel, WI, St. Mary, c/o Elcho, WI, Holy Family Church. (GB)
Picuris Indian Pueblo, NM, Taos Co., San Lorenzo Mission, c/o Penasco, NM, San Antonio de Padua Church. (SFE)
Piedmont, AL, Calhoun Co., St. Joachim, c/o Jacksonville, AL, St. Charles Church. (BIR)
Piedras Blancas, PR, Ntra. Sra. Reina de la Paz, c/o Aguada, PR, St. Francis of Assisi Church. (MGZ)
Pigeon Forge, TN, Sevier Co., Holy Cross, c/o Gatlinburg, TN, St. Mary Church. (KNX)
Piis, FM, c/o Lukunor, FM, Sacred Heart Church. (CI)
Pilar, NM, Taos Co., Nuestra Senora de los Dolores, c/o Dixon, NM, St. Anthony Church. (SFE)
Pima, AZ, Graham Co., Pima Mission, c/o Safford, AZ, St. Rose of Lima Church. (TUC)
Pin Oak, TX, Bastrop Co., St. Mary's, c/o Giddings, TX, St. Margaret Church. (AUS)
Pine Bluff, AR, Jefferson Co., St. Raphael's, c/o Pine Bluff, AR, St. Peter's Church. (LR)
Pine Mountain, GA, Harris Co., Christ the King, c/o [3] Columbus, GA, St. Anne Church. (SAV)
Pine Point, ME, Scarborough Co., St. Jude, c/o Scarborough, ME, St. Maximilian Kolbe Church. (PRT)
Pine Springs, AZ, St. Rose, c/o Houck, AZ, St. John Church. (GLP)
Pinedale, CA, Fresno Co., St. Agnes, c/o [2] Fresno, CA, Holy Spirit Church. (FRS)
Pineville, KY, Bell Co., St. Anthony, c/o Middlesboro, KY, St. Julian Church. (LEX)
Pineville, WV, Wyoming Co., Holy Cross, c/o Mullens, WV, St. John the Evangelist Church. (WH)
Pingree, ND, St. Michael, c/o Jamestown, ND, The Basilica of St. James Church. (FAR)
Pinhook, IA, St. Bridget, c/o Sumner, IA, Immaculate Conception Church. (DUB)
Pinon, AZ, Navajo Co., St. Mary of the Rosary, c/o Chinle, AZ, Our Lady of Fatima, Indian Mission Church. (GLP)
Pinos Altos, NM, Holy Cross, c/o Silver City, NM, St. Vincent de Paul Church. (LSC)
Pinos Wells, NM, Torrance Co., c/o Vaughn, NM, St. Mary Church. (SFE)
Pintada, NM, Guadalupe Co., c/o Santa Rosa, NM, St. Rose of Lima Church. (SFE)
Piru, CA, Ventura Co., San Salvador, c/o Fillmore, CA, St. Francis of Assisi Church. (LA)
Pisarach, FM, St. Catherine of Siena, c/o Fefan, FM, Sacred Heart Church. (CI)
Pittsburg, OK, Pittsburg Co., St. Edwards, c/o McAlester, OK, St. John Church. (TLS)

Pittsfield, MA, Berkshire Co., All Souls, c/o [3] Pittsfield, MA, Our Lady of Mt. Carmel Church. (SPR)
Pittsfield, VT, Rutland Co., St. Denis, c/o Bethel, VT, St. Anthony Church. (BUR)
Pittston, PA, Luzerne Co., St. Mary of the Assumption, c/o [6] Pittston, PA, St. Mary, Help of Christians Church. (SCR)
Pittstown, NJ, Hunterdon Co., St. Catherine of Siena, c/o Clinton, NJ, Immaculate Conception Church. (MET)
Placita, NM, Taos Co., Nuestra Senora de la Asuncion Mission, c/o Penasco, NM, San Antonio de Padua Church. (SFE)
Placitas, NM, Sandoval Co., c/o Bernalillo, NM, Our Lady of Sorrows Church. (SFE)
Placitas, NM, Rio Arriba Co., c/o El Rito, NM, San Juan Nepomuceno Church. (SFE)
Placitas, NM, San Lorenzo, c/o Truth or Consequences, NM, Our Lady of Perpetual Help Church. (LSC)
Plains, TX, Yoakum Co., Sacred Heart, c/o Denver City, TX, St. William Church. (LUB)
Plainview, SD, Meade Co., Our Lady of Victory, c/o Faith, SD, St. Joseph Church. (RC)
Plaisance, LA, St. Andrew, c/o Grand Prairie, LA, St. Peter Church. (LAF)
Plaquemine Point, LA, St. Agnes, c/o Lawtell, LA, Holy Family Church. (LAF)
Plasi, NE, Saunders Co., SS. Cyril and Methodius, c/o Prague, NE, St. John's Church. (LIN)
Platteville, CO, Weld Co., St. Nicholas, c/o Fort Lupton, CO, St. William Church. (DEN)
Playas, NM, St. Augustine, c/o Lordsburg, NM, St. Joseph Church. (LSC)
Playita Cortada, PR, San Patricio, c/o Santa Isabel, PR, St. James Church. (PCE)
Plaza, ND, Mountrail Co., Sacred Heart, c/o Parshall, ND, St. Bridget Church. (BIS)
Plaza Blanca, NM, Rio Arriba Co., c/o Los Ojos, NM, San Jose Church. (SFE)
Pleasant Hill, MO, Cass Co., St. Bridget, c/o Harrisonville, MO, Our Lady of Lourdes Church. (KC)
Pleasant Valley, PA, Blair Co., Our Lady of the Assumption, c/o [7] Altoona, PA, Our Lady of Mt. Carmel Church. (ALT)
Pleasanton, CA, Alameda Co., St. Elizabeth Seton, c/o Pleasanton, CA, St. Augustine Church. (OAK)
Pleasantville Park, NY, Westchester Co., Our Lady of Pompeii, c/o Pleasantville, NY, Holy Innocents Church. (NY)
Plena, PR, San Jose, c/o Salinas, PR, Our Lady of Monserrat Church. (PCE)
Plevna, MT, St. Anthony, c/o Baker, MT, St. John the Evangelist Church. (GF)
Plum Bayou, AR, Jefferson Co., St. Mary's, c/o Pine Bluff, AR, St. Joseph's Church. (LR)
Plum Island, MA, St. James, c/o Newburyport, MA, Immaculate Conception Church. (BO)
Plunketville, OK, McCurtain Co., St. Henry, c/o Idabel, OK, St. Francis De Sales Church. (TLS)
Plush, OR, St. Thomas, c/o Lakeview, OR, St. Patrick's Church. (BAK)
Plymouth, CA, Amador Co., St. Mary of the Mountains, c/o Sutter Creek, CA, Immaculate Conception Church. (SAC)
Plymouth Rock, IA, St. Agnes, c/o Cresco, IA, St. Joseph's Church. (DUB)
Pocahontas, PA, Somerset Co., St. Mary's, c/o West Salisbury, PA, St. Michael's Church. (ALT)
Pocono Summit, PA, Monroe Co., St. Joan of Arc, c/o Mount Pocono, PA, St. Mary of the Mount Church. (SCR)
Point Blank, TX, St. Stephen the Martyr, c/o New Waverly, TX, St. Joseph Church. (GAL)
Point Comfort, TX, St. Ann, c/o Port Lavaca, TX, Our Lady of the Gulf Church. (VIC)
Polvadera, NM, Socorro Co., c/o Socorro, NM, San Miguel Church. (SFE)
Pompano Beach, FL, Broward Co., St. Joseph, c/o [10] Miami, FL, Notre Dame d'Haiti Church. (MIA)
Ponce, P.R., La Dolorosa, c/o [2] Ponce, PR, Christ the King Church. (PCE)
Ponce, PR, Our Lady of Carmel, c/o [3] Ponce, PR, Church of the Resurrection Church. (PCE)
Ponce, PR, Saint Joseph, c/o [3] Ponce, PR, Church of the Resurrection Church. (PCE)
Pond Creek, OH, Scioto Co., Holy Trinity, c/o West Portsmouth, OH, Our Lady of Sorrows Church. (COL)
Pond Creek, OK, Grant Co., St. Joseph's, c/o Medford, OK, St. Mary's Church. (OKL)
Pond Eddy, NY, Sullivan Co., Sacred Heart, c/o Yulan, NY, St. Anthony of Padua Church. (NY)
Ponderosa, NM, Sandoval Co., c/o Jemez Pueblo, NM, San Diego Indian Missions Church. (SFE)
Ponsford, MN, Becker Co., St. Theodore, c/o White Earth, MN, St. Benedict Church. (CR)
Pontotoc, MS, Pontotoc Co., St. Christopher, c/o New Albany, MS, St. Francis of Assisi Church. (JKS)
Poplarville, MS, Pearl River Co., St. Joseph, c/o Lumberton, MS, Our Lady of Perpetual Help Church. (BLX)
Porcupine, ND, Sioux Co., St. James, c/o Fort Yates, ND, St. Peter - Catholic Indian Mission Church. (BIS)
Port Deposit, MD, Cecil Co., St. Teresa, c/o Perryville, MD, Church of the Good Shepherd Church. (WIL)
Port Norris, NJ, St. Anthony, c/o Cedarville, NJ, St. Michael's Church. (CAM)
Port O'Connor, TX, St. Joseph, c/o Port Lavaca, TX, Our Lady of the Gulf Church. (VIC)
Port Orford, OR, Curry Co., St. John the Baptist, c/o Bandon, OR, Holy Trinity Church. (P)
Port St. Joe, FL, Gulf Co., San Blas Catholic Mission, c/o Port St. Joe, FL, St. Joseph Church. (PT)
Portage, ME, Our Lady of the Lakes, c/o Ashland, ME, St. Mark's Church. (PRT)
Portal, ND, Burke Co., St. John the Baptist, c/o Bowbells, ND, St. Joseph Church. (BIS)
Portales, NM, Roosevelt Co., University Catholic Center, c/o Portales, NM, St. Helen Church. (SFE)
Porterville, CA, Our Lady of Guadalupe, c/o Porterville, CA, St. Anne Church. (FRS)
Portland, PA, Northampton Co., St. Vincent de Paul, c/o Bangor, PA, Our Lady of Good Counsel Church. (ALN)
Poston, AZ, Kateri Tekawitha Indian Mission, c/o Parker, AZ, Sacred Heart Church. (TUC)
Potash, LA, Plaquemines Parish, St. Joseph, c/o Port Sulphur, LA, St. Patrick Church. (NO)
Potatoe Creek, SD, Jackson Co., St. Henry, c/o Wanblee, SD, Ignatius Loyola Church. (RC)
Potter Place, NH, Merrimack Co., Immaculate Conception, c/o New London, NH, Our Lady of Fatima Church. (MAN)
Pottersville, NY, St. Pius X, c/o North Creek, NY, St. James Church. (ALB)
Power, MT, Guardian Angel, c/o Dutton, MT, St. William Church. (HEL)
Powers, OR, Coos Co., St. Bridget, c/o Coquille, OR, Holy Name Church. (P)
Powers Lake, ND, Burke Co., St. James, c/o Stanley, ND, Queen of the Most Holy Rosary Church. (BIS)
Prairie, IA, St. Joseph, c/o Peosta, IA, St. John the Baptist Church. (DUB)
Prairie Center, NE, Buffalo Co., St. Mary, c/o Pleasanton, NE, St. Mary's Church. (GI)
Prairie Laurent, LA, St. Jules, c/o Leonville, LA, St. Catherine Church. (LAF)
Prairie Ronde, LA, Sacred Heart, c/o Lawtell, LA, St. Bridget Church. (LAF)
Prairie View, AR, Logan Co., St. Meinrad, c/o Scranton, AR, St. Ignatius Church. (LR)
Prentiss, MS, Jefferson Davis Co., St. Mary's, c/o Bassfield, MS, St. Peter Church. (BLX)
Primghar, IA, O'Brien Co., St. Anthony of Padua, c/o Sutherland, IA, Sacred Heart Church. (SC)
Primrose, NE, Boone Co., St. Mary, c/o Cedar Rapids, NE, St. Anthony Church. (OM)
Princeton, CA, Colusa Co., St. Joseph, c/o Colusa, CA, Our Lady of Lourdes Church. (SAC)
Proctorsville, VT, Windsor Co., Holy Name of Mary, c/o Chester, VT, St. Joseph Church. (BUR)
Promise, SD, Dewey Co., St. Catherine, c/o Eagle Butte, SD, All Saints Church. (RC)
Promise, SD, Dewey Co., St. Catherine, c/o Eagle Butte, SD, Cheyenne River Reservation Church. (RC)
Promised Land, PA, Monroe Co., Our Lady of Fatima, c/o Canadensis, PA, St. Bernadette Church. (SCR)
Prudence Island, RI, Newport, Our Lady of Prudence, c/o Bristol, RI, St. Mary Church. (PRO)
Pueblitos, NM, Valencia Co., c/o Belen, NM, Our Lady of Belen Church. (SFE)
Pueblo West, CO, Pueblo Co., St. Paul the Apostle, c/o [16] Pueblo, CO, St. Pius X Church. (PBL)
Puerto de Luna, NM, Guadalupe Co., c/o Santa Rosa, NM, St. Rose of Lima Church. (SFE)
Puerto Plata, PR, Jayuya Co., San Juan, c/o Jayuya, PR, Our Lady of Monserrate Church. (PCE)
Puerto Real, PR, Our Lady of Mt. Carmel, c/o Cabo Rojo, PR, St. Michael Church. (MGZ)
Pulaski, VA, St. Edward, c/o Wytheville, VA, St. Mary's Church. (RIC)
Pulguillas, PR, Coamo Co., Christ the King, c/o Coamo, PR, St. Blase Church. (PCE)
Pulusuk, FM, Our Lady of Fatima, c/o Tol, FM, Assumption of the Blessed Virgin Mary Church. (CI)
Pulusuk, FM, Our Lady of Fatima, c/o Puluwat, FM, Santiago Church Church. (CI)
Puluwat, FM, c/o Tol, FM, Assumption of the Blessed Virgin Mary Church. (CI)
Punaluu, HI, St. Joachim, c/o Kahuku, HI, St. Roch Church. (HON)
Punlap, FM, Sacred Heart, c/o Tol, FM, Assumption of the Blessed Virgin Mary Church. (CI)
Punlop, FM, Sacred Heart, c/o Puluwat, FM, Santiago Church Church. (CI)
Punta de Agua, NM, Torrance Co., c/o Mountainair, NM, St. Alice Church. (SFE)
Punto Oro, PR, Ponce Co., Ntra. Sra. del Pilar, c/o [11] Ponce, PR, San Jose Obrero Church. (PCE)
Pursglove, WV, Monongalia Co., St. Ursula, c/o Westover, WV, St. Elizabeth Ann Seton Church. (WH)
Puuiki, HI, St. Peter, c/o Hana, HI, St. Mary Church. (HON)

Q

Quartz Hill, CA, Los Angeles Co., St. Elizabeth, c/o Lancaster, CA, Blessed Junipero Serra Church. (LA)
Quartzsite, AZ, Queen of Peace, c/o Parker, AZ, Sacred Heart Church. (TUC)
Quebrada Ceiba, PR, Milagrosa, c/o Penuelas, PR, St. Joseph Church. (PCE)
Quebrada Honda, PR, Nuestra Senora, c/o Guayanilla, PR, Immaculate Conception Church. (PCE)
Quebrada Larga, PR, Sgdo. Corazon de Jesus, c/o Aguada, PR, St. Francis of Assisi Church. (MGZ)
Quebradas, PR, Sacred Heart, c/o Yauco, PR, Holy Rossary Church. (PCE)
Quebradas, PR, San Francisco de Asis, c/o Guayanilla, PR, Immaculate Conception Church. (PCE)
Queen Creek, AZ, Maricopa Co., Our Lady of Guadalupe, c/o Gilbert, AZ, St. Anne Church. (PHX)
Queensbury, NY, Our Lady of the Assumption, c/o Lake George, NY, Sacred Heart Church. (ALB)
Queenstown, MD, Queen Anne Co., St. Peter, c/o Centreville, MD, Mother of Sorrows Church. (WIL)
Quemado, TX, Maverick Co., Our Lady of Guadalupe, c/o Eagle Pass, TX, Our Lady of Refuge Church. (SAT)
Quimby, IA, Cherokee Co., St. John the Baptist, c/o Holstein, IA, Our Lady of Good Counsel Church. (SC)
Quinault, WA, Grays Harbor & Jefferson Cos., Our Lady of the Olympics, c/o Hoquiam, WA, Our Lady of Good Help Church. (SEA)
Quinlan, TX, Hunt Co., Our Lady of Fatima, c/o Greenville, TX, St. William Church. (DAL)
Quitman, MS, Good Shepherd, c/o Meridian, MS, St. Patrick Church. (JKS)

R

Raeville, NE, Boone Co., St. Bonaventure, c/o Petersburg, NE, St. John the Baptist Church. (OM)
Ragley, LA, Beauregard Parish, St. Pius X, c/o De Quincy, LA, Our Lady of La Salette Church. (LKC)
Rainsville, NM, Mora Co., c/o Mora, NM, St. Gertrude Church. (SFE)
Raleigh, MS, St. Paul, c/o Magee, MS, St. Stephen Church. (JKS)
Ralph, SD, Harding Co., St. Isidore, c/o Buffalo, SD, St. Anthony Church. (RC)
Ralston, PA, Lycoming Co., St. Aloysius, c/o Canton, PA, St. Michael Church. (SCR)
Ramey-Maleza, PR, Los Santos Reyes, c/o Aguadilla, PR, San Jose Obrero Church. (MGZ)
Ramirez, TX, Duval Co., Our Lady of Guadalupe, c/o Premont, TX, St. Theresa of the Infant Jesus Church. (CC)
Ranchester, WY, Sheridan Co., St. Edmund, c/o Sheridan, WY, Holy Name Church. (CHY)
Ranchitos, NM, Rio Arriba Co., c/o San Juan Pueblo, NM, St. John the Baptist Church. (SFE)
Rancho Murieta, CA, c/o Elk Grove, CA, St. Joseph Church. (SAC)
Randsburg, CA, Kern Co., Santa Barbara, c/o Ridgecrest, CA, St. Ann Church. (FRS)
Rangeley, ME, St. Luke, c/o Oquossoc, ME, Our Lady of the Lakes Church. (PRT)
Rangely, CO, Rio Blanco Co., St. Ignatius, c/o Meeker, CO, Holy Family Church. (DEN)
Rankin, IL, Vermilion Co., Holy Trinity, c/o Penfield, IL, St. Lawrence's Church. (PEO)
Rankin, TX, Upton Co., St. Thomas, c/o Big Lake, TX, St. Margaret of Cortona Church. (SAN)
Rapid City, SD, Pennington Co., Indian Health Service, Sioux San Hospital and Pennington County Jail, c/o [4] Rapid City, SD, St. Isaac Jogues Church. (RC)
Rasselas, PA, Elk Co., Holy Cross, c/o Wilcox, PA, St. Anne Church. (E)
Ray, ND, Williams Co., St. Michael, c/o Tioga, ND, St. Thomas Church. (BIS)
Raymond, CA, Madera Co., St. Anne, c/o Madera, CA, St. Joachim Church. (FRS)
Raymond, MS, Immaculate Conception, c/o Clinton, MS, Holy Savior Church. (JKS)
Raynesford, MT, St. Mary, c/o Belt, MT, St. Mark the Evangelist Church. (GF)
Reading, PA, Berks Co., Holy Rosary Chapel, c/o [6] Reading, PA, Holy Rosary Church. (ALN)
Realitos, TX, Duval Co., Sacred Heart, c/o Hebbronville, TX, Our Lady of Guadalupe Church. (CC)
Rector, AR, Clay Co., St. Henry's, c/o Paragould, AR, St. Mary's Church. (LR)
Red Cliff, CO, Eagle Co., Our Lady of Mt. Carmel, c/o Minturn, CO, St. Patrick's Church. (DEN)

Red Feather Lakes, CO, Larimer Co., Our Lady of the Lakes, c/o [1] Fort Collins, CO, St. Joseph Church. (DEN)
Red Owl, SD, Meade Co., St. Anthony, c/o Faith, SD, St. Joseph Church. (RC)
Red River, NM, Taos Co., c/o Questa, NM, St. Anthony Church. (SFE)
Red Scaffold, SD, Ziebach Co., Sacred Heart, c/o Eagle Butte, SD, All Saints Church. (RC)
Red Scaffold, SD, Ziebach Co., Sacred Heart, c/o Eagle Butte, SD, Cheyenne River Reservation Church. (RC)
Red Shirt Table, SD, Shannon Co., St. Bernard, c/o Pine Ridge, SD, Holy Rosary Church. (RC)
Red Springs, NC, Robeson Co., St. Andrew, c/o Lumberton, NC, St. Francis De Sales Church. (R)
Reddick, IL, St. Mary, c/o Cabery, IL, St. Joseph Church. (JOL)
Redfield, NY, Oswego Co., St. Paul, c/o Florence, NY, St. Mary Church. (SY)
Redford, TX, San Jose, c/o Presidio, TX, Santa Teresa de Jesus Church. (ELP)
Redwood City, CA, San Mateo Co., St. Joseph the Workman, c/o [1] Menlo Park, CA, St. Anthony Church. (SFR)
Reeder, ND, Adams Co., Sacred Heart, c/o Hettinger, ND, Holy Trinity Church. (BIS)
Reeves, LA, Sacred Heart Parish, St. Maurice, c/o Kinder, LA, St. Philip Neri Church. (LKC)
Reform, AL, Dickens Co., St. Robert, c/o Tuscaloosa, AL, Holy Spirit Church. (BIR)
Regent, ND, Hettinger Co., St. Henry's, c/o New England, ND, St. Mary Church. (BIS)
Reidsville, GA, Tattnall Co., St. Andrew the Apostle, c/o Vidalia, GA, Sacred Heart Church. (SAV)
Reilly Settlement, IA, Sacred Heart, c/o Little Turkey, IA, Assumption of the B. V. M. Church. (DUB)
Remer, MN, St. Paul, c/o Longville, MN, St. Edward's Church. (DUL)
Reserve, NM, St. Francis, c/o Aragon, NM, Santo Nino Church. (GLP)
Retsof, NY, Livingston Co., St. Lucy, c/o Leicester, NY, St. Thomas Aquinas Church. (ROC)
Reva, SD, Harding Co., Our Lady of the Prairie, c/o Buffalo, SD, St. Anthony Church. (RC)
Rhame, ND, Bowman Co., St. Mel, c/o Bowman, ND, St. Charles Church. (BIS)
Rhinecliff, NY, Dutchess Co., St. Joseph, c/o Rhinebeck, NY, The Good Shepherd Church. (NY)
Rich Hill, MO, Bates Co., St. Bridget's, c/o Butler, MO, St. Patrick's Church. (KC)
Richardton, ND, Stark Co., St. Stephen, c/o Richardton, ND, St. Mary Church. (BIS)
Richey, MT, St. Francis de Sales, c/o Circle, MT, St. Francis Xavier Church. (GF)
Richgrove, CA, Tulare Co., St. Vincent, c/o Delano, CA, St. Mary's of the Miraculous Medal Church. (FRS)
Richland, NJ, Atlantic Co., St. Joseph, c/o [5] Vineland, NJ, St. Mary's Church. (CAM)
Richmond, KY, St. Stephen the Martyr, c/o Richmond, KY, St. Mark Church. (LEX)
Richmond, VA, St. Joseph Tridentine Community, c/o [7] Richmond, VA, St. Benedict Church. (RIC)
Rico, CO, Dolores Co., Immaculate Heart of Mary Chapel, c/o Mancos, CO, St. Rita Church. (PBL)
Rideau Settlement, LA, Sacred Heart, c/o Lebeau, LA, Immaculate Conception Church. (LAF)
Ridge Manor, FL, Hernando Co., St. Anne, c/o Brooksville, FL, St. Anthony Church. (SP)
Ridgebury, PA, Bradford Co., Our Lady of Perpetual Help, c/o Bentley Creek, PA, St. Ann's Church. (SCR)
Ridgefield, WA, Clark Co., St. Mary of Guadalupe, c/o Woodland, WA, St. Philip's Church. (SEA)
Ridgeview, SD, Dewey Co., St. Joseph, c/o Eagle Butte, SD, All Saints Church. (RC)
Ridgeview, SD, Dewey Co., St. Joseph, c/o Eagle Butte, SD, Cheyenne River Reservation Church. (RC)
Riegelwood, NC, Christ the King, c/o Southport, NC, Sacred Heart Church. (R)
Riley, NM, Socorro Co., c/o Socorro, NM, San Miguel Church. (SFE)
Rileyville, PA, Wayne Co., St. Joseph, c/o Honesdale, PA, St. John the Evangelist Church. (SCR)
Rimersburg, PA, Clarion Co., St. Richard, c/o East Brady, PA, St. Eusebius Church. (E)
Rincon, NM, Our Lady of All Nations, c/o Hatch, NM, Our Lord of Mercy Church. (LSC)
Ringgold, LA, Bienville Parish, Blessed Sacrament, c/o Minden, LA, St. Paul Church. (SHP)
Rio, WI, St. Joseph's, c/o Doylestown, WI, St. Patrick Church. (MAD)
Rio Canas, PR, Rio Canas Abajo, San Judas, c/o Juana Diaz, PR, St. Raymond Nonato Church. (PCE)
Rio Chiquito, NM, Rio Arriba Co., Sagrado Corazon, c/o Chimayo, NM, Holy Family Church. (SFE)
Rio Chiquito, PR, Ponce Co., Nino Jesus de Praga, c/o [2] Ponce, PR, Christ the King Church. (PCE)
Rio Chiquito, PR, Ponce Co., San Vicente, c/o [14] Ponce, PR, San Vicente-Cantera Church. (PCE)
Rio en Medio, NM, Sante Fe Co., Our Lady of Sorrows, c/o [2] Santa Fe, NM, Our Lady of Guadalupe Church. (SFE)
Rio Grande, PR, Nuestra Senora de Fatima, c/o Rio Grande, PR, Nuestra Senora del Carmen Church. (SJN)
Rio Grande, PR, Perpetuo Socorro, c/o Aguada, PR, St. Francis of Assisi Church. (MGZ)
Rio Grande, PR, San Pedro, c/o Rio Grande, PR, Nuestra Senora del Carmen Church. (SJN)
Rio Grande-Playa, PR, Ntra. Sra. del Carmen, c/o Aguada, PR, St. Francis of Assisi Church. (MGZ)
Rio Hondo, PR, San Carlos y San Antonio, c/o [6] Mayaquez, PR, Sacred Heart Church. (MGZ)
Rio Jueyes, PR, Coamo Co., Our Lady of Lourdes, c/o Coamo, PR, St. Blase Church. (PCE)
Rio Lucio, NM, Taos Co., Sagrado Corazon Mission, c/o Penasco, NM, San Antonio de Padua Church. (SFE)
Rio Piedras, PR, N. Sra. de la Paz, c/o [58] San Juan, PR, Santisimo Salvador Church. (SJN)
Rio Piedras, PR, San Jose de Calasanz, c/o [58] San Juan, PR, Santisimo Salvador Church. (SJN)
Rio Piedras, PR, Santa Teresita de Nino Jesus, c/o [47] San Juan, PR, Nuestra Senora del Pilar Church. (SJN)
Rio Prieto, PR, Milagrosa, c/o Castaner, PR, Our Lady of the Miraculous Medal Church. (PCE)
Rio Rancho, NM, Sandoval Co., Church of the Incarnation, c/o Rio Rancho, NM, St. Thomas Aquinas Church. (SFE)
Rio Rancho, NM, Sandoval Co., St. John Vianney, c/o Rio Rancho, NM, St. Thomas Aquinas Church. (SFE)
Rio Verde, AZ, St. Dominic, c/o Fountain Hills, AZ, Ascension Church. (PHX)
Rios, TX, Duval Co., St. Francis of Assisi, c/o Premont, TX, St. Theresa of the Infant Jesus Church. (CC)
Ripley, NY, Chautauqua Co., St. Thomas More, c/o Westfield, NY, St. James Church. (BUF)
Ripley, TN, Lauderdale Co., Ave Maria, c/o Covington, TN, St. Alphonsus Church. (MEM)
Rising Sun, MD, Cecil Co., St. Agnes, c/o Perryville, MD, Church of the Good Shepherd Church. (WIL)
Ritter, SC, Colleton Co., St. James, c/o Walterboro, SC, St. Anthony's Church. (CHR)
Riverside, CA, Our Lady of Guadalupe, c/o [11] Riverside, CA, St. Thomas the Apostle Church. (SB)
Riverside, MT, Sacred Heart, c/o Wolf Point, MT, Immaculate Conception Church. (GF)
Riverton, NE, Franklin Co., St. Catherine's, c/o Red Cloud, NE, Sacred Heart Church. (LIN)
Rivesville, WV, Marion Co., Our Lady of the Assumption, c/o Grant Town, WV, St. Anthony's Church. (WH)
Riviera, TX, Kleberg Co., Our Lady of Guadalupe, c/o Vattman, TX, Our Lady of Consolation Church. (CC)
Roanoke, AL, Randolph Co., Immaculate Conception, c/o Lanett, AL, Holy Family Church. (BIR)
Robbins, IL, Cook Co., St. Peter Claver, c/o Blue Island, IL, St. Benedict Church. (CHI)
Robbins, NC, Moore Co., Blessed Juan Diego, c/o Pinehurst, NC, Sacred Heart Church. (R)
Robbinsville, NC, Graham Co., Prince of Peace, c/o Andrews, NC, Holy Redeemer Church. (CHL)
Robert Lee, TX, Coke Co., Our Lady of Guadalupe, c/o Ballinger, TX, St. Mary Star of the Sea Church. (SAN)
Roberts, IL, Immaculate Conception, c/o Piper City, IL, St. Peter Church. (JOL)
Roberts, MT, St. Thomas Aquinas, c/o Red Lodge, MT, St. Agnes Church. (GF)
Robinson Township, MI, St. Anthony, c/o Grand Haven, MI, St. Patrick's Church. (GR)
Roby, MO, Texas Co., St. Vincent de Paul, c/o Houston, MO, St. Mark Church. (SPC)
Rochester, VT, Windsor Co., St. Elizabeth, c/o Bethel, VT, St. Anthony Church. (BUR)
Rociada Abajo, NM, San Miguel Co., Santo Nino, c/o Las Vegas, NM, Our Lady of Sorrows Church Church. (SFE)
Rock City Falls, NY, St. Paul, c/o Greenfield Center, NY, St. Joseph Church. (ALB)
Rock Hall, W. Main St., MD, Kent Co., St. John, c/o Chestertown, MD, Sacred Heart Church. (WIL)
Rock Lake, ND, Towner Co., c/o Rolla, ND, St. Joachim's Church. (FAR)
Rock Lake, PA, Wayne Co., St. Juliana's, c/o Pleasant Mount, PA, St. James Church. (SCR)
Rock Point, MD, Charles Co., St. Francis de Sales, c/o Issue, MD, Holy Ghost Church. (WDC)
Rockvale, CO, Fremont Co., St. Patrick, c/o Florence, CO, St. Benedict Church. (PBL)
Rockville, MD, Montgomery Co., Our Lady of China, c/o [3] Rockville, MD, St. Mary Church. (WDC)
Rockville, NE, Sherman Co., St. Mary's, c/o Ravenna, NE, Our Lady of Lourdes Church. (GI)
Rockwood, ME, Somerset Co., St. Joseph's, c/o Greenville, ME, Holy Family Church. (PRT)
Rocky Boy Indian Reservation, MT, St. Mary, c/o Big Sandy, MT, St. Margaret Mary Church. (GF)
Rockyford, SD, Shannon Co., St. Peter's, c/o Manderson, SD, St. Agnes Church. (RC)
Rodarte, NM, Taos Co., Santa Barbara Mission, c/o Penasco, NM, San Antonio de Padua Church. (SFE)
Rodeo, NM, San Felipe, c/o Lordsburg, NM, St. Joseph Church. (LSC)
Rogue River, OR, Jackson Co., Rogue River Catholic Community, c/o Grants Pass, OR, St. Anne Church. (P)
Roland, OK, Sequoyah Co., Blessed Kateri Tekakwitha, c/o Sallisaw, OK, St. Francis Xavier Church. (TLS)
Romanum, FM, St. Joseph, c/o Udot, FM, St. Francis Assisi Church. (CI)
Romeo, CO, Conejos Co., Our Lady of the Immaculate Conception, c/o Capulin, CO, St. Joseph Church. (PBL)
Romero, PR, Sagrado Corazon, c/o Villalba, PR, Our Lady of Mt. Carmel Church. (PCE)
Roosevelt Lake, AZ, Gila Co., St. Theresa, c/o Miami, AZ, Our Lady of the Blessed Sacrament Church. (TUC)
Ropesville, TX, Hockley Co., San Francisco de Asis, c/o Brownfield, TX, St. Anthony's Church. (LUB)
Rosario, PR, Nuestra Senora del Rosario, c/o Rosario, PR, Rosary Church. (MGZ)
Rosario, PR, San Jose, c/o [6] Mayaquez, PR, Sacred Heart Church. (MGZ)
Roscoe, IL, Winnebago Co., Church of the Holy Spirit, c/o South Beloit, IL, St. Peter Church. (RCK)
Roscoe, NY, Sullivan Co., Gate of Heaven, c/o Livingston Manor, NY, St. Aloysius Church. (NY)
Roscoe, TX, Nolan Co., St. Albert the Great, c/o Sweetwater, TX, Immaculate Heart of Mary Church. (SAN)
Rosebud, SD, Todd Co., St. Bridget, c/o St. Francis, SD, Rosebud Reservation Church. (RC)
Roseton, NY, Orange Co., Our Lady of Mercy, c/o Marlboro, NY, St. Mary Church. (NY)
Rosita, TX, Santa Rosa de Lima, c/o Escobares, TX, Sacred Heart Church. (BWN)
Rossie, NY, St. Lawrence Co., St. Patrick, c/o Hammond, NY, St. Peter Church. (OG)
Rotten Bayou, MS, Harrison Co., St. William, c/o DeLisle, MS, The Catholic Church in DeLisle Church. (BLX)
Roulette, PA, Potter Co., St. Mary, c/o Port Allegany, PA, St. Gabriel the Archangel Church. (E)
Round Lake, MI, St. Joseph, c/o Custer, MI, St. Mary's Church. (GR)
Round Mountain & Fish Lake, NV, St. Barbara/Our Lady of Guadalupe, c/o Tonopah, NV, St. Patrick Church. (LAV)
Round Rock, AZ, Our Lady of Guadalupe, c/o Lukachukai, AZ, St. Isabel Mission for Navajo Indians Church. (GLP)
Rouseville, PA, Venango Co., St. Venantius, c/o [1] Oil City, PA, Assumption of the Blessed Virgin Mary Church. (E)
Rowe, NM, San Miguel Co., c/o Pecos, NM, St. Anthony Church. (SFE)
Roxbury, CT, Litchfield Co., St. Patrick's, c/o Washington Depot, CT, Our Lady of Perpetual Help Church. (HRT)
Roxbury, NY, Our Lady of Good Counsel, c/o Margaretville, NY, Sacred Heart Church. (ALB)
Roxbury Pond, ME, St. Mary's Chapel, c/o Rumford, ME, St. Athanasius-St. John Church. (PRT)
Rubidoux, CA, Riverside Co., Our Lady of Guadalupe, c/o [8] Riverside, CA, St. John the Evangelist Church. (SB)
Rudyard, MT, Holy Family Center, c/o Chester, MT, St. Mary's Church. (GF)
Rural Linton, ND, Emmons Co., St. Michael's, c/o Strasburg, ND, Sts. Peter and Paul Church. (BIS)
Rush Springs, OK, Grady Co., St. Francis of Assisi, c/o Duncan, OK, Assumption Church. (OKL)
Rushville, NE, Sheridan Co., Immaculate Conception, c/o Gordon, NE, St. Leo's Church. (GI)
Rushville, NY, Ontario Co., St. Mary, c/o Stanley, NY, St. Theresa Church. (ROC)
Rusk, TX, Cherokee Co., Sacred Heart, c/o Jacksonville, TX, Our Lady of Sorrows Church. (TYL)
Russell, NY, St. Lawrence Co., St. Rene Goupil, c/o De Kalb Junction, NY, St. Henry Church. (OG)
Rutherford, CA, Holy Family, c/o Yountville, CA, St. Joan of Arc Church. (SR)
Rutten, ND, Ramsey Co., St. Benedict, c/o Devils Lake, ND, St. Joseph's Church. (FAR)
Ryan, OK, Jefferson Co., San Jose, c/o Duncan, OK, Assumption Church. (OKL)
Rye, CO, Pueblo Co., St. Aloysius, c/o [3] Pueblo, CO, Holy Family Church. (PBL)
Ryegate, MT, St Mathias, c/o Roundup, MT, St. Benedict's Church. (GF)

S

Sa'ilele, AS, c/o [5] Pago Pago, AS, Church of St. Peter and Paul Church. (SPP)
Sabana, PR, San Jose, c/o Aguada, PR, St. Francis of Assisi Church. (MGZ)

Sabana Eneas, PR, San Judas Tadeo, c/o San German, PR, San German de Auxerre Church. (MGZ)
Sabana Llana, PR, Perpetuo Socorro, c/o Salinas, PR, Our Lady of Monserrat Church. (PCE)
Sabin, MN, Clay Co., St. Cecilia, c/o Barnesville, MN, Assumption Church. (CR)
Sabinal, NM, Socorro Co., San Antonio, c/o La Joya, NM, Our Lady of Sorrows Church. (SFE)
Sabinoso, NM, San Miguel Co., c/o Roy, NM, Holy Family-St. Joseph Church. (SFE)
Sacaton, AZ, St. Anthony, c/o Bapchule, AZ, St. Peter's Church. (PHX)
Sacaton Flats, AZ, Our Lady of Victory, c/o Bapchule, AZ, St. Peter's Church. (PHX)
Saco, MT, St. Francis of Assisi, c/o Malta, MT, St. Mary's Church. (GF)
Saegertown, PA, Crawford Co., St. Bernadette, c/o Meadville, PA, St. Agatha Church. (E)
Sagamore, MA, Barnstable Co., St. Theresa, c/o Sandwich, MA, Corpus Christi Church. (FR)
Saginaw, MN, St. Philip Neri, c/o Proctor, MN, St. Rose Catholic Church Church. (DUL)
Saguache, CO, St. Agnes, c/o Center, CO, St. Francis Jerome Church. (PBL)
Sahuarita, AZ, Pima Co., St. Martin de Porres, c/o Green Valley, AZ, Our Lady of the Valley Church. (TUC)
St. Anne, IN, Jennings Co., St. Anne, c/o St. Joseph, IN, St. Joseph Church. (IND)
St. Anthony, ND, Rolette Co., St. Anthony, c/o Turtle Mountain Reservation, ND, (Chippewa Indians) Church. (FAR)
St. Augustine, FL, St. Johns Co., Prince of Peace, c/o [1] St. Augustine, FL, Cathedral of St. Augustine Church. (STA)
St. Augustine, FL, Protection of the Mother of God, c/o Ormond Beach, FL, Holy Dormition Church. (PSC)
St. Augustine, FL, St. Johns Co., St. Benedict the Moor, c/o [1] St. Augustine, FL, Cathedral of St. Augustine Church. (STA)
St. Augustine, TX, San Augustine Co., San Augustine, c/o Hemphill, TX, St. Pius I Church. (TYL)
St. Boniface, PA, Cambria Co., St. Boniface Chapel, c/o Hastings, PA, St. Bernard Church. (ALT)
St. Charles, IL, Kane Co., St. Patrick, c/o St. Charles, IL, St. Patrick Church. (RCK)
St. David, IL, Fulton Co., St. Michael, c/o Lewistown, IL, St. Mary's Church. (PEO)
St. Denis, IN, Jennings Co., St. Denis, c/o Millhousen, IN, Immaculate Conception Church. (IND)
St. Francis, SD, c/o St. Francis, SD, St. Charles Church. (RC)
St. Francis, SD, Todd Co., St. Charles, c/o St. Francis, SD, Rosebud Reservation Church. (RC)
Saint Helena Island, SC, Beaufort Co., Holy Cross, c/o Beaufort, SC, St. Peter's Church. (CHR)
St. Landry, LA, St. Theresa, c/o Pine Prairie, LA, St. Peter Church. (LAF)
St. Mary, NE, Johnson Co., St. Mary's, c/o Tecumseh, NE, St. Andrew's Church. (LIN)
St. Michaels, AZ, St. Michael's Mission for Navajo Indians, c/o St. Michaels, AZ, St. Michael Church. (GLP)
St. Michaels, MD, St. Michael, c/o Easton, MD, SS. Peter and Paul Church. (WIL)
St. Paul, MN, Ramsey Co., Hispanic Ministry, c/o [10] St. Paul, MN, Sacred Heart Church. (STP)
St. Paul, TX, St. Paul, c/o Sinton, TX, Sacred Heart Church. (CC)
St. Petersburg, FL, The Mercy of God Polish Mission, c/o [7] St. Petersburg, FL, St. Paul Church. (SP)
St. Petersburg, FL, Pinellas Co., Vietnamese Martyrs Mission, c/o [5] St. Petersburg, FL, St. Joseph Church. (SP)
St. Pius, IN, Ripley Co., St. Pius, c/o Milan, IN, St. Charles Borromeo Church. (IND)
St. Thomas, ND, Pembina Co., St. Thomas, c/o Drayton, ND, St. Edward's Church. (FAR)
St. Vincent de Paul, IN, c/o St. Vincent de Paul, IN, St. Vincent de Paul Church. (IND)
St. Xavier, MT, St. Francis Xavier, c/o Crow Agency, MT, St. Dennis Church. (GF)
Saipan, MP, Santa Soledad Mission, c/o San Vicente Village, District 10, MP, San Vicente Ferrer Parish Church. (CHK)
Salado, TX, St. Stephen, c/o Jarrell, TX, Holy Trinity Church. (AUS)
Salem, IN, Washington Co., St. Patrick, c/o Scottsburg, IN, American Martyrs Church. (IND)
Salem, OR, Marion Co., San Jose, c/o Salem, OR, St. Joseph Church. (P)
Salem Township, OH, Wyandot Co., St. Joseph, c/o Carey, OH, Our Lady of Consolation, Basilica-National Shrine Church. (TOL)
Saliente, PR, Jayuya Co., San Francisco, c/o Jayuya, PR, Our Lady of Monserrate Church. (PCE)
Salinas-Providencia, PR, Divina Providencia, c/o Ensenada, PR, Sacred Heart Church. (PCE)
Salineno, TX, St. Joseph, c/o Roma, TX, Our Lady of Refuge Church. (BWN)
Salon Usos Multiples-April Gardens, PR, Las Piedras, c/o Las Piedras, PR, Inmaculada Concepcion Church. (CGS)
Salt River Indian, AZ, St. Francis, c/o [4] Tempe, AZ, St. Margaret Church. (PHX)
Saltillo, MS, St. Thomas Aquinas, c/o Tupelo, MS, St. James Church. (JKS)
Salto, PR, Jayuya Co., Santos Reyes, c/o Jayuya, PR, Our Lady of Monserrate Church. (PCE)
Salyersville, KY, Magoffin Co., St. Luke's, c/o Prestonsburg, KY, St. Martha Church. (LEX)
San Acacio, CO, Costilla Co., San Acacio, c/o San Luis, CO, Sangre de Cristo Church. (PBL)
San Antonio, CO, San Antonio de Padua, c/o Conejos, CO, Our Lady of Guadalupe Church. (PBL)
San Antonio, NM, Socorro Co., c/o Socorro, NM, San Miguel Church. (SFE)
San Antonio, NM, Bernalillo Co., c/o Tijeras, NM, Holy Child Church. (SFE)
San Antonio, NM, San Miguel Co., Los Vigiles (Our Lady of Refuge), c/o Las Vegas, NM, Immaculate Conception Church. (SFE)
San Antonio, TX, Bexar Co., Byzantine Catholic Mission, c/o Houston, TX, St. John Chrysostom Church. (PBR)
San Antonio, TX, Bexar Co., Purisima Concepcion, c/o [32] San Antonio, TX, St. Cecilia Church. (SAT)
San Antonio, TX, Bexar Co., San Francesco di Paola, c/o [1] San Antonio, TX, Cathedral of San Fernando Church. (SAT)
San Antonio, TX, Bexar Co., Santa Cruz, c/o [17] San Antonio, TX, Our Lady of Guadalupe Church. (SAT)
San Antonio, TX, Santa Maria Goretti, c/o [47] San Antonio, TX, St. Jude Church. (SAT)
San Antonio, TX, St. Catherine, c/o [52] San Antonio, TX, St. Margaret Mary Church. (SAT)
San Antonio, TX, St. Francis Cabrini, c/o [69] San Antonio, TX, San Francisco de la Espada Church. (SAT)
San Ardo, CA, Monterey Co., Our Lady of Ransom, c/o San Miguel, CA, San Miguel Church. (MRY)
San Benito, TX, St. Joseph, c/o San Benito, TX, Our Lady, Queen of the Universe Church. (BWN)
San Cristobal, NM, Taos Co., c/o Arroyo Seco, NM, Holy Trinity Church. (SFE)
San Diego, CA, San Diego Co., SDSU Newman Center, c/o [3] San Diego, CA, Blessed Sacrament Church. (SD)
San Diego, PR, Coamo Co., San Diego, c/o Coamo, PR, St. Blase Church. (PCE)
San Felipe, NM, Sandoval Co., Indian Pueblo, c/o Pena Blanca, NM, Nuestra Senora De Guadalupe Church. (SFE)
San Felipe, PR, St. Martin de Porres, c/o Aguirre, PR, Sacred Heart Church. (PCE)
San Felipe, TX, Austin Co., c/o [1] Harlingen, TX, Our Lady of the Assumption Church. (BWN)
San Francisco, CO, Costilla Co., St. Francis of Assisi, c/o San Luis, CO, Sangre de Cristo Church. (PBL)
San Ignacio, NM, Guadalupe Co., c/o Santa Rosa, NM, St. Rose of Lima Church. (SFE)
San Ignacio, TX, Zapata Co., St. Ignatius, c/o Zapata, TX, Our Lady of Lourdes Church. (CC)
San Ildefonso, NM, Sante Fe Co., Indian Pueblo, c/o [1] Santa Fe, NM, The Cathedral of San Francisco de Asis Church. (SFE)
San Isidro, CO, Costilla Co., St. Isidro, c/o San Luis, CO, Sangre de Cristo Church. (PBL)
San Isidro, NM, San Isidro, c/o Dona Ana, NM, Our Lady of the Purification Church. (LSC)
San Isidro Norte, NM, San Miguel Co., c/o Ribera, NM, San Miguel Del Vado Church. (SFE)
San Isidro Sur, NM, San Miguel Co., c/o Ribera, NM, San Miguel Del Vado Church. (SFE)
San Joaquin, CA, Fresno Co., St. Vincent de Paul, c/o Tranquillity, CA, St. Paul Church. (FRS)
San Jon, NM, Quay Co., Our Lady of Guadalupe, c/o Tucumcari, NM, St. Anne Church. (SFE)
San Jose, AZ, Graham Co., San Jose, c/o Solomon, AZ, Our Lady of Guadalupe Church. (TUC)
San Jose, FL, Lee Co., Jesus the Worker, c/o [5] Fort Myers, FL, St. Francis Xavier Church. (VEN)
San Jose, NM, San Miguel Co., c/o Ribera, NM, San Miguel Del Vado Church. (SFE)
San Jose, NM, Arrey, c/o Garfield, NM, San Isidro Church. (LSC)
San Jose Ranch, TX, Duval Co., St. Joseph, c/o Benavides, TX, St. Rose of Lima Church. (CC)
San Juan, NM, San Miguel Co., c/o Ribera, NM, San Miguel Del Vado Church. (SFE)
San Juan, NM, San Juan, c/o Hurley, NM, Infant Jesus Church. (LSC)
San Juan, PR, Capilla San Conrado, c/o [18] San Juan, PR, San Francisco de Asis Church. (SJN)
San Juan, PR, Egida del Maestro, c/o [16] San Juan, PR, Ntra. Sra. de Fatima Church. (SJN)
San Juan, PR, Jesus de Nazaret, c/o [24] San Juan, PR, Jesus Maestro Church. (SJN)
San Juan, PR, La Inmaculada, c/o [62] San Juan, PR, San Vicente de Paul Church. (SJN)
San Juan, PR, La Milagrosa, c/o [28] San Juan, PR, San Juan Bosco Church. (SJN)
San Juan, PR, Medalla Milagrosa, c/o [9] San Juan, PR, Santa Catalina Laboure Church. (SJN)
San Juan, PR, Nra. Sra. del Altagracia, c/o [37] San Juan, PR, Maria Auxiliadora Church. (SJN)
San Juan, PR, Ntra. Senora de la Caridad del Cobre, c/o [38] San Juan, PR, Santa Maria de Los Angeles Church. (SJN)
San Juan, PR, Ntra. Sra. de Fatima, c/o [37] San Juan, PR, Maria Auxiliadora Church. (SJN)
San Juan, PR, Ntra. Sra. de la Caridad, c/o [43] San Juan, PR, San Pablo Church. (SJN)
San Juan, PR, Ntra. Sra. de la Providencia, c/o [14] San Juan, PR, Nuestra Senora de la Esperanza Church. (SJN)
San Juan, PR, Ntra. Sra. del Rosario, c/o [28] San Juan, PR, San Juan Bosco Church. (SJN)
San Juan, PR, Nuestra Senora del Buen Consejo, c/o [4] San Juan, PR, San Antonio Church. (SJN)
San Juan, PR, Sagrada Familia, c/o [61] San Juan, PR, Santa Teresita Del Nino Jesus Church. (SJN)
San Juan, PR, Sagrado Corazon, c/o [37] San Juan, PR, Maria Auxiliadora Church. (SJN)
San Juan, PR, San Fernando, c/o [23] San Juan, PR, Inmaculado Corazon de Maria Church. (SJN)
San Juan, PR, San Francisco de Asis, c/o [30] San Juan, PR, San Juan Evangelista Church. (SJN)
San Juan, PR, San Jose, c/o [62] San Juan, PR, San Vicente de Paul Church. (SJN)
San Juan, PR, San Martin de Porres, c/o [8] San Juan, PR, Nuestra Senora del Carmen Church. (SJN)
San Juan, PR, San Martin de Porres, c/o [28] San Juan, PR, San Juan Bosco Church. (SJN)
San Juan, PR, San Martin de Porres-Sierra Maestra, c/o [27] San Juan, PR, San Jose Obrero Church. (SJN)
San Juan, PR, San Pablo, c/o [9] San Juan, PR, Santa Catalina Laboure Church. (SJN)
San Juan, PR, Santa Ana, c/o [42] San Juan, PR, Ntra. Sra. de la Monserrate Church. (SJN)
San Juan, PR, Santa Catalina, c/o [62] San Juan, PR, San Vicente de Paul Church. (SJN)
San Juan, PR, Santisima Trinidad, c/o [37] San Juan, PR, Maria Auxiliadora Church. (SJN)
San Juan, PR, Santo Domingo, c/o [11] San Juan, PR, Corpus Christi Church. (SJN)
San Judas Tadeo, PR, Playuelas, c/o Aguadilla, PR, La Milagrosa Church. (MGZ)
San Lorenzo, NM, San Lorenzo, c/o Bayard, NM, Our Lady of Fatima Church. (LSC)
San Lucas, CA, Monterey Co., St. Luke, c/o King City, CA, St. John the Baptist Church. (MRY)
San Luis, AZ, Yuma Co., San Judas Tadeo, c/o Somerton, AZ, Immaculate Heart of Mary Church. (TUC)
San Luis, NM, Saint Aloysius Gonzaga, c/o Cuba, NM, Immaculate Conception Church. (GLP)
San Manuel, TX, St. Anne, c/o San Carlos, TX, St. Joseph the Worker Church. (BWN)
San Marcos, TX, Hays Co., Guadalupe Chapel, c/o San Marcos, TX, St. John the Evangelist Church. (AUS)
San Miguel, CO, San Miguel, c/o Conejos, CO, Our Lady of Guadalupe Church. (PBL)
San Patricio, NM, St. Jude Thaddeus, c/o Ruidoso, NM, St. Eleanor Church. (LSC)
San Patricio, TX, San Patricio Co., St. Patrick, c/o Mathis, TX, Sacred Heart Church. (CC)
San Pedro, CO, Costilla Co., SS. Peter and Paul, c/o San Luis, CO, Sangre de Cristo Church. (PBL)
San Pedro, FL, Collier Co., c/o [3] Naples, FL, St. Peter the Apostle Church. (VEN)
San Pedro, NM, c/o Santa Cruz, NM, Holy Cross Church. (SFE)
San Pedro, TX, San Pedro, c/o [5] Brownsville, TX, Our Lady of Good Counsel Church. (BWN)
San Perlita, TX, Sacred Heart, c/o Raymondville, TX, St. Anthony Church. (BWN)
San Rafael, CO, San Pedro y San Rafael, c/o Conejos, CO, Our Lady of Guadalupe Church. (PBL)
San Saba, TX, Lampass Co., Izoro, c/o San Saba, TX, St. Mary's Church. (AUS)
San Simon, AZ, Cochise Co., Our Lady of Perpetual Help, c/o Willcox, AZ, Sacred Heart Church. (TUC)
San Ysidro, NM, Sandoval Co., c/o Jemez Pueblo, NM, San Diego Indian Missions Church. (SFE)
Sand Springs, IA, Immaculate Conception, c/o Hopkinton, IA, St. Luke's Church. (DUB)
Sandersville, GA, Washington Co., St. William, c/o Dublin, GA, Immaculate Conception Church. (SAV)
Sandia Indian Pueblo, NM, Sandoval Co., c/o Bernalillo, NM, Our Lady of Sorrows Church. (SFE)
Sandy Valley, NV, St. Catherine of Siena, c/o [2] Las Vegas, NV, Christ the King Church. (LAV)
Sangerville, ME, Holy Family, c/o Dover-Foxcroft, ME, St. Thomas Church. (PRT)
Santa Ana, NM, Sandoval Co., c/o Jemez Pueblo, NM, San Diego Indian Missions Church. (SFE)
Santa Ana, PR, Coamo Co., Santa Ana, c/o Coamo, PR, St. Blase Church. (PCE)
Santa Catalina, PR, Coamo Co., Miraculous Virgin, c/o Coamo, PR, St. Blase Church. (PCE)
Santa Catalina, PR, Coama Co., Sacred Heart, c/o

Coamo, PR, St. Blase Church. (PCE)
Santa Clara, NM, Rio Arriba Co., Indian Pueblo, c/o [1] Santa Fe, NM, The Cathedral of San Francisco de Asis Church. (SFE)
Santa Clara, NY, St. Peter, c/o Saint Regis Falls, NY, St. Ann Church. (OG)
Santa Cruz, AZ, St. Catherine, c/o Laveen, AZ, St. John The Baptist Church. (PHX)
Santa Maria, AZ, Our Lady of Guadalupe, c/o Cashion, AZ, St. William Church. (PHX)
Santa Maria, TX, St. Margaret Ann, c/o Progreso, TX, Holy Spirit Church. (BWN)
Santa Monica, TX, Santa Monica, c/o Lyford, TX, Prince of Peace Church. (BWN)
Santa Rita, NM, San Miguel Co., c/o Ribera, NM, San Miguel Del Vado Church. (SFE)
Santan, AZ, St. Anne, c/o Bapchule, AZ, St. Peter's Church. (PHX)
Santiago, FM, c/o Tol, FM, Assumption of the Blessed Virgin Mary Church. (CI)
Santiago-Talco, NM, Mora Co., c/o Mora, NM, St. Gertrude Church. (SFE)
Santo Domingo, NM, Sandoval Co., Indian Pueblo, c/o Pena Blanca, NM, Nuestra Senora De Guadalupe Church. (SFE)
Santo Nino, NM, c/o Santa Cruz, NM, Holy Cross Church. (SFE)
Sapello, NM, San Miguel Co., Our Lady of Guadalupe, c/o Las Vegas, NM, Our Lady of Sorrows Church Church. (SFE)
Sapphire Valley, NC, Transylvania Co., St. Jude, c/o Brevard, NC, Sacred Heart Church. (CHL)
Sapwuahfik, FM, c/o Kolonia, FM, Our Lady of Mercy Church. (CI)
Saragosa, TX, Our Lady of Guadalupe, c/o Balmorhea, TX, Christ the King Church. (ELP)
Saratoga Lake, NY, Saratoga Co., St. Isaac Jogues, c/o Stillwater, NY, St. Peter the Apostle Church. (ALB)
Sardis, MS, St. John the Baptist, c/o Batesville, MS, St. Mary Church. (JKS)
Sargent, NE, Custer Co., Assumption of the Blessed Virgin Mary, c/o Burwell, NE, Sacred Heart Church. (GI)
Sartwell, PA, McKean Co., St. Mary, c/o Eldred, PA, St. Raphael Church. (E)
Saspamco, TX, Bexar Co., Our Lady of Perpetual Help, c/o Elmendorf, TX, St. Anthony Church. (SAT)
Satin, TX, Satin Falls Co., Santa Rita, c/o [2] Waco, TX, St. Francis on the Brazos Church. (AUS)
Satowan, FM, c/o Lukunor, FM, Sacred Heart Church. (CI)
Saugus, CA, Los Angeles Co., Blessed Kateri Tekakwitha Mission, c/o Canyon Country, CA, St. Clare Church. (LA)
Sault Sainte Marie, MI, Chippewa Co., St. Isaac Jogues, c/o Brimley, MI, St. Francis Xavier Church. (MAR)
Savage, MT, St. Michael, c/o Sidney, MT, St. Matthew Church. (GF)
Savannah, NY, Wayne Co., St. Patrick, c/o Clyde, NY, St. John the Evangelist Church. (ROC)
Savoy, LA, St. Thomas, c/o Richard, LA, St. Edward Church. (LAF)
Sawmill, AZ, Apache Co., St. Francis Mission, c/o Navajo, NM, St. Berard Church. (GLP)
Sawyer, MI, St. Agnes, c/o Three Oaks, MI, St. Mary of the Assumption Church. (KAL)
Sawyer, MN, SS. Mary & Joseph, c/o Cloquet, MN, Holy Family Church. (DUL)
Sawyer, MN, Carlton Co., SS. Mary and Joseph, c/o Duluth, MN, Indian Missions Church. (DUL)
Sawyer's Bar, CA, Siskiyou Co., St. Joseph, c/o Fort Jones, CA, Sacred Heart Church. (SAC)
Saxtons River, VT, Windham Co., St. Edmund of Canterbury, c/o Putney, VT, Our Lady of Mercy Church. (BUR)
Sayre, OK, Beckham Co., Queen of All Saints, c/o Elk City, OK, St. Matthew's Church. (OKL)
Schenectady, NY, Schenectady Co., St. Teresa Carmelite Monastery, c/o [11] Schenectady, NY, St. Luke Church. (ALB)
Schenevus, NY, Otsego Co., St. Mary, c/o Worcester, NY, St. Joseph Church. (ALB)
Schley, IA, Holy Cross, c/o Protivin, IA, Holy Trinity Church. (DUB)
Schodack Landing, NY, Assumption of B.V.M., c/o Castleton-on-Hudson, NY, Sacred Heart Church. (ALB)
Schodack Landing, NY, Shrine of St. Jude, c/o Castleton-on-Hudson, NY, Sacred Heart Church. (ALB)
Schoolcraft, NE, Madison Co., St. Francis de Sales, c/o Battle Creek, NE, St. Patrick's Church. (OM)
Scio, NY, Allegany Co., St. Joseph, c/o Belmont, NY, St. Mary Church. (BUF)
Scotia, NE, Greeley Co., St. Patrick, c/o Greeley, NE, Sacred Heart Church. (GI)
Scotland, CT, Windham Co., St. Margaret, c/o Willimantic, CT, St. Joseph Church. (NOR)
Scotland Neck, NC, Halifax Co., St. Anne, c/o Ahoskie, NC, St. Charles Borromeo Church. (R)
Scotts Mills, OR, Marion Co., Holy Rosary, c/o Mt. Angel, OR, St. Mary Church. (P)
Scranton, ND, Bowman Co., Sacred Heart, c/o Hettinger, ND, Holy Trinity Church. (BIS)
Scranton, PA, Lackawanna Co., Holy Cross, c/o [21] Scranton, PA, St. Patrick's Church. (SCR)
Scranton, PA, Lackawanna Co., St. John the Baptist, c/o [21] Scranton, PA, St. Patrick's Church. (SCR)
Scranton, PA, Lackawanna Co., St. Stanislaus, c/o [9] Scranton, PA, Holy Rosary Church. (SCR)
Scranton, PA, St. Stephen's, c/o [9] Scranton, PA, Holy Rosary Church. (SCR)
Scriba, NY, Sacred Heart, c/o [6] Oswego, NY, St. Peter Church. (SY)
Scribner, NE, Dodge Co., St. Lawrence, c/o Hooper, NE, St. Rose of Lima Church. (OM)
Seabrook Beach, NH, Rockingham Co., St. Elizabeth's, c/o Hampton, NH, Our Lady of the Miraculous Medal Church. (MAN)
Seadrift, TX, St. Patrick, c/o Port Lavaca, TX, Our Lady of the Gulf Church. (VIC)
Seagraves, TX, Gaines Co., St. Paul's, c/o Seminole, TX, St. James Church. (LUB)
Seama, NM, St. Anne, c/o Laguna, NM, St. Joseph Church. (GLP)
Seaside, OR, Clatsop Co., St. Peter the Fisherman, c/o Seaside, OR, Our Lady of Victory Church. (P)
Seat Pleasant, MD, St. Matthias, c/o Seat Pleasant, MD, St. Margaret Church. (WDC)
Seatonville, IL, Bureau Co., St. Gertrude, c/o Ladd, IL, St. Benedict's Church. (PEO)
Seattle, WA, Maronite Catholic Community, c/o Portland, OR, Saint Sharbel Church. (OLL)
Sebastian, TX, Willacy Co., St. Martin, c/o Lyford, TX, Prince of Peace Church. (BWN)
Seco Mines, TX, Maverick Co., Our Lady of Lourdes, c/o Eagle Pass, TX, Our Lady of Refuge Church. (SAT)
Sedillo, NM, Bernalillo Co., San Isidro, c/o Tijeras, NM, Holy Child Church. (SFE)
Seeley, CA, Holy Spirit, c/o Imperial, CA, St. Anthony of Padua Church. (SD)
Seeley Lake, MT, Missoula Co., Living Water Mission, c/o Bonner, MT, St. Ann Church. (HEL)
Segundo, CO, Las Animas Co., St. Ignatius, c/o Trinidad, CO, Most Holy Trinity, Trinidad Area Catholic Community (Trinidad Cluster) Church. (PBL)
Seiling, OK, Dewey Co., St. Thomas, c/o Okeene, OK, St. Anthony's Church. (OKL)
Seldovia, AK, St. James the Apostle, c/o Homer, AK, St. John the Baptist Church. (ANC)
Selinsgrove, PA, Snyder Co., Selinsgrove Center, c/o Selinsgrove, PA, St. Pius X Church. (HBG)
Selz, ND, Pierce Co., c/o Harvey, ND, St. Cecilia's Church. (FAR)
Sena, NM, San Miguel Co., c/o Villanueva, NM, Our Lady of Guadalupe Church. (SFE)
Seneca, OR, St. Charles, c/o John Day, OR, St. Elizabeth's Church. (BAK)
Seneca, SC, Oconee Co., St. Paul the Apostle, c/o Clemson, SC, St. Andrew Church. (CHR)
Servilleta, NM, Taos Co., c/o El Rito, NM, San Juan Nepomuceno Church. (SFE)
Seville-Creston, OH, Jesus Emmanuel, c/o Litchfield, OH, Our Lady Help of Christians Parish Church. (CLV)
Shafter, TX, Sgdo. Corazon de Jesus, c/o Presidio, TX, Santa Teresa de Jesus Church. (ELP)
Shamrock, TX, St. Patrick, c/o Wellington, TX, Our Mother of Mercy Church. (AMA)
Sharon, GA, Talifero Co., Purification, c/o Washington, GA, St. Joseph's Church. (ATL)
Sharon Springs, NY, St. Mary, c/o Cobleskill, NY, St. Vincent de Paul Church. (ALB)
Shasta Lake City, CA, Shasta Co., St. Michael, c/o Redding, CA, St. Joseph Church. (SAC)
Shattuck, OK, Ellis Co., Holy Name, c/o Woodward, OK, St. Peter's Church. (OKL)
Shawmut, MT, Wheatland Co., Blessed Sacrament, c/o Harlowton, MT, St. Joseph Church. (HEL)
Sheffield, TX, Pecos Co., Good Shepherd, c/o Ozona, TX, Our Lady of Perpetual Help Church. (SAN)
Shelby, IN, Lake Co., St. Theresa, c/o Lowell, IN, St. Edward Church. (GRY)
Sheldon, ND, St. Mary & Our Lady of the Scapular, c/o Enderlin, ND, St. Patrick's Church. (FAR)
Sheldon Point, AK, St. Peter's, c/o Alakanuk, AK, St. Ignatius Church. (FBK)
Shelton, NE, Sacred Heart, c/o Wood River, NE, St. Mary's Church. (GI)
Sheridan, AR, Grant Co., Holy Cross, c/o Fordyce, AR, Good Shepherd Church. (LR)
Sherman Station, ME, Penobscot Co., St. Joseph's Church, c/o Benedicta, ME, St. Benedict's Church. (PRT)
Sherwood, ND, Renville Co., St. James, c/o Mohall, ND, St. Jerome Church. (BIS)
Shickley, NE, Fillmore Co., St. Mary, c/o Geneva, NE, St. Joseph's Church. (LIN)
Shidler, OK, Osage Co., St. Ann, c/o Pawhuska, OK, Immaculate Conception Church. (TLS)
Shingletown, CA, Shasta Co., Mary Queen of Peace, c/o Anderson, CA, Sacred Heart Church. (SAC)
Shoreham, VT, Addison Co., St. Genevieve, c/o Orwell, VT, St. Paul Church. (BUR)
Shoshone-Tecopa, CA, Inyo Co., St. John the Baptist, c/o Lone Pine, CA, Santa Rosa Church. (FRS)
Shoshoni, WY, Fremont Co., St. Joseph, c/o Riverton, WY, St. Margaret's Church. (CHY)
Shubert, NE, Richardson Co., St. Ann's, c/o Dawson, NE, St. Mary's Church. (LIN)
Sidnaw, MI, Houghton Co., St. Francis Xavier, c/o Ewen, MI, Sacred Heart Church. (MAR)
Sieper, LA, St. Jude, c/o Glenmora, LA, St. Louis Church. (ALX)
Sierra Alta, PR, St. Lucy, c/o Yauco, PR, Holy Rossary Church. (PCE)
Sierra Blanca, TX, Our Lady of Miracles, c/o Van Horn, TX, Our Lady of Fatima Church. (ELP)
Sierra City, CA, Sierra Co., St. Thomas, c/o Downieville, CA, Immaculate Conception Church. (SAC)
Sigel, PA, Jefferson Co., St. Dominic, c/o Brookville, PA, Immaculate Conception Church. (E)
Sile, NM, Sandoval Co., c/o Pena Blanca, NM, Nuestra Senora De Guadalupe Church. (SFE)
Siletz, OR, Lincoln Co., St. Mary, c/o Newport, OR, Sacred Heart Parish Church. (P)
Silt, CO, Garfield Co., Sacred Heart, c/o Rifle, CO, St. Mary's Church. (DEN)
Silver Lake, PA, Susquehanna Co., St. Augustine, c/o Friendsville, PA, St. Joseph's Church. (SCR)
Silver Springs, NV, Our Lady of the Blessed Sacrament, c/o Fernley, NV, St. Robert Bellarmine Church. (RNO)
Silverton, CO, San Juan Co., St. Patrick, c/o Ouray, CO, St. Daniel the Prophet Church. (PBL)
Silverton, TX, Briscoe Co., Our Lady of Loreto, c/o Tulia, TX, Church of the Holy Spirit Church. (AMA)
Simpson, PA, Lackawanna Co., Holy Trinity, c/o Simpson, PA, St. Michael's Church. (SCR)
Slim Butte, SD, Shannon Co., Our Lady of Lourdes, c/o Pine Ridge, SD, Holy Rosary Church. (RC)
Smith Valley, NV, Lyon Co., St. John the Baptist, c/o Yerington, NV, Holy Family Church. (RNO)
Smith's Landing, NY, St. Mary's, c/o Catskill, NY, St. Patrick Church. (ALB)
Smithfield, NE, Gosper Co., St. John's, c/o Holdrege, NE, All Saints Church. (LIN)
Smiths Corners, MI, Hurenco Co., Holy Trinity, c/o Rapson, MI, St. Joseph Church. (SAG)
Smiths Creek, MI, St. Clair Co., Holy Rosary, c/o Columbus, MI, St. Philip Neri Church. (DET)
Sodus Point, NY, Wayne Co., St. Rose, c/o Sodus, NY, Epiphany Church. (ROC)
Soileau, LA, Allen Parish, St. Joseph, c/o Oberlin, LA, St. Joan of Arc Church. (LKC)
Solana Beach, CA, San Diego Co., St. Leo, c/o Solana Beach, CA, St. James Church. (SD)
Soldier Creek, SD, St. Rose, c/o Rosebud, SD, St. Bridget Church. (RC)
Soldier Creek, SD, Todd Co., St. Rose, c/o St. Francis, SD, St. Charles Church. (RC)
Soldier Creek, SD, Todd Co., St. Rose, c/o St. Francis, SD, Rosebud Reservation Church. (RC)
Soledad, CA, Monterey Co., Nuestra Senora de la Soledad, c/o Soledad, CA, Our Lady of Solitude Church. (MRY)
Solen, ND, Sioux Co., Sacred Heart, c/o Selfridge, ND, St. Philomena Church. (BIS)
Solomon's Gap, PA, Luzerne Co., St. Catherine, c/o Mountaintop, PA, St. Jude's Church. (SCR)
Somers, MT, St. Ann, c/o Bigfork, MT, St. Catherine Church. (HEL)
Sonoita, AZ, Santa Cruz Co., Our Lady of Angels, c/o Patagonia, AZ, St. Theresa Church. (TUC)
Sonsorol, FM, c/o Koror, FM, Sacred Heart Church. (CI)
South Byron, NY, Genesee Co., St. Michael, c/o [2] Batavia, NY, St. Joseph Church. (BUF)
South Centerville, NY, Orange Co., Holy Cross, c/o Middletown, NY, Our Lady of Mt. Carmel Church. (NY)
South Chatham, MA, Barnstable Co., Our Lady of Grace, c/o Chatham, MA, Holy Redeemer Church. (FR)
South Colton, NY, St. Lawrence Co., St. Paul, c/o Colton, NY, St. Patrick Church. (OG)
South Fork, CO, Rio Grande Co., Holy Family, c/o Del Norte, CO, Holy Name of Mary Church. (PBL)
South Hampton Twp., NJ, Vincentown Co., St. Jude, c/o Roebling, NJ, St. Nicholas Church. (PSC)
South Harpswell, ME, St. Mary-by-the-Sea, c/o Brunswick, ME, St. Charles Church. (PRT)
South Hartford, NY, St. Philip, c/o Fort Ann, NY, St. Ann Church. (ALB)
South Lee, MA, Berkshire Co., St. Francis of Assisi, c/o Lee, MA, St. Mary's Church. (SPR)
South Royalston, MA, Worcester Co., Our Lady Queen of Heaven, c/o Athol, MA, Our Lady Immaculate Church. (WOR)
South Royalton, VT, Windsor Co., St. Matthew, c/o Bethel, VT, St. Anthony Church. (BUR)
South Salem, NY, Westchester Co., S. Salem Presbyterian Church, c/o Katonah, NY, St. Mary of the

Assumption Church. (NY)
South Sterling, PA, Wayne Co., St. Mary Magdalene, c/o Gouldsboro, PA, St. Rita Church. (SCR)
South Strafford, VT, Orange Co., Our Lady of Light, c/o Bradford, VT, Our Lady of Perpetual Help Church. (BUR)
South Tucson, AZ, Pima Co., St. Nicholas Indian Center, c/o [2] Tucson, AZ, Blessed Kateri Tekakwitha Church. (TUC)
South Vallejo, CA, Solano Co., St. Louis Bertrand, c/o Vallejo, CA, St. Vincent Ferrer Church. (SAC)
South Wayne, WI, St. John, c/o Gratiot, WI, St. Joseph Church. (MAD)
Southton, TX, Bexar Co., St. Ann, c/o [71] San Antonio, TX, San Juan Capistrano Church. (SAT)
Southwest Oswego, NY, St. Joseph, c/o Hannibal, NY, Our Lady of the Rosary Church. (SY)
Spangler, PA, St. Jude Chapel, c/o Elmora, PA, St. Jude Church. (ALT)
Spanish Lake, LA, St. Anne, c/o Natchitoches, LA, Holy Cross Church. (ALX)
Sparta, NC, Alleghany Co., St. Frances of Rome, c/o Jefferson, NC, St. Francis of Assisi Church. (CHL)
Spartansburg, PA, Crawford Co., Our Lady of Victory, c/o Corry, PA, St. Elizabeth Church. (E)
Spelter, WV, Harrison Co., Holy Family, c/o Shinnston, WV, St. Ann's Church. (WH)
Spencer, OH, Jesus Our Savior, c/o Litchfield, OH, Our Lady Help of Christians Parish Church. (CLV)
Spencer Mountain, NC, St. Helen, c/o Belmont, NC, Queen of the Apostles Church. (CHL)
Spencerville, OH, Allen Co., St. Patrick, c/o Landeck, OH, St. John Baptist Church. (TOL)
Spiro, OK, Leflore Co., St. Elizabeth Seton, c/o Poteau, OK, Immaculate Conception Church. (TLS)
Split Rock, NY, St. Peter, c/o Onondaga Hill, NY, St. Michael Church. (SY)
Spofford Junction, TX, Kinney Co., St. Blaise, c/o Brackettville, TX, St. Mary Magdalen Church. (SAT)
Spotsylvania, VA, Spotsylvania Co., St. Matthew, c/o Chancellorsville, VA, St. Patrick's Church. (ARL)
Spring Creek, SD, Todd Co., St. Patrick, c/o St. Francis, SD, St. Charles Church. (RC)
Spring Creek, SD, Todd Co., St. Patrick, c/o St. Francis, SD, Rosebud Reservation Church. (RC)
Spring Lake, NJ, Monmouth Co., St. Margaret, c/o Spring Lake, NJ, St. Catharine Church. (TR)
Spring Lake Twp., MN, Scott Co., St. Catherine, c/o Cedar Lake, MN, St. Patrick Church. (STP)
Springfield, GA, St. Boniface, c/o Port Wentworth, GA, Our Lady of Lourdes Church. (SAV)
Springfield, MA, Center for South East Asian Apostolate, c/o [20] Springfield, MA, St. Thomas Aquinas Church. (SPR)
Springfield, SC, Orangeburg Co., St. Theresa, c/o Orangeburg, SC, Holy Trinity Church. (CHR)
Springfield Center, NY, Blessed Sacrament, c/o Cherry Valley, NY, St. Thomas the Apostle Church. (ALB)
Springhill, LA, Webster Parish, Sacred Heart, c/o Minden, LA, St. Paul Church. (SHP)
Spurlington, KY, Taylor Co., St. Frances de Sales, c/o Calvary, KY, Holy Name of Mary Church. (L)
Squaw Valley, CA, Fresno Co., St. Rita, c/o Orange Cove, CA, St. Isidore the Farmer Church. (FRS)
Staatsburg, NY, Dutchess Co., St. Paul, c/o Hyde Park, NY, Regina Coeli Church. (NY)
Staffordville, CT, Tolland Co., St. Joseph, c/o Stafford Springs, CT, St. Edward Church. (NOR)
Stamford, VT, Bennington Co., St. John Bosco, c/o Readsboro, VT, St. Joachim Church. (BUR)
Standish, NY, Clinton Co., St. Michael, c/o Lyon Mountain, NY, St. Bernard Church. (OG)
Stanfield, AZ, Pinal Co., St. Mary, c/o Casa Grande, AZ, St. Anthony Church. (TUC)
Stanton, KY, Powell Co., Our Lady of the Mountains, c/o Ravenna, KY, St. Elizabeth Church. (LEX)
Star Lake, NM, San Ignacio, c/o Crownpoint, NM, St. Paul Church. (GLP)
Starks, LA, St. Michael, c/o Vinton, LA, St. Joseph Church. (LKC)
Starkweather, ND, Ramsey Co., Assumption of the Blessed Virgin Mary, c/o Devils Lake, ND, St. Joseph's Church. (FAR)
Starr School, MT, Sacred Heart, c/o Browning, MT, Church of the Little Flower Church. (HEL)
Starrucca, PA, Wayne Co., St. Paul, c/o Jackson, PA, St. Martin of Tours Church. (SCR)
Staten Island, NY, St. Nicholas, c/o [230] Staten Island, NY, St. Teresa Church. (NY)
Steele, ND, Kidder Co., St. Francis de Sales, c/o Tappen, ND, St. Paul's Church. (FAR)
Steilacoom, WA, Pierce Co., Immaculate Conception, c/o [4] Tacoma, WA, St. John Bosco Church. (SEA)
Stephentown, NY, St. Joseph, c/o Berlin, NY, Sacred Heart Church. (ALB)
Stephentown, NY, St. Joseph's, c/o New Lebanon, NY, Immaculate Conception Church. (ALB)
Stepstone, KY, Pendleton Co., Immaculate Conception, c/o California, KY, Sts. Peter and Paul Church. (COV)
Sterling, CT, Windham Co., St. Joseph, c/o Moosup, CT, All-Hallows Church. (NOR)
Sterling, OK, Comanche Co., Our Lady of Perpetual Help, c/o Elgin, OK, St. Ann Church. (OKL)
Sterling City, TX, Sterling Co., St. Paschal Baylon, c/o Carlsbad, TX, St. Therese of the Child Jesus Church. (SAN)
Stevenson, WA, Skamania Co., Star of the Sea, c/o Camas, WA, St. Thomas Church. (SEA)
Stevinson, CA, Merced Co., St. Mary, c/o Hilmar, CA, Holy Rosary Church. (FRS)
Stigler, OK, Haskell Co., St. Joseph, c/o Poteau, OK, Immaculate Conception Church. (TLS)
Stinnett, TX, St. Ann's, c/o Borger, TX, St. John the Evangelist Church. (AMA)
Stockton, MO, Cedar Co., St. Peter the Apostle, c/o El Dorado Springs, MO, St. Elizabeth Church. (SPC)
Stockton, NJ, Hunterdon Co., St. Agnes, c/o Lambertville, NJ, St. John the Evangelist Church. (MET)
Stone City, IA, St. Joseph, c/o Anamosa, IA, St. Patrick's Church. (DUB)
Stoneham, CO, Morgan Co., St. John, c/o Brush, CO, St. Mary Church. (DEN)
Stonehan, TX, Grimes Co., St. Joseph, c/o Plantersville, TX, St. Mary Church. (GAL)
Stonewall, LA, DeSoto Parish, St. Ann, c/o [9] Shreveport, LA, St. Mary of the Pines Church. (SHP)
Stonyford, CA, Colusa Co., St. Mary of the Mountain, c/o Maxwell, CA, Sacred Heart Church. (SAC)
Story, WY, Sheridan Co., Our Lady of the Pines, c/o Sheridan, WY, Holy Name Church. (CHY)
Stowell, PA, Wyoming Co., St. Anthony, c/o Wyalusing, PA, St. Mary's Assumption Church. (SCR)
Strandquist, MN, Marshall Co., St. Edward the Confessor, c/o Stephen, MN, St. Stephen's Church. (CR)
Stratford, CA, Kings Co., St. Joseph, c/o Lemoore, CA, St. Peter Church. (FRS)
Stratton, ME, St. John, c/o Oquossoc, ME, Our Lady of the Lakes Church. (PRT)
Stratton, NE, Hitchcock Co., St. Joseph's, c/o Benkelman, NE, St. Joseph's Church. (LIN)
Stratton Mountain, VT, Windham Co., Chapel of the Snows, c/o Putney, VT, Our Lady of Mercy Church. (BUR)
Strawn, IL, Livingston Co., St. Rose, c/o Colfax, IL, St. Joseph's Church. (PEO)
String Prairie, TX, Bastrop Co., Assumption of the Blessed Virgin Mary, c/o Rockne, TX, Sacred Heart Church. (AUS)
Stroud, OK, Lincoln Co., St. Louis, c/o Chandler, OK, Our Lady of Sorrows Church. (OKL)
Stuart, FL, Martin Co., St. Andrew, c/o Stuart, FL, St. Joseph Church. (PMB)
Sturgeon Bay, WI, c/o Sturgeon Bay, WI, Corpus Christi Church. (GB)
Sturgeon Lake, MN, St. Isidore's, c/o Willow River, MN, St. Mary's Church. (DUL)
Sugar Island, MI, Chippewa Co., Sacred Heart, c/o Brimley, MI, St. Francis Xavier Church. (MAR)
Sugar Notch, PA, Luzerne Co., St. Charles Borromeo, c/o Sugar Notch, PA, Holy Family Church. (SCR)
Sugarloaf Shores, FL, Sugarloaf Firehouse, c/o Big Pine Key, FL, St. Peter Church. (MIA)
Sugarloaf U.S.A., ME, Richard H. Bell Memorial Chapel, c/o Oquossoc, ME, Our Lady of the Lakes Church. (PRT)
Sullivan City, TX, St. William, c/o La Joya, TX, Our Lady, Queen of Angels Church. (BWN)
Sulphur, LA, Calcasieu Parish, St. Peter Claver, c/o [3] Sulphur, LA, Our Lady of Prompt Succor Church. (LKC)
Sunapee, NH, Sullivan Co., St. Joachim, c/o Newport, NH, St. Patrick Church. (MAN)
Sunburst, MT, St. Thomas Aquinas, c/o Shelby, MT, St. William Church. (HEL)
Sundance, WY, Crook Co., St. Paul, c/o Newcastle, WY, Corpus Christi Church. (CHY)
Sundown, TX, Hockley Co., San Isidro, c/o Levelland, TX, St. Michael's Church. (LUB)
Sunray, TX, Moore Co., Christ the King, c/o Dumas, TX, SS. Peter and Paul Church. (AMA)
Sunrise Beach, TX, Burnet Co., Our Lady of the Lake, c/o Kingsland, TX, St. Charles Borromeo Church. (AUS)
Superior, MT, St. Mary Queen of Heaven, c/o Frenchtown, MT, St. John the Baptist Church. (HEL)
Superior, WY, Sweetwater Co., St. Vivian, c/o Rock Springs, WY, Our Lady of Sorrows Church. (CHY)
Superior, WY, St. Vivian, c/o Rock Springs, WY, Our Lady of Sorrows/Sts. Cyril & Methodius Church. (CHY)
Suquamish, WA, Kitsap Co., St. Peter, c/o Poulsbo, WA, St. Olaf Church. (SEA)
Surf City, NJ, Ocean Co., St. Thomas of Villanova, c/o Brant Beach, NJ, St. Francis of Assisi Church. (TR)
Susquehanna, PA, Snyder Co., Susquehanna University, c/o Selinsgrove, PA, St. Pius X Church. (HBG)
Susua, PR, La Resurreccion, c/o Sabana Grande, PR, Church of San Isidro Church. (MGZ)
Swartz, LA, St. Lawrence, c/o [3] Monroe, LA, Our Lady of Fatima Church. (SHP)
Sweet Lake, LA, St. Patrick's, c/o Big Lake, LA, St. Mary of the Lake Church. (LKC)
Sweet Springs, MO, Saline Co., Holy Family, c/o Marshall, MO, St. Peter Church. (JC)

T

Ta, FM, c/o Lukunor, FM, Sacred Heart Church. (CI)
Tabor, MN, Polk Co., Holy Trinity Catholic, c/o Warren, MN, SS. Peter and Paul Church. (CR)
Tabor, NE, Colfax Co., St. Mary, c/o Heun, NE, Holy Trinity Church. (OM)
Tache Indian Reservation, CA, Kings Co., St. Rosa, c/o Lemoore, CA, St. Peter Church. (FRS)
Taconite, MN, St. Joseph's, c/o Marble, MN, St. Mary's Church. (DUL)
Tahoka, TX, Lynn Co., St. Jude, c/o O'Donnell, TX, St. Pius X Church. (LUB)
Tajique, NM, Torrance Co., c/o Moriarty, NM, Estancia Valley Catholic Parish Church. (SFE)
Talihina, OK, Leflore Co., St. Catherine of Siena, c/o Hartshorne, OK, Holy Rosary Church. (TLS)
Tallaboa Alta, PR, Santa Ana St. Domingo, Carmen, c/o Penuelas, PR, St. Joseph Church. (PCE)
Talpa, NM, Taos Co., N.S. de San Juan de Los Lagos, c/o Ranchos De Taos, NM, San Francisco de Asis Church. (SFE)
Tamatam, FM, Maria Lourdes, c/o Tol, FM, Assumption of the Blessed Virgin Mary Church. (CI)
Tamatam, FM, Maria Lourdes, c/o Puluwat, FM, Santiago Church Church. (CI)
Tampa, FL, Hillsborough Co., St. Joseph Vietnamese Mission, c/o [3] Tampa, FL, Epiphany Church. (SP)
Tampa, KS, Marion Co., Holy Redeemer, c/o Marion, KS, Holy Family Church. (WCH)
Tanama, PR, Sagrado Corazon, c/o Adjuntas, PR, St. Joachim Church. (PCE)
Taos, NM, Taos Co., St. Jerome, c/o Taos, NM, Nuestra Senora De Guadalupe Church. (SFE)
Taos Pueblo, NM, c/o Taos, NM, Nuestra Senora De Guadalupe Church. (SFE)
Tapia, NM, San Miguel Co., c/o Moriarty, NM, Estancia Valley Catholic Parish Church. (SFE)
Tatum, NM, Our Lady of the Holy Rosary, c/o Lovington, NM, St. Thomas Aquinas Church. (LSC)
Tatum, TX, Rusk£anola Co., San Pedro the Fisherman, c/o Marshall, TX, St. Joseph Church. (TYL)
Taylorsville, KY, Spencer Co., All Saints Church, c/o Fairfield, KY, St. Michael Church. (L)
Taylorsville, NC, Alexander Co., Holy Trinity, c/o Lenoir, NC, St. Francis of Assisi Church. (CHL)
Teague, TX, Freestone Co., St. Mary, c/o Fairfield, TX, St. Bernard of Clairvaux Church. (TYL)
Tecolotito, NM, San Miguel Co., c/o Anton Chico, NM, San Jose Church. (SFE)
Tehama, CA, Tehama Co., St. Stanislaus, c/o Corning, CA, Immaculate Conception Church. (SAC)
Temple, PA, Berks Co., St. Anthony, c/o [5] Reading, PA, Holy Guardian Angels Church. (ALN)
Tenino, WA, Thurston Co., St. Peter, c/o Yelm, WA, St. Columban Church. (SEA)
Tennessee, IL, McDonough Co., Sacred Heart, c/o Macomb, IL, St. Paul's Church. (PEO)
Terlingua, TX, Brewster Co., St. Mary, c/o Alpine, TX, Our Lady of Peace Church. (ELP)
Terra Alta, WV, Preston Co., St. Edward, c/o Kingwood, WV, St. Sebastian's Church. (WH)
Terra Bella, CA, Blessed Miguel Agustin Pro, c/o Porterville, CA, St. Anne Church. (FRS)
Terrebonne, MN, Red Lake Co., St. Anthony, c/o Red Lake Falls, MN, St. Joseph's Church. (CR)
Terry, MT, Sacred Heart, c/o Miles City, MT, Sacred Heart Church. (GF)
Tesuque, NM, Sante Fe Co., Indian Pueblo, c/o [1] Santa Fe, NM, The Cathedral of San Francisco de Asis Church. (SFE)
Tesuque, NM, Santa Fe Co., San Ysidro, c/o [2] Santa Fe, NM, Our Lady of Guadalupe Church. (SFE)
Texico, NM, Curry Co., c/o Clovis, NM, Our Lady of Guadalupe Church. (SFE)
Texline, TX, Dallum Co., St. Mary's, c/o Dalhart, TX, St. Anthony's Church. (AMA)
Thatcher, AZ, Graham Co., Neuman Center, c/o Safford, AZ, St. Rose of Lima Church. (TUC)
Thayer, MO, Oregon Co., Sacred Heart, c/o West Plains, MO, St. Mary Church. (SPC)
Thedford, NE, Thomas Co., St. Thomas of Canterbury, c/o Mullen, NE, St. Mary's Church. (GI)
Theresa, NY, Jefferson Co., St. Theresa of Avila, c/o Evans Mills, NY, St. Mary Church. (OG)
Thomas, OK, Custer Co., Blessed Sacrament, c/o Weatherford, OK, St. Eugene's Church. (OKL)
Thomaston, GA, Upson Co., St. John the Baptist, c/o Griffin, GA, Sacred Heart Church. (ATL)
Thomaston, ME, Knox Co., St. James, c/o Rockland, ME, St. Bernard's Church. (PRT)
Thomasville, AL, Clarke Co., St. Joseph, c/o Grove Hill, AL, Sacred Heart Church. (MOB)

Thompson, ND, Grand Forks Co., St. Jude, c/o Reynolds, ND, Our Lady of Perpetual Help Church. (FAR)
Thorne Bay, AK, c/o Craig, AK, St. John by the Sea Church. (JUN)
Thornhurst, PA, Luzerne Co., St. Mark, c/o Bear Creek Township, PA, St. Elizabeth Church. (SCR)
Thornton, CA, San Joaquin Co., Mater Ecclesiae, c/o Lodi, CA, St. Anne Church. (STO)
Thornwell, LA, Jefferson Davis Parish, St. Francis of Assisi Chapel, c/o Lake Arthur, LA, Our Lady of the Lake Church. (LKC)
Three Rivers, CA, Tulare Co., St. Clair, c/o Woodlake, CA, St. Frances Cabrini Church. (FRS)
Three Rivers, NM, St. Patrick, c/o Mescalero, NM, St. Joseph Church. (LSC)
Three Rocks, CA, Fresno Co., Our Lady of Lourdes, c/o Mendota, CA, Our Lady of Guadalupe Church. (FRS)
Throop, PA, Lackawanna Co., St. Bridget, c/o Throop, PA, St. John the Baptist Church. (SCR)
Throop, PA, St. Mary, c/o Throop, PA, St. John the Baptist Church. (SCR)
Thunder Butte, SD, Ziebach Co., St. Luke, c/o Eagle Butte, SD, All Saints Church. (RC)
Thunder Butte, SD, Ziebach Co., St. Luke, c/o Eagle Butte, SD, Cheyenne River Reservation Church. (RC)
Tijeras, NM, San Antonito, c/o Tijeras, NM, Holy Child Church. (SFE)
Tilden, TX, McMullen Co., St. Joseph, c/o Charlotte, TX, St. Rose of Lima Church. (SAT)
Timpson, TX, Shelby Co., Epiphany, c/o Center, TX, St. Therese Church. (TYL)
Tinaja, NM, Colfax Co., c/o Springer, NM, St. Joseph Church. (SFE)
Tioga, PA, Tioga Co., St. Mary, c/o Mansfield, PA, Holy Child Church. (SCR)
Tionesta, PA, Forest Co., St. Anthony, c/o Tidioute, PA, St. John Church. (E)
Tipton, OK, Tillman Co., Sacred Heart, c/o Frederick, OK, St. Helen Church. (OKL)
Tishomingo, OK, Johnston Co., St. Anthony, c/o Sulphur, OK, St. Francis Xavier Church. (OKL)
Toa Alta, PR, Cristo de los Milagros, c/o [3] Toa Alta, PR, San Jose Church. (SJN)
Toa Alta, PR, La Resurreccion, c/o [5] Toa Alta, PR, N. Sra. de la Providencia Church. (SJN)
Toa Alta, PR, N. Sra. de Fatima, c/o [5] Toa Alta, PR, N. Sra. de la Providencia Church. (SJN)
Toa Alta, PR, Ntra. Sra. del Camino, c/o [3] Toa Alta, PR, San Jose Church. (SJN)
Toa Alta, PR, Nuestra Senora del Carmen, c/o [4] Toa Alta, PR, Nuestra Senora de la Medalla Milagrosa Church. (SJN)
Toa Alta, PR, Sagrada Familia, c/o [3] Toa Alta, PR, San Jose Church. (SJN)
Toa Alta, PR, Sagrado Corazon, c/o [3] Toa Alta, PR, San Jose Church. (SJN)
Toa Alta, PR, Sagrado Corazon de Jesus, c/o [4] Toa Alta, PR, Nuestra Senora de la Medalla Milagrosa Church. (SJN)
Toa Alta, PR, San Antonio, c/o [2] Toa Alta, PR, San Fernando Church. (SJN)
Toa Alta, PR, San Judas Tadeo, c/o [2] Toa Alta, PR, San Fernando Church. (SJN)
Toa Alta, PR, Santa Teresa, c/o [4] Toa Alta, PR, Nuestra Senora de la Medalla Milagrosa Church. (SJN)
Toa Alta, PR, Santa Teresita, c/o [3] Toa Alta, PR, San Jose Church. (SJN)
Toa Alta, PR, Virgen del Carmen, c/o [3] Toa Alta, PR, San Jose Church. (SJN)
Toa Baja, PR, Cristo Rey, c/o [2] Toa Baja, PR, Ntra. Sra. de la Candelaria Church. (SJN)
Toa Baja, PR, N. Sra. del Carmen, c/o [3] Toa Baja, PR, Espiritu Santo Church. (SJN)
Toa Baja, PR, Ntra. Sra. de Lourdes, c/o [1] Toa Baja, PR, Nuestra Senora de Covadonga Church. (SJN)
Toa Baja, PR, Ntra. Sra. del Carmen, c/o [4] Toa Baja, PR, Jose Obrero Church. (SJN)
Toa Baja, PR, San Martin de Porres, c/o [1] Toa Baja, PR, Nuestra Senora de Covadonga Church. (SJN)
Toa Baja, PR, San Martin de Porres, c/o [4] Toa Baja, PR, Jose Obrero Church. (SJN)
Toa Baja, PR, Santa Maria, c/o [2] Toa Baja, PR, Ntra. Sra. de la Candelaria Church. (SJN)
Toa Baja, PR, Santisima Trinidad, c/o [2] Toa Baja, PR, Ntra. Sra. de la Candelaria Church. (SJN)
Tobias, NE, Saline Co., St. Joseph's, c/o Wilber, NE, St. Wenceslaus Church. (LIN)
Tohono O'Odham, AZ, St. Lucy, Paloma Ranch, c/o Gila Bend, AZ, St. Michael Church. (PHX)
Tok, AK, Holy Rosary, c/o Delta Junction, AK, Our Lady of Sorrows Church. (FBK)
Tokio, ND, Benson Co., Christ the King, c/o Fort Totten, ND, Seven Dolors Church. (FAR)
Tokio, ND, Christ the King, c/o Fort Totten Reservation, ND, (Sioux Indians) Church. (FAR)
Tolna, ND, Nelson Co., St. Joseph, c/o Lakota, ND, St. Mary's Church. (FAR)
Tompkinsville, KY, Monroe Co., Christ the King, c/o Edmonton, KY, Christ the Healer Church. (L)
Tonopah, NV, Our Lady of Guadalupe, c/o Tonopah, NV, St. Patrick Church. (LAV)
Tonyville, CA, St. Anthony, c/o Lindsay, CA, Sacred Heart Church. (FRS)
Tornillo, TX, Santa Rita, c/o Fabens, TX, Our Lady of Guadalupe Church. (ELP)
Torrance, CA, Los Angeles Co., St. Joseph, c/o Torrance, CA, Nativity Church. (LA)
Torreon, NM, Torrance Co., c/o Mountainair, NM, St. Alice Church. (SFE)
Torrey, UT, Wayne Co., St. Anthony of the Desert, c/o Richfield, UT, St. Elizabeth's Church. (SLC)
Toston, MT, Broadwater Co., Immaculate Conception, c/o Townsend, MT, Holy Cross Church. (HEL)
Touhy, NE, Saunders Co., St. Vitus, c/o Weston, NE, St. John Nepomucene Church. (LIN)
Toulon, IL, Stark Co., St. John, c/o Wyoming, IL, St. Dominic's Church. (PEO)
Townsend, TN, Blount Co., St. Francis of Assisi, c/o Alcoa, TN, Our Lady of Fatima Church. (KNX)
Townshend, VT, Windham Co., Our Lady of the Valley, c/o Putney, VT, Our Lady of Mercy Church. (BUR)
Toyah, TX, St. Emily, c/o Pecos, TX, St. Catherine Church. (ELP)
Trail City, SD, Corson Co., Holy Rosary, c/o Timber Lake, SD, Holy Cross Church. (RC)
Trampas, NM, Taos Co., San Jose de Gracia, c/o Chimayo, NM, Holy Family Church. (SFE)
Trapper Creek, AK, St. Philip Benizi, c/o Talkeetna, AK, St. Bernard Church. (ANC)
Traver, CA, Tulare Co., St. John the Baptist Educational Center, c/o Kingsburg, CA, Holy Family Church. (FRS)
Tremonton, UT, Box Elder Co., Santa Ana, c/o Brigham City, UT, St. Henry Church. (SLC)
Trenton, MO, Mercer Co., Immaculate Heart of Mary Church, c/o Trenton, MO, St. Joseph's Church. (KC)
Trenton, ND, Williams Co., St. John the Baptist, c/o Williston, ND, St. Joseph Church. (BIS)
Tres de Jayuya, PR, Santa Teresita, c/o Adjuntas, PR, St. Joachim Church. (PCE)
Tres Piedras, NM, Taos Co., c/o El Rito, NM, San Juan Nepomuceno Church. (SFE)
Triadelphia, WV, Ohio Co., Our Lady of Seven Dolors, c/o [11] Wheeling, WV, St. Vincent de Paul's Church. (WH)
Trichel, LA, St. Joseph, c/o Campti, LA, Nativity of The Blessed Virgin Mary Church. (ALX)
Trinchera, CO, Las Animas Co., Sacred Heart, c/o Trinidad, CO, Most Holy Trinity, Trinidad Area Catholic Community (Trinidad Cluster) Church. (PBL)
Trinidad, CA, Holy Trinity, c/o McKinleyville, CA, Christ the King Church. (SR)
Trout Lake, MI, Chippewa Co., St. Mary, c/o Rudyard, MI, St. Joseph Church. (MAR)
Troy, MT, Immaculate Conception, c/o Libby, MT, St. Joseph Church. (HEL)
Troy, NY, Rensselaer Co., Hallmark Nursing Home, c/o [8] Troy, NY, St. Michael the Archangel Church. (ALB)
Troy, PA, Bradford Co., St. John Nepomucene, c/o Canton, PA, St. Michael Church. (SCR)
Truchas, NM, Rio Arriba Co., Holy Rosary, c/o Chimayo, NM, Holy Family Church. (SFE)
Trujillo, CO, St. James, c/o Pagosa Springs, CO, Immaculate Heart of Mary Church. (PBL)
Trujillo, NM, San Miguel Co., San Isidro, c/o Las Vegas, NM, Our Lady of Sorrows Church Church. (SFE)
Trujillo Alto, PR, El Divino Pastor, c/o [5] Trujillo Alto, PR, San Judas Tadeo Church. (SJN)
Trujillo Alto, PR, La Inmaculada Concepcion, c/o [3] Trujillo Alto, PR, San Francisco de Asis Church. (SJN)
Trujillo Alto, PR, La Milagrosa, c/o [3] Trujillo Alto, PR, San Francisco de Asis Church. (SJN)
Trujillo Alto, PR, Ntra. Sra. del Carmen, c/o [5] Trujillo Alto, PR, San Judas Tadeo Church. (SJN)
Trujillo Alto, PR, San Jose de la Montana, c/o [3] Trujillo Alto, PR, San Francisco de Asis Church. (SJN)
Trujillo Creek, CO, Mount Carmel, c/o Aguilar, CO, St. Anthony Church. (PBL)
Truman, WI, Immaculate Conception, c/o Belmont, WI, St. Philomena Church. (MAD)
Truro, MA, Barnstable Co., Sacred Heart, c/o Wellfleet, MA, Our Lady of Lourdes Church. (FR)
Tsaile, AZ, St. Ann, c/o Lukachukai, AZ, St. Isabel Mission for Navajo Indians Church. (GLP)
Tsis, FM, c/o Fefan, FM, Sacred Heart Church. (CI)
Tucson, AZ, Cristo Rey, c/o [2] Tucson, AZ, Blessed Kateri Tekakwitha Church. (TUC)
Tucson, AZ, Pima Co., Our Lady of Guadalupe, c/o [21] Tucson, AZ, Santa Cruz Church. (TUC)
Tucson, AZ, San Ignacio, c/o [2] Tucson, AZ, Blessed Kateri Tekakwitha Church. (TUC)
Tucson, AZ, Pima Co., Santa Catalina, c/o [18] Tucson, AZ, Saint Odilia Church. (TUC)
Tucson, AZ, Pima Co., Santa Rosa, c/o [2] Tucson, AZ, Blessed Kateri Tekakwitha Church. (TUC)
Tucson, AZ, Pima Co., Santa Rosa, c/o [3] Tucson, AZ, Holy Family Church. (TUC)
Tucson, AZ, Pima Co., St. Anthony's Catholic Instruction Center and Capilla, c/o [21] Tucson, AZ, Santa Cruz Church. (TUC)
Tucson, AZ, St. Mary of the Desert, c/o [6] Tucson, AZ, Our Lady of Fatima Church. (TUC)
Tulalip, WA, Snohomish Co., Tulalip Indian Reservation, St. Anne, c/o Marysville, WA, St. Mary's Church. (SEA)
Tule Indian Reservation, CA, Tulare Co., Mater Dolorosa, c/o Porterville, CA, St. Anne Church. (FRS)
Tullytown, PA, Bucks Co., Sacred Heart of Jesus, c/o Bristol, PA, St. Ann Church. (PH)
Tunica, MS, Tunica Co., St. Anthony of Padua, c/o Walls, MS, Sacred Heart Church. (JKS)
Tuolumne, CA, Tuolumne Co., St. Joseph, c/o Twain Harte, CA, All Saints Church. (STO)
Turquillo, NM, Mora Co., c/o Mora, NM, St. Gertrude Church. (SFE)
Turtle Lake, ND, McLean Co., St. Catherine, c/o Underwood, ND, St. Bonaventure Church. (BIS)
Tuscaloosa, AL, Tuscaloosa Co., St. John, c/o Tuscaloosa, AL, Holy Spirit Church. (BIR)
Tuscon, AZ, Pima Co., San Martin, c/o [2] Tucson, AZ, Blessed Kateri Tekakwitha Church. (TUC)
Twin Bridges, MT, Jefferson Co., Notre Dame, c/o Whitehall, MT, St. Teresa Church. (HEL)
Twin Buttes, ND, Dunn Co., St. Joseph, c/o Mandaree, ND, St. Anthony Church. (BIS)
Twin Sisters, TX, Blanco Co., Our Lady Help of Christians, c/o Blanco, TX, St. Ferdinand's Church. (AUS)
Twin Valley, MN, Norman Co., St. William, c/o [1] Crookston, MN, Cathedral of the Immaculate Conception Church. (CR)
Twin Valley, MN, Norman Co., St.William, c/o Ada, MN, St. Joseph's Church. (CR)
Two Inlets, MN, c/o Park Rapids, MN, St. Peter's Church. (CR)
Tyler, TX, Smith Co., Our Lady of Guadalupe, c/o [1] Tyler, TX, Cathedral of the Immaculate Conception Church. (TYL)
Tylertown, MS, Walthall Co., St. Paul the Apostle, c/o Columbia, MS, Most Holy Trinity Church. (BLX)
Tynan, TX, Bee Co., St. Francis Xavier, c/o Skidmore, TX, Immaculate Conception Church. (CC)

U

Uhland, TX, Hays Co., St. Michael's, c/o San Marcos, TX, St. John the Evangelist Church. (AUS)
Ulster, PA, Bradford Co., Immaculate Conception, c/o Towanda, PA, SS. Peter and Paul Church. (SCR)
Ulupalakua, HI, St. James the Less, c/o Kula, HI, Our Lady Queen of the Angels Church. (HON)
Unadilla, NY, Otsego Co., St. Ambrose, c/o Sidney, NY, Sacred Heart Church. (ALB)
Unalaska, AK, St. Christopher, c/o Dillingham, AK, Holy Rosary Church. (ANC)
Union, WV, Monroe Co., St. Andrew, c/o Ronceverte, WV, St. Catherine of Siena Church. (WH)
Union City, MI, Our Lady of Fatima, c/o Coldwater, MI, St. Charles Church. (KAL)
Union Springs, AL, Bullock Co., Bullock County Correctional Facility, c/o Eufaula, AL, Holy Redeemer Church. (MOB)
Union Springs, AL, Bullock Co., St. Piux X, c/o Eufaula, AL, Holy Redeemer Church. (MOB)
Unionville, MO, Putnam Co., St. Mary, c/o Milan, MO, St. Mary Church. (JC)
Unionville, NY, Orange Co., Our Lady of the Scapular, c/o Middletown, NY, Our Lady of Mt. Carmel Church. (NY)
Unity, OR, St. Joseph's, c/o [1] Baker, OR, Cathedral of St. Francis De Sales Church. (BAK)
Universal, IN, Vermillion Co., St. Joseph, c/o Clinton, IN, Sacred Heart Church. (IND)
Upper Black Eddy, PA, Bucks Co., St. Joseph, c/o Ottsville, PA, St. John the Baptist Church. (PH)
Upper Cutmeat, SD, Sacred Heart, c/o Parmelee, SD, St. Agnes Church. (RC)
Upper Cutmeat, SD, Todd Co., Sacred Heart, c/o St. Francis, SD, Rosebud Reservation Church. (RC)
Upper Little Caillou, LA, Our Lady of Prompt Succor, c/o Chauvin, LA, St. Joseph Church. (HT)
Upton, WY, Weston Co., St. Anthony, c/o Newcastle, WY, Corpus Christi Church. (CHY)
Urb. Santa Teresita, PR, Ponce Co., Santa Teresita, c/o [2] Ponce, PR, Christ the King Church. (PCE)
Uriah, AL, Monroe Co., Our Lady of Mount Carmel, c/o Monroeville, AL, Annunciation Church. (MOB)
Urich, MO, Henry Co., Holy Trinity, c/o Montrose, MO, Immaculate Conception Church. (KC)
Ute, IA, Monona Co., St. Mary's, c/o Charter Oak, IA, St. Boniface Church. (SC)
Utica, NE, Seward Co., St. Patrick's, c/o Beaver Crossing, NE, Sacred Heart Church. (LIN)
Utulei, AS, c/o [2] Pago Pago, AS, Co-Cathedral of St. Joseph the Worker Church. (SPP)

V

Vadito, NM, Taos Co., Nuestra Senora de los Dolores Mission, c/o Penasco, NM, San Antonio de Padua Church. (SFE)
Vado, NM, Dona Ana Co., San Pedro Del Cerro, c/o La Mesa, NM, San Jose Church. (LSC)
Vail, CO, Eagle Co., The Interfaith Chapel, c/o Minturn, CO, St. Patrick's Church. (DEN)
Valdez, NM, Taos Co., c/o Arroyo Seco, NM, Holy Trinity Church. (SFE)
Valentine, TX, Sacred Heart, c/o Van Horn, TX, Our Lady of Fatima Church. (ELP)
Valiant, OK, McCurtain Co., Good Shepherd, c/o Idabel, OK, St. Francis De Sales Church. (TLS)
Vallecitos, NM, Rio Arriba Co., c/o El Rito, NM, San Juan Nepomuceno Church. (SFE)
Valley Falls, NY, Our Lady of Good Counsel, c/o Schaghticoke, NY, St. John the Baptist Church. (ALB)
Van Alstyne, TX, Grayson Co., Holy Family, c/o McKinney, TX, St. Michael Church. (DAL)
Van Buren, ME, Aroostock Co., St. Rose Chapel, c/o Van Buren, ME, St. Bruno - St. Remi Church. (PRT)
Van Buren, MO, Carter Co., St. George, c/o Piedmont, MO, St. Catherine of Siena Church. (SPC)
Vanceboro, ME, Guardian Angel, c/o Lincoln, ME, St. Mary Church. (PRT)
Vandalia, NY, Cattaraugus Co., St. John the Baptist, c/o Allegany, NY, St. Bonaventure Church. (BUF)
Vanderpool, TX, Bandera Co., St. Mary, c/o Sabinal, TX, St. Patrick's Church. (SAT)
Variadero, NM, San Miguel Co., Holy Family, c/o Las Vegas, NM, Our Lady of Sorrows Church Church. (SFE)
Veblen, SD, Marshall Co., St. Matthew, c/o Sisseton, SD, St. Catherine Church. (SFS)
Vegas Abajo, PR, La Milagrosa, c/o Adjuntas, PR, St. Joachim Church. (PCE)
Vegas Arriba, PR, Sta. Ana, c/o Adjuntas, PR, St. Joachim Church. (PCE)
Veguita, NM, Socorro Co., San Juan, c/o La Joya, NM, Our Lady of Sorrows Church. (SFE)
Velarde, NM, Rio Arriba Co., Nuestra Senora de Guadalupe, c/o Dixon, NM, St. Anthony Church. (SFE)
Venice, LA, Plaquemines Parish, St. Anthony, c/o Buras, LA, Our Lady of Good Harbor Church. (NO)
Verdigre, NE, Knox Co., St. William, c/o Verdigre, NE, St. Wenceslaus Church. (OM)
Verdunville, LA, Immaculate Conception, c/o Franklin, LA, St. Jules Church. (LAF)
Verona, ND, LaMoure Co., St. Raphael, c/o Oakes, ND, St. Charles Borromeo Church. (FAR)
Verona Beach, NY, Oneida Co., St. Mary, c/o North Bay, NY, St. John Church. (SY)
Versailles, MO, Morgan Co., St. Philip Benizi, c/o Laurie, MO, Shrine of St. Patrick Church. (JC)
Viburnum, MO, Iron Co., St. Philip Benizi, c/o Ironton, MO, Ste. Marie Du Lac Church. (SPC)
Victor, CO, Teller Co., St. Victor's, c/o Woodland Park, CO, Our Lady of the Woods Church. (COS)
Victoria, TX, Victoria Co., Holy Trinity, c/o [4] Victoria, TX, Our Lady of Sorrows Church. (VIC)
Vida, MT, St. Ann, c/o Wolf Point, MT, Immaculate Conception Church. (GF)
Vidrine, LA, Holy Spirit, c/o Mamou, LA, St. Ann Church. (LAF)
Vigil, CO, St. Isidore, c/o Trinidad, CO, Most Holy Trinity, Trinidad Area Catholic Community (Trinidad Cluster) Church. (PBL)
Villa del Carmen, PR, Ponce Co., San Martin de Porres, c/o [4] Ponce, PR, Our Lady of Mt. Carmel Church. (PCE)
Villard, MN, Pope Co., St. Bartholomew, c/o West Union, MN, St. Alexius Church. (SCL)
Vintondale, PA, SS. Timothy & Mark Chapel, c/o Twin Rocks, PA, SS. Timothy & Mark Church. (ALT)
Viola, IL, Mercer Co., St. John, c/o Matherville, IL, St. Anthony's Church Church. (PEO)
Virginia Beach, VA, Virginia Beach Co., Our Lady of Perpetual Help, c/o Williamsburg, VA, Ascension of Our Lord Church. (PSC)
Volcano, CA, Amador Co., St. Bernard, c/o Jackson, CA, St. Patrick's Church. (SAC)
Vredenburgh, AL, Monroe Co., St. Martin de Porres, c/o Monroeville, AL, Annunciation Church. (MOB)

W

Waco, TX, c/o [4] Waco, TX, St. John the Baptist Church. (AUS)
Wadena, IA, St. Joseph, c/o Elkader, IA, St. Joseph's Church. (DUB)
Wadesboro, NC, Sacred Heart, c/o Monroe, NC, Our Lady of Lourdes Church. (CHL)
Wadsworth, TX, Sacred Heart, c/o Bay City, TX, Holy Cross Church. (VIC)
Waelder, TX, Gonzales Co., St. Patrick, c/o Gonzales, TX, St. James Church. (SAT)
Wahneta, FL, Polk Co., Our Lady of Guadalupe, c/o Bartow, FL, St. Thomas Aquinas Church. (ORL)
Waiakoa, HI, Holy Ghost, c/o Kula, HI, Our Lady Queen of the Angels Church. (HON)
Waikapu, HI, St. Joseph, c/o Waihee, HI, St. Ann Church. (HON)
Waimea, HI, Sacred Hearts of Jesus & Mary, c/o Kekaha, HI, St. Theresa Church. (HON)
Waimea Bay, HI, SS. Peter and Paul, c/o Waialua, HI, St. Michael Church. (HON)
Wakefield, VA, Infant of Prague, c/o Franklin, VA, St. Jude Church. (RIC)
Wakita, OK, Grant Co., St. Mary's Assumption, c/o Medford, OK, St. Mary's Church. (OKL)
Wakpala, SD, Corson Co., St. Bede, c/o McLaughlin, SD, St. Bernard Church. (RC)
Wakpala, SD, Corson Co., St. Bede, c/o Standing Rock, SD, Standing Rock Reservation Church. (RC)
Walden, CO, Grand Co., St. Ignatius, c/o Kremmling, CO, St. Peter Church. (DEN)
Waldron, AR, Scott Co., St. Jude Thaddeus, c/o Mena, AR, St. Agnes Church. (LR)
Wales, MA, Hampden Co., St. Monica, c/o Brimfield, MA, St. Christopher's Church. (SPR)
Walhalla, SC, Oconee Co., St. Francis of Assisi, c/o Clemson, SC, St. Andrew Church. (CHR)
Walker, CA, Mono Co., Our Lady of the Valley, c/o Mammoth Lakes, CA, St. Joseph Church. (STO)
Walker, MN, Ah-Gwah-Ching State Nursing Home, c/o Duluth, MN, Indian Missions Church. (DUL)
Walker Valley, NY, Ulster Co., Our Lady of the Valley, c/o Pine Bush, NY, The Infant Saviour Church. (NY)
Wallace, KS, Wallace Co., St. Peter, c/o Sharon Springs, KS, Holy Ghost Church. (SAL)
Wallace, NC, Transfiguration, c/o Burgaw, NC, St. Joseph Church. (R)
Wallkill, NY, Ulster Co., St. Benedict, c/o Walden, NY, Most Precious Blood Church. (NY)
Wallowa, OR, St. Pius X, c/o Enterprise, OR, St. Katherine's Church. (BAK)
Walnut Ridge, AR, Lawrence Co., Immaculate Heart of Mary, c/o Engelberg, AR, St. John the Baptist Church. (LR)
Walpole, NH, Cheshire Co., St. Joseph, c/o North Walpole, NH, St. Peter Church. (MAN)
Wamsutter, WY, Sweetwater Co., Catholic Community, c/o Rock Springs, WY, Our Lady of Sorrows Church. (CHY)
Wamsutter, WY, St. Anthony, c/o Rock Springs, WY, Our Lady of Sorrows/Sts. Cyril & Methodius Church. (CHY)
Wanette, OK, Pottawatomie Co., St. Mary, c/o Konawa, OK, Sacred Heart Church. (OKL)
Warba, MN, St. Paul's, c/o Hill City, MN, St. John Church. (DUL)
Wardsboro, VT, Windham Co., Our Lady of Hope, c/o Putney, VT, Our Lady of Mercy Church. (BUR)
Warm Springs, GA, Meriwether Co., St. Elizabeth Seton, c/o LaGrange, GA, St. Peter's Church. (ATL)
Warm Springs, OR, Jefferson Co., Blessed Kateri Tekakwitha, c/o Madras, OR, St. Patrick's Church. (BAK)
Warner Springs, CA, San Diego Co., St. Francis, c/o Santa Ysabel, CA, Santa Ysabel Indian Mission Church. (SD)
Warren, AR, Bradley Co., St. Luke, c/o Monticello, AR, St. Mark Church. (LR)
Warren, NH, St. John Vianney, c/o Woodsville, NH, St. Joseph Church. (MAN)
Warrenton, NC, Warren Co., St. Joseph, c/o Henderson, NC, St. James the Greater Church. (R)
Warrenton, TX, Fayette Co., St. Martin's, c/o Fayetteville, TX, St. John's Church. (AUS)
Warrior, AL, Jefferson Co., St. Henry, c/o Gardendale, AL, St. Elizabeth Ann Seton Church. (BIR)
Washburn, ME, St. Catherine, c/o Caribou, ME, Holy Rosary Church. (PRT)
Washburn, ND, McLean Co., St. Edwin, c/o Wilton, ND, Sacred Heart Church. (BIS)
Washington, VA, Rappahannock Co., St. Peter, c/o Culpeper, VA, Precious Blood Church. (ARL)
Waskom, TX, Harrison Co., St. Lawrence Brindisi, c/o Jefferson, TX, Immaculate Conception Church. (TYL)
Wataga, IL, Knoxville Co., St. Aloysius, c/o Alexis, IL, St. Theresa's Church. (PEO)
Watauga, SD, Corson Co., St. Michael, c/o Lemmon, SD, St. Mary's Church. (RC)
Waterproof, LA, St. Francis of Assisi, c/o St. Joseph, LA, St. Joseph Church. (ALX)
Watonga, OK, Blaine Co., St. Rose of Lima, c/o Kingfisher, OK, SS. Peter and Paul Church. (OKL)
Watrous, NM, Mora Co., c/o Wagon Mound, NM, Santa Clara Church. (SFE)
Watson, MI, Allegan Co., Sacred Heart, c/o Dorr, MI, St. Stanislaus Church. (KAL)
Wauneta, NE, Chase Co., St. John's, c/o Imperial, NE, St. Patrick's Church. (LIN)
Waurika, OK, Jefferson Co., St. Thomas Aquinas, c/o Walters, OK, St. Patrick Church. (OKL)
Wayland, MO, Clark Co., St. Martha, c/o Kahoka, MO, St. Michael the Archangel Church. (JC)
Waynoka, OK, Woods Co., Our Mother of Mercy, c/o Alva, OK, Sacred Heart Church. (OKL)
Webbers Falls, OK, Muskogee Co., St. Joseph, c/o Sallisaw, OK, St. Francis Xavier Church. (TLS)
Weirs Beach, NH, Belknap, St. Helena, c/o Lakeport, NH, Our Lady of the Lakes Church. (MAN)
Welch, OK, Craig Co., St. Ann, c/o Miami, OK, Sacred Heart Church. (TLS)
Welches, OR, Clackamas Co., St. John the Evangelist, c/o Sandy, OR, St. Michael the Archangel Church. (P)
Weldona, CO, Morgan Co., St. Francis of Assisi, c/o Fort Morgan, CO, St. Helena Church. (DEN)
Wellfleet, NE, Lincoln Co., St. William's, c/o Curtis, NE, St. James Church. (LIN)
Wells, NV, St. Thomas Aquinas, c/o Elko, NV, St. Joseph's Church. (RNO)
Wells, VT, Rutland Co., St. Paul, c/o Middletown Springs, VT, St. Anne Church. (BUR)
Wells River, VT, Orange Co., St. Eugene, c/o Bradford, VT, Our Lady of Perpetual Help Church. (BUR)
Wellton, AZ, Yuma Co., St. Joseph the Worker, c/o Yuma, AZ, Immaculate Conception Church. (TUC)
Wenden, AZ, St. John the Baptist, c/o Parker, AZ, Sacred Heart Church. (TUC)
Wendover, UT, Tooele Co., San Felipe, c/o Tooele, UT, St. Marguerite's Church. (SLC)
Wesby, MT, St. Elizabeth, c/o Plentywood, MT, St. Joseph's Church. (GF)
Weslaco, TX, St. Jude Chapel, c/o Weslaco, TX, San Martin de Porres Church. (BWN)
West Alton, MO, St. Charles Co., Immaculate Conception, c/o Portage Des Sioux, MO, St. Francis Church. (STL)
West Bangor, NY, Franklin Co., St. Edward, c/o North Bangor, NY, St. Augustine Church. (OG)
West Barnstable, MA, Barnstable Co., Our Lady of Hope, c/o Centerville, MA, Our Lady of Victory Church. (FR)
West Castleton, VT, Rutland Co., St. Matthew of Avalon, c/o Fair Haven, VT, Our Lady of Seven Dolors Church. (BUR)
West Charleston, VT, Orleans Co., St. Benedict Labre, c/o Derby Line, VT, St. Edward Church. (BUR)
West Columbia, TX, Brazoria Co., St. John the Apostle, c/o Sweeny, TX, Our Lady of Perpetual Help Church. (GAL)
West Covina, CA, St. Christopher Korean Catholic Community, c/o West Covina, CA, St. Christopher Church. (LA)
West Forks, ME, SS. Philip & James, c/o Bingham, ME, St. Peter's Church. (PRT)
West Gilgo Beach, NY, Suffolk Co., c/o Babylon, NY, St. Joseph's Church. (RVC)
West Glacier, MT, Flathead Co., c/o Columbia Falls, MT, St. Richard Church. (HEL)
West Haven, CT, Our Lady of Mt. Carmel Chapel, c/o [5] West Haven, CT, St. Paul's Church. (HRT)
West Mount Vernon, AL, Mobile Co., St. Theresa, c/o Chastang, AL, St. Peter the Apostle Church. (MOB)
West Pawlet, VT, Rutland Co., St. Frances Cabrini, c/o Middletown Springs, VT, St. Anne Church. (BUR)
West Peru, NY, Clinton Co., St. Patrick, c/o Peru, NY, St. Augustine Church. (OG)
West Point, CA, Calaveras Co., Our Lady of Fatima, c/o San Andreas, CA, St. Andrew Church. (STO)
West Point, IL, Hancock Co., St. Mary, c/o Carthage, IL, Immaculate Conception Church. (PEO)
West Point, KY, Hardin Co., St. Patrick Church, c/o [2] Valley Station, KY, Our Lady Help of Christians Church. (L)
West Point, OH, Columbiana Co., St. Agatha, c/o Lisbon, OH, St. George Church. (Y)
West Ridge, IA, St. John the Baptist, c/o Waukon, IA, St. Patrick's Church. (DUB)
West Shokan, NY, Ulster Co., St. Augustine, c/o West Hurley-Woodstock, NY, St. John Church. (NY)
West Springfield, MA, Hampden Co., St. Ann, c/o [9] Springfield, MA, Our Lady of Mt. Carmel Church. (SPR)
West Wareham, MA, Plymouth Co., St. Anthony, c/o Wareham, MA, St. Patrick's Church. (FR)
Westfield, IN, Hamilton Co., St. Maria Goretti, c/o Carmel, IN, Our Lady of Mount Carmel Church. (LFT)
Westfield, PA, Tioga Co., St. Catherine, c/o Elkland, PA, St. Thomas the Apostle Church. (SCR)
Westfield, WI, Marquette Co., Good Shepherd, c/o Montello, WI, St. John the Baptist Church. (MAD)
Westhoff, TX, St. Aloysius, c/o Meyersville, TX, SS. Peter & Paul Church. (VIC)
Westhope, ND, Bottineau Co., St. Andrew, c/o Bottineau, ND, St. Mark's Church. (FAR)
Westminster, CO, Adams Co., Our Lady of Visitation, c/o Westminster, CO, Holy Trinity Church. (DEN)
Weston, CO, Las Animas Co., Our Lord of Esquipula, c/o Trinidad, CO, Most Holy Trinity, Trinidad Area Catholic Community (Trinidad Cluster) Church. (PBL)

Westover, MD, Somerset Co., St. Elizabeth, c/o Pocomoke City, MD, Holy Name of Jesus Church. (WIL)
Westport, WA, St. Paul, c/o Aberdeen, WA, St. Mary's Church. (SEA)
Westville, NY, Franklin Co., Our Lady of Fatima, c/o Constable, NY, St. Francis of Assisi Church. (OG)
Westway, TX, El Paso Co., Immaculate Heart of Mary, c/o Canutillo, TX, St. Patrick Church. (ELP)
Wetumpka, AL, Elmore Co., St. Mark's, c/o Millbrook, AL, St. Elizabeth Ann Seton Church. (MOB)
Wewahitchka, FL, Gulf Co., St. Lawrence, c/o Blountstown, FL, St. Francis of Assisi Church. (PT)
Wewoka, OK, Seminole Co., St. Joseph, c/o Konawa, OK, Sacred Heart Church. (OKL)
Wheatfields, AZ, Our Lady of the Lake, c/o Lukachukai, AZ, St. Isabel Mission for Navajo Indians Church. (GLP)
Wheatland, CA, Yuba Co., St. Daniel, c/o Lincoln, CA, St. Joseph Church. (SAC)
Wheatville, NY, Genesee Co., St. Patrick, c/o Oakfield, NY, St. Cecilia Church. (BUF)
Wheelwright, MA, Hardwick Co., St. Augustine, c/o Barre, MA, St. Joseph's Church. (WOR)
Whetstone, AZ, Cochise Co., Good Shepherd, c/o Sierra Vista, AZ, St. Andrew Church. (TUC)
White Church, MO, Howell Co., St. Joseph, c/o Willow Springs, MO, Sacred Heart Church. (SPC)
White Horse, SD, Dewey Co., St. Therese, c/o Eagle Butte, SD, All Saints Church. (RC)
White Horse, SD, Ziebach Co., St. Therese, c/o Eagle Butte, SD, Cheyenne River Reservation Church. (RC)
White Horse Beach, MA, St. Catherine's Chapel, c/o [2] Plymouth, MA, St. Bonaventure Church. (BO)
White Lake, NY, Sullivan Co., St. Anne, c/o Monticello, NY, St. Peter Church. (NY)
White River, SD, Mellette Co., St. Ignatius, c/o St. Francis, SD, Rosebud Reservation Church. (RC)
White Rock, NM, Los Alamos Co., c/o Los Alamos, NM, Immaculate Heart of Mary Church. (SFE)
White Shield, ND, McLean Co., Sacred Heart, c/o Mandaree, ND, St. Anthony Church. (BIS)
White Sulphur, KY, Scott Co., St. Francis de Sales, c/o Georgetown, KY, St. John's Church. (LEX)
Whitesboro, TX, Grayson Co., St. Francis of Assisi, c/o Sherman, TX, St. Mary Church. (DAL)
Whitesville, WV, Boone Co., St. Joseph the Worker, c/o Beckley, WV, St. Francis De Sales Church. (WH)
Whiteville, LA, Resurrection, c/o Morrow, LA, St. Peter Church. (LAF)
Whitewater, MT, St. John, c/o Malta, MT, St. Mary's Church. (GF)
Wibaux, MT, St. Peter, c/o Glendive, MT, Sacred Heart Church. (GF)
Wibaux, MT, St. Philip, c/o Glendive, MT, Sacred Heart Church. (GF)
Wichita Falls, TX, Wichita Co., The Assumption of Mary, c/o Wichita Falls, TX, Sacred Heart Church. (FWT)
Wiggins, CO, Morgan Co., Our Lady of Lourdes, c/o Roggen, CO, Sacred Heart Church. (DEN)
Wilburton, OK, Latimer Co., Sacred Heart, c/o Hartshorne, OK, Holy Rosary Church. (TLS)
Wildwood, FL, Sumter Co., St. Vincent de Paul Mission, c/o Bushnell, FL, St. Lawrence Church. (ORL)
Wilkes-Barre, PA, Luzerne Co., St. Francis of Assisi, c/o [2] Wilkes-Barre, PA, Blessed Sacrament Church. (SCR)
Wilkes-Barre, PA, Luzerne Co., St. John The Baptist, c/o [2] Wilkes-Barre, PA, Blessed Sacrament Church. (SCR)
Wilkes-Barre, PA, Luzerne Co., St. John the Evangelist, c/o [18] Wilkes-Barre, PA, Sacred Heart of Jesus Church. (SCR)
Wilkes-Barre, PA, Luzerne Co., St. Joseph, c/o [14] Wilkes-Barre, PA, St. Mary's Church of the Immaculate Conception Church. (SCR)
Wilkeson, WA, Pierce Co., Our Lady of Lourdes, c/o Buckley, WA, St. Aloysius Church. (SEA)
Willacoochee, GA, Atkinson Co., Holy Family, c/o Douglas, GA, St. Paul's Church. (SAV)
Willard, NM, Torrance Co., c/o Mountainair, NM, St. Alice Church. (SFE)
Williams, CA, Colusa Co., Annunciation, c/o Maxwell, CA, Sacred Heart Church. (SAC)
Williams, MN, Lake of the Woods Co., St. Joseph, c/o Baudette, MN, Sacred Heart Church. (CR)
Williamsfield, IL, Knox Co., St. James, c/o Brimfield, IL, St. Joseph's Church. (PEO)
Williamstown, NY, St. Patrick, c/o Parish, NY, St. Ann Church. (SY)
Williamstown, PA, Dauphin Co., Sacred Heart of Jesus, c/o Lykens, PA, Our Lady Help of Christians Church. (HBG)
Williamstown, VT, Orange Co., St. Edward, c/o Graniteville, VT, St. Sylvester Church. (BUR)
Williamsville, MO, Wayne Co., Our Lady of Sorrows, c/o Piedmont, MO, St. Catherine of Siena Church. (SPC)
Willow, AK, St. Christopher, c/o Talkeetna, AK, St. Bernard Church. (ANC)
Willow City, ND, Bottineau Co., Notre Dame, c/o Rolette, ND, Sacred Heart Church. (FAR)
Wills Creek, OH, Coshocton Co., Our Lady of Lourdes, c/o Coshocton, OH, Sacred Heart Church. (COL)
Wills Point, TX, Van Zandt Co., St. Luke, c/o Canton, TX, St. Theresa Church. (TYL)
Wilmington, NY, Essex Co., St. Margaret, c/o Keene, NY, St. Brendan Church. (OG)
Wilson, TX, Lynn Co., Blessed Sacrament Church, c/o Slaton, TX, St. Joseph's Church. (LUB)
Wilton, MN, Beltrami Co., Sacred Heart, c/o Red Lake, MN, St. Mary's Mission Church Church. (CR)
Wimauma, FL, Our Lady of Guadalupe, c/o Ruskin, FL, St. Anne Church. (SP)
Wimauma, FL, Hillsborough Co., Our Lady of Guadalupe Catholic Mission, c/o Sun City Center, FL, Prince of Peace Church. (SP)
Wimbledon, ND, Barnes Co., c/o Sanborn, ND, Sacred Heart Church. (FAR)
Wind Gap, PA, Northampton Co., St. Joseph, c/o Pen Argyl, PA, St. Elizabeth of Hungary Church. (ALN)
Winder, GA, Barrow Co., St. Matthew, c/o Snellville, GA, St. Oliver Plunkett Church. (ATL)
Windsor, CO, Weld Co., Our Lady of the Valley, c/o Johnstown, CO, St. John the Baptist Church. (DEN)
Windsor, MO, Henry Co., St. Bartholomew, c/o Clinton, MO, Holy Rosary Church. (KC)
Wing, ND, Burleigh Co., St. Ignatius, c/o Wilton, ND, Sacred Heart Church. (BIS)
Wingdale, NY, Dutchess Co., Our Lady of Solace Mission, c/o Dover Plains, NY, St. Charles Borromeo Church. (NY)
Winifred, MT, Holy Family, c/o Lewistown, MT, St. Leo's Church. (GF)
Winn, ME, Sacred Heart, c/o Lincoln, ME, St. Mary Church. (PRT)
Winn, MI, Isabella Co., St. Leo, c/o Shepherd, MI, St. Vincent De Paul Church. (SAG)
Winnett, MT, St. Aloysius, c/o Roundup, MT, St. Benedict's Church. (GF)
Winnsboro, SC, Fairfield Co., St. Theresa, c/o [2] Columbia, SC, St. Joseph Church. (CHR)
Winnsboro, TX, Wood Co., St. Ann, c/o Sulphur Springs, TX, St. James Church. (TYL)
Winona, MS, Sacred Heart, c/o Lexington, MS, St. Thomas Church. (JKS)
Winston-Salem, NC, Forsyth Co., Our Lady of Fatima, c/o Winston-Salem, NC, Our Lady of Mercy Church. (CHL)
Winter Harbor, ME, St. Margaret, c/o Ellsworth, ME, St. Joseph's Church. (PRT)
Winter Park, CO, Grand Co., St. Bernard, c/o Grand Lake, CO, St. Anne Church. (DEN)
Winterhaven, CA, Imperial Co., St. Mary, c/o Winterhaven, CA, St. Thomas Church. (SD)
Wisdom, MT, Beaverhead Co., Our Lady of Wisdom, c/o Dillon, MT, St. Rose of Lima Church. (HEL)
Wishek, ND, McIntosh Co., St. Patrick, c/o Zeeland, ND, St. Andrew's Church. (FAR)
Wolbach, NE, St. Joseph's, c/o St. Libory, NE, St. Libory's Church. (GI)
Wolf Creek, MT, Lewis and Clark Co., Sacred Heart, c/o [3] Helena, MT, Our Lady of the Valley Church. (HEL)
Wolfforth, TX, Lubbock Co., St. Francis of Assisi, c/o Woodrow, TX, San Ramon Church. (LUB)
Wood, SD, Melette Co., Our Lady of Good Counsel, c/o White River, SD, St. Ignatius Church. (RC)
Wood, SD, Mellette Co., Our Lady of Good Counsel, c/o St. Francis, SD, Rosebud Reservation Church. (RC)
Woodville, CA, Tulare Co., St. Francis of Assisi, c/o Tipton, CA, St. John Church. (FRS)
Woodville, FL, Leon Co., St. Stephen the Protomartyr, c/o Medart, FL, St. Elizabeth Ann Seton Church. (PT)
Woodward, IA, Dallas Co., St. Ann, c/o Granger, IA, Assumption of the Blessed Virgin Mary Church. (DM)
Woodworth, LA, Mary, Mother of Jesus, c/o Lecompte, LA, St. Martin Church. (ALX)
Wounded Knee, SD, Shannon Co., Sacred Heart, c/o Manderson, SD, St. Agnes Church. (RC)
Wounded Knee, SD, Sacred Heart, c/o Porcupine, SD, Church of Christ the King Church. (RC)
Wright, WY, Campbell Co., Blessed Sacrament, c/o Gillette, WY, St. Matthew's Church. (CHY)
Wrightsville, PA, York Co., Mother of Holy Purity, c/o Columbia, PA, St. Peter Church. (HBG)
Wyanet, IL, Bureau Co., St. Margaret Mary, c/o Sheffield, IL, St. Patrick's Church. (PEO)
Wyola, MT, Blessed Kateri Tekakwitha, c/o Lodge Grass, MT, Our Lady of Loretto Church. (GF)

Y

Yacolt, WA, Clark Co., St. Joseph the Workman, c/o Battle Ground, WA, Sacred Heart Church. (SEA)
Yadkinville, NC, Yadkin Co., Cristo Rey Catholic Hispanic Center of Yadkin Valley, c/o Clemmons, NC, Holy Family Church. (CHL)
Yahuecas, PR, Virgen del Carmen, c/o Adjuntas, PR, St. Joachim Church. (PCE)
Yancy, TX, Medina Co., Immaculate Heart of Mary, c/o D'Hanis, TX, Holy Cross Church. (SAT)
Yarmouth Port, MA, Barnstable Co., Sacred Heart Chapel, c/o Hyannis, MA, St. Francis Xavier's Church. (FR)
Yarnell, AZ, Yavapai Co., St. Mary's, c/o Prescott, AZ, Sacred Heart Church. (PHX)
Yellowstone, WI, St. Michael, c/o Argyle, WI, St. Joseph Church. (MAD)
Yellowstone National Park, WY, Park Co., c/o Cody, WY, St. Anthony Church. (CHY)
Yellville, AR, Marion Co., St. Andrew's, c/o Mountain Home, AR, St. Peter the Fisherman Church. (LR)
Yolo, CA, Yolo Co., Our Lady of Guadalupe, c/o Woodland, CA, Holy Rosary Church. (SAC)
York Beach, ME, St. Mary, Star of the Sea, c/o York Harbor, ME, St. Christopher-by-the-Sea Church. (PRT)
Yorktown, TX, San Luis, c/o Yorktown, TX, Holy Cross Church. (VIC)
Youngsville, NM, Rio Arriba Co., c/o Abiquiu, NM, St. Thomas Apostle Church. (SFE)
Yuma, AZ, Yuma Co., Our Lady of Guadalupe, c/o Yuma, AZ, Immaculate Conception Church. (TUC)

Z

Zama, PR, Jayuya Co., Santa Cecila, c/o Jayuya, PR, Our Lady of Monserrate Church. (PCE)
Zamora, CA, Yolo Co., St. Agnes, c/o Knights Landing, CA, St. Paul Church. (SAC)
Zia, NM, Sandoval Co., c/o Jemez Pueblo, NM, San Diego Indian Missions Church. (SFE)
Zolfo Springs, FL, Hardee Co., San Alfonso Catholic Center, c/o Wauchula, FL, St. Michael Church. (VEN)
Zortman, MT, St. Joseph, c/o Hays, MT, St. Paul's Indian Mission Church. (GF)

Index for Religious Institutes of Men

Religious Institutes of Men

The Conference of Major Religious Superiors of Men, U.S.A., 8808 Cameron St., Silver Springs, MD 20910. Tel: 301-558-4030. Fax: 301-587-4575. An association of the major Superiors of religious communities and institutes for the purpose of promoting the spiritual and apostolic welfare of Priests and Brothers. Rev. Steven Henrich, O. S.C., Exec. Dir.; Bro. John Klein, F.M.S., Pres.; Bro. Stephen Glodek, S.M., Vice Pres.; Rev. Dennis D. Thiessen, S.D.S., Sec. & Treas.

[0100] (C.R.M.)—ADORNO FATHERS
(Clerics Regular Minor)

General Motherhouse: Via Alpi Apuane 1, Monte Sacro, Rome, Italy.

U.S. Foundation (1936): *St. Michael's Seminary,* 575 Darlington Ave., Ramsey, NJ 07446. Tel: 201-327-7375. Rev. Nicholas Capetola, C.R.M., Supr.

Priests 10.

Represented in the Archdiocese of Newark and in the Diocese of Charleston.

[0110] (S.M.A.)—SOCIETY OF AFRICAN MISSIONS
(Societas Missionum ad Afros)

Founded Dec. 8, 1856 with the approval of Pope Pius IX. A clerical society of apostolic life.

General Motherhouse: Via della Nocetta 111, 00164, Rome, Italy. Very Rev. Daniel Cardot, S.M.A.; Revs. Kiernan O'Reilly, S.M.A., Vicar Gen.; Lorenzo Mandirola, S.M.A., Gen. Councillor.

American Province (1941): 23 Bliss Ave., Tenafly, NJ 07670. Tel: 201-567-0450; 567-9085; Fax: 201-567-7156. Very Rev. Douglas B. Gilbert, S.M.A., Prov. Supr.; Revs. Ulick Bourke, S.M.A., Vice Prov.; Brendan Darcy, S.M.A., Prov. Councillor.

Legal Title: *Society of African Missions, Inc. N.J.*

Priests 45; Lay Missionary in temporary commitment 9; Lay Missionary in permanent commitment 1; Priest Associates 2.

Represented in the Archdioceses of Boston, Newark and Washington.

[0120] (C.F.A.)—ALEXIAN BROTHERS
(Congregatio Fratrum Cellitarum seu Alexianorum)

Generalate: Signal Mountain, TN 37377. Tel: 423-886-2969. Bros. Dominic Walsh, Supr. Gen.; Warren Longo, Asst. Gen., 3910 Ohio, St. Louis, MO 63118; Kamillus Bonn, Gen. Councillor, 52001 Aachen, Germany; Dominick Champagne, Gen. Councillor, B-2530 Boechout, Belgium.

General Motherhouse: Congregation of Alexian Brothers, Aachen, Germany.

United States Province (1866): 600 Alexian Way, Elk Grove Village, IL 60007. Tel: 847-640-7550; Fax: 847-981-5561. Bro. Edward Walsh, Prov. Supr. Prov. Councillors: Bros. Thomas Keusenkothen; Eugene Gizzi; Lawrence Krueger; Andrew Thome, Dir. Vocations; Bro. John Howard, Dir. of Novices, *Novitiate of Alexian Brothers* 6007 North Kenmore Ave., Chicago, IL 60660.

Professed Brothers 46; Novice Brothers 7.

Properties owned and or sponsored: General Hospitals 2; Life Care Centers 2; Novitiates 2; Nursing Homes 2; Residental AIDS Facility 2; Mobile Clinic (Davao, Philippines) 1.

Represented in the Archdioceses of Chicago, Milwaukee and St. Louis and in the Dioceses of Knoxville and San Jose. Also in Davao, Philippines.

[0130] (A.A.)—ASSUMPTIONISTS
(Augustinians of the Assumption)

General House: via San Pio V, 55, Rome, Italy, 00165. Very Rev. Claude Marechal, A.A., Supr. Gen.

Province of North America (1946): 330 Market St., Brighton, MA 02135. Tel: 617-783-0400. Very Rev. John L. Franck, A.A., Prov. Supr. Councillors: Revs. Donald Espinosa, A.A.; Richard Lamoureux, A.A.; Peter Precourt, A.A.; Stephen Goguen, A.A., Prov. Treas.

Priests 53; Brothers 22.

Parishes 3; Shrines 1; Colleges 1; Formation Centers 1; Novitiates 1; Residences 8.

Represented in the Archdioceses of Boston and New York and in the Dioceses of St. Petersburg, Nashville and Worcester. Also in Jerusalem, Kenya, Mexico, Russia and Canada.

[0140] (O.S.A.)—THE AUGUSTINIANS
(Ordo Fratrum Sancti Augustini)

Founded in 1244, first American foundation 1796.

Generalate: Via Paolo VI, 25, 00193, Rome, Italy. Most. Rev. Miguel Angel Orcasitas, O.S.A., Gen.

Province of St. Thomas of Villanova (1796): *Saint Augustine Friary,* 214 Ashwood Rd., P.O. Box 338, Villanova, PA 19085-0338. Tel: 610-527-3330. (The Brothers of the Order of Hermits of St. Augustine, a corporation in the state of Pennsylvania; Very Rev. John E. Deegan, O.S.A., Prior Prov.; Revs. John E. Rotelle, O.S.A., Prov. Sec.; Anthony P. Burrascano, O.S.A., Prov. Treas. Prov. Councillors: Revs. Arthur D. Johnson, O.S.A.; Kail C. Ellis, O.S.A.; Bro. Robert M. Thornton, O.S.A.; Revs. Richard D. Appicci, O.S.A.; James R. Flynn, O.S.A.; Peter M. Donohue, O.S.A.; Mr. David Piazza, Dir. Devel. Office; Revs. Joseph A. Jordan, O.S.A., Dir. Augustinian Guild; Richard D. Appicci, O.S.A., Dir. Mission Office; John E. Rotelle, O.S.A., Dir. Communications & Augustinian Press; Alfred E. Murphy, O.S.A., Archivist.

Legal Title: *The Brothers of the Order of Hermits of Saint Augustine.*

Priests 253; Students in Theology 6; Brothers 16; Permanent Deacon 1.

Parishes 34; (USA 30; Japan 4); Major Seminary 1; Colleges 1; Universities 1; Preparatory Schools and High Schools 3; Foreign Missions 2.

Represented in the Archdioceses of Boston, Miami, New York, Philadelphia and Washington and in the Dioceses of Albany, Orlando and Venice.

Province of Our Mother of Good Counsel (Order of St. Augustine) (1941): *Tolentine College & Center,* 20300 Governors Hwy., Olympia Fields, IL 60461-1081. Tel: 708-748-9500; Fax: 708-481-2090. Very Rev. David L. Brecht, O.S.A., Prior Prov.; Rev. G. Jerome Knies, O.S.A., Asst. Prov. & Personnel Dir.; Bros. Kenneth D. Mehn, O.S.A., Prov. Sec.; Bruce A. Jendraszak, O.S.A., Prov. Treas.; Rev. W. Timothy Cuny, O.S.A., Personnel Dir. & Vocation Dir.

Fathers 102; Bishops 2; Permanent Deacons 1; Professed Brothers 22; Professed Students 3.

Parishes 13; High Schools 4; Retreat Centers 1; Residences 9.

Represented in the Archdioceses of Chicago, Detroit, Milwaukee and St. Louis and in the Dioceses of Fort Worth, Joliet, Kalamazoo, Lansing and Tulsa. Also in Hamilton, Ontario, Canada, and Peru.

Province of St. Augustine: 1605 28th St., San Diego, CA 92102-1417. Tel: 619-235-0247; 282-2028. Very Rev. James A. Mott, O.S.A., Prov. Counselors: Revs. Patrick Keane, O.S.A.; James P. Clifford, O.S.A.; John D. Keller, O.S.A.; Gary E. Sanders, O.S.A.; Robert Gavotto, O.S.A., Sec.

Priests 30; Deacons 3; Brothers 4.

Parishes 7; High Schools 2; Retreat Centers 1; Low-Income Housing 2; Orphanages 1.

Legal Holdings or Titles: *St. Augustine High School,* San Diego, CA, *Monica House,* San Diego, CA, *Tierra del Sol,* Boulevard, CA, *Rita de Cascia House,* San Francisco, CA, *Rancho Camarillo,* Camarillo, CA, *Villanova Preparatory School,* Ojai, CA, *Austin House - House of Formation,* San Diego, CA.

Represented in the Archdioceses of Los Angeles and Portland (OR) and in the Dioceses of Oakland and San Diego.

Order of St. Augustine Province of St. Joseph: P.O. Box 333, King City, Ontario L0G 1K0. Canada.

U.S. Address: *Mother of Consolation Monastery,* 3103 Arlington Ave., Bronx, NY 10463. Tel: 718-548-0888. Revs. Cyril Smetana, O.S.A., Prov.; Leo Cameronosa, O.S.A.; Blaise Pelerine, O.S.A.; Lawrence MacQuarrie, O.S.A.; Othmar Mussmaecher, O.S.A.; S. K. Treu, O.S.A.; Arnold C. Diederich, O.S.A., Treas.

Priests 26; Professed Brothers 18; Seminarians 6.

Represented in the Archdiocese of New York.

Province of St. Thomas Villanova: *St. Augustine Preparatory School,* Richland, NJ 08350. Tel: 609-697-2600; Fax: 609-697-8389. Revs. Paul Galetto, O.S.A.; Stephen LaRosa, O.S.A.; James Cassidy, O.S.A.; Ronald Hamaday, O.S.A.; Cherubin F. Kerr, O.S.A.; Bro. Frank Cucinotta, O.S.A.

St. Augustine Preparatory School.

Represented in the Archdiocese Philadelphia and in the Diocese of Camden.

Region U.S.A. (1993): Christo Rey Church, 767 Ave. A, Beaumont, TX 77701. Tel: 409-835-7788. 767 Ave. A, Beaumont, TX 77701. Tel: 409-835-7788. Rev. Luis Urriza, O.S.A., Reg. Delegate.

Fathers 6; Parishes 5.

Represented in the Archdiocese of San Antonio and in the Diocese of Beaumont.

[0150] (O.A.R.)—ORDER OF THE AUGUSTINIAN RECOLLECTS
(Ordo Augustinianorum Recollectorum)

General Motherhouse: Rome, Italy. viale dell' Astronomia 27 (E.U.R.); Most Rev. Javier Pipaon, O.A.R., Prior Gen.

Province of St. Augustine (1944): *Augustinian Recollects,* 29 Ridgeway Ave., West Orange, NJ 07052. Tel: 973-731-0616; Fax: 973-731-1033. Very Rev. Francis E. Peluso, O.A.R., Prior Prov.; Revs. Gerard Cosgayon, O.A.R., 1st Councillor, Vicar of Prov.; Anthony Palos, O.A.R., 2nd Councillor; Bro. Michael Stechmann, O.A.R., 3rd Councillor & Prov. Sec.; Rev. Edward Fagan, O.A.R., 4th Councillor.

Priests 40; Brothers 10; Professed Clerics 9; Novices 4; Prepostulants 17.

Represented in the Archdioceses of Los Angeles, Newark and New York and in the Diocese of Orange.

Province of St. Nicholas of Tolentine (U.S.A. Delegation): 2800 Schurz Ave., Bronx, NY 10465. Tel: 718-823-0460. Rev. Jose Luis Duenas, O.A.R., Prov. Delegate.

Priests 24.

Represented in the Archdioceses of Newark & New York and the Diocese of El Paso and Las Cruces.

[0160] (C.R.S.P.)—CLERICS REGULAR OF ST. PAUL
(Barnabite Fathers)
(Ordo Clericorum Regularium Sancti Pauli)

Founded in Milan, Italy in 1533. First foundation in the United States in 1952 in Buffalo, NY.

Historical Motherhouse: *Church of St. Barnabas, Milan,* since 1545.

General Motherhouse: Via Giacomo Medici, 15, Rome, Italy. Rt. Rev. Luigi M. Villa, C.R.S.P., Supr. Gen.

North American Province: *Provincial Motherhouse,* 1023 Swann Rd., Youngstown, NY 14174. Tel: 716-754-7489. Very Rev. Julio M. Ciavaglia, C.R.S.P., Prov.

Legal Title: *Barnabite Fathers, Inc.*

Priests 16; Theology Students 2.

Fathers staff and serve: Parishes 4; Marian Shrine 1; Colleges 1; Philippine Mission 1; Spiritual Center 1.

Properties Owned: *Our Lady of Fatima Shrine and Barnabite Fathers Seminary,* Youngstown, NY *Barnabite Spiritual Center,* Bethlehem, PA.

Represented in the Dioceses of Allentown, Buffalo and San Diego. Also in Ontario, Canada and the Philippines.

[0170] (C.S.B.)—BASILIAN FATHERS
(Congregatio Presbyterorum a S. Basilio)

General Curia: *Cardinal Flahiff Basilian Centre,* 95 St. Joseph St., Toronto, Ont, M5S 3C2. Canada. Tel: 416-921-6674; Fax: 416-920-3413. Very Rev. Ronald P. Fabbro, C.S.B., Supr. General.

Casa San Basilio, 1910 W. Alabama, Houston, TX 77098. Tel: 713-522-1736. Rev. Alvin A. Sinasac, C.S.B., U.S. Gen. Councillor.

Eastern U.S.: 445 King's Hwy., Rochester, NY 14617. Tel: 716-266-1288.

[0180] (O.S.B.M.)—ORDER OF ST. BASIL THE GREAT
(Ordo Sancti Basilii Magni)

General Superior "Protoarchimandrita": Rt. Rev. Dionysius Lachovicz, O.S.B.M., Rome, Italy, 00153 (Aventino). Via San Giosafat 8.

American Province (1948): 31-12 30th St., Long Island City, NY 11106. Tel: 718-278-6622; Fax: 718-726-0686. Very Rev. Christopher Woytyna, O.S.B.M., Prov.

Fathers 24; Scholastics 8; Brothers 3; Novices 2.

Parishes 7; Community Houses 7; House of Studies; Novitiate; Monasteries 3; Retreat House; Library.

Represented in the Byzantine Rite Archdiocese of Philadelphia and in the Byzantine Rite Dioceses of Chicago, Parma, Passaic and Stamford.

[0190] (B.S.O.)—BASILIAN SALVATORIAN FATHERS

General Motherhouse: *Holy Savior Monastery, Saida,* Lebanon. Rt. Rev. Salim Ghazal, B.S.O., Supr. Gen.

American Headquarters: *Basilian Salvatorian Fathers,* 30 East St., Methuen, MA 01844. Rt. Rev. Gerasimos Murphy, B.S.O., J.C.D., Prov. Supr.; Revs. Simon Hage, B.S.O.; Lawrence Tumminelli, B.S.O.; John Jadaa, B.S.O.; Youssef Aziz, B.S.O.; Adib Badaoui, B.S.O.; George Dagher, B.S.O.; Eugene Mitchell, B.S.O., General Economos; Martin A. Hyatt, B.S.O.; Fuad Nasre, B.S.O., Local Supr.

Fathers in American Region 22.

Novitiate and House of Studies: *St. Basils Seminary,* Methuen, MA.

Parishes: Canada 4; U.S.A. 7.

Represented in the Archdioceses of Atlanta, Boston and Miami and in the Dioceses of Cleveland, Manchester, Newton and Norwich.

[0200] (O.S.B.)—BENEDICTINE MONKS

(Ordo Sancti Benedicti)

American Cassinese Congregation (Established by Pope Pius IX, Aug. 24, 1855)

Headquarters: *Newark Abbey,* 520 Dr. M.L. King Blvd., Newark, NJ 07102. Tel: 201-733-2822; Fax: 201-643-6922. Rt. Rev. Melvin J. Valvano, O.S.B., Abbot Pres.

President's Council: Rt. Rev. Douglas Nowicki, O.S.B., Saint Vincent Archabbey; Rt. Rev. Hugh Anderson, O.S.B., Saint Procopius Abbey; Revs. Claude Peifer, O.S.B., Saint Bede Abbey, Daniel Ward, O.S.B., Saint John Abbey, Roman Galiardi, O.S.B., Saint Procopius Abbey.

The Abbeys and Priories belonging to this Congregation are as follows:.

St. Vincent Archabbey: 300 Fraser Purchase Rd., Latrobe, PA 15650-2686. Tel: 412-532-6600. Rt. Rev. Douglas R. Nowicki, O.S.B., Archabbot; Rt. Rev. Paul R. Maher, O.S.B., Archabbot (Resigned); Rt. Rev. Egbert H. Donovan, O.S.B., Archabbot (Resigned); Most Rev. Rembert G. Weakland, O.S.B., Archbishop of Milwaukee.

Legal Title: *The Benedictine Society of Westmoreland County; Saint Vincent College Corporation; The Wimmer Corporation; The Saint Vincent Cemetery Corporation.*

Priests 147; Deacons 3; Solemn Professed Choir-Monks 24; Junior Professed Monks 12; Brothers 7; Choir Novices 4.

Represented in the Archdiocese of Baltimore and in the Dioceses of Altoona-Johnstown, Erie, Greensburg, Pittsburgh, Richmond and Savannah.

St. John's Abbey: P.O. Box 2015, Collegeville, MN 56321-2015. Tel: 320-363-2011; Fax: 320-363-3082.

Monastery founded in 1856 and raised to an Abbey in 1866; Rt. Rev. Timothy Kelly, O.S.B., Abbot; Very Rev. Geoffrey Fecht, O.S.B., Prior; Very Ven. Alan Reed, O.S.B., Subprior.

Fathers 148; Professed Brothers 63; Novices 3.

Abbeys 1; Dependent Priories 2; Parishes 19; Chaplaincies 11; Indian Mission Residences 1; Japanese Residences 2; School of Theology 1; University 1; High Schools 2; Novitiates 1.

Legal Holdings: *Saint John's Seminary; Saint John's University; Saint John's Preparatory School; Saint John's Abbey.*

Represented in the Archdiocese of St. Paul-Minneapolis and the Dioceses of Crookston, Duluth, Metuchen, New Ulm, St. Cloud and San Bernardino. Also in Austria, Switzerland, Japan, The Bahamas and Republic of China.

St. Benedict's Abbey: Atchison, KS 66002. Tel: 913-367-5341; Fax: 913-367-6230.

Founded in 1857 and raised to an Abbey in 1876; Rt. Rev. Barnabas Senecal, O.S.B., Abbot; Rt. Rev. Owen Purcell, O.S.B., Retired Abbot; Rt. Rev. Ralph Koehler, O.S.B., Retired Abbot; Very Revs. Michael Santa, O.S.B., Prior & Dir. Formation; Rev. Meinrad Miller, Subprior.

Bishops 1; Fathers 49; Brothers Professed 19; Novices 2.

Abbeys 1; Parishes 11; Missions 3; Foreign Missions 1; Chaplaincies 3; Colleges 1; High Schools 1.

Represented in the Archdiocese of Kansas City in Kansas and the Dioceses of Lansing and Springfield-Cape Girardeau. Also in Brazil.

St. Mary's Abbey: Delbarton, Morristown, NJ 07960. Tel: 201-538-3231.

Monastery founded in 1857 and raised to an Abbey in 1884; Rt. Rev. Gerard P. Lair, O.S.B., Abbot; Very Rev. Elias R. Lorenzo, O.S.B., Prior; Bro. Paul J. Diveny, O.S.B., Subprior.

Priests 42; Brothers 9.

Parishes 2; Schools Preparatory School 1.

Represented in the Archdiocese of Newark and in the Dioceses of Paterson and Trenton.

Newark Abbey: 528 Dr. Martin Luther King, Jr. Blvd., Newark, NJ 07102. Tel: 201-643-4800; Fax: 201-643-6922.

Priory founded 1857, Abbey in 1884; title transferred from Newark to Morristown, N.J. in 1956; became Abbey again in 1968 and known as Newark Abbey under the patronage of the Immaculate Conception; Rt. Rev. Melvin J. Valvano, O.S.B., Abbot; Very Revs. Mark M. Payne, O.S.B., Prior; Boniface J. Treanor, O.S.B., Subprior.

Priests 20; Brothers 7.

Legal Holding: *St. Benedict Preparatory School,* Newark, NJ.

Abbeys 1; Dependent Priories 1; Parishes 1; Preparatory (High) School 1.

Represented in the Archdioceses of Indianapolis and Newark.

Belmont Abbey: 100 Belmont-Mount Holly Rd., Belmont, NC 28012-1802. Tel: 704-825-6675; Fax: 704-825-6680.

Monastery founded in 1876, raised to an Abbey in 1884 and erected into an Abbey Nullius in 1910; Abbey Nullius suppressed January 1, 1977 and incorporated into Diocese of Charlotte; Rt. Rev. Oscar C. Burnett, O.S.B., Abbot; Rt. Rev. Walter A. Coggin, O.S.B., Retired Abbot; Very Rev. Christopher A. Kirchgessner, O.S.B., Prior & Novice Master; Very Rev. David G. Brown, O.S.B., Subprior.

Priests 18; Brothers 2.

Legal Title: *Southern Benedictine Society of North Carolina, Incorporated.*

Properties owned or sponsored: *Belmont Abbey College,* Belmont, NC.

St. Bernard Abbey (1891): Cullman, AL 35055. Tel: 205-734-8291; Fax: 205-734-2925. Rt. Rev. Cletus D. Meagher O.S.B., Abbot; Very Rev. Thomas O'Connor, O.S.B., Prior; Ven. Bro. Leo Borelli, O.S.B., Subprior.

Legal Title: *Benedictine Society of Alabama, Inc.*

Priests 24; Brothers 12.

Represented in the Archdiocese of Mobile and the Diocese of Birmingham.

St. Procopius Abbey: 5601 College Rd., Lisle, IL 60532. Tel: 630-969-6410; Fax: 630-969-6426.

Monastery founded in 1885 and raised to an Abbey in 1894; Rt. Rev. Hugh Anderson, O.S.B., Abbot; Very Ven. Columban Trojan, O.S.B., Prior; Revs. James Flint, O.S.B., Subprior; Kevin Sheeran, O.S.B., Procurator & Business Mgr.

Legal Holdings or Titles: *Benedictine University,* Lisle, IL, *Benet Academy,* Lisle, IL; *Benedictine Chinese Missions,* Lisle, IL; *Slav Mission,* Lisle, IL; *King of Martyrs Priory,* Fifield, WI; *St. Scholastica Mission House, Inc.,* Naperville, IL; *St. Procopius Abbey Endowment,* Lisle, IL.

Bishops 1; Priests 36; Brothers 14; Oblates 3.

Represented in the Archdiocese of Denver and in the Dioceses of Alexandria, Joliet and Superior. Also in Taiwan.

St. Gregory's Abbey: Shawnee, OK 74801. Tel: 405-878-5491; Fax: 405-878-5189.

Monastery founded in 1875 and raised to an Abbey in 1896.

Legal Title: *Benedictine Fathers of Sacred Heart Mission, Inc.*

Rt. Rev. Charles Massoth, O.S.B., Resigned Abbot; Rt. Rev. Philip Berning, O.S.B., Resigned; Rt. Rev. Adrian Vorderlandwehr, O.S.B., Resigned; Rt. Rev. Martin Lugo, O.S.B., Abbot; Very Rev. Patrick McCool, O.S.B., Prior; Rev. Joachim Spexarth, O.S.B., Subprior.

Properties owned or sponsored: *National Shrine of the Infant of Prague,* Prague, OK; *Mabee-Gerrer Museum of Art,* Shawnee, OK; *St. Gregory's University,* Shawnee, OK.

Ministries in 18 Parishes.

Priests 24; Brothers 10; Deacons 1.

Represented in the Archdioceses of Los Angeles and Oklahoma City and in the Diocese of Tulsa.

St. Leo Abbey: Saint Leo, FL 33574.

Founded in 1889 and raised to an Abbey in 1902; Rev. Simeon J. Thole, O.S.B., Apostolic Admin.

Legal Title: *Order of St. Benedict of Florida, Inc.*

Fathers 13; Brothers 20; Internal Oblates 1.

Represented in the Dioceses of Covington, Phoenix and St. Petersburg.

Assumption Abbey: P.O. Box A, Richardton, ND 58652. Tel: 701-974-3315.

Founded in 1893 and raised to an Abbey in 1903; Rt. Rev. Patrick Moore, O.S.B., Abbot; Rt. Rev. Lawrence Wagner, O.S.B., Resigned Abbot; Rt. Rev. Robert West, O.S.B., Resigned Abbot; Very Rev. Valerian Odermann, O.S.B., Prior; Rev. Thomas Wordekemper, O.S.B., Subprior; Bro. Alban Petesch, O.S.B., Formation Dir.

Priests 36; Brothers 23.

Properties owned or sponsored: Abbey; Dependent Priory; Parishes 9; Chaplaincies 4; Indian Mission.

Represented in the Dioceses of Bismarck, Fargo, Great Falls and Indianapolis. Also in Colombia.

St. Bede Abbey: Peru, IL 61354. Tel: 815-223-3140.

Monastery founded and raised to an Abbey in 1910; Rt. Rev. Marion Balsavich, O.S.B., Resigned Abbot; Rt. Rev. Roger Corpus, O.S.B., Abbot; Very Ven. Nathaniel Grossman, O.S.B., Prior; Very Rev. John Fitzgerald, O.S.B., Subprior.

Priests 29; Brothers 6.

Legal Title: *The Benedictine Society of Saint Bede.*

Properties owned or sponsored: Parishes 5.

Represented in the Archdiocese of Chicago and in the Diocese of Peoria.

St. Martin's Abbey: 5300 Pacific Ave. S.E., Lacey, WA 98503-1297.

Monastery founded in 1895 and raised to an Abbey in 1914; Rt. Rev. Neal G. Roth, O.S.B.; Rt. Rev. Conrad R. Rausch, O.S.B., Resigned Abbot; Rt. Rev. Adrian Parcher, O.S.B., Resigned Abbot; Very Revs. Urban C. Feucht, O.S.B., Prior; Nicholas B. Rausch, O.S.B., Subprior; Rev. Sean R. Malvey, O.S.B., Formation Dir.; Rev. Alfred J. Hulscher, O.S.B., Treasurer & Financial Dir.

Legal Holdings or Titles: *St. Martin's Abbey, St. Martin's College.*

Priests 29; Brothers 16.

Represented in the Archdioceses of Seattle and Portland in Oregon and in the Dioceses of Spokane and Yakima.

Holy Cross Abbey: P.O. Box 1510, Canon City, CO 81215-1510. Tel: 719-275-8631.

Founded in 1886 and raised to an Abbey in 1925; Revs. Kenneth Hein, O.S.B., Admin.; Ignatius Smith, O.S.B., Prior.

Fathers 18; Brothers 6; Oblates 2.

Parishes 4; Chaplaincies 2; Missions 1.

Represented in the Archdiocese of Denver and in Dioceses of Cheyenne, Colorado Springs and Pueblo.

St. Anselm Abbey: 100 St. Anselm Dr., Manchester, NH 03102-1310. Tel: 603-641-7000; Fax: 603-641-7116.

Monastery founded in 1889 and raised to an Abbey in 1927; Rt. Rev. Matthew K. Leavy, O.S.B., Abbot; Most Rev. Joseph J. Gerry, O.S.B., 3rd Abbot, Tenth Bishop of Portland, ME; Rt. Rev. Gerald F. McCarthy, O.S.B., 2nd Abbot, Resigned; Very Rev. John R. Fortin, O.S.B., Prior; Very Rev. Peter J. Guerin, O.S.B., Subprior.

Legal Title: *Order of Saint Benedict of New Hampshire.*

Bishops 1; Abbots 2; Fathers 31; Brothers 7.

Represented in the Archdiocese of San Francisco and the Diocese of Manchester.

St. Andrew Abbey: 10510 Buckeye Rd., Cleveland, OH 44104. Tel: 216-721-5300.

Founded in 1922 and raised to an Abbey in 1934; Rt. Rev. Roger Gries, O.S.B., Abbot; Very Rev. Joachim Pastirik, O.S.B., Prior; Ven. Bro. Peter Ancell, O.S.B., Subprior.

Legal Holdings or Titles: *Benedictine Order of Cleveland, Benedictine High School.*

Priests 26; Brothers 13; Simple Vows 1; Novices 1.

Abbeys 1; Parishes 2; High School; Chaplaincies 4.

Represented in the Dioceses of Cleveland and Great Falls-Billings.

St. Maur Priory: 4615 N. Michigan Rd., Indianapolis, IN 46228. Tel: 317-925-9095. Very Rev. Charles W. Henry, O.S.B., Prior.

Priests 2; Professed Brothers 4.

Represented in the Archdiocese of Indianapolis.

Holy Trinity Monastery: P.O. Box 990, Butler, PA 16003. Tel: 412-287-4461. Rt. Rev. Leo R. Schlosser, O.S.B., Hegumen.

Monks 12.

Represented in the Byzantine Archdiocese of Pittsburgh.

Benedictine Priory: P.O. Box 13577, 6502 Seawright Dr., Savannah, GA 31406. Tel: 912-356-3520; Fax: 912-356-3527.

Founded 1877, dependent priory of St. Vincent Archabbey, Latrobe, PA; Very Rev. Meinrad Lawson, O.S.B., Prior.

Priests 7; Brothers 3.

High Schools 1.

Represented in the Diocese of Savannah.

Woodside Priory: 302 Portola Rd., Portola Valley, CA 94028. Tel: 415-851-8220.

Founded in 1956, erected as Conventual Priory 1958, became a dependent Priory upon St. Anselm's Abbey, Manchester, NH, 1976; Very Rev. William J. Sullivan, O.S.B., Prior; Very Rev. Martin J. Mager, O.S.B., Subprior.

Priests 6; Brothers 2.

Legal Title: *Benedictine Fathers of the Priory, Inc.*

High Schools 1; Middle Schools 1.

Represented in the Archdiocese of San Francisco.

Benedictine Abadia de San Antonio Abad: P.O. Box 729, Humacao, PR 00792. Tel: 809-852-1616; 852-1766; Fax: 809-852-1920.

Monastery founded in 1947 and became an abbey in 1984; Rt. Rev. Oscar Rivera, O.S.B., Abbot; Rev. Eduardo Torrellas, O.S.B., Prior; Bro. Aristides Pacheco, Subprior.

Priests 10; Brothers 6.

Mary Mother of the Church Abbey: 12617 River

Rd., Richmond, VA 23233. Tel: 804-784-3508; Fax: 804-784-3508, Ext. 245.
Community founded in 1911 and became an Abbey in 1989; Rt. Rev. Benedict R. McDermott, O.S.B., Abbot; Very Rev. Theophile Brown, O.S.B., Prior & Novice Master.
Priests 9; Brothers 5.
Abbeys 1; Parishes 1; Chaplaincies 2; High Schools 1.
Legal Holdings: *Benedictine High School of Richmond; Mary Mother of the Church Abbey.*
Represented in the Diocese of Richmond.

Swiss-American Congregation
Founded by Pope Pius IX, 1870, and Pope Leo XIII, April 5, 1881.
The Abbeys and Priories belonging to this Federation are as follows:.

St. Meinrad Archabbey: St. Meinrad, IN 47577. Tel: 812-357-6611; Fax: 812-357-6551.
Founded 1854; raised to an Abbey in 1870; Rt. Rev. Lambert Reilly, O.S.B., Archabbot; Rt. Rev. Bonaventure Knaebel, O.S.B., Retired Archabbot; Very Rev. Martin Dusseau, O.S.B., Prior.
Archbishops 1; Priests 95; Brothers 31; Novices 8.
Parishes 19; Schools of Theology 1; Colleges 1; Chaplaincies 8.
Represented in the Archdioceses of Chicago, Cincinnati, Indianapolis, and Washington, and in the Dioceses of Baton Rouge, Evansville, Fargo, Hartford, Helena, Little Rock, Memphis, Owensboro, Sioux Falls and Venice.

Conception Abbey: Conception, MO 64433. Tel: 660-944-2211; Fax: 660-944-2800.
Founded December 8, 1873; Abbey April 5, 1881; Rt. Rev. Gregory Polan, O.S.B., Abbot; Rt. Rev. Anselm Coppersmith, O.S.B., Retired Abbot; Rt. Rev. James Jones, O.S.B., Retired Abbot; Very Rev. Kenneth Reichert, O.S.B., Prior; Bro. Michael Marcotte, O.S.B., Subprior.
Legal Title: *Conception Abbey, Inc.*
Archbishops 1; Fathers 55; Brothers 21.
Parishes 14; Seminary College 1; Chaplaincies 7.
Represented in the Archdiocese of Omaha and the Dioceses of Cheyenne, Des Moines, Dodge City, Kansas City-St. Joseph, Salina and Springfield-Cape Girardeau.

Mount Michael Abbey: 22520 Mount Michael Rd., Elkhorn, NE 68022-3400. Tel: 402-289-2541; Fax: 402-289-4539. Rt. Rev. Theodore Wolff, O.S.B., Abbot; Very Rev. Robert Halter, O.S.B., Prior; Bro. Jerome Kmiecik, Subprior.
Legal Holdings & Titles: *Benedictine Fathers, Inc.*; Mount Michael Benedictine High School, Elkhorn, NE; *Mt. Michael Foundation, Inc.*
Fathers 17; Brothers 9.
Monks serve & staff: Parishes 4.
Represented in the Archdiocese of Omaha and the Diocese of Pueblo.

Subiaco Abbey: Subiaco, AR 72865. Tel: 501-934-4295; Fax: 501-934-4328. Rt. Rev. Jerome Kodell, O.S.B., Abbot; Revs. David Bellinghausen, O.S.B., Prior; David McKillin, O.S.B., Subprior.
Legal Title: *Subiaco Abbey,* Subiaco, AR 72865.
Fathers 35; Perpetually Professed Brothers 29; Temporarily Professed Brothers 5.
Properties staffed or sponsored: Parishes 12; High School 1; Missions 1.
Represented in the Dioceses of Fort Worth and Little Rock. Also in Belize City-Belmopan.

St. Joseph Abbey: St. Benedict, LA 70457. Tel: 504-892-1800. Rt. Rev. Patrick Regan, O.S.B., Abbot; Very Rev. Gregory Boquet, O.S.B., Prior; Rev. Dominic Braud, O.S.B., Subprior.
Fathers 31; Brothers 17.
Legal Holdings: *St. Joseph Seminary College,* St. Benedict, LA.
Parishes 4; Novitiates 1; Seminary College 1.
Represented in the Archdiocese of New Orleans.

Mt. Angel Abbey: St. Benedict, OR 97373. Tel: 503-845-3030; Fax: 503-845-3594.
Founded on Oct. 30, 1882, from Engelberg in Switzerland and raised to an abbey on March 24, 1904; Rt. Rev. Joseph Wood, O.S.B., Abbot; Very Rev. Paul Thomas, O.S.B., Prior; Very Rev. Paschal Cheline, O.S.B., Subprior.
Legal Holdings or Titles: *Mt. Angel & Jerome, Ascension Priory,* Jerome, ID, *Our Lady of the Angels,* Cuernavaca, Morelos, Mexico.
Finally Professed Monks:: Priests 58; Brothers 26; Temporarily Professed Monks:; Brothers 8; Novices 9.

Marmion Abbey: 850 Butterfield Rd., Aurora, IL 60504. Tel: 630-897-7215.
Founded as Dependent Priory of St. Meinrad's Abbey, June 20, 1943; Abbey since March 21, 1947; Rt. Rev. Vincent de Paul Bataille, O.S.B., Abbot; Rt. Rev. Gerald Benkert, O.S.B., Abbot Emeritus; Rt. Rev. David J. Cyr, O.S.B., Abbot Emeritus; Very Rev. Kenneth Theisen, O.S.B., Prior; Ven. Bro. Anselm Mangano, O.S.B., Subprior.
Priests 33; Brothers 12.
Properties staffed or sponsored: Parishes 2; High Schools 2.
Represented in the Dioceses of Rockford and Sioux Falls. Also in Quetzaltenango, Guatemala.

St. Benedict's Abbey: Benet Lake, WI 53102. Tel: 414-396-4311.
Monastery founded in 1945 and raised to an Abbey in 1952; Rt. Rev. Leo Ryska, O.S.B., Abbot; Rt. Rev. Robert Schoofs, O.S.B., Abbot Resigned; Rt. Rev. Andrew Garber, O.S.B., Abbot Resigned; Very Rev. Edmund Boyce, O.S.B., Prior; Bro. Richard Aplington, O.S.B., Subprior.
Legal Title: *Benedictine Monks, Inc., St. Benedict's Home Missionary Society.*
Priests 13; Brothers 16.
Represented in the Archdiocese of Milwaukee. Also in Mexico.

Glastonbury Abbey: 16 Hull St., Hingham, MA 02043. Tel: 781-749-2155; Fax: 781-749-7236. Rt. Rev. Nicholas J. Morcone, O.S.B., Abbot.
Property owned: Lincoln School Apartments for the Elderly & Handicapped, Hingham, MA.
Monks in Solemn Vows 9; Monks in Simple Vows 2.
Represented in the Archdiocese of Boston.

Blue Cloud Abbey: Marvin, SD 57251-0098. Tel: 605-432-5528; Fax: 605-432-4754.
Monastery founded June 24, 1950; raised to a Priory August 5, 1952; raised to an Abbey March 21, 1954; Rt. Rev. Thomas Hillenbrand, O.S.B., Abbot. Retired Abbots: Rt. Rev. Alan Berndt, O.S.B.; Rt. Rev. Denis Quinkert, O.S.B.; Rev. George Lyon, O.S.B., Prior.
Legal Title: *Blue Cloud Abbey, Inc.*
Priests 25; Brothers 11.
Represented in the Dioceses of Sioux Falls. Also in Guatemala.

Corpus Christi Abbey: HCR 2, Box 6300, Sandia, TX 78383. Tel: 512-547-3257; Fax: 512-547-5184. Rt. Rev. Louis Hacker, O.S.B., Abbot; Very Rev. Michael De Leon, O.S.B., Prior.
Fathers 10; Professed Brothers 11.
Property owned: Benedictine Retreat Center, Sandia, TX.
Represented in the Diocese of Corpus Christi.

Prince Of Peace Abbey: 650 Benet Hill Rd., Oceanside, CA 92054. Tel: 760-430-1305; 430-1306. Rt. Rev. Charles Wright, O.S.B., Abbot; Rt. Rev. Claude Ehringer, O.S.B., Abbot (Retired); Very Rev. Basil Mattingly, Prior.
Fathers 11; Brothers 15; Postulants 2.

St. Benedict Abbey: 252 Still River Rd., P.O. Box 67, Still River-Harvard, MA 01467. Tel: 978-456-3221; Fax: 978-456-8181. Rt. Rev. Gabriel Gibbs, O.S.B., Abbot; Very Rev. Xavier Connelly, O.S.B., Prior.
Priests 8; Brothers 12; Oblates 1.
Represented in the Diocese of Worcester.

Congregation of St. Ottilien For Foreign Missions

St. Paul's Abbey: Newton, NJ 07860. Tel: 973-383-2470; Fax: 973-383-5782. (Benedictine Missionaries).
Monastery established March 15, 1924; elevated to an Abbey June 9, 1947; Very Rev. Joel P. Macul, O.S.B., Abbot; Rt. Rev. Justin E. Dzikowicz, O.S.B., Resigned Abbot; Rt. Rev. Augustine J. Hinches, O.S.B., Resigned Abbot; Rt. Rev. Charles V. Coriston, O.S.B., Resigned Abbot.
Solemnly professed monks 13 (11 priests).
Represented in the Diocese of Paterson.

Christ The King Priory - Benedictine Mission House: Schuyler, NE 68661. Tel: 402-352-2177; Fax: 402-352-2176. Revs. Germar Neubert, O.S.B., Prior; Volker Futter, O.S.B.; Herman Kornbrust, O.S.B.; Thomas Leitner, O.S.B.
Fathers 4; Brothers 6.
Represented in the Archdiocese of Omaha.

Congregation of The Annunciation

St. Andrew's Abbey: Valyermo, CA 93563. Tel: 805-944-2178. Rt. Rev. Francis Benedict, O.S.B., Abbot; Revs. Luke Dysinger, O.S.B., Prior; Simon O'Donnell, O.S.B., Subprior.
Monks solemn vows 16; Simple vows 4; Novices 2.
Represented in the Archdiocese of Los Angeles.

Houses Not In Congregations

Mount Saviour Monastery: (Elmira) Pine City, NY 14871. Tel: 607-734-1688; Fax: 607-734-1689.
Monastery founded in 1950, raised to Independent Priory 1957; Very Rev. Martin Boler, O.S.B., Prior; Rev. James Cronin, O.S.B., Subprior.
Professed Monks 16; Oblates 1.
Represented in the Diocese of Rochester.

Conventual Priory of St. Gabriel the Archangel (1953): 58 Priory Hill Rd., Weston, VT 05161. Tel: 802-824-5409; Fax: 802-824-3573. (Weston Priory of Benedictine Monks; Very Rev. Richard Iaquinto, O.S.B., Prior.
Monks 16.
Represented in the Diocese of Burlington.

Camaldolese Benedictine Congregation
(Congregatio Camaldulensis Ordinis Sancti Benedicti)

General Motherhouse: The Sacred Hermitage and Monastery of Camaldoli, Arezzo, Italy. Most Rev. Emanuele Bargellini, O.S.B.Cam., Prior Gen.

U.S. Foundation (1958): *New Camaldoli Hermitage,* New Camaldoli, Big Sur, CA 93920. Tel: 408-667-2456. Very Rev. Robert Hale, O.S.B.Cam., Prior.
Fathers 10; Professed Brothers 13.
Represented in the Dioceses of Manchester, Monterey and Oakland.

English Benedictine Congregation

St. Anselm's Abbey: 4501 S. Dakota Ave. N.E., Washington, DC 20017. Tel: 202-269-2300; Fax: 202-269-2312. Rt. Rev. Aidan Shea, O.S.B., Abbot.
Legal Title: *Benedictine Foundation at Washington DC.*
Solemnly Professed Monks 25.

Abbey of St. Gregory the Great: Cory's Ln., Portsmouth, RI 02871. Tel: 401-683-2000; Fax: 401-683-5888. Rt. Rev. Mark Serna, O.S.B., Abbot; Rt. Rev. Matthew Stark, O.S.B., Abbot Emeritus; Very Rev. Ambrose Wolverton, O.S.B., Prior.
Choir Religious 19.

Abbey of St. Mary and St. Louis: 500 S. Mason Rd., St. Louis, MO 63141-8500. Tel: 314-434-2557; Fax: 314-434-0795.
Founded as a dependent Priory 1955, granted independence 1973, raised to status of Abbey 1989; Rt. Rev. W. Thomas Frerking, O.S.B., Abbot.
Solemnly professed monks 17 (13 priests); Simply professed monks 2; Novices 2; Oblates 1.

Benedictines—Sylvestrine Congregation
(Monachorum Silvestrinorum, O.S.B.)

General Motherhouse: Rome, Italy. S. Stefano del Cacco 26; Rt. Rev. Andrew Pantaloni, O.S.B., Abbot Gen.

Foundations in U.S. (1910): Saint Benedict Priory, 2711 E. Drahner Rd., Oxford, MI 48370. Tel: 248-628-2249. Very Rev. Daniel Homan, O.S.B., Conventual Prior, *St. Sylvester Monastery,* 17320 Rosemont Rd., Detroit, MI 48219. Tel: 313-532-6064; *Holy Face Monastery,* 1697 State Hwy. S-3, Clifton, NJ 07012. Tel: 201-778-1177.
Brothers 6; Priests 9; Novices 1.
Represented in the Archdiocese of Detroit and in the Diocese of Paterson.

Olivetan Benedictines
(Congregatio Sanctae Mariae Montis Oliveti Ordinis Sancti Benedicti)

General Motherhouse: *The Archabbey of Monte Oliveto Maggiore,* Monte Oliveto, Siena, Italy. Most Rev. Michelangelo M. Tiribilli, O.S.B., Abbot Gen.

U.S. Foundations: *Holy Trinity Monastery,* P.O. Box 298, St. David, AZ 85630. Tel: 602-720-4642; 720-4902. Revs. Louis B. Hasenfuss, O.S.B., Prior; Alcuin Almasy, O.S.B.; Lawrence Fedor, O.S.B.; James Liprie, O.S.B.; Henri Capdeville O.S.B.; Alexander Mills O.S.B.; Bartolome Johnston O.S.B.
Solemnly Professed 12; Temporarily Professed 3; Novices 3.
Represented in the Diocese of Tucson.

Our Lady of Guadalupe Abbey: Pecos, NM 87552. Tel: 505-757-6415. Order of St. Benedict; Rt. Rev. Andrew J. Miles, O.S.B., Abbot; Rev. James Liprie, O.S.B., Supr.; Rev. Paul Meaden, O.S.B., Prior.
Priests 10; Brothers 6; Novices 1.
Represented in the Archdiocese of Santa Fe.

Benedictine Monastery of Hawaii: 67-290 Farrington Hwy., P.O. Box 490, Waialua, HI 96791. Tel: 808-637-7887; Fax: 808-637-8601. Rev. David Barfknecht, O.S.B., Supr.
Priests 3; Brothers 1; Postulants 1.

Benedictines Subiaco Congregation

Monastery of Christ in the Desert (1964): Abiquiu, NM 87510. Tel: 505-470-4515. Independent Abbey 1983; Very Rev. Philip Lawrence, O.S.B., Abbot.
Monks 39.
Represented in the Archdiocese of Santa Fe. Also in Mexico.

Saint Mary's Monastery (1987): P.O. Box 345, Petersham, MA 01366. Tel: 978-724-3350. Dependent Monastery 1987; Rev. Dom Anselm Atkinson, O.S.B., Supr.
Monks 6.
Represented in the Diocese of Worcester.

[0220] (S.S.S.)—CONGREGATION OF THE BLESSED SACRAMENT

(Congregatio Sanctissimi Sacramenti)

General Motherhouse: 46 Via Giovanni Battista de Rossi, Rome, 00161. Italy. Very Rev. Norman Pelletier S.S.S., Supr. Gen.

Province of St. Ann (1931): 5384 Wilson Mills Rd., Cleveland, OH 44143. Tel: 440-442-6311. Very Rev. Anthony Schueller S.S.S., Prov.; Rev. Edward Stapleton, S.S.S., Consultor & Prov. Treas. Consultors: Revs. Ernest Falardeau S.S.S., Vicar Provincial; Eugene LaVerdiere, S.S.S., Consultor for Formation; Michael Arkins S.S.S.

Bishops 1; Priests 59; Permanent Deacons 1; Clerics 4; Brothers 20.
Properties staffed or owned: Parishes 8; Seminary 1; Community Houses 9; Novitiate 1.
Represented in the Archdioceses of Chicago, New York, San Antonio and Santa Fe and in the Dioceses of Cleveland, Green Bay, Galveston-Houston and Salt Lake City.

[0230] (Er. Cam.)—CAMALDOLESE HERMITS OF THE CONGREGATION OF MONTE CORONA

(Eremitae Camaldulenses Congregationis Montis Coronae)

General Motherhouse: *Sacro Eremo Tuscolano*, 00044, Frascati (Roma), Italy. Rt. Rev. Lanfranco Longhi, Er. Cam., Father Major.
U.S. Foundation (1959): *Holy Family Hermitage*, 1501 Fairplay Rd., Bloomingdale, OH 43910-7971. Tel: 614-765-4511. Very Rev. Basil Corriere, Er. Cam., Prior.
Hermit Priests 3; Professed 3; Oblates 1.
Represented in the Diocese of Steubenville.

[0240] (O.S.CAM.)—CAMILLIAN FATHERS AND BROTHERS or ORDER OF ST. CAMILLUS

(Order of the Servants of the Sick)
(Ordo Ministrantium Infirmis)

General Motherhouse: *Casa Generalizia*, Ministri degli Infermi, C.P. 643, 00100, Roma Centro, Italy. Most. Rev. Angelo Brusco, O.S.Cam., Supr. Gen.; Very Rev. Richard O'Donnell, O.S.Cam., Vicar Gen.; Rev. Laurent Zougrana, O.S.Cam., Sec. of Formation; Rev. Anselmo Zambotti, O.S.Cam., Sec. of Missions; Rev. Ademar Rover O.S.Cam., Sec. of Ministry.
North American Province (1923): *Provincialate*, 10101 W. Wisconsin Ave., Wauwatosa, WI 53226. Tel: 414-259-4511; Fax: 414-258-4707. Very Rev. William F. Cronin, O.S.Cam., Prov.; Rev. Stephen E. Braddock, O.S.Cam., Ph.D, Chm. Bd.-St. Camillus Campus. Counselors: Revs. Louis Lussier, O.S.Cam.; James Francis Kovarik, O.S.Cam.; Bro. Nelson Edward Deloria, O.S.Cam.; Bro. Thomas Farrell, O.S.Cam.
Legal Title: *St. Camillus Nursing Home*, Whitinsville, MA; *St. Camillus Institute*, Whitinsville, MA; *St. Camillus Health Center Inc.*, Wauwatosa, WI; *St. Camillus Institute*, Wauwatosa, WI *San Camillo, Inc.*, Wauwatosa, WI; *St. Camillus Ministries Inc.*, Wauwatosa, WI; *St. Camillus Ministries Inc.*, Milwaukee, WI; *St. Camillus Formation House*, St. Francis, WI; *St. Camillus Communities Inc.*, Wauwatosa, WI.
Fathers 16; Professed Brothers 7; Temporary Professed 1; Novices 1.
Represented in the Archdiocese of Milwaukee and the Dioceses of Madison and Worcester.

[0250] (C.R.L.)—CANONS REGULAR OF THE LATERAN

(Ordo Canonicorum Regularium S. Augustini Congregations Ss. Salvatoris Lateranensis)

General House: *Curia Generalizia dei Canonicio Regolari Lateranensi*, Piazza S. Pietro in Vincoli, 4A, 00184, Roma, Italy.
United States: *Canons Regular of the Lateran*, 2317 Washington Ave., Bronx, NY 10458. Tel: 212-295-9600. Rev. Jose L. Biain, C.R.L., Supr. Tel: 212-994-1477.
Priests 6; Brothers 4.
Represented in the Archdiocese of New York and in the Diocese of Arecibo.

[0260] (O.C.D.)—DISCALCED CARMELITE FRIARS

(Ordo Carmelitarum Discalceatorum)

Founded Mt. Carmel, Palestine in the 13th Century.
Generalate: *Carmelitani Scalzi*, Corso d'Italia, 38, 00198, Rome, Italy. Very Rev. Camilo Maccise, O.C.D., Supr. Gen.
California-Arizona Province (1983): *Provincial House*, 926 E. Highland Ave., P.O. Box 2178, Redlands, CA 92373. Tel: 909-793-0424; Fax: 909-335-1304. Very Rev. Gerald Werner, O.C.D., Prov.
Legal Title: *Discalced Carmelite Province of California.*
Fathers 31; Brothers 2; Students 5; Novices 7.
Properties owned, staffed, or sponsored: Parishes 4; Retreat House; Novitiate; House of Studies; House of Prayer; Institute of Spirituality.
Represented in the Archdioceses of Los Angeles and Seattle and the Dioceses of Oakland, San Jose, San Bernardino, Santa Rosa and Tucson.
Province of St. Therese of Oklahoma (1935): *Provincial House-Monastery of Marylake*, 515 Marylake Drive, Little Rock, AR 72206-9424. Tel: 501-888-5827. Very Rev. Aloysius Deeney, O.C.D., Prov.
Fathers 25; Brothers 3\2; Students of Philosophy 2; Students of Theology 2; Novices 3.
Properties staffed or sponsored: Parishes 3; Community Houses 1; Novitiate 1; Student House 1.
Represented in the Archdioceses of San Antonio, New Orleans and Oklahoma City and in the Dioceses of Dallas and Little Rock.
Province of the Immaculate Heart of Mary (1947): *Discalced Carmelites*, 1233 S. 45th St., Milwaukee, WI 53214. Tel: 414-672-7212; Fax: 414-672-3138. Very Rev. Phillip R. Thomas, O.C.D., Prov.
Fathers 6; Brothers 2; Temporary Professed Brothers 2.
Polish Province of the Holy Spirit, Poland (1949): *Monastery of Our Lady of Mt. Carmel*, 1628 Ridge Rd., Munster, IN 46321. Tel: 219-838-7111; Fax: 219-838-7214. Rev. Thomas I. Balys, O.C.D., Prior.
Priests 10; Brothers 1; Postulants 2.
Represented in the Diocese of Gary.

[0270] (O.CARM.)—CARMELITE FATHERS & BROTHERS

(Ordo Fratrum Beatissimae Virginis Mariae de Monte Carmelo)

General Curia: 00184, Rome, Italy. Via Giovanni Lanza, 138; Most Rev. Joseph Chalmers, O.Carm., Prior Gen.
Province of the Most Pure Heart of Mary (1864): 1317 Frontage Rd., Darien, IL 60561. Tel: 630-971-0050; Fax: 630-971-0195. Very Rev. Leo McCarthy, O.Carm., Prior Prov.
Carmelite Provincials: 1317 Frontage Rd., Darien, IL 60561. Tel: 630-971-0050; Fax: 630-971-0195. Very Rev. Leo McCarthy, O.Carm., Prov., *Midwest Commissary Provincial;* Rev. Raymond Clennon, O.Carm., 8419 Bailey Rd., Darien, IL 60561. Tel:30-960-4934; *Western Commissary Provincial;* Rev. Ronald Oakham, O.Carm., 1540 E. Glenn St., Tuscan, AZ 85719; *Eastern Commissary Provincial;* Rev. Robert Wolfe, O.Carm., 158 Prospect St., Englewood, NJ 07631. Tel: 201-568-5612.
Provincial Officers: Revs. Daniel O'Neill, O.Carm., Prov. Treas.; John Welch, O.Carm., Dir. of Education. Councillors: Revs. Farrell Kane, O.Carm.; David Simpson, O.Carm.; Paul Schweizer, O.Carm.; Frederick Tillotson, O.Carm.; Peter Byrth, O.Carm., Lay Carmelite Dir.; Robert Colaresi, O.Carm., Dir. Little Flower Society; Rev. John Malley, O.Carm., Dir., *Carmelite Mission Office;* Revs. Jphn Malley, O. Carm., Dir.
Priests 234; Clerics 16; Pre-Novitiate College Students 10; Novices 2; Brothers 19.
Properties owned: Spiritual Centers 4; Shopping-center Chapels 2; *Carefree Leisure Village*, residence for senior citizens, Darien, IL High Schools 5 Community Houses 38 House of Study 2.
Ministries in 36 Parishes.
Represented in the Archdioceses of Boston, Chicago, Kansas City in Kansas, Los Angeles, Louisville, Newark and Washington and in the Dioceses of Galveston-Houston, Joliet, Pittsburgh, Phoenix, Sacramento, Stockton, Tucson and Venice.
Province of St. Elias (1931): P.O. Box 3079, Middletown, NY 10940-0890. Tel: 914-344-2223. Very Rev. Mario Esposito, O.Carm., Prov.
Legal Holdings or Titles: *The Missionary Society of Our Lady of Mt. Carmel of the State of New York; The Carmelite Fathers, Inc. of New York; Carmelite Fathers, Inc. of the Commonwealth of Massachusetts; Mt. Carmel Hermitage; Order of Carmelites of Palm Beach, Inc.; National Shrine of Our Lady of Mount Carmel, Inc.*
Fathers 67; Clerics 5; Brothers 2; Pre-Novices 2.
Properties staffed, owned, or sponsored: Parishes 10; Priories 14; House of Study 2; Retreat Houses 1; Novitiate 1; High Schools 1; Hermitages 2; Shrines 1.
Represented in the Archdioceses of Miami, New York and Washington and in the Dioceses of Albany, Brooklyn, Greensburg, Palm Beach, Rochester, Sioux Falls, Springfield (MA) and Trenton.
Mt. Carmel Hermitage: Pineland, R.D. 3, Box 36, New Florence, PA 15944. Tel: 412-235-2157.
Founded in 1970, became dependent upon St. Elias Province in 1995; Revs. Bede Mulligan, O.Carm.; Simeon Marro, O.Carm.
Fathers 2.
Represented in the Diocese of Greensburg.

[0275] (C.M.I.)—CARMELITES OF MARY IMMACULATE

(Congregatio Fratrum Carmelitarum B.V. Mariae Immaculatae)

Founded by Blessed Kuriakose Elias Chavara and Companions at Mannanam, Kerala, India in 1831.
Generalate: *Prior General's House*, P.B. No. 1056 Ernakulam, Cochin 682 011, Kerala, India. Tel: 484-360-137. Very Rev. Alex Ukken, C.M.I., Prior Gen.
North American Headquarters: 21 Nassau Ave., Brooklyn, NY 11222. Tel: 718-388-4866. Rev. Sebastian Kochupurackal, C.M.I., Reg. Coord.
Legal Title: *Carmelites of Mary Immaculate, Inc.*
Priests in the United States and Canada 50.
Ministries in Parishes; Hospitals; Universities; Prisons; Mission to the Syro-Malabar catholics.
Represented in the Archdioceses of New York and Philadelphia and the Dioceses of Beaumont, Brooklyn, Joliet, Lafayette, Lake Charles, Nashville, Syracuse, Toledo and Tyler. Also in Canada.

[0280] (O.CART.)—ORDER OF CARTHUSIANS

(Ordo Cartusianorum)

Motherhouse: Grande Chartreuse, St. Pierre de Chartreuse (Isere), France. Rev. Father Andre Poisson, Supr. Gen.
U.S. Charterhouse of the Transfiguration (1951): *Carthusian Foundation*, R.R. 2, Box 2411, Arlington, VT 05250. Tel: 802-362-2550. Rev. Lorenzo Maria T. De La Rosa, Jr., O.Cart., Rector.
In Community 23.
Legal Title: *Carthusian Foundation in America, Inc., Carthusian Foundation, Association Fraternelle Romande.*
Represented in the Diocese of Burlington.

[0290] (F.C.)—BROTHERS OF CHARITY

(Congregatio Fratrum Caritate)

General Motherhouse (1807): Via G.B. Pagano 35, C.P. 9082, 00167, Roma, Italia. Bro. Waldebert Devestal, F.C., Supr. Gen.
American District (1963): *District of Our Lady of Charity*, 7720 Doe Ln., Laverock, PA 19038. Bro. Michael Lonsway, District Supr.
Represented in the Archdiocese of Philadelphia.

[0300] (I.C.)—INSTITUTE OF CHARITY

Rosminians
Institutum Charitatis

General Motherhouse: Collegio Rosmini Via Porta Latina 17, Rome, Italy. Very Rev. James Flynn, I.C., Supr. Gen.
U.S. Foundation (1877): 2327 W. Heading Ave., Peoria, IL 61604. Tel: 309-676-6341. Very Rev. Christopher Fitzgerald, I.C., Prov.
Fathers in the U.S. 18.
Novitiate 1; Parishes 8.
Represented in the Dioceses of Peoria, St. Petersburg and Venice.

[0310] (C.F.C.)—CONGREGATION OF CHRISTIAN BROTHERS

(Christian Brothers Institute)

Founded in Ireland in 1802. First foundation in the United States in 1906.
General Motherhouse: *Fratelli Cristiani*, Via della Maglianella, 375, 00166, Roma, Italia. Very Rev. Bro. Edmund M. Garvey, Congregational Leader.
Eastern U.S. American Province (1916): 21 Pryer Terrace, New Rochelle, NY 10804. Tel: 914-636-6194. Bros. James B. Moffett, Prov.; Brian M. Walsh, Deputy Prov. Consultors: Bros. L. Alphonsus Killelea; J. Edward Roepke; V. Gregory McNally; Mr. Vincent J. Dougherty, Prov. Treas.
Brothers 220.
Properties owned, staffed, or sponsored: College 1; High Schools 15; Grade Schools 3; Migrant Education Center 1; Care Center 1.
Represented in the Archdioceses of Boston, Miami, Newark and New York and in the Dioceses of Albany, Charlotte, Owensboro, Providence, Rochester, St. Petersburg and Venice.
Brother Rice Province (Western United States): *Brother Rice Provincialate*, 958 Western Ave., Joliet, IL 60435-6954. Tel: 815-723-5464. Bros. Charles J. Gattone, Prov.; Robert N. Brouillette, Deputy Prov. Consultors: Bros. Charles D. McKenna; D. Dominic Murray; Michael S. Segvich; Bros. Paul Ickes, Vocations; George A. Gremley, Prov. Bursar.
Development Office: Christian Brothers Association, P.O. Box 42903, Evergreen Park, IL 60805-0903. Tel: 312-233-2949. Bro. Robert N. Brouillette, Dir.
Legal Title: *The Christian Brothers of Ireland, Inc.*
Properties administered: *Brother Rice High School (The Christian Bros. Inst. of Mich., Inc.)*, Bloomfield, MI; *Brother Rice High School (Brother Rice High School, Inc.)*, Chicago, IL; *Damien Memorial High School (The Congregation of Christian Bros. of Hawaii, Inc.)*, Honolulu, HI; *Palma Junior-Senior High School (The Christian Brothers Institute of California, Inc.)*, Salinas, CA; *St. Laurence High School, (St. Lawrence High School, Inc.)*, Oak Lawn, IL.
Brothers under Vows 101.
Represented in the Archdioceses of Chicago, Detroit

and Seattle and in the Dioceses of Helena, Honolulu, Joliet, Monterey and Owensboro. Also in Peru and West Africa.

[0320] (F.I.C.)—BROTHERS OF CHRISTIAN INSTRUCTION

La Mennais Brothers

(Institutum Fratrum Instructionis Christianae)

General Motherhouse: *Casa Generalizia*, Via della Divina Provvidenz, 44, 00166, Rome, Italy. Tel: 66.41.5618; Fax: 66.41.5652. Rev. Jose Antonio Obeso Vega, F.I.C., Supr. Gen.

American Province (1946): *Notre Dame Province-Notre Dame Institute*, P.O. Box 159, Alfred, ME 04002. Tel: 207-324-0067. Bro. Francis Blouin, F.I.C., Prov.

Brothers 49.

College 1; High Schools 2; Retreat Center 1; Houses of Study (Scholasticate-Novitiate) 1.

Represented in the Dioceses of Fairbanks, Fall River, Ogdensburg, Portland (ME) and Youngstown.

[0330] (F.S.C.)—BROTHERS OF THE CHRISTIAN SCHOOLS

(Fratres Scholarum Christianarum)

General Motherhouse: *Casa Generalizia*, Via Aurelia 476, CP 9099, 00100, Roma, Italia. Bros. John Johnston, F.S.C., Supr. Gen.; Alvaro Rodriquez Echeverria, Vicar Gen.

Christian Brothers Conference: *USA/Toronto Region*, 4351 Garden City Dr., Ste. 200, Landover, MD 20785-2248. Tel: 800-433-7593; 301-459-9410. Bros. Kevin Gilhooly, F.S.C., Exec. Sec.; Theodore Drahmann, F.S.C., Dir. Education; John Linhardt, F.S.C., Dir. Formation.

Organizations served by this office: *Regional Conference of USA-Toronto Brothers Provincial Regional F.S.C. Education Board Regional F.S.C. Finance Board Regional F.S.C. Vocation and Formation Board F.S.C. Publication Board.*

Organizations associated with this office: *Christian Brothers Major Superiors.*

Properties owned and or sponsored: *Bethlehem University of the Holy Land*, P.O. Box 9, Bethlehem, via Israel (Incorporated in the State of New Jersey).

Province of Baltimore (1845): *The Provincialate*, Box 29, Adamstown, MD 21710. Tel: 301-874-5188; Fax: 301-874-5674. Bros. Benedict Oliver, F.S.C., Prov., Visitor; Robert Schieler, F.S.C., Auxiliary-Visitor; Timothy Froehlich, F.S.C., Dir. Finance; Charles Lackes, F.S.C., Dir. St. LaSalle Auxiliary; David Trichtinger, F.S.C., Dir. Vocations; Martin Fahey, F.S.C., Sec.

Brothers 208.

Legal Holdings or Titles: *Christian Brothers of Frederick, Inc.; Ammendale Normal Institute of Prince George's County, Inc.; Christian Brothers Community Support Charitable Trust.*

Represented in the Archdioceses of Baltimore, Newark, Philadelphia and Washington and in the Dioceses of Camden and Pittsburgh.

Brothers Of The Christian Schools (Midwest Province - 1995): 200 S. Frontage Rd., Ste. 300, Burr Ridge, IL 60521-6953. Tel: 630-323-3725; Fax: 630-323-3779. Bros. Thomas Johnson, F.S.C., Prov. Visitor; Francis Carr, F.S.C., Aux. Visitor; Michael Fehrenbach, F.S.C., Aux. Visitor; Edwin Dupre, F.S.C., Dir. Development; Joseph Saurbier, F.S.C., Dir. Finance; Thomas Sullivan, F.S.C., Dir. Vocations/Formation; Nicholas Schumer, F.S.C., Dir. St. La Salle Auxiliary.

Legal Title: *The Christian Brothers of the Midwest, Inc.; The Christian Brothers of Illinois; Brothers of the Christian Schools of the St. Louis District; The Christian Brothers of Minnesota.*

Brothers 247; Aspirants 1.

Properties owned, staffed, or sponsored: Communities 32; Universities 3; High Schools 17; Retreat Houses 3; Group Homes 2; Publishing House 1.

Represented in the Archdiocese of Chicago, St. Louis, St. Paul-Minneapolis, and in the Dioceses of Green Bay, Gaylord, Jackson, Jefferson City, Joliet, Kansas City-St. Joseph, Memphis, Tulsa and Winona.

Province of New York (1848): *La Salle Provincialate Inc.*, 800 Newman Springs Rd., Lincroft, NJ 07738. Tel: 732-842-7420; Fax: 732-530-3504. Bros. Michael Corry, F.S.C., Prov. & Chm. Bd.; Stephen McCabe, F.S.C., Aux. Prov., Vice Pres. & Dir. Devel. Office; Robert Carnaghi, F.S.C., Aux. Prov. & Vice Pres.; John Martin, F.S.C., Treas.; Edward Cleary, F.S.C., Sec.; William Martin, F.S.C., Dir.-St. La Salle Auxiliary, P.O. Box 228, Lincroft, NJ 07738. Direct all inquiries to Bro. Michael Corry, F.S.C., Prov. All of these Brothers constitute the Board Members of St. Joseph Normal Institute, De La Salle Institute, Hillside Hall and De La Salle College.

Brothers 208.

College 1; High Schools 10; Elementary Schools 2; Welfare Schools 1; Community Houses 18; House of Study and Formation 1.

Represented in the Archdioceses of Detroit, Newark and New York and in the Dioceses of Albany, Buffalo, Syracuse and Trenton.

Province of Long Island-New England (1957): *Christian Brothers' Center-Provincial Offices, St. La Salle Auxiliary and Office of Public Information and Development*, Narragansett, RI 02882-1314. Tel: 401-789-0244; Fax: 401-783-5303. Bros. William Mann, F.S.C., Prov.-Visitor; Daniel Casey, F.S.C., Auxiliary Prov. Continuing-Initial Formation/Education; Peter Clifford, F.S.C., Dir. Finance & Devel.; Robert Hazard, F.S.C., Vocation Counselor; Peter Iorlano, F.S.C., Vocation & Formation Counselor; Leo Kane, F.S.C., Coord.- Elderly & Infirm; Eugene O'Gara, F.S.C., Archivist.

Legal Title: *Brothers of the Christian Schools, Province of the Long Island-New England, Inc.*

Organizations served by this office: *The Familiares Ocean Tides, Inc.* (1975; Bro. Brendan Gerrity, F.S.C., Pres. Tel: 401-789-1016.

Brothers 104; Aspirants 5; Postulants 1.

Properties owned, staffed, or sponsored: High Schools 5; Schools Elementary Schools 2; Community Houses 10.

Represented in the Dioceses of Brooklyn, Providence and Rockville Centre.

Province of San Francisco (1868): *Brothers of the Christian Schools Provincial Office*, P.O. Box 3720, Napa, CA 94558-0372. Tel: 707-252-0222. Bro. David Brennan, F.S.C., Prov.

Brothers 144.

College 1; High Schools 10; Community Houses 14; House of Study 1; Retreat & Conference Center 1.

Represented in the Archdioceses of Los Angeles, Portland (OR) and San Francisco and in the Dioceses of Fresno, Monterey, Oakland, Sacramento, Santa Rosa and Yakima. Also in India, Italy, Israel, Mexico, Philippines, Kenya, Tijuana, and England.

Province of New Orleans-Santa Fe (1921): *De La Salle - Christian Brothers Provincialate*, 1522 Carmel Dr., Lafayette, LA 70501. Tel: 318-234-1973. Bros. Clarence Fioke, F.S.C., Prov.; James Brown, F.S.C., Auxiliary Prov. & Finance Dir.

Legal Holdings or Titles: *Brothers of the Christian Schools of Lafayette, LA., Inc.; St. La Salle Auxiliary, New Orleans-Santa Fe Retirement Plan; The Christian Brothers of J.K. Mullen High School; J.K. Mullen High School Corporation, Christian Brothers Foundation; Christian Brothers Retirement Trust.*

Brothers 123.

Properties owned, staffed, or sponsored: College; High Schools 6; Elementary Schools 2.

Represented in the Archdioceses of Denver, New Orleans and Santa Fe and in the Dioceses of El Paso and Lafayette (LA).

[0340] (O.CIST.)—CISTERCIAN FATHERS

(Ordo Cisterciensis)

Headquarters: Piazza del Tempio di Diana 14, I-00153, Rome, Italy. Most Rev. Maurus Esteva, O.Cist., S.T.D., Abbot Gen.

Cistercian Abbey: *Our Lady of Spring Bank*, 17304 Haverwood Rd. - Rte. 3, Box 211, Sparta, WI 54656. Tel: 608-269-8138; Fax: 608-269-2800. Rt. Rev. Gregory Norman, O.Cist., Abbot; Rt. Rev. Blaise J. Fuez, O.Cist., Abbot Emeritus; Very Rev. Bernard McCoy, O.Cist., Sub-Prior; Rev. Robert Keffer, O.Cist., Dir.-Vocations & Formation.

Professed Priests 4; Solemnly Professed 4; Postulants 5; Novices 1.

Cistercian Monastery: *Our Lady of Dallas*, 1 Cistercian Rd., Irving, TX 75039. Tel: 972-438-2044. Rt. Rev. Denis Farkasfalvy, O.Cist., Abbot; Revs. Peter Verhalen, O.Cist., Prior; Bernard Marton, O.Cist., Subprior.

Priests 25.

Staff: Universities 2; Preparatory School 1; Novitiate 1; Chaplaincies 3.

Properties owned: Abbey & Preparatory School.

Represented in the Dioceses of Dallas and Fort Worth.

Cistercian Monastery: 564 Walton Ave., Mt. Laurel, NJ 08054. Tel: 609-235-1330. Revs. Lino Parente, O.Cist., Prior; Anselmo Florio, O.Cist.; Maurizio Nicoletti, O.Cist.

Established in 1961 as a dependent Monastery of the Congregation of Casamari (Italy).

Property owned: *Fatima House and the Monastery.*

Cistercian Conventual Priory: St. Mary's Priory, R.D. No. 1, Box 206, New Ringgold, PA 17960. Tel: 717-943-2645. Very Rev. Luke Anderson, O.Cist., Ph.D., Prior.

Legal Title: *The Cistercian Monastery of Pennsylvania.*

Monks 3.

[0350] (O.C.S.O.)—THE CISTERCIAN ORDER OF THE STRICT OBSERVANCE (TRAPPISTS)

(Ordo Cisterciensium Strictioris Observantiae)

General Motherhouse: *Casa Generalizia*, O.C.S.O., 33 Viale Africa, Rome, 00144. Italy. Most Rev. Dom Bernardo Olivera, O.C.S.O., Abbot Gen.

Abbey of Gethsemani (1848): Trappist, KY 40051. Tel: 502-549-3117. Rt. Rev. Timothy Kelly, O.C.S.O., Abbot.

Priests 18; Brothers 55; Novices 1.

Abbey of Our Lady of New Melleray (1849): 6500 Melleray Cir., Peosta, IA 52068. Tel: 319-588-2319. Rt. Rev. Brendan Freeman, O.C.S.O., Abbot; Revs. Thomas MacMaster, O.C.S.O., Prior; Daniel Lenihan, O.C.S.O., Subprior.

Professed Monks 51 (30 are Priests).

St. Joseph's Abbey (1825): Spencer, MA 01562-1233. Tel: 508-885-8700; Fax: 508-885-8701. Rt. Rev. Damian Carr, O.C.S.O., Abbot.

Legal Title: *Cistercian Abbey of Spencer, Inc.*

Total in community 82 (37 are Priests); Solemnly Professed 78; Simply Professed 3; Novices 1.

Monastery of The Holy Spirit, Inc. (1944): 2625 Hwy 212 S.W., Conyers, GA 30094. Tel: 770-483-8705; Fax: 770-760-0989. Rt. Rev. Bernard Johnson, O.C.S.O., Abbot; Rt. Rev. Dom Augustin, O.C.S.O., Retired Abbot.

Professed Monks 54; Priests 32; Novices 3.

Represented in the Archdiocese of Atlanta.

Abbey of Our Lady of Guadalupe (1947): Lafayette, OR 97127. Tel: 503-852-7174; Fax: 503-852-7748. Rt. Rev. Peter McCarthy, O.C.S.O., Abbot; Very Rev. John-Baptist Hasbrouck, O.C.S.O., Prior; Bro. Phillip Wertman, O.C.S.O., Subprior.

Solemnly Professed 36; Priests 16.

Abbey of Our Lady of the Holy Trinity (1947): Huntsville, UT 84317. Tel: 801-745-3784. Rt. Rev. Leander Dosch, O.C.S.O., Abbot.

Priests 13.

Abbey of The Genesee (1951): P.O. Box 900, Piffard, NY 14533. Tel: 716-243-0660. Rt. Rev. John Eudes Bamberger, O.C.S.O., Abbot; Rev. Francis Steger, O.C.S.O., Prior; Bro. Anthony Weber, O.C.S.O., Novice Master.

Retreat House. Tel: 716-243-2220.

Professed Monks 27; Professed Priests 13; Oblates 1.

Mepkin Abbey (1949): 1098 Mepkin Abbey Road, Moncks Corner, SC 29461. Tel: 803-761-8509; Fax: 803-761-6719. Rt. Rev. Francis Kline, O.C.S.O., Abbot; Bro. Stephen Petronek, O.C.S.O., Prior; Bro. Stan Gumula, O.C.S.O., Business Mgr.; Rt. Rev. Christian Aidan Carr, O.C.S.O., (Retired Abbot).

Priests 10; Monks in Community 28.

Abbey of Our Lady of the Holy Cross (1950): Rte. 2, Box 3870, Berryville, VA 22611-9526. Tel: 540-955-1425; Fax: 540-955-4006. Bro. Benedict Simmonds, O.C.S.O., Supr.

Legal Title: *Community of Cistercians of the Strict Observance, Inc.*

Solemnly Professed 22; Simply Professed 2; Novices 1; Priests 12.

Assumption Abbey: Rte. 5, Box 1056, Ava, MO 65608. Tel: 417-683-5110. Rt. Rev. James Conner, O.C.S.O., Abbot; Rt. Rev. Cyprian Harrison, O.C.S.O., Abbot (Retired); Rt. Rev. Robert Matter, O.C.S.O., Abbot (Retired).

Priests 8; Professed 15.

Abbey of New Clairvaux (1955): *Trappist-Cistercian Abbey*, Vina, CA 96092. Tel: 530-839-2161. Rt. Rev. Thomas X. Davis, O.C.S.O., Abbot.

Legal Title: *Abbey of New Clairvaux, Inc.*

Solemn Vows 24; Simple Vows 2.

St. Benedict's Monastery (1956): 1012 Monastery Rd., Snowmass, CO 81654. Tel: 970-927-3311. Rt. Rev. Joseph Boyle, O.C.S.O., Abbot; Bros. Raymond Roberts, O.C.S.O., Prior; Charles Albanese, O.C.S.O., Subprior.

Professed Monks 14; Novices 1.

[0360] (C.M.F.)—CLARETIAN MISSIONARIES

Missionary Sons of the Immaculate Heart of Mary

(Congregatio Missionariorum Filiorum Immaculati Cordis Beatae Mariae Virginis.)

General Headquarters: Rome, Via Sacro Cuore di Maria 5, Italy. Very Rev. Aquilino Bocos, C.M.F., Supr. Gen.

Western Province: *Provincial Headquarters*, 1119 Westchester Pl., Los Angeles, CA 90019. Tel: 213-734-1824; Fax: 213-737-0301. Rev. Ralph Berg, C.M.F., Prov.

Legal Title: *Claretian Missionaries-Western Province, Inc.*, A not-for-profit corporation under the laws of the State of California having as its purpose the support of any Roman Catholic benevolent, charitable, educational or missionary undertakings of the Claretian Missionaries - Western Province, Inc.

Other Corporations: *Dominguez Seminary, Inc.*, Compton, CA, *Claretian Educational and Renewal Center, Inc.*, Los Angeles, CA, *Claretian Tape Ministry, Inc.*, Los Angeles, CA.

Fathers 77; Brothers 7; Students 10; Deacons 1.

Ministries in the following areas: Newman Centers; Parishes; Novitiate; House of Study; Centers for Spanish; Speaking; Renewal Centers; Education; Spiritual Direction.

Represented in the Archdioceses of Los Angeles and San Antonio and in the Dioceses of Austin, Fresno, Lubbock, Oakland, Orange and Phoenix.

Eastern Province: *Headquarters*, 400 N. Euclid Ave., Oak Park, IL 60302. Tel: 708-848-2076; Fax: 708-848-2069. Very Rev. Theodore Cirone, C.M.F., Prov.; Revs. Mark Brummel, C.M.F., Vicar Prov. & Treas.; Greg Kenny, C.M.F., Consultor; Ronald Stua, C.M.F., Consultor; Thomas Joyce, C.M.F., Consultor & Sec.

Legal Holdings or Titles: *The Congregation of Sons of the Immaculate Heart of Mary of the Eastern Province, Inc., Claret Center*, Chicago, IL; *Claretian Lay Volunteer Program*, Chicago, IL; *Claretian Associates Neighborhood Development Office*, Chicago, IL; *U.S. Catholic Bookstore*, Chicago, IL; *Claretians, Inc., St. Jude League, Inc., Claret Hills, Inc., St. Jude Seminary, Inc.*

Fathers 44; Brothers 4; Novices 1.

House of Study 1.

Represented in the Archdioceses of Atlanta and Chicago and in the Dioceses of Metuchen and Springfield-Cape Girardeau. Also in Guatemala.

[0370] (S.S.C.)—SOCIETY OF ST. COLUMBAN

(Societas Sancti Columbani pro missionibus ad Exteros)

Central Administration (1918): *St. Columban's*, Grange Rd., Donaghmede, Dublin, 13. Ireland. Very Rev. Nicholas Murray, S.S.C., Supr. Gen.

Members 644.

Region of the United States: P.O. Box 10, St. Columbans, NE 68056. Tel: 402-291-1920. Very Rev. Brendan O'Sullivan, S.S.C., Dir.; Rev. James J. Hastings, S.S.C., Vice Dir. Council: Revs. Mark Mengel, S.S.C., Regional Vocation & Lay Missionaries Coord.; Thomas P. Reynolds, S.S.C., Education Coord.; William Morton, S.S.C.; Charles O'Rourke, S.S.C.; Rev. William Sweeney, Reg. Treas.

Legal Title: *St. Columban's Foreign Mission Society, The Columban Fathers.*

Fathers 107; Student Members and Candidates 2.

Represented in the Archdioceses of Boston, Chicago, Los Angeles, Omaha, and Washington, and in the Dioceses of Brooklyn, Dallas, El Paso, Orange, Providence, and San Bernadino.

[0380] (M.C.C.J.)—COMBONI MISSIONARIES OF THE HEART OF JESUS

(Verona Fathers)
Missionarii Comboniani Cordis Jesu
(A Pontifical World Missionary Congregation Of Priests And Brothers)

Founded by Blessed Bishop D. Comboni in 1867. First foundation in United States in 1939.

General Motherhouse: *Missionari Comboniani*, Via Luigi Lilio, 80, 00142, Rome, Italy. Very Rev. David Glenday, M.C.C.J., Supr. Gen.

North American Province (1950): *Comboni Mission Center*, 8108 Beechmont Ave., Cincinnati, OH 45255-3194. Tel: 513-474-4997; Fax: 513-474-0382. Revs. John Converset, M.C.C.J., Prov.; Paul Donohue, M.C.C.J., Editor, *Comboni Mission Newsletter and Comboni Press Feature Service.*

Legal Title: *Comboni Missionaries of the Heart of Jesus, Inc.*

Priests 36; Brothers 2; College Students 3; Scholastics 18.

Home Mission Parishes 4; Mission Centers 5.

Represented in the Archdioceses of Chicago, Cincinnati, Los Angeles and Newark.

[0390] (I.M.C.)—CONSOLATA MISSIONARIES

(Institutum Missionum a Consolata)

General Motherhouse: Rome, Viale delle Mura Aurelie, 11, Italy. Very Rev. Peter Trabucco, Supr. Gen.

Headquarters in the U.S.: P.O. Box 5550, 2301 Rte. 27, Somerset, NJ 08875. Tel: 908-297-9191; Fax: 908-940-3121. Rev. Anthony Bellagamba, I.M.C., Reg. Supr.

Legal Title: *Consolata Society for Foreign Missions, Mission International, Inc.*

Priests 17; Brothers 1.

Properties owned: Mission Community House 4; House of Studies for Philosophy.

Represented in the Archdiocese of Washington and the Dioceses of Buffalo, Metuchen, and San Bernardino.

[0400] (O.S.C.)—CANONS REGULAR OF THE ORDER OF THE HOLY CROSS

(Crosier Fathers and Brothers)
Canonici Regulares Ordinis Sanctae Crucis
(Cruciferi)

Generalate: *Generalatus Ordinis S. Crucis*, Via del Velabro 19, Rome, Italy, 00186. Very Rev. Rein Vaanhold, O.S.C., Master Gen.; Pierre-Paul Walraet, OSC, Gen. Asst./Procurator Gen.; James Hentges, OSC, Gen. Asst./Gen. Archivist.

United States Province: *Province of St. Odilia*, Crosier National Headquarters, 3510 Vivian Ave., Shoreview, MN 55126-3852. Tel: 612-486-7456; Fax: 612-486-7589. Very Rev. John J. Neville, O.S.C., Prov. Provincial Councillors: Revs. Dale Ehrman, O.S.C.; Eugene Plaisted, O.S.C.; Albert Becker, O.S.C.; Michael Van Sloun, O.S.C.; Rev. Thomas E. O'Brien, O.S.C., Prov. Econome.

Legal Title: *Crosier Fathers and Brothers Province, Inc., Canons Regular of the Order of the Holy Cross.*

Bishops 1; Fathers 85; Professed Clerics 2; Brothers 26.

Properties owned, sponsored, or staffed: Monasteries 9; Novitiates 2; Parishes 12; Chaplaincies 6; Foreign Mission 1.

Represented in the Archdioceses of Baltimore, Chicago, Detroit, New York, St. Paul-Minneapolis and Washington and the Dioceses of Duluth, Lincoln, Phoenix and St. Cloud. Also in Tokyo, Japan, Indonesia and the Democratic Republic of the Congo.

[0410] (F.D.P.)—SONS OF DIVINE PROVIDENCE

(Filiorum Divinae Providentiae)

General Motherhouse: Via Efruria 6, Roma, Italy.

Founded in 1893 by Blessed Don Louis Orione; Very Rev. Roberto Simionato, F.D.P., Supr. Gen.

Delegation of Our Lady Queen of the Universe-U.S. Foundation (1953): III Orient Ave., E. Boston, MA 02128. Tel: 617-569-2100; Fax: 617-561-1138. Very Rev. Angelo Quadrini, F.D.P., Supr.

Priests 10.

Properties staffed or owned: Parishes 1; Nursing Home 2; Shrine 1.

Represented in the Archdioceses of Boston and New York and the Diocese of Evansville.

[0420] (S.V.D.)—SOCIETY OF THE DIVINE WORD

(Societas Verbi Divini)

General Motherhouse: *Collegio del Verbo Divino*, Via Dei Verbiti 1, Rome, Italy. Very Rev. Henry Barlage, S.V.D., Supr. Gen.

Founded 1897, with Headquarters at St. Mary's Mission House (Divine Word Seminary) Techny, Illinois; later separating into four provinces. In 1985 the Eastern and Northern Provinces combined.

Chicago Province (1985): *Province of Blessed Joseph Freinademetz*, S.V.D.,, Province Center, 1985 Waukegan Rd., P.O. Box 6038, Techny, IL 60082-6038. Tel: 847-272-2700; Fax: 847-272-2517. Very Rev. Stanley Uroda, S.V.D., Prov.; Bro. Douglas Edmonds, S.V.D., Vice Prov.; Rev. Thomas Griffith, S.V.D., Treas.

Priests 167; Brothers 48; Theologians 31; Minor Seminarians: College 110; Student Brothers 4; Novices 12; Associates 9.

Properties owned: Theologate; College; Retreat House; House of Studies; Conference Center; Chaplaincies 1; Retirement Homes 2.

Legal Title: *Divine Word Funds, Inc.*, 1835 Waukegan Rd., P.O. Box 6099, Techny, IL 60082-6099. Tel: 847-272-7600. Revs. Thomas Krosnicki, S.V.D., Pres.; Francis Kamp, S.V.D., Treas.; Walter Bracken, S.V.D., Delegate Supr.-Missionaries on Leave.

Legal Titles: *Divine Word Missionaries, Inc.; S.V.D. Catholic Universities, Inc.; Divine Word International*, 2001 Waukegan Rd., P.O. Box 176, Techny, IL 60082-0176; *Hlasy z domova A Z missii (Slovak Department); Missionarze Slowa Bozego, Werbisci (Polish Department); S.V.D. Funds, Inc.; Blessed Arnold Charitable Trust.*

Represented in the Archdioceses of Boston, Chicago, Dubuque, Indianapolis, Milwaukee, Newark, St. Louis, Washington and the Dioceses of Pittsburgh, Trenton and Wheeling-Charleston. Also in Canada, Jamaica and the West Indies.

Eastern Province: Amalgamated with Northern Province. See Chicago Province.

Southern Province (1940): *Southern Province of St. Augustine Provincial Residence*, 201 Ruella Ave., Bay St. Louis, MS 39520. Tel: 228-467-4322; 467-3815. Very Rev. Clifton Labbe, S.V.D., Prov.; Rev. Thomas James, S.V.D., Vice. Prov.; Bro. Richard Chanbers, S.V.D., Treas., Address applications for Retreats and Missions to; Rev. William Kelley, S.V.D.

Fathers 48; Brothers 8.

Parishes 23; Mission Stations 3; Elementary Schools 5.

Represented in the Archdiocese of New Orleans and in the Dioceses of Baton Rouge, Biloxi, Galveston-Houston, Jackson, Lafayette (LA) and Little Rock.

Western Province (1964): *Province of St. Therese of the Child Jesus*, 2737 Pleasant St., Riverside, CA 92507. Tel: 909-781-0940. Very Rev. Gerald W. Leonard, S.V.D., Prov.; Rev. Bernard Donaghey, S.V.D., Vice Prov.

Fathers 51; Brothers 6; House of Study 6.

Properties staffed, sponsored, or owned: High Schools 1; Parishes 9; Retreat Centers 1; House of Study 1.

Represented in the Archdioceses of Los Angeles and San Francisco and in the Dioceses of Las Cruces, Oakland, Orange, San Bernardino and Tucson.

[0430] (O.P.)—ORDER OF PREACHERS

Dominicans
Fratres Sacri Ordinis Praedicatorum

Generalitia: *Convento Santa Sabina*, Piazza Pietro d' Illiria, Aventino, 00153, Rome, Italy. Most Revs. Timothy J. Radcliffe, O.P., Master Gen.; D. M. Hynous, O.P., Procurator Gen.

Dominican Province of St. Joseph-Eastern (1805): 869 Lexington Ave., New York, NY 10021. Tel: 212-737-5757; Fax: 212-861-4216.

Corporate Title: *Dominican Fathers Province of St. Joseph*; Very Rev. Urban Voll, O.P., Prov.; Revs. R. A. Morris, O.P., Vicar Prov. & Socius to Prov.; E. T. Myers, O.P., Prov. Econ. Admin.; K. J. Pritzl, O.P., Regent of Studies; G. N. Ingham, O.P., Archivist; J. J. Reid, O.P., Vocation Dir.; P. J. Allen, O.P., Dir. Dominican Laity; J. P. McGuire, O.P., Dir. Angelicum Fund; J. A. McMahon, O.P., Dir.-Health Affairs; T. B. Confer, O.P., Sec. for Nuns; R. F. Halligan, O.P., Dir.-Continuing Formation; W. A. Newman, O.P., Promoter Rosary; J. A. McKeon, O.P., Promoter of Preaching; N. Haddad, O.P., Promoter of Social Justice; G. L. Concordia, O.P., Promoter of the Holy Name & Dir., *St. Jude Shrine;* E. L. Martin, O.P., Dir.,, *Deserving Poor Boys Priesthood Assn. & Dominican Friars Guilds;* bro. T. A. Dolan, O.P., Sec. of Missions & Dir. St. Jude Dominican Mission.

Fathers 261; Cooperator Brothers 15; Professed Clerics 20; Novices 4.

Properties owned, staffed, or sponsored: Parishes 20; Colleges 1; House of Study 1; Retreat Houses 1; Novitiates 1.

Legal Title: *Pension Plan, Dominican Fathers, Province of St. Joseph, Deserving Poor Boys Priesthood Association, Inc., Dominican Friars' Guilds, Inc., St. Jude Dominican Missions, Inc., Dominican Foreign Missions, Handicapped Children's Fund, Peru, St. Martin de Porres Guild, Inc.*

Represented in the Archdioceses of Boston, Cincinnati, Detroit, Hartford, Louisville, Newark, New York, Philadelphia and Washington and in the Dioceses of Columbus, Metuchen, Providence, Richmond, Rockville Centre and Youngstown.

Province of the Most Holy Name of Jesus-Western Dominican Province (1912): 5877 Birch Ct., Oakland, CA 94618. Tel: 510-658-8722; Fax: 510-658-1061. Very Rev. Daniel Syverstad, O.P., Prior Prov.; Very Rev. Robert Christian, O.P., Vicar Prov. & Socius; Very Rev. Reginald E. Martin, O.P., Dir.-Shrine of St. Jude, & Asst. Prov. Treas., Dir.-Devel.; Revs. Donald Bramble, O.P., Dir.-Mission Foundation; Jordan Bradshaw, O.P., Sec.-Dominican Family; Luke D. Buckles, O.P., Regent of Studies; G. Albert Buckley, O.P., Dir.-Preaching; Anthony G. Cordeiro, O.P., Treas.

Legal Title: *Province of the Holy Name, Inc.*

Fathers 120; Brothers 8; Professed Clerics 17; Novices 11.

Parishes 11; Newman Centers/Personal Parishes 9; Retreat House; House of Studies; Novitiates.

Represented in the Archdioceses of Anchorage, Los Angeles, Portland in Oregon, San Francisco and Seattle and in the Dioceses of Norwich, Oakland, Phoenix, Providence, Sacramento, Salt Lake City, San Bernardino, San Jose and Tucson. Also in Mexico, Kenya, Guatemala and Rome.

Province of St. Albert the Great-Central Dominican Province (1939): 1909 S. Ashland Ave., Chicago, IL 60608. Tel: 312-666-3244; Fax: 312-829-8471. Very Revs. Edward M. Ruane, O.P., Prov.; David F. Wright, O.P., Socius, Vicar Prov. - Archivist; Gerald L. Stookey, O.P., Vicar Prov.; Revs. Michael A. Winkels, O.P., Economic Admin.; Louis S. Morrone, O.P., Promoter of Vocations; Charles W. Dahm, O.P., Promoter of Social Justice; Dennis R. Zuzy, O.P., Regent; Benjamin J. Russell, O.P., Dir. Society Vocational Support; Bro. Regis R. Hovald, O.P., Prov. Rep. to Dominican Laity; Revs. Bede R. Jagoe, O.P., Dir. St. Dominic Mission Society & Shrine of St. Jude; Michael A. Winkels, O.P.,

Dir. of Dominican Conference Center, 7200 W. Division St., River Forest, IL 60305.

Legal Title: *Dominicans, Province of St. Albert the Great, U.S.A., Shrine of St. Jude Thaddeus, Inc., Society for Vocational Support, Inc., St. Dominic Mission Society, Dominican Social Action Fund, Dominican Laity, Dominican Central Productions, Fra Angelico Art Foundation.*

Fathers 187; Professed Clerics 24; Novices 7; Brothers 24.

Properties owned, staffed, or sponsored: Parishes 8; Convents 8; Houses 11; Houses of Studies 2; Novitiates 2; High Schools 1.

Represented in the Archdioceses of Chicago, Denver, Detroit, the Military Services, St. Louis, St. Paul-Minneapolis and Santa Fe and in the Dioceses of Dallas, Des Moines, Duluth, Fort Wayne-South Bend, Grand Rapids, Joliet, Las Cruces, Madison, Peoria, St. Cloud, Springfield (IL), Superior, Venice, and Winona.

Southern Dominican Province (1979): 1421 N. Causeway Blvd., Ste. 200, Metairie, LA 70001-4144. Tel: 504-837-2129; Fax: 504-837-6604. Very Revs. Alberto Rodriguez, O.P., Prov.; Carl B. Trutter, O.P., Vicar Prov.; James A. McDonough, O.P., Econ. Admin.; Wayne A. Cavalier, O.P., Promoter for Community Life and Permanent Formation; John J. Markey, O.P., Regent of Studies; Henry B. Groover, O.P., Promoter of Vocations.

Legal Holdings or Titles: *Southern Dominican Foundation, Retirement and Community Support Plan, Southern Province, U.S.A., Shrine of St. Martin de Porres.*

Fathers 114; Professed Clerics 13; Brothers 9; Novices 7.

Properties owned, staffed, or sponsored: Parishes 12; Priories 6; Houses 7.

Represented in the Archdioceses of Denver, Los Angeles, Miami, New Orleans, St. Louis, San Antonio, Santa Fe, Washington and the Dioceses of Austin, Baton Rouge, Beaumont, Dallas, Galveston-Houston, Houma-Thibodaux, Knoxville, Memphis, Nashville, Pensacola-Tallahassee, Raleigh, and Tyler.

U.S. Foundation (1926): Province of Spain, P.O. Box 279, San Diego, TX 78384. Tel: 512-279-3596. Very Rev. Candido Aniz, O.P.

Priests 4.

Parishes 3; Missions 3.

Represented in the Diocese of Corpus Christi.

[0440] (S.S.E.)—SOCIETY OF SAINT EDMUND

(Societas Sancti Edmundi)

General Motherhouse: *Edmundite Generalate,* 270 Winooski Park, Colchester, VT 05439. Tel: 802-654-3400; Fax: 802-654-3409. Very Rev. Joseph L. Hart, S.S.E., Supr. Gen. Councillors: Revs. Richard M. Myhalyk, S.S.E.; David G. Cray, S.S.E., Dir. Vocation Ministries; David G. Theroux, S.S.E.; Michael P. Cronogue, S.S.E.; Adalbert Wolski, T.O.R., Procurator Gen.

Legal Titles: Society of St. Edmund, Inc., Bishop Perry Middle School, New Orleans, LA.

Bishops 1; Fathers 51; Brothers 8; Scholastics 2.

Properties owned, staffed, or sponsored: Parishes 13; Missions 5; College 1; Retreat House; Novitiate; Middle School.

Represented in the Archdioceses of Detroit, Mobile and New Orleans and in the Dioceses of Burlington, Norwich and Venice.

[0450] (C.J.M.)—CONGREGATION OF JESUS AND MARY

(Congregatio Jesu et Mariae)
(Eudist Fathers)

General Motherhouse: Via dei Querceti, 15, 00184, Rome, Italy. Very Rev. Pierre Drouin, C.J.M., Supr. Gen.

North American Province: 6125 Premiere Ave., Charlesbourg, Quebec G1H 2V9. Canada. Tel: 418-626-6494. Very Rev. Bernard Cantin, C.J.M., Prov.

U.S. Region Eudist Community: 36 Flohr Ave., W. Seneca, NY 14224-1818. Tel: 716-825-4475.

Bishops 1; Fathers 101; Laymen 5.

Represented in the Dioceses of Buffalo and San Diego.

[0460](C.F.P.)—BROTHERS OF THE POOR OF ST. FRANCIS

(Congregatio Fratrum Pauperum)

Generalate: Aachen, Germany. Very Rev. Bro. Mark Gastel, C.F.P., Min. Gen.

Province of St. Joseph: *Provincial Business Office,* P.O. Box 187, Burlington, IA 52601-0187. Tel: 319-752-0050; Fax: 319-752-5605. Rev. Bro. James Phelan, C.F.P., Prov. Supr. Tel: 606-431-7667; Fax: 606-581-5796.

Professed Brothers 24.

Brothers serve and staff: Development Office 1; High Schools 1; Elementary Schools 5; AIDS Social Service Agency 1; Hospices Social Service Agency 1; Homes for Senior Citizens 2; Group Homes 2.

Brothers' Special Mission:Care & education of neglected youth; elementary & secondary education; human services.

Properties owned: Morris School for Boys, Searcy, AR.

Represented in the Archdioceses of Boston, Cincinnati, Denver, Newark and in the Dioceses of Covington, Davenport, El Paso, Jefferson City, and Little Rock.

[0470] (O.F.M.CAP.)—THE CAPUCHIN FRIARS

(Ordinis Fratrum Minorum Capuccinorum)

Generalate: Curia Generalis Ord. Min. Cap. via Piemonte 70, Roma, Italy, 00187. Most Rev. John Corriveau, O.F.M.Cap., General Min.

Province of St. Joseph (1857): 1740 Mt. Elliott Ave., Detroit, MI 48207-3496. Tel: 313-579-2100; Fax: 313-579-2275. Revs. Daniel Fox, O.F.M.Cap., Prov. Minister; Perry McDonald, O.F.M.Cap., Prov. Vicar. Councillors: Revs. Daniel Crosby, O.F.M.Cap.; Loran Miller, O.F.M.Cap.; John Scherer, O.F.M.Cap.; T.L. Michael, O.F.M.Cap., Dir.-Capuchin Publications; Mr. Mark McDonough, Prov. Treas.; Revs. James C. Wolf, O.F.M.Cap., Sec. Corporations; David Schwab, O.F.M.Cap., Sec.-Religious Affairs; Edward Foley, O.F.M.Cap., Prov. Dir. of Continuing Education; Richard Hart, O.F.M.Cap., Prov. Dir. of Preaching; Ulric Buening, O.F.M.Cap., Prov. Asst. to Secular Franciscan Order; Michael H. Crosby, O.F.M.Cap., Corp. Responsibility Agent; Bro. Larry LaCross, O.F.M.Cap., Dir. Public Relations & Devel., 1820 Mt. Elliott Ave., Detroit, MI 48207-3496. Bro. Richard Merling, O.F.M.Cap., Dir. The Father Solanus Guild, 1780 Mt. Elliott Ave., Detroit, MI 48207-3496. Tel: 313-579-2100. Bro. Leo Wollenweber, O.F.M.Cap., Vice Postulator for the Cause of Ven. Father Solanus Casey, O.F.M.Cap.

Legal Title: *Province of St. Joseph of the Capuchin Order, Inc.*

Priests 183; Perpetually Professed Lay Friars 53; Professed Friars in Temporary Vows 3.

Properties owned, staffed, or sponsored: Parishes 40; Chaplaincies 19; Retreat Houses 4; House of Prayer 1; Novitiates 1; Preparatory Seminary 1; Mission for the Cheyenne Indians; Mission for the Crow Indians; Foreign Missionaries in The Vicariate of Bluefields, Nicaragua and in dioceses of Panama City, Panama; Agana, Guam; Naha, Japan; Australia, Costa Rica, Honduras, & Brisbane.

Represented in the Archdioceses of Chicago, Detroit, Los Angeles, Milwaukee, New York, St. Paul-Minneapolis and in the Dioceses of Brooklyn, Fort Wayne-South Bend, Great Falls-Billings, Green Bay, LaCrosse, Las Cruces, Madison, Marquette, Oakland, Pittsburg, Saginaw and San Bernardino.

Province of St. Augustine (1873): *Provincial Office,* 220 37th St., Pittsburgh, PA 15201. Tel: 412-682-6011; Fax: 412-682-0506. Headquarters of Capuchin Franciscan Volunteer Corps., Inc.; St. Augustine Province of the Capuchin Order; National Headquarters of Archconfraternity of Christian Mothers; Mission Office of Seraphic Mass Association; Secular Franciscan Order of St. Augustine, Province; Capuchin Friars Sick and Elderly Trust Fund; St. Fidelis, Inc.; Capuchin Friars Formation and Education Trust Fund. Very Rev. William J. Wiethorn, O.F.M.Cap., Definitor Gen.; Very Rev. Philip Fink, O.F.M.Cap., Prov. Min.; Very Rev. Gregory Chervenak, O.F.M.Cap., Vicar Prov. Definitors: Revs. Joseph Mindling, O.F.M.Cap.; Vernon Busch, O.F.M.Cap.; John Pavlik, O.F.M.Cap.; William Graham, O.F.M.Cap., Exec. Sec. & Sec. for Finances; Richard Lubomski, Asst. Sec. Finances; Brendon Malloy, O.F.M.Cap., Sec. Communications.

Legal Title: *Province of St. Augustine of the Capuchin Order.*

Bishops 1; Priests 131; Brothers 37; Professed in Formation 7; Novices 3; Postulants 3.

Properties owned, staffed, or sponsored: Parishes 29; Formation Houses 2; Novitiate 1; Friaries 17; Postulancy Houses 3; Hospital Chaplains 12; Military Chaplain 1; Foreign Missions 2.

Represented in the Archdioceses of Baltimore, Philadelphia and Washington and in the Dioceses of Altoona-Johnstown, Cleveland, Columbus, Greensburg, Harrisburg, Pittsburgh and Wheeling-Charleston. Also in Papua New Guinea and Puerto Rico.

Province of St. Mary (1952): *St. Conrad Friary,* 30 Gedney Park Dr., White Plains, NY 10605. Tel: 914-761-3008; Fax: 914-948-6429. Very Rev. Bernard Smith, O.F.M.Cap., Minister Prov. Definitors: Revs. Regis Armstrong, O.F.M.Cap.; John Gallagher, O.F.M.Cap.; Francis Gasparik, O.F.M.Cap.; Bro. Louis Esposito, O.F.M.Cap.

Legal Title: *The Province of St. Mary of the Capuchin Order, Capuchin Friars International, Inc.*

Development Office: St. John Friary, 210 W. 31st St., New York, NY 10001.

Bishops 2; Priests 146; Professed Clerical Brothers 5; Professed Lay Brothers 43; Novices 2.

Properties staffed or sponsored: Parishes 13; Chaplaincies 26; Major Seminaries 1; Novitiate 1; Foreign Missions 3.

Represented in the Archdioceses of Agana and New York and the Dioceses of Bridgeport, Brooklyn, Honolulu, Manchester, Norwich, Portland (ME), Rochester, Rockville Centre and Springfield (MA). Also in Japan.

Province of the Sacred Stigmata of St. Francis (1918): *Our Lady of Guadalupe Friary,* 319 - 36th St., P.O. Box 809, Union City, NJ 07087. Tel: 201-865-0611; Fax: 201-866-7035. Revs. Robert Grix, O.F.M.Cap., Prov. Min.; Cyprian Rosen, O.F.M.Cap., Prov. Vicar. Definitors: Bro. Kellen Mears, O.F.M.Cap.; Revs. Vincent Fortunato, O.F.M.Cap.; Achilles Cassiere, O.F.M.Cap.; Francis Sariego, O.F.M.Cap., Prov. Sec.

Priests 47; Brothers 17; Temporary Professed 3; Novices 3; Postulants 2.

Parishes 10; Friaries 5; Retreat House 1; Hospital Chaplaincies 1.

Represented in the Archdioceses of Newark and New York and in the Dioceses of Charlotte, Paterson, St. Petersburg and Wilmington.

Our Lady of Angels, Western American Province: 1345 Cortez Ave., Burlingame, CA 94010. Revs. Ronald Talbott, O.F.M.Cap., Prov. Definitors: Revs. Christopher Kearney, O.F.M.Cap.; Michael Mahoney, O.F.M.Cap.; Harold Snider, O.F.M.Cap.; David Lapierre, O.F.M.Cap.; Revs. Camillus MacRory, O.F.M.Cap., Spiritual Asst. to Secular Franciscans; Flavian Welstead, O.F.M.Cap., Dir. of Devel. Finances; Cyril Kelleher, O.F.M.Cap., Foreign Mission Office Dir.

Priests 46; Brothers 13; Brothers in Formation 6; Novices 1; Postulants 1.

Ministries in Parishes; High Schools; Novitiates; Chaplaincies; House of Study; Retreats; Foreign Missions.

Represented in the Archdioceses of Los Angeles and San Francisco and in the Dioceses of Baker, Fresno and Oakland. Also in Mexico.

Province of SS. Stanislaus and Adalbert (1948): *St. Stanislaus Friary,* 2 Manor Dr., Oak Ridge, NJ 07438. Tel: 201-697-7757. Revs. Henry T. Krajewski, O.F.M.Cap., Supr.; Francis Z. Majewski, O.F.M.Cap., Asst. Supr.

Fathers 9.

Represented in the Dioceses of Metuchen, and Paterson.

Vice Province of Texas: 5604 Bernal Dr., Dallas, TX 75212. Tel: 214-631-6267. Rev. Ignacio Cizur, O.F.M.Cap., Vice Prov.

Fathers 14; Brothers 2.

Parishes 4; Cursillo Centers 2.

Represented in the Dioceses of Dallas and Fort Worth.

Province of Mid-America (1977): *St. Francis of Assisi Friary,* 3553 Wyandot St., Denver, CO 80211-2948. Tel: 303-477-5436; 477-5542; Fax: 303-477-6925.

Legal Title: *Capuchin Province of Mid-America, Inc., St. Francis Seminary Endowment Foundation, Inc.;* Revs. David Gottschalk, O.F.M.Cap., Prov.; Gene Emrisek, O.F.M.Cap., Vicar Prov.; Duane Reinert, O.F.M.Cap., Councillor & Coord. Ongoing Formation; Michael Scully, O.F.M.Cap., Councillor; James Moster, O.F.M.Cap., Councillor; Revs. Harvey P. Dinkel, O.F.M.Cap., Exec. Sec. & Treas.; John Lager, O.F.M.Cap., Sec.-Missions & Dir.-Devel.; Jeff Ernst, O.F.M.Cap., Coord.-Initial Formation; William Kraus, O.F.M.Cap., Dir. Vocation Programs; Blaine Burkey, O.F.M.Cap., Communications Dir.; Christian Fey, O.F.M.Cap., Archivist.

Bishops 3; Priests 49; Students 1; Brothers 7.

Represented in the Archdioceses of Denver, Kansas City in Kansas and St. Louis and in the Diocese of Salina.

Vice Province of St. John The Baptist (1905): *Vice Provincial Offices,* 216 Arzuaga St., P.O. Box 21350, Rio Piedras, PR 00928-1350. Tel: 787-764-3090; Fax: 787-764-4070. Bros. John Bednarik, O.F.M.Cap., Vice Prov. Min.; Jose A. Cruz, O.F.M.Cap., First Councillor; Alberto A. Figueroa, O.F.M.Cap., Second Councillor; Jorge Macias de Cespedes, O.F.M.Cap., Vice Prov. Sec., Treas., Public Rels. Dir. Postnovitiate; Joseph McCarthy, O.F.M.Cap., Dir. Capuchin Mass Assoc.

Legal Title: *Asociacion de Frailes Capuchinos, Inc.*

Friars 26; Postulants 4.

Properties owned, staffed and sponsored: Formation Fraternites 3; Parishes 4; Retreat Center 1; Friaries 6; Mission Office 1.

Represented in the Archdiocese of San Juan and the Dioceses of Arecibo and Ponce.

[0480] (O.F.M.CONV.)—CONVENTUAL FRANCISCANS

(Friars Minor Conventual)
(Ordo Fratrum Minorum S. Francisci Conventualium)

General Curia: Piazza SS. Apostoli, 51, Rome, 00187. Italy. Most Rev. Agostino Gardin, O.F.M.Conv.; Most Rev. William Robison, O.F.M.Conv., Asst. Gen.

Province of the Immaculate Conception B.V.M. (1852): *Provincial House-Immaculate Conception Friary*, Rensselaer, NY 12144. Very Rev. Canice Connors, O.F.M.Conv., Minister Prov.; Rev. Paul Lininger, O.F.M.Conv., Treas.; Bros. John-Joseph Dolan, O.F.M.Conv., Guardian & Sec.; Andre Picotte, O.F.M.Conv., Dir. Cemeteries; Stephen Merrigan, O.F.M.Conv., Archivist.

Legal Title: *Order of Friars Minor Conventual Immaculate Conception, Province Charitable Trust.*

Fathers 108; Professed Clerics 5; Professed Brothers 21.

Parishes 21; Friaries 17; Chaplaincies 8; Filial Houses 2.

Represented in the Archdioceses of Newark, New York, Philadelphia, and Washington, and in the Dioceses of Albany, Charlotte, Metuchen, Raleigh, Syracuse and Trenton.

Province of St. Anthony of Padua (1906): Provincial House, 12300 Folly Quarter Rd., Ellicott City, MD 21042-1419. Tel: 410-531-9200; Fax: 410-531-4881. Very Rev. Mark L. Curesky, O.F.M.Conv., Minister Prov.; Revs. Gregory Moore, O.F.M.Conv., Vicar Prov.; Robert Twele, O.F.M.Conv., Prov. Sec. & Treas. Definitors: Revs. Donald Grzymski, O.F.M.Conv.; Michael Kolodziej, O.F.M.Conv.; John Koziol, O.F.M.Conv.; Dennis Grumsey, O.F.M.Conv.

Legal Title: *St. Francis High School of Athol Springs, NY, Inc.; The Father Justin Rosary Hour, Inc.; Franciscan Fathers Minor Conventuals of Buffalo, NY, Inc.; The Franciscan Center, Inc.; St. Anthony of Padua Province, Franciscan Fathers Minor, Conventual, U.S.A., Inc; The Friars Knights of the St. Francis High School, Inc.; Order of Friars Minor Conventual, Inc.; Conventual Franciscan Friars, St. Anthony of Padua Province, Franciscan Mission Association, Inc; Franciscan Fathers Minor Conventual, St. Anthony of Padua, Province U.S.A., MA. Inc; Franciscan Friars, St. Anthony of Padua Province, Education, Fund, Inc; Franciscan Friars, St. Anthony of Padua Province, Fund for the, Aged and Infirm, Inc; Franciscan Minor Conventuals of Maryland, of Ellicott, City, MD, Inc; The Franciscan Fathers, Minor Conventuals, of St. Stanislaus, Church of Baltimore City, MD. Inc; St. Francis of Assisi Community, Inc.; Order of Friars Minor Conventual, St. Anthony of Padua, Province, U.S.A., Inc; St. Stanislaus Cemetery, Inc.*

Priests 170; Brothers in Solemn Vows 20; Clerics in Temporary Vows 4.

Friaries 36; Filial Houses 3.

Apostolates owned, staffed, or sponsored: Novitiates 1; College 1; House of Study 1; Parishes 43; Campus Ministries 3; High Schools 5; Youth-Crisis Shelter 1; Sisters' Chaplaincies 2; Hospital-Nursing Home Chaplaincies 4; Apostolates Radio Apostolate; Healing Ministry; Apostolates Preaching Apostolate; Foreign Missions 3; Candidate House 1; Youth Ministry.

Represented in the Archdioceses of Atlanta, Baltimore, Boston and Hartford and in the Dioceses of Altoona-Johnstown, Birmingham, Bridgeport, Brooklyn, Buffalo, Erie, Fall River, Harrisburg, Norwich, Ogdensburg, Palm Beach, Paterson, Portland (ME), Rochester, Savannah, Springfield (MA) and Trenton.

St. Bonaventure Province (1939): 6107 Kenmore Ave., Chicago, IL 60660-2797. Tel: 312-274-7681; Fax: 312-274-9751. Very Rev. Anthony Labedis, O.F.M.Conv., Min. Prov.; Very Rev. Justin Kusibab, O.F.M. Conv., Vicar Prov. & Sec.; Bro. Thomas Surmam, Treas. Definitors: Revs. Patrick Greenough, O.F.M.Conv.; James Ciaramitaro, O.F.M.Conv.; Luke Poczworowski, O.F.M.Conv.; Michael Suszynski, O.F.M.Conv., Mission Promoter & Prov. Spiritual Asst. for Secular Franciscans.

Legal Title: *Conventual Franciscans of St. Bonaventure Province, Franciscan Friars Educational Corp., Conventual Franciscan Friars of Marytown, Shrine of St. Maximillian Kolbe, St. Hedwig Cemetery and Mausoleum, The Conventual Franciscans of Saint Bonaventure Province, Charitable Continuing Care Trust Fund.*

Fathers 34; Professed Clerics 3; Brothers 20.

Parishes 5; Chaplaincies 2; Marian Center 1; Shrine 1.

Represented in the Archdioceses of Chicago, Detroit and Milwaukee and in the Dioceses of Peoria and Rockford. Also in Mexico.

Province of Our Lady of Consolation (1926): 101 Anthony Dr., Mount St. Francis, IN 47146. Tel: 812-923-8444. Very Rev. Kent Biergans, O.F.M.Conv., Min. Prov.; Rev. Richard Kaley, O.F.M.Conv., Vicar Prov.; Bro. Jeff Hines, O.F.M.Conv., Sec.

Fathers 121; Brothers 30; Professed Clerics 2; Candidates 5; Novices 3.

Friaries 24; Parishes 22; Houses of Formation 3; Retreat-Renewal Centers 3; Missions 15; Chaplaincies 2.

Province of St. Joseph of Cupertino (1981): *Cupertino Heights*, P.O. Box 820, Arroyo Grande, CA 93421-0820. Tel: 805-489-1012; Fax: 805-489-8303. Very Rev. Allen Ramirez, O.F.M.Conv., Min. Prov; Rev. Victor Abegg, O.F.M.Conv., Vicar Prov.; Bro. James Reiter, O.F.M.Conv., Prov. Sec.; Revs. Paul Fazio, O.F.M.Conv., Custos Capitularis; Stephen Gross O.F.M.Conv., Definitor & Prov. Spitirual Asst. for Secular Franciscan Order; Christopher Deitz, O.F.M.Conv., Definitor; John Heinz, O.F.M.Conv., Definitor; Father Alexander Lewis, O.F.M. Conv., Prefect of Formation.

Legal Title: *Conventual Franciscans of California, Inc.*

Parishes 11; Shrines 1; Chaplaincies 5; High Schools 1; Houses of formation 3; Missions 3.

Priests 39; Brothers 14; Clerics (Professed Seminarians) 12; Novices 7; Candidates 11.

Represented in the Archdiocese of Los Angeles, Military Archdiocese, Portland in Oregon, San Francisco and in the Dioceses of Fresno, Monterey, Oakland, Reno, and San Bernardino.

[0490] (O.S.F.)—CONGREGATION OF THE RELIGIOUS BROTHERS OF THE THIRD ORDER REGULAR OF ST. FRANCIS

Franciscan Brothers of Brooklyn

Generalate (1858): *St. Francis Monastery*, 135 Remsen St., Brooklyn, NY 11201-4212. Tel: 212-858-8217; Fax: 718-858-8306. Bros. Kevin Smith O.S.F., Supr. Gen.; Joseph Moloney O.S.F., Asst. Supr. Gen.; Gerald Carrino, O.S.F., Master of Novices.

Legal Titles and Holdings: St. Francis Monastery, Franciscan Brothers' Generalate, Franciscan Brothers, Inc., Brooklyn, NY, *Mount Alvernia, Inc., St. Francis Center, Inc.*, Rockville Centre, NY.

Brothers 106.

Ministries in the field of Education at all levels; Pastoral Ministries, Social Services; Spirituality Centers.

Represented in the Archdioceses of Newark and St. Louis and the Dioceses of Brooklyn, Paterson, Raleigh and Rockville Centre.

[0500] (O.S.F.)—FRANCISCAN BROTHERS OF CHRIST THE KING

General Motherhouse and Novitiate (1961): 3737 N. Marybelle Ave., Peoria, IL 61615. Tel: 309-688-0094; 0093. Bro. Francis A. Skube, Supr. Gen.

Professed Brothers 4; Novices 1.

Represented in the Diocese of Peoria.

[0510] (F.F.S.C.)—FRANCISCAN BROTHERS OF THE HOLY CROSS

Generalate: St. Josefshaus, Hausen, Linz Rhein, West Germany. Bro. David Sarnecki, Supr. Gen.

American Region (1924): 2500 St. James Rd., Springfield, IL 62707. Tel: 217-544-4876, Ext. 222. Bros. John Francis Tyrrell, F.F.S.C., Pres.; Stephen Bissler, F.F.S.C., Vice Pres.; Joseph Havrilka, Board Member; Raphael Kreikemeier, Exec. Dir.; Joel Marc Roussea; Kuke Morin.

Properties owned, staffed, or sponsored: Home for Mentally Handicapped; Adult Training Center for Mentally Handicapped; Schools Elementary School; Novitiate.

Brothers 17.

Represented in the Dioceses of Jefferson City, Madison and Springfield (IL).

[0515] (O.S.F.)—FRANCISCAN BROTHERS OF THE THIRD ORDER REGULAR

Generalate: Franciscan Brothers' Generalate, Mountbellew, Ireland.

United States Region: 2117 Spyglass Trail W., Oxnard, CA 93030. Tel: 805-485-5002; Fax: 213-487-5275. Mailing Address: 4522 Gainsborough Ave., Los Angeles, CA 90027. Bro. Hilarion O'Connor, Reg. Supr.

Brothers 15.

Ministries in the field of secondary education.

Represented in the Archdioceses of Los Angeles and New York.

[0520] (O.F.M.)—FRANCISCAN FRIARS

(Ordinis Fratrum Minorum)

General Headquarters: Via S. Maria Mediatrice, 25, 00165, Rome, Italy. Curia Generalizia dei Frati Minori. Most Rev. Giacomo Bini, O.F.M., Min. Gen. Tel: 011-39-6-68491-203. Very Rev. Estevao Ottenbreit, O.F.M., Vicar Gen.; Bro. Sean Collins, O.F.M., English-Speaking General Councillor. Tel: 011-39-6-68491-290.

English-Speaking Conference of the Order of Friars Minor: 1615 Vine St., Cincinnati, OH 45210-1220. Tel: 513-721-4700; Fax: 513-421-9672. Bro. Ronald Bolfeta, O.F.M., Exec. Dir., Includes Order of Friars Minor Provinces 12; Vice Province 1; Custodies 2: of the United States, Canada, England, Ireland and Malta. Associate Member: Commissariat of the Holy Land, Washington DC.

Province of St. John the Baptist (1844): 1615 Vine St., Cincinnati, OH 45210-1222. Tel: 513-721-4700; Fax: 513-421-9672. Revs. John Bok, O.F.M., Prov.; Alan Hirt, O.F.M., Prov. Vicar. Councillors: Revs. Nicholas Lohkamp, O.F.M.; Joseph Rayes, O.F.M.; Frank Jasper, O.F.M.; Rock Travnikar, O.F.M.; Jeffrey Scheeler, O.F.M.; Bro. Ronald Bolfeta, O.F.M.; Bro. Gene Mayer, O.F.M., Prov. Sec.; Revs. Kenan Freson, O.F.M., Prov. Treas.; James Bok, O.F.M., Dir.-Devel.; Maynard Tetreault, O.F.M., Bldg. Coord.; Nicholas Lohkamp, O.F.M., Coord. of Ministry of the Word; Francis Tebbe, O.F.M., Dir. Continuing Education/Formation. Tel: 313-432-5300. Henry Beck, O.F.M., Dir.-Office of Peace, Justice & Integrity of Creation; Bro. Scott Obrecht O.F.M., Dir.-Franciscan Missionary Union; Revs. David Crank, O.F.M., Dir.-Office of Senior Friars; Daniel Anderson, O.F.M., Prov. Archivist & Librarian; Marcan Hetteberg, O.F.M., Prov. Archivist & Libriarian; Loren Connell, O.F.M., Prov. Spiritual Asst. for Secular Order; Stanley Bir, O.F.M., Personnel Advr. Vocation Dirs.: Rev. Rock Travnikar, O.F.M.; Bro. Allan Schmitz, O.F.M. Tel: 513-825-1082.

Priests 155; Temporary Professed 4; Deacons 3; Novices 4; Brothers 57.

Represented in the Archdioceses of Chicago, Cincinnati, Detroit, Indianapolis, Louisville, New Orleans, Santa Fe and the Dioceses of Baton Rouge, Brownsville, Gallup, Galveston-Houston, Gary, Houma-Thibodaux, Lafayette (LA), Lafayette (IN), Las Cruces, Lexington, Marquette, Palm Beach, Peoria, Shreveport, St. Augustine, and Stubenville.

Province of The Sacred Heart (1858): 3140 Meramec St., St. Louis, MO 63118. Tel: 314-353-3421. Very Rev. Kurt Hartrich, O.F.M., Prov. Minister; Rev. John Doctor, O.F.M., Prov. Vicar. Councillors: Revs. Arthur Anderson, O.F.M.; Michael Cusato, O.F.M.; Louis Davino, O.F.M.; John Eaton, O.F.M.; Thomas Nairn, O.F.M.; Bro. Herbert Rempe, O.F.M.; Bro. Christopher Lambert, O.F.M., Prov. Sec.; Bro. Thomas Smith, O.F.M., Prov. Spiritual Asst. of Secular Franciscan Order; Revs. Allan DaCorte, O.F.M., Prov. Treas.; Henry Willenborg, O.F.M., Prov. Dir. of Formation - Dir.-Franciscan Vocation Center, 4860 W. 29th St., Cicero, IL 60650. Michael Crosby, O.F.M., Office of Friar Formation; Thomas Gardner, O.F.M., Prov. Promoter of the Missions, Commissary of the Holy Land.

Legal Title: *An Association of Franciscan Fathers of the State of Illinois; Franciscan Fathers of the State of Missouri; Friars Minor of the Order of St. Francis, Cleveland; Franciscan Fathers of the State of Wisconsin, Inc.; Franciscan Press, Franciscan Tertiary Province of the Sacred Heart, Incorporated; Mayslake Village; Franciscan Mayslake Village; Cloister Courts; Chariton Apartments; Employees of the Franciscan Orders.*

Solemnly Professed:; Priests 245; Brothers 84; Simply Professed: Brothers 7; Permanent Deacons 2.

Properties owned, sponsored or staffed: Friaries 40; Parishes 38; Missions 30; Institutional Chaplaincies 20; Chaplaincies for Religious 9; Formation Houses 2; Novitiates 1; Colleges 1; High Schools 2; Publishing House 1.

Represented in the Archdioceses of Chicago, Indianapolis, New Orleans, St. Louis, St. Paul-Minneapolis and San Antonio and in the Dioceses of Cleveland, Fairbanks, Fort Worth, Gaylord, Jefferson City, Joliet, Knoxville, Little Rock, Memphis, Nashville, Shreveport, Springfield (IL), Superior and Victoria.

Province of the Assumption of the Blessed Virgin Mary (1887): *Provincial Office*, Pulaski, WI 54162. Tel: 920-822-5422; Fax: 920-822-5423. Very Rev. Paul Reczek, O.F.M., Prov.; Rev. Thomas Luczak, O.F.M., Vicar. Definitors: Revs. Leslie Hoppe, O.F.M.; Thomas Wojciechowski, O.F.M.; Placid Strolk, O.F.M.; John Puodziwnas, O.F.M.; Andrew Brophy, O.F.M.; Revs. Richard Tulko, O.F.M., Prov. Sec.; John Puodziunas, O.F.M., Comptroller; Hugh Zurat, O.F.M., Dir. of Evangelization Center; James Buda, Prov. Spiritual Asst. of Secular Franciscan Order.

Legal Holdings or Titles: *St. Francis Friary & Retreat Center,* Burlington, WI, *Holy Name Friary,* Chicago, IL, *Assumption of B.V.M. Friary,* Pulaski, WI.
Priests 142; Professed Clerics 2; Professed Brothers 56.
Properties owned or staffed: Parishes 20; Friaries 16.
Represented in the Archdioceses of Chicago, Detroit, Milwaukee, New York and Philadelphia and in the Dioceses of Brownsville, Burlington, Camden, Cleveland, Fort Wayne-South Bend, Gary, Gaylord, Green Bay, Jackson, Joliet, Pittsburgh, Rochester, Rockford, Saginaw, and St. Petersburg.

Province of Our Lady of Guadalupe (1985): San *Antonio Friary,* 1350 Lakeview Rd., S.W., Albuquerque, NM 87105. Tel: 505-877-5425; Fax: 505-877-1440. Very Rev. Gilbert Schneider, O.F.M., Prov. Min.; Revs. Salvador Aragon, O.F.M., Prov. Vicar; Gino Correa, O.F.M., Sec.-Formation & Studies. Councillors; Sean Murnan, O.F.M.; Gerald Grantner, O.F.M., Archivist; Jack Clark Robinson, O.F.M.; Wayne Gibbeaut, O.F.M.; Don Billiard, O.F.M., Prov. Treas.; Lawrence Schreiber, O.F.M., Sec. & Vocation Dir.; Bruce Michalek, O.F.M., Sec. Missionary Evangelization; Larry Dunham, O.F.M., Prov. Devel. & FMC Dir.; Dale Jamison, O.F.M., FMC Dir.
Legal Title: *The Province of Our Lady of Guadalupe of the Order of Friars, Minor, Inc; Southwest Franciscan Missions, Inc., Southwest Franciscan Services, Inc.*
Priests 63; Brothers 16; Temporary Professed 2; Postulants 1; Novices 1.
Represented in the Archdioceses of Denver and Santa Fe and the Dioceses of Gallup and Las Cruces. Also in Mexico and Peru.

Order of Friars Minor of the Province of the Most Holy Name (Legal Title) **(1901):** 126 West 32nd St., New York, NY 10001-3202. Tel: 212-967-6300; Fax: 212-967-6344. Very Rev. John M. Felice, O.F.M., Prov. Minister; Very Rev. Charles J. Miiller, O.F.M., Prov. Vicar. Provincial Councillors: Revs. Hugh Hines, O.F.M.; David Hyman, O.F.M.; Daniel McLellan, O.F.M.; Kevin Mullen, O.F.M.; John O'Connor, O.F.M.; Ronald Pecci, O.F.M.; Bro. F. Edward Coughlin, O.F.M., Prov. Sec.; Revs. Vincent Grogan, O.F.M., Legal & Canonical Counsel; Cassian A. Miles, O.F.M., Dir. Communications; Joseph Hertel, O.F.M., Dir. Office of Devel. & Public Rels.; Dennis Wilson, O.F.M., Treas.; Bro. Gordon (Denis) Clark, O.F.M., Promoter of the Missions & Sec.-Missionary Evangelization; Revs. Peter Brophy, O.F.M., Dir. Vocations; Matthew Gaskin, O.F.M., Prov. Spiritual Asst. for Secular Franciscan Order.
Solemn Profession: Bishops 3; Priests 395; Brothers 99; Permanent Deacons 3; Temporary Profession: Brothers 10; Clerics 9; Novices 6; Affiliates 11.
Properties owned or sponsored: Province Parishes 31; Missions 1; Urban Ministry Centers 4; University 1; Colleges 1; Community Houses-Residences 45; Houses of Formation 5; Shrine Churches 2.
Chaplaincies 17 Military Chaplain 2; Campus Ministry 8.
Represented in the Archdioceses of Atlanta, Baltimore, Boston, Chicago, Denver, Hartford, Kansas City in Kansas, Los Angeles, Miami, Newark, New York, Philadelphia, Santa Fe, Washington and the Dioceses of Albany, Bridgeport, Buffalo, Camden, Charleston, Charlotte, Corpus Christi, Las Cruces, Ogdensburg, Palm Beach, Paterson, Raleigh, Rockville Centre, Sacramento, San Diego, Scranton, St. Petersburg, Steubenville, Trenton, Wilmington and Youngstown.

Province of St. Barbara (1915), *The Franciscan Friars of California* (1900): 1500 34th Ave., Oakland, CA 94601. Tel: 510-536-3722; Fax: 510-536-3970. Very Rev. Finian McGinn, O.F.M., Prov.; Rev. Stephen Barnufsky, O.F.M., Vicar Prov. Definitors: Revs. Richard McManus, O.F.M.; Ben Innes, O.F.M.; Miguel Obregon, O.F.M.; John Hardin, O.F.M.; Bros. Ed Dunn, O.F.M.; William Short, O.F.M.; Rev. Melvin A. Jurisich, O.F.M., Prov. Sec.
Legal Title: *Franciscan Friars of California; Franciscan Fathers of Arizona; Franciscan Fathers of Oregon; Franciscan Fathers of Washington.*
Priests 156; Solemnly Professed Lay Brothers 78; Simply Professed Brothers 16; Novices 3; Pre-novitiate 8.
Represented in the Archdioceses of Los Angeles, Portland (OR), and San Francisco and in the Dioceses of Fresno, Gallup, Las Cruces, Monterey, Oakland, Orange, Phoenix, Las Vegas, Sacramento, Salt Lake City, San Diego, San Jose, Spokane and Tucson.

Province of the Immaculate Conception (Friars Minor of the Order of St. Francis) (1871): 125 Thompson St., New York, NY 10012. Tel: 212-674-4388. Very Rev. Robert M. Campagna, O.F.M., Prov.; Rev. Steven M. Sysol, O.F.M., Vicar Prov. Definitors: Revs. Blaise Tranchida, O.F.M.; Armand Padula, O.F.M.; Primo Piscitello, O.F.M.; Antonio Nardoianni, O.F.M.; Michael Bercik, O.F.M.; Simeon Distefano, O.F.M., Prov. Sec.; Claude Scrima, O.F.M., SFO Prov. Spiritual Asst.; Alban Montella, O.F.M., Promoter of the Franciscan Missions; Madeline Bonnici, Exec. Dir., *Franciscan Mission Associates,* 274-280 W. Lincoln Ave., Mount Vernon, NY 10550. Rev. Robert M. Campagna, O.F.M., *Pious League of St. Anthony.*
Fathers 155; Bishops 3; Brothers 29; Permanent Deacons 3.
Properties owned or staffed:: Parishes 38; Residences 22.
Represented in the Archdioceses of Boston, Hartford and New York and in the Dioceses of Albany, Bridgeport, Brooklyn, Fall River, Manchester, Metuchen, Pittsburgh, Portland (ME), Trenton, Wheeling-Charleston and Youngstown. Also in Toronto and Italy.

Commissariat of The Holy Cross (1912): 14246 Main St., P.O. Box 608, Lemont, IL 60439. Tel: 630-257-2494; Fax: 630-257-8559. Rev. Blase Chemazar, O.F.M., Custos. Councillors: Revs. Vendelin Spendov, O.F.M.; Bernard Karmanocky, O.F.M.; Bro. Robert Hochevar, O.F.M.
Legal Title: *The Slovene Franciscan Fathers; Order of Friars Minor; Commissariat of the Holy Cross,* Lemont, IL; *St. Mary's Retreat House,* Lemont, IL.
Fathers 14; Brothers 1.
Parishes 4; Monastery 1; Retreat House 1; Mission Center 1.
Represented in the Archdioceses of Chicago and New York and in the Diocese of Altoona-Johnstown.

Vice Province of the Holy Savior: Provincial House-Holy Family Friary, 232 S. Home Ave., Pittsburgh, PA 15202. Tel: 412-761-2550; 761-8470. Friar. David Kohut, O.F.M., Prov.; Friar John Joseph Gonchar, O.F.M., Vicar Prov. Councillors: Friar Michael Dubec, O.F.M.; Friar Richard Portasik, O.F.M.; Friar Mark Hudak, O.F.M.; Friar David Moczulski, O.F.M.
Fathers 19; Brothers 8.
Friaries 4.
Represented in the Dioceses of Allentown, Greensburg and Pittsburgh.

Franciscan Friars: Mt. Alverna Friary, 517 S. Belle Vista Ave., Youngstown, OH 44509. Tel: 330-799-1888. Revs. John Reiss, O.F.M., Vicar; Sandor Krupa, O.F.M., Guardian.
Represented in the Diocese of Youngstown.

Croatian Franciscan Custody of the Holy Family of U.S. & Canada (1926): 4848 S. Ellis Ave., Chicago, IL 60615. Tel: 312-536-0552; Fax: 312-536-0552. Rev. Slavko Soldo, O.F.M., Custos. Councillors: Revs. Matthew Ruyechan, O.F.M.; Jozo Abramovic, O.F.M.; Jozo Grubisic, O.F.M.; Paul Maslac, O.F.M.
Fathers 34; Cleric 1.
Friaries 1; Parishes 9; Missions in Canada 9; Printery 1.
Represented in the Archdioceses of Chicago, Detroit, Milwaukee, New York and St. Louis and in the Dioceses of Allentown and Erie. Also in Canada.

Lithuanian Franciscan Vice-Province of St. Casimir: Franciscan Friary, P.O. Box 980, Kennebunkport, ME 04046. Tel: 207-967-2011; Fax: 207-967-5721. Very Rev. Placid Barius, O.F.M., Prov. Minister; Rev. Augustine Simanavicius, O.F.M., Prov. Vicar. Councillors: Revs. Francis Giedgaudas, O.F.M.; Raphael Sakalys, O.F.M.; John Bacevicius, O.F.M.; Benedict Jurcys, O.F.M.
Bishops 1; Fathers 34; Brothers 4; Seminarians 14.
Properties owned or sponsored: Parishes 4; Summer Camps 1; Guest House; Retreat House 1; Printery 1.
Represented in the Dioceses of Brooklyn, Portland (ME), and St. Petersburg. Also in Toronto, Canada.

U.S. Foundation (1940): *Province of the Holy Gospel,* Roger Bacon College, 2400 Marr St., El Paso, TX 79903. Rev. Alberto Hernandez, O.F.M.
Priests 3; Brothers 1.
Represented in the Diocese of El Paso.

Commissariat of the Holy Land, Franciscan Monastery Of Mt. St. Sepulchre: 1400 Quincy St., N.E., Washington, DC 20017. Tel: 202-526-6800; Fax: 202-529-9889. Bro. Callistus Welch, O.F.M., Guardian & Commissary of the Holy Land; Revs. Mark Hurst, O.F.M., Moderator - Knights; James Brabandt, O.F.M., Dir.-Postulants; Stephen F. Sabbagh, O.F.M., Prov. Spiritual Asst. to the Secular Franciscan Order; Joshua Doyle, O.F.M.; Sabin Plechta, O.F.M.; Kevin Treston, O.F.M., Public Rels., Editor of Cursador's Almanac; Francis Sihuay, O.F.M. (Peru); Manuel Ybarra, O.F.M., Vicar, Vice Commissary, Treas.; Patrick Flanigan, O.F.M.
Priests 9; Brothers 14; Solemnly Professed 23.
Represented in the Archdiocese of Washington.

Franciscan Custody of St. Mary of the Angels (Byzantine-Slavonic Rite): *Holy Dormition Monastery,* P.O. Box 270, Sybertsville, PA 18251. Tel: 717-788-1212; Fax: 717-788-2431. Very Rev. James Carroll, O.F.M., Protohegumen.
Represented in the Byzantine Rite Dioceses of St. Nicholas in Chicago, Parma, Passaic, Philadelphia, Pittsburgh and Stamford.

Academy of American Franciscan History: 1712 Euclid Ave., Berkeley, CA 94709.
Legal Title: *Academy of American Franciscan History;* Dr. John F. Schwaller, Dir.

Franciscan Vocation Conference (F.V.C.) (1944): *Sacred Heart Province,* 4860 W. 29th St., Cicero, IL 60804. Tel: 708-656-2570. Rev. Henry V. Willenborg, O.F.M., Pres., Franciscan Society organized nationally to promote cooperative and unified vocational effort in the Franciscan Provinces, Vice-Provinces and Custodies of the U.S.A.

National Fraternity of the Secular Franciscan Order, U.S.A. (formerly North American Federation, Third Order of St. Francis): 3307 Quail Meadows Dr., Santa Maria, CA 93455. William Wicks, S.F.O., Natl. Minister.
Founded by St. Francis of Assisi in 1209, to give secular, clergy and laity, an opportunity to live according to the Gospel through the observance of an approved rule of life. In 1921 the Fraternities in the United States united in Secular Franciscan Provinces, and are officially known as the National Fraternity of the Secular Franciscan Order, U.S.A. Present membership in the United States is 18,000 in 720 local fraternities and 31 regional fraternities.

[0530] (S.A.)—FRANCISCAN FRIARS OF THE ATONEMENT

(Societas Adunationis T.O.R.)

Generalate: St. James Friary, P.O. Box 5, Garrison, NY 10524-0005. Tel: 914-424-3539. Very Rev. Emil F. Tomaskovic, S.A., Minister Gen.; Rev. Thomas Gumprecht, S.A., Vicar Gen. & Procurator Gen. to the Holy See; Bro. Raymond Saville, S.A., Sec. Gen. General Councillors: Revs. Elias Mallon, S.A.; Henry Marchese, S.A.; Dennis Polanco, S.A.; Rev. Bernard Palka, S.A., Treas. Gen.
Motherhouse: St. Paul's Friary, Graymoor, Garrison, NY 10524. Tel: 914-424-3671.
Legal Title: *St. Chistopher's Inn, St. James Friary, St. Paul's Friary, St. Francis of Assisi Novitiate.*
Priests 96; Professed Seminarians 6; Professed Brothers 47.
Friaries 13; Novitiates 1; Parishes (U.S. and Canada) 11; Overseas Ministries: England, Italy, and Japan; Ecumenical Institute 1; Pastoral Center 1; Campus Ministries; Retreat and Conference Center 1; Rehabilitation Center for Alcoholics 1; Shelter for Homeless men; Military Chaplaincies 2.
Represented in the Archdioceses of Boston, Los Angeles, New York and Washington and in the Dioceses of Arlington, Monterey, Ogdensburg and Raleigh.

[0533](F.F.I.)—FRANCISCAN FRIARS OF THE IMMACULATE

General Motherhouse: Benevento, Italy.
Founded 1990.
Our Lady's Chapel: *Marian Friary of Our Lady Queen of the Seraphic Order,* 600 Pleasant St., New Bedford, MA 02740-6299. Tel: 508-996-8274. P.O. Box 3003, New Bedford, MA 02741-3003. Rev. Peter Damian Mary Fehlner, F.F.I., American Supr.
Legal Title: *Marian Friary of Our Lady of Guadalupe,* Baltic, CT.
Represented in the Dioceses of Fall River and Norwich.

[0535] (C.F.R.)—FRANCISCAN FRIARS OF THE RENEWAL

Central House: *Saint Crispin Friary,* 420 E. 156th St., Bronx, NY 10455. Tel: 718-665-2441. Revs. Andrew Apostoli, C.F.R., Community Servant; Robert Stanion, C.F.R., Vicar. Counselors; Benedict J. Groeschel, C.F.R.; Glenn Sudano, C.F.R.
Represented in the Archdiocese of New York.

[0540] (O.S.F.)—FRANCISCAN MISSIONARY BROTHERS OF THE SACRED HEART OF JESUS

(Fratres Missionarii sti Francisci de Sso. Corde Jesu)

Motherhouse (1927): *Our Lady of Angels Monastery,* St. Joseph Rd., Eureka, MO 63025. Tel: 314-587-3661. Bros. Matthew Gallagher, O.S.F., Dir. Gen.; Damien De Braekeleer, O.S.F., Asst. Dir. Gen.
Legal Holdings or Titles: *The Black Madonna Shrine and Grottos (Our Lady of Czestoehowa), St. Joseph's Hill Infirmary, Inc., Price Memorial,* Eureka, MO, *Merkle-Knipprath Nursing Home & Apartment Community,* Clifton, MO.
Brothers 13.
Represented in the Archdiocese of St. Louis and the Diocese of Joliet.

[0560] (T.O.R.)—THIRD ORDER REGULAR OF SAINT FRANCIS

(Tertius Ordo Regularis de Poenitentia)

General Motherhouse: SS. Cosmas and Damian, Via dei Fori Imperiali, 1, Rome, Italy. Very Rev. Bonaventure Midili, T.O.R., Minister Gen.

Province of the Most Sacred Heart of Jesus (1910): *Provincial Residence,* 215 57th St., Pittsburgh, PA 15201. Tel: 412-781-8333; Fax: 412-781-1219. Very Rev. Edmund F. Carroll, T.O.R., Minister Prov.; Rev. Christian R. Oravec, T.O.R., Vicar Prov. Councillors: Revs. Michael Scanlan, T.O.R.; Thomas Bourque, T.O.R.; Daniel Sinisi, T.O.R.; Bro. Mark McBride, T.O.R., Treas. & Dir.-Missions; Revs. Fidelis Weber, T.O.R., Prov. Sec. Formation; Terence Henry, T.O.R., Dir.-Postulants; Peter A. Lyons, T.O.R., Dir. Post-Novitiate Formation; Michael Higgins, T.O.R., Novices Master; Richard Davis, T.O.R., Dir.-Vocations; Bernard Tickerhoof, T.O.R., Secular Franciscans Prov. Spiritual Asst.

Fathers 120; Professed Clerics 11; Brothers 30; Novices 2; Postulants 6.

Legal Title: *Province of the Most Sacred Heart of Jesus, Third Order Regular of Saint Francis (USA), Loretto, PA.*

Ministry in Ministries in Parishes; Universities and Colleges; High School; Chaplaincies; Foreign Mission in Brazil & Republic of South Africa; House of Study 1; Novitiates 1; Laymen's Retreat League.

Represented in the Archdioceses of Philadelphia and Washington and in the Dioceses of Altoona-Johnstown, Arlington, Fort Worth, Harrisburg, Pittsburgh, St. Augustine, St. Petersburg, Sioux Falls, Steubenville, Trenton, Venice and Wheeling-Charleston.

Province of The Immaculate Conception: San Pedro Center, 2400 Dike Rd., Winter Park, FL 32792. Tel: 407-677-6406; Fax: 407-677-6489. Very Rev. Robert J. D'Aversa, T.O.R., Minister Prov.; Very Rev. Theodore Midile, T.O.R., Vicar Prov.; Revs. Carl Vacek, T.O.R.; Alexis Nagle, T.O.R.; Anthony Criscitelli, T.O.R.; Guy Noonan, T.O.R. Prov. Councillors: Rev. Patrick Quinn, T.O.R., Prov. Sec.; Most Rev. Bonaventure Midili, Minister Gen. of the Order, Rome, Italy; Rev. Cyprian Mercieca, South Africa.

Legal Title: *Third Order Regular of St. Francis, Province of the Immaculate, Conception (USA).*

Priests 52; Brothers 9; Permanent Deacons 1; Student Friars 2.

Represented in the Archdioceses of Miami, St. Paul-Minneapolis, Washington, and the Dioceses of Altoona-Johnstown, Davenport, Orlando, Owensboro, Scranton, Wheeling-Charleston and Wilmington.

U.S.A. Franciscan Commissariate T.O.R., of The Spanish Province (1924): 301 Jefferson Ave., Waco, TX 76701. Tel: 817-752-8434; Fax: 817-752-2415. Very Rev. Joseph A. Martorell, T.O.R., Commissary. Councillors: Revs. Lawrence Soler, T.O.R.; Antonio Terrassa, T.O.R.

Fathers 12.

Parishes 6.

Represented in the Archdiocese of Newark and in the Dioceses of Austin and Fort Worth.

[0570] (Glmy.)—THE GLENMARY HOME MISSIONERS

(Societas Missionariorum Domesticorum Americas)
(The Home Missioners of America)

General Headquarters: P.O. Box 465618, Cincinnati, OH 45246-5618. Tel: 513-874-8900. Revs. Jerry Dorn, Pres.; Will Steinbacher, 1st Vice Pres.; Bros. Jack Henn, 2nd Vice Pres.; Mike Springer, Senior Member Coord.; Mr. Bob Knueven, Treas. Senior Members: Revs. Joseph Gartner; Robert Healy; Joseph Dean; Del Holmes; James P. Kelly; George Mathis; Raymond Orlett; Frank Schenk; William Smith; Ed Haggerty; Pat O'Donnell; Charles Hughes; John McNearney; John Otterbacher; Bob Berson; Bros. George Sauer; Paul Wilhelm; Tom Kelly; Bob Hoffman; Vincent Wilmes.

Vocation Center: P.O. Box 465618, Cincinnati, OH 45246. Rev. Mike Caroline, Dir. Vocations.

Houses of Formation: Glenmary House of Studies and Glenmary Novitiate, 1323 Quincy St., N.E., Washington, DC 20017. Tel: 202-526-1337. Rev. Chet Artysiewicz, Dir. House of Studies; Rev. Mike Kerin, Dir. Novitiate.

Glenmary Research Center, 235 E. Ponce de Leon Ave., Ste. 226, Decatur, GA 30030. Tel: 404-377-7010. Sr. Mary Priniski, O.P., Interim Dir., Works exclusively in the rural missionary apostolate, to serve the needs of the Catholic Church as a whole in small town and rural America.

Glenmary Department of Pastoral Services, 1312 Fifth Ave. N., Nashville, TN 37208. Tel: 615-256-1900. Rev. Dennis Holly, Dir., Assists in educational programs, teacher training, parish evaluations and long range planning. Maintains extensive library of publications and audio visuals.

Fathers 61; Students in Theology 3; Professed Brothers 19.

Properties owned, sponsored or staffed: Mission Bases 38; Houses of Study 2; Vocational Centers.

Represented in the Archdioceses of Atlanta, Cincinnati and Washington and in the Dioceses of Birmingham, Charlotte, Covington, Jackson, Knoxville, Lexington, Little Rock, Nashville, Owensboro, Richmond, Savannah, Tulsa, Tyler and Wheeling-Charleston.

[0580] (B.G.S.)—LITTLE BROTHERS OF THE GOOD SHEPHERD

Villa Mathias: Foundation House: Little Brothers of The Good Shepherd, 901 Bro. Mathias Pl. N.W., P.O. Box 389, Albuquerque, NM 87102. Tel: 505-243-4238; Fax: 505-764-9721.

General Headquarters (1987): *Good Shepherd Centre,* 412 Queen St. East, Toronto, Ontario , Canada, M5A 1T3. Tel: 416-869-3619. Rev. Bros. David Lynch, B.G.S., Supr. Gen.; Gerard Sullivan, B.G.S., Vicar Gen. & Dir. of Novices; Savio Charron, B.G.S., Sec. Gen.; Richard MacPhee, B.G.S., Gen. Treas.

Legal Holdings and Titles: ***Little Brothers of The Good Shepherd, Inc.***, New Mexico; ***Good Shepherd Center, Inc.***, Albuquerque, NM; ***Caritas Deus, Inc.***, New Mexico, ***Charity Unlimited, Inc.***, New Mexico; ***Villa Mathias, Inc.***, New Mexico; ***Brother Mathias Barrett, Inc.***, New Mexico; ***Brothers of Good Shepard, Inc.***, Pennsylvania; ***Little Brothers of Good Shepard, Inc.***, Illinois; ***Brothers of Good Shepard, Inc.***, Florida; ***Camillus House, Inc.***, Florida; ***Camillus Health Concern, Inc.***, Florida; ***Charity Unlimited, Inc.***, Florida; ***Brothers Mathias Barrett, Inc.***, Illinois.

Professed Brothers 38; Novice Brothers 5.

Properties owned and/or sponsored: temporary shelters for marginalized men & women 14; residences for the elderly 2; shelter for battered women & children 3; residences for persons with AIDS 1.

Professed Brothers 38; Novice Brothers 5.

Represented in the Archdioceses of Miami, Philadelphia and Santa Fe and the Diocese of Joliet.

[0590] (M.Ss.A.)—MISSIONARIES OF THE HOLY APOSTLES

General Administration: Missionaries of the Holy Apostles, 8594 rue Berri, Montreal, Quebec, Canada, H2P 2G4. Tel: 514-387-2222. Very Rev. Yvon Archambault, M.Ss.A., Supr. Gen. Adminator.

Missionaries of the Holy Apostles Headquarters: Provincial Administration, 33 Prospect Hill Rd., Cromwell, CT 06416. Tel: 203-632-3039; Fax: 203-632-3035. Very Rev. Benedict Klucinec, M.Ss.A., Prov. Animator; Rev. Martin D. Rooney, M.Ss.A., Sec.

Priests 48; Brothers 7.

Properties owned, staffed, or sponsored: Holy Apostles College and Seminary, 6 Parishes Hermitage 3 Hospital Chaplaincies.

Represented in the Archdioceses of Denver, Washington and the Dioceses of Norwich, Pennsacola-Tallahassee and Wheeling-Charleston.

[0600] (C.S.C.)—BROTHERS OF THE CONGREGATION OF HOLY CROSS

(Congregatio A Sancta Cruce)

Generalate: Congregazione di Santa Croce, Via Framura, 85, 00168, Rome, Italy. Rev. Claude Grou, Supr. Gen.; Bro. Patrick Sopher; Rev. Robert Morin; Bro. Joel Giallanza; Rev. Leo D'Souza.

Midwest Province of the Brothers of Holy Cross (1841): *Provincial House,* Box 460, Notre Dame, IN 45656. Tel: 219-239-8311; Fax: 219-289-0487. Bros. William Geenen, C.S.C., Prov. Supr.; Donald Gibbs, C.S.C., Asst. Prov.; Robert Fillmore, C.S.C., Sec.; Donald Bailer, C.S.C., Steward & Treas.; Bro. Richard Gilman, C.S.C., Councillor.

Legal Title: *Notre Dame, Ind. Brothers of Holy Cross, Inc.*

Professed Brothers 236; Temporarily Professed 1; Aspirants 7.

Properties owned, staffed, or sponsored: Community Houses 2; Junior College; High Schools 9; Boarding Military Grade School; Scholasticates 2; Foreign Mission Schools 3.

Represented in the Archdioceses of Anchorage, Chicago, Detroit, Indianapolis, Los Angeles, Miami, Milwaukee, New Orleans, Portland (OR), San Antonio and Washington and in the Dioceses of Austin, Cleveland, Colorado Springs, Erie, Evansville, Fort Wayne-South Bend, Gary, Grand Rapids, Lansing, Nashville, Oakland, Phoenix, Providence, St. Petersburg, Savannah, Scranton and Venice.

South-West Province of the Brothers of Holy Cross (1956): *Brother John Baptist Province Center,* St. Edward University, No. 1046, Austin, TX 78704. Tel: 512-442-7856. Bros. Donald Blauvelt, C.S.C., Prov.; Matthew Lyons, C.S.C., Asst. Prov.; Richard Critz, Sec.; Harold Ehlinger, C.S.C., Steward. Councillors: Bros. Stanley Culotta; Richard Daly; Stephen Walsh.

Professed Brothers 128; Temporarily Professed 7.

Properties owned, staffed, or sponsored: Colleges 1; High Schools 7; Home for Boys 1; Schools Foreign Mission Schools 2.

Represented in the Archdioceses of Los Angeles, Louisville, New Orleans, Portland (OR), San Antonio and Santa Fe and in the Dioceses of Austin, Beaumont, Cheyenne, Cleveland, Fort Wayne-South Bend, Knoxville, Lake Charles, Oakland, San Jose and Savannah.

Eastern Province of the Brothers of Holy Cross (1956): 85 Overlook Cir., New Rochelle, NY 10804. Tel: 914-632-4468; 4469; Fax: 914-632-2490. Bros. John Gleason, C.S.C., Prov.; Stephen LaMendola, C.S.C., Asst. Prov. & Councillor for schools; Mark Knightly, C.S.C., Sec.; Peter Martin, C.S.C., Councillor for Financial Services; John Thornton, C.S.C., Councillor; Paul Bednarcyzk, C.S.C., Councillor.

Legal Title: *Brothers of the Holy Cross of the Eastern Province of the United States of America, Inc.*

Professed Brothers 127; Temporarily Professed 5; Novices 1.

High Schools 4; Foreign Mission Houses 6; Schools Middle School; Spiritual Life Center; Boys Home.

Represented in the Archdioceses of Hartford, New York, San Antonio, Washington and in the Dioceses of Albany, Austin, Brooklyn, Savannah, Syracuse, and Wilmington.

[0610] (C.S.C.)—PRIESTS OF THE CONGREGATION OF HOLY CROSS

Congregatio a Sancta Cruce

Generalate: *Curia Generalizia di Santa Croce,* Via Framura 85, 00168, Rome, Italy. Rev. Claude Grou, C.S.C., Supr. Gen. General Assts.: Bro. Patrick Sopher, C.S.C.; Rev. Robert Morin, C.S.C.; Bro. Joel Giallanza, C.S.C.; Rev. Leo D'Souza, C.S.C.

Congregation of Holy Cross, Indiana Province (1841): *Provincial House,* 1304 E. Jeffersen Blvd., South Bend, IN 46617. Tel: 219-289-6850. Revs. William E. Dorwart, C.S.C., Prov. Supr.; Robert L. Epping, C.S.C., First Asst. Prov.; James F. Flanigan, C.S.C., Prov. Sec.; Mark B. Thesing, C.S.C., Secong Asst. Prov. & Steward. Prov. Councillors: Revs. David L. Guffey, C.S.C.; Peter A. Jarret, C.S.C.; Wilson D. Miscamble, C.S.C.; Robert S. Pelton, C.S.C.; David T. Tyson, C.S.C.; Bro. John J. Platte, C.S.C.

Legal Title: *Priests of Holy Cross, Indiana Province, Inc.*

Fathers 313; Professed Clerics 6; Temporarily Professed Clerics 23; Novices 9; Candidates 39; Professed Brothers 22.

Properties owned, sponsored, or staffed: College Seminary; Theological Seminary; Novitiate; Mission Center; Provincial House; Postulate; Universities 2; Colleges 2; High Schools 2; Parishes 15; 19 Chaplaincies; Home Mission Band; Publishing House; Retreat House.

Holy Cross Associates Lay Missionary Program, P.O. Box 668, Notre Dame, IN 46556. Mr. John Pinter, Dir.

Holy Cross Association, Box K, Notre Dame, IN 46556. Rev. Herbert C. Yost, C.S.C., Dir.

Represented in the Archdioceses of Anchorage, Chicago, Los Angeles, New Orleans, New York, Portland (OR), San Antonio, San Francisco, Washington and in the Dioceses of Austin, Colorado Springs, Fall River, Fort Wayne-South Bend, Gary, Kalamazoo, Monterey, Oakland, Phoenix, San Bernardino, San Diego and San Jose.

Congregation of Holy Cross—Eastern Province, Inc. (1952): *Provincial Headquarters,* 835 Clinton Ave., Bridgeport, CT 06604. Tel: 203-367-7252; 367-1152; Fax: 203-366-7886. Revs. Hugh W. Cleary, C.S.C., Prov. Supr.; Wilfred J. Raymond, C.S.C., Asst. Prov. Supr.; Leo Polselli, C.S.C., Treas. Prov. Councillors: Revs. Thomas P. Looney, C.S.C.; Bartley MacPhaidin, C.S.C.; George B. Mulligan, C.S.C.; Thomas J. O'Hara, C.S.C.; John P. Phalen, C.S.C.; Bro. Herman Zaccarelli, C.S.C.

Fathers 135; Temporarily Professed Clerics 9; Candidates 15; Novices 4; Brothers Professed 15.

Properties owned, sponsored, or staffed: Colleges 2; Mission Houses; Parishes 11; Retreat House; Chaplaincies 22; Campus Ministry 8; Family Rosary Crusade; Family Theater.

Represented in the Archdioceses of Boston, Hartford, Los Angeles, New York and Washington and in the Dioceses of Albany, Bridgeport, Brooklyn,

Burlington, Fall River, Norwich, Orlando, Portland (ME), Rochester and Scranton.

Southern Province (1968): *Holy Cross, Southern Province, Provincial House,* 2111 Brackenridge St., Austin, TX 78704. Tel: 512-443-3886; Fax: 512-416-1216. Revs. John S. Korcsmar, C.S.C., Prov. Supr.; Bro. Thomas G. Krieter, C.S.C., Asst. Prov. & Steward; Revs. Joseph M. Moyer, C.S.C., Prov. Sec.; Barry E. Cabell, Prov. Councillor; L. Peter Logsdon, C.S.C., Prov. Councillor.

Legal Title: *Congregation of Holy Cross, Southern Province, Inc.*

Fathers 30; Professed Brothers 1; Temporarily Professed 4; Novices 3.

Ministries in Parishes; Foreign Missions; Chaplaincies; Social Service.

Represented in the Archdioceses of New Orleans, St. Louis and San Antonio and in Dioceses of Austin, Baton Rouge, Fort Wayne-South Bend, Lafayette (LA) and Las Cruces.

[0620] (F.S.E.)—BROTHERS OF THE HOLY EUCHARIST

Founded in the United States 1957.

General Motherhouse and Novitiate: P.O. Box 25, Plaucheville, LA 71362. Tel: 318-922-3630; 922-3401. Rev. Bro. Andre M. Lucia, F.S.E., Supr. Gen.

Represented in the Diocese of Alexandria.

[0630] (M.S.F.)—CONGREGATION OF THE MISSIONARIES OF THE HOLY FAMILY

(Congregatio Missionariorum a Sacra Familia)

General Motherhouse: Via Odoari Beccari, 41, I-00154, Rome, Italy. Tel: 011-39-6-57-55-192; Fax: 011-39-6-57-55-208. Very Rev. Wim van der Weiden, M.S.F., Supr. Gen.

General Mission Office - M.S.F., Inc.: P.O. Box 918 - 260 W. Euclid Blvd., West Point, VA 23181. Tel: 804-843-2622; Fax: 804-843-3182. Rev. John Brieffies, M.S.F., Exec. Dir.

MSF Center: Provincialate USA of the Missionaries of the Holy Family, 210 El Rancho Way, San Antonio, TX 78209. Tel: 210-826-9815; Fax: 210-826-3393. Very Rev. Robert E. O'Hara, M.S.F., Prov. Supr.; Rev. John Dowling, M.S.F., Prov. Treas.

Fathers 52; Theology Students 4; Brothers 8.

Ministries in House of Study 2; Parishe 16.

Represented in the Archdioceses of St. Louis, and San Antonio, and in the Dioceses of Brownsville, Corpus Christi, Duluth and Richmond. Also in Canada and Mexico.

[0640] (S.F.)—SONS OF THE HOLY FAMILY

(Congregatio Filiorum Sacrae Familiae)

General Motherhouse: Entenza 301, Barcelona, 08029. Spain. Very Rev. Jose Roca, Gen. Superior.

U.S. Foundation (1920): 401 Randolph Rd., P.O. Box 4138, Silver Spring, MD 20914. Tel: 301-622-1184. Rev. Luis Picazo, S.F., Vice Prov.

Fathers 16.

Represented in the Archdioceses of Santa Fe, Washington, and the Archdiocese for the Military Services, U.S.A.

[0650] (C.S.SP.)—HOLY GHOST FATHERS

(Congregation of the Holy Ghost and of the Immaculate Heart of Mary)

(Congregatio Sancti Spiritus sub tutela Immaculati Cordis Beatissimae Virginis Mariae)

Generalate: Clivo di Cinna 195, Rome, 00136. Italy. Very Rev. Pierre Schouver, C.S.Sp., Supr. Gen.

Eastern Province of the United States (1872): 6230 Brush Run Rd., Bethel Park, PA 15102. Tel: 412-831-0302; Fax: 412-831-0970. Revs. Christopher P. Promis, C.S.Sp., Prov. Supr. Councillors: Revs. William R. Headley, C.S.Sp.; James P. McCloskey, C.S.Sp.; Donald McEachin, C.S.Sp.; John Sawicki, C.S.Sp.; David L. Smith, C.S.Sp.; Thomas P. Tunney, C.S.Sp.

Legal Holdings: *Archconfraternity of the Holy Ghost, Provincial Residence, Duquesne University, Holy Ghost Preparatory School, Bethel Holy Ghost Animation Center.*

Fathers in U.S. 83; Professed Theologians 2; Professed Brothers 1.

Properties owned, sponsored, or staffed: Parishes 14; Theologate; Home for Homeless Boys; Retirement Residences 3.

Represented in the Archdioceses of Chicago, Cincinnati, Detroit, New York, Philadelphia, Washington and in the Dioceses of Arlington, Charlotte, Pittsburgh, Providence, and Venice. Also in Puerto Rico.

Western Province of the United States (1964): *Congregation of the Holy Ghost,* 1700 W. Alabama St., Houston, TX 77098-2808. Tel: 713-522-2882; Fax: 713-522-8063. Very Rev. Donald S. Nesti, C.S.Sp., Prov. Supr. Prov. Councillors: Rev. Silvio A. D'Ostilio, C.S.Sp., 1st Asst.; Bro. Michael E. Suazo, C.S.Sp., 2nd Asst. & Prov. Sec.; Rev. Frankie L.G. Santos, C.S.Sp.; Rev. Daniel L. Walsh, C.S.Sp.; Rev. Joseph Gaglione, C.S.Sp., Prov. Bursar.

Priests 56; Professed Brothers 2; Lay Associates 10; Scholastics 10.

Properties owned, sponsored, or staffed: *Holy Spirit Provincialate & Holy Ghost Hall,* Houston, TX; *Libermann House at Spiritan Renewal Center,* New Braunfels, TX; *Casa Laval and Holy Ghost Novitiate,* Hemet, CA; *Iglesia de Santa Ana Maison Brottier,* Natchitoches, LA; Mision San Juan Bautista Staff: Parishes 13; Training Centers 3.

Represented in the Archdioceses of New Orleans, and San Antonio and in the Dioceses of Alexandria, Amarillo, Fresno, Galveston-Houston, Lafayette (LA), Little Rock, Phoenix, Pittsburgh, San Bernardino and San Diego. Also in Mexico.

Holy Ghost Fathers of Ireland (1971): Very Rev. Vincent O'Connell, C.S.Sp., Prov. Delegate U.S.A. East, 4849 37th St., Long Island City, NY 11101. Tel: 718-729-5273; Fax: 718-729-6949. Very Rev. Francis Mulloy, C.S.Sp., Prov. Delegate U.S.A. West, St. Dunstan's Church, 1133 Broadway, Mill Brae, CA 94030. Very Rev. Matthias Moore, C.S.Sp., Prov. Delegate Louisiana, St. John the Baptist Church, 1139 Dryades St., New Orleans, LA 70113. Councillors: Revs. Cornelius C. Woulfe, C.S.Sp.; Michael McCarthy, C.S.Sp.; Peter Nolan, C.S.Sp.; Andrew F. Duffy, C.S.Sp.; James Delaney, C.S.Sp.

Fathers 69.

Represented in the Archdioceses of Boston, Miami, New Orleans, New York and San Francisco and in the Dioceses of Brooklyn, Fargo, Metuchen, Palm Beach and St. Augustine.

[0660] (M.Sp.S.)—MISSIONARIES OF THE HOLY SPIRIT

General Motherhouse: Av. Universidad 1702, 04010, Mexico, D.F., Mexico. Tel: 5-658-74-33; 5-658-7851. Very Rev. Melecio Picazo, M.Sp.S., Supr. Gen.

American Headquarters: Our Lady of Guadalupe, 500 N. Juanita Ave., P.O. Box 1091, Oxnard, CA 93030. Tel: 805-483-0987.

Priests 17; Professed 17; Novices 16.

Parishes 5; House of Study 1; Novitiates 1; Theologate 1.

Represented in the Archdiocese of Los Angeles and the Diocese of Fresno.

[0670] (O.H.)—HOSPITALLER BROTHERS OF ST. JOHN OF GOD

General Motherhouse: Hospitaller Brothers of St. John of God, via della Nocetta 263, Rome, Italy, 00164. Most Rev. Bro. Pascual Piles, O.H., Prior Gen.

Order founded by St. John of God at Granada, Spain, in 1537.

American Province of Our Lady Queen of Angels (1970): *Villa Maria-Provincial Curia,* 2425 S. Western Ave., Los Angeles, CA 90018. Tel: 213-734-0233; 731-0641; Fax: 213-731-5987. Bro. Edward Francis McEnroe, O.H., Prov.

Brothers 32; Solemn Professed 30; Simple Professed 2; Priests 2.

Legal Holdings: *St. John of God Retirement and Care Center, Los Angeles, CA St. Joseph Health & Retirement Center, Ojai, CA St. John of God Health Care Services, Victorville, CA.*

Represented in the Archdiocese of Los Angeles and the Dioceses of Camden and San Bernardino.

[0680] (I.H.M.)—BROTHERS OF THE IMMACULATE HEART OF MARY

General Motherhouse (1948): 609 N. 7th St., Steubenville, OH 43952. Tel: 614-283-2462. Bro. Dominic Carroll, I.H.M., Supr. Gen.; Bro. Anthony Motto, I.H.M., Novice Master.

Professed Brothers 5.

Novitiate 1; Bishop's Residence; CCD Center 1; Pastoral Associates 3; Diocesan Office 1.

Represented in the Diocese of Steubenville.

[0690] (S.J.)—JESUIT FATHERS AND BROTHERS

(Societas Jesu)

Generalate: Casella Postale 6139, 00195, Rome, Italy. Very Rev. Peter-Hans Kolvenbach, S.J., Gen.; Revs. Hans Zwiefelhofer, Sec.; Francis E. Case, S.J., U.S. Assistant.

Jesuit Conference: The Society of Jesus in the United States National Offices, 1616 P Street, Suite 400, Washington, DC 20036-1405. Tel: 202-462-0400; Fax: 202-328-9212. Revs. Bradley M. Schaeffer, S.J., Pres.; James F. Lafontaine, S.J., Exec. Sec. & Sec. Formation; Richard J. Ryscavage, S.J., Sec. Int'l & Social Ministries and Jesuit Refugee Services; British Robinson, S.J., Dir.-Social Ministries; Thomas M. Rochford, S.J., Sec. for Communications.

Maryland Province (1833): 5704 Roland Ave., Baltimore, MD 21210. Tel: 410-532-1400; Fax: 410-532-1419. Very Rev. James R. Stormes, S.J., Prov.; Revs. James A. Casciotti, S.J., Supr. & Socius to the Prov.; J. Donald Freeze, S.J., Treas.; Charles L. Currie, S.J., Asst. Prov. for Higher Ed.; Daniel K. Lahart, S.J., Asst. Prov. for Secondary Ed.; Clement J. Petrik, S.J., Asst. Prov. for Pastoral Min.; Thomas P. Gaunt, S.J., Asst. Prov. for Jesuit Students; Hugh A. Kennedy, S.J., Assist. Sec. to Prov.; Ms. Suzanne M. Geaney, Dir. Social Ministries; Revs. William F. Lamm, S.J., Asst. Treas. & Sec.; Thomas P. Martin, S.J., Asst. Treas.; Francis H. McGauley, S.J., Health Care Coord.; William K. McGroarty, S.J., Asst. Treas. for Properties; Mr. James S. Schaefer, Bus. Mgr.; Revs. Francis R. Carmody, S.J., Dir. Mission Bureau & Jesuit Seminary Guild, Maryland Province; Richard J. Colgan, S.J., Asst. Dir.; Herbert F. Smith, S.J., Sec. Gen. of the League of the Sacred Heart; Joseph S. Costantino, S.J., Dir. Vocations; Gerald P. Fogarty, S.J., Archivist; James A. O'Brien, S.J., Promoter, Christian Life Communities; Brian O. McDermott, S.J., Tertian Instructor.

Legal Title: *Corporation of the Roman Catholic Clergymen, Maryland.*

Jesuit Volunteer Corps, East, 17th & Thompson Sts., Philadelphia, PA 19121.

Fathers 415; Scholastics 37; Brothers 27.

Properties owned, sponsored, or staffed: Parishes 12; Universities 4; Colleges 1; High Schools 5; Houses of Retreats 2; Residences 9.

Represented in the Archdioceses of Baltimore, Philadelphia and Washington and in the Dioceses of Allentown, Arlington, Camden, Charlotte, Erie, Pittsburgh, Raleigh, Richmond, Scranton, Wheeling-Charleston and Wilmington.

Province of New York (1943): 39 E. 83rd St., New York, NY 10028. Tel: 212-774-5500; Fax: 212-774-5510.

Legal Title: *The New York Province of the Society of Jesus, New York, N.Y.;* Very Rev. Kenneth J. Gavin, S.J., Prov.; Rev. Thomas E. Smith, S.J., Exec. Asst. to Prov.; Bro. Gilbert J. Scott, S.J., Asst. to the Prov.; Revs. J. Raymond Johnson, S.J., Prov. Treas.; J. Raymond Johnson, S.J., Auditor & American Rep. for the Missions of the Society of Jesus, Vatican City; Thomas P. Gaunt, S.J., Asst. for Formation; Frederick J. O'Brien, S.J., Asst. for Sec. Education; James F. Joyce, S.J., Asst. for Social & Pastoral Ministries; William T. Wood, S.J., Asst. for Intl. Apostolate; Joseph S. Costantino, S.J., Dir. of Vocations; William J. Scanlon, S.J., Dir. of the Jesuit Seminary & Mission Bureau.

Fathers 521; Scholastics 89; Brothers 34.

Properties owned, sponsored, or staffed: Parishes 8; Universities 1; Colleges 3; High Schools 8; Houses for Laymen's Retreats 4; House of Study 1; Novitiates 2; Community Houses 4.

Represented in the Archdioceses of Newark and New York and in the Dioceses of Albany, Brooklyn, Buffalo, Paterson, Rochester, Rockville Centre and Syracuse. Also in Guam, the Caroline Islands, Chalan Kanoa, and the Prefecture Apostolic of Marshall Islands.

The Jesuits of the Missouri Province (Missouri Province of the Society of Jesus): Province Offices, 4511 W. Pine Blvd., St. Louis, MO 63108-2191. Tel: 314-361-7765 Mon.-Fri. 9-5; Fax: 314-758-7164. Very Rev. Frank Reale, S.J., Prov.; Revs. Philip G. Steele, S.J., Socius 2nd Asst. for Secondary Ed.; Robert F. Weiss, S.J., Treas.; John A. Apel, S.J., Asst. for Jesuits in Pastoral and Intl. Apostolates; William T. Oulvey, S.J., Asst. for Prov. Planning and Vocation Dir.; L. Gene Martens, S.J., Assoc. Dir. Jesuit Devel. Office; David L. Fleming, S.J., Dir. of Publications & Editor, *The Jesuit Bulletin.* Tel: 314-977-2631. William B. Faherty, S.J., Prov. Archivist.

Fathers 278; Students in Major Seminary 26; Novices 7; Brothers 32.

Legal Title: ***Regis Jesuit High School Corporation,*** Aurora, CO; *Jesuit Novitiate - The Jesuits of the Missouri Province, Regis University,* Denver, CO; *Rockhurst University, Rockhurst High School,* Kansas City, KS; *The Province - The Jesuits of the Missouri Province; Bellarmine House of Studies - The Jesuits of the Missouri Province; Fusz Pavilion - The Jesuits of the Missouri Province; Institute of Jesuit Sources - The Jesuits of the Missouri Province; Jesuit Mission Bureau - The Jesuits of the Missouri Province; Review for Religious - The Jesuits of the Missouri Province; DeSmet Jesuit High School; Jesuit Community Corporation at St. Louis University, Saint Louis University; St. Louis University High School; The Sacred Heart Program, Inc.; White House Retreat, Inc.;* St. Louis, MO; *So-*

ciety of Jesus in Belize, Inc.; St. John's College, Inc., Belize; *Jesuit Retreat House,* Sedalia.
Ministries in Parishes; Universities; High Schools; Colleges; Novitiates; Curia; Retreat Houses.
Represented in the Archdioceses of Denver, Kansas City in Kansas and St. Louis and the Dioceses of Belleville, Cheyenne, Colorado Springs, Dodge City, Jefferson City, Kansas City-St. Joseph, Pueblo, Springfield-Cape Girardeau, Springfield in Illinois, Tulsa and Wichita.

Province of New Orleans (1907): 500 S. Jefferson Davis Pky., New Orleans, LA 70119-7192. Tel: 504-821-0334; Fax: 504-822-5322.
Legal Title: *Catholic Society of Religious and Literary Education, A Louisiana Corporation;* Very Rev. James P. Bradley, S.J., Prov.; Revs. Donald J. Martin, S.J., Asst. for Parishes & Retreat Apostolate; Michael S. Gallagher, S.J., Asst. for Social Apostolate; John F. Armstrong, S.J., Socius & Asst. for Secondary Education; Robert J. Ratchford, S.J., Staff Assist.; Bro. Lawrence J. Lundin, S.J., Treas.
Fathers 222; Students in Major Seminary 27; Novices 10; Brothers 32.
Properties owned, sponsored, or staffed: Parishes 14; Universities 1; Colleges 1; High Schools 4; Novitiate 1; Houses of Retreat 5.
Represented in the Archdioceses of Atlanta, Miami, New Orleans, San Antonio and Santa Fe and in the Dioceses of Alexandria, Amarillo, Austin, Baton Rouge, Charleston, Corpus Christi, Dallas, El Paso, Fort Worth, Galveston-Houston, Gallup, Lafayette (LA), Las Cruces, Little Rock, Mobile, Nashville, Orlando, Palm Beach, Pensacola-Tallahassee, St. Augustine, St. Petersburg and Venice.

California Province (1909): Executive Assistant, 300 College Ave., P.O. Box 519, Los Gatos, CA 95031-0519. Tel: 408-354-6143.
Legal Title: *The California Province of the Society of Jesus;* Very Rev. John A. Privett, S.J., Prov.; Revs. John T. Mitchell, S.J., Exec. Asst. & Dir. Vocations; Gerdenio M. Manuel, S.J., Asst. for Formation; Alfred E. Naucke, S.J., Asst. for Secondary Education; John A. Baumann, S.J., Asst. for Social Ministries; Thomas G. Piquado, S.J., Asst. for Pastoral Ministries; Paul A. Soukup, S.J., Dir. Studies; Robert L. St. Clair, S.J., Prov. Treas.; William J. Maring, S.J., Prov. Dir.-Devel.; Bros. Thomas A. Marshall, S.J., Prov. Archivist; Jack A. Hughes, S.J., Asst. Sec.; Revs. Paul J. Bernadicou, S.J., Tertian Instructor; James D. Erps, S.J., Ecclesial Asst., *Christian Life Communities;* Theodore T. Taheny, S.J., Dir., *California Jesuit Missionaries* 284 Stanyan St., San Francisco, CA 94118-4299. Tel: 415-221-1588. George M. Twigg-Porter, S.J., Apostleship of Prayer; Andrew F. Maginnis, S.J., Dir. Jesuit Seminary Association & Editor—""The Western Jesuit".
Legal Title: *JVC Center,* P.O. Box 23404, Oakland, CA 94623-9991. Tel: 510-465-5016.
Fathers 400; Brothers 35; Scholastics 46; Scholastic Novices 14.
Properties owned, sponsored, or staffed: Parishes 14; Universities 3; High Schools 5; Novitiates 1; Theologate 1; Retreat Center 2.
Represented in the Archdioceses of Los Angeles and San Francisco and in the Dioceses of Fresno, Honolulu, Monterey, Orange, Phoenix, Reno, Sacramento, Salt Lake City, San Bernardino, San Diego, San Jose, Santa Rosa, Stockton and Tucson.

New England Province (1926): 771 Harrison Ave., Boston, MA 02118-2311. Tel: 617-266-7233; Fax: 617-536-8074. Rev. Robert J. Levens, S.J., Prov.; Rev. Mr. William R. Campbell, S.J., Prov. Liaison for Pastoral Ministries, Revs. Thomas J. Gibbons, S.J., Asst. for Prov. Finances; William C. McInnes, S.J., Prov. Liaison for Continuing Education; John P. Murray, S.J., Socius, Asst. for Secondary Ed. & Liaison for Formation; William C. Russell, S.J., Asst. for Devel. & Dir.-Vocations; Thomas H. Schneider, S.J., Liaison for Intrnatl. Ministries; James F. Walsh, S.J., Liaison for Social Ministries.
Legal Title: *The Society of Jesus of New England.*
Fathers 430; Scholastics 33; Brothers 24.
Parishes 3; Universities 2; Colleges 1; High Schools 3; Houses of Retreats 2; Seminaries 1; Novitiates 1; Residences 1.
Represented in the Archdioceses of Baltimore, Boston, Detroit, Hartford, Los Angeles, Louisville, Miami, Milwaukee, New York, Philadelphia, St. Louis, St. Paul-Minneapolis, San Francisco, Washington, and in the Dioceses of Altoona-Johnstown, Bridgeport, Buffalo, Burlington, Charleston, Cleveland, Columbus, Fairbanks, Fall River, Honolulu, Kansas City-St. Joseph, Manchester, Norwich, Oakland, Orange, Pensacola-Tallahassee, Portland (ME), Rapid City, San Diego, San Jose, Scranton, Spokane, Tucson, Wheeling-Charlestown and Worcester.

Chicago Province - Society of Jesus (S.J.) (1928): 2050 N. Clark St., Chicago, IL 60614. Tel: 773-975-6363; Fax: 773-975-0230. Very Rev. Richard J. Baumann, S.J., Prov.; Revs. Richard H. McGurn, S.J., Exec. Asst. & Asst. for Formation; Daniel L. Flaherty, S.J., Prov. Treas. and Asst. for Bus. and Finance; James A. Stoeger, S.J., Asst. Secondary Education; Brian G. Paulson, S.J., Asst. for Vocation Promotion; Paul V. Robb, S.J., Asst. Treas.; Gerald P. Grace, S.J., Asst.-Intl. Apostolates; Dir.-Jesuit Intl. Missions; Asst.-Social Min.; William O. Madden, S.J., Asst. for Records & Research; James P. Gschwend, S.J., Asst. for Continuing Education & Asst. for Jesuits in Diaspora; John F. Costello, S.J., Coord.-Planned Giving; John J. Foley, S.J., Asst. to Devel. Dir. for Jesuit Seminary Assoc.; John A. McGrail, S.J., Dir. Apostleship of Prayer.
Jesuit Development Office, 2059 N. Sedgwick St., Chicago, IL 60614. Tel: 773-975-8181; Fax: 773-975-2042.
Quarterly Publication: *Company Magazine,* Offices, 3441 N. Ashland Ave., Chicago, IL 60657. Tel: 773-281-1534; Fax: 773-281-2667.
Legal Title: *Chicago Province of the Society of Jesus.*
Fathers 217; Scholastics 25; Brothers 18; Scholastic Novices 7.
Properties Sponsored: Parishes 4; Universities 2; High Schools 5; Retreat Houses 2; Diocesan Major Seminary 1; Residences 9; House of Writers 1.
Represented in the Archdioceses of Chicago, Cincinnati, Indianapolis and Louisville and in the Dioceses of Covington, Evansville, Fort Wayne-South Bend, Gary, Joliet, Lafayette (IN), Peoria and Rockford.

Oregon Province - Society of Jesus (1932): 2222 N.W. Hoyt, Portland, OR 97210. Tel: 503-226-6977. Very Rev. Robert B. Grimm, S.J., Prov.; Rev. Michael A. Tyrrell, S.J., Treas.; Revs. Brad R. Reynolds, S.J., Exec. Asst. to Prov.; Socius and Legal Sec.; Charles E. Schmitz, S.J., Province Coord.-Intl. Apostolate; Gary N. Smith, S.J., Province Coord. Social Ministries.
Legal Title: *Society of the Jesus, Oregon Province,* Portland, OR, *The Pioneer Educational Society,* Spokane, WA, *Montana Catholic Missions, SJ.*
Fathers 243; Scholastics 30; Brothers 20.
Properties owned, sponsored, or staffed: Parishes 8; Universities 2; High Schools 4; House of Study 1; Novitiates 1.
Represented in the Archdioceses of Anchorage, Portland in Oregon and Seattle and in the Dioceses of Baker, Boise, Fairbanks, Great Falls-Billings, Helena, Spokane and Yakima.

Detroit Province- Society of Jesus (S.J.) (1955): 7303 W. Seven Mile Rd., Detroit, MI 48221. Tel: 313-861-7500; Fax: 313-861-4230. Very Rev. John F. Libens, S.J., Prov. Supr.; Revs. Keith J. Esenther, S.J., Exec. Asst.; Walter L. Farrell, S.J., Treas.; Richard H. Twohig, S.J., Asst.-Intl. Apostolates & Vocation Training; John E. Dister, S.J., Asst for Pastoral & Social Ministries; Timothy J. Shepard, S.J., Asst. Formation.
Fathers 163; Scholastics 17; Brothers 250.
Properties owned, sponsored, or staffed: Parishes 8; Universities 2; High Schools 5; Retreat Houses 3.
Legal Title: *Detroit Province of the Society of Jesus, Colombiere Center,* Clarkston, MI; *Jesuit Retreat House of Cleveland, Ohio; Jesuit Seminary Association; Jesuit International Missions; John Carroll University of Cleveland, Ohio; John Carroll Jesuit Community Corporation; Loyola High School,* Detroit, MI; *Loyola of the Lakes Jesuit Retreat House, Inc.; Manresa Jesuit Retreat House; Patna Jesuit Mission Society, Inc.; St. Ignatius High School of Cleveland, Ohio; St. John's Jesuit High School of Toledo, Ohio; University of Detroit Mercy; The Jesuit Community Corporation at the University of Detroit; University of Detroit Jesuit High School and Academy; Walsh Jesuit High School.*
Represented in the Archdioceses of Boston, Chicago, Cincinnati, Detroit, New York, Washington and the Dioceses of Buffalo, Cleveland, Columbus, Davenport, Fort Wayne-South Bend, Lexington, Oakland, Richmond, Saginaw, Toledo, Wheeling-Charleston and Worcester.

Wisconsin Province- Society of Jesus (S.J.) (1955): 3400 W. Wisconsin Ave., P.O. Box 08277, Milwaukee, WI 53208-0277. Tel: 414-937-6949; Fax: 414-937-6950.
Legal Title: *Wisconsin Province of the Society of Jesus;* Very Rev. D. Edward Mathie, S.J., Prov. & Coord. for Higher Education; Revs. James E. Grummer, S.J., Asst. Prov. & Asst. for Intl. Ministries; Asst. for Secondary Education; James M. Kubicki, S.J., Asst.-Formation; J. Robert Hilbert, S.J., Asst.-Pastoral & Retreat Ministries; Eugene M. Dutkiewicz, S.J., Asst.-Finance; Warren J. Sazama, S.J., Pres.-Jesuit Partnership; Robert M. Frommelt, S.J., Asst. Pres.-Jesuit Partnership.
Fathers 324; Students in Major Seminary 29; Novices 6; Brothers 18.
Properties owned, sponsored, or staffed: Parishes 5; Universities 2; High Schools 3; Middle Schools 2; Community Houses 19; Novitiate; Native American Missions 3; Negro Mission; Ethnic Parishes 2; Retreat Houses 3.
Represented in the Archdioceses of Milwaukee, Omaha and St. Paul-Minneapolis and in the Dioceses of Green Bay, La Crosse, Rapid City, Winona, and Cheyenne.

Province of the Antilles (1947): Correa y Cindron, 28; P.O. Box 76, Santo Domingo, Dominican Republic. Tel: 809-532-5628.
U.S. Address: 13339 S.W. 9 Terrace, Miami, FL 33184. Very Rev. Benjamin Gonzalez-Buetta, S.J., Prov.; Revs. Pedro Suarez, S.J., Miami Reg. Supr.; Eduardo Alvarez, S.J., Supr.
Fathers 101; Scholastics 46; Brothers 18.
High Schools: Loyola in Dominican Republic Belen Jesuit Prep in Miami; Novitiate 1; House of Retreat 3 in Santo Domingo; Juan Pablo II in Miami; Residences 2.
Represented in the Archdiocese of Miami. Also in Santo Domingo.

[0700] (S.S.J.)—ST. JOSEPH'S SOCIETY OF THE SACRED HEART

(The Josephites)
(Societas Sancti Joseph SSmi Cordis)

Central House of Administration: 1130 N. Calvert St., Baltimore, MD 21202. Tel: 410-727-3386; Fax: 410-385-2331. Very Rev. Robert M. Kearns, S.S.J., Supr. Gen.
Fathers 121; Brothers 10; Students in House of Studies 4; Seminarians 4.
Legal Title: *St. Joseph's Society of the Sacred Heart, Inc.*
Properties owned, staffed, or sponsored: Parishes 57; Elementary Schools 18; High School; House of Study; Major Seminary; Novitiate; Missions 6.
Represented in the Archdioceses of Baltimore, Los Angeles, Mobile, New Orleans and Washington and in the Dioceses of Arlington, Baton Rouge, Beaumont, Biloxi, Birmingham, Fort Worth, Galveston-Houston, Lafayette (LA), Lake Charles, Jackson, and Wilmington.

[0710] (C.J.)—JOSEPHITE FATHERS

(Congregatio Iosephitarum Gerardimontensium)

General Motherhouse: Melle (Ghent), Belgium. Very Rev. Richard Lear, C.J., Supr. Gen.
U.S. Foundation (1963): *St. Joseph Seminary, Provincialate and Novitiate,* 180 Patterson Road, Santa Maria, CA 93455. Tel: 805-937-5378. Very Rev. Edward Jalbert, Prov. Supr.
Fathers 14; Brothers 1.
Ministry in Parishes; Academic Education; Military Chaplaincy.
Represented in the Archdiocese of Los Angeles.

[0720] (M.S.)—THE MISSIONARIES OF OUR LADY OF LA SALETTE

(Congregatio Missionariorum Vulgo ""De la Salette")

General House: Piazza Madonna Della Salette 3, Rome, 00152. Italy. Very Rev. Isidro Perin, M.S., Supr. Gen.
American Region was established 1892; Canonically erected 1934; Divided into other Provinces in 1945, 1958 and 1967.

Province of Our Lady of Seven Dolors (1934): 915 Maple Ave., Hartford, CT 06114-2330. Tel: 860-956-8870. Very Rev. James H. Kuczynski, M.S., Prov.; Revs. James H. Henault, M.S., Asst. & Vicar; Joseph M. O'Neil, M.S., Asst. & Treas.
Legal Title: *Missionaries of LaSalette Corp., Religious Trust of the Missionaries of Our Lady of La Salette, Province of Our Lady of Seven Dolors.*
Priests 84; Brothers 18; Oblate Brothers 1.
Represented in the Archdioceses of Atlanta, Boston, Hartford, New York, St. Paul-Minneapolis and Washington and in the Dioceses of Albany, Manchester, Norwich, Orlando, Raleigh, Springfield (MA) and Worcester.

Province of the Immaculate Heart of Mary (1945): *Missionaries of Our Lady of La Salette,* 947 Park St., P.O. Box 2965, Attleboro, MA 02703-0965. Tel: 617-222-7171; Fax: 508-222-6178. Very Rev. Dennis J. Loomis, M.S., Prov. Supr.; Revs. Bernard B. Baris, M.S., Vicar; Roland S. Nadeau, M.S., Councillor & Sec.; Bro. Claude Rheaume, M.S., Treas.
Priests 52; Brothers 23; Oblates 1.
Missionaries (priests and brothers) serve: Parishes 7; Shrines 2; Retreat House 1; Hospital Chaplaincies 3; College Chaplaincies 2.
Properties owned: La Salette Shrine, Provincial House and Center for Christian Living, Attleboro, MA La Salette Shrine, Enfield, NH.
Represented in the Dioceses of Burlington, Fall River, Manchester and Tucson. Also in Canada.

Province of Mary Queen (1958): *La Salette Missionaries,* 4650 S. Broadway, St. Louis, MO 63111-1303. Tel: 314-353-5000; Fax: 314-353-4582. Very

Rev. Dennis J. Meyer, M.S., Prov. Supr.; Revs. Peter D. Kohler, M.S., Prov. Vicar; Sec. & Treas.; Eduardo Nevares, M.S., Prov. Asst.; John Nuelle, M.S., Mission Procurator.

Legal Title: *Missionaries of La Salette Corporation of Missouri.*

Fathers 37; Professed Brothers 5; Oblate Brothers 2.

Parishes 14; Religious Houses 5; Chaplaincies 4.

Represented in the Archdiocese and St. Louis and in the Dioceses of Beaumont, Galveston-Houston, Jefferson City, Lake Charles, and Tyler.

Province of Mary, Queen of Peace (1967): P.O. Box 250, Twin Lakes, WI 53181. Tel: 414-877-3123. Revs. James Stajkowski, M.S., Prov.; Terrence Niziolek, M.S., Vicar; Bro. Adam Mateja, M.S., Councillor; Rev. Thaddeus Galuszka, M.S., Treas.

Priests 16; Missionary Brothers 4; Oblate Brothers 1.

Represented in the Archdiocese of Milwaukee and the Diocese of Peoria.

[0730] (L.C.)—LEGIONARIES OF CHRIST

Founded in Mexico 1941, first foundation in United States 1965.

General Headquarters: Via Aurelia 677, Rome, Italy. Very Rev. Marcial Maciel, L.C., Founder and Supr. Gen.

U.S. Headquarters: 393 Derby Ave., Orange, CT 06477. Tel: 203-795-2800; Fax: 203-795-2808. Rev. Anthony Bannon, L.C., Natl. Dir.

Novitiate and Juniorate, 475 Oak Ave., Cheshire, CT 06410. Tel: 203-271-0805. Rev. Julio Marty, L.C., Rector.

Priests 52; Religious 57; Novices 90; Juniors 36.

Represented in the Archdioceses of Atlanta, Detroit, Hartford, Los Angeles, New York Washington and the Dioceses of Dallas, Lincoln, Manchester, Madison and Providence.

[0740] (M.I.C.)—CONGREGATION OF MARIANS OF THE IMMACULATE CONCEPTION

(Congregatio Clericorum Marianorum sub titulo Immaculatae Conceptionis Beatae Mariae Virginis)

General Motherhouse: via Corsica no. 1, Rome, Italy. Very Rev. Adam Boniecki, M.I.C.; Very Rev. Vaclovas Aliulis, M.I.C., Vicar Gen.

American Province of St. Casimir (1913): 6336 S. Kilbourn Ave., Chicago, IL 60629-5588. Tel: 773-582-8191; Fax: 773-582-8961. Very Rev. Donald Petraitis, M.I.C., Prov.; Revs. Victor Rimselis, M.I.C.; Timothy Roth, M.I.C.; Boniface Vaisnoras, M.I.C.; Bro. Donald Schaefer, M.I.C., Prov. Treas.

Fathers 32; Seminarians 7; Brothers 3.

Parishes 6; High School 1; Community Houses 8.

Represented in the Archdioceses of Chicago and Milwaukee and in the Dioceses of Joliet, Norwich and Worcester. Also in Argentina.

St. Stanislaus Kostka Province: Eden Hill, Stockbridge, MA 01262-0951. Tel: 413-298-3931. Very Rev. Walter Dziordz, M.I.C., Prov. Supr. Councilors: Revs. Kazimierz Chwalek, M.I.C.; Seraphim Michalenko, M.I.C.; Mark Lamprich, M.I.C.; Bro. Andrew Maczynski, M.I.C., Dir. Marian Helpers Center.

Legal Holdings: *Marian Helpers Center Marian Scholasticate Divine Mercy International John Paul II Institute of Divine Mercy Shrine of Divine Mercy.*

Fathers 23; Brothers 7; Seminarians 7; Novices 3.

Properties owned, staffed or sponsored: 4 Community Houses; Novitiate; Filial House; 1 Residence.

Represented in the Archdioceses of Detroit and Washington and the Dioceses of Charlotte and Springfield. Also in Portugal.

[0750] (C.M.M.)—CONGREGATION OF MARIANNHILL MISSIONARIES, MARIANNHILL FATHERS AND BROTHERS

(Congregatio Missionariorum de Mariannhill)

Generalate: Via S. Giovanni Eudes 91, 00163, Rome, Italy. Very Rev. Yves LaFontaine, C.M.M., Supr. Gen.

American-Canadian Province (1938): Our Lady of Grace Monastery, 23715 Ann Arbor Trail, Dearborn Hts., MI 48127. Tel: 313-561-7140; Fax: 313-563-6716. Revs. Aloysius Blonigen, C.M.M., American Reg.; Timothy Mock, C.M.M., Procurator.

Fathers 12; Brothers 4.

Legal Holdings: *Mariannhill Retreat Center,* Dearborn MI.

Represented in the Archdiocese of Detroit.

[0760] (S.M.)—SOCIETY OF MARY

(Marianists—Brothers of Mary)

(Societas Mariae—Marianistae)

General Motherhouse: Via Latina 22, 00179 Rome. Italy. Very Rev. David Fleming, S.M., Supr. Gen.

Province of Cincinnati (1849): *Marianist Provincialate,* 4435 E. Patterson Rd., Dayton, OH 45430-1095. Tel: 937-429-0794; Fax: 937-429-3195. Bro. Joseph H. Kamis, S.M., Prov. Supr. Councillors: Revs. Joseph H. Lackner, S.M.; Joseph P. Tedesco, S.M.; Bros. Robert J. Metzger, S.M.; Bernard J. Ploeger, S.M.

Legal Holdings or Titles: *Mount St. John, Bergamo Center; University of Dayton; Chaminade-Julienne High School; Marianist Mission,* Dayton OH; *Governor's Island,* Huntsville, OH; *Marianist Communities,* Cleveland, OH, Cincinnati, OH, Dayton, OH, Portage, MI, Pittsburgh, PA.

Fathers 58; Brothers 161; Brothers Perpetual Professed 143; Temporary Professed 18; Novices 15; Aspirants 8.

Properties owned, sponsored, or staffed: Universities 1; High Schools 5; Parishes 5; Apostolic Centers 1; Novitiates 2.

Represented in the Archdiocese of Cincinnati and in the Dioceses of Cleveland, Kalamazoo and Pittsburgh.

Province of St. Louis (1908): *Marianist Provincialate,* P.O. Box 23130, St. Louis, MO 63156. Tel: 314-367-0390; Fax: 314-361-3131. Rev. Timothy Dwyer, S.M., Prov. Supr.; Bros. Jerome Bommer, S.M., Asst. Prov.; Richard Dix, S.M., Temporalities; Revs. John Moder, S.M., Councillor; Alvin McMenamy, S.M., Religious Life.

Fathers 61; Brothers 179; Novices 20.

Members serve and staff: Parishes 6; University 1; High Schools 5; Retreat House 1; Missions in India & Mexico.

Properties owned: St. Mary's University, San Antonio, TX Central Catholic Marianist High School, San Antonio, TX Chaminade Preparatory, St. Louis, MO Vianney High School, St. Louis, MO Marianist Retreat & Conference Center, Eureka, MO.

Represented in the Archdioceses of New Orleans, St. Louis and San Antonio and in the Dioceses of Belleville, Fort Worth and Galveston-Houston.

Province of the Pacific (1948): *Marianist Provincial Residence,* 22825 San Juan Rd., Cupertino, CA 95014-3934. P.O. Box 1775, Cupertino, CA 95015-1775. Tel: 408-253-4841; Fax: 408-253-5280. Very Rev. John Russi, S.M., Prov. & Religious Life; Bros. Gary Morris, S.M., Asst. Prov.; John Haster, S.M., Temporalities.

Legal Title: *Marianist Province of the Pacific, a Hawaii Corp.*

Fathers 30; Brothers 85; Parishes 2; University 1; High Schools 4; Middle Schools 1.

Legal Holdings: *Marianist Community,* Santa Clara, CA, *Marianist Community,* San Jose, CA, *Marianist Center, Villa St. Joseph, Marianist Provincialate,* Cupertino, CA.

Represented in the Archdioceses of Los Angeles and San Francisco and in the Dioceses of Honolulu, Monterey and San Jose. Also in Korea.

Province of New York (1961): *Marianist Provincial House,* 4301 Roland Ave., Baltimore, MD 21210. Tel: 410-366-1300. Bro. Stephen M. Glodek, S.M., Prov.; Rev. George J. Cerniglia, S.M., Asst. Prov. Councillors: Bros. Frank J. O'Donnell, S.M.; Francis M. Ouellette, S.M.; Rev. Theodore K. Cassidy, S.M.

Legal Titles & Holdings: Marianist Society, Inc. - A Maryland Corporation; Marianist Society of Floria, Inc. - A Florida Corporation; *Marianist Provincial House,* Baltimore, MD; *Marianist Community Residence,* Baltimore, MD; *Marianist Family Center,* Cape May Point, NJ; *Marianist Community Residence,* Vernon, CT; *Marianist Community Residence,* Hollywood, FL; *Chaminade/Madonna High School,* Hollywood, FL; *Mission Noell,* Villalba, PR; *Colegio San Jose,* Rio Piedras, PR.

Fathers 27; Brothers 59.

Properties owned, sponsored, or staffed: High Schools 2; Orphanage 1; Parishes 2; Apostolic Centers 3.

Represented in the Archdioceses of Baltimore, Boston, Hartford, Miami, Philadelphia, and San Antonio, and the Dioceses of Brooklyn, Camden, Fort Wayne-South Bend, Norwich, Orange, Raleigh, and Rockville Centre. Also in the Archdiocese of San Juan and the Diocese of Ponce.

Province of Meribah (1976): *Marianist Provincial Residence,* 240 Emory Rd., Mineola, NY 11501. Tel: 516-742-5555. Bro. George E. Endres, S.M., Prov.; Rev. Thomas A. Cardone, S.M., Asst. Prov. & Asst. for Rel. Life; Bro. Kenneth M. Hoagland, S.M., Asst. for Education; Rev. Philip K. Eichner, S.M., Asst. for Temporalities; Bro. Michael J. Gillen, S.M., Councillor; Rev. Francis T. Keenan, S.M., Councillor; Bro. Michael J. McAward, S.M., Councillor.

Legal Holdings: *Chaminade High School,* Mineola, NY, *Kellenberg Memorial High School,* Uniondale, NY.

Fathers 6; Brothers 33.

Properties owned, sponsored, or staffed: High Schools 2; Retreat Houses 2.

[0770] (F.M.S.)—THE MARIST BROTHERS

(Fratres Maristae a Scholis)

Generalate: Rome, Italy. Rev. Bro. Benito Arbues, F.M.S., Supr. Gen.; Rev. Bro. Sean D. Sammon, F.M.S., Vicar Gen.

Province of Esopus (1959): *Provincial Office,* 1241 Kennedy Blvd., Bayonne, NJ 07002. Tel: 201-823-1115; Fax: 201-823-2232. Bros. John Klein, F.M.S., Prov.; Leo Shea, F.M.S., Asst. Prov. Councillors: Bros. Vincent Damian; John McDonnell; Robert Clark; Stephen Schlitte; John Venturella; Joseph Sacino, F.M.S., Prov. Treas.; Michael Sheerin, F.M.S., Vocation Dir.

Brothers 148.

Represented in the Archdioceses of Boston, Miami, Newark, New York and in the Dioceses of Albany, Austin, Brooklyn, Brownsville, Corpus Christi, Manchester, Rockville Centre, Savannah and Wheeling-Charleston.

Poughkeepsie Province (1959): *Provincial Administration,* 26 First Ave., Pelham, NY 10803. Tel: 914-738-0740. Bros. Patrick Mcnamara, F.M.S., Prov.; Dermot Healy, F.M.S., Vice Prov.; Joseph Sacino, F.M.S., Prov. Treas.; Hugh Turley, F.M.S., Devel.; Patrick Tyrrell, F.M.S., Dir. Marist Foreign Missions. Councillors: Bros. Vito Aresto, F.M.S.; Richard Carey, F.M.S.; Donnell Neary, F.M.S.

Brothers 119.

High Schools 8; Community Houses 19; Junior High School 1; Two community schools located in Japan.

Represented in the Archdioceses of Boston, Chicago, Miami, New York and in the Diocese of Houma-Thibodau, Manchester and Wheeling-Charleston.

[0780] (S.M.)—MARIST FATHERS

(Societas Mariae)

General Motherhouse: via Alessandro Poerio 63, Rome, 00152. Italy. Very Rev. Joaquin Fernandez, S.M., Supr. Gen.; Rev. John Harhager, S.M., Treas. Gen., The first Marist foundation in the United States was in 1863, St. Michael's in Convent, Louisiana. The first Marist Province in the United States was established in 1889 under the name of American Province. This Province was subdivided in 1924 into the Washington Province and the Boston Province; On January 1, 1962, the San Francisco Province was established.

Washington Province (1924): 815 Varnum St., N.E., Washington, DC 20017-2199. Tel: 202-529-4800. Very Rev. William F. Rowland, S.M., Prov.; Revs. Joel Konzen, S.M., Vicar Prov.; H. Joseph Wilhelm, S.M., Prov. Treas.; Timothy F. Sugrue, S.M., Business Mgr. & Mission Promoter. Prov. Council: Revs. Thomas E. Ellerman, S.M.; Edwin L. Keel, S.M.; Andrew G. McCormack, S.M., Dir. Vocations; Peter R. Blanchard, S.M., Dir. Third Order of Mary; John J. Jazwiecki, S.M.

Legal Holdings & Titles: Marist Society, Inc., Marist College, Marist Provincial House, Washington, DC, *Marist Society of OH,* Cleveland, OH, *Marist Society of LA, Marist Community,* New Orleans, LA, *Marist Society of PA,* Philadelphia, PA.

Fathers 83; Brothers 9; Scholastics 2.

Properties owned, sponsored, or staffed: Community Houses 3; Parishes 10; Diocesan Seminaries/Houses of Study 1; and High School 1.

Represented in the Archdioceses of Atlanta, Chicago, US Military Services, New Orleans, New York, Philadelphia, St. Paul-Minneapolis, Washington and the Dioceses of Austin, Baton Rouge, Brooklyn, Brownsville, Cleveland, Orlando St. Petersburg, Savannah and Wheeling-Charleston.

Boston Province (Marist Fathers) (1924): *Marist Provincial House,* 27 Isabella St., Boston, MA 02116-5216. Tel: 617-426-5297; Fax: 617-482-1570. Very Rev. Kenneth Thibodeau, S.M., Prov.; Rev. Albert DiIanni, S.M., Vicar Prov. & Prov. Dir. of Third Order of Mary & Vocation Dir. Prov. Council: Revs. Philip Parent, S.M.; John Sajdak, S.M.; Gerard Demers, S.M.; Raymond Arsenault, S.M., Prov. Treas.; Robert Graham, S.M., Prov. Archivist; J. Armand Robichaud, S.M., Marist Missions & Council; Gerard Caron, S.M., Dir. Paratours Inc. & Lourdes Center. Tel: 617-247-2533.

Legal Title: *Marist Fathers of Boston, Marist Fathers of Detroit, Inc., Marist Fathers of New York.*

Fathers 73; Brothers 6; Seminarians 3.

Properties owned, sponsored, or staffed: Community Houses 7; Parishes 10; High Schools 2; Retreat House 1.

Represented in the Archdioceses of Anchorage, Boston, Hartford, Detroit and the Dioceses of Brooklyn, Burlington, Honolulu, Portland (ME), Rapid City, and St. Petersburg.

Third Order of Mary: Envisioned as the Third or Lay Branch of the Society of Mary by its Founder, Father Jean-Claude Colin. The Third Order of Mary was approved in 1850 for lay men and women, as well as for members of the Diocesan Clergy. The rule was written by Rev. Jean Claude

Colin, founder of the Society of Mary, the Marist Fathers and Brothers. It was approved by the Holy See in 1836. There are confraternities throughout the world. New styles of confraternities are being formed to help evangelize the world after the spirit of Jesus and Mary. Information concerning this Third Order of Mary or the Marist Laity Movement may be obtained from: Third Order of Mary-Marist Laity, 518 Pleasant St., Framingham, MA 01701-2898. Tel: 508-875-6075; 879-1620; Fax: 508-879-0719. Rev. Albert Dilanni, S.M., Dir.

San Francisco Western Province (1962): *Marist Center Provincial House*, 625 Pine St., San Francisco, CA 94108-3210. Tel: 415-398-3543. Very Rev. John F. McGregor, S.M., Prov.; Very Rev. Dennis J. Steik, S.M., Vicar Prov.; Revs. Etienne Siffert, S.M., Archivist; Francis Springer, S.M., Mission Promoter; Thomas Hamilton, S.M., Prov. Councillor, Vocation Dir. & Formation Dir. Prov. Councillors: Revs. Dennis Steik, S.M.; Bruce Lery, S.M.; James Pratt, S.M.; Rene Iturbe, S.M.; Rev. Bro. Ernest Morasci, S.M.

Fathers 20; Brothers 6; Deacon 2; Students in Theology 3.

Properties owned, sponsored, or staffed: Parishes 5; Preparatory Seminaries 1.

Represented in the Archdioceses of Portland (OR) and the Dioceses of Boise, Honolulu, Oakland, and Monterey.

[0785] (C.M.L.M.)—THE CONGREGATION OF MARONITE LEBANESE MISSIONARIES

Founded at the Monastery of Kreim-Ghosta (Mountain of Lebanon), in the year 1865. Established in the United States March of 1991: Agreement between Archbishop Zayek of the Diocese of St. Maron and the Congregation to serve the parishes of San Antonio, Dallas and Houston.

U.S. Headquarters: *Saint George Maronite Church*, 6070 Babcock Rd., San Antonio, TX 78240. Tel: 210-690-9569; Fax: 210-690-5093. Rev. Abdallah Zaidan, C.M.L.M.; Supr.

Bishops 2; Priests 65; Brothers 1; Seminarians 25; Novices 3; Postulants 10.

Represented in the Dioceses of Our Lady of Lebanon.

[0790] (O.Mar.)—CONGREGATION OF MARONITE MONKS

Monastery of the Most Holy Trinity: 67 Dugway Rd., Petersham, MA 01366-0605. Tel: 978-724-3347. Rt. Rev. William J. Driscoll, O. Mar., Abbot; Revs. Giles R. Goyette, O. Mar., 1st Councillor; Michael Cermak, O. Mar., Vicar.

Priests 5; Brothers 4.

Monastery of the Holy Nativity: (a dependency of Holy Trinity Monastery, Petersham, MA) Bethlehem, SD 57708. Tel: 605-787-4606. Rev. Louis Marie Dauphinais, O.Mar., Supr.

Priests 5.

Represented in the Diocese of St. Maron, Brooklyn.

[0800] (M.M.)—MARYKNOLL

Catholic Foreign Mission Society of America, Inc.

U.S. Foundation (1911): *Maryknoll Society Center & Admin. Offices*, Maryknoll, NY 10545-0305. Tel: 914-941-7590; Fax: 914-762-0316. Revs. Raymond J. Finch, M.M., Supr. Gen.; Jeremiah R. Burr, M.M., Vicar Gen. Assts. General: Revs. Thomas P. Henehan, M.M.; Michael J. Snyder, M.M.; Bro. Wayne J. Fitzpatrick, M.M.

Legal Title: *Catholic Foreign Mission Society of America Incorporated.*

Training Center: *Maryknoll Society Center*, Maryknoll, NY 10545.

Houses in Archdioceses and Dioceses

Boston: Maryknoll Fathers and Brothers, 80 Emerson Rd., East Walpole, MA 02032. Tel: 508-668-6831; Fax: 508-660-0252.

Buffalo: Maryknoll Fathers and Brothers, 71 Jewett Pkwy., Buffalo, NY 14214-2396. Tel: 716-834-6065.

Chicago: Maryknoll Fathers and Brothers, 3600 Seeley Ave., Chicago, IL 60609-1148. Tel: 773-927-9257; Fax: 773-927-7305.

Seminary Residence: 5508 S. Cornell Ave., Chicago, IL 60637. Tel: 773-288-3143; Fax: 773-288-3950.

Cincinnati: Maryknoll Fathers and Brothers, 104 Elm Ave. (Wyoming), Cincinnati, OH 45215. Tel: 513-761-5888; Fax: 513-761-5887.

Cleveland: Maryknoll Fathers and Brothers, 10309 Edgewater Dr., Cleveland, OH 44102. Tel: 216-651-2121; Fax: 216-651-8242.

Denver: Maryknoll Fathers and Brothers, 4460 Federal Blvd., Denver, CO 80211. Tel: 303-455-5669; Fax: 303-455-5753.

Detroit: Maryknoll Fathers and Brothers, 12709 Pembroke Ave., Detroit, MI 48235. Tel: 313-342-0330.

Galveston-Houston: Maryknoll Fathers and Brothers, 2360 Rice Blvd., Houston, TX 77005. Tel: 713-529-1912; Fax: 713-529-0372.

New York: Maryknoll Fathers and Brothers, 121 E. 39th St., New York, NY 10016. Tel: 212-697-4470; Fax: 212-697-4472.

Los Angeles: Maryknoll Fathers and Brothers, 745 W. Adams Blvd., Los Angeles, CA 90007. Tel: 213-747-9676; Fax: 213-747-8923.

Philadelphia: Maryknoll Fathers and Brothers, 6367 Overbrook Ave., Philadelphia, PA 19151. Tel: 215-477-5892; Fax: 215-477-3088.

Rockville Centre: Maryknoll Fathers and Brothers, 813 Myrna Dr., West Hempstead, NY 11552. Tel: 516-489-7799.

St. Augustine: Maryknoll Fathers and Brothers, 2243 Saragossa Ave., Jacksonville, FL 32217-2685. Tel: 904-739-1112; Fax: 904-739-1250.

St. Louis: Maryknoll Fathers and Brothers, 4542 W. Pine Blvd., St. Louis, MO 63108. Tel: 314-361-7729; Fax: 314-361-0718.

St. Paul: Maryknoll Fathers and Brothers, 10345 Portland Ave. S., Minneapolis, MN 55420. Tel: 612-884-7743; Fax: 612-884-7744.

San Francisco: Maryknoll Fathers and Brothers, 2555 Webster St., San Francisco, CA 94115. Tel: 415-921-1100; Fax: 415-775-8261; *Casa Maryknoll*, 453 Miller Ave., So. San Francisco, CA 94080. Tel: 415-952-5500.

San Jose: Maryknoll Residence, 23000 Cristo Rey Dr., Los Altos, CA 94024. Tel: 650-967-3822; Fax: 650-965-3473.

Seattle: Maryknoll Fathers and Brothers, 958 16th Ave., E., Seattle, WA 98112. Tel: 206-322-8831; Fax: 206-324-6909.

Washington: Maryknoll Fathers and Brothers, 4834 16th St., N.W., Washington, DC 20011. Tel: 202-726-4252; 726-4281; Fax: 207-726-0466.

Priests 559; Students in Theology 15; Brothers 71; Priests Associates 8.

Properties owned or sponsored: Major Society Center; House of Formation; U.S. Community Houses 24.

Represented in the Archdioceses of Boston, Chicago, Cincinnati, Denver, Detroit, Los Angeles, New York, Philadelphia, St. Louis, St. Paul-Minneapolis, San Francisco, Seattle, Washington and in the Dioceses of Buffalo, Cleveland, Galveston-Houston and San Jose.

[0810] (F.M.M.)—BROTHERS OF MERCY

General Motherhouse: 56410 Montabaur, West Germany. Bro. Stephen Geisslen, F.M.M., Supr. Gen.

American Province: 4520 Ransom Rd., Clarence, NY 14031. Tel: 716-759-8341. Bros. Jude Holzfoerster, F.M.M., Prov. Supr. Councillors: Bros. John McGrath, F.M.M.; Fidelis Verrall, F.M.M.

Brothers 15; Novices 2; Candidate 3.

Legal Holdings or Titles: *Brothers of Mercy Nursing Home Co., Inc., Brothers of Mercy Housing Co., Inc., Brothers of Mercy Sacred Heart Home, Inc.*

Represented in the Diocese of Buffalo.

[0820] (C.P.M.)—CONGREGATION OF THE FATHERS OF MERCY

(Congregatio Presbyterorum a Misericordia)

Generalate and Novitiate (1808): South Union, KY 42283. Tel: 502-542-4146. Very Rev. William Casey, C.P.M., Supr. Gen. Consultors: Revs. Joseph Burgdorf, C.P.M.; John O'Brien, C.P.M.; David Wilton, C.P.M.; Louis Caproiccio, C.P.M.

Priests 14; Novices 3; Students 10.

Represented in the Archdiocese of Louisville and in the Dioceses of Lafayette (LA), and Owensboro.

[0825] M.S.S.—MISSIONARIES OF THE BLESSED SACRAMENT

Missionaries of the Blessed Sacrament

Regional Headquarters: P.O. Box 4337, Corpus Christi, TX 78469. Tel: 512-881-5025; Fax: 512-883-1581. Revs. Martin V. Lucia, M.S.S., Supr.

Fathers 4.

Ministries in Special Apostolate: Promotion of perpetual Eucaristic adoration.

Represented in the Dioceses of Alexandria, Baton Rouge, Corpus Christi, Lafayette, and Lake Charles.

[0830] (M.H.M.)—MILL HILL MISSIONARIES

St. Joseph's Missionary Society of Mill Hill

International Headquarters: St. Joseph's College, Mill Hill, London NW7 4JX, England. Very Rev. Maurice McGill, M.H.M., Supr. Gen.

American Headquarters: Mill Hill Missionaries, 222 W. Hartsdale Ave., Hartsdale, NY 10530-1667. Tel: 914-682-0645; Fax: 914-682-0862. Very Rev. Terence J. Lee, M.H.M., Reg. Rep.

Legal Title: *Mill Hill Fathers, Inc.*

Fathers 17; Brothers 2; Associates 1.

Represented in the Archdioceses of Los Angeles & New York.

[0835] (O.M.)—MINIM FATHERS

General Motherhouse: Via S. Andrea delle Fratte, 1, 00184, Rome, Italy. Tel: 011-39-6-678-0407; Fax: 011-39-6-678-0752. Very Rev. Giuseppe Morosini, O.M., Supr. Gen.

North American Delegation (1970): 3431 Portola Ave., Los Angeles, CA 90032. Tel: 213-223-1101. Friar Constantino Mandarino, O.M., Delegate Gen.

Legal Title: *Minim Fathers.*

Priests 3.

Vocation Center: 6043 N. Barranca Ave., Azusa, CA 91702.

Represented in the Archdiocese of Los Angeles.

[0840] (S.T.)—MISSIONARY SERVANTS OF THE MOST HOLY TRINITY

(Missionarii Servi Sanctissimae Trinitatis)
(Trinity Missions)

Generalate-Missionary Servants of the Most Holy Trinity: 1215 N. Scott St., Arlington, VA 22209-3097. Tel: 703-276-8646; Fax: 703-522-2656. Revs. Dominigo Rodriguez, S.T., Gen. Custodian; Revs. John P. McSpiritt, S.T., Vicar Gen. & Vicar for Personnel; Jesus Rivera, S.T., Gen. Councillor & Vicar for Spanish-speaking Personnel &, Apostolates; John S. Edmunds, S.T., Gen. Councillor; Bros. Hilary Mettes, S.T., Sec. Gen.; Alexis Norton, S.T., Treas. Gen.; Jordan Baxter, S.T., Asst. Treas. Gen.; Paul Michalenko, S.T., Gen. Councillor & Vicar for Apostolates.

Legal Title: *Missionary Servants of The Most Holy Trinity (a.k.a) Trinity Missions, Missionary Servants Charitable Trust, Father Judge Charitable Trust.*

Priests 95; Brothers 37; Student Brothers 14; Novices 5; Candidates 52.

Ministry in the following areas: Missionary Cenacles; Parishes; Missions; Stations and Specialized Apostolates; Lay Apostolate Secretariat; Halfway House; Auxiliary Military Chaplaincies; Counseling Centers; Hospitals and Rest Home Chaplains; AA Programs; Protective Institutions; Prison Chaplains; V.A. Chaplains; Community Centers; Elementary Schools.

Properties owned and or sponsored: Generalate, Arlington, VA; Parish, rectory and school, Holy Trinity, AL; Apostolic Center, New Orleans, LA, Philadelphia, PA, Rio Piedras, PR; Seminary and Fund Raising Office Buildings, Silver Spring, MD; School Buildings, Camden, MS; St. Joseph Shrine, Stirling, NJ; Trinity Ministries Center, Stirling, NJ; Former minor seminary building, Monroe, VA; Residences, Harpers Ferry, WV, Sound Beach, NY; Senior Ministry Residence, Adelphi, MD; Residence Post-Novitiate Formation House, Adelphi, MD; Holy Trinity Missionary Cenacle, University Park, MD.

Represented in the Archdioceses of Boston, Chicago, Indianapolis, Los Angeles, Military Services-USA, Mobile, Newark, New Orleans, Philadelphia, St. Paul-Minneapolis and Washington and in the Dioceses of Arlington, Biloxi, Birmingham, Boise, Cleveland, Jackson, Orange, Paterson, Richmond, St. Augustine, San Bernardino, San Diego, Savannah, and Tucson. Also in Mexico, Puerto Rico, Costa Rica, and Colombia.

[0850] (M.AFR.)—MISSIONARIES OF AFRICA

(Societas Missionariorum Africae)

Generalate: 269 via Aurelia, C.P. 9078, I-00165, Rome, Italy. Rev. Gotthard Rosner, M.Afr., Supr. Gen.

Province of North America: 1624 21st St., N.W., Washington, DC 20009-1055. Tel: 202-232-5154; Fax: 202-332-8640. Revs. William Moroney, M.Afr., Asst. Prov.; David J. Goergen, M.Afr., Treas.; Roger L. Bisson, M.Afr., Dir. of Planned Giving Dept.; Pierre Benson, M.Afr., Coord.-Justice & Peace.

Priests 29; Brothers 2.

Represented in the Archdioceses of Chicago, Los Angeles and Washington, and in the Diocese of St. Petersburg and Little Rock.

[0853] (M.S.C.)—MISSIONARY SERVANTS OF CHRIST

Founded in the United States in 1979 by Bro. Edwin Baker.

Headquarters and Novitiate: St. Anthony in the Hills, P.O. Box 1932, Ocean City, MD 21843. Tel: 610-268-2747; Fax: 610-268-2747. Bro. Edwin Baker, M.S.C., Supr.

Professed Brothers 10; Novices 2; Postulants 1.

Represented in the Diocese of Wilmington.

[0854] (M.S.P.)—MISSIONARY SOCIETY OF ST. PAUL OF NIGERIA

Generalate: Gwagwalada P.O. Box 23,, , Abuja, Nigeria. Very Rev. Felix Elosi, M.S.P., Supr. Gen.

U.S. Region: Missionary Society of St. Paul, Inc., 12606 Crosby-Lynchburg Rd. - P.O. Box 3200, Barrette Station, TX 77532-2200. Tel: 713-328-8931; Fax: 713-328-7306. Rev. Paul N. Ofoha, M.S.P., Local Supr.

Universal number of Priests 104; Priests in U.S. 17.

Legal Title: Missionary Society of St. Paul, Inc., Barrette Station, TX.

Represented in the Diocese of Galveston-Houston.

[0855] (F.M.M.)—MISSIONARY FRATERNITY OF MARY

General Headquarters: 6A Calle 48-98, Zona 7-Apartado Postal 623-I, Zona 7, Guatemala, Central America. Rev. Msgr. Eduardo Aguirre-Oestmann, General Moderator.

U.S. Foundation (1991): 340 Pine St., Seaford, DE 19973. Tel: 302-629-5705; Fax: 302-629-7403. Revs. Ruben A. Soto, F.M.M., U.S. Regional Vicar; Juan Vicente Hidalgo, F.M.M.

Represented in the Archdiocese of Miami and in the Dioceses of Beaumont, TX and Wilmington, De.

[0860] (C.I.C.M.)—MISSIONHURST CONGREGATION OF THE IMMACULATE HEART OF MARY

(Congregatio Immaculati Cordis Mariae)
Foreign and home missions

General Motherhouse: Casa Generalizia C.I.C.M., Via S. Giovanni Eudes, 95, 00163, Roma, Italy. Very Rev. Jacques Thomas, C.I.C.M., Supr. Gen.

U.S. Province (1946): *Missionhurst*, 4651 N. 25th St., Arlington, VA 22207. Tel: 703-528-3800; Fax: 703-528-5355. Rev. Joseph Lapauw, C.I.C.M., Prov. Supr.

Legal Title: *American I.H.M. Province, Inc., Immaculate Heart Missions, Inc., Missionhurst, Inc.*

Fathers 55; Brothers 10.

Ministries in Parishes and Hospital Pastoral Work.

Represented in the Archdioceses of Detroit, Hartford, New York, Philadelphia and San Antonio and in the Dioceses of Arlington, Brooklyn and Brownsville.

[0870] (S.M.M.)—MONTFORT MISSIONARIES

(Missionaries of the Company of Mary)
(Societas Mariae Montfortana)

Generalate: Viale Dei Monfortani 65, Rome, 12. Italy. Very Rev. William J. Considine, S.M.M.

United States Province (1948): *Montfort Missionaries*, 101-18 104th St., Ozone Park, NY 11416. Tel: 718-849-5885; Fax: 718-849-7518. Very Rev. Gerald J. Fitzsimmons, S.M.M. Counselors: Revs. Richard Schebera, S.M.M.; Donald LaSalle, S.M.M.; Eugene Lynch, S.M.M.; Matthew Considine, S.M.M.

Fathers 32; Brothers 3.

Parishes 2; Community Houses 6.

Represented in the Archdioceses of Hartford, St. Louis and in the Dioceses of Brooklyn, and Rockville Centre.

[0895] (O.Ss.S.)—BRIGITTINE MONKS

(The Order of the Most Holy Savior)

Monastery of Our Lady of Consolation: 23300 Walker Ln., Amity, OR 97101. Tel: 503-835-8080; Fax: 503-835-9662. Bro. Benedict Kirby, O.Ss.S., Prior.

Professed Monks 12; Novices 1.

Represented in the Archdiocese of Portland in Oregon.

[0897] (M.E.P.)—PARIS FOREIGN MISSION SOCIETY

(Societas Parisiensis Missionum Ad Exteros)
Society of secular priests, without vows, of Pontifical Right

Headquarters: 128 Rue du Bac, Paris, France. Very Rev. Raymond Rossignol, Supr. Gen.; Rev. Jean-Baptiste Etcharren.

U.S. Establishment: Paris Foreign Mission Society, 930 Ashbury St., San Francisco, CA 94117. Tel: 415-664-6747. Rev. Jacques R. Didier, M.E.P., Dir.

Legal Title: *American Auxiliary of Paris Foreign Missions, Inc.*

Priests 3.

Represented in the Archdiocese of San Francisco.

[0900] (O. PRAEM.)—CANONS REGULAR OF PREMONTRE

(Norbertines, Order of St. Norbert, Premonstratensians)
(Ordo Canonicorum Regularium Praemonstratensium)
Founded in France in the 12th century. First foundation in the United States in 1893.

Abbot General: Most Rev. Hermenegild J. Noyens, O.Praem, Norbertine Generalate, 27 Viale Giotto, 00153, Rome, Italy. Tel: 011-39-6-57-46-979; 011-39-6-57-42-397; Fax: 011-39-6-574-0241.

United States: St. Norbert Abbey, 1016 N. Broadway, De Pere, WI 54115-2697. Tel: 920-337-4300; Fax: 920-337-4328. Rt. Rev. E. Thomas De Wane, O.Praem., Abbot; Rt. Rev. Sylvester M. Killeen, O.Praem., Abbot Emeritus; Rt. Rev. Jerome G. Tremel, O.Praem., Abbot Emeritus; Rt. Rev. Benjamin T. Mackin, O.Praem., Abbot Emeritus; Very Rev. David F. Strensk O.Praem., Prior; Donald C. Noel, O.Praem., Sub Prior; Revs. James T. Baraniak, O.Praem., Vocation Coord.; Robert K. Finnegan, O.Praem., Provisor/Sec.-Treas.; Alan D. Scheib, O.Praem., Dir.-Norbertine Center for Spirituality.

Legal Title: *The Premonstratensian Fathers, NORBERT & CO., a nominee of The Premonstratensian Fathers, Norbertine Fathers, St. Norbert Abbey, Inc., The Walnut Markets, Inc., Los Amigos del Peru, Inc., Norbertine Generalate, Inc.*

Fathers 86; Seminarians 4; Brothers 6.

Properties owned, staffed, or sponsored: Dependent Priories 4; House of Studies 1; Colleges 1; Chaplaincies 5; Parishes 12.

Represented in the Archdioceses of Boston, Chicago, Military Services for the U.S.A., and Santa Fe and in the Dioceses of Green Bay, Jackson, Madison and Providence. Also in Peru.

Daylesford Abbey: Norbertine Fathers and Brothers, 220 S. Valley Rd., Paoli, PA 19301-1900. Tel: 610-647-2530. Rt. Rev. Ronald J. Rossi, O.Praem., Prior; Revs. John J. Novielli, O.Praem., Sub Prior; Andrew D. Ciferni, O.Praem., Supr.; Theodore J. Antry, O.Praem, Vocation Dir.; Joseph P. McLaughlin, O.Praem., Master of Novices; Joseph A. Serano, O.Praem., Treas.

Legal Title: *Norbertine Fathers, Inc.*

Fathers 24; Brothers 3; Novice 1.

Properties owned, staffed, or sponsored: Chaplaincies 1; Dependent Priories 1; Seminary; Parishes 4.

Represented in the Archdioceses of Philadelphia, and the Dioceses of Harrisburg.Fort Also in Peru.

St. Michael's Abbey: 19292 El Toro Rd., Silverado, CA 92676. Tel: 714-858-0222; Fax: 714-858-4583.

Legal Title: *The Norbertine Fathers of Orange, Inc.;* Rt. Rev. Eugene J. Hayes, O.Praem., Abbot; Very Rev. Hugh Barbour, O.Praem., Prior; Rev. John Caronan, O.Praem., Treas.

Pious Association (Aid to the Church in Need, Inc.), P.O. Box 819, El Toro, CA 92630. Tel: 714-858-0222.

Priests 42; Clerics 11; Postulants 4; Novices 2.

Properties owned: St. Michael's College Preparatory High School, Orange, CA Summer Camp, Orange, CA.

Represented in the Archdiocese of Los Angeles and in the Diocese of Orange.

[0910] (O.M.I.)—OBLATES OF MARY IMMACULATE

General House: Oblati di Maria Immacolata, C.P. 9061, 00100, Roma-Aurelio-Italy; Most Rev. Marcello Zago, O.M.I., Supr Gen.; Very Rev. Daniel Corijn, O.M.I., Vicar Gen.

U.S. Consulate: 290 Lenox Ave., Oakland, CA 94610. Tel: 510-452-1550; Fax: 510-452-3421. Rev. Ronald Carignan, O.M.I., General Councillor.

Legal Title: *Western Oblates Support Trust Fund, Oblate Fathers Western Province, Inc.*

Southern U.S. Province (1904): Provincial Admin. Office, 7711 Madonna Dr., San Antonio, TX 78216-6696. Tel: 210-349-1475; Fax: 210-349-7411. Very Rev. Charles Banks, O.M.I., Prov.; Revs. Salvatore DeGeorge, O.M.I., Vicar Prov.; Warren Brown, O.M.I., Consultor; F. Kelly Nemeck, O.M.I., Consultor; Robert Wright, O.M.I., Consultor & Prov. Archivist; Rufus Whitley, O.M.I., Bursar.

Fathers 138; Brothers 4; Scholastics 20.

Properties owned, staffed, or sponsored: Retreat Centers; Religious Residences & Houses.

Represented in the Archdioceses of New Orleans, San Antonio, Washington and in the Dioceses of Austin, Beaumont, Brownsville, Corpus Christi, Dallas, Galveston-Houston, Juneau, Lubbock, San Angelo, Springfield (IL) and Tucson. Also in Zambia.

Eastern American Province (1883): *Our Lady of Hope*, 391 Michigan Ave., N.E., Washington, DC 20017. Revs. William Sheehan, O.M.I., Prov.; William O'Donnell, O.M.I., Vicar Prov. Councillors: Revs. Henry Lemoncelli, O.M.I.; Stephen Conserva, O.M.I.; Thomas Coughlin, O.M.I.; James Fee, O.M.I.; John Madigan, O.M.I.

Fathers 111; Brothers 8; Professed Clerics 9.

Staff and-or serve: Parishes 21; Prisons 2; Hospitals 2; Community Houses 5; Pre-Novitiate 1.

Represented in the Archdioceses of Boston, Miami, New York, Washington and in the Dioceses of Buffalo, Columbus, Juneau, Lexington, Palm Beach and Pensacola-Tallahassee. Also in Puerto Rico.

The Northern U.S. Province (St. John the Baptist) (1921): 61 Burns Hill Rd., Hudson, NH 03051-4423. Tel: 603-883-3233; Fax: 603-883-6089. Very Rev. Arthur Obin, O.M.I., Prov.; Rev. Charles Breault, O.M.I., Treas. Councillors: Revs. Roger E. Lamoureux, O.M.I.; Daniel Nassaney, O.M.I.; Thomas Horan, O.M.I.; James Robichaud, O.M.I.

Legal Title: *Missionary Oblates of Mary Immaculate.*

Fathers 79; Scholastics (Theology) 1; Brothers 12.

Ministries in Parishes; Retreat Houses; Hospital Chaplaincies; Men's Correctional Institutions; Nursing Home Res. Chaplains; Religious Community Resident Chaplains; Special; Ministries; U.S. Military.

Legal Holdings: Oblate Provincial House, Hudson, NH; *Andre Garin Residence*, Lowell, MA; *St. Paul Center*, Augusta, ME; *Oblate Seminary Residence*, Brighton, MA; *Shrine of Our Lady of Grace*, Colebrook, NH; *Oblate Retreat House*, Hudson, NH; *Oblate Foreign Missions Office*, Lowell, MA; *Oblate Ministry Development Office*, Lowell, MA; *St. Joseph the Worker Shrine & Center*, Lowell, MA; *Ephpheta House*, Manville, RI; *Immaculata Retreat House*, Willimantic, CT; *St. Joseph Cemetery*, East Chelmsford, MA; *Andre Garin Resident*, Lowell, MA; *St. Eugene House*, Lowell, MA.

Represented in the Archdioceses of Boston, Miami, New Orleans, Washington and the Dioceses of Manchester, Norwich, Oakland, Ogdensburg, Portland (ME), Providence, Richmond and Worcester. Also in Canada and French Polynesia.

Central U.S. Province (1924): 267 E. 8th St., St. Paul, MN 55101; Fax: 612-292-8769. Revs. David A. Kalert, O.M.I., Prov.; Thomas J. Singer, O.M.I., Vicar Prov. & Personnel Dir.; William P. Clark, O.M.I.; James F. Allen, O.M.I.; Louis B. Studer, O.M.I.; Joseph H. Hitpas, O.M.I.; William L. Johnson, O.M.I.; Robert F. Moobrugger, O.M.I., Treas.

Priests 122; Brothers 16; Scholastics 8; Novices 2; Post College Seminarians 2.

Ministries in Parishes; House of Study and Retreat Houses.

Represented in the Archdioceses of Chicago, St. Paul-Minneapolis and St. Louis and in the Dioceses of Belleville, Crookston, Duluth, Green Bay, Superior, Sioux Falls, Springfield-Cape Girardeau and Springfield (IL).

Western Province (1953): 290 Lenox Ave., Oakland, CA 94610. Tel: 510-452-1550; Fax: 510-452-3421. Very Rev. David Ullrich, O.M.I., Prov.; Revs. Thomas Rush, O.M.I., Vicarr; Leo Dummer, O.M.I., Bursar; Richard Haslam, O.M.I.; William Antone, O.M.I.; Paul Waldie, O.M.I.

Fathers 50; Scholastic Brothers 2; Brothers 2.

Legal Title: *Western Oblates Support Trust Fund, Oblate Fathers Western Province Inc.*

Ministries in Parishes; Missions; Retreat Houses; Chaplaincies.

Represented in the Archdioceses of Los Angeles, Portland (OR), Seattle and the Dioceses of Boise, Fresno, Monterey, Oakland and San Diego. Also in Mexico.

[0920] (O.S.F.S.)—OBLATES OF ST. FRANCIS DE SALES

(Congregatio Oblatorum Sancti Francisci Salesii)

General Motherhouse: Via Dandolo 49, Rome, Italy. In July 1966, the American Province divided into two provinces.

Wilmington-Philadelphia Province (1906): 2200 Kentmere Pky., Box 1452, Wilmington, DE 19899. (Direct all communications to Box 1452, Wilmington, DE 19899; Very Rev. Joseph G. Morrissey, O.S.F.S., Prov. Councillors: Revs. Edward T. Fitzpatrick, O.S.F.S.; Francis W. Danella, O.S.F.S.; James J. Behan, O.S.F.S., Prov.; Thomas B. Curran, O.S.F.S. Provincial Staff: Revs. Edward T. Fitzpatrick, O.S.F.S., Dir. Personnel; Francis W. Danella, O.S.F.S., Asst. Prov.; Robert A. Mancini, O.S.F.S., Treas.; Richard R. De Lillio, O.S.F.S., Dir. Development; Joseph P. Jocco, O.S.F.S., Dir. Vocations; John J. Hurley, O.S.F.S., Dir. Missions; Nicholas R. Waseline, O.S.F.S., Formation Advisor.

Fathers 212; Scholastics 14; Brothers 26.

Properties owned, staffed, or sponsored: Parishes 23; Colleges 1; Scholasticates 1; Novitiates 1; High Schools 6; Retreat Houses 1; Armed Forces 3; Chaplaincies 20; Foreign Missions 10.

Properties owned: Provincial Residence, Wilmington,

DE Salesianum School, Wilmington, DE DeSales House, Wilmington, DE Center for New Life, Childs, MD Oblate Novitiate, Wyndmoor, PA Villa St. Joseph, Newfield, NJ Oblate Residence, Cape May, NJ Brisson Seminary, Center Valley, PA DeSales Theological Center, Washington, DC Deshairs House, Washington, DC.

Represented in the Archdioceses of Philadelphia and Washington and in Dioceses of Allentown, Arlington, Camden, Charlotte, Harrisburg, Providence, Raleigh, Richmond, Trenton, Venice and Wilmington.

Toledo-Detroit Province (1966): 2056 Parkwood Ave., Toledo, OH 43620-1616. Tel: 419-243-5105; Fax: 419-243-8827. Very Rev. James F. Cryan, O.S.F.S., Prov.; Revs. John J. Loughran, O.S.F.S., Asst. Prov.; Richard E. Morse, O.S.F.S., Treas. Prov. Councillors: Revs. Richard E. Morse, O.S.F.S.; Ronald W. Olszewski, O.S.F.S.; Rev. Francis J. Gross, O.S.F.S., Oblate Mission Procurator, 259 4th St., Niagra Falls, NY 14303.

Legal Title: *Oblates of St. Francis de Sales, Inc.*

Priests 73; Brothers 14; Professed Scholastics 1; Novices 1.

Properties owned, staffed, or sponsored: *Provincial Residence,* Toledo, OH; *St. Francis de Sales High School,* Toledo, OH; *Oblate Residence,* Jackson, MI; *Oblate Residence,* Toronto, Canada; *Oblate Residence,* Lewiston, NY; *Oblate Residence,* Livonia, MI; *Oblate Residence,* Buffalo, NY.

Ministries in Parishes; Highschools; Chaplaincies; Armed forces; Senior Citizens Residence.

Represented in the Archdioceses of Detroit, Miami, Military Services, Oklahoma City and Philadelphia, and in the Dioceses of Buffalo, Erie, Lansing, Oakland, Saginaw, Salt Lake City, Stockton and Toledo. Also in Canada and the Virgin Islands.

[0930] (O.S.J.)—OBLATES OF ST. JOSEPH

(Congregatio Oblatorum S. Joseph)

Founded in Italy in 1878. Founder: Blessed Bishop Joseph Marello (1844-1895). Cause of Beatification introduced May 28, 1948. Beatified 1993. First foundation in U.S. in 1929.

Motherhouse: Corso Alfieri 384, Asti, Italy.

General House: Via Boccea, 364, Rome, Italy. Very Rev. Vito Calabrese, O.S.J., Supr. Gen.; Very Rev. Vito Accettura, O.S.J., Vicar Gen.; Very Rev. Tarcisio Stramare, O.S.J., Procurator Gen.

Oblates of St. Joseph Eastern Province: Rte. 315, R.R. 4, Box 14, Pittston, PA 18640; Fax: 717-654-8621. Rev. Joseph D. Sibilano, O.S.J., Prov. Councillors: Revs. Gregory T. Finn, O.S.J.; Paul A. McDonnell, O.S.J.

Priests 12.

Parishes 4; Community Houses 5; Houses of Studies 1.

Properties owned: St. Joseph's Oblate Seminary, Pittston, PA.

Represented in the Dioceses of Norwich and Scranton.

California Province: 544 W. Cliff Dr., Santa Cruz, CA 95060. Tel: 408-457-1868; Fax: 408-457-1317. Rev. Philip Massetti, O.S.J., Prov. Councillors: Revs. Larry Toschi, O.S.J.; Brian Crawford, O.S.J.

Legal Title: *Oblates of St. Joseph.*

Priests 15; Brothers 4; Deacons 1; Temporary Professed Clerical Student 2; Postulants 1; Aspirants 6.

Parishes 4; Community Houses 6; Houses of Study 2; Shrines 1.

Properties owned: St. Joseph House of Studies, Berkeley, CA Mount St. Joseph Seminary, Loomis, CA Shrine of St. Joseph, Guardian of the Redeemer, Santa Cruz, CA Blessed Marello House of Studies, Oxnard CA St. Joseph's Villa, Soda Springs, CA.

Represented in the Archdiocese of Los Angeles and in the Dioceses of Fresno, Monterey and Sacramento.

[0940] (O.M.V.)—OBLATES OF THE VIRGIN MARY

(Congregation of the Oblates of the Virgin Mary)
(Congregatio Oblatorum Beatae Mariae Virginis)

Generalate: Viale XXX Aprile, 17, 00153, Rome, Italy. Very Rev. Patrice Veraquia, O.M.V., Rector Major.

St. Ignatius Province: 2 Ipswich St., Boston, MA 02215-3607. Tel: 617-536-7471. Rev. Timothy Gallagher, O.M.V., Prov.

Priests in U.S. 39; Brothers 3.

Legal Holdings: *St. Clement's Eucharistic Shrine,* Boston, MA; *St. Joseph House,* Milton, MA; *St. Ignatius Province of the Oblates of the Virgin Mary, Inc.,* Boston, MA.

Ministries in Parishes; Hospital and Prison Chaplaincies; Retreats & Parish Missions; Novitiate; Community Houses; College Seminary Shrine Chaplaincies.

Represented in the Archdioceses of Boston and Los Angeles and in the Dioceses of Metuchen and Springfield. Also in the Philippines.

[0950] (C.O.)—ORATORIANS

(Confederatio Oratorii S. Philippi Nerii)

A Confederation of Autonomous Houses first founded in Rome, 1575

General Confederation: Confederazione dell'Oratorio S. Philippi Neri, Via S. Girolamo della Carita 63, 00186, Roma, Italia. Revs. Edoardo Cerrato, C.O., Procurator Gen.; Antonio Chavez Rios, C.O., Delegate of the Holy See, The Oratory, La Professa, Isabel La Catolica, 21 Apartado Postal 7113, Mexico, DF 06000.

The Oratory of Rock Hill: P.O. Box 11586, Rock Hill, SC 29731. Tel: 803-327-2097. Very Rev. Joseph Wahl, C.O., Father Provost.

Fathers 9; Brothers 4; Novices 2.

Represented in the Diocese of Charleston.

The Oratorian Community of Monterey: P.O. Box 1688, Monterey, CA 93942. Tel: 408-373-0476. Very Rev. Peter C. Sanders, Provost & Major Supr.; Revs. Michael P. Drury, Vicar; Lidio Limon, Sec. & Assoc. Vocational Apostolate; Thomas A. Kieffer, Treas.

Total in community 4.

Oratorian Foundation Inc., Arizona, P.O. Box 241, Yarnell, AZ 85362. An outreach of the Oratorian Community in Monterey.

Represented in the Diocese of Monterey.

The Pittsburgh Oratory: Congregation of the Oratory of St. Philip Neri, 4450 Bayard Street, Pittsburgh, PA 15213-1506. Tel: 412-681-3181. Very Rev. Bryan F. Summers, C.O., Provost; Revs. Drew P. Morgan, C.O., Vicar; David S. Abernethy, C.O., Treas.

Fathers 5; Novices 1.

Represented in the Diocese of Pittsburgh.

The Oratory of Pharr: P.O. Box II, Pharr, TX 78577-1235. Tel: 956-843-8217; Fax: 956-843-2946. Residence, end of S. Jackson Rd., FM 2061, near Hidalgo. Very Rev. Leo Francis Daniels, C.O., Provost; Rev. Jose Encarnacion Losoya, C.O., Sec. Treas.; Deacon Mario Aviles Campos, C.O., Asst. Sec.; Rev. David Garcia, C.O., In Residence; Very Rev. Antonio Rios, C.O., Delegate of the Holy See.

Properties owned: Casa Maria of the Oratory, Pharr, TX Oratory Academy-Academia Oratoriana, Pharr, TX Pharr Oratory of St. Philip Neri of Pontifical Right.

Ministries in Parish work; Services to the poor; promotion of Mexican-American cultural services.

Secular Oratory, Lay Institute founded by St. Philip Neri. Principal Work:.

Federacion Mexicana del Oratorio de San Felip Neri, American Office, The Oratory, Rte. 1, Box 118, Pharr, TX 78577. Rev. Antonio Ortega, C.O., Natl. Procurator, The Pharr Oratory is a member of the Mexican Federation of Oratories, and at present serves as the American office of all eleven houses.

Represented in the Diocese of Brownsville. Also in Mexico and Costa Rica.

The Oratory of St. Philip Neri: 109 Willoughby St., Brooklyn, NY 11201. Tel: 718-875-2096; Fax: 718-875-4678. Very Rev. Dennis M. Corrado, C.O., Provost.

Fathers 4; Brothers 2.

[0960] (F.S.R.)—BROTHERS OF THE CONGREGATION OF OUR LADY OF THE HOLY ROSARY

Founded in the United States in 1957.

General Motherhouse and Novitiate: 232 Sunnyside Dr., Reno, NV 89505-3510. Tel: 702-747-4441. Bros. Philip Napolitano, F.S.R., Supr.; Matthew Cunningham, F.S.R., Asst. Supr.

Brothers 3.

Ministries in the field of Education and Pastoral Ministry.

Represented in the Diocese of Reno.

[0970] (O.de.M.)—ORDER OF OUR LADY OF MERCY

(Mercedarians Friars)
(Ordo de Beatae Mariae Virginis de Mercede)
(Founded in Barcelona, Spain on August 10, 1218)

Generalate: Curia Generalizia dei PP. Mercedari,, Via Monte Carmelo 3, 00166, Rome, Italy. Most Rev. Emilio Aguirre Herrera, O.de.M., Master Gen.

U.S. Vicariate: St. Rocco Rectory, 3205 Fulton Rd., Cleveland, OH 44109. Tel: 216-961-8331. Rev. Marino Frascati, O.de.M., Vicar Prov.

Priests 16; Brothers 4; Clerics 4; Novices 2.

Properties owned: St. Raymond Nonnatus Novitiate, Le Roy, NY Monastery of Our Lady of Mercy, Philadelphia, PA Saint Peter Nolasco Residence, St. Petersburg, FL.

Represented in the Archdiocese of Philadelphia and in the Dioceses of Buffalo, Cleveland and St. Petersburg.

[0975] (S.O.L.T.)—SOCIETY OF OUR LADY OF THE MOST HOLY TRINITY

Headquarters: Casa San Jose, 109 W. Avenue F, P.O. Box 152, Robstown, TX 78380. Tel: 512-387-2754. Rev. James H. Flanagan, S.O.L.T., Gen. Priest Servant.

Priests 72; Deacons 3; Novices 21; Seminarians 81.

Pastoral Ministries: Community House; House of Study-Novitiate; Migrant Ministry.

Represented in the Archdioceses of Hartford and Santa Fe and in the Dioceses of Albany, Cheyenne, Corpus Christi, Gallup, Kansas City-St. Joseph, Lafayette, Norwich and Wheeling-Charleston.

[0980] (C.F.M.M.)—BROTHERS OF OUR LADY, MOTHER OF MERCY

(Congregatio Fratrum Beatae Mariae Virginis, Matris Misericordiae)

Generalate: Gasthuisring 54, 5041 DT, Tilburg, The Netherlands.

U.S. Region: 2336 S. C St., Oxnard, CA 93033. Tel: 805-486-3692. Bro. C. W. Gresnigt, C.F.M.M., Reg. Supr.

Brothers 8.

Represented in the Archdiocese of Los Angeles.

[0990] (S.A.C.)—SOCIETY OF THE CATHOLIC APOSTOLATE

(Pallottines)

Generalate: Pallottines, Piazza S.V. Pallotti 204, 00186, Rome, Italy.

Province of the Immaculate Conception (Eastern) (1953): P.O. Box 979, South Orange, NJ 07079. Tel: 201-762-2926. 204 Raymond Ave., South Orange, NJ 07079. Very Rev. Peter T. Sticco, S.A.C., Prov.; Revs. Frank Amato, S.A.C., 1st Consultor; Frank Gaetano, S.A.C., Bursar & Consultor. Consultors: Revs. Louis Micca, S.A.C.; Oreste Pandola, S.A.C.

Fathers 22; Professed Clerics 1; Professed Brothers 3.

Properties owned, sponsored, or staffed: Parishes 4; Seminary; High School; Novitiate; Shrine of St. Jude, Pallottine Center for Apostolic Causes.

Represented in the Archdioceses of Baltimore, Newark and Washington and in the Dioceses of Brooklyn and Camden.

Mother of God Province (1946): *Pallottine Father and Brothers, Inc.,* 5424 W. Blue Mound Rd., Milwaukee, WI 53208. Tel: 414-259-0688; Fax: 414-258-9314. Very Rev. Robert V. Carney, S.A.C., Prov.; Revs. Leon Martin, S.A.C., 1st Consultor; Harold J. Liebl, S.A.C., Consultor & Prov. Treas.; Francis Hueller, S.A.C., Consultor; Richard J. Gunderman, S.A.C., Consultor.

Fathers 18; Brothers 1.

Ministries in Parishes; Retreat House; Hospital Chaplaincies; High School.

Represented in the Archdiocese of Milwaukee and the Diocese of Fargo.

Irish Province (1909): Homestead, Sandyford Rd., Dundrum, Dublin 16, Republic of Ireland. Very Rev. William Hanly, S.A.C., Prov.

U.S. Foundation: 3352 4th St., P.O. Box 249, Wyandotte, MI 48192. Very Rev. Philip McNamara, S.A.C., Prov. Delegate.

Fathers 20.

Parishes 19; Missions 10.

Represented in the Archdiocese of Detroit and in the Diocese of Fort Worth, Lubbock and Reno-Las Vegas.

Queen of the Apostles Province (1909): Via Giuseppe Ferrari, 1-Rome, Italy. Very Rev. Gaetano Iann, S.A.C., Prov.

U.S. Foundation: Our Lady of Mt. Carmel Shrine and Church, 448 E. 116th St., New York, NY 10029. Tel: 212-534-0681. Very Rev. Terzo Vinci, S.A.C., Prov. Delegate.

Our Lady of Mt. Carmel, 70 Park Hill Ave., Yonkers, NY 10701.

Fathers 8.

Parishes 4.

Represented in the Archdiocese of New York and the Diocese of Albany and Pensacola-Tallahassee.

Infant Jesus Delegature of Christ The King Province: Mission House and Infant Jesus Shrine, 3452 Niagara Falls Blvd., North Tonawanda, NY 14120. Rev. Anthony Zemula, S.A.C., Supr. & Prov. Delegate, Motherhouse, Poznan, Poland; *Society of the Catholic Apostolate.*

Priests 11.

Represented in the Dioceses of Brooklyn and Buffalo.

[1000] (C.P.)—CONGREGATION OF THE PASSION

(Congregatio Passionis Jesu Christi)

Founded in Italy in 1720 by St. Paul of the Cross. First foundation in United States in 1853.

General Motherhouse: SS. Giovanni e Paolo Monastery, Rome, 00184. Italy. Most Rev. Jose A. Orbegozo, C.P., Supr. Gen.

Eastern Province, Province of St. Paul of the Cross (1852): *Province Pastoral Center*, 80 David St., South River, NJ 08882. Tel: 732-257-7177. Very Revs. Robert Joerger, C.P., Prov.; Lucian Clark, C.P., 1st Consultor; Paul Ruttle, C.P., 2nd Consultor; Richard Burke, C.P., 3rd Consultor; Terence Kristofak, C.P., 4th Consultor; Victor Hoagland, C.P., 5th Consultor; Paul Fagan, C.P., 6th Consultor; Rev. Dominic Papa, C.P., Dir., Office of Preaching Ministry.

Legal Title: *St. Paul's Benevolent, Educational and Missionary Institute of West Hoboken, New Jersey; Passionist Missions, Inc.; Passionist Missionaries, Inc.*

Fathers 192; Professed Clerics 2; Brothers 31.

Properties owned, sponsored, or staffed: Parishes 12; Community Houses 24; House of Study; Novitiate.

Represented in the Archdioceses of Atlanta, Baltimore, Boston, Hartford, Newark, New York and Philadelphia and in the Dioceses of Altoona-Johnstown, Brooklyn, Metuchen, Palm Beach, Pittsburgh, Raleigh, Rockville Centre, Scranton, Springfield (MA), Wheeling-Charleston and Worcester. Also in Canada.

Western Province, Province of the Holy Cross: Passionist Provincial Office, 5700 N. Harlem Ave., Chicago, IL 60631. Tel: 773-631-6336.

Legal Title: *Congregation of the Passion, Holy Cross Province;* Very Rev. Michael J. Stengel, C.P., Prov. Consultors: Revs. Michael Higgins, C.P., Assist. Prov.; Blaise Czaja, C.P., Prov. Consultor; Clemente Barron, C.P.; James Thoman, C.P., Consultor.

Fathers 122; Brothers 20.

Properties owned or sponsored: Passionist Provincial Office Stauros International Immaculate Conception Monastery Daneo Hall Passionist Community CTU Immaculate Conception Parish, Chicago, IL.

Represented in the Archdioceses of Chicago, Detroit, Los Angeles, Louisville, San Antonio and in the Dioceses of Birmingham, Galveston-Houston, Orlando and Sacramento.

[1010] (O.S.P.P.E.)—PAULINE FATHERS

(Ordo Sancti Pauli Primi Eremitae)

Founded in Hungary in the 13th Century. First foundation in the United States in 1953.

General Motherhouse: Ojcowie Paulini - Jasna Gora ul. Kordeckiego 2, 42-200, Czestochowa, Poland. Very Rev. Stanislaw Turek, O.S.P.P.E., Supr. Gen.; Very Rev. Lucius Turasinski, O.S.P.P.E., Prov.

American Province (1984): Beacon Hill, P.O. Box 2049, Ferry Rd., Doylestown, PA 18901. Tel: 215-345-0607; Fax: 215-345-8071; *Provincial Motherhouse - Monastery - Shrine of Our Lady of Czestochowa;* Revs. George Maj, O.S.P.P.E., Prior; Revs. Stephen Wozniczka, Shrine Dir.; John Kolmaga, O.S.P.P.E., Sub-Prior.

Priests in U.S. 17; Brothers 4.

Represented in the Archdioceses of New York, Philadelphia and in the Dioceses of Greensburg and Norwich.

[1020] (S.S.P.)—PAULINE FATHERS AND BROTHERS

Society of St. Paul for the Apostolate of Communications

General Motherhouse: Via della Fanella 39, 00148, Rome, Italy. Very Rev. Silvio Pignotti, S.S.P., Supr. Gen.; Very Rev. Teofilo Perez, S.S.P., Vicar Gen.

New York Province (1932): P.O. Box 139, Ellsworth, OH 44416-0139. Tel: 330-533-7427. Very Rev. Matthew R. Roehrig, S.S.P., Prov. Supr.; Bro. Aloysius W. Milella, S.S.P., Vicar Prov.; Rev. Ignatius W. Staniszewski, S.S.P., Publishing Editor, *Alba House*. Tel: 718-761-0047. Rev. Timothy Chenevey, S.S.P., Editor, *Pastoral Life Magazine, Alba House*. Tel: 216-533-5503. Bro. Dismas Beique, S.S.P., Editor, *Alba House AV Communications*. Tel: 216-533-5503. Bro. Peter C. Lyne, S.S.P., Vocation Dir. Tel: 718-698-3698.

Priests 12; Brothers 23; Juniors 2; Novices 2.

Represented in the Archdioceses of Detroit, New York and in the Diocese of Youngstown.

Los Angeles Province: 112 S. Herbert Ave., Los Angeles, CA 90063. Tel: 213-269-9814; 268-5010 (Bookstore); Fax: 213-268-4583. Revs. Gonzalo Ponce, S.S.P., Supr.; Gilberto Martinez, S.S.P., Vice Supr.; Valeriano Giachino, S.S.P.; Thomas Martinez, S.S.P.; Everardo Monroy, S.S.P.

Priests 5.

[1030] (C.S.P.)—PAULIST FATHERS

(Societas Missionaria a S. Paulo Apostolo)

Paulist Fathers Motherhouse (1858): 86-11 Midland Pkwy., Jamaica Estates, NY 11432. Tel: . Very Rev. Frank P. DeSiano, C.S.P., Pres.

Legal Title: *Missionary Society of St. Paul the Apostle in the State of New York.*

Fathers 205; Students in Major Seminary 13; Novices 4.

Properties owned or sponsored: Newman Campus Chaplaincies; Information Centers; Paulist Press; Paulist Radio-TV-Film Communications Svcs. Paulist National Catholic Evangelization Association; House of Study; Novitiate.

Represented in the Archdioceses of Boston, Chicago, Denver, Los Angeles, New York, Portland (OR), St. Paul-Minneapolis, San Francisco and Washington and in the Dioceses of Austin, Charleston, Columbus, Grand Rapids, Knoxville, Memphis, Oakland, Paterson, San Diego, Tucson and Wheeling-Charleston.

[1040] (SCH.P.)—PIARIST FATHERS

(Ordo Clericorum Regularum Pauperum Matris Dei Scholarum Piarum)

General Motherhouse: San Pantaleo, Piazza De Massimi, 4, Rome, Italy, 00186. Most Rev. Joseph M. Balcells, Sch.P., Supr. Gen.

U.S. Province (1975): *Devon Preparatory School*, 363 Valley Forge Rd., Devon, PA 19333. Tel: 215-688-7337; 688-6807. Very Rev. Richard S. Wyzykiewicz, Sch.P., Prov. Supr.

Legal Titles and Holdings: *Piarist Fathers, Inc.; Order of the Pious Schools, Inc.; Piarist Fathers House of Studies, Washington, DC; Piarist Fathers Residence,* Derby, NY; *Piarist Fathers Residence,* Martin, KY; *Devon Preparatory School,* Devon, PA.

Priests 25.

Represented in the Archdioceses of Miami, Philadelphia and Washington and the Dioceses of Buffalo, Lexington and Paterson.

New York-Puerto Rico Vice Province: Seminario Escolapio, P.O. Box 118, Playa Sta., Ponce, PR, 00734. Tel: 809-840-0610; Fax: 809-841-6861. Rev. Joseph Mateo, Sch.P., Vice Prov.

Priests 21; Cleric Students 1.

Houses 5; Parishes 3; High Schools 2; Schools 4.

Represented in the Archdioceses of New York and San Juan and the Diocese of Ponce Also, Calasanzian Fathers and Padres Escolapios de P.R.

Californias' Vice Province Piarist Fathers: Piarist Fathers, 3940 Perry St., Los Angeles, CA 90063. Tel: 213-261-1386; Fax: 213-269-0883. Rev. Antonio Tort, Sch.P., Vice Prov.

Properties owned, staffed, or sponsored: Parishes 5; Grammar Schools 2; House of Formation 3.

Priests 21; Novices 3; Prenovices 10; Seminarians 14.

Represented in the Archdiocese of Los Angeles.

[1050] (P.I.M.E.)—PONTIFICAL INSTITUTE FOR FOREIGN MISSIONS (P.I.M.E.), Inc.

General Motherhouse: Via F. D. Guerrazzi 11, Rome, Italy, 00152. Very Rev. Franco Cagnasso, P.I.M.E., Supr. Gen.

U.S. Region: 17330 Quincy Ave., Detroit, MI 48221. Tel: 313-342-4066; Fax: 313-342-6816. Very Rev. Bruno Piccolo, P.I.M.E., Prov. Supr.

Fathers 21; Brothers 1; Seminarians 5.

Legal Titles and Holdings: P.I.M.E. Mission Center, Newark, OH, *PIME Missionaries - PIME Mission Center, PIME College Community,* Detroit, MI, *PIME Missionaries,* Wayne, NJ, Tequesta, FL.

Formation Communities 1; Parishes 1; Mission Houses 3.

Represented in the Archdiocese of Detroit and the Dioceses of Paterson, Columbus and Palm Beach.

[1060] (C.PP.S.)—SOCIETY OF THE PRECIOUS BLOOD

(Congregatio Missionariorum Pretiosissimi Sanguinis Domini Nostri Jesu Christi)

General Motherhouse: Viale di Porta Ardeatina 66, Rome, Italy, 00154. Very Rev. Barry Fischer, C.PP.S., Moderator.

Cincinnati Province: 431 E. Second St., Dayton, OH 45402. Tel: 513-228-9263. Very Rev. Kenneth F. Pleiman, C.PP.S., Prov. Dir. Prov. Council: Revs. James F. McCabe, C.PP.S., Vice Prov.; Clarence Williams, C.PP.S.; William O'Donnell, C.PP.S.; James Seibert, C.PP.S.; Bros. Joseph Fisher, C.PP.S., Treas. & Mission Procurator; Benjamin Basile, C.PP.S.

Fathers 187; Brothers 36; Students in Major Seminaries 8; Students in Preparatory Seminary 11.

Ministries in Parishes; Missions; Chaplaincies; Shrine; Community Houses; Houses of Study; Military Chaplains.

Represented in the Archdioceses of Chicago, Cincinnati, Detroit, Military Services and in the Dioceses of Cleveland, Columbus, Fort Wayne-South Bend, Gary, Harrisburg, Lafayette in Indiana, Lansing, Orlando, Pensacola-Tallahassee, Steubenville, Toledo and Youngstown.

Kansas City Province: Precious Blood Society Provincial Office, P.O. Box 339, Liberty, MO 64069-0339. Tel: 816-781-4344; Fax: 816-781-3639. Very Rev. Mark Miller, C.PP.S., Prov. Dir.; Revs. William Walter, C.PP.S., 1st Consultor; Joseph Nassal, C.PP.S., 2nd Consultor; Ronald Will, C.PP.S., 3rd Consultor; William Miller, C.PP.S., 4th Consultor; Ronald Will, C.PP.S., Prov. Sec.; William Dineen, C.PP.S., Prov. Treas.

Bishops 1; Fathers 67; Brothers 5; Deacons 2; Seminarians 2.

Ministries in Parishes; Missions; Houses of Study; Community House; Chaplaincies.

Represented in the Archdioceses of Cincinnati, Kansas City in Kansas and in the Dioceses of Davenport, Dodge City, Jefferson City, Kansas City-St. Joseph, Salina, San Angelo, Superior, Toledo and Wichita.

Province of the Pacific of the Precious Blood: Society of the Precious Blood, 2337 134th Ave. West, San Leandro, CA 94577-4132. Tel: 510-357-4982; Fax: 510-357-4036. Very Rev. James Franck, C.PP.S., Prov. Dir. Councillors: Revs. Ronald Wiecek, C.PP.S., Vice Prov.; Gregory Comella, C.PP.S.; James Sloan, C.PP.S.; Jeffrey Finley, C.PP.S.; Joseph Brown, C.PP.S., Treas.; John Klopke, C.PP.S., Sec.; Jeffrey Finley, C.PP.S., Vocation Dir.

Fathers 22.

Ministries in Parishes; Chaplaincies; Community Houses; Center of Spirituality.

Represented in the Archdioceses of Los Angeles, St. Louis, San Francisco and the Dioceses of Des Moines, Oakland, and Salt Lake City.

Atlantic Province: Society of the Precious Blood, Provincial House, 13313 Niagara Pkwy., Niagara Falls, Ontario L2G 6R5. Canada. Tel: 416-658-3735. Very Rev. Peter Nobili, C.PP.S., Prov.; Rev. John Colacino, C.PP.S., Sec.

Priests in the U.S. 9.

Represented in the Archdioceses of Miami, Washington and the Dioceses of Buffalo, Rochester and Youngstown. Also in Canada.

[1065] (F.S.S.P.)—PRIESTLY FRATERNITY OF ST. PETER

Founded in Switzerland in 1988. First foundation in United States in 1991.

General Motherhouse: Priesterseminar Sankt Petrus, Kirchstrasse 20, 88145, Opfenbach-Wigratzbad, Germany. Tel: 49-8385/645; Fax: 49-8385/1840. Very Rev. Josef Bisig, F.S.S.P., Supr. Gen.

U.S. Headquarters and House of Formation: Our Lady of Guadalupe Seminary, Griffin Rd. - P.O. Box 196, Elmhurst, PA 18416. Tel: 717-842-4000; Fax: 717-842-4001. Revs. Arnaud J. Devillers, F.S.S.P., District Supr.; Nathan R. Vail, F.S.S.P., Rector; James B. Buckley, F.S.S.P., Novice Master; Dennis M. Duvelius, F.S.S.P., Admin. Asst. & Dir.-Admissions.

Priests 22; Seminarians 46; Novices 13.

Properties owned or sponsored: Houses 12; Elementary & High Schools.

Represented in the Archdioceses of Atlanta, Denver, Kansas City, New York, Oklahoma City, Omaha, and the Dioceses of Corpus Christi, Dallas, Lincoln, Little Rock, Paterson, Rapid City, Scranton, Tulsa, and Youngstown.

[1070] (C.SS.R.)—REDEMPTORIST FATHERS

(Congregatio Sanctissimi Redemptoris)
(Redemptorist Fathers and Brothers)

Generalate: Sant' Alphonso, Via Merulana 31. C.P. 2458, 1-00100, Roma, Italia. tleMost Rev. Joseph Tobin, C.Ss.R., Supr. Gen.; Very Rev. George Darlix, C.Ss.R., Vicar Gen.; Rev. Jose Sousa, C.Ss.R., Proc. Gen.

Province of Baltimore (1850): *Provincial Residence*, 7509 Shore Rd., Brooklyn, NY 11209. Tel: 718-833-1900. Very Rev. George J. Keaveney, C.Ss.R., Prov. Supr.; Revs. Patrick F. Woods, C.Ss.R., Prov. Vicar; Francis J. O'Rourke, C.Ss.R., Prov. Consultor; Very Rev. Francis Nelson, C.Ss.R., Prov. Procurator; Bro. Albert R. Schreiber, C.Ss.R., Prov. Sec.; Revs. Carl Hoegerl, C.Ss.R., Prov. Archivist; Gerard Knapp, C.Ss.R., Asst. Procurator.

Bishops 3; Priests 234; Brothers 25; Novices 4; Minor Seminarians 12.

Properties owned, staffed, or sponsored: Parishes 35; Residences 6; Retreat Houses 4; Community Houses 40.

Represented in the Archdioceses of Baltimore, Boston, Hartford, New York, Philadelphia and Washington and in the Dioceses of Albany, Brooklyn, Harrisburg, Rockville Centre, Toledo, Trenton and

Wilmington. Also in St. Thomas, V.I. and West Indies.

Richmond Vice Province (1942): *Vice Provincial Headquarters*, 313 Hillman St., P.O. Box 1529, New Smyrna Beach, FL 32170. Tel: 904-427-3094. Very Rev. Edward J. Gray, C.Ss.R., Vice Prov.; Revs. Eugene S. Daigle, C.Ss.R., Vicar. Consultors; Joseph Majewski, C.Ss.R.; Michael Koncik, C.Ss.R., Vocation Dir.; Bro. Thomas Kuhn, C.Ss.R., Vice Prov. Procurator.

Legal Title: *Congregation of the Most Holy Redeemer.*

Priests 55; Brothers 2; Professed Students 3.

Properties owned, staffed, or sponsored: Parishes 9; Retreat Houses 2; Retirement Home 1; Residences 1; Missions 7.

Represented in the Archdiocese of Atlanta and the Dioceses of Charleston, Charlotte, Orlando, Richmond, St. Augustine, St. Petersburg and Venice.

The Redemptorist-Denver Province (1875): *The Redemptorists Provincial Residence*, 2130 E. Fourteenth Ave. - Box 300399, Denver, CO 80203-0399. Tel: 303-370-0035; Fax: 303-370-0036. Very Rev. Richard Thibodeau, C.Ss.R., Prov. Supr.; Revs. J. Robert Fenili, C.Ss.R., Prov. Vicar; Stephen Meyer, C.Ss.R., Prov. Consultor; John Steingraeber, C.Ss.R., Co-Dir. - Office of Fin. Services Comptroller; Bro. Tom Wright, C.Ss.R., C0-Dir. - Office of Fin. Services.

Total in community Priests 21; Brothers 2.

Properties owned, sponsored or staffed: Parishes 15; Retreat Houses 3; Residences 5; Community Houses 19.

Represented in the Archdioceses of Chicago, Denver, Detroit, Milwaukee, Omaha, St. Louis and St. Paul-Minneapolis and in Dioceses of Davenport, Grand Rapids, Kansas City-St. Joseph and Wichita. Also in Foreign Missions.

Bangkok Vice-Province: Redemptorist Fathers, 123-19 Ruam Rudi Lane, Bangkok, 10500. Thailand. Very Rev. Philip Banchong Chaiyara, C.SS.R., Vice Prov.

Manaus Vice-Province: Padres Redentoristas, Caixa Postal 217, 69.011 Manaus, Amazonas, Brazil, South America. Very Rev. Jacson Rodrigues, C.SS.R., Vice Prov.

New Orleans Vice-Province: Redemptorist Fathers and Brothers, 5354 Plank Rd.-P.O. Box 53900, Baton Rouge, LA 70892-3900. Tel: 504-355-2600; Fax: 504-355-6200. Very Rev. Monroe G. Perrier, C.Ss.R., Vice Prov.; Revs. Samuel Maranto, C.Ss.R., Vice Prov. Consultor, Local Supr. & Archivist; Joseph L. Buhler, C.Ss.R., Vice Prov. Archivist Emeritus; Bro. Charles E. Fucik, C.Ss.R., Vice Prov. Treas.; Revs. Eugene E. Staub, C.Ss.R.; John C. Vargas, C.Ss.R., (Redemptorist Generalate - Rome); Bro. Steven E. Fruge, C.Ss.R.

Priests 56; Brothers 6; Professed Students 4.

Properties owned, staffed, or sponsored: Parishes 6; Retreat House; Residences.

Represented in the Archdioceses of New Orleans, San Antonio and the Dioceses of Amarillo, Baton Rouge, Biloxi, Corpus Christi, Galveston-Houston, Lafayette (LA) and San Angelo.

[1080] (C.R.)—CONGREGATION OF THE RESURRECTION

(Congregatio a Resurrectione Domini Nostri Jesu Christi)

Generalate: Via San Sebastianello 11, 00187, Rome, Italy. Very Rev. Sutherland MacDonald, C.R., Supr. Gen.

U.S. of America Province: 2250 North Latrobe Ave., Chicago, IL 60639. Tel: 773-637-0999. Very Rev. John H. Nowak, C.R., Prov. Supr. Councillors: Revs. Joseph Glab, C.R.; C. Frank Phillips, C.R., Dir. of Vocations; Eugene Szarek, C.R.; Manuel Williams, C.R.; Bro. William Hallas, C.R.; Rev. Marion Wroblewski, C.R., Treas.

Fathers 72; Brothers 5.

Ministries in Parishes; Missions; High Schools; Retreat House; Chaplaincies.

Represented in the Archdioceses of Chicago, Mobile, St. Louis and the Dioceses of Pensacola-Tallahassee, Rockford and San Bernardino. Also in Oaxaca, Mexico, St. George's & Bermuda.

Ontario Kentucky Province:.

U.S. Address: St. Cecilia House, 338 N. 25th St., Louisville, KY 40212. Tel: 502-772-3694; Fax: 502-772-3695. Revs. Ray Hofmann, C.R.; Ernest Schumacher, C.R.; John Lesousky, C.R.

Provincialate: Resurrection College, Waterloo, Ontario , Canada, N2L 3G7; Fax: 519-885-4951. Revs. Lory A. Keasey, C.R.; Charles Fedy, C.R. Councillors: Revs. Robert Liddy, C.R.; Larry Bordonaro, C.R.; James Link, C.R.; Bro. D. Taylor, C.R., Bursar.

Properties owned, sponsored, or staffed: Resurrection College Parishes 2 University High Schools 3 Community Houses 15 House of Study.

Represented in the Archdiocese of Louisville.

[1090] (R.C.J.)—ROGATIONIST FATHERS

Congregatio Rogationis-a-Corde-Jesu

Generalate:: via Tuscolana 167, 00182, Roma, Italy. Very Rev. Pietro Cifuni, R.C.J., Supr. Gen.

U.S.A. Delegation: 2688 S. Newmark Ave., Box 37, Sanger, CA 93657. Tel: 209-875-5808; 875-2025; Fax: 209-875-1281. Rev. John Bruno, R.C.J., Delegation Supr.

U.S. Foundations: St. Mary's Church, 828 O St., P.O. Box 335, Sanger, CA 93657. Tel: 209-875-2025. Revs. Salvatore Ciranni, R.C.J.; John Bruno, R.C.J.; Loji Pilones, R.C.J.

Vocation Center, 9815 Columbus Ave., North Hill, CA 91343. Tel: 818-894-2546. Revs. Rodolfo D'Agostino, R.C.J.; Vincent Buccheri, R.C.J.

Legal Title: *Congregation of Rogationists, Inc.*

Priests 7.

Ministries in Parishes; Vocation Center; Formation House; Social Service Center.

Represented in the Archdiocese of Los Angeles and the Diocese of Fresno.

[1100] (S.C.)—BROTHERS OF THE SACRED HEART

(Societas Fratrum Sacris Cordis)

Founded in Lyons, France in 1821. First foundation in the United States in Mobile in 1847.

Generalate: Piazza Sacro Cuore, No. 3, Rome, Italy, 00152. Bro. Bernard Couvillion, S.C., Supr. Gen. Provinces.

New Orleans Province (1847): *Provincial Office*, 4540 Elysian Fields Ave., New Orleans, LA 70122. Tel: 504-282-5693; Fax: 504-288-9920. Bro. Paul Montero, S.C., Prov. Prov. Councillors: Bros. Matthias Amos, S.C.; Ivy LeBlanc, S.C.; Francis David, S.C.; Xavier Werneth, S.C.; Donnan Berry, S.C., Treas.

Perpetual Professed 76; Temporary Professed 3; Ordained Brothers 6.

Incorporated Schools: Brother Martin High School, New Orleans, LA Catholic High School, Baton Rouge, LA Saint Stanislaus College, Bay St. Louis, MS.

Legal Title: *Brothers of the Sacred Heart, (a Louisiana Corporation); Vocational Development Fund of the Brothers of the Sacred, Heart, Inc.*

Represented in the Archdioceses of Mobile and New Orleans and the Dioceses of Baton Rouge, Biloxi and Houma-Thibodaux.

New England Province (1945): *Provincial House - Brothers of the Sacred Heart*, 685 Steere Farm Rd., Pascoag, RI 02859-4601. Tel: 401-568-3361; Fax: 401-568-9810. Bro. Robert F. Breault, S.C., Prov. Supr. Councillors: Bros. Robert Croteau, S.C.; Donald Tardif, S.C.; Raymond Reinsant, S.C.; Frederick U. Bouchard, S.C.; Edward Breault, S.C., Prov. Sec.; Louis Laperle, S.C., Exec. Asst. Finances; Paul Hebert, S.C., Missions Procurator; Willie Morin, S.C., Dir.-Community Volunteer Services.

Brothers 97.

Properties owned: Brothers of the Sacred Heart Provincial House, Pascoag, RI Mt. St. Charles Academy, Woonsocket, RI Bishop Guertin High School, Nashua, NH St. John Residence, Woonsocket, RI Brothers of the Sacred Heart Residence, Nashua, NH.

Represented in the Archdiocese of Hartford and in the Dioceses of Burlington, Manchester and Providence. Also in England, Lesotho, Zambia, Zimbabwe, and Uganda.

Province of New York (1960): *Brothers of the Sacred Heart Provincial House*, 141-11 123 Ave., South Ozone Park, NY 11436-1426. Tel: 718-322-3309; Fax: 718-529-6004. Bro. Joseph Rocco, S.C., Prov.

Final Professed Brothers 42; Temporary 1; Novices 1; Candidates 1.

Ministries in the field of Education; Spiritual Centers; Kenya Missions.

Properties owned: Sacred Heart Center, Belvidere, NJ Msgr. McClancy High School, East Elmhurst, NY St. Joseph High School, Metuchen, NJ.

Represented in the Dioceses of Brooklyn, Metuchen and Rockville Center. Also in Kenya.

[1110] (M.S.C.)—MISSIONARIES OF THE SACRED HEART

(Societas Missionariorum Sacratissimi Cordis Jesu)

General Motherhouse: Via Asmara 11, 00199, Rome, Italy. Very Rev. Michael Curran, M.S.C., Supr. Gen.

United States Province (1939): P.O. Box 270, 305 S. Lake St., Aurora, IL 60507. Tel: 630-892-8400; 892-2371; Fax: 630-892-3071. Very Rev. Mark McDonald, M.S.C., Prov. Supr. Consultors: Revs. David Foxen, M.S.C., Vice Prov.; Eugene Jung, M.S.C.; Peter Campbell, M.S.C.; Tony Ripp, M.S.C.; John Kavcak, M.S.C.

Legal Title: *Society of the Missionaries of the Sacred Heart.*

Fathers 71; Brothers 22; Foreign Missionaries 18; Professed Students 3.

Properties owned, staffed, or sponsored: Renewal Centers 1; Residential Houses 6; Parishes 9; Chaplaincies 5; Foreign Missions 2.

Represented in the Archdioceses of Baltimore, Chicago, Philadelphia and Washington and in the Dioceses of Allentown, Gary, Ogdensburg, Providence, Rockford, San Bernardino, Toledo and Youngstown. Also in Colombia, Papua New Guinea, Namibia and Slovakia.

U.S. Section of the Irish Province for California and Southern States: Sectional Headquarters, 237 W. Magnolia Ave., San Antonio, TX 78212-2916. Tel: 210-737-6394; Fax: 210-737-0327. Very Rev. Christopher Coleman, M.S.C., Sectional Supr. Sectional Consultors: Revs. Patrick O'Shea, M.S.C.; James Dudley, M.S.C.; James A. Harnan, M.S.C.; Aidan O'Donovan, M.S.C.

Priests 20.

Represented in the Archdioceses of Los Angeles, San Antonio and Washington and the Dioceses of Beaumont, Corpus Christi, Dallas and San Angelo.

[1120] (M.SS.CC.)—MISSIONARIES OF THE SACRED HEARTS OF JESUS AND MARY

(Missionarii a Sacris Cordibus Jesus et Mariae)

Founded in Italy in 1833.

General Motherhouse: Via dei Falegnami 23, Rome, Italy. Very Rev. Anthony Palmiero, M.SS.CC., Supr. Gen.

American Headquarters: 2249 Shore Rd., Linwood, NJ 08221. Tel: 609-927-5600; Fax: 609-927-5262. Revs. Anthony Patrizio, M.SS.CC., Reg. Supr.; John Perdue, M.SS.CC., Mission Procurator.

Legal Title: *Villa Pieta*, Linwood, NJ.

Priests 10; Brothers 2; Novices 2; Postulants 1.

Represented in the Dioceses of Camden and Harrisburg.

[1130] (S.C.J.)—CONGREGATION OF THE PRIESTS OF THE SACRED HEART

(Priests of the Sacred Heart)

(Congregatio Sacerdotum a Corde Jesu)

General Motherhouse: Curia Generalizia, S.C.J., Via Casale S. Pio v, no. 20, 00165, Rome, Italy. Very Rev. Virginio Domingo Bressanelli, S.C.J., Supr. Gen.

United States Province (1933): *Provincialate Offices*, P.O. Box 289, Hales Corners, WI 53130-0289. Tel: 414-425-6910. Very Rev. John Czyzynski, S.C.J., Prov. Supr.

Bishops 2; Priests 103; Clerics 6; Brothers 23; Deacons 1.

Represented in the Archdioceses of Chicago, Milwaukee and San Antonio and in the Dioceses of Brownsville, Galveston-Houston, Green Bay, Jackson, Memphis, Rapid City, St. Petersburg and Sioux Falls.

[1140] (SS.CC.)—CONGREGATION OF THE SACRED HEARTS OF JESUS AND MARY

(Congregatio Sacrorum Cordium)

General Motherhouse: Casa Generalizia-Padri Dei Sacri Cuori-via Rivarone 85, 00166, Rome, Italy. Very Rev. Enrique Losada, SS.CC., Supr. Gen.

Legal Title: *Congregation of the Sacred Hearts of Jesus and Mary.*

Eastern Province (1946): *Provincial House*, Box 111, Fairhaven, MA 02719-0111. Tel: 508-993-2442; Fax: 508-996-5499. Very Rev. Patrick Fanning, SS.CC., Prov.; Revs. William Heffron, SS.CC., Vicar Prov. Councillors; Thomas McElroy, SS.CC.; David Reid, SS.CC.; Stanley Kolasa, SS.CC.

Priests 64; Novices 3; Brothers 7.

Properties owned or staffed: Parishes 8; Community Houses 3; House of Studies 1.

Represented in the Archdiocese of Washington and the Dioceses of Brownsville, and Fall River.

Western United States Province (1970): *Congregation of the Sacred Hearts of Jesus and Mary*, 2150 Damien Ave., La Verne, CA 91750. Tel: 909-593-5441; Fax: 909-593-3971. Very Rev. Martin P. O'Loghlen, SS.CC., Prov.

Priests 20.

Ministries in the field of Religious and Academic Education; Parishes; Chaplaincies.

Represented in the Archdiocese of Los Angeles and the Dioceses of Oakland, and San Bernardino. Also in the Philippines.

Hawaii Province: Sacred Hearts Center, Box 797, Kaneohe, Oahu, HI 96744. Tel: 808-247-5035; Fax: 808-235-8849. Very Rev. Clyde Guerreiro, SS.CC., Prov.

Fathers 35; Brothers 7.

Properties owned, staffed, or sponsored: Churches 10; Mission 1; Chaplaincies 2.

[1144] (L.B.S.F.)—LITTLE BROTHERS OF SAINT FRANCIS

Founded in the United States in 1970 by Bro. James Curran, L.B.S.F.

Regional Fraternity and Novitiate (1970): 785-789 Parker St., Roxbury, MA 02120. Tel: 617-442-2556.

Legal Title: *Little Brothers of Saint Francis - Franciscan Fraternity of, Peace and Love, Inc.*

Professed Brothers 3; Novices 2; Postulants 3.

Represented in the Archdiocese of Boston.

[1150] (C.S.J.)—CONGREGATION OF ST. JOSEPH

(Congregatio Sancti Joseph)

Founded in Turin, Italy in 1873. First foundation in United States in 1951.

General Motherhouse: Via Belvedere Montello 77, 00166, Rome, Italy. Very Rev. Luigi Pierini, C.S.J., Supr. Gen.

U.S. and Mexico Vice Province: 338 N. Grand Ave., San Pedro, CA 90731. Tel: 310-547-2969. Rev. John Trimaglio, C.S.J., Prov. Supr.

Priests 25.

Properties owned, staffed, or sponsored: Parishes 5; High Schools 2; Center for troubled youths.

Properties owned: St. Leonard House, Avon, OH.

Represented in the Archdiocese of Los Angeles and the Diocese of Cleveland. Also in Mexico.

[1160] (F.S.P.)—BROTHERS OF ST. PATRICK

(Patrician Brothers)

Founded in Ireland 1808 by Bishop Daniel Delaney.

U.S. Foundation (1948): *St. Patrick's Novitiate,* 7820 Bolsa Ave., Midway City, CA 92655. Tel: 714-897-8181; Fax: 714-898-9020. Bro. Aquinas Cassin, F.S.P., Prov.

Brothers 8.

Represented in the Archdiocese of Los Angeles and Diocese of Orange.

[1170] (S.P.S.)—ST. PATRICK'S MISSIONARY SOCIETY

(St. Patrick Fathers)

Founded March 17, 1932 with the approval of Pope Pius XI. A Pontifical Society of secular priests devoted entirely to the missionary needs of the Church.

International Headquarters: St. Patrick's, Kiltegan, Wicklow , Ireland. Very Rev. Kieran Birmingham, S.P.S., Supr. Gen.; Very Rev. Timothy J. Barry, S.P.S., Vicar Gen. & Supr. for North America; Very Rev. James Birmingham, S.P.S., Proc. Gen.-Rome.

Total number of Priests 370; Priests in the U.S. 17.

U.S. Foundations (1965): *St. Patrick's,* 70 Edgewater Rd., Cliffside Park, NJ 07010. Tel: 201-943-6575; Fax: 201-943-9426. Very Rev. James Barry, S.P.S., Supr., *St. Patrick's,* (1967), 19536 Eric Dr., Saratoga, CA 95070. Tel: 408-253-3135. Rev. Eamonn Hayden, S.P.S., Supr., *St. Patrick's,* (1968), 1347 W. Granville Ave., Chicago, IL 60660. Tel: 312-973-3737. Rev. Karl Langsdord, S.P.S., Supr.

Legal Title: *St. Patrick Missionary Society, Camden, N.J.*

Represented in the Archdioceses of Chicago, New Orleans, Newark and San Francisco and in the Dioceses of Palm Beach, Paterson and San Jose.

[1180] (C.S.P.X.)—BROTHERS OF SAINT PIUS X

Founded in the United States in 1952.

Motherhouse: P.O. Box 217, DeSoto, WI 54624. Tel: 608-648-2087. Bro. Charles Bisenius, Dir.

Ministries in the field of Religious and Academic Education; Health Care; Community services and Administration.

Represented in the Diocese of La Crosse.

[1190] (S.D.B.)—SALESIANS OF DON BOSCO

Societas Sancti Francisci Salesii

Generalate: Salesian D. Bosco, via Della Pisana, 1111, C.P., 9092-00163, Roma-Aurelio, Italy. Very Rev. Juan Vecchi, S.D.B., Vicar. Gen.

Province of St. Philip the Apostle (1902): 148 Main St., New Rochelle, NY 10802. Tel: 914-636-4225. Very Rev. Patrick Angelucci, S.D.B., Prov.; Revs. Francis X. Aracil, S.D.B., Sec. & Dir.-Social Communication; David Gonder, S.D.B., Prov. Economer & Councillor; James Heuser, S.D.B., Vice Prov.; Steven Shafran, S.D.B., Dir. of Formation & Councillor; James Marra, S.D.B., Mission Procurator; Bro. Emile Dube, S.D.B., Dir. of Religious Education & Councillor.

Legal Title: *Salesian Society, Inc.,* New Rochelle, NY.

Fathers 156; Professed Clerics 15; Students in Major Seminaries 7; Coadjutor-Brothers 47.

Ministries in Parishes; High Schools; Trade Schools; Technical Schools; Boys Clubs; Camps.

Represented in the Archdioceses of Boston, Miami, Newark, New Orleans and New York and in the Dioceses of Birmingham, Columbus, Palm Beach, Passaic, Paterson, St. Petersburg and Scranton. Also in Canada.

San Francisco Province (1926): *Salesian Society - San Francisco,* 1100 Franklin St., San Francisco, CA 94109. Tel: 415-441-7144; Fax: 415-441-7155. Very Rev. Nicholas Reina, S.D.B., Prov.; Rev. Carmine Vairo, S.D.B., Vice Prov. Councillor: Revs. John Roche, S.D.B.; Joseph Boenzi, S.D.B.; David Purdy, S.D.B.; Bro. Joseph Lockwood, S.D.B., Treas.

Fathers 80; Professed Clerics 12; Professed Brothers 28; Novices 2; Students in Seminaries 2.

Ministries in Parishes; High Schools; Retreat House; Youth Centers.

Represented in the Archdioceses of Los Angeles, Santa Fe, San Francisco and the Dioceses of Corpus Christi, Monterey, Oakland, San Bernardino, San Diego, Santa Rosa, Stockton, and Van Nuys. Also in Canada and Sierra Leone.

[1200] (S.D.S.)—SOCIETY OF THE DIVINE SAVIOR

Salvatorian Fathers and Brothers

(Salvatorians - Societas Divini Salvatoris)

General Headquarters: Curia Generalizia dei Salvatoriani, Via della Conciliazione 51, 00193, Rome, Italy. Very Rev. Karl Hoffman, S.D.S., Supr. Gen.

U.S.A. Province (1896): *Salvatorian Provincial Residence,* 1735 Hi-Mount Blvd., Milwaukee, WI 53208-1720. Tel: 414-258-1735; Fax: 414-258-1934. Very Rev. Dennis D. Thiessen, S.D.S., Prov.; Revs. Michael A. Shay, S.D.S., Vicar; Jean F. Blais, S.D.S., Dir. Personnel; Joseph Rodrigues, S.D.S., Dir. Planning & Communications.

Legal Title: *Camp St. Charles, Inc.; Society of the Divine Savior; Society of the Divine Savior Ongoing Community Support Trust.*

Fund Raising and Public Relations Center: Salvatorian Center, New Holstein, WI 53061.

Fathers 103; Professed Clerics 2; Brothers 52.

Properties owned, staffed, or sponsored: Parishes 5; Houses of Study and Formation 2.

Represented in the Archdioceses of Baltimore, Chicago, Louisville, Milwaukee, New York, Portland, San Francisco, Washington and the Dioceses of Camden, Birmingham, Bismarck, Erie, Fresno, Gallup, Green Bay, LaCrosse, Mobile, Nashville, Oakland, Orlando, Phoenix, Sacramento, Savannah, Tucson, Wilmington and Richmond.

[1210] (C.S.)—MISSIONARIES OF ST. CHARLES-SCALABRINIANS

(Congregatio Missionariorum A Sancto Carolo)

General Motherhouse: Via Calandrelli, 42, 00153, Rome, Italy. Very Rev. Luigi Favero, C.S., Supr. Gen.

Province of St. Charles Borromeo (1888): Provincial Curia, 27 Carmine St., New York, NY 10014. Tel: 212-675-3993; Fax: 212-727-2866. Very Rev. Joseph Fugolo, C.S., Prov. Supr.; Revs. Joseph Cogo, C.S., Vicar & 1st Councillor; Charles Zanoni, C.S., Sec. & 2nd Councillor; Ezio Marchetto, C.S., 3rd Councillor; Dominic Rodighiero, C.S., Treas. & 4th Councillor.

Legal Title: *The Pious Society of the Missionaries of St. Charles Borromeo, Inc.*

Fathers 96; Brothers 3.

Properties staffed or owned:: Parishes 30; Missions 7; Homes for Aged 2; Seminaries 3; Center for Migration Studies; Assistance Agency for Migrants.

Represented in the Archdioceses of Boston, Hartford, Newark, New York and Washington and the Dioceses of Brooklyn, Buffalo, Palm Beach, Providence, Syracuse and Venice. Also in Eastern Canada, Venezuela, Colombia, the Dominican Republic and Haiti.

Province of St. John Baptist (1903): *Missionaries of St. Charles - Fathers of St. Charles,* 546 N. East Ave., Oak Park, IL 60302. Tel: 708-386-4430; Fax: 708-386-4457. Very Rev. Livio Stella, C.S., Prov.

Legal Title: *The Fathers of Saint Charles; Scalabrinian Community Support Corp.; Scalabrinian Community Formation Corp.*

Fathers 75; Brothers 4.

Ministries in 25 Parishes; 2 Homes for the Aged; 3 Missions; 4 Seminaries; 4 Centers for Migrants and Refugees.

Represented in the Archdioceses of Chicago, Cincinnati and Los Angeles and the Dioceses of Galveston-Houston, Kansas City-St. Joseph, San Diego and San Jose. Also in Canada, Mexico and Italy.

[1220] (S.C.)—SERVANTS OF CHARITY

(Guanellians)

(Congregatio Servorum a Charitate)

General Motherhouse: Vicolo Clementi 41, Rome, Italy. Very Rev. Nino Minetti, Supr. Gen.

U.S. Headquarters: Servants of Charity, 16195 Old U.S. 12, Chelsea, MI 48118-9646. Tel: 313-475-8430; Fax: 313-475-0310. Rev. Silvio De Nard, S.C., Supr. USA Province.

Priests 12; Brothers 1; Theologian 1; Novices 1.

Legal Title: *Pious Union of St. Joseph,* Publication: *Now and At the Hour.*

Ministry for the suffering and dying; Schools for mentally handicapped boys 2; Residences for mentally handicapped adults 2; Parishes 1; House of Formation 1; Group Home 1; Chaplaincies 1.

Represented in the Archdioceses of Chicago and Philadelphia and in the Dioceses of Lansing and Providence.

[1230] (s.P.)—SERVANTS OF THE PARACLETE

Generalate & U.S. Motherhouse (1952): *Foundation House,* Jemez Springs, NM 87025. Tel: 505-829-3586; Fax: 505-829-3706. Very Rev. Liam Hoare, s.P., Servant Gen.; Revs. Michael Foley, s.P., Vicar Gen.; Benedict Livingston, s.P., Dir. Formation & Treas. Gen.

Professed Priests 26; Professed Brothers 5.

Represented in the Archdioceses of St. Louis and Santa Fe and the Diocese of San Bernardino.

[1240] (O.S.M.)—SERVITES

Order of Friar Servants of Mary

(Ordo Fratrum Servorum Beatae Virginis Mariae)

Generalate: Curia Generalizia dei Servi di Maria, Piazza San Marcello al Corso, 5, 00187, Rome, Italy.

Eastern Province (1967): *Servite Friars-Eastern Province,* 3121 W. Jackson Blvd., Chicago, IL 60612. Tel: 773-533-0360; Fax: 773-533-8307. Very Rev. Michael M. Guimon, O.S.M., Prior Prov.; Revs. Joseph M. Chamblain, O.S.M., Asst. Prov. Councillors; Conrad M. Borntrager, O.S.M., Archivist & Historian; Paul M. Cullen, O.S.M.; Paul M. Novak, O.S.M.; Bro. Edmund M. Baran, O.S.M., Prov. Treas.; Bro. Michael M. Callary, O.S.M., Prov./Corporate Sec.; Bro. Donald M. Siple, O.S.M., Natl. Vocation Dir.

Legal Title: *Servite Friars-Eastern Province, Inc.,* Chicago, IL; *Servite Friars-Eastern Province Retirement Trust,* Chicago, IL; *St. Anthony Pucci Charitable Trust,* Chicago, IL; *Servants of Mary, Inc.,* Chicago, IL.

Parishes 10; Residences 8; Hospital Chaplaincies; Military Chaplaincies 1.

Priests 55; Professed Brothers 9; Temporary Professed Friars 2.

Represented in the Archdioceses of Chicago, Detroit, Military Services, Portland (OR), St. Louis, Santa Fe and the Dioceses of Orange, Orlando, St. Petersburg, Springfield-Cape Girardeau and Tucson. Also in Germany, Ireland, and South Africa.

Western Province (1967): *Servite Provincial Center,* 5210 Somerset St., Buena Park, CA 90621-1498. Tel: 714-523-5810; Fax: 714-523-8129. Revs. Peregrine M. Graffius, O.S.M., Prov.; Ignatius M. Kissel, O.S.M., Asst. Prov.; Prov. Treas., Sec. & Archivist. Councillors: Revs. Eugene M. Smith, O.S.M.; Joseph M. Cheah, O.S.M.; John M. Topper, O.S.M.; Donald M. Siple, O.S.M., Vocation Dir.

Legal Title: *The Western Province of the Servites, Inc.; The Western Province of the Servites Inc. Charitable Trust.*

Fathers 31; Professed Brothers 4; Temporarily Professed Brothers 1.

Properties owned, staffed, or sponsored: Parishes 9; High Schools 1; Community Houses 9; Hospital Chaplaincies 3.

Represented in the Archdioceses of Denver, Los Angeles and Portland in Oregon and in the Dioceses of Oakland, Orange and Tucson.

[1250] (C.R.S.)—SOMASCAN FATHERS

(Clericorum Regularium Somaschensium)

Order of St. Jerome Aemilian

General Motherhouse: Largo Alessandria del Carretto, 00040, Morena - Rome, Italy. Most Rev. Bruno Luppi, C.R.S., Ph.D., Father Gen.

U.S. Foundation: Pine Haven Boys Center, River Rd., P.O. 162, Suncook, NH 03275. Tel: 603-485-7141. Rev. Julian Gerosa, C.R.S., Supr.

Priests 9.

Represented in the Archdiocese of Hartford and in the Dioceses of Galveston-Houston and Manchester.

[1260] (S.Ch.)—SOCIETY OF CHRIST

(Societas Christi Pro Emigrantibus Polonis)

General Motherhouse: 60-962 Poznan Ulica Panny Marii 4, Poland. Very Rev. Tadeusz Winnicki,

S.Ch., Supr. Gen.; Rev. Marian Burniak, Procurator Gen., Via Botteghe Oscure 15, 00186, Rome, Italy.

American-Canadian Province: Provincial Residence, 3000 Eighteen Mile Rd., Sterling Heights, MI 48314. Tel: 810-939-5022. Very Rev. Andrzej Maslejak, S.Ch., Prov.; Revs. Stanislaw Kuczaik, S.Ch., Vice-Prov.; Gerald Grupczynski, S.Ch., Treas.

Priests 50.

Represented in the Archdioceses of Baltimore, Chicago, Detroit, Hartford, Los Angeles, Miami, Portland (OR), St. Paul-Minneapolis, San Francisco, Seattle, Washington and the Dioceses of Dallas, Galveston-Houston, Joliet, Passaic, San Diego, San Jose and Toledo. Also in Canada.

[1270] (F.M.S.I.)—SONS OF MARY MISSIONARY SOCIETY

Sons of Mary, Health of the Sick
(Filii Mariae Salutis Infirmorum)

General Headquarters: 567 Salem End Rd., Framingham, MA 01702. Tel: 508-879-6711. Bro. Kevin Courtney, Major Coord.; Revs. John Coss, Financial Coord.; Henry Cicale, F.M.S.I., Councilor.

Professed 12.

Represented in the Archdiocese of Boston. Also in the Philippines.

[1280] (C.S.S.)—STIGMATINE FATHERS AND BROTHERS

(Congregation of the Sacred Stigmata)

General Motherhouse: Via Mazzarino No. 16, Rome, Italy. Very Rev. Jose Luiz Nemes, C.S.S., Supr. Gen.; Rev. Giampietro DePaoli, C.S.S., Vicar Gen.

North American Province (1940): 554 Lexington St., Waltham, MA 02154. Tel: 781-894-7713; Fax: 781-894-9785. Very Rev. Robert S. White, C.S.S., Prov. Supr.

Priests 40; Brothers 4.

Legal Title: *Stigmatine Fathers & Brother, Inc.*

Properties owned, staffed, or sponsored: Parishes 6; Retreat & Conference Center.

Represented in the Archdioceses of Boston, New York, and the Dioceses of Springfield (MA) and Worcester.

[1290] (S.S.)—SOCIETY OF THE PRIESTS OF SAINT SULPICE

(Societas Presbyterorum a S. Sulpitio)

General Motherhouse: 6 rue du Regard, Paris, 75006. France. Very Rev. Lawrence B. Terrien, S.S., Supr. Gen.

U.S. Provincial House: 5408 Roland Ave., Baltimore, MD 21210. Tel: 301-323-5070; Fax: 410-433-6524. Very Rev. Ronald D. Witherup, S.S., Prov.; Mr. Joseph M. Reynolds, Exec. Asst. to Prov. & Operations Mgr.; Revs. Louis M. Reitz, S.S., Prov. Treas.; Melvin C. Blanchette, S.S., Dir. Formation & Personnel Services; Thomas R. Ulshafer, S.S., Prov. Sec. & Dir. Discernment & Admissions.

Legal Title: *The Associated Sulpicians of the United States.*

Fathers 85.

Represented in the Archdioceses of Baltimore, San Antonio, San Francisco, Seattle, Washington and the Dioceses of Honolulu and San Jose.

[1300] (C.R.)—THEATINE FATHERS

(Congregatio Clericorum Regularium)

General Motherhouse: Sant' Andrea della Valle, Piazza Vidoni, 6, 00186, Rome, Italy. Most Rev. Gabriele Darida, C.R., Supr. Gen.

U.S. Headquarters: 1050 S. Birch St., Denver, CO 80222. Tel: 303-756-5522. Very Rev. Patrick Valdez, C.R.

Fathers 17; Clerics 5.

Parishes 9; House of Formation 1; Provincial House 1.

Represented in the Archdioceses of Denver and New York and in the Diocese of Pueblo.

[1310] (O.SS.T.)—ORDER OF THE MOST HOLY TRINITY

Holy Trinity Fathers, Inc.
(Ordo Sanctissimae Trinitatis; *The Trinitarians*)

Founded in France in 1198 by St. John De Matha for the ransom of Christian slaves. First settlement in the United States in 1911.

General Curia: Via Massimi, 114C, 00136, Rome, Italy. Most Rev. Jose Hernandez Sanchez, Minister Gen.

U.S.A. Province (1950): *Province of the Immaculate Heart of Mary*, P.O. Box 5719, 8400 Park Heights Ave., Baltimore, MD 21282-0742. Tel: 410-486-5171. Very Rev. John L. Dorn, O.SS.T., Minister Prov.; Rev. Thomas N. Cerlo, O.SS.T., Vicar Prov. Prov. Councillors: Revs. William Axe, O.SS.T.; Thomas Burke, O.SS.T.; Joseph Gidaro, O.SS.T.; Albert Anuszewski, O.SS.T., Dir.-Vocation; Charles J. Flood, O.SS.T., Sec. & Treas.

Trinitarian Communities in the U.S. 14; Fathers 51; Brothers 13; Novices 2.

Ministries in 12 parishes; Seminary Facility Positions; High Schools; Prison Chaplaincies; Hospital Chaplaincies; Social Apostolate to the Homeless; Seminary; Faculty Members; India Foundation; Mission for Persecuted Christians.

Properties owned: DeMatha Catholic High School, Hyattsville, MD Holy Trinity Monastery, Pikesville, MD Redeemer House, Baltimore, MD Trinity House, Victoria, TX.

Represented in the Archdioceses of Baltimore, Los Angeles, New Orleans, Philadelphia, New York, Washington and in the Dioceses of Corpus Christi, Dallas, Trenton, Rockville Centre, Memphis, Palm Beach, Savannah, Trenton and Victoria. Also in India.

[1320] (C.S.V.)—CLERICS OF ST. VIATOR

(Congregatio Clericorum Sancti Viatoris)

General Motherhouse: Via Padre A. Paoli, 41, Rome, Italy. Casella Postale 10793, 00144, Roma, Italia. Very Rev. Leonard Audet, C.S.V., Supr. Gen.

Province of Chicago (1882): 1212 East Euclid St., Arlington Heights, IL 60004. Tel: 708-398-1354. Very Rev. Robert M. Egan, C.S.V., Prov.; Revs. Richard A. Rinn, C.S.V., Councillor and Asst. Prov.; Robert E. Erickson, C.S.V., Prov. Treas.

Fathers 93; Brothers 21.

Properties owned, staffed, or sponsored: Parishes 15; High Schools 4; Formation Houses 2.

Represented in the Archdioceses of Chicago, Kansas City in Kansas, Military Services and the Dioceses of Arlington, Joliet, Manchester, Monterey, Oakland, Peoria, Las Vegas, Rockford, San Diego, San Jose, Springfield (IL) and Tucson. Also in Colombia and Italy.

[1330] (C.M.)—CONGREGATION OF THE MISSION

Vincentians
(Congregatio Missionis Sti. Vincentii a Paulo)

Founded in France in 1625. First foundation in the United States in 1818.

General Motherhouse: Curia Generalizia, Via dei Capasso, 30, 00164, Roma, Italia. Very Rev. Robert P. Maloney, C.M., Supr. Gen.

Eastern Province of the U.S.A. (1888): St. Vincent's Seminary, 500 E. Chelten Ave., Philadelphia, PA 19144. Tel: 215-848-1985; Fax: 215-844-2085. Very Rev. Joseph L. Levesque, C.M., Prov.; Revs. Thomas F. McKenna, C.M., Asst. Prov.; John W. Gouldrick, C.M., Prov. Treas. Consultors: Revs. William W. Sheldon, C.M.; John Kettelberger, C.M.; Michael J. Carroll, C.M.; Stephen M. Grozio, C.M., Prov. Planner; Bro. Peter A. Campbell, C.M.

Legal Title: *Congregation of the Mission of St. Vincent de Paul in Germantown, Inc.*

Fathers 191; Brothers 11; Students in Major Seminaries 10; College Seminarians 5; Novices 6.

Properties owned, sponsored, or staffed: Parishes 14; Missions in Republic of Panama 9; Universities 2; Major Seminary Residences 2; College Seminary Residences 1; Novitiates 2; Retreat Houses 2; Hospitals 2.

Represented in the Archdioceses of Baltimore, New York, Mobile, Philadelphia, Washington and the Dioceses of Albany, Allentown, Birmingham, Brooklyn, Buffalo, Charleston, Charlotte, Grand Rapids, Metuchen, Palm Beach, Rockville Centre, St. Augustine and Wheeling-Charleston.

Midwest Province - Vincentians (1888): 13663 Rider Trail N., Earth City, MO 63045-1512. Tel: 314-344-1184; Fax: 314-344-2989. (Motherhouse St. Mary's Seminary, Perryville, MO.; Very Rev. William E. Hartenbach, C.M., Prov.; Rev. Michael P. Joyce, C.M., Prov. Asst.; Bro. F. Joseph Hess, C.M., Prov. Treas.

Priests 139; Brothers 18.

Serving in 18 (arch)dioceses: Universities; Foreign Mission Stations; Houses of Apostolic Activity.

Represented in the Archdioceses of Chicago, Denver, Kansas City in Kansas, Milwaukee, San Francisco, St. Louis, and the Dioceses of Belleville, Buffalo, Cheyenne, Colorado Springs, Evansville, Galveston-Houston, Jefferson City, Kansas City-St. Joseph, Phoenix, Pueblo, Salt Lake City and Springfield-Cape Girardeau. Also in Marsabit and Nairobi, Kenya.

The New England Province of the Vincentian Fathers (1975): *Vincentian Provincial House*, 234 Keeney Street, Manchester, CT 06040-7048. Tel: 860-643-2828; Fax: 860-533-9462. Very Rev. John S. Sledziona, C.M., Prov.

Fathers 33; Brothers 4.

Legal Title: *New England Province of the Congregation of the Mission, Inc., Charitable Trust of the New England Province of the Congregation of the Mission.*

Parishes 7.

Represented in the Archdiocese of Hartford and the Dioceses of Brooklyn, Manchester, and Portland (ME).

American Italian Branch (Naples, Italy) (1922): *Our Lady of Pompei Church*, 3600 Claremont St., Baltimore, MD 21224. Tel: 301-675-7790. Rev. Luigi Esposito, C.M., Supr.

Legal Title: *Vincentian Fathers of the Neapolitan Province of Maryland Charities, Inc.*

Fathers 3.

Represented in the Archdiocese of Baltimore.

American Spanish Branch (Barcelona, Spain): 234 Congress St., Brooklyn, NY 11201. Tel: 718-624-3425. Rev. Gabriel Del-Real, C.M., Supr.

Fathers 7.

Represented in the Diocese of Brooklyn.

American Spanish Branch (Zaragoza, Spain) (1926): *Holy Agony Church*, 1834 3rd Ave., New York, NY 10029. Tel: 212-289-5589; Fax: 212-289-8321. Revs. Victor Elia, C.M.; Candido Arrizurieta, C.M.; Santiago Lluch, C.M.

Legal Title: *Padres Paules Community - Vincentians Inc.*

Fathers 13.

Represented in the Archdioceses of Los Angeles, & New York.

(Vincentian) Province of the West (1975): 650 W. 23rd St., Los Angeles, CA 90007-2036. Tel: 213-749-1865; Fax: 213-749-1554. Very Rev. Bernard J. Quinn, C.M., Prov.

Fathers 51; Brothers 3; Permanent Deacons 3; Major Theologians 3.

Members serve and staff: Four Parishes, two Seminaries, two evanglization centers and staff 10 community houses.

Legal Title: *Congregation of the Mission in California, A Corporation; Vincentian Community Charitable Trust; Vincentian Foreign Mission Society; DePaul Center Corp. (Formerly St. Vincent's Seminary Corp.); Vincentians Province of the West Support Trust Fund.*

Properties owned: *DePaul Center*, Montebello, CA; *St. Mary's Seminary*, Santa Barbara, CA; *Amat House*, Los Angeles, CA.

Represented in the Archdioceses of Chicago and Los Angeles, and the Dioceses of Fresno, Phoenix, San Jose and Stockton. Also in Belgium.

The Congregation of the Mission Southern Province (1975): 3826 Gilbert Ave., Dallas, TX 75219-4346. Tel: 214-526-2421 & 526-0234; Fax: 214-526-3477. Very Rev. George Weber, C.M., Prov.; Rev. Miles Heinen, C.M., Treas.

Priests 32; Brothers 1.

Properties owned, sponsored, or staffed: Parishes 9; Community Houses 5; Mission Churches 3.

Represented in the Archdioceses of New Orleans, St. Louis, San Antonio and the Dioceses of Alexandria, Gallup, Galveston-Houston, Dallas, and Little Rock.

[1335] (V.C.)—VINCENTIAN CONGREGATION

Vincentians

Founded by Rev. Fr. Varkey Kattarath at Thottakom, Kerala, India in 1904.

Generalate: Vincentian Generalate, P.B. No. 2250 - Edappally Kochi, 682 024, Kerala, India. Very Rev. Antony Plackal, V.C., Supr. Gen.

St. Joseph Province: Vincentian Provincial House, S.H. Mouont P.O., 686 006, Kottayam, Kerala, India. Tel: 481-563-559. Very Rev. George Arackal, V.C., Supr. Gen.

North American Headquarters : Vincentian House, P.O. Box 252, Emery, SD 57332-0252. Rev. Joseph Thalanany, V.C., Reg. Coord.

Fathers 5.

Represented in the Archdioceses of St. Paul-Minneapolis and in the Dioceses of Sioux Falls and Trenton.

[1340] (S.D.V.)—VOCATIONIST FATHERS

(Society of The Divine Vocations)

Generali: Via Cortina D'Ampezzo, 138, 00135, Rome, Italy. Very Rev. James Capraro, S.D.V., Supr. Gen.

American Headquarters: 90 Brooklake Rd., Florham Park, NJ 07932. Tel: 201-966-6262. Rev. Mario

Muccitelli, S.D.V., Delegate of Supr. Gen. for U.S.A.

U.S. Foundations: Our Lady of Perpetual Help Center, 170 Broad St., Newark, NJ 07104. Revs. Louis Caputo, S.D.V., Pastor-Religious Supr. & Vocation Dir.; Giosue DiCesare, S.D.V.; Felix Antonitti, S.D.V.; Bro. Harold Hernandez, S.D.V.; Revs. Antonio da Silva, S.D.V.; Anthony Basso, S.D.V.

Represented in the Archdiocese of Newark and the Diocese of Paterson.

[1350] (C.F.X.)—BROTHERS OF ST. FRANCIS XAVIER

(Congregatio Fratrum Sti Francisci Xaverii)

Generalate - Xaverian Brothers: 4409 Frederick Ave., Baltimore, MD 21229. Tel: 410-644-0034; Fax: 410-644-2762. Bros. Matthew Burke, C.F.X., Supr. Gen.; Cornelius E. Hubbuch, C.F.X., Vicar & Dir. Staff Formation; Lawrence Harvey, C.F.X., Dir. Xaverian Sponsored Schools; Richard Mazza, C.F.X., Dir. Pastoral Care.

Legal Titles: *Xaverian Brothers USA Inc.; American Northeastern Province of the Xaverian Brothers Inc.; Isadore Charitable Trust.*

Brothers 277.

Ministries in the field of Religious and Academic Education at all levels; Diocesan Offices; Pastoral Ministry; Mission Schools; Communities; Houses and House of Formation.

Represented in the Archdioceses of Baltimore, Boston, Chicago, Los Angeles, Louisville, Hartford, Milwaukee, Newark, New Orleans, New York, St. Louis, Santa Fe, Washington and the Dioceses of Birmingham, Brooklyn, Charleston, Fairbanks, Fort Wayne-South Bend, Houma-Thibodaux, Jackson, Memphis, Richmond, Rapid City, Rockville Centre, Scranton, St. Augustine, St. Petersburg, Venice and Worcester. Also inn Bolivia, Belgium, Congo, England, Haiti, Kenya and Uganda.

[1360] (S.X.)—XAVERIAN MISSIONARY FATHERS

Saint Francis Xavier Foreign Mission Society

(Pia Societas Sancti Francisci Xaverii pro Exteris Missionibus)

General Motherhouse: *Istituto Saveriano Missioni Estere,* Viale Vaticano 40, 00165, Rome, Italy. Very Rev. Francesco Marini, S.X., Supr. Gen.

U.S. Province: *Xaverian Missionary Fathers,* 12 Helene Ct., Wayne, NJ 07470. Tel: 973-942-2975; Fax: 973-942-5012. Very Rev. Francis Signorelli, S.X., Prov.

Fathers 21; Seminarians 9.

Mission Houses 2; Houses of Formation 2.

Represented in the Archdioceses of Boston, Chicago and Milwaukee and in the Diocese of Paterson.

Index for Religious Institutes of Women

Religious Institutes of Women

Leadership Conference of Women Religious of the United States of America—National Office: 8808 Cameron St., Silver Spring, MD 20910. Tel: 301-588-4955. Sr. Mary Christine Fellerhoff, C.S.A., Exec. Dir.; Sr. Mary Waskowiak, R.S.M., Pres.; Sr. Camille D'Arienzo, R.S.M., Vice Pres.; Sr. Mary Finnerty, S.H.Sp., Sec.; Sr. Frances Mlocek, I.H.M., Treas.
Council Major Superiors of Women Religious in the United States of America—4200 Harewood Rd., N.E., P.O. Box 4467, Washington, DC 20017-0467. Tel: 202-832-2575; Fax: 202-832-6325. Mother Mary Bernard Nettle, L.S.P., Chm.

(The initial* D *or* P *indicates Diocesan or Pontifical Jurisdiction)

[0100] (A.S.C.)—ADORERS OF THE BLOOD OF CHRIST P

Founded in Acuto, Italy, in 1834. First foundation in the United States in 1870.
General Motherhouse: Via Beata Maria De Mattias 10, Rome, 00183. Italy. Sr. Giuseppina Fragasso, A.S.C., Supr. Gen.
Province of Ruma (1876): *Provincial House*, 2 Pioneer Ln., Red Bud, IL 62278. Tel: 618-282-3848; 282-6229. Sr. Margaret Mary Kopish, A.S.C., Prov. Supr.
Professed Sisters 205.
Sisters serve and staff: Colleges, Secondary & Elementary Schools, Special and Religious Education; Hospitals; Pastoral Care; Nursing Homes; Domestic Service in Communities and Institutions; Administration in Religious Orders and Parishes; Prayer Ministry; Retreat Ministry; Social Service; Pastoral and Chaplaincy Ministry; Prison and Minority Ministries.
Properties owned: *St. Clement Hospital*, Red Bud, IL; *St. Vincent Memorial Hospital*, Taylorville, IL; *MariaCare*, Red Bud, IL.
Represented in the Archdioceses of St. Louis, and San Antonio and the Dioceses of Belleville, Dodge City, Fort Wayne-South Bend, Gallup, Harrisburg, Jefferson City, Joliet, Springfield-Cape Girardeau, Oakland, Springfield (IL) and Tucson.
Province of Wichita (1929): *Provincial House*, 1400 S. Sheridan, Wichita, KS 67213-1394. Tel: 316-943-1203. Sr. Charlotte Rohrbach, A.S.C., Prov. Supr.; Sr. Helen Streck, Community Archivist.
Finally Professed Sisters 228; Scholasticates 7; Postulants 1; Novices 1.
Sisters Serve and Staff: College and Universities; High Schools; Elementary Schools; CCD-Parish Ministry; Social Work; Diocesan Offices; Hospitals-Clinics; Prayer Center; Homes for the Aged; Foreign Missions.
Properties owned: *Villa Maria*, Mulvane, KS; *Kansas Newman College*, Wichita, KS; *St. Joseph's Villa*, David City, NE.
Represented in the Archdioceses of Kansas City in Kansas, Oklahoma City, St. Louis, San Antonio and Washington and the Dioceses of Beaumont, Brownsville, Dodge City, El Paso, Fort Worth, Gallup, Jefferson City, Kansas City - St. Joseph, Las Cruces, Lincoln, Oakland, Owensboro, Salina, San Angelo, Springfield (IL), Tulsa and Wichita.
Province of Columbia (1925): *Adorers of the Blood of Christ Provincial House*, 3950 Columbia Ave., Columbia, PA 17512-9714. Tel: 717-285-4536. Sr. Agatha Marie Groft, A.S.C., Prov. Coord.
Legal Title: *Adorers of the Blood of Christ, Province of Columbia, PA, Inc.*
Total number in community 85.
Ministry in the field of Academic and Religious Education through College; Home for the; Aged; Home Nursing; Independent Living Retirement Village; Domestic Service at; Bishops' Residence; Religious Education Resource Center; Retreat House; Pastoral Assistants; Hospital Chaplaincy; Ministry to Abused Children and; Children with AIDS.
Properties owned: *St. Joseph Convent-Provincial House; Precious Blood Spiritual Center; St. Anne's Home for the Aged, Inc.; De Mattias Residence; St. Anne's Independent Living Retirement Village*, Columbia, PA.
Represented in the Archdioceses of Baltimore, Chicago, New York, Newark and St. Louis and the Dioceses of Altoona-Johnstown, Harrisburg, Savannah, Wilmington and Youngstown. Also in Guatemala and Slovak Republic.

[0110] (A.P.B.)—THE SISTERS ADORERS OF THE PRECIOUS BLOOD P
(Cloistered Contemplative Order)

American Federation: Consisting of six autonomous monasteries: 166 State St., Portland, ME 04101-3794. Sr. Mary Jo Divney, A.P.B., Pres. American Federation.
New York: 54th & Ft. Hamilton Pkwy., Brooklyn, NY 11219. Tel: 718-438-6371.
New Hampshire: 700 Bridge St., Manchester, NH 03104. Tel: 603-623-4264.
Indiana: 1106 State St., Lafayette, IN 47905. Tel: 317-742-8227.
New York: 400 Pratt St., Watertown, NY 13601. Tel: 315-788-1669.
Maine: 166 State St., Portland, ME 04101. Tel: 207-774-0861.
Canada: 9415 - 165th St., Edmonton, Alberta , Canada, T5R 2S5. Tel: 403-484-6691.
Professed Sisters 80; Novices 6; Postulants 2.
Represented in the Dioceses of Brooklyn, Lafayette (IN), Manchester, Ogdensburg and Portland (ME).

[0130] (A.S.C.J.)—APOSTLES OF THE SACRED HEART OF JESUS P

Founded in Italy in 1894. First foundation in United States 1902.
General Motherhouse: Via Germano Sommeiller, No. 38 Rome, Italy. Mother Auxiliadora deGodoy, Supr. Gen.; Sr. Leopoldina Euclidi, Archivist.
U.S. Provincial Motherhouse: *Mt. Sacred Heart*, 265 Benham St., Hamden, CT 06514. Tel: 203-248-4225; Fax: 203-230-8341.
Professed Sisters 189.
Ministry in the field of Education, Health Care, Parishes and Adult Day Care.
Properties owned: *Mary, Mother of the Church Convent*, Hamden, CT; *Mount Sacred Heart College for Sisters; Sacred Heart Academy; Sacred Heart Manor; Sacred Heart Manor Kindergarten and Nursery; Clelian Adult Day Care*, Hamden, CT; *Sacred Heart on the Lake*, Higganum, CT; *Cor Jesu Academy, Sacred Heart Villa Nursery*, St. Louis, MO; *Our Lady Queen of Apostles (Convent & Nursery)*, Imperial, MO; *Clelian Heights School for Exceptional Children*, Greensburg, PA; *Sacred Heart Private Elementary School*, Bronx, NY.
Represented in the Archdioceses of Hartford, Newark, New York and St. Louis and in the Dioceses of Bridgeport, Greensburg, Metuchen, Norwich, Palm Beach, Pensacola-Tallahassee, Pittsburgh, Providence, and Sacramento.

[0140] (S.A.A.)—SISTERS AUXILIARIES OF THE APOSTOLATE D

Founded in Canada in 1903. First United States foundation in 1911.
General Motherhouse: *Ss. Peter and Paul*, P.O. Box 9086, 689 Maple Terr., Monongah, WV 26555-9086. Tel: 304-534-3081. Sr. Angela Marie Pastore, Supr.
Total in Congregation 6; Professed Sisters 6.
Legal Holdings: *Ss. Peter and Paul Catholic School.*
Represented in the Diocese of Wheeling-Charleston.

[0150] (S.A.S.V.)—SISTERS OF THE ASSUMPTION P

Founded in Saint-Gregoire, P.Q., Canada in 1853. First foundation in the United States in 1891.
General Motherhouse: Nicolet, P.Q. Canada. Sr. Aline Vadnais, S.A.S.V., Supr. Gen.
United States Region: Regional Office, 316 Lincoln St., Worcester, MA 01605. Sr. Muriel Lemoine, S.A.S.V., Prov. Supr. Tel: 508-856-9383. Sr. Lorraine Normand, S.A.S.V., Regional Treas. Tel: 508-856-9450.
Total in Province 114; Total Professed 113; Junior Professed 1.
Ministry in all levels of education.
Legal Holdings: *Assumption Residence of the Sisters of the Assumption of the Blessed Virgin*, Petersham, MA; *Harper Residence*, Worcester, MA.
Represented in the Archdioceses of Boston, Hartford and the Dioceses of Fall River, Manchester, Portland in Maine, Providence, Springfield (MA) and Worcester. Missions in Japan, Brazil and Ecuador.

[0160] (O.S.A.)—AUGUSTINIAN NUNS OF CONTEMPLATIVE LIFE P

Augustinian Contemplative Nuns: *Mother of Good Counsel Convent*, 4328 Westminster Pl., St. Louis, MO 63108. Sr. Mary Grace, O.S.A., Prioress.
Total number in community 5.
Legal Title: *Augustinian Cloistered Nuns, Inc.*
Represented in the Archdiocese of St. Louis her Marguerite Derome, O.S.B., Prioress.
Total in Congregation 290; Total in community 14.
Represented in the Diocese of Burlington.

[0170] (O.S.B.)—BENEDICTINE NUNS OF THE CONGREGATION OF SOLESMES P

Order originated in Italy, c. 529. Congregation of Solesmes formed in France in 1837.
U.S. Establishment (1981): *Monastery of the Immaculate Heart of Mary*, H.C.R. #13, Box 11, Westfield, VT 05874. Tel: 802-744-6525. Rev. Mother Marguerite Derome, O.S.B., Prioress.
Total in Congregation 290; Total in community 14.
Represented in the Diocese of Burlington.

[0180] (O.S.B.)—BENEDICTINE NUNS OF THE PRIMITIVE OBSERVANCE P

First founded in Italy in about 529. First United States establishment in 1948.
Abbey of Regina Laudis: Bethlehem, CT 06751. Tel: 203-266-7727; Fax: 203-266-5915. Rt. Rev. Mother Benedict Duss, O.S.B., Abbess.
Professed Nuns 29; Sisters in First Vows 4; Novices 3; Postulants 1.

[0190] (O.S.B.)—BENEDICTINE SISTERS P

First founded in Italy c.529. Founded in the United States in 1931 from St. Walburg Abbey, Eichstatt, Bavaria, Germany.
The Sisters of St. Benedict of Westmoreland County: *St. Emma Monastery*, 1001 Harvey Ave., Greensburg, PA 15601-1494. Tel: 724-834-3060; Fax: 724-834-5772. Mother Mary Anne Noll, O.S.B., Prioress.
Professed Sisters 18; Postulants 1; Novices 1.
Ministry in Monastic Life; Benedictine hospitality extended through adjacent St. Emma Retreat House.
Represented in the Diocese of Greensburg.
Benedictine Nuns: *Abbey of St. Walburga*, 32,109 N. U.S. Hghwy 287, Virginia Dale, CO 80536-8942. Tel: 970-472-0612. Mother Maria-Thomas Beil, O.S.B., Abbess.
Sisters 22; Postulants 1.
Represented in the Archdiocese of Denver.

[0200] (O.S.B.)—BENEDICTINE SISTERS D
(Regina Pacis)

The first Monastery was founded 1680 in Kaunas, Lithuania by a Polish Abbess Eufemia Skorulska.
Founded in United States in 1957 by Mother M. Raphaela Simonis, O.S.B.
U.S. Foundation: Regina Pacis Benedictine Sisters, 333 Wallace Rd., Bedford, NH 03110. Tel: 603-472-3239. Mother M. Raphaela Simonis, O.S.B., Supr.
Novitiate; Kindergarten and Nursery School.
Represented in the Diocese of Manchester.

[0210] (O.S.B.)—MISSIONARY BENEDICTINE SISTERS P

The Congregation of Missionary Benedictine Sisters is of Pontifical Jurisdiction. Its Constitutions were approved by Rome on June 25, 1934; Revised approval June 29, 1983.
Generalate: Rome, Italy.
Provincial Motherhouse and Novitiate: *Immaculata Convent*, (1923), 300 N. 18th St., Norfolk, NE 68701-3687. Tel: 402-371-3438; Fax: 402-379-2877. Sr. M. Agnes Salber, O.S.B., Prioress.
Professed Sisters 49; Juniorates 9; Postulants 2; Novices 1.

Ministry in the fields of Education; Health & Hospitals; Nursing Homes.

Legal Holdings or Titles: *Immaculata Convent*, Norfolk, NE; *Our Lady of Lourdes Hospital*, Norfolk, NE; *St. Joseph Nursing Home*, Norfolk, NE; *Providence Medical Center*, Wayne, NE; *Graceville Missionary Benedictine Sisters, Inc., dba Holy Trinity Hospital - Grace Home*, Graceville, MN.

Represented in the Archdiocese of Omaha and the Diocese of New Ulm.

[0220] (O.S.B.)—CONGREGATION OF THE BENEDICTINE SISTERS OF PERPETUAL ADORATION OF PONTIFICAL JURISDICTION P

Founded from Maria Rickenbach, Switzerland, in 1874 with first monastery at Clyde, MO. Congregation erected by decree of the Holy See on June 16, 1936. Generalate, Novitiate and Healthcare community transferred to St. Louis in 1966.

General Motherhouse and Novitiate: *Benedictine Monastery of Perpetual Adoration*, 8300 Morganford Rd., St. Louis, MO 63123. Tel: 314-638-6427. Sr. Mary Jane Romero, Prioress Gen., General Council; Sr. M. Bede Luetkemeyer; Sr. Sarah Schwartzberg; Sr. Joan Therese Anderson; Sr. Cathleen Marie Timberlake, Public Rels. Dir.

Total number in community: Professed 130; Novices 2.

Interdependent Monasteries: R.R. 1, Box 101, Clyde, MO 64432. 800 N. Country Club Rd., Tucson, AZ 85716. Osage Monastery, 18701 W. Monastery Rd., Sand Springs, OK 74063. San Benito Monastery, Box 520, Dayton, WY 82836.

Ministry in Monastic/Contemplative/Eucharistic Apostolate of Prayer; Liturgy of the Hours four times daily in Choir; Contemplative Prayer and Monastic Atmosphere Shared with Others; Prayer Days and Retreats for Sisters; Editing and Publishing Bimonthly Magazine: ""Spirit & Life"; Production and Distribution of Altar Breads; Liturgical Vestments; Correspondence.

Represented in the Archdiocese of St. Louis and the Dioceses of Cheyenne, Kansas City-St. Joseph, Tucson and Tulsa.

[0230] (O.S.B.)—BENEDICTINE SISTERS OF PONTIFICAL JURISDICTION P

(I) The Federation of St. Scholastica:

Erected by Decree of the Holy See, Feb. 25, 1922, with final approbation by Decree of June 10, 1930.

Twenty-two Motherhouses in the United States and two in Mexico. Total number in the Federation 1,288; Sr. Regina Crowley, O.S.B., Pres., residing at 5807 N. Kolmar Ave., Chicago, IL 60646. Tel: 773-973-6845.

Benedictine Sisters of Baltimore, Inc.: *Emmanuel Monastery*, 2229 W. Joppa Rd., Lutherville, MD 21093. Tel: 410-821-5792. Sr. Patricia Kirk, O.S.B., Prioress.

Total number in community 15.

Ministry in the field of Education; Parish Ministry; Retreats and Spiritual Direction; Justice Ministry; Social Services; Hospice Chaplaincy.

Represented in the Archdioceses of Baltimore and Newark.

Benedictine Sisters of the Byzantine Rite (1969): *Queen of Heaven Monastery*, 8640 Squires Ln., N.E., Warren, OH 44484. Tel: 330-856-1813. Sr. Margaret Mary Schima, O.S.B., Prioress.

Professed Sisters 12.

Legal Holding: *BEL-Center (Benedictine Early Learning Center).*

Ministry in Religious and Academic Education; Pastoral Ministry; Child Care; Administration.

Represented in the Archdiocese of Pittsburgh Byzantine Rite.

Mount St. Scholastica, Inc. (1863): *Motherhouse of the Sisters of St. Benedict*, 801 S. Eighth St., Atchison, KS 66002-2778. Tel: 913-367-6110; Fax: 913-367-3866. Sr. Mary Agnes Patterson, O.S.B., Prioress.

Total number in community 234.

Legal Holdings: *Dooley Center, Inc.*; *The Mount Community Center, Inc.*; *Mount St. Scholastica, Inc.*, Atchison, KS.

Ministry in the field of Academic Education at all levels; Special Education; Music Conservatory; Pastoral Ministry; Counseling; Retreats; Spirituality Center; Spiritual Direction; Social Services; Diocesan Offices; Ministry to the Aged; Hospitality; Community & Conference Center Work; Special Services to the needy; Ministry to the sick; Missionary Work in Brazil.

Represented in the Archdioceses of Chicago, Kansas City in Kansas, New Orleans, St. Louis, Washington and the Dioceses of Des Moines, Kansas City-St. Joseph, Arlington, and Tulsa. Also in Brazil.

Sisters Benedict of Colorado, Inc.: 4264 Ponds View Dr., Denver, CO 80123. Tel: 303-795-2378. Sr. Judith Elms, O.S.B., Supr.

Benedictine Sisters of Elk Co. (1852): *St. Joseph Monastery*, St. Marys, PA 15857. Tel: 814-834-2267. Sr. Raphael Baker, O.S.B., Prioress.

Professed Sisters 48.

Ministry in the fields of Academic and Religious Education; Pastoral Ministry; Child Welfare; Retreats.

Benedictine Sisters of Erie (1856): *Mt. St. Benedict Monastery*, 6101 East Lake Rd., Erie, PA 16511. Tel: 814-899-0614; Fax: 814-898-4004. Sr. Phyllis Schleicher, O.S.B., Prioress.

Total in congregation 144; Professed sisters 137; In formation 7.

Sisters serve and staff: High Schools; Elementary Schools; Colleges; Day Care Centers; Residence for Elderly and Handicapped; Hospitals; Social Services; Diocesan Offices; Pastoral Ministry; Religious Education.

Properties owned: *Mount Saint Benedict Monastery Glinodo Center*; *St. Benedict Education Center; Benet Center Om Shanti*; *St. Scholastica Priory Kraus House*, Erie, PA; *Holy Family Priory*, Benet Lake, WI; *St. Walburga Priory*; *Sophia House Benedita Riepp Priory*, Erie, PA.

Represented in the Archdiocese of Chicago, Milwaukee and the Dioceses of Cleveland, Dodge City, Erie, Orlando and Syracuse.

Benedictine Sisters of Chicago O.S.B. (1861): *St. Scholastica Monastery*, 7430 Ridge Blvd., Chicago, IL 60645. Tel: 773-764-2413. Sr. Karen Bland, Prioress; Sr. Vivian Ivantic, Community Archivist.

Professed Sisters 88; Scholastics 2.

Ministry in Graduate Programs; High Schools; Elementary Schools; Pastoral Ministry; Religious Education; University staff; Management Consultant; Campus Ministry; Spiritual Direction; Peace and Shelter Ministry; Community Center Work; Social Service; Counseling.

Properties owned: *St. Scholastica Monastery*, Chicago, IL; *St. Scholastica High School*, Chicago, IL; *St. Scholastica Academy*, Canon City, CO.

Represented in the Archdioceses of Chicago and the Diocese of Pueblo.

Benedictine Sisters of the Sacred Heart O.S.B. (1895): *Sacred Heart Monastery*, 1910 Maple Ave., Lisle, IL 60532-2184. Tel: 630-969-7040. Sr. Judith Ann Heble, O.S.B., Prioress.

Legal Title: *Benedictine Sisters of the Sacred Heart Charitable Trust.*

Professed Sisters 51.

Sisters serve and staff: High Schools; Elementary Schools; Colleges; Queen of Peace Retirement Center; Religious Education; Pastoral Ministry; Nurses Administration; P.A.D.S.; Independent Positions involving Secretarial, Counseling, Liturgical Works, Occupational Therapy, Internal Ministry and Altar Bread Baking.

Represented in the Archdiocese of Chicago and the Diocese of Joliet.

Benedictine Sisters of Elizabeth, NJ O.S.B. (1868): *St. Walburga Monastery and Novitiate*, 851 N. Broad St., Elizabeth, NJ 07208. Tel: 201-352-4278. Sr. Germaine Fritz, O.S.B., Prioress.

Professed Sisters 72.

Legal Holdings and Titles: *Benedictine Hospital*, Kingston, NY; *Benedictine Academy*, Elizabeth, NJ; *Bender Memorial Academy*, Elizabeth, NJ.

Represented in the Archdioceses of New York, Newark and Washington and the Dioceses of Paterson and Trenton.

Benedictine Sisters of Pittsburgh, PA. O.S.B. (1870): *St. Benedict Monastery*, 4530 Perrysville Ave., Pittsburgh, PA 15229-2296. Tel: 412-931-2844. Sr. Roberta Campbell, O.S.B., Prioress.

Professed Sisters 89.

Ministry in the field of Education in all levels; Religious and Special Education; Pastoral Ministry; Childcare; House of Prayer; Social Service; Campus Ministry; Hospital Chaplaincy; Art Education; Ministry Resource; Peace & Justice Commission; Outreach with Poor; Benedictine Center for Senior Citizens; Adult Day Care.

Properties owned: *Saint Benedict Academy*, Pittsburgh, PA; *Pittsburgh Benedictine Ministries, Inc.*

Represented in the Dioceses of Greensburg, Lexington and Pittsburgh.

Sisters of Benedict O.S.B. (1968): *Red Plains Monastery*, 1132 N.W. 32nd, Oklahoma City, OK 73118. Tel: 405-528-7965; 528-2715. Sr. Marie Ballmann, O.S.B., Prioress.

Professed Sisters 12.

Ministry in the fields of Education, CCD and Adult Religious Education; Spiritual Formation; Spiritual Direction; Retreats.

Properties owned: Benedictine Spirituality Center, Piedmont, OK.

Represented in the Archdiocese of Oklahoma City.

Benedictine Sisters O.S.B. (1879): *St. Joseph Monastery, Priory and Novitiate*, 2200 S. Lewis, Tulsa, OK 74114-3100. Tel: 918-742-4989. Sr. Barbara Austin, O.S.B., Prioress; Sr. Anita Marie Gilpin, O.S.B., Archivist.

Professed Sisters 36; In Formation 2.

Ministry in the field of Academic Education; Catechetics; Evangelization; Nursing; Pastoral Ministry; Social Civic & Ecumenical Group Work; Counselling & Spiritual Direction; Prison Ministry; Religious Education & Religious Formation.

Legal Titles & Holdings: *Congregation of the Benedictine Sisters of the Sacred Hearts Monte Cassino School.*

Represented in the Archdiocese of Oklahoma City and the Diocese of Tulsa.

Benedictine Sisters of Pontifical Jurisdiction O.S.B. (1857): *St. Gertrude Monastery*, 14259 Benedictine Ln., Ridgely, MD 21660. Tel: 301-634-2497.

Professed Sisters 39; Temporary Professed 3.

Ministry in Special Schools and Elementary & Secondary Education; Job Training Center for the Mentally Handicapped; Open Community Houses for Mentally Handicapped; Do-It-Yourself Retreat Facility: Berg Center; Outreach facility for the poor: St. Martin's Barn.

Legal holdings & titles: *The Benedictine School for Exceptional Children*; *Berg Retreat Facility*; *St. Martin's Barn*; *St. Martin House*, Ridgely, MD; St. Benedict, Wilmington, DE.

Represented in the Archdiocese of Washington and the Diocese of Wilmington and the Diocese of Camden, NJ.

St. Walburg Monastery of Benedictine Sisters of Covington, KY. O.S.B. (1859): *St. Walburg Monastery*, 2500 Amsterdam Rd., Villa Hills, KY 41017-5316. Tel: 606-331-6324; Fax: 606-331-2136. Motherhouse and Novitiate. Sr. M. Catherine Wenstrup, O.S.B., Prioress; Sr. Teresa Wolking, O.S.B., Community Archivist.

Professed Sisters 104.

Sisters serve and staff: Diocesan Offices; Hospitals; Pastoral and Social Ministry; Home or Public Health Care; Seminary; all levels of academic education.

Legal titles & holdings: *Madonna Manor Nursing-Senior Citizens Home*; *Villa Madonna Early Learning Center*; *Villa Madonna Academy*; *Villa Madonna Center - Spirituality Center.*

Represented in the Archdiocese of Cincinnati and the Dioceses of Covington, Lexington and Pueblo.

Benedictine Sisters (1902): *Sacred Heart Monastery*, Cullman, AL 35056. Tel: 205-734-2199; 734-4622; Fax: 205-734-3835. Sr. Treva Heinberg, O.S.B., Prioress; Sr. Benedicta Karter, O.S.B., Community Archivist.

Professed Sisters 62.

Sisters staff and serve: in all levels of Academic Education; Pastoral Ministry; Diocesan Offices; Retirement Homes; Conference Centers.

Properties owned: *Benedictine Spirituality and Conference Center*; *Benedictine Manor Retirement Home.*

Represented in the Archdioceses of Atlanta, and the Dioceses of Birmingham and Orlando.

Benedictine Sisters of Virginia O.S.B. (1868): *St. Benedict Monastery*, Bristow, VA 20136-1217. Tel: 703-361-0106. Sr. Cecilia Dwyer, O.S.B., Prioress.

Total in Congregation 44; Professed Sisters 42.

Legal Holdings and Titles: *Benedictine Sisters of Virginia, Inc.*; *St. Gertrude High School*, Richmond, VA; *Linton Hall School*; *Benedictine Pastoral Center*; *Benedictine Counseling Services*, Bristow, VA.

Represented in the Dioceses of Arlington and Richmond.

Benedictine Sisters (1911): *St. Scholastica's Monastery and Novitiate*, 416 W. Highland Dr., Boerne, TX 78006. Tel: 210-249-2645. Sr. Mary Agnes Zinni, O.S.B., Prioress.

Total number in community 24.

Properties owned: *St. Scholastica Monastery*; *St. Albert Early Learning Center*, Boerne, TX; *Benedictine Resource Center*, San Antonio, TX, Convents 4.

Represented in the Archdiocese of San Antonio, and the Dioceses of Austin and Gallup.

Benedictine Sisters of St. Lucy's Priory Inc. O.S.B. (1956): *St. Lucy's Priory*, 19045 E. Sierra Madre Ave., Glendora, CA 91741. Tel: 818-335-1682. Sr. Elizabeth Brown, O.S.B., Prioress.

Professed Sisters 26.

Sisters serve & staff: all levels of Academic Education; Continuing Education; Home for Developmentally Disabled Adults; Pastoral Ministry; Hospital Chaplaincy.

Legal holdings: *St. Lucy's Priory High School*; *St. Lucy's Benedictine Child Development Center.*

Represented in the Archdiocese of Los Angeles and the Diocese of San Diego.

Benedictine Sisters of Florida (1889): *Holy Name Monastery*, P.O. Box 2450, St. Leo, FL 33574-2450. Tel: 904-588-8320; Fax: 904-588-8319. Sr. Ger-

maine Bevans, O.S.B., Prioress; Sr. M. Dorothy Neuhofer, O.S.B., Community Archivist.
Professed Sisters 25; Temporary Professed 1; Novices 2.
Represented in the Diocese of St. Petersburg.
Sisters of St. Benedict (1963): *Benet Hill Monastery-Motherhouse,* 2555 N. Chelton Rd., Colorado Springs, CO 80909-1399. Tel: 719-633-0655; Fax: 917-471-0403. Sr. Anne Stedman, O.S.B., Prioress; Sr. Diane Liston, Community Archivist.
Total number in community 47.
Properties owned: Benet Hill Center; Benet Pines Retreat Center.
Represented in the Archdiocese of Denver and the Dioceses of Colorado Springs, Salina, and Pueblo. Also in Jamaica.
Benedictine Sisters O.S.B. (1989): Queen of Angels Monastery, 23411 N.E. 100th St., Liberty, MO 64068. Tel: 816-750-4631; 781-6246. Sr. Imelda Koch, O.S.B., Prioress.
Professed Sisters 4; Temporary Professed 2; Novices 1; Pre-Novitiate 2.
Ministry in Residential Care Facility for Developmentally Disabled Women.
Represented in the Diocese of Kansas City-St. Joseph.
(II) The Federation of St. Gertrude:
Erected by Decree of the Apostolic See on April 14, 1937, with final approbation by Decree of April 4, 1950; *Federation Office,* Sacred Heart Monastery, P.O. Box 364, Richardton, ND 58652. Tel: 701-974-2121; Fax: 701-974-2124. Sr. Ruth Fox, O.S.B., Federation Pres.
Total in the Federation 1,168. Eighteen member monasteries form this Federation as follows:
Sisters of St. Benedict of Beech Grove, Ind., Inc.: *Our Lady of Grace Monastery,* (1956), 1402 Southern Ave., Beech Grove, IN 46107. Tel: 317-787-3287; Fax: 317-780-2368. Sr. Rachel Best, O.S.B., Prioress.
Total Professed Sisters 85.
Ministry in Education; Parish Ministries; Retirement Home; Educational Center; Religious Education; Hospitals.
Properties owned and sponsored: *Our Lady of Grace Monastery; Beech Grove Benedictine Center; St. Paul Hermitage; Regina Retreat.*
Legal Title: *Sisters of St. Benedict of Beech Grove, Ind., Inc.; Charitable Trust of the Monastery of Our Lady of Grace; Sisters of the Order of St. Benedict.*
Represented in the Archdioceses of Cincinnati and Indianapolis and the Diocese of Evansville.
Benedictine Sisters of Belcourt O.S.B.: *Queen of Peace Monastery,* (1963), P.O. Box 370, Belcourt, ND 58316. Tel: 701-477-6167; Fax: 701-477-5575. Sr. Judith Emge, O.S.B., Prioress.
Professed Sisters 6.
Ministry in Counselling; Religious Education; Parish Ministry and Administration; Home Ministry.
Benedictine Sisters O.S.B.: *Our Lady of Peace Monastery,* 3710 West Broadway, Columbia, MO 65203. Tel: 573-446-2300; Fax: 573-446-2312. Sr. JoAnn Schmidt, O.S.B., Prioress.
Professed Sisters 13.
Ministry in Education; Home Health Care; Parish & Social Ministries; Counseling.
Represented in the Dioceses of Jefferson City, Kansas City-St. Joseph, Little Rock, Springfield in Illinois and Springfield-Cape Girardeau.
Monastery of St. Gertrude (1882): HC 3 Box 121, Cottonwood, ID 83522-9408. Tel: 208-962-3224; Fax: 208-962-7212.
Legal Title: *Idaho Corporation of Benedictine Sisters;* Sr. Mary Kay Henry, O.S.B., Prioress.
Professed Sisters 90.
Sisters serve in: Education; Parish Ministry; Foreign Mission; Health Care; Retreat Ministry; Social Work; Counseling; St. Gertrude's Museum.
Sisters sponsor: *St. Benedict's Family Medical Center,* Jerome, ID.
Represented in the Archdioceses of Los Angeles, Portland (OR) and Seattle and the Dioceses of Bismarck, Boise, Springfield, (MA) and Spokane.
Sisters of St. Benedict of Crookston O.S.B.: *Mount St. Benedict Monastery,* (1919), 620 E. Summit Ave., Crookston, MN 56716-2799. Tel: 218-281-3441; Fax: 218-281-3441. Sr. Michelle McGurran, O.S.B., Prioress.
Professed Sisters 147.
Sisters serve and staff: Elementary, High Schools, Colleges; Nursing Homes; Board, Care and Assisted Living Home; Religious Education Center; Adult Education; Parish Ministry; Pastoral Care; Retreat Centers & Social Services; Child Care; Nursery School.
Legal Holding: *Villa St. Vincent,* Crookston, MN.
Represented in the Dioceses of Brownsville, Crookston, New Ulm and St. Cloud.
Benedictine Sisters O.S.B.: *Monastery Immaculate Conception,* (1867), 802 E. 10th St., Ferdinand, IN 47532-9239. Tel: 812-367-1411; Fax: 812-367-2313. Sr. Kathryn Huber, O.S.B., Prioress.
Professed Sisters 228.
Legal Title: *Sisters of St. Benedict of Ferdinand, Indiana, Inc.*
Sisters serve and staff: on all levels of Academic Education; Religious Education Centers; Parish Ministry; Special Education Centers; Hospitals; Public Health-Social Service Agencies; Diocesan Offices; Foreign Missions; Retreat House.
Dependent Monasteries: *Monasterio Paz de la Cruz,* Morropon, Peru, *Monasterio Reina de la Paz,* Coban, Guatemala.
Sisters Sponsor: *Marian Heights Academy; Kordes Enrichment Center,* Ferdinand, IN.
Represented in the Archdioceses of Chicago, Indianapolis, Louisville, and the Dioceses of Evansville, Fort Wayne-South Bend, Joliet, Lafayette (IN), Memphis, Owensboro, and Richmond.
Benedictine Sisters, O.S.B. of St. Scholastica Monastery: *St. Scholastica Monastery,* (1879), P.O. Box 3489, Fort Smith, AR 72913. Tel: 501-783-4147; Fax: 501-782-4352. Sr. Elise Forst, O.S.B., Prioress.
Professed Sisters 120.
Ministry in the fields of Elementary and Religious Education; Retreat Center; Parish Ministry; Hospital Chaplaincy; House of Prayer; Spiritual Direction.
Dependent Monastery: *St. Benedict Monastery,* Canyon, TX.
Represented in the Dioceses of Amarillo, Little Rock, and Tulsa.
Sisters of St. Benedict of Riverside, Inc.: *Holy Spirit Monastery,* (1972), 22791 Pico St., Grand Terrace, CA 92313-5750. Tel: 909-783-4446; Fax: 909-783-3525. Sr. Carolyn Gries, O.S.B., Prioress.
Professed Sisters 11.
Ministry in Elementary Education; Parish Ministry; Counseling and Spiritual Direction; Hospital Chaplaincy; Work with the Elderly; Retreat Centers; Educating the Handicapped.
Represented in the Dioceses of Orange and San Bernardino.
Benedictine Sisters: *Spirit of Life Monastery,* 10760 W. Glennon Dr., Lakewood, CO 80226. Tel: 303-986-9234. Sr. Charlotte Redpath, O.S.B., Prioress.
Corporate Minsitry: *Spirit of Life Center.*
Sisters serve in: Retreat and Prayer Ministry; Counseling and Spiritual Direction.
Professed Sisters 2.
Sisters of St. Benedict of Madison, Wisconsin, Inc.: *Monastery of St. Benedict Center,* (1897), P.O. Box 5070, Madison, WI 53705-0070. Tel: 608-836-1631; Fax: 608-831-9312. Sr. Mary David Walgenbach, O.S.B., Prioress.
Professed Sisters 6.
Sisters serve: Community Building, Prayer, Education, Retreat and Conference Ministries.
Corporate Ministries: *St. Benedict Center.*
Legal Title: *Sisters of St. Benedict, Sioux City, Iowa, Inc.; Sisters of St. Benedict of Madison, Wisconsin, Inc.*
Represented in the Dioceses of Madison and Sioux City.
Benedictine Sisters of Mt. Angel, Oregon: *Queen of Angels Monastery,* (1882), 840 S. Main St., Mt. Angel, OR 97362. Tel: 503-845-6141; Fax: 503-845-6585. Sr. Jeanette von Herrmann, O.S.B., Prioress.
Professed Sisters 58.
Sisters serve: Elementary and High Schools; Colleges; Parish Ministry; Retreat and Prayer Ministry; Nursing; Counseling and Spiritual Direction; Work with Handicapped and Aging; Home Health Care; Hospital Chaplaincy; Ministry to Poor and Hispanics.
Corporate Ministries: *Shalom Prayer Center; St. Joseph's Shelter,* Mt. Angel, OR.
Institution Sponsors: *Benedictine Nursing Center,* Mt. Angel, OR.
Represented in the Archdiocese of Portland (OR) and the Diocese of Boise, and Honolulu. Also in Victoria, B.C.
Benedictine Convent of St. Martin: St. Martin Monastery, (1889), 2110-C St. Martin's Dr., Rapid City, SD 57702. Tel: 605-343-8011; Fax: 605-399-2723. Sr. Florence McManamen, O.S.B., Prioress.
Professed Sisters 43.
Properties owned: *St. Martin's Academy Learning Center and Retreat Center.*
Sisters serve and staff: Elementary Schools; Retreat Center; C.C.D. Center; Adult Religious Education; Parish Ministries; Chancery and Catholic Social Services; Hospital Chaplaincies, Nursing and Medical Records.
Dependent Monastery: *Epiphany Monastery,* Columbia Falls, MT.
Represented in the Archdiocese of Seatlle and Dioceses of Great Falls-Billings, Helena, Madison, Orange, and Rapid City.
Benedictine Sisters of Richardton, O.S.B.: *Sacred Heart Monastery,* (1916), P.O. Box 364, Richardton, ND 58652. Tel: 701-974-2121; Fax: 701-974-2124. Sr. Paula Larson, O.S.B., Prioress.
Professed Sisters 40.
Ministry in the fields of Academic Education; Summer Vacation Schools; Hospital Chaplaincy; Indian ministry; Parish ministry; Health Care.
Legal titles or holdings: *St. Vincent's Nursing Home, Inc.; Marillac Manor, Inc.; Subiaco Manor Inc.; Sacred Heart Benedictine Foundation.*
Represented in the Diocese of Bismarck.
The Benedictine Sisters of Mother of God Monastery O.S.B.: *Mother of God Monastery,* (1961), 110 S.E. 28th Ave., Watertown, SD 57201. Tel: 605-882-6600; Fax: 605-882-6658. Sr. Sandra Meek, O.S.B., Prioress.
Professed Sisters 80.
Sisters serve and staff: in Elementary and College Education; CCD Centers; Social Justice Center; Parish Ministry; Social Services; Hospitals and Hospices; Retreat Center; Homes for Aged; Juvenile Services; Continuing Education Center; Native American Ministeries; Hispanic Ministries; Foreign Mission in Guatemala; and Congregate Housing for Elderly.
Legal Title: *The Benedictine Sisters of Mother of God Monastery,* Watertown, SD; *St. Ann's Corporation (includes Benet Place),* Watertown, SD; *Harmony Hill Corporation,* Watertown, SD.
Represented in the Archdioceses of Chicago, Omaha, St. Paul-Minneapolis and the Dioceses of Arlington, Bismarck, Boise, Crookston, Fargo, Lincoln, Sioux Falls, Tyler, Winona and Yakima. Also in Guatemala and Germany.
St. Benedict's Monastery (1912): 225 Masters Ave., Winnipeg, Manitoba , Canada, R4A 2A1. Tel: 204-338-4601; Fax: 204-339-8775. Sr. Virginia Evard, O.S.B., Prioress.
Professed Sisters 50.
Ministry in Retreat Center; Education and Health Care.
Represented in the Dioceses of Calgary, St. Boniface and Winnipeg in Canada.
Benedictine Convent of the Sacred Heart: *Sacred Heart Monastery,* (1880), 1005 W. 8th St., Yankton, SD 57078. Tel: 605-668-1011; Fax: 605-668-1559. Sr. Jacquelyn Ernster, O.S.B., Prioress.
Professed Sisters 167.
Sisters serve and staff: in Health Care Institutions; all levels of Academic Education; Social Services; Parish Ministry; Pastoral Care; Diocesan Offices; Counseling & Religious Education.
Represented in the Archdiocese of Denver, Omaha and the Dioceses of Bismarck, Lincoln, Pueblo, and Sioux Falls.
Benedictine Sisters, O.S.B.: *The Dwelling Place Monastery,* (1993), 150 Mt. Tabor Rd., Martin, KY 41649. Tel: 606-886-9624. Sr. Judy Yunkers, O.S.B., Prioress.
Professed Sisters 5.
Sisters serve and staff: Elementary and Adult Education; Mentally Handicapped; Retreat Center; Parish; Volunteer Program.
Represented in the Diocese of Lexington.
Benedictine Sisters of Nanaimo: *House of Bread Monastery,* (1993), 2329 Arbot Rd., Nanaimo, British Columbia , Canada, V9R 6S8. Tel: 250-753-1763; Fax: 250-753-6742. Sr. Jean Ann Berning, O.S.B., Prioress.
Sisters serve:: Counselling; Retreat and Prayer Ministry; Nursing; Artist; Corporate Ministries:; Bethlehem Retreat Centre; Bethlehem Counselling Centre.
Represented in the Diocese of Victoria, Canada.
Professed Sisters 10.
(III) The Federation of St. Benedict:.
Erected by decree of the Holy See March 24, 1947; *St. Benedict Convent,* 104 Chapel Lane, St. Joseph, MN 56374. Tel: 612-363-7070; Fax: 612-363-7130. Sr. Colleen Haggerty, O.S.B., Federation Pres.
Legal title: *Federation of St. Benedict.*
Total number of Sisters in Federation 970. Eleven monasteries form this Federation; *St. Benedict Monastery,* (1988), St. Benedict Monastery, No. 10, Ln. 34, Hsueh Fu Rd., Tanshui, Taipei, 25114, Taiwan, R.O.C. Tel: 011-886-2-621-2241. Sr. Beppo Wang, O.S.B. Prioress.
Professed sisters 8.
Sisters serve and staff: Retreat Center, Student's Activity Center, Girl's Hostel.
Represented in the Archdiocese of Taipei; *Sisters of St. Benedict,* 1994, St. Martin Monastery, Box N 940, Nassau, NP , Bahamas. Tel: 809-323-5517. Sr. Clare Rolle, O.S.B. Prioress.
Professed sisters 16.
Sisters serve and staff: Diocesan-sponsored education on all levels,: K-college extension program and Supt. of Education, parish ministry, social; services and various other apostolic work. Represented in the Diocese of; Nassau; *Sisters of St. Benedict,*

(1994), Mt. Benedict Priory, 309 E. 5450 South, Ogden, UT 84405. Tel: 801-479-7582. Sr. Mary Zenzen, O.S.B., Prioress.
Professed sisters 11.
Sisters serve and staff: Health Care; Campus Ministry; Diocesan: Offices—Retreat Center, Vocation Director.
Represented in the Diocese of Salt Lake City.
Sisters of the Order of St. Benedict-O.S.B. (1857): *St. Benedict's Convent-Motherhouse and Novitiate*, St. Joseph, MN 56374-0277. Tel: 612-363-7100. Sr. Ephrem Hollermann, O.S.B., Prioress; Sr. Ruth Boedigheimer, O.S.B., Archivist.
Total Sisters in Congregation 459.
Legal Title: *Sisters of the Order of St. Benedict*, St. Joseph, MN.
Ministry in the field of Education at all levels; Indian Missions; Hospitals; Nursing Homes; Dependent Priory; Individual Apostolates; Diocesan Marriage Tribunal; Diocesan Newspaper; Parish Ministry; Social Work; Counseling.
Represented in the Archdioceses of Mobile, St. Paul-Minneapolis Seattle and Washington and the Dioceses of Caguas (PR), Crookston, Duluth, La Crosse, Madison, Manchester, New Ulm, St. Cloud, Salt Lake City, San Diego and San Jose. Also in Brazil, Canada and Thailand.
Sisters of St. Benedict - St. Scholastica Monastery O.S.B. (1892): 1001 Kenwood Ave., Duluth, MN 55811. Tel: 218-723-6555. Sr. Danile Lynch, O.S.B., Prioress; Sr. Aelred Roehl, Archivist.
Total number in community 169.
Ministry in the field of Academic Education at all levels; Religious Education; Indian Ministry; Residence for Elderly; Nursing Homes; Hospitals; Pastoral Care and Parish Ministries; Prison Ministry; Peace and Justice; Retreat Center.
Properties owned and/or sponsored: *McCabe Renewal Center*, Duluth, MN; *College of St. Scholastica*; *St. Mary's Medical Center*, Duluth, MN; *Benedictine Foundation, Inc.*, Duluth, MN; *Benedictine Health Center*; *Polinsky Rehabilitation Center*, Duluth MN; *St. Joseph's Medical Center*, Brainerd, MN; *St. Mary's Regional Health Center*, Detroit Lakes, MN; *St. Francis Regional Medical Center*, Shakopee, MN; *St. Mary's Hospital*, Cottonwood, ID; *Tekakwitha Nursing Center, Inc.*, Sisseton, SD; *Madonna Towers of Rochester, Inc.*, Rochester, MN; *Dickinson Nursing Center*; *Ellendale Nursing Center*; *Garrison Nursing Home*; *LaMoure Healthcare*; *Manor Wahpeton Healthcare Center*, ND; *Aberdeen Living Center*, SD; *Benedictine Sisters Benevolent Association*; *Benedictine Health System*, Duluth, MN; *St Mary's Hospital of Superior*, Superior, WI; *St. Anne Hospice, Inc.*, Winona, MN; *St. Gertrude's Health Center*, Shakopee, MN; *Evergreen Place*, Ellendale, ND; *Benedictine Living Communities Foundation*, Bismarck, ND.
Represented in the Archdioceses of Chicago, Milwaukee, St. Paul-Minneapolis, Seattle and the Dioceses of Bismarck, Boise, Crookston, Duluth, Fargo, New Ulm, Phoenix, St. Cloud, Superior, Sioux Falls, and Winona.
St. Bede Priory (1948): 1190 Priory Rd., P.O. Box 66, Eau Claire, WI 54702. Tel: 715-834-3176. Sr. Margaret Michaud, O.S.B., Prioress; Sr. Lorayne Andre, O.S.B., Archivist.
Total number in community 50.
Properties owned and sponsored: *St. Bede Priory - Motherhouse St. Bede Retreat and Conference Center*.
Represented in the Archdioceses of San Antonio and St. Paul-Minneapolis and the Dioceses of La Crosse and Springfield-Cape Girardeau. Also in Jamaica.
Sisters of the Order of St. Benedict O.S.B. (1874): *St. Mary Monastery*, Nauvoo, IL 62354. Tel: 217-453-2227. Sr. Ruth Ksycki, O.S.B., Prioress; Sr. Antoinette Fineran, Archivist.
Total number in community 71.
Ministry in the field of Religious and Academic Education; Pastoral Care; Parish Ministry.
Represented in the Dioceses of Davenport, Gary, and Peoria.
Benedictine Sisters of the Annunciation, BVM (1947): *Annunciation Priory*, 7520 University Dr., Bismarck, ND 58504-9653. Tel: 701-255-1520. Sr. Susan Berger, O.S.B., Prioress.
Professed Sisters 98.
Ministry in Hospitals; Parish Ministry and Catechetical Work; Education and Health Care.
Represented in the Dioceses of Bismarck and Fargo.
Sisters of St. Benedict (1948): *St. Paul's Monastery*, 2675 Larpenteur Ave. E., St. Paul, MN 55109. Tel: 612-777-8181; Fax: 612-777-4442. Sr. Marie Fujan, O.S.B., Prioress.
Professed Sisters 89.
Sisters serve and staff: School on all levels; Hospitals; Homes for the Aged; Business, Child Care; Retreat Center; Parish Ministry; Social Service and various other apostolic work.
Represented in the Archdiocese of St. Paul-Minneapolis and the Dioceses of Great Falls, and Jacksonville.
Sisters of St. Benedict O.S.B. (1952): *St. Placid Priory*, 500 College St., N.E., Lacey, WA 98516-5338. Tel: 360-438-1771. Sr. Sharon McDonald, O.S.B., Prioress.
Professed Sisters 24.
Sisters serve in the field of Education;: Spirituality Centers.
Represented in the Archdiocese of Seattle.

[0233] (O.S.B.)—BENEDICTINE NUNS
Subiaco Congregation

St. Scholastica Priory: *Benedictine Nuns (Cloistered)*, Box 606, 271 N. Main St., Petersham, MA 01366-0606. Tel: 508-724-3213; Fax: 508-724-3574. Very Rev. Mother Mary Clare Vincent, O.S.B., Prioress; Sr. Mary Frances Wynn, O.S.B., Sub-Prioress.
Nuns in Solemn vows 10; Simple vows 1; Novices 1; Claustral Oblates 1.

[0235] (O.S.B.Cam.)—CAMALDOLESE BENEDICTINE SISTERS
Subiaco Congregation

First founded in Italy in the 11th century, affiliated with monastery in Rome founded in 1722; United States foundation in 1988.
Transfiguration Monastery: Camaldolese Benedictine Sisters, 701 NY Rte 79, Windsor, NY 13865. Tel: 607-655-2366. Sr. Donald Corcoran, O.S.B.Cam., Prioress.
Professed Nuns 4.
Monastic life and Benedictine hospitality.
Represented in the Diocese of Syracuse.

[0240] (O.S.B.)—OLIVETAN BENEDICTINE SISTERS D

Established in the Diocese of Little Rock in 1887.
Motherhouse and Novitiate (1887): *Holy Angels Convent*, P.O. Drawer 130, Jonesboro, AR 72403. Tel: 501-935-5810; Fax: 501-935-4210. Sr. M. Henrietta Hockle, O.S.B., Prioress.
Professed Sisters 55.
Sisters serve and staff: High Schools; Grammar Schools; Diocesan Office; CCD Centers & Parish Services.
Properties owned: *Little Angels Day Care Center*, Little Rock, AR; *Immaculate Heart Convent*, Pocahontas, AR; *St. Bernards Regional Medical Center*, Jonesboro, AR.
Represented in the Dioceses of Fort Worth and Little Rock.

[0250] (C.V.D.)—SISTERS OF BETHANY P

Founded in El Salvador in 1928.
General Motherhouse: *Instituto Bethania*, Santa Tecla, El Salvador, C.A.. Mother Dolores de Maria Zea, Mother foundrees; Madre Luz Elena Ordonez, Supr. Gen.
U.S. Address (1949): *Bethany House*, 850 N. Hobart Blvd., Los Angeles, CA 90029. Tel: 213-669-9411; 665-6937. Sr. Maria de Jesus Diaz, Superiora.
Professed Sisters 19.
Ministry in Social Service Centers; Parish Work.
Represented in the Archdiocese of Los Angeles.

[0260] (S.B.S.)—THE SISTERS OF THE BLESSED SACRAMENT FOR INDIANS AND COLORED PEOPLE P

Founded in the United States in 1891.
General Motherhouse: St. Elizabeth's Convent, Bensalem, PA 19020-8502. Tel: 215-244-9900. Sr. Monica Loughlin, Pres.
Professed Sisters 266.
Sisters serve and staff in: the field of Education on all levels; Catechetical Schools; Houses for Catechetical; Adult Education and Social Service; House of Prayer; Spiritual Center; Evangelization Center.
Properties owned: *St. Catherine Indian School*, Santa Fe, NM; *St. Michael Indian School*, St. Michael's, AZ; *Xavier Prep*, New Orleans, LA.
Represented in the Archdioceses of Atlanta, Boston, Chicago, Los Angeles, New Orleans, New York, Philadelphia and Santa Fe and the Dioceses of Camden, Gallup, Lafayette (LA), Palm Beach, Savannah and Tucson. Also in Haiti.

[0270] (C.B.S.)—CONGREGATION OF BON SECOURS P

Founded in France in 1824. First foundation in the United States in 1881.
Generalate: Maison Mere du Bon Secours, 18, rue N.D. des Champs, 75006 Paris, France. Sr. Justine Cyr, C.B.S., Supr. Gen.
United States Province: *Provincial House and Novitiate*, 1525 Marriottsville Rd., Marriottsville, MD 21104. Tel: 410-442-1333; Fax: 410-442-1394. Sr. Anne Marie Mack, Pres.
Total Sisters in U.S. Province 46.
Sisters own and operate: *Bon Secours Spiritual Center Bon Secours Health System, Inc.*
Represented in the Archdioceses of Baltimore, Detroit, Miami, Philadelphia and the Dioceses of Altoona-Johnstown, Charleston, Richmond, St. Petersburg and Venice.

[0280] (O.SS.S.)—THE BRIGITTINE SISTERS P

Founded in Sweden in 14th century.
Motherhouse: Rome, Italy.
Convent and Novitiate (1957): *Convent of St. Birgitta*, Vikingsborg, 4 Runkenhage Rd., Darien, CT 06820. Tel: 203-655-1068. Sr. M. Sabina Kavanadi, O.SS.S., Supr. Monastic tradition, more contemplative than active
Legal Title: *Order of the Most Holy Savior of St. Bridget.*
Professed Sisters 9.
Represented in the Diocese of Bridgeport.

[0300] (O.CARM.)—CALCED CARMELITES P

Carmelite Nuns of the Ancient Observance, Strictly Cloistered, belonging to the Second Order of Carmel.
Founded in Naples, Italy in 1536. First foundation in the United States in 1931.
Carmelite Monastery of St. Therese: *Little Flower of Jesus and St. M. Magdalen Di Pazzi*, St. Therese's Valley, 3551 Lanark Rd., Coopersburg, PA 18036-9324. Mother Joseph Marie, O.Carm., Prioress.
Professed Sisters 12.
Legal Title: *The Carmelite Sisters of St. Therese's Valley, Incorporated.*
Represented in the Dioceses of Allentown, Fargo, San Angelo and Superior.

[0315] (C.C.W.)—CARMELITE COMMUNITY OF THE WORD D

Motherhouse & Novitiate (1971): 1304 13th Ave., Altoona, PA 16601. Tel: 814-247-6362; Fax: 814-247-6362. Sr. Marilyn Welch, C.C.W., Gen. Admin.
Total number in the community 21.
Ministries in Diocesan Administration; the field of Religious and Academic Education at all levels; Pastoral Care to the Imprisoned, Institutionalized, Elderly, Mentally Handicapped, Family Life Support Groups and the Poor; Parish Ministry.
Represented in the Diocese of Altoona-Johnstown.

[0320] (O.CARM.)—CARMELITE NUNS OF THE ANCIENT OBSERVANCE P

Carmelite Nuns of the Ancient Observance: Strictly Cloistered, belonging to the Second Order of Carmel Founded in Guelder, Holland, in 1453. First Foundation in the United States in 1930.
Carmel Of Mary (1954): 17765 78th St., S.E., Wahpeton, ND 58075. Tel: 701-642-2360. Mother Margaret Mary of the Sacred Heart, O.Carm., Prioress.
Total number in community 16.
Represented in the Diocese of Fargo.
Monastery of Our Lady of Grace (1989): 1 Saint Joseph Place, San Angelo, TX 76905. Tel: 915-651-4959.
Professed Sisters 5; Novices 1; Postulants 1.
Represented in the Diocese of San Angelo.
Carmel Of The Sacred Heart (1963): 430 Laurel Ave., Hudson, WI 54016. Tel: 715-386-2156. Sr. Gemma Angelo, O.Carm., Prioress; Sr. Lucia LaMontagne, O.Carm., Archivist.
Professed Sisters 6.
Legal Title: *Carmelite Nuns of the Diocese of Superior, Inc.*
Represented in the Diocese of Superior.

[0330] (O.CARM.)—CARMELITE SISTERS FOR THE AGED AND INFIRM P

Founded in 1929 in New York.
Foundress: Mother M. Angeline Teresa, O.Carm.
Motherhouse and Novitiate: *St. Teresa's Motherhouse and Novitiate*, 600 Woods Rd., Avila on the Hudson, Germantown, NY 12526. Mother Mary Suzanne, O.Carm., Supr. Gen.
Professed Sisters 270.
Legal Holdings: *St. Patrick Home*, Bronx, NY; *Sacred Heart Manor*, Philadelphia, PA; *Villa Teresa*, Harrisburg, PA; *St. Raphael Home*, Columbus, OH; *St. Rita's Home*, Columbus, OH; *St. Margaret's Hall*, Cincinnati, OH; *Carmel Manor*, Fort Thomas, KY; *Kahl Home for the Aged*, Davenport, IA; *St. Patrick's Manor*, Framingham, MA; *Marian Manor*,

Boston, MA; *St. Patrick's Residence*, Naperville, IL; *Lourdes - Noreen McKeen Residence*, West Palm Beach, FL; *Our Lady's Manor*, Dublin, Ireland.

Represented in the Archdioceses of Boston, Cincinnati, New York and Philadelphia and the Dioceses of Albany, Altoona-Johnstown, Bridgeport, Brooklyn, Fall River, Harrisburg, Manchester, Scranton and Syracuse.

[0340] (C.aCh.)—CARMELITE SISTERS OF CHARITY P

Founded in 1826.

Motherhouse: Vic, Spain.

Generalate: Carlo Zucchi, 12, 00165 Rome, Italy. Tel: 06-662-03-52.

Provincial/Formation House: *Carmelite Sisters of Charity*, 701 Beacon Rd., Silver Spring, MD 20903. Tel: 301-434-6344. Sr. Maria Pilar Chamorro, Prov.

Ministry in Health Clinics; Parishes; Higher Education; Immigrants, Hispanics and Homeless, Educational Centers.

Properties owned or sponsored: *Mount Carmel House Formation House.*

Represented in the Archdiocese of Washington and the Diocese of Brooklyn.

[0350] (O.CARM.)—CARMELITE SISTERS (CORPUS CHRISTI) P

First foundation in the United States in 1920.

General Motherhouse: Tunapuna, Trinidad, West Indies. Sr. Antoinette Dickie, O.Carm., Supr. Gen.

U.S. Address: *Mount Carmel Home-Keens' Memorial*, 412 W. 18th, Kearney, NE 68847. Tel: 308-237-2287. Sr. Emerentiana, O.Carm., Reg. Supr.

Professed Sisters 105.

Ministry in Home and foreign missions; Academic and Religious Education; Social Work.

Represented in the Dioceses of Grand Island and Providence.

[0360] (Carmel D.C.J.)—CARMELITE SISTERS OF THE DIVINE HEART OF JESUS P

Founded in Germany in 1891. First Convent in the United States in 1912.

General Motherhouse: Sittard, Netherlands. Mother M. Katharina, Supr. Gen.

Northern Province: 1230 Kavanaugh Pl., Milwaukee, WI 53213. Tel: 414-453-4040; Fax: 414-453-6503. Sr. M. Immaculata, Prov. Supr.

Central Province: 10341 Manchester Rd., St. Louis, MO 63122. Tel: 314-965-7616. Sr. M. Angelina, Prov. Supr.

South Western Province: 8585 La Mesa Blvd., La Mesa, CA 92041. Tel: 619-466-3116. Sr. M. Angela Therese, Prov. Supr.

Professed Sisters Worldwide 480; Total in U.S. 90; Novices 40; Postulants 16.

Sisters minister to Homes for Children 3; Homes for the Aged 9; Day Nurseries 4; Mission work in Africa, Nicaragua, Venezuela & Brazil.

Represented in the Archdioceses of Detroit, Milwaukee, St. Louis and San Antonio and the Dioceses of Gary, Grand Rapids, Jefferson City, Owensboro and San Diego.

[0370] (O.C.D.)—CARMELITE SISTERS OF THE MOST SACRED HEART OF LOS ANGELES P

General Motherhouse & Novitiate: *Carmelite Sisters of the Most Sacred Heart of Los Angeles*, 920 E. Alhambra Rd., Alhambra, CA 91801. Tel: 626-289-1353; Fax: 626-308-1913. Mother Vincent Marie, O.C.D., Supr. Gen.; Sr. Mary Consolata, O.C.D., Archivist.

Total number in community 129.

Legal Title: *Sacred Heart Retreat House Santa Teresita Hospital.*

Sisters serve and staff: Grammar Schools; General Hospital; Skilled Nursing Facility for the care of the Aged; Nursery Schools With Day Care Centers and Kindergarten; Retreat House; Directors of Religious Education; Ministry to elderly, sick and convalescents.

Represented in the Archdioceses of Los Angeles and Miami and the Dioceses of Cleveland and Tucson.

[0380] (C.S.T.)—CARMELITE SISTERS OF ST. THERESE OF THE INFANT JESUS D

Founded in the United States in 1917 at Bentley, OK.

General Motherhouse: *Villa Teresa*, 1300 Classen Dr., Oklahoma City, OK 73103-2447. Tel: 405-232-7926. Sr. Immaculata Commet, C.S.T., Gen. Supr.

Legal Title: *Carmelite Sisters of St. Therese of the Infant Jesus Motherhouse.*

Properties owned and sponsored: *Villa Teresa School*, Oklahoma City, OK; *Villa Teresa Moore*, Oklahoma City, OK.

Total number in community 28.

Ministry in the field of Academic Education; Religious Education and Parish Ministry.

Represented in the Archdiocese of Oklahoma City.

[0390] (C.M.S.T.)—MISSIONARY CARMELITES OF ST. TERESA P

Founded in Mexico City in 1903.

General Motherhouse: Fresno 150, 06400. Mexico, D.F.. Mother Carmen Margarita Pratt, Supr. Gen.

U.S. Holy Family Province (1983): 9548 Deer Trail Dr., Houston, TX 77038. Tel: 281-445-5520; Fax: 281-445-5748. Sr. Victoria Alvarez, Prov. Supr.

Professed Sisters 66.

Ministry in Pastoral; Hospital Chaplaincy; Domestic and Retreats.

Represented in the Archdioceses of Los Angeles, St. Louis, Oklahoma City and the Dioceses of Corpus Christi, Galveston-Houston, and Little Rock.

[0400] (O.CARM.)—CONGREGATION OF OUR LADY OF MOUNT CARMEL P

Founded in France in 1824. First foundation in the United States in 1833.

Generalate: P.O. Box 476, Lacombe, LA 70445. Sr. Rose Marie Penouilh, O.Carm., Pres.; Sr. Therese Gregoire, O.Carm., Archivist; Sr. M. Hyacinth Breaux, O.Carm., Asst. Archivist; Sr. Andree Marie Bindewald, O.Carm., Devel. Dir.

Professed Sisters 106.

Ministry in the field of Education on all levels; Hospitals; Social Service; Religious Education; Pastoral Ministry and Retreat Work.

Represented in the Archdiocese of New Orleans, Washington and the Diocese of Houma-Thibodaux, Joliet, and Lafayette (LA). Also in the Philippines.

[0410] (O.CARM.)—INSTITUTE OF THE SISTERS OF OUR LADY OF MOUNT CARMEL P

(Istituto delle Suore di Nostra Signora del Carmelo)

Founded in Italy in 1854, First foundation in the United States, 1947.

General Motherhouse: Istituto di Nostra Signora del Carmelo, Via dei Baglioni 10, Roma, Italy.

U.S. Headquarters: *Carmelite Sisters*, 5 Wheatland St., Peabody, MA 01960. Tel: 508-531-4733. Sr. Benedetta Zaccardi, Supr.

Professed Sisters 7.

Ministry in Holy Childhood Nursery and Kindergarten.

Represented in the Archdioceses of Boston and Washington.

[0420] (O.C.D.)—DISCALCED CARMELITE NUNS P

Founded in Spain in 1562. First foundation in the United States in 1790 in Charles County, Maryland; later this monastery was moved to Baltimore.

The Monasteries listed here are strictly contemplative and belong to the Order of Discalced Carmelites.

Carmelite Monastery (1790): 1318 Dulaney Valley Rd., Towson, Baltimore, MD 21286-1399. Tel: 410-823-7415. Sr. Veronica Emmick, O.C.D., Prioress; Sr. Constance FitzGerald, O.C.D., Community Archivist.

Professed Sisters 16.

Legal Title: *Carmelite Sisters of Baltimore.*

Carmel of St. Joseph (1863): 9150 Clayton Rd., Ladue, St. Louis County, MO 63124-1898. Tel: 314-993-6899; Fax: 314-993-5039. Mother Mary Joseph of Divine Providence, O.C.D., Prioress.

Professed Cloistered Nuns 8; Professed Extern sisters 1.

Monastery of St. Joseph and St. Teresa (1877): *Discalced Carmelite Nuns*, 73530 River Rd., Covington, LA 70435-2206. Carmelite Nuns, Discalced (O.C.D.; Mother Mary Alice Grace, O.C.D., Prioress.

Total number in community 9.

Discalced Carmelite Monastery (1890): 61 Mt. Pleasant Ave., Boston, MA 02119. Tel: 617-442-1411; Fax: 617-442-0203. Sr. Mary Teresa Wisniewski, O.C.D., Prioress.

Total number in community 12.

Carmelite Monastery (1902): 66th Ave. and Old York Rd. (Oak Lane), Philadelphia, PA 19126. Tel: 215-424-6143; Fax: 215-424-6143-5*. Mother Pia of Jesus Crucified, O.C.D., Prioress.

Professed Nuns 9.

Monastery of Our Lady of Mt. Carmel (1907): 745 St. John's Pl., Brooklyn, NY 11216. Mother Josefa Marie, Prioress.

Carmelite Monastery of the Infant Jesus (1908): 1000 Lincoln St., Santa Clara, CA 95050. Tel: 408-296-8412. Sr. Emmanuel of Bethlehem, O.C.D., Prioress.

Sisters Solemn Vows 16; Novices 1.

St. Joseph's Carmelite Monastery (1908): 2215 N.E. 147th, Shoreline, WA 98155. Sr. Michael Marie, Prioress.

Professed Sisters 9; Novices 1.

Legal Title: *Carmelite Monastery of Seattle.*

Carmel of the Queen of Heaven (Formerly known as Regina Coeli Monastery) (1911): 17937 250th St., Eldridge, IA 52748. Tel: 319-285-8387. Sr. Mary Joan Loebig, O.C.D., Prioress.

Professed Sisters 12; Novices 2; Postulants 1.

Discalced Carmelite Nuns (1930): *Monastery of Mary Immaculate and St. Joseph*, 1740 Newburg Rd., Louisville, KY 40205. Tel: 502-451-6796. Mother Francis, Prioress; Sr. Clare, Archivist.

Professed Sisters 11; Novices 1; Postulants 2.

Legal Title: *Carmelite Monastery of Louisville, Inc.*

Order of Discalced Carmelites O.C.D. (1913): *Carmel of St. Teresa of Los Angeles, Inc.*, 215 E. Alhambra Rd., Alhambra, CA 91801. Tel: 626-282-2387; Fax: 626-282-2053. Mother Maria, O.C.D., Prioress.

Total number in community 15.

Carmelite Monastery (1916): 4300 Mount Carmel Dr., N.E., Ada (Parnell), MI 49301. Mother Elizabeth Ann, O.C.D., Prioress.

Cloistered Nuns 20; Externs 3.

Discalced Carmelite Nuns (1920): *Carmelite Monastery*, 139 DePuyster Ave., Beacon, NY 12508-3540. Tel: 914-831-5572. Sr. Marjorie Robinson, Prioress.

Total number in community 10.

Discalced Carmelite Monastery of St. Therese of the Child Jesus (1920): 75 Carmel Rd., Buffalo, NY 14214. Tel: 716-837-6499. Mother Miriam of Jesus, O.C.D., Prioress.

Cloistered Professed Sisters 15; Extern Professed Sisters 3; Novices 1.

Monastery of Discalced Carmelites (1922): 2500 Cold Spring Rd., Indianapolis, IN 46222. Tel: 317-926-5654. Sr. Joanne DeWald, O.C.D., Prioress.

Legal Title: *Monastery of the Resurrection, Discalced Carmelites Sisters of Our Lady of Mount Carmel Carmelite Monastery.*

Contemplative Professed Nuns 14; Novices 3.

Carmel of the Holy Family (1923): 3176 Fairmount Blvd., Cleveland Heights, OH 44118-4199. Tel: 216-321-6568. Sr. Mary Lavin, O.C.D., Prioress.

Contemplative Professed Nuns 16; Vowed Religious Transfer Sisters in Formation 2.

Discalced Carmelite Nuns of Schenectady, NY, Inc. (1923): *Monastery of St. Teresa of Jesus*, 428 Duane Ave., Schenectady, NY 12304. Mother Mary St. John of the Cross, O.C.D., Prioress.

Professed Nuns 12; Postulants 1.

Discalced Carmelites of the Order of Our Lady of Mount Carmel O.C.D. (1925): *Monastery of Our Lady and St. Therese*, 27601 Hwy. 1, Carmel, CA 93923. Tel: 408-624-3043; Fax: 408-624-5495. Mother Francisca of the Holy Spirit, O.C.D., Prioress.

Professed Sisters 14.

Legal Title: *Carmelite Monastery of Carmel, California, Inc.*

Discalced Carmelites O.C.D. (1926): *Monastery of the Most Blessed Virgin Mary of Mount Carmel*, 189 Madison Ave., Morristown, NJ 07960. Mother Mary Michael, O.C.D., Prioress.

Professed Sisters 7; Novices 1.

Order of Discalced Carmelites O.C.D. (1926): *Carmelite Monastery of the Trinity*, 5158 Hawley Blvd., San Diego, CA 92116. Tel: 619-280-5424. Sr. Yvonne Hanke, O.C.D., Prioress.

Professed Nuns 14.

Monastery of St. Therese of the Child Jesus (1926): 35750 Moravian Dr., Clinton Township, MI 48035-2138. Tel: 810-790-7255. Mother Therese Marie, O.C.D., Prioress.

Professed Nuns 8; Professed Extern Sisters 2; Extern Novice 1.

Carmel of St. Therese of Lisieux, Inc. (1927): *Discalced Carmelite Nuns*, P.O. Box 57, Loretto, PA 15940-0057. Tel: 814-472-8620. Mother John of the Cross, O.C.D., Prioress.

Professed Nuns 10; Postulants 1; Extern Sisters 1.

Discalced Carmelite Nuns O.C.D. (1928): *Carmelite Monastery of Cristo Rey*, 721 Parker Ave., San Francisco, CA 94118-4297. Mother Mary Joseph, O.C.D., Prioress; Sr. Maria de la Immaculada, O.C.D., Archivist.

Total number in community 16.

Monastery of Discalced Carmelites (1928): 600 Flowers Ave., Dallas, TX 75211. Reverend Mother Prioress, O.C.D.

Professed Nuns 9.

Discalced Carmelite Nuns (1930): *Monastery of Our Lady and St. Joseph*, 1931 W. Jefferson Rd.,

Pittsford, NY 14534. Tel: 716-427-7094. Mother Miriam of the Angels, Prioress.
Professed Nuns with Solemn Vows 8; Professed Extern Sisters 1; Novices 1.
Legal Title: *Carmelite Monastery of Rochester.*
Monastery of Discalced Carmelites O.C.D. (1930): *Monastery of Our Lady of Mount Carmel and St. Therese of the Child Jesus,* Watson Ave. at Nayatt Rd., Barrington, RI 02806. Tel: 401-245-3421. Sr. Genevieve Lawler, O.C.D., Prioress.
Total number in community 14.
Discalced Carmelite Nuns O.C.D. (1934): *Monastery of the Infant Jesus of Prague and Our Lady of Guadalupe,* 6301 Culebra & St. Joseph Way, San Antonio, TX 78238-4909. Tel: 210-680-1834. Mother Therese Leonard, Prioress.
Total number in community 10.
Carmel of the Holy Family and St. Therese (1935): 6981 Teresian Way, P.O. Box 1720, Georgetown, CA 95634. Tel: 916-333-1617. Mother Christine, Prioress.
Total number in community 14.
Discalced Carmelite Nuns O.C.D. (1936): *Monastery of Mary, Mother of Grace,* 1250 Carmel Ave., Lafayette, LA 70501. Tel: 318-232-4651. Mother Mary John Billeaud, O.C.D., Prioress.
Total number in community 21.
Discalced Carmelite Nuns O.C.D. (1939): *Carmel of St. Joseph,* 20,000 N. County Line Rd., Piedmont, OK 73078. Sr. Therese Ranallo, O.C.D., Prioress.
Total number in community 13.
Discalced Carmelite Nuns of Milwaukee O.C.D. (1940): *Carmel of the Mother of God,* W267 N2517, Meadowbrook Rd., Pewaukee, WI 53072. Tel: 414-691-0336. Sr. Mary Agnes Kramer, Prioress.
Total number in community 9.
Carmelite Monastery (1943): 716 Dauphin Island Pkwy., Mobile, AL 36606; Fax: 334-471-3991. Mother Agnes of the Infant Jesus, Prioress.
Solemnly Professed Nuns 6.
Discalced Carmelite Monastery (1945): 49 Mount Carmel Rd., Santa Fe, NM 87501-4597. Tel: 505-983-7232. Mother Rose Teresa, O.C.D., Prioress.
Total number in community 14.
Discalced Carmelite Monastery (1946): 275 Pleasant St., Concord, NH 03301-2590. Tel: 603-225-5791. Sr. Thomas Aquinas, O.C.D., Prioress.
Solemnly Professed Nuns 11.
Monastery of Discalced Carmelites O.C.D. (1947): *Monastery of St. Joseph,* Terre Haute, IN, 59 Allendale, Terre Haute, IN 47802-4751. Tel: 812-299-1410; Fax: 812-299-5820. Mother Joseph McKenzie, O.C.D., Prioress.
Professed Nuns 13; Postulants 1.
Discalced Carmelite Nuns of Colorado, Inc. (1948): *Carmel of Holy Spirit,* 6138 S. Gallup St., Littleton, CO 80120-2702. Tel: 303-798-4176. Mother Judith of the Immaculate Heart, D.C., Prioress.
Professed Nuns 9.
Carmel of St. Joseph of Santa Ynez Valley, Inc. O.C.D. (1949): 1883 Ringsted Dr., P.O. Box 379, Solvang, CA 93463. Tel: 805-686-4292. Mother Mary Veronica Arakaki, O.C.D., Prioress.
Professed Sisters 11.
Order of Discalced Carmelites O.C.D. (1949): *Carmel of Mary Immaculate and St. Mary Magdalen,* P.O. Box 785, Flemington, NJ 08822. Mother Anne of Christ, O.C.D., Prioress.
Total in community 14.
Discalced Carmelite Nuns O.C.D. (1950): *Monastery of the Infant Jesus of Prague,* 3501 Silver Lake Rd., Traverse City, MI 49684-8949. Tel: 616-946-4960. Mother Teresa Margaret, O.C.D., Prioress and Archivist.
Total number in community 10.
Carmelite Monastery of Christ, the Exiled King (1950): 68 Rincon Rd., Kensington, CA 94707. Sr. Mary Magdalen, Prioress.
Professed Nuns of Solemn Vows 6.
Discalced Carmelite Nuns O.C.D. (1951): *Monastery of the Holy Cross,* Hwy. U.S. 2, P.O. Box 397, Iron Mountain, MI 49801. Tel: 906-774-0561. Mother Pauline Marie of Jesus Crucified, O.C.D., Prioress.
Total number in community 18.
Discalced Carmelite Nuns O.C.D. (1950): *Monastery of the Immaculate Heart of Mary,* R.R. 2, Box 4784, Barre, VT 05641. Tel: 802-476-8362. Sr. Jeanne Gonyon, O.C.D., Prioress.
Total number in community 10.
Discalced Carmelite Nuns O.C.D. (1950): *Monastery of St. Teresa of Jesus,* 7201 W. 32nd St., Little Rock, AR 72204-4716. Tel: 501-565-5121. Sr. Therese Stewart, O.C.D., Prioress.
Professed Sisters 13.
Legal Title: *Discalced Carmelite Nuns of Little Rock.*
Discalced Carmelite Nuns O.C.D. (1951): *Monastery of Our Lady of Mount Carmel and The Little Flower,* 2155 Terry Rd., Jackson, MS 39204. Tel: 601-373-1460. Sr. Dona Marie Degnan, O.C.D., Prioress.
Professed Nuns 3; Temporary Professed 1.
Carmel of the Immaculate Heart of Mary (1952): 5714 Holladay Blvd., Salt Lake City, UT 84121-1599. Tel: 801-277-6075. Mother Margaret Mary Miller, O.C.D., Prioress; Sr. Mary Ann Krajicek, O.C.D., Archivist.
Solemn Vows 6; Finally Professed Externs 1.
Discalced Carmelite Nuns (1952): *St. Joseph's Monastery,* 68 Franklin Ave., Saranac Lake, NY 12983. Tel: 518-891-0655. Sr. Marie Gertrude Haughney, O.C.D., Prioress.
Total number in community 11.
Discalced Carmelite Nuns of St. Paul (1952): *Carmel of Our Lady of Divine Providence,* 8251 De Montreville Trail N., Lake Elmo, MN 55042-9547. Tel: 612-777-3882. Sr. Paula of the Eucharist, O.C.D., Prioress.
Professed Sisters 8; Novices 2; Postulants 1.
Discalced Carmelite Nuns O.C.D. (1953): 70 Monastery Rd., Elysburg, PA 17824-9697. Tel: 717-672-2935. Sr. Christine O'Brien, O.C.D., Prioress; Sr. Joan Lundy, O.C.D., Archivist.
Professed Sisters 18.
Discalced Carmelite Nuns O.C.D. (1954): *Monastery of Our Lady of the Mountains,* 1950 La Fond Dr., Reno, NV 89509-3099. Tel: 702-323-3236; Fax: 702-322-1532. Sr. Ann Weber, O.C.D., Prioress.
Professed Nuns 14.
Carmel of Maria Regina O.C.D. (1957): 87609 Green Hill Rd., Eugene, OR 97402. Tel: 541-345-8649. Mother Elizabeth Mary, O.C.D., Prioress; Sr. Maria Teresa, O.C.D., Community Archivist.
Total number in community 11.
Monastery of the Holy Family (1957): 510 E. Gore Rd., Erie, PA 16509. Mother Emmanuel of the Mother of God, Prioress.
Professed Sisters 6; Novices 2; Postulants 1.
Discalced Carmelite Nuns (1958): *Coffee Bluff,* 11 W. Back St., Savannah, GA 31419-3219. Tel: 912-925-8505. Sr. Angela Collins, O.C.D., Prioress.
Total number in community 6.
Monastery of the Most Holy Trinity (1958): 5801 Mt. Carmel Dr., Arlington, TX 76017. Tel: 817-468-1781. Mother Anne Teresa of Jesus Kulinski, O.C.D., Prioress.
Total number in community 11.
Discalced Carmelite Nuns O.C.D. (1958): *Carmel of the Most Holy Trinity,* 1100 Parthenon Pl., Roman Forest, New Caney, TX 77357. Sr. Angel Teresa Sweeney, O.C.D., Prioress; Sr. Mary Ann Harrison, O.C.D., 1st Council Sister.
Total number in community 12.
Monastery of Discalced Carmelites (1959): River Rd. and Central, Des Plaines, IL 60016. Tel: 708-298-4241. Mother Catherine of the Mother of God, Prioress.
Total number in community 18.
Order of Discalced Carmelites O.C.D. (1958): *Carmel of St. Therese,* 15 Mt. Carmel Rd., Danvers, MA 01923-3796. Tel: 978-774-3008. Mother Michael of Christ the King, O.C.D., Prioress.
Total number in community 17.
Legal Title: *Discalced Carmelite Nuns of Danvers.*
Discalced Carmelite Nuns O.C.D. (1960): *Monastery of The Sacred Heart and St. Joseph,* 2201 W. Main St., Jefferson City, MO 65109. Tel: 573-636-3364. Mother Therese, O.C.D., Prioress.
Solemnly Professed Nuns 8; Temporary Professed Nuns 1.
Carmel of the Assumption (1961): R.D. 6, Box 28, Center Dr., Latrobe, PA 15650. Tel: 412-539-1056. Sr. Barbara Sitter, O.C.D., Prioress.
Professed Sisters 14.
Discalced Carmelite Nuns, Inc. (1962): *Monastery of the Discalced Carmelite Nuns,* 2901 S. Cecelia St., Sioux City, IA 51106-3299. Tel: 712-276-1680. Mother Therese of the Spirit of Love, O.C.D., Prioress.
Total number in community 15.
Carmelite Monastery of the Mother of God (1965): 530 Blackstone Dr., San Rafael, CA 94903. Tel: 479-6872; Fax: 415-491-4964. Mother Anna Marie, O.C.D., Prioress.
Total number in community 7.
Discalced Carmelite Nuns O.C.D. (1965): *Carmel of St. Anne,* 424 E. Monastery St., Springfield, MO 65807. Tel: 417-881-2115. Mother Mary Charles, O.C.D., Prioress.
Total number in community 6.
Carmel of the Holy Trinity: 6301 Pali Hwy., Kaneohi, HI 96744. Tel: 808-261-6542. Mother Mary Agnes Tse, O.C.D., Prioress.
Total number in community 8.
Discalced Carmelite Nuns of the Byzantine Rite (1980): *Holy Annunication Monastery,* R.R. No. 1, Box 1336, Sugarloaf, PA 18249. Tel: 717-788-1205; Fax: 717-788-3329. Mother Marija of the Holy Spirit, O.C.D., Prioress.
Professed Nuns 11; Novices 1.
Represented in the Diocese of Passaic.
Carmel of Port Tobacco: 4035-A Mt. Carmel Rd., Port Tobacco, MD 20646-9611.
Professed 9; Simple Professed 1.

[0430] (B.V.M.)—SISTERS OF CHARITY OF THE BLESSED VIRGIN MARY P

Founded in America in 1833.
BVM Center: *Mount Carmel,* 1100 Camel Dr., Dubuque, IA 52003. Tel: 319-588-2351; Fax: 319-588-4832. Sr. Dolores Marie McHugh, B.V.M., Pres.
Total number in Congregation 936.
Sisters staff and serve in: the field of Academic Education on all levels; Health Care-Aging; Religious Education; Chaplaincies; Pastoral Ministry; Diocesan School Offices; Diocesan Services-Administration; Social Work; Homeless Shelters; Aids Ministry; Secretarial; Social Justice; Adult Day Care; Extended Day Care.
Represented in the Archdioceses of Atlants, Chicago, Denver, Dubuque, Indianapolis, Los Angeles, Omaha, Miami, Milwaukee, Mobile, Portland (OR), St. Louis, St. Paul-Minneapolis, San Francisco, Santa Fe, Seattle and the Dioceses of Belleville, Brooklyn, Biloxi, Davenport, Des Moines, Fort Wayne-South Bend, Fresno, Green Bay, Helena, Honolulu, Jackson, Joliet, Kansas City-St. Joseph, Knoxville, Lafayette, Lexington, Lincoln, Memphis, Oakland, Orange, Orlando, Peoria, Pensacola-Tallahassee, Phoenix, Reno-Las Vegas, Rockford, Rockville Centre, San Diego, San Bernardino, San Jose, Santa Rosa, Sioux City, Springfield-Cape Girardeau, Springfield (IL), Stockton, Tucson, Venice, Wichita and Winona. Also in Africa,Ecuador, and Guatemala.

[0440] (S.C.)—SISTERS OF CHARITY OF CINCINNATI, OHIO P

Founded by Saint Elizabeth Ann Seton, Emmitsburg, MD 1809. The Cincinnati Community became independent in 1852, Papal approval in 1939.
General Motherhouse (1852): Mount St. Joseph, Mt. Joseph, OH 45051. Tel: 513-347-5201; Fax: 513-347-5228. Sr. Mary Ellen Murphy, Pres.
Legal Title: *Sisters of Charity of Cincinnati-Charitable Trust,* Cincinnati, OH.
Professed Sisters 666.
Sisters serve and staff: Colleges; Secondary and Elementary Schools; Parishes; Healthcare Facilities and School of Nursing; Foreign Missions; Home for Profoundly Retarded Children; Senior Care Services; Social Services; Congregational Services.
Represented in the Archdioceses of Boston, Chicago, Cincinnati, Denver, Detroit, Indianapolis, Louisville, Newark, New Orleans, New York, St. Louis, San Francisco, Santa Fe, Washington and the Dioceses of Brownsville, Cleveland, Colorado Springs, Columbus, Covington, El Paso, Fort Wayne-South Bend, Galveston-Houston, Gaylord, Grand Rapids, Helena, Knoxville, Las Cruces, Las Vegas, Lansing, Memphis, Oakland, Orlando, Palm Beach, Phoenix, Pueblo, Rapid City, Raleigh, Reno, Savannah, Saginaw, St. Petersburg, Spokane, Toledo, and Wichita. Also in Armenia, Poland, Ecuador and Gautemala.

[0450] (S.C.I.C.)—SISTERS OF CHARITY OF THE IMMACULATE CONCEPTION OF IVREA P

Founded in Italy in the 18th Century. First Foundation in the United States in 1961.
General Motherhouse: della Renella 85, Rome, Italy. Tel: 396-5818145. Sr. Grazia Raffaella Rossi, Supr. Gen.
Total number in Congregation 1,387.
U.S. Foundation (1961): *Immaculate Virgin of Miracles Convent,* R.D. 2, Box 348, Mount Pleasant, PA 15666. Tel: 412-887-6753. Sr. Gemma Mancini, Reg. Supr. Tel: 412-887-0220.
Professed Sisters in the U.S.A. 13.
Sisters serve and staff: Kindergarten and Elementary Schools; Parish Services; Religious Education; Pastoral Ministry.
Properties owned: *Verna Montessori Children's House & Elememtary School; Immaculate Virgin of Miracles Convent,* Mt. Pleasant, PA.
Represented in the Diocese of Greensburg and Norwich.

[0460] (C.C.V.I.)—CONGREGATION OF THE SISTERS OF CHARITY OF THE INCARNATE WORD P

Founded in 1869 at San Antonio, Texas.
Generalate: 4503 Broadway, San Antonio, TX 78209-6209. Tel: 210-828-2224. Sr. Carol Ann Jokerst, Gen. Supr.

U.S. Motherhouse, Provincial and Retirement Center: 4707 Broadway, San Antonio, TX 78209-6200. Tel: 210-829-0987; Fax: 210-828-9741. Sr. Bridgid Marie Clarke, Prov. Supr.
Universal Total in Congregation 631; U.S. Province 386.
Properties owned and sponsored: Universities 1; Highschools 2; Hospitals 6; Temporary shelter for homeless women & children 1; Retirement Center 1.
Ministry in the field of Academic Education at all levels; Pastoral Ministry; Nursing Homes; Diocesan Offices; Social Service Agencies; Health Service Agencies.
Represented in the Archdioceses of Boston, Chicago, New Orleans, St. Louis, San Antonio, San Francisco and Santa Fe and the Dioceses of Amarillo, Austin, Brownsville, Corpus Christi, Fort Worth, Galveston-Houston, Jackson, Jefferson City, Lubbock, Springfield-Cape Girardeau, San Angelo, Spokane, Tucson, Tyler and Victoria. Also in Mexico, Peru, Guatemala and El Salvador.

[0470] (C.C.V.I.)—CONGREGATION OF THE SISTERS OF CHARITY OF THE INCARNATE WORD, HOUSTON, TEXAS P

Founded in the United States in 1866, St. Mary's Infirmary, Galveston, Texas.
Motherhouse: *Villa de Matel*, 6510 Lawndale Ave., P.O. Box 230969, Houston, TX 77223-0969. Tel: 713-928-6053; Fax: 713-928-8148. Sr. Elizabeth Ann Hayes, Gen. Supr.
Total number in congregation 244.
Legal Title: *Incarnate Word Charitable Trust.*
Sisters serve and staff: Hospitals; Homes for Aged; Elementary Schools; Social Services.
Represented in the Archdiocese of Los Angeles and the Dioceses of Alexandria, Beaumont, Brownsville, Galveston-Houston, Lake Charles, Little Rock, Salt Lake City, San Bernardino, Shreveport, Tulsa and Tyler. Also in Ireland, Guatemala, San Salvador and Kenya.

[0480] (S.C.L.)—SISTERS OF CHARITY OF LEAVENWORTH, KANSAS P

Founded in the United States in 1858.
Community Offices and Motherhouse: 4200 S. Fourth St., Leavenworth, KS 66048-5054. Tel: 913-758-6501; Fax: 912-682-2128. Sr. Mary Kathleen Stefani, Community Dir.; Sr. Helen Forge, Archivist.
Total number in community 447.
Properties owned and sponsored: *Saint Mary College*, Leavenworth, KS; *Residential and Day Treatment Centers for Children: Mount St. Vincent Home*, Denver, CO; *Saint John's Child Study Center*, Santa Monica, CA; Health Facilities: *Sisters of Charity of Leavenworth Health Services Corporation*, Cantwell Hall, Leavenworth, KS; *Saint John's Hospital & Health Center*, Santa Monica, CA; *Saint Joseph Hospital*, Denver, CO; *St. Mary's Hospital & Medical Center*, Grand Junction, CO; *Saint John Hospital*, Leavenworth, KS; *St. Francis Hospital and Medical Center*, Topeka, KS; *Saint Vincent Hospital & Health Center*, Billings, MT; *St. James Community Hospital*, Butte, MT; *Marian Clinic*, Topeka, KS; *Marillac Clinic*, Grand Junction, CO; *Providence Medical Center*, Kansas City, KS; *Caritas Clinic, Inc.*, Kansas City, KS.
Sisters serving in Elementary, Secondary, and Higher Education: Nursing Education; Special Education; Religious Education; Ministry Training; Hospitals; Latin American Missions; Diocesan Offices; Parish Administration and Pastoral Ministry; Liturgy-Music Ministry; Campus Ministry; Spiritual Direction; Communications; Social Justice; Housing.
Ministries to AIDS Victims; Cross-culture; Elderly; Prisoners, Handicapped Adults and Youth; Health Service Agencies; Mental Health; Native Americans; and Social Service Agencies.
Represented in the Archdioceses of Denver, Kansas City in Kansas, Los Angeles, Oklahoma City, Omaha, Santa Fe, San Antonio, Washington and the Dioceses of Cheyenne, Gallup, Great Falls-Billings, Helena, Jefferson City, Kansas City-St. Joseph, Oakland, Orange, Pueblo, St. Cloud, San Angelo, Spokane, and Tucson. Also in Peru and Ecuador.

[0490] (S.G.M.)—SISTERS OF CHARITY OF MONTREAL (Grey Nuns) P

Founded in 1737 by Saint Marguerite d'Youville at Montreal, Canada. First foundation in the United States 1855.
Generalate: *General Administration*, 138 Rue Saint-Pierre, Montreal, Quebec H2Y 2L7. Canada. Tel: 514-842-9411. Bernadette Poirier, S.G.M., Supr. Gen.
St. Joseph Province - U.S.A.: *Provincial Administration*, 10 Pelham Rd., Lexington, MA 02173. Tel: 617-862-4700. Sr. June Ketterer, S.G.M., Prov. Supr.; Sr. Helene Georges, S.G.M., Contact Person - Formation Team.
Legal Title: *The Grey Nuns Charities, Inc.*
Total number in community 68.
Ministry in Hospitals; Schools of Nursing; Nursing Homes; Parish Ministry; Adult Day Health Care; Social Day Care; Social Justice; Pastoral Care; Foreign Missions; Housing for the Elderly & Handicapped; Nutrition Programs for Poor; Elder Health Center; Shelter for Homeless; Emergency Satellite Facilities.
Represented in the Archdiocese of Boston and the Dioceses of Manchester, Portland (ME) and Toledo. Also in Bogota, Colombia.

[0500] (S.C.N.)—SISTERS OF CHARITY OF NAZARETH P

Founded in the United States in 1812.
SCN Center: P.O. Box 172, Nazareth, KY 40048. Tel: 502-348-1555; Fax: 502-348-1502. Sr. Elizabeth Wendeln, S.C.N., Pres.
Legal Title: *Nazareth Literary & Benevolent Institution.*
Total number in Congregation 799.
Properties owned or sponsored: *Nazareth Hospital, Mokama, India Educational Facilities Spalding University*, Louisville, KY; *Presentation Academy*, Louisville, KY; *Our Lady of Nazareth Academy*, Wakefield, MA; *Nazareth Montessori Children's Center*. Retreat Facilities: *Catherine Spalding Center*, Nazareth, KY; *Bethany Spring*, New Haven, KY; *Camp Maria*, Leonardtown, MD. Facilities for the Elderly and Handicapped: *Nazareth Village I Nazareth Village II*, Nazareth, KY; *Nazareth Home*, Louisville, KY. Missions: SCN Missions.
Louisville Region: Regional Office, 676 Atwood, P.O. Box 17545, Louisville, KY 40217. Tel: 502-636-0411. Sr. Elizabeth Blandford, S.C.N., Reg. Rep.
Final professed sisters 252.
Sisters serve and staff the field of Academic Education on all levels: Special Educational Services; Social Services; Public Library; Counseling; Campus Ministry; Archdiocesan Offices; Health Care Institutions; Pastoral Ministry; Literacy Council and Retirement Center.
Represented in the Archdiocese of Louisville and the Diocese of Evansville.
Southern Region: 126 Suburban Ct., Lexington, KY 40503. Tel: 606-277-4744. Sr. Anne Rita Mauck, S.C.N., Reg. Rep.
Final professed sisters 273.
Sisters serve and staff in the field of Academic Education on all levels: Literacy Program; Parish Ministry; Diocesan Centers; Social Services; Retirement Centers; Retreat Centers; Peace & Justice Center; Department of Human Resources; Counseling; Health Care Agencies.
Represented in the Archdioceses of Chicago, Cincinnati, Indianapolis, Louisville and St. Louis and the Dioceses of Baton Rouge, Birmingham, Brownsville, Covington, Charleston, Jackson, Little Rock, Lexington, Memphis, Nashville, Owensboro, Palm Beach, St. Petersburg and San Jose. Also in Belize City and Independence, Belize.
Northern Region: *Regional House*, 169 Fenno St., Quincy, MA 02170. Tel: 617-479-4909. Sr. Gwen McMahon, S.C.N., Reg. Rep.
Final professed sisters 82.
Sisters serve and staff in the field of Academic Education on all levels: Social Services; Parish Ministry; Diocesan Center; Health Care Institutions; Retreat Centers; Retirement Centers and Seminary.
Represented in the Archdioceses of Boston, Philadelphia and Washington and the Dioceses of Arlington, Columbus, Richmond, Steubenville, Wheeling-Charleston and Youngstown.
India Region: *Regional House*, E. Boring Canal Rd., Post Box 219, Patna, Bihar 800-001. India. Tel: 011-91-612-2341-21. Sr. Bridget Kappalumackal, S.C.N., Prov.
Final professed sisters 149. Central Leadership Team:.
Final professed sisters 3.

[0510] (O.L.M.)—SISTERS OF CHARITY OF OUR LADY OF MERCY D

Founded in Charleston, South Carolina in 1829.
Generalate and Motherhouse: 424 Fort Johnson Rd. - P.O. Box 12410, Charleston, SC 29422. Tel: 803-795-6083; 795-2866. Sr. Anne Francis Campbell, O.L.M., Gen. Supr.
Total number in community 32.
Sisters serve and staff: Parishes; High School; Elementary Schools; Hospital; Social Services.
Legal Title: *The Sisters of Charity of Our Lady of Mercy Charitable Trust.*
Properties owned: *Motherhouse, May Forest*, Charleston, SC; *Our Lady of Mercy Convent*, Charleston, SC; *Our Lady of Mercy Community Outreach Services, Inc.*, Johns Island, SC.
Represented in the Diocese of Charleston.

[0520] (S.C.M.M.)—SISTERS OF CHARITY OF OUR LADY, MOTHER OF MERCY P

Founded in Holland 1832. First foundation in the United States in 1874.
General Motherhouse: Den Bosch, Netherlands.
Universal number in Congregation 1,406.
U.S. Provincial House: 520 Thompson Ave., East Haven, CT 06512. Tel: 203-469-7872. Sr. Mary Ellen Ryley, S.C.M.M., Prov.
Total number in community 21.

[0530] (S.C.M.C.)—SISTERS OF CHARITY OF OUR LADY, MOTHER OF THE CHURCH P

First foundation in the United States in 1970.
General Motherhouse: Baltic, CT 06330. Tel: 860-822-8241; Fax: 860-822-9842.
Mother M. Theresita, Supr. Gen.
Professed Sisters 78; Junior Professed 10; Novices 3; Postulants 1.
Properties owned, staffed or sponsored: High Schools 2; Middle School 1; Elementary Schools 9; Nursing Home 1; Home for Aged 3; Home for Dependent Children 1; Catechetical Schools 18; Housekeepers at Bishops' Residence 1; Shelter for the Homeless 1; Hispanic Ministry 1.
Represented in the Archdioceses of Hartford and the Dioceses of Manchester, Madison and Norwich.

[0540] (S.C.O.)—SISTERS OF CHARITY, OF OTTAWA (Grey Nuns of the Cross) P

Founded in Ottawa, Canada, in 1845. First foundation in the United States in 1857.
General Motherhouse: 9 Bruyere St., Ottawa, Ontario K1N 5C9, Canada. Mother Claire Malette, S.C.O., Gen. Supr.
Total number of Sisters in Congregation based in Ottawa 858.
American Province (1950): *St. Joseph*, 975 Varnum Ave., Lowell, MA 01854. Tel: 978-453-4993. Sr. Gabrielle L. Jean, Prov. Supr.; Sr. Jeannie Bernier, Archivist.
Professed U.S. Sisters 52.
Sisters staff: High Schools; Grammar Schools; CCD Parish Services; Health Care and Pastoral Ministries; Apostolate of Aging.
Properties owned: *D'Youville Manor*; *Bachand Hall*; *St. Joseph Residence*, Lowell, MA.
Legal Title: *Sisters of Charity of Ottawa.*
Represented in the Archdioceses of Boston and Newark.

[0560] (S.C.Q.)—SISTERS OF CHARITY OF QUEBEC (Grey Nuns) P

Founded in Quebec, Canada, in 1849. First foundation in the United States in 1890.
General Motherhouse: 2655 Le Pelletier St., Beauport, Quebec GIC 3X7, Canada. Tel: 418-628-8860, Sr. Denise Marcoux, Gen. Supr.
U.S. House (1908): *Franco - American School*, 357 Pawtuckert St., Lowell, MA 01854. Tel: 508-937-8672. Sr. Monique Morin, Supr.
U.S. House (1917): *Sacred Heart Nursing Home*, 359 Summer St., New Bedford, MA 02740. Tel: 508-996-6751. Sr. Blandine D'Amours, Supr.
Professed U.S. Sisters 13.
Sisters serve and staff: The field of education and care of the elderly; *Franco-American School*, Lowell, MA; *Sacred Heart Nursing Home*, New Bedford, MA.
Represented in the Archdioceses of Boston and the Diocese of Fall River.

[0570] (S.C.)—SISTERS OF CHARITY OF SEATON HALL, GREENSBURG, PENNSYLVANIA P

Foundation from Cincinnati, Ohio to Altoona, Pennsylvania in 1870.
Generalate: Mt. Thor Rd., Greensburg, PA 15601. Tel: 412-836-0406; Fax: 412-836-8280. Sr. Gertrude Foley, S.C., President; Sr. Mary Catherine Seli, S.C., Archivist.
Total number in the community 545.

Ministry in the field of Academic Education at all levels; Day Care Centers; Community Service Center; Adult Day Care Center; Special Education for Persons with Handicaps.
Properties owned: *Elizabeth Seaton Center,* Pittsburgh, PA; *Doran Hall,* Greensburg, PA.
Represented in the Archdioceses of Baltimore, Chicago, Cincinnati, Los Angeles, Santa Fe, and Washington and the Dioceses of oston and the Dioceses of Altoona-Johnstown, Brooklyn, Erie, Greensburg, Hartford, Orlando, Paterson, Phoenix, Pittsburgh, Steubenville, Tucson, and Wheeling-Charleston. Also in South Korea and Israel.

[0580] (C.S.A.)—SISTERS OF CHARITY OF ST. AGUSTINE D

Founded in Cleveland, Ohio in 1851.
Motherhouse: *Mount Augustine,* 5232 Broadview Rd., Richfield, OH 44286. Sr. Mary Denis Maher, C.S.A., Archivist.
Total number in Congregation 104.
Properties owned and sponsored: *CSA Health Network,* Cleveland, OH; *Providence Hospital,* Columbia, SC; *Regina Health Center,* Richfield, OH; *Saint Ann Foundation,* Cleveland, OH; *Saint Augustine Academy,* Lakewood, OH; *Saint Vincent Charity Hospital & Health Center,* Cleveland, OH; *Sisters of Charity of St. Augustine Health System, Inc.,* Cleveland, OH; *Timken Mercy Medical Center,* Canton, OH; *Westlake Health Campus Association, dba St. John West Shore Hospital,* Westlake, OH.
Represented in the Dioceses of Charleston, Cleveland and Youngstown.

[0590](S.C.)—SISTERS OF CHARITY OF SAINT ELIZABETH, CONVENT STATION P

Founded in Newark, New Jersey in 1859.
General Motherhouse: *Convent of St. Elizabeth - Administration Building,* P.O. Box 476, Convent Station, NJ 07961-0476. Tel: 973-290-5000; Fax: 973-290-5335. Sr. Barbara Conroy, Gen. Supr.; Sr. Elizabeth McLoughlin, Archivist; Sr. Miriam Teresa League of Prayer.
Legal Titles and Properties: *Sisters of Charity of Saint Elizabeth Academy of Saint Elizabeth,* Convent Station, NJ; *Saint Vincent Academy,* Newark, NJ; *Academy of the Sacred Heart,* Hoboken, NJ; *Saint Frances Residence,* Paterson, NJ.
Total number in Congregation 693.
Southern Province (1967): *Provincial House,* 139 Gregory Ave., West Orange, NJ 07052. Tel: 973-731-5425. Sr. Edna Francis Hersinger, S.C., Prov.
Professed Sisters 256.
Ministry in the field of Elementary & High School Education; Hospital & Homes for Aged; Health and Welfare Services.
Represented in the Archdioceses of Boston, Newark, Omaha, and in the Dioceses of Jackson, Palm Beach, Paterson, Pensacola-Tallahassee, Providence, St. Petersburg, Trenton, Wilmington and Wheeling-Charleston. Also in the Virgin Islands.
Sisters of Charity of Saint Elizabeth - Western Province (1967): *Western Provincial House,* 31 Jackson St., Paterson, NJ 07501. Tel: 201-278-1424. Sr. Maureen Dunne, Prov. Supr.
Total number in Prvince 234.
Ministry in the field of Education; Diocesan/Parish Ministry; Hospitals; Homes for Aged/Residences for the Aged; Health Care; Social Services.
Represented in the Archdioceses of Boston, Newark and New York and of the Dioceses of Metuchen, Paterson, Richmond, Rochester, St. Petersburg, Scranton, Trenton, Wheeling, and Wilmington. Also in the Virgin Islands.

[0600] (S.C.S.J.A.)—SISTERS OF CHARITY OF ST. JOAN ANTIDA P

Founded in France in 1799 by Saint Joan Antida Thouret. First foundation in the U.S. 1932.
General Motherhouse: *Suore della Carita di Santa Giovanna Antida,* Via S. Maria in Cosmedin 5, 00153, Roma, Italia. Sr. M. Antoine Henriot, Supr. Gen.
North American Province (1976): *Regina Mundi Provincial House,* 8560 N. 76th Pl., Milwaukee, WI 53223. Tel: 414-354-9233; Fax: 414-355-6463. Sr. Jennifer L. Daul, S.C.S.J.A., Prov.
Total number in Congregation 48.
Properties owned and sponsored: *St. Joan Antida High School, Inc.; St. Joan Antida High School Foundation, Ltd.; St. Joan Antida Home, Inc.; Hope Nursing Home, Inc.; Guardian Angel Learning Center, Inc.; St. Joan Antida Day Care Center, Inc.*
Ministry also in prisons; neighborhood services and parishes.
Represented in the Archdioceses of Milwaukee and the Diocese of Amarillo.

[0610] (S.C.S.H.)—SISTERS OF CHARITY OF ST. HYACINTHE (Grey Nuns) P

Founded in 1840 in St. Hyacinthe, P.Q., Canada. First United States foundation in 1878.
Legal Title: The Society of Charity, Lewiston, ME.
General House: 16470 Avenue Bourdages, SUD, St. Hyacinthe, P.Q., Canada, J2T 4J8. Sr. Jeannie Daoust, S.C.S.H., Supr. Gen.; Sr. Monique Duhamel, S.C.S.H., Gen. Sec.
Universal number in Congregation 269.
U.S. Regional Administration: 98 Campus Ave., P.O. Box 701, Lewiston, ME 04243-0701. Tel: 207-784-2340. Sr. Diane Beaudoin, Pres.; Sr. Marguerite Carignan, Sec.
Total number in U.S. 12.
Sisters staff: *St. Joseph's Manor,* Portland, ME; *Catholic Medical Center,* Manchester, NH.
Properties owned: *St. Peter's Home,* Manchester, NH.
Represented in the Diocese of Manchester, Portland (ME), Boston (Lowell, MA). Also in Canada and Haiti.

[0620] (S.C.S.L.)—SISTERS OF CHARITY OF ST. LOUIS P

Founded in France in 1803. First foundation in the United States in 1910.
Generalate: Casa Generalizia Via Pecori Giraldi 67, Roma, Italia. Sr. Geraldine Hagel, Supr. Gen.
Total universal number in Congregation 796.
American Region: 4907 S. Catherine St., Plattsburgh, NY 12901. Tel: 518-563-7410; Fax: 518-563-0383. Sr. Bernadette Ducharme, Reg. Supr.
Total number in community 17.
Properties owned and sponsored: *Our Lady of Victory Convent* the former *Our Lady of Victory Secretarial School,* Ogdensburg, NY; *House of Formation,* Albany, NY.
Represented in the Dioceses of Albany and Ogdensburg.

[0630] (V.Z.)—SISTERS OF CHARITY OF ST. VINCENT DE PAUL OF ZAGREB P

Founded in Croatia (Austria-Hungary) in 1845. First U.S. Foundation in 1955.
General Motherhouse: Zagreb, Croatia. Mother Maria Agneta Tadic-Sutra, Supr. Gen.
U.S. Foundation: *Sisters of Charity Convent,* 171 Knox Ave., West Seneca, NY 14224. Tel: 716-825-5859; Sr. Maria Mirna Matic, V.Z., Supr., U.S. Delegate.
Professed Sisters 25.
Sisters staff: Nursery Schools; CCD Centers and Parish Services; Hospital & Health Services.
Properties owned: Nursery Schools 2.
Represented in the Archdiocese of Chicago and the Diocese of Buffalo.

[0640] (S.C.)—SISTERS OF CHARITY OF ST. VINCENT DE PAUL, HALIFAX P

Founded by Saint Elizabeth Ann Seton, Emmitsburg, Maryland in 1809. Congregation at Halifax became independent in 1856, Papal approval in 1908.
Motherhouse: *Mount Saint Vincent,* 150 Bedfird Hwy., Halifax, N.S. B3M 3J5, Canada. Tel: 902-457-3500; Fax: 902-457-3506. Sr. Mary Louise Brink, Congressional Leader; Sr. Frances Teresa Martin, Archivist.
Legal Title: *Sisters of Charity (Halifax).*
Total universal number in Congregation 840.
Boston Province: *Sisters of Charity of Saint Vincent De Paul, Inc.,* 125 Oakland St., Wellesley Hills, MA 02181. Tel: 617-237-2161. Sr. Mary Louise Brink, S.C., Gen. Supr.
Boston Province: Provincial Office, 26 Phipps St., Quincy, MA 02169. Tel: 617-773-6085; Fax: 617-773-4794. Sr. Esther Plefka, Councillor.
Legal Title: *Boston Province, Sisters of Charity of Saint Vincent De Paul, Inc. Elizabeth Seton Residence, Inc.,* Quincy, MA.
New York Province: 84-32 63rd Ave., Middle Village, NY 11379. Tel: 718-779-6284; Fax: 718-651-5645. Sr. Joan Holmberg, Councillor.
Legal Title: *New York Province, Sisters of Charity, Halifax, Inc.*
Ministry in Education at Elementary, Secondary and University Levels; Hospitals; Homes for the Aging; Parish Ministry; Spiritual Directors/Retreats; House of Prayer; Social Services; Pastoral Ministry; Administration.
Represented in the Archdioceses of Boston, New York, and Washington, and the Dioceses of Brooklyn, Manchester and Rockville Center. Also in Canada and Bermuda. Missionary Region in Dominican Republic and Peru.

[0650] (S.C.)—SISTERS OF CHARITY OF ST. VINCENT DE PAUL, OF NEW YORK D

Founded in Emmitsburg, MD in 1809 by Saint Elizabeth Ann Seton.
General Motherhouse: *Sisters of Charity Center, Mount Saint Vincent-on-Hudson,* 6301 Riverdale Ave., Bronx, NY 10471. Tel: 718-549-9200; Fax: 718-884-3013. Sr. Elizabeth A. Vermaelen, Pres.
Total number in Congregation 570.
Sisters serve and staff: Colleges; High Schools; Elementary Schools; Secretarial Science School; Child Caring Homes; General Hospitals; Foundling Hospital; Schools of Nursing; Residence for Senior and Invalid Sisters; Mental Health Divisions; Rest House for Community use; Housing for Homeless.
Represented in the Archdioceses of Atlanta, Baltimore, Newark, New York and Washington and the Dioceses of Albany, Bridgeport, Brooklyn, Camden, Charlotte, Gary, Oakland, Rockville Center, and Shreveport. Also in the Bahamas, Guatemala and Puerto Rico.

[0660] (S.C.C.)—SISTERS OF CHRISTIAN CHARITY P

Daughters of the Blessed Virgin Mary of the Immaculate Conception

Founded in Germany in 1849. First foundation in the United States in 1873.
Generalate: *Suore della Carita Cristiana Casa Generalizia,* Via di Boccea, 671, 00166, Roma (Casalotti), Italia. Tel: 011-396-6156-0829. Mother Gregoris Michels, Supr. Gen.
Total universal number in Congregation 960.
North American Eastern Province (1927): *Mallinckrodt Convent,* Mendham, NJ 07945. Tel: 973-543-6528. *(Div. of North American Province 1927);* Sr. Mary Edward Spohrer, Prov.; Sr. Mary Pierre Koesters, Archivist.
Professed Sisters 316.
Ministry in Academic Education; Retreat House; Catechetical Centers; Religion Coordinators; and Hospital work.
Properties owned and/or sponsored: *Villa Pauline, Retreat House,* Mendham, NJ; *Divine Providence Hospital,* Williamsport, PA; *Holy Spirit Hospital,* Campus Hill, PA; *Mallinckrodt Convent Motherhouse,* Mendham, NJ; Holy Family Convent
North American Western Province: *Sisters of Christian Charity—Daughters of the Blessed Virgin Mary of the Immaculate Conception,* 1041 Ridge Rd., Wilmette, IL 60091-1560. Tel: 847-853-3400; Fax: 847-251-0482. Sr. M. Judith Moran, Prov.; Sr. Joann Kelzer, Archivist.
Professed Sisters 145.
Ministry in the field of Academic Education at all levels; Abused and Neglected Children; Religious Education; Parish Ministry; Ministry to Aged; Prayer Ministry; Ministry to the Poor; Multi-Cultural Ministry.
Properties owned and sponsored: *Maria Immaculate Convent, Sacred Heart Convent,* Wilmette, IL; *Josephinum High School and Convent,* Chicago, IL; *Mallinckrodt College of the North Shore,* Wilmette, IL.
Represented in the Archdioceses of Chicago, New Orleans, St. Louis and Santa Fe and the Dioceses of Jefferson City, Lansing, Rapid City, Tucson and Brownsville.

[0670] (O.C.S.O.)—CISTERCIAN NUNS OF THE STRICT OBSERVANCE P

Founded at Citeaux, France, in 1125. First foundation in the United States in 1949.
Generalate: Viale Africa 33, 00144, Rome, Italy.
Total universal number of nuns in Order 1,908. Contemplative.
U.S. Establishments:
Mount St. Mary's Abbey: 300 Arnold St., Wrentham, MA 02093. Tel: 508-528-1282. Rev. Mother M. Agnes Day, O.C.S.O., Abbess.
Total number in community 53.
Represented in the Archdioceses of Boston.
Our Lady of the Mississippi Abbey: 8400 Abbey Hill Rd., Dubuque, IA 52003. Tel: 319-582-2595; Fax: 319-582-5511. Rev. Mother Gail Fitzpatrick, O.C.S.O., Abbess.
Total number in community 29.
Legal Title: *Trappistine Nuns, Inc.; Iowa Cistercians of the Strict Observance.*
Represented in the Archdioceses of Dubuque.
Santa Rita Abbey: HC 1, Box 929, Sonoita, AZ 85637-9705. Tel: 602-455-5595. Mother M. Beverly Aitken, O.C.S.O., Prioress.
Legal Title: *Cistercian Nuns of the Strict Observance.*
Total number in community 13.
Represented in the Diocese of Tucson.

Our Lady of the Redwoods Abbey: Whitethorn, CA 95589. Tel: 707-986-7419. Sr. Diane Foster, O.C.S.O., Abbess.
Total number in community 11.
Represented in the Diocese of Santa Rosa.
Our Lady of the Angel Monastery: 3365 Monastery Dr., Crozet, VA 22932. Tel: 804-823-1452; Fax: 804-823-6379. Mother Marion Rissetto, O.C.S.O., Prioress.
Legal Title: *Cistercian Nuns of the Strict Observance in Virginia, Inc.*
Total number in community 9.
Represented in the Diocese of Richmond.

[0680] (O.CIST.)—CISTERCIAN NUNS P

Headquarters: Piazza del Tempio di Diana, 14, Roma, Italia, 00153. Most Rev. Mautus Esteva, O. Cist., Abbot General.
U.S. Headquarters: *Valley of Our Lady Monastery,* E. 11096 Yanke Dr., Prairie du Sac, WI 53578. Tel: 608-643-3520; Fax: 608-643-3520. Rev. Mother Paula Hannah, O. Cist., Prioress.
Total number in community 14.

[0685] (R.M.I.)—CLARETIAN MISSIONARY SISTERS P

Religious of Mary Immaculate Claretian Missionary Sisters.
Founded in Santiago de Cuba, August 23, 1855. Established in the United States in 1956.
Generalate: Via Calandrelli 16, 00153, Roma, Italy. Eusebia Pizarro, Supr. Gen.
U.S. Delegation: 9600 W. Atlantic Ave., Delray Beach, FL 33446. Sr. Regina Tutzo, Superior Delegate.
Sisters in the World 600; Sisters in Florida 11.
Legal Title: *Claretian Missionary Sisters of Florida, Inc.*
Ministry in Religious Education; Theological formation in Pastoral Institutes and Seminaries; Social Ministries; Parish and Diocesan Ministries; Parrochial School.
Represented in the Archdiocese of Miami and the Diocese of Palm Beach.

[0690] (C.M.S.)—COMBONI MISSIONARY SISTERS P

Founded in Italy in 1872. An international congregation of 1,845 sisters serving in the mission fields of Africa, Latin America and the Middle East. First United States Foundation in 1950.
Generalate: Rome, Italy. Mother Mariangela Sardi, Supr. Gen.
American Headquarters: 1307 Lakeside Ave., Richmond, VA 23228. Tel: 804-262-8827; Fax: 804-264-2906. Sr. Ruth Ann Bryden, Prov. Supr.
Legal Titles & Holdings: *Provincial House Holy Angels Day Care Center Comboni Missionary Sisters, Inc.,* Richmond, VA.
Represented in the Archdioceses of Chicago and Philadelphia and the Diocese of Richmond.

[0700] (O.D.N.)—COMPANY OF MARY P

Founded in Bordeaux, France, April 7, 1607, by St. Jeanne de Lestonnac. First foundation in the United States in 1926, in Douglas, Arizona.
General Motherhouse: Rome, Italy. Sr. Margarita Maria Pedraz, O.D.N., Supr. Gen.
Universal number in Congregation 2,290.
U.S. Motherhouse (1926): Company of Mary Provincial House, 16791 E. Main St., Tustin, CA 92680. Tel: 714-541-3125. Sr. Mary Salud Estrada, O.D.N., Prov. Supr.; Sr. Kathy Schneider, O.D.N., Community Archivist.
Total number in U.S. 60.
Sisters serve and staff: Kindergartens; Grammar Schools; Religious Instruction Centers; Residences; Parishes & Retreat Centers; Medical Clinic.
Properties owned: *St. Jeanne de Lestonnac Kindergarten & Day Nursery,* Los Angeles, CA; *Divine Providence Kindergarten & Day Nursery,* Los Angeles, CA; *St. Joseph Residence for Women,* Los Angeles, CA; *St. Jeanne De Lestonnac School,* Tustin, CA; *Lestonnac Kindergarten & Day Nursery,* Douglas, AZ.
Represented in the Archdiocese of Los Angeles and the Dioceses of Orange, San Bernardino, and Tucson.

[0710] (C.S.)—THE COMPANY OF THE SAVIOR D

Founded in Spain in 1952. First United States foundation in 1962.
General Motherhouse: Aravaca Madrid-23, Spain. Mother Carmen Aige, Supr. Gen.
Total universal number in congregation is approximately 984.
U.S. Foundation: 820 Clinton Ave., Bridgeport, CT 06604. Tel: 203-368-1875.
Professed Sisters 51; Novices 1.
Represented in the Diocese of Bridgeport.

[0720] (M.C.)—CONSOLATA MISSIONARY SISTERS P

Founded in Italy in 1910. First foundation in United States in 1954.
Motherhouse: Istituto Suore Missionarie della Consolata, Via Cassia Km. 37, 01036 NEPI, Viterbo, Italy. Mother Rina Carla Salsa, Supr. Gen.
Total universal number in congregation is approximately 984.
U.S. Headquarters: Consolata Missionary Sisters, 6801 Belmont Rd., P.O. Box 371, Belmont, MI 49306. Tel: 616-361-2072; Fax: 616-361-2049. Sr. Cecilia Clara Zamboni, M.C. Supr.
Total number in community 22.
Sisters serve and staff: Grammar Schools; Apostolate among Minorities; Catechetical and Pastoral Work.
Represented in the Dioceses of Birmingham and Grand Rapids.

[0725](M.C-M.)—CORDI-MARIAN MISSIONARY SISTERS CONGREGATION P

Founded in Mexico City in 1921. First United States foundation in 1926.
General Motherhouse: Apdo. Postal #1109, Toluca, Mexico C.P., 50091. Sr. Maria Cibrian, M.C-M., Supr. Gen.
U.S. Provincial House: 11624 FM 471, Apt. 402, San Antonio, TX 78253. Tel: 210-688-3889. Sr. Mary Catalina Marquez, M.C-M., Prov. Supr.
Total number in Congregation 122; Total number in U.S. community 41.
Properties Owned: *Cordi-Marian Villa—Retreat Center and Provincial House,* San Antonio, TX; *East St. Louis Catholic Day Care Center and Convent,* East St. Louis, IL.
Ministry in Catechetical Centers; Pastoral Ministry Programs; Elementary Education; Kindergarten and Day Care Centers; Retreat Center; Social Service; Migrant Ministry; Prison Ministry; Vestment and Banner Making.
Represented in the Archdioceses of Chicago, Kansas City and San Antonio ans the Dioceses of Austin, Belleville and Galveston-Houston.

[0730] (Fd.CC.)—CANOSSIAN DAUGHTERS OF CAHRITY Canossian Sister P

Founded in Verona, Italy in 1808.
General Motherhouse: Via della Stazione di Ottavia 70, Rome, Italy, 00135.
U.S. Provincial House: Crista Rey Convent, 5625 Isleta Blvd., S.W. Albuquerque, NM 87105.
Sisters in the U.S. 33.
Ministry in Evangelization; Integral Promotion of the Person; Visiting the Sick; Intermediate Care Facility for Handicapped Children.
Represented in the Archdioceses of San Francisco and Sante Fe and the Diocese of Sacramento. Also in Canada and Mexico.

[0740] (D.C.P.B.)—DAUGHTERS OF CHARITY OF THE MOST PRECIOUS BLOOD P

Founded in Pagani, Italy in 1872. First foundation in United States in 1908.
Generalate: Via Vigna Fabbri 45, Rome, Italy. Sr. Ofelia Marzocca, Mother Gen.
U.S. Address: Daughters of Charity of the Most Precious Blood, 1482 North Ave., Bridgeport, CT 06604. Tel: 203-334-7000. Sr. Rosaria Carlino, D.C.P.B., Supr.
Total number in community 20.
Represented in the Dioceses of Albany, Bridgeport and Paterson.

[0750] (F.C.S.C.J.)—DAUGHTERS OF THE CHARITY OF THE SACRED HEART OF JESUS P

Founded in France at La Salle de Vihiers in 1823. First founded in the United States at Newport, Vermont in October 1905.
Generalate: Montgeron, France.
General Motherhouse: La Salle de Vihiers, France. Sr. Collette Lussier, Supr. Gen.
Mount Sacred Heart Provincial House: Daughters of the Charity of the Sacred Heart, (1949), Grove St., P.O. Box 642, Littleton, NH 03561-0642. Tel: 603-444-5346; Fax: 603-444-5348. Sr. Rosina Bechard, F.C.S.C.J., Prov. Supr.; Sr. Lucille Grandpre, F.C.S.C.J., Sr. Yvette Beloin, F.C.S.C.J., Local Suprs.
Total number in province 73.
Sisters serve and staff: Grammar Schools and Kindergarten; Catechetical Centers; Spiritual Directors; Pastoral Ministry; Foreign Missions.
Represented in the Archdiocese of Boston and the Dioceses of Burlington, Fall River, Manchester, Ogdensburg and Portland (ME, Lafayette, LA.

[0760] (F.C.S.C.J.)—DAUGHTERS OF CHARITY OF ST. VINCENT DE PAUL P

Founded in France in 1633. First foundation in the United States in 1809 by Saint Elizabeth Ann Seton, Emmitsburg, MD.
General Motherhouse: Paris, France. Sr. Juana Elizondo, Supr. Gen.
Emmitsburg Province (Southeast) (1809): *St. Joseph's Provincial House,* Emmitsburg, MD 21727. Tel: 301-447-3121; Fax: 301-447-6038. Sr. Virginia Ann Brooks, Prov.; Bonnie Weatherly, Archivist.
Legal Title: *Sisters of Charity of St. Joseph's.*
Total number in province 285.
Sisters serve and staff: High Schools; Elementary Schools; Medical Clinics; Hospitals; Nursing Homes; Homes for unmarried Mothers; Child Caring Homes; Social Service Centers; Catholic Charities; Parish Ministries; Hispanic Ministry; Dining Rooms for the Homeless; Retreat Center.
Represented in the Archdioceses of Baltimore and Washington and the Dioceses of Arlington, Charleston, Charlotte, Pensacola-Tallahassee, Raleigh, Richmond, Savannah, St. Augustine and Wheeling-Charleston.
West Central Province (1910): *Marillac Provincial House,* 7800 Natural Bridge Rd., St. Louis, MO 63121-4694. Tel: 314-382-2800; Fax: 314-382-8392. Sr. Nannette Gentile, Prov.; Sr. Genevieve Keusenkothen, Archivist.
Total number in the community 246.
Ministry in the field of Religious and Academic Education at all levels; Seminary Education; Hospitals; Leprosarium; Psychiatric Hospitals; Parish Ministry; Social Service Centers; Schools of Nursing; Day Care Centers; Clinics; Homes for Children and Young Women; Housing for the Homeless; Catholic Charities Offices; Refugee Resettlement; Housing; Peace and Justice; Diocesan Offices; Hospice; State Health Care; Home Health Care; Emergency Relief Centers; Spiritual Direction and Retreats.
Sponsors: *Clinics—Centro San Vicente,* El Paso, TX; *Daughters of Charity Services of San Antonio, Inc. Daughters of Charity Services of San Antonio-El Carmen Div.,* San Antonio, TX; *Daughters of Charity Services of San Antonio-De Paul Div.,* San Antonio, TX; *Daughters of Charity Services of New Orleans; Daughters of Charity Community Services of El Paso (DCCS-EP) Daughters of Charity Healthservices of Austin - Seaton East,* Austin, TX; *Daughters of Charity Health Services of Austin - Seaton South,* Austin, TX; *Hospitals—Seaton Medical Center,* Austin TX; *Seaton Northwest,* Austin, TX; *St. Paul Medical Center,* Dallas, TX; *Providence Health Center - De Paul Center,* Waco, TX; *Support Services—Daughters of Charity National Health System, West Central, Inc.,* St. Louis, MO; *Daughters of Charity National Health System,* St. Louis, MO; *Daughters of Charity National Health System, West Central, Data Center,* Dallas, TX.
Represented in the Archdioceses of Kansas City in Kansas, New Orleans, St. Louis, San Antonio and the Dioceses of Austin, Amarillo, Baton Rouge, Brownsville, Dallas, El Paso, Kansas City-St. Joseph, Little Rock, San Angelo and Springfield-Cape Girardeau.
East Central Province - Evansville (1969): *Daughters of Charity of St. Vincent de Paul of Indiana, Inc.,* 9400 New Harmony Rd., Evansville, IN 47720. Tel: 812-963-3341; Fax: 812-963-7589. Sr. Catherine Madigan, D.C., Prov. Supr.; Sr. Margaret Flynn, D.C., Archivist.
Total number in the community 195.
Sponsored Works: Home for Retired Sisters; General Hospitals; Skilled Nursing Facilities; Clinics; Home Health Care; Day Care Centers and Neighborhood Services; Childrens' Residence; Services to Elderly.
Sponsored Organizations: *Daughters of Charity National Health System, Inc. Daughters of Charity Regional Information Services, Inc.* Local Development Corporations. Shared ownership in Health Maintenance Organizations and Preferred Provider Organizations.
Legal Title: *Mater Dei Provincialate, Inc.*
Ministries of Insertion Religious and Academic Education at all levels; Campus Ministry; Parish Ministry; Social Services in parishes; Catholic Charities Office; Shelters for homeless; Residences for Elderly.
Represented in the Archdioceses of Chicago, Detroit, Indianapolis, Milwaukee, Mobile and the Dioceses

of Belleville, Biloxi, Birmingham, Evansville, Lafayette (IN), Nashville, Jackson, Peoria, Saginaw and Springfield (IL).

Northeast Province (1969): *De Paul Provincial House,* 96 Menands Rd., Albany, NY 12204-1499. Sr. Louise Gallahue, Prov. Supr.; Sr. Elaine Wheeler, Archivist.

Total number in the community 232.

Ministry in the field of Academic Education at all levels; Hospital; Specialized Hospitals; Homes for Unmarried Mothers; Child Caring Homes; Day Care Centers; Social Service Centers; Parish Centers.

Represented in the Archdioceses of Boston, Newark, New York, Philadelphia and in the Dioceses of Albany, Allentown, Bridgeport, Brooklyn, Buffalo, Metuchen, Ogdensburg, Rochester, Syracuse and Wilmington.

Province of the West (Los Altos Hills) (1969): *Seton Provincialate,* 26000 Altamont Rd., Los Altos Hills, CA 94022-4317. Tel: 650-941-4490; Fax: 650-949-3874. Sr. Joyce Weller, D.C., Prov.

Total number in the community 157.

Properties owned and sponsored: *Seton Medical Center,* Daly City, CA; *Seton Provincialate,* Los Altos Hills, CA; *St. Vincent Medical Center,* Los Angeles, CA; *St. Vincent's Senior Citizen Nutrition Program,* Los Angeles, CA; *St. Francis Medical Center,* Lynwood, CA; *Maryvale, Rosemead,* CA; *Mount St. Joseph-St. Elizabeth,* San Francisco, CA; *O'Connor Hospital,* San Jose, CA; *St. Louise Hospital,* Morgan Hill, CA; *St. Vincent's,* Santa Barbara, CA; *Robert F. Kennedy Medical Center,* Hawthorne, CA.

Represented in the Archdioceses of Los Angeles, San Francisco and in the Dioceses of Fresno, Gallup, Monterey, Oakland, Phoenix, Salt Lake City, San Jose, and Gallup.

[0770] (D.C.)—DAUGHTERS OF THE CROSS D

Founded in France in 1640. First foundation in the United States in 1855.

Motherhouse: *Daughters of the Cross Motherhouse,* 1000 Fairview St., Shreveport, LA 71104. Tel: 318-869-3482. Sr. Mary Louise Parisy, Supr. Gen.

Total number in community 9.

Represented in the Diocese of Shreveport.

[0780] (F.C.)—DAUGHTERS OF THE CROSS OF LIEGE P

Founded in Liege, Belgium in 1833. First foundation in the United States in 1958.

Principal House: *St. Bernard Convent,* 165 W. Eaton Ave., Tracy, CA 95376. Sr. M. Eugene Hagan, F.C., Supr.

Total number in community 9.

Represented in the Diocese of Stockton.

[0790] (F.D.C.)—DAUGHTERS OF DIVINE CHARITY P

Founded in Austria on Nov. 21, 1868. First founded in the United States on Oct. 8, 1913, in New York City.

General Motherhouse: Grottaferrata, Rome, Italy. Sr. Nicolina Hendges, Supr. Gen.

St. Joseph Province (1921): *St. Joseph Provincialate,* 205 Major Ave., Staten Island, NY 10305. Tel: 718-720-4377. Sr. Josita DiVita, F.D.C., Prov.; Sr. Marie Claire Weaver, F.D.C., 1st Prov. Councilor.

Total number universally 1,490.

Ministry in Education; Nursing; Residences for Women; Working with the Homeless and the Elderly.

Properties owned: *St. Mary's Residence,* New York, NY; *St. Joseph Hill Academy,* Staten Island, NY; *Villa Madonna,* Hackettstown, NJ.

Represented in the Archdioceses of Newark and New York and the Dioceses of Bridgeport, Metuchen, San Bernardino and San Diego.

[0793] (D.D.L.)—DAUGHTERS OF DIVINE LOVE

Founded in Ukpor, Nigeria in 1969. First United States Foundation in 1990.

General House: Fifth Avenue, P.O. Box 546, Enugu, Enugu State , Nigeria. Tel: 042-559071; 042-554450. Rev. Mother M. Chilota Elochukwu, D.D.L., Mother Gen.

Total Professed Sisters 563.

U.S. Regional House: 140 North Ave., Highwood, IL 60040. Tel: 847-432-9003. Sr. Mary Paul Asoegwu, D.D.L., Reg. Supr. & Vicar Gen.

Professed Sisters in U.S. 38.

Ministry in the field of Administration; Religious and Academic Education at all levels; Special Education; Health Services; Parish and Diocesan Services; Retreat Work; Social Work.

Represented in the Archdioceses of Chicago, New York and the Dioceses of Brooklyn and Springfield, IL.

[0794] (F.D.P.)—DAUGHTERS OF DIVINE PROVIDENCE

General Motherhouse: Daughters of Divine Providence, Via Matteo Bartoli 255, 00143, Rome, Italy. Mother Damiana DiLauro, F.D.P., Supr. Gen.

U.S. Delegation: Daughters of Divine Providence, 3100 Mumphrey Rd., Chalmette, LA 70043. Tel: 504-279-4617; Fax: 504-279-4617. Sr. Piercarla Barone, F.D.P., Local Supr.

Total number in community 5.

Represented in the Archdiocese of New Orleans.

[0795] (F.D.Z.)—DAUGHTERS OF DIVINE ZEAL

Founded in Messina, Italy in 1887 by Blessed Hannibal Maria DiFrancia. First foundation in the United States in 1951.

Generalate: *Figlie Del Divino Zelo,* Circonvallazione Appia 144, 00179, Rome, Italy. Mother Ferdinanda Reale, Supr. Gen.

Total universal number in the congregation 1,000.

U.S. Headquarters: *Hannibal House Spiritual Center,* 1526 Hill Rd., Reading, PA 19602. Tel: 610-375-1738 & 375-9072; Fax: 610-375-2188. Sr. Gesulmina Micali, F.D.Z., Supr.

Total number in community 6.

Ministry in the field of Religious and Academic Education; Parish and Youth Ministry; Retreat, Vocation, Prayer and Apostolate.

Represented in the Diocese of Allentown.

St. Mary Province (1950): *Provincial Motherhouse and Novitiate,* 39 N. Portage Path, Akron, OH 44303-1183. Tel: 330-867-4960. Sr. Maria Bakich, Prov. Supr.

Total number in community 22.

Ministry in the field of Education; Home for Working Girls; Home for elderly senior Women and Men.

Properties owned: *Daughters of Divine Charity, Inc.; Leonora Hall Convent; Leonora Hall Residence; Francesca Residence.*

Represented in the Archdioceses of Miami, Milwaukee and the Diocese of Cleveland.

Holy Trinity Province (1972): *Provincial House,* 1315 N. Woodward Ave., Bloomfield Hills, MI 48304. Tel: 313-645-5318. Sr. M. Paschal Grand, Prov. Supr.

Professed Sisters 34.

Ministry in Education; Foster Care Residence; Homes for the Aged.

Represented in the Archdiocese of Detroit and the Diocese of Fort Wayne-South Bend.

[0810](D.H.M.)—DAUGHTERS OF THE HEART OF MARY P

Founded in France in 1790. First United States foundation in 1851.

Generalate: 39 rue Notre Dame des Champs, 75006, Paris, France.

Provincialate: 1339 Northampton St., Holyoke, MA 01040-1913. Tel: 413-532-7406; Fax: 413-533-4217. Sr. Miriam Najimy, D.H.M., Prov.

Properties owned: *Marian Center & Residence,* Holyoke, MA; *Maryhill Retreat Center,* St. Paul, MN; *Nardin Academy, Buffalo,* NY; *Heart of Mary Center,* St. Louis, MO; *St. Isaac Jogues Center,* Philadelphia, PA; *Regina Maria Retreat House,* Plattsburgh, NY; *St. Joseph's School for the Deaf,* Bronx, NY; *Ephpheta Center,* Oak Park, IL.

Professed Sisters 136; Novices 1; Postulants 2; Aspirants 2.

Represented in the Archdioceses of Chicago, New York, Philadelphia, St. Louis and St. Paul-Minneapolis and the Dioceses of Buffalo, Ogdensburg, Springfield (MA) and Trenton.

[0820] (D.H.S.)—DAUGHTERS OF THE HOLY SPIRIT P

Founded in France in 1706. First foundation in the U.S. in 1902.

General Motherhouse: St. Brieuc, Cotes du Nord, Bretagne, France. Sr. Yvette LeGrand, F.S.E., Supr. Gen.

Provincial House: *Daughters of the Holy Spirit, Inc.,* 72 Church St., Putnam, CT 06260. Tel: 860-928-0891. Sr. Bonnie Morrow, D.H.S., Prov.

Total number in the community 192.

Ministry in the field of Academic Education at all levels; Home for Aged; Home/District Nursing; Nursing Home for Daughters of the Holy Spirit; and various social and pastoral ministries of service.

Represented in the Archdioceses of Boston, Hartford, Mobile, New York, Philadelphia and in the Dioceses of Birmingham, Bridgeport, Burlington, Fall River, Fresno, Norwich, Ogdensburg, Portland in Maine, Providence, Richmond, Sacramento, Springfield (MA), Stockton and Worcester.

[0830] (F.J.)—CONGREGATION OF THE DAUGHTERS OF JESUS (LES FILLES DE JESUS) P

Founded in France in 1834. First foundation in the U.S. in 1903.

Motherhouse: Kermaria, 56500, Locmine, France.

Generalate: 11, rue d'Arras, 75005, Paris, France. Sr. Ellen Martin, Supr. Gen.

Total universal number in Congregation 2,138.

Western Province (1902): 9040 84th Ave., Edmonton, Alberta T6C 1E4. Canada. Tel: 403-466-6527. Sr. Irene Magnan, Prov. Supr.

U.S. Address: 4209 3rd Ave. S., Great Falls, MT 59405. Tel: 406-452-7231.

Total number in community 3.

Represented in the Diocese of Great Falls.

[0840] (F.I.)—DAUGHTERS OF JESUS P

Founded in Spain in 1871. First foundation in the U.S. in 1950.

General Motherhouse: Rome, Italy.

U.S. Foundation: 2021 Stuart Ave., Baton Rouge, LA 70808. Tel: 504-344-7131. Sr. Ana Maria Lopez, F.I., Prov.

Professed Sisters 5.

Represented in the Diocese of Baton Rouge.

[0850] (F.M.A.)—DAUGHTERS OF MARY HELP OF CHRISTIANS P

Salesian Sisters of St. John Bosco

Founded in Mornese, Italy, in 1872. First foundation in the U.S. in 1908 at Paterson, New Jersey.

General Motherhouse: Via Ateneo Salesiano, 81, 00139, Rome, Italy. Very Rev. Mother Marinella Castagno, F.M.A., Mother Gen.

Total universal number in Congregation 16,701.

Province of St. Philip, Apostle: Provincial House, 655 Belmont Ave., Haledon, NJ 07508-2398. Tel: 201-790-7964; 7965. Mother Theresa Kelly, F.M.A., Prov.

Legal Title: *Missionary Society of the Salesian Sisters, Inc.; Salesian Sisters of Tampa, Inc.*

Properties owned: *Provincial House,* Haledon, NJ; *Mary Help of Christians Academy,* North Haledon, NJ; *Sacred Heart Center,* Newton, NJ; *Villa Madonna School-Salesian Sisters of Tampa, Inc.,* Tampa, FL; *Camp Auxilium Learning Center,* Newton, NJ.

Total number in the community 150.

Ministry in the field of Education; Day Nurseries; CCD Centers; Youth Ministry.

Represented in the Archdioceses of Miami, Newark, New York and the Dioceses of Birmingham, Paterson and St. Petersburg.

Province of Mary Immaculate: *FMA Provincial House,* 6019 Buena Vista, San Antonio, TX 78237. Tel: 210-432-0089; 0090; Fax: 210-432-4016. Mother Martina Ponce, F.M.A., Prov.

Legal Title: *Institute of the Daughters of Mary Help of Christians - Salesian Sisters of St. John Bosco,* San Antonio, TX; *Salesian Sisters - Mary Help of Christians Youth Center, Inc.,* Corralitos, CA.

Properties owned: *FMA Provincial House & St. John Bosco School,* San Antonio, TX; *Mary Help of Christians School,* Laredo, TX; *Salesian Sisters School - Salesian Sisters: MHC Youth Center, Inc.,* Corralitos, CA.

Total number in community 115.

Ministry in Education; Youth Ministry and Religious Education.

Represented in the Archdioceses of Los Angeles, New Orleans, San Antonio and San Francisco and the Dioceses of Austin, Corpus Christi, Monterey and Phoenix.

[0860] (D.M.)—DAUGHTERS OF MARY OF THE IMMACULATE CONCEPTION P

Founded in New Britain in 1904.

General Motherhouse and Novitiate: 314 Osgood Ave., New Britain, CT 06053. Tel: 203-225-9406. Mother Mary Mark, Supr. Gen.

Total number in community 69.

Legal Title: *Congregation of the Daughters of Mary of the Immaculate Conception, Inc.*

Ministry in the field of Education; Child Day Care Center; Home for the Aged; Homes for Working Girls and Students; Skilled Care Facilities; Catechetical Centers.

Properties owned: *St. Lucian's Home; Our Lady of Rose Hill Day Care Center; Marian Educational Clinic; Monsignor Bojnowski Manor; Mary Immaculate Academy Motherhouse and Novitiate Complex,* New Britain, CT; *St. Joseph's Home,* NY; *St. Agnes Residence,* NY; *Our Lady's Guild House,*

Boston, MA; *Sancta Maria Nursing Facility,* Cambridge, MA.
Represented in the Archdioceses of Boston, Hartford and New York and in the Diocese of Springfield (MA).

[0870] (F.M.I.)—CONGREGATION OF THE DAUGHTERS OF MARY IMMACULATE P
Marianist Sisters
Founded in France in 1816.
Motherhouse: Rome, Italy. Mother M. Blanca Jamar, Supr. Gen.
U.S. Foundation (1949): *Our Lady of the Pillar Convent,* 251 W. Ligustrum Dr., San Antonio, TX 78228. Tel: 210-433-5501; Fax: 210-431-9611. Sr. Evangeline Escobar, Prov. Supr.
Total number in community 22.
Properties owned: *Our Lady of the Pillar Convent,* San Antonio, TX; *Novitiate House,* Dayton, OH.
Represented in the Archdioceses of Cincinnati and San Antonio and the Diocese of Toledo.

[0880] (D.M.J.)—DAUGHTERS OF MARY AND JOSEPH P
Founded in Belgium in 1817. First U.S. Foundation in 1926.
Generalate: Via Rivarone, 100, 00166, Rome, Italy. Sr. Agnes Charles, Supr. Gen.
Novitiate: 5300 Crest Rd., Rancho Palos Verdes, CA 90275. Tel: 310-541-8194; Fax: 310-544-0387. Sr. Julia Costello, Formation Dir.
Provincialate: 5300 Crest Rd., Rancho Palos Verdes, CA 90274. Tel: 310-377-9968. Sr. Catherine McShane, Prov.
Professed Sisters 73.
Legal Title: *Daughters of Mary and Joseph, California.*
Sisters staff: Grammar & High Schools; Parish Ministry; Health Ministry; Missionary Work; Detention Ministry; Retreat Work; House of Prayer.
Represented in the Archdioceses of Los Angeles and San Francisco and in the Dioceses of San Bernardino and San Diego.

[0890] (D.M.)—DAUGHTERS OF OUR LADY OF MERCY P
Founded in Italy in 1837 by Saint Mary Joseph Rossello. First foundation in the United States in 1919.
Generalate: Via Monte Grappa, No. 7., Savona, Italy. Rev. Mother M. Celsa Benneti, Supr. Gen.
Provincialate and Novitiate: *Villa Rossello,* 1009 Main Rd., Newfield, NJ 08344. Tel: 609-697-2983. Sr. Grace Marie Scandale, Mother Prov.; Sr. Loretta Marie Stevens, D.M., Community Archivist.
Total number in community 65.
Ministry in the field of Education; Health Services; Day Nursery; Convalescent Hospital; C.C.D. and Parish Work.
Legal Holdings: *Misericordia Convalescent Home,* York, PA; *Holy Child Nursery,* York, PA; *Our Lady of Mercy Academy,* Newfield, NJ.
Represented in the Dioceses of Camden, Harrisburg, Scranton and Springfield (MA).

[0900] (F.D.N.S.C.)—DAUGHTERS OF OUR LADY OF THE SACRED HEART P
Founded in France in 1882.
Motherhouse: Via Casale S. Pio. V, 37, Rome, Italy. Sr. Mary Ringnalda, Supr. Gen.
U.S. Foundation (1955): *St. Francis de Sales Convent,* 424 E. Browning Rd., Bellmawr, NJ 08031. Tel: 609-931-8973; Fax: 609-931-7018.
Professed Sisters in U.S. 14.
Represented in the Archdiocese of Philadelphia and the Dioceses of Camden.

[0910] (Bethl.)—BETHLEMITA, DAUGHTER OF THE SACRED HEART OF JESUS P
Founded in Guatemala in 1861. First foundation in United States in Dallas, Texas.
Motherhouse: Bogota, Colombia, S.A.
U.S. Foundation: *St. Joseph Residence,* 330 W. Pembroke St., Dallas, TX 75208. Tel: 214-948-3597. Sr. Adelaide Bocanegra, Admin.
Professed Sisters 6.
Represented in the Diocese of Dallas.

[0920] (D.S.F.)—DAUGHTERS OF ST. FRANCIS OF ASSISI P
Founded in Austro, Hungary, 1894. First foundation in United States in 1946.
Motherhouse: *St. Joseph's Convent,* 507 N. Prairie St., Lacon, IL 61540. Tel: 309-246-2175. Sr. M. Vaclava Ballon, D.S.F., Prov. Supr.
Professed Sisters 30.
Represented in the Dioceses of Davenport, Peoria and Springfield-Cape Girardeau.

[0930] (F.S.J.)—RELIGIOUS DAUGHTERS OF ST. JOSEPH P
Founded in Gerona, Spain in 1875.
General Motherhouse: General Asensio Cabanillas, 18, Madrid, 28003. Spain. Mother Carmen Vela, Supr. Gen.
Total universal number in Congregation 880.
Provincial House, Calzada Ermita Istapalapa, Mexico; Sr. Pilar Soto, Prov.
U.S. Foundation: *Santa Marta Hospital,* 319 N. Humphreys Ave., Los Angeles, CA 90022. Sr. Eulalia Yepez, F.S.J., Supr.
Legal Title: *Daughters of St. Joseph of California, Inc.*
Total number in community 8.
Represented in the Archdiocese of Los Angeles.

[0940] (D.S.M.P.)—DAUGHTERS OF ST. MARY OF PROVIDENCE P
Founded in Italy in 1881. First foundation in the U.S. in 1913.
Generalate: Rome, Italy. Mother Elena Salarici, Supr. Gen.
Novitiate: *Daughters of St. Mary,* 24955 North Highway 12, Lake Zurich, IL 60047. Tel: 847-438-5050. Sr. Caryn Haas, Formation Dir.
Provincialate: *St. Mary of Providence,* 4200 N. Austin Ave., Chicago, IL 60634. Tel: 773-545-8300; 2596. Sr. Bernardine Kauffmann, Prov.
Professed Sisters 100.
Represented in the Archdioceses of Boston, Chicago, Detroit and Philadelphia and the Dioceses of Camden, Gary, Lansing, New Ulm, and Sioux Falls.

[0950] (F.S.P.)—PIOUS SOCIETY DAUGHTERS OF ST. PAUL P
(Missionary Sisters of the Media of Communications)
Founded in Alba, Piedmont, Italy, on June 15, 1915. First founded in the United States on June 28, 1932, in New York.
General Motherhouse: Rome, Italy. Sr. Giovanna Maria Carrara, Supr. Gen.
Total universal number in Congregation 2,607.
Provincial House, Novitiate, Juniorate, Publishing House: 50 St. Paul's Ave., Boston, MA 02130. Tel: 617-522-8911. Sr. Linda James Smith, F.S.P., Prov. Supr.; Sr. Cecilia Paula Livingston, F.S.P., Local Supr.
Legal Title: *Daughters of St. Paul, Inc.*
Properties owned: *St. Paul Book and Media Centers,* situated in 18 locations throughout the States (see list of (Arch)Dioceses where represented) *Provincialate,* Boston, MA; *St. Thecla Retreat House,* Billerica, MA.
Total number in community 158.
Represented in the Archdioceses of Boston, Chicago, Los Angeles, Miami, New Orleans, New York, Philadelphia, St. Louis, San Antonio, San Francisco and the Dioceses of Arlington, Charleston, Cleveland, Honolulu, Memphis, Metuchen and San Diego. Also in Canada.

[0960] (D.W.)—DAUGHTERS OF WISDOM P
Founded in France in 1703. First foundation in the United States in 1904.
General Motherhouse: St. Laurent-sur-Sevre, Vendee, France.
Superior General Headquarters located in Rome, Italy
U.S. Province (1949): *Provincial House,* 385 Ocean Ave., Islip, NY 11751-4600. Tel: 516-277-2660; Fax: 516-277-3274. Sr. Evelyn Eckhardt, D.W., Prov.
Professed Sisters 143.
Ministry in all levels of Education; Retreat House; Hospital & Health Services; Orphanage; Social Work; Pediatrics Clinic.
Properties owned: *Wisdom House Center for Spirituality,* Litchfield, CT; *Our Lady of Perpetual Help Convent* (Rest Home for Sisters), Sound Beach, NY; *Provincial House,* Islip, NY; *Our Lady of Wisdom Convent,* St. Agatha, ME.
Represented in the Archdioceses of Denver, Hartford, Mobile, Washington and the Dioceses of Brooklyn, Burlington, Charleston, Metuchen, Portland (ME), Raleigh, Richmond, Rockville Centre, St. Augustine, St. Petersburg and Wheeling-Charleston.

[0965] (D.L.J.C.)—DISCIPLES OF THE LORD JESUS CHRIST
Motherhouse: P.O. Box 17, Channing, TX 79018. Tel: 806-534-2312; Fax: 806-534-2223. Mother Bernadette Beamsley, Supr. Gen.

[0970] (R.D.C.)—SISTERS OF THE DIVINE COMPASSION D
Founded in the United States in 1886.
General Motherhouse: *Good Counsel Convent,* 52 N. Broadway, White Plains, NY 10603. Tel: 914-949-2950; Fax: 914-949-5169. Sr. Helen Coldrick, R.D.C., Gen. Supr.
Total number in community 125.
Legal Holdings and Titles: *Academy of Our Lady of Good Counsel High School and Elementary School,* White Plains, NY; *Preston High School,* New York, NY; *Divine Compassion Center for Spiritual Renewal,* NY; *Migrant Ministry,* Goshen, NY; *Residence,* Hampton Bays, NY; *RDC Center for Counselling and Human Development.*
Ministry in Pre-school, Elementary, Secondary, College and University Education; Religious Education; Educational Consultation; Adult Education; Special Education; Pastoral Ministry; Retreat Work and Spiritual Direction; Counseling; Social Services; Migrant Ministry; Health Services; Administration and Business Services.
Represented in the Archdiocese of New York.

[0980] (P.D.D.M.)—PIOUS DISCIPLES OF THE DIVINE MASTER P
Founded in 1924. First foundation in the United States in 1948.
General Motherhouse: Rome, Italy. Mother Mary Paola Mancini, Supr. Gen.
Universal number in Congregation 1,400.
U.S. Headquarters: 60 Sunset Ave., Staten Island, NY 10314. Tel: 718-494-8597; Fax: 718-494-8521. Sr. M. Lucille Van Hoogmoed, P.D.D.M., Reg. Supr.
Total number in region 47.
Ministry is a Three Dimensional Mission: Eucharistic, Priestly, Liturgical.
Represented in the Archdioceses of Boston, Los Angeles, and New York and the Dioceses of Fresno and San Jose.

[0990] (C.D.P.)—SISTERS OF DIVINE PROVIDENCE P
Founded in Germany in 1851. First foundation in United States in 1876.
General Motherhouse: Rome, Italy.
St. Peter's Province (1876): Provincial House, 9000 Babcock Blvd., Allison Park, PA 15101. Tel: 412-931-5241; Fax: 412-635-5416. Sr. Mary Ellen Rufft, Prov.
Total number in community 272.
Properties owned and sponsored: *La Roche College Providence Heights Alpha,* Allison Park, PA; *Transfiguration House of Prayer,* Butler, PA; *Kearns Spirituality Center,* Allison Park, PA; *Providence Connections, Inc.; Providence Child Care Center - South,* Castle Shannon, PA; *Providence Child Care Center, North,* Pittsburgh, PA; *Providence Family Support Center,* Pittsburgh, PA; *Amelia House - Safe House, Clarion,* PA.
Ministry in the fields of Education; Social Services; Pastoral Ministry; and Health Care Services.
Represented in the Archdioceses of Atlanta, Baltimore, Chicago, Denver, Detroit, Kansas City in Kansas, New York, Philadelphia, Santa Fe and the Dioceses of Altoona-Johnstown, Bismarck, Brownsville, Charleston, Charlotte, Cleveland, Columbus, Davenport, Erie, Greensburg, Orlando, Phoenix, Pittsburgh, Raleigh, Wheeling-Charleston, Wilmington, Yakima and Youngstown. Also in Puerto Rico, Italy and the Dominican Republic.
St. Louis Province (1930): *Provincial Center - Sisters of Divine Providence,* 8368 Latty Ave., St. Louis, MO 63042. Tel: 314-524-3803; Fax: 314-524-7203. Sr. Janet Folkl, C.D.P., Prov. Supr.
Total number in community 56.
Legal Title: *Providence Charitable Trust,* Normandy, MO.
Properties owned and sponsored: *Room at the Inn,* St. Louis, MO; *La Posada Providencia,* San Benito, TX; *St. Elizabeth Medical Center,* Granite City, IL.
Ministry in the fields of Education; Health Services; Parish Ministry; Social Work; Services to Refugees and Homeless People.
Represented in the Archdioceses of Chicago and St. Louis and the Dioceses of Brownsville, Jefferson City, Nashville, Springfield-Cape Girardeau, and Springfield (IL).
Our Lady of Divine Providence Province (1957): 363 Bishops Hwy., Kingston, MA 02364. Tel: 781-585-1745. Sr. Claudia Ward, C.D.P., Prov. Supr.

Total number in the community 46.
Sisters minister in: the field of Education at all levels; Hospital and other Health Services; Parish Ministries; Diocesan Administration; Elderly Care; Education for Mentally Handicapped; Alcohol Rehabilitation Ministry.
Properties owned: *Provincial Residence; Sacred Heart Junior-Senior High School Sacred; Heart Elementary and PrePrimary School; Visitation Camp Mishannock,* Kingston, MA.
Represented in the Archdiocese of Boston and the Dioceses of Fall River and Richmond.

[1000] (C.D.P.)—CONGREGATION OF DIVINE PROVIDENCE, MELBOURNE, KENTUCKY P

Founded in France in 1762. First foundation in the United States in 1889.
General Motherhouse: *St. Jean de Bassel,* 57930 Fenetrange, France. Sr. Marie Therese Seyler, Supr. Gen.
American Provincial House (1889): *St. Anne Convent,* Melbourne, KY 41059. Tel: 606-441-0679. Sr. Lynn Stenken, C.D.P., Prov. Supr.; Sr. Mary Joan Dohmen, C.D.P., Archivist.
Total number in community 189.
Ministry in the field of Academic Education at all levels; Montessori Schools; Home for Working Women; Retreat Center; Religious Education & Pastory Ministry; Health & Social Services.
Represented in the Archdioceses of Baltimore, Cincinnati, Louisville, New York and Washington and the Dioceses of Charleston, Covington, Duluth, Gallup, Lafayette in Indiana, Lexington, Providence, Savannah and Toledo. Also in West Africa.

[1010] (C.D.P.)—CONGREGATION OF DIVINE PROVIDENCE, SAN ANTONIO, TEXAS P

Founded in France in 1762. First Foundation in the United States in 1866.
The Generalate: P.O. Box 197, 18811 Scenic Loop Rd., Helotes, TX 78023. Tel: 210-695-8721; Fax: 210-695-6033. Sr. Lora Ann Quinonez, Supr. Gen., Councilors; Sr. Ann Umscheid; Sr. Regina Decker; Sr. Rose Kruppa; Sr. Lourdes Leal; Sr. Suzanne Dancer, Treas.; Sr. Margaret Riche, Community Archivist.
Legal Titles & Holdings: *Congregation of Divine Providence, Inc. Providence Trust,* Helotes, TX.
Novitiate and Formation: Formation/Vocation Office, 515 S.W. 24th St., San Antonio, TX 78207-4600. Tel: 210-431-3587.
Total number in community 344.
Properties owned: *The Generalate, Helotes,* TX; *Moye Center,* Castroville, TX; *Our Lady of the Lake Retirement Center,* San Antonio, TX.
Ministry in all levels of Education; Catechetical Centers; Hospitals, Clinics; Diocesan Offices; Retreat Houses; Spiritual Direction-Counseling; Pastoral; Social Work; Chaplaincies in Public Institutions; Home-Health Care; Administration.
Represented in the Archdioceses of Chicago, Denver, Milwaukee, New Orleans, Oklahoma City, San Antonio, San Francisco and in the Dioceses of Alexandria, Austin, Baton Rouge, Beaumont, Brownsville, Corpus Christi, Dallas, El Paso, Fort Worth, Fresno, Gallup, Galveston-Houston, Lafayette (LA), Lake Charles, Lexington, St. Petersburg, San Angelo, Savannah, Shreveport, Springfield-Cape Giradeau, Tucson, Tulsa and Victoria. Also in Brazil, Ghana, and Mexico.

[1020] (S.D.R.)—SISTERS OF THE DIVINE REDEEMER P

Founded in 1849 at Niederbronn, France. First founded in the United States on Oct. 6, 1912 at McKeesport, Pennsylvania.
Generalate: Rome, Italy. Sr. M. Emelia Grabner, Gen. Supr.
American Province (1922): *Divine Redeemer Motherhouse,* 999 Rock Run Rd., Elizabeth, PA 15037. Tel: 412-751-8600; Fax: 412-751-0355. Sr. M. Monica Kosztolnyik, Prov. Supr.; Sr. Bernard Szeman, Archivist.
Total number in province 58.
Legal Titles and Holdings: *Sisters of the Divine Redeemer Charitable Trust Divine Redeemer Health Care Ministries Corp.,* Elizabeth, PA.
Sisters serve and staff: Elementary Schools; Personal Care Home; CCD Centers; Parish Ministry; Nursing Home.
Represented in the Archdiocese of Philadelphia and the Dioceses of Buffalo, and Pittsburgh.

[1030] (S.D.S.)—SISTERS OF THE DIVINE SAVIOR P

Founded in Tivoli, Italy, in 1888. First foundation in the United States in 1895.
General Motherhouse: Rome, Italy. Viale Mura Gianicolensi 67; Sr. Jean Schafer, Supr. General.
North American Province: *Sisters of the Divine Savior,* 4311 N. 100 St., Milwaukee, WI 53222-1393. Tel: 414-466-0810; Fax: 414-466-4335. Sr. Grace Mary Croft, S.D.S., Prov. Supr.; Sr. Monica Lietz, Archivist.
Total number in U.S. Community 139.
Ministry in Novitiate; all levels of Education; Pastoral and Social Services; Health Care; and Homes for the Aged.
Properties owned or sponsored: *St. Anne's Home for the Elderly; St. Mary's Nursing Home; Divine Savior Holy Angels High School,* Milwaukee, WI; *Divine Savior Hospital and Nursing Home,* Portage, WI; *Divine Savior Holy Angels High School Endowment Foundation, Inc.,* Milwaukee, WI; *St. Mary's Convent,* St. Nazianz, WI.
Represented in the Archdioceses of Baltimore, Chicago and Milwaukee and the Dioceses of Birmingham, Green Bay, Jackson, La Crosse, Lexington, Madison, Phoenix, Rapid City, Saginaw, Sioux Falls and Tucson.

[1040] (C.D.S.)—CONGREGATION OF THE DIVINE SPIRIT D

First foundation in Erie, Pennsylvania in 1956.
Motherhouse: 409 W. Sixth St., Erie, PA 16507. Tel: 814-455-3590. Mother Patricia O'Connor, Supr. Gen.
Membership 47.
Sisters serve and staff: Parochial Schools 1; CCD Activities 1; Home for Aged 1; Social Work.
Represented in the Dioceses of Erie and Youngstown.

[1050] (O.P.)—DOMINICAN CONTEMPLATIVE NUNS P

(The Nuns of the Order of Preachers)

Founded in France in 1206. First foundation in the United States in 1880. Monastic contemplative branch of the Order of Preachers. Papal cloister.
Monastery of St. Dominic: 375 13th Ave., Newark, NJ 07103. Tel: 973-622-6622. Sr. Catherine Mary, O.P., Prioress.
Total number in community 20.
Nuns of the Order of Preachers O.P.: Corpus Christi Monastery, 1230 Lafayette Ave., Bronx, NY 10474. Tel: 718-328-6996. Sr. Lee, O.P., Prioress.
Total number in community 23.
Monastery of the Blessed Sacrament, (Contemplative, Cloistered): *Dominican Nuns of Perpetual Adoration,* 29575 Middlebelt, Farmington Hills, MI 48334-2311. Tel: 248-626-8321; 8253; Fax: 248-626-8724. Sr. Mary Thomas, O.P., Prioress.
Cloistered Professed Nuns 37; Extern Professed Sisters 3.
Monastery of the Angels: *Cloistered Dominican Nuns of Perpetual Adoration,* 1977 Carmen Ave., Los Angeles, CA 90068. Tel: 213-466-2186. Sr. Mary Raymond, O.P., Prioress.
Sisters 25.
Legal Title: *The Monastery of the Angels.*
Daughter Houses:
Monastery of the Angels Karachi, Pakistan. Mother Mary Augustine, O.P., Prioress.
Sisters 18.
Queen of Angels Monastery Bocaue, Bulacan, Philippines. Sr. Mary of Jesus, O.P., Prioress.
Sisters 22.
Corpus Christi Monastery: 215 Oak Grove Ave., Menlo Park, CA 94025. Tel: 650-322-1801; Fax: 650-322-6816. Sr. Mary of the Holy Family, O.P., Prioress.
Cloistered Total number in community 24.
Dominican Nuns O.P.: *Monastery of the Mother of God,* 1430 Riverdale St., West Springfield, MA 01089-4698. Tel: 413-736-3639; Fax: 413-736-0850 Ext: 18. Sr. Mary St. John, O.P., Prioress.
Total number in community 26.
Dominican Contemplative Nuns of the Perpetual Rosary: *Monastery of Our Lady of the Rosary,* 335 Doat St., Buffalo, NY 14211-2199. Tel: 716-892-0066. Mother Rose of St. Mary, O.P., Prioress.
Legal Title: *Dominican Nuns of the Perpetual Rosary.*
Professed 30; Postulants 5.
Monastery of Our Lady of Grace: North Guilford, CT 06437. Tel: 203-457-0599. Sr. Mary Ann, O.P., Prioress.
Legal Title: *Dominican Nuns of North Guilford, CT Inc.*
Total number in community 46.
Monastery of the Infant Jesus: *Dominican Contemplative Nuns O.P.,* 1501 Lotus Ln., Lufkin, TX 75904. Tel: 409-634-4233; Fax: 409-634-2156. Sr. Mary John, O.P., Prioress.
Total number in community 27.
Monastery of Our Lady of the Rosary (Rosary Shrine): Morris Ave. & Springfield Ave., Summit, NJ 07901. Tel: 908-273-1228. Sr. Mary Martin de Porres of Jesus, O.P., Prioress.
Professed Choir Sisters 19; Novices 1; Postulants 1.
Nuns of the Order of Preachers O.P.: *Monastery of Mary the Queen,* 1310 W. Church St., Elmira, NY 14905. Tel: 607-734-9506; Fax: 607-734-1452. Sr. Mary of the Sacred Heart, O.P., Prioress.
Total number in community 13.
Monastery of the Dominican Nuns of the Perpetual Rosary (Cloistered): 14th St. & West St., Union City, NJ 07087. Tel: 201-866-7004. Mother Mary Clare, O.P., Prioress.
Professed Sisters 8; Novices 1.
Monastery of the Perpetual Rosary: 1500 Haddon Ave., Camden, NJ 08103. Mother M. Immaculate Heart, O.P., Prioress.
Professed Nuns 7.
St. Dominic's Monastery (Contemplative): 4901 16th St. N.W., Washington, DC 20011-3839. Sr. Mary Dominic, O.P., Prioress.
Nuns 10.
The Dominican Nuns of the Perpetual Rosary (Cloistered-Contemplative): *Monastery of the Immaculate Heart of Mary,* 1834 Lititz Pike, Lancaster, PA 17601-6585. Tel: 717-569-2104; Fax: 717-569-1598. Mother Mary Veronica, O.P., Prioress.
Solemnly Professed 12; Temporarily Professed 2; Novices 2; Postulants 1.
Dominican Monastery of the Perpetual Rosary: 802 Court St., Syracuse, NY 13208. Tel: 315-471-6762. Sr. Mary Augustine, O.P., Prioress, Solemn Vows, Papal enclosure.
Total number in community 11.
Dominican Monastery of St. Jude: P.O. Box 170, Marbury, AL 36051. Tel: 205-755-1322. Dominican Nuns of Perpetual Rosary and Adoration; Mother Mary Aimee of the Holy Spirit, O.P., Prioress.
Professed Nuns 9.

[1060] (O.P.)—DOMINICAN CONTEMPLATIVE SISTERS D

(Cloistered Contemplative)

Founded in Calais, France in 1880.
Monastery of the Dominican Sisters of the Perpetual Rosary (Cloistered): 217 N. 68th St., Milwaukee, WI 53213. Tel: 414-258-0579. Mother Miriam Leonard, O.P., Prioress.
Professed Sisters 13; /qdepartm.

[1070] (O.P.)—DOMINICAN SISTERS

1There are thirty Congregations of the Dominican Sisters of the Third Order of St. Dominic in the United States. The list of General Motherhouses follows in the order of seniority. If the Congregation is known under a more familiar name, that name is given under the name of the Congregation.

[1070-01] CONGREGATION OF ST. CATHARINE OF SIENA (1822) P

The first American Foundation of the Dominican Sisters in the United States founded in Kentucky in 1822.
General Motherhouse: *Congregational Offices of St. Catharine of Siena,* 2645 Bardstown Rd., St. Catharine, KY 40061. Tel: 606-336-9303; Fax: 606-336-9306. Sr. Joan Scanlon, O.P., Pres.; Sr. Louise Quinlan, O.P., Archivist.
Legal Title: *The Literary Society of Saint Catharine of Siena.*
Total number in community 301.
Sisters serve and staff: Colleges and Universities; High Schools; Elementary Schools; Foreign Missions; Health Care-Facilities; Diocesan Offices; Pastoral Associates-Assistants; Parish Ministry; Chaplain-Pastoral Care; Directors Religious Education, and Human Services.
Properties owned: *Rosary Manor,* Watertown, MA; *Dominican Sisters,* Plainville, MA; *St. Mel Independent School,* Gloucester, MA; *Sansbury Memorial Infirmary; St. Catharine Motherhouse; St. Catharine College,* St. Catharine, KY; *St. Agnes Academy-St. Dominic School*, Memphis, TN.
Represented in the Archdioceses of Boston, Chicago, Louisville, New York, Omaha, St. Louis and the Dioceses of Bismarck, Brooklyn, Brownsville, Covington, Fort Wayne-South Bend, Grand Island, Jackson, Joliet, Lincoln, Lubbock, Manchester, Memphis, Norwich, Providence, Rockford, Saginaw, St. Petersburg, Shreveport, Springfield (MA) and Trenton.

[1070-02] CONGREGATION OF ST. MARY OF THE SPRINGS (1830) P

General Motherhouse: *Dominican Sisters - St. Mary of the Springs Motherhouse,* 2320 Airport Dr., Columbus, OH 43219-2098. Tel: 614-252-2137; Fax:

614-252-7435. Sr. Mary Faith Geelan, O.P., Major Supr.
Total number in community 330.
Properties owned and sponsored: Dominican Academy, New York, NY Ohio Dominican College, Columbus, OH St. Mary's Montessori Pre-school & Kindergarten, Columbus, OH Albertus Magnus College, New Haven, CT.
Ministry in Diocesan Offices; the field of Academic Education at all levels; Religious Education; Adult Education Programs; Congregational Infirmary; Hospitals; Home Health Care Agencies; Care of the Elderly; Parish Ministry; Pastoral Care; Justice and Peace Ministry; Family Care; Liturgy Preaching and Spirituality Programs; Research Programs; Missionaries; Counseling and Canon Law Ministry; Campus Ministry; Social Work.
Represented in the Archdioceses of Baltimore, Cincinnati, Denver, Detroit, Hartford, New Orleans, New York, Santa Fe, Seattle, Washington and the Dioceses of Brooklyn, Bridgeport, Columbus, Fort Wayne-South Bend, Gary, Green Bay, Harrisburg, Lexington, Norwich, Pittsburgh, Providence, Rockford, Steubenville, St. Petersburg, Venice and Wheeling-Charleston. Also in Puerto Rico, Peru, Italy and Bolivia.

[1070-03] SINSINAWA DOMINICAN CONGREGATION OF THE MOST HOLY ROSARY (1847) P

Generalate: Sinsinawa, WI 53824. Tel: 608-748-4411. Sr. Jean McSweeney, O.P., Prioress of the Congregation.
Interdependent Provinces (1987):
Eastern Province 533 Ashland Ave., River Forest, IL 60305. Tel: 708-366-0282. Sr. Marise Barry, O.P., Prov.
Southern Province 719 Penn Ave. N.E., Atlanta, GA 30308-1501. Tel: 404-892-6814. Sr. Patricia Caraher, O.P., Prov.
Western Province 3330 Kendall St., Wheat Ridge, CO 80033-4944. Tel: 303-462-0200. Sr. Carol Coenen, O.P., Prov.; Sr. Marjorie Buttner, O.P., Archivist.
Total number in community 919.
Novitiate: Manchester, MO. Tel: 3142-391-4934.
Properties owned or Institutions sponsored: *Sinsinawa Dominicans, Inc. Dominican University,* River Forest, IL; *Bethlehem Academy,* Faribault, MN; *Dominican High School,* Whitefish Bay, WI; *Queen of Peace High School,* Burbank, IL; *Trinity High School,* River Forest, IL; *Dominican Motherhouse,* Sinsinawa, WI; *St. Dominic Villa,* Dubuque, IA; *Camp We-Ha-Kee,* Winter, WI; *The Bridge,* Denmark, WI; *Edgewood Campus School; Edgewood High School; Edgewood College,* Madison, WI.
Ministry in a variety of cultures in Preaching & Evangelization; Elementary, Secondary and Higher Education; Medical, Legal and Social Services; Adult and Religious Education; Diocesan and Parish Administration, Spiritual Direction and Counseling; Rural, Migrant and Native American Services; Writing Research.
Represented in the Archdioceses of Anchorage, Atlanta, Chicago, Denver, Dubuque, Indianapolis, Los Angeles, Miami, Milwaukee, Mobile, New Orleans, New York, Oklahoma City, Omaha, St. Louis, St. Paul-Minneapolis, San Antonio, San Francisco, Santa Fe, Seattle, Washington and the Dioceses of Altoona-Johnstown, Austin, Baker, Beaumont, Birmingham, Brownsville, Camden, Charleston, Charlotte, Cheyenne, Columbus, Crookston, Dallas, Des Moines, Fairbanks, Fort Wayne-South Bend, Gallup, Gary, Gaylord, Grand Island, Great Falls-Billings, Green Bay, Helena, Honolulu, Jackson, Joliet, Juneau, Kansas City-St. Joseph, La Crosse, Lexington, Madison, Memphis, Nashville, New Ulm, Oakland, Ogdensburg, Orange, Orlando, Owensboro, Palm Beach, Pensacola-Tallahassee, Peoria, Phoenix, Richmond, Rockford, Sacramento, Saginaw, San Angelo, San Diego, San Jose, St. Augustine, St. Petersburg, Santa Rosa, Spokane, Superior, Tucson, Tulsa, Venice and Wheeling-Charleston. Also in Bolivia, Guatemala, Switzerland, Italy, and Trinidad.

[1070-04] CONGREGATION OF THE MOST HOLY NAME (1850) P

Generalate: *Dominican Sisters of San Rafael,* 1520 Grand Ave., San Rafael, CA 94901. Tel: 415-453-8303; Fax: 415-453-8367. Sr. Patricia Simpson, O.P., Prioress Gen.
Total number in community 156.
Legal Holdings and Titles: *Justin Siena High School,* Napa, CA; *Siena High School,* Napa, CA; *San Domenico School,* San Anselmo, CA; *Santa Sabina Retreat Center,* San Rafael, CA; *St. Rose Academy,* San Francisco, CA; *St. Joseph's HealthCare Corporation St. Joseph's Medical Center,* Stockton, CA; *St. Mary's Health Care Corporation St. Mary's Regional Medical Center,* Reno, NV; *Sisters of St. Dominic, Congregation of the Most Holy Name,* San Rafael, CA; *Mission Holding Corporation,* San Rafael, CA.
Represented in the Archdioceses of Los Angeles, San Francisco and in the Dioceses of Oakland, Reno, Sacramento, San Jose, Santa Rosa and Stockton. And also in Canada and Mexico.

[1070-05] CONGREGATION OF THE HOLY CROSS (1853) D

General Motherhouse: *Queen of the Rosary Motherhouse,* Albany Ave., Amityville, NY 11701. Tel: 516-842-6000; Fax: 516-842-0240. Sr. Mary Hughes, O.P., Prioress; Sr. Margaret Clines, O.P., Archivist.
Total number in community 754.
Sisters are engaged in the ministry of: Education at all levels; Catechetical Schools; Handicapped, Adult and Continuing Education; Hospitals; Homes for the Aged; Residence for Senior Citizens; Spiritual Life Centers; Chaplaincy; Advocacy; Communications; Social Service Institutions; Shelters; Pastoral Services; Prison ministry; Retreats; Health Services.
Represented in the Archdioceses of Baltimore, Hartford, Newark, New York, San Francisco, Seattle and Washington and in Dioceses of Albany, Brooklyn, Kalamazoo, Orlando, Paterson, Providence, Rochester, Rockville Centre, St. Augustine, St.Petersburg, and Trenton. Also in Puerto Rico, and Colombia.

[1070-07] CONGREGATION OF ST. CECILIA (1860) P

General Motherhouse: *St. Cecilia Convent,* 801 Dominican Dr., Nashville, TN 37228-1909. Tel: 615-256-5486; Fax: 615-726-1333. Mother Christine Born, O.P., Prioress Gen.; Sr. Rose Marie Masserano, Archivist.
Professed sisters in community 135; Novices 9; Postulants 7.
Ministry in the field of Academic Education at all levels.
Legal Holdings and Titles: *Aquinas College,* Nashville, TN.
Represented in the Archdioceses of Baltimore, Cincinnati, Denver, Washington and the Dioceses of Arlington, Birmingham, Knoxville, Memphis, Nashville and Richmond.

[1070-08] CONGREGATION OF ST. MARY (1860) P

General Motherhouse: *Dominican Sisters,* 580 Broadway, New Orleans, LA 70118. Tel: 504-861-8183; Fax: 504-861-8184. Sr. Therese Leckert, O.P., Prioress.
Total number in community 73.
Ministry in Education and Social Apostolates.
Legal Holdings: *St. Mary's Dominican High School,* New Orleans, LA; *Dominican Conference Center,* New Orleans, LA; *Rosaryville Retreat Center,* Ponchatoula, LA.
Represented in the Archdiocese of New Orleans, Dioceses of Baton Rouge and Houma-Thibodeaux.

[1070-09] CONGREGATION OF ST. CATHERINE OF SIENA (1862) P

General Motherhouse: *Convent of St. Catherine,* Siena Center, 5635 Erie St., Racine, WI 53402-1900. Tel: 414-639-4100. Tel: 414-639-9702. Sr. Evelyn Lins, O.P., Pres.; Sr. Diane Kenel, Archivist.
Total number in community 266.
Sisters minister in the areas of Elementary, Secondary, Higher and Music-Cultural Education; Adult Education; Religious Education; Administration; Parish and Pastoral Ministry; Prison Ministry; Communications; Social Justice; Campus Ministry; Social Services, Hospital and Health Services; Writing-Research; Hospital Chaplains; Diocesan Services; Retreats-Prayer Programs; Community Services.
Legal Holdings and Titles: *Sisters of St. Dominic,* Racine, WI; *Dominican College of Racine, Inc.,* Racine, WI; *St. Catherine's High School of Racine, Inc.,* Racine, WI; *Racine Dominican Ministries, Inc.,* Racine, WI; *Our Lady of the Oaks Convent,* Pewaukee, WI; *St. Catherine's Infirmary, Inc.,* Racine, WI.
Properties sponsored by the Franciscan Sisters, Daughters of the Sacred Hearts of Jesus and Mary, Wheaton, IL and the Sisters of St. Dominic, Racine, WI: Catherine Marian Housing, Inc. Villa St. Anna, Inc., Racine, WI.
Represented in the Archdioceses of Chicago, Detroit, Milwaukee, Newark, New York, St. Louis, Santa Fe, Washington and in the Dioceses of Arlington, Brownsville, Gallup, Jackson, Green Bay, La Crosse, Las Vegas, Lexington, Lansing, Madison, Marquette, Nashville, St. Cloud, Salt Lake City, Toledo and Wilmington Also in Kenya.

[1070-10] DOMINICAN SISTERS OF SPRINGFIELD IN ILLINOIS (1873) P

General Motherhouse: *Sacred Heart Convent,* 1237 W. Monroe St., Springfield, IL 62704. Tel: 217-787-0481; Fax: 217-787-8169. Sr. Rose Miriam Schulte, O.P., Prioress Gen.
Total number in community 349.
Ministry in elementary, secondary schools and college religious & academic education; daycare and learning center; hospices, hospitals, nursing homes, congregations' infirmary, and retirement centers; retreat & renewal centers; administrative positions in parishes and diocesan offices; parish liturgist/musician & pastoral associates; prison ministry; social services; and; foreign missions.
Legal Holdings or Titles: *Dominican Sisters of Springfield, Illinois; Alfred Fortin Villa and Day Care Learning Center,* Bourbonnais, IL; *Benincasa-Dominican Renewal Center,* Riverton, IL; *Marian Catholic High School,* Chicago Heights, IL; *Rosary High School,* Aurora, IL; *Sacred Heart-Griffin High School,* Springfield, IL; *St. Dominic-Jackson Memorial Hospital,* Jackson, MS.
Represented in the Archdioceses of Chicago and St. Paul-Minneapolis and the Dioceses of Baton Rouge, Belleville, Duluth, La Crosse, Little Rock, Jackson, Joliet, Peoria, Rockford, and Springfield (IL). Also in Peru.

[1070-11] CONGREGATION OF OUR LADY OF THE ROSARY (1876) D

General Motherhouse and Novitiate: *Dominican Convent of Our Lady of the Rosary,* Sparkill, NY 10976. Tel: 914-359-6400. Sr. Kathleen Kane, O.P., Pres.
Legal Title: *Dominican Congregation of Our Lady of the Rosary.*
Total number in community 475.
Ministry in High Schools and Elementary Schools; Parish Associates; Religious Education; Hospital Ministry; Colleges; House of Prayer; Housing and Community Centers; Foreign Missions; Substance Abuse Recovery.
Represented in the Archdioceses of New York Newark, St. Louis and the Dioceses of Belleville, Bridgeport, Brooklyn, Great Falls-Billings, Helena, Jefferson City, Metuchen, Oakland, Paterson, Phoenix, Rockville Centre, Rockford, San Diego, St. Petersburg, Scranton, Trenton and Wilmington. Also in Pakistan and Peru.

[1070-12]CONGREGATION OF THE QUEEN OF THE HOLY ROSARY (1876) P

General Motherhouse: *Dominican Convent,* P.O. Box 3908, Mission San Jose, CA 94539. Tel: 510-657-2468; Fax: 510-657-1734. Sr. Rose Marie Hennessy, Prioress Gen.; Sr. M. Evangela Balde, Community Archivist.
Legal Title: *Dominican Sisters of Mission San Jose, a Corporation Queen of the Holy Rosary College, a Corporation,* Mission San Jose, CA; *St. Catherine's Military School, a corp.,* Anaheim, CA; *Immaculate Conception Academy, a corp.,* San Francisco, CA; *Flintridge Sacred Heart Academy, a corp.,* La Canada-Flintridge, CA.
Total number in community 253.
Ministry in Parishes; Colleges; High Schools and Elementary Schools; Kindergarten and Music School.
Represented in the Archdioceses of Los Angeles, Portland (OR) and San Francisco and the Dioceses of Oakland, Orange, San Jose and Tucson.

[1070-13] CONGREGATION OF THE MOST HOLY ROSARY (1892) P

General Motherhouse: 1257 Siena Heights Dr., Adrian, MI 49221. Tel: 517-265-5135; Fax: 517-265-4733. Sr. Patricia Walter, O.P., Prioress.
Mission Chapters (1982):
Florida Mission Chapter 810 N. Olive Ave., West Palm Beach, FL 33401. Tel: 407-832-6521. Sr. Marie Carleen Maly, O.P., Chapter Prioress.
Great Lakes Mission Chapter 9400 Courville, Detroit, MI 48224. Tel: 313-882-8484. Sr. Rosemary Asaro, O.P., Chapter Prioress.
Mid-Atlantic Mission Chapter 5735 Dawsonville Hwy., Gainesville, GA 30506. Tel: 770-844-1370. Sr. Mary Kathryn Cliatt, O.P., Chapter Prioress.
Midwest Dominican Mission Chapter 8925 S. Kostner Ave., Hometown, IL 60456. Tel: 708-636-7566. Sr. Joella Miller, O.P., Chapter Prioress.

Motherhouse Mission Chapter 1257 Siena Heights Dr., Adrian, MI 49221. Tel: 517-265-5135. Sr. Marianne O'Neill, O.P., Chapter Prioress.
Nokomis Mission Chapter 7506 Inkster Rd., Dearborn Heights, MI 48127. Tel: 313-274-3543. Sr. Nancyann Turner, O.P., Chapter Prioress.
Overseas Mission Chapter 1257 Siena Heights Dr., Adrian, MI 49221. Tel: 517-265-5135. Sr. Mary Patricia Dewey, O.P., Chapter Prioress.
Pacific West Mission Chapter P.O. Box 2235, Santa Cruz, CA 95062. Tel: 408-457-7117. Sr. Molly Giller, O.P., Chapter Prioress.
South East Adrian Mission Chapter 15021 Twelve Mile Rd., Warren, MI 48093. Tel: 810-777-0105. Sr. Arlene Seckel, O.P., Chapter Prioress.
Southwest Mission Chapter 6126 E. Ensenada St., Mesa, AZ 85205. Tel: 602-985-7920. Sr. Virginia Kleckner, O.P., Chapter Prioress.
Upper Midwest Mission Chapter 8925 S. Kostner Ave., Hometown, IL 60456. Tel: 708-636-8178. Sr. Patricia Brady, O.P., Chapter Prioress.

Total number in community 1,206.

Legal Holdings or Titles: *Benefit Trust of the Adrian Dominican Congregation,* Adrian, MI; *Adrian Dominican Sisters Office of Development,* Adrian, MI; *Dominican High School,* Detroit, MI; *Dominican Santa Cruz Hospital,* Santa Cruz, CA; *Maria Health Care Center,* Adrian, MI; *Regina Dominican High School,* Wilmette, IL; *Rosarian Academy,* West Palm Beach, FL; *Siena Heights College,* Adrian, MI; *St. Joseph Academy,* Adrian, MI; *St. Rose Dominican Hospital,* Henderson, NV; *Weber Retreat Center,* Adrian, MI.

Sisters minister in the areas of Formal Education - as administrators, teachers and consultants at elementary, secondary, college, state and diocesan levels; Pastoral Ministry - parishes, hospitals and campuses; Religious Education - coordinators and teachers; Social Services - case workers, administrators, counselors, therapists, consultants, caregivers for elderly and staff for retirement centers; Health Services - administrators, nurses, therapists, doctors, physician assistants, psychologists, technologists, pharmacists and dietitians; Business Services - directors, accountants, secretaries, administrative assistants, typists, bookkeepers, office managers, office staff, drivers and housekeeping staff; Spiritual Direction - retreat work, formation, Congregation leadership and as diocesan Vicars for Religious; Social Justice - coordinators, staff and community organizers; other ministries including research, law, science, public relations, art, communications and full-time study.

Represented in the Archdioceses of Atlanta, Boston, Chicago, Cincinnati, Detroit, Indianapolis, Kansas City in Kansas, Los Angeles, Louisville, Miami, Milwaukee, New Orleans, New York, Oklahoma City, Philadelphia, St. Louis, San Antonio, San Francisco, Santa Fe, Seattle and Washington and the Dioceses of Austin, Birmingham, Charleston, Cleveland, Columbus, Des Moines, Duluth, El Paso, Erie, Fresno, Fort Wayne-South Bend, Gallup, Galveston-Houston, Gary, Gaylord, Grand Rapids, Green Bay, Helena, Jackson, Joliet, Kalamazoo, Knoxville, La Crosse, Lafayette, Lansing, Lexington, Madison, Marquette, Monterey, Oakland, Orange, Orlando, Palm Beach, Pensacola-Tallahassee, Peoria, Phoenix, Pittsburgh, Portland (ME), Providence, Pueblo, Raleigh, Rapid City, Reno, Richmond, Rockville Centre, Rockford, Saginaw, St. Augustine, St. Cloud, St. Petersburg, Salt Lake City, San Bernardino, San Diego, San Jose, Santa Rosa, Savannah, Springfield (IL), Toledo, Tucson, Venice, Wheeling-Charleston and Youngstown. Also in Belgium, Canada, Dominican Republic, Puerto Rico and South Africa.

[1070-14] CONGREGATION OF OUR LADY OF THE SACRED HEART (1877) P

General Motherhouse: *Marywood,* 2025 E. Fulton St., Grand Rapids, MI 49503. Tel: 616-459-2910; Fax: 616-454-6105. Sr. Barbara Hansen, O.P., Prioress; Sr. Michael Ellen Carling, O.P., Archivist.

Legal Holdings or Titles: *Sisters of the Order of St. Dominic of Grand Rapids; Marywood Academy; Sisters of St. Dominic of the Congregation of Our Lady of the Sacred Heart Charitable Trust; Dominican Land Company.*

Total number in community 349.

Sisters are involved in: Elementary and Secondary Education; Liturgy; Religious Education; Pastoral Ministry; Diocesan Offices; Health Care; Congregational Services; Social Work; Foreign Missions; Justice Advocacy.

Represented in the Archdioceses of Baltimore, Chicago, Denver, Detroit, Milwaukee, Mobile, New Orleans, New York, Omaha, St. Louis, Santa Fe, Seattle, Washington and in the Dioceses of Albany, Brownsville, Cleveland, El Paso, Gallup, Gaylord, Grand Rapids, Kalamazoo, Lafayette, Lansing, Lexington, Manchester, Providence, Rockville Centre, Saginaw, St. Cloud, Shreveport, Sioux Falls, Toledo and Wheeling-Charleston. Also in Peru.

[1070-15] CONGREGATION OF SAINT DOMINIC (1878) D

General Motherhouse: *Sisters of Saint Dominic of Blauvelt,* New York, 496 Western Hwy., Blauvelt, NY 10913-2097. Tel: 914-359-5600; Fax: 914-359-5773. Sr. Barbara Werner, O.P., Pres.; Sr. Judith Campbell, O.P., Archivist.

Total number in community 236.

Sisters serve and staff: Elementary; Secondary; Higher Education; Special Education; Hospital Care; Pastoral Care; Parish Ministry; Retreat Work; Child Care; Neighborhood Services; Services to Migrants; Services to Chemically Dependent.

Represented in the Archdioceses of Newark and New York and in the Dioceses of Orlando, Paterson, Providence, Rockville Centre and San Bernardino. Also in Jamaica.

[1070-16] DOMINICAN SISTERS OF THE SICK POOR - CONGREGATION OF THE IMMACULATE CONCEPTION (1879) D

General Motherhouse: *Mariandale - Queen of the Rosary Convent,* 299 N. Highland Ave., Ossining, NY 10562. Tel: 914-941-4455. Sr. Kathleen Hebbeler, O.P., Pres.

Total number in community 53.

Legal Titles and Holdings: *Dominican Sisters of the Sick Poor Ministry Trust.*

Sisters minister in low income areas providing health, social, community and pastoral services.

Represented in the Archdioceses of Cincinnati, Denver, Detroit, Newark, New York, Philadelphia and Washington and the Dioceses of Allentown, Jackson, Richmond and Rockville Centre.

[1070-17] CONGREGATION OF ST. CATHERINE DE RICCI (1880) P

General Motherhouse: *Fanjeaux,* 750 Ashbourne Rd., Elkins Park, PA 19027-2596. Tel: 215-635-6027. Sr. Mary Ellen Bennett, O.P., Pres.-elect.

Professed Sisters 94; Novices 5.

Sisters serve and staff: Retreat Houses; CCD Centers and Parish Services; Hospital; Pastoral Ministry; College; Diocesan Offices; Residence for Women; Campus Ministry; Special Services; Residence for Aging; Spiritual Direction; Counselling Center; House of Prayer; Liturgical Art Studio.

Properties owned: *Dominican Retreat House/Convent of Our Lady of Prouille,* Elkins Park, PA; *St. Dominic Hall,* Elkins Park, PA; *Dominican Retreat, Immaculate Heart of Mary Convent,* McLean, VA; *Dominican Retreat House/Our Lady of Grace Convent,* Schenectady, NY; *Dominican Retreat House/Queen of Apostles Convent,* Miami, FL; *The Lucy Eaton Smith Residence,* Philadelphia, PA; *St. Catherine Hall Efharisto Studio, Inc.,* Baltimore, MD.

Represented in the Archdioceses of Baltimore, Cincinnati, Detroit, Miami, Newark, Philadelphia, Santa Fe and the Dioceses of Albany, Arlington, Biloxi, Camden, Harrisburg, Orlando, Palm Beach, Providence, Raleigh, St. Petersburg, and Scranton.

[1070-18] SISTERS OF ST. DOMINIC OF THE AMERICAN CONGREGATION OF THE SACRED HEART OF JESUS (1881) D

Dominican Motherhouse: 1 Ryerson Ave., Caldwell, NJ 07006. Tel: 973-403-3331; Fax: 973-228-9611. Sr. Joan Doyle, O.P., Prioress; Sr. Helen Marguerite, O.P., Archivist.

Total number in community 221.

Legal Title: *Sisters of St. Dominic of Caldwell, N.J.*

Properties owned: *Caldwell College,* Caldwell, NJ; *Mount Saint Dominic Academy,* Caldwell, NJ; *St. Dominic Academy,* Jersey City, NJ; *Lacordaire Academy,* Upper Montclair, NJ.

Ministry in Education at all levels; Pastoral Ministry; Health and Human Services.

Represented in the Archdioceses of Boston, Newark, Portland, and the Dioceses of Alexandria, Metuchen, Orange, Paterson, Savannah, Springfield (IL) and Trenton.

[1070-19] DOMINICAN SISTERS OF HOUSTON, TEXAS (CONGREGATION OF THE SACRED HEART) (1882) P

General Motherhouse & Novitiate: *Dominican Sisters,* 6501 Almeda Rd., Houston, TX 77021. Tel: 713-747-3310; Fax: 713-747-4707. Sr. Paula Enderle, O.P., Prioress.

Legal Title: *Dominican Sisters of Houston, Texas, Inc. (aka Sacred Heart Convent of Houston).*

Total number in community 146.

Properties owned and sponsored: *St. Agnes Academy; St. Agnes Academy Foundation; St. Pius X High School; St. Pius X High School Foundation, Inc.; The Sacred Heart Convent Retirement Trust.*

Ministry in the field of Academic Education at all levels and Parish Ministry.

Represented in the Archdioceses of Baltimore, Los Angeles, San Antonio, St. Louis, Seattle and the Dioceses of Austin, Beaumont, Galveston-Houston, Lake Charles, San Angelo, San Bernardino, San Jose and Tyler. Also in Guatemala.

[1070-20] CONGREGATION OF ST. THOMAS AQUINAS (1888) P

Motherhouse: *Tacoma Dominican Center,* 935 Fawcett Ave. S., Tacoma, WA 98402-5605. Tel: 253-272-9688; Fax: 253-272-8790. Sr. Agnes Huck, O.P., Pres.

Total number in community 84.

Ministry in a variety of apostolacies.

Legal Holdings and Titles: *Sisters of St. Dominic, Tacoma Dominican Center; Sisters of St. Dominic - Tacoma Charitable Trust.*

Represented in the Archdioceses of Los Angeles, San Francisco, Seattle and the Dioceses of Baker, Fresno, St. Augustine, San Diego, San Bernardino, and Yakima. Also in Canada.

[1070-21] DOMINICAN SISTERS CONGREGATION OF HOLY CROSS (1890) P

General Motherhouse & Novitiate: *Rosary Heights,* P.O. Box 280, Edmonds, WA 98020. Tel: 206-542-7511; 542-3212. Sr. Judy Byron, O.P., Prioress.

Total number in community 71.

Sisters minister in: Elementary, Secondary and University Education; Diocesan, Parish and Hospital Pastoral Ministry; Health Care; Mental Health; Detention; Political; Direct Service and Advocacy with Women and Children; Housing; Peace and Justice; Community Service.

Represented in the Archdioceses of Los Angeles, St. Paul-Minneapolis, San Francisco, Santa Fe, Seattle and the Dioceses of Boise, Fairbanks and San Diego.

[1070-23] CONGREGATION OF ST. ROSE OF LIMA (1896) D
THE SERVANTS OF RELIEF FOR INCURABLE CANCER IN THE U.S.

General Motherhouse: *Rosary Hill Home,* Hawthorne, NY 10532. Tel: 914-769-0114. Mother Marie Edwards, O.P., Mother Gen.

Total number in community 80.

The work of these sisters is confined entirely to the incurable cancerous poor.

Represented in the Archdioceses of Atlanta, New York, Philadelphia and St. Paul-Minneapolis and in the Dioceses of Cleveland and Fall River.

[1070-24] DOMINICAN SISTERS OF GREAT BEND (1902) P

Motherhouse & Novitiate: *Immaculate Conception Convent,* 3600 Broadway, Great Bend, KS 67530. Tel: 316-792-1232. Sr. Betty Werner, O.P., Prioress.

Total number in community 130.

Legal Title: *The Nuns of the Third Order of St. Dominic.*

Sisters serve in: Grade Schools, Secondary Schools; Colleges; Special Education; CCD Centers and Centers for Retreats and Spirituality; Hospitals; Nursing Homes; Infirmary; Home Health Services; Health Care Ministries; Foreign Missions; Ministry to Minorities; Ministry to Aging; Housing; Parish Ministry; Office of Mission and Ministry.

Properties owned: *Central Kansas Medical Center,* Great Bend, KS; with campus at *St. Joseph Memorial Hospital,* Larned, KS; and *St. Rose Campus,* Great Bend, KS; *St. Catherine Hospital,* Garden City, KS; *Hospitality House,* Wichita, KS; *Several Residential Convents Pilgrim House of Praise,* Great Bend, KS; *Heartland Farm,* Pawnee Rock, KS; *Novitiate House,* Great Bend, KS.

Properties owned and sponsored: *Heartland Center for Spirituality,* Great Bend, KS; *St. Martin de Porres Association Dominican Retreat Center,* Great Bend, KS; *Cedar Park Place, Inc.* (Low and Middle Income Housing for Elderly and Handicapped), Great Bend, KS; *Heartland Center for Wholistic Health Association,* Great Bend, KS; *Office of Mission and Ministry,* Great Bend, KS; *Art of Learning Center,* Wichita, KS.

Represented in the Archdioceses of Denver, Kansas City in Kansas, Mobile, Oklahoma City and St. Louis and in the Dioceses of Dodge City, Phoenix,

Pueblo, Salina, San Angelo and Wichita. Also in Africa.

[1070-25] CONGREGATION OF THE DOMINICAN SISTERS OF ST. CATHERINE OF SIENA OF KENOSHA (1911) P

General Motherhouse & Novitiate: P.O. Box 1288, Kenosha, WI 53141. Tel: 414-694-2067; Fax: 414-694-6542. sr. Susan Anne Snyder, O.P., Prioress.

Legal Title: *Congregation of the Dominican Sisters of St. Catherine of Siena of Kenosha, Inc.*

Total number in community 29.

Properties owned: *Holy Rosary Medical Center,* Ontario, OR; *Our Lady of Fatima Villa,* Saratoga, CA; *Mercy Hospital,* Merced, CA.

Represented in the Archdioceses of Milwaukee and San Francisco and the Dioceses of Baker, Columbus, and Fresno. Also in Ecuador.

[1070-26] CONGREGATION OF ST. ROSE OF LIMA (1923) D

General Motherhouse: *St. Joseph's Convent,* 775 Drahner Rd., Box 167, Oxford, MI 48371-0167. Tel: 248-628-2872. Sr. Frances Mary Kernasovich, O.P., Pres.; Sr. Teresita Lipar, O.P., Vice Pres.; Sr. Susan McMahon, O.P., Vice Pres.

Total number in community 47.

Properties owned and sponsored: *St. Mary's Retreat House,* Oxford, MI; *St. Jude Home,* Waterford, MI; *Dominican Center* (Retreat House for teenagers), Oxford, MI; *Lourdes Nursing Home Fox Manor,* Waterford, MI.

Sisters minister in Elementary Schools; Nursing Homes; Retreat House; Parish Ministry; Religious Education; Senior Citizens Residence; Hospital Ministry; Pastoral Assistant.

Represented in the Archdiocese of Detroit and the Dioceses of Gaylord, Lansing and Saginaw.

[1070-27] CONGREGATION OF THE IMMACULATE CONCEPTION (1929) D

Provincial House: *Immaculate Conception Provincial House,* 9000 W. 81st. St., Justice, IL 60458. Tel: 708-458-3040. Mother M. Columba, O.P., Prov. Supr.

Total number in community 25.

Represented in the Archdioceses of Chicago and Milwaukee. Also in Canada.

[1070-28] CONGREGATION OF THE SISTERS OF ST. DOMINIC OF THE IMMACULATE HEART OF MARY (1929) D

General Motherhouse: *Our Lady of the Elms Convent,* 1230 W. Market St., Akron, OH 44313-7185. Tel: 330-836-4908; Fax: 330-836-5913. Sr. Bernadine Baltrinic, O.P., Pres.; Sr. Rebecca Betz, O.P., Archivist.

Total number in community 108.

Properties owned: *Our Lady of the Elms High School; Our Lady of the Elms Elementary School; Our Lady of the Elms Preschool.*

Represented in the Archdioceses of Chicago, Portland, OR, Seattle, St. Louis, and the Dioceses of Cleveland, Fort Wayne-South Bend, Lansing, Little Rock, Phoenix, St. Augustine, St. Petersburg, Toledo and Youngstown. Also in Central America.

[1070-29] DOMINICAN SISTERS OF SPOKANE D

Dominican Center: W. 3102 Ft. George Wright Dr., Spokane, WA 99204. Tel: 509-328-8033; Fax: 509-325-9877. Sr. Judith Nilles, O.P., Prioress.

Total number in community 36.

Legal Holdings or Titles: *Dominican Outreach Services; Dominican Outreach Foundation.*

Represented in the Diocese of Spokane.

[1070-30] DOMINICAN SISTERS OF OAKFORD P

Motherhouse: *Oakford Priory,* P.O. Verulam, Natal, Republic of South Africa. Sr. Gisela Wittershagen, O.P., Supr. Gen.

U.S. Regional Center: 1855 Miramonte Ave., Mountain View, CA 94040. Tel: 650-965-1903; Fax: 650-965-1456. Sr. Ursula Bomholt, O.P., Reg. Supr.

Total number in community 19.

Ministries in Care for the Aged; Pastoral Care; Community Services; Parish Work; Adult Education.

Properties owned: *Villa Siena* (Home for the Aged), Mountain View, CA; *Regional Center,* Mountain View, CA; *Formation House,* San Leandro, CA; *St. Catherine's Convent,* Sunnyvale, CA.

Represented in the Dioceses of Oakland, Phoenix and San Jose.

[1100] (O.P.)—DOMINICAN SISTERS OF CHARITY OF THE PRESENTATION OF THE BLESSED VIRGIN P

Founded in France in 1696. First foundation in the United States in 1906.

Motherhouse: 15 Quai Portillon, 37023, Tours Cedex, France.

Universal total in Congregation 3,377.

Provincial House: 3012 Elm St., Dighton, MA 02715. Tel: 508-669-5425. Tel: 508-669-5023. Sr. Joanna Fernandes, O.P., Prov. Supr.

Total number in province 42.

Ministry in Hospitals; Homes For the Aged; Residence for Working Women & Students; Dispensaries; Migrant Clinic; Education; Pastoral Ministry.

Represented in the Archdiocese of Washington and the Dioceses of Brownsville, Fall River and Providence. Also in India, Haiti, Korea, Peru, Bolivia, Columbia and Mexico.

[1105] (O.P.)—DOMINICAN SISTERS OF HOPE P

Founded July 20, 1995, as a merging of three former Congregations: Dominican Sisters of the Congregation of the Most Holy Rosary of Newburgh, NY; Dominican Sisters of the Sick Poor of Ossining

General Administrative Offices: *Dominican Sisters of Hope,* 299 N. Highland Ave., Ossining, NY 10562. Tel: 914-941-4420; Fax: 914-941-1125. Sr. Catherine Walsh, O.P., Prioress.

Total number in community 329.

Legal Titles and Holdings: *Dominican Sisters of Hope Ministry Trust.*

in Religious & Academic Education at all levels; Health, social, community and pastoral services in low income area; Parish service, counseling, retreats and spiritual direction.

Represented in the Archdioceses of Cincinnati, Denver, Detroit, Hartford, Newark, New York, Oklahoma City, Philadelphia, Washington and the Dioceses of Albany, Allentown, Arlington, Bridgeport, Brooklyn, Burlington, Camden, Fall River, Gallup, Jackson, Lexington, Metuchen, Ogdensburg, Palm Beach, Paterson, Providence, Richmond, Ro.

[1110] (O.P.)—DOMINICAN SISTERS OF OUR LADY OF THE ROSARY AND OF SAINT CATHERINE OF SIENA, CABRA P

Founded in Ireland in 1644.

General Motherhouse: Cabra, Dublin 7, Ireland.

Region of Louisiana established in 1978

Regional House: *Dominican Sisters,* Cabra, 1930 Robert E. Lee, New Orleans, LA 70122. Tel: 504-288-1593. Sr. Elizabeth Ferguson, O.P., Reg. Vicar.

Total number in local community 11.

Ministry in Academic and Religious Education; Parish Ministry; Neighborhood Social Service Agency; Diocesan Tribunal; Prison Ministry; Adult Education; Social Apostolate; Retreats; Spiritual Direction.

Represented in the Archdiocese of New Orleans and the Dioceses of Fort Worth and Houma-Thibodeaux.

[1120] (O.P.)—DOMINICAN SISTERS OF THE ROMAN CONGREGATION P

Founded in France in 1621. First United States foundation in 1904.

General Motherhouse: Rome, Italy. Sr. Rosario de Meer, Supr. Gen.

Universal total in Congregation 734.

U.S. Provincial Office: 304 Oberlin St., Iowa City, IA 52245. Sr. Jacqueline Provencher, O.P., Prov. Prioress.

Total number in community 34.

Properties owned: Retreat House; Residences 5.

Ministry in the field of Religious & Academic Education; Adult Education; Indian Reservation; Pastoral Ministry; Health Care; Social Work.

Represented in the Archdioceses of Chicago, New York and Portland (OR) and in the Dioceses of Davenport, Des Moines, Gallup, Phoenix and Portland (ME).

[1140] (O.P.)—EUCHARISTIC MISSIONARIES OF ST. DOMINIC D

Founded in Louisiana in 1927.

Eucharistic Missionaries of St. Dominic: General Motherhouse, 3801 Canal St. - Suite 400, New Orleans, LA 70119. Tel: 504-486-1133; Fax: 504-486-6547. Sr. Dorothy Trosclair, O.P., Pres.

Perpetually Professed Sisters 46; Missions 20.

Properties owned: *Regina Coeli Retreat Center,* Covington, LA.

Sisters Staff and Serve: Parish and Diocesan Religious Education; Parish and Diocesan Social Services; Parish Administrators; Home Health Nursing; Literacy ministry to immigrants; Hospital Chaplaincy and Parish ministry.

Represented in the Archdiocese New Orleans and the Dioceses of Baton Rouge, Beaumont, Biloxi, Houma-Thibodeaux, Lafayette (LA), Palm Beach, Phoenix, St. Petersburg and Tucson.

[1145] (O.P.)—RELIGIOUS MISSIONARIES OF ST. DOMINIC

General Motherhouse: Via di Val Cannuta 138, 00166, Rome, Italy. Mother Catalina Civit, O.P., Supr. Gen., 2237 Waldron Rd., Corpus Christi, TX 78418. Tel: 512-939-8102; Fax: 512-939-8203. Sr. Maria Purificacion Palis, O.P., Delegate of the Supr. Gen.

Total number in congregation 570; Sisters in the United States 32.

Represented in the Archdiocese of Los Angeles, and the Diocese of Corpus Christi.

[1150] (E.F.M.S.)—EUCHARISTIC FRANCISCAN MISSIONARY SISTERS D

Founded in Mexico in 1943. Mother Maria Gemma de Jesus Aranda, Founderess & Supr. Gen.

Motherhouse: *Our Lady's Convent,* 943 S. Soto St., Los Angeles, CA 90023. Tel: 213-264-6556. 1421 Cota Ave., Torrance, CA 90501. Tel: 213-328-6725. Sr. Gloria de Jesus, E.F.M.S., Gen. Sec.

Total number in community 26.

Legal Title: *Eucharistic Franciscan Missionary Sisters of Los Angeles.*

Sisters serve and staff: The field of Education; Missionary Activities; Catechetics; Social Work; Diocesan and Administration offices.

Represented in the Archdiocese of Los Angeles and the Diocese of Stockton.

[1170] (C.S.S.F.)—FELICIAN SISTERS P
(Congregation of Sisters of St. Felix of Cantalice, of the III Order of St. Francis)

Founded in Poland in 1855. First foundation in the United States in 1874.

General Motherhouse: Via del Casaletto 540, 00151, Rome, Italy. Sr. Mary Cynthia Strzalkowski, C.S.S.F., Min. Gen.

Presentation of the B.V.M. Province (1874): *Motherhouse and Novitiate-Provincialate,* 36800 Schoolcraft Rd., Livonia, MI 48150. Tel: 313-591-1730; Fax: 313-591-1710. Sr. Mary Dennis Glonek, C.S.S.F., Prov. Min.

Professed 250; Novices 3.

Ministry in the Field of Academic Education at all levels; Catechetical Center; CCD Programs; Archival and Secretarial Services in Seminary; Diocesan Nursing Home; Youth Ministry Center; Pastoral Ministry Programs; DRE Offices; Hospital; Health Care Centers; Nursing Homes; Assisted Living; Archdiocesan Tribunal and Office of Delegate for Religious; Parish Soup Kitchen; Hospice Inpatient and Home Care Program; Day Care Centers; Retreat Centers; House of Prayer; Senior Clergy Residence.

Properties owned: *Madonna University; Ladywood High School; Montessori Center of Our Lady; St. Mary Hospital,* Livonia, MI; *St. Joseph Day Care; Presentation Prayer Center,* Jackson, MI; *Maryville Center,* Holly, MI; *Angela Hospice Home Care and Inpatient Facility; Marian Professional Building,* Livonia, MI.

Represented in the Archdiocese of Detroit and the Dioceses of Fort Wayne-South Bend, Gaylord, Kalamazoo, Lansing, Saginaw and Toledo.

Immaculate Heart of Mary Province (1900): *Novitiate-Villa Maria,* 600 Doat St., Buffalo, NY 14211. Tel: 716-892-4141. Sr. Mary Raymond Kasprzak, C.S.S.F., Prov. Minister; Sr. Mary Simplicia Wytrwal, C.S.S.F., Prov. Archivist.

Total number in community 331.

Ministry in the field of Academic Education on all levels; Day Care Center; School for Mentally and Multiply Handicapped; Institute of Music; Religious Education Centers; Outreach Centers; Diocesan Office.

Properties owned: *Villa Maria College of Buffalo; Villa Maria Academy; Villa Maria Institute of Music,* Buffalo, NY.

Represented in the Dioceses of Buffalo, Charleston, Erie, Syracuse and Wilmington. Also in Canada, and Italy.

Mother of Good Counsel Province (1910): *Mother of Good Counsel Provincialate, Novitiate, & Convent,* 3800 W. Peterson Ave., Chicago, IL 60659. Tel: 773-463-3020. Sr. Mary Barbara Ann Bosch,

C.S.S.F., Prov. Minister; Sr. M. Adolphine Ksioszk, C.S.S.F., Community Archivist.
Total number in the community 274.
Ministry in the field of Academic and Religious Education at all levels; Homes for Aged; Independent Living for the Elderly; Assisted Living for the Elderly; Pastoral Ministry; Social Workers; Family Therapists; Day Care Centers; Hospitals; Infirmary for Sisters; Foreign Missions; Recreation House for Children.
Represented in the Archdioceses of Chicago and Milwaukee and the Dioceses of Belleville, Green Bay, Joliet, La Crosse and Rockford.

Immaculate Conception Provincial House (1913): *Motherhouse and Novitiate-Immaculate Conception Convent,* 260 S. Main St., Lodi, NJ 07644-2196. Tel: 973-473-7447; Fax: 973-473-7126. Sr. Mary Antonelle Chunka, C.S.S.F., Prov. Minister; Sr. Mary Alicia Adametz, Prov. Sec.; Sr. Mary Raphael Monczewska, Archivist.
Total number in community 242.
Properties sponsored: *Immaculate Conception High School; Felician College; Felician College Day Care Center; Felician School for Exceptional Children,* Lodi, NJ; *Felician Retreat Center; Our Lady of Grace Home; St. Ignatius Nursing Home.*
Sisters Serve and Staff: Colleges; High Schools; Elementary Schools; Hospitals; Home for Neglected Children; Home for Aged; Infirmary for Sisters; Day Care Center; School for Exceptional Children; Religious Education; Parish Ministries.
Represented in the Archdioceses of Newark and Philadelphia and the Dioceses of Arlington, Camden, Metuchen, Paterson, Trenton and Wilmington.

Our Lady of the Sacred Heart Province (1921): *Provincial House and Novitiate, Felician Sisters of Pennsylvania,* 1500 Woodcrest Ave., Coraopolis, PA 15108. Tel: 412-264-2890; Fax: 412-264-7047. Sr. Mary Cabrini Procopio, C.S.S.F., Prov. Min.
Total number in community 144.
Ministry in the field of Academic Education at all levels; Hospital Work; Religious Education; CCD Centers; Youth and Pastoral Ministry; Home for Mentally Retarded Children; Infirmary and Home for Aged; Missionary Work.
Legal Holdings and Titles: *Felician Sisters of Pennsylvania Our Lady of the Sacred Heart High School.*
Represented in the Dioceses of Altoona-Johnstown, Charleston, Greensburg, Harrisburg, Pittsburgh, and Venice. Also in Kenya.

Our Lady of the Angels Province (1932): *Felician Sisters, Provincial Hse./Novitiate, Our Lady of the Angels Convent,* 1315 Enfield St., Enfield, CT 06082-4929. Tel: 860-745-7791; Fax: 860-741-0819. Sr. Mary Laureann Alexandrowicz, C.S.S.F., Prov. Minister.
Universal total 2,500; Sisters in province 146; Novices 2.
Properties owned and sponsored: *Montessori School The Felician Adult Day Care,* Enfield, CT; *St. Joseph Hospital,* Bangor, ME.
Ministry in the field of Religious and Academic Education on all levels; Pastoral Ministry; Social Services; Healthcare.
Represented in the Archdioceses of Boston, Hartford, New York and the Dioceses of Albany, Manchester, Norwich, Portland (ME), Providence, Springfield (MA) and Worcester.

Assumption of the B.V.M. Province (1953): *Provincial House - Novitiate,* 4210 Meadowlark Ln., S.E., Rio Rancho, NM 87124-1021. Sr. Rosemarie Goins, C.S.S.F., Prov. Min.
Total number in community 78.
Legal Titles and Holdings: *Felician Sisters of the Southwest, Inc.; St. Felix Pantry Inc.*
Sisters serve and staff: High Schools; Elementary Schools; Foreign and Rural Missions; Religious Education Centers & Classes; Health Care; Pastoral Care; Food & Clothing Pantry; Youth Ministry; Adult Education.
Represented in the Archdioceses of Los Angeles, San Antonio, Santa Fe and the Diocese of Fort Worth. Also in Mexico.

[1180] (O.S.F.)—FRANCISCAN SISTERS OF ALLEGANY, NEW YORK P

Founded in the United States in 1859.

General Motherhouse (1859): *St. Elizabeth Motherhouse,* Allegany, NY 14706. Tel: 716-373-0200; Fax: 716-372-5774. Sr. Margaret Mary Kimmins, O.S.F., Gen. Minister; Sr. Marigene Kennedy, O.S.F., Local Minister.
Total number in community 446.
Legal Titles and Holdings: *Franciscan Sisters of Allegany, NY, Inc. Franciscan Center, Inc.,* Tampa, FL; *Dwelling Place, Inc.,* New York, NY; *St. Joseph Villa,* Catskill, NY.
Ministry to Evangelization in all levels of Education; Health Care; Social Services; Pastoral and Campus Ministries; Spiritual Ministries and Social Advocacy.
Represented in the Archdioceses of Boston, Hartford, Miami, Newark, New York and Philadelphia and the Dioceses of Albany, Buffalo, Camden, Fall River, Metuchen, Orlando, Palm Beach, Paterson, Rochester, Rockville Centre, St. Petersburg, Scranton, Springfield(MA), Syracuse, Trenton, Venice and Wilmington. Also in Bolivia, Brazil and Jamaica.

Region I Office: *Franciscan Sisters of Allegany,* (1984), 115 E. Main St., Allegany, NY 14706. Tel: 716-373-1888. Sr. Rosemary Higgins, O.S.F., Region I Minister.
Represented in the Dioceses of Albany, Buffalo, Rochester and Syracuse. Also in Bolivia.

Region II: *Franciscan Sisters of Allegany,* (1972), 168 Hopkins Ave., Haddonfield, NJ 08033. Tel: 609-429-1739. Sr. Victoria Masterpaul, O.S.F., Region II Minister.
Represented in the Archdioceses of Boston, Hartford, Newark, New York and Philadelphia and the Dioceses of Camden, Fall River, Metuchen, Paterson, Rockville Centre, Springfield (MA), Trenton and Wilmington.

Region III: *Franciscan Sisters of Allegany,* (1972), 631 - 11th St., No., St. Petersburg, FL 33705. Tel: 813-824-0857. Sr. Gladys Sharkey, O.S.F., Region III Minister.
Represented in the Archdiocese of Miami and in Dioceses of Orlando, Palm Beach, St. Petersburg and Venice. Also in Bolivia.

Region IV: *Franciscan Sisters of Allegany,* 152 Constant Spring Rd., Box 1654, Kingston, Jamaica, West Indies. Tel: 876-924-1719. Tel: 876-924-2141. Sr. Teresita Marie De Souza, O.S.F., Region IV Minister.

Region V: *Franciscan Sisters of Allegany,* C.P. 322, 75001-970 Anapolis, Goias, Brazil, South America. Tel: 011-55-62-321-0805. Sr. Maria do Socorro de Rosal, O.S.F., Region V Minister.

[1190] (S.A.)—FRANCISCAN SISTERS OF THE ATONEMENT P

Founded in the United States in 1898.

Motherhouse: *St. Francis Convent,* R1 Box 163B Graymoor, Garrison, NY 10524. Tel: 914-424-3623; Fax: 914-424-3298. Sr. Diane Bernier, S.A., Congregational Min.; Sr. Mary Annunciata Griffitts, S.A., Archivist.
Total number in community 227.
Properties owned: *St. Francis Convent - Complex, Garrison,* NY; *Mother Lurana House,* Garrison, NY; *Washington Retreat House,* Washington, DC.
Represented in the Archdioceses of Boston, Detroit, Newark, New York, Washington and the Dioceses of Albany, Brooklyn, Bridgeport, Burlington, Fresno, Manchester, Metuchen, Monterey, Norwich, Ogdensburg, Paterson, Pittsburgh, Portland (ME), Raleigh, Reno-Las Vegas, Sacramento, Salt Lake City, Syracuse and Trenton. Also in Canada, Brazil, Ireland, Italy and Japan.

[1200] (O.S.F.)—THE FRANCISCAN SISTERS OF BALTIMORE P

Founded in England in 1868. First foundation in the United States in 1881.

General Motherhouse: 3725 Ellerslie Ave., Baltimore, MD 21218. Tel: 410-235-0139; Fax: 410-243-2569. Sr. Ritamary Tan, O.S.F., Dir. Gen.
Total number in community 50.
Legal Title: *Franciscan Sisters of Baltimore, Inc.*
Sisters serve and staff: Parochial Schools; Schools of Special Education; Emergency Welfare Center; Youth Center; Religious Education Centers; Pastoral Ministry; Lay Volunteer Program; Chaplaincy Programs; Retreat Centers; Infant Aids Programs; Hispanic & African-American Evangelization.
Properties owned: Residences for the Mentally Handicapped: St. Elizabeth School, Inc. Francis House, Inc. Franciscan Center, Inc. General Motherhouse, Baltimore, MD.
Represented in the Archdioceses of Baltimore, New York, Washington and the Dioceses of Brownsville and Trenton.

[1210] (O.S.F.)—FRANCISCAN SISTERS OF CHICAGO P

Founded in Chicago, Illinois in 1894 by Mother Mary Theresa (Josephine Dudzik) Venerable Servant of God.

General Motherhouse: *Our Lady of Victory Convent,* 14700 Main St., Lemont, IL 60439-0956. Tel: 708-257-7776; Fax: 708-257-7887. Sr. M. Francis Clare Radke, Gen. Supr.; Sr. Emilie Marie Lesniak, Archivist.
Total number in community 147.
Sisters serve and staff: Elementary Schools 3; CCD Programs 5.
Properties owned: *Madonna High School,* Chicago, IL; *St. Anthony Medical Center, Inc.,* Crown Point, IN; *St. Anthony Home, Inc.,* Crown Point, IN; *St. Joseph Home of Chicago, Inc.,* Chicago IL; *Mount Alverna Home, Inc.; Mount Alverna Home Annex, Inc.,* Parma, OH; *Mother Theresa Home, Inc.; Franciscan Village,* Lemont, IL; *St. Francis House of Prayer Franciscan Sisters of Chicago Service Corp.; Our Lady of Victory Convent,* Lemont IL.
Represented in the Archdiocese of Chicago and the Dioceses of Cleveland and Gary.

[1230] (O.S.F.)—FRANCISCAN SISTERS OF CHRISTIAN CHARITY P

Founded in the United States in 1869.

Motherhouse: *Holy Family Convent,* 2409 S. Alverno Rd., Manitowoc, WI 54220. Tel: 920-682-7728; Fax: 920-682-4195. Sr. Paula Vanden Hogen, Community Dir.; Sr. Donna Marie Kessler, Community Archivist.
Total number in community 535.
Properties owned or sponsored: *Holy Family Convent,* Manitowoc, WI; *Holy Family Memorial Medical Center,* Manitowoc, WI; *St. Francis Memorial Hopital,* West Point, NE; *Good Samaritan Medical Center,* Zanesville, OH; *St. Joseph Retirement Community,* West Point, NE; *St. Paul Home,* Kaukauna, WI; *Silver Lake College,* Manitowoc, WI; *St. Paul Manor Franciscan Sisters of Christian Charity HealthCare Ministry, Inc.,* Manitowoc, WI; *Holy Family Conservatory of Music,* Manitowoc, WI; *St. Clare Convent, Manitowoc,* WI; *St. Francis Convent,* Manitowoc, WI; *San Damiano Convent,* Slinger, WI.
Represented in the Archdioceses of Chicago, Los Angeles, Milwaukee, Omaha and in the Dioceses of Columbus, Gaylord, Green Bay, Jackson, Honolulu, Lexington, Marquette, Phoenix, Steubenville, Superior, and Tucson. Also in Peru.

[1235] (F.H.M.)—FRANCISCAN SISTERS DAUGHTERS OF MERCY

Franciscanas Hijas de la Misericordia

Founded in Pina, Mallorca, Spain in 1856. First U.S. establishment in 1962.

General Motherhouse: Calle Moral 4, 07001 Palma de Mallorca, Spain. Sr. Antonia Barrilero Canadas, Supr. Gen.
Universal number in Congregation 447.
U.S. Regional Delegation: 612 N. 3rd St., Waco, TX 76701. Tel: 817-753-5565. Sr. Francisca Riutord, Reg. Delegate.
Professed Sisters 9.
Ministry in Kingergarten; Catechetical Work; Pastoral Work; Social Work.
Represented in the Diocese of Austin.

[1240] (O.S.F.)—FRANCISCAN SISTERS, DAUGHTERS OF THE SACRED HEARTS OF JESUS AND MARY P

Founded in Germany in 1860. First foundation in the United States in 1872.

Generalate: Via di Sant' Alessio, 22-24, 00153, Rome, Italy. Sr. Carola Thomann O.S.F., Gen. Dir.
Universal number in Congregation 940.

St. Clara's Province (1877): *Convent of Our Lady of the Angels, Motherhouse and Novitiate,* P.O. Box 667, Wheaton, IL 60189. Tel: 630-462-7422. Sr. Mary Ellen McAleese, Prov. Dir.
Total number in province 131.
Sisters serve and staff: Hospitals; Housing Development; Grammar Schools; Universities; Parish Ministry; Spirituality Center; Home Health Care; Corporate Offices; System Ministries; Long-term Care; Social Services; Wellness; Spiritual Direction; Campus Ministry; Foreign Mission.
Legal Holdings and Titles: *Oak Park Hospital,* Oak Park, IL; *Clare Gardens, Inc.; Francis Heights, Inc.; Francis of Assisi Foundation of Colorado, Inc.,* Denver, CO; *S.F.H., Inc.; Covenant Medical Center, Inc.; Covenant Foundation, Inc.; Mercy Hospital of Franciscan Sisters, Inc.; Covenant Health System, Inc.,* Waterloo, IA; *St. Elizabeth Hospital Inc.; St. Elizabeth Hospital Community Foundation, Inc.; Affinity Health System,* Appleton, WI; *Assisi Homes of Neenah, Inc.,* Neenah, WI; *Marianjoy, Inc.; Marian Park, Inc.; Wheaton Franciscan Sisters Corporation; WFSI-Illinois Wheaton Franciscan Sisters Religious Charitable Trust Wheaton Franciscan Services, Inc.; Franciscan Ministries, Inc.; Clara Pfaender Fund, Inc.,* Wheaton, IL; *St. Joseph's Hospital of Franciscan Sisters of Milwaukee, Inc.,* Milwaukee, WI; *St. Michael Hospital of*

Franciscan Sisters of Milwaukee, Inc., Milwaukee, WI; *Elmbrook Memorial Hospital*, Brookfield, WI; *Marian Catholic Center, Inc.; Franciscan Shared Laboratory, Inc.; M.F.S.I., Inc.; O.S.F. Services, Inc.; St. Michael Hospital Community Foundation, Inc.*, Milwaukee, WI; *St. Mary's Medical Center, Inc.*, Racine, WI; *Marian Center of Racine, Inc.*, Racine, WI; *Marian Housing Center, Inc.*, Racine, WI; *All Saints Visiting Nurse Association & Hospice of Racine, Inc.; S.E.T. Ministry, Inc.; All Saints Healthcare Foundation, Inc.; Franciscan Home Health, Inc.; WFSI-Milwaukee Foundation, Inc.; Marian Franciscan Center, Inc.; Assisi Homes of Wisconsin, Inc.; S.F.A. of Racine, Inc.; Assisi Community/Organization, Inc.*, Milwaukee, WI; *Assisi Homes of Illinois, Inc.*, Wheaton, IL; *All Saints Healthcare System, Inc.*, Racine, WI; *Villa St. Anna, Inc. Covenant Healthcare System, Inc. St. Francis Health Care Corporation of Racine*, Racine, WI; *Franciscan Care Center, Inc.*, Appleton, WI.

Represented in the Archdioceses of Chicago, Denver, Dubuque, Milwaukee and St. Louis and the Dioceses of Green Bay, Joliet and Springfield-Cape Girardeau. Also in Brazil, Italy and Nigeria.

[1250] (F.S.E.)—THE INSTITUTE OF THE FRANCISCAN SISTERS OF THE EUCHARIST P

Founded December 2, 1973.

Motherhouse: *John Lateran Center*, 405 Allen Ave., Meriden, CT 06450. Tel: 203-237-0841. Team Members: Mother Rosemae Pender, Mother Gen.; Mother Shaun Vergauwen, Mother Asst.; Mother Rita Brunner; Mother Mary Ann Schmitz; Mother Mary Michael Costello; Mother Mona Brunner.

Total number in community 76.

Legal Title: *Franciscan Sisters of the Eucharist, Incorporated.*

Schools and programs operated under: Franciscan Life Center Network, Incorporated.

Represented in the Archdioceses of Hartford, Portland (OR), Seattle, Washington, and the Dioceses of Boise, Duluth and Grand Rapids. Also in Israel and Italy.

[1260] (F.H.M.)—FRANCISCAN HANDMAIDS OF THE MOST PURE HEART OF MARY D

Founded in the United States in 1916.

General Motherhouse: 15 W. 124th St., New York, NY 10027. Tel: 212-289-5655.

Novitiate 444 Woodvale Ave., Pleasant Plains, Staten Island, NY 10309. Sr. Loretta Theresa, Supr. Gen.; Sr. Maria Goretti, Dir. Formation; Sr. Jacqueline, Community Archivist.

Total number in community 23.

Properties owned: *St. Benedict Day Nursery; Camp Saint Edward; Franciscan Handmaids of Mary Novitiate; Franciscan Handmaids of Mary Motherhouse.*

Ministry in the field of Education, Social Work and Pastoral Care.

Represented in the Archdiocese of New York.

[1270] (F.H.I.C.)—FRANCISCAN HOSPITALLER SISTERS OF THE IMMACULATE CONCEPTION P

Founded in Portugal in 1876.

General Motherhouse: Linda-a-Pastora,, Portugal. Sr. Maria Isilda Freitas, F.H.I.C., Supr. Gen.

U.S. Foundation (1960): *St. Joseph Novitiate*, 300 S. 17th St., San Jose, CA 95112-2245. Tel: 408-998-2896; Fax: 408-998-3407. Sr. Lucinda D. Fonseca, Supr.

Total number in community 19.

Sisters serve and staff: Parishes; Schools; Hospitals; Social Work.

Represented in the Dioceses of Fresno, Monterey and San Jose.

[1280] (O.S.F.)—FRANCISCAN SISTERS OF THE IMMACULATE CONCEPTION P

First foundation in United States in 1928.

General Motherhouse: Kloster Bonlanden, Germany. Sr. M. Fredigundis Fratz, O.S.F., Supr. Gen.

Province of the Blessed Virgin Mary: 291 W. North St., Buffalo, NY 14201; Fax: 716-881-1578. Sr. M. Bernard, O.S.F., Prov.

Professed Sisters 7.

Represented in the Archdiocese of New York and the Diocese of Buffalo.

[1300] (O.S.F.)—FRANCISCAN SISTERS OF THE IMMACULATE CONCEPTION AND ST. JOSEPH FOR THE DYING D

Founded in the United States in December, 1919 at San Carlos Parish, Monterey, California.

General Motherhouse: St. Joseph's Convent, 485 Church St., Monterey, CA 93940. Tel: 408-372-3579. Sr. M. Constance, O.S.F., Supr. Gen.; Sr. M. Bernadette, O.S.F., Archivist.

Total number in community 7.

Legal Holding: Ave Maria Convalescent Hospital, Monterey, CA.

Represented in the Diocese of Monterey.

[1302] (F.I.H.M.)—FRANCISCAN OF THE IMMACULATE HEART OF MARY D

General Motherhouse: *Immaculate Heart of Mary Generalate*, St. Theress St., Pondicherry, India, 6500-01. Sr. Regina Savarinathan, F.I.H.M. Supr. Gen.

Province in the U.S.: *St. Catherine's Convent*, 49 King St., Hillside, NJ 07205. Tel: 908-354-9131. Sr. Urmila Selvi, F.I.H.M., Supr.

Total number in community.

Represented in the Archdiocese of Newark.

[1310] (O.S.F.)—FRANCISCAN SISTERS OF LITTLE FALLS, MINNESOTA P

Founded in the United States in 1891.

General Motherhouse: *St. Francis' Convent*, Little Falls, MN 56345. Tel: 320-632-2981. Sr. Rose Margaret Schneider, O.S.F., Pres.; Sr. Sabina Collins, Archivist.

Total number in community 252.

Ministry in the field of Academic Education at all levels; Health Care in Nursing Homes, Hospitals, Apartment for the Elderly, Children's Home, Clinics; Religious Education; Parish Ministry; Retreat Ministries; Liturgical Music; Music Center; Wholistic Growth Center; Ministry to Refugees; Health and Recreation Center; Diocesan Offices; Social Services; Counseling-Spiritual Direction; Consulting; Ministry to the Poor; Ministry to Migrants; Ministry to the Hearing Impaired; Altar Bread-making, and Craft Activities; Ministry in Ecology; Social Justice and Nonviolent Activities; Spirituality Farm; Native Americans.

Properties owned or sponsored: *Wholistic Growth Resources Program; St. Francis Music Center; St. Francis Health & Recreation Center; Clare's Well.*

Represented in the Archdioceses of Chicago, Los Angeles, Milwaukee, New York, St. Louis, St. Paul-Minneapolis, Sante Fe, San Antonio, and the Dioceses of Arlington, Belleville, Birmingham, Buffalo, Brownsville, Charleston, Crookston, Fargo, Jackson, La Crosse, Madison, Manchester, Memphis, New Ulm, Oakland, St. Cloud, St. Petersburg, Scranton, Sioux Falls, Spokane, Tucson, Tyler and Winona. Also in Ecuador, Cameroon, and Tanzania.

[1320] (O.S.F.)—FRANCISCAN MISSIONARY SISTERS FOR AFRICA P

Generalate: *Franciscan Convent*, Mount Oliver, Dundalk Co. Louth, Ireland.

American Headquarters: 172 Foster St., P.O. Box 35095, Brighton, MA 02135. Tel: 617-254-4343. Sr. Nora Doyle, O.S.F.

Total number in community 7.

Represented in the Archdiocese of Boston.

[1330] (S.F.M.A.)—FRANCISCAN MISSIONARY SISTERS OF ASSISI P

General Motherhouse: Via San Francesco 13, Assisi, Italy. Sr. Serena Picchio, Mother Gen.

U.S. Foundation (1961): *St. Francis Convent*, 1039 Northampton St., Holyoke, MA 01040. Tel: 413-532-8156.

Total number in community 11.

Represented in the Diocese of Buffalo and Springfield (MA).

[1340] (F.M.D.C.)—FRANCISCAN MISSIONARY SISTERS OF THE DIVINE CHILD D

First founded in the United States on August 15, 1927 in Buffalo, New York.

Motherhouse: *Franciscan Missionary Sisters of the Divine Child Motherhouse*, 6380 Main St., Williamsville, NY 14221. Tel: 716-632-3144; Fax: 716-626-1332. Sr. Margaret Krantz, F.M.D.C., Minister Gen.

Total number in community 32.

Sisters serve and staff: Catechetical Centers; CCD Coordinators; Education in Elementary, High School and College; Parish Ministry; Vocation Formation Director.

Represented in the Diocese of Buffalo.

[1350] (O.S.F.)—FRANCISCAN SISTERS OF THE IMMACULATE CONCEPTION P

Founded in Mexico in 1874. First foundation in the United States in 1926.

Provincial House: 11320 Laurel Canyon Blvd., San Fernando, CA 91340. Tel: 818-365-2582. Sr. Maria de la Paz Ulloa, O.S.F., Prov. Supr.; Sr. Mary Gabriel De Leon, O.S.F., Community Archivist.

Total number in community 105.

Legal Holdings and Titles: *Franciscan Missionary Sisters of the Immaculate Conception, Inc.; Poverello of Assisi Retreat House*, San Fernando, CA; *St. Francis Home*, Santa Ana, CA; *Mother Gertrude Balcazar Home*, San Fernando, CA; *Immaculate Conception Home*, Los Angeles, CA.

Ministry in the field of Education and Religious Education to Children and Adults; Health Care in Hospitals and Home Visitation to the Sick.

Represented in the Archiocese of Los Angeles and the Dioceses of Gallup and Orange.

[1360] (M.F.I.C.)—MISSIONARY FRANCISCAN SISTERS OF THE IMMACULATE CONCEPTION P

Founded in the United States in 1873 in Belle Prairie, Minnesota.

General Motherhouse: Rome, Italy. Sr. Marian Bandille, M.F.I.C., Gen. Minister.

Provincialate: *Immaculate Conception Convent*, 790 Centre St., Newton, MA 02158. Tel: 617-527-1004; Fax: 617-527-2528. Sr. Mary Michele Craig, M.F.I.C., Prov.

Total number in province 261.

Represented in the Archdioceses of Boston, Hartford, Newark, New York, Philadelphia, Washington and the Dioceses of Bridgeport, Brooklyn, St. Petersburg, Savannah, Syracuse and Venice.

[1365] (F.M.I.J.)—FRANCISCAN MISSIONARY SISTERS OF THE INFANT JESUS P

Founded in Aquila, Italy in 1879 by Sr. Maria Giuseppa Micarelli. First Foundation in the U.S. in 1961.

Generalate: Piazza Nicoloso da Recco 13, Rome, Italy, 00154. Tel: 6-575-8358. Mother Maria Felicita Decio, F.M.I.J., Supr. Gen.

U.S. Province and Novitiate: 1215 Kresson Rd., Cherry Hill, NJ 08003. Tel: 609-428-7930; Fax: 609-428-7930. Sr. Chiara Lilia Ferrario, F.M.I.J., Delegate Supr.

Ministries of Evangelization; Education; Health Care; Social-Pastoral Services.

Professed Sisters 19; Junior Professed 1.

Represented in the Dioceses of Camden and Trenton.

[1370] (F.M.M.)—THE FRANCISCAN MISSIONARIES OF MARY P

Founded in India in 1877. First foundation in the United States in 1904.

General Motherhouse: 12 via Giusti, Rome, Italy. Sr. Christiane Megarbane, F.M.M., Supr. Gen.

Franciscan Missionaries of Mary -U.S. Province (1920): 3305 Wallace Ave., Bronx, NY 10467. Tel: 718-547-4604. Sr. Mary Petrosky, F.M.M., Prov.

Total number in community 202.

Educational Projects among Minority Group of Immigrants; Child Care Agencies; Cardiac and General Hospital; General Pediatric Hospital with Rehabilitation Specialty; Chaplaincy; Retreat Work; Day Care for Elderly; Catechetics; Home Visiting & Community Development.

Represented in the Archdioceses of Boston, Chicago, New York, St. Louis, San Francisco and in the Dioceses of Fall River, Las Cruces, Providence, Rockville Centre, Savannah, and St. Petersburg.

[1380] (O.S.F.)—FRANCISCAN MISSIONARIES OF OUR LADY P

Founded in Calais, France in 1854. First U.S. foundation in 1913.

General Motherhouse: Desvres, France.

Generalate: Paris, France.

Provincial and Novitiate House: *Maryville Novitiate*, 4200 Essen Ln., Baton Rouge, LA 70809. Tel: 504-926-1627; Fax: 504-926-4846. Sr. Brendan M. Ronayne, Supr.

Total number in community 30.

Properties owned and sponsored: *Our Lady of the Lake Regional Medical Center, Inc.*, Baton Rouge, LA; *Ollie Steele Burden Manor, Inc.*, Baton Rouge, LA; *Our Lady of Lourdes Regional Medical Center, Inc.*, Lafayette, LA; *St. Francis Medical Center, Inc.*, Monroe, LA; *FMOL Health System, Inc.*, Baton Rouge. LA.

Represented in the Dioceses of Baton Rouge, Lafayette (LA) and Shreveport.

[1390] (O.S.F.)—FRANCISCAN MISSIONARY SISTERS OF OUR LADY OF SORROWS D

Founded in Hunan China in 1939. First United States foundation in 1950.

Community Headquarters: Our Lady of Peace Retreat House, 3600 S.W. 170th Ave., Beaverton, OR 97006. Tel: 503-649-7127; Fax: 503-649-8382. Sr. Anne Marie Warren, O.S.F., Supr. Gen.

Total number in community 50.

Legal Titles and Holdings: *Our Lady of Peace Retreat,* Beaverton, OR; *St. Clare Retreat House,* Soquel, CA; *Our Lady of Mt. Carmel Group Home,* Gallup, NM.

Ministry in religious and academic education and foreign missions.

Represented in the Archdioceses of Portland (OR), San Francisco, and the Dioceses of Gallup and Monterey.

[1400] (F.M.S.C.)—FRANCISCAN MISSIONARY SISTERS OF THE SACRED HEART P

Founded in Italy in 1861. First foundation in the U.S. in New York City (1865).

General Motherhouse: Rome, Italy. Sr. Ines Pavan, Supr. Gen.

St. Francis Province (1869): *Mt. St. Francis,* 250 South St., Peekskill, NY 10566. Tel: 914-737-5409; Fax: 914-736-9614. Sr. M. Rose Cecilia Bozzo, F.M.S.C., Prov.

Universal number in Congregation 782; Number in United States Province 58.

Legal Title: *Missionary Sisters of the Third Order of St. Francis.*

Ministry in Religious and Academic Education; Health Care for Retired Sisters; Pastoral Ministry; Prison Apostolate; Hospital Ministry.

Represented in the Archdioceses of Newark, New York and in Dioceses of Brooklyn and Paterson.

[1410] (F.M.S.J.)—MILL HILL SISTERS P

Franciscan Missionaries of St. Joseph

Founded in 1883. First United States foundation in 1952.

Generalate: *St. Joseph's Convent,* Worsley Manchester, England. Sr. Theodora Slot, F.M.S.J., Supr. Gen.

American Headquarters: *Franciscan House,* 1006 Madison Ave., Albany, NY 12208. Tel: 518-482-1991. Sr. Judith Dever, F.M.S.J., Reg Supr.

Total number in community 12.

Represented in the Dioceses of Albany and Norwich.

[1415] (F.S.M.)—FRANCISCAN SISTERS OF MARY P

Founded in the United States in 1872.

Administrative Offices & Novitiate: *Franciscan Sisters of Mary,* 1100 Bellevue Ave., St. Louis, MO 63117-1883. Tel: 314-768-1824; Fax: 314-768-1880. Sr. Jacqueline Motzel, F.S.M., Pres.

Total number in community 210.

Properties owned or sponsored: *St. Mary of the Angels,* St. Louis, MO; *St. Mary's Ringling,* Baraboo, WI.

Ministry in Hospitals; Skilled Nursing Facilities; Rehabilitation Unit; Hospice; Foreign Missions; Birthing Centers; Pastoral Services; Consultation Services.

Represented in the Archdioceses of Chicago, Oklahoma City, San Francisco, St. Louis and the Dioceses of Albany, Belleville, Brownsville, Charleston, Jefferson City, Kansas City-St. Joseph, Lexington, Madison, St. Petersburg and Springfield-Cape Girardeau. Also in Brazil and South Africa.

[1420] (F.S.R.)—FRANCISCAN SISTERS OF RINGWOOD D

Founded in the United States in Passaic, New Jersey on Nov. 21, 1929.

General Motherhouse and Novitiate: *Mt. St. Francis,* Ringwood, NJ 07456. Tel: 973-962-7411; Fax: 973-962-0445. Sr. Annette Lucchese, Gen. Coord.

Total number in community 32.

Ministry in the field of academic and religious education and as pastoral associates.

Represented in the Archdioceses of Newark and the Diocese of Paterson.

[1425] (F.S.P.)—FRANCISCAN SISTERS OF PEACE D

Sisters of St. Francis of Peace: Congregation Center, 20 Ridge St., Haverstraw, NY 10927. Tel: 914-942-2527. Sr. Margaret Gaffikin, F.S.P., Congregation Minister.

Total number in the community 92.

Legal Titles and Holdings: *Our Lady of Hope Convent,* Cortlandt Manor, NY; *St. Joseph's Villa by the Sea,* Ventnor, NJ; *Congregation Center,* Haverstraw, NY.

Ministry in Youth & Campus Ministries; Care for the Aged; Pastoral; Education; Nursing; Catechetical; Social Work; Prison Ministry; Ministry to Unwed mothers and the Native American Indians in Arizona; New Mexico.

Represented in the Archdioceses of Newark, New York, Philadelphia, San Francisco and the Diocese of Albany, Charleston, Gallup, Madison, Paterson, and Rockville Centre.

[1430] (O.S.F.)—FRANCISCAN SISTERS OF OUR LADY OF PERPETUAL HELP P

Founded in the United States in 1901.

Motherhouse and Novitiate: *Villa St. Joseph,* 201 Brotherton Ln., St. Louis (Ferguson), MO 63135. Tel: 314-522-6800. Sr. Monica Marie Laws, O.S.F., Supr. Gen.; Rev. Larry Nickels, O.F.M., Chap.

Total number in community 163.

Legal Holdings and Titles: *Villa St. Joseph Motherhouse and Novitiate,* St. Louis, MO; *Villa St. Joseph Child Care and Education Center,* St. Louis, MO; *St. Francis Health Care Centre,* Green Springs, OH; *Perpetual Help Charitable Trust,* St. Louis, MO.

Ministry in Education; Nursing Homes; Rehabilitation Hospital; Child Day Care Center; Indian Missions.

Represented in the Archdioceses of Chicago, Kansas City in Kansas, Milwaukee, St. Louis, Santa Fe and the Dioceses of Belleville, El Paso, Great Falls-Billings, Las Cruces, Phoenix, Shreveport, Toledo and Wichita.

[1440] (S.F.P.)—FRANCISCAN SISTERS OF THE POOR P

Founded in Aachen, Germany in 1845. First foundation in the United States in 1858.

Congregational Office: 133 Remsen St., Brooklyn, NY 11201. Tel: 718-643-1919; Fax: 718-643-9710. Sr. Jeanne M. Glisky, S.F.P., Congregational Min.

Total number in community 197.

Congregation Sponsors Franciscan Sisters of the Poor.

U.S. Region: 1 McWilliams Pl., Rm. 305, Jersey City, NJ 07302. Tel: 201-418-2151. Sr. Marilyn Trowbridge, S.F.P., Reg. Min.

U.S. Region Sponsors: *St. Joseph Franciscan House, Inc.,* Brooklyn, NY; *Franciscan Sisters of the Poor Foundation, Inc.; Franciscan Sisters of the Poor Health System, Inc.,* Brooklyn Heights, NY; *Franciscan Health Services, Inc.,* Cincinnati, OH; *Parent: Franciscan Health System of Central Ohio, Inc.—Subsidiaries: St. Anthony Medical Center, Inc.,* Columbus, OH; *St. Anthony Mercy Hospital,* Columbus, OH; *Providential Corp., Inc.; MedOne Health Plan, Inc.; Parent: Franciscan Health System of Cincinnati, Inc.—Subsidiaries: Emerson A. North Hospital, Inc.; Providence Hospital, Inc.; St. Francis-St. George Hospital, Inc.; St. John Social Service Center, Inc.; West Park Retirement Community, Inc.,* Cincinnati, OH; *St. Raphael Social Service Center, Inc.,* Hamilton, OH; *West Park II, Inc.; Franciscan Health Network, Inc.; Franciscan Home Development, Inc.; St. Clare Retirement Community, Inc.; Parent: Franciscan Health System of Dayton, Inc.—Subsidiaries: St. Elizabeth Medical Center, Inc.,* Dayton, OH; *St. Leonard Center,* Centerville, OH; *Mary Black Schroder Home for the Aging, Inc.,* Hamilton, OH; Parent: *Franciscan Health System of Illinois, Inc.—Subsidiaries: St. Mary Hospital Health Development Association of Quincy,* Quincy, IL; Parent: *Franciscan Health System of New Jersey, Inc.— Subsidiaries: St. Francis Hospital, Inc.,* Jersey City, NJ; *St. Mary Hospital, Inc.; F+A+I+T+H Services, Inc.,* Hoboken, NJ; Parent: *Franciscan Health System of New York, Inc.—Subsidiaries: Frances Schervier Home & Hospital,* Bronx, NY; *Franciscan Community Services of NY, Inc. Frances Schervier Housing Development Fund Corporation Frances Schervier Nutrition Services, Inc. Frances Schervier Child Care and Learning Center, Inc. Parent: Franciscan Health System of South Carolina, Inc.—Subsidiaries: St. Francis Hospital, Inc., Greenville, SC. Parent: Franciscan Health System of Kentucky, Inc.—Subsidiaries: Our Lady of Bellefonte Hospital, Inc.,* Ashland, KY; —Subsidiaries: *St. Anthony Community Hospital, Inc. Mt. Alverno Center & Convent,* Warwick, NY; *Mt. Alverno Residency Corp. Inc.; Mercy Community Hospital,* Port Jarvis, NY; *Mt. Alverno Catering Service; St. Francis Center at the Knolls, Inc.; Villa Frances at the Knolls.* Co-sponsors: *St. Clare Holding Company,* Schenectady, NY; *St. Clare Hospital; St. Clare Foundation; St. Clare Center Regional House; Brazil Regional House* and *Frascati Complex,* Italy.

Represented in the Archdioceses of Cincinnati, Detroit, Newark, New York, Philadelphia and Santa Fe and the Dioceses of Albany, Brooklyn, Charleston, Columbus, Gallup, Lansing, Lexington, Phoenix and Springfield (IL). Also in Italy, Senegal and Brazil.

[1450] (O.S.F.)—FRANCISCAN SISTERS OF THE SACRED HEART P

Congregation of the Franciscan Sisters of the Sacred Heart. Founded in Germany 1866. Established in the United States in 1876 00/foun.

Motherhouse, Novitiate, Postulancy, Sacred Heart Residence and Portiuncula Center for Prayer: St. Francis Woods, 9201 W. St. Francis Rd., Frankfort, IL 60423-8335. Tel: 815-469-4895; Fax: 815-464-3809. Sr. Karen Marie Lanigan, Gen. Supr.

Legal Title: *An Association of Franciscan Sisters of the Sacred Heart; The Franciscan Sisters of the Sacred Heart in California.*

Legal Titles for Health Care entities: Franciscan Sisters Health Care Corporation St. Anne's Maternity Home St. Francis Medical Center of Santa Barbara Franciscan Foundation.

Sisters sponsor: *St. Joseph Medical Center,* Joliet, IL; *St. Joseph Hospital,* Elgin, IL; *St. Francis Medical Center,* Santa Barbara, CA; *St. Joseph College of Nursing,* Joliet, IL; *Villa Franciscan,* Joliet, IL; *Sacred Heart Home,* Avilla, IN; *LaVerna Terrace,* Avilla, IN; *St. Anne's Maternity Home,* Los Angeles, CA; *United Samaritans Medical Center,* Logan Campus-Danville, IL; *United Samaritans Medical Center,* Sager Campus-Danville, IL; *St. Therese Medical Center,* Waukegan, IL; *Franciscan Sisters Health Care Foundation,* Frankfort, IL.

Total number in community 156.

Sisters serve and staff: Elementary Schools; High School; Religious Education Centers; Neighborhood Health Care Centers; Foreign Mission Centers; Direct Domestic Work at Retreat Houses; Canon Lawyer; Diocesan Offices; Retreat Centers; Clinics, Home Health Agencies, Health Care Systems, Hospitals, Schools of Nursing, Nursing and Retirement Homes; Home for Unwed Mothers; Apartments-Well Elderly; Parish & Youth Ministry; Hispanic Ministry; Liturgical Ministry; Social Work; Congregate Care Facility.

Represented in the Archdioceses of Chicago and Los Angeles and the Dioceses of Fort Wayne-South Bend, Gary, Joliet, Peoria and Rockford. Also in Brazil.

[1460] (F.S.S.E.)—FRANCISCAN SISTERS OF ST. ELIZABETH P

(Suore Franciscane Elisabettine)

First founded in Naples, Italy, 1865. Founded in United States in Newark, New Jersey in 1919.

General Motherhouse: Via Marsico Nuovo 35, Rome, Italy. Mother Enrichetta Casa, Supr. Gen.

Delegate House: 499 Park Rd., Parsippany, NJ 07054. Tel: 201-539-3797. Mother Gina Maria Amico, Delegate Gen.

Total number in U.S. 66; Total in Community 300.

Ministry in Day Nurseries; Mission Houses; Elementary Schools and Montessori Schools.

Sister serve Christ in the person of the poor in Orphanages; Schools; Day Nursery Schools; Catechetical Instruction; Hospitals; Homes for the Poor, Aged, and Physically Handicapped.

Represented in the Archdiocese of Newark and the Diocese of Paterson. Also in India, Italy, Panama, and Philippines.

[1470] (F.S.S.J.)—FRANCISCAN SISTERS OF ST. JOSEPH P

Founded in the United States in 1897.

General Motherhouse: *Immaculate Conception Convent,* 5286 S. Park Ave., Hamburg, NY 14075. Tel: 716-649-1205; Fax: 716-649-5958. Sr. Mary Andrea Ciszewski, F.S.S.J., Gen. Min.

Total number in community 204.

Properties owned: *St. Clare Convent,* Hamburg, NY; *Immaculata Academy,* Hamburg, NY; *Hilbert College,* Hamburg, NY; *Marycrest Manor,* Livonia, MI; *St. Joseph Hospital,* Cheektowaga, NY.

Ministry in Education; Health Care; Home and Foreign Mission Work and other diverse ministries.

Represented in the Archdioceses of Baltimore, Detroit, Milwaukee and in the Dioceses of Bridgeport, Brooklyn, Buffalo, Harrisburg, Norwich, Saginaw, Savannah, Springfield (MA) and Trenton. Also in Brazil.

[1480] (F.S.S.J.)—FRANCISCAN SISTERS OF ST. JOSEPH D

Founded in Mexico.

Motherhouse: Ave. Revolucion No. 431, Delegacion Benito Juarez, Mexico, D.F, 03801. Tel: 277-29-66. Rev. Madre Maria del Rocio Garcia Guzman, H.F.J.

U.S. Address: *St. Paul's College,* 3015 4th St., N.E., Washington, DC 20017-1199. Tel: 202-832-6262; 269-2515.

Total number in community 5.

Ministry in domestic areas.

Represented in the Archdiocese of Washington.

[1485] (O.S.F.)—FRANCISCAN SISTERS OF ST. PAUL, MN. P

Franciscan Sisters of the Blessed Virgin Mary of the Holy Angels (Beatae Mariae Virginis Angelorum)

Founded in Germany in 1863. First foundation in the United States in St. Paul in 1923.

General Motherhouse (1863): *St. Marienhaus,* Waldbreitbach, bei Neuwied, Rhine, Germany. Sr. Irmgard Schmitt, O.S.F., Supr. Gen.

Universal total in Congregation 580.

U.S. Foundation: *Franciscan Regional Center,* 1388 Prior Ave. S., St. Paul, MN 55116. Tel: 612-690-1501; Fax: 612-690-2509. Sr. Antonice Delury, Prov.

Total number in community 12.

Represented in the Archdiocese of St. Paul-Minneapolis.

[1490] (O.S.F.)—SISTERS OF THE THIRD FRANCISCAN ORDER P

Founded in the United States in 1860.

Generalate Offices: *Sisters of the Third Franciscan Order,* 2500 Grant Blvd., Syracuse, NY 13208-1794; Fax: 315-425-0610. Sr. Grace Anne Dillenschneider, Gen. Supr.

Motherhouse: *St. Anthony Convent,* 1024 Court St., Syracuse, NY 13208-1794.

Total number in community 351.

Ministry in Academic Education at all levels; Hospitals; Schools of Nursing; Religious Education & Pastoral Ministry; Retreat House; Rehabilitation Centers; Intentional Communities; Home for Dying; Adult & Child Day Care.

Legal Holding: *Sisters of the Third Franciscan Order-Retirement Trust Fund.*

Properties Owned and/or Sponsored: *Sister Patricia Ann Preschool dba Gingerbread House,* Syracuse, NY; *St. Anthony Convent and Motherhouse,* Syracuse, NY; *St. Joseph Hospital,* Syracuse, NY; *St. Elizabeth Hospital,* Utica, NY; *Stella Maris Retreat Center,* Skaneateles, NY; *St. Francis Social Adult Day Service,* Syracuse, NY; *St. Francis Medical Center,* Honolulu, HI; *St. Francis Medical Center, West,* Ewa Beach, HI; *The Sister Maureen Keleher Hospice,* Honolulu, HI; *St. Francis School,* Honolulu, HI; *Mercy Rehabilitation Center,* Auburn, NY.

Represented in the Archdioceses of Boston, Los Angeles, Newark, New York, Philadelphia, San Antonio, Washington and the Dioceses of Albany, Camden, Harrisburg, Honolulu, Las Cruces, Metuchen, Orange, Orlando, Richmond, Rochester, San Diego, St. Petersburg, Scranton, Syracuse, Trenton, and Venice. Also in Peru.

[1500] (F.M.I.)—FRANCISCAN SISTERS OF MARY IMMACULATE OF THE THIRD ORDER OF ST. FRANCIS OF ASSISI P

Founded in Switzerland in the 16th Century. First founded in the United States on Aug. 15, 1932 at Amarillo, Texas.

General Motherhouse: Carrera 79 No. 40A-20, Bogota, Colombia, South America. Sr. Ana Margarita Untersander, F.M.I., Supr. Gen.

Universal total in congregation 659.

U.S. Provincial House and Novitiate (1964): *St. Francis Convent (1932),* 4301 N.E. 18th Ave., Amarillo, TX 79107. Tel: 806-383-5769. Sr. Geraldine Duran, F.M.I., Prov. Supr.

Total number in community 42.

Represented in the Archdioceses of Los Angeles and Santa Fe and the Diocese of Amarillo.

[1505] (O.S.F.)—ST. FRANCIS MISSION COMMUNITY

Established 1981 in the United States of America in Amarillo, Texas, as an autonomous province of the Franciscan Sisters of Mary Immaculate.

General Motherhouse: *St. Francis Convent,* 4305 54th St., Lubbock, TX 79413-4617. Tel: 806-793-9859. Sr. Celine Thames, O.S.F., Mission Community Coord.

Professed Sisters 22.

Ministry in the field of Religious and Academic Education in Elementary and Middle Schools; Parish Work; Pastoral Care in Hospitals.

Properties owned: *La Verna Convent,* Amarillo, TX; *St. Francis Convent,* Lubbock, TX; 105 acres of real estate.

Represented in the Archdiocese of Los Angeles and the Dioceses of Amarillo and Lubbock. Also in Mexico.

[1510] (O.S.F.)—SISTERS OF ST. FRANCIS D

Sisters of St. Francis of the Mission of the Immaculate Virgin. Founded in New York in 1893.

General Motherhouse: *Sisters of St. Francis-Immaculate Conception Motherhouse,* 49 Jackson Ave., Hastings-on-Hudson, NY 10706-3217. Tel: 914-478-3930; Fax: 914-478-5470. Sr. Marie Bernadette Wyman, Gen. Minister.

Total number in community 84.

Properties sponsored: *St. Francis Hospital,* Poughkeepsie, NY; *Nazareth Day Nursery,* New York, NY.

Ministry in Education; Day Nurseries; Hospitals and Parishes.

Represented in the Archdiocese of New York.

[1520] (O.S.F.)—SISTERS OF ST. FRANCIS OF CHRIST THE KING P

Founded in Austria in 1869. First founded in the United States at Kansas City, Kansas, in 1909.

General Motherhouse: Rome, Italy. Sr. Natalia Alvarenga, Supr. Gen.

Universal number in congregation 1,400.

St. Francis of Assisi of Christ the King Province (1926): *Mt. Assisi Convent,* 13900 Main St., Lemont, IL 60439. Tel: 630-257-7495. Sr. M. Ann Barbara Plavac, Prov. Supr.

Total number in community 80.

Properties owned and sponsored: *Mount Assisi Convent and Academy,* Lemont, IL; *Alvernia Manor,* Lemont, IL.

Ministry in Education and Care in Homes for the Aged.

Represented in the Archdioceses of Chicago and Milwaukee and the Diocese of Joliet.

[1530] (O.S.F.)—SISTERS OF ST. FRANCIS OF THE CONGREGATION OF OUR LADY OF LOURDES, SYLVANIA, OHIO P

Founded in the United States in 1916 at Sylvania, Ohio. Foundation from Rochester, Minnesota.

General Motherhouse: Convent and Novitiate, 6832 Convent Blvd., Sylvania, OH 43560-2897. Tel: 419-882-2016; Fax: 419-885-8643. Sr. Ruth Marie Kachelek, Minister Gen.

Total number in the Congregation 297.

Properties owned and sponsored: *Lourdes College,* Sylvania, OH; *Franciscan Services Corporation, Hospital System,* Sylvania, OH; Sponsored Facilities: *St. Francis Health Center,* Madisonville, TX; *Providence Hospital, Inc.,* Sandusky, OH; *Burleson St. Joseph Health Center,* Caldwell, TX; *Trinity Community Medical Center,* Brenham, TX; *St. Joseph Regional Health Center,* Bryan, TX; *Franciscan Shelters (Bethany House),* Toledo, OH; *Franciscan Center,* Sylvania, OH; *Convent Park Apartments,* Sylvania, OH; *Providence Care Center, Sandusky,* OH; *The Commons of Providence,* Sandusky, OH; *Trinity Medical Center East and Trinity Medical Center West,* Steubenville, OH.

Ministry in the field of Religious and Academic Education at all levels; Healthcare; Communications, Media, Producing; Counseling; Parish Ministries; Retreat Center; Social Services.

Represented in the Archdioceses of Atlant, Detroit, Los Angeles, Milwaukee, New Orleans, Portland (OR), St. Paul-Minneapolis, Santa Fe, Washington and the Dioceses of Austin, Biloxi, Cleveland, Columbus, Dallas, Grand Rapids, Jackson, Knoxville, Lansing, Lafayette, Raleigh, Richmond, St. Cloud, Springfield-Cape Girardeau, Shreveport, Steubenville, Toledo, Wheeling-Charleston, and Winona.

[1540] (O.S.F.)—SISTERS OF SAINT FRANCIS, CLINTON, IOWA P

Founded in the United States in 1868.

General Motherhouse: *Administrative Center,* 588 N. Bluff Blvd., Clinton, IA 52732. Tel: 319-242-7611; Fax: 319-243-0007. Sr. Marilyn Huegerich, O.S.F., Pres.

Total number in community 113.

Legal Holdings and Properties: *Mount St. Clare College; The Alverno Health Care Facility; Mount St. Clare Speech and Hearing Center Sisters of St. Francis, Clinton, Iowa Charitable Trust,* Clinton, IA; *The Canticle Clinton,* IA.

Ministry in the field of Academic Education at all levels; Health Care in Centers and Homes for the aged; Hospitals; Pastoral Ministry; Hospital Chaplaincy; Religious Education and Spiritual Direction; Ministry to the Poor in Legal Aid and Housing as well as to Persons with AIDS.

Represented in the Archdioceses of Chicago, Detroit, Dubuque, Indianapolis, Louisville, St. Louis and the Dioceses of Belleville, Charleston, Davenport, Des Moines, Joliet, Lansing, Lexington, Kansas City-St. Joseph, Oakland, Peoria, Portland, Phoenix, San Bernardino, San Diego, Sioux City, and Toledo. Also in the Bahamas and Peru.

[1550] (O.S.F.)—SISTERS OF ST. FRANCIS OF THE HOLY CROSS D

Founded in Wisconsin in 1881.

Motherhouse and Novitiate: *St. Francis Convent,* 3025 Bay Settlement Rd., Green Bay, WI 54311-7301. Tel: 920-468-1828; Fax: 920-468-1207. Sr. Sally Ann Brickner, O.S.F., Pres.

Total number in community 98.

Legal Title: *Sisters of St. Francis of the Holy Cross, Inc. Francis & Co.*

Ministries in the following areas: Education; Pastoral Ministry and Religious Education; Ministry to the Elderly; Health Care; Retreat Work; Foreign Missions.

Represented in the Archdioceses of Milwaukee, Washington and the Dioceses of Baton Rouge, Green Bay, and Jackson. Also in Nicaragua.

[1560] (O.S.F.)—SISTERS OF ST. FRANCIS OF THE HOLY EUCHARIST D

Founded in Grimmenstein, Switzerland in 1378. First foundation in United States in 1892.

Motherhouse, Novitiate and Prayer Center: *St. Francis Convent,* 2100 N. Noland Rd., Independence, MO 64050. Tel: 816-252-1673; Fax: 816-252-5574. Sr. M. Connie Boulch, O.S.F., Supr.; Sr. M. Lucy Lang, O.S.F., Vicar; Sr. Doris Engeman, Vocation Dir.

Total number in community 22.

Ministry in the following areas: Education at all levels; Retreat; Evangelization; Pastoral; Health Care.

Legal Title: *Franciscan Prayer Center,* Independence, MO; *Sisters of St. Francis of the Holy Eucharist Foundation,* Independence, MO.

Represented in the Archdiocese of Kansas City in Kansas and the Diocese of Kansas City-St. Joseph.

[1570] (O.S.F.)—SISTERS OF ST. FRANCIS OF THE HOLY FAMILY P

Founded in Germany in 1864. First foundation in the United States in 1875.

Motherhouse and Novitiate: *Mount St. Francis,* 3390 Windsor Ave., Dubuque, IA 52001-1311. Tel: 319-583-9786; Fax: 319-583-3250. Sr. Margaret Jungers, Pres.; Sr. Elvira Kelley, Community Archivist.

Total number in community 474.

Ministry in the following areas: Elementary and High Schools; Intercommunity High Schools; Religious Education-Parish Ministry; Health-Pastoral Care; Diocesan Offices; Social Service-Social Justice Centers; Food Service-Dietary; Communication Centers; Clerical Work-Business; Administration; Campus Ministry; Deaf Ministry; Art Studios; Foreign Missions.

Properties owned and sponsored: *Briar Cliff College,* Sioux City, IA; *Stonehill Care Center, Home for Aging; Alverno Apartments, Residence for the Elderly; Shalom Retreat Center and Mercy Health Center (co-sponsors),* Dubuque, IA; *Sisters of St. Francis of the Holy Family Charitable Trust,* Dubuque, IA.

Represented in the Archdioceses of Anchorage, Atlanta, Baltimore, Chicago, Detroit, Dubuque, Indianapolis, Omaha, Philadelphia, Portland (OR), St. Paul-Minneapolis, San Antonio, San Francisco, Santa Fe, Washington and the Dioceses of Allentown, Austin, Bismarck, Charleston, Charlotte, Colorado Springs, Columbus, Davenport, Des Moines, Erie, Fort Wayne-South Bend, Jackson, Joliet, LaCrosse, Las Cruces, Lafayette, Lexington, Madison, Manchester, New Ulm, Orlando, Owensboro, Phoenix, Providence, Pueblo, Rapid City, Rockford, Richmond, St. Cloud, St. Petersburg, San Jose, Santa Rosa, Sioux City, Springfield-Cape Girardeau, Springfield (IL), Stockton, Tucson, Tulsa, Tyler and Winona. Also in Central America, Africa, and Poland.

[1580] (O.S.F.)—SISTERS OF ST. FRANCIS OF THE IMMACULATE CONCEPTION D

Founded in the United States in 1891.

Motherhouse: *Immaculate Conception Convent Inc.,* 2408 W. Heading Ave., West Peoria, IL 61604-5096. Tel: 309-674-6168. Sr. Mary Barbara Buckley, Pres.; Sr. Mary Virginia Butkovich, Archivist.

Total number in community 60.

Properties owned and sponsored: *Immaculate Conception Convent,* Peoria, IL; *St. Joseph's Home of Peoria; St. Joseph's Home of Springfield in Illinois.*

Represented in the Dioceses of Joliet, Peoria, Rapid City and Springfield (IL).

[1590] (O.S.F.)—SISTERS OF ST. FRANCIS OF THE IMMACULATE HEART OF MARY (HANKINSON, NORTH DAKOTA) P

Founded in 1241 in Bavaria. First founded in the United States in 1913 at Collegeville, Minnesota.

General Motherhouse: Rome, Italy. Mother M. Irmtraud Eichelbronner, Supr. Gen.

Province of Hankinson (1928): *Sisters of St. Francis Motherhouse,* Hankinson, ND 58041. Tel: 701-242-7197. Sr. Ann Marie Friederichs, Prov.

Professed Sisters 70.

Legal Holdings or Titles: *St. Gerard's Community Nursing Home,* Hankinson, ND; *Oakes Community Hospital,* Oakes, ND; *St. Anne's Guest Home,* Grand Forks, ND.

Ministry in the field of Religious and Academic Education; Health Care in Hospitals; Homes for the Aged.

Represented in the Diocese of Fargo.

[1600] (O.S.F.)—SISTERS OF ST. FRANCIS OF THE MARTYR ST. GEORGE P

Founded in Thuine, Germany. First United States foundation in 1923.

General Motherhouse: Thuine, Germany. Mother Margaretha Maria Brand, Supr. Gen.

American Province St. Elizabeth: *Provincial Motherhouse, St. Francis Convent and Novitiate,* 2120 Central Ave., P.O. Box 9020, Alton, IL 62002-9020. Tel: 618-463-2750; 463-2755. Mother M. Ingeborg Rohner, O.S.F., Prov.

Worldwide Total 1,900.

Total in American Province 157.

Properties owned and sponsored: *Saint Anthony's Hospital,* Alton, IL; *St. Francis Day Care Center,* Alton, IL; *Mother of Good Counsel Home,* St. Louis, MO; *Saint Clare Hospital in Alton,* Illinois.

Sisters serve and staff: Hospitals; Home for Chronically ill; Social Service Center; Foreign Missions; Day Care Centers; Retirement Homes for the Aged; Grade & High Schools; Retirement Homes for Priests.

Represented in the Archdioceses of St. Louis and Washington and the Dioceses of Lincoln, Metuchen, Peoria, Springfield (IL) and Tulsa.

[1620] (O.S.F.)—SISTERS OF SAINT FRANCIS OF MILLVALE, PENNSYLVANIA P

Motherhouse and Novitiate (1871): *St. Francis Convent,* Mt. Alvernia, 146 Hawthorne Rd., Millvale P.O., Pittsburgh, PA 15209. Tel: 412-821-2200; Fax: 412-821-3318. Sr. Eileen Magill, O.S.F., Community Min.; Sr. M. Thomasita Heller, O.S.F., Community Archivist.

Total number in community 245.

Properties owned: *Mt. Alvernia High School,* Millvale, PA; *Mt. Alvernia Day Care & Learning Center,* Pittsburgh, PA.

Sponsored or managed facilities: *St. Francis Health System; St. Francis Hospital,* New Castle, PA.

Ministry in the following areas: Parochial Schools; Academic High Schools; Catechetical Centers; Hospitals; Consolidated Elementary Schools; Schools of Nursing; Day Care and Learning Center; Montessori School.

Represented in the Archdioceses of Baltimore, Buffalo, Chicago, Los Angeles, Miami, Newark, Santa Fe, San Juan, Washington and the Dioceses of Altoona-Johnstown, Caguas, Erie, Gaylord, Grand Rapids, Greensburg, Lansing, Lubbock, and Pittsburgh. Also in Canada and Nigeria.

[1630] (O.S.F.)—SISTERS OF ST. FRANCIS OF PENANCE AND CHRISTIAN CHARITY P

(aka Sisters of St. Francis of the Holy Name Province).

Founded in Holland in 1835. First Foundation in the U.S. in 1874.

General Motherhouse: Rome, Italy. Sr. Christina Pecoraro, Gen. Min.

Universal number in Congregation 2,484.

Holy Name Province (1928): *Sisters of St. Francis,* 4421 Lower River Rd., Stella Niagara, NY 14144. Tel: 716-754-4312; Fax: 716-754-7657. Sr. Mary McCarrick, O.S.F., Prov. Minister.

Total number in community 213.

Legal Holdings: *Stella Niagara Education Park,* Stella Niagara, NY; *Buffalo Academy of the Sacred Heart,* Eggertsville, NY.

Ministry in the field of Academic Education at all levels; Foreign Mission Work; Health and Hospital Care; Social Work; Pastoral Ministry.

Represented in the Archdioceses of Chicago, Cincinnati, Louisville, Miami, Sante Fe, Seattle and the Dioceses of Buffalo, Columbus, Fort Wayne-South Bend, Orlando, Paterson, Raleigh St. Petersburg, Trenton, Venice, and Wheeling-Charleston.

Sacred Heart Province (1939): Provincial Motherhouse-Marycrest, 2851 W. 52nd Ave., Denver, CO 80221. Tel: 303-458-6270. Sr. Gloria Shuffer, Prov. Minister.

Total number in community 84.

Sisters Serve and Staff: High Schools, Grammar Schools; Parish Ministries; Apostolate of Aging; Diocesan Biblical School; Hospital Pastoral Ministry; Emergency Housing; Home for Neglected Children; Retreat Ministry; Hospital; Formation Programs; Administrative.

Legal Holdings or Titles: *Kenmare Community Hospital,* Kenmare, ND; *St. Joseph's Hospital; St. Joseph's Hospital Foundation; St. Elizabeth Convent,* Minot, ND; *Marycrest Motherhouse Queen of Peace Convent; House of Prayer Damen House - Home for Single Women & Children; Marycrest Health System Sisters of St. Francis Foundation-Sacred Heart Province,* Denver, CO; *St. Anthony's Hospital St. Anthony's Convent,* O'Neill, NE; *St. Francis Home, (Home for Abused Native American Children),* Manderson, SD; *St. Mary's Home, (Home for the Aged),* St. Paul, MN; *Marian Residence, Convent for Retired Sisters,* Alliance, NE; *St. Francis Convent; St. Clare Convent,* Alliance, NE; *Franciscan Health Community,* St. Paul, MN.

Represented in the Archdioceses of Denver, Omaha, St. Paul-Minneapolis and Sante Fe and the Dioceses of Bismarck, Grand Island, Oakland, Rapid City, Las Vegas and Tulsa.

St. Francis Province (1939): *Mt. Alverno,* 3910 Bret Harte Dr., P.O. Box 1028, Redwood City, CA 94064. Tel: 650-369-1725. Sr. Maria Elena Martinez, Prov. Minister.

Total number in community 105.

Legal Title: *Sisters of St. Francis Charitable Trust Sisters of St. Francis - Mount Alverno.*

Ministry in the following areas: Grammar Schools; Formation House; Colleges; Diocesan Offices; Parish Ministry; Pastoral Ministry; Catholic Social Services Agencies; Education Programs; Secondary Education; Hospitals; Residence for Retired Men and Women; Day Home; CCD Centers; Retreat-Conference Centers; Apostolic Projects; ESL.

Represented in the Archdioceses of Los Angeles, Portland (OR), San Francisco, Seattle and the Dioceses of Monterey, Oakland, Reno, Phoenix, Sacramento, San Diego, San Jose and Stockton.

[1640] (O.S.F.)—SISTERS OF ST. FRANCIS OF PERPETUAL ADORATION P

Founded in Germany in 1863. First foundation in the United States in 1875.

Generalate: Olpe, Westfalen, West Germany. Sr. Xaveria Kronen, Supr Gen.

Universal total in congregation 799.

Province of the Immaculate Heart of Mary (1875): *Provincial House and Novitiate,* St. Francis Convent, Box 766, Mishawaka, IN 46546-0766. Tel: 219-259-5427. Sr. M. Rose Agnes Pfautsch, O.S.F., Prov.

Total number in community 166.

Ministry in the field of Academic Education at all levels; Health Care in Hospitals and Nursing Homes.

Properties owned: *Sisters of St. Francis of Perpetual Adoration, Inc.; St. Francis Convent,* Mishawaka, IN; *St. Francis College of Fort Wayne, Inc.,* Fort Wayne, IN; *Sisters of St. Francis Health Services, Inc.; Alverno Administrative Services Alverno Health Corporation,* Mishawaka, IN; *Sisters of St. Francis Health Services, Inc.,* Corporate Office, Mishawaka, IN, owns the following: *St. Elizabeth Healthcare Center,* Delphi, IN; *St. Francis Hospital & Health Centers,* Beech Grove, IN; *St. James Hospital and Health Centers,* Chicago Heights, IL; *St. Francis Hospital, Evanston,* IL; *St. Margaret Mercy Health Care Centers, North Campus,* Hammond, IN; *St. Margaret Mercy Health Care Centers, South Campus,* Dyer, IN; *St. Elizabeth Hospital Medical Center,* Lafayette, IN; *St. Joseph Hospital and Health Centers,* Memphis, TN; *St. Anthony Hospital and Health Centers,* Michigan City, IN; *St. James-Hospital Medical Clinic,* Beecher, IL; *St. James Manor,* Crete, IL; *St. Francis Extended Care,* Evanston, IL; *Franciscan Health Care Center,* Louisville, KY; *St. Joseph Family Health Center,* Memphis, TN; *St. Joseph Family Health Center, Fraser Blvd.,* Memphis, TN; *Alverno Administrative Services,* Beech Grove, IN; *St. Francis Health Center,* Lincolnwood, IL; *Suburban Heights-St. James Hospital Medical Clinic,* Frankfort, IL; *St. James Hospital Medical Clinic,* Lansing, IL. *Alverno Health Corporation* owns the following: *Northern Indiana Medical Laboratory Services,* Michigan City, IN.

Represented in the Archdioceses of Chicago, Indianapolis, Louisville and New Orleans and the Dioceses of Fort Wayne-South Bend, Gary, Joliet, Lafayette (IN) and Memphis.

Province of St. Joseph (March 19, 1932): *Provincial House and Formation House-Mt. St. Francis,* 7665 Assisi Heights, Colorado Springs, CO 80919. Tel: 719-598-5486. Sr. Clarice Gentrup, Prov.

Professed Sisters 115.

Ministry in Education; Hospitals; Homes for the Aged; Parish/Pastoral Ministry; Religious Education Centers.

Represented in the Archdioceses of Denver, Omaha, Santa Fe and the Dioceses of Colorado Springs, Grand Island, and Lincoln.

[1650] (O.S.F.)—THE SISTERS OF ST. FRANCIS OF PHILADELPHIA P

Founded in the United States in 1855.

Congregational Motherhouse: *Convent of Our Lady of Angels,* Aston, PA 19014. Tel: 215-459-4125. Sr. Marie Lucey, O.S.F., Congregational Min.; Sr. Esther Anderson, O.S.F., Asst. Congregational Min.; Sr. Eileen Valerie Kulacz, O.S.F., Congregational Sec.; Sr. M. Andrew, O.S.F., Archivist.

Total number in community 962.

Properties owned: *Formation House,* Puerto Rico; *Sisters of St. Francis,* Sea Isle City, NJ; *Franciscan Residence,* Hamilton Square, NJ; *Bay House,* Tacoma, WA; *Marion House,* Tacoma, WA; *St. Ann Convent,* Tacoma, WA; *Neumann College,* Aston, PA; *Assisi House,* Aston, PA; *Catholic Health Initiatives,* Denver, CO; *Portiuncula Convent,* Aston, PA; *St. Mary Convent,* Langhorne, PA; *St. Francis Convent,* Lancaster, PA; *Franciscan Residence,* Langhorne, PA; *St. Agnes Convent,* Philadelphia, PA; *Neumann Convent,* Reading, PA; *The Catholic High School of Baltimore,* Baltimore, MD; *St. Joseph Counseling Center,* Spokane, WA; *Convent of Our Lady of Angels,* Portland, OR; *Portiuncula Convent,* Philadelphia, PA; *Franciscan Renewal Center,* Portland, OR; *Sisters of St. Francis of Philadelphia, Canticle House,* Philadelphia, PA; *Sisters of St. Francis of Philadelphia, TAU Convent,* Aston, PA; *St. Clare Renewal Center,* Aston, PA; *Sisters of St. Francis of Philadelphia, Our Lady of the Valley,* Aston, PA; *Mt. Alvernia Convent,* Aston, PA; *St. Clare Convent,* Trenton, NJ.

Ministry in Health Care; Eldercare; Academic and Religious Education at all Levels; Specialized Education; Parish Ministry; Social Services; Family Centers; Renewal Centers; Seminaries; Diocesan Offices; Retreat Ministry; National Organizations.

Represented in the Archdioceses of Baltimore, Boston, Chicago, Hartford, Los Angeles, Miami, Mobile, New Orleans, New York, Philadelphia, Portland (OR), San Juan, Santa Fe, Seattle, Washington and the Dioceses of Allentown, Baker, Birmingham, Buffalo, Caguas (PR), Camden, Charleston, Cheyenne, El Paso, Fairbanks, Fort Wayne-South Bend, Gallup, Harrisburg, Las Cruces, Lexington, Metuchen, Oakland, Orlando, Pensacola-Tallahassee, Raleigh, Scranton, San Bernardino, San Diego, Spokane, Trenton, Venice, Wheeling-Charleston and Wilmington. Also in Ireland, Central America, England, Zambia, Kenya, Ethiopia, West Indies and Dominican Republic.

[1660] (O.S.F.)—SISTERS OF SAINT FRANCIS OF THE PROVIDENCE OF GOD P

Founded in Pittsburgh in 1922.

Motherhouse: *St. Francis Convent,* 3603 McRoberts Rd., Pittsburgh, PA 15234-2398. Tel: 412-882-9911; Fax: 412-885-7210. Sr. Joanne Brazinski, O.S.F., Gen. Supr.

Total professed 114.

Properties owned and sponsored: *Sisters of St. Francis of the Providence of God Sisters of St. Francis,* Mt. Vernon IL, Inc.; *Sisters of St. Francis of the Providence of God Ministries Corporation; St. Francis Academy Franciscan Child Day Care; Center Franciscan Spirit and Life Center.*

Ministry in the field of Education; Health Care; Social Service; Pastoral, Parish & Retreat Ministries;

Retreat Directors; Prison Chaplains; Foreign Mission work in Brazil & Lithuania.

Represented in the Archdiocese of Newark and the Dioceses of Albany, Buffalo, Galveston-Houston, Grand Rapids, Paterson, and Pittsburgh.

[1670] (O.S.F.)—SISTER OF ST. FRANCIS OF SAVANNAH, MO. P

Founded in Austria, 1850. Founded in the United States, August 22, 1922.

Provincial House and Novitiate: La Verna Heights, Box 488, 104 E. Park, Savannah, MO 64485-0488. Tel: 816-324-3179; Fax: 816-324-6512. Sr. Kathleen Reichert, Prov. Supr.

Total number in community 29.

Ministry in the field of Education; CCD Centers; Health Care and Hospital Work; Housing for Elderly, Persons with Aids, Abuse Victims and Unwed Mothers; Pastoral Care; Food Pantry.

Legal Holdings and Titles: *Sisters of St. Francis of Savannah, Inc. Maintenance and Custodial Care Trust of the Franciscan Sisters of Savannah; La Verna Village Apartment Units for Senior Citizens and Handicapped; La Verna Village Nursing Home, Inc.; La Verna Heights Provincial House and Retirement Center.*

Represented in the Dioceses of Jefferson City and Kansas City-St. Joseph.

[1680] (O.S.F.)—SCHOOL SISTERS OF ST. FRANCIS P

Founded in the United States in 1874.

General Motherhouse: 1501 S. Layton Blvd., Milwaukee, WI 53215. Tel: 414-384-4105; Fax: 414-645-7198. Sr. Frances Brenner, O.S.F., Pres.; Sr. Phyllis Vater, First Vice Pres.; Sr. Raphaela Munch, Vice Pres.; Sr. Alida Lopez, Vice Pres.; Sr. Charlita Foxhoven, Treas.; Sr. Constance Halbur, Archivist.

Total in Congregation 1,590; Total in U.S. 1,040.

Properties owned: *St. Joseph Convent,* Milwaukee, WI; *Generalate-School Sisters of St. Francis, Inc.; School Sisters of St. Francis of St. Joseph's Convent, New Castle, Inc.*

U.S. Province: 1515 S. Layton Blvd., Milwaukee, WI 53215. Tel: 414-384-1515. Provincial Team: Sr. Celestine Schall; Sr. Therese Thoenen; Sr. Jane Elyse Russell.

Sisters serve and staff: Universities, Colleges, Seminaries, High Schools, Grade Schools, Pre Schools, Adult and Special Education; National and Diocesan Offices; Hospitals and Nursing Homes; School & Parish Musicians; Retreat and Spiritual Direction; Social Ministries; Campus Ministry; Psychotherapy; Home Health Care Service; Religious Education and CCD; Pastoral Ministry; Pastoral Associate; Health Pastoral Care; Retirement Homes; Overseas Missions; Mission Projects; Special Service to Women; Fine Arts; Home Missions.

Properties owned and sponsored: *Alverno College,* Milwaukee, WI; *Clement Manor,* Greenfield, WI; *Villa Clement,* West Allis, WI; *Maryhill Manor,* Niagra, WI; *New Cassel,* Omaha, NE; *Clare Towers I,* Milwaukee, WI; *Clare Towers II,* Milwaukee, WI; *Telos, Inc.,* Milwaukee, WI; *St. Clare Management, Inc.,* Milwaukee, WI; *Marian Hall,* Milwaukee, WI; *Sacred Heart Center,* Milwaukee, WI; *St. Joseph Convent,* Campbellsport, WI; *School Sisters of St. Francis Foundation, Inc.,* Omaha, NE; *School Sisters of St. Francis of St. Joseph's Convent, Milwaukee, Wisconsin, Inc.; Convergence, Inc.,* Milwaukee, WI; *Vision Ministries,* Milwaukee, WI; *The School Sisters of Saint Francis of St. Joseph's Convent, Milwaukee, Wisconsin, Inc - Congregational Support Charitable Trust,* Milwaukee, WI.

Represented in the Archdioceses of Anchorage, Chicago, Denver, Dubuque, Indianapolis, Los Angeles, Milwaukee, New York, Oklahoma City, Omaha, Portland-OR, St. Paul-Minneapolis, San Antonio, Santa Fe, Washington and the Dioceses of Buffalo, Charleston, Dodge City, Davenport, Des Moines, El Paso, Gallup, Great Falls, Green Bay, Jackson, Jefferson City, Joliet, Kansas City-St. Joseph, Knoxville, La Crosse, Lexington, Lincoln, Madison, Memphis, Nashville, New Ulm, Orange, Palm Beach, Phoenix, Rapid City, Rockford, St. Cloud, San Bernardino, San Diego, Santa Rosa, Springfield (IL), St. Petersburg, Superior, Trenton, Tucson, Venice, Wheeling-Charleston and Winona.

[1690] (O.S.F.)—SCHOOL SISTERS OF THE THIRD ORDER OF ST. FRANCIS (PITTSBURGH, PA.) P

First foundation in the U.S. in 1913.

General Motherhouse: Rome, Italy.

Motherhouse and Novitiate: *Mount Assisi Convent,* 934 Forest Ave., Bellevue, Pittsburgh, PA 15202. Tel: 412-761-6004. Sr. Elaine Hromulak, O.S.F., Prov. Supr. Tel: 412-761-2855.

Total number in community 88.

Legal Title: *School Sisters of the Third Order of St. Francis; School Sisters of the Third Order of St. Francis, of Texas.*

Ministry in the following areas: the field of academic education at all levels; CCD Centers; Pastoral Ministry; Pastoral Associate; Residence Home for Aged Women; Mission Work in Chile & South Africa; Hospital Ministry; Campus Ministry; House of Prayer.

Represented in the Archdiocese of San Antonio and the Dioceses of Erie, Greensburg, Phoenix, Pittsburgh and San Angelo. Also in South Africa and Chile.

[1695] (O.S.F.)—SCHOOL SISTERS OF THE THIRD ORDER OF ST. FRANCIS (PANHANDLE, TEXAS) P

Founded in Austria, 1723; The Vienna Foundation in 1845. First founded in the United States, 1931.

General Motherhouse: Vienna, Austria.

American Center and Novitiate: P.O. Box 906, Panhandle, TX 79068. Tel: 806-537-3182. Mother M. Bernadette, Supr.

Total number in U.S. 26.

Ministry in the following areas: Grammar Schools; Confraternity Classes; Home for the Aged.

Represented in the Dioceses of Amarillo and Victoria.

[1700] (O.S.F.)—SCHOOL SISTERS OF THE THIRD ORDER OF ST. FRANCIS (BETHLEHEM, PA.) P

Founded in Austria, 1843. First founded in the United States, 1913.

General Motherhouse: Rome, Italy.

Bethlehem Province and Novitiate: 395 Bridle Path Rd., Bethlehem, PA 18017. Tel: 610-866-2597; Fax: 610-861-7478. Sr. M. Xavier Bomberger, Prov. Supr.

Sisters 62.

Properties owned: *St. Francis Academy Kindergarten; St. Francis Day Care; St. Francis Center for Renewal,* Bethlehem, PA.

Represented in the Archdiocese of Newark and the Dioceses of Allentown, Metuchen, Paterson, Scranton and Springfield (MA). Also in Chile, India and Rome, Italy.

[1705] (O.S.F.)—THE SISTERS OF ST. FRANCIS OF ASSISI P
(Sisters of Penance and Charity)

Founded in the United States in 1849.

General Motherhouse: *St. Francis Convent,* 3221 S. Lake Dr., St. Francis, WI 53235-3799. Tel: 414-744-1160; Fax: 414-744-7193. Sr. Marita Maschmann, O.S.F., Dir.

Total number in community 365.

Legal Titles: *The Sisters of St. Francis of Assisi; The Ongoing Community Support Fund of the Sisters of St. Francis.*

Goals of the Congregation are: to bring the healing, teaching, reconciling and liberating power of Jesus into the human situations in which we live and minister; to be in solidarity with the poor through the work of justice and peace; to appreciate and affirm and to encourage the development of each community member and each community apostolate for the sake of full effectiveness in the ministry of the Church; and to work effectively toward implementing co-responsibility, subsidiarity and accountability at all levels within the Congregation.

Sponsored Corporations: *St. Ann Center for Intergenerational Care,* St. Francis, WI; *St. Mary's Academy,* Milwaukee, WI; *Cardinal Stritch University,* Milwaukee, WI; *St. Coletta's of Wisconsin,* Jefferson, WI; *St. Coletta School Foundation of Jefferson Charitable Trust,* Jefferson, WI; *St. Coletta's of Illinois,* Palos Park, IL; *The Lt. Joseph P. Kennedy Jr. School for Exceptional Children,* Palos Park, IL; *St. Coletta's of Illinois Foundation,* Palos Park, IL; *St. Coletta's of Massachusetts: Cardinal Cushing School and Training Center,* Hanover, MA; *Cushing Residence, Inc.,* Hanover, MA; *The Cardinal Cushing School Foundation of Hanover Charitable Trust,* Hanover, MA; *St. Coletta Day School,* Braintree, MA. Services to the Elderly: *Alverno Housing Corporation,* Jefferson, WI; *Canticle Court, Inc.; Juniper Court, Inc.,* Milwaukee, WI.

Represented in the Archdioceses of Boston, Chicago, Denver, Los Angeles, Milwaukee, Philadelphia, San Antonio, San Francisco, Santa Fe and the Dioceses of Birmingham, Cheyenne, Davenport, Des Moines, Duluth, Fall River, Joliet, Gary, Green Bay, La Crosse, Madison, Nashville, Palm Beach, Peoria, Phoenix, Portland-ME, Reno, Rockford, San Diego, Santa Rosa, Steubenville, Superior, Toledo, Tucson and Winona. Also in Taiwan.

[1710] (O.S.F.)—CONGREGATION OF THE THIRD ORDER OF ST. FRANCIS OF MARY IMMACULATE, JOLIET, IL P

Founded in the United States, Joliet, Illinois, in 1865.

General Motherhouse: *St. Francis Convent,* 520 Plainfield Ave., Joliet, IL 60435. Tel: 815-727-3686. Sr. Mary Jean Morris, O.S.F., Pres.; Sr. Marian Voelker, O.S.F., Community Archivist.

Total number in community 334.

Legal Title: *Congregation of the Third Order of St. Francis of Mary Immaculate,* Joliet, IL; *Retirement Plan Trust of the Congregation of the Third Order of St. Francis of Mary Immaculate,* Joliet, IL.

Ministry in the following areas: School and Adult Education; Home for Emotionally Disturbed Children; Retirement Home; House of Prayer. Also engaged in Religious Education; Social Services; Spiritual Direction; Nursing and Health Services; Hospital and Parish Ministry; Food Service; and Prison ministry.

Represented in the Archdioceses of Boston, Chicago, Cincinnati, Denver, Los Angeles, Miami, Milwaukee, Omaha, St. Louis, Washington, and the Dioceses of Cleveland, Colorady Springs, Columbus, Fort Wayne-South Bend, Gary, Green Bay, Joliet, Lansing, Lexington, Palm Beach, Phoenix, Peoria, Rockford, St. Cloud, San Diego, St. Petersburg, Springfield-Cape Girardeau, Springfield (IL), Stockton, Superior, Toledo, Tucson, Venice and Youngstown. Also in Agana, Guam and Brazil.

[1720] (O.S.F.)—SISTERS OF THE THIRD ORDER REGULAR OF ST. FRANCIS OF THE CONGREGATION OF OUR LADY OF LOURDES P

Founded in the United States in 1877.

Administration Center: *Assisi Heights,* Rochester, MN 55903. Tel: 507-282-7441; Fax: 507-282-7762. Sr. Valerie Usher, O.S.F., Pres./Community Min. Tel: 507-280-2198. Sr. Mary Lonan Reilly, Community Archivists.

Total number in community 403.

Properties owned and sponsored: *Tau Center,* Winona, MN; *Assisi Heights,* Rochester, MN.

Ministry in the following areas: Education Services; Pastoral Concerns Development; Religious Life Development; Spiritual Life Development; Community Life Development; Social Concerns Development; Business Services; Health Care Services; Support Services.

Represented in the Archdioceses of Baltimore, Chicago, Denver, Dubuque, Indianapolis, Newark, St. Paul-Minneapolis, Santa Fe, Seattle and Washington and the Dioceses of Brownsville, Charleston, Charlotte, Columbus, Colorado Springs, Covington, Duluth, Fargo, Gallup, Great Falls-Billings, Helena, Joliet, La Crosse, Las Cruces, Lexington, Madison, Memphis, New Ulm, Orange, Owensboro, Phoenix, Pueblo, St. Cloud, San Bernardino, San Diego, Sioux City, Sioux Falls, Springfield-Cape Girardeau, Springfield (IL), Superior, Tucson and Winona. Also in Thailand, Colombia, Peru and Kenya.

[1730] (O.S.F.)—CONGREGATION OF THE SISTERS OF THE THIRD ORDER OF ST. FRANCIS, OLDENBURG, IN. P

Founded in U.S., Oldenburg, Indiana in 1851.

General Motherhouse and Novitiate: *Convent of the Immaculate Conception,* Oldenburg, IN 47036. Tel: 812-934-2475. Sr. Amy Kistner, Congregational Minister.

Total number in community 372.

Sisters serve & staff:: Liberal Arts College, Academy, High Schools, Elementary Schools; Navajo, Crow Indian and Cheyenne Missions; Religious Education Centers; Hospital & Parish Ministry; Apostolate of Aging; Diocesan Offices; Retreat & Counseling Ministry; Hispanic Ministry; Justice & Peace Offices; Clerical Staff; Social Services; Foreign Missions: Mexico & New Guinea.

Properties owned: *Marian College,* Indianapolis, IN; *ICA Academy,* Oldenburg, IN.

Represented in the Archdioceses of Chicago, Cincinnati, Detroit, Indianapolis, Los Angeles, New York, St. Louis and the Dioceses of Charleston, Cleveland, Columbus, Covington, El Paso, Evansville, Fort Wayne, Gallup, Great Falls-Billings, Helena, Jefferson City, Lexington, Peoria, Springfield-IL, St. Augustine, St. Petersburg and Wheeling-Charleston. Also in Korea and Mexico.

[1760] (O.S.F.)—SISTERS OF THE THIRD ORDER OF ST. FRANCIS OF PENANCE AND OF CHARITY P

Founded in Tiffin, Ohio in 1869.

General Motherhouse: *St. Francis Convent,* St. Francis Ave., Tiffin, OH 44883. Tel: 419-447-0435; Fax: 419-448-1612. Sr. Jacquelyn Doepker, Community Minister.

Total number in community 148.

Legal Title: *Sisters of St. Francis of Tiffin, OH.*

Properties Owned or Sponsored: *St. Francis Villas, Inc.; St. Francis Home, Inc.,* Tiffin, OH.

Ministry in the following areas: Parochial Schools; Ministry to the Aged; Parish Ministry; Retreat and Renewal Centers; Diocese Offices; Health Care; Health-Pastoral Care; Administration.

Represented in the Archdioceses of Cincinnati, Los Angeles and Santa Fe and the Dioceses of Brownsville, Columbus, Charlotte, Davenport, Jackson, Lansing, Lexington, Owensboro, Toledo, Venice and Wheeling-Charleston. Also in Mexico.

[1770] (O.S.F.)—THE SISTERS OF THE THIRD ORDER OF ST. FRANCIS (EAST PEORIA, ILLINOIS.) P

Founded in the United States in 1877.

Motherhouse: 1175 St. Francis Lane, East Peoria, IL 61611-1299. Tel: 309-699-7215. Sr. Mary Ellen Flannery, Major Supr.

Total number in community 71.

Properties owned and sponsored: *Saint Francis Medical Center,* Peoria, IL; *St. Joseph Medical Center,* Bloomington, IL; *St. Mary Medical Center,* Galesburg, IL; *Saint James Hospital,* Pontiac, IL; *Saint Anthony Medical Center,* Rockford, IL; *Saint Francis Hospital,* Escanaba, MI; *St. Francis Continuation Care and Nursing Home Center,* Burlington, IA; *Saint Joseph Hospital,* Belvidere, IL; *St. Anthony's Continuing Care Center,* Rock Island, IL; *St. Mary of the Angels Convent,* Rock Island, IL; *OSF Healthcare System,* Peoria, IL; *OSF Healthcare Foundation,* Peoria, IL; *Motherhouse,* East Peoria, IL.

Represented in the Dioceses of Davenport, Marquette, Peoria and Rockford.

[1780] (F.S.P.A.)—CONGREGATION OF THE SISTERS OF THE THIRD ORDER OF ST. FRANCIS OF PERPETUAL ADORATION P

(Francisan Sisters of Perpetual Adoration)

Founded in the United States in 1849.

Generalate: 912 Market St., La Crosse, WI 54601. Tel: 608-782-5610; Fax: 608-782-6301. Sr. Marla Lang, Pres.; Sr. Jolyce Greteman, Archivist.

Total number in Congregation 511.

Properties owned and sponsored: *St. Joseph Memorial Hospital, Inc.,* Hillsboro, WI; *St. Anthony Regional Hospital, Inc.,* Carroll, IA; *Viterbo College, Inc.,* La Crosse, WI.

Central Region of Franciscan Sisters of Perpetual Adoration (1966): P.O. Box 190, Hiawatha, IA 52233-0190. Tel: 319-393-5982; Office Sec. 393-6092. Sr. Karen Flottmeier, Reg. Admin.

Total number in region 178.

Ministry in the field of Academic Education at all Levels; Religious Education and Parish Centers; Health Care; Hospital and Parish Ministry; Diocesan Offices; Mission Centers.

Represented in the Archdioceses of Chicago, Dubuque, Milwaukee, Mobile, Oklahoma City, Santa Fe, St. Louis and St. Paul-Minneapolis and the Dioceses of Belleville, Davenport, Des Moines, El Paso, Jackson, La Crosse, Little Rock, Madison, Oakland, Peoria, Reno-Las Vegas, St. Cloud, Sioux City, Springfield-Cape Girardeau and Winona. Also in Caroline-Marshall Islands, Guatemala, Mexico and Zimbabwe.

Western Region (1985): *Mary of the Angels,* 4624 E. Jamieson, Spokane, WA 99223-2028. Tel: 509-448-0674. Sr. Patricia Gordon, Reg. Admin.

Professed Sisters 63.

Properties owned: *Clare Center,* Spokane, WA.

Sisters serve and staff: Religious Education; Education-University, College, High School, Elementary, Special Education; Home Health Care; Pastoral Ministry; Religious Education-Administrative, Adult, Consultative, Secondary, Elementary; Secretarial; Social Services; Health Services; Spiritual Direction.

Represented in the Archdioceses of Denver, Los Angeles, Portland (OR), Santa Fe and Seattle and the Dioceses of Boise, Helena, Honolulu, La Crosse, Oakland, Orange, Phoenix, Reno-Las Vegas, San Jose, Spokane and Tuscon. Also in Guam and El Salvador.

[1800] (O.S.F.)—SISTERS OF ST. FRANCIS OF THE THIRD ORDER REGULAR (WILLIAMSVILLE, NEW YORK) P

Motherhouse: *St. Mary of the Angels Convent of Perpetual Adoration,* 400 Mill St., P.O. Box 275, Williamsville, NY 14231. Tel: 716-632-2155; Fax: 716-632-0339. Sr. Patricia Burkard, Gen. Minister.

Total number in community 137.

Sisters serve and staff: Universities; High Schools Grammar Schools; Hospitals; Nursing Homes & Homes for the Aged; Pastoral Ministry in Parishes, Hospitals & Nursing Homes; Diocesan Offices.

Properties owned and/or sponsored: *Mount St. Mary's LTC Facility, Inc.,* Niagara Falls, NY; *Holy Family Home,* Williamsville, NY.

Represented in the Archdioceses of Chicago, San Juan and the Dioceses of Buffalo, Charleston, Harrisburg, Ogdensburg, Palm Beach, Rochester, and Syracuse. Also in Africa.

[1810] (O.S.F.)—BERNARDINE FRANCISCAN SISTERS P

Founded in the United States in 1894.

Generalate: 403 Allendale Rd., King of Prussia, PA 19406. Tel: 610-337-3864; Fax: 610-337-4359. Sr. Mary Margaret Jackson, O.S.F., Gen. Min.

Total number in community 555.

Bernardine Sisters OSF - Bernardine Franciscan Sisters: *United States Province Offices,* 460 St. Bernardine St., Reading, PA 19607-1737. Tel: 610-777-4174; Fax: 610-777-3973. Sr. Deborah Ann Surgot, O.S.F., Co-Dir., Office of Communications; Sr. Patrice Marie Klausing, O.S.F., Co-Dir., Office of Communications; Sr. Kateri Peake, O.S.F., Dir. Personnel; Sr. Dolorice Domin, O.S.F., Dir. Life Development; Sr. Rosemary Stets, O.S.F., Dir. Vocations and Assocs.; Sr. Miriam Keises, O.S.F., Dir. Finance and Health Benefits Office.

Total number in province 471.

Ministry in the field of academic education at all levels - preschool to college; religious education of children & adults; hospitals, health & home care; retreat work; social work.

Represented in the in 25 Archdioceses and Dioceses and 5 Overseas Dioceses.

Our Lady of the Rosary Province (Area 1): 27405 W. 10 Mile Rd., Farmington Hills, MI 48336. Tel: 810-476-3576; Fax: 810-476-6950. Sr. Maria Christine Keller, Prov. Minister.

Total number in province 110.

Properties owned: *Provincial House Mary's Manor, (Residence Home for retired sisters).*

Sisters engaged in Education in Elementary and High Schools; Special Education; Directing and Teaching Religious Education; Pastoral Ministry; Pastoral Care; Adult Ministry; Spiritual Direction and Retreat Ministry; Gerontology; Business & Clerical Ministry to the homeless; Hospital & Health Care Ministry; Day Care.

Represented in the Archdioceses of Detroit, Los Angeles and San Antonio and the Dioceses of Dallas and Saginaw.

Our Lady of Grace Convent (Area 2): 106 S. Seventh Ave., West Reading, PA 19611. Tel: 610-372-3390; Fax: 610-777-3973. Sr. Mary Sninsky, O.S.F., Provincial Min.

Our Lady of Grace Convent (Area 3): 106 S. Seventh Ave., West Reading, PA 19611. Tel: 610-372-3544; Fax: 610-777-3973. Sr. Lynn Rachelle Pascoe, O.S.F., Provincial Min.

Represented in the Archdioceses of Boston, Hartford, Newark, and the Dioceses of Bridgeport, Metuchen, Providence, Saginaw, and Scranton.

Properties owned and sponsored in the U.S.: *Alvernia Montessori School,* Reading, PA; *Bernardine Franciscans, Delaware County,* Villanove, PA; *Heart of Mary Covenant,* Stamford, CT; *Lt. Joseph P. Kennedy Memorial School,* Hyde Park, MA; *Mary's Home,* Farmington, MI; *Our Lady of Grace Covenant,* West Reading, PA; *Our Lady of the Rosary Covenant,* Farmington, MI; *Sacred Heart Covenant - Retirement Facility for Bernardine Sisters,* Reading, PA; *St. Joseph Villa,* Reading, PA; *St. Clare Covenant,* Reading, PA; *Villa Maria Retreat Center,* Stamford, CT; *Villa Maria Education Center,* Stamford, CT; *Villa of Our Lady of the Poconos Retreat House,* Mt. Pocono, PA. Sponsored: *Alvernia College,* Reading, PA; *Hazleton-St. Joseph Medical Center,* Hazleton, PA; *Mary Immaculate Hospital,* Newport News, VA.

Sisters engaged in the field of Religious and Academic education at all levels; Parish and Pastoral ministry; Sipritual Direction and Retreat House; Ministry to women, the poor, homeless, mentally and physically challenged; Gerontology, Hospital and Health Care; Day care; Overseas Missions; Business & Clerical.

[1820] (O.S.F.)—HOSPITAL SISTERS OF THE THIRD ORDER OF ST. FRANCIS P

Founded in Germany in 1844. First foundation in the United States in 1875.

General Motherhouse: Muenster in Westphalia, Germany. Sr. Mary Ann Minor, O.S.F., Gen. Supr.

American Province (1875): *St. Francis Convent, Motherhouse and Novitiate,* Box 19431, Springfield, IL 62794. Tel: 217-522-3386. Sr. Bernadine Gutowski, O.S.F., Prov. Supr.; Sr. Maureen O'Connor, O.S.F., Prov. Sec.

Total number in the community 222.

Sisters serve and Staff:: Hospitals; Home Health Services; Catechetical; Care of Chemically Dependent; Social Ministries; Pastoral Ministries; Overseas Missions.

Properties Owned or Sponsored: Residence 18; *St. Francis Convent, Motherhouse, Novitiate,* Springfield, IL; *Hospital Sisters Services, Inc.; Hospital Sisters of St. Francis Foundation Hospital; Sisters Health System; St. John's Hospital; St. John's College of Nursing,* Springfield, IL; *St. Mary's Hospital,* Decatur, IL; *St. Anthony Memorial Hospital,* Effingham, IL; *St. Joseph's Hospital,* Highland, IL; *St. Francis Hospital,* Litchfield, IL; *St. Elizabeth's Hospital,* Belleville, IL; *St. Joseph's Hospital,* Breese, IL; *St. Mary's Hospital Medical Center St. Vincent Hospital,* Green Bay, WI; *St. Joseph's Hospital; L.E. Phillips Treatment Center for the Chemically Dependent; Hospital Sisters Health Care West, Inc.; Transitus House,* Chippewa Falls, WI; *Sacred Heart Hospital; St. Francis Apartments,* Eau Claire, WI; *St. Nicholas Hospital,* Sheboygan, WI; *St. Mary's Hospital,* Streator, IL.

Represented in the Archdioceses of Chicago, Milwaukee, Santa Fe, and the Dioceses of Belleville, Green Bay, La Crosse, Peoria and Springfield (IL). Also in Taiwan, Japan and Haiti.

[1830] (R.G.S. - C.G.S.)—THE SISTERS OF THE GOOD SHEPHERD P

Congregation of Our Lady of Charity of the Good Shepherd

Founded in France in 1835. First foundation in the United States in Louisville, KY 1842.

Generalate for the Provinces: *Suore del Buon Pastore,* via Raffaello Sardiello 20, 00165, Rome, Italy. Sr. Liliane Tauvette, Supr. Gen.

Province of Cincinnati (Carthage) (1857): 2849 Fischer Pl., Cincinnati, OH 45211. Tel: 513-661-1833. Sr. Dolores Kalina, Prov.

Legal Titles: *The Sisters of the Good Shepherd, Cincinnati Province; The Congregation of Our Lady of Charity of the Good Shepherd Community Support Trust,* Cincinnati, OH.

Professed Sisters 51.

Ministry in Adolescent Treatment Centers; Parish Ministry; Social Service and Education Agencies.

Properties Owned and Sponsored: *Good Shepherd Provincialate and Gilead House,* Cincinnati, OH; *The Sisters of the Good Shepherd, Cincinnati Province Inc. aka Good Shepherd Pelletier, Inc.; Sisters of the Good Shepherd, Grand Rapids,* Grand Rapids, MI, *Sisters of the Good Shepherd of Detroit aka Vista Maria,* Dearborn Heights, MI; *Sisters of the Good Shepherd of the City of Cleveland aka Marycrest,* Independence, OH; *House of the Good Shepherd of Columbus aka Rosemont,* Columbus, OH; *Sisters of the Good Shepherd, Maryhurst, Inc. aka Maryhurst,* Louisville, KY.

Contemplatives of the Good Shepherd 1400 Morgan Pl., Grand Rapids, MI 49504. 7800 Brookside Rd., Independence, OH 44131. 20651 W. Warrne Ave., Dearborn Heights, MI 48127.

Professed sisters 43.

Represented in the Archdioceses of Cincinnati, Detroit, Louisville and in the Dioceses of Cleveland, Columbus, Covington and Grand Rapids.

Province of New York (1857): *Sisters of the Good Shepherd,* 82-31 Doncaster Pl., Jamaica, NY 11432. Tel: 718-380-3270; Fax: 718-591-9376. Sr. Helene Hayes, Prov.

Legal Title: *Sisters of the Good Shepherd, Province of New York.*

Professed Active Sisters 112; Contemplative Sisters 74.

Ministry in Counseling Centers; Social Service Agencies; Special Education Schools; Neighborhood Family Services; Adolescent Residential Programs; Human Services Workshops; Pastoral Ministry; Prison Ministry; Hospital Chaplaincy.

Legal Holdings or Titles: *Sisters of the Good Shepherd,* New York, NY; *House of the Good Shepherd, Villa Loretto,* Peekskill, NY; *Sisters of the Good Shepherd,* Albany, NY; *Sisters of the Good Shepherd,* Huntington, NY; *House of the Good Shepherd in the City of Hartford,* Hartford, CT; *Good Shepherd Association,* Springfield, MA; *Sisters of the Good Shepherd,* Marlboro, MA; *Madonna Hall,*

Marlboro, MA; *Maria Droste Services (Madonna Hall).*
Programs Sponsored: Good Shepherd Services, New York, NY; Maria Droste Services (St. Germaine's Services), New York, NY; Good Shepherd Center (Sisters of the Good Shepherd of New Jersey), Morristown, NJ; Collier Services, Wickatunk, NJ Good Shepherd Volunteers (St. Germaine's Services).
Represented in the Archdioceses of Boston and New York and the Dioceses of Albany, Brooklyn, Fall River, Metuchen, Paterson, Rockville Centre, Springfield (MA) and Trenton.
Province of Washington, DC (1850): *Sisters of the Good Shepherd,* 504 Hexton Hill Rd., Silver Spring, MD 20904-3300. Tel: 301-384-1169; Fax: 301-384-8889. Sr. Mary Brigid Lawlor, Prov.
Legal Title: *Sisters of the Good Shepherd of the City of Washington, D.C.*
Professed Sisters 71.
Ministry in the field of Adolescent Residential and Day Treatment Centers; Neighborhood Justice Center; Counseling and Referral Center for Families and Children; Family & Youth Services; Parish Ministry; Spousal Abuse Center; Refugee Services; Children's Shelter; Women-in-Transition; Women-with-AIDS.
Properties owned or sponsored: *Good Shepherd Corporation,* Clarks Summit, PA; *Lourdesmont Good Shepherd Youth & Family Services,* Clarks Summit, PA; *CORA Services, Inc.,* Philadelphia, PA; *Euphrasia House, Inc.,* Philadelphia, PA; *Good Shepherd Corporation,* Philadelphia, PA; *Good Shepherd Neighborhood House, Mediation Program,* Philadelphia, PA; *House of the Good Shepherd,* Baltimore, MD; *Good Shepherd Center,* Baltimore, MD; *Sisters of the Good Shepherd, A Corporation,* Baltimore, MD; *Sisters of the Good Shepherd of the City of Washington, DC; Good Shepherd Corporation (dba Shepherd's Dwelling),* Washington, DC; *Good Shepherd Services,* Atlanta, GA; *Good Shepherd Corporation of Orlando, Inc. ALEE Shelter and Children's Shelter,* Agana, GU; *Proyecto Nino,* Washington, DC.
Contemplative Sisters of the Good Shepherd 4100 Maple Ave., Baltimore, MD 21227-4099. Tel: 410-247-1485; Fax: 410-242-5890. Sr. Clare Szlachetka, Supr.
Sisters 9.
Contemplative Sisters of the Good Shepherd 715 Susquehanna Rd., Philadelphia, PA 19111-1396. Tel: 215-722-3970; Fax: 215-722-0786. Sr. Mary Euphrasia, Supr.
Sisters 14.
Represented in the Archdioceses of Agana, Atlanta, Baltimore, Philadelphia, Washington and in the Dioceses of Orlando, Raleigh and Scranton.
Province of St. Louis (1849): Provincialate, 7654 Natural Bridge Blvd., St. Louis, MO 63121. Tel: 314-381-3400; Fax: 314-381-6449. Sr. Nora Patricia O'Flannigan, Prov.
Legal Title: *Sisters of the Good Shepherd St. Louis Province.*
Professed Sisters 83; Contemplatives 25.
Properties owned and staffed: *Good Shepherd Shelter (for battered women with children),* Los Angeles, CA; *Gracenter (Women in Need),* San Francisco, CA; *Droste Residence (Women in need),* St. Louis, MO; *House of the Good Shepherd (Battered women with children),* Chicago, IL; *Immaculate Heart Convent (Retired Good Shepherd Sisters),* St. Louis, MO; *Good Shepherd Provincialate,* St. Louis, MO.
Ministry in parishes and prisons.
Represented in the Archdioceses of Chicago, Los Angeles, New Orleans, St. Louis and San Francisco and the Dioceses of Gallup, and Memphis. Also in Guam.
Contemplative Sisters of the Good Shepherd 2711 Mullanphy Lane, Florissant, MO 63031. Tel: 314-837-1719. Sr. Magdalen Clark, C.G.S., Supr.
Total number in the community 25.
Province of St. Paul (1868): Provincialate, 5100 Hodgson Rd., St. Paul, MN 55126. Tel: 612-482-5251. St. Joan Spiering, Prov.
Professed Sisters 51.
Represented in the Archdioceses of Denver, Omaha, Portland (OR), St. Paul-Minneapolis and Seattle.
Contemplative Sisters of the Good Shepherd 5104 Hodgson Rd., St. Paul, MN 55126. Tel: 612-482-5240. Sr. Teresita Mater, Supr.
Total number of Professed Sisters 31.
Represented in the Archdioceses of St. Paul-Minneapolis and Omaha.

[1840] (G.N.S.H.)—GREY NUNS OF THE SACRED HEART P

General Motherhouse (1921): 1750 Quarry Rd., Yardley, PA 19067-3998. Tel: 215-968-4236; Fax: 215-968-6656. Sr. Jean Liston, Supr. Gen.; Sr. R. Patricia Smith, Archivist; Sr. Mary O'Connell, Dir. Congregational Advancement Committee.
Total number in community 185.
Sisters staff: College, Secondary and Elementary Education; Hospitals; Nursing Homes; Rehabilitation Care of Aging; Pastoral Care; Personal Care Home; CCD-Parish Services; Diocesan Offices; Campus Ministry; Prison Ministry; Homeless Housing.
Properties owned: *Holy Angels Academy,* Buffalo, NY; *Motherhouse Complex,* Yardley, PA.
Represented in the Archdioceses of Anchorage, Atlanta, Baltimore, Newark, New York, Philadelphia and the Dioceses of Brooklyn, Buffalo, Erie, Manchester, Metuchen, Ogdensburg, Paterson, Richmond, Rochester, Rockville Centre and Trenton. Also in Canada.

[1845] (M.G.Sp.S.)—GUADALUPAN MISSIONARIES OF THE HOLY SPIRIT P

(Misioneras Guadalupanas del Espiritu Santo)
Founded in Morelia, Michoacan, Mexico in 1930 by Rev. Felix de Jesus Rougier, M.Sp.S.
General Motherhouse: Soja #44 Col. Esmeralda, Del. Iztapalapa 09810, Mexico, D.F.. Sr. Felicitas Almanza, Supr. Gen.
U.S. Delegation Headquarters: 2483 S.W. 4th St., Miami, FL 33135-2907. Tel: 305-642-9544.
U.S. Novitiate 758 S. Dunsmuir Ave., Los Angeles, CA 90036-3811. Tel: 213-936-0135.
Legal Title: *Missionary Guadalupanas of the Holy Spirit, Inc.*
Total Sisters in U.S. 43; Novices 3.
Ministry in Religious Education; Pastoral and Parish Ministries.
Represented in the Archdiocese of Los Angeles and Miami and the Dioceses of Fall River, Palm Beach and Venice. Also in San Juan, Puerto Rico.

[1850] (S.A.C.)—SISTERS OF THE GUARDIAN ANGEL

Founded in Quillan, France in 1839.
General Motherhouse: Avda, del Valle, 42, Madrid 3, Spain. Sr. Sagrario Escudero, S.A.C., Supr. Gen.
U.S. Foundation: 1245 S. Van Ness, Los Angeles, CA 90019. Tel: 213-732-7881.
Represented in the Archdiocese of Los Angeles.

[1855] (H.H.C.J.)—CONGREGATION OF THE HANDMAIDS OF THE HOLY CHILD JESUS P

Founded in Nigeria in 1931 by Sister Mary Magdalen Charles Walker. Canonically erected in 1937 by Bishop Joseph Moynagh.
General Motherhouse: Ifuho, Ikot Ekpene, Akwa Ibom State, Nigeria. Sr. Mary Langley, H.G.C.J., Supr. Gen.
Congregation of the Handmaids of the Holy Child Jesus: *U.S. Headquarters,* 1707 Bryant Ave., N., Minneapolis, MN 55411. Tel: 612-521-3127. Sr. Caroline Mbonu, H.H.C.J., Asst. Gen. & Contact Person.
Total Sisters in U.S. 26.
Ministry in elementary and higher education Parish ministry; Health care and social ministry.
Represented in the Archdioceses of St. Paul-Minneapolis, and the Dioceses of Alexandria, Beaumont and St. Petersburg.

[1860] (H.P.B.)—HANDMAIDS OF THE PRECIOUS BLOOD P

Founded in Jemez Springs, New Mexico in 1947.
Motherhouse and Novitiate: *Cor Jesu Monastery,* P.O. Box 90, Jemez Springs, NM 87025. Tel: 505-829-3906. Mother John Paul, Prioress.
Professed Sisters 34.
Ministry as Contemplative, Life of Eucharistic Adoration (Perpetual); for the sanctification of priests and for the entire world.
Represented in the Archdioceses of Chicago and Santa Fe. Also in Italy.

[1870] (A.C.J.)—THE HANDMAIDS OF THE SACRED HEART OF JESUS P

Founded in Spain in 1877. First Foundation in the United States in 1926.
General Motherhouse: Largo dei Monti Parioli, 3, 00197, Rome, Italy. Sr. Rita Burley, Supr. Gen.
Universal total in Congregation 1,700.
Provincial Motherhouse: 616 Coopertown Rd., Haverford, PA 19041. Tel: 610-642-5715; Fax: 610-642-3879. Sr. Gloria Petrone, A.C.J., Prov. Supr.
Total number in community 47.
Sisters serve and staff: Elementary Schools; Retreat Center; Mission Center; Parish Ministry; CCD; Diocesan Offices; Hispanic Pastoral Ministry; Vietnamese Pastoral Ministry; Hospital Chaplaincy.
Properties owned: *St. Raphaela Center,* Haverford, PA; *Ancillae Assumpta Academy,* Wyncote, PA.
Represented in the Archdioceses of Atlanta, Miami, Philadelphia and the Diocese of Beaumont.

[1880] (A.R.)—HANDMAIDS OF REPARATION OF THE SACRED HEART OF JESUS P

Founded in Messina, Italy in 1918.
U.S. Foundation (1958): *Sacred Heart Villa,* 36 Villa Dr., Steubenville, OH 43953-7129. Tel: 614-282-3801. Sr. Rosalba Putrino, A.R., Supr.
Total number in U.S. 6.
Apostolic Work in Religious & Academic Education Education All Levels; Religious Education; Parish and Diocesan Ministry; CCD Work; Orphanages; Missionary Work in Brazil and Africa.
Represented in the Dioceses of Arlington and Steubenville. Also in Africa, Brazil and Italy.

[1890] (H.H.S.)—SOCIETY OF HELPERS P

Founded in France in 1856. First foundation in the U.S. in 1892.
Generalate: 16 rue St. J. Baptiste de la Salle, Paris, France, 75006. Sr. Silvia Conde, Supr. Gen.
American Province (1921): 303 W. Barry Ave., Chicago, IL 60657.
Provincial Office: 2956 S. Lowe Ave., Chicago, IL 60616. Tel: 312-842-1039. Sr. Mary Therese Harrington, Prov. Supr.
Total number in U.S. province 55.
Legal Title: *Society of the Helpers of the Holy Souls; Helpers of the Holy Souls; Province of the Helpers of the Holy Souls in the United States.*
Represented in the Archdioceses of Chicago, New York, St. Louis, San Francisco and the Dioceses of Fort Wayne-South Bend and San Jose.

[1900] (H.C.G.)—HERMANAS CATEQUISTAS GUADALUPANAS P

Founded in Saltillo, Coahuila, Mexico in 1923. First United States foundation in 1950.
Motherhouse and Novitiate: Saltillo, Coahuila , Mexico.
U.S. Address: *Hermanas Catequistas Guadalupanas Convents,* 4110 S. Flores., San Antonio, TX 78214. Tel: 210-532-9344. Sr. Margarita Vasquez, Reg. Delegate.
Total number in the U.S. 19.
Represented in the Archdioceses of Oklahoma City, San Antonio and the Diocese of Fort Worth.

[1910] (H.J.)—HERMANAS JOSEFINAS P

General Motherhouse: Condor 336, Col. las Aguilas, Delg. Alvaro Obregon, 01710. Mexico D.F.. Mother Cointa Quijas, H.J., Supr. & Mother Gen.
U.S. Address: *Assumption Seminary,* 2600 W. Woodlawn Ave., P.O. Box 28240, San Antonio, TX 78284. Tel: 210-734-0039.
Sisters 8.
Represented in the Archdioceses of Chicago, Denver, Los Angeles and San Antonio and the Diocese of El Paso.

[1920] (C.S.C.)—CONGREGATION OF THE SISTERS OF THE HOLY CROSS P

Founded at Le Mans, France in 1841. First foundation in the U.S. in 1843.
General Administration: *Sisters of the Holy Cross Generalate,* Bertrand Hall-Saint Mary's, Notre Dame, IN 46556. Tel: 219-284-5550; Fax: 219-284-5779. Sr. Catherine O'Brien, C.S.C., Pres.; Sr. M. Genevra (Rolf), C.S.C., Gen. Sec.
Professed Members 644; Temporarily Professed 34; Novices 8; Candidates 8.
Legal Title: *Sisters of the Holy Cross, Inc.; Sisters of the Holy Cross, Inc. dba CSC Consultation Services; Holy Cross Services Corporation; Holy Cross Health System Corporation; Sisters of the Holy Cross of California,* Ventura, CA; *Havican Insurance Company Havcan-Vermont Insurancy Company; The Academy of the Holy Cross, Inc., MD; The Corporation of Saint Mary's College,* Notre Dame, IN; *Sociedade Civil Irmas da Santa Cruz,* Brasil, SA; *Society of the Congregation of the Sisters of the Holy Cross,* Bangladesh.
Areas and Coordinators:
Area I - USA West Sunland, CA. Tel: 818-353-3589; Fax: 818-352-3077. Sr. Mary Eliza Martin, C.S.C., Coord.
Area II - USA Midwest Notre Dame, IN. Tel: 219-232-2683; Fax: 219-232-7669. Sr. Joy O'Grady, C.S.C., Coord.

Area III - USA South & Mexico Austin, TX. Tel: 512-441-6693; Fax: 512-441-6693. Sr. Judith Hallock, C.S.C., Coord.

Area IV - USA East Wheaton, MD. Tel: 301-942-8549; Fax: 301-942-8549. Sr. Camilla Fitzgerald, C.S.C., Coord.

Area V - USA Retired Notre Dame, IN. Tel: 219-288-8271; Fax: 219-284-5596. Sr. Joseph Cecile, C.S.C., Coord.

Area VI - South America Sao Paulo, Brazil. Tel: 011-55-11-604-0229; Fax: 011-55-11-871-3430. Sr. Michael Mary Nolan, C.S.C., Coord.

Area VII - East Africa Jinja, Uganda, East Africa. Tel: 011-256-433-0127; Fax: 011-256-433-0127. Sr. Mary Alice Bowler, C.S.C., Coord.

Area VIII - Asia Dhaka, Bangladesh. Tel: 011-880-2-912-9600; Fax: 011-880-2-813-123. Sr. Joseph Mary, C.S.C., Coord.

Sisters staff and serve:: Colleges; High Schools; Grade Schools; Adult Education Centers; Social Service Centers; Prayer Centers; Counseling Centers; Human Rights Centers; Women's Development Center; Hospitals and other Health Ministries including Administration of Health Systems, Primary Health Care and Long Term Health Care; Parish Ministry; Diocesan Catechetical Services; Other Parish and Diocesan Ministries; Retirement Homes; Senior Citizen Residences; Pastoral Ministry with the Deaf.

Represented in the Archdioceses of Baltimore, Boston, Chicago, Cincinnati, Denver, Indianapolis, Los Angeles, Louisville, Newark, Portland (OR), San Antonio, San Francisco, Seattle, Washington and the Dioceses of Arlington, Austin, Boise, Brownsville, Columbus, Colorado Springs, Corpus Christi, Covington, Des Moines, Fall River, Fort Wayne-South Bend, Fresno, Gary, Harrisburg, Joliet, Kalamazoo, Knoxville, Lafayette (IN), Lexington, Monterey, Oakland, Orange, Palm Beach, Peoria, Raleigh, Richmond, Rockford, Rockville Centre, St. Cloud, St. Petersburg, Salt Lake City, San Diego, Spokane, Stockton, Tucson, Venice and Wheeling-Charleston. Also in Brasil, Peru, Ghana, Uganda, Mexico, Bangladesh, India, Lebanon and Italy.

[1930] (C.S.C.)—SISTERS OF HOLY CROSS P

Founded in Le Mans, France in 1841. First foundation in Canada in 1847.

General Administration: 905 rue Basile-Moreau, St-Laurent, Montreal, Quebec H4L 4A1. Canada. Sr. Liette Finnerty, C.S.C., Supr. Gen.

Universal total in congregation 1,203.

American Regional Office: 377 Island Pond Rd., Manchester, NH 03109. Tel: 603-622-9504. Sr. Lucille Cantin, C.S.C., Reg. Rep.

Total number in region 245.

Ministry in the field of Academic Education at all levels; Religious Education Centers; Social and Family Services; Counselor-Therapist; Parish Ministry; Youth and Hospital Chaplaincies; Administrative Positions; Diocesan Services; Hispanic Ministry; Ministry to Abused Women and Children; Social Work and Elderly Assistance.

Properties owned: *Notre Dame College Holy Cross Kindergarten,* Manchester, NH; *St. George Manor,* Manchester, NH; *Our Lady of the Sacred Heart Convent,* West Franklin, NH; *Londonderry House,* Londonderry, NH; *Sisters of the Holy Cross,* 454 Island Pond Rd., Manchester, NH 03109; 136 Lynwood Ln., Manchester, NH 03109; 113 Wedgewood Ln., Manchester, NH 03109; 969 & 971 Chestnut St., Manchester, NH 03104; 377 Island Pond Rd., Manchester, NH; Fairview Rd., R.R. 1, Box 191, Pittsfield, NH 03263.

Represented in the Archdioceses of Boston and New York and the Dioceses of Burlington, Fall River, Manchester, Norwich, Rochester and St. Petersburg. Also in Bangladesh, Cameroon, Costa Rica, Haiti, Mali and Peru.

[1940] (C.H.F.)—CONGREGATION OF THE SISTERS OF THE HOLY FAITH P

Founded in Ireland in 1856. First foundation in U.S. in 1953. St. John of God School, 13817 Pioneer Blvd., Norwalk, California, 90650.

Motherhouse: Glasnevin, Dublin, Ireland.

U.S. Province: 12322 S. Paramount Blvd., Downey, CA 90242. Tel: 562-869-6092; Fax: 310-869-4609. Sr. M. Victoire Haran, Reg. Supr.

Total number in community 255.

Represented in the Archdioceses of Los Angeles, New Orleans and San Francisco and the Diocese of Sacramento.

[1950] (S.S.F.)—CONGREGATION OF THE SISTERS OF THE HOLY FAMILY P

Founded in the New Orleans, Louisiana, in 1842.

Motherhouse: 6901 Chef Menteur Hwy., New Orleans, LA 70126. Tel: 504-242-8315. Mother M. de Chantal St. Julien, S.S.F., Supr. Gen.

Total number in community 179.

Ministry in Secondary and Elementary Schools; Day Care Centers; Pastoral and Social Services; Nursing Home and Apartments for the Elderly, Disabled and Handicapped.

Represented in the Archdioceses of Los Angeles, New Orleans and Washington and in the Dioceses of Alexandria, Baton Rouge, Galveston-Houston, and Lafayette (LA). Also in Belize, Central America.

[1960] (S.H.F.)—SISTERS OF THE HOLY FAMILY P

Founded in San Francisco, California, in 1872.

General Motherhouse: P.O. Box 3248, Mission San Jose, CA 94539. Tel: 510-624-4500; Fax: 510-624-4537. Sr. Elaine Marie Sanchez, Congregational Pres.

Total number in community 143.

Ministry in the following areas: Day Care Centers; Religious Education Program; Teacher Training for Laity; Parish Homevisiting; Parent Education; Family Programs; Pastoral Ministry; Religious Education Classes for Developmentally Disabled; Associate Pastors; Directors of Hispanic Ministry; Directors of Retreats; Counselling; Convalescent-Rest Home Visiting.

Properties owned: *St. Elizabeth's Day Home,* San Jose, CA; *Holy Family Renewal Center,* Pleasant Hill, CA.

Represented in the Archdioceses of Anchorage, Los Angeles, Louisville, San Antonio, San Francisco, Seattle, and the Dioceses of Fresno, Honolulu, Juneau, Monterey, Oakland, Reno, Portland, Sacramento, Salt Lake City, San Diego, San Jose and Stockton.

[1970] (C.S.F.N.)—SISTERS OF THE HOLY FAMILY OF NAZARETH P

Founded in Italy in 1875. First foundation in the United States in 1885.

General Motherhouse: Rome, Italy. Mother Maria Teresa Jasionowicz, Supr. Gen.

Sacred Heart Province (1885): 310 N. River Rd., Des Plaines, IL 60016-1211. Tel: 847-298-6760; Fax: 847-803-1941. Sr. M. Lucille, Prov. Supr.; Sr. M. Gemma, Archivist.

Total number in community 177.

Properties owned: *St. Mary of Nazareth Hospital Center; Holy Family Medical Center; Holy Family Health Center Nazarethville.*

Ministry in Academic Education; Hospitals and Health Care.

Represented in the Archdiocese of Chicago.

Blessed Frances Siedliska Province (1962): *Sisters of The Holy Family of Nazareth,* 1814 Egyptian Way, Box 530959, Grand Prairie, TX 75053. Tel: 972-641-4496. Sr. M. Ancilla Sojka, Prov. Supr.

Total number in community 45.

Legal Holdings or Titles: *Bethania Regional Health Care Center, Wichita Falls, TX; Trinity Mother Frances Health System,* Tyler, TX; *Blessed Frances Siedliska Province Charitable Trust Fund,* Dallas, TX.

Ministry in Education; Health Care; Parish Ministry; Religious Education.

Represented in the Dioceses of Dallas, Fort Worth and Tyler.

Immaculate Conception BVM Province (1918): *Sisters of the Holy Family of Nazareth Provincial House and Academy,* 4001 Grant Ave., Philadelphia, PA 19114-2999. Tel: 215-637-6464; Fax: 215-637-8475. Sr. M. Michaelann Delaney, Prov. Supr.; Sr. Mary Frances, Community Archivist.

Total number in community 180.

Properties owned: *Holy Family College Nazareth Academy Mount Nazareth,* Philadelphia, PA; *St. Mary Villa,* Ambler, PA; *Villa Nazareth,* Meadowbrook, PA.

Ministry in the field of Academic Education at all levels; Child-caring Institution; Hospitals; Nursing Homes; Sisters Retirement Home.

Represented in the Archdioceses of Baltimore, Miami, Philadelphia, San Juan and the Dioceses of Allentown and Scranton.

Saint Joseph Province (1918): 285 Bellevue Rd., Pittsburgh, PA 15229-2195. Tel: 412-931-4775; Fax: 412-931-9746. Sr. Maria Kruszewski, C.S.F.N., Prov. Supr.

Professed sisters in provincialate 39; Professed sisters 151.

Sisters serve and staff: High Schools; Elementary Schools; Religious Education Centers; Hospitals; Parish Pastoral Ministry; Housing Counseling; Low-Income Home Ownership; Family Counseling; Family Life Education; Senior Citizen Apartments; Home for the Elderly; Home for Children; Learning Centers.

Legal Holdings and Titles: *Mt. Nazareth Center, Inc.,* Pittsburgh, PA; *Holy Family Institute,* Emsworth, PA; *St. Leonard's Home, Inc.,* Hollidaysburg, PA; *Mercy Hospital,* Altoona, PA.

Represented in the Archdiocese of Detroit and the Dioceses of Altoona-Johnstown, Cleveland, Erie, Pittsburgh and Steubenville.

Immaculate Heart of Mary Province (1959): Sisters of Holy Family of Nazareth Provincial Residence - Marian Heights, 1428 Monroe Turnpike, Monroe, CT 06468. Tel: 203-268-7646; Fax: 203-452-9947. Sr. M. Janice Kobierowski, Prov. Supr.

Legal Title: *C.S.F.N. Congregation of the Sisters of the Holy Family of Nazareth.*

Total number in Province 114.

Ministry in Education; Child Care; Health Care; Religious Education; Retreat Work; House of Prayer; Pastoral Ministry and Hospital Chaplaincy; Prison Ministry.

Represented in the Archdioceses of Hartford and New York and the Dioceses of Bridgeport, Brooklyn, Rockville Centre, Syracuse, Trenton and Worcester.

[1980] (O.S.F.)—CONGREGATION OF THE SERVANTS OF THE HOLY CHILD JESUS OF THE THIRD ORDER REGULAR OF SAINT FRANCIS P

Founded in Germany in 1855. First founded in the United States on April 9, 1929, at Staten Island, New York.

General Motherhouse (1855): Kloster Oberzell, Wuerzburg, Germany. Mother M. Reginarda Holzer, Supr. Gen.

Regional House: *Villa Maria,* 641 Somerset St., North Plainfield, NJ 07060-4909. Tel: 908-757-3050. Rev. Sr. M. Dominic Ritter, Reg. Supr.

Total number in community 36.

Properties owned: Villa Maria Sanitarium, Inc., North Plainfield, NJ.

Ministry in Social Work; Health Care; Teaching.

Represented in the Archdiocese of Newark and Diocese of Metuchen.

[1990] (S.N.J.M.)—SISTERS OF THE HOLY NAMES OF JESUS AND MARY P

Founded by Marie Rose Durocher, in Longueuil, Quebec, Canada in 1843. First foundation in the U.S. in 1859.

Generalate: 80, rue Saint-Charles Est, Longueuil, Quebec , Canada, J4H 1A9. Tel: 514-651-8104. Sr. Mary Pat LeRoy, Supr. Gen.

Oregon Province (1859): *Provincial Administration,* Box 25, Marylhurst, OR 97036. Tel: 503-635-3621. Sr. Eileen Brown, Prov. Dir.

Total number in community 238.

Properties owned: *Provincial House,* Marylhurst, OR; *St. Mary's Academy,* Portland, OR.

An international congregation of 1,852 religious women with missions in Lesotho, Mexico, Nicaragua, Haiti and Brazil. Congregational sponsored works include colleges; adult centers; secondary, elementary and pre-schools; and health clinics.

Sisters ministering in works sponsored by other institutions/agencies include; Formal Education in Universities, Secondary, Elementary and Preschools; Adult Basic Education/Literacy; Administration in Diocesan Offices; Campus Ministry; Pastoral Ministry; Religious Education, Health Care and Social Services.

Represented in the Archdioceses of Detroit, Los Angeles, Portland (OR), San Francisco, Seattle and Washington and the Dioceses of Albany, Baker, Fairbanks, Jackson, Monterey, Oakland, Orlando, Palm Beach, Richmond, San Jose, Spokane, St. Petersburg, Venice and Yakima.

California Province (1868): *Provincial Administration,* P.O. Box 907, Los Gatos, CA 95031. Tel: 408-395-5150. Sr. Sally Slyngstad, Prov.

Total number in community 271.

Properties owned or sponsored: *Provincial House Casa Maria Montessori School,* Los Gatos, CA; *Holy Names College Holy Names High School,* Oakland, CA; *Ramona Convent Secondary School,* Alhambra, CA; *Villa Maria Del Mar,* Santa Cruz, CA; *Next Step Learning Center,* Oakland, CA.

New York Province (1865): *Provincial Administration,* 1061 New Scotland Ave., Albany, NY 12208. Tel: 518-489-5469; Fax: 518-489-5804. Sr. Virginia Bonan, Prov. Dir.

Total number in community 115.

Properties owned: *Provincial Center Academy of the Holy Names*, Albany, NY; *Sisters of the Holy Names*, Silver Spring, MD; *Academy of the Holy Names*, Tampa, FL.

Washington Province (1962): *Provincial Administration*, 2911 W. Fort Wright Dr., Spokane, WA 99224. Tel: 509-328-7470; Fax: 509-328-9824. Sr. Shirley Roberg, Prov. Dir.

Total number in community 209.

Properties owned: *Provincial House*, Spokane, WA; *Holy Names Academy*, Seattle, WA.

[2000] (C.S.R.)—SISTERS OF THE HOLY REDEEMER P

First foundation in the United States on March 19, 1924 in Baltimore, Maryland.

General Motherhouse (1866): Wuerzburg, Germany. Sr. M. Veronika Stauch, Supr. Gen.

American Province of the Immaculate Conception: 521 Moredon Rd., Huntingdon Valley, PA 19006. Tel: 215-938-0540; Fax: 215-938-7759. Sr. M. Regina Heilman, C.S.R., Prov. Supr.

Legal Holdings and Titles: *Holy Redeemer Health Care Corporation and Foundation; Holy Redeemer Health System,—Subsidiaries: Drueding Center (program for homeless women with children); Holy Redeemer Hospital and Medical Center; Holy Redeemer Foundation; HRH Management Corporation; Holy Redeemer Home Health Services; HR Physician Services; Holy Redeemer Visiting Nurse Agency, PA; Holy Redeemer Hospice, PA; Holy Redeemer Visiting Nurse Agency, Inc. NJ; Redeemer-Nazareth Medical Supply Co., Inc.; Redeemer Village & Redeemer Village II; St. Joseph's Manor The Lafayette-Redeemer Redeemer Center; Holy Redeemer Managed Care Organization; Holy Redeemer Transitional Care Unit Convents—Provincialate Emmaus Convent; Angelus Convent Emmanuel Convent; Our Lady of Peace Convent; St. Elizabeth Convent.*

Represented in the Archdiocese of Philadelphia and the Dioceses of Camden and Trenton.

[2010] (O.SS.R.)—ORDER OF THE MOST HOLY REDEEMER P
(Redemptoristine Nuns)

Founded 1731 by St. Alphonsus de Liguori and Ven. Marie Celeste. (Contemplative).

Rule approved 1750 by Pope Benedict XIV.

First United States Monastery (1957) Esopus, New York.

Mother of Perpetual Help Monastery: *Redemptoristine Nuns*, P.O.Box 220, Esopus, NY 12429-0220. Tel: 914-384-6533; Fax: 914-384-6533. Sr. Paula Schmidt, O.SS.R., Prioress. Solemn Vows, Papal Enclosure.

Total number in community 13.

Monastery of St. Alphonsus (1960): *Order of the Most Holy Redeemer*, 200 Liguori Dr., Liguori, MO 63057. Tel: 314-464-1093; Fax: 314-464-9446. Sr. Joan Calver, O.SS.R., Prioress.

Total number in community 16; Novices 1.

Represented in the Archdioceses of New York and St. Louis.

[2020] (C.H.S.)—COMMUNITY OF THE HOLY SPIRIT D

U.S. Foundation (1970): 6151 Rancho Mission Rd. - #205, San Diego, CA 95108. Tel: 619-584-0809. Sr. Susann Kernaghan, C.H.S., General Coord.

Total number in community 17.

Ministry in the field of Education; Health Care; and Social Services.

Represented in the Dioceses of Oakland, Orange, Portland (OR), Reno-Las Vegas, San Diego and San Jose.

[2030] (C.S.Sp.)—SISTERS OF THE HOLY SPIRIT D

Founded in the United States 1929; Decree of Establishment 1932.

Motherhouse and Novitiate: 10102 Granger Rd., Garfield Heights, OH 44125. Sr. Mary Assumpta, Supr. Gen.

Total number in community 9.

Represented in the Diocese of Cleveland.

[2040] (S.H.S.)—SISTERS OF THE HOLY SPIRIT D

Founded in the United States in 1913 at Donora, Pennsylvania.

Motherhouse: 5246 Clarwin Ave., Ross Township, Pittsburgh, PA 15229-2208. Tel: 412-931-1917. Sr. Marita Juras, S.H.S., Gen. Supr.

Total number in community 66.

Sisters serve and staff: Elementary Schools; Religious Education; Health and Social Services; Adult Day Care and Child Day Care; Care Facilities for the Aged.

Facilities owned and staffed: *Corporation of Sisters of the Holy Spirit of Pittsburgh; Marian Manor, Inc.; Martina Spiritual Renewal Center Corporation.*

Represented in the Dioceses of Greensburg, and Pittsburgh.

[2050] (S.H.Sp.)—SISTERS OF THE HOLY SPIRIT AND MARY IMMACULATE P

Founded in America in 1893. Papal Approbation 1930; final Approbation, 1938.

General Motherhouse: *Convent of the Holy Spirit and Mary Immaculate*, 301 Yucca St., San Antonio, TX 78203. Tel: 210-533-5149. Sr. Anne Finnerty, S.H.Sp., Gen. Supr.

Professed Sisters 130.

Legal Holdings: *Holy Spirit Trust Holy Spirit Motherhouse Healy Murphy Center, Inc.*; San Antonio, TX; *Mother of Perpetual Help Nursing Home*, Brownsville, TX.

Ministry in the following areas Education; Health Care; Pastoral Ministry; Catechetical Centers; Social Apostolate Centers; Retreats.

Represented in the Archdioceses of New Orleans and San Antonio and the Dioceses of Beaumont, Biloxi, Brownsville, Corpus Christi, Dallas, Fort Worth, Galveston-Houston, Houma-Thibadoux, Jackson, Lafayette (LA) and Shreveport. Also in Mexico and Zambia.

[2060] (O.SS.T.)—SISTERS OF THE MOST HOLY TRINITY P

Founded in Rome in 1198. First foundation in the United States in 1920.

General Motherhouse: Rome, Italy.

Provincial House: *Immaculate Conception Province*, 21281 Chardon Rd., Euclid, OH 44117. Tel: 216-481-8232; Fax: 216-481-6577. Sr. M. Valentine, Reg. Delegate.

Total number in community 27.

Properties owned: *Our Lady of Lourdes Shrine*, Euclid, OH.

Represented in the Archdiocese of Philadelphia and the Diocese of Cleveland.

[2070] (S.U.S.C.)—HOLY UNION SISTERS P

Founded in France in 1826. First foundation in the United States in 1886.

Generalate: Rome, Italy. Sr. Pauline Cowie, Supr. Gen.

Holy Union Fall River Province: *Provincial House*, 550 Rock St., Fall River, MA 02720-3436. Tel: 508-678-3616; Fax: 508-324-0686. Sr. Theresa M. Horvath, S.U.S.C., Prov.; Sr. Grace Donovan, S.U.S.C., Archivist.

Total number in community 115.

Ministry in the field of Religious and Academic Education; Social Services; Pastoral Care; Pastoral Ministry; Spiritual Renewal; Day Care; Business; Ministry Education; Family Ministry; Nursing; Peace & Justice; Spanish Apostolate; Legal Services; Foreign Mission work in Tanzania.

Represented in the Archdioceses of Baltimore, Boston, Miami, New York, Washington and the Dioceses of Albany, Brooklyn, Fall River, Jackson Lexington, Orlando, Pensacola-Tallahassee, Providence, and Rockville Centre.

Sacred Heart Province: Box 993, Main St., Groton, MA 01450. Tel: 978-448-6049. Sr. Alice Arsenault, S.U.S.C., Prov. Supr.; Sr. Rita Beaudoin, S.U.S.C., Archivist.

Professed Sisters 84.

Legal Title: *Holy Union of the Sacred Hearts Province of the Sacred Heart, Inc.*

Ministry in the fields of Education; Religious Education; Parish Ministry; Handicapped & Refugee Ministry; Foreign Missions; Clerical & Secretarial.

Properties owned: *Country Day School*, Groton, MA; *Convent of the Holy Union*, Lowell, MA.

Represented in the Archdiocese of Boston and the Dioceses of Fall River and Providence. Also in Cameroon, Africa.

[2080] (G.H.M.S.)—HOME MISSION SISTERS OF AMERICA D
Glenmary Sisters

Founded July 16, 1952.

Motherhouse: *Glenmary Sisters - Glenmary Center*, P.O. Box 22264, Owensboro, KY 42304-2264. Tel: 502-686-8401. Sr. Christine Beckett, Pres.

Total number in community 14.

Ministry in Social Outreach; Evangelization and Catechesis; Promotional Center.

Represented in the Dioceses of Lexington, Owensboro and Savannah.

[2090] (H.V.M.)—SISTERS HOME VISITORS OF MARY D

Founded in Detroit, Michigan in 1949.

Motherhouse: 121 E. Boston Blvd., Detroit, MI 48202. Tel: 313-869-2160. Sr. Barbara Dakoske, H.V.M., Admin.

Total number in community 15.

Ministry in Urban Parishes; Senior Citizen; Prisons; Sojourner Spiritual Affirmation Center; Seminary Staff; Intercultural Center; Pre-Schools; Religious Education, RCIA.

Represented in the Archdiocese of Detroit and the Diocese of Tucson.

[2100] (C.H.M.)—CONGREGATION OF THE HUMILITY OF MARY P

Founded in France in 1854. First United States foundation in 1864.

Motherhouse: *Humility of Mary Center*, Davenport, IA 52804. Tel: 319-323-9466; Fax: 319-323-5209. Sr. Jude Fitzpatrick, Pres.

Legal Title: *Congregation of the Humility of Mary; Humility of Mary Shelter, Inc.; Congregation of the Humility of Mary Charitable Trust.*

Total number in community 181.

Ministry in Schools and Colleges; Religious Education Centers; Migrant Programs; Pastoral Ministry; Social Services; Inner City Programs; Health Services; and Ministry to the Elderly.

Represented in the Archdioceses of Chicago, Denver, Dubuque, Los Angeles, Seattle and Washington and the Dioceses of Biloxi, Colorado Springs, Davenport, Des Moines, Dodge City, Fresno, Great Falls-Billings, Helena, Jackson, Joliet, Kansas City, Lexington, Peoria, New Ulm, Richmond, Rockford, St. Cloud, San Angelo, San Jose, Sioux City, Springfield (IL), Tyler, Wheeling-Charleston and Yakima. Also in Panama, Mexico.

ID# ROW-0391 Page 1

[2110] (H.M.)—SISTERS OF THE HUMILITY OF MARY P

Founded in France in 1854. First foundation in the United States in 1864 at Villa Maria, Lawrence County, Pennsylvania, 16155.

Motherhouse: Villa Maria Community Center, P.O. Box 914, Villa Maria, PA 16155-0914. Tel: 724-964-8861; Fax: 724-964-8082. Sr. Ruthmary Powers, H.M., Major Supr.; Sr. Mary-Joanna Huegle, H.M., Community Archivist.

Total number in community 255.

Ministry in the field of Academic and Religious Education at all levels; Hospitals and Nursing Home, Assisted Living; Parish and Pastoral Ministries; Publishing of Education Materials; Diocesan Offices; Legal Services; Social Services; Ministry to Native Americans, Migrants, Hispanics, Haitians; Housing Ministry to Rural Poor, Single Parents, Independent Elderly; Ministry to Deaf and to Prisoners; Retreat Ministry; Spirituality and Counseling; Advocacy for Eco-justice; Marketing of Creative Arts; Foreign Missions.

Legal Holdings and Titles: *Sisters of the Humility of Mary (Motherhouse)*, Villa Maria, PA; *Sisters of the Humility of Mary Charitable Trust*, Villa Maria, PA; *Humility of Mary Health Care Corporation*, Middleburg Heights, OH; *HM Health Services*, Youngstown, OH; *The Assumption Village*, North Lima, OH; *Humility of Mary Information Systems*, Youngstown, OH; *Community Health Partners of Ohio*, Lorain, OH; *Community Health Partners Foundation*, Lorain, OH; *Laurel Lake Retirement Communnity*, Hudson, OH; *Magnificat High School*, Rocky River, OH; *Villa Montessori Center*, Cleveland, OH; *The Center for Learning*, Villa Maria, PA; *Villa Maria Education Center*, Villa Maria, PA; *Humility of Mary Housing Program, Inc.*, Akron, OH; *HM Housing Development Corporation*, Akron, OH; *HM Life Opportunity Services*, Akron, OH; *Villa Residential Services (Villa Maria Apartments)*, Villa Maria, PA; *Christa Center*, Cleveland, OH; *Heartbeats*, Cleveland, OH; *Common Ground Center for Community Renewal*, Oberlin, OH.

Represented in the Archdioceses of Chicago, Cincinnati, San Antonio, Washington and the Dioceses of Charleston, Cleveland, Grand Island, Lansing, Palm Beach, Pittsburgh, Richmond, Spokane, Trenton, Tucson, Venice, Wheeling-Charleston and Youngstown.

[2120] (C.I.C.)—SISTERS OF THE IMMACULATE CONCEPTION D

Founded in the United States in 1874.

General Motherhouse and Convent of the Immaculate Conception: P.O. Box 50426, New Orleans, LA 70185-0426. Tel: 504-486-7426. Sr. Ada Missler, C.I.C., Contact Person.

Total number in community 17.

Ministry in Pastoral Ministry.

Represented in the Archdiocese of New Orleans and the Diocese of Houma-Thibodaux.

[2130] (R.C.M.)—SISTERS OF THE IMMACULATE CONCEPTION P

Founded in Spain in 1892.

General Motherhouse: Princesa 19 y 21, 28008, Madrid, Spain. Mother Maria Mateu, Mother Gen.

U.S. Delegation House (1962): 2230 Franklin, San Francisco, CA 94109. Tel: 415-474-0159.

Represented in the Archdiocese of San Francisco and the Diocese of Fresno.

[2140] SISTERS OF THE IMMACULATE CONCEPTION OF THE BLESSED VIRGIN MARY (LITHUANIAN) D

Founded in Marijampole, Lithuania in 1918. First foundation in the United States in 1936.

American Headquarters: *Immaculate Conception Convent and Novitiate,* 600 Liberty Hwy., Putnam, CT 06260-2503. Tel: 860-928-7955; Fax: 860-928-1930. Sr. Mary Paul Savickas, Prov. Supr.

Total number in community 30.

Ministry in Nursing Homes; Retreat House; Catechetical Work in Parishes; Summer Camp for Children and Young Adults; Day Nursery and Kindergarten.

Legal Titles & Holdings: *Immaculate Conception Convent Matulaitis Nursing Home,* Putnam, CT; *Camp Neringa,* Marlboro, VT.

Represented in the Archdiocese of Chicago and the Dioceses of Burlington and Norwich. Also in Canada.

[2145] (O.S.A.)—CONGREGATION OF AUGUSTINIAN SISTERS SERVANTS OF JESUS AND MARY P

Generalate: via Nomentana 514, Rome, Italy. Mother Atanasia Buhagiar, Gen.

Malta Province: 208 Fleur-de-Lys, B'Kara, Malta. Mother Miriam Grech, Mother Prov.

U.S. Foundation: *St. John School,* 513 E. Broadway, Brandenburg, KY 40108. Sr. Lydia Falzon, Supr.

Total number in community 4.

Represented in the Archdiocese of Louisville.

[2150] (I.H.M.)—SISTERS, SERVANTS OF THE IMMACULATE HEART OF MARY P

Founded in the United States in 1845.

SSIHM Leadership Council: 610 W. Elm, Monroe, MI 48162-7909. Tel: 734-241-0092. Sr. Mary M. McCann, Pres.; Sr. Rose Matthew Mangini, Archivist.

Total number in Congregation 733.

Ministry in Academic and Religious Education at all levels; Pastoral Ministry (parish, healthcare, campus and prison settings); Diocesan and Parish Administration; Peace and Justice; Social Service and Counseling; Spiritual Growth and Development; Overseas Ministries.

Legal Titles: *Marygrove College,* Detroit, MI; *Immaculate Heart of Mary High School,* Westchester, IL; *Marian High School,* Bloomfield Hills, MI; *St. Mary Center,* Monroe, MI; *Visitation House of Prayer,* Monroe, MI; Co-Sponsor: *Groundwork for a Just World,* Detroit, MI.

Represented in the Archdioceses of Atlanta, Chicago, Cincinnati, Detroit, Louisville, Miami, Milwaukee, Mobile, New York, Oklahoma City, St. Louis, St. Paul-Minneapolis, San Antonio, Santa Fe, Washington and the Dioceses of Albany, Allentown, Cleveland, Columbus, Duluth, Fort Wayne-South Bend, Gaylord, Grand Rapids, Joliet, Juneau, Kalamazoo, Kansas City-St. Joseph, Knoxville, Lansing, Lexington, Manchester, Marquette, Oakland, Orlando, Palm Beach, Pensacola-Tallahassee, Phoenix, Pittsburgh, Raleigh, Rockville Centre, Saginaw, St. Augustine, St. Petersburg, San Diego, San Jose, Toledo, Tucson, Tulsa, Venice, and Worcester. Also in Brazil, Canada, Italy, Honduras, Mexico, Uganda, and South Africa.

[2160] (I.H.M.)—SISTERS, SERVANTS OF THE IMMACULATE HEART OF MARY P

Founded in 1845. Established in Scranton, Pennsylvania in 1871.

General Motherhouse: *Immaculate Heart of Mary Center,* 2300 Adams Ave., Scranton, PA 18509. Tel: 717-342-6850; Fax: 717-346-5439. Sr. Anne Munley, I.H.M., Congregation Admin.

Total number in community 674.

Properties owned: *IHM Center Marian Convent Marywood University,* Scranton, PA; *Marian Community Hospital,* Carbondale, PA; *St. Joseph's Center,* Scranton, PA; *Our Lady of Grace Center,* Manhasset, NY.

Ministry in the field of Academic Education; Hospitals; Early Childhood Education Centers; Congregation Retirement and Health Care Centers; Spiritual Renewal Center; Directors of Religious Education; Pastoral Ministries; Social Services; Campus Ministry; Peace and Justice Center; Volunteer Services; Family Ministry; Drug and Alcohol Counseling; Ministry to Hispanics; Diocesan Offices; Vicar for Religious; Ministry to Persons with AIDS.

Represented in the Archdioceses of Baltimore, Boston, Los Angeles, Miami, Newark, New York, Philadelphia, Santa Fe, Washington and the Dioceses of Albany, Altoona-Johnstown, Bridgeport, Brooklyn, Camden, Harrisburg, Grand Rapids, Jackson, Norwich, Pittsburgh, Raleigh, Rockville Centre, St. Augustine, St. Petersburg, Scranton, Syracuse, Trenton, Venice, Wheeling-Charleston, Wilmington and Worcester Also in Canada and Peru.

[2170] (I.H.M.)—SISTERS, SERVANTS OF THE IMMACULATE HEART OF MARY P

Founded in 1845. Established in West Chester, Pennsylvania in 1872.

General Motherhouse: Villa Maria, Immaculata, PA 19345. Tel: 610-647-2160; Fax: 610-889-4874. Sr. Marie Angela Natoli, I.H.M., Supr. Gen.

Total number in congregation 1,313.

Ministry in the field of Academic Education at all levels in the U.S. as well as; Peru and Chile and Infirmary work.

Represented in the Archdioceses of Atlanta, Boston, Hartford, Miami, Philadelphia and San Francisco and the Dioceses of Allentown, Camden, Harrisburg, Metuchen, Richmond, San Jose, Savannah and Trenton.

[2180] (I.H.M.)—SISTERS OF THE IMMACULATE HEART OF MARY P

Founded in Spain in 1848. First foundation in United States in 1871.

General Motherhouse: Rome, Italy.

U.S. Province: 4100 Sabino Canyon Rd., Tucson, AZ 85750-6503. Tel: 520-886-4273. Sr. Alice M. Martinez, Prov. Supr.; Sr. Barbara Ann Gamboa, Sec. & Community Archivist.

Total number in community 32.

Ministry in the field of Academic and Religious Education.

Represented in the Archdiocese of Miami and the Dioceses of Oakland and Tucson.

[2185] (I.H.M.)—SISTERS OF THE IMMACULATE HEART OF MARY OF WICHITA

Founded in Olot, Spain, in 1848. First foundation in United States in 1871. Wichita foundation in 1979.

Motherhouse: 605 N. Woodchuck, Wichita, KS 67212. Tel: 316-722-9316. Mother M. Giovanni Oliveri, I.H.M., Gen. Supr.

Total number in community 12.

Apostolate: Contemplation of the Word and the spread of His Message of salvation through the various works and levels of education and retreat work:.

Represented in the Diocese of Wichita.

[2190] (C.V.I.)—CONGREGATION OF THE INCARNATE WORD AND BLESSED SACRAMENT P

Founded in France in 1625. First foundation in the United States in 1853.

Motherhouse and Novitiate: *Incarnate Word Convent,* 3400 Bradford Pl., Houston, TX 77025-1398. Tel: 713-668-0423. Sr. Brigid Cummins, Supr.; Sr. Dympna Lyons, Archivist; Sr. Brendan O'Donnell, Archivist.

Total number in community 66.

Ministry in the field of Academic and Religious Education; Social Service; Administration; Hispanic Ministry; Diocesan Ministry (Secretariat for Christian Formation, Department of Aging, Pastoral Care); Parish Ministry; Renewal Work.

Represented in the Dioceses of Austin, Beaumont and Galveston-Houston.

[2200] (I.W.B.S.)—CONGREGATION OF THE INCARNATE WORD AND BLESSED SACRAMENT P

Founded in France in 1625. First founded in the United States in 1853.

Motherhouse and Novitiate: *Incarnate Word Convent,* 1101 N.E. Water St., Victoria, TX 77901-9298. Tel: 512-575-2266; Fax: 512-575-2165. Sr. M. Stephana Marbach, Supr. Gen.; Sr. M. Andrea Hubnik, Community Archivist.

Total number in commuity 118.

Legal Titles: *Sisters of the Incarnate Word and Blessed Sacrament of Victoria; Texas Medical and Retirement Trust,* Victoria, TX; *Jeanne Chezard de Matel Fund,* Victoria, TX.

Properties owned or sponsored: *Nazareth Academy,* Victoria, TX; *Blessed Sacrament Academy,* San Antonio, TX.

Ministry in the field of Education; CCD Centers; Hospitals.

Represented in the Archdiocese of San Antonio and the Dioceses of Beaumont, Dallas, Galveston-Houston and Victoria. Also in Africa.

[2205] (I.W.B.S.)—SISTERS OF THE INCARNATE WORD AND BLESSED SACRAMENT P

Founded in France in 1625. First Founded in the United States in 1853.

Motherhouse and Novitiate: *Incarnate Word Convent,* 2930 S. Alameda St., Corpus Christi, TX 78404. Tel: 512-882-5413; Fax: 512-880-4152. Sr. Michelle Marie Kuntscher, Supr. Gen.

Legal Title: *Convent Academy of the Incarnate Word Incarnate Word Academy Foundation.*

Sisters 69.

Sisters serve and staff: Private High Schools; Private Kindergartens; Montessori; Private Middle Schools; Parochial and Private Elementary Schools; Other ministries include Religious Education; Hospital Ministry; Vocation Ministry; Diocesan Offices; Adult Education; General Administration; Retreat Ministry; Parish Ministry.

Represented in the Dioceses of Brownsville, Corpus Christi, Beaumont and Galveston-Houston. Also in Nakuru, Africa.

[2210] (S.I.W.)—SISTERS OF THE INCARNATE WORD AND BLESSED SACRAMENT D

Founded in France in 1625. First foundation in the United States in 1853.

Motherhouse and Novitiate: 6618 Pearl Rd., (Parma Heights-U.S. Rd. 42), Cleveland, OH 44130. Tel: 216-886-6440. Sr. Margaret Taylor, Congregational Leader.

Total number in community 41.

Ministry includes Evangelization; Elementary and Religious Education; Spiritual Ministry (Retreat and Spiritual Direction); Pastoral Ministry in Parishes, Hospitals and Nursing Homes.

Represented in the Diocese of Cleveland.

[2230] (C.I.J.)—CONGREGATION OF THE INFANT JESUS D

Founded in France in 1835. First foundation in the United States in 1905.

General Motherhouse: 310 Prospect Park W., Brooklyn, NY 11215. Tel: 718-965-7300 or. Tel: 516-823-3800. Tel: 516-594-0476. Sr. Dolores Castellano, Supr. Gen.

Total number in community 76.

Corporate Title: *Nursing Sisters of the Sick Poor Inc.* Congregation sponsors one Hospital and one Home Health Agency.

Ministry in the fields of Nursing; Social Work; Physical Therapy; Services to Disabled Persons; Pastoral Care; Chaplains; Retreat Work; Teaching; Parish Ministry; and other works related to Health Services.

Represented in the Dioceses of Brooklyn and Rockville Centre.

[2240] (I.J.)—SISTERS OF THE INFANT JESUS P

Founded in Rouen, France in 1662. First United States foundation in 1950.
Motherhouse: 8 Rue Abbe Gregoire, Paris, France, 75006.
Generalate: Via Trionfale, 8062-Palazzina D, Roma, Italy, 00135. Sr. Daniel Ee, Supr. Gen.
U.S. Foundation: *Holy Angels School,* 20 Reiner St., Colma, CA 94014.
Represented in the Archdiocese of San Francisco.

[2250] (O.S.B.)—CONGREGATION OF BENEDICTINES OF JESUS CRUCIFIED P

Founded in France in 1930. First foundation in the United States in 1955.
General Motherhouse: Brou-sur-Chantereine, France. Mother Godefrieda Bouwman, O.S.B., Prioress Gen.
U.S. Foundations: *Regina Mundi Priory,* 550 S. Waterloo Rd., Devon, PA 19333-1798. Tel: 610-688-5130; Fax: 610-995-0477. Sr. Marie Zita Wenker, O.S.B., Prioress.
St. Paul's Priory Newport, RI 02840. Sr. Marie-Agathe Karunaratne, O.S.B., Prioress.
Total number in the U.S. 29.
Represented in the Archdiocese of Philadelphia and the Diocese of Providence.

[2260] (A.D.)—SISTERS OF THE LAMB OF GOD D

Founded in France 1945.
General Motherhouse: *Institute of the Lamb of God,* 85 Rt du Vieux Saint Marc, Brest, France, 29283. Sr. Claire Marie Ducraux, A.D., Supr. Gen.
U.S. Foundation (1958): *House of Formation,* 2063 Wyandotte Ave., Owensboro, KY 42301. Tel: 502-281-5450. Sr. Mary Raymande, Supr.; Sr. Audrey Gold, Formation Dir.
Sisters 5; Novices 3.
Other Address *9534 Ky. 144, Philpot KY, 42366.* Tel: 502-281-5450. Sr. Mary Raymonde, Supr.
Sisters 4.
Represented in the Diocese of Owensboro.

[2270] (L.C.M.)—SISTERS OF THE LITTLE COMPANY OF MARY P

Founded in England in 1877. First foundation in the United States in 1893.
Generalate: Little Company of Mary Generalate, 28 Trinity Crescent, Tooting Bec London, England, SW17 7AE.
Universal total for the congregation 464.
Provincial Office: Province of the Immaculate Conception, The Little Company of Mary, 9350 S. California Ave., Evergreen Park, IL 60805. Tel: 708-422-0130. Sr. Carol Pacini, L.C.M., Prov.
Total number in community 31.
Properties owned: *Little Company of Mary Hospital and Health Care Centers,* Evergreen Park, IL; *Bay Harbor Hospital,* Harbor City, CA; *Memorial Hospital and Health Care Center,* Jasper, IN; *Little Company of Mary Health Services (Little Company of Mary Hospital - Torrance, California and San Pedro Peninsula Hospital - San Pedro, California).*
Ministry in Hospitals and Health Care; Pastoral/Parish areas.
Represented in the Archdioceses of Chicago, Los Angeles and the Dioceses of Evansville, Orange and Toledo.

[2280] (P.F.M.)—LITTLE FRANCISCANS OF MARY (U.S.) P

Founded in the United States in 1889.
General Motherhouse: Baie St. Paul, (Charlevoix), Diocese of Quebec, P.Q. Canada. Sr. Carmen Gravel, Supr. Gen.
American Region: *St. Francis,* 2 Dupont St., Worcester, MA 01604. Tel: 508-755-0878. Sr. Rena Mae Gagnon, Reg. Supr.
Total number in congregation including Canada and the United States 310.
Represented in the Dioceses of Portland (ME) and Worcester.

[2290] (L.M.S.C.)—LITTLE MISSIONARY SISTERS OF CHARITY P

Founded in Italy in 1915.
Generalate: Via Monte Acero, 5, 00141, Rome, Italy.
U.S. Address: *Immaculate Conception Convent,* 120 Orient Ave., East Boston, MA 02128. Tel: 617-569-2100; Fax: 617-569-2061. Sr. Mary Loreto, L.M.S.C., Contact Person.
Professed Sisters 3.
Represented in the Archdiocese of Boston.

[2300] (L.S.I.C.)—LITTLE SERVANT SISTERS OF THE IMMACULATE CONCEPTION P

Founded in Poland on May 3, 1850. First founded in the United States in Reading, Pennsylvania on December 8, 1926.
General Motherhouse: Stara Wies, Brzozow, Poland. Mother Mariola Karas, L.S.I.C., Mother Gen.
Universal total in Congregation 1,500.
Holy Trinity Province: *Little Servants Sisters of the Immaculate Conception Provincialate-Novitiate,* 1000 Cropwell Rd., Cherry Hill, NJ 08003. Tel: 609-424-1962. Mother Mary Leonarda, L.S.I.C., Prov.; Sr. M. Philomena, L.S.I.C., Archivist.
Legal Titles: *St. Joseph's Catholic Nursing Homes,* Woodbridge, NJ; *St. Joseph's Residences,* Woodbridge, NJ; *Edmund Child Education Center,* Cherry Hill, NJ; *Congregation of the Little Servant Sisters of the Blessed Virgin Mary of the Immaculate Conception.*
Professed Sisters 74.
Ministry in Religious and Academic Education; Nursery Schools; Senior Day Care Center; House of Study; Guest House and Retreat House; Homes for Aged; Nursing Homes; Home Nursing Service; Prayer Groups; Youth Ministry; Parish Ministry; Archbishops Residence.
Represented in the Archdioceses of Newark, Philadelphia and Dioceses of Camden and Metuchen.

[2310] (L.S.A.)—LITTLE SISTERS OF THE ASSUMPTION P

Founded in France in 1865. First foundation in the United States in 1891.
General Motherhouse: Paris, France. Sr. Celine Heon, Supr. Gen., 57 rue Violet, Paris, France, 75015.
United States Province: *Little Sisters of the Assumption Provincialate,* 214 E. 30th St., New York, NY 10016. Tel: 212-889-4310. Sr. Jean McCormack, Prov. Coord.
Total number in community 47.
Ministry in Home Health; Community Development Supportive Family Services Located in Poverty Areas; Services are predominantly provided in the Home Setting.
Represented in the Archdioceses of Boston, New York and Philadelphia and in the Diocese of Worcester.

[2315] (L.S.G.)—LITTLE SISTERS OF THE GOSPEL D

Founded in 1963 in France by Rev. Rene Voillaume. First foundation in the United States in 1972 in New York.
Generalate: *La Courneuve,* France, 93120. Tel: 1-48361814.
U.S. House: Box 305, Mott Haven Sta., Bronx, NY 10454. Tel: 718-292-2867.
Residence: 308 Willis Ave., Bronx NY, 10454.
Professed Sisters 78; Novices 6.
Ministry in Prison Ministry; Service to the Poor and Underserved.
Represented in the Archdiocese of New York.

[2320] (P.S.S.F.)—THE LITTLE SISTERS OF THE HOLY FAMILY P

Les Petites Soeurs de la Sainte Famille

Founded in Canada in 1880. First foundation in the United States in 1900.
General Motherhouse: *Mont Sainte-Famille,* 1820 Ouest, Rue Galt, Sherbrooke, Quebec , Canada, J1K 1H9. Tel: 819-823-0345. Sr. Jeannine Ferland, Supr. Gen.
U.S. Headquarters: *Marie Leonie Residence,* 285 Andover St., Lowell, MA 01852-1446. Tel: 508-454-7481. Sr. Alice Corbin, P.S.S.F., Supr.
Total number in U.S. 48.
Sisters dedicated to the service of priests by prayer and domestic work in rectories.
Represented in the Archdioceses of Boston, Chicago, San Francisco and Washington and the Diocese of Manchester. Also at the Apostolic Nunciature.

[2330] (L.S.J.)—LITTLE SISTERS OF JESUS P

Founded in the Sahara in 1939. First foundation in the United States in 1952.
General Motherhouse: Rome, Italy. Sr. Iris Mary of Jesus, Prioress Gen.
Universal total in congregation 1,400.
U.S. Regional House: 400 N. Streeper St., Baltimore, MD 21224-1230. Tel: 410-327-7863. Sr. Cathy of Jesus, Reg. Dir.
Total number in U.S. 25.
Represented in the Archdioceses of Anchorage, Baltimore, Chicago, Washington and the Dioceses of Altoona-Johnstown, and Fairbanks.

[2331] (L.S.J.M.)—LITTLE SISTERS OF JESUS AND MARY D

Founded in the United States in 1974. Sr. Mary Elizabeth, Foundress.
Joseph House: P.O. Box 1755, Salisbury, MD 21802. Tel: 410-543-1645. Sr. Mary Elizabeth Gintling, Dir.
Total in the community 8.
Represented in the Archdiocese of Baltimore and the Diocese of Wilmington.

[2340] (L.S.P.)—LITTLE SISTERS OF THE POOR P

Founded in France in 1839. First foundation in the United States in 1868.
General Motherhouse: *La Tour St. Joseph,* St. Peran, France, 35190. Mother Celine de la Visitation, Supr. Gen.
Universal total in congregation 3,709.
Province of Brooklyn (1868): *Queen of Peace Residence,* 110-30 221st St., Queens Village, NY 11429. Sr. Genevieve Regina, Prov.
Total number in province 182.
Ministry in Homes for the Aged.
Represented in the Archdioceses of Boston, Hartford, Philadelphia and New York and the Dioceses of Albany, Brooklyn, Metuchen, Paterson, Providence and Scranton. Also in Montreal.
Province of Baltimore: *Little Sisters of the Poor,* 601 Maiden Choice Ln., Baltimore, MD 21228-3698. Tel: 410-744-9367; Fax: 410-747-0601. Sr. Mary Bernard du St. Esprit, Prov.
Total number in province 154.
Ministry in Homes for the Aged.
Represented in the Archdioceses of Baltimore, Cincinnati, Indianapolis, Mobile, New Orleans and Washington and the Dioceses of Cleveland, Pittsburgh, Richmond, Toledo and Wilmington.
Province of Chicago: *Little Sisters of the Poor,* Chicago Province, Inc., 80 W. Northwest Hwy., Palatine, IL 60067-3582. Tel: 847-358-5700; Fax: 847-934-6852. Sr. Margaret Regina, Prov.
Total number in province 140.
Ministry in Homes for the Aged.
Represented in the Archdioceses of Chicago, Denver, Los Angeles, Louisville, St. Louis, St. Paul-Minneapolis and San Francisco and the Dioceses of Evansville, Gallup, and Kansas City-St. Joseph.

[2345] (P.O.S.C.)—LITTLE WORKERS OF THE SACRED HEARTS P

Founded in Italy in 1892. First Foundation in the U.S. in 1948.
General House: Via dei Pamphili 3, 00152, Rome, Italy.
Motherhouse and Novitiate: *Our Lady of Grace Convent,* 635 Glenbrook Rd., Stamford, CT 06906. Tel: 203-348-5531. Mother Lillian Cairo, P.O.S.C., Supr.
Ministry in Day Care Centers; Catechetics.
Represented in the Archdioceses of Philadelphia and Washington and the Diocese of Bridgeport.

[2350] (S.L.W.)—SISTERS OF THE LIVING WORD D

Founded in the United States in 1975.
General Motherhouse: *The Living Word Center,* 800 N. Fernandez Ave. B, Arlington Heights, IL 60004-5316. Tel: 708-577-5972; Fax: 708-577-5980. Sr. Mary Ann Zrust, Coord. of Spirituality.
Total number in community 80.
Ministry in the field of Academic and Religious Education; Hospitals; Parish Ministry and Social Services.
Represented in the Archdioceses of Chicago, Detroit, New Orleans, St. Louis and St. Paul-Minneapolis and the Dioceses of Biloxi, Brownsville, Jackson, Joliet, Lansing, Orlando, Rockford, San Angelo and Sioux City.

[2360] (S.L.)—SISTERS OF LORETTO AT THE FOOT OF THE CROSS P

Founded in America in 1812.
General Motherhouse & Novitiate: *Loretto Motherhouse and Novitiate,* Nerinx, KY 40049. Tel: 502-865-5811.
Administrative Office: 300 E. Hampden Ave., Suite 400, Englewood, CO 80110-2661. Tel: 303-783-

0450; Fax: 303-783-0611. Sr. Mary Ann Coyle, S.L., Pres.
Legal Title: *Loretto Literary and Benevolent Institution.*
Total number in congregation 425.
Ministry in the field of Academic and Religious Education at all levels; Seminaries; Specialized Education; Health Care-Aging; Community Administration; Pastoral Ministry; Social Justice-Social Service; Administration; Diocesan Offices; Medicine and Nursing; Prayer Retreats; Clerical Offices; Consultants; Spirituality Center.
Represented in the Archdioceses of Atlanta, Chicago, Cincinnati, Denver, Indianapolis,Los Angeles, Louisville, Mobile, New Orleans, New York, St. Louis, San Antonio, San Francisco, Santa Fe and the Dioceses of Cheyenne, Colorado Springs, El Paso, Galveston-Houston, Kansas City-St. Joseph, Nashville, Oakland, Pueblo, Rockford, San Diego and San Jose.

[2370] (I.B.V.M.)—INSTITUTE OF THE BLESSED VIRGIN MARY (LORETTO SISTERS) P

Founded in St. Omer, Belgium, 1609. First foundation in Canada in 1847; in the United States in 1880.
General Motherhouse North America: *Loretto Abbey,* 101 Mason Blvd., Toronto, Ontario , Canada, M5M 3E2. Sr. Jane McDonell, Supr. Gen.
Universal total in congregation 244.
Regional Office Canada: *Canadian Regional Government,* Loretto College, 70 St. Mary St., Toronto, Ontario , Canada, M5S 1J3. Sr. Anne Murray, Reg. Supr.-Canada.
Regional Office United States: *American Regional Administration, Loretto Convent,* P.O. Box 508, Wheaton, IL 60189. Tel: 708-665-3814; Fax: 708-653-4886. Sr. Barbara Nelson, Reg. Supr.
Total number in community 99.
Properties owned: *Loretto High School,* Sacramento, CA; *Loretto Development Office Loretto Convent,* Wheaton, IL; *Loretto Early Childhood Center,* Wheaton, IL; *Loretto Sisters Novitiate,* Ontario, Canada; *Loretto Conference Center,* Wheaton, IL.
Sisters serve and staff: High Schools; Grammar Schools; Missionary Work; Correspondence School; University; Pastoral Ministry; Adult Education; Social Work; Retreat Ministry; Diocesan Office; Director of Religious Education.
Represented in the Archdiocese of Chicago and the Dioceses of Joliet, Marquette, Fairbanks, Phoenix, Sacramento, St. Petersburg and San Bernardino. Also in the West Indies.

[2380] (I.B.V.M.)—INSTITUTE OF THE BLESSED VIRGIN MARY (LORETO SISTERS) P

Founded in St. Omer, Belgium, in 1609. Foundation in Arizona, 1954 from the diocese of Meath, Ireland.
Motherhouse: Rathfarnham, Dublin, Ireland.
Generalate: Viale Appio Claudio, 10, Rome, Italy. Sr. Noni Mitchell, Supr. Gen.
Total number in congregation 1,036.
U.S. Regional: *Mary Ward House,* 2521 W. Maryland Ave., Phoenix, AZ 85017. Tel: 602-433-0659. Sr. Christine Gilsenan, Reg. Supr.
Total number in community 18.
Represented in the Diocese of Phoenix.

[2390] (L.H.C.)—LOVERS OF THE HOLY CROSS SISTERS D

Founded in 1670 in Viet Nam by Bishop Pierre Lambert de la Motte. First foundation in the United States in 1976. Established as an autonomous institute of Consecrated Life of Diocesan Right in 1992.
General Motherhouse (1976): *Holy Cross Convent,* 14700 South Van Ness Ave., Garden, CA 90249. Tel: 310-768-1906 or 516-0271; Fax: 310-352-6435. Sr. Monica Phi Tran, L.H.C., Supr. Gen.
Legal Title: *Lovers of the Holy Cross Sisters, Inc.*
Sisters 40; Novices 9; Postulants 7; Aspirants 22; Oblates 2.
Represented in the Archdioceses of Los Angeles and New Orleans and the Diocese of Orange.

[2400] (M.S.)—MARIAN SISTERS OF THE DIOCESE OF LINCOLN D

Marycrest Motherhouse: Marian Center, R.R. No. 1, Box 108, Waverly, NE 68462. Tel: 402-786-2750. Sr. Ann Divis, M.S., Major Supr.
Total number in community 35.
Ministry in the field of Education; Specialized Education; Health Care; Catechetics.
Represented in the Diocese of Lincoln.

[2410] (M.S.C.)—CONGREGATION OF THE MARIANITES OF HOLY CROSS P

Founded in France in 1841. First foundation in the United States in 1843.
Congregational Administration Headquarters: 1011 Gallier St., New Orleans, LA 70117. Tel: 504-945-1620. Sr. Mary Kay Kinberger, M.S.C., Congregational Leader.
Total number in North America 205.
Legal Holdings or Titles:: *Our Lady of Holy Cross Convent,* New Orleans, LA; *Our Lady of Holy Cross College,* New Orleans, LA; *Prompt Succor Nursing Home,* Opelousas, LA; *C'est la Vie (Senior Citizen Independent Living Units),* Opelousas, LA; *Our Lady of Princeton Convent,* Princeton, NJ.
Ministry in Parishes; Social & Health Services; and the field of Education.
Represented in the Archdioceses of New Orleans, New York, and the Dioceses of Alexandria, Baton Rouge, Biloxi, Camden, Houma-Thibodeaux, Juneau, Lafayette (LA), Lake Charles, Manchester, Paterson, Rochestesr and Trenton. Also in Bangladesh, Canada, Central America and Mexico.

[2420] (S.M.S.M.)—MARIST MISSIONARY SISTERS (MISSIONARY SISTERS OF THE SOCIETY OF MARY) INC. P

Founded in France in 1845-1857. First foundation in the United States in Boston, Massachusetts 1922.
Motherhouse: *Via Cassia,* 1243, Roma, Italia, 00189.
Universal total in congregation 630.
North American Province: *Provincial Office,* 349 Grove St., Waltham, MA 02154. Tel: 781-893-0149; Fax: 781-894-7610. Sr. Rosalie Warpeha, S.M.S.M., Prov., *Vocation Promotion House,* 5142 S. Blackstone, Chicago, IL 60615. Sr. Claire Rheaume, S.M.S.M.
Represented in the Archdioceses of Boston, Chicago, San Francisco and the Dioceses of Brownsville, Davenport, Fairbanks, Honolulu, Little Rock, Memphis, St. Petersburg, Peoria, Providence, Rochester, Shreveport and Venice.

[2430] (S.M.)—MARIST SISTERS/CONGREGATION OF MARY P

Founded in France 1824 by Venerable John Claude Colin and Jeanne Marie Chavoin.
General Motherhouse: Via Aurelia 292, Rome, Italy, 00165. Sr. Gail Reneker, S.M., Supr. Gen.
Universal total in Congregation 500.
U.S. Foundation (1993): *Marist Sisters - Congregation of Mary,* 810 Peach, Abilene, TX 79602. Tel: 915-675-5806. Tel: 915-675-5127. Sr. Andrena Mulligan, S.M., Prov. Supr.
Total number in the community 18.
Ministry in Elementary & Adult Education; Pastoral Ministry; Counseling; Pastoral Care in Hospitals;
Physical Therapy; Seminary Formation; Social Ministry.
Represented in the Archdioceses of Chicago, Detroit and the Dioceses of Saginaw, San Angelo and Wheeling-Charleston.

[2440] (S.M.I.)—SISTERS OF MARY IMMACULATE P

Catechist Sisters of Mary Immaculate, Help of Christians

Founded in India in 1948 by the late Bishop Louis LaRavoire Morrow, Bishop of Krishnagar, India.
General Motherhouse: Krishnagar, Nadia Dist., West Bengal, India, 741 101. Sr. Marie Pothanamala, Supr. Gen.
Universal total in Congregation 475.
U.S. Foundation (1981): Sisters of Mary Immaculate, R.D. No.5, Box 1231, Leechburg, PA 15656. Tel: 412-845-2828; 836-0449. Sr. Gratia Kuttianickal, S.M.I., Delegation Supr.; Sr. Tracy Vattakuzhiyil, S.M.I., Supr.
Total number in the community 6.
Legal Holdings & Titles: *St. Joseph Hall Convent,* Greensburg, PA; *Bishop Morrow Personal Care Home,* Leechburg, PA.

[2450] (S.M.P.)—SISTERS OF MARY OF THE PRESENTATION P

Founded in France. First foundation in the United States in 1903.
General Motherhouse: Broons, Cotes-du-Nord, France. Sr. Anne Grall, Supr. Gen.
U.S. Provincial House & Novitiate At Maryvale: 11550 River Rd., Valley City, ND 58072. Tel: 701-845-2864. Sr. Marlyss Dionne, Prov.
Total number in the community 60.
Ministry in the field of Religious and Academic Education at all levels; Parish Ministry; Hospitals and Home Health Agencies.
Represented in the Archdiocese of St. Paul-Minneapolis and the Dioceses of Fargo, Peoria and Rockford.

[2460] (S.M.R.)—SOCIETY OF MARY REPARATRIX P

Founded in France in 1857. First foundation in the United States in 1908. Total International Membership: 1,000 Sisters.
Generalate: *Society Di Maria Riparatrice,* Via dei Lucchesi 3, Roma, Italia, 00187. Sr. Mary Henihan, Supr. Gen.
U.S. Province: 225 E. 234th St., Bronx, NY 10470. Tel: 718-324-2252. Sr. Ann Kasparek, Prov. Supr.
Total number in the community 40.
Represented in the Archdioceses of Detroit, Miami, New York and San Juan and the Dioceses of Albany and Brooklyn.

[2470] (M.M.)—MARYKNOLL SISTERS OF ST. DOMINIC P

Founded in New York 1912.
Center: *Maryknoll Sisters Center,* Maryknoll, NY 10545-0311. Tel: 914-941-7575. Sr. Helene O'Sullivan, M.M., Community Pres.; Sr. Rosemary Healy, Center Coord.; Sr. Ellen Pierce, M.M., Archivist.
Orientation Program: *Maryknoll Sisters.* Co-Dirs.: Sr. Rita Burdzy, M.M.; Sr. Christelle Zabalerio, M.M.
Legal Titles and Holdings: *Maryknoll Sisters of St. Dominic, Inc.; Maryknoll Mission Institute.*
Total number in the Congregation 712.
Represented in the Archdioceses of Baltimore, Boston, Chicago, Cincinnati, Detroit, Hartford, Los Angeles, Louisville, Newark, New York, Philadelphia, Portland (OR), St. Louis, San Francisco, Washington and and the Dioceses of Albany, Baker, Brownsville, Brooklyn, Gallup, Honolulu, Galveston-Houston, Kansas City-St. Joseph, Las Cruces, Madison, Manchester, Oakland, Palm Beach, Phoenix, Providence, Raleigh, Rochester, Rockville Centre, Sacramento, St. Augustine, St. Petersburg, San Bernardino, San Diego, San Jose, Scranton, Springfield, Stockton and Winona. Also in Samoa.

[2480] (M.M.M.)—MEDICAL MISSIONARIES OF MARY P

Founded in Ireland in 1937. First United States Foundation in 1950.
General Motherhouse: *Rosemount,* Booterstown Ave., Blackrock, Co. Dublin, Ireland. Mother Mary Martin, M.M.M., Foundress; Sr. Philomena Sheerin, Supr. Gen.
Zonal Center: 563 Minneford Ave., City Island, NY 10464-1118. Tel: 718-885-0945; Fax: 718-885-0010. Sr. Joanne Bierl, M.M.M., Coord.
Total number in the Congregation 436.
Represented in the Archdioceses of Boston, Chicago and New York and the Dioceses of Richmond and San Diego.

[2490] (M.M.S.)—MEDICAL MISSION SISTERS P

Generalate: London, England. Sr. Elizabeth Koonthanam, M.M.S., Society Coord.
Universal total in the Congregation 688.
North American Headquarters (1925): 8400 Pine Rd., Philadelphia, PA 19111. Tel: 215-742-6100; Fax: 215-342-3948. Sr. Maria Hornung, M.M.S., North American Coord.
Legal Titles: *Society of Catholic Medical Missionaries, Inc.; Society of Catholic Medical Missionaries Generalate, Inc.*
Total number in North America 149.
Represented in the Archdioceses of Anchorage, Baltimore, Boston, Chicago, Cincinnati, Hartford, Louisville, New Orleans, New York, Philadelphia, St. Louis, Washington and the Dioceses of Arlington, Harrisburg, Las Cruces, Memphis, Palm Beach, Richmond, St. Augustine, St. Petersburg, San Jose, San Diego, Savannah, Trenton, and Tucson. Also in Mexico.

[2500] (M.S.J.)—MEDICAL SISTERS OF ST. JOSEPH P

Founded in Kerala, South India, 1946.
General Motherhouse: Dharmagiri, P.O. Kothamangalam, Kerala, South India, 686691. Mother Nora, M.S.J., Supr. Gen.
U.S. Foundation (1985): *Medical Sisters of St. Joseph,* 3435 E. Funston, Wichita, KS 67218. Tel: 316-686-4746. Sr. Audrey, M.S.J., Supr.
Total number in Congregation 700.

Ministry as Health Care Apostolates.
Represented in the Diocese of Wichita.

[2515] (C.M.S.)—CASHEL MERCY SISTERS D

U.S. Foundation (St. Mel's Convent): *Congregation of the Sisters of Mercy of Ireland,* P.O. Box 1180, Fair Oaks, CA 95628. Tel: 916-967-9504. Sr. Kathleen Hanley, Supr.
Represented in the Diocese of Sacramento.

[2516] (S.M.)—SISTERS OF MERCY P

Founded in Ireland in 1831.
Motherhouse: **Convent of Mercy,** Carrick-on-Suir, Ireland.
U.S. Foundation (1956): St. John's Convent of Mercy, 11154 San Pablo Ave., El Cerrito, CA 94530. Tel: 415-233-6769.
Other U.S. Convents (1960): St. Nicholas Convent, 12816 S. El Monte Ave., Los Altos Hills CA, 94022. Tel: 415-948-0775.
Professed Sisters 10.
Represented in the Dioceses of Oakland, San Jose, Santa Rosa and Sioux Falls.

[2517] SISTERS OF MERCY P

Founded in Dublin, 1831.
Headquarters: Dublin, Ireland.
Holy Infant Convent: 239 Nancy Pl., Ballwin, MO 63021. Tel: 314-391-1528. Sr. Agnes Nolan, Facilitator.
Total number in the community 4.
Legal Title: *Sisters of Mercy, Ireland.*
Ministry in Education & Pastoral Ministries.
Represented in the Archdiocese of St. Louis.

[2519] (R.S.M.)—RELIGIOUS SISTERS OF MERCY OF ALMA, MICHIGAN P

The Religious Sisters of Mercy of Alma was officially founded on September 1, 1973; Diocesan approval on Jan. 25, 1974; Constitutions of Community approved March 17, 1978; Pontifical Status fully approved June 18, 1982. Final approval of constitution May 31, 1991.
Motherhouse and Novitiate: *Religious Sisters of Mercy,* 1835 Michigan Ave., Alma, MI 48801. Tel: 517-463-6035. Mother Mary Quentin Sheridan, R.S.M.
Total number in the community 53.
Represented in the Archdiocese of Hartford and the Dioceses of Lansing, Portland, Saginaw and Winona. Also in Canada, Germany and Italy.

[2520] (R.S.M.)—SISTERS OF MERCY P

Founded in the United States in 1960.
General Motherhouse: *Congregation of the Sisters of Mercy,* Elblano Ave., Dun Laoghlaire, Dublin, 01-2800448. Ireland. Sr. Dervilla Byrne, Supr. Gen.
U.S. Foundation: *St. Joan of Arc,* 500 S.W. Fourth St., Boca Raton, FL 33432. Tel: 407-368-6655. Sr. Kathleen Sweeney, Supr.
Professed Sisters 5.
Represented in the Diocese of Palm Beach.

[2523] (R.S.M.)—SISTERS OF MERCY OF ARDAGH & CLONMACNOIS

Founded in Dublin, Ireland in 1831.
General Motherhouse: Villa Maria, Ardagh Co., Longford, Ireland. Sr. Elizabeth Manning, Mother Gen.
U.S. Foundation (1962): *Little Flower Convent,* 1280 Casazza Dr., Reno, NV 89502.
Professed Sisters 4.
Represented in the Dioceses of Orlando, Palm Beach and Reno-Las Vegas.

[2530] SISTERS OF MERCY D

Founded in Dublin, Ireland in 1831.
Mercy Generalate: Dundalk Co. Louth, Ireland. Sr. M. Rosarii Carville.
U.S. Foundation: *Mailing Address:* P.O. Box 360937, Melbourne, FL 32936-0937; *Ascension School,* P.O. Box E.G. 937, Melbourne, FL 32935. Sr. M. Joseph Barden, Local Supr.
Represented in the Diocese of Orlando.

[2535] (R.S.M.)—SISTERS OF MERCY (IRELAND)

Founded in Ireland in 1831. First Foundation in United States in 1969.
Generalate: Dublin, Ireland. Sr. Dervila Byrne, Supr. Gen.
U.S. Address: 2766 Navajo Rd., El Cajon, CA 92020. Tel: 619-465-2233.
Ministry in Hospital, Schools and Parishes.
Professed Sisters 7.
Represented in the Diocese of San Diego.

[2540] (R.S.M.)—SISTERS OF MERCY P

General Motherhouse: *Congregation of the Sisters of Mercy,* Elblano Ave., Dun Laoghlaire, Dublin, 01-2800448. Ireland. Sr. Dervilla Byrne, Supr. Gen.
Novitiate and Religious Education Center (1971): 1172 S.W. 26th Ave., Deerfield Beach, FL 33442. Tel: 305-480-8511. Sr. Teresa O'Connell, Reg. Supr.
Total number in the community 13.
Ministry in the field of Education; Parish Work.
Represented in the Archdiocese of Miami and the Diocese of Palm Beach.

[2549] (R.S.M.)—SISTERS OF MERCY (SLIGO) P

Founded in Ireland in 1846. First foundation in United States in 1956.
Generalate: St. Peter's Convent, Athlone Roscommon, Ireland. Sr. Patricia Kelly, Supr. Gen.
American Region: 4825 H St., San Bernardino, CA 92447. Tel: 909-886-6172; Fax: 909-883-5954. Sr. Maura Feeley, Reg. Supr.
Total number in the community 25.
Ministry in the field of Religious and Academic Education; Parishes; Social Services; Diocesan Offices.
Represented in the Dioceses of Orange, San Bernardino and San Diego.

[2550] (R.S.M.)—SISTERS OF MERCY D

General Motherhouse: Convent of Mercy, St. Mary Limerick, Ireland. Sr. Clare Stapleton, Supr. Gen.
U.S. Addresses: *St. Pius X Convent,* 3012 Cottage Hill Rd., #395, Mobile, AL 36606. Tel: 205-470-8453.
Total number in community 1.
St. Mary Convent, Rockledge, FL 32955. Tel: 407-636-1341.
Total number in community 6.
Represented in the Archdiocese of Mobile and the Diocese of Orlando.

[2560] SISTERS OF MERCY D

Founded in Ireland.
General Motherhouse: *Sisters of Mercy - U.S. Province,* Redlands, CA 92374.
U.S. Address (1963): *St. James School,* 603 West Ave., Gulfport, MS 39507. Tel: 288-896-6631. Sr. Teresa O'Connell, Prov.
Total number in the community 8.
Represented in the Diocese of Biloxi.

[2575] (R.S.M.)—SISTERS OF MERCY OF THE AMERICAS

Catherine McAuley founded the Sisters of Mercy in Dublin, Ireland, in 1831. Ten years later, she received confirmation of the Rule by Pope Gregory XVI. In 1843 the Sisters of Mercy established their first U.S.A. foundation in Pittsburgh. In 1929 several of the independent congregations amalgamated to form the Sisters of Mercy of the Union. In 1991 the members of the nine provinces of the Union and of 16 other Mercy congregations founded the Sisters of Mercy of the Americas, with its 25 regional communities.
Universal total in the Congregation 6,177.
Institute Administrative Offices: 8300 Colesville Rd., #300, Silver Spring, MD 20910-3243. Tel: 301-587-0423; Fax: 301-587-0533. Sr. Doris Gottemoeller, R.S.M., Pres.
Mercy Action, Inc. is separately incorporated to foster innovative works of mercy.
McAuley Institute, Inc. is separately incorporated to foster the development of low-income housing ministry as a work of mercy.
Mercy Corps, Inc. is separately incorporated to conduct a volunteer lay ministry program to further the works of mercy.

Albany P

Regional Community of Albany (1863): *Convent of Mercy,* 310 S. Manning Blvd., Albany, NY 12208. Tel: 518-437-3000; Fax: 518-437-3030. Sr. Rosemary J. Sgroi, R.S.M., Pres.
Total number in the community 176.
Properties owned or sponsored: *Maria College St. Peter's Hospital.*
Ministry in the field of Education; Health Services; Pastoral Ministry; Social Services.
Represented in the Archdioceses of Anchorage, Hartford and Newark and the Dioceses of Albany and Syracuse.

Auburn P

Auburn Regional Community: *Institute of the Sisters of Mercy of the Americas,* 535 Sacramento St., Auburn, CA 95603. Tel: 530-887-2000. Sr. Susan McCarthy, R.S.M., Pres.
Total number in the community 89.
Properties owned, staffed or sponsored: *Our Lady of Mercy Convent,* Auburn, CA; *McAuley Convent Russell House Mercy Convent,* Sacramento, CA; *Mercy Convent,* Redding, CA; *Mercy San Juan Convent,* Fair Oaks, CA; *Mercy Convent,* Folsom, CA; *Mercy Convent,* Carmichael, CA.
Ministry in the field of Education; Parishes; Diocesan Offices; Hospitals; Convalescent Units; Clinics; Pastoral Ministries; Senior Housing; Social Ministries.
Represented in the Diocese of Sacramento.

Baltimore P

Sisters of Mercy, Regional Community of Baltimore: *House of Mercy, Inc.,* P.O. Box 11448, Baltimore, MD 21239. Tel: 410-435-4400. Sr. Margaret Downing, R.S.M., Pres.
Total number in community 241.
Legal Holdings and Titles: *Sisters of Mercy, Baltimore, Inc. The Villa, Inc.,* Baltimore, MD.
Sisters serve and staff: Elementary Schools; High Schools; Institutions of Higher Education; Multi-Level Long-Term Care Facility; Diocesan Child Care Homes; Pastoral Ministry Programs in Parishes; Diocesan Offices; National Conference of Catholic Bishops; United States Catholic Conference; Inner-City Literacy Programs.
Properties Owned or Sponsored: High Schools 3; Hospitals 4; Retirement Facilities for Sisters 4; Leisure-Retreat Houses for Sisters 3; Residential Program for Homeless Women 1.
Represented in the Archdioceses of Atlanta, Baltimore, Mobile and Washington and the Dioceses of Birmingham, Pensacola-Tallahassee, Savannah and Wilmington. Also in Belize.

Brooklyn P

Brooklyn Regional Community (1855): 273 Willoughby Ave., Brooklyn, NY 11205. Tel: 718-622-5750. Sr. Camille D'Arienzo, Pres.
Total number in the community 266.
Ministry in the field of Education and Child Care Institutions.
Represented in the Dioceses of Brooklyn and Rockville Centre. Also in Panama.

Buffalo P

Regional Community of Buffalo: 5245 Murphy Rd., Orchard Park, NY 14127. Tel: 716-662-9836; 662-5120; Fax: 716-662-9766. Sr. Peggy Gorman, R.S.M., Pres.
Total number in the community 205.
Legal Holdings and Titles, Sponsored Works: *Trocaire College Mount Mercy Academy,* Buffalo, NY; *Mercy Health System of Western New York,* Buffalo, NY; *Kenmore Mercy Hospital,* Kenmore, NY; *Mercy Hospital,* Buffalo, NY; *St. Jerome Hospital,* Batavia, NY; *Mercy Home Care of Western New York,* Lockport, NY; *Ignatia House,* Buffalo, NY. *Co-sponsor: The McAuley Seton Home Care Agency,* Cheektowaga, NY; *Eastern Mercy Health System,* Radnor, PA; *Catholic Health East,* Radnor, PA.
Ministry in the field of Education at all levels; Catholic Charities; Parish Ministry; Community Table.
Represented in the Archdiocese of Washington and the Dioceses of Buffalo, Providence and Rochester. Also in the Philippines.

Burlingame P

Regional Community of Burlingame (1854): 2300 Adeline Dr., Burlingame, CA 94010-5599. Tel: 650-340-7410; Fax: 650-347-2550. Sr. Judith Carle, Pres.; Sr. Marilyn Gouailhardou, Archivist.
Total number in the community 215.
Legal Title: *Sisters of Mercy,* Burlingame, California.
Ministry in Health Care; Religious and Academic Education; Spirituality and Conference Center; Foreign Missions; Social Services including housing; Retreats; Diocesan Offices.
Represented in the Archdioceses of Los Angeles and San Francisco and the Dioceses of Fresno, Oakland, Orange, Phoenix, San Diego, San Jose and Santa Rosa. Also in Peru.

Cedar Rapids P

Regional Community of Cedar Rapids: *Sacred Heart Convent Motherhouse,* 1125 Prairie Dr., N.E., Cedar Rapids, IA 52402-4737. Tel: 319-364-5196; Fax: 319-364-7383. Sr. Susan O'Connor, R.S.M., Pres.; Sr. Delores Marie Hannon, R.S.M., Vice Pres.
Total number in the community 108.

Ministry in the field of Academic and Religious Education at all levels; Parish Ministry; Pastoral Care; Foreign Mission work; Social Services; Hospitals; Literacy Programs; Transitional Housing; Aids Ministry; Social Justice Ministries; Home for Aged.

Properties owned or sponsored: Mount Mercy College Mercy Medical Center Sisters of Mercy Charitable Trust Catherine McAuley Center for Women, Cedar Rapids, IA.

Represented in the Archdioceses of Chicago, Cincinnati, Detroit, Dubuque, Indianapolis, Milwaukee, St. Louis, St. Paul-Minneapolis, Washington and the Dioceses of Davenport, Des Moines, Fall River, Helena, Kansas City-St. Joseph, Lincoln, Madison, Sioux City, St. Cloud, Springfield, Wheeling-Charleston. Also in Peru.

Chicago P

Regional Community of Chicago: *Administrative Center,* 10024 S. Central Park Ave., Chicago, IL 60655-3132. Tel: 773-779-6011; Fax: 773-779-6094. Sr. Lucille McKillop, R.S.M., Pres.

Total number in community 354.

Sisters serve and staff: Education at all Levels; Social Services; Pastoral Services; Health Care; Spirituality; Foreign Missions.

Legal Holdings and Titles: *Sisters of Mercy of the Americas, Regional Community of Chicago Mercy Housing Corporation, Chicago,* IL; *The Warde Corp. Sisters of Mercy of the Americas, Regional Community of Chicago Charitable Trust.*

Properties Owned and Sponsored: University 1; High Schools 1; Hospitals 3; Residence 2; Retreat Houses 1; Health Care and Rehabilitation Centers 2.

Represented in the Archdioceses of Boston, Chicago, Milwaukee, San Antonio, St. Louis and the Dioceses of Colorado Springs, Davenport, Des Moines, Joliet, Knoxville, Peoria, Phoenix, Rockford, St. Petersburg, Springfield (IL) and Superior. Also in Honduras.

Cincinnati P

Regional Community of Cincinnati: *Sisters of Mercy Regional Center,* 2335 Grandview Ave., Cincinnati, OH 45206. Tel: 513-221-1800; Fax: 513-221-0207. Sr. Marie Hartmann, R.S.M., Pres.

Total number in community 379.

Sisters staff and serve: Academic Education at all levels; Parish & Diocesan Ministry; Health and Child-Care; Hospitals and Schools of Nursing; Homes for the Aged; Retreat and Renewal Center; Special Education.

Represented in the Archdioceses of Cincinnati and Louisville and the Dioceses of Cleveland, Knoxville, Lexington, Memphis, Nashville, Owensboro and Toledo. Also in Jamaica and West Indies.

Connecticut P

Regional Community of Connecticut: *Sisters of Mercy of the Americas,* 249 Steele Rd., West Hartford, CT 06117. Tel: 860-232-8602; Fax: 860-233-0065. Sr. Judith A. Carey, R.S.M., Reg. Pres.; Sr. Dolores Liptak, Archivist.

Total number in the community 265.

Legal Title: *Sisters of Mercy of Connecticut, Inc.*

Properties owned and sponsored: *Mercyknoll, Inc. Saint Mary Home, Inc. McAuley Center, Inc. The Academy of Our Lady of Mercy - Lauralton Hall, Inc. Saint Joseph College, Inc. Our Lady of Mercy School, Inc. Mercy Housing and Shelter, Inc. Mercy Center, Inc. Mercy Community Health, Inc. Mercy Community Homecare, Inc.*

Ministry in the field of Religious and Academic Education at all levels; School for Exceptional Children; Spirituality and Retreat Work; Social Services and; Health Care.

Represented in the Archdioceses of Boston, Hartford, New York, Washington and the Dioceses of Bridgeport, Burlington, Lexington, Manchester, Norwich, Pittsburgh, Portland (ME), Providence, Richmond, Springfield, Wheeling-Charleston, Wichita, and Worcester. Also in Belize, Guatemala and Haiti.

Dallas P

Regional Community of Dallas: *Administrative Office,* P.O. Box 369, Dallas, PA 18612-0369. Tel: 717-675-1966; Fax: 717-675-9051. Sr. Maureen McCann, R.S.M., Pres.; Sr. Susan Marie Nowalis, R.S.M., Community Archivist.

Total number in community 371.

Properties owned or sponsored: *Mercy Center College Misericordia Mount Aloysius College Mercy Center Pre School Catherine McAuley Center Neuman Housing Services, Inc. Project REMAIN.*

Ministry in the field of Education; Hospital & Health Care; Art; Communications; Retirement Homes; Housing; Pastoral Services; Social Services; South American Ministries; European Ministries (overseas ministry).

Represented in the Archdioceses of Baltimore, Miami, Newark, New York, Philadelphia, St. Louis, Washington and the Dioceses of Altoona-Johnstown, Brooklyn, Camden, Charlotte, Greensburg, Harrisburg, Madison, Pittsburgh, Palm Beach, Rockville Centre, St. Cloud, St. Petersburg, Scranton, Springfield-Cape Girardeau and Wheeling-Charleston. Also in Guyana, & Honduras.

Detroit P

Regional Community of Detroit: *Sisters of Mercy,* 29000 Eleven Mile Rd., Farmington Hills, MI 48336. Tel: 248-476-8000; Fax: 248-467-4222. Sr. Gretchen Elliott, R.S.M., Pres.; Sr. Michaeline Lewandowski, R.S.M., Archivist.

Total number in community 295.

Legal Title: *Sisters of Mercy - Regional Community of Detroit Sisters of Mercy of the Americas, Regional Community of Detroit, Charitable Trusts I and II.*

Properties Sponsored: Universities 1; High Schools 2; Mercy Health Services and 8 Subsidiaries & 14 Health Care Systems; Mercy Center.

Represented in the Archdioceses of Baltimore, Denver, Detroit, Dubuque, Hartford, Milwaukee, Oklahoma City, Seattle and the Dioceses of Burlington, Charlotte, Cleveland, Columbus, Dodge City, Gaylord, Grand Rapids, Greensburg, Kalamazoo, LaCrosse, Lansing, Orlando, Owensboro, Saginaw, and St. Petersburg. Also in Argentina, & Chile.

Erie P

Regional Community of Erie: 444 E. Grandview Blvd., Erie, PA 16504. Tel: 814-824-2516; Fax: 814-824-2127. Sr. JoAnne Courneen, Reg. Pres.; Sr. Edith Langiotti, Archivist.

Total number in the community 82.

Legal Title: *Institute of the Sisters of Mercy of the Americans - Regional Community of Erie.*

Properties owned and or sponsored: *Mercyhurst College; Mercyhurst Preparatory School Mercy Center for the Arts,* (Pre-school) *Mercy Center on Aging Mercy Terrace Apartments,* (Housing for Elderly) *Mercy Center for Women.*

Ministry in the field of Religious and Academic Education at all levels; Prison Ministry; Health Care Ministry; Diocesan Marriage Tribunal; Social Services.

Represented in the Archdioceses of Detroit, Washington and the Dioceses of Erie, Little Rock, Pittsburgh and Savannah.

Merion P

Regional Community of Merion: *Motherhouse of The Sisters of Mercy,* Merion, PA 19066. Tel: 610-664-6650; Fax: 610-664-3429. Sr. Christine McCann, R.S.M., Reg. Pres.; Sr. Juliet Ferrari, R.S.M., Local Coord.

Total number in the community 444.

Legal Title: *Sisters of Mercy of Merion, Pennsylvania.*

Properties owned, staffed, or sponsored: *Gwynedd Mercy College; McAuley Convent; Merion Mercy Academy; Waldron Mercy Academy; Gwynedd Mercy Academy; Mercy Vocational High School; St. Mary Residence; Mercy Catholic Medical Center; Walsingham Academy; Mercy Health System.*

Sisters serve and staff: Religious and academic education at all levels; Hospices; House of Prayer; Social service organizations.

Represented in the Archdioceses of Anchorage, Atlanta, Baltimore, Chicago, Cincinnati, Miami, New York, Philadelphia, St. Louis, Washington and the Dioceses of Allentown, Biloxi, Buffalo, Camden, Gallup, Grand Rapids, Orlando, Raleigh, Richmond, Scranton, Toledo, Trenton, Tucson, Wheeling-Charleston and Wilmington. Also in Italy, Peru, Bolivia and Canada.

New Hampshire P

Motherhouse of the Sisters of Mercy Inc.: *Sisters of Mercy of the Americas-Regional Community of New Hampshire,* (1858), 21 Searles Rd., Windham, NH 03087-1297. Tel: 603-893-6550; Fax: 603-893-2413. Sr. Patricia Sullivan, Pres.

Total number in the community 187.

Properties Owned or Sponsored: *Castle College,* Windham, NH; *Marian Court College,* Swampscott, MA; *Mount St. Mary Early Childhood Center,* Manchester, NH; *Manchester Convent of the Sisters of Mercy Mount Saint Mary Corporation of the Sisters of Mercy Frances Warde House, Inc.,* Manchester, NH; *Warde Health Center, Inc.,* Windham, NH.

Ministry in the field of Academic Education at all levels; Nursing Homes; Hospitals.

Represented in the Archdioceses of Baltimore, Boston, and the Dioceses of Brooklyn, Fall River, Orlando, Manchester, Portland (ME), Providence, Pueblo, St. Augustine and St. Cloud.

New Jersey P

Regional Community of New Jersey: 1645 U.S. Hwy 22, W., Watchung, NJ 07060-6587. Tel: 908-756-5348; Fax: 908-754-0164. Sr. Diane Szubrowski, R.S.M., Reg. Pres.; Sr. Innocent Dolan, R.S.M., Archivist.

Total number in the community 324.

Legal Title: *Sisters of Mercy of New Jersey.*

Properties owned or sponsored: *McAuley Hall McAuley School for the Exceptional Child,* Watchung, NJ; *Georgian Court College of the Sisters of Mercy,* Lakewood, NJ; *Mount Saint Mary Academy,* Watchung, NJ; *Mount Saint Mary House of Prayer Mercy Center,* Asbury Park, NJ; *Center for Peace and Justice.*

Ministry in the field of Religious and Academic Education at all levels; Catholic Charities; Health Care and Hospital Chaplaincy; Diocesan and Tribunal Adminstration; Parish and Prison Ministry; School for Special Education; Day Center for Senior Citizens; Child Day Care Center; House of Prayer.

Represented in the Archdioceses of Detroit, New York, Newark, Philadelphia, Washington and the Dioceses of Camden, Charlotte, Las Cruces, Metuchen, Paterson, Rochester, Santa Rosa and Trenton.

New York P

Regional Community of New York: *Sisters of Mercy,* 150 Ridge Rd., Hartsdale, NY 10530. Tel: 914-328-3200; Fax: 914-328-3761. Sr. Patricia Wolf, R.S.M., Reg. Pres.

Total number in community 222.

Properties owned and sponsored: *Our Lady of Victory Academy,* NY; *St. Catharine Academy,* NY; *Nazareth Home for Boys,* Leicester, MA; *Uihlein Mercy Center (Skilled Nursing Facility),* Lake Placid, NY; *Mercy Healthcare Center, Inc.,* Tupper Lake, NY; *St. Joseph's Home,* Worcester, MA; Co-Sponsor: *Mercy Community Hospital,* Port Jervis, NY.

Ministry in the field of Academic Education at all levels; Health and Child care; Special Education; Social Services; Spirituality and Counseling centers; Catechetical services; Pastoral Ministry.

Represented in the Archdioceses of Boston, Hartford, Los Angeles, New York and the Dioceses of Ogdensburg, Rockville Centre, St. Petersburg and Worcester.

North Carolina P

Sisters of Mercy of the Americas - Regional Community of North Carolina: *Mercy Administration Center,* 101 Mercy Dr., Belmont, NC 28012. Tel: 704-829-5260; Fax: 704-829-5267. Sr. Mary Rosalind Picot, R.S.M., Pres.; Sr. Mary Andrew Ray, R.S.M., Community Archivist.

Total number in the community 135.

Legal Title: *Sisters of Mercy of NC, Inc.*

Ministry in the field of Religious and Academic Education at all levels; Aids Ministry; Pastoral Ministry; Hospitals; Developmental Center for Handicapped Children; Social Work; Religious and Academic Education in the Region of Guam, Saipan and Rota; Daycare and Preshool Centers; Transitional Housing for homeless women and children; Psycho-Spiritual Programs.

Represented in the Archdiocese of Agana, Miami and the Dioceses of Caroline Islands, Chalan Kanoa, Charlotte, Charleston, Lexington, Orlando, Pensacola-Tallahassee, and Wheeling-Charleston.

Omaha P

Regional Community of Omaha: *Sisters of Mercy Regional Office,* 7262 Mercy Rd., Omaha, NE 68124. Tel: 402-393-8225; Fax: 402-393-8145. Sr. Patricia McDermott, R.S.M., Pres.; Sr. Rita Connell, R.S.M., Community Archivist.

Total number in community 265; Associates 97.

Ministry in the field of Education at all levels; Hospitals; Nursing Centers and Long Term Care Facilities for the Aged; Diocesan and Parish programs & services; Social Service; Housing for Families and Elderly.

Properties owned or sponsored: *Knowles Mercy Center,* Waterloo, NE; *Mercy High School,* Omaha, NE; *Health and Retirement Plan of the Sisters of Mercy of the Americas Regional Community of Omaha.* Co-sponsor: *Catholic Health Initiatives,* Denver, CO; *Mercy Housing Inc.,* Denver, CO; *Health System of Mercy,* Omaha, NE; *McAuley Fund,* Omaha, NE.

Represented in the Archdioceses of Chicago, Dubuque, Denver, Detroit, Kansas City in Kansas, Omaha, Philadelphia, Portland (OR), Santa Fe, Seattle, St. Louis, St. Paul-Minneapolis, San Francisco, Washington and the Dioceses of Bismarck, Boise, Cheyenne, Colorado Springs, Des Moines,

Fargo, Fresno, Great Falls-Billings, Kansas City-St. Joseph, Lincoln, Las Cruces, Phoenix, Pueblo, Rochester, Sacramento, Salt Lake City, San Diego, and Springfield-Cape Girardeau. Also in Mexico.

Pittsburgh P

Regional Community of Pittsburgh (1843): 3333 Fifth Ave., Pittsburgh, PA 15213. Tel: 412-578-6225; Fax: 412-578-6180. Sr. Sheila Carney, R.S.M., Pres.; Sr. Patricia Hodge, R.S.M., Community Archivist.

Total number in the community 229.

Ministry in the field of Education and Health Services.

Legal Titles & Holdings: *Carlow College Pittsburgh Mercy Health System, Inc.; The Mercy Hospital of Pittsburgh; Pittsburgh Mercy Foundation; Mercy Center for Chemical Dependency; Mercy Psychiatric Institute; St. Joseph Nursing and Health Care Center, Inc.; St. Pius X Residence,* Pittsburgh, PA; *Holy Cross Health Corporation, Inc.; Holy Cross Hospital,* Fort Lauderdale, FL.

Represented in the Archdioceses of Boston, Baltimore, Hartford, Miami and Washington and the Dioceses of Charleston, Erie, Greensburg, Orlando, Pittsburgh, Raleigh and Richmond. Also in Guatemala, Peru and Puerto Rico.

Portland P

Regional Community of Portland: *St. Joseph's Convent Motherhouse,* 605 Stevens Ave., Portland, ME 04103. Tel: 207-797-7861; Fax: 207-797-0146. Sr. Mary Laboure Morin, R.S.M., Pres.; Sr. Mary Shaun Sevigny, R.S.M., Community Archivist.

Total number in the community 138.

Ministry in the field of Education; Health Services; Catechetical Centers; Social Services.

Represented in the Archdiocese of New York and the Diocese of Portland (ME). Also in the Bahamas and Peru.

Providence P

Regional Community of Providence: *Sisters of Mercy of the Americas,* Highland View Rd., Cumberland, RI 02864. Tel: 401-333-6333; Fax: 401-333-6450. Sr. Barbara Riley, R.S.M., Pres.; Sr. Catherine Felton, R.S.M., Community Archivist.

Total number in community 410.

Sisters serve and staff: Houses of Prayer; Hospitality Houses; Transitional House; Literacy Centers; Nursing Home; University; High Schools; Elementary Schools; Office of Peace and Justice; Diocesan Offices; Pre-School and Day Care; Education for Special Groups; Health Services; Pastoral Care; Religious Education; Parish Ministry Centers; Social Service; Spirituality and Counseling Services; Foreign Missionary work.

Legal Holdings or Titles: *Sisters of Mercy of Providence, Inc.; Mount St. Rita Health Centre, Inc.; Mercymount Country Day School; Mercy Lodge House of Hospitality,* Cumberland, RI; *St. Mary Academy,* East Providence, RI; *Salve Regina University,* Newport, RI; *McAuley House McAuley Village,* Providence, RI.

Represented in the Archdioceses of Baltimore, Boston, Chicago, Hartford, Philadelphia, St. Louis, Washington and the Dioceses of Fall River, Ogdensburg, Phoenix, Pittsburgh, Providence, Richmond and St. Petersburg. Also in Australia, Belize, Ireland and Honduras.

Rochester P

Regional Community of Rochester (1857): 1437 Blossom Rd., Rochester, NY 14610. Tel: 716-228-2710; Fax: 716-288-2756. Sr. Sheila Stevenson, R.S.M., Pres. Tel: 716-482-0552.

Total number in the community 210.

Properties owned: *Our Lady of Mercy High School,* Rochester, NY; *Mercy Prayer Center,* Rochester, NY; *Mercy Motherhouse,* Rochester, NY.

Ministry in the field of Education at all levels; Inner City and Urban Renewal Programs; Religious Education Coords.; Parish Associates; Campus Ministry; Social Work; Rural Ministry; Prayer Ministry; Ministry with the Aging; Hospital Ministry; Parish Visitation; Health Apostolates; AIDS Ministry; Foreign Missions (Chile); Care of Foster Children; Ministry to Pregnant Women; Counselling; Supportive Therapeutic Community for Women Religious.

Represented in the Archdioceses of Atlanta and the Dioceses of Buffalo, Jackson, Phoenix, Rochester and San Jose. Also in Guam and Chile.

St. Louis P

Regional Community of St. Louis: *Sisters of Mercy,* 2039 N. Geyer Rd., St. Louis, MO 63131-3399. Tel: 314-966-4313. Sr. Richard Mary Burke, R.S.M., Reg. Pres.

Total number in community 348.

Ministry in the following areas: Hospitals; Ambulatory Health Care Center; Long Term Care; Social Work Centers; Education Centers; Care and Counseling; Ministry to Elderly; Parish Ministry-Pastoral Care-Lay Ministry; Universities and Colleges; High Schools; Elementary Schools; Education Research Programs; Schools for Exceptional Children; Adult Education; Parish Directors of Religious Education-Coordinator of Religious Education; staffing of Diocesan Offices; Retreat-Renewal; Basic Formation; On-Going Development; Vocation Offices; Novitiate; Creative Spirituality Department/Office of Mercy/Associates-Volunteers.

Properties owned or sponsored: *Mercy Center,* St. Louis, MO. Hospitals: *Sisters of Mercy Health System, St. Louis, Inc. St. Edward Health Facilities of Logan County-dba North Logan Mercy Hospital,* Paris, AR; *St. Edward Mercy Medical Center,* Fort Smith, AR; *St. Edward Health Facilities of Franklin County dba Mercy Hospital/Turner Memorial,* Ozark, AR; *Harbor View Mercy Hospital,* Fort Smith, AR; *Saint Joseph's Regional Health Center, Inc.,* Hot Springs, AR; *St. Edward Health Facilities of Scott County-dba Mercy Hospital of Scott County; Pinewood Nursing Home; Mercy Village,* Waldron, AR; *Mercy Hospitals of Kansas, Inc.-dba Mercy Hospital of Fort Scott,* Fort Scott, KS; *St. Mary's Hospital,* Enid, OK; *Mercy Hospital of Independence,* Independence, KS; *St. John's Mercy Medical Center,* St. Louis, MO; *St. John's Regional Health Center,* Springfield, MO; *St. John's Mercy Hospital,* Washington, MO; *Mercy Health Center, Inc.,* Oklahoma City, OK; *Mercy Hospital of Laredo dba Mercy Regional Medical Center,* Laredo, TX. High Schools: *Mount St. Mary Academy,* Little Rock, AR; *Mount St. Mary High School,* Oklahoma City, OK; *Mercy Crest Housing, Inc.,* Barling, AR.

Convent Corporations: *Sisters of Mercy of the St. Louis Regional Community, Inc.; Sisters of Mercy Education System, St. Louis, Inc.*

Represented in the Archdioceses of Baltimore, Cincinnati, Hartford, Mobile, New Orleans, Oklahoma City, Omaha, St. Louis and San Antonio and in the Dioceses of Amarillo, Baton Rouge, Biloxi, Brownsville, Corpus Christi, Covington, Houma-Thibodaux, Jackson, Jefferson City, Lafayette (LA), Little Rock, Lubbock, Oakland, Pittsburgh, St. Cloud, Springfield-Cape Girardeau and Wichita. Also in Ghana, South Africa.

Vermont P

Regional Community of Vermont: *Mt. St. Mary Motherhouse and Novitiate,* 100 Mansfield Ave., Burlington, VT 05401. Tel: 802-863-6835. Sr. Jeannine Mercure, R.S.M., Pres.

Total number in the community 89.

Properties owned or sponsored: *Trinity College of Vermont, Inc.; Institute for Spiritual Development Mater Christi School Inc.,* Burlington, VT.

Ministry in the field of Education; Parish Ministry.

Represented in the Archdioceses of Hartford and Washington and the Dioceses of Burlington, Ogdensburg and San Bernardino.

[2590] (H.M.S.S.)—SISTERS OF MERCY OF THE BLESSED SACRAMENT P

(Sisters of Mercy of the Blessed Sacrament)

Founded in Mexico in 1910. First foundation in the United States in 1926.

General Motherhouse: Fernandez Leal #130, Coyoacan 04330, Mexico. Mother Guadalupe Aguilar Cancino, H.M.S.S., Supr. Gen.

Regional House: *Blessed Sacrament Convent,* 222 W. Cevallos St., San Antonio, TX 78204. Tel: 210-223-5013; 222-1354. Sr. Dolores Munoz, H.M.S.S., Reg. Supr.

Professed Sisters in U.S. 35; Postulants 1.

Represented in the Archdiocese of San Antonio and the Dioceses of Cleveland, Corpus Christi, San Bernardino and San Diego.

[2600] (S.M.)—SISTERS OF MERCY (CORK AND ROSS) D

General Motherhouse: *St. Columba Convent,* Bishopstown Ave., West Cork, Ireland. Sr. M. Imelda O'Shaughnessy, Supr. Gen.

U.S. Address: *Sacred Heart Convent,* 6240 105th St., Jacksonville, FL 32244. Tel: 904-771-3858. Sr. Regina Fahy, Contact Person.

Represented in the Diocese of St. Augustine.

[2610] (S.M.D.C.)—SISTERS OF MERCY DAUGHTERS OF CHRISTIAN CHARITY OF ST. VINCENT DE PAUL OF (HUNGARY) P

Founded in Hungary in 1842. Mother M. Klara Both, Supr. Gen.

U.S. Foundation: *St. Joseph Home and Convent and Novitiate,* Rte. 1, Box 353 A, 240 Longhouse Dr., Hewitt, NJ 07421. Tel: 201-853-7212. Sr. Mary Louise Horvath, Supr.

Represented in the Diocese of Paterson.

[2630] (S.C.S.C.)—SISTERS OF MERCY OF THE HOLY CROSS P

Founded in Switzerland in 1856. First foundation in the U.S. in 1912.

General Motherhouse: Ingenbohl, Switzerland. Sr. Louise-Henri Kolly, S.C.S.C., Supr. Gen.

U.S. Provincial Residence: *Holy Cross Sisters,* 501 South Center Ave., Merrill, WI 54452; Fax: 715-539-5012. Sr. Mary Anthony Menting, S.C.S.C., Prov.

Total number in community 51.

Legal Title: *Bell Tower Residence, Inc.; Sisters of Mercy of the Holy Cross of Merrill WI Inc.*

Ministry in the following areas: Schools; Hospitals; Home Nursing; Social Ministries; Parishes and Diocesan Offices; Retirement Homes; Adult Education; Campus Ministries.

Represented in the Archdioceses of Cincinnati, Milwaukee, New Orleans, St. Louis and the Dioceses of Belleville, Baton Rouge, Bismarck, Des Moines, Gaylord, Great Falls-Billings,Green Bay, Peoria, Steuvenville and Superior.

[2655] SISTERS OF MERCY OF PORTLAND D

Motherhouse: *Diocesan Sisters of Mercy of Portland,* 265 Cottage Rd., South Portland, ME 04106. Tel: 207-767-5804. Sr. Eunice Boyd, R.S.M.

[2670] (S.O.L.M.)—SISTERS OF OUR LADY OF MERCY

(Mercedarians)

General Motherhouse: via Ostriana 24, Rome, Italy. Mother Luisa Sanchez, Supr. Gen.

Brooklyn: *Most Precious Blood,* 133 27th Ave., Brooklyn, NY 11214. Sr. Doloretta, Supr.

Sisters 4.

St. Edward, Pine Hill NJ, 08021. Sr. Leonilla, Supr.

Sisters 6.

Represented in the Dioceses of Brooklyn and Camden.

[2675] (C.F.M.M.)—MINIM DAUGHTERS OF MARY IMMACULATE P

Founded in Leon, Guanajuato, Mexico 1886. Came to the United States in 1926.

U.S. Regional House: *Minim Daughters of Mary Immaculate,* 555 Patagonia Hwy., Nogales, AZ 85628. Tel: 520-287-3377; Fax: 520-287-2910. Sr. Rosa Maria Ruiz, C.F.M.M., Reg. Supr.

Ministry in Academic and Religious Education and Health Care.

Properties owned: *Our Lady of Lourdes High School,* Nogales, AZ.

Total Sisters in the U.S. 23.

Represented in the Diocese of Tucson.

[2677] (S.M.M.I)—SISTERS MINOR OF MARY IMMACULATE D

First foundation in the United States June 13, 1989. Active- contemplative Franciscan Religious Congregation following the spirituality of St. Maximilian Mary Kolbe, O.F.M.Conv.

Central Motherhouse & Novitiate: Via Germanico 198, 00192 Rome, Italy. Tel: 011-39-6-324-2036. Mother Maria Elisabetta Patrizi, S.M.M.I., Foundress.

American Headquarters - St. Francis Villa: *Vice Province of the Immaculate Conception,* 138 Brushy Hill Rd., Danbury, CT 06810-8431. Tel: 203-744-8041. Sr. Theresa Marie Kovacs, S.M.M.I., Vice Prov. Supr.

Legal Title: *Sisters Minor of Mary Immaculate; Holy Name of Jesus Convent.*

Ministry in the field of Academic and Religious Education; Health Care; Pastoral Care; Newman Centers.

Represented in the Diocese of Bridgeport and Springfield (MA).

[2680] (S.M.)—MISERICORDIA SISTERS P

Founded in Canada in 1848. First foundation in the United States in 1887.

General Motherhouse: 12435 Misericorde Ave., Montreal, Que, Canada, H4J 2G3. Tel: 514-332-0550. Sr. Jeannine Vallieres, Supr. Gen.

U.S. Address: 820 Jungles Ave., Aurora, IL 60505.

Represented in the Archdioceses of Chicago, Milwaukee and New York.

[2690] (M.C.D.P.)—MISSIONARY CATECHISTS OF DIVINE PROVIDENCE, SAN ANTONIO, TEXAS P

Autonomy with Pontifical status granted December 12, 1989.

Administrative House: *St. Andrew's Convent,* 2318 Castroville Rd., San Antonio, TX 78237. Tel: 210-432-0113; Fax: 210-432-1709. Sr. Carmen Therese Lazo, Supr.

Properties owned or sponsored: Benitia Family Center, San Antonio, TX.

Total number in community 52 Novices 1 Candidates 2.

Represented in the Archdiocese of Anchorage, San Antonio and the Dioceses of Austin, Brownsville, Corpus Christi, Dallas, El Paso, Fort Worth, Fresno, Galveston-Houston, Little Rock, Monterey, Oakland, and San Angelo.

[2700] (M.C.SS.CC.J.M.)—MISSIONARY CATECHISTS OF THE SACRED HEARTS OF JESUS AND MARY D

Founded in Mexico City, D.F. in 1918. U.S. foundation in 1943 in Victoria, Texas.

Central House: Mexico City, Mexico. Sr. Hermila Pena, Supr. Gen.

U.S. Provincial Office: 805 S. Liberty St., Victoria, TX 77901. Tel: 512-578-9302. Sr. Eva Sanchez, Prov. Supr.

Total number in U.S. Region 60.

Catechetical familiy ministry in parishes and missions.

Represented in the Dioceses of Fort Worth, Galveston-Houston, Lubbock, Metuchen, Trenton and Victoria.

[2710] (M.C.)—MISSIONARIES OF CHARITY P

Founded in India, 1950.

General Motherhouse: 54A AJC Bose Rd., Calcutta 700016, India. Sr. M. Nirmala, M.C., Supr. Gen.

U.S. Foundation & Office (1971): *Missionaries of Charity,* 335 E. 145th St., Bronx, NY 10451. Tel: 718-292-0019. Sr. M. Sabita, M.C., Reg. Supr.

Professed sisters in congregation 4,500.

Legal Title: *Missionaries of Charity, Inc.*

Sisters serve and staff: Soup Kitchens; Emergency Shelters for Women; Homes for Unwed Mothers; Shelters for Unwed Mothers; Shelters for Men; Religious Education Programs; After-School and Summer Camp Programs for Children; Homes for AIDS Patients; Prison Ministry; Nursing Homes; Hospital and Shut-in Ministry; Family Counseling and Ministry; Home for Infants for Adoption; Foreign Missionary Work.

Represented in the Archdioceses of Atlanta, Baltimore, Boston, Chicago, Denver, Detroit, Los Angeles, Miami, New York, Newark, Philadelphia, San Francisco, St. Louis, Washington and the Dioceses of Baton Rouge, Brooklyn, Charlotte, Dallas, Fall River, Gallup, Lafayette, Lexington, Little Rock, Peoria, Phoenix and Memphis. Also in Canada and Mexico.

[2715] (M.S.C.K.)—MISSIONARY SISTERS OF CHRIST THE KING D

Founded in Poland in 1959 by Father Ignacy Posadzy. First foundation in the U.S. 1978.

General Motherhouse: *Siostry Misjonarki Chrystusa Krola,* ulica Siostr Misjonarek 10, 61-680 Poznan, Poland. Sr. Teresa Ambroza, M.Chr., Supr. Gen.

Delegation Superior in the U.S.: *St. Ferdinand Parish,* 5936 W. Barry Ave., Chicago, IL 60634-5130. Tel: 773-889-7937; Fax: 773-889-7937. Sr. Veronica Ilnicka, M.Chr., Gen. Supr.; Sr. Irena Gertrude Szymanska, M.Chr., Sec.; Sr. Ewa Biniek, M.Chr., Treas.

Legal Title: *Missionary Sisters of Christ the King for Polonia.*

Total in Congregation 198; Professed in U.S. and Canada 22.

Ministry among Polish immigrants and people of Polish heritage.

Represented in the Archdioceses of Chicago, Detroit, Los Angeles and in the Diocese of San Jose. Also in Toronto, Canada.

[2717] (M.D.P.V.M.)—MISSIONARY DAUGHTERS OF THE MOST PURE VIRGIN MARY P

Founded in Mexico. First foundatioin in the United States in the Diocese of Corpus Christi 1916.

General Motherhouse: *Heroe de Nacocariz,* 72 Sur, Aguascalientes, Mexico. Mother Maria Christina Duran Herera, M.D.P.V.M.., Supr. Gen.

Missionary Daughters of the Most Pure Virgina Mary: 919 N. 9th St., Kingsville, TX 78363. Tel: 512-595-1087. Sr. Consuelo Ramirez, M.D.P.V.M.., Supr.; Sr. Carmen Villalpando, M.D.P.V.M., Sec.; Sr. Vicenta Aquilar, M.D.P.V.M., Treas.; Sr. Maria Amada Villarreal, M.D.P.V.M., Mission Dir.

Legal Title: *Missionary Daughters of the Most Pure Virgin Mary.*

Total in Congregation 500; Present in U.S. 31.

in the field of Religious and Academic Education at the elementary level; Pastoral Ministry.

Represented in the Diocese of Camden, Corpus Christi, Brownsville, and Yakima.

[2720] (M.H.S.H.)—MISSION HELPERS OF THE SACRED HEART P

Founded in the United States in 1890.

Mission Helper Center: 1001 W. Joppa Rd., Baltimore, MD 21204-3787. Tel: 410-823-8585; Fax: 410-825-6355. Sr. Catharine Dages, M.H.S.H., Pres.

Total number in community 111.

Legal Title: *Institute of Mission Helpers of Baltimore City.*

Represented in the Archdioceses of Atlanta, Baltimore, Boston, Cincinnati, Detroit, Indianapolis, New York, San Juan (PR), San Antonio, San Francisco, Washington and the Dioceses of Erie, Norwich, Orlando, Raleigh, Richmond, Pensacola-Tallahassee, Pittsburgh, Rochester, St. Petersburg, Tucson, Wilmington, and Youngstown. Also in Venezuela.

[2730] (M.S.H.R.)—MISSIONARY SISTERS OF THE HOLY ROSARY P

Generalate (1924): 23 Cross Ave., Blackrock County Dublin, Ireland. Sr. Monica Devine, Supr. Gen.

U.S. Regional Headquarters (1954): *Missionary Sisters of the Holy Rosary,* 741 Polo Rd., Bryn Mawr, PA 19010. Tel: 610-520-1974. Sr. Paula Molloy, M.S.H.R., Reg. Rep. (U.S. Region).

Total number in community 460.

Represented in the Archdiocese of Philadelphia.

[2740] (M.S.Sp.)—MISSION SISTERS OF THE HOLY SPIRIT D

Motherhouse and Novitiate: 1030 N. River Rd., Saginaw, MI 48609. Tel: 517-781-0934. Sr. Margo Tafoya, Community Coord.

Total number in community 12.

Legal Title: *Society of the Mission Sisters of the Holy Spirit of the Diocese of Saginaw Holy Spirit Sisters Charitable Trust,* Saginaw, MI.

Ministry in Social Services; Religious Education at all levels including Mentally Retarded and Deaf; Pastoral Ministry; Pastoral Administrator.

Represented in the Diocese of Saginaw.

[2750] (I.C.M.)—MISSIONARY SISTERS OF THE IMMACULATE HEART OF MARY P

Founded in India in 1897. First foundation in the United States in 1910.

Generalate: *Via di Villa Troili,* 30, Rome, Italy, 00163. Sr. M. Therese De Coninck, I.C.M., Supr. Gen.

Universal total of congregation 988.

American Province: 238 E. 15th St., New York, NY 10003. Tel: 212-677-2959. Sr. Alene Grothues, I.C.M., Prov.

Total number in community 31.

Missionaries Minister in Education; Catechetical; Pastoral and Social Ministry; Health Care; Ecology; Leprosaria; International Justice and the Promotion of Human Dignity.

Represented in the Archdioceses of Los Angeles, New York and Philadelphia and the Dioceses of Albany and Brownsville. Also in Belgium, Brazil, Burundi, Cameroon, Guatemala, Hong Kong, India, Italy, Philippines, Taiwan, Mongolia, Tchad, Virgin Islands, West Indies and Congo.

[2760] (S.M.I.C.)—MISSIONARY SISTERS OF THE IMMACULATE CONCEPTION OF THE MOTHER OF GOD P

Founded in Brazil in 1910. First foundation in the United States in 1922.

Generalate: 48 Garden Ave., West Paterson, NJ 07424-3325. Tel: 201-279-1484. Sr. Luci Fontenele, S.M.I.C., Coord. Gen.

U.S. Province (1960): *Provincialate of the Immaculate Conception,* P.O. Box 3026, Paterson, NJ 07509-3026. Tel: 201-279-3790; Fax: 201-742-8231. Sr. Margaret Reid, S.M.I.C., Prov. Coord.

Professed Sisters 65.

Properties owned: *Holy Family Residence,* Paterson, NJ.

Sisters serve and staff: Elementary Schools; Universities, Religious Education; Health and Social Services; Sheltered Care Facility for Aged Men and Women.

Represented in the Archdioceses of Newark, San Antonio and Washington and the Dioceses of Austin, El Paso, Gallup, Galveston-Houston, Paterson, Portland (ME), San Bernardino, and Trenton.

[2770] (M.J.M.J.)—MISSIONARIES OF JESUS, MARY AND JOSEPH P

Founded in Spain in 1942. First foundation in United States in 1956. Mother Maria Dolores de la Cruz Domingo, Foundress.

Motherhouse: Plaza de la In. Concepcion No. 1, Madrid, Spain, 28019. Sr. Mary Amparo Munoz Martin, M.J.M.J., Supr. Gen.

Delegation Headquarters and Formation House: 12940 Up River Rd., Corpus Christi, TX 78410. Tel: 512-241-1955. Sr. Avelina Sosa, M.J.M.J., Delegation Supr.; Sr. Angelez Berrozpe, M.J.M.J., Community Supr.

Sisters 25.

Properties owned: *Joseph of the Valley Pre-School,* El Paso, TX.

Represented in the Archdiocese of San Antonio and the Dioceses of Corpus Christi, El Paso. Also in Mexico.

[2780] (M.SS.S.)—MISSIONARY SISTERS OF THE MOST BLESSED SACRAMENT P

General Motherhouse: San Lucas 7, Madrid, Spain. Mother Socorro Musveta, Mother Gen.

U.S. Foundation: *Convent of Mary Immaculate,* 1111 Wordin Ave., Bridgeport, CT 06605. Sr. Presentacion Zabala, Prov.

Formation Center: 1109-1111 Wordin Ave., Bridgeport, CT 06605.

Represented in the Archdioceses of Boston and Newark and the Diocese of Bridgeport.

[2790] (M.S.B.T.)—MISSIONARY SERVANTS OF THE MOST BLESSED TRINITY P

Founded in United States in 1912.

Motherhouse-Generalate-Novitiate and Candidacy: 3501 Solly Ave., Philadelphia, PA 19136. Tel: 215-335-7550. Sr. Siena Marie Wahl, M.S.B.T., Gen. Custodian.

Total number in community 275.

Properties owned and sponsored: *Blessed Trinity Mother Missionary Cenacle,* Philadelphia, PA; *St. Patrick's School,* Phenix City, AL; *Blessed Trinity Shrine Retreat Cenacle,* Holy Trinity, AL; *Trinita Ecumenical Retreat Center,* New Hartford, CT; *Blessed Trinity Missionary Cenacle,* Stirling, NJ; *Blessed Trinity Mother Missionary Cenacle,* Philadelphia, PA.

Represented in the Archdioceses of Boston, Chicago, Hartford, Los Angeles, Newark, Mobile, New York and Philadelphia and the Dioceses of Arlington, Biloxi, Birmingham, Brooklyn, Charleston, Camden, Charlotte, Cleveland, Fall River, Gallup, Harrisburg, Metuchen, Jackson, Paterson, Pensacola-Tallahassee, Raleigh, Richmond, Rockford, Savannah and Syracuse. Also in Puerto Rico and Mexico.

[2800] (M.S.C.)—MISSIONARY SISTERS OF THE MOST SACRED HEART OF JESUS (OF HILTRUP) P

Founded in Germany in 1899. First foundation in the United States in 1908.

Generalate: *Via Martiri di Via Fani,* Sutri (Viterbo), Italy. Sr. MaryAnne Bigos, M.S.C.

American Province-Motherhouse (1908): *St. Michael's Convent,* 51 Seminary Ave., Reading, PA 19605. Tel: 610-929-5751. Sr. Joanne Leblanc, M.S.C., Coord.; Sr. Theresa Lepera, M.S.C., Coord.

MSC Province Center, 2811 Moyers Ln., Reading PA, *19605.* Tel: 610-929-5944. Sr. Marie Clark, M.S.C., Prov.

Total number in U.S. Province 135.

Legal Title: *Missionary Sisters of the Most Sacred Heart of Jesus, Inc.*

Ministry in Education; Health Care; Home Health Care; Parish Ministry; Prison Ministry; Counseling; Social Ministry; Spiritual Ministry.

Properties owned or sponsored: *St. Mary's Hospital,* Athens, GA; *MSC Province Center St. Michael Convent,* Reading, PA.

Represented in the Archdioceses of Atlanta, Philadelphia, Washington, and the Dioceses of Allentown, Galveston-Houston, Harrisburg, Jackson, Venice and Wheeling-Charleston.

[2810] (M.S.M.G.)—MISSIONARY SISTERS OF MOTHER OF GOD D
(Byzantine Ukrainian Rite-Stamford)
Motherhouse: 711 N. Franklin St., Philadelphia, PA 19123. Tel: 215-627-7808; *Novitiate,* 111 W. North St., Stamford, CT 06902. Tel: 203-323-1237. Sr. Josepha, M.S.M.G., Admin.
Total number in community 11.
Ministry in the field of Education.
Represented in the Ukrainian Archdiocese of Philadelphia and in the Ukrainian Diocese of Stamford.

[2820] (M.S.O.L.A.)—MISSIONARY SISTERS OF OUR LADY OF AFRICA P
(Sisters of Africa)
Founded in Algiers, N. Africa, in 1869. First foundation in the United States in 1929.
General Motherhouse: Rome, Italy. Sr. Marie McDonald, Supr. Gen.
Universal total in congregation 1,330.
American Headquarters: 47 West Spring St., Winooski, VT 05404. Tel: 802-655-4003. Sr. Nora Indelicato, M.S.O.L.A., District Supr.
Total number in U.S. 15.
Represented in the Archdiocese of Washington and the Diocese of Burlington.

[2830] (M.O.M.)—MISSIONARY SISTERS OF OUR LADY OF MERCY D
Founded in Piaui, Brazil in 1938. First foundation in United States at Lackawanna, New York 1955.
General Motherhouse: Salvador, Bahia, Brazil. Mother Felicidade Santos, M.O.M., Supr. Gen.
U.S. Headquarters: *Rainbow K,* 388 Franklin St., Buffalo, NY 14202. Tel: 716-854-5198. Sr. M. Neves, M.O.M., Supr.
Total number in community 3.
Represented in the Diocese of Buffalo.

[2840] (M.C.)—POOR CLARE MISSIONARY SISTERS P
Founded in Mexico by Mother Maria Ines Teresa Arias.
General Motherhouse: *Via Cardinale Garampi 17,* Pineta Sachetti, Rome, Italy. Mother Maria Teresa Botello, Gen. Supr.
U.S. Foundation: *Regional House and Novitiate,* 1019 N. Newhope, Santa Ana, CA 92703.
Total number in community 42.
Ministry in Day Nurseries; Schools and; Retreat House.
Represented in the Archdiocese of Los Angeles and the Diocese of Orange.

[2850] (C.P.S.)—MISSIONARY SISTERS OF THE PRECIOUS BLOOD P
Founded in South Africa on Sept. 8, 1885. First founded in the United States at Princeton, New Jersey on August 15, 1925.
Generalate: Casa Generalizia, Suore Missionarie del Preziosissimo Sangue Mariannhill, Via San Giovanni Eudes 93, Roma, Italia, 00163.
Universal number in congregation 970.
American Province: *Novitiate-Precious Blood Convent,* P.O. Box 97, Reading, PA 19607-0097. Tel: 610-777-1624. Precious Blood Convent, 1094 Welsh Rd., Reading, PA 19607. Sr. M. Francis Bisland, C.P.S., Prov. Supr.
Total number in community 24.
Represented in the Diocese of Allentown and Gallup.

[2860] (M.S.C.)—MISSIONARY SISTERS OF THE SACRED HEART OF JESUS P
(Cabrini Sisters)
Founded in Italy in 1880, by Saint Frances Xavier Cabrini. First foundation in the United States 1889.
Motherhouse: *Viale Cortina D'Ampezzo,* 269, Rome, Italy, 00135. Sr. Lina Colombini, M.S.C., Supr. Gen.
Provincial Office: 222 E. 19th St., 5B, New York, NY 10003. Sr. Diane Dalle Molle, M.S.C., Prov. Supr.
Professed Sisters 137; Total in Congregation 600.
Ministry in the field of Education; Hospitals; Nursing Home; Child Care; Parish Ministry; Pastoral Work; Parish Work.
Represented in the Archdioceses of Chicago, Denver, New Orleans, New York, Philadelphia and Seattle and in the Diocese of Brooklyn. Also in Argentina, Australia, Brazil, Central America, England, France, Italy, Philippines, Portugal, Spain, Swaziland and Taiwan.

[2865] (M.S.C.Gpe.)—MISSIONARIES OF THE SACRED HEART OF JESUS AND OUR LADY OF GUADALUPE
National Address: 1212 E. Euclid Ave., Arlington Heights, IL 60004. Tel: 708-398-1350. Sr. Piedad Fernandez, Pres.; Sr. Esperansa Hernandez, Sec.; Sr. Zoila Alcala, Treas.
Ministry in Schools; Nursing Homes; Seminaries and Foreign Missions.
Represented in the Archdiocese of Boston, Chicago, San Francisco and Washington and the Diocese of Rockford.

[2880] (S.S.C.)—MISSIONARY SISTERS OF ST. COLUMBAN P
(Columban Sisters)
Founded in Ireland in 1922. First Foundation in the United States in 1930.
General Motherhouse: Wicklow, Ireland. Sr. Mary Nolan, Congregational Leader.
U.S. Region: *Missionary Sisters of St. Columban,* 73 Mapleton St., Brighton, MA 02135. Tel: 617-782-5683; Fax: 617-789-3569. Sr. Ruth F. Duckert, S.S.C., Reg. Coord.
Professed Sisters 27.
Represented in the Archdioceses of Boston, and the Diocese of Buffalo.

[2890] (M.S.S.A.)—MISSIONARY SERVANTS OF ST. ANTHONY D
Founded in the United States in 1929.
General Motherhouse: 100 Peter Baque Rd., San Antonio, TX 78209-1805. Tel: 210-824-4553. Sr. Mary Ann Domagalski, M.S.S.A., Supr. Gen.
Total number in community 5.
Represented in the Archdiocese of San Antonio.

[2900] (M.S.C.S.)—MISSIONARY SISTERS OF ST. CHARLES BORROMEO
(Scalabrini Sisters)
Founded in Italy in 1895. First United States in 1941.
Motherhouse: *Via Monte del Gallo 68,* Rome, Italy, 00165. Sr. Marisonia Daltoe, Gen.
Universal total in congregation 820.
North American Provincial House: *Bishop Scalabrini Community and Provincial House,* 1414 N. 37th Ave., Melrose Park, IL 60160. Tel: 708-343-2162; Fax: 708-343-6452. Sr. Marciana Zambiasi, M.S.C.S., Prov.
Total number in community 63.
Ministry in the fields of Education; Pastoral Care of the Sick; Catechesis; Social Service.
Represented in the Archdioceses of Chicago, New York and Washington and the Diocese of San Jose. Also in Canada, Mexico and the Philippines.

[2920] (M.D.)—MOTHERS OF THE HELPLESS D
Founded in Malaga, Spain in 1881. Founded in the United States in 1916.
General Motherhouse: *Avda. San Jose de la Montana No.15,* Valencia, Spain, 46008. Mother Esperanza Ordonez, Supr. Gen.
U.S. Address: *Sacred Heart Residence,* 432 W. 20th St., New York, NY 10011. Mother Guadalupe Sordo, M.D., Dir.
Professed Sisters in U.S. 9.
Properties owned and sponsored: San Jose De La Montana Day Nursery Sacred Heart Residence.
Represented in the Archdiocese of New York.

[2930] (I.H.M.)—THE CALIFORNIA INSTITUTE OF THE SISTERS OF THE MOST HOLY AND IMMACULATE HEART OF THE BLESSED VIRGIN MARY P
Founded in Spain in 1848. First foundation in the United States in 1871.
Generalate, Novitiate and Retreat House: 3431 Waverly Dr., Los Angeles, CA 90027. Tel: 213-664-1124.
Professed Sisters 28.
Properties staffed: High Schools; Grammar Schools 2.
Represented in the Archdiocese of Los Angeles.

[2940] (M.H.S.)—SISTERS OF THE MOST HOLY SACRAMENT P
Founded in France in 1851. First foundation in the United States in 1872. Pontifical Approbation 1935.
Generalate: *Sisters of the Most Holy Sacrament,* 313 Corona Dr., P.O. Box 90037, Lafayette, LA 70509-0037. Tel: 318-981-8475. Sr. Judine Theriot, M.H.S., Major Supr.
Total number in community 45.
Legal Title: *St. Augustine Trust Fund,* Lafayette, LA; *Bethany Health Care Center,* Lafayette, LA.
Ministry in the field of Education; Homes for the Aged; Pastoral Care.
Represented in the Archdiocese of New Orleans and the Dioceses of Baton Rouge, Biloxi, Gallup, and Lafayette (LA).

[2950] (N.D.S.)—CONGREGATION OF NOTRE DAME DE SION P
Founded in France in 1850. First foundation in the United States in 1892.
Generalate: Rome, Italy. Sr. Patricia Watson, N.D.S., Supr. Gen.
Universal Total in Congregation 800.
Notre Dame de Sion: 3823 Locust St., Kansas City, MO 64109. Tel: 816-531-1374.
Total number in community 2.
Represented in the Archdiocese of Chicago and the Dioceses of Brooklyn and Kansas City-St. Joseph.

[2960] (N.D.)—NOTRE DAME SISTERS P
Founded in Czechoslovakia, Europe, in 1853. First foundation in the United States in 1910.
General Motherhouse: Hradec Kralove, Czech Republic. Mother M. Purissima Kazdova, Supr. Gen.
U.S. Provincial Motherhouse: *Notre Dame Convent,* 3501 State St., Omaha, NE 68112-1709. Tel: 402-455-2994. Sr. Mary Ann Zimmer, N.D., Prov. Supr.
Total number in community 70.
Sisters staff and serve: Elementary and Secondary Education; Hispanic Ministry; Pastoral Care; Housing for low income elderly; Social Work; Religious Education; Youth Ministry; Chemical Dependency Counseling; Health Care; TEC; Adult Education; Family Life-Diocesan Offices; Community Administration and Services.
Represented in the Archdioceses of Denver, Dubuque, Kansas City in Kansas, Omaha and the Dioceses of Davenport, Kansas City-St. Joseph, Lincoln, Pueblo, Rapid City and Springfield-Cape Girardeau.

[2970] (S.S.N.D.)—SCHOOL SISTERS OF NOTRE DAME P
Founded in Germany in 1833. First foundation in the United States in 1847.
General Motherhouse: Rome, Italy. Sr. Rosemary Horwath, Supr. Gen.
Milwaukee Province (1850) Milwaukee; (1959) Mequon; (1983) Milwaukee: *Motherhouse,* 13105 Watertown Plank Rd., Elm Grove, WI 53122-2291. Tel: 414-782-9850; Fax: 414-782-5725. Sr. Marilyn Kesler, S.S.N.D., Leader.
Total number in community 620.
Legal Title: School Sisters of Notre Dame at Milwaukee, Wisconsin, Inc. School Sisters of Notre Dame at Milwaukee, Wisconsin, Inc. Charitable Trust.
Properties owned: *Mount Mary College,* Milwaukee, WI; *Notre Dame of Elm Grove,* Elm Grove, WI; *Our Lady of Mt. Carmel Convent,* Mt. Calvary, WI.
Various ministries to Women, Youth, the Poor, Sick and Elderly; all levels of Academic Education; D.R.E.s; Pastoral Associates.
Represented in the Archdioceses of Chicago, Detroit, Milwaukee, St. Paul-Minneapolis, Seattle, St. Louis, and the Dioceses of Baker, Davenport, Evansville, Fort Wayne-South Bend, Gary, Gallup, Grand Rapids, Green Bay, Joliet, La Crosse, Lafayette (IN), Lexington, Madison, Marquette, Phoenix, Rockford, Saginaw, Sioux City, Superior, Tulsa, Wheeling-Charleston and Yakima. Also in Africa, Caroline-Marshall Islands, Central America and Guam.
Baltimore Province (1876): *School Sisters of Notre Dame,* 6401 N. Charles St., Baltimore, MD 21212-1099. Tel: 410-377-7774; Fax: 410-377-5363. Sr. Jane Burke, S.S.N.D., Prov. Leader.
Total number in community 417.
Legal Titles and Properties Owned: *School Sisters of Notre Dame in the City of Baltimore; Maria Health Care Center, Inc.; Villa Assumpta-Motherhouse of Baltimore; Province College of Notre Dame of Maryland; Notre Dame Preparatory School; Institute of Notre Dame,* Baltimore, MD.
Ministries to the Needy and Elderly; Teaching and Administering in the field of Academic Education at all levels; D.R.E.'s and Pastoral Associates.
Represented in the Archdioceses of Baltimore, Boston, Hartford, Los Angeles, Miami, Milwaukee, Newark, Philadelphia, St. Louis, San Antonio, Washington and the Dioceses of Arlington, Birmingham, Camden, Charleston, Gary, Greensburg, Harrisburg, Jackson, Lexington, Paterson, Palm Beach, Pittsburgh, Richmond, Rockville Centre, St. Petersburg, Trenton, Tucson, Venice and Wilmington. Also in Boliva, Ghana, Italy, El Salvador and Nigeria.

St. Louis Province (1895): *School Sisters of Notre Dame,* 320 E. Ripa Ave., St. Louis, MO 63125. Tel: 314-544-0455; Fax: 314-544-6754. Sr. Kathleen Wegman, Prov. Supr.

Legal Title: *The School Sisters of Notre Dame of St. Louis.*

Total number in community 686.

Represented in the Archdioceses Atlanta, Baltimore, Boston, Louisville, Los Angeles, New Orleans, Oklahoma City, St. Louis, St. Paul-Minneapolis, San Antonio, Washington and the Dioceses of Albany, Austin, Belleville, Bismarck, Charleston, Dallas, Davenport, Evansville, Fresno, Gallup, Jefferson City, Knoxville, Little Rock, La Crosse Monterey, Orange, Peoria, Rapid City, San Angelo, San Bernardino, San Diego, Shreveport, Sioux City, Springfield-Cape Girardeau, Springfield in Illinois, Tucson, Venice and Winona. Also in Canada, Guatemala, Ghana, Honduras, Japan, Kenya, Mexico, Nepal, South America, Rome and Sierra Leone.

Mankato Province (1912): *School Sisters of Notre Dame,* 170 Good Counsel Dr., Mankato, MN 56001-3138. Tel: 507-389-4200; Fax: 507-345-6679. Sr. Katherine Du Val, Prov.; Sr. Irene Feltz, Community Archivist.

Total number in community 485.

Legal Title: *School Sisters of Notre Dame at Mankato, Minnesota, Inc.; School Sisters of Notre Dame at Mankato, Minnesota, Inc. - Charitable Trust School Sisters of Notre Dame Cooperative Investment Fund.*

Represented in the Archdioceses of Chicago, Dubuque, Miami, Milwaukee, New Orleans, New York, St. Louis, St. Paul-Minneapolis, Seattle, Santa Fe, Washington and the Dioceses of Albany, Alexandria, Bismarck, Brownsville, Bridgeport, Charlotte, Dallas, Duluth, Fargo, Forth Worth, New Ulm, Phoenix, Richmond, Rockford, Sioux City, Sioux Falls, Superior, St. Cloud, Tyler, and Winona. Also in Guatemala and Kenya.

Northeastern Province (1957): *School Sisters of Notre Dame,* Wilton, CT 06897. Tel: 203-762-1220; Fax: 203-762-9434. Sr. Marie Jeannette Blatz, Prov. Leader.

Total number in community 411.

Legal Holdings and Titles: *The Northeastern Province of the School Sisters of Notre Dame in the State of Connecticut Motherhouse and Lourdes Health Care Center,* Wilton, CT; *Academy of the Holy Angels,* Demarest, NJ.

Represented in the Archdioceses of Baltimore, Boston, Hartford, Miami, Newark, New York, Philadelphia and Washington and the Dioceses of Albany, Allentown, Bridgeport, Brooklyn, Camden, Manchester, Metuchen, Norwich, Paterson, Providence, Richmond, Rochester, Rockville Centre and Venice. Also in Brazil, Cape Coast, Chile, Dominican Republic, Ghana, Peru and Puerto Rico.

Dallas Province (1961): *Notre Dame of Dallas - School Sisters of Notre Dame,* P.O. Box 227275, Dallas, TX 75222. Tel: 214-330-9152; Fax: 214-330-9197. Sr. Elizabeth Newman, Prov. Leader.

Total number in community 199.

Legal Title: *School Sisters of Notre Dame of Dallas Charitable Trust.*

Represented in the Archdioceses of New Orleans and San Antonio and in the Dioceses of Alexandria, Biloxi, Baton Rouge, Brownsville, Dallas, El Paso, Fort Worth, Galveston-Houston, Gallup, Houma-Thibodaux, Jackson, Lafayette (LA), Little Rock, Phoenix, San Angelo, Tucson, Tyler and Victoria. Also in Guatemala, Hungary, and West Africa.

Chicago Province: *School Sisters of Notre Dame,* 1431 Euclid Ave., Berwyn, IL 60402. Tel: 708-749-1380. Sr. Catherine Sarther, S.S.N.D., Prov. Leader.

Total number in the community 160.

Properties Owned: *Academy of Our Lady,* Chicago, IL.

Ministry in the field of Academic, Special and Religious Education; Day Care Centers; Foreign Mission work; Nurses; Pastoral Work; Apostolate of the Aging; Vicar for Women Religious.

Represented in the Archdioceses of Baltimore, Chicago, Los Angeles, Miami, Milwaukee, St. Louis, Washington and the Dioceses of Joliet, Lafayette, Peoria and Rockford. Also in Rome, Brazil, Japan and Paraguay.

[2980] (C.N.D.)—SISTERS OF THE CONGREGATION DE NOTRE DAME P

Founded in Canada in 1653. First Foundation in United States in 1860. American Novitiate established at Ridgefield, Connecticut; House of Formation in Staten Island, New York.

General Motherhouse: 4873 Westmount Ave., Montreal, Quebec , Canada.

Generalate: 2330 Sherbrooke St., W., Montreal, Quebec , Canada. Sr. Lorraine Caza, C.N.D., Congregational Leader.

U.S. Province (1946): *Blessed Sacrament Province,* 223 W. Mountain Rd., Ridgefield, CT 06877. Tel: 203-438-5282; Fax: 203-438-3150. Sr. Anne Leonard, C.N.D., Prov. Leader.

Total number in the U.S. Province 199.

Represented in the Archdioceses of Boston, Chicago, Hartford and New York and the Dioceses of Albany, Bridgeport, Brooklyn, Brownsville, Charlotte, Fall River, Jackson, Joliet, Gallup, Pensacola-Tallahassee, Providence, Rapid City, Richmond and Scranton.

[2990] (S.N.D.)—SISTERS OF NOTRE DAME P

Founded in Germany in 1850. First foundation in the United States in 1874.

Generalate: Rome, Italy. Sr. Mary Joell, Supr. Gen.

Universal total in congregation 2,679.

Cleveland Province (1874): *Notre Dame Educational Center - Provincial House, Juniorate, & Novitiate,* 13000 Auburn Rd., Chardon, OH 44024-9330. Tel: 440-286-7101; Fax: 440-286-3377. Sr. Mary Frances Murray, Prov. Supr.; Sr. M. Helen Louise Kist, Prov. Sec.

Legal Titles: *The Corporation of the Sisters of Notre Dame of Cleveland, Ohio The Sisters of Notre Dame Charitable Trust.*

Total number in community 465.

Properties owned and sponsored: *Notre Dame Cathedral Latin School,* Chardon, OH; *Notre Dame College of Ohio,* South Euclid, OH; *Notre Dame Elementary School,* Chardon, OH; *Notre Dame Montessori School,* Chardon, OH; *Regina High School,* Cleveland, OH; *Julie Billiart School,* Lyndhurst, OH.

Ministry in the field of Academic Education at all levels; Special Education for Exceptional Children; Foreign Mission Work; Religious Education; Pastoral Ministry; Diocesan and National Offices; Pastoral Associate and D.R.E.; Adult Literacy; Spiritual Life Ministries; Hispanic & Refugee Outreach; Sick and Elderly in Hospitals and Nursing Homes; Youth Ministry; Campus Ministry; Writing Textbooks for Religion Series.

Represented in the Archdioceses of Chicago, Detroit, Washington and the Dioceses of Arlington, Cleveland, Cincinnati, Lexington, Little Rock, Orlando, Raleigh, St. Petersburg, Scranton, Springfield-Cape Girardeau, Venice and Youngstown.

Covington Province (1924): *Provincial House and Novitiate of the Sisters of Notre Dame,* 1601 Dixie Hwy., (St. Joseph Heights), Covington, KY 41011. Tel: 606-291-2040; Fax: 606-291-1774. Sr. Mary Shauna, S.N.D., Prov.

Total number in the community 182.

Legal Title: Sisters of Notre Dame of Covington, KY Inc.

Ministry in the field of Education; Hospital and Health Care Services; Child Care.

Properties sponsored and owned: *St. Claire Medical Center,* Morehead, KY; *St. Charles Care Center and Village,* Covington, KY; *Notre Academy,* Covington, KY.

Represented in the Archdiocese of Cincinnati and the Dioceses of Birmingham, Covington and Lexington. Also in Hoima, Uganda, and East Africa.

Province of Toledo (1924): *Notre Dame Provincialate, Juniorate & Novitiate,* 3837 Secor Rd., Toledo, OH 43623. Tel: 419-474-5485. Sr. Constance Marie Suchala, S.N.D., Prov. Supr.

Total number in community 303.

Properties owned and sponsored: *Notre Dame Academy; Ladyfield School Maria Child Care Mary Immaculate School Notre Dame School of Music,* Toledo, OH; *Lial Elementary School, Convent & Renewal Center,* Whitehouse, OH; *Holy Trinity Mission,* Papua New Guinea.

Ministry in the field of Education; Specialized Education; Foreign Mission Work; Vocational School.

Represented in the Archdiocese of Detroit and the Dioceses of Fort Wayne-South Bend, Joliet, Lafayette (IN), St. Augustine and Toledo.

Province of Los Angeles (1924): *Notre Dame Provincialate, Juniorate & Novitiate,* 1776 Hendrix Ave., Thousand Oaks, CA 91360. Tel: 805-496-3243; Fax: 805-379-3616. Sr. Mary Amy, Prov. Supr.

Total number in province 90.

Legal Title: *Corporation of the Sisters of Notre Dame of Los Angeles; Notre Dame Academy High School; Notre Dame Academy Elementary School,* Los Angeles, CA; *Notre Dame Center La Reina High School,* Thousand Oaks, CA.

Ministry in the field of Education and Parish Ministry; Catechetics; Foreign Mission Work.

Represented in the Archdiocese of Los Angeles.

[3000] (S.N.D.deN.)—SISTERS OF NOTRE DAME DE NAMUR P

Founded in France in 1804. First foundation in the United States in 1840.

Generalate: Suore di Nostra Signora di Namur, Via Raffaello Sardiello 20, 00165, Rome, Italy. Tel: 011-39-6-6641-8704. Sr. Ellen Gielty, S.N.D.deN., Gen. Moderator.

Office of the General Treasurer: Generalate Offices in the U.S., *Notre Dame Congregational Center,* 30 Jeffrey's Neck Rd., Ipswich, MA 01938. Tel: 978-356-2159; Fax: 978-356-1034. Sr. Marie Kellyn, S.N.D.deN.

Boston Province (1973): *Sisters of Notre Dame de Namur,* 351 Broadway, Everett, MA 02149. Tel: 617-387-2500; Fax: 617-387-1303. Prov. Team: Sr. Lorraine Connell, S.N.D.deN.; Sr. Patricia Conner, S.N.D.deN.; Sr. Noel Doyle, S.N.D.deN.

Total number in community 235.

Legal Title: *The Boston Province of the Sisters of Notre Dame de Namur, Inc.*

Properties owned and sponsored: *Notre Dame Academy,* Worcester, MA; *Notre Dame Children's Class,* Wenham, MA.

Ministry in the field of Academic Educational at all levels; Adult Education Programs; Parish Ministries; Religious Education Programs; and Social Services.

Represented in the Archdioceses of Boston, Hartford, Louisville, New York and Washington and the Dioceses of Albany, Fall River, Gallup, Galveston-Houston, Honolulu, Manchester, Orlando, Portland (ME), Saginaw, Springfield (MA) and Worcester.

Ipswich Province (1973): *Sisters of Notre Dame de Namur Provincialate,* 30 Jeffrey's Neck Rd., Ipswich, MA 01938. Tel: 978-356-4381; Fax: 978-356-9759. Prov. Admin. Team: Sr. Mary A. Farren, S.N.D.deN.; Sr. Marie A. McDonald, S.N.D.deN.; Sr. Therese J. Fitzmaurice, S.N.D.deN.

Total number in community 272.

Legal Title: *Notre Dame Training School, Inc.*

Ministry in all fields of Education; Pastoral Ministry; Health, Social and Community Services; Retreat Work.

Properties owned and sponsored: *Academy of Notre Dame,* Tyngsboro, MA; *Julie Country Day School,* Leominster, MA; *Notre Dame Academy,* Hingham, MA; *Notre Dame Long Term Health Care Facility,* Worcester, MA; *Notre Dame Education Center,* Lawrence, MA; *Cuvilly Arts and Earth Center,* Ipswich, MA.

Represented in the Archdiocese of Boston, Washington, and the Dioceses of Birmingham, Fall River, Manchester, Nashville, Springfield (MA) and Worcester.

Connecticut Province (1959): *The Connecticut Province of the Sisters of Notre Dame de Namur, Inc.,* Sisters of Notre Dame de Namur Province Center, 468 Poquonock Ave., Windsor, CT 06095-2473. Tel: 203-688-1832. Prov. Admin. Team: Sr. Joan Farley, S.N.D.; Sr. Elizabeth McLaughlin, S.N.D.; Sr. Marilyn Pechillo, S.N.D.

Total number in community 162.

Sisters Serve and Staff: Colleges, High Schools, Grammar Schools.

Sisters Engaged in Specialized Educational Programs: Pastoral Ministry and Religious Education, Social Health and Community Services, Diocesan Offices.

Represented in the Archdioceses of Boston, Hartford and the Dioceses of Bridgeport, Burlington, Norwich, Providence, St. Augustine, Springfield (MA) and Worcester.

Baltimore Province (1934): *Sisters of Notre Dame de Namur, Maryland Province Center,* 1531 Greenspring Valley Rd., Stevenson, MD 21153. Tel: 410-486-5599. Sr. Bernadette Glodek, S.N.D., Prov. Moderator. Leadership: Sr. Jeanne McGlone, S.N.D.; Sr. Patricia Loome, S.N.D.

Total in community 154.

Properties owned and sponsored: *Trinity School Maryland Province Center,* Ellicott City, MD; Villa Julie Infirmary. Stevenson, MD; *Maryvale Preparatory School,* Brooklandville, MD; *Notre Dame Academy,* Villanova, PA; *Julie Billiart Residence,* Washington, DC; *The Development Center,* a joint activity of the Maryland, Chesapeake & Notre Dame Base Communities Provinces.

Represented in the Archdioceses of Atlanta, Baltimore, Philadelphia, Washington and the Dioceses of Brooklyn, Portland (ME), Rockville Centre and Wilmington. Also in Japan, Italy and Kenya.

Chesapeake Province (1990): *Sisters of Notre Dame de Namur Provincial Offices,* 305 Cable St., Baltimore, MD 21210-2511. Tel: 410-243-1993; Fax: 410-243-2279. Administrative Team: Sr. Agnes Rose McNally; Sr. Mary Margaret Pignone.

Total number in community 80.

Represented in the Archdioceses of Baltimore, Cincinnati, Miami, New York, Philadelphia and Washington and the Dioceses of Brooklyn, Fort

Wayne-South Bend, Metuchen, Raleigh, Richmond, and Wheeling-Charleston. Also in Brazil, Kenya, Mexico, Peru, Rome and Zaire.

Ohio Province (1840): *Sisters of Notre Dame de Namur Provincial House,* 701 E. Columbia Ave., Cincinnati, OH 45215. Tel: 513-821-7448. Sr. Claire Foley, Prov.

Total number in community 267.

Legal Title: *St. Mary's Educational Institute at Cincinnati; Sisters of Notre Dame de Namur, Ohio Province, Charitable Trust.*

Ministry in the field of Education at all levels; Montessori; Reading Centers; Pastoral Ministry; Administration and Services; Social Services; Communication; Health Care; Community Services.

Represented in the Archdioceses of Boston, Chicago, Cincinnati, Detroit, Indianapolis, Louisville and St. Louis and the Dioceses of Austin, Buffalo, Columbus, Covington, Gallup, Joliet, Lafayette, Lincoln, Memphis, Palm Beach, Phoenix, Saginaw, Salt Lake City, Sioux Falls, Tucson and Trenton. Also in Brazil, Nicaragua, Nigeria, Rome and Zimbabwe.

California Province (1851): *Provincial House Sisters of Notre Dame de Namur,* 14800 Bohlman Rd., Saratoga, CA 95070. Tel: 408-741-0324; Fax: 408-741-5809. Provincial Team: Sr. Claudia McTaggart, S.N.D.deN.; Sr. Jean Stoner, S.N.D.deN.; Sr. Barbara Thiella, S.N.D.deN.

Total number in community 176.

Legal Title: *Sisters of Notre Dame de Namur California Province; Raggio Memorial Trust.*

Ministries Include: Counselors; Convalescent Hospital Ministry; Campus Ministry; Diocesan Administrative Positions; Directors of Religious Education; Health Ministry; Hospice Services; Missionary Work; Parish Ministry; Education at all levels; Religious Education for Adults; Retreat Work; Social Services.

Represented in the Archdioceses of Los Angeles, San Francisco, Seattle and the Dioceses of Baker, Burlington, Des Moines, Fairbanks, Honolulu, Monterey, Oakland, Sacramento, San Jose, Stockton and Wheeling-Charleston.

Base Communities Province (1989): *Sisters of Notre Dame de Namur Base Communities Province Office,* 3037 Fourth St., N.E., Washington, DC 20017. Tel: 202-832-8770. Communications Network: Sr. Marlene Cunningham; Sr. Ann Gormly; Sr. Theresa Kreibick.

Total in Province 50.

Legal Titles: *Sisters of Notre Dame de Namur Base Communities, Inc. S.N.D.B.C. Charitable Trust.*

Ministry in Formal Education; Health Care; Social Services/Community Development; Pastoral Ministry.

Represented in the Archdioceses of Baltimore, Hartford, Philadelphia and Washington and the Dioceses of Brooklyn, Charleston, Harrisburg, Orlando, Richmond and Wilmington.

[3010] (O.S.B.S.)—OBLATE SISTERS OF THE BLESSED SACRAMENT — D

Founded in 1935 by Rev. Sylvester Eisenman, O.S.B.

Motherhouse: *St. Sylvester's Convent,* P.O. Box 217, Marty, SD 57361. Tel: 605-384-3305; Fax: 605-384-5886. Sr. Patricia Mylott, O.S.B.S., Supr.

Associate & Formation House: *Kateri Convent,* 624 Adams St., Rapid City, SD 57701. Tel: 605-343-6261.

Total number in community 7.

Represented in the Dioceses of Rapid City and Sioux Falls.

[3020] (O.B.T.)—SISTERS OBLATES TO THE BLESSED TRINITY — D

Founded in Italy in 1923. First foundation in the United States in 1987.

General House: New York, NY.

U.S. Novitiate: *St. Aloysius Gonzaga Novitiate,* Beekman Rd., Hopewell Junction, NY 12533. Tel: 914-226-5671. Mother Gloria Castro, Supr. Gen.

Total number in community 42.

Represented in the Archdiocese of New York and the Diocese of Madison. Also in Archdiocese of San Juan and the Diocese of Ponce, PR.

[3030] (O.SS.R.)—OBLATES OF THE MOST HOLY REDEEMER — P

Founded in Madrid in 1864.

Motherhouse: Ciempozuelos, Madrid, Spain. Analita Albani, Mother Gen.

U.S. Foundation: *Our Lady of the Way Residence,* 60-80 Pond St., Jamaica Plain, MA 02130. Tel: 617-524-1640. Sr. Matilde Murillo, Supr.

Total number in community 3.

Represented in the Archdioceses of Boston and New York. Also in Puerto Rico.

[3035] (O.M.O.)—OBLATES OF THE MOTHER OF ORPHANS — P

Founded in Italy on September 8, 1945.

General Motherhouse: via Amundsen 10, Milano, Italy. Sr. Lucilla Passoni, General Supr.

Universal Total in Congregation 200.

U.S. Address: 20 E. 72nd St., New York, NY 10021. Sr. Maria Isabel Reina, O.M.O., Supr.

Total in community 3.

Represented in the Archdiocese of New York. Also in Cameroon, Colombia, El Salvador, Guatemala and Italy.

[3040] (O.S.P.)—OBLATE SISTERS OF PROVIDENCE — P

Founded in the United States in 1829.

General Motherhouse: *Our Lady of Mount Providence Convent,* 701 Gun Rd., Baltimore, MD 21227. Tel: 410-242-8500. Sr. Mary Claudina Sanz, O.S.P., Supr. Gen.; Sr. Mary Alexis Fisher, O.S.P., Asst. Supr. Gen.; Sr. Naomi Smith, O.S.P., Sec. Gen.; Sr. Mary Joetta McGill, O.S.P., Treas. Gen.

Professed Sisters 135.

Legal Title: *The Oblate Sisters of Providence of the City of Baltimore.*

Sisters serve as: Pastoral Ministry-Associates; in the field of Education; Reading Centers; Day Care Centers; Teaching; Counseling; Hispanic & Migrant ministry.

Represented in the Archdioceses of Baltimore, Chicago, Detroit, Mobile, Philadelphia and Washington and the Dioceses of Buffalo, Charleston, Rockford and Trenton. Also in Costa Rica and the Dominican Republic.

[3050] (O.S.H.J.)—OBLATE SISTERS OF THE SACRED HEART OF JESUS — P

Founded in 1894. First foundation in the United States in 1949.

General Motherhouse: Rome, Italy.

American Headquarters: *Villa Maria Teresa,* 50 Warner Rd., Hubbard, OH 44425. Tel: 330-759-8468; Fax: 330-759-7290. Sr. Joyce Candidi, O.S.H.J., Supr.

Total number in the community 22.

Represented in the Dioceses of Pittsburgh and Youngstown.

[3060] (O.S.F.S.)—OBLATE SISTERS OF ST. FRANCIS DE SALES — P

Founded in France in 1866. First foundation in the United States in 1951.

General Motherhouse: 10 rue des Terrasses, Troyes, France.

American Headquarters: *Villa Aviat Convent,* Childs, MD 21916. Tel: 410-398-3699. Sr. Anne Elizabeth, O.S.F.S., Supr.

Total number in the community 14.

Ministry in the field of Academic and Religious Education; Retreat work; Summer Camp.

Represented in the Archdiocese of Philadelphia and the Diocese of Wilmington.

[3070] (N.A.U.-O.L.C.)—NORTH AMERICAN UNION SISTERS OF OUR LADY OF CHARITY — P

Founded in Caen, France in 1641, by St. John Eudes. First foundation in the United States in 1855.

The primary work of the Sisters of Our Lady of Charity, is to devote themselves to the needs of women and girls in residential and non-residential settings, also nursing homes, day care centers, teaching, pastoral ministries, CCD program, parish ministry, English and Spanish speaking.

The Autonomous Houses were Federated in 1944 and March 21, 1979 the North American Union of the Sisters of Our Lady of Charity was established and approved by Rome.

North American Union of the Sisters of Our Lady of Charity.

Administration Office: 154 Edgington Ln., Wheeling, WV 26003-1535. Tel: 304-242-0042; Fax: 304-242-8981. Sr. Deana Kohlman, Supr. Gen.

Madison

General Motherhouse and Administrative Centre, Box 327, Wisconsin Dells, WI 53965.

Total Sisters Membership 141.

Legal Title: *North American Union of the Sisters of Our Lady of Charity, Inc.*

Canonical Formation, Wisconsin Dells, WI.

North American Union Sisters of Our Lady of Charity, 1930 Illion St., San Diego, CA 92110. Tel: 619-275-0764.

North American Union Sisters of Our Lady of Charity, St. Andrew's Retreat House, 257 St. Andrew's Rd., Walden, NY 12586. Tel: 914-778-5941. Sr. Ellen Patrick Stapleton, Business Mgr.

North American Union Sisters of Our Lady of Charity 2140 Cottage St., Fort Myers, FL 33901. Tel: 813-337-4550. Sr. Rosa Hernandez, Local Supr.

Represented in the Archdioceses of New York and San Antonio and the Diocese of Buffalo, El Paso, Erie, Green Bay, Madison, Pittsburgh, Rochester, San Diego, Venice and Wheeling-Charleston. Also in Canada and Mexico.

Buffalo

North American Union of the Sisters of Our Lady of Charity: 3800 Howard Rd., Hamburg, NY 14075. Tel: 716-648-4988. Sr. Rosemary Toth, Local Supr.

Legal Title: *Sisters of Our Lady of Charity of Refuge, Inc.*

El Paso

North American Union of Our Lady of Charity: 415 N. Glenwood Dr., El Paso, TX 79905. Tel: 915-722-0737. Sr. Yolanda Martinez, Local Supr.

San Juan Day Care Centre, Inc., 5636 Frutas Ave., El Paso, TX 79905. Tel: 915-772-1681. Sr. Cruz Cecilia Gomez, Admin.

Legal Title: *North American Sisters of Our Lady of Charity, Inc.*

Erie

North American Union of the Sisters of Our Lady of Charity (1934): 4635 East Lake Rd., Erie, PA 16511. Tel: 814-899-1052. Sr. Carol Pregno, Local Supr.

Legal Title: *Gannondale Residential Center for Girls,* Erie, PA; *North American Union Sisters of Our Lady of Charity, Inc.*

Green Bay

North American Union of the Sisters of Our Lady of Charity: 2560 Shawano Ave. - P.O. Box 10357, Green Bay, WI 54307. Tel: 920-494-8747. Sr. Barbara Jean Arnsmeyer, Local Supr.

Legal Title: *Sisters of Our Lady of Charity of the North American Union, Inc. McClosky Program, Inc.*, Green Bay, WI.

Pittsburgh

North American Union of the Sisters of Our Lady of Charity: *Nativity Convent,* 4100 Vinceton St., Pittsburgh, PA 15214. Tel: 412-931-2299. Sr. Thomas Aul, Local Supr.

Legal Title: *North American Union Sisters of Our Lady of Charity, Inc.; Eudes Institute.*

Rochester

North American Union Sisters of Our Lady of Charity: 1280 Winton Rd. N., Rochester, NY 14609. Tel: 716-654-8600. Sr. Frances Aguillon, Local Supr.

Legal Title: *Sisters of Our Lady of Charity of Refuge, Inc.*

San Antonio

North American Union Sisters of Our Lady of Charity (1897): 1900 Montana St., San Antonio, TX 78203. Tel: 210-534-1231. Sr. Agnes O'Mahony, Local Supr.

Legal Title: *North American Union Sisters of Our Lady of Charity, Inc.; Our Lady of Victory School.*

Walden

North American Union of the Sisters of Our Lady of Charity: 257 St. Andrew's Rd., Walden, NY. Tel: 914-778-5941. Sr. Ellen Patrick Stapleton, Business Mgr.

Legal Title: *St. Andrew's Retreat House.*

Wheeling

North American Union Sisters of Our Lady of Charity: 141 Edgington Ln., Wheeling, WV 26003. Tel: 304-242-7070. Sr. Martha Teresa Gomez, Local Supr.

Legal Title: *North American Union Sisters of Our Lady of Charity, Inc.*

[3071] (O.L.C.)—SISTERS OF OUR LADY OF CHARITY — P

Mt. St. Michael Convent of Our Lady of Charity: 4500 W. Davis St., Dallas, TX 75211. Tel: 214-331-1754. Sr. Margaret McCaffrey, Supr.

Total number in the community 17.

Legal Holding: *Mt. St. Michael Spiritual Life Center.*

[3072] (R.O.L.C.)—OUR LADY OF CHARITY OF REFUGE — P

Monastery of Our Lady of Charity of Refuge: 1125 Malvern Ave., Hot Springs, AR 71901. Tel: 501-623-9651. Sr. Theresa Marie Lalancette, Supr.

Total number in the community 13; Professed Novices 1.

[3073] (O.L.C.)—SISTERS OF OUR LADY OF CHARITY P

Sisters of Our Lady of Charity: 620 Roswell Rd., N.W., Carrollton, OH 44615-9399. Tel: 216-627-7647; Fax: 216-627-4411. Sr. Mary Kevin Crain, Supr.

Total number in community 19.

[3080] (R.C.D.)—SISTERS OF OUR LADY OF CHRISTIAN DOCTRINE D

Founded in New York in 1910 for the work of religious education and social service.

Central Office: *Marydell Center,* 23 Haskell Ave., Suffern, NY 10901. Tel: 914-357-0046. Sr. Virginia Johnson, R.C.D., Pres.

Total number in the community 38.

Ministry in the field of Religious Education in Parish Centers and Parishes; Social Work and Counseling.

Represented in the Archdioceses of Chicago and New York and the Diocese of Manchester. Also in the Dominican Republic.

[3090] (C.L.H.C.)—CONGREGATION OF OUR LADY, HELP OF THE CLERGY D

Maryvale Sisters

Founded in the United States in 1961.

Motherhouse: *Maryvale Motherhouse,* 2522 June Bug Rd., Vale, NC 28168. Tel: 704-276-2626. Mother Mary Louis, Supr.

Total number in the community 5.

Represented in the Diocese of Charlotte.

[3100] (R.S.R.)—CONGREGATION OF OUR LADY OF THE HOLY ROSARY P

Founded in Rimouski, P.Q., Canada, in 1874. First Foundation in the United States in 1899.

General Motherhouse: 300 Alle du Rosaire, Rimouski, P. Q. Canada, G5L 3E3. Tel: 418-724-5940. Sr. Ida Cote, R.S.R., Supr. Gen.

U.S. Address: *Our Lady of the Holy Rosary,* 20 Thomas St., Portland, ME 04102. Tel: 207-774-3756; 772-3130 (Office). Sr. Carole Jean Lappa, R.S.R., Reg. Supr.

Total number in the region 10.

Our Lady of the Holy Rosary Regional House, 25 Portland Ave., Old Orchard Beach, ME 04064. Tel: 207-934-0592.

Ministry in the fields of Education; Diocesan Ministry; Retreat Ministry.

Represented in the Diocese of Portland (ME).

[3105] (S.O.L.T.)—OUR LADY OF THE MOST HOLY TRINITY CONVENT D

General Mother House: P.O. Box 189, Skidmore, TX 78389. Tel: 512-287-3146. Sr. Mary of the Redemption Mansfield, S.O.L.T., Gen. Sister Servant.

Professed Sisters 50; Novices 14; Candidates 6.

Represented in the Archdiocese of Santa Fe and in the Dioceses of Corpus Christi and Kansas City-St. Joseph.

[3110] (R.C.)—CONGREGATION OF OUR LADY OF THE RETREAT IN THE CENACLE P

Founded in France in 1826. First foundation in the United States in 1892.

Generalate: Piazza Madonna del Cenacolo, 15, Rome, Italy, 00136.

Eastern Province N.A. (1892): *The Cenacle of St. Regis, Inc.,* 310 Cenacle Rd. - P.O. Box 2429, Ronkonkoma, NY 11779-0408. Tel: 516-471-6270. Sr. Kathleen O'Brien, R.C., Prov.

Total number in community 105.

Properties owned and sponsored: *Cenacle of St. Regis, Inc.,* Rockville Centre, NY; *The Religious of Our Lady of the Cenacle of New Brunswick, NJ,* Metuchen, NJ; *Cenacle Center for Spiritual Renewal,* Brooklyn, NY; *Convent of Our Lady of the Cenacle of Rochester, NY,* Rochester, NY; *Ronkonkoma Cenacle, Inc.,* Rockville Centre, NY; *The Cenacle Convent of Palm Beach Co., Inc.,* Palm Beach, FL.

Represented in the Archdioceses of Atlanta, Boston and New York and the Dioceses of Arlington, Brooklyn, Metuchen, Rochester, Rockville Centre, Palm Beach and Wheeling-Charleston. Also in Ghana.

Midwestern Province (1946): *Congregation Of Our Lady of the Cenacle,* 513 Fullerton Pkwy., Chicago, IL 60614. Tel: 773-528-6300. Sr. Marguerite Gautreau, Prov.

Total number in community 91.

Properties owned and sponsored: *Cenacle Convent, Inc.,* Chicago, IL; *Cenacle Convent, Inc.,* Houston, TX; *Convent of Our Lady of the Cenacle,* Metairie, LA; *Warrenville Cenacle Retreat House,* Warrenville, IL; *Cenacle Retreat House,* Wayzata, MN.

Represented in the Archdioceses of Chicago, Milwaukee, New Orleans, San Antonio, St. Louis, St. Paul-Minneapolis and the Dioceses of Denver, Galveston-Houston, Joliet, Madison, Oakland and Sacramento. Also in Canada, Ghana and Rome, Italy.

[3120] (O.L.S.)—SISTERS OF OUR LADY OF SORROWS P

Founded in Italy in 1839. First foundation in the United States in 1947.

General Motherhouse: *Viale Vaticano 90,* Rome, Italy, 00165. Mother Vilge Terzanelli, O.L.S., Supr. Gen.

American Headquarters: *Sisters of Our Lady of Sorrows Convent,* 9894 Norris Ferry Rd., Shreveport, LA 71106; Fax: 318-797-7003. Sr. Mavis Champagne, O.L.S., Supr.

Total number in community 33.

Ministry in the field of Education; Work with people with mental retardation; Outreach to the poor; Pastoral Ministry; CCD & Adult Education.

Represented in the Dioceses of Alexandria and Shreveport.

[3130] (O.L.V.M.)—OUR LADY OF VICTORY MISSIONARY SISTERS P

Founded in the United States in 1922.

Motherhouse: *Victory Noll,* Box 109, Huntington, IN 46750. Tel: 219-356-0628; Fax: 219-356-0628. Sr. Lucy Regalado, Pres.

Total number in the community 209.

Legal Holding: *Victory Noll Sisters Community Support Trust.*

Represented in the Archdioceses of Chicago, Cincinnati, Denver, Detroit, Dubuque, Kansas, Los Angeles, Louisville, Miami, Milwaukee, Oklahoma City, Omaha, San Antonio, Santa Fe and the Dioceses of Austin, Belleville, Charlotte, Cheyenne, Cleveland, Fort Wayne-South Bend, Gary, Helena, Jefferson City, Kansas City-St. Joseph, Las Cruces, Lubbock, Oakland, Orlando, Phoenix, Pueblo, Salt Lake City, San Bernardino, San Diego, Toledo and Tucson.

[3140] (C.S.A.C.)—SISTERS OF THE CATHOLIC APOSTOLATE (PALLOTTINE) P

Founded in Italy in 1835. First foundation in the United States in 1889.

General Motherhouse: Viale Kennedy No. 62, Grottaferrata, Rome, Italy. Mother M. Ivete Garlet, C.S.A.C., Supr. Gen.

Universal total in congregation 650.

Provincial Motherhouse in America: *St. Patrick's Villa,* Harriman Heights, P.O. Box 118, Harriman, NY 10926. Tel: 914-783-9007. Sr. Michele Ruggiero, C.S.A.C., Prov. Moderator.

Novitiate , Pallottine House of Formation, Box 350, Harriman, NY 10926. Tel: 914-774-7585.

Total number in the community 70.

Ministry in the field of Academic and Religious Education at Elementary and Secondary Levels; Pastoral Services.

Represented in the Archdioceses of Newark and New York and the Diocese of Brooklyn.

[3150] (S.A.C.)—PALLOTTINE MISSIONARY SISTERS - QUEEN OF APOSTLES PROVINCE P

(Missionary Sisters of the Catholic Apostolate)

Founded in Rome, Italy, in 1838. First founded in the United States in 1912.

General Motherhouse: Rome, Italy. Sr. Maria Knaus, S.A.C., Supr. Gen.

American Provincialate: *Pallottine Renewal Center,* 15270 Old Halls Ferry Rd., Florissant, MO 63034. Tel: 314-837-7100; Fax: 314-837-2385. Sr. M. Elisabeth Heptner, S.A.C., Prov.; Sr. Phyllis Carpenter, S.A.C., Community Archivist.

Total number in the community 720.

Properties Owned: *Pallottine Renewal Center,* Florissant, MO; *Frascati Convent,* Londell, MO; *St. Mary's Hospital & Convent,* Huntington, WV; *Vincent Pallotti House,* Huntington, WV; *St. Joseph's Hospital & Convent,* Buckhannon, WV; *St. Vincent Pallotti Convent, High School & Child Care Center,* Laurel, MD.

Sisters minister in the fields of Health Care; Child Day Care; Education; Retreat and Renewal Ministry; Social Services; Counseling; Parish and Pastoral Work.

Represented in the Archdioceses of St. Louis and Washington and the Diocese of Wheeling-Charleston.

[3160] (P.V.M.I.)—PARISH VISITORS OF MARY IMMACULATE P

Founded in New York City in 1920 for family visitation and religious education.

Motherhouse, Juniorate and Novitiate: *Marycrest,* P.O. Box 658, Monroe, NY 10950-0658. Tel: 914-783-2251. Sr. Carole Marie Troskowski, Gen. Supr.; Sr. Rita Mairelenes, Juniorate Dir.; Sr. Frances Walter, Gen Sec.

Total number in community 77.

Serving the Church in the Pastoral Ministry as a bridge between the people and their pastor and associates; Visitation and Religious Education in Parishes and Catechetical Centers.

Represented in the Archdiocese of New York and the Dioceses of Brooklyn, Burlington, Norwich, Ogdensburg, Scranton and Syracuse. Also in the Diocese of Okigwe, Nigeria.

[3170] (C.P.)—RELIGIOUS OF THE PASSION OF JESUS CHRIST P

(Passionist Nuns)

Founded in Italy in 1771, by St. Paul of the Cross. First foundation in the United States in 1910.

Our Lady of Sorrows Convent of the Passionist Nuns (Contemplative): 2715 Churchview Ave., Pittsburgh, PA 15227. Tel: 412-881-1155. Mother Mary Ann, C.P., Supr.

Total number in community 9.

The Religious of the Passion of Jesus Christ (Contemplative) (1926): *St. Gabriel's Monastery,* 631 Griffin Pond Rd., Clarks Summit, PA 18411. Tel: 717-586-2791. Sr. Helen Gallagher, C.P., Pres.

Professed Sisters 15.

Legal Holding: *St. Gabriel's Monastery and Retreat Center.*

Sisters serve and staff: Retreats and other Programs for Women and Men of all Faiths; Clergy and Religious; Ecumenical Groups; Business and Civic Groups.

Passionist Nuns (Cloistered Contemplative) (1946): *St. Joseph's Monastery,* 8564 Crisp Rd., Whitesville, KY 42378. Tel: 502-233-4571. Sr. Mary Agnes, C.P., Supr.

Professed Nuns 18.

Passionist Nuns (Contemplative) (1947): *Monastery of the Sacred Passion,* 1151 Donaldson Hwy., Erlanger, KY 41018. Tel: 606-371-8568. Sr. Margaret Mary, C.P., Supr.

Legal Title: *Passionist Nuns of Covington, KY.*

Total number in community 9.

Passionist Nuns (Cloistered) (1947): *Immaculate Conception Monastery,* 15700 Clayton Rd., Ellisville, MO 63011-2300. Tel: 314-227-5275. Mother Mary Salvador, C.P., Supr.

Total number in community 13.

[3180] (C.P.)—SISTERS OF THE CROSS AND PASSION P

(Passionist Sisters)

Founded in 1852. First foundation in the United States 1924. Generalate located at 17 Elwes Way, Great Billing, Northampton, NNE 4EA England. Mother Margaret Mary Sheehy, Supr. Gen.

Motherhouse-American Provincial Office: *Holy Family Convent,* One Wright Ln., North Kingstown, RI 02852. Tel: 401-294-3554. Sr. Eileen Fucito, C.P., Prov.

Professed Sisters 47.

Sisters minister in Retreat Houses; Elementary and Secondary Education; Hospital Chaplaincy; Parish Ministry; Religious Education; Chancery and Tribunal Offices.

Properties owned and operated: *Our Lady of Calvary Retreat,* Farmington, CT.

Represented in the Archdioceses of Hartford, Los Angeles, New York and the Dioceses of Providence and Rockville Centre. Also in Jamaica, West Indies.

[3190] (A.P.)—NUNS OF THE PERPETUAL ADORATION OF THE BLESSED SACRAMENT P

Founded in Rome in 1807. First foundation in United States in 1925.

El Paso: *Expiatory Shrine of Christ the King and Monastery of Perpetual Adoration,* 145 N. Cotton Ave., El Paso, TX 79901. Tel: 915-533-5323. Mother Maria de Jesus, A.P., Supr.

Sisters 20.

Represented in the Archdioceses of Anchorage and San Francisco and the Diocese of El Paso.

San Francisco: *Monastery of Perpetual Adoration,* 771 Ashbury St., San Francisco, CA 94117. Tel: 415-566-2743. Mother Rosalba Maria, A.P., Supr.

Sisters 23.

Represented in the Archdiocese of San Francisco. Also in Africa, Chile, Mexico and Spain.

[3195] (A.P.G.)—SISTER OF PERPETUAL ADORATION OF GUADALUPE, INC. P

U.S. Foundation: 2403 W. Travis, San Antonio, TX 78207. Tel: 210-227-5546. Sr. Luz del Carmen Sanchez, A.P.G., General Counsel.
Total number in community 7.

[3200] (Sch.P.)—SISTERS OF THE PIOUS SCHOOLS (Escolapias) P

Founded in Figueras, Spain in 1829.
Universal total in congregation 844.
General Motherhouse: Via Crescenzio 77, Rome, Italy, 00193. Mother Isolina Vasquez, Sch.P., Supr. Gen.
U.S. Headquarters (1954): 17601 Nordhoff St., Northridge, CA 91325. Tel: 818-882-5265; Fax: 818-718-6752. Sr. Maria Jesus Jurado, Sch.P., Vice Prov.
Total number in community 26.
Ministry in Religious Education; Parish Schools.
Represented in the Archdiocese of Los Angeles.

[3210] (P.C.P.A.)—POOR CLARES OF PERPETUAL ADORATION P

Founded in France, 1854. First foundation in the United States at Cleveland, Ohio, 1921.
Poor Clares of Perpetual Adoration, cloistered, contemplative, solemn vows. Object: Perpetual Adoration in spirit of Praise and Thanksgiving, and Gospel living. Solemn Exposition day and night. Each monastery is autonomous
Sancta Clara Monastery (1946): 4200 N. Market Ave., Canton, OH 44714. Sr. Kay Marie, Abbess.
Total number in community 13.
Saint Joseph Adoration Monastery (1956): 2311 Stockham Ln., Portsmouth, OH 45662-3049. Tel: 614-353-4713. Mother M. Agnes, Abbess.
Total number in community 7.
Legal Holdings and Titles: *Poor Clares of Perpetual Adoration; St. Joseph Adoration Monastery.*
Adoration Monastery (1921): 4108 Euclid Ave., Cleveland, OH 44103. Tel: 216-361-0783. Mother Mary James, P.C.P.A., Abbess.
Total number in community 23 Novices 1.
Poor Clares of Perpetual Adoration (1954): Our Lady of the Most Blessed Sacrament Monastery, 3900 13th St., N.E., Washington, DC 20017. Tel: 202-526-6808. Mother Margaret Mary, P.C.P.A., Abbess.
Total number in community 10.
Our Lady of the Angels Monastery: 5817 Old Leeds Rd., Birmingham, AL 35210. Tel: 205-956-5987; Fax: 205-271-2927. Mother M. Angelica, P.C.P.A., Abbess & Pres.
Total number in community 32: Novices 3; Postulants 2; Members of the Lay Missionaries of the Eternal Word 50.
Properties owned or sponsored: *Eternal Word Television Network, Inc. (EWTN); WEWN Shortwave Radio Network; EWTN Catholic Publisher, global television, radio and book apostolates.*
Legal Titles: *Eternal Word Television Network, Inc. (EWTN); WEWN Shortwave Radio Network.*
Represented in the Diocese of Birmingham.

[3220] (P.C.J.)—SISTERS OF THE POOR CHILD JESUS P

Founded on February 2, 1844 in Germany. First founded in the United States on July 2, 1924 at Parkersburg, West Virginia.
General Motherhouse: *Haus Loreto,* Simpelveld, Netherlands. Rev. Mother Clare Angela, P.C.J., Supr. Gen.
Universal number in congregation 850.
American Region and Novitiate: *Our Lady of Bethlehem Convent,* 4567 Olentangy River Rd., Columbus, OH 43214. Tel: 614-451-3900; Fax: 614-451-4745. Sr. Frances Teresa Holzberger, P.C.J., Reg. Supr.
Total number in community 7.
Ministry in the field of Education.
Properties owned: Kindergarten and a Day Care Center.
Represented in the Dioceses of Columbus and Wheeling-Charleston.

[3230] (P.H.J.C.)—POOR HANDMAIDS OF JESUS CHRIST P

(The Ancilla Domini Sisters)

Founded in Germany in 1851. First foundation in the United States in 1868.
General Motherhouse: Dernbach, Westerwald, Germany. Sr. M. Germaine Hustedde, P.H.J.C., Supr. Gen.
American Province-Provincialate: *Convent Ancilla Domini,* Donaldson, IN 46513. Tel: 219-936-9936; Fax: 219-935-1785. Sr. Jolise May, P.H.J.C., Prov. Councilors: Sr. Mary Josef Shingler, P.H.J.C.; Sr. Shirley Bell, P.H.J.C.; Sr. Joetta Huelsman, P.H.J.C.; Sr. Margaret Anne Henss, P.H.J.C., Treas.; Ms. Mary Chudzynski, Dir. Devel.; Sr. M. Cecelia Bianchino, P.H.J.C., Archivist.
Professed Sisters 216.
Properties owned or sponsored: *Ancilla Domini College; Convent Ancilla; Domini Maria Center; Catherine Kasper Home; Lindenwood Retreat & Ministry Center Earthworks, Inc.; Poor Handmaids of Jesus Christ Community Support Trust,* Donaldson, IN; *Ancilla Domini Convent,* Milwaukee, WI; *Ancilla Domini Hospitals Self Insurance Trust St. Catherine Convent,* East Chicago, IN; *Annunciation Convent,* Hoffman Estates, IL; *Poor Handmaids of Jesus Christ,* 1916 S. Clarence Ave., Berwyn, IL 60402; *Mary Katherine Convent,* Cairo, IL; *Marian Convent St. Joseph Medical Center,* Fort Wayne, IN; *Beacon House,* Burlington, IA; *Catherine Kasper Center, St. Mary Hospital, St. Mary Convent,* East St. Louis, IL; *Ancilla Systems, Inc. St. Mary Medical Center,* Hobart, IN; *St. Elizabeth Hospital,* Chicago, IL; *St. Catherine Hospital,* East Chicago, IL; *St. Joseph Mishawaka Health Services, Inc.,* Mishawaka, IN.
Ministry in the field of Academic Education at all levels; Hospitals; Parish Ministries; Retreat Ministries; Child Care Institutions; and Retirement Homes.
Represented in the Archdioceses of Chicago, Cincinnati, Milwaukee, St. Paul-Minneapolis and the Dioceses of Belleville, Covington, Davenport, Fort Wayne-South Bend, Gary, Joliet, Lansing, Peoria, Savannah, Springfield (IL), Springfield-Cape Girardeau, and Wilmington. Also in Brazil, Germany and Mexico.

[3240] (C.J.C.)—POOR SISTERS OF JESUS CRUCIFIED AND THE SORROWFUL MOTHER D

Founded in the United States in 1924.
General Motherhouse and Novitiate: *Our Lady of Sorrows Convent,* 261 Thatcher St., Brockton, MA 02402-3997. Sr. Celestine Stakutis, C.J.C., Supr. Gen.
Total number in community 61.
Properties owned: *St. Joseph Manor Nursing and Extended Care Facility; Mater Dei Adult Day Health Program; Our Lady of Sorrows Convent,* Brockton, MA; *St. Mary's Villa Nursing Home,* Elmhurst, PA; *St. Peter's Convent,* South Boston, MA.
Ministry in Nursing Homes; Education Center; Elementary Schools; Inter-Community High Schools; Nursing Homes; and Pastoral Ministry.
Represented in the Archdiocese of Boston and in the Dioceses of Allentown and Scranton.

[3242] (P.S.N.)—POOR SISTERS OF NAZARETH P

Founded in England by Mother St. Basil.
Motherhouse: *Nazareth House,* Hammersmith,, London, W6 8DB. England. Mother Mary Bernard, Supr. Gen.
U.S. Region and Novitiate (1924): 3333 Manning Ave., Los Angeles, CA 90064. Tel: 310-839-2361. Mother Margaret Clare, Reg. Supr.
Professed Sisters 35.
Represented in the Archdioceses of Los Angeles and San Francisco and the Dioceses of Fresno, Madison and San Diego. Also in American Samoa.

[3250] (P.S.S.J.)—POOR SISTERS OF ST. JOSEPH

Founded in Buenos Aires, Argentina, 1880.
General Motherhouse: Leon Gallardo 734, Muniz, Buenos Aires, Argentina. Mother Agueda Magdalena Padros, Mother Gen.
U.S. Foundation: *Casa Belen,* 305 E. Fourth St., Bethlehem, PA 18015. Tel: 610-867-4030.
U.S. Motherhouse: *St. Gabriel Convent,* 4319 Sano St., Alexandria, VA 22312. Tel: 703-354-0395.
Casa Nazaret 5321 Spruce St., Reading, PA 19602. Tel: 610-378-1947.
Total number in community 15.
Represented in the Dioceses of Allentown and Arlington.

[3260] (C.PP.S.)—SISTERS OF THE PRECIOUS BLOOD (DAYTON, OHIO) P

Founded in Switzerland in 1834. First foundation in the United States in 1844.
Generalate: 4000 Denlinger Rd., Dayton, OH 45426. Tel: 937-837-3302. Sr. Joyce Langhals, C.PP.S., Pres.; Sr. Nancy Raley, C.PP.S., Vice Pres. & Councilor; Sr. Judy Kroeger, C.PP.S., Sec. & Councilor; Sr. Joyce Lehman, C.PP.S., Councilor; Sr. Benita Volk, C.PP.S., Councilor; Sr. Barbara Brown, C.PP.S., Treas.
Total Membership 319.
Properties owned and sponsored: *Generalate,* Dayton, OH; *Salem Heights Convent,* Dayton, OH; *Maria Stein Center,* Maria Stein, OH; *San Luis Rey Academy, Inc.,* San Luis Rey, CA.
Universities, High Schools, Elementary Schools & Seminaries; Diocesan Offices; Pastoral Ministry in Hospitals and Long-term Care Centers; Religious and Adult Education; Nursing Care; Homemaking Services in Homes for the Aged; Ethnic Minorities and Marginalized Peoples; Retreat and Music Ministry; Missionary and Volunteer Services.
Represented in the Archdioceses of Cincinnati, Denver, Detroit, Kansas City in Kansas, Los Angeles, Philadelphia, St. Paul-Minneapolis, Washington and the Dioceses of Altoona-Johnstown, Cleveland, Columbus, Covington, Dallas, Davenport, Gallup, Grand Rapids, Kalamazoo, Lafayette (IN), Lansing, Lexington, Marquette, Oakland, Phoenix, Saginaw, San Bernardino San Diego, Toledo and Tucson. Also in Chile, and Guatemala.

[3270] (C.PP.S.)—SISTERS OF THE MOST PRECIOUS BLOOD (O'FALLON, MO.) P

Founded in Switzerland in 1845. First foundation in the United States in 1870.
General Motherhouse: *St. Mary's Institute,* 204 N. Main St., O'Fallon, MO 63366-2299. Tel: 314-240-3420; Fax: 314-272-5031. Sr. Andree Fries, C.PP.S., Supr. Gen. Gen. Councilors: Sr. Susan Borgel; Sr. Cecile Gunelson; Sr. Eileen Schieber; Sr. Marjorie Cordes; Sr. Janice Bader, Treas.; Sr. Charlene Grieshaber, Sec.; Sr. Virginia Volkerding, Community Archivist.
Total number in community 296.
Properties Owned: *St. Mary's Institute, Inc. Charitable Trust, Sisters of the Most Precious Blood of O'Fallon, MO,* O'Fallon, MO; *Linda Vista Catholic School,* Chesterfield, MO; *St. Elizabeth Academy,* St. Louis, MO; *St. Elizabeth Adult Day Care Center,* St. Louis, MO; *Centers for Professional and Pastoral Services - Sisters of the Most Precious Blood,* O'Fallon, MO.
Ministry in the field of Education; Care of the Elderly; Pastoral and Parish Ministry; Ecclesiastical Art; Foreign Missions; Social Services; Prayer/Presence.
Represented in the Archdioceses of Anchorage, Baltimore, Chicago, Military Services, St. Louis and the Dioceses of El Paso, Jefferson City, Kansas City-St. Joseph, Kansas City (KS), Las Cruces, Lexington, Lincoln, Nashville, Sioux City, Springfield-Cape Girardeau, Springfield (IL) and Wheeling-Charleston.

[3310] (P.M.)—SISTERS OF THE PRESENTATION OF MARY P

Founded in France in 1796. First foundation in the United States in 1873.
General Motherhouse: *Presentazione di Maria,* Viale PIO XI, 29 C.P. 104, Castelgandolfo, Italy, 00040. Mother Carmen Barbe, Supr. Gen.
Inter-Provincial Novitiate: 180 Lowell Rd., Hudson, NH 03051. Sr. Colette Barbeau, Dir. Tel: 603-880-8186.
Manchester Province: *Provincial Administration,* 495 Mammoth Rd., Manchester, NH 03104. Tel: 603-669-1080. Sr. Mariette Plante, Prov. Supr.
Sisters 235.
Ministry in the field of Education at all levels; Pastoral Ministry; Youth Ministry; Ministry for Persons with Disabilities.
Properties owned: *Rivier College,* Nashua, NH; *Presentation of Mary Academy,* Hudson, NH; *Provincial House St. Joseph Residence St. Marie Residence,* Manchester, NH; *Our Lady of Hope House of Prayer,* New Ipswich, NH; *Bethany House,* Manchester, NH; *Presentation of Mary Novitiate,* Hudson, NH; *Emmanuel House,* Woonsocket, RI.
Represented in the Dioceses of Manchester and Providence.
Methuen Province: *Provincial Administration,* 209 Lawrence St., Methuen, MA 01844. Tel: 978-687-1369; 685-0980. Sr. Helene Bissonnette, C.PP.S., Prov.
Total number in Province 163.
Ministry in High Schools; Elementary Schools; Montessori Kindergartens; Montessorri Day Nurseries; Religious Instruction Centers; Spiritual Retreat Center.
Properties owned: *Montessori Kindergartens, Montessori Day Nurseries, Marie Joseph Spiritual Cen-*

ter, Biddeford, ME; *Presentation of Mary Academy,* Methuen, MA.
Represented in the Archdiocese of Boston and the Dioceses of Portland (ME), Springfield (MA) and Worcester.

[3320] (P.B.V.M.)—SISTERS OF THE PRESENTATION OF THE B.V.M. P

Founded in Ireland in 1775. First foundation in San Francisco CA in 1854.
Represented in the United States in the following Archdioceses and Dioceses.

Dubuque

P

Mt. Loretto Convent, Motherhouse and Novitiate: 2360 Carter Rd., Dubuque, IA 52001-2997. Tel: 319-588-2008; Fax: 319-588-4463. Sr. Mary Jacqueline Quillin, Congregational Leader.
Legal Title: *Sisters of the Presentation of the B.V.M.,* Dubuque, IA.
Total number in community 178.
Ministry in the field of Religious and Academic Education; Hospital & Prison Chaplaincy; Elder Care; Parish & Campus Ministries; South American Mission; Mission in Guatemala; Diocesan/Metropolitan Offices; Retreat & Spiritual Direction; Property Manager for Housing Project; Food Service; Lobbyist; Photo Editor.
Represented in the Archdioceses of Chicago, Denver Dubuque, Indianapolis, St. Paul-Minneapolis, Washington and the Dioceses of Austin, Brownsville, Covington, Davenport, Jackson, Kansas City (KS), Kansas City-St. Joseph Knoxville, Orlando, Pensacola-Tallahassee, Rapid City and Sioux City. Also in Bolivia and Guatemala.

New York

P

Mt. St. Joseph Administration Center: *Sisters of the Presentation of the Blessed Virgin Mary,* 880 Jackson Ave., New Windsor, NY 12553. Tel: 914-564-0513; Fax: 914-567-0219. Sr. Catherine Cleary, C.PP.S., Pres.; Sr. Luke Mulraney, C.PP.S., Community Archivist.
Total number in community 196.
Ministry in the field of Academic Education at all levels; Pastoral Services; Health Care, and Social Services.
Represented in the Archdioceses of Newark, New York, Washington, and the Dioceses of Bridgeport, Brooklyn, Dallas, Manchester, Metuchen, Norwich, Paterson, Providence and Worcester. Also in Bolivia and Ghana.

Our Lady of the Presentation, Motherhouse and Novitiate: 419 Woodrow Rd., Staten Island, NY 10312. Tel: 718-356-2121. Sr. Mary O'Keefe, Congregation Leader.
Professed Sisters 33.
Ministry in Elementary and High Schools; University; Campus Ministry; Pastoral Counseling; Adult Education; Healing & Parish Ministry.
Represented in the Archdioceses of New York and Philadelphia.

San Francisco

P

Presentation Convent-Motherhouse: 2340 Turk Blvd., San Francisco, CA 94118. Tel: 415-751-0406. Sr. Rosina Conrotto, P.B.V.M., Pres.; Sr. Kathleen Griffin, Archivist.
Legal Title: *Sisters of the Presentation of the Blessed Virgin Mary.*
Total number in community 152.
Ministry in the field of Religious and Academic Education at all levels; Parish Ministry; Social and Health Ministry; College and University Teaching; Retreat Work; Church Related Administrative Positions; Missionary Work; Internal Ministry.
Represented in the Archdioceses of Los Angeles, San Francisco and Washington and the Dioceses of Marquette, Monterey Oakland, San Jose, San Diego and Santa Rosa.

Albany

P

St. Colman's Presentation Convent, Motherhouse and Novitiate: *Sisters of the Presentation of the Blessed Virgin Mary PVBM,* Watervliet, NY 12189. Tel: 518-273-4911; Fax: 518-273-3312. Mother Mary Carmel, Supr.
Total number in community 48.
Ministry in the field of Academic Education; Day Care Center; Child Caring Institution; Resident School for Autistic & Emotionally Disturbed Children; Parish Ministry; Residential School for Mentally Retarded; Pre-School Handicapped Program.
Represented in the Diocese of Albany.

Fargo

P

Sacred Heart Convent, Motherhouse and Novitiate: *Sisters of Presentation of the Blessed Virgin Mary PBVM,* 1101 32nd Ave., S., Fargo, ND 58103. Tel: 701-237-4857. Sr. Paula Ringuette, Pres.; Sr. Mary Jo Hasey, Archivist.
Total number in community 64.
Sponsored Ministries: *Presentation Prayer Center,* Fargo, ND; *Riverview Place,* Fargo, ND; *Presentation Center,* Fargo, ND; *Friendship, Fargo,* ND; *St. Ansgar's Hospital,* Park River, ND; *Carrington Health Center,* Carrington, ND.
Represented in the Archdioceses of Portland (OR), St. Louis and the Dioceses of Bismarck, Columbus, Crookston, Fargo, Knoxville, Lexington, Rapid City and Springfield-Cape Girardeau. Also in Peru & Africa.

Sioux Falls

P

Presentation Convent, Motherhouse and Novitiate: *Sisters of the Presentation of the Blessed Virgin Mary,* Aberdeen, SD 57401. Tel: 605-225-0420. Sr. Joyce Meyer, Pres.; Sr. Lois Ann Sargent, Congregation Archivist.
Total number in community 166.
Ministry in the field of Academic Education at all levels; Hospitals; Homes for the Aged; Parish Pastoral Ministry; Missionary Ministry in Mexico.
Represented in the Diocese of Sioux Falls.

Worcester

P

Presentation Convent of the Presentation of the B.V.M.: 99 Church St., Leominster, MA 01453. Sr. Catherine Cleary, Pres.
Total number in community 196.
Sisters Staff or Sponsor: Elementary and High School Education; Spanish Apostolate; Pastoral Ministry; Social Services; Nursing.
Represented in the Archdiocese of Boston, Newark, New York and the Dioceses of Brooklyn, Manchester, Metuchen, Norwich, Paterson, Providence, Rockville Centre, Springfield and Worcester. Also in Bolivia.

[3330] (P.B.V.M.)—UNION OF THE SISTERS .OF THE PRESENTATION OF THE BLESSED VIRGIN MARY P

The Congregation of the Presentation was founded in Cork, Ireland, 1775. By decree of the Sacred Congregation for Religious, the Union of Sisters of the Presentation was established in Ireland in 1976. First U.S.A. Province in 1989.

Generalate: Monasterevan Co. Kildare, Ireland. Tel: 045-525-335. Sr. Wiona Engel, P.B.V.M., Supr. Gen.

Provincialate: 729 W. Wilshire Dr., Phoenix, AZ 85007. Tel: 602-271-9687. Sr. Catherine Burke, P.B.V.M., Prov.; Sr. Betty O'Dowd, P.B.V.M., Treas.
Novitiate 5151 Evergreen Ave., Cypress, CA 90630. Tel: 714-527-4844.
Perpetual Profession 93.
Sisters serve and staff: Elementary and Religious Education; Parish Ministry; Health & Hospital Services; Social Services.
Represented in the Archdioceses of Los Angeles, Mobile, New Orleans, San Antonio and San Francisco and the Dioceses of Birmingham, Biloxi, Oakland, Orange, Phoenix, Sacramento, San Bernadino, Savannah and Tucson.

[3340] (S.P.)—SISTERS OF PROVIDENCE P

Founded in Kingston, Canada in 1861. First foundation in the United States in 1873. Became independent, diocesan foundation in 1892.

Providence Motherhouse: Gamelin St., Holyoke, MA 01040-4083. Tel: 413-536-7511; Fax: 413-536-7917. Sr. Ruth McGoldrick, S.P., Congregation Pres.
Professed Sisters 138.
Legal Holdings and Titles: *Sisters of Providence, Inc.,* Holyoke, MA; *Sisters of Providence Health System, Inc.,* Springfield, MA. Hospitals: *Mercy Hospital,* Springfield, MA; *Providence Hospital,* Holyoke, MA; *Sisters of Providence Care Centers, Inc.* including: *Queen of Peace Centennial House; Beaven Kelly Home; St. Luke's Home, Inc.; Mt. St. Vincent Nursing Home,* Holyoke, MA; *Farren Care Center, Inc.,* Turners Falls, MA; *St. Joseph of the Pines Hospital, Inc.,* Southern Pines, NC; *Brightside for Children & Families, Inc.,* West Springfield, MA. Family Services: *Providence Ministries for the Needy, Inc.,* Holyoke, MA. Retreat House: *Genesis Spiritual Life Center,* Westfield, MA.
Represented in the Archdiocese of Boston and the Dioceses of Raleigh, Springfield (MA) and Worcester.

[3350] (S.P.)—SISTERS OF PROVIDENCE P

Founded in Montreal in 1843. First foundation in the United States in 1856.

General Motherhouse and Novitiate: 12055 Grenet St., Montreal, Quebec , Canada, H4J 2J5. Sr. Gloria Keylor, Supr. Gen.

Province of the Sacred Heart (1856): *Province and Sisters of Providence-Pariseau Association,* P.O. Box 11038, Seattle, WA 98111-9038. Tel: 206-464-3355. Sr. Judith Desmarais, S.P., Acting Prov. Supr.; Loretta Zwolak Greene, Archivist. Tel: 206-937-4600.
Novitiate-Vocation House, 4727 Stanley Rd. SW, Calgary, Alberta T25 293. Canada. Tel: 403-287-2863.
Total number in community 1,369; Sisters in Sacred Heart Province 158.
Ministry in the field of Academic Education; Health Care Services; Hospitals & Skilled Nursing Facilities; Outpatient Health Care Services; Home, Health and Hospice; Retirement Homes; Children's Nursing Centers; Senior and Handicapped Housing Facilities; Shelters for Homeless Women with Children; Transitional Housing for Women.
Sisters of Providence System Office, P.O. Box 11038, Seattle, WA 98111-9038. Tel: 206-464-3355. Sr. Karin Dufault, S.P., Chm. Bd.; Mr. Henry Walker, Pres. & CEO.
Properties, entities and divisions owned or operated: Sisters of Providence in Washington— *Providence Alaska Medical Center,* Anchorage, AK; *Providence Extended Care Center,* Anchorage, AK; *Providence Seward Medical Center,* Seward, AK; *Providence Kodiak Island Medical Center,* Kodiak, AK; *Mary Conrad Center,* Anchorage, AK; *Providence General Medical Center,* Everett, WA; *System Office Providence Medical Center Heritage House at the Market (leased) Hospice of Seattle Providence Mount St. Vincent,* Seattle, WA; *Vincent House,* Seattle, WA; *Providence St. Peter Hospital Providence Marianwood, Issaquah Providence Mother Joseph Care Center,* Olympia, WA; *Providence Centralia Hospital,* Centralia, WA; *Providence SoundHomeCare,* Olympia, WA; *Providence Yakima Medical Center,* Yakima, WA; *Providence Hospital,* Toppenish, WA. Sisters of Providence in Oregon— *Oregon Regional Office Providence, St. Vincent Medical Center Providence Portland Medical Center Providence Child Center,* Portland, OR; *Providence Milwaukie Hospital,* Milwaukie, OR; *Providence Newberg Hospital,* Newberg, OR; *Providence Seaside Hospital (leased),* Seaside, OR; *Providence Medford Medical Center,* Medford, OR. Sisters of Providence in California— *Providence High School, Saint Joseph Medical Center,* Burbank, CA. Sisters of Providence-Pariseau Association— *Saint Joseph Residence, Providence Holy Cross Medical Center,* Mission Hills, CA; *Providence St. Elizabeth Care Center,* North Hollywood, CA; *Providence Hospitality House Sojourner Place The Gamelin Association—Providence House,* Yakima, WA; *The Gamelin-Oregon Association—Emilie House,* Portland, OR; *The Gamelin-California Association—Providence House,* Oakland, CA.
Represented in the Archdioceses of Anchorage, Los Angeles, Portland (OR) and Seattle and the Dioceses of Oakland and Yakima.

Province of St. Ignatius (1891): *Sisters of Providence,* 9 E. Ninth Ave., Spokane, WA 99202-1295. Tel: 509-455-4884; Fax: 509-455-4882. Sr. Eileen Croghan, S.P., Prov. Supr.
Total number in province 97.
Properties owned or sponsored: *University of Great Falls, Inc.; Columbus Hospital Corporation; St. Thomas Child and Family Center,* Great Falls, MT; *St. Patrick Hospital Corporation,* Missoula, MT; *St. Joseph Hospital Corporation,* Polson, MT; *St. Mary Medical Center,* Walla Walla, WA; *Holy Family Hospital, Holy Family Adult Day Health; Sacred Heart Medical Center; St. Brendan Nursing Home; St. Joseph Care Center; Sisters of Providence; St. Ignatius Province,* Spokane, WA; *Mount Carmel Hospital,* Colville, WA; *St. Joseph's Hospital,* Chewelah, WA.
Represented in the Dioceses of Boise, Great Falls-Billings, Helena and Spokane.

Province of Elizabeth (1911): *Sisters of Charity of Providence, Maryville Convent,* 353 N. River Rd., Des Plaines, IL 60016. Tel: 708-299-7808. Sr. Imelda Caissie, Supr. Tel: 708-299-7808; *Maryville Academy,* 1150 N. River Rd., Des Plaines, IL 60016. Tel: 708-824-6126.
Represented in the Archdioceses of Chicago and Newark and the Dioceses of Burlington and Manchester.

[3360] (S.P.)—SISTERS OF PROVIDENCE OF SAINT MARY-OF-THE-WOODS, INDIANA P

Founded in France in 1806. First foundation in the United States in 1840.

General Administration: *Sisters of Providence,* St. Mary-of-the-Woods, IN 47876-1089. Tel: 812-535-

4193. Sr. Diane Ris, S.P., Gen. Supr.; Sr. Eileen Ann Kelley, S.P., Congregation Archivist.
Legal Titles and Sponsored Institutions: *Mother Theodore Guerin High School,* River Grove, IL; *Saint Mary-of-the-Woods College,* St. Mary-of-the-Woods, IN; *Woods Day Care/Pre-School, Inc.,* St. Mary-of-the-Woods, IN; *Providence Self-Sufficency Ministries, Inc.,* New Albany, IN.
Sisters of Providence Community Support Trust (1969) Foundation to provide support for the aged and infirm members of the Congregation.
Total Number Professed Sisters 668.
Ministry in the fields of Education at all levels; Diocesan Offices; Parish and Pastoral Ministry; Health Care and Retirement Facilities; Congregation Administration; Social Services; Therapeutic/Rehabilitative/Mental Health Services.
Represented in the Archdioceses of Atlanta, Boston, Chicago, Cincinnati, Indianapolis, Louisville, Los Angeles, Mobile, Omaha, St. Paul-Minneapolis, San Antonio, San Francisco, Washington and the Dioceses of Arlington, Belleville, Corpus Christi, Covington, Evansville, Fort Wayne-South Bend, Fresno, Galveston-Houston, Gary, Helena, Jackson, Joliet, La Crosse, Lafayette (LA), Lafayette (IN), Lexington, Manchester, Norwich, Oakland, Ogdensburg, Oklahoma, Orange, Owensboro, Palm Beach, Peoria, Rockford, St.Petersurg, San Bernadino, San Jose, Springfield, Trenton, Venice and Wheeling-Charleston. Also in China, Singapore and Antigua, West Indies.
Area of Taiwan: *Providence University,* 200 Chung Chi Rd., Shalu 433, Taichung County, Taiwan, Republic of China. Tel: 011-886-4-631-1182. Sr. Marilyn Baker, S.P., Area Rep.
Total number in community 9.
Ministry in the field of Education; Opportunity Center for Mentally Handicapped.
Property Owned: Mother Marie Gratia Spirituality Center.
Represented in the Archdiocese of Taipei and the Dioceses of Taichung and Tainan.

[3380] (R.A.)—RELIGIOUS OF THE APOSTOLATE OF THE SACRED HEART OF JESUS P
Religiosas del Apostolado del Sagrado Corazon
General Motherhouse: San Esteban de Gormaz 32, Madrid, Spain, 28033. Leonor Micheo, Mother Gen.
St. Lazaro Convent: 1310 W. 42nd Pl., Hialeah, FL 33012. Tel: 305-823-3232.
Represented in the Archdiocese of Miami. Also in Puerto Rico.

[3390] (R.A.)—RELIGIOUS OF THE ASSUMPTION P
Founded in France in 1839. Established in the United Stats of America in 1919.
Generalate: 17 rue de l'Assomption, 75016, Paris, France.
Universal total in Congregation 1,423.
Represented in the 31 countries through Europe, Africa, Asia, North America, Central America, and South America.
North American Province: *Provincial House,* 227 N. Bowman Ave., Merion Station, PA 19066. Tel: 610-664-3074. Sr. Ann-Francoise Salaun, R.A., Prov. Supr.
Total number in province 21.
Represented in the Archdiocese of Philadelphia and the Diocese of Worcester.
Ministry in Spiritual Formation; Counselling; Campus Ministry; Pastoral and Social Ministry; Education.

[3400] (R.S.C.)—RELIGIOUS SISTERS OF CHARITY P
Founded in Dublin, Ireland in 1815. Sisters in entire congregation 650.
Motherhouse: *Caritas,* 15 Gilford Rd., Sandymount, Dublin 4, Ireland. Sr. Una O'Neill, Supr. Gen.
U.S. Headquarters & Novitiate (1953): *Regional Residence,* 10664 St. James' Dr., Culver City, CA 90230. Tel: 310-559-0176; Fax: 310-838-9647. Sr. Carmel Noone, R.S.C., Reg. Supr.
Total in U.S. community 34.
Represented in the Archdiocese of Los Angeles and the Diocese of Orange.

[3410] (R.C.E.)—RELIGIOUS OF CHRISTIAN EDUCATION P
Founded in France in 1817. First foundation in the United States in 1905.
General Motherhouse: France.
Provincial Residence: 55 Parkwood Dr., Milton, MA 02186. Tel: 617-696-7732; Fax: 617-696-9405. Sr. Martha Brigham, R.C.E., Prov. Supr.
Total number in community 37.
Legal Title: *Religious of Christian Education, Inc.*
Ministry in Religious Education Centers; Pastoral Associates; Teaching; Home Care.
Represented in the Archdiocese of Boston and the Dioceses of Fall River and Springfield, MA.

[3420] (R.E.)—RELIGIOUS OF THE EUCHARIST P
(formerly Society of Perpetual Adoration)
Founded in Belgium in 1857. First Foundation in U.S. in 1900.
General Motherhouse: Watermael, near Brussels, Belgium, . Very Rev. Mother Marie Virginie, Supr. Gen.
American Foundation: *Convent of the Religious of the Eucharist,* 2907 Ellicott Terrace, N. W., Washington, DC 20008. Tel: 202-966-3111. Sr. Patricia, Supr.
Ministry in the fields of Education; General.
Professed Sisters 5.
Represented in the Archdiocese of Washington.

[3430] (M.P.F.)—RELIGIOUS TEACHERS FILIPPINI P
(Maestre Pie Filippini)
Founded in Italy in 1692. First foundation in the United States in 1910.
General Motherhouse: *Villa Maria Regina,* Via Stazione Ottavia, 72, Rome, Italy. Sr. Mary DeBacco, M.P.F., Supr. Gen.
St. Lucy Filippini Province: *Villa Walsh,* Morristown, NJ 07960-4928. Tel: 973-538-2886. Sr. Frances Lauretti, Prov. Supr.; Sr. Clare Testa, Community Archivist.
Total number in community 274.
Properties owned and sponsored: *Villa Walsh,* Morristown, NJ; *Villa Victoria,* Trenton, NJ; *St. Joseph by The Sea,* South Mantoloking, NJ.
Ministry in the field of Religious and Academic Education in elementary; and secondary schools; Child Care Centers; Parish Ministry; Pastoral Care; Foreign Mission Work; Special Education; House of Prayer; Retreat House.
Represented in the Archdioceses of Newark and Philadelphia and the Dioceses of Albany, Brooklyn, Cleveland, Camden, Metuchen, Paterson, Pittsburgh, Scranton and Trenton.
Queen of Apostles Province: *Religious Teachers Filippini M.P.F.,* 474 East Rd., Bristol, CT 06010. Tel: 203-584-2138. Sr. Christine Spirito, M.P.F., Prov.; Sr. Josephine Riccio, M.P.F., Community Archivist.
Total number in community 49.
Ministry in the field of Education; Pastoral Ministry; Catechetical Centers; Youth Retreats; Foreign Mission Work.
Represented in the Archdioceses of Hartford and Washington and the Dioceses of Bridgeport, Norwich, Orlando and Providence.

[3449] (C.V.I.)—RELIGIOUS OF THE INCARNATE WORD P
Founded in Lyon, France, in 1625. First foundation in United States in 1853, in Mexico 1894.
General Motherhouse: Mexico City, Industria #1-Col.Toriello Guerra, Deleg. Tlalpan, Mexico, D.F., 14050. Sr. Marta Patricia Ochoa, C.V.I., Gen. Supr.
U.S. Vice Provincial House: 153 Rainier Ct., Chula Vista, CA 91911. Tel: 619-420-0231. Sr. Camille Crabbe, C.V.I., Vice Prov.
Total number in Congregation 490.
Ministry in Parishes; Schools; Diocesan Offices and Missions.
Represented in the Diocese of San Diego. Also in Africa, Argentina, France, Guatemala, Mexico & Spain.

[3450] (R.J.M.)—RELIGIOUS OF JESUS AND MARY P
Founded at Lyons, France, 1818. First foundation in the U.S. in 1877.
Motherhouse: Via Nomentana 325, Rome, Italy. Rev. Mother Aurora Tralleno, R.J.M., Supr. Gen.
Universal number in Congregation 1,683.
United States Province Provincialate: 3706 Rhode Island Ave., Mount Rainier, MD 20712. Tel: 301-277-3794; Fax: 301-277-8656. Sr. Rosemary Mangan, R.J.M., Prov.; Sr. Yvette Beaulieu, R.J.M., Archivist.
Legal Title: *Religious of Jesus and Mary, Inc.*
Total in community 151.
Ministry in the field of Academic and Religious Education; Pastoral Ministry; Social Services; QUEST Volunteer Program.
Represented in the Archdioceses of Boston, Los Angeles, New York, Washington and the Dioceses of El Paso, Fall River, Manchester, Providence and San Diego. Also in Haiti and Mexico.

[3460] (R.M.I.)—RELIGIOUS OF MARY IMMACULATE P
Founded in Madrid, Spain in 1876.
Mother House: Madrid, Spain.
Generalate: Rome, Italy.
U.S. Foundation (1954): *Villa Maria,* 719 Augusta St., San Antonio, TX 78215. Tel: 210-226-0025; Fax: 210-226-3305. Sr. Clara Echeverria, Local Supr.
Total number in community 14.
Headquarters: *Centro Maria,* 539 West 54th St., New York, NY 10019. Tel: 212-581-5273. Sr. Maria del Rosario Merin, Local Supr.
Total number in community 8.
Represented in the Archdioceses of New York, San Antonio and Washington.

[3465] (R.S.H.M.)—RELIGIOUS OF THE SACRED HEART OF MARY P
Founded in France in 1848. First foundation in the United States in 1877.
Generalate: Via Adelaide Ristori 26, Curia Generalizia, Rome, Italy, 00197. Sr. Catherine Dolan, R.S.H.M., Gen. Supr.
Universal number in Congregation 1,145.
Eastern American Province (1907): 50 Wilson Park Dr., Tarrytown, NY 10591. Tel: 914-631-8872; 631-2630. Sr. Letizia Pappalardo, R.S.H.M., Prov.
Total number in community 250.
Ministries including Education; Pastoral Ministry; Retreat and Spiritual Direction; Health Care and Social Work.
Represented in the Archdioceses of Baltimore, New York and St. Louis and the Dioceses of Arlington, Brooklyn, Norwich, Oakland, Palm Beach, Richmond, Rockville Centre, Trenton, Venice and Winona. Also in Africa and Europe.
Western American Province (1959): *Religious of the Sacred Heart of Mary R.S.H.M.,* R.S.H.M. Provincial Center, 441 N. Garfield Ave., Montebello, CA 90640-2901. Tel: 213-887-8821; Fax: 213-887-8952. Sr. Mary Milligan, R.S.H.M., Prov.
Total number in community 88.
Legal titles or holdings: *Religious of the Sacred Heart of Mary, California Province, a California corporation; Marymount School, a California corporation.*
Ministry in the field of Academic Education at all levels; Diverse Pastoral Ministries.
Represented in the Archdioceses of Los Angeles, San Francisco and the Dioceses of San Bernardino, San Diego and San Jose. Also in Mexico.

[3470] (S.R.C.M.)—SISTERS OF REPARATION OF THE CONGREGATION OF MARY, INC. D
Motherhouse and Novitiate: *St. Zita's Villa,* Monsey, NY 10952. Tel: 914-356-2011. Sr. Maureen Francis, S.R.C.M.
Total number in the community 12.
Represented in the Archdiocese of New York.

[3480] (C.R.)—SISTERS OF THE RESURRECTION P
Founded in Rome, Italy, in 1891. First foundation in the United States in 1900.
General Motherhouse: Via Marcantonio Colonna 52A, Rome, Italy. Rev. Mother Dolores Stepien, C.R., Supr. Gen.
Universal total in Congregation 586.
Western Province Provincialhouse and Novitiate: 7432 Talcott Ave., Chicago, IL 60631. Tel: 773-792-6363. Sr. Virginia Ann Wanzek, C.R., Prov. Supr.
Total number in community 79.
Properties owned or sponsored: *Resurrection Medical Center; Our Lady of Resurrection Medical Center; Resurrection Nursing and Rehabilitation Center; Resurrection Retirement Community; Resurrection Day Care Center; Resurrection High School; Resurrection Health Care Corporation; Queen of Resurrection House of Prayer.*
Represented in the Archdioceses of Chicago, Milwaukee and Mobile.
Eastern Province Provincialhouse and Novitiate: *Sisters of the Resurrection - Mount St. Joseph,* 35 Boltwood Ave., Castleton-on-Hudson, NY 12033. Tel: 518-732-2226; Fax: 518-732-2898. Sr. Jeanne Marie Harla, C.R., Prov. Supr.
Total number in community 76.
Legal Title: *Sisters of the Resurrection, New York, Inc.*
Ministry in Nursing Homes; Elementary Schools; Christian Doctrine Centers; High School for Girls; Day Care Centers; Pre-schools.

Represented in the Archdiocese of New York and the Dioceses of Albany, Bridgeport, Fall River and Trenton.

[3490] (O.S.S.)—RELIGIOUS OF THE ORDER OF THE BLESSED SACRAMENT AND OF OUR LADY P
Sacramentine Nuns

Cloistered Contemplative.
Founded in France in 1639. First foundation in the United States in 1912. The Sisters devote their lives to the perpetual adoration of Christ in the Eucharist.
Blessed Sacrament Monastery: 23 Park Ave., Yonkers, NY 10703. Tel: 914-963-0913. Sr. Mary Veronica, O.S.S., Prioress.
Professed sisters 19.
Monastery of Perpetual Adoration (1951): U.S. 31, P.O. Box 86, Conway, MI 49722. Tel: 616-347-0447. Sr. Rosalie, O.S.S., Prioress.
Professed Sisters 4.
Represented in the Archdiocese of New York and the Diocese of Gaylord.

[3499] (S.J.S.)—SISTERS SERVANTS OF THE BLESSED SACRAMENT P

Founded in Mexico in 1904. First foundation in the United States in 1926.
General Motherhouse: Juan Bernardino 650, Guadalajara, Jalisco , Mexico, 45000. Sr. M. Concepcion Cervantez, S.J.S., Supr. Gen.
U.S. Vice Province: 215 Lomita St., El Segundo, CA 90245. Tel: 310-615-0766; Fax: 310-615-0571. Sr. Ana Rosa Aceves, S.J.S., Vice Prov.
Total number in the community 59.
Legal Title: *Sisters Servants of the Blessed Sacrament, Inc.*
Ministry in the field of Education.
Represented in the Archdiocese of Los Angeles and the Diocese of Fresno, Sacramento and San Diego.

[3500] (S.S.S.)—SERVANTS OF THE BLESSED SACRAMENT P

Founded in France in 1858; First foundation in the United States in 1947.
General Motherhouse: Via Aurelia, 145-Int. C-2, Rome, Italy, 00165.
American Provincial House: *St. Charles Borromeo Parish,* 1818 Coal Pl. S.E., Albuquerque, NM 87106. Tel: 505-242-3692. Sr. Catherine Marie Caron, S.S.S., Prov.
Total number in the community 22.
Represented in the Archdiocese of Santa Fe and the Dioceses of Portland (ME) and Pueblo.

[3510] (S.S.C.K.)—SISTER SERVANTS OF CHRIST THE KING D

Founded in the United States in 1936.
General Motherhouse: *Loretto Convent,* N. 8114 Calvary St., Mt. Calvary, WI 53057. Tel: 920-753-3211. Mother Mary Rose, Supr.
Professed Sisters 9.
Represented in the Archdiocese of Milwaukee and the Diocese of Fargo.

[3520] (S.S.C.M.)—SERVANTS OF THE HOLY HEART OF MARY P

Founded in Paris, France in 1860. First foundation in the United States in 1889.
Generalate: 2029 rue Holy Cross, Montreal, Quebec , Canada, H4E 2A4. Sr. Fernande Dionne, S.S.C.M., Gen. Supr.
United States Region-Holy Family Province: Provincialate, 145 S. Fourth Ave., Kankakee, IL 60901-3603. Tel: 815-937-2380. Sr. Kathleen Mulchay, S.S.C.M., Prov. Supr.
Total number in region 60.
Legal Title: *ServantCor; HealthCor; Service Cor, Inc.; Servants United Foundation.*
Ministry in Grammar Schools; Nursing Homes; Health Care; Education; Pastoral Ministry; Parishes; Ministry to the Aged; and Home Missions.
Represented in the Archdioceses of Chicago and Washington and the Dioceses of Joliet, Peoria and Rockford.

[3530] (S.Sp.S.)—MISSIONARY SISTERS SERVANTS OF THE HOLY SPIRIT P

Founded in Holland in 1889. First foundation in the United States in 1901.
General Motherhouse: *Convento dello Spirito Santo,* Via Cassia 645, Roma, Italy, 00189. Sr. Agada Brand, S.Sp.S., Supr. Gen.
Universal total in Congregation 3,750.
American Motherhouse (1901): *Convent of the Holy Spirit,* Techny, IL 60082-6026. Tel: 847-272-5930; Fax: 847-272-0113. Sr. Priscilla Burke, S.Sp.S., Prov.
Total number in the community 131.
Affiliates: *Missionary Sisters Sponsorship, Inc.,* Techny, IL; *Missionary Sisters Health Care System,* McHenry, IL; *Sacred Heart Home, Inc.,* Hyattsville, MD; *Arnold Janssen Foundation,* Techny, IL.
Ministry in Schools; Health Care; Home for the Aged; Central Houses for Catechetical Work; Parish Ministry & Administration.
Represented in the Archdioceses of Chicago, Dubuque, Los Angeles and Washington.

[3540] (S.Sp.S.deA.P.)—SISTER-SERVANTS OF THE HOLY SPIRIT OF PERPETUAL ADORATION P

Cloistered Contemplative.
Founded in Holland in 1896. First foundation in the United States in 1915.
Generalate: Convent of the Most Holy Trinity, Bad Driburg, Germany. Mother Mary Aurora, S.Sp.S.deA.P., Supr. Gen.
U.S. Novitiate House: *Convent of Divine Love,* 2212 Green St., Philadelphia, PA 19130. Tel: 215-567-0123. Sr. Mary Catherine, S.Sp.S.deA.P., Supr.
Mount Grace Convent, 1438 E. Warne Ave., St. Louis, MO. Tel: 314-381-5686. Sr. Mary Gemma, S.Sp.S.deA.P., Supr.
Professed Sisters 26.
Mount Grace Convent, 1438 E. Warne Ave., St. Louis, MO. Tel: 314-381-5686. Sr. Mary Gemma, S.Sp.S.deA.P., Supr.
Professed Sisters 29.
Convent of the Blessed Sacrament, 4105 Ocean Dr., Corpus Christi, TX 78411. Tel: 512-852-6212. Sr. Mary Margaret, S.Sp.S.deA.P., Supr.
Professed Sisters 10.
Adoration Convent of Christ the King Church, 1040 S. Cotner Blvd., Lincoln, NE 68510. Tel: 402-489-0765. Sr. Mary Henrita, S.Sp.S.deA.P., Supr.
Professed Sisters 9.

[3550] (S.C.I.M.)—SERVANTS OF THE IMMACULATE HEART OF MARY P
Good Shepherd Sisters of Quebec

Founded in Canada in 1850. First foundation in the United States in 1882.
Generalate: 2550, rue Marie-Fitzbach, Ste-Foy, Quebec , Canada. Sr. Helen Pelletier, S.C.I.M., Supr. Gen.
Universal total in Congregation 857.
Provincial House: St. *Joseph Province at Bay View,* 313 Seaside Ave., Saco, ME 04072. Tel: 207-283-3433; Fax: 207-282-7376. Sr. Theresa Rounds, S.C.I.M., Prov. Supr.
Total number in community 109.
Ministry in High Schools; Grammar Schools; Adoption Agency; Group Homes for Unmarried Mothers; Group Home for Troubled Adolescents; C.C.D. Centers; Youth (Retreat Work); Apostolate to the Elderly and Homeless.
Represented in the Archdiocese of Boston and the Diocese of Portland (ME).

[3570] (O.S.M.)—MANTELLATE SISTERS, SERVANTS OF MARY OF BLUE ISLAND P

Founded in Italy in 1861. First foundation in the United States in 1916.
Generalate and Novitiate: Rome, Italy.
U.S. Motherhouse & Novitiate: *Convent of Our Mother of Sorrows,* 13811 S. Western Ave., Blue Island, IL 60406. Tel: 708-385-2103. Sr. M. Gabriel Cossa, O.S.M., Prov.
Professed Sisters 22.
Grammar Schools 1; Nursery and Kindergartens 1; Catechetical Work 1.
Represented in the Archdiocese of Chicago.

[3572] (O.S.M.)—MANTELLATE SISTERS SERVANTS OF MARY OF PLAINFIELD

Founded October 6, 1861 in Treppi, Italy. First founded in the United States 1916.
Universal number of Mantellate Sisters 800.
Mantellate Sisters Servants of Mary of Plainfield (1977): 16949 S. Drauden Rd., Plainfield, IL 60544-9219. Tel: 815-436-5796. Sr. Francis Gresser, O.S.M., Reg. Supr.
Sisters 12.
Ministry in the field of Academic Education; Parish Ministry; Social Work; Nursing; Homes for the Aged; Foreign Missions.
Represented in the Archdiocese of Chicago and the Diocese of Joliet.

[3580] (O.S.M.)—SERVANTS OF MARY P

Founded in Italy in the 13th Century. First foundation in the United States in 1893.
General Motherhouse: 89, St. Bernard's Rd., Solihull, B92 7DG. England. Sr. M. Felicity McKeon, O.S.M., Prioress Gen.
American Province (1893): *Provincial Motherhouse, Convent of Our Lady of Sorrows,* 7400 Military Ave., Omaha, NE 68134-3398. Tel: 402-571-2547; Fax: 402-573-6055. Sr. Terese Lux, O.S.M., Prov.
Total number in community 122.
Ministry in the field of Religious and Academic Education at all levels; Parishes; Social Service Agencies; Diocesan Offices; Hospital Pastoral Care; Counseling Agencies; Peace and Justice Offices; Campus Ministry; Hospice; Jail Ministry; Development; Health Care Services; Medical Research; Consulting; Spiritual Direction; Retreat Work; Missionary Work in Foreign Countries and in the United States.
Properties owned: *Marian High School,* Omaha, NE; *Our Lady of Sorrows Convent,* Omaha, NE.
Represented in the Archdioceses of Denver, Detroit, Kansas City in Kansas, Omaha, Portland (OR), St. Paul-Minneapolis and the Dioceses of Colorado Springs, Des Moines, Gaylord, Grand Island, Lexington, Metuchen, Ogdensburg, Salina, St. Cloud, Sioux City, and Tucson. Also in Jamaica and West Indies.

[3590] (O.S.M.)—SERVANTS OF MARY (SERVITE SISTERS) D

Founded in Italy in the 13th Century. First United States foundation in 1912.
General Motherhouse: *Servants of Mary,* 1000 College Ave. W., Ladysmith, WI 54848. Tel: 715-532-3364; Fax: 715-532-6153. Sr. Anita C. Swansen, O.S.M., Pres.
Total number in community 90.
Ministry in the field of Academic Education; Parish and Pastoral Ministry; Health Care; Social Services, Law; and Administration.
Represented in the Archdioceses of Boston, Chicago, Louisville, Milwaukee and St. Paul-Minneapolis and the Dioceses of Duluth, Fresno, Gary, Green Bay, Joliet, La Crosse, Orange, Orlando, Superior, St. Petersburg, Tucson and Wheeling-Charleston.

[3595] (S.S.J.)—SERVANTS OF ST. JOSEPH P

Founded in Spain in 1874.
Motherhouse: Salamanca, Spain.
General House: Rome, Italy. Mother Josefa Somoza, Supr. Gen.
U.S. Address (1957): *Servants of St. Joseph,* 203, Falls Church, VA 22046. Tel: 703-533-8441. Sr. Fabiola Ospina, Supr. Tel: 703-534-9549.
Total number in community 16.
Represented in the Archdiocese of Newark and Diocese of Arlington.

[3600] (S.M.)—SISTERS SERVANTS OF MARY P
(Ministers to the Sick)

Founded in Madrid, Spain by St. Maria Soledad Torres, August 15, 1851. First foundation in the United States in 1914. Total Membership 1,950 Sisters.
General Motherhouse: via Antonio Musa 16, Rome, Italy. Mother Josefa Oyarzabal, S.M., Supr. Gen.
Provincial Motherhouse: 800 N. 18th St., Kansas City, KS 66102. Sr. Alfonsa Bellido, S.M., Prov. Supr.; Sr. Mercedes Rodriguez, S.M., Locale Supr.; Sr. Carmela Sanz, S.M., Community Archivist; Sr. Victoria P. Villarreal, S.M., Treas.
Total number in the province 251.
Represented in the Archdioceses of Kansas City in Kansas, Los Angeles, New Orleans and New York.

[3610] (S.S.M.I.)—SISTERS SERVANTS OF MARY IMMACULATE P

Founded in Zuzel, Ukraine on August 28, 1892. Approved by the Holy See, 1932. Arrived in the United States on August 15, 1935 at Stamford, Connecticut.
Generalate: Via Cassia Antica 104,, Rome, Italy, 00191. Sr. Teresa Kito, S.S.M.I., Supr. Gen.
Sisters Servants of Mary Immaculate: Sisters Servants Ln., 9 Emmanuel Dr., P.O. Box 6, Sloatsburg, NY 10974-0006. Tel: 914-753-2840. Sr. Michele Yakymovitch, S.S.M.I., Prov. Supr.; Sr. Thadea Nykolayow, S.S.M.I., Prov. Archivist.
Total number in community 52.
Properties owned: *Home of Divine Providence,* Philadelphia, PA; *Immaculate Conception Provincialate & Novitiate; St. Joseph's Home (for the aged); Saint Mary's Villa Spiritual, Cultural and Educational Center,* Sloatsburg, NY.

Ministry in the field of Education; Parish and Pastoral ministry; Health Care; Administration; Hospitality; Holy Dormition Pilgrimage.
Represented in the Ukrainian and Byzantine Rite Catholic Dioceses of the United States.

[3620] (S.S.M.I.)—SISTERS SERVANTS OF MARY IMMACULATE P

First founded in Poland 1878.
General Motherhouse: Mariowka-Opoczynska, Poland. Mother Maria Floryn, Mother Gen.
Universal total in Congregation 1,100.
American Province (1935): 1220 Tugwell Dr., Catonsville, MD 21228. Tel: 410-747-1353. Sr. Bernadette Kozyra, S.S.M.I., Prov. Supr.; Sr. Marianna Danko, Community Archivist.
Total in the community 34.
Represented in the Archdioceses of Baltimore and Washington and the Diocese of Cleveland.

[3630] (S.S.C.J.)—SERVANTS OF THE MOST SACRED HEART OF JESUS P

Founded in Poland in 1894.
General Motherhouse: Garncarska St., Cracow, Poland. Mother Szczesna Niemiec, Supr. Gen.
Sister Servants of the Most Sacred Heart of Jesus (1959): *Sacred Heart Province,* 866 Cambria St., Cresson, PA 16630-1713. Sr. Theresa Marie, S.S.C.J., Prov. Supr.
Total number in U.S. Province 32.
Represented in the Archdiocese of Philadelphia and the Dioceses of Altoona-Johnstown and Metuchen.

[3640] (S.M.G.)—POOR SERVANTS OF THE MOTHER OF GOD P

Founded in London, England in 1869. First foundation in the United States in 1947.
General Motherhouse: Maryfield, Roehampton, London S.W. 15, England. Sr. Rosarii O'Connor, S.M.G., Supr. Gen.
American Foundations: *Maryfield Nursing Home,* High Point, NC 27260. Tel: 910-886-2444. Sr. Elizabeth Crehan, S.M.G., Reg. Supr.
Total number in the community 26.
Ministry in Hospitals; Nursing Homes; Schools; Retreat House.
Represented in the Archdiocese of Philadelphia and the Dioceses of Charlotte, Metuchen, Richmond and Tulsa.

[3650] (S.R.C.)—SERVANTS OF OUR LADY, QUEEN OF THE CLERGY D

Founded in Canada December 8th, 1929. First foundation in the United States in 1934.
General Motherhouse: 57 Jules-A. Brillant, Rimouski, Quebec G5L 1X1. Canada. Tel: 418-722-4402. Mother Pierrette Pelletier, S.R.C., Supr. Gen.
Sisters working in the United States 4.
Sister serve in the area of Domestic work.
Represented in the Dioceses of Fall River, Manchester and Providence.

[3658] (S.S.H.J.)—SISTERS OF THE SACRED HEART OF JESUS P

Founded in Ragusa, Italy in 1889. First foundation in the United States in 1950. Generalate House: Instituto Sacro Cuore di Ragusa, Via Cassia 1714, 00123 Rome, Italy. Universal total in Congregation 605.
Motherhouse: *Instituto Sacro Cuore,* Via Suor Maria Schinina 2, 97100 Ragusa, Italy.
American Headquarters: *Sacred Heart Villa School & Convent,* 5269 Lewiston Rd., Lewiston, NY 14092. Tel: 716-284-8273. Sr. M. Terenzia Giudice, S.S.H.J., Supr.
Legal Title: Sacred Heart Villa School & Convent, Lewiston, NY Saint Frances Cabrini Nursery and Convent, North Haven, CT.
Ministry in the field of Religious and Academic Education at all levels; Hospitals; Homes for the Aged; Orphanages; Parish Ministry; Youth Ministry; Foreign Missions; Social Services.
Represented in the Archdiocese of Hartford and the Diocese of Buffalo.

[3660] (S.S.H.J.P.)—SERVANTS OF THE SACRED HEART OF JESUS AND OF THE POOR P

Founded in Leon, Gto., Mexico in 1885. First foundation in U.S. in 1907.
Motherhouse: Apartado 92, Puebla, Pue, Mexico. Tel: 01152-22-42-1869. Mother Guadalupe Lucia Bertoglio, Mother Gen.
U.S. Address: *Sacred Heart Children's Home Convent,* 3310 S. Zapata Hwy., Laredo, TX 78046. Sr. Maria Teresa Grajeda, S.S.H.J.P., Admin.
Professed Sisters in U.S. 45.
Ministry in in academic and religious education at all levels; Children's Home.
Represented in the Dioceses of Corpus Christi and El Paso.

[3670] (S.S.C.J.)—SISTERS OF THE SACRED HEART OF JESUS OF SAINT JACUT P

Founded in France in 1816. First foundation in the United States in 1903.
Generalate: Paris, France.
Motherhouse: St. Jacut, Brittany, France.
USA\Mexico Province (1916): *Mt. Sacred Heart Convent,* 5922 Blanco Road, San Antonio, TX 78216. Tel: 210-344-4805 & 7203. Sr. Juana Villescas, S.S.C.J., Prov.
Total number in community 63.
Properties owned or sponsored: *Mount Sacred Heart Convent; Mount Sacred Heart School; Mount Sacred Heart School for Girls,* San Antonio, TX; *Casa Angelique, Mexico; Casa San Antonio,* San Antonio, TX.
Ministry in Education; Pastoral Work; Schools of Religion; Health Care; Mexico Missions.
Represented in the Archdioceses of San Antonio and Santa Fe and the Dioceses of Amarillo, Brownsville and Galveston-Houston. Also in Mexico City.

[3680] (S.H.J.M.)—SISTERS OF THE SACRED HEARTS OF JESUS AND MARY P

Founded in France in 1866. First foundation in United States in 1953.
Motherhouse: Essex, England.
Regional House: 8644 Don Carlo Dr., El Cerrito, CA 94530. Tel: 415-527-3328.
Total number in community 260.
Represented in the Dioceses of Fresno, Oakland, Sacramento and Stockton.

[3690] (SS.CC.)—CONGREGATION OF THE SACRED HEARTS AND OF PERPETUAL ADORATION P

Founded in France in 1800 as a Congregation of men and women. Members are consecrated to the Hearts of Jesus and Mary. Special Ministries are Perpetual Adoration, the education of youth, especially the poor, parish work and foreign missions. First Catholic missionaries to Hawaii in 1827: Sisters started Catholic Schools for girls in Hawaii 1859. First foundation in the continental United States in 1908.
Generalate: Via Aurelia 145, Scala C-Int 10-14-00165, Rome, Italy. Mother Jeanne Cadiou, SS.CC., Supr. Gen.
Pacific Province: *Sisters of the Sacred Hearts,* 1120 Fifth Ave, Honolulu, HI 96816. Tel: 808-737-5822. Sr. Regina Mary Jenkins, SS.CC., Prov.
Total number in community 43.
Legal Holdings and Titles: *Sisters of the Sacred Hearts Corporation; Regina Pacis Convent; Sacred Hearts Academy Corporation; Saint Anthony Home Corporation; Malia O Ka Malu Community,* Honolulu, HI.
East Coast Region: *Sisters of the Sacred Hearts of Jesus and Mary and of Perpetual Adoration,* 35 Huttleston Ave., Fairhaven, MA 02719-3154. Tel: 508-994-9341; Fax: 508-990-1967. Sr. Dolores Pavao, SS.CC., Reg. Supr.
Total number in community 14.
Represented in the Diocese of Fall River.

[3710] (C.S.A.)—CONGREGATION OF SISTERS OF SAINT AGNES P

Founded in the United States in 1858.
General Motherhouse: *St. Agnes Convent,* 475 Gillett St., Fond du Lac, WI 54935. Tel: 920-923-2121. Sr. Mary Mollison, C.S.A., Gen. Supr.; Sr. Patricia Hayes, C.S.A., Gen. Vicar. Councillors: Sr. Anita Henning,, C.S.A.; Sr. Deborah Walter, C.S.A.
Total number in congregation 410.
Properties owned or sponsored: *Hazotte Ministries, Inc.; Nazareth Heights, Inc.; Marian College of Fond du Lac; St. Agnes Hospital; St. Francis Home,* Fond du Lac, WI; *Waupun Memorial Hospital,* Waupun, WI; *The Monroe Clinic* (corporate title: *St. Clare Hospital*), Monroe, WI.
Ministry in the field of Academic and Religious Education; Hospitals; Homes for Aged; Parish Ministry; Foreign Missions; Social Services; Healthcare.
Represented in the Archdioceses of Chicago, Cincinnati, Denver, Miami, Milwaukee, Mobile, New York, Philadelphia, St. Paul-Minneapolis, Washington, and the Dioceses of Allentown, Altoona-Johnstown, Fort Wayne-South Bend, Gallup, Gary, Grand Island, Green Bay, Jackson, Joliet, Lafayette, Lexington, Madison, Marquette, Memphis, Oakland, Orlando, Passaic, Phoenix, Raleigh, Rockford, Salina, St. Petersburg, Superior, Toledo, Tucson and Wichita. Also in Nicaragua, & Honduras.

[3718] (S.S.A.)—SISTERS OF ST. ANN P

Founded in Italy in 1834.
General Motherhouse: V.d. Aldobrandeschi, 100-00163, Rome, Italy. Franceschina Milanesio, S.S.A., Supr. Gen.
Universal total in Congregation 1,500.
U.S. Delegation (1952): *Mount St. Ann,* Ebensberg, PA 15931. Tel: 814-472-9354. Sr. Anna Maria Lorenzon, S.S.A., Delegate; Sr. Melany Pereira, S.S.A., Community Archivist.
Total number in Community 9.
Ministry in the field of Education; Retreat Ministry; Foreign Mission; Pastoral Ministry.
Represented in the Dioceses of Altoona-Johnstown and Corpus Christi.

[3720] (S.S.A.)—SISTERS OF SAINT ANNE P

Founded in Vaudreuil, Province of Quebec, Canada, 1850. First foundation in the United States in 1866.
Legal Title: *The Community of the Sisters of St. Anne.*
General Motherhouse: 1950 Provost St., Lachine, Quebec , Canada. Sr. Yvette Bellerose, S.S.A., Supr. Gen.
Saint Marie Province (1887): 720 Boston Post Rd. East, Marlboro, MA 01752. Tel: 508-485-3791. Prov. Leaders: Sr. Therese Noury, S.S.A.; Sr. Michele Jacques, S.S.A. Tel: 508-481-4934.
Total number in province 157; In Community 962.
Properties owned: *Saint Anne Convent; Mary Martha House,* Marlboro, MA; *Emmanuel House,* Wayland, MA; *Esther House,* Worcester, MA; *Marie Esther Health Center, Inc.,* Marlboro, MA.
Ministry in the field of Academic and Religious Education at all levels; Center for Spiritual Renewal; Campus Ministry; Various Apostolates; Retreat Work; Pastoral Ministry; Ministry to the Aged, Shut-ins and the Poor; Hospital and Infirmary Nursing; Prison and Hospital Chaplaincies; Foreign Missions.
Represented in the Archdioceses of Anchorage, Boston and Washington and the Dioceses of Fall River, Manchester, Norwich, Providence, St. Petersburg, Springfield (MA), Venice, Wheeling-Charleston and Worcester.

[3730] (O.S.B.M.)—SISTERS OF THE ORDER OF ST. BASIL THE GREAT P

(International Byzantine Rite)

Founded in Cappadocia in the 4th Century by St. Basil the Great and his sister St. Macrina. First foundation in the United States in 1911.
Basilian Generalate: Via San Alessio 26,, Roma, Italy, 00153. Sr. M. Dia Stasiuk, Gen. Supr.

(Philadelphia-Ukrainian Byzantine Rite)

Provincial and Motherhouse: 710 Fox Chase Rd., Fox Chase Manor, PA 19046. Tel: 215-379-2817; 663-9153; Fax: 215-728-6129. Sr. Dorothy Ann Busowski, O.S.B.M., Prov.
Solemnly Professed Sisters 71.
Ministry in Education at all levels; Pastoral Ministry.
Represented in the Ukrainian Archdiocese of Philadelphia and the Ukrainian Dioceses of Chicago, Parma and Stamford.

Pittsburgh Ruthenian Byzantine Rite

Motherhouse and Novitiate: *Mount St. Macrina,* 500 W. Main St., P.O. Box 878, Uniontown, PA 15401. Tel: 412-438-8644. Sr. Ruth Plante, O.S.B.M., Prov.
Professed Sisters 96.
Sisters serve in: Diocesan, Parish and Religious Education Ministry; Health Care; Pastoral Ministry.
Declaration of the Sisters of the Order of St. Basil the Great Endwoment Trust.
Declaration of Trust of the Sisters of the Order of St. Basil the Great Community Support Program. A charitable trust established to provide funding of retirement responsibilities for the sisters. (Byzantine-Ruthenian Rite).
Represented in the Byzantine Archdiocese of Pittsburgh and the Dioceses of Parma, Passaic and Van Nuys.

[3735] (C.S.B.)—CONGREGATION OF ST. BRIGID P

Founded in Ireland in 1807.

U.S. Foundation (1953): *St. Brigid's Convent,* 5118 Loma Linda Dr., San Antonio, TX 78201. Tel: 210-733-0701. Sr. Teresa Carter, C.S.B., Reg. Coord.

Total number in community 19.

Properties owned: *Regional House St. Brigid's Kindergarten,* San Antonio, TX.

Ministry in Pastoral Ministry in Seminary, Detention and Hospitals; Academic Education at all levels; Ministry among immigrants and overseas; Music Ministry.

Represented in the Archdioceses of Boston and San Antonio.

[3740] (S.S.C.)—SISTERS OF ST. CASIMIR P

Founded by Mother Maria Kaupas in the United States in 1907.

General Motherhouse: 2601 W. Marquette Rd., Chicago, IL 60629. Tel: 773-776-1324; Fax: 773-776-8755. Sr. Marilyn Kuzmickus, S.S.C., Gen. Supr.; Sr. M. Christella, S.S.C., Archivist.

Total number in community 199.

Properties owned: *Maria High School Holy Cross Hospital,* Chicago, IL; *Villa Joseph Marie High School,* Holland, PA; *St. Joseph Home for the Aged,* Holland, PA.

Ministry in the field of Academic Education; Foreign Missions; Hospitals; Homes for the Aged; Pastoral Ministry.

Represented in the Archdioceses of Baltimore, Chicago, Miami, Philadelphia and Washington and the Dioceses of Allentown, Joliet and Las Cruces. Also in Argentina.

[3750] (S.S.Ch.)—SISTERS OF ST. CHRETIENNE P

Founded in France in 1807. First foundation in the United States in 1903.

General Motherhouse: Metz (Moselle), 57000, France.

Provincial House: 297 Arnold St., Wrentham, MA 02093-1798. Tel: 508-384-8066; Fax: 508-384-3170. Sr. Suzanne Beaudoin, S.S.Ch., Prov. Supr. Tel: 508-384-7841.

Total number in community 74.

Legal Titles: *St. Chretienne Educational Institute, Inc.,* Marlboro, MA; *St. Chretienne Educational Institute Trust,* Wrentham, MA.

Properties Owned: *Nazareth Spiritual Enrichment Center,* Newport, RI; *Retirement Home and Infirmary,* Marlboro, MA; *Our Lady Pre-school Learning Center,* Marlboro, MA.

Represented in the Archdiocese of Boston and the Dioceses of Lexington, Manchester, Portland (ME), Providence, and St. Petersburg.

[3760] (P.C.C. or O.S.C.)—ORDER OF ST. CLARE P

Poor Clares—Poor Clares of the Primitive Observance—:

Founded in Assisi, Italy in 1212. First foundation in the United States in 1875.

Motherhouse: *Monastery of St. Clare,* Assisi, Italy, is called the Motherhouse of the Order, but the Abbess of said Monastery has no jurisdiction over other Communities of Poor Clares. Some Monasteries, such as those at Omaha, Evansville, New Orleans, Memphis, Jamaica Plain, Greenville, Lowell and Spokane, are subject to a Father General and to the Provincial of the Franciscan Province in which the Monastery is located. Monasteries at Aptos, Cleveland, Kokomo. Los Altos Hills, Newport News, Rockford, Roswell and Santa Barbara are Colettines

Franciscan Monastery of St. Clare: 3626 N. 65th Ave., Omaha, NE 68104-3299. Tel: 402-558-4916. Sr. Veronica Leubbert, O.S.C., Abbess.

Solemnly Professed Sisters 8.

St. Clare's Monastery of the Blessed Sacrament O.S.C.: 720 Henry Clay Ave., New Orleans, LA 70118. Tel: 504-895-2019. Sr. Elizabeth Mortell, O.S.C., Abbess.

Cloistered. Total number in community 11.

Franciscan Monastery of St. Clare O.S.C.: 6825 Nurrenbern Rd., Evansville, IN 47712. Tel: 812-425-4396. Sr. Jeanne A. Maffet, O.S.C., Supr.; Sr. Mary Martha, O.S.C., Community Archivist.

Total number in community 19.

Monastery of St. Clare (1932): 1310 Dellwood Ave., Memphis, TN 38127. Tel: 901-357-6662. Sr. Mary Helen Kelley, O.S.C., Abbess.

Solemnly Professed Cloistered. Total number in community 11.

The Franciscan Monastery of St. Clare: 920 Centre St., Jamaica Plain, MA 02130. Tel: 617-524-1760. Sr. Teresa J. Dericks, O.S.C., Abbess.

Total number in community 23.

Monastery of St. Clare O.S.C.: 201 Crosswicks St., Bordentown, NJ 08505. Tel: 609-298-0016. Sr. Mary McCourt, O.S.C., Abbess.

Total number in community 15.

Franciscan Monastery of Saint Clare: 1271 Langhorne-Newtown Rd., Langhorne, PA 19047-1297. Tel: 215-968-5775; Fax: 215-968-6254. Sr. Mary Alfred Beattie, O.S.C., Abbess.

Total number in community 14.

Franciscan Monastery of St. Clare, Spokane, Washington: *Poor Clare Nuns,* 4419 N. Hawthorne St., Spokane, WA 99205. Tel: 505-327-4479. Solemn Vows, Papal Enclosure *Franciscan Province of Santa Barbara.* Mother Bentivoglio Federation of Poor Clares; Sr. Mary Rita Dolan, O.S.C., Abbess; Sr. Patricia Proctor, O.S.C., Community Archivist.

Professed Nuns 8.

Monastery of St. Clare: 142 Hollywood Ave., Bronx, NY 10465. Tel: 718-822-7271; Fax: 718-822-7271. Sr. Mary Bernadette Quinn, O.S.C., Abbess, Solemn Vows, Papal Enclosure.

Total number in community 15.

St. Clare's Monastery: 421 S. Fourth St., Sauk Rapids, MN 56379. Tel: 320-251-3556. Mother Mary Peter, O.S.C., Abbess.

Solemn Professed Cloistered. Total number in community 14.

St. Clare's Monastery of the Infant Jesus (1953): *Franciscan Poor Clare Nuns,* 8650 Russell Ave. S., Minneapolis, MN 55431-1998. Tel: 612-881-4766. Sr. Mary Helen Weier, O.S.C., Abbess.

Legal Title: Franciscan Poor Clare Nuns.

Total number in community 13.

Monastery of Poor Clares: *Order of St. Clare-Poor Clare Colettine Nuns P.C.C.,* 3501 Rocky River Dr., Cleveland, OH 44111-2998. Tel: 216-941-2820. Mother Mary St. Paul, P.C.C., Abbess, Poor Clare Nuns (Colettines), observing the Primitive Rule of St. Clare. Strictly cloistered, Solemn Vows, Perpetual Exposition of the Most Blessed Sacrament.

Total number in community 28.

St. Joseph Monastery of the Poor Clares Colettines P.C.C.: 1671 Pleasant Valley Rd., P.O. Box 160, Aptos, CA 95001-0160. Tel: 408-761-9659. Mother Mary Clare, Abbess, (Reform of St. Colette) Daily Exposition of the Most Blessed Sacrament.

Total number in community 15 Postulants 1 Novices 2.

Corpus Christi Monastery (Solemn Vows, Papal Enclosure): *Poor Clare Colettines P.C.C.,* 2111 S. Main St., Rockford, IL 61102. Tel: 815-963-7343. Mother Mary Annette, P.C.C., Abbess.

Cloistered. Total number in community 26.

Monastery of Poor Clares-P.C.C. (1928): 215 E. Los Olivos St., Santa Barbara, CA 93105. Tel: 805-682-7670. Mother M. Clare of Jesus, Abbess.

Total number in community 16.

Monastery of St. Clare: 460 River Rd., Andover, MA 01810-4260. Tel: 978-851-6743; Fax: 978-851-2320. Sr. Therese Lacroix, O.S.C., Abbess.

Cloistered. Total number in community 14.

Poor Clare Monastery of Our Lady of Guadalupe: 809 E. 19th St., Roswell, NM 88201. Tel: 505-622-0868. Mother M. Francis, Abbess.

Legal Title: *Community of the Poor Clares of New Mexico, Inc.*

Cloistered. Total number in community 33.

Immaculate Heart Monastery of Poor Clares: 28210 Natoma Rd., Los Altos Hills, CA 94022. Tel: 415-948-2947. Mother Maura, P.C.C., Abbess.

Total number in community 18.

Monastery of St. Clare: 1916 N. Pleasantburg Dr., Greenville, SC 29609-4080. Tel: 864-244-4514; Fax: 864-268-9379. Sr. Rucia Rauton, O.S.C., Abbess.

Cloistered. Total number in community 18.

Monastery of Poor Clares Colettine P.C.C.: 28 Harpersville Rd., Newport News, VA 23601. Tel: 804-596-5942. Solemn Vows. Mother Mary Colette, P.C.C., Abbess; Sr. Mary Agnes, P.C.C., Archivist.

Cloistered. Total number in community 14.

Maria Regina Mater Monastery P.C.C.: *Poor Clare Nuns,* 1175 N., 300 W., Kokomo, IN 46901. Tel: 765-457-5743. Mother Miriam, Abbess.

Cloistered. Total number in community 10.

Christ the King Monastery of St. Clare O.S.C.: 3900 Sherwood Blvd., Delray Beach, FL 33445. Tel: 561-498-3294. Sr. Mary Veronica Butler, O.S.C., Abbess.

Total number in community 12.

Monastery of St. Clare of the Immaculate Conception O.S.C.: *Poor Clares,* 200 Marycrest Dr., St. Louis, MO 63129. Tel: 314-846-2618. Mother Mary Leo Hoffmann, O.S.C., Abbess.

Legal Title: Nuns of the Order of St. Clare of St. Louis.

Total number in community 9.

Monastery of St. Clare (Solemn Vows, Papal Enclosure): 6029 Estero Blvd., Fort Myers Beach, FL 33931-4325. Tel: 941-463-5599; Fax: 941-463-4993. Sr. Mary Emmanuel Kilkenny, O.S.C., Abbess.

Cloistered Sisters 4.

Monastery of St. Clare: 9300 Hwy. 105, Brenham, TX 77833. Tel: 409-836-2444; Fax: 409-836-9652. Sr. Mary Angela Chandler, O.S.C., Abbess.

Sisters in Community 10.

[3765] (O.S.C.CAP.)—CAPUCHIN POOR CLARES P

Federation of Our Lady of the Angels in North America (1991): *Monastery of the Blessed Sacrament,* 4201 N.E. 18th St., Amarillo, TX 79107. Tel: 806-383-6771; Fax: 806-383-9877. Mother Catalina de Maria Banuelos, Pres.

[3770] (O.S.C.)—SISTERS OF ST. CLARE P

Generalate: 63 Harold's Cross Rd., Dublin 6W, Ireland. Sr. Helen Conway, Abbess Gen.

Regional Superior California: *St. Francis Convent,* 326 Santa Clara Dr., Vista, CA 92083. Sr. Madeline Fitzgerald, O.S.C., Reg. Supr.

Regional Superior Florida: *St. Vincent De Paul Convent,* 2109 Tilogia Ct., Holiday, FL 34690. Sr. Josephine Rooney, O.S.C., Reg. Supr.

Ministry in the Fields of Academic and Religious Education at All Levels; Pastoral Ministry; Youth Ministry; Retreat Ministry.

Represented in the Dioceses of Orange, St. Petersburg, San Bernadino and San Diego. Also in Australia, El Salvador, England, Ireland and Wales.

[3780] (SS.C.M.)—SISTERS OF SAINTS CYRIL AND METHODIUS P

Founded in the United States in 1909.

General Motherhouse: *Villa Sacred Heart,* Danville, PA 17821-1698. Tel: 717-275-3581; Fax: 717-275-5997. Sr. M. Paracleta, Gen. Supr.

Total number in community 195.

Properties owned or sponsored: *St. Cyril Academy; Villa Sacred Heart; Sacred Heart Institute; Maria Hall; Maria Joseph Manor; The Meadows at Maria Joseph Manor,* Danville, PA; *Villa St. Cyril,* Highland Park, IL.

Ministry in the field of Education; Parish Ministry and Religious Education; Retreat/Spiritual Direction; Hospital Chaplaincy; Prison Ministry; Deaf Apostolate; Homes for the Aged; Music Conservatory; Education Resource Centers; Continuing Care Retirement Community.

Represented in the Archdioceses of Chicago, Detroit, Hartford and the Dioceses of Allentown, Bridgeport, Charleston, Gary, Harrisburg, Scranton and Syracuse.

[3790] (S.S.D.)—INSTITUTE OF THE SISTERS OF ST. DOROTHY P

Founded in Italy in 1834. First foundation in the United States in 1911.

General Motherhouse: Via del Gianicolo 4-a, Rome, Italy, 00165. Sr. Teresa Lopez, Gen. Coord.

Province of United States of America (1920): *Mt. St. Joseph,* 13 Monkeywrench Lane, Bristol, RI 02809. Tel: 401-253-7835. Sr. Eileen Egan, S.S.D., Prov. Coord.

Total number in community 59.

Properties owned or sponsored: *Villa Fatima,* Taunton, MA; *Mt. St. Joseph,* Bristol, RI; *Our Lady of Fatima High School,* Warren, RI; *St. Dorothy Academy,* Staten Island, NY.

Ministry in the fields of Education; Spiritual Life Centers; Social work with immigrants.

Represented in the Archdiocese of New York and the Dioceses of Brownsville, Fall River and Providence.

[3810] (X.S.)—SOCIETY OF CATHOLIC MISSION SISTERS OF ST. FRANCIS XAVIER, INC. D

(Xavier Sisters)

Founded in the United States in 1946.

Convent: 37179 Moravian Dr., Clinton Township, MI 48036. Tel: 810-465-5082. Sr. Miriam Kennedy, Coord.

Total number in community 3.

Represented in the Archdiocese of Detroit.

[3820] (C.S.J.B.)—SISTERS OF ST. JOHN THE BAPTIST P

Founded in Italy in 1878. First foundation in the United States in 1906.

Legal Title: *Sisters of St. John the Baptist, Inc.*
General Motherhouse: Rome, Italy. Mother John Marie White, C.S.J.B., Supr. Gen.
U.S. Provincial House: 3308 Campbell Dr., Bronx, NY 10465-1358. Tel: 718-518-7820. Sr. Mary Cecile Swanton, C.S.J.B., Prov. Supr.
Total number in community 125.
Legal Titles and Holdings: *Mt. St. John Convent,* Purchase, NY; *St. John Villa Academy,* Staten Island, NY; *Providence Rest Nursing Home,* Bronx, NY; *St. Lucy School,* Newark, NJ; *Mt. St. John Convent,* Gladstone, NJ; *St. Joseph Villa,* Peapack, NJ.
Ministry in the field of Education; Health Care for Aged Women & Men; Child Day Care; Private Guest House.
Represented in the Archdioceses of Newark, New York and the Dioceses of Albany, Metuchen and Paterson.

[3830] (C.S.J. or S.S.J.)—SISTERS OF ST. JOSEPH

The Independent Motherhouses of the Sisters of St. Joseph are represented in the United States in the following Archdioceses and Dioceses:.

[3830-01] **BOSTON** D

Motherhouse of the Congregation of the Sisters of St. Joseph of Boston-CSJ (1873): 637 Cambridge St., Brighton, MA 02135. Tel: 617-783-9090; Fax: 617-783-8246. Sr. Kathleen McCluskey, C.S.J., Pres.; Sr. Therezon Sheerin, C.S.J., Community Archivist.
Total number in community 764.
Legal Holdings or Titles: *Motherhouse of the Sisters of Saint Joseph of Boston,* Brighton, MA; *Bethany Health Care Center, Inc.; Bethany Hill School, Inc.,* Framingham, MA; *Fontbonne Hall,* Framingham, MA; *Retreat Center,* Cohasset, MA; *The Merrimack Montessori School,* Haverhill, MA; *Walnut Park Montessori School,* Newton, MA; *Jackson School Continuous Progress Elementary,* Newton, MA; *Fontbonne Academy,* Milton, MA; *Mount Saint Joseph Academy,* Brighton, MA; *Aquinas College,* Milton, MA; *Aquinas College,* Newton, MA; *Regis College,* Weston, MA.
Ministry in the field of Education at all levels; Health and Hospital services; Human Services and Pastoral Ministries.
Represented in the Archdioceses of Boston and Santa Fe.

[3830-02] **CHICAGO** D

Sisters of St. Joseph of La Grange CSJ (1899): 1515 W. Ogden Ave., La Grange Park, IL 60526. Tel: 708-354-9200. Leadership Team: Sr. Carol Crepeau, Pres.; Sr. Peter Mary Hettling; Sr. Terry Middendorf; Sr. Marlene Schemmel; Sr. Ethel Yaca; Sr. Kathleen Lucas.
Total number in community 113.
Ministry in the field of Education; School Administration; Nursing; Pastoral Care in Hospitals; Nursing Homes; Work with the Elderly; Parish Ministry; Archdiocesan Administration; Spiritual Direction and Retreats.
Legal Titles and Holdings: *Bethlehem Woods Retirement Living Center; Nazareth Academy; Sisters of St. Joseph of LaGrange Charitable Trust,* La-Grange Park, IL.
Represented in the Archdioceses of Chicago and the Dicceses of Cheyenne, Fort Wayne-South Bend, Jackson, Joliet, New Ulm, Rockford and Springfield-Cape Girardeau.

[3830-03] **ORANGE** P

Motherhouse of the Sisters of St. Joseph of Orange CSJ: 480 S. Batavia St., Orange, CA 92668. Tel: 714-633-8121; Fax: 714-744-3165. Sr. Nancy O'Connor, Gen. Supr.; Sr. Annette Bachand, C.S.J., Community Archivist.
Total number in community 240.
Ministry in the field of Education; Health & Hospital Services; Pastoral and Social Services.
Legal Holdings and Titles: *St. Joseph Hospital of Orange,* Orange, CA; *St. Joseph Health System, A Sisters of St. Joseph of Orange Corporation,* Orange, CA; *St. Jude Medical Center,* Fullerton, CA; *Center for Spiritual Development,* Orange, CA; *St. Joseph College,* Orange, CA; *Santa Rosa Memorial Hospital,* Santa Rosa, CA; *St. Joseph Hospital of Eureka,* Eureka, CA; *Redwood Memorial Hospital,* Fortuna, CA; *Queen of the Valley Hospital of Napa,* Napa, CA; *St. Mary of the Plains Hospital,* Lubbock, TX; *St. Joseph Health System Foundation,* Orange, CA; *St. Jude Memorial Foundation,* Fullerton, CA; *Redwood Memorial Foundation,* Fortuna, CA; *St. Jude Hospital Yorba Linda,* Yorba Linda, CA; *Sisters of St. Joseph Healthcare Foundation,* Orange, CA; *Mission Hospital Regional Medical Center; St. Mary Desert Valley Hospital,* Apple Valley, CA.
Represented in the Archdioceses of Los Angeles and San Francisco and the Dioceses of El Paso, Lubbock, Oakland, Orange, San Bernardino, San Diego and Santa Rosa. Also in El Salvador, Mexico, Hungary, Israel and Australia.

[3830-05] **ROCKVILLE CENTRE** D

St. Joseph's Convent - Congregation of the Sisters of Saint Joseph of Brentwood, NY CSJ: Brentwood, NY 11717. Tel: 516-273-4531. Sr. Angela Gannon, Gen. Supr.; Sr. Edna McKeever, Community Archivist.
Total number in community 970.
Ministry in the field of Education; Health & Hospital Services.
Represented in the Dioceses of Brooklyn and Rockville Centre. Also in Puerto Rico.

[3830-06] **BUFFALO** P

Generalate - Congregation of the Sisters of St. Joseph SSJ: 23 Agassiz Cir., Buffalo, NY 14214. Tel: 716-838-4400. Sr. Bea Manzella, Pres.; Sr. Mary Anne Butler, S.S.J., Community Archivist.
Total number in community 156.
Properties owned or sponsored: *Mt. St. Joseph Academy Administrative Office; Sisters of St. Joseph Residence.*
Ministry in the field of Education at all levels; Hospital; Infant Home; School for Deaf; Youth Ministry; Justice Ministry; Pastoral Ministry; Hospital Chaplaincy; Prison Ministry; Spirituality Center.
Represented in the Archdioceses of Cincinnati, Detroit and the Dioceses of Buffalo, Pensacola-Tallahassee, and Tucson. Also in Peru.

[3830-07] **BURLINGTON** D

Sisters of St. Joseph SSJ: 129 Convent Ave., Rutland, VT 05701. Tel: 802-775-0665. Sr. Miriam Francis Preedom, Pres.
Total number in community 51.
Properties owned or sponsored: *St. Joseph Residence; Kervic Home Fontbonne Hall; St. Francis Residence Guest House; Avilla Hall; Marion Hall Residence; Mt. St. Joseph Academy,* Rutland, VT; *St. Joseph Convent,* Bennington.
Ministry in the field of Education; Pastoral Ministry; Health Care; Social Services.
Represented in the Diocese of Burlington.

[3830-08] **CLEVELAND** D

St. Joseph Convent - Sisters of St. Joseph CSJ: 3430 Rocky River Dr., Cleveland, OH 44111. Tel: 216-252-0440. Executive Team: Sr. Barbara Green; Sr. Donna Hawk; Sr. Marietta Starrie; Sr. Ruth Rogers, Community Archivist.
Total number in community 163.
Legal Holdings & Titles: *Saint Joseph Academy; Sisters of Saint Joseph Community Support Charitable Trust Fund.*
Ministry in the field of Academic and Religious Education at all levels; Parish and Pastoral Ministry; Deaf Apostolate; Parish Team Member; Justice Work; Health Care; Social Services; Bookstores and Radio; Social Concerns; Retreat Work; House of Prayer.
Represented in the Archdiocese of Miami and Washington and the Dioceses of Cleveland, Colorado Springs, Columbus, Galveston-Houston, Oakland, Stuebenville, Venice and Wheeling-Charleston.

[3830-09] **ERIE** D

Sisters of St. Joseph SSJ: *Villa Maria,* 5031 W. Ridge Rd., Erie, PA 16506-1249. Tel: 814-838-4100; Fax: 814-838-5167. Sr. Mary Fromknecht, Congregational Admin.
Total number in the community 179.
Legal Title: *Sisters of St. Joseph of Northwestern Pa.*
Institutions sponsored: Saint Vincent Health Center; St. Mary's Home of Erie; Villa Maria Elementary; Villa Maria Academy; Villa Maria Center.
Ministry in the field of Education at all levels; Social Ministries; Nursing Home; Health Care; Pastoral Work and other Diocesan Ministries.
Represented in the Archdioceses of Chicago, Louisville, Miami, Milwaukee, Washington and the Dioceses of Arlington, Buffalo, Cleveland Memphis, Pittsburgh and Rochester.

[3830-10] **LAFAYETTE-IN-INDIANA** D

St. Joseph Center - Sisters of St. Joseph of Tipton CSJ: 1440 W. Division Rd., Tipton, IN 46072. Tel: 765-675-6203; Fax: 765-675-7471. Sr. Dorothy Gall, Pres.
Total number in community 53.
Ministry in Education; Health Care; Pastoral Ministry; Social Service; Evangelization.
Represented in the Archdiocese of Indianapolis and the Dioceses of Baker and Lafayette (IN). Also in Haiti.

[3830-11] **KALAMAZOO** P

Motherhouse and Novitiate - Sisters of St. Joseph of Nazareth SSJ: Nazareth, MI 49074. Tel: 616-381-6290; Fax: 616-381-4909. Leadership Team: Sr. Janet Fleischhacker, Pres.; Sr. Christine Parks; Sr. Rita Ann Teichman; Sr. Judy Schroeder.
Total number in community 346.
Properties owned or sponsored: Hospitals; Holding Companies for Health Service Corporation; Nursing Homes; Day Care Center for handicapped and senior citizens; Residence for Senior Citizens; Home Health Care Organizations; Ambulatory Care Services; Residential Treatment Center; Family Clinic; Gerontology Research Center; Outpatient Mental Health Clinic.
Ministry in the field of Educational; Social Services; Parish and Church-related Ministries; Foreign Missions.
Represented in the Archdioceses of Chicago Detroit, Los Angeles, New Orleans, Omaha, Sante Fe and Washington and the Dioceses of Gary, Gaylord, Grand Rapids, Jackson, Jefferson City, Kalamazoo, Lafayette in Indiana, Lansing, Memphis, Phoenix, Saginaw, and St. Petersburg. Also in Peru and France.

[3830-12] **OGDENSBURG** D

Motherhouse of the Society of the Sisters of St. Joseph SSJ: 1425 Washington St., Watertown, NY 13601. Tel: 315-782-3460. Sr. Annunciata Collins, Supr. Gen.; Sr. Mary Joseph Meichelbeck, Community Archivist.
Total number in community 77.
Ministry in the field of Education at all levels.
Represented in the Diocese of Ogdensburg.

[3830-13] **PITTSBURGH** P

Sisters of St. Joseph CSJ - Motherhouse & Mt. Gallitzin Academy: Baden, PA 15005. Tel: 724-869-2151. Leadership Team: Sr. Jeanette Bussen; Sr. Cynthia Comiskey; Sr. Anna Marie Gaglia; Sr. Dolores Montini; Sr. Patricia Phillips; Sr. Helen Marie Shrift, Community Archivist.
Total number in community 324.
Properties owned: Motherhouse and 8 residences for sisters.
Ministry in the field of Religious and Academic Education; Campus Ministry; Hospital Ministry; Health Care; Social Work; Parish Social and Pastoral Ministry; Family Life Ministry; Missionary Work; Housing Managers; Prison Ministry; Diocesan Administrative Services.
Represented in the Archdioceses of Baltimore, Boston, Hartford, Miami, Mobile, New York, Washington and the Dioceses of Altoona-Johnstown, Arlington, Charlotte, Cheyenne, Columbus, Covington, Fresno, Greensburg, Harrisburg, Jackson, Pittsburgh, Richmond, and Wheeling-Charleston. Also in and Jamaica and London.

[3830-14] **ROCHESTER** P

Sisters of St. Joseph SSJ - Motherhouse: 4095 East Ave., Rochester, NY 14618-3798. Tel: 716-586-1000; Fax: 716-586-1193. Sr. Rosemary St. Peter, Congregational Pres.; Sr. Jeanne Agnes Michaud, Archivist.
Total number in community 461.
Properties owned and sponsored: *Nazareth Academy; Nazareth Hall; Nazareth Academy; Convent Motherhouse; St. Joseph Convent Infirmary.*
Ministry in the field of Education at all levels; Homes for Aging; Health Care; Pastoral Ministry; School for Special Children and Adults; Homes for Emotionally Disturbed Children; Parish and Diocesan Evangelization; College Campus Ministry; Social Service; Justice and Peace Offices; Drug Dependency Programs; Prison Ministry.
Sisters sponsor: 2 Foster Care Homes, 1 Food Kitchen and 1 Community Neighborhood Center.
Represented in the Archdioceses of Boston and Mobile and the Dioceses of Albany, Buffalo and Rochester and Syracuse. Also in Brazil.

[3830-15] **SALINA** P

General Administration Office (1884): *Sisters of St. Joseph of Concordia CSJ,* 215 Court St., P.O. Box 279, Concordia, KS 66901. Tel: 785-243-2149. Sr. Christine Doman, Pres.
Motherhouse: Sisters of St. Joseph, 1300 Washington St., Concordia, KS 66901. Tel: 785-243-2113.

Total sisters in community 241; Postulants 2.
Properties owned: *Medaille Center,* Salina, KS; *Manna House of Prayer,* Concordia, KS; *Saint Joseph Foundation for Apostolic and Charitable Purposes, Inc.*
Ministries: Care for Elderly; Homeless; Education; Parish and Diocesan Evangelization; Social Services; Justice and Peace Offices; Marriage and Family Counseling; Youth Formation; Handicapped Adults; Healthcare; College Campus Ministry; Drug Dependency Programs; Prisons; Consultants; Refugees; Continuous Prayer.
Represented in the Archdioceses of Atlanta, Boston, Chicago, Denver, Kansas City in Kansas, St. Louis, St. Paul-Minneapolis and the Dioceses of Davenport, Dodge City, El Paso, Fargo, Grand Island, Jackson, Jefferson City, Kansas City-St. Joseph, Las Cruces, Marquette, Oakland, Phoenix, Pueblo, Rockford, St. Cloud and Salina.

[3830-16] SPRINGFIELD (MA) D

Motherhouse: *Mont Marie - Sisters of St. Joseph of Springfield SSJ,* Holyoke, MA 01040. Tel: 413-536-0853; Fax: 413-533-3275. Sr. Constance Quinlan, Pres.; Sr. Rita Morey, Archivist.
Total number in community 399.
Legal Holdings and Titles: *Mont Marie Child Care Center, Inc.; Mont Marie Health Care Center, Inc.; Mont Marie Conference Center,* Holyoke, MA.
Ministry in the field of Education at all levels; Spiritual Direction; Retreat Work; Diocesan Administration; Pastoral Ministry; Campus Ministry; Hospital Chaplaincy; Ministry to the Elderly; Youth Ministry; Counseling; Social Services; Health Care; Peace and Justice; Spanish Apostolate and Communications.
Represented in the Archdioceses of Hartford and Washington and the Dioceses of Fall River, Lake Charles, Providence, Springfield (MA) and Worcester. Also in Tanzania.

[3830-17] WHEELING D

Motherhouse: *Mt. St. Joseph-Sisters of St. Joseph of Wheeling SSJ,* Pogue Run Rd., Wheeling, WV 26003. Tel: 304-232-8160. Sr. Marguerite O'Brien, Pres.; Sr. Mary Thomas Camilletti, Community Archivist.
Total number in community 108.
Legal Holdings and Titles: *Sisters of St. Joseph Ministries Support Fund, Inc.; Sisters of St. Joseph of Wheeling Foundation; St. Joseph Hospital,* Parkersburg, WV.
Ministry the following areas: Parish Ministry; Pastoral Services; Elementary, Secondary, College Education; Health Care; Social Services; Spiritual Formation, Direction and Retreat Ministries; Diocesan; Administration and Service.
Represented in the Diocese of Wheeling-Charleston.

[3830-18] WICHITA P

Motherhouse: *Mt. St. Mary Convent - Sisters of St. Joseph of Wichita, CSJ,* 3700 E. Lincoln St., Wichita, KS 67218. Tel: 316-686-7171; Fax: 316-689-4056. Sr. Veronice Born, Pres.; Sr. Denise Sevart, Archivist.
Total number in community 201.
Legal Holdings and Titles: *Mt. St. Mary Convent* (Motherhouse), Parent organization for: 5 residences, Wichita, KS; 1 residence, Pittsburg, KS; 1 residence, Ponca City, OK; 1 residence, Hayward, CA; *Via Christi Health System, Inc.,* (Parent organization) for: *Via Christi Regional Medical Center, Inc.; St. Francis Campus; St. Joseph Campus Via Christi Rehabilitation Hospital, Inc. - Lourdes Campus; GeorgeTown Village, Inc.,* Wichita, KS; *Mount Carmel Medical Center, Inc.* Parent organization for: *Mount Carmel Foundation,* Pittsburg, KS; *Mount Joseph Senior Community, Inc.; St. Joseph Senior Community, Inc.,* Manhattan, KS; *St. Joseph Regional Medical Center of Northern Oklahoma, Inc.; Hayward Sisters Hospital, dba St. Rose Hospital.* Parent organization for: *St. Rose Medical Building, Inc.; St. Rose Hospital Foundation,* Hayward, CA.
Ministry in the field of Religious and Academic Education; Adult Religious Correspondence Courses; Diocesan Program for the Handicapped; School of Special Education; Day Nursery; Home for Aged; Pro-Life Ministry to Women; ESL Language School; G.E.D. Program; Home Hospice; Hospital and Clinical Care; Pastoral Ministry; Campus Ministry.
Represented in the Archdioceses of Kansas City in Kansas, Oklahoma City and the Dioceses of Oakland, Salina and Wichita. Also in Japan.

[3840] (C.S.J.)—SISTERS OF ST. JOSEPH OF CARONDELET P

Founded in France in 1650. First foundation in the United States in 1836.
Congregational Offices: 2307 S. Lindbergh Blvd., St. Louis, MO 63131. Sr. Helene Wilson, C.S.J., Congregational Dir. for the Provinces and Vice Province listed below.
Province of St. Louis (1836): *St. Joseph's Provincial House,* 6400 Minnesota Ave., St. Louis, MO 63111. Tel: 314-481-8800; Fax: 314-481-2366; 351-3111. Sr. Barbara Dreher, C.S.J., Prov. Dir. Team Members: Sr. Paulette Gladis, C.S.J.; Sr. Suzanne Giblin, C.S.J.
Total number in community 616.
Sponsored Institutions: Colleges 2; Academies 2; Hospitals 3; Institute for the Deaf 1; Long Term Care Facility 1.
Legal Title: *Sisters of St. Joseph ofa Carondelet, St. Louis Province.*
Ministries in the field of Academic Education; Pastoral Ministries; Diocesan Offices; Health Care; Child Care; Geriatric Care; Foreign Missions; Social Servies; Community Services; Special Services; Fine Arts.
Represented in the Archdioceses of Atlanta, Boston, Chicago, Denver, Indianapolis, Kansas City in Kansas, Los Angeles, Miami, Mobile, New Orleans, Oklahoma City, St. Louis, St. Paul-Minneapolis, Seattle and the Dioceses of Brownsville, Charleston, Colorado Springs, Davenport, El Paso, Evansville, Green Bay, Helena, Jackson, Kansas City-St. Joseph, Lansing, Marquette, Nashville, Palm Beach, Peoria, Reno-Las Vegas, St. Petersburg, San Diego, San Jose, Savannah, Shreveport, Springfield-Cape Girardeau, Steubenville, Syracuse, Tucson, Venice and Wilmington. Also in Canada.
Province of St. Paul (1851): *St. Joseph's Administration Center,* 1884 Randolph Ave., St. Paul, MN 55105. Tel: 612-690-7000; Fax: 612-690-7039. Province Admin. Team: Sr. Ann Vivia Walton, C.S.J.; Sr. Margaret Belanger, C.S.J.; Sr. Margaret L. Kvasnicka, C.S.J.; Sr. Mary Kraft, C.S.J., Archivist.
Total number in community 454.
Legal Holdings or Titles: *St. Joseph of Carondelet - St. Paul Province Provincial House; The College of St. Catherine Bethany Convent for Retired Sisters,* St. Paul, MN.
Ministry in the fields of Education; Health; Social Services; Spirituality.
Represented in the Archdioceses of Los Angeles, New York, Portland (OR), St. Paul-Minneapolis, Seattle and the Dioceses of Brownsville, Charlotte, Duluth, El Paso, Fargo, Fort Worth, Helena, Jackson, Jefferson City, Kalamazoo, New Ulm, Pittsburgh and Superior.
Province of Albany (1858): *St. Joseph's Provincial House,* 385 Watervliet-Shaker Rd., Latham, NY 12110-4799. Tel: 518-783-3500. Sr. Sean C. Peters, C.S.J., Prov. Dir.; Sr. Anne L. Clark, C.S.J., Prov. Archivist.
Total number in community 620.
Novitiate 369 Watervliet-Shaker Rd., Latham, NY 12110. Tel: 518-783-3536.
Ministry in the fields of Academic and Special Education at all levels; Hospital and Infirmary Services; Hospital Pastoral Ministries; Parish Ministry and Religious Education; Diocesan Offices; Youth Ministry; Counseling; Retreat and Spiritual Direction; Social and Community Services; Fine Arts.
Represented in the Archdioceses of Anchorage, Boston, Cincinnati, Detroit, Indianapolis, Los Angeles, New York, St. Louis, St. Paul-Minneapolis, Seattle, San Francisco, Washington and the Dioceses of Albany, Arlington, Birmingham, Brooklyn, Buffalo, Erie, Fairbanks, Fall River, Harrisburg, Honolulu, Kansas City-St. Joseph, Lafayette, Manchester, Ogdensburg, Orange, Orlando, Palm Beach, Pensacola-Tallahassee, Pittsburgh, Providence, Rochester, Rockville Centre, Scranton, Spokane, Syracuse, Trenton, and Tucson. Also in Chile, Japan and Peru.
Province of Los Angeles (1878): *St. Mary's Provincialate and Carondelet Center,* 11999 Chalon Rd., Los Angeles, CA 90049-1524. Tel: 213-272-8016; Fax: 310-476-5253. Sr. Joyce Marie Gaspardo, Prov. Supr.; Sr. Mary Ellen Sprouffske, C.S.J., Archivist.
Professed Sisters 500.
Legal Titles or Holdings: *Sisters of St. Joseph in California; Sisters of St. Joseph in Arizona; Sisters of St. Joseph Ministerial Services.*
Sisters serve in the fields of Education, Health and Hospital services; Social Services; and other related services.
Represented in the Archdioceses of Boston, Chicago, Los Angeles, San Francisco, Seattle and Washington and the Dioceses of Boise, Fresno, Honolulu, Monterey, Oakland, Orange, Phoenix, Sacramento, San Bernardino, San Diego, San Jose, Santa Rosa, Spokane, Stockton, Tucson and Yakima.
Hawaii Vice-Province (1956): *Sisters of St. Joseph of Carondelet,* Carondelet Convent, 5311 Apo Dr., Honolulu, HI 96821-1829. Tel: 808-373-2096. Sr. Brenda Lau, C.S.J., Vice-Prov. Supr.
Legal Title: *Sisters of St. Joseph of Carondelet-Hawaii Vice-Province.*
Professed Sisters 43.
Ministries Include: Elementary and Secondary Schools; Pastoral Associates; Prayer & Spirituality; Hispanic Ministry; Administering Diocesan Offices; Religious Education Directors; Campus Ministry; Social Ministry.
Represented in the Diocese of Honolulu. Also in Chile.

[3850] (C.S.J.)—SISTERS OF ST. JOSEPH OF CHAMBERY P

Founded in France in 1650. First foundation in United States in 1885.
Generalate: Via Calandrelli 7, 00153, Rome, Italy. Sr. Lorraine Delaney, C.S.J., Supr. Gen.
Provincial House: *Convent of Mary Immaculate,* 27 Park Rd., West Hartford, CT 06119. Tel: 860-233-5126; 232-8252. Sr. Mary Kelly, C.S.J., Prov. Supr.
Total number in community 194.
Legal Title: *Sisters of St. Joseph Corporation.*
Ministry in the field of Academic and Religious Education at all levels; Social Services; Pastoral and Parish Ministries; Prisons; Law and Business; Child Day Care Center; Foreign Missions; Hospitals and Health Care.
Represented in the Archdioceses of Baltimore, Hartford, Miami, Mobile, New York, Washington and the Dioceses of Bridgeport, El Paso, Fairbanks, Lexington, Norwich, Springfield (MA) and Trenton.

[3860] (S.J.C.)—SISTERS OF ST. JOSEPH OF CLUNY P

Founded in France in 1807.
Generalate: Paris, France. Sr. Marie Noel LeFrancios, Supr. Gen.
American Novitiate: *Mary Immaculate Queen Novitiate,* 20955 Halldale Ave., Torrance, CA 90501. Tel: 310-328-1807.
Provincialate Brenton Rd., Newport, RI 02840. Tel: 401-846-4757. Sr. Mary J. Glynn, Prov. of U.S. & Canada.
Professed Sisters in U.S. & Canada 45.
Legal Title: *Sisters of St. Joseph of Cluny, Inc.*
Represented in the Archdiocese of Los Angeles and the Dioceses of Orange, Providence and Wheeling-Charleston. Also in Canada.

[3870] (C.S.J.)—SISTERS OF ST. JOSEPH OF LYONS, FRANCE P

Founded in France October 15, 1650. First foundation in United States in 1906 in Jackman, Maine.
General Motherhouse: Lyons, France. Sr. Joelle Peillon, Supr. Gen.
Maine Province: *Sisters of St. Joseph,* 93 Halifax St., Winslow, ME 04901. Tel: 207-873-4512; Fax: 207-873-1976. Sr. Janet Gagnon, Prov.
Total number in community 55.
Properties owned and sponsored: *Mount St. Joseph Nursing Home,* Waterville, ME; *St. Joseph Child Care Center,* Auburn, ME.
Ministry in Catechetical Centers; Nursing Homes; Day Care Centers; Renewal Center; Pastoral Ministry; Education; Drug and Substance Abuse; Rehabilitation.
Represented in the Dioceses of El Paso, Fairbanks, and Portland (ME).

[3880] (C.S.J.)—SISTERS OF ST. JOSEPH OF MEDAILLE P

Founded in France in 1650. First foundation in the United States in 1855. Classified as an American Congregation November 30, 1977.
Central Office: *Congregation of the Sisters of Saint Joseph of Medaille,* 1821 Summit Rd., Suite 210, Cincinnati, OH 45237. Tel: 513-761-2888; Fax: 513-761-9957. Sr. Lucy Silvio, Pres.; Sr. Maria Hill, Vice Pres. General Councilors: Sr. Joan Hartlaub; Sr. Janice Miller.
Total number in community 200.
Legal Title: *Sisters of St. Joseph of Medaille, Ohio Corporation.*
Ministry in the field of Academic Education at all levels; Hospital and Clinic Care; Pastoral Ministry; Religious Education; Foreign Missions; Social Service; Centers for Christian Renewal; Services to Poor and Minorities; Community Service; Diocesan Offices; Activities Programs for Retired-Elderly; Chemical Dependency; Adult Mentally Retarded; Care for Retired Sisters.
Represented in the Archdioceses of Cincinnati, New Orleans, St. Paul-Minneapolis and Washington and the Dioceses of Baton Rouge, Crookston, El

Paso, Fargo, Fort Wayne-South Bend, Green Bay, Houma-Thibodaux, St. Petersburg and Superior. Also in Managua, Nicaragua.

[3890] (C.S.J.P.)—SISTERS OF ST. JOSEPH OF PEACE P

Founded in England 1884. First United States foundation 1885.

Generalate: *Sisters of St. Joseph of Peace Generalate, Inc.*, 3043 Fourth St. N.E., Washington, DC 20017. Tel: 202-832-5333; Fax: 202-832-5327. Sr. Ann Rutan, C.S.J.P., Congregation Leader.

St. Joseph Province-Eastern Province (1885; Sr. Mary Rattigan, C.S.J.P., Prov.; Sr. Nora Molyneux, C.S.J.P., Vice Prov.

Total number in the community 384, Total number in the province 179.

Ministry in the field of Education; Health and Social Services.

Properties owned or sponsored: *St. Joseph's Home for the Blind; The Kenmare School; St. Ann's Home for The Aged; St. Mary's Residence; Stella Maris Retreat House, School of Nursing; Senior Sisters Residence; St. Joseph's Home Messenger; The Guild for the Sisters of St. Joseph of Peace; Retirement Trust Fund for St. Joseph Province (Eastern); St. Joseph Province Offices, Shalom Center,* Englewood Cliffs, NJ; Affiliated Corporations: *St. Joseph's Village; Englewood Cliffs College; Holy Name Hospital; St. Joseph's School for the Blind; St. Michael's Villa; Villa Marie Claire; Holy Name Health Care Foundation; St. Joseph's Home for the Blind-Sisters of St. Joseph of Peace; St. Joseph's Home,* Jersey City, NJ; *The Nurturing Place (York Street Child Development Center).*

Represented in the Archdioceses of Baltimore, Los Angeles, Newark, New York and Washington and the Dioceses of Camden, Metuchen, Paterson, St. Petersburg and Trenton.

Our Lady Province (Western) (1909): *St. Mary's Provincialate,* 1663 Killarney Way, Box 248, Bellevue, WA 98009-0248. Tel: 425-451-1770; Fax: 425-462-9760. Sr. Kathleen Pruitt, C.S.J.P., Prov. Leader.

Properties owned: *St. Mary's Residence and Novitiate,* Bellevue, WA; *Prospect House,* Seattle, WA; *St. Theres Residence,* Seattle, WA; *Grace House,* Seattle, WA; *Alicia Park House,* Seattle, WA; *Eugene Residence,* Eugene, OR.

Corporate Titles: *Sisters of St. Joseph of Peace; Our Lady Province (Western); Sisters of St. Joseph of Peace; Charitable Trust Health and Hospital Services; Sisters of St. Joseph of Peace,* Bellevue, WA; *Jubilee Women's Center,* Seattle, WA.

Total number in community 102.

Ministry in the field of Education; Health and Hospital; Services; Social Services; Religious Education; Parish Ministry, Retreat Ministry, Social and Minority Ministry.

Represented in the Archdioceses of Anchorage, Los Angeles, Portland (OR), San Francisco and Seattle and the Dioceses of Juneau, San Diego, Spokane and Yakima. Also in Canada.

[3893] (S.S.J.)—SISTERS OF SAINT JOSEPH OF CHESTNUT HILL, PHILADELPHIA P

Founded in France in 1650. First foundation in Philadelphia in 1847.

Motherhouse (1847): *Mount St. Joseph Convent,* Chestnut Hill, Philadelphia, PA 19118-2694. Tel: 215-248-7200. Sr. Margaret Fleming, Supr. Gen.; Sr. Lawrence Joseph Murphy, Community Archivist.

Total number in congregation 1,361.

Legal Holdings or Titles: *Saint Joseph Villa; Saint Joseph Guild; Bethelehem Retirement Village,* Flourtown, PA; *Academy Village,* McSherrystown, PA; *Saint Joseph Housing Corporation; Saint Mary by-the-Sea Convent,* Cape May Point, NJ; *Cecilian Academy,* Philadelphia, PA; *Mount Saint Joseph Academy,* Flourtown, PA; *Norwood-Fontbonne Academy for Boys and Girls,* Philadelphia, PA; *Holy Family Academy,* Bayonne, NJ; *Chestnut Hill College,* Philadelphia, PA; *Saint Joseph Academy,* McSherrystown, PA; T*he Convent of the Sisters of St. Joseph,* Chestnut Hill, PA.

Ministry in the field of Academic and Religious Education at all levels; Institutes for Dependent Children; Pastoral Ministry; Campus Ministry; Care of the Aged; Social Services; Prison Ministry; Health Care; Psychologists; Hospice Ministry; Hospital Chaplaincy; Spiritual Directors; Drug and Alcohol Counsellors; Legal Services Ministry; Delegates for Religious.

Represented in the Archdioceses of Baltimore, Chicago, Mobile, Newark, Philadelphia, San Antonio, Washington and the Dioceses of Albany, Allentown, Altoona-Johnstown, Arlington, Belleville, Camden, Charlotte, Corpus Christi, Fort Wayne-South Bend, Harrisburg, Jackson, Juneau, Lexington, Metuchen, Paterson, Raleigh, Rockville Centre, St. Petersburg, Savannah, Scranton, Trenton and Wilmington. Also in Canada, Peru, and the Dominican Republic.

[3900] (S.S.J.)—SISTERS OF ST. JOSEPH OF ST. AUGUSTINE, FLORIDA D

Founded in France in 1650. First foundation in the United States in 1866. Classified as an American Congregation in 1899.

Motherhouse: *St. Joseph Convent,* 241 St. George St. P.O. Box 3506, St. Augustine, FL 32085. Tel: 904-824-1752. Sr. Florence Bryan, S.S.J., General Supr.; Sr. Mary Albert Lussier, S.S.J., Community Archivist.

Legal Title: *The Sisters of St. Joseph Continuing Community Support Trust Fund.*

Total number in community 110.

Ministry in Hospital-Health Care Services; Social Services; Hospital Pastoral Care; Care of Aged; Academic and Religious Education at all levels; Parish Ministry; Diocesan Office Administration; House of Prayer; Ministry to the Handicapped.

Represented in the Archdiocese Miami and the Dioceses of Orlando, Palm Beach, Pensacola-Tallahassee, St. Augustine and St. Petersburg.

[3910] (S.J.S.M.)—SISTERS OF ST. JOSEPH OF ST. MARK D

Founded in France in 1845. First foundation in the United States in October, 1937.

Generalate: Colmar, France. Sr. Sophie Moog, Gen. Supr.

Universal total number in Congregation 256.

Youngstown Diocese: *Community Center,* 2337 Reno Dr., Louisville, OH 44641. Tel: 330-875-5946. Sr. M. Leo Hauck, Supr.

Total number in U.S. 9.

General Motherhouse (Cleveland) (1939): 21800 Charden Rd., Euclid, OH 44117. Mother Mary Therese Trunk, Supr. Gen.

Represented in the Diocese of Cleveland.

[3920] (S.J.W.)—SISTERS OF ST. JOSEPH THE WORKER D

General Motherhouse: *St. William Convent,* 1 St. Joseph Ln., Walton, KY 41094. Mother Ellen Curran, S.J.W., Supr.

Total number in the community 21.

Properties owned and operated: *Taylor Manor Nursing Home,* Versailles, KY; 16-acre property in Walton, KY: *Motherhouse Formation House.*

Represented in the Dioceses of Covington and Lexington.

[3930] (SSJ-TOSF)—SISTERS OF ST. JOSEPH OF THE THIRD ORDER OF ST. FRANCIS P

Founded in the United States in 1901.

Corporate Office: P.O. Box 305 - 1300 Maria Dr., Stevens Point, WI 54481-0305. Tel: 715-341-8457; Fax: 715-341-8830. Sr. Jeanne Conzemius, S.S.J.-T.O.S.F., Pres.; Sr. Beth Konkol, S.S.J.-T.O.S.F., Vice Pres.; Sr. Katherine Wyszynski, S.S.J.-T.O.S.F., Vice Pres.; Sr. Mary Allice Jarosz, S.S.J.-T.O.S.F., Vice Pres.

Total number in the Congregation 543.

Ministries in the following areas: Academic Education at all levels; Pastoral Ministry; Health Care Services; Ministry abroad in South Africa, South America and Puerto Rico; 8th Day Center for Justice; Social Services.

Sponsors: 1 Learning Center; 3 High Schools; 1 Health Care Facility.

Represented in the Archdioceses of Chicago, Denver, Detroit, Hartford, Los Angeles, Milwaukee, Newark, St. Paul-Minneapolis and the Dioceses of Cleveland, Fort Wayne-South Bend, Gary, Grand Island, Green Bay, Harrisburg, Jackson, Joliet, Kalamazoo, Knoxville, La Crosse, Lansing, Madison, Norwich, Oakland, Phoenix, Rockford, Superior, Toledo and Youngstown.

[3935] (S.S.L.)—THE CONGREGATION OF THE SISTERS OF ST. LOUIS, JUILLY - MONAGHAN P

Founded in France in 1842. First foundation in the United States in 1949.

General Motherhouse: Louisville Monaghan, Ireland. Sr. Maud Murphy, S.S.L., Supr. Gen.

Regional House: *Louisville Convent,* 22300 Mulholland Dr., Woodland Hills, CA 91364. Tel: 818-883-1678. Sr. Bernadette Murphy, S.S.L., Reg. Supr.

Legal Title: *Sisters of St. Louis (Monaghan), Inc.*

Finally Professed Sisters 79.

Ministry in the field of Education; Pastoral and Social Ministries.

Represented in the Archdioceses of Indianapolis, Los Angeles, Washington and the Dioceses of Oakland, Orange, Raleigh and Salt Lake City.

[3950] (S.S.M.N.)—SISTERS OF SAINT MARY OF NAMUR P

Founded in Namur, Belgium, in 1819. First foundation in the United States in 1863.

General Motherhouse: Namur, Belgium; Sr. Marie Julianne Farrington, Gen. Supr.

Universal Total in Congregation 421.

Eastern Province: *Provincial House,* 250 Bryant, Buffalo, NY 14222. Tel: 716-884-8221; Fax: 716-884-2950. Sr. Maureen Quinn, S.S.M.N., Prov. Supr.

Total number in community 111.

Legal Holdings or Titles: *St. Joseph Convent,* Lockport, NY.

Ministry in the field of Religious and Academic Education; Pastoral Ministry; Social Services; Diocesan and Health related services; Refugee Assistance.

Represented in the Archdiocese of Boston and the Dioceses of Buffalo, Charleston, Jackson, Rochester, Savannah and Syracuse.

Western Province: *Provincial House - Our Lady of Victory Center,* 909 W. Shaw St., Fort Worth, TX 76110. Tel: 817-923-8393. Sr. Gabriela Martinez, Prov. Supr.

Total number in community 75.

Properties owned or sponsored: *Our Lady of Victory Center,* Fort Worth, TX; *Our Lady of Victory Elementary School,* Fort Worth, TX; *Casa de Esperanza,* Houston, TX; *Sisters of St. Mary of Namur,* Fort Worth, TX; *Notre Dame Convent Mercy Convent,* Wichita Falls, TX.

Ministry in the field of Religious and Academic Education; Diocesan Offices; Pastoral Ministry; Social Services; Health Care.

Represented in the Dioceses of Dallas, Fort Worth, Galveston-Houston, Richmond and Victoria.

[3960] (S.S.M.O.)—SISTERS OF ST. MARY OF OREGON P

Founded in Oregon in 1886.

General Motherhouse: *St. Mary of the Valley,* 4440 S.W. 148th Ave., Beaverton, OR 97007. Tel: 503-644-9181. Sr. Delores Adelman, Supr. Gen.

Total number in Congregation 98.

Properties owned or sponsored: *St. Mary of the Valley School & Convent; Valley Catholic School; Maryville Nursing Home; Little Flower Development Center,* Beaverton, OR.

Ministry in the field of Education; Nursing Homes; and Parish Services.

Represented in the Archdioceses of Los Angeles, Portland (OR) and Seattle and the Dioceses of Baker, Helena and Sacramento.

[3980] (S.P.C)—SISTERS OF SAINT PAUL DE CHARTRES P

Founded in France in 1696.

General House: 193 Via della Vignaccia, Rome, I-00163. Italy. Sr. Anne-Marie Audet, S.P.C., Supr. Gen.

Universal total in Congregation 4,000.

U.S. Province: 1300 County Rd. 492, Marquette, MI 49855. Tel: 906-226-3932; 226-2139. Sr. Mary Anne Laurin, S.P.C., Prov. Supr.

Total number in community 21.

Legal Holding: *Bishop Noa Home for Senior Citizens,* Escanaba, MI.

Ministry in the field of Academic and Religious Education; Campus Ministry; Pastoral Associates; Ministry to the Aged.

Represented in the Archdiocese of Washington and the Diocese of Marquette.

[3990] (S.S.P.C.)—MISSIONARY SISTERS OF ST. PETER CLAVER P

Founded in 1894. First Foundation in the United States, 1914.

Legal Title: *The Sodality of St. Peter Claver for the African Missions.*

General House: 16 via dell' Olmata, Rome, Italy. Mother M. Elizabeth Adamiak, S.S.P.C., Supr. Gen.

American Headquarters: 667 Woods Mill Rd. S., P.O. Box 1058, Chesterfield, MO 63006-0401. Tel: 314-434-8084. Sr. M. Irene Brahmakulath, S.S.P.C., Supr.

Total number in community 26.

Represented in the Archdioceses of Chicago, St. Louis and St. Paul-Minneapolis.

[4010] (O.S.A.)—SISTERS OF ST. RITA D

General Motherhouse: F. Spee Str., Wurzburg, 87. Germany. Sr. M. Dolores Schneider, Gen.

Universal total in Congregation 190.

U.S. Address: *St. Monica's Convent,* 3920 Green Bay Rd., Racine, WI 53404. Tel: 414-639-1766. Sr. Hanika, Supr.

Represented in the Archdiocese of Milwaukee.

[4020] (S.T.J.)—SOCIETY OF ST. TERESA OF JESUS P
(Teresian Sisters)

Founded in Spain in 1876. First foundation in the United States in 1910. Total Membership 1,854.

Generalate: Rome, 00166, Italy Via Valcannuta, 134.

Provincial House: *St. Francis de Sales Province,* 18080 St. Joseph's Way, Covington, LA 70435-5623. Tel: 504-893-1470; Fax: 504-893-2476.

Formation House: 18158 St. Joseph's Way, Covington, LA 70435-5623. Tel: 504-893-1557. Sr. Martha L. Gonzalez, Community Archivist.

Total number in community 53.

Ministry in the field of Academic Education at all levels; Education in underdeveloped areas; Youth Centers.

Properties owned: *St. Teresa's Academy,* San Antonio, TX; *Henry de Osso Convent,* San Antonio, TX; *Provincialate,* Covington, LA.

Represented in the Archdioceses of Miami, New Orleans and San Antonio.

[4030] (S.S.T.V.)—CONGREGATION OF SISTERS OF ST. THOMAS OF VILLANOVA P

Founded in France in 1661. First foundation in the United States in 1948.

General Motherhouse: 52 Blvd. d'Argenson, Neuilly-sur-Seine, France.

Universal total in Congregation 400.

Sisters of St. Thomas of Villanova Convent: Rocks Rd., Norwalk, CT 06851. Tel: 203-847-2885. Mother Edmond, Supr.

Total number in the community 4.

Properties owned: *Notre Dame Convalescent Home.*

Represented in the Dioceses of Bridgeport.

[4040] (S.U.)—SOCIETY OF ST. URSULA P

Founded in Dole, France, in 1606. First foundation in the United States in 1902.

General Motherhouse: St. Cyr-Loire, France. Sr. Marie Bernard, Supr. Gen.

Provincialate: *Linwood Spiritual Center,* 139 S. Mill Rd., Rhinebeck, NY 12572. Tel: 914-876-4178; 876-4512. Sr. Mary Isaac Jogues Koenig, Prov.

Total number in the community 36.

Ministry in the field of Education; Parish Ministry; Social Work.

Represented in the Archdioceses of Boston, Hartford, New York, Washington and the Dioceses of Providence and Raleigh.

[4048] (F.C.J.)—SOCIETY OF THE SISTERS, FAITHFUL COMPANIONS OF JESUS P

Founded in France in 1820. First founded in United States 1895.

General Motherhouse: *Stella Maris Convent,* Northforeland, Broadstairs Kent, England.

American Province: *St. Philomena Convent,* Cory's Ln., Portsmouth, RI 02871. Tel: 401-683-2222. Sr. Paula Terroni, F.C.J., Supr. Gen.; Sr. Carmel Hamilton, F.C.J., Local Supr.; Sr. Susan Donohue, F.C.J., Prov. Supr.; Sr. Marie Therese Dyer, Novice Dir.

Sisters 18.

[4050] (S.D.S.H.)—SISTERS OF THE SOCIETY DEVOTED TO THE SACRED HEART D

Founded in Hungary in 1940.

Motherhouse (1956): 9814 Sylvia Ave., Northridge, CA 91324. Tel: 818-772-9961; Fax: 818-772-2742. Sr. Jane Stafford, Supr. Gen.; Sr. Ida Peterfy, Foundress.

Novitiate House 10480 Winnetka, Chatsworth, CA 91313. Tel: 818-831-9710.

Total number in community 53.

Ministry in Parish Religious Education Centers; Catechist Formation Centers; Camp for year-round Retreats and summer Family Retreats Camps; Catechesis; Youth Leadership Programs; Day Retreat Center for Children and Adults; Catechesis in Parochial Schools and Catholic High Schools; "Sacred Heart Kids' Club" Video Catechesis; Hispanic, Chinese and Korean Catechetical Centers; Catechetical Programs on Military Bases; Catechetical Missions to Dioceses; Far East Mission in Taiwan; Mission in Hungary.

Properties owned: *Heart of Jesus Retreat Center,* Santa Ana, CA; *Sacred Heart Retreat Camp,* Big Bear Lake, CA; *Sacred Heart Novitiate,* Chatsworth, CA.

Represented in the Archdiocese of Los Angeles and Dioceses of Orange, and San Bernardino. Also in Taiwan and Hungary.

[4060] (S.H.C.J.)—SOCIETY OF THE HOLY CHILD JESUS P

Founded in England in 1846. First foundation in the United States in 1862.

Motherhouse: Via della Maglianella 379, Rome, Italy 00166. Sr. Mary Ann Buckley, Supr. Gen.

American Province: *Provincial Offices,* 460 Shadeland Ave., Drexel Hill, PA 19026-2312. Tel: 610-626-1400. Sr. Susan Slater, Prov.; Sr. Dorothy Cropper, Archivist, 1341 Montgomery Ave., Rosemont, PA 19010.

Total number in province 265.

Properties owned or sponsored: *Connelly School of the Holy Child,* Potomac, MD; *Cornelia Connelly School,* Anaheim, CA; *Mayfield Junior School of the Holy Child Jesus; Mayfield Senior School of the Holy Child Jesus,* Pasadena, CA; *Oak Knoll School of the Holy Child,* Summit, NJ; *Old Westbury School of the Holy Child,* Old Westbury, NY; *Rosemont School of the Holy Child,* Rosemont, PA; *School of the Holy Child,* Drexel Hill, PA; *School of the Holy Child,* Rye, NY; *Providence Center,* Philadelphia, PA.

Sisters minister in a variety of Educational and Pastoral Work.

Represented in the Archdioceses of Boston, Chicago, Cincinnati, Hartford, Los Angeles, Louisville, Milwaukee, Newark, New Orleans, New York, Philadelphia, Portland (OR) and Washington and the Dioceses of Baker, Brooklyn, Camden, Charlotte, Las Cruces, Metuchen, Orange, Paterson, Pueblo, Rockville Centre, Sacramento, San Diego, Trenton, Toledo, Venice, Wheeling-Charleston, and Wilmington.

[4070] (R.S.C.J.)—SOCIETY OF THE SACRED HEART P

Founded in France in 1800. First foundation in the United States in 1818.

Generalate: Via Tarquinio Vipera, 16, 00152, Rome, Italy. Sr. Patricia Garcia de Quevedo, Supr. Gen.

United States Provincial House: 4389 W. Pine Blvd., St. Louis, MO 63108. Tel: 314-652-1500; Fax: 314-534-6800. Sr. Barbara Dawson, Prov.; Sr. Elizabeth Farley, Prov. Archivist.

Total number in the Province 527.

Province Corporations: *California Province of the Society of the Sacred Heart, Inc.; Society of the Sacred Heart, Chicago Province, Inc.; Religious of the Sacred Heart, Washington Province, Inc.; Religious of the Sacred Heart, New York Province, Inc.; Ladies of the Sacred Heart, MO; Religious of the Sacred Heart in Massachusetts, Inc.*

Network of Sacred Heart Schools, Inc. 860 Beacon St., Newton, MA 02159-1879. Tel: 617-244-9260.

Ministry in the field of Religious and Academic Education at all levels; Adult Education; Parish, Pastoral, Social and Health Care Ministries.

Represented in the Archdioceses of Boston, Chicago, Detroit, Miami, New Orleans, New York, Omaha, St. Louis, San Francisco, Seattle and Washington and the Dioceses of Albany, Bridgeport, Galveston-Houston, Lafayette (LA), Richmond, San Diego, San Jose, Trenton and Venice.

[4080] (S.S.S.)—SISTERS OF SOCIAL SERVICE OF LOS ANGELES, INC. P

Founded in Hungary. Established in the United States at Los Angeles, California in 1926.

General Motherhouse: 1120 Westchester Pl., Los Angeles, CA 90019. Tel: 213-731-2117; Fax: 213-733-3374. Sr. Simone Campbell, Gen. Dir.

Total number in the community 104.

Legal Title: *Sisters of Social Service of Los Angeles; Sisters of Social Service Support Trust Fund.*

Social Service Work in Parishes and in Diocesan Agencies; Leadership Training of Youth and Adults; Summer Camps for Children and Families; Programs for the Elderly; Peace and Justice Work; Religious Education; Settlement Houses; Health Programs; Low Cost Legal Services; Family Counseling Services; International houses in Mexico, Philippines and Taiwan.

Represented in the Archdioceses of Los Angeles, Portland (OR), San Francisco and Seattle and the Dioceses of Baton Rouge, El Paso, Great Falls-Billings, Oakland, Sacramento and San Diego.

[4090] (S.S.S.)—SISTERS OF SOCIAL SERVICE D

Founded in Budapest, Hungary in 1923; Sr. Margaret Slachta, Foundress.

Generalate Residence: 296 Summit Ave., Buffalo, NY 14214. Tel: 716-834-0197. Sr. Anne Lehner, S.S.S., General Moderator.

U.S. Residence: 440 Linwood Ave., Buffalo, NY 14209. Tel: 716-883-0112. Sr. Angela Homoki-Szabo, S.S.S., District Moderator.

Total number in the United States 20.

Social Work in private and public agencies; Religious Education; Parish Ministry; Ministry for Justice and Human Rights; Spanish Apostolate.

Represented in the Archdiocese of Miami and the Dioceses of Buffalo and Ponce, PR.

[4100] (S.S.M.)—SISTERS OF THE SORROWFUL MOTHER (THIRD ORDER OF ST. FRANCIS) P

Founded in Italy in 1883. First foundation in the United States in 1889.

General Motherhouse: *Casa Generalizia della Suore dell'Addolorata,* Via Paolo III, 7-9, I-00165, Roma, Italy. Sr. Helen Malolepsy, S.S.M., Supr. Gen.

U.S./Caribbean Province: *Our Lady of Sorrows Convent,* 17600 E. 51st St., Broken Arrow, OK 74012. Tel: 918-355-1148; Fax: 918-355-3534. Sr. Dorothy Ann M. Dirkx, S.S.M., Prov. Supr.

Total number in the U.S. community 223.

Legal Holding: *Sisters of the Sorrowful Mother - US Health System, Inc.; Sisters of the Sorrowful Mother - US/Caribbean Province, Inc.*

Ministry in the fields of Religious and Academic Education; Nursing Homes; Social Work; Hospitals and Hospital Administration.

Represented in the Archdiocese of Milwaukee and the Dioceses of El Paso, Green Bay, La Crosse, Paterson, Superior, Tulsa, Wichita and Winona. Also in Dominican Republic, Trinidad, Grenada and Castries.

[4110] (O.S.U.)—URSULINE NUNS P
(Roman Union)

Founded in Italy in 1535. First foundation in the United States New Orleans, Louisiana in 1727.

Generalate: Via Nomentana, 236, Rome, 00162. Italy. Mother Colette Lignon, O.S.U., Prioress Gen.

Eastern Province of the U.S. (1900): *Ursuline Provincialate-St. Mary's Hall,* 323 E. 198th St., Bronx, NY 10458. Tel: 718-365-7410; Fax: 718-733-4498. Sr. Marie-Celine Miranda, O.S.U., Prov.

Total number in the province 217.

Legal Title: *Ursuline Provincialate, Eastern Province of the United States, Inc.; Marian Residence Fund, Bronx, NY; OSU Charitable Trust,* Bronx, NY.

Ministry in the field of Academic Education at all levels; Varied Pastoral and Social Services.

Represented in the Archdioceses of Baltimore, New York and Washington and the Dioceses of Ogdensburg, Orlando, Raleigh, and Wilmington.

Central Province of the U.S.: *Ursuline Provincialate,* 210 Glennon Heights Rd., Crystal City, MO 63019. Tel: 314-937-6206; Fax: 314-937-7627. Sr. Elisa Ryan, O.S.U., Prov. Prioress.

Total number in the community 231.

Ministry in the field of Religious and Academic Education.

Represented in the Archdioceses of New Orleans, St. Louis, St. Paul-Minneapolis, San Antonio and the Dioceses of Corpus Christi, Dallas, Galveston-Houston, Springfield-Cape Girardeau and Springfield (IL).

Western Province U.S. (1932): *Ursuline Provincialate,* 639 Angela Dr., Santa Rosa, CA 95403-1793. Tel: 707-545-6811; Fax: 707-579-8571. Sr. Francis Xavier Porter, O.S.U., Prov. Prioress.

Total number in the province 48.

Ministry in the field of Elementary and Secondary Education; Work with the Eskimos, American Indians, Hispanics & Blacks; Parish Ministry; Catechetical Coordinators; Blind Apostolate; Spiritual Growth Center; Counseling Services.

Represented in the Archdioceses of Anchorage, Los Angeles and San Francisco and the Dioceses of Boise, Fairbanks, Great Falls-Billings, Oakland, San Jose and Santa Rosa.

Northeastern Province: *Ursuline Provincialate,* 45 Lowder St., Dedham, MA 02026-4200. Tel: 617-326-6219; Fax: 617-326-7296. Sr. Dorothy Doyle, O.S.U., Prov.

Total number in the community 68.

Ministry in the field of Education.

Represented in the Archdiocese of Boston and the Diocese of Portland (ME).

[4120] (O.S.U.)—URSULINE NUNS, OF THE CONGREGATION OF PARIS P

Founded in Italy in 1535. First foundation in the United States in New Orleans, Louisiana in 1727.

Motherhouse (1845): Immaculate Heart of Mary Convent, 20860 St. Rte. 251, St. Martin, OH 45118-9705. Tel: 513-875-2020. Sr. Nancy Vollman, O.S.U., Supr.

Total number in the community 40.

Ministry in the field of Academic Education at all levels; Special Education; Adult Education; Catechetical Instruction; Administration; Retreats; Counseling; Organization Consultation; Social-Inner City & Rural; Hospital; Senior Services; Campus and Parish Ministry.

Legal Title: *St. Ursula Literary Institute; Ursulines of Brown County; Ursuline Academy of Cincinnati; Chatfield College.*

Represented in the Archdiocese of Cincinnati and the Dioceses of Covington, Trenton and Toledo.

[4120-01] **Cincinnati** P

Motherhouse: *Ursulines of Cincinnati, St. Ursula Convent,* 1339 E. McMillan St. (Walnut Hills), Cincinnati, OH 45206. Tel: 513-961-3410. Sr. Elizabeth Lang, O.S.U., Supr.

Total number in the community 29.

Legal Title: *Ursulines of Cincinnati.*

Ministry in the field of Academic Education at all levels; Administration; Adult Education; Pastoral Ministry; Catholic Social Services; Hospice.

Properties Owned and Operated: *St. Ursula Convent,* Cincinnati, OH.

Represented in the Archdiocese of Cincinnati and the Diocese of Covington.

[4120-02] **Kansas City in Kansas** D

Ursuline Convent of Our Lady of Lourdes: 901 E. Miami St., Paola, KS 66071. Tel: 913-294-2349. Sr. Pat Lynch, O.S.U., Supr.

Total number in the community 37.

Legal Title: *Ursuline Sisters, Inc.; Ursuline Sisters, Inc. Charitable Trust.*

Ministry in the field of Academic Education at all levels; Parish and Diocesan Services.

Represented in the Archdioceses of Kansas City in Kansas and New Orleans and the Dioceses of Kansas City-St. Joseph and Sacramento.

[4120-03] **Louisville** P

Ursuline Motherhouse of the Immaculate Conception: 3115 Lexington Rd., Louisville, KY 40206. Tel: 502-893-0125; Fax: 502-896-3913. Sr. Sarah Stauble, O.S.U., Pres.; Sr. Amelia Dues, O.S.U., Community Archivist.

Total number in the community 227.

Legal Title: *Ursuline Society and Academy of Education aka Ursuline Sisters.*

Properties owned and sponsored: *Sacred Heart Academy; Sacred Heart Model School; Ursuline Montessori; Ursuline Child Development Center; Ursuline School of Music & Drama; Marian Home,* Louisville, KY.

Ministry in the field of Academic Education; Child Care; Pastoral Ministry; Social Services; Health Care.

Represented in the Archdioceses of Baltimore, Indianapolis, Louisville, Philadelphia and the Dioceses of Charleston, Cheyenne, Davenport, Evansville, Grand Island, Jackson, Lexington, Pittsburgh, Richmond, St. Petersburg and Wheeling-Charleston.

[4120-04] **Cleveland** P

Ursuline Motherhouse and Educational Center: 2600 Lander Rd., Cleveland, OH 44124; Fax: 440-449-3588. Sr. Virginia DeVinne, O.S.U., Supr. Gen.; Sr. Joann Kessler, O.S.U., Community Archivist.

Total number in the community 281.

Legal Title: *The Ursuline Academy of Cleveland; The Ursuline Nuns of Cleveland.*

Properties sponsored: *Ursuline College Beaumont High School.*

Ministry in the field of Academic Education at all levels; Parish Ministry; Diocesan Offices; Seminary; Social Service Agency; Hospital Ministry; Foreign Mission.

Represented in the Archdiocese of Indianapolis and the Dioceses of Buffalo, Cleveland, Columbus, Fort Wayne-South Bend, Great Falls, Kansas City-St. Joseph, and Pittsburgh.

[4120-05] **Owensboro** P

Mt. St. Joseph Ursuline Motherhouse: Maple Mount, KY 42356. Tel: 502-229-4103. Sr. Rose Marita O'Bryan, O.S.U., Major Supr.

Total number in community 222.

Legal Holdings & Titles: *St. Joseph Female Ursuline Academic, Inc.; Brescia College; Mount St. Joseph Center,* Maple Mount, KY.

Ministry in Colleges; High Schools; Elementary Schools; Pastoral Ministries; Retreat Care; Pastoral Care; Social Services; Chancellor, Diocesan Offices.

Represented in the Archdioceses of Cincinnati, Louisville, St. Louis, Santa Fe, Washington and the Dioceses of Beaumont, Brownsville, Evansville, Gallup, Kansas City-St. Joseph, Lincoln, Memphis, Owensboro, and Springfield-Cape Girardeau.

[4120-06] **Toledo** P

Ursuline Convent of the Sacred Heart Offices: 4045 Indian Rd., Toledo, OH 43606. Tel: 419-536-9587. Sr. Nancy Mathias, Gen. Supr.

Total number in the community 103; Associates 101.

Legal Title: Ursuline Convent of the Sacred Heart.

Properties owned or sponsored: St. Ursula Academy, Toledo, OH.

Ministry in the field of Administration; Religious and Academic Education; Health Care; Counseling Services; Diocesan Education Office; Pastoral Ministry; Pastoral Care; Retreat Work; Spiritual Direction; Education in Music; Home Health Care.

Represented in the Archdiocese of Washington and the Dioceses of Fresno and Toledo. Also in Lima, Peru.

[4120-07] **Youngstown** P

Motherhouse: *Ursuline Motherhouse and Educational Center,* 4250 Shields Rd., Canfield, OH 44406. Tel: 330-792-7636. Sr. Nancy Dawson, Gen. Supr.

Total number in the community 80.

Legal Title: *Ursuline Sisters of Youngstown.*

Properties Owned: *Ursuline Motherhouse; Ursuline Center; Ursuline Preschool & Kindergarten; Beatitude House.*

Ministry in the field of Religious and Academic Education at all levels; Parish Ministry; Diocesan Offices; Social Services; Hospital Services; Single Parenting; AIDS Ministry; Preschool; Kindergarten; Nursing Home Administration; Nursing Home Service; Audiology; Speech Pathology; Music.

Represented in the Dioceses of Cleveland,and Youngstown.

[4130] (O.S.U.)—URSULINE SISTERS OF THE CONGREGATION OF TILDONK, BELGIUM P

International Congregation.

Founded in Italy in 1535 by St. Angela Merici (Ursulines). Congregation of Tildonk founded in Belgium in 1832. First foundation in the United States in Ozone Park, New York, in 1924.

Generalate: Brussels, Belgium. Sr. Judith O'Connor, O.S.U., Gen. Supr.

Ursuline Provincialate: 81-15 Utopia Pkwy., Jamaica, NY 11432. Tel: 718-591-0681. Sr. Catherine Talia, O.S.U., Prov. Supr.

Properties owned: *St. Ursula Center, (Convent & Retreat Center),* Blue Point, NY; *Ursuline Provincialate,* Jamaica, NY.

Total number in the community 69.

Ministry in the field of Education in all its aspects.

Represented in the Archdioceses of Hartford and New York and the Dioceses of Bridgeport, Brooklyn, Burlington, Richmond and Rockville Centre.

[4140] (O.S.U.)—URSULINE SISTERS OF BELLEVILLE D

Founded in Italy in 1535. First foundation in the United States in 1910. Newly established as Diocesan Community August 13, 1983.

Central House: 1026 N. Douglas Ave., Belleville, IL 62220-4198. Tel: 618-234-3326. Sr. Dorothy Helbling, O.S.U., Community Leader.

Total number in the community 18.

Ministry in the field of Religious and Academic Education; Retreat Work; Pastoral Ministry.

Represented in the Diocese of Belleville.

[4155] (M.T.G.)—VIETNAMESE ADORERS OF THE HOLY CROSS P

Founded in 1670 in Viet Nam by Bishop Pierre Lambert de la Motte. First foundation in the United States 1976.

General Motherhouse: *Vietnamese Adorers of the Holy Cross,* Holy Cross Convent, 7408 S.E. Adler, Portland, OR 97215. Tel: 503-254-3284. Sr. Mary Kim Phuong T. Nguyen, M.T.G., Supr.

Sisters 14; Novices 5; Candidates 10.

Legal Title: *Vietnamese Adorers of the Holy Cross,* Portland, OR.

Represented in the Archdiocese of Portland, OR and in the Diocese of Arlington.

[4160] (V.S.C.)—VINCENTIAN SISTERS OF CHARITY P

First foundation in the United States in 1902.

General Motherhouse and Novitiate: *St. Vincent Hill,* 8200 McKnight Rd., Pittsburgh, PA 15237. Tel: 412-364-3000; Fax: 412-364-9055. Sr. Rita Gesue, Supr. Gen.

Professed sisters 184.

Properties owned or sponsored: *Vincentian Child Care Center; Vincentian High School; Vincentian Home, Inc.; Villa de Marillac Nursing Home; Regency Hall Nursing Home and Adult Day Care; St. Louise De Marillac Mission Convent,* Talara, Peru.

Ministry in the Field of Education at All Levels; Health Care in Nursing Homes; Child Care Center; Adult Day Care; Catechetical Centers; Social Apostolates; Montessori; Pastoral Ministries.

Represented in the Archdiocese of Mobile and in Dioceses of Altoona-Johnstown, Greensburg, Pittsburgh, Springfield-Cape Girardeau, Steubenville, Venice, Wheeling-Charleston and Youngstown. Also in Canada, Peru.

[4170] (V.S.C.)—VINCENTIAN SISTERS OF CHARITY D

Founded in Bedford in 1928.

Motherhouse & Novitiate: *Villa San Bernardo,* 1160 Broadway, Bedford, OH 44146-4523. Tel: 440-232-4755; Fax: 440-232-7832. Sr. Margaret Mach, Gen. Supr.; Sr. Dorothy Ann Blatnica, Dir. Formation; Sr. Ruthann Rody, Vocation Contact Person.

Professed 75.

Ministry in the field of Education at all levels; Pastoral Ministry and Counseling; Social Services; Nursing; Care of the Elderly; Marian Shrine and Poustinia; Hospice; Poor in Appalachia; Facility for Elderly - Independent and Assisted Living; Light of Hearts Villa (Assisted Living Facility).

Represented in the Dioceses of Cleveland, and Lexington.

[4180] (M.P.V.)—RELIGIOUS VENERINI SISTERS P

Founded in Italy in 1685. First foundation in the United States in 1909.

General Motherhouse: via Gioachino Belli 31, Rome, Italy. Rev. Mother Marcella Lorenzetti, Supr. Gen.

Universal total in Congregation 480.

Provincialhouse for the U.S.: 23 Edward St., Worcester, MA 01605. Sr. Hilda Ponte, Prov.

Total number in the community 34.

Legal Holdings: *Venerini Academy,* Worcester, MA.

Ministry in the field of Education; Health Care; Social Services; Parish and Diocesan Ministry; Foreign Missions.

Represented in the Dioceses of Albany, Fall River, St. Petersburg and Worcester.

[4190] (V.H.M.)—VISITATION NUNS P

Founded in France in 1610. First foundation in the United States in Georgetown, Washington, DC in 1799.

First Federation of North America

Major pontifical enclosure. Mother Mary Jozefa, Federation Pres., residing at the Monastery of Visitation, Snellville GA.

Listed in the Order of Foundation established.

Monastery of the Visitation (1833): 2300 Springhill Ave., Mobile, AL 36607-3202. Tel: 334-473-2321. Sr. Rose Marie Kinsella, Supr.

Total number in the community 13.

Monastery of the Visitation: 14 Beach Rd.-P.O. Box 432, Tyringham, MA 01264. Tel: 413-243-3995. Mother Mary Francis Metz, V.H.M., Supr.

Legal Title: *Visitation of Holy Mary.*

Total number in the community 19.

Monastery of the Visitation: 12221 Bienvenue Rd., Rockville, VA 23146. Tel: 804-749-4885. Mother Margaret Mary McGuire, Supr.

Legal Title: *Visitation of Holy Mary.*

Professed Sisters 17; Novices 3.

Monastery of the Visitation: 5820 City Ave., Philadelphia, PA 19131-1295. Tel: 215-473-5888. Mother Frances de Sales Paganelli, Supr.

Legal Title: *Sisters of the Visitation of Philadelphia.*

Professed Sisters Cloistered 11; Externs: Professed 1; Novices 1; Postulants 1.

Monastery of the Visitation (Contemplative): 1745 Parkside Blvd., Toledo, OH 43607. Tel: 419-536-1343. Mother Sharon Elizabeth Gworek V.H.M., Supr.

Professed Sisters 14; In formation 3.

Monastery of the Visitation (Strictly Cloistered): 2055 Ridgedale Dr., Snellville, GA 30278. Tel: 404-972-1060. Mother Mary Jozefa Kowalewski, Supr.

Legal Title: *Order of the Visitation.*
Professed Sisters 14; Novices 1; Postulants 1.

Second Federation of North America

Sister Anne Madeleine Godefroy residing at Monastery of the Visitation, St. Louis, Missouri.
Total number of nuns in this federation 160.

Monastery of the Visitation of Georgetown: 1500 35th St., N.W., Washington, DC 20007. Tel: 202-337-0305; Fax: 202-965-3845. Mother Mary de Sales McNabb, Supr.; Sr. Mada-anne Gell, Community Archivist.
Legal Titles & Holdings: *Sisters of the Visitation of Georgetown; Georgetown Visitation Preparatory School.*
Total number in the school community 423; Total number in religious community 29.

Monastery of the Visitation (1833): 3020 N. Ballas Rd., St. Louis, MO 63131. Tel: 314-432-5353. Sr. Anne Madeleine Godefroy, Supr.
Total number in the community 24.
Ministry in Education.
Legal Holdings: *Visitation Academy of St. Louis County Monastery of the Visitation,* St. Louis, MO.

Monastery of the Visitation (1846): 200 E. Second St., Frederick, MD 21701. Tel: 301-622-3322. Mother Marguerite Therese Leary, V.H.M., Supr.
Total number in the community 5.
Legal Holdings or Titles: *Monastery of the Visitation - Frederick, Maryland; Frederick Academy of the Visitation Cloistered Contemplative Order with Elementary School as Apostolate.*

Sisters of the Visitation of Holy Mary of Mount de Chantal, Inc. (1848): Wheeling, WV 26003. Tel: 304-232-1283. Sr. Mary Grace Flynn, V.H.M., Supr.
Total number in the community 29.
Legal Holdings or Titles: *Sisters of the Visitation of Holy Mary of Mount de Chantal, Inc.; Mount de Chantal Visitation Academy, Inc.*
Ministry in the field of Education.

Monastery of the Visitation (1855): 8902 Ridge Blvd., Brooklyn, NY 11209-5716. Tel: 718-745-5151. Sr. Marie Anatrella, V.H.M., Supr.
Professed Sisters 25.
Ministry: Comtemplative Prayer and limited participation in Elementary School.

Villa de Chantal Monastery of the Visitation Mailing Address: 2936 36th St., Rock Island, IL 61201. Sr. Mary Veronica Haronik, V.H.M., Pres.
Monastery located at 2000 16th Ave., Rock Island, IL 61201. Tel: 314-432-5353.
Legal Title: *Sisters of the Visitation.*
Ministry in Spiritual and Educational Center.

Monastery of the Visitation: 2455 Visitation Dr., Mendota Heights, MN 55120. Tel: 612-683-1700. Sr. Mary Denise Villaume, V.H.M., Supr.
Total number in the community 20.
Ministry in Prayer and Education.

[4200] (S.V.M.)—SISTERS OF THE VISITATION OF THE CONGREGATION OF THE IMMACULATE HEART OF MARY D

Founded in France in 1610. First foundation in the United States in 1799.

Visitation Convent: 2950 Kaufmann Ave., Dubuque, IA 52001-1655. Tel: 319-556-2440. Sr. Ruth Jackson, Pres.
Total number in community 9.
Ministry in Elementary & Higher Education; Adult Education; Parish Ministry.
Represented in the Archdiocese of Dubuque and the Dioceses of Fort Wayne-South Bend and Oakland.

[4210] (S.D.V.)—VOCATIONIST SISTERS P (Sisters of the Divine Vocations)

Founded in Italy in 1921. First established in the United States in 1967.

General Motherhouse: Corso Duca D'Aosta, 22 Pianura, 80126, Naples, Italy. Sr. Giannina Di Francia, S.D.V., Mother Supr. Gen.

U.S. Foundation: *Perpetual Help Day Nursery,* 172 Broad St., Newark, NJ 07104. Tel: 201-484-3535. Sr. Luisa Gargione, S.D.V., Supr.
Total number in community 5.
Ministry in Nursery Schools & Kindergartens; CCD Program and Parish Services.
Represented in the Archdiocese of Newark.

Sister Joanna Formation House: 88 Brooklake Rd., Florham Park, NJ 07932. Tel: 201-966-9762. Sr. Anna Maria Mancino, Delegate; Sr. Gelsomina Mosca, Supr.
Total number in community 9.
Ministry in Nursery School; Formation House.
Represented in the Diocese of Paterson.

[4230] (X.M.M.)—XAVERIAN MISSIONARY SOCIETY OF MARY, INC. P

Founded in Italy in 1945. First established in the United States in 1954.

General Motherhouse: Missionarie Saveriane Di Maria, Via Omero 4, Parma, Italy. Sr. Giuseppina Caccia, X.M.M., Supr. Gen.
Total Membership 250.

U.S. Headquarters: *Xaverian Missionary Society of Mary,* 242 Salisbury St., Worcester, MA 01609. Tel: 508-757-0514. Sr. Rita Davoli, X.M.M., Gen. Delegate.
Ministry to Hispanics; Elderly; Families; CCD Programs and Mission Education.
Represented in the Archdiocese of New York and the Diocese of Worcester.

COLLEGES AND UNIVERSITIES

ALABAMA

Mobile
Archdiocese of Mobile

Spring Hill College (1830)
4000 Dauphin St.
Mobile, AL 36608
Tel: 334-380-4000; Fax: 334-460-2195
Web Site: www.shc.edu
Revs.:
GREGORY LUCEY, S.J., Pres.
JOHN R. PAYNE, S.J., Rector of Jesuit Community
FREDERICK W. GUNTI (LR)
J. WILLIAM HARMLESS, S.J.
WALTER L. FURMAN, S.J.
DAVID BORBRIDGE, S.J.
EVERETT H. LARGUIER, S.J.
GERALD T. REGAN, S.J (Wisconsin)
ROBERT B. RIMES, S.J.
SIDNEY A. TOMSMEIRE, S.J.
MICHAEL A. WILLIAMS, S.J (Maryland)
STEPHEN CAMPBELL, S.J.
CHRISTOPHER J. VISCARDI, S.J.
Bros.:
FERRELL BLANK
CLAUDE L. ORY, S.J.
Priests of Faculty 8
Brothers 2
Lay Teachers 54
Students 960

CALIFORNIA

Belmont
Archdiocese of San Francisco

College of Notre Dame
1500 Ralston Ave.
Belmont, CA 94002
Tel: 650-593-1601; Fax: 650-637-0493
Web Site: www.cnd.edu
Sisters of Notre Dame de Namur
Dr. MARGARET A. HUBER, Pres.
LUCILLE H. SANSING, Ph.D., Vice Pres., Academic Affairs
JOHN BOLLARD, Dir. Campus Ministry
Priests 1
Sisters 10
Lay Faculty 53
Students 1,694

Fremont
Diocese of Oakland

Queen of the Holy Rosary College
Mailing Address:
P.O. Box 3908
Mission San Jose, CA 94539
Tel: 510-657-2468; Fax: 510-657-1734
Legal Title: *Queen of the Holy Rosary College*
Dominican Sisters of Mission San Jose
Sr. ROSE MARIE HENNESSY, O.P., Pres.
Sr. MARY PAUL MEHEGAN, O.P., Dean
Priests 1
Sisters 18
Lay Teachers 2
Total Enrollment 252

Los Angeles
Archdiocese of Los Angeles

Loyola Marymount University
7900 Loyola Blvd.
Los Angeles, CA 90045-2699
Tel: 310-338-2700
Sponsored by the Society of Jesus (Jesuit Fathers), Religious of Sacred Heart of Mary, Sisters of St. Joseph of Orange
Revs.:
THOMAS P. O'MALLEY, S.J., Pres.
DONALD P. MERRIFIELD, S.J., Chancellor
PATRICK J. CAHALAN, S.J., Assoc. Chancellor
Dr. JOSEPH G. JABBRA, Academic Vice Pres.
Mr. JOHN R. OESTER, Vice Pres. Business and Finance
Rev. JOHN S. ROGERS, Vice Pres. University Relations
Dr. LANE BOVE, Vice Pres. Student Affairs
Rev. RICHARD A. ROBIN, S.J., Asst. to the Pres.
Mr. DAVID G. TRUMP, Vice Pres. Facilities Mgmt.
Mr. GERALD T. MCLAUGHLIN, Dean, Law School
Ms. ROSENIA ST. ONGE, Registrar
Mr. MATTHEW FISSINGER, Dir. Admissions
Ms. DONNA PALMER, Dir. Financial Aid
Mr. FRANK MOMALVO, Dir. Personnel Svcs.
Mr. FERNANDO D. MORENO, Dir. Campus Ministry
Dr. JOHN T. WHOLIHAN, Dean of Business Admin.
Dr. GERALD S. JAKUBOWSKI, Dean of Science and Engrg.
THOMAS KELLY, Dean of Communication & Fine Arts
Dr. RENE HARRANGUE, Interim Dean, Liberal Arts
Jesuit Community
P.O. Box 45041
Los Angeles, CA 90045-8427
Tel: 310-338-7445
Very Rev. MICHAEL ENGH, S.J., Rector
Rev. TERRANCE L. MAHAN, S.J.
In res.,
Revs.:
CLINTON E. ALBERTSON, S.J.
JAMES ARENZ, S.J.
JOHN L. BOYLE, S.J.
ANTHONY B. BRZOSKA, S.J.
THOMAS E. BUCKLEY, S.J.
PETER BURNS, S.J.
ROBERT I. BURNS, S.J.
WILLIAM F. CAIN, S.J.
ROBERT V. CARO, S.J.
JOHN P. DALY, S.J.
GEORGE H. DUNNE, S.J.
MICHAEL E. ENGH, S.J.
Bro. WILLIAM C. FARRINGTON, S.J.
Revs.:
D. THEODORE FISHER, S.J.
JOHN J. FLYNN, S.J.
WILLIAM J. FULCO, S.J.
THOMAS P. HIGGINS, S.J.
FLOYD A. JENKINS, S.J.
CHARLES L. JURGENSMEIER, S.J.
CHARLES J. KAVANAGH, S.J.
JAMES H. KEENE, S.J.
JOHN F. KILLEEN, S.J.
LOUIS E. LIBBEY, S.J.
TERRANCE L. MAHAN, S.J.
THOMAS J. MALONEY, S.J.
SHANE P. MARTIN, S.J.
DONALD P. MERRIFIELD, S.J.
THOMAS P. O'MALLEY, S.J.
THOMAS P. RAUSCH, S.J.
RICHARD A. ROBIN, S.J.
RICHARD W. ROLFS, S.J.
HERBERT J. RYAN, S.J.
ERNEST S. SWEENEY, S.J.
ROBERT H. TAYLOR, S.J.
RICHARD H. TRAME, S.J.
Bro. RAYMOND W. UPTON, S.J.
Revs.:
RICHARD P. VAUGHAN, S.J.
CLARENCE J. WALLEN, S.J.
HANFORD E. WECKBACH, S.J.
MICHAEL F. WEILER, S.J.
ROBERT J. WELCH, S.J.
JOHN B. WELING, S.J.
Priests 29
Brothers 1
Sisters 7
Lay Teachers 245
The Sacred Heart of Mary and Sisters of St. Joseph of Orange
7900 Loyola Blvd.
Los Angeles, CA 90045
Tel: 310-338-2700; 641-4682
Legal Title: *Communities of the Religious of the Sacred Heart of Mary and Sisters of St. Joseph of Orange*
Loyola School of Law
919 S. Albany St., P.O. Box 15019
Los Angeles, CA 90015
Tel: 213-736-1000
Mr. GERALD T. MCLAUGHLIN, Dean

Mount St. Mary's College
E-mail: kkennelly@msmc.la.edu
Web Site: www.msmc.la.edu
Chalon Campus
12001 Chalon Rd.
Los Angeles, CA 90049-1599
Tel: 310-954-4000; Fax: 310-954-4379
Doheny Campus
10 Chester Pl.
Los Angeles, CA 90007
Tel: 213-477-2500; Fax: 213-477-2689
Conducted by the Sisters of St. Joseph of Carondelet
Resident and non-resident students.
Sr. KAREN M. KENNELLY, Pres.
Dr. JANE LINGUA, Vice Pres. for Student Affairs
Mr. LARRY SMITH, Asst. Vice Pres. for Info. Support Services
Dr. JACQUELINE DOWD, Academic Vice Pres.
Mr. WILLIAM EVERHART, Vice Pres. for Business & Finance
Sr. KATHLEEN KELLY, Vice Pres. Doheny Campus and Dean Graduate and Assoc. Divisions
PAMELA HILLMAN, Vice Pres. for Institutional Advancement
Ms. KATY MURPHY, Executive Dir. of Enrollment Mgt.
Sisters 32
Priests 2
Lay Teachers 212
Students 1,966

Moraga
Diocese of Oakland

St. Mary's College
Moraga, CA 94575
Tel: 510-631-4000
Legal Title: *Saint Mary's College of California*
Brothers of the Christian Schools
Coed. Resident and Non-Resident Students.
Bros.:
T. MEL ANDERSON, F.S.C., Pres.
JEROME WEST, F.S.C., Vice Pres., College Rels.
Saint Mary's College Community:
Bros.:
ARNOLD STEWART, F.S.C., Dir.
RICHARD LEMBERG, F.S.C., Sub-Dir.
Alemany Community:
Bro. ROBERT LEE F.S.C., Dir.
Rev. JOHN MCDONOUGH, Chap. & Dir. Campus Ministry
Campus Ministers:
Rev. MICHAEL CAREY, O.P.
Sr. INGRID CLEMMENSEN, O.P.
Revs.:
DAVID DEIBEL
SALVATORE RAGUSA, S.D.S.
Faculty:
Rev. OWEN CARROLL (Canada)
Rev. Msgr. EDGAR P. MCCARREN (RVC)
Revs.:
JOHN MORRIS, O.P.
MICHAEL MORRIS, O.P.
MICHAEL A. RUSSO (NEW)
Sr. CLARE WAGSTAFFE
Priests 9
Sisters 2
Brothers 35
Professors 221
Total Enrollment 4,318

Oakland
Diocese of Oakland

Holy Names College (1868)
3500 Mountain Blvd.
Oakland, CA 94619
Tel: 510-436-1000
Chartered 1880. Resident and Non-Resident Students.
Sisters of the Holy Names of Jesus and Mary
Legal Title: *Sisters of the Holy Names of Jesus and Mary, A Corporation*
Legal Title: *Holy Names College, A Corporation*
Administration:
MARY ALICE MUELLERLEILE, Pres.
JUDIE GRAFFIN WEXLER, Vice Pres. for Academic Affairs
Sr. CAROL SELLMAN, S.N.J.M., Assoc. Dean
LISA LEMON, Assoc. Dean, Academic Affairs
ROBERT D. HITE, Vice Pres. for Finance
MICHAEL A. PETRINI, Vice Pres. for College Advancement
XAVIER E. ROMANO, Vice Pres. for Student Services
Administrative Staff:
LUCY HOLMAN, Dir., Residence Life
BETH HOENNINGER, Dir., Development
MARIANNE STICKEL, Registrar
FRANCES HUI, Dir., Library Services
TO AHN NGUYEN, Dir., Financial Aid
SHARON CASEY, Dir., Campus Ministry
Religious Faculty:
Sr. ELIZABETH ADAMS, S.N.J.M.
Sr. MARY ANDERSON, S.N.J.M.
Sr. MARGARET CAMPBELL, S.N.J.M.
Sr. DEBORAH CHURCH, S.N.J.M.
Rev. JAMES CONLON
Sr. ROSE ELEANOR EHRET, S.N.J.M.
MARCIA FRIDEGER
Sr. JEAN ELIZABETH GRIFFIN, S.N.J.M.
Sr. MAUREEN HESTER, S.N.J.M.
Sr. DONNA MAYNARD, S.N.J.M.
Sr. JUNE KEARNEY, S.N.J.M.
Rev. HENRY ORMOND, O.Carm.
Sr. JOANNE QUINLIVAN, S.N.J.M.
Sr. DELORES RASHFORD, S.N.J.M.
Sr. NANCY TESKEY, S.N.J.M.
Sr. CHRISTINE PATRINOS, S.N.J.M.
Sr. ETHEL MARY TINNEMANN, S.N.J.M.
Sr. FRANCESCA CABRINI WEBER, S.N.J.M.

Sr. Irene Woodward, C.F.C.
Religious Staff:
Sr. Sylvia Bartheld, S.N.J.M.
Sr. Marguerite Kirk, S.N.J.M.
Sr. Mary Christine Fleitz, S.N.J.M.
Sr. Ann Martinovich, S.N.J.M.
Priests 2
Sisters 17
Lay Professors 55
Students 923

Orange
Diocese of Orange in California

St. Joseph College, Orange
480 S. Batavia St.
Orange, CA 92868
Tel: 714-633-8121; Fax: 714-744-3165
Branch Campus of University of San Francisco; St. Joseph College Library.

Rancho Palos Verdes
Archdiocese of Los Angeles

Marymount College, Palos Verdes, California
30800 Palos Verdes Dr., E.
Rancho Palos Verdes, CA 90275-6299
Tel: 310-377-5501
E-mail: shart@marymountpv.edu
An Independent and Catholic Co-Educational Two-Year Liberal Arts College; Resident and Non-Resident.
Dr. Thomas M. McFadden, Pres.
Dr. Robert Matthes, Dean of Academic Affairs
Mr. James Reeves, Vice Pres. of College Opererations & Student Svcs.
Mr. Ed Ogle, Registar
Rev. Sean Cronin, Chap.
Sisters 3
Lay Teachers 72
Students 1,008

Rosemead
Archdiocese of Los Angeles

Don Bosco Technical Institute
(Junior College)
1151 San Gabriel Blvd.
Rosemead, CA 91770-4299
Tel: 626-307-6500; Fax: 626-280-9316
Two-year college program leading to Associate in Science degree in seven technical areas. (Staffed by Salesians of St. John Bosco).
Revs.:
Carmine Vairo, S.D.B., Pres.
Michael Gergen, S.D.B., Admin. Vice Pres.
Peter Bui, S.D.B.
Marc Rougeau, S.D.B., Dir.
Bros.:
Patrick Barbariol, S.D.B.
Jose Lucero, S.D.B.
Gene Mylan, S.D.B.
Joseph Nguyen, S.D.B.
Michael Touchstone, S.D.B.
Priests 4
Brothers 5
Lay Teachers 29
Students 128
Don Bosco High School
Rev. Michael Alvarez, S.D.B., Prin.
Priests 4
Brothers 8
Sisters 1
Lay Teachers 77
Students 784

San Diego
Diocese of San Diego

Austin House - House of Formation
1605 28th St.
San Diego, CA 92102
Tel: 619-233-9141 (Prov. Office)
E-mail: osagartII@aol.com
Very Rev. James A. Mott, O.S.A., Prior Prov. & Vocation Dir., Tel: 619-235-0247; Fax: 619-231-2814
Revs.:
Walter P. Vogel, O.S.A., Prior
Jerome Bevilacqua, O.S.A.
Deacon Richard Hardick, O.S.A.

University of San Diego
5998 Alcala Park
San Diego, CA 92110-2492
Tel: 619-260-4600
Dr. Alice Bourke Hayes, Pres.
Dr. Francis M. Lazarus, Vice Pres. and Provost
Sr. Maureen Cronin, R.S.C.J., Assoc. Provost and Dir. Institutional Research
Dr. Patrick Drinan, Dean, College of Arts and Sciences
Dr. Curtis Cook, Dean, School of Business Administration
Dr. Edward F. De Roche, Dean, School of Education
Grant Morris, Acting Dean, School of Law
Dr. Janet Rodgers, Dean, Hahn School of Nursing
University Ministers:
Revs.:
John D. Keller, O.S.A., Dir. of Univ. Ministry
Vincent Walsh
Paul A. Donovan, S.J.
Sr. Irene Cullen, R.S.C.J.
Bro. Tom Thing, O.F.M.
Mike McIntyre
Kathy Valdivia
Annette Welsh
Mr. Edward P. Starkey, Librarian
Dr. Jane Gorman, Dir., Institute for Christian Min.
Rev. Msgr. William L. Shipley
Revs.:
Stephen Dunn
Dennis W. Krouse
James W. McGray
Ronald A. Pachence (SAV)
Norbert J. Rigali, S.J.
Matthew D. Spahr
Kenneth del Priore
Faculty:
Priests 8
Sisters 4
Lay Faculty 555
Students 6,694
Graduate Division:
Students 1,207
School of Law:
Grant Morris, Acting Dean
Lay Teachers 105
Students 1,131

San Francisco
Archdiocese of San Francisco

**University of San Francisco*
2130 Fulton St.
San Francisco, CA 94117-1080
Tel: 415-422-5555; Fax: 415-422-2303
Jesuit Fathers
Established 1855; Chartered by State, 1859.
Revs.:
John P. Schlegel, S.J., Pres.
John J. LoSchiavo, S.J., Chancellor
Charles W. Dullea, S.J., Chancellor Emeritus
John W. Clark, S.J., Provost & Vice Pres. Academic Affairs
Robert F. Curran, S.J., Vice Pres. for Legal Affairs
Philip P. Callaghan, S.J., Sec. of the Univ.
Dr. Carmen A. Jordan-Cox, Vice Pres. Student Affairs
Mr. Willard H. Nutting, Vice Pres. Business & Finance
Mr. Alfred P. Alessandri, Vice Pres. Univ. Rels.
Mr. David F. MacMillan, Vice Pres. Devel.
Maureen L. Pryor, Dir. of Campus Ministry
The following are the Schools and Colleges that compose the University:
College of Arts and Sciences—
Dr. Stanley D. Nel, Dean
McLaren School of Business—
Dr. Gary G. Williams, Dean
School of Nursing—
Dr. Norma L. Chaska, Dean
School of Education—
Dr. Paul B. Warren, Dean
School of Law—
Dr. H. Jay Folberg, Dean
College of Professional Studies—
Dr. Betty E. Taylor, Dean
Priests 19
Sisters 5
Lay Faculty 263
Students 7,803

San Rafael
Archdiocese of San Francisco

Dominican College
50 Acacia Ave.
San Rafael, CA 94901-2298
Tel: 415-457-4440; Fax: 415-485-3205
An Independent and Catholic Coeducational Liberal Arts College.
Dr. Joseph R. Fink, Pres.
Dr. Katherine Henderson, Vice Pres. for Academic Affairs
Resident and non-resident students.
Sisters 6
Lay Teachers 146
Students 1,479

Santa Clara
Diocese of San Jose in California

Santa Clara University
500 El Camino Real
Santa Clara, CA 95053-0001
Tel: 408-554-4764; Fax: 408-554-2700
E-mail: username@mailer.scu.edu
Web Site: www.scu.edu
Mission Santa Clara. Founded in 1777. University established in 1851 and chartered by the State in 1855.
Society of Jesus
Administrators:
Rev. Paul L. Locatelli, S.J., Pres.
Mr. Robert Warren, Vice Pres. Finance Admin.
Rev. Stephen A. Privett, S.J., Provost
Dr. Peter A. Facione, Dean, College of Arts and Sciences
Dr. Barry Posner, Dean, Leavey School of Business Administration
Dr. Terry E. Shoup, Dean, School of Engrg.
Dr. Mack A. Player, Dean, School of Law
Rev. Mario J. Prietto, S.J., Dir. Campus Ministry
Priest Teachers 33
Brothers 1
Sisters 3
Scholastics 3
Lay Teachers 367
Students 7,863
Jesuit Community
500 El Camino Real
Santa Clara, CA 95053-1600
Tel: 408-554-4124; Fax: 408-554-4795
Legal Title: *Jesuit Community at Santa Clara University, Inc.*
Revs.:
Gerald L. McKevitt, S.J., Rector
Peter F. Filice, S.J., Min. & Contact
Louis I. Bannan, S.J.
Luis F. Calero, S.J.
Paul G. Crowley, S.J.
Albert J. DiUlio, S.J.
William F. Donnelly, S.J.
Carlo A. Farina, S.J.
James W. Felt, S.J.
Paul J. Fitzgerald, S.J.
James J. Fleming, S.J.
Daniel V. Germann, S.J.
Paul J. Goda, S.J.
Pablo Guerrero, S.J.
Carl H. Hayn, S.J.
John R. LeVecke, S.J.
Arthur F. Liebscher, S.J.
Paul L. Locatelli, S.J.
Norman F. Martin, S.J.
Dennis R. Parnell, S.J.
Charles T. Phipps, S.J.
Mario J. Prietto, S.J.
Stephen A. Privett, S.J.
James W. Reites, S.J.
Theodore J. Rynes, S.J.
Stephen R. Schloesser, S.J.
Robert M. Senkewicz, S.J.
Thomas E. Shanks, S.J.
Anthony E. Sholander, S.J.
Francis R. Smith, S.J.
Dennis C. Smolarski, S.J.
Paul A. Soukup, S.J.
Robert L. St. Claire, S.J.
Gerald P. Sullivan, S.J.
Salvatore A. Tassone, S.J.
Frederick P. Tollini, S.J.
Edward V. Warren, S.J.
Tennant C. Wright, S.J.
Bro. Thomas C. Bracco, S.J.
Mr. Thomas J.E. Schwarz, S.J., (Scholastic)
Mr. Joseph A. Thomas
Mr. Michael M. Turnacliff
Priests 38
Brothers 1
Scholastics 3

Santa Paula
Archdiocese of Los Angeles

Thomas Aquinas College
10000 N. Ojai Rd.
Santa Paula, CA 93060
Tel: 805-525-4417
Four-year undergraduate program in the Liberal Arts leading to the B.A. Degree; Coeducational.
Dr. Thomas E. Dillon, Pres.
Dr. R. Glen Coughlin, Dean
Mr. Peter L. DeLuca, III, Vice Pres. Finance and Admin.
Mr. Daniel J. Grimm, Vice Pres. Devel.
Chaplains:
Revs.:
Bartholomew de la Torre, O.P.
Thomas V. Conn, S.J.

WILFRED F. BORDEN, O.M.I.
Lay Teachers 24
Students 217

COLORADO

Denver
Archdiocese of Denver

Regis University
3333 Regis Blvd.
Denver, CO 80221-1099
Tel: 303-458-4100
A university conducted under the auspices of the Society of Jesus.
Revs.:
WILLIAM J. FORTUNE, Chm. Board of Trustees
MICHAEL J. SHEERAN, S.J., Pres.
DAVID M. CLARKE, S.J., Chancellor
Dr. ALLAN L. SERVICE, Vice Pres. Academic Affairs
Dr. JAMES R. SCHOEMER, Vice Pres. Admin.
Dr. THOMAS E. REYNOLDS, Vice Pres. Student Life
Mr. JOHN A. ALEXANDER, Vice Pres. Devel. & Public Affairs
Dr. STEPHEN DOTY, Dean, Regis College
Dr. WILLIAM J. HUSSON, Dean, School for Professional Studies
Dr. PATRICIA A. LADEWIG, Dean, School for Health Care Professions
Mr. ANDREW D. SCRIMGEOUR, Dean Libraries
Ms. KATHLEEN M. SCHAEFER, Dir. Campus Ministry
Priests 16
Sisters 3
Lay Teachers 500
Students 10,155

CONNECTICUT

Bridgeport
Diocese of Bridgeport

St. Vincent's College
2800 Main St.
Bridgeport, CT 06606
Tel: 203-576-5235
E-mail: svcadmin@snet.net
ANNE T. AVALLONE, M.A., Pres.
BARBARA B. DAVIS, M.S., Dean/Provost
ROBERT S. TROJANOWSKI, M.B.A., J.D., CFO
JANICE NOLAN FAYE, Dir. Admin. Svcs.
JO ANN LOFTUS, B.S., Registrar
ANITA K. MCCAIN, Ed.D., Assoc. Dean of Academic Svcs.
TRACEY S. CHAVIS, M.A., Assoc. Dean & Enrollment Management
Students 177

Fairfield
Diocese of Bridgeport

**Fairfield University*
(Coed)
1073 N. Benson Rd.
Fairfield, CT 06430-5195
Tel: 203-254-4000; Fax: 203-254-4007
Web Site: www.fairfield.edu
The Society of Jesus. College of Arts and Sciences; School of Business; School of Continuing Education; School of Nursing; BEI School of Engineering; Graduate School of Education & Allied Professions; Graduate Program in Financial Management; Graduate Program in Nursing; and Masters in Business Administration.
Revs.:
ALOYSIUS P. KELLEY, S.J., Pres.
TIMOTHY E. TOOHIG, S.J.
CHARLES H. ALLEN, Exec. Asst. to Pres.
Mr. L. WILLIAM MILES, Vice Pres. Admin.
Dr. ROBERT E. WALL, Academic Vice Pres.
Mr. ROBERT C. RUSSO, University Registrar
Mr. STEPHEN P. JAKAB, Assoc. Vice Pres. Admin.
Rev. W. LAURENCE O'NEIL, S.J., Dir. Student Support Svcs.
Dr. WALTER RYBA, Dean School of Business
Dr. THERESA M. VALIGA, Dean School of Nursing
Dr. ORIN L. GROSSMAN, Dean of Arts & Sciences
Dr. EVANGELOS HADJIMICHAEL, Dean, BEI, School of Engrg.
Dr. J. MICHAEL SWEENEY, Dean of Continuing Education
Dr. MARGARET DEIGNAN, Acting Dean of Graduate School of Education & Allied Professions
Rev. HENRY J. MURPHY, S.J., Dean of Freshmen
Ms. MARY SPIEGEL, Dir. Admissions
Mrs. SUSAN KADIR, Dir. of Financial Aid
Mr. JAMES ESTRADA, University Librarian
Mr. WILLIAM P. SCHIMPF, Vice Pres. Student Svcs.
Dr. GWENDOLYN M. VENDLEY, Dean of Students
Dr. SUSAN BIRGE, Dir. Counseling Svcs.
Mr. JAMES D. FITZPATRICK, Assoc. Dean of Students & Dir. University Activities
Rev. PAUL E. CARRIER, S.J., University Chap.
Mr. ROBERT W. CARTER, S.J., Asst. University Chap.
Revs.:
GREGG GROVENBURG, Asst. Chap.
RICHARD J. STANLEY, S.J., Asst. Chap.
Mr. GEORGE E. DIFFLEY, Vice Pres. Advancement
Mr. MURRAY FARBER, Dir. Public Rels.
Ms. JANET CANEPA, Dir. Alumni Rels.
Mr. FREDRIC WHEELER, Assoc. Vice Pres. Devel.
Mr. WILLIAM J. LUCAS, Vice Pres. Finance
Mr. MICHAEL S. MACCARONE, Controller
Revs.:
JAMES R. BLAETTLER, S.J.
VINCENT M. BURNS, S.J.
ALBERT A. CARDONI, S.J.
WILLIAM F. CARR, S.J.
JOHN W. ELDER, S.J.
G. SIMON HARAK, S.J.
VICTOR F. LEEBER, S.J.
FRANCIS W. LEWIS, S.J.
DONALD D. LYNCH, S.J.
JOSEPH F. MACDONNELL, S.J.
Mr. MICHAEL CROWLEY, S.J.
Mr. LUIS A. TAMPE, S.J.
Mr. MICHAEL F. ANDREWS, S.J.
Revs.:
JAMES J. MAYZIK, S.J.
G. PAUL PETERSON, S.J.
ALBERT F. REDDY, S.J.
THOMAS J. REGAN, S.J.
MAURICE WONG, S.J.
Sisters 1
Lay Teachers 191
Students 5,179
(See separate listing for Fairfield College Prep).

**Sacred Heart University*
5151 Park Ave.
Fairfield, CT 06432-1000
Tel: 203-371-7999
E-mail: QUINNM@sacredheart.edu
Web Site: sacredheart.edu
Coeducational and Comprehensive University. Courses offered year round, day & evening.
Dr. ANTHONY J. CERNERA, Pres.
Dr. DAVID HARNETT, Provost & Vice Pres. for Academic Affairs
Dr. DONNA DODGE, S.C., Vice Pres. Mission & Planning
Mr. JAMES M. BARQUINERO, Vice Pres. Enrollment, Planning & Student Affairs
Dr. PAUL K. MADONNA, Vice Pres. Admin. & Finance
Dr. JAMES LYDDY, Vice Pres. Institutional Advancement
Priests 1
Sisters 3
Lay Teachers 403
Students 5,549

Hamden
Archdiocese of Hartford

Mt. Sacred Heart College
265 Benham St.
Hamden, CT 06514-2801
Tel: 203-248-4225; Fax: 203-230-8341
Chartered by the State of Connecticut for Sisters of Community of Apostles of the Sacred Heart of Jesus.
Sr. DEBORAH LOPEZ, A.S.C.J., Pres./Dean
Sisters 3
Students 1

New Haven
Archdiocese of Hartford

Albertus Magnus College
700 Prospect St.
New Haven, CT 06511-1189
Tel: 203-773-8500; Fax: 203-785-8652
E-mail: admissions@albertus.edu
Web Site: www.albertus.edu
Dominican Sisters (St. Mary of the Springs, Columbus, OH)
Dr. JULIA M. MCNAMARA, Pres.
Sr. CHARLES MARIE BRANTL, O.P., Vice. Pres.
BETSEY PARLATO, Vice Pres. Inst. Advancement
JEANNE MANN, Treas.
EILEEN PERILLO, Registrar
MAUREEN MORRISON, Dean Student Svcs.
SUSAN GALLAGHER, Dir. Public Rels.
Sisters 2
Lay Teachers 45
Total Enrollment 1,497

West Hartford
Archdiocese of Hartford

Saint Joseph College
1678 Asylum Ave.
West Hartford, CT 06117
Tel: 860-232-4571; Fax: 860-233-5695
E-mail: info@mercy.sjc.edu
Web Site: www.sjc.edu
Women.
Sisters of Mercy
Chartered by the State of Connecticut.
WINIFRED E. COLEMAN, M.A., Pres.
MARK KOSINSKI, Ph.D., Assoc. Dean
Dr. KAREN RISTAU, Ed.D., Vice Pres. Academic
Dr. MAUREEN REARDON, Exec. Vice Pres., COO & Contact
MARY C. DEMO, Dean of Students
IRENE RIOS, Registrar
Revs.:
DAVID CINQUEGRANI, C.P.
JOHN J. STACK, S.T.D.
JOHN W. MCHUGH
CHARLES J. TOPPER, Ed.D.
TERENCE KRISTOFAK, C.P.
JAMES F. LEARY, M.A.
Priests 6
Sisters 12
Lay Teachers 71
Students 1,943
Undergraduates:
Women 1,210
Men 41
Graduates Coed 692
School for Young Children 84
Gengras Center for Exceptional Children 125

DISTRICT OF COLUMBIA

Washington
Archdiocese of Washington

Catholic University of America, The (1887)
Nugent Hall/Executive Offices
Washington, DC 20064
Tel: 202-319-5000
E-mail: webmaster@cua.edu
His Eminence JAMES CARDINAL HICKEY, Chancellor (Ex Officio)
His Eminence BERNARD CARDINAL LAW, Chm., Bd. of Trustees
Bro. F. PATRICK ELLIS, F.S.C., Ph.D., Pres.
JOHN J. CONVEY, Ph.D., Provost
Rev. Msgr. DENNIS MAHON, Ph.D., Vice Pres. Development
RALPH H. BEAUDOIN, Vice Pres. Finance and Treas.
SUSAN D. PERVI, M.A., Vice Pres. Admin.
Rev. ROBERT M. FRIDAY, S.T.D (PIT) Vice Pres. Student Affairs
Mr. VINCENT P. WALTER, JR., M.M., Sec. of the University, Bd. of Trustees & Chief of Staff
Rev. RAYMOND F. COLLINS, S.T.D., Dean, School of Religious Studies
JUDE P. DOUGHERTY, Ph.D., Dean, School of Philosophy
ANTANAS SUZIEDELIS, Ph.D., Dean, School of Arts and Sciences
WILLIAM E. KELLY, D. Civil Eng., Dean, School of Engrg.
BERNARD DOBRANSKI, J.D., Dean, Columbus School of Law
Sr. MARY JEAN FLAHERTY, S.C., Ph.D., Dean, School of Nursing
ELAINE R. WALTER, Ph.D., Dean, Benjamin T. Rome School of Music
ELIZABETH SMITH EVERSA, Ph.D., Dean, School of Library and Information Science
Sr. ANN PATRICK CONRAD, D.S.W., Dean, National Catholic School of Social Svc.
GREGORY K. HUNT, A.I.A., Dean, School of Architecture and Planning
JAMES S. PULA, Ph.D., Dean, Metropolitan College
Rev. HOWARD P. BLEICHNER, S.S., D.Th., Rector, Theological College
INGRID MERKEL, Ph.D., Vice Provost for Undergraduate Studies
Rev. JOHN E. LYNCH, C.S.P., Ph.D., Vice Provost for Graduate Studies
JAMES W. MAYO, Assoc. Provost for Sponsored Research
Rev. MICHAEL MANNION (CAM) Univ. Chap. & Dir. Campus Ministry
ADELE CHWALEK, M.S.L.S., Dir. Libraries
G. KENDALL RICE, Ph.D., Registrar
ANNE SMITH, Exec. Dir., Office of Public Affairs
Rev. EUGENE HEMRICK, Dir., Diocesan Rels.
DAVID J. MCGONAGLE, Dir., CUA Press
KATHERINE S. LAFRANCE, Dean, Amissions and Financial Aid
Priests Associated with the University Full-Time:
Revs.:
C. GERARD AUSTIN, O.P., S.T.D.
JOHN P. BEAL, J.C.D.
CHRISTOPHER T. BEGG, S.T.D., Ph.D.
HOWARD P. BLEICHNER, S.S., D.Th.
ANDREW C. BUECHELE, Sch.P., Ph.D.

WILLIAM CENKNER, O.P., Ph.D.
RAYMOND F. COLLINS, S.T.D.
ALEXANDER A. DI LELLA, O.F.M., Ph.D.
ROBERT B. ENO, S.S., S.T.D.
JOHN T. FORD, C.S.C., S.T.D.
ROBERT M. FRIDAY, S.T.D (PIT)
JOHN P. GALVIN, D.Th (BO)
ALBERT C. GIAQUINTO, S.S., M.A., S.T.L.
FRANCIS T. GIGNAC, S.J., D.Phil.
PATRICK GRANFIELD, O.S.B., J.D., Ph.D., S.T.D.
THOMAS J. GREEN, J.C.D (BGP)
JACQUES GRES-GAYER, Dr.Th (France)
SIDNEY H. GRIFFITH, S.T., Ph.D.
THOMAS P. HALTON, Ph.D (Ireland)
DONALD J. HEET, O.S.F.S.
STEPHEN W. HAPPEL, S.T.D., Ph.D.
THOMAS R. HURST, S.S., Ph.D.
KEVIN W. IRWIN, S.T.D (NY)
JOSEPH JENSEN, O.S.B., S.T.D.
DAVID W. JOHNSON, S.J., Ph.D.
THOMAS C. KANE, O.P., S.T.D.
ROBERT T. KENNEDY, J.U.D (NY)
JOSEPH A. KOMONCHAK, Ph.D (NY)
LOUIS M. LAFAVIA, C.PP.S., Ph.D.
JOHN E. LYNCH, C.S.P., Ph.D.
MICHAEL MANNION, C.A.M.
BERARD L. MARTHALER, O.F.M.Conv., Ph.D., S.T.D.
FRANK J. MATERA, Ph.D (HRT)
JOHN P. MEIER, S.S.D (NY)
RAYMOND C. O'BRIEN, J.D.
EDWARD G. PFNAUSCH, J.C.L.
PETER C. PHAN, Ph.D., S.T.D (DAL)
DAVID N. POWER, O.M.I., S.T.D.
KURT PRITZL, O.P., Ph.D.
JAMES H. PROVOST, J.C.D (HEL)
PAUL G. ROBICHAUD, C.S.P., Ph.D.
BRIAN J. SHANLEY, O.P., Ph.D.
ROBERT S. SOKOLOWSKI, Ph.D (HRT)
RAYMOND STUDZINSKI, O.S.B., Ph.D.
ROBERT F. TRISCO, H.E.D (CHI)
JOHN J. TUOHEY, Ph.D (SPR)
WILLIAM VIOLA, S.S., S.T.M., S.T.L.
Rev. Msgr. JOHN WIPPEL, Ph.D (STU)
Rev. JAMES A. WISEMAN, O.S.B., S.T.D.
Priests Associated with the University Part-Time:
Very Rev. SEELY BEGGIANI, S.T.D (SAM)
Revs.:
WILLIAM J. CONLAN, O.P.
PETER J. DALY, J.D.
GEORGE T. DENNIS, S.J., S.E.D.
COLUMBA J. ENRIGHT, T.O.R.
JOSEPH A. FITZMYER, S.J., Ph.D.
BERNARD K. HARKINS, O.P.
Rev. Msgr. GEORGE G. HIGGINS, Ph.D (CHI)
Revs.:
WILLIAM J. HILL, O.P., S.T.D.
JOHN FREDERICK HINNEBUSCH, O.P.
Rev. Msgr. FREDERICK R. MCMANUS, J.C.D., L.L.D (BO)
Rev. Msgr. ROBERT PAUL MOHAN
Revs.:
THOMAS PATER (CIN)
RAYMOND H. POTVIN, Ph.D (SPR)
WILLIAM J. ROONEY (CHI)
JOHN F. SMOLKO (BGP)
Clerical Members, Board of Trustees:
Most Rev. Robert J. Banks; His Eminence, Anthony Cardinal Bevilacqua; Rev. Msgr. Michael Bransfield; Most Rev. Daniel M. Buechlein; Most Rev. Charles J. Chaput; Most Rev. Thomas V. Daily; Most Rev. Harry J. Flynn; Most Rev. Francis E. George; His Eminence, James Cardinal Hickey, Chancellor (Ex-Officio); His Eminence, William Cardinal Keeler; His Eminence, Bernard Cardinal Law, Chm.; Most Rev. John J. Leibrecht; Rev. Msgr. Paul A. Lenz; Most Rev. William J. Levada; Most Rev. Oscar H. Lipscomb; Most Rev. William E. Lori; His Eminence, Adam Cardinal Maida; Most Rev. Theodore E. McCarrick; Most Rev. Robert E. Mulvee; Most. Rev. William Francis Murphy; His Eminence, John Cardinal O'Connor; Most Rev. Daniel E. Pilarczyk; Most Rev. Frances B. Shulte; Most Rev. Terry J. Steib; Most Rev. Donald W. Wuerl; Most Rev. Philip M. Hannan, (Emeritus).
Religious 52
Lay Teachers 318
Students 5,974

**Georgetown University* (1789)
37th and O Sts., N.W.
Washington, DC 20057
Tel: 202-687-0100
E-mail: umhoferm@gunet.georgetown.edu
Web Site: http://www.georgetown.edu
Rev. LEO J. O'DONOVAN, S.J., Pres.
KATHLEEN CURRY SANTORA, Univ. Sec.
WILLIAM E. COOPER, Ph.D., Exec. Vice Pres., Main Campus
SAM WIESEL, M.D., Exec. Vice Pres., Health Sciences
KENNETH BLOEM, C.E.O., Medical Center
JUDITH AREEN, Exec. Vice Pres. for Law Center Affairs & Dean of the School of Law
JAMES M. WAGNER, Vice Pres. for Admin. & Facilities
NICOLE MANDEVILLE, Vice Pres. & Treas.
JOSEPH PETTIT, Ph.D., Vice Pres. Planning and Inst. Research
KATHLEEN T. JONES, Vice Pres. Alumni & Univ. Rels.
Rev. ADAM BUNNELL, O.F.M., University Chap.
JAMES A. DONAHUE, Dean Student Affairs
The following are the Schools and Colleges which compose the University:
Rev. ROBERT B. LAWTON, S.J., Dean
College of Arts and Sciences (1789)—
Graduate School:
RICHARD B. SCHWARTZ, Ph.D., Dean
School of Medicine (1851)
3900 Reservoir Rd., N.W.
Washington, DC 20007
WILLIAM MAXTED, M.D., Dean
Law Center (1870)
600 New Jersey Ave., N.W.
Washington, DC 20001
JUDITH AREEN, Esq., Dean
School of Nursing (1903)
3700 Reservoir Rd., N.W.
Washington, DC 20007
ELAINE L. LARSON, Ph.D., Dean
Edmund A. Walsh School of Foreign Service (1919).
School of Business (1958)—
KASRA FERDOWS, Acting Dean
School for Summer and Continuing Education (1954)—
MICHAEL J. COLLINS, Ph.D., Dean
Georgetown University Hospital
3800 Reservoir Rd., N.W.
Washington, DC 20007
SHARON FLYNN HOLLANDER, Chief Exec.
Undergraduate Admissions and Records—
CHARLES A. DEACON, M.A., Dean
Lauinger Memorial Library—
SUSAN K. MARTIN, M.S.L.S., Librarian
Alumni Associates:
Alumni House
3604 O St., N.W.
Washington, DC 20057
Affirmative Action Programs
3800 Reservoir Rd., N.W.
Washington, DC 20007
ROSEMARY KILKENNY, M.A., Special Asst. to Pres. for AAP
Jesuits 70
Sisters 1
Lay Teachers 2,085
Total Enrollment 12,629

Trinity College
Michigan Ave. and Franklin St., N.E.
Washington, DC 20017
Tel: 202-939-5000
Sisters of Notre Dame de Namur
PATRICIA A. MCGUIRE, Pres.
Sr. CATHERINE MARIE LEE, S.N.D., Community Rep.
Dr. PATTY WEITZEL-O'NEILL, Vice Pres. Academic Affairs
Priests 2
Sisters 6
Lay Professors 44
Students 1,450

FLORIDA

Miami
Archdiocese of Miami

Barry University
President's Office
11300 N.E. 2nd Ave.
Miami, FL 33161
Tel: 305-899-3000
Web Site: www.barry.edu
Sisters of St. Dominic (Adrian, MI)
Sr. JEANNE O'LAUGHLIN, O.P., Ph.D., Pres.
Sr. PEGGY ALBERT, O.P., Ph.D., Exec. Asst. Pres.
Dr. J. PATRICK LEE, Ph.D., Provost & Senior Vice Pres. Academic Affairs
Sr. CORINNE SANDERS, O.P., Ed.D., Dir. of Mission & Ministry
Mrs. GRACE MERINO SCHOLLMEYER, Dean Records & Registrar
Mr. TIMOTHY H. CZERNIEC, Senior Vice Pres. Business & Finance
Dr. GEORGE J. WANKO, Ph.D., Vice Pres. Student Svcs.
Sr. MARGARET JOHNSON, O.P., Vice Pres. Planning, Research & Evaluation
Sr. LORETTA MULRY I.H.M., Ed.D., Dean School of Adult & Continuing Education
Dr. EILEEN MCDONOUGH, Assoc. Vice Pres. Student Svcs.
Revs.:
MARK WEDIG, O.P.
DANIEL P. MADDEN, O.P.
PEDRO A. SUAREZ, S.J.
JOHN F. O'GRADY, S.S.D., S.T.D (ALB)
EMILIANO ZAPATA, O.P.
Bro. EDWARD VAN MERRIENBOER, O.P.
Sr. EVELYN PICHE, O.P., Ph.D., Dean of School of Education
Mr. GREGORY MILLER, Dean of Admissions & Enrollment Planning
Sr. JOHN KAREN FREI, O.P., Ph.D., Assoc. Vice Pres. Research & Dean School of Natural & Health Science
CHESTER A. EVANS, D.P.M., Assoc. Vice Pres. & Dean, School of Podiatric Medicine
LEWIS W. LASH, Ph.D., Dean, School of Business
LAURA S. ARMESTO, Ph.D., Assoc. Vice Pres. Undergraduate Studies & Dean, School of Arts & Sciences
HUGH W. RIPLEY, M.S.L.S., Dean, Library Svcs.
JUDITH A. BALCERSKI, Ph.D., Dean, School of Nursing
STEPHEN M. HOLLOWAY, Ph.D., Assoc. Vice Pres. Graduate Studies & Dean, School of Social Work
WILLIAM FENTON, Vice Pres., Institutional Advancement & Chm. Capital Campaign
Sr. SARAH CAVANAUGH, O.P., M.S., Assoc. Vice Pres. Institutional Advancement
G. JEAN CERRA, Ph.D., Assoc. Vice Pres. Academic Svcs. & School of Human Performance & Leisure Science
Priests 5
Brothers 1
Sisters 31
Lay Teachers 239
Students 7,218

Opa Locka
Archdiocese of Miami

St. Thomas University
(Coed)
16400 N.W. 32nd Ave.
Opa Locka, FL 33054
Tel: 305-625-6000; Fax: 305-628-6511
Web Site: www.stu.edu
Board of Trustees:
THOMAS A. BASTIAN, C.P.A.
C. CLYDE ATKINS
ROBERT V. GLASER
JOSEPH M. CATANIA
EILEEN CORNACCHIA
RONALD E. FRAZIER
WILLIAM O. CULLOM
FRANK R. ESPOSITO, Trustee Emeritus
GEORGE GOLDBLOOM
STEVEN D. HAYWORTH
Rev. Msgr. WILLIAM HENNESSEY, V.G.
Most Rev. ROBERT N. LYNCH
MARIO MARTINEZ
Very Rev. TOMAS M. MARIN
SAMUEL L. HIGGINBOTTOM
Rev. Msgr. GERARD T. LACERRA
MARIA C. LEIVA
ANN P. MACHADO
CORINNE H. RIEDER
VICTOR H. MENDELSON
Revs.:
GUSTAVO J. MIYARES
JOSE P. NICKSE
HERMAN J. RUSSOMANO, Esq., Chair
RALPH A. SANCHEZ
STEPHEN HAROLD SCHOTT
Dr. P. ALAN SMURFIT
Sr. ELIZABETH ANNE WORLEY, S.S.J.
The Member:
Most Rev. JOHN CLEMENT FAVALORA
Of Counsel:
J. PATRICK FITZGERALD
Administration:
Rev. GARY N. MCCLOSKEY, O.S.A., Ph.D., Vice Pres. for Academic Affairs
Mr. NORMAN BLAIR, Vice Pres. for Admin. & Treas.
ANA GLORIA RIVAS-VASQUEZ, Esq., Vice Pres. for Devel. & External Affairs
Mr. STEPHEN CONDON, Vice Pres. Student Affairs
Dr. JOSEPH IANNONE, Dean of the School of Graduate Studies
DANIEL MORRISSEY, Esq., Dean of the School of Law
Rev. EDWARD A. BLACKWELL, Dir. of Campus Ministry
Clergy and Religious Full-Time Faculty:
Revs.:
JORGE SARDINAS
RAYMOND E. GEISSER, O.S.A.
JAMES GAUGHAN
DANIEL KENT
JAMES L. MACDOUGALL, O.S.A.
Sr. HELEN ROSENTHAL, R.S.C.J.
Priests 8
Sisters 2
Lay Teachers 80
Students 3,359

St. Leo
Diocese of St. Petersburg

Saint Leo College
Mailing Address:
P.O. Box 6665
St. Leo, FL 33574
Tel: 352-588-8200
An Independent and Catholic Coeducation Liberal Arts College.
Dr. ARTHUR F. KIRK, JR., Pres.
Sr. CANDICE TUCCI, O.S.F., Asst. to Pres. for Campus Ministry
Rev. ANTHONY KISSEL, Asst. Dir. Campus Ministry
Legal Title: *Saint Leo College, Inc.*
Legal Title: *Saint Leo College Educational Fund, Inc.*

HAWAII

Honolulu
Diocese of Honolulu

**Chaminade University of Honolulu*
3140 Waialae Ave.
Honolulu, HI 96816
Tel: 808-735-4711
E-mail: cuhadm@lava.net
Web Site: www.chaminude.edu
MARY C. WESSELKAMPER, Pres.
Campus Ministry:
Rev. HERMAN GOMES, SS.CC.
Bro. THOMAS HEINLE, S.M.
Priests 6
Brothers 4
Sisters 1
Lay Teachers 49
Students 2,592

ILLINOIS

Chicago
Archdiocese of Chicago

De Paul University
One E. Jackson Blvd.
Chicago, IL 60604
Tel: 312-362-8000
Conducted by the Priests of the Congregation of the Mission (Vincentian Fathers and Brothers)
Campuses: Downtown, Lincoln Park, O'Hare, Naperville, South Suburban.
Revs.:
JOHN P. MINOGUE, C.M., Pres.
JOHN T. RICHARDSON, C.M., Chancellor
Dr. RICHARD J. MEISTER, Exec. Vice Pres. Academic Affairs
Rev. EDWARD R. UDOVIC, C.M., Senior Exec. Univ. Mission
Mr. KENNETH A. MCHUGH, Exec. Vice Pres. & Chief Fin. Officer
Ms. ELAINE M. WATSON, Sec. Univ. & Vice Pres. Admin.
Ms. MARYANN AHAMD, Spec. Asst. to Pres. on Diversity
Rev. Msgr. JOHN J. EGAN, Spec. Asst. to Pres., Office of Community Affairs
Ms. CAROLE SCHOR, Vice Pres. Human Resources
Mr. JAMES R. DOYLE, Vice Pres. Student Affairs
Mr. DAVID KALSBEEK, Vice Pres. Enrollment Mgmt.
Mr. JAMES R. LOONEY, Vice Pres. Advancement
Ms. SUSAN H. WALLACE, Controller
Mr. ROBERT L. KOZOMAN, Treas. Univ.
Mr. DAVID O. JUSTICE, Vice Pres. Lifelong Learning & Suburban Campuses
Priests 20
Brothers 3
Sisters 12
Faculty 527
Students 17,769
College of Liberal Arts and Sciences
2320 N. Kenmore Ave.
Chicago, IL 60614
Dr. MICHAEL L MEZEY, Dean
College of Law
One E. Jackson Blvd.
Chicago, IL 60604
Dr. TEREE E. FOSTER, Dean
College of Commerce
One E. Jackson Blvd.
Chicago, IL 60604
Dr. RONALD J. PATTEN, Dean
School of Music
804 W. Belden
Chicago, IL 60614
Dr. DONALD E. CASEY, Dean
School for New Learning Computer Science and Telecommunication Center
243 S. Wabash Ave.
Chicago, IL 60604-2302
Dr. SUSANNE M. DUMBLETON, Dean
School of Computer Science, Telecommunication and Information Systems Vice President for Information Services. Computer Science and Telecommunication Center
243 S. Wabash Ave.
Chicago, IL 60604-2302
Dr. HELMUNT P. EPP, Dean
The Theatre School
2135 N. Kenmore Ave.
Chicago, IL 60614
Dr. JOHN R. WATTS, Ph.D., Dean
School of Education
2320 N. Kenmore Ave.
Chicago, IL 60614
Dr. BARBARA SIZEMORE, Dean

Jesuit Community at Loyola University of Chicago
Jesuit Residence, 6525 N. Sheridan Rd.
Chicago, IL 60626
Tel: 773-508-8800; Fax: 773-508-2098
Legal Title: *The Jesuit Community Corporation at Loyola University*
Revs.:
LAWRENCE REUTER, S.J., Rector
DENNIS P. AHERN, S.J.
RICHARD W. ANDERSON, S.J.
M. SELVAN AUGUSTINE, S.J.
RAYMOND C. BAUMHART, S.J.
FRANS J. VAN BEECK, S.J.
ROBERT L. BIRELEY, S.J.
PETER W. BRESLIN, S.J.
DONALD E. BRUGGER, S.J.
JOHN CHRYSOSTOM, S.J.
Bro. BRUTUS J. CLAY, S.J.
Revs.:
RICHARD F. COSTIGAN, S.J.
WILLIAM E. CREED, S.J.
MATTHEW E. CREIGHTON, S.J.
WILLIAM A. DEHLER, S.J.
JOHN T. DILLON, S.J.
EUGENE F. DWYER, S.J.
RONALD J. FERGUSON, S.J.
KEVIN T. FITZGERALD, S.J.
PETER D. FOX, S.J.
EUGENE M. GEINZER, S.J (MAR)
Bro. MICHAEL J. GRACE, S.J.
Revs.:
PAUL F. HARMAN, S.J.
WILLIAM J. HARMLESS, S.J (NOR)
DANIEL F. HARTNETT, S.J.
JOHN C. HAUGHEY, S.J (MAR)
F. TORRENS HECHT, S.J.
WILLIAM H. HOGAN, S.J.
JOHN J. KILGALLEN, S.J.
STEVEN KIMMONS, S.J (NOR)
JOHN J. KINSELLA, S.J.
ALLAN F. KIRK, S.J.
WALTER P. KROLIKOWSKI, S.J.
MARK J. LINK, S.J.
CARLOS LLAGAS, S.J (PH)
JAMES F. MAGUIRE, S.J.
FRAZER MASCARENHAS, S.J.
ROBERT W. MULLIGAN, S.J.
JOHN P. MURPHY, S.J.
JOHN J. O'CALLAGHAN, S.J.
JEROME T. OVERBECK, S.J.
BRIAN G. PAULSON, S.J.
EGERTON PERERA, S.J.
AUGUSTINE PERUMALIL, S.J (PAT)
GENE D. PHILLIPS, S.J.
JOHN J. PIDERIT, S.J (NY)
JOHN J. POWELL, S.J.
EDWARD J. QUINNAN, S.J (NY)
JOHN E. REILLY, S.J.
JOHN H. REINKE, S.J.
LIBORIUS REPSCHINSKI, S.J.
HUGH B. RODMAN, S.J.
CHARLES E. RONAN, S.J.
THEODORE C. ROSS, S.J (DET)
DONALD F. ROWE, S.J.
THOMAS SARJUMANARSA, S.J.
ROBERT T. SEARS, S.J.
MYLES N. SHEEHAN, S.J.
AMADEUS SHIRIMA, S.J.
WILLIAM J. SPINE, S.J.
PETER STEELE, S.J (AUS)
JAMES A. STOEGER, S.J.
LEO C. SWEENEY, S.J.
THOMAS H. TOBIN, S.J.
THEODORE J. TRACY, S.J.
J. RICHARD VANDEVELDE, S.J.
MUREL R. VOGEL, S.J.
GERALD C. WALLING, S.J.
EARL A. WEIS, S.J (DET)
JARED W. WICKS, S.J (DET)
ROBERT J. WILLMES, S.J.

Loyola University-Chicago
6525 N. Sheridan Rd.
Chicago, IL 60626
Tel: 773-274-3000
Mailing Address:—President's Office
820 N. Michigan Ave.
Chicago, IL 60611
Tel: 312-915-6400
Legal Title: *Loyola University of Chicago, Illinois*
FRANK W. CONSIDINE, Chm. Bd.
Rev. JOHN J. PIDERIT, S.J., Pres.
Dr. RONALD E. WALKER, Exec. Vice Pres.
Dr. ANTHONY L. BARBATO, Pres. & C.E.O, Loyola Univ. Medical Center
Dr. JOSEPH SANDMAN, Vice Pres. Advancement
Dr. SHERRI COE-PERKINS, Vice Pres. Student Affairs
Mr. ALLAN O. BALDWIN, Vice Pres. Information Technologies
Rev. LAWRENCE REUTER, S.J., Vice Pres. University Ministry
Dr. JAMES L. WISER, Senior Vice Pres. & Dean Faculties
Mr. JOHN KAMBANIS, Vice Pres. Human Resource Mgmt.
Dr. MARJORIE BEANE, Vice Pres. Admin. Coorindation
Mr. DAVID MEAGHER, Vice Pres. Finance & Treas.
Mrs. ELLEN KANE MUNRO, Vice Pres. and General Counsel
The following are the Schools and Colleges which compose the University:
The College of Arts and Sciences (1870)
Lake Shore Campus
6525 N. Sheridan Rd.
Chicago, IL 60626
Water Tower Campus
820 N. Michigan Ave.
Chicago, IL 60611
Dr. KATHLEEN MCCOURT, Dean
The School of Law (1908)
1 E. Pearson St.
Chicago, IL 60611
NINA APPEL, Dean
The Stritch School of Medicine (1909)
2160 S. First Ave.
Maywood, IL 60153
Dr. DANIEL H. WINSHIP, Dean
School of Social Work (1914)
820 N. Michigan Ave.
Chicago, IL 60611
Dr. JOSEPH WALSH, Dean
Mundelein College of Loyola
6525 N. Sheridan Rd.
Chicago, IL 60626
Dr. STEPHEN FREEDMAN, Dean
The School of Business Administration (1922)
820 N. Michigan Ave.
Chicago, IL 60611
Dr. WILLIAM BRYAN, Dean
The Graduate School (1926)
820 N. Michigan Ave.
Chicago, IL 60611
Dr. JAMES BRENNAN, Dean
The School of Nursing (1935)
6525 N. Sheridan Rd.
Chicago, IL 60626
Dr. SHIRLEY DOOLING, Dean
The School of Education (1969)
Mallinkrodt Campus, 1041 Ridge Rd.
Wilmette, IL 60091
Dr. MARGARET FONG, Dean
Total University enrollment 13,759
Total full-time faculty 1,135
St. Joseph's Seminary
6551 N. Sheridan Rd.
Chicago, IL 60631
Rev. DENNIS J. LYLE, Academic Dean
Mallinckrodt Campus
1041 Ridge Rd.
Wilmette, IL 60091

Saint Xavier University
3700 West 103rd St.
Chicago, IL 60655
Tel: 773-298-3000
Dr. RICHARD A. YANIKOSKI, Pres.
Sisters of Mercy of the Union in the U.S. 10
Order of St. Francis 1
Sisters of Charity of Blessed Virgin Mary 1
Lay Teachers 262
Students 4,100

Vincentian Community at DePaul University
2233 N. Kenmore Ave.
Chicago, IL 60614
Tel: 312-880-2968
Legal Title: *Society of Priests of the Congregation of the Mission of Chicago*
Rev. PAUL OTTO SCHNEEBECK, C.M., Supr.
Mr. MICHAEL WALSH, Treas.
Members of the Vincentian Community (Congregation of the Mission):
Rev. WILLIAM V. BRENNAN, C.M.
Bros.:
PAUL P. JOSEPH, C.M.
LEO KEIGHER, C.M.

Revs.:
JOHN HICKEY, C.M.
JAY JUNG, C.M.
THOMAS J. MEIK, C.M.
AUSTIN F. MINOGUE, C.M.
JOHN P. MINOGUE, C.M.
PATRICK MULLINS, C.M.
THOMAS P. MUNSTER, C.M.
MANUEL J. PELLETERI, C.M.
MARTIN J. CULLIGAN, C.M.
DONALD OURS, C.M.
ANTHONY DOSEN, C.M.
JOHN F. CAWLEY, C.M.
WILLIAM A. RYAN, C.M.
EDWARD J. TOMASIEWICZ, C.M.
CHARLES J. WELTER, C.M.
RAYMOND F. WHITE, C.M.

Joliet
Diocese of Joliet in Illinois

College of St. Francis
500 N. Wilcox
Joliet, IL 60435
Tel: 815-740-3360
Web Site: http://www.stfrancis.edu
A coed resident and commuter school.
Dr. JAMES A. DOPPKE, Pres.
Sr. DOLORES ZEMONT, O.S.F., Dir. Campus Ministry
Priests 1
Sisters of St. Francis of Mary Immaculate 1
Lay Teachers 67
Students 5,203
Total Staff 193
Saint Joseph College of Nursing (1988) (Coed Commuter College)
290 N. Springfield Ave.
Joliet, IL 60435
Tel: 815-741-7123; Fax: 815-741-7131
Dr. JAMES A. DOPPKE, Pres.
ALBERTTA DAVID, Dean
Lay Teachers 14
Students 221

Lake Forest
Archdiocese of Chicago

Barat College
700 Westleigh Rd.
Lake Forest, IL 60045
Tel: 708-234-3000
Dr. LUCY S. MORROS, Pres.
Dr. DAVID THROGMORTON, Dean of College & Vice Pres. Academic Affairs
Religious of the Sacred Heart 2
Lay Teachers 88
Students 731

Lisle
Diocese of Joliet in Illinois

Benedictine University
5700 College Rd.
Lisle, IL 60532-0900
Tel: 630-829-6000; Fax: 630-960-1126
Rt. Rev. HUGH R. ANDERSON, O.S.B., Chancellor
Dr. WILLIAM J. CARROLL, Pres.
Mr. SAM ROSS, Vice-Pres. Univ. Advancement
CHARLES GREGORY, Vice Pres. Enrollment Mgmt & Mktg.
Dr. PHYLLIS M. KITTEL, Vice Pres. for Academic Affairs
Mr. ROBERT HEAD, Vice-Pres. Finance & Admin.
DAVID TURNER, Univ. Chap.
Revs.:
KEVIN J. SHEERAN, O.S.B., Sec. & Treas.
STANLEY G. VESELY, O.S.B.
PHILIP S. TIMKO, O.S.B.
CHRISTIAN W. CEPLECHA, O.S.B.
MICHAEL E. KOMECHAK, O.S.B.
ODILO CRKVA, O.S.B.
THEODORE D. SUCHY, O.S.B.
JOHN PALMER, C.S.V.
JAMES FLINT, O.S.B.
PASCHAL D. HONNER, O.S.B.
Bros.:
SEBASTIAN KUHN, O.S.B.
AUGUSTINE MALLAK, O.S.B.
ROBERT L. LORITZ, O.S.B.
Fathers 12
Brothers 3
Sisters 1
Lay Teachers 190
Administrators 102
Students 2,842

Quincy
Diocese of Springfield in Illinois

Quincy University (1860)
1800 College Ave.
Quincy, IL 62301
Tel: 217-222-8020; 228-5318
Web Site: www.quincy.edu
Franciscan Friars, Sacred Heart Province
Revs.:
EUGENE R. KOLE, O.F.M.Conv (NY) Pres.
VICTOR KINGERY, O.F.M., Librarian
KENNETH CAPALBO, O.F.M., Guardian
Bros.:
GREGORY BUMM, O.F.M.
JAMES EDMISTON, O.F.M.
JAMES FINNEGAN, O.F.M.
JACK HARDESTY, O.F.M.
Rev. PHILIBERT HOEBING, O.F.M.
Bro. HERMAN JOE JAMES, O.F.M.
Revs.:
RICHARD M. JESKE, O.F.M., Chap., Illinois Veteran's Home
WILLIAM BURTON, O.F.M.
JOHN J. LAKERS, O.F.M.
Bros.:
JAMES LAMMERS, O.F.M.
THOM SMITH O.F.M., Campus Min.
Revs.:
JOSEPH TAN DOAN NGUYEN, O.F.M.
DENNIS SCHAFER, O.F.M.
HARRY SPECKMAN, O.F.M., Exec. Vice Pres. & Dir., Radio Station
RICHARD BENDORF, O.F.M.
GEORGE WINDOLPH, O.F.M.
JOSEPH ZIMMERMAN, O.F.M.
Bros.:
JACK CARNAGHI, O.F.M.
DAN PIASECKI, O.F.M.
SCOTUS REN, O.F.M.
Rev. IRENAEUS KIMMINU, O.F.M.
Sr. DAWN NOTHWEHR, O.S.F.
Priests 15
Brothers 7
Sisters 1
Lay Faculty - Administrators 97
Students 1,147

River Forest
Archdiocese of Chicago

Dominican University (Formerly Rosary College)
7900 W. Division St.
River Forest, IL 60305
Tel: 708-366-2490
Legal Title: *Dominican University*
Dominican Sisters of Sinsinawa, WI
Dr. DONNA M. CARROLL, Pres.
Sr. DIONA MCNICHOLS, O.P., Prioress
Dr. NORMAN CARROLL, Vice Pres. of Academic Affairs
Rosary College of Arts and Sciences at Dominican University
Dr. PRUDENCE DALRYMPLE, Dean
School of Business
Dr. MOLLY BURKE, Dean
School of Education
Sr. COLLEEN MCNICHOLAS, Dean
Graduate School of Library and Information Science
Dr. PEGGY SULLIVAN, Dean
Sisters 12
Lay Teachers 60
Students 1,800

Romeoville
Diocese of Joliet in Illinois

Lewis University
(Coed University)
Rt. 53
Romeoville, IL 60446
Tel: 815-838-0500
Web Site: http://www.lewisu.edu/
Bros.:
JAMES GAFFNEY, F.S.C., Pres.
ROBERT MURPHY, O.Carm., Dir. University Ministry
Priests 4
Sisters 3
Brothers of the Christian Schools 15
Lay Teachers 131
Students 4,264

Springfield
Diocese of Springfield in Illinois

Springfield College in Illinois
1500 N. Fifth St.
Springfield, IL 62702
Tel: 217-525-1420
Sr. SUZANNE SIMS, O.S.U., Ph.D., Pres.
Rev. DAVID S. LANTZ, Dir.
Priests 1
Ursuline Sisters 2
Lay Teachers 46
Students 525

INDIANA

Donaldson
Diocese of Fort Wayne - South Bend

Ancilla Domini College
Mailing Address:
P.O. Box 1
Donaldson, IN 46513
Poor Handmaids of Jesus Christ (Ancilla Domini Sisters)
Dr. WILLIAM J. SHUSTOWSKI, JR., Pres.
RAYMOND GIRRES, Business Officer
Dr. MARCIA MITTELSTADT, Academic Dean
SHARON BLUBAUGH, Registrar
MARK RINGENBERG, Dir. of Student Svcs.
GLENDA BOCKMAN, Head Librarian
JILL PARMLEY, Dir. Inst. Advancement
Sisters 5
Lay Teachers 37
Students 608

Fort Wayne
Diocese of Fort Wayne - South Bend

University of St. Francis
2701 Spring St.
Fort Wayne, IN 46808-3994
Tel: 219-434-3100; Fax: 219-434-3183; 434-3194
E-mail: ekriss@sfc.edu
Web Site: http://www.sfc.edu
Conducted by Sisters of St. Francis of Perpetual Adoration.
Sr. M. ELISE KRISS, O.S.F., Pres.
Rev. JAMES SAPP (WH) Residence Chap.
Priests 1
Sisters 10
Lay Teachers 42
Students 992

Indianapolis
Archdiocese of Indianapolis

Marian College
(Coed)
3200 Cold Spring Rd.
Indianapolis, IN 46222
Tel: 317-955-6000; Fax: 317-955-6048
Web Site: http://www.marian.edu
Sisters of the Third Order Regular of St. Francis
Sr. NORMA ROCKLAGE, O.S.F., Ph.D., Vice Pres. Mission Effectiveness & Planning
C. EDWARD BALOG, Ph.D., Dean of Academic Affairs
DANIEL A. FELICETTI, Ph.D., Pres.
Revs.:
FRANCIS E. BRYAN
LEOPOLD KEFFLER, O.F.M.Conv.
Priests 2
Sisters 10
Lay Teachers 67
Students 1,418

Notre Dame
Diocese of Fort Wayne - South Bend

Holy Cross College, Holy Cross College, Inc.
1801 N. Michigan, P.O. Box 308
Notre Dame, IN 46556-0308
Tel: 219-239-8400; Fax: 219-233-7427
E-mail: richard.b.gilman.1@nd.edu
Web Site: http://www.hcc-nd.edu
Legal Title: *Holy Cross College, Inc.*
Bros.:
RICHARD GILMAN, C.S.C., Pres.
JAMES BLUMA, C.S.C., Dean of Student Life
R. DOUGLAS IRVINE, Dir. Financial Aid
MARK P. MULLANEY, Vice Pres. Finance
Bro. CHARLES GREGG, C.S.C., Librarian
JOSEPH GOEPFRICH, Vice Pres. Advancement
CHRISTOPHER J. RUHE, Dir. Residence Life
RICHARD J. SULLIVAN, Registrar
VINCENT M. DUKE, Dir. Admissions
Sr. ANNA MAE GOLDEN, C.S.C., Academic Dean
Sr. NANCY MILLER, O.S.F., Coord. Academic Advising
ROBERT KLOSKA, Dir. Campus Ministry
Priests 5
Sisters 5
Brothers 12
Lay Professors 26
Students 507

Saint Mary's College
Notre Dame, IN 46556
Tel: 219-284-4000; Fax: 219-284-4716
E-mail: 1hitch@saintmarys.edu
An institution of higher education for women.
Sisters of the Holy Cross
MARILOU ELDRED, Pres.
Sisters 3
Lay Professors 109

Students 1,416

**University of Notre Dame Du Lac* (1842)
Corby Hall
Notre Dame, IN 46556
Tel: 219-631-5000
Web Site: http://www.nd.edu/ndhomepage/ndhomepage.html
The Graduate School (29 departments). The Law School. The Undergraduate School (four colleges, 36 departments). Institutes and Radiation Laboratory, Center for Study of Man, Institute for Urban Studies and Institute for International Studies.
Officers Group:
Rev. EDWARD A. MALLOY, C.S.C., Pres. & C.S.C. Faculty and Personnel
NATHAN O. HATCH, Ph.D., Provost
Revs.:
E. WILLIAM BEAUCHAMP, C.S.C., Exec. Vice Pres.
TIMOTHY R. SCULLY, C.S.C., Vice Pres. & Senior Assoc. Provost
Dr. PATRICIA O'HARA, Vice Pres. Student Affairs
JEFFREY C. KANTOR, Ph.D., Vice Pres. & Assoc. Provost
CAROL A. MOONEY, J.D., Vice Pres. & Assoc. Provost
Dr. WILLIAM P. SEXTON, Vice Pres. Univ. Rels.
JAMES L. MERZ, Ph.D., Vice Pres. Graduate Studies & Research
JAMES J. LYPHOUT, Assoc. Vice Pres. for Business Operations
SCOTT C. MALPASS, Assoc. Vice Pres. for Finance
Rev. RICHARD V. WARNER, C.S.C.
CAROL C. KAESEBIER, J.D., Vice Pres. & General Counsel
Mr. MATTHEW S. CULLINAN, Asst. to Pres.
Rev. RICHARD V. WARNER, C.S.C., Counselor to the Pres., Dir. of Campus Ministry
Administrative Group:
COLLIN MESSINER, Asst. Provost
Dr. ANTHONY HYDER, Assoc. Vice Pres. Graduate School
Dr. THOMAS L. SWEENEY, Asst. Vice Pres. Research
Dr. JAMES H. POWELL, Asst. Vice Pres. & Dir. Summer Session
DANIEL J. SARACINO, Asst. Provost for Enrollment
JENNIFER YOUNGER, Dir. Univ. Libraries
ROGER V. MULLINS, Assoc. Vice Pres. for Human Resources
MICHAEL A. WADSWORTH, Dir. Athletics
RICHARD W. CONKLIN, Assoc. Vice Pres. Univ. Rels.
IRIS OUTLAW, Dir. Minority Students
Asst. Vice Presidents for Student Affairs:
WILLIAM W. KIRK
Sr. JEAN LENZ, O.S.F.
Rev. PETER D. ROCCA, C.S.C.
C.S.C. Faculty & Personnel:
Most Rev. MARK MCGRATH, C.S.C.
Revs.:
ROBERT AUSTGEN, C.S.C.
NICHOLAS AYO, C.S.C.
LEONARD N. BANAS, C.S.C.
ERNEST J. BARTELL, C.S.C.
MICHAEL BAXTER, C.S.C.
E. WILLIAM BEAUCHAMP, C.S.C.
THOMAS E. BLANTZ, C.S.C.
WILLIAM A. BOTZUM, C.S.C.
RICHARD S. BULLENE, C.S.C.
DAVID B. BURRELL, C.S.C.
CHARLES M. CAREY, C.S.C.
AUSTIN I. COLLINS, C.S.C.
JOHN E. CONLEY, C.S.C.
RAYMOND F. COUR, C.S.C.
ALFRED F. D'ALONZO, C.S.C.
PAUL F. DOYLE, C.S.C.
Deacon THOMAS P. DOYLE
Revs.:
JOHN S. DUNNE, C.S.C.
CLARENCE R. DURBIN, C.S.C.
MARK J. FITZGERALD, C.S.C.
JAMES F. FLANIGAN, C.S.C.
JAMES K. FOSTER, C.S.C.
PATRICK GAFFNEY, C.S.C.
DAVID A. GARRICK, C.S.C.
THOMAS E. GAUGHAN, C.S.C.
MARK R. GHYSELINCK, C.S.C.
Bro. FRANCIS GORCH, C.S.C.
Revs.:
GREGORY A. GREEN, C.S.C.
ROBERT GRIFFIN, C.S.C.
CARL G. HAGER, C.S.C.
THEODORE M. HESBURGH, C.S.C.
Bro. LOUIS HURCIK, C.S.C.
Revs.:
JOHN I. JENKINS, C.S.C., Religious Supr.
DANIEL R. JENKY, C.S.C.
EDMUND P. JOYCE, C.S.C.
THOMAS P. KING, C.S.C.
JEROME E. KNOLL, C.S.C.
JAMES MARTIN LIES, C.S.C.
Bro. EDWARD LUTHER, C.S.C.
Revs.:
PATRICK H. MALONEY, C.S.C.
JAMES E. MCDONALD, C.S.C., Steward
JAMES J. MCGRATH, C.S.C.
Most Rev. MARK G. MCGRATH, C.S.C.
Revs.:
DONALD P. MCNEILL, C.S.C.
JOSE M. MARTELLI, C.S.C.
LEON J. MERTENSOTTO, C.S.C.
Bro. DENNIS MEYERS, C.S.C.
Revs.:
MATTHEW M. MICELI, C.S.C.
WILSON D. MISCAMBLE, C.S.C.
ROBERT H. MOSS, C.S.C.
MICHAEL J. MURPHY, C.S.C.
STEPHEN P. NEWTON, C.S.C.
MARTIN LAM NGUYEN, C.S.C.
EDWARD D. O'CONNOR, C.S.C.
JOHN H. PEARSON, C.S.C.
ROBERT S. PELTON, C.S.C.
MARK L. POORMAN, C.S.C.
LOUIS J. PUTZ, C.S.C.
HERMAN R. REITH, C.S.C.
JAMES L. RIEHLE, C.S.C.
JAMES A. RIGERT, C.S.C.
JOSEPH D. ROSS, C.S.C.
GEORGE A. ROZUM, C.S.C.
Bro. BEATUS SCHLENKER, C.S.C.
Revs.:
DAVID J. SCHEIDLER, C.S.C.
TIMOTHY R. SCULLY, C.S.C.
WILLIAM D. SEETCH, C.S.C.
THOMAS G. STREIT, C.S.C.
MICHAEL BRUCE SULLIVAN, C.S.C.
THOMAS TALLARIDA, C.S.C.
MERWYN J. THOMAS, C.S.C.
JAMES W. THORNTON, C.S.C.
WILLIAM A. WACK, C.S.C.
JOSEPH L. WALTER, C.S.C.
CHARLES F. WEIHER, C.S.C.
OLIVER F. WILLIAMS, C.S.C.
GEORGE C. WISKIRCHEN, C.S.C.
Non-C.S.C. Religious Faculty:
Rev. JOSEPH P. AMAR (SAM)
Sr. ELEANOR BERNSTEIN, C.S.J.
Sr. JURIS BINDER, O.P.
Rev. PAUL F. BRADSHAW
Sr. SUSAN BRUNO, O.S.F.
Sr. KATHLEEN CANNON, O.P.
Sr. REGINA COLL, C.S.J.
Revs.:
BRIAN DALEY, S.J.
MICHAEL DRISCOLL
Sr. CARRINE ETHERIDGE, I.H.M.
Rev. PATRICK TIMOTHY FITZGERALD
Rt. Rev. ASTRIK L. GABRIEL
Rev. THOMAS GEDEON, S.J.
Sr. JOANN HANEY, O.S.F.
Sr. MARY CATHERINE HIKERT, O.P.
Revs.:
ROBERT LEE KERBY
EUGENE F. LAUER
RICHARD P. MCBRIEN
ERNAN MCMULLIN
RICHARD A. MCCORMICK, S.J.
JOHN A. MELLOH, S.M.
GEORGE MINAMICKI, S.J.
Sr. MARY ANN MUENINGHOFF, O.P.
Rev. JEROME H. NEYREY, S.J.
Sr. MARY CATHERINE NOLAN, O.P.
Revs.:
MARVIN O'CONNELL
THOMAS O'MEARA, O.P.
HUGH H. PAGE
FREDERICK W. PFOTENHAUER
Bro. BONAVENTURE SCULLY, C.F.X.
Revs.:
LOURDES SHEEHAN, R.S.M.
PAUL PHILIBERT, O.P.
JAMES F. WHITE
D. REGINALD WHITT, O.P.
Priests 48
Sisters 7
Total Staff 1,256
Total Enrollment 10,359

Rensselaer
Diocese of Lafayette in Indiana

Saint Joseph's College
Rensselaer, IN 47978
Tel: 219-866-6000
The Society of the Precious Blood
Dr. ALBERT SHANNON, Ph.D., Pres.
Revs.:
CHARLES H. BANET, C.PP.S., (Retired)
RAYMOND M. CERA, C.PP.S., (Retired)
JAMES E. FROELICH, C.PP.S.
DOMINIC B. GERLACH, C.PP.S.
PHILIP F. GILBERT, C.PP.S.
LAWRENCE F. HEIMAN, C.PP.S.
DENNIS J. KINDERMAN, C.PP.S.
LEONARD J. KOSTKA, C.PP.S., (Retired)
WILLIAM J. KRAMER, C.PP.S., (Retired)
EDWARD P. MCCARTHY, C.PP.S., (Retired)
TIMOTHY D. MCFARLAND, C.PP.S.
CHARLES J. ROBBINS, C.PP.S., (Retired)
JOSEPH V. RODAK, C.PP.S.
CHARLES R. RUEVE, C.PP.S.
WILLIAM J. STANG, C.PP.S.
RALPH C. VERDI, C.PP.S.
PAUL R. WHITE, C.PP.S., (Retired)
Diocesan Priests:
Rev. JAMES CHALLANCIN (MAR) Chap.
Bros.:
TIMOTHY P. HEMM, C.PP.S., Religious Supr.
HUGH HENDERSON, C.PP.S.
Sr. CATHERINE FAY, B.V.M.
Sr. PATRICIA ROBINSON, B.V.M.
Priests 18
Sisters 2
Lay Teachers 70
Brothers 2
Students 927

Saint Mary-of-the-Woods
Archdiocese of Indianapolis

Saint Mary-of-the-Woods College
Saint Mary-of-the-Woods, IN 47876
Tel: 812-535-5151; Fax: 812-535-4613
E-mail: smeier@woods.smwc.edu
Web Site: http://woods.smwc.edu
Dr. BARBARA DOHERTY, S.P., Pres.
Priests 1
Sisters of Providence 7
Sisters of St. Francis 1
Lay Teachers 50
Students 1,267

St. Meinrad
Archdiocese of Indianapolis

St. Meinrad Seminary-College of Liberal Arts
St. Meinrad, IN 47577
Tel: 812-357-6611; Fax: 812-357-6964
E-mail: @saintmeinrad.edu
Web Site: www.saintmeinrad.edu
Very Rev. MARK O'KEEFE, O.S.B., Pres. & Rector
Revs.:
DAMIAN SCHMELZ, O.S.B., Vice Rector & Provost
BEDE CISCO, O.S.B.
PATRICK COONEY, O.S.B (BEL)
SIMEON DALY, O.S.B.
GUERRIC DEBONA, O.S.B.
JONATHAN FASSERO, O.S.B.
THEODORE HECK, O.S.B.
EUGENE HENSELL, O.S.B.
COLUMBA KELLY, O.S.B.
JEREMY KING, O.S.B.
MICHEAS LANGSTON, O.S.B.
ISAAC MCDANIEL, O.S.B.
GUY MANSINI, O.S.B.
NOEL MUELLER, O.S.B.
MATTHIAS NEUMAN, O.S.B.
DAVID RABENECKER, O.S.B.
DENIS ROBINSON, O.S.B (MEM)
CHRISTOPHER SHAPPARD, O.S.B.
DONALD WALPOLE, O.S.B.
CAJETAN WHITE, O.S.B.
Deacon THOMAS HOLSWORTH (EVN)
Other Faculty and Staff 24
Sisters 5
Lay Women 6
Lay Men 13
Students 47

Whiting
Diocese of Gary

Calumet College of St. Joseph
2400 New York Ave.
Whiting, IN 46394
Tel: 219-473-7770
Web Site: www.ccsj.edu
Dr. DENNIS RITTENMEYER, Pres.
Rev. ERNEST KRANTZ, C.PP.S., Chap.
Bros.:
BENJAMIN BASILE, C.PP.S., Religious Supr., Registrar
JAMES BALLMANN, C.PP.S., Dir. Computer Svcs.
GABRIEL BRIDGES, C.PP.S., Dir. Information Svcs., Campus Ministry
In res.,
Bros.:
JEROME SCHULTE, C.PP.S
GERARD VON-HAGEL, C.PP.S.
Priests 1
Brothers 3
Sisters 2
Lay Teachers 65
Total Staff 110
Enrollment 1,035

IOWA

Cedar Rapids
Archdiocese of Dubuque

Mount Mercy College
1330 Elmhurst Dr., N.E.
Cedar Rapids, IA 52402
Tel: 319-363-8213; Fax: 319-368-6492
E-mail: admission@mmc.mtmercy.edu
Web Site: http://www.mtmercy.edu
Dr. THOMAS R. FELD, Pres.
MARGARET JACKSON, J.D., Registrar
Dr. JEAN F. SWEAT, Vice Pres. Academic Affairs
Sisters 1
Lay Teachers 63
Students 1,200

Clinton
Diocese of Davenport

Mt. St. Clare College
(Coed)
Bluff Blvd. & Springdale Dr.
Clinton, IA 52732
Tel: 319-242-4023
E-mail: admissns@clare.deu
Web Site: www.clare.edu
Sisters of St. Francis, Clinton, IA
Dr. JAMES J. ROSS, Pres.
Sisters 4
Lay Teachers 56
Students 582
Total Staff 75

Davenport
Diocese of Davenport

St. Ambrose University
Davenport, IA 52803-2898
Tel: 319-333-6300; Fax: 319-333-6243
EDWARD ROGALSKI, Ph.D., Pres.
DONALD J. MOELLER, Provost
ANN FREEBERG, Ph.D., Vice Pres. Inst. Research
EDWARD J. HENKHAUS, Vice Pres. Finance
Rev. DRAKE R. SHAFER, Vice Pres. Univ. Ministry
Rev. Msgr. CLETUS P. MADSEN, Asst. to Pres.
STEVEN R. GOEBEL, Vice Pres. Univ. Rels.
SHEILA FUNDERBURK, Campus Min.
Priest Faculty:
Revs.:
CHARLES A. ADAM
EDWARD A. BOTKIN
WILLIAM F. DAWSON, Ph.D.
JOSEPH DE FRANCISCO, Ph.D (BEA)
EDMOND J. DUNN, Ph.D.
ROBERT L. GRANT
JOSEPH KOKJOHN, Ph.D.
GEORGE MCDANIEL, Ph.D.
DRAKE R. SHAFER
BRIAN MICLOT, Ph.D.
Priests 7
Lay Teachers 117
Total Staff 210
Students 2,776

Des Moines
Diocese of Des Moines

Mercy College of Health Sciences
928-6th Ave.
Des Moines, IA 50309-1239
Tel: 515-247-3180; Fax: 515-362-6698
E-mail: mercy@mchs.edu
Web Site: http://www.mchs.edu
Sponsored by Sisters of Mercy of the Americas (Omaha Province).
DEANNE REMER, R.N., M.S., M.A., CEO
DAVID THUENTE, Ph.D., Academic Dean
KATHLEEN CLAUSON, M.A., Dir. Student Svcs.
LINDA PARKER, Ph.D., Dir. Inst. Research
BRIAN TINGLEFF, B.A., Dir. Inst. Advancement
SUZANNE MAINS, R.N., M.S., Registrar
Lay Teachers 44
Students 478

Dubuque
Archdiocese of Dubuque

Clarke College
1550 Clarke Dr.
Dubuque, IA 52001
Tel: 319-588-6300; Fax: 319-588-6789
Web Site: www.clarke.edu
Liberal Arts College. (Coed)
Conducted by Sisters of Charity, B.V.M.
Sr. CATHERINE DUNN, B.V.M., Ph.D., Pres.
Sr. EUGENA SULLIVAN, B.V.M., Registrar
Bro. JOHN WOZNIAK, F.S.C., Vice Pres. Academic Affairs
LOUISE OTTAVI, Academic Dean
KATE ZANGER, Vice Pres. Student Life
GAIL NAUGHTON, Vice Pres. of Institutional Advancement
BOBBE AMES, Mktg.
JAMES PRINCE, Business & Finance
LAURA KESTNER, Dir. Career Center & Placement
JOHN MOSHER, Dir. of Campus Ministry
Brothers 1
Sisters 22
Lay Teachers 67
Students 1,150

Loras College
1450 Alta Vista St., P.O. Box 178
Dubuque, IA 52004-0178
Tel: 319-588-7100; Fax: 319-588-7964
(Accredited by the North Central Assoc. of Colleges and Secondary Schools)
Dr. JOACHIM FROEHLICH, Pres.
Dr. RONALD BECHT, Vice Pres. of Academic Affairs
Dr. SUZANNE DEXTRAS, Vice Pres. for Student Affairs/ Dean of Students
JAMES COLLINS, Vice Pres. for Institutional Advancement
KENNETH J. TEKIPPE, Vice Pres. Finance & Admin. Svcs.
TEDDI JOYCE, Dean of Admissions & Financial Planning
KATHY BLAU, Career Center
Mr. JON CHRISTY, Registrar
LINDA CROSSETT, Dir. Graduate Division & Continuing Ed.
Rev. DAVID H. O'CONNOR, Chap.
JAMES M. GOODMANN, Dir. of Campus Ministry
College Faculty:
Revs.:
ROBERT R. BECK, D.Min.
DENNIS J. COLTER
JOHN C. FRIEDELL, Ph.D.
JOHN J. MCDERMOTT, S.S.L.
MARK A. RESSLER, Ph.D.
RICHARD L. SCHAEFER, M.A.
KARL G. SCHROEDER, M.A., (Oxon)
DOUGLAS O. WATHIER, S.T.D.
WILLIAM E. WILKIE, Ph.D.
Rev. Msgr. ROBERT R. VOGL, M.A.
Priests 8
Sisters 1
Lay Teachers 112
Students 1,776

Sioux City
Diocese of Sioux City

Briar Cliff College
3303 Rebecca St., P.O. Box 2100
Sioux City, IA 51104-2100
Tel: 712-279-5321; Fax: 712-279-5410
E-mail: rasmuss@briar-cliff.edu
Web Site: www.briar-cliff.edu
Sisters of St. Francis of the Holy Family of Dubuque, Iowa
Liberal Arts College. Coed. Day and Resident Students.
Sr. MARGARET WICK, Pres.
RICK OLESKI, Registrar
LAURIE GROTHAUS, Admissions Dir.
Revs.:
ROBERT M. CONDON
TIMOTHY A. FRIEDRICHSEN
BRIAN C. HUGHES
Priests 1
Sisters 16
Lay Teachers 58
Lay Admins. and Staff 95
Students 1,011

KANSAS

Atchison
Archdiocese of Kansas City in Kansas

Benedictine College
Atchison, KS 66002
Tel: 913-367-5340; Fax: 913-367-3673
E-mail: peylar@raven.benedictine.edu
Web Site: http://www.benedictine.edu
DANIEL J. CAREY, Ph.D., Pres.
WAYNE VALENTINE, Business Mgr.
BEV MCCONNOUGHY, Registrar
Revs.:
BERTRAND LANOUE, O.S.B.
DENIS MEADE, O.S.B.
BLAINE SCHULTZ, O.S.B.
EUGENE DEHNER, O.S.B.
MARK BROSKI, O.S.B.
MEINRAD MILLER, O.S.B.
Bro. LAWRENCE BRADFORD, O.S.B.
Coed College of St. Benedict's & Mount St. Scholastica.
Priests 1
Brothers 1
Benedictine Sisters 7
Laypeople 37
Students 964

Kansas City
Archdiocese of Kansas City in Kansas

Donnelly College
608 N. 18th St.
Kansas City, KS 66102
Tel: 913-621-6070; Fax: 913-621-0354
Dr. JOHN MURRY, Pres.
FRANCES SANDERS, Dean
Mrs. PEGGY HOYTAL, Registrar
Benedictine Sisters 7
Other Order Sisters 5
Lay Teachers 28
Students 718

Leavenworth
Archdiocese of Kansas City in Kansas

Saint Mary College
Leavenworth, KS 66048
Tel: 913-682-5151; Fax: 913-758-6140
Rev. RICHARD MUCOWSKI, O.F.M., Ph.D., Pres.
Dr. EDGAR SCHICK, Interim Academic Vice Pres.
Lay Teachers 28
Sisters of Charity of Leavenworth 11
Notre Dame Sisters 1
Students 561

Wichita
Diocese of Wichita

Kansas Newman College
3100 McCormick Ave.
Wichita, KS 67213
Tel: 316-942-4291; Fax: 316-942-4483
E-mail: thompsong@ksnewman.edu
Web Site: WWW.KSNEWMAN.EDU
Sr. TARCISIA ROTHS, A.S.C., Ph.D., Pres.
ANDREW BOGNER, Ph.D., Vice Pres. Academic Affairs
EDWARD G. LITTIG, Ph.D., Vice Pres. Advancement
MARK DRESSELHAUS, Vice Pres. Finance & Admin.
KIM MILLER JACOBS, Vice Pres. Student Affairs
SHIRLEY RUEB, Registrar
Coeducational liberal arts college, founded in 1933 by the Sisters Adorers of the Blood of Christ. (Accredited by the North Central Association of Colleges and Secondary Schools).
Sisters 20
Lay Teachers 80
Students 1,857

KENTUCKY

Covington
Diocese of Covington

Thomas More College
(Coed)
Crestview Hills
Covington, KY 41017-3495
Tel: 606-341-5800; Fax: 606-344-3345
E-mail: clevesw@thomasmore.edu
Web Site: www.thomasmore.edu
Rev. WILLIAM F. CLEVES, Ph.D., Pres.
Mr. GARY R. BOCKELMAN, Vice Pres. Admin. & Finance
MARY B. FISHER, Vice Pres. for Institutional Advancement
LAURA A. KOEHL, Vice Pres. for Enrollment Management & Planning
Dr. RAYMOND G. HEBERT, Vice Pres. Academic Affairs & Dean of College
Dr. DALE MYERS, Assoc. Vice Pres. for Graduate Programs & Continuing Educ.
Rev. GERALD TWADDELL, Chap.
Mr. VICTOR GRAY, Dean of Students
Mr. JAMES MCKELLOGG, Dir. Library
Ms. PATSY KENNER, Registrar
Ms. MICHIALE SCHNEIDER, Dir. Financial Aid
Ms. BARBARA DAVIS, Dir. Student Support Svcs.
Sr. RITA MARIE MUELLER, S.N.D., Dir. Inst. Research
Priests 4
Lay Teachers 70
Sisters 4
Administration:
Priests 1
Sisters 5
Lay People 23
Students 1,505

Louisville
Archdiocese of Louisville

Bellarmine College
2001 Newburg Rd.

Louisville, KY 40205-0671
Tel: 502-452-8211
Administration Officers:
Most Rev. THOMAS C. KELLY, O.P., J.C.D., Archbishop of Louisville, Chancellor
Dr. JOSEPH J. MCGOWAN, JR., Pres.
Mr. ROBERT ZIMLICH, Acting Vice Pres. Admin. & Finance
Dr. FRED W. RHODES, Vice Pres. Student Affairs & Dean of Students
Dr. LEONARD MANIACI, Ph.D., Vice Pres. Inst. Advancement
Dr. SUSAN HOCKENBERGER, Dean of the Lansing Nursing
Mr. TIM STURGEON, Acting Vice Pres. for Enrollment Mgmt.
Dr. TOM OPPELT, Acting Dean of the College of Arts and Sciences
Dr. EDWARD POPPER, Dean of the Rubel School of Business
Revs.:
NELSON BELIZARIO
CLYDE F. CREWS
W. FREDERICK HENDRICKSON
GEORGE A. KILCOURSE
EUGENE L. ZOELLER
Priests 5
Sisters 3
Students 2,180

Spalding University
851 S. 4th St.
Louisville, KY 40203
Tel: 502-585-9911; Fax: 502-585-7158
THOMAS R. OATES, Pres.
Mr. ISHMON BURKS, Exec. Vice Pres.
Mr. EDWARD GALANIF, Vice Pres. for Finance
M. JANICE MURPHY, Provost & Dean of Graduate Studies
BYRON WUNDERLICH, Registrar
PHYLLIS PASSAFIUME, Dean, College of Arts & Sciences
MARY BURNS, S.C.N., Dean, School of Education
Dr. CYNTHIA CRABTREE, Dean, School of Nursing & Health Sciences
Dr. M. DUNCAN STANTON, Dean School of Professional Psychology & Social Work
VANDELIA VANMETER, Dir. Library
DEBORAH A. FORD, Dean Student Life & Devel.
EMILY WHALIN, Dir. Public Rels.
BRIAN KESSE, Dir. of Enrollment Mgmt.
DOROTHY ALLEN, Dir. Admissions
BETTY HARLAN, Dir. Student Financial Aid
Priests 1
Sisters 5
Brothers 1
Lay Teachers 68
Students 1,564

Owensboro
Diocese of Owensboro

Brescia College
717 Frederica St.
Owensboro, KY 42301
Tel: 502-685-3131
Web Site: http://brescia.edu
Sr. VIVIAN MARIE BOWLES, O.S.U., Pres.
Sr. JOANN MARK, A.S.C., Dean
Sr. HELENA FISCHER, O.S.U., Registrar
Sr. ROSE JEAN POWERS, O.S.U., Campus Min.
Revs.:
LEONARD J. ALVEY
ANTHONY J. SHONIS
Priests 1
Sisters 6
Lay Teachers 30
Students 750

St. Catharine
Archdiocese of Louisville

St. Catharine College
2735 Bardstown Rd.
St. Catharine, KY 40061
Tel: 606-336-5082
Dominican Sisters
Mr. BILL HUSTON, Pres.
Sr. MARINA GIBBONS, O.P., Vice Pres. & Academic Dean
Priests 1
Sisters 1
Lay Teachers 20
Students 364

LOUISIANA

Baton Rouge
Diocese of Baton Rouge

Our Lady of the Lake College
5345 Brittany Dr.
Baton Rouge, LA 70808-4398
Tel: 504-768-1710; Fax: 504-768-1726
Web Site: www.ololcollege.cc.la.us
Dr. JAMES W. FIRNBERG, Pres.
Lay Teachers 36
Students 961

New Orleans
Archdiocese of New Orleans

Loyola University (1912)
6363 St. Charles Ave.
New Orleans, LA 70118-6195
Tel: 504-865-2011; Fax: 504-865-3851
Revs.:
BERNARD P. KNOTH, S.J., Pres.
JAMES C. CARTER, S.J., Chancellor
Dr. DAVID C. DANAHAR, Provost/Vice Pres. for Academic Affairs
Revs.:
ROBERT S. GERLICH, S.J., Rector
ROBERT L. ANDERSON, S.J.
JOHN F. ARMSTRONG, S.J.
EDWARD B. ARROYO, S.J.
EMMETT M. BIENVENU, S.J.
THOMAS CLANCY, S.J.
HAROLD F. COHEN, S.J.
JOSEPH A. CURRIE, S.J.
GREGORY F. CURTIN, S.J.
STEPHEN DUFFY, S.T.D.
GERALD M. FAGIN, S.J.
ERNEST FERLITA, S.J.
ALVIN J. HOLLOWAY, S.J.
THEODORE M. KALAMAJA, S.J.
JOHN F. KELLER, S.J.
MARVIN C. KITTEN, S.J.
JOHN J. KONICEK, S.J.
C. FRANKLYN LYNETTE, S.J.
RANSOM MARLOW, S.J.
LAWRENCE MOORE, S.J.
THOMAS MULCRONE, S.J.
LEO A. NICOLL, S.J.
CHARLES E. O'NEILL, S.J.
ROBERT J. RATCHFORD, S.J.
W. WAYNE ROCA, S.J.
PETER S. ROGERS, S.J.
RAYMOND A. SCHROTH, S.J.
JOHN L. VESSELS, S.J.
GEORGE F. WILTZ, S.J.
BENJAMIN L. WREN, S.J.
Dr. DAVID A. BOILEAU
Dr. KENNETH P. KEULMAN
Dr. BERNARD J. LEE, S.M.
Dr. ROBERT J. ROWLAND, JR., Dean, College of Arts and Sciences
Dr. DAVID SWANZY, Dean, College of Music
MARCEL GARSAUD, Interim Dean, School of Law
Dr. J. PATRICK O'BRIEN, Dean, College of Business Admin.
Dr. MARCEL DUMESTRE, Interim Dean, City College
Priests 30
Brothers 1
Lay Teachers 407
Students 5,530

Our Lady of Holy Cross College
4123 Woodland Dr.
New Orleans, LA 70131-7399
Tel: 504-394-7744; Fax: 504-391-2421
Rev. THOMAS E. CHAMBERS, C.S.C., Ph.D., Pres.
Dr. GERALD F. DELUCA, Vice Pres. Academic Affairs
Mr. THOMAS O. PORTEOUS, JR., Vice Pres. Business Affairs
Ms. JUNE H. AMUNDSON, Registrar
Rev. THOMAS ELLERMAN, S.M., Chap.
Priests 2
Brothers 1
Congregation of the Sisters Marianites of Holy Cross 11
Sisters 2
Lay Teachers 28
Students 1,300
Total Staff 92

Xavier University of Louisiana
Palmetto and Pine Sts.
New Orleans, LA 70125-1098
Tel: 504-486-7411; Fax: 504-485-7904
Web Site: www.xavier.xula.edu
(Coed)
Dr. NORMAN C. FRANCIS, Pres.
Dr. DEIDRE LABAT, Vice Pres. Academic Affairs
Dr. HAROLD VINCENT, Dean, College of Arts and Sciences
Mr. JOSEPH BYRD, Vice Pres., Student Svcs.
ANTHONY M. RACHAL, JR., Exec. Vice Pres. Emeritus
CALVIN S. TREGRE, Vice Pres., Finance and Admin.
Mr. JOHN PECOUL, Acting Vice Pres., Devel.
Dr. MARCELLUS GRACE, Dean, College of Pharmacy
Mrs. LISA LEWIS MCCLAIN, Dir., Office of Campus Ministry
Rev. BRYAN J. FONTENOT, O.P., Assoc. Dir. & Chap.
Priests 3
Brothers 1
Sisters of the Blessed Sacrament 9
Lay Teachers 215
Students 3,512

MAINE

Standish
Diocese of Portland (In Maine)

Saint Joseph's College
278 Whites Bridge Rd.
Standish, ME 04084-5263
Tel: 207-893-7711; Fax: 207-893-7867
Dr. DAVID B. HOUSE, Pres.
Sr. MARY ELLEN MURPHY, R.S.M., Vice Pres. for Academic Affairs and Dean
Dr. TIMOTHY O'LEARY, Vice Pres. for Student Affairs
Sr. MARY KNEELAND, R.S.M., Treas.
Rev. JOHN TOPAK, O.F.M.Cap., Campus Min.
Sr. SYLVIA COMER, R.S.M.
Rev. EMMANUEL SULLIVAN, O.C.D (BO) Assoc. Prof. Religious Studies
Priests 1
Sisters 19
Lay Professors 90
Students 1,105
Undergraduate Students in Distance Education 2,350
Graduate Students 1,330

MARYLAND

Baltimore
Archdiocese of Baltimore

College of Notre Dame of Maryland
4701 N. Charles St.
Baltimore, MD 21210
Tel: 410-435-0100
School Sisters of Notre Dame
Sr. JANE BURKE, S.S.N.D., Chm. of the Bd. of Trustees
Dr. MARY PAT SEURKAMP, Ph.D., Pres.
Dr. LEONARD BROWN, Ph.D., Vice Pres. Academic Affairs
PATRICIA A. GREGA, Registrar
Dr. JEANNE ORTIZ, Dean of Students
PATRICIA BOSSE, Vice Pres. for Inst. Advancement
Sr. KATHLEEN JAGER, S.S.N.D., Campus Min.
Priests 1
Sisters 13
Lay Professors 74
Students 3,109
Residents 364
Total Staff 220

**Loyola College*
4501 N. Charles St.
Baltimore, MD 21210
Tel: 410-617-2000
Web Site: www.loyola.edu
Other locations at which courses are offered: For information call Graduate Admissions.
Tel: 410-617-5012, Ext. 5012
I-97 Business Park
1110 Benfield Blvd., Ste F
Millersville, MD 21108
Harford County, H.E.A.T. Center
5336 Churchville Rd.
Aberdeen, MD 21001
Hunt Valley
Longview Executive Park, 311 International Cir.
Hunt Valley, MD 21031
Cecil County - Booth Street Center
Elkton, MD 21921
Loyola College Business Center
7135 Minstrel Way
Columbia, MD 21045
College Established 1852. Combined with Mt. St. Agnes College 1971.
Legal Title: *Loyola College in Maryland, Inc.*
Rev. HAROLD E. RIDLEY, S.J., Pres.
Dr. THOMAS SCHEYE, Academic Vice Pres. & Provost
Dr. JOHN HOLLWITZ, Dean, College of Arts and Sciences
Dr. PETER LORENZI, Dean, Sellinger School of Business & Mgmt.
Revs.:
RONALD J. ANTON, S.J.
CHARLES BORGES, S.J.
JOHN L. BRUNETT, S.J.
TIMOTHY B. BROWN, S.J.
EDWIN H. CONVEY, S.J.
WILLIAM M. DAVISH, S.J.
PATRICK F. EARL, S.J.
MICHAEL D. FRENCH, S.J.
C. KEVIN GILLESPIE, S.J.
EDGAR B. GRAHAM, S.J.

JOHN H. GRAY, S.J.
FRANK R. HAIG, S.J.
FRANCIS G. HILTON, S.J.
ROBERT K. JUDGE, S.J.
JOSEPH M. KENNEDY, S.J.
WILLIAM K. MCGROARTY, S.J.
FRANCIS G. MCMANAMIN, S.J.
FRANCIS J. NASH, S.J.
HAROLD E. RIDLEY, S.J.
JOSEPH S. ROSSI, S.J.
PETER F. RYAN, S.J.
WILLIAM J. SNECK, S.J.
JOSEPH A. SOBIERAJSKI, S.J.
JAMES F. SALMON, S.J.
PAUL SUN, S.J.
LAWRENCE YOM, S.J.
Students 6,241
Priests 9
Sisters 1
Lay Teachers 215
Jesuit Community of Loyola College, Inc.
Revs.:
PATRICK F. EARL, S.J., Rector
JOHN H. GRAY, S.J., Asst. to the Rector
EDGAR B. GRAHAM, S.J., Treas.
Mount St. Agnes College (Merged to Loyola College. Corporation remains in existence.)
Sisters of Mercy of the Americas
Sr. ANGELA MARIE EBBERWEIN, R.S.M., Chm. of the Board of Trustees

Emmitsburg
Archdiocese of Baltimore

Mount Saint Mary's College (1808)
Emmitsburg, MD 21727
Tel: 301-447-6122
GEORGE R. HOUSTON, JR., Pres.
Dr. STEPHEN ROCKWOOD, Librarian
Mr. LEO B. TOPPER, Vice Pres. Finance and Admin.
Mr. JOSEPH P. ZANELLA, Dir. Financial Aid
Dr. CAROL L. HINDS, Vice Pres. & Dean of College
Dr. WILLIAM J. CRAFT, Dean of Undergraduate Studies
Dr. BYRON STAY, Assoc. Dean
Mr. STEPHEN P. NEITZ, Dir. Admissions
Mr. JOHN C. GILL, Registrar
Dr. CHRISTOPHER B. SMITH, Dean of Student Devel.
Rev. KEVIN RHOADES, Vice Pres. & Rector of the Seminary
Rev. Msgr. ROBERT R. KLINE, Ph.D (SCR) Pres. Emeritus
Rev. Msgr. HUGH J. PHILLIPS, Chap. of the Grotto Shrine and Pres. Emeritus
Revs.:
GERARD FRANCIK, Chap.
DANIEL C. NUSBAUM (ALB)
JAMES T. DELANEY (WIL)
PAUL V. REDMOND (ALB)
DAVID W. SHAUM, Ph.D.
JOHN J. ZEC (TR)
CARL J. FIVES (SCR)
THOMAS J. BYRD
ROBERT TERENTIEFF (BGR)
JAMES DONOHUE, C.R.
Priests 16
Sisters 5
Lay Teachers 110
Total Enrollment 1,800
Priests 16
Sisters 5
Lay Teachers 112
Total Enrollment 1,900

MASSACHUSETTS

Boston
Archdiocese of Boston

Emmanuel College
400 The Fenway
Boston, MA 02115
Tel: 617-277-9340; 735-9825
Sr. JANET EISNER, S.N.D., Ph.D., Pres. Sisters of Notre Dame de Namur
Rev. RICHARD CLANEY, Campus Min.
Priests 1
Sisters 13
Lay Teachers 42
Students 1,560

Chestnut Hill
Archdiocese of Boston

**Boston College*
(Coed)
Chestnut Hill, MA 02167
Tel: 617-552-8000
Web Site: http://www.bc.edu
Revs.:
WILLIAM P. LEAHY, S.J., Pres.
WILLIAM B. NEENAN, S.J., Academic Vice Pres.
Students 14,652
College of Arts and Sciences.
Students 5,589
Rev. J. ROBERT BARTH, S.J., Dean
Summer Session.
Rev. JAMES A. WOODS, S.J., Dean
Graduate School of Arts and Sciences.
Students 1,088
Dr. MICHAEL A. SMYER, Dean
School of Law.
Students 826
AVIAM SOIFER, J.D., Dean
College of Advancing Studies.
Students 1,012
Rev. JAMES A. WOODS, S.J., Dean
Graduate School of Social Work.
Students 569
Dr. JUNE G. HOPPS, Dean
School of Management.
Students 2,276
Dr. JOHN J. NEUHAUSER
Graduate School of Management.
Students 928
School of Nursing.
Students 250
Dr. BARBARA HAZARD MUNRO, Dean
School of Education.
Students 806
Priests 36
Sisters 1
Lay Teachers 578
Dr. MARY M. BRABECK, Dean
Graduate School of Nursing
Students 152
Dr. BARBARA HAZARD MUNRO, Dean
Graduate School of Education
Students 955
Dr. MARY M. BRABECK, Dean

Chicopee
Diocese of Springfield in Massachusetts

College of Our Lady of the Elms
Chicopee, MA 01013
Tel: 413-594-2761; Fax: 413-592-4871
E-mail: keating@elms.edu
Web Site: www.elms.edu
Sisters of St. Joseph
Most Rev. THOMAS L. DUPRE, Bishop of Springfield
Sr. KATHLEEN C. KEATING, S.S.J., Pres.
Dr. JOHN FREED, Vice Pres. Academic Affairs & Academic Dean
Sisters 28
Professors 52
Lay Teachers 45
Students 1,132
Total Staff 114

North Andover
Archdiocese of Boston

Merrimack College
North Andover, MA 01845
Tel: 978-837-5000
Revs.:
ROBERT M. BURKE, O.S.A., Treas., Our Mother of Good Counsel Monastery
THOMAS M. CASEY, O.S.A.
KEVIN F. DWYER, O.S.A.
GEORGE R. MORGAN, O.S.A.
JOSEPH F. GILLIN, O.S.A.
JOSEPH L. FARRELL, O.S.A.
SCOTT C. NESS, O.S.A.
RICHARD M. JACOBS
Priests 8
Lay Teachers 120
Students 2,000
Continuing Education 1,000
Our Mother of Good Counsel Monastery (1947)
Tel: 978-837-5168
In res.,
Revs.:
SALVATORE S. BONACCORSI, O.S.A., Sacristan
THOMAS C. KENNY, O.S.A., Prior
JOHN V. CASEY, O.S.A.
CARMEN J. COLETTA, O.S.A., (Chicago Prov.)
ALBERT P. MACPHERSON, O.S.A.
WILLIAM J. WYNNE, O.S.A., Librarian
JAMES T. DEERY, O.S.A.
EDWARD C. DOHERTY, O.S.A.
JOSEPH X. O'CONNOR, O.S.A.

North Easton
Diocese of Fall River

Holy Cross Fathers Religious
480 Washington St.
North Easton, MA 02356
Tel: 508-238-5942; Fax: 508-238-1297
Revs.:
R. BRADLEY BEAUPRE, C.S.C., Supr.
RICHARD E. GRIBBLE, C.S.C., Asst. Supr.
GENARO P. AGUILAR, C.S.C.
DAVID J. ARTHUR, C.S.C.
THOMAS C. BERTONE, C.S.C.
FOSTER J. BURBANK, C.S.C.
RUDOLPH V. CARCHIDI, C.S.C.
JAMES W. CHICHETTO, C.S.C.
Bros.:
RONALD L. CHRISTESON, C.S.C.
STEPHAN CLARKE, C.S.C.
Revs.:
ALBERT J. CROCE, C.S.C.
JOHN F. DENNING, C.S.C.
JAMES M. DUANE, C.S.C.
HARRY B. EICHORN, C.S.C.
THOMAS M. FEELEY, C.S.C.
THOMAS P. GARIEPY, C.S.C.
THOMAS M. HALKOVIC, C.S.C.
FRANCIS J. HURLEY, C.S.C.
DANIEL J. ISSING, C.S.C.
LAWRENCE A. JERGE, C.S.C.
ROBERT J. KRUSE, C.S.C.
BARTLEY J. MACPHAIDIN, C.S.C.
Bro. JAMES W. MADIGAN, C.S.C.
Revs.:
LOUIS A. MANZO, C.S.C.
JOHN E. MCCARTHY, C.S.C.
JOHN J. MURPHY, C.S.C.
AUGUSTINE J. PEVERADA, C.S.C.
JAMES T. PRESKENIS, C.S.C.
G. MICHAEL SCULLY, C.S.C.
RICHARD J. SEGREVE, C.S.C.
KEVIN P. SPICER, C.S.C.
DENIS B. SUGHRUE, C.S.C.
JAMES E. TOBIN, C.S.C.
FRANCIS M. WALSH, C.S.C.
PETER J. WALSH, C.S.C.
FRANCIS T. ZLOTKOWSKI, C.S.C.

Stonehill College
North Easton, MA 02357
Tel: 508-238-1081; Fax: 508-230-3732
Revs.:
FRANCIS M. WALSH, C.S.C., Supr., Tel: 508-238-7838; Fax: 508-230-7455
BARTLEY J. MACPHAIDIN, C.S.C., Pres.
DANIEL J. ISSING, C.S.C., College Chap.
DAVID J. ARTHUR, C.S.C.
F. JAMES BURBANK, C.S.C.
RUDOLPH V. CARCHIDI, C.S.C.
JAMES W. CHICHETTO, C.S.C.
ANTHONY J. DECONCILIIS, C.S.C.
HARRY B. EICHORN, C.S.C.
THOMAS M. FEELEY, C.S.C.
THOMAS P. GARIEPY, C.S.C.
RICHARD E. GRIBBLE, C.S.C.
THOMAS M. HALKOVIC, C.S.C.
FRANCIS J. HURLEY, C.S.C.
ROBERT J. KRUSE, C.S.C.
JOHN E. MCCARTHY, C.S.C.
LOUIS A. MANZO, C.S.C.
Priests 9
Sisters 2
Lay Teachers 109
Students 2,882

Paxton
Diocese of Worcester

Anna Maria College
Paxton, MA 01612
Tel: 508-849-3300; Fax: 508-849-3334
E-mail: rzukowsk@anna-maria
Web Site: http://www.anna-maria.edu
A Coeducational Catholic College.
Sisters of St. Anne
Dr. BERNARD PARKER, Pres.
Sr. ROLLANDE QUINTAL, S.S.A., Registrar
Lay Teachers 32
Total Staff 125
Students 1,927

Weston
Archdiocese of Boston

Regis College
Wellesley St.
Weston, MA 02193
Tel: 617-893-1820
Sr. SHEILA E. MEGLEY, Ph.D., Pres.
Sr. MILDRED CROWLEY, S.C., Campus Min.
Sisters of St. Joseph 15
Lay Teachers 106
Students 1,121

Worcester
Diocese of Worcester

Assumption College
500 Salisbury St.

Worcester, MA 01615-0005
Tel: 508-767-7000; Fax: 508-756-1780
E-mail: info@ave.assumption.edu
Web Site: http://www.assumption.edu
A Catholic Liberal Arts College under the Auspices of the Augustinians of the Assumption (Assumptionists).
Dr. JOSEPH H. HAGAN, Pres.
Revs.:
WILFRID J. DUFAULT, A.A., Chancellor
LOUIS F. DION, A.A., Vice Chancellor
FRANCIS P. GURLEY, Exec. Vice Pres.
CHARLES L. FLYNN, Provost
Vice Presidents:
RICHARD P. BURKE
ROBERT D. BRILL
J. RICHARD CHRISTIANSEN
Rev. ROLAND O. GUILMAIN, A.A., Vice Pres. Religious Affairs & Dir. Campus Ministry
DAVID AALTO, Registrar
Priests 6
Sisters 2
Lay Teachers 104
Students 2,244

College of the Holy Cross, Inc
Worcester, MA 01610
Tel: 508-793-2011
A College for Boarders and Day Scholars.
Revs.:
GERARD REEDY, S.J., Pres.
WILLIAM J. O'HALLORAN, S.J., Vice Pres.
Priests 25
Sisters 3
Lay Teachers 203
Students 2,710
Jesuit Teachers 13

MICHIGAN

Adrian
Diocese of Lansing

Siena Heights College - President
1247 E. Siena Heights Dr.
Adrian, MI 49221-1796
Tel: 517-263-0731; Fax: 517-264-7702
RICHARD B. ARTMAN, Ph.D., Pres.
Sr. SHARON R.. WEBER, O.P., Ph.D., Academic Dean
Sisters 14
Brothers 1
Priests 1
Faculty 72
Staff 118
Students 2,026
Sponsored by the Adrian Dominican Sisters.

Detroit
Archdiocese of Detroit

Marygrove College
8425 W. McNichols Rd.
Detroit, MI 48221
Tel: 313-862-8000
(Coed)
Dr. JOHN E. SHAY, JR., Pres.
Sr. ANDREA LEE, I.H.M., Exec Vice Pres.
Dr. JOHN R. NOVAK, Academic Dean
Faculty:
I.H.M. Sisters 9
Sisters 2
Priests 1
Lay 66
Students 2,381
Incorporated.
Sisters, Servants of the Immaculate Heart of Mary

University of Detroit Mercy
McNichols Campus, 4001 W. McNichols Rd. at Livernois
Detroit, MI 48219-0900
Tel: 313-993-1000
Outer Drive Campus
8200 W. Outer Dr.
Detroit, MI 48219-0900
Law School
851 E. Jefferson
Detroit, MI 48226
Dental School
8200 E. Outer Dr.
Detroit, MI 48219-0900
Dr. MAUREEN FAY, O.P., Pres.
Dr. GEORGE F. LUNDY, Vice Pres. Academic Affairs & Provost
Mr. JOE CLARK, Vice Pres. Business & Finance
Ms. BARBARA MILBAUER, Vice Pres. University Advancement
Dr. KENNETH MENOLD, Vice Pres. Student Affairs
Dr. LINDA WERTHMAN, R.S.M., Assoc. Vice Pres. for Academic Studies & Provost, Urban Health Educ. Center
Priests 24
Sisters 17
Lay 895
Students 7,284

Grand Rapids
Diocese of Grand Rapids

Aquinas College
1607 Robinson Rd., S.E.
Grand Rapids, MI 49506
Tel: 616-459-8281
HARRY J. KNOPKE, Ph.D., Pres.
GARY G. KONOW, Ph.D., Academic Vice Pres.
MARIBETH WARDROP, B.A., Vice Pres. Devel.
Sr. M. AQUINAS WEBER, O.P., M.A., Chancellor
MICHAEL C. KELLER, M.S.A., Vice Pres. Enrollment Mgmt.
JOYCE MCNALLY, D.B.A., Dean Graduate Studies
LOIS B. KALMAN, B.A., Registrar
Sisters 8
Lay Teachers 70
Students 2,385

Livonia
Archdiocese of Detroit

Madonna University
36600 Schoolcraft Rd.
Livonia, MI 48150
Tel: 734-432-5300; Fax: 734-432-5393
Coeducational, resident and non-resident.
Conducted by the Felician Sisters.
Sr. M. FRANCILENE VAN DE VYVER, C.S.S.F., Pres.
Sr. M. LAURIANA GRUSZCYNSKI, C.S.S.F., Vice Pres. Univ. Advancement
Dr. ERNEST NOLAN, Vice Pres. Academic Affairs
Sr. NANCY MARIE JAMROZ, C.S.S.F., Vice Pres. Student Life
Sr. ALICIA BOMYA, Registrar
Mr. LEONARD WILHELM, Vice Pres. Finance
Mr. FRANK KRIBAR, Dir. Enrollment Mgmt.
Ms. DONNA BERRY, Dir. Admin. Computer Center & Inst. Research
Mr. CHRIS ZIEGLER, Dir. Financial Aid
Deacon EUGENE DESJARLAIS, Dir. Campus Ministry
Rev. FRANCIS TEBBE, O.F.M., Vice Pres. Planning and Mission Effectiveness
Priests 7
Sisters 25
Lay Staff 475
Students 3,294

Orchard Lake
Archdiocese of Detroit

Saint Mary's College
3535 Indian Trail
Orchard Lake, MI 48324
Tel: 248-682-1885
(Coed, resident and non-resident)
Rev. Msgr. STANLEY E. MILEWSKI, Chancellor of the Orchard Lake Schools and Centers
THADDEUS C. RADZILOWSKI, Pres.
RONALD P. MULLER, Ph.D., Academic Dean
MICHAEL LOEFFLER, Business Office
Rev. FRANCIS B. KOPER (WIL) Dir. Prog. of Priestly Formation
DEBORAH GRACZYK, Dir. Financial Aid & Dir. Admissions
JOANNE BELLAIRE, Dean of Students
Rev. JAMES K. MAZUREK (PIT) Exec. Sec. Natl. Alumni Assn.
NANCY WARD, Dir. Library
DEBORAH GRACZYK, Ph.D., Registrar Faculty
Faculty 34
Students 276

MINNESOTA

Collegeville
Diocese of St. Cloud

St. John's University (1857)
(Men)
Collegeville, MN 56321-2000
Tel: 320-363-2011; Fax: 320-363-2504
Web Site: http://www.csbsju.edu
Sponsored by the Collegeville Benedictine Monks as a division of the corporate Order of St. Benedict, Collegeville, MN.
The Graduate School of Theology (Coed)/Saint John's Seminary (Men): M.A. in Theology, Liturgical Studies, Liturgical Music, Pastoral Ministry and a Master of Divinity. The Undergraduate College of Liberal Arts and Sciences (Men), in full coordinate academic relation with the College of St. Benedict, St. Joseph (Women), offers forty departments, ten pre-professional and ten special academic programs.
Rt. Rev. TIMOTHY KELLY, O.S.B., M.A., Abbot, Chancellor
Sponsored Programs: The Hill Monastic Manuscript Library, the College of St. Benedict/Saint John's University Bahamas Campus, the Interfaith Sexual Trauma Institute, the Saint John's Pottery.
Officers Group:
Bro. DIETRICH REINHART, O.S.B., Pres.
Dr. CLARK HENDLEY, Provost, Academic Affairs
Dr. GAR KELLOM, Vice Pres., Student Devel.
Mr. WARREN JANZEN, Vice Pres., Admin. Svcs.
Mr. JOHN CROSBY, Institutional Advancement
MARY MILBERT, Dean of Admissions
Bro. BENEDICT LEUTHNER, O.S.B., Corp. Treas.
Rev. DALE LAUNDERVILLE, O.S.B., Dean, School of Theology
CHERYL KNOX, Dean of the College
Administrative Group:
Rev. ALBERIC CULHANE, O.S.B., Exec. Asst. to the Pres. for Univ. Rels.
Mr. HERB TRENZ, Dir. Human Resources
Mr. JAMES HARDWICK, Assoc. Dean of Students
Bro. ISAAC CONNOLLY, O.S.B., Dean of Students
Rev. TIMOTHY BACKOUS, O.S.B., Chap., Dir. Campus Ministry
Dr. BERNARD EVANS, The Butler Family's Virgil Michel Ecumenical Chair in Rural Social Ministries
Dr. DANIEL RUSH FINN, The William & Virginia Clemens Chair in Economics and the Liberal Arts
Dr. CHARLES THORNBURY, The Michael Blecker Professorship
Mr. MICHAEL WHITE, Dir. Financial Aid
Dr. DAVID BENNETTS, Dir. Summer Academic Prog.
Mr. MICHAEL KATHMAN, Dir. Libraries and Media
Mr. JAMES KOENIG, Dir. Computing Svcs.
Mr. DAVID LYNDGAARD, Registrar
Revs.:
ROBERT PIERSON, O.S.B., Rector, St. John's Seminary
JONATHAN LICARI, O.S.B., Vice Rector, Saint John's Seminary
ERIC HOLLAS, O.S.B., Dir. Hill Monastic Manuscript Library
ROMAN PAUR, O.S.B., Dir. Interfaith Sexual Trauma Institute
Mr. RICHARD BRESNAHAN Potter, The St. John's Pottery
Mr. JOSE BOURGET, Dir. of Intercultural Programs
Mr. JAMES SMITH, Dir. Athletics
Dr. GENE SANDS, Exec. Dir. Public Affairs
Mr. ROBERT COLLIGAN, Acting Dir. Devel. and Univ. Rels.
Bros.:
LINUS ASCHEMAN, O.S.B., Dir. Buildings and Grounds
DAVID KLINGEMAN, O.S.B., Archivist
Priests 21
Brothers 3
Sisters 3
Faculty 105
Administrators 101
Students 1,823
Bahamas Campus Students 213

Duluth
Diocese of Duluth

College of St. Scholastica
1200 Kenwood Ave.
Duluth, MN 55811
Tel: 218-723-6000; Fax: 218-723-6290
A coed Benedictine college for resident and day students.
Dr. DANIEL H. PILON, Ed.D., Pres.
Sr. MARY ODILE CAHOON, O.S.B., Senior Vice Pres.
STEVE LYONS, Dean of Student Affairs
Sisters 9
Lay Faculty 116
Students 1,749

Minneapolis
Archdiocese of St. Paul and Minneapolis

The College of St. Catherine-Minneapolis
601 25th Ave. S.
Minneapolis, MN 55454
Tel: 612-690-7702
E-mail: dajohnson@stkate.edu
Web Site: http://www.stkate.edu
MARY E. BRODERICK, Interim Pres.
DAN JOHNSON, Acting Academic Dean & Campus Admin.
Coed Health Occupation Human Service and Continuing Education Programs.
Total Staff 64
Students 1,029

St. Joseph
Diocese of St. Cloud

College of St. Benedict (1913)
(Women)
37 S. College Ave.
St. Joseph, MN 56374-2099
Tel: 320-363-5407 (Public Affairs); Fax: 320-363-5136 (Public Affairs)
Legal Title: *College of Saint Benedict*
Affiliation: Roman Catholic, established for the undergraduate education of women by the Sisters of the Order of Saint Benedict.
Sisters of the Order of St. Benedict
Partnership: In 1964 CSB began its first faculty exchange with Saint John's University (SJU) for men. Its present partnership with SJU offers complete coeducational academics, and a variety of coed social, cultural and spiritual programs. Sponsored Programs: CSB/SJU Bahamas Campus; corporate sponsors of Minnesota Public Radio (KNSR).
Officers Group:
MARY E. LYONS, Pres.
W. CLARK HENDLEY, Provost, Academic Affairs
KATHLEEN ALLEN, Vice Pres. Student Devel.
MIRIAM ARDOLF, Vice Pres. of Fin.
BARB CARLSON, Vice Pres. of Institutional Advancement
MARY MILBERT, Dean of Admission
RITA KNUESEL, Dean of the College
Administrative Group:
HERB TRENZ, Dir. Human Resources
MARY GELLER, Dean of Students
JODY TERHAAR, Dir. of Residence Life/Housing
MARY HOLICKY, Dir. Campus Ministry
JANE HAUGEN, Dir. of Fin. Aid
MICHAEL KATHMAN, Dir. of Libraries and Media
JAMES KOENIG, Dir. of Computing Svcs.
DAVID LYNDGAARD, Registrar
MICHELLE SAUER, Dir. of Academic Advising
JOSE BOURGET, Dir. of Cultural Enrichment
STEPHEN BURMEISTER-MAY, Dir. of Intl. Education
CAROL HOWE-VEENSTRA, Dir. of Athletics
MARY HARLANDER-LOCKE, Dir. of Career Svcs.
GENE SANDS, Exec. Dir. of Public Affairs
CONNIE CROSS, Dir. of Public Affairs
GREG HOYE, Dir. of Publications
MIKE DURBIN, Dir. of Sports Information
ANN RUFF, Exec. Dir. Devel.
PAMELA NOVAK, Dir. of Purchasing/Facility Coord.
SUSAN HARRISON, Archivist
Sisters 16
Faculty 111
Administrators 113
Students 1,980
Bahamas Campus Students 213

St. Paul
Archdiocese of St. Paul and Minneapolis

College of St. Catherine
2004 Randolph Ave.
St. Paul, MN 55105
Tel: 612-690-6000
Web Site: www.stkate.edu
MARY E. BRODERICK, Ph.D., Interim Pres.
JEAN CAMERON, Ph.D., Academic Dean
WILLIAM HALLORAN, Vice Pres. Business and Financial Affairs
RANDI S.N. YODER, Vice Pres. Institutional Advancement
COLLEEN HEGRANES, Dean of Students & Vice Pres. Student Affairs
DAN JOHNSON, Academic Dean, CSC-Minneapolis
SUSAN HAMES, Co-Dir. Campus Ministry
CATHY STEFFENS, Co-Dir. Campus Ministry
MICHELLE PLOMBON, Assoc. Dir. Campus Ministry
Sisters of St. Joseph of Carondelet 14
Total Staff 428
Students 3,935

University of St. Thomas
2115 Summit Ave.
St. Paul, MN 55105
Tel: 612-962-5000; Fax: 612-962-6504
Rev. DENNIS J. DEASE, Pres.
Rev. Msgr. TERRENCE J. MURPHY, Chancellor
Dr. CHARLES J. KEFFER, Provost
Dr. MIRIAM Q. WILLIAMS, Assoc. Vice Pres. Academic Affairs
Dr. PAULINE LAMBERT, Exec. Asst. to the Pres.
Dr. NOREEN CARROCCI, Dean of the College
Dr. RALPH PEARSON, Vice Pres. Academic Affairs
Dr. MICHAEL SULLIVAN, Vice Pres. Business Affairs
Mr. GREGORY ROBERTS, Vice Pres. Students Affairs
Dr. JEROME HALVERSON, Dean, New College
Dr. TED FREDRICKSON, Dean, Graduate School of Business
Mr. QUENTIN J. HIETPAS, Senior Vice Pres. External Affairs
Dr. NONA MASON, Dir., Masters in Business Communications
Dr. BERNICE FOLZ, Dir., Graduate Program in the Software Design and Devel. Dept.
Mr. ALAN SICKBERT, Dean of Student Life
Dr. RONALD BENNETT, Chair, Manufacturing Systems Engineering Dept.
JEAN WALSTROM HALEY, Assoc. Provost for Info. Technology
Rev. PHILLIP J. RASK, Vice Pres. & Rector of St. Paul Seminary School of Divinity
Dr. VICTOR KLIMOSKI, Dean, St. Paul Seminary School of Divinity
Rev. Msgr. JAMES M. LAVIN, Alumni Affairs
Rev. Msgr. ROBERT L. PROBST, Computing & Communication Svcs.
Rev. Msgr. JOHN P. SANKOVITZ, Theology Dept.
Revs.:
RONALD BOWERS, J.C.D., Assoc. Prof. of Canon Law, Vice Rector
J. MICHAEL BYRON, M.Div., Instructor, Dogmatic Theology
PETER F. CHRISTENSEN, Rector, St. John Vianney Seminary
KEVIN CONNOR, S.T.L., Instructor in Theology
THOMAS J. CONROY, Asst. Prof. Theology
DOUGLAS E. DANDURAND, M.Div., Spiritual Formation Advisor
JEROME M. DITTBERNER, S.T.D., Prof. Dogmatic Theology
JOHN ECHERT, S.S.L., Instructor, Sacred Scripture
PAUL F. FEELA, M.A., Instructor, Sacramental Theology & Liturgy
PETER E. FELDMEIER, Ph.D., Instuctor, Dogmatic Theology
JAY M. HARRINGTON, O.P., Prior, St. Albert the Great
JAN MICHAEL JONCAS, Dept. Theology, School of Divinity
ARTHUR L. KENNEDY (BO) Dept. Theology
THOMAS KRENIK, Spiritual Dir.
JOHN M. MALONE, Assoc. Prof. Business
WILLIAM C. MCDONOUGH, Asst. Prof. Moral Theology
JAMES R. MOTL, O.P., Ph.D., Assoc. Prof. Homiletics
LEE PICHE, Asst. Prof. Theology
THADEUS J. POSEY, O.F.M.Cap., Assoc. Prof. of Theology
JAMES REIDY, Dept. English
DOMINIC SERRA, Asst. Prof. Sacramental Theology & Liturgy
PAUL D. SIRBA, Spiritual Dir.
DAVID W. SMITH, Prof. Philosophy
JAMES S. STROMBERG, Dept. Philosophy
XAVIER THELAKKART, Spiritual Dir.
GREGORY TOLAAS, Campus Ministry
JOHN UBEL, Co-Dir. of Vocations
ROBERT B. WELLISCH, Dept. English
Students 10,324

Winona
Diocese of Winona

Saint Mary's University of Minnesota
(Coed)
700 Terrace Hts.
Winona, MN 55987-1399
Tel: 507-452-4430; 800-635-5987; Fax: 507-457-1633
E-mail: admissions@smumn.edu
Web Site: http://www.smumn.edu
DeLaSalle Christian Brothers
Bro. LOUIS DE THOMASIS, F.S.C., Pres.
Dr. JEFFREY HIGHLAND, Vice Pres., Academic Affairs & Dean, College of Liberal Arts
Mr. ANTHONY PISCITIELLO, Exec. Vice Pres., Admissions
SHARON GOO, Vice Pres., Student Devel.
MARY C. FOX, Vice Pres. Univ. Rels.
Dr. DANIEL MALONEY, Vice Pres. & CEO, Minneapolis Campus
CYNTHIA MAREK, Vice Pres., Financial Affairs
LORAS SIEVE, Vice Pres., Corporate and Community Rels.
TIM BURCHILL, Pres., Metanoia
ANN MERCHLEWITZ, Vice Pres., General Counsel
Dr. JAMES TOWERS, Dean, School of Education
LAWRENCE GORRELL, Dean, School of Arts and Humanities
JAMES BEDTKE, Dean, School of Business and Social Sciences
Priests 6
Brothers 15
Sisters 10
Lay Faculty 513
Students 5,126

MISSOURI

Kansas City
Diocese of Kansas City-St. Joseph

Avila College
11901 Wornall Rd.
Kansas City, MO 64145-1698
Tel: 816-942-8400; Fax: 816-942-3362
Web Site: www.avila.edu
Dr. LARRY KRAMER, Ed.D., Pres.
Mr. THOMAS LEASE, Vice Pres. & Dean for Student Affairs
Sr. MARIE JOAN HARRIS, C.S.J., Ph.D., Vice Pres. & Dean for Academic Affairs
Mr. NORMAN GERHART, Vice Pres. for Fiscal Affairs
Dr. JAMES T. "TIM" BARRY, Ed.D., Vice Pres. Advancement
Rev. DANIEL TORSON, C.PP.S., Dir. Campus Ministry & Chap.
Sisters of St. Joseph of Carondelet 12
Lay Teachers 56
Students 1,245

Rockhurst College
1100 Rockhurst Rd.
Kansas City, MO 64110-2561
Tel: 816-501-4000; Fax: 816-501-4588
JANET WATSON SHEERAN, Ph.D., Interim Pres.
Ms. ROBIN STRACHAN, Vice Pres. Inst. Advancement
JOHN HAYES, Chm., Board of Trustees
ROGER MCCOY, Chief Financial Officer
NANCY TONJES, Dir. Enrollment Svcs.
JEAN LANGDON, Dir. of the Library
RISE MCGARVEY, Controller
Revs.:
E. EDWARD KINERK, S.J., Rector
FRANCIS L. PEDROTTI, S.J.
College of Arts & Sciences:
COREY SIMMONDS, Dean
ELIZABETH KRAMER, Dean of Students
School of Professional Studies:
NANCY TONJES, Dean
School of Management:
TOM LYON, Interim Dean
Research College of Nursing:
NANCY DEBASIO, Pres./Dean
2316 E. Meyer Blvd.
Kansas City, MO 64123
Tel: 816-276-4700
Rockhurst College Continuing Education Center/National Seminars Group:
MARK TRUITT, Exec. Dir.
GARY TRUITT, Mng. Dir.
6901 West 63rd St.
Kansas City, KS 66205
Tel: 913-432-7755
Revs.:
E. EUGENE ARTHUR, S.J.
JULES M. BRADY, S.J.
MARTIN J. BREDECK, S.J.
EDWARD K. BURGER, S.J.
ROBERT R. BURKE, S.J.
MICHAEL P. CARUSO, S.J.
THOMAS J. CASEY, S.J.
THOMAS F. DENZER, S.J.
JOSEPH M. FREEMAN, S.J.
JOSEPH E. GOUGH, S.J.
WILFRED L. LACROIX, S.J.
FRANCIS J. MURPHY, S.J.
WALTER G. NESBIT, S.J.
LOUIS J. OLDANI, S.J.
JAMES D. WHEELER, S.J.
Bros.:
JOHN R. OLSON, S.J.
GERARD A. SCHROEDER, S.J.
Sisters 2
Priests 22
Lay Professors 180
Students 2,867

St. Louis
Archdiocese of St. Louis

Fontbonne College
6800 Wydown Blvd.
St. Louis, MO 63105
Tel: 314-862-3456
E-mail: sking@fontbonne.edu
Web Site: www.fontbonne.edu
DENNIS C. GOLDEN, Ed.D., Pres.
Sisters 3
Lay Teachers 48
Students 1,970

Saint Louis University
Corporate Title: St. Louis University
221 N. Grand Blvd., DB 261
St. Louis, MO 63103-2097
Tel: 314-977-2222
Mr. MICHAEL F. SHANAHAN, SR., Chm. Bd. of Trustees

Rev. LAWRENCE H. BIONDI, S.J., Pres.
RICHARD D. BRESLIN, Ph.D., Exec. Vice Pres. & Provost
Revs.:
PAUL C. REINERT, S.J., Chancellor Emeritus
J. BARRY MCGANNON, S.J., Chancellor
Vice Presidents:
Rev. MICHAEL J. GARANZINI, S.J., Academic Vice Pres.
ROBERT ALTHOLZ, Acting Vice Pres. for Business and Finance
DONALD J. WHELAN, JR., Interim Vice Pres. Devel. & Univ. Rels.
KATHLEEN T. BRADY, Vice Pres. Facilities Mgmt. & Civic Affairs
WILLIAM R. KAUFFMAN, J.D., Vice Pres. & General Counsel
JAMES R. KIMMEY, M.D., Vice Pres. Health Sciences
KATHY G. HAGEDORN, Vice Pres. Human Resource Mgmt.
RICK L. CHANEY, Ph.D., Vice Pres. Madrid Campus
Revs.:
PAUL V. STARK, S.J., Vice Pres. Student Devel.
A. JAMES BLUMEYER, S.J., Vice Pres. Univ. Mission & Ministry
Deans:
Allied Health Professions, School of
FRANCES L. HORVATH, M.D., Dean
Arts and Sciences, College of
SHIRLEY M. DOWDY, Ph.D., Dean
Business and Administration, School of
NEIL E. SEITZ, Ph.D., Dean
Graduate School
DONALD C. BRENNAN, Ph.D., Dean
Medicine, School of
PATRICIA L. MONTELEONE, M.D., Dean
Nursing, School of
JOAN HRUBETZ, Ph.D., R.N., Dean
Parks College of Engineering and Aviation
CHARLES C. KIRKPATRICK, Ph.D., Dean
Philosophy and Letters, College of
GARTH L. HALLETT, S.J., Dean
Professional Studies, School of
ROBERT L. HASENSTAB, Ph.D., Dean
Public Health, School of
RICHARD S. KURZ, Ph.D., Dean
Social Service, School of
SUSAN C. TEBB, Ph.D., Dean
Academic Services
JOHN G. SEVERSON, Ph.D.
Leadership and Public Services
JAMES F. GILSINAN, Ph.D.
Pius XII Memorial Library
FRANCES BENHAM, Ph.D.
Student Educational Services Center
CELERSTINE B. JOHNSON, Ed.D.
Other Jesuits Associated with the University:
Revs.:
ALBERT AGRESTI, S.J.
A. JAMES BLUMEYER, S.J.
JAMES H. BAKER, S.J.
MICHAEL D. BARBER, S.J.
Bro. WILLIAM BIERNATZKI
Revs.:
LAWRENCE BIONDI, S.J.
JOSEPH E. BROWN, S.J.
FRANCIS X. CLEARY, S.J.
ANTHONY C. DALY, S.J.
DENIS E. DALY, S.J.
TERRENCE E. DEMPSEY, S.J.
MICHAEL J. DOODY, S.J.
ROBERT FLACK, S.J.
JOHN B. FOLEY, S.J.
IGNATIUS FUTO, S.J.
MICHAEL J. GARANZINI, S.J.
EUGENE E. GROLLMES, S.J.
GARTH L. HALLETT, S.J.
CHARLES HEISER, S.J.
ROBERT HURD, S.J.
JOHN J. KAVANAUGH, S.J.
THOMAS E.J. KELLY, S.J.
EDWIN J. LISSON, S.J.
MICHAEL MAHER, S.J.
MICHAEL K. MAY, S.J.
BARRY MCGANNON, S.J.
FREDERICK G. MCLEOD, S.J.
MAURICE MCNAMEE, S.J.
JOHN J. MUELLER, S.J.
CLAUDE N. PAVUR, S.J.
ROBERT PHILLIPS, S.J.
ROBERT POIRER, S.J.
DONALD W. RECK, S.J.
Bro. WILLIAM R. REHG, S.J.
Revs.:
PAUL REINERT, S.J.
RALPH C. RENNER, S.J.
LARS REUTER, S.J.
ALBERT C. ROTOLA, S.J.
JAMES A. SEBESTA, S.J.
JOHN F.X. SHEEHAN, S.J.
PAUL V. STARK, S.J.
WILLIAM V. STAUDER, S.J.
JAMES V. VELTRIE, S.J.
Priests 26
Brothers 1
Sisters 4
Lay Teachers 1,047
Total Staff 3,697
Total Enrollment 11,038

MONTANA

Great Falls
Diocese of Great Falls - Billings

University of Great Falls (1932)
1301 20th St. S.
Great Falls, MT 59405
Tel: 406-761-8210
E-mail: adminrec@ugf.edu
Web Site: www.ugf.edu
Sponsored by the Sisters of Providence
Dr. FREDERICK GILLIARD, Pres.
Dr. B. LEE COOPER, Academic Vice Pres.
AUDREY THOMPSON, Vice Pres. Student Svcs.
JAMES B. WASHBURN, JR., Vice Pres. Admin. & Finance
BILL COYLE, Vice Pres. Institutional Advancement
JO MARIE EINAN, Dir. of Campus Ministry
Rev. JAMES SIKORA, Chap.
Sr. LAWRENCE CROWLEY, S.P., Grants Coord.
Assoc. Professors of Religious Studies:
Revs.:
JAMES R. SIKORA
JON TAYLOR, A.B.D.
Sr. MARY KAYE NEALEN, S.P.
Priests 3
Lay Teachers 48
Students 1,253

Helena
Diocese of Helena

Carroll College (1909)
Tel: 406-447-4300; Fax: 406-447-4533
Four year Diocesan College of Liberal Arts and Sciences.
Dr. MATTHEW J. QUINN, Pres.
Dr. JAMES TRUDNOWSKI, Vice Pres. Academic Affairs
Ms. LYNN ETCHART, Vice Pres. Business Affairs
Mr. THOMAS J. MCCARVEL, Vice Pres. Inst. Advancement
Mr. ROBERT PASTOOR, Vice Pres. Student Affairs
Revs.:
JOSEPH D. HARRINGTON
WILLIAM GREYTAK
DANIEL P. HILLEN
JEREMIAH LOWNEY
J. EUGENE PEOPLES
LEO G. PROXELL
DANIEL B. SHEA
JEREMIAH T. SULLIVAN
In res.,
Revs.:
HUMPHREY J. COURTNEY, (Retired)
GERALD J. LYNAM, (Retired)
Priests 9
Lay Professors 68
Students 1,418
Total Staff 114

NEBRASKA

Omaha
Archdiocese of Omaha

College of St. Mary
1901 S. 72 St.
Omaha, NE 68124
Tel: 402-399-2400
E-mail: enroll@csm.edu
Web Site: www.csm.edu
Sr. MARYANNE STEVENS, R.S.M., Pres.
Dr. CLAUDE WYNN, Vice-Pres. for Academic Affairs & Dean of the College
Sr. SYLVIA SWANKE, R.S.M., Dir. of Campus Ministry
JENNIFER M. SAND, Media Relations Coord.
Sisters 1
Lay Teachers 54

**Creighton University*
2500 California Plaza
Omaha, NE 68178
Tel: 402-280-2700
E-mail: fmm@creighton.edu
Web Site: http:www.creighton.edu
Rev. MICHAEL G. MORRISON, S.J., Pres. & Contact
The University is comprised of the following schools:
College of Arts and Sciences—
Rev. MICHAEL PROTERRA, S.J., Dean
College of Business Administration—
Dr. ROBERT E. PITTS, Dean
Graduate School—
Dr. BARBARA J. BRADEN, Dean
School of Law—
LAWRENCE RAFUL, J.D., Dean
University College/Summer Sessions—
Ms. SUZANNE M. ALLEGRETTI, Acting Dean
School of Dentistry—
Dr. WAYNE W. BARKMEIER, Dean
School of Medicine—
Dr. RODERICK NAIRN, Interim Dean
School of Nursing—
Dr. EDITH K. KITCHENS, Dean
School of Pharmacy and Allied Health Professions—
Dr. SIDNEY J. STOHS, Dean
Priests 14
Sisters 1
Lay Teachers 596
Students 6,292

NEW HAMPSHIRE

Manchester
Diocese of Manchester

Notre Dame College
2321 Elm St.
Manchester, NH 03104
Tel: 603-669-4298; Fax: 603-644-8316
Founded by Sisters of Holy Cross.
Sr. CAROL J. DESCOTEAUX, C.S.C., Ph.D., Pres.
Sr. EDIE DALY, S.N.D.deN., Dir. Campus Ministry
Sisters 17
Lay Teachers 110
Students 1,240

Saint Anselm College
Manchester, NH 03102
Tel: 603-641-7000
Order of St. Benedict
Rt. Rev. MATTHEW K. LEAVY, O.S.B., Ph.D., Chancellor
Rev. JONATHAN P. DEFELICE, O.S.B., J.C.L., Pres. Admin. & Faculty
Priests 4
Lay Teachers 109
Sisters 2
Students 2,007

Merrimack
Diocese of Manchester

The Thomas More College of Liberal Arts
6 Manchester St.
Merrimack, NH 03054
Tel: 603-880-8308; Fax: 603-880-9280
PETER V. SAMPO, Pres.
Total Staff 8
Students 63

Nashua
Diocese of Manchester

Rivier College
Nashua, NH 03060
Tel: 603-888-1311
E-mail: poneil@rivier.edu
Web Site: www.rivier.edu
Sisters of the Presentation of Mary
Sr. LUCILLE C. THIBODEAU, P.M., Ph.D., Pres.
Rev. PAUL R. DEMERS, S.C., Chap.
Presentation Sisters 35
Teaching Sisters 8
Teaching Priests 2
Lay Teachers 196
Students 2,840

Warner
Diocese of Manchester

Magdalen College
511 Kearsarge Mountain Rd.
Warner, NH 03278-9206
Tel: 603-456-2656
JOHN D. MEEHAN, Pres.
MARY L. PRIETO, Dean of Students
Dr. GEORGE N. STANCIU, Academic Dean
Rev. THOMAS J. SPARKS, Chap.
Lay Teachers 9
Total Staff 19
Students 70

Windham
Diocese of Manchester

Castle College
23 Searles Rd.
Windham, NH 03087-1200
Tel: 603-893-6111
E-mail: ccadmin@ultranet.com

Degree-Granting Program: Associate in Business Science (A.B.S.), Associate in Early Childhood Education (A.E.C.E.), Associate of Science in Human Services (A.H.S.S.), Associate Degree in Recreation Therapy (A.R.T.), collaborative program with St. Joseph Healthcare.
Sisters of Mercy
Sr. OLIVIA KIDNEY, R.S.M., Pres.
Sisters 1
Lay Teachers 3
Students 170

NEW JERSEY

Caldwell
Archdiocese of Newark

Caldwell College
9 Ryerson Ave.
Caldwell, NJ 07006
Tel: 973-228-4424
Incorporated under the laws of the State of New Jersey with full power to confer degrees.
College Faculty:
Sr. PATRICE WERNER, O.P., Ph.D., Pres.
Dr. WILLIAM ALEXANDER, Ph.D., Vice Pres., Dean for Academic Affairs
MATTHEW GREELEY, Coord. of Campus Ministry
Priests 4
Sisters 2
Sisters of St. Dominic 9
Lay Teachers 115
Students 1,826

Haledon
Diocese of Paterson

Salesian College
655 Belmont Ave.
Haledon, NJ 07508
Sr. THERESA KELLY, F.M.A., Pres., Dean
Sr. IDA OSSI, F.M.A., Registrar
Students 15

Jersey City
Archdiocese of Newark

Saint Peter's College
2641 Kennedy Blvd.
Jersey City, NJ 07306-5997
Tel: 201-915-9000; Fax: 201-451-0036
Rev. JAMES N. LOUGHRAN, S.J., Pres.
EILEEN L. POIANI, Ph.D., Exec. Asst. to the Pres.
Dr. GEORGE E. MARTIN, Academic Vice Pres.
Mr. FRANK J. BARLETTA, Vice Pres. Finance and Admin. Svcs.
Mr. EDWARD W. REUTER, Vice Pres. Student Affairs
Mr. MICHAEL F. LARKIN, Vice Pres. Advancement
Dr. PETER ALEXANDER, JR., Academic Dean-Day Session
Mr. MARK JOHN HOESLY, Dean of Freshmen
Ms. SUSAN E. NELSON, Dean of Upperclassmen
Dr. KATHERINE M. RESTAINO, Dean of Undergraduate Evening & Summer Sessions
Ms. BARBARA PENNIPEDE, Assoc. Dean, Englewood Cliffs Campus
Mr. WILLIAM MORRISON, Asst. Dean-Evening Session
Mr. BEN SCHOLZ, Co-Acting Dir. Admissions
Ms. STEPHANIE M. DECKER, Co-Acting Dir. Admissions
Ms. JOAN Z. SHIELDS, Registrar
Priests 36
St. Peter's College Jesuit Community
Gothic Towers, 50 Glenwood Ave.
Jersey City, NJ 07306-4606
Tel: 201-433-2527; Fax: 201-432-7397
Jesuit Center
St. Peter Hall, 2652 Kennedy Blvd.
Jersey City, NJ 07306
Tel: 201-433-2527; 2528 (Rector's Office); Fax: 201-433-7139
Revs.:
WILLIAM M. ABBOTT, S.J.
THOMAS BLESSIN
EDWARD W. BRANDE, S.J.
JOHN M. BUCKLEY, S.J.
CLAUDIO M. BURGALETA, S.J.
LAURENCE L. CASSIDY, S.J.
EUGENE J. CULHANE, S.J.
JAMES H. DAHLINGER, S.J.
MARK T. DESTEPHANO, S.J.
EUGENE J. DEVLIN, S.J.
JUAN DIAZ VILAR
JAMES DOLAN
Bro. PATRICK T. FLANAGAN
Revs.:
CHARLES A. GALLAGHER, S.J.
EDWARD B. GILLEN, S.J.
JEROME H. GRUSZCZYK
EDWARD J. HEAVEY, S.J.
JOSE KADANKEVIL, S.J.
JOSEPH KALLEPALLIL, S.J.
JOSEPH A. KELLY
ROBERT E. KENNEDY, S.J.
JAMES N. LOUGHRAN, S.J.
JOSEPH W. LUX, S.J.
T. PATRICK LYNCH
DONAL T. MACVEIGH, S.J.
OSCAR G. MAGNAN
WILLIAM F.X. MAHER, S.J.
EDMUND W. MAJEWSKI, S.J.
CARSTEN P. MARTENSEN, S.J.
ROBERT E. MCCARTY, S.J.
WILLIAM A. MCKENNA, S.J.
AIDAN C. MCMULLEN
JOHN J. O'BRIEN
JOHN P. RUANE, S.J.
JOHN P. ST. GEORGE, S.J.
DAVID X. STUMP, S.J.
THOMAS L. SHERIDAN, S.J.
JOHN P. WRYNN
Full Time Faculty:
Priests 15
Lay Teachers 103
Students 3,698

Lakewood
Diocese of Trenton

Georgian Court College
900 Lakewood Ave.
Lakewood, NJ 08701-2697
Tel: 732-364-2200; Fax: 732-367-3920
Sisters of Mercy
Sr. BARBARA WILLIAMS, R.S.M., Pres.
Sr. MARIE COOK, R.S.M., Academic Dean
Rev. NORMAN DEMECK, C.P.
Priests 1
Sisters 16
Lay Teachers 170
Students 2,422

Lodi
Archdiocese of Newark

Felician College
262 S. Main St.
Lodi, NJ 07644
Tel: 201-778-1190; Fax: 201-778-4111
E-mail: petersen@inet.felician.edu
Web Site: www.felician.edu
Sr. THERESA MARY MARTIN, C.S.S.F., Pres.
Rev. DAMIAN COLICCHIO, O.F.M.Cap., Dir. of Campus Ministry
Priests 1
Sisters 26
Lay Teachers 109
Students 1,231

Mendham
Diocese of Paterson

Assumption College for Sisters
Mendham, NJ 07945
Fax: 973-543-9459
E-mail: socc@tsa.net
Conducted by Sisters of Christian Charity.
Sr. JULITTA HEINEN, S.C.C., Pres.
Sr. HELEN MARIE CRONIN, S.C.C., Academic Dean
Sr. CATHERINE KEMPER, S.C.C., Registrar
Religious 24
Students 24

Morristown
Diocese of Paterson

College of Saint Elizabeth
2 Convent Rd.
Morristown, NJ 07961
Tel: 973-290-4000
Web Site: http://www.st-elizabeth.edu
Sisters of Charity
Sr. FRANCIS RAFTERY, S.C., Pres.
Dr. JOHANNA GLAZEWSKI, Vice Pres. for Academic Affairs and Dean of Studies
MARIA CAMMARATA, Vice Pres. for Finance & Admin. and Treas.
Mrs. ROSEMARIE GENCO, Comptroller
Mrs. KATHERINE SHILENOR-MCKINLEY, Registrar
Mrs. DONNA YAMANIS, Dean of Admissions and Financial Aid
Rev. ANTHONY J. CIORRA, O.F.M.Cap., Chap.
Tel: 973-290-4210
Full-time Admin. and Faculty:
Priests 1
Religious 25
Lay Teachers 55
Students 2,087

South Orange
Archdiocese of Newark

Seton Hall University (1856)
400 South Orange Ave.
South Orange, NJ 07079
Tel: 973-761-9000; Fax: 973-275-2361
Rev. THOMAS R. PETERSON, O.P., S.T.D., Ph.D., Chancellor
Rev. Msgr. ROBERT T. SHEERAN, S.T.D., Pres.
Officers of University:
MARY MEEHAN, Vice Pres. & Asst. to the Pres.
PETER G. AHR, Ph.D., Interim Provost
KIMBERLY CLINE, Ed.D., Vice Pres. Finance & Admin.
JOHN H. SHANNON, J.D., Vice Pres. University Affairs
LAURA A. WANKEL, Ed.D., Vice Pres. Student Affairs
DENNIS BARBINI, M.B.A., Asst. to Pres. for Technology
Rev. Msgr. WILLIAM C. HARMS, D.Min., Vice Pres. Planning
CATHERINE KIERNAN, Vice Pres. & University Counsel
Administrators:
LISA GRIDER, Asst. Vice Pres. Public Rels.
JANE V. NORTON, Ed.D., Asst. Provost for Academic Svcs.
PATRICIA L. BURGH, M.A., Asst. Provost for Enrollment Mgmt.
FRANCISCO MORALES, Dir. Special Academic Programs
CHERYL NOTARI, Acting Dean, Freshman Studies
ARTHUR W. HAFNER, Ph.D., Dean University Libraries
MARY ELLEN FARRELL, Registrar
MICHAEL MENENDEZ, Dir. Financial Aid
EDWIN MILLAR, Chief Financial Mgr.
DEBORAH KROEGER, Dir. Human Resources
DANIEL MURRAY, Dir. Alumni Rels.
Dr. ROBERT HALLISSEY, Dir. Grants & Contracts
SUE REGAN, Dir. University Athletics
Revs.:
JOHN F. MORLEY, Ph.D., Min. to Priest Community
JAMES F. SPERA, M.Div., Dir. Campus Ministry
ROBERT S. MEYER, S.T.L., Asst. to Vice Pres. Student Affairs
Rev. Msgr. ANDREW T. CUSACK, Ph.D., Dir. National Inst. for Clergy Formation
College of Arts and Sciences
JAMES VAN OOSTING, Ph.D., Dean, Tel: 973-761-9022
School of Business
SHELDON EPSTEIN, Ph.D., Interim Dean, Tel: 973-761-9013
College of Education and Human Services
SYLVESTER KOHUT, JR., Ph.D., Dean, Tel: 973-761-9025
College of Nursing
BARBARA A. BEEKER, R.N. Ed.D., Dean, Tel: 973-761-9014
School of Law
RONALD J. RICCIO, J.D., Dean
One Newark Center
Newark, NJ 07102
Tel: 973-642-8750
School of Theology
Rev. JOHN W. FLESEY, S.T.D., Rector/Dean, Tel: 973-761-9016
School of Graduate Medical Education
JOHN PATERSON, D.D.S., Dean, Tel: 973-761-9710
College Seminary
Rev. Msgr. ARTHUR J. SERRATELLI, S.T.D., Rector, Tel: 973-761-9420
University College
JANE V. NORTON, Ed.D. Tel: 973-761-9430
Priest Community:
Rev. JOHN F. MORLEY, Ph.D., Min. to Priest Community
Rev. Msgr. ROBERT F. COLEMAN, J.C.D.
Rev. Msgr. ANDREW T. CUSACK, Ph.D.
Rev. Msgr. WILLIAM N. FIELD, M.L.S., M.A.
Rev. Msgr. EDWARD J. FLEMING, Ph.D., (Retired)
Rev. Msgr. JOHN W. FLESEY, S.T.D.
Rev. Msgr. WILLIAM C. HARMS, D.Min.
Rev. Msgr. RICHARD M. LIDDY, Ph.D.
Rev. Msgr. ROBERT T. SHEERAN, S.T.D.
Rev. Msgr. EDWIN V. SULLIVAN, Ph.D., (Retired)
Rev. Msgr. JAMES C. TURRO, S.T.L., S.S.L., A.M., Ph.D., (Retired)
Rev. Msgr. ROBERT J. WISTER, S.T.M.
Revs.:
JOHN M. BALLWEG, M.A., Holy Spirit, Union, NJ
W. JEROME BRACKEN, Ph.D.
JAMES M. CAFONE, S.T.D.
ALFRED V. CELIANO, Ph.D., (Retired)
GABRIEL B. COSTA, Ph.D.
EUGENE J. COTTER, D.Lett
DECLAN J. CUNNIFF, Th.M., M.L.S., D.Min.
WALTER A. DEBOLD, M.A., (Retired)
ARNOLD P. DE ROSA, Ph.D.

MARTIN J. FORAN, M.A., (Retired)
LAWRENCE E. FRIZZELL, D.Phil.
FRANCIS T. GAVIN, M.A., (Retired)
NICHOLAS S. GENGARO, S.T.D.
THOMAS G. GUARINO, S.T.D.
KEVIN M. HANBURY, Ed.D.
PAUL A. HOLMES, S.T.D.
CHRISTOPHER J. HYNES, Ed.S.
PETER F. LENNON, Ph.D.
GERALD H. MCCARREN, S.T.D.
ROBERT S. MEYER, S.T.L.
DANIEL A. MURPHY, Ph.D., (Retired)
RICHARD M. NARDONE, Ph.D.
ROBERT P. NESTOR, Ed.D.
MARTIN F. O'BRIEN, M.S.
THOMAS R. PETERSON, O.P., S.T.D., Ph.D.
LAWRENCE B. PORTER, O.P., Ph.D.
JOHN J. RANIERI, Ph.D.
JOHN F. RUSSELL, O.Carm., S.T.D.
HENRY J. SCHREITMUELLER, Ed.D.
ARTHUR J. SERRATELLI, S.T.D.
WILLIAM P. SHERIDAN, M.Div.
DONALD C. SMITH, M.A.
JAMES F. SPERA, M.Div.
C. ANTHONY ZICCARDI, S.T.L., S.S.L.
In res.,
Revs.:
JOSEPH R. CHAPEL, S.T.D.
DOUGLAS J. MILEWSKI, S.T.L.
THOMAS P. NYDEGGER, M.Div.
JOSEPH F. WORTMANN, M.A.
Priests 51
Lay Teachers 343
Students 9,528

NEW MEXICO

Santa Fe
Archdiocese of Santa Fe

College of Santa Fe (1947)
(Coed Four Year Liberal Arts College)
Santa Fe, NM 87501
Tel: 505-473-6011
Brothers of the Christian Schools
Dr. JAMES FRIES, Pres.
Dr. JIM LAWRENCE, Sr. Vice Pres. & Dean of the College
DALE REINHART, Dir. Admissions and Enrollment Mgmt.
Ms. YVONNE RUSSELL, Dean of Students
Revs.:
LEONA STUCKY-ABBOTT, Dir. Campus Ministry
JAMES CRONIN
Brothers 7
Lay Teachers 110
Students 1,600

NEW YORK

Albany
Diocese of Albany

The College of Saint Rose
(Corporate Name)
432 Western Ave.
Albany, NY 12203
Tel: 518-454-5111; 800-657-8556; Fax: 518-458-5447
Founded by the Sisters of St. Joseph of Carondelet in 1920.
Dr. MARK SULLIVAN, Pres.
Sr. ANNE CLARK, Acting Vice Pres. for Academic Affairs and Provost
KATHLEEN M. SINEL, Vice Pres. for Finance & Admin.
Ms. JEANNE KOBUSZEWSKI, Vice Pres. Devel. & Alumni Rels.
CHARLES E. GREENE, JR., Comptroller
JUDITH A. KELLY, Registrar
MARGARET KIRWIN, Dean of Studies
DENNIS MCDONALD, Dean of Student Svcs.
MICHAEL FISHBEIN, Dean of Instructional Resources
MARY GRONDAHL, Dean of Enrollment Svcs.
Revs.:
CHRISTOPHER DEGIOVINE, Chap. & Dir. of Campus Ministry
ANTHONY D. GULLEY, Non-Resident Priest
Priests 2
Sisters 14
Lay Teachers 125
Students 3,800

Maria College
700 New Scotland Ave.
Albany, NY 12208
Two Year College
Sr. LAUREEN FITZGERALD, Pres.
Sr. JOSEPHINE REYNOLDS, Dean for Academic Affairs
Ms. LAURIE GILMORE, Dir. Admissions
Ms. DEBORAH CORRIGAN, Dean Students
Mrs. FRANCES BERNARD, Dir. Business Affairs
Revs.:
MICHAEL HOGAN
PAUL R. SMITH
THOMAS F. BERARDI
Sisters of Mercy 16
Lay Teachers 34
Students 815

St. Bernard's Institute at Albany
Extension Program of St. Bernard's Institute, Rochester, NY.
40 N. Main Ave.
Albany, NY 12203
Tel: 518-453-6760
Graduate School of Theology & Ministry Studies.
Sr. MARGERY HALPIN, R.S.M., Dir.

Bronx
Archdiocese of New York

**Fordham University* (1841)
Fordham Rd.
Bronx, NY 10458
Fax: 718-817-4925
Second campus and Branch campus at Lincoln Center, New York, NY 10023 and Marymount College, Tarrytown, NY 10591. Chartered by the Legislature of the State of New York.
Revs.:
JOSEPH A. O'HARE, S.J., Pres.
GERARD C. REEDY, S.J., Vice Pres. Academic Affairs
Dr. BARBARA ELLEN BLACK, Financial Vice Pres. and Treas.
Mr. BRUNO M. SANTONOCITO, Vice Pres. Devel. & Univ. Rels.
Revs.:
GEORGE J. MCMAHON, S.J., Vice Pres. Lincoln Center
JOHN J. SHEA, S.J., Vice Pres. Students Affairs
Dr. BRIAN BYRNE, Vice Pres. Admin.
Dr. JOHN W. HEALEY, Vice Pres. Planning & Budget
Mr. RICHARD T. WALDRON, Vice Pres., Institutional Research
Dr. ROBERT F. HIMMELBERG, Dean of Graduate School of Arts and Sciences
Rev. JOSEPH M. MCSHANE, S.J., Dean of Fordham College
Dr. SHARON SMITH, Dean of College of Business Admin.
Mr. WILLIAM SMALL, Dean of Graduate School of Business Admin.
Dr. MAX WEINER, Dean of Graduate School of Education
JOHN D. FEERICK, LL.B., Dean of School of Law
Dr. MARY ANN QUARANTA, Dean of Graduate School of Social Service
Dr. EDWARD BRISTOW, Dean of College at Lincoln Center
Dr. MICHAEL GILLAN, Dean of Ignatius College
Rev. VINCENT M. NOVAK, S.J., Dean of Graduate School of Religion and Religious Education
Sr. MONICA KEVIN, O.S.U., Dean of Summer Session

Manhattan College
Manhattan College Pkwy.
Bronx, NY 10471
Tel: 718-862-7200; 800-MC2-XCEL
Web Site: http://www.manhattan.edu
Bro. THOMAS SCANLAN, F.S.C., Pres.
Priests 1
Brothers 4
Sisters 1
Lay Staff 160
Total Enrollment 3,076

Brooklyn
Diocese of Brooklyn

**St. Francis College*
180 Remsen St.
Brooklyn, NY 11201
Tel: 718-489-5200
Dr. FRANK MACCHIAROLA Pres.
Brothers 3
Sisters 1
Students 2,136

**St. Joseph's College*
245 Clinton Ave.
Brooklyn, NY 11205
Tel: 718-636-6800
Branch Campus
155 Roe Blvd.
Brooklyn, NY 11772
Tel: 516-447-3200
Under supervision of Board of Trustees.
Sr. ELIZABETH A. HILL, C.S.J., Pres.
Sr. MARY FLORENCE BURNS, C.S.J., Ph.D., Academic Vice Pres.
Sr. MARGARET BUCKLEY, C.S.J., Ed.D., Academic Dean
THOMAS G. TRAVIS, Ph.D., Dean, Div. General Studies
Sisters 18
Lay Teachers 31
Students 1,381

Buffalo
Diocese of Buffalo

Canisius College
2001 Main St.
Buffalo, NY 14208-1098
Tel: 716-883-7000; Fax: 716-888-2525
E-mail: cookev@canisus.edu
Web Site: http://www.canius.edu
Revs.:
VINCENT M. COOKE, S.J., Pres.
JAMES P. HIGGINS, S.J., Sec., Bd. Trustees
Sr. MARLENE G. BUTLER, G.N.S.H., Dir., Campus Min.
Dr. RICHARD A. WALL, Interim Vice Pres. for Student Affairs
Mr. JOHN J. HURLEY, Vice Pres. for College Relations & Gen. Counsel
Dr. LAURENCE W. FRANZ, Vice Pres. of Business & Finance & Treas.
Dr. HERBERT J. NELSON, Vice Pres. for Academic Affairs
Dr. ELLEN O. CONLEY, Dean, College of Arts & Sciences
Dr. RICHARD A. SHICK, Dean, Wehle School of Business
Dr. JAMES M. MCDONNELL, Acting Dean, School of Educ. & Human Svcs.
Mr. GEORGE M. TELATNIK, Dir. Library
Dr. JOEL A. COHEN, Dir., Information Technology Svcs.
Priests 17
Lay Teachers 178
Total Enrollment 4,615

**D'Youville College*
320 Porter Ave.
Buffalo, NY 14201
Tel: 716-881-3200; Fax: 716-881-7780
E-mail: bordercb@dyc.edu
Web Site: www.dyc.edu
Grey Nuns of the Sacred Heart.
Sr. DENISE A. ROCHE, G.N.S.H., Ph.D., Pres.
Bro. JAMES SARACH, D.T.O.R., Chap. (Dir. Campus Ministry)
Priests 3
Sisters 7
Lay Teachers 158
Total Staff 318
Students 1,870

Trocaire College
360 Choate Ave.
Buffalo, NY 14220
Tel: 716-826-1200
Web Site: www.trocaire.edu
Sr. BARBARA CIARICO, R.S.M., Pres.
Sisters 13
Lay Teachers 73
Students 1,135
Total Staff 56

Villa Maria College of Buffalo
240 Pine Ridge Rd.
Buffalo, NY 14225-3999
Tel: 716-896-0700; Fax: 716-896-0705
Web Site: www.villa.edu
Sr. MARCELLA MARIE GARUS, Pres.
NATALIE J. MOUDGIL, Ph.D., Vice Pres. Academic Affairs
Sr. MARY DE ANGELIS NOWAK, Vice Pres. Business Affairs
Sr. MARY MARCINE BOROWIAK, Vice Pres. Devel.
Sr. MARY LOUIS RUSTOWICZ, Vice Pres. Student Affairs
Sisters 1
Lay Teachers 17
Students 356
Total Staff 71

Dobbs Ferry
Archdiocese of New York

Mercy College in Dobbs Ferry
541 Broadway
Dobbs Ferry, NY 10522
Tel: 914-693-4500

Hamburg
Diocese of Buffalo

Hilbert College
5200 S. Park Ave.

Hamburg, NY 14075
Tel: 716-649-7900
Franciscan Sisters of Saint Joseph
Sr. Edmunette Paczesny, F.S.S.J., Pres.
Rev. Bernard Olszewski, O.F.M.Conv., Chap.
Priests 2
Sisters 3
Lay Teachers 65
Students 892
Total Staff 134

Jamaica
Diocese of Brooklyn

St. John's University
8000 Utopia Pkwy.
Jamaica, NY 11439
Tel: 718-990-6161; Fax: 718-990-5886
Web Site: http://www.stjohns.edu
Sponsored by the Vincentian Priests and Brothers Eastern Province of the Congregation of the Mission.
Rev. Donald J. Harrington, C.M., Pres.
Officers of Administration:
Robert J. Crimmins, Exec. Vice Pres.
Tony H. Bonaparte, Ph.D., Provost
Rev. Michael J. Carroll, C.M., Vice Pres. Campus Ministry & Rome Campus
Cecilia S. Chang, Ed.D., Vice Pres. Intl. Rels.
John P. Connolly, Jr., Vice Pres. Administrative Svcs.
Rev. Joseph V. Daly, C.M., Asst. to the Pres.
Susan L. Ebbs, Ed.D., Vice Pres. Student Life
Dorothy E. Habben, Ph.D., Vice Pres. & Univ. Sec.
Suzanne M. Halpin, Vice Pres. Communications
Rev. James F. Kiernan, C.M., Senior Vice Pres., Staten Island Campus
James P. Pellow, Vice Pres. Finance & Treas.
Joseph Sciame, Vice Pres. Govt. & Community Rels.
Rev. Bernard M. Tracey, C.M., Vice Pres. Inst. Advancement
Priests 21
Sisters 2
Lay Teachers 559
Total Enrollment 16,384 (undergraduate and graduate of Queens and Staten Island campuses)
Queens campus enrollment 14,002

Loudonville
Diocese of Albany

Siena College
Loudonville, NY 12211
Tel: 518-783-2300
Founded in 1937 by the Franciscan Friars, Order of Friars Minor, Province of the Most Holy Name of Jesus.
Revs.:
Kevin E. Mackin, Pres.
James Toal, Vice Pres.
Dr. Timothy Lederman, Vice Pres. Academic Affairs
Anthony Pondillo, Vice Pres. Finance & Admin.
Dr. Gregory Stahl, Vice Pres. for Inst. Advancement
Noel Hogan, Dean of Enrollment Mgmt.
Ned Jones, Dir. of Admissions
Rev. John C. Frambes, O.F.M., Vice Pres. for Student Affairs
Dr. Frederick J. DeCasperis, Dean of Continuing Education
Rev. Francis X. Gunn, O.F.M., Dir. of Campus Ministry
Ann White, Dir. Financial Aid
Dr. Kenneth Wittig, Asst. Vice Pres. Inf. & Tech. Svcs.
William Kelley, Dir. of Physical Plant
James A. Serbalik, Registrar
Thomas Denhan, Dir. Career Resources
Legal Title: *Siena College*
Students 3,021
The Friary:
Bro. John P. Mahon, O.F.M., Guardian
Revs.:
Capistran J. Hanlon, O.F.M., Vicar
Callistus M. Bamberg, O.F.M., Dir. Northway Mall Chapel
Bros.:
Romuald Chinetsky, O.F.M.
Gary Maciag, O.F.M.
Michael Harlan, O.F.M.
James Sabak, O.F.M.
Revs.:
Matthew T. Conlon, O.F.M.
Julian A. Davies, O.F.M.
William DeBiase, O.F.M.
Daniel P. Dwyer, O.F.M.
Peter A. Fiore, O.F.M.
John C. Frambes, O.F.M.
Berard A. Giblin, O.F.M.
Francis X. Gunn, O.F.M.
Kevin E. Mackin, O.F.M.
Henry L. Madden, O.F.M.
William E. McConville, O.F.M.
Daniel C. Nelson, O.F.M.
Luke A. O'Connell, O.F.M.
Kenneth Paulli, O.F.M.
Laurence P. Rainville, O.F.M.
Reginald J. Reddy, O.F.M.
Blaise R. Reinhart, O.F.M.
Sennen C. San Fratello, O.F.M.
Dennis Tamburello, O.F.M.
James Toal, O.F.M.
John E. Van Hook, O.F.M.

New Rochelle
Archdiocese of New York

**College of New Rochelle*
29 Castle Pl.
New Rochelle, NY 10805
Tel: 914-654-5000; Fax: 914-654-5290
E-mail: info@cnr.edu
Web Site: http://www.cnr.edu
Founded in 1904 by the Religious of the Order of St. Ursula. Chartered by the Regents of the University of the State of New York. The College is composed of four schools: School of Arts and Sciences (Women); Graduate School; School of New Resources; School of Nursing (Coed).
Dr. Stephen Sweeny, Pres.
Dr. Joan Bailey, Senior Vice Pres. Academic Affairs
Dr. Laura Ellis, Dean, Graduate School
Dr. Connie Vance, Dean, School of Nursing
Dr. Bessie Blake, Dean of School of New Resources
Walter McCarthy, Vice Pres. Financial Affairs
Rev. John Rathschmidt, O.F.M.Cap., Chap.
Mrs. Mary Naughton, Dir., Campus Ministry
Rev. Bernard McMahon, Asst. Chap.
Sr. Patricia McLoughlin, S.C., Dir. Grants
Priests 2
Sisters 12
Lay Teachers 630
Students 7,169

Iona College
715 North Ave.
New Rochelle, NY 10801
Tel: 914-633-2000
E-mail: webmaster@iona.edu
Web Site: http://www.iona.edu
(Coed)
Branch Orangeburg Campus
One Dutch Hill Rd.
Orangeburg, NY 10962
Tel: 914-359-2252
Branch Manhattan Campus
St. Michael High School, 425 W. 33rd St.
New York, NY 10001
Tel: 212-630-0270
Education in the tradition of the Christian Brothers. Independent College.
Bro. James A. Liguori, Ed.D., Pres.
Dr. Judson R. Shaver, Vice Pres. for Academic Affairs/Provost
Mr. John Braunstein, Vice Provost for Enrollment Management
Dr. Michael McGrath, Vice Provost for Student Devel.
Ms. Dixie K. Norris, Vice Pres. Finance & Administration
Mr. James Link, Vice Pres. for Advancement
Dr. Warren Rosenberg, Dean of School of Arts & Sciences
Dr. Nicholas Beutell, Dean of the Hagan School of Business
Ms. Joy Collins, Dir. of Libraries
Priests 3
Brothers 27
Sisters 11
Lay Teachers 468
Students 4,897

New York
Archdiocese of New York

College of Mount Saint Vincent
(Coed)
6301 Riverdale Ave.
New York, NY 10471-1093
Tel: 718-405-3200; Fax: 718-549-2603
E-mail: cfinegan@cmsv.edu
Web Site: http://www.cmsv.edu
Founded by the Sisters of Charity of Saint Vincent de Paul. Chartered by the University of the State of New York.
Mary C. Stuart, Ph.D., Pres.
Michael J. McGovern, Ed.D., Vice Pres., Academic Affairs
Theresa D. Whitesell, C.F.R.E., Vice Pres. Institutional Advancement
Brothers 1
Sisters 8
Lay Faculty 64
Total Enrollment 1,563

Marymount Manhattan College
Chartered by the Univ. of the State of NY.
221 E. 71st St.
New York, NY 10021
Tel: 212-517-0400
Dr. Regina S. Peruggi, Pres.
Paula Mayhew, Vice Pres. Academic Affairs
Rosemarie Dackerman, Vice Pres. Student Affairs
Arnold Dimond, Vice Pres. Business & Financial Affairs
Mary Kay Demetry-Jeynes, Dean Courses for Adults
Diana Zwirn, Dir. College Rels. & Inst. Advancement
Sisters 4
Students 1,330

Newburgh
Archdiocese of New York

Mt. St. Mary College (1954)
Newburgh, NY 12550
Tel: 914-561-0800
E-mail: coyne@msmc.edu
Web Site: http://www.msmc.edu
(Coed)
Sr. Ann Sakac, O.P., Pres.
Sr. Agnes Boyle, O.P., Academic Dean
Gerald Jilbert, Registrar
Rev. James Gilhooley, Chap.
Divisions: Arts & Letters; Education; Business; Nursing; Natural Sciences; Mathematics & Computer Science; Philosophy & Religious Studies; Social Sciences.
Sisters 8
Lay Teachers 46
Students 1,950

Niagara University
Diocese of Buffalo

Niagara University
Lewiston Rd.
Niagara University, NY 14109-2015
Tel: 716-285-1212; Fax: 716-286-8355
E-mail: jbm@niagara.edu
Web Site: www.niagara.edu
Rev. Paul L. Golden, C.M., Pres.
Susan E. Mason, Ph.D., Vice Pres. for Academic Affairs
David M. Alexander, Vice Pres. for Bus. Affairs
Rev. Francis X. Prior, C.M., Vice Pres. Devel. & Univ. Rels., Emeritus
Sheila L. Hausrath, M.S.Ed., Vice Pres. for Student Life
Richard S. Hopkins, B.S., Vice Pres. for Univ. Advancement
Rev. Vincent J. O'Malley, C.M., Senior Asst. to the Pres. for Mission
Dr. Judith S. Willard, Asst. Pres. for Planning
Dolores A. Bower, R.N., Ph.D., Dean, College of Nursing
Nancy E. McGlen, Ph.D., Acting Dean, College of Arts & Science
Keith T. Miller, Ph.D., Dean, College of Business Administration
Rev. Daniel F. O'Leary, O.M.I., Dean, College of Education
George C. Pachter, Jr., M.S.Ed., Dean, Enrollment Management
JoAnne E. Wray, M.S., Dean, Division of Lifelong Learning
Mark D. LaRoach, M.S., Asst. Vice Pres. for Academic Affairs
Patricia G. Kinner, M.A., Dir., Academic Support
Leslie Morris, M.L.S., Dir. Library
Sandra H. Olsen, Ph.D., Dir. Castellani Art Museum
Maureen Salfi, M.S.Ed., Dir. Fin. Aid
John B. Stranges, Ph.D., Univ. Prof.
James Williams, Ed.D., Chair, Center for Study and Stabilization of Black Families
David J. Boyda, M.S.Ed., Dir., Campus Activities
Mary Beth Coates, M.S., Dir. Campus Min.
Joseph H. Cuda, M.A., Dean Student Affairs
Maureen L. Dever-Bumba, N.P., Dir. Health Svcs.
Blake H. Dye, M.P.A., Dir. Multicultural Student Affairs
Thomas McDermott, M.S., Dir. Counseling Svcs.
Martha E. Troia, M.S., Dir. Career Dev.
Kimberly J. Zukowski, M.S.Ed., Dir. University Housing
Sandra Mann Ormsby, B.A., Alumni Dir.
Linus L. Ormsby, M.S.Ed., Dir. Public Relations
Jeannine Brown Miller, M.A., Dir. Human Resources
Revs.:
John C. Bowes, C.M., Assistant Prof. of Rel. Studies

Kevin G. Creagh, C.M., Campus Min.
Patrick S. Flanagan, C.M., Campus Min.
William L. Green, C.M., Dir. SELF
Joseph G. Hubbert, C.M., Asst. Prof. Rel. Studies
John Kettelberger, C.M., Supr. of Vincentian Community
Gregory L. Klein, O.Carm., Asst. Prof. of Rel. Studies
Thomas P. McGourty, C.M., Adjunct Prof. of Rel. Studies
Louis P. Trotta, C.M., Asst. Pres. Alumni Relations
Garvey C. Meade, Adjunct Prof. of Foreign Language
Bros.:
Stephen J. Kennedy, C.M., Dir. St. Vincent de Paul
Martin Schneider, C.M., Coordinator Conv.
Augustine D. Towey, C.M., Prof. of English and Theatre Studies
Meade Hall:
In res.,
Revs.:
Michael J. Tumulty, C.M.
Peter A. Fitzgerald, C.M.
Martin J. Sleasman, C.M.
John J. Trainor, C.M.
Thomas P. Mallaghan, C.M.
Priests 4
Brothers 1
Lay Teachers 112
Sisters 2
Students 3,075
Total Staff 261
Founded in 1856 by the Congregation of the Mission (Vincentian Community of Priests & Brothers). Niagara University is composed of the College of Arts & Sciences; Business Education; Nursing; The Division of Lifelong Learning; and The Institute of Travel & Hotel- Restaurant Administration

Ogdensburg
Diocese of Ogdensburg

Mater Dei College
5428 State Hwy. 37
Ogdensburg, NY 13669
Tel: 315-393-5930; Fax: 315-393-5056
Leigh Wilcox, D.V.M., Interim Pres.
Sr. M. Bethany Fitzgerald, S.S.J., Chap.
In res.,
Rev. Charles J. Richard
Sisters of St. Joseph 3
Lay Teachers 30
Students 508

Orangeburg
Archdiocese of New York

Dominican College of Blauvelt
Orangeburg, NY 10962
Tel: 914-359-7800
Web Site: http://www.dc.edu
Chartered by Univ. of the State of NY.
Sr. Kathleen Sullivan, O.P., Pres.
Dr. Leigh Holt, Dean
Sr. M. Noel Dwyer, O.P., Registrar
Sisters 15
Lay Teachers 55
Students 1,725

Patchogue
Diocese of Rockville Centre

St. Joseph's College
155 W. Roe Blvd.
Patchogue, NY 11772-2399
Tel: 516-447-3200; Fax: 516-654-1782
Sr. Loretta McGrann, C.S.J.
Priests on Faculty:
Revs.:
Angelo Ditta
Thomas Petriano
Frank Pizzarelli, S.M.M.
Sisters 16
Lay Teachers 52
Students 2,398

Poughkeepsie
Archdiocese of New York

Marist College
(Coed)
Poughkeepsie, NY 12601-1328
Tel: 914-575-3000
E-mail: hmaltmi@marista.marist.edu
Web Site: http://www.marist.edu
Dennis J. Murray, Ph.D., Pres.
Rev. Luke W. Cann, Ph.D., Chap.
Priests 2
Brothers 8
Lay Teachers 160
Students 4,300
Marist Foreign Missions
Bro. Paul Ambrose, F.M.S.

Rochester
Diocese of Rochester

St. Bernard's Institute
1100 S. Goodman St.
Rochester, NY 14620
Tel: 716-271-3657
Dr. Patricia A. Schoelles, S.S.J., Pres.
Margery Halpin, Dir. at Albany
Dr. Stephen Graff, Coord.Certificate Designated Ministry,Perm. Diaconate Formation & Dir. Admission
Dr. Cy Young, Dir. of Development
Judith Ann Kollar, Dir. Continuing Education
Dr. Marvin Mich, Dean
Ms. Mary Ann LaCour, Dir. Business Affairs
Dr. Devadasan Premnath, Registrar
Rev. Robert Kennedy, Coord. of Student Formation
Total Staff 10
Total enrollment 152

Rockville Centre
Diocese of Rockville Centre

Molloy College
1000 Hempstead Ave.
Rockville Centre, NY 11571-5002
Tel: 516-678-5000; 888-4-MOLLOY
Web Site: http://molloy.edu
Martin D. Snyder, Ph.D., Pres.
Sr. Patricia Morris, O.P., Ph.D., Vice Pres. Academic Affairs (Academic Dean)
Sr. Dorothy Anne Fitzgibbons, O.P., Ed.D., Exec. Asst. to Pres.
Sr. Joan Garvey, O.P.
Catherine C. Krein, M.A., Vice Pres. External Affairs
Tony Mancaluso, C.F.O. & Treas.
Wayne F. James, M.S., Assoc. Vice Pres. Enrollment Management
James A. O'Reilly, Jr., M.A., Registrar
Lisa Kandell, Dir. Financial Aid
Sr. Doris Nevitt, O.P., M.A., Dir. Student Financial Svcs.
Rev. John A. Madigan, O.P., M.B.A., Chap. for Sisters
John Southard, Chief Information Officer
Joan Merlo, Dir. Planning & Research
Priests 3
Ministers 4
Sisters of St. Dominic (Amityville Community) 32
Lay Teachers 240
Students 2,298

Sparkill
Archdiocese of New York

St. Thomas Aquinas College
Sparkill, NY 10976
Tel: 914-398-4000; Fax: 914-359-8136
Founded by Dominican Sisters of Sparkill in 1952. Senior coed college, chartered by Univ. of the State of New York.
Sr. Margaret M. Fitzpatrick, S.C., Ed.D., Pres.
Dr. Peter O'Connor, Vice Pres. Academic Affairs
Priests 1
Sisters 9
Lay Professors 65
Students 2,100

St. Bonaventure
Diocese of Buffalo

St. Bonaventure University
St. Bonaventure, NY 14778
Tel: 716-375-2000; Fax: 716-375-2055
E-mail: fstorms@sbu.edu
Web Site: http://www.sbu.edu
Franciscan Friars, Province of the Holy Name, Order of Friars Minor.
School of Arts and Sciences, School of Education, Business School of Journalism/Mass Communication; Franciscan Studies and the Franciscan Institute; Graduate Studies.
Administration:
Robert J. Wickenheiser, Ph.D., Pres.
Edward K. Eckert, Ph.D., Vice Pres. Academic Affairs
Donald L. Zekan, Ed.D., Vice Pres. Business & Finance
Rev. Anthony M. Carrozzo, O.F.M., D.Min., Vice Pres. for the Franciscan Charism
George F. Solan, M.S., Vice Pres. Student Life
Mary E. Freeman, B.A., Vice Pres. Public Relations
David L. Diles, Ed.D., Vice Pres. & Dir. Athletics
Rev. Francis Storms, O.F.M., M.A., Asst. to Pres.
James P. White, Ph.D., Dean, School of Arts & Sciences
Rev. Anthony M. Carrozzo, O.F.M., D.Min., Dean, School of Franciscan Studies; Dir. The Franciscan Institute
John H. Burns, Ph.D., Dean, School of Business & Graduate Studies
Carol Anne Pierson, Ph.D., Dean, School of Educ.
Lee Coppola, J.D., Dean, Russel J. Jandoli School of Journalism & Mass Communication
John V. Apczynski, Ph.D., Dean, Clare College
Jon Boeckenstedt, B.A., Dean, Enrollment Mgmt.
Alex P. Nazemetz, M.S., Dir. Admissions
Mary K. Piccioli, M.B.A., Dir. Financial Aid
Barbara Russell, M.S., Registrar
Sharon D. Hannah, M.S.Ed.D., N.C.C., Dir. Counseling & Career Development
Stephen Plesac, M.S., Dir. Student Activities
John Frazier, M.A.E.D., Dir. Residence Life
Joseph Flanagan, M.S., Dir. Alumni Services
June T. Solan, M.S., Dir. Human Resources
Margaret T. Bryner, M.S., Dir. Higher Educ. Opportunities Program (HEOP)
Jean T. Ehman, M.A., Dir. The Teaching & Learning Center
Rajeev N. Parikh, Ph.D., Lifelong Learning
Alice F. Sayegh, M.S., Advisor, International Student Advisement
Gordon F. Murray, B.S., Exec. Dir. Technology Svcs.
Paul J. Spaeth, M.L.S., M.A., Dir. Library
Constance F. Whitcomb, M.S.Ed., Dir. Career Devel.
Sr. Mary Kathryn Dougherty, O.S.F.,, M.A., Dir. of University Ministries
Rev. Jack Zilbert, O.F.M., Ph.D., Guardian of the Friary
Priests 20
Brothers 7
Sisters 5
Lay Professors 149
Students 2,822
Friar Community
St. Bonaventure, NY 14778
Bros.:
Thomas Cole, O.F.M.
David Haack, O.F.M.
Anthony J. LoGalbo, O.F.M., Vicar
Michael Montgomery, O.F.M.
Adrian A. Riester, O.F.M.
Julian Riester, O.F.M.
Basil Valente, O.F.M.
Revs.:
Giles Bello, O.F.M.
Michael Blastic, O.F.M.Conv.
Thomas Blow, O.F.M.
J. Gregory Brennan, O.F.M.
Anthony M. Carrozzo, O.F.M.
Mathias F. Doyle, O.F.M.
Regis Duffy, O.F.M.
Richard Flaherty, O.F.M.
Gedeon Gal, O.F.M.
Peter Schneible, O.F.M.
Xavier Seubert, O.F.M.
Robert Stewart, O.F.M.
Francis Storms, O.F.M.
Alphonus A. Trabold, O.F.M.
Allen Weber, O.F.M.
Robert H. White, O.F.M.
Gervase F. White, O.F.M.
Alan Wolter, O.F.M.
Jack Zibert, O.F.M., Guardian
Holy Peace Friary
Mt. Irenaeus
West Clarksville, NY 14786-0100
Bro. Joseph A. Kotula, O.F.M.
Revs.:
James Falduti, O.F.M.
Daniel A. Hurley, O.F.M.
Louis M. McCormick, O.F.M.
Daniel P. Riley, O.F.M., Guardian, Dir.

Staten Island
Diocese of Brooklyn

St. John's University, Staten Island Campus
300 Howard Ave.
Staten Island, NY 10301
Tel: 718-390-4545; Fax: 718-816-4520
Web Site: http://www.stjohns.edu
Sponsored by the Vincentian Priests and Brothers Eastern Province of the Congregation of the Mission.
Rev. Donald J. Harrington, C.M., Pres.
Officers of Administration:
Robert J. Crimmins, Exec. Vice Pres.
Tony H. Bonaparte, Ph.D., Provost
Rev. Michael J. Carroll, C.M., Vice Pres. Campus

Ministry & Rome Campus
Cecilia S. Chang, Ed.D., Vice Pres. Intl. Rels.
John P. Connolly, Jr., Vice Pres. Administrative Svcs.
Rev. Joseph V. Daly, C.M., Asst. to the Pres.
Susan L. Ebbs, Ed.D., Vice Pres. Student Life
Dorothy E. Habben, Ph.D., Vice Pres. & Univ. Sec.
Suzanne M. Halpin, Vice Pres. Communications
Rev. James F. Kiernan, C.M., Senior Vice Pres., Staten Island Campus
James P. Pellow, Vice Pres. Finance & Treas.
Joseph Sciame, Vice Pres. Govt. & Community Rels.
Rev. Bernard M. Tracey, C.M., Vice Pres. Inst. Advancement
Priests 21
Sisters 2
Lay Teachers 559
Staten Island Campus Enrollment 2,382
Total Undergraduate & Graduate Enrollment 16,384

Archdiocese of New York

St. John's University Staten Island Campus
300 Howard Ave.
Staten Island, NY 10301
Tel: 718-390-4545; Fax: 718-816-4520
Vincentian Community
Very Rev. Donald J. Harrington, C.M., Pres.
Rev. James F. Kiernan, C.M., Senior Vice Pres.-Staten Island
Dr. Judith Dwyer, Assoc. Vice Pres. & Dean Notre Dame College
Donna Narducci, Asst. Dean & Dir. Programs Colleges of Business
Kathleen MacDonald, Dean St. Vincent's College
Dr. Stephen Kuntz, Asst. Dean, School of Education, Graduate Div.
Mr. James R. Guilbert, Dean, Office of Student Life

Syracuse
Diocese of Syracuse

Le Moyne College
Syracuse, NY 13214
Rev. Robert A. Mitchell, S.J., Pres.
Dr. Kurt F. Geisinger, Academic Vice Pres.
Dr. Michael W. Yost, Vice Pres. Student Life
Dr. W. Richard Merriman, Jr., Vice Pres. for Institutional Advancement
Ms. Genevieve R. Saya, Vice Pres. Campus Svcs. & Asst. to Pres.
Mr. Thomas E. O'Neil, Vice Pres. for Finance & Treasurer
Mrs. Barbara M. Maylone, Assoc. Dean Student Life/Dir. Campus Activities
Mr. C. Joseph Behan, Asst. Dean of Student Life
Rev. Edmund G. Ryan, S.J., Special Asst. to the Pres. for Mission & Planning
Dr. Marcia Rowe, Academic Dean
Miss Dorothy A. Namishia, Registrar
Mr. Dennis R. DePerro, Dean of Enrollment Management

Tarrytown
Archdiocese of New York

Marymount College
Tarrytown, NY 10591
Tel: 914-631-3200
E-mail: admiss@mmt.marymt.edu
Web Site: http://www.marymt.edu
Founded by the Religious of the Sacred Heart of Mary. Women Resident and non-resident.
Sr. Brigid Driscoll, R.S.H.M., Ph.D., Pres.
Roberta Matthews, Ph.D., Vice Pres. Academic Affairs & Dean of Faculty
Sisters 4
Lay Teachers 52
Students 1,229

NORTH CAROLINA

Belmont
Diocese of Charlotte

Belmont Abbey College
100 Belmont-Mount Holly Rd.
Belmont, NC 28012-2795
Tel: 704-825-6700; Fax: 704-825-6670
E-mail: schup@crusader.bac.edu
Web Site: bac.edu
(Coed) Liberal Arts Senior College.
Dr. Robert A. Preston, Pres.
Rt. Rev. Oscar Burnett, O.S.B., Chancellor
Rev. Placid D. Solari, O.S.B., Academic Dean
Margaret Skidmore, Registrar
Dr. Elizabeth Sechler, Dir. Campus Ministry
Dr. Mike McLeod, Dean, Student Life
Mr. James Schuppenhauer, Vice Pres. Admin. & Finance
Mr. Denis M. Stokes, Vice Pres. Enrollment Mgmt.
Marjorie C. McDermott, Librarian
Priests 4
Lay Teachers 33
Students 902
The Ecumenical Institute of Wake Forest University and Belmont Abbey College
Mrs. Margaret Arndt, Dir.
P.O. Box 2143
Blowing Rock, NC 28605

Sacred Heart College
100 Mercy Dr.
Belmont, NC 28012
Tel: 704-829-5110; Fax: 704-829-5137
Sisters of Mercy
Sr. M. Rosalind Picot, R.S.M., Pres.
College ceased academic operation, effective August 1987. Corporation intact.

NORTH DAKOTA

Bismarck
Diocese of Bismarck

University of Mary
7500 University Dr.
Bismarck, ND 58504-9652
Tel: 701-255-7500
E-mail: marauder@umary.edu
Web Site: http://www.umary.edu
Sr. Thomas Welder, O.S.B., Pres.
Thomas P. Johnson, Vice Pres. Academic Affairs
Revs.:
Daniel Maloney, O.S.B.
Richard Wilhelmi, O.S.B.
Denis Fournier, O.S.B.
Victor Feser, O.S.B.
Valerian Odermann, O.S.B., Chap.
Priests 3
Sisters 5
Lay Teachers 72
Students 2,148

OHIO

Cincinnati
Archdiocese of Cincinnati

College of Mount St. Joseph
5701 Delhi Rd.
Cincinnati, OH 45233-1670
Tel: 513-244-4200
E-mail: greggrady@mail.msj.edu
Web Site: www.msj.edu
Coed. Chartered by the State of Ohio.
Sr. Francis Marie Thrailkill, O.S.U., Pres.
Sr. John Miriam Jones, Ph.D., Academic Dean
Rev. Angelo A. della Picca (Italy)
Faculty:
Sisters 4
Lay Teachers 97
Students 2,205

Xavier University
3800 Victory Pkwy. at Dana Ave.
Cincinnati, OH 45207
Tel: 513-745-3000
Rev. James E. Hoff, S.J., Pres.
Vice Presidents:
Revs.:
J. Leo Klein, S.J.
Michael J. Graham, S.J.
Dr. James E. Bundschuh
Dr. Ronald Slepitza
Dr. J. Richard Hirte
Mr. John F. Kucia
Revs.:
Joseph A. Bracken, S.J., Rector, Jesuit Community
Richard W. Bollman, S.J., Pastor, Bellarmine Chapel
Mr. David Sauter, Registrar
Valerie Withiam, Assoc. V.P. for Marketing
Dr. Max Keck, Dean, College of Arts & Sciences
Rev. Thomas P. Kennealy, S.J., Assoc. Dean, College of Arts & Sciences and College of Social Sciences
Dr. Michael Webb, Dean, College of Business Admin.
Dr. James Brodzinski, Assoc. Dean, College of Business Administration
Dr. Neil R. Heighberger, Dean, College of Social Sciences
Ms. Susan G. Wideman, Dean, Center for Adult and Part-Time Students
Dr. Charles A. Edington, Assoc. Vice Pres. Enrollment Svcs.
Enrollment: College of Arts & Sciences:
Students 1,869
College of Business Administration:
Students 684
College of Social Sciences:
Students 1,038
Center for Adult and Part-Time Students:
Students 324
Graduate Programs:
Students 2,589
Permanent Staff:
Priests 15
Sisters 2
Faculty (full-time):
Priests 9
Lay Teachers 255

Cleveland
Diocese of Cleveland

John Carroll Jesuit Community
E-mail: jesuits@jcvaxa.jcu.edu
John Carroll University
University Heights
Cleveland, OH 44118
Tel: 216-397-1886; Fax: 216-397-4228
Revs.:
Peter J. Fennessy, S.J., Rector
John A. Knapek, S.J., Min.
William M. Bichl, S.J.
Casimir R. Bukala, S.J.
Emmanuel M. Carreira, S.J. (Spain)
Gregory N.P. Konz, S.J.
Stephen T. Krupa, S.J.
Francis P. Lihvar, S.J.
William H. Nichols, S.J.
Joseph P. Owens, S.J.
Daniel T. Reim, S.J.
Francis X. Ryan, S.J.
Gerald J. Sabo, S.J.
Richard P. Salmi, S.J.
Joseph O. Schell, S.J.
Thomas L. Schubeck, S.J.
John J. Shea, S.J.
Francis J. Smith, S.J.
Ernest G. Spittler, S.J.
Michael J. Vjecha, S.J.
Bros.:
Michael L. Nusbaum, S.J.
Donald J. Dunbar, S.J., Scholastic
Priests 20
Brothers 1
Scholastics 1

John Carroll University
North Park & Miramar Blvd.
Cleveland, OH 44118
Tel: 216-397-1886
Web Site: http://www.jcu.edu
Rev. John J. Shea, S.J., Pres.
Mr. W. D. Bookwalter, Vice Pres. & Asst. to the Pres.
Revs.:
Peter Fennessy, S.J., Vice Pres. & Dir. Campus Ministry, Religious Affairs
Richard P. Salmi, S.J., Vice Pres. Student Affairs
Mr. Paul Kantz, Vice Pres. Devel.
Mr. Jonathan Ivec, Vice Pres. Business
Mr. John T. Reali, Vice Pres. Services
Dr. David M. LaGuardia, Asst. Academic Vice Pres.
Dr. Frederick F. Travis, Provost and Academic Vice Pres.
Dr. Donald Czapski, Special Asst. to Pres.
Dr. Frank J. Navratil, Dean, Boler School of Business
Dr. Nick Baumgartner, Dean, College of Arts & Sciences
Dr. Sally Wertheim, Dean of Graduate School
Dr. Joseph B. Miller, Assoc. Dean, College of Arts & Sciences
Rev. William M. Bichl, S.J., Asst. Dean, College of Arts & Sciences
Mrs. Martha A. Mackie, Asst. Dean, College of Arts & Sciences
Dr. James Daley, Assoc. Dean, Boler School of Business
Priests 15
Sisters 1
Lay Faculty 215
Students 4,391

Notre Dame College of Ohio
(Women)
E-mail: ndc.edu
Web Site: www.ndc.edu
4545 College Rd.
South Euclid, OH 44121
Tel: 216-381-1680; Fax: 216-381-3802
Anne L. Deming, Ph.D., Pres.
Sr. Margaret Gorman, S.N.D., Exec. Vice Pres.
Marilyn Jones, Ph.D., Vice Pres. Academic Affairs
Priests 1
Sisters of Notre Dame 10
Lay Teachers 27
Total Staff 105

Students 685

Ursuline College
2550 Lander Rd.
Pepper Pike, OH 44124
Tel: 440-449-4200; Fax: 440-646-8102
E-mail: urspub@aol.com
Web Site: www.ursuline.edu
Diana Stano, Ph.D., Pres.
JoAnne Podis, Ph.D., Vice Pres. Academic Affairs
Valerie A. Hughes, Vice Pres. Fin. & Admin.
Deanne Hurley, Dean Students
Sr. Anna Margaret Gilbride, O.S.U., Ph.D., Asst. to the Pres.
Kathleen Burke, Ph.D., Interim Dean Graduate Studies
Ursuline Nuns of Cleveland 14
Lay Professors 56
Students 1,233

Columbus
Diocese of Columbus

Ohio Dominican College
1216 Sunbury Rd.
Columbus, OH 43219
Tel: 614-253-2741; Fax: 614-252-0776
E-mail: admissions@odc.edu
Web Site: http://www.odc.edu
Dominican Sisters of the Third Order of St. Dominic
Sr. Mary Andrew Matesich, O.P., Pres.
Andrew Keogh, Vice Pres. Academic Affiars
James Sagona, Vice Pres. Admissions & Student Svcs.
Michael D. Bromberg, Vice Pres. Business Affiars
Lynda Huey, Vice Pres. College Advancement
James Grove, Dir. Campus Ministry & Lecturer in Theology Studies
Sisters 11
Lay Teachers 104
Students 1,949

Dayton
Archdiocese of Cincinnati

The University of Dayton (1850)
(Coed)
300 College Park Ave.
Dayton, OH 45469-1624
Tel: 937-229-1000
Web Site: www.udayton.edu
Bro. Raymond L. Fitz, S.M., Pres.
Rev. James L. Heft, S.M., Chancellor & Prof. of Faith
Dr. John O. Geiger, Provost
Dr. Patrick F. Palermo, Assoc. Provost, Faculty & Academic Affairs
Mr. Christopher Munoz, Assoc. Provost, Enrollment Mgmt.
Bro. Bernard J. Ploeger, S.M., Senior Vice Pres.-Admin.
Mr. Thomas E. Burkhardt, Vice Pres. for Financial Affairs & Treas.
Mr. Theodore L. Kissell, Dir. of Athletics
Dr. William C. Schuerman, Vice Pres. Student Devel. & Dean of Students
Rev. Eugene J. Contadino, S.M., Rector
Ms. Lisa Rismiller, Exec. Asst. to the Pres.
Mr. Richard T. Ferguson, Asst. to the Pres. for Regional & Government Relations
Mr. Herman A. Cole, Dir. Facilities Mgmt.
Mr. Thomas J. Westendorf, Registrar
Mr. Myron H. Achbach, Dir. Admissions
Mrs. Joyce J. Wilkins, Dir. Financial Aid
Revs.:
Norbert C. Burns, S.M.
Gerald T. Chinchar, S.M.
Matthew F. Kohmescher, S.M.
William P. Frost
Joseph F. Kozar, S.M.
Robert J. Hater
James L. Heft, S.M.
Paul F. Vieson, S.M.
Theodore A. Koehler, S.M.
Joseph H. Lackner, S.M.
Thomas A. Schroer, S.M.
John S. Putka, S.M.
Bertrand A. Buby, S.M.
Christopher W. Conlon, S.M., Dir., Campus Ministry
John A. McGrath, S.M.
Johann B.G. Roten, S.M.
Thomas A. Schoen, S.M.
Thomas A. Thompson, S.M., Dir. and Curator, Marian Library
Joseph D. Massucci
Sr. Nancy H. Bramlage, S.C.
Sr. Laura M. Leming, F.M.I., (On Leave)
Sr. Kathleen A. Rossman, O.S.F.
Sr. Judith G. Martin, S.S.J.
Sr. Jody O'Neil, S.P.
Sr. Pamela L. Thimmes, O.S.F.
Sr. Frances M. Trampiets, S.C.
Sr. Angela Ann Zukowski, M.H.S.H.
Sr. M. Jean Frisk
Sr. Monica M. Gundler, S.C.
Sr. Mary Louise Foley, F.M.I.
Sr. Eileen J. Cehyra, F.M.I.
Sr. Judith Keehnen, C.S.J.
Sr. Leanne M. Jablonski, F.M.I.
Sr. Ellen M. Murphy, O.P.
Society of Mary (Marianists)
College of Arts and Sciences
Dr. Paul J. Morman, Dean
Dr. Fred P. Pestella, Assoc. Dean
Dr. Mary Jo Vesper, Assoc. Dean
Mr. Sam F. Johnson, Asst. Dean
Mrs. Rae Ellen Huff, Asst. Dean.
Professors 224
Students 3,176
Graduate Studies and Research
Dr. Gordon A. Sargent, Vice Pres. Graduate Studies & Research and Dean of Graduate School
Dr. Katy E. Marre, Assoc. Dean of the Grad. School
Ms. Carol M. Shaw, Dir. Center for Competitive Change
Students 3,321
School of Business Administration
Dr. Sam Gould, Dean
Dr. John E. Rapp, Assoc. Dean
Dr. E. James Dunne, Assoc. Dean & Dir., MBA Prog.
Professors 46
Students 1,100
School of Education
Dr. Patricia F. First, Dean
Dr. Joseph F. Rogus, Assoc. Dean for Graduate Studies
Dr. Donald J. Frericks, Asst.
Dr. James R. Biddle, Assoc. Dean
Professors 42
Students 839
School of Engineering
Dr. Blake E. Cherrington, Dean
Dr. Donald L. Moon, Assoc. Dean for Graduate Engineering Programs & Research
Dr. Richard J. Kee, Interim Asst. Dean
Professors 71
Students 1,214
School of Law
Francis J. Conte, Dean
Mr. Richard P. Perna, Assoc. Dean for Academic Affairs
Mr. Charles Roboski, Asst. Dean and Dir. of Admissions and Financial Aid
Mr. Timothy P. Stonecash, Asst. Dean of Law School Development
Professors 21
Students 483
Libraries and Information Technologies
Dr. Edward D. Garten, Dean of Libraries and Information Technology
Total Enrollment 10,320
Faculty 404
The Marian Library / International Marian Research Institute (IMRI)
Revs.:
Johann B.G. Roten, S.M., S.T.D., Dir.
Thomas A. Thompson, S.M., Dir. & Curator
Theodore A. Koehler, S.M., S.T.D., Dir. Emeritus
University of Dayton
Dayton, OH 45469-1390
Tel: 937-229-4214

North Canton
Diocese of Youngstown

Walsh University
(Coed)
2020 Easton St., N.W.
North Canton, OH 44720-3396
Tel: 330-499-7090
Web Site: http://www.walsh.edu
Brothers of Christian Instruction
Rev. Donald A. Miller, O.F.M., Ph.D., (St. John the Baptist Province)
Sr. Carol Herbert, S.S.J., Campus Min.
Kenneth N. Hamilton, Jr., Ph.D., Pres.
Mr. Dale Howard, Vice Pres. for Student Affairs
James C. Foster, Ph.D., Vice Pres. Academic Affairs & Dean of the College
Doug Swartz, Dir. Admissions
Priests 1
Brothers 5
Sisters 1
Lay Teachers 124
Total Staff 203
Students 1,306

Saint Martin
Archdiocese of Cincinnati

Chatfield College
Brown County Ursulines, 20918 State Rte. 251
Saint Martin, OH 45118
Tel: 937-875-3344; Fax: 937-875-3912
Sr. Margaret Anne Dougherty, R.S.M.
Students 300

Steubenville
Diocese of Steubenville

Franciscan University of Steubenville
University Blvd.
Steubenville, OH 43952
Tel: 740-283-3771
E-mail: admissions@franuniv.edu
Web Site: www.franuniv.edu
Rev. Michael Scanlan, T.O.R., Pres.
Mr. David Skiviat, Vice Pres. Finance & Admin.
Dr. Michael J. Healy, Dean of Faculty
Mr. Nicholas Healy, Jr., Vice Pres. Univ. Rels.
Mr. John Madigan, Vice Pres. Community Rels.
Mr. Randall Cirner, Dean of Students
Ms. Sharon Kilzer, Sec. of the Univ.
Revs.:
Thomas Bourque, T.O.R., Provost
Brian Cavanaugh, T.O.R., Student Svcs.
Richard Davis, T.O.R., Community Rels.
Jose Del Toro, T.O.R., Admissions Counselor
Giles Dimock, O.P., (Austria) Assoc. Prof.
Conrad Harkins, O.F.M., Assoc. Prof.
Robert Hilz, T.O.R.
Stanley Holland, T.O.R., Dir. of Works of Mercy
Joseph Lehman, T.O.R., Res. Hall Chap.
Ronald Mohnickey, T.O.R., Religious Admin.
Aidan Mullaney, T.O.R., (Austria) Campus Ministry
Daniel Pattee, T.O.R, Lecturer
David Pivonka, T.O.R., Campus Ministry & Lecturer
Dominic Scotto, T.O.R., Univ. Chap.
Daniel Sinisi, T.O.R., Assoc. Prof.
Edmund J. Sylvia (Austria) (BGP) Student Life
David Testa (ALB) Campus Min.
Laurence Uhlman, T.O.R., Chap.
Priests 5
Lay Teachers 86
Students 1,997

Sylvania
Diocese of Toledo

Lourdes College
6832 Convent Blvd.
Sylvania, OH 43560
Tel: 419-885-3211
E-mail: rturek@lourdes.edu
Web Site: www.lourdes.edu
Sisters of St. Francis of the Congregation of Our Lady of Lourdes, (O.S.F.).
Sr. M. Ann Francis Klimkowski, O.S.F., Pres.
Sr. M. Cabrini Warpeha, O.S.F., Vice Pres. Academic Affairs
Sr. Nancy Ann Surma, O.S.F., Vice Pres. Admin. Svcs.
Robert Turek, Vice Pres. Student Svcs.
G. Patrick Williams, Vice Pres. Inst. Advancement
Sue Bucher, Registrar
Sisters 16
Full-time faculty 70
Lay instructors 51
Enrollment 1,535

OKLAHOMA

Shawnee
Archdiocese of Oklahoma City

St. Gregory's University
(Coed)
Shawnee, OK 74801
Tel: 405-878-5100; Fax: 405-878-5170
Liberal Arts and Sciences.
Benedictine Monks
Mr. Frank Pfaff, Ph.D., Pres.
Priests 8
Brothers 2
Sisters 2
Lay Teachers 30
Students 600

OREGON

Marylhurst
Archdiocese of Portland in Oregon

Marylhurst College
Marylhurst, OR 97036

Tel: 503-636-8141
E-mail: president@marylhurst.edu
Web Site: http://www.marylhurst.edu
Dr. NANCY WILGENBUSCH, Pres.
DENIS LAWRENCE, Vice Pres. Academic Affairs & Contact Person
Sisters 8
Lay Teachers 212
Students 2,763

Portland
Archdiocese of Portland in Oregon

**University of Portland*
5000 N. Willamette Blvd.
Portland, OR 97203
Tel: 503-283-7911
E-mail: webmaster@uofport.edu
Web Site: www.uofport.edu
Endowed by the Congregation of Holy Cross; established 1901.
Exec. Officers of the Univ.:
Rev. DAVID T. TYSON, C.S.C., Pres.
Dr. ARTHUR A. SCHULTE, JR., Special Asst. to the Pres. & Exec. Vice Pres. Emeritus
Bro. DONALD J. STABROWSKI, C.S.C., Academic Vice Pres.
Mr. ANTHONY J. DISPIGNO, Vice Pres. Univ. Rels.
Dr. JOHN GOLDRICK, Interim Vice Pres. Student Svcs.
Dr. ROY HEYNDERICKX, Financial V.P.
Faculty Staff:
Revs.:
RICHARD F. BERG, C.S.C.
GEORGE C. BERNARD, C.S.C.
JAMES CONNELLY, C.S.C., Religious Supr.
MICHAEL M. DELANEY, C.S.C.
BARRY J. HAGAN, C.S.C.
THOMAS HOSINSKI, C.S.C.
WILLIAM HUND, C.S.C.
JOHN KURTZKE, C.S.C.
EDWIN OBERMILLER, C.S.C.
DENNIS O'HARE, C.S.C.
CLAUDE POMERLEAU, C.S.C.
RICHARD RUTHERFORD, C.S.C.
JEFFREY SCHNEIBEL, C.S.C.
CHARLES D. SHERRER, C.S.C.
JEFFREY SOBOSAN, C.S.C.
PHILIP SOPKE, C.S.C.
ARTHUR F. WHEELER, C.S.C.
In res.,
Revs.:
FREDERICK BARR, C.S.C.
GEORGE C. BERNARD, C.S.C.
THOMAS BILL, C.S.C.
G. JAMES BRADY, C.S.C.
HARRY BRIDE, C.S.C.
PAUL FRYBERGER, C.S.C.
CHESTER PRUSYNSKI, C.S.C.
ADRIEN STE. MARIE, C.S.C.
ARTHUR SCHOENFELDT, C.S.C.
STEPHEN J. SEDLOCK, C.S.C.
Bros.:
KEN ALLEN, C.S.C.
FULGENCE DOUGHERTY, C.S.C.
DANIEL MALLON, C.S.C.
FREDERICK WILLIAMS, C.S.C.
Priests 27
Brothers 5
Sisters 5
Lay Teachers 126
Adjunct Faculty 104
Students 2,821
Following is the Academic Structure of the University:
College of Arts and Sciences—
Dr. MARLENE MOORE, Dean
School of Nursing—
Dr. SUSAN MOSCATO, Dean
School of Business Administration—
Dr. RONALD HILL, Dean
School of Engineering—
Dr. ZIA J. YAMAYEE, Dean
School of Education—
Sr. MARIA CIRIELLO, O.P., Dean
Graduate School—
Dr. KARL J. WETZEL, Dean

PENNSYLVANIA

Aston
Archdiocese of Philadelphia

Neumann College
One Neumann Dr.
Aston, PA 19014-1298
Tel: 610-459-0905
E-mail: neumann@smtpgate.neumann.edu
Web Site: http://www.neumann.edu
Opened September 1965.
Sponsored by the Sisters of St. Francis of Philadelphia
Dr. ROSALIE M. MIRENDA, D.N.Sc., Pres.
Rev. JUDE MICHAEL KRILL, O.F.M.Conv., Chap.
Priests 1
Sisters 29
Administrators 35
Faculty and Staff 137
Adjuncts 89
Lay Teachers 45
Students 1,256

Center Valley
Diocese of Allentown

Allentown College of St. Francis de Sales
2755 Station Ave.
Center Valley, PA 18034-9568
Tel: 610-282-1100
Coeducational liberal arts college conducted by the Oblates of St. Francis de Sales (1965); Accredited.
Very Rev. DANIEL G. GAMBET, O.S.F.S., Ph.D., Pres.
Revs.:
ALEXANDER T. POCETTO, O.S.F.S., Ph.D., Senior Vice Pres.
BERNARD F. O'CONNOR, O.S.F.S., Ph.D., Academic Dean
JOHN HANLEY, O.S.F.S., Dir. Campus Ministry
JOHN F. MCGINLEY, O.S.F.S., M.A., Vice Pres. for Continuing Education
Mrs. MARGARET KENDER, M.A., Vice Pres. Student Svcs.
Mr. GEORGE KELLY, Vice Pres. Enrollment Mgmt.
Mrs. JAN HOLLY, Registrar
Mr. WILLARD CRESSMAN, Treasurer
Mr. DENNIS CAMPBELL, Vice Pres. Devel.
Mr. MICHAEL THOMPSON, Vice Pres. Admin.
Dr. KAREN DOYLE WALTON, Vice Pres. Academic Affairs
Revs.:
JOHN F. HARVEY, O.S.F.S., S.T.D.
JAMES P. FINNEGAN, O.S.F.S., Ph.D.
GERARD H. SCHUBERT, O.S.F.S., Ph.D.
BERNARD F. DONAHUE, O.S.F.S., Ph.D.
PETER LEONARD, O.S.F.S., M.A.
A. ROBERT MCGILVARY, O.S.F.S., Ph.D.
THOMAS F. DAILEY, O.S.F.S., S.T.L.
JACOB WELLE, M.S.C., M.A.
ROBERT M. RUTLEDGE, O.S.F.S.
Priests on Faculty 14
Lay Teachers 99
Students 1,670

Cresson
Diocese of Altoona-Johnstown

Mount Aloysius College
7373 Admiral Peary Hwy.
Cresson, PA 16630
Tel: 814-886-4131
E-mail: cindymi@mtaloy.edu
Web Site: www.mtaloy.edu
Sisters of Mercy
Sr. MARY ANN DILLON, R.S.M., Pres.
Ms. SYLVIA HIRSCH, Dean Enrollment Mgmt.
Dr. DANIEL FREDRICKS, Acting Academic Dean Academic Affairs
Ms. BEIRNE B. COFIELD, Dean Inst. Advancement
Rev. GEORGE J. VALKO, M.A., M.Div., Chap.
Sisters 1
Lay Teachers 51
Total Staff 117
Students 2,673

Dallas
Diocese of Scranton

College Misericordia
Dallas, PA 18612
Tel: 717-674-6400
Web Site: www.miseri.edu
Religious Sisters of Mercy of the Americas.
Administration:
ALBERT B. ANDERSON, Ph.D., Pres.
Mr. JOHN RISBOSKIN, Vice Pres. of Financial & Admin.
Rev. MICHAEL M. BRYANT, M.Th., Chap.
Sr. MARY GLENNON, R.S.M., Ed.D., Vice Pres. of Academic Affairs & Dean of the College
Ms. MARILYN SANTARELLI, Exec. Dir., Institutional Advancement
Sr. JEAN MESSAROS, R.S.M., Dean of Students
Mrs. JANE DESSOYE, M.S., Exec. Dir., Admissions & Financial Aid
Mr. EDWARD LAHART, M.S., Registrar
Ms. JENNIFER A. MCCARTHY, Dir., Career Svcs.
Ms. GERALDINE WALL, M.S., Dir., Counseling Svcs.
Mr. JOSEPH MACK, M.B.A., Dir., Mgmt. Information Svcs.
Sr. MARY SHARON GALLAGHER, R.S.M., M.S.L.S., Dir., Library Svcs.
Ms. KATHLEEN A. FOLEY, B.S., M.S., Asst. Dean of Students
Mr. RONALD HROMISIN, C.P.A., Comptroller
Mr. JOSEPH J. HAYER, M.B.A., Business Mgr.
Mrs. GAIL SMALLWOOD, Dir. of Public Information
Priests 1
Sisters Teaching 8
Students 1,695

Erie
Diocese of Erie

Gannon University
University Square
Erie, PA 16541
Tel: 814-871-7000
Rev. Msgr. DAVID A. RUBINO, Ph.D., Pres.
Rev. Msgr. ADDISON YEHL, M.S.
Rev. Msgr. GERALD L. ORBANEK, M.A.
Very Rev. JOSEPH C. GREGOREK, V.F.
Revs.:
CHARLES H. DREXLER, S.T.D.,V.F.
JOHN P. SCHANZ, Censor Librorum
PAUL J. DESANTE, Ph.D.
SCOTT P. DETISCH, Ph.D.
GILIO L. DIPRE, Ph.D.
ROBERT G. FIN, Ph.D., (Retired)
EDWARD C. KRAUSE, C.S.C., Ph.D.
ROBERT J. LEVIS, Ph.D.
JAMES MCCULLOUGH, M.S.
NICHOLAS J. ROUCH
ROBERT P. SUSA, M.A.
CASIMIR J. WOZNIAK
MICHAEL KESICKI
CHRISTOPHER HAMLETT
RONALD E. GMEREK
Priests 18
Sisters 7
Lay Teachers 280
Students 3,327

Mercyhurst College
501 E. 38th St. Blvd.
Erie, PA 16546
Tel: 814-824-2000
E-mail: jgower@paradise.mercy.edu
Web Site: www.mercy.edu
Dr. WILLIAM P. GARVEY, Pres.
Dr. JOSEPH F. GOWER, Dean
Rev. STEPHEN A. ANDERSON, Chap.
Priests 3
Sisters 2
Lay Teachers 112
Students 2,850

Greensburg
Diocese of Greensburg

Seton Hill College
Greensburg, PA 15601
Tel: 724-834-2200; Fax: 724-830-4611
Sisters of Charity of Seton Hill
Dr. JOANNE W. BOYLE, Pres.
MARY ANN GAWELEK, Ed.D., Vice Pres. Academic Affairs & Dean of College
Rev. ANTHONY CARBONE, Chap.
Sisters 4
Lay Teachers 45
Students 1,080

Gwynedd Valley
Archdiocese of Philadelphia

Gwynedd-Mercy College
Gwynedd Valley, PA 19437
Tel: 215-646-7300; Fax: 215-641-5509
Rev. JOSEPH B. SMITS, C.I.C.M., Chap.
Sisters of Mercy 29
Lay Teachers 161
Students 1,979

Immaculata
Archdiocese of Philadelphia

Immaculata College
Immaculata, PA 19345
Tel: 610-647-4400
Web Site: http://www.immaculata.edu
Sisters, Servants of the Immaculate Heart of Mary
Sr. MARIE ROSEANNE BONFINI, I.H.M., Pres.
Sr. GEORGINE MARIE, I.H.M., Registrar
Sr. M. CARROLL ISSELMANN, Vice Pres. for Academic Affairs
Rev. HANS A.L. BROUWERS, Chap.
Priests 1
Sisters 30
Lay Teachers 144
Day Students 2,296

Jenkintown
Metropolitan Archdiocese of Philadelphia Ukrainian

Manor Junior College
700 Fox Chase Rd.
Jenkintown, PA 19046
Tel: 215-885-2360; Fax: 215-576-6564
Approved by the Commonwealth of Pennsylvania and accredited by the Middle States Association of Colleges and Secondary Schools.
Sisters of St. Basil the Great
Sr. M. CECILIA JURASINSKI, O.S.B.M., Pres.
SALLY MYDLOWEC, Academic Dean
OLGA UDVARI, Contact Person

Latrobe
Diocese of Greensburg

St. Vincent College
300 Fraser Purchase Rd.
Latrobe, PA 15650-2690
Tel: 724-539-9761
Legal Title: *Saint Vincent College Corporation*
Rt. Rev. DOUGLAS R. NOWICKI, O.S.B., Chancellor
Rev. MARTIN R. BARTEL, O.S.B., Pres.
Bro. NORMAN W. HIPPS, O.S.B., Provost
Priests 17
Brothers 6
Lay Teachers 53
Students 1,222

Loretto
Diocese of Altoona-Johnstown

St. Francis College
P.O. Box 600
Loretto, PA 15940-0600
Tel: 814-472-3000
Rev. CHRISTIAN R. ORAVEC, T.O.R., Pres.
Dr. RICHARD CRAWFORD, Asst. to the Pres.
Dr. KATHLEEN OWENS, Vice Pres. Academic Affairs
Rev. CARL A. SZURA, T.O.R., Dir. Campus Ministry
Dr. F. DENNIS RIEGELNEGG, Vice Pres. Student Devel.
Mr. RICHARD GAJEWSKI, Vice Pres. Finance
Ms. MARY ANN JACOBS, Acting Dir. Continuing Education
Mr. RAYMOND PONCHIONE, Dir. Devel.
Mr. RANDY FRYE, Dir. M.B.A. Prog.
Dr. WILLIAM DURYEA, Dir. M.M.S. Prog.
Ms. GLENDA GRIFFITH, Dir. Residence Life
Ms. PATRICIA SEROTKIN, Dir. Library
Mr. MICHAEL SARAKA, Dir. Career Devel.
Rev. JOSEPH A. CHANCLER, T.O.R., Dir. Computer Svcs.
Dr. PHILIP BENHAM, Dir. Graduate School Human Resource Mgmt./Industrial Rels.
Mr. DOMINICK PERUSO, Dir. Student Activities
Ms. DENISE KOVACH, Dir. Learning Resource Center
Mr. FRANK PERGOLIZZI, Dir. Athletics
Ms. KATHLEEN GILMOUR, Dir. Public Rels.
Mr. DAVID WILSON, Dir. Counseling
Revs.:
BEDE F. HINES, T.O.R.
THOMAS CARAPELLA, T.O.R.
EMIL C. RESCONICH, T.O.R., (Retired)
OLIVER J. HEBERT, T.O.R.
THOMAS BOURQUE, T.O.R.
CARL A. SZURA, T.O.R.
MICHAEL HIGGINS, T.O.R.
JOSEPH A. CHANCLER, T.O.R.
Priests 1
Sisters 1
Lay Professors 76
Students 1,853

Philadelphia
Archdiocese of Philadelphia

Chestnut Hill College
Philadelphia, PA 19118
Tel: 215-248-7000; Fax: 215-248-7155
Web Site: www.chc.edu
Sr. CAROL JEAN VALE, Ph.D., Pres.
Sisters 19
Lay Teachers 34
Students 1,340

Holy Family College (1954)
Grant and Frankford Aves.
Philadelphia, PA 19114
Tel: 215-637-7700; Fax: 215-637-3787
E-mail: fonley@hslc.org
Congregation of the Sisters of the Holy Family of Nazareth
Sr. FRANCESCA ONLEY, C.S.F.N., Pres.
Rev. ALBERT J. SMITH, O.S.F.S., Chap. & Campus Minister
In res.,
Rev. JAMES J. COLLINS, S.O.E.D., Dept. of Religious Studies
Priests 8
Sisters 14
Lay Faculty 217
Undergraduate Students 2,124
Graduate 466

LaSalle University
1900 W. Olney Ave.
Philadelphia, PA 19141
Tel: 215-951-1000; Fax: 215-951-1783
(Incorporated under the auspices of the Brothers of the Christian Schools)
Bros.:
JOSEPH F. BURKE, F.S.C., Ph.D., Pres.
DANIEL C. PANTALEO, Ph.D., Provost
RAYMOND P. HEATH, Ph.D., Vice Pres. Student Affairs
DAVID C. FLEMING, M.B.A., Vice Pres. Business Affairs
FRED J. FOLEY, JR., Ph.D., Vice Pres. Devel.
RAYMOND A. RICCI, Ed.M., Vice Pres. Enrollment Svcs.
BARBARA C. MILLARD, Ph.D., Dean of the School of Arts and Sciences
JOSEPH A. KANE, Ph.D., Dean of the School of Business Admin.
MARYANNE R. BEDNAR, Ph.D., Interim Dean, School of Continuing Studies
Bros.:
CHRISTOPHER LYDON, Dir., Admissions
CHARLES ECHELMEIER, F.S.C., Dir. Campus Ministry
GLORIA A. DONNELLY, Ph.D., Dean, School of Nursing
Brothers 24
Priests 5
Sisters 1
Lay Teachers 194
Students 5,376

St. Joseph's University
5600 City Ave.
Philadelphia, PA 19131
Tel: 610-660-1000; Fax: 610-660-1201
Jesuit Fathers
Tel: 610-660-1400
Under the direction of the Jesuit Fathers. Incorporated January 29, 1852.
Revs.:
NICHOLAS J. RASHFORD, S.J., Pres.
JAMES W. MOORE, S.J., Assoc. Dean College of Arts and Sciences
JOSEPH A. ARROYO, S.J., (Spain) Assoc. Dean, College of Business and Admin.
JOHN E. BENNETT, S.J., Campus Min.
ANTHONY J. BERRET, S.J.
H. CORNELL BRADLEY, S.J.
FRANCIS F. BURCH, S.J.
JOSEPH CHORPENNING, O.S.F.S.
DONALD G. CLIFFORD, S.J.
JEROME B. COLL, S.J.
MARK J. CONNELLY, S.J.
CHARLES L. CURRIE, S.J.
JOSEPH J. FEENEY, S.J.
GERALD F. FINNEGAN, S.J.
VINCENT J. GENOVESI, S.J.
JOSEPH J. GODFREY, S.J.
HOWARD J. HEIM, S.J.
FREDERICK A. HOMANN, S.J.
MICHAEL A. HRICKO, S.J.
ALBERT H. JENEMANN, S.J.
JOSEPH M. KAKALEC, S.J.
JOSEPH L. LOMBARDI, S.J.
MICHAEL A. MCELNEE, S.J.
DENNIS E. MCNALLY, S.J.
SCOTT R. PILARZ, S.J.
MARTIN R. TRIPOLE, S.J.
Bro. JOHN J. MCLANE S.J.
Sr. ANN BERNADETTE, G.N.S.H.
Sr. NORMANDIE GAITLEY, S.S.J.
Sr. FRANCES HART, S.S.J.
Sr. FRANCIS JOSEPH, R.A.
Sr. ELIZABETH ANN LINEHAN, R.S.M.
Sr. ANNE MCCOY, S.S.J.
Priests 26
Sisters 4
Lay Teachers 360
Students 6,502

Pittsburgh
Diocese of Pittsburgh

Carlow College
3333 5th Ave.
Pittsburgh, PA 15213
Tel: 412-578-6000
Sisters of Mercy
Sr. GRACE ANN GEIBEL, R.S.M., Ph.D., Pres.
MARIE IMMACULEE DANA, R.S.M., Ph.D., Vice Pres. for Academic Affairs
Sisters 5
Lay Teachers 65
Students 2,377

Duquesne University of the Holy Ghost
600 Forbes Ave.
Pittsburgh, PA 15282
Tel: 412-396-6000; Fax: 412-396-5785
Dr. JOHN E. MURRAY, JR., Pres.
Holy Ghost Fathers
Revs.:
CHARLES J. FENNER, C.S.Sp., Univ. Sec.
DAVID T. COTTINGHAM, C.S.Sp.
WILLIAM CROWLEY, C.S.Sp.
REGINALD DEFOUR, C.S.Sp.
EDWARD A. BUSHINSKI, C.S.Sp.
JOSEPH A. DUCHENE, C.S.Sp.
WILLIAM R. HEADLEY, C.S.Sp.
J. CLIFTON HILL, C.S.Sp.
SEAN M. HOGAN, C.S.Sp., Exec. Vice Pres. Student Life
SEAN KEALY, C.S.Sp.
DONALD MCEACHIN, C.S.Sp.
RAYMOND FRENCH, C.S.Sp.
EDWARD L. MURRAY, C.S.Sp.
JOSEPH PUDICHERY
DAVID L. SMITH, C.S.Sp.
WILLIAM SMITH, C.S.Sp.
EDMUND R. SUPPLE, C.S.Sp.
RICHARD F. WERSING, C.S.Sp.
ADRIAN VAN KAAM, C.S.Sp.
DAVID F. KELLY
MICHAEL SLUSSER
THOMAS SCHAEFER, C.S.Sp.
JOCELYN GREGORIE, C.S.Sp.
MICHAEL GREY, C.S.Sp.
FRANCIS MALINOWSKI, C.S.Sp.
GERALD WALSH, C.S.Sp.
Priests 26
Sisters 6
Lay Teachers 350
Students 9,285
The University is coeducational and comprises the following Colleges and Schools and Institutes:
College of Library Arts—
Dr. CONSTANCE RAMIREZ, Dean, College & Graduate School of Liberal Arts
School of Business Administration—
Mr. THOMAS J. MURRIN, Dean
School of Music—
D. MICHAEL KUMER, Dean
School of Law—
NICHOLAS CAFARDI, Dean
Division of Continuing Education—
Dr. BENJAMIN HODES, Dean
School of Education—
Dr. JAMES E. HENDERSON, Interim Dean
School of Nursing—
Dr. MARY DE CHESNAY, Dean
School of Pharmacy—
Dr. DOUGLAS H. KAY, Dean
School of Health Sciences—
Dr. JEROME L. MARTIN, Dean
Dr. HEINZ MACHATZKE, Dean, School of Natural & Environmental Sciences
Dr. MICHAEL P. WEBER, Provost and Academic Vice Pres.
Mr. ISADORE R. LENGLET, Executive Vice Pres. Mgmt. and Business
Dr. PAUL J. PUGLIESE, Librarian
Dr. FRANK YINING LIU, Law Librarian

La Roche College
9000 Babcock Blvd.
Pittsburgh, PA 15237
Tel: 412-367-9300
Sisters of Divine Providence
Rev. Msgr. WILLIAM A. KERR, Ph.D., Pres.
Sr. CAROLYN WINSCHEL, C.D.P., Ph.D., Exec. Vice Pres.
Rev. W. PETER HORTON, M.A., M.Div., Campus Minister
PATRICIA D. O'DONOGHUE, Ph.D., Vice Pres. Academic Affairs & Academic Dean
ROGER CAROTHERS, Vice Pres. Business Affairs
ARTHUR SHUKER, Vice Pres. Finance
Rev. PATRICK O'BRIEN, S.T.D., M.S.Ed., Div. Chair Humanities
Priests 3
Sisters 10
Lay Teachers 145
Students 1,641

Radnor
Archdiocese of Philadelphia

Cabrini College (1957)
610 King of Prussia Rd.
Radnor, PA 19087
Tel: 610-902-8100
Missionary Sisters of the Sacred Heart
Dr. ANTOINETTE IADAROLA, Pres.
Campus Ministers:
JOHN DIMUCCI

ARLENE SMITH
Lay Teachers 150
Students 2,119

Reading
Diocese of Allentown

Alvernia College
Reading, PA 19607
Tel: 610-796-8200; Fax: 610-777-6632
Bernardine Sisters of the Third Order of St. Francis
LAURENCE W. MAZZENO, Ph.D., Pres.
Priests 1
Sisters 2
Lay Teachers 53
Students 1,201

Rosemont
Archdiocese of Philadelphia

Rosemont College of the Holy Child Jesus
Rosemont, PA 19010-1699
Tel: 610-526-2984; Fax: 610-527-0341
E-mail: jfrogers@rosemont.edu
Web Site: www.rosemont.edu
MARGARET M. HEALY, Pres.
Sr. KATHY RONEY, S.H.C.J., Campus Minister
Sisters of the Holy Child Jesus 7
Full Time Lay Teachers 34
Part Time Lay Teachers 74
Students 1,210

Scranton
Diocese of Scranton

Marywood University
Scranton, PA 18509
Tel: 717-348-6211
E-mail: mreap@ac.marywood.edu
Web Site: http://www.marywood.edu
Sisters, Servants of the Immaculate Heart of Mary
Sr. MARY REAP, I.H.M., Ph.D., Pres.
Sr. PATRICIA ANN MATTHEWS, I.H.M., Ph.D., Vice Pres., Academic Affairs
Mr. STEVEN D. KARCHER, M.S.A., C.P.A., Vice. Pres., Business Affairs
Dr. CLAYTON N. PHEASANT, Vice Pres., College Advancement
Dr. RAYMOND P. HEATH, Vice Pres., Student Life
Dr. JANET R. REOHR, Dean, Undergraduate School
Dr. JAMES L. GEARITY, Dean, Graduate School of Arts & Sciences
Dr. WILLIAM H. WHITAKER, Dean, School of Social Work
Dr. EDNA FARACE WILSON, Dean, School of Continuing Educ.
ANN BOLAND-CHASE, M.A., Acting Registrar
MARY ANNE FEDRICK, M.S.L.S., M.A., Asst. Vice Pres., Academic Affairs
Dr. BARBARA R. SADOWSKI, Dir., Planning & Institutional Research
Faculty:
Sisters 21
Lay Teachers 122
Students 2,948

University of Scranton
(Society of Jesus)
18510
Tel: 717-941-7533
Web Site: http://www.uofs.edu
Rev. JOSEPH A. PANUSKA, S.J., Pres.
Dr. RICHARD H. PASSON, Provost & Academic Vice Pres.
Rev. BRENDAN G. LALLY, S.J., Rector of the Jesuit Community
Mr. DAVID E. CHRISTIANSEN, Vice Pres., Finance & Treas.
Mr. ROBERT J. SYLVESTER, Vice Pres., Inst. Advancement
Ms. SUSAND G. IKERD, Assoc. Provost for Enrollment Mgt.
Rev. THOMAS D. MASTERSON, S.J., Vice Pres., Univ. Ministries
Dr. JOSEPH H. DREISBACH, Dean of the College of Arts and Sciences
Dr. RONALD D. JOHNSON, Dean of the School of Mgmt.
Dr. SHIRLEY M. ADAMS, Dean of the Dexter Hanley College
Dr. ROBERT E. POWELL, Dean of the Graduate School
Mr. ROBERT FETTERHOFF, Registrar
Dr. JAMES J. PALLANTE, Dean, College of Health, Education & Human Resources
Dr. SUSAN WILLIAMS-QUINLAN, Dir., Counseling Center
Dr. JAMES T. BRYAN, Vice Pres., Student Affairs
Dr. LAWRENCE J. MORTON, Asst. to Vice Pres., Student Affairs
Mr. MARTIN L. LANGAN, Assoc. Vice Pres., Admin. Svcs.
Mr. CHARLES E. KRATZ, Dir., Library
Mr. GERALD C. ZABOSKI, Exec. Asst. to the Pres.
Miss MARILYN COAR, Sec. of the University
Revs.:
JOSEPH D. AYD, S.J.
JOHN J. BEGLEY, S.J.
PAUL R. BEINING, S.J.
PATRICK T. BRANNAN, S.J.
ROYDEN B. DAVIS, S.J.
JOHN H. DUGGAN, S.J.
HARRY J. GENSLER, S.J.
JOSEPH M. HAMERNICK, S.J., Subminister, Campion Hall
WILLIAM B. HILL, S.J.
MICHAEL A. HRICKO, S.J.
HERBERT B. KELLER, S.J., Pres., Scranton Prep
FRANCIS J. KOWNACKI, S.J.
JOHN W. LANGE, S.J.
JOHN J. LEVKO, S.J.
KENNETH G. LOFTUS, S.J.
FRANCIS J. MACENTEE, S.J.
LEONARD A. MARTIN, S.J.
THOMAS D. MASTERSON, S.J.
RICHARD S. MCCOUCH, S.J.
WILLIAM J. MCGRATH, S.J.
BERNARD R. MCILHENNY, S.J., Min. Jesuit Community
RONALD H. MCKINNEY, S.J.
NEIL P. MCLAUGHLIN, S.J.
ROBERT J. MCTEIGUE, S.J.
J. PATRICK MOHR, S.J.
OLIVER J. MORGAN, S.J.
G. DONALD PANTLE, S.J.
JOSEPH A. PANUSKA, S.J.
EDWARD R. POWERS, S.J.
JOHN J. QUINN, S.J.
JOSEPH L. QUINN, S.J.
RICHARD W. ROUSSEAU, S.J.
THOMAS F. SABLE, S.J.
GEORGE J. SCHEMEL, S.J.
THOMAS R. SLON, S.J.
FREDERICK P. ZAGONE, S.J.
Bro. JAMES C. LEMON, S.J.
Mr. PATRICK D. ROGERS
Priests 36
Students 4,906
Center for Eastern Christian Studies
University of Scranton
Scranton, PA 18510
Tel: 717-941-6116
Revs.:
JOHN J. LEVKO, S.J., Dir.
THOMAS F. SABLE, S.J., Editor Diakonia
Sr. JOAN L. ROCCASALVO, C.S.J., Coord. & Mng. Editor

Villanova
Archdiocese of Philadelphia

Villanova University
Villanova, PA 19085
Tel: 610-519-4500; Fax: 610-519-4514
Founded 1842 by the Augustinians, Province of St. Thomas of Villanova. Colleges of Liberal Arts and Sciences, Engineering, Commerce and Finance, Nursing, University College (part time), Graduate Studies and the School of Law.
E-mail:fmcguire@email.vill.edu
Board of Trustees:
Revs.:
EDMUND J. DOBBIN, O.S.A., Pres.
GEORGE F. BURNELL, O.S.A.
THOMAS M. CASEY, O.S.A.
JOHN E. DEEGAN, O.S.A.
JOHN M. DRISCOLL, O.S.A.
KEVIN F. DWYER, O.S.A.
DONALD F. REILLY, O.S.A.
JOSEPH F. WIMMER, O.S.A.
EDSON J. WOOD, O.S.A.
Mr. LAWRENCE E. BATHGATE, II
JAMES R. BIRLE
ROBERT M. BIRMINGHAM
DAVID R. COOK
NANCE K. DICCIANI, Ph.D.
JAMES A. DROBILE
ROSA M. GATTI
JOHN G. GILFILLAN, III, ESQ.
ARTHUR J. HALLERAN, JR.
HARRY R. HALLORAN, JR.
HAZEL W. JOHNSON-BROWN, Ph.D.
JOHN H. KOLMER, JR.
ANDREW J. MARKEY, JR.
MAUREEN H. MCCULLOUGH, Esq.
JOSEPH M. MCNAMARA
MICHAEL P. MONACO
ANTHONY T. RANDAZZO
EMILY C. RILEY
Dr. MARIELLEN WHELAN
Administration:
Dr. JOHN R. JOHANNES, Vice Pres. Academic Affairs
Dr. HELEN K. LAFFERTY, Univ. Vice Pres.
Mr. GARY B. FENNER, Vice Pres., Fin. Affairs
Rev. PATRICK J. RICE, O.S.A., Vice Pres. Admin.
Mr. JOHN M. ELIZANDRO, Vice Pres. Inst. Advancement
Dr. RICHARD A. NEVILLE, Vice Pres. Student Life
Rev. GEORGE F. RILEY, O.S.A., Special Asst. to Pres./Alumni & External Affairs
STEVEN P. FRANKINO, J.D., Dean of the School of Law
Rev. KAIL C. ELLIS, O.S.A., Dean of Liberal Arts and Sciences
Dr. M. LOUISE FITZPATRICK, Dean of Nursing
Dr. ROBERT LYNCH, Dean of Engrg.
Rev. WILLIAM A. MCGUIRE, O.S.A., Dean of Enrollment Mgmt.
Dr. THOMAS F. MONAHAN, Dean of Commerce of Finance
Rev. JOHN P. STACK, O.S.A., Dean of Students
Dr. DANIEL J. ZIEGLER, Dean, Graduate School of Liberal Arts & Sciences
Dr. EDWARD L. COLLYMORE, Dir.. Multicultural Affairs
Revs.:
EDWARD T. HASTINGS, O.S.A., Exec. Dir., Campus Ministry
T. SHAWN TRACY, O.S.A., Campus Ministry
KEVIN J. KEELEN, O.S.A., Campus Ministry
JOHN P. BETONI, O.S.A., Asst. Registrar
JOHN F. MCATEE, O.S.A.
Revs.:
FRANCIS A. FARSACI, O.S.A., Residence Life
DENNIS J. GALLAGHER, O.S.A., Archivist
THOMAS J. MAHONY, O.S.A., Facilities Mgmt.
FRANCIS CHAMBERS, O.S.A., Office of Undergraduate Admission
Clerical Faculty:
Revs.:
DONALD X. BURT, O.S.A.
JAN H. BUSCH, O.S.A.
ARTHUR B. CHAPPELL, O.S.A.
PETER M. DONOHUE, O.S.A.
DANIEL E. DOYLE, O.S.A.
FRANCIS A. EIGO, O.S.A.
EDWARD J. ENRIGHT, O.S.A.
JOHN J. FARRELL, O.S.A.
ALLAN D. FITZGERALD, O.S.A.
JOHN J. HAGEN, O.S.A.
OWEN R. JACKSON, O.S.A.
CHARLES P. LAFERTY, O.S.A.
BERNARD A. LAZOR, O.S.A.
JOSEPH LOYA, O.S.A.
LEE J. MAKOWSKI, O.S.A.
THOMAS MARTIN, O.S.A.
JAMES J. MCCARTNEY, O.S.A.
NEIL J. MCGETTIGAN, O.S.A.
JOHN J. MCKENZIE, O.S.A.
ROBERT J. MURRAY, O.S.A.
MICHAEL J. SCANLON, O.S.A.
RALPH C. SHURER, O.S.A.
DENNIS G. WILDE, O.S.A.
Bros.:
RICHARD CANNULI, O.S.A.
JOHN STAGLIANO, O.S.A.
Full-Time Enrollment 6,271
Part-Time Enrollment 449
Total Enrollment 10,156
Priests 42
Brothers 2
Sisters 2
Lay Teachers 486
Students 10,156

Wilkes-Barre
Diocese of Scranton

**Kings College*
Wilkes-Barre, PA 18711
Tel: 717-826-5900
Web Site: http://www.kings.edu
Officers of the College:
Rev. JAMES R. LACKENMIER, C.S.C., Pres.
Dr. DONALD W. FARMER, Vice Pres., Academic Affairs
Mr. STEVEN H. SEITCHIK, Vice Pres., Business Affairs & Treas.
Rev. EUGENE F. GORSKI, C.S.C., Vice Pres., Student Affairs
Mr. TERRENCE F. MECH, Vice Pres., Information & Instructional Technologies & Dir., Corgan Library
Mr. FRANK J. PASQUINI, Vice Pres., Development
Rev. JOHN R. GERACCI, C.S.C., College Chap. & Dir., Campus Ministry
Dr. EDWARD J. SCHOEN, Dean of the William J. McGowan School of Business
Dr. WILLIAM A. SHERGALIS, Dean of the College of Arts and Sciences
Mr. CHARLES O. BACHMAN, Dean of Enrollment Management
Dr. JEAN P. ANDERSON, Registrar
Rev. JOSEPH A. SIDERA, C.S.C., Religious Supr.
Holy Cross Community
Revs.:
THOMAS F. CARTEN, C.S.C.
JOHN R. GERACCI, C.S.C.

Eugene F. Gorski, C.S.C.
Anthony R. Grasso, C.S.C.
Donald J. Grimes, C.S.C.
James E. Kelly, C.S.C.
Charles J. Kociolek, C.S.C.
James R. Lackenmier, C.S.C.
Thomas P. Looney, C.S.C.
Thomas J. O'Hara, C.S.C.
William R. Ribando, C.S.C.
John J. Ryan, C.S.C.
Joseph A. Sidera, C.S.C.
Ronald J. Wasowski, C.S.C.
Bros.:
James H. Miller, C.S.C.
Thomas Sawyer, C.S.C.
In res.,
Revs.:
James J. Doyle, C.S.C.
Joseph J. Long, C.S.C.
Clement J. Podskoch, C.S.C.
Bros.:
Jerome Matthews, C.S.C.
Harold J. Rogan, C.S.C.
Priests 17
Brothers 4
Lay Teachers 95
Students 2,201

PUERTO RICO

Ponce
Diocese of Ponce, Puerto Rico

The Pontifical Catholic University of Puerto Rico
2250 Avenida de las Americas
Ponce, PR 00731-6382
Tel: 787-841-2000
The University is composed of the following: College of Arts and Humanities and Graduate Studies in Hispanic Studies; College of Business Administration and Graduate Studies; College of Education and Graduate Studies; College of Science and Graduate Studies; School of Law; Institute of Graduate Studies in Behavioral Science and Community Affairs; Institute of Social Doctrine of the Church; Program for Special Services; Post-Baccalaureate Achievement Program; Upward Bound Program.
Administration:
Most Revs.:
Fremiot Torres Oliver, D.D., Chancellor
Ricardo A. Surinach, Vice Chancellor
Mrs. Marcelina Velez de Santiago, Interim Pres. & Vice Pres. for Academic Affairs
Mrs. Irma Rodriguez, Assoc. Vice Pres. for Academic Affairs
Mr. Carl B. Sauder, Vice Pres. for Student Affairs
Mrs. Lisania Morales de Aulet, Special Asst. to the Vice Pres. for Student Affairs
Dr. Enid Miranda, Dean, College of Arts and Humanities
Mr. Jaime Santiago Canet, Dean, College of Business Admin.
Dr. Lillian Negron, Dean, College of Education
Mr. Julio Rivera, Dean, College of Science
Jose Alberto Morales, Esq., Dean, School of Law
Mr. Ivan E. Davila, Registrar
Mrs. Caridad C. de Frau, Dir., Admissions
Mrs. Amelia M. Velazquez, Interim Dir., Freshmen Prog.
Mrs. Gladys M. Vidal, Dir., Guidance Ctr.
Mrs. Esther Irizarry, Dir. Libraries
Noelia Padua, Esq., Dir. Law Library
Faculty:
Rev. Msgr. Joaquin A. Alicea
Rev. Msgr. Herminio de Jesus
Rev. Msgr. Roberto Garcia
Revs.:
Tosello Giangiacomo, C.S.Sp.
Felix Lazaro, Sch.P.
Jose Luis Larreategui, Sch.P.
Perfecto Alvarez, O.S.A.
Jose M. Herrero
Abel A. Di Marco
Brian W. Harrison, O.S.
Moises Navascues, Sch.P.
Adalin Rivera
Alvaro Huerga, O.P.
Esteban Santaella
Alfredo Alvarez Lacruz
Ponce:
Revs.:
Alexio Jose de Armas, O.C.D.
Segismundo Cintron
Carmelo de Jesus, O.C.D.
Juan Rodriguez
Vicente Salas, O.M.
Isidro Gonzales Ferreras
Jose Luis Alonso, O.P.
Miguel Alvarez, Sch.P.
Jesus R. Diez Antonanzas
Francisco Sirvent-Dominguez
Jesus Pacho
Arecibo:
Revs.:
Serapio Fernandez, O.F.M.
Cesar E. Santos
Luis Rios Capiello
Antonio J. Vazquez
Alfredo E. Guzman, S.J.
Guayama:
Revs.:
Rafael Alvarado De Jesus
Antonio A. Hernandez, C.SS.R.
Jose C. Vargas Oliveras
Mayaguez:
Revs.:
Jose Francisco Baez
Juan Lamela, C.M.
Jose R. Linares
Edgardo Lopez
Luis Alberto Rodriguez
Delroy E. Thomas
Priests 41
Sisters 3
School of Law 34
Lay Teachers 473
Students 10,801

RHODE ISLAND

Newport
Diocese of Providence

Salve Regina University
Newport, RI 02840-4192
Tel: 401-847-6650; Fax: 401-847-0372
E-mail: sruadmis@salve.edu
Web Site: www.salve.edu
Legal Title: *Salve Regina University*
Sisters of Mercy of the Americas
Dr. M. Therese Antone, R.S.M., Pres.
Dr. Judith Mills, Vice Pres. for Academic Affairs
Dominic C. Varisco, Exec. Vice Pres.
William B. Hall, Vice Pres. for Business and Financial Affairs
Thomas P. Flanagan, Vice Pres. for Admin./Services and Community Relations
John J. Rok, Vice Pres. for Student Life
Laura E. McPhie, Dean of Enrollment Svcs.
Frederick C. Promades, Dir. Institutional Research
Lucile Flanagan, Dir. Financial Aid
Michael Semenza, Vice Pres. Institutional Advancement
David Kim, Dean of Library Sciences
John Quinn, Dean of Students
Thomas H. Brennan, Dir. of Information Systems
Revs.:
Donald L. Paradis, M.S.
Michael T. Malone, C.S.Sp.
Priests 2
Brothers 4
Sisters 20
Lay Teachers 89
Students-Men 761
Women 1,347

Providence
Diocese of Providence

Providence College
River Ave. & Eaton St.
Providence, RI 02918
Tel: 401-865-1000; Fax: 401-865-2057
E-mail: pcadmiss@providence.edu
Web Site: http://www.providence.edu
Legal Title: *Providence College*
Conducted by the Dominican Friars.
Revs.:
Philip A. Smith, O.P.
Terence J. Keegan, O.P., Exec. Vice Pres.
Thomas L. Canavan, O.P., Vice Pres. Academic Admin.
Mr. Michael V. Frazier, Vice Pres. Finance & Business
Rev. J. Stuart McPhail, O.P., Vice Pres. Student Svcs.
Mr. Joseph P. Brum, Vice Pres. Alumni/Devel.
Mr. Edward J. Caron, Vice Pres. College Relations
Rev. Robert E. Bond, O.P., Dean Undergraduate Studies
Dr. Richard E. Farmer, Dean School of Continuing Education
Revs.:
Robert J. Hennessey, O.P., Dir. Academics for Graduate Religious Studies Prog.
James A. Driscoll, O.P., Dir. Promotions and Publicity of the Grad. School of Rel. & Biblical Studies
Richard J. Barranger, O.P., Chap.
Mr. Edgar C. Bailey, Jr., Dir. Library
Dominican Priests Teaching 31
Diocesan Priests Teaching 4
Sisters Teaching 5
Lay Professors 284
Enrollment-Day School:
Men 1,535
Women 2,092
Graduate School:
Men 361
Women 666
Evening Division:
Men 415
Women 604

SOUTH DAKOTA

Aberdeen
Diocese of Sioux Falls

Presentation College
Aberdeen, SD 57401
Tel: 605-225-1634; Fax: 605-229-8430
Sisters of the Presentation of the B.V.M.
Dr. Lorraine M. Hale, Pres.
Rev. Joseph Sheehan, O.Carm., Chap.
Priests 1
Sisters 6
Lay Teachers 26
Students 384

Yankton
Diocese of Sioux Falls

Mount Marty College
1105 W. 8th St.
Yankton, SD 57078
Fax: 605-668-1357
Benedictine Sisters
Dr. Mark Hurtubise, Pres.
Priests 1
Sisters 15
Lay Teachers 42
Students 1,142

TENNESSEE

Memphis
Diocese of Memphis

**Christian Brothers University* (1871)
(Coed)
650 E. Parkway S.
Memphis, TN 38104
Tel: 901-321-3000
Legal Title: *Christian Brothers Univ. of Memphis, Tenn.*
Bro. Michael J. McGinniss, Pres.
Four-Year university with Schools of Business, Engineering, Liberal Arts, and Science-Mathematics. Graduate programs in Business and Engineering.
Dr. Mark Smith, Vice Pres. Academic Affairs
Mr. J. Christopher Mathis, Vice Pres. Admin. Affairs
Mr. Nick Scully, Vice Pres. Institutional Advance
Bro. Frank Osage, F.S.C., Vice Pres. Student Affairs
Mrs. Debra Czestochowski, Dir. University Rels.
Ms. Betty McWillie, Dir. Career Devel. & Placement
Bro. John Edward Doody, F.S.C., Dir. Grants & Proposals
Deacon John Hivner, Dir. Campus Ministry
Mr. Thomas Faulkner, Business Office Mgr.
Sr. Sue Russell, R.S.M., Campus Minister
Brothers 21
Sisters 2
Lay Teachers 130
Students 1,784

Nashville
Diocese of Nashville

Aquinas College
4210 Harding Rd.
Nashville, TN 37205
Tel: 615-297-7545
Web Site: www.aquinas-TN.edu
Dominican Sisters of St. Cecilia Congregation
Mother Christine Born, O.P., Chm.
Sr. Mary Evelyn Potts, O.P., Pres.
Sr. Mary Justin Halton, Academic Dean
Sisters 9
Lay Teachers 33
Students 385

TEXAS

Austin
Diocese of Austin

St. Edward's University (1881)
3001 S. Congress Ave.

Austin, TX 78704
Tel: 512-448-8400
Officers:
Dr. PATRICIA A. HAYES, Pres.
Sr. DONNA JURICK, S.N.D., Vice Pres. Academic Affairs
Dr. SANDRA PACHECO, Dean Student Devel.
JOHN LUCAS, Vice Pres. Student Svcs.
DAVID A. DICKSON, JR., Vice Pres. Financial Affairs
Faculty:
Dominican Priests 1
Holy Cross Brothers 11
Sisters 2
Lay Professors 233
Students 3,101

Houston
Diocese of Galveston—Houston

University of St. Thomas
3800 Montrose Blvd.
Houston, TX 77006-4696
Tel: 713-522-7911
E-mail: basil.stthom.edu
E-mail: basil.stthom.edu
Founded in 1947, Graduate Division (Four Schools). Undergraduate Division (21 Departments). Center for Thomistic Studies. Center for International Studies.
Rev. J. MICHAEL MILLER, C.S.B., Pres.
Dr. LEE WILLIAMES, Vice Pres., Academic Affairs
Rev. WILLIAM J. YOUNG, C.S.B., Pres. Emeritus; Dir., Community Svcs. of the Univ.
RODNEY CROWL, Inst. Advancement
Deacon RICHARD GLOR, Registrar
Mrs. ELSIE BIRON, Dir., Admission
Mr. JAMES PICCININNI, Dir., Doherty Library
Rev. LOUIS BRUSATTI C.M., Dean, School of Theology
Dr. YHI MIN HO, Dean, Cameron School of Business
Dr. ANNA DEWALD, Dean, School of Education
Dr. JOHN FREED, Dean, Special Progams
Dr. RONALD HATCHETT, Dir., Center for Intl. Studies
Ms. LINDA BALLARD, Dir., Financial Aid
Mr. JACK HANK, Dean, Student Svcs.
Rev. MARK GAZIN, C.S.B., Coord., Campus Ministry
Mr. JAMES RODREGUEZ, Dir., Alumni Relations
Rev. EDWARD A. BADER, C.S.B., Curator, University Art Collection
Dr. KHALIL YAZDI, Asst. Vice Pres. Academic Affairs & Dir. of Institutional Research
Mr. JAMES BOOTH, Vice Pres., Finance
Dr. JEROME KRAMER, Assoc. Vice Pres., Academic Affairs; Dean Arts & Sciences;Acting Dir., Center, for Thomistic Studies (Graduate Philosophy)
Dr. JANICE GORDON-KELTER, Dean Special Programs (Acting)
Ms. MARIE-PIERRE STIEN, Dir., Human Resources
Dr. DEBORAH BAKER, Dir., Counseling and Testing Services
Priests 22
Sisters 5
Lay Professors 180
Total Staff 119
Students 2,506

Irving
Diocese of Dallas

University of Dallas
President's Office, 1845 E. Northgate
Irving, TX 75062
Tel: 972-721-5000; Fax: 972-721-5017
Administrative Officers:
Most Rev. CHARLES V. GRAHMANN, D.D., Grand Chancellor
Rev. Msgr. MILAM JOSEPH, Pres.
Mr. ROBERT GALECKE, Vice Pres. Admin.
Dr. GLEN E. THUROW, Provost & Dean
Dr. PAULA HUGHES, Acting Dean
Mrs. SYBIL NOVINSKI, Assoc. Provost
Dr. FRED ZUKER, Dean of Students
Rev. THOMAS CLOHERTY, Chap.
Diocesan Priests:
Rev. ENRIQUE NARDONI, S.S.D.
Cistercian Priests:
Revs.:
DAVID BALAS, O.Cist.
PLACID CSIZMAZIA, O.Cist.
JAMES LEHRBERGER, O.Cist.
ROBERT MAGUIRE, O.Cist.
Lay Teachers 205
Students 2,897

San Antonio
Archdiocese of San Antonio

Oblate School of Theology (1903)
(Coed) (Graduate Theology)
285 Oblate Dr.
San Antonio, TX 78216-6693
Tel: 210-341-1366; Fax: 210-341-4519
Conducted by the Missionary Oblates of Mary Immaculate
Rev. J. WILLIAM MORELL, O.M.I., M.Div., Pres.
Mrs. CHRISTIANE B. SCHEEL, Dir. Admissions, Registrar
Mr. HECTOR RODRIGUEZ, Dir. Finance
Mrs. PEGGY PIPER, Admin. Asst. Pres.
Faculty:
Revs.:
WARREN BROWN, O.M.I., L.C.L., M.C.L.
KEVIN COLLINS, O.M.I., M.Div., Dir. Oblate Renewal Center
VAUGHN J. FAYLE, O.M.I., Dir. Phil. Program
MARK A. GARRETT, O.S.A.
KEN HANNON, O.M.I., Ph.D.
JAN HEEMROOD, O.M.I., S.S.L.
JOHN JOYCE, O.M.I., M.Div.
JOHN KEMPER, S.S., D.Min.
ROBERT E. LAMPERT, Ph.D (STL)
JOSE A. LOPEZ
JOHN M. MAKOTHAKAT, Ph.D., J.C.D., S.T.D.
FRANCIS KELLY NEMECK, O.M.I., S.S.D.
LEOPOLDO PEREZ, O.M.I., S.T.D., Co-Dir. M.Div.
FREDERICK SACKETT, O.M.I., J.C.D.
STEPHEN K. SHERWOOD, C.M.F., S.T.D.
JAMES K. SULLIVAN, M.A (SPC) Dir. Ministry to Ministers Prog.
ROBERT E. WRIGHT, O.M.I., Ph.D.
Ms. MARGARET ESCOBEDO, M.T.S., Dir. Lay Ministry
Priests 24
Sisters 2
Lay Professors 12
Students 272

Our Lady of the Lake University
411 S.W. 24th
San Antonio, TX 78207-4689
Tel: 210-434-6711; Fax: 210-436-0824
E-mail: mahos@lake.OLLUSA.edu
Sponsored by Sisters of Divine Providence
SALLY MAHONEY, M.S., Pres.
Dr. ROBERT E. GIBBONS, Ph.D., Exec. Vice Pres.
Dr. HOWARD BENOIST, Ph.D., Vice Pres. & Dean Academic Affairs
ALLEN R. KLAUS, B.B.A., C.P.A., Vice Pres. Finance and Facilities
MARY ELLEN SMITH, M.S., Vice Pres. & Dean of Student Life
Ms. LORETTA A. SCHLEGEL, M.Ed., Vice Pres. Enrollment Mgmt.
FRED D. SCOTT, M.A., Inst. Research Officer
Dr. SANTOS H. HERNANDEZ, Ph.D., Dean, Worden School of Social Svcs.
Sr. ISABEL BALL, C.D.P., Ph.D., Dean, College of Arts & Sciences
Dr. W. EARL WALKER, Ph.D., Dean, School of Business & Public Admin.
Dr. JACQUELYN ALEXANDER, Ph.D., Dean, School of Education & Clinical Studies
Campus Ministry Team:
Rev. MIGUEL BRISENO, O.F.M.Conv.
WAYNE ROMO, M.T.S.
Sisters 21
Full-time Faculty 170
Lay Teachers 149
Students 3,666

St. Mary's University of San Antonio, Texas (1852)
(Coed)
One Camino Santa Maria
San Antonio, TX 78228-8572
Tel: 210-436-3011
E-mail: jmoder@alvin.stmarytx.edu
Web Site: www.stmarytx.edu
Conducted by the Society of Mary
Rev. JOHN J. MODER, S.M., Pres.
Dr. CHARLES COTRELL, Academic Vice Pres.
Ms. RUTH RODGERS, Vice Pres. Student Devel.
Mr. DANIEL J. WHITE, Vice Pres. Admin. & Finance
Rev. CHARLES H. MILLER, S.M., Dean, School of Humanities and Social Sciences
Dr. DAVID MANUEL, Dean, School of Business
Dr. ANTHONY J. KAUFMANN, Dean, School of Science, Engrg. and Technology
Dr. RONALD MERRELL, Dean, Graduate School
BARBARA BADER ALDAVE, Dean, School of Law
LOUISA AVITUA-TREVINO, Registrar
Mr. RICHARD CASTILLO, Dir. Admissions
Dr. H. PALMER HALL, Dir. Academic Library
Mr. ROBERT L. SUMMERS, JR., Dir. Law Library
Revs.:
WILLIAM MEYERS, S.M., Dir. Campus Ministry
JOHN RECHTEIN, S.M.
W. FRANZ SCHORP, S.M.
CONRAD J. KACZKOWSKI, S.M.
JOHN MODER, S.M.
CHARLES H. MILLER, S.M.
JOHN A. LEIES, S.M.
J. WILLIS LANGLINAIS, S.M.
NORBERT C. BROCKMAN, S.M.
GEORGE MONTAGUE, S.M.
WILLIAM ELLOS, S.J.
ROBERT E. HOGAN, S.M.
CHRIS JANSON, S.M.
Priests 14
Brothers 15
Sisters 5
Lay Teachers 177
Students 4,096

The United Colleges of San Antonio
(A Consortium of Catholic Colleges in San Antonio)
285 Oblate Dr.
San Antonio, TX 78216
Revs.:
J. WILLIAM MORELL, O.M.I.
JOHN MODER, S.M.
Dr. LOUIS AGNESE, JR., Ph.D.
Ms. SALLY MAHONEY
San Antonio, TX 78212
Tel: 210-341-1366

University of the Incarnate Word
4301 Broadway
San Antonio, TX 78209
Tel: 210-829-6000
Dr. LOUIS J. AGNESE, JR., Ph.D., Pres.
Sr. MARGARET PATRICE SLATTERY, C.C.V.I., Ph.D., Chancellor
Dr. EDUARDO PADERON, Ph.D., Vice Pres. Academic Affairs
DOUGLAS B. ENDSLEY, M.B.A, Vice Pres. Business & Finance
THOMAS PLOFCHAN, M.A., Vice Pres. Inst. Advancement
FRANK AYALA, Ph.D., Vice Pres. Student Affairs
DAVID JURENOVICH, Ph.D., Vice Pres. Mktg. and Planning
GILBERT HINOJOSA, Ph.D., Dean of Arts and Sciences
REGINALD TRAYLOR, Ph.D., Dean of Graduate Studies
WILLARD PLATZER, Ph.D., Dean of Professional Studies
RENEE MOORE, Dean of Student Life
BRIAN DALTON, Dean of Student Enrollment
Sr. MARGARET SNYDER, C.C.V.I., Dir. Campus Ministry
Rev. GREGORY NEVLUD, Chap.
Sr. EILISH RYAN, Ph.D., Dir. Pastoral Institute
BOBBYE FRY, Registrar
Priests 1
Sisters of the Incarnate Word 15
Lay Faculty 342
Students 3,312

VERMONT

Burlington
Diocese of Burlington

Trinity College of Vermont
President's Office, 208 Colchester Ave.
Burlington, VT 05401
Tel: 802-658-0337
Dr. LORNA DUPHINEY EDMUNDSON, Ed.D., Pres.
Priests 1
Sisters 3
Lay Teachers 36
Students 829

Colchester
Diocese of Burlington

St. Michael's College
Winooski Park
Colchester, VT 05439
Tel: 802-654-2211; Fax: 802-654-2701
E-mail: mcormier@smcvt.edu
Web Site: www.smcvt.edu
Dr. MARC A. VANDERHEYDEN, Pres.
Mr. WILLIAM H. CHADWICK, Chm. of the Board
Ms. MARILYN CORMIER, Asst. to Pres.
Mr. ROBERT P. KENNY, Interim Vice Pres., Academic Affairs
Mr. MICHAEL D. SAMARA, Vice Pres. for Student Affairs
Mr. JOHN T. GUTMAN, Vice Pres. for Admin.
Mr. RICHARD V. DIVENERE, Assoc. Vice Pres. Alumni Relations & Devel.
Dr. JOHN P. KENNEY, Dean of the College
Mr. JERRY E. FLANAGAN, Vice Pres. for Admissions & Enrollment Mgmt.
Mr. JOHN D. SHEEHEY, Registrar
Dr. BONNIE TANGALOS, Dean of the School for Intl. Studies
Dr. SUSAN W. KUNTZ, Dean of the Prevel School
Dr. EDWARD MAHONEY, Chm. Graduate Theology & Pastoral Ministry Prog.
Rev. MICHAEL P. CRONOGUE, S.S.E., Dir. Edmundite Campus Ministry
Ms. DIANE FOSTER, Edmundite Campus Min. (Religious Education)

Ms. ANN GIOMBETTI, Dir. of Volunteer Programs
Priests 4
Lay Teachers 142
Students 2,658

Rutland
Diocese of Burlington

College of St. Joseph in Vermont
71 Clement Rd.
Rutland, VT 05701-3899
Tel: 802-773-5900
Dr. FRANK G. MIGLORIE, JR., Pres.
Lay Teachers 13
Students 518

VIRGINIA

Arlington
Diocese of Arlington

Marymount University
2807 N. Glebe Rd.
Arlington, VA 22207
Tel: 703-522-5600
E-mail: admissions@marymount.edu
Web Site: www.marymount.edu
Religious of the Sacred Heart of Mary
Resident and Non-resident coed students.
Sr. EYMARD GALLAGHER, R.S.H.M., Pres.
Sisters 11
Layfaculty & Staff 366
Students 3,845

Front Royal
Diocese of Arlington

Christendom College
Tel: 540-636-2900
Resident and Non-resident students.
TIMOTHY T. O'DONNELL, S.T.D., Pres.
In res.,
Rev. ROBERT A. SKERIS, Adjunct Prof., Theology
Priests 3
Lay Teachers 27
Students 214

WASHINGTON

Lacey
Archdiocese of Seattle

St. Martin's College
5300 Pacific Ave., S.E.
Lacey, WA 98503
Tel: 360-491-4700
Order of St. Benedict College of Liberal Arts and Sciences.
Dr. DAVID R. SPANGLER, Pres.
Dr. LILLIAN CADY, Interim Vice Pres. Academic Affairs
Resident and non-resident students.
Main Campus 1,033
Extension Campuses 496
Priests 5
Brothers 2
Lay Teachers 64

Seattle
Archdiocese of Seattle

Seattle University
900 Broadway
Seattle, WA 98122
Tel: 206-296-6000
Web Site: http://www.seattleu.edu
Revs.:
STEPHEN V. SUNDBORG, S.J., Pres.
ALEXIUS W. BYRNE, S.J.
PHILIP BOROUGHS, S.J., Rector
EMMETT H. CARROLL, S.J.
GERALD T. COBB, S.J.
PETER B. ELY, S.J.
JOHN F. FOSTER, S.J.
RONALD R. FUNKE, S.J.
THEODORE N. FORTIER, S.J.
ROGER S. GILLIS, S.J.
JAMES M. HARBAUGH, S.J.
PATRICK J. HOWELL, S.J.
PAUL A. JANOWIAK, S.J.
MICHAEL M. KELLIHER, S.J.
WILLIAM F. LEROUX, S.J.
DAVID J. LEIGH, S.J.
FRANCIS A. LOGAN, S.J.
PHILIP J. LUCID, S.J.
JAMES N. MEEHAN, S.J.
JOSEPH O. MCGOWAN, S.J.
PATRICK B. O'LEARY, S.J.
IGNATIUS OHNO, S.J.
LAMMERT B. OTTEN, S.J.
JAMES B. REICHMANN, S.J.
RICHARD R. ROACH, S.J.
JOHN D. WHITNEY, S.J.
JOSEF V. VENKER, S.J (MIS)
Bros.:
JAMES P. SELINSKY, S.J.
FREDERICK O. MERCY, S.J.
Revs.:
ROBERT J. SPITZER, S.J.
JOSEPH R. STOCKING, S.J.
WILLIAM J. SULLIVAN, S.J.
MICHAEL J. TAYLOR, S.J.
L. JOHN TOPEL, S.J.
THEODORE E. ZEMBAL, S.J (BGP)
Mr. GEORGE H. WATSON, Scholastic
Priests 36
Sisters 3
Brothers 2
Scholastics 1
Lay Teachers 223
Students 5,990

Spokane
Diocese of Spokane

Gonzaga University
Spokane, WA 99258
Tel: 509-328-4220
College of Arts and Sciences, and Schools of Law, Engineering, Education, Business Administration, Graduate School. Professional Studies Education conducted by the Fathers of the Society of Jesus.
Revs.:
PATRICK J. FORD, S.J., Academic Vice Pres.
ROBERT J. ARAUJO, S.J.
DONALD R. CADDEN, S.J.
J. ALFRED CARROLL, S.J.
TIMOTHY R. CLANCY, S.J.
SCOTT W. COBLE, S.J.
MICHAEL J. CONNOLLY, S.J (New England)
MICHAEL L. COOK, S.J.
FRANK B. COSTELLO, S.J.
BERNARD J. COUGHLIN, S.J (Missouri)
TIMOTHY F. CRONIN, S.J.
ROBERT R. DORIN, S.J (New England)
ROBERT J. EGAN, S.J.
JOHN J. EVOY, S.J.
FRANCIS J. FALSETTO, S.J.
GERALD R. GORDON, S.J.
DONALD E. HIGHBERGER, S.J (Missouri)
JOHN F. HURLEY, S.J.
CLIFFORD KOSSEL, S.J.
KENNETH R. KRALL, S.J.
STEPHEN R. KUDER, S.J.
WALTER F. LEEDALE, S.J.
ANTHONY LEHMANN, S.J.
ROBERT LYONS, S.J.
JAMES M. MCDONOUGH, S.J.
MICHAEL C. MCFARLAND, S.J.
HOWARD L. MORAN, S.J.
ALFRED MORISETTE, S.J.
GEORGE O. MORRIS, S.J.
JOHN P. MOSSI, S.J (California)
MICHAEL E. MOYNAHAN, S.J.
ARMAND M. NIGRO, S.J.
JAMES G. POWERS, S.J.
KENNETH J. RUDNICK, S.J.
WILLIAM F. RYAN, S.J.
FREDRIC SCHLATTER, S.J.
MICHAEL SICONOLFI, S.J (New York)
LEONARD F. SITTER, S.J.
M. DELMAR SKILLINGSTAD, S.J.
J. PATRICK STEWART, S.J.
MICHAEL TRELEAVEN, S.J.
RICHARD E. TWOHY, S.J.
BERNARD J. TYRRELL, S.J.
GARY D. UHLENKOTT, S.J.
ANTHONY P. VIA, S.J.
J. KEVIN WATERS, S.J.
CHARLES W. WEISS, S.J.
Bros.:
DONALD A. JELLISON, S.J.
EDWARD S. JENNINGS, S.J.
THOMAS J. O'SHEA, S.J.
MAURICE C. PAQUET, S.J.
STEPHEN J. SOUZA, S.J.
BENJAMIN A. TRAUTMAN, S.J.
ADAM C. WEISGERBER, S.J.
Priests 23
Sisters 7
Lay Teachers 220
Students 4,370

Mater Dei Institute
(at Gonzaga University)
E. 405 Sinto Ave.
Spokane, WA 99202
Tel: 509-328-8332; Fax: 509-325-4011
Rev. ARMOND NIGRO, S.J., Devel. Dir.
RICHARD TROMAN, Ph.D.
Mrs. DIANE IMES, Bus. Mgr.

Toppenish
Diocese of Yakima

**Heritage College*
(Interdenominational University with an Independent Board)
3240 Fort Rd.
Toppenish, WA 98948
Tel: 509-865-2244
Web Site: www.heritage.edu
Sisters 5
Lay Teachers 39
Students 1,244

WEST VIRGINIA

Wheeling
Diocese of Wheeling-Charleston

Wheeling Jesuit University
316 Washington Ave.
Wheeling, WV 26003-6295
Jesuit Fathers
Tel: 304-243-2000
E-mail: acKer@WJUedu
Web Site: http://www.wju.edu
Very Rev. JOSEPH J. HAYDEN, S.J., Rector, Jesuit Community
Revs.:
THOMAS S. ACKER, S.J., Pres., University
FRANK C. BOURBON, S.J.
WALTER A. BUCKIUS, S.J.
JOHN J. COLL, S.J.
JOSEPH A. BURKE, S.J.
JOSEPH C. FORTIER, S.J.
JOHN J. KARWIN, S.J.
JOSEPH E. KOLB, S.J.
VINCENT J. LAGOMARSINO, S.J.
JAMES A. O'BRIEN, S.J.
JOSEPH P. SANDERS, S.J.
JOHN J. ROCK, S.J.
DONALD M. SERVA, S.J.
MICHAEL F. STELTENKAMP, S.J.
CARL L. PIEBER, C.M.
Bro. NOAH A. KACUR, S.J.
Priests 16
Brothers 1
Sisters 1
Lay Teachers 79
Students 1,556

WISCONSIN

De Pere
Diocese of Green Bay

St. Norbert College
De Pere, WI 54115-2099
Tel: 920-403-3181
E-mail: opatpjcsncad.snc.edu
Web Site: http://www.snc.edu
Legal Title: *St. Norbert College, Inc.*
Dr. THOMAS A. MANION, Pres.
Dr. THOMAS J. TREBON, Vice Pres. Academic Affairs & Dean of College
Mr. WILLIAM C. KOMSI, Vice Pres., Business & Finance
Dr. RICHARD RANKIN, Vice Pres. Student Life
Mr. DONALD L. SALMON, Vice Pres., Institutional Advancement
Revs.:
GERY G. MEEHAN, O.Praem, Dir. Campus Min. & Pastor St. Norbert College Parish
DENNIS M. BURKE, O.Praem., S.T.D., J.C.D., LL.D., Chancellor Emeritus
Faculty:
Revs.:
RICHARD M. VER BUST, Ph.D.
ROBERT J. CORNELL, O.Praem.
JOHN P. KASTENHOLZ, O.Praem.
DAVID M. KOMATZ, O.Praem.
Priests 5
Sisters 2
ROTC 1
Lay Teachers 142
Students 2,100
St. Norbert College Summer School
Tel: 920-403-3051
Dr. JOHN SUTTON, Assoc. Dean Instructional Svcs.

Fond du Lac
Archdiocese of Milwaukee

Marian College of Fond du Lac
45 S. National Ave.
Fond du Lac, WI 54935
Tel: 414-923-7600
Dr. RICHARD I. RIDENOUR, Pres.
Dr. GARY J. BOELHOWER, Academic Dean
Rev. ROY A. MATELJAN, Chap.

Sr. MARIE SCOTT, C.S.A., Campus Min.
Sisters of the Congregation of St. Agnes 3
Lay Teachers 66
Students 2,099
Total Staff 107

La Crosse
Diocese of La Crosse

Viterbo College
815 S. 9th St.
La Crosse, WI 54601-8802
Tel: 608-796-3000; Fax: 608-796-3050
A Catholic four-year coed liberal arts college founded by the Franciscan Sisters of Perpetual Adoration. Fully accredited Resident, Day and Evening Students.
Dr. WILLIAM J. MEDLAND, Ph.D., Pres.
LORILEE REBHAN, Vice Pres. Inst. Advancement
JANET LINDERBAUM, Registrar
Dr. ROLAND NELSON, Ph.D., Dir. Admissions
Rev. THOMAS M. O'NEILL, Chap. & Dir. Campus Ministry, Tel: 608-796-3804
Sisters 9
Lay Teachers 148
Students 1,700
Nursing Department
Students 409

Madison
Diocese of Madison

Edgewood College
855 Woodrow St.
Madison, WI 53711
Tel: 608-257-4861
Dominican Sisters, Sinsinawa, WI
Dr. JAMES A. EBBEN, Pres.
Sr. MAUREEN McDONNELL, O.P., Campus Minister
Sr. MARGARET HOPKINS, O.P., Dir., Church Relations
STEPHEN BULLOCK, Campus Ministry
Sisters 22
Lay Teachers 153
Students 2,056

Manitowoc
Diocese of Green Bay

Silver Lake College of the Holy Family
2406 S. Alverno Rd.
Manitowoc, WI 54220-9319
Tel: 920-684-6691; Fax: 920-684-7082
E-mail: adm@sl.edu
Web Site: http://sl.edu/slc
Connected with Holy Family Motherhouse of Franciscan Sisters of Christian Charity.
Sr. BARBARA BELINSKE, O.S.F., Pres.
Rev. JUSTIN A. PIERCE, S.D.S., Chap.
Priests 13
Sisters 64
Lay Teachers 140
Students 3,000

Milwaukee
Archdiocese of Milwaukee

Alverno College
3401 S. 39th St., P.O. Box 343922
Milwaukee, WI 53234-3922
Tel: 414-382-6000; Fax: 414-362-6354
Mr. GUY A. OSBORN, Chm., Bd. of Trustees
Sr. JOEL READ, O.S.F., Pres.
Sr. AUSTIN DOHERTY, O.S.F., Vice Pres. Academic Affairs
Mr. JAMES OPPERMANN, Vice Pres., Finance & Mgmt. Svcs.
Sisters 15
Lay Teachers 97
Students 2,157
Total Staff 217

Cardinal Stritch University
6801 N. Yates Rd.
Milwaukee, WI 53217
Tel: 414-352-5400
Web Site: www.ocs.stritch.edu
Conducted by Sisters of St. Francis of Assisi
Sr. MARY LEA SCHNEIDER, O.S.F., Pres.
Dr. MARNA BOYLE, Vice Pres. Academic Affairs
Revs.:
JAMES E. LOBACZ, Office of Campus Ministry
RICHARD C. BREITBACH
Sisters 7
Priests 2
Lay Teachers 68
Students 5,526
Total Staff 406

**Marquette University*
P.O. Box 1881
Milwaukee, WI 53201-1881
Tel: 414-288-7250
Web Site: www.mu.edu
Legal Title: *Marquette University*
Opened in 1881. Conducted under the auspices of the Society of Jesus.
DAVID A. STRAZ, JR., Chm. Bd. of Trustees
Rev. ROBERT A. WILD, S.J., Pres.
Dr. JERRY A. VISCIONE, Exec. Vice Pres.
Internet Address: WildR@VMS.CSD.MU.EDU
Revs.:
PATRICK J. BURNS, S.J., Corp. Vice Pres., & Asst. to the Pres.
JOHN P. RAYNOR, S.J., Chancellor
Dr. DAVID R. BUCKHOLDT, Vice Pres. Academic Affairs
Mr. KENNETH H. SMITS, Finance & Administrative Svcs.
Mr. NORBERT J. TLACHAC, Asst. to Pres. Emeritus
Dr. MARY FEELEY, Dir. Univ. Min.
The University is comprised of the following divisions:
College of Arts and Sciences—
Dr. THOMAS E. HACHEY, Dean
College of Business Administration—
Dr. LEWIS MANDELL, Dean
School of Dentistry—
Dr. WILLIAM K. LOBB, Dean
School of Education—
Dr. MARY P. HOY, Dean
College of Engineering—
Dr. ROBERT L. REID, Dean
Graduate School—
Rev. THADDEUS J. BURCH, S.J., Dean
College of Communication—
Dr. WILLIAM R. ELLIOT, Dean
Law School—
Mr. HOWARD B. EISENBERG, Dean
College of Nursing—
Dr. MADELINE WAKE, Dean
College of Health Sciences—
Dr. JACK C. BROOKS, Dean
MU College of Professional Studies—
Dr. ROBERT J. DEAHL, Dean
Division of Continuing Education—
Ms. LORRAINE LOMBARDI, Dir.
Priests 25
Sisters 3
Lay Staff 520
Students 10,400
Total Staff 1,680

Mount Mary College
2900 N. Menomonee River Pkwy.
Milwaukee, WI 53222-4545
Tel: 414-258-4810
Web Site: www.mtmary.edu
Sponsored by the School Sisters of Notre Dame
Most Rev. REMBERT G. WEAKLAND, O.S.B., D.D., Chancellor
PATRICIA D. O'DONOGHUE, Pres.
Rev. DENNIS DIRKX, Th.M., Campus Minister
Sisters 40
Lay Teachers 60
Students 1,309
Total Staff 298

HOSPITALS

ALABAMA

Birmingham
Diocese of Birmingham

St. Vincent's Hospital
P.O. Box 12407
Birmingham, AL 35202-2407
Tel: 205-939-7000
E-mail: apurdy@stv.org
Web Site: www.stv.inter.net
810 St. Vincent's Dr.
Birmingham, AL 35205
Sponsored by Daughters of Charity
Mr. VINCENT CAPONI, Pres./CEO
Sisters 7
Full-Time Nurses 359
Patients assisted annually 122,764
Beds 338

Seton Health Corporation of North Alabama
P.O. Box 12407
Birmingham, AL 35202-2407
Tel: 205-939-8600
Daughters of Charity
Mr. VINCENT CAPONI, Pres.
Full-Time Nurses 265
Patients assisted annually 880,527

Mobile
Archdiocese of Mobile

Providence Foundation
6701 Airport Blvd., Ste. C-130, P.O. Box 850429
Mobile, AL 36608
Tel: 334-639-2050
THOMAS T. ZIEMAN, JR., Chm. of the Board
BETH MCFADDEN ROUSE, Vice Chm. of the Board
GAVIN J. BENDER, Sec.
FRANK J. LOTT, JR., Treas.
Patients assisted annually 182,750
Total Staff 2,011
Nurses 511

Providence Healthcare Services
6801 Airport Blvd., P.O. Box 850429
Mobile, AL 36608
Tel: 334-633-1000; Fax: 334-633-1679
Sr. ELISE BOUDREAUX, D.C., Chm.
JOHN R. ROEDER, Pres.
W. CARL MARTIN, Sec. & Treas.
Patients assisted annually 182,750
Nurses 511
Total Staff 2,011

Providence Hospital
6801 Airport Blvd., P.O. Box 850429
Mobile, AL 36608
Tel: 334-633-1000; Fax: 334-633-1679
JOHN R. ROEDER, Pres. & CEO
Sr. ELISE BOUDREAUX, D.C., Chm.
Rev. LEO WEISHAAR, Chap.
Daughters of Charity of St. Vincent de Paul 8
Beds 349
Patients assisted annually 182,750
Nurses 511
Total Staff 2,011

Seton Health Corp. of South Alabama
6801 Airport Blvd., P.O. Box 850429
Mobile, AL 36608
Tel: 334-633-1660; Fax: 334-633-1679
Sr. ELISE BOUDREAUX, D.C., Chm. Bd.
JOHN R. ROEDER, Pres.
Sr. MARY LOUISE YEEND, D.C., Sec.
Patients assisted annually 182,750
Nurses 511
Total Staff 2,011

Seton Medical Management, Inc.
6801 Airport Blvd., P.O. Box 850429
Mobile, AL 36608
Tel: 334-633-1000
Sr. ELISE BOUDREAUX, D.C., Chm.
JOHN R. ROEDER, Pres.
Mr. ROBERT B. ANDREWS, Sec. & Treas.
Patients assisted annually 182,750
Nurses 511
Total Staff 2,011

ALASKA

Anchorage
Archdiocese of Anchorage

Providence Alaska Foundation
3200 Providence Dr., P.O. Box 196604
Anchorage, AK 99519
Tel: 907-261-3600; Fax: 907-261-3048
REBECCA PARKER, Pres.

Providence Alaska Medical Center
3200 Providence Dr., P.O. Box 196604
Anchorage, AK 99519
Tel: 907-562-2211; Fax: 907-261-3041
Mr. GENE O'HARA, Admin.
MONICA ANDERSON, Mission Integration/Spiritual Care
Sr. KAYE BELCHER, S.P., Admin. Mission Integration Svcs.
Bed Capacity 341
Patients assisted annually 287,000
Staff 1,700

Ketchikan
Diocese of Juneau

Ketchikan General Hospital
3100 Tongass
Ketchikan, AK 99901
Tel: 907-225-2173; Fax: 907-228-8322
EDWARD F. MAHN, Admin.
Licensed Bed Capacity 92
Patients assisted annually 46,505
Island View Nursing Home

ARIZONA

Nogales
Diocese of Tucson

Holy Cross Hospital, Inc.
Div. of Carondelet Health Care Corporation,
1171 W. Target Range Rd.
Nogales, AZ 85621
Tel: 520-287-2771; Fax: 520-287-7314; 287-8015
Sr. ST. JOAN WILLERT, C.S.J., CEO
CAROL A. FIELD, C.P.A., Senior Corp. Dir. & Admin.
BETH BEBEE, Chap.
Beds 31
Patients assisted annually 42,200
Holy Cross Geriatric Center
Patients assisted annually 49
Total Acute Patients Days 4,702
Admissions 1,841

Phoenix
Diocese of Phoenix

Mercy Services Corporation
350 W. Thomas Rd.
Phoenix, AZ 85013
Skilled Nursing, Rehabilitation, Restorative & Custodial Care, Home Care, Senior Services, Functional Assessment, Psychological Services.
MICHAEL NANKO, Ph.D., Vice Pres.

St. Joseph's Hospital and Medical Center
350 W. Thomas Rd., P.O. Box 2071
Phoenix, AZ 85001
Tel: 602-285-3000
MARY YARBROUGH, Pres. & CEO
Chaplaincy Services:
THERESA M. EHRSAM, Dir.
Rev. MILTON N. ADAMSON, C.S.C.
MICHAEL CENERINI
Sr. M. LAURANA GROSE, R.S.M.
Sr. DIANA DURLING, S.C.
Deacon ED BURKE
MICHAEL HUNDEMER
Sisters of Mercy 7
Beds 570
Patients assisted annually 311,481
Total Staff 3,665

Tucson
Diocese of Tucson

Carondelet Health Network
1601 W. St. Mary's Rd.
Tucson, AZ 85745-2682
Sr. ST. JOAN WILLERT, C.S.J., Pres. & CEO
St. Joseph and St. Mary Hospitals and Health Centers
1601 W. St. Mary's Rd.
Tucson, AZ 85745-2682
St. Joseph Hospital Div. of Carondelet Health Network.
350 N. Wilmot Rd., P.O. Box 12069
Tucson, AZ 85711-2678
Tel: 520-296-3211
Sr. ST. JOAN WILLERT, C.S.J., Pres. & CEO
Rev. JAMES A. FREEMAN
Mrs. BETH BEBEE, Dir. Chaplain Svcs.
Sisters of St. Joseph of Carondelet 7
Beds 303
Bassinets 30
Patients assisted annually 123,358
St. Mary's Hospital Div. of Carondelet Health Network.
1601 W. St. Mary's Rd.
Tucson, AZ 85745-2682
Tel: 520-622-5833
Sr. ST. JOAN WILLERT, C.S.J., CEO
Revs.:
JOSEPH SABA
JAMES MODEEN
Sisters of St. Joseph 15
Beds 374
Patients assisted annually 134,232
Carondelet Foundation
P.O. Box 13190
Tucson, AZ 85732-3170
M. GARDEA BRACAMONTE, Chm.
Holy Family Center, Inc.
1802 W. St. Mary's Rd.
Tucson, AZ 85745
Tel: 520-628-1991
CRAIG HOOVER, Admin.
Sisters of St. Joseph of Carondelet 1
Beds 150
Total Assisted 5,721
Sisters of St. Joseph in Arizona
1601 W. St. Mary's Rd.
Tucson, AZ 85745
Sr. JOYCE MARIE GASPARDO, C.S.J., Pres.

St. Elizabeth of Hungary Out-Patient Clinic
140 W. Speedway Blvd.
Tucson, AZ 85705
Tel: 520-628-7871
E-mail: stelizccs@aol.com
Sr. BARBARA ANNE STOWASSER, C.S.J., Exec. Dir., Admin.
Patients assisted annually 23,000

ARKANSAS

Fort Smith
Diocese of Little Rock

Northside Community Health Center
3202 North 6th
Fort Smith, AR 72904
Tel: 501-782-1456
Operated and sponsored by St. Edward Mercy Medical Center

St. Edward Mercy Medical Center
7301 Rogers Ave.
Fort Smith, AR 72917
Tel: 501-484-6000; Fax: 501-452-1770
Mr. MICHAEL MORGAN, Pres. & CEO
Rev. VINCENT E. MAGUIRE, Chap., Tel: 501-484-6082
Beds 343
Patients assisted annually 110,566
St. Edward Mercy Foundation
2713 S. 74th St., Ste. 103
Fort Smith, AR 72903
Tel: 501-484-6040

St. Edward Mercy Medical Center, dba Harbor View Mercy Hospital and Counseling Center
10301 Mayo Rd., P.O. Box 17000
Fort Smith, AR 72917-7000
Tel: 501-484-5550
Mr. RON SUMMERHILL, Admin.
Mr. MICHAEL MORGAN, Pres. & CEO
Beds 80
Patients assisted annually 1,100

Hot Springs National Park
Diocese of Little Rock

St. Joseph's Regional Health Center
300 Werner St.
Hot Springs National Park, AR 71913
Tel: 501-622-1000; Fax: 501-622-1199
E-mail: tjmmcvey@htsp.smhs.com
RANDALL J. FALE, Pres. & CEO
Rev. ALAN ROSENAU, Priest Chap.
Patients assisted annually 227,408
Bed Capacity 317
Sisters of Mercy of St. Joseph Convent of Hot Springs, Arkansas, Inc.

Jonesboro
Diocese of Little Rock

St. Bernard's Regional Medical Center
224 E. Matthews St.

Jonesboro, AR 72401
Tel: 870-972-4100
BEN E. OWENS, Pres.
Rev. NICHOLAS FUHRMAN, O.S.B., Chap.
Olivetan Benedictine Sisters 9
Patients assisted annually 111,909
Beds 375

Little Rock
Diocese of Little Rock

St. Vincent Infirmary Medical Center
No. 2 St. Vincent Circle
Little Rock, AR 72205
Tel: 501-660-3000; Fax: 501-671-4241
DIANA HUETER, Pres. & CEO
Rev. IGNATIUS GOMES, S.F.X., Chap.
Sisters 17
Beds 691
Patients assisted annually 176,986
Sisters of Charity of Nazareth, KY

Morrilton
Diocese of Little Rock

Conway County Hospital
#4 Hospital Dr.
Morrilton, AR 72110-4510
Tel: 501-354-3512; Fax: 501-354-2830
JOHNSON L. SMITH, Admin.
Sponsored by St. Vincent Infirmary Medical Center, a division of the Sisters of Charity of Nazareth, KY.
Patients assisted annually 20,996
Beds 84

Ozark
Diocese of Little Rock

St. Edward Health Facilities of Franklin County, dba Mercy Hospital/Turner Memorial
801 W. River St.
Ozark, AR 72949
Tel: 501-667-4138; Fax: 501-667-4751
Mr. MICHAEL MORGAN, CEO
Mr. JOHN NEAL, Admin.
Patients assisted annually 8,045
Beds 39

Paris
Diocese of Little Rock

St. Edward Health Facilities of Logan Co., dba North Logan Mercy Hospital
500 E. Academy
Paris, AR 72855
Mr. MICHAEL MORGAN, CEO
JIM L. MADDOX, Admin., Tel: 501-963-6101, FAX: 501-963-6155
Patients assisted annually 22,285
Beds 16

Rogers
Diocese of Little Rock

St. Mary-Rogers Memorial Hospital
72756
Tel: 501-636-0200, Ext. 705; Fax: 501-936-2906
Rev. STANISLAUS OLEKSY, Chap.
Mr. MICHAEL J. PACKNETT, Pres. & CEO
1119 W. Poplar St.
Rogers, AR,
Tel: 501-636-2548
Sisters of St. Dominic 9
Beds 165
Patients assisted annually 76,787
St. Mary Hospital Foundation
Tel: 501-636-0200

Waldron
Diocese of Little Rock

St. Edward Health Facilities of Scott County dba Mercy Hospital
Hwy. 71 & 80, Box 2230
Waldron, AR 72958
Tel: 501-637-4135; Fax: 501-637-3523
Sr. MARY ALVERA SIMON R.S.M., Admin.
Sr. MARITA POZEK, V.S.C., Asst. Admin.
Mr. MICHAEL L. MORGAN, CEO
Vincentian Sisters of Charity 1
Patients assisted annually 26,719
Beds 24
Pinewood Nursing Home, Waldron (Skilled nursing facility)
Beds 105
Patients assisted annually 145
Mercy Village (Assisted Living) (Residential care facility)
Apartments 22
Patients assisted annually (Mercy Village) 31

CALIFORNIA

Apple Valley
Diocese of San Bernardino

St. Mary Regional Medical Center
18300 Hwy. 18, P.O. Box 7025
Apple Valley, CA 92307.
Tel: 760-242-2311; Fax: 760-242-9750
St. Joseph Health System
Sr. DIANE HEJNA, Pres. & CEO
Sisters 3
Brothers 2
Beds 195
St. Mary Regional Medical Center Auxiliary
St. Mary Desert Valley Hospital Foundation

Bakersfield
Diocese of Fresno

Mercy Healthcare Bakersfield
2215 Truxtun Ave.
Bakersfield, CA 93301
Tel: 805-632-5000; Fax: 805-327-2592
Web Site: www.chw.edu
Mailing Address:
P.O. Box 119
Bakersfield, CA 93302
BERNARD J. HERMAN, Pres.
Rev. ROY BURKHART, C.S.Sp., Chap.
Mercy Southwest Hospital
400 Old River Rd.
Bakersfield, CA 93311
Tel: 805-663-6000
Mailing Address:
P.O. Box 119
Bakersfield, CA 93302
Mercy Foundation - Bakersfield
2215 Truxtun Ave.
Bakersfield, CA 93301
Tel: 805-632-5683
Mailing Address:
P.O. Box 119
Bakersfield, CA 93302
SID SHEFFIELD, Exec. Dir.
Patients assisted annually 155,000
Beds 261
Sisters 4
Staff 1,491

Burbank
Archdiocese of Los Angeles

Providence Health System
(Los Angeles Service Area)
501 S. Buena Vista St.
Burbank, CA 91505
Tel: 818-365-8051; Fax: 818-898-4569
Sisters of Providence
MICHAEL J. MADDEN, CEO
Rev. KENNETH O. MCCABE, SS.CC., Chap.
Sr. COLLEEN SETTLES, O.P., D.Min., Dir. Chaplaincy Svcs.
Bed Capacity 309
Sisters 6
Patients assisted annually 98,000
Providence Care Center
10425 Magnolia Blvd.
N. Hollywood, CA 91601
Tel: 818-980-3872
Providence St. Joseph Medical Center
501 Buena Vista St.
Burbank, CA 91505
Tel: 818-843-5111; Fax: 818-843-0641
Sisters of Providence
MICHAEL J. MADDEN, CEO
GERALD FITZGERALD, Spiritual Care
Sisters 13
Bed Capacity 454
Patients assisted annually 182,000
Providence Holy Cross Medical Center
Chaplains:
Rev. JOSEPH ECWEARIRI
Bro. JOE MCTAGGART, C.S.C.
Sr. EMILY DEMUTH, C.S.C.
JOSUE DELGADO
Bed Capacity 257
Patients assisted annually 60,000
Total Staff 1,086

Providence Saint Joseph Medical Center
501 S. Buena Vista
Burbank, CA 91505
Tel: 818-843-5111; Fax: 818-843-0641
Conducted by the Sisters of Providence Health System
Revs.:
JAMES TOAL
HAROLD J. FREE, S.J.
DAN HUDSON
RICK MOLDEN
Sr. MARY PRENDERGAST
Rev. MARION KOZLOWSKI
Deacon GERALD FITZGERALD, Dir. of Spiritual Care
Rev. BRENDA MITCHELL, (Protestant)
Bed Capacity 455
Patients assisted annually 163,560
Total Staff 2,199

Carmichael
Diocese of Sacramento

Mercy American River/Mercy San Juan Hospital/ Mercy American River Campus
4747 Engle Rd.
Carmichael, CA 95608
Tel: 916-484-2222
MICHAEL UBOLDI, Vice Pres., COO
NORM HARRIS, Dir. Ancillary and Support Svcs.
KATHY RICHERSON, Dir. Inpatient Svcs.
Sr. CLARE DALTON, R.S.M., Mission Svcs. and Chaplaincy
Sisters of Mercy 4
Nurses 200
Beds 100
Patients assisted annually 30,000
Affiliated with Mercy Healthcare Sacramento.
Mercy San Juan Campus
6501 Coyle Ave.
Carmichael, CA 95608
Tel: 916-537-5000
Sisters of Mercy 5
Beds 220
Nurses 350
Inpatients 70,000
MICHAEL UBOLDI, Vice Pres., COO
NORM HARRIS, Dir. Ancillary snd Support Svcs.
KATHY RICHERSON, Dir. Inpatient Svcs.
Sr. CLARE DALTON, R.S.M., Mission Svcs. and Chaplaincy

Daly City
Archdiocese of San Francisco

Seton Medical Center
1900 Sullivan Ave.
Daly City, CA 94015
Tel: 650-992-4000
Daughters of Charity of St. Vincent de Paul
BARBARA O'BRIEN, Interim Vice-Pres. & CEO
RICHARD OLSEN, Chap. Svcs.
Daughters of Charity 12
Patients assisted annually 261,546
Catholic Healthcare West
Seton Health Services Foundation
San Francisco Heart Institute
Seton Institute for International Development
Seton Medical Center
Daughters of Charity of St. Vincent de Paul
2000 Sullivan Ave.
Daly City, CA 94015
Sisters 12
Sr. NOREEN MCPARTLAND, D.C., Supr.

Duarte
Archdiocese of Los Angeles

Santa Teresita Hospital
819 Buena Vista St.
Duarte, CA 91010
Tel: 818-359-3243; Fax: 818-357-7166
E-mail: sth@santa-teresita.org
Web Site: www.santa-teresita.org
MICHAEL J. COSTELLO, JR., CEO
Mother VINCENT MARIE, O.C.D., Pres. Bd. Directors
Chaplains:
Revs.:
FELIX MAIZA, S.J.
ROBERT GRIFFIN, S.J.
Bed Capacity 253
Sisters 44
Total Staff 410
Patients assisted annually 47,074

Eureka
Diocese of Santa Rosa in California

St. Joseph Hospital of Eureka
2700 Dolbeer St.
Eureka, CA 95501
Tel: 707-445-8121
Sisters of St. Joseph of Orange
Mr. PAUL CHODKOWSKI, Area Pres. & CEO
KEN MEECE, Area Dir. of Pastoral Care
ADRIENNE BENSEN, Area Chap.
Rev. JAMES THOTTAPALLY (India)
Bed capacity 140
Priests 1
Sisters 4
Employees 800
Patients assisted annually 172,909

Folsom
Diocese of Sacramento

Mercy Hospital of Folsom
1650 Creekside Dr.
Folsom, CA 95630
Tel: 916-983-7400
E-mail: cgrittner@chw.edu.
DON HUDSON, Vice Pres., Chief Oper. Officer
Sisters of Mercy 2
Beds 95
Nurses 150
Patients assisted annually 18,734
Attended by St. John the Baptist, Folsom.
Corporate Name: Mercy Hospital of Folsom

Fortuna
Diocese of Santa Rosa in California

Redwood Memorial Hospital
3300 Renner Dr.
Fortuna, CA 95540
Tel: 707-725-3361; Fax: 707-725-7212
Sisters of St. Joseph of Orange
Mr. WILLARD G. FOOTE, Interim Area Pres. & CEO
Sisters 3
Staff 184
Bed capacity 46
Patients assisted annually 33,447
Redwood Memorial Foundation
JOANN CENTER, Pres.

Fresno
Diocese of Fresno

Saint Agnes' Medical Center
1303 E. Herndon
Fresno, CA 93720
Tel: 209-449-3000
Sisters of the Holy Cross
Sr. RUTH MARIE NICKERSON, C.S.C., Pres. & CEO
Mr. SAMUEL REEVES, Chm., Bd. of Trustees
Chaplains:
Revs.:
MICHAEL KENDALL, S.D.S.
JAMES E. CAIRNS, C.M.
SERGIO P. NEGRO, Ethicist Consultant
Sisters 11
Nurses 629
Priests 3
Bed Capacity 326
Patients assisted annually 361,663
Professional Office Corporation
Saint Agnes Medical Center, 1303 E. Herndon Ave.
Fresno, CA 93720
Tel: 209-449-3000
Sr. RUTH MARIE NICKERSON, C.S.C., CEO
THOMAS MAC MICHAEL, Chm. Bd. of Trustees

Fullerton
Diocese of Orange in California

St. Jude Medical Center
101 E. Valencia Mesa Dr.
Fullerton, CA 92834
Tel: 714-871-3280
SHARON RICHARDSON, L.C.S.W., Admin. Dir. Patient/Family Support Svcs.
Chaplains:
Revs.:
WILLIAM PATRICK
GIL MANGAMPO
Sr. DOROTHY MORRIS, C.S.J.
Sr. DOLORES MIKULA, C.S.J.O.F.
Rev. JEAN WATKINS
Mr. JIM ERIXSON
Beds 347
Nurses 607
Staff 1,448
Patients assisted annually 14,484

St. Jude Memorial Foundation
P.O. Box 4138
Fullerton, CA 92834
Tel: 714-992-3033; Fax: 714-738-0691

Hawthorne
Archdiocese of Los Angeles

**Hawthorne Community Hospital, Inc.*
711 Grevilles Ave.
Hawthorne, CA 90250

Hayward
Diocese of Oakland

St. Rose Hospital
27200 Calaroga Ave.
Hayward, CA 94545-4383
Tel: 510-264-4000
Affiliated with Via Christi Health System, Inc.
Sisters of St. Joseph of Wichita, Kansas
Mr. MICHAEL MAHONEY, Pres.
Sr. MARY ALICE GIRRENS, C.S.J., Dir. of Mission Services
Chaplains:
Revs.:
ROY V. ECO
BRUCE J. KLIKUNAS, O.S.M.
Sr. DONALDA WINFREY, C.S.J.
SALLY HUSSEY
JOAN M. SILVA
Religious 5
Beds 175
Total Staff 710
Patients assisted annually 80,000
St. Rose Medical Office Bldg.
27200 Calaroga
Hayward, CA 94545
Tel: 510-264-4000
St. Rose Hospital Foundation
Sr. ANTOINETTE YELEK, C.S.J., Exec. Dir.
27200 Calaroga Ave.
Hayward, CA 94545-4383
Tel: 510-264-4008
Silva Pediatric Clinic
680 W. Tennyson Rd.
Hayward, CA 94544
Tel: 510-782-4470

Inglewood
Archdiocese of Los Angeles

Daniel Freeman Memorial Hospital
Division of Daniel Freeman Hospitals, Inc.
333 N. Prairie Ave.
Inglewood, CA 90301
Tel: 310-674-7050; 678-0361; Fax: 310-419-8273
PETER F. BASTONE, CEO
BRITT BERRETT, COO and Admin.
Sr. REGINA CLARE SALAZAR, C.S.J., Corp. Vice Pres. Sponsorship and Mission
G. ARNOLD MULDER, M.D., Chief of Staff
Rev. FRANCIS X. CHRYSOSTOM (Sri Lanka) Chap.
Sr. JEAN O'LEARY, C.S.J., Dir. of Pastoral Care
Sisters of St. Joseph of Carondelet 25
Bed Capacity 360
Patients assisted annually 107,279
Total Staff 1,863
Sisters of St. Joseph of Carondelet in California
Sr. KATHLEEN MARY MCCARTHY, C.S.J., Chm.
Freeman Hospitals Foundation
Sr. MARY ESTHER MCCANN, C.S.J., Pres. Emeritus
BRIAN GAUTHIER, Vice Pres.
BERNIE SKLAR, Chm.

Long Beach
Archdiocese of Los Angeles

St. Mary Medical Center
1050 Linden Ave.
Long Beach, CA 90813

St. Mary Medical Center Foundation
P.O. Box 887
Long Beach, CA 90801
Bed Capacity 551
Total Assisted Annually 35,000
Total Staff 1,600

St. Mary Professional Building, Inc.
1045 Atlantic Ave.
Long Beach, CA 90813
JAMES RIEDEL, Sec., Tel: 310-491-9010
TAMMIE MCMANN BRAILSFORD, Pres.

Los Angeles
Archdiocese of Los Angeles

Queen of Angels-Hollywood Presbyterian Medical Center
A California Corporation is the lessee-operator of the Hospital at:
1300 N. Vermont Ave.
Los Angeles, CA 90027
Rev. STEVE RYAN, O.S.M., Dir. of Chaplains
Mr. S. M. GRAFF, Admin.
Chaplains:
Revs.:
GEORGE WHEDBEE, C.M.F.
CARLOS C. CASTILLO, C.M.F.
JOHN HUBBARD, Presbyterian Chap.
Mrs. INGE FAMULARO, Presbyterian Chap.
Sr. DIANE MARTIN, O.S.F.
Sr. MAGDALENE MYLANG
Sisters 2
Bed Capacity 427
Patients assisted annually 150,000

St. Vincent Medical Center
2131 W. 3rd St.
Los Angeles, CA 90057
Tel: 213-484-7111
Daughters of Charity of St. Vincent de Paul
Mr. VINCENT F. GUINAN, JR., Pres.
Revs.:
FRANCIS ELDRIDGE
FRANCISCO AYLA
Chaplains:
Rev. JOHN P. FAHEY
FELIPE MARTINEZ
FRANK GODILLO
CAROL DETRANA
Sisters 14
Bed Capacity 320
Nurses 327
Patients assisted annually 50,000

Santa Marta Hospital
319 N. Humphreys Ave.
Los Angeles, CA 90022
Tel: 213-266-6500; Fax: 213-260-8641 (Admin.)
Mr. JAMES G. OVIEDA, Pres. & CEO
Sr. CATHERINE MARIE KRETA, C.S.J., Vice Pres. Mission
Sponsored by Carondelet Health System, which is Sponsored by Sisters of St. Joseph of Carondelet.
Bed Capacity 110
Patients assisted annually 31,000
Total Staff 430

Lynwood
Archdiocese of Los Angeles

Catholic Health Care West-Southern California
3630 E. Imperial Hwy.
Lynwood, CA 90262
Tel: 310-603-6000
DIANE CARTER, Esquire, Tel: 415-438-5610
Operating Divisions:
Robert F. Kennedy Medical Center
4500 W. 116th St.
Hawthorne, CA 90250
Patients assisted annually 5,409
Total Staff 550
Bed Capacity 274
St. Bernadine Medical Center (San Bernadino Diocese)
St. Francis Medical Center
St. Mary Medical Center
St. Vincent Medical Center

St. Francis Medical Center
3630 E. Imperial Hwy.
Lynwood, CA 90262
Tel: 310-603-6000
GERALD T. KOZAI, Pharm.D., Admin./Chief Operating Officer
Bro. RICHARD HIRBE, B.F.C.C., Dir. Pastoral Care
Revs.:
JAMES CLEARY, O.F.M., Assoc. Chap.
BOCTOR BISHARA, Assoc. Chap.
Sponsered by the Daughters of Charity of St. Vincent de Paul. (Member of CHW Southern California Region)
Patients assisted annually 133,385
Bed Capacity 520
Total Staff 1,650

Manteca
Diocese of Stockton

St. Dominic's Hospital
(Sub. of St. Joseph's Regional Health System) Member of Catholic Healthcare West
1777 W. Yosemite Ave., P.O. Box 1307
Manteca, CA 95337
Tel: 209-825-3500
Acute care community hospital.
EDWARD G. SCHROEDER, Pres. & CEO
Beds 63
Staff 226
Patients assisted 36,014

Marina Del Rey
Archdiocese of Los Angeles

Daniel Freeman Marina Hospital
Division of Daniel Freeman Hospitals, Inc.
4650 Lincoln Blvd.
Marina Del Rey, CA 90292
Tel: 310-823-8911
Mailing Address:—c/o Daniel Freeman Hospitals, Inc.
333 N. Prairie
Inglewood, CA 90301
JOSEPH W. DUNN, Ph.D., CEO, D.F. Marina Hospital
CHRISTOPHER GRAY, M.D., Chief of Staff
Sr. ANNA MARY MEYER, C.S.J., Dir. Pastoral Care
Priests 1
Sisters 6
Bed Capacity 184

Patients assisted annually 24,300

Merced
Diocese of Fresno

Mercy Hospital & Health Services
2740 M St.
Merced, CA 95340
Tel: 209-384-6444; Fax: 209-722-2902
Mr. Edward G. Schroeder, Pres.
Catholic Healthcare West and San Joaquin-Sierra Region
Sacramental Ministry by Priests of Merced.
Sponsored by the Sisters of Mercy, Auburn and Burlingame Regional Communities, Adrian Dominican Sisters; Daughters of Charity, Province of the West; Sisters of the Incarnate Word of Houston, Texas; Dominican Sisters of San Rafael; Dominican Sisters of St. Catherine of Siena of Kenosha, Wisconsin; Franciscan Sisters of the Sacred Heart, Frankfort, Illinois; Sisters of St. Francis of Redwood City, California
Mercy Home Care
Annually assisted 23,000
Sisters 5
Beds 101
Patients assisted annually 60,000

Mission Viejo
Diocese of Orange in California

Mission Hospital Regional Medical Center
27700 Medical Center Rd.
Mission Viejo, CA 92691
Tel: 714-364-1400
E-mail: srma@0103.stjoe.org
Sponsored by Sisters of St. Joseph of Orange
Peter Bastone, Pres. & CEO
Staff 1,350
Patients assisted: Inpatient days 54,533
Outpatients 101,969
Bed Capacity 271

Morgan Hill
Diocese of San Jose in California

O'Connor Hospital dba Saint Louise Hospital & Health Center
Admin. Office, 18500 Saint Louise Dr.
Morgan Hill, CA 95037
Tel: 408-779-1500
Member of Catholic Healthcare West
Rev. Walter Johnson, M.M., Pastoral Care Svcs.
Joan A. Bero, Acting CEO
Sisters 3
Staff 183
Beds 60
Patients assisted annually 31,965

Moss Beach
Archdiocese of San Francisco

Seton Medical Center Coastside
600 Marine Blvd.
Moss Beach, CA 94038
Tel: 650-728-5521
Daughters of St. Vincent de Paul
Deborah E. Stebbins, Pres. & CEO
Katy Innerst, R.N., Mgr.
Sr. Ann D.C., Patient Advocate
Religious 1
Patients assisted annually 8,451

Mt. Shasta
Diocese of Sacramento

Mercy Medical Center
914 Pine St., P.O. Box 239
Mt. Shasta, CA 96067
Tel: 916-926-6111
Web Site: ntmhn1.mercy.org
Mr. James Hoss, Pres.
Beds 80
Patients assisted annually 39,400
Staff 254

Napa
Diocese of Santa Rosa in California

Queen of the Valley Hospital of Napa
1000 Trancas St.
Napa, CA 94558
Tel: 707-252-4411; Fax: 707-257-4073
Sisters of St. Joseph of Orange, California
Howard LeVant, Pres.
Chaplains:
Rev. Gerard Heintzelman (HBG)
Priests 1
Sisters 6
Lay Staff 1,200
Bed Capacity 159
Patients assisted annually 40,398

Orange
Diocese of Orange in California

St. Joseph Health System
440 S. Batavia St.
Orange, CA 92868
Tel: 714-997-7690
Sr. Marianna Gemmet, C.S.J., Chm. of the Board
Mr. Richard Statuto, Pres. & CEO
St. Joseph Hospital of Orange
110 W. Stewart Dr., P.O. Box 5600
Orange, CA 92868-3995
Tel: 714-633-9111
Larry Ainsworth, Pres. & CEO
Rev. Elly S. Tavarro (Phillipines) Contact Person
Patients assisted annually 34,448
Beds 457
Other Employees 2,061
Nurses 806
St. Jude Hospital Yorba Linda
St. Joseph Health System, 440 S. Batavia St.
Orange, CA 92868-3995
Mr. Patrick Kapsner, CEO
SRM Alliance Hospital Services
St. Joseph Health System, 440 S. Batavia St.
Orange, CA 92868-3995
Susan Whittaker, Contact Person

**Sisters of St. Joseph Healthcare Foundation*
Sisters of St. Joseph of Orange, 480 S. Batavia St.
Orange, CA 92868-3995
Sr. Diane Hejna, C.S.J., Exec. Dir.

Oxnard
Archdiocese of Los Angeles

St. John's Regional Medical Center
1600 N. Rose Ave.
Oxnard, CA 93030
Tel: 805-988-2500
Daniel Herlinger, Pres. & CEO
Christine Picchi, Dir. Mission Svcs.
Elizabeth Cook, Clinical Pastoral Education Mgr.
Sisters of Mercy 4
Bed Capacity 264
Patients assisted annually 104,006
Total Staff 1,336
St. John's Pleasant Valley Hospital
2309 Antonio Ave.
Camarillo, CA 93010
Daniel Herlinger, Pres. & CEO
Sisters 4
Acute Beds 81
Skilled Nursing 99
Patients assisted annually 43,022
Total Staff 645

Rancho Cordova
Diocese of Sacramento

Mercy Healthcare Sacramento
10540 White Rock Rd.
Rancho Cordova, CA 95670
Tel: 916-851-2000
Michael Erne, Pres.
(Parent Company - Catholic Healthcare West)
Corporate Office
1700 Montgomery St., Ste. 300
San Francisco, CA 94111
Tel: 415-397-9000
Mr. Richard Kramer, Pres.
Sponsored by Sisters of Mercy of Burlingame; Sisters of Mercy of Auburn; Adrian Dominican Sisters; Daughters of Charity, Province of the West; Congregation of the Sisters of Charity of the Incarnate Word, Houston, Texas; Dominican Sisters of San Rafael; Dominican Sisters of St. Catherine of Siena of Kenosha, WI; Franciscan Sisters of the Sacred Heart of Frankfort, IL; Sisters of St. Francis of Penance and Christian Charity of Redwood City, CA.
This organization provides regional management and support functions for the following affiliated non-profit organizations: Mercy General Hospital of Sacramento; Mercy American River/Mercy San Juan Hospital, Carmichael (these hospitals are now operating under a single license); Mercy Hospital of Folsom; and the subsidiary corporations of Mercy McMahon Terrace and Mercy Medical Foundation.

Red Bluff
Diocese of Sacramento

St. Elizabeth Community Hospital Mercy Healthcare North
2550 Sr. Mary Columba Dr.
Red Bluff, CA 96080-4397
Tel: 916-529-8000; Fax: 916-529-8009
Mr. George A. Govier, Pres. & CEO
Mr. Thomas F. Grimes, Exec. Vice Pres. & COO
Sisters of Mercy 3
Nurses 157
Beds 76
Patients assisted annually 50,000
Total Staff 443
Attended by Sacred Heart, Red Bluff.

Redding
Diocese of Sacramento

Mercy Medical Center
Clairmont Heights, P.O. Box 496009
Redding, CA 96049
Tel: 916-225-6000
Mr. George A. Govier, Pres. & CEO
Rev. Michael Brennan, C.P., Chap.
Sisters of Mercy 6
Beds 256
Patients assisted annually 49,000
Corporate Name: Mercy Healthcare North dba Mercy Medical Center of Redding

Sacramento
Diocese of Sacramento

Mercy General Hospital
4001 J St.
Sacramento, CA 95819
Tel: 916-453-4545
Mr. Thomas A. Peterson, Vice Pres., COO
Margaret Mette, Vice Pres. Cardiovascular Serv.
Rev. John J. Healy, Chap.
Sisters of Mercy 14
Sisters of St. Francis 1
Nurses 689
Patients assisted annually 85,000
Beds 395
Mercy Care
862 39th St.
Sacramento, CA 95819

San Bernardino
Diocese of San Bernardino

St. Bernardine Medical Center
2101 N. Waterman Ave.
San Bernardino, CA 92404
Tel: 909-883-8711; Fax: 909-881-4546
Margo Winter, Admin. & CEO
Revs.:
Bernard Donaghey, S.V.D., Chap.
Barnabas Laubach, O.S.B., Chap. & Dir. Pastoral Care
Sisters 8
Beds 443
Patients assisted annually 403,000

San Diego
Diocese of San Diego

Mercy Hospital and Medical Center dba Mercy Healthcare San Diego
4077 Fifth Ave.
San Diego, CA 92103
Tel: 619-294-8111; Fax: 619-686-3530
E-mail: sisterJ@Mercvsd.com
Nancy Wilson, Sr. Vice Pres., Rgl. Admin.
Sr. JoCeal Young, Dir. Mission Svcs.
Revs.:
Francis W. McDonnell
Benjamin Bachmeier
Robert White
N.A.C.C. Certified Chaplains:
Benjamin Bachmeier
Michael Harkay
Elaine Martin
Sr. Barbara Checkhart, R.S.M.
Josie Rodriquez
John Gillman
Sr. Mary Sutherland, R.S.C.J.
Bed Capacity 520
Patients assisted annually 308,108
Mercy Clinic (Mercy Hospital)
Sisters of Mercy
Mercy Clinic Out Patients 33,587
Mercy Hospital Foundation
San Diego Mercy Hospital Auxiliary

San Francisco
Archdiocese of San Francisco

St. Mary's Medical Center
450 Stanyan St.
San Francisco, CA 94117
Tel: 415-668-1000
Mr. John G. Williams, Pres. & CEO

Chaplains:
Revs.:
ANTHONY BAUMANN, O.F.M.
EDWARD MURRAY
Sr. JOSEPH MARY GALLI, R.S.M.
Sr. SHARON KRENN, R.S.M.
Sr. KATHLEEN SICKLEY, P.B.V.M.
Priests 2
Religious 18
Patients assisted annually 182,405

San Jose
Diocese of San Jose in California

Alexian Brothers Hospital
225 N. Jackson Ave.
San Jose, CA 95116
Tel: 408-259-5000
Legal Title: *Alexian Brothers of San Jose, Inc.*
Parent Corporation: Alexian Brothers of California, Inc.
Congregation of Alexian Brothers, Immaculate Conception Province
Bro. EDWARD WALSH, C.F.A., Prov.
Mr. STEVE BARRON, CEO
Bros.:
JIM CLASSON, C.F.A., Dir., Alexian Bros. Community
JAMES JOHNSTON, C.F.A., Info. Desk
LARRY LOOBY, C.F.A., Nursing Dept.
Rev. ADEL GHALI
Sr. ROSALINE LIEU NGUYEN, L.H.C., Pastoral Care Dept.
Rev. ARTURO MATEO, M.S.C.
Sr. FRANCES WEIBERGER, S.N.D.
Sr. CHRISTINE LE, Q.M.H.C.
Priests 2
Brothers 3
Sisters 3
Pastoral Care Volunteers 40
Staff 428
Bed Capacity 204
Patients assisted annually 101,665
Employees 1,301

O'Connor Hospital
2105 Forest Ave.
San Jose, CA 95128
Tel: 408-947-2500
Legal Title: *O'Connor Hospital*
Member of Catholic Healthcare West
JOAN A. BERO, Acting CEO
Revs.:
ROBERT CARY, Pastoral Care Svcs.
TORIBIO IVES ANIBAN
Sisters 5
Total Staff 999
Beds 360
Patients assisted annually 139,885
O'Connor Foundation
2105 Forest Ave.
San Jose, CA 95128
Tel: 408-947-2717
MARIE BERNARDY, Vice Pres.

San Pedro
Archdiocese of Los Angeles

San Pedro Peninsula Hospital
(Affiliate of Little Company of Mary Health Services)
1700 W. Seventh St.
San Pedro, CA 90732
Tel: 310-832-3311
Patients assisted annually 36,962
Total Staff 1,200

Santa Barbara
Archdiocese of Los Angeles

St. Francis Medical Center of Santa Barbara
601 E. Micheltorena St.
Santa Barbara, CA 93103
Tel: 805-962-7661; Fax: 805-966-5704
Franciscan Sisters of the Sacred Heart
Mr. RON BISCARO, Pres. & CEO
Rev. Msgr. JOHN A. RAWDEN, Chap.
P.O. Box 4654
Santa Barbara, CA 93103
Sisters 5
Bed Capacity 110
Patients assisted annually 17,533

Santa Cruz
Diocese of Monterey in California

Dominican Santa Cruz Hospital
(Acute and Rehabilitation Services)
1555 Soquel Dr.
Santa Cruz, CA 95065
Tel: 408-462-7700; Fax: 408-462-7555
Sisters of St. Dominic (Adrian, MI)
Sr. JULIE HYER, O.P., Pres. & CEO
610 Frederick St.
Santa Cruz, CA 95062
Tel: 408-462-7700
Bed Capacity 375
Total Assisted in Hospital 116,693
Total Staff 1,300

Santa Maria
Archdiocese of Los Angeles

Marian Medical Center
1400 E. Church St.
Santa Maria, CA 93454
Tel: 805-739-3000
Sponsored by Sisters of St. Francis of Penance and Christian Charity
MICHAEL A. SCAVOTTO, CEO
CHARLES J. COVA, Exec. Vice Pres.
Deacon ZENON L. NAWROCIK, Dir. Pastoral Care
Sisters 9
Bed Capacity 130
Patients assisted annually 54,665
Total Staff 795
Marian Medical Center Extended Care Facility Skilled Nursing Facility.
Beds 95
Marian Medical Center Day Care Facility for Children
Capacity 52
Marian Residence Retirement Home
124 S. College Dr.
Santa Maria, CA 93454
Tel: 805-922-7731
Marian Medical Center Foundation
1406 E. Main St., Ste. E.
Santa Maria, CA 93454
Tel: 805-349-9486

Santa Monica
Archdiocese of Los Angeles

Saint John's Health Center
1328 22nd St.
Santa Monica, CA 90404
Tel: 310-829-5511; Fax: 310-315-6134
Sisters of Charity of Leavenworth
Sr. MARIE MADELEINE SHONKA, Pres.
Mr. BRUCE LAMOUREUX, C.E.O.
Rev. PATRICK COMERFORD, Chap.
Sisters 11
Bed Capacity 317
Patients assisted annually 200,000
Total Staff 1,440
Saint John's Health Center Foundation
The Michael Burke Foundation
The Hope Guild
The Irene Dunne Guild
John Wayne Cancer Institute Benefactors
John Wayne Cancer Institute Auxiliary
The ABC's, Associates for Breast Cancer Studies

Santa Rosa
Diocese of Santa Rosa in California

Santa Rosa Memorial Hospital
1165 Montgomery Dr.
Santa Rosa, CA 95405
Tel: 707-546-3210
Sisters of St. Joseph of Orange Corporation
Mr. ROBERT FISH, Pres. & CEO
Rev. MARK G. O'LEARY, O.P., Chap.
Rev. Msgr. PATRICK MCCOY (England) Chap.
Priests 2
Sisters 5
Employees 1,246
Bed capacity 219
Patients assisted annually 78,255

Stockton
Diocese of Stockton

Catholic Healthcare West System San Joaquin-Sierra Region
1800 N. California St., P.O. Box 213008
Stockton, CA 95213-9008
Tel: 209-943-2000
Sponsored by the Sisters of Mercy, Auburn and Burlingame Regional Communities; Adrian Dominican Sisters; Daughters of Charity, Province of the West; Sisters of Charity of the Incarnate Word of Houston, Texas; Dominican Sisters of San Rafael; Dominican Sisters of St. Catherine of Siena of Kenosha, Wisconsin; Franciscan Sisters of the Sacred Heart, Frankfort, Illinois; Sisters of St. Francis of Redwood City, California
Mr. EDWARD G. SCHROEDER, Pres. & CEO
This organization provides regional management and support functions for the following affiliated non-profit organizations: St. Joseph's Medical Center of Stockton; St. Dominic's Hospital of Manteca; Mark Twain St. Joseph's Hospital of San Andreas; St. Joseph's Behavioral Health Center of Stockton and Mercy Hospital and Health Services of Merced.
Active Medical Staff 470
Licensed Acute Beds 492
Full-Time Employees 2,589

St. Joseph's Behavioral Health Center
(Sub. of St. Joseph's Regional Health System)
2510 N. California St.
Stockton, CA 95204
Tel: 209-948-2100
Psychiatric and chemical dependency care hospital.
NORMA BROWN, Admin.
DON WILEY
Beds 35
Staff 157
Patients assisted 2,650

St. Joseph's Medical Center of Stockton
(Sub. of St.Joseph's Regional Health System) Member of Catholic Healthcare West
1800 N. California St., P.O. Box 213008
Stockton, CA 95213-9008
Tel: 209-943-2000
Acute care community hospital.
EDWARD G. SCHROEDER, Pres. & CEO
Beds 294
Staff 2,005
Patients assisted 286,500

Susanville
Diocese of Sacramento

Lassen Community Hospital
560 Hospital Ln.
Susanville, CA 96130
Tel: 916-257-5325
St. Mary's Health Care Corp. Affiliate.
235 W. Sixth St.
Reno, NV 89520
Mr. DAVID S. ANDERSON, Admin.
Beds 59
Bassinets 5
Patients assisted annually 25,100
Total Staff 180
Corporate Name: Lassen Community Hospital, Inc.

Torrance
Archdiocese of Los Angeles

Little Company of Mary Health Services
4101 Torrance Blvd.
Torrance, CA 90503
Tel: 310-543-5803; Fax: 310-540-7659
Little Company of Mary Hospital
4101 Torrance Blvd.
Torrance, CA 90503
Tel: 310-540-7676
Conducted By: Sisters of Little Company of Mary.
Sr. CAROL PACINI, L.C.M., Chm.
MARK COSTA, Pres.
Sr. GLORIA HARPER, L.C.M., Dir. Pastoral Care
Chaplains:
Deacon RICHARD PRUITT
Mrs. JUANITA MELLER, C.C., Ph.D.
Bed Capacity 356
Pavilion - Little Company of Mary Hospital Skilled nursing facility.
4320 Maricopa St.
Torrance, CA 90503
Tel: 310-543-5900
Conducted By: Sisters of Little Company of Mary
Sr. CAROL PACINI, L.C.M., Chm.
MARK COSTA, Pres.
Sr. GLORIA HARPER, L.C.M., Dir. Pastoral Care
Chaplains:
Deacon RICHARD PRUITT
Mrs. JUANITA MELLER, C.C., Ph.D.
Bed Capacity 121
San Pedro Peninsula Hospital
1700 W. 7th St.
San Pedro, CA 90732
Tel: 310-832-3311
Conducted By: Sisters of Little Company of Mary
Sr. CAROL PACINI, L.C.M., Chm.
JOHN M. WILSON, Pres.
Sr. MARY BABCOCK, L.C.M., Dir. Pastoral Care
Rev. FRANCIS SHIGO, S.V.D., Chap.
Bed Capacity 387
Pavilion - San Pedro Peninsula Hospital Skilled nursing facility.
1322 W. Sixth St.
San Pedro, CA 90732
Tel: 310-514-5270
Conducted By: Sisters of Little Company of Mary.
Sr. CAROL PACINI, L.C.M., Chm.
JOHN M. WILSON, Pres.
Sr. MARIE BABCOCK, L.C.M., Dir. Pastoral Care

Rev. Francis L. Shigo, S.V.D., Chap.
Bed Capacity 128
Bay Harbor Hospital
1437 W. Lomita Blvd.
Harbor City, CA 90710
Tel: 310-325-1221
Conducted By: Sisters of Little Company of Mary.
Sr. Carol Pacini, L.C.M., Chm.
Jack Weiblen, Pres.
Sr. Gloria Harper, L.C.M., Dir. Pastoral Care
Chaplains:
Rev. Ernest Montoya
Mrs. Ginny Harney
Bed Capacity 134
Bay Harbor Hospital West Skilled nursing facility.
3620 W. Lomita Blvd.
Torrance, CA 90505
Tel: 310-378-8587
Conducted By: Sisters of Little Company of Mary.
Sr. Carol Pacini, L.C.M., Chm.
Jack Weiblen, Pres.
Sr. Gloria Harper, L.C.M., Dir. Pastoral Care
Chaplains:
Rev. Ernest Montoya
Mrs. Ginny Harney
Bed Capacity 212

West Covina
Archdiocese of Los Angeles

Citrus Valley Health Partners, Queen of the Valley Campus
1115 S. Sunset Ave., P.O. Box 1980
West Covina, CA 91793
Tel: 818-962-4011; Fax: 818-814-2482
E-mail: vip.pm@cvhp.org
Web Site: cvhp.com
Mr. Peter Makowski, CEO
Bed Capacity 263
Patients assisted annually 121,483
Staff 850

COLORADO

Canon City
Diocese of Pueblo

Centura Health-St. Thomas More Hospital
An operating unit of Catholic Health Initiatives Mountain Region (an affiliate of Catholic Health Initiatives).
1338 Phay Ave.
Canon City, CO 81212
Tel: 719-269-2000; Fax: 719-269-2016
Ray Honaker, Admin.
Chaplains:
Rev. Martin Muheim, O.S.B.
Sr. Virginia Knopp, O.S.B.
Beds 245
Patients assisted annually 72,252

Colorado Springs
Diocese of Colorado Springs

Centura Health-Penrose-St. Francis Health Services
Penrose Hospital An operating unit of Catholic Health Initiatives Mountain Region (an Affiliate of Catholic Health Initiatives).
2215 N. Cascade Ave.
Colorado Springs, CO 80907
Tel: 719-776-5000; Fax: 719-776-2494
Revs.:
Gerald H. Bruggeman, Sacramental Min.
Alan Filippi, Protestant Chap.
Tom Stella
Chaplains:
Michael Crino
Sr. Jane Grosheider, S.C.
Sr. Lucille Krippel, O.S.F., Dir. Spiritual Care
Ginger Morgan
Sr. Immaculata Park, O.S.F.
John Zay
Sisters 3
Penrose Community Hospital An operating unit of Catholic Health Initiatives Mountain Region (an Affiliate of Catholic Health Initiatives).
3205 N. Academy Blvd.
Colorado Springs, CO 80917
Tel: 719-776-3000; Fax: 719-591-3477
Sr. Joan Crocker, S.C.

Penrose-St. Francis Healthcare Foundation
A division of Catholic Health Initiatives Mountain Region Foundation.
7606 N. Union Blvd., Ste. D
Colorado Springs, CO 80920
Tel: 719-528-5883

St. Francis Health Center
An operating unit of Catholic Health Initiatives Mountain Region (an Affiliate of Catholic Health Initiatives).
825 E. Pikes Peak Ave.
Colorado Springs, CO 80903
Tel: 719-776-8800; Fax: 719-636-8871
Sr. Lucille Krippel, O.S.F., Dir. Spiritual Care
Sisters 1

Denver
Archdiocese of Denver

**Centura Health*
1601 Lowell Blvd.
Denver, CO 80204
Gardens at St. Elizabeth
2835 W. 32nd Ave.
Denver, CO 80211
Tel: 303-477-4442; Fax: 303-964-2340
An operating unit of Sisters of Charity Health Services Colorado.
Centura Senior Life Center
1601 Lowell Blvd.
Denver, CO 80204
Tel: 303-825-2190; Fax: 303-899-5059
An operating unit of Sisters of Charity Health Services Colorado.
Centura Adult Day Care
4165 Eaton St.
Denver, CO 80033
Tel: 303-422-9000
An operating unit of Sisters of Charity Health Services Colorado.

Mercy Medical Center
1650 Fillmore St.
Denver, CO 80206
Affiliate of Catholic Health Initiatives.

Provenant Acute Long Stay Hospital
1601 Lowell Blvd.
Denver, CO 80204
Affiliate of Catholic Health Initiatives.

Provenant Home Health and Eldercare Services
1560 Meade St.
Denver, CO 80204
Affiliate of Catholic Health Initiatives.

St. Anthony Hospital Central
4231 W. 16th Ave.
Denver, CO 80204
Affiliate of Catholic Health Initiatives.

St. Anthony Hospital North
2551 W. 84th Ave.
Denver, CO 80030
Affiliate of Catholic Health Initiatives.

St. Joseph Hospital
1835 Franklin St.
Denver, CO 80218
Tel: 303-837-7111
Sr. Marianna Bauder, Pres. & CEO
Rev. R. Philip Negele, O.C.S.O.
Sisters of Charity of Leavenworth 14
Bed Capacity 601
Patients assisted annually 109,795
Outpatients assisted annually 264,878

The Villas at Sunny Acres
2501 E. 104th Ave.
Denver, CO 80233
Affiliate of Catholic Health Initiatives.

Durango
Diocese of Pueblo

Centura Health-Mercy Medical Center
An affiliate of Catholic Health Initiatives.
375 E. Park Ave.
Durango, CO 81301
Tel: 970-247-4311; Fax: 970-382-1082
Mr. Renato V. Baciarelli, Senior Vice Pres., Admin.
Chaplains:
Rev. Michael L. McCleary
Sr. Sharon Ekler, Vice Pres., Mission & Ministry
Beds 111
Patients assisted annually 203,170

Grand Junction
Diocese of Pueblo

Marillac Clinic, Inc.
600 Center Ave., Bldg. 3A
Grand Junction, CO 81501
Ms. Janet K. Cameron, Exec. Dir.
Legal Title: *Sisters of Charity of Leavenworth, Health Services Corp.*

St. Mary Hospital and Medical Center
P.O. Box 1628
Grand Junction, CO 81502
Tel: 970-244-2273; Fax: 970-244-7510
Sr. Lynn Casey, S.C.L., Pres.
Rev. Aloysius J. Bertrand, Chap.
Sisters of Charity of Leavenworth, Kansas 10
Beds 354
Patients assisted annually 296,238

Pueblo
Diocese of Pueblo

Centura Health-St. Mary-Corwin Hospital
An operating unit of Catholic Health Initiatives Mountain Region (an affiliate of Catholic Health Initiatives).
1008 Minnequa Ave.
Pueblo, CO 81004
Tel: 719-560-4000; Fax: 719-560-5823
John Sackett, Admin.
Chaplains:
Rev. Michael C. DeSciose
Sr. Margaret Donnelly, S.C.
Sr. Darlene Mahoney, O.S.F.
Revs.:
Phil Sorinson
Robert Frimpong-Manso, Coord., Spiritual Care
Beds 200
Patients assisted annually 303,204

CONNECTICUT

Bridgeport
Diocese of Bridgeport

St. Vincent's Development Corporation
2800 Main St.
Bridgeport, CT 06606
Tel: 203-576-5459
Mr. William Riordan, Chm.
Mr. Richard D'Aquila, Pres. & CEO

St. Vincent's Health Services Corporation
2800 Main St.
Bridgeport, CT 06606
Tel: 203-576-5455
Sr. Margaret John Kelly, D.C., Chm.
Mr. William J. Riordan, Pres. & CEO

St. Vincent's Medical Center
2800 Main St.
Bridgeport, CT 06606
Tel: 203-576-6000
Daughters of Charity of St. Vincent de Paul (Albany, NY)
Sr. Margaret John Kelly, D.C., Chm.
Mr. William J. Riordan, Pres. & CEO
Revs.:
Robert DeLeon, C.S.C., Dir.
Natalie Shiras
Robert Malone, C.S.C.
John V. Borgo, S.J.
Daniel Kennelly
Thomas Elliott, C.S.C.
St. Vincent's College
Students 201
Saint Vincent's Special Needs Center, Inc.
95 Merritt Blvd.
Trumball, CT 06611

St. Vincent's Medical Center Foundation
2800 Main St.
Bridgeport, CT 06606
Tel: 203-576-5451
Mr. Joseph H. Maloney, Chm.
Mr. Ronald J. Bianchi, Pres.

Hartford
Archdiocese of Hartford

Saint Francis Hospital and Medical Center
114 Woodland St.
Hartford, CT 06105-1299
Tel: 860-714-4000; Fax: 860-714-7809
Dr. David D'Eramo, Pres. & CEO
Chaplains:
Revs.:
Liam C. Casey, Dir. Pastoral Care
Mark Bonsignore
Thomas Puthiyadom
Licensed Beds 617
Bassinets 65
Out-Patient Visits 273,911
In-Patient Visits 128,319
Staff 3,804
The Women's Auxiliary of Saint Francis Hospital and Medical Center
Mrs. Ranjana Chawla, Pres.
Asylum Hill Family Medicine Center, Inc.
Woodland Physician Associates, Inc.

Camillus Corporation
The One Thousand Corporation
One Thousand One Corporation
Saint Francis Hospital and Medical Center Foundation, Inc.
114 Woodland St.
Hartford, CT 06105
The Rehabilitation Hospital of Connecticut, Inc.
480 Blue Hills Ave.
Hartford, CT 06112
Tel: 714-548-4000
Nurses School
260 Ashley St.
Hartford, CT 06105
Student Nurses 54

New Haven
Archdiocese of Hartford

Hospital of St. Raphael
1450 Chapel St.
New Haven, CT 06511
Tel: 203-789-3000; Fax: 203-789-3653
Sisters of Charity (Convent Station)
JAMES J. CULLEN, Pres.
CINDY VON BEREN, Admin. & Contact
Chaplains:
Revs.:
CHACKO KUMPLAMTHANAM
ROBERT STRUMINSKI, S.M.
GREGORY M. ALTERMATT
SANDY BELCHER
Sr. MARJORIE CREANI, S.C.
Sr. COLETTE HANLON, S.C., Dir. Pastoral Care
JANICE LABAS
RABBI STEVE STEINBERF
Chaplains 8
Sisters 12
Bed Capacity 511
Bassinets 22
Patients assisted annually 110,000
Staff 3,000
Legal Holdings: Saint Raphael Healthcare System; Saint Raphael Foundation, Inc.; DePaul Health Services Corporation; Seton Real Estate, Inc.; Saint Regis Health Center, Inc. (Non-profit charitable corporations affiliated with the Hospital of Saint Raphael).

Saint Regis Health Center, Inc.
1354 Chapel St.
New Haven, CT 06511
Tel: 203-867-8300
ROBERT HELLRIGEL, Exec. Dir. & Contact
125-bed skilled nursing facility.

Stamford
Diocese of Bridgeport

St. Joseph Medical Center
128 Strawberry Hill Ave.
Stamford, CT 06904-1222
Tel: 203-353-2001
Most Rev. WILLIAM J. RIORDAN, Bd. Chm.
PHILIP D. CUSANO, Pres. & CEO

St. Joseph Medical Center Foundation, Inc.
128 Strawberry Hill Ave.
Stamford, CT 06904
Mr. JACKSON E. SPEARS, K.S.G., Pres.

Waterbury
Archdiocese of Hartford

St. Mary Hospital
56 Franklin St.
Waterbury, CT 06706
Tel: 203-574-6000; Fax: 203-597-3238
Sisters of St. Joseph of Chambery
Sr. MARGUERITE WAITE, C.S.J., Pres.
Revs.:
ROBERT J. GRANT
STANLEY R. STARON
Sisters 13
Bed Capacity 347
Bassinets 32
Patients assisted annually 203,056
The Slocum Corporation-St. Mary's Hospital Foundation, Inc., Non-profit corporations for the exclusive benefit of St. Mary Hospital.

West Hartford
Archdiocese of Hartford

McAuley Center, Inc.
275 Steele Rd.
West Hartford, CT 06117
Tel: 860-236-6300
MICHAEL ESCAMILLA, Exec. Dir. & Contact
Continuing care retirement community; Sisters of Mercy. 255 residential apartment units for individuals age 55 and over. Nursing care at St. Mary's Home included.

DELAWARE

Wilmington
Diocese of Wilmington

St. Francis Hospital, Inc.
7th and Clayton Sts., P.O. Box 2500
Wilmington, DE 19805-0500
Tel: 302-575-8300
STEVEN C. BJELICH, Pres./Chief Exec. Officer
Sr. MARGARET ALOYSIUS MCGRAIL, O.S.F., V.P. Mission & Ministry
Rev. JOSEPH NARIMATTAM, Chap.
Beds 395
Staff 1,500
Patients assisted annually 311,000

DISTRICT OF COLUMBIA

Washington
Archdiocese of Washington

Center for Life of Providence Hospital
1150 Varnum St., N.E.
Washington, DC 20017
Non-Profit Corporation to Render Service, Support and Assistance in the Provision of Community Services Which Foster Human Dignity, Family Unity and Respect for Life. Services Include: Reduced Fee Maternity Programs.
Total Assisted 109,400
Total Staff 1,571

De Paul Foundation, Inc.
1150 Varnum St., N.E.
Washington, DC 20017
De Paul Foundation, Inc. was Organized to Provide Fund Development, Financial and Other Assistance to Provide Hospital and Other Subsidiaries of De Paul Foundation for the Health Care, Medical, Educational and Human Needs of the District of Columbia and Vicinity, by Functioning as a Charitable Nonprofit, Nonstock Corporation.
Providence Health Foundation
1150 Varnum St., N.E.
Washington, DC 20017
Providence Health Foundation, Inc. (PHF), a District of Columbia Charitable Nonprofit Corporation, was Organized to Support the Mission of Providence Hospital by Conducting Fundraising and Development Activities, by Receiving and Managing Donations, by Making Grants, and by Promoting Educational Activities and Scientific Research.

Georgetown University Hospital
3800 Reservoir Rd., N.W.
Washington, DC 20007
Tel: 202-784-3000
SHARON FLYNN HOLLANDER, Hopital Chief Exec.
Rev. JAMES M. SHEA, S.J., Dir. Pastoral Care
Chaplains:
Sr. SARA-ANN BUCKLEY, S.N.D.
Revs.:
JAMES J. DENN, C.S.C.
GUSTAAF M. KEPPENS, S.J.
Bed Capacity 535
Patients assisted annually 150,000

Providence Health Services, Inc.
1150 Varnum St., N.E.
Washington, DC 20017
Ambulatory-Outpatient Care, Promote Wellness and Carry Out of Educational Activities and Scientific Research.

FLORIDA

Clearwater
Diocese of St. Petersburg

St. Michael's Housing Corporation dba Casa Miguel
Independent Living.
2285 State Rd. #580
Clearwater, FL 33763
Tel: 813-797-8551
Mrs. JOANN LUNGARO, Admin.
Total Staff 5
Residents 82

The Tepeyac Corporation dba/La Clinica Guadalupana
1215 Drew St., Ste. 7B
Clearwater, FL 34615
Tel: 813-461-7730
E-mail: laclinica@compuserve.com
Rev. PETER SCHWEITZER, Pres.
Annually Assisted 890
Staff 1

Fort Lauderdale
Archdiocese of Miami

Holy Cross Hospital
4725 N. Federal Hwy.
Fort Lauderdale, FL 33308
Tel: 954-771-8000; Fax: 954-492-5741
ROBERT GRANGER, Acting Pres. & CEO
Chaplains:
Revs.:
WILLIAM MUNIZ
WILLIAM HOURAN
Sr. ANN DRISCOLL, R.S.M.
Sr. MARGARET RITCHIE, R.S.M.
Ms. BARBARA OUELLETTE
Sisters of Mercy 14
Staff 2,000
Bed Capacity 587
Patients assisted annually 366,632 (includes Home Health & Holy Cross Medical Group Visits)
Holy Cross Health Ministries, Inc.
Holy Cross Hospital, Inc.
Holy Cross Long Term Care, Inc.

Jacksonville
Diocese of St. Augustine

St. Vincent's Medical Center, Inc.
Member Baptist/St. Vincent's Health System.
1800 Barrs St., P.O. Box 2982
Jacksonville, FL 32203
Tel: 904-308-7300
Web Site: www.Baptist-Stvincents.com/
Daughters of Charity of St. Vincent de Paul
Revs.:
ROBERT GALCHUS, O.M.
EDWARD MCQUILLAN, C.M.
LESTER DEMOTT, C.M., Chap.
Nurses 724
Beds 528
Bassinets 15
Outpatients 168,453
Inpatient 24,247
St. Vincent's Foundation, Inc.
Baptist/St. Vincent's Primary Care System
The Heart And Lung Institute, Inc.
St. Catherine Laboure Manor, Inc.

Miami
Archdiocese of Miami

Mercy Hospital
3663 S. Miami Ave.
Miami, FL 33133
Tel: 305-854-4400
Sponsored by the Sisters of St. Joseph of St. Augustine, FL
Sr. ELIZABETH ANNE WORLEY, S.S.J., Chm. Board of Trustees, Contact
Sr. LORRAINE KRAVERATH, S.S.J., Dir. Mission and Ministry
Mercy Mission Services (Subsidiary of Mercy Hospital)
Chaplains:
Revs.:
CARL T. MORRISON
LUIS MARQUINA
FABIO ARANGO
ANTHONY ACEVEDO
Sisters 10
Staff 2,230
Bed Capacity 512
Patients assisted annually 206,566

Pensacola
Diocese of Pensacola-Tallahassee

The Mother Seton Guild of Sacred Heart Hospital, Inc.
Pensacola, FL 32504
Mr. DONALD HOLLAND, Pres.

Sacred Heart Foundation, Inc.
4475 Bayou Blvd.
Pensacola, FL 32503
P.O. Box 2700
Pensacola, FL 32513-2700
CHARLES ALCOTT, III, Pres.

Sacred Heart Hospital of Pensacola
5151 N. Ninth Ave.
Pensacola, FL 32504
Tel: 850-416-7000
PATRICK J. MADDEN, Pres. & CEO
Annual Admissions 20,269
Staff 2,411

Port Charlotte
Diocese of Venice

Bon Secours-St. Joseph Hospital
2500 Harbor Blvd.
Port Charlotte, FL 33952
Tel: 941-625-4122
E-mail: jim_hoff@bshsi.com
Mr. MICHAEL HARRINGTON, EVP/Admin.
Sisters 9
Beds 212
Patients assisted annually 54,439
Total Staff 832
Bon Secours-St. Joseph Healthcare Group, Inc.
2500 Harbor Blvd.
Port Charlotte, FL 33952
Sr. ROSE MARIE JASINSKI, C.B.S., Pres.
Mr. MICHAEL HARRINGTON, EVP/Admin.
Chaplains:
Revs.:
PAUL ORTNER, S.S.J.
OTMAR GALLAGHER, O.F.M.Cap.
ARTHUR B. SCHUTE, NACC Cert.
Sr. KATHLEEN MORONEY, C.B.S., NACC Cert.
JAMES E. HOFF, Coord., NACC Cert.
KAREN RILEY, Coord. Parish Nurse, NACC Cert.

**Bon Secours-St. Joseph Healthcare Group Foundation, Inc.*
Bon Secours-St. Joseph Home Health Agency, Inc.
Bon Secours-St. Joseph Nursing Care Center
Sr. MARY ADELE WIECZORKOWSKI, C.S.S.F.
Bon Secours Hospice
Sr. DOROTHY BROGAN, C.B.S., NACC Cert.

St. Petersburg
Diocese of St. Petersburg

**Bon Secours-Maria Manor Nursing Care Center, Inc.*
10300 Fourth St., N.
St. Petersburg, FL 33716
Tel: 813-576-1025
Sisters of Bon Secours
Mr. MICHAEL WARD, Admin.
Sr. KARLA BOGNAR, S.N.D., Dir. Pastoral Care
Rev. PETER ZEMANICK, O.C.S.O., Chap., Tel: 813-576-6370
JANET KELLER, Asst. Admin.
Bed Capacity 274
Total Annually Assisted 259
Total Staff 295

Holy Cross Housing dba Casa Santa Cruz
7825 54th Ave. N.
St. Petersburg, FL 33709
Mr. JOSEPH A. DIVITO, Registered Agent
Total Staff 4
Total in Residence 81

St. Anthony's Hospital, Inc.
1200 Seventh Ave., N.
St. Petersburg, FL 33705
Tel: 813-825-1100
Chaplains:
Revs.:
TERRENCE K. FLEMMING
JIM JONES, O.F.M.
Franciscan Sisters of Allegany
Licensed Beds 415
Employees 1,448
Patients assisted annually 73,466
Legal Title: *St. Anthony's Hospital, Inc.*
Legal Title: *St. Anthony's Ancillary Services, Inc.*
Legal Title: *St. Anthony's Professional Buildings and Services, Inc.*
Legal Title: *St. Anthony's Health Care Foundation, Inc.*

Tampa
Diocese of St. Petersburg

Christ the King Housing II, Inc. dba Kings Manor
2946 W. Columbus Dr.
Tampa, FL 33607
Tel: 813-875-0139; Fax: 813-875-6061
Mr. PATRICK O'SULLIVAN, Admin.
Residents 125
Total Staff 4

Christ the King Housing, Inc. dba Kings Arms
4125 N. Lincoln Ave.
Tampa, FL 33607
Tel: 813-873-0234
Mr. PATRICK O'SULLIVAN, Admin.
Total Staff 4
Total in Residence 89

St. Joseph's Hospital, Inc.
3001 W. Martin Luther King Blvd.
Tampa, FL 33607
Mailing Address:
P.O. Box 4227
Tampa, FL 33677
Tel: 813-870-4000
Chaplains:
Revs.:
KENNETH GERTH, M.C.C.J.
JOHN BECKLEY, S.M.
Franciscan Sisters of Allegany
Legal Title: *St. Joseph's Hospital, Inc.*
Legal Title: *St. Joseph's Ancillary Services, Inc.*
Legal Title: *St. Joseph's Health Care Center, Inc.*
Legal Title: *St. Joseph's Hospital of Tampa Foundation, Inc.*
St. Francis Residence, Inc.

St. Patrick's Housing Corporation dba Patrician Arms
4516 S. Manhattan Ave.
Tampa, FL 33611
Tel: 813-835-8227
Total Staff 4
Total in Residence 85

Venice
Diocese of Venice

Bon Secours-Venice Healthcare Corp.
540 The Rialto
Venice, FL 34285
Tel: 941-483-7664
E-mail: roy_hess@BSHSI.com
Web Site: www.bshsi-florida.com
Sr. MARY CATHERINE ROGERS, C.B.S., Pres.
Mr. ROY HESS, Exec. Vice Pres.
Sisters 1
Total Beds 462
Total Patients 177,102
Total Staff 1,396

West Palm Beach
Diocese of Palm Beach

St. Mary's Hospital, Inc.
901 45th St.
West Palm Beach, FL 33407-2495
Tel: 561-881-2865; Fax: 561-881-2864
Mailing Address:
P.O. Box 24620
West Palm Beach, FL 33416-4620
Rev. Msgr. RONALD BESHARA, Dir. Pastoral Care
Chaplains:
Rev. Msgr. RONALD N. BESHARA, Dir. Mission Integration
Revs.:
EMMETT MULLIGAN, O.F.M.
DOMINIC NOVOA (HRT)
CHARLES H. MUZZEY (WDC)
Franciscan Sisters of Allegany 9
Beds 460
Patients assisted annually 268,877
Total Discharges 15,826
Affiliated Support Organizations:
St. Mary's Medical Center, Inc.
St. Mary's Hospital Foundation, Inc.
St. Mary's Ancillary Services, Inc.
St. Mary's Imaging Center, Inc.
St. Mary's Care Services, Inc.
St. Mary's Pain Center, Inc.
St. Mary's A.S.C., Inc.
St. Mary's Women's Health Services
Mid-County Medical Center, Inc.
United Medical Management

GEORGIA

Athens
Archdiocese of Atlanta

St. Mary's Hospital
1230 Baxter St.
Athens, GA 30606-3791
Tel: 706-354-3033; Fax: 706-354-3197
Missionary Sisters of the Most Sacred Heart of Jesus
Mr. EDWARD J. FECHTEL, JR., Pres. & CEO
Sr. M. GEORGETTE, M.S.C., Community Care Coord.
Nursing Sisters 3
Other Sister Personnel 4
Nurses 325
Beds 196
Patients assisted annually 114,463

Atlanta
Archdiocese of Atlanta

Saint Joseph's Hospital of Atlanta, Inc.
5665 Peachtree Dunwoody Rd., N.E.
Atlanta, GA 30342
Tel: 404-851-7001
Sisters of Mercy of Americas, Baltimore Regional Community.
RONALD P. HOGAN, CEO
Sisters 16
Total Staff 2,000
Bed Capacity 346
Patients assisted annually 18,273

Augusta
Diocese of Savannah

St. Joseph Center For Life, Inc.
2260 Wrightsboro Rd.
Augusta, GA 30910
WILLIAM PAUGH, Pres./CEO

St. Joseph Hospital, Augusta, GA, Inc.
2260 Wrightsboro Rd.
Augusta, GA 30910
Tel: 706-481-7400; Fax: 706-481-7599
J. WILLIAM PAUGH, Pres./CEO
Rev. DANIEL M. MUNN, Dir. Mission Effectiveness
Deacon GREGORY BERNARD, Dir. Pastoral Care
Bed Capacity 144
Patients assisted annually 110,000
Staff Chaplains 5
Sisters 5

Columbus
Diocese of Savannah

St. Francis Hospital
2122 Manchester Expwy., P.O. Box 7000
Columbus, GA 31908-7000
Tel: 706-596-4000
MICHAEL E. GARRIGAN, FACHE Pres.
Rev. HUGH MARSHALL, S.T., Chap.
Beds 376
Patients assisted annually 82,000

Savannah
Diocese of Savannah

St. Joseph's Hospital
11705 Mercy Blvd., P.O. Box 60129
Savannah, GA 31419-1791
Tel: 912-925-4100
Mr. PAUL P. HINCHEY, Pres./C.E.O., Tel: 912-927-5404
Sr. BERNADETTE LAFLAMME, R.S.M., Dir. Pastoral Care, Tel: 912-927-5582
Sr. GRACE MARIE DILLARD, R.S.M., Vice Pres., Mission Effectiveness, Tel: 912-925-4100
Rev. RODOLFO P. ROXAS, Chap.
Sisters of Mercy of the Americas 7
Bed Capacity 305
Bassinets 20
Patients assisted annually 89,620

HAWAII

Honolulu
Diocese of Honolulu

St. Francis Healthcare System of Hawaii
P.O. Box 30100
Honolulu, HI 96820
Tel: 808-566-4783
Web Site: www.sfhs.hi.org
Sr. BEATRICE TOM, O.S.F., CEO
Total Staff 163
St. Francis Medical Center
2230 Liliha St.
Honolulu, HI 96817
Tel: 808-547-6011
Sr. GRETCHEN GILROY, O.S.F., CEO
Chaplains:
Revs.:
EDWARD POPISH, SS.CC.
PAULO TUUGUSAMUSU
Bed Capacity 308
Patients assisted annually 358,054
Total Staff 1,449
Women's Addiction Treatment Center
2230 Liliha St.
Honolulu, HI 96817
Patients assisted annually 204
Bed Capacity 14
St. Francis Medical Center - West
91-2141 Fort Weaver Rd.
Ewa Beach, HI 96706
Tel: 808-678-7000
Sr. GRETCHEN GILROY, O.S.F., CEO
Rev. GORDON COMBS, O.F.M.Cap., Chap.
Bed Capacity 100
Patients assisted annually 35,961
Total Staff 627
St. Francis Healthcare Foundation of Hawaii
P.O. Box 30100
Honolulu, HI 96820
Mr. EUGENE TIWANAK, Pres.
Total Staff 5

The Sister Maureen Keleher Center (Hospice)
24 Puiwa Rd.
Honolulu, HI,
Tel: 808-595-7566
Sr. Francine Gries, O.S.F., Dir.
Bed Capacity 12
Patients assisted annually 717
St. Francis Health Centers (Iwilei, Downtown, Pali)
Patients assisted annually 9,517
Health Services for Senior Citizens
1149 Bethel St.
Honolulu, HI 96813
Patients assisted annually 30,194
Northern Koolau Health Education Center
54-316 Kamehameha Hwy.
Honolulu, HI 96717
Patients assisted annually 1,620

IDAHO

Boise
Diocese of Boise

St. Alphonsus Regional Medical Center, Inc.
1055 N. Curtis Rd.
Boise, ID 83706
Tel: 208-378-2121
Sandra Barrett Bruce, Pres. & CEO
Rev. Morse A. Later, Priest Chap.
Sisters of the Holy Cross 4
Bed Capacity 281
Patients assisted annually 296,000
Legal Title: *St. Alphonsus Regional Medical Center.*
Legal Title: *St. Alphonsus Building Co., Inc.*
Legal Title: *St. Alphonsus Diversified Care.*

Cottonwood
Diocese of Boise

St. Mary's Hospital
(Sub. of Benedictine Health System)
Cottonwood, ID 83522
Tel: 208-962-3251; Fax: 208-962-3722
Mrs. Casey Uhling, Admin.
Rev. Norbert Lemke, S.J., Chapl.
Iris Hawley, D.N.S., Dir., Nursing
Sponsored by Sisters of St. Benedict, Duluth, MN
Sisters 1
Bed Capacity 28
Patients assisted annually 25,000

Jerome
Diocese of Boise

St. Benedict Family Medical Center
709 N. Lincoln
Jerome, ID 83338
Tel: 208-324-4301
Mr. David Farnes, Admin.
Sponsored by Sisters of St. Benedict, Cottonwood, ID
Sisters 2
Bed Capacity 40
Patients Assisted Annually 43,674
Skilled Nursing Facility in connection with Medical Center.

Lewiston
Diocese of Boise

St. Joseph Regional Medical Center
415 6th St., P.O. Box 816
Lewiston, ID 83501
Tel: 208-743-2511
Howard A. Hayes, Pres. & CEO
Sr. Mary Ann Farley, S.N.J.M., Dir., Pastoral Care
Sisters of St. Joseph of Carondelet 2
Bed Capacity 161
Patients assisted annually 102,394
Nursing Education is in affiliation with Lewis-Clark State College and with Walla-Walla Community College, Clarkston Branch.

Nampa
Diocese of Boise

Mercy Medical Center
1512 12th Avenue Rd.
Nampa, ID 83686
Tel: 208-467-1171
Joseph A. Messmer, Pres. & CEO
Revs.:
John J. Tivenan (BRK) Vice Pres., Mission Effectiveness
Charles Foltz, Chap.
Sr. Alice Marie Schmid, O.P.
Cheri Wissenbach, M.A., Patient Advisor
Sr. Maura C. Lark, R.S.M.
Rev. Joseph Newcomer, Min. Supvr.
Sisters 2
Bed Capacity 152
Patients assisted annually 119,048

ILLINOIS

Alton
Diocese of Springfield in Illinois

Saint Anthony's Health Center
Saint Anthony's Way, P.O. Box 340
Alton, IL 62002-0340
Tel: 618-465-2571
Two Campuses: Saint Anthony's Hospital and Saint Clare's Hospital.
William E. Kessler, Pres.
Rev. Craig MacMahon, O.M.V., Chap.
Sisters of St. Francis of the Martyr St. George 18
Bed Capacity 292
Patients assisted annually 142,706
Staff 825

Aurora
Diocese of Rockford

Mercy Health Corporation
1325 N. Highland Ave.
Aurora, IL 60506
Tel: 630-859-2222; Fax: 630-859-9014
Mr. John K. Barto, Jr., Pres.
Mrs. D. Van Dyke, Pastoral Assoc.
Chaplains:
Revs.:
Joseph M. Lessard (PHX)
Ron Leinen, M.S.C.
Beds 340
Patients assisted annually 94,000
The following are subsidiaries of Mercy Health Corporation: Mercy Center for Health Care Services; McAuley Medical Properties; Bennett Operating Company.

Belleville
Diocese of Belleville

St. Elizabeth Hospital
211 S. Third St.
Belleville, IL 62222
Tel: 618-234-2120; Fax: 618-234-4391
Hospital Sisters of the Third Order of St. Francis
Clinically Affiliated with Southern Illinois University School of Medicine.
Mr. Gerald M. Harman, Exec. Vice Pres.
Rev. Dennis F. Voss, Chap.
Sisters 5
Bed Capacity 498
Patients assisted annually 94,025

Belvidere
Diocese of Rockford

Saint Joseph Hospital
1005 Julien St.
Belvidere, IL 61008
Tel: 815-544-3411; Fax: 815-547-5977
Mr. David A. Schertz, Admin.
Rev. Robert Jackson, Chap.
O.S.F. Healthcare System.
Beds 72
Inpatient Days 13,566
Outpatient Visits 12,926

Bloomington
Diocese of Peoria

OSF St. Joseph Medical Center
2200 E. Washington
Bloomington, IL 61701
Tel: 309-662-3311; Fax: 309-662-7143
Mr. Kenneth J. Natzke, Admin.
Sr. M. Grace, O.S.F., Supr.
Rev. Msgr. Joseph McGowan, Chap.
Sisters of the Third Order of St. Francis 2
Beds 182

Blue Island
Archdiocese of Chicago

St. Francis Hospital and Health Center
12935 S. Gregory St.
Blue Island, IL 60406
Tel: 708-597-2000
Owned and operated by SSM Health Care Corporation. Member of SSM Health Care
Mr. Jay Kreuzer, Pres.
Chaplains:
Sr. Doris Ashcraft, F.S.M.
Sr. Virginia Conway, O.P.
H. Kay Ernst, R.N., M.P.C.
Revs.:
Edward J. Glanzmann, O.S.B.
Robert Perez
Bro. Patrick Varilla, C.F.C.
Sisters 2
Bed Capacity 410
Patients assisted annually 97,909
St. Francis Family Health Center
13000 S. Maple Ave.
Blue Island, IL 60406

Breese
Diocese of Belleville

St. Joseph Hospital
9515 Holy Cross Ln.
Breese, IL 62230
Tel: 618-526-4511
Hospital Sisters of the Third Order of St. Francis
Jacolyn M. Schlautman, Exec. Vice Pres.
Sr. Virginia Klein, S.C.S.C., Pastoral Care
Sisters 2
Bed Capacity 85
Patients assisted annually 50,000

Centralia
Diocese of Belleville

St. Mary's Hospital
400 N. Pleasant Ave.
Centralia, IL 62801
Tel: 618-532-6731
Mr. James W. McDowell, Pres. & CEO
Rev. Joel Burget, O.F.M.Conv., Chap.
Sisters 10
Bed Capacity 276
Patients assisted annually 125,852

Chicago
Archdiocese of Chicago

Columbus Hospital
Daughters of Charity of St. Vincent de Paul & Missionary Sisters of the Sacred Heart.
2520 N. Lakeview Ave.
Chicago, IL 60614
Legal Title: *Catholic Health Partners Services.*
Mr. Jeffrey Frerichs, Board Chm.
Sr. Theresa Peck, D.C., Pres. & C.E.O.
Gordon Bass, C.O.O.
Rev. Theodore Ploplis, Dir. Pastoral Care Dept.
Chaplains:
Rev. Richard B. Bartz
Sr. Joan Bernich
Sisters 9
Bassinets 28
Bed Capacity 535
Patients assisted annually 82,359
Chicago Institute for Neuro Surgery & Neuro Research (Affiliate)
420 W. Deming Pl.
Chicago, IL 60614
Tel: 773-883-8585
Leonard Cerullo, M.D., Dir.

Holy Cross Hospital
2701 W. 68th St.
Chicago, IL 60629
Tel: 312-471-8000
Legal Title: *Holy Cross Hospital*
Sisters of St. Casimir of Chicago.
Mark C. Clement, Pres. & CEO
Alice Kilgallon, Dir. Pastoral Care
Chaplains:
Rev. Arubraj Ambrose
Sr. Dolores Cavalli, O.P.
Revs.:
Erwin J. Dodge, O.S.A.
Thomas Griffin, O.S.A.
Mark Menzel, S.S.C.
Thomas A. Morrison, O.P.
Donna Mulvenna
Revs.:
Pablo Mora, S.J.
Gerald Van Overbeel, O.S.A.
Arturo Perez
Michael Hogan, O.S.A.
Sr. Agnese Chapp, Patient Visitor
Sisters 26
Licensed Beds 400
Patients assisted annually 185,123
Holy Cross Hospital and Sisters of St. Casimir Foundation

Mercy Hospital and Medical Center
Fiscal Management.
2525 S. Michigan Ave.
Chicago, IL,
Stevenson Expwy. at King Dr.
Chicago, IL 60616
Tel: 312-567-2100; Fax: 312-567-6575
Winkle Lee, Pres.

LILIA ZAMAR, Chief Financial Officer, Tel: 312-567-2012
Rev. MARTIN J. HEBDA, Dir. Pastoral Care, Tel: 312-567-2045
Sisters 11
Bed Capacity 386
Bassinets 30
Patients assisted annually 371,287
Affiliates:
Mercy Diagnostic & Treatment Center
Mercy Health Care Corp.
Mercy Services Corp.
Mercy Foundation, Inc.
Mercy Health Care & Rehabilitation Center
Mercy Medical at Presidential Towers (Outpatient Satellite Facility & Alcohol-Drug Dependency Program)
Tower Three, 614 W. Madison St.
Chicago, IL 60606
Tel: 312-902-4000
Ms. PAT O'NEILL, Admin.
Ms. MARY KAY KACMAREK, Admin.
Mercy Medical in Chinatown (Outpatient Satellite Facility)
2347 S. Wentworth
Chicago, IL 60616
Tel: 312-842-0100
Mercy Medical in Justice (Ambulatory Care & Alcohol-Drug Dependency Program)
81st & Kean Ave.
Chicago, IL 60458
Tel: 708-594-3500
Mercy Medical on Pulaski (Outpatient Satellite Facility & Alcohol-Drug Dependency Program)
5635 S. Pulaski
Chicago, IL 60629
Tel: 312-585-1955
St. Patrick's Family Health Center (Outpatient Satellite Facility)
3344 S. Halsted
Chicago, IL 60608
Tel: 312-523-9550
Mercy Medical in Chicago Ridge (Outpatient Satellite Facility)
9830 S. Ridgeland
Chicago, IL 60415
Tel: 708-636-8200
Mercy Medical in Little Village (Outpatient Satellite Facility)
3649 W. 26th St.
Chicago, IL 60623
Tel: 312-521-2080
Mercy Medical on Michigan (Outpatient Satellite Facility)
2930 S. Michigan Ave.
Chicago, IL 60616
Tel: 312-808-0400
Mercy Medical in Mt. Greenwood, Chicago
11055 S. St. Louis Ave.
Chicago, IL 60655
Tel: 312-445-5800
Mercy Works on Ashland
3316 S. Ashland
Chicago, IL 60608
Tel: 312-890-2489
Arlington Heights (Alchohol, Drug Dependency Program)
115 S. Wilke Rd., Ste. 101
Arlington Heights, IL 60005
Tel: 708-398-0045
Hazel Crest (Alcohol, Drug Dependency Program)
17577 S. Kedzie Ave., Ste. 204
Hazel Crest, IL 60429
Tel: 708-922-1983
Mercy Medical in Lincoln Park, Chicago
990 W. Fullerton, Ste. 495
Chicago, IL 60616
Tel: 312-327-8848
Mercy Medical in Chatham
8529-33 S. State St.
Chicago, IL 60619
Bryn Mawr
8610 W. Bryn Mawr
Chicago, IL 60631
Tel: 312-380-0400

**Our Lady of the Resurrection Medical Center*
5645 W. Addison
Chicago, IL 60634
Tel: 773-282-7000
Sisters of the Resurrection
JOSEPH F. TOOMEY, Pres.
JOHN SULLIVAN, CEO
Chaplains:
Revs.:
LEON GRANTZ, C.P.
JEROME ANDRACKI, C.R.
Sr. LYDIA MARY YOKIEL, C.R.
Sr. MARY LEONETTE KLAFETA, C.R.
Sisters 2
Bed Capacity 286
Patients assisted annually 66,987

Resurrection Medical Center
7435 Talcott Ave.
Chicago, IL 60631
Tel: 773-774-8000
Sisters of the Resurrection
JOSEPH F. TOOMEY, Pres.
Sr. DONNA MARIE, C.R., CEO
Sr. MARY FLORENCE, C.R., Supr.
Chaplains:
Revs.:
WILLIAM BILINSKY
ROBERT KOWNACKI (SAT)
CHESTER UBOWSKI
GORDON VAN HOOF, O.S.C.
Sisters 15
Bed Capacity 428
Patients assisted annually 243,780
Student Nurses affiliated with Nurses-Triton College 40
Students Nurses, Oakton Community College 20
Chicago Board of Education 12
Affiliates:
Resurrection Health Care Corporation
Resurrection Ambulatory Care Services
Resurrection Development Foundation

St. Anthony Hospital
Daughters of Charity of St. Vincent de Paul & Missionary Sisters of the Sacred Heart.
2875 W. 19th St.
Chicago, IL 60623
Tel: 773-521-1710
Legal Title: *Catholic Health Partners Services*
Mr. JEFFREY FRERICHS, Board Chm.
Sr. THERESA PECK, D.C., Pres. & C.E.O.
Rev. THEODORE PLOPLIS, Dir. Pastoral Care Dept.
Chaplains:
Rev. DONALD CRAIG
Sr. BENIGNA MORAIS, M.S.C., Dir. of Pastoral Care
Missionary Sisters of the Sacred Heart 3
Bassinets 28
Bed Capacity 184
Patients assisted annually 45,246

St. Basil Health Service - Free People's Clinic
1850 W. Garfield
Chicago, IL 60609
Tel: 773-436-4758
Patients assisted annually 4,500

St. Bernard Hospital & Health Care Center
326 W. 64th St.
Chicago, IL 60621
Tel: 773-962-3900
Legal Title: *St. Bernard Hospital*
Religious Hospitallers of St. Joseph
Sr. JANET WAHLEITHNER, R.H.S.J., Supr.
Sr. ELIZABETH VAN STRATEN, R.H.S.J., Pres. & CEO
Sr. JANET WAHLEITHMER, R.H.S.J., Dir. Pastoral Care Dept.
Sisters 2
Bed Capacity 233
Patients assisted annually 101,000

St. Elizabeth's Hospital
1431 N. Claremont Ave.
Chicago, IL 60622
Tel: 773-278-2000
Legal Title: *St. Elizabeth's Hospital of Chicago, Inc.*
Operated by the Ancilla Systems, Inc.
JOANN BIRDZELL, CEO
Bed Capacity 276
Patients assisted annually 149,172

St. Joseph Hospital
Daughters of Charity of St. Vincent de Paul & Missionary Sisters of the Sacred Heart.
2900 N. Lake Shore Dr.
Chicago, IL 60657
Tel: 773-665-3000
Legal Title: *Catholic Health Partners Services*
Daughters of Charity of St. Vincent de Paul of Indiana, Inc.
Mr. JEFFREY FRERICHS, Board Chm.
Sr. THERESA PECK, D.C., Pres. & CEO
MARGARET SULLIVAN MCDERMOTT, C.O.O.
Rev. THEODORE PLOPLIS, Dir. Pastoral Care Dept.
Chaplains:
Revs.:
ANTHONY J. ADDUCCI
JOHN GOMES
ROBERT LUCAS, C.M.
ROBERT A. WALSH
Sr. ALVERDA BONIFAS, O.F.
Rabbi NORMAN LEWISON
Sisters 4
Bassinets 33
Bed Capacity 492
Patients assisted annually 114,428
Seton Health Care of Northern Illinois Affiliate.

St. Mary of Nazareth Hospital Center
2233 W. Division
Chicago, IL 60622
Tel: 312-770-2000
Sisters of the Holy Family of Nazareth
Sr. KATHLEEN ANN STADLER, C.S.F.N., Supr.
Sr. STELLA LOUISE, C.S.F.N., Pres.
Revs.:
JOHN KOBUS
DENIS CARNEIRO
ABRAHAM MILLER
Sisters 22
Bed Capacity 421
Bassinets 32
Patients assisted annually 192,587

Chicago Heights
Archdiocese of Chicago

Alverno Lakeside Corporation
1423 Chicago Rd.
Chicago Heights, IL 60411
Lincoln Hwy. at Chicago Rd.
Chicago Heights, IL 60411
Sisters 2

St. James Hospital and Health Centers
1423 Chicago Rd.
Chicago Heights, IL 60411
Tel: 708-756-1000
Legal Title: *Sisters of St. Francis Health Services, Inc., Mishawaka, Indiana*
Sisters of St. Francis of the Perpetual Adoration
Mr. PETER J. MURPHY, Pres. & CEO
Sr. MARLENE SHAPLEY, O.S.F., Vice Pres. Resource Mgmt. Svcs.
Sr. M. RUTH LUTHMAN, O.S.F., Vice Pres. Mission Services
Rev. RONALD L. KONDZIOLKA, Chap.
Sisters 3
Bed Capacity 361
Patients assisted annually 82,886

Crestwood
Archdiocese of Chicago

St. Francis Family Health Center
13755 Cicero Ave.
Crestwood, IL 60445

Danville
Diocese of Peoria

United Samaritans Medical Center
812 N. Logan
Danville, IL 61832
Tel: 217-443-5000; Fax: 217-443-1965
Legal Title: *Div. of Franciscan Sisters Health Care Corp.*
DENNIS J. DORAN, Pres.
Rev. ROBERT G. MANN, Chap.
Franciscan Sisters of the Sacred Heart 4
Capacity 359
Patients assisted annually 93,814
Franciscan Home Health
812 N. Logan Ave.
Danville, IL 61832
United Samaritans Medical Center Foundation
600 Sager Ave.
Danville, IL 61832
United Samaritans Medical Center Apothecary
800 N. Logan Ave.
Danville, IL 61832
Family Care Center
Danville, IL 61832
Catlin Family Practice
P.O. Box 380
Catlin, IL 61817
JOHN MASON, P.A.-C
Chrisman Clinic
139 N. Monroe
Chrisman, IL 61924
MICHAEL GIBSON, P.A.-C
East Main Family Practice
1415 E. Main
Danville, IL 61832
WILLIAM HENSOLD, M.D.
RUSTY MARTIN, P.A.-C
Family Practice Center
7 N. Virginia
Danville, IL 61832
JAMES HENSOLD, M.D.
WILLIAM HENSOLD, M.D.
TIMOTHY HORNER, M.D.
RUSTY MARTIN, P.A.-C
Westville Family Practice
302 N. State
Westville, IL 61883
BRUCE FERGUSON, P.A.-C
800 N. Logan, Suite 204
Danville, IL 61832
DAVID HURLEY, JR., M.D.
ROBERT KLAUSNER, M.D.

800 N. Logan Ave.
Danville, IL 61832
DAVID LEHMAN, M.D.
VICTORIA BIGNAL, M.D.
806 N. Logan Ave.
Danville, IL 61832
KARUNA KONERU, M.D.
MARVIN HOOVIS, M.D.
Franciscan Home Health
812 N. Logan
Danville, IL 61832
United Samaritans Medical Center Apothecary
800 N. Logan Ave.
Danville, IL 61832

Decatur
Diocese of Springfield in Illinois

St. Mary's Hospital
1800 E. Lake Shore Dr.
Decatur, IL 62521
Tel: 217-464-2966; Fax: 217-464-1616
KEITH L. CALLAHAN, Exec. Vice Pres.
Hospital Sisters of the Third Order of St. Francis 7
Patients assisted annually 142,000
Bed Capacity 374
Staff 1,176

Des Plaines
Archdiocese of Chicago

Holy Family Medical Center
100 N. River Rd.
Des Plaines, IL 60016
Tel: 847-297-1800; Fax: 847-297-1863
Legal Title: *Holy Family Medical Center*
Sisters of the Holy Family of Nazareth
Sr. PATRICIA ANN KOSCHALKE, C.S.F.N., Pres. & CEO
Revs.:
ROBERT MILLER, O.P.
STANLEY FERNANDO
Sisters 8
Bed Capacity 252
Patients assisted annually 120,703

Dolton
Archdiocese of Chicago

St. Francis Family Health Center
13826 S. Lincoln Ave.
Dolton, IL 60419

East St. Louis
Diocese of Belleville

St. Mary's Hospital
129 N. 8th St.
East St. Louis, IL 62201
Tel: 618-274-1900
Sponsored by the Poor Handmaids of Jesus Christ. Affiliate of Ancilla Systems, Inc.
RICHARD MARK, Pres. & CEO
Sisters 2
Bed Capacity 169
Patients assisted annually 33,037

Effingham
Diocese of Springfield in Illinois

St. Anthony's Memorial Hospital
503 N. Maple St.
Effingham, IL 62401
Tel: 217-342-2121
ANTHONY D. PFITZER, Admin.
Sr. HELEN MARIE PLUMMER, O.S.F., Religious Leader
Rev. ALEXIS PRUEMER, O.F.M., Chap.
Hospital Sisters of the Third Order of St. Francis 5
Bed Capacity 146
Patients assisted annually 66,195

Elgin
Diocese of Rockford

St. Joseph Hospital
77 N. Airlite St.
Elgin, IL 60123
Tel: 847-695-3200
Legal Title: *Franciscan Sisters Health Care Corp.*
Sponsored by Franciscan Sisters of the Sacred Heart, Frankfort, IL.
Mr. LARRY NARUM, Pres.
EDWARD J. HUNTER, Dir., Pastoral Care
Rev. DOMINIC J. CASSIDY (DAV) Chap.
Sisters 4
Beds 259
Patients assisted annually 232,530
St. Joseph Hospital Foundation
St. Joseph Hospital Auxiliary
Franciscan Home Health of St. Joseph Hospital

Elk Grove Village
Archdiocese of Chicago

Alexian Brothers Medical Center, Inc.
800 Biesterfield Rd.
Elk Grove Village, IL 60007-3397
Tel: 847-437-5500
Congregation of Alexian Brothers, Immaculate Conception Province
Associated with Stritch School of Medicine of Loyola University.
MICHAEL J. SCHWARTZ
Chaplains:
Sr. SUSAN HART, O.P., Chap. Supvr.
Revs.:
JAMES W. KELLY, O.P.
RICHARD C. LAPATA, O.P.
WILLIAM E. VEITH
Brothers 13
Licensed Beds 473
Lay Staff 2,200
Patients assisted annually 159,200
Parent: Alexian Brothers of Illinois, Inc.

Evanston
Archdiocese of Chicago

Saint Francis Hospital of Evanston
355 Ridge Ave.
Evanston, IL 60202
Tel: 847-316-4000
Legal Title: *Sisters of St. Francis Health Services Inc., Mishawaka, IN*
Legal Title: *Alverno-Evanston Corporation*
Headquarters Address, St. Francis Provincialate
P.O. Box 766
Mishawaka, IN 46544
Sisters of St. Francis of Perpetual Adoration.
Chaplains:
Revs.:
DANIEL J. COLLINS
JAMES DUNLAP
HERBERT MAXWELL
RABBI ILENE MELEMAD
Deacon ARTHUR METALLO
Sr. ALOYSIUS ALBERT, O.S.F.
CAROL ANN JARECKI
OWEN DOUGHERTY
Sisters 4
Bed Capacity 367
Patients assisted annually 250,000
St. Francis School of Nursing
Students 12

Evergreen Park
Archdiocese of Chicago

Little Company of Mary Hospital and Health Care Centers
2800 W. 95th St.
Evergreen Park, IL 60805
Tel: 708-422-6200; Fax: 708-425-9369
Legal Title: *The Little Company of Mary Hospital and Health Care Centers*
Sr. KATHLEEN MCINTYRE, L.C.M., Pres.
Ms. ROSEANN KELLER, Dir. Pastoral Care Svcs.
Chaplains:
Revs.:
LAMBERT KEMPKES, C.M.M.
LAWRENCE COLLINS
JAMES GALLAHER
MICHAEL SLATTERY, O.S.A.
Mr. DALE LAWSON, Baptist Min.
Mr. MICHAEL KUSH
Sr. ELIZABETH DONLAN, S.F.C.C.
MARGARET SCHNEIDER
Sisters of the Little Company of Mary 32
Bed Capacity 403
Bassinets 24
Patients assisted annually 175,221
Affiliates:
Little Company of Mary Auxiliary
2800 W. 95th St.
Evergreen Park, IL 60805
Tel: 708-229-5066
Little Company of Mary Affiliated Services, Inc.
2800 W. 95th St.
Evergreen Park, IL 60805
Tel: 708-422-6200, Ext. 5100
Oak Lawn Care Station
5660 W. 95th St.
Oak Lawn, IL 60453
Tel: 708-499-2273
Burbank Care Station
4901 W. 79th St.
Burbank, IL 60459
Tel: 708-424-2273
Mary Potter Pavilion
2850 W. 95th St.
Evergreen Park, IL 60805
Little Company of Mary Hospital Foundation
2800 W. 95th St.
Evergreen Park, IL 60805
Tel: 708-229-5022
MARY JO MAY, Exec. Dir.

Galesburg
Diocese of Peoria

St. Mary Medical Center
3333 N. Seminary St.
Galesburg, IL 61401-1299
Tel: 309-344-3161; Fax: 309-344-9494
Sr. M. BERNARDA, O.S.F., Supr.
Rev. MICHAEL R. VAN ACKER, Chap.
Sisters of the Third Order of St. Francis 3
Capacity 156
Patients assisted annually 39,000
Total Staff 550
The Galesburg St. Mary Medical Center Foundation
3333 N. Seminary St.
Galesburg, IL 61401

Granite City
Diocese of Springfield in Illinois

St. Elizabeth Medical Center
2100 Madison Ave.
Granite City, IL 62040
Tel: 618-798-3000; Fax: 618-798-3508
Sr. M. THOMAS, C.D.P., Chm. Bd.
TED EILERMAN, Pres.
Rev. FINIAN MCMULLIN, O.F.M., Chap.
Sisters of Divine Providence, IL 8
Patients assisted annually 222,873
Bed Capacity 403

Highland
Diocese of Springfield in Illinois

St. Joseph's Hospital
1515 Main St.
Highland, IL 62249
Tel: 618-654-7421; Fax: 618-654-2012
Hospital Sisters of the Third Order of St. Francis 4
Patients assisted annually 33,800
Bed Capacity 106
Staff 275

Joliet
Diocese of Joliet in Illinois

St. Joseph Medical Center
Franciscan Sisters Health Care Corporation.
333 N. Madison St.
Joliet, IL 60435
Tel: 815-725-7133
DAVID W. BENFER, Pres.
Deacon ED PETAK, Dir. Pastoral Care
Sisters 13
Chaplains 9
Bed Capacity 542
Patients assisted annually 398,459
Total Staff 2,300
Industrial Rehab Center
Rte. 59
Joliet, IL 60435
Franciscan Home Health
333 N. Madison St.
Joliet, IL 60435
St. Joseph College of Nursing
290 N. Springfield Ave.
Joliet, IL 60435
VIRGINIA E. KECK, Ph.D., R.N., Pres.
Coal City Family Health Center
410 N. Broadway St.
Coal City, IL 60416
New Lenox Family Health Center
305 Vine St.
New Lenox, IL 60451
Mokena Family Health Center
19401 Wolf Rd.
Mokena, IL 60448
St. Joseph Medical Center Foundation
333 N. Madison St.
Joliet, IL 60435
St. Joseph Medical Center Women Auxiliary
333 N. Madison St.
Joliet, IL 60435
St. Joseph Medical Center Physical Rehabilitation and Sports Injury Center
2400 Glenwood Ave.
Joliet, IL 60435
Plainfield Family Health Center
138 S. Division St.
Plainfield, IL 60544
Wheatland Family Health Center
24024 W. Brancaster Dr.
Naperville, IL 60564
Weber Road Family Health Center
1280 Windham Pkwy.
Romeoville, IL 60441

Ottawa Cardiology Clinic
1301 Gemini
Ottawa, IL,

Kankakee
Diocese of Joliet in Illinois

St. Mary's Hospital
500 West Court St.
Kankakee, IL 60901
Tel: 815-937-2490
Servants of the Holy Heart of Mary.
Sr. Virginia Marie Derk, Supr., Tel: 815-937-2384
Mr. Allan C. Sonduck, Pres.
Rev. Edward Poff, Chap.
Bed Capacity 222
Patients assisted annually 145,507
Staff 992

Litchfield
Diocese of Springfield in Illinois

St. Francis Hospital
1215 Franciscan Dr., P.O. Box 1215
Litchfield, IL 62056
Tel: 217-324-2191
Michael Sipkoski, Admin.
Rev. Theodosius A. Schelich, O.F.M., Chap.
Sr. Paulette Collings, O.S.F., Religious Coord.
Hospital Sisters of the Third Order of St. Francis 3
Patients assisted annually 65,000
Bed Capacity 138
Staff 350

Maywood
Archdiocese of Chicago

Foster G. McGaw Hospital of Loyola University of Chicago
2160 S. First Ave.
Maywood, IL 60153
Tel: 708-216-9056
Revs.:
Thomas M. Heskin, O.S.M.
John P. Coakley, S.J.
Mr. Jerry Kaelin
Revs.:
Allan F. Kirk, S.J.
James J. Creighton, S.J., CPE Supvr.
Ms. Linda Bronersky, M.P.S., Supvr.
Mr. David Corcoran, M.Ed.
Sr. Kathleen Conway, B.V.M.
Sr. Joanetta Bruene, O.P.
Ms. Beth Butler
Marie Coglianese, M.P.S., Dir.
JoElla Doggett, M.P.S.
Deacon Albin Wegner
Rev. Keenan Schuler, Evangelical Free Church
Bed Capacity 561
Patients assisted annually 275,000

Mount Vernon
Diocese of Belleville

Good Samaritan Regional Health Center
605 N. 12th St.
Mount Vernon, IL 62864
Tel: 618-242-4600
Member of SSM Health Care.
Leo F. Childers, Jr., Pres.
Sr. Denise Sharp, S.S.J., Chap.
Sisters 3
Bed Capacity 175
Patients assisted annually 83,160

Murphysboro
Diocese of Belleville

St. Joseph Memorial Hospital
2 S. Hospital Dr.
Murphysboro, IL 62966
Tel: 618-684-3156
A service of Southern Illinois Healthcare.
Adorers of the Blood of Christ.
Ms. Betty Gaffney, Senior Vice Pres. & Admin.
Sr. Mildred Gross, A.S.C., Corporate Dir. of Spritual Care
Sr. Mary Bede, A.S.C., Dir. of Pastoral Care
Sisters 3
Bed Capacity 59
Patients assisted annually 23,403

Oak Park
Archdiocese of Chicago

Oak Park Hospital
520 S. Maple Ave.
Oak Park, IL 60304
Tel: 708-383-9300
Legal Title: *Oak Park Hospital*
Wheaton Franciscan Sisters
Mr. Leonard J. Muller, Pres. & CEO
Ms. Lee Kotnour, EVP
Chaplains:
Rev. Raymond Zsolczai, O.F.M.
Bro. Michael May, O.F.M.
Sylvia Fromme
Bed Capacity 296
Patients assisted annually 45,306
Oak Park Hospital Endowment Fund Affiliate.

Peoria
Diocese of Peoria

OSF Healthcare System
800 N.E. Glen Oak Ave.
Peoria, IL 61603-3200
Web Site: OSFHEALTHCARE.org
Sr. Frances Marie Masching, O.S.F., Pres. of OSF Healthcare System
OSF Healthcare Foundation
800 N.E. Glen Oak Ave.
Peoria, IL 61603-3200
Mr. Kevin Schoeplein, Pres.
Total Annually Assisted 26,850,000
Total Staff 6,505

St. Francis' Medical Center
530 N.E. Glen Oak Ave.
Peoria, IL 61637
Tel: 309-655-2000; Fax: 309-655-2347
Sr. M. Canisia, O.S.F., Admin.
Mr. Kevin Steffen, Assoc. Admin.
Sr. M. Ildefonsa, O.S.F., Supr.
Revs.:
Thomas Mizeur, Dir.
Michael Bliss
Capacity: Beds 590
Patients assisted annually 439,600
Saint Francis Medical Center College of Nursing Students 156

Pontiac
Diocese of Peoria

Saint James Hospital
610 E. Water
Pontiac, IL 61764
Tel: 815-842-2828; Fax: 815-842-4912
David T. Ochs, Admin.
Sr. M. Gaudentia, O.S.F., Supr.
Rev. David Roche, Chap.
Sisters of the Third Order of St. Francis 5
Capacity 81
Patients assisted annually 72,033
Total Staff 400

Red Bud
Diocese of Belleville

St. Clement Health Services
One St. Clement Blvd.
Red Bud, IL 62278
Tel: 618-282-3831; Fax: 618-282-6101
Adorers of the Blood of Christ
Mary Salois, Dir. of Pastoral Care
Mr. Michael McManus, Pres.
Rev. William J. Kane, S.J., Chap.
Sisters 1
Bed Capacity 105
Patients assisted annually 1,964

Rockford
Diocese of Rockford

Saint Anthony College of Nursing
5658 E. State St.
Rockford, IL 61108
Tel: 815-395-5090
Terese A. Burch, Ph.D., R.N., Dean
Students 95

Saint Anthony Medical Center
5666 E. State St.
Rockford, IL 61108
Tel: 815-226-2000
Mr. David Schertz, Admin.
Rev. William R. Wentink, Chap. & Dir., Pastoral Care
Center for cancer care.
Sisters of the Third Order of St. Francis (Peoria, IL) 4
Beds 285
Patients assisted annually 118,630

Spring Valley
Diocese of Peoria

St. Margaret's Hospital
600 E. First St.
Spring Valley, IL 61362
Tel: 815-664-5311; Fax: 815-664-1335
Web Site: http://www.St.Margarets.com
Timothy Muntz, Pres.
Sr. Frances Ann Bellmare, Chap.
Sisters of Mary of the Presentation 7
Bed Capacity 127
Patients assisted annually 65,578
Total Staff 570

Springfield
Diocese of Springfield in Illinois

St. John's Hospital
800 E. Carpenter St.
Springfield, IL 62769
Tel: 217-544-6464
E-mail: alaabs@st-johns.org
Mr. Alison C. Laabs, Exec. Vice Pres.
Susal Lied, Dir. Pastoral Care
Patients assisted annually 207,534
Bed Capacity 606
Staff 3,652
St. John's College of Nursing
Jane Schachtsiek, R.N., Ph.D., Chancellor
Students 98

Streator
Diocese of Peoria

St. Mary's Hospital
111 E. Spring St.
Streator, IL 61364
Tel: 815-673-2311; Fax: 815-673-4541
Hospital Sisters of St. Francis.
James F. Dover, Executive Vice Pres.
Thomas Whelan Asst. Admin.
Sisters 2
Patients assisted annually 41,353
Bed Capacity 251
Bassinets 28
Total Staff 469

Taylorville
Diocese of Springfield in Illinois

St. Vincent Memorial Hospital
201 E. Pleasant St.
Taylorville, IL 62568
Tel: 217-824-3331; Fax: 217-824-2099
Rev. Richard Trutter, Chap.
Adorers of the Blood of Christ 6
Patients assisted annually 28,649
Bed Capacity 129
Bassinets 8
Extended care facility 50
Staff 480

Tinley Park
Archdiocese of Chicago

St. Francis Family Health Center
17148 S. Harlem Ave.
Tinley Park, IL 60477

Urbana
Diocese of Peoria

Covenant Medical Center of Champaign/Urbana
1400 W. Park St.
Urbana, IL 61801
Tel: 217-337-2000; Fax: 217-337-4541
Servants of the Holy Heart of Mary
Sr. Charlene Cesario, S.S.C.M., Supr.
Sr. Evelyn Var Boncouer, S.S.C.M., Bd. Chm.
Mr. Joseph Beard, Pres.
Chaplains:
Sr. Mary Robert Morton, S.S.C.M., Dir.
Vera Duncanson
Ginny Conron
Peter Dyck
Bob Mulligan
Harry Litzenberg
Sisters 7
Capacity 280
Patients assisted annually 117,962
Total Staff 1,425

Waukegan
Archdiocese of Chicago

Saint Therese Medical Center
2615 Washington St.
Waukegan, IL 60085
Tel: 847-249-3900
Legal Title: *Franciscan Sisters Health Care Corp.*
Sponsored by Franciscan Sisters of the Sacred Heart (Frankfort, IL).
Timothy Selz, Pres.
Sr. M. Norma Janssen, O.S.F., Bd. Chm.

Sr. JEANETTE PIERCE
Sisters 2
Bed Capacity 388
Patients assisted annually 41,489
Franciscan Sisters Health Care Corp. Affiliate

Worth
Archdiocese of Chicago

St. Francis Family Health Center
11415 S. Harlem Ave.
Worth, IL 60482

INDIANA

Anderson
Diocese of Lafayette in Indiana

Saint John's Health System
2015 Jackson St.
Anderson, IN 46016
Tel: 765-649-2511
Mr. JERRY D. BRUMITT, Interim Pres. & CEO
Ms. BONNIE J. BURNETT, Dir. Center for Spiritual Care
Sisters of the Holy Cross 5
Bed Capacity 332

Beech Grove
Archdiocese of Indianapolis

St. Francis Hospital and Health Centers
1600 Albany St.
Beech Grove, IN 46107
Tel: 317-787-3311
Sisters of St. Francis Health Services, Inc.
Mr. ROBERT J. BRODY, Pres. & CEO
Chaplains:
Revs.:
FREDERICK J. DETERS
RUTA A. CABAZI (Tanzania)
JOHN H. MANNION (LFT)
Sisters 5
Staff 2,299
Beds 540
Patients assisted annually 173,259

Crown Point
Diocese of Gary

St. Anthony Medical Center, Inc.
1201 S. Main St.
Crown Point, IN 46307-8483
Tel: 219-738-2100
Mr. STEPHEN O. LEURCK, Pres.
Pastoral Care Team:
Revs.:
ANTHONY F. JANIK, O.F.M.
CARMEN SCUDERI, O.F.M.
Franciscan Sisters of Chicago 24
Beds 411
Total Staff 981
Patients assisted annually 96,353

Dyer
Diocese of Gary

St. Margaret Mercy Healthcare Centers, South Campus
(Div. of the Sisters of St. Francis Health Services, Inc.)
24 Joliet
Dyer, IN 46311
Tel: 219-932-2300
Rev. MICHAEL MAGINOT
Sisters of St. Francis of Perpetual Adoration 2
Beds 319
Bassinets 16
Total Staff 1,017
Patients assisted annually 45,659

East Chicago
Diocese of Gary

St. Catherine Hospital
4321 Fir St.
East Chicago, IN 46312
Tel: 219-392-1700; Fax: 219-392-7002
Sponsored by the Poor Handmaids of Jesus Christ.
Affiliates of Ancilla Systems.
JOANN BIRDZELL, Pres. & CEO
MARK ROGERS, Chief Oper. Officer & Chief Fin. Officer
Sr. STEPHEN BOUGGEMAN, P.H.J.C., Vice Pres. Mission Effectiveness
Sisters 4
Beds 290
Bassinets 20
Total Staff 612
Patients assisted annually 46,318
St. Catherine Hospital Foundation, Inc.
Transitional Care Unit (TCU)
Nazareth Home

Elwood
Diocese of Lafayette in Indiana

St. Vincent Mercy Hospital, Inc.
1331 South A St.
Elwood, IN 46036-1942
Tel: 765-552-4600; Fax: 765-552-4700
ROSEMARY J. COUGHLIN, C.S.J., Chap.
Daughters of Charity National Health System
Bed Capacity 40
Patients assisted annually 33,285
Staff 144

Evansville
Diocese of Evansville

St. Mary's Medical Center of Evansville, Inc.
3700 Washington Ave.
Evansville, IN 47750
Tel: 812-485-4000
RICHARD BREON, Pres. & CEO
Sr. CATHERINE KELLY, D.C., Vice Pres. Mission Svcs.
Rev. RALPH SCHIPP, Chap.
Daughters of Charity of St. Vincent de Paul 4
Beds 502
Patients assisted annually 222,167

Fort Wayne
Diocese of Fort Wayne - South Bend

St. Joseph Medical Center
700 Broadway
Fort Wayne, IN 46802
Tel: 219-425-3000; Fax: 219-425-3222
Sponsored by the Poor Handmaids of Jesus Christ.
Affiliate of Ancilla Systems Incorporated.
JOHN T. FARRELL, SR., CEO & Pres.
Sr. M. CONRAD KIRCHHOFF, P.H.J.C., Vice Pres. Mission Effectiveness
GEORGIA K. FLOYD, D.Min., Dir. Pastoral Care
Rev. MATTHEW S. KAFKA, Priest Chap.
Staff Chaplains:
Sr. MARY RUTH KRACK, O.S.B.
Rev. JOSEPH W. ANDREWS
Deacon FRANCIS C. WALSH
JANE F. TILL
Sisters 5
Bed Capacity 191
Nursery beds 20
Licensed 191
Patients assisted annually 125,362

Hammond
Diocese of Gary

St. Margaret Mercy Healthcare Centers - North Campus
5454 Hohman Ave.
Hammond, IN 46320
Tel: 219-932-2300
Sisters of St. Francis Health Services, Inc.
Rev. GREGORY HOLICKY
Sisters of St. Francis of Perpetual Adoration 5
Beds 487
Bassinets 45
Total Staff 2,003
Patients assisted annually 84,766

Hobart
Diocese of Gary

St. Mary Medical Center
1500 S. Lake Park Ave.
Hobart, IN 46342
Tel: 219-942-0551; Fax: 219-947-6037
Sponsored by the Poor Handmaids of Jesus Christ.
Affiliate of Ancilla Systems, Inc.
MILTON TRIANA, CEO
Sr. MARY ELLEN GOELLER, PHJC, Regl. Vice Pres. Mission Effectiveness
Rev. JOSEPH J. MONTORO, Chap.
Sisters 4
Beds 184
Bassinets 12
Total Staff 753
Patients assisted annually 41,204
St. Mary Medical Center Foundation, Inc.
The Linden House of Hobart, Inc.

Indianapolis
Archdiocese of Indianapolis

St. Vincent Hospital and Health Care Center, Inc.
2001 W. 86th St.
Indianapolis, IN 46260
Tel: 317-338-7000; Fax: 317-338-7005
E-mail: jbford@stvincent.org
Web Site: www.stvincent.org
Daughters of Charity of St. Vincent de Paul.
DOUGLAS D. FRENCH, Pres. & CEO
Sr. SHARON RICHARDT, D.C., Vice Pres. Mission Svcs.
Revs.:
CHARLES W. HENRY, O.S.B.
GEORGE F. PLASTER (LAF)
JOSEPH F. RAUTENBERG (IND)
DONALD J. EVRARD (IND)
Ms. JOAN M. BUMPUS, Dir. Pastoral Care
Sisters 8
Bed Capacity 749
Total Staff 5,663
Inpatient Admissions 32,863
Outpatient Visits 872,860
Emergency Visits 68,682
Chaplains 17

**St. Vincent New Hope, Inc.*
8405 N. Payne Rd.
Indianapolis, IN 46268
Tel: 317-872-4210
Daughters of Charity of St. Vincent de Paul.

Seton Health Corporation of Central Indiana
2001 W. 86th St.
Indianapolis, IN 46260
Tel: 317-338-7000; Fax: 317-338-7005
E-mail: jbford@stvincent.org
Web Site: www.stvincent.org
Daughters of Charity of St. Vincent de Paul.
Sr. LUCILLE MARIE BEAUCHAMP, D.C., Chm.

**St. Vincent Cardiac Services, Inc.*
2001 W. 86th St.
Indianapolis, IN 46260
Tel: 317-338-7000; Fax: 317-338-7005
Mr. SCOTT C. MALANEY, Chm.

Jasper
Diocese of Evansville

Memorial Hospital and Health Care Center, Little Company of Mary of Indiana, Inc.
800 W. Ninth St.
Jasper, IN 47546
Tel: 812-482-2345
Sr. MARY ADRIAN DAVIS, L.C.M., Pres. & CEO
Sr. MAURA BECKMAN, O.S.B., Chap.
Sisters of the Little Company of Mary 2
Beds 131
Patients assisted annually 98,261
Hospice Patients 68

Memorial Hospital Foundation, Inc.
Jasper, IN 47546
WILLIAM RUBINO, Pres.

Kokomo
Diocese of Lafayette in Indiana

Saint Joseph Hospital & Health Center of Kokomo, Indiana, Inc.
1907 W. Sycamore St.
Kokomo, IN 46901
Tel: 765-452-5611
Mailing Address:
P.O. Box 9010
Kokomo, IN 46904-9010
KATHLEEN M. KORBELAK, Pres. & CEO
Dr. DWIGHT G. LEE, Dir. Pastoral Care
Total Staff 908
Sisters 1
Bed Capacity 157
Patients assisted annually 89,423
Saint Joseph Foundation of Kokomo, Indiana, Inc.

Lafayette
Diocese of Lafayette in Indiana

St. Elizabeth Medical Center
1501 Hartford St., P.O. Box 7501
Lafayette, IN 47903
Tel: 765-423-6011
Legal Title: *Sisters of St. Francis Health Services, Inc., Mishawaka, IN*
Mr. DOUGLAS W. EBERLE, Pres.
Sr. ANNETTE CRONE, O.S.F., Senior Vice Pres.
Revs.:
JEFFREY BRAMBORA
PAUL GRAF
Sisters of St. Francis of Perpetual Adoration 5
Operational Beds 210
Patients assisted annually 85,059
Staff 1,175
School of Nursing
Students 165

Michigan City
Diocese of Gary

St. Anthony Hospital and Health Centers
301 W. Homer St.
Michigan City, IN 46360
Tel: 219-879-8511
Web Site: www.sahhc.org
Sisters of St. Francis Health Services, Inc.
Rev. Larry Henry, C.S.C., Chap.
Sisters of St. Francis of Perpetual Adoration 3
Beds 190
Bassinets 20
Total Staff 731
Patients assisted annually 246,044

Mishawaka
Diocese of Fort Wayne - South Bend

**St. Joseph Community Hospital*
215 W. 4th St.
Mishawaka, IN 46544
Tel: 219-259-2431
E-mail: khabgood@skynet.net
Web Site: http://www.specialtymile.com/ancillahealthcare/index.html
Poor Handmaids of Jesus Christ
Affiliate of Ancilla Systems Incorporated.
Stephen Crain, Pres. & CEO
Sr. Pauline Bridegroom, P.H.J.C., Vice Pres. Mission Effectiveness
Bed Capacity 125
Total Staff 697
Patients assisted annually 79,676

Plymouth
Diocese of Fort Wayne - South Bend

Saint Joseph's Hospital of Marshall County, Inc.
1915 Lake Ave., P.O. Box 670
Plymouth, IN 46563
Tel: 219-936-3181
Sponsored by Congregation of Sisters of the Holy Cross
Brian Dietz, Pres. & C.O.O.
Mary Coursey, Vice Pres. Support Svcs.
Mr. Jeff Nixa, N.A.C.C. Cert., Chap.
Lori Price, Vice Pres. Patient Care Svcs.
Catherine Lohmuller, Vice Pres., Mission Integration
Staff 297
Bed Capacity 58
Patients assisted annually 50,000

South Bend
Diocese of Fort Wayne - South Bend

Saint Joseph's Medical Center, Inc.
801 E. LaSalle St.
South Bend, IN 46617
Tel: 219-237-7111
E-mail: breedenm@sjcg.org
Robert L. Beyer, Pres. & CEO
Martin G. Breeden, Vice Pres., Mission Services
Alan Bowman, Dir. Chaplaincy Services
Sisters 13
Bed Capacity 339
Staff 1,849
Patients assisted annually 114,027

St. Mary Community Hospital
2515 E. Jefferson Blvd.
South Bend, IN 46615
Tel: 219-288-8311
E-mail: khobgood@skynet.net
Web Site: http://www.specialtymile.com/ancillahealthcare/index.html
Poor Handmaids of Jesus Christ (Affiliate of Ancilla Systems Incorporated)
Stephen Crain, Pres. & CEO
Sr. Pauline Bridegroom, P.H.J.C., Vice Pres. Mission Effectiveness
Total Assisted 19,956
Total Staff 97

IOWA

Carroll
Diocese of Sioux City

St. Anthony Regional Hospital
Carroll, IA 51401
Tel: 712-792-3581
Gary P. Riedmann, Pres.
Rev. Robert L. Leiting, Chap.
Franciscan Sisters of Perpetual Adoration 3
Bed Capacity 99
Patients assisted annually 43,364
St. Anthony Regional Nursing Home
Rev. Robert L. Leiting, Chap.
Orchard View, Inc.
S. Clark St.
Carroll, IA 51401
Tel: 712-792-3581

Cedar Rapids
Archdiocese of Dubuque

Mercy Medical Center, Cedar Rapids, Iowa
(Sub. of Mercy Care Service Corp.)
701 Tenth St., S.E.
Cedar Rapids, IA 52403
Tel: 319-398-6011
E-mail: mercylib@crpl.cedar-rapids.lib.ia.us
Web Site: http.//www.mercycare.org
Sponsored by the Sisters of Mercy, Cedar Rapids Regional Community.
A. James Tinker, CEO
Rev. John R. Gallagher, Res. Chap.
Sr. Mary Lou Podzimek, R.S.M., Dir. Pastoral Care Office
Chaplains:
Rev. Gary DeVries
Sr. Bernice Kurt, R.S.M.
Sr. Madonna Schmitt, O.S.B.
Staff 1,120
Bed Capacity 382
Patients assisted annually 123,926

Mercy Medical Center, Cedar Rapids, Iowa, Endowment Foundation, Inc.
701 Tenth St., S.E.
Cedar Rapids, IA 52403
Tel: 319-398-6278
Sr. Mary Augustine Roth, Pres.

Mercycare Service Corporation
(Parent Corp.)
701 10th St., S.E.
Cedar Rapids, IA 52403
Tel: 319-398-6011
Sponsored by the Sisters of Mercy, Cedar Rapids Regional Community.
A. James Tinker, CEO

Centerville
Diocese of Davenport

St. Joseph's Mercy Hospital
One St. Joseph's Dr.
Centerville, IA 52544
Tel: 515-437-4111
E-mail: stjocvil@se-iowa.net
William C. Assell, Pres.
Owned by Mercy Hospital Medical Center, Des Moines.
Attended from St. Mary's, Centerville.
Legacies, The Foundation of St. Joseph's Mercy Hospital
Tel: 515-437-3434
Beds 60
Patients assisted annually 72,268
Total Staff 225

Clinton
Diocese of Davenport

Samaritan Health System, Inc.
A subsidiary of Mercy Health Services.
1410 N. Fourth St.
Clinton, IA 52732
Tel: 319-244-5555
Thomas J. Hesselmann, Pres.
Revs.:
Horst Hehr, Chap.
John J. Stack
Beds 201
Staff 1,016
Samaritan Hospital South
638 S. Bluff Blvd.
Clinton, IA 52732
Tel: 319-244-5555
Samaritan Hospital North
1410 N. Fourth St.
Clinton, IA 52732
Tel: 319-244-5555
Samaritan Services for Aging
Bluff Terrace Nursing Home, 638 S. Bluff Blvd.
Clinton, IA 52732
Beds 64
Wyndcrest Nursing Home
600 14th Ave. N.
Clinton, IA 52732

Corning
Diocese of Des Moines

Mercy Midlands: Mercy Hospital
Rosary Dr., P.O. Box 368
Corning, IA 50841
Tel: 515-322-3121; Fax: 515-322-4872
James C. Ruppert, Admin.
Rev. Dan Siepker, Chap.
Patients assisted annually 3,342

Council Bluffs
Diocese of Des Moines

Bergan Mercy-Alegant Health System: Mercy Hospital
800 Mercy Dr.
Council Bluffs, IA 51502
Tel: 712-328-5000; Fax: 712-328-5202
Sisters of Mercy of the Americas
The Mercy Center
Mercy Medical Office Bldgs., Inc.
Revs.:
Dennis Trausch
Charles Scott
Chaplains 5
Beds 284
Patients assisted annually 47,925

Des Moines
Diocese of Des Moines

Mercy Hospital Medical Center
400 University Ave.
Des Moines, IA 50314
Tel: 515-247-3121
Sisters of Mercy of the Americas (Omaha Province)
Sr. Pauline Tursi, C.H.M., Dir., Pastoral Care
Chaplains:
Revs.:
Robert Aubrey
Dan Krettek
Paul Solomia (Philippines)
Braulio Tolosa (Philippines)
Sisters 29
Patients assisted annually 143,767
Mercy Clinics, Inc.
Mercy Court
Mercy College of Health Sciences
Clark Street House of Mercy

Dubuque
Archdiocese of Dubuque

Mercy Health Center-St. Joseph's Unit
(Div. of Mercy Health Services)
250 Mercy Dr.
Dubuque, IA 52001
Tel: 319-589-8000; Fax: 319-589-8073
Russell Knight, Pres.
Sr. Marilyn Schlosser, O.P., Dir. Pastoral Care Dept.
Chaplains:
Rev. Stephen A. Lundgren
Sr. Rosalyn Ulfers, P.B.V.M.
Joan Haug
Bed Capacity 402
Total Staff 1,110
Patients assisted annually 43,412

Dyersville
Archdiocese of Dubuque

Mercy Health Center-St. Mary's Unit
(Div. of Mercy Health Services)
1111 Third St., S.W.
Dyersville, IA 52040
Tel: 319-875-7101; Fax: 319-875-2957
Russell Knight, Pres.
Bed Capacity 49
Total Staff 73
Patients assisted annually 4,440

Estherville
Diocese of Sioux City

Holy Family Hospital
826 N. Eighth St.
Estherville, IA 51334
Tel: 712-362-2631
Sisters of the Presentation of the B.V.M. (Aberdeen, S.D.)
Bed Capacity 58
Patients assisted annually 39,780
Total Staff 220
Holy Family Hospital Foundation.

Iowa City
Diocese of Davenport

Mercy Hospital
Iowa City, IA 52240
Tel: 319-339-0300; Fax: 319-339-3788
Ronald R. Reed, Admin.
Chaplains:
Revs.:
Andrew E. Kelly

Francis E. Bass
Sisters 3
Beds 222

Mason City
Archdiocese of Dubuque

North Iowa Mercy Health Center
(Div. of Mercy Health Services)
1000 4th St. S.W.
Mason City, IA 50401
Tel: 515-422-7000; Fax: 515-422-7827
David H. Vellinga, Pres. & CEO
Chaplains:
Rev. Kenneth B. Gehling
Sr. Agnes Coveney, O.S.U., Mission & Ethics
Sr. Emily Devine, R.S.M.
Sr. Elaine Frank, O.S.F.
Rose Schleuter
Rev. Kirk Johnson, (Protestant)
Barbara McCaulley, (Protestant)
Bed Capacity 350
Patients assisted annually 635,547

New Hampton
Archdiocese of Dubuque

St. Joseph Community Hospital
(Div. of Mercy Health Services)
308 N. Maple Ave.
New Hampton, IA 50659
Tel: 515-394-4121; Fax: 515-394-5628
Thomas R. Thompson, Pres. & CEO
Marge Tekippe, Chm. Board, Community Health Care System
Rev. John Harpel, S.V.D., Chap.
Staff 150
Bed Capacity 49
Patients assisted annually 19,300

Oelwein
Archdiocese of Dubuque

Mercy Hospital of Franciscan Sisters
Oelwein, IA 50662
Tel: 319-283-6000; Fax: 319-283-6004
Franciscan Sisters. Daughters of the Sacred Hearts of Jesus and Mary, Wheaton, IL
Richard Schrupp, Pres. & C.E.O.
Chaplains:
Sr. Alice Maiers, R.S.M.
Rev. Frederick Fangman
Bed Capacity 64
Patients assisted annually 42,732
Staff 163

Sioux City
Diocese of Sioux City

Marian Health Center
801 Fifth St.
Sioux City, IA 51101
Tel: 712-279-2010; Fax: 712-279-2034
E-mail: mccrudep@mercyhealth.com
Web Site: www.mercyhealth.com arian
Mercy Health Services, Regional Community of Detroit.
Ms. Deborah VandenBroeck, Pres. & CEO
Chaplains:
Rev. Richard A. Sitzmann
Sr. Marlys Becker, O.S.F.
Rev. John Lee, Lutheran Chap.
Deacon Patrick McCruden
Sisters 3
Total Staff 1,500
Bed Capacity 484
Patients assisted annually 298,000

Waterloo
Archdiocese of Dubuque

Covenant Medical Center
3421 W. Ninth St.
Waterloo, IA 50702
Tel: 319-272-8000
Franciscan Sisters. Daughters of the Sacred Hearts of Jesus and Mary, Wheaton, IL
Mr. Raymond Burfeind, Pres.
Rev. Paul C. McManus, Chap.
Sartori Memorial Hospital, Inc. (Formerly known as S.F.H., Inc.)
515 College St.
Cedar Falls, IA 50613
Tel: 319-266-3584
Ms. Verna Klinkenborg, Pres.
Total Staff 335
Bed Capacity 101
Patients assisted annually 1,757
Covenant Health System, Inc.
3421 W. Ninth St.
Waterloo, IA 50702
Tel: 319-272-7302
Raymond F. Burfeind, Pres.
Covenant Foundation, Inc.
3421 W. Ninth St.
Waterloo, IA 50702
Tel: 319-236-4030
Don L. Hoth, Exec. Dir.
Sisters 1
Staff 2,116
Bed Capacity 346
Patients assisted annually 11,066

KANSAS

Fort Scott
Diocese of Wichita

Mercy Health System of Kansas, Inc.
821 Burke St.
Fort Scott, KS 66701
Tel: 316-223-7057; Fax: 316-223-5327
Susan Barrett, Admin.
Rev. Eugene Grabner
Sisters of Mercy 26
Lay Staff 450
Bed Capacity 110
Bassinets 15
Patients assisted annually 26,396
Home Health Visits 28,578

Garden City
Diocese of Dodge City

St. Catherine Hospital
410 E. Walnut
Garden City, KS 67846-5672
Tel: 316-272-2222; Fax: 316-272-2566
Affiliated with Catholic Health Initiatives.
Gary L. Rowe, Pres. & CEO
Mark Steadham, Sr. Vice Pres. Operations
Leanne Irsik, Vice Pres. of Patient Svcs.
Susan Steele, Chap. & Interim Exec. Assistant Mission
Shannon Borchert, Chap.
Mark Tozzio, Chief Development & Marketing
John Ostram, Human Resources Dir.
Terry Stofferson, CFO
Bed Capacity 100
Patients assisted annually 69,480

Great Bend
Diocese of Dodge City

Central Kansas Medical Center
3515 Broadway
Great Bend, KS 67530
Tel: 316-792-2511
Sisters of the Third Order of St. Dominic
Gary L. Barnett, Pres. & CEO
Joyce Young, R.N., Vice Pres. Patient Care Svcs.
Tom Sommers, Vice Pres. Fiscal Svcs.
Sr. Jeanine Tisot, R.S.M., Vice Pres. Mission Effectiveness
Darlene Redden, Vice Pres. Human Resources
Sisters 9
Bed Capacity 302
Total Staff 620
Patients assisted annually 51,000

Independence
Diocese of Wichita

Mercy Health Systems of Kansas, Inc.-Independence
800 W. Myrtle St.
Independence, KS 67301
Tel: 316-331-2200
E-mail: abrau@mhsk.smhs.com
Web Site: terraworld.net/mercy/
Susan Barrett, CEO
Sisters of Mercy 3
Bed Capacity 93
Patients assisted annually 51,274
Home Health Visits 23,017

Kansas City
Archdiocese of Kansas City in Kansas

Providence Medical Center
8929 Parallel Pkwy.
Kansas City, KS 66112
Fax: 913-596-4098
An affiliate of the Sisters of Charity of Leavenworth Health Services Corporation.
Mr. Frank Creeden, Pres. & CEO
Sisters 3
Bed Capacity 400
Bassinets 13
Employees 970
Physicians 300
Patients assisted annually 59,308

Larned
Diocese of Dodge City

Central Kansas Medical Center, St. Joseph Campus
923 Carroll St.
Larned, KS 67550
Tel: 316-285-3161
Gary Barnett, Pres. & CEO
Bed Capacity 69
Total Staff 95

Leavenworth
Archdiocese of Kansas City in Kansas

St. John Hospital
3500 S. 4th St.
Leavenworth, KS 66048
Tel: 913-680-6000
Mr. Frank Creeden, Pres.
Sisters of Charity of Leavenworth 3
Bed Capacity 76
Patients assisted annually 49,957

Pittsburg
Diocese of Wichita

Mount Carmel Medical Center; Mount Carmel Foundation
1102 E. Centennial
Pittsburg, KS 66762
Tel: 316-231-6100
Dan Lingor, Pres. & CEO
Sisters of St. Joseph 3
Bed Capacity 188
Patients assisted annually 79,337

Topeka
Archdiocese of Kansas City in Kansas

St. Francis Hospital and Medical Center
1700 W. 7th St.
Topeka, KS 66606
Tel: 785-295-8000
Sr. Loretto Marie Colwell, S.C.L., Pres.
Sisters of Charity of Leavenworth 3
Bed Capacity 378
Total Staff 1,603
Patients assisted annually 227,411

Wichita
Diocese of Wichita

Via Christi Regional Medical Center, Inc.
Web Site: www.Via-Christi.org
St. Francis Campus
929 N. St. Francis
Wichita, KS 67124
Tel: 316-268-5000
St. Joseph Campus
3600 E. Harry
Wichita, KS 67218
Tel: 316-685-1111
Mr. Randall G. Nyp, Pres. & CEO
Sr. Helene Lentz, C.S.J., Vice Pres. Mission Svcs.
Bed Capacity 1222
Outpatients assisted annually 240,510
Inpatients assisted annually 40,731
Total Staff 4,155

Via Christi Rehabilitation Center, Inc.
Our Lady of Lourdes Campus, 1151 N. Rock Rd.
Wichita, KS 67208
Tel: 316-634-3400
Mr. Anthony Isaac, Chm.
Ms. Laurie Labarca, COO
Mr. Tim Lytle, Pastoral Svcs.
Staff 208
Bed Capacity 60
Patients assisted annually 1,095

KENTUCKY

Ashland
Diocese of Lexington

Our Lady of Bellefonte Hospital, Inc.
St. Christopher Dr.
Ashland, KY 41101
Tel: 606-833-3333; Fax: 606-833-3695
(Member of Franciscan Health System of Kentucky, Inc.).
Rev. John P. Noe, Chap.
Franciscan Sisters of the Poor 3
Beds 189
Patients assisted annually 61,957

Bardstown
Archdiocese of Louisville

Flaget Memorial Hospital
Bardstown, KY 40004

Tel: 502-348-3923, Ext. 4641
Sisters of Charity of Nazareth Health System
Suzanne Reasbeck, Pres. & CEO
Sisters 5
Bed Capacity 52
Bassinets 8
Patients assisted annually 43,148
Attended from St. Joseph Church.

Covington
Diocese of Covington

St. Elizabeth Medical Center, North
401 E. 20th St.
Covington, KY 41014-1585
Tel: 606-292-4000; Fax: 606-292-4487
Mr. Joseph W. Gross, Pres. & CEO
Mr. Marc A. Hoffman, Senior Vice Pres. & COO
Ms. Jane Swain, Vice Pres. Nursing
Mr. Michael Arthur, Vice Pres. Finance
Mr. Thomas Horton, Vice Pres. Human Resources
Mr. Len Puthoff, Vice Pres. General Svcs.
Mr. Thomas E. Saalfield, Vice Pres. Professional Svcs.
Mr. Michael J. Walters, Vice Pres. Systems Devel.
Mr. Allen Zobay, M.D., Vice Pres. Medical Affairs
Chaplains:
Rev. Robert J. Ross, S.J., Dir. Pastoral Care
Res.,
2028 Mackoy St.
Covington, KY 41014-1543
Rev. Robert Rosing
Res.,
Marydale Retreat Center, 945 Donaldson Hwy.
Erlanger, KY 41018-1093
Beds 127
Patients assisted annually 95,315
St. Elizabeth Medical Center Foundation, Inc.

Edgewood
Diocese of Covington

St. Elizabeth Medical Center, South
One Medical Village Dr.
Edgewood, KY 41017-3441
Tel: 606-344-2000; Fax: 606-344-3968
Mr. Joseph Gross, Pres. & CEO
Mr. Marc A. Hoffman, Senior Vice Pres. & COO
Chaplains:
Revs.:
Robert J. Ross, S.J., Dir. Pastoral Care
John P. Werner
Beds 358
Patients assisted annually 228,087

Frenchburg
Diocese of Lexington

Menifee Medical Center
P.O. Box 49
Frenchburg, KY 40322
Tel: 606-768-2191
(Div. of St. Claire Medical Center).
David Bolt, Vice Pres.
Patients assisted annually 13,551

Irvine
Diocese of Lexington

Marcum and Wallace Memorial Hospital
60 Mercy Ct.
Irvine, KY 40336
Tel: 606-723-2115; Fax: 606-723-2951
(Member of Mercy Health System, Cincinnati, OH).
Christopher M. Goddard, Admin.
Beds 26
Patients assisted annually 27,500

Lexington
Diocese of Lexington

St. Joseph Hospital
1 St. Joseph Dr.
Lexington, KY 40504
Tel: 606-278-3436
(Member of Catholic Health Initiatives)
Thomas Murray, Pres. & CEO
Mr. Mark Dundon, Pres. & CEO, Sisters of Charity of Nazareth Health System
Revs.:
Herb Osborne, Dir. Chap. Svcs.
Joseph E. Whalen (GI) Chap.
Sisters of Charity of Nazareth 12
Bed Capacity 468
Patients assisted annually 61,314

London
Diocese of Lexington

London, Marymount dba Marymount Medical Center
310 E. Ninth St.
London, KY 40741
Tel: 606-878-6520
(Member of Catholic Health Initiatives)
Mr. Lowell Jones, Pres. & CEO
Robert Reh, Acting Pres.
Bed Capacity 100
Patients assisted annually 150,401

Louisville
Archdiocese of Louisville

Caritas Medical Center
1850 Bluegrass Ave.
Louisville, KY 40215
Tel: 502-361-6000
Sisters of Charity of Nazareth
Rev. Joseph H. Stoltz, Chap.
Sisters 11
Bed Capacity 331
Patients assisted annually 107,154

Martin
Diocese of Lexington

Our Lady of the Way Hospital, Inc.
Box 910
Martin, KY 41649
Tel: 606-285-5181
Sisters of Charity, Cincinnati, OH
Mr. Lowell Jones, Admin.
Beds 39
Patients assisted annually 26,028

Morehead
Diocese of Lexington

Saint Claire Medical Center
Morehead, KY 40351
Tel: 606-784-6661
Sisters of Notre Dame
Mr. Mark Neff, Pres. & CEO
Sisters 6
Beds 159
Bassinets 10
Patients assisted annually 345,388
Patients with Primary Care Centers 77,592

Olive Hill
Diocese of Lexington

Carter County Medical Clinic
P.O. Box 1268, U.S. 60 W.
Olive Hill, KY 41164
Tel: 606-286-4152
(Div. of St. Claire Medical Center).
David Bolt, Vice Pres.
Patients assisted annually 23,951

Owingsville
Diocese of Lexington

Bath County Medical Clinic
632 Slate Ave.
Owingsville, KY 40360
Tel: 606-674-6386
(Div. of St. Claire Medical Center).
Mr. David Bolt, Vice Pres.
Patients assisted annually 20,076

Paducah
Diocese of Owensboro

Lourdes Hospital
1530 Lone Oak Rd., P.O. Box 7100
Paducah, KY 42002-7100
Tel: 502-444-2444
Robert P. Goodwin, Pres.
Sr. Marie Moore, Vice. Pres. of Mission Svcs.
Legal Title: *Lourdes Hospital, Inc.*
Beds 389
Patients assisted annually 85,000

Sandy Hook
Diocese of Lexington

Elliot County Medical Clinic
P.O. Box 748
Sandy Hook, KY 41171
Tel: 606-738-5155
(Div. of St. Claire Medical Center).
Mr. David Bolt, Vice Pres.
Patients assisted annually 11,781

Williamstown
Diocese of Covington

St. Elizabeth Medical Center, Grant County
238 Barnes Rd.
Williamstown, KY 41097-9482
Tel: 606-824-2400; Fax: 606-823-0951
Mr. Joseph Gross, Pres. & CEO
Mr. Marc A. Hoffman, Senior Vice Pres. & COO
Mr. Chris Carle, Admin.
Rev. Robert J. Ross, S.J., Chap. & Dir. Pastoral Care
Beds 30
Patients assisted annually 17,591

LOUISIANA

Alexandria
Diocese of Alexandria

St. Frances Cabrini Hospital
3330 Masonic Dr.
Alexandria, LA 71301
Tel: 318-487-1122
Sr. Olive Bordelon, C.C.V.I., Admin. & CEO
Revs.:
Christudas Nayak (India) Dir. Pastoral Care
Ferreolus D'Cruz (India) Chap.
Sisters of Charity of the Incarnate Word 9
Bed Capacity 302
Patients assisted annually 131,845
St. Frances Cabrini Hospital Foundation of Alexandria, Inc.
3330 Masonic Dr.
Alexandria, LA 71301

Baton Rouge
Diocese of Baton Rouge

Our Lady of the Lake Regional Medical Center
5000 Hennessy Blvd.
Baton Rouge, LA 70808-4398
Tel: 504-765-6565; Fax: 504-766-5645
Franciscan Missionaries of Our Lady (North American Province)
Sr. Brendan Mary Ronayne, O.S.F., Supr.
Mr. Robert C. Davidge, Pres.
Revs.:
George E. Goodbout (STU) Dir. Pastoral Care
Anthony Walter, O.F.M., Chap.
Francis Ferrier, S.J.
Daniel P. Lemoine
Bed Capacity 838
Sisters 9
Patients assisted annually 200,000
Tau Center
8080 Margaret Ann Dr.
Baton Rouge, LA 70809-3444
Tel: 504-767-1320; Fax: 504-767-1327

Lafayette
Diocese of Lafayette

Our Lady of Lourdes Regional Medical Center, Inc.
611 St. Landry St., P.O. Box 4027
Lafayette, LA 70502
Tel: 318-289-2100
E-mail: ololexec@popalexl.linknet.net
Web Site: www.lourdes.net
Mr. Robert Traham, Chm. of the Governing Board
Mr. Dudley Romero, CEO
Revs.:
Thomas Kamenski, O.F.M.
Lawrence N. Abara
Franciscan Missionaries of Our Lady 3
Beds 293
Patients assisted annually 83,107
St. Mary's Imaging Center, Inc.
P.O. Box 4424
Lafayette, LA 70502
Patients assisted annually 15,100
A wholly owned, nonprofit subsidiary of Our Lady of Lourdes Regional Medical Center, Inc. Operating as an outpatient diagnostic facility.

Lake Charles
Diocese of Lake Charles

St. Patrick Hospital of Lake Charles
524 S. Ryan St.
Lake Charles, LA 70601
Tel: 318-436-2511
Owned and operated by the Sisters of Charity of the Incarnate Word (Houston, TX).
J. William Hankins, Admin.
Revs.:
Brian M. King, Dir. Pastoral Care & Chap.
Samuel Osuji, Chap.
Sisters 9
Beds 257
Patients assisted annually 104,497
Total Staff 1,300

Monroe
Diocese of Shreveport

St. Francis Medical Center
P.O. Box 1901

Monroe, LA 71210-1901
Tel: 318-327-4000; Fax: 318-327-4142
Mr. H. Gerald Smith, Pres. & CEO
Revs.:
Joseph Puthuppally (India) Chap.
Zacharias Prakuzhy, C.M.I., (India) Chap.
Franciscan Missionaries of Our Lady 4
Beds 400
Patients assisted annually 80,000
Total Staff 1,559
Hospice & Ancillary Care
30,163
Total Staff 204

**St. Francis Specialty Hospital* (1995)
309 Jackson St., P.O. Box 1532
Monroe, LA 71210
Tel: 318-327-4600
E-mail: ryanm@stfran.com
Web Site: http://www.specialtyhospital.com
Mr. Michael G. Ryan, Pres. & CEO
Licensed Beds 50
Physicians 128
Employees 170
Patient admissions 350

New Orleans
Archdiocese of New Orleans

Daughters of Charity Services of New Orleans
3900 S. Carrollton Ave.
New Orleans, LA 70118-4712
Tel: 504-482-2080; Fax: 504-483-6016
Mr. David J. Ward, Pres. & CEO

Inter-Community Health Care, Inc.
1011 Gallier St.
New Orleans, LA 70117-6111
Tel: 504-945-1620; Fax: 504-944-0756
Sr. Marjorie Herbert, M.S.C., Pres.

St. John's Place of New Orleans, Inc. dba Mercy Family Center
3816 Bienville St.
New Orleans, LA 70119-5206
Tel: 504-482-6600; Fax: 504-482-6125
4444 York St., Ste. 101
Metairie, LA 70001
Tel: 504-779-5500; Fax: 504-779-5505
Mr. Bernard A. Duco, Pres.

Shreveport
Diocese of Shreveport

Schumpert Medical Center (1907)
One St. Mary Pl., P.O. Box 21976
Shreveport, LA 71120-1976
Tel: 318-681-4500
Sisters of Charity of the Incarnate Word
Dr. Arthur Gonzalez, P.H., CEO & Pres.
Sr. Rose Marie McDermott, Senior Vice Pres., Mission
Betsy Williams, Chap., Dir. of Pastoral Care
Chaplains:
Rev. Gonzalo Ferrer, T.O.R. (Spain)
Rev. Msgr. Norman C. Buvens
Sisters 9
Beds 350
Patients assisted annually 130,546
Total Staff 2,300

MAINE

Bangor
Diocese of Portland (In Maine)

St. Joseph Hospital
360 Broadway
Bangor, ME 04401
Tel: 207-262-1000
Sr. Mary Edith, C.S.S.F., Supr.
Sr. Mary Norberta, C.S.S.F., Pres.
Felician Sisters 9
Nursing Sisters 1
Lay Nurses 198
Patients assisted annually 69,840
Pastoral Care Dept.
360 Broadway
Bangor, ME 04401
Rev. Richard V. Rokos

Bucksport
Diocese of Portland (In Maine)

Bridgewell, Inc.
Box 836
Bucksport, ME 04416
Sr. Miriam Devlin, Contact Person
Health Care Facility.

Lewiston
Diocese of Portland (In Maine)

Community Clinical Services, Inc.
(Formerly: Metropolitan Rehabilitation Institute)
100 Campus Ave, Ste. #1
Lewiston, ME 04240
Tel: 207-777-8841
Lawrence A. Cross, Dir.

Sisters of Charity Health System, Inc.
97 Campus Ave.
Lewiston, ME 04240
Tel: 207-777-8802
James E. Cassidy, Pres. & CEO
Lifeline
Serving 500
Covenant 50
Subscribers 9,000
Genesis Residential Treatment Facility Facility for Adolescent Boys.
Chez Enfant Residential Program for Children 3 months to 12 years old.
WorkMed Occupational Health Program.
Health & Wellness Program

**St. Mary's Regional Medical Center*
Campus Ave., P.O. Box 291
Lewiston, ME 04243-0291
Tel: 207-777-8100
Chaplains:
Sr. Huguette Allard, S.G.M.
Sr. Madeleine Normand, P.M.
Sr. Sharon Leavitt, S.C.I.M.
Sally A. Brochu, Dir.
Kenn Rancourt
Rev. Bertrand R. Poussard, Sacramental Min.
Sisters 3
Nurses 233
LPN 11
CNA 43
Beds 233
Patients assisted annually 72,872

Portland
Diocese of Portland (In Maine)

**Mercy Hospital*
144 State St.
Portland, ME 04101
Tel: 207-879-3000
Mr. Howard R. Buckley, Pres.
Rev. Donald McAllister, Chap.
Lay Nurses (RN's and LPN's) 305
Beds 200
Patients assisted annually 78,360
School of Radiology Students 17

MARYLAND

Baltimore
Archdiocese of Baltimore

Bon Secours Baltimore Health Corporation, Inc.
2000 W. Baltimore St.
Baltimore, MD 21223
Tel: 410-362-3000
E-mail: bobknott@bshsi.com
Sisters of Bon Secours
Jane Durney Crowley, CEO
Sr. Mary Skopal, S.S.J., Dir. of Pastoral Care
Sisters 13
Beds 490
Sub-acute beds 32
Patients assisted annually 142,637
Total Staff 1,798
Bon Secours Hospital Baltimore, Inc.
Bon Secours Community Health Services, Inc.
Bon Secours Facilities, Inc.
Bon Secours Housing, Inc.
Bon Secours Housing II, Inc.
Unity Properties, Inc.
Bon Secours of Maryland Foundation, Inc.

**Liberty Medical Center, Inc.*

**Urban Medical Institute, Inc.*

**The Urban Medical Institute Foundation, Inc.*
Primary Care:
Bon Secours Family Care Center
Fall Lane Medical Center
Hilton Community Medical Center
Imani Center
Park Circle Health Center
Washington Village Community Medical Center
Community Health Services:
Bon Secours Renal Dialysis Center (Glen Burnie)
Bon Secours Renal Dialysis Center (Charing Cross)
Bon Secours Dialysis at North Charles
Bon Secours Home Health/Hospice
Community Institute of Behavorial Services (CIBS)
New Hope Treatment Center
New Phases
Next Passage
Community Outreach:
Bon Secours Apartments
Bon Secours Hollins Terrace (Apts. for the Elderly)
Bon Secours Benet House (Apts. for the Elderly)
Community Support Center
St. Jerome's Head Start
Urban Medical Institute (UMI)

Mercy Medical Center, Inc.
301 St. Paul Pl.
Baltimore, MD 21202
Tel: 410-332-9000; Fax: 410-962-1303
Institute of the Sisters of Mercy of the Americas
Sr. Helen Amos, R.S.M., Pres. & CEO
Chaplains:
Revs.:
Theodore E.A. Brady, S.J.
Bernard A. Suppe, S.J.
Francis L. Duffy, S.J.
Sr. M. Benedict Brady, R.S.M.
Sr. Mary Harper, R.S.M.
Sr. Judith Montone, R.S.M.
Sr. Naomi Zerhusen, R.S.M.
Sisters 15
Employees 2,042
Patients assisted annually 436,853
Mercy Medical Center Subsidiaries: St. Paul Place Specialists, Inc.; Mercy Home Health Services, Inc.; Mercy Primary Care Group, Inc.; Mercy Ventures, Inc.; Northeast Medical Center; Mercy Southern; Mercy Little Italy; Mercy Basilica Place; Healthcare for the Homeless; Mercy Family Care; Fellowship House; New Song Health Center; South Baltimore Health Center (Cherry Hill); Maryland Personal Physicians, Inc.; Mercy Transitional Care; Stella Maris Hospice at Mercy; Stella Maris, Inc.; Cardinal Shehan Center, Inc.

St. Agnes HealthCare, Inc.
900 Caton Ave.
Baltimore, MD 21229-5299
Tel: 410-368-6000
E-mail: info@stagnes.org
Web Site: www.stagnes.org
Daughters of Charity of St. Vincent de Paul
Robert E. Pezzoli, Pres. & CEO
Rev. Daniel Free, C.P., Chap.
Sisters 13
Bed Capacity 383
Patients assisted annually 287,504
Total Staff 2,909
St. Agnes Foundation, Inc. (Subsidiary of St. Agnes HealthCare, Inc.)

St. Joseph Medical Center, Inc.
7620 York Rd.
Baltimore, MD 21204
Tel: 410-337-1109; Fax: 410-337-1024
Sisters of St. Francis of Philadelphia
John S. Prout, Pres. & CEO
Nancy Conner, Dir. Spiritual Care
Chaplains:
Revs.:
Samuel Lupico
Gilberto Liboroni-Pierozzi
Sr. Evelyn Jane Grudza, O.S.F.
Sr. Anne Conrad Koerner, O.S.F.
Joan Manning
Pamela Wicklein
Maureen O'Brien
Sisters 23
Nurses 640
Beds 460
Patients assisted annually 70,550
Total Staff 2,343
Affiliate of Catholic Health Initiatives.

Cumberland
Archdiocese of Baltimore

Sacred Heart Hospital of the Western Maryland Health System
900 Seton Dr.
Cumberland, MD 21502
Tel: 301-759-4200
Daughters of Charity of St. Vincent de Paul
William T. Bradel, Exec. Dir.
Sr. Mary Patricia Winters, D.C.
Rev. Alfred Cutajar, S.J., Chap.
Beds 240
Sisters 11
Nurses 250
Patients assisted annually 142,040

Silver Spring
Archdiocese of Washington

Holy Cross Hospital of Silver Spring, Inc.
1500 Forest Glen Rd.
Silver Spring, MD 20910
Tel: 301-754-7000; Fax: 301-754-7012
Sisters of the Holy Cross
Mr. NEAL MCKELVEY, Interim C.E.O.
Sr. VIRGINIA MCLAUGHLIN, C.S.C., Dir. Pastoral Care
Revs.:
ELIOT NITZ, S.D.S.
LOUIS A. TOU
Sisters 15
Bed Capacity 434
Patients assisted annually 202,651
Total Staff 2,300

MASSACHUSETTS

Boston
Archdiocese of Boston

Daughters of Charity National Health System - Boston, Inc.
(Formerly The Carney Hospital)
2100 Dorchester Ave.
Boston, MA 02124
Tel: 617-296-4000
MATTHIAS D. MAGUIRE, Pres.
Sr. DECHANTAL LAROW, D.C., Chm. Bd.
Rev. LUCIEN A. SAWYER, O.M.I.
Daughters of Charity of St. Vincent de Paul 12
Bed Capacity 285
Patients treated during the year 111,326

Brighton
Archdiocese of Boston

St. Elizabeth's Hospital of Boston
736 Cambridge St.
Brighton, MA 02135
Tel: 617-789-3000
School of Nursing.
3 Year course (4 years of complete day high school).
Mr. THEODORE DRUHOT, Pres.
Revs.:
BRIAN F. MCMAHON, Chap.
JAMES J. FOLEY, Asst. Chaplain
Rev. Msgr. CHARLES W. MCCARTHY
Sr. VIRGINIA MURRAY, C.S.J.
Sr. IVAN CADIGAN, C.S.J.
Sr. REATA KELLEHER, C.S.J.
Sr. MARGARET SHEEHAN, C.S.J.
Sr. LOUISE MURRAY, C.S.J.
Student Nurses 160
Bed Capacity 350
Bassinets 30
Patients treated during the year 176,302

Brockton
Archdiocese of Boston

Good Samaritan Medical Center
235 N. Pearl St.
Brockton, MA 02401
Tel: 508-427-3000; 427-3151
FRANK J. LARKIN, Pres. & CEO
Sisters of Charity of Nazareth 1
Sisters of Jesus Crucified 1
Holy Union Sisters 1
Revs.:
RICHARD W. VISBISKY, Chap. & Dir. of Pastoral Care
SUZANNE HIGGINS, (Congregational)
Mr. RICHARD MESSING, (Rabbi)
Total Assisted 107,500
Total Staff 1,350

Fall River
Diocese of Fall River

Saint Anne's Health Care Management Services, Inc.
795 Middle St.
Fall River, MA 02721-1798
JOSEPH W. WILCZEK, Pres.

Saint Anne's Health Care System, Inc.
795 Middle St.
Fall River, MA 02721-1798
JOSEPH W. WILCZEK, Pres.

Saint Anne's Hospital
795 Middle St.
Fall River, MA 02721-1798
Tel: 508-674-5741
Dominican Sisters of Charity of the Presentation of the Blessed Virgin Mary
JOSEPH W. WILCZEK, Pres.
Rev. ROBERT A. ROCHON
Sisters 6
Total Staff 873
Bed Capacity 165
Patients assisted annually 54,062

Lowell
Archdiocese of Boston

Saints Memorial Health System, Inc.
P.O. Box 30
Lowell, MA 01852
Tel: 508-458-1411; Fax: 508-458-8369
THOM CLARK, Pres. & CEO
Sisters of Charity of Ottawa
Bed Capacity 225
Total Assisted 11,000
Total Staff 1,250

Methuen
Archdiocese of Boston

Holy Family Hospital and Medical Center
Caritas Christi, Inc.
70 East St.
Methuen, MA 01844-4597
Tel: 978-687-0151
Web Site: http://www.holyfamilyhosp.org
WILLIAM L. LANE, Pres.
Rev. JOHN T. CRABB, S.J., Chap.
Bed Capacity 241
Bassinets 30
Patients assisted annually 150,000
Affiliating Hospital for: St. Anselm's Collegiate School of Nursing; Northern Essex Community College; University of Lowell; Salem State College; Boston University School of Public Health; Essex Agricultural School; New Hampshire Technical School; Massachusetts Bay Community College; Northeastern University; Rivier College; Woodmill Nursing Home; Greater Lowell Vocational School; Whittier Regional Vocational Technical School; Greater Lawrence Vocational School; and Salem High School.
Priests 1
Holy Family Hospital Auxiliary
70 East St.
Methuen, MA 01844-4597

Springfield
Diocese of Springfield in Massachusetts

CHE - Mercy Mass. Hosp. Corp.
271 Carew St.
Springfield, MA 01120
Tel: 413-748-9000
VINCENT J. MCCORKLE, Pres.

Mercy Hospital
271 Carew St., Box 9012
Springfield, MA 01102-9012
Tel: 413-748-9000
VINCENT J. MCCORKLE, Pres. & CEO
Sr. MARGARET M. MCCARTHY, S.N.D., Dir. Dept. of Pastoral Care
Chaplains:
Revs.:
HERBERT C. BALOGA, O.F.M.Conv.
WILLIAM J. DOHERTY, M.S.
Sr. THERESA DUBE, S.A.S.V.
Sr. MADELINE JOY, S.D.
SANDRA MATTUCCI
SUZANNE NOLAN
JAMES LORD
Sisters of Providence 3
Beds 313
Patients annually assisted 124,000
Nurses:
RNs 292
LPNs 36
Providence Hospital Campus of Mercy Hospital
1233 Main St.
Holyoke, MA 01040
Pastoral Care Dept. 1
Beds 113
Staff 260

Turners Falls
Diocese of Springfield in Massachusetts

Farren Care Center, Inc.
340 Montague City Rd.
Turners Falls, MA 01376
Tel: 413-774-3111
WILLIAM E. CASPER, Pres.
JAMES T. CLIFFORD, Admin.
Sisters of Providence 7
Beds 122
Total Staff 195
Total Assisted 140

Worcester
Diocese of Worcester

Our Lady of Mercy Health Care Center, Inc.
101 Barry Rd.
Worcester, MA 01609
Tel: 508-798-3727
Sr. SUZANNE ELLIOTT, R.S.M., Board Chair
Sr. ANNA MARIA TAG, R.S.M., Licensed Admin.

Pernet Family Health Service
237 Millbury St.
Worcester, MA 01610
Tel: 508-755-1228
Mission of the Little Sisters of the Assumption.
Certified Home Health and Social Service Agency. Focus of services toward the parent and young child. Parenting groups, family activities available, Early Childhood Development services also available.
SHEILAH DOOLEY, Exec. Dir.
Total Staff 33
Little Sisters of the Assumption 3
Total Volunteers 4

Saint Vincent Hospital, Inc.
25 Winthrop St.
Worcester, MA 01604
Tel: 508-798-1234; Fax: 508-798-1240
Mr. ROBERT MAHER, CEO
Rev. PETER R. BEAULIEU, Dir. Pastoral Care
Chaplains:
Rev. FRANCIS J. ROACH
Sr. MARY O'LEARY, S.P.
Deacon MATTEO PAGANO
Sisters 1
Beds 329
Patients assisted annually 174,661
Saint Vincent Healthcare System, Inc.
25 Winthrop St.
Worcester, MA 01604

MICHIGAN

Ann Arbor
Diocese of Lansing

Catherine McAuley Health Services Corporation
(Subsidiary of Mercy Health Services)
5305 E. Huron River Dr., P.O. Box 992
Ann Arbor, MI 48106
Tel: 313-712-3789
Health Care Center, Ancillary Care Systems: (Primary Care Physician Practices)
HELEN V. BERG, Pres.
Staff 135
Patients assisted annually 57,860

Catherine McAuley Health System
(Sponsored by Mercy Health Services - A unit of Mission Health Corporation)
5305 E. Huron River Dr., Box 992
Ann Arbor, MI 48106
Tel: 313-712-4025
BRIAN CONNOLLY, CEO
Beds 918
Gen. Hospitals 3
Staff 4,324
Annually Assisted 644,152

McAuley Clinic Corporation
(Subsidiary of Mercy Health Services)
5333 McAuley Dr., Box 994
Ann Arbor, MI 48106
Tel: 313-712-3788
ROBERT L. RAVIN, Pres.
Health Care Center, Ancillary Care Systems:
Staff 8
Patients assisted annually 6,323

St. Joseph Mercy Hospital
(A Unit of Mission Health Corporation)
5301 E. Huron River Dr., P.O. Box 995
Ann Arbor, MI 48106
Tel: 313-712-3456
Mr. GARRY C. FAJA, CEO
Sr. FRANCES GERHARD, R.S.M., Consultant, Mission Services
Chaplains:
Revs.:
TIMOTHY DOMBROWSKI
MICHAEL BRAND, C.S.B.
Beds 905
Gen. Hospitals 1
Total Staff 4,751
Patients assisted annually 822,937

Sisters of St. Joseph Health Services Corp.
455 E. Eisenhower, Ste. 300
Ann Arbor, MI 48108

Tel: 313-741-1700

Sisters of St. Joseph Health System, Inc.
455 E. Eisenhower, Ste. 300
Ann Arbor, MI 48108
Tel: 313-741-1700
Mr. JOHN LORE, Pres. & CEO
Beds 3,154 (acute care) 887 (Nursing Home)
Total Staff 22,000

Battle Creek
Diocese of Kalamazoo

Battle Creek Health System
300 North Ave.
Battle Creek, MI 49016
Tel: 616-966-8000; Fax: 616-966-8010
Div. of Sisters of Mercy Health Corp.
Mr. STEPHEN L. ABBOTT, Pres. & CEO
Bed Capacity 490
Patients assisted annually 140,391

Cadillac
Diocese of Gaylord

Mercy Hospital
Mercy Health Services North, Division of Sisters of Mercy Health Corp., Sisters of Mercy Detroit Prov.
400 Hobart St.
Cadillac, MI 49601
Tel: 616-779-7200
Mr. DENNIS RENANDER, Pres. & CEO
Bed Capacity 174
Patients assisted annually 56,899

Clinton Township
Archdiocese of Detroit

Mercy Mount Clemens Corporation
(Acting under the assumed name of St. Joseph's Mercy of Macomb or St. Joseph's Mercy Hospitals and Health Services). A subsidiary of Mercy Health Services.
15855 Nineteen Mile Rd.
Clinton Township, MI 48038
Tel: 810-263-2707
Provides acute care hospital services, home health care services, outpatient medical center services, hospice care services, long term service and fund-raising services.
MICHAEL A. SLUBOWSKI, Pres. & C.E.O.
DEBORA MURRAY, Dir., Spiritual Care Svcs.
Bed Capacity 512 acute care
St. Joseph's Mercy - West
15855 Nineteen Mile Rd.
Clinton Township, MI 48038
Tel: 810-263-2300; 263-2330
St. Joseph's Mercy - East
215 North Ave.
Mt. Clemens, MI 48043
Tel: 810-466-9300
St. Joseph's Mercy - North
80650 Van Dyke
Romeo, MI 48065
Tel: 810-752-3551
Additional divisional operations:
St. Joseph's HomeCare
St. Joseph's Medical Centers
St. Joseph's Mercy Foundation
St. Joseph's Mercy Healthier Image

Detroit
Archdiocese of Detroit

Holy Cross Hospital
4777 E. Outer Dr.
Detroit, MI 48234
Tel: 313-369-9100
Sisters of St. Joseph (Nazareth, MI)
JAMES E. KOERPER, Pres.
Sisters 4
Bed Capacity 229
Patients assisted annually 30,850

Mercy Family Care Program Unit
5555 Conner Ave.
Detroit, MI 48213
Tel: 313-579-4300
TOMMYE H. ARNOLD, Vice Pres. Ambulatory Svcs.
Mercy-Family Practice Center, St. Joseph Center, Chandler Center, Mercy-Nurse Managed Center, Gratiot Center.

Mercy Hospital
A division of Sisters of Mercy Health Corporation.
5555 Conner Ave.
Detroit, MI 48213
Tel: 313-579-4000
BRENITA CRAWFORD SEARCY, Pres. & CEO
KATHY GARBARINO, Dir. Pastoral Care
Bed Capacity 268
Patients assisted annually 224,708

St. John Hospital and Medical Center
(Subsidiary of St. John Health System)
22101 Moross Rd.
Detroit, MI 48236
Tel: 313-343-4000
ANTHONY R. TERSIONI, Pres. & CEO
Sr. SUZANNE ZIESKE, S.S.J., Vice Pres. Sponsorship
Sisters of Saint Joseph (Nazareth) 12
Bed Capacity 607
Patients assisted annually 154,939
Outpatients 66,007
Affiliates:
St. John Ambulatory Care, Detroit
St. John Dialysis Center, Detroit
Eastwood-Oxford Network of Care, Detroit
Affiliated Health Services, Inc., Detroit
St. John Hospital-Macomb Center, Harrison Township
St. John-Bon Secour Senior Community, Detroit
Saratoga Community Hospital, Detroit
Holy Cross Hospital, Detroit
Oakland General Hospital, Madison Heights
River District Hospital, East China

Dowagiac
Diocese of Kalamazoo

Lee Memorial Hospital
420 W. High St.
Dowagiac, MI 49047
Tel: 616-782-8681; Fax: 616-782-7611
Mr. FRITZ FAHRENBACHER, CEO
Bed Capacity 74
Patients assisted annually 34,000

Escanaba
Diocese of Marquette

O.S.F. St. Francis Hospital
Escanaba, MI 49829
Tel: 906-786-3311
O.S.F. Healthcare System.
Mr. ROGER BURGESS, Admin.
Sisters 4
Patients assisted annually 66,670
Beds 110

Flint
Diocese of Lansing

Center for Gerontology
An affiliate of Genesys Health System.
303 W. Water St., Ste. 100
Flint, MI 48503
Tel: 810-767-7080
Provides adult day care, care management programs, and educational training.
Annually Assisted 716
Total Staff 37

Genesys Ambulatory Health Services, Inc.
An affiliate of Genesys Health System.
302 Kensington Ave.
Flint, MI 48503
Tel: 810-232-9900
Provides private duty home care services and manages shared services. Also provides outpatient psychiatric services.
Annually Assisted 6,521
Total Staff 496

Genesys Home Health & Hospice
An affiliate of Genesys Health System.
100 S. Dort Hwy.
Flint, MI 48503
Tel: 810-762-7500
Provides professional home care and rehabilitation services.

Genesys Regional Medical Center/Flint Osteopathic Campus
An affiliate of Genesys Health System.
3921 Beecher Rd.
Flint, MI 48532-3699
Tel: 810-762-4000
MICHAEL S. DEMING, Acting Pres. & CEO
Beds 297
Annually Assisted 125,053

Genesys Regional Medical Center/St. Joseph Campus
An affiliate of Genesys Health System.
302 Kensington Ave.
Flint, MI 48503-2000
Tel: 810-762-8000
MICHAEL S. DEMING, Acting Pres. & CEO
KATHLENE O'DONNELL, S.S.J., Dir. Pastoral Care
Bassinets 39
Beds 374
Patients assisted annually 209,227

Goodrich
Diocese of Lansing

Genesys Hospice
(Affiliate of Genesys Health System)
7280 S. State Rd.
Goodrich, MI 48438
Tel: 810-636-5000
LAVERNE MCCOMBS, Admin. & Contact Person
Provides in-home and residential hospice care.
Beds 30

Grand Blanc
Diocese of Lansing

Genesys Convalescent Center, Grand Blanc, Inc.
An affiliate of St. Genesys Health Systems.
8481 Holly Rd.
Grand Blanc, MI 48439-1899
Tel: 810-694-1711
Nursing Home
Beds 140
Patients assisted annually 222
Total Staff 180

Genesys Health System
One Genesys Pkwy.
Grand Blanc, MI 48439
Tel: 810-606-6600
Mr. MICHAEL S. DEMING, Acting Pres. & CEO
Sr. ELIZABETH GRANGER, S.S.J., Vice Pres., Mission Effectiveness

Genesys Regional Medical Center
An affiliate of Genesys Health System.
One Genesys Pkwy.
Grand Blanc, MI 48439
Tel: 810-606-5000
MICHAEL S. DEMING, Acting Pres. & CEO
Beds 379
Annually Assisted 329,241
Total Staff 2,400

Grand Rapids
Diocese of Grand Rapids

St. Mary's Health Services
200 Jefferson, S.E.
Grand Rapids, MI 49503
Tel: 616-752-6090
Religious Sisters of Mercy (Detroit Regional Community)
DAVID AMEEN, Pres. & CEO
Revs.:
AYUB NOSOC
ROBERT GERL
Beds 300
Patients assisted annually 184,469
Mercy Central School of Nursing
Affiliation with U of D Mercy, Detroit.

Grayling
Diocese of Gaylord

Mercy Hospital
Mercy Health Services North, Division of Sisters of Mercy Health Corp., Sisters of Mercy Detroit Prov.
1100 Michigan Ave.
Grayling, MI 49738
Tel: 517-348-5461; Fax: 517-348-4839
DENNIS RENANDER, Pres. & CEO
Bed Capacity 130
Patients assisted annually 57,264

Grosse Pointe
Archdiocese of Detroit

Bon Secours Hospital
468 Cadieux Rd.
Grosse Pointe, MI 48230
Tel: 313-343-1000
HENRY DEVRIES, CEO
GARY A. JANKOWSKI, Chief Finance Officer
Sr. ANNE MARIE MACK, C.B.S., V.P. Mission Effectiveness
MARY ALICE PURCELL, Dir. of Pastoral Care
Sisters of Bon Secours 4
Sisters 1
Registered Nurses 450
Practical Nurses 102
Bed Capacity 311
Bassinets 28
Patients assisted annually 130,000

**Bon Secours of Michigan Health Care System, Inc.*
Bon Secours of Michigan Foundation
VANU BAGCHI, Vice Pres.

MICHAEL SERILLA, Vice Pres. Operation

Howell
Diocese of Lansing

McPherson Hospital
(A unit of Mission Health Corporation)
620 Bryon Rd.
Howell, MI 48843-1093
Tel: 517-546-1410
ROBERT B. CARBECK, M.D., Pres. & CEO
Beds 136
Gen. Hospitals 1
Patients assisted annually 155,160
Total Staff 503

Kalamazoo
Diocese of Kalamazoo

Borgess Medical Center
1521 Gull Rd.
Kalamazoo, MI 49001
Tel: 616-226-7000; Fax: 616-226-7396
Mr. R. TIMOTHY STACK, Pres.
Rev. A. THOMAS FERNANDO (India) Chap.
542 W. Michigan Ave.
Kalamazoo, MI 49007
Sisters of St. Joseph 4
Bed Capacity 469
Patients assisted annually 391,569

Lansing
Diocese of Lansing

St. Lawrence Hospital and Healthcare Services
1210 W. Saginaw St.
Lansing, MI 48915
Tel: 517-372-3610; Fax: 517-377-0382
(A Division of Mercy Health Services)
ARTHUR A. KNUEPPEL, Pres. & CEO
Chaplains:
Revs.:
FRANCIS MARTIN
STANLEY CZARNOTA
Sr. MERCITA LOGAN, R.S.M., Coord. of Pastoral Ministry
Sr. KATHLEEN BOTSFORD, R.S.M.
MATT PARLMER
DORIS STRIFE
JOAN TIRAK
Rev. REBECCA EBB-SPEESE, Lutheran (ELCA)
Beds 257
Patients assisted annually 286,119
Total Staff 1,314

Livonia
Archdiocese of Detroit

Marian Village Corporation
36475 Five Mile Rd.
Livonia, MI 48154
Tel: 313-464-4800, Ext. 2300
Sr. MARY MODESTA PIWOWAR, C.S.S.F., Pres. & C.E.O.
Marybrook Manor (Assisted Living)
36975 W. Five Mile Rd.
Livonia, MI 48154
Tel: 313-464-9667

St. Mary Hospital
36475 W. Five Mile Rd.
Livonia, MI 48154
Tel: 313-655-4800
Sr. MARY MODESTA, C.S.S.F., Pres.
Sr. MARY RENETTA C.S.S.F., Exec. Vice Pres.
Revs.:
JOHN ANTHONY PARENZA
KAZIMIERZ JASINSKI
Sisters 17
Bed Capacity 304
Patients assisted annually 182,508
RN's 333
LPN's 25
Congregation of the Sisters of St. Felix Felician Sisters
36800 Schoolcraft
Livonia, MI 48150

Muskegon
Diocese of Grand Rapids

Mercy Hospital
1500 E. Sherman Blvd., P.O. Box 358
Muskegon, MI 49443
Tel: 616-739-9341; Fax: 616-733-0957
Sisters of Mercy (Detroit Regional Community)
ROGER SPOELMAN, Pres. & CEO
LYNNE GORDON, Dir. Pastoral Care
Sisters 2
Beds 175
Patients assisted annually 125,533
Amicare Home Health Services-Western Michigan, Inc.
1500 E. Sherman Blvd.
Muskegon, MI 49444
Tel: 616-733-4064

Okemos
Diocese of Lansing

Majorie J. Gardner Wellness Center for Women
5100 Marsh Rd.
Okemos, MI 48864
Patients assisted annually 6,281

Pontiac
Archdiocese of Detroit

St. Joseph Mercy - Oakland
(Div. of Mercy Health Services)
900 Woodward Ave.
Pontiac, MI 48341-2985
Tel: 248-858-3000
Sponsored Work of the Sisters of Mercy Regional Community of Detroit.
A community healthcare system comprised of: Mercy Bellbrook Living Center, Rochester Hills; Alexander Living Center, Royal Oak; Orchard Hills Living Center, Pontiac; Amicare, West Bloomfield; Mercy Cranbrook Hospice, West Bloomfield; Seven Clinics & St. Joseph Mercy Hospital, Pontiac, MI.
THOMAS L. FEURIG, Pres. & CEO
RICHARD L. BROCHU, B.A., Th.M., Dir. Mission/Values & Ethics
Chaplains:
Revs.:
JOSEPH SZEWCZYK
DONALD WORTHY
JAMES VON DREHLE
FREDERICK B. MOORE
Sr. DIANE RONDEAU, R.S.M.

Port Huron
Archdiocese of Detroit

Mercy Hospital of Port Huron
(Div. of Sisters of Mercy Health Corporation)
2601 Electric
Port Huron, MI 48060-6518
Tel: 810-985-1500
MARY R. TRIMMER, Pres. & CEO
Sr. IMELDA SHERRETT, R.S.M., Dir. Resource Devel.
Chaplains:
Rev. C. PAUL HIGDON
EVELYN DENEAU
Sr. MARGARET WEBER, R.S.M.
Sr. FRANCIS VILLEROT, R.S.M., Patient Rep.
Bed Capacity 119
Patients assisted annually 26,409

Saginaw
Diocese of Saginaw

St. Mary's Medical Center of Saginaw, Inc.
830 S. Jefferson Ave.
Saginaw, MI 48601-2594
Daughters of Charity of St. Vincent de Paul, East Central Province, Evansville, IN
FREDERIC L. FRAIZER, Pres. & CEO
Sr. DINAH WHITE, D.C., Vice Pres. Mission Svcs.
Chaplains:
Rev. RAYMOND MOEGGENBERG
Sr. ADELAIDE CURTIS, D.C., Patient Rep.
DELMAR SMOLINSKI
RICHARD MCCOOL
DIANE SMILEY
Sisters 3
Beds 268
Patients assisted annually 67,100
Field Neurosciences Institute
830 S. Jefferson Ave.
Saginaw, MI 48601
FREDERIC L. FRAIZER, Chm.

Saline
Diocese of Lansing

Saline Community Hospital
(A unit of Mission Health Corporation)
400 W. Russell
Saline, MI 48176
Tel: 313-429-1600
GARRY FAJA, CEO
Beds 82
Gen. Hospitals 1
Patients assisted annually 85,000
Total Staff 286

Southfield
Archdiocese of Detroit

Providence Hospital
(A unit of Mission Health Corporation)
16001 W. Nine Mile Rd., P.O. Box 2043
Southfield, MI 48037
Tel: 810-424-3000
BRIAN M. CONNOLLY, Pres.
Sr. JANE BURGER, D.C., Vice Pres., Mission/Ethics Services
Rev. GEORGE HAZLER, Vice Pres. Mission Health Mission Svcs.
Chaplains:
Revs.:
KENT HAJDUK, O.F.M.
RONALD HEIDELBERGER
JOHN GAGALA
JOSEPH DROGOWSKI
FELIX ALSOLA
Ms. CAROL CROWLEY
Sr. ANGELE HINKEY, D.C.
Daughters of Charity of St. Vincent de Paul 4
Bed Capacity 440
Bassinets 65
Lay Staff 2,888
Patients assisted annually 809,721
Medical and Surgical Residences.

Tawas City
Diocese of Gaylord

**Saint Joseph Huron Home Health and Hospice*
716 German St., Ste. B, P.O. Box 208
Tawas City, MI 48764
Tel: 517-362-4611
ANN BALFOUR, Pres.
Patients assisted annually 789

Tawas St. Joseph Hospital
200 Hemlock, M-55
Tawas City, MI 48764-0659
Tel: 517-362-3411; Fax: 517-362-7277
Mr. PAUL SCHMIDT, Pres.
Sr. MARGOT EDER, S.S.J., Chap.
Sr. PATRICIA MULLEN, S.S.J., Vice Pres. Sponsorship
Sisters of St. Joseph (Nazareth, MI) 2
Bed Capacity 60
Patients assisted annually 108,016

MINNESOTA

Albany
Diocese of St. Cloud

Albany Area Hospital
300 Third Ave.
Albany, MN 56307
Tel: 320-845-2121
BEN KOPPELMAN, Admin.
Chaplains:
Sr. LORETTO SCHNEIDER, O.F.M.
WINI HERDA
Sisters of St. Francis 2
Beds 17
Patients assisted annually 5,987

Baudette
Diocese of Crookston

Lakewood Health Centers
Rte. 1, Box 2120
Baudette, MN 56623
Tel: 218-634-2120; Fax: 218-634-1307
SHARRAY PALM, Pres. & CEO
Bed Capacity 18
Staff 57
Patients assisted annually 15,561
Affiliate of Catholic Health Initiatives.
Lakewood Care Center
410 Third Ave. S.E., Rte. 1, Box 1180
Baudette, MN 56623
Tel: 218-634-2120; Fax: 218-634-1589
Sisters 1
Beds 52
Staff 49
Residents assisted annually 61
Affiliate of Catholic Health Initiatives.

Brainerd
Diocese of Duluth

St. Joseph's Medical Center
523 N. Third St.
Brainerd, MN 56401
Tel: 218-829-2861; Fax: 218-828-3103
Sr. GENEVIEVE VAN DRIEL, O.S.B., Chap.
Sr. LYNNETTE BOUTA, V.P. Operations
Sr. VIVIAN ARTS, Dir. of Mission
VERN BROUGHTON, Dir. Pastoral Care

Sisters of St. Benedict 4
Nurses 225
Patients assisted annually 23,976
Beds 162

Breckenridge
Diocese of St. Cloud

St. Francis Medical Center
415 Oak St.
Breckenridge, MN 56520
Tel: 218-643-3000
David Nelson, Pres.
Karen Stokes, Pastoral Care Dir.
Rev. Stanley Wieser, Chap.
Sisters 3
Beds 95
Patients assisted annually 22,000

Detroit Lakes
Diocese of Crookston

**St. Mary's Regional Health Center*
(Sub. of Benedictine Health System)
1027 Washington Ave.
Detroit Lakes, MN 56501
Tel: 218-847-5611; Fax: 218-847-7674
John Solheim, CEO
Rev. Stephen Wagman, O.S.B.
St. Mary's EMS (Sub. of St. Mary's Regional Health Center)
1240 Washington Ave., P.O. Box 1410
Detroit Lakes, MN 56502
Tel: 218-847-1631; Fax: 218-847-0673
John Solheim, CEO
Beds: Acute 87
Long Term Care 100
Nursing Home Residents 100
Patients Treated Annnually:
Hospital Inpatients 2,078
Hospital Outpatients 11,234
St. Mary's Hillview Home of Waubun (Sub. of St. Mary's Regional Health Center)
1011 Central Ave., Rte. 1, Box 17
Waubun, MN 56589
Tel: 218-473-3115
John Solheim, CEO
Beds 18
Residents 6

Duluth
Diocese of Duluth

St. Mary's Medical Center
407 E. Third St.
Duluth, MN 55805
Tel: 218-726-4000; Fax: 218-726-4383
Sr. Kathleen Hofer, O.S.B., Pres.
John Gibbs, Chap., Dir. of Chaplaincy Svcs.
Sisters 6
Nurses 778
Patients assisted annually 134,095
Beds 286
Bassinets 43

Graceville
Diocese of New Ulm

Graceville Health Center dba Holy Trinity Hospital and Grace Home
115 W. 2nd St.
Graceville, MN 56240-0157
Tel: 320-748-7223
Hospital:
Beds 32
Inpatients 300
Outpatients 7,450
Clinic Patients 6,500
Staff 36
Nursing Home:
Beds 60
Patients assisted annually 93
Staff 49
Board & Lodging:
Beds 13

Hastings
Archdiocese of St. Paul and Minneapolis

Regina Medical Center
1175 Nininger Rd.
Hastings, MN 55033
Tel: 612-480-4100
Lynn W. Olson, Admin.
Rev. James J. Dunne, S.S.C., Chap.
Bed capacity 57
Patients assisted annually 22,648
Other Sister Personnel 3
Personnel 477

Ivanhoe
Diocese of New Ulm

Divine Providence Health Center
312 E. George St., P.O. Box G
Ivanhoe, MN 56142-0136
Tel: 507-694-1414; Fax: 507-694-1191
Schoenstatt Sisters of Mary (Waukesha, WI)
James Rossow, Admin.
Rev. Marion G. Casey, Chap.
Sisters 6
Lay Workers 115
Aged Residents 51
Other Nurses 22
Patients assisted annually 180
Bed Capacity 18

Little Falls
Diocese of St. Cloud

St. Gabriel's Hospital
815 S.E. Second St.
Little Falls, MN 56345
Tel: 320-632-5441; Fax: 320-632-1190
Larry A. Schulz, Admin.
Bea Britz, Chap.
Sisters 3
Beds 55
Bassinets 10
Patients assisted annually 21,557

New Prague
Archdiocese of St. Paul and Minneapolis

Queen of Peace Hospital
302 Second St., N.E.
New Prague, MN 56071
Tel: 612-758-4431; Fax: 612-758-5009
Web Site: http://www.np.k12.mn.us/[]qofp.htm
Sr. Jean Juenemann, O.S.B., Admin.
Mr. Loy J. Jeffrey, Dir. Pastoral Care, Chap.
Ann Schoenbauer, Chap.
Sisters 3
Bed Capacity 28
Bassinets 6
RNs 63
LPNs 14
Other Personnel 153
Patients assisted annually 80,796

Park Rapids
Diocese of Crookston

St. Joseph Area Health Services
600 Pleasant Ave.
Park Rapids, MN 56470
Tel: 218-732-3311
Mr. David R. Hove, Pres./CEO
Sisters 2
Bed Capacity 50
Patients assisted annually 23,632
Affiliate of Catholic Health Initiatives.

Rochester
Diocese of Winona

Poverello Foundation
St. Marys Hospital, 1216 S.W. Second St.
Rochester, MN 55902
Tel: 507-255-5158
Sr. Generose Gervais, O.S.F., Pres.

**Saint Marys Hospital*
Rochester, MN 55902-1970
Tel: 507-255-5123; Fax: 507-255-3125
Gerald T. Mahoney, Admin.
Sisters of the Third Order Regular of St. Francis of the Congregation of Our Lady of Lourdes 32
Bed Capacity 1,157
Patients assisted annually 44,467

Shakopee
Archdiocese of St. Paul and Minneapolis

St. Francis Regional Medical Center
1455 St. Francis Ave.
Shakopee, MN 55379
Tel: 612-403-3000; Fax: 612-403-3820
Subsidiary of Benedictine Health System.
Venetia Kudrle, Pres.
Sr. Antonice Delury, O.S.F., Dir., Pastoral Care
Mary Beckfeld, Chap.
Sisters of St. Francis 1
Nurses 132
Bed Capacity 40
Patients assisted annually 36,000

St. Cloud
Diocese of St. Cloud

St. Cloud Hospital
1406 Sixth Ave. N.
St. Cloud, MN 56303
Tel: 320-251-2700
John Frobenius, Pres.
Rev. Roger Botz, O.S.B., Chap.
Sisters of St. Benedict 7
Students 17
Beds 320
Bassinets 40
Patients assisted annually 115,413

St. Peter
Diocese of New Ulm

St. Peter Regional Treatment Center
100 Freeman Dr.
St. Peter, MN 56082-1599
Tel: 507-931-7104
Rev. Bill Bowles, Chap.
Developmental Disabilities Division:
Patients assisted annually 935
Bed Capacity 662
Total Staff 800

Wabasha
Diocese of Winona

St. Elizabeth's Hospital
1200 5th Grant Blvd., W.
Wabasha, MN 55981
Tel: 612-565-4531
Mr. Thomas Crowley, Pres.
Rev. Joseph R. McGinnis
Sisters of the Third Order of St. Francis of the Sorrowful Mother 5
Beds 31
Patients assisted annually 18,150
Staff 150

Winsted
Diocese of New Ulm

St. Mary's Care Center
551 4th St. N., P.O. Box 750
Winsted, MN 55395-0750
Tel: 320-485-2151; Fax: 320-485-4241
Rev. Martin Rath, O.S.B., Chap.
Helen J. Guggemos, Admin.

MISSISSIPPI

Jackson
Diocese of Jackson

St. Dominic-Jackson Memorial Hospital
969 Lakeland Dr.
Jackson, MS 39216
Tel: 601-982-0121
Sr. Mary Karen O'Kelly, Prioress
Mr. Claude W. Harbarger, Pres.
Rev. Robert Olivier, Res. Chap.
Sisters of St. Dominic of Springfield, IL 10
Beds 571
Patients assisted annually 68,195

Tutwiler
Diocese of Jackson

Tutwiler Clinic, Inc.
205 Alma St., P.O. Box 462
Tutwiler, MS 38963-0462
Tel: 601-345-8334; Fax: 601-345-8336
E-mail: sabrooks@pol.net
Sr. Anne Brooks, S.N.J.M., D.O., Dir.
Patients assisted annually 7,655

MISSOURI

Blue Springs
Diocese of Kansas City-St. Joseph

St. Mary's Hospital of Blue Springs
201 W. R.D. Mize Rd.
Blue Springs, MO 64014
Tel: 816-228-5900; Fax: 816-228-7555
Sponsored by the Sisters of St. Joseph of Carondelet. Acute care facility, having medical, surgical, obstetrical and pediatric services.
Mr. Richard M. Abell, Pres. & CEO
Sisters 4
Bed Capacity 121
Patients assisted annually 52,371
Staff 650

Bridgeton
Archdiocese of St. Louis

De Paul Health Center
12303 De Paul Dr.

Bridgeton, MO 63044
Tel: 314-344-6000
Member of SSM Health Care.
ROBERT G. PORTER, Pres.
Chaplains:
Revs.:
JULES G. YALLALY, C.M.
LAWRENCE F. ASMA, C.M.
FREDERICK LENCZYCKI (JOL)
Sisters 6
Patients assisted annually 114,456
Staff 1,762
DePaul General Hospital Division
(Operating) Excluding Nursery-Including 14 Bed Acute Rehabilitation Unit 219
(Licensed) Excluding Nursery-Including 14 Bed Acute Rehabilitation Unit 344
St. Anne Division
12303 De Paul Dr.
Bridgeton, MO 63044
Tel: 314-344-6000
Skilled Nursing Facility, Certified for Medicare, for Men and Women.
Operating 94
Licensed 96
St. Vincent Division
12303 De Paul Dr.
Bridgeton, MO 63044
Tel: 314-344-6000
Pre-Adolescent, Adolescent, Adult & Gero Psychiatric Care and Chemical Dependency.
Operating 59
Licensed 98

Cape Girardeau
Diocese of Springfield-Cape Girardeau

**St. Francis' Medical Center*
211 St. Francis Dr.
Cape Girardeau, MO 63703
Tel: 573-335-1251
(Owned and operated by a lay board with Diocesan sponsorship)
Mr. JAMES J. SEXTON, CEO
Chapel St. Francis.
Mr. JOHN CANTORE, C.M., Chap.
Sisters 1
Bed Capacity 264
Inpatients 8,996
Outpatients 63,143
St. Francis Medical Center
211 St. Francis Dr.
Cape Girardeau, MO 63703
St. Francis Foundation
211 St. Francis Dr.
Cape Girardeau, MO 63703
St. Francis Continuing Care Center
211 St. Francis Dr.
Cape Girardeau, MO 63703
St. Francis Hospital of Franciscan Sisters
211 St. Francis Dr.
Cape Girardeau, MO 63703

Creve Coeur
Archdiocese of St. Louis

St. John's Mercy Medical Center
615 S. New Ballas Rd.
Creve Coeur, MO 63141
Tel: 314-569-6000; Fax: 314-569-6910
Conducted by the Religious Sisters of Mercy of the Americas-St. Louis Region
(See Branch Unit under Washington, MO)
Mr. MARK F. WEBER, Pres. & CEO
Chaplains:
Revs.:
DAVID D. SULLIVAN
LOWRIE DALY, S.J.
PHILIP G. KRAHMAN
Deacon KEN POTZMAN
Sisters 25
Other Nurses 984
Bed Capacity 892
Patients assisted annually 482,015
Capacity Includes: Chemical Dependency Unit of 35 beds
Skilled Nursing facility of 120 Beds

Jefferson City
Diocese of Jefferson City

St. Marys Health Center
100 St. Marys Medical Plaza
Jefferson City, MO 65101
Tel: 573-761-7000
Owned and operated by SSM Health Care Central Region, a Member of SSM Health Care
JOHN S. DUBIS, Pres.
Chaplains:
Revs.:
ERWIN R. KONRAD
JAMES CARTER, American Baptist Min., C.O.C. Certified Chap.
Ms. JAN SCHUPP, NACC Certified Chap. Dept. Mgr.
Sr. EVELYN MARIE PETERMAN, F.S.M.
Bed Capacity 167
Patients assisted annually 117,463
Clinics 14
Clinic visits 128,056
Home health visits 23,099

Joplin
Diocese of Springfield-Cape Girardeau

St. John's Regional Health Center, Mercy LifeCare Systems, Inc.
2727 McClelland Blvd. J
Joplin, MO 64804
Tel: 417-885-2000; Fax: 417-888-8730
Sisters of Mercy Health System (St. Louis)
Mr. ALLEN L. SHOCKLEY, Pres.
Rev. ANTHONY SHIDLER, O.S.B., Chap.
Sisters 11
Bed Capacity 866
Patients assisted annually 136,537

St. John's Regional Medical Center; Mercy Lifecare Systems, Inc.
Affiliates of Catholic Health Initiatives.
2727 McClelland Blvd.
Joplin, MO 64804
Tel: 417-781-2727; Fax: 417-625-2910
Sisters of Mercy (Omaha)
Mr. ROBERT G. BRUECKNER, Pres.
Rev. BENEDICT W. HARTER, Chap.
Sisters 6
Bed Capacity 367
Patients assisted annually 63,000
Mercy Regional Health Foundation, Inc.
2727 McClelland Blvd.
Joplin, MO 64804

Kansas City
Diocese of Kansas City-St. Joseph

Saint Joseph Health Center
1000 Carondelet Dr.
Kansas City, MO 64114
Tel: 816-942-4400
Sponsored by the Sisters of St. Joseph of Carondelet.
Mr. RICHARD M. ABELL, Pres. & CEO
CAROL NASH, Chap.
Sisters 11
Bed Capacity 300
Nurses 228
Total Staff 1,007
Patients assisted annually 109,872
Parent Corporation:
Carondelet Health
P.O. Box 8510
Kansas City, MO 64114
Tel: 816-943-5698
Parent Co. Sponsored by the Sisters of St. Joseph of Carondelet.
RICHARD M. ABELL, Pres. & CEO
Divisions:
Saint Joseph Health Center Foundation
1000 Carondelet Dr.
Kansas City, MO 64114
Tel: 816-942-4400
Sponsored by the Sisters of St. Joseph of Carondelet.
KENNETH MELLARD, Chm.
Mr. RICHARD M. ABELL, Pres. & CEO
Carondelet Manor
621 Carondelet Dr.
Kansas City, MO 64114
Tel: 816-943-4777
DIANNE DOCTOR, Admin.
Bed Capacity 180
Legal Title: *Carondelet Long Term Care Facilities, Inc.*
Owned and operated by Carondelet Long Term Care Facilities, Inc. Sponsored by Sisters of St. Joseph of Carondelet.
Carondelet Home Care Services Inc.
11050 Roe Ave., Ste. 120
Kansas City, KS 66211
Tel: 816-943-4700
KAREN STEFFEN, Admin.
Home health agency affiliated with Carondelet Health.
Villa Saint Joseph
11901 Rosewood
Overland Park, KS 66209
Tel: 913-345-1745
KATHARINE ENSIGN, Admin.
Bed Capacity 120

Kirkwood
Archdiocese of St. Louis

St. Joseph Hospital of Kirkwood
525 Couch Ave.
Kirkwood, MO 63122
Tel: 314-966-1601
Member of SSM Health Care.
CARLA S. BAUM, Pres.
Rev. MARK L. FULLER, Supr. & Chap.
Bed Capacity 281
Sisters 2
Nurses 311
Patients assisted annually 50,000

Lake St. Louis
Archdiocese of St. Louis

St. Joseph Hospital West
100 Medical Plaza
Lake St. Louis, MO 63367
Tel: 314-625-5200; Fax: 314-625-5314
Member of SSM Health Care.
Mr. KURT L. WEINMEISTER, Pres.
Rev. JEROME G. STOWELL, C.P., Chap.
Bed Capacity 100
Patients assisted annually 38,614
Staff 309

Maryville
Diocese of Kansas City-St. Joseph

St. Francis Hospital & Health Services
2016 S. Main
Maryville, MO 64468
Tel: 660-562-2600; Fax: 660-562-7911
A member of the SSM Health Care System. Sponsored by Franciscan Sisters of Mary, St. Louis, MO. Acute care facility.
MICHAEL BAUMGARTNER, Pres.
Rev. PHILIP SCHUSTER, O.S.B., Chap.
Priests of the deanery serve as chaplains.
Sisters 3
Bed Capacity 90
Total Staff 360
Patients assisted annually 32,500

Mountain View
Diocese of Springfield-Cape Girardeau

St. Francis Hospital
P.O. Box 82
Mountain View, MO 65548
Tel: 417-934-2246; Fax: 417-934-6024
Daughters of St. Francis of Assisi
Sr. M. CORNELIA BLASKO, D.S.F., Admin., C.E.O.
Sisters 5
Bed Capacity 42
Patients assisted annually 15,482

Pilot Knob
Diocese of Springfield-Cape Girardeau

Arcadia Valley Hospital
P.O. Box 548
Pilot Knob, MO 63663
Tel: 573-546-3924; Fax: 573-546-2918
Owned & Operated by SSM Health Care System. A member of the SSM Health Care System.
Rev. ANTHONY M. GAYDOS, O.S.M., Chap.
Sisters 5
Bed Capacity 60

St. Charles
Archdiocese of St. Louis

St. Joseph Health Center
300 First Capitol Dr.
St. Charles, MO 63301
Tel: 314-947-5000; Fax: 314-947-5090
Member of SSM Health Care.
Mr. KURT WEINMEISTER, Pres.
Mr. DAVE W. FITZGERALD, Dir. of Pastoral Care
Rev. RAY HAMPE
Sisters 3
Bed Capacity 316
Patients assisted annually 79,133
Staff 967

St. Louis
Archdiocese of St. Louis

Alexian Brothers Hospital
3933 S. Broadway
St. Louis, MO 63118
Tel: 314-865-3333
Legal Title: *Alexian Brothers Hospital*
Congregation of The Institute of the Sisters of Mercy of the Americas, Regional Community of St. Louis

DAVID SEIFERT, Pres.
Bed Capacity 203
Patients assisted annually 52,000
Total Staff 798
A member of the Unity Health System.

Lafayette Grand Hospital
3545 Lafayette
St. Louis, MO 63104
Tel: 314-865-6500; Fax: 314-865-6526
Conducted by the Congregation of Sisters of Charity of the Incarnate Word.
JOAN I. HOLDEN, C.C.V.I., D.Min.
LINDA M. ALLIN, CEO
Sisters 2
Other Nurses 151
Bed Capacity 336
Patients assisted annually 29,524
Total Staff 1,500

St. Anthony's Medical Center
10010 Kennerly Rd.
St. Louis, MO 63128
Tel: 314-525-1000
E-mail: solamsestlo.smhs.com
Owned by the Sisters of Mercy Health System (of St. Louis).
Beds 914
Patients assisted annually 194,965
Staff 2,364
A member of the Unity Health System.

Saint Louis University Hospital
3635 Vista Ave., P.O. Box 15250
St. Louis, MO 63110-0250
Tel: 314-577-8000, Ext. 8066; Fax: 314-577-8003 (Exec. Office)
Owned and Operated by St. Louis University, Society of Jesus.
MARY LOU BENNETT, Dir.
Chaplains:
Revs.:
ROBERT J. CHENOWETH (JC)
GREGORY G. KIRSCH
PAUL MANDZIUK, M.S.
Sr. ANN JOHNSTON, O.P.
Deacon LOUIS A. MENARD
MARY SALOIS
SANDRA SPENCER
Rev. KATHY SPIVEY
KATHY HERRON, Pastoral Care Asst.
Nurses 537
Bed Capacity 356
Patients assisted annually 139,019

St. Mary's Health Center
6420 Clayton Rd.
St. Louis, MO 63117
Tel: 314-768-8000; Fax: 314-768-8011
Member of SSM Health Care
MICHAEL ZILM, Pres.
Rev. NICHOLAS J. RUTKOWSKI, Chap.
Franciscan Sisters of Mary 5
Bed Capacity 679
Patients assisted annually 99,338
Total Staff 1,945

Washington
Archdiocese of St. Louis

St. John's Mercy Hospital
200 Madison Ave.
Washington, MO 63090
Tel: 314-239-8000
Rev. TIMOTHY J. TOOHEY, Chap.
TERRY M. ROSE, Admin.
Beds 185
Staff 700
(See Listing Under Creve Coeur, MO)

MONTANA

Billings
Diocese of Great Falls - Billings

Saint Vincent Hospital and Health Center
1233 N. 30th St., P.O. Box 35200
Billings, MT 59107-5200
Tel: 406-657-7000
Sisters of Charity of Leavenworth, Kansas
Mr. JAMES T. PAQUETTE, Pres.
Pastoral Care:
LUKE LARSON, Dir.
Revs.:
MARTIN FISHER
ANTHONY J. OZIMEK, O.S.B.
ROBERT H. KOERNER
Sisters 5
Beds 302
Patients assisted annually 12,000

Butte
Diocese of Helena

St. James Community Hospital, Inc.
400 S. Clark St.
Butte, MT 59701
Mailing Address:
P.O. Box 3300
Butte, MT 59702
Tel: 406-723-2500; Fax: 406-782-1967
ROBERT ROGERS, Admin.
Rev. JAMES C. MCCARTHY, Chap.
Sr. JOY DUFF, S.C.L., Pastoral Care
Bed Capacity 156
Sisters of Charity of Leavenworth 7
Lay Staff 441
Patients assisted annually 38,171

Great Falls
Diocese of Great Falls - Billings

Benefis Health Care
500-15th Ave. S., P.O. Box 5013
Great Falls, MT 59403
Tel: 406-727-3333
Sisters of Providence
Rev. JAMES E. BIRKMAIER, Dir. Pastoral Care & Chap.
LLOYD V. SMITH, FACHE-Pres. & CEO
Sisters 2
Student Nurses 60
Patients assisted annually 94,271

Miles City
Diocese of Great Falls - Billings

Holy Rosary Health Center
2600 Wilson St.
Miles City, MT 59301
Tel: 406-233-2600; Fax: 406-233-2601
Sponsored by Sisters of Charity of Levenworth
Mr. H. RAY GIBBONS, Pres.
Sisters 1
Beds: Acute Care 44
Extended Care 107
Patients assisted annually 16,000
Home Care 2,400

Missoula
Diocese of Helena

St. Patrick Hospital Corporation
500 W. Broadway
Missoula, MT 59802
Web Site: www.saintpatrick.org
Mailing Address:
P.O. Box 4587
Missoula, MT 59806
Tel: 406-543-7271; Fax: 406-329-5693
Mr. LAWRENCE L. WHITE, JR., Pres.
Rev. ROGER E. BLANCHETTE, S.J., Chap.
Pastoral Care:
Sr. MARIE L. CORR, B.V.M.
Sr. ELIZABETH OLSEN, B.V.M.
Sr. CATHERINE PALMATIER, S.P.
Rev. HENRY LITTLEHALES, (Presbyterian)
Sisters 3
Lay Staff 1,213
Bed Capacity 213
Patients assisted annually 123,433

Polson
Diocese of Helena

St. Joseph Hospital Corporation
Skyline Dr., P.O. Box 1010
Polson, MT 59860
Tel: 406-883-5377; Fax: 406-883-4388
JOHN W. GLUECKERT, Admin.
Deacon WES VERT
Sr. MARY K. CUMMINGS, S.P., Pastoral Care
Sisters 1
Bed Capacity 24
Lay Staff 121
Patients assisted annually 19,793

NEBRASKA

Grand Island
Diocese of Grand Island

Saint Francis Medical Center
2620 W. Faidley Ave., P.O. Box 9804
Grand Island, NE 68802
Tel: 308-384-4600; Fax: 308-389-5589
E-mail: dsanders@sfmc-gi.org
Web Site: www.sfmc-gi.org
Mr. MICHAEL GLOOR, Pres.
Catholic Health Initiatives.
Beds 198
Bassinets 17
Patients assisted annually 59,303
Total Staff 749

Kearney
Diocese of Grand Island

Good Samaritan Health Systems dba Good Samaritan Hospital
10 E. 31st St., P.O. Box 1990
Kearney, NE 68848-1990
Tel: 308-865-7100
WILLIAM W. HENDRICKSON, Pres.
Sisters 3
Beds 187
Patients assisted annually 76,985
Richard H. Young Hospital
4600 17th Ave.
Kearney, NE 68847
Tel: 308-865-2000
Beds 80
Patients assisted annually 1,040

Lincoln
Diocese of Lincoln

St. Elizabeth Community Health Center
555 S. 70th St.
Lincoln, NE 68519
Tel: 402-489-7181
Mr. ROBERT LANIK, Pres.
Rev. PATRICK MURPHY, B.A., Chap.
Priests 1
Sisters 3
Beds 208
Patients assisted annually 181,740
Affiliate of Catholic Health Initiatives.

Nebraska City
Diocese of Lincoln

St. Mary's Hospital
1314 3rd Ave.
Nebraska City, NE 68410
Tel: 402-873-3321
DANIEL J. KELLY, CEO, Admin.
Beds 38
Patients assisted annually 26,546
Affiliate of Catholic Health Initiatives.

Norfolk
Archdiocese of Omaha

Faith Regional Health Services
1500 Koenigstein Ave.
Norfolk, NE 68701
Tel: 402-371-3402; Fax: 402-644-7468
The Missionary Benedictine Sisters
Sr. MARY JAMES UHING, O.S.B., Pres.
Sr. M. AGNES SALBER, O.S.B., Prioress
Rev. DUANE LUKES, Chap.
PATRICK ROCHE, Contact & Vice Pres. for Mission Effectiveness
Sisters 4
Beds 185
Patients assisted annually 54,627
New Born 935

O'Neill
Archdiocese of Omaha

St. Anthony's Hospital
O'Neill, NE 68763
Tel: 402-336-2611; Fax: 402-336-2815
E-mail: sahml@inetnebr.com
Sisters of St. Francis of Penance and Christian Charity
RONALD J. CORK, Pres. & C.E.O.; Contact
Beds 44
Bassinets 10
Patients assisted annually 16,095
Attended by St. Patrick Church.

Omaha
Archdiocese of Omaha

Alegent Health - Bergen Mercy Health System
1010 N. 96th St., Ste. 200
Omaha, NE 68114
Tel: 402-343-4430; Fax: 402-343-4337
Sr. NORITA COONEY, R.S.M., Board Chair
Affiliate of Catholic Health Initiatives.

**Archbishop Bergan Mercy Medical Center*
7500 Mercy Rd.
Omaha, NE 68124
Tel: 402-398-6060; Fax: 402-398-6920
RICHARD A. HACHTEN, II, Pres.
Chaplains:

Revs.:
ROBERT E. BRODZELLER, S.J.
HARRY EGLSAER, S.J.
Sr. ELAINE ABELS, R.S.C.J.
KATHY KASHER
MARY LOU RUH
MARY SUE STURGEON
Deacon TOM MURPHY
MARY EILEEN ANDREASEN, Congregational Nurse Min.
MARIAN STANDEVEN, Dir. Mission Svcs./Community Affairs
PEGGY O'MALLEY, Coord. Health Ministry Prog.
Priests 2
Sisters 1
Bed Capacity 656
Inpatients assisted annually 14,623
Outpatients assisted annually 121,398
Affiliate of Catholic Health Initiatives.
Bergan Mercy Foundation, Inc.
RICHARD A. HACHTEN, II, Pres.
MARIAN STANDEVEN, Contact

Boys Town National Research Hospital
555 N. 30 St.
Omaha, NE 68131
Tel: 402-498-6511; Fax: 402-498-6357
Dr. PATRICK BROOKHOUSER, Dir.

Catholic Health Corp.
Under Catholic Health Initiatives.
920 S. 107 Ave.
Omaha, NE 68114
Tel: 402-393-7661
ELEANOR G. CLAUS, Interim CEO & Contact
Catholic Health Care Federation
Catholic Health Corporation Retirement Plan
Health Services Self Protection Fund
Health Facilities, Inc.

Wayne
Archdiocese of Omaha

Providence Medical Center
1200 Providence Rd.
Wayne, NE 68787
Missionary Benedictine Sisters
MARCILE THOMAS, Admin.
Sr. KEVIN HERMSEN, Asst. Admin.
Sr. MONICA BACKES, Supr.
Rev. DONALD M. CLEARY, Chap.
Sr. GERTRUD MARIE WOLFER, O.S.B., Pastoral Care
Sr. KEVIN HERMSEN, Contact
Beds 34
Patients assisted annually 6,900

West Point
Archdiocese of Omaha

Franciscan Care Services, Inc., dba St. Francis Memorial Hospital
430 N. Monitor St.
West Point, NE 68788-1595
Tel: 402-372-2404; Fax: 402-372-2360
E-mail: fc70656@navix.net
Franciscan Sisters of Christian Charity
RONALD O. BRIGGS, CEO & Contact
Revs.:
GARY L. OSTRANDER
CHARLES R. UHLIK
Sisters 6
Bed Capacity 49
Patients assisted annually 60,386

NEVADA

Henderson
Diocese of Las Vegas

St. Rose Dominican Hospital
102 Lake Mead Dr.
Henderson, NV 89015
Tel: 702-564-2622
Sisters of the Third Order of St. Dominic, Congregation of the Most Holy Rosary (Adrian, MI)
Mr. ROD A. DAVIS, Pres. & CEO
Affiliated with the University of Nevada-Las Vegas School of Nursing Affiliated with the University of Nevada-Las Vegas School of Nursing-Paramedic Program-Vo-Tech. & Community College of South Nevada.
Sisters 13
Beds 147
Total Staff 790
Patients assisted annually 89,420

Reno
Diocese of Reno

St. Mary's Regional Medical Center
235 W. Sixth St.
Reno, NV 89520-0108
Tel: 702-323-2041; Fax: 702-789-3963
Dominican Sisters of San Rafael
Sr. JEREMY CARMODY, O.P., Congregational Rep.
JEFF K. BILLS, Pres. & CEO, Tel: 702-789-3004
BENEDICT DASHER, Chm.
JULIANA JERVIS, Natural Family Planning
Deacon RANDOL G. BATSON, Mgr. Chaplaincy Svcs.
Chaplaincy Services:
Revs.:
JOHN COEN, S.A.C.
WILLIAM FAUST
Sr. MARRIANNA HARRISON, O.P.
GINGER AYALA, Admin.
Sisters 3
Beds 367
Patients assisted annually 142,566

NEW HAMPSHIRE

Manchester
Diocese of Manchester

Catholic Medical Center of Manchester, NH, Inc.
100 McGregor St.
Manchester, NH 03102
Tel: 603-668-3545
Sr. ANDREA MCDONALD, R.S.M., Dept. Dir.
Sisters 4
Beds 330
Inpatient Admissions 9,861
Outpatient Admissions 103,114

Nashua
Diocese of Manchester

St. Joseph Hospital
172 Kinsley St.
Nashua, NH 03061
Tel: 603-882-3000
KENNETH FERRON, Vice Pres./COO
Sr. JOSEPHINE PATTIGASH, Vice Pres., Mission Integration
Dr. JOHN A. GIANINO, Pastoral Care Mgr.
Deacon JOHN MARTIN, Staff Chap.
Grey Nuns 2
Beds 218
Total Staff 1,089
Patients assisted annually 2,299
Rivier-St. Joseph School of Nursing
Students 635

NEW JERSEY

Camden
Diocese of Camden

Our Lady of Lourdes Medical Center, Inc.
(Formerly Our Lady of Lourdes Hospital).
1600 Haddon Ave.
Camden, NJ 08103
Tel: 609-757-3500
Revs.:
WARREN RECTOR, O.F.M.
ARTHUR T. ANDERSON
Our Lady of Lourdes Associates Foundation, Inc.
853 Haddon Ave.
Collingswood, NJ 08108
Tel: 609-858-5097
Lourdes HomeHealth Services
1600 Haddon Ave.
Camden, NJ 08103
Tel: 609-869-0900
Haddon HealthCare
900 Haddon Ave., Suite 318
Camden, NJ 08108
Tel: 609-869-0800
Osborn Family Health Center, Inc.
1601 Haddon Ave.
Camden, NJ 08103
Tel: 609-757-3700
Lourdes Ancillary Services, Inc.
1565 Vesper Blvd.
Camden, NJ 08103
Tel: 609-757-3500
Our Lady of Lourdes School of Nursing, Inc.
1565 Vesper Blvd.
Camden, NJ 08103
Tel: 609-757-3730
Our Lady of Lourdes Medical Center, Inc. Auxiliary
1600 Haddon Ave.
Camden, NJ 08103
Tel: 609-757-3500
Our Lady of Lourdes Health Care Services, Inc.
1600 Haddon Ave.
Camden, NJ 08103
Tel: 609-757-3500
Patients assisted annually 165,000
Staff 2,000
Beds 375

Saint Luke's Catholic Medical Services, Inc.
511 State St.
Camden, NJ 08102
Tel: 609-365-4642
Rev. MARK C. AITA, S.J., M.D., Medical Dir.
Patients assisted annually 2,000
Staff 8

Denville
Diocese of Paterson

Northwest Covenant Medical Center
25 Pocono Rd.
Denville, NJ 07834
(Parent Corp.: Via Caritas Health System, Inc.)
Sr. CATHERINE MARIE BELONGIA, S.S.M., Chm.
Sr. KATHRYN MCDONAGH, Pres. & CEO
Affiliates:
St. Clares-Riverside Campus-Denville
St. Clares-Riverside Campus-Boonton Township
St. Clares-Riverside Campus-Sussex
Dover General Campus-Dover
Chaplains:
Revs.:
THOMAS A. HEFFERNAN
CHARLES LOVATO, S.F.
STUART BAER
JEREMIAH O'RIORDAN
NOEL CLARKE
Deacons:
ED LALLY
FRANK PADDEN
Sisters of the Sorrowful Mother 10
Bed Capacity 927
Patients assisted annually 318,000

Sisters of the Sorrowful Mother Ambulatory Care Corp.
c/o 25 Pocono Rd.
Denville, NJ 07834
(Parent Corp.: Via Caritas Health System, Inc.)
Sr. M. JOHNICE THONE, S.S.M., Chm.
JOSEPH TRUNFIO, Ph.D., Pres. & CEO
Affiliates:
St. Clares-Riverside Foundation, Inc.
St. Francis Life Care Corporation
St. Francis Assisted Living Corporation
St. Francis Health Resort, Inc.
Wallkill Valley Health Care Foundation, Inc.
Sisters of the Sorrowful Mother Housing Corporation I, Inc.
Sisters of the Sorrowful Mother Housing Corporation II, Inc.

Elizabeth
Archdiocese of Newark

St. Elizabeth Hospital
225 Williamson St.
Elizabeth, NJ 07207
Tel: 908-527-5000; Fax: 908-820-0554
E-mail: seam5122@aol.com
Sisters of Charity of Saint Elizabeth
Sr. ELIZABETH ANN MALONEY, S.C., Pres. & CEO
Sr. DOROTHY APPRICH, S.S.J., Dir. Pastoral Care
Chaplains:
Revs.:
EDWARD HABER
VIRGILIO P. CHAGAS (Philippines)
Sisters 16
Bed Capacity 329
Bassinets 31
Patients assisted annually 105,094

**Marillac Corp.*
240 Williamson St.
Elizabeth, NJ 07207
Tel: 908-527-5122; Fax: 908-820-0554
Sr. ELIZABETH ANN MALONEY, Pres.
Sr. EDNA FRANCIS HERSINGER, S.C., Vice Pres.
Sr. MARCELLA NOLAN, S.C., Sec. & Treas.

New Brunswick
Diocese of Metuchen

St. Peter's Medical Center
254 Easton Ave.
New Brunswick, NJ 08901
Tel: 732-745-8600; Fax: 732-745-9888
JOHN E. MATUSKA, Pres.
Chaplains:
Revs.:
CECILIO E. SIPACO (Philippines)
GUY I. MCPARTLAND, O.Carm.
JAMES DE URIES, Dir.
RAYNARD SMITH
Sr. BREDA BOYLE, C.S.J.P.
Sr. CLAIRE MACDONALD, O.P.
Sr. MARY JO O'CONNOR, D.W.
Sr. BARBARA ORTMANN, O.P.
Beds 416

Bassinets 95
Patients assisted annually 172,380

Newark
Archdiocese of Newark

Catholic Community Services (C.C.S.) Mt. Carmel Guild Hospital
1160 Raymond Blvd.
Newark, NJ 07102
Tel: 973-596-4084
Rev. Msgr. DENNIS J. MAHON, Exec. Dir., C.C.S.
LEONARD S. ALTAMURA, D.S.W., Dir. Behavioral Healthcare
AMBROSE MGBAKO, M.D., Medical Dir.
Operated by Catholic Community Services. The hospital has two adult units: Psychiatric Unit; Substance Abuse Detoxification Unit. Also available are Extensive outpatient and day treatment services in the area of substance abuse and mental health for adults.
Bed Capacity 20
Staff 27
Patients assisted annually 555

St. James Hospital
155 Jefferson St.
Newark, NJ 07105
Tel: 973-589-1300
CEU CIRNE-NEVES, Admin.
OLIMPIA ESCUDERO, Vice Pres. Operations
Chaplains:
Sr. DOLORES CERVI
Rev. KENNETH MARTIN
ALAN GOLDFEDER, M.D., Pres. Medical Staff
Bed Capacity 189
Bassinets 23
Staff 550
Patients assisted annually 30,000

Saint Michael's Medical Center
268 Dr. Martin Luther King. Jr. Blvd.
Newark, NJ 07102-9880
Tel: 973-877-5411; Fax: 973-877-2714
DOMINICK R. CALGI, Admin.
Rev. MANUEL CRUZ, Mgr. Pastoral Care
JAMES AMATO, M.D., Pres. Medical Staff
Division of Cathedral Health Services, Inc.
Bed Capacity 411
Sisters 5
Bassinets 32
Admissions 11,713
Outpatient Visits 82,000

Orange
Archdiocese of Newark

Saint Mary Life Center, Inc. - Pope John Paul II Pavilion
Skilled nursing facility, comprehensive personal care.
135 S. Center St.
Orange, NJ 07050
Tel: 973-266-3000
MICHAEL SHIPLEY, Admin.
Skilled nursing facility, comprehensive personal care.

Passaic
Diocese of Paterson

St. Mary's Hospital
211 Pennington Ave.
Passaic, NJ 07055
Tel: 973-470-3000
(Parent Corp.: Via Caritas Health System, Inc.)
PATRICIA PETERSON, Pres. & CEO
Rev. VINCENT LIUZZO, O.F.M.Cap., Dir. Pastoral Care
Sisters of Charity of St. Elizabeth, NJ 10
Bed Capacity 229
Patients assisted annually 67,683
St. Mary Health Corporation
Sr. BARBARA CONROY, S.C.
St. Mary's Hospital Corporation
PATRICIA PETERSON, Pres.
Gillen Property Holding Corporation
PATRICIA PETERSON, Pres.

Paterson
Diocese of Paterson

St. Joseph's Hospital and Medical Center
703 Main St.
Paterson, NJ 07503
Tel: 973-754-2000
(Parent Corp.: Via Caritas Health System, Inc.)
Sr. JANE FRANCES BRADY, Pres.
Revs.:
FRANCIS HANUDEL, O.F.M.
WILLIAM CRAMER
Sisters of Charity of St. Elizabeth, NJ 35
Bed Capacity 787
Patients assisted annually 315,607

Teaneck
Archdiocese of Newark

Holy Name Hospital
718 Teaneck Rd.
Teaneck, NJ 07666
Tel: 201-833-3000; Fax: 201-833-3230
Sisters of St. Joseph of Peace
MICHAEL MARON, Pres. & CEO
Bed Capacity 361
Bassinets 36
School of Nursing
Sr. CLARE TYNAN C.S.J.P., Senior Vice Pres.
Pastoral Care:
Sr. LOIS JABLONSKI, S.S.J., M.S., Dir.
Chaplains:
Rev. PATERNO GOROSPE
CONSTANCE FORCILLO, R.N.
MARY ELLEN DORAN, M.S.
JANE SELINSKE, Ed.D., M.S.W.
Sisters 12

Trenton
Diocese of Trenton

St. Francis Medical Center
601 Hamilton Ave.
Trenton, NJ 08629
Tel: 609-599-5000; Fax: 609-695-2744
Affiliate of Catholic Health Initiatives.
Sisters of St. Francis of Philadelphia 10
Bed Capacity 412
Patients assisted annually 143,858
Bassinets 27
Schools for Nurses
JUDITH M. PERSICHILLI, Pres. & C.E.O.
BONNIE ROSS, Dir. School of Nursing
Revs.:
JOEL F. SZYDLOWSKI, O.F.M., Dir. Pastoral Care
LINUS E. KOPCZEWSKI, O.F.M.
RUDOLPH WIESZCZEK, O.F.M.
Student Nurses 40

NEW MEXICO

Albuquerque
Archdiocese of Santa Fe

St. Joseph Healthcare System
E-mail: ConeM@SJHS.ORG
Mailing Address:
P.O. Box 25555
Albuquerque, NM 87125-0555
7850 Jefferson N.E.
Albuquerque, NM 87109
Tel: 505-727-2804; Fax: 505-727-2814
Affiliate of Catholic Health Initiatives.
STEPHEN J. SMITH, Pres.
Sr. MARIE RAPHAEL MORELL, O.P., Dir. Spiritual Care
Priests 2
Chaplains 8
Patients assisted annually 17,621
Beds 677
Total Staff 2,162

St. Joseph Medical Center
E-mail: ConeM@SJHS.ORG
Mailing Address:
P.O. Box 25555
Albuquerque, NM 87125-0555
601 Dr. Martin Luther King Jr. Ave., N.E.
Albuquerque, NM 87102
Tel: 505-727-2804; Fax: 505-727-2814
Affiliate of Catholic Health Initiatives.
C. VINCENT TOWNSEND, JR.
Sr. MARIE RAPHAEL MORELL, O.P., Dir. Spiritual Care
Priests 1
Chaplains 5
Beds 255
Patients assisted annually 10,141
Total Staff 945

St. Joseph Northeast Heights Hospital
E-mail: ConeM@SJHS.ORG
Mailing Address:
P.O. Box 25555
Albuquerque, NM 87125-0555
4701 Montgomery, N.E.
Albuquerque, NM 87109
Tel: 505-727-2804; Fax: 505-727-2814
Affiliate of Catholic Health Initiatives.
MARY LOU COORS, Admin.
Sr. MARIE RAPHAEL MORELL, O.P., Dir. Spiritual Care
Priests 1
Chaplains 1
Beds 112
Patients assisted annually 3,839
Total Staff 230

St. Joseph Rehabilitation Hospital
E-mail: ConeM@SJHS.ORG
Mailing Address:
P.O. Box 25555
Albuquerque, NM 87125-0555
505 Elm St., N.E.
Albuquerque, NM 87102
Tel: 505-727-2804; Fax: 505-727-2814
Affiliate of Catholic Health Initiatives.
MARY LOU COORS, Admin.
Sr. MARIE RAPHAEL MORELL, O.P., Dir. Spiritual Care
Priests 1
Beds 63
Patients assisted annually 897
Total Staff 207

St. Joseph West Mesa Hospital
E-mail: ConeM@SJHS.ORG
Mailing Address:
P.O. Box 25555
Albuquerque, NM 87125-0555
10501 Golf Course Rd.
Albuquerque, NM 87114
Tel: 505-727-2804; Fax: 505-727-2814
Affiliate of Catholic Health Initiatives.
MARY LOU COORS, Admin.
Sr. MARIE RAPHAEL MORELL, O.P., Dir. Spiritual Care
Chaplains/Priests available 1
Beds 112
Patients assisted annually 2,631
Total Staff 196

NEW YORK

Albany
Diocese of Albany

Mercycare Corporation
315 S. Manning Blvd.
Albany, NY 12208
Tel: 518-454-1084; Fax: 518-454-1520

Mercycare Corporation, St. Peter's Hospital
315 S. Manning Blvd.
Albany, NY 12208
Tel: 518-454-1540
Mr. STEVEN P. BOYLE, Pres. & CEO
Rev. JOHN YANAS, Chap.
Bed Capacity 437
Patients assisted annually 193,077
Hospice
Tel: 518-454-1563
Sr. JEAN ROCHE, R.S.M., Contact Person
Hospice of Rensselaer Co.
258 Broadway
Albany, NY 12180
Tel: 518-271-1901
Sr. MARLENE HORRIGAN, C.S.J., Contact Person
Our Lady of Mercy Life Center
2240 Western Ave.
Guilderland, NY 12084
Tel: 518-464-8100
WESLEY I. HALE, Exec. Dir.

Amsterdam
Diocese of Albany

St. Mary's Hospital
427 Guy Park Ave.
Amsterdam, NY 12010
Tel: 518-842-1900
Mr. PETER E. CAPOBIANCO, Pres. & CEO
Rev. JOSEPH J. DWORAK, Chap.
Sisters of St. Joseph of Carondelet 14
Bed Capacity 143
Patients assisted annually 150,355

Auburn
Diocese of Rochester

Mercy Health & Rehabilitation Center Nursing Home Co., Inc. (1972)
St. Anthony St.
Auburn, NY 13021
Tel: 315-253-0351; Fax: 315-258-3904
E-mail: dfdonnelly@attmail
Sr. MARY NORBERT STANG, Dir. Pastoral Care
Sr. LINDA ANN PALMISANO, CEO
Sisters of the Third Franciscan Order
Nursing Facility Beds 297

Batavia
Diocese of Buffalo

St. Jerome Hospital
16 Bank St.
Batavia, NY 14020
Tel: 716-343-3131
Mr. CHARLES W. SMITH, Admin.
LINDA PROUTY, R.N., Dir. Nursing Services
Sisters of Mercy 4
Capacity 96
Patients assisted annually 78,961
Total Staff 343

Beacon
Archdiocese of New York

St. Francis Hospital
Delavan Ave.
Beacon, NY 12508
Tel: 914-831-3500
LAWRENCE M. WITTE, FACHE

Binghamton
Diocese of Syracuse

Our Lady of Lourdes Memorial Hospital
169 Riverside Dr.
Binghamton, NY 13905
Tel: 607-798-5111
Mr. MICHAEL GULEY, Pres.
Daughters of Charity of St. Vincent de Paul 9
Beds 277
Patients assisted annually 316,481

Buffalo
Diocese of Buffalo

McAuley Mercy Corporation
515 Abbott Rd.
Buffalo, NY 14220
Tel: 716-828-2750
Sr. SALLY MALONEY, R.S.M., Chairperson
Sponsored by the Sisters of Mercy of the Buffalo Diocese.

Mercy Health System of Western New York
Marian Professional Center
515 Abbott Rd., Ste. 508
Buffalo, NY 14220
Tel: 716-828-2750
ROBERT V. STANEK, Pres./ C.E.O.
Annually Assisted 581,114
Total Staff 2,932

Mercy Hospital
565 Abbott Rd.
Buffalo, NY 14220
Tel: 716-826-7000
E-mail: mercyhosp@aol.com
JAMES W. CONNOLLY, Admin.
SHIRLEY A. HEINTZ, Nursing Svcs.
Sisters of Mercy 10
Patients assisted annually 291,016
Outpatients 274,886
Admissions 16,130
Beds 349
Skilled Nursing Beds 74
Bassinets 60
Total Staff 2,144

Sisters Hospital Foundation, Inc.
2130 Main St.
Buffalo, NY 14214
Tel: 716-862-2533

Sisters of Charity Hospital of Buffalo, NY
2157 Main St.
Buffalo, NY 14214
Tel: 716-862-1000; Fax: 716-862-1899
E-mail: mdougher@sisters-buffalo.org
Web Site: http://www.sisters-buffalo.org81
Chaplains:
Revs.:
LOUIS S. KLEIN
RICHARD E. ZAJAC
Sr. MARGARET DOUGHERTY, D.C., Dir., Pastoral Care
Sr. M. CAROLINE HRICZKO, D.C.
Sr. DIANE LOUTTIT, D.C.
Deacon KAREN GOUGH
Ms. JUDITH MILLER
Ms. TERESA MAIKISCH
Daughters of Charity of St. Vincent de Paul 12
Bed Capacity 493
Bassinets 60
Patients assisted annually 317,000
Total Staff 2,000
School for Nurses
Student Nurses 62

Cheektowaga
Diocese of Buffalo

McAuley-Seton Home Care
14 Appletree Business Park
Cheektowaga, NY 14227
Tel: 716-685-4870
JAMES CORRIGAN, Pres.

St. Joseph Hospital
2605 Harlem Rd.
Cheektowaga, NY 14225-4097
Tel: 716-891-2400; Fax: 716-891-2616
Franciscan Sisters of St. Joseph
Bed Capacity 208
Patients assisted annually 143,100
Total Staff 895

Elmira
Diocese of Rochester

St. Joseph's Health System, Inc. (Formerly St. Joseph's Hospital)
55 E. Market St.
Elmira, NY 14902
Tel: 607-733-6541
Web Site: www.stjosephs.org
Sisters of St. Joseph
Skilled Nursing Facility.
Sr. MARIE CASTAGNARO, Pres.
Total Staff 1,087
Bed Capacity 224
Skilled Nursing Facility 31
Patients assisted annually 105,994

St. Joseph's Hospital Foundation, Inc.
555 E. Market St.
Elmira, NY 14902
Tel: 607-737-7004; Fax: 607-737-7837
DAVID P. SULLIVAN, Pres.

Hornell
Diocese of Rochester

St. James Mercy Hospital
411 Canisteo St.
Hornell, NY 14843
Tel: 607-324-8000
PAUL E. SHEPHARD, CEO
Sr. ANN MILLER, Spiritual Care
Sisters of Mercy 3
Total Staff 201
Bed Capacity 232
Patients assisted annually 4,674

Jamaica
Diocese of Brooklyn

Catholic Medical Center of Brooklyn & Queens
88-25 153rd St.
Jamaica, NY 11432
Tel: 718-558-6900
Corporate Staff:
Most Rev. JOSEPH M. SULLIVAN, Chm.
WILLIAM D. MCGUIRE, Pres. & CEO
RICHARD BIRRER, M.D., Vice Pres. Physician Svcs. & CMO
Sr. ANNELLE FITZPATRICK, Ph.D., Vice Pres. Mission
Ms. KATHLEEN GALVIN, Vice Pres. Strategy & Network
STEPHEN MCCLELLAN, Ph.D., Vice Pres. Public Affairs & Devel.
MALCOLM MURRAY, Vice Pres. Information System
DANIEL J. RINALDI, Vice Pres. & Chief Fin. Officer
KATHLEEN M. SCHER, Vice Pres. Nursing & Human Resources
MILDRED A. SHANLEY, Vice Pres. Legal Affairs
JOSEPH SKARZYNSKI, M.D., Medical Dir. Quality & Risk Mgmt.
MARGARET FERNANDEZ, Admin. Asst. to the Pres.
Mary Immaculate Hospital Division
152-11 89th Ave.
Jamaica, NY 11432
Tel: 718-558-2000
St. John's Queens Hospital Division
90-02 Queens Blvd.
Elmhurst, NY 11373
Tel: 718-558-1000
St. Joseph's Hospital Division
158-40 79th Ave.
Flushing, NY 11366
Tel: 718-558-6200
St. Mary's Hospital of Brooklyn Affiliate
170 Buffalo Ave.
Brooklyn, NY 11213
Tel: 718-221-3000
Mary Immaculate Hospital Home Health Agency
95-25 Queens Blvd.
Rego Park, NY 11374
Tel: 718-830-4500
CATHERINE BARBERA, Exec. Dir., Home Care Agency
St. Mary's Hospital of Brooklyn Home Health Agency
170 Buffalo Ave.
Brooklyn, NY 11213
Tel: 718-221-3844
CATHERINE BARBERA, Exec. Dir., Home Care Agency
St. Mary's Hospital of Brooklyn Long Term Home Health Program
170 Buffalo Ave.
Brooklyn, NY 11213
Tel: 718-221-3844
CATHERINE BARBERA, Exec. Dir., Home Care Agency
St. Anthony Health Professions & Nursing Institute
175-05 Horace Harding Expwy.
Fresh Meadows, NY 11365
Tel: 718-357-0500, Ext. 104
ANTHONY SHALLASH, M.D., Dir. Allied Health
Catholic Medical Center Physician Assistant Program
175-05 Horace Harding Expwy.
Fresh Meadows, NY 11365
Tel: 718-805-7599
JOANN DEASY, M.P.H., PA-C, Dir.
Catholic Medical Center School of Nursing
175-05 Horace Harding Expwy.
Fresh Meadows, NY 11365
Tel: 718-805-5602
ELISA DALMAN-HESS, Dir.
Catholic Medical Center Program of Medical Technology
175-05 Horace Harding Expwy.
Fresh Meadows, NY 11365
Tel: 718-357-0500, Ext. 111
ANN PAULA ZERO, Dir.
Catholic Medical Center Program of Radiography
175-05 Horace Harding Expwy.
Fresh Meadows, NY 11365
Tel: 718-357-0500, Ext. 112
Ms. BARBARA WILSON CHAKMAKJIAN, M.S., R.T., Dir.
Catholic Medical Center Emergency Medical Services Institute
175-05 Horace Harding Expwy.
Fresh Meadows, NY 11365
Tel: 718-357-0500, Ext. 181
MICHAEL TRETOLA, Mgr. Allied Health Educ.
Catholic Medical Center Pathology Assistants Program
152-11 89th Ave.
Jamaica, NY 11432
Tel: 718-558-6731
USHA RUDER, M.D., Dir.
Catholic Medical Center Catholic Hospital Administration Personnel (CHAP) Program
88-25 153rd St.
Woodhaven, NY 11432
Tel: 718-558-7102
Sr. ANNELLE FITZPATRICK, C.S.J., Ph.D., Dir.
Co-sponsored with St. John's University.

Kenmore
Diocese of Buffalo

Kenmore Mercy Foundation Inc.
2950 Elmwood Ave.
Kenmore, NY 14217
Tel: 716-879-6204
Bed Capacity 184
Total Staff 800

Kenmore Mercy Hospital
2950 Elmwood Ave.
Kenmore, NY 14217
Tel: 716-447-6100; Fax: 716-447-6090
Sisters of Mercy
Sr. MARY JOEL SCHIMSCHEINER, R.S.M., CEO
Chaplains:
Rev. VINCENT J. FERRARO
DONNA KROPIDLOWSKI, Dir.
Bed Capacity 219
Total Staff 845
Outpatient Visits 170,000
Admissions 7,000

Kingston
Archdiocese of New York

Benedictine Hospital
105 Mary's Ave.
Kingston, NY 12401
Tel: 914-338-2500
Sr. MARY FEEHAN, O.S.B., Senior Vice Pres., Mission Effectiveness
Sr. MARY DOROTHY HUGGARD, O.S.B., Dir., Pastoral Care
Revs.:
MARTIN SVITAN
LIONEL G. TRUDEL, M.M.
Sisters of St. Benedict (Federation of St. Scholastica) 6
Capacity 222
Patients assisted annually 59,428

Total Staff 682

Lackawanna
Diocese of Buffalo

Our Lady of Victory Hospital
55 Melroy at Ridge Rd.
Lackawanna, NY 14218
Tel: 716-825-8000; Fax: 716-825-4681
Mr. JOHN P. DAVANZO, Pres./CEO
Revs.:
FRANCIS N. MILLER, Dir. Emeritus
ROBERT J. MCARTNEY, Dir. Pastoral Care
RAYMOND MAHAR
Rev. Msgr. ROBERT C. WURTZ, Chm.
Sisters of St. Joseph 4
Capacity 242
Patients assisted annually 72,939
Total Staff 951
Affiliated Programs:
BOCES
Food & Nutritional Services, Nursing Asst., LPN.
Daemen College
Medical Technology, Medical Records Admin., Physical Therapy.
D'Youville College
Physical Therapy, Nutritional Services, Registered Nurses.
Edinboro University of PA
Speech-Language Pathology.
Erie Community College
Dietetic Technology, Emergency Medical Technology.
Genesee Community College
Physical Therapy.
Niagara Community College
Physical Therapy Asst.
Trocaire College
Registered Nurses, Medical Records, EKG/Cardiac Monitor Technology, Surgical Technology, Phlebotomy, Radiologic Technology.
S.U.N.Y. at Buffalo
Speech Language Technology, Dietary, Physical Therapy, Pharmacy, Social Work, Clinical Nutrition.
S.U.N.Y. at Alfred
Medical Records.

Our Lady of Victory Hospital Auxiliary
55 Melroy Ave.
Lackawanna, NY 14218
Tel: 716-825-8000; Fax: 716-825-4583

Lewiston
Diocese of Buffalo

Mount St. Mary's Hospital of Niagara Falls
5300 Military Rd.
Lewiston, NY 14092-1997
Tel: 716-297-4800
Daughters of Charity National Health System - East
ANGELO G. CALBONE, Pres./CEO
Rev. PAUL C. SCHRECK, Chap.
Sr. MARY AGNES O'NEIL, D.C., Chm. Bd. Dir.
Capacity 179
Bassinets 22
Patients assisted annually 155,570
Total Staff 798

Lockport
Diocese of Buffalo

Niagara Homemaker Services, dba Mercy Home Care of Western New York
111 Main St.
Lockport, NY 14094
Tel: 716-434-2388
Directors:
J. THOMAS BRIODY
ROBERT STANEK
PATRICK EDGEN
Sr. MARY ANN WELDON
Sr. SALLY MALONEY

New York
Archdiocese of New York

Bayley Seton Hospital
75 Vanderbilt Ave.
Staten Island, NY 10304
Tel: 718-390-6000
Web Site: http://www.schcs.com
Annually Assisted 59,000
JOHN DEPIERRO, Pres.
Rev. EDWARD J. DATTY, S.A., Chap.

Cabrini Medical Center (Cabrini Development Council, Inc.)
227 E. 19th St.
New York, NY 10003
Tel: 212-995-6000
Mr. JEFFREY FRERICHS, Pres.
Sr. ARLENE PRIMUS, M.S.C., Asst. to the Pres. for Mission & Chaplaincy Svcs.
Bed Capacity Acute Hospital 493
Skilled nursing facility at Dobbs Ferry 304
Home Care 150
New York City, Beds 240 (Cabrini Nursing Home)
Missionary Sisters of the Sacred Heart 11
Patients assisted annually 44,588
Cabrini Hospice Program (home care) 710
Stuyvesant Polyclinic, Inc.
Tel: 212-674-0220
Patients assisted annually 45,382

Our Lady of Mercy Medical Center
233rd St. Division
600 E. 233 St.
Bronx, NY 10466
Tel: 718-920-9000
Florence D'Urso Pavilion
1870 Pelham Pkwy. S.
Bronx, NY 10461
Tel: 718-430-6000
Acute Care General Hospital.
Mr. GARY S. HORAN, Pres. & CEO
Revs.:
FREDERICK J. BECKER, Vice Pres. Pastoral Svcs.
THOMAS P. D'ANGELO, Catholic Chap.
BERNARD IHEOHA, Catholic Chap.
Capacity 612
Patients assisted annually 271,994
Total Staff 2,349
Rosalie Hall Shelter for Unwed Mothers
DIANE PRUSINSKI, S.M., Dir.
Capacity 28

St. Clare's Hospital and Health Center
415 W. 51st St.
New York, NY 10019
Tel: 212-586-1500
RICHARD N. YEZZO, Pres.
Rev. JOHN J. DONAHUE, C.S.C., Chap.
Bed Capacity 250
Patients assisted annually 15,903

St. Vincent's Hospital and Medical Center of New York
153 W. 11th St.
New York, NY 10011
Tel: 212-604-7000
KARL P. ADLER, M.D., Pres. & CEO
Sr. KAREN HELFENSTEIN, Senior Vice Pres. Mission
Chaplains:
Revs.:
TIMOTHY COLON, O.S.C., Supvr.
JEFFERSON HAMMER
PRAXID DESILVA
MARTIN RAJU
Sr. EILEEN LAMBERT O.S.F.
Sr. PATRICIA LAWLOR, S.C.
Sr. BERNADETTE BAER, S.C.
Sr. ALBERTA JUREWICZ, C.S.F.N.
Bros.:
JOHN CONWAY, O.F.M.
MICHAEL MORAN, C.P.
Sisters of Charity, Mt. St. Vincent on Hudson 31
Capacity 813
Patients assisted annually 195,000
School of Nursing: Students 140

Saint Vincent's Medical Center of Richmond
355 Bard Ave.
Staten Island, NY 10310
Tel: 718-876-1234
Sisters of Charity of St. Vincent de Paul of NY 2
Capacity 440 beds
Patients assisted annually 70,000
School of Nursing Students 110
School of Nursing Staff 23
Total Staff 2,500
Sr. CATHERINE SHERRY, S.C., Treas.
Sr. THERESE MONAGHAN, O.P., Ed.D., Dir. Pastoral Care
Chaplains:
Revs.:
RALPH DAWIS
DOROTHY CALDWELL, M.Div., C.P.E.
Sr. MARY ALICE DUGGAN, O.S.U.
Rabbi MORRIS ZACHARISH
Rabbi GERALD SUSSMAN
Revs.:
JOANNA WHITE, M.Div., C.P.E.
JOSEPH NIETLONG
Priests from Our Lady of Mt. Carmel.

Port Jefferson
Diocese of Rockville Centre

St. Charles Hospital, Port Jefferson, New York
Port Jefferson, NY 11777
Tel: 516-474-6000
Founded by the Daughters of Wisdom.
BARRY ZEMAN, Pres. & CEO
Revs.:
JUNIPER JONES THOMAS
JAMES C. MILLER
Chaplains:
Sr. MARTHA WINUM, D.W.
Sr. MONA GUERRETTE, D.W.
Patients assisted annually 93,800
Beds 271
Bassinets 41
Staff 980

Port Jervis
Archdiocese of New York

Mercy Community Hospital
160 E. Main St.
Port Jervis, NY 12771
Tel: 914-856-5351; Fax: 914-858-5402
MARIE T. DROEGE, Site Admin.
Capacity 141
Sisters of Mercy 1
SNF Beds 46
Patients assisted annually 67,926
Total Staff 473

Poughkeepsie
Archdiocese of New York

St. Francis Hospital
North Rd.
Poughkeepsie, NY 12601
Tel: 914-471-2000
Sisters of St. Francis of Hastings-on-Hudson
DONALD F. MURPHY, Exec. Vice Pres.
Sr. M. ANN ELIZABETH, O.S.F., Pres.
Rev. THOMAS A. MCDONALD, Dir. Pastoral Care
Capacity 295
St. Francis Health Care Foundation
North Rd.
Poughkeepsie, NY 12601
Sr. M. ANN ELIZABETH, Pres.
Saint Francis Hospital, Beacon
Delavan Ave.
Beacon, NY 12538
Tel: 914-831-3500
LAWRENCE M. WITTE, Exec. Dir.
Capacity 116 beds
Total Annually Assisted 150,000
Total Staff 1,300

Rochester
Diocese of Rochester

Unity Health System
89 Genesee St.
Rochester, NY 14611
Tel: 716-464-3000; Fax: 716-464-0044
(An Alliance of St. Mary's Hospital and Park Ridge Health System)
TIMOTHY MCCORMICK, Pres. & CEO
Sr. BETSY MACKINNON, D.C., V.I.P. of Mission
Rev. COSGROVE
Daughters of Charity of St. Vincent de Paul 7
Total Staff 4,000
Bed Capacity 1,000
Beds 839
Patients assisted annually 107,000

Rockville Centre
Diocese of Rockville Centre

Catholic Health Services of Long Island, Inc.
50 N. Park Ave.
Rockville Centre, NY 11570
Tel: 516-678-5800, Ext. 528

Catholic Healthcare Network of Long Island
50 N. Park Ave.
Rockville Centre, NY 11570
Tel: 516-678-5800
DONNA M. O'BRIEN, Contact Person

Mercy Medical Center
1000 N. Village Ave.
Rockville Centre, NY 11570
Tel: 516-255-0111
Founded by The Congregation of the Infant Jesus (Nursing Sisters of the Sick Poor).
HENRY W. DWYER, Chm.
VINCENT DI RUBBIO, Pres. & CEO
PATRICK F. CARONE, M.D., Dir. Psychiatry
CHRISTINE LEFLOWITZ, M.P.S., R.N., Vice Pres. & Dir. Behavioral Health & Substance Abuse Svcs.
Chaplains:
Revs.:
DENIS J. SHERIDAN
ASIR ANTONY
Patients assisted annually 362,170

Total Staff 1,599
Legal Title: *Mercy Medical Center*

Roslyn
Diocese of Rockville Centre

St. Francis Hospital
100 Port Washington Blvd.
Roslyn, NY 11576
Tel: 516-562-6000
Founded by the Franciscan Missionaries of Mary.
PATRICK J. SCOLLARD, Pres. & CEO
Sr. LOIS VAN DELFT, F.M.M., Asst. to the CEO Pastoral Care
Annual Admissions 12,695
Bed Capacity 247
Staff 1,952

Schenectady
Diocese of Albany

St. Clare's Holding Company, Inc.
600 McClellan St.
Schenectady, NY 12304

St. Clare's Hospital
600 McClellan St.
Schenectady, NY 12304
Tel: 518-382-2000
PAUL CHODKOWSKI, Pres. & CEO
Rev. RICHARD J. LESKOVAR, Chap., Dir. Pastoral Care
Sr. DONNA MARIE IRVINE, S.S.N.D.
Sr. MIRIAM NATALE, O.S.F.
Bed Capacity 200
Patients assisted annually 159,153

Suffern
Archdiocese of New York

Good Samaritan Hospital of Suffern
Suffern, NY 10901
Tel: 914-368-5000
JAMES A. MARTIN, Pres.
Sr. MARGARET STRAUCH, S.S.N.D., Dir. Pastoral Care
Chaplains:
Revs.:
GEORGE MATTIONI, O.A.R.
FRANCIS A. CREGAN, O.A.R.
Bro. GERARDO J. DE FILLIPPO, O.A.R.
Sr. ANNE VERONICA TONNE, S.C.
Sr. SHEILA M. MULLINS, O.P.
Sisters of Charity of St. Elizabeth 3
Capacity 370
Patients assisted annually 165,000
Total Staff 1,600

Syracuse
Diocese of Syracuse

St. Joseph's Hospital Health Center
301 Prospect Ave.
Syracuse, NY 13203
Tel: 315-448-5111; Fax: 315-448-6161
Mr. THEODORE M. PASINSKI, Pres. & CEO
Chaplains:
Revs.:
FIRMIN FINN, O.F.M.Conv.
ROBERT AMRHEIN, O.F.M.Conv.
Sisters of the Third Franciscan Order 25
Bed Capacity 431
Patients assisted annually 240,000
School for Nurses
Students 203

Troy
Diocese of Albany

Seton Health System, Inc.
1300 Massachusetts Ave.
Troy, NY 12180
Tel: 518-272-5000
Daughters of Charity of St. Vincent de Paul
Dr. EDWARD MURPHY, Pres. & CEO
Sr. ELLEN BOYLE, R.S.M., Dir. Spiritual Care
Rev. TIMOTHY HARRISON, Priest Chap.
Sr. DE CHANTAL LAROW, D.C., Chm. Bd. of Dir.
Sisters 11
Bed Capacity 201
Patients assisted annually 315,000
Legal Title: *Seton Health System, Inc.*

Utica
Diocese of Syracuse

St. Elizabeth Hospital
2209 Genesee St.
Utica, NY 13501
Tel: 315-798-8100
Sr. ROSE VINCENT GLEASON, CEO
Sr. M. JOHANNA DELELYS, COO
Rev. JOHN H. COMESKEY
Sisters of the Third Franciscan Order 18
Beds 201
Patients assisted annually 214,913
College of Nursing
Students 105

Warwick
Archdiocese of New York

St. Anthony Community Hospital, Inc.
Franciscan System of Warwick, Inc.
15-19 Maple Ave.
Warwick, NY 10990
Tel: 914-986-2276
JAMES GIORDANO, Site Admin.
LEAH CERKVENIK, R.N., Vice Pres. Mission
Sr. ROSEMARY CORK, O.P., Dir. Pastoral Care
Rev. EDWARD SULLIVAN, O.F.M., Chap.
Capacity 73
Patients assisted annually 34,262

West Islip
Diocese of Rockville Centre

Good Samaritan Hospital Medical Center
1000 Montauk Hwy.
West Islip, NY 11795
Tel: 516-376-4001
DANIEL P. WALSH, Pres. & CEO
Revs.:
LAWRENCE BELLEW, C.P., Dir.
VINCENT P. CUNNINGHAM, S.M.M.
BERNARD M. BLOOD, S.M.M.
PAUL DAHM, Assoc. Dir.
Annually Assisted 110,640
Staff 2,400
Good Samaritan Nursing Home
Patients Cared For 160
Good Samaritan Chronic Dialysis Center
Treatments 34,064
Good Samaritan Certified Home Health Agency
Visits 96,547
Good Samaritan Long Term Home Health Care Program
Visits 21,892
Martin Luther King Jr. Health Center
Visits 36,214

White Plains
Archdiocese of New York

St. Agnes Hospital and Children's Rehabilitation Center
305 North St.
White Plains, NY 10605
Tel: 914-681-4500; Fax: 914-681-4974
GARY S. HORAN, Pres. & CEO
Sr. MARY VIRGINIA R.D.C., Dir. Pastoral Care
Capacity 184
Childrens Rehabilitation Center 34,751
Hospital 61,014
Total Staff 864

Yonkers
Archdiocese of New York

St. Joseph's Medical Center
127 S. Broadway
Yonkers, NY 10701
Tel: 914-378-7000; Fax: 914-965-4838
E-mail: SJMCgen@interactive.net
Web Site: http://saintjosephs.org
Sr. MARY LINEHAN Pres.
Rev. THOMAS MURPHY, O.F.M.Cap.
Sr. CAROLINE PARKER, Dir. of Pastoral Care
Beds 194
Nursing Home Beds 200
Sisters of Charity of St. Vincent de Paul 9
Patients assisted annually 9,000

NORTH CAROLINA

Asheville
Diocese of Charlotte

St. Joseph's Health Services Corporation
345 Biltmore Ave.
Asheville, NC 28801
Sr. M. VERONICA SCHUMACHER, R.S.M., CEO
G. JOHN COLI, Ph.D., Pres. & COO

St. Joseph's Hospital
428 Biltmore Ave.
Asheville, NC 28801
Tel: 704-255-3100
Sr. MARY VERONICA SCHUMACHER, R.S.M., Sec. & Treas.
JEFFREY A. GOULD, Vice Chm.
Mr. J. LEWIS DANIELS, Pres. & CEO
Sisters 7
Beds 275
Patients assisted annually 69,157

St. Joseph's Urgent Care, Inc.
345 Biltmore Ave.
Asheville, NC 28801
Tel: 704-258-6569
Patients assisted annually 138,235

Charlotte
Diocese of Charlotte

Selwyn Life Center at Mercy
1921 Vail Ave.
Charlotte, NC 28207
Tel: 704-379-5005
RUTH HUEY, R.N., M.S.N., Dir.
Adult Health Facility.

Southern Pines
Diocese of Raleigh

St. Joseph of the Pines
590 Central Dr.
Southern Pines, NC 28387
Tel: 910-692-2212
Web Site: www.sjp.org
Legal Title: *St. Joseph of the Pines, Inc.*
Mr. GEORGE KECATOS, Pres. & CEO
Beds 190
Staff 1,500

NORTH DAKOTA

Bismarck
Diocese of Bismarck

St. Alexius Medical Center
P.O. Box 5510
Bismarck, ND 58502
Tel: 701-224-7000; Fax: 701-224-7284
Sisters of St. Benedict
RICHARD A. TSCHIDER, Admin. & CEO
Sr. RENAE ZASTOUPIL, Dir. Pastoral Care
Priests 1
Sisters 14
Bed Capacity 287
Total Staff 1,416
Patients assisted annually 147,767

Bottineau
Diocese of Fargo

St. Andrew's Health Center
316 Ohmer St.
Bottineau, ND 58318
Tel: 701-228-2255
Sr. CORINNE S.M.P., Supr.
KEITH KORMAN, Pres.
Sisters of Mary of the Presentation 3
Beds 67
Staff 80
Bassinets 4
Patients assisted annually 5,000

Carrington
Diocese of Fargo

Carrington Health Center
Catholic Health Initiatives.
800 N. Fourth St.
Carrington, ND 58421
Tel: 701-652-3141
BRIAN J. MCDERMOTT, CEO
Acute Beds 30
LTC Beds 40
Staff 143
Patients assisted annually 654

Devils Lake
Diocese of Fargo

Mercy Hospital
1031 Seventh St.
Devils Lake, ND 58301
Tel: 701-662-2131; Fax: 701-662-4862
MARLENE KREIN, Pres.
In res.,
Rev. DENNIS L. SCHUE
Sisters of Mercy of the Americas 2
Staff 223
Beds 50
Bassinets 7
Patients assisted annually 15,649

Dickinson
Diocese of Bismarck

St. Joseph's Hospital and Health Center
30 W. Seventh St.

Dickinson, ND 58601
Tel: 701-225-7271
GREG HANSON, Pres. & CEO
Nurses 190
Total Staff 365
Beds 109
Patients assisted annually 40,236

Garrison
Diocese of Bismarck

Garrison Memorial Hospital
P.O. Box 39
Garrison, ND 58540
Tel: 701-463-2275
RICHARD SPILOVOY, Admin.
Sisters of St. Benedict (Bismarck) 4
Nurses 45
Total Staff 110
Bed Capacity 56
Patients assisted annually 1,353

Harvey
Diocese of Fargo

St. Aloisius Medical Center
325 E. Brewster St.
Harvey, ND 58341
Tel: 701-324-4651
Sisters of Mary of the Presentation.
RONALD J. VOLK, Admin./Pres.
SHEILA ERICKSON, CFO
Staff 295
Beds 49
Nursing Home 116
Patients assisted annually 5,370

Kenmare
Diocese of Bismarck

**Kenmare Community Hospital*
P.O. Box 697
Kenmare, ND 58746
Tel: 701-385-4296
Sisters of St. Francis of Penance and Christian Charity (Denver)
VERLIN BUECHLER, Pres. & CEO
Nurses 38
Total Staff 75
Bed Capacity 42
Patients assisted annually 13,870

Minot
Diocese of Bismarck

St. Joseph's Hospital dba UniMed Medical Center
Attn: Administration, P.O. Box 5001
Minot, ND 58702
Tel: 701-857-2000; Fax: 701-839-8947
Rev. PAUL D. BECKER, Res. Chap.
Sr. LONA THORSON, Interim CEO
Priests 1
Sisters of St. Francis of Penance and Christian Charity 1
Nurses 160
Bed Capacity 186
Patients assisted annually 54,000

UniMed Medical Center Foundation
407 3rd St., S.E.
Minot, ND 58701
Tel: 701-857-2070
BRUCE CHRISTENSON, Dir. Devel.
Total Staff 2

Oakes
Diocese of Fargo

Oakes Community Hospital
314 S. Eighth St.
Oakes, ND 58474
Tel: 701-742-3291
Sr. M. DIANNA HELL, O.S.F., Supr.
Sr. SUSAN MARIE LOEFFEN, O.S.F., Admin.
Sisters of St. Francis of the Immaculate Heart of Mary (Hankinson, ND) 5
Beds 30
Bassinets 4
Patients assisted annually 28,278

Park River
Diocese of Fargo

St. Ansgar's Health Center
115 Vivian St.
Park River, ND 58270
Tel: 701-284-7500
Mr. MICHAEL MAHRER, CEO
Staff 82
Beds 30
Patients assisted annually 5,995

Rolla
Diocese of Fargo

Presentation Medical Center
213 N.E. Third St.
Rolla, ND 58367
Tel: 701-477-3161
KIMBER L. WRAALSTAD, Pres. & CEO
Sisters of Mary of the Presentation 3
Beds 54
Patients assisted annually 6,000

Valley City
Diocese of Fargo

Mercy Hospital
Catholic Health Initiatives.
570 Chautauqua Blvd.
Valley City, ND 58072
Tel: 701-845-0440
Mr. GREG HANSON, Pres.
Beds 74
Bassinets 15
Patients Assisted 15,253
Staff 185

Williston
Diocese of Bismarck

Mercy Hospital
1301 15th Ave. W.
Williston, ND 58801
Tel: 701-774-7400; Fax: 701-774-7409
Sisters of Mercy
DUANE JERDE, CEO
Sr. JEANINE SALAK, R.S.M., Dir. Pastoral Care
Sisters 2
Bed Capacity 134
Total Staff 449
Patients assisted annually 25,919

Mercy Medical Center - Affiliate of Catholic Health Initiatives
1301 15th Ave., W.
Williston, ND 58801
Tel: 701-774-7401
DUANE JERDE, Pres.

Mercy Medical Foundation
1301 15th Ave., W.
Williston, ND 58801
Tel: 701-774-7404
KELLY S. BUECHLER, Dir.

Mercy Recovery Center
1301 15th Ave. W.
Williston, ND 58801
Tel: 701-774-7409; Fax: 701-774-7479
Mr. DONALD WAHUS, Dir.
Bed Capacity 14

OHIO

Batavia
Archdiocese of Cincinnati

Clermont Mercy Hospital
3000 Hospital Dr.
Batavia, OH 45103
Tel: 513-732-8200
Sisters of Mercy
KAREN S. EHRAT, Ph.D., Pres.
Sr. KATHY GREEN, R.S.M., Vice Pres., Mission Svcs.
Bed Capacity 157
Patients assisted annually 24,938

Cincinnati
Archdiocese of Cincinnati

Franciscan Hospital, Mt. Airy Campus
A member of the Franciscan Health System of the Ohio Valley, Inc.
2446 Kipling Ave.
Cincinnati, OH 45239
Tel: 513-853-5000
R. CHRISTOPHER WEST, Pres.
Sr. ARLENE MCGOWAN, Vice Pres. Mission & Support Svcs.
DON ROHLING, Dir. Mission
Chaplains:
Revs.:
MICHAEL PARANIUK
DOMINIC WACHTEL, O.F.M.
Sr. MARGARET SCHLSTEDT, M.M.
Sr. DONNA DE MANGE, O.S.F.
Sr. YVONNE FACKLER, S.F.P.
Sisters 3
Beds 299
Patients assisted annually 85,000

Franciscan Hospital, Western Hills Campus
A member of the Franciscan Health System of Cincinnati.
3131 Queen City Ave.
Cincinnati, OH 45238
Tel: 513-389-5000
R. CHRISTOPHER WEST, Pres. & CEO
Sr. ARLENE MCGOWAN, Vice Pres. of Mission & Support Svcs.
DON ROHLING, Dir. Spiritual Care
Chaplains:
Sr. JOANNE BURKHART, S.F.P.
Sr. ADRIENNE COLSON, O.P.
Sr. LAURENE HAGMAN, O.P.
Mrs. JOAN OWENS
Ms. ALBERTA UTRUP
Revs.:
PAUL WALSMAN, O.F.M.
AQUINAS SCHNEIDER, O.F.M.
Sisters 8
Beds 281
Patients assisted annually 90,000

Good Samaritan Hospital
375 Dixmyth Ave.
Cincinnati, OH 45220
Tel: 513-872-1400; Fax: 513-872-3435
Catholic Health Initiative (CHI).
Sr. MYRA JAMES BRADLEY, S.C., CEO
Revs.:
GERALD R. NIKLAS
EUGENE J. NEVINS, S.J.
BRODIE HENRY, (Protestant)
Bed Capacity 673
Bassinets 62
Long-term Care 15
Patients assisted annually 200,000
Registered Training School for Nurses
Students 250

Mercy Hospital Anderson
7500 State Rd.
Cincinnati, OH 45255
Tel: 513-624-4500
Sisters of Mercy
KAREN S. EHRAT, Ph.D., Pres.
Sr. KATHY GREEN, R.S.M., Vice Pres., Mission Svcs.
Rev. DAVID J. KELLEY, Chap.
Bed Capacity 186
Patients assisted annually 10,946

Cleveland
Diocese of Cleveland

Marymount Hospital, Inc.
12300 McCracken Rd.
Cleveland, OH 44125
Tel: 216-581-0500
Mr. THOMAS J. TRUDELL, Pres.
JUDITH SHEMKOVITZ, Dir. Pastoral Care
Rev. JOSEPH O'DONNELL, Chap. & Coord. Sacramental Svcs. & Priest Chaplains
Staff Chaplains:
Rev. WILLIAM SEVERT
Sr. ANNE MASLANKA, S.S.J.-T.O.S.F.
Sr. BERNICE THERESE, S.S.J.-T.O.S.F.
Sisters of St. Joseph of Third Order of St. Francis 5
Bed Capacity (med/surg) 259 (skilled nursing) 20
Bassinets 18
Patients assisted annually 134,076
Total Staff 1,289

St. Alexis Hospital Medical Center
5163 Broadway Ave.
Cleveland, OH 44127

St. John Hospital
2351 E. 22nd St.
Cleveland, OH 44115
Tel: 216-696-5560
Sr. MARY PATRICIA BARRETT, C.S.A., Chm. Bd. of Trustees

Columbus
Diocese of Columbus

Holy Cross Care Services, Inc. dba Northland Terrace Medical Center
5700 Karl Rd.
Columbus, OH 43229
Tel: 614-846-5420; Fax: 614-846-3247
LUKE SUTHERLAND, Admin.

Mohun Health Care Center
2320 Airport Dr.
Columbus, OH 43219
Tel: 614-253-8517
E-mail: springscomm@juno.com

Web Site: http://www.odc.edu/sisters
Sr. Jacqueline Baum, O.P., Admin.
Total Staff 92
Bed Capacity 75
Patients assisted annually 91

Mount Carmel Health System
793 W. State St.
Columbus, OH 43222
Tel: 614-234-5423; Fax: 614-234-5985
Dale St. Arnold, Pres. & CEO
Beds 945
Staff 6,300
Patients assisted annually 750,000
Legal Holdings:
Mount Carmel Health System
Mount Carmel Medical Center - Medical Center
Mount Carmel East Hospital - General Hospital
Mount Carmel Health Continuum Businesses
Mount Carmel College of Nursing
Mount Carmel Auxiliary
St. Ann's Hospital
St. Ann's Hospital - General Hospital
St. Ann's Auxiliary
Niagara Health Corporation
Mount Carmel Health System Foundation

Dayton
Archdiocese of Cincinnati

Franciscan Medical Center - Dayton Campus
One Franciscan Way
Dayton, OH 45408
Tel: 513-229-6000
A facility of the Franciscan Health System of the Ohio Valley, Inc.
Sponsored by Franciscan Sisters of the Poor
Mr. James M. Strieby, CEO
R. Christopher West, Pres.
Chaplains:
Revs.:
Allen Weimer, D.Min., Dir.
Gary M. Scherer, C.PP.S.
Thomas Beischel, C.PP.S.
Craig Schneider, M.Div.
Edna Lewis, M.Div.
Jackie Geyer
Myra Wentworth
Sisters 1
Bed Capacity 622
Bassinets 30
Patients assisted annually 300,468

Good Samaritan Hospital
2222 Philadelphia Dr.
Dayton, OH 45406
Tel: 937-278-2612
Affiliated with Catholic Health Initiative.
Mr. Douglas Deck, Pres.
Bed Capacity 560
Patients assisted annually 200,000

Fairfield
Archdiocese of Cincinnati

Mercy Ambulatory Surgery Center
2990 Mack Rd.
Fairfield, OH 45014
Tel: 513-874-6440
Patty Clark, Dir. & Admin.
Ambulatory Surgery Center.

Hamilton
Archdiocese of Cincinnati

Mercy Hospital of Hamilton-Fairfield
100 Riverfront Plaza, P.O. Box 418
Hamilton, OH 45011
Tel: 513-867-6400; Fax: 513-867-9043
3000 Mack Rd.
Fairfield, OH 45014
Tel: 513-870-7000; Fax: 513-870-7065
Sisters of Mercy of Hamilton, OH
Mr. David A. Ferrell, Pres.
Sr. Monica Marie Knipfer, Mission Regional Dir.
Sisters 6
Bed Capacity 326
Patients assisted annually 153,413

Lima
Diocese of Toledo

St. Rita's Medical Center
730 W. Market St.
Lima, OH 45801
Tel: 419-227-3361
Mr. James P. Reber, Pres.
Mr. Kenneth G. Payne, Vice Pres. Finance
Mr. Mark Skaja, Vice Pres. Mission Svcs.
Chaplains:
Revs.:
Vincent Hoying, C.PP.S.
Ben Lowell
Greta Wagner
Sr. Natalie Haas, R.S.M.
Sr. Noel Frey, R.S.M.
Deacon Walt Miller
Sisters 2
Bed Capacity 424
Patients assisted annually 223,400
Total Staff 2,042

Lorain
Diocese of Cleveland

Community Health Partners of Ohio
3700 Kolbe Rd.
Lorain, OH 44053-1161
Tel: 440-960-3000
Mr. Brian C. Lockwood, Pres. & CEO

Lorain Community/St. Joseph Regional Health Center
205 W. 20th St.
Lorain, OH 44052

Oregon
Diocese of Toledo

St. Charles Mercy Hospital
2600 Navarre Ave.
Oregon, OH 43616
Tel: 419-698-7200; Fax: 419-698-7328
Sisters of Mercy of the Americas
Cathleen K. Nelson, Pres. & CEO
Chaplains:
Revs.:
George M. Koerber
Charles Denny
Don Corbin, Pastoral Care Dir.
Sisters 4
Bed Capacity 386
Patients assisted annually 121,696
Total Staff 1,460

Sandusky
Diocese of Toledo

Providence Hospital Inc.
1912 Hayes Ave.
Sandusky, OH 44870
Tel: 419-621-7000
Sisters of St. Francis of Sylvania, Ohio
Sr. Nancy Linenkugel, O.S.F., Pres. & CEO
Rev. John R. Laudick, Chap.
Providence Hospital School of Nursing
Student Nurses 74
Providence Hospital School of Radiology
Student Radiology Technicians 14
Providence Care Center
2025 Hayes Ave.
Sandusky, OH 44870
Tel: 419-627-2273
Sisters 2
Bed Capacity 138
Patients assisted annually 208
Total Staff 152
Rick Ryan, Admin.
The Commons of Providence Apartment assisted living facility.
5000 Providence Dr.
Sandusky, OH 44870
Tel: 419-624-1171
Bed Capacity 56
Residents 56
Total Staff 18
Jan Gluth, Admin.
Sisters 6
Bed Capacity 270
Patients assisted annually 52,300
Total Staff 700

Springfield
Archdiocese of Cincinnati

Mercy Medical Center
1343 N. Fountain Blvd.
Springfield, OH 45501-1380
Tel: 937-390-5000; Fax: 937-890-5507
Sisters of Mercy
Mr. Jerrold Maki, Pres. & CEO
Sr. Macrina Dorrian, R.S.M., Mission Services
Rev. Marvin R. Hackman, Chap.
Sisters 5
Bed Capacity 329
Patients assisted annually 130,000

Steubenville
Diocese of Steubenville

Trinity Health System
Trinity Medical Center, West
4000 Johnson Rd.
Steubenville, OH 43952
Tel: 740-264-8000; Fax: 740-264-8620
Chaplains:
Sr. LaDonna Pinkelman, O.S.F.
Rev. John McCoy
Trinity Medical Center, East
380 Summit Ave.
Steubenville, OH 43952
Tel: 740-283-7000
Chaplains:
Sr. Maria Consuelo, O.S.F.
Rev. John McCoy
Beds 632
Sisters 6
Nursing Sisters 4
RNs 263
LPNs 26
Nurse Anesthetists 9
Patients Assisted Annually:
Admissions 11,276
Outpatients 167,723
Emergency Room 52,948
Births 765

Tiffin
Diocese of Toledo

Mercy Hospital
Sr. Janet Hay
Tiffin, OH 44883
Tel: 419-447-3130
Sisters of Mercy of the Americas
Sisters 2
Bed Capacity 70
Patients assisted annually 54,848
Total Staff 431

Toledo
Diocese of Toledo

Mercy Hospital
2200 Jefferson Ave.
Toledo, OH 43624-9988
Tel: 419-259-1500
Sisters of Mercy of the Americas
Cathleen K. Nelson, Pres.
Sisters 8
Mercy College of Northwest Ohio
Student Nurses 174
Bed Capacity 311
Patients assisted annually 78,000
Total Staff 960

Riverside Mercy Hospital
1600 N. Superior St.
Toledo, OH 43604
Tel: 419-251-0713
H. Terrence Smith, Statutory Agent
Daryll R. Lippman, Pres. & CEO

St. Vincent Medical Center
2213 Cherry St.
Toledo, OH 43608
Tel: 419-321-3232; Fax: 419-321-3810
Sisters of Mercy
Affiliated with Mercy Health System.
Mr. Steven L. Mickus, Pres. & CEO
Chaplains:
Revs.:
William Foster, Dir. Pastoral Care
Joel Buchman
Sr. Sharon Belisle
Sr. Elaine Ladd
Sisters 6
Patients assisted annually 272,242
Bed capacity 588

Urbana
Archdiocese of Cincinnati

Mercy Memorial Hospital
904 Scioto St.
Urbana, OH 43078
Tel: 937-653-5231
Sisters of Mercy
Sisters 3
Bed Capacity 73

Warren
Diocese of Youngstown

St. Joseph Health Center
667 Eastland Ave., S.E.
Warren, OH 44484
Tel: 330-841-4000; Fax: 330-841-4019
Mr. Robert W. Shroder, COO
Rev. George Popovich, Chap.
Ms. Beth Jacob, Vice Pres. Mission Integration
Sisters of the Humility of Mary 4

Bed capacity 237
Bassinets 17
Patients assisted annually 130,925
Total Staff 813

Willard
Diocese of Toledo

Mercy Hospital of Willard
110 E. Howard St.
Willard, OH 44890
Tel: 419-933-2931
Sisters of Mercy of the Americas
Mr. JAMES O. DETWILER, Pres.
Sisters 1
Bed Capacity 63
Total Staff 200
Patients assisted annually 43,905

Youngstown
Diocese of Youngstown

HM Health Services
4964 Belmont Ave.
Youngstown, OH 44505-1046
Tel: 330-759-7484
KEVIN E. NOLAN, Pres. & CEO
Beds 877
Patients assisted annually 475,496
Lay Staff 3,196

HM Health Services, St. Elizabeth Health Center
1044 Belmont Ave., Box 1790
Youngstown, OH 44501
Tel: 330-480-3570
NANCY VOITUS, Dir. of Social Work
MICHAEL S. SENCHAK, Vice Pres. Shared & Support Svcs.
Sisters of the Humility of Mary 8
Bed Capacity 580
Bassinets 60
Patients assisted annually 253,748
Total Staff 2,122

St. Elizabeth Health Resources, Inc.
P.O. Box 207
Youngstown, OH 44501
Patients assisted annually 3,190
Total Staff 120
5211 Mahoning Ave.
Austintown, OH 44515
2460 Elm Rd., Ste. 300
Warren, OH 44483

Zanesville
Diocese of Columbus

Good Samaritan Medical Center
800 Forest Ave.
Zanesville, OH 43701
Tel: 614-454-5000
Mr. THOMAS L. SIEBER, Pres.
Franciscan Sisters of Christian Charity 7
Bed Capacity 368
Patients assisted annually 156,461

OKLAHOMA

Ardmore
Archdiocese of Oklahoma City

Mercy Memorial Health Center, Inc. (MMHC)
1011 14th Ave., N.W.
Ardmore, OK 73401
Tel: 580-221-6611
Mr. BOBBY THOMPSON, Pres. & CEO
Beds 278
Patients assisted annually 83,849

Enid
Archdiocese of Oklahoma City

St. Mary Mercy Hospital
305 S. 5th St., Box 232
Enid, OK 73701
Tel: 580-233-6100
FRANK LOPEZ, Pres.
Sisters 8
Beds 277
Patients assisted annually 96,975

Oklahoma City
Archdiocese of Oklahoma City

Hillcrest Health Center, Inc.
2129 S.W. 59th St.
Oklahoma City, OK 73119
Tel: 405-685-6671; Fax: 405-680-2817
Mr. RAY BRAZIER, Pres.
A member of SSM Health Care.
Beds 203
Patients assisted annually 43,881

Mercy Memorial Health Center
4300 W. Memorial Rd.
Oklahoma City, OK 73120
Tel: 405-755-1515
Owned and operated by Sisters of Mercy Health System, St. Louis.
BRUCE F. BUCHANAN, Pres. & CEO
Revs.:
CLETUS BASH
GARY W. KAYLER
JOHN TUOHEY
Sisters 3
Beds 396
Patients assisted annually 131,323
Chaplains 8

St. Anthony Hospital
1000 N. Lee St., P.O. Box 205
Oklahoma City, OK 73101
Tel: 405-272-7000; Fax: 405-272-7075
Franciscan Sisters of Mary (St. Louis, MO)
Mr. STEVEN HUNTER, Pres.
Rev. JOSEPH S. VAS, Chap.
A member of SSM Health Care.
Sisters 6
Beds 664
Patients assisted annually 214,074
Bone and Joint Hospital
1111 N. Dewey Ave.
Oklahoma City, OK 73103
Patients assisted annually 5,680
A member of SSM Health Care.

Ponca City
Archdiocese of Oklahoma City

St. Joseph Regional Medical Center
14th and Hartford
Ponca City, OK 74602
Tel: 580-765-3321; Fax: 580-765-0379
Sisters of St. Joseph of Wichita/Sisters of the Sorrowful Mother of Broken Arrow, OK
GARRY L. ENGLAND, Pres.
Sr. CLARITA WANER, C.S.J., Dir. Pastoral Care
Sr. MARY KAY LISTON, C.S.J., Asst. Admin. Mission Devel.
Sisters 3
Beds 169
Patients assisted annually 80,000

Tulsa
Diocese of Tulsa

Marian Health System, Inc.
P.O. Box 4753
Tulsa, OK 74159-0753
Sr. M. THERESE GOTTSCHALK, Pres.

Saint Francis Hospital, Inc.
6161 S. Yale Ave.
Tulsa, OK 74136
Tel: 918-494-2200
JOHN L. LUCAS, M.D., C.E.O & Pres.
Revs.:
DENIS CASEY, Dir. Pastoral Care
URBAN J. KRAMER, S.J.
JOSEPH W. HOWELL
Sisters of Charity of the Incarnate Word (Houston) 4
Beds 897
Bassinets 94
Patients assisted annually 403,051

St. John Health System, Inc.
1923 S. Utica
Tulsa, OK 74104
Fax: 918-744-2716
Sr. M. THERESE GOTTSCHALK, Pres.

St. John Medical Center, Inc.
1923 S. Utica Ave.
Tulsa, OK 74104
Tel: 918-744-2345
Sisters of the Sorrowful Mother (Third Order of St. Francis)
Sr. MARY THERESE GOTTSCHALK, C.E.O. & Pres.
Chaplains:
Revs.:
DANIEL A. PERLINSKI
JOHN WADE
LAWRENCE P. COURTRIGHT
Sisters 12
Beds 572
Patients assisted annually 130,094

OREGON

Baker City
Diocese of Baker

St. Elizabeth Health Services, Inc.
3325 Pocahontas Rd.
Baker City, OR 97814
Tel: 541-523-6461 (Hospital); 523-4452 (Nursing Care); Fax: 541-523-1794
ROBERT MANNIX, Pres. & COO
Sisters of St. Francis of Philadelphia 2
Bed Capacity 42
Nursing Home Beds 112
Patients assisted annually 22,314

Bend
Diocese of Baker

St. Charles Medical Center
2500 N.E. Neff Rd.
Bend, OR 97701
Tel: 541-382-4321; Fax: 541-388-7723
Sisters of St. Joseph
Sr. CATHERINE HELLMANN, C.S.J., Pres. Emeritus
Mr. JIM LUSSIER, Pres., CEO
JEROID ROUSSELL, JR., D.Min., Pastoral Care Coord.
Bed Capacity 181
Patients assisted annually 110,000

Eugene
Archdiocese of Portland in Oregon

**Sacred Heart Medical Center*
1255 Hilyard St., P.O. Box 10905
Eugene, OR 97440
Tel: 541-686-7300
Div. of Peace Health.
Sisters of St. Joseph of Peace
ANDREW MCCULLOCH, Admin. & CEO
Chaplains:
ROBERT V. SCHERI, Dir. Pastoral Care
Rev. J. NOEL HICKIE (BAK)
Sr. KATHERINE MCCARRY, C.S.J.P.
Sr. RITACLARE JOHNSON, O.S.F.
Sr. VIVIAN RIPP, S.N.J.M.
Sisters 4
Bed Capacity 432
Patients assisted annually 286,846

Florence
Archdiocese of Portland in Oregon

Peace Harbor Hospital
400 Ninth St.
Florence, OR 97439
Tel: 503-997-8412
Acute care hospital owned and operated by Peace Health, Bellevue, WA.
JAMES BARNHART, Admin.
Sr. NOREEN TERRAULT, C.S.J.P., Pastoral Care
Bed Capacity 21
Patients assisted annually 94,431

Medford
Archdiocese of Portland in Oregon

Providence Medford Medical Center
1111 Crater Lake Ave.
Medford, OR 97504-6225
Tel: 541-732-5000
Legal Title: *Sisters of Providence in Oregon.*
Mr. CHARLES T. WRIGHT, Chief Executive, Southern Oregon Service Area
Mr. BART RODRIGUES, Dir. Mission Integration, Ethics & Spiritual Care
Rev. JOSEPH E. SHIREY, S.J., (Part-time)
Sr. THERESE KOHLES, S.P., Sr. Representative to Foundation Board (on call)
Sr. PATRICIA MARIE LANDIN, S.S.M.O., Chap.
Sisters 2
Bed Capacity 168
Patients assisted annually 61,000

**Providence Community Health Foundation, Medford*

Milwaukie
Archdiocese of Portland in Oregon

**Providence Milwaukie Hospital*
10150 S.E. 32nd Ave.
Milwaukie, OR 97222
Tel: 503-652-8300
Legal Title: *Sisters of Providence in Oregon.*
CAMELIA HANEMANN, Dir. Pastoral Care
Bed Capacity 56
Patients assisted annually 70,000

**Providence Milwaukie Foundation, Milwaukie*

Newberg
Archdiocese of Portland in Oregon

Providence Newberg Hospital
501 Villa Rd.
Newberg, OR 97132
Tel: 503-537-1701
MARK MEINERT, CEO
Bed Capacity 35
Patients assisted annually 72,550

Ontario
Diocese of Baker

The Dominican Sisters of Ontario, Inc. dba Holy Rosary Medical Center
351 S.W. Ninth St.
Ontario, OR 97914
Tel: 541-881-7000; Fax: 541-881-7184
Mr. BRUCE JENSEN, Admin.
Mr. LEONARD SHERMAN, D.V.M., Chm.
Rev. CLETUS KIRKPATRICK, Chap.
Dominican Sisters of St. Catherine of Siena (Kenosha, WI) 4
Bed Capacity 92
Patients assisted annually 73,825

Pendleton
Diocese of Baker

St. Anthony Hospital
1601 S.E. Court Ave.
Pendleton, OR 97801
Tel: 541-276-5121
E-mail: kuhl@chiwest.com
JEFFREY DROP, Pres.
Sisters of St. Francis of Philadelphia 6
Bed Capacity 49
Patients assisted annually 25,600

Portland
Archdiocese of Portland in Oregon

Providence Portland Medical Center
4805 N.E. Glisan St.
Portland, OR 97213
Tel: 503-215-1111
Legal Title: *Providence Health Systems, Oregon Region*
Revs.:
HERBERT WHEATLEY, O.F.M.
JON BUFFINGTON (EST)
ELAINE K. FORREST, CPE Supervisor (Protestant)
JOHN HUBBARD, Presbyterian Chap.
CINDY MCNUTT-KAESTNER, Methodist Staff Chaplain (Protestant)
Sr. KATHLEEN KIRCHER, S.N.J.M., Dir. Pastoral Care & Contact Person
Sr. ROSALIE ORR, S.N.J.M., Geriatrics
Sr. MAUREEN NIEDERMEYER, O.S.B., Cardiology
Sr. BRIGID CAREY, P.B.V.M., Staff Chaplain
Lay Chaplains:
MICHELE SAKURAI, Oncology
JOSEPH JOYCE, Addiction Treatment
BONITA STILLER, Hospice Home Health (Protestant)
Bed Capacity 483
Sisters 8
Patients assisted annually 264,113
Providence Medical Foundation
4805 N.E. Glisan
Portland, OR 97213
BRYCE STRANG, Exec. Dir.

Providence St. Vincent Medical Center
9205 S.W. Barnes Rd.
Portland, OR 97225
Tel: 503-297-4411; Fax: 503-291-2468
Providence Health System.
Legal Title: *Providence Health System.*
RUSS DANIELSON, Admin. Health Care Oper., Providence Health System
DONALD S. ELSOM, Admin., Providence St. Vincent Medical Center
Sr. LUCY ST. HILAIRE, S.P., Sister Rep.
Sr. FARROEL RICHARDSON, S.N.J.M., Dir. Pastoral Svcs.
Revs.:
EDWARD P. MCTIGHE, S.J., Chap.
JOSEPH REEVES
Bro. LARRY ESCHWEILER, O.H.
Sr. MARY LOUISE OLBERDING, O.S.B.
Sr. SCHOLASTICA LEE, S.P.
Ms. SHIELA SCHAEFFER, Catholic Chap.
Mr. TIMOTHY G. SERBAN, Catholic Chap.
Mrs. EILEEN NORRIS
Ms. JOANNE FLANNIGAN, Catholic Chap.
Ms. THERESA VITHAYATHIL, Catholic Chap.
Ms. PAT WOLFE, Protestant Chap. (Presbyterian)
Patients assisted annually 480,864
Bed Capacity 451
Sisters 5
Brothers 1

**St. Vincent Medical Foundation, Portland*

Roseburg
Archdiocese of Portland in Oregon

Mercy Medical Center, Inc.
2700 Stewart Pkwy.
Roseburg, OR 97470
Tel: 541-673-0611; Fax: 541-677-4830
VICTOR J. FRESOLONE, Pres. & CEO
JANET BUCHANAN, Dir. Mission Devel.
Bed Capacity 111
Patients assisted annually 143,160
Mercy Healthcare, Inc.
2700 Stewart Pkwy.
Roseburg, OR 97470
Tel: 541-673-0611
SANDRA R. PEARSON, Exec. Asst., Tel: 541-677-2467
Mercy Foundation, Inc.
2700 Stewart Pkwy.
Roseburg, OR 97470
Tel: 541-677-4818
Linus Oakes, Inc.
2700 Stewart Pkwy.
Roseburg, OR 97470
Tel: 541-677-4800
Mercy Rehabilitation and Care Center
2700 Stewart Pkwy.
Roseburg, OR 97470
Tel: 541-677-2198

Seaside
Archdiocese of Portland in Oregon

Providence Seaside Hospital
725 S. Wahanna Rd.
Seaside, OR 97138-7735
Tel: 503-717-7000; Fax: 503-717-7505
RON SWANSON, Admin.
Sr. JERI RENNER, O.P., Spiritual Care
Legal Title: *Sisters of Providence in Oregon.*
Bed Capacity 34
Extended Care 22
Patients assisted annually 60,000

**Providence Seaside Hospital Foundation, Inc.*

PENNSYLVANIA

Allentown
Diocese of Allentown

Sacred Heart Hospital
421 Chew St.
Allentown, PA 18102-3490
Tel: 610-776-4500
JOSEPH M. CIMEROLA, Pres. & CEO
Rev. MICHAEL J. VASTI, M.S.C., Chap. & Dir. Pastoral Care
Sisters 7
Beds 277
Total Staff 1,116
Patients assisted annually 359,792

Altoona
Diocese of Altoona-Johnstown

Bon Secours Holy Family Regional Health System
2500 Seventh Ave.
Altoona, PA 16602
Web Site: www.mercynet.org
Mr. DAVID DAVIES, CEO
Patients assisted annually 105,502
Total Staff 712
Bed Capacity 183

Camp Hill
Diocese of Harrisburg

Holy Spirit Hospital and Community Mental Health Center
503 N. 21st St.
Camp Hill, PA 17011-2288
Tel: 717-763-2100; Fax: 717-763-2183
E-mail: mcicco@hsh.org
Sisters of Christian Charity
Sr. ROMAINE NIEMEYER, S.C.C., Pres.
Legal Title: *Sisters of Christian Charity Health Care Corporation.*
Legal Title: *Comfort Care of Holy Spirit Hospital, Inc.*
Legal Title: *Holy Spirit Ventures, Inc.*
Legal Title: *Holy Spirit Corporation.*
Legal Title: *West Shore ALS, Inc.*
Legal Title: *Holy Spirit Hospital.*
Legal Title: *Spirit Physician Services, Inc.*
Patients assisted annually 12,807
Bed Capacity 335
Bassinets 14
Sisters 26
Total Staff 1,700

Carbondale
Diocese of Scranton

Marian Community Hospital
100 Lincoln Ave.
Carbondale, PA 18407
Tel: 717-281-1000; Fax: 717-281-7177
Sr. JEAN COUGHLIN, I.H.M., Pres. & CEO
WILLIAM ROE, Vice Pres. & CFO
Rev. LEO P. CUMMINGS, Chap.
Sisters, Servants of the Immaculate Heart of Mary
Bed Capacity 112
Patients assisted annually 67,300
Sisters 12

Marian Community Hospital Foundation
100 Lincoln Ave.
Carbondale, PA 18407
Tel: 717-281-1000

Maxis Medical Services
100 Lincoln Ave.
Carbondale, PA 18407
Tel: 717-281-1000

Cranberry Township
Diocese of Pittsburgh

St. Francis Nursing Center-North
One St. Francis Way
Cranberry Township, PA 16066
Tel: 412-772-5350
JOHN L. SPIELER, Ph.D., Admin.
Rev. JOHN GALLAGHER, Chap.
Bed Capacity 150
Total Staff 117
Patients assisted annually 218

Darby
Archdiocese of Philadelphia

Mercy Catholic Medical Center
Fitzgerald Mercy Hospital, Lansdowne Ave. and Baily Rd.
Darby, PA 19023
Tel: 215-237-4000
Opened July 1, 1933. Incorporated May 1, 1969.
Sr. RITA POWELL, R.S.M., Chm. Bd.
PLATO A. MARINAKOS, Pres. of the Center
Chaplains:
Revs.:
LAWRENCE H. HANSEN
WILLIAM R. CRAIG, O.Praem.
JOSEPH C. LAENEN, O.Praem.
Sisters of Mercy 10
Bed Capacity 469
Patients assisted annually 96,905

Erie
Diocese of Erie

**Saint Vincent Health Center*
232 W. 25th St.
Erie, PA 16544
Tel: 814-452-5000
Sr. CATHERINE MANNING, S.S.J., Corp. Leader
Revs.:
RAYMOND GRAMATA, Chap.
DENNIS A. MARTIN, Chap.
Saint Vincent Health System
Sr. CATHERINE MANNING, S.S.J., Pres. & CEO, St. Vincent Health System

Haverford
Archdiocese of Philadelphia

Mercy Haverford Hospital
2000 Old West Chester Pike
Haverford, PA 19083
Tel: 215-645-3600
Opened Haverford Hospital in 1958; Haverford Community Hospital in 1977; Mercy Haverford Hospital June 28, 1991.
FRANK C. VIDEON, SR., Chm. Bd.
JOHN BUCKLEY, SR., Vice Pres. & CEO
Attended by Local Parishes.
Sisters of Mercy
Bed Capacity 107
Patients assisted annually 27,208

Hazleton
Diocese of Scranton

Hazleton-Saint Joseph Medical Center
687 N. Church St.

Hazleton, PA 18201
Tel: 717-459-4444
E-mail: pward@ptd.net
Web Site: www.ghha.org
Mr. Bernard C. Rudegeair, Pres.
Sr. M. Francesca, O.S.F., Supr.
Rev. Austin E. Flanagan, Chap.
Bernardine Sisters of the Third Order of St. Francis 12
Beds 111
Patients assisted annually 157,713

Huntingdon Valley
Archdiocese of Philadelphia

Holy Redeemer Foundation
521 Moredon Rd.
Huntingdon Valley, PA 19006
Tel: 215-938-0505; Fax: 215-938-8717
E-mail: foundtn@phillynet.com
Web Site: www.holyredeemer.com
Subsididary of Holy Redeemer Health System, Inc.; Sponsor: Sisters of the Holy Redeemer, C.S.R.
Communications Department
c/o 1648 Huntingdon Pike
Meadowbrook, PA 19046
Foundation solicits and manages funds for future growth and development.

HRH Management Corporation
727 Welsh Rd.
Huntingdon Valley, PA 19006
Tel: 215-938-0180; Fax: 215-938-1237
Subsidiary of Holy Redeemer Health System, Inc. Sponsor: Sisters of the Holy Redeemer, C.S.R.
Communications Department
c/o 1648 Huntingdon Pike
Meadowbrook, PA 19046

Jeannette
Diocese of Greensburg

Jeannette District Memorial Hospital
Jefferson Ave.
Jeannette, PA 15644
Tel: 724-527-3551
Mr. Robert J. Bulger, Pres. & CEO
Revs.:
Dominic J. Petroy, O.S.B., Chap.
Justin Withrow, O.S.B., Assoc. Chap.
Sisters of Charity of Seton Hill 5
Bed Capacity 170

Johnstown
Diocese of Altoona-Johnstown

Good Samaritan Medical Center
1020 Franklin St.
Johnstown, PA 15905
Tel: 814-533-1000; 533-1410; Fax: 814-533-1819
E-mail: stucker@conemaugh.org
Mr. Timothy J. Karnes, Pres. & CEO
Revs.:
Andrew C. Stanko
Bernard V. Grattan
Leonard Blostic, T.O.R.
Beds 175
Bassinets 12
Patients assisted annually 113,519
Nursery 374
Skilled Nursing Care Center Beds 73
Patients assisted annually 143
Total Staff 573

Lancaster
Diocese of Harrisburg

St. Joseph Hospital and Health Care Center
(Affiliate of Catholic Health Initiatives)
250 College Ave., P.O. Box 3509
Lancaster, PA 17604
Tel: 717-291-8211; Fax: 717-291-8516
Sisters of St. Francis of Philadelphia
John K. Tolmie, Pres.
Barbara R. McLaughlin, M.Div., Regional Dir. of Pastoral Care
Rev. Emmanuel Camilleri, Chap.
Bed Capacity 309
Sisters 3
Total Staff 1,231
Patients assisted annually 194,430
Accredited Schools:
School of Respiratory Therapy 28
Paramedic Institute 28
Affiliate of Catholic Health Initiatives.

Langhorne
Archdiocese of Philadelphia

St. Mary Medical Center
Langhorne-Newton Rd.
Langhorne, PA 19047
Tel: 215-750-2000
Sisters of St. Francis of Philadelphia 18
Bed Capacity 287
Total Staff 1,164
Patients assisted Annually 83,000
Opened February 21, 1973.
Sr. Clare Carty, O.S.F., Pres.
Rev. George Wallace, S.M., Chap.
Affiliate of Catholic Health Initiatives.

Meadowbrook
Archdiocese of Philadelphia

Holy Redeemer Hospital and Medical Center
1648 Huntingdon Pike
Meadowbrook, PA 19046
Tel: 215-947-3000
Subsidiary of Holy Redeemer Health System, Inc.
Sponsor: Sisters of the Holy Redeemer, C.S.R.
Mark Jones, Pres.
Chaplains:
Revs.:
Michael C. Bolesta
Timothy M. Judge
Acute care community hospital, providing broad spectrum of services, including preventive, rehabilitative, emergency and obstetrical care plus pastoral counseling.
Total Assisted 11,800
Total Staff 1,200

Muncy
Diocese of Scranton

Muncy Valley Hospital
215 E. Water St.
Muncy, PA 17756
Tel: 717-546-4242
E-mail: Lcioffi:@shscares.org
Kirby O. Smith, Pres.
Sr. Sharon Hartman, S.C.C., Dir., Pastoral Care
Capacity 174
Patients assisted annually 69,901

Nanticoke
Diocese of Scranton

Mercy Special Care Hospital
128 W. Washington St.
Nanticoke, PA 18634
Tel: 717-735-5000; Fax: 717-740-5220
Robert D. Williams, Admin.
Bed Capacity 94
Patients assisted annually 30,000

New Castle
Diocese of Pittsburgh

St. Francis Hospital of New Castle
(Affiliate of St. Francis Health System)
1000 S. Mercer St.
New Castle, PA 16101
Tel: 412-658-3511
Sr. Donna Zwigart, O.S.F., CEO
Sisters of St. Francis of Millvale 11
Total Staff 617
Bed Capacity (includes 45 skilled nursing beds) 193
Patients assisted annually 73,230
Chaplains:
Rev. Frank G. Erdeljac
Sr. Jane Fisher
Schools:
Nursing 75
Radiology 15
St. Francis Hospice of New Castle:
Total Staff 4
Patients assisted annually 478
St. Francis Home Health of New Castle:
Total Staff 39
Patients assisted annually 20,454

Norristown
Archdiocese of Philadelphia

Sacred Heart Hospital and Rehabilitation Center
1430 DeKalb St.
Norristown, PA 19401
Tel: 215-278-8200
Opened 1936.
Missionary Sisters of the Most Sacred Heart of Jesus
Sr. M. Eileen, M.S.C., Coord.
Mr. J. Russell Walsh, Pres.
Chaplains:
Revs.:
Joseph F. Sabadish
John F. Lipp, O.S.A.
Bed Capacity 256
Student Nurses 40
Patients assisted annually 7,000

Philadelphia
Archdiocese of Philadelphia

Mercy Hospital of Philadelphia
501 S. 54th St.
Philadelphia, PA 19143
Tel: 215-748-9000
Opened July 2, 1918. Incorporated May 1, 1969.
Sr. Christine McCann, Chm. Bd.
Plato A. Marinakos, Pres. & CEO
Bernadette M. Mangan, Senior Vice Pres. & CEO
Chaplains:
Revs.:
Lawrence H. Hansen
Matthew Michael
Sisters of Mercy 14
Bed Capacity 266
Patients assisted annually 37,642
Attended from Transfiguration of Our Lord Church & St. Carthage Church.

Nazareth Hospital
2601 Holme Ave.
Philadelphia, PA 19152
Tel: 215-335-6000
Daniel J. Sinnott, Pres.
Revs.:
Edward V. Avery
Michael Kerper
Affiliate of Catholic Health Initiatives.
Bed Capacity 328
Total Staff 900
Patients assisted annually 164,000

St. Agnes Medical Center
1900 S. Broad St.
Philadelphia, PA 19145
Tel: 215-339-4100
Opened May 15, 1888.
Daniel J. Sinnott, Pres.
Rev. John P. Gutekunst, Chap.
Affiliate of Catholic Health Initiatives.
Bed Capacity 240
Total Staff 653
Annually Assisted 64,807

Pittsburgh
Diocese of Pittsburgh

Mercy Hospital of Pittsburgh
1400 Locust St.
Pittsburgh, PA 15219
Tel: 412-232-8111
Web Site: www.mercylink.org
Howard A. Zaren, M.D., Exec. Vice Pres., Acute Care & Hospital Svcs.
Total Assisted 201,379
Total Staff 2,486

Mercy Providence Hospital
1004 Arch St.
Pittsburgh, PA 15212
Tel: 412-323-5600; Fax: 412-323-5685
Sr. Susanne Cherney, Dir. Pastoral Care
Rev. Bob Mellott, Chap.
Sisters 12
Bed Capacity 160
Patients assisted annually 22,721

Pittsburgh Mercy Foundation
Forbes-Stevenson Bldg., 1401 Locust St., Ste. 2, 3rd Fl.
Pittsburgh, PA 15219-5125
Web Site: www.mercylink.org
Total Assisted 10,000
Total Staff 3,000

Pittsburgh Mercy Health System, Inc.
1400 Locust St.
Pittsburgh, PA 15219
Tel: 412-232-7510
E-mail: jmastal@mercy.PMHS.org
Web Site: www.mercylink.org
Sr. Joanne Marie Andiorio, R.S.M., Dr.P.H., Pres. & CEO
Parent company of the following subsidiaries:
The Mercy Hospital of Pittsburgh
Pittsburgh Mercy Foundation
Mercy Life Center Corporation
St. Joseph Nursing and Health Care Center, Inc.
St. Pius X Residence, Inc.
Brighton Woods, Inc.
Mercy Providence Hospital, Inc. (Formerly Divine Providence Hospital of Pittsburgh)
Beds 868
Total Assisted 228,966
Total Staff 3,082

St. Francis Central Hospital
(Affiliate of St. Francis Health System)

1200 Centre Ave.
Pittsburgh, PA 15219
Tel: 412-562-3301
Ms. Robin Z. Mohr, CEO
Chaplains:
Reverend Father John Walsh
Sr. Germaine Convery
Sisters of St. Francis of Millvale 1
Bed Capacity 202
Total Staff 555
Patients assisted annually 48,588

St. Francis Medical Center
(Affiliate of St. Francis Health System)
400 45th St.
Pittsburgh, PA 15201
Tel: 412-622-4343
Sr. Florence Brandt, O.S.F., CEO
Chaplains:
Rev. Robert Craig, O.F.M.Cap.
Sr. Mary Joseph Trimbur
Rev. Bonaventure Stefun, O.F.M.Cap.
Reverend Fathers:
Anthony Ngwatu
Charles Karatta
Schools:
Professional Nursing 46
Practical Nursing 15
Anesthesia 16
Respiratory Care 8
Sisters 5
Sisters of St. Francis of Millvale 25
Bed Capacity 630
Total Staff 2,533
Patients assisted annually 316,259

St. Francis Nursing Center-East
745 N. Highland Ave.
Pittsburgh, PA 15206
Tel: 412-362-6622
Harry E. Ayres, Admin.
Chaplains:
Reverend Father Edward Hoffman
Sr. M. Sara Magaldi
Sisters of St. Francis of Millvale 1
Bed Capacity 150
Sisters 1
Total Staff 138
Patients assisted annually 187

∗*St. Francis Health System*
4401 Penn Ave.
Pittsburgh, PA 15224-1380
Tel: 412-622-4343
Web Site: www.sfhs.edu
Sr. M. Rosita Wellinger, O.S.F., Pres. & CEO
Sr. M. Sylvia Schuler, Consultant & Pres. Emeritus
Parent company for the following affiliates:
St. Francis Medical Center
St. Francis Nursing Center-North
St. Francis Nursing Center-East
St. Francis Hospital of New Castle
St. Francis Central Hospital

∗*St. Francis Plaza, Inc.*

∗*St. Francis Health Foundation*

∗*St. Francis Financial Corporation*

∗*St. Francis Health Care Services*
Beds 1,325
Total Assisted 459,517
Total Staff 3,973

Pottsville
Diocese of Allentown

Good Samaritan Regional Medical Center
700 E. Norwegian St.
Pottsville, PA 17901
Tel: 717-621-4000; Fax: 717-622-7950
Mr. Gino J. Pazzaglini, Pres.
Sr. Helen Edward Dodd, Dir. of Spiritual Care
Rev. James Morgan, Chap.
Daughters of Charity 12
Beds 221
Bassinets 20
Patients assisted annually 129,496
Good Samaritan Health Corporation
700 E. Norwegian St.
Pottsville, PA 17901
Tel: 717-621-4003
Good Samaritan Foundation, Inc.
700 E. Norwegian St.
Pottsville, PA 17901
Tel: 717-621-4252
Good Samaritan Regional Medical Center Auxiliary
700 E. Norwegian St.
Pottsville, PA 17901
Tel: 717-621-4242

Reading
Diocese of Allentown

Bornemann Health Corporation
c/o Saint Joseph Hospital, 12th St. & Walnut St., P.O. Box 316
Reading, PA 19603
Tel: 610-378-2300
Mr. Philip G. Dionne, Pres. & CEO
Total Staff 77
Bed Capacity 92

CHI Community General Hospital
215 N. 12th St., Box 316
Reading, PA 19603
Tel: 610-358-4215
Mr. Patrick F. Roche, Pres.

Saint Joseph Medical Center
215 N. 12th St., P.O. Box 316
Reading, PA 19603
Tel: 610-378-2000
Opened Aug. 26, 1873.
Patrick F. Roche, Pres. & CEO
Rev. Thomas Kuller, S.J., Chap.
Sisters of St. Francis of Philadelphia 17
Beds 289
Bassinets 16
Patients assisted annually 183,362

Scranton
Diocese of Scranton

Mercy Hospital
Mercy Health System Northern Region.
746 Jefferson Ave.
Scranton, PA 18501
Tel: 717-348-7100
John L. Nespoli, Pres. & CEO
Sr. JoMarie Kaczanowski, R.S.M., Local Coord.
Rev. John C. Ruth, Chap.
Sisters of Mercy 14
Bed Capacity 362
Bassinets 18
Total Capacity 380
Patients assisted annually 252,996

Wilkes-Barre
Diocese of Scranton

Mercy Hospital
Mercy Health System Northeast Region.
25 Church St., P.O. Box 658
Wilkes-Barre, PA 18765
Tel: 717-826-3100; Fax: 717-831-8989
John L. Nespoli, Pres. & CEO
Sr. Carol Gallagher, R.S.M., Sisters Liasion
Rev. Joseph C. Streit, Chap.
Sisters of Mercy 1
Bed Capacity 223
Bassinets 24
Patients assisted annually 79,255

Mercy Med-Care, Inc.
25 Church St., Box 658
Wilkes-Barre, PA 18765
Tel: 717-826-3100

Williamsport
Diocese of Scranton

Divine Providence Hospital of the Sisters of Christian Charity
1100 Grampian Blvd.
Williamsport, PA 17701
Tel: 717-320-7007
E-mail: Lcioffi@shscares.org
Kirby O. Smith, Pres.
Sr. Grace Kerekes, S.C.C., Supr.
Rev. James Patrick Kelly, O.S.F.S., Chap.
Bed Capacity 213
Bassinets 20
Patients assisted annually 123,006

∗*Grampian Health Services, Inc.*
1201 Grampian Blvd.
Williamsport, PA 17701
Tel: 717-326-8214

Providence Foundation
1100 Grampian Blvd.
Williamsport, PA 17701
Tel: 717-321-5467
E-mail: gharrington@shscares.org
Web Site: shscares
Geoffrey Harrington, Exec. Dir.

Providence Health System, Inc.
1100 Grampian Blvd.
Williamsport, PA 17701
Tel: 717-320-7007
E-mail: Lcioffi@shscares.org
Web Site: shscares
Kirby O. Smith, Pres. DPH/MVH

Sisters of Christian Charity Healthcare Corporation
1100 Grampian Blvd.
Williamsport, PA 17701
Tel: 717-326-8181
E-mail: Lcioffi@shscares.org
Web Site: shscares

∗*Susquehanna Regional Home Health & Services*
1201 Grampian Blvd.
Williamsport, PA 17701
Tel: 717-323-9891
E-mail: Lcioffi@shscares.org
Web Site: shscares
Patients assisted annually 49,752

PUERTO RICO

Rio Piedras
Archdiocese of San Juan, Puerto Rico

Hospital del Maestro
Calle Flamboyanes #218, Hyde Park
Rio Piedras, PR 00929
Tel: 809-763-8383
Rev. Msgr. Angel Valdes, Chap.

San German
Diocese of Mayaguez, Puerto Rico

Hospital of the Immaculate Conception
Box 285
San German, PR 00683
Sisters of Charity
Sr. Maria Teresa Diaz Bird, Supr.
Rev. Urian J. Perez Zapata, Chap.
Jaime Maestre, Admin.
Sisters 10
Beds 124
Patients assisted annually 113,123

San Juan
Archdiocese of San Juan, Puerto Rico

Centro Medico de P.R.
Calle 10 #1030, Pto Nuevo, 00920. Apdo. 347
San Juan, PR 00936
Tel: 809-763-7272
Revs.:
Pedro L. Zaballa, Chap.
Manuel Garcia, Chap. Hospital Municipal
Calle E., I-90; Urb. Costa de Oro
San Juan, PR 00646
Tel: 809-766-2222; 796-3418 (Res.)
Rev. Florentino Zans, Chap., Tel: 809-754-2525; 790-2014 (Res.)

Our Lady of Providence
Dispensary and Health Center.
Mailing Address:
P.O. Box 9020614
San Juan, PR 00902-0614
Tel: 787-725-5358
Sisters Oblates of the Most Holy Redeemer 2
Annually Assisted 92

VA Medical Center
One Veterans Plaza
San Juan, PR 00927-5800
Tel: 809-758-7575, Ext. 3324
Revs.:
Jose E. Colon, Chief Chap. Serv.
Hector Diaz Estrada, Chap.

Santurce
Archdiocese of San Juan, Puerto Rico

Hospital de Diego
Ave. de Diego #310, Pda. 22
Santurce, PR 00908
Tel: 809-724-1700
Rev. Jesus Vallejo, Chap.

RHODE ISLAND

North Providence
Diocese of Providence

St. Joseph Health Services of Rhode Island - Our Lady of Fatima Hospital
200 High Service Ave.
North Providence, RI 02904
Tel: 401-456-3000
Web Site: www.saintjosephri.com

Mr. H. JOHN KEIMIG, Pres.
Rev. JOHN PETROCELLI, Dir. Pastoral Care
Chaplains:
Revs.:
ARMAND V. VENTRE
M.J. BERNARD DORE (India)
Miss ELIZABETH DECOSTA, R.N., Dir. School of Nursing
Student Nurses 100
Beds 386
Births 485
Patients assisted annually 201,000

Providence
Diocese of Providence

St. Joseph Health Services of Rhode Island - St. Joseph Hospital for Specialty Care
21 Peace St.
Providence, RI 02907
Tel: 401-456-3000
Web Site: www.saintjosephri.com
Mr. H. JOHN KEIMIG, Pres.
Rev. C. LEON KACHEL, Chap.
Includes:
Southern New England Rehabilitation Center
Tel: 401-456-4500
JON A. MUKAND, M.D., Medical Dir.
A joint venture of St. Joseph Hospital and Rhode Island Hospital.
Corporate Care Occupational Health and Safety Services
Tel: 401-456-4020
RANDALL UPDEGROVE, M.D., M.P.H., Medical Dir.
St. Joseph Center for Health & Human Services
Tel: 401-456-4321
MUNAWAR AZAM, M.D., Medical Dir.
St. Joseph Center for Psychiatric Services
Tel: 401-456-4232
RONALD GOBEIL, M.D., Medical Dir.

SOUTH CAROLINA

Charleston
Diocese of Charleston

Bon Secours-St. Francis Xavier Hospital
2095 Henry Tecklenburg Dr.
Charleston, SC 29414
Tel: 843-402-1000
Sponsored by the Sisters of Bon Secours, Marriottsville, MD.
Sr. ANNE MACK, C.B.S., Pres., Sisters of Bon Secours USA
Mr. ALLEN P. CARROLL, CEO
Sr. MARY GEMMA NEVILLE, C.B.S., Dir. Pastoral Svcs. & Clinical Pastoral Education
Rev. TIMOTHY J. WATTERS, Chap.
Sr. KATHLEEN OWEN, O.P., Assoc. Dir. Pastoral Svcs.
Sr. CHARLOTTE MCAULIFFE, O.L.M., Pastoral Visitor
Bed Capacity 141
Staff 600
Patients assisted annually 168,432

**St. Francis Xavier Home Health Care, Inc.*

Dillon
Diocese of Charleston

Saint Eugene Community Hospital
301 E. Jackson St., P.O. Box 1327
Dillon, SC 29536-1327
Tel: 843-774-4111; Fax: 843-774-1563
Owned and operated by SSM Health Care Corporation. Member of SSM Health Care.
Mr. RONALD W. WEBB, FACHE, Pres.
CINDY MARTHERM, Chap.
Franciscan Sisters of Mary (St. Louis, MO) 1
Bed Capacity 92
Patients assisted annually 33,008

Greenville
Diocese of Charleston

**Franciscan Health System of South Carolina, Inc.*
One St. Francis Dr.
Greenville, SC 29601
Tel: 864-255-1000

**St. Francis Hospital, Inc.*
Mr. RICHARD NEUGENT, Pres.
MARY ANN. BENNETT, Dir. of Mission Services
Franciscan Sisters of the Poor 1
Bed Capacity 319
Patients assisted annually 197,814

SOUTH DAKOTA

Aberdeen
Diocese of Sioux Falls

St. Luke's Midland Regional Medical Center
Aberdeen, SD 57401
Tel: 605-622-5000
DALE STEIN, Pres. & CEO
Rev. CHARLES EMEZIE (Nigeria)
ELAINE VAN DOVER, Dir. Pastoral Care
Sisters of the Presentation of the B.V.M. (Aberdeen, SD) 16
Bed Capacity 225
Bassinets 20
Annually Assisted 174,418
Staff 892

Gettysburg
Diocese of Sioux Falls

Gettysburg Medical Center
57442
Tel: 605-765-2488
BRIAN J. MCDERMOTT, CEO
Gettysburg Day Care Center
700 E. Garfield
Gettysburg, SD 57442
Tel: 605-765-2541
Staff 4
Children 25
BETTY BROWN, Dir.
Beds 67
Residential Living Units 12

Milbank
Diocese of Sioux Falls

St. Bernard Providence Hospital
Milbank, SD 57252
Tel: 605-432-4538
E-mail: sbphosp@tnics.com
Rev. RAY OTTO, O.S.B., Chap.
Sr. GENEVIEVE KARELS, D.S.M.P., Supr.
Daughters of St. Mary of Providence 5
Bed Capacity 35
Staff 77

Mitchell
Diocese of Sioux Falls

Queen of Peace Hospital
525 N. Foster
Mitchell, SD 57301
Tel: 605-995-2000; Fax: 605-995-2441
Sisters of the Presentation of the B.V.M.
RON JACOBSON, Admin.
Sisters 3
Beds 204
Staff 624
Patients assisted annually 15,964

Parkston
Diocese of Sioux Falls

St. Benedict Health Care Center; Bormann Manor; Parkston Supervised Living
Parkston, SD 57366
Tel: 605-928-3311
GALE N. WALKER, Admin.
Benedictine Sisters (Yankton, SD) 2
Bed Capacity 105

Pierre
Diocese of Sioux Falls

Maryhouse Residential Nursing Facility
800 E. Dakota, P.O. Box 1023
Pierre, SD 57501
Guests 105

Parkwood Retirement Apartments
400 Parkwood Dr.
Pierre, SD 57501
Units 60

St. Mary's Foundation
800 E. Dakota
Pierre, SD 57501
Tel: 605-224-3451
E-mail: StMary'sSD@aol.com
Web Site: www.ST-Marys.com
ELLEN J. LEE, Exec. Dir.

St. Mary's Healthcare Center of Pierre, South Dakota
800 E. Dakota, P.O. Box 1023
Pierre, SD 57501
Tel: 605-224-3100
JAMES D.M. RUSSELL, CEO
Benedictine Sisters 7
Beds 86
Staff 400
Annnually Assisted 24,509

Sioux Falls
Diocese of Sioux Falls

McKennan Hospital
Sioux Falls, SD 57110-5045
Tel: 605-322-8000
Mr. FREDRICK W. SLUNECKA, Pres. & CEO
Mr. JEREMIAH MURPHY, Chm. Bd. of Trustees
Sr. NORMA NORTON, O.S.B., Dir. Pastoral Care
Rev. GARY TERNES (Nigeria) Chap.
Sisters of the Presentation of the B.V.M. (Aberdeen, SD) 7
Bed Capacity 429
Patients assisted annually 195,000

Tyndall
Diocese of Sioux Falls

St. Michael's Hospital
Tyndall, SD 57066
Tel: 605-589-3341
CAROL DEURMIER, CEO
Bed Capacity 25
Nursing Home Beds 9
Annually Assisted

Yankton
Diocese of Sioux Falls

Sacred Heart Health Services
501 Summit
Yankton, SD 57078
Tel: 605-668-8000
MICHAEL T. HEALY, Acting Pres.
Sisters 5
Beds 144
St. James Nursing Home Beds 113

TENNESSEE

Chattanooga
Diocese of Knoxville

Memorial Hospital (1952)
(Div. of Sisters of Charity of Nazareth Health Corp., S.C.N.H.C.)
2525 DeSales Ave.
Chattanooga, TN 37404
Tel: 423-495-2525
Mr. CLARK TAYLOR, Pres. & CEO
Rev. LOUIS J. JUNOD, Chap.
Sisters 10
Bed Capacity 337
Patients assisted annually 118,056
Total Staff 1,720

Knoxville
Diocese of Knoxville

St. Mary's Medical Center, Inc. (1930)
900 E. Oak Hill Ave.
Knoxville, TN 37917
Tel: 423-545-8000
Conducted by Sisters of Mercy of the Americas
RICH WILLIAMS, Pres.
Rev. BERTRAND DEMERS, Chap.
Sisters 6
Bed Capacity 531
Patients assisted annually 199,872
Total Staff 2,134
St. Mary's Health System, Inc.
St. Mary's Foundation, Inc.

Memphis
Diocese of Memphis

St. Joseph Hospital (1889)
220 Overton Ave.
Memphis, TN 38105
Tel: 901-577-2700; Fax: 901-577-3620
Title of Incorporation: Sisters of St. Francis Health Services, Incorporated.
JOAN M. CARLSON, CEO
Sr. ELIZABETH ANN SCHILDMEYER, O.S.F., Pastoral Care Dir.
Beds 440
Patients assisted annually 25,168
School for Nurses
Students 131
Teaching Personnel 12
Graduate Nurses 47
Staff 5

Nashville
Diocese of Nashville

St. Thomas Hospital (1898)
4220 Harding Rd.
Nashville, TN 37205
Tel: 615-222-2111
Legal Title: *St. Thomas Hospital.*
Daughters of Charity of St. Vincent de Paul, (East Central Prov., Evansville, IN)
JOHN F. TIGHE, Pres. & CEO

Sr. PRISCILLA GRIMES, D.C., Supr.
Sisters 5
Beds 541
Chaplains 6
Patients assisted annually 153,760
Saint Thomas Foundation

TEXAS

Amarillo
Diocese of Amarillo

**Baptist St. Anthony Health System*
1600 Wallace Blvd.
Amarillo, TX 79106
Tel: 806-358-3151
Sisters of Charity of the Incarnate Word (C.C.V.I.)
Mr. LEE ROARK, Dir. Pastoral Care
Sr. HELEN ANN COLLIER, C.C.V.I., Coord. Mission & Ministry
Rev. Msgr. HAROLD L. WALDOW, Chap.

**St. Anthony's Campus*
200 N.W. Seventh St., P.O. Box 950
Amarillo, TX 79176
Tel: 806-376-4411

**The Auxiliary of St. Anthony's Hospital, Inc.*

**St. Anthony's Health Corporation*

St. Anthony's Hospice and Life Enrichment Center
600 N. Tyler, P.O. Box 950
Amarillo, TX 79176
Tel: 806-378-6777; Fax: 806-378-5031
LEZLIE ROBERSON Dir.

Austin
Diocese of Austin

Seton East Community Health Center
2811 E. Second St.
Austin, TX 78702
Tel: 512-323-4930
Mr. LARRY MEJIA, Dir.
Total clients assisted annually 30,000

Seton Medical Center
1201 W. 38th St.
Austin, TX 78705
Tel: 512-323-1000
Daughters of Charity Health Services of Austin
Mr. CHARLES J. BENNETT, Pres. & CEO
Rev. JIM DENHAM, Dir. Pastoral Care
Chaplains:
Revs.:
DON OLIVER WEERAKKODY
JOSEPH GENIESSE
LAWRENCE J. STEHLING
Daughters of Charity of St. Vincent de Paul 10
Bed Capacity 585
Patients assisted annually 30,053
Equivalent Patients 7,307

Seton Northwest Hospital
11113 Research Blvd.
Austin, TX 78759
Tel: 512-795-1000
E-mail: choke@dcnhs-wc.edu
Daughters of Charity Health Services of Austin
CAROL A. HOKE, Senior Vice Pres. Admin.
JIM DENHAM, Dir. Pastoral Care
Bed Capacity 82
Patients assisted annually 53,431
Staff 307

Seton South Community Health Center
3706 S. First St.
Austin, TX 78704
Tel: 512-323-4940
Mr. LARRY MEJIA, Dir.
Patients assisted annually 10,000

Beaumont
Diocese of Beaumont

St. Elizabeth Hospital of Beaumont
2830 Calder Ave., P.O. Box 5405
Beaumont, TX 77726-5405
Tel: 409-892-7171
Operated by Sisters of Charity of the Incarnate Word
Sr. M. FATIMA MCCARTHY, C.C.V.I., Admin.
Chaplains:
Revs.:
JAMES DEMPSEY
JOSEPH BERTRAND
Sisters 9
Bed Capacity 461
Patients assisted annually 249,204

Beeville
Diocese of Corpus Christi

Spohn Bee County Hospital
1500 E. Houston Hwy.
Beeville, TX 78102
Tel: 512-354-2125
ANDREW E. ANDERSON, JR., Contact Person
Total Staff 300

Brenham
Diocese of Austin

Trinity Community Medical Center of Brenham
700 Medical Pkwy.
Brenham, TX 77833
Tel: 409-836-6173
JOHN SIMMS, Admin.
Sr. GERALDINE PALUSZAK, O.S.F., Dir. Pastoral Care
Attended from St. Mary's Church.
Sisters of St. Francis of Sylvania, OH 3
Bed Capacity 60
Patients assisted annually 24,000
Staff 287

Bryan
Diocese of Austin

Burleson Lease Corp. Inc./dba Burleson St. Joseph Health Center
2801 Franciscan Dr.
Bryan, TX 77802
Tel: 409-776-2464
E-mail: info@mail.st-joseph.org
Web Site: http://www.st-joseph.org
WILLIAM F. HYER, JR., Sec.
Patients assisted annually 13,765
Total Staff 102

St. Joseph Regional Health Center
2801 Franciscan Dr.
Bryan, TX 77802
Tel: 409-776-3777
E-mail: info@mail.st-joseph.org
Web Site: http://www.st-joseph.org
Sr. GRETCHEN KUNZ, O.S.F., Pres.
Rev. Msgr. JOHN C. MALINOWSKI, Chap.
JAMES W. STEGALL, Chm. Bd.
Bed Capacity 204
Patients assisted annually 133,977
Total Staff 1,485
Sisters of St. Francis of Sylvania, OH 7

St. Joseph Services Corp.
2801 Franciscan Dr.
Bryan, TX 77802
Tel: 409-776-3777
E-mail: info@mail.st-joseph.org
Web Site: http://www.st-joseph.org
BILLIE H. MAGEE, Chm. Bd.

Corpus Christi
Diocese of Corpus Christi

Spohn Hospital
600 Elizabeth St.
Corpus Christi, TX 78404
Tel: 512-881-3000; Fax: 512-881-3149
JAKE HENRY, JR., Pres. & CEO
GARY DEER, Admin.
Chaplains:
Revs.:
JOSE M. GUTIERREZ
ROBERT FRIMTONG-MANSO
TERENCE A. HOLACHEK, O.P.
Sr. MARY EUSTACE FARRELL, C.C.V.I.
Staff 1,655
Beds 458
Sisters 7
Patients assisted annually 113,670

Spohn Hospital South
5950 Saratoga Blvd.
Corpus Christi, TX 78414
Tel: 512-985-5000; Fax: 512-985-5109
Sisters of Charity of the Incarnate Word (San Antonio, TX)
JAKE HENRY, Pres. & CEO
ANDY HARRIS, Admin.
Sr. JUNE Chap.
A member of the Spohn Health System.
Sisters 1
Staff 350
Beds 102
Patients assisted annually 30,000

Spohn Memorial Hospital
Mailing Address:
P.O. Box 5280
Corpus Christi, TX 78465-5280
2620 Hospital Blvd.
Corpus Christi, TX 78405-1818
Tel: 512-902-4000; Fax: 512-902-4949
Mr. ANTHONY W. HEEP, Admin.

Dallas
Diocese of Dallas

Parkland Hospital
5201 Harry Hines Blvd.
Dallas, TX 75235
Tel: 214-590-8512
Pastoral Care:
Sr. CARMEN AVILA, M.C.D.P.

St. Paul Medical Center
5909 Harry Hines Blvd.
Dallas, TX 75235
Tel: 214-879-1000
Sr. MARY ANGELYN PERA, D.C., Supr.
Mr. FRANK TIEDEMANN, Pres., CEO & Community Mgr.
Mr. MICHAEL AUSTIN, Admin.
Sr. NOREEN CREAN, D.C., Vice Pres. Mission Affairs
Department of Chaplain Services,
Revs.:
F. PATRICK HANSER, C.M., Dir.
JOHN ALPHONSO (India)
RUDY RENTERIA (FWT)
GARY CARRUTH, Lay Chap.
ROYCE TAYLOR, Baptist Chap.
Sr. EDITH THOMPSON, D.C.
Sr. MICHAEL FRIEBE, D.C.
Sr. MARY ANGELYN PERA, D.C., Volunteer
Daughters of Charity of St. Vincent de Paul 11
Bed Capacity 600

St. Paul Medical Center
5909 Harry Hines Blvd.
Dallas, TX 75235
(Texas Non-Profit Corp.)

St. Paul Medical Center Foundation Inc.
2777 Stemmons Fwy., #957
Dallas, TX 75207
(Texas Non-Profit Corp.)
BITSY HENDERSON, Pres.

El Paso
Diocese of El Paso

Centro San Vicente
(Affiliated with Daughters of Charity National Health System)
8061 Alameda
El Paso, TX 79915
Tel: 915-859-7545
JIM C. PARKER, Exec. Dir.
Legal Title: *Centro San Vicente*
Community Oriented Primary Health Care Center (Medical Care).
Total Assisted 23,000

La Clinica Guadalupana, Inc.
901 Ascencion
El Paso, TX 79927
Tel: 915-852-3328
Sr. PEGGY DENEWETH, Contact Person
Sr. JANET GILDEA, M.D., Staff Physician & Medical Dir.

Houston
Diocese of Galveston—Houston

St. Joseph Hospital
1919 LaBranch
Houston, TX 77002
Tel: 713-757-1000
Operated by Sisters of Charity of the Incarnate Word, Houston, Texas.
RAYMOND KHOURY, Admin.
Chaplains:
Revs.:
BEN MEYER, O.P.
RICHARD MARTIN PATRICK, O.P.
Bed Capacity 792
Patients assisted annually 163,809

Sisters of Charity of the Incarnate Word, Houston, Texas
2600 N. Loop W.
Houston, TX 77092
Tel: 713-681-8877
Sr. CHRISTINA MURPHY, Pres. & CEO
SCH Corporate Offices
SCH Health Care System
SCH Employee Benefit Plans
Sisters of Charity of the Incarnate Word Retirement Trust

Sisters of Charity/City of Houston Southwest Community Health Clinic
SCH Liability Retention Trust
St. Elizabeth Hospital of Houston, Texas, 2600 N. Loop West
Houston, TX 77092

Jasper
Diocese of Beaumont

Jasper Memorial Hospital
1275 Hancock Dr.
Jasper, TX 75951
Operated by the Sisters of Charity of the Incarnate Word.
GEORGE MILLER, Admin.
Bed Capacity 95
Patients assisted annually 15,461

Kingsville
Diocese of Corpus Christi

Spohn-Kleberg Memorial Hospital
1300 General Cavazos Blvd.
Kingsville, TX 78363
Tel: 512-595-1661; Fax: 512-595-9888
Mr. ANDREW HARRIS, Admin.
Operated by the Sisters of Charity of the Incarnate Word (San Antonio, TX).
Beds 100
Patients assisted annually 41,798

Laredo
Diocese of Corpus Christi

Mercy Regional Medical Center
1515 Logan, P.O. Box 2068
Laredo, TX 78044
Tel: 210-718-6222; Fax: 210-718-6904
MARK STAUDER, Pres. & CEO
Chaplains:
Revs.:
HERNANDO RAMIREZ, S.J.
THOMAS P. O'DONOVAN
Deacon GUILLEMO DE LA GARZA
AUDELIA BUSTAMANTE
Sisters of Mercy of the St. Louis Region of South Texas 3
Beds 326
Staff 1,243
Patients assisted annually 185,594

Lubbock
Diocese of Lubbock

St. Mary of the Plains Hospital
4000 24th St.
Lubbock, TX 79410-1894
Tel: 806-796-6000; Fax: 806-796-6081
Sisters of St. Joseph of Orange, CA
Mr. CHARLEY TRIMBLE, CEO
DAVID HARTMAN, Dir. Pastoral Care
Sr. MARY C. GERRIOR, O.P., CPE Supvr.
Chaplains:
Revs.:
JAMES FURLONG
GEORGE THEKKEDAM
Sisters 6
Bed Capacity 420
Total Staff 2,448
Patients assisted annually 391,647

Madisonville
Diocese of Galveston—Houston

Madison Acquisition Company dba St. Francis Health Center
P.O. Box 698 - 100 W. Cross St.
Madisonville, TX 77864-0698
WILLIAM F. HYER, JR., Trustee & Contact Person
Bed Capacity 52

Nassau Bay
Diocese of Galveston—Houston

St. John Hospital
2050 Space Park Dr.
Nassau Bay, TX 77058
Tel: 281-333-5503; Fax: 281-333-8891
Operated by Sisters of Charity of the Incarnate Word, Houston, Texas.
Rev. THOMAS F. MCNAMARA, M.S., Chap.
THOMAS PERMETTI, Admin.
Bed Capacity 135
Patients assisted annually 102,181
Total Staff 669

Paris
Diocese of Tyler

St. Joseph Hospital and Health Center
820 Clarksville St., P.O. Box 9070
Paris, TX 75461
Tel: 903-785-4521; Fax: 903-737-3848
Mr. MONTY MCLAURIN, Pres./CEO
Sisters 6
Beds 212
Patients assisted annually 18,269
Staff 753
Health Care Centers, Ancillary Care Systems 4
Patients Assisted Annually at St. Joseph's Family Clinic:
4,250 at Cooper, TX
2,532 at Honey Grove, TX
722 at DePort, TX
1,927 at Paris, TX
St. Joseph's Foundation of Paris, Texas

Port Arthur
Diocese of Beaumont

St. Mary Hospital
3600 Gates Blvd., P.O. Box 3696
Port Arthur, TX 77643
Tel: 409-985-7431; Fax: 409-985-9404
Sisters of Charity of the Incarnate Word
Sr. MAURA THERIOT, C.C.V.I., Treas.
Mr. JIM GARDNER, Admin.
Rev. DONALD E. DONAHUGH (RCK) Chap.
Sisters 6
Bed Capacity 200
Patients assisted annually 108,938

San Antonio
Archdiocese of San Antonio

Incarnate Word Health System
9311 San Pedro #1250
San Antonio, TX 78216-4496
Tel: 210-524-4100
E-mail: iwhs@iwhs.org
Web Site: www.incarnatewordhealth.org
JOSEPH BLASKO, JR., Pres. & CEO
IWHS Forth Worth Health Care Corporation
9311 San Pedro #1250
San Antonio, TX 78216
Tel: 210-524-4100
St. John's Hospital and Health Center
9311 San Pedro #1250
San Antonio, TX 78216

Santa Rosa Children's Hospital
519 W. Houston St.
San Antonio, TX 78207-3198
Tel: 210-704-2011
A Division of Santa Rosa Health Care.
RICHARD WAYNE, MD, CEO
Licensed Beds 262
Anually Assisted 85,562

Santa Rosa Health Care System
519 W. Houston St.
San Antonio, TX 78207-3198
Tel: 210-704-2011
Web Site: www.santarosahealth.org
Sisters of Charity of the Incarnate Word
BILL FINLAYSON, Pres. & CEO
RICH WOODLEY, Dir. Pastoral Ministry
Revs.:
MICHAEL NORTON, C.PP.S.
PALMER MAXWELL, O.C.D.
Health related activities.
Nurses 636 (Full time registered & licensed)
Patients assisted annually 170,068
Sisters 22
Santa Rosa Home Health
5115 Medical Dr., Cottage E.
San Antonio, TX 78229
Tel: 210-705-5200
JOYCE DAVEY, Dir.
Santa Rosa Hospice
5115 Medical Dr.
San Antonio, TX 78229
Tel: 210-705-5252
KIMBERLY CAMP, Dir.
Rev. MARK SCHEFFLER, C.S.S.R.

Santa Rosa Hospital
519 W. Houston St.
San Antonio, TX 78207-3198
Tel: 210-704-2011
A Division of Santa Rosa Health Care.
Patients assisted annually 35,000
Licensed Beds 442

Santa Rosa Northwest Hospital
2827 Babcock Rd.
San Antonio, TX 78229
Tel: 210-705-6300
A Division of Santa Rosa Health Care.
RICH WOODLEY, Dir. Pastoral Ministry
Licensed Beds 137
Villa Rosa Hospital
5115 Medical Dr.
San Antonio, TX 78229
Tel: 210-705-5600
A Division of Santa Rosa Health Care.
Licensed Beds 136
Santa Rosa Rehabilitation Hospital
2827 Babcock
San Antonio, TX 78229
Tel: 210-705-6100
A Division of Santa Rosa Health Care.
Beds 34

Santa Rosa Skilled Nursing Facility
519 W. Houston St.
San Antonio, TX 78207-3198
Tel: 210-704-2011
WANDA LEDFORD, Dir.
Licensed Beds 20

Texarkana
Diocese of Tyler

St. Michael Health Care Center
2600 St. Michael Dr.
Texarkana, TX 75503
DON A. BEELER, CEO
Operated by Sisters of Charity of the Incarnate Word, Houston, TX.
General Hospital
Annually Assisted 11,407
Staff 1,232
Bed Capacity 239

St. Michael Rehabilitation Hospital
2400 St. Michael Dr.
Texarkana, TX 75503
E-mail: gormert@smh.sch.org
CHRISTOPHER KARAM, Admin.
Operated by Sisters of Charity of the Incarnate Word, Houston, Texas.
Health Care Centers, Ancillary Care Systems:
Annually Assisted 1,061
Staff 229
Bed Capacity 80

Tyler
Diocese of Tyler

Trinity Mother Frances Health System
800 E. Dawson St.
Tyler, TX 75701
Tel: 903-593-8441
Mr. J. LINDSEY BRADLEY, JR., Pres.
Rev. Msgr. JOHN BRENNAN, V.G., Chap.
Sisters of the Holy Family of Nazareth 8
Bed Capacity 358
Staff 2,300
Annually Assisted 550,436

Waco
Diocese of Austin

Providence Health Center
6901 Medical Pkwy., P.O. Box 2589
Waco, TX 76702-2589
Tel: 254-751-4764
KENT A. KEAHEY, Pres.
Sr. ROSEMARY BURKE, C.C.V.I., Dir. Chaplain Services
Sr. CECILE MATUSHEK, D.C., V.P. Mission
Medical & Surgical acute care; DePaul Center - Psychiatric care; St. Catherine's Center - Long Term care; Providence Medical Clinics; Providence Home Health/Hospice.
Daughters of Charity of St. Vincent de Paul 6
Bed Capacity 429
Patients assisted annually 124,402
Total Staff 1,154

Wichita Falls
Diocese of Fort Worth

Bethania Regional Health Care Center
1600 Eleventh St.
Wichita Falls, TX 76301
Tel: 817-723-4111
Sisters of the Holy Family of Nazareth
Mr. DAVID D. WHITAKER, FACHE, Pres. & CEO
Sr. M. IRENA, C.S.F.N., Supr.
Rev. AIDAN DONLON, S.A.C., Chap.
Sisters 5
Bed Capacity 242
Patients assisted annually 60,000

UTAH

Murray
Diocese of Salt Lake City

Holy Cross Ministries
Mailing Address:

P.O. Box 57672
Murray, UT 84157-0672
404 E. 5600 South
Murray, UT 84107-6218
Tel: 801-281-1457; Fax: 801-281-1602
Sr. ALICE MARY QUINTANA, C.S.C., Exec. Dir.
Outreach Programs, Health Center, Wellness & Literacy Programs, Seniors, Children, Women.
Total Staff 18
Total Annually Assisted 8,651

Ogden
Diocese of Salt Lake City

The St. Benedict's Foundation
319 E. Ridgeline Dr.
Ogden, UT 84405-6925
Tel: 801-479-1800; Fax: 801-479-3216
ESTELLE G. DAHLKEMPER, Exec. Dir.
STEVE SPURLOCK, Foundation Bd. Chm.

VIRGINIA

Newport News
Diocese of Richmond

Mary Immaculate Hospital
2 Bernardine Dr.
Newport News, VA 23602-4499
Tel: 757-886-6600
KIRBY H. SMITH, JR., CEO
Sr. BERNARD MARIE MAGILL, O.S.F., M.S., Dir. Pastoral Care Dept.
Rev. CHARLES A. SAGLIO, Chap.
Bernardine Franciscan Sisters Foundation, Inc.
3 Bernardine Dr.
Newport News, VA 23602
The Bernardine Sisters of the Third Order of St. Francis 13
Beds 110
Nurses 252
Patients assisted annually 65,880

Norfolk
Diocese of Richmond

Bon Secours - DePaul Health Foundation
150 Kingsley Ln.
Norfolk, VA 23505

Bon Secours De Paul Medical Center, Inc.
150 Kingsley Ln.
Norfolk, VA 23505
Tel: 757-889-5000
Sisters of Bon Secours
DAVID J. MCCOMBS, Exec. Vice Pres./Admin.
Clinic is connected with hospital.
Sisters 2
Beds 366
Patients assisted annually 8,808
Nursing School
Students 36
Legal Title: *Bon Secours DePaul Medical Center*
Legal Title: *Bon Secours DePaul Health Foundation*
Legal Title: *Bon Secours Bayley Properties*

Norton
Diocese of Richmond

St. Mary's Hospital, Inc.
P.O. Box 620
Norton, VA 24273
Tel: 540-679-9100
Poor Servants of the Mother of God
GARY L. DELFORGE, Admin.
Sisters 6
Beds 133
Patients assisted annually 58,753
Nurses 172

Portsmouth
Diocese of Richmond

Maryview Medical Center
3636 High St.
Portsmouth, VA 23707
Tel: 757-398-2200
Legal Title: *Maryview Hospital*
Sisters of Bon Secours
H. WAYNE JONES, Exec. Vice Pres./Admin.
MARYANN CHICHESTER, Dir. Pastoral Care
Chaplains:
Rev. PANTALEON O. MANALO
Sr. GRACE MALONZO
KATHY KOFRON
Beds 321
Patients assisted annually 134,608

Richmond
Diocese of Richmond

St. Mary's Hospital
5801 Bremo Rd.
Richmond, VA 23226
Tel: 804-285-2011
Sisters of Bon Secours
CHRISTOPHER M. CARNEY, CEO
Sr. PATRICIA A. ECK, V.P., Pres.
Sisters 4
Beds 391
Patients assisted annually 216,757
Bon Secours-Richmond Health Corporation
Bon Secours-Maryview Health Corporation

**Bon Secours-Maryview Foundation, Inc.*
Bon Secours-St. Mary's Health Care Foundation
Bon Secours-Stuart Circle Hospital
Bon Secours-Richmond Community Hospital
Bon Secours-Richmond Health System

WASHINGTON

Bellingham
Archdiocese of Seattle

St. Joseph Hospital
2901 Squalicum Pkwy.
Bellingham, WA 98225
Tel: 360-734-5400; Fax: 360-738-6393
Sisters of St. Joseph of Peace and PeaceHealth
NANCY BITTING, Admin.
Sr. JUDY TRALNES, C.S.J.P., Dir. Values Integration/ Spiritual Care
Sisters 4
Beds 253
Patients assisted annually 76,490

Centralia
Archdiocese of Seattle

Providence Centralia Hospital
914 S. Scheuber Rd.
Centralia, WA 98531
Tel: 360-736-2803
Legal Title: *Sisters of Providence in Washington*
Sr. MAUREEN COMER, O.P., Admin.
Sisters 3
Patients assisted annually 117,000
Beds 206

Chewelah
Diocese of Spokane

St. Joseph's Hospital of Chewelah
E. 500 Webster
Chewelah, WA 99109
Tel: 509-935-8211
GARY V. PECK, CEO
Pastoral Care:
Sr. HUMILITAS LAMBER, O.P.
Sr. ALBERTA NETT, O.P.
Sr. MARY TOECKES, O.P.
Ms. MARGARET RETHERFORD
Sisters 3
Bed Capacity 65
Patients assisted annually 15,113

Colville
Diocese of Spokane

Mount Carmel Hospital
982 E. Columbia, Box 351
Colville, WA 99114
Tel: 509-684-2561
GLORIA P. COOPER, CEO
Sisters 3
Bed Capacity 55
Patients assisted annually 27,642

Deer Park
Diocese of Spokane

Deer Park Health Center and Hospital
Mailing Address:
5633 N. Lidgerwood
Spokane, WA 99207
CATHY J. SIMCHUK, R.N., COO
Bed capacity 26
Patients assisted annually 21,304

Everett
Archdiocese of Seattle

Providence General Medical Center
14th & Colby, P.O. Box 1147
Everett, WA 98206
Tel: 206-261-2000
Rev. RAYMOND F. CRERAND, CEO
Mr. MEL PYNE, Opers. Admin.
Sisters 4
Patients assisted annually 117,581
Beds 475

Federal Way
Archdiocese of Seattle

St. Francis Hospital of Federal Way
3415 9th Ave. S.
Federal Way, WA 98003
Tel: 206-927-9700; 838-9700
Sisters of St. Francis of Philadelphia
MAGGIE LONG, COO
Patients assisted annually 59,321
Beds 110

Lakewood
Archdiocese of Seattle

St. Clare Hospital
11315 Bridgeport Way S.W.
Lakewood, WA 98499
Tel: 206-588-1711; Fax: 206-584-3001
Sisters of St. Francis of Philadelphia
SYD BERSANTE, Vice Pres. Opers.
Sr. JUDE CONNELLY, O.S.F., Vice Pres., Mission & Ministry
Sisters 1
Beds 86
Patients assisted annually 50,254

Longview
Archdiocese of Seattle

Peace Health, St. John Medical Center
1614 E. Kessler Blvd.
Longview, WA 98632
Tel: 360-423-1530; Fax: 360-414-7550
Sisters of St. Joseph of Peace and PeaceHealth
MARK MCGOURTY, Regl. CEO
Sisters of St. Joseph of Peace 4
Patients assisted annually 124,573
Beds 198

Olympia
Archdiocese of Seattle

Providence St. Peter Hospital
413 Lilly Rd., N.E.
Olympia, WA 98506
Tel: 360-491-9480
Legal Title: *Sisters of Providence in Washington*
Mr. SCOTT BOND, Admin.
Chaplains:
Revs.:
URBAN FEUCHT, O.S.B.
KIERAN P. CUNNINGHAM, O.S.B.
Beds 390
Patients assisted annually 166,382

Pasco
Diocese of Spokane

Our Lady of Lourdes Health Center
520 N. Fourth Ave., P.O. Box 2568
Pasco, WA 99302
Tel: 509-547-7704
THOMAS CORLEY, Admin.
In res.,
Rev. JOHN BIRK
Sisters of St. Joseph of Carondelet 5
Bed capacity 132
Patients assisted annually 38,701

Richland
Diocese of Yakima

Carondelet Behavioral Health Center
1175 Carondelet Dr.
Richland, WA 99352
Tel: 509-943-9104
BARBARA MEAD, Asst. Admin., Behavorial Health
Beds 32
Patients assisted annually 23,374
Total Staff 133

Seattle
Archdiocese of Seattle

Providence Seattle Medical Center
500 17th Ave., Box 34008
Seattle, WA 98124
Tel: 206-320-2000
Web Site: www.proups.org
Legal Title: *Sisters of Providence in Washington*
NANCY GUINTO, Admin.
Sr. SUSANNE HARTUNG, S.P., Dir., Mission & Ethics
Rev. AUGUSTINE HARTMAN, O.P., Chap.
Sisters of Providence 2
Patients assisted annually 120,000
Beds 436

Spokane
Diocese of Spokane

Holy Family Hospital
N. 5633 Lidgerwood St.

Spokane, WA 99207
Tel: 509-482-0111
Mr. Ron Schurra, Pres.
Mr. Richard Spinal, Dir. Pastoral Care
Chaplains 5
Sisters 3
Bed capacity 272
School of Radiology
Students 18

Holy Family Hospital Adult Day Health
c/o Dominican Network
N. 5633 Lidgerwood
Spokane, WA 99207
Tel: 509-482-2475
Mrs. Marie Raschko, Exec. Dir.
Purpose: to perform and provide health care services to the elderly and disadvantaged.

Sacred Heart Medical Center
W. 101 Eighth Ave., TAF-C9
Spokane, WA 99220
Tel: 509-455-3131
Mr. Ryland P. Davis, Pres.
Priest Chaplains:
Revs.:
Donald R. Cadden, S.J.
Gerald R. Gordon, S.J.
Michael D. Venneri
Chaplains 21
Bed Capacity 623
Patients assisted annually 10,553

Tacoma
Archdiocese of Seattle

St. Joseph Medical Center
1717 S. J St.
Tacoma, WA 98401-2197
Tel: 253-627-4101
Sisters of St. Francis of Philadelphia
Helen Batie, Mgr. Pastoral Care
Revs.:
Michael Feeney, O.S.B., Chap.
James E. Poole, S.J.
Emmanuel Iweh (Nigeria)
Sisters 9
Beds 340
Patients assisted annually 154,380

Toppenish
Diocese of Yakima

Providence Hospital
504 W. 4th Ave., P.O. Box 672
Toppenish, WA 98948
Tel: 509-865-3105
Mr. Steve Burdick, Operations Admin.
Sr. Betty Kane, C.S.J.P., Dir. Pastoral Care
Patients assisted annually 48,000
Beds 63
Total Staff 197

Walla Walla
Diocese of Spokane

St. Mary Medical Center
401 W. Poplar St.
Walla Walla, WA 99362
Tel: 509-525-3320
Sisters of Providence
Mr. John A. Isely, Pres.
Bed capacity 142
Patients assisted annually 56,000

Yakima
Diocese of Yakima

Providence Yakima Medical Center
110 S. 9th Ave.
Yakima, WA 98902
Tel: 509-575-5000
Barbara Hood, CEO
Sr. Patricia Glen, Dir., Spiritual Care
Revs.:
Justin D. McCreedy, O.S.B.
John T. Rashford, S.J.
Sisters of Providence 3
Patients assisted annually 244,495
Beds 226

WEST VIRGINIA

Buckhannon
Diocese of Wheeling-Charleston

St. Joseph's Hospital of Buckhannon, Inc.
1 Amalia Dr.
Buckhannon, WV 26201
Tel: 304-473-2000
Mr. Wayne B. Griffith, Admin.
Sisters of the Pallottine Missionary Society 4
Bed Capacity 95
Patients assisted annually 42,799
Home Health Care & Hospice Patients
Attended by Marist Fathers
St. Joseph's Foundation of Buckhannon, Inc.
1 Amalia Dr.
Buckhannon, WV 26201

Huntington
Diocese of Wheeling-Charleston

Pallottine Health Services, Inc.
2900 First Ave.
Huntington, WV 25702
Tel: 304-526-1028
E-mail: bushee@citynet.net
Web Site: http://www.ST.MARYS.org
Sponsored by the Pallottine Missionary Sisters.
Parent Corp. for:
St. Mary's Hospital of Huntington, Inc.
2900 First Ave.
Huntington, WV 25702
Tel: 304-526-1234
St. Joseph's of Buckhannon, Inc.
1 Amelia Dr.
Buckhannon, WV 26201
Tel: 304-473-2000

St. Mary's Hospital of Huntington, Inc.
2900 First Ave.
Huntington, WV 25702
Tel: 304-526-1234
J. Thomas Jones, Exec. Dir.
Pallottine Missionary Sisters 13
Bed Capacity 440
Patients assisted annually 126,631
School of Nursing
Student Nurses 113

Pineville
Diocese of Wheeling-Charleston

Children's Health Care, Inc.
Pineville Children's Clinic, Box 1419
Pineville, WV 24874
Tel: 304-732-7069
E-mail: ecatters@MARShall.EDU
Sr. Eileen Catterson, D.W.M.D., Dir.

Rhodell
Diocese of Wheeling-Charleston

Rhodell Health Clinic
P.O. Box 158
Rhodell, WV 25915
Tel: 304-683-4318
Legal Title: *Appalachian Health Cooperative, Inc.*

Wheeling
Diocese of Wheeling-Charleston

Bishop Joseph H. Hodges Continuous Care Center
Medical Park
Wheeling, WV 26003
Tel: 304-243-3800
Deborah A. Cox, R.N., B.S.N., Admin.
Bed Capacity 120
Skilled and Intermediate Care.

Children's Health Care, Inc.
1300 Byron St.
Wheeling, WV 26003

Wheeling Hospital
Medical Park
Wheeling, WV 26003
Tel: 304-243-3000
Donald H. Hofreuter, M.D., Admin.
Rev. Gregory Monahan, T.O.R., Pastoral Care Dir.
Sisters of St. Joseph 3
Marist Brother 1
Bed Capacity 276
Patients assisted annually 123,731

WISCONSIN

Antigo
Diocese of Green Bay

Langlade Memorial Hospital
112 E. 5th Ave.
Antigo, WI 55409
Tel: 715-623-2331; Fax: 715-623-9359
Religious Hospitallers of St. Joseph
Sr. Dolores Demulling, R.H.S.J., Supvr., Mission and Philosophy Advocate & Trustee, Dir. of LeRoyer Hospice
Mr. David Schneider, Exec. Dir.
Sr. Jean Bricco, Dir. Pastoral Care, Trustee & Contact Person
Sr. Adele Demulling, Coord. LeRoyer Hospice
Rev. Omer Kelley, Part-time Chap.
Sisters Res.
644 Longlade Rd.
Antigo, WI 55409
Tel: 715-623-4615
Sisters 3
Priests 1
Bed Capacity 49
Patients assisted annually 46,100

Appleton
Diocese of Green Bay

St. Elizabeth Hospital
1506 S. Oneida St.
Appleton, WI 54915-1305
Tel: 920-738-2665; Fax: 920-738-0949
Legal Title: *St. Elizabeth Hospital, Inc.*
Mr. Otto L. Cox, Pres.
Rev. James M. Gilsoul, Chap.
Sr. Johnette Marek, Dir. Spiritual Svcs. & Contact Person
Priests 1
Franciscan Sisters, Daughters of the Sacred Hearts of Jesus and Mary (Wheaton, IL) 5
Bed Capacity 135
Patients assisted annually 165,494

Arcadia
Diocese of La Crosse

Franciscan Skemp Healthcare, Mayo Health System, Arcadia Campus Hospital
464 S. St. Joseph Ave.
Arcadia, WI 54612
Tel: 608-323-3341
Franciscan Sisters of Perpetual Adoration and Mayo Foundation
Robert Tracey, Admin.
Chaplains:
Rev. Robert F. Polcyn, O.F.M.
Sr. Arlene Melder, F.S.P.A.
Total Staff 200
Bed Capacity 26
Patients assisted annually 19,853

Baraboo
Diocese of Madison

St. Clare Hospital and Health Services
707 14th St.
Baraboo, WI 53913
Tel: 608-356-5561
Owned and operated by SSM Health Care Corporation, Member of the SSM Health Care.
David Jordahl, Pres.
Rev. William Beers, Ph.D.
Franciscan Sisters of Mary (St. Louis, MO) 3
Bed Capacity 100
Patients assisted annually 40,000
Staff 294

Brookfield
Archdiocese of Milwaukee

Elmbrook Memorial Hospital, Inc.
19333 W. North Ave.
Brookfield, WI 53045
Tel: 414-785-2000
Franciscan Sisters, Daughters of the Sacred Hearts of Jesus and Mary (Wheaton, IL)
Kimry A. Johnsrud, Pres.
Rev. Robert J. Artmann, Chap.
Bed Capacity 166
Patients assisted annually 77,283
Total Staff 634

Chippewa Falls
Diocese of La Crosse

St. Joseph's Hospital
2661 County Hwy. I
Chippewa Falls, WI 54729
Tel: 715-723-1811
Hospital Sisters Health System.
Hospital Sisters of the Third Order of St. Francis
David B. Fish, Exec. Vice Pres.
Sr. Frances E. Schmitz, O.S.F., Local Coord.
Sisters 6
Bed Capacity 147
Patients assisted annually 134,314

Eau Claire
Diocese of La Crosse

Sacred Heart Hospital
900 W. Clairemont Ave.

Eau Claire, WI 54701-5105
Tel: 715-839-4121
MATTHEW W. HUBLER, Exec. Vice Pres.
Rev. EDMUND J. KLIMEK, Chap.
Sr. AUGUSTA SPERL, O.S.F., Dir. Pastoral Care
Hospital Sisters of the Third Order of St. Francis 6
Bed Capacity 344
Patients assisted annually 96,259

Fond du Lac
Archdiocese of Milwaukee

Agnesian HealthCare, Inc.
430 E. Division St.
Fond du Lac, WI 54935
Tel: 414-929-2300; Fax: 414-929-1866
Mr. ROBERT A. FALE, Pres. & CEO
Sisters 5
Bed Capacity 161
Patients assisted annually 214,666
Total Staff 870

Green Bay
Diocese of Green Bay

Libertas Treatment Center for Chemically Dependent
1701 Dousman St.
Green Bay, WI 54303-3282
Tel: 920-498-8600
Hospital Sisters Health System.
Hospital Sisters of the Third Order of St. Francis
DAVID B. FISH, Exec. Vice Pres.
PATRICK W. RYAN, Prog. Dir.
Bed Capacity 24
Patients assisted annually 600

St. Mary's Hospital-Medical Center
1726 Shawano Ave.
Green Bay, WI 54303-3282
Tel: 920-498-4200; Fax: 920-498-1861
Hospital Sisters of Third Order of St. Francis
Mr. JAMES G. COLLER, Admin.
DAVID J. SCHMIDT, Dir. Pastoral Care & Social Svc. Depts.
Revs.:
JOHN H. VAN DEUREN, Dir. Clinical Pastoral Education
FRANK P. SCHRAGE, Chap.
Bed Capacity 158
Patients assisted annually 85,161

St. Vincent Hospital
P.O. Box 13508
Green Bay, WI 54307-3508
Tel: 920-433-0111; 433-8162; Fax: 920-431-3215
Mr. JOSEPH J. NEIDENBACH, Exec. Vice Pres. & CEO
MARY J. BUSH, Dir. Pastoral Care
Chaplains:
Revs.:
WILLIAM J. STENGEL
CAMPION KLUCZYNSKI, O.F.M.
JAY FOSTNER, O.Praem.
Sr. IRENE BUSHMAN, O.S.F.
Sr. MARILYN HERR, O.S.F.
Hospital Sisters of the Third Order of St. Francis 2
Bassinets 25
Beds 547
Patients assisted annually 113,656

Hillsboro
Diocese of La Crosse

St. Joseph's Memorial Hospital, Inc.
400 Water Ave., P.O. Box 527
Hillsboro, WI 54634
Tel: 608-489-2211
Franciscan Sisters of Perpetual Adoration
Sr. RUTH BERRA, F.S.P.A., Dir. Pastoral Care
Rev. JAMES E. ENNIS, Chap.
Sisters 1
Bed Capacity 34
Patients assisted annually 3,440
Connected with the hospital is a home for the aged. Under care 65 infirm and aged men and women.

Kenosha
Archdiocese of Milwaukee

St. Catherine's Hospital
3556 Seventh Ave.
Kenosha, WI 53140
Tel: 414-656-3011
Sponsored by Franciscan Sisters and Daughters of the Sacred Hearts of Jesus and Mary, Wheaton, IL
Mr. ROBERT M. LOVELL, Pres. & CEO
JOHN OLIVERIO, Sec., Board of Directors
JILL HOFFMAN, Chap.
Legal Title: *St. Catherine's Hospital, Inc.*
Bed Capacity 247
Patients assisted annually 154,811
Total Staff 836

Kewaunee
Diocese of Green Bay

St. Mary Kewaunee Area Memorial Hospital
810 Lincoln St., P.O. Box 117
Kewaunee, WI 54216-0117
Tel: 920-388-2210; Fax: 920-388-2302
STEVEN SPENCER, Admin.
Patients assisted annually 14,005

La Crosse
Diocese of La Crosse

Franciscan Skemp Healthcare, Mayo Health System, La Crosse Campus Medical Center
700 West Ave. S.
La Crosse, WI 54601-4796
Tel: 608-785-0940; Fax: 608-791-9429
BRIAN CAMPION, M.D., CEO
Rev. PAUL L. SANKOORIKAL, Chap.
Franciscan Sisters of Perpetual Adoration and Mayo Foundation
Sisters 7
Total Staff 1,130
Bed Capacity 345
Patients assisted annually 52,400

Madison
Diocese of Madison

St. Marys Hospital Medical Center
707 S. Mills St.
Madison, WI 53715
Tel: 608-251-6100
Owned and operated by SSM Health Care Corporation, Member of SSM Health Care.
Franciscan Sisters of Mary (St. Louis, MO)
Mr. GERALD W. LEFERT, Pres.
Sisters 4
Capacity 440
Patients assisted annually 65,247
Pastoral Care Department:
Revs.:
GARRETT KEEGSTRA, O.F.M.Cap.
TED LINDQUIST, Lutheran Minister, Evangelical Lutheran Church of America
HUGO WREISNER, O.P.
LEO PETRIMOUIX, O.F.M.Cap.
Sr. MARY ELLEN LEWIS, F.S.M., Dir.
Sr. CLEMENT SABOL, V.S.C.
JOAN CARLSON, Chap.
PAULA MCKENZIE

Manitowoc
Diocese of Green Bay

Holy Family Memorial, Inc.
2300 Western Ave., P.O. Box 1450
Manitowoc, WI 54221-1450
Tel: 920-684-2011; Fax: 920-684-2522
Mr. DANIEL MCGINTY, Pres.
Deacon RAHLF PROULX, Dir. Pastoral Care
Chaplains:
Revs.:
RICHARD H. KLINGEISEN
KEVIN ORI
Sr. JEAN HERMAN DYKSTRA
Bro. JOE MARCO
MOLLY LA FOND
Franciscan Sisters of Christian Charity Sisters 9
Licensed Beds 303
Bassinets 26
Patients assisted annually 60,760

Marshfield
Diocese of La Crosse

St. Joseph's Hospital
611 St. Joseph Ave.
Marshfield, WI 54449
Tel: 715-387-1713
MICHAEL SCHMIDT, Pres. & CEO
Sr. ANTONIENNE THOMA, O.S.F., Acting Mgr.
Chaplains:
Rev. DONALD F. WILGER
MARY ELLA COLLINS, Catholic Lay Chap.
RITA AUSTIN
Protestant Chaplains:
Revs.:
STEVEN E. SUTTERER
LINDEN NELSON
Sisters of the Sorrowful Mother 4
Bed Capacity 524
Patients assisted annually 57,590
Training School for Nurses (Affiliated with U.W.-Eau Claire).

Mequon
Archdiocese of Milwaukee

St. Mary's Hospital Ozaukee, Inc.
13111 N. Port Washington Rd.
Mequon, WI 53097
Tel: 414-243-7300; 800-848-2844; Fax: 414-243-7416
THERESE PANDL, Sr. Vice Pres.
Rev. JOHN R. PACZESNY, Chap.
Bed Capacity 82
Patients assisted annually 147,965

Merrill
Diocese of Superior

Good Samaritan Health Center of Merrill, Wisconsin, Inc.
601 S. Center Ave.
Merrill, WI 54452
Tel: 715-536-5511
MICHAEL HAMMER, Pres. & CEO
Bed Capacity 73
Patients assisted annually 33,627
Good Samaritan Health Center Foundation of Merrill, Wisconsin, Inc.
A not-for-profit corporation for the purpose of soliciting and receiving contributions for the benefit of Good Samaritan Health Center of Merrill, Wisconsin, Inc.
Bed Capacity 73
Patients assisted annually 33,627
Affiliate of Catholic Health Initiatives.

Milwaukee
Archdiocese of Milwaukee

St. Francis Hospital
3237 S. 16th St.
Milwaukee, WI 53215
Tel: 414-647-5000
Sponsored by the Congregation of the Sisters of St. Felix of Cantalice of the United States of America, Chicago Province (Felician Sisters).
GREG BANASZYNSKI, Pres.
Chaplains:
Revs.:
JOSEPH L. BISOFFI, O.S.Cam.
GEORGE BALDERRAMA, S.C.J.
Sisters 7
Bed Capacity 260
Patients assisted annually 139,000
Total Staff 1,615

St. Joseph's Hospital of Franciscan Sisters, Milwaukee, Inc.
5000 W. Chambers St.
Milwaukee, WI 53210
Tel: 414-447-2000
JON L. WACHS, Pres.
Chaplains:
Revs.:
DAVID J. HANSER
NEAL DURHAM, S.D.S.
NORMAN R. SCHWARTZ
Corporate title: St. Joseph Hospital of Franciscan Sisters, Milwaukee, Inc.
Franciscan Sisters, Daughters of the Sacred Hearts of Jesus and Mary (Wheaton, IL) 8
Bed Capacity 567
Patients assisted annually 175,431
Total Staff 2,678

St. Mary's Hospital of Milwaukee
2323 N. Lake Dr., P.O. Box 503
Milwaukee, WI 53201-0503
Tel: 414-291-1000; Fax: 414-291-1444
CHARLES LOBECK, CEO
Chaplains:
Revs.:
JOHN R. PACZESNY
RUSSELL F. TIKALSKY
ALLEN BRATKOWSKI, O.S.Cam.
Sr. ROSALYNN DZIKONSKI, O.S.F.
Sr. MARGARET WENZEL, F.S.P.A.
Sr. MARGARET ANN ARNOLD, S.S.S.F.
Corporate title: St. Mary's Hospital of Milwaukee.
Daughters of Charity of St. Vincent de Paul 6
Bed Capacity 294
Patients assisted annually 344,195

St. Michael Hospital of Franciscan Sisters of Milwaukee, Inc.
2400 W. Villard Ave.
Milwaukee, WI 53209
Tel: 414-527-8000
Mr. JEFFREY K. JENKINS, Pres.
Sr. JOELISE RESTLE, Dir. of Pastoral Care Dept.
Corporate title: St. Michael Hospital of Franciscan Sisters, Milwaukee, Inc.
Franciscan Sisters, Daughters of the Sacred Hearts of Jesus and Mary (Wheaton, IL) 6

Bed Capacity 405
Patients assisted annually 103,709
Total Staff 1,386

Monroe
Diocese of Madison

St. Clare Hospital of Monroe, Wisconsin, Inc., dba The Monroe Clinic, Inc.
515 22nd Ave.
Monroe, WI 53566
Tel: 608-324-1000
Sisters of the Congregation of St. Agnes
Kenneth E. Blount, Pres. & CEO
Chaplains:
Rev. Thomas F. Campion
Sr. Agnes Kircher
Bed Capacity 221
Nurses 179
Patients assisted annually 212,800

New Richmond
Diocese of Superior

Holy Family Hospital
535 Hospital Rd.
New Richmond, WI 54017
Tel: 715-246-2101
Jean Needham, Pres.
Sr. Marian Schmit C.S.J., Pastoral Care
Sisters of St. Joseph of Carondelet 1
Bed Capacity 40
Patients assisted annually 15,000

Oshkosh
Diocese of Green Bay

Mercy Medical Center
631 Hazel St., P.O. Box 1100
Oshkosh, WI 54902-1100
Tel: 920-236-2000; Fax: 920-231-5677
Mr. Otto Cox, CEO
Sr. Johnette Marek, S.S.M., Dir. Spiritual Svcs.
Sr. Rita Schmidt, S.S.J., Chap.
Sisters of the Sorrowful Mother 4
Bed Capacity 209
Bassinets 14
Patients assisted annually 208,112

Portage
Diocese of Madison

Divine Savior Hospital & Nursing Home, Inc.
1015 W. Pleasant St.
Portage, WI 53901
Tel: 608-742-4131; Fax: 608-742-6098
Sisters of the Divine Savior
Mr. Michael Decker, Pres. & CEO
Chaplains:
Levonne Tappa
Sr. Kathleen Dooley, S.D.S.
Sisters 4
Bed Capacity 69
Patients assisted annually 40,000

Racine
Archdiocese of Milwaukee

St. Mary's Medical Center, Inc.
3801 Spring St.
Racine, WI 53405
Tel: 414-636-4011; Fax: 414-636-4540
Mr. Edward P. DeMeulenaere, Pres.
Rev. William J. Dietzler, Dir. Pastoral Care & Chap.
Corporate Title: St. Mary's Medical Center, Inc.
Franciscan Sisters, Daughters of the Sacred Hearts of Jesus and Mary 4
Bed Capacity 226
Patients assisted annually 191,000
Total Staff 1,100
Ambulatory Clinics
Patients assisted annually 410,000
Total Staff 678
All Saints Medical Group-Northwestern Campus
2405 Northwestern Ave.
Racine, WI 53404
All Saints Medical Group-Spring St. Campus
3807 Spring St.
Racine, WI 53405
All Saints Medical Group- Union Grove Campus
1120 Main St.
Union Grove, WI 53182
Family Practice Associates of Kenosha
3535 30th Ave.
Kenosha, WI 53144

Rhinelander
Diocese of Superior

Sacred Heart-St. Mary's Hospitals, Inc.
1044 Kabel Ave.
Rhinelander, WI 54501
Tel: 715-369-6600
Mr. Kevin J. O'Donnell, Pres.
Sisters of the Sorrowful Mother Ministry Corporation
Bed Capacity 99
Annually Assisted 34,428

Sheboygan
Archdiocese of Milwaukee

St. Nicholas Hospital
1601 N. Taylor Dr.
Sheboygan, WI 53081
Tel: 920-459-8300
Michael J. Stenger, Exec. Vice Pres. & Admin.
Sr. Renelle Brueggemann, O.S.F., Rel. Coord.
Mary Fleischman, Dir. Spiritual Devel.
Hospital Sisters of the Third Order of St. Francis 3
Bed Capacity 185
Patients assisted annually 105,932
Total Staff 585

Sparta
Diocese of La Crosse

Franciscan Skemp Healthcare, Mayo Health System, Sparta Campus Hospital
310 W. Main St.
Sparta, WI 54656-2142
Tel: 608-269-2132
Franciscan Sisters of Perpetual Adoration and Mayo Foundation
William P. Sexton, M.H.A., Admin.
Total Staff 185
Bed Capacity 49
Patients assisted annually 36,776

Stanley
Diocese of La Crosse

**Victory Medical Center, Inc.*
230 E. Fourth Ave.
Stanley, WI 54768
Tel: 715-644-5571; Fax: 715-644-5665
Mrs. Cynthia Eichman, CEO
Sr. Pat Belongia, Dir. Spiritual Svcs.
Ministry Health Care
Beds 127
Patients assisted annually 26,528

Stevens Point
Diocese of La Crosse

St. Michael's Hospital and School for Med. Technology
900 Illinois Ave.
Stevens Point, WI 54481
Tel: 715-346-5000; Fax: 715-346-5077
Mr. Jeffrey L. Martin, Pres. & CEO
Rev. Robert W. Greatorex, Chap.
Mr. David C. Baker, Dir. Spiritual Services
Mrs. Janet Jacoby, Spiritual Services
Sr. Mary Lee Slowey, S.S.M., Patient Concerns Rep.
Sisters of the Sorrowful Mother 2
Bed Capacity 144
Patients assisted annually 60,000

Superior
Diocese of Superior

St. Mary's Hospital of Superior
3500 Tower Ave.
Superior, WI 54880
Tel: 715-392-8281
E-mail: tjacobson@smdl.org
Mr. Terry R. Jacobson, Admin.
Bed Capacity 42
Patients assisted annually 25,106

Tomahawk
Diocese of Superior

Sacred Heart-St. Mary's Hospitals, Inc.
216 N. 7th St.
Tomahawk, WI 54487
Tel: 715-453-7700
Sisters of the Sorrowful Mother Ministry Corporation (Third Order of St. Francis)
Mr. Kevin J. O'Donnell, Pres.
Bed Capacity 60
Patients assisted annually 8,318

Waupun
Archdiocese of Milwaukee

Waupun Memorial Hospital
Waupun, WI 53963
Tel: 414-324-5581
James E. Baer, Pres. & Admin.
Bed Capacity 49
Patients assisted annually 39,599
Staff 265
Corporate title: Franciscan Sisters Hospital, Inc.

SPECIAL CARE FACILITIES

ALABAMA

Daphne
Archdiocese of Mobile

Mercy Medical
A Corporation.
P.O. Box 1090
Daphne, AL 36526
Tel: 334-626-2694
E-mail: info@mercymedical.com
Web Site: www.mercymedical.com
Sr. MARY EILEEN WILHELM, R.S.M., Admin.
Rev. Msgr. J. EDWIN STUARDI, Chap.
Acute Rehabilitation Hospital, Hospice, Home Health Service.
The Birches—An assisted living facility.
McAuley Place—An assisted living facility.
Portier Place—An independent living facility.
Sisters of Mercy 6
Nursing Sisters 1
Professional Nurses 200
Beds 157
Daughters of Wisdom 1
Congregation of St. Joseph 1
Patients assisted annually 4,402
Residential Care Units 120

Marbury
Archdiocese of Mobile

Resurrection Catholic Nursing Home
165 County Rd. 20 E., P.O. Box 89
Marbury, AL 36051-0089
Skilled Nursing Facility.
Rev. MANUEL WILLIAMS, C.R., Dir.
Registered Nurses 1
Licensed Practical Nurses 4
Beds 20
In-Patients 20

Mobile
Archdiocese of Mobile

Allen Memorial Home Skilled Nursing Facility
735 S. Washington Ave.
Mobile, AL 36603
Tel: 334-433-2642
Sr. MARILYN MOORE, D.C., Admin.
Daughters of Charity of St. Vincent de Paul 3
Beds 119
Patients assisted annually 170
Total Staff 137

Cathedral Place
351 Conti St.
Mobile, AL 36602
Tel: 334-434-1590
Mrs. JO ANN SCANLAND, Mgr.
Sr. DELPHINE FLEMING, D.C., Asst. Social Dir.
Residents 185
Total Staff 4

Little Sisters of the Poor, Home For the Aged, Inc.
Sacred Heart Residence, 1655 McGill Ave.
Mobile, AL 36604
Tel: 334-476-6335; Fax: 334-478-6519
Rev. LOUIS M. SUFFREDINI, Chap.
Sr. JUDITH MARY, L.S.P (STP) Supr. & Admin.
Rev. Msgr. JOSEPH G. MCARDLE
Rev. Msgr. JAMES MADIGAN
Rev. Msgr. GEORGE C. ROYER
Revs.:
JAMES MELDRUM, O.C.D.
MICHAEL FINBAR DESMOND
Sisters 12
Residents 84

St. Mary's Home
4350 Moffat Rd.
Mobile, AL 36618
Tel: 334-344-7733
Mr. PHILLIP A. WYNNE, Admin.
Dependent Children 48

Montgomery
Archdiocese of Mobile

City of St. Jude, Inc., The
2048 W. Fairview Ave.
Montgomery, AL 36108
Tel: 334-265-6791
Rev. MATTHEW A. SINDIK
Includes:
St. Jude Administration Building
St. Jude Church and Rectory
St. Jude Elementary and High School
St. Jude Exceptional Children's Center
St. Jude Head Start
St. Jude Social Services Center
Vincentian Sisters' Convent
The Old Convent
Central Alabama Laubach Literacy
St. Jude Apartments

Father Purcell Memorial Exceptional Children Center
2048 W. Fairview Ave.
Montgomery, AL 36108
Tel: 334-834-5590; Fax: 334-834-5592
Deacon FRANK J. MAY, JR., Admin.
Bed Capacity 58
Patients assisted annually 58

Father Walter Memorial Center for Handicapped Children
2815 Forbes Dr.
Montgomery, AL 36199
Tel: 334-262-6421; Fax: 334-262-2265
Rev. MANUEL WILLIAMS, C.R., Dir.
AUDREY C. WRIGHT, R.D., Admin.
BETTY THOMAS, Asst. Admin.
A skilled nursing facility for the mentally and physically handicapped child. Operated by The Resurrection Catholic Missions.
R.N. 7
L.P.N. 8
Beds 54
Patients assisted annually 54
Total Staff 73

Laboure Complex Foundation
P.O. Box 3074
Montgomery, AL 36109
Tel: 334-277-5213
Board of Directors:
LARRY NEUHOFF, Pres.
BARBARA DUKE, Vice Pres.
EDWARD AZAR, Sec. & Treas.

St. Bede's Children's Center
3840 Atlanta Hwy.
Montgomery, AL 36109
Total Assisted 56
Total Staff 13

St. John Resurrection Early Childhood Center
2815 Forbes Dr.
Montgomery, AL 36110
Sr. INEZ THERESA, O.S.P., Prin.
Licensed by Alabama State Dept. of Human Resources for 45 Students, Ages 2 1/2 to 5 years.

Seton Haven
3721 Wares Ferry Rd.
Montgomery, AL 36109
Tel: 334-272-4000
Sr. MARY CAROL MAUTEMPS, D.C., Admin.
Sr. MARILLAC CLARKE, D.C., Admin. Asst.
Residents 101
Total Staff 14

Prichard
Archdiocese of Mobile

Queen's Court I Apartments
W. Clark Ave.
Prichard, AL 36610
Mailing Address:
c/o Archdiocese of Mobile, P.O. Box 1966
Mobile, AL 36633
Tel: 334-434-1585

ALASKA

Anchorage
Archdiocese of Anchorage

**Mary Conrad Center*
9100 Centennial Dr.
Anchorage, AK 99504
Tel: 907-333-8100; Fax: 907-338-6789
Mr. KARL GARBER, Admin.
Sr. FRANCESCA KOLLER, O.P., Spiritual Care Coord.
Patients assisted annually 89
Staff 140
A long term care facility for the elderly, owned by Cook Inlet Housing Development Corporation and managed by Sisters of Providence in Washington.

Providence Extended Care Center
4900 Eagle St.
Anchorage, AK 99503
Tel: 907-562-2281
THOMAS E. BOLING, Admin.
Sr. PATRICIA COLLINS, R.S.M., Mission Integration
Legal Title: *Sisters of Providence in Washington.*
Patients assisted annually 380
Staff 340
Bed Capacity 224

Juneau
Diocese of Juneau

St. Ann's Care Center, Inc.
415 Sixth St.
Juneau, AK 99801
Tel: 907-586-3883
Skilled and intermediate care facility.
Bed Capacity 45

ARIZONA

Avondale
Diocese of Phoenix

Vianney Villas Apartments
(Retirement)
750 S. Fourth St.
Avondale, AZ 85323
Tel: 602-932-2036

Kingman
Diocese of Phoenix

Kingman Heights Apartments
(Retirement)
1020 Detroit Ave.
Kingman, AZ 86401
Tel: 602-753-2425

Lake Havasu City
Diocese of Phoenix

Becket House Apartments
(Retirement)
865 Cashmere Dr.
Lake Havasu City, AZ 86403
Tel: 602-855-7178

Phoenix
Diocese of Phoenix

Desert Crest Apartments
(Retirement)
2101 E. Maryland Ave.
Phoenix, AZ 85016
Tel: 602-264-6427

Senior Village
3541 W. Vogel
Phoenix, AZ 85051
Tel: 602-843-3008

Sweetwater Gardens Apartments
(Handicapped)
2035 E. Sweetwater
Phoenix, AZ 85022
Tel: 602-867-4549

Wickenburg
Diocese of Phoenix

Padua Hills Apartments
(Retirement)
460 S. West Rd.
Wickenburg, AZ 85390
Tel: 602-684-7034

Williams
Diocese of Phoenix

St. Agnes Apartments
(Retirement)
200 S. Ninth
Williams, AZ 86046
Tel: 602-635-2913

ARKANSAS

Barling
Diocese of Little Rock

Mercy Crest of Arkansas, Inc.
1300 Strozier Ln.
Barling, AR 72923
Tel: 501-478-3000; Fax: 501-478-3006
Sponsored by the Religious Sisters of Mercy.
Retirement Facility:

DON'T BLAME THE BARTENDER

Tonight Was a Long Time Coming

Could this priest be heading for his car? Let's hope not. Clearly, he's been drinking and he'd be putting in harm's way not only himself, but every occupant of every car on the road he drives.

Maybe he intends to walk. In which case, he might very well meet members of his congregation along the way. They can't fail to notice his unsteady gait and unfocused eyes. Will they feel shock or disappointment? More likely, what they'll feel is a sudden sense of abandonment.

Who's to blame? Alcoholism is a disease. The victim seldom is able to shake its tenacious grasp without a helping hand. Think about it. Didn't you notice, or at least suspect, *before* tonight, that Father had a chemical dependency problem? What steps have you taken?

One Out of Ten

Chemical dependency is a problem so widespread that at least ten percent of the Catholic clergy is afflicted. The popular impression is that men who are not treated are left to suffer the horrid consequences alone. That's simply not true. They don't suffer alone. Members of their dioceses fall victims, too.

If this priest decides tonight to drive in his impaired condition and has a serious accident, it could cost his diocese tens of thousands of dollars in legal fees and lawsuits – programs will have to be eliminated, parish improvements canceled, needy people deprived.

Shame shared.

You Need to Act Now

Time and time again, the court says, "They're your employees. You're responsible." ***If they get in an accident, the diocese is going to pay.***

As for those parishioners the priest may encounter if he instead decides to walk – no monetary system can repay the damage done them.

No Priest Is an Island

In the end, of course, it's not a moral issue for the alcoholic, but for you. We're only following our Faith in giving troubled clergy the "hand up" they require to continue their work with success and sobriety. They need us. More importantly, we need them. Denial by the priest or deacon is generally part of the problem, so contact us at Guest House for help on how to proceed. Call now. We are able to provide a complete spiritual, psychological and medical evaluation at no charge.

GuestHouse®

Ph: 1-800-634-4155

4800 48th Street N.E.
Rochester, Minnesota 55903

the miracle of GUEST HOUSE

If It Wasn't For This...

Over 90% recovery rate

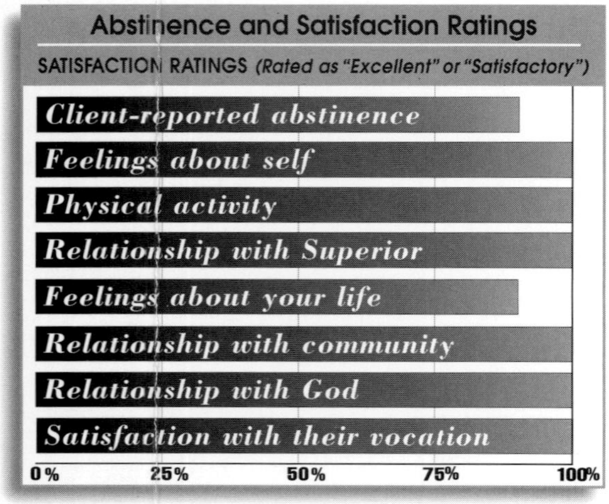

Five years ago, Guest House began admitting Catholic women religious for chemical abuse treatment at its Lake Orion, Michigan campus. Male clergy are treated separately at Guest House's Minnesota facility. How successful has the Lake Orion Guest House program for women been? Periodic surveys conducted at six months, twelve months and eighteen months following discharge show a consistent abstinence rate of 90% or higher.

...There Wouldn't Be This.

Clothing for the needy

Helping an uneasy young mother feel welcomed, this sister has an unusual bond with people down on their luck. She's a recovering alcoholic. One night not long ago, she was too drunk to make it back to her community. It was a homeless person who saw to it that she was taken to an emergency room. Today, she's a graduate of Guest House, living a sober, successful life. If you know of a sister suffering from chemical dependencies, our free evaluation program could be of great help.

GuestHouse®
For Women Religious

Call, write or fax for more information. Ask for our free brochure.

Ph: 1-800-626-6910 • Fax: (248) 391-0210 • E-mail: ghouse@ic.net

P.O. Box 68 • 1840 West Scripps Rd. • Lake Orion, MI 48361

Beds 60
Patients assisted annually 48
Residential Care Facility for the Elderly.

Hot Springs National Park
Diocese of Little Rock

Monastery of Our Lady of Charity of Refuge (Good Shepherd)
1125 Malvern Ave.
Hot Springs National Park, AR 71901
Tel: 501-623-9651
Sr. THERESA MARIE LALANCETTE, Supr.
Rev. ANDREW J. DUFAULT, M.Afr., Chap.
Sisters 13
Novices 1

St. Michael's School
1125 Malvern Ave.
Hot Springs National Park, AR 71901
Tel: 501-623-9651
Sr. THERESA MARIE LALANCETTE, Supr.
Sisters of Our Lady of Charity of Refugee (Good Shepherd) 14
Elementary students 51
Kindergarten 15
Day Care Center 82

Little Rock
Diocese of Little Rock

ABBA House, Missionaries of Charity
1014 S. Oak St.
Little Rock, AR 72204
Tel: 501-666-9718
Home for expectant mothers.
Missionaries of Charity 4

Catherine's House c/o Sisters of Mercy Health System
1020 W. 14th St.
Little Rock, AR 72202
Tel: 501-370-9100
Home for the first time expectant mothers or parenting teenagers.
Ms. AUDREY COLEMAN, Dir.
Number Served 40
Lay Personnel 15

AS

Pago Pago
Diocese of Samoa-Pago Pago

Nazareth House
P.O. Box 1510
Pago Pago, AS 96799
Tel: 684-699-2101; Fax: 684-699-1459
Conducted by Poor Sisters of Nazareth.
Sr. ENID HEALY, Dir.
Sisters 4
Aged Residents 15
Special Care Children 11
Montessori Early Education 144
Day Care Center 105

CALIFORNIA

Campbell
Diocese of San Jose in California

Susan House
100 El Caminito Ave.
Campbell, CA 95008-3412
Tel: 408-374-8684
Sr. CLAIRE SPELLMAN, S.N.D., Contact
Sisters of Notre Dame de Namur
Home for the Developmentally Disabled ages 18-59
Total Assisted 4
Staff 2

Chatsworth
Archdiocese of Los Angeles

Rancho San Antonio
21000 Plummer St.
Chatsworth, CA 91311
Tel: 818-882-6400
Sponsored by Catholic Archdiocese of Los Angeles.
Directed by the Brothers of Holy Cross.
Bro. JOHN CROWE, C.S.C., Exec. Dir.
In res.,
Rev. JAMES BLANTZ, C.S.C.
Brothers 4
Boys (13-17 yrs.) 102

Culver City
Archdiocese of Los Angeles

Marycrest Manor, Convalescent Home
10664 St. James Dr.
Culver City, CA 90230-5498
Tel: 310-838-2778
Religious Sisters of Charity.
Skilled Nursing Facility attended by priests from Loyola University and St. Augustine Parish.
Mrs. ESTHER MOSSE, Admin.
Sr. FRANCIS MARIA, Admin. Asst.
Pastoral Care Sisters 2
Bed Capacity 57
Residents 57
Total Staff 85

Fresno
Diocese of Fresno

Nazareth House
2121 N. First St.
Fresno, CA 93703
Tel: 209-237-2257
Sr. TERESA GRANT, P.S.N., Supr.
Rev. MICHAEL O'SHEA, O.F.M.Cap.
Poor Sisters of Nazareth of Fresno Inc. 7
Residential Care 85
Skilled Nursing 39
Total Staff 79

La Mesa
Diocese of San Diego

Little Flower Haven
8585 La Mesa Blvd.
La Mesa, CA 91941
Tel: 619-466-3163
Sr. BARBARA LEARY, D.C.J., Adm.
Sr. CARMELA LOVATO, Co-Adm.
Rev. PHILIP BRONK, S.T., Chap.
Postulants 2
Aged Residents 76

Los Angeles
Archdiocese of Los Angeles

Convent of the Good Shepherd-Good Shepherd Shelter
2561 Venice Blvd.
Los Angeles, CA 90019
Tel: 213-737-6111
Conducted by Sisters of the Good Shepherd.
Shelter for Battered Women and Their Children.
Sisters 10
Women Assisted Annually 40
Children 166

Franciscan Health Center
2859 Glassell St.
Los Angeles, CA 90026
Tel: 213-413-1050
ROSIE ORTEGA, Clinic Mgr.
Community Clinic Offering Surgical, Medical, OB-GYN, Optometry, Ophthalmology, Pediatrics, & Dental patients. Payment based on ability to pay.
A United Way Agency. Sponsored by Franciscan Sisters of the Sacred Heart.
Patients assisted annually 5,700

Immaculate Conception Home for Girls
1923 Micheltorena St.
Los Angeles, CA 90039
Tel: 213-664-7070
Sr. BENIGNA, Dir. Franciscan
Missionary Sisters of the Immaculate Conception.
Capacity 10

Knights of Malta Free Clinic, Inc.
2222 W. Ocean View #112
Los Angeles, CA 90057
Tel: 213-384-4323; Fax: 213-384-4097
Conducted by Knights of Malta Inc.
Primary Health Care for Senior Citizens.
DAVID FRELINGER, M.D., K.M., Medical Dir.
DAVID JOHNSON, Admin.
Visitation 7,500

Little Flower Missionary House
2434 Gates St.
Los Angeles, CA 90031
Tel: 213-221-9248
E-mail: be629@lafn.org
Web Site: www.yeocities.com/athens/acropolis/7053/sst.html
Sr. MARY JEANNE CODERRE, O.C.D., Supr., Ctr. Admin.
Mrs. CATHERINE CATANO, Dir. & Prin.
Attended by Salesian priests.
Child and Kindergarten Care Center.
Sisters 10
Lay Teachers 10
Capacity 197
Kindergarten Capacity 50

Missionary Brothers of Charity
1345 Alvarado Ter.
Los Angeles, CA 90006
Tel: 213-251-9707
Day Center and Residence for Homeless Youth.

Nazareth House
3333 Manning Ave.
Los Angeles, CA 90064
Tel: 310-839-2361; Fax: 310-839-4204
Conducted by the Poor Sisters of Nazareth.
Sr. FINTAN KEAVENEY, Supr.
Rev. PAUL PETERSON, S.S.C., Chap.
In res.,
Sisters 10
Retired Priests 18
Total Staff 185
Residents 150

St. Anne's
155 N. Occidental Blvd.
Los Angeles, CA 90026
Tel: 213-381-2931; Fax: 213-381-7804
E-mail: stannes@ix.netcom.com
Web Site: www.stannes.org
Residential care and community counseling programs for pregnant and parenting adolescents.
Sponsored by the Franciscan Sisters of the Sacred Heart
TOM OWENSON, Pres. & CEO
Rev. WILLIAM BRAND, O.F.M., Chap.
Beds Licensed for Children Under 18 years of age 96
Children Served Annually in Residential Care 300
St. Anne's also provides community counseling centers at the following locations to serve pregnant/parenting young women in their homes:
155 N. Occidental Blvd.
Los Angeles, CA 90026
Tel: 213-381-2931
11401 Valley Blvd., #102
El Monte, CA 91731
Tel: 818-443-2577
2301 Daily Dr., #202
Camarillo, CA 93010
Tel: 805-383-7277
Support groups include:
St. Anne's Foundation
St. Anne's Guild
St. Anne's Guild of Ventura
St. Anne's Junior Guild
Roney League
Helen Clark Auxiliary
Mabel Mosler Auxiliary
Loretta Young Auxiliary
Sister Winifred Auxiliary
Total Assisted 240
Total Staff 109

St. John of God Retirement and Care Center
2035 W. Adams Blvd.
Los Angeles, CA 90018
Tel: 213-731-0641
JOHN WILLIAMS, Admin.
Bros.:
STEPHEN DE LA ROSA, O.H., Local Supr.
EDWARD FRANCIS MCENROE, O.H., Prov.
STEPHEN DE LA ROSA, O.H., Novice Master
Brothers 14
Bed Capacity 215
SNF 131
Residential Care 33
Independent Living 51
Patients assisted annually 258
Supporting Organizations:
Hospitaller Foundation of California, Inc.
Tel: 213-731-7141
Bro. PATRICK CORR, O.H., Pres.
Women's League of St. John of God, Inc., Helpers Club of St. John of God, Inc.

Monterey
Diocese of Monterey in California

Ave Maria Convalescent Hospital
1249 Josselyn Canyon Rd., P.O. Box 1977
Monterey, CA 93940
Tel: 408-373-1216
Rev. FELIX MIGLIAZZO, Chap.
Franciscan Sisters of the Immaculate Conception 7
Bed Capacity 31
Patients assisted annually 46
Total Staff 46

Mountain View
Diocese of San Jose in California

Villa Siena
1855 Miramonte Ave.
Mountain View, CA 94040
Tel: 415-961-6484
Residential Care and Skilled Nursing Facility.
Mr. CARL BRAGINSKY, Admin.
Sr. URSULA BOMHOLT, O.P., Pres.

Rev. Salvatore M. DiNardo, O.P., Chap.
Dominican Sisters of Oakford, dedicated to St. Catherine of Siena. S.A. Motherhouse.
Professed Sisters 9
Residents 46
In Nursing Care 20
Nursing Staff 47
Total Staff 47

Newbury Park
Archdiocese of Los Angeles

Mary Health of the Sick Convalescent and Nursing Hospital
2929 Theresa Dr.
Newbury Park, CA 91320
Tel: 805-498-3644; Fax: 805-498-5112
Sisters Servants of Mary
Skilled Nursing Facility.
Sr. Purificacion Ferrero, S.M., Supr./Exec. Dir.
Sisters 16
Bed Capacity 61
Residents Assisted Annually 90
Total Staff 90

Oakland
Diocese of Oakland

Bishop Begin Villa
(Retired Priests)
3418 E. 18th St.
Oakland, CA 94601
Rev. Msgr. Martin E. Walsh
Revs.:
Edmund L. Hayburn
Adrian L. Murray
Thomas B. Gallagher
Residents 4
Total Assisted 4

Mercy Retirement and Care Center
3431 Foothill Blvd.
Oakland, CA 94601
Tel: 510-534-8540; Fax: 510-261-7551
Else Marie Kiefer, Pres.
Sr. Patrick Curran, Vice Pres.
Sponsored by the Sisters of Mercy.
Sisters of Mercy 4
Sisters of the Holy Names 2
Employees 160
Convalescent Hospital - Skilled Nursing Facility
Residential Care, Assisted Living, Personal Care.
Bed capacity 135
Retirement Facility for Priests in the Oakland Diocese Extensive community services.

Ojai
Archdiocese of Los Angeles

St. Joseph's Health and Retirement Center
2464 E. Ojai Ave., P.O. Box 760
Ojai, CA 93024
Tel: 805-646-1466
Hospitaller Brothers of St. John of God.
Bros.:
Pascal Barry, Prior
Michael Bassemier, O.H., Admin.
Andre Arculetta, O.H., Res. Mgr.
Rev. Carroll Laubacher, S.J.
Capacity 28
Independent Living 25 elderly
Total Staff 50

Palm Desert
Diocese of San Bernardino

La Paz Villas
P.O. Box 1962
Palm Desert, CA 92261
Tel: 619-346-6033
Units 24

Rosemead
Archdiocese of Los Angeles

Maryvale
P.O. Box 1039
Rosemead, CA 91770-1003
Tel: 626-280-6510; 213-283-9311; Fax: 626-288-8903
Sr. Linda Ann Cahill, D.C., Exec. Dir.
Daughters of Charity of St. Vincent de Paul 6
Children:
Residential Treatment 85
Day Care 80
The Los Angeles Orphan Asylum
7600 E. Graves Ave.
Rosemead, CA 91770
Los Angeles Orphanage Guild
7600 E. Graves Ave.
Rosemead, CA 91770

Sacramento
Diocese of Sacramento

Mercy-McMahon Terrace
3865 J St.
Sacramento, CA 95816
Tel: 916-733-6510; Fax: 916-733-6515
Sr. Mary St. John, R.S.M., Admin.
Licenced Units 189
Total Assisted 118
Total Staff 45

San Bernardino
Diocese of San Bernardino

St. Bernardine Plaza
550 W. Fifth St.
San Bernardino, CA 92401
Tel: 909-888-0153; Fax: 909-381-1589
Staff 4
Units 150

San Diego
Diocese of San Diego

Cathedral Plaza
1551 Third Ave.
San Diego, CA 92101
Tel: 619-234-0093
Legal Title: *Cathedral Plaza Development Corp. A California Nonprofit Corporation*
Mr. & Mrs. Herman T. Geelhoed, Res. Mgrs.
Apartments 222
In Residence 256

Guadalupe Plaza
4142 42nd St.
San Diego, CA 92105
Tel: 619-584-2414
Legal Title: *Guadalupe Plaza Development Corp., A California Nonprofit Corporation*
Mr. & Mrs. George Pettinga, Res. Mgrs.
Apartments 127
In Residence 130

Nazareth House
6333 Rancho Mission Rd.
San Diego, CA 92108
Tel: 619-563-0480
Sr. Margaret Brody, P.S.N., Supr.
Poor Sisters of Nazareth 9
Dependent Children 9
Day Students 358

Nazareth House Retirement Home
6333 Rancho Mission Rd.
San Diego, CA 92108
Tel: 619-563-0480
Retired Priests Residential and Nursing
Rev. Msgr. William Wilson, Chap.
Rev. Harry Murphy
Sr. Fidelis McCormack, P.S.N., Mgr.
Capacity 139
Priests 25
Poor Sisters of Nazareth of San Diego 10

St. John's Plaza
8150 Broadway
Lemon Grove, CA 91945
Tel: 619-466-5354
Legal Title: *Calexico Plaza Development Corp., A California Nonprofit Corporation*
Mr. & Mrs. Robert Partiss, Res. Mgrs.
Residences 99
Total In Residence 106

San Fernando
Archdiocese of Los Angeles

Mother Gertrude Home for Senior Citizens
(Franciscan Missionary Sisters of the Immaculate Conception, Inc.)
11320 Laurel Canyon Blvd.
San Fernando, CA 91340
Tel: 818-898-1546; Fax: 818-365-3159
Capacity 98
Total Staff 19
Total in Residence 36

San Francisco
Archdiocese of San Francisco

Alexis Apartments of St. Patrick's Parish
390 Clementina St.
San Francisco, CA 94103
756 Mission St.
San Francisco, CA 94103
Tel: 415-495-3690; Fax: 415-495-3629
Brenda Thomas, Property Admin.
Residents 218

The Good Shepherd Gracenter
1310 Bacon St.
San Francisco, CA 94134
Tel: 415-586-2822
Jean Marie Fernandez, Dir.
A treatment program for chemically dependent women.
Sisters 4
Lay Staff 8
Residence capacity 13

Home for the Aged of the Little Sisters of the Poor
St. Anne's Home, 300 Lake St.
San Francisco, CA 94118
Tel: 415-751-6510; Fax: 415-751-0650
Sr. Maria Christine Lynch, L.S.P., Supr.
In res.,
Rev. Msgr. Edwin J. Kennedy
Revs.:
Joseph Sanchez, Chap.
Ralph Carpenter, C.S.P.
Joseph Jaszovsky
Anthony Lee
David I. Walsh
Religious 14
Residents 90

Madonna Residence
1055 Pine St.
San Francisco, CA 94109
Tel: 415-928-0743
Cathy Koger, Mgr.
Total in Residence 37
Nonprofit residence for women over 60 with low income. Meal program, social services program.

Mercy Terrace Corporation Apartments
333 Baker St.
San Francisco, CA 94117
Tel: 415-931-2325
E-mail: mercyterrace@msn.com
Mr. Todd Landreneau, Admin.
The purpose of this corporation is to develop, construct, own, and operate housing for low and moderate income persons and families.
Units 155

Mount St. Joseph-St. Elizabeth (1976)
100 Masonic Ave.
San Francisco, CA 94118
Tel: 415-567-8370; Fax: 415-292-5531
Michael M. Sullivan, Exec. Dir.
Successor Corporation to Mount St. Joseph Home for Girls and St. Elizabeth Infant Hospital.
Sisters 7
Mount St. Joseph Program-Benita House Residential group homes for abused and neglected girls, ages 11-19, with emotional and behavioral problems.
Number assisted 34
St. Elizabeth Adolescent Parenting Program Residential care for pregnant teens, teen mothers, and their children.
Girls 34
Babies 24
Shelter Nursery for Drug Exposed Babies
Individuals assisted 42
Simpatico School On-site junior-senior high school offering basic education and vocational training to school-age residents of our group home and adolescent parenting programs.
Students 40
Epiphany Center for Families in Recovery Comprehensive support and reunification program for the parents and family members of drug-exposed infants.
Families served 80

San Jose
Diocese of San Jose in California

Giovanni Center, Inc.
85 S. Fifth St.
San Jose, CA 95112
Tel: 408-288-7436
E-mail: EdnCarol@aol.com
Carol George, Admin.
Lay Staff 3
Residents 40
A California nonprofit charitable, public-benefit, housing project for low-income elderly. Sponsored by the Roman Catholic Bishop of San Jose, a corporation sole.

Jeanne d'Arc Manor
85 S. Fifth St.
San Jose, CA 95112
Tel: 408-288-7421; Fax: 408-288-7264
Housing project for low-income elderly and handicapped. Sponsored by the Roman Catholic Bishop of San Jose, A Corporation Sole.

CAROL GEORGE, Admin.
Lay Staff 13
Residents 145
Units 87

San Pedro
Archdiocese of Los Angeles

Little Sisters of the Poor
Jeanne Jugan Residence, 2100 S. Western Ave.
San Pedro, CA 90732
Tel: 310-548-0625
Sr. MARGARET CHARLES, Supr.
Legal Title: *Little Sisters of the Poor of Los Angeles. A Corporation*
Sisters 12
Residents 62
Total Staff 45

San Rafael
Archdiocese of San Francisco

Nazareth House
245 Nova Albion Way
San Rafael, CA 94903
Tel: 415-479-8282
Sr. MARY ANTOINETTE FARRELL, P.S.N., Supr.
Rev. PATRICK F. CONWAY, C.S.Sp., (Ireland) Chap.
Poor Sisters of Nazareth 5
Residents 151
In res.,
Rev. Msgr. THOMAS I. KENNEDY
Rev. Msgr. GEORGE MONAGHAN
Rev. Msgr. CLYDE TILLMAN
Rev. Msgr. ANDRE TOURNEIR
Revs.:
THOMAS KEFFER
ANTHONY SPIKA

Santa Barbara
Archdiocese of Los Angeles

St. Vincent Residence
4200 Calle Real, P.O. Box 669
Santa Barbara, CA 93102-0669
Tel: 805-683-6381; Fax: 805-967-7508
For female youthful offenders, ages 12-17.
Daughters of Charity of St. Vincent de Paul Sisters 4
Residents 21
Total Assisted 35
Total Staff 55

Santa Cruz
Diocese of Monterey in California

Dominican Health Services
1555 Soquel Dr.
Santa Cruz, CA 95065
Tel: 408-462-7700; Fax: 408-462-7555
Sr. JULIE HYER, O.P., Pres.
Total in Residence 350
Total Staff 130

Santa Maria
Archdiocese of Los Angeles

Marian Residence
124 S. College Dr.
Santa Maria, CA 93454
Conducted by Sisters of St. Francis of Penance and Christian Charity.
Sisters 29
Residents 33
Total Staff 42

Santa Rosa
Diocese of Santa Rosa in California

**Vigil Light Apartments (The Vigil Light, Inc.)*
1945 Long Dr.
Santa Rosa, CA 95405
Tel: 707-544-2810
Sr. ERNESTINA MOLINARI, B.V.M., Mgr.
Sisters 2
Residents 54

Saratoga
Diocese of San Jose in California

Our Lady of Fatima Villa
20400 Saratoga-Los Gatos Rd.
Saratoga, CA 95070
Tel: 408-741-2950; Fax: 408-741-4930
E-mail: ourlady@earthlink.com
Provides skilled nursing care for aged women and men and Special Alzheimer's Unit.
Dominican Sisters of St. Catherine of Siena, Saratoga: Congregation of St. Catherine of Siena, Kenosha, Wisconsin.
Affiliate: Catholic Health Initiative
SUSAN SNYDER, O.P., Prioress
Sr. ANDREA MENDOZA, O.P., Pastoral Care
Sr. GERTRUDE BORACCA, O.P.
Rev. LEONARD TRAVERSO, Chap.
Religious 3
Residents 85

Spring Valley
Diocese of San Diego

Noah Homes
12526 Campo Rd.
Spring Valley, CA 91978
Tel: 619-660-6200; Fax: 619-660-1481
E-mail: NoahHomes@Juno.com
Sr. KATHRYN JENNINGS, O.S.B., Exec. Dir.

Stockton
Diocese of Stockton

Casa Manana Inn
3700 N. Sutter St.
Stockton, CA 95204
Tel: 209-466-4046
PHYLLIS WILLIAMS, Mgr.
Total in Residence 162
Total Staff 4

Garden Oaks
3334 Wagner Heights Rd.
Stockton, CA 95209
Tel: 209-956-3401
Assisted living facility.
Sisters of the Third Order of St. Dominic, Congregation of the Most Holy Name.
PENNY LEAL-MALLETTE, Dept. Mgr.
Total Staff 12
Units 48

St. Joseph's Regional Housing Corp.
1805 N. California St., Ste. 407
Stockton, CA 95204
Tel: 209-467-6312
O'Connor Woods Housing Corp. dba Garden Oaks
3334 Wagner Heights Rd.
Stockton, CA 95209
Tel: 209-956-3400
O'Connor Woods, A Calif. Corp.
3400 Wagner Heights Rd.
Stockton, CA 95209
Tel: 209-3400
St. Joseph's Regional Health System provides regional management and support functions for St. Joseph's Regional Housing Corp. Sponsored by the Sisters of the Third Order of St. Dominic, Congregation of the Most Holy Name, this non-profit Corp. provides a residential community for seniors offering a variety of living arrangements from active to assisted, and coordinates skilled nursing and rehabilitation services with St. Joseph's Medical Center's subsidiary operation, MEADOWOOD.
SCOTT SINCLAIR, Exec. Dir.
Total Assisted 322
Total Staff 113

Sun Valley
Archdiocese of Los Angeles

Villa Scalabrini
10631 Vinedale St.
Sun Valley, CA 91352
Tel: 818-768-6500; Fax: 818-767-1410
E-mail: mrainen@aol.com
Retirement Center and Special Care Unit.
Missionary Fathers of St. Charles
MARLENE RAINEN, Admin. Retirement Center
WILLIAM CLOONAN, Admin. Skilled Nursing Facility
Rev. AUGUSTO FECCIA, C.S., Exec. Dir.
Sisters of the Poor of St. Catherine of Siena.
Bed Capacity 188
Retirement Center 130
Skilled Nursing Unit 58

COLORADO

Canon City
Diocese of Pueblo

Centura Health-Progressive Care Center
An operating unit of Catholic Health Initiatives Mountain Region (an affiliate of Catholic Health Initiatives).
1338 Phay Ave.
Canon City, CO 81212
Tel: 719-269-2000; Fax: 719-269-2016

Colorado Springs
Diocese of Colorado Springs

Centura Health-Namaste Alzheimer Center
An operating unit of Catholic Health Initiatives Mountain Region (an affiliate of Catholic Health Initiatives).
2 Penrose Blvd.
Colorado Springs, CO 80906
Tel: 719-560-2000
Beds 64

The Medalion (East)
An operating unit of Catholic Health Initiatives Mountain Region (an affiliate of Catholic Health Initiatives).
1719 E. Bijou St.
Colorado Springs, CO 80909
Tel: 719-471-4800; Fax: 719-471-4807
Skilled Nursing 45
Assisted Living 25
Apartments 79
Rev. LEONARD WEEKS

The Medalion (West)
An operating unit of Catholic Health Initiatives Mountain Region (an affiliate of Catholic Health Initiatives).
417 E. Kiowa St.
Colorado Springs, CO 80903
Tel: 719-471-2578; Fax: 719-471-4807
Assisted Living 32
Apartments 89
Rev. LEONARD WEEKS

**St. Francis Nursing Center*
7550 Assisi Heights
Colorado Springs, CO 80920
Tel: 719-598-1336
Sisters of St. Francis.
NORMA FISHER, N.H.A., Admin.
Staff 95
Beds 107

Denver
Archdiocese of Denver

Archdiocesan Housing Committee
1544 Pearl St.
Denver, CO 80203
Tel: 303-830-0215; Fax: 303-830-2885
Archdiocesan Family Housing, Inc., Housing for Low-Income Families:
3700 Humboldt
Denver, CO 80205
1900 S. Raritan
Denver, CO 80223
1300 S. Irving
Denver, CO 80219
800 S. Monaco
Denver, CO 80224
Cathedral Plaza Inc.
1575 Pennsylvania St.
Denver, CO 80203
Tel: 303-837-1424
Housing for Low-Income Elderly:
Holy Family Plaza, Inc.
4300 Vrain
Denver, CO 80212
Tel: 303-455-4433
Marian Plaza, Inc.
1818 Marion St.
Denver, CO 80218
Tel: 303-837-1818
Higgins Plaza, Inc.
1380 Detroit St.
Denver, CO 80206
Tel: 303-320-4990
Madonna Plaza, Inc.
6275 Kearney St.
Commerce City, CO 80022
Tel: 303-289-2626
St. Martin Plaza, Inc.
1300 Bruce Randolph Ave.
Denver, CO 80205
Tel: 303-297-1414
Colorado Affordable Catholic Housing Corporation
1544 Pearl St.
Denver, CO 80203
Tel: 303-830-0215

Clare Gardens, Inc.
2626 Osceola St.
Denver, CO 80212
Tel: 303-433-6268
Franciscan Sisters, Daughters of the Sacred Hearts of Jesus and Mary (Wheaton, IL)
Rev. DECLAN A. MADDEN, O.F.M.Conv., Chap.
LINDA HILTON, Prop. Mgr.
Housing Ministry, low-income family units.
Housing Units 128
Residents 600

Damen House
P.O. Box 11580
Denver, CO 80211

Tel: 303-433-4280
Shelter and Safehouse for Homeless Women and Children.
Sr. DONNA BAIOCCO, Contact person
Total Staff 11
Total Assisted 81

Dayspring Villa, Inc.
3777 W. 16th Ave.
Denver, CO 80211
Tel: 630-455-5066
CAROLE HULL, Admin.
Total Assisted 56
Total Staff 20

Francis Heights, Inc.
2626 Osceola St.
Denver, CO 80212
Tel: 303-433-6268
Franciscan Sisters, Daughters of the Sacred Hearts of Jesus and Mary, (Wheaton, IL).
Rev. DECLAN A. MADDEN, O.F.M.Conv., Chap.
LINDA HILTON, Property Mgr.
Housing Ministry, Senior Citizens and Handicapped.
Housing Units 384
Residents 411

**Gardens at St. Elizabeth*
(Men and Women)
2835 W. 32nd Ave.
Denver, CO 80211
Tel: 303-477-4442
Web Site: www.centura.org
A division of Centura Health.
Sisters of St. Francis of Colorado Springs (O.S.F.)
CINDY HOGAN, Admin.
Rev. CHARLES P. SALMON, Res. Chap.
Sisters 5
Aged Residents 320

Hospice of Peace
1601A Lowell Blvd.
Denver, CO 80204-1545
Tel: 303-575-8393; 575-8350
Home Hospice Care.
ANN LUKE, Dir.

Mullen Home
3629 W. 29th Ave.
Denver, CO 80211
Tel: 303-433-7221; Fax: 303-455-9184
Sr. PATRICIA FRIEL, Supr.
Rev. Msgr. J. HARLEY SCHMITT, Chap.
Little Sisters of the Poor 11
Aged Residents 70

Florence
Diocese of Pueblo

Centura Health-St. Joseph Manor
An operating unit of Catholic Health Initiatives Mountain Region (an affiliate of Catholic Health Initiatives).
600 W. 3rd St.
Florence, CO 81226-1117
Tel: 719-784-4893; Fax: 719-784-4308
Rev. BERNARD GERVAIS, O.S.B., Chap.
Ms. ANN GENOVA, N.H.A.
Clearview of Colorado, Tertiary Substance Abuse Facility

Pueblo
Diocese of Pueblo

Villa Pueblo
An operating unit of Catholic Health Initiatives Mountain Region (an affiliate of Catholic Health Initiatives).
1111 Bonforte Blvd.
Pueblo, CO 81001
Tel: 719-646-5911; Fax: 719-544-1354
Rev. RAY HAWKINS, Chap.

Westminster
Archdiocese of Denver

Clare of Assisi Homes - Westminster, Inc.
2451 W. 82 Pl.
Westminster, CO 80003
Tel: 303-427-4406; 462-9271 (Corporate)

Villa Maria, Inc.
2461 W. 82nd Pl.
Westminster, CO 80030-4065
Tel: 303-426-1518; Fax: 303-426-4301
CINDY FRICK, Admin.
Total Assisted 40

CONNECTICUT

Bethel
Diocese of Bridgeport

Augustana Homes/Bishop Curtis Homes
Simeon Rd.
Bethel, CT 06801
Tel: 203-743-2508
BERNARD E. REIDY, K.C.S.G., Exec. Dir.
CLAIRE HIPP, Project Mgr.

Bridgeport
Diocese of Bridgeport

Augustana Homes Bishop Curtis Homes - Danbury
238 Jewett Ave.
Bridgeport, CT 06606
BERNARD E. REIDY, K.C.S.G., Exec. Dir.

Augustana Homes/Bishop Curtis Homes
525 Palisade Ave.
Bridgeport, CT 06610
Tel: 203-366-4333; Fax: 203-576-6790
Mr. JAMES J. CASEY, Manager
Mrs. LILLIAN ARAUJO, Site Mgr.

Augustana Homes/Bishop Curtis Homes
280 Jewett Ave.
Bridgeport, CT 06606
Tel: 203-374-5346
Mr. JAMES J. CASEY, Mgr.
Mrs. NILDA ALAMO, Site Mgr.

Augustana Homes/Bishop Curtis Homes - East Bridgeport
238 Jewett Ave.
Bridgeport, CT 06606
Tel: 203-372-4301; Fax: 203-371-8698
Mr. BERNARD E. REIDY, Contact Person

Bridgeport Diocesan Health Care Corporation
238 Jewett Ave.
Bridgeport, CT 06606
Tel: 203-372-4301
Mr. CARLETON H. PEMBER, III, Dir.

The Pope John Paul II Foundation, Inc.
238 Jewett Ave.
Bridgeport, CT 06606
Most Rev. EDWARD M. EGAN, Chm.
Mr. BERNARD REIDY, K.C.S.G., Exec. Dir.

Roncalli Apartments
430 Grant St.
Bridgeport, CT 06610
Tel: 203-384-9984
Rev. EDWARD C. DOHERTY, M.SS.A., Pres.
MARIANN CALLAHAN, L.P.N., Admin.
Affiliate of the Roncalli Institute, Supervised Apartments for the Elderly & Handicapped.

St. Camillus Home Foundation, Inc.
238 Jewett Ave.
Bridgeport, CT 06606
Fax: 203-353-0550
BERNARD E. REIDY, K.C.S.G., Exec. Dir.

Danbury
Diocese of Bridgeport

The Pope John Paul II Center for Health Care, Inc.
33 Lincoln Ave.
Danbury, CT 06810
Tel: 203-797-9300; Fax: 203-790-4645
Mrs. DIANE A. PIMENTEL, Admin.
Rev. Msgr. DANIEL J. FOLEY, Chap.
Sr. FRANCES SMALKOWSKI, C.F.S.N., Co-Dir. Pastoral Care

Deep River
Diocese of Norwich

Mount St. John
135 Kirtland St.
Deep River, CT 06417
Tel: 203-526-5391; Fax: 203-526-3846
Bro. K. PAUL MCGLADE, C.F.C., Exec. Dir.
Rev. THADDEUS (TED) SWERTZ, C.S.C.
In res.,
Rev. NOEL G. AHREN, O.Carm.
Lay Staff 100
Boys 77

Enfield
Archdiocese of Hartford

The Home for the Aged of the Little Sisters of the Poor
Incorporated Operating as St. Joseph's Residence
1365 Enfield St.
Enfield, CT 06082-4900
Tel: 860-741-0791
Rev. ANDREW SCOPP, S.J.
Little Sisters of the Poor 15
Residents 93
Senior Day Center 15
Total Assisted 27

Fairfield
Diocese of Bridgeport

Augustana Homes/Bishop Curtis Homes
1677 Post Rd.
Fairfield, CT 06430
Mr. JAMES J. CASEY, Manager, Tel: 203-576-0823

Meriden
Archdiocese of Hartford

Franciscan Family Care Center
267 Finch Ave.
Meriden, CT 06450
Tel: 203-237-8084
Legal Title: *Franciscan Family Care Center, Inc.*
Sr. SHAUN VERGAUWEN, F.S.E., Dir.
Sr. SUZANNE GROSS, F.S.E., Dir. Franciscan Home Care & Contact, Tel: 203-238-1441
Franciscan Sisters of the Eucharist 8
Total Assisted 390
Total Staff 90

New Britain
Archdiocese of Hartford

Marian Educational Clinic
314 Osgood Ave.
New Britain, CT 06053
Tel: 860-223-0501
Daughters of Mary of the Immaculate Conception
Sr. MARY EDMUNDA, D.M., Dir. & Contact
Sisters 2

Monsignor Bojnowski Manor, Inc.
50 Pulaski St.
New Britain, CT 06053
Fax: 860-229-3252
Owned and operated by the Daughters of Mary of the Immaculate Conception.
Sr. MARY DEBORAH, D.M., Exec. Dir.
Skilled Nursing Beds 54
Total Staff 99

St. Lucian's Home for the Aged
532 Burritt St.
New Britain, CT 06053
Tel: 860-223-2123
Daughters of Mary of the Immaculate Conception
Rev. GILBERT WDZIECZNY, O.F.M.Conv., Chap.
Sisters 2
Residents 42

New Haven
Archdiocese of Hartford

St. Francis Home for Children, Inc.
651 Prospect St.
New Haven, CT 06511
Tel: 203-777-5513; Fax: 203-777-0644
Residential, day treatment, group home, special education, preschool, foster placement adoptions
Sisters of Mercy, Sisters of Notre Dame
Rev. JEREMIAH N. MURASSO, Exec. Dir. & Contact
Sisters 3
Lay Staff 105
Children 52
Intensive Day Treatment 25
Preschool 25

Norwalk
Diocese of Bridgeport

Notre Dame Convalescent Home
76 W. Rocks Rd.
Norwalk, CT 06851
Tel: 203-847-5893
Sisters of St. Thomas of Villanova
Mother EDMOND, S.S.T.V., Supr.
Mr. JOHN FARLING, Admin.
Rev. ALBERT W. WATTS, Chap.
Sisters 4
Patients assisted annually 60

Riverside
Diocese of Bridgeport

Augustana Homes of Greenwich/Bishop Curtis Homes
1040 E. Putnam Ave.
Riverside, CT 06878

Mr. JAMES J. CASEY, Manager, Tel: 203-576-0823

Stamford
Diocese of Bridgeport

Augustana Homes/Bishop Curtis Homes - Glenbrook
352 Glenbrook Rd.
Stamford, CT 06902
Tel: 203-576-0823
Mr. JAMES J. CASEY, Manager

St. Camillus Health Center
494 Elm St.
Stamford, CT 06902
Tel: 203-353-0550; Fax: 203-325-0200
Ms. ANNA BURKE, Admin.
LIZ MONTELLI, Asst. Admin.
Rev. PAUL B. LALIC, Chap.
St. Camillus Auxiliary Committee
494 Elm St.
Stamford, CT 06902
Tel: 203-325-0200
St. Camillus Adult Day Care
494 Elm St.
Stamford, CT 06902
Tel: 203-325-0200
MARY SPENCER, Dir.

Trumbull
Diocese of Bridgeport

Carmel Ridge
6454 Main St.
Trumbull, CT 06611
Tel: 203-261-2229
Mr. PETER CADY, Site Mgr.

St. Joseph's Housing Corporation
Teresian Towers & Carmel Ridge Estates, 6448 Main St.
Trumbull, CT 06611
Tel: 203-261-2229
Mr. PETER CADY, Site Mgr.

St. Joseph's Manor
6448 Main St.
Trumbull, CT 06611
Tel: 203-268-6204; Fax: 203-268-5271
Sr. MICHELLE ANNE REHO, O.Carm., Admin.
Rev. ALFRED E. RUSSO, Chap.
Rev. Msgr. THOMAS HENAHAN
Revs.:
CHARLES L. HEWITT (HRT)
JOHN R. O'CONNOR
CHARLES T. KENNEDY (HRT)
PATRICK SPEER (HRT)
Carmelite Sisters for the Aged and Infirm 8
Capacity 297

West Hartford
Archdiocese of Hartford

Saint Agnes Home, Inc.
104 Mayflower St.
West Hartford, CT 06110
Tel: 860-521-7516; Fax: 860-521-6160
E-mail: safc@aol.com
For adolescent single mothers and their infants
M. KEEGAN, Exec. Dir.
Bed Capacity 16
Patients assisted annually 53
Total Staff 31

Saint Mary Home
2021 Albany Ave.
West Hartford, CT 06117
Tel: 860-236-1924
Mrs. MAUREEN KOLACZENKO, Admin.
Mrs. BONNIE MCMAHON, R.N., Dir. Nursing Svcs.
Mr. JAMES CASEY, Assoc. Admin.
Rev. HERBERT CLARKIN, Res. Chap.
Sisters of Mercy 16
Sisters in Res. 6
Residents 98
Patients assisted annually 217
St. Mary Home, II, Inc.
2021 Albany Ave.
West Hartford, CT 06117
Adult Day Care 21
Staff 6

Willimantic
Diocese of Norwich

Holy Family Home and Shelter, Inc.
88 Jackson St., P.O. Box 884
Willimantic, CT 06226
Tel: 860-423-7719; Fax: 860-423-7719
BONNIE REILEIN, Exec. Dir.
In res.,
Rev. STEPHEN FRONCKEWICZ, O.S.B.
Residents 23
Total Assisted 132
Total Staff 8

Windham
Diocese of Norwich

St. Joseph Living Center
14 Club Rd.
Windham, CT 06280
Tel: 860-456-1107; Fax: 860-450-7114
PATRICIA HAMILL, M.S., Admin.
Dr. MICHAEL KEENAN, Medical Dir.
DEBBIE MOYNIHAN, Dir. Nursing Svcs.
CATHY RAUCHLE, Dir. Admissions
PAULA HANEY, Dir. Rehabilitation Svcs.
JANET GRISWOLD, Dir. Day Care
Rev. WILLIAM J. FLYNN, Chap.
Sisters 1
Lay Staff 164
Capacity 120
Total Assisted 120
Total Staff 165

DELAWARE

Claymont
Diocese of Wilmington

Children's Home, Inc.
2901 Green St.
Claymont, DE 19702
Tel: 302-798-0601
BARBARA GRIECO, M.C., Deputy Dir. & Dir. of Children's Services
Capacity:
Children 40

Hockessin
Diocese of Wilmington

Franciscan Health System/Care at Brackenville
100 St. Clare Dr.
Hockessin, DE 19707
Tel: 302-234-5420

Newark
Diocese of Wilmington

Jeanne Jugan Residence
185 Salem Church Rd.
Newark, DE 19713
Conducted by the Little Sisters of the Poor
Sr. ANDREA MUNARRIZ, L.S.P., Supr.
Rev. ANTHONY T. SCHELICH, O.S.F.S.
Residents 82
Sisters 12

Marydale Retirement Village
135 Jeandell Dr.
Newark, DE 19713
Tel: 302-368-2784
Bro. ROBERT GILROY, C.S.C., Admin.
Sr. ALICE PENROSE, S.H.C.J., Pastoral Care Coord.
Apartments for Elderly
Apartments 108
Residents 120

Our Lady of Grace Home for Children, Inc.
487 E. Chestnut Hill Rd.
Newark, DE 19713
Tel: 302-738-4658; 737-6650
Sr. MARY ANTONEA SLOWIK, C.S.S.F., Admin. & Supr.
Sr. MARY CHARLOTTE WSZOLEK, C.S.S.F., Supr.
Felician Sisters 5
Children 10
Total Assisted 29

Wilmington
Diocese of Wilmington

The Antonian
1701 W. 10th St.
Wilmington, DE 19805
Tel: 302-421-3758
Mrs. CHRISTINE T. SPAGNOLO, Mgr.
Rev. MARIO BUGLIOSI, O.S.F.S., Chap.
Congregate Housing for the Elderly
Residents 143
Apartments 136

Franciscan Health System/Care at Wilmington
801 N. Broom St.
Wilmington, DE 19806
Tel: 302-652-3861

Home of Divine Providence, Inc.-Bayard House
300 Bayard Ave.
Wilmington, DE 19805
Tel: 302-654-1184
EILEEN M. POORTEN, Dir.
Pregnant Teens & Women (12-35)
Residents 25
Staff 13
Total Assisted Annually 400

Ministry of Caring, Inc.
506 N. Church St.
Wilmington, DE 19801-4812
Tel: 302-652-5523; Fax: 302-652-1919
Rev. RONALD GIANNONE, O.F.M.Cap., Exec. Dir.
Ms. LOUISA TEOLI, Office Mgr. & Asst.
DEBBE DUNPHY, Exec. Asst.
Sr. FIDES MILWICZ, C.S.S.F., Dir. of Human Resources & Sec.
Child Care Center
221 N. Jackson St.
Wilmington, DE 19805-3649
Tel: 302-652-8992; Fax: 302-652-8945
Child care for homeless children, from infancy to 5 years old.
KAREN SLIZGI, Dir.
St. Clare Medical Outreach
7th & Clayton Sts.
Wilmington, DE 19805-3156
Mobile Medical Van which provides health services for the poor.
THOMAS SCOTT, M.D.
MARYANN FAGAN, R.N.
Mary Mother of Hope House Transitional Residence
818 Jefferson St.
Wilmington, DE 19801-1432
Tel: 302-427-9170
Transitional Residence for single women.
Sr. MARY ANNE MATARESE, O.S.B., Dir.
Capacity 8
House of Joseph II
7-9 W. 18th St.
Wilmington, DE 19802-4833
Hospice for men with AIDS.
Capacity 8
Bro. KEVIN O'LOUGHLIN, O.F.M. Cap., Dir.
Pierre Toussaint Dental Office
830 Spruce St.
Wilmington, DE 19801-4205
Dental office for the homeless.
DOROTHY MILLER, Sec.
Angela Merici House
1105 W. 8th St.
Wilmington, DE 19806-4605
Tel: 302-655-4817
Residence for Sisters of St. Francis 3
St. Francis Transitional Residence
103-107 & 111 N. Jackson St.
Wilmington, DE 19805-3648
Transitional living for women and children.
EMMA TERRELL, Dir.
House of Joseph Transitional Residence
704 West St.
Wilmington, DE 19801-1523
Transitional residence for men.
Bro. KEVIN O'LOUGHLIN, O.F.M.Cap., Dir.
Samaritan Outreach
1410 N. Claymont St.
Wilmington, DE 19802-5227
Tel: 302-652-0969
Sr. LYNN ZAWACKA, C.S.S.F., Mgr.
Social outreach for the homeless.
Mary Mother of Hope House I
1103 W. 8th St.
Wilmington, DE 19806-4605
Tel: 302-652-8532
Sr. MARY ANNE MATARESE, O.S.B., Dir.
Emergency shelter for homeless women.
Capacity 21
Mary Mother of Hope House II
121 N. Jackson St.
Wilmington, DE 19805-3670
Tel: 302-652-1935
Ms. ELLEN ROBB, Mgr.
Emergency shelter for women with children.
Capacity 23
Mary Mother of Hope House III
515 N. Broom St.
Wilmington, DE 19805-3114
Tel: 302-652-0970
Ms. LINDA MYRIE, Mgr.
Emergency shelter for women with children.
Capacity 21
Job Placement Center
1100 Lancaster Ave.
Wilmington, DE 19805-4009
Tel: 302-652-0917
Ms. JUANITA BEAUFORD, Dir.
Employment agency to assist the poor.
House of Joseph I
1328 W. Third St.
Wilmington, DE 19805-3662
Tel: 302-652-0904
JOHN SMITH, Acting Mgr.

Shelter for homeless employable men who are seeking employment.
Capacity 13
Capuchin Friars 1
Emmanuel Dining Room, West
121 N. Jackson St.
Wilmington, DE 19805-3670
Tel: 302-652-3228; Fax: 302-652-2576
Bro. ROBERT LONGO, O.F.M.Cap., Dir.
Ms. MARY TAGGART, Co-Mgr.
Sr. BERNADETTE MCGOLDRICK, O.S.F., Co-Mgr.
Sr. CHRISTINA SEMINATORE, C.D.P., Sec.
Emmanuel Dining Room, East
226 N. Walnut St.
Wilmington, DE 19801-3934
Tel: 302-652-2577
Mr. ODELL PARKER, Mgr.
Emmanuel Dining Room, South
500 Rogers Rd.
New Castle, DE 19720
Tel: 302-577-2951
Ms. EMMA MITCHELL, Mgr.
Ministry of Caring Distribution Center
1410 N. Claymont St.
Wilmington, DE 19802-5227
Tel: 302-652-0969
Mr. EUGENE MCLAUGHLIN, Dir.
Ministry of Caring Guild
506 N. Church St.
Wilmington, DE 19801
BARBRA ANDRISANI, Pres.
ROBERTA CAMPBELL, Treas.

St. Patrick's House, Inc.
115 E. 14th St.
Wilmington, DE 19801
Tel: 302-654-6908
Rev. JAMES F. TRAINOR, Chm. of Board
Affiliated with St. Patrick Parish. Congregate Independent Living Facility for the elderly
Capacity 16

Seton Villa, Inc.
800 Bellevue Rd.
Wilmington, DE 19809
Tel: 302-762-2982
BARBARA GRIECO, M.C., Deputy Dir. & Dir. Children's Services
Capacity:
Children (ages 5-18) 28

Siena Hall, Inc.
2307 Kentmere Pkwy.
Wilmington, DE 19806
Tel: 302-656-2183
BARBARA GRIECO, M.C., Deputy Dir. & Dir. Children's Services
Capacity:
Children (ages 5-18) 30

Vianney House
905 Milltown Rd.
Wilmington, DE 19808
Tel: 302-636-0200
MARYANN BLATT, Dir.
Rev. CHRISTOPHER H. PLOKHOOY, Diocesan Liaison

DISTRICT OF COLUMBIA

Washington
Archdiocese of Washington

Cardinal O'Boyle Residence for Priests
1150 Varnum St., N.E.
Washington, DC 20017
In res.,
Revs.:
JOSEPH A. O'BRIEN, Rector
JOSEPH BUI-TRANG-NGHIEM, Tribunal
Rev. Msgr. ARMANDO JIMENEZ
Rev. Msgr. JOSEPH W. HARTMAN
Rev. Msgr. LEONARD F. HURLEY, Chap., Carroll Manor
Revs.:
ROBERT H. WHARTON
ROGER P. GALLAGHER
JOHN A. LUBEY
J. EDWARD STUDNEY

Jeanne Jugan Residence-St. Joseph's Villa
4200 Harewood Rd., N.E.
Washington, DC 20017-1554
Tel: 202-269-1831
Little Sisters of the Poor
Sr. CHRISTINE KREUPER, L.S.P., Admin.
Rev. Msgr. E. ROBERT ARTHUR, Chap.
Sisters 21
Residents 80
Apartments 8
Total Staff 140

FLORIDA

Daytona Beach
Diocese of Orlando

Casa San Pablo
401 N. Ridgewood Ave.
Daytona Beach, FL 32114
Tel: 904-253-2828; Fax: 904-253-0842
ROBERTA RYAN, Admin.
Total Staff 3
Total in Residence 65

Fort Myers
Diocese of Venice

Villa Francisco
2140 Cottage St.
Fort Myers, FL 33901
Tel: 941-332-3229
Very Rev. THOMAS M. ANGLIM, V.G., Pres.
Sr. MARIE VINCENT CHIARAVALLE, O.S.F., Admin.
Total in Residence 73
Total Staff 2

Jacksonville
Diocese of St. Augustine

All Saints Home
5888 Blanding Blvd.
Jacksonville, FL 32246
ALICE WILBUR, Admin.
Rev. B. BUTLER, Chap.
Physical Therapy, Speech Therapy & Occupational Therapy Available.
Total Staff 110
Total Assisted 120

St. Catherine Laboure Manor
1750 Stockton St.
Jacksonville, FL 32204
Tel: 904-308-4700
Long term health care Skilled Nursing Facility.
Beds 240
Sisters 3
Total Staff 239
Patients assisted annually 884

Melbourne
Diocese of Orlando

Ascension Manor
2960 Pineapple Ave.
Melbourne, FL 32935
Tel: 407-757-9828
JACKIE HAYNES, Mgr.
Total Staff 4
Total in Residence 85

Miami
Archdiocese of Miami

Camillus House, Inc.
P.O. Box 11829
Miami, FL 33101-1829
726 N.E. 1st Ave.
Miami, FL 33132
Tel: 305-374-1065; Fax: 305-372-1402
Bro. PAUL JOHNSON, B.G.S., Exec. Dir., Contact
Provides services to the homeless: emergency services, substance abuse rehabilitation, transitional housing
Camillus Health Concern, Inc.
P.O. Box 12408
Miami, FL 33101-2408
708 N.E. 1st Ave.
Miami, FL 33132
Tel: 305-577-4840; Fax: 305-372-0478
Provides medical and social services to the homeless
Charity Unlimited of Florida, Inc.
Provides buildings and grounds for charitable works.
Brothers of the Good Shepherd, Inc.
A religious congregation
Priests 1
Brothers 4
Total Staff 58
Grand Total Assisted 480,952

Gift of Hope, Missionaries of Charity
724 N.W. 17 St.
Miami, FL 33136
Tel: 305-326-0032
Sr. NIRMALA, Supr. Gen.
Women's and Children's Shelter
Total Women Assisted 375
Total Children Assisted 156
Soup Kitchen for Men
Total Assisted 46,783
Total Staff 6

Ocala
Diocese of Orlando

Trinity Villas I, Inc.
3728 N.E. 8th Pl.
Ocala, FL 34470-1093
Tel: 904-694-5507; Fax: 904-694-7434
DEBRA CRAWFORD, Mgr.
Total Staff 5
Total in Residence 98

Trinity Villas II, Inc.
3728 N.E. 8th Pl.
Ocala, FL 34470-1093
Tel: 904-694-5507; Fax: 904-694-7434
DEBRA CRAWFORD, Mgr.
Total Staff 3
Total in Residence 64

Orlando
Diocese of Orlando

Monsignor Bishop Manor Apts., Inc.
824 Borders Cir.
Orlando, FL 32808
Tel: 407-293-3339; Fax: 407-293-0085
E-mail: Bishopmanor@juno.com
Total Staff 6
Total in Residence 174

Ormond Beach
Diocese of Orlando

Prince of Peace Villas, Inc.
664 S. Nova Rd.
Ormond Beach, FL 32174
Tel: 904-673-5080; Fax: 904-673-2008
SUE TYSON, Mgr.
Total in Residence 70

Pensacola
Diocese of Pensacola-Tallahassee

Haven of Our Lady of Peace
5203 N. Ninth Ave.
Pensacola, FL 32504
Tel: 850-477-0531; Fax: 850-477-6782
Daughters of Charity of St. Vincent de Paul
Mr. J. BRENT WATSON, Admin.
Guests 89
Total Staff 92

Port Charlotte
Diocese of Venice

Bon Secours-St. Joseph Nursing Care Center, Inc.
2370 Harbor Blvd.
Port Charlotte, FL 33952
Tel: 941-624-5966; Fax: 941-624-3963
SCOTT MIXER, Admin.
Patients assisted annually 37,960
Total Staff 130

St. Charles Housing I, Inc.
(aka Villa San Carlos)
2550 Easy St.
Port Charlotte, FL 33952
Tel: 941-624-2266
LYNN STEPHENS, Pres.
Total in Residence 55
Total Staff 8

St. Charles Housing II, Inc.
(dba Villa San Carlos II)
22250 Vick St.
Port Charlotte, FL 33980
Tel: 941-624-4404; Fax: 941-624-5556
Sr. FRANCES KOWALSKI, O.S.F., Resident Mgr.
Ms. LYNN STEPHENS, Pres.
Total in Residence 55
Total Staff 9

Port Orange
Diocese of Orlando

Epiphany Manor
4792 S. Ridgewood Ave.
Port Orange, FL 32127
Total Staff 5
Total in Residence 72

Sarasota
Diocese of Venice

St. Martha's Housing II, Inc.
(Casa Santa Marta II)
800 N. Lemon Ave.
Sarasota, FL 34236
Tel: 941-365-7913; Fax: 941-365-8887

Rev. FAUSTO STAMPIGLIA, S.A.C., Pres.
CORA BEALS, Site Mgr.
Total in Residence 54
Total Staff 2

St. Martha's Housing, Inc.
(Casa Santa Marta)
1576 Eighth St.
Sarasota, FL 34236
Tel: 941-366-4448
Rev. FAUSTO STAMPIGLIA, S.A.C., Pres.
Total in Residence 82
Total Staff 5

Tallahassee
Diocese of Pensacola-Tallahassee

Casa Calderon, Inc.
800 W. Virginia St.
Tallahassee, FL 32304
Tel: 850-222-4026
E-mail: karkoel@aol.com.
Rev. Msgr. JAMES AMOS, V.G., Pres.
Mrs. CONNIE BROWN, Mgr.

West Palm Beach
Diocese of Palm Beach

Noreen McKeen Residence for Geriatric Care
315 Flagler Dr., S.
West Palm Beach, FL 33401
Tel: 561-655-8544
Sr. FIDELIS M. REGAN, O.Carm., Admin.
Rev. EUGENE BANNIN, S.J., Chap.

Winter Haven
Diocese of Orlando

Episcopal Catholic Apartments
500 Ave. L N.W.
Winter Haven, FL 33881
Tel: 941-299-4481
SAM P. PLAINES, JR., Admin.
Total Staff 15
Total in Residence 199

GEORGIA

Atlanta
Archdiocese of Atlanta

Our Lady of Perpetual Help Home
760 Washington St. S.W.
Atlanta, GA 30315
Tel: 404-688-9515
Sisters of St. Dominic
Legal Title: *Servants of Relief for Incurable Cancer*
Nursing Home for Free Care of Cancer Patients.
Sr. M. FLORENCE GILMORE, O.P., Supr.
Rev. RICHARD LOPEZ, Res. Chap.
Sisters 9
Bed Capacity 45
Patients assisted annually 202

Saint Joseph's Mercy Care Services
60 Eleventh St.
Atlanta, GA 30309-3970
Tel: 404-249-8600
Division of Saint Joseph's Health System. Operates Mercy Mobile Health Care (Atlanta, Georgia). Operates Mercy Senior Care (Rome, Georgia).
Total Staff 102
Sisters 5
Total Assisted 20,000

Rome
Archdiocese of Atlanta

Mercy Senior Care, Inc.
212 W. Third St.
Rome, GA 30165
Sr. ANGELA MARIE EBBERWEIN, R.S.M., Vice Pres.

Savannah
Diocese of Savannah

St. Mary's Home
E. Victory Dr., P.O. Box 3627, Sta. B
Savannah, GA 31404
Tel: 912-236-7164; Fax: 912-236-9699
Sisters of Mercy of the Americas
Sr. MARY ALVIN SEUBOTT, R.S.M., Admin
Sisters 3
Lay Staff 25
Residents 42

HAWAII

Kalaupapa, Molokai
Diocese of Honolulu

Kalaupapa Settlement
Kalaupapa, Molokai, HI 96742
Operated by the State Dept. of Health for treatment of Leprosy.
Mrs. FE AUSTRIA-SCHWIND, Nursing Supvr.
Dr. W. PHILIP JONES, Medical Dir. Settlement
Rev. NOBINCIO FERNANDEZ, SS.CC., Pastor
Franciscan Sisters of the Third Order 3
Bed Capacity 14
Patients assisted annually 56
CareHome nursing care/assistance and home visits annually 16,016

ILLINOIS

Alton
Diocese of Springfield in Illinois

Catholic Children's Home
1400 State St.
Alton, IL 62002
Tel: 618-465-3594; Fax: 618-465-4023
E-mail: cch1400@ezl.com
Mr. LAWRENCE DRURY, Dir.
STEVEN ROACH, Admin.
Children under care 135
Total Staff 43

Marian Heights Apartments
20 Marian Heights Dr.
Alton, IL 62002
Tel: 618-462-0363
Residence for the Elderly.
Sr. M. ANGELA, O.S.F., Supr.
SUSAN E. BARNETT, Operations Mgr.
Rev. JOHN SHEAHAN, Chap.
Sisters of St. Francis of the Martyr St. George 2
Residents 130
Total Staff 5

Aurora
Diocese of Rockford

Fox Knoll (Retirement Community)
421 N. Lake St.
Aurora, IL 60506
Tel: 630-844-0380
A Mercy Retirement Community.
Sr. DOROTHY BURNS, R.S.M., Exec. Dir.
Total Staff 50
Total in Residence 165

McAuley Manor
400 W. Sullivan Rd.
Aurora, IL 60506
Tel: 630-859-3700; Fax: 630-264-1862
Sisters of Mercy
Mrs. MARY A. BURNELL, Admin.
Total Staff 130
Bed Capacity 85
Total assisted 138

Bartlett
Archdiocese of Chicago

Bartlett Learning Center
801 W. Bartlett Rd.
Bartlett, IL 60103
Tel: 630-289-4221
Legal Title: *Bartlett Learning Center, Inc.*
RUSSELL E. CONRAD, Admin.
Sisters 7
Lay Staff 65
Students 120
Day school program for developmentally delayed and multiple handicapped individuals ages 3 to 21. Accept youth identified LD, BD, EMH, & TMH, Speech/Language Impaired, Autistic.
Sponsored by the Sisters of St. Joseph, Third Order of St. Francis.

Belleville
Diocese of Belleville

Charles and Bertha Hincke Residence for Priests and Sense Residence
2620 Lebanon Ave.
Belleville, IL 62221
Tel: 618-234-5722
Owned by Diocese of Belleville.
CAROL KIEFER, Admin.
Guests 15

Meredith Memorial Home
16 S. Illinois St.
Belleville, IL 62220
Tel: 618-233-8780; Fax: 618-233-9602
Owned by the Diocese of Belleville.
Mr. ROBERT L. WEBER, Admin.
Rev. Msgr. LEONARD A. BAUER, Chap., Tel: 618-234-2773
Guests 71

Our Lady of the Snows Apartment Community Retirement Home
726 Community Dr.
Belleville, IL 62223
Tel: 618-397-6700
D. ROBERT MCCARDLE, Exec. Vice Pres.
LUCY NILE, Dir. of Pastoral Care
Revs.:
LINUS J. GARITY (MIL)
ANDY CHALKEY, O.M.I.
ANDREW G. CHALKEY, O.M.I.
Guests 175

Bourbonnais
Diocese of Joliet in Illinois

Our Lady of Victory Nursing Home
20 Briarcliff Ln.
Bourbonnais, IL 60914
Tel: 815-937-2022; Fax: 815-936-3231
Servants of the Holy Heart of Mary
CHERYL GUILD, Admin.
Rev. FRANK CZERWIONKA, C.S.V., Chap.
Bed Capacity 107

Chicago
Archdiocese of Chicago

Big Sisters
721 N. LaSalle St., Room 434
Chicago, IL 60610
Tel: 312-751-0111
Dr. JOAN E. O'MALLEY, Pres.
Mrs. CHRISTINE BEDNAREK, Exec. Sec.
Patients assisted annually 200

Catholic Home Care
721 N. LaSalle St.
Chicago, IL 60610
Tel: 312-655-7415
Home health agency, Medicare certified, JCAHO accredited, providing health care to individuals in their homes in Cook and Lake Counties.
ANNE DEMKE, Exec. Dir.

Catholic Home Care Home Services
721 N. LaSalle St.
Chicago, IL 60610
Tel: 312-655-7415
Home health agency, private duty, JCAHO accredited
ANNE DEMKE, Exec. Dir.

Cortland Manor Retirement Home
1900 N. Karlov
Chicago, IL 60639
Tel: 773-235-3670
Catholic Charities Housing Development Corporation.
MAUREEN SCHOLLE, Admin.
Capacity 48

**Dehon House*
6451 N. Greenview
Chicago, IL 60626
Tel: 773-465-1526; Fax: 773-465-9422
Sr. LOIS MCGOVERN, O.P., Exec. Dir.
A collaborative ministry of the Sacred Heart Fathers and Brothers, Dominican Sisters of St. Catherine (KY), School Sisters of St. Francis and Felician Sisters, Chicago Province.
Shelter for homeless families
Capacity: 9 Families

House of the Good Shepherd
1114 W. Grace St.
Chicago, IL 60613
Tel: 773-935-3434; Fax: 773-935-3523
Legal Title: *House of the Good Shepherd*
Sisters of The Good Shepherd
Sisters 7
Part time social workers 6
Capacity: 14 Families
Abused Women with children.

Jugan Terrace
2300 N. Racine
Chicago, IL 60614
Tel: 773-935-9600; Fax: 773-935-4291
Legal Title: *Little Sisters of the Poor, North Side Chicago, Inc., (HUD subsidized)*
Sr. MARCEL JOSEPH, L.S.P., Admin.
Senior Housing Apts. 50

Little Sisters of the Poor Center for the Aging
2325 N. Lakewood Ave.
Chicago, IL 60614
Tel: 773-935-9600; Fax: 773-935-9614
Legal Title: *Little Sisters of the Poor of Chicago, Inc.*
Sr. MARIA CHRISTINE, L.S.P., Admin. & Supr.

Rev. WALTER HUPPENBAUER, Chap.
Sisters 15
Residents 96
Intermediate and skilled care facility.

Misericordia Home South
2916 W. 47th St.
Chicago, IL 60632
Tel: 773-254-9595
Sr. ROSEMARY R.S.M., Dir.
Sisters of Mercy 9
Patients assisted annually 110
Respite Beds 2
Handicapped children under 22 years of age: Bed Capacity for Children 110

Misericordia / Heart of Mercy Center
6300 N. Ridge
Chicago, IL 60660
Tel: 773-973-6300
Children and young adults with developmental disabilities.
Sr. ROSEMARY CONNELLY, R.S.M., Dir.
Sisters 25
Residents 548

Resurrection Retirement Community
7262 W. Peterson Ave.
Chicago, IL 60631
Tel: 773-792-7930
Division of Resurrection Health Care Corporation.
Sr. MARY PAUL SCHULTZ, C.R.. Exec. Dir.
Apartments 472

St. Joseph Home of Chicago, Inc.
2650 N. Ridgeway Ave.
Chicago, IL 60647
Tel: 773-235-8600; Fax: 773-235-2933
Legal Title: *St. Joseph Home of Chicago, Inc.*
Franciscan Sisters of Chicago
JANE D. WINTER, Admin.
Rev. CHARLES MROWINSKI, C.R., Chap.
Sisters 6
Licensed Beds 173

St. Joseph's Carondelet Child Center
739 E. 35th St.
Chicago, IL 60616
Tel: 773-624-7443; Fax: 773-624-7676
Legal Title: *St. Joseph's Carondelet Child Center*
Treatment, rehabilitation and education of the dependent emotionally disturbed children and youth.
Sisters of St. Joseph of Carondelet
Mr. JAMES B. MCLAUGHLIN, Pres. & CEO
Rev. CHARLES T. RUBEY, Chap.
Sisters 2
Children 92

St. Mary of Providence
4200 N. Austin Ave.
Chicago, IL 60634
Tel: 773-545-8300; Fax: 773-545-8035
Operated by the Daughters of St. Mary of Providence.
Sr. NANCY MCLENNON, Admin.
Sr. PATRICIA MCCAFFERTY, Dir.
Rev. SALVATORE J. OGNIBENE, Chap.
Sisters 13
Staff 142
Students 70
Adults 96
Legal Title: *Daughters of St. Mary of Providence*
Education and residential care of developmentally disabled boys, girls and young adults.

Clifton
Diocese of Joliet in Illinois

Merkle-Knipprath Countryside Home
1190 E. 2900 N Rd.
Clifton, IL 60927-9705
Tel: 815-694-2306
Bro. DAMIEN DEBRAEKELEER, O.S.F., Admin.
Religious 4
Total in Nursing Care 100
Apartment Living 30
Apartment Community and Nursing Center.

Crete
Diocese of Joliet in Illinois

St. James Manor
1251 Richton Rd.
Crete, IL 60417
Tel: 708-672-6700
DIANNE STRUTYNSKI, Admin.
Beds 110
Total Assisted Annually 32,832
Total Staff 109
Care of the Elderly.

Darien
Diocese of Joliet in Illinois

Carmelite Carefree Retirement Village
8419 Bailey Rd.
Darien, IL 60561-5361
Tel: 630-960-4060
Rev. RAYMOND J. CLENNON, O.Carm., Dir.
Residents 98

Des Plaines
Archdiocese of Chicago

Holy Family Health Center
2380 Dempster
Des Plaines, IL 60016
Tel: 847-296-3335
Sr. M. ELIZABETH, C.S.F.N., Admin.
Licensed Bed Capacity 362
Intermediate and skilled nursing care facility.
Sponsored by the Sisters of the Holy Family of Nazareth

Nazarethville
300 N. River Rd.
Des Plaines, IL 60016
Tel: 847-297-5900
Sr. M. AMATA SWEENEY, C.S.F.N., Admin.
Total under care 83
Sponsored by the Sisters of the Holy Family of Nazareth

Freeport
Diocese of Rockford

St. Joseph Adult Day Care Center
659 E. Jefferson St.
Freeport, IL 61032
Tel: 815-232-6181; Fax: 815-232-6143
Mrs. KELLY SCHLEICH, Prog. Dir.
Rev. CLARENCE J. THENNES, Chap.
Sisters 1

St. Joseph Center
659 E. Jefferson St.
Freeport, IL 61032
Tel: 815-232-6181; Fax: 815-232-6143
Under auspices of Provena Senior Services.
Mr. RICHARD RIMKUS, Admin.
Rev. CLARENCE J. THENNES, Chap.
Sisters 1
Aged Residents 120

Glenview
Archdiocese of Chicago

Maryhaven Inc.
1700 East Lake Ave.
Glenview, IL 60025
Tel: 847-729-1300; Fax: 847-729-9202
Legal Title: *Maryhaven Inc.*
Home for Aged, intermediate and skilled care facilities, Medicare, Therapy.
Mr. PAUL M. ASSELIN, Admin.
Rev. JOHN E. FLAVIN, Pres.
Capacity 138

Homewood
Archdiocese of Chicago

Mercy Health Care and Rehabilitation Center
19000 S. Halsted St.
Homewood, IL 60430
Tel: 708-957-9200; Fax: 708-799-4787
Affiliate of Mercy Hospital and Medical Center.
Sponsored by the Religious Sisters of Mercy
JANICE L. PODWIKA, Admin.
Pastoral Care:
Sr. BERNADETTE MADDEN, R.S.M.
Sr. JOANNE VALLERO, C.S.J.
Bed Capacity 259
Total under care 245

Joliet
Diocese of Joliet in Illinois

Guardian Angel Home
1550 Plainfield Ave.
Joliet, IL 60435
Tel: 815-729-0930; Fax: 815-744-6087
E-mail: sas726@aol.com
Sponsored by the Sisters of St. Francis of Mary Immaculate.
Child and family welfare agency: residential treatment, therapeutic school, foster care, domestic violence shelter, child abuse prevention center, and counselling.

Our Lady of Angels Retirement Home
1201 Wyoming
Joliet, IL 60435
Tel: 815-725-6631
Sisters of St. Francis of Mary Immaculate
Sr. MARGARET ROSE SCZESNIAH, Local Coord.
In res.,
Rev. PATRICK GLEESON, Chap.
Sr. PHYLLIS PITZ, Admin.
Sister Staff 15
Lay Employees 173
Retired Sisters 82
Residents 103

St. Elizabeth Home
704 W. Marion St.
Joliet, IL 60436
Tel: 815-727-0125
Sr. ELLEN THOMAS, R.C., Senior Prog. Dir.
In Residence 11

Villa Franciscan, Franciscan Sisters Health Care Corp.
210 N. Springfield
Joliet, IL 60435
Tel: 815-725-3400; Fax: 815-725-2160
DIANE MIKES, Admin.
Bed Capacity 176
Extended, Intermediate, and Skilled Care, Respite Care, Alzheimer Unit.

Justice
Archdiocese of Chicago

Rosary Hill Home
9000 W. 81st St.
Justice, IL 60458
Tel: 708-458-3040
Operated by the Dominican Sisters of Chicago
Sr. M. NATALIE, O.P., Supr.
Rev. JOSEPH MIKA, O.F.M., Chap.
Sisters 9
Bed Capacity 48
Number under care 48

Lacon
Diocese of Peoria

St. Joseph's Nursing Home
801 Ninth St.
Lacon, IL 61540
Tel: 309-246-2175
Daughters of St. Francis of Assisi
Sr. CATHERINE Admin.
Rev. MICHAEL MENNER, Chap.
Sisters 17
Bed Capacity 93
Total Staff 100

Lake Zurich
Archdiocese of Chicago

Mt. St. Joseph Home
24955 North Hwy. 12
Lake Zurich, IL 60047
Tel: 847-438-5050; Fax: 847-438-1561
Intermediate care for developmentally developed women.
Operated by the Daughters of St. Mary of Providence.
Sr. JANET KOSMAN, Admin.
Rev. ALOYSIUS ROMANSKI, O.F.M.Conv.
Sisters 9
Lay Assistants 200
Residents 130

Lemont
Archdiocese of Chicago

Alvernia Manor
13950 Main St.
Lemont, IL 60439
Tel: 708-257-7721
Sr. GEORGINE HROMA, O.S.F., Admin.
Sisters of St. Francis of Christ King 7
Guests 50

Holy Family Villa
12375 McCarthy Rd.
Lemont, IL 60439
Sisters of St. Casimir
ROBERTA MAGURANY, Admin.
Sisters 3
Residents 99

Mother Theresa Home
1270 Franciscan Dr.
Lemont, IL 60439
Tel: 708-257-5801; Fax: 708-257-1328
Conducted by the Franciscan Sisters of Chicago.
THERESA D. KOLAZ, Admin.
Sisters 5

Residents 150

Lisle
Diocese of Joliet in Illinois

Queen of Peace Center
1910 Maple Ave.
Lisle, IL 60532
Tel: 630-852-5360
Retirement home.
Mr. GLENN TREMBLEY, Admin.
Lay Staff 7
Residents 32

Momence
Diocese of Joliet in Illinois

Good Shepherd Manor
P.O. Box 260
Momence, IL 60954
Tel: 815-472-6492; Fax: 815-472-2160
Adult Male DD-MR.
Dr. JAMES CZERWIONKA, Pres. & CEO
DORIS WILLIAMSON, Admin.
Bro. ALPHONSUS BROWN, B.G.S., Asst. Admin.
Rev. ARTHUR LEMRISE, C.S.V., Chap.
Brothers of the Good Shepherd 3
Bed Capacity 120
Permanent Residents 120

Naperville
Diocese of Joliet in Illinois

St. John Vianney Villa
1464 Green Trails Dr.
Naperville, IL 60540-8359
Tel: 630-983-0533
Retirement home for priests.
Revs.:
PATRICK MORAN
WILLIAM RYAN
EUGENE DOHERTY
THOMAS CORLEY
THOMAS FLEMING
RAYMOND GRASSO
Residents 6

St. Patrick's Residence
1400 Brookdale Rd.
Naperville, IL 60563-2125
Tel: 630-416-6565
Sr. M. ANTHONY DELOURDES, O.Carm., Admin.
Rev. PHILIP DEDERA, Chap.
Carmelite Sisters 10
Beds 210
Residents 210
Total Assisted 288
Total Staff 222

Niles
Archdiocese of Chicago

St. Andrew Home for the Aged
7000 N. Newark Ave.
Niles, IL 60714-4497
Tel: 847-647-8332
Felician Sisters
JUDY PITZEK, Admin.
Sr. MARY AGNES, C.S.S.F., Supr.
Sisters 13
Number under care 177

St. Benedict Home for the Aged
6930 W. Touhy Ave.
Niles, IL 60714
Tel: 847-647-0003
Legal Title: *St. Benedict Home for the Aged (Catholic Charities of Chicago)*
Sisters of St. Benedict (Lisle, IL)
ARLENE H. WAJDA, Admin.
Rev. EDWARD JARZYNSKI, Chap.
Priests 14
Sisters 5
Residents 129

Northlake
Archdiocese of Chicago

Villa Scalabrini Home for the Aged
480 N. Wolf Rd.
Northlake, IL 60164-1667
Tel: 708-562-0040
Missionaries of St. Charles Scalabrinians
VIRGINIA BARRY, Admin.
Rev. JOHN DIVITO, C.S., Chap.
Sisters 10
Residents 265

Oak Brook
Diocese of Joliet in Illinois

Mayslake Village
1801 35th St.
Oak Brook, IL 60521
Tel: 630-654-3280
E-mail: mayslakvlg@aol.com
Including Mayslake Villas, Mayslake Manor, and Cloisters Courts.
Senior Citizen Retirement Community.
Rev. LARRY DREFFEIN, O.F.M., Pres.
Mr. MICHAEL A. FRIGO, Admin.
Units 630
Residents 750
Total Staff 45

Oak Park
Archdiocese of Chicago

Ephpheta Center and Hearing Conservation Service
119 S. Harvey Ave.
Oak Park, IL 60302
Legal Title: *Ephpheta Center and Hearing Conservation Service*
Under the direction of the Daughters of the Heart of Mary.
Sr. ANITA BAIRD, D.H.M., Supr.
Sisters 8

Olympia Fields
Archdiocese of Chicago

Mercy Residence at Tolentine Center
20300 Governors Hwy.
Olympia Fields, IL 60461
Tel: 708-748-9500; Fax: 708-481-2090
Sr. ARMELLA GUINEY, R.S.M., Admin.
Sr. CONLETH FOLEY, R.S.M., Asst. Admin.
Sisters 4
Residents 48
Senior citizen housing.

Palatine
Archdiocese of Chicago

St. Joseph's Home for the Elderly
80 W. Northwest Hwy.
Palatine, IL 60067
Tel: 847-358-5700; Fax: 847-358-5763
Legal Title: *Little Sisters of the Poor, Palatine, Inc.*
Operated by the Little Sisters of the Poor
Sr. MARY ANTHONY POWER, Supr.
Rev. ROBERT F. PIEPER, O.P.
Sisters 16
Guests 61

Palos Park
Archdiocese of Chicago

St. Coletta's of Illinois
123rd and Wolf Rd.
Palos Park, IL 60464
Tel: 708-448-6520
Sponsored by the Sisters of St. Francis of Assisi. Residential care, education, job training & job placement for developmentally disabled children and adults.
Mr. WAYNE A. KOTTMEYER, Exec. Dir.
Residents 138
Students 100
Job Training Clients 165
Infants & Toddlers 18
Divisions:
Lt. Joseph P. Kennedy Jr. School, Palos Hills
Kennedy Job Training Center, Bedford Park
St. Coletta's of Illinois Foundation Affiliate

Park Ridge
Archdiocese of Chicago

Resurrection Nursing and Rehabilitation Center
1001 N. Greenwood
Park Ridge, IL 60068
Tel: 708-692-5600; Fax: 708-692-2305
Legal Title: *Resurrection Health Care*
PATRICIA TIERNAN, Admin.
Skilled Care Bed Capacity 295

Peoria
Diocese of Peoria

Cabrini Hall Maternity Home
2900 W. Heading Ave.
Peoria, IL 61604
Tel: 309-671-5743
For Care of Unwed Mothers.
Staff 12
Capacity 10
Served 29

St. Augustine Manor
1301 N.E. Glendale Ave.
Peoria, IL 61603
Tel: 309-674-7069
Mr. DICK LANGJAHR, Admin.
In res.,
Most Rev. EDWARD W. O'ROURKE, D.D.
Rev. Msgr. BERNARD A. RENDER
Revs.:
E. C. BLOUGH
GEORGE RAYMOND SPRAGUE
MARIO W. SHAW
Residents 80
Total Staff 30

St. Joseph's Home of Peoria
2223 W. Heading Ave.
Peoria, IL 61604
Tel: 309-673-7425
Sisters of St. Francis of the Immaculate Conception
Co-Administrators:
Sr. MARY PAUL MAZZORANA
Sr. MARY DRIES
Rev. RICHARD SOSEMAN, Chap.
In res.,
Rev. Msgr. GEORGE A. CARTON
Sisters 10
Residents 175
Retired Sisters 11
Total Assisted 57
Total Staff 109

Red Bud
Diocese of Belleville

Maria Care
350 W. South First St.
Red Bud, IL 62278
Tel: 618-282-3891
Under the Co-sponsorship of the Adorers of the Blood of Christ & Sisters of Mercy.
BARBARA WAGNER, Admin.
MARY SALOIS, Dir. of Pastoral Care
Guests 115

Rock Island
Diocese of Peoria

St. Anthony's Continuing Care Center
767 30th St.
Rock Island, IL 61201
Tel: 309-788-7631
Rev. RAPHAEL FABISH
Sisters 3
Beds 145
Total Assisted 110
Total Staff 108

Rockford
Diocese of Rockford

Cor Mariae Center
3330 Maria Linden Dr.
Rockford, IL 61114
Servant Cor owned and operated retirement center for religious and laypersons assisted living/nursing home.
Rev. MELVYN J. VLASZ, Sacramental Min.
Ms. CHERYL STOUT, Admin.
Number Assisted 55

St. Anne Center
4405 Highcrest Rd.
Rockford, IL 61107
Tel: 815-229-1999
Servants of the Holy Heart of Mary
Ms. JUDY K. LARSON, Admin.
Total Staff 165
Bed Capacity 179

St. Anne Place
4444 Brendenwood Rd.
Rockford, IL 61107
Tel: 815-399-6167
Senior Retirement Community.
ERIC VANDENBERGH, Admin.
Total Staff 35
Total Residences
Total in Residence 120

Vianney Oaks
7712 E. McGregor Rd.
Rockford, IL 61102
Tel: 815-965-0910
Office:
1245 N. Court St., P.O. Box 7044
Rockford, IL 61126
Tel: 815-962-3709
A retirement home for priests conducted by the Diocese of Rockford.
Total Full-time Staff 1
Total in Residence 6

Springfield
Diocese of Springfield in Illinois

Brother James Court
2500 St. James Rd.

Springfield, IL 62707
Tel: 217-544-4876
E-mail: bjcicfdd@aol.com
Residence for Mentally Retarded Male Adults.
Franciscan Brothers of the Holy Cross
Bro. RAPHAEL KREIKEMEIER, F.F.S.C., Exec. Dir.
Franciscan Brothers of the Holy Cross 3
Bed Capacity 93
Residents 93

Pope John Paul Apartments
1 Pope John Paul Plaza
Springfield, IL 62703
Tel: 217-528-1771; Fax: 217-528-5110
Residence for the Elderly.
Sr. M. BARBARA, O.S.F., Supr.
NORMA JEAN CAPRANICA, Proj. Mgr.
Mr. THOMAS E. REISER, Admin.
Sisters of St. Francis of the Martyr St. George 2
Residents 160
Staff 8

St. Joseph's Home
3306 S. Sixth St. Rd.
Springfield, IL 62703
Tel: 217-529-5596
Residence for the Elderly.
Sr. JUDITH MORRIS, O.S.F., Admin.
Sr. M. PATRICIA MASTERSON, O.S.F., Asst. Admin.
Rev. Msgr. JOHN W. BRETZ, Chap.
Sisters of St. Francis of the Immaculate Conception 5
Residents 110
Staff 95

St. Monica's Center
109 E. Lawrence Ave.
Springfield, IL 62704
Tel: 217-523-7922; Fax: 217-525-8241
Maternity Home For Care of Unwed Mothers & Residential Care for Adolescent Women.
JUDITH A. COMERIO, Admin.
Bed Capacity 17
Patients assisted annually 49
Staff 19

West Peoria
Diocese of Peoria

Catholic Social Service Foster Care Program
2900 W. Heading Ave.
West Peoria, IL 61604
Tel: 309-671-5750; Fax: 309-671-1046
Ms. PEGGY A. ARIZZI, Exec. Dir.
Mr. JEFF TURNBULL, Assoc. Dir.
Ms. TRISH FOX, Asst. Dir. for Child Welfare
Clients placed in Foster Care during year 1,300
Total in Residence 1,100
Total Staff 119

Guardian Angel Home
2900 W. Heading Ave.
West Peoria, IL 309-671-5760
PEGGY ARIZZI, Exec. Dir.
Treatment for Abused and Neglected Youth.
Staff 45
Capacity 22
Served 58

St. Anne Residential Treatment Center
2900 W. Heading Ave.
West Peoria, IL 61604
Tel: 309-671-5755
PEGGY ARIZZI, Exec. Dir.
For Single Mothers and Infants/Children.
Staff 35
Capacity 16
Served:
Mothers 32
Children 29

Wheaton
Diocese of Joliet in Illinois

Marian Park, Inc.
26 W. 171 Roosevelt Rd., P.O. Box 667
Wheaton, IL 60187
Tel: 630-665-9100
Franciscan Sisters, Daughters of the Sacred Hearts of Jesus and Mary, (Wheaton, IL)
RAY WOJCIK, Pres. Housing Ministry
Apartments 208
Senior Citizen Residents 117
Low Income Family Units 91
Residents 470

Wheeling
Archdiocese of Chicago

Addolorata Villa
555 McHenry Rd.
Wheeling, IL 60090
Tel: 847-537-2900; Fax: 847-215-5805
Sponsored by the Franciscan Sisters of Chicago
Home for the aged and independent living apartments.
Mr. GERALD B. KINNEY, CFACHCA, CEO & Pres.
Sr. PATRICIA A. FERGUSON, O.S.M., Asst. Admin.
Ms. NANCY LABIAK, Dir. Mission Services
Mrs. BETTY SKONIECZNY, Pastoral Care Coord.
Rev. MARION J. SNIEG, Chap.
Servants of Mary 20
Skilled 80
Intermediate 10
Sheltered 45
Independent Living Apartments 100

INDIANA

Avilla
Diocese of Fort Wayne - South Bend

LaVerna Terrace Apartments
517 N. Main St.
Avilla, IN 46710
Tel: 219-897-2093
Conducted by Franciscan Sisters Health Care Corp.
SHARON MASEAR, Mgr.
In res.,
Rev. DANIEL LEEUW Tel: 219-897-3922
Total Staff 2
Apartments 51
Total Assisted 51

Sacred Heart Home
515 N. Main St.
Avilla, IN 46710-9602
Tel: 219-897-2841
Legal Title: *Franciscan Sisters Health Care Corporation*
NANCY K. SCHENKEL, Admin.
Sr. MARY WILLIAM HUGHES, O.S.F., Religious Supr.
Rev. DANIEL LEEUW, Chap.
Staff 160
Total assisted 133

Beech Grove
Archdiocese of Indianapolis

St. Paul Hermitage
501 N. 17th Ave.
Beech Grove, IN 46107
Tel: 317-786-2261
Sisters of St. Benedict of Beech Grove, IN, Inc.
Sr. PATRICIA DEDE, O.S.B., Admin.
Rev. RALPH LYNCH, O.S.B.
Sisters 10
Total Staff 95
Residents 100

Crown Point
Diocese of Gary

St. Anthony Home, Inc.
203 Franciscan Dr.
Crown Point, IN 46307-4824
Tel: 219-757-6281
STEPHEN J. BARDOCZI, Pres.
Rev. MYRON LOWISZ, O.F.M., Pastoral Care
Priests 1
Franciscan Sisters of Chicago 22
Total Staff 620
Residents 229

Delphi
Diocese of Lafayette in Indiana

St. Elizabeth Healthcare Center
701 Armory Rd.
Delphi, IN 46923
Fax: 765-564-6384
Rev. RICHARD W. PUETZ, Chap.
Managed by St. Elizabeth Hospital, Lafayette. Owned by Sisters of St. Francis Health Services, Inc.
Total Assisted 270
Total Staff 92

East Chicago
Diocese of Gary

Carmelite Home for Girls
4840 Grasselli Ave.
East Chicago, IN 46312
Tel: 219-397-1085; Fax: 219-392-3574
Sr. MARIA GIUSEPPE MOXLEY, Supr.
Carmelite Sisters of the Divine Heart of Jesus 4
Total Staff 30
Girls 61

Evansville
Diocese of Evansville

The Regina Continuing Care Center
3900 Washington Ave.
Evansville, IN 47714
Tel: 812-485-4226
Mrs. ANN M. MORROW, Admin.
Beds 128
Nursing Patients 128

St. John's Home for the Aged
1236 Lincoln Ave.
Evansville, IN 47714
Tel: 812-464-3607
Sr. MARY MICHAEL NICKLES, L.S.P., Supr.
Rev. Msgr. CLARENCE LINDAUER, Chap.
Little Sisters of the Poor 12
Residents 70

Seton Residence
9200 New Harmony Rd.
Evansville, IN 47720-8918
Tel: 812-963-7600
Home for the Senior Sisters of the Daughters of Charity of St. Vincent de Paul.
Sr. ANTHONY PRUGGER, Admin.
Sr. GERTRUDE BASTNAGEL, Supr.
Rev. GLENNON E. FIGGE, C.M., Chap.
Senior Sisters 51

Fort Wayne
Diocese of Fort Wayne - South Bend

Saint Anne Home & Retirement Community
1900 Randallia Dr.
Fort Wayne, IN 46805
Tel: 219-484-5555
A Service of the Fort Wayne-South Bend Diocese, Inc.
MARY E. HAVERSTICK, Admin.
Rev. FRANK KRONEWITTER, Chap.
In res.,
Rev. LOUIS ZENZ
Staff 185
Residents 204

St. Anne Home of the Diocese of Fort Wayne - South Bend
1900 Randalia Dr.
Fort Wayne, IN 46805
Tel: 219-422-4611
Rev. Msgr. JAMES J. WOLF, Contact Person
Purpose: Nursing Home and Independent Living Units.

Hammond
Diocese of Gary

Albertine Home
1501 Hoffman St.
Hammond, IN 46327
Tel: 219-937-0575
Sr. LORETTA SOJA, Dir.
Albertine Sisters 11
Guests 35

Carmelite Home for Boys
4007 Sheffield Ave.
Hammond, IN 46327
Tel: 219-931-6451
Sr. M. LUCY CarmelD.C.J., Supr.
Sr. M. FRANCIS XAVIER, Carmel.D.C.J., Admin.
Carmelite Sisters of the Divine Heart of Jesus 4
Total Staff 47
Boys (4-18 yrs.) 62

Indianapolis
Archdiocese of Indianapolis

St. Augustine Home, Little Sisters of the Poor
2345 W. 86th St.
Indianapolis, IN 46260
Tel: 317-872-6420
Sr. CHARLES MARIE, S.S.P.
Rev. ADRIAN FIGUEROLA, Chap.
Sisters 13
Total Staff 93
Residents 100

Jasper
Diocese of Evansville

Providence Home, Nursing Home for the Needy
520 W. Ninth St.
Jasper, IN 47546
Tel: 812-482-6603
Conducted by the Sons of Divine Providence.
Revs.:
THADDEUS J. SZTUCZKO, F.D.P., Admin.

Angelo Quadrini, Supr.
Priests 4
Residents 60

Lafayette
Diocese of Lafayette in Indiana

St. Anthony Health Care
1205 N. 14th St.
Lafayette, IN 47904
Tel: 765-423-4861; Fax: 765-742-8790
Rev. John A. Bach, Chap.
Total Staff 110
Bed Capacity 120
Residents 115

New Albany
Archdiocese of Indianapolis

Mercy Long Term Care Initiatives dba Providence Retirement Home
703 E. Spring St.
New Albany, IN 47150
Tel: 812-945-5221; Fax: 812-945-2614
Sisters of Mercy
Jane F. Cook, Admin.
Priests 1
Sisters 4
Total Staff 62
Residents 103

Notre Dame
Diocese of Fort Wayne - South Bend

University Health Services
Notre Dame, IN 46556
Tel: 219-239-8013
Rev. Joseph Fey, C.S.C., Health Center Chap.
Total Staff 47
Patients assisted annually 20,500

San Pierre
Diocese of Gary

Holy Cross Care Services dba Little Company of Mary Health Facility, Inc.
7520 S. U.S. Hwy. 421
San Pierre, IN 46374-4275
Tel: 219-828-4111; Fax: 219-828-4172
Comprehensive Nursing Care Home.
Mr. Steven J. Minniear, Admin.
Edward B. Newman, Pres. & CEO
Rev. William J. Spranger, Chap.
Priests 1
Beds 200
Patients assisted annually 214

Schererville
Diocese of Gary

Hoosier Boys' Town
7403 Cline Ave.
Schererville, IN 46375
Tel: 219-838-7723
A residential care facility for abused, neglected boys from 10-18 years of age.
Boys 68

Terre Haute
Archdiocese of Indianapolis

Gibault School for Boys
6301 S. U.S. Hwy. 41, P.O. Box 2316
Terre Haute, IN 47802-0316
Tel: 812-299-1156
School for delinquent boys, sponsored by the Knights of Columbus of Indiana.
Mr. Daniel P. McGinley, A.C.S.W., Exec. Dir.
Boys 190
Total Staff 220

IOWA

Burlington
Diocese of Davenport

St. Francis Continuation Care and Nursing Home
Burlington, IA 52601
Tel: 319-752-4564
Sr. Bernadette Duman, C.D.P., Admin.
Sr. M. Dolorita, O.S.F., Supr.
Rev. Thomas J. Reilman, Chap.
Sisters of the Third Order of St. Francis 3
Bed Capacity 88
Independent Living Unit 12
Patients assisted annually 170

**Young House Family Services, Inc.*
Central Office, 724 N. 3rd St., P.O. Box 845
Burlington, IA 52601
Tel: 319-752-4000; Fax: 319-752-6933
Jack Escorcia, Admin.
Lynnda Stogdill, Asst. Admin./Controller
Woodlands Treatment Center
Sullivan Slough Rd.
Burlington, IA 52601
Tel: 319-753-0700
John Korb, Coord.

**Christamore House Incorporated*
701 Broadway St.
Burlington, IA 52601
Tel: 319-385-3330
Jon Coon, Coord.
Total Assisted 45
Total Staff 30

Carroll
Diocese of Sioux City

St. Anthony Nursing Home
406 E. Anthony St.
Carroll, IA 51401
Tel: 712-792-3581
Gary Riedmann, Admin.
Rev. Robert L. Leiting, Chap.
Total Staff 45
Residents 79

Cedar Rapids
Archdiocese of Dubuque

Hallmar-Mercy Medical Center
701 Tenth St., S.E.
Cedar Rapids, IA 52403
Sisters of Mercy
Cedar Rapids Regional, owned and operated by Mercy Medical Center. Home for Aged.
Mr. A. James Tuiker, CEO
Total Assisted 34
Total Staff 30
Residents 59

Clinton
Diocese of Davenport

The Alverno Health Care Facility
Clinton, IA 52732
Tel: 319-242-1521; Fax: 319-243-3016
E-mail: ruthcox@sanasys.com
Sr. Ruth A. Cox, O.S.F., Pres. & CEO
Rev. Thomas H. Mohr
Sisters of St. Francis, Clinton, IA 3
Bed Capacity 138
Total Assisted 219
Total Staff 185

Arch Office
Box 278
Clinton, IA 52733-0278
Tel: 319-243-9035
E-mail: larchia@clinton.net
Arch I
402 S. Fourth St.
Clinton, IA 52732
Tel: 319-243-3980
Arch II
734 Fifth Ave. S.
Clinton, IA 52732
Tel: 319-242-5082
Arch III
505 7th Ave. S.
Clinton, IA 52732
Tel: 319-242-8740
Total Assisted 18
Total Staff 10

Cresco
Archdiocese of Dubuque

Elder Hospitality of Iowa, Inc.
Village Apartments, 301 First Ave.
Cresco, IA 52136
Tel: 319-547-3325
Mailing Address:—c/o Archdiocese of Dubuque
P.O. Box 479
Dubuque, IA 52004-0479
Bonnie Felten, Housing Coord.
Richard Berendes, Admin./Extended Care
Franciscan Sisters of Perpetual Adoration, La Crosse, Wisconsin and Mayo Foundation, Rochester, MN
Elderly housing for low income. HUD section 202.
Units 12
Elder Hospitality of Iowa II, Inc.
Village Apartments, 509 Goose Island Dr.
Decorah, IA 52101
Tel: 319-382-2863
Mailing Address:—c/o Archdiocese of Dubuque
P.O. Box 479
Dubuque, IA 52004-0479
Bonnie Felten, Housing Coord.
Richard Berendes, Admin./Extended Care
Elderly housing for low income. HUD section 202.
Units 24

Davenport
Diocese of Davenport

Kahl Home for the Aged and Infirm
1101 W. Ninth St.
Davenport, IA 52804
Tel: 319-324-1621
Carmelite Sisters for the Aged and Infirm
Sr. M. Paul Anthony, O.Carm., Supr. & Admin.
In res.,
Revs.:
Pasquale Ferrara
Joseph A. Hratz
Herman A. Strub
Richard J. Von Ah
Sisters 6
Beds 134
Total Assisted 190
Total Staff 140

Des Moines
Diocese of Des Moines

House of Mercy
1409 Clark St.
Des Moines, IA 50314-1964
Tel: 515-362-6500; Fax: 515-243-0318
Mr. Todd Beveridge, Dir.

Dubuque
Archdiocese of Dubuque

Holy Family Hall Infirmary
3340 Windsor Ave.
Dubuque, IA 52001-1300
Tel: 319-583-9786; Fax: 319-583-3250
E-mail: mtstfran@mwci.net
Web Site: www.osfdbg.org
Sisters of St. Francis, Dubuque
Rev. William E. Wilkie, Chap.
Sr. Marge Staudt, O.S.F., Dir. Sister Support Svcs.
Bed Capacity 98
Professed Sisters 89
Patients assisted annually 145

Marian Hall Infirmary
1050 Carmel Dr.
Dubuque, IA 52003
Tel: 319-556-5474
Sr. Mary Agnes O'Connor, B.V.M., Admin.
Rev. Msgr. Robert R. Vogl, Chap.
Professed Sisters 133
Bed Capacity 133

Padre Pio Health Care Center, Inc. dba Stonehill Care Center
3485 Windsor Ave.
Dubuque, IA 52001-1312
Tel: 319-557-7180; Fax: 319-557-8934
John Schmidt, Pres.
Sr. Dolores Ullrich, O.S.F., Admin.
Sisters of St. Francis of the Holy Family 10
Staff 250
Residents 248
Stonehill Benevolent Foundation
George Freund, Pres. Stonehill Benevolent Foundation Board
Sponsored by Sisters of St. Francis of the Holy Family.

St. Dominic Villa
Cardiff St. and Mazzuchelli Heights
Dubuque, IA 52001-7399
Community infirmary and staff residence.
Dominican Sisters (Sinsinawa, WI)
Sr. Margaret Mary O'Neill, O.P., Prioress
Sr. Marian De Grood, O.P., Asst. Prioress
Sr. Maryann Tranel, O.P., Admin.
Part-time Chaplains:
Revs.:
Brian Bricker, O.P.
Joseph Fogarty, O.P.
Sisters 15
Lay Staff 126
Patients assisted annually 110

Villa Raphael
1235 Mt. Loretta Ave.
Dubuque, IA 52003
Tel: 319-583-4904
Administered by the Archdiocese of Dubuque.
Sr. Mary Pierre Kollasch, P.B.V.M., Coord.
Accommodations for 16 priests.
Total Staff 6

Total in Residence 14

Dyersville
Archdiocese of Dubuque

Mercy Health Center St. Mary's Unit-Oakcrest Manor
(Div. of Mercy Health Services)
1111 Third St., S.W.
Dyersville, IA 52040
Tel: 319-875-7101; Fax: 319-875-2957
RUSSELL KNIGHT, Pres.
Bed Capacity 40
Total Staff 26
Patients assisted annually 60

Fort Dodge
Diocese of Sioux City

The Marian Home
2400 Sixth Ave. N.
Fort Dodge, IA 50501
Mr. GERALD BRUENING Admin.
Rev. EUGENE F. WALDING
Guests 97
Total in Residence 29
Total Staff 112

Johnston
Diocese of Des Moines

Bishop Drumm Retirement Center
Affiliate of Catholic Health Initiatives.
5837 Winwood Dr.
Johnston, IA 50131
Tel: 515-270-1100; Fax: 515-276-1714
Mr. BRIAN E. FARRELL, Admin.
In res.,
Rev. THOMAS M. DECARLO, Res. Chap.
Sisters of Mercy of the Americas (Omaha Province) 8
Care Center Residents 150
Apartment Residents 81
McAuley Terrace Apts.
5921 Winwood Dr.
Johnston, IA 50131
Tel: 515-270-6640
Sr. SUE SELLERS, C.H.M.
Martina Place Assisted Living Residence
5815 Winwood Dr.
Johnston, IA 50131
Tel: 515-251-7999
Mrs. CATHERINE BERRY, Dir.

Sioux City
Diocese of Sioux City

Holy Spirit Retirement Home
1701 W. 25th St.
Sioux City, IA 51103
Tel: 712-252-2726
PATRICK J. TOMSCHA, Admin.
Rev. LEROY L. SEUNTJENS
Total in Residence 28
Total Assisted 85
Total Staff 95

St. Anthony's Orphanage
(Iowa Corporation)
Mailing Address:—Catholic Charities of the Diocese of Sioux City
1601 Military Rd., P.O. Box 2025
Sioux City, IA 51104
Tel: 712-252-4547

KANSAS

Concordia
Diocese of Salina

Mount Joseph Senior Community
Concordia, KS 66901
Tel: 785-243-1347; Fax: 785-243-1907
Owned & operated by the Sisters of St. Joseph of Wichita, via Christi, Inc., Wichita, KS.
JANET G. CHAPMAN, CEO & Admin.
Rev. HENRY KIEFFER, Chap.
Sisters 2
Residents 87
Retirement Apartments 12

Hays
Diocese of Salina

St. John's New Horizons
2225 Canterbury
Hays, KS 67601
Tel: 785-628-8742
GEORGE GATSCHET, Admin.
Sr. VERA BITTEL
Residents 45

St. Elizabeth of Hungary Home Health Agency
Semi-independent Living Apartments 10
Assisted Living Units 43

Kansas City
Archdiocese of Kansas City in Kansas

Marian Hall
1920 Tauromee
Kansas City, KS 66102
Tel: 913-621-4302
LYNNE SERRANO, S.C.L., Admin.
Total in Residence 53
Total Staff 10

Providence Place
8909 Parallel
Kansas City, KS 66112
Tel: 913-596-4200
Sisters 1
Total Staff 60
Total Residents 77

St. Joseph Care Center, Inc.
LTC
759 Vermont Ave.
Kansas City, KS 66101
Tel: 913-621-6800
Mr. FRANK T. TRIMBOLI, Admin.
Owned and operated by Catholic Housing Services, Inc.
Intermediate and skilled nursing care and independent boarding.
In res.,
Most Rev. MARION F. FORST
Rev. PATRICK FITZGERALD
Sisters of Charity of Leavenworth 4
Total Staff 225
Total Residents 240

Manhattan
Diocese of Salina

St. Joseph Senior Community, Inc.
2423 Kimball Ave.
Manhattan, KS 66502
Tel: 785-539-7671
Web Site: www.talk2u.com/sjsc
Owned & operated by the Via Christi Health System of Wichita.
Residents 80

Mulvane
Diocese of Wichita

Villa Maria
116 S. Central
Mulvane, KS 67110
Tel: 316-777-1129; Fax: 316-777-4406
CHARLENE MATHIS, Admin.
Home for Aging Men and Women.
Adorers of the Blood of Christ 7
Guests 66

Overland Park
Archdiocese of Kansas City in Kansas

Villa St. Joseph Nursing Home
11901 Rosewood
Overland Park, KS 66209
Tel: 913-345-1745
Ms. KATHARINE ENSIGN, Admin.
Total Staff 284
Total Assisted 211

Victoria
Diocese of Salina

St. John's Rest Home
701 Seventh St.
Victoria, KS 67671
Tel: 785-735-2208
Rev. FRANK GRINKO, O.F.M.Cap., Chap.
Residents 90

Wichita
Diocese of Wichita

Catholic Care Center, Inc.
6700 E. 45th St., N.
Wichita, KS 67226
Tel: 316-744-2020
FRED HERMES, CEO
Rev. RONALD M. GILMORE, Chap.
Sisters 11
Residents 178
Operated by Catholic Diocese of Wichita.

Georgetown Village, Inc.
1655 Georgetown St.
Wichita, KS 67218
Tel: 316-685-0400; Fax: 316-685-0174
Staff 70
Residences 200
Residents 215

KENTUCKY

Cold Spring
Diocese of Covington

Campbell Lodge Boys Home
150 Skyline Dr.
Cold Spring, KY 41076-2099
Tel: 606-781-1214; Fax: 606-781-1511
Ms. KATHY LEE KIRST, Dir.
Boys 50

Covington
Diocese of Covington

Diocesan Catholic Children's Home
Orphanage Rd., P.O. Box 17007
Fort Mitchell, KY 41017-2730
Sisters of Notre Dame 6
Lay Staff 43
Children in Residence 28
Students 21
Sr. JEAN MARIE HOFFMAN, S.N.D., Exec. Dir. & Religious Supr.
Sr. PAMELA MAE GEIGER, S.N.D., Prin.

Madonna Manor, Inc.
2344 Amsterdam Rd.
Villa Hills, KY 41017-3712
Tel: 606-341-3981
Sisters of St. Benedict 11
Patients assisted annually 60
49 Independent living apartments with 54 residents
Sr. CHARLES WOLKING, O.S.B., Admin.
Rev. JOSEPH BROERING, Chap.

St. Charles Care Center, Inc.
500 Farrell Dr.
Covington, KY 41011-3798
Tel: 606-331-3224; Fax: 606-578-2065
Sr. MARY LUANN BENDER, S.N.D., Admin.
Rev. CHARLES E. WEBER, Chap.
Sisters of Notre Dame 7
Beds 149
Assisted Living Apartments 60
Independent Living Apartments 12
Independent Living Cottages 35
Total Assisted 371
Adult Day Health Program & Licensed Physical Therapy Department.

Fort Thomas
Diocese of Covington

Carmel Manor
100 Carmel Manor Rd.
Fort Thomas, KY 41075-2395
Tel: 606-781-5111; Fax: 606-781-2337
Carmelite Sisters for the Aged and Infirm
Sr. MARY DAVID, O.Carm., Admin.
Rev. GARY A. MILLER, Chap.
153
Residents 145

Regina Cleri Home for Retired Priests
100 Carmel Manor Rd.
Fort Thomas, KY 41075-2395
Tel: 606-781-5111; Fax: 606-781-2337
Carmelite Sisters for the Aged and Infirm
Sr. ANN BROWN, O.Carm., Admin.
Rev. GARY A. MILLER, Chap.
Residents 6

Knottsville
Diocese of Owensboro

Bishop Soenneker Home
9545 Kentucky 144
Philpot, KY 42366
Tel: 502-281-4881
Sr. MARY RAYMONDE CARRAT, A.D., Admin.
Residents 63

Louisville
Archdiocese of Louisville

Boys' Haven
2301 Goldsmith Ln.
Louisville, KY 40205
Tel: 502-458-1171; Fax: 502-451-2161
For dependent, neglected, or abused boys, 12 to 18 years of age.
Mr. JEROME A. WEBER, Exec. Dir.

Rev. JAMES C. MALONEY, Chap.
Number of Boys in Home 30

Caritas Health Services, Inc. dba Caritas Peace Center
2020 Newburg Rd.
Louisville, KY 40205
Tel: 502-451-3330
Hospital for Psychiatric Illness.
Nazareth Health, Inc.
Sisters 7
Bed Capacity 416
Patients assisted annually 2,300

Franciscan Health Care Center/Retirement Center
3625 Fern Valley Rd.
Louisville, KY 40219
Rev. WILLIAM BROWNING, Chap.
Nursing Facility Beds 150
Legal Title: *Sisters of St. Francis Health Services, Inc. dba Franciscan Health Care Center*

Marian Home
3105 Lexington Rd.
Louisville, KY 40206
Tel: 502-893-0121; Fax: 502-896-3925
Sr. ASSUMPTA DEVINE, O.S.U., Admin.
Rev. JOSEPH T. MERKT, Chap.
Staff Sisters 8
Residents 70

Maryhurst
1015 Dorsey Ln.
Louisville, KY 40223
Tel: 502-245-1576; Fax: 502-245-4737
Sisters of the Good Shepherd
Sr. GLYNIS MARY MCMANAMON, R.G.S., Supr.
JUDITH LAMBETH, Exec. Dir.
Sisters 3
Students 79

Nazareth Home
2000 Newburg Rd.
Louisville, KY 40205
Tel: 502-459-9681; Fax: 502-456-9077
Sisters of Charity of Nazareth
JOYCE DENCZEK, CEO & Admin.
Rev. GERMAIN LEGERE, C.P., Chap.
In res.,
Revs.:
LINUS T. GIESLER
PAUL M. RUSSELL
WILLIAM A. SPALDING
Staff Sisters 15
Residents 168

Sacred Heart Home, Inc.
(Rudd-Taylor Memorial)
2120 Payne St.
Louisville, KY 40206
Tel: 502-895-9888; 895-9425; Fax: 502-894-9619
Sisters of Mercy
Catholic Healthcare Partners, Cincinnati, OH.
LESLIE A. WILSON, Admin.
Rev. LOUIS MILLER, Chap.
Sisters 3
Residents 111
Capacity 162
Mercy Assoc. 1

St. Joseph Catholic Orphan Society
2823 Frankfort Ave.
Louisville, KY 40206
Tel: 502-893-0241; Fax: 502-896-2394
Mr. DENNIS DAVIS, Exec. Dir.
Mr. ROBERT BEAM, Pres.

St. Joseph Children's Home
2823 Frankfort Ave.
Louisville, KY 40206
Tel: 502-893-0241; Fax: 502-896-2394
Mr. DENNIS DAVIS, Exec. Dir.
Ursuline Sisters 1
Children 62

St. Joseph Home for the Aged
15 Audubon Plaza Dr.
Louisville, KY 40217
Fax: 502-636-2239
Sr. ROSE MARIE MAYOCK, Admin.
In res.,
Revs.:
MARK SANFORD, O.F.M.
DONALD FISHER
SIMON SAUER, O.F.M.Conv.
Legal Title: *Home for the Aged of the Little Sisters of the Poor*

St. Thomas Orphan Society, Inc.
P.O. Box 1073
Louisville, KY 40201

St. Vincent's Orphan Society, Inc.
P.O. Box 1073
Louisville, KY 40201

Owensboro
Diocese of Owensboro

Carmel Home
2501 Old Hartford Rd.
Owensboro, KY 42303
Tel: 502-683-0227
Carmelite Sisters of the Divine Heart of Jesus
Sr. M. FRANCIS TERESA SCULLY, Carmel.D.C.J., Supr.
Rev. JOSEPH RHODES, Chap.
Sisters 4
Residents 101

Versailles
Diocese of Lexington

Taylor Manor Nursing Home
300 Berry Ave.
Versailles, KY 40383
Tel: 606-873-4201
Sr. MARY CHRISTINA MURRAY, S.J.W., Admin.
Rev. MAURICE J. BRINKER, Chap.
Sisters of St. Joseph the Worker 4
Patients assisted annually 82

LOUISIANA

Alexandria
Diocese of Alexandria

Our Lady's Manor, Inc.
402 Monroe St.
Alexandria, LA 71301
Tel: 318-473-2560
Mrs. JOANN BARONNE, Admin.
Apartments 114

St. Mary's Residential Training School, Inc.
P.O. Box Drawer 7768
Alexandria, LA 71306
Tel: 318-445-6443; Fax: 318-449-8520
Congregation of the Sisters of Our Lady of Sorrows of the U.S.A., Inc.
Sr. SERAPHINE RICCI, O.L.S., Admin.
Sisters 5
Lay Staff 270
Beds 152
Students 152

Baton Rouge
Diocese of Baton Rouge

Assisi Homes, Inc., of Our Lady of the Lake Medical Center
5000 Hennessy Blvd.
Baton Rouge, LA 70808-4398
Tel: 504-765-6565
Mr. ROBERT C. DAVIDGE, Pres. & CEO
Assisi Village, Inc., of Our Lady of the Lake Medical Center
7585 Bishop Ott Dr.
Baton Rouge, LA 70806-8922
Tel: 504-927-5070
Senior citizens' residence.
Calais House, Inc., of Our Lady of the Lake Medical Center
7545 Bishop Ott Dr.
Baton Rouge, LA 70806-8900
Tel: 504-927-1889
Senior citizens' residence.
Villa St. Francis, Inc., of Our Lady of the Lake Medical Center
7575 Bishop Ott Dr.
Baton Rouge, LA 70806-8906
Tel: 504-927-0070
Housing facilities for elderly and handicapped persons.

Ollie Steele Burden Manor
4250 Essen Ln.
Baton Rouge, LA 70809-2196
Tel: 504-926-0091; Fax: 504-926-4937
Our Lady of the Lake Regional Medical Center, Our Lady of the Lake Pastoral Care.
Staff 170
Bed Capacity 184

Belle Chasse
Archdiocese of New Orleans

Padua Community Services Pediatric Residential Program
200 Beta St.
Belle Chasse, LA 70037-1499
Tel: 504-392-0502; Fax: 504-392-5411
Residential Facility for Severely-Profoundly Retarded and Multihandicapped Children
PASHENA CASIMIRE, Admin.

Forest Hill
Diocese of Alexandria

Our Lady of Guadalupe Mission
10 Butter Cemetery Rd.
Forest Hill, LA 71430
Mailing Address:
4400 Coliseum Blvd.
Alexandria, LA 71303
Rev. PEDRO J. SIERRA-POSADA
Franciscan Religious of Our Lady of Refuge 3

La Place
Archdiocese of New Orleans

Place Dubourg, Inc.
201 Rue Dubourg
La Place, LA 70068-2433
Tel: 504-652-1981; Fax: 504-651-6147
Ms. CHRISTINE PALMISANO, Admin.
Units 115
Total Staff 8
Total in Residence 118

Lafayette
Diocese of Lafayette

Bethany M.H.S. Health Care Center
P.O. Box 2308
Lafayette, LA 70502
Tel: 318-234-2459
Sisters of the Most Holy Sacrament 12
Bed Capacity 42

Village du Lac, Inc.
1404 Carmel Ave.
Lafayette, LA 70501
Tel: 318-234-5106
Community housing for the handicapped and elderly with low income. Sponsored by the Diocese.
Mr. J. BERNEL FONTENOT, Dir.
Residents 200

Mandeville
Archdiocese of New Orleans

Rouquette Lodge
St. Tammany Manor, Inc.
4300 Hwy. 22
Mandeville, LA 70448-2824
Tel: 504-626-5217; Fax: 504-626-9226
Residence for Senior Citizens
Bro. HAROLD EHLINGER, C.S.C., Admin.
Residential Units 120
Total in Residence 170
Total Staff 8
Rouquette II
Residential Units 51

Marrero
Archdiocese of New Orleans

Hope Haven Center (1925)
1101 Barataria Blvd.
Marrero, LA 70072-3085
Tel: 504-347-5581; Fax: 504-340-2075
Residential Treatment Center and School
Mr. ROBERT GUASCO, Asst. Admin.

Villa D'Ames Apartments
6305 Fourth St.
Marrero, LA 70072-1513
Tel: 504-347-0474; Fax: 504-347-0476
Ms. YVONNE STEWART, Admin.
Units 200

Wynhoven Apartments and Wynhoven II
4600-10th St.
Marrero, LA 70072-3048
Tel: 504-347-8443; Fax: 504-340-6076
Private Non-Profit Residence for Senior Citizens Sponsored by the Archdiocese
Sr. EMMA DUNNE, S.S.N.D., Admin.
Sr. MARTIN MARIE BULLARD, S.S.N.D., Mgr., Wynhoven II
Sisters 4
Residents 375
Total Staff 13

Wynhoven Health Care Center
1050 Medical Center Blvd.
Marrero, LA 70072-3170
Tel: 504-347-0777; 347-3443 (Convent); Fax: 504-341-7240
Mr. JOHN TIEPERMAN, Admin.
Total Assisted 200
Total Staff 173

Meraux
Archdiocese of New Orleans

St. Bernard Manor, St. Bernard II, and St. Bernard III
2400 Archbishop Hannan Blvd.
Meraux, LA 70075-2640
Tel: 504-277-2441; Fax: 504-277-6300
Ms. DIANE JOHNSON, Admin.
Residents 235
Total Staff 11

Metairie
Archdiocese of New Orleans

Cascades Apartments, Walmsley Housing Corp.
2212 N. Arnoult Rd.
Metairie, LA 70001-1807
Tel: 504-835-2998; Fax: 504-835-3647
Mrs. THELMA AGUILAR, Admin.
Units 120

Metairie Manor, Metairie II, and Metairie III
4929 York St.
Metairie, LA 70001-1013
Tel: 504-456-1467; Fax: 504-887-3718
Sr. MARY ALOYSIUS OTT, O.P., Admin.
Sr. MARY GRIGNON BAUDOUIN, O.P., Asst. Admin.
Rev. JOHN A. POWERS, O.P., Chap.
Residential Units 287

Rock Creek Apartments, Walmsley Housing Corp.
4817 York St.
Metairie, LA 70001-1168
Tel: 504-455-3886; Fax: 504-455-3888
Ms. DIANA LAMBERT, Admin.
Units 160

Monroe
Diocese of Shreveport

St. Joseph Home
2301 Sterlington Rd., P.O. Box 6057
Monroe, LA 71211-6057
Tel: 318-323-3426
Operated by the Sisters of Charity of the Incarnate Word, Houston, TX
Mrs. JOY HUFF, Admin.
Licensed Capacity 132
Sisters 2
Total Staff 120

Moreauville
Diocese of Alexandria

St. John's Village
116 Beridon St.
Moreauville, LA 71355-3004
Tel: 318-985-2948
Rev. Msgr. JOHN TIMMERMANS, Admin.
Apartments 50

New Iberia
Diocese of Lafayette

Consolata Home
2319 E. Main St.
New Iberia, LA 70560
Tel: 318-365-8226
Mr. DAVID LANDRY, Admin.
Rev. RAYMOND ROBITAILLE, Chap., Tel: 318-365-7477
Residents 114
Bed Capacity 114

New Orleans
Archdiocese of New Orleans

The 1540 House
1540 N. Johnson St.
New Orleans, LA 70116-1721
Tel: 504-945-0253
Mr. MATTHEW ROBINSON, III, Admin.
Residents 12

Annunciation Inn
1220 Spain St.
New Orleans, LA 70117-8369
Tel: 504-944-0512; Fax: 504-944-0514
Residence for Elderly
Sr. HELEN I. BREAUX, S.F.C.C., Admin.
Units 106
Total Staff 8
Residents 111

Boys Hope
4128 Baudin St.
New Orleans, LA 70119-6815
Tel: 504-486-6030
E-mail: boyshope-girlshope@charitiesusa.com
Web Site: www.boyshopegirlshope.org
4233 Banks St.
New Orleans, LA 70119-6714
Tel: 504-486-5223
2726 Esplanade
New Orleans, LA 70119-3333
Tel: 504-484-7744; Fax: 504-484-6120
Group Homes for Boys. Jesuit Program for Living and Learning
Rev. ROBERT C. ALLANACH, O.M.I., Ph.D., Dir.
Total Staff 9
Boys 16

Carriage House Apartments, Pontchartrain Housing Corp. I
10151 Curran Blvd.
New Orleans, LA 70127-1390
Mrs. SHERRI TARDIFF, Admin.
Units 216
Total Staff 5
Residents 214

Chateau de Notre Dame
2832 Burdette St.
New Orleans, LA 70125-2596
Tel: 504-866-2741; Fax: 504-866-6769
Residence and Nursing Home
Ms. PATRICIA ANN GAUTREAUX, Admin.
Rev. EDWARD J. LAWLOR, S.S.J., Chap.
Residential Units 106
Nursing Beds 180
Priests 1
Sisters 4
Lay Staff 215

Christopher Inn Apts.
2110 Royal St.
New Orleans, LA 70116-1693
Tel: 504-949-0312; Fax: 504-945-2634
Private Non-Profit Residence for Senior Citizens Sponsored by the Archdiocese
Ms. EVANGELINE WASHINGTON, Acting Admin.
Residents 148

**Covenant House*
611 N. Rampart St.
New Orleans, LA 70112-3540
Tel: 504-584-1111; 800-999-9999 (Hotline); Fax: 504-584-1171
Home for Runaway, Abused & Homeless Youth
Mrs. MAUDELLE CADE, Exec. Dir.

DeLille Inn
6924 Chef Menteur Hwy.
New Orleans, LA 70126-5260
Tel: 504-241-4877; Fax: 504-241-1828
Sr. M. TEKAKWITHA VEGA, S.S.F., Admin.
Total Staff 5
Residents 55

Haydel Heights Apartments
4402 Reynes St.
New Orleans, LA 70126
Tel: 504-242-4438; Fax: 504-242-4061
Ms. LINDA CHAPMAN, Admin.
Units 65
Total Assisted 225
Total Staff 2

Josephine Apartments
1410 St. Andrew St., Apt. #6
New Orleans, LA 70130-5344
Tel: 504-522-5425; Fax: 504-522-5446
Mrs. ROSALYN W. TRIPPS, Mgr.
Residents 93

Lafon Nursing Home of the Holy Family
6900 Chef Menteur Hwy.
New Orleans, LA 70126-5296
Tel: 504-246-1100; Fax: 504-241-6672
Sisters of the Holy Family
Sr. ANN ELISE SONNIER, S.S.F., Admin.
Sisters 8
Residents 171
Total Staff 154

Mary-Joseph Residence for the Elderly (1868)
4201 Woodland Dr.
New Orleans, LA 70131-7398
Tel: 504-394-2200; Fax: 504-391-3347
Sr. JOSEPH GRENON, L.S.P., Supr.
Rev. FRANCIS WHATLEY, O.SS.T., Chap.
Sisters 12
Total Staff 140
Residents 110

Nazareth II
9640 Hayne Blvd.
New Orleans, LA 70127-4725
Tel: 504-246-9640; Fax: 504-241-9631
Sr. TERESA CARONIA, S.S.N.D., Dir.
Apartments 120
Total Staff 5
Total in Residence 122

Nazareth Inn
9630 Hayne Blvd.
New Orleans, LA 70127-1260
Tel: 504-241-9630; Fax: 504-241-9631
Legal Title: *Nazareth Manor, Inc.*
Sr. ANNA MARY CARONIA, S.S.N.D., Dir.
Sisters 2
Apartments 150
Total Staff 9
Total in Residence 158

St. John Berchmans Manor
3400 St. Anthony St.
New Orleans, LA 70122-3098
Tel: 504-943-9343; Fax: 504-947-6090
Sr. M. ROSE DE LIMA HAZEUR, S.S.F., Admin.
Rev. VINCENT THEOBALD, S.V.D., Chap., Tel: 504-948-4425
Units 150
Residents 158
Total Staff 11

St. Margaret's Daughters' Home
6220 Chartres St.
New Orleans, LA 70117-1595
Tel: 504-279-6414; Fax: 504-277-1834
Mrs. PATRICIA G. HEINTZ, Admin.
GAETANA MANGIN, Asst. Admin.
Residents 113
Total Staff 110
Total Assisted 115

St. Martin Manor
1501 N. Johnson St.
New Orleans, LA 70116-1720
Tel: 504-945-7728; Fax: 504-945-1645
Sr. M. CAMILLUS DURALD, S.S.F., Admin.
Residential Units 140
Total Staff 12
Total in Residence 145

Timber Ridge Apartments Pontchartrain Housing Corp. III
6364 Woodland Hwy.
New Orleans, LA 70131-7474
Tel: 504-391-9841; Fax: 504-391-9996
Legal Title: *Christopher Homes Inc.*
Ms. JOANN ROBERT, Admin.
Units 152

Villa St. Maurice
500 St. Maurice Ave.
New Orleans, LA 70117-1568
Tel: 504-277-8477; Fax: 504-277-8493
Residence for Senior Citizens & Handicapped
Mrs. JUANITA C. JONES, Admin.
Residential Units 110
Residents 193
Total Staff 10

Villa St. Maurice II (Villa Additions)
6101 Douglas St.
New Orleans, LA 70117-2100
Tel: 504-277-8731; Fax: 504-277-8493
Residence for Senior Citizens & Handicapped.
Mrs. CAROL MOTEN, Asst. Admin.
Residential Units 75
Residents 80
Total Staff 2

Opelousas
Diocese of Lafayette

C'est La Vie Center of the Sisters Marianites of Holy Cross
749 E. Prudhomme Ln.
Opelousas, LA 70570
Tel: 318-942-8154
Independent living for the elderly and handicapped.
Sr. KAY KINBERGER, M.S.C., Pres.
Sr. MARY ZITA GUIDRY, M.S.C., Coord.
Sr. JOYCELYN F. LEE, Admin.
Sisters 2

Our Lady of Prompt Succor Home
751 E. Prudhomme Ln.
Opelousas, LA 70570
Tel: 318-948-3634
Mrs. JOCELYN FORET LEE, Admin.
Sisters 5
Patients assisted annually 120

Shreveport
Diocese of Shreveport

Holy Angels Residential Facility
10450 Ellerbe Rd.

Shreveport, LA 71106-7712
Tel: 318-797-8500; 797-9070; Fax: 318-798-0159
Sisters of Our Lady of Sorrows
Sr. CONCETTA SCIPIONE, O.L.S., Admin.
Sr. GEMMA FORLANI, O.L.S., Supr.
Most Rev. WILLIAM B. FRIEND, D.D., Pres.
Sisters 5
Lay Personnel 265
Residents 184

St. Rose
Archdiocese of New Orleans

River Road Apartments, Pontchartrain Housing Corp. II
100 A East Club Dr.
St. Rose, LA 70087-9411
Tel: 504-464-0326; Fax: 504-466-1987
Ms. JO ANN ANDRY, Admin.
Units 320
Total Staff 7

MAINE

Bangor
Diocese of Portland (In Maine)

St. Xavier's Home
119 Somerset St.
Bangor, ME 04401
Tel: 207-942-4815
Mailing Address:—St. John Parish
207 York St.
Bangor, ME 04401-5442
GERARD G. GOSSELIN, Contact Person
Units 19

Biddeford
Diocese of Portland (In Maine)

St. Andre Health Care Facility
407 Pool St.
Biddeford, ME 04005-9716
Tel: 207-282-5171
Sr. MADELEINE D'ANJOU, Admin.
Sponsored by Servants of the Immaculate Heart of Mary S.C.I.M. Good Shepherd, Quebec, Canada
Beds 96

Lewiston
Diocese of Portland (In Maine)

Maison Marcotte
(Formerly: Marcotte Congregate Housing)
100 Campus Ave.
Lewiston, ME 04240
Tel: 207-786-0062
CECILE Y. MATHIEU, Dir.
Total In Res. 128
Total Staff 4

**St. Marguerite d'Youville Pavilion*
(Formerly: Marcotte Nursing Home)
102 Campus Ave.
Lewiston, ME 04240
Tel: 207-777-4200
Rev. RAYMOND CORRIVEAU, O.P., Chap.
Beds 280
Patients assisted annually 94,000

Portland
Diocese of Portland (In Maine)

Deering Pavilion Apartment House for Senior Citizens
880 Forest Ave.
Portland, ME 04103
Tel: 207-797-8777
Mr. OREN W. SCHROEDER, Admin.
Residents 235
Apartments 200

St. Joseph's Manor
1133 Washington Ave.
Portland, ME 04103
Tel: 207-797-0600; Fax: 207-797-4168
Most Rev. JOSEPH J. GERRY, O.S.B., Pres.
Mr. RONALD G. TARDIF, Dir.
FAITH STILPHEN, R.N., Dir. Nurses
Bed Capacity 200

Waterville
Diocese of Portland (In Maine)

Mt. St. Joseph Holistic Care Community
Highwood St.
Waterville, ME 04901
Tel: 207-873-0705
PATRICIA BERGER, Admin.
Sisters of St. Joseph of Lyons, C.S.J.
Bed Capacity 138

Seton Village Inc.
1 Carver St.
Waterville, ME 04901
Tel: 207-873-0178
Most Rev. JOSEPH J. GERRY, Bishop of Portland, Pres.
DAVID P. TWOMEY, Treas.
ARMAND CARON, Chm.
Ms. PAMELA HALL, Admin.
Units 140
Guests 150

MARYLAND

Baltimore
Archdiocese of Baltimore

Dismas House East
1415 N. Caroline St.
Baltimore, MD 21213
Tel: 410-539-2520
Rev. JOSEPH R. WENDEROTH, Exec. Dir.
Non-Sectarian-Use Diocesan Property Rehabilitation center under contract to the Maryland Division of Corrections to provide inmate svcs.
Total Staff 18
Total in Residence 45
Total Assisted 155

Dismas House West
105 S. Mount St., P.O. Box 4435
Baltimore, MD 21223
Tel: 410-566-9400; Fax: 410-233-1622
Rev. JOSEPH R. WENDEROTH, Exec. Dir
Non-Sectarian Rehabilitation center under contract to the Maryland Division of Corrections to provide inmate svcs.
Total Staff 47
Total in Residence 90
Total Assisted 155

St. Charles Villa
603 Maiden Choice Ln.
Baltimore, MD 21228
Tel: 410-747-1211
Revs.:
LAWRENCE A. BENDER, S.S.
JOHN W. BOWEN, S.S.
JAMES H. BRENNAN, S.S.
FREDERICK V. CHUDZINSKI, S.S.
CHARLES P. DILLON, S.S.
CLAUDE H. DUKEHART, S.S.
VINCENT M. EATON, S.S.
JAMES J. HEALY, S.S.
RAYMOND F. HESLER, S.S.
WILLIAM J. LEE, S.S.
JOHN F. MATTINGLY, S.S.
WILLIAM S. MORRIS, S.S.
WILLIAM T. O'KEEFFE, S.S., Supr. & Dir.
WILLIAM A. THIELEMANN, S.S.
JOHN A. WARD, S.S.
J. PAUL WELCH, S.S.
JOSEPH L. WHITE, S.S.
Total in Residence 17
Total Staff 10

St. Elizabeth Rehabilitation and Nursing Center
3320 Benson Ave.
Baltimore, MD 21227-1088
Tel: 410-644-7100; Fax: 410-644-2154
Legal Title: *The Jenkins Memorial Nursing Home, Inc.*
Sponsored by Associated Catholic Charities.
Ms. PATRICIA A. SUPIK, Admin.
Sisters 3
Beds 162
Total Assisted 420
Total Staff 210

St. Joseph's Nursing Home
1222 Tugwell Dr.
Baltimore, MD 21228
Tel: 410-747-0026; Fax: 410-747-0386
Legal Title: *Sisters Servants of Mary Immaculate, Inc.*
Sr. CAROLYN CARNE, Admin.
Rev. JOSEPH SIELSKI, M.I.C., Chap.
Sisters 11
Residents 40
Total Assisted 49
Total Staff 55

St. Martin's Home for Aged, Little Sisters of the Poor
601 Maiden Choice Ln.
Baltimore, MD 21228
Tel: 410-744-9367
Rev. ROBERT G. HAWKINS, Chap.
Sisters 21
Intermediate Care Beds 62
Assisted Living 22
Apartments 18
Aged Residents 104
Total Staff 130

Beltsville
Archdiocese of Washington

Ammendale Normal Institute of Prince George's County-La Salle Hall (1880)
6001 Ammendale Rd.
Beltsville, MD 20705
Tel: 301-210-7443
Brothers of the Christian Schools
Bros.:
KEVIN ERB, F.S.C., Dir.
LEO QUINN, F.S.C., Assoc. Dir.
Residence for Retired and Convalescent Brothers.
Brothers 20

Ellicott City
Archdiocese of Baltimore

St. Agnes Nursing and Rehabilitation Center
(Subsidiary of St. Agnes HealthCare)
3000 N. Ridge Rd.
Ellicott City, MD 21043
Tel: 410-461-7577; Fax: 410-461-6695
Daughters of Charity of St. Vincent De Paul
MICHAEL R. BAKER, Admin.
Pastoral Care:
Sr. GENEVIEVE KURTH, Coord.
FRITZ GOLLERY, Chap.
Sisters 1
Beds 187
Total Assisted 260
Total Staff 178

Hyattsville
Archdiocese of Washington

Sacred Heart Home Inc.
5805 Queens Chapel Rd.
Hyattsville, MD 20782
Tel: 301-277-6500
Missionary Sisters, Servants of the Holy Spirit
Sr. MARY AGNES FAHRLAND, S.Sp.S., Admin.
Rev. ROBERT MERTES, S.V.D.
Sisters 3
Residents 102

St. Ann's Infant and Maternity Home
4901 Eastern Ave.
Hyattsville, MD 20782
Tel: 301-559-5500; Fax: 301-853-6985
Daughters of Charity
Sr. JOSEPHINE Admin.
Sr. PAULA Local Supr.
Sisters 7
Residential Children 57
Maternity Program 18
Day Care 85
After Care Program:
Mothers 14
Infants 14

Mitchellville
Archdiocese of Washington

Villa Rosa Nursing Home, Inc.
3800 Lottsford Vista Rd.
Mitchellville, MD 20721-4026
Tel: 301-459-4700; Fax: 301-459-0754
Rev. CARMELO NEGRO, C.S., Dir.
Mr. EUGENE L. ZIBRAT, Admin.
Sr. REINALDA STRAPAZZON, M.S.S.C., Supr.
Sisters 6
Residents 100
Comprehensive Care Nursing Facility.

Ridgely
Diocese of Wilmington

St. Martin's Ministries
14259 Benedictine Ln.
Ridgely, MD 21660
Tel: 410-634-2497
Sisters of St. Benedict
Sr. PATRICIA GAMGORT, O.S.B., Exec. Dir.
St. Martin's Barn
14376 Benedictine Ln.
Ridgely, MD 21660
Tel: 410-634-1140
Volunteers 20
Staff 5
Total Assisted 10,254
Sr. FRANCES WALKER, O.S.F., Dir.
St. Martin's House
14374 Benedictine Ln.
Ridgely, MD 21660

Tel: 410-634-2537
Volunteers 3
Staff 4
Total Assisted 28
Ms. JUDITH BATES, Dir.

Timonium
Archdiocese of Baltimore

Stella Maris Operating Corporation
2300 Dulaney Valley Rd.
Timonium, MD 21093
Tel: 410-252-4500; Fax: 410-560-9675
Sr. LOUIS MARY BATTLE, R.S.M., Pres. Emeritus
Sr. HELEN AMOS, R.S.M., Pres. & CEO
Sr. KAREN MCNALLY, R.S.M., Chief Admin. Officer
Rev. LAWRENCE M. JOHNSON, Dir. of Pastoral Care
The management corporation for all programs of the Center. Long-term care; subacute care; home health; rehabilitative services; hospice services; hospice inpatient; home/hospice care; outreach ministries program; independent living; group home; and counseling/bereavement services for adults and children. All applications for the facilities of the Center are processed directly through the Admissions Office at Stella Maris.
Lay Personnel 680
Sisters 12
Residents 416
Saint John Hall-Long Crandon
Rev. Msgr. ANTHONY SAUERWEIN
Revs.:
GERALD BRODERICK
JOHN C. COLLOPY
PAUL F. DOLAN
JOSEPH KAISER
JOSEPH A. KENNEY
CHARLES QUINN
Stella Maris
Revs.:
WILLIAM M. DRISCOLL, S.J.
LEON KACZKOWSKI
St. Elizabeth Hall
Rev. Msgr. ROBERT A. BOZEL
Revs.:
THOMAS FANNON
CHARLES MEISEL
MYLES MULLER
Cardinal Shehan Center, Inc.

MASSACHUSETTS

Boston
Archdiocese of Boston

Don Orione Nursing Home
111 Orient Ave.
East Boston, MA 02128
Tel: 617-569-2100
Revs.:
LAWRENCE TOSATTO, F.D.P., Supr., Dir. and Admin.
ROCCO CRESCENZI, F.D.P., Vicar & Treas.
GINO MARCHESANI, F.D.P., Counselor
JOHN KILMARTIN, F.D.P., Rector of the Shrine & Counselor
Sons of Divine Providence (Don Orione Fathers) 4
Guests 190
Total Assisted 185
Total Staff 195

Franciscan Children's Hospital and Rehabilitation Center
30 Warren St.
Brighton, MA 02135
Tel: 617-254-3800
E-mail: fch@fch.com
Web Site: http://www.fch.com
General Pediatrics, Rehabilitation, Special Education, Mental Health Services & Home Care.
PAUL DELLA ROCCO, Pres. & C.E.O.
Bed Capacity 100
Number under care 58,815
Day Program 90

Marian Manor (1954)
130 Dorchester St.
South Boston, MA 02127
Tel: 617-268-3333
Sr. PAULINE ROSS, Admin.
Revs.:
JOSEPH M. KANE, Chap.
HERBERT J. CLEARY, S.J., Assoc. Chap.
Priests 2
Carmelite Sister for the Aged and Infirm 14
Guests 366

St. Joseph Nursing Care Center
321 Centre St.
Dorchester, MA 02122
Tel: 617-825-6320; Fax: 617-825-7410
PAUL F. SHANNON, Admin.
Rev. JOHN J. JENNINGS, Chap.
123 Bed Nursing Care Center.
St. Joseph Nursing Care Center, Inc.
Sisters 2

St. Mary's Women and Infants Center
90 Cushing Ave.
Dorchester, MA 02125
Center for pregnant women.
(See Guidance Centers for more information.)

Brighton
Archdiocese of Boston

St. John of God Hospital
296 Allston St.
Brighton, MA 02146
Tel: 617-277-5750
WILLIAM K. BRINKERT, Pres.
Rev. JOSEPH K. COLEMAN, Chap., Dir. Pastoral Care, Chronic and Rehabilitation Hospital.
A member of Caritas Christi, the Catholic Health Care System of the Archdiocese of Boston.
Bed Capacity 70
Total Staff 119

Brockton
Archdiocese of Boston

St. Joseph Manor Nursing & Extended Care Facility
215 Thatcher St.
Brockton, MA 02402-3999
Tel: 508-583-5834; Fax: 508-583-8551
THOMAS J. BROWN, CEO
ANNE M. TERI, Admin.
Rev. AUSTIN NAGLE, SS.CC., Chap.
Adult Day Health Center
Total Assisted 30
Total Staff 5
Sisters of Jesus Crucified and the Sorrowful Mother 9
Residents 118

Cambridge
Archdiocese of Boston

**Youville Healthcare Center, Inc.*
1575 Cambridge St.
Cambridge, MA 02138-4398
Tel: 617-876-4344
Mr. T. RICHARD QUIGLEY, Pres. & CEO
Sr. JOAN COYNE, Admin.
Ms. MARSHA V. WHELAN, Vice Pres. Mission Integration
Chaplains:
Revs.:
WILLIAM L. MULLIGAN, S.J., Chap.
JENNIFER CASSTEVENS
Ms. PATRICIA KENNEDY, Dir., Pastoral Care Services
Ms. ELIZABETH WALSH
Priests 1
Sisters of Charity (Grey Nuns) 3
Member of Youville Lifecare, Inc.
Bed Capacity 140
Patients assisted annually 1,267
Staff 166

**Youville Hospital & Rehabilitation Center, Inc.*
1575 Cambridge St.
Cambridge, MA 02138-4398
Tel: 617-876-4344
Mr. T. RICHARD QUIGLEY, Pres. & CEO
Ms. MARSHA V. WHELAN, Vice Pres. Mission Integration
Chaplains:
Revs.:
WILLIAM L. MULLIGAN, S.J.
JENNIFER CASSTEVENS
Ms. PATRICIA KENNEDY, Dir. Pastoral Care Services
Ms. ELIZABETH WALSH
Priests 1
Sisters of Charity (Grey Nuns) 3
School of Practical Nursing
Ms. HELEN M. BARRETT, R.N., M.S., Dir.
Member of Youville Lifecare, Inc.
Bed Capacity 146
Patients assisted annually 7,255
Staff 383
Youville Place
10 Pelham Rd.
Lexington, MA 02173-5799
Tel: 617-861-3535; Fax: 617-862-5477
Sr. JUNE L. KETTERER, S.G.M., Pres.

Fairhaven
Diocese of Fall River

Our Lady's Haven of Fairhaven Inc.
71 Center St.
Fairhaven, MA 02719
Tel: 508-999-4561
JEAN M. GOLITZ, Admin.
Rev. ROY YURCO, SS.CC., Chap.
Sr. MARIA CRAVEDI, M.P.V., Dir. Pastoral Care
Residents 117

Fall River
Diocese of Fall River

Catholic Memorial Home Inc.
2446-2474 Highland Ave.
Fall River, MA 02720-4599
Tel: 508-679-0011; Fax: 508-672-5858
Sr. NINA AMARAL, O.Carm., Supr. & Admin.
Rev. ARTHUR K. WINGATE, Chap.
Sr. ELAINE HEFFERNAN, R.S.M., Dir. Pastoral Care
Carmelite Sisters 5
Total Assisted 300
Total Staff 400

Rose Hawthorne Lathrop Home
(Servants of Relief for Incurable Cancer)
1600 Bay St.
Fall River, MA 02724
Tel: 508-673-2322; Fax: 508-679-5830
Dominican Sisters of the Congregation of St. Rose of Lima
Rev. DENNIS M. MCNELIS, C.S.C., Chap.
Total Assisted 120
Sisters 7
Total Staff 30
Bed Capacity 35
Patients assisted annually 120

Framingham
Archdiocese of Boston

Carmel Terrace
933 Central St.
Framingham, MA 01701
Tel: 508-788-8000
Sr. M. JOSEPH AUGUSTINE, Dir.
Carmelite Sisters for the Aged and Infirm 3
Apartments for Assisted Living of the Elderly 62
Total Staff 35

St. Patrick's Manor, Inc.
863 Central St.
Framingham, MA 01701
Tel: 508-879-8000; Fax: 508-626-1604
Sr. SEAN DAMIEN FLYNN, Admin.
Rev. JOHN FENTON FOLEY, S.J., Chap.
Carmelite Sisters for the Aged and Infirm 31

Holyoke
Diocese of Springfield in Massachusetts

Mont Marie Health Care Center, Inc.
34 Lower Westfield Rd.
Holyoke, MA 01040
Tel: 413-536-0853; Fax: 413-533-3275
Sr. ELIZABETH SULLIVAN, S.S.J., Admin.
In res.,
Rev. Msgr. EUGENE GUERIN
Rev. Msgr. PAUL REIDL
Total Staff 83
Total Assisted 72
Total Resident Days 26,193
Total Census 72 residents

Sisters of Providence Care Centers, Inc.
35 Holy Family Rd.
Holyoke, MA 01040-2758
Mr. WILLIAM E. CASPER, Pres.
Beaven Kelly Home
25 Brightside Dr.
Holyoke, MA 01040
Tel: 413-532-4892
Residents 55
Mrs. CYNTHIA BROWN, Admin.
Mount St. Vincent Nursing Home
35 Holy Family Rd.
Holyoke, MA 01040-2758
Tel: 413-532-3246
Sisters of Providence 1
Persons under care 125
In res.,
Revs.:
JOSEPH MOYNAHAN (Worchester, MA)
EUGENE OZIMEK
CASIMIR S. SWITALSKI (SPR)
Sr. MARY HORGAN, S.P., M.Div., Chap. (Staff)
Mr. DENNIS K. MCKENNA, Admin.
St. Luke's Home
85 Spring St.
Springfield, MA 01105
Tel: 413-736-5494
Residents 89
Sr. DOROTHY YOUNG, S.P., Pastoral Care Dir. (Staff)
Sr. GERALDINE NOONAN, S.P., Admin.

In res.,
Rev. ZENO WIERZBINSKI, (Granby Friar)
Sr. MABEL WITHAM, R.C.E.
Sr. PATRICIA DOLAN, S.S.J.
Sr. JOSEPHINE AHEARN, R.C.E.
Center for Rehabilitation and Nursing Care
217 Westfield St.
West Springfield, MA 01089
Tel: 413-746-0390
Residents 120
DAVID IANACONE, Admin.
Sr. JOAN MANNING, S.P., (CNA - Staff)
Sr. MARY DOLARETTA, S.P., (Pastoral Care-Staff)
Sr. AGNES REICHLIN, (3-11 RN Supvr.) - Staff
In res.,
Sr. MARY KWALA, O.P.
Sr. FRANCIS LESIAK
Bro. JOSEPH MULLIGAN
Providence Care Centers (Washington)
1462 Lovers Lane Rd.
Washington, MA 01223
Tel: 413-623-8936
Residents 57
Mr. JOHN WYSOCKI, Admin.
Providence Care Centers (Springfield)
388 Central St.
Springfield, MA 01105
Tel: 413-734-4986
Residents 75
Ms. CONSTANCE HENNING, Admin.
Total Staff 505
Total Assisted 464

Lawrence
Archdiocese of Boston

**M.I. Adult Day Health Center, Inc.*
189 Maple St.
Lawrence, MA 01841
Tel: 508-682-7575
Sisters of Charity of Montreal (Grey Nuns)
BARBARA E. GRANT, Pres. & C.E.O.
Adult day health and social day care for Senior Citizens.
Total in Residence 100
Total Staff 16

M.I. Nursing-Restorative Center, Inc.
172 Lawrence St.
Lawrence, MA 01841
Tel: 508-685-6321
Sisters of Charity Montreal (Grey Nuns)
THOMAS L. LUCAS, Pres. & CEO
JOANNE MUKERJEE, Admin.
Multi-level Skilled Nursing Facility.
Member of Convenant Health System, Lexington, MA. Unit of: Mary Immaculate Health Care Services.
Residents 250
Total Staff 340

M.I. Residential Community II, Inc.
191 Maple St.
Lawrence, MA 01841
Tel: 508-682-7575
Sisters of Charity of Montreal (Grey Nuns)
THOMAS L. LUCAS, Pres. & CEO
BARBARA E. GRANT, Admin.
Independent & assisted living for Elderly and Handicapped.
Units 106
Total in Residence 120
Total Staff 35

M.I. Residential Community III, Inc.
193 Maple St.
Lawrence, MA 01841
Tel: 508-682-7575
Sisters of Charity of Montreal (Grey Nuns)
THOMAS L. LUCAS, Pres. & CEO
BARBARA E. GRANT, Admin.
Independent & assisted living for Elderly and Handicapped.
Units 88
Total in Residence 95
Total Staff 35

M.I. Residential Community, Inc.
189 Maple St.
Lawrence, MA 01841
Tel: 508-682-7575
Sisters of Charity of Montreal (Grey Nuns)
THOMAS L. LUCAS, Pres. & CEO
BARBARA E. GRANT, Admin.
Independent & assisted living for Elderly and Handicapped.
Units 110
Total in Residence 121
Total Staff 35

**M.I. Transportation, Inc.*
189 Maple St.
Lawrence, MA 01841
Tel: 508-682-7575
Sisters of Charity of Montreal (Grey Nuns)
BARBARA E. GRANT, Admin.
GENE GOODWIN, Dir. of Plant
Total Assisted 75
Total Staff 5

Leominster
Diocese of Worcester

Presentation Health Care Center
99 Church St.
Leominster, MA 01453-3147
Tel: 978-537-7856
Sr. CATHERINE CLEARY, P.B.V.M., Pres.
Total in Residence 19
Total Staff 30
Purpose: To operate and maintain a nursing home for aged and/or infirmed persons at Presentation Convent.

Lowell
Archdiocese of Boston

D'Youville Manor
981 Varnum Ave.
Lowell, MA 01854
Tel: 508-454-5681
Sisters of Charity of Ottawa (Grey Nuns of the Cross)
STEVE JOHNSON, CEO
Rev. FRANK DOLAN, O.M.I., Chap.
Priests 4
Sisters 5
Total Assisted 196
Total Staff 260
Adult Day Health Care Capacity 22
Total Staff 6

Marlboro
Archdiocese of Boston

Marie Esther Health Center, Inc.
720 Boston Post Rd.
Marlboro, MA 01752
Tel: 508-485-3791
Total Assisted 56
Total Staff 45

Millbury
Diocese of Worcester

Providence House Nursing Home of Millbury
29 Main St.
Millbury, MA 01527
Tel: 508-865-6106
Member of Saint Vincent Healthcare System, Inc.
Beds 138
Total Assisted 138
Total Staff 180

New Bedford
Diocese of Fall River

Sacred Heart Home
359 Summer St.
New Bedford, MA 02740
Tel: 508-996-6751
Sr. BLANDINE D'AMOURS, S.C.Q., Supr. & Admin.
Sisters of Charity of Quebec 8
Total Staff 324
Residents 217

North Attleboro
Diocese of Fall River

Madonna Manor Inc.
85 N. Washington St.
North Attleboro, MA 02760
Tel: 508-699-2740; Fax: 508-699-0481
Mrs. SUSAN L. CALDWELL, Admin.
Rev. RAYMOND MOQUIN, M.S.
Sr. CONSTANCE PERRON, D.H.S., Dir. of Pastoral Care
Total Staff 180
Residents 129

Somerville
Archdiocese of Boston

Jeanne Jugan Pavilion
190 Highland Ave.
Somerville, MA 02143
Mailing Address:
186 Highland Ave.
Somerville, MA 02143
Apartments for the Elderly 27
Residents 27
Total Staff 3

Jeanne Jugan Residence
186 Highland Ave.
Somerville, MA 02143
Tel: 617-776-4420; Fax: 617-623-0707
Rev. JOSEPH J. DOWNEY, Chap.
Senior Citizen Total in Residence 84
Total Staff 100
Little Sisters of the Poor 16
Residents 84

Southbridge
Diocese of Worcester

Providence House Nursing Home of Southbridge
84 Chapin St.
Southbridge, MA 01550
Tel: 508-765-9133
Member of Saint Vincent Healthcare System, Inc.
Beds 226

Springfield
Diocese of Springfield in Massachusetts

St. Michael's Residence
86 Wendover Rd.
Springfield, MA 01118
Tel: 413-783-6773
In res.,
Revs.:
THOMAS S. GREENE
MANUEL ROCHA
JOHN TOKARZ
JOHN J. SEXTON
FRANCIS J. SULLIVAN
Rev. Msgr. ROGER VIAU
Total Staff 2
Total in Residence 6

Taunton
Diocese of Fall River

Bethany House Adult Day Care
72 Church Green
Taunton, MA 02780
Tel: 508-822-9200
Mr. THOMAS F. HEALY, Admin.
Total Assisted 30
Total Staff 6

Marian Manor Inc.
33 Summer St.
Taunton, MA 02780
Tel: 508-822-4885
Mr. THOMAS F. HEALY, Admin.
Rev. HUGH J. MUNRO, Chap.
Sr. PAULINA CARDENAS, O.P., Dir. Pastoral Care
Dominican Sisters of Charity of the Presentation of the Blessed Virgin Mary 46
Total Staff 165
Guests 182

Waltham
Archdiocese of Boston

Maristhill Nursing & Rehabilitation Center
66 Newton St.
Waltham, MA 02154
Tel: 781-893-0240; Fax: 781-894-6330
JANET C. MURPHY, Admin.
A member of Covenant Health Systems, offering skilled and rehabilitative nursing care.
Priests 2
Sisters 6
Residents 123
Total Staff 132

West Springfield
Diocese of Springfield in Massachusetts

The Brightside for Families & Children
Private, Non-Profit Agency.
2112 Riverdale St.
Springfield, MA 01089
Tel: 413-788-7366
Sisters of Providence
Sr. KATHLEEN POPKO, S.P., Ph.D., Chm., Bd. of Trustees
RALPH B. SPERRY, Ph.D., Pres.
Children in Residence 114
Children in Day Treatment Program 25
Placement Services:
Children in Foster Homes 10
Adoption Services 50
Pregnant Parenting Youth Services 100
Outpatient Mental Health Clinic 5,000
Family Stabilization Team 100
Acute Residential Treatment 325

Whitinsville
Diocese of Worcester

St. Camillus Hospice, Inc.
447 Hill St.
Whitinsville, MA 01588
Tel: 508-234-7306; Fax: 508-234-7597
Rev. JOHN J. GALLAGHER, O.S.Cam.
Bro. THOMAS J. FARRELL, O.S.Cam., Treas.

St. Camillus Nursing Home Inc.
447 Hill St.
Whitinsville, MA 01588
Tel: 508-234-7306
Mr. DAVID C. TURNER
Bro. THOMAS FARRELL, O.S.Cam., Dir. Pastoral Care
Priests 1
Brothers 2
Beds 123
Patients assisted annually 43,070
St. Camillus Institute
497 Hill St.
Whitinsville, MA 01588
St. Camillus Rectory
495 Hill St.
Whitinsville, MA 01588
Rev. JACK GALLAGHER, O.S.Cam.

Worcester
Diocese of Worcester

Notre Dame Long Term Care Center
559 Plantation St.
Worcester, MA 01605
Tel: 508-852-3011; Fax: 508-852-0397
KATHERINE LEMAY, Admin.
Beds 123
Employees 180
Total Assisted 166
Total Staff 277

Providence Extended Care Center
119 Providence St.
Worcester, MA 01604
Tel: 508-860-5000
Member of Saint Vincent Healthcare System, Inc.
Rev. THOMAS M. BARRY, Chap.
Beds 160
Patients assisted annually 1,000
Total Staff 270

Vianney House
222 June St.
Worcester, MA 01602
Tel: 508-791-0311
Retired Priests' Home.
Most Rev. BERNARD J. FLANAGAN
Rev. Msgr. THOMAS J. DALEY
Rev. Msgr. EDMOND G. HADDAD
Rev. Msgr. RICHARD HANNIGAN
% 49 Elm St.
Worcester, MA 01609
Revs.:
WILLIAM W. MCGOVERN
CYRIL A. LEBEAU
JOHN F. CAHILL, Admin.
JOSEPH ASH
Total Staff 3

MICHIGAN

Allen Park
Archdiocese of Detroit

Little Sisters of the Poor
P.O. Box 610
Allen Park, MI 48101
Sr. MARY JOSEPH, L.S.P., Supr.

Battle Creek
Diocese of Kalamazoo

Mercy Pavilion Skilled Nursing Home and Senior Care Residence
80 N. 20 St.
Battle Creek, MI 49015
Tel: 616-964-5400; Fax: 616-964-5559
Sub. of Battle Creek Health System.
Mr. MICHAEL C. RICHARDS, Admin.
Bed Capacity 77
Senior Care Residence Beds 64

Bloomfield Hills
Archdiocese of Detroit

St. Elizabeth's Briarbank
1315 N. Woodward Ave.
Bloomfield Hills, MI 48304
Tel: 248-644-1011
Daughters of Divine Charity
Sr. M. PASCHAL, Admin.
Sisters 15
Aged Residents 44

Villa Francesca
565 W. Long Lake Rd.
Bloomfield Hills, MI 48302
Tel: 248-644-5390
Daughters of Divine Charity
Sr. MARY AURELIA GEGUS, F.D.C., Admin.
Sisters 3
Lay Staff 2
Employees 2
Under Care 15

Clinton Twp.
Archdiocese of Detroit

A Friends House Adult Day Care Center
16931 19 Mile Rd., Ste. 140
Clinton Twp., MI 48038
Tel: 810-412-8494
Daytime care for older adults. Support services for care giving families. A service of Catholic Services of Macomb.
JOYCE MCCRACKEN, L.P.N., Dir.

Dearborn Heights
Archdiocese of Detroit

Vista Maria
20651 W. Warren Ave.
Dearborn Heights, MI 48127
Tel: 313-271-3050
Sr. M. ELISE KRAMER, Exec. Dir.
Residential and community-based treatment programs for adolescent girls in conflict. Sponsored by the Sisters of the Good Shepherd.
Sisters 4
Girls Residential 145
Lay Staff 270
S.F.C. 41
Independent Living 6

Detroit
Archdiocese of Detroit

Christ Child House
15751 Joy Rd.
Detroit, MI 48228
Tel: 313-584-6077; Fax: 313-584-1148
JOHN YABLONKY, ACSW, Exec. Dir.

Don Bosco Hall, Inc.
10001 Petosky
Detroit, MI 48204
Tel: 313-834-8677
CHARLES SMALL, Dir.
Residential treatment center for boys, ages 12-17, in need of care, guidance and therapy.
Lay Staff 41
Residents 23
Emergency Shelter Program 12
Transitional Services 180
Mentoring Program 155

St. Catherine's House
1641 Webb Ave.
Detroit, MI 48206
Tel: 313-868-4505
MARY CONNORS, Mgr.
For elderly-ambulatory & younger disabled ambulatory women.
Capacity 12

St. Joseph's Home
4800 Cadieux Rd.
Detroit, MI 48224
Tel: 313-882-3800; Fax: 313-882-6944
Carmelite Sisters of the Divine Heart of Jesus
Sr. MARY MAGDALENE Admin.
Sisters 5
Lay Staff 68
Aged Residents 104

St. Mary's Residence
2120 Orleans St.
Detroit, MI 48207
Tel: 313-259-6874; 259-0459
Sr. M. FIDELIS, F.D.C., Admin.
Rev. WILLIAM LUNNON
A residence for women desiring home-like surroundings.
Daughters of Divine Charity
Sisters 6
Residents 60

Dimondale
Diocese of Lansing

St. Lawrence Dimondale Center
4000 N. Michigan Rd. (M-99)
Dimondale, MI 48821
Tel: 517-646-6258
Rev. STANLEY CZARNOTA, Chap. in res., Tel: 517-646-0408; Fax: 517-646-7578
DIANNE WEAVER, Admin.
Sr. MARY KATHLEEN BOTSFORD, R.S.M., Pastoral Care Asst. Nursing Home
Nursing Home Residents 178
Total Staff 272
Total Assisted 177

Dowagiac
Diocese of Kalamazoo

Dowagiac Nursing Home
610 Uneta St.
Dowagiac, MI 49047
Tel: 616-782-3471
Sisters of St. Joseph 2
Bed Capacity 100

Escanaba
Diocese of Marquette

Bishop Noa Home for Senior Citizens
2900 3rd Ave., S.
Escanaba, MI 49829
Tel: 906-786-5810; Fax: 906-786-5372
Sisters of St. Paul de Chartres
In res.,
Revs.:
EMIL J. BEYER, Assoc. Chap.
GILBERT N. NEUROHR, Chap.
Sisters of St. Paul de Chartres 5
Residents 123

Farmington Hills
Archdiocese of Detroit

Marillac Programs
A Division of St. Vincent and Sarah Fisher Center, 22255 Greenfield, Ste. 330
Southfield, MI 48334
Tel: 810-559-2272; Fax: 810-559-2226
JEAN VICKERS, Exec. Dir.
CHERYL BUKOFF, Dir.
Outreach case management and counseling services for pregnant and parenting teens in the tri-county area. Eight beds for the transitional housing of eighteen mothers 16-18 years of age and eight homeless babies 0-18 months of age.

Mercy Services for Aging
34605 Twelve Mile Rd.
Farmington Hills, MI 48331-3221
Tel: 248-305-7920
KAREN STRUVE, Pres. & CEO

St. Vincent and Sarah Fisher Center
27400 W. Twelve Mile Rd.
Farmington Hills, MI 48334
Tel: 313-538-6000; 810-626-7527
JEAN M. VICKERS, Exec. Dir.
Licensed capacity for: Residential care 60 (ages 4-15), Specialized Foster Care 120 (ages 0-17), Seton Preschool & Child Care Center 49 (ages 2 weeks-5 yrs.).
Pregnancy and Parenting For Teen Parents (Ages 16-19) Outreach Program:
Residential 41

Seton Nursery School and Infant-Toddler Child Care Center
29475 Inkster Rd.
Farmington Hills, MI 48018
Tel: 810-626-6990
ANN COYLE Dir.
Center licensed for 80 children, 8 weeks-5.5 years.
In Day Care 68
Legal Title: *Seton Nursery School and Infant-Toddler Child Care Center - St. Vincent Sara Fisher Center*

Flint
Diocese of Lansing

Marian Hall
529 Martin Luther King Ave.
Flint, MI 48502
Tel: 810-238-7646
SHARON DUCKWORTH, Admin.
Sisters of the Precious Blood 3
Residents 80

Grand Rapids
Diocese of Grand Rapids

Contemplative Sisters of the Good Shepherd
1355 Walker Ave., N.W.
Grand Rapids, MI 49504

Tel: 616-454-6268
Sr. HEART OF MARY FILLION, C.G.S., Supr.
Total Sisters 6
Sisters of the Good Shepherd
Rev. Msgr. CHARLES D. BROPHY, Chap.
Res.,
1247 Rennslaer, N.W.
Grand Rapids, MI 49504
Sisters of the Good Shepherd 2

St. Ann's Home
2161 Leonard St., N.W.
Grand Rapids, MI 49504
Tel: 616-453-7715; Fax: 616-453-7359
Carmelite Sisters of the Divine Heart of Jesus
Sisters 5
Residents 134

Kalamazoo
Diocese of Kalamazoo

Borgess Nursing Home
537 Chicago Ave.
Kalamazoo, MI 49001
Tel: 616-382-2392; Fax: 616-382-0843
Mrs. RUTH M. OLECH, Admin.
Bed Capacity 121

Lake Orion
Archdiocese of Detroit

Guest House for Women Religious
1840 W. Scripps Rd., Box 68
Lake Orion, MI 48360
Tel: 248-391-3100; Fax: 248-391-1553
A state licensed and JCAHO accredited endorsed residential treatment center for Catholic sisters and women in formation.
Sr. MAE KIERANS, C.S.J., Prog. Dir.
Bed Capacity 20
Central Admissions Office, from U.S. & Canada call: 800-626-6910.
Office of Guest House, Inc. Management Services Offices
1601 Joslyn Rd., P.O. Box 420
Lake Orion, MI 48361
Tel: 248-391-4445

Livonia
Archdiocese of Detroit

Marybrook Manor
36975 W. Five Mile Rd.
Livonia, MI 48154
Tel: 313-464-9667
Sr. MARY MODESTA PIWOWAR, C.S.S.F., Pres.
Sr. MARY RENETTA, C.S.S.F., Exec. Vice Pres.
Sr. ELIZABETH ANN C.S.S.F., N.H.A., Admin.
Residents 29

Marycrest Manor
15475 Middlebelt Rd.
Livonia, MI 48154
Tel: 313-427-9175
Sr. M. INNOCENT, F.S.S.J., Admin. Skilled nursing facility
Ownership: Franciscan Sisters of St. Joseph.
Sisters 3
Residents 55
Served by Marianhill Fathers.

Marywood Nursing Care Center
36975 W. Five Mile Rd.
Livonia, MI 48154
Tel: 313-464-0600
Long-term care Facility.
Sr. MARY MODESTA PIWOWAR, C.S.S.F., Pres.
Sr. MARY RENETTA C.S.S.F., Exec. Vice Pres.
Sr. ELIZABETH ANN C.S.S.F., N.H.A., Admin.
Sisters 3
Capacity 91

Ryan Senior Residences of the Archdiocese of Detroit. Inc.
Central Office, 36800 Schdolcraft
Livonia, MI 48150
Tel: 313-953-5873
EDEL DUNNE O'TOOLE, Exec. Dir.
Madonna Villa
17825 Fifteen Mile Rd.
Clinton Township, MI 48035
Tel: 810-792-0358
Total Staff 18
Number of Units 90
Number of Persons Served in 12 Month Period 1,080
SUZANNE SZCZEPANSKI-WHITE, Admin.
Casa Maria
600 Maple Vista
Imlay City, MI 48444
Tel: 810-724-6300
Total Staff 16
Number of Units 90
Number of Persons Served in 12 Months Period 1,080
PAUL WALKER, Admin.
Villa Marie
15131 Newburgh
Livonia, MI 48154
Tel: 313-464-9494
Total Staff 15
Number of Units 90
Number of Persons Served in 12 Month Period 1,080
Sr. LUCILLE BLIZMAN, O.P., Admin.
Marian Place
408 W. Front St.
Monroe, MI 48161
Tel: 313-241-2414
Total Staff 11
Number of Units 53
Number of Persons Served in 12 Month Period 636
KAREN MORRIN, Admin.
Kundig Center
3300 Jeffries Fwy.
Detroit, MI 48208
Tel: 313-894-0555
Total Staff 18
Number of Units 160
Number of Persons Served in 12 Month Period 1,680
THOMAS MCCUISH, Admin.
Stapleton Center
9341 Agnes
Detroit, MI 48214
Tel: 313-822-0397
Total Staff 15
Number of Units 59
Number of Persons Served in 12 Month Period 708
JENNIE BOYD, Admin.
Marian Oakland-West
29250 W. Ten Mile Rd.
Farmington Hills, MI 48336
Tel: 810-474-7204
Total Staff 14
Number of Units 90
Number of Persons Served in 12 Month Period 1,080
ELAINE MACDERMOTT, Admin.
Marydale Center
3147 Tenth Ave.
Port Huron, MI 48060
Tel: 810-985-9683
Total Staff 11
Number of Units 59
Number of Persons Served in 12 Month Period 708
Sr. ANN CHRISTINE CHARRON, Admin.
Maryhaven
11350 Reeck Road
Southgate, MI 48195
Tel: 313-287-2111
Total Staff 18
Number of Units 90
Number of Persons Served in 12 Month Period 1,080
Sr. PAULA COONEY, I.H.M., Admin.

Mount Clemens
Archdiocese of Detroit

St. Joseph Mercy Living Care Center
A Division of Mercy Mt. Clemens Corp.
37700 Harper
Mount Clemens, MI 48043
Tel: 810-468-0827
ROBERT L. BEYER, Pres.
Bed Capacity 264

Nazareth
Diocese of Kalamazoo

Dillon Complex for Independent Living, Inc.
Nazareth, MI 49074
Tel: 616-342-0263
Sponsored by the Sisters of St. Joseph
Sr. RUTH A. HEYN, S.S.J., Mgr.
Residents 77

Northville
Archdiocese of Detroit

Our Lady of Providence Center
16115 Beck Rd.
Northville, MI 48167
Tel: 313-453-1300
Sr. LINDA WILLETTE, Supr., Admin.
Rev. STANISLAUS C. KUKULSKI, Chap.

Otsego
Diocese of Kalamazoo

Otsego Senior Apts., Inc.
Baraga Manor, 301 Washington St.
Otsego, MI 49078
Tel: 616-694-9711
Mrs. DONNA M. HOLMES, Res. Mgr.
Managed by Catholic Family Services, Diocese of Kalamazoo.
1819 Gull Rd.
Kalamazoo, MI 49001
Apartments 48

Saginaw
Diocese of Saginaw

St. Francis Nursing Home
915 N. River Rd.
Saginaw, MI 48609
Fax: 517-781-3791
Sr. JANE MARIE LEBIEDZINSKI, C.S.S.F., Admin.
Rev. EDWARD TROMBLEY, Chap.
Felician Sisters (Livonia, MI) 4
Residents 100

St. Vincent Home-Boysville of Michigan, Inc.
925 N. River Rd.
Saginaw, MI 48609
Tel: 517-781-2780; Fax: 517-781-5422
RICK BOONE, M.S.W., C.S.W., Regl. Dir.
Mr. JOE MARTINUS, Pastoral Min.
Youth 56
Residential and community based treatment programs for troubled youth and families with facilities located throughout the state of Michigan and one in Ohio, under the auspices of the Brothers of the Holy Cross at Notre Dame.
Holland House
614 E. Holland Ave.
Saginaw, MI 48601
Tel: 517-755-5397
Boys 14
Boysville's Family & Community Support Program
925 N. River Rd.
Saginaw, MI 48609
Tel: 517-781-2780
Boys 32
Girls 24
Includes Specialized Foster Care, Supervised Independent Living, In-Home Treatment, Families First, and Nokomis Challenge.
Curtis House
P.O. Box 309
Frankenmuth, MI 48734
Tel: 517-652-3212
Boys 14

Southfield
Archdiocese of Detroit

Boysville of Michigan, Inc.
Community Resource Office, 17117 W. Nine Mile Rd., Ste. 1111
Southfield, MI 48075
Tel: 248-569-6630; Fax: 248-569-8171
Residential and communtiy based treatment programs for troubled youth and families with facilities located throughout the state of Michigan and one in the state of Ohio under the auspices of the Brothers of Holy Cross at Notre Dame.
Bro. FRANCIS BOYLAN, C.S.C., Exec. Dir.
Associate Executive Directors:
EDWARD J. OVERSTREET
PAUL S. NEITMAN
Andre House
7001 Burlingame
Detroit, MI 48204
Tel: 313-935-0769
Boys 17
Bowman House / Boysville of Michigan, Inc.
17200 Rowe St.
Detroit, MI 48205
Tel: 313-372-7320
Girls 17
Boysville's Family & Community Support Program
19403 W. Chicago
Detroit, MI 48228
Tel: 313-838-7500
Includes specialized foster care, supervised independent living, in-home family treatment, & Families First.
Bro. FRANCIS BOYLAN, C.S.C., Exec. Dir.
LYNNE ALEXANDER, Regl. Dir.
Cabrini Center / Boysville of Michigan, Inc.
23915 Elmira
Redford, MI 48239
Tel: 313-537-7868
Girls 19
Hitchcock Center / Boysville of Michigan, Inc.
5675 Larkins
Detroit, MI 48210
Tel: 313-895-5119
Boys 16
Holy Cross Center / Boysville of Michigan, Inc.
5690 Cecil
Detroit, MI 48210
Tel: 313-895-2200
Day treatment, education, recreation program for

Detroit region.
Johnson House / Boysville of Michigan, Inc.
7798 W. Fort St.
Detroit, MI 48209
Tel: 313-554-1700
Boys 102
King House / Boysville of Michigan, Inc.
24455 Crocker Blvd.
Mt. Clemens, MI 48043
Tel: 810-463-7130
Boys 14
Moreau Center / Boysville of Michigan, Inc.
3500 Comboni Way
Monroe, MI 48162
Tel: 313-242-5898
Boys 67
GEORGE BIRKAM, Reg. Dir.
St. Cecilia House / Boysville of Michigan, Inc.
7001 Burlingame St.
Detroit, MI 48204
Tel: 313-372-7320
Boys 18
St. Thomas Assessment Center / Boysville of Michigan, Inc.
8333 Townsend
Detroit, MI 48213
Tel: 313-579-1600
Sisters 1
Boys 218
Xavier Center / Boysville of Michigan, Inc.
27652 W. Outer Dr.
Ecorse, MI 48229
Tel: 313-381-5845
Boys 22

St. Francis Family Services
17500 W. Eight Mile Rd.
Southfield, MI 48075
Tel: 810-552-0750
RITA MONTGOMERY GRZELIK, Exec. Dir.
Foster home respite & adoption services for infants through 17 years.

Sheltering Arms
18310 W. 12 Mile
Southfield, MI 48076
Tel: 248-557-7373
Adult day care for the elderly. A service of Catholic Social Services of Oakland County.
Lay Staff 8
Volunteers 35
Patients assisted annually 71

St. Clair Shores
Archdiocese of Detroit

Sisters of Bon Secours Nursing Care Center
26001 E. Jefferson
St. Clair Shores, MI 48081
Tel: 810-779-7000
HENRY DEVRIES, CEO
ANNE SADLER, Admin.
GARY JANKOWSKI, Chief Finance Officer
Sr. ANNE MARIE MACK, C.S.B., V.P., Mission Effectiveness
Sr. PATRICIA SALTSZ, I.H.M., Dir. Spiritual Care
Long Term Care Facility.
Sisters 3
Bed Capacity 195

Sisters of Bon Secours Nursing Care Center
26001 E. Jefferson
St. Clair Shores, MI 48081
Tel: 810-779-7000
ANNE SADLER, Admin.
A member of the Bon Secours of Michigan Healthcare Systems, Inc. operated by the Sisters of Bon Secours. The center provides short and long term nursing, residential care and rehabilitative services for older adults.
Bed Capacity 200

Waterford
Archdiocese of Detroit

Fox Manor, Inc.
2350 Watkins Lake Rd.
Waterford, MI 48238
Tel: 810-674-9590
Dominican Sisters
Residential facility for independent senior citizens of moderate or limited means.
Sr. VIRGINIA BERAK, Admin.

Lourdes Nursing Home
Dominican Sisters of Oxford, MI
2300 Watkins Lake Rd.
Waterford, MI 48328
Tel: 810-674-2241
Sr. SUSAN MCMAHON, O.P., Admin.
Rev. JEROME L. KRIEG, Res. Chap.
Skilled & basic nursing facility for men and women; 24 hour nursing care.
Residents 108

St. Jude Home, Inc.
2270 Marwood
Waterford, MI 48328
Tel: 248-673-5179
SAM YAKER, Pres.
Dominican Sisters residential facility for those over 60 years of age requiring supervisory care, but not skilled nursing.
Religious 1
Lay Staff 6
Residents 6
McFadden Home
2150 Watkins Lake Rd.
Waterford, MI 48328
Tel: 248-673-3347
Religious 2
Lay Staff 2
Residents 6

MINNESOTA

Albany
Diocese of St. Cloud

Mother of Mercy Nursing Home and Retirement Center
Box 676
Albany, MN 56307
Tel: 320-845-2195
BOB WIKAN, Admin.
Rev. JOHN EIDENSCHINK, O.S.B., Chap.
Guests 114

Austin
Diocese of Winona

Sacred Heart Hospice, Inc.
1200 Twelfth St., S.W.
Austin, MN 55912
Tel: 507-433-1808
REBECCA MATHEWS HALVERSON, Admin.
Rev. FRANK E. ENRIGHT, Chap.
Sisters of the Third Order of St. Francis of the Congregation of Our Lady of Lourdes 1
Bed Capacity 59
Residents 59
Adult Day Care (client days) 4,348
Alzheimer's Day Program (client days) 2,445

Breckenridge
Diocese of St. Cloud

St. Francis Home
Breckenridge, MN 56520
Tel: 218-643-7661
DAVID NELSON, CEO
Rev. STANLEY WIESER, Chap.
KAREN STOKES, Pastoral Care Dir.
Residents 124

Cold Spring
Diocese of St. Cloud

Assumption Court
615 1st St. N.
Cold Spring, MN 56320
Tel: 320-685-4110
Sr. MARY ROGER, O.S.B., Admin.
Rev. JULIAN SCHMEISING, O.S.B., Chap.
Residents 34

Assumption Home
715 N. First St.
Cold Spring, MN 56320
Tel: 320-685-3693; Fax: 320-685-7044
Sr. MARY ROGER ANDERT, O.S.B., Admin.
Rev. JULIAN SCHMEISING, O.S.B., Chap.
Sisters of St. Benedict 2
Residents 95

John Paul Apartments
200 Eighth Ave. N.
Cold Spring, MN 56320
Tel: 320-685-4429
Pioneer Housing Development, Inc.
Sr. MARY ROGER ANDERT, O.S.B., Admin.
Rev. JULIAN SCHMEISING, O.S.B., Chap.
Apartments 61

Mother Teresa Home
101 Tenth Ave.
Cold Spring, MN 56320
Tel: 320-685-8626
Mr. STEVEN P. BRESNAHAN, Exec. Dir.
JOHN KRUEGER, Dir. Residential Svcs.
Supervised Living Situation for Persons with Developed Mental Disabilities
Residents 4

St. Ann's Home
103 10th Ave. N.
Cold Spring, MN 56320
Tel: 320-685-7898
Mr. STEVEN P. BRESNAHAN, Exec, Dir,
JOHN KRUEGER, Dir. Residential Svcs.
Supervised Living Situation for Persons with Developed Mental Disabilities
Residents 4

St. Luke's Home
411 Eighth Ave. N.
Cold Spring, MN 56320
Tel: 320-685-7750
Mr. STEVEN P. BRESNAHAN, Exec. Dir.
JOHN KRUEGER, Dir. Residential Svcs.
Adults with mild to moderate developmental disabilities.
Residents 4

Cold Springs
Diocese of St. Cloud

Bethany Home
13 8th Ave. S.
Cold Springs, MN 56320
Tel: 320-685-7899
Mr. STEVEN P. BRESNAHAN, Exec. Dir,
JOHN KRUEGER, Dir. Residential Svcs.
Supervised Living Situation for Persons with Developed Mental Disabilities

Crookston
Diocese of Crookston

Villa St. Vincent
516 Walsh St.
Crookston, MN 56716
Mr. MICHAEL D. SIEKAS, Admin.
Sisters of St. Benedict 3
Board and Care Beds 32
Assisted Living Beds 27
Skilled Nursing Beds 104
Residents 136

Detroit Lakes
Diocese of Crookston

St. Mary's Nursing Center
Detroit Lakes, MN 56501
Mr. DAVE ARMSTRONG, Admin.
Residents 100
Attended by Staff of St. Mary's Regional Health Center.

Duluth
Diocese of Duluth

Benedictine Health Center
(Sub. of Benedictine Health System)
935 Kenwood Ave.
Duluth, MN 55811
Tel: 218-723-6408; Fax: 218-723-6449
Rev. BERNARD BRENNAN, Chap.
Sr. MARY SUSAN DEWITT, O.S.B., Dir. of Chaplaincy Svcs.
Rehabilitation services and respite care.
Permanent Guests 120
Day Care:
Adults 44
Children 89

St. Ann's Senior Residence
330 E. Third St.
Duluth, MN 55805
Tel: 218-727-8831; Fax: 218-727-8833
Mr. FREDERICK OLSEN, Admin.
Rev. ROBERT BESTER, Chap.
Sisters of St. Benedict 2
Residents 185

Fergus Falls
Diocese of St. Cloud

Catholic Charities Intensive Treatment Unit
Box 1006
Fergus Falls, MN 56538-1006
Tel: 218-739-9325; Fax: 218-739-2242
Mr. STEVEN BRESNAHAN, Exec. Dir. in St. Cloud
JOHN KRUEGER, Dir. Residential Svc. in St. Cloud
Children 14

Hastings
Archdiocese of St. Paul and Minneapolis

Regina Convalescent and Nursing Care and Retirement Center
Hastings, MN 55033

Tel: 612-480-4333
Rev. JAMES J. DUNNE, S.S.C., Res. Chap.
Regina Healthcare
Number under care 75
Convalescent and Nursing Care 61
Retirement Center 43
Boarding Care 32
Total Staff 72

Little Falls
Diocese of St. Cloud

Alverna Apartments
(An Affiliate of Catholic Health Initiatives.)
300 Eighth Ave., S.E.
Little Falls, MN 56345
Tel: 320-632-1246
BEA BRITZ, Chap.
Residents 64

St. Camillus Place
1100 S.E. Fourth St.
Little Falls, MN 56345
Tel: 320-632-1212
CORY GLAD, Admin.
RANDAL FOSSUM, Dir.
BEA BRITZ, Chap.
Beds 14

St. Otto's Care Center
920 S.E. 4th St.
Little Falls, MN 56345
Tel: 320-632-9281; Fax: 320-632-1120
CORY GLAD, Vice Pres.
BEA BRITZ, Chap.
Residents 150

Minneapolis
Archdiocese of St. Paul and Minneapolis

St. Joseph's Home for Children
1121 E. 46th St.
Minneapolis, MN 55407
Tel: 612-827-6241
Mr. DOUGLAS GOKE, Admin.
In res.,
Rev. Msgr. J. JEROME BOXLEITNER
Intake; Emergency Shelter; Diagnostic and Assessment; Serving 3,821 Children Yearly; Residential Treatment (services 81); Day Treatment (services 49); Family Stability (outreach) Serving 120 Families Yearly; 3 Community Homes Serving 115 Yearly.
Lay persons 205

Morris
Diocese of St. Cloud

Villa of St. Francis Nursing Home
1001 Scott Ave.
Morris, MN 56267
Tel: 320-589-1133
CAROL ABELE, Admin.
Guests 138

Parkers Prairie
Diocese of St. Cloud

St. William's Living Center
P.O. Box 30
Parkers Prairie, MN 56361
Tel: 218-338-4671; Fax: 218-338-5917
PAUL BAER, Admin.
Guests 90

Pierz
Diocese of St. Cloud

St. Mary's Villa Inc.
Pierz, MN 56364
Tel: 320-468-6405
Rev. KENNETH BRENNY
VIRGINIA M. MEYER, Admin.
Guests 101

Rochester
Diocese of Winona

Guest House
4800 48th St., N.E., P.O. Box 954
Rochester, MN 55903
Tel: 800-634-4155; 507-288-4693
E-mail: ghousemn@infonet.isl.net
Web Site: http://ic.net/[]ghouse/ghouse.html
WILLIAM C. MORGAN, Dir.
A State licensed, JCAHO accredited and ecclesiastically endorsed residential treatment center for priests, brothers, deacons and seminarians. (Corporate headquarters located in Lake Orion, MI 48361)
Bed Capacity 39

Madonna Towers of Rochester, Inc.
4001 19th Ave., N.W.
Rochester, MN 55901
Tel: 507-288-3911; Fax: 507-288-0393
Subsidiary of Benedictine Health System.
MARK CAIRNS, Admin.
Rev. CATHAL J. GALLAGHER, S.S.C.
Guests 183
Total Staff 180
Chapel of the Immaculate Conception
Health Care Endowment Fund
4001 19th Ave., N.W.
Rochester, MN 55901

Sleepy Eye
Diocese of New Ulm

Divine Providence Community Home & Lake Villa Maria Senior Apts.
700 3rd Ave. N.W.
Sleepy Eye, MN 56085-1099
Tel: 507-794-3011; 794-5333
E-mail: divine@prairie.lake.com
Daughters of St. Mary of Providence
Sr. SHARON WILLIAMS, D.S.M.P., Admin. & Supr.
Sisters 4
Lay Workers 76
Aged Residents 58
Tenants 26

St. Cloud
Diocese of St. Cloud

Caritas Family Services, Catholic Charities Community Services
305 N. Seventh Ave.
St. Cloud, MN 56303
Tel: 320-252-4121; Fax: 320-259-8761
Mr. STEVEN P. BRESNAHAN, Exec. Dir.

Community Services of Catholic Charities
205 Seventh Ave. N.
St. Cloud, MN 56303
Tel: 320-259-8757; Fax: 320-240-3339
Community Service of Catholic Charities: SILS (Semi-Independent Living Skills), Community Support for Mentally Ill and Related Services to Persons with Disabilities.
Mr. STEVEN P. BRESNAHAN, Exec. Dir.

Day Treatment Services
1712 Seventh Ave. S.
St. Cloud, MN 56301
Tel: 320-251-3647
Mr. STEVEN P. BRESNAHAN, Exec. Dir.
JOHN KRUEGER, Dir. Residential Svcs.
Students 24

In-Home Family Services, Catholic Charities Community Services
700 Mall Germain
St. Cloud, MN 56302
Tel: 320-251-1404; Fax: 320-252-8180
Mr. STEVEN P. BRESNAHAN, Exec. Dir.

LaPaz Community Inc.
1730 Seventh Ave., S.
St. Cloud, MN 56301
Tel: 320-253-9470
Mr. STEVEN P. BRESNAHAN, Exec. Dir.
HARVEY SCHMITT, Dir. Housing Svcs.

St. Benedict's Center
1810 Minnesota Blvd., S.E.
St. Cloud, MN 56304
Tel: 320-252-0010; Fax: 320-654-2351
LINDA DOERR, Exec. Dir.
ROBIN THEIS, Admin., Housing and Community Svcs.
Rev. MEINRAD DINDORF, O.S.B., Chap.
Corporate Division of the St. Cloud Hospital. Operated under the auspices of the local Catholic Church of St. Cloud.
Residential Homes for residents with Alzheimers. All Benedict Homes are managed by St. Benedict's Center. A division of the St. Cloud Hospital. Operated under the auspices of the local Catholic Church of St. Cloud.
Residents 222
Benedict Village
2000 15th Ave., S.E.
St. Cloud, MN 56304
Tel: 320-252-4380
LINDA DOERR, Exec. Dir.
ROBIN THEIS, Admin., Housing and Community Svcs.
Rev. MEINRAD DINDORF, O.S.B., Chap.
Managed by St. Benedict's Center. A Division of the St. Cloud Hospital. Operated under the auspices of the local Catholic Church of St. Cloud.
Residents 115
Benedict Homes
Isaiah House
2052 15th Ave., S.E.
St. Cloud, MN 56304
Tel: 320-252-0010
Ruth House
1342 Minnesota Blvd., S.E.
St. Cloud, MN 56304
Tel: 320-252-0010
Rebekah House
1346 Minnesota Blvd., S.E.
St. Cloud, MN 56304
Tel: 320-252-0010
Sarah House
2060 15th Ave., S.E.
St. Cloud, MN 56304
Tel: 320-252-0010
Daniel House
1344 Minnesota Blvd., S.E.
St. Cloud, MN 56304
Tel: 320-252-0010
Timothy House
1348 Minnesota Blvd., S.E.
St. Cloud, MN 56304
Tel: 320-252-0010
Residential Homes for residents with Alzheimers. All Benedict Homes are managed by St. Benedict's Center. A division of the St. Cloud Hospital. Operated under the auspices of the local Catholic Church of St. Cloud.
Day Break
2056 15th Ave., S.E.
St. Cloud, MN 56304
Tel: 320-252-0010
Adult day care for individuals with memory loss located outside of Center but on Campus. Operated under the auspices of the local Catholic Church of St. Cloud.
Staff 2
Participants 18
Day Break II
2044 15th Ave., S.E.
St. Cloud, MN 56304
Tel: 320-252-0010
Adult day care for frail elderly in residential setting on campus. Operated under the auspices of the local Catholic Church of St. Cloud.
Staff 5
Participants 10
Benedict Court
1980 15 Ave., S.E.
St. Cloud, MN 56304
Tel: 320-252-0010
Assisted living apartments.
Residents 39
LINDA DOERR, Exec. Dir.
ROBIN THEIS, Admin., Housing and Community Svcs.
Sr. JUDITH SCHAFFER, Benedict Court Dir.
Rev. MEINRAD DINDORF, O.S.B., Chap.
Managed by St. Benedict's Center. A Division of the St. Cloud Hospital. Operated under the auspices of the local Catholic Church of St. Cloud.
Staff 12
Residents 31

**Benet Place*
1420 Minnesota Blvd., S.E.
St. Cloud, MN 56304
Tel: 320-252-2557
Subsidized apartments with supportive services for older adults only. Operated under the auspices of the local Catholic Church of St. Cloud.
Staff 4
Tenants 43

St. Cloud Children's Home of the Diocese of St. Cloud
1726 Seventh Ave. S.
St. Cloud, MN 56301
Tel: 320-251-8811; Fax: 320-251-3198
Mr. STEVEN P. BRESNAHAN, Exec. Dir.
JOHN KRUEGER, Dir. Residential Svcs.
Children 78
Youth Learning Center
374 Fourth Ave. S.
St. Cloud, MN 56301
Tel: 320-253-6614
Cottage 7 - St. Cloud Children's Home
1700 Seventh Ave. S.
St. Cloud, MN 56301
Tel: 320-251-9101

St. Elizabeth Home
306 15th Ave., N.
St. Cloud, MN 56301
Tel: 320-252-8350
Mr. STEVEN P. BRESNAHAN, Exec. Dir.
JOHN KRUEGER, Dir. of Residential Svcs.
Board and Lodging Home for Functionally Impaired Adults.

Residents 18

St. Paul
Archdiocese of St. Paul and Minneapolis

Bethany Convent for Retired Sisters
1870 Randolph
St. Paul, MN 55105
Tel: 612-690-7050
Sr. MARY CALDER, C.S.J., Dir. of Community
Sr. GEORGE ANN BOHL, C.S.J., Assoc. Dir. of Community
Sisters of St. Joseph of Carondelet
Total Staff 90
Total in Residence 150

Franciscan Health Community
1925 Norfolk Ave.
St. Paul, MN 55116
Tel: 612-696-8400
JOSEPH STANISLAV, Pres. & CEO
Clergy:
Rev. Msgr. FRANCIS J. FLEMING
Revs.:
MARTIN M.P. FLEMING
JOHN R. FLEMING (NU)
Sisters 4
Aged Residents 223

Holy Family Residence
330 S. Exchange St.
St. Paul, MN 55102
Tel: 612-227-0336
Sr. MARGUERITE MC CARTHY, Supr.
Rev. ROBERT H. FITZGERALD, S.J., Chap.
Little Sisters of the Poor 12
Aged Residents 75
Apartments 32
Total Staff, all facilities 130

Our House of Minnesota, Inc. I
1846 Dayton Ave.
St. Paul, MN 55104
Tel: 612-644-6650
Office
Tel: 612-646-1104
DENNIS HOLMAN, Admin.
Staff 8
Mentally Handicapped Adults 6

Our House of Minnesota, Inc. II
1846 Portland
St. Paul, MN 55104
Tel: 612-644-2411
Office:
Tel: 612-646-1104
DENNIS HOLMAN, Admin.
Staff 14
Mentally Handicapped Adults 6

Our Lady of Good Counsel Home
2076 St. Anthony Ave.
St. Paul, MN 55104
Tel: 612-646-2797
Sisters of St. Dominic. Servants of Relief for Incurable Cancer
Sr. M. JOSEPH, O.P., Supr.
Rev. JAMES W. JACKSON
Nursing Sisters 9
Bed capacity 40
Patients assisted annually 175
Total Assisted 175
Total Staff 35

Staples
Diocese of St. Cloud

Mary Rondorf Retirement Home of Sacred Heart Parish
Staples, MN 56479
Tel: 218-894-2124
Mrs. VIRGINIA ROLLINS, Admin.
Guests 45

Wabasha
Diocese of Winona

St. Elizabeth's Health Care Center
626 Shields Ave.
Wabasha, MN 55981
Tel: 612-565-4581
(Conducted in connection with St. Elizabeth's Hospital)
THOMAS CROWLEY, Admin.
Rev. JOSEPH R. MCGINNIS
Skilled Beds 100
Admissions 84
St. Elizabeth's Nursing Home
1200 5th Grant Blvd., W.
Wabasha, MN 55981
(Conducted in connection with St. Elizabeth's Hospital)
THOMAS CROWLEY, Pres.
Rev. JOSEPH MCGINNIS
Beds 50
Residents 50

Waite Park
Diocese of St. Cloud

St. Francis Home
25 Second St. N.
Waite Park, MN 56387
Tel: 320-251-7630
Supervised living situation for Persons with Developed Disabilities
Mr. STEVEN P. BRESNAHAN, Exec. Dir.
JOHN KRUEGER, Dir. Residential Svcs.
Residents 4

West St. Paul
Archdiocese of St. Paul and Minneapolis

Guild Incorporated
1025 Dodd Rd.
West St. Paul, MN 55118
Tel: 612-450-2220
Programs owned by The Guild of Catholic Women. A variety of housing and support services for adults who have experienced serious and persistant mental illness. Apartments and group living available.
Capacity for clients:
St. Paul 160
Total Assisted 300
Total Staff 50

Winona
Diocese of Winona

St. Anne Hospice, Inc.
1347 W. Broadway
Winona, MN 55987
Tel: 507-454-3621
RICHARD BOYD, Admin.
Rev. Msgr. J. RICHARD FEITEN, Chap.
Bed Capacity 134
Residents 134
Adult Day Care (patient days) 900
Forget Me Not Adult Day Center (Guest days) 1,052
Nursing Care for the aged, chronically ill or invalid (resident days) 48,732
Total Staff 414

St. Francis Community Programs of Minnesota, Inc.
725 W. Broadway
Winona, MN 55987
Tel: 507-454-7711
Amethyst House
428 W. Broadway
Winona, MN 55987
Tel: 507-452-8877
A 14-bed transitional living adult alcohol and chemical abuse home in two locations.
Hiawatha Hall
725 W. Broadway
Winona, MN 55987
Tel: 507-454-7711
A 13-bed mental health residential treatment facility.
Wenonah Hall
221 E. Fourth St.
Winona, MN 55987
Tel: 507-452-1191
10-bed capacity for the mentally ill.
Carillian House
1623 Fourth St., N.W.
Rochester, MN 55901
Tel: 507-281-3000
An 18-bed transitional living alcohol and chemical abuse home for adults.
Total Assisted 130
Total Staff 29

MISSISSIPPI

Bay St. Louis
Diocese of Biloxi

Notre Dame de la Mer Retirement Apartments
292 Hwy. 90
Bay St. Louis, MS 39520
Tel: 228-467-2885; Fax: 228-466-6300
Ms. MICHELE TINE, Mgr.
Total Staff 8
Total in Residence 62

Biloxi
Diocese of Biloxi

Gabriel Manor
2321 Atkinson Rd.
Biloxi, MS 39531
Tel: 228-388-1013; Fax: 228-388-1176
Ms. LOUISE CUMMINS, Mgr.
Total Staff 1
Total in Residence 51

Santa Maria Retirement Apartments
674 Beach
Biloxi, MS 39530
Tel: 228-432-1289; Fax: 228-435-0380
E-mail: santa.maria.del.mar@worldnet.attnet
Ms. PATTY ROBERTS, Mgr.
Total Staff 7
Total in Residence 223

Gulfport
Diocese of Biloxi

Carlow Manor
15195 Barbara Dr.
Gulfport, MS 39503
Tel: 228-539-0707; Fax: 228-539-0704
PHYLLIS GORDON, Mgr.
Total Staff 2
Total in Residence 39

Jackson
Diocese of Jackson

D'Evereaux Hall Home, Inc.
P.O. Box 2248
Jackson, MS 39225
Tel: 601-355-8634
Mrs. LINDA RAFF

St. Mary Orphan Home, Inc.
P.O. Box 2248
Jackson, MS 39225
Tel: 601-355-8634
Mrs. LINDA RAFF

Ocean Springs
Diocese of Biloxi

Samaritan House
642 Jackson Ave.
Ocean Springs, MS 39564
Tel: 228-875-1087; Fax: 228-872-9500
JUDY HIGGINS, Mgr.
Total Staff 2
Total in Residence 51

Villa Maria Retirement Apartments
921 Porter Ave.
Ocean Springs, MS 39564
Tel: 228-875-8811; Fax: 228-875-8889
Mrs. CINDY A. LADNIER, Mgr.
Total Staff 15
Total in Residence 225

Petal
Diocese of Biloxi

Caritas Manor
145 W. 10th Ave.
Petal, MS 39465
Tel: 601-545-7744; Fax: 601-545-7740
CINDY HOPKINS, Mgr.
Total Staff 2
Total in Residence 32

MISSOURI

Blue Springs
Diocese of Kansas City-St. Joseph

St. Mary's Manor
111 Mock Ave.
Blue Springs, MO 64014
Tel: 816-228-5655
PAT BAKER, Admin.
Rev. JOACHIM SCHIEBER, O.S.B., Chap.
Long term care facility with skilled nursing care and residential care.
Skilled care 132
Residential care 45

Eureka
Archdiocese of St. Louis

Price Memorial
Forby Rd., P.O. Box 476
Eureka, MO 63025
Tel: 314-587-3200
Bro. JOHN SPILA, O.S.F., Admin.
A skilled nursing facility conducted by the Franciscan Missionary Brothers of St. Joseph's Hill Infirmary.
Brothers 3

Residents 120

St. Joseph Hill Infirmary, Inc.
St. Joseph Rd.
Eureka, MO 63025
Tel: 314-587-3661
Bro. BERNARDO TROSA, O.S.F., Admin.
A skilled nursing facility conducted by the Franciscan Missionary Brothers of the Sacred Heart of Jesus.
Brothers 11
Residents 127
Total Assisted 120
Total Staff 55

Florissant
Archdiocese of St. Louis

Father Dunne's Newsboys Home
853 Dunn Rd.
Florissant, MO 63031
Tel: 314-837-0513
Corporate Title: Father Dunne's Newsboys' Home and Protectorate
WILLIAM J. DONLEY, Exec. Dir.
Emergency and long-term residential care to homeless, neglected and abused boys, status offenders and boys with family problems. Ages 12-21.
Children 30
Total in Residence 87
Total Staff 27

Marygrove Services, Inc.
2705 Mullanphy Ln.
Florissant, MO 63031
Tel: 314-837-1702; Fax: 314-830-6258
E-mail: mgrove@swb.net
Owned and operated under the auspices of Catholic Charities.
Sr. HELEN NEGRI, D.C., Admin.
Residential treatment for emotionally disturbed males and females (ages 6-21). Special education, therapy and medical services. Overnight emergency care: males and females (Birth-18).
Bed Capacity 87
Total Assisted 2,689
Total Staff 125
Sequoia House - Mullanphy
Group Home for Females Ages 17-21.
Beds 10
Sycamore House
Bed Capacity 3
Overnight Emergency Care: Bed Capacity 8

Jefferson City
Diocese of Jefferson City

St. Joseph's Home
1306 W. Main St.
Jefferson City, MO 65109
Tel: 573-635-0166
Conducted by the Carmelite Sisters of the Divine Heart of Jesus.
GRACE HOFFMANN, Admin.
Sr. LYDIA ANN BRAUN, Supr.
DENISE SOMMERER, Dir. Nurses
Rev. Msgr. CHARLES PATTERSON, Chap.
Sisters 5
Residents 90

Villa Marie Skilled Nursing Facility
1030 Edmonds St.
Jefferson City, MO 65109
Tel: 573-761-6700
Owned and operated by SSM Health Care Central Region. Member of SSM Health Care
JOHN H. SCHULTE, Admin.
Ms. BARBARA L. LOWRY, Dir. Nursing Svcs.
Rev. HUGH F. BEHAN, Chap.
Franciscan Sisters of Mary, St Louis 4
Bed Capacity 120

Kansas City
Diocese of Kansas City-St. Joseph

Brighton Place
2429 Brighton
Kansas City, MO 64127
Tel: 816-231-3211
CHUCK JAMES, Mgr.
A 31-unit residence for the elderly and disabled.

Cathedral Square Towers
444 W. 12th St.
Kansas City, MO 64105
Tel: 816-471-6555
Apartment residence for the elderly and handicapped.
Mrs. SANDRA CARLSON, Mgr.
Ms. CATHERINE ANCONA, Asst. Mgr.
Mr. NEAL D. COLBY, JR., Diocesan Liaison
Units 156
Total in Residence 167
Total Staff 10

Columbus Park Plaza
801 Pacific
Kansas City, MO 64106
Tel: 816-472-0887
ALICE MCGAN, Mgr.
Mr. NEAL D. COLBY, Diocesan Liaison
Apartment residence for elderly and handicapped.
Units 56
Total in Residence 55
Total Staff 2

Jeanne Jugan Center
8745 James A. Reed Rd.
Kansas City, MO 64138
Tel: 816-761-4744; Fax: 816-761-4724
Legal Title: *Little Sisters of the Poor*
Little Sisters of the Poor
Sr. MAUREEN WEISS, Supr.
Rev. FRANCIS J. SCHUELE, Chap.
Sisters 15
Apartments 33
Beds 78
Total in Residence 112
Total Staff 90

Marlborough Manor
1818 E. 79th St.
Kansas City, MO 64132
Tel: 816-221-4377
DONNA QUICK, Mgr.
Rental housing for low income (a 31-unit apartment residence for the elderly and disabled).

Red Bridge Place
11300 Colorado
Kansas City, MO 64137
Tel: 816-761-4667
JAN CARSON, Mgr.
Total in Residence 48
Total Staff 3

Redemptorist Retirement Home
207 W. Linwood
Kansas City, MO 64111-1327
Tel: 816-561-3025
E-mail: solnnette@IX.netcom.com
Sr. M. ANNETTE SCHORMAN, C.S.J., Dir.
Guests 19
Total Staff 10

Tremont Place
6161 N. Chatham
Kansas City, MO 64151
Tel: 816-587-7707
TERRI JONES, Mgr.
A 50-unit apartment residence for the elderly and disabled.

Kirkwood
Archdiocese of St. Louis

St. Agnes Home for the Elderly
10341 Manchester Rd.
Kirkwood, MO 63122
Tel: 314-965-7616; Fax: 314-965-3179
Sr. M. ANGELINA Finnel, Carmel.D.C.J., Admin.
Rev. Msgr. BERNARD GRANICH
In res.,
His Eminence JOHN JOSEPH CARDINAL CARBERRY, Former Archbishop of St. Louis
Conducted for Elderly Ladies, Gentlemen and Couples by the Carmelite Sisters of the Divine Heart of Jesus.
Legal Title: *Carmelite Sisters of the Divine Heart of Jesus of Missouri*
Sisters 10
Guests 124
Total Staff 110

Liberty
Diocese of Kansas City-St. Joseph

Immaculata Manor Foundation
2101 Hughes Rd.
Liberty, MO 64068-9397
Tel: 816-781-4332; Fax: 816-781-8820
Residential Care Center for women with developmental disabilities.
NANCY MILLER, Exec. Dir.
WILLIAM WEBB, Pres.
Operated by the Immaculata Board of Directors.
Residents 26
Total Staff 28

Our Lady of Mercy Country Home
2205 Hughes Rd.
Liberty, MO 64068
Tel: 816-781-5711
Mercedarian Missionaries of Berriz
Sr. BETTY PRESTON, M.M.B., Pres.
Guests 110
Sisters 33

Mehlville
Archdiocese of St. Louis

Nazareth Living Center
2 Nazareth Ln.
Mehlville, MO 63129
Tel: 314-487-3950
Residential and Skilled Nursing Care Facility.
Sisters of St. Joseph of Carondelet and General Public
Sr. AUDREY OLSON, C.S.J., Supr.
Rev. THOMAS GRAHAM, Chap.
BARBARA PROSSER, Admin.
Total Assisted 267
Total Staff 264

Normandy
Archdiocese of St. Louis

Maria Droste Residence
7660 Natural Bridge Rd.
Normandy, MO 63121
Tel: 314-383-5553
Sisters of the Good Shepherd
For Women in Need.
Capacity 12
Total Assisted 68
Total Staff 6

St. Vincent Home for Children
7401 Florissant Rd.
Normandy, MO 63121
Tel: 314-261-6011
Legal Title: *The German St. Vincent Orphan Association*
Sr. JOANN KELZER, S.C.C., Exec. Dir.
Sr. PAULINE SHAFER, Supr.
Rev. MARTIN MANNION, Chap.
Sisters of Christian Charity 6
Children 48
Chapel of the Sacred Heart.

Savannah
Diocese of Kansas City-St. Joseph

La Verna Heights Retirement Center, Inc.
104 E. Park Ave., P.O. Box 488
Savannah, MO 64485-0488
Tel: 816-324-3179
MICHAEL BURAK, Admin.
Sisters of St. Francis of Savannah
Guest Capacity 39
Total Assisted 72
Total Staff 52

La Verna Village Apartments
1000-1005 Hall Ave.
Savannah, MO 64485
Tel: 816-324-3179
Sisters of St. Francis of Savannah
Rev. WALTER HEENEY, O.S.B., Chap.
DOYLE MCCUSH, Mgr.
Apartments for the elderly and handicapped.
Units 20
Total in Residence 22

La Verna Village Nursing Home
904 Hall Ave., P.O. Box 279
Savannah, MO 64485
Tel: 816-324-3185; Fax: 816-324-4097
MICHAEL BURAK, Admin.
Sisters of St. Francis of Savannah
Sr. M. MAGDALENE, O.S.F., Asst. Admin.
Guest Capacity 120
Total Assisted 161
Total Staff 124

Springfield
Diocese of Springfield-Cape Girardeau

St. John's Mercy Villa
1100 E. Montclair
Springfield, MO 65807
Tel: 417-888-8500; Fax: 417-888-8532
Sisters of Mercy Healthcare System (St. Louis)
Skilled Care of Long Term Nursing Home, for the Aged and Chronically Ill.
Mr. DON SWAFFORD, Admin.
Rev. WAYNE J. BARRON, C.M.F., Chap.
Sisters 2
Bed Capacity 150

St. Charles
Archdiocese of St. Louis

St. Joseph Carmelite Home
723 First Capitol Dr.
St. Charles, MO 63301
Tel: 314-946-4140
E-mail: stjoseph@primary.net
Rev. ALBERT F. DANTER, Chap.
Conducted by the Carmelite Sisters of the Divine Heart of Jesus
Legal Title: *Carmelite Sisters of the Divine Heart of Jesus of Missouri*
Sisters 5
Guests 150
Total Staff 117

St. Louis
Archdiocese of St. Louis

Alexian Brothers Lansdowne Village
4624 Lansdowne
St. Louis, MO 63116
Tel: 314-351-6888; Fax: 314-351-5825
Total Assisted 435
Total Staff 150

Alexian Brothers Sherbrooke Village
4005 Ripa Ave.
St. Louis, MO 63125
Tel: 314-544-1111; Fax: 314-544-5134
C. MICHAEL ROTH, Pres.
Total in Residence (Assisted Living) 43
Total Assisted (Nursing Care) 113
Total Staff 112

Boys Hope / Girls Hope of St. Louis, Inc.
755 S. New Ballas Rd., Ste. 120
St. Louis, MO 63141
Tel: 314-692-7477; Fax: 314-692-7810
JULIE SHERIDAN, Exec. Dir.
Residential Care for Adolescent Boys and Girls, Troubled by Family Disruptions, who are Capable of College Preparatory High School Work. Ages 7-18.
Total Assisted 16
Total Staff 5

Cardinal Glennon Children's Hospital
1465 S. Grand Blvd.
St. Louis, MO 63104
Tel: 314-577-5600; Fax: 314-268-6468
Member of SSM Health Care.
Mr. DOUGLAS A. RIES, Pres.
Sr. JUDITH CARRON, R.S.M., Dir. of Pastoral Care
Sisters 4
Bed Capacity (for Children) 190
Patients assisted annually 170,538

Cathedral Tower
325 N. Newstead Ave.
St. Louis, MO 63108
Tel: 314-531-0511
Ms. RUTH RAITHEL, Admin.
Residence for Women, Men and Girls. Operated by Catholic Charities.
Sisters 9
Residents 127

Chariton Apartments
4249 Michigan Ave.
St. Louis, MO 63111
Tel: 314-352-7600
Retirement Home for the Elderly, Conducted by the Third Order of St. Francis, Franciscan Tertiary Province of Missouri, Inc.
Residents 136
Apartments 122

Father Dempsey's Hotel, Inc.
3427 Washington Ave.
St. Louis, MO 63103
Rev. Msgr. CHARLES A. MOTTIN, Dir.
Total in Residence 47
Total Staff 3

Father Jim's Home
3427 Washington Ave.
St. Louis, MO 63103
Tel: 314-535-7221
Rev. Msgr. CHARLES A. MOTTIN, Gen. Mgr.
Under Care 81
Total in Residence 47
Total Staff 4

Fusz Pavilion
3601 Lindell Blvd.
St. Louis, MO 63108
Tel: 314-534-1201
A Retirement Home for Jesuits.
Rev. PAUL C. PILGRAM, S.J., Rector
Bro. ROBERT L. AUG, S.J., Asst. Rector
Revs.:
JOHN R. ALLEN, S.J.
LAWRENCE E. BARRY, S.J.
JOHN C. CHOPPESKY, S.J.
DARYL G. CORNISH, S.J.
FREDERICK T. DALY, S.J.
VINCENT F. DAUES, S.J.
ANDREW J. DEEMAN, S.J.
JOHN G. FLANNIGAN, S.J.
GEORGE E. GANSS, S.J.
LOUIS J. HANLON, S.J.
ROBERT J. HENLE, S.J.
FRANCIS R. LEIKER, S.J.
EDWARD P. MANHARD, S.J.
LEONARD M. MURRAY, S.J.
J. PAUL O'CONNOR, S.J.
JOHN R. PADBERG, S.J.
GEORGE M. PIEPER, S.J.
BERNARD C. SCHULTE, S.J.
EDWARD A. THRO, S.J.
EDWARD H. WINTERGALEN, S.J.
JEROME A. ZUMMACH, S.J.
Bros.:
LAWRENCE W. EILERT, S.J.
PAUL M. HOFER, S.J.
ROBERT H. NILGES, S.J.
PHILIP G. MALONE, S.J.
JOHN J. SCHWENDEMANN, S.J.
Priests 22
Brothers 6
Total Assisted 26
Total Staff 25

Little Sisters of the Poor, Home for the Aged
3225 N. Florissant Ave.
St. Louis, MO 63107
Tel: 314-421-6022
Sr. MARY SYLVIA KARL, L.S.P., Supr.
Rev. SIMON BRZOZOWSKI, M.S.F., Chap.
Sisters 13
Residents 110
Total assisted 120
Total Staff 122

Marian Hall Agencies
1340 Partridge Ave.
St. Louis, MO 63130
Tel: 314-726-3339
Sr. PATRICIA JOHNSON, C.S.J., Admin.
Residential Care to Homeless, Neglected and Abused Adolescent Girls (ages 11-18) with Emotional and/or Behavioral Problems.
Legal Title: *Managers of the Roman Catholic Orphan Asylums of St. Louis*
Sisters 2
Lay Staff 17
Capacity 24

Marian Hall Emergency Shelter
325 N. Newstead
St. Louis, MO 63108
Tel: 314-531-0511
Emergency Shelter in a Residential Setting for Runaway, Homeless or Abused Adolescent Girls (ages 11-18), with Emotional and/or Behavioral Problems.
Legal Title: *Managers of the Roman Catholic Orphan Asylums of St. Louis*
Lay Staff 8
Capacity 10
Total Assisted 300

Mary Queen and Mother Center
7601 Watson Rd.
St. Louis, MO 63119
Tel: 314-961-8485
A part of Cardinal Carberry Living Center

Mary, Queen and Mother Nursing Center
7601 Watson Rd.
St. Louis, MO 63119
Rev. JOHN P. COMER
Sr. SUZANNE WESLEY, C.S.J., Exec. Dir.
Total Assisted 510
Total Staff 250
A part of Cardinal Carberry Living Center.

Mother of Good Counsel Home
6825 Natural Bridge Rd., (St. Louis Co.)
St. Louis, MO 63121
Tel: 314-383-4765
Sr. M. STEPHANIE BELGERI, O.S.F., Admin.
Rev. BERNARD F. HUHN, Chap.
Skilled Nursing Facility for Men and Women.
Conducted by Sisters of St. Francis of the Martyr St. George
Sisters 10
Residents 114
Total Staff 156

Mother of Perpetual Help Residence
7609 Watson Rd.
St. Louis, MO 63119
Tel: 314-961-8000
A part of Cardinal Carberry Living Center

Our Lady of Life Apartments, Inc.
7655 Watson Rd.
St. Louis, MO 63119
Tel: 314-968-9447
A part of Cardinal Carberry Living Center.

Queen of Peace Center
325 N. Newstead Ave.
St. Louis, MO 63108
Tel: 314-531-0511
CONSTANCE S. NEUMANN, Admin.
Substance Abuse Treatment and Rehabilitation for Drug-Affected Women and their Children. Three levels of Care: Outpatient and Inpatient Residential, Medicaid Provider, Therapeutic Daycare and Nursery. Focus on High-Risk Pregnant Women. DMH certified.
Beds 42
Outpatient 150
Total Assisted 1,093
Total Staff 82

Regina Cleri Residence
7850 Kenrick Rd.
St. Louis, MO 63119
Tel: 314-968-2240
A Residence for Retired Diocesan Priests of the Archdiocese of St. Louis. Conducted by the Archdiocese of St. Louis.
Sr. GERALDINE VOGEL, C.PP.S., Admin.
Sisters of the Most Precious Blood of O'Fallon, MO 4
Franciscan Sisters of Our Lady of Perpetual Help 1
Priests 34
Total Staff 24

Rosati Group Home, Inc.
4532 Lindell Blvd.
St. Louis, MO 63108
Tel: 314-367-5500
JOHN M. LALLY, Pres.
Group Home and Stabilization Center for homeless mentally ill adults.

Rosati Stabilization Center
4224 N. Grand Ave.
St. Louis, MO 63107
Tel: 314-534-6624
Residential Transitional Facility for Mentally Ill Homeless.
Managed by the St. Patrick Center.
Capacity 15
Total Assisted 72
Total Staff 9

St. Joseph's Home for Boys
4753 S. Grand Blvd.
St. Louis, MO 63111-1459
Tel: 314-481-9121; Fax: 314-481-5605
E-mail: stjoehome@stl.unitedway.org
JAMES M. SINCLAIR, SR., Exec. Dir.
Emergency and Long-Term Residential Treatment Center for Young Men (ages 6-14) with Moderate to Severe Behavioral, Emotional, Family, and/or Educational Problems. Majority are Survivors of Neglect and/or Abuse. Day Treatment Program for Grades 1-8, Residents and Day Students.
Legal Title: *Managers of the Roman Catholic Orphan Asylums of St. Louis*
Sisters of St. Joseph of Carondelet 2
Lay Staff 55
Residential 46
Day Treatment 30
Total Assisted 136

St. Martha's Hall
P.O. Box 4950
St. Louis, MO 63108
Tel: 314-533-1313
MICHELLE SCHILLER-BAKER, Dir.
Provides Shelter, Advocacy and Support to Abused Women & their Children.
Capacity 25
Total Assisted 241

St. Philippine Duchesne Shelter
1015 Goodfellow Blvd.
St. Louis, MO 63112
Tel: 314-454-1012
MARY CARROLL, M.S.W., Coord.
ARNETTA HARRIS, Dir.
Serves homeless families & their children.
Emergency Shelter:
Total Assisted 571

Total Staff 7

SSM Rehab
6420 Clayton Rd., #600
St. Louis, MO 63117
Tel: 314-768-5300; Fax: 314-768-5355
Member of SSM Health Care.
MELINDA CLARK, Pres.
For rehabilitation of pediatrics, adolescents and adults
Bed Capacity:
St. Mary's Health Center, St. Louis 80
St. Joseph Health Center, St. Charles 20
Outpatient Locations 14

Villa Maria Center
8351 Florissant Rd.
St. Louis, MO 63121
Tel: 314-521-2255
Ms. MARY PATTON, M.S.
Under the Auspices of Catholic Services for Children and Youth. Comprehensive Program for Unmarried Parents; Provides Individual and Group Counseling, Arranges Obstetrical and Pediatric Care, Provides Educational Services Including Academic and Personal Growth and Development, Training in Parenting and Living Skill.
Capacity 13
Total Assisted 49
Total Staff 13

Stoutsville
Diocese of Jefferson City

Columbia Nursing Home Ministry
R.R. #1, P.O. Box 103-BC
Stoutsville, MO 65283
E-mail: rhunkins@trib.net
Rev. RICHARD C. HUNKINS, Dir.

NEBRASKA

Boys Town
Archdiocese of Omaha

**Father Flanagan's Boys' Home*
Boys Town, NE 68010
Tel: 402-498-1111
Rev. VALENTINE J. PETER, Exec. Dir.
Dr. PATRICK McGINNIS, Dir. Education
Rev. EUGENE McREYNOLDS, O.S.B.
High School:
Dr. RICHARD LOHMEIER, Prin.
Teachers 28
Students 449
Grade School:
CATHY DESALVO, Prin.
Teachers 14
Students 121
Boys Town USA
DON WEBER, Special Deputy, Public Policy Advisor
Dr. DAVID COUGHLIN, Deputy Exec. Dir. Youth Care
Dr. DAN DALY, Dir. Home Campus & Midwest Region
Boys Town National Research & Training Center
TOM DOWD, Dir.
MARK GRAHAM, Dir. of Operations
Managed Care Division
KAREN AUTHIER, Dir.
Boys Town Research Division
Dr. DAN DALY, Dir.
Boys Town National Research Hospital for Children
Dr. PATRICK BROOKHOUSER, Dir.
Boys Town Crisis Hotline
Tel: 800-448-3000
CONSTANCE GARRETT, Coord.
Boys Town Religious Education Program
TOM EVERSON, Dir.
KATHY SORENSEN, Assoc. Dir.
Total Assisted 29,802
Total Staff 1,806

David City
Diocese of Lincoln

St. Joseph's Villa, Inc.
927 7th St.
David City, NE 68632
Tel: 402-367-3045; Fax: 402-367-3730
Sisters Adorers of the Blood of Christ (Wichita, KS)
JOYCE STEWART, Admin.
Residents 65

Kearney
Diocese of Grand Island

Mount Carmel Home-Keens' Memorial
412 W. 18th St.
Kearney, NE 68847
Tel: 308-237-2287
Sr. EMERANTIANA, O.Carm., Supr.
Carmelites 16
Guests 78
Total Staff 95

Lincoln
Diocese of Lincoln

Bonacum House
3301 Sheridan Blvd.
Lincoln, NE 68506
Residence for retired priests.
Rev. Msgr. WILLIAM J. REZABEK
Rev. Msgr. DENIS L. BARRY
Rev. Msgr. CHARLES J. KEENAN
Rev. Msgr. CLARENCE P. REISDORFF
Revs.:
ERNEST O. SLOUP
PATRICK J. LYONS
JOHN W. KELLY

Madonna Rehabilitation Hospital
5401 South St.
Lincoln, NE 68506
Tel: 402-489-7102
Physical Medicine and Rehabilitation, Outpatient Services, Long-Term Care, and Adult Day Care.
Rev. STANLEY REDMERSKI, Chap.
Sisters 9
Beds 252
Patients assisted annually 2,826

Norfolk
Archdiocese of Omaha

St. Joseph Nursing Home
401 N. 18th St.
Norfolk, NE 68701
Tel: 402-371-9404
E-mail: stjoeadm@ncfcomm.com
KIM CROMWELL, Exec. Sec. & Contact
Missionary Benedictine Sisters 3
Aged Residents 99

Omaha
Archdiocese of Omaha

**Bergan Mercy Care Center*
1870 S.75th St.
Omaha, NE 68124
Tel: 402-398-6800
Sisters of Mercy of the Americas
MARY KERRES, Contact Person
S. DOTTIE BROWN, Svc. Leader
Subacute Care/Skilled Nursing Facility.
Beds 246
Average Daily Census 220
Affiliate of Catholic Health Initiatives.

Mercy Villa
1845 S. 72 St.
Omaha, NE 68124
Retirement Home for the Sisters of Mercy of the Americas.
Sr. JOHNEEN OWENS, R.S.M., Coord.
Rev. EDWARD SCHAD, Chap.
Resident Sisters 36

New Cassel Retirement Center
900 N. 90th St.
Omaha, NE 68114
Tel: 402-393-2277
School Sisters of St. Francis
Mr. JOSEPH H. SCHULTE, Dir.
Rev. JAMES R. TIEGS
MARY ANN KRESS, Dir. Pastoral Care
JOSEPH H. SCHULTE, Contact
Sisters 2
Aged Residents 165

West Point
Archdiocese of Omaha

Franciscan Care Services, Inc., (d.b.a. St. Joseph Retirement Community)
320 E. Decatur
West Point, NE 68788
Tel: 402-372-3477
Sr. ANGELINE HENSEN, Admin. & Contact
Franciscan Sisters of Christian Charity, Manitowoc, WI 7
Residents 72

NEW HAMPSHIRE

Allenstown
Diocese of Manchester

Pine Haven Boys Center
River Rd., P.O. Suncook
Allenstown, NH 03275
Somascan Fathers
Revs.:
JOHN VITALI, C.R.S., M.Ed., Dir.
GIULIANO GEROSA, C.R.S., M.A., Supr.
PAOLO RIVA, C.R.S.
ZANATTA REMO, C.R.S.
Total Staff 38
Children 20

Berlin
Diocese of Manchester

St. Vincent de Paul Nursing Home
29 Providence Ave.
Berlin, NH 03570
Tel: 603-752-1820
STEVEN WOODS, Admin.
Rev. JOSEPH A. COTE, Chap.
Sr. THERESA RICHARD, S.P.
Sisters of Charity of Providence 6
Aged residents 80

Dover
Diocese of Manchester

St. Ann Home
Dover, NH 03820
Tel: 603-742-2612; Fax: 603-743-3055
Rev. FREDERICK J. PENNETT, Chap.
Total Staff 87
Aged Residents 54

Jaffrey
Diocese of Manchester

Good Shepherd Nursing Home
20 Plantation Dr.
Jaffrey, NH 03452
Tel: 603-532-8762
JUDITH A. LEBLANC, Admin.
Total Staff 126
Total Assisted 83

Laconia
Diocese of Manchester

Bishop Bradley Apartments
406 Court St.
Laconia, NH 03246
Total Staff 1
Aged residents 25
Apartments 25

St. Francis Home for the Aged
Laconia, NH 03246
Tel: 603-524-0466; Fax: 603-527-0884
Mrs. JULIEANN R. FAY, Admin.
Rev. RAYMOND A. DEMERS, Chap.
Total Staff 72
Aged residents 51

Manchester
Diocese of Manchester

Carpenter Center, Inc.
323 Franklin St.
Manchester, NH 03101
CAROL HAEBLER, Mgr.
Apartments 96
DBH Shelter, Inc.
DBH Shelter II, Inc.
Apartments 8
DBH Shelter III, Inc.
Apartments 28
DBH Management, Inc.
Total Staff 10
Total Assisted 132

Frances Warde House, Inc.
435 Union St.
Manchester, NH 03103
Residents 26

Mt. Carmel Nursing Home
235 Myrtle St.
Manchester, NH 03104
Tel: 603-627-3811
Carmelite Sisters for the Aged and Infirm
Sr. JACINTA MARY, O.Carm., Supr. Admin.
Rev. ALBERT L. BOULANGER
Sisters 7
Total Staff 175
Aged residents 120
Total Assisted 145

St. Peter's Home
Manchester, NH 03102-3093
Tel: 603-625-9313; Fax: 603-625-1910
Sr. FLORENCE THERRIEN, S.C.S.H., Dir.

Mrs. DONNA M. VACHON, Asst. Dir.
Sr. RITA BEAULIEU, S.C.S.H., Treas.
Sisters of Charity (Grey Nuns) 4
Total Staff 75
Children 309

St. Teresa's Manor & Bishop Primeau Apartments
519 Bridge St.
Manchester, NH 03104
Tel: 603-668-2373
STEPHEN V. FULCHINO, Admin.
LINDA ILLG, Apt. Mgr.
Rev. J. KIERAN O'CONNOR
Sisters 1
Aged Residents 5
Total Staff 72

Nashua
Diocese of Manchester

Marguerite's Place
87 Palm St.
Nashua, NH 03060
Tel: 603-598-1582
Sr. MARY SHARON WALSH, G.N.S.H., CEO
Total Staff 14
Total in Residence 25

Rochester
Diocese of Manchester

St. Charles Children's Home
19 Grant St.
Rochester, NH 03867
Sisters of Charity of Our Lady, Mother of The Church
Mother M. PAUL MARIE
Rev. MAURICE R. BOULANGER, Chap.
Sisters 6
Dependent Children 28

Windham
Diocese of Manchester

Warde Health Center
21 Searles Rd.
Windham, NH 03087
Fax: 603-890-1293
Sisters of Mercy
Ms. MONIQUE DOSOGNE, Admin.
Sisters 30
Total Staff 40
Total Assisted 40

NEW JERSEY

Cape May
Diocese of Camden

Victorian Towers Associates
608 Washington St.
Cape May, NJ 08204
Tel: 609-884-5883
Total in Residence 270
Total Staff 7

Cherry Hill
Diocese of Camden

The Manor at St. Mary's
220 St. Mary's Dr.
Cherry Hill, NJ 08003
Sr. FRANCES SZYMANSKA, L.S.I.C., Admin.
Total in Residence 86
Total Staff 48

Marian Residence
1000 Cropwell Rd.
Cherry Hill, NJ 08003
Tel: 609-424-1131
Sr. M. MELCHIOR, L.S.I.C., Supvr.
Total in Residence 5
Total Staff 3

St. Mary's Nursing Home
210 St. Mary's Dr.
Cherry Hill, NJ 08003
Tel: 609-424-9521; Fax: 609-424-5143
Little Servant Sisters of the Immaculate Conception
Sr. MARY FRANCES SZYMANSKA, Supr.
Sr. M. BEATRIX WIECZOREK, Admin.
Revs.:
JAMES J. HEINZ, Assoc. Admin.
WILLIAM D. TITMAS, Chap.
Sisters 6
Residents 315

Village Apartments of Cherry Hill, NJ, Inc.
212 Lourdes Ct.
Cherry Hill, NJ 08003
Tel: 609-424-7913
Mr. MILTON BECK, Supt.
Total in Residence 168
Total Staff 6

Denville
Diocese of Paterson

Franciscan Oaks Independent Living Units & Health Center
21 Pocono Rd.
Denville, NJ 07834
Staffed by Sisters of the Sorrowful Mother.

St. Francis Health Resort
Denville, NJ 07834
Fax: 973-625-9245
E-mail: billmili@aol.com
Rest and Residential Home
Mr. WILLIAM MILIANES, Admin.
Rev. WILLIAM J. FREESWICK, Chap.
Sisters of the Sorrowful Mother 16
Bed Capacity 100
Apartments 63
Guests 150

Hoboken
Archdiocese of Newark

Good Counsel, Inc. (St. Francis Home)
303 Madison St.
Hoboken, NJ 07030
Tel: 201-798-9059; 795-0637; 800-723-8331 (Hotline); Fax: 201-795-0809
Rev. BENEDICT J. GROESCHEL, C.F.R., Chm.
CHRISTOPHER R. BELL, Exec. Dir.
Housing, counseling and referrals for single women who are pregnant or single mothers with children.
Good Counsel, Inc.
P.O. Box 6068
Hoboken, NJ 07030
Tel: 201-795-0637
Residences for single mothers and children.
Rev. BENEDICT J. GROESCHEL, C.F.R., Chm.
CHRISTOPHER R. BELL, Exec. Dir.

Hopewell
Diocese of Trenton

St. Michael's Orphanage and Industrial School
Mailing Address:—c/o the Diocese of Trenton
701 Lawrenceville Rd.
Trenton, NJ 08648

Jersey City
Archdiocese of Newark

St. Ann's Home for the Aged
198 Old Bergen Rd.
Jersey City, NJ 07305
Tel: 201-433-0950
Sr. NORAH CLARKE, C.S.J.P., LNHA Admin.
HENRY WOJTOWICZ, Pastoral Care
Sisters of St. Joseph of Peace 5
Total Staff 166
Under Care 106

St. Joseph's Home
81 York St.
Jersey City, NJ 07302
Tel: 201-413-9280
Sr. KRISTIN FUNARI, C.S.J.P., Dir.
Total Staff 13
Total Assisted 111
Transitional housing for homeless women and children.
The Nurturing Place
Sr. BARBARA MORAN, C.S.J.P., Dir., Tel: 201-413-1982
Total Staff 19
Total Assisted 110
A developmental child care center for disadvantaged youngsters.

St. Joseph's Home for the Blind
537 Pavonia Ave.
Jersey City, NJ 07306
Tel: 201-653-8300
Sisters of St. Joseph of Peace
Sr. ANN TAYLOR, C.S.J.P., Admin.
Rev. JOHN CAVANAUGH, Chap.
Sisters 3
Total Staff 140
Nursing Home Patients 129

St. Mary's Residence for Business and Professional Women
240 Washington St.
Jersey City, NJ 07302
Tel: 201-432-6289
Sisters of St. Joseph of Peace
Sr. MARY DONOHUE, C.S.J.P., Admin.
Total Staff 7
Total Assisted 40

Kearny
Archdiocese of Newark

New Jersey Boystown
499 Belgrove Dr.
Kearny, NJ 07032
Tel: 201-991-3770
Family Counseling Services.
Rev. FRANCIS T. MAIONE, Ed.S., Dir.
Pregnancy Counselling and Adoption
Tel: 201-991-3770

Lawrenceville
Diocese of Trenton

Morris Hall-Saint Lawrence, Inc.
Morris Hall - St. Mary's Residence.
1 Bishops' Dr., P.O. Box 6498
Lawrenceville, NJ 08648-0498
Tel: 609-896-0006
Mr. CHARLES L. BRENNAN, CEO
Mrs. ROSALIE DANEK, R.N., Admin.
In res.,
Revs.:
EDWARD ATZERT
JUSTIN J. HERBST, Chap.
ROBERT P. MURRAY
EARL A. GANNON
EDWIN DZIENKIEWICZ
Guests 180
Beds 220

Morris Hall / Saint Lawrence, Inc.
St. Lawrence Rehabilitation Center.
2381 Lawrenceville Rd.
Lawrenceville, NJ 08648
Tel: 609-896-9500
Mr. CHARLES L. BRENNAN, Admin.
Rev. JUSTIN J. HERBST, Chap.
Sr. CLAIRE DESTEFANO, S.S.J., Dir. Pastoral Care
Bed Capacity 116
Bed Licensure 116

Morris Hall / Saint Lawrence, Inc.
Morris Hall - St. Joseph's Nursing Center.
1 Bishops' Dr.
Lawrenceville, NJ 08648-0498
Tel: 609-896-0006
Mrs. ROSALIE DANEK, Admin.
Skilled Nursing Care Facility for the Chronically Ill.
Residences for Senior Citizens
Bed Capacity 220
Total in Residence 180

Montclair
Archdiocese of Newark

Mother Seton Residence
51 Washington St.
Montclair, NJ 07042
Tel: 973-783-1400
Sisters of Charity of St. Elizabeth
Sr. ROSE VINCENT, Admin.
Residents 23

St. Vincent's Nursing Home
(Div. of St. Joseph's Hospital and Medical Center)
45 Elm St.
Montclair, NJ 07042
Tel: 973-754-4800; Fax: 973-746-2362
Conducted by Sisters of Charity of St. Elizabeth
Mr. THOMAS P. SHEEHY, JR., Admin.
Sisters 5
Capacity: Long term care beds 141

Newark
Archdiocese of Newark

Queen of Peace
60 Jay St.
Newark, NJ 07103
Tel: 973-481-9056
Total Staff 4
Total Assisted 330
Missionaries of Charity

Newfield
Diocese of Camden

Mater Dei Nursing Home
176 Rte. 40
Newfield, NJ 08344
Tel: 609-358-2061
Marianites of Holy Cross
Sr. ANNE EBERSOLD, Admin.

Rev. SEBASTIAN V. ANNINO, Chap.
Sisters 4
Bed Capacity 64
Residents assisted annually 64
Total Staff 100

North Plainfield
Diocese of Metuchen

Villa Maria Sanitarium
641 Somerset St.
North Plainfield, NJ 07060-4909
Tel: 908-757-3050; Fax: 908-754-4939
Home for the aged (with infirmary).
KAREN UEBELE, Admin.
Rev. SEVERIN DIETRICH, O.F.M.Conv., Chap., Tel: 908-757-3050
Patients and Residents 86

Paramus
Archdiocese of Newark

Mount St. Andrew Villa
55 W. Midland Ave.
Paramus, NJ 07652
Tel: 201-261-5950
Sr. JOANN BROMLEY, S.C.
Sisters of Charity of St. Elizabeth 2
Residents 55

Paterson
Diocese of Paterson

St. Joseph Rest Home for Aged Women
Conducted by Daughters of Charity of the Most Precious Blood
46 Preakness Ave.
Paterson, NJ 07522
Sr. MARIA GORETTI CHALOUX, Supr.
Residents 25

Pleasantville
Diocese of Camden

Our Lady's Residence
1100 Clematis Ave.
Pleasantville, NJ 08232
Hospitaler Sisters of Mercy
Sr. M. AURELIA Admin.
Sr. ANN MARIA K. MATHEW, H.S.M., Supr.
Rev. ROBERT T. MCDADE, M.SS.CC., Chap.
Sisters 7
Beds 214
Patients assisted annually 214
Total Staff 236

Red Bank
Diocese of Trenton

Collier Group Home
180 Spring St.
Red Bank, NJ 07701
Tel: 732-842-8337
Mr. PAUL DESANTIS, Dir.
24 hour program-Therapy and Educational Services. Provided Under the Supervision of the Sisters of the Good Shepherd.
Capacity 10

Saddle River
Archdiocese of Newark

Villa Marie Claire
12 W. Saddle River Rd.
Saddle River, NJ 07458
Residence for retired, independent men & women.
Sisters of St. Joseph of Peace 12
Residents 30

Somerset
Diocese of Metuchen

McCarrick Care Center
15 Dellwood Ln.
Somerset, NJ 08873
Tel: 732-545-4200
JAMES F. CARON, Admin.
Rev. MAURICE T. CARLTON, Chap.
In res.,
Rev. Msgr. JOSEPH R. BRZOZOWSKI
Rev. RICHARD ABRAMOWICZ
Sisters 2
Patients assisted annually 142

Totowa
Diocese of Paterson

St. Joseph's Home for the Elderly
140 Shepherd Ln.
Totowa, NJ 07512
Tel: 973-942-0300
Conducted by Little Sisters of the Poor
MARY VINCENT, L.S.P.
Rev. RAYMOND BEACH, O.F.M., Chap.
Sisters 17
Residents 131

Trenton
Diocese of Trenton

Cathedral Square Housing, Inc.
26 W. Hanover Pl.
Trenton, NJ 08608
Tel: 609-392-1111
Most Rev. JOHN M. SMITH, Dir.
Senior Citizen Housing Project.

Sister Georgine School
544 Chestnut Ave.
Trenton, NJ 08611
Tel: 609-396-5444
Sisters of St. Francis

Vineland
Diocese of Camden

Bishop McCarthy Residence
1045 E. Chestnut Ave.
Vineland, NJ 08360
Hospitaler Sisters of Mercy
Sr. LUCIA MAROOR, L.N.H.A., Admin.
Sr. ELETTA FELLI, Supr.
Rev. EDWARD P. SOMMERS, Chap.
Sisters 5
Beds 182
Patients assisted annually 182

Wickatunk
Diocese of Trenton

Collier Services
Collier High School, Conover Rd.
Wickatunk, NJ 07765
Tel: 732-946-4771
Ms. AIDEEN BUGLER, Program Dir.
Sr. ELLEN KELLY, Exec. Dir.
Adolescent Boys and Girls.
Capacity 136
Mrs. JOAN KEELER, Prog. Dir. of Kateri Center, Tel: 732-946-9694
Mrs. LYNDA SHERIDAN, Prog. Dir., Shepherd Center for Child Care, Tel: 908-946-4323
Full-day Early Childhood Program for children 6 weeks through age 12. Full-day Kindergarten. School Age Care for Summer.
Capacity 98

Woodbridge
Diocese of Metuchen

St. Joseph Assisted Living Residence
One St. Joseph Terr.
Woodbridge, NJ 07095
Tel: 732-634-0004
Sr. MARY LOUISE, L.S.I.C., Admin.
Little Servant Sisters 17
Residents 60

NEW MEXICO

Albuquerque
Archdiocese of Santa Fe

Casa Angelica
5629 Isleta Blvd., S.W.
Albuquerque, NM 87105
Tel: 505-877-5763
The Daughters of Charity of Canossa
Home for developmentally disabled children.
Sisters 1
Residents 16
Lay Staff 47

Good Shepherd Center, Inc.
218 Iron St., S.W., P.O. Box 749
Albuquerque, NM 87103
Tel: 505-243-2527
Direct Service Agency for the Homeless.
R. J. SCHAEFER, Pres.
Total Staff 8

Good Shepherd Manor
10127 Guadalupe Tr., N.W., P.O. Box 10248
Albuquerque, NM 87184
Tel: 505-898-0177
Bro. SAVIO CHARRON, B.G.S., M.H.A., Admin.
Sponsored by Bro. Mathias Barrett, Inc. of New Mexico. Shelter Care Facility for aged adults.
Residents 40
Staff 21

Marie Amadea Shelter for Unwed Mothers
(Alternative to Abortion)
P.O. Box 708
Albuquerque, NM 87103
Tel: 505-242-1516
Mrs. DOROTHY WICKENS, Dir.
Home for unwed expectant women.
Total Assisted 26
Total Staff 8

Carlsbad
Diocese of Las Cruces

St. Mary's Health Care Center
(Sub. of St. Mary of the Plains Hospital)
2330 West Pierce
Carlsbad, NM 88220
Tel: 505-887-0516; Fax: 505-885-8239
ROBERT GOODE, Dir.

Hobbs
Diocese of Las Cruces

St. Mary Medical Center
(Sub. of St. Mary of the Plains Hospital)
2410 North Fowler
Hobbs, NM 88240
Tel: 505-392-5572; Fax: 505-392-4848
ROBERT GOODE, Dir.

St. Mary's Family Health Care Center
(Sub. of St. Mary of the Plains Hospital)
515 East Main
Hobbs, NM 88240
Tel: 505-393-1096; Fax: 505-393-3758
ROBERT GOODE, Dir.

Santa Fe
Archdiocese of Santa Fe

Villa Therese Catholic Clinic
219 Cathedral Pl.
Santa Fe, NM 87501
Tel: 505-983-8561
Sr. PATRICK MARIE BERNARD, S.C., Dir.
Sisters of Charity of Cincinnati, Ohio 1
Patients assisted annually 5,000

NEW YORK

Albany
Diocese of Albany

Arbor House
302 Western Ave.
Albany, NY 12203
Tel: 518-489-6030
Legal Title: *Arbor House, Inc.*

Bishop Broderick Apartments Housing Development Fund Co., Inc.
50 Prescott St.
Albany, NY 12205
Tel: 518-869-7441; Fax: 518-869-0443
Senior Citizen and Handicapped Housing.
JANE LAX, Dir.

C.S.C. Housing Development Fund Co., Inc., dba Sanderson Court Senior Apts.
6 Carondelet Dr.
Watervliet, NY 12189
Tel: 518-436-0156; 782-1123; Fax: 518-782-1125
MICHELE KRAMM, Dir.

DePaul Management Corp.
41 N. Main Ave.
Albany, NY 12203
Tel: 518-459-0183; Fax: 518-459-0202
Sr. GRACE R. DIAZ, S.N.J.M., Exec. Dir.
ROSALIE MACE, Assoc. Exec. Dir.
Managing diocesan sponsored housing for persons of low income who are elderly or mobility impaired.

LaSalle School, Inc.
391 Western Ave.
Albany, NY 12203
Tel: 518-242-4731; Fax: 518-242-4747
Brothers of the Christian Schools 8
Mr. WILLIAM WOLFF, Exec. Dir.
Residential and day programs, independent living program, sexual victim/offender program, licensed substance abuse treatment program, and preventative services for boys (ages 12-18) and their families in New York State. Registered New York State Junior and Senior High School and certified School of Special Education.

Prevention Families 60
Resident Students 100
Day Students 30
The La Salle School Foundation of Albany

Saint Anne Institute
160 N. Main Ave.
Albany, NY 12206
Tel: 518-437-6500
RALPH F. FEDULLO, Exec. Dir.
Residential and Community-based Preventive Service Center. Regents accredited and certified junior and senior H.S. for the emotionally handicapped and Preschool program for 3-4 year olds who are speech impaired and emotionally disturbed. Residential care and Day Treatment for young women ages 12-18. Family Services, Vocational Training, Sex Abuse Prevention and Juvenile Sex Offender Programs for male and female adolescents in crisis and their families.
Capacity:
Residential 124
Day Treatment 40
Juvenile Sex Offender & Sex Abuse Prevention Families 90

Saint Catherine's Center for Children
40 N. Main Ave.
Albany, NY 12203
Tel: 518-453-6700; Fax: 518-453-6712
Ms. HELEN HAYES, Exec. Dir.
Residential and day treatment, group homes and foster family programs for children with special needs. Community based prevention programs; Parent aides; Parent Training; Transitional Program for Homeless Families.
Individuals assisted 1,250
The Foundation for St. Catherine's Center for Children

St. Vincent Apartments Housing Development Fund Co., Inc.
475 Yates St.
Albany, NY 12208
Tel: 518-482-8915; Fax: 518-489-1220
E. BYRL MOORE, Building Dir.

Teresian House (1974)
200 Washington Ave. Ext.
Albany, NY 12203
Tel: 518-456-2000
Corporate Title: Teresian House Nursing Home Co., Inc.
Carmelite Sisters for the Aged and Infirm
Sr. PAULINE BRECANIER, O.Carm., Admin.
Sr. JOAN LEWIS, O.Carm., Coord. Pastoral Care
Rev. GERARD LEE, O.F.M., Chap.
Bed Capacity 300
Teresian House Foundation

Villa Mary Immaculate
301 Hackett Blvd.
Albany, NY 12208
Tel: 518-482-3363
S.N.F. and long term skilled care nursing home.
Franciscan Sisters of Allegany, NY
Allegany Health System
JAMES A. REYNOLDS, Pres. & CEO
Revs.:
ROBERT J. DONNELLY
FRANCIS J. GILCHREST
Sr. MARY PATRICIA NERF, R.S.M.
Sr. BARBARA DUDLEY, R.S.M.
Sr. PATRICIA MILLS, S.N.J.M.
Sr. ROSE ANN FERRARA, S.N.J.M.
Sisters 4
Bed Capacity 160
Patients assisted annually 252

Amityville
Diocese of Rockville Centre

Dominican Village, Inc.
565 Albany Ave.
Amityville, NY 11701
Tel: 516-842-6091
Sr. HELEN BUTLER, Pres. & CEO
Sr. VIRGINIA MAGUIRE, Vice Pres.
Housing Units 266
Staff 92

Amsterdam
Diocese of Albany

Mt. Loretto Nursing Home
302 Swart Hill Rd.
Amsterdam, NY 12010
Tel: 518-842-6790; Fax: 518-843-5993
Health Care Facility, 24 Hour Skilled Nursing Care, Hospice, IV Therapy & Rehab. Conducted by the Sisters of the Resurrection.
Sr. PATRICIA ANNE CORBETT, C.R., Admin.
Sr. MARY LUCILLE BOROWSKI, C.R., Supr. & Chap.
Rev. RAYMOND S. PIECHOCKI, Priest In Res.
Capacity 120

Auburn
Diocese of Syracuse

Mercy Housing Development Fund Co., Inc.
Mercy Apartments, 1 Thornton Ave.
Auburn, NY 13021
Tel: 315-253-2015
40 one bedroom units for the elderly and handicapped. Christopher Community, Inc., (Managing Agent).

Baldwinsville
Diocese of Syracuse

Smokey Hollow Housing Development Fund Company, Inc.
Mailing Address:—St. Mary's Apartments, Baldwinsville
1654 W. Onondaga St.
Syracuse, NY 13204
Tel: 315-424-1821
Christopher Community, Inc., (Managing Agent).

Batavia
Diocese of Buffalo

St. Luke Manor
17 Wiard St.
Batavia, NY 14020
Tel: 716-343-8806
JOHN R. DURNO
Bed Capacity 20
Patients assisted annually 20

Bayside
Diocese of Brooklyn

Ozanam Hall of Queens Nursing Home, Inc.
42-41 201st St.
Bayside, NY 11361
Tel: 718-423-2000
Sr. M. PHILIP ANN, O.Carm., Admin.
Chaplains:
Revs.:
MARTIN J. O'SULLIVAN
DANIEL J. SHEEHAN
Carmelite Sisters for the Aged and Infirm
Sisters 18
Residents 432

Blauvelt
Archdiocese of New York

St. Dominic Home
10913
Tel: 914-359-3400; Fax: 914-359-4253
Sr. JOSEPH MARY, O.P., Exec. Dir.
Capacity: Boys 12
Girls 12
In Foster Homes 690
Group Homes 57
Boys 26
Girls 31
AOBH Girls 6
Sisters 15
New York Offices
343 E. 137th St.
Bronx, NY 10454
Tel: 718-993-5765
Special education program for emotionally disturbed mentally ill children ages 6-15.
Capacity 72
Preschool ages 3-5
Capacity 48
Community residences for developmentally disabled
Capacity 81
Community residences for emotionally handicapped
Capacity 36
TORCH (To Reach Children)
2340 Andrews Ave.
Bronx, NY 10463
Tel: 718-365-7238
Friends of St. Dominic
500 Western Hwy.
Blauvelt, NY 10913
Tel: 212-563-4939
Sr. JOSEPH MARY MAHONEY, O.P.

Brewerton
Diocese of Syracuse

Bartell Road Housing Development Fund Co., Inc.
Bartell Rd.
Brewerton, NY 13029
c/o Christopher Community
1654 W. Onondaga St.
Syracuse, NY 13204
20 units, one bedroom apartments. Christopher Community, Inc., (Managing Agent).

Bronx
Archdiocese of New York

Franciscan Health System of New York, Inc.
2975 Independence Ave.
Bronx, NY 10463-4699
Tel: 718-548-1700; Fax: 718-601-3384
JEANNE LEE, Pres. & CEO
Rev. ALBERT PELLICANE, C.P., Chap.
Legal Title: *Frances Schervier Home and Hospital*
Legal Title: *Frances Schervier Housing Development Fund Corporation*
Legal Title: *Frances Schervier Nutrition Services, Inc.*
Legal Title: *Frances Schervier Child Care and Learning Center*
Legal Title: *Frances Schervier Long Term Home Health Care Program*
Franciscan Sisters of the Poor Health System, Inc.
708 Third Ave., Ste. 200
New York, NY 10017
Tel: 212-818-1987; Fax: 212-808-0096
Franciscan Sisters of the Poor Foundation, Inc.
708 Third Ave., Ste. 200
New York, NY 10017
Tel: 212-818-1987; Fax: 212-808-0096
Total Assisted 523
Total Staff 456

Jeanne Jugan Residence
3200 Baychester Ave.
Bronx, NY 10475
Fax: 718-671-0305
Sr. BERNICE MARIE WALL, L.S.P., Supr.
Little Sisters of the Poor 14
Bed Capacity 92
Adult Care 32
Nursing Home 60

Medical Missionaries of Mary
563 Minneford Ave.
Bronx, NY 10464-1118
Tel: 718-885-0945; Fax: 718-885-0010
E-mail: mmmci@aol.com
Web Site: http://www.medical-missionaries.com
Sr. PHILOMENA SHEERIN, M.M.M., Supr. Gen.
Sr. JOANNE BIERL, M.M.M., Zonal Coord. of the Americas

Providence Rest
3304 Waterbury Ave.
Bronx, NY 10465
Tel: 718-931-3000
Sr. SELINE MARY FLORES, Admin.
Sr. LUCILLE VERGA
Sisters of St. John the Baptist 19
Bed Capacity 200
Total Assisted 168
Total Staff 228

Saint Dominic's Home - Prevention Program (ASTAAN)
2345 University Ave.
Bronx, NY 10468
Tel: 718-584-4407
Parent Aide Counseling Advocacy Information and Referral.
Families 100
Families Served 200

St. Patrick's Home for the Aged and Infirm
66 Van Cortlandt Park S.
Bronx, NY 10463
Tel: 718-519-2800
Carmelite Sisters for the Aged and Infirm
Sr. M. PATRICK MICHAEL, O.Carm., Admin.
Rev. GERARD ORLANDO, C.P., Dir. Pastoral Care
Sisters 16
Bed Capacity 264
Total Assisted 378
Total Staff 350

Brooklyn
Diocese of Brooklyn

Bishop Francis J. Mugavero Center for Geriatric Care, Inc.
155 Dean St.
Brooklyn, NY 11217
Tel: 718-694-6700
ANN C. CARROLL, Admin.
Affiliated with Catholic Medical Center.
Total Staff 340
Total Assisted 288

Holy Family Home
1740 84th St.

Brooklyn, NY 11214
Tel: 718-232-3666
Affiliated with Catholic Medical Center.
MARY ANNE ROSE, Admin.
Sr. ANNE SHEEHAN, C.S.J., Dir. Pastoral Care Office
Deacon FRANK ROSATI
Total Staff 224
Total Assisted 188

SS. Joachim & Anne Residence, Inc.
2720 Surf Ave.
Brooklyn, NY 11224
Tel: 718-714-4800
MARIE FERRARA, Admin.

Buffalo
Diocese of Buffalo

The Franciscan Center, Inc.
1910 Seneca St.
Buffalo, NY 14210-1842
Tel: 716-822-8017; Fax: 716-822-8537
Emergency & Transitional Shelters for Adolescent Males 16-20.
Rev. JOSEPH BAYNE, O.F.M.Conv., Exec. Dir. & Guardian
Total Assisted 120
Total Staff 14
St. Joseph, Foster Parent, Friary
Tel: 716-826-6714

German Roman Catholic Orphan Home
795 Main St.
Buffalo, NY 14203
Temporarily Inactive

Nazareth Nursing Home
291 North St.
Buffalo, NY 14201
Tel: 716-881-2323
Sr. M. BERNARD KEANE, O.S.F.
Mr. KEVIN B. KENNEDY, Admin.
Franciscan Sisters of the Immaculate Conception 7
Bed Capacity 125
Patients assisted annually 125
Total Staff 220
Legal Title: *Nazareth Nursing Home of the Franciscan Sisters of the Immaculate Conception*
Attended by Chapel attended by Oblate Fathers of Holy Angels Church.

St. Francis Geriatric and Healthcare Services, Inc.
(Formerly known as St. Francis Hospital).
2787 Main St.
Buffalo, NY 14214
Tel: 716-837-4200; Fax: 716-837-4218
Sr. JEANNE WEISBECK, O.S.F., CEO
Rev. JOSEPH MORENO, Chap.
Sr. MARILYN PERKINS, D.C., Chm. & Prov. Supr.
Daughters of Charity 7
Patients assisted annually 230
Bed Capacity 120
Total Assisted 229
Total Staff 195

Castleton
Diocese of Albany

Resurrection Nursing Home
(Corporate Name: Resurrection Nursing Home, Inc.)
Castleton, NY 12033
Tel: 518-732-7617; Fax: 518-732-4211
Nursing Home (Established 1962).
Conducted by Sisters of Resurrection
Bed Capacity 80

Catskill
Diocese of Albany

St. Joseph's Villa
38 Prospect Ave.
Catskill, NY 12414
Tel: 518-943-5701
Sr. ROBERTA F. BRUNNER, O.S.F., Admin.
An Adult Care Facility for Men and Women.

Cicero
Diocese of Syracuse

Cicero Housing Development Fund Company Inc.
Mailing Address:
1654 W. Onondaga St.
Syracuse, NY 13204
Tel: 315-424-1821
Sacred Heart Apartments
Cicero, NY 13039
Christopher Community, Inc., (Managing Agent).

Clarence
Diocese of Buffalo

Brothers of Mercy Housing Co., Inc.
10500 Bergtold Rd.
Clarence, NY 14031
Tel: 716-795-2122
Ms. LENORE MAURER, Admin.
Bro. JUDE HOLZFOERSTER, Pres.
Bed Capacity 100
Total in Residence 117
Total Staff 4

Brothers of Mercy Nursing & Rehabilitation Center
10570 Bergtold Rd.
Clarence, NY 14031
Tel: 716-759-6985
Mr. DANIEL J. KENNY, Admin.
Bro. JUDE HOLZFOERSTER, F.M.M., Pres.
Rev. JOHN J. SARDINA, Chap.
In res.,
Bro. HUGH DENOMME, F.M.M., Dir. Pastoral Care
Bed Capacity 240

Brothers of Mercy Sacred Heart Home, Inc.
4520 Ransom Rd.
Clarence, NY 14031
Tel: 716-759-2644
Mr. MICHAEL J. MALONEY, Admin.
Bro. JUDE HOLZFOERSTER, F.M.M., Pres. of Board
Rev. JOHN J. SARDINA, Chap.
Bed Capacity 80
Total in Residence 80
Total Staff 46

Clifton Park
Diocese of Albany

Halfmoon Housing Development Fund Co., Inc. dba Bishop Hubbard Senior Apartments/De Paul Management Corp.
54 Katherine Dr.
Clifton Park, NY 12065
Tel: 518-383-2705
MARILYN D. HAGGERTY, Dir.

Dobbs Ferry
Archdiocese of New York

St. Cabrini Nursing Home
115 Broadway
Dobbs Ferry, NY 10522
Tel: 914-693-6800
Sr. SUZANNE POULIN, C.N.D., Dir. Pastoral Care
Missionary Sisters of the Sacred Heart 5
Bed Capacity 304
Total Assisted 474
Total Staff 437

Dunkirk
Diocese of Buffalo

St. Vincent's Home for the Aged
319 Washington Ave.
Dunkirk, NY 14048
Tel: 716-366-2066; Fax: 716-366-0545
Catholic Charities of Buffalo, Inc.
ELAINE J. SZCZERBACKI, Admin.
Residents 40
Total Staff 25

Fayetteville
Diocese of Syracuse

Redfield South Housing Development Fund Co., Inc.
Redfield Village Apartments, 380 Salt Springs Rd.
Fayetteville, NY 13066
Tel: 315-637-8280
50 one bedroom units. Christopher Community, Inc., (Managing Agent).

Garrison
Archdiocese of New York

St. Christopher's Inn
P.O. Box 150
Garrison, NY 10524-0150
Tel: 914-424-3616
Temporary shelter for homeless men.
Atonement Friars
Rev. BERNARD PALKA, S.A., Dir.
Total Assisted 3,200
Total Staff 35

Harrison
Archdiocese of New York

St. Vincent's Hospital and Medical Center of New York, Westchester Branch
275 North St.
Harrison, NY 10528
Tel: 914-967-6500; Fax: 914-925-5157
BRIAN L. FITZSIMMONS, Ph.D.
Psychiatric Hospital.
Clergy Consultation Program
Capacity 133
Patients assisted annually 2,226
Sisters of Charity of St. Vincent de Paul 3
All outpatient program admissions 1,734
Partial Hospital 240
Methadone Maintenance Treatment Program 130

Hawthorne
Archdiocese of New York

Rosary Hill Home
Hawthorne, NY 10532
Tel: 914-769-0114
Legal Title: *The Servants of Relief for Incurable Cancer*
Free home for incurable cancer patients.
Sr. M. DOMINIC, Admin.
Sr. MIRIAM O.P., Supr.
Rev. JOHN PROPPE, O.F.M.Cap., Chap.
Professed Sisters of St. Dominic 25
Capacity 72
Patients assisted annually 401

Huntington
Diocese of Rockville Centre

St. Joseph's Guest Home for the Aged, Inc.
350 Cuba Hill Rd.
Huntington, NY 11743
Tel: 516-368-9528
Missionary Sisters of St. Benedict
Sr. M. BOGUSLAWA KAPUSTA, O.S.B.
In res.,
Rev. THOMAS P. CURRY

Jamaica
Diocese of Brooklyn

Msgr. James H. Fitzpatrick Pavilion for Skilled Nursing Care
152-11 89th Ave.
Jamaica, NY 11432
Tel: 718-558-2800
Affiliated with Catholic Medical Center.
GREGORY BRADLEY, Admin.
Total Staff 109
Total Assisted 115
Residents 115

Kenmore
Diocese of Buffalo

KMH Homes, Inc.
Administrative Offices
2950 Elmwood Ave.
Kenmore, NY 14217
Residential Health Care Facility
Sponsored by the Sisters of Mercy.
Bed Capacity 160
Total Assisted 160
Total Staff 152

Lackawanna
Diocese of Buffalo

Baker Victory Services
(formerly known as Baker Hall, Our Lady of Victory Infant Home, St. Joseph Orphanage and St. John's Protectory)
780 Ridge Rd.
Lackawanna, NY 14218
Tel: 716-828-9500; 888-287-1160
Rev. Msgr. ROBERT C. WURTZ, Pres. of the Board
JAMES J. CASION, C.E.O.
JOSEPH J. COZZO, C.O.O.
J. BRENT HERMAN, Personnel Dir.
Staff 800
Total Assisted 2,500
Educational Services:
Toddler Development Group (ages birth to 3)
Therapeutic Preschool (ages 3-5)
Baker Hall School (ages 5-21)
Residential Services:
Dorothy Miler House (mother & child group residence)
Foster Family Boarding Home Care
Residential Treatment Facilities (phychiatric adolescent and young adult residence)
Special Services Program
Institutional Program
Group/Boarding Home Program
Services For The Developmentally Disabled:
Residential Services
Respite Program
Case Management
Other Services:
Prenatal Outpatient Maternity Program
Postpartum Aftercare Program
Domestic and International Adoption Services

Preventive Services
Outpatient Clinic
Day Treatment Program
Healthcare Center (general medicine, pediatrics, ob/gyn, and dental services)

Lake Placid
Diocese of Ogdensburg

St. Margaret Convent
420 Old Military Rd.
Lake Placid, NY 12946
Tel: 518-523-2929; Fax: 518-523-1401
Sisters of Mercy
Sr. M. CAMILLUS O'KEEFE, R.S.M., Supr.

Uihlein Mercy Center
420 Old Military Rd.
Lake Placid, NY 12946
Tel: 518-523-2464; Fax: 518-523-1401
Institute of the Sisters of Mercy of the Americas, Regional Community of New York.
DOUGLAS MENZIES, Admin.
Rev. PATRICK J. O'REILLY, Chap.
Skilled Nursing Facility.
Sisters 3
Total Staff 230
Total Assisted 216

Lancaster
Diocese of Buffalo

St. Elizabeth's Home
5539 Broadway
Lancaster, NY 14086
Tel: 716-683-5150; Fax: 716-683-4049
CAROL A. WANTUCH, Admin.
Rev. WILLIAM J. ROCHE, Chap.
Sisters of the Third Order of St. Francis 1
Residents 117
Total Staff 60

Latham
Diocese of Albany

Our Lady of Hope Residence
Little Sisters of the Poor
Jeanne Jugan Ln.
Latham, NY 12110
Tel: 518-785-4551
Rev. FIRMIN FINN, O.F.M.Conv.
Nursing Facility 70
Adult Care 30
Apartments for the Elderly 17

Lincolndale
Archdiocese of New York

Lincoln Hall
P.O. Box 600
Lincolndale, NY 10540
Tel: 914-248-7474; Fax: 914-248-5173
E-mail: pt.lincolnhall@worldnet.att.net
KATHLEEN T. O'KULA, C.S.W., Exec. Dir.
City Office
220 E. 23rd St.
New York, NY 10010
Capacity Boys 207
Total Staff 321
Total Assisted 406

Lockport
Diocese of Buffalo

St. Clare Manor
543 Locust St.
Lockport, NY 14094
Fax: 716-434-5900
Conducted by Catholic Charites of the Diocese of Buffalo.
Mr. JOHN DURNO, Admin.
Residents 28

Middletown
Archdiocese of New York

St. Teresa's Nursing Home
120 Highland Ave.
Middletown, NY 10940
Tel: 914-342-1033; Fax: 914-344-5631
Bed Capacity 98
Total Assisted 98
Total Staff 122

Millbrook
Archdiocese of New York

Cardinal Hayes Home for Children
North Ave., P.O. Box CH
Millbrook, NY 12545
Tel: 914-677-6363; Fax: 914-677-6691
FRED APERS, Exec. Dir.
Residential care for developmentally disabled children and young adults.
Franciscan Missionaries of Mary 5
Capacity of residential facilities:
Millbrook Intermediate Care Facility 45
Community Intermediate Care Facilities 50
Total assisted 105
Total Staff 250
In-home Respite Services.

Montrose
Archdiocese of New York

Kolping-on-Hudson
95 Montrose Point Rd.
Montrose, NY 10548
Tel: 914-737-9547
(Catholic Kolping Society New York, Inc.)
Total Assisted 2,000
Total Staff 10

Nanuet
Archdiocese of New York

St. Agatha Home of the New York Foundling Hospital
135 Convent Rd.
Nanuet, NY 10954
Tel: 914-623-3461
(Residential.)
Sisters of Charity of St. Vincent de Paul of New York.
ROSEMARIE CRISTELLO, Dir.
Rev. MICHAEL F. GANNON, Chap.
Bed Capacity 126
Diagnostic Facilities 26
In Foster Homes 38
Group Homes 99
Non-secure Detention 8 beds
Adult Intermediate Care facilities 65 beds
Family Support/Respite 10 beds
Runaway Youth Program.
Refugee Assistance Program.
Ulster County Prevention.

Nesconset
Diocese of Rockville Centre

Cleary Deaf Child Center, Inc.
301 Smithtown Blvd.
Nesconset, NY 11767
Tel: 516-588-0530 (Voice and TTY); Fax: 516-588-0016
E-mail: CatherineF@ClearySchool.org
Directed by Catholic Charities.
Day School (Infants thru 21 years).
Sr. CATHERINE FITZGIBBON, C.S.J., Supt.
Students 75

New York
Archdiocese of New York

Calvary Hospital
1740 Eastchester Rd.
Bronx, NY 10461
Tel: 718-863-6900
For advanced cancer patients.
FRANK A. CALAMARI, Exec. Dir.
Rev. MICHAEL J. ALESSANDRO, Chap.
MARY TERESA O'NEILL, Asst. Admin. & Dir. Pastoral Services
Pastoral Staff 16
Accommodations for 200
Patients assisted annually 3,300

Catholic Charities Department of Mental Health Services
1011 First Ave.
New York, NY 10022
Tel: 212-371-1000, Ext. 2000; Fax: 212-826-8377
Mr. JOHN J. HUGHES, Dir.
Inwood/Washington Hts.:
652 E. 187th St.
New York, NY 10033
Tel: 212-795-6860; Fax: 212-928-4351
Mr. JOHN J. HUGHES
Bronx:
2380 Belmont Ave.
Bronx, NY 10458
Tel: 718-364-7700; Fax: 718-364-1513
Dr. MARJORIE STUCKLE
Yonkers:
4 St. Mary's St.
Yonkers, NY 10701
Tel: 914-476-2700; Fax: 914-965-4241
Ms. POLLY KERRIGAN
Peekskill:
1045 Park St.
Peekskill, NY 10566
Tel: 914-737-7338; Fax: 914-737-1050
Ms. JULIA REDDY
Hudson Valley Counseling Corps:
Rockland County
Tel: 914-426-3436
Orange County
Tel: 914-561-3452
Dutchess County
Tel: 914-452-1400
Sullivan County
Tel: 914-791-6023
Ulster County
Tel: 914-340-9170

Catholic Guardian Society
1011 First Ave.
New York, NY 10022
Tel: 212-371-1000
Mr. JOHN FREIN, Exec. Dir.
Intermediate care facilities, individual residential alternatives and family support programs for mentally retarded, developmentally disabled adults. Group home program for boys and girls, ages 13-21 years; agency operated boarding homes and adoption services for boys and girls ages 0-16; provides foster homes for boys and girls ages 0-21; and specialized foster homes for children with AIDS.
Total Assisted 1,075
Total Staff 506

Catholic Guild for the Blind
1011 First Ave., 6th Floor
New York, NY 10022
Tel: 212-371-1000, Ext. 2017; Fax: 212-826-8377
Ms. ANN T. SNYDER, Dir.

Catholic Home Bureau
1011 First Ave.
New York, NY 10022
Tel: 212-371-1000
Sr. UNA MCCORMACK, O.P., Exec. Dir.
Placement of dependent and neglected boys and girls ages birth-18 in foster and adoptive homes and agency-operated boarding homes. Maternity Services Program provides free, confidential counseling, medical & shelter care to single and married parents seeking help in planning for their unborn children. Toll-free hotline 1-800-592-HELP.
Total Assisted 2,500
Total Staff 300

Centro Maria, Inc.
539 W. 54th St.
New York, NY 10019
E-mail: centroma@erols.com
For young students and working women.
Sr. MARY CHRISTINE LOPEZ, R.M.I., Supr.
Religious of Mary Immaculate 5
Bed Capacity 54

Cor Mariae
c/o 1011 First Ave., Rm. 1130
New York, NY 10022
Tel: 212-371-1000, Ext. 2435
Residence for formerly homeless senior women.

Covenant House Under 21
460 W. 41st St.
New York, NY 10036
(Runaway and Homeless Youth.)
Sr. MARY ROSE MCGEADY, D.C., Pres.

The Dwelling Place
409 W. 40th St.
New York, NY 10018
Tel: 212-564-7887
For homeless women.
Sr. NANCY CHIARELLO, O.S.F., Admin.
Total Assisted 100
Total Staff 5

El Carmelo Residence
249 W. 14th St.
New York, NY 10011
Tel: 212-242-8224
Sr. MODESTA PEREZ, Supr.

Good Shepherd Services
305 7th Ave., 9th Floor
New York, NY 10001
Tel: 212-243-7021
E-mail: palomonaco@aol.com
Web Site: http://www.goodshepherds.org
Sr. PAULETTE LOMONACO, Exec. Dir.
Provides foster care and adoption services (formerly McMahon Services for Children) and five residential programs for troubled adolescents, a training program for social service workers and a comprehensive range of neighborhood family services to individuals and youth from the South Brooklyn

community. These services include educational support, employment, counseling, crisis intervention, literacy, skills training and advocacy services.

Guild of the Infant Savior
1011 First Ave., Room 1287
New York, NY 10022
Tel: 212-371-1000, Ext. 2440

The Jeanne d'Arc Residence
253 W. 24th St.
New York, NY 10011
Tel: 212-989-5952
Women 18 to 40.
Sr. ROSE ANN MENKE, Admin.
Accommodations for 140
Sisters of Divine Providence 7

Kateri Residence
150 Riverside Dr.
New York, NY 10024-2201
Tel: 212-769-0744; Fax: 212-873-0658
E-mail: 1bond@chcn.org
Web Site: http://www.chcn.org/kateri
Skilled Nursing Care/Residential Health Care Facility for the Elderly.
LASCELLES L. BOND, Exec. Vice Pres. & Admin.
Asst. Admins.:
ROBERT G. SUSSINGHAM
M. EILEEN DOLPHIN
BRUCE L. ADLER, CFO
DORIS HUNG, Controller
ROBERT R. MORGAN, M.D., Medical Dir.
SARAH A. JERRO, R.N., Dir. of Nursing Services
BARBARA A. GAUGHAN, R.N., Dir. of R.U.G.S./Admissions
PATRICIA E. SCHNEIDER, R.N., Ph.D., Dir. QM/Staff Development
ROBERT J. GEIER, Dir. Recreation Therapy
NICKI MEADE, Dir. Volunteers/Development
Sr. PATRICIA GEOGHEGAN, P.B.V.M., Dir. Pastoral Care
Sr. MIRIAM POVEDA, R.S.H.M., Pastoral Care Assoc.
Sr. PADRAIC MARY MCGUINNESS, O.P., Pastoral Care Assoc.
Attended by Franciscan Friars from St. Francis of Assisi Friary.
In res.,
Rev. VINCENT MELE, O.F.M (Immaculate Conception Prov.)
Rev. Msgr. ROBERT LOFTUS
Rev. Msgr. JAMES J. HANLON
Rev. Msgr. STEPHEN KELLEHER
Bed Capacity 520
Total Assisted 768
Total Staff 610

Kennedy Child Study Center
151 E. 67th St.
New York, NY 10021
Tel: 212-988-9500
ANN WILLIAMS, Ph.D., Exec. Dir.
Preschool Special Education 125
Infant/Parent Services 50
Case Management Services
Family Support Services 40
Parent Program 60
Clinic Program 400
Bronx Site
1021 E. 178th St.
Bronx, NY 10460
Tel: 212-842-0200
Preschool Special Education 125
Infant/Parent Services 50
Case Management Services
Clinic Program 400
Family Support Services 40
Parent Program 60

Kolping Society of New York Men's Residence (Catholic Kolping Society New York, Inc.)
165 E. 88th St.
New York, NY 10128
Tel: 212-369-6647
For young Catholic men.
MARY MINARIK, Mgr.
Total in Residence 88
Total Staff 11

Kolping-on-Concourse
2916 Grand Concourse
Bronx, NY 10458
Tel: 212-733-6119
JORGE PARIS, Mgr.
(Catholic Kolping Society New York, Inc.)
Total in Residence 91
Total Staff 11

Lavelle School for the Blind
221st St. and Paulding Ave.
New York, NY 10469
Tel: 718-882-1212
Sisters of St. Dominic of Blauvelt.
Sr. LOUIS MARIE BAXTER, O.P., Supt.
Capacity 100

Leo House
332 W. 23rd St.
New York, NY 10011
Tel: 212-929-1010; Fax: 212-366-6801
For the Clergy, Sisters & Laity.
THOMAS E. FREEBURN, Exec. Dir.
Senior Citizens in Residence 8
Total Staff 36
Catholic Hotel for Travelers 10,912

Mary Manning Walsh Home
1339 York Ave.
New York, NY 10021
Tel: 212-628-2800
Carmelite Sisters for the Aged and Infirm.
Sr. SEAN WILLIAM O'BRIEN, Admin.
Rev. Msgr. JAMES J. MURRAY, Chap.
Rev. RICHARD PEIRIS, Asst. Chap.
Total Staff 488
Total Assisted 362

Mission of the Immaculate Virgin
Mount Loretto
Staten Island, NY 10309
Tel: 718-317-2600
STEPHEN RYNN, Exec. Dir.
In res.,
Rev. Msgr. JOSEPH C. ANSALDI
Rev. Msgr. JAMES F. BOLGER
Legal Title: *Mission of the Immaculate Virgin for the Protection of Homeless and Destitute Children*
Intermediate Care Facility:
Capacity 12
Community Residence:
Capacity 4
Day Care Center:
Capacity 45
Individual Residential Alternatives:
St. Matthew Cottage:
Capacity 8
108 Bedell St.:
Capacity 6
6532 Amboy Rd.:
Capacity 7
Residential & Day Care
Total Assisted 82
Total Staff 101

New York Catholic Deaf Center
1011 First Ave., 6th Floor
New York, NY 10022
Tel: 212-371-1000; Fax: 212-826-8377
Rev. Msgr. PATRICK P. MCCAHILL, Supvr.

New York Foundling Charitable Corp.
590 Avenue of the Americas
New York, NY 10011
Tel: 212-633-9300
Sr. ELIZABETH VERMAELEN, S.C., Pres.

New York Foundling Hospital for Pediatric, Medical and Rehabilitative Care, Inc.
590 Avenue of the Americas
New York, NY 10011
Tel: 212-633-9300
MICHAEL GARBER, Exec. Dir.
RUTH MULLER, Admin.
Sponsored by Sisters of Charity of St. Vincent de Paul of New York.
Children 136

New York Foundling Hospital, The
590 Avenue of the Americas
New York, NY 10011
Tel: 212-633-9300
(Children from Infancy to 21)
Sr. HELEN MURPHY, Exec. Dir.
Children cared for during the year
In the institution 469
In foster homes 1,937
In adoptive homes 244
Mothers cared for in St. Mary's Maternity Residence 261
Group residences 308
Diagnostic reception centers 228
Sisters of Charity of St. Vincent de Paul of New York 18
Family day care 243 children
Group day care 101
Mother and abusing parent and child program
Families 301
Children 534
Mother and child program 59 mothers and 59 babies
Community-based services
Families 350
Children 1,000
Programs for handicapped children 120
Foster Boarding Home Program
Children with AIDS 22
Total Assisted 6,300
Total Staff 1,200

Padre Pio Shelter for Homeless Men
419 E. 155th St.
Bronx, NY 10455
Tel: 718-292-3713
Total Assisted 18/night
Bros.:
JOSEPH EDWARDS, C.F.R., Dir.
FRANCIS EDKINS, C.F.R., Asst. Dir.

Pelletier School & Services
147 W. 70th St.
New York, NY 10023
MARY ELLEN MURPHY, Program Dir.
Day School-Day Treatment Program for girls and boys 13-17.
Bed Capacity 50

Pius XII Youth and Family Services, Inc.
Office of the Pres., 570 Lexington Ave., 33rd Fl.
New York, NY 10022
Tel: 212-319-0464
Bro. ROBERT FONTAINE, C.S.C., Pres. & CEO
Executive Offices.
The Victor J. Riley Jr. Center for Human Services
188 W. 230th St.
Bronx, NY 10463
Tel: 718-561-2073
Provides residential, community, chemical dependency and corporate services to over 25,000 people in New York State.
Residential Services:
Chester Campus
Gibson Hill Rd.
Chester, NY 10918
Tel: 914-469-2121
Complete residential services for troubled adolescent males.
Capacity 114
Sugar Loaf Union Free School District
Special Act School for youngsters at Chester Campus.
Rhinecliff Campus
Morton Rd.
Rhinecliff, NY 12574
Tel: 914-876-4084
Complete residential services for troubled adolescent males.
Capacity 96
Rhinecliff Union Free School District
Special Act School for youngsters at Rhinecliff Campus.
Group Homes
11 King Center
Middletown, NY 10940
Tel: 914-343-7487
Two group homes and two non-secure detention group homes for co-educational population, one each in Orange and Duchess Counties.
Capacity 40
Foster Boarding Homes & Adoption
188 W. 230th St.
Bronx, NY 10463
Tel: 718-562-7855
395 Ann St.
Newburgh, NY 12550
Tel: 914-565-4618
Placement for 500 infants, children and adolescents in New York City and the Hudson Valley. Offices provide services and medical care to natural families, children and foster parents and recruitment of new foster parents. Adoptive parents are sought for children freed for adoption.
Admission & Family Services
188 W. 230th St.
Bronx, NY 10463
Tel: 718-562-7855
Offices for referral contact and for services to the families of children in residential care. Includes aftercare and independent living services.
Community Services:
North Bronx Family Service Center
2190 University Ave.
Bronx, NY 10453
Tel: 718-365-1400
Preventive services center for local community.
Court Diversion Project
1967 Turnbull Ave.
Bronx, NY 10473
Tel: 718-931-2611
Bronx Family Court
900 Sheridan Ave.
Bronx, NY 10473
Tel: 718-681-0056
Counseling services to youngsters and families when a PINS petition has been filed in family court

to divert youngster from residential placement.
University Heights Day Care
2167 University Ave.
Bronx, NY 10453
Tel: 718-584-6400
On-site day care for preschool children and after-school care for school-age children. Office for family day care that provides in-home services for families.
Children 101
Goshen Day Care-Early Learning Center
59 St. John St.
Goshen, NY 10924
Tel: 914-294-7502
Montessori-based day care for 60, ages 3-5.
Employment Training and Job Placement
Snow House
135 Hall of Fame Terr.
Bronx, NY 10453
Tel: 718-365-7755
Training and placement in auto mechanics, word processing and secretarial skills. Special family support and resource program which coordinates job training with family services.
Young Adult Training Academy
320 E. 96th St.
New York, NY 10128
Educational opportunities for students in job training programs.
Student Services - Dropout Prevention
Theodore Roosevelt High School
500 E. Fordham Rd.
Bronx, NY 10458
Morris High School
166th St. & Boston Rd.
Bronx, NY 10456
South Bronx High School
701 St. Ann's Ave.
Bronx, NY 10455
I.S. 206B
2280 Aqueduct Ave.
Bronx, NY 10468
P.S. 79
125 E. 181st St.
Bronx, NY 10453
Intergenerational program between Jewish Home Hospital and P.S. 79.
P.S. 279
2100 Walton Ave.
Bronx, NY 10453
Adlai Stevenson High School
1980 Lafayette Ave.
Bronx, NY 10473
Walton High School
West 196 St. & Reservoir Ave.
Bronx, NY 10468
Counseling services to identified population of students considered high risk for dropping out of school.
After School Programs
Family Service Center
2190 Unviersity Ave.
Bronx, NY 10453
Supervised Latch-key program of classes, workshops and recreation for 6-18 year olds. Teen Program for adolescents provides recreational program year round.
Beacon Program
Middle School 45, 2502 Lorillard Pl.
Bronx, NY 10458
Tel: 718-367-9577
Community Center serving youths, children and adults in educational, recreational and social services after school, evenings, and weekends.
P.S. 91
220 Aqueduct Ave.
Bronx, NY 10453
Tutoring for students 6-18 who are one year or more behind grade level. G.E.D. program for high school equivalency. English as a second language classes.
"Aimin' High" Family Service Center
2190 University Ave.
Bronx, NY 10453
One hundred at-risk teens involved in sports and education programs with added community service.
Administrative Office
224 Main St.
Goshen, NY 10924
Tel: 914-294-5124
Chemical Dependency Services:
Chemical Dependency Clinics:
224 Main St.
Goshen, NY 10924
Tel: 914-294-5888
15 Lake St.
Newburgh, NY 12550
Tel: 914-562-8255
10 Orchard St.
Middletown, NY 10940
Tel: 914-343-7675
520 Rte. 17M
Monroe, NY 10950
Tel: 914-782-0295
150 Pike St.
Port Jervis, NY 12771
Tel: 914-856-8440
Medically supervised outpatient clinics for chemically dependent adults and their families.
Alcohol Clinic
440 Rte. 17M
Monroe, NY 10950
Tel: 914-782-6600
Specialized clinic for the treatment of alcoholics and their families.
School-based Services
Alternatives
14 Scotchtown Ave.
Goshen, NY 10924
Tel: 914-294-3501
Chemical dependency awareness and prevention program. Taught to school districts in Orange County. Summer and year-round programs in chemical dependency, AIDS, coping with behavioral problems and others.
Student Assistance Services.
Gateway Center
46 Roe St.
Newburgh, NY 12550
Tel: 914-569-0034
Chemical dependency outpatient clinic for Newburgh high school students, located on school grounds.
Employee Assistance Services.
Employee Assistance Services Office
14 Scotchtown Ave.
Goshen, NY 10924
Tel: 914-294-3501
Employee Assistance Programs for corporations, businesses, governments and groups. Provides confidential counseling, assessment and referral for employees on a self-initiated or supervisor-recommended basis. Training for supervisors and services provided in areas outside the office area.
Residential and Community Services:
Total Assisted 25,079
Total Staff 643

Sacred Heart Residence
432 W. 20th St.
New York, NY 10011
Tel: 212-929-5790
Congregation of Mothers of the Helpless
Working or studying young ladies ages 19-29.
Sr. GUADALUPE SORDO ECHEVERRIA, Admin.
Capacity 30

St. Agnes' Residence
237 W. 74th St.
New York, NY 10023
Tel: 212-874-1361
For students and working women under 40.
Sr. MARY JOACHIM Admin.
Daughters of Mary of the Immaculate Conception 2
Accommodations for 99
Franciscan Fathers of St. Francis Monastery.

St. Joseph's Immigrant Home
425 W. 44th St.
New York, NY 10036-4402
Tel: 212-246-5363
For students and working women.
Sr. MARY CELINE, Admin.
Daughters of Mary of the Immaculate Conception 2
Accommodations for 94

St. Mary's Residence
225 E. 72nd St.
New York, NY 10021
Tel: 212-249-6850
For students and young working women.
Sr. M. PERPETUA KODBA, F.D.C., Admin.
Sr. M. VIRGINIA SKARUPA, F.D.C., Dir. of Admissions
Daughters of Divine Charity 6
Accommodations for 145

St. Rose's Home
71 Jackson St.
New York, NY 10002
Tel: 212-677-8132
Legal Title: *The Servants of Relief for Incurable Cancer*
Free home for incurable cancer patients.
Sr. M. KEVIN O.P., Supr.
Sr. M. DENISE O.P., Admin.
Rev. GERARD MULVEY, O.F.M.Cap., Chap.
Dominican Sisters of the Congregation of St. Rose of Lima 10
Bed Capacity 60
Patients assisted annually 160

St. Vincent dePaul Residence
900 Intervale Ave.
New York, NY 10459
Tel: 718-589-6965
Mr. JORGE VASQUEZ, Dir.

St. Zita's Home for Adults
143 W. 14th St.
New York, NY 10011
Tel: 212-243-7200
Home for Women.
Sr. ANTHONY MARIE Supr.
Sisters of Reparation of the Congregation of Mary 12
Accommodations for 46 Women

Terence Cardinal Cooke Health Care Center
1249 Fifth Ave.
New York, NY 10029
Tel: 212-360-1000
E-mail: tccgen@chcn.org
Web Site: http://www.chcn.org
Mr. JAMES D. CAMERON, Pres. & CEO
Hospital for developmentally disabled.
Bed Capacity 50
Developmental Disabilities Clinic
1249 Fifth Ave.
New York, NY 10029
Comprehensive Outpatient medical, therapeutic and educational services.
Patients assisted annually 44,000
Hemodialysis
1249 Fifth Ave.
New York, NY 10029
22 End Stage Renal Dialysis Stations
Patients assisted annually 22,000
(For information concerning nursing home see Homes for Aged category.)

Terence Cardinal Cooke Health Care Center
1249 Fifth Ave.
New York, NY 10029
Tel: 212-360-1000; Fax: 212-289-2739
JAMES D. CAMERON, Pres. & CEO
Sr. MARY ANN DALY, S.C.
Skilled nursing facility.
Bed Capacity 523
Skilled Nursing Facility AIDS Program.
Bed Capacity 156
(See Special Hospitals Category for additional services offered from this Health Care Center.)

Thorpe Family Residence, Inc.
2252 Crotona Ave.
New York, NY 10457
Sr. BARBARA LENNIGER, O.P., Exec. Dir.
The Crotona-Thorpe Housing Development Fund Corporation (Sub of Thorpe Family Residence, Inc.),
Sr. MARY MURRAY, O.P., Pres.
Residents 65
Total Assisted 130
Total Staff 10

Niagara Falls
Diocese of Buffalo

Mount St. Mary's LTC Facility, Inc.
2600 Main St.
Niagara Falls, NY 14305
E-mail: jlomeo@aol.com
JOHN L. LOMEO, Admin.
JILL PARYZ, Dir. Nursing Svcs.
Sponsored by the Sisters of St. Francis.
Bed Capacity 131
Patients assisted annually 190
Total Staff 200

St. Mary's Manor
515 Sixth St.
Niagara Falls, NY 14301
Tel: 716-285-3236
JOHN M. DUNN, Admin.
THERESA A. THOMAS, Dir. Nursing Svcs.
Bed Capacity 119
Patients assisted annually 162
Total Staff 165

North Greenbush
Diocese of Albany

S.J. Housing Development Fund Company, Inc. dba St. Jude's Apartments
50 Dana Ave.
Wynantskill, NY 12198
Tel: 518-283-5690; Fax: 518-283-5893
MELISSA GILL, Dir.
Nonprofit housing facility for elderly and handicapped persons of very low income.
Apartments 50

North Syracuse
Diocese of Syracuse

Pitcher Hill-Christopher Housing Development Fund Co., Inc.
114 Elbow Rd.
North Syracuse, NY 13212
Engaged in the construction and operation of non-profit housing facilities for elderly and handicapped persons of low income. 100 units, one bedroom apartments. Christopher Community, Inc., (Managing Agent).

Ogdensburg
Diocese of Ogdensburg

St. Joseph's Home
420 Lafayette St.
Ogdensburg, NY 13669
Tel: 315-393-3780; Fax: 315-393-3847
WILLIAM L. O'REILLY, Admin.
Most Rev. PAUL S. LOVERDE, Chm.
Total Staff 95
Total Assisted 117

Olean
Diocese of Buffalo

St. Joseph Manor
2211 W. State St.
Olean, NY 14760
Fax: 716-373-4375
MARILYN J. GIBBIN, Admin.
Bed Capacity 22
Total Assisted 30
Total Staff 75

Orchard Park
Diocese of Buffalo

W.N.Y. Catholic LongTerm Care, Inc. dba Father Baker Manor
6400 Powers Rd.
Orchard Park, NY 14127
Tel: 716-667-0001; Fax: 716-667-0028
E-mail: ronz2977@aol.com
Nursing facility sponsored by Our Lady of Victory Hospital of Lackawanna, Mercy Hospital of Buffalo and St. Joseph Hospital of Cheektowaga.
Bed Capacity 160
Total Assisted 160
Total Staff 225

Ossining
Archdiocese of New York

The Cardinal McCloskey Emergency Residential School
155 N. Highland Ave.
Ossining, NY 10562
Mr. JOHN M. QUEENAN, Pres.

Oswego
Diocese of Syracuse

St. Luke's Housing Development Fund Co., Inc.
St. Luke's Apartments, W. First St.
Oswego, NY 13126
Engaged in the construction and operation of a non-profit housing facility for elderly and handicapped persons of low income. 100 units, one bedroom apartments. Christopher Community, Inc., (Managing Agent).

Saint Luke's Residential Health Care Facility Co., Inc.
299 E. First St.
Oswego, NY 13126
Tel: 315-342-3166
Mr. TERRENCE GORMAN, Admin.

Port Jefferson
Diocese of Rockville Centre

Maryhaven Center of Hope
Myrtle Ave.
Port Jefferson, NY 11777
Tel: 516-474-4100; Fax: 516-474-4110
Mr. LEWIS GROSSMAN, CEO
Sheltered Workshop
Consumers 372
Staff 67
Day Programs
Consumers 824
Staff 324
Residential Programs
Consumers 282
Staff 392
Provides svcs. to multi-handicapped children & adults; Vocational & sheltered workshop prog. for adults; day treatment prog. for adults; community residence prog. for adults; residential-day school for the mentally retarded emotionally disturbed (5-21 yrs).

Queens Village
Diocese of Brooklyn

Queen of Peace Residence
110-30 221st St.
Queens Village, NY 11429
Tel: 718-464-1800
Legal Title: *Home for the Aged, Little Sisters of the Poor*
Sr. GERTRUDE MARY, L.S.P., Admin.
Rev. Msgr. WILLIAM J. RODGERS, Chap.
In res.,
Revs.:
PAUL KLOHR
JOSEPH J. BIHLER
JOHN F. HUGHES
JAMES MEADE
ALFRED J. WEINLICH
JOHN STONEBRIDGE
MUELLER
HARTH
JOHN KEAN
Sisters 19

Rensselaer
Diocese of Albany

East Greenbush Housing Development Fund Co., Inc. dba Branson Manor Senior Apartment
3 Grandview Dr.
Rensselaer, NY 12144
Tel: 518-283-8280; Fax: 518-283-8292
GEORGETTE KNOTT-DEFOE, Exec. Dir.

Rhinebeck
Archdiocese of New York

Astor Home for Children, The
36 Mill St., P.O. Box 5005
Rhinebeck, NY 12572-5005
Tel: 914-876-4081; Fax: 914-876-2020
Sr. ROSE LOGAN, D.C., Exec. Dir.
Rev. GEORGE J. KUHN, Chap.
Daughters of Charity 4
Residential treatment facility for severe emotionally disturbed-mentally ill boys and girls, ages 5-12.
Bed Capacity 20
Residential Treatment Center (Rhinebeck):
Bed Capacity 55
Therapeutic Foster Boarding Homes 8
Family-Based Treatment 10
Child Guidance Clinics: Rhinebeck, Poughkeepsie, Beacon, Bronx, ages birth-18.
Capacity: unlimited
Day treatment programs ages 5-12:
Capacity Dutchess Co. 56
Bronx 156
Therapeutic Nursery, Bronx 40
Intensive Parenting Program, Bronx, ages birth-18:
Capacity 53 families
Head Start-Day Care Centers: Poughkeepsie, Beacon, Red Hook, Millerton, Wingdale, ages 3-5.
Capacity 350
Day Care Centers: Beacon, Red Hook, Millerton.
Capacity 45
Special Education Nursery, Wingdale, ages 3-5.
Capacity 10
Parent/Child Program.
Capacity 85
Total Assisted 4,010
Total Staff 525

Astor Learning Center, The
36 Mill St., P.O. Box 5005
Rhinebeck, NY 12572-5005
Tel: 914-876-4081; Fax: 914-876-2020
Special Education Program for emotionally disturbed, mentally ill children ages 6-13 in the Residential Treatment Center and local community.
Capacity 75
Total Assisted 123
Total Staff 38

Ferncliff Nursing Home
52 River Rd.
Rhinebeck, NY 12572
Tel: 914-876-2011; Fax: 914-876-2019
Carmelite Sisters for the Aged and Infirm
Sr. M. BERNADETTE THERESE REILLY, Admin.
Rev. PETER SMITH, Chap.
Bed Capacity 328

Rochester
Diocese of Rochester

St. Ann's Home for the Aged
1500 Portland Ave.
Rochester, NY 14621
Tel: 716-342-1700
Web Site: www.stannsrochester.org
Sisters of St. Joseph
BETTY MULLIN, Pres. & CEO
ROSEMARIE ZLOTNICK, Pastoral Assoc.
Rev. RICHARD KINSKY, C.S.B., Chap.
In res.,
Revs.:
ROBERT BRENNAN
JAMES O'CONNELL
Rev. Msgr. LESLIE G. WHALEN
Rev. Msgr. CHARLES BOYLE
Residents 354

St. Ann's Nursing Home Co., Inc.
(The Heritage)
1450 Portland Ave.
Rochester, NY 14621
Web Site: www.stannsrochester.org
BETTY MULLIN, Pres. & CEO
Residents 237

St. Joseph's Villa of Rochester
3300 Dewey Ave.
Rochester, NY 14616
Tel: 716-865-1550
ROGER C. BATTAGLIA, Pres. & C.E.O.
TERRENCE FINEGAN, Chm.
Total Staff 311
Total Assisted 577
LIFE
Substance Abuse Program.
Total Staff 16
Total Assisted 50

Rome
Diocese of Syracuse

C.N.C. Inc.
W. Thomas St.
Rome, NY 13440
Tel: 315-735-7545
Facility for ten deinstitutionalized chronically mentally ill individuals living in a group home.

Rome Mall Housing Development Fund Company, Inc.
Mailing Address:
1654 W. Onondaga St.
Syracuse, NY 13204
Tel: 315-424-1821
Rome Mall Apts.
Rome, NY 13440
40 one bedroom units for the elderly. Christopher Community, Inc., (Managing Agent).

Saranac Lake
Diocese of Ogdensburg

St. Joseph's Rehabilitation Center, Inc.
99 Glenwood Estates, P.O. Box 470
Saranac Lake, NY 12983
Tel: 518-891-3950; 891-4135 (Admissions); Fax: 518-891-3986
E-mail: stjoes@northnet.org
Alcoholism & Substance Abuse Rehab.
Revs.:
ARTHUR M. JOHNSON, S.A., Pres./CEO
DANIEL CALLAHAN, S.A., Chap.
Bros.:
ALAN LEMAY, S.A.
PASCHAL STEEN, S.A.
Franciscan Friars of the Atonement.
Priests 2
Brothers 2
Residents 62

Sayville
Diocese of Rockville Centre

Good Samaritan Nursing Home
Sayville, NY 11782
Tel: 516-244-2400
Sr. MARYAN E. RUSSO, C.I.J., Admin.
Chaplains:
Sr. ELIZABETH TOOHIG, S.C.
Rev. FRANCIS B. NUSS
Total Assisted 100
Total Staff 145

Silver Creek
Diocese of Buffalo

St. Columbans on the Lake, Home for the Aged
2546 Lake Rd.
Silver Creek, NY 14136
Tel: 716-934-4515
Sr. CORONA COLLEARY, Admin.
In res.,
Revs.:

PATRICK CASHMAN, S.S.C.
ANTHONY HASSETT, S.S.C.
EDMUND BAHL, S.S.C.
Columban Sisters 11
Aged Residents 50
Total Staff 35

Slingerlands
Diocese of Albany

Marie-Rose Manor HDFCI
100 Marquis Dr.
Slingerlands, NY 12159
Fax: 518-459-0204
GWEN FRIESEN, Dir.

Sloatsburg
Ukrainian Catholic Diocese of Stamford

St. Joseph's Home
125 Sisters Servants Ln., Box 25
Sloatsburg, NY 10974-0025
Tel: 914-753-2555
Sr. CHARLOTTE PIPPING, Admin.
Sisters Servants of Mary Immaculate 9
Residents 28
Staff 13

Springfield Gardens
Diocese of Brooklyn

Martin De Porres Group Homes
136-25 218th St.
Springfield Gardens, NY 11413
Bro. PHILIP ROFRANO, F.S.C., Exec. Dir.
Sr. VIRGINIA LACKER, R.S.M., A.F.S.C., Coord. Youth Care

Staten Island
Archdiocese of New York

Carmel Richmond Nursing Home, Inc.
88 Old Town Rd.
Staten Island, NY 10304-4299
Tel: 718-979-5000
Carmelite Sisters for the Aged and Infirm
Sr. M. STEPHEN MCBRIDE, O.Carm., Admin.
Rev. ERIC KYLE, O.F.M., Chap.
Bed Capacity 300
Friends of Carmel Richmond, Inc.
Total Assisted 300
Total Staff 358

Syosset
Diocese of Rockville Centre

St. Mary's Children and Family Services
525 Convent Rd.
Syosset, NY 11791-3864
Tel: 516-921-0808
Under the sponsorship of the Sisters of Mercy
LIZ GIORDANO, Exec. Dir.
Residential treatment center, non-secure detention, group homes, foster boarding homes, diagnostic assessment prog., preventive svc. prog. in Nassau Co. Residential treatment facility for mentally ill children.

Syracuse
Diocese of Syracuse

Bernardine Apartments, Inc.
417 Churchill Ave.
Syracuse, NY 13205
Tel: 315-469-7786
Mr. JAMES INTRONE, Pres.
TIM CARROLL, Mgr.

Christopher Community, Inc.
1654 W. Onondaga St.
Syracuse, NY 13204
Tel: 315-424-1821
Professional management and consultants of housing programs for the elderly, families and special populations.
Mr. PETER WHITE, Exec. Dir.
FRED ZOLNA, Housing Devel. Specialist

Churchill Manor, Inc.
750 E. Brighton Ave.
Syracuse, NY 13205
Tel: 315-424-1821
A non-profit corporation founded to provide housing for low and moderate income families and individuals.

Hawley Winton Housing Development Fund, Inc.
Walter Ludovico Apts., 340 Winton St.
Syracuse, NY 13203
Tel: 315-422-0475
33 one bedroom units occupied. Christopher Community, (Managing Agent).

Loretto
700 E. Brighton Ave.
Syracuse, NY 13205
Tel: 315-469-5561
Legal Title: *Loretto Rest Nursing Home Company, Inc.*
Mr. MICHAEL PALMIERI, Vice Pres., Admin. Cunningham Bldg.
Rev. WILBUR J. VOTRAW, Chap.

Loretto Geriatric Community Residences, Inc.
5018 S. Salina St.
Syracuse, NY 13205
Tel: 315-492-0896
4810 S. Salina St.
Syracuse, NY 13205
Tel: 315-469-8562
50 Syracuse St.
Baldwinsville, NY 13027
Tel: 315-635-1647
8659 Carpenter Rd.
Baldwinsville, NY 13027
Tel: 315-635-1763

Loretto Rest, Inc.
750 E. Brighton Ave.
Syracuse, NY 13205
Tel: 315-469-5061
Adult Home.
Mr. PATRICK DEPTULA, Exec. Vice Pres.
Rev. WILBUR J. VOTRAW, Chap.

Ludden Housing Development Fund Company, Inc.
1654 W. Onondaga St.
Syracuse, NY 13204
Tel: 315-424-1821
Fifty one bedroom apartments for the elderly and handicapped. Units opened in 1992 and are located on Fay Road, Town of Geddes. Christopher Community Inc., (Managing Agent).

Marcellus Apartments Housing Development Fund Company, Inc.
Mailing Address:
1654 W. Onondaga St.
Syracuse, NY 13204
Tel: 315-424-1821
Christopher Community, Inc., (Managing Agent).

Miller Road Housing Development Co., Inc.
(Brewerton)
Mailing Address:
1654 W. Onondaga St.
Syracuse, NY 13204
Tel: 315-424-1821
Housing for well elderly.

Mother Marianne Cope Housing Development Fund Co., Inc.
1654 W. Onondaga St.
Syracuse, NY 13204
Tel: 315-424-1821
E. Fayette St.
Syracuse, NY,
24 Units for HIV+ patients.

Mount St. James Corporation
1654 W. Onondaga St.
Syracuse, NY 13204
Tel: 315-424-1821
Engaged in the operation of a non-profit housing facility known as Mount St. James Apartments, at 338 Jamesville Ave., for persons of low to moderate income. Christopher Community, Inc., (Managing Agents).

Pompei Housing Development Fund Company, Inc.
c/o Christopher Community, Inc.
1654 W. Onondaga St.
Syracuse, NY 13204
Tel: 315-424-1821
50 one bedroom apartments for the elderly and handicapped. Christopher Community, Inc., (Managing Agent).

Pond St. Housing Development Fund Co., Inc.
Bishop Harrison Apartments, Pond St.
Syracuse, NY 13208
Operation of 48 units, one bedroom apartments for the elderly and handicapped. Christopher Community Inc., (Managing Agent).

Providence House Apartments
1700 W. Onondaga St.
Syracuse, NY 13204
Tel: 315-471-8427
Senior citizen housing, 100 units. Christopher Community, (Managing Agent).

St. Camillus Health & Rehabilitation Center
813 Fay Rd.
Syracuse, NY 13219
Tel: 315-488-2951
Mrs. AILEEN M. BALITZ, Pres.
Mr. RICK KING, Dir. Social Svcs.
St. Camillus Foundation
813 Fay Rd.
Syracuse, NY 13219
Mr. MARTIN M. DUGGAN, Chm.
KAROLAN PIZIO-MUNRO, Pres.

St. Peter's Italian Church Housing Development Fund Co., Inc. Villa Scalabrini Apts.
709 James St.
Syracuse, NY 13203
RAYMOND A. BANACH, Vice Pres. & Treas.
MARIO ROSSI, Sec.
Operation of a non-profit housing facility for aged, well persons of low income at the 800 Block of E. Willow St. in Syracuse. 120 units, one-bedroom apartments. Christopher Community, Inc., (Managing Agent).

Stoneleigh Housing Development Fund Co., Inc.
Stoneleigh Apartments, 400 Lamb Ave., Canastota
Syracuse, NY 13032
Engaged in the construction and operation of a non-profit housing facility for elderly and handicapped persons of low income. 100 units, one bedroom apartments. Christopher Community, Inc., (Managing Agent).

Tyson Place Housing Development Fund Company, Inc.
(40 apartments for the elderly)
Mailing Address:—Blessed Sacrament Apartments
1654 W. Onondaga St.
Syracuse, NY 13204
Tel: 315-424-1821
Christopher Community, Inc., (Managing Agent).

Town of Gates
Diocese of Syracuse

Steger Housing Development Fund Co., Inc.
4100 Lyell Rd.
Town of Gates, NY,
1654 W. Onondaga St.
Syracuse, NY 13204
Tel: 315-424-1821
56 apartments for well elderly.

Troy
Diocese of Albany

St. Mary's Woodland Village, Inc.
Upper Tibbits Ave.
Troy, NY 12180
Tel: 518-273-2040
Mrs. ROBIN SAGE, Admin.
Bed Capacity 155

Tupper Lake
Diocese of Ogdensburg

Mercy Healthcare Center, Inc.
114 Wawbeek Ave.
Tupper Lake, NY 12986
Tel: 518-359-3355; Fax: 518-359-9044
PAUL M. SCARPINATO, Admin.
Skilled Nursing Facility.
Sisters of Mercy of the Americas (Dobbs Ferry) 1
Capacity 80 Beds

Uniondale
Diocese of Rockville Centre

Mercy Hospice
St. Pius X Service Center, 122 Front St.
Uniondale, NY 11553
Tel: 516-485-3060
Total Annually Assisted 300
Staff 20
Volunteers 80

Utica
Diocese of Syracuse

Catherine St. Housing Development Fund Company, Inc.
Mailing Address:—Mt. Carmel Apartments
1654 W. Onondaga St.
Syracuse, NY 13201-0511
Tel: 315-424-1821
Christopher Community, Inc., (Managing Agent).

St. Joseph Nursing Home
2535 Genesee St.

Utica, NY 13501
Tel: 315-797-1230
Sr. BARBARA CONNOLLY, O.Carm., Admin.

Wading River
Diocese of Rockville Centre

Little Flower Children's Services of New York
Wading River, NY 11792
Tel: 516-929-6200
Directed by the Diocese of Brooklyn. Foster care, adoption & post-adoption svcs., intermediate care facilities, residential treatment center, Special Act school district, family day care, family care for MR/DD clients, foster homes for teen mothers & their babies.
Rev. Msgr. JOHN T. FAGAN, Exec. Vice Pres. (CEO)
Mrs. MARY G. RYDER, Exec. Dir. (COO)
Sisters of the Holy Family of Nazareth
Sr. RITA WASILEWSKI, C.S.F.N., Supr.

Warwick
Archdiocese of New York

Villa Frances at the Knolls
Franciscan System of Warwick, Inc.
20 Grand St.
Warwick, NY 10990
Tel: 914-986-2267
F. DENNIS HARRINGTON, Pres.
Rev. EDWARD SULLIVAN, Chap.
Capacity 120

Watervliet
Diocese of Albany

Carondelet Commons Senior Apartments
Delatour Housing Development Fund Company, Inc. dba, Carondelet Commons Senior Apartments.
2 Carondelet Dr.
Watervliet, NY 12189
Tel: 518-783-0444; Fax: 518-783-0456
DORIS SEIP, Building Dir.

Italian-American Housing Development Fund Co., Inc. dba Cabrini Acers Senior Apts.
4 Carondelet Dr.
Watervliet, NY 12189
Tel: 518-785-0050; Fax: 518-785-0110
DORIS SEIP, Building Dir.

St. Colman's Home
Watervliet, NY 12189
Tel: 518-273-4911; Fax: 518-273-3312
Sisters of the Presentation of the B.V.M.
Sr. M. VIRGINIA, P.B.V.M., Dir.
Rev. JOHN A. MOLYN, Chap.
Tel: 518-271-6784
Children 50

West Islip
Diocese of Rockville Centre

Good Samaritan Hospice
1000 Montauk Hwy.
West Islip, NY 11795
Tel: 516-376-4001
Admissions to Program 371

Our Lady of Consolation Geriatric Care Center
Short & long term nursing & rehabiliative care.
111 Beach Dr.
West Islip, NY 11795
Tel: 516-587-1600; Fax: 516-587-5960
Under the supervision of the Sisters of St. Dominic
Sr. AUDREY HARSEN, O.P.
Rev. ROBERT A. HYATT, Chap.
Total Assisted 450
Total Staff 625

West Park
Archdiocese of New York

St. Cabrini Home
West Park, NY 12493
Tel: 914-384-6500; Fax: 914-384-6001
JAMES J. LAVELLE, Exec. Dir.
Children 80
In Foster Homes 32
Agency Operated Boarding Home 12
Group Homes 108
Missionary Sisters of Sacred Heart 5
Served by Redemptionist Fathers
Cabrini-on-Hudson
An adult community.
Residents 60

White Plains
Archdiocese of New York

Cardinal McCloskey Services
Two Holland Ave.
White Plains, NY 10603
Tel: 914-997-8000
Mrs. MARJORIE MCLOUGHLIN, Exec. Dir.
Sisters 3
In Foster Homes 500
In Group Homes 38
In Family Day Care:
Site I: Capacity 540
Site II: Capacity 115
Site III: Capacity 145
Cardinal McCloskey Emergency Residential School
155 N. Highland Ave.
White Plains, NY 10562
Capacity 20

Williamsville
Diocese of Buffalo

Holy Family Home
410 Mill St.
Williamsville, NY 14221
Tel: 716-634-5400
Sr. PAULA MARIE NOTARTHOMAS, O.S.F., CEO
Sisters of St. Francis of the Third Order Regular 7
Residents 91
Total Staff 56

St. Francis Home of Williamsville
147 Reist St.
Williamsville, NY 14221
Tel: 716-633-5400; Fax: 716-663-6404
Legal Title: *St. Francis Home of Williamsville*
Skilled Nursing Facility
JAMES A. WALSH, Ph.D., Admin.
Rev. Msgr. HENRY J. GUGINO
Residents 142
Total Assisted 194
Total Staff 200

Yonkers
Archdiocese of New York

St. Eleanora's Home for Convalescents
127 S. Broadway
Yonkers, NY 10701
Tel: 914-378-7000
E-mail: sclegras@erols.com
Unit of St. Joseph's Nursing Home (Yonkers).

NORTH CAROLINA

Belmont
Diocese of Charlotte

**Holy Angels, Inc.*
6600 Wilkinson Blvd., P.O. Box 710
Belmont, NC 28012
Tel: 704-825-4161; Fax: 704-825-0553
Mrs. REGINA P. MOODY, M.Ed., Exec. Dir.
Mother MARY BENIGNUS HOBAN, R.S.M., Pres.
Sisters of Mercy 6
Capacity (All Programs) 174
Residential and developmental programs and services for children and adults with mental retardation and physical disabilities.
Holy Angels Specialized Community Residential Center (Children 0-20)
Little Angels Child Development Center
On-site integrated day care.
Great Adventures Social Club
Adults with mental retardation.
South Point
Children/Adult group home.
Belhaven
Adult group home.
Lakewood
Adult group home.
Fox Run ICF/MR Group Homes
Beds 18
Life Choices Vocational Program (Age 18+)
Cherubs Craft & Coffee Shop by Holy Angels (Age 18+)
Job coaching, work options.
Supported Living (Age 18+)
Camp Hope
Integrated Day Camp for Children/Adults with Developmental Disabilities.

Hayesville
Diocese of Charlotte

Good Shepherd Home Health & Hospice Agency, Inc.
P.O. Box 465
Hayesville, NC 28904
Tel: 704-389-6311; Fax: 704-389-9584
Mr. THOMAS J. TAAFFE, Exec. Dir
Home Health Care & Hospice.
Murphy Branch
104 E. Hwy. 64, W.
Murphy, NC 28906
Tel: 704-837-3430; Fax: 704-837-3485

High Point
Diocese of Charlotte

Maryfield Nursing Home
1315 Greensboro Rd.
High Point, NC 27260
Tel: 910-886-2444; Fax: 910-886-4036
Sr. LUCY HENNESSY, S.M.G., Admin.
Rev. JOHN B. MURPHY, O.S.F.S., Non-Res. Chap.
Poor Servants of the Mother of God 7
Beds 115

Rosman
Diocese of Charlotte

**Frances Warde Health Service*
Star Rte. 1, Box 581
Rosman, NC 28772
Tel: 704-884-7990; Fax: 704-966-9609
Sr. GRETCHEN HERMANNY, R.S.M., M.D., Medical Dir.
Sisters 4

NORTH DAKOTA

Bismarck
Diocese of Bismarck

Emmaus Place
1020 N. 26th St.
Bismarck, ND 58501
Tel: 701-258-2618
Priests retirement home.
Revs.:
CHARLES H. BACKES
BLAINE COOK
WILLIAM J. FAHNLANDER
JOHN H. KUHN
ALBERT R. LEARY
LADISLAUS C. BRYDL
WILLIAM A. RUSHFORD
JACOB J. SCHUMACHER
Total Staff 5
Total in Residence 8

Marillac Manor
1016 N. 28th St.
Bismarck, ND 58501
Tel: 701-258-8702; Fax: 701-223-3127
Sr. PHOEBE SCHWARTZE, O.S.B., Admin.
Retirement Apartments 78
Total Staff 11
Total in Residence 85

St. Vincent's Care Center
1021 N. 26 St.
Bismarck, ND 58501-3199
Tel: 701-223-6888
TIMOTHY N. BURCHILL, Admin.
Sisters of St. Benedict 1
Total Staff 160
Resident Patients 145

Edgeley
Diocese of Fargo

Manor St. Joseph
404 Fourth Ave.
Edgeley, ND 58433
Tel: 701-493-2477
TAMMY JANGULA, Admin.
Sister Servants of Christ the King 2
Guests 40
Bed Capacity 40
Staff 33

Ellendale
Diocese of Fargo

Ellendale Nursing Center
201 8th St. N.
Ellendale, ND 58436
Tel: 701-349-3312; Fax: 701-349-3944
Operated by Benedictine Health System Long Term Care Inc.
Mr. TONY HANSON, Admin.
Bed Capacity 74
Staff 92

Fargo
Diocese of Fargo

Riverview Place, Inc.
5300 12th St., S.
Fargo, ND 58103
Tel: 701-237-4700
THOMAS DONALDSON, CFO

Revs.:
ALBERT BINDER, (Retired)
JOHN STEARNS, (Retired)
VLADAS ALEKSONIS, (Retired)
PETER W. GRADY, (Retired)
JEROME E. FILTEAU, (Retired)
WILLIAM J. MEHOK, S.J., (Retired)
MAURICE M. MUELLER, (Retired)
JOHN MOORE, (Retired)
LAMBERT STUDZINSKI, (Retired)
Residents 180
Staff 60

Villa Nazareth dba Friendship, Inc.
3004 S. 11th St.
Fargo, ND 58103
Tel: 701-235-8217
Presentation Sisters (P.B.V.M.)
A community-based facility providing an array of educational, social and clinical services for children and adults with mental retardation and other developmental disabilities.

Grand Forks
Diocese of Fargo

St. Anne's Guest Home
524 N. 17th St.
Grand Forks, ND 58203
Tel: 701-746-9401
Sr. ELAINE MARIE ROGGENBUCK, O.S.F.
Sr. REBECCA METZGER, Admin.
Sisters of St. Francis of the Immaculate Heart of Mary (Hankinson, ND) 11
Staff 36
Guests 86

Hankinson
Diocese of Fargo

St. Gerard Community Nursing Home
613 First Ave. S.W.
Hankinson, ND 58041
Tel: 701-242-7891
Rev. PAUL L. KOEHLER, Chap.
Sr. ROSE MARIE FREUND, O.S.F., Admin.
Sisters of St. Francis of the Immaculate Heart of Mary (Hankinson, ND) 2
Beds 37
Patients assisted annually 37
Independent Living Unit Beds 11
Staff 65

La Moure
Diocese of Fargo

La Moure Healthcare Manor
Hwy. 13, P.O. Box 627
La Moure, ND 58458
Tel: 701-883-5363; Fax: 701-883-5711
Operated by Benedictine Health System Long Term Care, Inc.
Mr. TONY HANSON, Admin.
Bed Capacity 60
Staff 60

Rolette
Diocese of Fargo

Presentation Care Center
304 John St.
Rolette, ND 58366
Tel: 701-246-3786
KIMBER WRAALSTAD, Pres. CEO
Beds 48
Patients Assisted 65
Staff 75

Sentinel Butte
Diocese of Bismarck

Home On The Range
16351 I-94
Sentinel Butte, ND 58654-9500
Tel: 701-872-3745; Fax: 701-872-3748
Mr. RANDAL SATROM, Exec. Dir.
Rev. DAVID MORMAN, Chap.
Total Staff 105
Total Assisted 170

Wahpeton
Diocese of Fargo

Wahpeton Health Care Center
1307 N. Seventh St.
Wahpeton, ND 58075
Tel: 701-642-6667
Operated by Benedictine Health System Long Term Care, Inc.
KATHLEEN HOEFT, Admin.
Residents 180
Long-term Care Beds 164
Basic Care Beds 16
Staff 200

OHIO

Akron
Diocese of Cleveland

Francesca Residence
39 N. Portage Path
Akron, OH 44303
Tel: 330-867-6334
Sr. M. MARTIN GREEN, F.D.C., Admin.
Rev. THOMAS F. SULLIVAN, Chap.
Daughters of Divine Charity 8
Total Under Care 47
Total in Residence 44
Total Staff 12

Leonora Hall
39 N. Portage Path
Akron, OH 44303
Tel: 330-867-1752
Residence for Young Women.
Sr. M. ANTOINETTE, F.D.C., Admin.
Daughters of Divine Charity 2
Residents 21

Beachwood
Diocese of Cleveland

Villa Sancta Anna Home for the Aged, Inc.
25000 Chagrin Blvd.
Beachwood, OH 44122-5665
Tel: 216-464-9250
Sr. M. ELISABETH ANN RECHKA, V.S.C., Admin.
Rev. KENNETH J. KATRICAK, O.S.B., Chap. & Asst. Admin.
Vincentian Sisters of Charity (Bedford, Ohio) 3
Residents 68
Total Assisted 68
Total Staff 85

Bedford
Diocese of Cleveland

Light of Hearts Villa, Inc.
283 Union St.
Bedford, OH 44146
Tel: 216-232-1991
Sr. HELEN THERESE SCASNY, V.S.C., Exec. Dir.
Sr. KATHY THOMAS, C.S.J., Asst. Dir.
Total in Residence 86
Total Staff 50

Canton
Diocese of Youngstown

House of Loreto
2812 Harvard Ave., N.W.
Canton, OH 44709
Tel: 330-453-8137; Fax: 330-453-8140
Administered by the Congregation of the Divine Spirit.
Sr. GLADYS SPENGLER, C.D.S., Exec. Dir.
Sr. CLAIRE BATTERSON, C.D.S., Admin.
Rev. JOSEPH J. PHILLIPS, S.P., Chap.
In res.,
Rev. NORBERT R. WEST
Sisters of the Congregation of the Divine Spirit 15
Residents 91
Total Staff 70

Centerville
Archdiocese of Cincinnati

The Franciscan at St. Leonard
8100 Clyo Rd.
Centerville, OH 45458
Tel: 937-433-0480
A facility of the Franciscan Health System of Dayton, sponsored by the Franciscan Sisters of the Poor Health System, Inc. A residence for Senior Citizens.
Revs.:
JAMES VAN VURST, O.F.M., Dir. Pastoral Care
ANTHONY PERFETTO, S.M., Staff Chap.
SAMUEL ZEBRON, O.F.M., Moderator & Chap., Sunday Community
JUVENAL PFALZER, O.F.M., (Retired)
ROMAN PRALZER, O.F.M., (Retired)
Residents 480

Cincinnati
Archdiocese of Cincinnati

Archbishop Leibold Home for the Aged
476 Riddle Rd.
Cincinnati, OH 45220-2493
Tel: 513-281-8001
The Little Sisters of the Poor
Revs.:
JOVIAN C. WEIGEL, O.F.M., Chap.
AUGUST J. KNIEPP
BERARD GERBUS, O.F.M.
Sr. CECILIA SARTORIUS, L.S.P., Supr.
Sisters 15
Residents 115

The Franciscan at St. Clare
100 Compton Rd.
Cincinnati, OH 45215
Tel: 513-761-9036
A member of the Franciscan Health System of the Ohio valley.
R. CHRISOPHER WEST, Pres./CEO
SHARON K. THORNTON, Admin.
Pastoral Care Dept.:
Sr. ELLEN DURSO, S.F.P.
Residents 117
Retired Sisters 13
Retired Brothers 2
Retired Priests 9
Other Residents 116

The Franciscan at West Park
2950 West Park Dr.
Cincinnati, OH 45238
Tel: 513-451-8900
A Member of the Franciscan Health System of the Ohio Valley, Inc.
R. CHRISTOPHER WEST, Pres. & CEO
TIMOTHY C. DRESSMAN, Admin.
Sr. ARLENE MCGOWAN, Vice Pres. Mission
DON ROHLING, Dir. Mission Svcs.
Ms. ALBERTA UTRUP, Chaplain
Residents 310

Mercy St. Theresa Center
7010 Rowan Hill Dr., Ste. 200
Cincinnati, OH 45227
Tel: 513-271-7010; Fax: 513-527-0181
DEBORAH SAMPSIL, Vice Pres. Aging Svcs.
Rev. STEPHEN J. EMERICK, Chap.
Sisters 3
Permanent Residents 149

St. Aloysius Orphanage
4721 Reading Rd.
Cincinnati, OH 45237
Tel: 513-242-7600; Fax: 513-242-2845
For boys and girls ages 6-14.
Sisters of Notre Dame (Covington, KY)
DONNA SAUNDERS, Exec. Dir.
REGGIE BUTLER, Dir. Educ.
Sisters 4
Children 24

St. Joseph Infant and Maternity Home dba St. Joseph Home
10722 Wyscarver Rd.
Cincinnati, OH 45241
Tel: 513-563-2520
Sisters of Charity of Cincinnati, OH
Sr. MARIANNE VAN VURST, Admin.
Children and young adults with severe/profound mental and motor disabilities 47

St. Joseph Orphanage
Archdiocesan Children's Residential Center.
5400 Edalbert
Cincinnati, OH 45239
ROBERT J. WEHR, Ph.D., Exec. Dir.
A.C.T. Child Case Management
5400 Edalbert Dr.
Cincinnati, OH 54239
Tel: 513-245-9944; Fax: 513-245-9401
ROBERT J. WEHR, Ph.D., Exec. Dir.
Employees 51
St. Joseph Villa
5400 Edalbert
Cincinnati, OH 45239
Tel: 513-741-3100
Residential Treatment Children 6-18.
ROBERT J. WEHR, Ph.D., Exec. Dir.
Staff 78
Residents 55
Altercrest
274 Sutton Rd.
Cincinnati, OH 45230
Tel: 513-231-5010
Residential Treatment for Boys ages 12-18.
ROBERT J. WEHR, Ph.D., Exec. Dir.
Staff 46
Residents 61
C.A.R.E. Child Case Management
90 Lawn Ave.
Hamilton, OH 45013
Tel: 513-887-2100

ROBERT J. WEHR, Ph.D., Exec. Dir.
Staff 14
Family Ties Therapeutic Foster Care
5400 Edalbert
Cincinnati, OH 45239
Tel: 513-741-3100
ROBERT J. WEHR, Ph.D., Exec. Dir.
Staff 12
Total Assisted 60
Individualized Services
411 Oak St.
Cincinnati, OH 45219
Tel: 513-281-3700
Dr. ROBERT J. WEHR, Ph.D., Exec. Dir.
Staff 54
Total Assisted 160

St. Margaret Hall
1960 Madison Rd.
Cincinnati, OH 45206-1896
Tel: 513-751-5880; Fax: 513-751-9813
Sr. ANN M. DAILEY, O.Carm., Admin.
Rev. RODNEY MCDANIEL, Chap.
In res.,
Revs.:
CORNELIUS C. BERNING
BERNARD FELIX
PIUS WINTER O.F.M.
Carmelite Sisters for the Aged and Infirm 9
Residents 133

Sisters of Charity Senior Care Corp., dba Bayley Place
990 Bayley Place Dr.
Cincinnati, OH 45233
Tel: 513-347-5500; Fax: 513-347-5553
Sr. JEANNE ROACH, Admin.

Cleveland
Diocese of Cleveland

Christ Child - DePaul Day Care Center
2320 E. 24th St.
Cleveland, OH 44115
Tel: 216-687-0006; Fax: 216-687-0403
Day Care program co-sponsored by Catholic Social Services and Counseling of Cuyahoga County. Funded by United Way & Catholic Charities.
ELBERT W. CLARK, JR., M.A., L.S.W.

Holy Family Home
6707 State Rd.
Cleveland, OH 44134
Tel: 216-885-3100; Fax: 216-885-0644
Free nursing home for terminal cancer patients who are unable to pay.
Legal Title: *The Servants of Relief for Incurable Cancer*
Administered by Dominican Sisters of the Third Order, Congregation of St. Rose of Lima.
Sr. M. BARBARA, O.P., Supr.
Rev. JOSEPH F. CIOLEK, Chap., Tel: 216-842-1436
Sisters 9
Total Staff 55
Bed Capacity 50
Patients assisted annually 245

Jennings Hall Inc.
10204 Granger Rd.
Cleveland, OH 44125
Tel: 216-581-2900; Fax: 216-581-1517
E-mail: jenningshal@aol.com
Mrs. MARTHA M. KUTIK, Pres. & Exec. Dir.
Rev. KESTUTIS ZEMAITIS (Vilnius) Chap., Tel: 216-581-2900
Residential Long-Term Care Facility. Under Diocesan Auspices.
Sisters 5
Residents 150
Total Assisted 225
Total Staff 190

Mount Alverna Home, Inc. & Mount Alverna Home Annex, Inc.
6765 State Rd.
Parma, OH 44134
Tel: 216-843-7800; Fax: 216-843-7107
ROBERT J. SHERRIN, Admin.
Rev. ERIC GAUCHAT, Cap. O.F.M.
Capacity 203
Residents 203
Total Assisted 203
Total Staff 313

Mount St. Joseph
21800 Chardon Rd.
Cleveland, OH 44117
Tel: 216-531-7426; Fax: 216-531-4033
Sr. M. CECILIA ILLIG, NHA
Conducted by Sisters of St. Joseph of St. Mark - Mount St. Joseph.
Sisters 22
Bed Capacity 100
Residents 100
Total Assisted 100
Total Staff 160

Rose Mary, The Johanna Grasselli Rehabilitation and Education Center
19350 Euclid Ave.
Cleveland, OH 44117
Tel: 216-481-4823
Ms. PATRICIA A. COLOMBO, Exec. Dir.
Sisters of the Humility of Mary 1
Children 40
Residents 84
Bed Capacity 86
Total Staff 250

St. Augustine Manor
7801 Detroit Ave.
Cleveland, OH 44102
Tel: 216-634-7400; Fax: 216-634-7483
E-mail: p.gareau@worldnet.att.net
Affiliated with Catholic Charities.
Mrs. MARY DOYLE, Chm., Board of Trustees
Mr. PATRICK GAREAU, Pres. & CEO
Rev. JOSEPH A. ROMANSKY, Residence Chap.
Bed Capacity 248
Patients assisted annually 650
Total in Residence 242
Total Staff 400
Coterie of St. Augustine Manor, The
7801 Detroit Ave.
Cleveland, OH 44102
Tel: 216-634-7400
(Operates the Coterie Boutique)
Mrs. MARGARET LYNCH, Pres.

Sts. Mary and Joseph Home for the Aged
4291 Richmond Rd.
Cleveland, OH 44122-6199
Tel: 216-464-1222
Little Sisters of the Poor
Mother CHANTAL I.S.P.
In res.,
Revs.:
THOMAS CAREY, S.M.
EDWARD CORRIGAN, S.M.
CLAUDE GAEBELEIN
JOHN J. GERRITY
PAUL DUZINSKI, O.F.M.Conv.
STEPHEN TOWELL
Sisters 13
Fraternity Members 2
Bed Capacity 125

Columbus
Diocese of Columbus

Nazareth Towers
300 E. Rich St.
Columbus, OH 43215
Tel: 614-464-4780; Fax: 614-464-1733
Sr. MARY LOIS SCHMELTZER, O.P., Admin.
Total Staff 7
Total in Residence 229

Rosemont Center
2440 Dawnlight Ave.
Columbus, OH 43211
Tel: 614-471-2626
E-mail: rmarx@rosemont.org
Web Site: http://www.rosemont.org
ROBERT J. MARX, Exec. Dir.
Sisters of the Good Shepherd 10
Total Staff 125
Rosemont Center Endowment Fund

St. Raphael Home for the Aged, Inc.
1550 Roxbury Rd.
Columbus, OH 43212
Tel: 614-486-0436; Fax: 614-486-1640
Carmelite Sisters for Aged and Infirm
Sr. KATHLEEN DOMINICK, O.Carm., Admin. & Supr.
Rev. LARRY NOLAN, Chap.
Residents 78
Total Assisted 78
Total Staff 105

St. Rita Home
880 Greenlawn Ave.
Columbus, OH 43223
Tel: 614-443-9433; Fax: 614-443-1196
Sr. M. JACQUELINE O.Carm., Supr. & Admin.
Rev. THOMAS J. CADDEN, Chap.
Carmelite Sisters for Aged and Infirm 6
Total Staff 200
Guests 100
Total Assisted 150

Seton London, Inc.
350 Cambridge Dr.
London, OH 43140
Tel: 614-852-4233
Total in Residence 61
Total Staff 2

Seton South Columbus, Inc.
155 Highview Blvd.
Columbus, OH 43207
Tel: 614-492-9944

Seton Square North
1776 Drew Ave.
Columbus, OH 43235
Tel: 614-451-1995
CINDY FISHER, Gen. Mgr. Seton Projects
Total in Residence 240
Total Staff 4

Seton Washington Court House, Inc.
400 N. Glenn Ave.
Washington Court House, OH 43160
Tel: 614-335-2292
Total in Residence 42
Total Staff 2

Coshocton
Diocese of Columbus

Seton Coshocton, Inc.
377 Clow Ln.
Coshocton, OH 43812
Tel: 614-451-1995
Apartments 41
Total Staff 3

Dayton
Archdiocese of Cincinnati

The Maria Joseph Living Care Center
4830 Salem Ave.
Dayton, OH 45416
Tel: 937-278-2692; Fax: 937-278-9016
Skilled Nursing-Intermediate Nursing; Independent Living.
BONNIE G. LANGDON, Pres. & CEO
Rev. HARRY CAVANAUGH, C.PP.S., Chap.
Sr. BETTY MASSAREK, C.PP.S., Pastoral Care Coord.
Licensed/Certified Nursing Care 384
Independent Living 56

Mercy Siena Woods
235 W. Orchard Springs Dr.
Dayton, OH 45415
Tel: 937-278-8211; Fax: 937-278-8046
E-mail: shayes@erinet.com
Nursing Home, nonsectarian. A member of Catholic Healthcare Partners. Specialized Alzheimer's Center. Sponsored by the Religious Sisters of Mercy. 53 years of ministry.
SUSAN M. HAYES, Admin. & CEO
Rev. FRANCIS A. MASSARELLA, Res. Chap.
Sisters 1
Residents 99

Siena Springs
6215 N. Main St.
Dayton, OH 45415
Tel: 937-274-4790
Apartments, Independent Living for the Elderly.
Sponsored by the Sisters of Mercy
Sr. PATRICIA CONNOLLY, R.S.M., Admin.,Mgr. & CEO
Residents 45
Total Staff 2

Dover
Diocese of Columbus

Seton Square Dover, I, Inc.
501 James St.
Dover, OH 44622
Tel: 330-343-3611
CHARLES ERBE, Co-Mgr.
MYRTLE ERBE, Co-Mgr.
Total Staff 3
Total in Residence 50

Seton Square Dover, II, Inc.
139 Fillmore St.
Dover, OH 44622
Tel: 330-343-3611
A retirement residence for the elderly.
Total Staff 3
Total in Residence 41

Fairlawn
Diocese of Cleveland

St. Edward Home dba The Village at Saint Edward Nursing Care and Assisted Living
3131 Smith Rd.

Fairlawn, OH 44333
Tel: 330-666-1183
JOHN J. HENNELLY, Pres. & CEO
Rev. JOHN F. WILSON, Chap.
Sisters 3
Nursing Care Residents 100
Assisted Living Residents 26
Total Staff 138

St. Edward Housing Corporation dba The Village at St. Edward Independent Living
3125 Smith Rd.
Fairlawn, OH 44333
Tel: 330-668-2828
JOHN J. HENNELLY, Pres. & CEO
Rev. JOHN F. WILSON, Chap.
Total in Residence 161
Total Staff 38

Green Springs
Diocese of Toledo

St. Francis Health Care Center
401 N. Broadway St.
Green Springs, OH 44836
Tel: 419-639-2626; Fax: 419-639-6225
Owned by Franciscan Sisters of Our Lady of Perpetual Help (St. Louis, MO)
Operated by Franciscan Sisters of Our Lady of Perpetual Help of Ohio Corp.
GREGORY T. STORER, CEO
CHARLES HULL, M.D., Medical Dir.
Rev. DONALD R. MUELLER, Chap.
Sisters 6
Bed capacity 186
Total Staff 300

St. Francis Health Care Centre (ICF & Skilled)
401 N. Broadway St.
Green Springs, OH 44836
Tel: 419-639-2626; Fax: 419-639-3559
Owned by Franciscan Sisters of Our Lady of Perpetual Help (St. Louis, MO)
Operated by Franciscan Sisters of Our Lady of Perpetual Help of Ohio Corp.
GREGORY T. STORER, CEO
CHARLES HULL, M.D., Medical Dir.
Rev. DONALD R. MUELLER
Sisters 6
Bed capacity 150
Total under care 147

Hamilton
Archdiocese of Cincinnati

The Franciscan at Schroder
1302 Millville Ave.
Hamilton, OH 45013
Tel: 513-867-1300; Fax: 513-867-1415
A Facility of the Franciscan Health System of the Ohio Valley. Sponsored by the Franciscan Sisters of the Poor Health System, Inc. Special unit for Alzheimer Treatment.
Ms. MARCY MORGAN, Exec. Dir.
Residents 138

Hubbard
Diocese of Youngstown

Villa Maria Teresa
50 Warner Rd.
Hubbard, OH 44425
Tel: 330-759-9329 (Villa); 875-4635 (Emmaus House)
Retired Priests' Residence.
Residents 5

Independence
Diocese of Cleveland

Marycrest
7800 Brookside Rd.
Independence, OH 44131
Tel: 216-524-5280; Fax: 216-524-2127
Residential treatment and transitional living for adolescent girls and adolescent mothers and babies.
Sisters 3
Total Assisted 100
Total Staff 110

Kenton
Diocese of Columbus

Seton Kenton, Inc.
699 Morningside Dr.
Kenton, OH 43326
Tel: 419-673-7202
MARY LOU SWEET, Mgmt. Rep.
DAVID MANNS, Maintenance
Total Staff 2
Total in Residence 52

Lancaster
Diocese of Columbus

Seton Lancaster, Inc.
232 Gay St.
Lancaster, OH 43130
Tel: 614-681-1403

Louisville
Diocese of Youngstown

Emmaus House
1515 California Ave.
Louisville, OH 44641
Tel: 330-875-4635
Rev. WILLIAM B. KRAYNAK, Admin.
Retired Priests' Residence.
Residents 5
Total Staff 3

St. Joseph Care Center
2308 Reno Dr.
Louisville, OH 44641
Tel: 330-875-5562; Fax: 330-875-8947
JOHN T. BANKS, Admin.
Sisters of St. Joseph of St. Mark 4
Sisters of the Humility of Mary 1
Nursing Home 150
Assisted Living 50
Total Staff 160

Marion
Diocese of Columbus

Seton Square Marion, Inc.
255 Richland Rd.
Marion, OH 43302
Tel: 614-389-4746
DEBRA J. ERWIN, Office Mgr.
GARRY BAILEY, Maintenance
Total in Residence 112
Total Staff 3

North Lima
Diocese of Youngstown

The Assumption Village
9800 Market St.
North Lima, OH 44452
Tel: 330-549-0740; Fax: 330-549-0701
Sponsorship: Sisters of the Humility of Mary
Member: HM Health Partners.
Sr. ROSEMARY HAMMER, H.M., Pres. & CEO
PHYLLIS ANDERSON, R.N., Dir. Nursing & Health Svcs. Admin.
Special Care Unit for residents with Alzheimer's or Dementia.
Residents 48
Total Staff 20
Skilled Nursing Unit with Subacute Care Program
Total Assisted 150
Total Staff 176

The Assumption Village
9800 Market St.
North Lima, OH 44452
Tel: 330-549-0740; Fax: 330-549-0701
Sponsorship: Sisters of the Humility of Mary
Member: HM Health Partners.
Sr. ROSEMARY HAMMER, H.M., Pres. & CEO
PHYLLIS ANDERSON, R.N., Dir. Nursing & Health Svcs. Admin.
Skilled Nursing Unit with Subacute Care Program
Total Assisted 150
Total Staff 176
Special Care Unit for residents with Alzheimer's or cognitive impairment
Residents 48
Total Staff 20

Oregon
Diocese of Toledo

Sacred Heart Home
4900 Navarre Ave.
Oregon, OH 43616-3599
Tel: 419-698-4331; Fax: 419-698-1109
Little Sisters of the Poor
Sr. MARY JOSEPH L.S.P., Supr.
Revs.:
JOHN SHIFFLER
FERNAN J. BRENNAN, O.S.F.S.
JAMES O'GRADY
FREDERICK HUG
Sisters 12
Aged Residents 119
Independent Living Apartments 20
Total Staff 165

Parma
Diocese of Cleveland

Parmadale
6753 State Rd.
Parma, OH 44134
Tel: 216-845-7700; Fax: 216-845-5910
MICHAEL J. HAGGERTY, Exec. Dir.
THOMAS W. WOLL, Pres.
Rev. JOSEPH J. SEMINATORE, Chap.
In res.,
Rev. JAMES R. SEMONIN
Specialized Residential Services; Intensive Treatment Services; Partial Hospitalization; Community Flexible Clinical Response; Specialized Foster Care; Wrap-Around Services; Whole Family Treatment; In-Home Services; Outpatient Services; Day Care; Training and Consultation Services; and Volunteer Program.
Total Capacity 90
Total Staff 280
Children in Foster Care 210

Reynoldsburg
Diocese of Columbus

Seton Square East, Inc.
1235 Briarcliff Rd.
Reynoldsburg, OH 43068
Tel: 614-861-4860

Richfield
Diocese of Cleveland

Regina Health Center
5232 Broadview Rd.
Richfield, OH 44286-9608
Tel: 216-659-4161; Fax: 216-659-5113
Sr. NANCY HENDERSHOT, C.S.A., Pres.
Sponsored by Sisters of Charity of St. Augustine.
Nursing Home Beds 81
Assisted Living Units 74
Total in Residence 144
Total Assisted 65
Total Staff 136

Springfield
Archdiocese of Cincinnati

Oakwood Village Retirement Community
1500 Villa Rd.
Springfield, OH 45503
Tel: 937-390-9000; Fax: 937-390-9333

Tiffin
Diocese of Toledo

St. Francis Home Inc.
182 St. Francis Ave.
Tiffin, OH 44883
Mr. ANGELO VIVINO Admin.
Mr. WILLIAM BOOTH, Chm., Board of Trustees
Rev. RUSSELL F. GILLIG, Chap.
Residents 173
Total Staff 230

Toledo
Diocese of Toledo

St. Anthony Villa/Boysville of Michigan, Inc.
2740 W. Central Ave.
Toledo, OH 43606
Tel: 419-473-1353; Fax: 419-473-2963
E-mail: bv.mhs@compuserve.com
Web Site: www.boysville.org
Residential and community-based treatment programs for troubled youth and families with facilities located throughout the state of Michigan and one facility in the state of Ohio under the auspices of the Brothers of Holy Cross at Notre Dame.
Bro. FRANCIS BOYLAN, C.S.C., Exec. Dir.
VICKY PRIMER, Ph.D., Reg. Dir.
Deacon JOHN ALGEE, Pastoral Min.
Sisters 2
Lay Staff 100
Residential 75

Urbana
Archdiocese of Cincinnati

Mercy McAuley Center-Mercy Health Systems
906 Scioto St.
Urbana, OH 43078
Tel: 937-653-5432; Fax: 937-652-2072
RICHARD ZECHIEL, Admin.
Residents 129
Total Staff 130

Warren
Metropolitan Archdiocese of Pittsburgh, Byzantine

Infant of Prague Manor
169 Kenmore, N.E.
Warren, OH 44483
Tel: 330-372-4700
Sr. MARGARET MARY, O.S.B., Admin.
Apartments 46
Staff 4
In Residence 43
Housing for the elderly.

Wellston
Diocese of Columbus

Seton Square Wellston, Inc.
570 W. First St.
Wellston, OH 45692
Tel: 614-384-6174

Zanesville
Diocese of Columbus

Seton Housing, Inc.
516 Sheridan St.
Zanesville, OH 43701
Tel: 614-453-4422
Total Staff 2
Total in Residence 45

OKLAHOMA

Oklahoma City
Archdiocese of Oklahoma City

St. Ann's Home Inc.
9400 St. Ann's Dr.
Oklahoma City, OK 73162
Tel: 405-728-7888; Fax: 405-728-1302
Mrs. JOY ECKER, Admin.
Rev. DONALD C. MOORE, Chap.
Sisters 4
Beds 120
Total Assisted 119

Trinity Place Apartments
Associated Catholic Charities, 3825 N.W. 19th St.
Oklahoma City, OK 73107
Tel: 405-947-4143; Fax: 405-947-4199
Mr. TIMOTHY O'CONNOR, Contact Person
1501 N. Classen
Oklahoma City, OK 73106
58 low income apartments for senior citizens.

Villa Isenbart, Inc.
c/o Associated Catholic Charities, 1501 Classen Blvd.
Oklahoma City, OK 73106
3801 N.W. 19th St.
Oklahoma City, OK 73107
Tel: 405-947-4143; Fax: 405-947-4199
Mr. TIMOTHY O'CONNOR, Dir.
40 Apartment Residences for Low-Income Ederly.

Ponca City
Archdiocese of Oklahoma City

St. Mary's Housing Foundation
408 S. 8th St.
Ponca City, OK 74601
Rev. JOHN J. MICHALICKA, Pres.
Senior Citizens Residences 6

Westminster Village, Inc.
1601 Academy Rd.
Ponca City, OK 74604
Tel: 405-762-0927
Via Christi Health System.
RAY VERNON, Interim CEO
Nursing Care for Aged.
Residents 110

Tulsa
Diocese of Tulsa

Frances Streitel Senior Care Corporation
1923 S. Utica Ave.
Tulsa, OK 74104
Tel: 918-744-2471
CHARLES ANDERSON, Pres.

St. John Villas, Inc.
1923 S. Utica
Tulsa, OK 74104
Tel: 918-744-2180; Fax: 918-744-2716
Retirement Residence and Health Care Center for Intermediate Nursing Care.
Sisters of the Sorrowful Mother
Sr. CATHERINE MARIE HANEGAN, Pres.
Chaplains:
Revs.:
HARRY S. BARTNIK
PARICK M. BRANKIN
Beds 179
Apartments 66
Residents 208
Total Staff 130

OREGON

Beaverton
Archdiocese of Portland in Oregon

Maryville Nursing Home
14645 S.W. Farmington Rd.
Beaverton, OR 97007
Tel: 503-643-8626
Sr. GERALDINE BERNARDS, Admin.
RITA WILLIAMS, R.N., Dir. Nurses
Rev. JOHN M. DOMIN, Chap.
Sisters 8
Lay Workers 187
Guests 258
Little Flower Development Center
4415 S.W. 148th Ave.
Beaverton, OR 97007
Children 220

Mt. Angel
Archdiocese of Portland in Oregon

Benedictine Nursing Center
540 S. Main St.
Mt. Angel, OR 97362-9523
Tel: 503-845-6841
JOHN H. HOGAN, Admin.
Chaplains:
Sr. JOSEPH FENNIMORE
Revs.:
MARION DEL MONACO
KURT SMIDT-JERNSTROM, Pastor & Inter-faith Chap.
Home Health Agency
Staff 26
Patients assisted annually 600
Sisters 2
Patients assisted annually 469

North Bend
Archdiocese of Portland in Oregon

Evergreen Court for Retirement Living, Inc.
451 O'Connell St.
North Bend, OR 97459
Tel: 541-756-2545
WILLIAM J. HEALY, CEO
Affiliate of Catholic Health Initiatives.

St. Catherine's Residence and Nursing Center
9359 Sheridan Ave.
North Bend, OR 97459
Tel: 541-756-4151; Fax: 541-756-1049
WILLIAM J. HEALY, Pres. & CEO
Affiliate of Catholic Health Initiatives.
Sisters 10
Patients assisted annually 429
Bed Capacity 180

Portland
Archdiocese of Portland in Oregon

Mt. St. Joseph Residence and Extended Care Center
3060 S.E. Stark St.
Portland, OR 97214-3099
Tel: 503-232-6193; Fax: 503-235-2772
Operated by the Sisters of Mercy, Omaha Regional Community.
MARY KLEIN, Pres. & CEO & Contact Person
CATHY COLBY, Dir. Pastoral Care
Rev. STEPHEN STOBIE
Affiliate of Catholic Health Initiatives.
Sisters 15
Residents 298

PENNSYLVANIA

Allison Park
Diocese of Pittsburgh

Providence Connections, Inc.
Corporate Office, 9000 Babcock Blvd.
Allison Park, PA 15101
Tel: 412-931-5241; Fax: 412-635-5416
Sr. DONNA MARIE GRIBSCHAW, C.D.P., Exec. Dir.
Providence Day Care Center, North
Total Assisted 50
Total Staff 9
Providence Child Care Center, South
Total Assisted 37
Total Staff 5
Providence Family Support Center
Total Assisted 140
Total Staff 11
Amelia House
Total Assisted 30
Total Staff 1
Purpose: To engage in educational activities and operation of day care centers and other related services to women and children.

Regency Hall Nursing Home, Inc.
9399 Babcock Blvd.
Allison Park, PA 15101
Tel: 412-366-8540; Fax: 412-369-9789
Vincentian Sisters of Charity
Sr. DOROTHY DOLAK, V.S.C., Admin.
Revs.:
DAVID C. DIXON
GREGORY C. SWIDERSKI
Beds 143
Total Staff 200

Ambler
Archdiocese of Philadelphia

St. Mary's Villa for Children
701 Bethlehem Pike, P.O. Box 388
Ambler, PA 19002-0388
Tel: 215-242-0376; 643-7676
E-mail: csfn@juno.com
Sr. M. EUNICE, C.S.F.N., D.S.W., Admin.
Provides services for dependent-neglected children with emotional problems 5-12 and their families.
Sisters of the Holy Family of Nazareth 7
Capacity 70
Total Staff 70
Total Assisted 91

Aston
Archdiocese of Philadelphia

Assisi House
600 Red Hill Rd.
Aston, PA 19014
Tel: 215-459-8990
Home for retired Sisters of St. Francis of Philadelphia.
Sr. JEAN MARGARET MCDEVITT, O.S.F., Admin.
Rev. GERALD M. DOLAN, O.F.M., Chap.
Total Assisted 140
Total Staff 110

Audubon
Archdiocese of Philadelphia

St. Gabriel's Hall
Box 7280
Audubon, PA 19407-7280
Tel: 215-247-2776 (Philadelphia); 610-666-7970 (Audubon)
Bro. ROBERT KINZLER, F.S.C., A.C.S.W., Exec. Dir.
Mr. JOHN GAYNOR, Prog. Dir.
Mr. JAMES LOGAN, Asst. Program Dir.
Offers residential treatment for court-committed delinquent boys, ages 12-18.
Capacity 201
Total Staff 230
Total Assisted 200

Baden
Diocese of Pittsburgh

**Villa St. Joseph of Baden, Inc.*
1030 State St.
Baden, PA 15005
Tel: 412-869-6300
Sr. ANNA MARIE GAGLIA, C.S.J., Pres. & Contact Person
Sr. MICHELLE PRAH, C.S.J., N.H.A., Admin.
Purpose: to operate a 120 bed skilled/intermediate care licensed nursing home, striving to address not only medical needs, but to also maximize opportunities for physical activity and social interaction.
30 Beds for Patients with Dementia or Alzheimers
Total Staff 130

Bensalem
Archdiocese of Philadelphia

St. Francis Homes for Boys
857 Langstroth Ln.
Bensalem, PA 19020-5735
Tel: 215-638-9310
FRANCIS E. SWIACKI, JR., L.S.W., Admin.
Provides residential treatment in four campus-based group homes and seven community-based

group homes for boys, ages 12 to 18; also Supervised Living for boys 17 and older.
Total Assisted 150
Capacity 100
Total Staff 110

Bethlehem
Diocese of Allentown

Grace Mansion Personal Care Residence of Holy Manor
1200 Spring St.
Bethlehem, PA 18018
Tel: 610-865-6748
Rev. Msgr. DENNIS A. RIGNEY, Pres. & CEO
KAREN ABRUZZESE, Admin.
Mr. JIM POLASKI, Diocesan Dir.
Personal care facility for 25 elderly.
Total in Residence 25
Total Staff 12

Holy Family Adult Day Care
1200 Spring St.
Bethlehem, PA 18018
Tel: 610-865-5595
BARBARA FAHRINGER, Dir.
Day care for elderly clients 22

Holy Family Apartments
330-338 13th Ave.
Bethlehem, PA 18018
Tel: 610-866-4603
Rev. Msgr. DENNIS A. RIGNEY, Pres.
RAY LAUDENSLAGER, Mgr.
Catholic housing for the elderly.
Apartments 50
Residents 52

Holy Family Manor
1200 Spring St.
Bethlehem, PA 18018
Tel: 610-865-5595; Fax: 610-865-5866
Rev. Msgr. DENNIS A. RIGNEY, M.Div., L.S.W., A.C.S.W., Pres. & CEO
Mrs. MARY ANN CHAKLOS, N.H.A., Admin.
Rev. JOSEPH A. ROCK, Th.F., Chap.
Nursing Care for the Aged, Chronically Ill, or Invalid.
Total Assisted 314
Total Staff 275
Skilled and intermediate care facility.
Capacity 208
Total Staff 275
Patients assisted annually 314

Trexler Pavilion, Personal Care Residence of Holy Family Manor
1220 Prospect Ave.
Bethlehem, PA 18018
Tel: 610-868-7776
Rev. Msgr. DENNIS A. RIGNEY, Pres. & CEO
KAREN ABRUZZESE, Admin.
Mr. JAMES POLASKI, Diocesan Dir.
Personal care facility for 23 elderly.
Total in Residence 21
Total Staff 12

Columbia
Diocese of Harrisburg

St. Anne's Home
3952 Columbia Ave.
Columbia, PA 17512-9715
Tel: 717-285-5443
Adorers of the Blood of Christ
Sr. M. CARMELA GUITO, A.S.C., Admin.
Rev. JOHN HERBER, C.PP.S., Chap.
Sisters 19
Total Staff 214 (includes Personal Care)
Personal Care Staff 14
Residents 121
Cottages 36
Residents in Retirement Village 45
Personal Care 17

Dallas
Diocese of Scranton

Mercy Center Nursing Unit, Inc.
Lake St., Box 370
Dallas, PA 18612
Tel: 717-675-2131; Fax: 717-674-5658
Sr. SARA SWEENEY, R.S.M., Admin.
BEVERLY VESPICO, R.N., Dir. of Nursing
Rev. FRANCIS G. KULIG, Chap.

Danville
Diocese of Harrisburg

Holy Family Convent and Infirmary
One Montour St.
Danville, PA 17821
Tel: 717-275-3141
Home for the Aged Sisters of Christian Charity.
Sr. GEMMA STREIT, S.C.C., Supr.
Rev. LEONARD CASEY, Chap., Tel: 717-275-0103
Sisters of Christian Charity 93

Maria Hall
Maria Hall Dr.
Danville, PA 17821
Tel: 717-275-1120
Home for retired Sisters of SS. Cyril and Methodius.
Sr. M. ROSAMUND, SS.C.M., Admin.
Rev. FREDERICK A. FARACE, Chap.
Sisters 84

Maria Joseph Manor
875 Montour Blvd.
Danville, PA 17821
Tel: 717-275-4221; Fax: 717-275-4711
Sr. M. JEANETTE, SS.C.M., Exec. Dir.
Sr. M. MARGUERITE, SS.C.M., Admin.
Rev. FRANCIS TAMBURRO Tel: 717-275-8740
Nursing Home Beds 60
Personal Care Beds 37
Independent Living Units 100
Sisters 15
Total Staff 5
Residents 135
The Meadows at Maria Joseph Manor
875 Montour Blvd.
Danville, PA 17821
Tel: 717-271-1000; Fax: 717-275-4711
Sr. ELIZABETH ANN MATONAK, SS.C.M., Dir.

Darby
Archdiocese of Philadelphia

Little Flower Manor
1201 Springfield Rd.
Darby, PA 19023
Tel: 610-534-6000; Fax: 610-534-6039
Staffed by Sisters of the Divine Redeemer
All Skilled Nursing Care.
Rev. EDWARD J. CASEY, Chap.
Total Staff 200
Patients assisted annually 159

St. Francis Country House
1412 Lansdowne Ave.
Darby, PA 19023-1218
Tel: 610-461-6510; Fax: 610-461-3558
Opened June 30, 1913.
Mrs. JUDITH P. HORVATH, Admin.
Rev. EDWARD J. KENNEDY, Chap.
Total Assisted 273
Total Staff 360

Villa Saint Joseph
1436 Lansdowne Ave.
Darby, PA 19023-1298
Tel: 610-586-8535
Home for aged, infirm and convalescent priests of the Archdiocese of Philadelphia.
Rev. Msgr. FRANCIS A. MENNA, Rector
Rev. EDWARD J. CASEY, Asst. Rector
Sisters 1
Total Staff 43
Residents 51

Villa St. Teresa
1215 Springfield Rd.
Darby, PA 19023
Tel: 610-583-0700
Staffed by Sisters of the Divine Redeemer
Residential.
Sr. M. ANNE ANGELCYK, S.D.R., Admin.
Sr. M. COLOMBIERE HOFSTEDDER, S.D.R., Supr.
Total Staff 32
Residents 54

Downingtown
Archdiocese of Philadelphia

St. John Vianney Hospital
151 Woodbine Rd.
Downingtown, PA 19335
Tel: 610-269-2600
Center for Healing for Priests, Brothers, and Sisters.
LOUIS D. HORVATH, Admin.
Rev. CHARLES R. O'HARA, Chap.
Bed Capacity 54
Total Assisted 116
Total Staff 56

St. Martha Manor
470 Manor Ave.
Downingtown, PA 19335
Tel: 610-873-8490
COLLEEN PATRICIA FRANKFIELD, N.H.A., Admin.
Capacity 128
Total Staff 298
Total Assisted 188

Du Bois
Diocese of Erie

Christ the King Manor, Inc.
1100 W. Long Ave.
Du Bois, PA 15801
Tel: 814-371-3180
Rev. MARK S. SWOGER, Chap.
Residents 160

Easton
Diocese of Allentown

Antonian Towers
2405 Hillside Ave.
Easton, PA 18042
Tel: 610-258-2033
Total in Residence 50
Total Staff 2
Rev. Msgr. DENNIS A. RIGNEY, Pres.
Mrs. JUDITH KERN, Mgr.
Catholic housing for the elderly.
Apartments 50

Elmhurst
Diocese of Scranton

St. Mary's Villa Nursing Home
Elmhurst, PA 18416
Tel: 717-842-7621; Fax: 717-842-2953
COLLEEN M. LANDO, N.H.A., Admin./CEO
Sr. MARIE CONCEPTA, C.J.C., Convent Supr., Tel: 717-842-7466
Rev. JOSEPH C. OSTROWSKI, Chap.
Poor Sisters of Jesus Crucified and the Sorrowful Mother 9
Residents 112
Total Staff 175

Elverson
Archdiocese of Philadelphia

St. Mary of Providence Center
227 Isabella Rd.
Elverson, PA 19520
Tel: 610-942-4166
Sr. BERNARDINE UGOLINI, D.S.M.P., Supr.
Rev. GERARD J. HOFFMAN, Chap.
Residence for Senior Citizens. Center of Spirituality, Retreats and Days of Recollection.
Sisters 3
Capacity 39
Overnight and day retreats 110
Total in Residence 52

Emsworth
Diocese of Pittsburgh

Holy Family Institute
8235 Ohio River Blvd.
Emsworth, PA 15202
Tel: 412-766-4030
Sisters of the Holy Family of Nazareth
Sr. LINDA YANKOSKI, Exec. Dir.
Dedicated to helping children who are abandoned, abused or neglected, and to working with families in crisis. Teen parenting program, after school partial hospitalization program, special education services, and private counseling services.
Sisters 1
Total Assisted: Chidren 1,518
Families 402
Total Staff 278

Erie
Diocese of Erie

Bishop Michael J. Murphy Residence for Retired Priests
400 E. Gore Rd.
Erie, PA 16509
Tel: 814-825-0680
Rev. Msgr. ROBERT J. SMITH, J.C.L., Dir.

Community House Inc.
521 W. 7th St.
Erie, PA 16502
Tel: 814-459-5853; Fax: 814-452-3416
CARLEEN M. DAVIS, Exec. Dir.

Gannondale Residential Center for Girls
4635 E. Lake Rd.
Erie, PA 16511
Tel: 814-899-7659
North American Union of Sisters of Our Lady of

Charity-Erie
Sr. Martha Teresa Gomez, O.L.C., Supr.
Mr. Louis J. Grande, A.C.S.W., Exec. Dir.
Rev. Msgr. Lawrence E. Brandt, J.C.D. Ph.D., Chap.
Residents 45

Mercy Center for Women
1039 E. 27th St.
Erie, PA 16504
Tel: 814-453-3668
Tish Donze, Exec. Dir.

Mercy Terrace Apartments
430 E. Grandview Blvd.
Erie, PA 16504
Tel: 814-825-6791
Sr. M. Felice Duska, R.S.M., Mgr.
Sisters of Mercy of Erie

St. Mary's Home of Erie
607 E. 26th St.
Erie, PA 16504
Tel: 814-459-0621; Fax: 814-454-0909
Sr. Anastasia Valimont, S.S.J., Admin.
Rev. Msgr. Joseph Wardanski, Chap.
Sisters 20
Residents 131
Patients-Nursing Home 228

St. Patrick Haven, Inc.
147 E. 12th St.
Erie, PA 16501
Tel: 814-454-7219; 838-5430
Sr. Marie Eileen Moyer, Admin.

Flourtown
Archdiocese of Philadelphia

Bethlehem Retirement Village
100 W. Wissahickon Ave.
Flourtown, PA 19031
Tel: 215-233-0998
E-mail: j.grelise@juno.com
Staffed by the Sisters of St. Joseph
Sr. Joan Grelis, S.S.J., Mgr.
Apartments 100
Total Staff 4
Total in Residence 113

St. Joseph Villa
110 W. Wissahickon Ave.
Flourtown, PA 19031-1898
Tel: 215-836-4179
Chaplains:
Revs.:
Gerard M. Duff, O.S.A.
Bernard J. O'Dowd, O.S.A.
Sr. Marie Rudegeair, S.S.J., N.H.A., Admin.
Bed Capacity 324
Total Assisted 500
Total Staff 300

Sisters of St. Joseph of Philadelphia, St. Joseph Villa Staff
110 W. Wissahickon Ave.
Flourtown, PA 19031-1898
Sr. Mary Scherr, S.S.J., Contact

Greensburg
Diocese of Greensburg

Neumann House
2900 Seminary Dr.
Greensburg, PA 15601
Fax: 724-834-7351
Residence for retired Priests.
In res.,
Rev. Msgr. John L. Garred Tel: 724-837-1472
Rev. Msgr. Robert A. Hanicak Tel: 724-834-7991
Revs.:
Aloysius J. Bahleda Tel: 724-834-5953
Louis W. Cheatham Tel: 724-850-7619
Edward V. Curry Tel: 724-850-7647
Apolinary Murawski Tel: 724-834-0458
Patrick J. O'Connor Tel: 724-853-6884
Francis M. Ott Tel: 724-832-8345
Francis D. Pirulli Tel: 724-836-3827
Michael A. Bienia Tel: 724-836-1017

St. Anne Home
685 Angela Dr.
Greensburg, PA 15601
Tel: 724-837-6070; Fax: 724-837-6099
Rev. Edward J. Kretz, Chap.
Sr. Bernice M. Fiedor, C.S.S.F., Admin.
In res.,
Revs.:
Edwin H. Hirt Tel: 724-837-9443
Andrew J. Charnoki Tel: 724-853-8935
Felician Sisters 8
Capacity 125

Harborcreek
Diocese of Erie

**Benetwood Apartments for Persons Elderly and Handicapped*
641 Troupe Rd.
Harborcreek, PA 16421-1048
Tel: 814-899-0088
Sr. Mary Therese Wacker, O.S.B., Mgr.
Benedictine Sisters of Erie
Residents 81

Harborcreek Youth Services
5712 Iroquois Ave.
Harborcreek, PA 16421
Tel: 814-899-7664; Fax: 814-899-3075
Mr. James E. Henry, A.C.S.W., L.S.W., Dir.
William A. Kohler, M.A., Clinical Psychologist, Clinical Services Admin.
Children 190

Harrisburg
Diocese of Harrisburg

Villa Teresa Nursing Home
1051 Avila Rd.
Harrisburg, PA 17109
Tel: 717-652-5900; Fax: 717-652-5941
Carmelite Sisters
Sr. Timothy Anne, O.Carm., Admin.
Rev. Walter A. Sempko, Chap.
Sisters 7
Bed Capacity 184
Total Staff 250

Hermitage
Diocese of Erie

John XXIII Home
2250 Shenango Fwy.
Hermitage, PA 16148
Tel: 412-981-3200
Miss Roberta T. Lamont, Admin.
Rev. Msgr. Raymond Meier, Coord.
Residents 142

Holland
Archdiocese of Philadelphia

St. Joseph Home for the Aged
1182 Holland Rd.
Holland, PA 18966
Tel: 215-357-5511; Fax: 215-357-1701
Sisters of St. Casimir
Sr. M. Lawrence, Admin.
Rev. John A. Cannon, Chap.
Senior Residents 38
Total Staff 7
Nursing Care Total Assisted 38
Total Staff 33

Hollidaysburg
Diocese of Altoona-Johnstown

Dmitri Manor Priests' Residence
St. Mary's Ln.
Hollidaysburg, PA 16648
Rev. Msgr. Robert J. Saly, Admin.
Aged Residents 8
Staff 2

Garvey Manor
Logan Blvd.
Hollidaysburg, PA 16648
Tel: 814-695-5571
Sr. M. Joachim Anne Ferenchak, O.Carm., Admin.
Carmelite Sisters for the Aged and Infirm 9
Aged Residents 150
Patients assisted annually 210
Total Staff 215

St. Leonard's Home, Inc.
601 N. Montgomery St.
Hollidaysburg, PA 16648
Tel: 814-695-9581; Fax: 814-695-2606
Legal Title: *St. Leonard's Home, Inc.*
Sr. Dorothy M. Pawlus, C.S.F.N., Admin.
Sisters of the Holy Family of Nazareth 3
Aged Residents 23
Total Staff 14

Huntingdon Valley
Archdiocese of Philadelphia

Redeemer Long Term Care & Elder Services
727 Welsh Rd.
Huntingdon Valley, PA 19006
Tel: 215-938-0180; Fax: 215-938-1237
Subsidiary of Holy Redeemer Health System, Inc.
Mailing Address:—Communications Department c/o 1648 Huntingdon Pike
Meadowbrook, PA 19046
Sisters of the Holy Redeemer, C.S.R.
St. Joseph's Manor
1616 Huntingdon Pike
Meadowbrook, PA 19046
Tel: 215-938-4000
Rev. Msgr. Charles V. Gallen, Chap.
Personal and Long-term Nursing Care; Provides a full range of therapies and support services; Medicare approved comprehensive outpatient rehabilitation facility. (CORF).
The Lafayette Redeemer
8580 Verree Rd.
Philadelphia, PA 19111
Tel: 215-214-2800
Virginia A. Thompson, Pres. Long Term Care & Elder Svcs.
Independent living apartments, Personal care and long term nursing care.

Redeemer Village
1551 Huntingdon Pike
Huntingdon Valley, PA 19006
Tel: 215-947-8168
Mailing Address:—Communications Department
Holy Redeemer Health System, c/o 1648 Huntingdon Pike
Meadowbrook, PA 19046
Subsidiary of Holy Redeemer Health System, Inc.
Low income housing for the elderly or handicapped, subsidized by HUD.
Sisters of the Holy Redeemer, C.S.R.
Francis G. Hamel, Mgr., Redeemer Village
Apartments 151
Redeemer Village II
1551 Huntingdon Pike
Huntingdon Valley, PA 19006
Tel: 215-947-8168
Subsidiary of Holy Redeemer Health System, Inc.
Low income housing for the elderly or handicapped, subsidized by HUD.
Sisters of the Holy Redeemer, C.S.R.
Apartments 49

Immaculata
Archdiocese of Philadelphia

Camilla Hall Nursing Home
P.O. Box 100
Immaculata, PA 19345-0100
Tel: 610-644-1152
Sisters, Servants of the Immaculate Heart of Mary
Sr. Marie Jerome, I.H.M., Admin.
Mother Marie Genevieve, Supr.
Chaplains:
Rev. Michael L. Walsh
Rev. Msgr. Charles V. Gallen
Bed Capacity 248
Residents 210

Lansdale
Archdiocese of Philadelphia

St. Mary Manor
701 Lansdale Ave.
Lansdale, PA 19446
Tel: 215-368-0900; Fax: 215-362-2891
Immaculate Heart of Mary Sisters
Maureen Humphreys Heckler, Admin.
Rev. Joseph F. McCafferty, Chap.
Total Staff 200
Residents 210

Lebanon
Diocese of Harrisburg

Villa Vianney
915 S. Lincoln Ave.
Lebanon, PA 17042
Tel: 717-273-1295
Home for Convalescent and Retired Priests of the Diocese of Harrisburg.
Very Rev. David T. McAndrew, V.F., Admin.
In res.,
Rev. Msgr. Vincent J. Topper
Residences 9
Total Staff 4
Residents 3

Merion Station
Archdiocese of Philadelphia

McAuley Convent
517 Montgomery Ave.
Merion Station, PA 19066

Tel: 610-667-2775
Infirmary for Religious Sisters of Mercy.
Sr. THERESA MONAGHAN, R.S.M., Supr.
Sr. MARY BONAVENTURE, R.S.M., Dir.
Total Staff 40
Total Assisted 36

Nanticoke
Diocese of Scranton

Mercy Health Care Center
(Skilled Care Nursing Facility)
Newport St.
Nanticoke, PA 18634
Tel: 717-735-7300
ROBERT D. WILLIAMS, Vice Pres. of Aging Svcs.
LAURA REIDER NOVAKOWSKI, Admin.
Rev. BERNARD A. TOLOCZKO, Chap.
Bed Capacity 110
Patients assisted annually 110

New Philadelphia
Diocese of Allentown

Holy Family Apartments
Valley St. & Clay St.
New Philadelphia, PA 17959
Tel: 717-429-0699; Fax: 717-429-2368
Mailing Address:—c/o Neumann Apartments (Rental Office)
25 N. Nichols St.
Saint Clair, PA 17970
Rev. Msgr. DENNIS A. RIGNEY, Pres.
Mr. JOHN STILES, Mgr.
Catholic housing for the elderly.
Apartments 11
Total Staff 2

Orwigsburg
Diocese of Allentown

Holy Family Adult Day Care at St. Francis Center
900 W. Market St.
Orwigsburg, PA 17961
Tel: 717-366-2924
Rev. Msgr. DENNIS A. RIGNEY, Pres. & CEO
Mrs. LINDA HERB, Dir.
Day care for the elderly.
Clients 34

Holy Family Home Health and Hospice Care
Schuylkill County and Admin. Office, 900 W. Market St.
Orwigsburg, PA 17961
Tel: 717-366-0990; 800-726-8761
5 Hearthstone Ct., Ste. 201
Reading, PA 19606
Tel: 610-779-6432
ARLENE MONGRAIN, R.N., B.S., Exec. Dir.
Patients assisted annually 1,641

Holy Family Residence
900 W. Market St.
Orwigsburg, PA 17961
Tel: 717-366-2912
Rev. Msgr. DENNIS A. RIGNEY, Pres. & CEO
PATRICIA MISKE, Admin.
Mr. JAMES POLASKI, Diocesan Coord.
Personal care facility for 58 elderly of Holy Family Manor.
Total in Residence 52
Total Staff 22

Philadelphia
Archdiocese of Philadelphia

Catholic Home for Girls
(St. Joseph Catholic Home for Children)
5238 N. Broad St.
Philadelphia, PA 19141
Tel: 215-324-2610
Sr. LOUISE KANE, S.S.J., L.S.W., Admin.
Provides Therapeutic Group Home Care; Maternity Home Care; Mother/Baby Supervised Independent Living; Outreach School Social Work for Adolescent Girls. Mental Health services available on site for all residents.
Sisters of St. Joseph 4
Sisters of Mercy 1
Capacity 60

Holy Family Home
5300 Chester Ave.
Philadelphia, PA 19143-4993
Tel: 215-729-5153
Little Sisters of the Poor
Mother PAUL L.S.P., Supr.
Rev. DOUGLAS M. MCKAY, Chap.
Total Staff 120
Residents 110

Immaculate Mary Home
2990 Holme Ave.
Philadelphia, PA 19136-1829
Tel: 215-335-2100; Fax: 215-331-1016
Opened March 1976.
CARL N. CLINE, Admin.
Total Staff 317
Total Assisted 296

Mount Nazareth
2755 Holme Ave.
Philadelphia, PA 19152
Tel: 215-338-8992
Sisters of the Holy Family Of Nazareth
Home for retired and infirm sisters.
Sr. MARGARET MARY MACHOWSKI, C.S.F.N., Supr.
Rev. Msgr. CHARLES J. SCHAEFLEIN, Chap.
Resident Sisters 51
Total Staff 13
Total Assisted 42

Sacred Heart Free Home for Incurable Cancer
1315 W. Hunting Park Ave.
Philadelphia, PA 19140
Tel: 215-329-3222
Opened April 27, 1930.
Sisters of the Third Order of St. Dominic
Sr. M. JUDE, O.P., Supr.
Sr. M. LUKE, O.P., Admin.
Legal Title: *The Servants of Relief for Incurable Cancer*
Bed Capacity 45
Total Staff 45
Patients assisted annually 84
Attended by Oblates of St. Francis de Sales.

Sacred Heart Manor
6445 Germantown Ave.
Philadelphia, PA 19119
Tel: 215-438-5268
Carmelite Sisters for the Aged and Infirm
Sr. M. PATRICIA MICHAEL, O.Carm., Admin.
Rev. JOHN S. HEIM, Chap.
Nursing Care Residents 171
Independent Living Residents 72
Personal Care Boarding Home 24

St. Gabriel's System
Administrative Offices, 117 S. 17th St., Ste. 1701
Philadelphia, PA 19103
Tel: 215-665-8777; Fax: 215-665-8821
Bro. ROBERT J. KINZLER, F.S.C., A.C.S.W., Exec. Dir.
Administrative and Intake services for residential treatment; Group Home care and Day Treatment for Court-committed delinquent boys, ages 12-17. (See St. Gabriel's Hall, De LaSalle in Towne, De LaSalle Vocational and De LaSalle Aftercare).
Total Staff 420
Total Assisted 2,000

St. Ignatius Nursing Home
4401 Haverford Ave.
Philadelphia, PA 19104
Tel: 215-349-8800; Fax: 215-222-3078
Sr. MARY AGATHA CEBULA, C.S.S.F., N.H.A., Admin.
Attended from St. Ignatius Church.
Felician Sisters 6
Bed Capacity 176
Total Assisted 247
Total Staff 200
Total in Residence 176

St. John Neumann Nursing Home
10400 Roosevelt Blvd.
Philadelphia, PA 19116
Tel: 215-698-5600
Sisters of the Holy Famly of Nazareth
Rev. L. JAMES MULLEN, Chap.
Beds 226
Total Staff 294

St. Joseph Housing Corporation
Mount St. Joseph Convent
Philadelphia, PA 19118-2694
Tel: 215-248-7200
Total Staff 4
Total in Residence 107
Staffed by the Sisters of St. Joseph.

St. Joseph's House for Boys
4010-4012 Ashburner St.
Philadelphia, PA 19136-2801
Tel: 215-332-3490
Rev. FRANCIS R. DUFFY, C.S.Sp., Ph.D., Dir.
Provides community-based group home residential treatment for boys 8-18.
Capacity 40
Total Staff 39
Total Assisted 56

St. Vincent's Orphanage Tacony
7201 Milnor St.
Philadelphia, PA 19135
Tel: 215-624-5601
Revs.:
ENGELBERT G. MICHEL, Pres., Bd. of Mgrs.
EDUARDO G. MONTERO, J.C.L., Chap.
Provides Family Oriented residential care for children 2-12 years of age.
Residential program, 84 boys and girls; comprehensive emergency shelter.
Capacity 84
Total Staff 105

Metropolitan Archdiocese of Philadelphia Ukrainian

Ascension Manor, Inc.
911 N. Franklin St.
Philadelphia, PA 19123
Tel: 215-922-1116
Most Rev. STEPHEN SULYK, D.D., S.T.L., Pres.
Revs.:
JAMES MELNIC, Exec. Vice Pres.
MICHAEL HUTSKO, Sec. & Treas.
Directors:
Most Rev. WALTER PASKA
Rev. JOHN FIELDS
MICHAEL SMYLIE
Dr. JAROSLAW JARYMOWYCH
JEANNE KARBIWNYK
IHOR SHUST
MARIE J. HANUSEY, Gen. Mgr.
Ascension Manor I
911 N. Franklin St.
Philadelphia, PA 19123
Tel: 215-922-1116
ANNA SIWAK, Mgr.
Ascension Manor II
970 N. Seventh St.
Philadelphia, PA 19123
Tel: 215-923-3907
EWHENIA NOWAKIWSKY, Mgr.

Home of Divine Providence
209 W. Chestnut Hill Ave.
Philadelphia, PA 19118
Tel: 215-247-7107
Sr. BERNARDINE SYMIONOW, S.S.M.I., Admin.
Rev. VASYL SIVINSKI, Chap.
Home for the aged. Assisted living - personal care.
Sisters 11
Residents 30

Pittsburgh
Diocese of Pittsburgh

Franciscan Child Day Care Center
1401 Hamilton Rd.
Pittsburgh, PA 15234-2399
Tel: 412-882-5085
E-mail: srsosfprov@aol.com
CAROL A. UNRUE, Dir.
Sr. MARIAN BLODIS, O.S.F., Pres.
Total Assisted 100
Total Staff 30

Home for the Aged of the Little Sisters of the Poor
1028 Benton Ave.
Pittsburgh, PA 15212
Tel: 412-761-5373
Sr. MARGARET BANAR, Supr. & Admin.
Rev. JEROME A. DIXON, J.C.L.
Sisters 13
Total Staff 92
Residents 106

Marian Hall Home, Inc.
934 Forest Ave.
Pittsburgh, PA 15202
Tel: 412-761-1999; 761-2556; Fax: 412-761-2556
Personal care home for women.
Lay Staff 28
In Residence:
Sisters 22
Lay People 24

Marian Hall Home, Inc.
934 Forest Ave.
Pittsburgh, PA 15202-1118
Tel: 412-761-1999; Fax: 412-761-2556
Sr. MARY LOUISE VRANA, O.S.F., Admin.
Purpose: to provide programs, facilities, and services, including, but not limited to, residential personal care, and long-term care homes for the elderly, ill, or disabled, including supportive services.
Total in Residence 46
Total Staff 28

Marian Manor Corp.
2695 Winchester Dr.
Pittsburgh, PA 15220-4099
Tel: 412-563-6866 (Admin.); 563-1244 (Nursing Service)

Sr. EILEEN CHLEBOWSKI, N.H.A., Admin.
Rev. HENRY SZARNICKI, Chap.
Sisters of the Holy Spirit 13
Total Staff 292
Residents 212

Mt. Alvernia Day Care & Learning Center
146 Hawthorne Rd.
Pittsburgh, PA 15209
Provides infant care as well as before and after school care for school age children.
Total Assisted 110
Total Staff 17

Providence Child Care Center
400 Hoodridge Dr.
Pittsburgh, PA 15234
Tel: 412-562-3745
Sr. DONNA MARIE GRIBSCHAW, C.D.P., Exec. Dir.
Sr. MARIA FEST, Contact Person
Purpose: to engage in educational activities and operation of a day care program.

St. Joseph Nursing and Health Care Center, Inc.
5324 Penn Ave.
Pittsburgh, PA 15224-1798
Tel: 412-665-5100
ARTHUR L. NANCE, N.H.A., Admin.
Rev. GEORGE LEECH, M.Div.
Beds 158
Patients assisted annually 149
Total Assisted 1,789
Total Staff 180

St. Paul Manor
148 Monastery Ave.
Pittsburgh, PA 15203
Tel: 412-381-4744
GERTRUDE BUSCH, R.N., Admin.
Total Assisted 62
Total Staff 58

St. Pius X Residence, Inc.
2681 Waddington Ave.
Pittsburgh, PA 15226
Tel: 412-563-5040; Fax: 412-563-3776
MARY JO HUMMEL, Admin.
Rev. THOMAS M. MARPES, Chap.

**St. Francis Plaza, Inc.*
451 44th St.
Pittsburgh, PA 15201-1122
Tel: 412-683-6252; Fax: 412-683-4269
Sr. M. SYLVIA SCHULER, Chm.
Sisters 2
Residents 106

Villa De Marillac Nursing Home
5300 Stanton Ave.
Pittsburgh, PA 15206
Tel: 412-361-2833
Non-sectarian, skilled nursing home.
Sr. THERESA NOVAK, V.S.C., N.H.A., Contact
Rev. THOMAS MURPHY, Chap.
Vincentian Sisters of Charity 4
Total Staff 104
Bed Capacity 52
Total Assisted 71

Vincentian Child Care, Inc.
8200 McKnight Rd.
Pittsburgh, PA 15237
Tel: 412-366-8588
Sr. GEORGINE BIRES, V.S.C., Contact Person
Purpose: to engage in educational activities; operating a day care program; to perform any lawful acts to effectuate purposes of this corporation and in this pursuit to apply funds or incomes exclusively for charitable, religious, scientific, literary, and educational purposes.
Total Assisted 1,476
Total Staff 32

Vincentian Home Inc.
111 Perrymont Rd.
Pittsburgh, PA 15237
Tel: 412-366-5600
Vincentian Sisters of Charity
Sr. ANNE KULL, V.S.C., Admin.
Revs.:
GREGORY SWIDERSKI
DAVID DIXON
Sisters 9
Total Staff 273
Bed Capacity 221
Patients assisted annually 271

Pottsville
Diocese of Allentown

Queen of Peace Apartments
777 Water St.
Pottsville, PA 17901
Tel: 717-628-4504
Rev. Msgr. DENNIS A. RICHEY, Pres.
Mrs. MARY ANN STERNER, Mgr.
Catholic housing for the elderly.
Apartments 65
Total in Residence 65
Total Staff 1

Reading
Diocese of Allentown

Queen of Angels Apartment
22 Rothermel St., Hyde Park
Reading, PA 19605
Tel: 610-921-3115
Rev. Msgr. DENNIS A. RIGNEY, Pres.
Ms. VALERIE PHELPS, Mgr.
Catholic housing for the elderly.
Apartments 45
Total in Residence 44
Total Staff 2

Rosemont
Archdiocese of Philadelphia

St. Edmond's Home for Children
320 S. Roberts Rd.
Rosemont, PA 19010
Tel: 610-525-8800
Daughters of St. Mary of Providence
MARK E. FITZGERALD, Admin.
Rev. Msgr. EDWARD P. CULLEN, V.G., Chap.
Licensed I.C.F./M.R. care for severely/profoundly impaired, physically handicapped boys and girls 1-16 years of age at admission.
Capacity 40

Saint Clair
Diocese of Allentown

Neumann Apartments
25 N. Nichols St.
Saint Clair, PA 17970
Tel: 717-429-0699
Rev. Msgr. DENNIS A. RIGNEY, Pres.
Mr. JOHN T STILES, Mgr.
Catholic housing for the elderly.
Total in Residence 25
Total Staff 2
Apartments 25
Total in Residence 25
Total Staff 2

Scranton
Diocese of Scranton

Home for Aged of the Little Sisters of the Poor, Holy Family Residence
2500 Adams Ave.
Scranton, PA 18509
Tel: 717-343-4065; 346-5788; Fax: 717-347-1941
Sr. MONIQUE GALLAGHER, p.s.d.p., Supr. & Admin.
Rev. JOSEPH F. MEIGHAN, Chap.
Little Sisters of the Poor 16
Aged Residents 58
Residents in Independent Living Apts. 22

St. Joseph's Center
2010 Adams Ave.
Scranton, PA 18509
Tel: 717-342-8379; 961-1549
Sr. VINCENTIA DORSEY, I.H.M., Admin.
Rev. WILLIAM B. PICKARD, Chap.
Sisters, Servants of the Immaculate Heart of Mary 11
Bed Capacity 147
Patients assisted annually 163

Uniontown
Metropolitan Archdiocese of Pittsburgh, Byzantine

Mount Macrina Manor
520 W. Main St.
Uniontown, PA 15401
Tel: 412-437-1400; Fax: 412-430-1095
JOSEPH S. BIENIEK, N.H.A., R.H.P., Admin.
Sisters of St. Basil the Great 6
Beds 144

St. Basil's Home
530 W. Main St., Box 878
Uniontown, PA 15401
Tel: 412-437-7480; 437-5826
Sr. EVELYN SWEDA, O.S.B.M., Admin.
Sisters of St. Basil the Great 3
Residents 11

Ventnor
Archdiocese of Philadelphia

Villa St. Joseph by the Sea
114 S. Princeton Ave.
Ventnor, PA 08406
Tel: 609-822-7184
Summer residence for aged, infirm, and convalescent priests of the Archdiocese of Philadelphia.
Rev. Msgr. FRANCIS A. MENNA
Rev. EDWARD J. CASEY, Asst. Rector

Warminster
Archdiocese of Philadelphia

Regina Coeli Residence for Priests
685 York Rd.
Warminster, PA 18974
Tel: 215-441-4642
Rev. JAMES D. BEISEL, Admin.
Home for retired priests of the Archdiocese of Philadelphia.
Total Staff 5
Total in Residence 11

Wilkes-Barre
Diocese of Scranton

Little Flower Manor of the Diocese of Scranton
200 S. Meade St.
Wilkes-Barre, PA 18702
Tel: 717-823-6131
Sr. M. JEANETTE LINDSAY, O.Carm., Supr. & Admin.
Rev. W. JEFFREY PAULISH, Chap.
Conducted by the Carmelite Sisters for the Aged and Infirm.
Sisters 8
Aged Residents 133
Total Staff 190

Yardley
Archdiocese of Philadelphia

D'Youville Manor
1750 Quarry Rd.
Yardley, PA 19067
Tel: 215-579-1750
Operated by Grey Nuns of the Sacred Heart. Assisted living retirement residence for the elderly.
Sr. JACQUELINE WEIGLE, G.N.S.H., Dir.
Capacity 51
Total Staff 29
Total in Residence 75

York
Diocese of Harrisburg

Misericordia Convalescent Home
998 S. Russell St.
York, PA 17402
Tel: 717-755-1964
Daughters of Our Lady of Mercy
Sr. CARMEL MARIE, D.M., Admin.
Sisters 6
Bed Capacity 55
Total Staff 45
Total Assisted 45

PUERTO RICO

Arecibo
Diocese of Arecibo, Puerto Rico

Hogar de Ancianos San Vicente
Mailing Address:
P.O. Box 4196
Vega Baja, PR 00694
Bo. Almirante Sur-Carr 645 Km. 6.6
Vega Baja, PR 00763
Tel: 787-855-0487
Hermanas de la Presentacion 4
Guests 48

Hogar Sta. Maria Eufrasia
Calle Andres Garcia, No. 10
Arecibo, PR 00612
Tel: 878-5166
House for Unwed Mothers.
Good Shepherd Sisters 4
Unwed Mothers 12

La Milagrosa Home for Orphan Girls
Cotto Ave., No. 987
Arecibo, PR 00612
Tel: 809-878-6231
Sisters of Charity 7
Girls 20

San Rafael Home for Aged
00612

Hogar Geriatrico San Rafael
Calle Cervantes
Arecibo, PR 00612
Tel: 787-878-3813
Sisters of Charity 5
Guests 37

Dorado
Archdiocese of San Juan, Puerto Rico

Santuario del Espiritu Santo
Box 187
Dorado, PR 00646-0187
Tel: 809-796-2798
Revs.:
EDUARDO CARON, C.S.Sp.
JOSE ANTONIO ALAMO VILLEGAS, C.S.Sp.
IVAN SERRANO RIVERA, C.S.Sp.
JOSE WEHNING, C.S.Sp., (Retired)

Hato Rey
Archdiocese of San Juan, Puerto Rico

Jesuit Community - Casa Claver
398 Francisca Sein
Hato Rey, PR 00917
Mailing Address:
Apto. 22634 U.P.R. Sta.
San Juan, PR 00931-2634
Rev. FERNANDO PICO, S.J., Insular Supr.

Isabela
Diocese of Arecibo, Puerto Rico

Hogar Infantil Jesus Nazareno, Inc.
P.O. Box 1671
Isabela, PR 00662
Residential Care of Children 25

Lares
Diocese of Arecibo, Puerto Rico

Fundacion Irma Fe
Calle Comerio No. 52
Lares, PR 00669
Tel: 787-897-6090
Charity Sisters of St. Joseph (Mexico) 6
Guests 25

Ponce
Diocese of Ponce, Puerto Rico

Home for Aged and Infirm
Barrio Sabenetas, P.O. Box 2127
Ponce, PR 00731
Tel: 787-840-7575
Sr. ANGELA ESTEVEZ, Supr.
Rev. PERFECTO ALVAREZ, O.S.A., Chap.
Total Staff 16
Residents 209

Puerta De Tierra
Archdiocese of San Juan, Puerto Rico

Asylum For The Aged and Infirm
Hogar de la Providencia, Stop 5
Puerta De Tierra, PR 00906
Tel: 809-722-1331
Mailing Address:
P.O. Box 9066571
San Juan, PR 00906-6571
Sisters of the Poor
Sr. ANGELA ESTEVEZ, Supr.
Rev. OVIDIO ORTEGA, Chap.
Sisters 19
Patients assisted annually 275

Rio Piedras
Archdiocese of San Juan, Puerto Rico

Asylum For Orphan Girls
107 Jose de Diego St. S.
Rio Piedras, PR 00925
Tel: 809-765-6114
Daughters of Charity
Sr. VIRGINIA TORRES, H.C., Supr.
Rev. HIGINIO MADRAZO, C.M., Chap.
Sisters 15
Beds 70

Centro N. Sra. de la Providencia
Sisters of Notre Dame.
R.F.D. #2, Box 16T
Rio Piedras, PR 00928
Tel: 809-761-0273

Hogar Carmelitano
Julian Bengochea Final;
Urb. San Martin
Rio Piedras, PR 00924
Tel: 809-769-6510
Carmelite Sisters (Spain)
Sr. TERESA M. NEGRON, Supr.
Beds 3,200
Patients assisted annually 360

Hogar Santa Teresa Jornet for the Aged
Cupey Alto, Km. 3, Hm. 8, Box 21012
Rio Piedras, PR 00928
Tel: 787-761-5805
Sisters of the Poor
Sr. ANA MARIA HIDALGO, Mother Supr.
Rev. JOSE MARIA LOPEZ, Chap.
Sisters 18
Beds 210
Guests 220

Vega Alta
Diocese of Arecibo, Puerto Rico

Mision Juan XXIII
00692
Centro Geriatrico Juan de los Olivos
HC-91, Box 8983
Vega Alta, PR 00692-9606
Tel: 787-883-2370
Sisters of Charity 3
Guests 43

RHODE ISLAND

Cumberland
Diocese of Providence

Mount St. Rita Health Centre
15 Sumner Brown Rd.
Cumberland, RI 02864
Tel: 401-333-6352
Legal Title: *Mount St. Rita Health Centre Inc.*
Licenced Nursing Home.
Sr. JOAN BAILEY, R.S.M., Admin.
Residents 30

Newport
Diocese of Providence

St. Clare Home
309 Spring St.
Newport, RI 02840
Tel: 401-849-3204; Fax: 401-849-5780
Legal Title: *The Saint Clare Home*
Nursing Facility.
MARY BETH DAIGNEAULT, Admin.
Rev. TIMOTHY J. SULLIVAN
Sr. PHILOMENA MCCANN, Cluny Convent
Daughters of the Holy Spirit 1
R.N., Nursing Sisters 1
Lay Nurses 12
Lay Employees 73
Residents 46

North Kingstown
Diocese of Providence

Scalabrini Villa
860 N. Quidnessett Rd.
North Kingstown, RI 02852
Tel: 401-884-1802
E-mail: ejm@bdol.com
Legal Title: *Scalabrini Villa Inc.*
Full Skilled Nursing Facility.
Rev. EDWARD J. MARINO, C.S., Admin., Tel: 401-884-1802
Sr. WILMA LOPEZI, F.A.S., Supr., Tel: 401-884-4594
In res.,
Rev. Msgr. OSCAR A. GUILBAULT Tel: 401-884-1426
Franciscan Apostolic Sisters 4
Residents 120

North Smithfield
Diocese of Providence

St. Antoine Residence
400 Mendon Rd.
North Smithfield, RI 02896
Tel: 401-767-3500
Legal Title: *Saint Antoine Residence*
MARY ANN ALTRUI, Admin.
Rev. DONAT A. BARRETTE, Chap.
In res.,
Rev. Msgr. EDMUND J. BROCK
Rev. Msgr. DONAT J. FAGNANT
Rev. WILLIAM F. PYNE
Residents 260

Pawtucket
Diocese of Providence

Jeanne Jugan Apartments
310 Sayles Ave.
Pawtucket, RI 02860
Mailing Address:
964 Main St.
Pawtucket, RI 02860
Apartments for elderly 27
Residents 30
Total Staff 1

Jeanne Jugan Residence
964 Main St.
Pawtucket, RI 02860
Tel: 401-723-4314; Fax: 401-727-2885
Legal Title: *Jeanne Jugan Residence of the Little Sisters of the Poor*
Rev. Msgr. WILLIAM I. VARSANYI, J.C.D., Chap.
In res.,
Rev. Msgr. PAUL A. LLOYD
Rev. OVILA T. DOUCET
Little Sisters of the Poor 16
Residents 74

Providence
Diocese of Providence

St. Joseph Living Center
153 Dean St.
Providence, RI 02903
Tel: 401-272-3335
DIANE E. EVANS, R.N., B.S.N., Exec. Dir.
Assisted and independent living and respite care facility, a division of St. Joseph Health Services of Rhode Island.
Residents 60

Woonsocket
Diocese of Providence

Saint Francis House
167 Blackstone St.
Woonsocket, RI 02895
Tel: 401-762-5255
Legal Title: *Saint Francis House, Woonsocket RI*
HELEN STRADONE, Dir.
Rev. JOSEPH D. SHANLEY, Chap.
Residents 59
Total Staff 27

SOUTH CAROLINA

Charleston
Diocese of Charleston

Carter-May Home
1660 Ingram Rd.
Charleston, SC 29407
Tel: 843-556-8314
Mrs. JANINE N. BAUDER, Admin.
Residents 15

SOUTH DAKOTA

Aberdeen
Diocese of Sioux Falls

Aberdeen Living Center
(Operated by Benedictine Health System-Benedictine Living Communities, Inc.)
1700 N. Hwy. 281
Aberdeen, SD 57401
Tel: 605-225-7315
Total Assisted 290
Total Staff 160

Mother Joseph Manor, Nursing Care Facility
1002 N. Jay St.
Aberdeen, SD 57401
Tel: 605-622-5850
TOM SNYDER, Admin.
Rev. CHARLES EMEZIE (Nigeria)
Presentation Sisters of the B.V.M. (Aberdeen, SD) 2
Residents 81
Units for Apartment Living 57
Total Staff 117
Adult Day Care
Community Outreach
Respite Care
Health Screening Clinics
Family Support Council

Milbank
Diocese of Sioux Falls

St. William Home for the Aged
Milbank, SD 57252
Tel: 605-432-4538; Fax: 605-432-5412
Conducted by Daughters of St. Mary of Providence, Milbank
Rev. RAY OTTO, O.S.B.
Guests 60

Angela Hall Assisted Living Center
Guests 22
Sisters 5

Mitchell
Diocese of Sioux Falls

Queen of Peace Hospital dba Brady Memorial Home
500 S. Ohlman
Mitchell, SD 57301
Tel: 605-966-7701; Fax: 605-996-5726
Mrs. ROBERTA CLARK, Admin.
Rev. THOMAS J. MCPHILLIPS, Chap.
Presentation Sisters of the B.V.M. 1
Skilled Nursing Care Units 83
Senior Residences 9
Total Assisted 188
Total Staff 88
Bishop Hoch Villa
Units for Congregate Living 6
Additional Senior Units 3
Brady Day Services Adult Day Care.
Respite Care Bed 1

Sioux Falls
Diocese of Sioux Falls

Prince of Peace Retirement Community, Inc.
4500 Prince of Peace Pl.
Sioux Falls, SD 57103
Tel: 605-371-0700
Mr. GARY TUSCHEN, Admin.
Presentation Sisters of B.V.M. 1
Nursing Home Beds 90
Congregate Apartments 74
Assisted Living Apartments 32
Total Assisted 203
Total Staff 128

Sisseton
Diocese of Sioux Falls

Tekakwitha Nursing Center, Inc.
(sub. of Benedictine Health System)
6 E. Chestnut
Sisseton, SD 57262
Tel: 605-693-7693; Fax: 605-698-3091
PATRICK J. RAFFERTY, Admin.
Sr. COLETTA VAN HEEK, Dir. Pastoral Care
Residents 101
Total Staff 120
(Owned and operated by: Benedictine Health System)

TENNESSEE

Dyersburg
Diocese of Memphis

St. Joseph Manor
885 Hwy. 51, Byp. W., P.O. Box 151
Dyersburg, TN 38024
Tel: 901-285-8560
BEVERLY BATES, Mgr.

The Village Apartments
Box 151, Hwy. 51 Byp. W.
Dyersburg, TN 38024
Tel: 901-285-8560
BEVERLY BATES, Mgr.

Westgate Apartments
1405-8 Meeks
Dyersburg, TN 38024
Tel: 901-286-4874
Ms. ANGELA HARRIS, Mgr.

Germantown
Diocese of Memphis

Madonna Learning Center for Retarded Children
7007 Poplar Ave.
Germantown, TN 38138
Tel: 901-752-5767
Sisters of St. Benedict (Ferdinand, IN)
Sr. MARY MARK GRAF, O.S.B.
Sisters 2
Lay Teachers 8
Students 45

Humboldt
Diocese of Memphis

St. Matthew Manor
2575 Viking Dr.
Humboldt, TN 38343
Tel: 901-784-7229
Ms. ANNE M. SAIN, Acting Mgr.

St. Matthew Manor - West
2575 Viking Dr.
Humboldt, TN 38343
Tel: 901-824-3793

Jackson
Diocese of Memphis

St. Mary Manor
1771 Hwy. 45 By-Pass
Jackson, TN 38305
Tel: 901-668-5633
ANNE M. SAIN, Mgr.

Knoxville
Diocese of Knoxville

Columbus Home, Inc.
119 Dameron Ave.
Knoxville, TN 37917
Tel: 423-971-3570; Fax: 423-546-0433
DAVID C. DOTSON, Exec. Dir.
Total Assisted 400
Total Staff 22

Memphis
Diocese of Memphis

Diocese of Memphis Housing Corp.
P.O. Box 41705
Memphis, TN 38174-1705
Tel: 901-722-4761; 722-4772
Mr. DAVID FIELD, Dir. of Housing
Mrs. MICHELLE R. BURRELL, Asst. Dir. of Housing

Northwood Park Apartments
1130 N. Breedlove
Memphis, TN 38107
Tel: 901-526-3964
JOANN JONES, Mgr.

St. Peter Home for Children (1852)
3060 Baskin St.
Memphis, TN 38127-7799
Tel: 901-354-6300; Fax: 901-354-6343

St. Peter Manor
108 N. Auburndale
Memphis, TN 38104
Tel: 901-278-8200
Sr. MARILYN TERWILLIGER, S.S.J., Mgr.
Chaplains:
Tel: 901-725-2700
Revs.:
TOM KIRK
JOE KERRIGAN
St. Peter Chapel & Activity Center

St. Peter Villa
141 N. McLean
Memphis, TN 38104-2644
Tel: 901-276-2021
Diocesan Nursing Home.
Mrs. KAE WERKHOVEN, Admin.
Rev. DAVID FOLEY, Chap., Tel: 901-276-1412

Moscow
Diocese of Memphis

St. Mark Village Apartments
85 St. Mark Cove
Moscow, TN 38057
Tel: 901-877-3456
Ms. GEORGIA LAUGHTER, Mgr.

Nashville
Diocese of Nashville

St. Mary Orphanage, Inc. dba St. Mary Villa
30 White Bridge Rd.
Nashville, TN 37205
Mr. DAVID GLASCOE, Exec. Dir.
Rev. Msgr. GEORGE W. ROHLING, V.G., Chap.

St. Mary Villa Child Development Center
30 White Bridge Rd.
Nashville, TN 37205
Tel: 615-356-6336
JOANNE CHASE, Prog. Dir.
Staff 44
Children 220

St. Mary Villa Retirement Community, Inc.
2400 21st Ave.
Nashville, TN 37212

**St. Bernard After School Program*
2020 24th Ave. S.
Nashville, TN 37212
Tel: 615-298-1298
BRENDA DYE, Dir.
Lay Staff 10
Students 80

Villa Maria Manor, Inc. dba Villa Maria Manor
32 White Bridge Rd.
Nashville, TN 37205
Tel: 615-352-3084
Mailing Address:
2400 21st Ave.
Nashville, TN 37212
Mr. WILLIAM P. SINCLAIR, Mng. Agent
Residents 211

Signal Mountain
Diocese of Knoxville

Alexian Village Health Care Center (1938)
100 James Blvd.
Signal Mountain, TN 37377
Tel: 423-886-0100
Licensed Skilled & Intermediate Care Nursing Home.
Bro. EUGENE RATLEY, C.F.A., Dir. of Community
Rev. MARO CANNON, C.F.A., Chap.
Mrs. CHRIS TARZIERS, Admin.
Brothers 12
Bed Capacity 114
Patients assisted annually 103
Assisted Living 33

Alexian Village of Tennessee, Inc.
100 James Blvd.
Signal Mountain, TN 37377
Tel: 423-870-0101
Life Care Residences and Nursing Home.
Mr. DAN GRAY, Pres.
Life Care Units 277
Total In Residence 481
Total Staff 145

TEXAS

Arlington
Diocese of Fort Worth

Nuestro Hogar, Inc. Catholic Charities
709 Magnolia St.
Arlington, TX 76012
Tel: 817-261-0608
65 unit apartment complex for the elderly and disabled.
Total in Residence 68
Total Staff 3

Boerne
Archdiocese of San Antonio

Childrens' Inn
216 W. Highland
Boerne, TX 78006
Tel: 830-249-9456
Co-Directors:
Sr. KATHLEEN KEAN, S.S.J.
MARILYN HAIDER
Provides foster care for children with special needs in a holistic setting.

Brownsville
Diocese of Brownsville

Mother of Perpetual Help Nursing Home, Inc.
519 A East Madison St.
Brownsville, TX 78520
Tel: 956-546-6745; Fax: 956-546-0711
Owner: Sisters of the Holy Spirit and Mary Immaculate.
Ms. JANICE KLINE, Admin.
Beds 38
Chapel attended from Immaculate Conception Cathedral.

Corpus Christi
Diocese of Corpus Christi

Casa San Lucas
222 Ocean View
Corpus Christi, TX 78412
Tel: 512-857-5758
Care of infirm and aged priests.

Mount Carmel Home
4130 S. Alameda St.
Corpus Christi, TX 78411
Tel: 512-855-6243
Sr. MARY TERESA, Supr.
Rev. JOHN THOMAS KENNA, Chaplain
Sisters 9
Residents 92
Total Staff 29

Villa Maria, Inc.
3146 Saratoga Blvd.
Corpus Christi, TX 78415
Tel: 512-857-6171; Fax: 512-857-6173
Apartment complex for senior adults.
Total Staff 3
Total in Residence 59

Crowley
Diocese of Fort Worth

St. Francis Village, Inc.
1 Chapel Plaza
Crowley, TX 76036
Tel: 817-292-5786
(On shores of Lake Benbrook near Fort Worth)
Residence village for retirees and the elderly sponsored by Franciscan Tertiary Provinces Foundation & SFV, Inc. (Illinois).
Revs.:
J. MICHAEL EWERT, O.F.M., Pres.
VINCENT ELSEN, O.F.M., Chap.
In res.,
Revs.:
RAY BOBBER, O.F.M., (Retired)
PETER FRITZ, O.F.M., (Retired)
DONALD WERR, O.F.M.
RONALD J. AXEN
MATHIAS KIEMEN, O.F.M.
Residents 420
Franciscan Tertiary Provinces Foundation
1 Chapel Plaza
Crowley, TX 76036
Sponsor corporation of St. Francis Village (retirement village) in Crowley, TX.
Rev. J. MICHAEL EWERT, O.F.M., Pres.
Total Staff 17

El Paso
Diocese of El Paso

Nazareth Hall
4614 Trowbridge
El Paso, TX 79903
Tel: 915-565-4677; Fax: 915-566-7530
Sr. ELISA RODRIGUEZ, Admin. Nursing Center

Villa Maria
920 S. Oregon St.
El Paso, TX 79901
Tel: 915-533-5152
Home for Aged Women and Men.
Sr. MARY ANN HAMOR, C.S.J., Dir.
Women Residents 17
Men Residents 7

Fort Worth
Diocese of Fort Worth

Casa del Cor, Inc.
2701 Burchill Rd., N.
Fort Worth, TX 76105
Tel: 817-534-0814; Fax: 817-535-8779

Casa, Inc. Housing for the Elderly and Handicapped
3201 Sondra Dr.
Fort Worth, TX 76107
Tel: 817-332-7276
Units 200
Total in Residence 197
Total Staff 7

Hillje
Diocese of Victoria in Texas

Czech Catholic Home For The Aged
Rte. 3, Box 40
El Campo, TX 77437
Tel: 409-648-2628

Houston
Diocese of Galveston—Houston

Casa de Esperanza, De Los Ninos, Inc.
Mailing Address: P.O. Box 66581
Houston, TX 77006
Tel: 713-529-0639
Homes for children in crisis situations.
KATHLEEN FOSTER, Dir.
Mr. WILLIAM JONES, Assoc. Dir.
Sisters 8
Served 1,500
Total Assisted 135
Total Staff 40

Casa Juan Diego
4818 Rose
Houston, TX 77007
Tel: 713-869-7376
Mr. MARK ZWICK, Dir.
Houses 16
Patients assisted annually 263,700

Casa Maria de Guadalupe Medical Clinic and Social Service Center
(Catholic Worker)
6101 Edgemoor
Houston, TX 77081
Tel: 713-995-9414
Mailing Address:
P.O. Box 70113
Houston, TX 77270
Patients assisted annually 229,300

Covenant House Texas
1111 Lovett Blvd.
Houston, TX 77006
Tel: 713-523-2231
Sr. MARY ROSE MCGEADY, Pres.
CAROLYN LARSEN, Exec. Dir.
ANDREA METZGER, Pastoral Min.
Total Assisted 609
Total Staff 74

Pope John XXIII Priest Residence
2407 Holcombe Blvd.
Houston, TX 77021-2023
Tel: 713-748-4608
Revs.:
GABRE-TINSAYE ADHANA, (Retired), Tel: 713-748-4425
NICHOLAS C. ANTLE, (Retired), Tel: 713-748-1553
PETER CHU, (Retired), Tel: 713-747-8774
FELICIANO DEL VAL, (Retired), Tel: 713-747-2124
JOHN C. DEFORKE, (Retired), Tel: 713-748-6693
THOMAS A. DONOVAN, (Retired), Tel: 713-741-9471
EUGENE E. GILLECE, (Retired), Tel: 713-748-7201
TOM GRENNAN, (Retired), Tel: 713-741-0475
JACK B. JONES, (Retired), Tel: 713-747-1746
FRANK A. LAGANA, (Retired), Tel: 713-748-7022
LAWRENCE LEE, (Retired), Tel: 713-741-7267
JAMES J. MADDEN, (Retired), Tel: 713-748-1761
JAMES NELSON, (Retired), Tel: 713-748-8144
LAWRENCE PEGUERO, (Retired), Tel: 713-741-8326
GEORGE V. RHEIN, (Retired), Tel: 713-747-7308
CHARLES K. SCHOEPPE, (Retired), Tel: 713-748-4596
JOHN A. WEIHRER, (Retired), Tel: 713-748-3130
Residents 18
Total Staff 2

St. Dominic Nursing Home
St. Dominic Center, 2409 E. Holcombe Blvd.
Houston, TX 77021-2023
Tel: 713-741-8701
Mrs. RUTH WHIGHAM, Admin.
Aged Residents 130

St. Dominic Residence Hall
St. Dominic Diocesan Center, 2401 E. Holcombe Blvd.
Houston, TX 77021-2023
Tel: 713-741-8700
Ms. BILLIE J. COKER, Admin.
Total in Residence 137
Total Staff 26

Santa Maria Hostel
807 Paschall St.
Houston, TX 77009
Tel: 713-228-0125
Intensive residential treatment (substance abuse) for women ages 18 and above.
Ms. CHERYL EMPEY, Exec. Dir.
Residents 23
Patients assisted annually 226
Total Staff 13

Kenedy
Archdiocese of San Antonio

John Paul II Nursing Home
209 S. 3rd St., P.O. Box 359
Kenedy, TX 78119
Tel: 830-583-9841
Sr. MARIA LODZIANA, S.O.L.S., Admin.
Seraphic Sisters of Our Lady of Sorrows 5
Residents 63

Laredo
Diocese of Corpus Christi

Sacred Heart Children's Home
3310 S. Zapata Hwy.
Laredo, TX 78046
Tel: 210-723-3343
Servants of the Sacred Heart of Jesus and of the Poor
Mother MARIA TERESA GRAJEDA, Supr.
Sisters 17
Children 59

Panhandle
Diocese of Amarillo

St. Ann's Nursing Home
P.O. Box 1179
Panhandle, TX 79068
Tel: 806-537-3194
Rev. Msgr. MONROE J. MATTHIESEN, Dir.
Rev. Msgr. PETER MORSCH
JANA SCHICK, Admin.
School Sisters of St. Francis
Residents 56

St. Joseph's Home for Retired Priests
P.O. Box 1179
Panhandle, TX 79068
Pastor Emeriti:
Rev. Msgr. JAMES W. SONDERMAN
Rev. Msgr. CLIFTON J. CORCORAN
Rev. Msgr. MONROE J. MATTHIESEN, Dir.
Rev. J. ARNOLD CARLSON

San Antonio
Archdiocese of San Antonio

Casa De Padres
8520 Cross Mountain Tr.
San Antonio, TX 78255
Home for retired Priests of San Antonio.
Rev. Msgr. SHERRILL SMITH, No. 201, Tel: 210-698-8819
Revs.:
PABLO PANIAGUA, No. 401, Tel: 210-698-8036
ROGELIO MARTINEZ, No. 1101, Tel: 210-698-2243
Rev. Msgr. J. LEROY MANNING, No. 1102, Tel: 210-698-3183
Rev. Msgr. ROY RIHN, No. 301, Tel: 210-431-9903
Rev. Msgr. BERNARD C. MULLANEY, No. 402, Tel: 210-698-3975
Rev. Msgr. ALOIS J. GOERTZ, No. 402, Tel: 210-698-9067
In res.,
Rev. Msgr. TERENCE NOLAN, No. 701, Tel: 201-698-0349

Father Flanagan's Boys' Town of San Antonio
503 Urban Loop
San Antonio, TX 78204
Tel: 210-271-1010
Ms. DEBORAH WILSON, Site Dir.
Staff 47
Bed Capacity 48
Children Under Care 41
Residential Center (For Children under 18)
8400, 8401, 8402, 8405, 8406 Flanagan St.
San Antonio, TX 78249
Tel: 210-271-1010
Staff 18
Bed Capacity 30
Youth Shelter
503 Urban Loop
San Antonio, TX 78204
Tel: 210-271-3131
Staff 22
Bed Capacity 16
Total Assisted 400
Common Sense Parenting
503 Urban Loop
San Antonio, TX 78204
Tel: 210-271-1010
Staff 1
Total Assisted 200
Family Preservation Services
503 Urban Loop
San Antonio, TX 78204
Tel: 210-271-1010
Staff 5
Families Assisted 50

Incarnate Word Motherhouse and Retirement Center
4707 Broadway
San Antonio, TX 78209
Tel: 210-829-7561
For lay persons also.
Mr. RICHARD BOYD, Exec. Dir.
Rev. Msgr. THOMAS A. FRENCH, Chap.
Total in Residence 208

Marianist Residence: Skilled Nursing
520 Fordham Ln.
San Antonio, TX 78228-4821
Tel: 210-436-3771 (Nurses' Station)
Home for Infirm Marianist Brothers and Priests.
Bros.:
JOSEPH GREISHABER, S.M., Dir.
JAMES JAECKLE, S.M., Sub Dir., Health Care Oper.
Revs.:
RALPH J. DYER, S.M. Tel: 210-436-3288
HERBERT KRAMER, S.M.
JOHN G. LEIES, S.M. Tel: 210-436-3140

Louis Reile, S.M. Tel: 210-436-3764
Richard J. Schneider, S.M. Tel: 210-436-3165
Thomas M. Schelble, S.M. Tel: 210-436-3770
Infirm Brothers 20
Infirm Priests 6

Oblate Madonna Residence
5722 Blanco Rd.
San Antonio, TX 78216
Tel: 210-341-2350
Home for retired Priests and Brothers.
Missionary Oblates of Mary Immaculate
Revs.:
Clifford Blackburn, O.M.I., Dir.
Richard A. Houlahan, O.M.I., Asst. Dir.
Jose Azpiazu, O.M.I.
Charles Banks, O.M.I.
Alan Brelivet, O.M.I.
John Busch, O.M.I.
John Clarkson, O.M.I.
Edward J. Cronin, O.M.I.
James P. Delaney, O.M.I.
Laurent Dupuis, O.M.I.
Maximo Fuente, O.M.I.
Leo Gauvin, O.M.I.
Anthony Goossens, O.M.I.
Joseph Hamel, O.M.I.
Robert Koerner, O.M.I.
Joseph Lyons, O.M.I.
Galeb Mokarzel, O.M.I.
Sebastian Mozos, O.M.I.
Patrick O'Brien, O.M.I.
George O'Connell, O.M.I.
Alfred Prado, O.M.I.
Thomas Ryan, O.M.I.
Francis Schoutten, O.M.I.
Michael Slattery, O.M.I.
Donald Stavinoha, O.M.I.
Antonio Strano, O.M.I.
Roger Temme, O.M.I.
Bros.:
Emmanuel Hoffart, O.M.I.
Joseph Palazzo, O.M.I.
Priests 27
Brothers 2
Sisters of the Sacred Heart of Jesus 1

Padua Place
80 Peter Baque Rd.
San Antonio, TX 78209
Tel: 210-826-7721
Home for infirm and retired Priests and Brothers.
Sr. Rose Mary Martinez, M.S.S.A., Admin.
In res.,
Revs.:
James Coleman (SAN)
Ullric J. Proeller (FAR)
Andrew Coels, C.I.C.M.
Peter Vergauwen (SAN)
Theodore Clerx, C.I.C.M.
Francis Maas, M.S.F.
Eugene Janson (VIC)
Russell Schultz (SAN)
Francis Nelan, M.S.C.
Charles Larue (SAN)
Robert Timperman, C.I.C.M.
Rev. Msgr. Anthony J. Costantino
Rev. Msgr. Victor Schmidtzinsky (VIC)
Bro. Edward Kinsley, M.S.F.
Priests 12
Brothers 1

Providence Home & Family Services, Inc.
(Foster Home and Childcare for HIV Positive Children)
2650 Castroville Rd.
San Antonio, TX 78237
Tel: 210-434-2111; Fax: 210-433-2806
Patricia N. Kozar, Dir.
Sisters 4

St. Francis Nursing Home
630 W. Woodlawn
San Antonio, TX 78212
Tel: 210-736-3177; Fax: 210-783-2221
Home for the Aged and Convalescents.
Seraphic Sisters of Our Lady of Sorrows
Sr. Alfonsa Bobek, S.O.L.S., Pres. of Corp.
Sr. Elizabeth Dubicka, S.O.L.S., Admin.
Sisters 6
Bed Capacity 152
Total Staff 130

St. Peter & Joseph Childrens Home
919 Mission Rd.
San Antonio, TX 78210
Tel: 210-533-1203
Rev. Msgr. Marvin G. Doerfler, LMSW-AP, Exec. Dir.
House Parent Staff 12
Administrative & Support Staff 20
Bed Capacity 60
Children Under Care (ages 2-18) 60

Seton Home for Homeless, Pregnant Young Women
1115 Mission Rd.
San Antonio, TX 78210
Tel: 210-533-3504
Cathy Clough, Exec. Dir.
Bed Capacity 24

The South Texas Catholic Retirement Center, Inc.
P.O. Box 6290
San Antonio, TX 78209-0290
Tel: 210-829-7561; Fax: 210-826-6280
Sr. Kathleen Coughlin, C.C.V.I., Chm.
Purpose: A collaborative effort of twelve Religious Congregations, men and women, to provide a facility for elderly religious and lay men and women who are economically disadvantaged.

Visitation Hospitality House of San Antonio, Texas and La Posada Transitional Housing
945 W. Huisache
San Antonio, TX 78201
Tel: 210-735-6910
A non-profit corporation chartered under the laws of the State of Texas.
Operated by the Sisters of Charity of the Incarnate Word of San Antonio, TX
Sr. Yolanda Tarango, C.C.V.I., Dir.
Provides human services for homeless women and children on a temporary basis.
La Posada Transitional Housing

San Juan
Diocese of Brownsville

San Juan Home Health and Hospice
300 N. Nebraska, P.O. Box 2359
San Juan, TX 78589
Tel: 956-782-0333; Fax: 956-782-0335
Mrs. Olga Navarro, Admin.

San Juan Nursing Home
300 N. Nebraska, P.O. Box 1238
San Juan, TX 78589
Tel: 956-787-1771; Fax: 956-787-8091
Legal Title: *San Juan Nursing Home, Inc., of the Diocese of Brownsville, a Texas Non-Profit Corporation*
Most Rev. Raymundo J. Pena, Chm.
Mrs. Olga Navarro, Admin.
Board of Directors:
Ernesto Alvarado
Nieves Canales
Janice Kline
Sr. Angela Murdaugh, F.S.M.
Ex-Officios:
Revs.:
Armando Escobedo, Moderator of the Curia, (Upper Valley)
Juan Victor Heredia, Social Svcs. Commission
Bed Capacity 127

Stephenville
Diocese of Fort Worth

CASA Brendan and CASA II, Inc. Catholic Charities
1300 Hyman
Stephenville, TX 76401
Tel: 817-965-6964
86 unit apartment complex for the elderly and handicapped.
Total in Residence 86
Total Staff 6

Waco
Diocese of Austin

DePaul Center
301 Londonderry Dr.
Waco, TX 76712
Tel: 254-776-5970; 1-800-777-5043
Psychiatric Hospital
Sr. Mary Ann Ryan, Dir. Pastoral Care
Dr. Keith M. Hankins, Ed.D., Admin.; Vice Pres.
Daughters of Charity of St. Vincent de Paul
Daughters of Charity 1
Bed Capacity 64
Patients assisted annually 1,900

The Regis Retirement Home and St. Elizabeth Nursing Home
400 Austin Ave., P.O. Box 1909
Waco, TX 76703
Tel: 254-756-5441; Fax: 254-754-0133
Michael Sims, Admin.
Sisters of Charity of the Incarnate Word (Houston) 2
Residents 220

UTAH

Salt Lake City
Diocese of Salt Lake City

St. Joseph Villa
451 Bishop Federal Ln.
Salt Lake City, UT 84115-2295
Tel: 801-487-7557
Operated by Sisters of Charity of the Incarnate Word Health Care System
Galen K. Ewer, Pres. & CEO
Residents 300
Total in Residence 287
Total Assisted 723
Total Staff 285

VERMONT

Burlington
Diocese of Burlington

St. Joseph's Home for Aged
243 N. Prospect St.
Burlington, VT 05401
Tel: 802-864-0264
Operated by Vermont Catholic Charities.
Rev. Roland J. Rivard, Dir.
Esther MacPherson, Admin.
Rev. Msgr. Edward J. Gelineau
Revs.:
Omer L. Dufault
Edward J. Hart
Thomas J. Beary
Walter Wells
Robert Lapan
Sisters 1
Guests 30

Derby Line
Diocese of Burlington

Michaud Memorial Manor
Derby Line, VT 05830
Tel: 802-873-3152
Conducted by Vermont Catholic Charities.
Rev. Roland J. Rivard, Dir.
Mrs. Therese Fortin, Admin.
Guests 31

Rutland
Diocese of Burlington

Loretto Home for Aged
Rutland, VT 05701
Tel: 802-773-8840
Conducted by Vermont Catholic Charities.
Rev. Roland J. Rivard, Dir.
Terry Dion Cavacas, Admin.
Rev. Joseph Lagor, Res. Chap.
Guests 57

St. Joseph Assisted Living Residence/Kervick Home
131 Convent Ave.
Rutland, VT 05701
Tel: 802-775-5133
Sr. Miriam Francis Predom, S.S.J., Pres.
Sr. Mary Polworth, S.S.J., Vice. Pres.
Conducted by Covenant Health Systems, Inc.
Guests 34

VIRGINIA

Charlottesville
Diocese of Richmond

Our Lady of Peace
751 Hillsdale Dr.
Charlottesville, VA 22901
Tel: 804-973-1155
Mrs. Pamela Doshier, Admin.
Nursing Bed Capacity 30
Independent Units 64
Assisted Units 36

Hampton
Diocese of Richmond

Seton Manor
215 Marcella Rd.
Hampton, VA 23666
Tel: 757-827-6512
Ms. Reagan Weber, Mgr.
Residents 113

Lynchburg
Diocese of Richmond

McGurk House Apartments
2425 Tate Springs Rd.

Lynchburg, VA 24501
Independent Living for adults 62 yrs. or older, or mobility impaired.
Ms. MELISSA CROSIER, Property Mgr., Tel: 804-846-2425
Apartments 89

Nott Homes, Inc.
3009-3011 Roundelay Rd.
Lynchburg, VA 24502
CALVIN STATON, Dir., Tel: 804-239-0722

Newport News
Diocese of Richmond

St. Francis Nursing Center
4 Ridgewood Pkwy.
Newport News, VA 23602
PATRICIA N. MILLER, Admin., Tel: 757-886-6500
Total Assisted 115

Norfolk
Diocese of Richmond

Madonna Home
814 W. 37th St.
Norfolk, VA 23508
Tel: 757-623-6662
CHARLENE DAVIS, Dir.
Residents 14

St. Mary's Home for Disabled Children
317 Chapel St.
Norfolk, VA 23504
Tel: 757-622-2208
WILLIAM M. JOLLY, Admin.
Long term care for multiply handicapped children birth to eleven years old.
Daughters of Wisdom 2
Beds 88

Richmond
Diocese of Richmond

Marywood Apartments
1261 Marywood Ln.
Richmond, VA 23229
Tel: 804-740-5567
PATRICIA SCOTT, Res. Mgr.
Residents 126

Our Lady of Hope Health Center, Inc.
13700 N. Gayton Rd.
Richmond, VA 23233
Tel: 804-360-1960
MATTHEW FARMER, Admin.
Residents 127

St. Francis Home, Inc.
2511 Wise St.
Richmond, VA 23225-3952
Tel: 804-231-1043; Fax: 804-231-1065
Mr. DAVID CRAN, Dir.
Bed Capacity 63

St. Joseph's Home for the Aged
1503 Michael Rd.
Richmond, VA 23229
Tel: 804-288-6245
Sr. REGINA MARIE LOFTUS, L.S.P., Supr.
Rev. THOMAS W. STUMPF, O.S.B., Chap.
Little Sisters of the Poor 12
Guests 72
Attended by Benedictine Fathers.

St. Joseph's Villa
8000 Brook Rd.
Richmond, VA 23227-1338
Tel: 804-553-3200; Fax: 804-553-3259
RAMON E. PARDUE, Exec. Dir.
Children in Res. 12
Children in Day Care 155
Children in Extended Day Services 24
Children in Special Education 50
Children in Alternative Education 30
Children in Transitional Housing 40

St. Joseph's Villa Housing Corp.
8000 Brook Rd.
Richmond, VA 23227-1399
Tel: 804-553-3283; Fax: 804-553-3259
Mr. RAMON E. PARDUE, Exec Dir.
Apartments for Physically Challenged Adults.
Apartments 60
St. Joseph's Villa Housing Corp., II

St. Mary Wood's
1257 Marywood Ln.
Richmond, VA 23229
Tel: 804-741-8624
RANDY SCOTT, Admin.
Units 118

Roanoke
Diocese of Richmond

The Achievement Center-St. Vincent's Home, Inc.
Mailing Address:
P.O. Box 12368
Roanoke, VA 24025
Tel: 540-982-0128
615 N. Jefferson St.
Roanoke, VA 24016
BARBARA ANN WHITWELL, Dir.

De Paul Family Services, Inc.
4502 Starkey Rd., S.W.
Roanoke, VA 24014
Tel: 540-989-7355
Specialized Foster Care.
HERB BESKAR, Exec. Dir.

Our Lady of the Valley Retirement Community
650 N. Jefferson St.
Roanoke, VA 24016
Tel: 540-345-5111
Mr. MICHAEL BRUBAKEN, Admissions Counselor
Residents 85

Suffolk
Diocese of Richmond

Bon Secours-Maryview Nursing Care
4775 Bridge Rd.
Suffolk, VA 23435
Tel: 757-686-0488
DIANA L. JARRETT, Admin.
Bed Capacity 120
Martha W. Davis Cancer Center
Maryview Employee Assistance Program
Maryview MedCare Centers (Urgent Care)
Maryview Wellspring Home Health Agency
Maryview Hospice Program

Virginia Beach
Diocese of Richmond

Marian Manor
5345 Marian Ln.
Virginia Beach, VA 23462
Tel: 804-456-5018
IRVIN LAND, Admin.
Units 100
Nursing Beds 30

Our Lady of Perpetual Help Health Center, Inc.
4560 Princess Anne Rd.
Virginia Beach, VA 23462-7905

Russell House
900 First Colonial Rd.
Virginia Beach, VA 23454
Tel: 804-481-0770
ELEANOR OLSEN, Admin.
Units 119
Residents 126

WASHINGTON

Bellevue
Archdiocese of Seattle

Champion House
1800 145th Pl. S.E.
Bellevue, WA 98007
Tel: 206-644-4477

Elbert House
16000 N.E. 8th St.
Bellevue, WA 98008
Tel: 206-747-5111

Halcyon
1200 134th Ave. N.E.
Bellevue, WA 98005
Tel: 206-643-780; Fax: 206-746-0438

Bellingham
Archdiocese of Seattle

The Martin Center
2806 Douglas
Bellingham, WA 98225
Tel: 206-733-5804
Children 26

Bothell
Archdiocese of Seattle

Franciscan Health System West dba FHS Care Center at Bothell
10909 N.E. 185th St.
Bothell, WA 98011
Tel: 206-486-7174; 483-9905; Fax: 206-487-1313
CHI-Catholic Health Initiatives.
KEN BLOOMSTINE, Admin.
Beds 135

Chehalis
Archdiocese of Seattle

Providence Place
350 S.E. Washington Ave.
Chehalis, WA 98532
Tel: 360-740-8389

Chewelah
Diocese of Spokane

DominiCare
303 E. King St., P.O. Box 1070
Chewelah, WA 99109
Sr. SHARON STANGLER, O.P., CEO
A home care/chore service in Stevens County.

Clarkston
Diocese of Spokane

Austen Manor
30 apartments for senior citizens and mobility handicapped.
1222 Chestnut St.
Clarkston, WA 99403
CHARLES GRASSESCKI, Mgr.

Lewis and Clark District Council of St. Vincent de Paul
Office:
604 Second St.
Clarkston, WA 99403
Tel: 509-758-7061; Fax: 509-758-9545
Stores:
609 Third St.
Clarkston, WA 99403
3138 5th St.
Lewiston, ID 83501

Colville
Diocese of Spokane

The Rhodena, A Washington Non-profit Organization
Mailing Address:
P.O. Box 1453
Spokane, WA 99210-1453
A six unit affordable housing complex for families living in Colville, WA.

Dayton
Diocese of Spokane

St. Vincent de Paul Store
257 E. Main St.
Dayton, WA 99328
Tel: 509-382-4146
Mailing Address:
112 S. First St.
Dayton, WA 99328-1307

Everett
Archdiocese of Seattle

Providence Home Care and Hospice of Snohomish County
2731 Wetmore Ave., #520
Everett, WA 98201
Tel: 206-261-4800

Issaquah
Archdiocese of Seattle

Providence Marianwood
3725 Providence Point Dr., S.E.
Issaquah, WA 98027
Tel: 425-391-2800; Fax: 425-391-5440
Sisters of Providence Health System
Ms. ANN E. HUGHES, Admin.
MARY GOULD, Pastoral Care Svcs.
Sisters 1
Bed Capacity 120

Manito Station
Diocese of Spokane

Spokane Boys' Ranch, Inc.
(aka Morning Star Boys' Ranch)
P.O. Box 8087
Manito Station, WA 99203
Tel: 509-448-1411
Rev. JOSEPH M. WEITENSTEINER, Dir.
Children in residence 12
Total Assisted 35

Olympia
Archdiocese of Seattle

Providence Mother Joseph Care Center
3333 Ensign Rd., N.E.
Olympia, WA 98506
Tel: 360-493-4900; Fax: 360-493-4948
Mr. ROBERT WILDENHAUS, Admin.
Sr. JUDY RYAN, S.N.J.M., Pastoral Care

Providence Sound Home Care and Hospice
3706 Griffin Ln., S.E.
Olympia, WA 98501
Tel: 800-869-7062; 360-459-8311

Pasco
Diocese of Spokane

St. Vincent de Paul Store
1120 W. Sylvester
Pasco, WA 99301
Tel: 509-547-2341; Fax: 509-547-7804

Pullman
Diocese of Spokane

Pioneer Square
S.E. 220 Kamiaken
Pullman, WA 99163
Bed Capacity 45

Redmond
Archdiocese of Seattle

Emma McRedmond Manor
7960 169th N.E.
Redmond, WA 98052
Tel: 206-869-2424

Seattle
Archdiocese of Seattle

Chancery Place
910 Marion
Seattle, WA 98104
Tel: 206-343-9415

The Franciscan
15237 21st Ave. S.W.
Seattle, WA 98166
Tel: 206-431-8001

The Josephinum
1902 2nd Ave.
Seattle, WA 98101
Tel: 206-448-8500

Providence Home Services
425 Pontius Ave., N., Ste. 300
Seattle, WA 98109
Tel: 206-320-4848

Providence Mount St. Vincent
4831 35th Ave. S.W.
Seattle, WA 98126
Tel: 206-937-3700; Fax: 206-938-8999
Legal Title: *Sisters of Providence in Washington*
Ms. CHARLENE BOYD, Admin.
Rev. BRIAN MCGOVERN, Chap.
Sisters 3
Bed Capacity 174
Apartments 111

Providence Mount St. Vincent
4831 35th Ave. S.
Seattle, WA 98126
Tel: 206-937-3700

Vincent House
1423 First Ave.
Seattle, WA 98101
Tel: 206-682-9307
Sponsored by the Sisters of Providence.

The Westlake
2008 Westlake Ave.
Seattle, WA 98121
Tel: 206-340-0410

Spokane
Diocese of Spokane

Cathedral Plaza Apartments
W. 1120 Sprague Ave.
Spokane, WA 99204
Bed Capacity 150

Catholic Charities, Inc.
W. 1023 Riverside Ave., P.O. Box 1453
Spokane, WA 99210-1453
Tel: 509-358-4250
Mrs. DONNA HANSON, Bishop's Sec. for Social Ministries

Catholic Family Service
W. 1023 Riverside Ave., P.O. Box 1453
Spokane, WA 99210-1453
Tel: 509-358-4260
MICHAEL T. RYAN, Dir.

The Delaney
W. 242 Riverside Ave.
Spokane, WA 99201
Bed Capacity 84

Fahy Garden Apartments
W. 1403 Dean Ave.
Spokane, WA 99201
Bed Capacity 31

Fahy West Apartments
W. 1523 Dean Ave.
Spokane, WA 99201
Bed Capacity 54

Guse Summit View
Housing for single parents with children.
820 N. Summit Blvd.
Spokane, WA 99201
E-mail: sumview@gntech.net

House of Charity
Hospitality house for homeless men.
W. 9 Main Ave., P.O. Box 1453
Spokane, WA 99210-1453
Tel: 509-624-7821
ED MCCARRON, Dir.
Total Assisted 50,645

Miryam's House
A long-term residence for women in transition.
W. 1805 Ninth St.
Spokane, WA 99204
Total Assisted 25

The O'Malley
E. 707 Mission Ave.
Spokane, WA 99202
Bed Capacity 100

Rockwood Lane / Court
E. 221 Rockwood Blvd.
Spokane, WA 99202
KIM MOE, Property Mgr.
Bed Capacity 106
Residents 140

St. Anne's Children's Home
Therapeutic child care for abused/neglected children and assistance to their parents through parent education and counseling.
N. 707 Cedar St.
Spokane, WA 99201-1999
Tel: 509-325-7672
PAT WOLF, Dir.

St. Joseph Care Center
W. 20 Ninth Ave.
Spokane, WA 99204
Tel: 509-838-6437
ALICE ANDERSON, Admin.
Sisters of Providence 3
Residents 280

St. Joseph dba St. Brendan Continuing Care Center
(A Non-profit Corporation)
E. 17 Eighth Ave.
Spokane, WA 99202
Tel: 509-624-1161
Sisters of Providence
ALICE ANDERSON, Admin.
Beds 165

St. Joseph's Counseling Center
N. 1016 Superior St.
Spokane, WA 99202
Tel: 509-483-6495
E-mail: sjfc@icehouse.net
Sr. CARMEL GREGG, O.S.F., Dir., St. Joseph Family Center
Sisters of St. Francis of Philadelphia 7

St. Margaret's Shelter
Emergency shelter for single women & children.
P.O. Box 1453
Spokane, WA 99210
Tel: 509-624-7624
STEPHANIE KENNEDY, Dir.

St. Vincent de Paul Social Service Office
E. 2901 Trent Ave.
Spokane, WA 99202
Tel: 509-534-2824 (Social Svc.); 535-2491 (Main Store & Office)
SCOTT COOPER, Social Svc. Dir.
BRIAN TAYLOR, Mgr. Main Store & Business Office
Legal Title: *St. Vincent de Paul Social Service Office and Main Store St. Business Office*

St. Vincent de Paul Society
Spokane District Council
E. 2901 Trent Ave.
Spokane, WA 99202
Tel: 509-534-2824
Mrs. NICKY COOK, Pres.

Senior Citizen Housing
W. 242 Riverside Ave.
Spokane, WA 99201
Tel: 509-624-6060
Mr. RICHARD CUNNINGHAM, Dir.

Transitional Living Center
3128 N. Hemlock
Spokane, WA 92204
E-mail: tlc@cet.com
Housing for homeless families.

Women's Drop In Center
218 S. Howard
Spokane, WA 92204-1419
A safe place for women at risk.

Tacoma
Archdiocese of Seattle

Franciscan Health System West dba FHS Care Center at Tacoma
6220 S. Alaska
Tacoma, WA 98408
Tel: 253-473-2273
CHI-Catholic Health Initiatives.
LINDA LARSON, Admin.
Licensed skilled beds 123

Norm Fournier Court
112 S. 127th
Tacoma, WA 98444
Tel: 253-531-5087

Tumwater
Archdiocese of Seattle

Tumwater Apartments
5701 6th Ave., S.W.
Tumwater, WA 98501
Tel: 206-352-4321

Walla Walla
Diocese of Spokane

Catholic Children and Family Service
5 W. Alder St., Ste. 333
Walla Walla, WA 99362
Tel: 509-525-0572; Fax: 509-525-0576
RICHARD A. GARCIA, M.S.W., Dir.

Garden Court Apartments
Sixth & Alder Sts.
Walla Walla, WA 99362
Bed Capacity 20

Mike Foye Apartments
Sixth & Alder Sts.
Walla Walla, WA 99362
Bed Capacity 27

St. Vincent de Paul Store
308 W. Main St.
Walla Walla, WA 99362
Tel: 509-525-3903 (Store); 529-6778 (Office)
TERRY ADAMS, Store Mgr.
ALBERT TORRETTA, Society Pres.

WEST VIRGINIA

Clarksburg
Diocese of Wheeling-Charleston

Madonna Day Care Center
444 E. Pike St.
Clarksburg, WV 26031
Tel: 304-622-4453

Wheeling
Diocese of Wheeling-Charleston

Good Shepherd Nursing Home
159 Edgington Ln.
Wheeling, WV 26003

Tel: 304-242-1093
Mr. DONALD R. KIRSCH, Admin.
Rev. JOHN WEIGLEIN, S.M., Chap.
Sisters 3
Bed Capacity 192

Holy Family Child Care Center, Inc.
161 Edgington Ln.
Wheeling, WV 26003
Tel: 304-242-5222
PATRICIA GREEN, Dir.

St. John's Home for Children
141 Key Ave.
Wheeling, WV 26003-7412
Tel: 304-242-5633
TERENCE A. MCCORMICK, Exec. Dir.
Children 8

Welty Home for the Aged, Inc.
21 Washington Ave.
Wheeling, WV 26003-6261
Tel: 304-242-5233
Sr. SHEILA ROONEY, O.L.C., Dir.
Sisters 2
Residents 45
WELTRUST, INC.
P.O. Box 230
Wheeling, WV 26003
Trustees:
Most Rev. BERNARD W. SCHMITT, Pres.
Rev. JOHN R. GALLAGHER, V.G., Vice Pres. & Sec.
RICHARD G. HERNDON, ESQ., Treas.
Welty Retirement Apartments
1276 National Rd.
Wheeling, WV 26003
Tel: 304-242-5820

WISCONSIN

Appleton
Diocese of Green Bay

Franciscan Care and Rehabilitation Center, Inc.
2915 N. Meade St.
Appleton, WI 54911-1598
Tel: 920-831-8700; Fax: 920-731-3206
E-mail: osh.screech@affinity.com
MARGE RANKIN, Vice Pres. Operations/Admin.
Total assisted 215

Arcadia
Diocese of La Crosse

Franciscan Skemp Healthcare, Mayo Health System, Arcadia Campus Nursing Home
464 S. St. Joseph Ave.
Arcadia, WI 54612
Tel: 608-323-3341
Franciscan Sisters of Perpetual Adoration and Mayo Foundation.
DARLENE GOEHNER, Admin.
Chaplains:
Rev. ROBERT F. POLCYN, O.F.M. Cap. Tel: 608-539-3704
Sr. ARLENE MELDER, F.S.P.A.
Bed Capacity 75

Baraboo
Diocese of Madison

St. Clare Meadows Care Center
1414 Jefferson St.
Baraboo, WI 53913
Tel: 608-356-4838; Fax: 608-356-5441
Owned and operated by SSM Health Care Corporation, Member of the SSM Health Care.
Mr. CRAIG UBBELOHDE, Admin.

Eau Claire
Diocese of La Crosse

St. Francis Apartment
851 University Dr.
Eau Claire, WI 54701
Tel: 715-834-1388
DAVID B. FISH, Chm.
Legal Title: *Hospital Sisters Health Care-West, Inc.*
Units 60
Total in residence 65

Fond du Lac
Archdiocese of Milwaukee

St. Francis Home for Aged
365 Gillett St.
Fond du Lac, WI 54935
Tel: 920-923-7980; Fax: 920-923-7995
Sisters of St. Agnes, C.S.A.
Sr. M. IRENE KOHNE, C.S.A., Admin.
Rev. JOACHIM STRUPP, O.F.M.Cap., Chap.
Sisters 1
Residents 70
St. Clare Terrace
Residents 34
Independent Elderly Apartments 30
Total Staff 3

Green Bay
Diocese of Green Bay

McClosky Program, Inc.
2560 Shawano Ave., P.O. Box 10357
Green Bay, WI 54313
Tel: 920-434-8208
Sr. PATRICIA DOLAN, O.L.C., Dir.
Sr. ELLEN P. STAPELTON, Business Mgr.
A Community based residential facility for women 18 years old and over who are pregnant or in a crisis situation and in need of transitional supervision and guidance. Needs addressed are personal and family problems. Also, shelter offered during crisis or unemployment.
Total assisted 10

The McCormick Memorial Home for the Aged
212 Iroquois Ave.
Green Bay, WI 54301-1918
Tel: 920-437-0883; Fax: 920-437-2696
JAMES GENRICH, Admin.
Rev. THADDEUS J. KOSZAREK, Chap.
Sisters of St. Francis of the Holy Cross 1
Lay Helpers 28
Residents 60

Our Lady of Charity Center, Inc.
2560 Shawano Ave., P.O. Box 10357
Green Bay, WI 54313
Tel: 920-434-8208
Sr. BARBARA JEAN ARNSMEYER, O.L.C., Dir.
Sr. ELLEN PATRICK STAPELTON, Business Mgr.
Total assisted 20

Greenfield
Archdiocese of Milwaukee

Clement Manor Health Center
3939 S. 92nd St.
Greenfield, WI 53228
Tel: 414-321-1800
Sponsored by School Sisters of St. Francis
Corporate Title: Villa Clement, Inc.
WILLIAM H. LANGE, Pres. & CEO
Mr. DENNIS FERGER, Admin.
Rev. DANIEL T. MURPHY, Chap.
Sisters 3
Residents 168
Adult Day Care 50
Child Day Care 35

Clement Manor Retirement Community
9339-9405 W. Howard Ave.
Greenfield, WI 53228
Tel: 414-546-7375
Corporate Title: Villa Clement, Inc. Sponsored by the School Sisters of St. Francis
Mr. DENNIS FERGER, Admin.
DANIEL T. MURPHY, Chap.
Sisters 3
Residents 235
Apartments 201

Hillsboro
Diocese of La Crosse

St. Joseph's Nursing Home
P.O. Box 527
Hillsboro, WI 54634
(See Hospital Listing.)

Janesville
Diocese of Madison

St. Elizabeth Home
502 St. Lawrence Ave.
Janesville, WI 53545
Tel: 608-752-6709
Rev. JAMES J. MATTUCCI, Chap.
Aged Residents 43

Kaukauna
Diocese of Green Bay

St. Paul Home, Inc.
1211 Oakridge Ave.
Kaukauna, WI 54130-9961
Tel: 920-766-6020; Fax: 920-766-9161
Sr. PATRICIA SEVCIK, Pastoral Care Dir.
JAMES J. FETT, Admin.
Rev. PAUL SCHULZE, S.D.S., Chap.
Skilled care nursing home; 24 hour nursing service.
St. Paul Manor
509 W. Wisconsin Ave.
Kaukauna, WI 54130-1999
Tel: 920-766-6027
Franciscan Sisters of Christian Charity 5
Total Assisted 28
JAMES J. FETT, Admin.
Sr. MARY HUGH KERKHOF, O.S.F., Manor Service Coord.
Community based residential facility (CBRF): assisted living for men, women, and couples with no age limit.
Franciscan Sisters of Christian Charity 5
Licensed Capacity 129
Aged Residents 129

Kenosha
Archdiocese of Milwaukee

St. Joseph's Adult Day Care Center, Inc.
9244 29th Ave.
Kenosha, WI 53144
Tel: 414-694-6000
Ms. JOYCE MITCHELL, Dir.
Sponsored by: Carmelite Sisters of the Divine Heart of Jesus
Total Assisted 75
Total Staff 13

St. Joseph's Home for the Aged
9244 29th Ave.
Kenosha, WI 53143
Tel: 414-694-0080
E-mail: apanites@ix.netcom.com
Corporate Title: Carmelite Sisters of the Divine Heart of Jesus.
Sr. MARY EMMANUEL APANITES, D.C.J., Admin.
Sr. M. JACINTA CUSUMANO, D.C.J., Supr.
Rev. BRONISLAW SLODOWSKI
Sisters 5
Residents 93
Adult Day Care 45
Total Staff 150
St. Joseph's Villa, Independent living units
Apartments 44

La Crosse
Diocese of La Crosse

Bethany-St. Joseph Care Center
2501 Shelby Rd.
La Crosse, WI 54601
Tel: 608-788-5700
THOMAS RAND, Admin.
Rev. THOMAS J. SMITH, Chap., Tel: 608-788-4555
Bed Capacity 226
Patients assisted annually 247

Elder Care of North La Crosse, Inc. (Village on St. James)
800 St. James St.
La Crosse, WI 54603
Tel: 608-791-9784
RICHARD BERENDES, Admin. Extended Care
Units 24

Franciscan Elder Care, Inc.
800 West Avenue S.
La Crosse, WI 54601-4796
Tel: 608-791-9774
RICHARD D. ALLEN, Vice Pres.
RICHARD BERENDES, Admin. Extended Care
Total Staff 9
Subsidized Units 144
Village on Cass
225 S. 24th St.
La Crosse, WI,
Village on 9th
621 S. 9th St.
La Crosse, WI,
Village Apartments
Village Apartments

Franciscan Skemp Healthcare, Mayo Health System, La Crosse Campus Nursing Home
620 S. 11th St.
La Crosse, WI 54601
Tel: 608-791-9787
ROBERTA MESSER, Admin.
Bed Capacity 95
Patients assisted annually 215

St. Joseph's Nursing Home
2902 East Ave., S.
La Crosse, WI 54601
Tel: 608-788-9870
Operated by Catholic Residential Services, Inc., Diocese of La Crosse.
JAMES S. BIALECKI, Admin.

Rev. THOMAS J. SMITH, Chap., Tel: 608-788-4555
Patients assisted annually 80
Units 80

Lomira
Archdiocese of Milwaukee

Hope Nursing Home, Inc.
438 Ashford Ave., P.O. Box 280
Lomira, WI 53048-0280
Tel: 414-269-4386; Fax: 414-269-4616
Sr. ANN JOSEPHA LENCIONI, Admin.
Sisters of Charity of St. Joan Antida 2
Patients assisted annually 42
Total Staff 48

Madison
Diocese of Madison

St. Marys Care Center
1347 Fish Hatchery Rd.
Madison, WI 53715
Tel: 608-257-0781
Owned and operated by SSM Health Care Corporation, Member of the SSM Health Care.
WILLIAM BENDER, Admin.

Manitowoc
Diocese of Green Bay

Felician Village Inc.
1700 S. 18th St.
Manitowoc, WI 54220
Tel: 920-684-7171
Sr. MARY CLAUDE SZYPERSKI, C.S.S.F., Dir.
Apartments 134
Villagers 180

St. Mary's Home for the Aged
2005 Division St.
Manitowoc, WI 54220-5699
Tel: 920-684-7171; Fax: 920-684-0240
Sr. NOEL MARIE GABRIEL, C.S.S.F., Admin.
Rev. THOMAS WOJCIECHOWSKI, O.F.M., Chap.
Sisters 23
Aged Residents 266

Milwaukee
Archdiocese of Milwaukee

Adult Day Services and Resource Center
1919 N. 60th St.
Milwaukee, WI 53208
Tel: 414-464-8004
Sponsored by Catholic Charities of the Archdiocese of Milwaukee

Alexian Village of Milwaukee, Inc.
9301 N. 76th St.
Milwaukee, WI 53223
Tel: 414-355-9300
Congregation of Alexian Brothers, Immaculate Conception Province
Mr. GARY MOHN, CEO
Rev. JOE JAGODENSKY, S.D.S., Chap.
Nursing Home and Life Care Facility
Units 317
Residents 341
Brothers 3
Total Staff 278

Daystar, Inc.
P.O. Box 11709
Milwaukee, WI 53217
Tel: 414-228-8887
Transitional living program for battered women without children, for up to two years.
Residents 16
Total Staff 4

Marian Catholic Center, Inc.
3333 W. Highland Blvd.
Milwaukee, WI 53208
Tel: 414-344-8100
Corporate Title: Marian Catholic Center, Inc.
Sponsored by Franciscan Sisters, Daughters of the Sacred Hearts of Jesus and Mary, Wheaton, IL.
MICHAEL R. ZIMMERMAN, Admin.
Residents 309
Total Staff 357

Marian Franciscan Center, Inc.
9632 W. Appleton Ave.
Milwaukee, WI 53225
Tel: 414-461-8850
JAMES D. GRESHAM, Pres.
Franciscan Sisters, Daughters of the Sacred Hearts of Jesus and Mary, Wheaton, IL
Residents 329
Total Staff 416

**Milwaukee Catholic Home*
2462 N. Prospect Ave.
Milwaukee, WI 53211-4462
Tel: 414-224-9700
Mr. PAUL J. CONNOLLY, N.H.A., Exec. Dir.
Rev. CHARLES R. KEEFE, Dir. Pastoral Care
Corporate Title: Milwaukee Catholic Home, Inc.
Retirement Home Residents 131
Retirement Home Total Staff 92
Nursing Home Residents 72
Nursing Home Total Staff 45
Day Care (Adult) 3
Assisted Living 10

Rosalie Manor, Inc.
4803 W. Burleigh St.
Milwaukee, WI 53210
Tel: 414-449-2868
E-mail: rosaliemanor@aeronet
ROSEMARIE FISHER, Dir.
Community Programs for Single and First-Time Parents and an abstinence-based pregnancy prevention program for youth.
Franciscan Sisters Daughters of the Sacred Hearts of Jesus & Mary of Wheaton, IL.
Total Assisted 2,113 families per year
Total Staff 62

Sacred Heart Rehabilitation Institute, Inc.
2350 N. Lake Dr.
Milwaukee, WI 53211
Tel: 414-298-6700
Daughters of Charity of St. Vincent de Paul.
WILLIAM H. LANGE, Adm.
Sr. MARGARET ANN ARNOLD, Chap.
Sisters 1
Bed Capacity 81
Patients assisted annually 14,000
Total Staff 300
Satellite Locations:
Sacred Heart Rehabilitation Institute
Lakeland Medical Center, Hwy. NN
Elkhorn, WI 53121
Sacred Heart Rehabilitation Institute
Memorial Hosp. at Oconomowoc, 791 E. Summit Ave.
Oconomowoc, WI 53066

St. Ann Rest Home
2020 S. Muskego Ave.
Milwaukee, WI 53204
Tel: 414-383-2630
Conducted by the Dominican Sisters (Congregation of the Immaculate Conception)
Sr. M. COLUMBA, O.P., Admin.
Sisters 6
Residents 54
Total Staff 47

St. Anne's Home for the Elderly
3800 N. 92nd St.
Milwaukee, WI 53222
Tel: 414-463-7570; Fax: 414-463-2311
E-mail: mah@execpc.com
Web Site: www.wahsa.org/st.anne/index.html
Sisters of the Divine Savior
Mr. MICHAEL W. BERRY, Admin.
Rev. RUSSELL F. WITON, Chap.
Retired Priests 16
Terrace-Independent Living Apartments 16
Residents 106
Total Staff 180

St. Charles Youth and Family Services
151 S. 84th St., P.O. Box 14005
Milwaukee, WI 53214
Tel: 414-476-3710
E-mail: jamesms@aol.com
Mr. JAMES M. SAMPSON, Pres.
Residents 78
Girls in Holy Cross Group Home 12
Total Assisted 750
Total Staff 200

St. Mary's Nursing Home
3515 W. Hadley St.
Milwaukee, WI 53210
Tel: 414-873-9250; Fax: 414-873-6876
Corporate Title: St. Mary's Nursing Home of Milwaukee, Inc.
Sisters of the Divine Savior
Mr. MICHAEL BERRY
In res.,
Most Rev. ARNOLD COTY, S.D.S.
Rev. DANIEL CARROLL, S.D.S.
Residents 103
Total Staff 199

The Terrace at St. Francis, Inc.
3200 S. 20th St.
Milwaukee, WI 53215
Fax: 414-389-3300
Sponsored by the Congregation of the Sisters of St. Felix of Cantalice of the United States of America, Inc., Chicago Province (Felician Sisters).
Skilled Nursing Facility for Transitional & Extended Subacute Care.
Sr. M. RAMONA DOMBROWSKI, C.S.S.F., Pres.
Beds 81

Villa St. Francis, Inc.
1910 W. Ohio Ave.
Milwaukee, WI 53215
Fax: 414-649-2880
Sr. MARY RAMONA DOMBROWSKI, C.S.S.F., Pres.
Sponsored by the Congregation of the Sisters of St. Felix of Cantalice of the United States of America, Inc. Chicago Province (Felician Sisters)
Independent & Assisted Living Facility
Resident Apartments 142
Total Staff 63

Mount Calvary
Archdiocese of Milwaukee

Cristo Rey Ranch, Inc.
N8102 Calvary St.
Mount Calvary, WI 53057
Tel: 920-753-2026; 753-3211; Fax: 920-753-3100
Sister Servants of Christ the King
A day treatment and respite home to provide treatment and care of children/adolescents.
Total Assisted 50
Total Staff 5

Villa Loretto Nursing Home
N8114 Calvary St.
Mount Calvary, WI 53057
Tel: 920-753-3211; Fax: 920-753-3100
E-mail: sister@thesurf.com
Sr. MARY ROSE, Supr.
Sisters 7
Residents 52
Total Assisted 63
Total Staff 77
Corporate Title: Sister Servants of Christ the King, Inc. dba Villa Loretto.

Neenah
Diocese of Green Bay

Assisi Homes of Neenah, Inc.
210 Byrd Ave.
Neenah, WI 54946
Tel: 920-821-0336
SHERRI BEYER, Mgr.
(An independent living community for Seniors.)
Total in residence 38

Villa Saint Clare, Inc.
130 Byrd Ave.
Neenah, WI 54952
SHERRI BEYER, Mgr.
Special care facility, affordable housing with supportive accommodations in an independent setting for seniors 55+.
Total in Residence 45
Staff 12

New London
Diocese of Green Bay

St. Joseph Residence, Inc., New London
107 E. Beckert Rd.
New London, WI 54961
Tel: 920-982-5354
E-mail: sjradm@athenet.net
Mr. DANIEL W. ORR, CEO
Total in Residence 60
Staff 23
Nursing Care:
Total Assisted 107
Staff 163

Niagara
Diocese of Green Bay

Maryhill Manor (SNF)
501 Madison Ave.
Niagara, WI 54151
Tel: 715-251-3178; Fax: 715-251-1200
Sponsored by School Sisters of St. Francis, Milwaukee.
LARRY D. WELSH, CEO
Nursing Care:
Total Assisted 26,645
Staff 91
Elderly Residents 75

Onalaska
Diocese of La Crosse

Franciscan Skemp Healthcare, Mayo Health System, Onalaska Nursing Home
1600 Main St.
Onalaska, WI 54650
Tel: 608-783-4681
LARRY ALENS, Admin.
Beds 112
Patients assisted annually 259

Oshkosh
Diocese of Green Bay

The Convent Project, Inc.
435 High Ave.
Oshkosh, WI 54901
Tel: 920-235-6002
For victims of domestic abuse
BARBARA BAKER, Sec.
Total Assisted 28

Portage
Diocese of Madison

Divine Savior Nursing Home
715 W. Pleasant St.
Portage, WI 53901
Tel: 608-742-4131
(See Divine Savior Hospital, Portage.)
Aged Residents 124

Racine
Archdiocese of Milwaukee

Marian Housing Center, Inc
4105 Spring St.
Racine, WI 53405
Tel: 414-633-5807
STEVE KUKLIN, Pres.
Franciscan Sisters, Daughters of the Sacred Hearts of Jesus and Mary, Wheaton, IL.
HUD subsidized housing for the elderly
Residents 40

St. Monica's Senior Citizens Home, Inc.
3920 N. Green Bay Rd.
Racine, WI 53404
Tel: 414-639-5050
Non-Profit Corp.
Sr. IRENE HANIKA, O.S.A., Supr. and Admin.
Rev. RICHARD ZELONIS, S.C.J., Chap.
Sisters of St. Rita 6
Residents 110
Total Staff 45

South Milwaukee
Archdiocese of Milwaukee

Franciscan Villa of South Milwaukee, Inc.
3601 S. Chicago Ave.
South Milwaukee, WI 53172
Tel: 414-764-4100
ROGER L. DEMARK, Pres. & CEO
Catholic Health Corporation
Residents 150
Adult Day Care 30
Child Day Care 36
Affiliate of Catholic Health Initiatives.

Sparta
Diocese of La Crosse

Elder Care of Sparta, Inc.
622 S. Court
Sparta, WI 54656
Tel: 608-791-9774
RICHARD BERENDES, Admin. Extended Care
Units 24

Franciscan Skemp Healthcare, Mayo Health System, Sparta Campus Nursing Home
310 W. Main St., P.O. Box 529
Sparta, WI 54656-2142
Tel: 608-269-2132
SUSAN STEIVANG, Admin.
Rev. MARK A. WALLJASPER, Chap.
Bed Capacity 49

St. Francis
Archdiocese of Milwaukee

Canticle Court, Inc.
3201 S. Lake Dr.
St. Francis, WI 53235
Tel: 414-744-9959; Fax: 414-744-7636
E-mail: junipe29@mail.idt.net
An Apartment building sponsored by the Sisters of St. Francis of Assisi funded by HUD for low income elderly persons who can live independently
Units 48
Total in Residence 49
Total Staff 2

Juniper Court, Inc.
3209 S. Lake Dr.
St. Francis, WI 53235-3702
Tel: 414-744-5878; Fax: 414-744-7636
E-mail: junipe29@mail.idt.net
Sr. ANNE MARY RISCHAR, O.S.F., Pres.
An apartment building with congregate meal site for persons of low to moderate income who can live independently.
Sponsored by the Sisters of St. Francis of Assisi, St. Francis, WI.
Total in Residence 58
Total Units 53
Total Staff 2

St. Ann Center for Intergenerational Care, Inc.
3221 S. Lake Dr.
St. Francis, WI 53235
Tel: 414-482-1340; Fax: 414-482-9351
Sr. EDNA LONERGAN, O.S.F., Dir.
Sisters of St. Francis of Assisi, St. Francis, WI
Total Assisted 150
Total Staff 26

Stoughton
Diocese of Madison

Nazareth House
814 Jackson St.
Stoughton, WI 53589
Tel: 608-873-6448; Fax: 608-873-0829
Poor Sisters of Nazareth
Sr. MARGARET BRODY, P.S.N., Supr.
Sisters 6
Aged Residents 99

Superior
Diocese of Superior

St. Francis Home, Inc.
1800 New York Ave.
Superior, WI 54880
Tel: 715-394-5591
KURT GRAVES, CEO
Deacon PHIL L. MARTINEAU, Supvr. Pastoral Care
Bed Capacity 192

Two Rivers
Diocese of Green Bay

Sisters Treatment Group Home
3904 Martin Ln.
Two Rivers, WI 54241
Tel: 920-794-1524
Co-Directors:
Sr. IRMINA BULA, S.S.J.-T.O.S.F.
Sr. EDMUND ANTONIEWICZ, S.S.J.-T.O.S.F.
For physically and mentally handicapped.
Children 5
Adults 2
Staff 5
Total assisted 7

Watertown
Diocese of Madison

St. Joseph's Home
705 Clyman St.
Watertown, WI 53094
Tel: 414-261-4283
Sisters of Charity of Our Lady, Mother of the Church
Rev. RAYMOND ASHENBRENNER, O.P., Chap.
Sisters 3
Aged Residents 28

Wausau
Diocese of La Crosse

Marywood Convalescent Center
1821 N. 4th Ave.
Wausau, WI 54401
Tel: 715-675-9451
KATHRYN L. SPRAGUE, Admin.
Operated by Catholic Residential Services, Inc.
Units 90
Patients assisted annually 131

Wauwatosa
Archdiocese of Milwaukee

St. Camillus Health Center, Inc.
10101 W. Wisconsin Ave.
Wauwatosa, WI 53226
Tel: 414-258-1814
Skilled Nursing Home
Order of the Servants of the Sick (Order of St. Camillus)
Very Rev. WILLIAM F. CRONIN, O.S.Cam., M.S.W., Pres. & Prov.
RICK JOHNSON, CEO
Ms. KATHLEEN SULLIVAN, Dir. of Pastoral Care, C.P.E. Program Sup.
Chaplains:
Revs.:
CLAUDE PULVERMACHER, O.F.M.Cap.
CARLO NOTARO, O.S.Cam.
Ms. BARBARA BAUDHUIN
Ms. SALLY REDMOND
In res.,
Revs.:
GEORGE A. KOLANDA
JOHN O'BRIEN, S.J.
PETER T. AMRHEIN
LEON BRIELMAIER
WALTER GAWINEK
Patients assisted annually 386
Total Staff 638

San Camillo, Inc.
10200 W. Bluemound Rd.
Wauwatosa, WI 53226
Tel: 414-259-6300
Order of the Servants of the Sick (Order of St. Camillus)
Very Rev. WILLIAM CRONIN, O.S.Cam., M.S.W., Pres. & Prov. Supr.
MARIE D'AMICO, Vice Pres. Housing
Rev. CARLO NOTARO, O.S.Cam., Chap.
Independent living facilities for older adults.
Residents 560
Total Assisted 1,860
Total Staff 128

West Allis
Archdiocese of Milwaukee

St. Joan Antida Home, Inc.
6700 W. Beloit Rd.
West Allis, WI 53219
Tel: 414-541-6575; 541-9840; Fax: 414-541-8040
Mr. MAX TAGLIN, Admin.
Sr. ANNE-MARIE DOYLE, O.P., Chap.
Sisters of Charity of St. Joan Antida 3
Residents 73
Total Staff 100

Villa Clement Health Center
9047 W. Greenfield Ave.
West Allis, WI 53214
Tel: 414-453-9290
Corporate Title: Villa Clement Health Center
WILLIAM LANGE, Pres. & CEO
JAMES LEHMKUHL, Admin.
Rev. LUIS PACHECO-SANCHEZ, Chap.
Skilled Nursing Home
Sponsored by School Sisters of St. Francis
Sisters 12
Residents 194

WYOMING

Casper
Diocese of Cheyenne

St. Anthony Manor
211 E. Sixth St.
Casper, WY 82601
Tel: 307-237-0843
Rev. Msgr. JAMES O'NEILL
Administrators:
PATRICIA JOHNSTON
LOU ANN TOOKER
Total Staff 6
Total in Residence 64

Cheyenne
Diocese of Cheyenne

Holy Trinity Manor
2516 E. 18th St.
Cheyenne, WY 82001
Tel: 307-778-8850
Sr. RUTH ANN HEHN, S.C.L., Admin.
Total Staff 1
Total in Residence 30

Torrington
Diocese of Cheyenne

St. Joseph's Children's Home
Box 1117
Torrington, WY 82240-1117

Tel: 307-532-4197; Fax: 307-532-8405
E-mail: stjch@prairieweb.com

ROBERT C. MAYOR, Exec. Dir.
Children 62

Total Staff 133
Total Assisted 100

Diocesan Abbreviations

ARCHDIOCESES AND DIOCESES

(ALB) .... Albany (New York)
(ALN) .... Allentown (Pennsylvania)
(ALT) .... Altoona-Johnstown (Pennsylvania)
(ALX) .... Alexandria (Louisiana)
(AGN) .... Agana (Guam)
(AMA) .... Amarillo (Texas)
(ANC) .... Anchorage (Alaska)
(ARE) .... Arecibo (Puerto Rico)
(ARL) .... Arlington (Virginia)
(ARM) .... Armenian Catholic Exarchate (Pennsylvania)
(ATH) .... Apostolate To Hungarians (Washington, DC)
(ATL) .... Atlanta (Georgia)
(AUS) .... Austin (Texas)
(B) .... Boise (Idaho)
(BAK) .... Baker (Oregon)
(BAL) .... Baltimore (Maryland)
(BEA) .... Beaumont (Texas)
(BEL) .... Belleville (Illinois)
(BGP) .... Bridgeport (Connecticut)
(BIR) .... Birmingham (Alabama)
(BIS) .... Bismarck (North Dakota)
(BLX) .... Biloxi (Mississippi)
(BO) .... Boston (Massachusetts)
(BR) .... Baton Rouge (Louisiana)
(BRK) .... Brooklyn (New York)
(BUF) .... Buffalo (New York)
(BUR) .... Burlington (Vermont)
(BWN) .... Brownsville (Texas)
(CAM) .... Camden (New Jersey)
(CC) .... Corpus Christi (Texas)
(CGS) .... Caguas (Puerto Rico)
(CHI) .... Chicago (Illinois)
(CHK) .... Chalan Kanoa
(CHL) .... Charlotte (North Carolina)
(CHR) .... Charleston (South Carolina)
(CHY) .... Cheyenne (Wyoming)
(CI) .... Caroline Islands
(CIN) .... Cincinnati (Ohio)
(CLV) .... Cleveland (Ohio)
(COL) .... Columbus (Ohio)
(COS) .... Colorado Springs (Colorado)
(COV) .... Covington (Kentucky)
(CR) .... Crookston (Minnesota)
(DAL) .... Dallas (Texas)
(DAV) .... Davenport (Iowa)
(DEN) .... Denver (Colorado)
(DET) .... Detroit (Michigan)
(DM) .... Des Moines (Iowa)
(DOD) .... Dodge City (Kansas)
(DUB) .... Dubuque (Iowa)
(DUL) .... Duluth (Minnesota)
(E) .... Erie (Pennsylvania)
(ELP) .... El Paso (Texas)
(EST) .... Eparchy of Saint Thomas the Apostle
(EVN) .... Evansville (Indiana)
(FAR) .... Fargo (North Dakota)
(FBK) .... Fairbanks (Alaska)
(FgM) .... Foreign Mission Section
(FR) .... Fall River (Massachusetts)
(FRS) .... Fresno (California)
(FTW) .... Fort Wayne-South Bend (Indiana)
(FWT) .... Fort Worth (Texas)
(GAL) .... Galveston-Houston (Texas)
(GAY) .... Gaylord (Michigan)
(GB) .... Green Bay (Wisconsin)
(GBG) .... Greensburg (Pennsylvania)
(GF) .... Great Falls-Billings (Montana)
(GI) .... Grand Island (Nebraska)
(GLP) .... Gallup (New Mexico)
(GR) .... Grand Rapids (Michigan)
(GRY) .... Gary (Indiana)
(HBG) .... Harrisburg (Pennsylvania)
(HEL) .... Helena (Montana)
(HON) .... Honolulu (Hawaii)
(HRT) .... Hartford (Connecticut)
(HT) .... Houma-Thibodaux (Louisiana)
(IND) .... Indianapolis (Indiana)
(JC) .... Jefferson City (Missouri)
(JKS) .... Jackson (Mississippi)
(JOL) .... Joliet in Illinois
(JUN) .... Juneau (Alaska)
(KAL) .... Kalamazoo (Michigan)
(KC) .... Kansas City-St. Joseph (Missouri)
(KCK) .... Kansas City in Kansas
(KNX) .... Knoxville (Tennessee)
(L) .... Louisville (Kentucky)
(LA) .... Los Angeles (California)
(LAF) .... Lafayette (Louisiana)
(LAN) .... Lansing (Michigan)
(LC) .... La Crosse (Wisconsin)
(LEX) .... Lexington (Kentucky)
(LFT) .... Lafayette in Indiana
(LIN) .... Lincoln (Nebraska)
(LIT) .... Lithuanian Apostolate for Lithuanian Catholics
(LKC) .... Lake Charles (Louisiana)
(LR) .... Little Rock (Arkansas)
(LSC) .... Las Cruces (New Mexico)
(LUB) .... Lubbock (Texas)
(LAV) .... Las Vegas (Nevada)
(MAD) .... Madison (Wisconsin)
(MAN) .... Manchester (New Hampshire)
(MAR) .... Marquette (Michigan)
(MEM) .... Memphis (Tennessee)
(MET) .... Metuchen (New Jersey)
(MGZ) .... Mayaguez (Puerto Rico)
(MI) .... Marshall Islands
(MIA) .... Miami (Florida)
(MIL) .... Milwaukee (Wisconsin)
(MO) .... Military Services (Maryland)
(MOB) .... Mobile (Alabama)
(MRY) .... Monterey in California
(NEW) .... Newark (New Jersey)
(NO) .... New Orleans (Louisiana)
(NOR) .... Norwich (Connecticut)
(NSH) .... Nashville (Tennessee)
(NTN) .... Newton (Melkite, United States)
(NU) .... New Ulm (Minnesota)
(NY) .... New York (New York)
(OAK) .... Oakland (California)
(OG) .... Ogdensburg (New York)
(OKL) .... Oklahoma City (Oklahoma)
(OLD) .... Our Lady of Deliverance *Syriac* (Union City, New Jersey)
(OLL) .... Our Lady of Lebanon of Los Angeles (California)
(OM) .... Omaha (Nebraska)
(ORG) .... Orange in California
(ORL) .... Orlando (Florida)
(OWN) .... Owensboro (Kentucky)
(P) .... Portland in Oregon
(PAT) .... Paterson (New Jersey)
(PBL) .... Pueblo (Colorado)
(PBR) .... Pittsburgh *Byzantine* (Pennsylvania)
(PCE) .... Ponce (Puerto Rico)
(PEO) .... Peoria (Illinois)
(PH) .... Philadelphia (Pennsylvania)
(PHU) .... Philadelphia *Ukrainian* (Pennsylvania)
(PHX) .... Phoenix (Arizona)
(PIT) .... Pittsburgh (Pennsylvania)
(PMB) .... Palm Beach (Florida)
(PP) .... Personal Prelatures
(PRM) .... Parma *Byzantine* (Ohio)
(PRO) .... Providence (Rhode Island)
(PRT) .... Portland (Maine)
(PSC) .... Passaic *Byzantine* (New Jersey)
(PT) .... Pensacola-Tallahassee (Florida)
(R) .... Raleigh (North Carolina)
(RC) .... Rapid City (South Dakota)
(RCK) .... Rockford (Illinois)
(RIC) .... Richmond (Virginia)
(RNO) .... Reno (Nevada)
(ROC) .... Rochester (New York)
(ROM) .... Romanian (Byzantine) (Ohio)
(RVC) .... Rockville Centre (New York)
(SAC) .... Sacramento (California)
(SAG) .... Saginaw (Michigan)
(SAL) .... Salina (Kansas)
(SAM) .... St. Maron of Brooklyn (U.S.A.), Eparchy of
(SAN) .... San Angelo (Texas)
(SAT) .... San Antonio (Texas)
(SAV) .... Savannah (Georgia)
(SB) .... San Bernadino (California)
(SC) .... Sioux City (Iowa)
(SCL) .... St. Cloud (Minnesota)
(SCR) .... Scranton (Pennsylvania)
(SD) .... San Diego (California)
(SEA) .... Seattle (Washington)
(SFD) .... Springfield in Illinois
(SFE) .... Santa Fe (New Mexico)
(SFR) .... San Francisco (California)
(SFS) .... Sioux Falls (South Dakota)
(SHP) .... Shreveport (Louisiana)
(SJ) .... San Jose in California
(SJN) .... San Juan (Puerto Rico)
(SJP) .... St. Josaphat in Parma (Ohio)
(SLC) .... Salt Lake City (Utah)
(SP) .... St. Petersburg (Florida)
(SPC) .... Sprgfld-Cape Girardeau (Missouri)
(SPK) .... Spokane (Washington)
(SPP) .... Samoa-Pago Pago
(SPR) .... Springfield in Massachusetts
(SR) .... Santa Rosa in California
(STA) .... St. Augustine (Florida)
(STF) .... Stamford *Ukrainian* (Connecticut)
(STL) .... St. Louis (Missouri)
(STN) .... St. Nicholas in Chicago *Ukrainian*
(STO) .... Stockton (California)
(STP) .... St. Paul and Minneapolis (Minnesota)
(STU) .... Steubenville (Ohio)
(STV) .... St. Thomas, Virgin Islands
(SUP) .... Superior (Wisconsin)
(SY) .... Syracuse (New York)
(TLS) .... Tulsa (Oklahoma)
(TOL) .... Toledo (Ohio)
(TR) .... Trenton (New Jersey)
(TUC) .... Tucson (Arizona)
(TYL) .... Tyler (Texas)
(VEN) .... Venice (Florida)
(VIC) .... Victoria in Texas
(VNN) .... Van Nuys *Byzantine* (California)
(WCH) .... Wichita (Kansas)
(WDC) .... Washington (District of Columbia)
(WH) .... Wheeling-Charleston (West Virginia)
(WIL) .... Wilmington (Delaware)
(WIN) .... Winona (Minnesota)
(WOR) .... Worcester (Massachusetts)
(Y) .... Youngstown (Ohio)
(YAK) .... Yakima (Washington)

An Alphabetical List of Diocesan and Religious Priests of the United States

REPORTED TO THE PUBLISHERS FOR THIS ISSUE
(Cardinals, Archbishops, Bishops, Archabbots and Abbots are listed in previous section)
ABBREVIATIONS

aa.a. Assumptionists.
b.g.s. Little Brothers of the Good Shepherd.
b.s.o. Basilian Salvatorian Fathers.
c.f.a. Alexian Brothers.
c.f.c. Congregation of Christian Brothers.
c.f.m.m. Brothers of the Poor of St. Francis.
c.f.p. Brothers of the Poor of St. Francis.
c.f.r. Franciscan Friars of the Renewal.
c.f.x. Brothers of St. Francis Xavier.
c.i.c.m. Missionhurst Congregation of the Immaculate Heart of Mary.
c.j. Josephite Fathers.
c.j.m. Congregation of Jesus and Mary, Eudist Fathers.
c.m. Congregation of the Mission, Vincentian Fathers.
c.m.c. Congregation of Mother Coredemptrix.
c.m.f. Claretian Missionaries, Missionary Sons of the Immaculate Heart of Mary.
c.m.i. Carmelites of Mary Immaculate.
c.m.m. Congregation of Mariannhill Missionaries, Mariannhill Fathers and Brothers.
c.m.vd. Mekhitarist Fathers.
c.o. Oratorians.
c.p. Congregation of the Passion, Passionist Fathers.
c.p.m. Congregation of the Fathers of Mercy.
c.pp.s. Society of the Precious Blood.
c.r. Congregation of the Resurrection, Resurrectionist Fathers.
c.r. Theatine Fathers.
c.r.i.c. Canons Regular of the Immaculate Conception.
c.r.l. Canons Regular of the Lateran.
c.r.m. Adorno Fathers.
c.r.s. Somascan Fathers, Order of St. Jerome Aemilian.
c.r.s.p. Clerics Regular of St. Paul, Barnabite Fathers.
c.s. Missionaries of St. Charles-Scalabrinians.
c.s.b. Basilian Fathers.
c.s.c. Priests and Brothers of the Congregation of Holy Cross.
c.s.j. Congregation of St. Joseph.
c.s.p. Paulist Fathers.
c.s.p.x. Brothers of Saint Pius X.
c.s.s. Stigmatine Fathers and Brothers, Congregation of the Sacred Stigmata.
c.s.sp. Holy Ghost Fathers, Congregation of the Holy Ghost.
c.ss.r. Redemptorist Fathers.
c.s.v. Clerics of St. Viator, Viatorian Fathers.
d.l.p. Diocesan Labor Priests.
er.cam. Camaldolese Hermits of the Congregation of Monte Corona.
f.c. Brothers of Charity.
f.d.p. Sons of Divine Providence.
f.f.i. Franciscan Friars of the Immaculate
f.f.s.c. Franciscan Brothers of the Holy Cross.
f.i.c. Brothers of Christian Instruction.
f.j. Congregation of St. John.
f.m.j. The Monastic Fraternity of Jerusalem.
f.m.m. Brothers of Mercy.
f.m.s. Marist Brothers.
f.m.s.i. Sons of Mary Missionary Society.
f.s.c. Brothers of the Christian Schools.
f.s.e. Brothers of the Holy Eucharist.
f.s.p. Brothers of St. Patrick.
f.s.r. Brothers of the Congregation of Our Lady of the Holy Rosary.
glmy. The Glenmary Home Missioners.
i.c. Institute of Charity.
i.h.m. Brothers of the Immaculate Heart of Mary.
i.m.c. Consolata Missionaries.
l.b.s.f. Little Brothers of Saint Francis.
l.c. Legionaries of Christ.
m.afr. Missionaries of Africa.
m.c.b.s. Missionary Congregation of the Blessed Sacrament.
m.c.c.j. Comboni Missionaries of the Heart of Jesus.
m.d. Mercedarios Descalzos.
m.e.p. Paris Foreign Mission Society.
m.g. Guadalupe Missioners.
m.h.m. Mill Hill Missionaries.
m.i.c. Congregation of Marians of the Immaculate Conception.
m.j. Missionaries of St. Joseph.
m.m. Maryknoll Fathers, Catholic Foreign Mission Society of America.
m.s. The Missionaries of Our Lady La Salette.
m.s.c. Missionaries of the Sacred Heart.
m.s.c. Missionary Servants of Christ.
m.s.f. Congregation of the Missionaries of the Holy Family.
m.s.p. Missionaries of St. Paul.
m.sp.s. Missionaries of the Holy Spirit.
m.ss.a. Missionaries of the Holy Apostles.
m.ss.cc. Missionaries of the Sacred Hearts of Jesus and Mary.
o.a.r. Order of the Augustinian Recollects.
o.carm. Carmelite Fathers and Brothers.
o.cart. Order of Carthusians.
o.c.d. Discalced Carmelite Friars.
o.cist. Cistercian Fathers.
o.c.s.o. The Cistercians Order of the Strict Observance, Trappists.
o.de.m. Order of Our Lady of Mercy.
o.f.m. Franciscan Friars, Order of Friars Minor.
o.f.m.cap. The Capuchin Friars, Franciscan Fathers.
o.f.m-.conv. Conventual Franciscans, Friars Minor Conventual.
o.h. Hospitaller Brothers of St. John of God.
o.i.c. Order of the Imitation of Christ.
o.l.c. Brothers of Our Lady of Providence.
o.m. Minim Fathers.
o.mar. Congregation of Maronite Monks.
o.m.i. Oblates of Mary Immaculate.
o.m.v. Oblates of the Virgin Mary.
o.p. Order of Preachers, Dominican Fathers.
o.praem. Canons Regular of Premontre, Premonstratensians, Norbertines.
o.r.c. Operarios del Reina de Cristo.
o.s.a. The Augustinians.
o.s.b. Benedictine Monks, Olivetan Benedictines, Sylvestrine Benedictines.
o.s.b.cam. Camaldolese Hermits.
o.s.b.m. Order of St. Basil the Great.
o.s.c. Canons Regular of the Order of the Holy Cross, Crosier Fathers.
o.s.cam. Camillian Fathers and Brothers.
o.s.f. Religious Brothers of the Third Order Regular of St. Francis.
o.s.f. Franciscan Brothers of Christ the King.
o.s.f. Franciscan Brothers of the Third Order Regular.
o.s.f. Franciscan Missionary Brothers of the Sacred Heart of Jesus.
o.s.f.s. Oblates of St. Francis de Sales.
o.s.j. Oblates of St. Joseph.
o.s.m. Servite Fathers.
o.s.p.p.e. Pauline Fathers.
o.ss.s. Brigittine Monks.
o.ss.t. Order of the Most Holy Trinity, Trinitarian Fathers.
p.i.m.e. Pontifical Institute for Foreign Missions.
r.c.j. Rogationist Fathers.
s.a. Franciscan Friars of the Atonement.
s.a.c. Society of the Catholic Apostolate, Pallottine Fathers.
s.c. Brothers of the Sacred Heart.
s.c. Servants of Charity.
s.ch. Society of Christ.
sch.p. Piarist Fathers.
s.c.j. Congregation of the Priests of the Sacred Heart of Jesus.
s.d.b. Salesians of Don Bosco.
s.d.s. Society of the Divine Savior.
s.d.v. Vocationist Fathers, Society of the Divine Vocations.
s.f. Sons of the Holy Family.
s.f.c. Society of the Brothers of Charity.
s.f.m. Scarboro Foreign Missions.
s.j. Jesuit Fathers and Brothers, Society of Jesus.
s.l.t. Servants of Our Lady of the Most Holy Trinity.
s.m. Society of Mary, Marianists.
s.m. Marist Fathers.
s.m.a. Society of African Missions.
s.m.m. Montfort Missionaries.
s.m.p. Society of Our Mother of Peace.
s.o.cist. Cistercian Monks of the Strict Observance.
s.o.l.t. Society of Our Lady of the Most Holy Trinity.
s.p. Servants of the Paraclete.
s.p.s. St. Patrick's Missionary Society.
s.s. Society of the Priest of Saint Sulpice, Sulpician Fathers.
s.s.c. Society of St. Columban, St. Columban's Foreign Mission Society.
ss.cc. Congregation of the Sacred Hearts of Jesus and Mary.
s.s.e. Society of Saint Edmund.
s.s.j. St. Joseph's Society of the Sacred Heart, Josephite Fathers.
s.s.p. Pauline Fathers and Brothers, Society of St. Paul for the Apostolate of Communications.
s.s.s. Congregation of the Blessed Sacrament.
s.s.t. Missionary Society of St. Thomas the Apostle.
s.t. Missionary Servants of the Most Holy Trinity.
s.v.d. Society of the Divine Word.
s.x. Xaverian Missionary Fathers, St. Francis Xavier Mission Society.
t.o.r. Third Order Regular of Saint Francis.
v.c. Vincentian Congregation.

The letters in parentheses designate the diocese. See the "Diocesan Abbreviations". Numbers in brackets designate the numerical order of the Church in cities in which there are four or more Catholic Churches listed. Letters in brackets designate categories in the Institution Section.

A

Aaron, Andrew '96 (BAL) [70] Baltimore, MD Our Lady of Hope Church.
Aaron, James L. '54 (PIT) [78] Pittsburgh, PA Most Holy Name of Jesus Church.
Aaron, James R. '57 (SAN) Retired.
Aaron, Robert *o.m.i.* '72 (BEL) [H] Belleville, IL Retreat and Renewal Center.
Abad, Msgr. Federico '46 (PCE) On Duty Outside the Diocese.
Abad, Jose Antonio P. '82 (AGN) Tamuning, GU St. Anthony and St. Victor Church.
Abano, Edgardo D. '85 (MET) Piscataway, NJ St. Frances Cabrini Church.
Abara, Lawrence N. '78 (LAF) [F] Lafayette, LA Our Lady of Lourdes Regional Medical Center, Inc.
Abarrategui, Leandro *o.f.m.* '54 (SJN) [3] Carolina, PR Santa Clara de Asis Church.
Abarratelegui, Leanardo (SJN) [3] Carolina, PR Santa Clara de Asis Church.
Abate, Anthony P. *o.f.m.* '56 (NY) [DD] Mount Vernon, NY St. Bernardine of Siena Friary.
Abaya, Francisco (NY) Manhattan, NY New York University Medical Center.
Abbaticchio, Damian *o.s.b.* '45 (RIC) [6] Virginia Beach, VA St. Gregory the Great Church.
Abbatiello, Robert *o.f.m.cap.* '90 (NY) [DD] Garrison, NY St. Francis Friary.
Abbott, Donald '73 (BO) Wilmington, MA St. Dorothy Church.
Abbott, Donald S. '73 (CHR) On Duty Outside the Diocese.

Abbott, Eugene J. '57 (STP) Minneapolis, MN Minnesota Soldiers' Home; Special Assignment; Retired.
Abbott, Kerry *o.f.m.conv.* (MRY) [G] Arroyo Grande, CA St. Joseph Cupertino Province, Provincial Center.
Abbott, Walter M. *s.j.* '56 (BO) [W] Boston, MA Arrupe House.
Abbott, William M. *s.j.* '72 (NEW) [B] Jersey City, NJ Saint Peter's College; [N] Jersey City, NJ Jesuits of Saint Peter's College, Inc.
Abdella, Peter M. *c.s.p.* '85 (SD) [M] San Diego, CA University of California at San Diego (Campus Ministry).
Abdoo, Louis *i.m.c.* '73 (ORG) [2] Anaheim, CA St. Boniface Church.
Abdulmasih, Yousif '75 (OLD) [1] Newark, NJ Our Lady of Deliverance Church.
Abe, John Adam '84 (RIC) Staunton, VA St. Francis of Assisi Church.
Abegg, Victor *o.f.m.conv.* (SB) [11] Riverside, CA St. Thomas the Apostle Church.
Abegg, Victor *o.f.m.conv.* '74 (MRY) [G] Arroyo Grande, CA St. Joseph Cupertino Province, Provincial Center.
Abel, Robert M. '73 (L) [23] Louisville, KY St. Elizabeth Ann Seton Church; [53] Louisville, KY St. Mary Church.
Abele, Alan Carl '73 (ANC) On Duty Outside Archdiocese.
Abele, Joseph P. '49 (GI) Retired.
Abell, Donald E. '76 (BEL) Eldorado, IL St. Mary Church.
Abell, Edward '67 (GAL) [A] Houston, TX St. Mary's Seminary.
Abella, Ray *o.s.f.s.* (STO) Jamestown, CA Sierra Conservation Center.
Abella, Ray G. *o.s.f.s.* '93 (TOL) [K] Toledo, OH Oblates of St. Francis de Sales.
Abercrombie, Jamie M. *c.s.b.* '73 (GAL) Rosenberg, TX Our Lady of Guadalupe Church.
Abernethy, David S. *c.o.* '94 (PIT) [O] Pittsburgh, PA Congregation of the Oratory of St. Philip Neri; [R] Slippery Rock, PA Office for Campus Ministry.
Abert, Richard P. *s.j.* '76 (MIL) [64] Milwaukee, WI St. Patrick Church; [P] Milwaukee, WI Jesuit Community at Marquette University.
Abgali, Anthony '95 (DET) Detroit, MI Harper Hospital and Rehabilitation Center.
Abi-Sarkis, Elias '75 (SAM) Unassigned.
Ablahad, Najor '43 (EST) Retired.
Abler, Lawrence *o.f.m.cap.* '64 (DET) [K] Detroit, MI St. Mary's Friary.
Ablog, Frederick J. *s.s.s.* (CLV) [P] Cleveland, OH Congregation of the Blessed Sacrament Provincial House.
Aboody, Charles '62 (NTN) Retired.
Abosike, James O. '79 (DEN) [23] Denver, CO Presentation of Our Lady Church.
Abracinskas, Albert C. '40 (BO) Retired.
Abraham, Benedict *s.a.c.* '65 (VEN) [3] Sarasota, FL St. Martha Church.
Abraham, John J. '79 (WIL) Perry Point, MD Veterans Admin.
Abraham, Mussie *m.c.c.j.* '81 (CHI) [N] Chicago, IL Comboni Missionaries Theologate (M.C.C.J.), Verona Fathers.
Abraham, Thaddeus '90 (BRK) [178] Queens, NY Holy Family Church.
Abraham, Thomas J. '66 (LC) Hatley, WI St. Florian Church.
Abrahams, John '79 (BAL) [3] Baltimore, MD St. Agnes Church; Special Assignment.
Abrama, John L. '51 (BRK) [U] Douglaston, NY Bishop Mugavero Residence.
Abramovic, Joseph M. *o.f.m.* '60 (STL) [44] St. Louis, MO St. Joseph Church.
Abramowicz, Richard '86 (MET) [G] Somerset, NJ McCarrick Care Center.
Abramowicz, Richard B. '86 (MET) Retired.
Abramowicz, Msgr. Sylvester '46 (NEW) Retired.
Abrams, John L. '51 (BRK) Retired.
Abreu, John E. '74 (PRO) [9] Woonsocket, RI Our Lady, Queen of Martyrs Church.
Abruzzese, Msgr. John A. '74 (BO) On Duty Outside the Archdiocese.
Abruzzese, Joseph A. (PRO) Absent on Leave.
Abts, Cletus '44 (LC) Retired.
Abts, John J. *o.f.m.* (STL) [P] St. Louis, MO Franciscan Friary of St. Anthony of Padua.
Abts, John J. *o.f.m.* '84 (HON) [2] Honolulu, HI Co-Cathedral of St. Theresa of the Child Jesus.
Abucewicz, Msgr. John A. '44 (BO) Retired.
Abugel, Alexander G. '80 (BRK) [184] Queens, NY St. Joan of Arc Church.
Acaba, Jose A. '82 (MGZ) Cabo Rojo, PR St. Michael Church.
Accardi, Joseph N. '90 (PH) Levittown, PA St. Michael the Archangel Church.
Acciarito, Anthony J. '78 (BRK) [131] Brooklyn, NY Sacred Hearts of Jesus and Mary and St. Stephen Church.
Acebo, Jeff (OAK) [3] Oakland, CA St. Anthony's Church.
Acerbi, Luigi *p.i.m.e.* '50 (DET) [K] Detroit, MI P.I.M.E. Missionaries of SS. Peter and Paul.
Acerbi, Luigi *p.i.m.e.* '50 (PAT) [M] Wayne, NJ P.I.M.E. Missionaries Residence.
Acevedo, Anthony '73 (MIA) [G] Miami, FL Mercy Hospital.
Acevedo, Bertulfo '55 (ARE) [4] Vega-Baja, PR Our Lady of Carmen-Playa Church.
Acevedo, Joaquin *o.f.m.* '60 (ELP) [B] El Paso, TX St. Anthony's School of Theology.
Acevedo, Luis H. '51 (ELP) Retired.
Acevedo, Natividad *o.p.* '86 (SJN) [8] Bayamon, PR Invencion de la Santa Cruz Church.
Achi, Stephen *m.s.p.* '86 (WDC) [B] Washington, DC St. Joseph's Seminary.
Achonwa, Aloysius (WDC) [31] Washington, DC Nigerian Catholic Community Church.
Acker, Karl H. '63 (MIL) Saukville, WI Immaculate Conception Church.
Acker, Thomas S. *s.j.* (DET) [K] Detroit, MI Jesuit Provincial Office-Detroit Province of the Society of Jesus.
Acker, Thomas S. *s.j.* '63 (WH) [A] Wheeling, WV Wheeling Jesuit University.
Ackeret, Dennis R. '68 (MIL) [2] Wauwatosa, WI Christ King Church.
Ackerman, Donald K. '61 (EVN) [3] Vincennes, IN St. John the Baptist Church; [4] Vincennes, IN St. Thomas Church.
Ackerman, James Thomas, Jr. '97 (BIR) [4] Huntsville, AL Holy Spirit Church.
Ackerman, Phillip '78 (FAR) [2] Fargo, ND Holy Spirit Church; Fargo, ND Veterans Administration Facility.
Ackerman, Ray '91 (OKL) [1] Oklahoma City, OK Cathedral of Our Lady of Perpetual Help.
Ackerman, Raymond K. '91 (OKL) Special Assignment; [C] Oklahoma City, OK Mount St. Mary High School.
Ackerson, Msgr. Francis A. '46 (ALT) Retired.
Acklin, Thomas *o.s.b.* '80 (GBG) [A] Latrobe, PA St. Vincent Seminary; [H] Latrobe, PA Saint Vincent Archabbey.
Aclan, Alex '93 (LA) [16] Los Angeles, CA Immaculate Heart of Mary Church.
Acosta, Carlos Lopez '60 (NY) [139] Bronx, NY St. Francis of Assisi Church.
Acosta, Edgardo '83 (MGZ) Rincon, PR St. Rose of Lima Church.
Acosta, Francisco '70 (BWN) [1] McAllen, TX Our Lady of Perpetual Help Church.
Acosta, Humberto J. '74 (BWN) Absent.
Acquaria, Msgr. Paschal '48 (BUF) Lancaster, NY St. Mary of the Assumption Church.
Acquaro, Philip *c.s.b.* '70 (PHX) Special Assignment.
Acquaro, Philip A. *c.s.b.* '70 (VNN) Gilbert, AZ St. Thomas the Apostle Church; [A] Phoenix, AZ Congregation of Saint Basil.
Acquavia, Msgr. Paschal L. '48 (BUF) Retired.
Acrea, John W. '62 (DM) Creston, IA Holy Spirit Church.
Acri, John A. '65 (HBG) Enola, PA Our Lady of Lourdes Church.
Acton, Msgr. John '48 (LA) Glendora, CA St. Dorothy Church.
Acton, Thomas M. '57 (LA) Gardena, CA Maria Regina Church.
Adackapara, Matthew '60 (TR) Freehold, NJ St. Robert Bellarmine Church.
Adam, Charles A. '86 (DAV) [A] Davenport, IA St. Ambrose University Seminary; [B] Davenport, IA St. Ambrose University.
Adam, John *s.j.* '61 (NY) [HH] Bronx, NY Saint Jutta Foundation, Inc.
Adam, Nicholas '76 (DAV) Mount Pleasant, IA St. Alphonsus Church.
Adam, Richard A. '88 (SC) Absent on Leave.
Adamcik, Bryan F.J. '96 (NEW) Emerson, NJ Church of the Assumption.
Adamczyk, Stanley J. '48 (NEW) Retired.
Adamec, Joseph *c.ss.r.* '52 (BO) [13] Boston, MA Our Lady of Perpetual Help Church.
Adamiak, Leo '46 (SJP) [11] Youngstown, OH Holy Trinity Church.
Adamiak, Stephen (SJP) Retired.
Adamich, Albert R. '48 (CHI) Evergreen Park, IL Most Holy Redeemer Church.
Adamich, Albert R. '88 (CHI) Retired.
Adamko, Msgr. Cyril A. '53 (Y) Retired.
Adamo, Joseph A. '73 (WOR) [2] Worcester, MA Ascension Church.
Adamo, Joseph P. '42 (NY) Retired; [DD] New York, NY Our Lady of Consolation Residence.
Adamo, Msgr. Salvatore J. '45 (CAM) Haddon Township, NJ St. Vincent Pallotti Church; Retired.
Adams, Alvin J. '67 (PIT) [4] Munhall, PA St. Rita Church; [C] Pittsburgh, PA Canevin Catholic High School.
Adams, Archie H. '55 (MAD) Absent on Sick Leave.
Adams, Benedict *o.f.m.cap.* '57 (MAD) [M] Madison, WI San Damiano Friary.
Adams, Daniel '80 (P) On Duty Outside the Archdiocese.
Adams, Daniel '80 (SFR) [6] San Francisco, CA St. Benedict Parish at St. Francis Xavier Church; [47] San Francisco, CA Sacred Heart Church.
Adams, David A. '88 (TR) Mount Holly, NJ Sacred Heart Church.
Adams, David C. '61 (KAL) Benton Harbor, MI St. John-St. Bernard Church.
Adams, Dudley R.C. *s.j.* '92 (FgM) Provinces.
Adams, Edmond F. '52 (SC) Retired.
Adams, Msgr. George J. '50 (STU) Retired.
Adams, H. J., Jr. '68 (NO) [6] Metairie, LA St. Christopher the Martyr Church.
Adams, J.K. *s.j.* '95 (SPK) [6] Spokane, WA St. Aloysius Church; [E] Spokane, WA Gonzaga Preparatory School.
Adams, James P. '82 (ATL) Buford, GA Prince of Peace Church.
Adams, John '69 (WDC) [U] Washington, DC Community of Christ.
Adams, John *o.p.* '96 (ANC) [1] Anchorage, AK Holy Family Cathedral.
Adams, John E. '69 (WDC) Special Ministries.
Adams, Msgr. Michael '46 (CC) Retired.
Adams, Michael J. '59 (CHI) [131] Chicago, IL St. Mary, Star of the Sea Church.
Adams, Michael T. '68 (MRY) On Duty Outside the Diocese.
Adams, Patrick *o.f.m.* '42 (SP) [O] St. Petersburg, FL St. Anthony Friary.
Adams, Msgr. Raymond A. '51 (BUR) Retired.
Adams, Richard T. '65 (NY) [109] New York, NY St. Rose of Lima Church; Goshen, NY St. John the Evangelist Church.
Adams, Msgr. Robert '45 (OAK) Retired.
Adams, Rodney T. *o.p.* '91 (STL) [P] St. Louis, MO St. Dominic Priory.
Adams, Scott '95 (OKL) Guymon, OK St. Peter's Church.
Adams, Scott '97 (OKL) [K] Norman, OK Campus Ministry for the Archdiocese of Oklahoma City.
Adams, Stephen E. '81 (DEN) Johnstown, CO St. John the Baptist Church; Windsor, CO Our Lady of the Valley Church.
Adams, T. Edmund *o.s.b.* '89 (PRO) [P] Portsmouth, RI Abbey of St. Gregory the Great.
Adams, Thomas J. '64 (OM) [45] Omaha, NE St. Therese of the Child Jesus Church.
Adams, Walter C. '84 (NY) Military Chaplains.
Adams, William *s.v.d.* '45 (LA) [76] Los Angeles, CA St. Malachy Church.
Adams, William '78 (VEN) Arcadia, FL St. Paul Church.
Adamski, Donald J. *o.f.m.conv.* '75 (LSC) Hobbs, NM St. Helena Church.
Adamski, John S. '71 (ATL) [12] Atlanta, GA Shrine of the Immaculate Conception Church.
Adamsky, Raymond J. '58 (MIL) Retired.
Adamson, Fred '95 (PHX) [24] Phoenix, AZ St. Theresa Church.
Adamson, Joseph J. '90 (CAM) Runnemede, NJ St. Maria Goretti Church.
Adamson, Milton N. *c.s.c.* '66 (PHX) [C] Phoenix, AZ St. Joseph's Hospital and Medical Center; [F] Phoenix, AZ Holy Cross Congregation of Casa Santa Cruz.
Adan, Aurelio '69 (CGS) [B] Aibonito, PR Casa Manresa.
Adarve, Hernan '61 (SJN) [12] Bayamon, PR Nuestra Senora de la Milagrosa Church.
Adcock, Basil W. '80 (NTN) Leave of Absence.
Addari, Enzo *s.c.* '76 (LAN) [E] Chelsea, MI St. Louis Center for Exceptional Children & Adults.
Adducci, Anthony J. '76 (CHI) [J] Chicago, IL St. Joseph Hospital.
Adejoh, Patrick '92 (LA) [80] Los Angeles, CA St. Mary Magdalen Church.
Adelman, Norbert '56 (ORL) Longwood, FL Church of the Nativity.
Adelmann, Edward *o.carm.* '75 (JOL) [J] Darien, IL Carmelite Provincial Office.
Adelmann, Frederick J. *s.j.* '47 (BO) [W] Weston, MA Campion Health Center, Inc.
Adessa, Msgr. Domenick J. '47 (RVC) [O] Amityville, NY Queen of the Rosary, Motherhouse.
Adessa, Msgr. Dominick J. *p.e.* '47 (BRK) [204] Queens, NY Nativity of the Blessed Virgin Mary Church; Retired.
Adeyanju, Henry M. '96 (BO) [4] Waltham, MA St. Mary Church.
Adhana, Gabre-Tinsaye (GAL) [N] Houston, TX Pope John XXIII Priest Residence.
Adkins, Joseph H. '47 (BIS) Retired.
Adkins, Patrick J. *o.s.c.* '50 (PHX) Phoenix, AZ Good Samaritan Medical Center; [F] Phoenix, AZ Crosier Community of Phoenix (Canons Regular of the Order of the Holy Cross).
Adogamhe, Paul '76 (NY) [191] Bronx, NY St. Thomas Aquinas Church.
Adolf, Gregory P. '91 (TUC) Sierra Vista, AZ St. Andrew Church.
Adolfo, Hermengildo '68 (FRS) Tehachapi, CA California Correctional Institution.

Adolfo, Neil '68 (FRS) Tehachapi, CA St. Malachy Church.
Adomaitis, John J. '44 (GAY) Mackinaw City, MI St. Anthony of Padua Church; Retired.
Adonizio, Joseph J. '56 (SCR) West Pittston, PA Immaculate Conception Church.
Adorno, Anibal '92 (DAL) [1] Dallas, TX Cathedral-Santuario de Guadalupe.
Adragna, Joseph J. '65 (STL) Gardenville, MO St. George Church.
Adrian, Stephen J. '39 (NU) Retired.
Adrian, Stephen J. '68 (STP) [29] St. Paul, MN St. Matthew Church.
Adrians, Thomas M. '67 (PBL) [2] Pueblo, CO Christ the King Church.
Adu, Martin '75 (MIA) [34] Miami, FL St. Vincent De Paul Church.
Adversario, Efren F. '89 (AGN) Inarajan, GU St. Joseph Church.
Adzogba, Ben *c.s.sp.* (PIT) [40] Pittsburgh, PA St. Patrick-St. Stanislaus Kostka Church.
Aelavanthara, Antony '68 (ALX) St. Joseph, LA St. Joseph Church.
Aerts, Daniel C. '77 (GR) Reed City, MI St. Philip Neri Church.
Afanador, Hernan '82 (ORL) [8] Orlando, FL St. Isaac Jogues Church.
Affanoso, Joseph L. '56 (NEW) [1] East Orange, NJ Holy Name of Jesus Church; Retired.
Affelt, Francis *o.f.m.* '52 (FTW) [K] Mishawaka, IN St. Francis Provincialate.
Affonso, Alexander '68 (SJ) Los Altos, CA St. Simon Church.
Afful-Broni, Anthony '68 (NY) Cortlandt Manor, NY Holy Spirit Church.
Afunugo, Emmanuel '83 (AMA) On Duty Outside the Diocese.
Agambi, Isaac (NY) Mount Vernon, NY Mount Vernon Hospital.
Agan, Jose '70 (NEW) Glen Rock, NJ St. Catharine Church.
Agapito, John *c.p.m.* '89 (WH) [G] Morgantown, WV Our Lady of Good Counsel Franciscan Friary.
Agar, Bartholomew A. *o.praem.* '58 (GB) [I] De Pere, WI St. Norbert Abbey.
Agbakwuru, Emmanuel C. '73 (PIT) Duquesne, PA St. Joseph Church.
Agbor, Emmanuel *m.s.p.* '95 (GAL) [31] Houston, TX St. Francis Xavier Church.
Ageas, Cesar '83 (SAC) [11] Sacramento, CA St. Charles Borromeo Church.
Agede, Kenneth (PIT) [4] Donora, PA Our Lady of the Valley Church.
Ager, Fay W. '79 (OG) Chateaugay, NY St. Patrick Church.
Aggeler, Vince *c.ss.r.* '58 (FgM) Redemptorist Foreign Missions.
Aggugia, Steven '93 (BRK) [34] Brooklyn, NY St. Edmund's Church.
Agius, Grace '42 (DET) [50] Detroit, MI Most Holy Trinity Church.
Agnew, Francis H. *c.m.* '60 (STL) Sereno, MO Our Lady of Victory Church.
Agnew, John C. '90 (BO) [V] Cambridge, MA Opus Dei, Prelature of the Holy Cross and Opus Dei.
Agonis, Edwin *o.f.m.conv.* '41 (BGP) [14] Bridgeport, CT St. Michael the Archangel Church.
Agostinelli, Gianni *c.s.* '86 (BRK) [71] Brooklyn, NY St. Joseph Patron of the Universal Church.
Agostini, Sixtus *m.c.c.j.* '71 (CIN) [V] Cincinnati, OH The Comboni Lay Missionaries Association.
Agostino, Emil *o.carm.* '64 (NEW) Englewood, NJ St. Cecilia's Church.
Agostino, Joseph V. *c.m.* '83 (BRK) [66] Brooklyn, NY St. John the Baptist Church; [U] Brooklyn, NY St. John the Baptist Rectory.
Agostino, Sixtus *m.c.c.j.* '72 (CHI) [N] La Grange Park, IL Comboni Mission Center.
Agostino, Stephen J. *s.j.* '93 (CLV) [E] Cleveland, OH St. Ignatius High School.
Agresti, Albert *s.j.* (STL) [C] St. Louis, MO Saint Louis University.
Agresti, Albert *s.j.* '80 (STL) [P] St. Louis, MO Leo Brown Jesuit Community.
Agresti, Albert A. *s.j.* '80 (BO) [W] Boston, MA The Society of Jesus of New England-Provincial Offices.
Agudo, Teodoro *o.f.m.cap.* '54 (NO) [62] New Orleans, LA St. Theresa Of Avila Church.
Aguggia, Steven J. '93 (BRK) [103] Brooklyn, NY Our Lady of Miracles Church.
Aguilar, Arturo *s.s.c.* '84 (OM) [K] St. Columbans, NE St. Columban's Foreign Mission Society.
Aguilar, Benjamin *o.carm.* '94 (CHI) [D] Chicago, IL Mt. Carmel High School.
Aguilar, Genaro P. *c.s.c.* '83 (FR) [A] North Easton, MA Holy Cross Fathers Religious.
Aguilar, Jose '96 (NY) [160] Bronx, NY St. Luke Church.
Aguilar, Jose A. *s.j.* '82 (OAK) [N] Berkeley, CA Jesuit Community at Jesuit School of Theology at Berkeley.
Aguilar, Jose M. (NY) [65] New York, NY St. Jude Church.
Aguilar, Jose Maria *sch.p.* '59 (LA) [75] Los Angeles, CA St. Lucy Church.
Aguilar, Ricardo '95 (AUS) Temple, TX Our Lady of Guadalupe Church.
Aguilar, Rogelio Mur *o.carm.* '56 (MGZ) Anasco, PR St. Anthony Abbot Church.
Aguilera, George '83 (LA) [39] Los Angeles, CA St. Aloysius Gonzaga Church.
Aguilera, Salvador '84 (ELP) On Duty Outside of Diocese.
Aguirre, Ignacio *o.s.b.* '53 (CGS) Humacao, PR Maria Reina de la Paz Church.
Aguirre, Osmar '93 (YAK) Sunnyside, WA St. Joseph's Church.
Aguirre, Robert G. '72 (CHI) Wauconda, IL Transfiguration Church.
Aguirre-Garza, Jesus *o.f.m.* '96 (SAT) [50] San Antonio, TX St. Leonard's Church; [B] San Antonio, TX Franciscan Formation Program in San Jose Friary (Casa Juan Diego).
Aguirre-Garza, Jesus M. *o.f.m.* '96 (SAT) [70] San Antonio, TX San Jose y San Miguel Church.
Agumanu, Benedict '66 (LA) Claremont, CA Our Lady of the Assumption Church.
Agustin, Richard *m.m.* '85 (FgM) Maryknoll Foreign Missions.
Ahearn, Donald J. '51 (CHI) [112] Chicago, IL St. Juliana Church; Retired.
Ahearn, John F. *m.m.* '73 (FgM) Maryknoll Foreign Missions.
Ahearn, John S. *o.f.m.* '50 (PAT) [M] Butler, NJ St. Anthony Friary.
Ahearn, Kieran T. '64 (BGP) Leave of Absence.
Ahearn, Richard F. '60 (BO) Danvers, MA St. Mary of the Annunciation Church.
Ahearn, Thomas *m.m.* '68 (FgM) Maryknoll Foreign Missions.
Ahern, Bernard '54 (ALB) Retired.
Ahern, Dennis P. *s.j.* '70 (CHI) [C] Chicago, IL Jesuit Community at Loyola University of Chicago.
Ahern, Jack '79 (BO) [4] Brookline, MA St. Mary of the Assumption Church.
Ahern, Msgr. John B. (NY) [I] New York, NY The Catholic Charities of the Archdiocese of New York.
Ahern, Msgr. John B. '54 (NY) [88] New York, NY Our Lady of Loreto Church.
Ahern, John J. '48 (CHI) Retired.
Ahern, John J. '49 (CHI) Retired.
Ahern, John S. '54 (HRT) Norfolk, CT Immaculate Conception Church.
Ahern, John V. '67 (SY) [2] Liverpool, NY Immaculate Heart of Mary Church.
Ahern, Richard *c.s.s.* '54 (BO) [Z] Waltham, MA Stigmatine Fathers and Brothers.
Ahern, Thomas '54 (SJ) Retired.
Ahern, Thomas '94 (BRK) [190] Queens, NY St. Leo Church.
Ahern, Thomas W. '48 (NOR) Chester, CT St. Joseph Church.
Aherne, Greg *s.j.* '60 (SFR) [48] San Francisco, CA Star of the Sea Church.
Aherne, James *m.s.* '73 (HRT) [3] Hartford, CT Immaculate Conception Church; [7] Hartford, CT St. Anne Church.
Aherne, James J. *m.s.* '73 (HRT) [M] Hartford, CT Missionaries of LaSalette Provincial Secretary; [M] Hartford, CT Missionaries of LaSalette Provincial Secretary.
Aherne, John '57 (MOB) Semmes, AL Holy Name of Jesus Church.
Aherne, P. Vincent *c.m.* '52 (STL) [P] St. Louis, MO Vincentian Residence.
Ahlbach, William J. '62 (SFR) [3] San Mateo, CA St. Matthew Church.
Ahlemeyer, Richard J. '77 (BRK) [227] Queens, NY St. Pius V Church; [229] Queens, NY Presentation of the Blessed Virgin Mary Church.
Ahler, Richard H. *s.j.* '61 (MIL) [P] Milwaukee, WI Jesuit Community at Marquette University.
Ahles, Donald M. '71 (RCK) Cary, IL SS. Peter & Paul Church.
Ahles, Jerry *o.f.m.* '44 (MRY) [G] San Miguel, CA Franciscan Friars, O.F.M.
Ahlin, Robert J. '71 (PIT) Brentwood, PA St. Sylvester Church.
Ahlstrom, Michael P. '69 (CHI) Rolling Meadows, IL St. Colette Church.
Ahn, Michael '79 (SEA) Special Assignment.
Aho, Charles A. '70 (SY) Liverpool, NY Developmental Center; Special Assignment.
Ahrems, Noel G. *o.carm.* '53 (NOR) Middletown, CT Long Lane School.
Ahren, Noel G. *o.carm.* '46 (NOR) [D] Deep River, CT Mount St. John.
Ahrens, Giles *c.p.* '52 (BRK) [U] Jamaica, NY Immaculate Conception Monastery.
Ahrens, Noel *o.carm.* '53 (NEW) Englewood, NJ St. Cecilia's Church.
Ahrens, William B. '51 (STL) Concord Village, MO St. Simon the Apostle Church.
Ahrensfield, Michael E. '80 (ALN) Coplay, PA St. Peter Church.
Ahumanda, Jose E. *c.s.c.* '83 (FTW) [J] South Bend, IN Congregation of Holy Cross Indiana Province Provincial House.
Ahurwendeire, Emiliano '82 (DET) [53] Detroit, MI Our Lady of Good Counsel Church.
Aiardi, Reno *i.m.c.* '65 (SB) [7] Riverside, CA St. Francis de Sales Church.
Aichele, Raymond P. '58 (CIN) [B] Cincinnati, OH Mt. St. Mary's Seminary of the West; [B] Cincinnati, OH Mt. St. Mary's Seminary of the West.
Aidoo, Thomas '85 (NY) Nyack, NY St. Ann Church.
Aiello, Anthony '69 (DM) [2] Des Moines, IA All Saints Church.
Aiello, John A. '85 (MEM) [10] Memphis, TN Holy Rosary Church.
Aiello, John D. '69 (MIL) Special Assignment.
Aiello, Louis F. '77 (SY) Tully, NY St. Leo Church.
Aigner, Edward M. '72 (WIL) Princess Anne, MD University of Maryland, Eastern Shore; [O] Newark, DE Univ. of Delaware Newman Center.
Aigner, Edward M., Jr. '72 (WIL) Westover, MD Eastern Correctional Institution.
Aiken, Lloyd E. '70 (BAL) Glyndon, MD Sacred Heart Church.
Aiken, Richard J. '70 (MIL) Greendale, WI St. Alphonsus Church.
Aiken, Msgr. Roy F. '46 (CHR) Retired.
Aime, Moise '54 (RVC) Plainview, NY St. Pius X Church.
Aineto, Luis *s.d.b.* '61 (PMB) Belle Glade, FL St. Philip Benizi Church.
Aita, Mark C. *s.j.* '83 (CAM) [4] Camden, NJ Holy Name Church; [S] Camden, NJ Saint Luke's Catholic Medical Services, Inc.
Aitcheson, William '88 (ARL) Chancellorsville, VA St. Patrick's Church.
Aitcheson, William M. '88 (RNO) On Duty Outside the Diocese.
Ajamie, Albert '50 (IND) Retired.
Ajayi, Vincent O. '94 (NY) [2] Mt. Vernon, NY Our Lady of Victory Church.
Ajuria, Cruz *o.f.m.* '57 (SJN) [52] San Juan, PR Resurreccion del Senor Church.
Akabueze, Emeka (DM) West Des Moines, IA Sacred Heart Church.
Akalefu, Wisdom '83 (BRK) [153] Queens, NY Ascension Church.
Akano, Yoshi *c.s.s.r.* (NY) [150] Bronx, NY Immaculate Conception Church.
Akekee, Wlademer '49 (SAM) Retired.
Akers, Bert *s.j.* '61 (WIL) Ocean City, MD St. Mary, Star of the Sea Church.
Akhwesso, Huberti *s.m.* (BO) [59] Boston, MA Our Lady of Victories Church.
Akian, Mikael '35 (ARM) [A] La Crescenta, CA Mekhitarist School.
Akiki, Joseph '87 (SAM) Orlando, FL St. Jude Mission Church; [E] Williston, VT Blessed Rafka Retreat Center.
Akiona, Lane *ss.cc.* (HON) [4] Honolulu, HI St. Augustine Church.
Akkin, Florentinus '93 (CI) Dublon, FM St. Anthony's Church.
Akordor, Edmund '80 (NO) [46] New Orleans, LA St. Matthias Church.
Akpabio, Felix '78 (BRK) [238] Queens, NY Sacred Heart Church.
Akpan, Msgr. Godwin *m.s.p.* '60 (WDC) [B] Washington, DC St. Joseph's Seminary.
Akpan, Msgr. Goodwin *m.s.p.* (GAL) [66] Houston, TX St. Peter the Apostle Church.
Aksamit, Stanley J. '77 (SPR) Greenfield, MA Sacred Heart Church; Turners Falls, MA St. Mary's Church; Turners Falls, MA St. Anne Church.
Akwue, Francis *c.s.sp.* '71 (MIA) [17] Miami, FL St. Catherine of Siena Church.
Al-Badwi, Alfred '91 (OLL) Dayton, OH Saint Ignatius Mission Church.
Al-Nahal, Jean *m.l.m.* '93 (OLL) San Antonio, TX St. George Maronite Church.
Al-Nahal, John *m.l.m.* '93 (OLL) [A] San Antonio, TX The Congregation of Maronite Lebanese Missionaries.
Alabart, Francis X. '40 (FRS) Retired.
Alagia, Vincent *s.j.* '58 (CHL) Mars Hill, NC St. Andrew the Apostle Church.
Alagia, Vincent P. *s.j.* '58 (CHL) [J] Charlotte, NC Jesuit Community; [M] Hot Springs, NC Jesuit House of Prayer.
Alaharasan, V. Anthony J. '65 (NOR) Preston, CT St. Catherine of Siena Church.
Alamo, Emiliano *o.p.* '62 (NO) [P] New Orleans, LA Dominican Fathers & Brothers, Southern Dominican Province.
Alamo, Emiliano '66 (PCE) Villalba, PR Our Lady of Mt. Carmel Church.
Alamo Villegas, Jose Antonio *c.s.sp.* '85 (SJN) [F] Dorado, PR Santuario del Espiritu Santo.

Alapatt, Mathew *m.s.f.s.* '62 (CHR) Garden City, SC St. Michael Church.
Alappat, Joy (NEW) New Milford, NJ Ascension Church.
Alappat, Joy '60 (NEW) Plainfield, NJ Muhlenberg Medical Center.
Alarcon, Felix '63 (RVC) Priests Released from Diocesan Assignment.
Alarcon, Felix '63 (VEN) [3] Naples, FL St. Peter the Apostle Church.
Alava, Andres *o.a.r.* '63 (LSC) Anthony, NM St. Anthony's Church.
Alayon, Hermenegildo '79 (CGS) [13] Barrio Rio Canas, PR Maria Madre de la Iglesia Church.
Alba, Msgr. Jose M. '48 (NEW) [18] Jersey City, NJ St. Nicholas Church; Retired.
Alba, Ricardo de *m.sp.s.* '81 (LA) [3] Oxnard, CA Our Lady of Guadalupe Parish.
Albacete, Msgr. Lorenzo '73 (NY) [A] Yonkers, NY St. Joseph's Seminary.
Albacete, Msgr. Lorenzo '73 (WDC) On Duty Outside the Archdiocese.
Albaladejo, Juan A. '85 (MET) [3] New Brunswick, NJ Our Lady of Mt. Carmel Church.
Albamonti, Richard '76 (NOR) Westbrook, CT St. Mark Church.
Albano, Arturo '74 (SFR) Colma, CA Holy Angels Church.
Albano, George M. '44 (TR) Retired.
Albano, Peter J. *c.m.* '68 (BRK) [U] Jamaica, NY Vincentian Residence.
Albano, Vincent *s.o.l.t.* '72 (CC) Robstown, TX St. Anthony Church; [H] Robstown, TX Society of Our Lady of the Most Holy Trinity.
Albarano, Richard '68 (LA) Downey, CA St. Raymond Church.
Albee, Paul M. '84 (LA) Torrance, CA Nativity Church.
Albenesius, Paul M. '97 (OM) [33] Omaha, NE Our Lady of Lourdes Church.
Alber, Thomas L. '85 (JC) Milan, MO St. Mary Church.
Alberdi, Inmanol *c.p.* (SJN) [46] San Juan, PR Nuestra Senora de la Piedad Church.
Albero, Steven J. *o.praem.* '92 (PH) [D] Philadelphia, PA St. John Neumann High School; [AA] Philadelphia, PA St. Norbert Priory.
Albers, Austin *o.f.m.* '64 (SFD) [4] Quincy, IL St. Francis Solanus Church; [K] Quincy, IL St. Francis Solanus Friary.
Albers, Edwin O. *o.f.m.* '61 (SFD) Bishop Creek, IL St. Aloysius Church; Dieterich, IL Immaculate Conception Church; Island Grove, IL St. Joseph Church; [K] Teutopolis, IL St. Francis Assisi Friary.
Albers, George J. *c.pp.s.* '62 (CLV) [53] Cleveland, OH Our Lady of Good Counsel Church.
Albers, Paul C. '37 (DAV) Retired.
Albers, Robert J. *s.a.c.* '48 (MIL) [35] Milwaukee, WI Holy Cross Church.
Albers, Thomas *c.pp.s.* '67 (JC) Sedalia, MO St. Patrick Church.
Albert, Andrew R. *s.m.* '65 (BO) [59] Boston, MA Our Lady of Victories Church; [W] Boston, MA Marist Fathers of Our Lady of Victories (Boston Prov.).
Albert, Claude J., Jr. '64 (PRT) [3] Lewiston, ME Holy Family Church.
Albert, George S. *s.j.* '72 (BO) [W] Boston, MA The Society of Jesus of New England-Provincial Offices.
Albert, James R. '86 (PRT) Eagle Lake, ME St. Mary's Church; Wallagrass, ME St. Joseph's Church.
Albert, Leo W. '91 (LA) [4] Los Angeles, CA Ascension Church.
Albert, Msgr. Louis W. (WDC) [3] Bowie, MD St. Edward Church.
Albert, Msgr. Louis W. '34 (WDC) Retired.
Albert, Patrick L. '92 (SCR) Dickson City, PA Visitation of the Blessed Virgin Mary Church.
Albert, Xavier R. '63 (STL) [1] St. Charles, MO St. Charles Borromeo Church.
Alberte, Carl P. '58 (MIL) [1] Pewaukee, WI Queen of Apostles Church.
Alberth, Regis '80 (PIT) Beaver County, PA McGuire Memorial Home.
Alberth, Regis R. '80 (PIT) Beaver, PA SS. Peter and Paul Church.
Albertine, Richard P. *m.m.* '66 (LA) [R] Los Angeles, CA Maryknoll Fathers and Brothers.
Alberts, Edward T. '75 (NSH) Brentwood, TN Holy Family Church.
Alberts, Keith M. '94 (CLV) [1] Euclid, OH St. Christine Church.
Albertson, Clinton E. *s.j.* '49 (LA) [C] Los Angeles, CA Loyola Marymount University.
Albertson, Eric '86 (ARL) Military Chaplains.
Albertson, Lawrence '65 (KCK) [1] Overland Park, KS Church of the Ascension.
Albietz, Henry F. '74 (CIN) Bellefontaine, OH St. Patrick's Church.
Albino, Brian E. *s.j.* '79 (BO) [W] Boston, MA The Society of Jesus of New England-Provincial Offices.
Albino, Brian E. *s.j.* '79 (FR) [5] New Bedford, MA Our Lady of the Immaculate Conception Church.
Albino, Ramon E. '84 (MGZ) Aguadilla, PR La Milagrosa Church.
Albosta, John T. '64 (SCR) Waymart, PA St. Mary's Church.
Albrecht, Craig L. '95 (SAG) Merrill, MI Sacred Heart Church; Ryan, MI St. Patrick Church.
Albrecht, G.R. Keith '77 (CIN) [51] Cincinnati, OH St. Jude the Apostle Church; Leave of Absence.
Albrecht, James W. '58 (NEW) [M] South Orange, NJ Opus Dei.
Albrecht, Louis Henry '86 (BAK) La Grande, OR Our Lady of the Valley Church.
Albrecht, Walter H. '43 (SAC) Retired and in Senior Ministry.
Albright, Charles W. *c.s.p.* '49 (NY) [DD] Jamaica Estates, NY Paulist Fathers Generalate.
Albright, R. Gerard *s.j.* '58 (DET) [K] Detroit, MI Jesuit Community at the University of Detroit.
Albright, Robert E. '72 (BAL) Special Assignment; [O] Baltimore, MD Archdiocesan Office-Newman Center.
Alcantara, Miguel B. '65 (CHI) [134] Chicago, IL St. Matthias Church.
Alcazar, Emanuel '89 (ELP) [29] El Paso, TX St. Paul the Apostle Church.
Alciati, Paul J. '77 (SY) [6] Binghamton, NY St. John the Evangelist Church.
Alco, James J. '90 (SCR) [2] Hazleton, PA Church of the Most Precious Blood.
Alcocer, Jose '60 (ELP) [36] El Paso, TX San Jose Church.
Alcocer, Jose M. *m.ss.cc.* '64 (SJN) [1] Trujillo Alto, PR San Bartolome Church.
Aldana, Antonio '53 (NY) [169] Bronx, NY Our Lady of Angels Church.
Aldasoro, Msgr. Francisco '47 (SD) Retired.
Aldegunde, Jose R. '58 (BRK) [201] Queens, NY St. Michael Church.
Alder, Ronald J. '69 (DET) Dundee, MI St. Irene Church.
Alderson, George K. '71 (GBG) [1] Uniontown, PA St. John The Evangelist Church.
Alderson, John *o.f.m.* '66 (NEW) Fair Lawn, NJ St. Anne's Church.
Aldrich, Louis G. *s.j.* '86 (FgM) Provinces.
Aldrich, Ralph '53 (PEO) Retired.
Aldridge, William J. *o.p.* '46 (BR) [J] Ponchatoula, LA Rosaryville/Spirit Life Center.
Aldworth, Thomas '75 (CHI) [167] Chicago, IL St. Peter's Church; [N] Chicago, IL St. Peter's Friary.
Alecio, Freddy '91 (SJN) [11] Carolina, PR Jesus Mediador Church; [C] Rio Piedras, PR Seminario Menor San Jose.
Aleckna, John Mark *c.p.* '41 (HRT) [M] West Hartford, CT Holy Family Monastery/Retreat.
Alejunas, Richard '89 (BO) [E] Boston, MA Don Bosco Preparatory School.
Aleksa, Thomas M. '75 (E) Bradford, PA St. Bernard Church.
Aleksonis, Vladas '34 (FAR) Retired; [E] Fargo, ND Riverview Place, Inc.
Aleman, Msgr. Vernon P. '35 (NO) [56] New Orleans, LA St. Raphael the Archangel Church; Retired.
Alenchery, Siby J. '87 (RVC) Coram, NY St. Frances Cabrini Church.
Alesandro, Msgr. John A. '66 (RVC) Garden City, NY St. Joseph's Church; East Meadow, NY Nassau County Police Department.
Alessandrini, Raniero *c.s.* '57 (CHI) [N] Chicago, IL Scalabrini House of Theology.
Alessandro, Michael J. '44 (NY) Bronx, NY Calvary Hospital; Retired; [X] New York, NY Calvary Hospital.
Alexander, Andrew *s.j.* '79 (OM) [K] Omaha, NE Jesuit Community At Creighton University.
Alexander, Anthony F. '45 (CLV) Perry, OH St. Cyprian Church; Retired.
Alexander, F. Leon '66 (WH) South Charleston, WV Blessed Sacrament Church.
Alexander, Fred *o.c.d.* '82 (MIL) Holy Hill, WI St. Mary of the Hill Church; [P] Holy Hill, WI Discalced Carmelite Monastery.
Alexander, Jim *s.c.j.* '44 (MIL) [P] Franklin, WI Villa Maria.
Alexander, John D. *s.j.* '54 (NY) [DD] New York, NY Jesuit Community at Fordham University; [HH] New York, NY Brooklyn Prep Alumni Association.
Alexander, Jon *o.p.* '85 (LSC) Silver City, NM St. Francis Newman Center Parish.
Alexander, Joseph J. '73 (LAF) Eunice, LA St. Anthony of Padua Church.
Alexander, Marc R. '85 (HON) [A] Kaneohe, HI St. Stephen's Diocesan Center.
Alexandrunas, Albert *o.f.m.cap.* '65 (WH) Belle, WV St. John Church; [N] Charleston, WV Capuchins-St. Anthony Friary.
Alfano, Michael A.J. '87 (BO) Maynard, MA St. Bridget Church.
Alfaro, Juan '62 (SAT) [64] San Antonio, TX St. Rose of Lima Church.
Alfonso, Jairo *c.s.* '96 (BRK) [71] Brooklyn, NY St. Joseph Patron of the Universal Church.
Alicea, Adrian *s.s.s.* '90 (CGS) [5] Caguas, PR Santisimo Sacramento Church.
Alicea, Msgr. Joaquin '71 (PCE) Juana Diaz, PR St. Raymond Nonato Church.
Alicea, Msgr. Joaquin A. '71 (PCE) [B] Ponce, PR The Pontifical Catholic University of Puerto Rico.
Alicea, Luis Antonio '96 (CGS) Humacao, PR Dulce Nombre de Jesus Church.
Alisauskas, Peter J. '43 (SCR) Retired.
Alkire, Thomas J. *o.carm.* '63 (STO) [5] Stockton, CA St. Gertrude Church.
Alkire, Timothy M. '85 (LFT) [3] Lafayette, IN St. Boniface Church.
Allaire, Barry J. '61 (BUF) [D] Olean, NY Archbishop Walsh High School.
Allaire, Barry J. '72 (BUF) Hinsdale, NY St. Helen Church.
Allaire, Robert A. '61 (PRO) Absent on Leave.
Allanach, Robert C. *o.m.i.* '80 (NO) [K] New Orleans, LA Boys Hope; [S] New Orleans, LA Jesuit Program for Living and Learning of New Orleans, Inc.
Allard, George L. '60 (PRO) [2] West Warwick, RI Christ the King Church.
Allard, Gilles *i.m.c.* '63 (SB) [H] San Bernardino, CA Newman Catholic Fellowship.
Allard, Msgr. John C. '75 (PRO) [1] Woonsocket, RI St. Agatha Church; [10] Woonsocket, RI Precious Blood Church.
Allard, John E. *o.p.* '86 (BO) [W] Dover, MA St. Stephen Priory; [Y] Dover, MA St. Stephen Priory Spiritual Life Center.
Allard, Marcel M. '65 (MAN) Newton, NH Mary, Mother of the Church.
Allard, William '55 (OWN) [1] Owensboro, KY St. Stephen Cathedral.
Allbright, Brian V. *m.m.* '83 (SEA) [M] Seattle, WA Maryknoll Fathers.
Allega, Ernest P. '76 (WOR) Uxbridge, MA St. Mary's Church.
Allegra, Christopher '70 (L) [3] Springfield, KY Holy Trinity Church.
Allegretto, William M. *c.m.* '85 (MOB) Opelika, AL St. Mary of the Mission Church.
Alleman, Msgr. C. J. '49 (GAL) Retired.
Allen, A. Christopher '81 (PMB) Stuart, FL St. Joseph Church.
Allen, Charles H. '73 (BGP) [A] Fairfield, CT Fairfield University; [O] Fairfield, CT The Fairfield Jesuit Community-Fairfield University.
Allen, David E. '78 (BR) [13] Baton Rouge, LA St. Jude the Apostle Church.
Allen, David G. *s.j.* '79 (BAL) [M] Baltimore, MD Jesuit Fathers and Brothers Maryland Provincial Curia.
Allen, David W. '95 (DEN) [2] Aurora, CO St. Michael the Archangel Church.
Allen, Edward A. *s.s.c.* '30 (FgM) St. Columban's Foreign Mission.
Allen, Francis J. *s.m.m.* '51 (RVC) [N] Bay Shore, NY Montfort Missionaries.
Allen, Francis R. *s.j.* '56 (BGP) [O] Fairfield, CT The Fairfield Jesuit Community-Fairfield University.
Allen, James *o.m.i.* '65 (CHI) [N] Chicago, IL The Oblate House of Theology.
Allen, John Andrew '90 (PRT) Biddeford, ME St. Mary's Church.
Allen, John G. '70 (HBG) [7] Harrisburg, PA St. Margaret Mary Alacoque Church.
Allen, John R. *s.j.* '42 (STL) [O] St. Louis, MO Fusz Pavilion.
Allen, Joseph '81 (FAR) La Moure, ND Holy Rosary Church.
Allen, Joseph A. '53 (BIS) On Duty Outside the Diocese.
Allen, Joseph A. '53 (GR) Retired.
Allen, Joseph C. '50 (BIR) Athens, AL St. Paul's Church.
Allen, Joseph P. *o.p.* '67 (Y) [13] Youngstown, OH St. Dominic's Church.
Allen, Joseph P. '91 (CHI) Lansing, IL St. Ann Church.
Allen, Loren '94 (SR) Special Assignment; [B] Eureka, CA St. Bernard's High School.
Allen, Michael '71 (EVN) Jasper, IN St. Joseph Church.
Allen, Paul L. *s.j.* '38 (DET) [P] Clarkston, MI Colombiere Center.
Allen, Peter A. '71 (RVC) Cutchogue, NY Sacred Heart Church.
Allen, Philip J. '58 (WCH) Aleppo, KS Immaculate Conception Church; Garden Plain, KS St. Anthony Church.
Allen, Philip T. '59 (OG) Redford, NY Assumption of the B.V.M. Church.
Allen, Richard '54 (SP) [4] Tampa, FL Good Shepherd Church.
Allen, Msgr. Richard F. '56 (CHL) [4] Charlotte, NC St. Ann Church.
Allen, Richard J. '97 (E) Corry, PA St. Thomas The Apostle Church; Meadville, PA St. Agatha Church.
Allen, Richard L. '61 (GB) Neenah, WI St. Gabriel I Church.
Allen, Richard T. *o.s.a.* '63 (JOL) New Lenox, IL St. Jude Church.
Allen, Terry E. '61 (ALX) Pineville, LA Sacred Heart Church.

Allen, Thomas E. '48 (SPC) Lamar, MO St. Mary Church.
Allen, William F. '31 (SPR) Retired.
Allende, Santiago Rivera '83 (MGZ) Moca, PR Our Lady of Monserrate Church.
Allender, Raymond P. *s.j.* '75 (SJ) [D] San Jose, CA Bellarmine College Preparatory.
Allender, Thomas G. *s.j.* '71 (SJ) [M] Los Gatos, CA Sacred Heart Jesuit Center.
Aller, Domingo *o.s.a.* (SJN) [A] Bayamon, PR Bayamon Central University.
Aller, Domingo *o.s.a.* '61 (SJN) [15] Bayamon, PR Ntra. Sra. de la Monserrate Church.
Allessandro, Michael J. '44 (NY) [127] Bronx, NY St. Anthony Church.
Alletto, Nicholas P. '45 (ROC) Retired.
Alleyne, Msgr. Edward D. '60 (CAM) [6] Cherry Hill, NJ Queen of Heaven Church.
Alliata, Peter R. '61 (WDC) Mount Rainier, MD St. James Church.
Allie, Robert *o.m.i.* '51 (STP) [28] St. Paul, MN St. Mary Church; St. Paul, MN St. Paul-Ramsey Hospital; St. Paul, MN Gillette Children's Hospital.
Allie, Stanley J. '58 (ALB) On Duty Outside the Diocese.
Allie, Stanley J. '58 (ANC) Wasilla, AK Sacred Heart Church.
Alliegro, Msgr. Michael J. '73 (MET) East Brunswick, NJ St. Bartholomew Church; [N] Metuchen, NJ The Catholic Lawyers Guild of the Diocese of Metuchen, Inc.
Allin, R. Benedict *o.s.b.* '67 (STL) [1] Creve Coeur, MO St. Anselm Church; [P] St. Louis, MO The Abbey of St. Mary and St. Louis.
Alling, James '92 (PHX) Kingman, AZ St. Mary's Church.
Allison, Msgr. Bruce '61 (E) [C] Erie, PA Cathedral Preparatory School.
Allison, Jeffrey *c.s.c.* '96 (AUS) [13] Austin, TX St. Ignatius Martyr Church.
Allison, Joseph C. '56 (CIN) Morrow, OH St. Philip the Apostle Church.
Allison, Michael (PMB) On Duty Outside the Diocese.
Allison, Michael P. (E) [28] Erie, PA St. Paul Church.
Allison, Michael P. '91 (E) [P] Erie, PA Newman Centers and Campus Ministry.
Allman, Mark '96 (ALB) Guilderland, NY Christ the King Church.
Allman, Timothy J. '58 (SP) [2] Clearwater, FL Light of Christ Church; [F] Clearwater, FL Light of Christ Preschool.
Allmaras, Alfred '59 (FAR) Michigan, ND St. Lawrence O'Toole Church.
Allt, John F. '73 (TUC) [15] Tucson, AZ St. Joseph Church.
Almade, Frank D. '78 (PIT) [P] Allison Park, PA The Sisters of Divine Providence; [S] Pittsburgh, PA Christ Child Society of Pittsburgh.
Almango, R. Stephen *o.f.m.* '65 (PIT) [60] Pittsburgh, PA St. Pamphilus Church.
Almarza, Juan *o.a.r.* '65 (LSC) Anthony, NM St. Anthony's Church.
Almasy, Alcuin M. *o.s.b.* '60 (TUC) [F] St. David, AZ Holy Trinity Monastery.
Almazan, Jose A. *c.m.* '63 (CC) Premont, TX St. Theresa of the Infant Jesus Church.
Almeida, George F. '65 (FR) [4] Swansea, MA Our Lady of Fatima Church.
Almendariz, Jose J. '63 (MGZ) San Sebastian, PR San Sebastian Martir Church.
Almendra, Leoncio T. '60 (NOR) Retired.
Almendras, Joel '75 (MRY) Soledad, CA Correctional Training Facility.
Alminde, Joseph M. *s.j.* '62 (BAL) [C] Baltimore, MD Loyola High School.
Almonte, Alfred P. *c.s.* '61 (PRO) [4] Johnston, RI St. Rocco Church.
Almonte, Antonio '97 (NY) [53] New York, NY Incarnation Church.
Almy, Augustin '74 (BRK) [109] Brooklyn, NY Our Lady of Refuge Church.
Alonso, Armando '90 (MIA) [33] Miami, FL St. Timothy Church.
Alonso, Ignacio *c.m.* '60 (PCE) [8] Ponce, PR La Milagrosa Church.
Alonso, Jose A. *l.c.* '64 (PRO) [U] South Kingstown, RI "Mater Ecclesiae" International Formation Center.
Alonso, Msgr. Jose A. '68 (PAT) Absent on Leave.
Alonso, Jose Luis *o.p.* '61 (PCE) Yauco, PR Holy Rossary Church; [B] Ponce, PR The Pontifical Catholic University of Puerto Rico.
Alonso, Oscar *sch.p.* '68 (MIA) [C] Fort Lauderdale, FL Cardinal Gibbons High School.
Alonso, Santiago '50 (ELP) [35] El Paso, TX San Antonio Church.
Alookaran, Joy '80 (NEW) Scotch Plains, NJ St. Bartholomew Church.
Alphonso, John '68 (DAL) [I] Dallas, TX St. Paul Medical Center.
Alrutz, Paul W. *s.m.a.* '75 (BO) [W] Dedham, MA African Mission House.
Alsola, Felix '86 (DET) [H] Southfield, MI Providence Hospital.
Alt, Clement B. *c.pp.s.* '51 (CIN) Rockford, OH St. Teresa Church.
Alt, Kenneth G. *c.pp.s.* '78 (FTW) [11] Fort Wayne, IN Most Precious Blood Church.
Altamira, Francisco *m.sp.s.* '39 (LA) [3] Oxnard, CA Our Lady of Guadalupe Parish.
Altavilla, Philip A. '92 (SCR) [21] Scranton, PA St. Patrick's Church.
Altavista, Salvatore D. *m.s.* '64 (HRT) [M] Hartford, CT Missionaries of LaSalette Provincial Secretary.
Altenbaugh, Richard L. '60 (PT) [9] Pensacola, FL St. John the Evangelist Church.
Altermatt, Gregory '76 (HRT) [1] West Haven, CT Our Lady of Victory Church.
Altermatt, Gregory M. '76 (HRT) [I] New Haven, CT Hospital of St. Raphael.
Althoff, Arthur J. '55 (STL) Retired.
Altier, Robert J. '89 (STP) [12] St. Paul, MN St. Agnes Church.
Altine, Richard L. '95 (KAL) Byron Center, MI St. Mary's Visitation Church.
Altman, David *o.c.s.o.* '79 (SLC) [F] Huntsville, UT Abbey of Our Lady of the Holy Trinity of the Order of Cistercians.
Altman, Joseph W. '76 (CHI) Harvey, IL Ascension-St. Susanna Church.
Altmann, George '44 (BAL) Retired.
Altmann, Robert T. '62 (LC) [5] Wausau, WI St. Matthew Church.
Altrui, Ronald P. '81 (NY) Beacon, NY St. Joachim Church.
Altstock, Edward '59 (P) Molalla, OR St. James Church.
Altuna, Javier *s.j.* '66 (LA) Inglewood, CA St. John Chrysostom Church.
Alvar, Zosimo '89 (SFR) San Francisco, CA San Francisco General Hospital.
Alvar, Zosimo C., Jr. '89 (SFR) [44] San Francisco, CA St. Peter Church.
Alvarado, Felix Emilio '90 (PCE) [2] Ponce, PR Church San Patricio; Jayuya, PR Our Lady of Monserrate Church.
Alvarado, John P. '88 (MET) [3] Perth Amboy, NJ Holy Trinity Church; [5] Perth Amboy, NJ Our Lady of Hungary Church.
Alvarado, Marco Antonio '83 (OAK) [15] Oakland, CA Mary Help of Christians Church.
Alvarado, Robert *c.m.f.* '39 (SAT) [12] San Antonio, TX Immaculate Heart of Mary Church.
Alvarado, Roberto '89 (ELP) Pecos, TX Santa Rosa Church.
Alvares, Augustine '50 (P) Retired.
Alvarez, Abel *o.s.a.* '58 (NY) [49] New York, NY Holy Rosary Church; Bronx, NY Lincoln Medical and Mental Health Center.
Alvarez, Anthony M. '93 (MET) On Duty Outside the Diocese.
Alvarez, Antonio '85 (ARE) On Duty Outside the Diocese.
Alvarez, Armando '72 (SJN) [45] San Juan, PR Ntra. Sra. del Perpetuo Socorro Church.
Alvarez, Eduardo *s.j.* '74 (MIA) [D] Miami, FL Belen Jesuit Preparatory School; [H] Miami, FL Villa Javier.
Alvarez, Fred *s.a.* '61 (NY) [DD] Garrison, NY Franciscan Friars of the Atonement.
Alvarez, Isaias *o.s.a.* '76 (SJN) [15] Bayamon, PR Ntra. Sra. de la Monserrate Church.
Alvarez, Javier *o.f.m.* (SJ) [18] San Jose, CA Our Lady of Guadalupe Church.
Alvarez, Jay '81 (PMB) [F] Delray Beach, FL Opus Dei.
Alvarez, Julio '75 (WDC) Hyattsville, MD St. Mark Church.
Alvarez, Manuel '44 (SFE) Retired.
Alvarez, Michael *s.d.b.* '79 (LA) [C] Rosemead, CA Don Bosco Technical Institute.
Alvarez, Miguel *sch.p.* '61 (PCE) [4] Ponce, PR Our Lady of Mt. Carmel Church; [B] Ponce, PR The Pontifical Catholic University of Puerto Rico.
Alvarez, Miguel *c.s.* '96 (CHI) [122] Chicago, IL Santa Maria Addolorata Church.
Alvarez, Pablo *f.s.s.p.* '86 (SCR) [M] Elmhurst, PA Priestly Fraternity of St. Peter (F.S.S.P.), North American District Headquarters.
Alvarez, Pablo D. *f.s.s.p.* '86 (LR) [L] Little Rock, AR Priestly Fraternity of St. Peter.
Alvarez, Pablo D. '86 (PCE) On Duty Outside the Diocese.
Alvarez, Perfecto *o.s.a.* '52 (PCE) [15] Ponce, PR Church of the Sacred Heart; [B] Ponce, PR The Pontifical Catholic University of Puerto Rico; [D] Ponce, PR Home for Aged and Infirm.
Alvarez, Pompilio '60 (NY) [130] Bronx, NY St. Athanasius Church.
Alvarez, Porfirio '69 (LA) Santa Fe Springs, CA St. Pius X Church.
Alvarez, Rafael *o.f.m.* '95 (LA) [68] Los Angeles, CA Santa Isabel Church.
Alvarez, Ramon '82 (DAL) [25] Dallas, TX St. Pius X Church.
Alvarez, Victor *s.s.p.* (CHI) [A] Mundelein, IL University of St. Mary of the Lake-Mundelein Seminary.
Alvarez, Xavier '73 (AMA) Absent on Leave.
Alvernaz, Dennis M. '71 (FRS) Yosemite National Park, CA Our Lady of the Snows Church.
Alves, Eugene L. '61 (BO) [2] Gloucester, MA Our Lady of Good Voyage Church.
Alves, Francis *s.j.* '95 (WDC) [M] Washington, DC The Jesuit Community at Georgetown University.
Alves, Msgr. Joseph T. '53 (BO) Retired.
Alves, Ronald *c.m.f.* '72 (FRS) [8] Fresno, CA St. Anthony Claret Church.
Alvesteffer, Eugene '65 (GR) Retired.
Alvey, J. Paul '53 (SC) Retired.
Alvey, Leonard J. '58 (OWN) Non-Parochial Assignments; [A] Owensboro, KY Brescia College.
Alvez, Angel Oscar *l.d.* '96 (PCE) [18] Ponce, PR Church Santisimo Sacramento.
Alvsarez, Milton *c.m.f.* '77 (CHI) [80] Chicago, IL Holy Cross/Immaculate Heart of Mary Church.
Alzate, Alberto '77 (LAV) [6] Las Vegas, NV St. Anne Church.
Alzate, Alvaro (SAC) [11] Sacramento, CA St. Charles Borromeo Church.
Alzugaray, Msgr. Joseph '67 (SR) Petaluma, CA St. James Church; Petaluma, CA St. Vincent de Paul Church.
Amabile, Patsy C. '73 (CAM) [5] Cherry Hill, NJ St. Thomas More Church.
Amadee, Msgr. Francis J. '48 (HT) [6] Thibodaux, LA St. Luke Church.
Amadeo, Michael (DM) On Special Assignment.
Amador, Alfonso *c.ss.r.* (CGS) Fajardo, PR Santiago Apostol Church.
Amaldoss, G. '78 (NO) [8] Metairie, LA St. Edward the Confessor Church.
Amalfitano, Joseph A. '63 (PH) Marcus Hook, PA Immaculate Conception Church.
Amalraj, Loyola '81 (MIL) Muskego, WI St. Leonard Congregation Church.
Aman, Gerald W. *s.j.* '73 (FgM) Provinces.
Amanchukwu, Emeka Godfrey '89 (NY) Ardsley, NY Our Lady of Perpetual Help Church.
Amandolare, Msgr. Ronald A. '61 (PAT) Chatham, NJ St. Patrick's Church.
Amann, John J. '66 (BRK) [161] Queens, NY St. Catherine of Sienna Church.
Amann, Msgr. Robert A. '50 (CIN) [33] Cincinnati, OH Holy Angels Church.
Amann, Steven J. '74 (MIL) New Berlin, WI St. Elizabeth Ann Seton Church.
Amann, William '54 (ROC) Hamlin, NY St. Elizabeth Ann Seton Church.
Amantegui, Carmelo *s.j.* (NY) [152] Bronx, NY St. Jerome's Church.
Amantia, Damian-Vincent *t.o.r.* '90 (VEN) [2] Sarasota, FL Our Lady Queen of Martyrs Church.
Amanzeh, Augustine '74 (SAT) [7] San Antonio, TX Holy Redeemer Church; San Antonio, TX San Antonio State Hospital.
Amar, Joseph P. '74 (FTW) [B] Notre Dame, IN University of Notre Dame Du Lac.
Amar, Joseph P. '74 (SAM) On Duty Outside the Diocese.
Amar, Mubarak A. '91 (PEO) Depue, IL St. Mary's Church.
Amaral, Angelo '86 (NEW) [17] Newark, NJ St. James Church.
Amaral, Stephen P. (PRO) South Kingstown, RI St. Francis of Assisi Church.
Amarasekera, Giles '73 (AUS) Rockdale, TX St. Joseph's Church.
Amarco, Arlindo A. *c.s.sp.* '56 (PRO) [4] Pawtucket, RI Immaculate Heart of Mary Church.
Amarillas, Thomas R. *m.m.* '68 (FgM) Maryknoll Foreign Missions.
Amato, Antonio '61 (PRT) Dexter, ME St. Ann's Church.
Amato, Benet *o.s.b.* '79 (IND) Cannelton, IN St. Michael Church; Tell City, IN St. Paul Church; Troy, IN St. Pius Church; [J] St. Meinrad, IN St. Meinrad Archabbey.
Amato, Joseph '59 (ALB) Retired.
Amato, Joseph S. '59 (VEN) [3] Sarasota, FL St. Martha Church.
Amato, Msgr. Nicholas P. '70 (BAL) Parkton, MD Our Lady of Grace Church.
Amato, Salvatore '69 (BRK) [233] Queens, NY Resurrection-Ascension Church.
Amberger, Frank '96 (CIN) Coldwater, OH Holy Trinity Church.
Ambert, Jorge *s.j.* '66 (SJN) [22] San Juan, PR San Ignacio de Loyola Church; [D] Hato Rey, PR Renovacion Conyugal.
Ambosta, Dawson '75 (NY) Bronxville, NY St. Joseph Church.
Ambre, John T. '22 (GRY) [N] Gary, IN Indiana University Northwest.

Ambre, John T. '75 (GRY) [14] Gary, IN St. Mark Church.
Ambrogi, James J. '64 (PH) Malvern, PA St. Patrick Church.
Ambros, Joseph M. '46 (WDC) [B] Washington, DC Diocesan Laborer Priests, House of Studies.
Ambrose, Arubraj (CHI) [J] Chicago, IL Holy Cross Hospital.
Ambrose, C. '88 (NY) Mamaroneck, NY St. Vito Church.
Ambrose, Thomas E. *s.j.* '47 (NY) [DD] New York, NY Murray-Weigel Hall.
Ambrosio, Joseph '74 (NEW) [28] Newark, NJ Our Lady of Mt. Carmel Church.
Ambrosy, David J. '85 (DUB) [11] Dubuque, IA St. Joseph the Worker Church.
Ameche, William A. *s.j.* '81 (FgM) Provinces.
Amedee, Msgr. Francis J. '48 (HT) [1] Thibodaux, LA St. Joseph Co-Cathedral; [E] Thibodaux, LA St. Joseph Manor.
Ameling, Richard H. '66 (GRY) [2] Michigan City, IN Notre Dame Church.
Amen, Maurice E. *c.s.c.* '61 (FTW) [J] South Bend, IN Congregation of Holy Cross Indiana Province Provincial House.
Amengual, Miguel '46 (LA) Torrance, CA Nativity Church.
Ament, Msgr. Ernest P. '29 (DUB) Bellevue, IA St. Joseph's Church; Retired.
Ament, Richard J. '66 (DUB) Central City, IA St. Stephen's Church; Coggon, IA St. John the Evangelist Church; Prairieburg, IA St. Joseph's Church.
Ament, Robert J. '52 (DUB) Retired.
Amerando, Jerry (FRS) [H] Fresno, CA St. Paul Newman Center.
Amerando, Jerry '84 (FRS) [10] Fresno, CA St. Helen Church; [12] Fresno, CA St. Paul Church.
Amershek, Charles M., Jr. '75 (ALT) [7] Johnstown, PA St. Rochus Church.
Ames, Gregory K. '86 (DEN) Greeley, CO St. Peter Church; [P] Greeley, CO University of Northern Colorado (Greeley).
Ames, John J. '82 (PH) Conshohocken, PA St. Matthew Church; [D] Springfield, PA Cardinal O'Hara High School.
Amey, Robert G. '69 (WDC) [4] Silver Spring, MD St. Catherine Laboure Church.
Amezaga, Louis D. '96 (LSC) [1] Las Cruces, NM Cathedral of Immaculate Heart of Mary.
Amezcua, Alfonso *o.r.c.* '87 (PCE) Adjuntas, PR St. Joachim Church.
Amezcua, Pedro E. '86 (LA) [15] Los Angeles, CA Immaculate Conception Church.
Amico, Alexander D. '73 (E) Coalport, PA St. Basil the Great Church.
Amico, Charles R. '52 (BUF) [A] East Aurora, NY Christ the King Seminary.
Amico, Francis A. *c.s.b.* '75 (GAL) [Q] Sugar Land, TX Basilian Mission Center.
Amico, Nicholas H. '51 (DET) Oak Park, MI Our Lady of Fatima Church.
Amico, Msgr. Richard S. '60 (BUF) [5] Niagara Falls, NY St. Joseph Church.
Amidon, Philip *s.j.* '74 (OM) [23] Omaha, NE St. John Church.
Amidon, Philip R. *s.j.* '74 (OM) [K] Omaha, NE Jesuit Community At Creighton University.
Amiot, Ronald J. *s.j.* (BO) [W] Weston, MA Campion Center; [Y] Weston, MA Campion Renewal Center.
Amiro, Raymond M. '43 (SFE) Retired.
Amissah, Kofi '79 (ALB) [6] Albany, NY St. George Church.
Ammering, Bruce F. '54 (ROC) [8] Rochester, NY Blessed Sacrament Church.
Amo, Steven '92 (SPR) West Springfield, MA St. Thomas the Apostle Church.
Amodio, Francis *o.carm.* '82 (NY) [97] New York, NY Our Lady of the Scapular/St. Stephen Church.
Amora, Edito '77 (TR) Brick Town, NJ Visitation Church.
Amora, Silvano '77 (TR) Tuckerton, NJ St. Teresa Church.
Amore, Innocent *o.f.m.cap.* '34 (NY) [B] Beacon, NY St. Lawrence of Brindisi Friary.
Amoros, Juan Maria *o.carm.* '55 (MGZ) Anasco, PR St. Anthony Abbot Church.
Amos, Msgr. James '54 (PT) [3] Pensacola, FL Holy Spirit Church; [E] Tallahassee, FL Casa Calderon, Inc.
Amos, Msgr. John R. '73 (MOB) Mon Luis Island, AL St. Rose of Lima Church.
Amos, Martin J. '68 (CLV) Shaker Heights, OH St. Dominic Church.
Amponsah, Peter (BEL) Carbondale, IL St. Francis Xavier Church.
Amrhein, Peter T. '48 (MIL) Retired; [N] Wauwatosa, WI St. Camillus Health Center, Inc.
Amrhein, Quentin *c.p.* '53 (HRT) [M] West Hartford, CT Holy Family Monastery/Retreat.
Amrhein, Raphael *c.p.* '62 (PMB) [G] North Palm Beach, FL Our Lady of Florida Spiritual Center.
Amrhein, Robert *o.f.m.conv.* '62 (SY) [2] Syracuse, NY Assumption B.V.M. Church; Syracuse, NY St. Joseph's Hospital Health Center; [O] Syracuse, NY St. Joseph's Hospital Health Center.
Amsberry, John '97 (P) Milwaukie, OR St. John the Baptist Church.
Amundarain, Atanasio *c.p.* (SJN) [9] Carolina, PR Santa Gema Galgani Church.
Amundsen, Robert L. '69 (DEN) [3] Fort Collins, CO John XXIII University Parish; [P] Fort Collins, CO Colorado State University (Fort Collins).
Amy, Msgr. Peter L. '64 (LA) Sylmar, CA St. Didacus Church.
Amyot, Andrew J. '64 (OG) Norfolk, NY Visitation of the B.V.M. Church.
An, Andrew *c.m.c.* '87 (BO) [2] Chelsea, MA St. Rose of Lima Church.
An Ninh, Vincent Nguyen '71 (DET) Clawson, MI Guardian Angels Church.
Anable, Richard J. *s.j.* '45 (PAT) [I] Morristown, NJ Loyola House of Retreats.
Anadore, Charles E. '50 (BO) [1] Milton, MA St. Agatha Church; Retired.
Anandan, Elangovan '91 (TYL) Sulphur Springs, TX St. James Church.
Anandappa, Mahendra '85 (TYL) [1] Tyler, TX Cathedral of the Immaculate Conception; Jacksonville, TX Our Lady of Sorrows Church.
Anania, Alexis *o.f.m.* '58 (PIT) [O] McKeesport, PA Franciscan Friars.
Anastasia, Thomas '91 (SP) Pinellas Park, FL Sacred Heart Church.
Anastasio, Thomas '58 (BRK) [115] Brooklyn, NY St. Patrick Church.
Ancharski, John J. '83 (TUC) Solomon, AZ Our Lady of Guadalupe Church; Safford, AZ Conservation Center; Fort Grant Rural Station, AZ Fort Grant Training Center; Solomon, AZ Our Lady of Guadalupe.
Ancheril, Jose '86 (BEL) St. Libory, IL St. Liborius Church.
Ancona, Msgr. Gaspar F. '63 (GR) Byron Center, MI St. Sebastian's Church.
Anctil, Leo '43 (SUP) Retired.
Anctil, Peter Claude *o.s.b.* '67 (BUR) [E] Weston, VT Priory of Benedictine Monks.
Andalikiewicz, Charles '58 (KCK) [6] Kansas City, KS Sacred Heart Church; [12] Kansas City, KS St. John the Evangelist Church.
Andary, Edward J. '69 (PBL) Ignacio, CO St. Ignatius Parish.
Andary, John S. '51 (SAM) Retired.
Andary, Thomas M. '41 (MAR) Retired.
Andel, David '95 (SB) Palm Springs, CA St. Theresa Church.
Anderl, Henry *o.s.b.* '45 (SCL) [I] Collegeville, MN St. John's Abbey, of the Order of St. Benedict.
Anderlonis, Joseph J. '69 (PH) [49] Philadelphia, PA St. George Church.
Anders, Arnold '50 (VIC) Ganado, TX Assumption of the B.V.M. Church.
Anderson, Alexander R. '75 (STL) Eureka, MO Sacred Heart Church.
Anderson, Andrew '74 (MIA) [1] Miami, FL St. Mary's Cathedral.
Anderson, Anthony *s.o.l.t.* '91 (CC) Robstown, TX St. Anthony Church; [H] Robstown, TX Society of Our Lady of the Most Holy Trinity.
Anderson, Arthur *o.f.m.* '83 (CHI) [N] Chicago, IL St. Joseph Interprovincial Post-Novitiate Formation House.
Anderson, Arthur C. '62 (RVC) Brookville, NY St. Paul the Apostle Church.
Anderson, Arthur Edward '60 (SD) Retired.
Anderson, Arthur T. '58 (CAM) [9] Camden, NJ Sacred Heart Church; [H] Camden, NJ Our Lady of Lourdes Medical Center, Inc.
Anderson, B. Ernest '82 (B) Aberdeen, ID Blessed Sacrament Church; American Falls, ID St. Mary Church.
Anderson, Basil J. *o.s.b.* '54 (MIL) [P] Benet Lake, WI St. Benedict's Abbey.
Anderson, Bertil J. '74 (PRO) [8] Warwick, RI St. Rita Church.
Anderson, Daniel J. *o.f.m.* '76 (CIN) [M] Cincinnati, OH Pleasant Street Friary.
Anderson, Edward C. *c.s.v.* '50 (LAV) [D] Las Vegas, NV Clerics of St. Viator Retirement Home.
Anderson, Emil '64 (E) Retired.
Anderson, Emil '64 (SEA) Kirkland, WA Holy Family Church.
Anderson, Gabriel C. '89 (DUB) Walker, IA Sacred Heart Church.
Anderson, Garbiel C. '89 (DUB) Urbana, IA St. Mary Church.
Anderson, George M. *s.j.* '73 (NY) [80] New York, NY Nativity Church.
Anderson, Gregory H. *o.p.* '47 (SFR) [13] San Francisco, CA St. Dominic Church; [N] San Francisco, CA St. Dominic Priory.
Anderson, James B. '78 (GAL) [A] Houston, TX St. Mary's Seminary.
Anderson, James W. (LA) Port Hueneme, CA Naval Construction Battalion Center.
Anderson, John C. '59 (PEO) Special Assignment; [M] Henry, IL King's House of Retreats - Diocese of Peoria.
Anderson, John C. '93 (SUP) Hawkins, WI St. Mary Czestowchowa Church; Ladysmith, WI Our Lady of Sorrows Church; Tony, WI St. Anthony de Padua Church.
Anderson, John D. '62 (FAR) Hankinson, ND St. Philip's Church.
Anderson, John E. '66 (LSC) [2] Las Cruces, NM Holy Cross Church.
Anderson, John F. '50 (CLV) Chesterland, OH St. Anselm Church; Retired.
Anderson, John R. '96 (ATL) Alpharetta, GA St. Thomas Aquinas Church.
Anderson, Msgr. John V. '52 (DEN) [1] Denver, CO Cathedral of the Immaculate Conception.
Anderson, Jordan S. *o.praem* '96 (ORG) [D] Siverado, CA St. Michael's College Preparatory High School; [H] Silverado, CA Norbertine Fathers of Orange Inc.
Anderson, Joseph G. '63 (MIL) [2] South Milwaukee, WI St. John Church.
Anderson, Joseph K. *o.s.b.* '54 (LSC) Deming, NM Holy Family Church.
Anderson, Joseph R. '48 (SFS) Retired.
Anderson, Joseph W. '62 (PEO) [2] La Salle, IL St. Hyacinth's Church.
Anderson, Jude *o.s.b.* '94 (B) [C] Jerome, ID Ascension Priory.
Anderson, Kenneth J. '87 (RCK) Fulton, IL Immaculate Conception Church.
Anderson, Kevin '83 (SCL) [10] St. Cloud, MN Christ Church; [L] St. Cloud, MN Newman Center, Inc.
Anderson, Knute *o.s.b.* '56 (SCL) [I] Collegeville, MN St. John's Abbey, of the Order of St. Benedict.
Anderson, Kurt J. *m.m.* '72 (FgM) Maryknoll Foreign Missions.
Anderson, Louis L. '63 (GR) [17] Grand Rapids, MI St. Mary Magdalen Church.
Anderson, Luke *s.o.cist.* '54 (ALN) [K] New Ringgold, PA Cistercian Conventual Priory, St. Mary's Priory.
Anderson, Msgr. Marcel '57 (ALX) Retired.
Anderson, Mark R. '86 (E) Morrisdale, PA St. Agnes Church.
Anderson, Michael F. '83 (STP) [16] St. Paul, MN St. Bernard Church.
Anderson, R. Bentley *s.j.* '96 (BO) [W] Chestnut Hill, MA The Jesuit Community at Boston College.
Anderson, Richard W. *s.j.* '66 (CHI) [C] Chicago, IL Jesuit Community at Loyola University of Chicago.
Anderson, Robert L. *s.j.* '50 (NO) [C] New Orleans, LA Loyola University.
Anderson, Robert M. *o.s.m.* '65 (ORG) [H] Buena Park, CA Servite Fathers And Brothers.
Anderson, Ronald '72 (DET) Milford, MI St. Mary, Our Lady of the Snows Church.
Anderson, Ronald *s.j.* '83 (BO) [W] Chestnut Hill, MA The Jesuit Community at Boston College.
Anderson, Ronald *s.j.* '84 (BO) [W] Boston, MA The Society of Jesus of New England-Provincial Offices.
Anderson, Ronald C. '66 (BWN) Absent.
Anderson, Stephen A. '59 (E) [B] Erie, PA Mercyhurst College.
Anderson, Stephen A. '79 (E) [P] Erie, PA Newman Centers and Campus Ministry.
Anderson, Terence '84 (SFS) Faulkton, SD St. Thomas the Apostle Church.
Anderson, William (WH) Huttonsville, WV St. John Bosco Church.
Anderson, William A. '63 (WH) Coalton, WV St. Patrick Church; Elkins, WV St. Brendan Church.
Anderson, William C. '52 (TR) Holmdel, NJ St. Benedict Church.
Anderson, William R. '42 (BO) Retired.
Andert, Thomas *o.s.b.* '75 (SCL) [I] Collegeville, MN St. John's Abbey, of the Order of St. Benedict.
Andicoechea, Anselmo *c.p.* (SJN) [9] Carolina, PR Santa Gema Galgani Church.
Andonian, Rafael *c.m.vd.* '65 (BO) [5] Cambridge, MA Holy Cross Church.
Andonian, Raphael *o.m.ven.* '65 (ARM) Boston, MA Holy Cross Church.
Andracki, Jerome *c.r.* '42 (CHI) [D] Chicago, IL Weber High School; [J] Chicago, IL Our Lady of the Resurrection Medical Center.
Andrade, Anthony *o.s.b.* (STP) [27] St. Paul, MN St. Mark Church.
Andrade, Antonio L '63 (BO) Hudson, MA St. Michael Church.
Andrade, Bernardino '65 (OAK) Oakley, CA St. Anthony Church.
Andrade, Richard G. '83 (FR) Absent on Leave; [J] Fall River, MA St. John Vianney House.
Andrae, Henry C. '78 (E) Stoneboro, PA St. Columbkille Church.
Andraschko, Msgr. James F. '59 (SFS) [3] Sioux Falls, SD Holy Spirit Church.
Andrate, David M. '86 (FR) [15] Fall River, MA St. Jean Baptiste Church.

Andre, Leonard J. '61 (MIL) Retired.
Andre, Ludwig M. '57 (SJ) Los Altos, CA St. Simon Church.
Andreatta, Msgr. Tullio '38 (SB) Retired.
Andree, Daniel *c.ss.r.* '80 (WCH) [G] Wichita, KS Redemptorist Mission House.
Andree, Daniel H. *c.ss.r.* '80 (WCH) [14] Wichita, KS St. Joseph Church.
Andree, John *c.ss.r.* '68 (CHI) [9] Chicago, IL St. Alphonsus Church; [136] Chicago, IL St. Michael Church.
Andres, Edmundo *c.m.f.* '56 (CHI) [N] Oak Park, IL Claretian Fathers Headquarters of U.S.A. Eastern Province.
Andres, James R. *o.f.m.cap.* '63 (DET) [P] Washington, MI Capuchin Retreat.
Andres, Joseph P. '48 (CIN) Retired.
Andres, Timothy *o.carm.* '86 (JOL) [J] Joliet, IL St. Elias Carmelites.
Andreu, Ramon R. *s.j.* '55 (LA) [73] Los Angeles, CA St. Kevin Church.
Andrews, Alexander *o.s.b.* '69 (SCL) [I] Collegeville, MN St. John's Abbey, of the Order of St. Benedict.
Andrews, Dennis M. '65 (MIL) Brookfield, WI St. John Vianney Church.
Andrews, Dennis M. *c.s.b.* '70 (GAL) [Q] Houston, TX Residence of the Basilian Fathers of the University of St. Thomas.
Andrews, Edward *o.s.a.* '59 (CHI) [D] Chicago, IL St. Rita High School; [N] Chicago, IL St. Rita Monastery.
Andrews, Eric *c.s.p.* '95 (NY) [104] New York, NY St. Paul the Apostle Church.
Andrews, Gregory J. '76 (SP) [1] Clearwater, FL All Saints Church.
Andrews, John F. '62 (FR) Wellfleet, MA Our Lady of Lourdes Church.
Andrews, John S. '96 (OM) [40] Omaha, NE St. Robert Bellarmine Church.
Andrews, Lawrence W. '78 (OG) Absent on Leave.
Andrews, Mark J. *s.j.* (DET) [B] Berkley, MI Loyola House.
Andrews, Mark W. *s.j.* '92 (CHI) [N] Chicago, IL Chicago Province of the Society of Jesus-Provincial Office.
Andrews, Peter J. '88 (PRO) [1] Providence, RI Cathedral of SS. Peter and Paul.
Andrews, Robert F. *o.s.a.* '54 (NY) [216] Staten Island, NY Our Lady of Good Counsel Church.
Andrey, Roberto '83 (SFR) Daly City, CA St. Andrew Church.
Andrie, Donald A. *c.s.p.* '94 (COL) [J] Columbus, OH Campus Ministry.
Andriekus, Leonard *o.f.m.* '40 (PRT) [I] Kennebunkport, ME St. Anthony's Friary.
Andries, John W. '96 (ALX) Plaucheville, LA Mater Dolorosa Church.
Andrus, Albin '73 (PRT) [1] Portland, ME Cathedral of the Immaculate Conception; Portland, ME Maine Medical Center.
Andrus, Charles *s.s.j.* '76 (LA) [51] Los Angeles, CA St. Brigid's Church.
Andrus, David L. *s.j.* '79 (LAF) [A] Grand Coteau, LA St. Charles College.
Andrus, Richard R. *s.v.d.* '83 (STL) [53] St. Louis, MO St. Nicholas Church.
Andrushkiw, Vladimir '36 (STF) Retired.
Anduaga, Francisco J. *c.r.l.* '67 (ARE) Corozal-Palos Blancos, PR Christ the King Church.
Andujar, J. Iriarte *o.p.* '86 (PRO) [P] Providence, RI St. Thomas Aquinas Priory at Providence College.
Angadiath, Jacob '72 (DAL) [5] Garland, TX St. Thomas the Apostle Church.
Angelicchio, Paul F. '77 (SY) Fairmount, NY Holy Family Church.
Angelini, Joseph *o.f.m.conv.* '65 (ALB) [4] Albany, NY St. Casimir Church; [12] Albany, NY Our Lady of Angels Church.
Angelini, Joseph '67 (MIA) [35] Miami, FL Visitation Church.
Angell, Charles *s.a.* '60 (NY) [DD] Garrison, NY Franciscan Friars of the Atonement; [DD] Garrison, NY St. Christopher's Friary.
Angella, Ludovico '47 (NY) Middletown, NY St. Joseph Church.
Angelle, Msgr. Robert G. '56 (LAF) [14] Lafayette, LA St. Mary, Mother of the Church.
Angelo, Girard F. '55 (SCR) Harleigh, PA Sacred Heart of Jesus Church.
Angelo, Thomas M. '85 (NOR) Military Chaplains.
Angeloni, Michael A. '75 (WIL) Milford, DE St. John the Apostle Church.
Angeloni, Owen *o.f.m.* '62 (ALB) [A] Catskill, NY St. Anthony Friary.
Angelov, Kiril '89 (STF) Ludlow, MA SS. Peter and Paul Church; South Deerfield, MA Holy Ghost Church.
Angelovic, Michael '65 (SEA) [21] Seattle, WA Assumption Church.
Angelucci, Patrick *s.d.b.* '74 (PAT) [D] Paterson, NJ Don Bosco Technical High School.
Angelucci, Patrick *s.d.b.* '76 (FgM) Salesians of Don Bosco Foreign Missions.
Angelucci, Patrick *s.d.b.* '76 (NY) [DD] New Rochelle, NY Salesian Provincial House.
Anger, Raymond G. '57 (WOR) Retired.
Angers, Joseph *o.p.* '48 (NSH) [I] Nashville, TN St. Cecilia Convent.
Angert, James *t.o.r.* (ARL) Herndon, VA St. Joseph Church.
Angilella, Joseph T. *s.j.* '65 (SFR) [N] San Francisco, CA Jesuit Community at University of San Francisco.
Anginoli, Joseph T. '75 (PAT) Green Pond, NJ St. Simon the Apostle Church.
Angkel, Julio '83 (CI) Fefan, FM Sacred Heart Church; Lukunor, FM Sacred Heart Church.
Angle, Camillus *t.o.r.* '54 (ALT) [F] Newry, PA St. Bernardine Monastery.
Angles, Sebastian '44 (BRK) Retired.
Angles, Sebastian '44 (ORL) Retired.
Anglim, Ronald H. '65 (CHI) Antioch, IL St. Peter Church.
Anglim, Thomas M. '54 (VEN) [5] Fort Myers, FL St. Francis Xavier Church; [F] Fort Myers, FL Villa Francisco; [K] Fort Myers, FL St. Francis Xavier School Foundation.
Anglin, John *o.f.m.* '81 (BO) [W] Boston, MA Ministry of the Word.
Angotti, Joseph A. '91 (GRY) Highland, IN St. James the Less Church.
Anguiano, James '82 (LA) [D] Playa Del Rey, CA St. Bernard High School.
Angulo, Raul '85 (MIA) [8] Miami, FL Mother of Christ Church.
Anholzer, Daniel *o.f.m.cap.* '80 (SAG) [14] Saginaw, MI St. Joseph Church.
Aniban, Toribio Ives '66 (SJ) San Jose, CA O'Connor Hospital; [H] San Jose, CA O'Connor Hospital.
Anich, Kenneth *s.v.d.* '73 (DUB) [B] Epworth, IA Divine Word College.
Anichini, Albert *m.c.c.j.* '62 (FgM) Comboni Foreign Missions.
Aniello, Frederick M. '79 (HRT) Wethersfield, CT Incarnation Church.
Anifer, Jeffrey '67 (DET) Centerline, MI St. Clement Church.
Aniszczyk, Leon S. '73 (MET) Sayreville, NJ St. Stanislaus Kostka Church.
Ankenbrandt, Thomas F. *s.j.* '60 (DET) [P] Clarkston, MI Colombiere Center.
Ankenbrandt, Thomas W. '56 (TOL) Retired.
Anklan, Horecio Carlos *c.s.* '97 (MIA) Lighthouse Point, FL St. Paul the Apostle Church.
Annese, Joseph P. '62 (LAV) Boulder City, NV St. Andrew's Church.
Annese, Lucius *o.f.m.* '58 (BO) [3] Cambridge, MA St. Francis of Assisi Church.
Annie, Frederick P. '78 (WH) [1] Wheeling, WV St. Joseph's Cathedral.
Annino, Sebastian V. '61 (CAM) Rosenhayn, NJ St. Mary's Church; [I] Newfield, NJ Mater Dei Nursing Home.
Annunziato, Michael *ss.cc.* '53 (BWN) Edinburg, TX Sacred Heart Church.
Anoia, John '57 (SP) New Port Richey, FL Our Lady Queen of Peace Church.
Anoia, John '57 (SPR) Retired.
Anomah, Anthony *c.s.sp.* '97 (PIT) [78] Pittsburgh, PA Most Holy Name of Jesus Church.
Anosike, Donatus *m.s.p.* '90 (GAL) [53] Houston, TX St. Nicholas Church.
Ansaldi, Msgr. Joseph C. '62 (NY) [F] New York, NY St. Joseph by the Sea, High School; [G] New York, NY Seton Foundation for Learning, Inc.; [S] New York, NY Mission of the Immaculate Virgin.
Ansaloni, Edmund *o.f.m.* '49 (HRT) Canaan, CT St. Joseph's Church.
Ansbro, Msgr. Francis J. '51 (NY) Peekskill, NY Assumption Church.
Anschutz, Larry '82 (SFD) Mount Olive, IL Ascension Church; Mount Olive, IL Holy Trinity Church.
Anselment, Joseph '61 (ALB) Queensbury, NY Our Lady of the Annunciation Church.
Anselmi, Albert (ALT) Altoona, PA Altoona Hospital.
Anselmi, Albert '71 (ALT) [2] Altoona, PA Immaculate Conception Church.
Anselmi, Victor J. '74 (ALN) Ringtown, PA St. Mary Church; [7] Shenandoah, PA St. Stephen Church.
Anslow, Thomas C. *c.m.* '72 (LA) [R] Los Angeles, CA Vincentian Fathers and Brothers.
Anson, Cesar R. '77 (TR) Medford, NJ St. Mary of the Lakes Church.
Anstiss, Arthur '60 (SFE) Retired.
Anta, Antonio '55 (NEW) Retired.
Antal, Andras '68 (CLV) [21] Cleveland, OH St. Elizabeth Church.
Antall, Richard C. '80 (CLV) Painesville, OH St. Mary Church; [X] Cleveland, OH Diocesan Hispanic Office.
Antao, Msgr. John S. '60 (NEW) [15] Elizabeth, NJ Our Lady of Fatima Church.
Antczak, John '63 (JOL) Bradley, IL St. Joseph Church; Kankakee, IL Riverside Medical Center.
Antczak, Robert '64 (NEW) [26] Jersey City, NJ St. Paul's Church.
Antekeier, Charles R. '62 (GR) [6] Grand Rapids, MI St. Francis Xavier Church.
Anthamatten, Joseph *c.pp.s.* '43 (CIN) [B] Carthagena, OH St. Charles.
Anthony, Alphonse '92 (TYL) Paris, TX Our Lady of Victory Church.
Anthony, Angelo P. *c.pp.s.* '89 (CIN) [23] Dayton, OH Precious Blood Church; [M] Dayton, OH Provincial House of the Cincinnati Province of the Society of the Precious Blood; [U] Dayton, OH Community Support Charitable Trust.
Anthony, Edd *o.f.m.* '77 (STL) [P] St. Louis, MO Franciscan Friary of St. Anthony of Padua.
Anthony, Joseph L. '80 (LAV) [12] Las Vegas, NV St. Joseph, Husband of Mary Church.
Anthony, Msgr. Paul G. '61 (STL) Warson Woods, MO Ste. Genevieve Du Bois Church.
Anthony, Walter *c.s.p.* '56 (NY) [DD] Jamaica Estates, NY Paulist Fathers Generalate.
Antinarelli, Ronald A. '73 (ROC) Penfield, NY Holy Spirit Church.
Antipas, Douglas *o.f.m.cap.* (AGN) [E] Agana Heights, GU St. Fidelis Friary.
Antiporek, James W. '81 (JOL) Bolingbrook, IL St. Dominic Church.
Antl, Louis *o.f.m.* '48 (STL) [P] St. Louis, MO Franciscan Friary of St. Anthony of Padua.
Antl, Louis B. *o.f.m.* '48 (FgM) Franciscan Foreign Missions.
Antle, Nicholas C. (GAL) [N] Houston, TX Pope John XXIII Priest Residence.
Antle, Nicholas C. '59 (GAL) Retired.
Antoine, James *o.f.m.cap.* '67 (GF) Lodge Grass, MT Our Lady of Loretto Church.
Antolini, Vincenzo *o.m.v.* '58 (BO) [B] Boston, MA Oblate Provincialate.
Anton, Luciano *o.m.i.* '47 (LA) Pacoima, CA Mary Immaculate Church.
Anton, Ronald J. *s.j.* '83 (BAL) [B] Baltimore, MD Loyola College; [M] Baltimore, MD Jesuit Community of Loyola College, Inc.
Antonanzas, Msgr. Jesus R. Diez '57 (PCE) [A] Ponce, PR Diocesan Seminary.
Antoncic, Msgr. John J. '68 (BRK) [176] Queens, NY Holy Child Jesus Church.
Antone, William *o.m.i.* '80 (OAK) [N] Oakland, CA Oblate Provincial House & Procure.
Antonelli, Msgr. Louis '49 (CHK) Songsong Village, MP San Isidro Mission Parish.
Antonelli, Robert C. *c.s.c.* '65 (FTW) [J] South Bend, IN Congregation of Holy Cross Indiana Province Provincial House.
Antonellis, Joseph A. '72 (BO) [2] Revere, MA Immaculate Conception Church.
Antonicelli, Charles V. '93 (WDC) [1] Silver Spring, MD St. Andrew Apostle Church.
Antonio, William '88 (WDC) [B] Washington, DC Oblate College/Oblate Center for Mission Studies.
Antonucci, Richard J. *o.praem.* '72 (PH) [AA] Philadelphia, PA St. Norbert Priory.
Antony, Asir '82 (RVC) Rockville Centre, NY Mercy Medical Center; [I] Rockville Centre, NY Mercy Medical Center.
Antony, Charles '70 (NY) Absent on Leave.
Antony, John F. '91 (NY) Millbrook, NY St. Joseph Church.
Antony, John K. '96 (LR) [5] Little Rock, AR Christ the King Church.
Antony, Wilson Paul '92 (MIL) [17] Milwaukee, WI St. Catherine Church.
Antos, Paul J. '54 (ALB) [2] Watervliet, NY Immaculate Conception Church.
Antoun, Bernard '95 (OLD) Laval, St. Ephrem Church.
Antoun, Msgr. Elie '80 (SAM) Retired.
Antram, Cormac *o.f.m.* '54 (GLP) St. Michaels, AZ St. Michael Church.
Antry, Theodore J. *o.praem.* '66 (PH) [B] Paoli, PA Daylesford Abbey; [AA] Paoli, PA Daylesford Abbey.
Antunez, Roy *s.j.* '71 (P) [19] Portland, OR St. Ignatius Church.
Antus, Lawrence *o.m.i.* '58 (DUL) Duluth, MN Indian Missions Church.
Antus, Lawrence T. *o.m.i.* '53 (DUL) Cook, MN St. Mary's Church.
Antus, Lawrence T. *o.m.i.* '58 (DUL) Orr, MN Holy Cross Church.
Antus, Roland J. '62 (DUL) Brainerd, MN St. Francis Church.
Antweiler, Donald J. '73 (JC) St. Thomas, MO St. Thomas the Apostle Church.
Antwi, Dominic '81 (VIC) [5] Victoria, TX St. Mary's Church.
Anul, Salagunla Xavier '91 (NY) [1] New Rochelle, NY Blessed Sacrament Church.
Anumudu, Alphonsus '73 (NY) [89] New York, NY Our Lady of Lourdes Church.
Anuszewski, Albert M. *o.ss.t.* '91 (WDC) [M] Hyattsville, MD St. John de Matha Monastery, Order of Most Holy Trinity.
Anuszewski, Damian *o.ss.t.* '79 (BAL) [M] Baltimore, MD Holy Trinity Monastery.

Anuzis, Stanislovas '83 (LA) [54] Los Angeles, CA St. Casimir Church.
Anyaka, Godfrey (NY) Bronx, NY St. Barnabas Hospital.
Anyanwu, Celestine '83 (BRK) [170] Queens, NY St. Gabriel Church.
Anyanwu, Chris '80 (NEW) Newark, NJ St. Michael Medical Center.
Anyanwu, Chris '85 (NEW) [14] Newark, NJ Queen of Angels Church.
Anyimaduwireko, Joseph '81 (NY) Nanuet, NY St. Anthony Church.
Anziano, James J. '81 (PH) [21] Philadelphia, PA St. Bartholomew Church.
Anzoategui, Francisco J. *s.x.* '88 (BO) [3] Peabody, MA St. John the Baptist Church.
Apassa, Cyril '71 (RNO) [6] Reno, NV St. Therese Church of the Little Flower.
Apel, John A. *s.j.* '69 (FgM) Provinces.
Apel, John A. *s.j.* '69 (STL) [P] St. Louis, MO Jesuit Community Corporation at St. Louis University - Jesuit Hall; [P] St. Louis, MO The Jesuits of the Missouri Province.
Apoldite, Dennis A. '78 (TR) New Monmouth, NJ St. Mary Church.
Apolinares, Jaime G. '77 (NO) [44] New Orleans, LA St. Maria Goretti Church.
Aponte, Eliud '86 (PCE) Arroyo, PR Our Lady of Mt. Carmel Church.
Apostoli, Andrew D. *c.f.r.* '67 (NY) [18] Yonkers, NY Most Holy Trinity Church; [A] Yonkers, NY St. Joseph's Seminary; [DD] Yonkers, NY St. Felix Friary.
Apparcel, Gregora *c.s.p.* '83 (NY) [DD] Jamaica Estates, NY Paulist Fathers Generalate.
Appel, George '57 (BIR) On Duty Outside the Diocese.
Appelby, Gerald J. '59 (ROC) Pittsford, NY Church of the Transfiguration Church.
Appelt, Francis '52 (GRY) [J] Cedar Lake, IN Our Lady of Lourdes Friary.
Appicci, Richard D. *o.s.a.* '60 (FgM) Foreign Missions.
Appicci, Richard D. *o.s.a.* '60 (PH) [AA] Villanova, PA Provincial Offices of the Order of St. Augustine, Province of St. Thomas of Villanova; [AA] Villanova, PA St. Thomas Monastery.
Applegate, Gary '81 (KCK) [2] Leavenworth, KS Sacred Heart of Jesus Church; [3] Leavenworth, KS St. Casimir's Church.
Applegate, Msgr. P.A Bennett '45 (COL) Retired.
Appleyard, Msgr. George '68 (SJP) McKees Rocks, PA St. John the Baptist Church; Pittsburgh, PA St. George Church.
Appleyard, Joseph A. *s.j.* '62 (BO) [W] Chestnut Hill, MA The Jesuit Community at Boston College.
Appleyard, Joseph A. *s.j.* '66 (BO) [W] Boston, MA The Society of Jesus of New England-Provincial Offices.
Aquila, Samuel '76 (DEN) [1] Denver, CO Cathedral of the Immaculate Conception.
Aquino, James J. '65 (WOR) [11] Worcester, MA Our Lady of Loreto Church.
Aquino, Joe *m.s.* '69 (ORL) [2] Orlando, FL Blessed Trinity Church.
Aquino, Msgr. Oscar '64 (NY) [36] New York, NY St. Francis de Sales Church.
Aquino, Peter M. '69 (NEW) [13] Elizabeth, NJ SS. Peter and Paul's Church.
Aquwa, Jude (NY) Croton Falls, NY St. Joseph Church.
Aracich, Anthony S. *s.j.* '67 (NY) [80] New York, NY Nativity Church.
Aracil, Francis X. *s.d.b.* '34 (NY) [DD] New Rochelle, NY Salesian Cooperators of St. John Bosco.
Aracil, Javier *s.d.b.* '63 (NY) [DD] New Rochelle, NY Salesian Provincial House.
Arackal, Joseph J. *v.c.* '67 (STP) Vermillion, MN St. John the Baptist Church.
Arackal, Matthew *m.c.b.s.* '81 (SP) [1] Largo, FL St. Catherine of Siena Church.
Aragon, Ramon '50 (SFE) [8] Albuquerque, NM Our Lady of Guadalupe Church.
Aragon, Salvador *o.f.m.* '55 (SFE) [1] Santa Fe, NM The Cathedral of San Francisco de Asis; [J] Albuquerque, NM San Antonio Provincial Friary Franciscan Friars.
Aramburo, Eugenio '88 (MRY) Greenfield, CA Holy Trinity Church.
Aramburu, Jose A. *m.m.* '84 (NY) [DD] Maryknoll, NY Maryknoll Fathers and Brothers.
Arana, Francisco '64 (SJN) [1] Toa Baja, PR Nuestra Senora de Covadonga Church.
Arango, Fabio '66 (MIA) [G] Miami, FL Mercy Hospital.
Arango, Gilbert L. '93 (STO) Modesto, CA St. Stanislaus Church.
Arango, Gilberto (STO) Manteca, CA St. Anthony Church.
Arango, Miguel '65 (SAT) Asherton, TX Immaculate Conception Church.
Aranha, George '75 (SJ) [24] San Jose, CA Church of the Transfiguration.
Aranjaniyil, Hilarios *v.c.* '68 (SP) Sun City Center, FL Prince of Peace Church.
Araque, Alvaro U. '72 (STO) [8] Stockton, CA St. Mary of the Assumption Church.
Arata, Miguel A. '95 (NEW) On Duty Outside the Archdiocese.
Araudo, Robert J. *s.j.* '93 (STL) [P] St. Louis, MO Jesuit Community Corporation at St. Louis University - Jesuit Hall.
Araujo, Manuel *c.m.* '54 (MGZ) [8] Mayaquez, PR San Vicente Church.
Araujo, Robert J. *s.j.* '93 (BO) [W] Boston, MA The Society of Jesus of New England-Provincial Offices.
Araujo, Robert J. *s.j.* '93 (SPK) [C] Spokane, WA Gonzaga University.
Aravindassery, Anthony '75 (CHI) [165] Chicago, IL St. Patrick Church.
Araya-Morales, Reynord '89 (ORL) [4] Lakeland, FL St. Joseph's Church.
Arbanas, Harold P. '48 (GF) Retired.
Arbelaez, Ernesto *s.j.* '56 (SJ) [M] Los Gatos, CA Sacred Heart Jesuit Center.
Arbelaez, Ernesto '56 (STO) Hughson, CA St. Anthony Church.
Arbelaez, Mario '94 (SLC) [4] Midvale, UT St. Therese of the Child Jesus Church.
Arbizu, Juventino '44 (NO) Retired.
Arboleda, Vidal '55 (ORL) [9] Orlando, FL St. John Vianney Church; Retired.
Arcamo, Floro B. '65 (SFR) Belmont, CA St. Mark Church.
Arce, Aaron *o.p.* '80 (SAT) San Antonio, TX Methodist Hospital; [B] San Antonio, TX Dominican Priory of Juan Macias.
Arce, Robert P. '64 (NY) [162] Bronx, NY St. Margaret Mary Church.
Arceneaux, Chester '92 (LAF) Abbeville, LA St. Therese of the Child Jesus Church.
Arceneaux, Jules M. '90 (LAF) Eunice, LA St. Thomas More Church.
Arceneaux, Louis A. *c.m.* '66 (LAF) [J] Grand Coteau, LA Jesuit Spirituality Center.
Archambault, Donald '70 (DET) [26] Detroit, MI St. Gerard Church.
Archambault, Msgr. Henry N. (NOR) Jewett City, CT St. Mary Church.
Archambault, Msgr. Henry N. '59 (NOR) Taftville, CT Sacred Heart Church.
Archambault, James H. '67 (HRT) Retired.
Archambault, Paul A. '72 (PRO) Absent on Leave.
Archambault, Richard *m.afr.* '73 (FgM) Missionaries of Africa Foreign Missions.
Archambault, Richard L. '55 (NOR) [G] Putnam, CT Holy Spirit Provincial House.
Archer, Arthur A. '80 (NOR) Niantic, CT St. Agnes Church.
Archer, Richard R. *o.p.* '58 (BR) Ponchatoula, LA St. Joseph Church.
Archer, Scott '90 (PEO) Fairbury, IL St. John the Baptist Church.
Archer, W. Donald '48 (CR) Retired.
Archey, Eugene C. '40 (WOR) Retired.
Archuleta, Marvin *s.f.* '70 (WDC) [B] Silver Spring, MD Holy Family Seminary.
Arciga, Michael '92 (KC) Leave of Absence.
Arcilesi, Leonard '89 (OWN) Cadiz, KY St. Stephen Church; Oak Grove, KY St. Michael the Archangel Church.
Arciszewski, Gilbert G. '59 (MIL) [60] Milwaukee, WI Our Lady, Queen of Peace Church.
Arcuri, Carmen J. '61 (COL) [30] Columbus, OH St. Mary Magdalene Church.
Arcuri, Frank A. *s.j.* '56 (MIL) [P] Milwaukee, WI Jesuit Community at Marquette University.
Ardagh, Brian '95 (CHI) Orland Hills, IL St. Elizabeth Seton Church.
Ardis, John B. *c.s.p.* '90 (NY) [104] New York, NY St. Paul the Apostle Church.
Ardolf, Edward J. '64 (NU) North Mankato, MN Holy Rosary Church.
Ardolf, Paul C. '49 (STP) Norwood, MN Ascension Church.
Ardos, Msgr. George A. '59 (TR) Washington Crossing, NJ St. George Church; Trenton, NJ Mercer County Correction Center.
Ardouin, Beaubrun '93 (NEW) Roselle, NJ Church of St. Joseph the Carpenter.
Arejola, Rodolfo '68 (AGN) Asan, GU Holy Family, Nino Perdido Church.
Arel, Donald *o.m.i.* '64 (OAK) [A] Berkeley, CA The Jesuit School of Theology at Berkeley.
Arella, Msgr. Gerard J. '54 (BRK) [79] Brooklyn, NY St. Mark's Church.
Arenas, Msgr. Francisco '50 (SJN) [17] San Juan, PR Francisca Javiera Cabrini Church.
Arenas, Joseph Victor '70 (NY) [199] Staten Island, NY Blessed Sacrament Church.
Arens, John F. '74 (BO) [E] Needham, MA St. Sebastian's Country Day School, Inc.
Arentsen, Edwin F. '43 (BEL) Retired.
Arenz, James *s.j.* '65 (LA) [C] Los Angeles, CA Loyola Marymount University.
Ares, Francisco J. '83 (BRK) [236] Queens, NY St. Rose of Lima Church.
Aresseril, Xavier '64 (B) Pocatello, ID St. Anthony's Church.
Aresta, Frank *s.c.j.* '81 (MIL) [P] Franklin, WI Villa Maria.
Arevalo, Joseph '65 (RVC) Huntington Station, NY St. Hugh of Lincoln Church.
Argent, Robert W. '55 (STL) [16] St. Louis, MO Resurrection of Our Lord Church.
Argentino, Ralph '68 (SP) Pinellas Park, FL Sacred Heart Church.
Argue, Patrick *ss.cc.* '62 (LA) [D] Mission Hills, CA Alemany High School; [R] Mission Hills, CA Congregation of the Sacred Hearts.
Arguelles, Antonio G. (CC) Retired.
Arguelles, I. Anthony '74 (BLX) [5] Biloxi, MS St. John Church; [6] Biloxi, MS St. Louis Church.
Arguinzoniz, Francisco '54 (PCE) On Duty Outside the Diocese.
Argullo, Msgr. Michael A. '37 (CAM) Retired.
Argy, Msgr. William '40 (OG) Retired.
Argy, Msgr. William J. '40 (OG) [1] Ogdensburg, NY St. Mary's Cathedral; Lisbon, NY SS. Philip and James Church.
Aria, Evaristo Santa '79 (P) Cornelius, OR St. Alexander Church.
Ariano, Msgr. Joseph W. '51 (OM) Retired.
Arias, Ariel '85 (RNO) Carson City, NV Corpus Christi Church.
Arias, Guillermo *s.j.* '72 (SJN) [22] San Juan, PR San Ignacio de Loyola Church.
Arias, Herman '85 (PAT) [2] Passaic, NJ St. Anthony of Padua Church.
Arias, Hernan '83 (PAT) Paterson, NJ Passaic County Jail.
Arias, Jesus '92 (MIA) [4] Miami, FL Epiphany Church.
Arias, Jose *o.a.r.* '60 (NEW) [N] West Orange, NJ Augustinian Recollects.
Arias-Hurtado, Guillermo (NEW) [2] Newark, NJ St. Patrick's Pro-Cathedral.
Arico, Carl '60 (NEW) [5] Bayonne, NJ St. Vincent de Paul Church.
Aridas, Christopher '73 (RVC) Selden, NY St. Margaret of Scotland Church.
Arimond, James C.L. *s.j.* '70 (CHI) [D] Chicago, IL St. Ignatius Jesuit Community.
Arista, Gregario *o.a.r.* '96 (NY) [FF] Bronx, NY St. Joseph's Center.
Arista, Gregorio *o.a.r.* '96 (NY) [154] Bronx, NY St. John's Church.
Ariza, Campo E. (ARE) On Duty Outside the Diocese.
Ariza, Campo Emilio '75 (CGS) [14] Caguas, PR Divino Nino Church.
Ariza, Vicente '75 (SJN) [G] Guaynabo, PR Opus Dei.
Arizpe, Samuel '87 (BWN) San Carlos, TX St. Joseph the Worker Church.
Arizti, Fernando *s.j.* '71 (LA) [51] Los Angeles, CA St. Brigid's Church.
Arkins, Michael *s.s.s.* (SLC) Salt Lake City, UT County Youth Detention Center.
Arkins, Michael J. *s.s.s.* '73 (SLC) [7] Taylorsville, UT St. Martin de Porres Church.
Arko, Richard '90 (CLV) [4] Barberton, OH St. Mary's Church.
Arle, David '84 (VEN) [1] Fort Myers, FL St. Vincent de Paul Church.
Arledge, Joseph '97 (OKL) Woodward, OK St. Peter's Church.
Arledge, Thaddaeus R. *o.s.b.* '56 (SEA) [M] Lacey, WA St. Martin's Abbey.
Arlotta, Jack '92 (NY) Rye, NY Resurrection Church.
Armas, Calixto '43 (SFR) [48] San Francisco, CA Star of the Sea Church.
Armas, James '43 (SFR) Retired.
Armato, Robert J. '95 (BRK) [182] Queens, NY Incarnation Church.
Armbrust, Leo F. '77 (PMB) Special Assignment.
Armbruster, Julius *o.s.b.* '42 (SFS) [F] Marvin, SD Blue Cloud Abbey.
Armell, Francisco *o.c.* '68 (SJN) [61] San Juan, PR Santa Teresita Del Nino Jesus Church.
Armenio, Peter V. '80 (CHI) [W] Chicago, IL Opus Dei.
Armenta, Benito '87 (LA) South El Monte, CA Epiphany Church.
Armey, Charles R. '80 (WOR) [3] Southbridge, MA Sacred Heart Church.
Arminio, Alfonse M. '61 (NEW) Military Chaplains.
Arminio, Thomas G. '81 (NEW) Woodcliff Lake, NJ Our Lady Mother of the Church.
Armistead, John M. '71 (STO) [4] Stockton, CA St. George Church.
Arms, Michael M. '68 (STP) Inver Grove Heights, MN St. Patrick Church.
Armshaw, Joseph *c.ss.r.* '52 (BLX) [E] Biloxi, MS St. John Neumann Residence.
Armshaw, Msgr. Patrick J. '62 (RVC) Greenlawn, NY St. Francis of Assisi Church; [L] Bethpage, NY Central Council.
Armstrong, Christopher R. '80 (CIN) [89] Cincinnati, OH St. William Church.
Armstrong, Daniel F. '78 (IND) Retired.

Armstrong, James L. '77 (PIT) [3] Butler, PA St. Paul Church.
Armstrong, John F. *s.j.* '78 (NO) [C] New Orleans, LA Loyola University; [P] New Orleans, LA Jesuit Provincial Office.
Armstrong, Msgr. Peter G. '54 (SFR) Redwood City, CA St. Pius Church.
Armstrong, Regis *o.f.m.cap.* '67 (NY) [DD] White Plains, NY St. Conrad Friary.
Armstrong, Msgr. Robert A. '62 (BAL) [1] Baltimore, MD Cathedral of Mary Our Queen.
Armstrong, Rodney J. *s.s.j.* '91 (BEA) [3] Beaumont, TX Blessed Sacrament Church.
Armstrong, Steven A. *s.j.* '87 (SFR) [38] San Francisco, CA Our Lady of Fatima Byzantine Catholic Church; [N] San Francisco, CA Jesuit Community at University of San Francisco.
Arnao, Thomas V. '82 (RVC) Merrick, NY Cure of Ars Church.
Arnaud, Michael J. '75 (LAF) [13] Lafayette, LA St. Leo Church.
Arnberg, Todd '76 (LUB) O'Donnell, TX St. Pius X Church.
Arneson, James E. '67 (IND) Retired.
Arnheiter, Burkard *o.s.b.* '37 (SCL) [I] Collegeville, MN St. John's Abbey, of the Order of St. Benedict.
Arnhols, Msgr. Richard J. '73 (NEW) [10] Elizabeth, NJ St. Patrick's Church.
Arnholt, Joseph M. '73 (PH) Ardmore, PA St. Colman Church.
Arnister, Msgr. Edward A. '79 (TR) [4] Trenton, NJ Holy Cross Church.
Arnold, Andrew L. '59 (WH) Retired.
Arnold, Msgr. Daniel K. '75 (E) [2] Erie, PA Blessed Sacrament Church.
Arnold, Edward C. '57 (NSH) Franklin, TN St. Philip Church.
Arnold, Edward R. *m.m.* '63 (NY) [DD] Maryknoll, NY Maryknoll Fathers and Brothers.
Arnold, Friedrich *s.m.* '70 (FgM) Marist Foreign Missions.
Arnold, J. F. *o.p.* '56 (FgM) Dominican - Order of Preachers Foreign Missions.
Arnold, J. Ralph '41 (BEL) Retired.
Arnold, John D. *s.j.* '73 (STL) [P] St. Louis, MO De Smet Jesuit High School Community.
Arnold, Robert P. '75 (SCR) Luzerne, PA Sacred Heart Church.
Arnold, Roger S. *s.v.d.* '61 (CHI) [B] Techny, IL Divine Word Residence; [N] Chicago, IL Divine Word Theologate; [N] Techny, IL Society of the Divine Word, Provincial Headquarter-Chicago Prov.
Arnold, William L. '80 (COL) Dover, OH St. Joseph Church.
Arnoldt, David M. '68 (WIN) Military Chaplains.
Arnone, Leo F. '93 (ALT) [14] Johnstown, PA Our Mother of Sorrows Church.
Arnott, John J. '74 (BUR) Cambridge, VT St. Mary Church; [H] Burlington, VT University of Vermont-The Catholic Center at UVM.
Arnott, John J. '74 (PIT) On Duty Outside the Diocese.
Arnout, Eric R., Jr. '96 (ALN) [11] Allentown, PA St. Thomas More Church.
Arnsparger, Roger K. '77 (LEX) Corbin, KY Sacred Heart Church.
Arnzen, Kenneth '57 (B) Nezperce, ID Holy Trinity Church.
Arocho, Marcelino '88 (MGZ) San German, PR San German de Auxerre Church.
Arockiam, Michaelsami (CHI) [140] Chicago, IL St. Monica Church.
Arokiasamy, G. '79 (NEW) [34] Newark, NJ Sacred Heart Church.
Arokiasamy, Kulan-Daisamy '71 (DET) Eastpointe, MI St. Veronica Church.
Arong, Jose R. *o.m.i.* '66 (OAK) [21] Oakland, CA Sacred Heart Church.
Aronica, Paul *s.d.b.* '47 (NY) [DD] New Rochelle, NY Salesian Provincial House.
Aronyu, Cuthbert '72 (OAK) [5] Oakland, CA St. Benedict Church.
Arpie, Msgr. Robert A. '47 (NY) Retired.
Arpin, Fred *c.ss.r.* '81 (OAK) [N] Oakland, CA Redemptorists.
Arpin, Frederick *c.ss.r.* '81 (WCH) [G] Wichita, KS Redemptorist Community.
Arpin, Frederick L. *c.ss.r.* '81 (WCH) [I] Wichita, KS Spiritual Life Center.
Arputham, Michael A. '78 (NY) [201] Staten Island, NY St. Christopher Church.
Arquitt, William A. '50 (DUB) Retired.
Arraiza, Luis Gerardo *o.f.m.cap.* '88 (DAL) [8] Dallas, TX Our Lady of Lourdes Church.
Arrambide, James C. *c.ss.r.* '73 (GAL) [51] Houston, TX St. Raphael the Archangel Church.
Arrando, Angelo S. '71 (BGP) [1] Danbury, CT St. Gregory's Church.
Arredondo, Jesus *m.sp.s.* '52 (LA) Huntington Park, CA St. Martha Church.
Arregui Moso, Miguel '59 (CGS) Juncos, PR Inmaculada Concepcion Church.
Arresta, Frank *s.c.j.* '81 (MIL) [P] Hales Corners, WI Priests of the Sacred Heart.
Arriaga, Joaquin '97 (FRS) Los Banos, CA St. Joseph Church.
Arriage, Martin *o.f.m.* '74 (ELP) [B] El Paso, TX St. Anthony's School of Theology.
Arribas, Santiago *c.m.* '58 (ARE) [1] Manati, PR La Candelaria Church.
Arrien, Mariano *c.p.* '32 (ARE) Lares, PR St. Joseph Church.
Arrieta, David '62 (SJN) [19] San Juan, PR San Francisco de Monte Alvernia Church.
Arrilucea, Jesus Maria P. *o.a.r.* '65 (ELP) [8] El Paso, TX Guardian Angel Church.
Arrizurieta, Candido *c.m.* '54 (NY) [44] New York, NY Holy Agony Church; [DD] New York, NY Vincentian Fathers.
Arroyave, Jhon Jairo '95 (GAL) [29] Houston, TX St. Francis de Sales Church.
Arroygo, Peter '85 (BO) [69] Boston, MA Sacred Heart Church.
Arroyo, Brigido U. '61 (AGN) Tamuning, GU St. Anthony and St. Victor Church.
Arroyo, Edward B. *s.j.* '75 (FgM) Provinces.
Arroyo, Edward B. *s.j.* '75 (NO) [C] New Orleans, LA Loyola University.
Arroyo, Jose del Carmen (NY) [95] New York, NY Our Lady Queen of Martyrs Church.
Arroyo, Joseph A. *s.j.* '62 (PH) [C] Philadelphia, PA St. Joseph's University; [AA] Philadelphia, PA Jesuit Community at St. Joseph's University.
Arroyo, Mario J. '77 (GAL) Pasadena, TX St. Pius the Fifth Church.
Arruda, Henry S. '67 (FR) [6] New Bedford, MA Our Lady of Mt. Carmel Church.
Arsenault, Edward J. '91 (MAN) [14] Manchester, NH St. Patrick Church.
Arsenault, James M. '89 (RIC) West Point, VA Our Lady of the Blessed Sacrament Church.
Arsenault, Joseph B. *m.m.* '59 (NY) [DD] Maryknoll, NY Maryknoll Fathers and Brothers.
Arsenault, Raymond J. *s.m.* '51 (BO) [Y] Framingham Centre, MA The Marist House.
Arseneau, Vernon '72 (JOL) West Chicago, IL St. Mary Church.
Arseneault, David J. (ALT) Elmora, PA St. Jude Church; Spangler, PA Holy Cross Church.
Arter, Ronald L. '61 (COL) Lancaster, OH St. Mark Church.
Arthasseril, Jerome S. '66 (NEW) [1] East Orange, NJ Holy Name of Jesus Church.
Arthur, David J. *c.s.c.* '54 (FR) [A] North Easton, MA Stonehill College; [A] North Easton, MA Holy Cross Fathers Religious.
Arthur, E. Eugene *s.j.* '66 (KC) [B] Kansas City, MO Rockhurst College; [J] Kansas City, MO Rockhurst College - Jesuit Community.
Arthur, Msgr. E. Robert (WDC) Retired.
Arthur, Msgr. E. Robert '38 (WDC) [L] Washington, DC Jeanne Jugan Residence-St. Joseph's Villa.
Arthur, Francis '79 (SAG) [9] Bay City, MI St. Stanislaus Church.
Artiga, Steven E. *s.j.* '94 (LA) [R] Culver City, CA Ignatius House, The Novitiate of the California Province, Society of Jesus.
Artim, Michael '63 (VNN) Retired.
Artis, George *s.v.d.* '62 (JKS) [6] Jackson, MS Holy Ghost Church; [G] Jackson, MS Tougaloo College Newman Center.
Artmann, Robert J. '64 (MIL) [K] Brookfield, WI Elmbrook Memorial Hospital, Inc.
Arts, Paul-Louis '64 (SC) [4] Sioux City, IA St. Casimir Church; [5] Sioux City, IA St. Francis of Assisi Church; [6] Sioux City, IA Immaculate Conception Church.
Arturi, Bradley K. '62 (NY) [II] New Rochelle, NY Opus Dei (Prelature of the Holy Cross and Opus Dei).
Artuso, Grazioso '64 (BGP) [19] Bridgeport, CT St. Raphael's Church.
Artysiewicz, Chet '73 (WDC) [M] Washington, DC Glenmary House of Studies.
Artzer, James *s.v.d.* '50 (TR) [M] Bordentown, NJ Society of the Divine Word.
Arude, Aristide D. '58 (BO) Stoughton, MA Immaculate Conception Church.
Arul, John '70 (MRY) San Luis Obispo, CA San Luis Obispo Church.
Arul, Joseph *s.v.d.* '89 (CHI) [N] Chicago, IL Divine Word Theologate.
Arulappa, Devaraj '86 (TYL) Center, TX St. Therese Church; Nacogdoches, TX Sacred Heart Church.
Arvay, Alfred S. '58 (NEW) On Duty Outside the Archdiocese.
Arzela, Roberto *o.p.* '74 (SJN) [3] Bayamon, PR Catalina de Siena Church.
Asantey, Samuel '88 (NY) Carmel, NY St. James the Apostle Church.
Asare-Dankwah, John '94 (NO) [42] New Orleans, LA St. Julian Eymard Church.
Ascencio, Joseph A. '82 (COL) On Duty Outside the Diocese.
Ascheman, Thomas *s.v.d.* '82 (FgM) Society of the Divine Word Foreign Missions.
Aschenbrenner, George A. *s.j.* '54 (PH) [A] Wynnewood, PA Theological Seminary of St. Charles Borromeo, Overbrook.
Aschenbrenner, George A. *s.j.* '65 (ALN) [A] Wernersville, PA Novitiate of St. Isaac Jogues; [N] Wernersville, PA Jesuit Center for Spiritual Growth.
Aschenbrenner, George F. '42 (CHI) [4] Lemont, IL St. James at Sag Bridge Church; Retired.
Aschenbrenner, Ralph L. '61 (SAL) Lincoln, KS St. Patrick's Church.
Ascherl, Vincent (ELP) [25] El Paso, TX St. Joseph's Church.
Ascherl, Vincent '81 (ELP) Retired.
Aschmann, Karl '50 (CHL) Concord, NC St. James Church.
Ascolese, Robert J. '89 (MET) [6] Perth Amboy, NJ Most Holy Rosary Church; Perth Amboy, NJ Raritan Bay Medical Center.
Asencios-Pablo, Maximo *m.ss.a.* (HRT) [2] Waterbury, CT Immaculate Conception Church.
Asenjo, Jose Maria '65 (GAL) South Houston, TX Our Lady of Grace Church.
Ash, Joseph '58 (WOR) [M] Worcester, MA Vianney House.
Ash, Joseph H. '58 (WOR) Retired.
Ashbaugh, William A. (LAN) Westphalia, MI St. Mary Church.
Ashbeck, David '68 (GB) Isaar, WI St. Sebastian Church.
Ashe, Brendan '59 (CC) Orange Grove, TX St. John of the Cross Church.
Ashe, John F. '63 (NOR) Portland, CT St. Mary Church.
Ashe, Joseph C. '76 (NOR) [2] Middletown, CT St. John Church.
Ashe, Kevin P. '63 (NEW) [3] Jersey City, NJ St. Anne's Church; Special Assignment; [S] Union City, NJ Park Performing Arts, Inc.
Ashenbrenner, Raymond *o.p.* '51 (MAD) [H] Watertown, WI St. Joseph's Home.
Ashenbrenner, Robert D. *o.s.f.s.* '54 (PH) [AA] Philadelphia, PA Oblates of St. Francis De Sales.
Ashfeld, Bernard '82 (SFS) Sioux Falls, SD South Dakota State Penitentiary & Minnehaha County Jail.
Ashkar, Dominic F. '62 (SAM) Washington, DC Our Lady of Lebanon Church.
Ashley, Benedict M. *o.p.* '48 (STL) [P] St. Louis, MO Dominican Community of St. Louis.
Ashman, Robert F. '86 (NY) [190] Bronx, NY St. Theresa of the Infant Jesus Church; Tuckahoe, NY Immaculate Conception Church.
Ashton, Msgr. John P. '55 (Y) Campbell, OH St. Lucy's Church.
Ashurst, Peter '92 (OKL) Elgin, OK St. Ann Church.
Ashwell, G. Barry '69 (SEA) Oak Harbor, WA St. Augustine Church.
Asika, Raphael *m.s.p.* '92 (BEA) Ames, TX Our Mother of Mercy Church; Raywood, TX Sacred Heart Church.
Asip, Msgr. James W. '37 (BRK) [191] Queens, NY St. Luke Church; Retired; [L] Brooklyn, NY Catholic Charities.
Asir, Antony '82 (RVC) Lynbrook, NY Our Lady of Peace Church.
Asis, Alfonso '75 (AGN) Toto, GU Immaculate Heart of Mary Church.
Askew, Msgr. Prosper '53 (STV) [3] Estate Tutu, VI Holy Family Parish.
Asma, Lawrence F. *c.m.* '83 (STL) [K] Bridgeton, MO De Paul Health Center; [P] St. Louis, MO Vincentian Bellerive Residence.
Asmar, Maroun '93 (SAM) Somerset, NJ St. Sharbel Church.
Aspinall, Campion W. *c.j.* '61 (LA) Santa Maria, CA St. Louis de Montfort Church.
Aspiras, Jose '47 (SEA) Retired.
Assariparambil, John Mathai '97 (BIS) [5] Dickinson, ND St. Wenceslaus Church.
Assenheimer, Roy C. *m.m.* '65 (FgM) Maryknoll Foreign Missions.
Assenmacher, Hugh *o.s.b.* '58 (LR) [A] Subiaco, AR Subiaco Monastery.
Astorino, Robert F. *m.m.* '70 (FgM) Maryknoll Foreign Missions.
Astruc, Rene *s.j.* '54 (FBK) [E] St. Marys, AK Brother Joe Prince Jesuit Community.
Astudillo, Antonio P. '73 (LA) [7] Long Beach, CA Holy Innocents Church.
Asturi, Bruno '76 (PBR) Upper St. Clair, PA St. Gregory Nazianzus Church.
Astuto, Lucian S. '57 (OM) [34] Omaha, NE St. Patrick Church.
Asuncion, Leo '79 (OAK) El Cerrito, CA St. John the Baptist Church.
Atchely, Jonathan D. '88 (LA) Sick Leave.
Atcher, Joseph *o.carm.* '76 (NEW) Tenafly, NJ Our Lady of Mount Carmel Church.
Atchison, Donald W '57 (KAL) Retired.
Aten, Robert L. '79 (STL) Special Assignment; [P]

Centerville, MO Contemplative Heart of Mary Hermitage.
Atkins, Daniel '87 (IND) Bloomington, IN St. Paul Catholic Center Church; [N] Bloomington, IN Indiana University, Bloomington Newman Center.
Atkins, James '72 (RVC) East Northport, NY St. Anthony of Padua Church.
Atkins, James '81 (SFR) Retired.
Atkins, James P. '75 (ATL) On Duty Outside the Archdiocese.
Atkins, Tim *c.i.c.m.* '74 (FgM) Missionhurst Foreign Missions.
Atkinson, Anselm *o.s.b.* '82 (WOR) [N] Petersham, MA St. Mary's Monastery.
Atkinson, John V. '61 (MEM) [18] Memphis, TN St. Michael's Church.
Atkinson, Sean '69 (JKS) Leland, MS St. James Church.
Atkinson, William E. *o.s.a.* '74 (PH) [D] Drexel Hill, PA Monsignor Bonner High School.
Atomori, Paschal (CHI) [117] Chicago, IL St. Leo The Great Church.
Atonio, Falniko '92 (SPP) [6] Pago Pago, AS Church of the Holy Cross.
Atoyebi, John Bola '94 (CHI) Blue Island, IL St. Benedict Church.
Attak, Cyril '64 (PRM) Allen Park, MI St. Stephen Church.
Attanasio, Raymond V. '58 (MET) Laurence Harbor, NJ St. Lawrence Church.
Attanasio, Scott F. '95 (NEW) Kearny, NJ St. Stephen's Church.
Attea, Msgr. Antoine '58 (BUF) Jamestown, NY St. James Church.
Attridge, Terry '65 (NY) Dobbs Ferry, NY Sacred Heart Church.
Attumaly, Antony *m.ss.cc.* '88 (HBG) Blue Ridge Summit, PA St. Rita Church; Fairfield, PA Immaculate Conception of the Blessed Virgin Mary Church.
Atuk, George *s.d.b.* (NY) [72] New York, NY Mary Help of Christians Church.
Atwater, John T. '63 (BO) Groton, MA St. James Church; Groton, MA Sacred Heart Church.
Atwill, Msgr. William H. '44 (LA) Retired.
Atwood, Ray E. '94 (DUB) Dyersville, IA Basilica of St. Francis Xavier Church.
Atwood, Ronald E. '84 (OAK) Richmond, CA St. David of Wales Church.
Atwood, Ronald J. '69 (COL) [43] Columbus, OH St. Thomas the Apostle Church.
Atwood, Wilbur J. *s.s.j.* '58 (NO) [P] New Orleans, LA Josephite Fathers and Brothers.
Atzert, Edward '37 (TR) [L] Lawrenceville, NJ Morris Hall-Saint Lawrence, Inc.
Atzert, Edward P. '37 (TR) Retired.
Au, Thomas Y. '79 (LIN) Roseland, NE Sacred Heart Church.
Au, William A. '75 (BAL) [82] Baltimore, MD SS. Philip and James Church.
Aube, Paul L. '70 (MAN) Sabbatical.
Aubespin, Francis Borgin *s.v.d.* '65 (LAF) [4] Lafayette, LA Immaculate Heart of Mary Church.
Aubin, Msgr. Joseph '55 (OG) Keeseville, NY Church of the Immaculate Conception; Keeseville, NY St. John the Baptist Church.
Aubin, Joseph '61 (LAN) Durand, MI St. Mary Church.
Aubin, Pierre *m.s.c.* '58 (OG) Evans Mills, NY St. Mary Church; [J] Watertown, NY Mission Project Service; [J] Watertown, NY Sacred Heart Foundation.
Aubin, Ronald B. '81 (SP) Land O'Lakes, FL Our Lady of the Rosary Church.
Auble, Theodore J. '75 (ROC) [M] Rochester, NY Diocesan Office of Campus Ministry.
Aubrey, Robert (DM) [D] Des Moines, IA Mercy Hospital Medical Center.
Aubrey, Robert J. '71 (DM) Cumming, IA St. John Church.
Aubry, Donald W. *m.m.* '47 (NY) [DD] Maryknoll, NY Maryknoll Fathers and Brothers.
Aubry, Ronald J. '81 (COL) Millersburg, OH St. Peter Church.
Aubut, Charles E. '41 (BO) Retired.
Auby, John R. '94 (MAD) [8] Madison, WI St. James Church.
Auchter, Msgr. John A. '54 (ALN) Lake Harmony, PA St. Peter the Fisherman Church.
Aucoin, Msgr. Charles '47 (MOB) Retired.
Aucoin, Msgr. Robert H. '70 (OG) [A] Ogdensburg, NY Wadhams Hall.
Auda, Lawrence '60 (SFD) Benld, IL St. Joseph Church; Gillespie, IL SS. Simon and Jude Church.
Audet, Arthur J. '85 (HRT) Forestville, CT St. Matthew Church.
Audet, Dennis J. '78 (MAN) Merrimack, NH Our Lady of Mercy Church.
Audette, Albert D. '93 (BGP) Brookfield, CT St. Marguerite Bourgeoys Church.
Audibert, John I. '67 (PRT) Augusta, ME St. Mary's Church.
Audibert, John L. '67 (PRT) Whitefield, ME St. Denis Church.
Auer, Benedict L. *o.s.b.* '80 (SEA) [M] Lacey, WA St. Martin's Abbey.
Auer, John '79 (COS) [14] Colorado Springs, CO Saint Paul Church.
Auer, John J. '57 (BAL) Millersville, MD Our Lady of the Fields Church.
Auer, Joseph E. '57 (CHI) [4] Oak Lawn, IL St. Linus Church.
Auer, Paul '45 (SEA) Retired.
Auer, Peter (STO) Lodi, CA St. Anne Church.
Auer, Peter J. *s.o.l.t.* '93 (CC) [H] Robstown, TX Society of Our Lady of the Most Holy Trinity.
Auer, Robert F. '51 (DUB) Retired.
Aufdermauer, Joseph A. '68 (MIL) [75] Milwaukee, WI St. Stephen Church.
Aufieri, Robert J. '74 (NY) [161] Bronx, NY St. Margaret of Cortona Church.
Aufiero, Louis D. '65 (BRK) [178] Queens, NY Holy Family Church.
Auger, Gaston E. '32 (PRT) Retired.
Auger, George *c.s.v.* '61 (CHI) [N] Arlington Heights, IL Viatorian Province Center-Clerics of St. Viator.
Auger, Gerald E. '55 (MAN) Retired.
Auger, Raymond D. '56 (PRT) Sanford, ME St. Ignatius Martyr Church.
Auguste, Jean-Miguel (BRK) [57] Brooklyn, NY Holy Innocents Church.
Augustine, Kenneth J. '77 (MIL) Franklin, WI St. James Church.
Augustine, M. Selvan *s.j.* '90 (CHI) [C] Chicago, IL Jesuit Community at Loyola University of Chicago.
Augustine, Msgr. Roger J. '59 (SC) Moville, IA Immaculate Conception Church.
Augustine, Russell A. '89 (BGP) Brookfield, CT St. Joseph's Church.
Augustinowitz, Michael E. '75 (BUR) Greensboro Bend, VT St. Michael Church; Hardwick, VT St. Norbert Church.
Augustyn, Andrew M. '47 (GI) Retired.
Augustyn, James M. '63 (BUF) [6] Lackawanna, NY St. Michael the Archangel Church.
Augustyn, Richard H. '76 (BUF) [34] Buffalo, NY Immaculate Heart of Mary Church; Buffalo, NY Buffalo General Hospital.
Aultz, Gary C. '69 (OKL) Absent on Leave.
Auman, Robert '47 (SFE) Retired.
Aumann, J. *o.p.* (WDC) [11] Washington, DC St. Dominic Church & Priory Church.
Aumann, Jordan *o.p.* '45 (CHI) [N] River Forest, IL St. Thomas Aquinas Priory.
Aumen, Paul *c.pp.s.* '49 (CIN) [M] Dayton, OH Provincial House of the Cincinnati Province of the Society of the Precious Blood.
Aurilia, John C. *o.f.m.cap.* '66 (CHL) Hendersonville, NC Immaculate Conception Church.
Ausenbaugh, Andrew '95 (OWN) Henderson, KY Holy Name of Jesus Church.
Ausperk, Michael D. '89 (CLV) [1] Elyria, OH St. Agnes Church.
Austgen, Robert *c.s.c.* '58 (FTW) [B] Notre Dame, IN University of Notre Dame Du Lac.
Austgen, Robert J. *c.s.c.* '58 (FTW) [J] Notre Dame, IN Holy Cross Community, Corby Hall, University of Notre Dame.
Austin, C. Gerard *o.p.* '59 (WDC) [C] Washington, DC Catholic University of America, The.
Austin, John J. '97 (PRT) [3] Lewiston, ME Holy Family Church.
Austin, Jonathan G. '97 (DAL) [17] Dallas, TX St. Elizabeth Church.
Austin, Stephen E. '84 (TLS) Bartlesville, OK St. John's Church; Dewey, OK Our Lady of Guadalupe Church.
Austin, Walter J. '81 (NO) Chalmette, LA Prince of Peace Church.
Auth, James E. '61 (TOL) [13] Toledo, OH Regina Coeli Church.
Auth, William G. *o.s.f.s.* '69 (TOL) [K] Toledo, OH Oblates of St. Francis de Sales.
Auther, John *s.j.* '90 (PHX) [7] Phoenix, AZ SS. Anthony and Pius X Church.
Auve, Msgr. Perron Joseph '62 (YAK) Ellensburg, WA St. Andrew's Church.
Avallone, Paul P. *s.d.b.* '50 (PAT) [D] Paterson, NJ Don Bosco Technical High School.
Avau, Felix A. *c.i.c.m.* '54 (SAT) Poteet, TX St. Philip Benizi Church.
Avella, Alberto '80 (GLP) Show Low, AZ St. Rita Church.
Avella, Robert E. '75 (ARL) Fairfax, VA St. Leo's Church.
Avella, Steven M. '79 (MIL) Special Assignment.
Avella, William '50 (RNO) Retired.
Avellaneda, J. Armando, P. *m.ss.a.* '56 (ARL) Dale City, VA Holy Family Church.
Avello, Vicente Salas *o.de.m.* '66 (PCE) [13] Ponce, PR Santuario San Judas Tadeo Church.
Avendano, Alvaro D. '91 (ATL) [2] Atlanta, GA Holy Cross Church.
Averbeck, Ronald J. '61 (CIN) [83] Cincinnati, OH St. Stephen Church.
Averman, Melvin *o.f.m.cap.* '53 (PIT) [O] Herman, PA St. Mary's Friary.
Aversa, Alfred S. '88 (CAM) Glassboro, NJ St. Bridget's Church.
Aversa, Domenic R. *t.o.r.* '59 (ALT) [F] Hollidaysburg, PA St. Joseph Friary.
Avery, Edward V. '70 (PH) [74] Philadelphia, PA St. Jerome Church; [U] Philadelphia, PA Nazareth Hospital.
Avery, Joseph E. *m.m.* '49 (NY) [DD] Maryknoll, NY Maryknoll Fathers and Brothers.
Avery, Raymond '44 (MET) Retired; [H] Somerset, NJ Maria Regina Residence.
Avicolli, Maurice C. *o.praem.* '68 (PH) [AA] Paoli, PA Daylesford Abbey.
Avila, Daniel C. '87 (FRS) Hanford, CA St. Brigid Church.
Avila, Msgr. Lourenco '52 (SB) Ontario, CA St. Elizabeth Ann Seton Church.
Avila, Mark *o.m.v.* '87 (BO) [B] Boston, MA Oblate Provincialate.
Avila, Martin '57 (SFR) Novato, CA Our Lady of Loretto Church.
Aviles, Joe '90 (SAT) [56] San Antonio, TX St. Mary Magdalen Church.
Aviles, Victor (SJN) [8] Bayamon, PR Invencion de la Santa Cruz Church.
Avitabile, Camillo *m.s.* '53 (ORL) [2] Orlando, FL Blessed Trinity Church.
Avramenko, Alexander '96 (STN) San Francisco, CA Immaculate Conception Church; Santa Clara, CA St. Vladimir Church.
Awad, Msgr. Assad '57 (SAM) Unassigned.
Awalaka, Jude '80 (BRK) [245] Queens, NY St. Thomas Apostle Church.
Awalt, Msgr. William J. '47 (WDC) [3] Washington, DC St. Ann Church.
Award, Richard *c.p.* '81 (FgM) Passionist Foreign Missions.
Axe, Thomas R. '60 (CIN) [31] Cincinnati, OH Good Shepherd Church.
Axe, William J. *o.ss.t.* '74 (BAL) Jessup, MD St. Lawrence Church.
Axen, Ronald J. '40 (DUB) Retired.
Axen, Ronald J. '40 (FWT) [G] Crowley, TX St. Francis Village, Inc.
Axtmann, Joseph S. '44 (FAR) Munich, ND St. Mary's Church.
Ayala, Agustin Mateo '90 (WDC) Mount Rainier, MD St. James Church.
Ayala, Ricardo, III '94 (BWN) San Juan, TX Santuario de Nuestra Senora de San Juan del Valle Church; [I] San Juan, TX Virgen de San Juan del Valle Shrine.
Ayala, Saul '71 (SB) Mecca, CA Our Lady of Guadalupe Shrine Church.
Ayathupadam, Joseph '61 (CHL) Albemarle, NC Our Lady of the Annunciation Church.
Ayd, Joseph D. *s.j.* '54 (SCR) [C] Scranton, PA University of Scranton.
Aydt, Raymond A. '46 (BIS) Grenora, ND St. Boniface Church.
Ayers, Daniel '97 (COS) [12] Colorado Springs, CO St. Joseph's Church.
Ayers, J. Cameron *s.j.* '86 (PHX) [B] Phoenix, AZ Brophy College Preparatory.
Ayers, John J. '51 (SPR) Northfield, MA St. Patrick Church.
Ayla, Francisco '84 (LA) [K] Los Angeles, CA St. Vincent Medical Center.
Aylward, Gerard J. *c.s.p.* '53 (CHR) Clemson, SC St. Andrew Church.
Aylward, James W. '64 (SFR) Burlingame, CA St. Catherine of Siena Church.
Aylward, Richard A. *m.m.* '53 (FgM) Maryknoll Foreign Missions.
Aymanamkuzhy, Jacob '60 (PMB) Lantana, FL Holy Spirit Church.
Aymanathil, Mathew '59 (NEW) Emerson, NJ Church of the Assumption.
Ayo, Nicholas *c.s.c.* '59 (FTW) [B] Notre Dame, IN University of Notre Dame Du Lac; [J] Notre Dame, IN Holy Cross Community, Corby Hall, University of Notre Dame.
Ayoob, John '65 (PIT) Moon Township, PA St. Margaret Mary Church.
Ayotte, David J. '92 (LA) Lancaster, CA Sacred Heart Church.
Ayoub, Fawaz '79 (AUS) Mason, TX St. Joseph's Church.
Ayoub, Msgr. S. Paul '53 (BUF) [6] Cheektowaga, NY Mother of Divine Grace Church.
Ayuyu, Isaac '86 (CHK) Chalan Kanoa Village, MP Cathedral of Our Lady of Mt. Carmel.
Azadian, Joseph G. *s.j.* '52 (LA) El Segundo, CA St. Anthony Church.
Azar, Fahed '80 (SAM) Wilkes-Barre, PA St. George Church; Wilkes-Barre, PA St. Anthony Church.
Azar, John T., Jr. '88 (NTN) North Hollywood, CA St. Anne Church.
Azaro, Stanley *o.p.* '75 (FgM) Dominican - Order of Preachers Foreign Missions.

Azcoiti, Vicente '56 (BWN) [2] Mission, TX Our Lady of the Holy Rosary Church.
Azcoitia, Florentino *s.j.* '52 (MIA) [H] Miami, FL Villa Javier.
Azcona, Eric *o.f.m.cap.* '51 (FWT) [6] Fort Worth, TX Our Lady of Guadalupe Church.
Azevedo, Ferdinand T. *s.j.* '70 (FgM) Provinces.
Azhakatch, Mathew *o.c.d.* (CHI) [153] Chicago, IL Our Lady of Mercy Church.
Aziz, George *s.j.* '57 (SR) Sebastopol, CA St. Sebastian Church.
Azizo, Toma B. '54 (OLD) Farmington Hills, MI St. Toma Church.
Azoon, Philip '94 (NTN) Scranton, PA St. Joseph Church.
Azorji, Eugene E. '80 (NY) [220] Staten Island, NY Our Lady of Pity Church.
Azpericueta, Lucas '79 (FRS) Arvin, CA St. Thomas Church.
Azpiazu, Jose *o.m.i.* '28 (SAT) [K] San Antonio, TX Oblate Madonna Residence.
Azrak, Albert *c.s.s.* '60 (NY) [4] White Plains, NY Our Lady of Mt. Carmel Church.
Azzarone, Daniel M. '78 (PRO) [5] Cranston, RI St. Mary Church.
Azzarto, Anthony J. *s.j.* '69 (NEW) [C] Jersey City, NJ St. Peter's Preparatory School.

B

Ba Do, Ai '51 (ALN) [3] Bethlehem, PA Holy Ghost Church.
Baalman, William *c.p.* (DET) [K] Detroit, MI St. Paul of the Cross Community, Congregation of the Passion.
Babalya, Michael T. '86 (TR) Willingboro, NJ Corpus Christi Church.
Babb, James C. *s.j.* '46 (ATL) [K] Atlanta, GA Ignatius House.
Babbitt, William T. '70 (FR) North Attleboro, MA St. Mary's Church; Retired.
Babcock, David J. *o.f.m.* '53 (FgM) Franciscan Foreign Missions.
Babcock, James K. '81 (NTN) Fullerton, CA Holy Cross Church; San Bernardino, CA St. Philip Church.
Babcock, Timothy F. '68 (DET) Rochester, MI St. Andrew Church.
Babeu, Gill C. '87 (BGP) [2] Stamford, CT St. Bridget Church.
Babich, Ronald J. '77 (DET) Fraser, MI Our Lady Queen of All Saints Church.
Babicz, Edmund A. '84 (MAN) Sanbornville, NH St. Anthony Church.
Babiczuk, Freddie, Jr. '86 (FR) Wareham, MA St. Patrick's Church.
Babin, Albert *c.ss.r.* '52 (BLX) [E] Biloxi, MS St. John Neumann Residence.
Babin, Victor '75 (MIA) [15] Miami, FL St. Agatha Church.
Babineau, Alexis A. *a.a.* '45 (WOR) [N] Worcester, MA Assumptionists (Augustinians of the Assumption).
Babineau, William E. '68 (MAN) [4] Berlin, NH Guardian Angel Church.
Babinski, Donald E. '81 (RVC) Williston Park, NY St. Aidan's Church.
Babka, Robert H. '68 (STL) [7] St. Louis, MO Immaculate Heart of Mary Church.
Bablitch, Michael '37 (GB) Retired.
Babonas, Alphonse '62 (DET) [9] Detroit, MI St. Anthony Church.
Babowitch, John F. '96 (PH) [20] Philadelphia, PA St. Barnabas Church.
Babula, Benjamin S. '75 (GBG) [2] Connellsville, PA Holy Trinity Church.
Babulski, Robert E. '69 (NEW) Retired.
Bac, Isidore D.T. *c.m.c.* '70 (LIN) [3] Lincoln, NE Immaculate Heart of Mary Church.
Baca, Alfred S. '89 (ORG) [8] Santa Ana, CA St. Joseph's Church.
Baca, Paul M. '49 (SFE) [3] Albuquerque, NM Community of the Risen Saviour Church.
Bacalso, Felipe *s.j.* '90 (BO) [W] Chestnut Hill, MA The Jesuit Community at Boston College.
Baccaro, Gaetano T. '85 (SY) [3] Liverpool, NY St. John Church.
Baccellieri, Joseph '66 (P) [7] Portland, OR Assumption Church.
Bacchi, Lee F. '77 (JOL) Chebanse, IL SS. Mary and Joseph's Church; Clifton, IL St. Peter's Church.
Bacchi, Robert A. '77 (CHI) Maywood, IL St. Eulalia Church.
Bacevice, Joseph A. '77 (CLV) [25] Cleveland, OH St. George Church.
Bacevicius, John A. '36 (FAR) Kintyre, ND St. Boniface's Church.
Bacevicius, John J. *o.f.m.* '62 (PRT) [I] Kennebunkport, ME St. Anthony's Friary.
Bach, Msgr. Frank J. '56 (SPK) Retired.
Bach, Ignacio *o.c.d.* '50 (TUC) [21] Tucson, AZ Santa Cruz Church.
Bach, James Nguyen '94 (NO) Arabi, LA St. Louise De Marillac Church.
Bach, John A. '71 (LFT) [D] Lafayette, IN St. Anthony Health Care; [F] Lafayette, IN Monastery of the Precious Blood.
Bach, Lester *o.f.m.cap.* '57 (GB) [M] Appleton, WI Monte Alverno Retreat Center.
Bachand, Joseph G. *m.s.* '76 (WDC) [M] Washington, DC La Salette Community.
Bacher, Anthony A. *c.s.sp.* '46 (VEN) [G] Sarasota, FL Congregation of the Holy Ghost.
Bacher, Arthur A. '54 (CLV) Richfield, OH St. Victor Church.
Bacher, Msgr. Robert E. '48 (CLV) Clinton, OH St. George Church.
Bachkay, John M. '83 (PIT) [31] Pittsburgh, PA St. Louise de Marillac Church.
Bachman, Michael J. '84 (BGP) [17] Bridgeport, CT St. Patrick Church.
Bachmann, Leonard *s.t.* '55 (WDC) [M] University Park, MD Holy Trinity Missionary Cenacle.
Bachmeier, Benjamin '68 (SD) San Diego, CA Mercy Hospital; [F] San Diego, CA Mercy Hospital and Medical Center dba Mercy Healthcare San Diego.
Bachmeier, Bernard A. '68 (FAR) On Duty Outside the Diocese.
Bachmeier, Brian M. '97 (FAR) [4] Fargo, ND SS. Anne & Joachim Church; Kindred, ND St. Maurice Church.
Bachmeier, Mark V. '89 (P) Astoria, OR St. Mary, Star of the Sea Church.
Bachnak, Francis J. '43 (KC) Retired.
Bachner, James M. '96 (PIT) West View, PA St. Athanasius Church.
Bacia, Eliot *o.f.m.* '62 (MIL) [P] Milwaukee, WI Francis and Clare House.
Bacik, James '62 (TOL) [O] Toledo, OH U.T. Newman Foundation for Student Education and Development.
Bacik, James J. '62 (TOL) [5] Toledo, OH Corpus Christi, University of Toledo Church; [N] Toledo, OH University of Toledo Campus Ministry.
Bacik, Leonard M. '72 (CLV) [3] Lorain, OH Holy Trinity Church.
Bacino, Benjamin J. *o.f.m.* '75 (PBL) [3] Pueblo, CO Holy Family Church.
Backes, Charles H. '48 (BIS) Retired; [G] Bismarck, ND Emmaus Place.
Backes, Hugo G. '36 (BIS) Retired.
Backes, John J. '73 (NY) Garnerville, NY St. Gregory Barbarigo Church.
Backiel, Bernard *m.i.c.* (DET) Detroit, MI Detroit Receiving Hospital.
Backiel, Bernard *m.i.c.* '60 (DET) Detroit, MI Michigan Health Care Corporation.
Backiel, Bernard *m.i.c.* '60 (SPR) [I] Stockbridge, MA Congregation of Marians.
Backous, Timothy *o.s.b.* '86 (SCL) [B] Collegeville, MN St. John's University; [I] Collegeville, MN St. John's Abbey, of the Order of St. Benedict.
Bacleon, Misael '84 (NY) [52] New York, NY Immaculate Conception Church.
Bacovin, Ronald '66 (TR) Lakehurst, NJ St. John Church.
Badaoui, Adib '52 (NTN) Retired.
Baddick, Thomas D. '81 (ALN) [7] Reading, PA St. Joseph Church.
Badding, Joseph P. (BUF) Gasport, NY St. Mary Church; Middleport, NY St. Stephen Church.
Badeaux, Kevin '84 (BEA) Special Assignment.
Badem, Wendel J. '48 (MIL) Retired.
Baden, Robert D. '77 (RC) Kadoka, SD Our Lady of Victory Church; Wall, SD St. Patrick's Church.
Bader, Edward '82 (NY) [153] Bronx, NY St. Joan of Arc Church.
Bader, Edward A. *c.s.b.* '63 (GAL) [C] Houston, TX University of St. Thomas; [Q] Houston, TX Residence of the Basilian Fathers of the University of St. Thomas.
Bader, Paul A. '61 (CIN) [69] Cincinnati, OH Our Lady of the Rosary Church.
Bader, Paul L. '58 (ALN) Coplay, PA St. Peter Church.
Badger, Arthur '53 (TOL) Retired.
Badgerow, Rock J. '79 (GR) Evart, MI Sacred Heart Church; Marion, MI St. Agnes Church.
Badia, Leonard F. '60 (BRK) [168] Queens, NY St. Francis of Assisi Church.
Badillo, Juan Randell (WIN) [6] Rochester, MN St. John's Church.
Badillo, Robert *m.id.* '95 (NY) [180] Bronx, NY Santa Maria Church; [DD] Bronx, NY Idente Missionaries - Santa Maria Residence.
Badnerosky, Myron M. '56 (PSC) Levittown, PA Our Lady of Perpetual Help Church.
Bado, Walter *s.j.* '59 (LEX) [2] Lexington, KY The Newman Center, Holy Spirit Church; [L] Lexington, KY The Newman Center Holy Spirit Parish University of Kentucky.
Badovsky, Thomas '73 (PEO) Peru, IL St. Valentine's Church.
Badurina, Gabriel *t.o.r.* (WDC) [9] Washington, DC St. Blaise Church.
Badurina, Gabriel *t.o.r.* '62 (PIT) [O] Pittsburgh, PA Croatian Commissariate, T.O.R.
Baehr, David J. '64 (SY) [4] Oswego, NY St. Mary Church.
Baek, Gus W. *s.d.b.* '95 (NY) [2] Port Chester, NY Corpus Christi Church.
Baenziger, Edward J. *c.s.b.* '76 (GAL) [Q] Houston, TX Residence of the Basilian Fathers of the University of St. Thomas.
Baer, Campion *o.f.m.cap.* '56 (MIL) [B] Mount Calvary, WI St. Lawrence Seminary; [P] Mount Calvary, WI St. Lawrence Friary.
Baer, M. Stuart '92 (PEO) On Duty Outside the Diocese.
Baer, Robert W. *c.s.p.* '54 (NY) [DD] Jamaica Estates, NY Paulist Fathers Generalate.
Baer, Stuart (PAT) Denville, NJ St. Clare Hospital; [J] Denville, NJ Northwest Covenant Medial Center.
Baer, Timothy K. '96 (WDC) Hyattsville, MD St. Mark Church.
Baer, William '96 (STP) [8] St. Paul, MN The Nativity of Our Lord Church.
Baerwald, Jeffrey P. *s.j.* '89 (NY) [DD] New York, NY Jesuit Community at Fordham University.
Baeten, David '62 (GB) [11] Green Bay, WI St. Matthew Church.
Baeten, Lambert C. *o.praem.* '59 (GB) [I] De Pere, WI St. Norbert Abbey.
Baez, Jose Francisco (PCE) [B] Ponce, PR The Pontifical Catholic University of Puerto Rico.
Baeza, Manuel *m.c.c.j.* '96 (FgM) Comboni Foreign Missions.
Bafaro, Michael P. '53 (WOR) [13] Worcester, MA Our Lady of Mt. Carmel and St. Ann Church.
Baffa, Robert J. '66 (BUR) North Bennington, VT St. John the Baptist Church.
Bagan, Francis *o.m.i.* '52 (PT) Perry, FL Immaculate Conception Church.
Bagatin, Tarcisio *c.s.* '58 (SY) [21] Syracuse, NY St. Peter Church.
Bagdanavicius, Vytautas *m.i.c.* '36 (CHI) [N] Chicago, IL Congregation of Marian Fathers of the Immaculate Conception.
Bagdonis, Raymond *o.carm.* '94 (NY) Middletown, NY Our Lady of Mt. Carmel Church.
Bagert, Matthew A. '97 (DAL) Plano, TX St. Mark the Evangelist Church.
Baggarly, John D. *s.j.* '60 (CHI) [N] Chicago, IL Chicago Province of the Society of Jesus-Provincial Office.
Baggetta, Joseph J. (BO) Roslindale, MA Judge John J. Connelly Youth Center; Mattapan, MA Metropolitan Youth Service Center.
Baggetta, Joseph J. '74 (BO) [31] Boston, MA St. James the Greater Church.
Bagienski, Ronald A. '69 (BUF) [28] Buffalo, NY Holy Apostles SS. Peter and Paul Church.
Baginskis, Boleslaus *m.i.c.* '42 (CHI) [162] Chicago, IL Our Lady of Aglona Church.
Bagley, Gary J. '72 (BUF) [P] Williamsville, NY Franciscan Missionary Sisters of the Divine Child, Inc.; [S] Allegany State Park, NY Camp Turner.
Bagley, John J. '60 (WOR) North Grafton, MA St. Mary's Church.
Bagley, Ronald M. *c.j.m.* '77 (BUF) [1] West Seneca, NY St. Bonaventure Church; [O] West Seneca, NY St. Bonaventure.
Bagnato, James D. *o.praem.* '79 (WIL) [B] Claymont, DE Archmere Academy; [I] Claymont, DE Immaculate Conception Priory of the Canons Regular of Premontre.
Bahena, Jesus '95 (GAL) [24] Houston, TX St. Cyril of Alexandria Church.
Bahhuth, Albert '96 (LA) Whittier, CA St. Gregory the Great Church.
Bahl, Edmund *s.s.c.* '43 (BUF) [M] Silver Creek, NY St. Columbans on the Lake, Home for the Aged.
Bahleda, Aloysius J. '58 (GBG) Retired; [G] Greensburg, PA Neumann House.
Bahlinger, Donald G. *s.j.* '59 (FgM) Provinces.
Bahlinger, Donald G. *s.j.* '59 (GAL) [42] Houston, TX St. Joseph Church.
Bahning, Frederick C. '45 (DUB) Retired.
Bahr, Joseph E. '60 (DOD) Claflin, KS Immaculate Conception Church; Ellinwood, KS St. Joseph Church.
Baiardi, Sereno *o.f.m.* '66 (MIL) [P] Burlington, WI Queen of Peace Friary; [Y] Waterford, WI General Secretariat of the Franciscan Missions, Inc.
Baidoo, Joseph '85 (RVC) Deer Park, NY SS. Cyril and Methodius Church.
Baidoo, Raphael *o.ss.t.* '77 (VIC) Goliad, TX Immaculate Conception Church.
Baier, Donald E. '75 (VEN) Holmes Beach, FL St. Bernard's Church.
Baier, Donald M. '70 (RVC) Malverne, NY Our Lady of Lourdes Church.
Baier, William J. '82 (STL) Bridgeton, MO St. Mary Church.
Bailey, Casey *o.c.s.o.* '83 (P) [L] Lafayette, OR The Cistercian (Trappist) Abbey of Our Lady of Guadalupe.
Bailey, David P. '65 (BO) Sherborn, MA St. Theresa Church.
Bailey, Declan *o.f.m.* '44 (SP) [O] St. Petersburg, FL St.

Anthony Friary.
Bailey, Douglas *s.d.s.* '77 (ORL) [E] Melbourne, FL Florida Institute of Technology Campus Ministry.
Bailey, Fred K. '83 (ORG) Laguna Niguel, CA St. Timothy Church.
Bailey, Msgr. John L. '41 (WDC) [14] Washington, DC St. Francis Xavier Church; Retired.
Bailey, Msgr. Joseph G. '43 (OG) Retired; [A] Ogdensburg, NY Wadhams Hall.
Bailey, Justin J. *o.f.m.* '60 (NY) [DD] New York, NY Franciscan Friars, Order of Friars Minor, Holy Name Province.
Bailey, Larry (GF) Special Assignment.
Bailey, Lawrence '86 (SEA) Military Chaplains.
Bailey, Paul F. '58 (BO) [4] Plymouth, MA St. Peter Church.
Bailey, Richard L. *s.j.* '58 (STL) [F] St. Louis, MO De Smet Jesuit High School; [P] St. Louis, MO De Smet Jesuit High School Community.
Bailey, Robert L. '93 (PRO) [1] East Providence, RI St. Brendan Church.
Bailey, Scott *c.ss.r.* (BAL) [96] Baltimore, MD St. Wenceslaus Church.
Baillargeon, Albert G. '47 (MAN) Retired.
Bailleres, Anthony *l.c.* (HRT) [B] Cheshire, CT Novitiate of the Legion of Christ.
Bailleres, Anthony *l.c.* '81 (HRT) [V] Orange, CT Legion of Christ, Inc.
Bailon, Abelardo '58 (LA) Huntington Park, CA St. Matthias Church.
Bailon, Cirilo '93 (SB) Palm Springs, CA Our Lady of Solitude Church.
Baily, Harold E. '69 (PIT) Sewickley, PA St. James Church; Allegheny County, Pa Sewickley Valley Hospital; [R] Slippery Rock, PA Office for Campus Ministry.
Baima, Thomas A. '80 (CHI) Skokie, IL St. Peter Church.
Bain, Daniel '64 (RIC) Elkton, VA Holy Infant Church; Greene County, VA Shepherd of the Hills Church.
Bain, J.F. Michael (PHX) Williams, AZ St. Joseph's Church.
Bain, John K. '70 (RNO) Zephyr Cove, NV Our Lady of Tahoe Church.
Bain, Ken '90 (SFS) Clark, SD St. Michael Church.
Bain, Richard '80 (SFR) San Anselmo, CA St. Anselm Church; Special Assignment.
Bain, Thomas J. *s.j.* '56 (CLV) [E] Cleveland, OH St. Ignatius High School.
Baird, James R. '93 (DEN) Brush, CO St. Mary Church.
Baird, Joseph A. *o.s.f.s.* '68 (WIL) [I] Childs, MD Oblates of St. Francis De Sales.
Baird, Msgr. Lawrence J. '69 (ORG) Newport Beach, CA Our Lady Queen of Angels Church.
Baird, Stephen E. *s.j.* '96 (COS) [E] Sedalia, CO Sacred Heart Retreat House - Jesuit Community; [G] Sedalia, CO Sacred Heart Jesuit Retreat House.
Baistra, Jorge '74 (SAT) [71] San Antonio, TX San Juan Capistrano Church.
Bajek, Gerald '69 (NEW) Closter, NJ St. Mary's Church; Paramus, NJ Bergen Pines County Hospital.
Bajek, Mietek *o.m.i.* '81 (SFS) Sisseton, SD St. Catherine Church; Sisseton, SD St. Peter Church.
Bajkowski, Dennis (TR) [S] Princeton, NJ Campus Ministry for the Diocese of Trenton.
Bajkowski, Dennis W. '71 (CAM) Pine Hill, NJ St. Edward's Church.
Bajorek, James R. '80 (PH) [119] Philadelphia, PA Our Lady of Hope Church.
Bajorek, Joseph S. *s.d.b.* '45 (NEW) Mahwah, NJ Immaculate Heart of Mary Church.
Bak, Bernard '88 (BAL) Cockeysville, MD St. Joseph Church.
Bakatuinamina, Sebastien *c.i.c.m.* '83 (STP) Cedar Lake, MN St. Patrick Church.
Baker, Andrew R. (ALN) [O] Kutztown, PA Christopher House.
Baker, Andrew R. '91 (ALN) [C] Bethlehem, PA Bethlehem Catholic High School.
Baker, Bartley P. '93 (NEW) [20] Jersey City, NJ Our Lady of Mercy Church.
Baker, Donald C. '95 (NY) [141] Bronx, NY St. Frances de Chantal Church.
Baker, Donald H. '66 (WOR) [4] Gardner, MA Sacred Heart of Jesus Church.
Baker, Donald P. '80 (CHL) Absent On Leave.
Baker, George (NY) Manhattan, NY Mount Sinai Medical Center.
Baker, George E. '81 (NY) [76] New York, NY St. Monica Church.
Baker, Gerald H. '83 (OWN) Hopkinsville, KY SS. Peter and Paul Church.
Baker, Jack H. '93 (DET) Wayne, MI St. Mary Church.
Baker, James E. '63 (DOD) Deerfield, KS Christ the King Church; Garden City, KS St. Mary Church.
Baker, James H. *s.j.* (STL) [C] St. Louis, MO Saint Louis University.
Baker, James H. *s.j.* '69 (STL) [P] St. Louis, MO Jesuit Community Corporation at St. Louis University - Jesuit Hall.
Baker, Jay '92 (HT) Thibodaux, LA Nicholls State University.
Baker, Jay L. '92 (HT) [7] Thibodaux, LA St. Thomas Aquinas Church.
Baker, John C. '82 (PRO) Bristol, RI St. Elizabeth Church.
Baker, John Sims '94 (NSH) McEwen, TN St. Patrick Church; Tennessee Ridge, TN St. Elizabeth Ann Seton Church.
Baker, John W. '39 (SPC) Retired.
Baker, Joseph M. '85 (TUC) [3] Tucson, AZ Holy Family Church.
Baker, Msgr. Joseph W. '51 (STL) [37] St. Louis, MO St. Hedwig Church.
Baker, Joseph W. '69 (NY) [60] New York, NY St. John the Martyr Church.
Baker, Kenneth *s.j.* '62 (PAT) Pequannock, NJ Our Lady of Fatima Chapel (Tridentine) Church.
Baker, Kenneth R. '62 (CIN) [27] Dayton, OH St. Rita Church.
Baker, Mike '74 (LA) [53] Los Angeles, CA St. Camillus De Lellis Church.
Baker, Nicholas J. '63 (LIN) Crete, NE Sacred Heart Church.
Baker, Richard D. '90 (NY) [A] Bronx, NY St. John Neumann Residence.
Baker, Richard M. *m.m.* '71 (FgM) Maryknoll Foreign Missions.
Baker, Robert '70 (STA) [3] Jacksonville, FL Christ the King Church.
Baker, Robert R. *c.s.c.* '70 (FgM) Holy Cross Foreign Missions.
Baker, Robert R. *c.s.c.* '70 (NY) [188] Bronx, NY Sacred Heart Church.
Baker, Thomas E. '89 (LA) [24] Los Angeles, CA Our Lady of Guadalupe Church.
Baker, W. Pierre '78 (MAN) Keene, NH St. Bernard Church.
Baker, William '82 (FgM) Society of St. James the Apostle.
Baker, William F. '77 (FR) Absent on Leave.
Baker, William S. '55 (SY) Clayville, NY St. Patrick Church.
Baker, William T. '82 (ALN) On Duty Outside the Diocese.
Bakewell, Anderson E. *s.j.* '51 (SFE) [K] Santa Fe, NM Discalced Carmelite Monastery.
Bakewell, Donald V. '66 (DUB) Preston, IA St. Joseph's Church; Sabula, IA St. Peter Church; Springbrook, IA SS. Peter and Paul Church; [D] Bellevue, IA Marquette High School; [F] Bellevue, IA Bellevue Area Catholic Elementary School.
Bakh, Antoine '88 (OLL) Anaheim, CA St. John Maron Mission Church.
Bakke, Lawrence M. '75 (MAD) Sun Prairie, WI St. Albert the Great Church.
Bakker, Richard T. *s.m.a.* '59 (BO) [2] Malden, MA St. Joseph Church.
Bakle, John L. *s.m.* '67 (CIN) [M] Dayton, OH Marianist Provincialate.
Bakle, John L. *s.m.* '67 (COL) [2] Columbus, OH St. Agatha Church; [39] Columbus, OH Saint Stephen the Martyr Church.
Bakos, Stephen '36 (Y) Retired.
Baky, Isidore '72 (MIA) [7] Fort Lauderdale, FL St. Helen Church.
Bakyil, Alphonsus *s.o.l.t.* '85 (GAL) [52] Houston, TX St. Monica Church.
Bala, Paul '69 (SAG) Wilmot, MI St. Michael Church.
Bala, Paul W. '69 (SAG) Cass City, MI St. Pancratius Church.
Balaban, Oryst (SJP) Retired.
Balado, Armando '49 (MIA) [29] Miami, FL St. Raymond Church.
Balagapo, Victorio '31 (SFR) [11] San Francisco, CA St. Charles Borromeo Church.
Balagat, Arturo '75 (SB) Norco, CA St. Mel Church.
Balagtas, Rodel '91 (LA) Valinda, CA St. Martha Church.
Balas, Christopher *o.f.m.conv.* '57 (R) Burgaw, NC St. Joseph Church; [E] Wilmington, NC Conventual Franciscans O.F.M.Conv.
Balas, David *o.cist.* '53 (DAL) [B] Irving, TX University of Dallas.
Balas, David *o.cist.* '54 (DAL) [M] Irving, TX Cistercian Abbey of Our Lady of Dallas.
Balash, Michael D. '87 (Y) Ashtabula, OH Our Lady of Mt. Carmel Church.
Balasko, George J. '67 (Y) East Liverpool, OH St. Ann's Church; Wellsville, OH Immaculate Conception Church.
Balaun, George W. '72 (CLV) Brook Park, OH St. Peter the Apostle Church.
Balazs, Richard P. *c.r.* '65 (CHI) [D] Chicago, IL Weber High School.
Balazy, Edwin W. '62 (DET) [3] Dearborn Heights, MI St. John the Baptist Church.
Balbi-Port, Mario '47 (NEW) [3] Elizabeth, NJ St. Anthony's Church.
Balcerski, Duane *c.s.c.* '71 (FgM) Holy Cross Foreign Missions.
Balchunas, Henry A. '65 (HRT) Wolcott, CT St. Pius X Church.
Balcom, Gary E. '72 (BO) Health Leave.
Balczeniuk, Mark G. '83 (SCR) Dorrance, PA Our Lady Help of Christians Church.
Balczewski, Leslaw *s.j.* '59 (CHI) [N] Chicago, IL Sacred Heart Mission House; [N] Chicago, IL Sacred Heart Mission House.
Baldacchino, Peter '96 (NEW) Ridgewood, NJ Our Lady of Mount Carmel Church.
Balderas, Jose Luis '68 (SAT) La Pryor, TX St. Joseph Church.
Balderas, Msgr. Luis G. '44 (SD) Retired.
Balderrama, George *s.c.j.* '73 (MIL) [K] Milwaukee, WI St. Francis Hospital; [P] Hales Corners, WI Sacred Heart Monastery.
Baldonado, Angel *s.d.b.* '77 (OAK) [E] Richmond, CA Salesian High School.
Baldonado, Felipe *o.f.m.* '38 (ORG) [3] Huntington Beach, CA SS. Simon and Jude Church.
Baldonado, Luis *o.f.m.* '52 (PHX) [19] Phoenix, AZ St. Mary's Basilica Church; [23] Phoenix, AZ Sacred Heart Church.
Baldonieri, Thomas F. '90 (CHI) [198] Chicago, IL St. Tarcissus Church.
Baldovin, John F. *s.j.* '75 (OAK) [A] Berkeley, CA The Jesuit School of Theology at Berkeley; [N] Berkeley, CA Jesuit Community at Jesuit School of Theology at Berkeley.
Baldrick, James F. '63 (PH) [1] Norristown, PA Epiphany of Our Lord Church.
Balducelli, Roberto *o.s.f.s.* '36 (WIL) [3] Wilmington, DE St. Anthony of Padua Church.
Balduck, Walter *o.f.m.cap.* '73 (SAG) [9] Saginaw, MI St. Anthony of Padua Church; [G] Saginaw, MI Queen of Angels Friary and Retreat House.
Balduf, Raymond J. *s.j.* '51 (NEW) [C] Jersey City, NJ St. Peter's Preparatory School.
Baldus, Leonard M. *o.m.i.* '42 (SPC) Mansfield, MO Immaculate Heart of Mary Church.
Baldwin, Bradley *t.o.r.* '94 (STP) Brooklyn Park, MN St. Gerard Church.
Baldwin, David E. '77 (CHI) [28] Chicago, IL St. Benedict the African (East) Church.
Baldwin, Msgr. Edward J. '55 (DET) Bloomfield Hills, MI St. Owen Church.
Baldwin, John F. '59 (CHI) Military Chaplains.
Baldwin, Michael E. '83 (WCH) [20] Wichita, KS St. Vincent de Paul Church.
Baldwin, Paul C. '97 (DUB) [8] Dubuque, IA Holy Ghost Church.
Baldyga, William L. '69 (HRT) Suffield, CT St. Joseph's Church.
Bales, Robert J. '57 (MIL) Slinger, WI St. Peter Church.
Bales, Thomas E. '74 (RCK) Sterling, IL St. Mary Church.
Balestino, Francis P. '60 (ALT) [16] Johnstown, PA St. Francis of Assisi Church.
Balestrieri, Edward '59 (BEL) Vienna, IL St. Paul Church.
Balinong, Alfredo *s.j.* '64 (NY) [18] New York, NY Blessed Sacrament Church.
Balint, R. James '61 (DAL) Plano, TX Prince of Peace Church.
Balint, Stephen J. '65 (BGP) [3] Norwalk, CT St. Ladislaus Church.
Balio, Paul '72 (SD) [1] San Diego, CA St. Joseph Cathedral; San Diego, CA UCSD Medical Center.
Balistreri, Anthony '93 (SJP) [9] Rossford, OH St. Michael Church.
Balizan, Daniel '89 (SFE) Clovis, NM Our Lady of Guadalupe Church.
Balkan, Paschal *o.c.s.o.* '55 (ARL) [J] Berryville, VA Cistercian Abbey of Our Lady of the Holy Cross.
Balker, Msgr. Joseph W. '44 (FRS) Retired.
Ball, David '62 (CHI) Military Chaplains.
Ball, Edward *m.s.c.* '66 (RCK) [H] Aurora, IL Missionaries of the Sacred Heart Community.
Ball, Harry W. *s.j.* '42 (FgM) Provinces.
Ball, Matthew J. '91 (RVC) Absent on Leave.
Ball, Raymond A. '87 (MAN) [11] Manchester, NH St. John the Baptist Church; [C] Manchester, NH Trinity High School.
Ball, Richard D. '77 (SC) Merrill, IA Assumption Church; [B] Le Mars, IA Gehlen Catholic School.
Ball, Thomas J. '66 (BUR) [1] Burlington, VT Cathedral of the Immaculate Conception.
Ball, Wayne L. '89 (RIC) Roanoke, VA St. Gerard Church; Salem, VA Salem VA Medical Center.
Ballance, Harvey J. '57 (NEW) On Duty Outside the Archdiocese.
Ballard, Kevin D. *s.j.* '85 (FgM) Provinces.
Ballentine, Edgar S. '46 (NSH) Retired.
Ballester, Msgr. Buenaventura '43 (ARE) [2] Arecibo, PR Church of Sagrado Corazon de Jesus.
Ballester, Msgr. Pedro J. '58 (PCE) [6] Ponce, PR San Conrado Church.
Ballestrazzi, Libero *c.s.j.* '44 (CLV) [P] Avon, OH Congregation of St. Joseph.
Balleza, John '85 (SFR) Absent on Leave.

Balleza, John '85 (SJ) [13] San Jose, CA St. Julie Church.
Ballman, Thomas J. '43 (CIN) [4] Dayton, OH St. Anthony of Padua Church; Retired.
Ballor, Milton A. *c.pp.s.* '55 (CIN) St. Wendelin, OH St. Wendelin Church; Sharpsburg, OH St. Paul Church.
Balluff, John '88 (JOL) Elmhurst, IL Immaculate Conception Church.
Ballweber, Eugene L. (CHI) Retired.
Ballweg, John M. '56 (NEW) Union, NJ Holy Spirit Church; [B] South Orange, NJ Seton Hall University.
Ballweg, Msgr. Lawrence '40 (RVC) Retired.
Balmeo, Simeon '65 (AGN) Maina, GU Our Lady of the Purification Church.
Balog, John '67 (PSC) Wilkes-Barre, PA St. John's Church.
Balog, Robert A. '72 (RCK) Johnsburg, IL St. John the Baptist Church.
Baloga, Herbert *o.f.m.conv.* '38 (SPR) [10] Chicopee, MA St. Stanislaus Basilica Church.
Baloga, Herbert C. *o.f.m.conv.* '38 (SPR) [F] Springfield, MA Mercy Hospital.
Balogh, Donald J. '49 (CLV) [5] Parma, OH St. Francis de Sales Church; Retired.
Balogun, Patrick O. '94 (NY) Suffern, NY Sacred Heart Church.
Balquin, Don M. '93 (FBK) Delta Junction, AK Our Lady of Sorrows Church.
Balsam, John B. *o.p.* '47 (DAL) [M] Irving, TX Dominican Priory of St. Albert the Great.
Balser, Edward '56 (JKS) [5] Jackson, MS Holy Family Church.
Balser, Robert *c.ss.r.* '49 (GR) [3] Grand Rapids, MI St. Alphonsus Church.
Balskus, Charles '65 (CHI) [4] Oak Lawn, IL St. Linus Church.
Balta, Msgr. Raymond A. '69 (PBR) Johnstown, PA St. Mary's Church.
Baltazar, Ayala '43 (SJ) Retired.
Baltes, Gabriel *o.s.b.* '91 (JOL) Lisle, IL St. Joan of Arc Church; [J] Lisle, IL St. Procopius Abbey.
Baltes, Timothy '76 (SCL) [8] St. Cloud, MN St. Paul Church.
Baltrucki, Leon S. '40 (BRK) Retired.
Baltrusaitis, Gabriel *o.f.m.* '54 (PRT) [I] Kennebunkport, ME St. Anthony's Friary.
Baltrushunas, Anthony P. '37 (BO) Retired.
Baltz, Albert G. '70 (BUR) Bristol, VT St. Ambrose Church.
Baltz, David *m.c.c.j.* '67 (FgM) Comboni Foreign Missions.
Baltz, John P., Jr. '43 (NSH) Retired.
Baluyot, Michael Noel '97 (BEA) [9] Beaumont, TX St. Jude Thaddeus Church.
Balvanera, Andres (JOL) West Chicago, IL St. Mary Church.
Balvo, Msgr. Charles D. '76 (NY) On Duty Outside the Archdiocese.
Balwinski, Gerald E. '69 (SAG) [12] Bay City, MI Our Lady of the Visitation Church.
Balys, Thomas I. *o.c.d.* '63 (GRY) [J] Munster, IN Discalced Carmelite Fathers Monastery.
Balzer, Raymond J. '49 (FTW) Auburn, IN Immaculate Conception Church.
Bambenek, Oliver *o.f.m.cap.* '65 (MIL) [B] Mount Calvary, WI St. Lawrence Seminary; [P] Mount Calvary, WI St. Lawrence Friary.
Bamber, William J. *c.m.* '55 (PH) [AA] Philadelphia, PA Congregation of the Mission.
Bambera, Joseph C. '83 (SCR) [A] Dalton, PA Saint Pius X Seminary.
Bamberg, Callistus M. *o.f.m.* '61 (ALB) [B] Loudonville, NY Siena College.
Bambir, Vjekoslav *o.f.m.* '40 (CHI) [N] Chicago, IL Croatian Franciscan Custody of the Holy Family.
Bambol, John *o.f.m.conv.* '41 (BAL) [M] Ellicott City, MD Order of Friars Minor Conventual.
Bambol, John *o.f.m.conv.* '41 (SPR) [5] Holyoke, MA Mater Dolorosa Church.
Bambrick, John P. '91 (TR) Manalapan, NJ St. Thomas More Church.
Bambrick, John W. '70 (ALN) [3] Minersville, PA Our Lady of Mount Carmel Church.
Bambrick, Msgr. Kevin '47 (BLX) [6] Biloxi, MS St. Louis Church; Retired.
Banach, Henry S. '48 (WOR) Retired.
Banach, Joseph S. '56 (MET) Retired.
Banach, Msgr. Michael (WOR) On Duty Outside the Diocese.
Banach, Michael '88 (WOR) On Special or Other (Arch)Diocesan Assignment.
Banach, Walter F. '39 (LIN) Retired.
Banaga, Gregg *c.m.* '79 (CLV) [30] Cleveland, OH Holy Rosary Church.
Banas, James T. *c.s.c.* '57 (FgM) Holy Cross Foreign Missions.
Banas, Leonard N. *c.s.c.* '57 (FTW) [B] Notre Dame, IN University of Notre Dame Du Lac; [J] Notre Dame, IN Holy Cross Community, Corby Hall, University of Notre Dame.
Banazak, Gregory '85 (DET) [A] Orchard Lake, MI SS. Cyril and Methodius Seminary.
Banden, Joseph W. '69 (STL) [11] Florissant, MO Transfiguration Church.
Bandiera, Colombo F. '52 (WH) Retired.
Bandle, Ronald J. '68 (MIL) Special Assignment.
Bandurski, Pawel *s.ch.* '92 (SJ) [1] Sunnyvale, CA St. Albert Chmielowski Polish Catholic Pastoral Mission Church; [3] Sunnyvale, CA St. Cyprian Church.
Bane, Msgr. Raymond T. '51 (NO) Retired.
Banet, Charles *c.pp.s.* (GAL) Retired.
Banet, Charles H. *c.pp.s.* '49 (GAL) [2] Galveston, TX Holy Rosary Church.
Banet, Charles H. *c.pp.s.* '49 (LFT) [A] Rensselaer, IN Saint Joseph's College.
Banet, Paul H. *s.s.j.* '55 (GAL) [2] Galveston, TX Holy Rosary Church.
Banet, Stephen J. (IND) On Duty Outside the Archdiocese.
Bang, Le Huy *c.ss.r.* '46 (LA) [R] Baldwin Park, CA Vietnamese Redemptorist Mission.
Baniak, Walter '41 (ALB) Retired.
Banick, Msgr. Thomas V. '63 (SCR) [14] Wilkes-Barre, PA St. Mary's Church of the Immaculate Conception.
Banigan, Herbert '46 (DEN) Retired.
Banken, Robert L. '68 (STL) Military Chaplains.
Banker, Richard '88 (STP) Prior Lake, MN St. Michael Church.
Banko, John M. '72 (MET) Hillsborough, NJ Mary, Mother of God Church.
Banks, Charles *o.m.i.* '66 (SAT) [K] San Antonio, TX Oblate Madonna Residence; [M] San Antonio, TX Provincial Administration Office, Oblates of Mary Immaculate (Southern Prov.).
Banks, David A. '73 (SP) Homosassa, FL St. Thomas the Apostle Church.
Banks, Edward J. *s.j.* '50 (BO) Dedham, MA St. Mary Church; [W] Boston, MA The Society of Jesus of New England-Provincial Offices; [W] Weston, MA Campion Center.
Banks, Evan *o.f.m.* '50 (NEW) Fair Lawn, NJ St. Anne's Church.
Banks, Gary *s.t.* '76 (LA) Compton, CA Our Lady of Victory Church.
Banks, John P. *s.j.* '51 (FgM) Provinces.
Banks, Michael *o.f.m.cap.* '84 (NY) New Paltz, NY St. Joseph Church; [DD] New Paltz, NY St. Joseph Friary.
Bannan, Louis I. *s.j.* '44 (SJ) [B] Santa Clara, CA Santa Clara University.
Bannan, Msgr. Martin '56 (BRK) [U] Brooklyn, NY St. Joseph's Priest Residence.
Bannan, Peter F. '67 (NY) Pelham, NY St. Catharine Church.
Bannantine, Thomas E. *s.j.* '65 (OM) [K] Omaha, NE Jesuit Community At Creighton University.
Banner, Russell J. '67 (CLV) [7] Cleveland, OH Annunciation Church.
Bannin, Eugene *s.j.* '50 (PMB) [3] West Palm Beach, FL St. Ann Church; [E] West Palm Beach, FL Noreen McKeen Residence for Geriatric Care.
Bannon, Anthony *l.c.* (NY) [HH] Rye, NY Center for Family Life, Inc.
Bannon, Anthony *l.c.* '75 (HRT) [V] Orange, CT Legion of Christ, Inc.
Bannon, Msgr. Martin J. '56 (BRK) [115] Brooklyn, NY St. Patrick Church.
Banos, Felix '58 (ORL) Lake Wales, FL Holy Spirit Church.
Bantle, Charles *o.f.m.cap.* '48 (DET) [K] Detroit, MI St. Bonaventure Friary.
Bantle, Charles *o.f.m.cap.* '48 (FgM) Capuchin Foreign Missions.
Bantz, William E. '60 (Y) Maximo, OH St. Joseph Church.
Banuelas, Msgr. Arturo '76 (ELP) [30] El Paso, TX St. Pius X Church.
Banzin, Robert S. '64 (CHI) Niles, IL St. John Brebeuf Church.
Bao, Tran Quoc *c.ss.r.* '90 (LA) [R] Baldwin Park, CA Vietnamese Redemptorist Mission.
Baptista, Diego '69 (SR) Crescent City, CA St. Joseph Church.
Baptista, Michael *s.d.b.* '85 (LA) [F] Bellflower, CA St. John Bosco High School.
Baptiste, Chuck '96 (PIT) Center Township, PA St. Frances Cabrini Church.
Baptiste, Glen *c.r.* '91 (CHI) [N] Chicago, IL Provincial Office of the Congregation of the Resurrection.
Baraan, Geoffrey '97 (OAK) Pleasanton, CA St. Augustine Church.
Barachini, Nello A. *c.m.* '86 (BGP) [2] Bridgeport, CT St. Ambrose Church; Bridgeport, CT Bridgeport Hospital.
Barajas, Abel '96 (MIA) Plantation, FL St. Gregory Church.
Barajas, Msgr. Ricardo '52 (FRS) Mendota, CA Our Lady of Guadalupe Church.
Barak, Christopher L. '87 (LIN) Palmyra, NE St. Leo's Church.
Barakat, Jean Pierre '89 (OLL) Las Vegas, NV St. Sharbel Mission Church.
Baraki, Tesfamariam '75 (WDC) [15] Washington, DC St. Gabriel Church; [25] Washington, DC Kidane-Mehret Ge'ez Rite Catholic Church; [V] Washington, DC Ethiopian and Eritrean Catholic Mission, USA.
Baran, Blaise R. '82 (MET) Raritan, NJ St. Ann Church.
Baran, Jody '89 (PSC) Wilkes-Barre, PA St. Mary's Church.
Baran, John P. '84 (BGP) [2] Fairfield, CT Assumption Church.
Baran, Joseph L. '47 (MIL) Retired.
Baran, Volodymyr *c.ss.r.* '85 (PHU) Newark, NJ St. John the Baptist Church.
Baranek, Raymond '76 (CLV) Absent on Leave.
Baraniak, James T. *o. praem.* '93 (GB) [5] De Pere, WI Our Lady of Lourdes Church; [A] De Pere, WI St. Norbert Abbey; [I] De Pere, WI St. Joseph Priory.
Baranowski, Art '68 (DET) [T] Marysville, MI National Alliance of Parishes Restructuring into Communities.
Baranowski, Arthur R. '68 (DET) Marysville, MI St. Christopher Church.
Baranowski, David J. '73 (HRT) [7] Hamden, CT St. Stephen's Church.
Baranowski, Stanley A. '55 (MIL) Retired.
Baranowski, Xavier S. '34 (SPR) Retired.
Baranski, Andrew '92 (SY) Graduate Studies.
Baransky, Francis J. '79 (ALN) Coaldale, PA SS. Cyril and Methodius Church; Coaldale, PA St. John the Baptist Church; Coaldale, PA St. Mary of the Assumption Church.
Barasinski, John B. '81 (GRY) [1] Michigan City, IN St. Mary of the Immaculate Conception Church.
Barattini, John H. '44 (NO) Retired.
Barauskas, Peter *m.i.c.* '39 (NOR) [F] Thompson, CT Marian Fathers.
Barbato, Robert *o.f.m.cap* '81 (LA) Solvang, CA Old Mission Santa Ines Church.
Barbella, John J. '87 (MET) Flemington, NJ St. Magdalen de Pazzi Church.
Barber, Bradley (CC) [B] Corpus Christi, TX Bishop Garriga Middle School.
Barber, Bradley A. M. (CC) [5] Corpus Christi, TX Most Precious Blood Church.
Barber, Eugene J. *s.j.* '63 (BAL) [M] Baltimore, MD Jesuit Fathers and Brothers Maryland Provincial Curia.
Barber, Eugene J. *s.j.* '63 (FgM) Provinces.
Barber, Hal L. '61 (SFS) Dell Rapids, SD St. Mary's Church.
Barber, Michael *s.m.* '90 (STL) [P] St. Louis, MO Provincialate of the Society of Mary, Province of St. Louis.
Barber, Michael C *s.j.* '85 (SAC) [G] Carmichael, CA Jesuit High School Community of Sacramento.
Barber, Michael D. *s.j.* (STL) [C] St. Louis, MO Saint Louis University.
Barber, Michael D. *s.j.* '79 (STL) [P] St. Louis, MO Leo Brown Jesuit Community.
Barber, Michael L. *s.j.* '75 (PH) [AA] Philadelphia, PA Jesuit Community at St. Joseph's University.
Barber, Robert *o.f.m.* '84 (PRT) [I] Kennebunkport, ME St. Anthony's Friary.
Barbernitz, John '50 (MOB) Camden, AL St. Joseph Church; Orrville, AL Immaculate Conception Church.
Barbernitz, John P. '50 (BAL) [5] Baltimore, MD St. Alphonsus Church; Retired.
Barbetta, Philip '72 (BRK) Absent on Leave.
Barbian, Leonard M. '65 (MIL) Special Assignment.
Barbone, Joseph F. '72 (NEW) Plainfield, NJ St. Bernard's Church.
Barbour, Hugh C. *o.praem* '90 (ORG) [A] Silverado, CA St. Michael's Norbertine Postulancy, Novitiate and Juniorate; [H] Silverado, CA Norbertine Fathers of Orange Inc.
Barcellona, Thomas J. '95 (CAM) Bridgeton, NJ Immaculate Conception Church.
Barcelo, Jose *c.m.* '53 (BRK) [W] Brooklyn, NY Centro Evangelizacion San Vicente de Paul.
Barch, Howard C. '93 (PEO) Penfield, IL St. Lawrence's Church.
Barcio, Robert '47 (E) [1] Erie, PA St. Peter Cathedral.
Barcio, Robert G. '47 (E) Retired.
Barclay, Robert F. '75 (BRK) [170] Queens, NY St. Gabriel Church.
Barclift, Richard '66 (PEO) Moline, IL Christ the King Church.
Barcome, Earl '52 (GB) Retired.
Barczak, Rene *o.f.m.* '64 (PH) [D] Philadelphia, PA Archbishop Ryan High School; [AA] Philadelphia, PA St. Pius X Friary.
Barczyk, John '87 (TYL) Sulphur Springs, TX St. James Church.
Bardes, Msgr. George F. '44 (NY) Retired; [E] White Plains, NY Archbishop Stepinac High School.
Bardino, Jose '62 (MIA) [3] Hialeah, FL St. Benedict Church.
Bardon, John Brent '68 (TUC) [18] Tucson, AZ Saint Odilia Church.
Barerra, Luis A. (ORL) [1] Ocala, FL Blessed Trinity Church.

Barett, Robert '46 (SY) [S] Syracuse, NY St. Pius X Home, Inc.
Barfield, Daniel R. *s.j.* '67 (LSC) Alamogordo, NM St. Jude Church.
Barfknecht, David *o.s.b.* '89 (HON) [H] Waialua, Oahu, HI Benedictine Monastery of Hawaii.
Barga, Louis J. *c.pp.s.* '54 (CIN) Philothea, OH St. Mary's Church.
Bargielski, John C. '45 (GRY) Retired.
Baribeau, Donald G. *m.s.* '75 (R) Washington, NC Mother of Mercy Church.
Baril, Gerald *m.s.* '59 (FR) [J] Attleboro, MA La Salette Provincial House.
Barile, Ralph E. (BRK) [18] Brooklyn, NY St. Bernadette Church.
Barile, Ralph E. '82 (TR) On Duty Outside the Diocese.
Barille, Nicholas *s.t.* '95 (LA) Compton, CA Our Lady of Victory Church.
Baris, Bernard *m.s.* '69 (FR) Brewster, MA Our Lady of the Cape Church.
Barius, Placid *o.f.m.* '43 (PRT) [I] Kennebunkport, ME St. Anthony's Friary.
Barjacoba, Peter '60 (NY) Absent on Leave.
Barkemeyer, John H. '90 (CHI) [A] Mundelein, IL University of St. Mary of the Lake-Mundelein Seminary.
Barkenquest, Lehr *o.s.f.s.* '64 (LAN) Clarklake, MI St. Rita Church.
Barker, Barnabas *t.o.r.* '58 (DAV) Mount Pleasant, IA Mental Health Institute, St. Dymphna Chapel.
Barker, Brian '94 (BEL) West Frankfort, IL St. John the Baptist Church.
Barker, Harry O. '57 (SHP) Retired.
Barker, Jack D. '92 (SB) La Quinta, CA St. Francis of Assisi Church.
Barker, James '80 (BAL) Special Assignment; [Q] Baltimore, MD Serra Club Vocation Center.
Barker, James M. '80 (BAL) [63] Baltimore, MD St. Michael Church.
Barker, John A. '59 (L) Brandenburg, KY St. John the Apostle Church.
Barker, Joseph F. '53 (ALB) Johnstown, NY St. Patrick Church.
Barker, Richard '92 (GAL) [78] Houston, TX St. Vincent de Paul Church.
Barker, Ronald A. '75 (BO) [2] Revere, MA Immaculate Conception Church.
Barker, Virgil M. '88 (LFT) Peru, IN St. Charles Borromeo Church.
Barkett, James S. '91 (ARL) Dale City, VA Holy Family Church.
Barkey, Patrick C. '90 (PIT) Ross Township, PA St. Sebastian Church.
Barkin, Martin F. '77 (PIT) Unity, PA St. John the Baptist Church.
Barletta, Michael '66 (E) [M] Erie, PA Holy Family Monastery.
Barletta, Michael G. '66 (E) [27] Erie, PA St. Patrick/St. Hedwig Church.
Barley, Tom '91 (SAN) St. Lawrence, TX St. Lawrence Church.
Barlog, Raymond M. '55 (CHI) [209] Chicago, IL St. Turibius Church.
Barlow, James P. '73 (SAT) Military Chaplains.
Barlowski, Joseph R. '41 (HRT) Retired.
Barman, William '81 (ORG) [4] Santa Ana, CA Our Lady of Lourdes Church.
Barmasse, Gerald R. *c.s.c.* '76 (FgM) Holy Cross Foreign Missions.
Barmasse, Gerald R. *c.s.c.* '76 (FTW) [J] South Bend, IN Congregation of Holy Cross Indiana Province Provincial House.
Barnd, Donald *s.c.j.* '78 (MIL) [P] Franklin, WI Villa Maria.
Barnes, Bernard M. *o.s.m.* '48 (CHI) [N] Chicago, IL Servite Friars - Eastern Province.
Barnes, David J. '97 (BO) Wakefield, MA St. Joseph Church.
Barnes, Gavin *o.s.b.* '52 (IND) [J] St. Meinrad, IN St. Meinrad Archabbey.
Barnes, Gerard J. '62 (PH) Retired.
Barnes, James H. '69 (LA) [70] Los Angeles, CA St. Joan of Arc Church.
Barnes, John E. '55 (LR) Retired; [H] Little Rock, AR St. John Manor.
Barnes, John G. '52 (DUB) Retired.
Barnes, Joseph A. '57 (ALN) Retired; [J] Bethlehem, PA Holy Family Villa.
Barnes, Msgr. Joseph C. '58 (FRS) Tehachapi, CA St. Malachy Church.
Barnes, Robert *o.c.s.o.* '70 (ARL) [J] Berryville, VA Cistercian Abbey of Our Lady of the Holy Cross.
Barnes, Robert W. '80 (NOR) Occum, CT St. Joseph Church.
Barnes, Thomas C. '87 (COV) [6] Covington, KY Holy Cross Church.
Barnett, Fred J. '52 (JC) Laurie, MO Shrine of St. Patrick Church.
Barnett, James Q. *o.p.* '65 (CHI) [N] Chicago, IL Dominicans (Provincial Office).
Barnett, James Q. *o.p.* '65 (FgM) Dominican - Order of Preachers Foreign Missions.
Barnett, Larry *o.s.b.* '76 (SFS) [F] Marvin, SD Blue Cloud Abbey.
Barnett, Msgr. Stephen T. '70 (SFS) [1] Sioux Falls, SD St. Joseph Cathedral.
Barnhardt, Bruno *o.s.b.cam.* '66 (MRY) [G] Big Sur, CA New Camaldoli Hermitage.
Barnhart, Victor A. '90 (STL) Pagedale, MO St. Catherine of Siena Church.
Barnhill, Robert K. '85 (LIN) [8] Lincoln, NE St. Mary Church.
Barnickel, William *o.f.m.* '52 (SFD) [K] Sherman, IL Our Lady of Angels Friary.
Barnufsky, Stephen *o.f.m.* '76 (OAK) [N] Oakland, CA Franciscan Friars Provincial Office, Province of St. Barbara; [N] Oakland, CA Franciscan Friars Provincial Office, Province of St. Barbara.
Barnum, Martin '74 (CHI) On Duty Outside the Archdiocese.
Barnum, Martin '74 (MIL) [B] Hales Corners, WI Sacred Heart School of Theology.
Barnwell, Gerald P. '77 (FR) [2] Fall River, MA Blessed Sacrament Church.
Baron, John B. '73 (NEW) Lodi, NJ St. Francis de Sales Church; [Q] Teaneck, NJ Fairleigh Dickinson Univ.-Teaneck Campus.
Barona, German *m.s.c.* '86 (RCK) [H] Aurora, IL Missionaries of the Sacred Heart Community.
Barone, Frank '67 (BUF) Perrysburg, NY Wende Correctional Facility.
Barone, Frank E. '67 (BUF) [2] Lackawanna, NY St. Anthony Church.
Barone, Robert J. '67 (SCR) [3] Scranton, PA St. Anthony of Padua Church; [A] Dalton, PA Saint Pius X Seminary; [O] Scranton, PA Immaculate Heart of Mary Center, Marywood.
Baroni, Barry J. '79 (ALT) [20] Johnstown, PA St. Andrew's Church.
Baronti, David '73 (SPK) On Duty Outside the Diocese.
Baroody, Sami W. '94 (NTN) West Paterson, NJ St. Ann's Church.
Barousse, Raphael *o.s.b.* '55 (NO) [P] St. Benedict, LA St. Joseph Abbey.
Barozzi, Italo '65 (BRK) [33] Brooklyn, NY St. Dominic Church.
Barr, Brian Patrick '93 (RVC) West Hempstead, NY St. Thomas, the Apostle Church.
Barr, Eric R. '84 (RCK) [10] Rockford, IL St. Rita Church.
Barr, Frank *o.s.a.* (BO) [9] Lawrence, MA St. Mary Immaculate Conception Church.
Barr, Frederick *c.s.c.* '54 (P) [B] Portland, OR University of Portland; [L] Portland, OR Holy Cross Fathers & Brothers, C.S.C. - University of Portland.
Barr, Joseph F. '78 (BAL) Davidsonville, MD Holy Family Church.
Barr, Liam M. '74 (LIN) Valparaiso, NE Sts. Mary and Joseph's Church.
Barr, Philip R. '48 (PH) Retired.
Barr, Pierre J. '51 (CHI) [145] Chicago, IL Our Lady of Fatima Church; Retired.
Barr, Stanley J. (CAM) Retired.
Barr, Walter M. '59 (BEL) Christopher, IL St. Andrew Church.
Barragan, Juan Carlos '97 (AMA) Borger, TX St. John the Evangelist Church.
Barrand, James '89 (VNN) On Leave.
Barranger, Ralph '61 (ELP) Kermit, TX St. Thomas & St. Joseph Church; Monahans, TX St. John the Apostle and Evangelist Church.
Barranger, Richard J. *o.p.* '87 (PRO) [B] Providence, RI Providence College.
Barranger, Richard Joseph *o.p.* '87 (PRO) [P] Providence, RI St. Thomas Aquinas Priory at Providence College.
Barrango, Rogelio *s.d.b.* '61 (SJN) [37] San Juan, PR Maria Auxiliadora Church.
Barras, Greg '84 (BLX) [7] Biloxi, MS St. Mary Church.
Barras, Michael J. '73 (LKC) [1] Lake Charles, LA Immaculate Conception Cathedral.
Barras, Robert S. '80 (GAL) [17] Houston, TX St. Catherine of Siena Church.
Barre, Michael L. *s.s.* '70 (BAL) [A] Baltimore, MD St. Mary's Seminary and University.
Barreda, Giles *o.f.m.* '61 (NY) [DD] New York, NY Franciscan Province of the Immaculate Conception.
Barreneche, Franco *o.c.* '44 (SJN) [61] San Juan, PR Santa Teresita Del Nino Jesus Church.
Barrera, Albino F. *o.p.* '93 (PRO) [P] Providence, RI St. Thomas Aquinas Priory at Providence College.
Barrera, Gustave (BWN) [I] Harlingen, TX KMBH-TV 60/KHID-FM 88.1/KMBH-FM 88.9.
Barrera, Gustavo '79 (BWN) [10] Brownsville, TX Saint Mary, Mother of the Church.
Barres, John O. '89 (WIL) On Duty Outside the Diocese.
Barrett, Charles J. *s.m.* '42 (WDC) [M] Washington, DC Marist Provincial House.
Barrett, D. Oliver *c.s.sp.* '48 (PT) [7] Pensacola, FL St. Anne Church.
Barrett, Daniel J. (BO) Retired.
Barrett, David A. '97 (STP) Maplewood, MN Presentation of the Blessed Virgin Mary Church.
Barrett, David S. '64 (GB) Keshena, WI St. Michael Church; South Branch, WI St. Joseph of the Lake Church.
Barrett, Edward F. '61 (SCR) [10] Scranton, PA Immaculate Conception Church.
Barrett, Edward J. '57 (HBG) On Duty Outside the Diocese.
Barrett, Edward J. '75 (CHI) [1] Des Plaines, IL St. Mary Church.
Barrett, Emmett A. *o.f.m.* '55 (PAT) [M] Butler, NJ St. Anthony Friary.
Barrett, Msgr. Francis X. '55 (ALN) [5] Reading, PA Holy Guardian Angels Church.
Barrett, Gerard *o.m.i.* '64 (SAT) Del Rio, TX Sacred Heart Church.
Barrett, Msgr. Harry C. '73 (NY) On Special or Other (Arch)Diocesan Assignment.
Barrett, James L. '56 (KAL) Marshall, MI St. Mary Church.
Barrett, James L. '82 (CHI) Skokie, IL St. Joan of Arc Church.
Barrett, John '59 (JOL) Elmhurst, IL Mary, Queen of Heaven Church.
Barrett, John '78 (RVC) Setauket, NY St. James Church.
Barrett, John W. (WOR) Retired.
Barrett, Kevin S. '92 (PCE) On Duty Outside the Diocese.
Barrett, M. Stephen *s.s.* '79 (BAL) [M] Baltimore, MD Sulpician Provincial House.
Barrett, M. Stephen *s.s.* '79 (BGP) On Duty Outside the Diocese.
Barrett, Michael '84 (PH) [135] Philadelphia, PA St. Peter the Apostle Church.
Barrett, Michael *o.f.m.* '90 (SFD) [4] Quincy, IL St. Francis Solanus Church; [K] Quincy, IL St. Francis Solanus Friary.
Barrett, Michael D. '84 (MAN) On Duty Outside the Diocese.
Barrett, Michael F. '57 (HBG) [5] Lancaster, PA St. Joseph Church.
Barrett, Michael G. '76 (MIL) Grafton, WI St. Joseph Church.
Barrett, Michael J. '85 (GAL) [P] Houston, TX Opus Dei.
Barrett, Miles J. '82 (SC) On Duty Outside the Diocese.
Barrett, Patrick H. '57 (MET) [4] Carteret, NJ St. Elizabeth of Hungary Church.
Barrett, Patrick J. '52 (PRT) [1] Portland, ME Cathedral of the Immaculate Conception; Retired.
Barrett, Patrick J. '59 (GAY) Mapleton, MI St. Joseph Church.
Barrett, Robert E. '63 (BO) Permanent Disability.
Barrett, Robert P. '48 (Y) Retired.
Barrett, Thomas '88 (ORL) [7] Orlando, FL St. Charles Borromeo Church; Special Assignment.
Barrett, Thomas '93 (PMB) [B] West Palm Beach, FL Cardinal Newman High School.
Barrett, Thomas J. *c.ss.r.* '67 (TOL) [2] Lima, OH St. Gerard Church.
Barrett, Thomas M. '71 (BEL) New Baden, IL St. George Church.
Barrett, Tom '88 (ORL) [A] Orlando, FL Bishop Moore High School.
Barrett, Msgr. Walter C. '75 (RIC) [5] Norfolk, VA Basilica of St. Mary Church.
Barrett, William M. '59 (ROC) Lyons, NY St. Michael Church.
Barretta, Msgr. Anthony J. '47 (BRK) [212] Queens, NY Our Lady of Hope Church; Retired; [Y] Brooklyn, NY Holy Cross.
Barrette, Donat A. '54 (PRO) [M] North Smithfield, RI St. Antoine Residence.
Barrette, Eugene *m.s.* '67 (ATL) Smyrna, GA St. Thomas the Apostle Church.
Barricks, Robert '94 (P) [16] Portland, OR Holy Family Church.
Barrientos, Gustavo '87 (OM) [32] Omaha, NE Our Lady of Guadalupe Church.
Barrientos, Jesus H. *o.c.d.* '46 (CGS) [2] Caguas, PR San Jose Church.
Barrios, Diego *c.m.f.* '42 (LA) [R] Rancho Dominguez, CA Dominguez Seminary Inc.
Barrios, Eduardo '72 (MIA) [H] Miami, FL Villa Javier.
Barron, Cecil *c.m.f.* '42 (FRS) [8] Fresno, CA St. Anthony Claret Church.
Barron, Clemente *c.p.* '70 (CHI) [N] Chicago, IL Passionist Provincial Office.
Barron, Clemente *c.p.* '70 (SAT) [M] San Antonio, TX Casa Pasionista Guadalupe.
Barron, Dale F. *m.m.* '65 (FgM) Maryknoll Foreign Missions.
Barron, Daniel *o.m.v.* '96 (SFD) [2] Alton, IL Immaculate Conception-St. Mary's Church; [3] Alton, IL St. Patrick Church.
Barron, Donald L. '71 (SPR) [6] Springfield, MA Holy Name Church.
Barron, Edward M. '38 (CHI) Retired.
Barron, Gerald *o.f.m.cap.* '66 (LA) [B] Santa Ynez, CA

San Lorenzo Novitiate and Seminary.
Barron, Henry T. '88 (CHR) [11] Charleston, SC Church of the Nativity.
Barron, John P. *s.j.* '82 (ALN) [A] Wernersville, PA Novitiate of St. Isaac Jogues; [N] Wernersville, PA Jesuit Center for Spiritual Growth.
Barron, Robert E. '86 (CHI) [A] Mundelein, IL University of St. Mary of the Lake-Mundelein Seminary.
Barron, Stanley C. '74 (PAT) Ogdensburg, NJ St. Thomas of Aquin Church.
Barron, Wayne J. *c.m.f.* '58 (SPC) [D] Springfield, MO St. John's Mercy Villa; [E] Springfield, MO Claretians Missionaries' Residence-Villa Claret.
Barrons, Brian *m.m.* '84 (NY) [DD] Maryknoll, NY Maryknoll Fathers and Brothers.
Barrow, John '80 (PMB) [4] Delray Beach, FL St. Vincent Ferrer Church.
Barrow, Joseph A. '96 (NEW) [3] Newark, NJ Blessed Sacrament Church.
Barruetabena, Esteban (ARE) Lares, PR St. Joseph Church.
Barruetabena, Esteban *c.p.* '54 (SJN) [46] San Juan, PR Nuestra Senora de la Piedad Church.
Barruetabena, Felix *c.p.* (SJN) [9] Carolina, PR Santa Gema Galgani Church.
Barrus, Paul '78 (DAL) Plano, TX St. Elizabeth Ann Seton Church.
Barry, Bernard J. '39 (SPK) Retired.
Barry, David E. *s.j.* '78 (R) [1] Durham, NC Holy Cross Church; [E] Raleigh, NC Jesuit Community; [H] Durham, NC North Carolina Central University.
Barry, Msgr. Denis L. '35 (LIN) Retired; [E] Lincoln, NE Bonacum House.
Barry, Donald M. *s.j.* '66 (BGP) [D] Fairfield, CT Fairfield College Preparatory School; [O] Fairfield, CT The Fairfield Jesuit Community-Fairfield University.
Barry, Edward '73 (NY) Dover Plains, NY St. Charles Borromeo Church.
Barry, Francis '75 (SAV) Retired.
Barry, Garrett J. '66 (BO) [1] Quincy, MA St. Ann Church.
Barry, George F. *s.j.* '54 (BO) [W] Weston, MA Campion Health Center, Inc.
Barry, Gerard D. '50 (BO) [1] Newton, MA St. Bernard Church.
Barry, Gerard S. *s.j.* '63 (BAL) [M] Baltimore, MD Jesuit Fathers and Brothers Maryland Provincial Curia.
Barry, Gerard S. *s.j.* '63 (FgM) Provinces.
Barry, Henry F. '41 (BO) Rockland, MA Holy Family Church; Retired.
Barry, James '59 (NEW) [N] Cliffside Park, NJ St. Patrick's Missionary Society.
Barry, James *c.p.* '69 (CHI) [N] Chicago, IL Passionist Community-CTU.
Barry, James D. '61 (NU) Arlington, MN St. Mary Church; Henderson, MN St. Joseph Church; Jessenland, MN St. Thomas (Mission) Church.
Barry, James F. '67 (CAM) Clayton, NJ St. Catherine's Church.
Barry, James H. *s.j.* '40 (BO) [W] Weston, MA Campion Health Center, Inc.
Barry, James J. '69 (BO) [4] Chelsea, MA Our Lady of Grace Church.
Barry, John *c.ss.r.* '48 (ORL) New Smyrna Beach, FL Sacred Heart Church.
Barry, Msgr. John F. '61 (LA) Manhattan Beach, CA American Martyrs Church.
Barry, John M. '88 (WDC) Laurel, MD St. Nicholas Church.
Barry, Joseph A. '35 (STA) Retired.
Barry, Lawrence E. *s.j.* '58 (STL) [O] St. Louis, MO Fusz Pavilion.
Barry, Leo '51 (WOR) Retired.
Barry, Maurice J. '67 (HRT) Windsor, CT St. Gertrude's Church.
Barry, Msgr. Patrick J. '54 (NY) [5] Mt. Vernon, NY SS. Peter and Paul Church.
Barry, Paul '48 (WDC) Retired.
Barry, Peter J. *m.m.* '65 (FgM) Maryknoll Foreign Missions.
Barry, Raymond J. '65 (HRT) Branford, CT St. Therese Church.
Barry, Robert *o.p.* '73 (PEO) [2] Champaign, IL St. John's Catholic Chapel Church; [O] Champaign, IL St. John's Catholic Student Chapel and Newman Foundation, University of Illinois.
Barry, Robert L. *o.p.* '73 (CHI) [N] River Forest, IL St. Thomas Aquinas Priory.
Barry, Ronald '52 (RVC) Retired.
Barry, Thomas J. '67 (HRT) Newington, CT St. Mary Church.
Barry, Thomas M. '61 (WOR) [28] Worcester, MA St. Stephen's Church; [K] Worcester, MA Providence Extended Care Center.
Barry, Msgr. Thomas P. '39 (DEN) [1] Englewood, CO All Souls Church; Retired.
Barry, William J. '44 (LA) Retired.
Barsen, Msgr. Herman J. '40 (LAF) Retired.
Barszcz, Benedict *s.a.c.* (BRK) [43] Brooklyn, NY St. Frances de Chantal Church.
Barszcz, Benedict *s.a.c.* '90 (BUF) [O] North Tonawanda, NY Society of the Catholic Apostolate.
Barszczewski, Francis A. '68 (PH) Clifton Heights, PA Sacred Heart Church.
Barta, Ardel H. '63 (DUB) [3] Dubuque, IA St. Columbkille's Church; [5] Dubuque, IA St. Patrick's Church.
Barta, Msgr. James O. '55 (DUB) On Special or Other (Arch)Diocesan Assignment.
Barta, Wayne J. '60 (MIL) Ashford, WI St. Martin Church; St. Kilian, WI St. Kilian Church.
Bartak, James J. '89 (OM) Newcastle, NE St. Peter Church; Ponca, NE St. Joseph Church.
Bartchak, Mark L. '81 (E) [29] Erie, PA St. Stanislaus Church.
Bartczyszyn, Steve *c.r.* '86 (CHI) [D] Chicago, IL Weber High School.
Bartek, James F. '53 (OM) Retired.
Bartek, Valerian '82 (LIN) Grant, NE Mother of Sorrows Church.
Bartek, William C. '61 (OM) Retired.
Bartel, Franklin L. '70 (PHX) Litchfield Park, AZ St. Thomas Aquinas Church.
Bartel, Leo J. '58 (RCK) Morrison, IL St. Mary Church.
Bartel, Martin R. *o.s.b.* '85 (GBG) [B] Latrobe, PA St. Vincent College; [H] Latrobe, PA Saint Vincent Archabbey.
Bartell, Ernest J. *c.s.c.* '61 (FTW) [B] Notre Dame, IN University of Notre Dame Du Lac; [J] Notre Dame, IN Holy Cross Community, Corby Hall, University of Notre Dame.
Bartelme, James P. '82 (SUP) Gilman, WI SS. Peter and Paul Church; Lublin, WI St. Stanislaus Church.
Barter, Robert J. '61 (PRM) Detroit, MI St. Nicholas Church.
Barth, Msgr. Charles P. '56 (CAM) Merchantville, NJ St. Peter's Church.
Barth, J. Robert *s.j.* '61 (BO) [C] Chestnut Hill, MA Boston College; [W] Chestnut Hill, MA The Jesuit Community at Boston College.
Barth, John C. *m.m.* '91 (FgM) Maryknoll Foreign Missions.
Barth, Michael *s.t.* '79 (CLV) [P] Cleveland, OH Missionary Servants of the Most Holy Trinity.
Barth, Michael D. '94 (COV) Erlanger, KY St. Henry Church; [B] Erlanger, KY St. Henry District High School.
Barth, Michael K. *s.t.* '79 (CLV) [3] Cleveland, OH St. Agnes - Our Lady of Fatima Church.
Barth, Raymond J. '85 (KAL) Bridgman, MI Our Lady Queen of Peace Church.
Barthel, Charles '82 (STL) [63] St. Louis, MO St. Stephen, Protomartyr Church.
Barthelme, Frederick J. '34 (STP) Retired.
Bartko, Gerald *o.s.f.s.* '66 (BUF) [5] Lockport, NY St. Patrick Church.
Bartko, Gerald L. *o.s.f.s.* (BUF) [D] Niagara Falls, NY Niagara Catholic Junior-Senior School.
Bartko, Louis '90 (HT) [4] Houma, LA Our Lady of the Most Holy Rosary Church.
Bartkus, Msgr. Algimantas A. '65 (ALN) On Duty Outside the Diocese.
Bartlett, Albert P. *s.j.* '54 (NY) [145] Bronx, NY St. Helena Church; [DD] New York, NY Jesuit Community at Fordham University.
Bartlett, H. James *s.m.* '69 (CIN) [M] Dayton, OH Marianist Provincialate.
Bartlett, James *s.m.* '69 (CIN) [24] Dayton, OH Queen of Apostles Church.
Bartlett, Lee F. '72 (WOR) [16] Worcester, MA Sacred Heart Church.
Bartlett, Richard *c.m.f.* '50 (CHI) [N] Oak Park, IL Claretian Fathers Headquarters of U.S.A. Eastern Province.
Bartley, Denis *s.s.c.* '51 (LA) [R] Los Angeles, CA Columban Fathers, Procure House.
Bartley, Vincent '69 (NY) [223] Staten Island, NY St. Paul Church.
Bartman, Roch *o.f.m.conv.* '31 (MRY) [G] Arroyo Grande, CA St. Joseph's Cupertino Novitiate.
Bartnik, Harry S. '56 (TLS) Retired; [F] Tulsa, OK St. John Villas, Inc.
Bartnik, James T. '75 (BUF) [18] Buffalo, NY St. Casimir Church.
Bartnikowski, Raymond B. '63 (CLV) Maple Heights, OH St. Wenceslas Church.
Bartniski, William D. '67 (GAL) [5] Galveston, TX St. Peter the Apostle Church.
Bartok, Msgr. Charles '47 (ORL) Retired.
Bartollotta, Victor W., Jr. '90 (ROC) On Duty Outside the Diocese.
Bartolo, Salvador *o.carm.* '52 (FgM) Carmelite Foreign Missions.
Bartolo, Salvador *o.carm.* '52 (JOL) [J] Darien, IL Carmelite Provincial Office.
Bartolotta, Victor (DAL) [C] Dallas, TX Bishop Lynch High School.
Barton, Michael *m.c.c.j.* '75 (FgM) Comboni Foreign Missions.
Barton, Msgr. Raymond A. '66 (RIC) Charlottesville, VA Church of the Holy Comforter.
Bartone, Donald E. '48 (DET) Retired.
Bartos, Francis J. '54 (PH) Lansdale, PA St. Stanislaus Church.
Bartos, Msgr. John V. '52 (PH) Warminster, PA Nativity of Our Lord Church.
Bartos, Kris '85 (MIA) [13] Miami, FL Our Lady of Lourdes Church.
Bartosic, Mark '94 (CHI) [5] Chicago, IL St. Agnes of Bohemia Church.
Bartoszek, Justin *c.p.* '64 (FgM) Mission Procurators.
Bartoszek, Richard J. '89 (DET) Woodhaven, MI Our Lady of the Woods Church.
Bartoul, William '77 (SAM) On Duty Outside the Diocese.
Bartruff, Louis B. '45 (BRK) Retired; [U] Douglaston, NY Bishop Mugavero Residence.
Bartsch, Edward C. '49 (VIC) High Hill, TX Nativity of the Blessed Virgin Mary Church; Praha, TX St. Mary's Church.
Bartsch, Ken *o.f.m.conv.* (STP) [Q] Prior Lake, MN Franciscan Retreat House.
Bartz, Richard B. (CHI) [J] Chicago, IL Columbus Hospital.
Barusefski, Ronald '89 (PSC) Hazleton, PA St. Mary's Church.
Barwig, Regis N. '59 (GB) [I] Oshkosh, WI Community of Our Lady.
Barwin, John G. '80 (E) Mount Jewett, PA St. Joseph Church; Bradford, PA Federal Correction Institution.
Baryski, Wojciech *s.ch.* '65 (DET) Hamtramck, MI St. Florian Church.
Barzyk, Andrew A. '94 (CHI) Niles, IL St. John Brebeuf Church.
Barzyk, Msgr. Robert R. '58 (GAL) Retired.
Basa, Francis J. '71 (CLV) [4] Akron, OH Christ the King Church.
Basarab, John G. '79 (PSC) Annandale, VA Epiphany of Our Lord Church.
Bascio, Patrick *c.s.sp.* '55 (GAY) Whittemore, MI St. James Church.
Baseford, Paul '57 (SB) Retired.
Basetti-Sani, Giulio F. *o.f.m.* '35 (PAT) [M] Butler, NJ St. Anthony Friary.
Bash, Cletus '56 (OKL) Special Assignment; [E] Oklahoma City, OK Mercy Memorial Health Center.
Bashyam, Francis '86 (DUB) [10] Dubuque, IA Nativity Church.
Basil, John E. '62 (NEW) [22] Jersey City, NJ Our Lady of Victories Church.
Basile, Gioacchino '95 (NEW) West New York, NJ St. Joseph of the Palisades Church.
Basile, Nicholas F. '49 (NY) [174] Bronx, NY Our Lady of Mt. Carmel Church; Retired.
Basinow, Leonard '53 (SAM) West Palm Beach, FL Mary Mother of Light Maronite Mission Church.
Baskara Tulus Wardaya, Francis Xavier *s.j.* '92 (MIL) [P] Milwaukee, WI Jesuit Community at Marquette University.
Basler, Msgr. Howard B. '58 (BRK) [L] Brooklyn, NY Catholic Charities; [U] Brooklyn, NY St. Joseph's Priest Residence.
Basols, Jose Andres *sch.p.* '68 (SJN) [58] San Juan, PR Santisimo Salvador Church.
Bass, Francis E. '48 (DAV) Iowa City, IA Veteran's Administration Hospital; Retired; [J] Iowa City, IA Mercy Hospital.
Bass, Michael E. '87 (LR) Pocahontas, AR St. Paul the Apostle Church.
Bass, Msgr. Ricardo E. '74 (DET) [4] St. Clair Shores, MI St. Joan of Arc Church.
Bassano, Michael '75 (SY) On Duty Outside the Diocese.
Basso, Anthony *s.d.v.* (NEW) [25] Newark, NJ St. Michael's Church.
Basso, Richard '62 (SEA) [C] Bellevue, WA Eastside Catholic High School.
Basso, Settimo *c.s.* '41 (PRO) [4] Johnston, RI St. Rocco Church.
Bastia, Raymond B. '78 (PRO) [4] Providence, RI St. Ann Church.
Bastian, Robert J. '43 (CIN) Retired.
Bastianelli, Dan *s.s.j.* '64 (BEA) [3] Beaumont, TX Blessed Sacrament Church.
Bastides, Alexis '84 (NY) [18] New York, NY Blessed Sacrament Church.
Bastien, James R. '95 (BUF) Williamsville, NY St. Gregory the Great Church.
Bastos, Luiz '95 (ORL) Kissimmee, FL Holy Redeemer Church.
Basznianin, Richard '84 (TR) Brick Town, NJ St. Dominic Church.
Batch, Thomas A. '76 (SAC) Knights Landing, CA St. Paul Church.
Batcha, James '85 (PRM) Lorain, OH St. Michael Church; Lorain, OH St. Nicholas Church.
Batcheldor, C. Joseph '57 (L) Shelbyville, KY Annunciation of the Blessed Virgin Mary Church.
Batcho, Michael '73 (PHU) Absent on Leave.
Batcho, Robert J. '88 (STF) [2] Ansonia, CT SS. Peter and Paul Church.

Bateman, John '96 (HBG) [3] Harrisburg, PA St. Francis of Assisi Church.
Bates, Donald J. *o.s.a.* '60 (CHI) [N] Olympia Fields, IL Austin Friary.
Bates, James R. '63 (LFT) Noblesville, IN Our Lady of Grace Church.
Bates, Urban M. *o.p.* '53 (ANC) [1] Anchorage, AK Holy Family Cathedral.
Bath, Winston L. '72 (ALB) Hudson, NY Church of St. Mary.
Bathke, Joseph *c.pp.s.* '78 (KC) [3] St. Joseph, MO St. Francis Xavier Church.
Batista, George L. '83 (NEW) On Duty Outside the Archdiocese.
Batista, George L. '83 (PMB) Lake Worth, FL St. Luke Church.
Batkiewicz, Joseph '71 (CLV) Berea, OH St. Adalbert Church.
Batkiewicz, Joseph J. '35 (ALB) Retired.
Batson, Msgr. John R. '57 (MEM) Retired.
Batt, Dacian *o.f.m.* '58 (PEO) Metamora, IL St. Mary's Church; Washburn, IL St. Elizabeth Church.
Battafarano, Gregory *o.carm.* (GAL) [Q] Houston, TX Carmelite Priory.
Battafarano, Gregory *o.carm.* '67 (GAL) [58] Houston, TX Our Lady of Mt. Carmel Church.
Battaglia, Ignatius *c.s.* '59 (PRO) [16] Providence, RI Holy Ghost Church.
Batterberry, Michael J. '70 (SEA) [B] Seattle, WA John F. Kennedy Memorial High School.
Battiato, Patrick W. '76 (COS) Security, CO Holy Family Church.
Battiato, Ronald A. '61 (OM) Randolph, NE St. Frances de Chantal Church.
Battirossi, Bartholomew *m.c.c.j.* '42 (LA) [11] Los Angeles, CA Holy Cross Church.
Battista, Msgr. Leo '48 (WOR) Retired.
Battisti, Lewis A. '62 (CAM) Margate, NJ Blessed Sacrament Church.
Battle, Lawrence '49 (SB) Retired.
Battocletti, Richard '53 (STU) [7] Steubenville, OH St. Peter's Church; [9] Steubenville, OH St. Stanislaus Church.
Battolini, Ottaviano *o.f.m.* '43 (FgM) Franciscan Foreign Missions.
Batts, Peter M. *o.p.* '81 (WDC) [B] Washington, DC Dominican House of Studies.
Batule, Robert J. '85 (RVC) Mineola, NY Corpus Christi Church.
Batykefer, John J. '90 (PIT) Natrona Heights, PA Our Lady of the Most Blessed Sacrament Church.
Bau, Chau Xuan *c.ss.r.* '62 (LA) [R] Baldwin Park, CA Vietnamese Redemptorist Mission; [DD] Baldwin Park, CA The Redemptorist Vietnamese Mission Corporation.
Bau, Mark *c.m.c.* '77 (FWT) [15] Fort Worth, TX St. Rita Church.
Baudhuin, Robert F. *m.m.* '54 (FgM) Maryknoll Foreign Missions.
Baudone, Louis '59 (GR) Retired.
Bauer, Carl E. '63 (WH) Star City, WV St. Mary's Church.
Bauer, Charles A. '78 (MEM) Humboldt, TN Sacred Heart Church; Milan, TN St. Matthew Mission Church.
Bauer, Daniel *s.v.d.* '74 (FgM) Society of the Divine Word Foreign Missions.
Bauer, Donald J. '48 (SY) [3] Utica, NY Our Lady of Lourdes Church; Retired.
Bauer, Elmer, III *c.m.* '93 (FgM) Vincentian Foreign Missions.
Bauer, Erwin J. '75 (DET) Harsens Island, MI St. Mark Church; Retired.
Bauer, Francis '41 (EVN) Retired.
Bauer, Msgr. Henry '48 (KC) Retired.
Bauer, Jacob F. '48 (GI) Retired.
Bauer, John '73 (PIT) [6] Ambridge, PA Good Samaritan Church.
Bauer, John F. '65 (E) Sheffield, PA St. Anthony Church; Warren, PA Warren State Hospital.
Bauer, John M. '79 (STP) Deephaven, MN St. Therese Church.
Bauer, Joseph O. '53 (SAG) Retired.
Bauer, Karl A. '67 (NY) [142] Bronx, NY St. Frances of Rome Church.
Bauer, Lawrence T. *c.s.c.* '35 (FTW) [J] South Bend, IN Congregation of Holy Cross Indiana Province Provincial House.
Bauer, Msgr. Leonard A. '37 (BEL) [E] Belleville, IL Meredith Memorial Home; [J] Belleville, IL Serra Club of St. Clair County.
Bauer, Mark F. '86 (GR) Coopersville, MI St. Michael's Church; [K] Coopersville, MI Grand Valley State University Catholic Campus Ministry.
Bauer, Paul '91 (SD) [3] Chula Vista, CA St. Pius X Church.
Bauer, Ralph '47 (LR) Retired.
Bauer, Richard W. *m.m.* '85 (FgM) Maryknoll Foreign Missions.
Bauer, Robert *s.d.b.* '71 (COL) [H] Columbus, OH Salesian Center.
Bauer, Robert A. '87 (DET) Carleton, MI St. Patrick Church.
Bauer, Robert J. *s.d.b.* '71 (COL) [A] Columbus, OH Pontifical College Josephinum.
Bauer, Roy R. '59 (SFD) [8] Quincy, IL St. Peter Church.
Bauer, Stephan *o.s.c.* '92 (CHI) [N] Chicago, IL Crosier Community of Chicago.
Bauer, Stephen F. '77 (STL) Dutzow, MO St. Vincent de Paul Church.
Bauer, Steven *o.s.c.* '88 (CHI) [170] Chicago, IL SS. Peter and Paul Church.
Bauer, Sylvester (JC) Jefferson City, MO Missouri Intermediate Reformatory.
Bauer, Sylvester W. '42 (SPC) Retired.
Bauer, William M. '73 (ALB) Greenville, NY St. John the Baptist Church.
Bauerle, Bernhard *o.carm.* '64 (JOL) [C] Joliet, IL Joliet Catholic Academy; [J] Joliet, IL St. Elias Carmelites.
Bauernfeind, Thomas '63 (BAL) [5] Baltimore, MD St. Alphonsus Church.
Baugh, David G. '57 (CLV) [6] Euclid, OH St. William Church.
Bauhoff, Msgr. Richard C. '73 (RVC) Roslyn, NY St. Mary's Church.
Bauhs, Eugene J. '48 (MAD) Retired.
Bauler, Msgr. Gary P. '67 (LA) Pasadena, CA St. Philip the Apostle Church; Simi Valley, CA St. Peter Claver Church.
Baum, Boniface '46 (CHI) [N] Chicago, IL St. Peter's Friary.
Baum, Msgr. Charles J. '34 (CHR) Greenville, SC St. Mary's Church; Retired.
Baum, Dennis *o.f.m.* (NY) [13] New York, NY St. Anthony of Padua Church.
Baum, Jerome '47 (CHI) [N] Chicago, IL St. Peter's Friary.
Baum, Terrence A. *s.j.* (CHI) [D] Wilmette, IL Loyola Academy.
Bauman, Dale '82 (FTW) Albion, IN Blessed Sacrament Church; Ligonier, IN St. Patrick Church.
Bauman, John F. '69 (NEW) [26] Jersey City, NJ St. Paul's Church.
Bauman, Richard J. *s.j.* '75 (CHI) [N] Chicago, IL Chicago Province of the Society of Jesus-Provincial Office.
Bauman, Rodger R. '82 (STP) Richfield, MN St. Peter Church.
Bauman, William A. '60 (KC) [40] Kansas City, MO St. Thomas More Church.
Baumann, Anthony *o.f.m.* '44 (SFR) [5] San Francisco, CA St. Anthony Church; [J] San Francisco, CA St. Mary's Medical Center.
Baumann, Charles R. *s.j.* '80 (MIL) [P] Milwaukee, WI Jesuit Community at Marquette University.
Baumann, Gregory R. *s.j.* '93 (LA) [10] Los Angeles, CA Dolores Mission Church.
Baumann, Hugh *o.s.b.* '41 (NO) [P] St. Benedict, LA St. Joseph Abbey.
Baumann, John A. *s.j.* '69 (OAK) [N] Oakland, CA Murray Residence Community; [S] Oakland, CA Pacific Institute for Community Organization.
Baumann, Lawrence '64 (PHX) [4] Phoenix, AZ Immaculate Heart of Mary Church.
Baumann, Silas '51 (GB) [I] Appleton, WI St. Fidelis Friary.
Baumann, Steve '92 (ORL) Ormond Beach, FL St. Brendan Church.
Baumann, Theodore J. '67 (BEL) Bartelso, IL St. Cecilia Church.
Baumberger, Richard '89 (SFS) Kranzburg, SD Holy Rosary Church.
Baumberger, Rudolph *o.s.b.* '43 (SCL) [I] Collegeville, MN St. John's Abbey, of the Order of St. Benedict.
Baumbusch, Steven *p.i.m.e.* '83 (DET) [K] Detroit, MI P.I.M.E. Missionaries of SS. Peter and Paul.
Baumert, Frank J. '78 (OM) Neligh, NE St. Francis Church.
Baumgaertner, Msgr. William L. '46 (STP) Retired.
Baumgardner, Michael L. '95 (SD) Santee, CA Guardian Angels Church.
Baumgartel, David A. '73 (WIL) Newark, DE St. John the Baptist-Holy Angels Church; Wilmington, DE A.I. du Pont Institute.
Baumgartner, Msgr. A. Thomas '58 (BAL) [93] Baltimore, MD St. Ursula Church.
Baumgartner, Andrew *o.s.b.* '60 (B) [C] Jerome, ID Ascension Priory.
Baumgartner, Bernard *c.ss.r.* '44 (BAL) Annapolis, MD St. Mary Church; [M] Annapolis, MD Saint Mary Rectory.
Baumgartner, David '90 (CR) [1] Crookston, MN Cathedral of the Immaculate Conception.
Baumgartner, John N. '63 (MIL) [1] West Allis, WI St. Aloysius Church.
Baumhart, Raymond C. *s.j.* '57 (CHI) [C] Chicago, IL Jesuit Community at Loyola University of Chicago.
Baumiller, Robert C. *s.j.* '65 (CIN) [M] Cincinnati, OH Jesuit Community at Xavier Unversity.
Baumstein, Paschal M. *o.s.b.* '79 (CHL) [J] Belmont, NC Belmont Abbey.
Baur, Edward *s.v.d.* '55 (GAL) [1] Galveston, TX St. Mary's Cathedral Basilica Church; [K] Houston, TX The Catholic Chaplain Corps.
Baur, Joseph *o.f.m.* (OAK) [S] Berkeley, CA Multicultural Institute.
Baur, Joseph A. *o.f.m.* '52 (PHX) Guadalupe, AZ Our Lady of Guadalupe Church.
Baures, Steven H. '83 (LC) New Lisbon, WI St. Paul Church.
Baures, Steven M. '83 (LC) Germantown, WI Our Lady of the Lake Church.
Bausch, Michael J. '79 (ROC) Henrietta, NY Church of the Good Shepherd.
Bausch, William (TR) Retired.
Bauschka, Joseph C. '55 (GB) Elcho, WI Holy Family Church.
Bauta, Krzysztof T. '86 (CC) On Duty Outside the Diocese.
Bautch, Richard J. *s.j.* '94 (CHI) [N] Chicago, IL Chicago Province of the Society of Jesus-Provincial Office.
Bautista, Gaspar '75 (LA) San Gabriel, CA St. Anthony Church.
Bautista, Javier *m.s.c.* '95 (RCK) [H] Aurora, IL Missionaries of the Sacred Heart Community.
Bautista, Jose '91 (ORL) Melbourne, FL Our Lady of Lourdes Church.
Bauwens, Joseph P. *o.c.s.o.* '56 (DUB) [K] Peosta, IA New Melleray Abbey, Order of Cistercians of the Strict Observance.
Bauwens, Thomas E. '87 (OM) Walthill, NE St. Joseph Church; Winnebago, NE St. Augustine's Church; [O] Winnebago, NE St. Augustine's Indian Mission.
Bava, David '73 (WDC) [18] Washington, DC Holy Redeemer Church.
Bavaro, John D. *o.f.m.* '63 (BO) [P] Andover, MA Franciscan Center; [W] Andover, MA St. Francis Friary; [Y] Andover, MA Franciscan Center - Retreat House.
Baver, John J. '91 (PIT) [4] New Castle, PA St. Vitus Church.
Baver, Msgr. William F. '81 (ALN) [10] Allentown, PA St. Stephen of Hungary Church.
Bavero, Benvenute *o.f.m.* '44 (LA) [R] Santa Barbara, CA Franciscan Friary, Order of Friars Minor (Old Mission).
Bavinger, R. Bruce '78 (WDC) [2] Washington, DC St. Aloysius Church.
Bawiec, Edward J. '54 (PEO) Retired.
Bawyn, Anthony '82 (SEA) Special Assignment.
Baxa, Henry R. '90 (SAL) Beloit, KS St. John the Baptist Church.
Baxer, Joseph J. *m.s.* '71 (HRT) [3] Hartford, CT Immaculate Conception Church; [7] Hartford, CT St. Anne Church; [M] Hartford, CT Missionaries of LaSalette Provincial Secretary.
Baxter, Gregory P. '88 (OM) On Duty Outside the Archdiocese.
Baxter, Michael *c.s.c.* '85 (FTW) [B] Notre Dame, IN University of Notre Dame Du Lac.
Baxter, Michael J. *c.s.c.* (FTW) [J] Notre Dame, IN Holy Cross Community, Corby Hall, University of Notre Dame.
Baxter, Stephen R. '81 (WCH) Fredonia, KS Sacred Heart Church; Neodesha, KS St. Ignatius Church.
Baxter, Thomas A. *o.s.b.* '79 (CHI) [N] Chicago, IL Monastery of the Holy Cross.
Baxter, Thomas F. '76 (MAD) Lancaster, WI St. Clement Church.
Bay, Joseph N. '94 (COL) Graduate Studies.
Bayard, Nicholas R. '46 (CHR) Greer, SC Blessed Trinity Church.
Baybay, Felicito S. '74 (ORL) St. Cloud, FL St. Thomas Aquinas Church.
Bayer, Edward J. '56 (BAL) Randallstown, MD Holy Family Church; [Q] Baltimore, MD Cursillo Movement.
Bayer, Lawrence J. '58 (CLV) [2] Parma, OH St. Bridget Church.
Bayer, Leonard '51 (SFE) Retired.
Bayer, Peter T. '71 (ROC) [43] Rochester, NY St. Margaret Mary Church.
Bayer, Robert *o.f.m.conv.* '37 (IND) [I] Mount Saint Francis, IN Mount Saint Francis Friary and Retreat Center.
Bayer, Walter C. '42 (STA) Korona, FL St. Mary's Church.
Bayhi, M. Jeffrey '79 (BR) [2] Baton Rouge, LA St. Agnes Church.
Bayhi, W. Peter *s.j.* (DAL) [26] Dallas, TX St. Rita Church.
Baylis, Thomas J. '59 (HRT) [2] Milford, CT St. Ann's Church.
Bayne, David C. *s.j.* '52 (DET) [K] Detroit, MI Jesuit Provincial Office-Detroit Province of the Society of Jesus.
Bayne, Joseph *o.f.m.conv.* '85 (BUF) [J] Buffalo, NY The Franciscan Center, Inc.
Bayne, Robert C. *m.m.* '63 (FgM) Maryknoll Foreign Missions.

Baysinger, Leo A. *s.d.b.* '67 (AUS) [B] Waco, TX Reicher Catholic High School; [H] Waco, TX Salesians of Don Bosco.
Baz, Louis '81 (OLL) Detroit, MI St. Maron/St. Sharbel Church.
Bazan, Arnaldo '58 (MIA) Coral Gables, FL Little Flower Church.
Bazan, Msgr. Joaquin '62 (SFE) [21] Albuquerque, NM St. Anne Church.
Bazan, Msgr. Joaquin '62 (WDC) On Duty Outside the Archdiocese.
Bazan, Michael J. '84 (ARL) Warrenton, VA St. John the Evangelist Church.
Bazina, Basile (BO) Burlington, MA St. Margaret Church.
Bazton, Jose M. Garcia *m.ss.cc.* '62 (SJN) [10] Bayamon, PR San Juan Bautista de la Salle Church.
Bazzi, Michael J. '64 (EST) El Cajon, CA St. Peter Chaldean Parish.
Bazzi, Michael J. '64 (SD) El Cajon, CA St. Peter Church.
Bazzoli, Robert *o.s.f.s.* '89 (PH) [75] Philadelphia, PA St. Joachim Church.
Beach, Francis W. '76 (PH) [70] Philadelphia, PA Immaculate Heart of Mary Church; [D] Philadelphia, PA Roman Catholic High School for Boys.
Beach, Raymond *o.f.m.* '48 (PAT) [K] Totowa, NJ St. Joseph's Home for the Elderly.
Beach, Robert '50 (SFE) Retired.
Beachum, Edwin P. '84 (MOB) [2] Mobile, AL St. Catherine of Siena Church.
Beacom, John F. '37 (OM) Retired.
Beacom, Vincent L. '44 (SC) Retired.
Beain, Victorio *o.f.m.* '42 (SJN) [52] San Juan, PR Resurreccion del Senor Church.
Beal, John P. '74 (E) On Duty Outside Diocese.
Beal, John P. '74 (WDC) [C] Washington, DC Catholic University of America, The.
Beale, Kenneth R. '92 (NEW) Military Chaplains.
Beale, Robert P. (BO) Dedham, MA Norfolk County House of Correction.
Beall, John *o.praem.* '97 (SFE) [11] Albuquerque, NM Our Lady of Most Holy Rosary Church; [J] Albuquerque, NM Santa Maria de la Vid Priory.
Bean, Charles S. '62 (CAM) On Sick Leave; [M] Cherry Hill, NJ Vianney Villa.
Bean, Mark Doan Quang *c.m.c.* (BO) [62] Boston, MA St. Peter Church.
Beane, Raymond A. *o.f.m.* '38 (NY) [DD] New York, NY Franciscan Friars, Order of Friars Minor, Holy Name Province.
Beans, Elmer (FBK) Mountain Village, AK St. Lawrence Church.
Beard, Msgr. Raymond '41 (BAK) Retired.
Bearden, Clark '89 (BLX) Lumberton, MS Our Lady of Perpetual Help Church.
Beardsley, Frederick '60 (RIC) Retired.
Bearss, James M. '97 (GAY) Manistee, MI St. Joseph Church.
Beary, Thomas J. '62 (BUR) Retired; [D] Burlington, VT St. Joseph's Home for Aged.
Beasley, Msgr. Thomas J. '53 (BUF) [1] Orchard Park, NY Nativity Church.
Beat, Jerome A. '63 (WCH) [17] Wichita, KS St. Patrick Church.
Beath, James D. '79 (CHI) Skokie, IL St. Peter Church.
Beaton, Angus *c.j.m.* '56 (SD) [M] San Diego, CA San Diego State University Newman Center.
Beaton, Kevin J. '87 (SAM) Scranton, PA St. Ann Church.
Beattie, Msgr. James T. '61 (WDC) [1] Bethesda, MD St. Bartholomew Church.
Beattie, John A. *o.s.f.s.* '65 (VEN) [A] Fort Myers, FL Bishop Verot High School.
Beattie, Joseph A. *o.s.f.s.* '65 (VEN) [A] Fort Myers, FL Bishop Verot High School.
Beattie, Thomas '93 (SEA) Sequim, WA St. Joseph Church.
Beatty, James H. '74 (CLV) Avon Lake, OH Holy Spirit Church.
Beatty, Michael D. '64 (CIN) [82] Cincinnati, OH St. Simon the Apostle Church.
Beaubien, David W. '93 (WDC) [3] Washington, DC St. Ann Church.
Beauchamp, E. William *c.s.c.* '60 (FTW) [J] Notre Dame, IN Holy Cross Community, Corby Hall, University of Notre Dame.
Beauchamp, E. William *c.s.c.* '82 (FTW) [B] Notre Dame, IN University of Notre Dame Du Lac.
Beauchemin, Ronald A. *m.s.* '68 (TYL) Lufkin, TX St. Patrick Church.
Beauclair, Stephen G. *o.s.b.* '67 (STP) Hastings, MN St. Elizabeth Ann Seton Church.
Beaudet, Eugene J. '53 (OG) Star Lake, NY St. Hubert Church.
Beaudet, George W. '75 (PRT) East Millinocket, ME St. Peter's Church.
Beaudin, William *o.f.m.* (PRO) [P] Providence, RI St. Francis Friary.
Beaudin, William R. '82 (BUR) Montpelier, VT St. Augustine Church.
Beaudoin, Andrew *s.s.s.* '54 (CLV) [P] Cleveland, OH Congregation of the Blessed Sacrament Provincial House.
Beaudoin, Andrew *s.s.s.* '54 (SP) Spring Hill, FL St. Frances Xavier Cabrini Church.
Beaudoin, Hubert N. *o.praem.* '56 (PH) [D] Philadelphia, PA St. John Neumann High School; [AA] Philadelphia, PA St. Norbert Priory.
Beaudry, David '82 (GB) Alverno, WI St. Joseph Church; Northeim, WI St. Casimir Church.
Beaulieu, Earl '60 (SHP) Retired.
Beaulieu, Kerry '74 (ORG) [1] Huntington Beach, CA St. Bonaventure Church.
Beaulieu, Peter R. (WOR) [J] Worcester, MA Saint Vincent Hospital, Inc.
Beaulieu, Peter R. '83 (WOR) On Special or Other (Arch)Diocesan Assignment.
Beaulieu, Raymond '42 (PRO) Retired.
Beaulieu, Richard W. '71 (FR) [6] Fall River, MA Notre Dame de Lourdes Church.
Beaulieu, Robert J. '57 (HEL) Bozeman, MT Holy Rosary Church.
Beaumont, Gregory '96 (FRS) Visalia, CA St. Mary Church.
Beaumont, Msgr. Joachim B. '59 (NY) [31] New York, NY St. Elizabeth Church.
Beaumont, Richard '58 (FWT) [9] Fort Worth, TX St. Bartholomew Church.
Beaupre, R. Bradley *c.s.c.* '68 (FR) [A] North Easton, MA Holy Cross Fathers Religious.
Beauregard, David M. *o.m.v.* '80 (BO) [B] Boston, MA Our Lady of Grace Seminary.
Beauregard, James E. '70 (BUR) Readsboro, VT St. Joachim Church.
Beauregard, Paul *o.m.i.* (BO) [4] Lowell, MA Saint Jeanne d'Arc Church.
Beauregard, Thomas '51 (TOL) [24] Toledo, OH St. Hyacinth Church; Retired.
Beausang, Msgr. Charles C. '46 (CAM) Retired.
Beausoleil, Charles *o.m.i.* '56 (NY) [FF] Newburgh, NY Our Lady of Hope Center.
Beausoleil, Gerald L. *m.m.* '52 (FgM) Maryknoll Foreign Missions.
Beauvais, David E. '62 (RCK) [6] Rockford, IL St. James Church.
Beaven, Robert W. '68 (CHI) Grayslake, IL St. Gilbert Church.
Beaver, Nelson '76 (TOL) Norwalk, OH St. Mary, Mother of the Redeemer Church; Peru, OH St. Alphonsus Liguori Church.
Beaver, Reinard W. '56 (SPK) Retired.
Beaver, William A. *o.s.b.* '85 (GBG) Jeannette, PA Sacred Heart Church.
Beavers, Carl A. '68 (CHY) [1] Cheyenne, WY St. Mary's Cathedral; Cheyenne, WY U.S. Veterans Administration Hospital 1.
Bebak, Brian '86 (WCH) Fort Scott, KS Mary Queen of Angels Church.
Bebedik, Hilarion *o.s.b.m.* '48 (RVC) [N] Glen Cove, NY St. Josaphatis Monastery, Novitiate and Retreat House.
Bebek, Dominic L. '53 (LA) Sick Leave.
Bebel, Alfred J. '58 (SY) [8] Syracuse, NY Our Lady of Solace Church; Syracuse, NY University Hospital; Special Assignment.
Becera, Rafael *c.s.* '95 (GAL) [44] Houston, TX St. Leo the Great Church.
Becerra, Robert '89 (NEW) [1] Elizabeth, NJ St. Mary of the Assumption Church; Elizabeth, NJ Elizabeth General Medical Center.
Bechamps, Vincent *o.ss.t.* '66 (NO) [16] New Orleans, LA Our Lady Of Good Counsel Church; New Orleans, LA University Hospital.
Bechard, Bernard J. *s.s.e.* '49 (BUR) Sheldon Springs, VT St. Anthony Church.
Bechard, Dean P. *s.j.* '91 (NY) [DD] New York, NY Jesuit Community at Fordham University.
Bechard, Gerard V. '80 (DET) [5] Westland, MI SS. Simon and Jude Church.
Becherer, David '48 (MOB) On Duty Outside the Archdiocese.
Becherer, James R. '54 (CLV) Retired.
Becht, James '53 (RC) [D] Rapid City, SD Priest Retirement and Aid Association.
Becht, James D. '53 (RC) Bonesteel, SD Immaculate Conception Church; Fairfax, SD St. Anthony's Church.
Bechtel, James C. '71 (ALN) Gordon, PA Our Lady of Good Counsel Church.
Bechtold, Paul I. *c.p.* '41 (CHI) [N] Chicago, IL Immaculate Conception Monastery.
Beck, Aelred J. *o.s.b.* '48 (GBG) Youngstown, PA Sacred Heart Church; [H] Latrobe, PA Saint Vincent Archabbey.
Beck, Msgr. Albert J. '49 (GAL) [33] Houston, TX Holy Cross Chapel Church; On Special Assignment.
Beck, Charles L. '45 (MAD) Retired.
Beck, David J. '67 (TOL) Bluffton, OH St. Mary Church; [3] Lima, OH St. John the Evangelist Church.
Beck, Edward *c.p.* '85 (NY) [HH] New York, NY Passionist Residence.
Beck, Erwin G. *s.j.* '60 (NEW) [C] Jersey City, NJ St. Peter's Preparatory School.
Beck, Msgr. George A. '41 (GAL) [33] Houston, TX Holy Cross Chapel Church; Retired.
Beck, Henry *o.f.m.* '80 (CIN) [M] Cincinnati, OH St. Francis Seraph Friary.
Beck, Joseph '84 (PIT) Allegheny County, PA Greater Pittsburgh Rehab Hospital; Allegheny County, PA Independent Court of Monroeville; Allegheny County, PA Manorcare Health Services.
Beck, Joseph C. '84 (PIT) [5] Pittsburgh, PA St. Bede Church; Allegheny County, PA Forbes Nursing Center; Allegheny County, PA Kane Regional Center - Glen Hazel; Allegheny County, PA Woodhaven Convalescent Center.
Beck, Lawrence J. '88 (LA) Montebello, CA Our Lady of the Miraculous Medal Church.
Beck, Leo J. '37 (PIT) Retired; [O] Pittsburgh, PA St. John Vianney Manor.
Beck, Richard *o.m.i.* '67 (SAT) Eagle Pass, TX Our Lady of Refuge Church.
Beck, Richard P. '55 (MIL) Retired.
Beck, Richard W. '74 (SCR) Pleasant Mount, PA St. James Church.
Beck, Robert '66 (DUB) [L] Dubuque, IA Visitation Convent.
Beck, Robert P. '76 (BEA) Military Chaplains.
Beck, Robert R. '66 (DUB) [C] Dubuque, IA Loras College.
Becka, Robert *s.j.* '60 (FgM) Provinces.
Becker, Anthony J. '47 (RCK) Retired.
Becker, Arthur J. '73 (ALB) [1] Cohoes, NY St. Agnes-St. Patrick Church; [4] Cohoes, NY St. Marie Church.
Becker, Bruno *o.s.b.* '51 (P) [L] St. Benedict, OR Mt. Angel Abbey.
Becker, Charles J. *s.s.* '53 (CAM) [6] Camden, NJ St. Joseph's Church; Retired.
Becker, Charles P. '86 (CHI) Other Assignments.
Becker, Daniel '96 (WOR) [1] Worcester, MA St. Paul's Cathedral.
Becker, David R. '66 (ALT) Shade Gap, PA St. Mary's Church; Huntingdon, PA State Correctional Institution.
Becker, Dennis E. '62 (NU) Hutchinson, MN Church of St. Anastasia.
Becker, Donald W. '67 (BUF) [3] Batavia, NY St. Mary Church.
Becker, Franklyn W. '64 (MIL) On Leave.
Becker, Frederick J. '59 (NY) [159] Bronx, NY St. Lucy Church; Bronx, NY Our Lady of Mercy Medical Center; [W] New York, NY Our Lady of Mercy Medical Center.
Becker, George A. '53 (LC) Elmwood, WI Sacred Heart Church; Spring Valley, WI Sacred Heart of Jesus Church.
Becker, John (GB) [2] Oshkosh, WI St. Mary Church.
Becker, John J. '72 (GB) [1] Oshkosh, WI St. Peter Church.
Becker, John R. *s.j.* '56 (PHX) [B] Phoenix, AZ Brophy College Preparatory.
Becker, Joseph M. '39 (DET) [P] Clarkston, MI Colombiere Center.
Becker, Joseph P. *o.s.f.s.* '69 (ALN) Allentown, PA Lehigh Valley Hospital at Cedar Crest; [K] Center Valley, PA Oblates of St. Francis de Sales.
Becker, Luke *o.s.b.* '34 (KC) [J] Conception, MO Conception Abbey.
Becker, Michael '75 (ALT) Loretto, PA Basilica of St. Michael the Archangel Church.
Becker, Nicholas J. '38 (SC) Retired.
Becker, Paul D. '73 (BIS) Foxholm, ND St. Mary Church; [D] Minot, ND St. Joseph's Hospital dba UniMed Medical Center.
Becker, Richard F. '72 (PBL) [12] Pueblo, CO St. Joseph Church; Vineland, CO St. Therese Church.
Becker, Robert '79 (AUS) [9] Austin, TX Sacred Heart Church.
Becker, Robert T. '64 (SFD) [5] Springfield, IL St. Agnes Church.
Becker, Ronald '72 (TR) [13] Trenton, NJ St. Francis of Assisium Church.
Becker, Russell *o.f.m.* '72 (NY) [DD] New York, NY Franciscan Friars, Order of Friars Minor, Holy Name Province.
Becker, Thomas G. '80 (SCL) Glenwood, MN Sacred Heart Church.
Becker, Valentine A. *s.m.* '42 (WDC) [M] Washington, DC Marist Provincial House.
Becker, Vincent J. '62 (BUF) [46] Buffalo, NY St. Martin Church.
Becker, William M. '88 (WIN) [A] Winona, MN Immaculate Heart of Mary Seminary.
Beckers, Msgr. Henry F. '47 (ALX) Retired.
Beckfelt, John W. '74 (LC) Big River, WI Nativity of the Blessed Virgin Mary Church.
Beckley, Clarence *s.s.c.* '66 (FgM) St. Columban's Foreign Mission.
Beckley, John *s.m.* (SP) [K] Tampa, FL St. Joseph's Hospital, Inc.
Beckman, David M. '90 (DUB) Mason City, IA Holy

Family Church.
Beckman, David M. '92 (DUB) [G] Mason City, IA Newman Catholic.
Beckman, Msgr. Donald (RVC) Woodbury, NY Holy Name of Jesus Church.
Beckman, Gary L. '95 (DAV) Bettendorf, IA Our Lady of Lourdes Church.
Beckman, John J. *s.j.* '54 (CIN) [F] Cincinnati, OH St. Xavier High School.
Beckman, John J. *s.j.* '65 (CIN) [M] Cincinnati, OH Faber Jesuit Community.
Beckman, Joseph '54 (CIN) [B] Cincinnati, OH Mt. St. Mary's Seminary of the West.
Beckman, Joseph F. '54 (CIN) Retired.
Beckman, Mark '90 (NSH) Springfield, TN Our Lady of Lourdes Church.
Beckman, Martin A. '58 (STP) South St. Paul, MN St. John Vianney Church.
Beckman, Richard J. '56 (OKL) Newkirk, OK St. Francis of Assisi Church.
Beckman, Robert E. *s.j.* '56 (CHI) [N] Chicago, IL Chicago Province of the Society of Jesus-Provincial Office.
Beckman, Robert E. *s.j.* '56 (FgM) Provinces.
Beckmann, Msgr. Donald M. *d.min.* '70 (RVC) Davis Park, NY Most Precious Blood Church.
Becnel, Msgr. Terry B. '64 (NO) Buras, LA Our Lady of Good Harbor Church.
Becquet, Paul *c.pp.s.* '56 (SAL) Washington, KS St. Augustine's Church.
Bedard, Andre L. '57 (MAN) Bennington, NH St. Patrick Church.
Bedard, J. Raymond '53 (WOR) Retired.
Bedard, Paul *s.d.b.* (BO) [Y] Ipswich, MA Sacred Heart Retreat Center.
Bedard, Roland *m.s.* '46 (TUC) Tucson, AZ U.S. Veterans Hospital.
Bedenikovic, Stephen *o.f.m.* '85 (MIL) [72] Milwaukee, WI Sacred Heart Church.
Bedessem, Henry W. '59 (GB) Retired.
Bedillion, James R. '75 (PIT) [P] Bellevue, PA Mount Assisi Convent.
Bednar, Dwayne '91 (CLV) [3] Parma, OH St. Charles Borromeo Church.
Bednar, Dwayne A. '91 (CLV) [3] Parma, OH St. Charles Borromeo Church.
Bednar, Francis M. '74 (CLV) [69] Cleveland, OH Sacred Heart of Jesus Church.
Bednar, Gerald J. '83 (CLV) [A] Wickliffe, OH St. Mary Seminary and Graduate School of Theology.
Bednar, Martin *o.f.m.* '64 (SP) [O] Belleair Bluffs, FL St. James Friary.
Bednar, Thomas V. *c.s.c.* '85 (FgM) Holy Cross Foreign Missions.
Bednar, Thomas V. *c.s.c.* '85 (FTW) [J] South Bend, IN Congregation of Holy Cross Indiana Province Provincial House.
Bednarik, John *o.f.m.cap.* '68 (FgM) Capuchin Foreign Missions.
Bednarik, John *o.f.m.cap.* '68 (SJN) [C] Rio Piedras, PR Fraternidad Santa Maria de Los Angeles; [H] Rio Piedras, PR The Viceprovince of Saint John the Baptist, Puerto Rico, of the Order Friars Minor Capuchins.
Bednark, Walter '47 (SCL) Lake Henry, MN St. Margaret's Church; Retired.
Bednarski, Mitchell J. '44 (LAN) Retired.
Bednartz, Msgr. August C. '52 (BRK) Retired; [Y] Farmingdale, NY St. Charles.
Bednarz, Jan '72 (SLC) Vernal, UT St. James the Greater Church.
Bednarz, Matt A. '42 (CHI) [78] Chicago, IL St. Hilary Church; [201] Chicago, IL St. Thecla Church; Retired.
Bedoya, Carlos '90 (ORL) [9] Orlando, FL St. John Vianney Church.
Bedoya, Guillermo L. Corrales '89 (PRO) [6] Providence, RI Assumption of the Blessed Virgin Mary Church.
Bedoya, Hugo *c.m.* '56 (BRK) [243] Queens, NY St. Teresa Church.
Beebe, Msgr. Charles J. '70 (PEO) [9] Peoria, IL St. Jude's Church.
Beebe, David E. '61 (CAM) [O] Blackwood, NJ St. Pius X Spiritual Life Center.
Beechem, Joseph '40 (IND) Retired.
Beeching, Roy T. '74 (GRY) [6] Hammond, IN St. Joseph Church.
Beeda, Msgr. Francis J. '61 (SCR) [6] Hazleton, PA St. Joseph's Church.
Beeman, James W. '53 (HBG) Retired.
Beemster, John *s.v.d.* '40 (MIL) [P] East Troy, WI Divine Word Seminary.
Beemsterboer, Francis *s.v.d.* '51 (FgM) Society of the Divine Word Foreign Missions.
Beerntsen, Harold A. '61 (GB) Lena, WI Holy Cross Church.
Beers, J. Michael '79 (BAL) [A] Emmitsburg, MD Mount St. Mary's Seminary.
Beers, John Michael *s.s.l.* '79 (ALN) On Duty Outside the Diocese.
Beers, William (MAD) [G] Baraboo, WI St. Clare Hospital and Health Services.
Beeson, Msgr. Lawrence A. (DM) Atlantic, IA SS. Peter and Paul Church.
Beever, Carlton '74 (IND) [32] Indianapolis, IN St. Philip Neri Church.
Beez, John E. *s.j.* '61 (COL) [25] Columbus, OH Community of Holy Rosary and St. John Church.
Beezer, Arnold R. *s.j.* '64 (FgM) Provinces.
Beezer, Arnold R. *s.j.* '64 (P) [L] Portland, OR Colombiere Community.
Befort, Daryl '95 (WCH) [13] Wichita, KS St. Francis of Assisi Church.
Befort, Earl *o.f.m.cap.* (SAL) Hays, KS St. Joseph's Church; [D] Hays, KS St. Joseph's Friary.
Begay, Joseph N. *s.s.j.* '59 (WDC) [27] Washington, DC St. Luke Church.
Begg, Christopher T. '77 (WDC) [24] Washington, DC St. Joseph on Capitol Hill Church; Special Ministries; [C] Washington, DC Catholic University of America, The.
Beggane, Thomas P. '78 (LSC) [1] Las Cruces, NM Cathedral of Immaculate Heart of Mary.
Beggans, Msgr. Joseph A. '43 (NEW) [12] Jersey City, NJ St. John the Baptist Church; Retired.
Beggiani, Seely '61 (SAM) [A] Washington, DC Our Lady of Lebanon Maronite Seminary.
Beggiani, Seely '61 (WDC) [C] Washington, DC Catholic University of America, The.
Beggin, Thomas M. '79 (GF) Retired.
Begin, Daniel L. '75 (CLV) [16] Cleveland, OH St. Cecilia Church; [23] Cleveland, OH Epiphany Church.
Begin, Msgr. Raymond F. '52 (PRT) Retired.
Begin, Robert T. '64 (CLV) [17] Cleveland, OH St. Colman Church; Avon, OH Our Lady of the Wayside.
Begley, James J. '82 (RIC) Mechanicsville, VA Church of the Redeemer.
Begley, John J. *s.j.* '62 (BO) [W] Boston, MA The Society of Jesus of New England-Provincial Offices.
Begley, John J. *s.j.* '62 (SCR) [C] Scranton, PA University of Scranton.
Begley, Paul '55 (OM) [11] Omaha, NE St. Bridget Church; Retired.
Begley, Thomas B. '60 (SPR) Cheshire, MA St. Mary of the Assumption Church.
Begley, Thomas M. '89 (STL) [28] St. Louis, MO St. Boniface Church.
Begly, Mark S. '84 (ALT) New Baltimore, PA St. John the Baptist Church.
Begnaud, Adam *o.s.b.* '96 (NO) [A] St. Benedict, LA St. Joseph's Seminary College; [P] St. Benedict, LA St. Joseph Abbey.
Begolly, Michael J. '81 (GBG) Indiana, PA St. Thomas More University Parish.
Begue, Joseph E. *c.m.* '55 (STL) [P] St. Louis, MO Vincentian Henrietta Residence; [W] St. Louis, MO The Vincentian Press Religious Supply.
Behan, George P. '56 (PRO) [12] Warwick, RI St. William Church.
Behan, Harry P. '73 (NU) St. Peter, MN St. Peter Church.
Behan, Hugh F. '64 (JC) Jefferson City, MO Renz Correctional Facility; Jefferson City, MO Central Missouri Correctional Center; Special Assignments; [D] Jefferson City, MO Villa Marie Skilled Nursing Facility.
Behan, Jim *o.s.f.s.* '73 (R) Carolina Beach, NC Immaculate Conception Church.
Behan, Msgr. Philip A. '70 (SB) Hesperia, CA Holy Family Church.
Behan, Thomas W. *o.s.a.* '58 (OAK) Castro Valley, CA Our Lady of Grace Church.
Behen, John M. *c.pp.s.* '46 (JC) Sedalia, MO Sacred Heart Church.
Behl, Msgr. Richard A. '66 (MET) [1] Metuchen, NJ Cathedral of St. Francis.
Behler, Donald '47 (CIN) Retired.
Behman, Toma A. '54 (DET) [2] Southfield, MI St. Bede Church.
Behnen, Robert *o.f.m.* '60 (STL) Oakville, MO St. Francis of Assisi Church; [P] Oakville, MO St. Francis Friary.
Behnke, John J. *c.s.p.* '76 (STP) [29] Minneapolis, MN St. Lawrence Church; [N] Minneapolis, MN Paulist Fathers.
Behnke, Robert C. '73 (CHI) [19] Chicago, IL Assumption of the B.V.M./St. Catherine of Genoa Church; [169] Chicago, IL SS. Peter and Paul Church.
Behrens, Msgr. A.W. '45 (SC) Retired.
Behrens, James Stephen *o.c.s.o.* '74 (ATL) [I] Conyers, GA The Monastery of the Holy Spirit.
Behringer, William R. *s.m.* '60 (CIN) [M] Dayton, OH Marianist Provincialate.
Behrmann, Msgr. Elmer H. '38 (STL) Retired.
Beichner, Paul E. *c.s.c.* '39 (FTW) [J] South Bend, IN Congregation of Holy Cross Indiana Province Provincial House.
Beierschmitt, Msgr. Leo A. (HBG) [1] Lancaster, PA St. Anne Church.
Beierwaltes, Charles *c.ss.r.* '67 (FgM) Redemptorist Foreign Missions.
Beigel, Gerard '86 (OAK) [5] Fremont, CA St. Leonard Church.
Beighlie, James T. *c.m.* '79 (STL) [P] St. Louis, MO Vincentian Bellerive Residence.
Beilman, J. Brian '86 (OM) Humphrey, NE St. Francis Church.
Beining, Paul R. *s.j.* '55 (SCR) [C] Scranton, PA University of Scranton.
Beirne, Charles J. *s.j.* '69 (FgM) Provinces.
Beirne, Charles J. *s.j.* '69 (NY) [DD] New York, NY Jesuit Provincial's Office.
Beirne, Gerald E. '62 (PRO) Smithfield, RI St. Philip Church.
Beirne, M. Christen '69 (NEW) Mahwah, NJ Immaculate Conception Church.
Beirne, Robert M. '63 (PRO) [1] Central Falls, RI The Holy Spirit Catholic Community Church.
Beischel, Richard L. *c.pp.s.* '56 (CIN) [M] Dayton, OH Provincial House of the Cincinnati Province of the Society of the Precious Blood.
Beischel, Thomas *c.pp.s.* '58 (CIN) [K] Dayton, OH Franciscan Medical Center - Dayton Campus.
Beischel, Thomas J. *c.pp.s.* '58 (CIN) [U] Dayton, OH Community Support Charitable Trust.
Beisel, James D. '80 (PH) [D] Warminster, PA Archbishop Wood Catholic High School; [V] Warminster, PA Regina Coeli Residence for Priests.
Beitans, John '73 (IND) Starlight, IN St. John the Baptist Church.
Beiter, Eugene J. '64 (LAN) Leslie, MI SS. Cornelius and Cyprian Church.
Beiter, Msgr. Lambert M. '37 (ALT) Retired.
Beiter, Robert G. '64 (BUF) Brocton, NY St. Patrick Church.
Beiting, Msgr. Ralph '49 (LEX) Louisa, KY St. Jude Church.
Beitzinger, George J. '45 (MIL) Retired.
Bejgrowicz, Joseph S. '70 (NEW) Kenilworth, NJ St. Theresa's Church.
Bek, Robert *c.ss.r.* '64 (GAL) [34] Houston, TX Holy Ghost Church.
Bek, Viktor '92 (PHU) Millville, NJ St. Nicholas Church.
Beksha, Francis W. '46 (BO) Franklin, MA St. Mary Church; Retired.
Belair, Eugene '53 (SCL) Ogilvie, MN St. Kathryn's Church.
Belair, Eugene G. '53 (SCL) Mora, MN St. Mary's Church.
Belanger, Gerald R. '75 (MAN) Portsmouth, NH St. James Church.
Belanger, Leo J. *s.j.* '32 (DET) [P] Clarkston, MI Colombiere Center.
Belanger, Rene A. *s.s.s.* '50 (CLV) [P] Cleveland, OH Congregation of the Blessed Sacrament Provincial House.
Belanger, Thomas *o.m.i.* (DUL) International Falls, MN St. Thomas Aquinas Church.
Belanggoy, Plutarco *c.i.c.m.* '96 (BWN) La Joya, TX Our Lady, Queen of Angels Church.
Belanich, Giordano (NEW) Secaucus, NJ Hudson County Juvenile Detention Center.
Belanich, Giordano '75 (NEW) Fairview, NJ St. John the Baptist Church.
Belanich, Giordano '75 (PAT) On Duty Outside the Diocese.
Belauskas, August J. '68 (CHI) [A] Mundelein, IL University of St. Mary of the Lake-Mundelein Seminary.
Belcher, Francis H. *s.j.* '61 (BO) [W] Boston, MA Arrupe House.
Belcher, Paul F. *s.j.* '63 (SAC) [14] Sacramento, CA St. Ignatius of Loyola Church.
Belcher, Sandy (HRT) [I] New Haven, CT Hospital of St. Raphael.
Belchez, Caesar A. '95 (HBG) Gettysburg, PA St. Francis Xavier's Church.
Belczak, Edward A. '72 (DET) [1] Troy, MI St. Thomas More Church.
Belczak, Thomas A. '80 (DET) [4] Redford, MI St. Valentine Church.
Belda, Leo W. '42 (MIL) Retired.
Belen, Germain *o.f.m.conv.* '50 (SAV) St. Simons Island, GA St. Williams Church.
Belfield, John '58 (STU) Retired.
Belford, Msgr. William J. '74 (NY) Blauvelt, NY St. Catharine Church.
Belgarde, George H. *s.j.* '88 (NY) [DD] New York, NY Jesuit Provincial's Office.
Belgarde, George H. '88 (OG) [J] Hogansburg, NY St. Regis Mission.
Belhumeur, Paul *m.s.* '61 (BUR) Windsor, VT St. Francis of Assisi Church.
Belhumeur, Roger E. '61 (PRO) Retired.
Beligotti, Richard J. '68 (ROC) Leicester, NY St. Thomas Aquinas Church.
Beligotti, Robert L. '68 (ROC) [7] Auburn, NY St. Francis of Assisi Church.
Belinda, Augustine *t.o.r.* '93 (SFS) Wessington Springs, SD St. Joseph Church.
Belinski, Michael *c.s.c.* '89 (FTW) [9] South Bend, IN

Holy Cross Church.
Belisch, Carl L. *c.s.b.* '65 (GAL) [F] Houston, TX St. Thomas High School.
Belisle, Ronald H. '62 (SEA) Camas, WA St. Thomas Church.
Belitz, Justin *o.f.m.* '61 (IND) [12] Indianapolis, IN Sacred Heart of Jesus Church.
Belitz, Ronald C. '79 (GB) [8] Green Bay, WI St. Jude Church.
Beliveau, Richard '60 (BRK) Absent on Leave.
Belizario, Nelson '68 (L) [A] Louisville, KY Bellarmine College; [B] Louisville, KY St. Francis DeSales High School.
Bell, Brian T. '70 (TUC) On Duty Outside the Diocese.
Bell, Msgr. Carl F. '66 (LA) Encino, CA St. Cyril Church.
Bell, Edward H. '77 (PH) Lower Makefield, PA St. John the Evangelist Church.
Bell, Edward M. '64 (WH) Parkersburg, WV St. Margaret Mary Church.
Bell, Gerald L. '73 (L) Lebanon Junction, KY St. Benedict Church; Shepherdsville, KY St. Aloysius Church.
Bell, Gerard P. *s.j.* '57 (NY) [DD] New York, NY Jesuit Provincial's Office.
Bell, Gerard P. *s.j.* '57 (WDC) [V] Silver Spring, MD Apostleship of Prayer.
Bell, Ira J. '52 (STL) Retired.
Bell, Joseph W. '74 (SPK) [2] Spokane, WA Assumption of the Blessed Virgin Mary Church.
Bell, Michael J. '79 (SAG) Caro, MI Sacred Heart Church.
Bell, Michael T. '61 (MRY) San Luis Obispo, CA California Men's Colony West.
Bell, Milford C. '49 (FTW) Retired.
Bell, Milford C. '49 (WH) Retired.
Bell, Richard A. *m.m.* '57 (NY) [DD] Maryknoll, NY Maryknoll Fathers and Brothers.
Bellagamba, Anthony *i.m.c.* '52 (MET) [H] Somerset, NJ Consolata Society for Foreign Missions.
Bellantonio, Albert '69 (BRK) [111] Brooklyn, NY Our Lady of Solace Church.
Bellavista, Jose '35 (LA) Retired.
Bellavista, Jose '36 (LA) Los Nietos, CA Our Lady of Perpetual Help Church.
Bellefeuille, Albert A. '54 (MAN) Colebrook, NH St. Brendan Church.
Bellenoit, George C. '72 (FR) Mansfield, MA St. Mary's Church.
Belleque, Thomas A. '85 (SEA) Sumner, WA St. Andrew Church; Orting, WA U.S. Soldiers' Home.
Beller, Frederic J. *o.s.b.* '43 (JOL) [J] Lisle, IL St. Procopius Abbey.
Beller, Joseph '58 (Y) Retired.
Bellesorte, Anthony R. *o.c.s.o.* '69 (SAC) [A] Vina, CA Abbey of New Clairvaux, Trappist Seminary; [G] Vina, CA Abbey of New Clairvaux, Trappist.
Bellester, Msgr. Pedro J. '58 (PCE) Special Assignment.
Belletty, Emile '78 (LA) [12] Los Angeles, CA Holy Name of Jesus Church; [48] Los Angeles, CA St. Bernadette Church; [97] Los Angeles, CA Transfiguration Church.
Bellew, Msgr. Francis P. '66 (NY) Wappingers Falls, NY St. Mary Church.
Bellew, Lawrence *c.p.* '53 (BRK) [U] Jamaica, NY Immaculate Conception Monastery.
Bellew, Lawrence *c.p.* '53 (RVC) West Islip, NY Good Samaritan Hospital Medical Center; [I] West Islip, NY Good Samaritan Hospital Medical Center.
Belley, Bernard *o.m.i.* '54 (FgM) Oblates Foreign Missions.
Belleza, John A. '85 (SFR) On Duty Outside the Archdiocese.
Bellinghausen, David *o.s.b.* '86 (LR) [A] Subiaco, AR Subiaco Monastery.
Bellino, Samuel P. *s.j.* '88 (SFR) [E] San Francisco, CA St. Ignatius College Preparatory (Coed); [N] San Francisco, CA Jesuit Community at St. Ignatius College Preparatory.
Bellisario, Andrew E. *c.m.* '84 (STO) Patterson, CA Sacred Heart Church.
Bellittiere, David A. '89 (BUF) Snyder, NY Christ the King Church.
Belliveau, Gary J. '85 (MAN) Hudson, NH St. Kathryn Church.
Belliveau, Paul D. *m.m.* '69 (FgM) Maryknoll Foreign Missions.
Bello, David *o.p.* (OAK) [N] Oakland, CA Western Dominican Province.
Bello, Giles *o.f.m.* (BUF) [C] St. Bonaventure, NY St. Bonaventure University.
Bello, Giles F. *o.f.m.* '55 (BUF) [O] St. Bonaventure, NY St. Bonaventure Friary.
Bellon, John E. *c.ss.r.* '41 (DET) [33] Detroit, MI Holy Redeemer Church.
Bellopede, Louis P. '91 (PH) [3] Norristown, PA Holy Saviour Church.
Bellow, Richard '70 (CHL) [5] Charlotte, NC St. Gabriel Church.
Belluomini, Msgr. Ralph '60 (FRS) [2] Bakersfield, CA Our Lady of Perpetual Help Church.
Belmonte, John M. *s.j.* '96 (MIL) [E] Milwaukee, WI Marquette University High School; [P] Milwaukee, WI Pere Marquette House Jesuit Community.
Belogi, James '81 (ALB) Guilderland, NY St. Madeleine Sophie Church.
Beloin, Robert L. '73 (HRT) [R] New Haven, CT Yale University-St. Thomas More Catholic Center and Chapel.
Belongea, David *o.f.m.cap.* (GB) [3] Appleton, WI St. Joseph Church.
Belongia, David *o.f.m.cap.* '59 (GB) [I] Appleton, WI St. Joseph Friary.
Belschner, Wayne '95 (BO) [3] Woburn, MA St. Charles Church.
Belsole, Kurt J. *o.s.b.* '78 (GBG) [H] Latrobe, PA Saint Vincent Archabbey.
Belsome, Garland T. '90 (BR) [6] Baton Rouge, LA Christ the King Church; [K] Baton Rouge, LA Christ the King Parish and Catholic Student Center.
Belt, David D. '90 (OM) Wisner, NE St. Joseph Church.
Beltrami, Robert *o.f.m.* '62 (P) [25] Portland, OR Our Lady of Sorrows Church.
Beltran, Esteban *ss.cc.* '56 (SJN) [8] Guaynabo, PR Nuestra Senora de la Paz Church.
Beltran, Justo '69 (BRK) [143] Brooklyn, NY St. Vincent de Paul Church.
Beltzner, Lucian W. *o.carm.* '63 (NY) Middletown, NY Our Lady of Mt. Carmel Church.
Belzer, Msgr. Paul J. '54 (BUF) Pendleton, NY Good Shepherd Church.
Benacchio, Onorio *c.s.* '50 (VEN) Immokalee, FL Our Lady of Guadalupe Church.
Benack, Henry I. '51 (RVC) Glen Cove, NY St. Patrick's Church; Glen Cove, NY North Shore Community Hospital at Glen Cove.
Benak, Wes *o.s.a.* '92 (CHI) [N] Chicago, IL St. John Stone Friary.
Benakovic, Benedict *o.f.m.conv.* '49 (GRY) [12] Gary, IN St. Joseph The Worker Church.
Benarick, Juan (SJN) [4] San Juan, PR San Antonio Church.
Benas, Randy '85 (SJ) Los Altos, CA St. Simon Church.
Benavente, James L.G. '94 (AGN) [1] Agana, GU Dulce Nombre de Maria Cathedral - Basilica Church.
Benbenek, Gerald J. '66 (PEO) Farmer City, IL Sacred Heart Church.
Bench, John F. '64 (CHR) Absent On Leave.
Benda, Frank M. '57 (DUB) Earlville, IA St. Joseph's Church; Greeley, IA St. Joseph's Church.
Benda, Frederick J. *s.j.* '72 (CLV) [E] Cuyahoga Falls, OH Walsh Jesuit High School.
Benda, M. Eugene '60 (DAV) Tipton, IA St. Mary's Church.
Bendel, Eugene '57 (STL) [4] University City, MO St. Patrick Church.
Benden, Stephen *c.ss.r.* '89 (OM) [19] Omaha, NE Holy Name Church.
Bender, Arthur C. *s.j.* '78 (NY) [F] New York, NY Regis High School; [DD] New York, NY St. Ignatius Loyola Residence.
Bender, James W. *c.pp.s.* '52 (CIN) [M] Dayton, OH Provincial House of the Cincinnati Province of the Society of the Precious Blood.
Bender, Joseph J. '57 (ALT) Retired.
Bender, Lawrence *s.s.* '51 (WDC) Retired.
Bender, Lawrence A. *s.s.* '51 (BAL) [J] Baltimore, MD St. Charles Villa; [M] Baltimore, MD St. Charles Villa.
Bender, Philip M. '64 (ALT) State College, PA Good Shepherd Church.
Bender, Reginald G. *o.s.b.* '59 (GBG) [H] Latrobe, PA Saint Vincent Archabbey.
Bender, Msgr. Thomas G. '56 (COL) Bremen, OH St. Mary Church.
Bender, Thomas J. '61 (ALN) Unassigned.
Bendernagel, Cajetan *c.p.* '52 (HRT) [M] West Hartford, CT Holy Family Monastery/Retreat.
Bendik, Msgr. John J. '67 (SCR) [4] Pittston, PA St. John the Evangelist Church.
Bendixen, Arthur '76 (ORL) Sabbatical.
Bendorf, Richard *o.f.m.* '87 (SFD) [1] Quincy, IL St. Anthony of Padua Church; [6] Quincy, IL St. Joseph Church; [B] Quincy, IL Quincy University.
Bendyk, Marian '82 (CLV) [35] Cleveland, OH Immaculate Heart of Mary Church.
Bendzella, Sylvester J. '59 (ALT) Clarence, PA St. Michael's Church; Snow Shoe, PA St. Mary's Church.
Bene, Philip J. '94 (STL) Graduate Studies.
Benecki, Stanley '84 (COL) [7] Columbus, OH Sts. Augustine and Gabriel Church.
Benedict, Francis *o.s.b.* '76 (LA) [X] Valyermo, CA St. Andrew's Abbey Retreat House (All Groups).
Benedict, John *o.carm.* '77 (CHI) [68] Chicago, IL St. Gelasius Church.
Benedict, Joseph M. '97 (SJ) Campbell, CA St. Lucy Church.
Benedict, Msgr. Michael J. '43 (LAF) Retired.
Benedicto, Benjamin '62 (ORG) Newport Beach, CA Our Lady Queen of Angels Church.
Benedik, Hilarion *o.s.b.m.* '48 (STF) [B] Glen Cove, NY Basilian Fathers Novitiate of the Order of St. Basil the Great.
Benefiel, Msgr. Harry E. '60 (LAF) Retired.
Benen, John *c.pp.s.* (CIN) [B] Carthagena, OH St. Charles.
Benestad, Msgr. Thomas J. '70 (ALN) On Duty Outside the Diocese.
Benestad, Msgr. Thomas J. '70 (PH) [A] Wynnewood, PA Theological Seminary of St. Charles Borromeo, Overbrook.
Bengert, Anthony L. '65 (ELP) Absent on Leave.
Bengochea, Gerardo *s.j.* '63 (NY) [50] New York, NY Holy Trinity Church.
Benguria, Juan B. (SJN) [46] San Juan, PR Nuestra Senora de la Piedad Church.
Benguria, Juan Bautista '57 (SJN) [46] San Juan, PR Nuestra Senora de la Piedad Church.
Benham, Michael C. '76 (MIL) Burlington, WI St. Charles Church.
Benicewicz, Joseph *ofm conv.* '88 (BUF) [D] Athol Springs, NY St. Francis High School; [O] Athol Springs, NY St. Francis of Assisi Friary.
Beninati, Francis H. *m.m.* '55 (FgM) Maryknoll Foreign Missions.
Benintende, Joseph '70 (ALB) Ilion, NY Annunciation Church.
Benischeck, Bernard J. '53 (PH) [39] Philadelphia, PA St. Dominic Church.
Benish, William '72 (AUS) Cedar Park, TX St. Margaret Mary Church.
Benitez, Eduardo '66 (ORL) Retired.
Benjamin, Don *o.carm.* '67 (PHX) [F] Phoenix, AZ Carmelite Community.
Benjamin, Don *o.carm.* '86 (PHX) Special Assignment.
Benjamin, Don C. *o.carm.* (PHX) [I] Phoenix, AZ Kino Institute.
Benjamin, John '93 (SB) Lucerne Valley, CA St. Paul Church.
Benkert, Gerald *o.s.b.* '34 (FgM) American - Cassinese Congregation Foreign Missions.
Benkowski, Gregory '84 (OM) Fordyce, NE St. John the Baptist Church; Menominee, NE St. Boniface Church.
Benkowski, Gregory *s.m.* '84 (STL) [P] St. Louis, MO Provincialate of the Society of Mary, Province of St. Louis.
Benliro, Fernando C. '58 (OM) [29] Omaha, NE St. Mary Magdalene Church.
Benn, Walter J. '77 (PH) Downingtown, PA St. Joseph Church.
Bennett, Msgr. Austin P. '49 (BRK) Retired; [U] Brooklyn, NY Curial Residence.
Bennett, Christopher '90 (SJ) [11] San Jose, CA St. Christopher Church.
Bennett, Msgr. Donald T. '67 (RVC) Garden City, NY St. Joseph's Church.
Bennett, Gordon D. *s.j.* '75 (LA) [F] Los Angeles, CA Loyola High School.
Bennett, John E. *s.j.* '53 (PH) [C] Philadelphia, PA St. Joseph's University; [AA] Philadelphia, PA Jesuit Community at St. Joseph's University.
Bennett, Msgr. John F. '71 (RVC) Baldwin, NY St. Christopher Church.
Bennett, Joseph R. '66 (CHI) South Holland, IL Holy Ghost Church.
Bennett, Joseph T. *s.j.* '57 (BO) [E] Boston, MA Boston College High School & Jesuit Community.
Bennett, Melvin J. '69 (LFT) Crawfordsville, IN St. Bernard Church.
Bennett, Michael X. '71 (HBG) Absent on Leave.
Bennett, Noel I. '59 (MIA) [2] Miami Beach, FL St. Joseph Church.
Bennett, Norman S. *c.ss.r.* '71 (BRK) [107] Brooklyn, NY Our Lady of Perpetual Help Basilica Church.
Bennett, Richard L. '72 (JOL) [5] Joliet, IL Sacred Heart Church.
Bennett, Richard S. *c.ss.r.* '96 (PH) [25] Philadelphia, PA St. Boniface Church.
Bennett, Rolland *o.m.i.* '61 (PMB) Riviera Beach, FL St. Francis of Assisi Church.
Bennett, Msgr. Thomas '57 (COL) [22] Columbus, OH Immaculate Conception Church.
Bennett, Thomas F. '68 (HRT) Washington Depot, CT Our Lady of Perpetual Help Church.
Bennett, Msgr. Thomas M. '57 (COL) [C] Columbus, OH St. Charles Preparatory School.
Bennington, Msgr. J. Clement '45 (PH) Abington, PA Our Lady Help of Christians Church; Retired.
Beno, Brian M. '76 (MIL) Awaiting Assignment.
Beno, John R. '59 (PBL) Retired.
Beno, Joseph '57 (P) Retired.
Benoit, Adrian J. '65 (SPR) [7] Springfield, MA Immaculate Conception Church.
Benoit, Bryan *s.c.j.* '93 (MIL) [P] Hales Corners, WI Priests of the Sacred Heart.
Benoit, Lloyd F. '90 (LAF) Cecilia, LA St. Joseph Church.
Benoit, Louis R. '79 (RIC) Christiansburg, VA Holy Spirit Catholic Church; Pearisburg, VA Holy Family Church.
Benoit, Raymond (BO) Boston, MA Boston Medical Center.

Benoit, Raymond P. '89 (BO) [43] Boston, MA St. Margaret Church.
Benoit, Ronald H. '55 (BUR) Richmond, VT Our Lady of the Holy Rosary Church.
Benoit, Vincent *o.p.* '78 (P) [6] Eugene, OR St. Thomas More Church.
Benoit, Vincent *o.p.* '84 (P) [D] Eugene, OR Marist High School.
Benonis, Richard R. '58 (PH) Retired.
Benonis, William J. '52 (PH) Swarthmore, PA Notre Dame de Lourdes Church.
Bensman, Gerald E. '64 (CIN) McCartyville, OH Sacred Heart of Jesus Church.
Bensman, John L. '56 (CIN) Chickasaw, OH Most Precious Blood Church; St. Sebastian, OH St. Sebastian Church.
Benson, Gerard *o.carm.* '42 (VEN) [G] Venice, FL Carmel in Venice.
Benson, James A. *s.j.* '56 (BO) [3] Newton, MA St. Ignatius Church.
Benson, Msgr. John D. '47 (WDC) Retired.
Benson, Joseph A. '84 (NO) [4] Slidell, LA St. Margaret Mary Church; Slidell, LA Greenbriar Nursing & Convalescent Home; Slidell, LA Guest House of Slidell Nursing Home; Slidell, LA Greenery Neurologic Rehabilitation Center at Slidell.
Benson, Pierre *m.afr.* '70 (WDC) [M] Washington, DC Missionaries of Africa.
Benson, Richard *c.m.* '78 (LA) [A] Camarillo, CA St. John's Seminary; [A] Camarillo, CA St. John's Seminary.
Bentivegna, Salvatore A. *o.s.j.* '63 (SCR) [16] Scranton, PA St. Lucy's Church.
Bentivoglio, Louis '53 (VEN) Retired.
Bentley, David (ALB) Special Assignment.
Benton, James F. '73 (LIN) Seward, NE St. Vincent de Paul Church.
Bentz, John B. '66 (COL) Marysville, OH Our Lady of Lourdes Church; Marysville, OH Ohio Reformatory for Women.
Benwell, Msgr. William '80 (MET) Warren, NJ Our Lady of the Mount Church.
Benya, Edward G. *s.j.* '84 (FgM) Provinces.
Benya, Edward G. *s.j.* '84 (NO) [P] New Orleans, LA Jesuit Provincial Office.
Benz, David H. '75 (PH) Military Chaplains.
Benz, James J. '74 (STL) Richmond Heights, MO Little Flower, St. Teresa of the Infant Jesus Church.
Benz, Walter J. '50 (PIT) Glenshaw, PA St. Mary Church.
Benzinger, Oscar L. *s.j.* '67 (MIL) [P] Milwaukee, WI Jesuit Provincial Office, Wisconsin Province.
Benzoni, Martin *o.praem.* '81 (ORG) [1] Huntington Beach, CA St. Bonaventure Church.
Benzoni, Martin R. *o.praem.* '81 (ORG) [H] Silverado, CA Norbertine Fathers of Orange Inc.
Beof, Marlon *o.a.r.* '96 (NEW) [N] West Orange, NJ Augustinian Recollects.
Berancourt, Homero *s.d.b.* (SJN) Catano, PR San Francisco de Sales Church.
Berard, Aram *s.j.* '66 (ALN) [10] Reading, PA St. Paul Church.
Berard, Aram J. *s.j.* '66 (BO) [W] Boston, MA The Society of Jesus of New England-Provincial Offices.
Berardi, Msgr. Ferdinando (NY) [HH] New York, NY Committe for Mission Responsibility Society, Inc.
Berardi, Msgr. Ferdinando D. '77 (NY) [76] New York, NY St. Monica Church; [HH] New York, NY Catholic Medical Mission Board, Inc.
Berardi, James J. '59 (CLV) [1] Akron, OH Annunciation Church; Akron, OH Akron City Hospital.
Berardi, Thomas F. '76 (ALB) Cobleskill, NY St. Vincent de Paul Church; [B] Albany, NY Maria College.
Berbena, Christopher '80 (OAK) [2] Walnut Creek, CA St. John Vianney Church.
Berberian, David '74 (ALB) [9] Troy, NY Our Lady of Victory Church.
Berbian, David '74 (ALB) Special Assignment.
Berbig, Steven A. '87 (RVC) Mastic Beach, NY St. Jude Church.
Berbusse, Edward J. *s.j.* '45 (NY) [DD] New York, NY Murray-Weigel Hall.
Berchmanz, Anthony '67 (NEW) Military Chaplains.
Berciano, Jose '64 (MIA) [28] Miami, FL SS. Peter and Paul Church.
Bercier, Barry *a.a.* '85 (WOR) [N] Worcester, MA Assumptionists of Assumption College.
Bercik, G. Michael *o.f.m.* '79 (BO) [1] Marlboro, MA St. Ann Church.
Berding, Richard P. '84 (L) [48] Louisville, KY St. Luke Church.
Berdis, Donald E. '63 (E) [2] Farrell, PA Our Lady of Fatima Church.
Berdugo, Hernan (SJN) [10] Carolina, PR Inmaculata Concepcion Church.
Berdugo, Hernan '82 (SJN) Rio Grande, PR San Francisco de Asis Church.
Berean, Christopher H. '87 (NY) Saugerties, NY St. Mary of the Snow Church.
Bereda, Stanislaw J. '65 (GAY) Posen, MI St. Casimir Church.
Berendt, George *p.i.m.e.* '74 (FRS) Clovis, CA Our Lady of Perpetual Help Church.
Berendt, Msgr. James M. '55 (COL) [18] Columbus, OH Holy Cross Church.
Berendt, Peter *c.p.* '51 (CHI) [91] Chicago, IL Immaculate Conception Church.
Berendt, Peter *c.p.* '57 (CHI) [N] Chicago, IL Immaculate Conception Monastery.
Berens, Cyprian E. *o.f.m.* '51 (MAR) Calumet, MI St. Paul the Apostle Church.
Beretta, J. Christian '97 (WIL) [B] Wilmington, DE Salesianum School.
Beretta, John W. *o.s.a.* '45 (CHI) [N] Olympia Fields, IL The Augustinian Provincialate Tolentine Center.
Bereza, Stepan '93 (STF) [7] New Britain, CT St. Josaphat Church.
Berg, Msgr. Arnold J. '33 (NU) Retired.
Berg, Donald M. '47 (LC) Pittsville, WI St. Joachim Church; Spaulding-City Point, WI North American Martyrs Church.
Berg, John *f.s.s.p.* '97 (SCR) [M] Elmhurst, PA Priestly Fraternity of St. Peter (F.S.S.P.), North American District Headquarters.
Berg, John Leonard '83 (NU) Absent on Leave.
Berg, Paul '48 (DET) Retired.
Berg, Peter M. '71 (OG) Dannemora, NY St. Joseph Church; Dannemora, NY Clinton Correctional Facility.
Berg, Ralph *c.m.f.* '64 (LA) [R] Los Angeles, CA Missionary Sons of the Immaculate Heart of Mary; [R] Los Angeles, CA Claretian Retreat Center Community.
Berg, Ramon A. '82 (CHL) Retired.
Berg, Richard F. *c.s.c.* '63 (P) [38] Portland, OR St. Vincent de Paul Church; [B] Portland, OR University of Portland; [L] Portland, OR Holy Cross Fathers & Brothers, C.S.C. - University of Portland.
Berg, Richard V. '52 (STP) Retired.
Berg, Msgr. S. Theodore '61 (BUF) [63] Buffalo, NY St. Teresa Church.
Berg, Timothy '79 (SEA) Pe Ell, WA St. Joseph's Church; Toledo, WA St. Francis Xavier Church; Winlock, WA Sacred Heart Church.
Berg, Timothy '79 (SFE) On Duty Outside the Archdiocese.
Bergamo, John A. '65 (SCR) East Stroudsburg, PA St. Matthew's Church; [D] East Stroudsburg, PA Notre Dame Junior/Senior High School.
Bergbower, Daniel J. '88 (SFD) Effingham, IL Sacred Heart Church.
Berge, Frank J. '78 (DET) Macomb, MI St. Isidore Church.
Bergedick, Charles *s.m.* (CIN) [9] Dayton, OH Emmanuel Church.
Bergedick, Charles T. *s.m.* '57 (CIN) [M] Dayton, OH Marianist Provincialate.
Bergen, William J. *s.j.* '55 (NY) [51] New York, NY St. Ignatius Loyola Church.
Bergen, William J. *s.j.* '65 (NY) [DD] New York, NY St. Ignatius Loyola Residence.
Berger, Bernard M. '64 (GI) Burwell, NE Sacred Heart Church.
Berger, John G. '67 (NU) Gibbon, MN St. Willibrord Church.
Berger, Lawrence B. '66 (LC) [4] La Crosse, WI Holy Trinity Church.
Berger, Michel R. *f.s.s.p.* '94 (SCR) [M] Elmhurst, PA Priestly Fraternity of St. Peter (F.S.S.P.), North American District Headquarters.
Berger, Robert F. '62 (HBG) Myerstown, PA Mary, Gate of Heaven Church.
Bergeron, Albert G. '62 (HT) Retired.
Bergeron, Marc H. '70 (FR) [12] Fall River, MA St. Anne's Church.
Bergeron, Michael A. '96 (HT) [1] Thibodaux, LA St. Joseph Co-Cathedral.
Bergeron, Robert E. '52 (BO) Westford, MA St. Catherine of Alexandria Church.
Bergeur, John '45 (NEW) [N] Rutherford, NJ St. John Vianney Residence for Priests.
Bergeur, John X. '45 (NEW) Retired.
Bergewisch, Fred F. *s.j.* '55 (CHI) [N] Chicago, IL Chicago Province of the Society of Jesus-Provincial Office.
Bergewisch, Fred F. *s.j.* '55 (FgM) Provinces.
Berggreen, Msgr. Robert H. '64 (BR) [2] Baton Rouge, LA St. Agnes Church.
Berghammer, Robert J. '49 (MIL) Le Roy, WI St. Andrew Church.
Berghout, Paul A. '96 (ARL) Manassas, VA All Saints Church.
Bergin, Msgr. Clifford E. (CHI) Retired.
Bergin, James *s.v.d.* '69 (CHI) [B] Techny, IL Divine Word Residence; [N] Techny, IL Society of the Divine Word, Provincial Headquarter-Chicago Prov.
Bergin, John J. *s.v.d.* '67 (BO) [W] Duxbury, MA Society of the Divine Word.
Bergin, John J. *s.j.* '67 (STL) [P] St. Louis, MO De Smet Jesuit High School Community.
Bergin, Pascal '57 (CC) On Duty Outside the Diocese.
Bergin, Paschal '57 (SAT) Runge, TX St. Anthony's Church.
Bergin, Patrick A. *m.m.* '59 (NY) [DD] Maryknoll, NY Maryknoll Fathers and Brothers.
Bergin, Patrick A. *m.m.* '59 (RVC) Hampton Bays, NY St. Rosalie's Church.
Bergin, Patrick P. '57 (SAT) Kenedy, TX Our Lady of Peace Church.
Bergin, Robert D. '62 (HRT) Special and Other Archdiocesan Assignment; [N] West Hartford, CT Mercyknoll, Incorporated.
Bergin, Msgr. Thomas '61 (NY) [E] New York, NY Cathedral High School.
Bergin, Msgr. Thomas J. '61 (NY) [58] New York, NY St. John the Evangelist Church; [D] New York, NY Department of Education.
Bergin, Thomas J. '62 (ORL) New Smyrna Beach, FL Our Lady Star of the Sea Church.
Bergin, Msgr. William A. '42 (SD) Retired.
Bergkamp, Roger *o.m.i.* '64 (FgM) Oblates Foreign Missions.
Bergman, Charles B. '58 (PIT) Zelienople, PA St. Gregory Church.
Bergman, Msgr. Robert '71 (KCK) Shawnee, KS St. Joseph's Church.
Bergmann, F. Frederick *c.s.c.* '39 (FgM) Holy Cross Foreign Missions.
Bergner, David *s.d.s.* (WDC) [B] Silver Spring, MD Salvatorian Community.
Bergner, David J. *s.d.s.* '76 (RIC) [K] Richmond, VA Commonwealth Catholic Charities.
Bergquist, Patrick '90 (BAL) Special Assignment.
Bergquist, Patrick D. '90 (FBK) Galena, AK St. John Berchman Church.
Bergs, David J. '76 (LSC) Carrizozo, NM St. Rita Church.
Bergsbaken, Dennis (GB) Kimberly, WI Holy Name of Jesus Church.
Bergstadt, John (GB) [2] Appleton, WI St. Bernard Church.
Bergwall, John E. *m.m.* '59 (NY) [DD] Maryknoll, NY Maryknoll Fathers and Brothers.
Berinti, Ben *c.pp.s.* '85 (ORL) [6] Orlando, FL St. Andrew Church.
Beristain, Juan M. '71 (SJN) [6] Toa Baja, PR Santisima Trinidad Church.
Berk, Aloysius '67 (PIT) [7] Pittsburgh, PA St. Catherine of Siena Church.
Berkemeier, Charles A. '58 (IND) Retired.
Berkery, Patrick J. (HRT) [3] Ansonia, CT St. Anthony's Church.
Berkhout, Frans '87 (ALN) [C] Ashland, PA Cardinal Brennan Jr./Sr. High School.
Berkhout, Frans J. '87 (ALN) Ashland, PA St. Joseph Church; Ashland, PA St. Mauritius Church.
Berko, Matthew (ORL) Retired.
Berko, Matthew '62 (SJP) Apopka, FL St. Mary's Church; St. Petersburg, FL Epiphany of Our Lord Church; Spring Hill, FL St. Andrew Church.
Berland, Mark '74 (SAL) Grainfield, KS St. Agnes Church; Park, KS Sacred Heart Church.
Berling, Alban *o.s.b.* '45 (IND) [J] St. Meinrad, IN St. Meinrad Archabbey.
Berlo, Benedict *c.p.* '40 (NY) [FF] New York, NY Cardinal Spellman Retreat House.
Berlo, Benedict *c.p.* '57 (NY) [DD] New York, NY Passionist Spiritual Center.
Berlowski, Michael '95 (GAL) [22] Houston, TX St. Christopher Church.
Berman, Andrew J. '96 (WIN) [6] Rochester, MN St. John's Church.
Bermingham, Msgr. Charles E. '23 (RVC) Retired.
Bermingham, Msgr. Charles E. '32 (RVC) Williston Park, NY St. Aidan's Church.
Bermingham, Thomas V. *s.j.* '49 (NY) [DD] New York, NY Jesuit Community at Fordham University.
Bermudez, Alberto '86 (NO) [1] Marrero, LA Immaculate Conception Church.
Bermudez, Jose '80 (SPR) On Duty Outside the Diocese.
Bernabe, Humberto '92 (LA) Altadena, CA St. Elizabeth of Hungary Church.
Bernacki, Edward *c.s.sp.* (SB) [E] Hemet, CA Holy Ghost Fathers.
Bernacki, William J. *o.p.* '56 (CHI) [D] Oak Park, IL Fenwick High School; [N] River Forest, IL St. Thomas Aquinas Priory.
Bernadicou, Paul J. *s.j.* '65 (SFR) [N] San Francisco, CA Jesuit Community at University of San Francisco.
Bernal, Edward M. '87 (SAT) [43] San Antonio, TX St. John Berchmans Church.
Bernans, Arvids '64 (COL) [27] Columbus, OH St. Leo Church.
Bernans, Arvids '76 (TUC) Fort Huchuca, AZ Fort Huchuca Army Post.
Bernaola, Javier '85 (SJN) [G] Guaynabo, PR Opus Dei.
Bernard, Andre '71 (WOR) Absent on Leave.
Bernard, Andre '73 (SR) Scotia, CA St. Patrick Church.
Bernard, George C. *c.s.c.* '49 (P) [B] Portland, OR University of Portland; [L] Portland, OR Holy Cross

Fathers & Brothers, C.S.C. - University of Portland.
Bernard, Gerard *m.s.c.* '53 (PRO) Cranston, RI Rhode Island State Institutions.
Bernard, John P. '62 (BUF) Batavia, NY Veterans Hospital.
Bernard, John P. '62 (CAM) Retired.
Bernard, Msgr. M.J. '52 (LKC) Retired.
Bernard, Paul J. '41 (SPR) Retired.
Bernardi, Peter J. *s.j.* (DET) [K] Detroit, MI Jesuit Provincial Office-Detroit Province of the Society of Jesus.
Bernardin, Paul A. *o.p.* '61 (HRT) [14] New Haven, CT St. Mary's Priory Church.
Bernardo, Joaquin *o.p.* '84 (NY) [DD] New York, NY St. Vincent Ferrer Priory.
Bernardy, Patrick A. '60 (GB) Niagara, WI St. Anthony Church; Pembine, WI St. Margaret Church.
Bernas, Casimir *o.c.s.o.* '58 (SLC) [F] Huntsville, UT Abbey of Our Lady of the Holy Trinity of the Order of Cistercians.
Bernas, Elwood S. '84 (STU) Absent on Leave.
Bernas, Eugene '66 (NEW) Belleville, NJ St. Anthony's Church.
Bernas, Thomas A. '94 (CHI) Brookfield, IL St. Barbara Church; [U] Chicago, IL Catholic League for Religious Assistance to Poland.
Bernasconi, Gino '50 (VIC) Retired.
Bernatonis, John F. '45 (BO) Retired.
Bernauer, James '52 (CR) Retired.
Bernauer, James W. *s.j.* '75 (BO) [W] Chestnut Hill, MA The Jesuit Community at Boston College.
Bernbrock, John *s.j.* '56 (PHX) [2] Scottsdale, AZ Our Lady of Perpetual Help Church.
Bernbrock, John E. *s.j.* '56 (MIL) [P] Milwaukee, WI Jesuit Provincial Office, Wisconsin Province.
Berndt, Rudolph C. '76 (DAV) Buffalo, IA St. Peter's Church; Absent on Leave.
Berndt, Wayne *o.f.m.cap.* '83 (FgM) Capuchin Foreign Missions.
Bernelli, Matthew '64 (BGP) [13] Bridgeport, CT St. Mary's Church.
Berner, Albert J. '68 (NEW) [Q] Upper Montclair, NJ Montclair State University.
Berner, Francis '70 (NO) [64] New Orleans, LA St. Thomas The Apostle Church; New Orleans, LA Delgado College; New Orleans, LA Southern University in New Orleans; New Orleans, LA University of New Orleans.
Berner, Michael '86 (DM) Earling, IA St. Joseph Church.
Bernhardt, Gary *o.f.m.* (CHI) [D] Chicago, IL Hales Franciscan High School, Inc.
Bernier, Daniel L. '93 (MAN) Newport, NH St. Patrick Church.
Bernier, Lawrence J. '63 (SPR) East Longmeadow, MA St. Michael's Church.
Bernier, Paul *s.s.s.* (NY) [GG] New York, NY University Apostolate.
Bernier, Roland *m.s.* '57 (LKC) De Ridder, LA St. Joseph's Church.
Berning, Cornelius C. '31 (CIN) Retired; [L] Cincinnati, OH St. Margaret Hall.
Berning, James *s.d.b.* (NEW) [N] South Orange, NJ The Salesian Community.
Berning, James C. '91 (WIN) Slayton, MN St. Ann's Church.
Berning, John B. '34 (CIN) Retired.
Bernotas, Robert J. '83 (LFT) Earl Park, IN St. John the Baptist Church; Goodland, IN SS. Peter and Paul Church; Kentland, IN St. Joseph Church.
Bernott, Albert R. '43 (GR) Retired.
Bernott, Ernest J. '48 (GR) Retired.
Berns, Eric R. '95 (LC) [C] Chippewa Falls, WI McDonell Central Catholic High School.
Berns, Eric R. '96 (LC) Chippewa Falls, WI Notre Dame Church.
Berny, Paul W. '72 (ATL) Fayetteville, GA St. Gabriel Church.
Berran, Donald M. '60 (BRK) [158] Queens, NY Blessed Virgin Mary, Help of Christians Church.
Berres, Peregrin *o.s.b.* '57 (SCL) [I] Collegeville, MN St. John's Abbey, of the Order of St. Benedict.
Berret, Anthony J. *s.j.* '71 (PH) [C] Philadelphia, PA St. Joseph's University; [AA] Philadelphia, PA Jesuit Community at St. Joseph's University; [AA] Philadelphia, PA St. Alphonsus House.
Berrigan, Daniel J. *s.j.* '52 (NY) [DD] New York, NY West Side Jesuit Community.
Berrio, Augusto *s.j.* '63 (SD) [12] San Diego, CA Our Lady of Guadalupe Church.
Berrio, Ignacio (BO) [3] Lynn, MA St. Joseph Church.
Berrios, George '89 (BRK) [165] Queens, NY Corpus Christi Church.
Berrios, Israel '96 (CGS) Barranquitas, PR San Andres Apostol Church.
Berrueta, Jose *s.d.b.* '62 (NY) [72] New York, NY Mary Help of Christians Church.
Berruete, Joseph *s.d.b.* '62 (NY) [3] Port Chester, NY Our Lady of the Rosary Church.
Berry, Dennis *s.t.* (PAT) [P] Stirling, NJ Trinity Mission Center.
Berry, Dennis *s.t.* '74 (PAT) [P] Stirling, NJ Father Judge Apostolic Center.
Berry, James A. '75 (HON) Holualoa, HI St. Michael The Archangel Church.
Berry, Thomas *c.p.* '42 (MET) [H] South River, NJ Passionist Provincial Office.
Berry, William F. '66 (WDC) College Park, MD Holy Redeemer Church.
Berryman, Harold '58 (GB) [1] Appleton, WI St. Bernadette Church.
Berschied, Paul L. '86 (COV) Independence, KY St. Cecilia Church.
Berson, Bob *glmy.* '49 (CIN) [M] Fairfield, OH Headquarters of Glenmary Home Missioners.
Berson, Robert *glmy.* '53 (CIN) West Union, OH Holy Trinity Church.
Berson, Robert C. '53 (CIN) [U] Fairfield, OH Glenmary Home Missioners Charitable Trust.
Bertasius, Anthony '37 (ELP) Retired.
Bertasius, Msgr. Anthony '37 (PAT) [6] Paterson, NJ St. Casimir's Church.
Bertelli, Very James '59 (BO) Sudbury, MA St. Anselm Church.
Bertels, George '55 (KCK) Beattie, KS St. Malachy's Church; Marysville, KS St. Gregory's Church.
Bertels, Henry J. *s.j.* '62 (FgM) Provinces.
Bertels, Henry J. *s.j.* '62 (NY) [DD] New York, NY Jesuit Provincial's Office.
Bertha, Joseph '80 (PSC) Amherst, NY St. Stephen's Church.
Bertha, Joseph W. (BUF) Amherst, NY Millard Fillmore Suburban Hospital.
Berthelette, Ernest H. '74 (PRO) On Duty Outside the Diocese.
Berthiaume, Eugene F. '58 (WOR) Brookfield, MA St. Mary's Church.
Berthiaume, Gary D. '68 (CLV) Released from Diocesan Assignment.
Berthold, George C. '63 (BO) On Duty Outside the Archdiocese.
Bertin, Gerard (WOR) [C] Worcester, MA St. Peter-Marian Central Catholic Junior/Senior High School.
Bertin, Gerard L. '89 (WOR) [5] Worcester, MA Holy Name of Jesus Church.
Bertini, Angelo '73 (AUS) [7] Waco, TX St. Mary of the Assumption Church.
Bertino, Dominic V. '75 (GRY) Hobart, IN St. Bridget Church.
Bertiz, Santos '93 (NEW) Fairfield, NJ St. Thomas More Church.
Bertke, Erwin J. '43 (CIN) [52] Cincinnati, OH St. Lawrence Church; Retired.
Bertocchi, Luigi *o.s.b.* '70 (SCL) [I] Collegeville, MN St. John's Abbey, of the Order of St. Benedict.
Bertogli, John O. '77 (DM) Churchville, IA Assumption of the Blessed Virgin Mary Church; Irish Settlement, IA St. Patrick Church; St. Marys, IA Immaculate Conception Church.
Bertolotti, David '91 (BRK) [60] Brooklyn, NY Holy Spirit Church.
Bertolucci, John '65 (ALB) Latham, NY St. Ambrose Church.
Bertone, Thomas C. *c.s.c.* '81 (FR) [A] North Easton, MA Holy Cross Fathers Religious.
Bertoni, Albert *s.m.* '79 (RVC) [D] Uniondale, NY Kellenberg Memorial High School.
Bertoniere, Gabriel *o.c.s.o.* '58 (WOR) [N] Spencer, MA St. Joseph's Abbey.
Bertram, Michael *o.f.m.cap.* '88 (DET) Hazel Park, MI St. Mary Magdalen Church.
Bertrand, Aloysius J. '43 (PBL) [D] Grand Junction, CO St. Mary Hospital and Medical Center.
Bertrand, Armand J. '89 (SC) Fonda, IA Our Lady of Good Counsel Church; Varina, IA St. Columbkille's Church.
Bertrand, C. Conley '59 (LAF) Rynella, LA St. Marcellus Church.
Bertrand, Evarist *o.f.m.cap.* '63 (FgM) Capuchin Foreign Missions.
Bertrand, Joseph '60 (BEA) [C] Beaumont, TX St. Elizabeth Hospital of Beaumont.
Bertrand, Joseph E. *c.ss.r.* '55 (FgM) Redemptorist Foreign Missions.
Bertrand, Richard D. *s.j.* '79 (BO) [W] Boston, MA The Society of Jesus of New England-Provincial Offices.
Bertrand, Richard D. *s.j.* '79 (PRT) Auburn, ME St. Louis Church; [4] Lewiston, ME St. Mary's Church.
Bertrand, Victor E. '62 (CHI) [N] Arlington Heights, IL Viatorian Province Center-Clerics of St. Viator.
Bertrand, Victor E. *c.s.v.* '62 (LR) Little Rock, AR U.S. Veterans Administration Hospital; North Little Rock, AR U.S. Veterans Administration Hospital.
Bertrand, Vincent E. '87 (SPC) Marshfield, MO Holy Trinity Church.
Bertsche, Conrad J. '45 (BEL) Retired.
Berube, John J. '48 (BO) Retired.
Berube, Louis '47 (PRT) Retired.
Berube, Msgr. Louis D. '30 (OG) Retired.
Berube, Paul W. '60 (BO) Wayland, MA St. Zepherin Church.
Berube, Richard N. *s.s.e.* '70 (BUR) [E] Colchester, VT Society of St. Edmund.
Berube, Theodore E. '41 (NOR) Wauregan, CT Sacred Heart Church; Retired.
Berumen, Edward '80 (LA) Redondo Beach, CA St. James Church.
Berumen, Matthias '86 (LA) Valinda, CA St. Martha Church.
Besanceney, Paul H. *s.j.* '56 (FgM) Provinces.
Beseau, Steven (KCK) [B] Kansas City, KS Bishop Ward High School.
Beseau, Steven '95 (KCK) [1] Kansas City, KS Cathedral of St. Peter the Apostle.
Besendorfer, Ralph L. *j.c.d.* '59 (STA) Callahan, FL Our Lady of Consolation Church.
Beshara, Msgr. Ronald '71 (PMB) [D] West Palm Beach, FL St. Mary's Hospital, Inc.
Beshara, Msgr. Ronald M. '71 (SAM) On Duty Outside the Diocese.
Beshara, Msgr. Ronald N. '71 (PMB) [D] West Palm Beach, FL St. Mary's Hospital, Inc.
Beshoner, Sebastian *o.s.b.* '55 (LR) Paris, AR St. Joseph's Church.
Besinga, Dionisio '82 (LAV) Henderson, NV St. Peter the Apostle Church.
Besse, Joseph A. '45 (PRO) Retired.
Bessellieu, Mel '97 (FWT) Bedford, TX St. Michael Church.
Bessert, James W. '80 (SAG) Coleman, MI St. Philip Neri Church.
Best, Richard '61 (JOL) Absent on Sick Leave.
Best, Russell W. '86 (BO) [60] Boston, MA St. Patrick Church.
Best, Russell W.M., Jr. '86 (BO) [36] Boston, MA St. Joseph Church.
Bester, Robert '79 (CR) On Duty Outside the Diocese.
Bester, Robert '79 (DUL) [D] Duluth, MN St. Ann's Senior Residence.
Bestler, Joseph '57 (GB) Retired.
Beston, William J. *c.s.c.* '48 (FR) [O] Taunton, MA Paul A. Dever State School (For Retarded) Newman Center.
Beston, William J. *c.s.c.* '48 (FTW) [J] South Bend, IN Congregation of Holy Cross Indiana Province Provincial House.
Betan, Norbert *s.v.d.* '83 (CHI) [N] Chicago, IL Divine Word Theologate.
Betancur, Gonzalo (RVC) Freeport, NY Our Holy Redeemer Church.
Betancur, Nelson '75 (PAT) [8] Passaic, NJ Our Lady of Fatima Church.
Betancurt, Rigoberto *o.s.m.* '83 (SHP) [4] Monroe, LA St. Joseph Church.
Betchel, James '71 (ALN) [C] Ashland, PA Cardinal Brennan Jr./Sr. High School.
Bethancourt, Michael A. (MRY) Soledad, CA Salinas Valley State Prison.
Betit, John '94 (SPR) [8] Chicopee, MA St. Patrick's Church.
Betley, Michael E. '80 (GB) Plainfield, WI St. Paul Church.
Betoni, John P. *o.s.a.* '62 (PH) [C] Villanova, PA Villanova University; [AA] Villanova, PA St. Thomas Monastery.
Betowski, E. Paul *s.j.* '49 (BAL) [M] Baltimore, MD Jesuit Fathers and Brothers Maryland Provincial Curia.
Betrozoff, Larry (MRY) Tres Pinos, CA Immaculate Conception Church.
Bettendorf, James B. '59 (LAN) [8] Flint, MI St. Leo the Great Church.
Betti, Frederick G. *s.j.* '90 (ROC) [B] Rochester, NY McQuaid Jesuit High School.
Betti, Jose (ARE) Retired.
Betti, Mark J. '96 (R) New Bern, NC St. Paul Church.
Bettinger, Eugene *o.carm.* '76 (NEW) Demarest, NJ St. Joseph's Church.
Bettinger, Mark T. '93 (PBL) Grand Junction, CO St. Joseph Church.
Bettley, Emil L. '83 (NY) [E] New York, NY Cardinal Spellman High School.
Betts, John C. '68 (P) Albany, OR Our Lady of Perpetual Help Church.
Betz, James '71 (CAM) Military Chaplains.
Betz, James S. '89 (WDC) [1] Bowie, MD Ascension Church.
Betz, Kenneth '65 (EVN) Ireland, IN Annunciation of the Blessed Virgin Mary Church.
Betz, Robert L. '73 (MIL) [70] Milwaukee, WI St. Roman Church.
Betz, Thomas *o.f.m.cap.* '91 (PH) [79] Philadelphia, PA St. John the Evangelist Church.
Betzen, James G. *c.pp.s.* '81 (KC) [30] Kansas City, MO Sacred Heart-Guadalupe Church.
Beunen, Emmanuel *o.f.m.* '70 (CLV) Warrensville Heights, OH St. Jude Church; Cleveland, OH Cleveland House of Correction; Cleveland, OH Cuyahoga Hills Boys School; Cleveland, OH Dept. of Youth Services; Cleveland, OH Sunny Acres Skilled Nursing Facility; [P] Cleveland, OH St. Jude Friary.
Beuth, William J. *c.pp.s.* '59 (CIN) [M] Dayton, OH Provincial House of the Cincinnati Province of the

Society of the Precious Blood.
Beuther, Richard J. '96 (BRK) [199] Queens, NY St. Matthias Church.
Beutner, Edward F. '65 (SUP) On Leave.
Beuzer, Vincent J. *s.j.* '58 (ANC) [G] Anchorage, AK Holy Spirit Retreat House; [I] Anchorage, AK Holy Spirit Retreat House.
Bevan, James J., Jr. '75 (LAV) [9] Las Vegas, NV St. Francis de Sales Church.
Bevan, Norman E. *c.s.sp.* '63 (PH) [AA] Bensalem, PA Congregation of the Holy Ghost.
Bevan, Thomas R. '63 (BAL) Cumberland, MD St. Patrick Church.
Bevans, Stephan *s.v.d.* '71 (CHI) [N] Techny, IL Society of the Divine Word, Provincial Headquarter-Chicago Prov.
Bevans, Stephen B. *s.v.d.* '71 (CHI) [B] Chicago, IL The Catholic Theological Union at Chicago; [N] Chicago, IL Divine Word Theologate.
Bevard, Herbert A. '72 (PH) [17] Philadelphia, PA St. Athanasius Church.
Bevenour, Richard F. '57 (DAV) On Duty Outside the Diocese.
Bevens, Stephen *s.v.d.* '71 (CHI) [B] Techny, IL Divine Word Residence.
Beveridge, John P. '72 (SFD) [5] Quincy, IL St. John the Baptist Church.
Bevilacqua, Carlo *c.s.s.* '45 (BO) [Z] Waltham, MA Stigmatine Fathers and Brothers.
Bevilacqua, Jerome *o.s.a.* '65 (SD) [B] San Diego, CA Austin House - House of Formation; [H] San Diego, CA Augustinian Community.
Bevington, William S. '51 (NSH) Hendersonville, TN Our Lady of the Lake Church; [L] Hendersonville, TN Legion of Mary; [L] Hendersonville, TN Priests Eucharistic League.
Bevins, John J. '58 (HRT) [2] Waterbury, CT Immaculate Conception Church.
Beyenka, John T. '37 (CHI) [140] Chicago, IL St. Monica Church; Retired.
Beyer, Baldwin *o.f.m.cap.* '53 (SB) Twentynine Palms, CA Blessed Sacrament Church.
Beyer, Emil J. '40 (MAR) Retired; [D] Escanaba, MI Bishop Noa Home for Senior Citizens.
Beyer, Gregory *o.f.m.cap.* '62 (DEN) [3] Denver, CO Annunciation Church; Northglenn, CO Immaculate Heart of Mary Church; [M] Denver, CO Annunciation Friary.
Beyer, Lawrence A. '96 (DAL) Plano, TX Prince of Peace Church.
Beyer, Leroy O. '66 (WH) Retired.
Beyer, Richard J. '81 (DAV) On Duty Outside the Diocese.
Beyette, Paul V. '50 (OG) Retired.
Bezdicek, Valerian V. '39 (GF) Retired.
Bezunartea, Herman O. '58 (FRS) Bass Lake, CA St. Dominic Savio Church.
Bezuszka, Stanley J. *s.j.* '46 (BO) [W] Chestnut Hill, MA The Jesuit Community at Boston College.
Bezzina, Benjamin '77 (GLP) On Duty Outside of Diocese.
Biagi, Vincent L. *s.j.* '78 (NY) [F] New York, NY Regis High School; [DD] New York, NY St. Ignatius Loyola Residence.
Biain, Jose '48 (MIA) Retired; [H] Miami, FL Franciscan Fathers' Residence.
Bialas, Andrew A. *c.s.v.* '44 (JOL) [2] Kankakee, IL St. Patrick Church; Kankakee, IL Shapiro Development Center.
Bialkowski, David W. '88 (BUF) [3] Cheektowaga, NY St. John Gualbert Church.
Bialkowski, Henry A. '49 (NOR) Retired.
Bialkowski, Jacek '96 (SCR) [3] Williamsport, PA St. Boniface's Church.
Bialoncik, Emmanuel *o.f.m.* '73 (BWN) Elsa, TX Sacred Heart Church.
Biancalana, Angelo *m.c.c.j.* '58 (CHI) [N] La Grange Park, IL Comboni Mission Center.
Bianchi, Paul '64 (DM) Portsmouth, IA St. Mary Church.
Bianchi, Raymond S. '52 (TR) [1] Trenton, NJ St. Mary Cathedral.
Bianco, Anthony M. *c.r.s.p.* '51 (ALN) [K] Bethlehem, PA The Barnabite Fathers Barnabite Spiritual Center.
Biase, Justin *o.f.m.conv.* '70 (ALB) [A] Rensselaer, NY Conventual Franciscan Friars.
Biase, Justin *o.f.m.conv.* '84 (ALB) [L] Rensselaer, NY Provincialate, Immaculate Conception Friary - Order of Friars Minor Conventual.
Biase, Justin A. *o.f.m.conv.* '70 (NY) [B] New York, NY St. Francis Novitiate.
Biasio, Mariano *c.s.j.* '54 (LA) Lancaster, CA Blessed Junipero Serra Church.
Biasiol, Virgilio *o.f.m.* '42 (LA) [R] Santa Barbara, CA Franciscan Friary, Order of Friars Minor (Old Mission).
Biasiotto, Richard P. *o.f.m.* '64 (PAT) [M] Butler, NJ St. Anthony Friary.
Bibeault, Norbert P. *c.s.v.* '56 (LAV) [A] Las Vegas, NV Bishop Gorman High School; [D] Las Vegas, NV Clerics of St. Viator Retirement Home.
Biber, J. Morton '85 (RIC) Powhatan, VA St. John Neumann Church.
Bich, Tran Ngoc *c.ss.r.* '52 (LA) [R] Baldwin Park, CA Vietnamese Redemptorist Mission.
Bichl, William M. *s.j.* '67 (CLV) [C] Cleveland, OH John Carroll University; [C] Cleveland, OH John Carroll Jesuit Community.
Bichsel, William J. *s.j.* '59 (SEA) [C] Tacoma, WA Bellarmine Preparatory School.
Bickel, Timothy C. '92 (MIL) New Berlin, WI Holy Apostles Church.
Bickerstaff, Albert *o.s.b.* '67 (SAV) [B] Savannah, GA Benedictine Military School; [F] Savannah, GA The Benedictine Priory.
Bickett, Tony '83 (OWN) Hawesville, KY Immaculate Conception Church; Lewisport, KY St. Columba Church.
Bickle, John *o.f.m.* (NY) Manhattan, NY St. Vincent Hospital.
Bico, Anthony (NEW) Newark, NJ Essex County Youth Detention Center.
Bico, Anthony '93 (NEW) [15] Elizabeth, NJ Our Lady of Fatima Church.
Bicomong, Sergio '79 (SCR) Muncy, PA Resurrection Church.
Bicomong, Sergio '79 (TR) On Duty Outside the Diocese.
Bicsko, Stephen C. *c.m.* '70 (BRK) [U] Queens Village, NY DePaul Residence.
Bicz, Marian '88 (RVC) Franklin Square, NY St. Catherine of Sienna Church.
Biczak, Arkad '63 (SFE) [26] Albuquerque, NM St. John the Apostle Church.
Bida, John A. '73 (NY) Brewster, NY St. Lawrence O'Toole Church.
Bidawid, Kamal Warda '68 (EST) Turlock, CA St. Thomas Assyrian-Chaldean Parish.
Biddle, Ward *c.p.* '51 (FgM) Mission Procurators.
Bidinger, Bruce M. *s.j.* '86 (PH) [AA] Philadelphia, PA Jesuit Community at St. Joseph's University.
Bidwell, Michael L. '89 (CIN) [37] Cincinnati, OH Holy Trinity Church.
Bidwill, Joseph E. *o.p.* '55 (STP) [15] Minneapolis, MN St. Albert the Great Church.
Bie, Paul R. '83 (RVC) Riverhead, NY St. John the Evangelist Church.
Biebel, Msgr. William E. '62 (E) [1] Erie, PA St. Peter Cathedral.
Bieberle, Victor '51 (WCH) Retired.
Biecker, Thomas C. *s.j.* '40 (DET) [P] Clarkston, MI Colombiere Center.
Biedermann, Msgr. Arnold '45 (LA) Ventura, CA Sacred Heart Church.
Biedermann, Msgr. Arnold '49 (LA) Retired.
Bieganowski, Ronald R. *s.j.* '72 (MIL) [P] Milwaukee, WI Jesuit Community at Marquette University.
Biegler, Steven '93 (RC) McIntosh, SD St. Bonaventure's Church; McLaughlin, SD St. Bernard Church; Standing Rock, SD Standing Rock Reservation Church.
Bieh, John '63 (SPK) Pasco, WA St. Patrick Church.
Bielanski, Joseph J. '80 (STU) Absent on Leave.
Bielawa, Thomas G. *s.d.s.* '72 (PHX) Cashion, AZ St. William Church.
Bielby, Donald J. *c.s.c.* (FTW) [16] South Bend, IN St. Patrick Church.
Bielecki, Michael *o.s.a.* '83 (PH) Villanova, PA St. Thomas of Villanova Parish Community Church.
Bielek, Robert M. '74 (CLV) [43] Cleveland, OH St. Leo the Great Church.
Bielen, Msgr. Stephen A. '45 (MET) Hackettstown, NJ Assumption of the Blessed Virgin Mary Church; Retired.
Bielewicz, Harry R. '86 (PIT) [3] Butler, PA St. Paul Church.
Bielonko, Joseph '59 (WOR) Dudley, MA St. Andrew Bobola Church.
Bielskas, Edward J. '41 (GR) Retired.
Bielski, Francis V. '57 (PH) Willow Grove, PA St. David Church.
Bieluch, Chester A. '48 (HRT) Retired.
Bien, Francis P. '58 (BRK) [186] Queens, NY St. Josaphat Church.
Bien Quang Do, Joseph '64 (SD) [2] El Cajon, CA Our Lady of Grace Church.
Bienia, Michael A. '58 (GBG) Retired; [G] Greensburg, PA Neumann House.
Bieniek, Stanislaus '67 (GAL) [77] Houston, TX St. Thomas More Church.
Bienvenu, Emmett M. *s.j.* '44 (NO) [C] New Orleans, LA Loyola University; [P] New Orleans, LA Ignatius Residence.
Bienvenu, Kenneth '60 (LAF) St. Martinville, LA St. Martin of Tours Church.
Bienvenu, Paul G. '92 (LAF) Berwick, LA St. Stephen Church.
Bier, Louis C. '76 (PH) [4] Norristown, PA St. Patrick Church.
Biergans, Kent *o.f.m.conv.* (FgM) Conventual Franciscan Foreign Missions.
Biergans, Kent *o.f.m.conv.* (IND) St. Joseph Hill, IN St. Joseph Church.
Biergans, Kent *o.f.m.conv.* '67 (IND) [I] Mount Saint Francis, IN Mount Saint Francis Friary and Retreat Center; [J] Mount Saint Francis, IN Provincial Headquarters for the Conventual Franciscan Province.
Bierie, Elwyn L. '38 (DUB) Retired.
Bierman, Earl C. '57 (COV) Leave of Absence; Retired.
Biermann, John G. *s.a.c.* '69 (WDC) [B] West Hyattsville, MD Pallottine Seminary at Green Hill.
Biernacki, Jacob S. '67 (SPC) Sarcoxie, MO St. Agnes Church.
Biernat, Leon J. '92 (BUF) [1] Tonawanda, NY St. Amelia Church.
Biersack, Thomas E. '81 (MIL) New Munster, WI St. Alphonsus Church.
Bierschenk, Stephen W. '76 (DAL) [27] Dallas, TX St. Thomas Aquinas Church.
Bierster, Msgr. Leo N. '52 (HBG) Hershey, PA St. Joan of Arc Church.
Biesiada, Msgr. Louis W. (PAT) Retired.
Biesinger, Robert J. '56 (BUF) Absent on Leave; [O] Buffalo, NY Sheehan Residence for Priests.
Bietighofer, Alfred J. '65 (BGP) [4] Norwalk, CT St. Mary's Church.
Biffar, Cornelius *ss.cc.* '51 (FR) [J] Fairhaven, MA Sacred Hearts Provincial House.
Biffar, William *c.ss.r.* '47 (ORL) New Smyrna Beach, FL Sacred Heart Church.
Bigelow, William R. '67 (BUF) [30] Buffalo, NY Holy Family Church.
Biggers, Clarence J. *o.c.s.o.* '50 (ATL) [I] Conyers, GA The Monastery of the Holy Spirit.
Biggs, Anselm G. *o.s.b.* '40 (CHL) [J] Belmont, NC Belmont Abbey.
Bigley, Michael J. *s.d.s.* '87 (NSH) Lewisburg, TN St. John the Evangelist Church; Shelbyville, TN St. William Church.
Biglin, Martin J. '67 (NY) [5] New Rochelle, NY Holy Name of Jesus Church.
Bignall, Douglas J. '93 (DET) Farmington, MI Our Lady of Sorrows Church.
Bigot, Ross G. '48 (STP) Retired.
Bihler, Joseph J. '46 (BRK) Retired; [R] Queens Village, NY Queen of Peace Residence.
Bihr, Msgr. Louis J. '68 (PAT) [3] Wayne, NJ Immaculate Heart of Mary Church.
Bihuniak, Michael J. '89 (MET) Fords, NJ Our Lady of Peace Church.
Bik, Michael *o.s.b.* '93 (SCL) [I] Collegeville, MN St. John's Abbey, of the Order of St. Benedict.
Bikoma, Msgr. Edward J. '51 (EST) Chicago, IL St. Ephrem's Church; Chicago, IL Mart Mariam Parish.
Bilanych, Msgr. John '40 (PHU) [8] Philadelphia, PA Christ the King Church.
Bilicky, Louis S. '49 (BO) Maynard, MA St. Casimir Church.
Bilinsky, William (CHI) [J] Chicago, IL Resurrection Medical Center.
Bilinsky, William M. '65 (STN) Chicago, IL Resurrection and Our Lady of Resurrection.
Bill, J. Armand '56 (PRT) Retired.
Bill, Msgr. Ronald '57 (SY) Cicero, NY Sacred Heart Church.
Bill, Thomas *c.s.c.* '55 (P) [B] Portland, OR University of Portland; [L] Portland, OR Holy Cross Fathers & Brothers, C.S.C. - University of Portland.
Billac, Christopher A. *s.j.* '65 (GAL) [F] Houston, TX Strake, Jesuit College Preparatory Inc.
Biller, Andrew *s.v.d.* '61 (FgM) Society of the Divine Word Foreign Missions.
Biller, Harold N. '70 (ALT) [8] Johnstown, PA St. Patrick's Church.
Biller, Thomas P. '57 (TLS) [10] Tulsa, OK Church of the Madalene.
Billett, Robert *c.m.f.* '57 (LA) [R] Los Angeles, CA Claretian Retreat Center Community; [X] Los Angeles, CA Claretian Retreat Center (All Groups).
Billian, Michael '84 (TOL) [34] Toledo, OH St. Patrick Church.
Billian, Michael R. '84 (TOL) [B] Toledo, OH Central Catholic High School.
Billiard, Donald *o.f.m.* '83 (SFE) [J] Albuquerque, NM San Antonio Provincial Friary Franciscan Friars.
Billig, Maynard *o.f.m.* '39 (STL) [P] St. Louis, MO Franciscan Friary of St. Anthony of Padua.
Billimek, Alvin O. *c.ss.r.* '38 (STL) [P] Liguori, MO St. Clement Health Care Center.
Billinger, James J. '83 (WCH) [12] Wichita, KS St. Elizabeth Ann Seton Church.
Billings, Jerome D. '71 (STL) Shrewsbury, MO St. Michael Church.
Billman, George B. '72 (FAR) Fessenden, ND St. Augustine's Church.
Billotte, Philip J. '66 (ROC) Naples, NY St. Januarius Church.
Billotti, Joseph E. *s.j.* '63 (CI) [B] Pohnpei, FM PATS (Pohnpei Agriculture and Trade School).
Billotti, Joseph E. *s.j.* '63 (FgM) Provinces.
Billy, Dennis *c.ss.r.* '80 (WDC) [M] Washington, DC

Holy Redeemer College.
Billy, George '48 (PSC) Retired.
Bilodeau, Florent R. '57 (MAN) Hampstead, NH St. Anne Church.
Bilodeau, Leopold J. '73 (BUR) Burlington, VT Fletcher Allen Health Care.
Bilodeau, Roger '65 (MAN) Lincoln, NH St. Joseph Church.
Bilot, James '92 (DET) Bloomfield Hills, MI St. Hugo of the Hills Church.
Bilski, Harry '58 (AUS) Temple, TX V.A. Hospital.
Bilskie, Msgr. Maurilius '43 (EVN) [7] Evansville, IN Holy Rosary Church; Retired.
Bily, Msgr. Edward '51 (SAT) New Braunfels, TX SS. Peter and Paul Church.
Bily, John C. '58 (VIC) Weimar, TX St. Michael Church.
Bily, Lambert S. '63 (SAT) [20] San Antonio, TX Our Lady of Sorrows Church.
Binder, Albert (FAR) Retired.
Binder, Albert '51 (FAR) [E] Fargo, ND Riverview Place, Inc.
Binder, Mark '71 (SPC) Houston, MO St. Mark Church.
Bindner, Charles J. '58 (L) [31] Louisville, KY St. Helen Church.
Bingham, John K. *s.j.* '58 (BAL) [M] Baltimore, MD Jesuit Fathers and Brothers Maryland Provincial Curia.
Bingham, John K. *s.j.* '58 (FgM) Provinces.
Binh, John Phan Cong '51 (SHP) Retired.
Biniek, Joseph P. '78 (ARL) Dale City, VA Holy Family Church.
Biniszkiewicz, Msgr. Leonard E. '63 (BUF) [14] Niagara Falls, NY St. Teresa of the Infant Jesus Church.
Binkowski, Msgr. George '72 (STF) Fresh Meadows, NY Annunciation of the B.V.M. Church.
Binkowski, James P. '56 (LC) [I] La Crosse, WI Holy Cross (Seminary) Diocesan Center.
Binsfeld, Msgr. Michael A. '67 (RCK) Special Assignment.
Binsfeld, Steven '79 (SCL) [1] St. Cloud, MN St. Mary's Cathedral of St. Cloud.
Binzer, Joe '94 (CIN) On Duty Outside the Archdiocese.
Bionda, Bonaventure *o.f.m.* '59 (ALB) [3] Watervliet, NY Our Lady of Mt. Carmel Church.
Biondi, Lawrence *s.j.* (STL) [C] St. Louis, MO Saint Louis University.
Biondi, Lawrence H. *s.j.* '70 (STL) [C] St. Louis, MO Saint Louis University; [P] St. Louis, MO Jesuit Community Corporation at St. Louis University - Jesuit Hall.
Biondi, Nicholas A. '38 (PIT) Retired; [O] Pittsburgh, PA St. John Vianney Manor.
Biondino, Joseph P. '55 (ALB) [10] Schenectady, NY St. Joseph Church.
Biondino, Joseph P. '55 (BGP) Leave of Absence.
Biondolillo, Gabriel *o.m.i.* '56 (BEL) [F] Belleville, IL Shrine of Our Lady of the Snows.
Biosco, Emilio *o.f.m.cap.* '94 (FgM) Capuchin Foreign Missions.
Bir, Stanley *o.f.m.* '52 (CIN) [M] Cincinnati, OH St. Clement Friary.
Birarelli, Carl A. '58 (CIN) Retired.
Birch, Donald G. '67 (PH) [90] Philadelphia, PA St. Madeleine Sophie Church.
Birch, Keith L. '71 (DUB) Tama-Toledo, IA St. Patrick's Church.
Birch, Msgr. Thomas J. '59 (ALN) Shillington, PA St. John Baptist de la Salle Church; Retired.
Birchmeyer, Robert J. '73 (SY) Solvay, NY St. Cecilia Church.
Bircumshaw, Colin F. '75 (SLC) [3] Ogden, UT St. Joseph's Church; [C] Ogden, UT St. Joseph Regional School.
Bird, James F. '91 (E) Hermitage, PA Church of Notre Dame.
Bird, Stephen J. '76 (OKL) [15] Oklahoma City, OK St. Patrick Church; Special Assignment.
Birdsall, Anthony J. '60 (GB) Sturgeon Bay, WI Corpus Christi Church.
Birdsall, Hugh G. *s.d.s.* '62 (MIL) Greendale, WI St. Alphonsus Church; [B] Hales Corners, WI Sacred Heart School of Theology.
Birdsall, John M. '56 (RC) Retired.
Bireley, Robert L. *s.j.* '64 (CHI) [C] Chicago, IL Jesuit Community at Loyola University of Chicago.
Birge, George D. '56 (BGP) Newtown, CT St. Rose of Lima Church.
Biriruka, Ernest '81 (MIA) Pembroke Pines, FL St. Maximilian Kolbe Church.
Birk, John '61 (CHI) Brookfield, IL St. Barbara Church.
Birk, John '63 (SPK) Special Ministry; [G] Pasco, WA Our Lady of Lourdes Health Center.
Birk, John G. '63 (CHI) Chicago, IL Hines V.A. Hospital.
Birk, John W. '70 (L) [34] Louisville, KY Holy Name Church.
Birkel, John B. '96 (LIN) [8] Lincoln, NE St. Mary Church.
Birkel, Richard C. '96 (WDC) [G] Washington, DC Lt. Joseph P. Kennedy, Jr., Institute.
Birkel, Robert C. '49 (L) Retired.
Birkenfeld, Darryl '88 (AMA) On Duty Outside the Diocese.
Birkenhauer, Henry F. *s.j.* '45 (CLV) [E] Cleveland, OH St. Ignatius High School; [U] Cleveland, OH Jesuit Retreat House.
Birket, Dwight '72 (WCH) [16] Wichita, KS St. Margaret Mary Church.
Birkhead, Henry G. '56 (PH) [34] Philadelphia, PA Christ the King Church.
Birkle, Walter A. '58 (NY) [172] Bronx, NY Our Lady of Grace Church; [Q] Bronx, NY District Council of the Bronx.
Birkmaier, James E. '68 (GF) [G] Great Falls, MT Benefis Health Care.
Birkmeyer, John R. *c.s.c.* '57 (AUS) [H] Austin, TX Congregation of Holy Cross - Southern Province.
Birmingham, Kevin M. '97 (CHI) Blue Island, IL St. Benedict Church.
Birmingham, Robert F. '93 (HRT) Middlebury, CT St. John of the Cross Church.
Biron, Gerald R. *m.s.* '60 (SPR) [1] Westfield, MA Holy Trinity Church.
Biron, Robert G. '74 (MAN) Somersworth, NH St. Martin Church.
Biroschak, Robert V. '93 (LA) Graduate Studies.
Birringer, Raphael *s.d.s.* '51 (MIL) [P] Milwaukee, WI Salvatorian Provincial Residence.
Birzer, W. L. '39 (DOD) Retired.
Bisaillon, Rene '59 (HON) Waipahu, HI St. Joseph Church.
Bisbal, Pedro J. Silva *o.m.* '75 (CGS) Cayey, PR Nuestra Senora de la Asuncion Church.
Bisbee, Burnell B. *s.j.* '75 (OM) [C] Omaha, NE Creighton Preparatory School.
Bischko, Kenneth *t.o.r.* '64 (SP) [4] Clearwater, FL St. Cecelia Church.
Bischof, Donald R. (PIT) Beaver Falls, PA Divine Mercy Church.
Bischof, Simon *o.s.b.* '55 (SCL) [5] St. Cloud, MN St. Augustine Church.
Bischoff, Albert J. *s.j.* '56 (IND) [D] Indianapolis, IN Brebeuf Jesuit Preparatory School, Inc.
Bischoff, Msgr. Francis J. (PAT) Retired.
Bisenius, Thomas R. '54 (DUB) Garryowen, IA St. Patrick's Church.
Bisgrove, Charles *s.c.j.* '90 (MIL) Franklin, WI Sacred Hearts of Jesus and Mary Church; St. Martins, WI Holy Assumption Church.
Bishara, Boctor '51 (LA) [K] Lynwood, CA St. Francis Medical Center.
Bisharat, George Said '92 (NTN) North Hollywood, CA St. Anne Church.
Bishop, Benedict *o.c.d.* '54 (BO) [W] Brighton, MA Carmelite Monastery.
Bishop, E. Louis *s.j.* '64 (PHX) [B] Phoenix, AZ Brophy College Preparatory.
Bishop, Joseph E. '58 (SAC) Yuba City, CA St. Isidore Church.
Bishop, Patrick '45 (OAK) [2] Fremont, CA Holy Spirit Church.
Bishop, Patrick A. '74 (ATL) [4] Marietta, GA Church of the Transfiguration.
Bishop, Robert *c.m.f.* '71 (LA) [R] Rancho Dominguez, CA Dominguez Seminary Inc.
Bishop, Thomas A. '75 (CHI) Buffalo Grove, IL St. Mary Church.
Bishop, Thomas G. '70 (Y) [4] Canton, OH St. Anthony's Church.
Bisignano, Joseph J. '81 (NY) Beacon, NY St. John Evangelist Church.
Bismonte, Honesto '54 (LA) Gardena, CA St. Anthony of Padua Church.
Bisoffi, Joseph L. *o.s.cam.* '72 (MIL) [K] Milwaukee, WI St. Francis Hospital; [P] Wauwatosa, WI St. Camillus Community House.
Bispels, William J. '61 (PH) [74] Philadelphia, PA St. Jerome Church.
Bisson, Andrew R. '93 (PRT) [I] Kennebunkport, ME St. Anthony's Friary.
Bisson, Eddy N. '68 (MAN) Laconia, NH Sacred Heart Church.
Bisson, Joseph *s.v.d.* '63 (FgM) Society of the Divine Word Foreign Missions.
Bisson, Roger *m.afr.* '55 (WDC) [M] Washington, DC Missionaries of Africa.
Bissonette, James '88 (DUL) Carlton, MN St. Francis Church.
Bissonnette, Bernard (NOR) On Duty Outside the Diocese.
Bissot, Robert H. '57 (GAY) West Branch, MI St. Joseph Church.
Bistany, Msgr. Joseph '37 (SAM) Retired.
Bistricky, Frederick J. '65 (MIL) Retired.
Biszek, Msgr. Robert J. '65 (ALN) [4] Bethlehem, PA Holy Infancy Church.
Bitanga, Msgr. Fred A. '64 (SFR) [41] San Francisco, CA St. Patrick Church.
Bitangjol, Albert P. '56 (SFR) Retired.
Bitsko, Daniel J. (PSC) Westbury, NY St. Andrew the Apostle Church.
Bitsko, Daniel J. '65 (PSC) Smithtown, NY Resurrection Church.
Bittel, Patrick M. '82 (OWN) Morganfield, KY St. Ann's Church.
Bitterman, John L. *s.s.* '69 (BAL) [M] Baltimore, MD Sulpician Provincial House.
Bittmenn, David '94 (SLC) Milford, UT St. Bridget Church.
Bittner, Gregory T. '85 (BIR) Pell City, AL Our Lady of the Lake Church.
Bittner, Joseph A. *s.j.* '39 (BAL) [M] Baltimore, MD Jesuit Fathers and Brothers Maryland Provincial Curia.
Bittner, Joseph H. *s.j.* '39 (FgM) Provinces.
Bittner, Wayne W. '64 (MIL) Plymouth, WI St. John the Baptist Church.
Bitz, Al '69 (FAR) Casselton, ND St. Leo Church.
Biven, Louis Russell '57 (MOB) [17] Mobile, AL Our Savior Church.
Bizaca, Mate '73 (LA) San Pedro, CA Mary, Star of the Sea Church.
Bizkarra, Juan *s.j.* '35 (CI) Angaur, FM Holy Rosary Church.
Bjorklund, Brian '66 (DET) Military Chaplains.
Bjorum, James L. '76 (DET) [1] St. Clair Shores, MI St. Germaine Church.
Blacet, Msgr. William J. '46 (KC) [28] Kansas City, MO Our Lady of Good Counsel Church.
Blach, Leo M. '53 (DEN) Retired.
Black, Alvin *o.f.m.* '60 (SCR) [12] Wilkes-Barre, PA St. Joseph Church; [M] Wilkes-Barre, PA St. Joseph's Friary.
Black, Frank A. '80 (BRK) [154] Queens, NY St. Bartholomew's Church.
Black, James P. '88 (COL) [1] Columbus, OH St. Joseph Cathedral.
Black, Joseph '56 (P) Junction City, OR St. Helen Church; Monroe, OR St. Rose Church; Veneta, OR St. Catherine of Siena Church.
Blackall, John C. '51 (HRT) [9] Waterbury, CT St. Cecilia's Church; [T] Waterbury, CT Spanish-Speaking Center.
Blackall, L. Randall '54 (HRT) Glastonbury, CT St. Paul's Church.
Blackburn, Clifford *o.m.i.* '47 (SAT) [K] San Antonio, TX Oblate Madonna Residence; [M] San Antonio, TX Provincial Administration Office, Oblates of Mary Immaculate (Southern Prov.).
Blackburn, David *o.c.s.o.* '54 (SPC) [E] Ava, MO Assumption Abbey (Trappist).
Blackburn, Michael *o.f.m.* '86 (LAV) [10] Las Vegas, NV St. James the Apostle Church.
Blackowski, Theodore A. *o.f.m.* '45 (SP) [O] St. Petersburg, FL St. Anthony Friary.
Blackwell, Edward '76 (HBG) On Duty Outside the Diocese.
Blackwell, Edward A. '76 (MIA) [B] Opa Locka, FL St. Thomas University.
Blackwell, Maurice J. '74 (BAL) [29] Baltimore, MD St. Edward Church.
Blackwell, Michael J. '73 (WDC) Landover Hills, MD St. Mary's Catholic Church.
Blackwood, Wallace E. '67 (BO) [2] Peabody, MA St. Ann Church.
Bladt, Joel S. *s.t.* '61 (SAV) Bainbridge, GA St. Joseph's Church.
Blaes, James F. *c.s.c.* '55 (FTW) [17] South Bend, IN Faith & Hope & Charity Chapel Church; [J] South Bend, IN Congregation of Holy Cross Indiana Province Provincial House.
Blaes, Paul '51 (KC) Retired.
Blaeser, Alfred A. '32 (BRK) Retired.
Blaeser, Donald P. *o.f.m.* '70 (GRY) [J] Cedar Lake, IN San Damiano Friary.
Blaetter, James R. *s.j.* '80 (BGP) [O] Fairfield, CT The Fairfield Jesuit Community-Fairfield University.
Blaettler, James R. *s.j.* '80 (BGP) [A] Fairfield, CT Fairfield University.
Blaha, John (GB) [5] Appleton, WI St. Pius X Church.
Blaha, John F. '75 (GB) On Duty Outside the Diocese.
Blain, Lionel A. '54 (PRO) [7] Woonsocket, RI St. Joseph Church.
Blaine, James E. '77 (SLC) American Fork, UT St. Peter's Church; Draper, UT State Penitentiary.
Blaine, Michael '91 (PH) [D] Philadelphia, PA St. Maria Goretti High School.
Blaine, Michael J. '91 (PH) [110] Philadelphia, PA Nativity of the Blessed Virgin Mary Church.
Blair, Guy *s.c.j.* '82 (MIL) [P] Hales Corners, WI Sacred Heart Monastery.
Blair, Guy A. *s.c.j.* '82 (MAD) [9] Madison, WI Saint Joseph Church.
Blair, Msgr. Leonard P. '76 (DET) Grosse Pointe Farms, MI St. Paul Catholic Church.
Blair, Msgr. Raymond O. '60 (MAN) On Duty Outside the Diocese.
Blais, Denis *c.p.m.* '93 (OWN) [F] South Union, KY Fathers of Mercy.
Blais, George P. '90 (ORG) El Toro, CA Santiago de Compostela Church.

Blais, Jean *s.d.s.* '64 (MIL) [P] Milwaukee, WI Salvatorian Provincial Residence.
Blais, Melvin J. '42 (STP) Retired.
Blais, Robert L. '63 (PRO) Absent on Leave.
Blais, Robert R. *o.p.* '68 (L) [47] Louisville, KY St. Louis Bertrand Church.
Blais, Roger '50 (KC) On Duty Outside the Diocese.
Blais, Roland O. '44 (MAN) [9] Manchester, NH St. George Church; Retired.
Blake, Andrew P. '63 (RVC) Sag Harbor, NY St. Andrew's Church.
Blake, Carlyle *c.ss.r.* (OAK) [N] Oakland, CA Redemptorists.
Blake, David *o.f.m.* (BUF) [59] Buffalo, NY SS. Rita & Patrick Church.
Blake, David D. *o.f.m.* '95 (BUF) [O] St. Bonaventure, NY St. Bonaventure Friary.
Blake, John Vincent *o.p.* '51 (SFE) [29] Albuquerque, NM St. Thomas Aquinas University Parish.
Blake, Peter M. '84 (STL) Union, MO Immaculate Conception Church.
Blake, Philip C. *s.j.* '61 (SJ) [L] Los Altos, CA Jesuit Retreat House.
Blake, Richard *s.j.* '69 (BO) [W] Chestnut Hill, MA The Jesuit Community at Boston College.
Blake, Robert '77 (SR) Cloverdale, CA St. Peter's Church.
Blake, William B. '63 (SCR) Jessup, PA St. James Church.
Blakely, Leonard J. '80 (WIL) Chestertown, MD Sacred Heart Church; Chestertown, MD Washington College; [O] Chestertown, MD Washington College Newman Center; [O] Newark, DE Univ. of Delaware Newman Center.
Blakely, Paige A. '84 (ORL) DeBary, FL St. Ann's Church.
Blaker, John '96 (OAK) Dublin, CA St. Raymond Church.
Blanch, Jose Maria *s.f.* '51 (SFE) Santa Cruz, NM Holy Cross Church.
Blanchard, David *o.carm.* (WDC) [M] Washington, DC Carmelite Community.
Blanchard, David *o.carm.* '87 (WDC) [B] Washington, DC Whitefriars Hall.
Blanchard, Donald V. '69 (BR) [12] Baton Rouge, LA St. Jean Vianney Church.
Blanchard, John L. *s.j.* '48 (DET) [P] Clarkston, MI Colombiere Center.
Blanchard, Peter *s.m.* '67 (NO) [F] Covington, LA The St. Paul's School.
Blanchet, Leo '86 (MOB) Whistler, AL St. Bridget Church.
Blanchette, Brian D. '85 (PRT) Calais, ME Immaculate Conception Church.
Blanchette, Melvin C. *s.s.* '46 (BAL) [M] Baltimore, MD Sulpician Provincial House.
Blanchette, Michael '84 (JOL) Absent on Leave.
Blanchette, Oliver R. *a.a.* '44 (WOR) Fiskdale, MA St. Anne's and St. Patrick's Church.
Blanchette, Roger E. *s.j.* '64 (HEL) [5] Missoula, MT St. Francis Xavier Church; [E] Missoula, MT St. Patrick Hospital Corporation.
Blanchfield, David W. '82 (BGP) [1] Norwalk, CT St. Jerome Church.
Blanchfield, John P. '50 (HRT) Plantsville, CT St. Aloysius Church.
Blanchfield, Joseph J. '41 (PH) Norwood, PA St. Gabriel Church; Retired.
Blanco, Adalberto '77 (LA) Santa Monica, CA St. Anne Church.
Blanco, Gonzalo *o.s.b.* '92 (BIS) [A] Richardton, ND Assumption Abbey.
Blanco, Gonzalo *o.s.b.* '92 (FgM) American - Cassinese Congregation Foreign Missions.
Blanco, Ignacio *c.m.f.* '51 (SAT) [12] San Antonio, TX Immaculate Heart of Mary Church.
Blanco, John *s.d.b.* '64 (NY) [2] Port Chester, NY Corpus Christi Church.
Blanco, Joseph J. '84 (DEN) Roggen, CO Sacred Heart Church.
Blanco, Telesforo R. *o.s.a.* '60 (BEA) [1] Port Arthur, TX Our Lady of Guadalupe Church.
Bland, Thomas A. '74 (SAC) Auburn, CA St. Joseph Church.
Blanda, William C. '91 (LAF) Kaplan, LA Our Lady of the Holy Rosary Church.
Blandford, James T. '38 (LEX) Retired.
Blandino, Salvatore '53 (SJ) Retired.
Blaney, Jim *o.m.i.* '65 (JUN) Craig, AK St. John by the Sea Church.
Blaney, Robert M. '92 (BO) [3] Peabody, MA St. John the Baptist Church; Graduate Studies.
Blangiardi, B. Jeffrey *s.j.* '86 (BO) [W] Boston, MA The Society of Jesus of New England-Provincial Offices.
Blangiardi, Jeffrey *s.j.* '86 (ORG) Laguna Hills, CA St. Nicholas Church.
Blank, Godfrey *o.f.m.* '45 (SFE) [1] Santa Fe, NM The Cathedral of San Francisco de Asis.
Blank, Severius '58 (FWT) Burkburnett, TX St. Jude Thaddeus Church.
Blank, William H. '87 (NO) Franklinton, LA Holy Family Church.
Blankenship, John P. '63 (RIC) Colonial Heights, VA St. Ann Church; Petersburg, VA Federal Correctional Institution.
Blankinship, Calvin, Jr. '96 (B) Idaho Falls, ID Holy Rosary Church.
Blantz, James *c.s.c.* '56 (LA) [P] Chatsworth, CA Rancho San Antonio.
Blantz, Thomas E. *c.s.c.* '60 (FTW) [B] Notre Dame, IN University of Notre Dame Du Lac; [J] Notre Dame, IN Holy Cross Community, Corby Hall, University of Notre Dame.
Blaschko, Harvey *o.p.* '81 (CHI) [13] Chicago, IL Angel Guardian Croatian Catholic Mission Church; [N] Chicago, IL Croatian Dominican Fathers.
Blasco, Ignacio '62 (MIA) [21] Miami, FL St. Joachim Church.
Blascovich, Joseph D. '75 (HBG) Elizabethtown, PA St. Peter Church; [K] Harrisburg, PA Catholic Campus Ministry.
Blaser, John R. '64 (TOL) [30] Toledo, OH St. Louis Church; [41] Toledo, OH St. Thomas Aquinas Church.
Blasich, Bernard '67 (CHI) Evergreen Park, IL St. Bernadette Church.
Blaska, John A. '53 (DET) Clawson, MI Guardian Angels Church; Retired.
Blastic, Michael *o.f.m.conv.* (BUF) [C] St. Bonaventure, NY St. Bonaventure University.
Blastic, Michael *o.f.m.conv.* '73 (BUF) [O] St. Bonaventure, NY St. Bonaventure Friary.
Blaszczyk, Thaddeus J. '53 (DET) [2] Troy, MI St. Alan Church.
Blattner, Joseph H. '58 (PRT) Benedicta, ME St. Benedict's Church; Island Falls, ME St. Agnes Church.
Blattner, Joseph H. '58 (STL) On Duty Outside the Archdiocese.
Blaufuss, Tony '58 (KCK) Ottawa, KS Sacred Heart Church.
Blauvelt, Robert W. '59 (BRK) [233] Queens, NY Resurrection-Ascension Church.
Blay, Msgr. Roberto Garcia '86 (PCE) [3] Ponce, PR Church of the Resurrection.
Blazak, Camillus W. '51 (BIR) Scottsboro, AL St. Jude Church.
Blazejewski, Richard J. '74 (BUF) Perry, NY St. Stanislaus Kostka Church.
Blazejewski, Richard W. '74 (BUF) Perry, NY St. Joseph Church.
Blazek, David J. '97 (DET) Centerline, MI St. Clement Church.
Blazek, Eugene E. '76 (HON) Military Chaplains.
Blazek, James F. '79 (CHI) [94] Chicago, IL Immaculate Heart of Mary Church.
Blazek, John *c.s.c.* '58 (CLV) [E] Gates Mills, OH Gilmour Academy.
Blazewicz, William J. '59 (LC) Mondovi, WI Sacred Heart of Jesus Church.
Blazine, James A. '62 (BEL) [7] Belleville, IL St. Mary Church; Fayetteville, IL St. Pancratius Church.
Bleaux, Floyd J., Jr. '73 (OG) [1] Plattsburgh, NY Our Lady of Victory Church.
Blecha, Charles A. (LC) Menomonie, WI St. Joseph Church.
Blecha, Charles A. '40 (LC) Retired.
Blecha, Jordan R. *o.praem.* '39 (GB) [I] De Pere, WI St. Norbert Abbey.
Blee, Edward C. *s.m.* '55 (HON) [15] Honolulu, HI Star of the Sea Church.
Blee, Michael J. *s.j.* '37 (PH) [AA] Philadelphia, PA Jesuit Community at St. Joseph's University.
Blehl, Vincent F. *s.j.* '52 (NY) [DD] New York, NY Jesuit Provincial's Office.
Bleich, Msgr. Russell M. '60 (DUB) [4] Waterloo, IA St. Edward's Church; [D] Waterloo, IA Columbus High School.
Bleichner, Howard P. '67 (PIT) On Duty Outside the Diocese.
Bleichner, Howard P. *s.s.* '67 (WDC) [A] Washington, DC Theological College of the Catholic University of America; [C] Washington, DC Catholic University of America, The.
Bleiler, William C. '82 (CHR) Absent On Leave.
Bleiler, William James '66 (CAM) Cedarville, NJ St. Michael's Church.
Bleilevens, Msgr. Charles A. '50 (BRK) [153] Queens, NY Ascension Church; Retired.
Blenker, Ambrose J. '62 (LC) Plum City, WI St. John the Baptist Church.
Blenkle, Joseph A. '90 (NY) Cortlandt Manor, NY St. Columbanus Church.
Blesnuk, Donald J. '85 (BUF) On Duty Outside the Diocese.
Blesnuk, Donald J. *m.m.* '85 (FgM) Maryknoll Foreign Missions.
Blessin, Thomas '63 (NEW) [B] Jersey City, NJ Saint Peter's College.
Blessin, Thomas C. *s.j.* '63 (NEW) [N] Jersey City, NJ Jesuits of Saint Peter's College, Inc.
Blessing, Howard '76 (LAF) [14] Lafayette, LA St. Mary, Mother of the Church.
Blessing, Loren *o.f.m.* '81 (FRS) [7] Fresno, CA St. Anthony of Padua Church.
Blessinger, James C. '64 (EVN) [1] Vincennes, IN Sacred Heart Church.
Blessington, Msgr. William H. '43 (DUB) Retired.
Blethen, John '49 (SD) [H] San Diego, CA Augustinian Community.
Blewett, John E. *s.j.* '53 (MIL) [P] Milwaukee, WI Jesuit Provincial Office, Wisconsin Province.
Blewett, John E. *s.j.* '53 (STL) [P] St. Louis, MO Jesuit Community Corporation at St. Louis University - Jesuit Hall.
Blicharski, Michael *s.o.cist.* '93 (CHI) [N] Willow Springs, IL Cistercian Fathers.
Blick, Ned '92 (WCH) [19] Wichita, KS St. Thomas Aquinas Church.
Blickhan, Donald '74 (SFD) Military Chaplains.
Blighton, Francis E. '74 (ROC) [12] Rochester, NY St. Charles Borromeo Church.
Blind, Thomas '81 (NEW) Summit, NJ St. Teresa's Church.
Blinn, Mark R. '43 (CLV) [3] Garfield Heights, OH St. Therese Church; Retired.
Blinn, Richard J. *s.j.* '69 (SAC) Davis, CA St. James Church.
Bliss, Michael '91 (PEO) [J] Peoria, IL St. Francis' Medical Center.
Bliszcz, Michael '87 (SJP) Carnegie, PA Holy Trinity Church.
Bliven, Edmond '50 (P) Retired.
Bliven, Robert *o.s.c.* '56 (PHX) [4] Glendale, AZ St. Louis The King Church.
Bliven, Robert J. *o.s.c.* '56 (PHX) [F] Phoenix, AZ Crosier Community of Phoenix (Canons Regular of the Order of the Holy Cross).
Blizard, David '70 (WOR) Absent on Leave.
Blocher, James *c.s.b.* '75 (VIC) Wharton, TX Our Lady of Mt. Carmel Church.
Block, John G. (PMB) On Duty Outside the Diocese.
Blockley, Matthew '96 (CHK) San Jose Village, District 7, MP San Jose Parish.
Blocklinger, James L. '66 (DUB) [2] Cedar Rapids, IA All Saints Church.
Bloh, John F. '64 (CAM) Swedesboro, NJ St. Joseph's Church.
Bloh, Stephen R. '81 (PH) Absent on Sick Leave.
Blom, Gerald '79 (NY) Middletown, NY St. Joseph Church.
Blomberg, John '59 (STL) [21] St. Louis, MO St. Aloysius Gonzaga Church.
Bloms, Burton *o.s.b.* '45 (SCL) [I] Collegeville, MN St. John's Abbey, of the Order of St. Benedict.
Blong, Delbert F. '52 (PBL) Retired.
Blonigen, Aloysius *c.m.m.* '65 (DET) [K] Dearborn Heights, MI Our Lady of Grace Monastery.
Blonski, Joachim '92 (GLP) Waterflow, NM Sacred Heart Church.
Blood, Bernard M. *s.m.m.* '50 (RVC) West Islip, NY Good Samaritan Hospital Medical Center; [I] West Islip, NY Good Samaritan Hospital Medical Center; [N] Bay Shore, NY Montfort Missionaries.
Blood, Francis X. '79 (STL) [30] St. Louis, MO St. Cecilia Church.
Bloom, Phillip '71 (SEA) [24] Seattle, WA Holy Family Church.
Bloom, R. Frederick '52 (WDC) Retired.
Blostic, Leonard *t.o.r.* '63 (ALT) [10] Johnstown, PA St. Anthony's Church; [D] Johnstown, PA Good Samaritan Medical Center.
Blotsky, Hugo L. '88 (BIS) Garrison, ND St. Nicholas Church; [A] Richardton, ND Assumption Abbey.
Blottman, William P. '65 (FR) [2] Taunton, MA Our Lady of the Immaculate Conception Church.
Blough, E. C. '33 (PEO) Retired.
Blough, E. C. '37 (PEO) [L] Peoria, IL St. Augustine Manor.
Blough, William G. '58 (PIT) Retired.
Blout, Daniel L. '86 (GBG) [4] Greensburg, PA St. Paul Church; [C] Greensburg, PA Greensburg Central Catholic High School.
Blow, Thomas *o.f.m.* (BUF) [C] St. Bonaventure, NY St. Bonaventure University.
Blow, Thomas *o.f.m.* '87 (BUF) [O] St. Bonaventure, NY St. Bonaventure Friary.
Blowers, Leslie F. *m.m.* '63 (CIN) [M] Cincinnati, OH The Catholic Foreign Mission Society of America, Inc.; [V] Cincinnati, OH St. Andrew Kim Korean Catholic Society.
Blubaugh, Homer D. '69 (COL) Westerville, OH St. Paul the Apostle Church.
Bludnicki, Dennis G. '75 (BGP) [2] Bridgeport, CT St. Ambrose Church.
Blue, Peter W. *o.s.b.* '70 (FgM) Ottilien Congregation Foreign Missions.
Blue, Peter W. *o.s.b.* '70 (PAT) [M] Newton, NJ St. Paul's Abbey.
Blue Jacket, David '88 (DEN) Littleton, CO St. Mary Church.
Bluett, Anthony '69 (ORL) Winter Haven, FL St. Joseph's Church.
Bluett, James K. '67 (PT) Military Chaplains.

Bluett, John J. '63 (ORL) Winter Springs, FL St. Stephen Church.
Blum, John J. '96 (SP) Tarpon Springs, FL St. Ignatius Church.
Blum, Msgr. Orville '62 (AMA) Hereford, TX St. Anthony's Church.
Blum, Owen *o.f.m.* '38 (SFD) [K] Sherman, IL Our Lady of Angels Friary.
Blum, Stephen J. '76 (TOL) Vermilion, OH St. Mary Church.
Blum, William G. *c.s.c.* '65 (FTW) [L] Notre Dame, IN Holy Cross Mission House.
Bluma, Dacian *o.f.m.* '49 (MIL) [P] Burlington, WI Queen of Peace Friary.
Blume, Michael *s.v.d.* '72 (FgM) Society of the Divine Word Foreign Missions.
Blumeyer, A. James *s.j.* (STL) [C] St. Louis, MO Saint Louis University; [C] St. Louis, MO Saint Louis University.
Blumeyer, A. James *s.j.* '63 (STL) [P] St. Louis, MO Jesuit Community Corporation at St. Louis University - Jesuit Hall.
Blumm, John L. *m.s.* '45 (LKC) De Quincy, LA Our Lady of La Salette Church.
Blute, Robert H. '56 (BO) [1] Peabody, MA St. Adelaide Church.
Bly, Walter J. '64 (FTW) [7] South Bend, IN Corpus Christi Church; [C] South Bend, IN Saint Joseph's High School.
Blyman, Robert Y. '71 (RVC) [N] Uniondale, NY St. Pius X Residence.
Blyskosz, Joseph J. (FR) West Harwich, MA Holy Trinity Church.
Boackle, H. Paul '89 (SAM) Dover, NH St. George Church.
Boadt, Lawrence *c.s.p.* '69 (NEW) [S] Mahwah, NJ Paulist Press.
Boadt, Lawrence E. *c.s.p.* '69 (NY) [41] New York, NY Good Shepherd Church.
Boadt, Lawrence E. *c.s.p.* '69 (WDC) [B] Washington, DC St. Paul's College.
Boarman, Leon J. *c.s.c.* (AUS) [H] Austin, TX St. Joseph Hall.
Boarman, Leon J. *c.s.c.* '37 (AUS) [H] Austin, TX Congregation of Holy Cross - Southern Province.
Boateng-Mensah, John '73 (PT) [1] Tallahassee, FL Co-Cathedral of St. Thomas More.
Bobadilla, Tomas (NY) Haverstraw, NY St. Peter Church.
Bobal, Msgr. Joseph K. '63 (E) Ridgway, PA St. Leo the Great Church.
Boban, Dujo *o.f.m.* '69 (SJ) [26] San Jose, CA St. Mary of the Assumption Church.
Bobber, Ray *o.f.m.* '57 (FWT) [G] Crowley, TX St. Francis Village, Inc.
Bobber, Raymar *o.f.m.* '57 (FWT) [H] Crowley, TX St. Maximilian Kolbe Friary.
Bober, Bernard '62 (STU) Retired.
Bober, Charles S. '72 (PIT) [54] Pittsburgh, PA St. John Vianney Church.
Bober, Francis J. '69 (WDC) Retired.
Bober, Marjan L. '63 (CAM) Collings Lakes, NJ Our Lady of the Lakes Church.
Bober, Richard J. '57 (CLV) [2] Euclid, OH St. Felicitas Church.
Bobersky, Michael '35 (STN) Retired.
Bobrek, Edwin *o.f.m.* '51 (NY) [DD] New York, NY Franciscan Province of the Immaculate Conception.
Boburek, Aurelius *o.s.b.* '57 (IND) [J] St. Meinrad, IN St. Meinrad Archabbey.
Bocad, Deo '74 (NEW) East Orange, NJ East Orange Hospital; Orange, NJ Hospital Center at Orange.
Boccaccio, Michael A. '71 (BGP) [6] Norwalk, CT St. Philip Church.
Boccali, Ronald *p.i.m.e.* '60 (COL) [H] Newark, OH P.I.M.E. Mission & Prayer Center.
Boccardi, Raymond C. '52 (PIT) Coylesville, PA St. John Church.
Boccieri, Ronald J. *m.m.* '62 (ALB) [S] Saratoga, NY Skidmore College.
Boccieri, Ronald J. *m.m.* '62 (NY) [DD] Maryknoll, NY Maryknoll Fathers and Brothers.
Boccio, Msgr. Charles P. '61 (BRK) [181] Queens, NY Immaculate Conception Church.
Boccio, Msgr. Charles P. '61 (NY) Bronx, NY Veterans Administration Hospital.
Bochenek, Joseph G. '71 (BAL) [19] Baltimore, MD St. Brigid Church.
Bochicchio, Paul L. '71 (NEW) [1] Garfield, NJ Our Lady of Mt. Virgin Church.
Bochinski, Mark J. '58 (SCR) Avoca, PA SS. Peter and Paul Church.
Bochnak, Zenon A. '85 (MET) Martinsville, NJ Blessed Sacrament Church.
Bocian, Msgr. Ronald C. '72 (ALN) Cumbola, PA St. Anthony of Padua Church; [C] Pottsville, PA Nativity B.V.M. High School.
Bocianowski, Thaddeus Nicholas '71 (BUF) [2] Buffalo, NY St. Adalbert's Basilica Church.
Bocianski, Andrew B. '26 (SCR) Retired.
Bock, Lawrence R. '62 (HRT) Simsbury, CT St. Mary's Church.
Bockenfeld, Elgar *o.f.m.* '44 (STP) St. Benedict, MN St. Benedict Church; Union Hill, MN St. John the Evangelist Church.
Bocklage, Richard F. *s.j.* '55 (DEN) [M] Denver, CO Xavier Jesuit Center.
Bockskopf, Richard J. '70 (STL) Maryland Heights, MO St. Blaise Church.
Bocod, Dioscoro P. (NEW) [2] Orange, NJ Our Lady of the Valley Church.
Boczek, Zenon *s.d.s.* '96 (GRY) [J] Merrillville, IN Salvatorian Fathers (Society of the Divine Savior).
Bodah, Henry J. '78 (PRO) [20] Providence, RI St. Joseph Church; [S] Providence, RI Brown University.
Bodart, William D. '61 (TOL) Kirby, OH St. Mary Church; Upper Sandusky, OH St. Peter Church.
Bodde, Frederick A. '53 (DET) Retired.
Bodden, Charles J. *o.s.a.* '78 (CHI) [N] Olympia Fields, IL The Augustinian Provincialate Tolentine Center.
Bodden, Charles J. *o.s.a.* '78 (FgM) Foreign Missions.
Bodden, Clarence *c.ss.r.* '49 (LA) Whittier, CA St. Mary of the Assumption Church; [R] Whittier, CA Redemptorist Fathers Mission House.
Boddie, James R., Jr. '78 (STA) [20] Jacksonville, FL St. Pius the Fifth Church.
Boddie, John D. '88 (RIC) Mathews, VA Church of Francis de Sales; Middlesex County, VA Church of the Visitation.
Bodenschatz, Ronald *t.o.r.* '49 (ALT) [F] Loretto, PA Mount Assisi Friary.
Bodenstedt, James A. *m.m.* '56 (SJ) [M] Los Altos, CA Maryknoll.
Bodensteiner, Peter C. '45 (DUB) Retired.
Bodero, Fortunato *o.p.* '66 (PCE) Yauco, PR Holy Rossary Church.
Bodnar, Edward W. *s.j.* '52 (WDC) [M] Washington, DC The Jesuit Community at Georgetown University.
Bodo, Murray L. *o.f.m.* '64 (CIN) [M] Cincinnati, OH Pleasant Street Friary.
Bodziak, Charles F. '67 (ALT) [2] Barnesboro, PA St. Stanislaus Kostka Church; [4] Barnesboro, PA Christ the King Church.
Bodziony, Ralph A. '58 (CLV) [37] Cleveland, OH St. John Cantius Church.
Boeckman, Floyd B. *o.m.i.* '55 (BEL) [F] Belleville, IL Shrine of Our Lady of the Snows; [J] Belleville, IL Missionary Association of Mary Immaculate-Missionary Oblates of Mary Immaculate.
Boeckman, John R. '84 (E) [1] Farrell, PA Holy Trinity Church; [3] Farrell, PA St. Adalbert Church.
Boeding, Damian '52 (SPC) Retired.
Boedy, Thomas G. *s.j.* '70 (STP) Delano, MN St. Joseph Church; Delano, MN St. Peter Church; [N] Minneapolis, MN La Storta Jesuit Community.
Boeff, Dismas *o.s.b.* '76 (CLV) Brook Park, OH St. Peter the Apostle Church; Cleveland, OH SouthWest General Hospital; [P] Cleveland, OH Benedictine Order of Cleveland.
Boegel, Joseph L. *c.m.* '49 (PH) [AA] Philadelphia, PA Congregation of the Mission.
Boeglin, John '78 (EVN) Jasper, IN Holy Family Church.
Boehm, Claude L. *c.s.c.* '35 (FTW) [J] South Bend, IN Congregation of Holy Cross Indiana Province Provincial House.
Boehm, Msgr. James A. '58 (STU) Wintersville, OH Blessed Sacrament Church.
Boehm, Michael (STL) [W] St. Louis, MO Archdiocesan Stewardship Education Committee.
Boehm, Michael '75 (CHI) [4] Waukegan, IL Holy Family Church.
Boehm, Michael P. '94 (STL) Kirkwood, MO St. Peter Church.
Boehman, John R. *o.f.m.* '59 (CIN) [M] Cincinnati, OH St. Francis Seraph Friary.
Boehme, Arnold *o.c.d.* '68 (MIL) [P] Milwaukee, WI Provincial Offices - Discalced Carmelites.
Boehme, Ferdinand J. '97 (LIN) McCook, NE St. Patrick Church.
Boehme, Walter E. *s.j.* '70 (OM) [7] Omaha, NE St. Benedict the Moor Church; [K] Omaha, NE Jesuit Community At Creighton University.
Boehmicke, Roger A. '38 (L) [66] Louisville, KY St. Pius X Church; Louisville, KY Audubon Regional Medical Center; Retired.
Boehning, John A. '62 (NY) [118] New York, NY St. Thomas More Church.
Boeke, Aloysius B. '41 (CIN) Fort Loramie, OH St. Michael's Church; Retired.
Boeke, Anselm F. '43 (CIN) Piqua, OH St. Mary Church; Retired.
Boekelman, Timothy J. (SC) Duncombe, IA St. Joseph's Church.
Boekelman, Timothy J. '77 (SC) Moorland, IA Our Lady of Good Counsel Church.
Boel, Joseph H. *s.j.* (DET) [B] Berkley, MI Loyola House.
Boel, Joseph H. *s.j.* '59 (CHI) [N] Chicago, IL Chicago Province of the Society of Jesus-Provincial Office.
Boensch, Gregory A. '94 (CC) Freer, TX St. Mary Church.
Boenzi, Joseph *s.d.b.* '79 (OAK) [A] Berkeley, CA Dominican School of Philosophy and Theology; [N] Berkeley, CA Salesian Community.
Boes, Clair L. '65 (SC) Storm Lake, IA St. Mary's Church.
Boes, Marvin J. '62 (SC) [3] Sioux City, IA St. Boniface Church.
Boes, Steven (OM) [O] Winnebago, NE St. Augustine's Indian Mission.
Boes, Steven '85 (OM) Walthill, NE St. Joseph Church; Winnebago, NE St. Augustine's Church.
Boesche, Walfrid *o.f.m.* '38 (SFD) [K] Sherman, IL Our Lady of Angels Friary.
Boesel, Msgr. James E. '54 (RVC) Hicksville, NY Our Lady of Mercy Church.
Boeshans, Msgr. Francis G. '48 (NO) Lacombe, LA St. John of the Cross Church.
Boesmans, Camilo *c.i.c.m.* '47 (FgM) Missionhurst Foreign Missions.
Boessen, Msgr. Bernard H. '50 (STL) [1] St. Charles, MO St. Charles Borromeo Church; Retired.
Boettcher, John '91 (SR) On Duty Outside the Diocese.
Boettner, David '94 (KNX) [1] Knoxville, TN Cathedral of the Sacred Heart of Jesus.
Boever, Richard *c.ss.r.* '73 (WCH) [G] Wichita, KS Redemptorist Community.
Boever, Richard A. *c.ss.r.* '73 (CHI) [29] Chicago, IL Blessed Sacrament Church.
Bofenkamp, Andrew H. '45 (LC) Retired.
Boff, Bernard J. '61 (TOL) [1] Toledo, OH Queen of the Most Holy Rosary Cathedral; [L] Toledo, OH Ursuline Convent of the Sacred Heart; [O] Toledo, OH Office of Global Concerns.
Boffa, William L. '75 (FR) [3] Attleboro, MA St. Stephen's Church.
Bofto, Robert C. '63 (GF) Retired.
Bogart, Kenneth C. *s.j.* '56 (FgM) Provinces.
Bogda, Dennis M. '67 (PBR) Lyndora, PA St. John the Baptist Church.
Bogdan, Msgr. Henry S. '48 (TR) [6] Trenton, NJ Incarnation Church; Retired.
Bogdan, Palka *s.d.s.* '92 (NEW) [N] Verona, NJ The Salvatorian Fathers.
Bogdziewicz, Msgr. Anthony F. '49 (NEW) Summit, NJ St. Teresa's Church; Retired; [N] Rutherford, NJ St. John Vianney Residence for Priests.
Bogel, William A. *c.m.* '68 (STL) [P] St. Louis, MO Vincentian-St. Lazare Residence; [R] Normandy, MO Marillac Provincial House.
Bogert, James (RVC) Priests Released from Diocesan Assignment.
Bogetto, Clarence J. *c.m.* '45 (STL) [P] Perryville, MO Congregation of The Mission.
Boggs, Msgr. Dennis R. '86 (ALT) Lock Haven, PA Immaculate Conception Church.
Bognacki, Edward R. '91 (NEW) Roseland, NJ Our Lady of the Blessed Sacrament Church.
Bognanno, Msgr. Frank E. '65 (DM) [6] Des Moines, IA St. Augustin's Church.
Bogniak, Msgr. Casimir A. '57 (E) Meadville, PA St. Mary Church.
Bogolin, Leonard *o.f.m.* '34 (CHI) [N] Lemont, IL The Slovene Franciscan Fathers, Order of Friars Minor, Commissariat of the Holy Cross.
Bogovich, Msgr. Paul P. '41 (GRY) [2] East Chicago, IN Holy Trinity Church.
Boguslawski, Steven C. *o.p.* '87 (WDC) [B] Washington, DC Dominican House of Studies.
Bogusz, Dennis A. '79 (GBG) Point Marion, PA St. Hubert Church.
Bogusz, Joseph C. '75 (BO) Awaiting Assignment.
Bohan, Philip *o.f.m.cap.* '67 (BRK) [U] Brooklyn, NY St. Michael's Friary.
Bohan, Philip F. *o.f.m.cap.* '67 (BRK) [87] Brooklyn, NY St. Michael's Church.
Bohan, Philip F. *o.f.m.cap.* '67 (NY) [83] New York, NY Our Lady Queen of Angels Church.
Bohl, Ronald *o.f.m.conv.* '80 (IND) [I] Mount Saint Francis, IN Mount Saint Francis Friary and Retreat Center.
Bohlinger, Kenneth '76 (LFT) Leave of Absence.
Bohn, John Joseph '97 (JKS) Greenville, MS St. Joseph Church.
Bohn, Raymond G. '43 (BUF) Retired; [O] Buffalo, NY Sheehan Residence for Priests.
Bohnert, Edward A. '85 (SFR) [4] Menlo Park, CA St. Raymond Church.
Bohnsack, David *m.c.c.j.* '94 (FgM) Comboni Foreign Missions.
Boholnick, Theodore '53 (PHU) Simpson, PA SS. Peter and Paul Church.
Bohr, Msgr. David A. '71 (SCR) [A] Dalton, PA Saint Pius X Seminary.
Bohr, Gail G. *s.j.* '73 (OM) [K] Omaha, NE Jesuit Community At Creighton University.
Bohr, Luke *o.s.b.* '48 (RCK) [H] Aurora, IL Marmion Abbey-St. Augustine's Abbey.
Bohrer, John D. '78 (CAM) Glassboro, NJ Our Lady of Lourdes Church.

Bohula, Edwin V. '55 (CHI) [4] Lemont, IL St. James at Sag Bridge Church.
Boiko, John G. '87 (AUS) Elgin, TX Sacred Heart Church.
Boileau, David '56 (NO) [A] New Orleans, LA Notre Dame Seminary Graduate School of Theology.
Boileau, David A. '56 (NO) [15] New Orleans, LA Mater Dolorosa Church; [C] New Orleans, LA Loyola University.
Boisaubin, Robert D. '69 (STL) O'Fallon, MO Assumption Church.
Boisselle, Aime A. '59 (MAN) [3] Concord, NH Sacred Heart Church.
Boisvert, Gilbert O. '71 (OG) Altona, NY Holy Angels Church; Sciota, NY St. Louis Church.
Boisvert, Gregory *a.a.* '51 (BO) [W] Brighton, MA Assumptionist Center.
Boisvert, Gregory L. *a.a.* '51 (KNX) Alcoa, TN Our Lady of Fatima Church.
Boisvert, Marc *o.m.i.* '84 (FgM) Oblates Foreign Missions.
Boisvert, Marc '84 (ORG) El Toro, CA El Toro Marine Base.
Boisvert, Robert G. '58 (MAN) [15] Manchester, NH St. Pius X Church.
Boisvert, Russel L. '64 (NOR) Montville, CT St. John Church.
Boivin, Henry P. '57 (BO) Whitman, MA Holy Ghost Church.
Boivin, John '76 (CHI) [1] Chicago, IL Cathedral of the Holy Name.
Boivin, Louis R. '48 (FR) Retired.
Bojczuk, Thaddeus J. '73 (CHI) Summit, IL St. Joseph Church.
Boji, Manuel Y. '68 (EST) Southfield, MI Our Lady of Chaldeans Cathedral, Mother of God Chaldean Parish.
Bok, James *o.f.m.* '74 (CIN) [M] Cincinnati, OH St. Francis Seraph Friary; [M] Cincinnati, OH St. Clare Friary.
Bok, James M. *o.f.m.* (CIN) [O] Cincinnati, OH Friars Club.
Bok, John *o.f.m.* '62 (CIN) [M] Cincinnati, OH St. Francis Seraph Friary.
Bokenkotter, Thomas '50 (CIN) [12] Cincinnati, OH Assumption of the Blessed Virgin Mary Church.
Bokinskie, Richard '79 (SAG) Marlette, MI St. Elizabeth Church; Mayville, MI St. Joseph Church.
Bokota, Marek '81 (NEW) Wallington, NJ Most Sacred Heart of Jesus Church.
Boks, Lawrence E. '66 (GAY) Harrisville, MI St. Anne Church; Mikado, MI St. Raphael Church.
Bolan, John E. *c.pp.s.* '53 (CIN) [M] Dayton, OH Provincial House of the Cincinnati Province of the Society of the Precious Blood.
Bolan, John E. *c.pp.s.* '53 (CLV) Cleveland, OH Veterans Administration Hospitals, Brecksville V.A.
Boland, Eamonn '69 (DUL) Eveleth, MN Resurrection Church.
Boland, Edward F. '44 (PRO) Retired; [P] Providence, RI St. John Vianney Residence.
Boland, Edward G. '51 (PH) Retired.
Boland, Msgr. Eugene M. '63 (PAT) Totowa Borough, NJ St. James of the Marches Church.
Boland, Jeremiah M. '81 (CHI) Deerfield, IL Holy Cross Church.
Boland, John '75 (GLP) Seboyeta, NM Our Lady of Sorrows Church.
Boland, John P. '55 (PH) North Wales, PA St. Rose of Lima Church.
Boland, Msgr. John V. '65 (PAT) McAfee, NJ St. Francis de Sales Church.
Boland, Joseph B. '40 (JC) Retired.
Boland, Michael M. '86 (CHI) [1] Chicago, IL Cathedral of the Holy Name; [G] Chicago, IL Catholic Charities of the Archdiocese of Chicago-Archdiocesan Offices.
Boland, Patrick *t.o.r.* '41 (ARL) [J] Winchester, VA Sacred Heart Friary.
Boland, Steve *m.s.c.* '86 (FgM) Missionaries of the Sacred Heart Foreign Missions.
Boland, Steve *m.s.c.* '86 (RCK) [H] Aurora, IL Missionaries of the Sacred Heart Community.
Boland, Thomas L. '65 (L) [35] Louisville, KY Holy Spirit Church.
Bolcar, Andrew J. '65 (CAM) Westville, NJ St. Anne's Church.
Bolderson, John D. '81 (STL) [34] St. Louis, MO St. Francis de Sales Church.
Boldt, William J. '49 (NY) [230] Staten Island, NY St. Teresa Church.
Bolduc, John P. *s.m.* '70 (FgM) Marist Foreign Missions.
Bolduc, Marcel '39 (BO) [W] Lowell, MA Missionary Oblates of Mary Immaculate.
Bolduc, Marcel *o.m.i.* '39 (PRT) [I] Portland, ME.
Bolduc, Msgr. Norman, Jr. '79 (MAN) Auburn, NH St. Peter Church.
Bolduc, Paul (BO) Boston, MA Beth Israel Deaconess Medical Center, West Campus (Deaconess).
Bolduc, Richard *o.m.i.* '64 (FgM) Oblates Foreign Missions.
Boler, Martin *o.s.b.* '60 (ROC) [I] Pine City, NY Mount Saviour Monastery.
Bolerasky, Msgr. Peter E. '55 (PEO) [4] Streator, IL St. Stephen's Church.
Boles, John P. '63 (BO) [26] Boston, MA St. Gregory Church.
Boles, Joseph M. *v.f.* '65 (SCR) Dalton, PA Our Lady of the Abingtons Church.
Bolesta, Michael C. '89 (PH) [U] Meadowbrook, PA Holy Redeemer Hospital and Medical Center; [BB] Huntingdon Valley, PA Sisters of the Holy Redeemer Provincialate.
Boley, Edward J. '44 (GBG) On Duty Outside the Diocese.
Boley, Robert *o.carm.* '75 (JOL) [J] Darien, IL Carmelite Provincial Office.
Bolez, Edward C. '74 (ALN) [5] Bethlehem, PA St. John Capistrano Church.
Bolger, Anthony '69 (HON) Kihei, HI St. Theresa Church.
Bolger, James (NY) [209] Staten Island, NY St. John Neumann Church.
Bolger, Msgr. James '74 (NY) [F] New York, NY St. Joseph by the Sea, High School.
Bolger, Msgr. James F. (NY) [S] New York, NY Mission of the Immaculate Virgin.
Bolger, John '50 (SP) [9] St. Petersburg, FL Transfiguration Church.
Bolger, Michael J. '92 (RCK) [2] Freeport, IL St. Joseph Church; [B] Freeport, IL Aquin Central Catholic Junior-Senior High School.
Bolger, Richard T. '66 (PH) Willow Grove, PA St. David Church.
Bolger, Msgr. William '53 (SD) Retired.
Bolha, Jeremy *o.s.b.* '59 (E) St. Marys, PA Queen of the World Church.
Bolieau, Henry G. '72 (NOR) Absent on Leave.
Bolin, John *s.m.* '55 (HON) [D] Honolulu, HI St. Louis School; [H] Honolulu, HI Center Marianist Community.
Bolin, John F. *s.m.* '55 (HON) [J] Honolulu, HI Aina Kupaa O Maili.
Boll, John E. '70 (SAC) Woodland, CA Holy Rosary Church.
Boll, John J. *o.p.* '82 (NO) [25] New Orleans, LA St. Anthony Of Padua Church; [65] New Orleans, LA St. Thomas More Church; New Orleans, LA Tulane-Newcomb.
Bollea, Richard C. '62 (HRT) [7] Waterbury, CT Sacred Heart Church; Waterbury, CT Waterbury Hospital.
Boller, Robert J. '91 (STP) Retired.
Bolling, Joseph M. '91 (MOB) [13] Mobile, AL St. Matthew Church.
Bollman, Richard W. *s.j.* '69 (CIN) [78] Cincinnati, OH St. Robert Bellarmine Church; [D] Cincinnati, OH Xavier University; [M] Cincinnati, OH Jesuit Community at Xavier Unversity.
Bolman, Anthony P. '60 (SFE) [2] Albuquerque, NM Ascension Church.
Bologna, Anthony F. '43 (DET) [24] Detroit, MI St. Gabriel Church; Retired.
Bolser, Charles G. *c.s.v.* '73 (CHI) [D] Arlington Heights, IL St. Viator High School.
Bolser, Robert T. *c.s.v.* '95 (CHI) [210] Chicago, IL St. Viator Church.
Bolster, M. Thomas '82 (GR) [1] Grand Rapids, MI Cathedral of St. Andrew; On Special Assignment.
Bolte, George '38 (FAR) Retired.
Bolte, Richard '83 (COV) [B] Newport, KY Newport Central Catholic High School.
Bolte, Richard G. '83 (COV) [1] Newport, KY Holy Spirit Church.
Bolte, Thomas L. '80 (CIN) [38] Cincinnati, OH St. Ignatius Loyola Church.
Bolton, Bill *s.d.b.* '86 (LA) [X] Rosemead, CA St. Joseph's Salesian Youth Renewal Center.
Bolton, Donald *c.ss.r.* '52 (ORL) [F] New Smyrna Beach, FL St. Alphonsus Villa-Redemptorist Fathers and Brothers.
Bolton, Norman (SPR) [P] Amherst, MA University of Massachusetts and Amherst College, Newman Center.
Bolton, Norman B. '83 (SPR) West Springfield, MA St. Louis de France Church.
Bolton, Paul J. '62 (PRO) On Duty Outside the Diocese.
Bolvary, Paul L. '47 (PIT) Retired.
Boly, S.J., Craig '74 (SEA) [11] Seattle, WA St. Joseph Church.
Bomar, Msgr. Fred '60 (AUS) [20] Austin, TX St. Peter the Apostle Church.
Bomba, Paul M. '77 (WOR) Military Chaplains.
Bombardier, Dennis P. '68 (SPR) Millers Falls, MA St. John's Church.
Bombardier, Gerald W. '73 (BUR) Winooski, VT St. Stephen Church.
Bombardier, Paul A. '82 (SPR) Ware, MA Our Lady of Mt. Carmel Church.
Bombardier, Wilfrid F. '43 (MAN) Retired.
Bombera, Alex *t.o.r.* '46 (SFS) Plankinton, SD St. John Church; Plankinton, SD State Training School.
Bomberger, Ray *s.s.j.* '71 (BEA) [7] Beaumont, TX Our Mother of Mercy Church.
Bomeisl, Robert A. *s.j.* '52 (FgM) Provinces.
Bommarito, Vincent '77 (STL) [10] Florissant, MO St. Thomas the Apostle Church.
Bona, Joseph F. *s.j.* '72 (DEN) [M] Denver, CO Xavier Jesuit Center.
Bonacci, (Eugene) Thomas P. '72 (OAK) [3] Concord, CA St. Francis of Assisi Church.
Bonacci, Louis *s.j.* '62 (CIN) [Q] Cincinnati, OH Xavier University Campus Ministry.
Bonacci, Louis A. *s.j.* '73 (CIN) [M] Cincinnati, OH Jesuit Community at Xavier Unversity.
Bonacci, Paul (ROC) [M] Rochester, NY Diocesan Office of Campus Ministry.
Bonaccorsi, Salvatore S. *o.s.a.* '55 (BO) [C] North Andover, MA Merrimack College.
Bonacum, Thomas '79 (SB) Retired.
Bonadies, Kenneth P. '65 (HRT) [4] Hamden, CT St. Ann's Church.
Bonadio, Joseph *s.s.* '64 (BAL) [32] Baltimore, MD St. Francis of Assisi Church.
Bonadio, Joseph J. *s.s.* '64 (BAL) [M] Baltimore, MD Sulpician Provincial House.
Bonafed, Joseph E. '92 (GBG) [4] Uniontown, PA St. Therese, the Little Flower of Jesus Church.
Bonamo, James '70 (RIC) Absent On Leave.
Bonanno, Raphael *o.f.m.* (FgM) Custody of St. Mary of the Angels. Byzantine-Slavonic.
Bonano, Salvatore *c.m.f.* '84 (LA) [R] Rancho Dominguez, CA Dominguez Seminary Inc.
Bonanti, Thomas A. '85 (PT) [8] Pensacola, FL St. Anthony of Padua Church; [10] Pensacola, FL St. Joseph Church.
Bonar, Clyde A. '84 (ORL) Apopka, FL St. Francis of Assisi Church.
Bonarrigo, David *t.o.r.* '78 (ARL) Herndon, VA St. Joseph Church.
Bonavitacola, John M. '88 (PH) [131] Philadelphia, PA Our Mother of Mercy Prison Chaplaincy Church; [139] Philadelphia, PA St. Raymond of Penafort Church; Philadelphia, PA Philadelphia Prison System.
Bonczewski, Msgr. William D. '76 (OLL) [C] North Jackson, OH National Shrine of Our Lady of Lebanon.
Bond, Daniel '84 (RIC) Hopewell, VA St. James Church.
Bond, Ernest W. '88 (COS) Bailey, CO St. Mary's of the Rockies Church.
Bond, Robert *glmy.* '60 (TLS) Hugo, OK Immaculate Conception Church.
Bond, Robert E. *o.p.* '55 (PRO) [B] Providence, RI Providence College; [P] Providence, RI St. Thomas Aquinas Priory at Providence College.
Bond, Thomas Aquinas *o.c.s.o.* '39 (ROC) [I] Piffard, NY Abbey of the Genesee.
Bonderenko, Thomas '80 (BAL) Special Assignment.
Bondi, Paul '48 (ALB) Retired.
Bondi, Richard '74 (SPR) [3] Holyoke, MA Holy Family Church.
Bondi, Steven '86 (JOL) Wheaton, IL St. Michael Church.
Bondy, Alberto P. '86 (DET) [6] Livonia, MI St. Michael Church.
Boneck, Norman D. '62 (LC) [1] Wausau, WI Holy Name of Jesus Church.
Boned, Enrique '57 (MIA) [1] Hialeah, FL Immaculate Conception Church.
Bonelli, Charles *i.m.c.* '69 (MET) [H] Somerset, NJ Consolata Society for Foreign Missions; [N] Somerset, NJ Mission International, Inc.
Bonelli, Msgr. Theodore V. '61 (NEW) Retired.
Bonello, Joseph *o.f.m.* '85 (FgM) Franciscan Foreign Missions.
Bones, James J. '64 (PH) Levittown, PA Immaculate Conception B.V.M. Church.
Bonetti, Henry *s.d.b.* '73 (FgM) Salesians of Don Bosco Foreign Missions.
Boney, Vincent *c.p.* '57 (SCR) [M] Scranton, PA Saint Ann's Passionist Monastery.
Bonfadini, Leo '74 (PBL) Absent on Leave.
Bonfigilo, Anthony J. '48 (WDC) Retired.
Bonfiglio, David G. '63 (BO) [14] Cambridge, MA Sacred Heart of Jesus Church.
Bonfiglio, Gregory R. *s.j.* '93 (LA) [10] Los Angeles, CA Dolores Mission Church.
Bonfilgio, David G. (BO) Retired.
Bongard, Joseph W. '86 (PH) [6] Norristown, PA St. Titus Church; [D] Norristown, PA Kennedy-Kenrick Catholic High School.
Bonghanoy, Edgardo C. '80 (HON) Mountain View, HI St. Theresa Church.
Bongiorno, Angelo *s.d.b.* '42 (BO) [E] Boston, MA Don Bosco Preparatory School.
Bonham, Ray O. '94 (OM) Heun, NE Holy Trinity Church.
Bonian, Stephen J. *s.j.* '82 (BO) [W] Boston, MA The Society of Jesus of New England-Provincial Offices.
Boniface, Jeyarah *s.j.* '87 (BO) [W] Chestnut Hill, MA The Jesuit Community at Boston College.
Bonifas, Casper *c.pp.s.* '43 (CIN) [B] Carthagena, OH St. Charles.

Bonifas, Roger D. '45 (TOL) Ottoville, OH Immaculate Conception Church; Retired.
Bonifazi, Flavian *s.a.c.* '43 (BAL) [51] Baltimore, MD St. Jude Shrine Church.
Bonifazi, Remo J. *c.s.sp.* '45 (FgM) Holy Ghost Foreign Missions.
Bonikowski, Leon V. *o.s.f.s.* '65 (FgM) Oblates of St. Francis de Sales Foreign Missions.
Bonikowski, Leon V. *o.s.f.s.* '65 (PH) [AA] Philadelphia, PA Oblates of St. Francis De Sales.
Bonin, David L. '74 (ROC) Odessa, NY St. Benedict Church; Watkins Glen, NY St. Mary of the Lake Church.
Bonin, Harold A. '65 (CHI) [100] Chicago, IL St. Jerome Church.
Bonin, Richard G. '46 (NU) Gaylord, MN St. Michael Church; Winthrop, MN St. Francis de Sales Church.
Bonjean, Jerry *s.d.b.* '67 (SFR) [45] San Francisco, CA SS. Peter and Paul Church.
Bonjean, Richard '76 (MRY) Retired.
Bonk, Carl *s.j.* '82 (CLV) [E] Cleveland, OH St. Ignatius High School; [U] Cleveland, OH Jesuit Retreat House.
Bonke, James (IND) Greenwood, IN Our Lady of the Greenwood Church.
Bonke, James R. '70 (IND) [1] Indianapolis, IN SS. Peter and Paul Cathedral.
Bonn, Ferdinand C. '49 (JC) Retired.
Bonnaci, Paul '91 (ROC) Ithaca, NY Immaculate Conception Church.
Bonnar, David J. '88 (PIT) Bethel Park, PA St. Thomas More Church.
Bonneau, Normand *o.m.i.* '76 (FgM) Oblates Foreign Missions.
Bonneau, Roger (GAL) [14] Houston, TX St. Bernadette Soubirous Church.
Bonnell, Robert A. '49 (CLV) Oberlin, OH Sacred Heart Church; Retired.
Bonnell, Victor G. '60 (SLC) Layton, UT St. Rose of Lima Church.
Bonner, Charles E. '65 (PH) Yeadon, PA St. Louis Church.
Bonner, Dismas *o.f.m.* '58 (STL) [T] Dittmer, MO Il Ritiro-The Little Retreat.
Bonner, Joseph P. '53 (SCR) Weston, PA Sacred Heart Church.
Bonner, Michael J. *s.v.d.* '66 (CHI) [32] Chicago, IL St. Bronislava Church; [B] Techny, IL Divine Word Residence.
Bonner, Patrick J. *o.s.b.* '59 (PAT) [M] Newton, NJ St. Paul's Abbey.
Bonner, W. Richard '61 (NY) [DD] Esopus, NY Redemptorist Priests and Brothers C.Ss.R. (Province of Baltimore).
Bonner, William J. *s.v.d.* '67 (LA) [76] Los Angeles, CA St. Malachy Church.
Bonneville, Lionel '63 (SPR) Northampton, MA Veterans Administration Hospital.
Bonneville, Lionel E. '63 (SPR) [3] Ludlow, MA St. John the Baptist Church.
Bonnici, John S. '91 (NY) [34] New York, NY Epiphany Church; [D] New York, NY Department of Education.
Bonnici, William '67 (DET) [5] Roseville, MI Sacred Heart Church.
Bonnot, Bernard R. '67 (Y) On Duty Outside the Diocese.
Bono, Vincent *s.c.* '81 (NO) [P] New Orleans, LA Brothers of the Sacred Heart; [R] New Orleans, LA Center of Jesus the Lord; [R] Ponchatoula, LA Magnificat Center of the Holy Spirit.
Bonsall, D. Leo *o.s.b.* (FWT) [5] Arlington, TX St. Matthew Church.
Bonsignore, Dennis (ROC) [30] Rochester, NY St. John Evangelist Church.
Bonsignore, Mark '95 (HRT) [I] Hartford, CT Saint Francis Hospital and Medical Center.
Bonsignore, Mark J. '67 (HRT) Wallingford, CT Resurrection Church.
Bonsor, Jack '74 (SFR) On Duty Outside the Archdiocese.
Bonvouloir, Philip *a.a.* '57 (NY) [87] New York, NY Our Lady of Guadalupe Church.
Bonzagni, John (SPR) Graduate Studies.
Bonzagni, John J. '80 (SPR) Lenox Dale, MA St. Vincent de Paul's Church.
Book, Msgr. A. Joseph '63 (E) Greenville, PA St. Michael Church.
Boone, Kirby *c.f.x.* (FBK) Tanana, AK St. Aloysius Church.
Boone, Thomas A. '61 (CLV) Brook Park, OH Assumption of Mary Church.
Boor, Colin J. '50 (WCH) Hutchinson, KS Our Lady of Guadalupe Church; Hutchinson, KS Kansas State Industrial Reformatory.
Booth, Earl J. '44 (LR) Retired.
Booth, Earl J. '60 (LR) [H] Little Rock, AR St. John Manor.
Booth, Edward N. '74 (STA) [1] St. Augustine, FL Cathedral of St. Augustine.
Booth, John '82 (SY) Binghamton, NY Binghamton Psychiatric Hospital.
Booth, John A. '82 (SY) Deposit, NY St. Joseph Church.
Booth, Mark Thomas *ofm conv.* '85 (BUF) [D] Athol Springs, NY St. Francis High School.
Booth, Mark-Thomas *o.f.m.conv.* '85 (NOR) Stafford Springs, CT St. Edward Church.
Booth, Michael A. '89 (SD) Valley Center, CA St. Stephen Church.
Booth, Raymond '57 (ROC) Webster, NY St. Paul Church.
Booth, Stephen R. *m.m.* '86 (NY) [DD] Maryknoll, NY Maryknoll Fathers and Brothers.
Boothali, Anthony '89 (SCR) [3] Williamsport, PA St. Boniface's Church.
Bootkoski, Paul G. '71 (NEW) [1] Newark, NJ Cathedral Basilica of the Sacred Heart Church.
Boquet, Gregory M. *o.s.b.* '88 (NO) [A] St. Benedict, LA St. Joseph's Seminary College; [P] St. Benedict, LA St. Joseph Abbey.
Boquet, Shenan J. '93 (HT) Galliano, LA St. Joseph Church.
Boracco, John B. *p.i.m.e.* '30 (DET) [K] Detroit, MI P.I.M.E. Missionaries of SS. Peter and Paul.
Boras, Kurt '59 (CHI) Orland Park, IL St. Michael Church.
Borawski, Gerald J. '72 (LFT) Frankfort, IN St. Mary Church.
Borba, Joseph Anthony '97 (SB) Barstow, CA St. Joseph Church.
Borbely, James A. *s.j.* '76 (ALN) [A] Wernersville, PA Novitiate of St. Isaac Jogues; [N] Wernersville, PA Jesuit Center for Spiritual Growth.
Borbridge, David *s.j.* '63 (MOB) [B] Mobile, AL Spring Hill College.
Borbridge, David C. *s.j.* '63 (FgM) Provinces.
Borca, Dennis L. '81 (MAR) Munising, MI Sacred Heart of Jesus Church.
Borchardt, Edward '96 (SPK) [15] Spokane, WA St. Mary Church.
Borcherding, Martin '73 (LAF) [3] Lafayette, LA Holy Cross Church.
Borcic, John J. '76 (STL) Webster Groves, MO Mary, Queen of Peace Church.
Borcz, Casimir Adalbert *o.c.d.* '45 (GRY) [J] Munster, IN Discalced Carmelite Fathers Monastery.
Borda, Peter '42 (SD) National City, CA St. Anthony of Padua Church.
Borda, Peter Paul '42 (SD) Retired.
Bordages, Msgr. Martin '41 (BEA) [5] Port Arthur, TX St. James Church; Retired.
Bordeaux, Henry *o.c.d.* '62 (LR) [A] Little Rock, AR Marylake - Carmelite Novitiate.
Bordeleau, Normand G. '5 (BRK) Released from Diocesan Assignment.
Bordeleau, Normand G. '85 (MAN) Concord, NH N.H. State Hospital.
Bordelon, H. Gerald '56 (ALX) [2] Alexandria, LA Our Lady of Prompt Succor Church.
Bordelon, Lloyd '91 (LAF) Cow Island, LA St. Anne Church.
Bordelon, Msgr. Roland '50 (ALX) On Duty Outside the Diocese.
Borden, Wilfred F. *o.m.i.* '63 (LA) [C] Santa Paula, CA Thomas Aquinas College.
Bordenca, Charles '55 (BIR) Retired.
Bordignon, Angelo *c.s.* '51 (LA) [87] Los Angeles, CA St. Peter Church.
Bordignon, Narciso *c.r.s.* '67 (GAL) [11] Houston, TX Assumption Church.
Bordonaro, Joseph C. '89 (PH) Primos, PA St. Eugene Church; [D] Springfield, PA Cardinal O'Hara High School.
Boreczky, John V. '48 (CHI) Retired.
Borel, Albert W. '81 (LKC) Graduate Studies.
Boren, Edward Daniel *o.f.m.* '64 (VIC) Bay City, TX Our Lady of Guadalupe Church.
Borer, Gerard J. *s.j.* '59 (COS) [9] Colorado Springs, CO Our Lady of the Pines-Black Forest Church.
Borer, Robert D. '76 (STU) Cambridge, OH St. Benedict Church.
Boretto, Christopher '87 (SY) [9] Binghamton, NY St. Patrick Church; Binghamton, NY Our Lady of Lourdes Memorial Hospital.
Borg, Marcellinus *o.f.m.* '59 (NY) [DD] New York, NY Franciscan Province of the Immaculate Conception.
Borg, Ron *c.s.b.* '79 (DET) [43] Detroit, MI St. Louis the King Church.
Borgelt, Daniel '93 (TOL) Delphos, OH St. John the Evangelist Church.
Borger, Theodore R. '83 (DAV) Retired.
Borgerding, John *o.s.b.* '66 (LA) [R] Valyermo, CA St. Andrew's Abbey.
Borgerding, Terry J. '77 (STL) Apple Creek, MO St. Joseph's Church; Biehle, MO St. Maurus Church.
Borgers, Charles *o.m.i.* '41 (SAT) [M] San Antonio, TX Oblate Benson Residence (Southern Prov.).
Borges, Charles *s.j.* '81 (BAL) [B] Baltimore, MD Loyola College; [M] Baltimore, MD Jesuit Community of Loyola College, Inc.
Borges, Jose Angel *s.j.* '69 (SJN) [22] San Juan, PR San Ignacio de Loyola Church.
Borges, Laurence '59 (BO) [1] Weymouth, MA St. Albert the Great Church.
Borges, Mario L. '82 (OAK) [7] Oakland, CA St. Columba's Church.
Borgesen, Kenneth *o.ss.t.* '87 (NO) [16] New Orleans, LA Our Lady Of Good Counsel Church.
Borgia, Anthony A. '84 (TOL) Galion, OH St. Joseph Church.
Borgmeyer, Dean G. '81 (WH) Dunbar, WV Christ the King Church; Nitro, WV Holy Trinity Church.
Borgo, John V. *s.j.* '57 (BGP) [I] Bridgeport, CT St. Vincent's Medical Center; [O] Fairfield, CT The Fairfield Jesuit Community-Fairfield University.
Borgognoni, Msgr. Charles L. '48 (SY) Retired.
Borgonovo, Mario '51 (MGZ) Aguadilla, PR San Jose Obrero Church.
Borho, Charles D. '57 (P) St. Paul, OR St. Paul Church.
Borino, David J. '86 (HRT) [1] Meriden, CT Our Lady of Mount Carmel Church.
Bork, Vincent P. '95 (ARL) McLean, VA St. John's Church.
Borkowski, Aloysius J. '39 (GBG) Retired.
Borkowski, Edward *s.v.d.* '44 (CHI) [B] Techny, IL Divine Word Residence.
Borkowski, Francis '77 (NY) Military Chaplains.
Borkowski, John A. '49 (PRO) Retired.
Borkowski, Mark A. '96 (DET) [6] St. Clair Shores, MI St. Margaret of Scotland Church.
Borkowski, Raymond *o.f.m.conv.* '61 (NOR) Cromwell, CT St. John Church.
Borkowski, Tom '81 (KC) [4] Independence, MO St. Mary's Church.
Borkowski, Walter '85 (OAK) [2] Concord, CA St. Bonaventure Church.
Borlick, Daniel P. *c.m.* '76 (CHI) [138] Chicago, IL St. Michael Church.
Borman, Ron *o.f.m.conv.* '92 (IND) [3] Terre Haute, IN St. Benedict Church.
Bormann, Paul D. '85 (SC) Wesley, IA St. Joseph's Church.
Bornbach, Raymond H. '41 (LC) Retired.
Borntrager, Conrad M. *o.s.m.* '60 (CHI) [15] Chicago, IL Annunciata Church; [N] Chicago, IL Servite Friars - Eastern Province.
Borocz, Isaac *o.s.b.* '82 (WDC) [M] Washington, DC St. Anselm's Abbey.
Borodach, John J. '57 (PBR) Donora, PA St. Michael Church.
Borodach, Joseph '60 (PBR) Bradenville, PA St. Mary's Church.
Boronat, Francis *sch.p.* '54 (LA) [21] Los Angeles, CA Our Lady Help of Christians (Maria Auxiliadora) Church; [R] Los Angeles, CA Piarist Fathers.
Borosh, Carl '68 (STU) Retired.
Boroughs, Philip *s.j.* '78 (SEA) [A] Seattle, WA Seattle University.
Borowczyk, Martin R. '42 (CHI) [45] Chicago, IL St. Constance Church; [64] Chicago, IL St. Francis Borgia Church; Retired.
Borowiak, David J. '71 (BUF) [3] Depew, NY St. James Church.
Borowiak, Henry M. '44 (BUF) [3] Depew, NY St. James Church; Retired.
Borowiak, Kenneth A. '87 (LIN) Dwight, NE Assumption Church.
Borowik, John '66 (NEW) Lyndhurst, NJ St. Michael's Church.
Borowski, Charles E.J. '66 (WOR) West Warren, MA St. Stanislaus Church.
Borowski, Douglas V. '84 (BO) Absent on Leave.
Borowski, Ladislaus '48 (DET) Retired.
Borowski, Paul J. *c.ss.r.* '87 (BRK) [C] Whitestone, NY St. Alphonsus Formation Residence.
Borre, Robert J. (CHI) Chicago, IL V.A. Lakeside Medical Center.
Borrelli, Msgr. Anthony '54 (COL) [28] Columbus, OH St. Margaret of Cortona Church.
Borrero, Victor R. *s.e.m.v.* '89 (ARE) Hatillo, PR Our Lady of Guadalupe Church.
Borsari, John Peter '94 (GAL) [11] Houston, TX Assumption Church.
Borski, Charles *o.m.i.* '70 (GAL) [37] Houston, TX Immaculate Conception Church.
Borski, Msgr. Chester L. '67 (GAL) [A] Houston, TX St. Mary's Seminary.
Borski, Jerome *o.s.b.* '92 (PAT) [M] Morristown, NJ St. Mary's Abbey.
Borstelmann, James E. '67 (NY) Croton Falls, NY St. Joseph Church.
Borsuk, Msgr. Alan J. '59 (PSC) Hillsborough Township, NJ St. Mary's Church.
Borsuk, Ronald W. '58 (PBR) Conemaugh, PA Holy Trinity Church.
Bortolazzo, Peter *c.s.* '39 (BO) [67] Boston, MA Sacred Heart Church.
Borucki, Wallace T. '65 (BUF) Cattaraugus, NY St. Mary's Church; East Otto, NY St. Isidore Church; Little Valley, NY St. Mary Church.
Boruszewski, Msgr. Joseph A. '53 (BUF) Varysburg, NY St. Joseph Church.
Boruta, Alexander *o.f.m.* '60 (GAY) Skidway Lake, MI St. Stephen of Hungary Church.

Borycz, Edmund S. '69 (DET) Military Chaplains.
Borzaga, Rinaldo '47 (BRK) Retired.
Borzuchowski, John W. '68 (NY) [2] Kingston, NY Immaculate Conception Church; Castle Point, NY Veterans Administration Medical Center.
Borzych, Alexander J. '80 (GI) Military Chaplains.
Bosack, Albert J. '43 (BUF) Lyndonville, NY St. Joseph Church; Retired.
Bosch, John *c.pp.s.* '52 (CIN) [B] Carthagena, OH St. Charles.
Bosch, Stan *s.t.* '86 (LA) Compton, CA Our Lady of Victory Church.
Bosch, William J. *s.j.* '60 (SY) [S] Syracuse, NY Jesuits at LeMoyne, Inc.
Boschert, Hubert *s.j.* (WIN) Owatonna, MN St. Joseph's Church.
Boschert, Hubert G. *s.j.* '68 (MIL) [P] Milwaukee, WI Jesuit Provincial Office, Wisconsin Province.
Boschert, Joseph N. '60 (COV) California, KY Sts. Peter and Paul Church.
Boschetto, Danilo *s.x.* '70 (FgM) Xaverian Foreign Missions.
Boschetto, Danilo *s.x.* '70 (PAT) [M] Wayne, NJ Xaverian Missionary Fathers.
Bosco, Don (NY) [230] Staten Island, NY St. Teresa Church.
Bosco, John M. '71 (LAN) Milan, MI Immaculate Conception Church.
Boscoe, John L. *c.s.b.* '72 (GAL) [Q] Sugar Land, TX Basilian Mission Center.
Boscutti, Darrio L. '86 (CHI) [176] Chicago, IL St. Priscilla Church.
Bosio, August P. *s.d.b.* '46 (SP) [E] Tampa, FL Mary Help of Christians School.
Bosken, Robert E. *s.j.* '56 (STL) [P] St. Louis, MO De Smet Jesuit High School Community.
Boslett, Donald E. '59 (ALT) Renovo, PA St. Joseph's Church.
Bosnich, David A. '95 (PBR) Sheffield, PA St. Michael Church.
Bossa, Barry *s.a.c.* '81 (NY) [13] Yonkers, NY Our Lady of Mt. Carmel Church.
Bosse, Dennis *o.f.m.* '90 (CIN) [E] Cincinnati, OH Roger Bacon High School.
Bosse, Dennis *o.f.m.* '91 (CIN) [C] Cincinnati, OH St. Anthony Shrine, Francisan Candidacy.
Bosse, Roger *o.f.m.* '83 (CIN) [E] Cincinnati, OH Roger Bacon High School; [U] Cincinnati, OH Community Support Charitable Trust; [U] Cincinnati, OH Roger Bacon High School Endowment.
Bosse, Roger T. *o.f.m.* '83 (CIN) [M] Cincinnati, OH St. Clement Friary.
Bossi, Paul R. '69 (BUF) [14] Buffalo, NY Blessed Sacrament Church.
Bossi, Stephen E. *c.s.p.* '86 (P) [Q] Portland, OR Paulist Fathers Catholic Center for Evangelization.
Bossi, Stephen E.M. *c.s.p.* '85 (P) [28] Portland, OR St. Philip Neri Church.
Bossie, Robert *s.c.j.* '75 (MIL) [P] Hales Corners, WI Priests of the Sacred Heart.
Bossie, Robert W. *s.c.j.* '75 (CHI) [N] Chicago, IL Priests of the Sacred Heart.
Bossman, David M. *o.f.m.* '65 (NY) [DD] New York, NY Franciscan Friars, Order of Friars Minor, Holy Name Province.
Bosso, Stephen '78 (PMB) [A] Boynton Beach, FL St. Vincent de Paul Regional Seminary.
Bosso, Stephen C. '78 (PT) On Duty Outside the Diocese.
Bostwick, John '69 (RIC) Unassigned.
Bostwick, John *o.praem.* '76 (GB) [I] De Pere, WI St. Joseph Priory.
Botean, John Michael '86 (ROM) Canton, OH St. George Cathedral.
Boteju, Bernard '85 (TYL) Mineola, TX St. Peter the Apostle Church.
Boteler, William M. *m.m.* '68 (FgM) Maryknoll Foreign Missions.
Botenhagen, Paul *o.f.m.* '82 (LSC) Mescalero, NM St. Joseph Church.
Botia, Omar '90 (RNO) [6] Reno, NV St. Therese Church of the Little Flower.
Botik, Msgr. William A. '44 (DAL) [3] Dallas, TX Blessed Sacrament Church.
Botkin, Edward A. '73 (DAV) Delmar, IA St. Patrick's Church; Petersville, IA Immaculate Conception Church; Welton, IA St. Anne Church; [B] Davenport, IA St. Ambrose University.
Botsko, Jerome '82 (PBR) Brownsville, PA St. Nicholas Church.
Bottazo, Alex '43 (LAN) Retired.
Botte, Gregory *o.f.m.* '68 (NY) [DD] New York, NY Franciscan Province of the Immaculate Conception.
Botthof, Robert J. *o.p.* '87 (CHI) River Forest, IL St. Vincent Ferrer Priory Church.
Bottino, Msgr. Dominic J. '78 (CAM) Somerdale, NJ Our Lady of Grace Church.
Bottino, Msgr. Edward J. '52 (BRK) [197] Queens, NY Mary's Nativity Church.
Botton, Msgr. Pierre A. '56 (BGP) Retired.
Botz, Lawrence '40 (SCL) Elrosa, MN SS. Peter and Paul Church; Retired.
Botz, Paschal *o.s.b.* '31 (SCL) [I] Collegeville, MN St. John's Abbey, of the Order of St. Benedict.
Botz, Roger *o.s.b.* '60 (SCL) [G] St. Cloud, MN St. Cloud Hospital.
Botzum, William A. *c.s.c.* '43 (FTW) [17] South Bend, IN Faith & Hope & Charity Chapel Church; [B] Notre Dame, IN University of Notre Dame Du Lac; [J] Notre Dame, IN Holy Cross Community, Corby Hall, University of Notre Dame.
Bou, Pedro L. *s.v.d.* '74 (TR) Lakewood, NJ St. Anthony Claret Church.
Bou Sallem, George *m.l.m.* '91 (OLL) [A] San Antonio, TX The Congregation of Maronite Lebanese Missionaries.
Bou-Mehri, Gebran '88 (SLC) Salt Lake City, UT Veterans Administration Hospital.
Bou-Merhi, Gebran '88 (OLL) Murray, UT Saint Jude Church.
Bou-Merhi, Gebran '88 (SLC) [5] Murray, UT St. Jude Church.
Bou-Mssalem, Georges '96 (OLL) El Paso, TX St. Anthony of the Desert Mission Church.
Bouchaert, Paul *c.i.c.m.* '68 (FgM) Missionhurst Foreign Missions.
Bouchard, Charles E. *o.p.* '79 (STL) [B] St. Louis, MO Aquinas Institute of Theology; [P] St. Louis, MO Dominican Community of St. Louis.
Bouchard, Lucien *o.m.i.* '55 (FgM) Oblates Foreign Missions.
Bouchard, Marcel H. '72 (FR) Sandwich, MA Corpus Christi Church.
Bouchard, Norman '88 (PBL) Absent on Leave.
Bouchard, Msgr. Paul L. '72 (MAN) [7] Manchester, NH St. Edmund Church.
Bouchard, Robert '84 (PRT) [8] Portland, ME St. Christopher's Church.
Bouchard, Thomas '53 (DUL) Retired.
Bouchea, M. Lawrence *o.s.b.* '89 (BIR) [E] Cullman, AL St. Bernard Abbey.
Boucher, Clarence R. '40 (BO) Retired.
Boucher, Edward F. '60 (SAG) Retired.
Boucher, Gerard A. '53 (MAN) Plaistow, NH Holy Angels Church; Retired.
Boucher, Gilmond *o.m.i.* '58 (MAN) Claremont, NH St. Mary Church.
Boucher, Kevin J. '91 (FAR) Bottineau, ND St. Mark's Church; [I] Bottineau, ND Minot State University-Bottineau.
Boucher, Maurice U. *s.s.e.* '48 (BUR) Alburg, VT St. Amadeus Church; [I] Isle La Motte, VT St. Anne's Shrine.
Boucher, Nelson '53 (MAN) Retired.
Boucher, Richard R. *m.s.* '60 (HRT) [M] Hartford, CT Missionaries of LaSalette Provincial Secretary.
Boucher, Roger R. '73 (WOR) Military Chaplains.
Boucrees, Thaddeus *s.v.d.* '52 (BLX) [A] Bay St. Louis, MS St. Augustine's.
Boudoin, Burt '82 (SD) [2] El Cajon, CA Our Lady of Grace Church.
Boudreau, George *o.p.* '78 (STL) [B] St. Louis, MO Aquinas Institute of Theology.
Boudreau, George R. *o.p.* '83 (STL) [P] St. Louis, MO St. Dominic Priory.
Boudreau, Paul '83 (NOR) Coventry, CT St. Mary Church.
Boudreau, Thomas '56 (LA) [9] Los Angeles, CA Divine Saviour Church.
Boudreau, Thomas C. '95 (BO) [2] Woburn, MA St. Barbara Church.
Boudreaux, John S. '73 (LAF) On Duty Outside the Diocese.
Boudreaux, John S. '73 (MOB) [3] Mobile, AL Corpus Christi Church.
Boudreaux, Msgr. Roland J. '42 (HT) Retired; [E] Thibodaux, LA The Diocese of Houma-Thibodaux Historical Research Center.
Bouffard, Msgr. James F. '70 (NEW) Haworth, NJ Sacred Heart Church.
Bouffier, Robert *s.m.* '74 (BO) [11] Boston, MA St. Anthony Church.
Bouffier, Robert J. *s.m.* '74 (CIN) [M] Dayton, OH Marianist Provincialate.
Boufford, Thomas F. '81 (GR) Lake Odessa, MI St. Edward's Church.
Boughton, Michael *s.j.* '79 (BGP) [D] Fairfield, CT Fairfield College Preparatory School; [O] Fairfield, CT The Fairfield Jesuit Community-Fairfield University.
Bouhall, William G. '94 (CLV) [1] Parma, OH St. Anthony of Padua Church.
Boul, Walter '41 (STL) Retired.
Boulanger, Albert L. '62 (MAN) Manchester, NH Nursing Homes; [J] Manchester, NH Mt. Carmel Nursing Home.
Boulanger, Andre '65 (PHX) Unassigned.
Boulanger, Gerald *m.s.* '73 (NOR) Jewett City, CT St. Mary Church.
Boulanger, Maurice R. '47 (MAN) [H] Rochester, NH St. Charles Children's Home.
Boulanger, Raymond *s.m.* '51 (BO) [Y] Framingham Centre, MA The Marist House.
Boulden, Garry '77 (SPK) Absent on Leave.
Boule, Roland B. '32 (FR) Retired.
Boulet, Marshall '71 (LKC) Elton, LA St. Paul Church.
Boulet, Norman J. '69 (FR) Absent on Leave; [J] Fall River, MA Priests' Hostel.
Boulette, Michael J. '76 (SAT) Kerrville, TX Notre Dame Church.
Bouley, Allan *o.s.b.* '62 (SCL) [I] Collegeville, MN St. John's Abbey, of the Order of St. Benedict.
Boulos, Peter '93 (SAM) Atlanta, GA St. Joseph's Maronite Church.
Boulton, David G. *s.j.* '61 (BO) [W] Weston, MA Campion Center.
Boumans, Albert J. '52 (LAF) [2] New Iberia, LA Nativity of Our Lady Church.
Bourassa, Msgr. Stanley C. '55 (CR) Barnesville, MN Assumption Church.
Bourbon, Arthur '77 (PHX) Retired.
Bourbon, Frank C. *s.j.* '65 (WH) [A] Wheeling, WV Wheeling Jesuit University.
Bourcy, Robert Scott (ROC) Macedon, NY St. Patrick Church.
Bourdeau, Leo *s.m.* '42 (BO) [4] Methuen, MA St. Theresa Church.
Bourdon, Norman W. '73 (PRO) [2] Cumberland, RI St. Joan of Arc Church.
Bourek, David F. '79 (LIN) Hastings, NE St. Michael's Church; [L] Hastings, NE St. Cecilia High School Endowment Fund.
Bouressa, Donald J. '61 (PRO) Narragansett, RI St. Mary, Star of the Sea Church.
Bourg, Edwin (LAF) Retired.
Bourg, Rodney P. '78 (NO) [3] Slidell, LA St. Luke the Evangelist Church.
Bourgault, Ronald L. '63 (BO) [5] Quincy, MA St. Mary Church.
Bourgea, Roger *s.m.* '70 (BRK) [45] Brooklyn, NY St. Francis of Assisi-St. Blaise Church.
Bourgeois, Bernard W. '95 (BUR) Barre, VT St. Monica Church.
Bourgeois, Donald E. '85 (SY) Bainbridge, NY St. John the Evangelist Church.
Bourgeois, Francis L. '61 (LAF) Robert's Cove, LA St. Leo IV Church.
Bourgeois, Francois A. *m.s.* '54 (HON) Kekaha, HI St. Theresa Church.
Bourgeois, Henry *c.s.c.* '62 (BO) [X] Framingham, MA Fontbonne Hall.
Bourgeois, Msgr. Joseph E. '58 (NO) [3] Metairie, LA St. Ann Church and Shrine Church; Metairie, LA St. Ann Shrine Church.
Bourgeois, Msgr. Lloyd V. '57 (SD) [38] San Diego, CA San Rafael Church.
Bourgeois, Louis D. '59 (BO) Hamilton, MA St. Paul Church.
Bourgeois, Richard J. *o.s.b.* '76 (BO) [W] Hingham, MA Glastonbury Abbey.
Bourgeois, Roger *s.s.s.* '57 (SFE) [23] Albuquerque, NM St. Charles Borromeo Church.
Bourgeois, Roy L. *m.m.* '72 (NY) [DD] Maryknoll, NY Maryknoll Fathers and Brothers.
Bourget, Laurence *o.c.s.o.* '42 (WOR) [N] Spencer, MA St. Joseph's Abbey.
Bourgoin, Raymond *o.m.i.* '66 (FgM) Oblates Foreign Missions.
Bourke, Albert *o.c.d.* '39 (BO) [W] Brighton, MA Carmelite Monastery.
Bourke, Charles E. '70 (BO) Military & VA Chaplains.
Bourke, Msgr. Daniel J. '34 (SAV) [4] Savannah, GA Most Blessed Sacrament Church; Retired.
Bourke, John F. '60 (CAM) Berlin, NJ Our Lady of Mt. Carmel Church.
Bourke, Martin *s.s.c.* '74 (SEA) Des Moines, WA St. Philomena Church.
Bourke, Michael J. '60 (CAM) Washington Township, NJ SS. Peter and Paul Church.
Bourke, Msgr. Myles M. '42 (NY) [28] New York, NY Corpus Christi Church; Retired.
Bourke, Nathaniel J. '59 (GF) [7] Billings, MT St. Thomas the Apostle Church.
Bourke, Ulick *s.m.a.* '68 (NEW) [N] Tenafly, NJ Society of African Missions, Provincialate, S.M.A. Fathers.
Bourke, William D. *s.s.c.* '54 (FgM) St. Columban's Foreign Mission.
Bourne, Peter '61 (B) Salmon, ID St. Charles Church; [C] Lemhi, ID Hermitage of St. Joseph.
Bourque, Charles J. '62 (BO) [56] Boston, MA Our Lady of Lourdes Church.
Bourque, John R. '48 (SPR) Retired.
Bourque, Msgr. Joseph A. '55 (LKC) Westlake, LA St. John Bosco Church.
Bourque, Real *o.m.i.* '54 (FgM) Oblates Foreign Missions.
Bourque, Real *o.m.i.* '54 (MAN) [K] Hudson, NH Missionary Oblates of Mary Immaculate.
Bourque, Thomas *t.o.r.* '82 (ALT) [A] Loretto, PA St. Francis College.
Bourque, Thomas *t.o.r.* '82 (STU) [A] Steubenville, OH Franciscan University of Steubenville; [F] Steubenville, OH Holy Spirit Monastery.

Bourret, Philip L. *s.j.* '41 (SJ) [M] Los Gatos, CA Sacred Heart Jesuit Center.
Bouska, Jerome A. '56 (LA) South Gate, CA St. Helen Church.
Bousquet, Roland *s.t.l.* '54 (FR) [20] New Bedford, MA St. Theresa Church.
Bouterie, Thomas R. '80 (HT) [7] Houma, LA St. Louis Church.
Boutin, Emile R. '91 (BO) [1] Norwood, MA St. Catherine of Siena Church.
Bouton, Thomas F. '83 (BO) Absent on Leave.
Boutot, Michel *c.s.sp.* '93 (NO) [7] New Orleans, LA Holy Ghost Church.
Bova, Eugene R. '57 (BIS) Retired.
Bova Conte, Michael J. '71 (BO) Sudbury, MA Our Lady of Fatima Church.
Bovard, William R. '64 (PIT) Franklin Park Borough, PA St. John Neumann Church.
Bove, Ralph A. *c.s.* '78 (NY) [94] New York, NY Our Lady of Pompeii Church.
Bovee, Brian '81 (RCK) [7] Rockford, IL St. Mary Shrine, Institute of Christ the King Sovereign King Church.
Bovenzi, Robert *c.p.* '85 (SAT) [62] San Antonio, TX St. Philip of Jesus Church; [M] San Antonio, TX Casa Pasionista Guadalupe.
Bowab, Michael L. '60 (BO) Permanent Disability.
Bowden, John V. '62 (TR) Brick Town, NJ Epiphany Church.
Bowden, Lloyd '49 (JOL) Retired.
Bowe, John C. *c.r.* '68 (PBL) Pagosa Springs, CO Immaculate Heart of Mary Church.
Bowe, John F. '73 (PH) Sellersville, PA St. Agnes Church.
Bowe, Msgr. Martin (RVC) Riverhead, NY St. John the Evangelist Church.
Bowen, Daniel *c.ss.r.* '56 (ORL) [F] New Smyrna Beach, FL St. Alphonsus Villa-Redemptorist Fathers and Brothers.
Bowen, Donald J. '64 (FgM) Society of St. James the Apostle.
Bowen, Donald J. '64 (FR) Special Assignment.
Bowen, Gerard J. '77 (BAL) [13] Baltimore, MD St. Augustine Church.
Bowen, Henry G. '56 (WOR) [21] Worcester, MA St. Charles Borromeo Church.
Bowen, John W. *s.s.* '49 (BAL) [A] Baltimore, MD St. Mary's Seminary and University; [J] Baltimore, MD St. Charles Villa; [M] Baltimore, MD St. Charles Villa.
Bowen, Joseph D. '57 (PH) Abington, PA Our Lady Help of Christians Church.
Bowen, Robert *s.s.j.* '59 (NO) [P] New Orleans, LA Josephite Fathers and Brothers.
Bowens, Lorin M. '74 (MAD) Lime Ridge, WI St. Boniface Church.
Bower, Alan E. '89 (STA) Military Chaplains.
Bower, Lawrence C. '88 (BAK) Vale, OR St. Patrick's Church.
Bower, Robert F. '59 (E) Cambridge Springs, PA St. Anthony Church.
Bowering, Gerhard H. *s.j.* '70 (BGP) [O] Fairfield, CT The Fairfield Jesuit Community-Fairfield University.
Bowers, Phillip T. '64 (LFT) Fishers, IN Holy Spirit Church.
Bowers, Robert J. '87 (BO) [1] Milton, MA St. Agatha Church.
Bowers, Ronald '64 (STP) [A] St. Paul, MN The Saint Paul Seminary; [C] St. Paul, MN University of St. Thomas.
Bowers, Vernon J. '39 (RIC) Retired.
Bowes, Bruce O. '92 (NY) Hopewell Junction, NY St. Columba Church.
Bowes, Charles '71 (CIN) [43] Cincinnati, OH St. John the Baptist Church.
Bowes, David '46 (KNX) Retired.
Bowes, James J. *s.j.* (NY) [DD] New York, NY Jesuit Provincial's Office.
Bowes, James J. *s.j.* '66 (FgM) Provinces.
Bowes, John C. *c.m.* '85 (BUF) [C] Niagara University, NY Niagara University; [O] Niagara University, NY Vincentian Community at Niagara University.
Bowes, Vincent *o.c.d.* '61 (BO) [W] Brighton, MA Carmelite Monastery.
Bowes, Vincent *o.c.d.* '61 (MIL) [P] Milwaukee, WI Provincial Offices - Discalced Carmelites.
Bowker, Jeffrey *l.c.* '94 (HRT) [B] Cheshire, CT Novitiate of the Legion of Christ; [V] Orange, CT Legion of Christ, Inc.
Bowlds, Robert Kent '93 (JKS) Clarksdale, MS St. Elizabeth Church; Clarksdale, MS Immaculate Conception Church.
Bowler, James M. *s.j.* '74 (BO) [W] Boston, MA The Society of Jesus of New England-Provincial Offices.
Bowler, Joseph D. *o.s.f.s.* '45 (WIL) [I] Wilmington, DE DeSales House.
Bowler, Michael '57 (CHI) [209] Chicago, IL St. Turibius Church.
Bowles, Bill (NU) [F] St. Peter, MN St. Peter Regional Treatment Center.
Bowles, Richard J. '61 (PT) [12] Pensacola, FL St. Michael Church.
Bowles, William H. '91 (NU) Nicollet, MN St. Paul Church.
Bowling, Frederick T. '64 (BAL) Retired.
Bowling, George K. '47 (L) Retired.
Bowling, Robert A. '54 (RNO) [6] Reno, NV St. Therese Church of the Little Flower.
Bowling, Theodore B. *s.j.* '53 (FgM) Provinces.
Bowling, William Martin '97 (L) [66] Louisville, KY St. Pius X Church.
Bowman, James (RVC) Priests Released from Diocesan Assignment.
Bowman, James C. '65 (RVC) Military Chaplains.
Bowman, John '65 (SEA) Mercer Island, WA St. Monica Church.
Bowman, R. Peter '55 (CHI) [199] Chicago, IL St. Teresa Church.
Bowman, Ronald C. '82 (ALN) [4] Saint Clair, PA St. Mary Church.
Bowman, Ronald P. '82 (ALN) [4] Pottsville, PA St. Patrick Church; Frackville, PA State Prison.
Bowski, Eugene (GLP) Cuba, NM Immaculate Conception Church.
Boxleitner, Msgr. J. Jerome '56 (STP) Lino Lakes, MN Minnesota Correctional Facility; [I] Minneapolis, MN St. Joseph's Home for Children.
Boyack, Kenneth G. *c.s.p.* '79 (WDC) [B] Washington, DC St. Paul's College; [V] Washington, DC Paulist National Catholic Evangelization Assoc.
Boyce, Edmund J. *o.s.b.* '62 (MIL) [P] Benet Lake, WI St. Benedict's Abbey.
Boyce, James J. *o.carm.* '77 (NEW) Cresskill, NJ St. Therese of Lisieux Church.
Boyce, Thomas '66 (JKS) Batesville, MS St. Mary Church.
Boyd, C. Morris '78 (CHL) Asheville, NC St. Joan of Arc Church.
Boyd, Daniel A. *m.m.* '82 (FgM) Maryknoll Foreign Missions.
Boyd, Douglas A. '79 (PIT) [54] Pittsburgh, PA St. John Vianney Church.
Boyd, James A. '63 (BRK) Military Chaplains.
Boyd, John D. *s.j.* '47 (NY) [DD] New York, NY Jesuit Community at Fordham University.
Boyd, Joseph '50 (NY) Larchmont, NY SS. John and Paul Church.
Boyd, Norman *s.a.* '65 (NY) [DD] Garrison, NY Franciscan Friars of the Atonement.
Boyd, Richard '79 (CR) Park Rapids, MN St. Peter's Church.
Boyd, Rick *o.m.i.* '79 (CR) Two Inlets, MN St. Mary's Church.
Boyd, Theophane *o.c.s.o.* '55 (DEN) [M] Snowmass, CO St. Benedict's Monastery.
Boyea, Earl '78 (DET) [A] Detroit, MI Sacred Heart Major Seminary, Inc.
Boyer, Msgr. Leland '49 (LA) La Canada Flintridge, CA St. Bede the Venerable Church.
Boyer, Msgr. Leland J. '49 (LA) Retired.
Boyer, Mark G. '76 (SPC) Special Assignment.
Boyer, Millard G. (LAF) On Special Assignment.
Boyer, Thomas J. '68 (OKL) [1] Oklahoma City, OK Cathedral of Our Lady of Perpetual Help.
Boyer, Wayne M. '87 (JC) Martinsburg, MO St. Joseph Church; Wellsville, MO Resurrection Church.
Boyhan, J. Patrick '77 (NOR) [F] Cromwell, CT Missionaries of the Holy Apostles.
Boykins, Charles '65 (JKS) Vicksburg, MS St. Mary Church.
Boylan, Colman *o.f.m.cap.* '49 (NOR) [4] Middletown, CT St. Pius X Church.
Boylan, Dennis '74 (AMA) Childress, TX Holy Angels Church.
Boylan, John J. '56 (BRK) [176] Queens, NY Holy Child Jesus Church.
Boylan, Martin M. '80 (SCR) Gouldsboro, PA St. Rita Church.
Boyle, Andrew J. *o.s.a.* '54 (PH) [AA] Villanova, PA St. Thomas Monastery.
Boyle, Bernard J. *s.j.* '65 (BAL) [M] Baltimore, MD Jesuit Fathers and Brothers Maryland Provincial Curia.
Boyle, Bernard J. *s.j.* '65 (FgM) Provinces.
Boyle, Msgr. Charles '40 (ROC) [E] Rochester, NY St. Ann's Home for the Aged.
Boyle, Msgr. Charles V. '40 (ROC) Retired.
Boyle, Daniel J. '78 (SPR) Adams, MA Notre Dame des Sept Douleurs Church; Adams, MA St. Thomas Aquinas Church.
Boyle, Dennis P. '73 (PH) Military Chaplains.
Boyle, Edward F. *s.j.* '69 (BO) [E] Boston, MA Boston College High School & Jesuit Community.
Boyle, Eugene J. '46 (SJ) Retired.
Boyle, Msgr. Francis V. '55 (NY) [199] Staten Island, NY Blessed Sacrament Church.
Boyle, George J. '52 (PH) Manoa, PA Sacred Heart Church.
Boyle, Gregory J. *s.j.* '84 (LA) [10] Los Angeles, CA Dolores Mission Church.
Boyle, Howard '73 (BAL) Retired.
Boyle, James '61 (SEA) Puyallup, WA All Saints Church; Buckley, WA Rainier School.
Boyle, James A. '49 (FWT) Retired.
Boyle, James E. '66 (ROC) Fairport, NY St. John of Rochester Church.
Boyle, James F. *c.s.c.* '57 (SCR) [4] Wilkes-Barre, PA St. Casimir's Church.
Boyle, James M. '56 (HRT) Retired.
Boyle, John *s.j.* '60 (LA) [CC] Los Angeles, CA Archdiocesan Office for Campus Ministry.
Boyle, John '83 (NY) [226] Staten Island, NY St. Roch Church.
Boyle, John B. *v.f.* '76 (SCR) Tobyhanna, PA St. Ann Church.
Boyle, John J. (ALT) Retired.
Boyle, John L. *s.j.* '60 (LA) [C] Los Angeles, CA Loyola Marymount University.
Boyle, John P. '56 (DAV) [C] Iowa City, IA Catholic Chair of Religion.
Boyle, John T. '69 (CHI) [57] Chicago, IL St. Felicitas Church.
Boyle, Msgr. Lawrence P. '62 (CAM) Brigantine, NJ St. Thomas Church.
Boyle, Leo A. '44 (KC) Retired.
Boyle, Michael '95 (RVC) Hauppauge, NY St. Thomas More Church.
Boyle, Michael J. *c.m.* '59 (PHX) [26] Phoenix, AZ St. Vincent de Paul Church.
Boyle, Neil *s.s.c.* '43 (FgM) St. Columban's Foreign Mission.
Boyle, Patrick *o.f.m.* (NY) Dobbs Ferry, NY St. Cabrini Nursing Home.
Boyle, Patrick *o.s.m.* '56 (ORG) [H] Buena Park, CA Servite Fathers And Brothers.
Boyle, Patrick *o.c.s.o.* '67 (SLC) [F] Huntsville, UT Abbey of Our Lady of the Holy Trinity of the Order of Cistercians.
Boyle, Patrick D. *o.f.m.* '80 (NY) [DD] Mount Vernon, NY St. Bernardine of Siena Friary.
Boyle, Patrick J. *s.j.* '63 (CHI) [A] Mundelein, IL University of St. Mary of the Lake-Mundelein Seminary.
Boyle, Msgr. Patrick J. '65 (NY) [135] Bronx, NY St. Brendan Church.
Boyle, Msgr. Raymond J. '56 (PEO) Seneca, IL St. Patrick's Church.
Boyle, Richard *o.s.m.* '84 (P) [31] Portland, OR St. Rita Church.
Boyle, Richard M. *o.s.m.* '84 (P) [L] Portland, OR The Grotto, The National Sanctuary of Our Sorrowful Mother.
Boyle, Richard P. *s.j.* '75 (BO) [W] Boston, MA The Society of Jesus of New England-Provincial Offices.
Boyle, Richard P. *s.j.* '75 (TUC) [F] Tucson, AZ Jesuit Community of the Vatican Observatory.
Boyle, Robert J. (BO) Retired.
Boyle, Robert J. *s.j.* '50 (BUF) [50] Buffalo, NY St. Michael Church.
Boyle, Robert J. '51 (BO) Acton, MA St. Elizabeth of Hungary Church; [D] Brighton, MA Archdiocesan Central High Schools, Inc.
Boyle, Robert J. '63 (PIT) Bellevue, PA Assumption of the Blessed Virgin Mary on the Beautiful River Church.
Boyle, Robert R. *s.j.* '50 (MIL) [P] Wauwatosa, WI Jesuit Community at St. Camillus.
Boyle, Stephen M. *o.praem.* '90 (ORG) [H] Silverado, CA Norbertine Fathers of Orange Inc.
Boyle, Stephen M. *o.praem.* '92 (ORG) [D] Siverado, CA St. Michael's College Preparatory High School.
Boyle, Stephen M. '95 (BO) [2] Weymouth, MA St. Francis Xavier Church.
Boyle, Sylvan *o.carm.* '48 (GAL) [3] Houston, TX St. Albert of Trapani Church.
Boyle, Thomas '56 (PHX) Retired.
Boyle, Thomas '64 (ALB) Gloversville, NY Sacred Heart Church.
Boyle, Thomas S. '41 (CHI) [57] Chicago, IL St. Felicitas Church; Retired.
Boyle, Valentine L. *o.carm.* '46 (PHX) [16] Phoenix, AZ St. Luke Church; [F] Phoenix, AZ Carmelite Community.
Boyle, Victor J. '60 (BRK) Absent on Leave.
Boyle, William E. *s.j.* '45 (NY) [DD] New York, NY Jesuit Community at Fordham University.
Boyle, William M. '56 (ORL) [1] Orlando, FL Mary Queen of the Universe Shrine Church.
Boymer, Lloyd '43 (CLV) Brecksville, OH St. Basil the Great Church.
Boymer, Lloyd J. '43 (CLV) Macedonia, OH Our Lady of Guadalupe Church; Retired.
Bozada, Mark S. '81 (STL) Chesterfield, MO Incarnate Word Church.
Bozanic, Anton '77 (BRK) [203] Queens, NY Most Precious Blood Church; [T] Brooklyn, NY Catholic Migration & Refugee Office, Catholic Migration Services, Inc.
Bozek, Robert J. '78 (WDC) [5] Silver Spring, MD Christ the King Church; Pastoral Center Special Ministries.
Bozel, Msgr. Robert A. '48 (BAL) Retired; [J] Timonium, MD Stella Maris Operating Corporation.

Boznar, Joseph P. '70 (CLV) [76] Cleveland, OH St. Vitus Church.
Bozung, James M. '61 (GR) Belmont, MI Assumption of the Blessed Virgin Mary Church.
Bozza, Nicholas G. '77 (PAT) [7] Paterson, NJ St. George Church.
Bozzell, Richard '94 (BAL) Clarksville, MD St. Louis Church.
Bozzelli, Joseph V. '67 (WIL) Bear, DE St. Elizabeth Ann Seton Church.
Bozzo, Kenneth J. '80 (FRS) Kingsburg, CA Holy Family Church.
Braak, Thomas E. '59 (DUB) Marshalltown, IA St. Henry's Church; [F] Marshalltown, IA Marshalltown Area Consolidated Catholic School.
Braakhuis, Frits J. *c.m.* '49 (CHY) Riverton, WY St. Margaret's Church.
Braaten, James B. '89 (BIS) Mohall, ND St. Jerome Church.
Braband, James *s.v.d.* '80 (CHI) [B] Techny, IL Divine Word Residence; [N] Techny, IL Society of the Divine Word, Provincial Headquarter-Chicago Prov.
Brabandt, James *o.f.m.* '95 (WDC) [M] Washington, DC Commissariat of the Holy Land, Franciscan Monastery - Mount St. Sepulchre.
Bracci, Carlos A. '77 (NEW) Harrison, NJ Holy Cross Church.
Bracco, Theodore *o.f.m.* '66 (SFD) [K] Teutopolis, IL St. Francis Assisi Friary.
Bracht, Donald F. *s.m.* '43 (SJ) [M] Cupertino, CA The Marianist Mission.
Bracikowski, Felix *ofm conv.* '38 (BUF) [D] Athol Springs, NY St. Francis High School; [O] Athol Springs, NY St. Francis of Assisi Friary.
Bracke, James A. *c.s.c.* '80 (COS) [10] Colorado Springs, CO Sacred Heart Church.
Bracken, Jerome *c.p.* '68 (BRK) [U] Jamaica, NY Immaculate Conception Monastery.
Bracken, Msgr. John J. '67 (BRK) [233] Queens, NY Resurrection-Ascension Church.
Bracken, Joseph A. *s.j.* '62 (CIN) [D] Cincinnati, OH Xavier University; [M] Cincinnati, OH Jesuit Community at Xavier Unversity.
Bracken, W. Jerome *c.p.* '68 (NEW) [A] South Orange, NJ Immaculate Conception Seminary; [B] South Orange, NJ Seton Hall University.
Bracken, Walter *s.v.d.* '71 (CHI) [B] Techny, IL Divine Word Residence; [N] Techny, IL Society of the Divine Word, Provincial Headquarter-Chicago Prov.
Brackenridge, David F. '52 (PH) Upper Darby, PA St. Alice Church.
Bracket, Louis P. '47 (MAR) Retired.
Brackett, Anthony H. '59 (BUR) Retired.
Brackett, Christopher *l.c.* '93 (HRT) [B] Cheshire, CT Novitiate of the Legion of Christ.
Brackett, Joseph '57 (GLP) Retired.
Brackett, Richard M. *s.j.* '55 (BO) [W] Weston, MA Campion Health Center, Inc.
Brackin, James *s.c.j.* '75 (MIL) [P] Hales Corners, WI Sacred Heart Monastery.
Brackin, James D. *s.c.j.* '75 (MIL) [B] Hales Corners, WI Sacred Heart School of Theology.
Brackley, J. Dean *s.j.* '76 (FgM) Provinces.
Brackley, J. Dean *s.j.* '76 (NY) [DD] New York, NY Jesuit Provincial's Office.
Bracq, Edward E. '50 (MAN) Retired.
Bradbury, Henry M. *c.m.* '59 (BUF) [8] Niagara Falls, NY Our Lady of Lebanon Church.
Braden, Msgr. Leroy H. '53 (GAL) Pearland, TX St. Helen Church.
Braden, Patrick O. *c.s.b.* '52 (GAL) [Q] Houston, TX Residence of the Basilian Fathers of the University of St. Thomas.
Bradican, Msgr. Francis L. '36 (ARL) Annandale, VA Holy Spirit Church; Retired.
Bradler, Robert '62 (ROC) [L] Rochester, NY Holy Childhood Association.
Bradler, Robert C. '62 (ROC) [59] Rochester, NY St. Thomas the Apostle Church.
Bradley, Alfred *c.ss.r.* '88 (STV) [2] Christiansted, VI Church of the Holy Cross.
Bradley, Allan P. '72 (SUP) New Richmond, WI Immaculate Conception Church.
Bradley, Allan W. '70 (COV) Ludlow, KY Sts. Boniface and James Church.
Bradley, Bruce A. '78 (DAL) Allen, TX St. Jude Church.
Bradley, Daniel P. *m.s.* '93 (ORL) [3] Orlando, FL Good Shepherd Church.
Bradley, Denis J.M. '70 (WDC) Special Ministries.
Bradley, Dennis J. '77 (PIT) Midland, PA St. Blaise Church.
Bradley, Edward C. *s.j.* '79 (PH) [AA] Philadelphia, PA Jesuit Community at St. Joseph's University.
Bradley, Edward G. '66 (NEW) [1] Orange, NJ St. John's Church; [C] West Orange, NJ Seton Hall Preparatory School.
Bradley, Gary *s.j.* '75 (CHK) Garapan Village, District 11, MP Kristo Rai Parish.
Bradley, Gary J. *s.j.* '75 (FgM) Provinces.
Bradley, H. Cornell *s.j.* '69 (PH) [C] Philadelphia, PA St. Joseph's University; [AA] Philadelphia, PA Jesuit Community at St. Joseph's University.
Bradley, Harold C. '61 (STL) [P] St. Louis, MO Jesuit Community Corporation at St. Louis University - Jesuit Hall.
Bradley, Hugh J. '89 (CAM) [3] Vineland, NJ St. Francis of Assisi Church.
Bradley, J. Edward '75 (OWN) Henderson, KY Holy Name of Jesus Church.
Bradley, J. Richard '81 (TLS) Muskogee, OK Saint Joseph Church.
Bradley, James *s.d.s.* '61 (LA) Whittier, CA St. Bruno Church.
Bradley, James *o.s.f.s.* '61 (LAN) [B] Jackson, MI Lumen Christi High School.
Bradley, James F. '43 (PH) Media, PA Nativity of the Blessed Virgin Mary Church; Retired.
Bradley, James P. *s.j.* '58 (WDC) [M] Washington, DC Carroll House.
Bradley, James P. *s.j.* '67 (NO) [P] New Orleans, LA Jesuit Provincial Office.
Bradley, James P. '73 (BRK) [208] Queens, NY Our Lady of the Cenacle Church.
Bradley, John A. '65 (ORG) Capistrano Beach, CA San Felipe de Jesus Church.
Bradley, Msgr. John J. '42 (SB) Retired.
Bradley, John J. '67 (ALB) [3] Albany, NY Blessed Sacrament Church.
Bradley, John Paul '44 (CHL) Absent On Leave.
Bradley, Joseph '91 (SFR) [53] San Francisco, CA St. Vincent de Paul Church.
Bradley, Msgr. Joseph P. '38 (BAL) Retired.
Bradley, Jude C. *o.s.b.* '47 (PAT) [M] Newton, NJ St. Paul's Abbey.
Bradley, Matthew '72 (BO) [Y] Scituate, MA Foyer of Charity.
Bradley, Michael *o.m.i.* '66 (FgM) Oblates Foreign Missions.
Bradley, Michael J. '78 (CHI) [1] Cicero, IL St. Anthony Church.
Bradley, Msgr. Paul F. '41 (TR) Retired.
Bradley, Paul J. '71 (PIT) Ross Township, PA St. Sebastian Church.
Bradley, Richard S. *s.j.* '49 (SB) [E] Morongo Valley, CA St. Michael's of Morongo Valley, Inc.
Bradley, Richard W. *o.carm.* '59 (NEW) Paramus, NJ Carmelite Chapel of St. Therese Church.
Bradley, Robert *s.j.* '55 (AUS) [9] Austin, TX Sacred Heart Church.
Bradley, Robert '73 (CC) Retired.
Bradley, Robert M. '57 (LA) Retired.
Bradley, Theodore F.X. (SPK) Spokane, Wa U.S. Veterans Hospital.
Bradley, Theodore F.X. '58 (SPK) Retired.
Bradley, Thomas J. '93 (CHI) [179] Chicago, IL Queen of All Saints Basilica Church.
Bradley, Msgr. William J. '57 (NY) [1] New Rochelle, NY Blessed Sacrament Church.
Bradlo, Antoni *c.ss.r.* '57 (CHI) [82] Chicago, IL Holy Innocents Church.
Bradly, Michael '91 (TUC) Globe, AZ Holy Angels Church.
Bradower, Theodore J. *t.o.r.* '50 (FWT) [8] Fort Worth, TX St. Andrew Church.
Bradshaw, Alexander H. '85 (ROC) [23] Rochester, NY Holy Ghost Church.
Bradshaw, Jordan *o.p.* (OAK) [N] Oakland, CA Western Dominican Province.
Bradshaw, Joseph *o.p.* '92 (SEA) [22] Seattle, WA Blessed Sacrament Church.
Bradshaw, Paul F. '70 (FTW) [B] Notre Dame, IN University of Notre Dame Du Lac.
Bradshaw, Terry L. '80 (L) [12] Louisville, KY St. Bartholomew Church.
Bradt, Kevin M. *s.j.* '79 (OAK) [N] Berkeley, CA Jesuit Community at Jesuit School of Theology at Berkeley.
Bradtke, Thomas A. '62 (DEN) Absent on Leave.
Bradunas, John J. *o.s.f.s.* '73 (WIL) [I] Childs, MD Oblates of St. Francis De Sales.
Brady, Andrew J. *s.j.* '45 (NY) [DD] New York, NY Murray-Weigel Hall.
Brady, Charles '55 (SAC) [3] Sacramento, CA Holy Spirit Church.
Brady, Coman V. '59 (BRK) [144] Brooklyn, NY St. Vincent Ferrer Church.
Brady, Daniel J. '42 (NY) Armonk, NY St. Patrick Church; Retired.
Brady, Daniel J. '61 (CHI) [1] Mt. Prospect, IL St. Cecilia Church.
Brady, Daniel O. '84 (RIC) Pocahontas, VA St. Elizabeth Church; Tazewell, VA St. Theresa Church.
Brady, Daniel P. *o.p.* '48 (DAL) [M] Irving, TX Dominican Priory of St. Albert the Great.
Brady, Edmund P. '59 (BRK) [193] Queens, NY St. Margaret Mary Church; [216] Queens, NY Our Lady of Mount Carmel Church.
Brady, Edward J. *s.j.* '59 (BAL) [M] Baltimore, MD Jesuit Fathers and Brothers Maryland Provincial Curia.
Brady, Edward J. *s.j.* '59 (FgM) Provinces.
Brady, Msgr. Frank J. '46 (SC) Retired.
Brady, G. James *c.s.c.* '59 (P) Shaw, OR St. Mary Church; [B] Portland, OR University of Portland; [L] Portland, OR Holy Cross Fathers & Brothers, C.S.C. - University of Portland.
Brady, Gerald '83 (SPR) Hatfield, MA Holy Trinity Church.
Brady, Msgr. Gerard J. '59 (SR) Napa, CA St. Thomas Aquinas Church.
Brady, James *s.m.m.* '92 (BRK) [195] Queens, NY St. Mary Gate of Heaven Church; [U] Ozone Park, NY Montfort Missionaries Provincialate - for Nation Community.
Brady, James H.T. *s.o.l.t.* '89 (CC) [H] Robstown, TX Society of Our Lady of the Most Holy Trinity.
Brady, James H.T. *s.o.l.t.* '89 (WH) Grant Town, WV St. Anthony's Church.
Brady, James J. '53 (MIL) Retired.
Brady, James J. '72 (TR) Bradley Beach, NJ Ascension Church.
Brady, James R. '57 (ALN) Tremont, PA Immaculate Conception Church.
Brady, Jeremiah *s.s.j.* (WIL) Wilmington, DE St. Francis Hospital.
Brady, John '49 (LA) Van Nuys, CA St. Elisabeth Church.
Brady, John '55 (SFS) Retired.
Brady, Msgr. John B. '55 (WDC) Avenue, MD Holy Angels Church; [V] Pomfret, MD Ministr-O-Media, Inc.
Brady, John F. *s.j.* '48 (DEN) [31] Denver, CO St. Ignatius Loyola Church; [M] Denver, CO Loyola Parish - Jesuit Community.
Brady, Joseph '89 (SD) Poway, CA St. Gabriel Church.
Brady, Jude W. *o.s.b.* '80 (E) St. Marys, PA St. Mary Church.
Brady, Jules M. *s.j.* '53 (KC) [B] Kansas City, MO Rockhurst College; [J] Kansas City, MO Rockhurst College - Jesuit Community.
Brady, Leo Patrick *c.p.* (GAL) [S] Houston, TX Holy Name Retreat Center.
Brady, Martin D. *t.o.r.* '56 (ALT) [F] Newry, PA St. Bernardine Monastery.
Brady, Mel P. *o.f.m.* '50 (DET) [3] Detroit, MI St. Aloysius Church.
Brady, Patrick *o.m.i.* '48 (NY) [FF] Newburgh, NY Our Lady of Hope Center.
Brady, Patrick A. '61 (WIL) Rehoboth, DE St. Edmond Church; Retired.
Brady, Patrick J. '64 (CAM) [5] Atlantic City, NJ Our Lady Star of the Sea Church.
Brady, Patrick J. '93 (PH) [147] Philadelphia, PA Stella Maris Church.
Brady, Philip W. '43 (BGP) Retired.
Brady, Reginald '93 (DET) Royal Oak, MI Shrine of the Little Flower Church.
Brady, Richard J. '59 (BO) [5] Lawrence, MA St. Francis Church.
Brady, Msgr. Roger J. '58 (BO) Belmont, MA St. Luke Church.
Brady, Severin *o.f.m.* '66 (PRO) [P] Providence, RI St. Francis Friary.
Brady, Theodore E.A. *s.j.* '61 (BAL) [H] Baltimore, MD Mercy Medical Center, Inc.; [M] Baltimore, MD Ferdinand Wheeler Jesuit Community.
Brady, Msgr. Thomas C. '54 (RCK) South Beloit, IL St. Peter Church.
Brady, Thomas E. *s.j.* '47 (ALB) [O] Auriesville, NY Jesuit Retreat House for Priests, Religious and Lay People.
Brady, Msgr. Thomas F. '59 (BRK) [50] Brooklyn, NY Good Shepherd Church.
Brady, Vincent '67 (SAC) [1] Sacramento, CA Cathedral of the Blessed Sacrament.
Brady, Vincent M. '95 (PSC) Endicott, NY SS. Peter and Paul's Church.
Brady, William J. *o.p.* '42 (NO) [30] New Orleans, LA St. Dominic Church.
Brady, William J. '80 (SFR) [16] San Francisco, CA St. Emydius Church.
Braganza, Joe (NY) [1] Port Chester, NY Our Lady of Mercy Church.
Bragotti, Joseph *m.c.c.j.* '62 (CIN) [M] Cincinnati, OH Comboni Missionaries (Verona Fathers)-Comboni Mission Center.
Bragotti, Joseph *m.c.c.j.* '62 (FgM) Comboni Foreign Missions.
Brague, Robert J. '70 (VEN) Palmetto, FL Holy Cross Church.
Brahill, John *o.s.b.* '82 (FgM) American - Cassinese Congregation Foreign Missions.
Brahill, John *o.s.b.* '82 (RCK) [H] Aurora, IL Marmion Abbey-St. Augustine's Abbey.
Brahm, Harvey W. '51 (MIL) Brookfield, WI St. Luke Church.
Braida, Ernest E. '64 (DAV) Newton, IA Sacred Heart Church.
Brainard, Arthur *s.d.b.* '53 (OAK) [E] Richmond, CA Salesian High School.
Brainard, Ernest '45 (OAK) [2] Oakland, CA St. Andrew-St. Joseph Church.
Brainard, Ernest B. '45 (OAK) Retired.
Brainerd, Winthrop '84 (WDC) [12] Washington, DC

Epiphany Church.
Brajkovich, Thomas R. '61 (PEO) Wyoming, IL St. Dominic's Church.
Brakora, Anthony '35 (LAN) Retired.
Braley, James P. '75 (BO) [1] Norwood, MA St. Catherine of Siena Church.
Brambilla, Charles A. '71 (STP) Lindstrom, MN St. Bridget of Sweden Church.
Brambilla, Sigmund *o.f.m.* '55 (NY) [DD] New York, NY Franciscan Province of the Immaculate Conception.
Bramble, Donald *o.p.* '76 (OAK) [N] Oakland, CA Dominican Order (Western Province), St. Albert's Priory.
Bramble, Donald J. *o.p.* '76 (OAK) [N] Oakland, CA Western Dominican Province.
Brambora, Jeffrey '93 (LFT) [C] Lafayette, IN St. Elizabeth Medical Center.
Bramlage, Gregory '96 (IND) Milan, IN St. Charles Borromeo Church; Morris, IN St. Anthony of Padua Church; St. Nicholas, IN St. Nicholas Church; St. Pius, IN St. Pius Church.
Bramlage, James A. '64 (CIN) [1] Cincinnati, OH St. Peter in Chains Cathedral.
Bramlage, Vincent J. '43 (CIN) Retired.
Bramwell, Bevil *o.m.i.* '85 (BO) [W] Lowell, MA Missionary Oblates of Mary Immaculate.
Bramwell, Bevil *o.m.i.* '85 (MAN) [K] Hudson, NH Missionary Oblates of Mary Immaculate.
Branagan, Henry *f.m.s.i.* '63 (BO) [B] Framingham, MA Sylva Maria.
Brancaccio, Alberto A. *s.o.l.t.* '93 (CC) [H] Robstown, TX Society of Our Lady of the Most Holy Trinity.
Branch, Edward '74 (ATL) [L] Atlanta, GA Campus Ministry.
Branch, Edward B. '74 (L) On Duty Outside the Archdiocese.
Branch, Leslie '71 (WDC) Retired; [D] Washington, DC Archbishop Carroll High School.
Branche, John S. '54 (OG) Retired.
Branconnier, Gerard '78 (WOR) Absent on Leave.
Brand, Edmund H. *o.c.s.o.* '54 (ATL) [I] Conyers, GA The Monastery of the Holy Spirit.
Brand, Michael *c.s.b.* '73 (LAN) [F] Ann Arbor, MI St. Joseph Mercy Hospital.
Brand, William *o.f.m.* '74 (LA) [72] Los Angeles, CA St. Joseph Church; [P] Los Angeles, CA St. Anne's.
Brande, Edward W. *s.j.* '63 (NEW) [B] Jersey City, NJ Saint Peter's College; [N] Jersey City, NJ Jesuits of Saint Peter's College, Inc.
Brandenberger, Robert J. *c.m.* '52 (PH) [AA] Philadelphia, PA Congregation of the Mission.
Brandenhoff, Peter B. '70 (WIN) On Duty Outside the Diocese.
Brandes, John F. '51 (NU) Retired.
Brandes, John F. '51 (STP) On Duty Outside the Archdiocese.
Brandmeyer, William H. '37 (BEL) Retired.
Brando, Joseph J. '72 (KNX) Alcoa, TN Our Lady of Fatima Church.
Brandow, Stephen J. '96 (ALX) Pineville, LA Central Louisiana State Hospital.
Brandstrader, Frederick L. '68 (CHI) Wheeling, IL St. Joseph the Worker Church.
Brandt, Joseph D. '83 (PH) West Chester, PA St. Agnes Church; [D] West Chester, PA Bishop Shanahan High School.
Brandt, Msgr. Lawrence E. '69 (E) [H] Erie, PA Gannondale Residential Center for Girls.
Brandt, Paul C. '84 (PH) Roslyn, PA St. John of the Cross Church; [D] Wyncote, PA Bishop McDevitt High School.
Branigan, Francis H. '37 (GR) Retired.
Branigan, Patrick G. '43 (RVC) Retired.
Brankin, Anthony J. '75 (CHI) [206] Chicago, IL St. Thomas More Church.
Brankin, Parick M. '79 (TLS) [F] Tulsa, OK St. John Villas, Inc.
Brankin, Patrick '79 (TLS) Collinsville, OK St. Therese Church.
Brankin, Patrick M. '79 (CHI) On Duty Outside the Archdiocese.
Brannan, Patrick T. *s.j.* '63 (SCR) [C] Scranton, PA University of Scranton.
Brannen, Brett A. '91 (SAV) Macon, GA Holy Spirit Church.
Brannen, Charles J. *s.j.* '52 (CHI) [N] Chicago, IL Chicago Province of the Society of Jesus-Provincial Office.
Brannigan, Joseph E. *m.m.* '46 (NY) [DD] Maryknoll, NY Maryknoll Fathers and Brothers.
Brannon, Bernard *s.j.* '53 (SJ) [M] Los Gatos, CA Sacred Heart Jesuit Center.
Brannon, Robert F. '58 (GBG) West Newton, PA Holy Family Church.
Branon, Philip J. '51 (BUR) South Hero, VT St. Rose of Lima Church.
Bransfield, J. Brian '94 (PH) Newtown, PA St. Andrew Church.
Bransfield, Msgr. Michael J. '71 (PH) On Duty Outside the Archdiocese.
Bransfield, Msgr. Michael J. '71 (WDC) [Q] Washington, DC Basilica of the National Shrine of the Immaculate Conception.
Bransfield, Thomas A. '64 (BUR) Orleans, VT St. Theresa of Child Jesus Church.
Branson, Bernard E. '59 (KC) Smithville, MO Church of the Good Shepherd.
Branson, Dale '97 (TUC) [10] Tucson, AZ St. Ambrose Church.
Brant, David '65 (SEA) Edmonds, WA Holy Rosary Church.
Brant, Paul W. *s.j.* (R) Kinston, NC Holy Trinity-Our Lady of the Atonement Church.
Brant, Paul W. *s.j.* '77 (R) [E] Raleigh, NC Jesuit Community.
Brantley, Charles (CHL) Statesville, NC St. Philip the Apostle Church.
Brantman, Thomas E. '75 (RCK) Hampshire, IL St. Charles Borromeo Church.
Brantome, Oscar '88 (MIA) Miami Lakes, FL Our Lady of the Lakes Church; Absent on Sick Leave.
Braquet, David J. '94 (ALX) Lecompte, LA St. Martin Church.
Braquet, Patrick X. '97 (ALX) Natchitoches, LA Immaculate Conception Church; Powhatan, LA St. Francis Church.
Brashears, Bill '82 (AMA) Retired.
Brasher, C. John '75 (SFE) Springer, NM St. Joseph Church.
Brasley, Msgr. Lucian R. (CC) Retired.
Brassard, Leo *a.a.* '69 (BO) [W] Brighton, MA Assumptionist Center.
Brassard, Ronald E. '74 (PRO) [3] Cranston, RI Immaculate Conception Church.
Brassil, James A. '62 (RVC) Seaford, NY Maria Regina Church.
Brassil, Kevin J. '58 (PRO) Portsmouth, RI St. Barnabas Church.
Bratek, Martin *c.r.* '72 (PT) Panama City, FL St. John the Evangelist Church.
Brath, John A. '68 (SPC) Kimberling City, MO Our Lady of the Cove Church.
Bratko, Kenneth R. *c.r.* '64 (CHI) Schaumburg, IL St. Matthew Church.
Bratkowski, Allen (MIL) [48] Milwaukee, WI St. Margaret Mary Church.
Bratkowski, Allen *o.s.cam.* '89 (MIL) [K] Milwaukee, WI St. Mary's Hospital of Milwaukee.
Bratus, Walter N. '56 (GBG) Retired.
Braud, Dominic *o.s.b.* '61 (NO) [P] St. Benedict, LA St. Joseph Abbey.
Braud, Dominic R. *o.s.b.* '61 (NO) [A] St. Benedict, LA St. Joseph's Seminary College.
Braud, Ronald J. '64 (NO) Gretna, LA St. Joseph Church.
Braudis, Joseph M. '77 (ALN) Hamburg, PA St. Mary Church.
Brauer, Frank J. '86 (BAL) Edgewater, MD Our Lady of Perpetual Help Church.
Brauer, Mark S. '92 (DET) [16] Detroit, MI St. Christine Church; [25] Detroit, MI St. Gemma Galgani Church.
Braukman, Donald '86 (CR) Florian, MN Assumption Church; Greenbush, MN Blessed Sacrament Church.
Brault, Bernard *s.m.m.* '68 (BRK) [195] Queens, NY St. Mary Gate of Heaven Church.
Brault, Gilles '71 (MAR) Champion, MI Sacred Heart Church; Republic, MI St. Augustine Church; Marquette, MI Marquette General Hospital.
Brault, Laurence V. '77 (WOR) Upton, MA Holy Angels Church.
Brault, Y. David '77 (WDC) Poolesville, MD Our Lady of the Presentation Church.
Braun, David F. '54 (CHI) Retired.
Braun, David J. '55 (MIL) Lake Geneva, WI St. Francis de Sales Church.
Braun, David L. '81 (BEL) Wendelin, IL Holy Cross Church.
Braun, Dean E. '69 (BEL) Retired.
Braun, Donald B. '57 (MIL) Fox Lake, WI Immaculate Conception - St. Mary Church; Lost Lake, WI St. Mary Church; Randolph, WI St. Gabriel Church.
Braun, Edgar F. '40 (MIL) Retired.
Braun, Msgr. Francis '54 (BUF) [45] Buffalo, NY St. Mark Church.
Braun, Gary G. '77 (STL) [V] St. Louis, MO Washington University Newman Centers.
Braun, Gerard E. *s.j.* '46 (NY) [DD] New York, NY St. Ignatius Loyola Residence; [HH] New York, NY Jesuit Seminary and Mission Bureau, Inc.
Braun, H. Gerard '85 (FAR) Valley City, ND St. Catherine's Church.
Braun, John J. *m.afr.* '57 (FgM) Missionaries of Africa Foreign Missions.
Braun, John S. '87 (SPC) Monett, MO St. Lawrence Church.
Braun, Michael C. '61 (LC) Black River Falls, WI St. Joseph Church.
Braun, Msgr. Michael R. '67 (FRS) [2] Bakersfield, CA Our Lady of Perpetual Help Church; [H] Bakersfield, CA Bakersfield College Newman Center.
Braun, Norbert L. '57 (CIN) Retired.
Braun, Robert *o.m.i.* '51 (BEL) [F] Belleville, IL Shrine of Our Lady of the Snows.
Braun, Robert G. '59 (MIL) Eden, WI St. Mary Church.
Braun, Serran R. '55 (SAN) Retired.
Braun, Virgil '60 (SCL) Eden Valley, MN The Church of the Assumption.
Braun, Virgil R. '60 (NU) Eden Valley, MN St. Peter Church.
Braunreuther, Robert J. *s.j.* (BAL) [39] Baltimore, MD St. Ignatius Church; [E] Baltimore, MD St. Ignatius Loyola Academy.
Braunreuther, Robert J. *s.j.* '65 (BO) [W] Boston, MA The Society of Jesus of New England-Provincial Offices.
Bravo, Enrique *c.s.b.* '96 (SFE) [14] Albuquerque, NM Sacred Heart Church.
Bravo, Gregorio (SJN) [36] San Juan, PR Maria Madre de La Iglesia Church.
Bravo, Joseph '77 (SFR) Absent on Leave.
Bravo, Joseph A. '77 (SFR) Olema, CA Sacred Heart Church.
Bray, Kevin '67 (FRS) Absent on Sick Leave.
Bray, Kevin M. *o.s.b.* '51 (PAT) [M] Morristown, NJ St. Mary's Abbey.
Bray, William A. '54 (HRT) East Haven, CT St. Clare Church.
Brazaskas, Robert '66 (TUC) Green Valley, AZ Our Lady of the Valley Church.
Brazil, Sean *s.s.c.* '54 (ORG) Special Assignment; [G] Westminster, CA Korean Catholic Ministry; [H] Westminster, CA Columban Fathers.
Breaker, Donald J. '64 (CIN) Military Chaplains.
Bream, James I. '64 (SFS) Yankton, SD Sacred Heart Church.
Breau, Paschal *s.a.* '79 (NY) [DD] Garrison, NY Generalate of the Franciscan Friars of the Atonement-St. James Friary.
Breault, Charles *o.m.i.* '59 (BO) [W] Lowell, MA Missionary Oblates of Mary Immaculate.
Breault, Charles *o.m.i.* '59 (FgM) Oblates Foreign Missions.
Breault, Charles *o.m.i.* '59 (MAN) [K] Hudson, NH Missionary Oblates of Mary Immaculate.
Breault, William F. *s.j.* '62 (SAC) [G] Carmichael, CA Jesuit High School Community of Sacramento.
Breaux, Duane L. '90 (BR) Pierre Part, LA St. Joseph the Worker Church.
Breaux, Louis Allen '81 (LAF) Catahoula, LA St. Rita Church.
Breaux, O. Joseph '68 (LAF) Duson, LA St. Theresa of the Child Jesus Church; [K] Opelousas, LA Cursillo Center.
Brecheteau, Gabriel *c.p.* '48 (FgM) Mission Procurators.
Brecht, David L. *o.s.a.* '65 (CHI) [N] Olympia Fields, IL The Augustinian Provincialate Tolentine Center; [N] Olympia Fields, IL Tolentine Monastery at Tolentine Center.
Brecht, David L. *o.s.a.* '65 (FgM) Foreign Missions.
Brechtl, Joseph A. '44 (MAD) Retired.
Breckensiek, Marne *o.f.m.* '65 (PEO) [3] Peoria, IL Sacred Heart Church.
Bredeck, Martin J. *s.j.* '64 (KC) [B] Kansas City, MO Rockhurst College; [J] Kansas City, MO Rockhurst College - Jesuit Community.
Bredemann, George '83 (PHX) Unassigned.
Bredeweg, Frank H. *c.s.b.* '64 (DET) [E] Redford, MI Catholic Central High School.
Breedlove, Lawrence '56 (FWT) [4] Fort Worth, TX Holy Name of Jesus Church.
Breen, Bernard J. '72 (L) [49] Louisville, KY St. Margaret Mary Church.
Breen, Brendan *c.p.* '50 (BO) [24] Boston, MA St. Gabriel Church; [W] Brighton, MA St. Gabriel's Passionist Community.
Breen, Msgr. Edward J. '58 (BRK) [210] Queens, NY Our Lady of Fatima Church.
Breen, Francis J. *m.m.* '70 (FgM) Maryknoll Foreign Missions.
Breen, J. A. *o.p.* '63 (FgM) Dominican - Order of Preachers Foreign Missions.
Breen, James '80 (BGP) Wilton, CT Our Lady of Fatima Church.
Breen, John (NY) West Nyack, NY St. Francis of Assisi Church.
Breen, John F. '47 (NY) Retired.
Breen, John M. *m.m.* '51 (FgM) Maryknoll Foreign Missions.
Breen, Joseph P. '61 (NSH) [5] Nashville, TN St. Edward's Church.
Breen, Michael *s.s.c.* '47 (BO) [W] Quincy, MA St. Columban's Foreign Mission Society.
Breen, Philip M. '65 (NSH) [2] Nashville, TN St. Ann Church.
Breen, Robert H. '57 (PH) Riegelsville, PA St. Lawrence Church.
Breen, Stephen B. '55 (WIL) Retired.
Brehob, Keith *s.j.* '96 (LA) [CC] Los Angeles, CA Archdiocesan Office for Campus Ministry.
Breidenbach, John '87 (EVN) [4] Evansville, IN Corpus Christi Church.

Breier, Donald P. '69 (PIT) Castle Shannon, PA St. Anne Church.
Breig, Gary R. '76 (STL) Military Chaplains.
Breig, Gary R. '78 (FAR) Grand Forks, ND Grand Forks Air Force Base.
Breighner, Joseph F. '71 (BAL) [1] Baltimore, MD Cathedral of Mary Our Queen; Special Assignment.
Breis, Gary R. '78 (FAR) [I] Grand Forks, ND Air Force Base, Our Lady of the Snows Catholic Community.
Breit, Melvin P. '62 (MIL) [37] Milwaukee, WI Holy Rosary Church; [68] Milwaukee, WI St. Rita Church.
Breitbach, Richard C. '60 (MIL) Special Assignment.
Breitbach, Richard C. '61 (MIL) [C] Milwaukee, WI Cardinal Stritch University.
Breitenstein, Stephen '42 (P) Roy, OR St. Francis of Assisi Church.
Breitnauer, James L. '59 (BUF) [4] West Seneca, NY St. William Church.
Brelivet, Alan *o.m.i.* '31 (SAT) [K] San Antonio, TX Oblate Madonna Residence.
Brelsford, William J. '70 (LA) [94] Los Angeles, CA St. Timothy Church.
Brembos, Msgr. George M. '56 (MET) Far Hills, NJ St. Elizabeth Church; [N] Peapack, NJ Everitt Academy.
Brenberger, Thomas R. *c.pp.s.* '66 (CIN) Egypt, OH St. Joseph Church; Minster, OH St. Augustine's Church; [U] Dayton, OH Community Support Charitable Trust.
Brenda, William H. *o.p.* '49 (GAL) [36] Houston, TX Holy Rosary Church.
Brendel, John A. '39 (RVC) Retired.
Brenes-Chaves, Fabio R. '85 (NEW) [5] Elizabeth, NJ Immaculate Conception Church.
Brengartner, Robert E. '42 (Y) [4] Massillon, OH St. Mary's Church; Retired.
Brenk, Frederick E. *s.j.* '63 (MIL) [P] Milwaukee, WI Jesuit Provincial Office, Wisconsin Province.
Brenkert, Edward J. '72 (BRK) [164] Queens, NY St. Clement Pope Church.
Brenkle, Msgr. John J. '58 (SR) Saint Helena, CA St. Helena Church.
Brennan, Anthony V. *m.m.* '61 (FgM) Maryknoll Foreign Missions.
Brennan, Bernard '61 (SFR) Special Assignment.
Brennan, Bernard '65 (DUL) [D] Duluth, MN Benedictine Health Center.
Brennan, Bernard F. (OAK) Military Chaplains.
Brennan, Brian C. '79 (NY) [1] New York, NY Cathedral of St. Patrick.
Brennan, C. John '54 (SC) Retired.
Brennan, Cathal '52 (P) [9] Portland, OR Blessed Sacrament Church; [15] Portland, OR Holy Cross Church.
Brennan, Charles M. *o.s.m.* '48 (CHI) [N] Chicago, IL Servite Friars - Eastern Province.
Brennan, Msgr. Daniel H. '43 (ORG) Costa Mesa, CA St. John the Baptist Church.
Brennan, Denis J. '63 (ALB) Rotterdam Junction, NY St. Margaret of Cortona Church.
Brennan, Dennis J. '74 (LA) On Duty Outside the Archdiocese.
Brennan, Msgr. Dermot R. '56 (NY) Yorktown Heights, NY St. Patrick Church.
Brennan, Donald *o.s.a.* '68 (FWT) Pilot Point, TX St. Thomas Aquinas Church.
Brennan, Edmund J. '82 (ALN) Branchdale, PA St. Mary Star of the Sea Church; Newtown, PA Sacred Heart Church.
Brennan, Edward C. '63 (BRK) Released from Diocesan Assignment.
Brennan, Elmer F. '42 (CIN) Retired.
Brennan, Eugene P. '70 (STL) Warrenton, MO Holy Rosary Church.
Brennan, Eugene P. *m.s.* '80 (HRT) [M] Hartford, CT Missionaries of LaSalette Provincial Secretary.
Brennan, Fernan J. *o.s.f.s.* '41 (TOL) [J] Oregon, OH Sacred Heart Home; [K] Toledo, OH Oblates of St. Francis de Sales.
Brennan, Francis *s.j.* '58 (SPC) Kennett, MO St. Cecilia Church.
Brennan, Msgr. Francis M. '38 (NY) [204] Staten Island, NY Holy Child Church; Retired.
Brennan, Msgr. Francis P. '37 (NY) Retired.
Brennan, George *m.s.* '75 (FR) [J] Attleboro, MA La Salette Shrine.
Brennan, George '87 (VEN) [5] Sarasota, FL St. Patrick Church.
Brennan, Msgr. George J. '49 (BUF) Retired.
Brennan, George P. '68 (STL) [5] St. Louis, MO Holy Innocents Church.
Brennan, Gerald H. *o.f.m.* '46 (PRO) [P] Providence, RI St. Francis Friary.
Brennan, Gerard M. (BO) Retired.
Brennan, J. Gregory *o.f.m.* (BUF) [C] St. Bonaventure, NY St. Bonaventure University.
Brennan, J. Gregory *o.f.m.* '79 (BUF) Humphrey, NY St. Pacificus, Mission of St. Bonaventure University Friary Church; [O] St. Bonaventure, NY St. Bonaventure Friary.
Brennan, James '85 (DEN) [36] Denver, CO St. Rose of Lima Church.
Brennan, James F. '55 (BO) Permanent Disability.
Brennan, James H. *s.s.* '31 (BAL) [J] Baltimore, MD St. Charles Villa; [M] Baltimore, MD St. Charles Villa.
Brennan, James J. *m.a.* '89 (PH) [74] Philadelphia, PA St. Jerome Church; [M] Springfield, PA Divine Providence Village.
Brennan, James P. *c.ss.r.* '64 (NY) [23] New York, NY St. Cecilia Church.
Brennan, Msgr. John '55 (TYL) [A] Tyler, TX Trinity Mother Frances Health System.
Brennan, John D. '70 (PIT) Kennedy Township, PA St. Malachy Church.
Brennan, John J. *s.j.* '46 (LA) [6] Los Angeles, CA Blessed Sacrament Church.
Brennan, John J. '78 (SPR) [3] Westfield, MA St. Casimir's Church; [5] Westfield, MA St. Peter's Church.
Brennan, John P. *s.m.a.* '64 (LA) [A] Camarillo, CA St. John's Seminary.
Brennan, John W. *o.s.f.s.* '65 (WIL) [I] Childs, MD Oblates of St. Francis De Sales.
Brennan, Joseph *o.s.c.* '45 (SCL) [I] Onamia, MN Crosier Monastery.
Brennan, Joseph (Dennis) *o.s.b.* '74 (LA) [R] Valyermo, CA St. Andrew's Abbey.
Brennan, Joseph F. *s.j.* '56 (FgM) Provinces.
Brennan, Msgr. Joseph F. '56 (LA) Long Beach, CA Veterans Affairs Medical Center.
Brennan, Msgr. Joseph F. '56 (SD) Retired.
Brennan, Joseph L. *c.m.* '43 (LA) [95] Los Angeles, CA St. Vincent De Paul Church.
Brennan, Joseph P. '54 (ROC) Retired.
Brennan, Joseph T. *s.j.* '69 (CHI) [D] Chicago, IL St. Ignatius College Prep; [D] Chicago, IL St. Ignatius Jesuit Community.
Brennan, Joseph V. '80 (LA) Norwalk, CA St. Linus Church.
Brennan, Keith *s.d.s.* '70 (MIL) [5] Wauwatosa, WI St. Pius X Church.
Brennan, Keith R. '84 (STA) Special Assignment.
Brennan, Lawrence C. '76 (STL) [1] Lemay, MO Mary Queen of the Universe Church; [A] St. Louis, MO Kenrick-Glennon Seminary.
Brennan, Mark E. '76 (WDC) Pastoral Center Special Ministries.
Brennan, Matthew F. '62 (BIR) [5] Birmingham, AL Blessed Sacrament Church.
Brennan, Michael *c.p.* (SAC) [F] Redding, CA Mercy Medical Center.
Brennan, Michael *c.p.* '53 (MET) [H] South River, NJ Passionist Provincial Office.
Brennan, Michael J. '71 (BRK) [86] Brooklyn, NY St. Michael's Church.
Brennan, Patrick *c.p.* '73 (LA) [R] Pasadena, CA Passionist Community; [X] Sierra Madre, CA Mater Dolorosa Retreat Center.
Brennan, Patrick '77 (P) Special Assignment; [A] St. Benedict, OR Mount Angel Seminary.
Brennan, Patrick A. *o.s.a.* '63 (ORG) Buena Park, CA St. Pius V Church.
Brennan, Patrick J. '73 (CHI) Inverness, IL Holy Family Church.
Brennan, Paul '59 (ROC) [2] Auburn, NY Sacred Heart Church.
Brennan, Philip M. *o.s.m.* '41 (P) [L] Portland, OR The Grotto, The National Sanctuary of Our Sorrowful Mother.
Brennan, Pierce A. *s.j.* '76 (NY) [F] New York, NY Fordham Preparatory School; [DD] New York, NY Jesuit Community at Fordham University.
Brennan, Pierce A. *s.j.* '76 (RVC) Oceanside, NY St. Anthony Church.
Brennan, Msgr. Ralph '57 (AUS) Old Washington-on-the Brazos, TX Blessed Virgin Mary Church.
Brennan, Msgr. Ralph A. '57 (AUS) Brenham, TX St. Mary of the Immaculate Conception Church; [M] Brenham, TX Blinn College Catholic Student Union.
Brennan, Raymond *c.ss.r.* '59 (FgM) Redemptorist Foreign Missions.
Brennan, Robert (NY) Castle Point, NY Veterans Administration Medical Center.
Brennan, Robert (ROC) [E] Rochester, NY St. Ann's Home for the Aged.
Brennan, Robert '51 (CLV) Retired.
Brennan, Robert E. '45 (SY) [17] Syracuse, NY St. John the Baptist Church; Retired.
Brennan, Robert E. '66 (PH) [6] Norristown, PA St. Titus Church.
Brennan, Robert F. '51 (CLV) [64] Cleveland, OH SS. Philip and James Church.
Brennan, Robert J. '49 (NY) Retired.
Brennan, Robert J. *c.s.c.* '68 (ORL) [F] Cocoa Beach, FL Holy Cross Fathers, Eastern Priests Province.
Brennan, Msgr. Robert J. '89 (RVC) [1] Rockville Centre, NY St. Agnes Cathedral.
Brennan, Robert L. '64 (PH) [140] Philadelphia, PA Resurrection of Our Lord Church.
Brennan, Robert M. '65 (NEW) [1] Hackensack, NJ Holy Trinity Church.
Brennan, Roderick *o.f.m.cap.* '45 (FgM) Capuchin Foreign Missions.
Brennan, Ronan P. '50 (SAC) Sutter Creek, CA Immaculate Conception Church; Retired and in Senior Ministry.
Brennan, Msgr. Seamus F. '72 (MET) Edison, NJ St. Matthew Church.
Brennan, Terrence M. *s.j.* '76 (MIL) [E] Milwaukee, WI Marquette University High School; [P] Milwaukee, WI Pere Marquette House Jesuit Community.
Brennan, Thomas *s.j.* '63 (BO) [W] Chestnut Hill, MA The Jesuit Community at Boston College.
Brennan, Thomas '66 (TR) Bay Head, NJ Sacred Heart Church.
Brennan, Thomas *s.d.b.* '82 (MIA) [25] Miami, FL St. Kieran Church.
Brennan, Thomas '89 (LAN) Retired.
Brennan, Thomas J. '74 (PH) Quakertown, PA St. Isidore Church.
Brennan, Thomas N. *s.j.* '67 (MIL) [P] Milwaukee, WI Arrupe House Jesuit Community.
Brennan, Timothy J. *o.s.b.* '78 (PAT) [M] Morristown, NJ St. Mary's Abbey.
Brennan, Walter *s.j.* '60 (FgM) Provinces.
Brennan, Walter M. *o.s.m.* '61 (CHI) [N] Chicago, IL Servite Friars - Eastern Province.
Brennan, William B. '53 (DET) [8] Dearborn Heights, MI St. Sebastian Church.
Brennan, William J. '42 (SPK) Retired.
Brennan, William J. '49 (L) [49] Louisville, KY St. Margaret Mary Church; Retired.
Brennan, William J. *s.j.* '51 (LA) [6] Los Angeles, CA Blessed Sacrament Church.
Brennan, William P. '63 (CAM) [4] Cherry Hill, NJ St. Pius X Church.
Brennan, William V. *c.m.* '41 (CHI) [C] Chicago, IL Vincentian Community at DePaul University.
Brennell, John J. '78 (STL) Kirkwood, MO St. Peter Church.
Brenner, Raymond A. '69 (EVN) [10] Evansville, IN Resurrection Church.
Brenner, Msgr. Thomas R. '61 (HBG) Chambersburg, PA Corpus Christi Church; [K] Harrisburg, PA Catholic Campus Ministry.
Brennick, Stephen '59 (BO) [6] Somerville, MA Patronage of St. Joseph Church.
Brenny, Kenneth '63 (SCL) Pierz, MN St. Joseph's Church; [E] Pierz, MN Holy Trinity School; [H] Pierz, MN St. Mary's Villa Inc.
Brenon, Terence '91 (SAN) [4] San Angelo, TX St. Mary's Church.
Brensinger, Richard C. '92 (ALN) Sinking Spring, PA St. Ignatius Loyola Church.
Brentrup, Bruce *s.d.s.* '59 (MIL) [P] Milwaukee, WI Salvatorian Provincial Residence.
Brenza, William J. '70 (HRT) [9] New Haven, CT St. Francis Church.
Breski, Martin *o.f.m.conv.* '69 (BAL) [M] Ellicott City, MD Order of Friars Minor Conventual.
Breslawski, William G. '79 (RVC) Nesconset, NY Church of the Holy Cross.
Bresler, C. John '75 (SFE) Cimarron, NM Immaculate Conception Church.
Breslin, J. Michael '65 (RIC) Cape Charles, VA St. Charles Church.
Breslin, John *s.m.m.* '56 (BRK) [U] Ozone Park, NY Montfort Missionaries Provincialate - for Nation Community.
Breslin, John B. *s.j.* '73 (SY) [S] Syracuse, NY Jesuits at LeMoyne, Inc.
Breslin, Msgr. John E. '61 (PH) Doylestown, PA Our Lady of Mount Carmel Church.
Breslin, John S. '85 (CHI) [6] Chicago, IL St. Ailbe Church.
Breslin, Joseph W. '39 (SCR) Retired; [N] Dunmore, PA Villa St. Joseph.
Breslin, Msgr. Lawrence K. '57 (CIN) [7] Dayton, OH St. Charles Borromeo Church.
Breslin, Paul *o.f.m.* (CAM) [2] Camden, NJ St. Anthony of Padua Church.
Breslin, Peter W. *s.j.* '91 (CHI) [C] Chicago, IL Jesuit Community at Loyola University of Chicago.
Breslin, William E. '74 (DEN) [1] Aurora, CO Queen of Peace Church.
Bresnahan, James F. *s.j.* '59 (BO) [W] Boston, MA The Society of Jesus of New England-Provincial Offices.
Bresnahan, James F. *s.j.* '59 (CHI) [N] Chicago, IL Chicago Province of the Society of Jesus-Provincial Office.
Bresnahan, John E. *o.s.a.* '36 (PH) [AA] Villanova, PA St. Thomas Monastery.
Bresnahan, John J. *s.j.* '58 (FgM) Provinces.
Bresnahan, John J. '60 (CHI) Schiller Park, IL St. Beatrice Church.
Bresnahan, Richard F. '58 (PEO) Coal Valley, IL St. Maria Goretti Church.
Bresnahan, Thomas J. '40 (DET) Retired; [Q] Troy, MI Gabriel Richard Institute.
Bresnahan, Thomas J. '60 (MAN) Londonderry, NH St. Mark the Evangelist Church.
Bresnehan, Msgr. Paul M. '54 (BUR) Proctor, VT St. Dominic Church.

Brestel, Msgr. Joseph R. (PAT) [P] Paterson, NJ Riese Corporation.
Brestel, Msgr. Joseph R. '38 (PAT) Hawthorne, NJ St. Anthony's Church.
Brethour, Gary G. '89 (LIN) Curtis, NE St. James Church.
Bretl, James J. *s.d.s.* '65 (NSH) McMinnville, TN St. Catherine Church; Smithville, TN St. Gregory Church.
Breton, Albert E. '54 (SPR) Agawam, MA St. Theresa of the Child Jesus Church.
Breton, Denis R. '76 (BUR) Hyde Park, VT St. Teresa Church; Morrisville, VT Holy Cross Church.
Breton, Louis *o.s.m.* '49 (P) [L] Portland, OR The Grotto, The National Sanctuary of Our Sorrowful Mother.
Breton, Raymond G. '68 (OAK) [10] Oakland, CA St. Jarlath's Church.
Bretone, Richard '89 (BRK) [175] Queens, NY St. Helen Church.
Brett, Frank X. '59 (KNX) Norris, TN St. Joseph Church.
Brett, James D. '41 (CHI) Lake Forest, IL St. Mary Church; Retired.
Brett, James G. '44 (JKS) Retired.
Brett, Stephen F. *s.s.j.* '76 (WDC) [27] Washington, DC St. Luke Church.
Brett, Stephen J. *s.s.j.* '76 (PH) [A] Wynnewood, PA Theological Seminary of St. Charles Borromeo, Overbrook.
Bretz, Msgr. John W. '41 (SFD) Retired; [J] Springfield, IL St. Joseph's Home.
Bretzke, James T. *s.j.* '81 (MIL) [P] Milwaukee, WI Jesuit Provincial Office, Wisconsin Province.
Bretzke, James T. *s.j.* '81 (OAK) [A] Berkeley, CA The Jesuit School of Theology at Berkeley; [N] Berkeley, CA Jesuit Community at Jesuit School of Theology at Berkeley.
Breu, David L. '73 (NU) Ivanhoe, MN SS. Peter & Paul Church; Wilno, MN St. John Cantius Church.
Breunig, Robert L. '51 (DEN) Retired.
Breunig, Rudy *s.t.* '65 (FgM) Trinity Missions.
Breuning, Walter A. '54 (PEO) Henry, IL St. Joseph's Church; Henry, IL St. Mary's Church.
Brevetti, Adrian '42 (BRK) Retired.
Brew, Frederick A. *s.j.* '43 (ALN) [A] Wernersville, PA Novitiate of St. Isaac Jogues.
Brewczynski, Jacek '96 (DET) Waterford, MI Our Lady of the Lakes Church.
Brewer, Dexter S. '89 (NSH) Decherd, TN Good Shepherd Church.
Brewer, Gervase '43 (MAR) Retired.
Brewer, James P. '77 (PRT) Westbrook, ME St. Hyacinth Church.
Brewer, Martin L. *s.j.* '54 (LA) [2] Santa Barbara, CA Our Lady of Sorrows Church.
Brewer, Timothy M. '79 (WOR) [5] Leominster, MA Our Lady of the Lake Church.
Brewerton, Peter H. '40 (HT) Retired.
Brey, Christopher '97 (SFD) Effingham, IL St. Anthony of Padua Church.
Brey, Lawrence S. '53 (MIL) Retired.
Breza, Paul J. '63 (WIN) Hokah, MN St. Peter's Church.
Brezik, Victor B. *c.s.b.* '40 (GAL) [Q] Houston, TX Residence of the Basilian Fathers of the University of St. Thomas.
Brezinski, Blaine *c.p.* (RVC) Shelter Island, NY Our Lady of the Isle Church; [P] Shelter Island Heights, NY St. Gabriel's Youth House.
Breznikar, Victor '40 (SPK) Retired.
Brezovec, John F. '66 (ALT) [1] Johnstown, PA St. John Gualbert Cathedral.
Brian, Bertrand J. '50 (L) Retired; [M] St. Catharine, KY Sansbury Memorial Infirmary.
Brice, Donald '58 (WDC) [4] Washington, DC Annunciation Church.
Brice, Frederick J. '69 (MIA) Lighthouse Point, FL St. Paul the Apostle Church.
Brice, Steven J. '82 (LC) [2] Wausau, WI St. Anne Church.
Briceland, Alan *s.j.* (BRK) Queens, NY Elmhurst General Hospital.
Briceland, W. Alan *s.j.* '65 (NY) [DD] New York, NY West Side Jesuit Community.
Briceno, Joseph '81 (PHX) Unassigned.
Brichetto, James M. *s.j.* '63 (CIN) [M] Cincinnati, OH Faber Jesuit Community.
Brichetto, James N. *s.j.* '63 (CIN) [54] Cincinnati, OH St. Louis Church.
Brick, Daniel F. '42 (OM) [28] Omaha, NE St. Mary Church.
Brick, Maurice J. *o.f.m.* '45 (PAT) [M] Butler, NJ St. Anthony Friary.
Brick, Paul T. *s.d.s.* '63 (SAV) [4] Columbus, GA St. Benedict the Moor Church.
Bricker, Brian *o.p.* '89 (MAD) [J] Sinsinawa, WI Dominican Motherhouse.
Bricker, Brian *o.p.* '90 (DUB) [I] Dubuque, IA St. Dominic Villa.
Brickl, Joseph M. '37 (MAD) Retired.
Brickler, R. Richard '61 (ROC) [9] Rochester, NY St. Boniface Church.
Brickley, John J. '35 (DUB) Retired.
Brickman, Donald P. '81 (CLV) [1] Cleveland, OH Cathedral of St. John the Evangelist.
Brickner, Charles W. '75 (RIC) Woodlawn, VA St. Joseph's Church.
Brickner, Ronald J. '92 (TOL) On Duty Outside the Diocese.
Bride, Harry *c.s.c.* '49 (P) [B] Portland, OR University of Portland; [L] Portland, OR Holy Cross Fathers & Brothers, C.S.C. - University of Portland.
Bride, Msgr. Thomas R. (NOR) Jewett City, CT St. Mary Church.
Bride, Msgr. Thomas R. '67 (NOR) New London, CT St. Mary, Star of the Sea Church; On Special or Other (Arch)Diocesan Assignment.
Bridge, George *c.ss.r.* '48 (ALB) [L] Saratoga Springs, NY St. John Neumann Residence.
Bridge, George H. *c.ss.r.* '48 (VEN) Wauchula, FL St. Michael Church.
Bridge, Robert E. '72 (CHI) [168] Chicago, IL St. Peter Canisius Church.
Bridges, Clarence S. '88 (ALT) [1] Johnstown, PA St. John Gualbert Cathedral.
Bridges, Geoffrey *o.f.m.* (OAK) [S] Oakland, CA Missionaries of the Kingship of Christ.
Bridges, James P. '62 (SAN) [4] Midland, TX St. Stephen's Church.
Bridgman, Mark '96 (OM) [16] Omaha, NE Holy Cross Church.
Bried, William *o.f.m.* '79 (TR) Brant Beach, NJ St. Francis of Assisi Church.
Brieffies, John *m.s.f.* '56 (RIC) [L] West Point, VA Missionaries of the Holy Family, General Mission Office—M.S.F., Inc.
Brielmaier, Leon '77 (MIL) [N] Wauwatosa, WI St. Camillus Health Center, Inc.
Brielmaier, Leon J. '77 (MIL) Retired.
Brien, Paul *m.m.* '60 (DET) [K] Detroit, MI Maryknoll Fathers and Brothers.
Brien, Peter C. *m.m.* '60 (CHI) [N] Chicago, IL Maryknoll Fathers & Brothers.
Brienz, Edward '96 (Y) [16] Youngstown, OH St. Joseph Church.
Bries, Marvin J. '73 (DUB) Britt, IA St. Patrick's Church; Corwith, IA St. Mary's Church; Woden, IA Sacred Heart Church.
Briese, Dominic *o.p.* '96 (PHX) [5] Phoenix, AZ Most Holy Trinity Church.
Brietbach, Richard C. '61 (MIL) Whitefish Bay, WI St. Monica Church.
Brietske, Msgr. Richard C. '62 (TR) Willingboro, NJ Corpus Christi Church.
Briffa, Philip '60 (DET) [3] Warren, MI St. Cletus Church.
Briffa, Salvino '71 (DET) Allenton, MI St. John the Evangelist Church.
Brigandi, Msgr. Paul A. (SY) [W] Oswego, NY St. Peter & St. Paul.
Brigandi, Msgr. Paul A. '54 (SY) [8] Binghamton, NY St. Mary of the Assumption Church.
Brigandi, Stephen J., Jr. '97 (RVC) Valley Stream, NY Holy Name of Mary Church.
Briganti, Philip J. '73 (PAT) Military Chaplains.
Briggman, Michael J. '68 (ALN) Bally, PA Most Blessed Sacrament Church; Retired; [J] Bethlehem, PA Holy Family Villa.
Briggs, Everett F. '33 (WH) Retired.
Briggs, Michael J. *m.m.* '76 (FgM) Maryknoll Foreign Missions.
Brigham, Kenneth M. '61 (CHI) [150] Chicago, IL Our Lady Help of Christians Church.
Brighenti, Kenneth D. '88 (MET) Parlin, NJ St. Bernadette Church.
Brignac, Horace L., Jr. '83 (NO) [56] New Orleans, LA St. Raphael the Archangel Church.
Brimley, Wilfred *c.s.p.* '62 (NY) [DD] Jamaica Estates, NY Paulist Fathers Generalate.
Brimley, Wilfred A. *c.s.p.* '62 (STP) [29] Minneapolis, MN St. Lawrence Church; [N] Minneapolis, MN Paulist Fathers.
Brincat, George R. '57 (LA) Tujunga, CA Our Lady of Lourdes Church.
Brindamour, Albert H. '46 (PRO) [10] Woonsocket, RI Precious Blood Church; Retired.
Brindamour, Maurice L. '74 (PRO) [7] Woonsocket, RI St. Joseph Church.
Brink, Joseph C. '63 (COV) Alexandria, KY St. Mary of the Assumption Church.
Brinker, Brian J. '88 (RVC) North Merrick, NY Sacred Heart Church; East Meadow, NY Nassau County Medical Center.
Brinker, Louis B. '50 (COV) Cynthiana, KY St. Edward Church.
Brinker, Maurice J. '54 (LEX) Retired; [F] Versailles, KY Taylor Manor Nursing Home.
Brinker, Paul '36 (COV) Dayton, KY St. Bernard Church.
Brinker, Paul J. '36 (COV) Retired.
Brinker, William *c.s.c.* '46 (CHI) [D] Niles, IL Notre Dame High School.
Brinkman, Barry '91 (SAL) Educational Leave of Absence.
Brinkman, Charles J. '77 (PH) [3] Philadelphia, PA St. Agatha-St. James Church; [EE] Philadelphia, PA Newman Apostolate.
Brinkman, Don G. '67 (STL) Absent on Sick Leave.
Brinkman, Frederick C. *c.ss.r.* '75 (ROC) [K] Canandaigua, NY Notre Dame Retreat House.
Brinkman, James J. '81 (SUP) Farmington, WI Assumption of the Blessed Virgin Mary Church; Somerset, WI St. Anne Church.
Brinkman, John T. *m.m.* '71 (NY) [DD] Maryknoll, NY Maryknoll Fathers and Brothers.
Brinkman, Norbert C. '45 (CIN) Retired.
Brinkman, Terence *s.t.d.* '73 (GAL) Kingwood, TX St. Martha Church.
Brinkman, Terence P. (GAL) [U] Houston, TX Martha's Kitchen Food Services.
Brinkmann, Charles J. *c.ss.r.* '56 (RIC) [N] Hampton, VA Holy Family Retreat.
Brinkmann, Frederick C. *c.ss.r.* '75 (NY) [HH] Esopus, NY Holy Shroud Guild; [HH] Esopus, NY Holy Shroud Guild.
Brinkmann, Gerard J. *c.ss.r.* '61 (PH) [25] Philadelphia, PA St. Boniface Church.
Brinkmoeller, David E. '71 (CIN) [5] Dayton, OH Ascension Church.
Brinn, Adrian '97 (SB) Running Springs, CA St. Anne in the Mountains Church.
Brinn, John J. '62 (NY) [2] Poughkeepsie, NY St. Mary Church.
Brinsmade, John F. '81 (HRT) [2] West Haven, CT St. John Vianney Church.
Briody, Hugh J. '63 (SUP) On Duty Outside the Diocese.
Briody, Msgr. Thomas '39 (SD) Retired.
Brioschi, Thomas H. '86 (STP) [30] St. Paul, MN St. Pascal Baylon Church.
Brioso, Luis *c.m.* '93 (PCE) [14] Ponce, PR San Vicente-Cantera Church.
Brioso, Luis Renier *c.m.* (SJN) Loiza, PR Santiago Apostol, El Mayor Church.
Briscoe, Orville '84 (NSH) Retired.
Briseno, Miguel *o.f.m.conv.* '90 (SAT) [B] San Antonio, TX San Damiano Friary; [C] San Antonio, TX Our Lady of the Lake University; [M] San Antonio, TX San Damiano Friary.
Briseno, Pedro (BWN) [I] Harlingen, TX KMBH-TV 60/KHID-FM 88.1/KMBH-FM 88.9.
Briseno, Pedro '81 (BWN) [1] Harlingen, TX Our Lady of the Assumption Church; [2] Harlingen, TX Immaculate Heart of Mary Church; [I] Harlingen, TX KMBH-TV 60/KHID-FM 88.1/KMBH-FM 88.9.
Brisk, Ralph *c.p.* '29 (CHI) [N] Chicago, IL Immaculate Conception Monastery; [N] Chicago, IL Daneo Hall.
Briske, Larry F. '64 (MIL) Retired.
Brislin, Thomas *c.p.* '68 (FgM) Passionist Foreign Missions.
Brissette, Eugene C. *s.j.* '51 (BO) [W] Weston, MA Campion Health Center, Inc.
Brissette, Reginald R. '63 (PRT) Biddeford, ME St. Andre's Church.
Brisson, Robert A. '85 (NY) [II] New Rochelle, NY Opus Dei (Prelature of the Holy Cross and Opus Dei).
Brito, Cristiano *o.s.b.* '91 (GBG) [H] Latrobe, PA Saint Vincent Archabbey.
Britt, Jerome C. '82 (COV) Burlington, KY Immaculate Heart of Mary Church.
Britt, William J. '53 (STL) Retired.
Brittain, Gerald W. '62 (MIL) West Bend, WI Holy Angels Church.
Britto, Federico A. '82 (PH) [67] Philadelphia, PA St. Ignatius of Loyola Church.
Britz, Francis '55 (SCL) Mayhew Lake, MN Annunciation Church.
Britz, Gerald F. '48 (DET) Retired.
Brixius, Hilary R. '68 (WIN) St. James, MN St. James Church.
Brizzolara, Andrew *c.s.* '75 (NY) [64] New York, NY St. Joseph Church.
Broadhurst, T. Paul *c.s.b.* '60 (ROC) [I] Rochester, NY Basilian Residence.
Brobst, James *o.m.i.* '90 (SAT) [B] San Antonio, TX George Sexton House of Studies.
Brobst, Richard A. '65 (Y) [9] Youngstown, OH St. Brendan's Church.
Brocato, Francis W. *o.p.* '90 (PRO) [P] Providence, RI St. Thomas Aquinas Priory at Providence College.
Brocato, Robert S. '95 (SJ) [22] San Jose, CA Sacred Heart of Jesus Church.
Broccolo, Gerard T. '65 (CHI) On Duty Outside the Archdiocese.
Brochu, Albert E. *a.a.* '43 (NY) [87] New York, NY Our Lady of Guadalupe Church.
Brochu, Gerard H. '50 (BUR) Retired.
Brock, David F. '56 (DET) Retired.
Brock, Msgr. Edmund J. '36 (PRO) Retired; [M] North Smithfield, RI St. Antoine Residence.
Brock, Herald *c.f.r.* '94 (NY) [DD] Yonkers, NY St. Leopold's Friary.
Brock, John '62 (JKS) Natchez, MS Assumption of the

B.V.M. Church.
Brock, William '91 (DEN) [35] Denver, CO St. Mary Magdalene's Church.
Brockel, Kenneth E. '69 (JC) Perry, MO St. William Church.
Brockett, Norman L. '87 (HRT) Cheshire, CT Church of the Epiphany.
Brockhaus, Msgr. Edward '64 (SD) Lemon Grove, CA St. John of the Cross Church.
Brockhaus, Thomas Aq. *o.s.b.* '39 (P) [L] St. Benedict, OR Mt. Angel Abbey.
Brockland, John A. '91 (STL) Graduate Studies.
Brockland, Robert J. *c.m.* '74 (STL) [P] Perryville, MO Congregation of The Mission.
Brockman, Blaise '77 (LA) Tujunga, CA Our Lady of Lourdes Church.
Brockman, David D. '90 (R) [6] Raleigh, NC St. Luke the Evangelist Church.
Brockman, James P. '97 (DUB) Springville, IA St. Isidore's Church.
Brockman, Leon *o.c.s.o.* '55 (SPC) [E] Ava, MO Assumption Abbey (Trappist).
Brockman, Norbert *s.m.* '73 (SAT) [M] San Antonio, TX Marianist Woodlawn Community.
Brockman, Norbert C. *s.m.* '73 (CIN) [M] Dayton, OH Marianist Provincialate.
Brockman, Norbert C. *s.m.* '73 (SAT) [C] San Antonio, TX St. Mary's University of San Antonio, Texas.
Brockson, Scott D. '96 (PH) [32] Philadelphia, PA St. Cecilia Church.
Broderick, Francis *o.s.b.* '36 (KCK) Seneca, KS SS. Peter and Paul's Church.
Broderick, Gerald '42 (BAL) [J] Timonium, MD Stella Maris Operating Corporation.
Broderick, Msgr. Gerard W. '42 (BAL) Retired.
Broderick, James M. '60 (BO) [1] Haverhill, MA St. George Church.
Broderick, Msgr. John A. (BO) Retired.
Broderick, John F. *s.j.* '45 (BO) [W] Weston, MA Campion Center.
Broderick, Msgr. Kilian J. '67 (DAL) Coppell, TX St. Ann Church.
Broderick, Leo P. '56 (DET) Algonac, MI St. Catherine Church.
Broderick, Michael '87 (WOR) Whitinsville, MA St. Patrick's Church.
Broderick, Richard '70 (ALB) Crescent, NY St. Mary Church.
Broderick, William '49 (SAC) Carmichael, CA Our Lady of the Assumption Church; Retired and in Senior Ministry.
Brodersen, Msgr. Charles '48 (OM) [39] Omaha, NE St. Richard Church.
Brodersen, Charles F. '48 (OM) Retired.
Brodersen, Steven W. '85 (SC) Algona, IA St. Cecelia Church.
Broderson, Donald '68 (OAK) Retired.
Brodeur, Dennis A. '77 (PRO) On Duty Outside the Diocese.
Brodeur, Henry *m.s.* '66 (MAN) Lebanon, NH Sacred Heart Church.
Brodeur, Scott N. *s.j.* '90 (BO) [W] Boston, MA The Society of Jesus of New England-Provincial Offices.
Brodeur, Theodore J. '66 (MAR) Sault Sainte Marie, MI Holy Name of Mary Church.
Brodfuehrer, Robert S. (CHI) Retired.
Brodfuehrer, Robert S. '45 (CHI) [46] Chicago, IL St. Cornelius Church; [64] Chicago, IL St. Francis Borgia Church.
Brodie, Thomas *o.p.* '58 (BO) [W] Cambridge, MA Faber House.
Brodley, Thomas J. *s.j.* '72 (FgM) Provinces.
Brodniak, Anthony B. *m.m.* '54 (FgM) Maryknoll Foreign Missions.
Brodnick, Edward J. '76 (COV) Union, KY St. Timothy Church.
Brodnick, Joseph (ROC) Elmira, NY St. Joseph Hospital; Elmira, NY Elmira Correctional Facility, Center and Camp Monterey.
Brodnick, Joseph '69 (CLV) Absent on Leave.
Brody, Donald '47 (GB) [I] Appleton, WI St. Fidelis Friary.
Brodzeller, Robert E. *s.j.* '63 (OM) [C] Omaha, NE Creighton Preparatory School; [G] Omaha, NE Archbishop Bergan Mercy Medical Center.
Broering, Joseph '53 (COV) [I] Covington, KY Madonna Manor, Inc.
Broering, Raymond L. '53 (COV) Retired.
Broering, Victor F. '42 (CIN) Retired.
Brogan, Hugh T. '69 (WDC) Retired.
Brogan, John F. '75 (BRK) [80] Brooklyn, NY St. Martin of Tours-Fourteen Holy Martyrs Church; [T] Brooklyn, NY Catholic Migration & Refugee Office, Catholic Migration Services, Inc.
Brogan, John J. '75 (BRK) [Y] Douglaston, NY Society of the Immaculate Conception of Brooklyn.
Brogan, Leo T. '67 (PHX) On Duty Outside the Diocese.
Brogan, Malachy *o.f.m.* '57 (FgM) Franciscan Foreign Missions.
Brogan, Neal E. '66 (TLS) Henryetta, OK St. Michael Church.
Brogan, Paul '94 (LA) Woodland Hills, CA St. Bernardine of Siena Church.
Brogan, William '64 (NY) Absent on Leave.
Brogley, Charles F. *s.m.* '44 (WDC) [M] Washington, DC Marist Provincial House.
Broglio, Msgr. Timothy '77 (CLV) Released from Diocesan Assignment.
Brogus, Albert G. '45 (SCR) Retired.
Brohammer, Ronald '60 (MIA) Retired.
Brohead, Martin *t.o.r.* '42 (ARL) [J] Winchester, VA Sacred Heart Friary.
Broker, John A. *c.ss.r.* '44 (MIL) [S] Oconomowoc, WI Our Mother of Perpetual Help Retreat Center.
Broker, William *c.ss.r.* '49 (MIL) [S] Oconomowoc, WI Our Mother of Perpetual Help Retreat Center.
Brokman, James P. '97 (DUB) Marion, IA St. Joseph's Church.
Brom, D. Giles '96 (PEO) [14] Peoria, IL St. Thomas Church.
Bromenshenkel, Fintan *o.s.b.* '45 (FgM) American - Cassinese Congregation Foreign Missions.
Bromenshenkel, Fintan *o.s.b.* '45 (SCL) [I] Collegeville, MN St. John's Abbey, of the Order of St. Benedict.
Bromenshenkel, Silvan *o.s.b.* '47 (SCL) [I] Collegeville, MN St. John's Abbey, of the Order of St. Benedict.
Bromham, Frederick *o.f.m.* '33 (LA) [R] Santa Barbara, CA Franciscan Friary, Order of Friars Minor (Old Mission).
Bromley, Vincent M. '65 (SUP) Gordon, WI St. Anthony of Padua Church; Minong, WI St. Mary Church; Solon Springs, WI St. Pius X Church; Superior, WI Middle River Center.
Bromschwig, Arthur F. '50 (STL) [5] St. Charles, MO St. Peter Church.
Bronder, Joseph P. *o.s.b.* '69 (GBG) [H] Latrobe, PA Saint Vincent Archabbey.
Broniak, Leonard *c.ss.r.* '79 (SAT) [M] San Antonio, TX Redemptorists of Texas- San Antonio #1.
Bronk, Philip *s.t.* '51 (SD) La Mesa, CA Little Flower Haven; [G] La Mesa, CA Little Flower Haven.
Bronkiewicz, Msgr. Laurence R. '73 (BGP) Westport, CT Assumption Church.
Brooker, Richard L. *m.m.* '55 (FgM) Maryknoll Foreign Missions.
Brooks, Armand L. '97 (FAR) [1] Fargo, ND St. Mary's Cathedral; Argusville, ND St. William Church.
Brooks, Bryan V. '93 (TLS) Okmulgee, OK St. Anthony's Church.
Brooks, Charles '65 (GB) Mackville, WI St. Edward Church.
Brooks, David R. *s.j.* '78 (WDC) [E] Washington, DC Gonzaga College High School.
Brooks, Donald W. '61 (TLS) [1] Tulsa, OK Holy Family Cathedral; Special Assignment.
Brooks, Edwin J. *s.j.* '39 (NY) [DD] New York, NY St. Ignatius Loyola Residence.
Brooks, Jeddie P. '77 (SPR) Monson, MA St. Patrick's Church.
Brooks, John E. *s.j.* '59 (WOR) [N] Worcester, MA Jesuits of Holy Cross College, Inc.
Brooks, Msgr. John N. '49 (NY) Retired.
Brooks, Lawrence V. *s.j.* '74 (FgM) Provinces.
Brooks, Michael J. *ss.cc.* '61 (SB) Cathedral City, CA St. Louis Church.
Brooks, Robert '95 (SAC) Roseville, CA St. Rose of Lima Church.
Brooks, Robert C. '61 (ARL) Leesburg, VA St. John the Apostle Church.
Brooks, Thomas M. '78 (E) [11] Erie, PA Sacred Heart Church.
Brooks, William C. '76 (AUS) [3] Waco, TX St. Jerome Church.
Broom, Edward *o.m.v.* '86 (LA) Hawaiian Gardens, CA St. Peter Chanel Church.
Broome, Robert C. *s.j.* '43 (DET) [P] Clarkston, MI Colombiere Center.
Brophy, Msgr. Charles D. '39 (GR) Retired; [F] Grand Rapids, MI Contemplative Sisters of the Good Shepherd.
Brophy, Edward G. '93 (BRK) [163] Queens, NY St. Clare Church.
Brophy, John L. '69 (MIL) [67] Milwaukee, WI St. Philip Neri Church.
Brophy, Peter *o.f.m.* '85 (NY) [35] New York, NY St. Francis of Assisi Church.
Brophy, Peter V. *o.f.m.* '85 (NY) [DD] New York, NY The Franciscan Vocation Ministry of Holy Name Province.
Brophy, R. Michael *s.j.* '69 (CIN) [P] Milford, OH Milford Spiritual Center.
Brophy, Robert J. '56 (MAD) Retired.
Brosius, Alfred G. '50 (DUB) Retired.
Brosk, Steven J. '90 (NEW) Military Chaplains.
Broski, Mark *o.s.b.* '91 (ARL) [K] Bristow, VA St. Benedict Monastery.
Broski, Mark *o.s.b.* '91 (KCK) [A] Atchison, KS Benedictine College; [H] Atchison, KS St. Benedict's Abbey.
Brosmer, Thomas J. '69 (COL) Hilliard, OH St. Brendan Church.
Brosnan, Msgr. Dermot N. '57 (SAT) [T] San Antonio, TX The Patrician Movement.
Brosnan, Msgr. John R. '37 (LA) [43] Los Angeles, CA St. Ann Church; Retired.
Brosnan, Msgr. Liam P. '59 (SAT) [63] San Antonio, TX St. Pius X Church.
Brosnan, Thomas F. '81 (BRK) [21] Brooklyn, NY Blessed Sacrament Church.
Brost, Frederick '56 (SUP) Stetsonville, WI Sacred Heart of Jesus Church.
Brothersen, Maynard J. '48 (DAV) Retired; [M] Davenport, IA St. Vincent Center.
Brou, Francis R. *s.j.* '61 (BR) [11] Baton Rouge, LA Immaculate Conception Church; [K] Baton Rouge, LA Martin Luther King, Jr. Student Center.
Brouchoud, Earl '46 (GB) Retired.
Broudou, Joseph '96 (OM) [22] Omaha, NE St. Joan of Arc Church.
Broughan, Leonard *o'carm.* '55 (JOL) [J] Darien, IL Carmelite Provincial Office.
Brougher, Douglas C. '62 (NO) [38] New Orleans, LA St. James Major Church; New Orleans, LA Touro Infirmary.
Brouillard, Donald *s.s.s.* '50 (NY) [55] New York, NY St. Jean Baptiste Church.
Brouillard, John '56 (P) Retired.
Brouillard, Louis A. (AGN) Retired.
Brouillette, Thomas S. '96 (LIN) [11] Lincoln, NE St. Teresa's Church.
Brouke, Gabriel Vanden *ss.cc.* '48 (HON) [H] Honolulu, HI St. Patrick's Monastery.
Broussard, A. Rex '66 (LAF) Leroy, LA Our Lady of Perpetual Help Church.
Broussard, Dennis A. '91 (MAN) [1] Concord, NH St. John the Evangelist Church.
Broussard, F. David '93 (LAF) [2] Opelousas, LA Our Lady of Mercy Church.
Broussard, Henry J. '72 (LAF) Judice, LA St. Basil Church.
Broussard, Hubert C. '52 (HT) Retired.
Broussard, John S. *c.s.b.* '48 (GAL) Manvel, TX Sacred Heart of Jesus Church.
Broussard, Kenneth M. (LAF) Absent on Leave.
Broussard, Oris '60 (LKC) Jennings, LA Immaculate Conception Church; [C] Lake Charles, LA Holy City Community.
Broussard, Paul (LAF) Absent on Sick Leave.
Broussard, Ronald *v.g.* '88 (LAF) Duson, LA St. Benedict the Moor Church.
Broussard, Warren *s.j.* '88 (LAF) Grand Coteau, LA St. Charles Borromeo Church.
Broussard, Msgr. William L. '56 (AUS) [N] Austin, TX Texas Conference of Catholic Health Facilities.
Broussard, Msgr. William L. '56 (GAL) On Duty Outside the Diocese.
Brouwers, Hans A.L. '78 (PH) [C] Immaculata, PA Immaculata College.
Brovey, Steven L. '91 (CHR) Georgetown, SC St. Mary's Church; Georgetown, SC St. Cyprian Church.
Brown, Msgr. Anthony M. '49 (HEL) Retired.
Brown, Arnold *o.f.m.* '49 (SP) [O] St. Petersburg, FL St. Anthony Friary.
Brown, Arthur A. '57 (BO) [1] Norwood, MA St. Catherine of Siena Church.
Brown, Benedict J. '74 (L) Military Chaplains.
Brown, Bruce '63 (P) Milwaukie, OR St. John the Baptist Church.
Brown, Charles *s.c.j.* '84 (MIL) [P] Milwaukee, WI St. Joseph House of Formation.
Brown, Charles '87 (PSC) Retired.
Brown, Charles '89 (NY) On Duty Outside the Archdiocese.
Brown, Charles C. '58 (SFE) Los Alamos, NM Immaculate Heart of Mary Church.
Brown, Charles D. '93 (GR) Weare Twp., MI St. Joseph's Church.
Brown, Charles E. '71 (WDC) Burtonsville, MD Resurrection Parish.
Brown, Charles L. '73 (BRK) Absent on Leave.
Brown, Charles L., III '67 (WIL) Salisbury, MD St. Francis De Sales Church.
Brown, David *o.s.m.* '48 (CHI) [N] Chicago, IL Servite Friars - Eastern Province.
Brown, David G. *o.s.b.* '75 (CHL) [J] Belmont, NC Belmont Abbey.
Brown, David M. *o.s.m.* '48 (CHI) [18] Chicago, IL Assumption of the Blessed Virgin Mary Church.
Brown, Edward J. *m.s.* '81 (RVC) [Q] Rockville Centre, NY The Campus Parish of Long Island.
Brown, Eugene M. '60 (NU) [1] New Ulm, MN Cathedral of The Holy Trinity; [2] New Ulm, MN St. Mary Church.
Brown, Everett *s.m.m.* '61 (BRK) [U] Ozone Park, NY Montfort Missionaries Provincialate - for Nation Community.
Brown, Ferdinand L. *c.s.c.* '42 (FTW) [J] South Bend, IN Congregation of Holy Cross Indiana Province Provincial House.
Brown, Francis E. '64 (BO) On Duty Outside the Archdiocese.
Brown, George *o.m.i.* '64 (MAN) [K] Hudson, NH Missionary Oblates of Mary Immaculate.

Brown, Gerald *c.m.* '57 (FgM) Vincentian Foreign Missions.
Brown, Gerald L. *s.s.* '64 (BAL) [M] Baltimore, MD Sulpician Provincial House.
Brown, Gerard J. '46 (TR) Leave of Absence.
Brown, Harold C. *c.pp.s.* '59 (TOL) Glandorf, OH St. John the Baptist Church.
Brown, Henry '51 (IND) [24] Indianapolis, IN St. Lawrence Church; Indianapolis, IN Community Hospital North; Indianapolis, IN Winona Medical Center.
Brown, Isaac Jogues *o.s.b.* '84 (P) [L] St. Benedict, OR Mt. Angel Abbey; [N] St. Benedict, OR Mount Angel Abbey Retreat House.
Brown, James '62 (BWN) Pharr, TX St. Margaret Mary Church.
Brown, James '97 (NEW) New Milford, NJ Ascension Church.
Brown, James E. '72 (TOL) Marblehead, OH St. Joseph Church.
Brown, James J. '62 (L) On Duty Outside the Archdiocese.
Brown, James V. *o.a.r.* '46 (OM) [21] Omaha, NE St. James Church.
Brown, John J. '83 (BRK) [120] Brooklyn, NY Queen of All Saints Church.
Brown, John T. '48 (STP) Retired.
Brown, John T. *glmy.* '84 (TLS) Idabel, OK St. Francis De Sales Church.
Brown, Joseph *c.pp.s.* (DM) Westphalia, IA St. Boniface Church.
Brown, Joseph A. *s.j.* '72 (MIL) [P] Milwaukee, WI Jesuit Provincial Office, Wisconsin Province.
Brown, Joseph E. *s.j.* (STL) [C] St. Louis, MO Saint Louis University.
Brown, Joseph E. *s.j.* '56 (STL) [P] St. Louis, MO Jesuit Community Corporation at St. Louis University - Jesuit Hall.
Brown, Joseph L. *c.pp.s.* '97 (DM) Defiance, IA St. Peter Church.
Brown, Joseph L. *c.pp.s.* '97 (OAK) [N] San Leandro, CA Society of the Precious Blood.
Brown, Justin *o.s.b.* '90 (NO) [P] St. Benedict, LA St. Joseph Abbey.
Brown, Kenneth '77 (STL) [47] St. Louis, MO St. Margaret of Scotland Church.
Brown, Konstantin K. '88 (ROM) Leave of Absence.
Brown, Leonard J. *c.m.f.* '82 (MET) [4] Perth Amboy, NJ Our Lady of Fatima Church.
Brown, Lewis E. '67 (ROC) Military Chaplains.
Brown, Matthew F. '63 (SY) Vestal, NY Our Lady of Sorrows Church; Vestal, NY Binghamton Nursing Homes; Special Assignment.
Brown, Matthew J. *o.s.b.* '49 (OKL) Konawa, OK Sacred Heart Church; [I] Shawnee, OK St. Gregory Abbey.
Brown, Matthew J. *o.s.b.* '49 (TLS) Holdenville, OK St. Stephen's Church.
Brown, Michael '74 (TOL) Military Chaplains.
Brown, Michael R. '89 (ROC) Corning, NY St. Mary Church; Corning, NY St. Patrick Church; Corning, NY St. Vincent de Paul Church; Painted Post, NY Immaculate Heart of Mary Church.
Brown, Nicholas *s.c.j.* (SAT) [B] San Antonio, TX Priests of the Sacred Heart- House of Formation.
Brown, Nicholas *s.c.j.* '76 (SAT) San Antonio, TX St. Luke's Baptist Hospital; University Hospital; [M] San Antonio, TX Harcar House.
Brown, Patrick '66 (PAT) On Duty Outside the Diocese.
Brown, Patrick *o.c.s.o.* '74 (WOR) [N] Spencer, MA St. Joseph's Abbey.
Brown, Patrick E. '78 (PAT) Stirling, NJ St. Vincent de Paul Church; Morristown, NJ Morris County Jail.
Brown, Patrick M. *o.f.m.* '59 (PAT) [M] Butler, NJ St. Anthony Friary.
Brown, Phillip J. '89 (BIS) Graduate Studies.
Brown, Raymond E. *s.s.* '53 (MIA) Miami Shores, FL St. Rose of Lima Church.
Brown, Raymond E. *s.s.* '53 (STA) On Duty Outside the Diocese.
Brown, Richard '80 (DAL) Absent on Leave.
Brown, Richard *s.p.* '80 (STL) [P] St. Louis, MO Servants of the Paraclete; [T] Dittmer, MO Vianney Renewal Center.
Brown, Richard H. *s.j.* '58 (SD) [12] San Diego, CA Our Lady of Guadalupe Church.
Brown, Robert '63 (SC) Maple River, IA St. Francis of Assisi Church; Mount Carmel, IA Our Lady of Mt. Carmel Church.
Brown, Robert A. '42 (L) Howardstown, KY St. Ann Church; Retired.
Brown, Robert A. *o.s.f.s.* '67 (ARL) Reston, VA St. John Neumann Church.
Brown, Msgr. Robert L. '69 (NOR) Montville, CT St. John Church; On Special or Other (Arch)Diocesan Assignment.
Brown, Robert W. '66 (ORL) [10] Orlando, FL St. Joseph Church.
Brown, Roderick M. *o.p.* '79 (BUF) [19] Buffalo, NY SS. Columba & Brigid Church; [49] Buffalo, NY St. Martin de Porres Church.
Brown, Roderick M. *o.p.* '79 (CHI) [N] Chicago, IL Dominicans (Provincial Office).
Brown, Shaun '94 (NTN) Military Chaplains.
Brown, Stephan *s.v.d.* '93 (LAF) [4] Lafayette, LA Immaculate Heart of Mary Church.
Brown, Steven '77 (SJ) Special Assignment.
Brown, Steven P. '77 (SJ) Alviso, CA Our Lady, Star of the Sea Church.
Brown, Sylvester F. '56 (WIN) Janesville, MN St. Ann's Church.
Brown, Theophile *o.s.b.* '56 (SCL) [I] Collegeville, MN St. John's Abbey, of the Order of St. Benedict.
Brown, Theophile W. *o.s.b.* '50 (RIC) [L] Richmond, VA Mary Mother of the Church Abbey.
Brown, Thomas *o.m.i.* '55 (FgM) Oblates Foreign Missions.
Brown, Thomas E. '78 (E) Galeton, PA St. Bibiana Church.
Brown, Timothy B. *s.j.* '86 (BAL) [B] Baltimore, MD Loyola College; [M] Baltimore, MD Jesuit Community of Loyola College, Inc.
Brown, Timothy T. '88 (ROC) [1] Rochester, NY Sacred Heart Cathedral.
Brown, Victor *o.p.* '63 (NO) [30] New Orleans, LA St. Dominic Church.
Brown, Vincent A. '34 (BRK) Retired.
Brown, Vincent A. '57 (HRT) Branford, CT St. Mary Church.
Brown, W. P. '80 (PT) Bayou George, FL Our Lady of the Rosary Church.
Brown, W.T. St. John '92 (CC) [13] Corpus Christi, TX St. Anselm Anglican Use Community Church; Retired.
Brown, Walter W. '94 (JKS) Natchez, MS St. Mary Church.
Brown, Warren *o.m.i.* '82 (SAT) [C] San Antonio, TX Oblate School of Theology; [M] San Antonio, TX De Mazenod House.
Brown, Wayland Y. '77 (SAV) Special Assignment.
Brown, William *o.m.v.* '94 (BO) [B] Boston, MA Oblate Provincialate.
Brown, William A. '94 (STP) Stillwater, MN St. Mary Church.
Brown, William E. '88 (SFR) Redwood City, CA St. Pius Church.
Brown, William J. '55 (SY) [S] Syracuse, NY St. Pius X Home, Inc.
Brown, William P. '80 (PT) Fountain, FL Our Lady Queen of Peace Mission Church.
Browne, Denis P. *m.m.* '47 (FgM) Maryknoll Foreign Missions.
Browne, Msgr. Edward P. '51 (ARL) Annandale, VA St. Michael's Church.
Browne, Francis J. *c.ss.r.* '68 (HRT) [5] Enfield, CT St. Patrick's Church.
Browne, George E. *c.m.* '46 (PH) [AA] Philadelphia, PA Congregation of the Mission.
Browne, George T. '55 (DET) [1] Roseville, MI St. Angela Church.
Browne, Gerald '81 (MET) [3] Carteret, NJ Sacred Heart Church.
Browne, J. Patrick '67 (SJ) [1] San Jose, CA Cathedral Basilica of St. Joseph Church.
Browne, John T. *o.s.b.* '56 (NEW) Maplewood, NJ St. Joseph's Church; [N] Newark, NJ Newark Abbey.
Browne, Joseph *c.s.c.* '55 (P) [L] Portland, OR Holy Cross Fathers & Brothers, C.S.C. - University of Portland.
Browne, Joseph P. *c.s.c.* '55 (P) [8] Portland, OR St. Birgitta Church.
Browne, Joseph T. *s.j.* '56 (NY) [FF] Staten Island, NY Mount Manresa Jesuit Retreat House.
Browne, Michael E. *s.j.* '71 (NEW) [C] Jersey City, NJ St. Peter's Preparatory School.
Browne, Robert M. '61 (BO) Wilmington, MA St. Thomas of Villanova Church.
Browne, Ronald '88 (DET) Special Assignment.
Browne, Ronald '91 (DET) [A] Detroit, MI Sacred Heart Major Seminary, Inc.
Browne, Stanley (GB) Hollandtown, WI St. Francis Church.
Browne, Vincent T. '54 (MAD) Military Chaplains.
Brownell, Patrick '94 (KNX) [3] Chattanooga, TN St. Jude Church; [J] Chattanooga, TN Newman Foundation of Chattanooga, Inc.
Brownell, Robert A. '69 (RIC) [16] Richmond, VA St. Peter Church.
Brownfield, David '90 (DAV) DeWitt, IA St. Joseph's Church.
Brownfield, David L. '90 (DAV) Grand Mound, IA Church of St. Philip and James.
Brownfield, Frowin '56 (SPC) Retired.
Brownfield, Robert L. '92 (DAV) Retired; [M] Iowa City, IA O'Keefe Hall.
Brownholtz, George J. *o.s.f.s.* '69 (FgM) Oblates of St. Francis de Sales Foreign Missions.
Brownholtz, George J. *o.s.f.s.* '69 (WIL) [I] Childs, MD Oblates of St. Francis De Sales.
Browning, John E. *s.j.* '59 (NEW) [C] Jersey City, NJ St. Peter's Preparatory School.
Browning, John E. *s.j.* '59 (NY) [DD] New York, NY Murray-Weigel Hall.
Browning, Joseph E. *s.j.* '54 (NO) [P] New Orleans, LA Ignatius Residence.
Browning, Lawrence *c.p.* '55 (CHI) [N] Chicago, IL Immaculate Conception Monastery.
Browning, Thomas *s.s.c.* '90 (FgM) St. Columban's Foreign Mission.
Browning, William '49 (L) [K] Louisville, KY Franciscan Health Care Center/Retirement Center; [L] Louisville, KY Sacred Heart Retreat.
Brownsey, Brian K. '96 (PEO) Moline, IL Sacred Heart Church.
Brownstein, Donald '81 (COS) [13] Colorado Springs, CO St. Patrick's Church.
Broxmeyer, Dominic *o.s.b.* '45 (P) [L] St. Benedict, OR Mt. Angel Abbey.
Brozat, Charles *s.a.* '57 (NY) [DD] Garrison, NY Generalate of the Franciscan Friars of the Atonement-St. James Friary.
Brozena, Joseph M. '58 (SCR) [3] Old Forge, PA St. Michael's Church.
Brozonowicz, Gregorz P. '96 (NOR) Moosup, CT All-Hallows Church.
Brubaker, Claude E. '55 (VEN) [4] Sarasota, FL St. Michael the Archangel Church.
Brubaker, George J. '80 (WIL) On Duty Outside the Diocese.
Brubaker, Scott '82 (PHX) [22] Phoenix, AZ Our Lady of the Valley Church.
Bruce, Joseph J. *s.j.* '81 (BO) [W] Boston, MA Loyola House; [W] Boston, MA The Society of Jesus of New England-Provincial Offices.
Bruce, Robert '64 (Y) [12] Canton, OH St. Peter's Church.
Bruce, Robert J. '64 (Y) Retired.
Bruce, Terry '67 (KC) [1] Independence, MO St. Ann's Church.
Bruch, James A. '65 (SC) [10] Sioux City, IA Sacred Heart Church.
Bruch, Lynn '86 (SC) St. Benedict, IA St. Benedict's Church.
Bruch, Walter L. '50 (SC) Retired.
Bruck, Donald '68 (DM) Hamburg, IA St. Mary Church.
Bruck, Donald '82 (DM) Shenandoah, IA St. Mary Church.
Brucker, George W. '56 (ALB) [16] Schenectady, NY St. Paul the Apostle Church.
Bruckner, Ronald L. '65 (SFE) [1] Albuquerque, NM Annunciation Church.
Brucksch, James L. '69 (GAY) Oscoda, MI Sacred Heart Church.
Brucz, James M. *c.s.p.* '74 (CHR) Clemson, SC St. Andrew Church; [G] Clemson, SC Clemson University, Southern Wesleyan University.
Bruder, John W. *o.c.s.o.* '56 (BUR) Other Residence.
Brudzynski, Peter F. (BO) Retired.
Brudzynski, Peter F. '50 (VEN) [1] Venice, FL Epiphany Cathedral.
Bruecken, Albert *o.s.b.* '77 (KC) [A] Conception, MO Conception Seminary College; [J] Conception, MO Conception Abbey; [O] Conception, MO Conception Benedictine Trust.
Bruemmer, Joseph '48 (CIN) Withamsville, OH St. Thomas More Church.
Bruemmer, Joseph A. '48 (CIN) Retired.
Bruemmer, Joseph J. *o.s.c.* '47 (PHX) [F] Phoenix, AZ Crosier Community of Phoenix (Canons Regular of the Order of the Holy Cross).
Bruening, Allen '51 (CLV) Retired.
Bruening, Bernard H. '59 (CIN) Miamisburg, OH Our Lady of Good Hope Church.
Bruening, Joseph B. '53 (CIN) Franklin, OH St. Mary's Church.
Bruetsch, Joseph '70 (LFT) [1] Lafayette, IN St. Mary Cathedral.
Bruetsch, Joseph J. '70 (LFT) Retired.
Bruggeman, Donald R. '62 (DUB) [3] Cedar Rapids, IA St. Jude Church; [D] Cedar Rapids, IA Xavier High School dba Regis High School and LaSalle High School Center.
Bruggeman, Gerald H. '49 (COS) Retired; [B] Colorado Springs, CO Centura Health-Penrose-St. Francis Health Services.
Brugger, Craig F. '73 (PH) [54] Philadelphia, PA St. Helena Church.
Brugger, Donald E. *s.j.* '70 (CHI) [C] Chicago, IL Jesuit Community at Loyola University of Chicago.
Brugger, Msgr. Robert L. '68 (E) Meadville, PA St. Brigid Church.
Brugli, Msgr. Angelo F. '47 (BRK) Retired.
Brum, Louis L. '74 (BWN) Alamo, TX Resurrection Church.
Brumleve, Matthew '88 (KC) [6] St. Joseph, MO St. Patrick's Church; Easton, MO St. Joseph's Church.
Brummel, Mark J. *c.m.f.* '60 (CHI) [149] Chicago, IL Our Lady of Guadalupe Church; [N] Chicago, IL Claretian Missionaries, St. Jude League, Inc.; [N] Oak Park, IL Claretian Fathers Headquarters of U.S.A. Eastern Province.
Brummel, Thomas *c.m.f.* '59 (CHI) [N] Oak Park, IL Claretian Fathers Headquarters of U.S.A. Eastern Province.

Brummer, Lawrence *o.f.m.* '58 (SAT) [46] San Antonio, TX St. Joseph Church.
Brundage, John L. '70 (MET) Bridgewater, NJ St. Bernard Church.
Brundage, Thomas T. '88 (MIL) Special Assignment; [B] Hales Corners, WI Sacred Heart School of Theology.
Brune, James '48 (EVN) Retired.
Brune, Meinrad *o.s.b.* '61 (IND) [J] St. Meinrad, IN St. Meinrad Archabbey.
Brune, Theodore *o.s.b.* '75 (FAR) St. Michael, ND St. Michael's Church; St. Michael, ND St. Michael's Indian Mission Church.
Brune, Theodore *o.s.b.* '75 (IND) [J] St. Meinrad, IN St. Meinrad Archabbey.
Brunelle, J. Ernest *m.m.* '59 (FgM) Maryknoll Foreign Missions.
Brunelle, Richard *a.a.* '63 (BO) [W] Brighton, MA Assumptionist Center.
Brunet, Msgr. Frederic J. '60 (HT) Chauvin, LA St. Joseph Church.
Brunet, Gerald O. *o.m.i.* '57 (SEA) Forks, WA St. Anne Parish.
Brunet, Jules A. '55 (BR) White Castle, LA Our Lady of Prompt Succor Church.
Brunett, John L. *s.j.* '55 (BAL) [B] Baltimore, MD Loyola College; [M] Baltimore, MD Jesuit Community of Loyola College, Inc.
Brunette, Bernard M. *o.praem.* '51 (MAD) [9] Madison, WI Saint Joseph Church.
Bruney, J. Lawrence '84 (PIT) [4] New Castle, PA St. Vitus Church.
Brungardt, Aloysius '71 (SAL) Junction City, KS St. Francis Xavier's Church.
Brungs, Robert A. *s.j.* '64 (STL) [P] St. Louis, MO Jesuit Community Corporation at St. Louis University - Jesuit Hall; [W] St. Louis, MO Institute for Theological Encounter with Science & Technology (ITEST).
Bruni, John E. '76 (CAM) Blackwood, NJ St. Agnes Church.
Brunick, Charles J. *c.s.p.* '70 (CHI) [125] Chicago, IL Old St. Mary Church.
Bruning, David R. '78 (TOL) Bascom, OH St. Patrick Church; Liberty, OH St. Andrew Church.
Bruning, William '93 (KCK) Shawnee, KS St. Joseph's Church.
Brunkan, Msgr. Walter L. '56 (DUB) Greene, IA St. Mary's Church; Roseville, IA St. Mary Church.
Brunner, Frank J. '55 (WH) Retired.
Brunner, Msgr. James C. *v.g.* '54 (VIC) Bay City, TX Holy Cross Church.
Brunner, John H. '62 (NU) Fairfax, MN St. Andrew Church; Franklin, MN Sacred Heart Church.
Brunner, Thomas J. '74 (CIN) Troy, OH St. Patrick Church.
Brunner, William M. *s.s.c.* '62 (SB) Needles, CA St. Ann Church.
Brunnert, Edward J. *m.s.* '63 (STL) [P] St. Louis, MO La Salette Missionaries.
Brunnert, Jude *m.s.* '64 (LKC) Oberlin, LA St. Joan of Arc Church; Dequincy, LA Phelps Correctional Center.
Brunnert, Theodore J. '54 (STL) Sullivan, MO St. Anthony Church.
Bruno, Anthony J. '68 (HRT) [2] Enfield, CT St. Adalbert's Church; Suffield, CT Macdougall Correctional Institute.
Bruno, John *r.c.j.* '74 (FRS) Del Rey, CA St. Katherine Church; Sanger, CA St. Mary Church.
Brunovsky, Michael *o.s.b.* '93 (CLV) [E] Cleveland, OH Benedictine High School; [P] Cleveland, OH Benedictine Order of Cleveland.
Brunovsky, Stephen K. '92 (CLV) Hudson, OH St. Mary Church.
Bruns, Wilbert H. *c.m.* '51 (STL) [P] St. Louis, MO Vincentian Henrietta Residence.
Brunskill, Richard W. '83 (PEO) Chatsworth, IL SS. Peter and Paul Church; Cullom, IL St. John's Church.
Brunsman, Barry *o.f.m.* (OAK) [P] Danville, CA San Damiano Retreat.
Brunton, Daniel B. '60 (SPR) Lenox, MA St. Ann's Church; Lenox Dale, MA St. Vincent de Paul's Church.
Brusato, Martin '89 (SAC) Galt, CA St. Christopher Church.
Brusatti, Louis T. *c.m.* '75 (GAL) [A] Houston, TX St. Mary's Seminary; [C] Houston, TX University of St. Thomas.
Bruse, James C. '84 (ARL) Kilmarnock, VA St. Francis de Sales Church.
Brusky, David *s.d.s.* '52 (FgM) Salvatorian Foreign Missions.
Bruso, Robert D. '93 (WOR) Clinton, MA St. John the Evangelist Church.
Brutus, Ferry '80 (MIA) North Miami, FL Holy Family Church.
Bryan, Dunstan *o.f.m.conv.* '37 (IND) [I] Mount Saint Francis, IN Mount Saint Francis Friary and Retreat Center.
Bryan, Francis E. '62 (IND) [B] Indianapolis, IN Marian College.
Bryan, Kevin J. '76 (L) [67] Louisville, KY St. Raphael the Archangel Church.
Bryan, Paul *c.ss.r.* '59 (PH) [135] Philadelphia, PA St. Peter the Apostle Church.
Bryant, F. Michael '69 (WDC) [16] Washington, DC Holy Comforter—St. Cyprian Church; [V] Washington, DC District of Columbia Detention Facility.
Bryant, James M. '85 (STU) Chesapeake, OH St. Ann Church.
Bryant, Michael '69 (WDC) Special Ministries; [V] Hyattsville, MD Prison Outreach Ministry.
Bryant, Michael M. '78 (SCR) [C] Dallas, PA College Misericordia.
Bryce, Ambrose S. '61 (CAM) Waterford, NJ St. Anthony Church.
Bryce, Edward M. '60 (PIT) [5] Pittsburgh, PA St. Bede Church.
Bryce, Vincent *o.p.* '57 (GR) Edmore, MI St. Margaret Mary Church; Stanton, MI St. Bernadette of Lourdes Church.
Bryce, Vincent W. *o.p.* '57 (CHI) [N] Chicago, IL Dominicans (Provincial Office).
Bryda, Ronald J. '66 (CLV) Litchfield, OH Our Lady Help of Christians Parish.
Brydl, Ladislaus C. '31 (BIS) Retired; [G] Bismarck, ND Emmaus Place.
Bryerton, Robert R. '74 (TUC) Sierra Vista, AZ Our Lady of the Mountains Church.
Bryk, John J. '53 (CLV) [3] Lakewood, OH St. Hedwig Church.
Bryl, Thaddeus '66 (LIN) Grafton, NE St. Helena's Church; Sutton, NE St. Mary's Church.
Bryl, Thaddeus J. '66 (MIL) On Duty Outside the Archdiocese.
Brylinski, Bruce '83 (COV) Vanceburg, KY Holy Redeemer Church.
Brylinski, Bruce C. *glmy.* '83 (LEX) Grayson, KY Ss. John & Elizabeth Church.
Brylka, Vincent R. '65 (OAK) Martinez, CA St. Catherine of Siena Church.
Brynda, Msgr. Gerald J. '57 (TUC) Yuma, AZ Immaculate Conception Church.
Brynes, Msgr. Donald M. '55 (NO) Retired.
Bryon, Paul J. (R) Retired.
Bryon, Thomas C. '63 (STL) [49] St. Louis, MO St. Mary Magdalen Church.
Bryson, John *s.m.* '53 (DET) [E] Harper Woods, MI Notre Dame High School.
Bryson, John H. '50 (MAN) West Swanzey, NH St. Anthony Church.
Bryson, Robert C. (BO) Retired.
Bryson, Robert C. '46 (BO) Hingham, MA Resurrection of Our Lord and Saviour Jesus Christ Church.
Brzakowski, Jerome *s.v.d.* '45 (TR) [M] Bordentown, NJ Society of the Divine Word.
Brzek, Jon J. '83 (PIT) Military Chaplains.
Brzezicki, Zbigniew '88 (STF) Hamptonburgh, NY St. Andrew's Church.
Brzezinski, Hilary *o.f.m.* '76 (JKS) Greenwood, MS St. Francis of Assisi Church; Lexington, MS St. Thomas Church; [G] Greenwood, MS Holmes Community College Newman Center.
Brzezinski, Jerome A. '69 (DET) Auburn Hills, MI St. John Fisher Chapel University Parish; [S] Auburn Hills, MI St. John Fisher Chapel University Parish.
Brzezniak, Aurelian W. *ofm conv.* '45 (BUF) [D] Athol Springs, NY St. Francis High School; [O] Athol Springs, NY St. Francis of Assisi Friary.
Brzoska, Anthony B. *s.j.* '59 (LA) [C] Los Angeles, CA Loyola Marymount University.
Brzostowski, Hilary *o.f.m.conv.* '69 (NOR) Cromwell, CT St. John Church.
Brzozowski, Edward J. '44 (CHI) [143] Chicago, IL St. Nicholas of Tolentine Church; Retired.
Brzozowski, Msgr. Joseph R. '37 (MET) Fords, NJ Our Lady of Peace Church; Retired; [G] Somerset, NJ McCarrick Care Center.
Brzozowski, Simon *m.s.f.* (STL) [O] St. Louis, MO Little Sisters of the Poor, Home for the Aged.
Buby, Bertrand A. *s.m.* '64 (CIN) [D] Dayton, OH The University of Dayton; [M] Dayton, OH Marianist Provincialate.
Bucaria, James A. '72 (SP) Masaryktown, FL St. Mary, Our Lady of Sorrows Church.
Bucaro, Michael '80 (SB) Chino, CA Southern Conservation Center.
Buccafurni, Ferdinand '58 (PH) [40] Philadelphia, PA St. Donato Church; [112] Philadelphia, PA Our Lady of Angels Church.
Buccellato, Sebastian *o.f.m.* '51 (NY) [142] Bronx, NY St. Frances of Rome Church; [DD] New York, NY Padua Friary.
Buccheri, Vincenzo *r.c.j.* '79 (LA) [R] North Hills, CA Rogationist Fathers.
Bucchino, John *o.f.m.* '73 (NY) [DD] New York, NY Franciscan Province of the Immaculate Conception.
Bucci, Evan *o.f.m.conv.* (TR) Riverside, NJ St. Peter Church.
Bucci, Michael J. '62 (GBG) Retired.
Bucci, Richard A. '73 (PRO) [8] West Warwick, RI SS. Peter and Paul Church.
Bucciantini, Charles '72 (JKS) Cleveland, MS Our Lady of Victories Church; Rosedale, MS Sacred Heart Church; [G] Cleveland, MS Delta State University Newman Center.
Bucciarelli, Michael R. '75 (TUC) San Manuel, AZ St. Bartholomew Church.
Bucciarelli, Robert P. '60 (MIL) [O] Brookfield, WI Opus Dei-Prelature of the Holy Cross and Opus Dei.
Buccicone, Ananius G. *o.s.b.* '93 (E) St. Marys, PA Sacred Heart of Jesus Church.
Bucciferro, Eugene '63 (JOL) [17] Joliet, IL St. Patrick Church.
Bucciferro, William *s.d.b.* '83 (COL) [H] Columbus, OH Salesian Center.
Bucek, Timothy P. '76 (GAL) Bellville, TX SS. Peter & Paul Church.
Buchanan, Caleb A. '97 (BRK) [238] Queens, NY Sacred Heart Church.
Buchanan, David '93 (BIR) Eutaw, AL St. Mary Church; Livingston, AL St. Francis of Assisi Church; Tuscaloosa, AL Holy Spirit Church.
Buchanan, Donald '45 (SD) Lemon Grove, CA St. John of the Cross Church; Retired.
Buchanan, Donald E. '65 (IND) Military Chaplains.
Buchanan, J. Scott '97 (CHR) On Duty Outside the Diocese.
Buchanan, John J. '36 (STP) Retired.
Buchanan, Robert '68 (SB) On Duty Outside the Diocese.
Buchanan, Robert E. '68 (RNO) [2] Reno, NV Our Lady of the Snows Church.
Buchek, Basil '68 (STN) St. Joseph, MO St. Joseph's Church; Lincoln, NE St. George's Church; Omaha, NE Assumption of B.V.M. Church.
Bucher, Mel *o.f.m.* '61 (SD) [H] San Luis Rey, CA Mission San Luis Rey; [K] San Luis Rey, CA Mission San Luis Rey Retreat.
Bucher, Otto N. *o.f.m.cap.* '59 (MIL) [B] Hales Corners, WI Sacred Heart School of Theology; [P] Milwaukee, WI St. Conrad House.
Bucher, Msgr. Philip A. '61 (SPC) Branson, MO Our Lady of the Lake Church.
Bucher, Raymond J. *o.f.m.* '64 (OAK) [P] Danville, CA San Damiano Retreat.
Buchette, Anthony J. (BO) Retired.
Buchheit, Msgr. Jerome J. '51 (STL) Ballwin, MO Holy Infant Church.
Buchheit, Msgr. Richard A. '63 (STL) [29] St. Louis, MO St. Bridget of Erin Church.
Buchholz, Athanasius *o.s.b.* '54 (P) [L] St. Benedict, OR Mt. Angel Abbey.
Buchignani, Peter P. '65 (MEM) [8] Memphis, TN St. Francis of Assisi Church.
Buchignani, Richard G. '62 (NSH) Lawrenceburg, TN Sacred Heart Church; [L] Nashville, TN Diocesan Council of Catholic Women.
Buchleitner, Donald N. '70 (PIT) [50] Pittsburgh, PA Holy Innocents Church.
Buchman, Joel '91 (TOL) [14] Toledo, OH Sacred Heart of Jesus Church; Toledo, OH St. Vincent Medical Center; [H] Toledo, OH St. Vincent Medical Center.
Buchmeier, Francis X. *s.j.* '73 (FgM) Provinces.
Buchmeier, Robert P. '91 (WDC) Clinton, MD Church of St. John the Evangelist.
Buchmiller, Ronald J. '69 (SD) Military Chaplains.
Bucia, Msgr. Edward H. '62 (CAM) [6] Camden, NJ St. Joseph's Church.
Buck, Daniel P. '71 (CHI) [2] Cicero, IL St. Frances of Rome Church.
Buck, Francis C. *s.j.* '46 (GLP) Church Rock, NM St. Philip Benizi Church.
Buck, Franklin G. '85 (ORL) [4] Lakeland, FL St. Joseph's Church.
Buck, James '41 (SEA) Retired.
Buckalew, Jack '74 (SEA) Bremerton, WA Holy Trinity Church.
Bucke, Gerald L. '43 (BO) [35] Boston, MA St. Joseph Church.
Buckel, John J. '80 (IND) [A] St. Meinrad, IN St. Meinrad Seminary.
Bucki, John P. *s.j.* '79 (NY) [37] New York, NY St. Francis Xavier Church; [DD] New York, NY Xavier Jesuit Community.
Buckius, Walter A. *s.j.* '52 (WH) [A] Wheeling, WV Wheeling Jesuit University.
Buckles, David '88 (LFT) Special Assignment; [H] West Lafayette, IN St. Thomas Aquinas Parish and Foundation for Catholic Students Attending Purdue University.
Buckles, Luke *o.p.* (OAK) [N] Oakland, CA Western Dominican Province.
Buckles, Luke D. *o.p.* '78 (OAK) [A] Berkeley, CA Dominican School of Philosophy and Theology; [N] Oakland, CA Dominican Order (Western Province), St. Albert's Priory.
Buckley, Brendan *o.f.m.cap.* '81 (NY) [DD] White Plains, NY St. Conrad Friary.
Buckley, Charles *o.s.b.* '70 (OKL) [I] Shawnee, OK St. Gregory Abbey.
Buckley, Cornelius M. *s.j.* '62 (SFR) [N] San Francisco,

CA Jesuit Community at University of San Francisco.
Buckley, Msgr. Edwin T. '41 (BUR) Retired.
Buckley, Francis *s.j.* '58 (OAK) [A] Oakland, CA Graduate School of Theology, School of Applied Theology.
Buckley, Francis J. *s.j.* '58 (SFR) [N] San Francisco, CA Jesuit Community at University of San Francisco.
Buckley, Frederick J. '45 (BO) Retired.
Buckley, G. Albert *o.p.* (OAK) [N] Oakland, CA Western Dominican Province.
Buckley, George M. *m.m.* '39 (SJ) [M] Los Altos, CA Maryknoll.
Buckley, George P. *o.m.i.* '40 (BO) [Z] Tewksbury, MA Immaculate Heart of Mary Novitiate-Infirmary.
Buckley, Gerald A. *o.p.* '57 (SFR) [N] San Francisco, CA St. Dominic Priory.
Buckley, Gerald J. '57 (SY) [1] Binghamton, NY St. Andrew Church; Binghamton, NY Binghamton Psychiatric Hospital.
Buckley, Harold P. '53 (RVC) Retired.
Buckley, James '82 (GLP) Absent on Leave.
Buckley, James B. *f.s.s.p.* '65 (SCR) [M] Elmhurst, PA Priestly Fraternity of St. Peter (F.S.S.P.), North American District Headquarters.
Buckley, James F. '59 (FR) Chatham, MA Holy Redeemer Church.
Buckley, James M. '90 (OM) Plainview, NE St. Paul Church.
Buckley, John A. *s.s.c.* '68 (FgM) St. Columban's Foreign Mission.
Buckley, John E. '59 (BO) Burlington, MA St. Margaret Church.
Buckley, John J. *c.m.* '57 (FgM) Vincentian Foreign Missions.
Buckley, John J. *c.m.* '57 (PH) [AA] Philadelphia, PA Congregation of the Mission.
Buckley, John K. '47 (BO) Retired.
Buckley, John M. *s.j.* '56 (NEW) [B] Jersey City, NJ Saint Peter's College; [N] Jersey City, NJ Jesuits of Saint Peter's College, Inc.
Buckley, Joseph F. '43 (BRK) [28] Brooklyn, NY St. Cecilia Church; Retired.
Buckley, Lawrence J. *c.ss.r.* '49 (BO) [13] Boston, MA Our Lady of Perpetual Help Church.
Buckley, Michael *o.c.d.* '47 (SJ) [M] San Jose, CA Carmelite Monastery, Novitiate.
Buckley, Michael '55 (LA) Retired.
Buckley, Michael *s.j.* '62 (BO) [W] Chestnut Hill, MA The Jesuit Community at Boston College.
Buckley, Ramon J. '77 (STP) Clearwater, MN St. Luke Church.
Buckley, Robert L. '57 (ALB) Schuylerville, NY Notre Dame-Visitation Church.
Buckley, Thomas E. *s.j.* '70 (LA) [C] Los Angeles, CA Loyola Marymount University.
Buckley, Thomas E. *s.j.* '70 (OAK) [A] Berkeley, CA The Jesuit School of Theology at Berkeley.
Buckley, Thomas J. '61 (BO) Amesbury, MA Sacred Heart Church.
Buckley, Thomas J. *s.j.* '70 (OAK) [N] Berkeley, CA Jesuit Community at Jesuit School of Theology at Berkeley.
Buckley, Thomas J. *s.j.* '74 (WDC) [M] Washington, DC The Jesuit Community at Georgetown University.
Buckley, Thomas R. '76 (ALN) Limeport, PA St. Joseph Church.
Buckley, Thomas W. '55 (BO) Essex, MA St. John the Baptist Church.
Buckley, Timothy J. '92 (PH) Brookline, PA Annunciation B.V.M. Church.
Buckman, Franklin J. '63 (BAK) Klamath Falls, OR St. Pius Xth Church.
Buckman, Franklin J. '63 (ORG) On Duty Outside the Diocese.
Buckner, Christopher M. '80 (ARL) Fredericksburg, VA St. Mary Church.
Bucko, Raymond A. *s.j.* '83 (SY) [S] Syracuse, NY Jesuits at LeMoyne, Inc.
Buckon, Neal J. '95 (CLV) South Euclid, OH St. Margaret Mary Church.
Buckson, John R. '92 (OM) [15] Omaha, NE St. Francis Assisi Church; [32] Omaha, NE Our Lady of Guadalupe Church.
Bucolo, Joseph W. '54 (SCR) Pardeesville, PA St. Nazarius Church.
Buczynski, Edward '61 (DUL) Hill City, MN St. John Church.
Budai, Frank A. '88 (GLP) Retired.
Budde, John G. '77 (DET) Novi, MI Holy Family Church.
Budden, William A. '68 (RCK) Oregon, IL St. Mary Church.
Buddendorff, Kenneth *s.j.* '61 (LAF) [J] Grand Coteau, LA Our Lady of the Oaks Retreat House.
Budenholzer, Francis *s.v.d.* '72 (FgM) Society of the Divine Word Foreign Missions.
Budi, Hartono *s.j.* '94 (OAK) [N] Berkeley, CA Jesuit Community at Jesuit School of Theology at Berkeley.
Budka, Dennis G. '84 (MIL) [3] Waukesha, WI St. John Neumann Church.
Budnar, Randy J. '88 (MAD) Sun Prairie, WI Sacred Hearts of Jesus and Mary Church.
Budney, Msgr. David F. '57 (CAM) [5] Cherry Hill, NJ St. Thomas More Church.
Budnick, Austin J. *o.f.m.* '51 (ROC) [I] Watkins Glen, NY St. Anthony of Padua Friary.
Budovic, Francis X. *s.j.* '38 (DET) [61] Detroit, MI SS. Peter and Paul Jesuit Church.
Budwick, Msgr. John J. '64 (NY) [1] Newburgh, NY St. Patrick Church.
Budzikowski, Kenneth A. '80 (CHI) Park Ridge, IL St. Paul of the Cross Church.
Budzynski, Daniel A. '56 (MIL) Retired.
Buebendorf, Victor J. '64 (NY) [213] Staten Island, NY St. Mary Church.
Bueche, Charles C. *c.ss.r.* '53 (STL) [P] Liguori, MO Liguori Mission House/Redemptorists.
Bueche, Gary '70 (DET) Allen Park, MI St. Frances Cabrini Church.
Bueche, Walter *c.ss.r.* '38 (ORL) [F] New Smyrna Beach, FL St. Alphonsus Villa-Redemptorist Fathers and Brothers.
Bueche, William *c.ss.r.* (CHI) [29] Chicago, IL Blessed Sacrament Church.
Buechele, Andrew C. *sch.p.* '69 (WDC) [B] Washington, DC Queen of Pious Schools House of Studies-Piarist Fathers; [C] Washington, DC Catholic University of America, The.
Buehler, John A. '74 (SY) [9] Utica, NY St. John Church.
Buehler, Paul A. *c.pp.s.* '44 (CIN) [M] Dayton, OH Provincial House of the Cincinnati Province of the Society of the Precious Blood.
Buelt, Msgr. Edward L. '82 (DEN) On Duty Outside the Archdiocese.
Buenaventura, Cesar (OAK) Military Chaplains.
Buenger, Edward A. *c.s.c.* '53 (FTW) [J] South Bend, IN Congregation of Holy Cross Indiana Province Provincial House.
Buening, Robert B. '58 (CIN) [41] Cincinnati, OH St. James Church.
Buening, Ulric *o.f.m.cap.* '53 (MIL) [25] Milwaukee, WI St. Francis of Assisi Church; [Y] Milwaukee, WI Capuchin Franciscan Tertiary Province of St. Joseph of Wisconsin, Inc.
Bueno, Alberto *t.o.r.* '86 (SP) [10] Tampa, FL St. Lawrence Church.
Buentello, Michael A. *c.s.b.* '95 (GRY) [J] Merrillville, IN Basilian Fathers Residence.
Buenzli, August H. '53 (MAD) Briggsville, WI St. Mary Help of Christians Church.
Buerger, Francis J. '44 (CIN) Retired.
Buermann, Eric R. *o.s.b.* '45 (CGS) Humacao, PR Maria Reina de la Paz Church.
Buersmeyer, David A. '80 (DET) Lincoln Park, MI Christ the Good Shepherd Church.
Buerster, James A. '79 (BEL) [1] Belleville, IL Cathedral of St. Peter.
Buescher, David G. '71 (JC) Jefferson City, MO Capital Region Medical Center, Still Campus; Jefferson City, MO Capital Region Medical Center, Memorial Campus; [F] Jefferson City, MO Lincoln University-Newman Center.
Bueter, Paul '59 (FTW) Goshen, IN St. John the Evangelist Church; Milford, IN Our Lady of Guadalupe Church.
Bueter, Robert J. *s.j.* '73 (LEX) [A] Lexington, KY Lexington Catholic High School.
Buetow, Harold A. '44 (BRK) Retired; [U] Douglaston, NY Bishop Mugavero Residence.
Buettner, George '52 (BAL) Retired.
Buezyna, Andrew (JOL) Joliet, IL Silver Cross Hospital.
Buezyna, Andrew L. (JOL) [3] Lockport, IL St. John Vianney Church.
Buffardi, Joseph G. '76 (PAT) [10] Paterson, NJ St. Mary's Church.
Buffer, Thomas '91 (COL) [5] Columbus, OH St. Andrew Church.
Buffington, Jon '81 (EST) On Assignment Outside the Diocese.
Buffington, Jon '81 (P) [J] Portland, OR Providence Portland Medical Center.
Bugarin, Fred '75 (ANC) Kodiak, AK St. Mary's of Kodiak and the Islands Church.
Bugarin, Michael '91 (DET) Special Assignment.
Bugay, Stephen R. '84 (GBG) Clymer, PA Church of the Resurrection.
Bugayong, Demetrio '70 (LA) Carson, CA St. Philomena Church.
Buggert, Donald W. *o.carm.* '66 (WDC) [B] Washington, DC Whitefriars Hall.
Bugler, Henry J. '75 (NO) [58] New Orleans, LA St. Rita Church.
Bugler, Msgr. Joseph T. '38 (JC) Retired.
Bugliosi, Mario *o.s.f.s.* '43 (WIL) [3] Wilmington, DE St. Anthony of Padua Church; [G] Wilmington, DE The Antonian.
Bugman, Msgr. John H. '52 (BUF) [1] Lackawanna, NY Basilica of Our Lady of Victory Church; Retired.
Bugner, Joseph *s.v.d.* '63 (FgM) Society of the Divine Word Foreign Missions.
Bugno, Krzysztof *s.d.s.* '85 (BRK) [187] Queens, NY St. Joseph Church.
Bugno, Krzysztof *s.d.s.* '85 (NEW) [N] Verona, NJ The Salvatorian Fathers.
Buhl, Wilbert L. '60 (GB) Maplewood, WI St. Mary Church.
Buhler, Richard O. *s.j.* '70 (COS) [E] Sedalia, CO Sacred Heart Retreat House - Jesuit Community; [G] Sedalia, CO Sacred Heart Jesuit Retreat House.
Buhman, Leo T. '48 (JC) Retired.
Buholzer, Robert E. '56 (MAD) Palmyra, WI St. Mary Church.
Buhr, Eugene '54 (LA) Hawthorne, CA St. Joseph Church.
Buhrfeind, William J. '38 (CHI) [3] Mt. Prospect, IL St. Raymond de Penafort Church; [2] Oak Lawn, IL St. Gerald Church; Retired.
Buhrman, Donald A. '86 (GI) Lexington, NE St. Ann's Church.
Bui, Francis '90 (HT) Amelia, LA Thanh Gia Church.
Bui, Francis T. '75 (LA) [9] Long Beach, CA St. Lucy Church.
Bui, Joseph T.P. '97 (GAL) [12] Houston, TX St. Augustine Church.
Bui, Peter *s.d.b.* '90 (LA) [C] Rosemead, CA Don Bosco Technical Institute.
Bui, Phong (P) Sheridan, OR Federal Correctional Institution.
Bui, Tin Mahn '75 (SFE) [9] Albuquerque, NM Our Lady of Lavang Church.
Bui, Vincent '95 (LAN) On Duty Outside the Diocese.
Bui, Vincent D. '95 (BAL) [M] Baltimore, MD Sulpician Provincial House.
Bui-Trang-Nghiem, Joseph '73 (WDC) [L] Washington, DC Cardinal O'Boyle Residence for Priests.
Buitrago, Alejandro '67 (DAL) Richardson, TX St. Paul the Apostle Church.
Buitrago, Tarsicio '64 (ARL) [1] Alexandria, VA Blessed Sacrament Church.
Bujnak, George A. '65 (PSC) Nesquehoning, PA St. Mary's Church.
Bukala, Casimir R. *s.j.* '66 (CLV) [C] Cleveland, OH John Carroll Jesuit Community.
Bukase, Joseph *c.i.c.m.* '84 (BWN) Hidalgo, TX Sacred Heart Church.
Bukaty, Lawrence J. '76 (ALN) [3] Mahanoy City, PA St. Casimir Church; [C] Ashland, PA Cardinal Brennan Jr./Sr. High School.
Bukauskas, Anthony '46 (STL) Retired.
Bukofsky, James (BRK) [95] Brooklyn, NY Our Lady of Good Counsel Church.
Bukosk, Joseph, III *ss.cc.* '79 (HON) [H] Honolulu, HI St. Patrick's Monastery.
Bulfer, Stephen C. '73 (FRS) Mariposa, CA St. Joseph Church.
Bulger, Albion F. '56 (MAN) [9] Nashua, NH Resurrection Church.
Bulger, John '64 (SEA) Marysville, WA St. Mary's Church.
Bull, Albert D. '41 (CHI) Retired.
Bullene, Richard *c.s.c.* '83 (FTW) [J] Notre Dame, IN Holy Cross Community, Corby Hall, University of Notre Dame.
Bullene, Richard S. *c.s.c.* '83 (FTW) [B] Notre Dame, IN University of Notre Dame Du Lac.
Bullock, Gabriel G. *o.s.b.* '61 (PEO) [A] Peru, IL St. Bede Abbey and Academy.
Bullock, Myron F. '53 (BO) [4] Gloucester, MA Sacred Heart Church.
Bullock, Robert W. '56 (BO) Sharon, MA Our Lady of Sorrows Church.
Bullock, Scott E. '91 (DUB) St. Donatus, IA St. Donatus Church; [A] Dubuque, IA Seminary of St. Pius X.
Bullock, Sean '91 (DUB) St. Catherine, IA St. Catherine's Church.
Bulman, Msgr. Robert T. '40 (TR) Sea Girt, NJ St. Mark Church; Retired.
Bulovas, Msgr. Francis J. '43 (BRK) [247] Queens, NY Transfiguration Church; Retired.
Bultman, Robert S. '67 (EVN) Celestine, IN St. Celestine Church.
Bulto, Luis (MIL) [5] Kenosha, WI St. Mark Church; [Y] Kenosha, WI St. Mark Latin American Center.
Bulwith, Richard E. '67 (CHI) [30] Chicago, IL St. Bonaventure Church; [G] Chicago, IL Catholic Charities of the Archdiocese of Chicago-Archdiocesan Offices.
Bumbar, Philip '68 (SJP) Wheeling, WV St. Mary Church.
Bumbarger, Bruce *m.ss.cc.* '92 (CAM) [8] Camden, NJ Our Lady of Fatima and Mount Carmel Church.
Bump, James F. '78 (GBG) Masontown, PA All Saints Church.
Bumpus, Harold '63 (SP) Citrus Springs, FL St. Elizabeth Ann Seton Church.
Bunch, Timothy S. '79 (CIN) Fort Loramie, OH St. Michael's Church.
Bunchek, Edward P. '65 (PIT) [3] West Mifflin, PA Holy Trinity Church.
Bunda, Roland *s.m.* '78 (MRY) [G] Santa Cruz, CA

Society of Mary, Marianists; [J] Monterey, CA Department of Campus Ministry.
Bundz, Michael '81 (STF) Rome, NY St. Michael Church; Utica, NY St. Volodymyr the Great Church.
Bunger, Kevin J. '83 (SY) [2] Binghamton, NY St. Ann Church; Sanitaria Springs, NY St. Joseph Church.
Bungo, Samuel '77 (E) Frenchville, PA St. Mary of the Assumption Church.
Buni, Leon '75 (TR) Lakewood, NJ St. Mary of the Lake Church.
Bunn, James F. '64 (ALT) Ashville, PA St. Thomas Aquinas Church; Fallentimber, PA St. Mary Magdalen's Church; Fallentimber, PA St. Joan of Arc Church.
Bunnell, Adam *o.f.m.* (WDC) [C] Washington, DC Georgetown University.
Bunnell, Adam E. *o.f.m.conv.* '74 (WDC) [B] Washington, DC St. Bonaventure Friary.
Bunnell, Thomas J. *s.j.* '74 (FgM) Provinces.
Bunnell, Thomas J. *s.j.* '74 (P) [L] Portland, OR Jesuit Provincial Office (Society of Jesus, Oregon Prov.).
Bunnell, Thomas J. *s.j.* '74 (YAK) Special Assignment.
Bunny, Msgr. Michael '65 (LA) Newbury Park, CA St. Julie Billiart Church.
Bunofsky, Walter *s.v.d.* '60 (DUB) [B] Epworth, IA Divine Word College.
Bunse, Gerald L. '83 (SFD) Edwardsville, IL St. Mary Church.
Bunsic, Albert *o.c.d.* '67 (SJ) [M] San Jose, CA Carmelite Monastery, Novitiate.
Buntel, Richard A. '71 (BO) Awaiting Assignment.
Bunyk, Vasyl '93 (PHU) Passaic, NJ St. Nicholas Church.
Buonanno, Vito '81 (BRK) [153] Queens, NY Ascension Church.
Buongirno, Richard T. '84 (NOR) [1] Middletown, CT St. Francis Church.
Buono, Joseph *c.ss.r.* '43 (BRK) [107] Brooklyn, NY Our Lady of Perpetual Help Basilica Church.
Buote, Martin L. '60 (FR) [9] New Bedford, MA St. Anne Church.
Bur, George *s.j.* '72 (PH) [I] Philadelphia, PA The Gesu School; [AA] Philadelphia, PA Gesu School Jesuit Community and Outreach Center(S.J.).
Bur, George W. *s.j.* '72 (PH) [CC] Philadelphia, PA Urban House of Prayer.
Bur, Stanislaus '50 (SAG) Retired.
Bura, Msgr. John '71 (PHU) Chester, PA Holy Ghost Church.
Burak, Alex '62 (PHU) Edwardsville, PA St. Vladimir's Church; Wilkes-Barre, PA SS. Peter and Paul Church.
Burak, Paul '72 (CHI) Chicago Ridge, IL Our Lady of the Ridge Church.
Burakowski, Anthony E. '36 (HBG) Retired.
Burakowski, Wieslaw '92 (NSH) Clarksville, TN Immaculate Conception Church.
Buranosky, Dennis M. '72 (PIT) Imperial, PA St. Columbkille Church.
Burba, Edward A. '75 (CLV) Bedford, OH St. Mary Church.
Burbach, Jude *o.s.b.* '53 (KCK) Blaine, KS St. Columbkille Church; Lillis, KS St. Joseph's Church; Onaga, KS St. Vincent de Paul Church.
Burbach, Richard C. *s.j.* '88 (MIL) [P] Milwaukee, WI Jesuit Provincial Office, Wisconsin Province.
Burbach, Richard C. *s.j.* '88 (WDC) [M] Washington, DC Leonard Neale House.
Burbank, F. James *c.s.c.* '57 (FR) [A] North Easton, MA Stonehill College.
Burbank, Foster J. *c.s.c.* '57 (FR) [A] North Easton, MA Holy Cross Fathers Religious.
Burbank, Robert J. '64 (HRT) East Haven, CT St. Vincent de Paul's Church.
Burbank, William '62 (HRT) [17] New Haven, CT St. Rose of Lima Church.
Burbidge, Michael F. '84 (PH) [BB] Merion, PA Sisters of Mercy of the Americas, Merion Regional Community, Convent.
Burby, Clarence J. *s.j.* '67 (FgM) Provinces.
Burch, Francis F. *s.j.* '63 (PH) [C] Philadelphia, PA St. Joseph's University; [AA] Philadelphia, PA Jesuit Community at St. Joseph's University.
Burch, Michael (RCK) [10] Rockford, IL St. Rita Church.
Burch, Thaddeus J. *s.j.* '61 (MIL) [C] Milwaukee, WI Marquette University; [P] Milwaukee, WI Jesuit Community at Marquette University.
Burchell, Richard '75 (CLV) [1] Barberton, OH St. Augustine Church.
Burchfield, Michael '93 (FRS) Merced, CA Our Lady of Mercy/St. Patricks Church.
Burchianti, Leo R. '64 (PIT) Retired; [O] Pittsburgh, PA St. John Vianney Manor.
Burchill, John Patrick *o.p.* '65 (NY) [DD] New York, NY St. Vincent Ferrer Priory.
Burckhart, William C. '53 (BO) Belmont, MA St. Joseph Church.
Burden, George W. *s.s.j.* '91 (NO) Reserve, LA Our Lady of Grace Church.
Burden, Lewis E. '97 (SUP) Hudson, WI St. Patrick Church.
Burdess, James J. '88 (ALN) Orefield, PA St. Joseph The Worker Church.
Burdick, Thomas J. '84 (SB) [6] Riverside, CA St. Catherine of Alexandria Church.
Burdiek, Fabian F. *o.f.m.* '74 (STP) [10] St. Paul, MN Sacred Heart Church; St. Paul, MN St. John's Hospital.
Burdt, Eric *o.ss.t.* '65 (MEM) [C] Memphis, TN Christian Brothers High School.
Burdt, Eric T. *o.ss.t.* '65 (BAL) [M] Baltimore, MD Holy Trinity Monastery.
Burdt, Eric T. *o.ss.t.* '65 (MEM) [J] Memphis, TN Order of The Holy Trinity.
Bureau, Germain '53 (PRT) [I] Waterville, ME Mt. St. Joseph Priest Retirement Home.
Bureau, Germain H. '53 (PRT) Retired.
Burek, Frank J. '71 (CHI) Burbank, IL St. Albert the Great Church.
Bures, Francis *s.v.d.* '53 (FgM) Society of the Divine Word Foreign Missions.
Burg, Thomas R. '64 (CLV) Absent on Leave.
Burgaleta, Claudio M. *s.j.* '92 (NEW) [B] Jersey City, NJ Saint Peter's College; [N] Jersey City, NJ Jesuits of Saint Peter's College, Inc.
Burgdorf, Joseph H. *c.p.m.* '52 (OWN) [F] South Union, KY Fathers of Mercy.
Burge, Robert A. '71 (CLV) Litchfield, OH Our Lady Help of Christians Parish; [1] Parma, OH St. Anthony of Padua Church.
Burger, Edward K. *s.j.* '70 (KC) [B] Kansas City, MO Rockhurst College; [J] Kansas City, MO Rockhurst College - Jesuit Community.
Burger, Frank '69 (KCK) Olathe, KS Prince of Peace Church.
Burger, Frank J. '38 (KAL) Retired.
Burger, Herman N. '73 (CAM) Ventnor, NJ St. James Church.
Burger, John *s.s.c.* '73 (FgM) St. Columban's Foreign Mission.
Burger, Joseph W. '54 (OKL) Blackwell, OK St. Joseph's Church; Tonkawa, OK St. Joseph's Church; [K] Norman, OK Campus Ministry for the Archdiocese of Oklahoma City.
Burger, Mark '80 (CIN) [63] Cincinnati, OH St. Michael Church.
Burger, Mark J. '80 (CIN) [35] Cincinnati, OH Holy Family Church.
Burger, Matthias *o.s.b.* '47 (P) [2] Portland, OR St. Agatha Church; [L] St. Benedict, OR Mt. Angel Abbey.
Burger, Philip G. *v.f.* '83 (HBG) Coal Township, PA Our Lady of Hope Church; Trevorton, PA St. Patrick Church.
Burger, Raymond '60 (KCK) Lenexa, KS Holy Trinity Church.
Burger, Raymond O. *s.j.* '48 (LC) Prairie du Chien, WI St. John Nepomucene Church.
Burger, Robert '48 (KCK) Lenexa, KS Holy Trinity Church; Retired.
Burget, Joel *o.f.m.conv.* '66 (BEL) [D] Centralia, IL St. Mary's Hospital.
Burghardt, Walter J. *s.j.* '41 (WDC) [E] Washington, DC Gonzaga College High School; [V] Washington, DC Woodstock Theological Center.
Burghoff, Theodore '55 (STL) Kirkwood, MO St. Peter Church.
Burgoon, Charles E. '64 (STL) [36] St. Louis, MO St. Gabriel the Archangel Church.
Burgos, Adnel '88 (BRK) [243] Queens, NY St. Teresa Church.
Burgos, Juan *o.p.* (SJN) [6] Bayamon, PR Santo Domingo de Guzman Church.
Burgoyne, Sidney C. '54 (PH) Boothwyn, PA St. John Fisher Church.
Burian, Edward P. '65 (SFS) Ipswich, SD Holy Cross Church; Leola, SD Our Lady of Perpetual Help Church.
Burk, Bill *s.d.b.* '93 (NY) [3] Port Chester, NY Our Lady of the Rosary Church.
Burkard, Msgr. Paul J.E. '69 (BUF) [3] Orchard Park, NY Our Lady of the Sacred Heart Church.
Burkardt, Msgr. Harold J. '47 (ALT) Newry, PA St. Patrick's Church; Retired.
Burkart, Donald R. '58 (GB) Crivitz, WI St. Mary Church.
Burkart, James M. '93 (GAL) [76] Houston, TX St. Theresa Church.
Burkauskas, Peter (PH) [30] Philadelphia, PA St. Casimir Church.
Burkauskas, Peter M. '79 (PH) [10] Philadelphia, PA St. Andrew Church.
Burke, Adrian *o.s.b.* (IND) Fulda, IN St. Boniface Church; Siberia, IN St. Martin of Tours Church.
Burke, Adrian *o.s.b.* '93 (IND) St. Meinrad, IN St. Meinrad Church.
Burke, Adrian *o.s.b.* '97 (IND) [J] St. Meinrad, IN St. Meinrad Archabbey.
Burke, Alfred '69 (NEW) Berkeley Heights, NJ Church of the Little Flower.
Burke, Alfred M. *o.s.a.* '57 (CHI) [N] Olympia Fields, IL The Augustinian Provincialate Tolentine Center.
Burke, Alfred M. *o.s.a.* '57 (FgM) Foreign Missions.
Burke, Amadeus *o.f.m.* '35 (BO) [Z] Boston, MA Saint Anthony Residence.
Burke, Msgr. Ambrose J. '21 (DAV) Retired.
Burke, Christopher R. '86 (PBR) Trauger, PA St. Mary's Church.
Burke, Clement '61 (DUB) On Duty Outside the Archdiocese.
Burke, Clement J. '61 (STP) Minneapolis, MN Abbott-Northwestern Hospital.
Burke, David M. '42 (BO) [4] Milton, MA St. Pius Tenth Church.
Burke, Dennis M. *o.praem.* '29 (GB) [B] De Pere, WI St. Norbert College; [I] De Pere, WI St. Joseph Priory.
Burke, Donal *o.f.m.cap.* (FRS) Fresno, CA Community Hospital, Veterans' Hospital.
Burke, Edmund M. '77 (NY) [1] Kingston, NY Holy Name of Jesus Church; [4] Kingston, NY St. Mary Church.
Burke, Edward *o.f.m.* (NY) Callicoon, NY Community General Hospital.
Burke, Edward *o.f.m.* '62 (SP) [O] St. Petersburg, FL St. Anthony Friary.
Burke, Edward P. '73 (PH) [5] Philadelphia, PA All Saints Church.
Burke, Edward T. *s.j.* '56 (SJ) [M] Los Gatos, CA Sacred Heart Jesuit Center.
Burke, Edward W. '46 (DET) [P] Clarkston, MI Colombiere Center.
Burke, Msgr. Edwin F. '62 (BGP) [3] Norwalk, CT St. Ladislaus Church.
Burke, Eugene A. *c.s.c.* '53 (PHX) [F] Phoenix, AZ Holy Cross Congregation of Casa Santa Cruz.
Burke, Francis J. *s.j.* '60 (STP) [N] Minneapolis, MN La Storta Jesuit Community.
Burke, Geoffrey D. '74 (ALB) Special Assignment.
Burke, Geoffrey D. '79 (ALB) [M] Latham, NY Provincial House of the Sisters of St. Joseph of Carondelet (Albany Province).
Burke, Gilbert J. *o.s.b.* '62 (GBG) [H] Latrobe, PA Saint Vincent Archabbey.
Burke, Gregory '51 (HEL) Retired.
Burke, Harry '63 (NY) [E] New York, NY Cardinal Hayes High School.
Burke, Henry J. '45 (CHR) Retired.
Burke, Herbert '92 (WDC) Absent On Leave.
Burke, James *o.p.* (R) [E] Raleigh, NC De Porres House.
Burke, James *o.p.* '49 (R) [E] Raleigh, NC Dominican Community.
Burke, Msgr. James '64 (PMB) Palm Beach, FL St. Edward Church.
Burke, Msgr. James A. '56 (NEW) Westfield, NJ St. Helen Church.
Burke, James C. '64 (ROC) Avon, NY St. Agnes Church.
Burke, James E. '58 (NY) [227] Staten Island, NY Sacred Heart Church.
Burke, James F. *c.s.sp.* '52 (GAL) Plantersville, TX St. Mary Church.
Burke, James G. '77 (BO) Littleton, MA St. Anne Church.
Burke, James J. *c.ss.r.* '56 (VEN) Wauchula, FL St. Michael Church.
Burke, John C. *c.s.c.* '40 (FTW) [J] South Bend, IN Congregation of Holy Cross Indiana Province Provincial House.
Burke, Msgr. John D. '56 (NY) [204] Staten Island, NY Holy Child Church.
Burke, Msgr. John F. '46 (MAN) [13] Manchester, NH Our Lady of Perpetual Help Church; Retired.
Burke, John F. '55 (WOR) West Boylston, MA Our Lady of Good Counsel Church.
Burke, John R. '54 (E) On Duty Outside Diocese.
Burke, John R. '72 (L) [20] Louisville, KY Christ the King Church.
Burke, John W. *o.p.* '60 (WDC) [B] Washington, DC Dominican House of Studies.
Burke, Joseph A. *s.j.* '51 (WH) [A] Wheeling, WV Wheeling Jesuit University.
Burke, Joseph D. *c.s.c.* '65 (LA) Pacific Palisades, CA Corpus Christi Church.
Burke, Joseph F. *s.j.* '78 (BUF) [O] Buffalo, NY Canisius Jesuit Community.
Burke, Joseph F. *s.j.* '78 (NY) [5] New York, NY St. Aloysius Church.
Burke, Kevin F. *s.j.* '86 (BO) [W] Cambridge, MA Faber House; [W] Cambridge, MA Weston Jesuit Community.
Burke, Lawrence *o.f.m.* '41 (PAT) [N] Ringwood, NJ Mt. St. Francis.
Burke, Leonard J. '42 (BO) Retired.
Burke, Mark J. *s.j.* '93 (BGP) [O] Fairfield, CT The Fairfield Jesuit Community-Fairfield University.
Burke, Michael '50 (CC) Retired.
Burke, Michael *s.c.j.* '63 (CHI) [N] Chicago, IL Priests of the Sacred Heart.
Burke, Michael *s.c.j.* '63 (MIL) [P] Hales Corners, WI Priests of the Sacred Heart.
Burke, Michael '76 (PAT) [1] Passaic, NJ St. Nicholas Church.
Burke, Michael J. '62 (PH) Exton, PA SS. Philip and

James Church.
Burke, Michael L. '74 (MAD) [10] Madison, WI St. Maria Goretti Church.
Burke, Michael M. *o.p.* (R) [E] Raleigh, NC De Porres House.
Burke, Michael M. '50 (NY) Mt. Kisco, NY St. Francis of Assisi Church.
Burke, Michael M. *o.p.* '68 (R) [E] Raleigh, NC Dominican Community.
Burke, Paul A. '96 (ATL) [3] Marietta, GA St. Joseph Church.
Burke, Paul E. *o.s.f.s.* '54 (WIL) [B] Wilmington, DE Salesianum School.
Burke, Perry *o.f.m.cap.* (FRS) Fresno, CA Community Hospital, Veterans' Hospital.
Burke, Peter D. '65 (PH) East Lansdowne, PA St. Cyril of Alexandria Church.
Burke, Richard *c.p.* '76 (MET) [H] South River, NJ Passionist Provincial Office.
Burke, Richard *c.p.* '76 (SCR) [M] Scranton, PA Saint Ann's Passionist Monastery.
Burke, Richard P. *s.j.* '51 (WOR) [N] Worcester, MA Jesuits of Holy Cross College, Inc.
Burke, Robert E. '47 (DET) Birmingham, MI Holy Name Church.
Burke, Robert M. *o.s.a.* '55 (BO) [C] North Andover, MA Merrimack College.
Burke, Robert R. *s.j.* '64 (BO) [W] Boston, MA The Society of Jesus of New England-Provincial Offices.
Burke, Robert R. *s.j.* '64 (KC) [J] Kansas City, MO Rockhurst College - Jesuit Community.
Burke, Robert R. *s.j.* '65 (KC) [B] Kansas City, MO Rockhurst College.
Burke, Ronald A. '54 (SFR) San Bruno, CA St. Bruno Church.
Burke, Ronald J. '72 (HON) Waipahu, HI Resurrection of the Lord Church.
Burke, Sean P. *m.m.* '78 (FgM) Maryknoll Foreign Missions.
Burke, Terence '75 (AMA) [E] Amarillo, TX Catholic Family Service, Inc.
Burke, Thomas *c.ss.r.* '81 (ATL) Griffin, GA Sacred Heart Church.
Burke, Thomas J. *m.m.* '55 (FgM) Maryknoll Foreign Missions.
Burke, Thomas J. *o.ss.t.* '78 (BAL) [A] Baltimore, MD St. Mary's Seminary and University; [K] Baltimore, MD Trinitarian Counseling Services, Inc.; [M] Baltimore, MD Holy Trinity Monastery.
Burke, Msgr. Thomas P. '53 (CHL) Retired.
Burke, Vincent *s.v.d.* '61 (FgM) Society of the Divine Word Foreign Missions.
Burke, Vincent de Paul *o.s.f.s.* '57 (WIL) [B] Wilmington, DE Salesianum School.
Burke, Walter Deo (SAC) Quincy, CA St. John Church.
Burke, Walter E. '47 (DET) Retired.
Burke, Walter J. *o.praem* '44 (PH) Paoli, PA St. Norbert Church.
Burke, Walter J. *o.praem.* '44 (WIL) [I] Claymont, DE Immaculate Conception Priory of the Canons Regular of Premontre.
Burke, William '75 (MEM) [26] Memphis, TN Our Lady of Sorrows Church.
Burke, William *s.d.b.* '93 (NY) [FF] West Haverstraw, NY Don Bosco Retreat Center and Marian Shrine; [FF] West Haverstraw, NY Marian Shrine.
Burke, William A. '66 (CHI) Hometown, IL Our Lady of Loretto Church.
Burke, Msgr. William F. '43 (BRK) Retired.
Burke, Msgr. William F. '59 (BAL) [32] Baltimore, MD St. Francis of Assisi Church.
Burke, William T. *s.j.* '69 (ANC) [G] Anchorage, AK Holy Spirit Retreat House.
Burkemper, Robert W. '81 (STL) [5] Florissant, MO St. Dismas Church.
Burkert, Gerald F. '61 (IND) Beech Grove, IN Holy Name Church.
Burkert, William C. *s.t.* '71 (MIL) Brookfield, WI St. John Vianney Church.
Burkett, Thomas J. '97 (DEN) Louisville, CO St. Louis Church.
Burkey, Blaine *o.f.m.cap.* '61 (STL) [P] St. Louis, MO St. Crispin's Friary.
Burkhalter, Ross '94 (OM) South Sioux City, NE St. Michael Church.
Burkhard, John D. *o.f.m.conv.* '67 (WDC) [B] Washington, DC St. Bonaventure Friary.
Burkhardt, Alan T. '86 (LC) [3] Stevens Point, WI St. Joseph Church.
Burkhardt, Godfrey F. *o.s.b.* '45 (GBG) [H] Latrobe, PA Saint Vincent Archabbey.
Burkhardt, Odilo *o.s.b.* '50 (SFS) [F] Marvin, SD Blue Cloud Abbey.
Burkhart, John J. *o.s.a.* '56 (DET) Grosse Pointe Park, MI St. Clare of Montefalco Church.
Burkhart, Roy *c.s.sp.* '44 (FRS) [C] Bakersfield, CA Mercy Healthcare Bakersfield.
Burkholder, Robert '47 (DET) Retired.
Burkle, Raymond A. '90 (DUB) Jewell, IA Good Shepherd Church; Williams, IA St. Mary's Church.
Burkley, John T. '70 (CLV) [5] Euclid, OH St. Robert Bellarmine Church; [AA] Euclid, OH St. Robert's Holy Name Society Boosters.
Burks, William P. '86 (L) Pleasure Ridge Park, KY St. Polycarp Church.
Burkus, John '40 (ELP) Retired.
Burla, Frank J. '63 (NEW) Montclair, NJ Immaculate Conception Church.
Burlas, Anthony J. *o.s.b.* '58 (GBG) Forbes Road, PA St. Mary Church; [H] Latrobe, PA Saint Vincent Archabbey.
Burlton, Msgr. Francis H. '54 (BEA) [6] Beaumont, TX Our Lady of the Assumption Church.
Burmester, Edwin J. '40 (STL) [36] St. Louis, MO St. Gabriel the Archangel Church; Retired.
Burn, William C. '56 (CHR) Retired.
Burnell, George F. *o.s.a.* '45 (PH) [C] Villanova, PA Villanova University; [AA] Villanova, PA St. Thomas Monastery.
Burnell, Robert J. '70 (CHI) Morton Grove, IL St. Martha Church.
Burnet, Donald *o.m.i.* '66 (SAT) [M] San Antonio, TX Provincial Administration Office, Oblates of Mary Immaculate (Southern Prov.).
Burnet, Donald T. '66 (BEL) [J] Belleville, IL Scott Air Force Base.
Burnet, Jerome *o.m.i.* '53 (SAN) [2] Midland, TX Our Lady of Guadalupe Church.
Burnett, Eugene David *o.f.m.* '54 (LA) [72] Los Angeles, CA St. Joseph Church.
Burnett, Eugene David *o.f.m.* '54 (ORG) [C] Santa Ana, CA Mater Dei High School; [H] Santa Ana, CA Franciscan Fathers.
Burnett, George P. '61 (HRT) [1] Ansonia, CT Assumption Church.
Burnett, James '68 (JOL) [2] Naperville, IL Sts. Peter and Paul Church.
Burnett, James E. '74 (DAV) Military Chaplains.
Burnett, John C. '85 (SFD) [2] Springfield, IL Blessed Sacrament Church.
Burnett, Robert E. '55 (SCR) Plains, PA Sacred Heart Church.
Burnett, Timothy J. *o.s.b.* '80 (NO) [A] St. Benedict, LA St. Joseph's Seminary College; [P] St. Benedict, LA St. Joseph Abbey.
Burnette, Kurt '89 (SB) [5] Fontana, CA St. Nicholas Church.
Burnette, Kurt '89 (VNN) Fontana, CA St. Nicholas Church.
Burnham, Alfred S. '76 (LA) Culver City, CA St. Augustine Church.
Burnia, Scott '88 (SD) Jamul, CA St. Pius X Church.
Burnie, James H. *c.s.sp.* '93 (SB) Hemet, CA Our Lady of the Valley Church.
Burns, Msgr. A. Francis '63 (NY) [6] Yonkers, NY Christ the King Church.
Burns, Msgr. Bernard '38 (SFE) Retired.
Burns, Bernard J. '53 (SAC) Portola, CA Holy Family Church.
Burns, Charles D. *s.v.d.* '52 (OAK) [20] Oakland, CA St. Patrick's Church.
Burns, Charles E. '58 (GAL) Retired.
Burns, Charles F. *s.j.* '72 (STP) [6] St. Paul, MN The Immaculate Heart of Mary Church.
Burns, Clement *o.p.* '54 (CIN) [30] Cincinnati, OH St. Gertrude Church; [M] Cincinnati, OH St. Gertrude Priory.
Burns, Cyril J. '56 (SPR) South Hadley, MA St. Theresa of the Infant Jesus Church.
Burns, David E. '61 (GAL) Retired.
Burns, Dennis J. '50 (BO) Marblehead, MA Our Lady, Star of the Sea Church.
Burns, Donald W. '50 (STP) Retired.
Burns, Edward J. *o.s.a.* '40 (PH) [AA] Villanova, PA St. Thomas Monastery.
Burns, Edward J. '54 (FR) Retired.
Burns, Edward J. '83 (PIT) [A] Pittsburgh, PA Saint Paul Seminary.
Burns, Ernest '51 (HEL) Retired.
Burns, Eugene P. '55 (CHI) Retired.
Burns, Francis H. '48 (DET) Retired.
Burns, Msgr. G. Thomas '57 (NEW) Livingston, NJ St. Raphael Church.
Burns, Gerald H. '69 (BR) [3] Baton Rouge, LA St. Aloysius Church.
Burns, Msgr. Gerald J. '50 (SCR) Retired; [N] Dunmore, PA Villa St. Joseph.
Burns, Hugh D. *o.p.* '82 (NEW) [28] Jersey City, NJ Sacred Heart Church.
Burns, James '62 (GLP) Retired.
Burns, James P. '93 (STP) [20] St. Paul, MN St. Francis De Sales Church; [22] St. Paul, MN St. James Church.
Burns, John '90 (PEO) Kewanee, IL St. Francis of Assisi Church.
Burns, John '95 (MRY) [4] Salinas, CA Madonna Del Sasso Church.
Burns, John A. *c.s.sp.* '42 (ALX) [F] Natchitoches, LA Holy Ghost Fathers Home, Maison Brothier.
Burns, John A. '48 (BRK) [83] Brooklyn, NY Mary Queen of Heaven Church; Retired.
Burns, John F. '48 (BO) Retired.
Burns, John M. '82 (STP) [O] Lake Elmo, MN Carmel of Our Lady of Divine Providence; [T] Lake Elmo, MN Hermits of the Most Blessed Virgin Mary of Mount Carmel.
Burns, John R. '65 (ALB) South Kortright, NY Church of the Most Precious Blood of Jesus.
Burns, John T. '58 (CIN) Retired.
Burns, Joseph '55 (JOL) Steger, IL St. Liborius Church.
Burns, Joseph Clement *o.p.* '54 (CIN) [C] Cincinnati, OH Dominican Novitiate.
Burns, Joseph H. '60 (CAM) Hammonton, NJ St. Anthony of Padua Church.
Burns, Laurence J. '64 (SC) Carroll, IA St. Lawrence Church.
Burns, Msgr. Lawrence E. '56 (MAN) Portsmouth, NH St. Catherine of Siena Church.
Burns, Lawrence E. '62 (BUF) Blasdell, NY Our Mother of Good Counsel Church.
Burns, Lawrence J. *m.m.* '46 (BO) Wakefield, MA St. Joseph Church.
Burns, Leo J. *s.j.* '36 (MIL) [P] Wauwatosa, WI Jesuit Community at St. Camillus.
Burns, Malcolm J. '85 (RVC) Oyster Bay, NY St. Dominic's Church.
Burns, Michael (BO) [4] Brookline, MA St. Mary of the Assumption Church.
Burns, Michael J. '58 (SJ) Los Altos, CA St. William Church.
Burns, Michael J. '73 (TR) Bordentown, NJ St. Mary Church.
Burns, Norbert C. *s.m.* '53 (CIN) [D] Dayton, OH The University of Dayton; [M] Dayton, OH Marianist Provincialate.
Burns, Patrick G. '92 (BRK) [157] Queens, NY Blessed Sacrament Church.
Burns, Patrick J. *s.j.* '50 (MIL) [C] Milwaukee, WI Marquette University.
Burns, Patrick J. *s.j.* '63 (MIL) [P] Milwaukee, WI Jesuit Community at Marquette University.
Burns, Paul D. *c.s.s.* '62 (WOR) Milford, MA Sacred Heart Church.
Burns, Peter *s.j.* '92 (LA) [C] Los Angeles, CA Loyola Marymount University.
Burns, Robert A. *o.p.* '61 (TUC) [I] Tucson, AZ University of Arizona.
Burns, Robert I. *s.j.* '52 (LA) [C] Los Angeles, CA Loyola Marymount University.
Burns, Robert O. *s.j.* '57 (OM) [K] Omaha, NE Jesuit Community At Creighton University.
Burns, T. Lee '56 (PRT) Retired.
Burns, Thomas '44 (SFS) Retired.
Burns, Thomas E. (CAM) Retired.
Burns, Thomas J. '54 (SFR) Retired.
Burns, Thomas J. *m.m.* '69 (FgM) Maryknoll Foreign Missions.
Burns, Thomas L. *s.c.j.* '65 (JKS) Booneville, MS St. Francis of Assisi Church; Corinth, MS St. James Church.
Burns, Timothy L. '76 (BIR) [5] Huntsville, AL Our Lady Queen of the Universe Church.
Burns, Tom *m.s.c.* '65 (SB) Upland, CA St. Joseph Church.
Burns, Vincent M. *s.j.* '57 (BGP) [A] Fairfield, CT Fairfield University; [O] Fairfield, CT The Fairfield Jesuit Community-Fairfield University.
Burns, Vincent P. '67 (PH) Military Chaplains.
Burns, William A. '33 (ROC) Waverly, NY St. James Church; Retired.
Burns, William L. '85 (HRT) Naugatuck, CT St. Francis of Assisi Church.
Burr, Jeremiah R. *m.m.* '67 (FgM) Maryknoll(M.M.).
Burr, Jeremiah R. *m.m.* '67 (NY) [DD] Maryknoll, NY Maryknoll Fathers and Brothers.
Burr, Thomas E. '73 (RCK) McHenry, IL St. Mary Church.
Burr, Thomas W. '61 (ROC) Horseheads, NY St. Mary Our Mother Church.
Burrascano, Anthony P. *o.s.a.* '79 (FgM) Foreign Missions.
Burrascano, Anthony P. *o.s.a.* '79 (PH) Bryn Mawr, PA Our Mother of Good Counsel Church; [AA] Villanova, PA Provincial Offices of the Order of St. Augustine, Province of St. Thomas of Villanova.
Burrell, David B. *c.s.c.* '59 (FTW) [B] Notre Dame, IN University of Notre Dame Du Lac; [J] Notre Dame, IN Holy Cross Community, Corby Hall, University of Notre Dame.
Burrows, Michael *o.s.b.* '80 (RCK) [H] Aurora, IL Marmion Abbey-St. Augustine's Abbey.
Burruano, Albert J. (PH) [88] Philadelphia, PA St. Lucy Church.
Burrus, Barry '93 (LEX) Ashland, KY Holy Family Church.
Burshek, James J. *s.j.* '75 (DEN) [D] Aurora, CO Regis Jesuit High School.
Burshek, James J. *s.j.* '75 (OAK) [N] Berkeley, CA Jesuit Community at Jesuit School of Theology at Berkeley.
Burshnick, Francis J. *s.c.j.* '70 (JKS) Southhaven, MS Christ the King Church; Walls, MS Sacred Heart

Church; [E] Nesbit, MS St. Michael Community House.
Burson, James *c.j.m.* '63 (SD) [3] San Diego, CA Blessed Sacrament Church; San Diego, CA Alvarado, Grossmont and Kaiser Hospitals.
Burt, Donald X. *o.s.a.* '55 (PH) [C] Villanova, PA Villanova University; [AA] Villanova, PA St. Thomas Monastery.
Burt, Julian F. *o.s.b.* '41 (GBG) [H] Latrobe, PA Saint Vincent Archabbey.
Burtchaell, James T. *c.s.c.* '53 (TR) [N] Trenton, NJ; [N] Princeton, NJ Our Lady of Princeton.
Burtchaell, James T. *c.s.c.* '60 (FTW) [J] South Bend, IN Congregation of Holy Cross Indiana Province Provincial House.
Burtka, Joseph *l.c.* '97 (HRT) [B] Cheshire, CT Novitiate of the Legion of Christ.
Burton, C. Jeffries *s.j.* '67 (CAM) Pleasantville, NJ St. Peter's Church; [R] Mays Landing, NJ Atlantic Community College; [R] Pomona, NJ Richard Stockton College of New Jersey.
Burton, Charles '80 (KNX) Kingsport, TN St. Dominic Church.
Burton, John H. '72 (CAM) Villas, NJ St. Raymond Church.
Burton, Msgr. Richard '63 (WDC) [5] Washington, DC St. Anthony Church.
Burton, William *o.f.m.* '89 (SFD) [B] Quincy, IL Quincy University.
Burtschi, J. Richard *s.j.* '71 (STL) [P] St. Louis, MO Jesuit Community Corporation at St. Louis University - Jesuit Hall.
Burwinkel, Elmer J. '84 (IND) Retired.
Bury, Harold J. '55 (STP) On Duty Outside the Archdiocese.
Buryska, James '65 (WIN) [G] Rochester, MN Congregational Center of the Sisters of the Third Order Regular of St. Francis of the Congregation of Our.
Burzynski, Michael H. '89 (BUF) [3] Kenmore, NY St. John the Baptist Church.
Burzynski, Regis *o.f.m.* '55 (GAY) Mio, MI St. Mary Church.
Bus, Anthony *c.r.* '84 (CHI) [193] Chicago, IL St. Stanislaus Kostka Church.
Busca, Salvatore L. *s.p.* '55 (SB) [G] Cherry Valley, CA Servants of the Paraclete Guadalupe Retreat Center.
Busch, Msgr. Aloysius J. '52 (PAT) Highland Lakes, NJ Our Lady of Fatima Church.
Busch, Arthur A. '58 (WCH) [2] Wichita, KS All Saints Church.
Busch, August '56 (EVN) Retired.
Busch, James *c.p.* '42 (SAC) [G] Citrus Heights, CA Christ the King Retreat.
Busch, Jan H. *o.s.a.* '49 (PH) [C] Villanova, PA Villanova University; [AA] Villanova, PA St. Thomas Monastery.
Busch, John *o.m.i.* '40 (SAT) [K] San Antonio, TX Oblate Madonna Residence.
Busch, Joseph '80 (ALB) [1] Watervliet, NY St. Brigid Church.
Busch, Peter *t.o.r.* '45 (SP) Pinellas Park, FL Sacred Heart Church.
Busch, Robert '93 (AMA) [11] Amarillo, TX St. Thomas the Apostle Church; [K] Canyon, TX Catholic Student Center at West Texas A & M University.
Busch, Vernon *o.f.m.cap.* '60 (BAL) Cumberland, MD SS. Peter and Paul Church; [M] Cumberland, MD SS. Peter and Paul Friary.
Busch, Vincent J. *s.s.c.* '74 (FgM) St. Columban's Foreign Mission.
Buscher, Adelbert *o.s.b.* '41 (IND) [J] St. Meinrad, IN St. Meinrad Archabbey.
Buscher, Adelbert *o.s.b.* '41 (VEN) [2] Fort Myers, FL Church of the Resurrection of Our Lord.
Buschmiller, Robert J. '44 (CIN) [20] Cincinnati, OH St. Cecilia Church; Retired.
Busco, Msgr. John J. '40 (PH) [3] Norristown, PA Holy Saviour Church; Retired.
Buse, Harold J. '77 (OM) Norfolk, NE Sacred Heart Church.
Busemeyer, Louis *s.j.* '70 (CHI) [N] Chicago, IL Miguel Pro Jesuit Community.
Bush, Bernard J. *s.j.* '65 (SJ) [L] Los Altos, CA Jesuit Retreat House.
Bush, Edward E. '57 (PEO) Colona, IL St. Patrick's Church.
Bush, Frederick W. '51 (ROC) Penfield, NY Holy Spirit Church.
Bush, John H. '39 (LAN) Retired.
Bush, Robert '69 (SAN) [1] Abilene, TX Sacred Heart Church.
Bush, Scott '92 (HON) Hilo, HI St. Joseph Church.
Bush, William C. '62 (LEX) Nicholasville, KY St. Luke Church.
Bushee, Richard J. '88 (PRO) [12] Providence, RI St. Edward Church.
Bushell, Ralph *c.pp.s.* '49 (KC) [J] Liberty, MO Precious Blood Center.
Busher, Robert J. '76 (DAV) Oskaloosa, IA St. Mary's Church.
Bushinski, Edward A. *c.s.sp.* '50 (PIT) [B] Pittsburgh, PA Duquesne University of the Holy Ghost.
Bushy, Timothy F. '83 (CR) [1] Crookston, MN Cathedral of the Immaculate Conception; [B] Crookston, MN Cathedral - Religious Education/Faith Formation.
Bushy, Timothy F. '83 (FAR) On Duty Outside the Diocese.
Bussen, Robert J. '71 (SLC) Park City, UT St. Mary of the Assumption Church.
Bustamante, Arturo *o.f.m.* '81 (ELP) Presidio, TX Santa Teresa de Jesus Church.
Busteed, Francis '51 (SAT) Absent on Sick Leave.
Busteed, Robert T. '69 (SCR) Bastress, PA Immaculate Conception Church.
Bustinza, Pedro *o.ss.t.* '63 (ARE) Isabela, PR St. Anthony Church.
Butcavage, Leonard M. '72 (SCR) [5] Hazleton, PA Holy Trinity Church.
Butch, Brian '93 (TR) Princeton, NJ St. Paul Church.
Butera, George J. '68 (BO) Beverly, MA St. John the Evangelist Church.
Butkowski, Alto *o.s.b.* '41 (SCL) [I] Collegeville, MN St. John's Abbey, of the Order of St. Benedict.
Butkus, Casimir '46 (DET) Retired.
Butler, Allan L.W. '67 (BO) Abington, MA St. Bridget Church.
Butler, Arthur *o.f.m.* '43 (PAT) [M] Ringwood, NJ Holy Name Friary, Inc.
Butler, B. '44 (STA) [F] Jacksonville, FL All Saints Home.
Butler, Bede J. *o.s.b.* '51 (PBL) [F] Canon City, CO Holy Cross Abbey.
Butler, Daniel J. '66 (PT) Niceville, FL Holy Name of Jesus Church.
Butler, Donald J. (DET) [P] Clarkston, MI Colombiere Center.
Butler, Francis *s.s.j.* '85 (LAF) Church Point, LA Our Mother of Mercy Church.
Butler, Henry J. *s.j.* '40 (BO) [W] Weston, MA Campion Health Center, Inc.
Butler, James F. '69 (R) Southern Pines, NC St. Anthony of Padua Church.
Butler, Msgr. James M. '52 (ALN) [4] Bethlehem, PA Holy Infancy Church.
Butler, James P. '86 (BO) Health Leave.
Butler, John '60 (HON) On Duty Outside the Diocese.
Butler, John J. '54 (L) [M] Louisville, KY Ursuline Motherhouse of the Immaculate Conception.
Butler, John M. '72 (GBG) [3] Connellsville, PA St. John the Evangelist Church.
Butler, John R. '57 (MET) Colonia, NJ St. John Vianney Church.
Butler, Michael '85 (R) Morehead City, NC St. Egbert Church.
Butler, Michael C. '84 (COS) [3] Colorado Springs, CO Divine Redeemer Church.
Butler, Norman H. *m.s.* '75 (HRT) [M] Hartford, CT Missionaries of LaSalette Provincial Secretary.
Butler, Patrick J. '82 (ALB) Guilderland, NY Christ the King Church.
Butler, Paul '94 (FTW) [10] South Bend, IN Holy Family Church.
Butler, Paul F. '87 (RVC) Oyster Bay, NY St. Dominic's Church.
Butler, Rene J. *m.s.* '73 (SPR) [1] Westfield, MA Holy Trinity Church.
Butler, Richard J. '62 (BO) [4] Norwood, MA St. Timothy Church.
Butler, Robert E. *s.j.* '58 (LA) Alhambra, CA St. Thomas More Church.
Butler, Robert J. '62 (BO) Pepperell, MA St. Joseph Church.
Butler, Robert R. *m.s.* '69 (HRT) [M] Hartford, CT Missionaries of LaSalette Provincial Secretary.
Butler, Thomas *o.carm.* '50 (L) [60] Louisville, KY Our Lady of Mount Carmel Church.
Butler, Thomas D. *c.m.* '77 (MET) [J] Plainsboro, NJ Vincentian Renewal Center.
Butler, Thomas J. *c.m.* '77 (PH) [B] Philadelphia, PA DePaul Novitiate.
Butler, Thomas W. '82 (LAN) Hillsdale, MI St. Anthony Church.
Butler, Timothy A. '88 (BO) Military & VA Chaplains.
Butler, Victor *s.v.d.* '64 (TR) [M] Bordentown, NJ Society of the Divine Word.
Butler, Vincent E. *s.j.* '63 (NY) [F] New York, NY Xavier High School.
Butler, William *c.s.sp.* '44 (STA) Orange Park, FL St. Catherine's Church.
Butler, William L. '61 (BO) [4] Revere, MA St. Mary of the Assumption Church.
Butler, Xavier *s.a.* '47 (NY) [DD] Garrison, NY Franciscan Friars of the Atonement.
Butori, Harry '52 (HEL) [1] Butte, MT Butte Catholic Community North Church; [9] Butte, MT St. Joseph Church.
Butrie, Matthew Peter '95 (PSC) Somerset, NJ SS. Peter and Paul Church.
Butryn, Msgr. Richard E. '58 (E) Meadville, PA St. Brigid Church; Meadville, PA Crawford Country Home.
Butsch, Matthew *o.s.b.* '43 (P) [L] St. Benedict, OR Mt. Angel Abbey.
Butters, Craig (ORG) Mission Viejo, CA St. Kilian Church.
Butters, Joseph '65 (JOL) On Duty Outside the Diocese.
Butters, Joseph '65 (MRY) Arroyo Grande, CA St. Patrick Church.
Buttimer, Joseph '63 (SB) [E] Morongo Valley, CA St. Michael's of Morongo Valley, Inc.
Buttimer, Joseph J. '63 (SD) Leave of Absence.
Buttimer, Maurice L. *s.j.* '43 (BO) [W] Weston, MA Campion Health Center, Inc.
Buttinelli, Anthony '38 (NY) Retired.
Buttini, Mario S. *o.s.j.* '39 (SCR) [B] Pittston, PA St. Joseph's Oblate Seminary.
Buttino, James V. *m.m.* '47 (FgM) Maryknoll Foreign Missions.
Buttner, Michael '78 (CHL) Lenoir, NC St. Francis of Assisi Church.
Buttomer, Jeremiah R. *c.s.c.* '43 (AUS) [H] Austin, TX Congregation of Holy Cross - Southern Province.
Buttomer, Jeremiah R. *c.s.c.* '43 (FTW) [J] South Bend, IN Congregation of Holy Cross Indiana Province Provincial House.
Buttrick, Dean T. '63 (SUP) [3] Superior, WI St. Anthony Church; Lake Nebagamon, WI St. Anthony Church.
Butz, Joseph *c.ss.r.* '70 (FgM) Redemptorist Foreign Missions.
Buu, Francis X. '74 (NY) [52] New York, NY Immaculate Conception Church.
Buvala, Andrew *o.f.m.* '47 (GAY) Peshabestown, MI Blessed Kateri Tekakwitha Church.
Buvala, Medard *o.f.m.* '43 (JOL) [11] Joliet, IL St. John the Baptist Church; [J] Joliet, IL St. John the Baptist Friary.
Buvens, Msgr. Norman '64 (SHP) Bossier City, LA Christ the King Church.
Buvens, Msgr. Norman C. '64 (SHP) [B] Shreveport, LA Schumpert Medical Center.
Buxkemper, Msgr. Roland '65 (LUB) [8] Lubbock, TX St. Theresa's Church.
Buxman, Donald R. '70 (P) Oregon City, OR St. John the Apostle Church.
Buyansky, Timothy *o.s.b.* '69 (CLV) [E] Cleveland, OH Benedictine High School; [P] Cleveland, OH Benedictine Order of Cleveland.
Buzek, Joseph J. '42 (ORL) Retired.
Buzek, Joseph L. '42 (COL) Retired.
Buzga, John *glmy.* (TLS) Idabel, OK St. Francis De Sales Church.
Buzynski, Laurin *o.f.m.* '44 (SFD) [K] Sherman, IL Our Lady of Angels Friary.
Buzzelli, Aaron N. *o.s.b.* '77 (GBG) [H] Latrobe, PA Saint Vincent Archabbey.
Buzzerio, Joseph (NEW) Hackensack, NJ Bergen County Jail.
Byaruhanga, Frederick '89 (LA) [70] Los Angeles, CA St. Joan of Arc Church.
Bydlon, Msgr. Adam J. '46 (PH) [78] Philadelphia, PA St. John Cantius Church; Retired.
Byer, James M. '81 (CHL) Statesville, NC St. Philip the Apostle Church.
Byerley, E. Joseph '93 (CAM) Woodbury, NJ St. Patrick's Church.
Byerley, Timothy E. '85 (CAM) [4] Cherry Hill, NJ St. Pius X Church.
Byers, Dohrman W. '74 (CIN) Arnheim, OH St. Mary Church; Sardinia, OH St. Elizabeth Parish.
Byers, George *c.p.m.* '92 (LAF) Iota, LA St. Joseph Church.
Byers, John A. '95 (LAN) [1] Ann Arbor, MI St. Francis of Assisi Church.
Byington, Edward J. '70 (FR) Hyannis, MA St. Francis Xavier's Church.
Bykowski, Norbert H. '56 (CHI) Retired.
Bynon, Msgr. Joseph P. '56 (BRK) [233] Queens, NY Resurrection-Ascension Church.
Byrd, Freddie '88 (OWN) [7] Owensboro, KY SS. Joseph and Paul Church.
Byrd, Howard W. *s.s.j.* '75 (NO) [4] New Orleans, LA Blessed Sacrament Church.
Byrd, Thomas J. '50 (BAL) Retired; [B] Emmitsburg, MD Mount Saint Mary's College.
Byrider, Charles L. '41 (CLV) [5] Akron, OH St. Francis de Sales Church; [17] Akron, OH St. Sebastian Church; Retired.
Byrne, Albert F. '47 (STP) North St. Paul, MN St. Peter Church.
Byrne, Albert J. '79 (ALN) Frackville, PA St. Joseph Church; Maizeville, PA Our Lady of Siluva Church.
Byrne, Alexius W. *s.j.* '53 (SEA) [A] Seattle, WA Seattle University.
Byrne, Basil *o.c.s.o.* '76 (WOR) [N] Spencer, MA St. Joseph's Abbey.
Byrne, Bernard P. *m.m.* '56 (FgM) Maryknoll Foreign Missions.
Byrne, Christopher *s.p.s.* (SJ) [M] Saratoga, CA St. Patrick's Missionary Society.
Byrne, David J. '78 (CHI) Evergreen Park, IL St.

Bernadette Church.
Byrne, Edward *c.ss.r.* '44 (BRK) [107] Brooklyn, NY Our Lady of Perpetual Help Basilica Church.
Byrne, Edward G. '64 (NY) Ossining, NY St. Ann Church.
Byrne, Francis A. *c.m.* '62 (STL) [P] Perryville, MO Congregation of The Mission.
Byrne, Frederick *o.s.b.* '82 (ALT) [I] University Park, PA Penn State Catholic Community.
Byrne, Gary '87 (MRY) Hollister, CA Sacred Heart Church.
Byrne, George '69 (SD) Del Mar, CA St. William of York Church.
Byrne, Glen F. (BO) [11] Boston, MA St. Anthony Church.
Byrne, Glenn '75 (BAL) Special Assignment.
Byrne, Msgr. Harry J. '46 (NY) Retired.
Byrne, Harry M. *o.p.* '78 (STL) [B] St. Louis, MO Aquinas Institute of Theology.
Byrne, Msgr. Henry L. '37 (STL) Retired.
Byrne, Hugh A. '62 (BRK) [246] Queens, NY St. Thomas More-St. Edmund Church.
Byrne, James A.P. *s.j.* '47 (WDC) [E] North Bethesda, MD Georgetown Preparatory School.
Byrne, James F. '52 (IND) Retired.
Byrne, James O. '37 (CIN) St. Marys, OH Holy Rosary Church; Retired.
Byrne, James P. *o.s.f.s.* '60 (ALN) Robesonia, PA St. Francis de Sales Church.
Byrne, John F. *s.s.j.* '66 (BAL) [M] Baltimore, MD St. Joseph Society of the Sacred Heart House of Central Administration.
Byrne, John J. '25 (RVC) Retired; [N] Uniondale, NY St. Pius X Residence.
Byrne, Msgr. John T. '45 (STL) Retired.
Byrne, Joseph F. '69 (BO) [5] Waltham, MA Our Lady, Comforter of the Afflicted Church.
Byrne, Joseph L. '54 (HEL) Townsend, MT Holy Cross Church.
Byrne, Msgr. Laserian '48 (FRS) [7] Fresno, CA St. Anthony of Padua Church.
Byrne, Laurence *s.d.b.* '53 (OAK) [E] Richmond, CA Salesian High School.
Byrne, Luke J. *s.j.* '65 (STL) [P] St. Louis, MO White House Retreat Jesuit Community; [T] St. Louis, MO White House Retreat.
Byrne, Patrick J. '55 (COL) On Duty Outside the Diocese.
Byrne, Peter D. *s.j.* '75 (P) [N] Portland, OR The Jesuit Spirituality Center.
Byrne, Peter J. '84 (NY) [191] Bronx, NY St. Thomas Aquinas Church; [207] Staten Island, NY Immaculate Conception Church; [208] Staten Island, NY St. John the Baptist de La Salle Church.
Byrne, Pierce D. '53 (NEW) [2] Linden, NJ Holy Family Church.
Byrne, Raymond J. '57 (NY) Irvington-on-the-Hudson, NY Immaculate Conception Church.
Byrne, Robert H. '75 (SAG) Shields, MI Holy Spirit Church.
Byrne, Robert P. '50 (LA) Retired.
Byrne, Thomas '58 (DET) Retired.
Byrne, Thomas C. *o.s.b.* '49 (RIC) [L] Richmond, VA Mary Mother of the Church Abbey.
Byrne, Thomas H. *s.j.* '53 (SJ) [M] Los Gatos, CA Sacred Heart Jesuit Center.
Byrne, Thomas J. *s.j.* '53 (SJ) San Jose, CA Agnews State Hospital.
Byrne, Tom *c.s.sp.* '64 (GAL) [68] Houston, TX St. Philip Neri Church.
Byrne, W. Gordon '32 (NEW) Retired.
Byrne, William D. '94 (WDC) [2] Rockville, MD Shrine of St. Jude Church.
Byrnes, Christopher *o.carm.* '51 (NY) [97] New York, NY Our Lady of the Scapular/St. Stephen Church.
Byrnes, Donald M. '55 (NO) [4] Kenner, LA St. Jerome Church.
Byrnes, Edward M. '80 (MEM) [11] Memphis, TN Holy Spirit Church.
Byrnes, Francis J. '51 (BRK) Retired.
Byrnes, James J. '80 (STL) [1] Florissant, MO North American Martyrs Church.
Byrnes, James T. '86 (NY) [E] New York, NY Cardinal Hayes High School.
Byrnes, John (ALT) [20] Johnstown, PA St. Andrew's Church.
Byrnes, John D. '94 (ALT) [B] Johnstown, PA Bishop McCort High School.
Byrnes, John J. '66 (CAM) Bellmawr, NJ Mary, Mother of the Church; [A] Haddonfield, NJ Paul VI High School.
Byrnes, John P. '45 (TR) Retired.
Byrnes, John W. '47 (BRK) [183] Queens, NY SS. Joachim and Anne Church; Retired.
Byrnes, Michael J. '96 (DET) [4] St. Clair Shores, MI St. Joan of Arc Church.
Byrnes, Paul A. '62 (BAL) Frostburg, MD St. Michael Church.
Byrnes, Robert R. '67 (GBG) Leechburg, PA Church of the Assumption.
Byrnes, Thomas M. *c.m.* '50 (FgM) Vincentian Foreign Missions.
Byrnes, Timothy '52 (LAN) [3] Lansing, MI Holy Cross Church.
Byrns, Joseph P. '69 (BRK) [127] Brooklyn, NY St. Rose of Lima Church.
Byrolly, Bruce '58 (WIL) Cambridge, MD St. Mary Refuge of Sinners Church.
Byron, J. Michael (STP) [C] St. Paul, MN University of St. Thomas.
Byron, J. Michael '89 (STP) Graduate Studies.
Byron, J. Paul (R) [4] Durham, NC St. Matthew Church.
Byron, Patrick J. '58 (YAK) Retired.
Byron, William '62 (YAK) Roslyn, WA Immaculate Conception Church.
Byron, William J. *s.j.* '61 (WDC) [M] Washington, DC The Jesuit Community at Georgetown University.
Byrth, Peter *o.carm.* '59 (JOL) [J] Darien, IL Carmelite Community; [M] Darien, IL Provincial Office of Lay Carmelites and Scapular Confraternity.
Bzdyra, Stephen '79 (HRT) Wallingford, CT SS. Peter and Paul Church.
Bzdyra, Steven H. '79 (HRT) New Haven, CT Community Correctional Institution.

C

Caamano, Raphael '78 (BO) [V] Chestnut Hill, MA Opus Dei.
Cabala, Thomas S. '79 (CHI) South Holland, IL St. Jude the Apostle Church.
Caballero, Francisco '53 (TOL) Retired.
Caballero, Lloyd C. '40 (BR) Retired.
Cabarello, Francisco *o.de.m.* '90 (SB) Rancho Cucamonga, CA Our Lady of Mount Carmel Church.
Cabasino, Philip *c.ss.r.* '47 (BO) [13] Boston, MA Our Lady of Perpetual Help Church.
Cabasino, Philip A. *c.ss.r.* '47 (BO) Boston, MA Veterans Administration Hospital.
Cabazi, Ruta A. '65 (IND) [F] Beech Grove, IN St. Francis Hospital and Health Centers.
Cabell, Barry *c.s.c.* '89 (AUS) [13] Austin, TX St. Ignatius Martyr Church.
Cabello, Tomas (SJN) [23] Bayamon, PR Santa Maria Church.
Caboboy, Juan '76 (ORG) Laguna Hills, CA St. Nicholas Church.
Cabral, Clifford J. '79 (PRO) Burrilleville, RI St. Joseph Church.
Cabral, Kenneth J. '50 (OAK) Retired.
Cabrera, Sergio '73 (MIA) [29] Miami, FL St. Raymond Church.
Cabrerizo, Juan L. *sch.p.* '77 (PCE) [C] Coto Laurel, PR Colegio Ponceno.
Cabrita, Paul *s.m.* '86 (BR) [7] Baton Rouge, LA St. Francis De Sales Parish; Convent, LA St. Michael the Archangel Church.
Caccavale, Charles '91 (BRK) Graduate Studies.
Caccavalle, Paschal *o.f.m.cap.* (NEW) [4] Hackensack, NJ St. Francis Church.
Caccavalle, Paschal *o.f.m.cap.* '35 (NY) [151] Bronx, NY Immaculate Conception Church.
Caccavalle, Pius *o.f.m.cap.* '47 (NY) [DD] New York, NY Immaculate Conception Friary.
Cacciapuoti, Antonio '90 (LA) Goleta, CA St. Raphael Church.
Caceras, Marco Antonio *c.ss.r.* '67 (MET) [8] Perth Amboy, NJ La Asuncion Church.
Caceres, Alonso '59 (ORG) [2] Santa Ana, CA Our Lady of Guadalupe Church.
Caceres, Angel Diaz (SJN) [A] Bayamon, PR Bayamon Central University.
Cach, Mark '83 (P) Medford, OR Sacred Heart of Jesus Church.
Cachat, Leo P. *s.j.* '66 (FgM) Provinces.
Cadarso, Carmelo '59 (VEN) Bradenton, FL St. Joseph Church.
Cadden, Donald R. *s.j.* (SPK) [C] Spokane, WA Gonzaga University.
Cadden, Donald R. *s.j.* '58 (SPK) [G] Spokane, WA Sacred Heart Medical Center.
Cadden, Thomas J. '55 (COL) [G] Columbus, OH St. Rita Home.
Caddy, James L. '64 (CLV) Gates Mills, OH St. Francis of Assisi Church.
Cadena, Enrique '84 (ROC) [14] Rochester, NY Corpus Christi Church.
Cadera, James (FRS) Coalinga, CA Pleasant Valley State Prison.
Cadera, James R. '57 (MRY) On Duty Outside the Diocese.
Cadigan, Timothy J. *s.j.* '91 (WDC) [M] Washington, DC The Jesuit Community at Georgetown University.
Cadorette, Curtis R. *m.m.* '77 (NY) [DD] Maryknoll, NY Maryknoll Fathers and Brothers.
Cadri, Diego (PIT) Penn Hills, PA St. Bartholomew Church.
Cadusale, Jose '60 (BRK) Queens, NY Queens Hospital Center—Pastoral Care Office; [U] Jamaica, NY Parsons Manor.
Cadwallader, George B. '92 (PH) [13] Philadelphia, PA St. Anselm Church.
Cady, Frank G. '81 (TUC) Rio Rico, AZ Nativity of Our Lord Jesus Christ Church.
Caesar, Floyd '75 (ALN) Ashland, PA St. Joseph Church; Ashland, PA St. Mauritius Church.
Caesar, Roger J. *s.s.j.* '76 (BAL) [M] Baltimore, MD St. Joseph Society of the Sacred Heart House of Central Administration.
Cafarelli, Aquinas F. *o.s.b.* '65 (MAN) [K] Manchester, NH St. Anselm Abbey.
Caffe, John I. '62 (STL) St. Ann, MO St. Gregory Church.
Caffery, James *m.s.* '60 (ATL) Smyrna, GA St. Thomas the Apostle Church.
Caffrey, Benet W. *o.s.b.* '58 (PAT) [M] Morristown, NJ St. Mary's Abbey.
Caffrey, Edward F. '57 (SPK) Clayton, WA St. Joseph Church; Deer Park, WA St. Mary's Presentation Church.
Caffrey, Gerald *c.m.f.* '80 (PHX) Prescott, AZ United States Veterans Hospital (Prescott).
Caffrey, Joseph P. '63 (PT) Panama City, FL St. Dominic Church.
Caffrey, William J. *s.v.d.* '59 (LA) Lancaster, CA Sacred Heart Church; [D] Lancaster, CA Paraclete High School.
Cafiero, John Paul *o.f.m.* '95 (CHI) [D] Chicago, IL Hales Franciscan High School, Inc.
Cafone, James M. '65 (NEW) [B] South Orange, NJ Seton Hall University.
Caforio, Stephen *o.f.m.* '49 (NY) [DD] New York, NY St. Clare Friary.
Caggiano, Frank '87 (BRK) [72] Brooklyn, NY Shrine Church of St. Jude.
Caggiano, Kyrin *o.carm.* '62 (L) [B] Louisville, KY St. Francis DeSales High School.
Cagney, John M. *o.praem.* '48 (PH) [D] Philadelphia, PA St. John Neumann High School; [AA] Philadelphia, PA St. Norbert Priory.
Cahalan, Patrick J. *s.j.* '65 (LA) [C] Los Angeles, CA Loyola Marymount University; [F] Los Angeles, CA Loyola High School.
Cahalane, Msgr. Thomas P. '63 (TUC) [8] Tucson, AZ Our Mother of Sorrows Church.
Cahalane, Timothy *m.s.c.* '59 (LA) [50] Los Angeles, CA St. Brendan Church.
Cahill, Brendan J. '90 (GAL) On Duty Outside the Diocese.
Cahill, Clemente *c.ss.r.* '51 (CGS) [1] Caguas, PR Cathedral Dulce Nombre de Jesus Church.
Cahill, Daniel '73 (TR) Keansburg, NJ St. Ann Church.
Cahill, Msgr. Daniel P. '43 (SFR) [42] San Francisco, CA St. Paul Church.
Cahill, Msgr. Daniel R. '43 (SFR) Retired.
Cahill, Dennis H. '77 (DUB) Mason City, IA Holy Family Church; [G] Mason City, IA Newman Catholic.
Cahill, Donald C. '67 (CHI) Tinley Park, IL St. George Church.
Cahill, Edward B. '60 (PH) Springfield, PA Holy Cross Church.
Cahill, Frank '68 (MIA) Retired.
Cahill, J. Donald *s.m.* (STL) [F] Kirkwood, MO Vianney High School.
Cahill, J. Donald *s.m.* '61 (STL) [4] Creve Coeur, MO Our Lady of the Pillar Church.
Cahill, James P. '61 (CHL) Sylva, NC St. Mary Church.
Cahill, John F. '51 (WOR) [M] Worcester, MA Vianney House.
Cahill, John W. '63 (RCK) [2] Freeport, IL St. Joseph Church.
Cahill, John W. '73 (COV) [1] Covington, KY Cathedral, Basilica of the Assumption Church.
Cahill, Joseph W. '76 (PRT) Oakland, ME St. Theresa Church.
Cahill, Neil *s.j.* '56 (OM) [K] Omaha, NE Jesuit Community At Creighton University.
Cahill, Patrick *c.s.v.* '62 (SFD) Rochester, IL Church of St. Jude.
Cahill, Msgr. Paul J. '35 (PH) Lansdale, PA St. Stanislaus Church; Retired.
Cahill, Msgr. Richard (NY) New York, NY National Catholic Community Service.
Cahill, Msgr. Richard M. '58 (BUF) Grand Island, NY St. Stephen Church.
Cahill, Thomas *m.j.* '88 (PCE) [7] Ponce, PR Santa Maria Church.
Cahill, William C. '61 (SY) [5] Rome, NY Transfiguration Church; Mohawk, NY Oneida Correctional Facility I.; Special Assignment.
Cahoon, John E. '89 (GAL) [19] Houston, TX St. Charles Borromeo Church.
Cahouet, Eugene *o.p.* '62 (COL) [13] Columbus, OH Santa Cruz Church; [36] Columbus, OH St. Patrick Church.
Caiazzo, Gregory G. *c.s.p.* '76 (NY) [DD] Jamaica Estates, NY Paulist Fathers Generalate.
Caiazzo, Nicholas '92 (NOR) On Duty Outside the Diocese.
Caimi, Luke A. '58 (WDC) Retired.

Cain, Dennis R. '79 (DUB) Maquoketa, IA Sacred Heart Church; St. Catherine, IA St. Catherine's Church; St. Donatus, IA St. Donatus Church.
Cain, Frederick L. '70 (PIT) [2] Bridgeville, PA Holy Child Church.
Cain, Gervase *t.o.r.* '57 (ARL) Herndon, VA St. Joseph Church.
Cain, Harry J. *s.j.* '63 (BO) [W] Weston, MA Campion Center.
Cain, Msgr. James E. (STO) On Special or Other Diocesan Assignment.
Cain, James R. '56 (OM) Springfield, NE St. Joseph Church.
Cain, John C. '58 (CHI) Harwood Heights, IL St. Rosalie Church.
Cain, John F. '56 (SC) Retired.
Cain, John N. '47 (NSH) Retired.
Cain, John T. '44 (SPR) West Springfield, MA St. Thomas the Apostle Church.
Cain, Joseph P. *o.s.c.* '44 (PHX) [F] Phoenix, AZ Crosier Community of Phoenix (Canons Regular of the Order of the Holy Cross).
Cain, Randy '88 (CC) [12] Laredo, TX St. John Neumann Church.
Cain, Robert K.C. '95 (TLS) Hartshorne, OK Holy Rosary Church.
Cain, Thomas *m.s.c.* '65 (FgM) Missionaries of the Sacred Heart Foreign Missions.
Cain, Thomas *m.s.c.* '65 (RCK) [H] Aurora, IL Missionaries of the Sacred Heart Community.
Cain, Thomas M. *o.p.* '37 (DAL) [M] Irving, TX Dominican Priory of St. Albert the Great.
Cain, Urban A. *o.f.m.* '48 (BO) [Z] Boston, MA Saint Anthony Residence.
Cain, William F. *s.j.* '69 (LA) [C] Los Angeles, CA Loyola Marymount University.
Cain, William P. *s.j.* '76 (NY) [DD] New York, NY Xavier Jesuit Community.
Caine, Msgr. Martin J. '46 (BUF) Retired.
Cairns, James E. *c.m.* '69 (FRS) [C] Fresno, CA Saint Agnes' Medical Center.
Cairns, John L. '63 (ALB) Clifton Park, NY St. Edward the Confessor Church.
Cairns, Stephen P. (TOL) [10] Toledo, OH Little Flower of Jesus Church.
Cairns, Thomas '63 (BIR) Absent on Leave.
Cairone, A. Robert '64 (CAM) Magnolia, NJ St. Gregory's Church.
Cajes, Prisco '86 (OAK) [3] Oakland, CA St. Anthony's Church.
Calabrese, Charles L. '72 (FWT) [M] Fort Worth, TX Texas Christian University Catholic Community.
Calabrese, Charles L. '72 (STU) On Duty Outside the Diocese.
Calabrese, Daniel '87 (NY) Absent on Leave.
Calabrese, Peter M. *c.r.s.p.* (ALN) [K] Bethlehem, PA The Barnabite Fathers Barnabite Spiritual Center.
Calabrese, Robert *o.f.m.cap.* '83 (NY) [151] Bronx, NY Immaculate Conception Church.
Calabro, John E. '73 (PH) [44] Philadelphia, PA Epiphany of Our Lord Church.
Calabro, Nicholas J. '66 (BGP) [4] Greenwich, CT St. Roch Church.
Calais, Floyd J. (LAF) Retired.
Calamari, Joseph *s.s.j.* (MOB) Chastang, AL St. Peter the Apostle Church.
Calamari, Paul '80 (NO) On Duty Outside the Archdiocese.
Calamari, Paul '80 (WIL) Hockessin, DE St. Mary of the Assumption Church.
Calarco, Dominic *s.x.* '55 (BO) [W] Holliston, MA Xaverian Missionaries.
Caldara, John N. '46 (ALB) Retired.
Caldarella, James J. '71 (WOR) Princeton, MA Prince of Peace Church.
Caldas, Msgr. Constantino R. '51 (BGP) [15] Bridgeport, CT Our Lady of Fatima Church; Retired.
Calder, Kenneth J. '60 (BRK) [91] Brooklyn, NY Our Lady of Angels Church.
Calderon, Francisco '50 (MIA) [16] Miami, FL St. Brendan Church.
Calderon, Vicente, Jr. '63 (ELP) [31] El Paso, TX St. Raphael Church.
Calderone, Philip J. *s.j.* '56 (FgM) Provinces.
Calderwood, Vincent T. '44 (BRK) Retired.
Calderwood, Vincent T. '44 (MET) [H] Somerset, NJ Maria Regina Residence.
Caldognetto, Dominic *s.x.* '66 (MIL) [B] Franklin, WI Xaverian Missionary Fathers College Seminary.
Caldwell, Dorothy (NY) [W] New York, NY Saint Vincent's Medical Center of Richmond.
Caldwell, Msgr. Frank J. '81 (RVC) [1] Rockville Centre, NY St. Agnes Cathedral.
Caldwell, H. Fred '95 (DAL) [15] Dallas, TX St. Cecilia Church.
Caldwell, J. Ripley '54 (SJ) [M] Los Gatos, CA Sacred Heart Jesuit Center.
Caldwell, James V. '60 (SD) [28] San Diego, CA St. Jerome Church; Chula Vista, CA South Bay Detention Facility.
Caldwell, John A. '70 (L) Campbellsville, KY Our Lady of Perpetual Help Church; Finley, KY Our Lady of the Hills Church; Greensburg, KY Holy Redeemer Church.
Caldwell, Thomas A. *s.j.* '56 (MIL) [P] Milwaukee, WI Jesuit Community at Marquette University.
Caldwell, William '68 (KC) Excelsior Springs, MO St. Ann Church.
Caldwell, William T. '44 (L) Retired.
Calegari, Leonard J. '63 (SFR) Pacifica, CA St. Peter Church.
Calero, Luis F. *s.j.* '83 (SJ) [B] Santa Clara, CA Santa Clara University.
Calero, Nomar J. '91 (MGZ) [1] Mayaquez, PR Cathedral of Our Lady of Purification.
Calgaro, John *o.f.m.conv.* (CHI) [N] Chicago, IL Conventual Franciscans of St. Bonaventure Province.
Calgaro, John *o.f.m.conv.* '74 (FgM) Conventual Franciscan Foreign Missions.
Calhoun, C. John '64 (NY) Absent on Leave.
Calhoun, George *o.c.s.o.* '40 (WOR) [N] Spencer, MA St. Joseph's Abbey.
Calhoun, Gerald '61 (OWN) [1] Paducah, KY St. Francis de Sales Church; [2] Paducah, KY Rosary Chapel Church.
Calhoun, Ronald G. '72 (BO) Middleboro, MA Sacred Heart Church.
Calicchio, Isaac J. *o.f.m.* '56 (ALB) [1] Troy, NY St. Anthony of Padua Church.
Calicott, John W. '74 (CHI) [79] Chicago, IL Holy Angels Church.
Caligiuri, Msgr. Angelo M. '58 (BUF) [2] Cheektowaga, NY Infant of Prague Church.
Caligiuri, Msgr. Anthony J. '49 (BUF) Lewiston, NY St. Peter Church.
Calik, Joseph *s.ch.* '60 (SEA) [13] Seattle, WA St. Margaret of Scotland Church.
Calimeri, Anthony F. '47 (ROC) Retired.
Calise, Joseph '80 (BRK) [B] Elmhurst, NY Cathedral Preparatory Seminary of the Immaculate Conception.
Caliwan, Marc '72 (BRK) [215] Queens, NY Our Lady of the Miraculous Medal Church.
Calkins, Arthur B. '70 (NO) On Duty Outside the Archdiocese.
Calkins, Frank M. *o.s.m.* '30 (CHI) [N] Chicago, IL Servite Friars - Eastern Province.
Calkins, Gerard M. *o.s.m.* (ORG) [H] Anaheim, CA Servite Fathers and Brothers.
Calkins, Gerard M. *o.s.m.* '45 (ORG) [H] Orange, CA Servite Fathers and Brothers.
Calkins, Msgr. Howard W. '67 (NY) [HH] Bronx, NY Abraham House, Inc.
Calkins, John J. '49 (RCK) Loves Park, IL St. Bridget Church; Retired.
Calkins, Leroy *o.s.m.* '35 (P) Roseburg, OR U.S. Veterans' Administration Hospital.
Calkins, Martin J. *s.j.* (DET) [K] Detroit, MI Jesuit Provincial Office-Detroit Province of the Society of Jesus.
Calkins, Martin J. *s.j.* '94 (WDC) [M] Washington, DC The Jesuit Community at Georgetown University.
Calkins, Raymond J. '46 (SC) Retired.
Calkins, Ronald L. '78 (NO) Mandeville, LA Mary Queen of Peace Church.
Callaghan, Msgr. Aloysius R. '71 (ALN) On Duty Outside the Diocese.
Callaghan, George J. *o.s.a.* '56 (PH) [AA] Villanova, PA St. Thomas Monastery.
Callaghan, Michael '90 (BAL) [C] Severn, MD Archbishop Spalding High School.
Callaghan, Patrick *o.f.m.* (OG) Retired.
Callaghan, Patrick C. *o.f.m.* '46 (NY) [DD] New York, NY Franciscan Friars, Order of Friars Minor, Holy Name Province.
Callaghan, Philip P. *s.j.* '60 (SFR) [C] San Francisco, CA University of San Francisco.
Callahan, Msgr. Brian F. '65 (BRK) [141] Brooklyn, NY St. Thomas Aquinas Church.
Callahan, Daniel *s.a.* '87 (OG) [E] Saranac Lake, NY St. Joseph's Rehabilitation Center, Inc.
Callahan, Daniel P. *s.a.* '87 (OG) [F] Saranac Lake, NY Atonement Friars.
Callahan, David P. '87 (BO) Melrose, MA St. Mary of the Annunciation Church.
Callahan, Dennis D. '62 (MIL) Pell Lake, WI St. Mary Church.
Callahan, Edward M. '59 (SPR) [12] Springfield, MA Sacred Heart Church; Springfield, MA Wesson Memorial Hospital Unit; Springfield, MA Olympus Specialty Hospital.
Callahan, Edward R. *s.j.* '49 (BO) [W] Chestnut Hill, MA The Jesuit Community at Boston College.
Callahan, Francis F. *s.j.* '43 (BO) [W] Weston, MA Campion Health Center, Inc.
Callahan, Msgr. Francis J. *v.f.* '72 (SCR) [20] Wilkes-Barre, PA St. Therese's Church.
Callahan, Francis X. '49 (HRT) Woodmont, CT St. Agnes Church.
Callahan, Francis X. '63 (BAL) Bel Air, MD St. Margaret Church.
Callahan, James '44 (NEW) Retired.
Callahan, James A. '73 (PH) [153] Philadelphia, PA Transfiguration of Our Lord Church.
Callahan, James F. *s.m.a.* '75 (BO) [W] Dedham, MA African Mission House.
Callahan, James F. *s.m.a.* '75 (WIN) [2] Rochester, MN Pax Christi Church.
Callahan, James P. '74 (STL) [2] St. Charles, MO St. Cletus Church.
Callahan, Jerome *o.carm.* '52 (VEN) [6] Sarasota, FL St. Thomas More Church.
Callahan, John J. *s.j.* '70 (DEN) [M] Denver, CO Regis Jesuit Community (The Jesuits at Regis University).
Callahan, Joseph F. *c.s.c.* '70 (SCR) [4] Wilkes-Barre, PA St. Casimir's Church.
Callahan, Joseph H. '86 (CLV) El Salvador, C.A., OH Parroquial de Nuestra Senora de Guadalupe.
Callahan, Joseph W. '66 (PH) [152] Philadelphia, PA St. Timothy Church.
Callahan, Kevin G. '84 (STL) [5] Lemay, MO St. Martin of Tours Church.
Callahan, Leonard F. '69 (COV) On Duty Outside the Diocese.
Callahan, Michael J. '76 (BRK) [U] Jamaica, NY Vincentian Residence.
Callahan, Nelson J. '53 (CLV) Bay Village, OH St. Raphael Church.
Callahan, Raymond J. '48 (MIL) Retired.
Callahan, Richard B. *m.m.* '64 (NY) [DD] Maryknoll, NY Maryknoll Fathers and Brothers; [DD] Maryknoll, NY M.M.A.F. Charitable Trust; [EE] Maryknoll, NY Maryknoll Sisters Charitable Trust.
Callahan, Msgr. Richard J. '51 (CAM) Haddon Heights, NJ St. Rose's Church.
Callahan, Ronan *c.p.* '51 (HRT) [M] West Hartford, CT Holy Family Monastery/Retreat.
Callahan, Ronan P. *c.p.* (NOR) [A] Cromwell, CT Holy Apostles College and Seminary.
Callahan, Steven '87 (SD) [A] San Diego, CA St. Francis Seminary.
Callahan, Vincent '75 (CHI) [N] Chicago, IL St. Peter's Friary.
Callahan, William J. *s.j.* '72 (FgM) Provinces.
Callahan, William J. *s.j.* '72 (MIL) [P] Milwaukee, WI Jesuit Provincial Office, Wisconsin Province.
Callahan, William P. *o.f.m.conv.* '77 (MIL) [45] Milwaukee, WI Basilica of St. Josaphat Church.
Callahan, Zachary '58 (RVC) Uniondale, NY St. Martha Church.
Callam, Daniel D. *c.s.b.* '64 (GAL) [Q] Houston, TX Residence of the Basilian Fathers of the University of St. Thomas.
Callan, Dennis *s.v.d.* '87 (FgM) Society of the Divine Word Foreign Missions.
Callan, James B. '74 (ROC) [14] Rochester, NY Corpus Christi Church.
Callan, John '82 (MIA) [C] Fort Lauderdale, FL Cardinal Gibbons High School.
Callan, L. James '45 (ROC) Retired.
Callan, Patrick J. '61 (RVC) Bridgehampton, NY Queen of the Most Holy Rosary Church.
Callanan, Edward E. *s.j.* '58 (PHX) [11] Phoenix, AZ St. Francis Xavier Church.
Callanan, Jonas *i.c.* (PEO) Pontiac, IL Illinois State Penitentiary.
Callari, William P. '79 (MAR) Vulcan, MI St. Barbara Church.
Calle, Juan de la '54 (PMB) Retired.
Calleja, Msgr. Guido '53 (MOB) Magnolia Springs, AL St. John the Baptist Church.
Callery, Peter *s.j.* '72 (NO) [F] New Orleans, LA Jesuit High School.
Calles, Msgr. Robert S. '63 (ELP) [13] El Paso, TX Most Holy Trinity Church.
Callipare, Joseph '85 (PT) [13] Pensacola, FL St. Paul Church.
Callis, Elbert '76 (MEM) Dyersburg, TN Holy Angels Church.
Callone, Ivan *i.m.c.* '53 (CAM) Egg Harbor City, NJ St. Nicholas Church.
Callone, Ivan *i.m.c.* '53 (MET) [H] Somerset, NJ Consolata Society for Foreign Missions.
Calme, Stephen J. '54 (CIN) Retired.
Caloca-Rivas, Rigoberto *o.f.m.* (OAK) [S] Berkeley, CA Multicultural Institute.
Caloca-Rivas, Rigoberto *o.f.m.* '82 (OAK) [A] Berkeley, CA Franciscan School of Theology; [N] Oakland, CA Franciscan Friars.
Calovini, Msgr. Gerald E. '73 (STU) Wintersville, OH Blessed Sacrament Church; Wintersville, OH Our Lady of Lourdes Church; [J] Steubenville, OH Campaign for Human Development.
Calpin, Thomas J. '54 (PH) Retired.
Calter, Arthur M. '56 (BO) Hingham, MA Resurrection of Our Lord and Saviour Jesus Christ Church.
Caluda, Charles J. '62 (NO) Garyville, LA St. Hubert Church.
Calumba, Faron (HRT) Naugatuck, CT St. Francis of Assisi Church.
Calumba, Faron P. '79 (HRT) Newington, CT Holy Spirit Church.

Caluza, Ramon *c.i.c.m.* '79 (FgM) Missionhurst Foreign Missions.
Calvert, Roland *o.s.f.s.* '65 (LAN) [H] Adrian, MI Motherhouse of the Sisters of St. Dominic.
Calvo, Gabriel '52 (WDC) [B] Washington, DC Diocesan Laborer Priests, House of Studies.
Calvo, Msgr. Oscar (AGN) Retired.
Calvo, Randolph '77 (SFR) Redwood City, CA Our Lady of Mount Carmel Church.
Calvo Muniain, Jose M. '59 (CGS) Juncos, PR Inmaculada Concepcion Church.
Calzada, Teodoro *c.m.* '53 (SJN) [47] San Juan, PR Nuestra Senora del Pilar Church.
Camacho, Enrique '81 (YAK) Retired.
Camacho, Enrique L. '81 (YAK) Zillah, WA Resurrection Church.
Camacho, Gilbert '47 (ELP) Retired.
Camacho, Henry *o.p.* '60 (NEW) [28] Jersey City, NJ Sacred Heart Church.
Camacho, Jesus '75 (B) Jerome, ID St. Jerome's Church.
Camacho, Jose Fco. Baez '87 (MGZ) [3] Mayaquez, Mayaguez Ascension Church.
Camacho, Juan L.G. '55 (AGN) Tumon Bay, GU Blessed Diego Luis de San Vitores Church.
Camacho, Robert '79 (RCK) Carpentersville, IL St. Monica Church.
Camacho, Msgr. Zoilo L.G. '54 (AGN) Dededo, GU Santa Barbara Church.
Camadella, Christian F. *o.f.m.* '56 (NY) [35] New York, NY St. Francis of Assisi Church.
Camara, Michael *o.f.m.* (FR) [6] New Bedford, MA Our Lady of Mt. Carmel Church.
Camarda, Ronald A. (STA) Orange Park, FL St. Catherine's Church.
Cambra, Dan *m.i.c.* '86 (MIL) [9] Kenosha, WI St. Peter Church.
Cambra, Raymond '77 (FR) [14] Fall River, MA St. Elizabeth's Church.
Cameli, Louis J. '70 (CHI) [30] Chicago, IL St. Bonaventure Church.
Camera, Bede G. *o.s.b.* (MAN) [16] Manchester, NH St. Raphael Church.
Camera, Bede G. *o.s.b.* '88 (MAN) [K] Manchester, NH St. Anselm Abbey.
Cameron, Albert S. '57 (MAN) Retired.
Cameron, Ben *c.p.m.* '97 (OWN) Hopkinsville, KY SS. Peter and Paul Church.
Cameron, Hilary J. '64 (PRT) Berwick, ME Our Lady of Peace Church.
Cameron, Kevin '84 (DM) [13] Des Moines, IA Visitation Church.
Cameron, Peter John *o.p.* '86 (NY) [A] Yonkers, NY St. Joseph's Seminary; [DD] New York, NY St. Vincent Ferrer Priory.
Cameron, Robert '59 (KC) Special Assignment.
Cameron-Mowat, Andrew *s.j.* '92 (OAK) [N] Berkeley, CA Jesuit Community at Jesuit School of Theology at Berkeley.
Camille, Edward J. '58 (CLV) Brecksville, OH St. Basil the Great Church; Retired.
Camilleri, Emanuel M. *o.p.* '37 (NO) [P] New Orleans, LA Dominican Fathers & Brothers, Southern Dominican Province.
Camilleri, Emmanuel '66 (HBG) [F] Lancaster, PA St. Joseph Hospital and Health Care Center.
Camilleri, Joseph M. '74 (BR) Bayou Pigeon, LA St. Joan of Arc Church.
Camilleri, Roberto *o.f.m.* '75 (FgM) Franciscan Foreign Missions.
Camilli, E. Michael *m.s.c.* '60 (ALN) [A] Center Valley, PA Missionaries of the Sacred Heart.
Camilli, E. Michael *m.s.c.* '60 (BAL) [A] Baltimore, MD St. Mary's Seminary and University.
Camire, Bernard J. *s.s.s.* '66 (NY) [55] New York, NY St. Jean Baptiste Church; [HH] New York, NY Nocturnal Adoration Society of the United States.
Cammayo, Ruben '80 (NY) [131] Bronx, NY St. Augustine Church; Bronx, NY Bronx-Lebanon Hospital Center.
Cammisa, James N. '49 (TR) Retired.
Camorlinga, Angel *m.c.c.j.* '96 (FgM) Comboni Foreign Missions.
Camp, Alfred L. '57 (JKS) Natchez, MS St. Mary Church.
Camp, Steven '87 (RVC) Seaford, NY St. William, the Abbot Church.
Campagna, Robert M. *o.f.m.* '77 (NY) [DD] New York, NY Franciscan Province of the Immaculate Conception; [HH] Mount Vernon, NY Franciscan Mission Associates; [HH] Mount Vernon, NY St. Dymphna Devotion.
Campagnone, Msgr. Francis '48 (ORL) New Smyrna Beach, FL Our Lady Star of the Sea Church; Retired.
Campagnone, Msgr. Francis A. '48 (BGP) Retired.
Campagnone, Nicholas '65 (ALB) Retired.
Campana, Pedro '56 (SJN) [19] Bayamon, PR Santa Rosa de Lima Church.
Campana, Thomas J. '80 (CHI) [4] Oak Park, IL St. Giles Church.
Campbell, Andrew S. *o.s.b.* '81 (GBG) [H] Latrobe, PA Saint Vincent Archabbey.
Campbell, Bernard *c.s.p.* '68 (AUS) [11] Austin, TX St. Austin's Church; [M] Austin, TX University Catholic Center.
Campbell, Bernard '89 (STV) [1] Barrenspot, VI Church St. Ann Church.
Campbell, Bernard J. *o.f.m.cap* '68 (MAN) [2] Manchester, NH St. Anne Church.
Campbell, Colm '60 (BRK) [243] Queens, NY St. Teresa Church.
Campbell, Colm '63 (BRK) [T] Brooklyn, NY Catholic Migration & Refugee Office, Catholic Migration Services, Inc.
Campbell, Donald C. *c.s.p.* '62 (NY) [104] New York, NY St. Paul the Apostle Church.
Campbell, Douglas '76 (WCH) Lindsborg, KS St. Bridget of Sweden Church; McPherson, KS St. Joseph Church.
Campbell, Edward *o.s.b.* (PMB) Tequesta, FL St. Jude Church.
Campbell, Francis *o.m.i.* '42 (BO) [Z] Tewksbury, MA Immaculate Heart of Mary Novitiate-Infirmary.
Campbell, Msgr. Frank '53 (P) North Plains, OR St. Edward Church.
Campbell, Frederick F. '80 (STP) West St. Paul, MN St. Joseph Church.
Campbell, Gerard J. *s.j.* '51 (WDC) [20] Washington, DC Holy Trinity Church.
Campbell, Gerardo *c.ss.r.* '67 (CGS) [1] Caguas, PR Cathedral Dulce Nombre de Jesus Church.
Campbell, Howard W. '61 (PIT) [5] Munhall, PA St. Theresa of Lisieux Church.
Campbell, Hugh P. '61 (PH) Westtown, PA St. Maximilian Kolbe Church.
Campbell, James *m.s.c.* '72 (RCK) [H] Aurora, IL Missionaries of the Sacred Heart Community.
Campbell, James D. *o.p.* '62 (R) [E] Raleigh, NC Dominican Community; [E] Raleigh, NC De Porres House.
Campbell, James F. '57 (PEO) [N] Peoria, IL Immaculate Conception Convent.
Campbell, Msgr. James F. '64 (BUF) [1] Buffalo, NY St. Joseph's Cathedral.
Campbell, John '50 (SFD) Retired.
Campbell, Msgr. John '55 (ORG) San Juan Capistrano, CA (Old Mission) Church.
Campbell, John D. *s.j.* '76 (MIL) [29] Milwaukee, WI Gesu Parish.
Campbell, John J. *s.j.* '50 (DEN) [M] Denver, CO Xavier Jesuit Center.
Campbell, Msgr. John Michael '71 (STU) Minerva, OH St. Gabriel the Archangel Church.
Campbell, John P. *c.s.p.* '69 (BO) [P] Boston, MA Paulist Center; [W] Boston, MA Paulist Fathers Residence.
Campbell, John R. '58 (STL) Retired.
Campbell, Msgr. John S. '66 (ALN) [5] Minersville, PA St. Vincent de Paul Church.
Campbell, Joseph '60 (FAR) Retired.
Campbell, Joseph '60 (SPC) Caruthersville, MO Sacred Heart Church.
Campbell, Louis J. *f.s.s.p.* '61 (SCR) [19] Scranton, PA St. Michael's Church; [M] Elmhurst, PA Priestly Fraternity of St. Peter (F.S.S.P.), North American District Headquarters.
Campbell, Mark A. (SD) [10] San Diego, CA Mission Basilica San Diego De Alcala Church.
Campbell, Michael '79 (STL) [14] St. Louis, MO Our Lady of Sorrows Church.
Campbell, Michael J. '93 (ATL) Lilburn, GA St. John Neumann Church.
Campbell, Norbert J. '60 (PIT) [3] New Castle, PA St. Joseph the Worker Church.
Campbell, Paul B. *s.j.* '88 (SY) [S] Syracuse, NY Jesuits at LeMoyne, Inc.
Campbell, Paul F. '65 (WOR) Dudley, MA St. Anthony's Church.
Campbell, Paul J. *o.s.f.s.* '82 (WIL) [3] Wilmington, DE St. Anthony of Padua Church.
Campbell, Peter A. *c.m.* '85 (PH) [B] Philadelphia, PA DePaul Novitiate.
Campbell, Peter E. *m.s.c.* '60 (RCK) [H] Aurora, IL Missionaries of the Sacred Heart Community.
Campbell, Ralph C. *s.j.* '59 (ALN) [A] Wernersville, PA Novitiate of St. Isaac Jogues.
Campbell, Robert *m.s.* '55 (MAN) [K] Enfield, NH Shrine of Our Lady of La Salette.
Campbell, Robert *o.p.* '57 (SD) [1] San Diego, CA St. Joseph Cathedral.
Campbell, Robert *m.s.* '58 (MAN) [M] Enfield, NH La Salette Shrine and Center of Enfield.
Campbell, Robert B. *s.j.* '57 (FgM) Provinces.
Campbell, Robert I. *o.p.* '56 (CHI) [N] River Forest, IL St. Thomas Aquinas Priory.
Campbell, Stephen *s.j.* '85 (MOB) [B] Mobile, AL Spring Hill College.
Campbell, Theodore C. '72 (STP) Golden Valley, MN Good Shepherd Church.
Campbell, Thomas E. '80 (SAV) Retired.
Campbell, Thomas L. *c.s.c.* '48 (FR) [J] North Dartmouth, MA Holy Cross Mission House.
Campbell, Msgr. Thomas P. '17 (BRK) [168] Queens, NY St. Francis of Assisi Church.
Campbell, Msgr. Thomas P. '43 (BRK) Retired.
Campbell, Wayne '86 (OAK) [3] San Leandro, CA St. Felicitas Church.
Campbell, William D. '58 (SCR) [10] Scranton, PA Immaculate Conception Church.
Campbell, William G. '63 (FR) Marion, MA St. Rita's Church.
Campbell, William W. (BO) Retired.
Campechano, Francisco '95 (STO) Newman, CA St. Joachim Church.
Campellone, Joseph G. *o.s.f.s.* '96 (PH) [AA] Philadelphia, PA Father Judge Faculty House.
Campi, Vincent L. '45 (WH) Retired.
Campion, Msgr. John J. '51 (SD) Retired.
Campion, John R. '48 (HBG) Chambersburg, PA Corpus Christi Church; Doylesburg, PA Our Lady of Refuge Mission Church.
Campion, Joseph J. '73 (ALN) Catasauqua, PA St. Lawrence Church.
Campion, Joseph J. *s.s.j.* '91 (LAF) Rayne, LA Shrine of Our Mother of Mercy Church.
Campion, Joseph J. *s.s.j.* '91 (NO) [2] New Orleans, LA All Saints Church.
Campion, Owen F. '66 (NSH) On Duty Outside the Diocese.
Campion, Thomas B. '52 (HRT) Wethersfield, CT Corpus Christi Church; Wethersfield, CT Sacred Heart Church.
Campion, Thomas F. '57 (MAD) [G] Monroe, WI St. Clare Hospital of Monroe, Wisconsin, Inc., dba The Monroe Clinic, Inc.
Campion, William T. '77 (ALN) [2] Mahanoy City, PA St. Canicus Church; [4] Mahanoy City, PA St. Fidelis Church.
Campo, Lance (NO) [D] Metairie, LA Archbishop Chapelle High School.
Campo, Lance J. '93 (NO) [1] Metairie, LA Our Lady of Divine Providence Church.
Campo, Richard W. '85 (ALN) [3] Easton, PA St. Jane Frances de Chantal Church.
Campobello, Mark (RCK) Geneva, IL St. Peter Church.
Campoli, John F. (TR) On Duty Outside the Diocese.
Campoli, Timothy J. '74 (SPR) Greenfield, MA Blessed Sacrament Church.
Campos, George C. '97 (STO) San Andreas, CA St. Andrew Church.
Campos, Miguel *sch.p.* '96 (LA) [R] Los Angeles, CA Piarist Fathers.
Campuzano, J. Eduardo '46 (CAM) Retired.
Camuso, Robert '92 (SEA) [3] Seattle, WA St. Anne Church; [13] Seattle, WA St. Margaret of Scotland Church.
Can, Anselm Dinh Vuong *c.m.c.* '77 (GAL) [Q] New Canen, TX Congregation of the Mother Coredemptrix.
Canaan, Timothy '92 (OG) [2] Plattsburgh, NY St. John the Baptist Church.
Canal, Manuel '58 (MRY) [1] Salinas, CA Christ the King Church.
Canary, John F. '69 (CHI) [A] Mundelein, IL University of St. Mary of the Lake-Mundelein Seminary.
Canas, Eugene *o.m.i.* '64 (FgM) Oblates Foreign Missions.
Canavan, Edward P. *o.s.f.s.* (FgM) Oblates of St. Francis de Sales Foreign Missions.
Canavan, Francis P. *s.j.* '50 (NY) [DD] New York, NY Jesuit Community at Fordham University.
Canavan, Gerald D. '69 (PH) Eddystone, PA St. Rose of Lima Church.
Canavan, John D. (DET) Retired.
Canavan, Joseph T. '70 (BO) [3] Lynn, MA St. Joseph Church.
Canavan, Mark P. '71 (CHI) [2] Cicero, IL St. Frances of Rome Church.
Canavan, Msgr. Martin '68 (PHU) Absent on Leave.
Canavera, Lawrence J. '67 (GB) [14] Green Bay, WI St. Philip the Apostle Church.
Cancro, Francis T. '81 (CHL) Asheville, NC St. Eugene Church.
Candelaria, Ernest *c.s.j.* '58 (LA) Lancaster, CA Blessed Junipero Serra Church.
Candelas, Rafael '59 (SJN) [56] San Juan, PR Sagrado Corazon de Jesus Church.
Candreva, Thomas '63 (RVC) Great Neck, NY St. Aloysius Church.
Cane, Pere '93 (MIL) [5] Kenosha, WI St. Mark Church; [Y] Kenosha, WI St. Mark Latin American Center; [Y] Racine, WI Missionary Community of St. Paul the Apostle and Mary, Mother of the Church, Inc.
Cane-Gombau, Pere '93 (MIL) [5] Kenosha, WI St. Mark Church; Sick Leave.
Canepa, Jorge A. *c.s.c.* '56 (FTW) [J] South Bend, IN Congregation of Holy Cross Indiana Province Provincial House.
Canez, Jorge '79 (PHX) [3] Phoenix, AZ Holy Family Church; [10] Phoenix, AZ St. Edward Confessor Church.
Canfield, Francis E. *s.j.* '67 (TOL) [C] Toledo, OH St. John's Jesuit High School.
Canfield, Msgr. Francis X. '45 (DET) Retired.

Canfield, Joseph '58 (SUP) Retired.
Cangemi, Dominic *s.t.* '44 (BLX) Pearlington, MS St. Joseph Church.
Caniga, Branislav '97 (JOL) [10] Joliet, IL SS. Cyril and Methodius Church.
Canino, Louis *o.f.m.* '69 (CHL) [5] Greensboro, NC St. Pius X Church; [J] Greensboro, NC Franciscan Friary.
Canizares, Dwight '81 (GAL) [2] Spring, TX St. Edward Church.
Canjar, John A. '49 (DEN) Retired.
Cann, Hilarion V. '53 (WH) Retired.
Cann, Leslie '58 (PMB) Hobe Sound, FL St. Christopher Church.
Cann, Luke W. (NY) [C] Poughkeepsie, NY Marist College.
Canna, Joseph '70 (LA) [1] Long Beach, CA St. Anthony Church.
Cannan, Walter F. '68 (SY) Oriskany, NY St. Stephen, Protomartyr Church.
Cannariato, Paul A. '83 (NEW) [12] Jersey City, NJ St. John the Baptist Church.
Canniff, James B. '60 (BO) [46] Boston, MA St. Mary Church.
Canning, John *o.carm.* '55 (NY) [97] New York, NY Our Lady of the Scapular/St. Stephen Church.
Canning, John W. '50 (OG) Retired.
Canning, Wilfred S. *c.s.b.* '55 (GAL) [Q] Houston, TX Dominican Fathers and Brothers, St. Mark Priory, Inc.; [Q] Houston, TX Dillon House.
Cannizzo, Vito *c.s.s.* '43 (BO) [Z] Waltham, MA Stigmatine Fathers and Brothers.
Cannoles, Antonio *c.ss.r.* '69 (FgM) Redemptorist Foreign Missions.
Cannon, Hugh D. '66 (RVC) Plainview, NY St. Pius X Church.
Cannon, James *c.ss.r.* '48 (ALB) Saratoga Springs, NY St. Clement Church.
Cannon, John A. '48 (PH) [G] Holland, PA Villa Joseph Marie High School for Girls; [Y] Holland, PA St. Joseph Home for the Aged; [BB] Holland, PA Villa Joseph Marie.
Cannon, Maro *c.f.a.* '85 (KNX) [C] Signal Mountain, TN Alexian Village Health Care Center; [F] Signal Mountain, TN Alexian Brothers.
Cannon, Michael J. '81 (ORL) Altamonte Springs, FL Annunciation Church.
Cannon, Richard F. '86 (BO) [73] Boston, MA St. Vincent de Paul Church.
Cannon, Richard W. *s.s.c.* '54 (FgM) St. Columban's Foreign Mission.
Cannon, Robert R. '78 (VEN) [2] Venice, FL Our Lady of Lourdes Church.
Cannon, Msgr. Thomas (CAM) Retired.
Cannon, Msgr. Thomas *s.j.* '55 (ORL) De Land, FL St. Peter's Church.
Canny, Michael (SAC) Redding, CA Our Lady of Mercy Church.
Canny, Stephen J. '61 (SR) Cotati, CA St. Joseph Church.
Cano, Emilio '37 (PCE) Retired.
Cano, Nicolas '97 (FgM) American - Cassinese Congregation Foreign Missions.
Canonici, Msgr. Paul '57 (JKS) [A] Jackson, MS St. Joseph Catholic School.
Canterbury, Keith '94 (SAC) Weaverville, CA St. Patrick Church.
Canterna, Charles J. '76 (BAL) [95] Baltimore, MD St. Vincent de Paul Church; Baltimore, MD Maryland Correctional Adjustment Center; Special Assignment.
Cantillon, Joseph '76 (OAK) [5] Fremont, CA St. Leonard Church.
Cantley, Msgr. Michael J. '55 (BRK) [149] Queens, NY St. Anastasia Church.
Cantones, Joel P. '81 (NO) [24] New Orleans, LA St. Andrew the Apostle Church.
Cantore, John *c.m.* '63 (SPC) [C] Cape Girardeau, MO St. Francis' Medical Center.
Cantu, Oscar '94 (GAL) On Duty Outside the Diocese.
Cantwell, Edward '58 (ALB) Glens Falls, NY Hudson Correctional Facility.
Cantwell, Edward F. '58 (ALB) Hudson, NY Church of St. Mary.
Cantwell, James *o.f.m.conv.* '61 (L) [7] Louisville, KY St. Anthony Church.
Cantwell, John '69 (SAC) Citrus Heights, CA Holy Family Church.
Cantwell, Stephen F. *c.m.* '82 (PH) [69] Philadelphia, PA Immaculate Conception Church.
Cantwell, William J. *c.s.p.* '56 (NY) [DD] Jamaica Estates, NY Paulist Fathers Generalate.
Cantwell, William J. *c.s.p.* '56 (PMB) [G] Vero Beach, FL Paulist Fathers Retirement Home.
Canty, Richard J. '85 (SAV) Special Assignment.
Canuel, Paul E. '66 (FR) [2] New Bedford, MA Nuestra Senora de Guadalupe Church; [13] New Bedford, MA St. Hedwig Church; [15] New Bedford, MA St. John the Baptist Church; [M] Fall River, MA Special Apostolates, Department of.
Canzano, Ettore *c.s.s.* '47 (BO) [Z] Waltham, MA Stigmatine Fathers and Brothers.
Canzio, Celestino *o.f.m.* '73 (NY) [DD] New York, NY Franciscan Province of the Immaculate Conception.
Cao, John '89 (HT) On Duty Outside the Diocese.
Cao Phuong Ky, Joseph *s.s.* (SPC) [E] Carthage, MO Congregation of the Mother Co-Redemptrix, United States Assumption Province.
Cao Xuan Canh, Joseph M. *c.m.c.* (SPC) [E] Carthage, MO Congregation of the Mother Co-Redemptrix, United States Assumption Province.
Capacetti, Luis O. '87 (SJN) [5] Guaynabo, PR Maria Madre de la Misericordia Church.
Capacillo, Euben *o.a.r.* '75 (ORG) [5] Santa Ana, CA Our Lady of the Pillar Church.
Capalbo, Kenneth *o.f.m.* '74 (SFD) [B] Quincy, IL Quincy University.
Capato, Justin *o.s.b.* (TR) [P] Neptune, NJ The Upper Room Spiritual Center.
Capato, Justino *o.s.b.* '80 (PAT) [M] Morristown, NJ St. Mary's Abbey.
Capdepon, Federico '83 (MIA) [9] Miami, FL Mother of Our Redeemer Church.
Capdeville, Henri *o.s.b.* '93 (TUC) [F] St. David, AZ Holy Trinity Monastery.
Capece, Juniper *o.f.m.* (WDC) [B] Silver Spring, MD Holy Name College.
Capella, Joseph *s.a.c.* '90 (CAM) [C] Pennsauken, NJ Bishop Eustace Prep School.
Capelle, John J. *s.j.* '47 (NO) [F] New Orleans, LA Jesuit High School.
Capellupo, Frank '75 (BRK) [100] Brooklyn, NY Our Lady of Lourdes Church.
Capewell, Timothy J. '83 (TR) West Windsor, NJ Church of St. David the King.
Capiello, Luis Rios '81 (PCE) [B] Ponce, PR The Pontifical Catholic University of Puerto Rico.
Capik, Msgr. William J. '55 (MET) Basking Ridge, NJ St. James Church.
Capillo, John E. '69 (BRK) [64] Brooklyn, NY Immaculate Heart of Mary Church.
Capitani, Msgr. Anthony L. '46 (TR) Retired.
Capitani, Sylvan P. '64 (HBG) New Freedom, PA St. John the Baptist Church.
Capitolo, Mario L. *s.j.* '59 (SJ) [D] San Jose, CA Bellarmine College Preparatory.
Capitolo, Paul F. *s.j.* '69 (SFR) [E] San Francisco, CA St. Ignatius College Preparatory (Coed); [N] San Francisco, CA Jesuit Community at St. Ignatius College Preparatory.
Capizzi, Simeon *o.f.m.* '53 (SP) [O] St. Petersburg, FL St. Anthony Friary.
Caplice, Richard J. *s.j.* (NEW) [24] Jersey City, NJ Parish of the Resurrection Church.
Caplis, Roger J. '58 (CHI) [112] Chicago, IL St. Juliana Church.
Capo Iriarte, Rafael *sch.p.* '96 (SJN) [58] San Juan, PR Santisimo Salvador Church.
Capo', Msgr. Jaime '49 (SJN) [5] Guaynabo, PR Maria Madre de la Misericordia Church.
Capone, Albert L. '80 (BO) [10] Lowell, MA St. Michael Church.
Caponi, Francis J. *o.s.a.* '89 (PH) [B] Villanova, PA St. Augustine Friary; [AA] Villanova, PA Provincial Offices of the Order of St. Augustine, Province of St. Thomas of Villanova.
Caponi, Jerome '60 (VIC) Retired.
Caporali, Paul M. *s.d.b.* '54 (LA) Bellflower, CA St. Dominic Savio Church.
Caporiccio, Louis *c.p.m.* '97 (OWN) [3] Paducah, KY St. John the Evangelist Church.
Capoverdi, James D., Jr. '97 (PRO) Bristol, RI Our Lady of Mount Carmel Church.
Capozzelli, Anthony M. '73 (E) Retired; [O] Erie, PA Theophilus.
Capozzelli, Msgr. Emmanuel '49 (NEW) Retired.
Cappel, Charles H. *m.m.* '44 (FgM) Maryknoll Foreign Missions.
Cappel, Joseph H. *m.m.* '35 (FgM) Maryknoll Foreign Missions.
Cappelletti, Edward *s.d.b.* '50 (NY) [DD] New Rochelle, NY Salesian Provincial House.
Cappelletti, Joseph '82 (CLV) Lyndhurst, OH St. Clare Church.
Cappelli, Msgr. Angelo J. '48 (STU) Retired.
Cappelloni, David P. '79 (SCR) Muncy, PA Resurrection Church.
Cappelloni, David P. '86 (SCR) Muncy, PA Muncy Prison.
Cappelloni, Thomas A. '76 (SCR) Jackson, PA St. Martin of Tours Church.
Cappiello, Luis Rios '81 (ARE) [4] Arecibo, PR Santa Ana Church.
Cappo, Louis C. '46 (MAR) [1] Marquette, MI St. Peter Cathedral.
Cappucci, Chester *o.m.i.* '63 (GB) Baileys Harbor, WI St. Mary of the Lake Church; Sister Bay, WI St. Rosalia Church.
Cappuccino, Gregory J. '73 (RVC) Valley Stream, NY Blessed Sacrament Church.
Caprio, Albert Augustine *o.p.* '66 (NY) [DD] New York, NY St. Vincent Ferrer Priory.
Caprio, Robert J. *o.f.m.* '63 (BO) [P] Andover, MA Franciscan Center; [W] Andover, MA St. Francis Friary; [Y] Andover, MA Franciscan Center - Retreat House.
Capriolo, Victor R. '71 (MIL) [1] Wauwatosa, WI St. Bernard Church.
Capua, Msgr. Nicholas J. '56 (BRK) [191] Queens, NY St. Luke Church.
Capuci, John M. '90 (BO) Braintree, MA St. Thomas More Church; [D] Braintree, MA Archbishop Williams' High School.
Caputo, Louis *s.d.v.* '67 (NEW) [25] Newark, NJ St. Michael's Church.
Caputo, Ralph J. '75 (BRK) [231] Queens, NY Queen of Peace Church.
Caputo, Salvatore S. *s.s.c.* '76 (FgM) St. Columban's Foreign Mission.
Caraballo, Antonio '81 (ARE) [3] Camuy, PR Our Lady of Asumption Church.
Caraballo, Msgr. Benito '40 (HON) Retired.
Carabello, Francis J. '68 (NO) Gretna, LA St. Joseph Church.
Caracci, Christopher P. '94 (ORL) Altamonte Springs, FL Annunciation Church.
Carajal, Nelson *c.r.* (SP) Sun City Center, FL Prince of Peace Church.
Carapella, Thomas *t.o.r.* '92 (ALT) [A] Loretto, PA St. Francis College; [F] Loretto, PA St. Francis Friary, Third Order Regular of St. Francis of Penance; [H] Hollidaysburg, PA Campus Ministry.
Carathers, Patrick '81 (AMA) [7] Amarillo, TX St. Hyacinth's Church; Vega, TX Immaculate Conception Church.
Carawan, Thomas '77 (P) [A] St. Benedict, OR Mount Angel Seminary.
Carbajales, Ignacio '60 (MIA) On Duty Outside the Archdiocese.
Carberry, Francis J. (WOR) Retired.
Carberry, John '81 (SFD) [2] Quincy, IL St. Boniface Church.
Carbine, Francis A. '62 (PH) [1] Bensalem, PA St. Charles Borromeo Church.
Carbo, Eugene J. '62 (PH) Strafford, PA Our Lady of the Assumption Church.
Carbonaro, Dennis J. '81 (PH) [A] Wynnewood, PA Theological Seminary of St. Charles Borromeo, Overbrook.
Carbone, Angelo *c.s.* '56 (KC) [18] Kansas City, MO Holy Rosary Church.
Carbone, Anthony (GBG) [B] Greensburg, PA Seton Hill College.
Carbone, Joseph M. *o.s.m.* '59 (DEN) [22] Denver, CO Our Lady of Mt. Carmel Church.
Carbone, Roland *o.s.b.* '54 (KC) Parnell, MO St. Joseph's Church.
Carbone, Roland *o.s.b.* '56 (KC) [A] Conception, MO Conception Seminary College.
Carbone, Vito J. '62 (PH) [120] Philadelphia, PA Our Lady of Loreto Church.
Carbonneau, Robert *c.p.* '78 (CHI) [N] Chicago, IL Passionist Community-CTU.
Carboy, Daniel J. *c.ss.r.* '66 (CHL) Concord, NC St. James Church.
Carcerano, Michael J. '76 (LA) Simi Valley, CA St. Rose of Lima Church.
Carchidi, Rudolph V. *c.s.c.* '55 (FR) [A] North Easton, MA Stonehill College; [A] North Easton, MA Holy Cross Fathers Religious.
Carcich, G. John '45 (R) Retired.
Cardelli, Daniel E. '57 (OAK) Danville, CA St. Isidore's Church; [S] Oakland, CA Italian Catholic Federation.
Carden, Robert F. '56 (PBL) Vineland, CO St. Therese Church.
Carden, Robert J. '57 (NY) Absent on Leave.
Carden, Robert J. '57 (PBL) [12] Pueblo, CO St. Joseph Church.
Cardenas, David J. '61 (GAL) [72] Houston, TX Resurrection Church.
Cardenas, Eugenio *m.sp.s.* '82 (LA) Huntington Park, CA St. Martha Church.
Cardenas, Marco *c.m.f.* '91 (CHI) [166] Chicago, IL St. Paul Church.
Cardenas, Mario '94 (SAT) [62] San Antonio, TX St. Philip of Jesus Church.
Cardente, Edward S. '74 (PRO) [1] North Providence, RI St. Anthony Church.
Cardenzana, Philip A. '65 (DAV) Newton, IA Sacred Heart Church.
Cardiff, Msgr. John I. '45 (CHI) [4] Oak Lawn, IL St. Linus Church; Retired.
Cardillo, Clement *s.d.b.* (NEW) [N] South Orange, NJ The Salesian Community.
Cardinal, Maurice '50 (SB) Apple Valley, CA Our Lady of the Desert Church.
Cardinali, Fred '38 (FTW) Retired.
Cardona, George '53 (MIA) [5] Hialeah, FL St. John the Apostle Church; Retired.
Cardona, Jorge (CGS) Barranquitas, PR Church of St. Anthony of Padua.
Cardone, Christopher *o.p.* '86 (FgM) Dominican - Order of Preachers Foreign Missions.

Cardone, Joseph P. '87 (TOL) Sylvania, OH St. Joseph Church.
Cardone, Thomas A. *s.m.* '85 (RVC) [D] Uniondale, NY Kellenberg Memorial High School; [N] Mineola, NY Provincial Residence and Novitiate.
Cardoni, Albert A. *s.j.* '60 (BGP) [A] Fairfield, CT Fairfield University; [O] Fairfield, CT The Fairfield Jesuit Community-Fairfield University.
Cardoso, Luis A. '58 (FR) [18] Fall River, MA St. Michael's Church.
Cardoso, Reinaldo M. '60 (PRO) [1] West Warwick, RI St. Anthony Church.
Cardoza, Timothy N. '83 (FRS) Tulare, CA St. Rita Church.
Cardy, William E. *o.f.m.* '72 (FBK) Aniak, AK St. Theresa Church; Holy Cross, AK Holy Cross Church.
Cardy, William E. *o.f.m.* '72 (FgM) Franciscan Foreign Missions.
Carek, Peter P. '60 (MIL) [4] Wauwatosa, WI St. Jude the Apostle Church.
Carelli, Msgr. Richard J. '53 (WOR) Retired.
Carew, Lawrence F. '66 (BGP) [1] Trumbull, CT Christ the King Church.
Carey, Brian *c.s.sp.* '58 (STA) [3] Jacksonville, FL Christ the King Church.
Carey, Charles M. *c.s.c.* '35 (FTW) [B] Notre Dame, IN University of Notre Dame Du Lac; [J] Notre Dame, IN Holy Cross Community, Corby Hall, University of Notre Dame.
Carey, David M. '62 (BAL) Special Assignment; [N] Baltimore, MD The School Sisters of Notre Dame in the City of Baltimore (Baltimore Prov.).
Carey, Donald D. '96 (STL) [5] St. Charles, MO St. Peter Church.
Carey, J. Peter *s.j.* '64 (IND) [D] Indianapolis, IN Brebeuf Jesuit Preparatory School, Inc.
Carey, James H. '66 (SY) [14] Syracuse, NY St. Charles Church.
Carey, John *o.f.m.cap.* '53 (GBG) Export, PA St. Mary Church.
Carey, Joseph H. *c.s.c.* '69 (FTW) [J] South Bend, IN Congregation of Holy Cross Indiana Province Provincial House.
Carey, Msgr. Leo P. '51 (PAT) Retired; [P] Chester, NJ Nazareth Village.
Carey, Michael (OAK) [N] Oakland, CA Dominican Order, Siena House.
Carey, Michael *o.p.* '77 (OAK) [B] Moraga, CA St. Mary's College; [N] Moraga, CA Dominican Community.
Carey, Paul J. '42 (PH) New Hope, PA St. Martin of Tours Church; Retired.
Carey, Paul V. '71 (SY) Pompey, NY Immaculate Conception Church.
Carey, Raymond '70 (P) Special Assignment.
Carey, Richard '55 (LA) Pomona, CA St. Joseph Church.
Carey, Richard T. '65 (WOR) North Brookfield, MA St. Joseph's Church.
Carey, Robert *c.s.v.* '57 (SJ) San Jose, CA O'Connor Hospital.
Carey, Robert H. *c.s.v.* '58 (CHI) [N] Arlington Heights, IL Viatorian Province Center-Clerics of St. Viator.
Carey, Stephen '62 (CAM) Sea Isle City, NJ St. Joseph's Church.
Carey, Thomas *s.m.* '49 (CLV) [N] Cleveland, OH Sts. Mary and Joseph Home for the Aged.
Carey, Msgr. Thomas '49 (NEW) Retired; Retired.
Carey, Thomas F. '37 (PIT) Whitehall, PA St. Gabriel of the Sorrowful Virgin Church; Allegheny County, PA Mt. Lebanon Manor Convalescent Center; Allegheny County, PA Southwestern Nursing and Rehabilitation Center; Allegheny County, PA Manorcare Health Services; Retired.
Carey, Thomas G. *s.m.* '49 (WDC) [M] Washington, DC Marist Provincial House.
Carey, Thomas P. '34 (IND) Retired.
Carey, William F. '67 (BGP) Military Chaplains.
Carey, William G. '81 (BGP) [3] Stamford, CT St. Cecilia's Church.
Carey, William H. '59 (SHP) Many, LA St. John the Baptist Church.
Carey, Msgr. William J. (PRO) [2] Newport, RI Jesus Saviour Church.
Carey, Msgr. William J. '43 (PRO) Retired.
Carfagna, Frank A. '67 (Y) [8] Canton, OH St. Joseph's Church.
Carges, Bernard L. (ROC) Groton, NY St. Anthony Church.
Cargill, Msgr. Eugene '59 (GAL) League City, TX St. Mary Church.
Cargo, Thomas H. *c.m.* '78 (LA) [95] Los Angeles, CA St. Vincent De Paul Church.
Caridi, Michael A. '94 (PIT) Monroeville, PA St. Bernadette Church.
Carie, Giles *o.f.m.conv.* '61 (ELP) [17] El Paso, TX Our Lady of Mt. Carmel Church.
Cariglio, Msgr. Michael J. '70 (Y) [6] Youngstown, OH Our Lady of Mt. Carmel Church.
Carignan, Armand *o.m.i.* '53 (FgM) Oblates Foreign Missions.
Carignan, Raymond P. *s.s.j.* '61 (LAF) Crowley, LA St. Theresa Church.
Carignan, Ronald *o.m.i.* '59 (BEL) [F] Belleville, IL Missionary Oblates of Mary Immaculate - St. Henry's Oblate Residence.
Carillo, J.M. *m.c.c.j.* '40 (NEW) [N] Montclair, NJ Comboni Missionaries of the Heart of Jesus (Verona Fathers).
Carina, Chester H. '85 (MET) Bernardsville, NJ Our Lady of Perpetual Help Church; [K] Bernardsville, NJ Sacred Heart Chapel.
Carini, James P. '65 (NOR) Tolland, CT St. Matthew Church.
Carkenord, David '62 (FTW) Waterloo, IN St. Michael the Archangel Church.
Carkhuff, Thomas *o.s.c.* '76 (STP) [N] Shoreview, MN Crosier Community of Shoreview.
Carles, Alexander J. '88 (MET) Clinton, NJ Immaculate Conception Church.
Carleton, Robert J. *m.m.* '64 (NY) [DD] Maryknoll, NY Maryknoll Fathers and Brothers.
Carley, Edward B. '48 (WIL) Retired.
Carlin, Bernie *c.ss.r.* '78 (GR) [3] Grand Rapids, MI St. Alphonsus Church.
Carlin, George *s.o.l.t.* '84 (CC) [H] Robstown, TX Society of Our Lady of the Most Holy Trinity.
Carlin, Harry V. *s.j.* '48 (SFR) [E] San Francisco, CA St. Ignatius College Preparatory (Coed); [N] San Francisco, CA Jesuit Community at St. Ignatius College Preparatory.
Carlin, Msgr. John A. '39 (NY) [16] Yonkers, NY St. Peter Church; Retired.
Carlin, John T. '76 (CLV) [3] Parma, OH St. Charles Borromeo Church.
Carlin, Thomas F. *s.j.* '76 (FBK) St. Michael, AK St. Michael Church; Stebbins, AK St. Bernard Church; Unalakleet, AK Church of the Holy Angels; [E] St. Marys, AK Brother Joe Prince Jesuit Community.
Carlin, Warren *o.carm.* '58 (JOL) [J] Darien, IL Carmelite Provincial Office.
Carlino, Richard A. '79 (ALB) [13] Schenectady, NY Our Lady of the Assumption Church.
Carlo, Joseph C. '63 (BUF) [1] Niagara Falls, NY St. Charles Church.
Carlo, Raymond (RVC) Priests Released from Diocesan Assignment.
Carlo, Raymond J. '87 (STA) [1] Jacksonville, FL Assumption Church.
Carlone, Carmen A. '69 (CAM) Williamstown, NJ St. Mary's Church.
Carlos, Joseph '75 (STL) [P] St. Louis, MO Franciscan Friary of St. Anthony of Padua.
Carlos, Miguel '95 (LAN) [4] Jackson, MI Queen of the Miraculous Medal Church.
Carlsen, Jeffrey '72 (BAL) Jessup, MD Maryland House of Correction & Annex; Special Assignment.
Carlson, Curtis *o.f.m.cap.* (SAL) Hays, KS St. Joseph's Church.
Carlson, Curtis *o.f.m.cap.* '95 (SAL) [D] Hays, KS St. Joseph's Friary; [G] Hays, KS Comeau Catholic Campus Center at Fort Hays State University.
Carlson, Edward A. '83 (CHI) [52] Chicago, IL St. Edward Church.
Carlson, George F. '66 (BO) [10] Lawrence, MA St. Patrick Church.
Carlson, Gerald J. '97 (GI) Greeley, NE Sacred Heart Church.
Carlson, Gregory I. *s.j.* '74 (OM) [K] Omaha, NE Jesuit Community At Creighton University.
Carlson, J. Arnold '48 (AMA) Retired; [D] Panhandle, TX St. Joseph's Home for Retired Priests.
Carlson, James R. '73 (SAG) Munger, MI St. Norbert Church; Reese, MI St. Elizabeth Church.
Carlson, Richard D. '69 (NEW) Hillside, NJ Christ the King Church.
Carlson, Robert D. '63 (GAL) Galena Park, TX Our Lady of Fatima Church.
Carlson, Steven '96 (R) Clinton, NC Immaculate Conception Church.
Carlton, Maurice T. '68 (MET) South River, NJ Corpus Christi Church; [G] Somerset, NJ McCarrick Care Center.
Carlucci, F. Antonio *r.c.j.* '78 (LA) [R] Camarillo, CA Rogationist Fathers.
Carmichael, Eugene J. *s.j.* '73 (CIN) [M] Cincinnati, OH Jesuit Community at Xavier Unversity.
Carmichael, John F. '97 (BO) [7] Lynn, MA St. Pius Fifth Church.
Carmody, Emeric *o.carm.* '54 (NEW) Teaneck, NJ St. Anastasia's Church.
Carmody, Francis R. *s.j.* '55 (BAL) [M] Baltimore, MD Jesuit Fathers and Brothers Maryland Provincial Curia; [M] Baltimore, MD Ferdinand Wheeler Jesuit Community; [Q] Baltimore, MD Jesuit Mission Bureau, Maryland Province, Inc.; [Q] Baltimore, MD Jesuit Seminary Guild, Maryland Province, Inc.
Carmody, James '63 (RVC) Hicksville, NY St. Ignatius Loyola Church.
Carmody, James F. '70 (WOR) [17] Worcester, MA St. Andrew the Apostle Church.
Carmody, Lawrence W. '90 (COS) [2] Colorado Springs, CO Corpus Christi Church.
Carmody, Michael J. '83 (GAL) [71] Houston, TX Queen of Peace Church.
Carmody, Stephen F. *o.p.* '81 (PH) [61] Philadelphia, PA Holy Name of Jesus Church; [AA] Philadelphia, PA Holy Name Priory, Dominican Friars.
Carmola, Michael J. '64 (SY) Special Assignment; [U] Syracuse, NY Christ the King Retreat House.
Carmon, Dominic *s.v.d.* '60 (NO) [3] Kenner, LA St. Elizabeth Ann Seton Church.
Carmona, Edwardo (SB) [E] Riverside, CA Operarios Del Reino De Cristo, O.R.C.
Carmona, Henry (B) Rupert, ID St. Nicholas Church.
Carmona, Henry '78 (B) Rupert, ID St. Nicholas Church.
Carmona, Hugo '85 (PRO) [26] Providence, RI Our Lady of Mt. Carmel Church.
Carmone, Anthony F. '47 (PRO) Retired.
Carnago, William J. '88 (DET) [35] Detroit, MI Immaculate Heart of Mary Church; Special Assignment.
Carne, Joseph D. '71 (MAR) Bessemer, MI St. Sebastian Church.
Carneiro, Denis '68 (CHI) [161] Chicago, IL Our Lady of Victory Church; [J] Chicago, IL St. Mary of Nazareth Hospital Center.
Carnes, Matthew E. *s.j.* (SJ) [D] San Jose, CA Bellarmine College Preparatory.
Carnevale, John *o.f.m.* '66 (PAT) Pompton Lakes, NJ Our Lady of the Assumption Church.
Carnevale, Thomas J. '61 (PRO) Retired.
Carney, Aloysius S. '60 (NEW) Plainfield, NJ St. Mary Church; Plainfield, NJ Muhlenberg Medical Center.
Carney, Angus N. *o.s.a.* '43 (PH) [AA] Villanova, PA St. Thomas Monastery.
Carney, Christopher M. '71 (BAL) [63] Baltimore, MD St. Michael Church.
Carney, Edward '63 (PEO) Special Residence.
Carney, J. Michael '70 (SY) Clark Mills, NY Church of the Annunciation.
Carney, James R. *s.j.* '56 (NY) [F] New York, NY Regis High School; [DD] New York, NY St. Ignatius Loyola Residence.
Carney, John '70 (BAL) Retired.
Carney, John F. '91 (SFE) Tijeras, NM Holy Child Church.
Carney, John J. *c.m.* '82 (FgM) Vincentian Foreign Missions.
Carney, Joseph T. '68 (MIA) Miami Springs, FL Blessed Trinity Church.
Carney, Msgr. Patrick J. '55 (NY) [28] New York, NY Corpus Christi Church.
Carney, Ralph *o.f.m.* '53 (SEA) [4] Tacoma, WA St. John Bosco Church.
Carney, Richard F. '55 (KC) [33] Kansas City, MO Our Lady of Sorrows Church.
Carney, Robert *s.a.c.* '66 (MIL) [P] Milwaukee, WI St. Vincent Community.
Carney, Robert E. '91 (TUC) Douglas, AZ St. Luke Church; Pirtleville, AZ St. Bernard's Church.
Carney, Robert V. *s.a.c.* '66 (MIL) [D] Milwaukee, WI Pius XI High School; [P] Milwaukee, WI Pallotti House; [Y] Milwaukee, WI Pallottine Fathers and Brothers, Inc., Disability Trust; [Y] Milwaukee, WI Pallottine Fathers and Brothers, Inc., Educational and Apostolic Ministry Trust.
Carney, Thomas *m.s.c.* (Y) [A] Youngstown, OH Sacred Heart Retreat House & Renewal Center.
Carney, Thomas A. *m.s.c.* (Y) [20] Youngstown, OH St. Rose of Lima Church.
Carnicelli, Xavier *o.f.m.* '57 (NY) [DD] New York, NY Franciscan Province of the Immaculate Conception.
Caro, Ernesto '90 (CIN) [14] Dayton, OH Holy Family Church.
Caro, Jorge '89 (MGZ) Lajas, PR De la Merced Parish.
Caro, Robert V. *s.j.* '70 (LA) [C] Los Angeles, CA Loyola Marymount University.
Carod, Rogelio '35 (SJN) [17] San Juan, PR Francisca Javiera Cabrini Church.
Carola, Joseph A. *s.j.* '93 (NO) [P] New Orleans, LA Jesuit Provincial Office.
Carolan, Charles B. '55 (VIC) Flatonia, TX Sacred Heart Church.
Carolan, Craig '91 (BWN) [1] Harlingen, TX Our Lady of the Assumption Church; [2] Harlingen, TX Immaculate Heart of Mary Church.
Carolan, Emmit '62 (SAT) [41] San Antonio, TX St. James the Apostle Church.
Carolan, J. Lawrence '69 (SR) Calistoga, CA Our Lady of Perpetual Help Church.
Carolan, John J. '51 (CHI) [2] Oak Park, IL St. Catherine of Siena-St. Lucy Church; Retired.
Carolan, Thomas *o.f.m.* '58 (CLV) Warrensville Heights, OH St. Jude Church; [P] Cleveland, OH St. Jude Friary.
Carolin, Joeseph C. '66 (HBG) South Mountain, PA Restoration Center.
Carolin, William, J. '45 (LAN) Retired.
Carolin, William J. '45 (LAN) Brighton, MI St. Patrick Church.
Caroluzza, Msgr. Thomas J. '58 (RIC) [5] Virginia Beach, VA Holy Spirit Church.

Caron, Antonin R. '69 (PRT) Sabbatical.
Caron, David '89 (SPR) Graduate Studies.
Caron, Eduardo *c.s.sp.* '57 (SJN) [F] Dorado, PR Santuario del Espiritu Santo.
Caron, Gerard *s.m.* '54 (BO) [W] Boston, MA Marist Fathers Lourdes Residence; [BB] Boston, MA Chapel of Our Lady of Lourdes.
Caron, Gerard J. '94 (PRO) [1] Woonsocket, RI St. Agatha Church; [10] Woonsocket, RI Precious Blood Church.
Caron, Marc B. '89 (PRT) Special or Other Diocesan Assignment.
Caron, Paul A. '83 (FR) Acushnet, MA St. Francis Xavier's Church.
Caronan, John E. *o.praem.* '94 (ORG) [A] Silverado, CA St. Michael's Norbertine Postulancy, Novitiate and Juniorate; [H] Silverado, CA Norbertine Fathers of Orange Inc.
Carosella, Jerome A. '63 (VEN) Boca Grande, FL Our Lady of Mercy Church.
Carota, Peter '97 (STO) [4] Stockton, CA St. George Church.
Carotenuto, Anthony M. '68 (TR) New Egypt, NJ Assumption Church.
Carpena, Octavio R. '84 (MET) On Duty Outside the Diocese.
Carpender, John W. '53 (DUB) Monti, IA St. Patrick's Church; Ryan, IA St. Patrick's Church.
Carpender, Thomas J. '48 (DUB) Retired.
Carpenter, Christopher '95 (PHX) [2] Mesa, AZ Christ the King Church.
Carpenter, Edward C. '95 (ELP) [32] El Paso, TX St. Stephen, Deacon and Martyr Church.
Carpenter, Edward V. '43 (SC) Retired.
Carpenter, Ralph *c.s.p.* '44 (SFR) [K] San Francisco, CA Home for the Aged of the Little Sisters of the Poor.
Carpenter, Ralph T. *c.s.p.* '44 (NY) [DD] Jamaica Estates, NY Paulist Fathers Generalate.
Carpenter, William L. *c.s.v.* '77 (CHI) [210] Chicago, IL St. Viator Church.
Carpentier, Normand E. '71 (PRT) Old Orchard Beach, ME St. Margaret's Church.
Carpentier, Robert A. '67 (PRO) Absent on Leave.
Carpine, Eric *o.f.m.* '75 (NY) [35] New York, NY St. Francis of Assisi Church.
Carqueijo Se, Luiz Antonio *o.s.b.* '92 (GBG) [H] Latrobe, PA Saint Vincent Archabbey.
Carr, Alton T. *c.ss.r.* '50 (GAL) [34] Houston, TX Holy Ghost Church.
Carr, Andrew *c.ss.r.* '92 (BAL) [62] Baltimore, MD St. Michael Church.
Carr, Bernard '76 (LFT) On Duty Outside the Diocese.
Carr, Bernard J. '76 (SB) Anza, CA Sacred Heart Church.
Carr, Brendan T. '72 (BAL) Glen Burnie, MD Crucifixion, Church of the.
Carr, Charles T. '80 (BGP) Leave of Absence.
Carr, Cornelius *s.j.* (GB) [M] Oshkosh, WI Jesuit Retreat House.
Carr, David '80 (PMB) [B] West Palm Beach, FL Cardinal Newman High School.
Carr, David W. '80 (WOR) On Duty Outside the Diocese.
Carr, Ephrem *o.s.b.* '67 (IND) [J] St. Meinrad, IN St. Meinrad Archabbey.
Carr, Eugene R. '63 (SCR) [13] Scranton, PA St. John the Evangelist Church.
Carr, Gary M. '82 (SPC) On Duty Outside the Diocese.
Carr, Gerald F. *o.f.m.* '56 (NY) [35] New York, NY St. Francis of Assisi Church.
Carr, Msgr. James A. (CAM) Retired.
Carr, James M. '34 (ALN) Retired.
Carr, James P. *s.j.* '92 (BO) [E] Boston, MA Boston College High School & Jesuit Community.
Carr, James V. '69 (RIC) Portsmouth, VA Church of the Resurrection.
Carr, John A. *c.s.p.* '40 (NY) [DD] Jamaica Estates, NY Paulist Fathers Generalate.
Carr, John A. *c.s.p.* '40 (SFR) [31] San Francisco, CA Old St. Mary's Cathedral.
Carr, John F. '47 (BO) Retired.
Carr, Mark V. (BO) Retired.
Carr, Martin P. '74 (GB) Special Assignment.
Carr, Michael '68 (CHY) [3] Cheyenne, WY St. Joseph's Church.
Carr, Paul *f.s.s.p.* '92 (SCR) [E] Moscow, PA St. Gregory's Academy.
Carr, Paul S. *f.s.s.p.* '92 (SCR) [M] Elmhurst, PA Priestly Fraternity of St. Peter (F.S.S.P.), North American District Headquarters.
Carr, Peter *o.f.m.* '39 (SP) [O] St. Petersburg, FL St. Anthony Friary.
Carr, Raymond *s.m.* '63 (NO) [9] New Orleans, LA Holy Name Of Mary (Algiers) Church.
Carr, Robert J. '93 (BO) [2] Chelsea, MA St. Rose of Lima Church.
Carr, Walter F. '92 (AUS) Andice, TX Santa Rosa Church; Georgetown, TX St. Helen's Church.
Carr, William F. *s.j.* '56 (BGP) [A] Fairfield, CT Fairfield University; [O] Fairfield, CT The Fairfield Jesuit Community-Fairfield University.
Carr, William H. '69 (RIC) Williamsburg, VA St. Bede's Church.
Carr, William M. '59 (WCH) [1] Wichita, KS Cathedral of the Immaculate Conception.
Carranco, Juan '50 (SJ) San Jose, CA Santa Clara County Jail.
Carrano, Michael A. '70 (BRK) [12] Brooklyn, NY Assumption of the Blessed Virgin Mary Church; [E] Brooklyn, NY Office of Religious Education: Evangelization and Catholic Formation.
Carranza, Fernando '95 (NEW) [1] Newark, NJ Cathedral Basilica of the Sacred Heart Church.
Carranza, Riz. J. '80 (LA) Carson, CA St. Philomena Church.
Carrara, Christopher C. '94 (OG) Carthage, NY St. James Minor Church; Deferiet, NY St. Rita Church.
Carraro, Francesco '95 (NEW) Bergenfield, NJ St. John the Evangelist Church.
Carreira, Emmanuel M. *s.j.* '60 (CLV) [C] Cleveland, OH John Carroll Jesuit Community.
Carreiro, Walter A. (BO) [1] Cambridge, MA St. Anthony Church.
Carrella, Eugene J. '84 (NY) Crestwood, NY Church of the Annunciation.
Carreon, Albert S. '51 (GAL) Retired.
Carreras, Carlos *s.j.* '76 (ATL) [4] Atlanta, GA Immaculate Heart of Mary Church.
Carrero, Angel Dario (SJN) [A] Bayamon, PR Bayamon Central University.
Carrero, Dario *o.f.m.* '95 (SJN) [4] Toa Baja, PR Jose Obrero Church.
Carrico, Rui M. '87 (HRT) [4] Hartford, CT Our Lady of Fatima Church.
Carrier, Herve G. '47 (PRT) Retired.
Carrier, J. Victor '69 (SPR) [4] Chicopee, MA St. Anne's Church.
Carrier, Joseph S. '33 (PRT) Retired.
Carrier, Michael J. '95 (WIL) Elkton, MD Immaculate Conception Church.
Carrier, Paul E. *s.j.* '77 (BGP) [A] Fairfield, CT Fairfield University; [O] Fairfield, CT The Fairfield Jesuit Community-Fairfield University; [V] Fairfield, CT Newman Centers - Campus Ministry.
Carriere, David *o.f.m.* '63 (LA) [R] Santa Barbara, CA Franciscan Friary, Order of Friars Minor (Old Mission).
Carriere, Henry G. '46 (CR) Retired.
Carrieri, Leonard *m.ss.cc.* '36 (CAM) [M] Linwood, NJ Villa Pieta.
Carriero, John P. *s.j.* '63 (ROC) [B] Rochester, NY McQuaid Jesuit High School.
Carrigan, Fred (NY) Manhattan, NY Columbia Presbyterian Medical Center.
Carrigan, Fredrick '61 (PRT) On Duty Outside the Diocese.
Carrigan, John T. *o.p.* '38 (SPR) [J] West Springfield, MA Monastery of the Mother of God, Dominican Nuns (Contemplative).
Carrigan, Thomas '60 (SAC) Westwood, CA Our Lady of the Snows Church.
Carrigg, George A. '57 (BO) [19] Boston, MA St. Christopher Church.
Carrigg, William J. '56 (BO) On Duty Outside the Archdiocese.
Carrigg, William J. '56 (PRT) Fort Fairfield, ME St. Denis Church; Limestone, ME St. Louis Church.
Carrillo, Arhtur *c.p.* '70 (CHI) [N] Chicago, IL Passionist Provincial Office.
Carrillo, Msgr. Arsenio S. *v.g.* '56 (TUC) [1] Tucson, AZ St. Augustine's Cathedral; Special Assignment.
Carrillo, Ron *s.f.* '74 (SFE) Santa Cruz, NM Holy Cross Church.
Carrillo, Sergio '82 (MIA) [3] Miami, FL Corpus Christi Church.
Carrillo, Victor '87 (SAT) Floresville, TX Sacred Heart Church.
Carrington, Richard J. '76 (NEW) [1] Hoboken, NJ Our Lady of Grace Church.
Carrion, Jose A. *o.f.m.cap.* '92 (ARE) [1] Utuado, PR San Miquel Church.
Carrion, Michael W. '77 (BAL) [24] Baltimore, MD St. Clare Church.
Carrion, Patrick '82 (BAL) Special Assignment.
Carrion-Parroco, Jose Antonio '77 (SJN) [1] Toa Alta, PR San Esteban, Protomartir Church.
Carrol, Joseph '55 (HON) Retired.
Carrol, Joseph C. '55 (HON) Waihee, HI St. Ann Church.
Carrola, Rudolph T., Jr. '88 (SAT) Macdona, TX Our Lady Queen of Heaven Church; Von Ormy, TX Sacred Heart Church.
Carroll, Msgr. Aidan M. '63 (LA) Valinda, CA St. Martha Church; [D] La Puente, CA Bishop Amat Memorial High School.
Carroll, Alban *s.a.* (R) Apex, NC St. Andrew the Apostle Church.
Carroll, Brian '62 (JKS) Brandon, MS St. Paul Church.
Carroll, Brian *o.f.m.* '86 (NY) [35] New York, NY St. Francis of Assisi Church.
Carroll, Msgr. Daniel '37 (CHY) Retired.
Carroll, Daniel *s.d.s.* '44 (MIL) [N] Milwaukee, WI St. Mary's Nursing Home.
Carroll, Daniel *o.carm.* '60 (CHI) [D] Chicago, IL Mt. Carmel High School; [N] Chicago, IL Carmelite Priory of St. Cyril.
Carroll, Msgr. Donald M. '34 (CHI) Retired.
Carroll, Eamon R. *o.carm.* '46 (CHI) [N] Chicago, IL Brandsma House.
Carroll, Edmund F. *t.o.r.* '57 (FgM) T.O.R. Foreign Missions.
Carroll, Edmund F. *t.o.r.* '57 (PIT) [O] Pittsburgh, PA Franciscan Friars, T.O.R.; [O] Pittsburgh, PA Third Order Regular of Saint Francis - Province of the Most Sacred Heart of Jesus.
Carroll, Edward E. '50 (MIL) Retired.
Carroll, Edward G. '67 (BO) [2] Woburn, MA St. Barbara Church.
Carroll, Emmett *o.f.m. conv.* '54 (TR) Seaside Heights, NJ Our Lady of Perpetual Help Church.
Carroll, Emmett H. *s.j.* '62 (SEA) [A] Seattle, WA Seattle University.
Carroll, Francis *o.f.m.* '36 (PAT) [M] Ringwood, NJ Holy Name Friary, Inc.
Carroll, Francis B. *o.f.m.* '36 (BO) [Z] Boston, MA Saint Anthony Residence.
Carroll, Francis P. *s.s.c.* '62 (FgM) St. Columban's Foreign Mission.
Carroll, George A. *s.j.* '58 (SD) Jacumba, CA St. Mary Magdalene Church.
Carroll, Gilbert A. '41 (CHI) [207] Chicago, IL St. Timothy Church; Retired.
Carroll, Howard '54 (SFS) Retired; [I] Sioux Falls, SD The Berakkah House.
Carroll, J. Alfred *s.j.* '59 (SPK) [C] Spokane, WA Gonzaga University.
Carroll, Msgr. James '45 (COL) Retired.
Carroll, James '49 (JKS) Shelby, MS St. Mary Church; Parchman, MS Mississippi State Penitentiary.
Carroll, James *o.f.m.* '79 (PHU) [E] Sybertsville, PA Holy Dormition Monastery.
Carroll, James *o.f.m.* '79 (PSC) [A] Sybertsville, PA Holy Dormition Monastery.
Carroll, James J. '56 (NEW) Fairview, NJ St. John the Baptist Church.
Carroll, James M. '68 (BO) [6] Haverhill, MA St. Rita Church.
Carroll, John *t.o.r.* '38 (WDC) [M] Washington, DC St. Louis Friary.
Carroll, John A. *s.s.j.* '66 (WDC) [B] Washington, DC St. Joseph's Seminary.
Carroll, John J. *s.j.* '55 (FgM) Provinces.
Carroll, Msgr. John J. '66 (PAT) Kinnelon, NJ Our Lady of the Magnificat Church.
Carroll, Msgr. John P. '42 (BO) Retired.
Carroll, John P. '53 (BO) [6] Quincy, MA Most Blessed Sacrament Church.
Carroll, John R. (BO) Boston, MA Beth Israel Deaconess Medical Center, East Campus (Beth Israel).
Carroll, Joseph *s.j.* '42 (OAK) [17] Oakland, CA St. Mary, Immaculate Conception-St. Francis de Sales Church.
Carroll, Msgr. Joseph A. '74 (SD) [35] San Diego, CA St. Rita Church; [J] San Diego, CA St. Vincent de Paul Management Inc.; [N] San Diego, CA Catholic Committee on Scouting.
Carroll, Joseph D. '41 (ALN) Retired; [J] Bethlehem, PA Holy Family Villa.
Carroll, Joseph P. *s.j.* '41 (OAK) [N] Berkeley, CA Jesuit Community at Jesuit School of Theology at Berkeley.
Carroll, L. Patrick *s.j.* '67 (SPK) [6] Spokane, WA St. Aloysius Church.
Carroll, Lawrence J. '81 (BGP) [2] Stratford, CT St. James Church.
Carroll, Maurice E. '56 (NY) [122] New York, NY St. Vincent de Paul Church.
Carroll, Michael '67 (LA) Temple City, CA St. Luke the Evangelist Church.
Carroll, Michael '72 (SAC) [7] Sacramento, CA Presentation of the Blessed Virgin Mary Church.
Carroll, Michael A. '85 (RVC) East Rockaway, NY St. Raymond's Church.
Carroll, Michael J. *c.m.* (BRK) [D] Staten Island, NY St. John's University, Staten Island Campus; [D] Jamaica, NY St. John's University.
Carroll, Msgr. Michael J. '61 (PH) Rydal, PA St. Hilary of Poitiers Church.
Carroll, Michael J. *c.m.* '77 (BRK) [U] Jamaica, NY Vincentian Residence.
Carroll, Michael R. '70 (GB) Marion, WI St. Mary Church; Tigerton, WI St. Anthony Church.
Carroll, Norman P. '93 (WIL) Liftwood, DE Immaculate Heart of Mary Church.
Carroll, Owen '73 (NTN) Oakland, CA St. John The Theologian Church.
Carroll, Owen '73 (OAK) [A] Berkeley, CA Dominican School of Philosophy and Theology; [B] Moraga, CA St. Mary's College.
Carroll, Patrick *c.s.sp.* '66 (STA) Elkton, FL St. Ambrose Church.
Carroll, Patrick A. '43 (OM) Retired.
Carroll, Patrick A. *s.j.* '66 (YAK) [4] Yakima, WA St. Joseph's Church.

Carroll, Patrick J. '53 (NY) [88] New York, NY Our Lady of Loreto Church.
Carroll, Patrick J. '54 (ORL) Barefoot Bay, FL St. Luke Church.
Carroll, Patrick M. '71 (NY) [10] Yonkers, NY St. Joseph Church; [E] White Plains, NY Archbishop Stepinac High School.
Carroll, Msgr. Ralph E. '58 (NO) [7] Metairie, LA St. Clement of Rome Church.
Carroll, Msgr. Richard L. '59 (NO) [4] Slidell, LA St. Margaret Mary Church; Slidell, LA Greenbriar Nursing & Convalescent Home; Slidell, LA Guest House of Slidell Nursing Home; Slidell, LA Greenery Neurologic Rehabilitation Center at Slidell.
Carroll, Robert *o.carm.* '71 (CHI) [D] Mundelein, IL Carmel High School; [N] Mundelein, IL Carmelite Monastery.
Carroll, Msgr. Robert B. '63 (PAT) [1] Passaic, NJ St. Nicholas Church.
Carroll, Robert J. '75 (PH) [A] Wynnewood, PA Theological Seminary of St. Charles Borromeo, Overbrook.
Carroll, Roger F. '63 (STP) [14] St. Paul, MN St. Andrew Church.
Carroll, Thomas F. *o.p.* '58 (CIN) [30] Cincinnati, OH St. Gertrude Church; [M] Cincinnati, OH St. Gertrude Priory.
Carroll, Thomas J. *m.s.* '54 (ATL) Snellville, GA St. Oliver Plunkett Church.
Carroll, Thomas J. *s.j.* '84 (LA) [F] Los Angeles, CA Loyola High School.
Carroll, Thomas R. *sch.p.* '70 (LEX) [B] Martin, KY The Piarist School; [G] Prestonsburg, KY Piarist Fathers.
Carroll, Vincent *o.f.m.* '62 (BO) [BB] Boston, MA St. Anthony Shrine.
Carroll, William '50 (B) Retired.
Carroll, William C. *s.j.* '69 (BUF) [O] Buffalo, NY Canisius Jesuit Community.
Carroll, William R. '70 (BO) [1] Arlington, MA St. Agnes Church.
Carron, J. Walter '37 (ROC) Geneseo, NY St. Mary Church; Retired.
Carron, Malcolm *s.j.* '51 (DET) [K] Detroit, MI Jesuit Community at the University of Detroit.
Carrozza, Andrew P. '90 (NY) Mahopac, NY St. John the Evangelist Church.
Carrozzo, Anthony M. *o.f.m.* (BUF) [C] St. Bonaventure, NY St. Bonaventure University.
Carrozzo, Anthony M. *o.f.m.* '64 (BUF) [O] St. Bonaventure, NY St. Bonaventure Friary.
Carrozzo, Anthony M. *o.f.m., d.min.* '66 (BUF) [C] St. Bonaventure, NY St. Bonaventure University.
Carscallen, Edward C. '47 (TUC) Special Assignment; Retired.
Carson, David (ROC) Bath, NY Soliders' Home and Veterans' Hospital.
Carson, David L. *o.f.m.* '84 (NY) On Duty Outside the Archdiocese.
Carson, John '64 (NY) [3] Yonkers, NY St. Ann Church.
Carson, Paul C. '83 (KC) Retired.
Carson, Robert E. *o.praem.* '46 (GB) [I] De Pere, WI St. Norbert Abbey.
Carson, Msgr. Stanley B. '79 (ALT) [4] Altoona, PA Sacred Heart Church.
Carta, Umberto '35 (CAM) Retired.
Cartagena, Antonio '85 (CGS) [11] Barrio Rio Canas, PR San Juan Apostol y Evangelista Church.
Cartaya, Pedro *s.j.* '67 (MIA) [D] Miami, FL Belen Jesuit Preparatory School; [H] Miami, FL Villa Arrieta.
Carten, Thomas F. *c.s.c.* '79 (SCR) [C] Wilkes-Barre, PA Kings College.
Carter, Augustine *o.carm.* '51 (LA) [F] Encino, CA Crespi Carmelite High School.
Carter, Augustine W. *o.carm.* '51 (LA) [R] Los Angeles, CA Mount Carmel Priory, Carmelite Fathers and Brothers.
Carter, Daniel E. '79 (SFR) [26] San Francisco, CA St. James Church; San Francisco, CA Youth Guidance Center.
Carter, Edward W. *s.j.* '62 (CIN) [M] Cincinnati, OH Faber Jesuit Community.
Carter, Eli K., Jr. '75 (HON) Ewa, HI Immaculate Conception Church.
Carter, Francis T. '86 (HRT) [10] New Britain, CT St. Mary's Church.
Carter, Msgr. James A. '66 (CHR) [17] Charleston, SC Christ Our King Church.
Carter, James C. *s.j.* '58 (NO) [C] New Orleans, LA Loyola University.
Carter, John T. '49 (E) [16] Erie, PA St. George Church.
Carter, John T. '70 (BAL) Military Chaplains.
Carter, Joseph F. '97 (PRT) Biddeford, ME St. Joseph's Church; [M] Biddeford, ME University of New England.
Carter, Leo J. *o.s.b.* '53 (BIR) Cullman, AL Sacred Heart Church; Cullman, AL Sacred Heart Church; [E] Cullman, AL St. Bernard Abbey.
Carter, Mark *o.f.m.cap.* '92 (PIT) [O] Pittsburgh, PA St. Conrad Friary.
Carter, Martin J. *s.a.* '75 (BRK) [113] Brooklyn, NY Our Lady of Victory Church; [T] Brooklyn, NY Catholic Migration & Refugee Office, Catholic Migration Services, Inc.
Carter, Raymond J. '49 (COL) Retired.
Carter, Robert E. *s.j.* '63 (NY) [DD] New York, NY West Side Jesuit Community.
Carter, Stephen *o.f.m.cap.* '82 (WDC) [39] Washington, DC Shrine of the Sacred Heart Church.
Carton, A. Richard '93 (PAT) Mountain Lakes, NJ St. Catherine of Siena Church.
Carton, Msgr. George A. '44 (PEO) Retired; [L] Peoria, IL St. Joseph's Home of Peoria.
Carton, Leo F. '43 (CHI) Skokie, IL St. Peter Church; Retired.
Carton, Msgr. William J. '59 (TR) Sea Girt, NJ St. Mark Church.
Cartwright, Christopher M. *s.j.* '80 (SAC) [14] Sacramento, CA St. Ignatius of Loyola Church.
Carty, John A. *s.j.* '59 (FgM) Provinces.
Carty, John T. '50 (PRO) Retired.
Carty, Robert E. '54 (MAN) Retired.
Caruana, Alfred E. *s.j.* '71 (NY) [DD] New York, NY Xavier Jesuit Community; [HH] New York, NY Xavier Society for the Blind.
Carucci, David '95 (MOB) [5] Montgomery, AL St. John the Baptist Church; [K] Montgomery, AL Alabama State University Newman Center; [L] Montgomery, AL St. John's Soup Kitchen, Inc.
Caruso, Carmen A. '66 (JOL) On Duty Outside the Diocese.
Caruso, Carmen A. '66 (VEN) Sanibel, FL St. Isabel Church.
Caruso, Daniel M. '94 (SY) Johnson City, NY St. James Church.
Caruso, Gerardo M. '78 (PH) Norwood, PA St. Gabriel Church.
Caruso, Lawrence '51 (LA) [1] Long Beach, CA St. Anthony Church.
Caruso, Michael P. *s.j.* '82 (KC) [B] Kansas City, MO Rockhurst College; [J] Kansas City, MO Rockhurst College - Jesuit Community.
Caruso, Philip J. '78 (NY) [172] Bronx, NY Our Lady of Grace Church.
Caruso, Robert '80 (PHX) [1] Mesa, AZ All Saints Church.
Caruso, Vincent *o.de.m.* '27 (CLV) [57] Cleveland, OH Our Lady of Mount Carmel Church; [P] Cleveland, OH Mercedarians.
Carvajal, Damian '53 (SJN) [12] San Juan, PR Cristo Redentor Church.
Carvajal, Msgr. Felipe (PAT) Sabbatical.
Carvajal, Raul H. '65 (MRY) Retired.
Carvajel, Nelson *c.r.* '95 (SP) Ruskin, FL St. Anne Church.
Carvalho, David *o.s.b.* '57 (SD) [H] Oceanside, CA Prince of Peace Abbey, Benet Hill.
Carvalho, Gordian J., Jr. '85 (HON) Kalaheo, HI Holy Cross Church.
Carven, John W. *c.m.* '60 (PH) [B] Philadelphia, PA St. Vincent's Seminary; [AA] Philadelphia, PA Congregation of the Mission.
Carver, Dennis '94 (BLX) Pass Christian, MS Sacred Heart Church.
Carvill, Michael '89 (FR) [O] North Dartmouth, MA University of Massachusetts Dartmouth Catholic Campus Ministry.
Carvill, Michael '90 (FR) [17] Fall River, MA St. Louis Church; [P] Fall River, MA Priestly Fraternity of the Missionaries of St. Charles Borromeo, Inc.
Carville, John *s.t.d.* '63 (BR) [21] Baton Rouge, LA St. Thomas More Church.
Cary, Robert '57 (SJ) [H] San Jose, CA O'Connor Hospital.
Cary, Robert M. *c.s.p.* '84 (NY) [104] New York, NY St. Paul the Apostle Church.
Cary, William J. '58 (SUP) Retired.
Carzon, Thomas *o.m.v.* '96 (BO) [B] Boston, MA Our Lady of Grace Seminary; [BB] Boston, MA St. Francis Chapel.
Casabon, Luis '61 (MIA) [5] Hialeah, FL St. John the Apostle Church.
Casaclang, Joseph D. '64 (RVC) Manhasset, NY St. Mary's Church.
Casagram, Michael *o.c.s.o.* '82 (L) [L] Trappist, KY Abbey of Our Lady of Gethsemani, of the Order of Cistercians of the Strict Observance.
Casale, Charles '69 (FRS) Frazier Park, CA Our Lady of the Snows Church.
Casale, Msgr. Franklyn M. '67 (NEW) On Duty Outside the Archdiocese.
Casaleggio, Dave '81 (LAV) [4] Las Vegas, NV Our Lady of Las Vegas Church.
Casaliggi, John R. '36 (GBG) Retired.
Casares, Benigno Palomo *o.s.a.* '66 (SJN) [1] Bayamon, PR San Agustin Church.
Casari, Michael T. '95 (WIL) Absent on Sick Leave.
Casarotto, Secondo *c.s.* '66 (BUF) [9] Buffalo, NY St. Anthony of Padua Church.
Casaus, Vicente *sch.p.* '52 (LA) [75] Los Angeles, CA St. Lucy Church.
Casavantes, Carlos *f.s.s.p.* '86 (CC) [18] Corpus Christi, TX St. Paul the Apostle Church.
Casavantes, Carlos S. *f.s.s.p.* '85 (SCR) [M] Elmhurst, PA Priestly Fraternity of St. Peter (F.S.S.P.), North American District Headquarters.
Casavantes, Carlos S. *f.s.s.p.* '86 (CC) [16] Corpus Christi, TX St. Michael the Archangel Latin Mass Community Church.
Casazza, Msgr. David J. '43 (NEW) River Edge, NJ St. Peter the Apostle Church; Retired.
Cascelli, Msgr. George J. '55 (NY) [59] New York, NY St. John Nepomucene Church.
Cascelli, Msgr. George J. '59 (NY) [A] Yonkers, NY St. Joseph's Seminary.
Cascia, Philip J. '77 (HRT) Prospect, CT St. Anthony's Church.
Cascino, Marion *o.f.m.* (HRT) Canaan, CT St. Joseph's Church.
Cascino, Marion *o.f.m.* '49 (NY) [1] New York, NY Cathedral of St. Patrick; [DD] New York, NY Padua Friary.
Cascione, James *c.ss.r* (STV) [2] Christiansted, VI Church of the Holy Cross.
Cascione, James R. *c.ss.r.* '83 (STV) [2] Christiansted, VI Church of the Holy Cross; [B] St. Thomas, VI Miscellaneous Organizations.
Casciotti, James A. *s.j.* '78 (BAL) [M] Baltimore, MD Jesuit Fathers and Brothers Maryland Provincial Curia.
Casco, Jose M. '54 (ARE) [13] Arecibo, PR Church of Santa Cecilia.
Case, Francis E. *s.j.* '69 (P) [L] Portland, OR Jesuit Provincial Office (Society of Jesus, Oregon Prov.).
Case, Francis J. '66 (SY) New Berlin, NY St. Theresa of the Infant Jesus Church.
Case, Lowell D. *s.s.j.* '80 (WDC) [32] Washington, DC Our Lady of Perpetual Help Church.
Case, Richard D. *s.j.* '75 (FBK) Pilot Station, AK St. Charles Spinola Church; [E] St. Marys, AK Brother Joe Prince Jesuit Community.
Case, Msgr. Vincent T. '58 (NY) Tuckahoe, NY Immaculate Conception Church; Tuckahoe, NY Assumption Church.
Casella, David P. '75 (NY) [169] Bronx, NY Our Lady of Angels Church.
Casella, Thomas A. *c.m.* '71 (BRK) [U] Jamaica, NY St. Vincent's House.
Casellas, Ramon Jaime *o.f.m.cap.* '84 (SJN) [18] San Juan, PR San Francisco de Asis Church.
Caserta, Angelo C. '45 (CIN) Piqua, OH St. Boniface Church; Retired.
Caserta, Charles W. '45 (CIN) Retired.
Caserta, Thomas G. '79 (BRK) [B] Douglaston, NY Cathedral Residence of the Immaculate Conception.
Casey, Msgr. A. Robert '43 (SY) [S] East Syracuse, NY Bishop Grimes Priests Residence.
Casey, Anthony C. '58 (BRK) [30] Brooklyn, NY St. Columba Church.
Casey, Christopher C. *s.j.* (NY) [F] New York, NY Xavier High School.
Casey, Daniel *o.p.* '38 (DET) [20] Detroit, MI St. Dominic Church.
Casey, Daniel J. '58 (SAC) Roseville, CA St. Rose of Lima Church.
Casey, David J. *s.j.* '69 (NY) [DD] New York, NY Jesuit Community at Fordham University.
Casey, Denis '57 (TLS) [E] Tulsa, OK Saint Francis Hospital, Inc.
Casey, Diarmuid *c.s.sp.* '69 (SJ) Mountain View, CA St. Athanasius Church.
Casey, Donald A. '65 (SB) Retired.
Casey, Edward J. '79 (PH) [V] Darby, PA Villa Saint Joseph; [V] Ventnor, PA Villa St. Joseph by the Sea; [Y] Darby, PA Little Flower Manor.
Casey, Francis M. '64 (RVC) Seaford, NY Maria Regina Church; Retired.
Casey, Msgr. George T. '37 (SCR) Retired.
Casey, James E. '69 (WDC) Retired.
Casey, John *s.a.c.* '67 (LUB) Brownfield, TX St. Anthony's Church.
Casey, John D. '55 (HRT) [5] New Haven, CT St. Boniface's Church; [7] New Haven, CT St. Casimir's Church.
Casey, John F. *o.s.a.* '39 (PH) [AA] Villanova, PA St. Thomas Monastery.
Casey, Msgr. John F. '54 (BRK) [182] Queens, NY Incarnation Church.
Casey, Msgr. John H. '57 (CAM) Haddon Township, NJ St. Vincent Pallotti Church.
Casey, John J. '32 (LA) [R] Los Angeles, CA Amat House; [X] Montebello, CA DePaul Center.
Casey, John J. *m.m.* '56 (FgM) Maryknoll Foreign Missions.
Casey, John J. '84 (MET) North Plainfield, NJ St. Joseph Church.
Casey, John V. *o.s.a.* '39 (BO) [C] North Andover, MA Merrimack College.
Casey, John W. '45 (SCR) Retired.
Casey, Joseph H. *s.j.* '49 (BO) [W] Weston, MA Campion Center.
Casey, Joseph M. '66 (PAT) Morristown, NJ Assumption of the Blessed Virgin Mary Church; Morristown,

NJ Morristown Memorial Hospital.
Casey, Joseph M. '67 (DET) [P] Clarkston, MI Colombiere Center.
Casey, Kevin *c.p.* '67 (MET) [H] South River, NJ Passionist Provincial Office.
Casey, Kevin M. *c.p.* '56 (MET) Old Bridge, NJ St. Thomas the Apostle Church.
Casey, Leonard '52 (HBG) [G] Danville, PA Holy Family Convent and Infirmary.
Casey, Liam C. '62 (ALB) On Duty Outside the Diocese.
Casey, Liam C. '93 (HRT) [I] Hartford, CT Saint Francis Hospital and Medical Center.
Casey, Marion G. '34 (NU) Ivanhoe, MN Divine Providence Hospital & Home; Retired; [B] Ivanhoe, MN Divine Providence Health Center.
Casey, Martin J. *s.j.* '43 (WDC) [M] Washington, DC The Jesuit Community at Georgetown University.
Casey, Matthew *o.m.i.* '47 (WDC) [B] Washington, DC Oblate College/Oblate Center for Mission Studies.
Casey, Noah *o.s.b.* '76 (IND) [17] Indianapolis, IN St. Bernadette Church; [J] St. Meinrad, IN St. Meinrad Archabbey.
Casey, Patrick L. '65 (NU) Olivia, MN St. Aloysius Church; Renville, MN Holy Redeemer Church.
Casey, Patrick M. *s.j.* '72 (FgM) Provinces.
Casey, Patrick P. '97 (DET) New Baltimore, MI St. Mary Queen of Creation Church.
Casey, Patrick T. '80 (STP) [17] St. Paul, MN St. Casimir Church.
Casey, Paul E. *s.s.c.* '54 (OM) [K] St. Columbans, NE St. Columban's Foreign Mission Society.
Casey, Peter J. '68 (BO) [1] Somerville, MA St. Ann Church.
Casey, Richard L. '65 (BO) Awaiting Assignment.
Casey, Msgr. Robert A. '43 (SY) Retired.
Casey, Robert E. '87 (BO) Amesbury, MA Sacred Heart Church.
Casey, Robert G. '94 (CHI) [96] Chicago, IL Saint Ita Church.
Casey, Thomas J. *o.s.a.* (BO) [6] Lawrence, MA Holy Rosary Church.
Casey, Thomas J. *s.j.* '57 (STL) [P] St. Louis, MO Jesuit Community Corporation at St. Louis University - Jesuit Hall.
Casey, Thomas J. *s.j.* '62 (KC) [B] Kansas City, MO Rockhurst College; [J] Kansas City, MO Rockhurst College - Jesuit Community.
Casey, Thomas M. *o.s.a.* '65 (BO) [C] North Andover, MA Merrimack College.
Casey, Thomas M. *o.s.a.* '65 (PH) [C] Villanova, PA Villanova University.
Casey, Walter E. (BO) Retired.
Casey, William C. '69 (KNX) Greeneville, TN Notre Dame Church; Newport, TN Good Shepherd Church.
Casey, William J. *c.m.* '43 (PH) [AA] Philadelphia, PA Congregation of the Mission.
Casey, William P. *c.p.m.* '91 (OWN) [F] South Union, KY Fathers of Mercy.
Cash, Richard L. '89 (OWN) Aurora, KY St. Henry Church.
Cashel, Richard '54 (SFS) Dimock, SD SS. Peter and Paul Church.
Cashen, M.E. '91 (TLS) Cushing, OK SS. Peter and Paul Church.
Cashin, James '65 (SAT) Brackettville, TX St. Mary Magdalen Church.
Cashioli, Lawrence J. '82 (MET) Retired.
Cashman, Ambrose *c.p.* '67 (MET) [H] South River, NJ Passionist Provincial Office.
Cashman, Christopher '77 (BRK) [240] Queens, NY St. Sebastian Church.
Cashman, James *o.s.c.* '48 (SCL) Foreston, MN St. Louis Bertrand Church; [I] Onamia, MN Crosier Monastery.
Cashman, Jeremiah '55 (LC) Cornell, WI Holy Cross Church; Jim Falls, WI Sacred Heart Church.
Cashman, Joseph C. '60 (WIN) Absent on Leave.
Cashman, Msgr. Michael J. '75 (MET) Woodbridge, NJ St. James Church.
Cashman, Patrick *s.s.c.* '42 (BUF) [M] Silver Creek, NY St. Columbans on the Lake, Home for the Aged.
Cashnelli, Toni (CIN) [M] Cincinnati, OH St. Francis Seraph Friary.
Casillas, Rafael '72 (LA) [35] Los Angeles, CA Resurrection Church.
Casillas, Richard *s.v.d.* (SB) Indio, CA Our Lady of Perpetual Help Church.
Casillas, Richard *s.v.d.* '97 (SB) [A] Riverside, CA Divine Word Seminary.
Casimano, Santino '75 (GLP) On Duty Outside of Diocese.
Casio, Efrin (OAK) Pleasanton, CA Federal Correctional Institution.
Caskey, John '82 (SCL) Pearl Lake, MN Holy Cross Church; St. Nicholas, MN St. Nicholas Church.
Caskey, John U. '59 (L) [56] Louisville, KY Most Blessed Sacrament Church.
Caskey, John V. *c.ss.r.* '44 (CGS) Aguas Buenas, PR Church of Tres Santos Reyes.
Caslin, Msgr. Peter C. '41 (LA) [4] Long Beach, CA St. Bartholomew Church; Retired.
Casper, Christian J. *o.s.b.* '57 (PAT) [M] Morristown, NJ St. Mary's Abbey.
Casper, Kenneth R. *o.f.m.cap.* '80 (MIL) [B] Mount Calvary, WI St. Felix Friary.
Casper, Paul *s.c.j.* '57 (JKS) Holly Springs, MS St. Joseph Church.
Casper, Philip *o.f.m.cap.* '65 (MIL) [P] Mount Calvary, WI St. Lawrence Friary.
Casper, Robert '44 (MIL) [P] Milwaukee, WI Salvatorians - Jordan Hall.
Caspers, William A. '54 (CHY) Thermopolis, WY St. Francis Church.
Cassar, Edward A. '69 (BRK) [126] Brooklyn, NY St. Rosalia-Regina Pacis Church.
Cassar, Julian '77 (RVC) Hicksville, NY Holy Family Church.
Cassar, Mariano '74 (BR) [15] Baton Rouge, LA Most Blessed Sacrament Church.
Cassato, Msgr. David L. '72 (BRK) [105] Brooklyn, NY Shrine of Our Lady of Mount Carmel Church.
Cassel, Harry A. *o.s.a.* '50 (PH) Bryn Mawr, PA Our Mother of Good Counsel Church.
Cassella, John J. '58 (PIT) [4] Swissvale, PA Madonna del Castello Church.
Cassem, Ned H. *s.j.* '70 (BO) [W] Weston, MA Campion Center.
Cassem, Ned H. *s.j.* '70 (MIL) [P] Milwaukee, WI Jesuit Provincial Office, Wisconsin Province.
Casserly, Eugene D. '69 (PT) [11] Pensacola, FL St. Mary Church.
Cassese, Anthony '77 (CLV) [36] Cleveland, OH St. Jerome Church.
Cassese, John-Marie *o.f.m.* '50 (NY) [DD] New York, NY Padua Friary.
Cassidy, Bernard F. *s.j.* '63 (HON) [H] Honolulu, HI Jesuit Fathers House.
Cassidy, Msgr. Charles C. (PAT) Retired.
Cassidy, Daniel H. *s.s.j.* '43 (BAL) [M] Baltimore, MD St. Joseph's Manor.
Cassidy, Daniel J. *o.p.* '57 (PRO) [P] Providence, RI St. Thomas Aquinas Priory at Providence College.
Cassidy, Daniel J. '78 (CHI) [172] Chicago, IL St. Philomena Church.
Cassidy, Dominic J. '74 (DAV) On Duty Outside the Diocese.
Cassidy, Dominic J. '74 (RCK) [D] Elgin, IL St. Joseph Hospital.
Cassidy, Felix F. *o.p.* '54 (SFR) [13] San Francisco, CA St. Dominic Church; [N] San Francisco, CA St. Dominic Priory.
Cassidy, Francis '59 (LA) Monrovia, CA Immaculate Conception Church.
Cassidy, Francis P. '57 (CHI) [143] Chicago, IL St. Nicholas of Tolentine Church.
Cassidy, James (STP) Minneapolis, MN Metropolitan Medical Center.
Cassidy, James *o.s.a.* '90 (CAM) [C] Richland, NJ St. Augustine Preparatory School.
Cassidy, James E. *o.s.f.s.* '55 (WIL) [I] Childs, MD Oblates of St. Francis De Sales.
Cassidy, James G. *o.s.b.* '84 (MAN) [K] Manchester, NH St. Anselm Abbey.
Cassidy, James M. '61 (CLV) Ashland, OH St. Edward Church.
Cassidy, Msgr. James P. '51 (NY) Cortlandt Manor, NY Holy Spirit Church; [HH] New York, NY Catholic Foundation for the Dominican Republic.
Cassidy, Jeremiah *o.f.m.cap.* '56 (FgM) Capuchin Foreign Missions.
Cassidy, John M. '58 (CHI) [48] Chicago, IL St. Daniel the Prophet Church.
Cassidy, John T. '79 (PT) [15] Pensacola, FL St. Thomas More Church.
Cassidy, John V. '69 (LC) Eastman, WI St. Wenceslaus Church.
Cassidy, Joseph '45 (NEW) [N] Rutherford, NJ St. John Vianney Residence for Priests.
Cassidy, Joseph L. '45 (NEW) Retired.
Cassidy, Kevin W. '60 (MAD) Wisconsin Dells, WI St. Cecilia Church.
Cassidy, Laurence L. *s.j.* '61 (NEW) [B] Jersey City, NJ Saint Peter's College; [N] Jersey City, NJ Jesuits of Saint Peter's College, Inc.
Cassidy, Martin J. '57 (MIA) [1] Pompano Beach, FL Assumption Church.
Cassidy, Patrick '47 (RIC) Retired.
Cassidy, Richard '67 (BUF) [A] East Aurora, NY Christ the King Seminary.
Cassidy, Richard '67 (DET) On Duty Outside the Archdiocese.
Cassidy, Robert T. '58 (STP) Edina, MN Our Lady of Grace Church.
Cassidy, Terry '67 (PEO) Chenoa, IL St. Joseph's Church.
Cassidy, Theodore K. *s.m.* '68 (CIN) [C] Dayton, OH Marianist Novitiate; [M] Dayton, OH Marianist Provincialate.
Cassidy, Thomas *s.v.d.* '45 (FgM) Society of the Divine Word Foreign Missions.
Cassidy, Msgr. Thomas J. '57 (ARL) Purcellville, VA St. Francis de Sales Church.
Cassiere, Achilles *o.f.m.cap.* '52 (NEW) [4] Orange, NJ Mt. Carmel Church; [N] Union City, NJ Capuchin Friars - Province of the Sacred Stigmata of St. Francis.
Cassiero, Daniel '68 (NY) Absent on Leave.
Cassin, Msgr. Andrew J. '54 (WDC) Waldorf, MD St. Peter Church.
Cassion, Kieran A. *o.f.m.* '45 (PAT) [M] Butler, NJ St. Anthony Friary.
Cassista, Fern *m.s.* '65 (FR) [L] Attleboro, MA La Salette Center for Christian Living.
Casstevens, Jennifer (BO) Cambridge, MA Youville Lifecare, Inc.; [R] Cambridge, MA Youville Hospital & Rehabilitation Center, Inc.; [U] Cambridge, MA Youville Healthcare Center, Inc.; [FF] Cambridge, MA The Youville House, Inc.
Castaldi, Joseph '63 (NOR) New London, CT St. Joseph Church.
Castaldo, John '87 (BGP) New Fairfield, CT St. Edward the Confessor Church.
Castaneda, Heiber '94 (MRY) Watsonville, CA St. Patrick Church.
Castaneda, Mario '95 (STO) Tracy, CA St. Bernard's Church.
Castaneda, Oscar '87 (MIA) Opa Locka, FL Our Lady of Perpetual Help Church.
Castaneda, Severiano '71 (LA) [62] Los Angeles, CA San Francisco Church.
Castaneda-Cerna, Antonio '97 (YAK) Sunnyside, WA St. Joseph's Church.
Casteel, Michael J. '84 (SPC) Leave of Absence.
Casteig, Alfonso *o.f.m.cap.* '56 (DAL) [9] Dallas, TX Our Lady of Perpetual Help Church; [10] Dallas, TX Our Lady of San Juan De Los Lagos and St. Theresa Church.
Castellani, John J. '48 (HRT) Retired.
Castellani, Paul A. '96 (PH) [60] Philadelphia, PA Holy Innocents Church.
Castellano, Francis J. *v.f.* '60 (SCR) [5] Williamsport, PA Mater Dolorosa Church.
Castellanos, Ricardo C. '70 (MIA) [2] Pompano Beach, FL San Isidro Church.
Castellino, Albert *c.ss.r.* '61 (CHI) [136] Chicago, IL St. Michael Church.
Castelot, John '42 (DET) [3] Livonia, MI St. Edith Church; Retired.
Castelow, Ralph T. '89 (WIL) Dover, DE Holy Cross Church.
Caster, Gary '92 (PEO) [B] Peoria, IL Notre Dame High School.
Castillejo-Llusia, Jorge J. '89 (SJN) [4] Carolina, PR Santo Cristo de la Agonia Church.
Castillo, Carlos '83 (OKL) Edmond, OK St. Monica Church.
Castillo, Carlos C. *c.m.f.* '73 (LA) [K] Los Angeles, CA Queen of Angels-Hollywood Presbyterian Medical Center; [R] Los Angeles, CA Claretian Retreat Center Community.
Castillo, Domingo '91 (AMA) Hereford, TX San Jose Church.
Castillo, Francisco '67 (BWN) Weslaco, TX St. Joan of Arc Church.
Castillo, Jose '80 (SD) [30] San Diego, CA St. Jude Church; National City, CA St. Mary Church.
Castillo, Rene '89 (RIC) [9] Richmond, VA St. Edward The Confessor Church.
Castillo, Rolando '94 (MIA) Coconut Grove, FL St. Hugh Church.
Castillo, Rolo '92 (RIC) [5] Virginia Beach, VA Holy Spirit Church.
Castle, Nathan *o.p.* '76 (PHX) [H] Phoenix, AZ Office of Youth and Young Adult Ministries.
Castle, Nathan G. *o.p.* '85 (PHX) [F] Tempe, AZ Dominicans (Dominican Community-Jordan House).
Castles, Patrick J. '69 (TR) Hightstown, NJ St. Anthony of Padua Church.
Castrillo, Jesus '49 (LA) El Monte, CA Our Lady of Guadalupe Church.
Castrillo, Jesus Saez *o.de.m.* '69 (CGS) Cayey, PR Nuestra Senora de la Merced Church.
Castrillon, Heriberto Mejias '84 (CGS) Las Piedras, PR Inmaculada Concepcion Church.
Castro, Anthony A. '84 (GAL) Deer Park, TX St. Hyacinth Church.
Castro, John G. *o.m.i.* '62 (BWN) [8] Brownsville, TX St. Joseph Church.
Castro, Pablo *s.j.* '96 (BAL) [M] Baltimore, MD Jesuit Fathers and Brothers Maryland Provincial Curia.
Castro, Patrick *o.f.m.cap.* '87 (FgM) Capuchin Foreign Missions.
Castro, Patrick *o.f.m.cap.* '88 (AGN) Yona, GU San Francisco d'Assisi Church.
Castro, Robert '85 (SR) Sonoma, CA St. Francis Solano Church.
Castronovo, Edmund A. '76 (SY) Sherburne, NY St. Malachy Church; Georgetown, NY Camp Georgetown; South Plymouth, NY Camp Pharsalia.
Caswell, Thomas C. '66 (SPK) Pullman, WA Sacred Heart Church.
Catagnus, James N. '70 (PH) [9] Philadelphia, PA St. Ambrose Church.

Catala, Felix E. *c.ss.r.* '75 (MGZ) [2] Mayaquez, PR Our Lady of Mt. Carmel Church.
Catalana, Mark '91 (SJ) Cupertino, CA St. Joseph of Cupertino Church.
Catalano, James *o.s.j.* '63 (FRS) [1] Bakersfield, CA Our Lady of Guadalupe Church.
Catalano, James A. *s.j.* '95 (NY) [DD] New York, NY Xavier Jesuit Community.
Catallo, Sylvester *o.f.m.cap.* '54 (NY) [B] Beacon, NY St. Lawrence of Brindisi Friary.
Catanach, Richard '88 (LSC) Ruidoso, NM St. Eleanor Church.
Catanello, Ignatius '66 (BRK) [178] Queens, NY Holy Family Church.
Catania, Thomas M. '73 (BRK) [158] Queens, NY Blessed Virgin Mary, Help of Christians Church; Released from Diocesan Assignment.
Catanzaro, Albert *c.p.* '45 (BRK) [U] Jamaica, NY Immaculate Conception Monastery.
Catarise, Joseph '82 (ROC) [M] Rochester, NY Diocesan Office of Campus Ministry.
Cataudo, Anthony I. *o.p.* '60 (CAM) [M] Camden, NJ Dominican Sisters of the Perpetual Rosary Chaplain's Residence.
Catellani, Remus A. *m.c.c.j.* '47 (NEW) [N] Montclair, NJ Comboni Missionaries of the Heart of Jesus (Verona Fathers).
Catoir, John T. (PAT) [P] Passaic, NJ St. Jude Media Ministries.
Catoir, John T. '60 (PAT) [3] Passaic, NJ Assumption of the Blessed Virgin Mary Church.
Catucci, Thomas F. '82 (SY) Kirkwood, NY St. Mary Church; Special Assignment.
Catullo, Pasquale R. '63 (PH) [12] Philadelphia, PA Annunciation B.V.M. Church; Retired.
Catuso, Orville J. *s.j.* (GB) [M] Oshkosh, WI Jesuit Retreat House.
Caufield, Msgr. John J. '48 (PH) Retired.
Caufield, Kenneth J. *s.j.* (NY) [B] Bronx, NY Ciszek Hall.
Caul, Robert F. '61 (PRO) [R] Narragansett, RI Our Lady of Peace Spiritual Life Center.
Cauley, Robert W. '42 (CLV) Retired.
Cauley, Thomas F. '81 (PMB) Port St. Lucie, FL Holy Family Church.
Caulfield, John '59 (ORL) [4] Lakeland, FL St. Joseph's Church.
Caulfield, John F. *s.j.* '44 (BO) [W] Chestnut Hill, MA The Jesuit Community at Boston College.
Caulfield, Msgr. John J. (PH) [1] Philadelphia, PA Cathedral Basilica of SS. Peter and Paul Church.
Caulfield, Msgr. John J. '48 (PH) Exton, PA SS. Philip and James Church.
Caulfield, Sean '49 (B) Lewiston, ID St. Stanislaus Church; [F] Lewiston, ID Lewis and Clark State College.
Cautela, Mauro '74 (PIT) Ellwood City, PA Purification of the Blessed Virgin Mary Church.
Cauterucci, Francis J. '90 (PH) [3] Drexel Hill, PA St. Charles Borromeo Church.
Cavagnaro, Camillus *o.f.m.* '46 (FgM) Franciscan Foreign Missions.
Cavagnaro, John A. '75 (CAM) Sea Isle City, NJ St. Joseph's Church.
Cavagnaro, Mark R. '70 (CAM) Marmora, NJ The Church of the Resurrection.
Cavagnuolo, Salvatore F. '67 (HRT) Yalesville, CT Our Lady of Fatima Church.
Cavalier, Robert C. '72 (NO) [4] Kenner, LA St. Jerome Church.
Cavalier, Wayne *o.p.* '93 (NO) [25] New Orleans, LA St. Anthony Of Padua Church; [P] New Orleans, LA Dominican Fathers & Brothers, Southern Dominican Province.
Cavallaro, Msgr. Galliano J. '42 (PRO) Retired.
Cavalli, Victor *o.p.* '21 (SAC) Benicia, CA St. Dominic Church.
Cavalluzzi, Kevin P. '93 (BRK) [155] Queens, NY St. Benedict Joseph Labre Church.
Cavanagh, Brian '58 (LA) Covina, CA Sacred Heart Church.
Cavanagh, David '85 (BO) [V] Chestnut Hill, MA Opus Dei.
Cavanagh, Gerald F. *s.j.* '64 (DET) [K] Detroit, MI Jesuit Community at the University of Detroit.
Cavanagh, Msgr. James M. '52 (BRK) [91] Brooklyn, NY Our Lady of Angels Church.
Cavanagh, Joseph A. *s.j.* '62 (FgM) Provinces.
Cavanagh, Michael J. '59 (PBL) Retired.
Cavanaugh, Brian *t.o.r.* '82 (STU) [A] Steubenville, OH Franciscan University of Steubenville; [F] Steubenville, OH Holy Spirit Monastery.
Cavanaugh, Daniel J. '60 (BO) Awaiting Assignment.
Cavanaugh, Daniel J. '66 (PH) Ambler, PA St. Joseph Church; Ridley Park, PA St. Madeline Church.
Cavanaugh, Harry *c.pp.s.* '54 (CIN) [L] Dayton, OH The Maria Joseph Living Care Center.
Cavanaugh, James K. '51 (Y) Retired.
Cavanaugh, John (NEW) [I] Jersey City, NJ St. Joseph's Home for the Blind.
Cavanaugh, John *c.ss.r.* '46 (ORL) New Smyrna Beach, FL Sacred Heart Church.
Cavanaugh, John '90 (FAR) West Fargo, ND Blessed Sacrament Church.
Cavanaugh, John L. '51 (NY) Retired; [E] White Plains, NY Archbishop Stepinac High School.
Cavanaugh, John L. '56 (CIN) Retired.
Cavanaugh, John R. '55 (ROC) [I] Rochester, NY Basilian Residence.
Cavanaugh, Kevin P. '86 (HRT) Military Chaplains.
Cavanaugh, Michael *o.s.f.s.* (ARL) [D] Fairfax, VA Paul VI High School.
Cavanaugh, Michael *o.s.f.s.* '76 (ARL) [J] Fairfax, VA Oblates of St. Francis de Sales Residence.
Cavanaugh, Paul K. *c.m.* (BRK) [Y] Jamaica, NY Vincentian Service Corps.-East Inc.
Cavanaugh, Peter M. '66 (PRO) [7] Warwick, RI St. Peter Church.
Cavazos, Gilberto *o.f.m.* '85 (STL) [P] St. Louis, MO Franciscan Friary of St. Anthony of Padua.
Caveglia, Patrick *o.s.b.* '94 (KC) [A] Conception, MO Conception Seminary College; [J] Conception, MO Conception Abbey.
Cavell, Lawrence A. '89 (HT) [1] Houma, LA Cathedral of St. Francis De Sales.
Cavellier, Richard '87 (DET) [6] Clinton Twp., MI St. Valerie of Ravenna Church.
Caverly, Msgr. J. Bernard '65 (SP) [8] St. Petersburg, FL St. Raphael Church.
Caverly, Patrick J. '61 (ORL) Altamonte Springs, FL Annunciation Church.
Caverte, Rolando '62 (SFR) [17] San Francisco, CA Church of the Epiphany.
Cavey, Donald J. '76 (RIC) Hampton, VA VA Medical Center.
Caviglia, Caesar '55 (LAV) Retired.
Cavoto, Joseph F. *s.a.* '80 (NY) Harrison, NY St. Vincent Hospital and Medical Center of New York; [DD] New York, NY Atonement Friars.
Cawley, John F. *c.m.* '65 (CHI) [C] Chicago, IL Vincentian Community at DePaul University.
Cawley, Joseph A. *s.j.* '42 (PH) [AA] Philadelphia, PA Jesuit Community at St. Joseph's University.
Cawley, Martin *o.c.s.o.* '61 (P) [L] Lafayette, OR The Cistercian (Trappist) Abbey of Our Lady of Guadalupe.
Cawley, Patrick '70 (GR) Retired.
Cawley, Thomas *c.m.* '57 (KC) [J] Kansas City, MO Vincentian Parish Mission Center.
Cawley, Thomas *c.m.* '57 (KCK) Nortonville, KS St. Joseph's Church.
Cawley, Msgr. Thomas J. '36 (SCR) Retired; [N] Dunmore, PA Villa St. Joseph.
Cawley, William '73 (GF) On Duty Outside of the Diocese.
Cawley, William M. '73 (HBG) [3] York, PA St. Patrick Church; [A] York, PA York Catholic High School.
Cayer, John B. '96 (PT) Panama City, FL St. Dominic Church.
Caylor, Dennis J. '75 (CIN) Mount Carmel, OH St. Veronica Church.
Cazayoux, Clair M. *s.j.* '62 (NO) [P] New Orleans, LA Ignatius Residence.
Cazenavette, John J. *s.j.* '53 (SP) [C] Tampa, FL Jesuit High School.
Cebula, Joseph S. '75 (ALB) Stamford, NY Sacred Heart Church.
Cebula, Richard S. *o.s.b.* '41 (SEA) [6] Tacoma, WA St. Joseph's Church; [13] Tacoma, WA Holy Rosary Church; [M] Lacey, WA St. Martin's Abbey.
Cebula, Thomas '68 (Y) [1] Massillon, OH St. Barbara's Church.
Cebulka, Peter R. '93 (MET) East Brunswick, NJ St. Bartholomew Church.
Cecchini, Franco *c.r.s.* '70 (HRT) [6] Hartford, CT Sacred Heart Church.
Cecere, Michael *c.m.f.* '43 (SAT) [12] San Antonio, TX Immaculate Heart of Mary Church.
Cecero, John J. *s.j.* '89 (BAL) [M] Baltimore, MD Jesuit Fathers and Brothers Maryland Provincial Curia.
Cecero, John J. *s.j.* '89 (BGP) [O] Fairfield, CT The Fairfield Jesuit Community-Fairfield University.
Cecil, Bruce *c.s.c.* '92 (PHX) Tolleson, AZ Blessed Sacrament Church.
Cecil, Ivo E. '54 (L) Retired.
Cecil, Patrick G. '78 (CHI) Wadsworth, IL St. Patrick Church.
Ceckowski, Robert J. '55 (SPR) Three Rivers, MA SS. Peter and Paul Church.
Cedillo, Bruno (BWN) [7] Brownsville, TX St. Eugene De Mazenod Church.
Cedolia, Robert J. '78 (PIT) Holiday Park, PA Our Lady of Joy Church.
Cedrone, Laurence C. (BO) Retired.
Cegielka, Francis A. *s.a.c.* '31 (BUF) [O] North Tonawanda, NY Society of the Catholic Apostolate.
Ceja, Miguel '90 (SB) Palm Springs, CA Our Lady of Solitude Church.
Cejudo, Serafin '56 (GAL) [4] Galveston, TX St. Patrick Church.
Celano, Joseph G. '87 (MET) [1] New Brunswick, NJ St. Peter Apostle Church; [M] New Brunswick, NJ Catholic Center at Rutgers University.
Celano, Leo J. *o.praem.* '72 (ORG) [H] Silverado, CA Norbertine Fathers of Orange Inc.
Celano, Leo John *o.praem.* '72 (LA) Norwalk, CA California Youth Authority.
Celeste, Charles R. '80 (ALB) [4] Little Falls, NY Holy Family Church.
Celia, Joseph A. '67 (HBG) Selinsgrove, PA St. Pius X Church; Selinsgrove, PA Selinsgrove Center; [K] Harrisburg, PA Catholic Campus Ministry.
Celiano, Alfred V. '53 (NEW) [B] South Orange, NJ Seton Hall University.
Celino, Anthony '97 (ELP) [1] El Paso, TX St. Patrick's Cathedral.
Celino, Juventino C. '82 (ELP) [32] El Paso, TX St. Stephen, Deacon and Martyr Church.
Cell, Robert *m.s.c.* '47 (RCK) [H] Aurora, IL Missionaries of the Sacred Heart Community.
Cellini, Ronald R. '79 (CHR) Beaufort, SC St. Peter's Church; [G] Beaufort, SC University of South Carolina, Beaufort Extension Newman Center.
Cellini, Ronald R. '79 (PIT) On Duty Outside the Diocese.
Cellucci, Carl D. '53 (PH) Retired.
Celso, Thomas B. '79 (ROC) On Duty Outside the Diocese.
Cembor, Thomas M. '79 (NEW) [2] Irvington, NJ St. Leo's Church.
Cencula, Leonard '63 (STU) Dillonvale, OH St. Adalbert Church.
Cenefeldt, Harry E. '54 (TR) [8] Trenton, NJ Our Lady of Good Counsel Church.
Cenkner, William *o.p.* '58 (WDC) [C] Washington, DC Catholic University of America, The.
Centala, Theodore *o.c.d.* '65 (WDC) [B] Washington, DC Monastery of Our Lady of Mount Carmel.
Centner, David *o.c.d.* '71 (OAK) [N] Berkeley, CA Carmelite (Discalced) House of Studies.
Centrella, Msgr. Arthur J. '54 (PH) [3] Norristown, PA Holy Saviour Church.
Centrella, Dismas *o.f.m.* '55 (BO) [42] Boston, MA St. Leonard of Port Maurice Church.
Cepeda, Abraham *s.d.b.* (SJN) Catano, PR San Francisco de Sales Church.
Cepeda, Jose Arturo '96 (SAT) [1] San Antonio, TX Cathedral of San Fernando.
Cepeda, Ray '79 (AGN) On Duty Outside the Archdiocese.
Cepeda, Santos A. *s.d.b.* '89 (ARE) Orocovis, PR San Juan Bautista Church.
Ceperley, Eugene F. (SC) Retired.
Ceplecha, Christian W. *o.s.b.* '53 (JOL) [A] Lisle, IL Benedictine University; [J] Lisle, IL St. Procopius Abbey.
Cepress, Adalbert J. '44 (NU) Retired.
Cera, James B. '64 (MIL) Kansasville, WI St. Mary-Dover Church.
Cera, Raymond M. *c.pp.s.* '46 (LFT) [A] Rensselaer, IN Saint Joseph's College.
Cerank, Gerald A. '72 (OG) Mooers, NY St. Joseph Church; Mooers Forks, NY St. Ann Church.
Ceranowski, Albert B. '64 (TOL) Oregon, OH St. Ignatius Church.
Ceranowski, Gerald L. '67 (TOL) [26] Toledo, OH St. Joan of Arc Church.
Cerbin, Walter A. *s.s.j.* '55 (BR) Donaldsonville, LA St. Catherine of Siena Church.
Cerbone, James L. *s.d.b.* '80 (NY) [3] Poughkeepsie, NY Holy Trinity Church.
Cercone, Raymond A. '48 (PIT) Retired.
Ceresko, Anthony R. *o.s.f.s.* '70 (TOL) [K] Toledo, OH Oblates of St. Francis de Sales.
Cerezo, Alberto F. '60 (YAK) On Duty Outside the Diocese.
Ceriello, Joseph A. '78 (BRK) Military Chaplains.
Cerio, Frank '86 (ORL) [7] Orlando, FL St. Charles Borromeo Church.
Cerkas, John W. (GB) Newald, WI St. Hubert Church.
Cerkas, John W. '70 (GB) Laona, WI St. Leonard Church; Long Lake, WI St. Norbert Church.
Cernaj, Emil *s.v.d.* '51 (CHI) [B] Techny, IL Divine Word Residence; [N] Techny, IL Society of the Divine Word, Provincial Headquarter-Chicago Prov.
Cernaj, Emil *s.v.d.* '51 (FgM) Society of the Divine Word Foreign Missions.
Cernak, Michael *o.mar.* '95 (SAM) [C] Petersham, MA Most Holy Trinity Monastery.
Cernauskas, Daniel '54 (MIA) Tamarac, FL St. Malachy Church.
Cerne, Joze '92 (CLV) [47] Cleveland, OH St. Mary Church.
Cernich, Joseph '83 (SFD) Absent on Leave.
Cerniglia, Francis J. '53 (CHI) Elk Grove Village, IL Queen of the Rosary Church; Retired.
Cerniglia, George J. *s.m.* '69 (BAL) [M] Baltimore, MD Society of Mary (Marianists); [Q] Baltimore, MD Marianist Conference.
Cernoch, Gerard '64 (VIC) Shiner, TX SS. Cyril and Methodius Church.
Cerny, George F. '64 (CHI) [23] Chicago, IL St. Bartholomew Church.

Cerpich, Richard J. '61 (MIL) Adell, WI St. Patrick Church; Cascade, WI St. Mary- Cascade Church; Dacada, WI St. Nicholas Church; Mitchell, WI St. Michael Church; Random Lake, WI St. Mary- Random Lake Church.
Cerrito, Msgr. Albert J. '51 (PRO) Retired.
Cerrone, Michael, III '81 (AUS) Copperas Cove, TX Holy Family Church.
Cerrone, Michael J. *u.s.a.* '81 (SAV) Military Chaplains.
Cerullo, Fritz J. *o.s.a.* '71 (BO) Andover, MA St. Augustine Church.
Cerulo, Thomas N. *o.ss.t.* '78 (WDC) [M] Hyattsville, MD St. John de Matha Monastery, Order of Most Holy Trinity.
Cervantes, Fidel '55 (ELP) [13] El Paso, TX Most Holy Trinity Church.
Cervantes, Leo '62 (RIC) Emporia, VA St. Richard Church; Emporia, VA St. Peter the Apostle Church.
Cervantes, Leo T. (RIC) Lake Easton, VA St. Peter The Apostle Church.
Cervantes, Lucius F. *s.j.* '46 (STL) [P] St. Louis, MO Jesuit Community Corporation at St. Louis University - Jesuit Hall.
Cervantes, Rhenne A. '92 (NO) [3] Slidell, LA St. Luke the Evangelist Church.
Cervella, Albert T. '79 (ALN) [J] Bethlehem, PA Holy Family Villa.
Cervenak, Andrew '78 (TR) Retired.
Cervera, Pascual '87 (NY) [149] Bronx, NY Holy Spirit Church.
Cervero, Joseph '89 (BGP) Darien, CT St. John Church.
Cervini, John I. '68 (RVC) Wyandanch, NY Our Lady of the Miraculous Medal Church.
Cervinski, Paul L. '61 (BIS) [5] Minot, ND St. Theresa, the Little Flower Church.
Cervoni, Stephen F. '67 (CAM) Woodstown, NJ St. Joseph's Church.
Cerwonka, Clarence G. '61 (PBL) Military Chaplains.
Cerwonka, Clarence J. '61 (SY) [8] Binghamton, NY St. Mary of the Assumption Church.
Cerwronka, Francis *c.s.v.* '59 (JOL) [2] Kankakee, IL St. Patrick Church.
Cesanek, Damian *o.f.m.* '69 (PEO) [2] Bloomington, IL St. Mary's Church.
Cesario, Victor *o.f.m.* '39 (NY) [DD] New York, NY Franciscan Province of the Immaculate Conception.
Cesaro, Nicholas J. '54 (HRT) [8] Hartford, CT St. Augustine Church.
Cesarone, Jeffrey T. *o.praem.* '94 (WIL) [B] Claymont, DE Archmere Academy; [I] Claymont, DE Immaculate Conception Priory of the Canons Regular of Premontre.
Cesta, James M. (SY) [2] Oswego, NY St. Joseph Church.
Cestare, Gerald '95 (RVC) West Babylon, NY Our Lady of Grace Church.
Cestaro, Joseph A. '62 (BRK) [34] Brooklyn, NY St. Edmund's Church.
Cestaro, Joseph J. '46 (NEW) Belleville, NJ St. Anthony's Church; Retired; [N] Rutherford, NJ St. John Vianney Residence for Priests.
Cestero, Luis '36 (CGS) [2] Caguas, PR San Jose Church.
Ch'e, James '54 (AGN) Tamuning, GU St. Anthony and St. Victor Church.
Chaanine, Georges '96 (OLL) Wheeling, WV Our Lady of Lebanon Church.
Chaback, Msgr. Michael J. '70 (ALN) [2] Bethlehem, PA SS. Cyril and Methodius Church.
Chaback, Msgr. Michael J. '70 (PH) [A] Wynnewood, PA Theological Seminary of St. Charles Borromeo, Overbrook.
Chabak, Robert M. '72 (NEW) Bloomfield, NJ St. Valentine Church.
Chabala, Brian J. '77 (DET) Farmington Hills, MI St. Fabian Church.
Chabot, Bertrand R. '46 (FR) Retired.
Chabot, Peter L. *m.m.* '65 (NY) [DD] Maryknoll, NY Maryknoll Fathers and Brothers.
Chabot, Robert *s.s.s.* '66 (SFE) [23] Albuquerque, NM St. Charles Borromeo Church.
Chabot, Roger P. '65 (PRT) Auburn, ME St. Philip's Church.
Chachlowski, Marek '82 (NEW) [4] Linden, NJ St. Theresa of the Child Jesus Church.
Chacko, Joseph C. (MET) Lyons, NJ U.S. Veterans Medical Center.
Chacko, Sebastian '76 (SPP) [7] Pago Pago, AS Church of the Immaculate Conception.
Chacon, Frank '89 (GLP) Concho, AZ San Rafael Church; St. Johns, AZ St. John the Baptist Church.
Chacon, Gilbert *s.j.* (PHX) [11] Phoenix, AZ St. Francis Xavier Church.
Chacon, Jorge '74 (NEW) North Bergen, NJ St. Brigid Church.
Chadwick, John '95 (NEW) Cedar Grove, NJ St. Catherine of Siena Church.
Chadwick, Lawrence A. '75 (RVC) Dix Hills, NY St. Matthew Church.
Chaffman, Charles '84 (LA) [4] Los Angeles, CA Ascension Church.
Chagas, Virgilio P. '67 (NEW) Elizabeth, NJ St. Elizabeth Hospital; [G] Elizabeth, NJ St. Elizabeth Hospital.
Chagnon, Robert J. '40 (HRT) Retired.
Chaguaceda, Juan Manuel *o.s.a.* '53 (NY) [49] New York, NY Holy Rosary Church.
Chaisson, John C. '66 (BO) [1] Peabody, MA St. Adelaide Church.
Chaisson, Louis '65 (HT) On Leave.
Chaiyara, Yarat *s.d.b.* '94 (OAK) [N] Berkeley, CA Salesian Community.
Chakian, Joy '78 (FAR) Forman, ND St. Mary's Church.
Chalany, Robert (WH) On Duty Outside the Diocese.
Chalhoub, Maximos '39 (NTN) Retired.
Chalifour, Gerald F. '52 (MAN) Retired.
Chalkey, Andrew G. *o.m.i.* '56 (BEL) [E] Belleville, IL Our Lady of the Snows Apartment Community Retirement Home; [F] Belleville, IL Missionary Oblates of Mary Immaculate - St. Henry's Oblate Residence.
Chalkey, Andy *o.m.i.* '56 (BEL) [E] Belleville, IL Our Lady of the Snows Apartment Community Retirement Home.
Challancin, James '68 (LFT) [A] Rensselaer, IN Saint Joseph's College.
Challancin, James '68 (MAR) On Duty Outside the Diocese.
Challinor, Michael '91 (NY) Stony Point, NY Immaculate Conception Church.
Challman, Stephen G. '96 (NY) [206] Staten Island, NY Holy Rosary Church.
Chalmers, H. Edward '79 (WOR) [2] Fitchburg, MA St. Bernard's Church.
Chaloult, Msgr. Gilman '47 (PRT) Caribou, ME Holy Rosary Church; Retired.
Chaloux, Joseph '94 (ATL) Athens, GA St. Joseph's Church.
Chalupa, Fred '73 (AUS) On Duty Outside the Diocese.
Chamberlain, Charles M. *o.s.f.s.* '93 (WIL) [B] Wilmington, DE Salesianum School.
Chamberlain, Francis M. *s.j.* '68 (FgM) Provinces.
Chamberlain, Henry T. *s.j.* '61 (CHI) [N] Chicago, IL Chicago Province of the Society of Jesus-Provincial Office.
Chamberlain, Msgr. Michael J. '66 (DEN) [17] Denver, CO Mother of God Church.
Chamberlain, Robert '54 (Y) Retired.
Chamberlain, Robert F. '57 (GI) Retired.
Chamberlain, Msgr. Robert J. '64 (DM) [9] Des Moines, IA St. Joseph's Church.
Chamberland, Gary *c.s.c.* (FTW) [6] South Bend, IN Christ the King Church.
Chamberlin, Gregory D. *o.s.b.* '65 (EVN) [14] Evansville, IN St. Benedict Church.
Chamberlin, Gregory D. *o.s.b.* '65 (IND) [J] St. Meinrad, IN St. Meinrad Archabbey.
Chamberlin, Mark '68 (CC) [22] Corpus Christi, TX St. Theresa Church; Portland, TX Our Lady of Mount Carmel Church.
Chambers, Francis E. *o.s.a.* '78 (PH) [AA] Villanova, PA St. John Stone Friary.
Chambers, Henry C. '65 (BO) Millis, MA St. Thomas the Apostle Church.
Chambers, James *s.j.* '55 (IND) [20] Indianapolis, IN St. Joan of Arc Church.
Chambers, John E. *s.j.* '64 (FgM) Provinces.
Chambers, Leonard R. '65 (SPC) Joplin, MO St. Peter Church.
Chambers, Thomas E. *c.s.c.* '61 (NO) [22] New Orleans, LA Sacred Heart Of Jesus Church; [C] New Orleans, LA Our Lady of Holy Cross College.
Chamblain, Joseph M. *o.s.m.* '84 (CHI) [159] Chicago, IL Our Lady of Sorrows, Basilica of Church; [N] Chicago, IL Servite Friars - Eastern Province.
Champagne, Dennis V. '71 (SEA) Snohomish, WA St. Michael's Church.
Champagne, Michael '94 (LAF) [M] Lafayette, LA Community of Jesus Crucified.
Champagne, Rene *c.p.* '49 (DET) [K] Detroit, MI St. Paul of the Cross Community, Congregation of the Passion; [P] Detroit, MI St. Paul of the Cross Retreat Center.
Champagne, Robert *s.m.* (BO) Boston, MA Metro West Medical Center.
Champagne, Robert E. *s.m.* '51 (BO) [Y] Framingham Centre, MA The Marist House.
Champigny, Richard *o.carm.* '65 (NY) [DD] Middletown, NY St. Albert's Priory.
Champigny, Richard *o.carm.* '65 (SPR) [K] Williamstown, MA Mount Carmel Retreat Center.
Champigny, Roger G. '60 (PRO) [2] Warwick, RI St. Catherine Church.
Champigny, Thomas R. '81 (SPR) Easthampton, MA Our Lady of Good Counsel Church.
Champion, James D. '76 (WOR) Blackstone, MA St. Paul's Church.
Champlin, Msgr. Joseph M. '56 (SY) [1] Syracuse, NY The Cathedral of the Immaculate Conception.
Champlin, Michael A. *o.p.* '66 (SUP) [I] Webster, WI Thomas More Center for Preaching and Prayer, Inc.
Champlin, William E. '93 (WOR) [8] Worcester, MA Our Lady of the Angels Church.
Champoux, Thomas C. '67 (YAK) Richland, WA Christ the King Church.
Chan, Albert *s.j.* '47 (SFR) [N] San Francisco, CA Jesuit Community at University of San Francisco; [U] San Francisco, CA The Ricci Institute for Chinese-Western Cultural History at the Center for the Pacific Rim.
Chan, Paul '50 (NY) [HH] New York, NY Chinese Catholic Information Center.
Chan-Kyu, Simeon Je '50 (JOL) Itasca, IL St. Andrew Kim Church.
Chancler, Joseph A. *t.o.r.* '83 (ALT) [A] Loretto, PA St. Francis College; [A] Loretto, PA St. Francis College; [F] Loretto, PA St. Francis Friary, Third Order Regular of St. Francis of Penance.
Chancy, Richard F. '91 (BO) [CC] Dorchester, MA University of Massachusetts at Boston Campus Ministry.
Chandler, Anthony L. '89 (L) [33] Louisville, KY Holy Family Church.
Chandler, John W. *s.j.* '64 (LA) [R] Culver City, CA Ignatius House, The Novitiate of the California Province, Society of Jesus.
Chandonnet, A. J. *c.ss.r.* '50 (GAL) [34] Houston, TX Holy Ghost Church; Retired.
Chandrankunnel, Mathew '64 (NEW) Dumont, NJ St. Mary's Church; Englewood, NJ Englewood Hospital.
Chane, Lawrence J. '62 (BO) Dracut, MA St. Therese Church.
Chaney, Robert E. '88 (SAV) [2] Savannah, GA St. Anthony's Church.
Chang, Benedict '63 (SFR) [48] San Francisco, CA Star of the Sea Church.
Chang, Cornelius P. *o.s.b.* '62 (GBG) [H] Latrobe, PA Saint Vincent Archabbey.
Chang, Francis X. *s.j.* '49 (GAL) [10] Houston, TX Ascension Chinese Mission Church.
Chang, Gordon '84 (LA) Hacienda Heights, CA St. John Vianney Church.
Chang, Joseph *o.s.b.* '57 (JOL) [J] Lisle, IL St. Procopius Abbey.
Chang, Simeon '49 (SFR) [34] San Francisco, CA St. Monica Church; Retired.
Chant, William S. '88 (BUR) Graniteville, VT St. Sylvester Church.
Chao, Joseph '48 (P) Retired.
Chao, Joseph '61 (NY) [54] New York, NY St. James Church.
Chap, Robert W. *c.m.* '66 (FgM) Vincentian Foreign Missions.
Chapdelaine, Gerard E. *s.j.* '66 (SEA) [C] Tacoma, WA Bellarmine Preparatory School.
Chapeau, Mary Paul *o.cart.* '45 (BUR) [E] Arlington, VT Carthusian Foundation, Charterhouse of the Transfiguration.
Chapel, Joseph R. '92 (NEW) [B] South Orange, NJ Seton Hall University.
Chapell, Norbert A. '48 (CHI) Hickory Hills, IL St. Patricia Church; Retired.
Chapin, Daniel L. '72 (OG) Clayton, NY St. Mary of Clayton Church; Lafargeville, NY St. John the Evangelist Church.
Chaplin, John G. *c.s.c.* '68 (E) Houtzdale, PA Christ the King Church.
Chapman, A. James '39 (PH) [72] Philadelphia, PA Saint Irenaeus Church; Retired.
Chapman, Gerard C. '91 (PH) Doylestown, PA Our Lady of Mount Carmel Church.
Chapman, Lawrence J. '77 (MIL) [D] Burlington, WI Catholic Central High School.
Chapman, Michael A. '82 (PH) [154] Philadelphia, PA St. Veronica Church.
Chapman, Michael L. '69 (OKL) Weatherford, OK St. Eugene's Church; [K] Norman, OK Campus Ministry for the Archdiocese of Oklahoma City.
Chapman, Robert J. '67 (PH) Lansdowne, PA St. Philomena Church.
Chappell, Arthur B. *o.s.a.* '69 (PH) [C] Villanova, PA Villanova University.
Chappell, James T. '67 (DUB) [7] Dubuque, IA Sacred Heart Church.
Chappetto, Raymond F. *v.e.* '71 (BRK) [2] Brooklyn, NY St. Agatha's Church.
Charankat, Peter '59 (OAK) [3] Walnut Creek, CA St. Mary's Church; Walnut Creek, CA Kaiser-Permanente Medical Center.
Charboneau, Damian *o.s.m.* '50 (ORL) Palm Bay, FL Our Lady of Grace Church.
Charbonneau, Damian M. *o.s.m.* '50 (CHI) [N] Chicago, IL Servite Friars - Eastern Province.
Charbonneau, Roger L. '71 (BUR) Colchester, VT Holy Cross Church.
Charbonneau, William R. '73 (HRT) On Duty Outside the Archdiocese.
Charest, Anthony *s.m.* '40 (BO) [10] Cambridge, MA Our Lady of Pity Church.
Charest, Edmund P. '60 (BO) Emergency Response Group.
Charest, Roger M. *s.m.m.* '42 (RVC) [N] Bay Shore, NY

Montfort Missionaries.
Charipar, Henry W. '68 (DUB) Dorchester, IA St. Mary's Church; Hanover, IA St. Mary's Church; New Albin, IA St. Joseph's Church.
Charland, George A. '60 (WOR) Westminster, MA St. Edward the Confessor Church.
Charland, Paul A. '71 (PRO) Foster, RI St. Paul the Apostle Church.
Charlebois, Msgr. John J. '54 (GRY) Valparaiso, IN St. Paul Church.
Charlebois, Msgr. Robert L. '57 (GRY) On Duty Outside the Diocese.
Charles, Frank A. *s.v.d.* '67 (LAF) [8] Lafayette, LA St. Anthony Church.
Charlot, Lucien '61 (BRK) Brooklyn, NY Kings County Hospital Center.
Charlton, Robert *ss.cc.* '88 (FR) Fairhaven, MA St. Mary's Church.
Charlton, Terrence P. *s.j.* '76 (FgM) Provinces.
Charm, Robert W. '77 (OAK) [11] Oakland, CA St. Lawrence O'Toole Church.
Charman, Eugene J. '71 (HRT) Southington, CT Immaculate Conception Church; Special and other (Arch)Diocesan Assignment.
Charnley, George '76 (DET) Canton, MI Saint John Neumann Church.
Charnoki, Andrew J. '43 (GBG) Retired; [G] Greensburg, PA St. Anne Home.
Charnoki, John J. '45 (PIT) [35] Pittsburgh, PA St. Raphael Church; Retired.
Charnoki, Msgr. William G. *j.c.l.* '65 (GBG) Indiana, PA St. Bernard Church.
Charpentier, Alfred *o.m.i.* '71 (FgM) Oblates Foreign Missions.
Charpentier, Dale '83 (HT) On Leave.
Charters, Thomas S. '75 (OWN) Elkton, KY St. Susan Church; Guthrie, KY Sts. Mary & James Church.
Charvet, Louis *o.s.b.* '45 (FgM) American - Cassinese Congregation Foreign Missions.
Chase, Charles E. '79 (OG) Copenhagen, NY St. Mary Church.
Chase, Kenneth M. '84 (DET) [30] Detroit, MI St. Hedwig Church.
Chase, Lee P. '93 (ROC) Penfield, NY St. Joseph Church.
Chase, Martin L. *s.j.* (DET) [K] Detroit, MI Jesuit Provincial Office-Detroit Province of the Society of Jesus.
Chase, Martin L. *s.j.* '91 (FgM) Provinces.
Chase, Maurice '53 (SD) Retired.
Chase, P. Geoffrey *o.s.b.* '59 (PRO) [P] Portsmouth, RI Abbey of St. Gregory the Great.
Chase, Raymond '78 (BAL) Special Assignment; [G] Timonium, MD Villa Maria Treatment Center.
Chase, Terrence R. '84 (GRY) [2] Merrillville, IN St. Andrew Church.
Chassaniol, Warren F. '65 (HT) Grand Isle, LA Our Lady of the Isle Church.
Chasse, Joseph S. *s.m.* '52 (PRT) Hamlin, ME St. Joseph Church; Van Buren, ME St. Bruno - St. Remi Church.
Chasse, Lucien *s.m.* '43 (BO) [59] Boston, MA Our Lady of Victories Church; [W] Boston, MA Marist Fathers of Our Lady of Victories (Boston Prov.).
Chateau, Paul F. '66 (DET) Oak Park, MI Our Lady of Fatima Church.
Chatham, Msgr. Donald '65 (AUS) On Duty Outside the Diocese.
Chatigny, Donat W. *m.m.* '34 (NY) [DD] Maryknoll, NY Maryknoll Fathers and Brothers.
Chau, Peter Do Quang '73 (NSH) Ashland City, TN St. Martha Church.
Chaumont, James '77 (SAN) Fort Stockton, TX St. Joseph's Church; Sanderson, TX St. James Church.
Chaupetta, Victor *m.s.* '70 (BGP) [P] Wilton, CT Lourdes Health Care Center.
Chaupetta, Victor W. *m.s.* '70 (BGP) [P] Wilton, CT School Sisters of Notre Dame Motherhouse (Northeastern Province).
Chauvin, David M. '64 (BR) Vacherie, LA St. Philip Church.
Chavarin, Jose '79 (SFR) [1] San Francisco, CA Cathedral of St. Mary (Assumption).
Chavarin, Jose' '79 (SFR) San Francisco, CA St. Thomas More Society.
Chavarria, Horacio '66 (BWN) [3] Brownsville, TX Church of the Good Shepherd.
Chavarria, Juan *c.m.* '95 (FgM) Vincentian Foreign Missions.
Chavarriq, Jerome *c.ss.r.* '84 (ATL) Griffin, GA Sacred Heart Church.
Chaves, David *l.c.* '74 (PRO) [G] Warwick, RI Overbrook Academy at Our Lady of Providence Center.
Chaves, David *l.c.* '94 (PRO) [E] Smithfield, RI Immaculate Conception Academy.
Chavez, Msgr. Adolphus '56 (SB) [5] San Bernardino, CA Our Lady of Guadalupe Church; Loma Linda, CA Jerry Pettis Memorial Hospital.
Chavez, Carlos '84 (SFE) Clovis, NM Sacred Heart Church.
Chavez, Don J. '89 (SFE) Abiquiu, NM St. Thomas Apostle Church.
Chavez, Frank '76 (SAN) [1] Odessa, TX Holy Redeemer Church.
Chavez, Gerald F. '73 (FRS) Bishop, CA Our Lady of Perpetual Help Church.
Chavez, Johnny Lee '76 (SFE) Moriarty, NM Estancia Valley Catholic Parish.
Chavez, Jose *c.ss.r.* '84 (SAT) [M] San Antonio, TX Redemptorists of Texas- San Antonio #1.
Chavez, Jose '96 (MRY) Nipomo, CA St. Joseph Church.
Chavez, Leopoldo *c.ss.r.* '96 (DEN) [33] Denver, CO St. Joseph's Church.
Chavez, Luis N. '91 (TUC) Douglas, AZ Immaculate Conception Church.
Chavez, Manuel '96 (SR) Windsor, CA Our Lady of Guadalupe Church.
Chavez, Patrick J. '68 (SFE) El Rito, NM San Juan Nepomuceno Church.
Chavez, Phillip *s.o.l.t.* '93 (CC) [H] Robstown, TX Society of Our Lady of the Most Holy Trinity.
Chavez, Ricardo A. '63 (OAK) Pittsburg, CA St. Peter Martyr of Verona Church.
Chavez, Scott '97 (OAK) Livermore, CA St. Michael's Church.
Chavez, Vincent P. '91 (SFE) Arroyo Seco, NM Holy Trinity Church.
Cheah, Joseph *o.s.m.* '92 (P) Milwaukie, OR Christ the King Church.
Cheah, Joseph M. *o.s.m.* '92 (ORG) [H] Buena Park, CA Servite Fathers And Brothers.
Cheah, Joseph P. *o.s.m.* '92 (ORG) Fullerton, CA St. Juliana Falconieri Church; [L] Fullerton, CA California State University Fullerton, Newman Center.
Cheatham, Louis W. '45 (GBG) Retired; [G] Greensburg, PA Neumann House.
Checchio, James '92 (CAM) [M] Blackwood, NJ Bishop's Residence.
Checchio, James F. (CAM) On Educational Leave of Absence.
Check, Paul N. '97 (BGP) Graduate Studies.
Checon, Amarilho '57 (BRK) [T] Brooklyn, NY Catholic Migration & Refugee Office, Catholic Migration Services, Inc.
Cheeramkuzhy, Matthew *c.m.i.* '75 (NSH) Loretto, TN Sacred Heart Church; Saint Joseph, TN St. Joseph Church; [K] Liberty, TN Carmelites of Mary Immaculate Center of Spirituality.
Cheesman, Robert *c.ss.r.* '57 (NY) [EE] Hastings-on-Hudson, NY Sisters of St. Francis.
Cheetham, William J. '46 (PIT) [36] Pittsburgh, PA St. Regis Church.
Cheikho, John Hanna '68 (EST) West Bloomfield, MI St. Thomas Chaldean Catholic Parish.
Chelena, Thomas '68 (PRM) Absent on Leave.
Chelick, James A. '76 (GR) [23] Grand Rapids, MI St. Thomas the Apostle Church.
Cheline, Paschal *o.s.b.* '64 (P) [L] St. Benedict, OR Mt. Angel Abbey.
Chemazar, Blase *o.f.m.* '53 (CHI) [194] Chicago, IL St. Stephen Church; [N] Lemont, IL The Slovene Franciscan Fathers, Order of Friars Minor, Commissariat of the Holy Cross.
Chembakassery, Vincent '80 (BIS) Stanley, ND Queen of the Most Holy Rosary Church.
Chemino, Stephen Scott '93 (ALX) Plaucheville, LA Mater Dolorosa Church.
Chen, Anthony K. '52 (CHI) Retired.
Chen, John '86 (DAL) Richardson, TX Mission of the Sacred Heart of Jesus Church.
Chen, Raphael '52 (AMA) Retired.
Chen, Vincent P. '57 (MET) Phillipsburg, NJ SS. Philip and James Church; Phillipsburg, NJ Warren Hospital.
Chenevey, Anthony L. *s.s.p.* '58 (Y) [A] Canfield, OH Society of St. Paul.
Cheney, Edmund K. *s.j.* '42 (WOR) [N] Worcester, MA Jesuits of Holy Cross College, Inc.
Cheney, James '95 (FAR) Cooperstown, ND St. George's Church.
Cheney, Jesse C. '43 (LR) Retired; [H] Little Rock, AR St. John Manor.
Cheng, Joseph *s.d.b.* '59 (LA) [52] Los Angeles, CA St. Bridget's Chinese Catholic Center Church; [R] Los Angeles, CA Dominic Savio Salesian Residence.
Chengazcheril, George '86 (SAN) On Duty Outside the Diocese.
Chenot, Paul *c.p.* '51 (BRK) Queens, NY Creedmoor Psychiatric Center; [U] Jamaica, NY Immaculate Conception Monastery.
Chenoweth, Robert '63 (JC) Retired.
Chenoweth, Robert J. '63 (STL) [K] St. Louis, MO Saint Louis University Hospital.
Cheol Soo Lee, Stephanus (SFR) [32] San Francisco, CA St. Michael Korean Church.
Cheong, Mark H.S. '83 (LA) [14] Los Angeles, CA Holy Trinity Church.
Chepaitis, Peter S. '72 (NY) [DD] New York, NY Franciscan Friars, Order of Friars Minor, Holy Name Province.
Chepanis, Anthony J. '48 (PMB) Highland Beach, FL St. Lucy Church; Retired.
Cheplic, Msgr. Peter A. '72 (NEW) [2] Jersey City, NJ St. Aloysius Church.
Chepponis, James '85 (PIT) Kennedy Township, PA St. Malachy Church.
Cheri, Fernand (NSH) [H] Nashville, TN Franciscan Friars.
Cheri, Fernand J., III *o.f.m.* '78 (NSH) [13] Nashville, TN St. Vincent de Paul Church.
Cherry, Athanasius C. *o.s.b.* '68 (GBG) [H] Latrobe, PA Saint Vincent Archabbey.
Cherry, Richard W. *s.j.* '69 (FgM) Provinces.
Cherubini, Perry A. '85 (CAM) Northfield, NJ St. Bernadette Church.
Cherukarakunnel, Alexander J. '63 (HRT) North Haven, CT St. Therese's Church.
Cherup, Michael A. '81 (PT) [1] Pensacola, FL Cathedral of the Sacred Heart.
Cheruparambil, Francis '82 (TR) Union Beach, NJ Holy Family Church.
Chervenak, Gregory *o.f.m.cap.* '79 (PIT) [O] Pittsburgh, PA St. Augustine Friary.
Chervenak, Stephen M. '60 (PIT) White Oak Boro, PA St. Angela Church.
Chesebrough, Charles S. '67 (IND) Bloomington, IN St. Charles Borromeo Church.
Chesney, Michael E. *s.j.* '91 (SP) [C] Tampa, FL Jesuit High School.
Chess, Msgr. Edwin R. '37 (CHI) Retired.
Chester, Thomas '95 (TR) Lawrenceville, NJ St. Ann Church.
Chethipuzha, Varghese '69 (NY) [125] Bronx, NY St. Ann Church; Bronx, NY North Central Bronx Hospital.
Chetock, James J. '93 (WH) Charles Town, WV St. James Church.
Chetwynde, Clyde H. '80 (BO) Townsend, MA St. John Church.
Chevalier, Martin G. '83 (DM) Adel, IA St. John Church.
Chevalier, Thomas H. '80 (ALB) [10] Albany, NY St. Margaret Mary Church.
Chevedden, James *s.j.* '78 (FgM) Provinces.
Chevedden, James N. *s.j.* '78 (SJ) [M] Los Gatos, CA Sacred Heart Jesuit Center.
Chew, Randolf G. '71 (PRO) [7] Cranston, RI St. Paul Church.
Chi, Msgr. John '42 (SEA) [31] Seattle, WA Our Lady of Mount Virgin Church.
Chi, Paul Chu Van '75 (ORG) Garden Grove, CA St. Callistus Church.
Chia, Luis '59 (GAL) Highlands, TX St. Jude Thaddeus Church.
Chiang, John B. '53 (NY) [116] New York, NY St. Teresa Church; On Duty Outside the Archdiocese.
Chiang, Joseph S. '59 (NEW) Paramus, NJ Our Lady of the Visitation Church.
Chiang, Joseph S. '59 (NY) [HH] New York, NY Chinese Clergy & Religious Association in North America.
Chiara, Msgr. Peter A. '48 (RVC) East Islip, NY St. Mary's Church; Retired.
Chiaramonte, Anthony '65 (ALB) Special Assignment.
Chiaravalle, Dominic M. '65 (PH) [44] Philadelphia, PA Epiphany of Our Lord Church.
Chiarilli, Msgr. Patrick S. '61 (CAM) [3] Vineland, NJ St. Francis of Assisi Church.
Chiasson, Arthur B. *m.afr.* '38 (LR) St. Vincent, AR St. Mary Church.
Chiasson, Ron *o.m.i.* '76 (SD) San Diego, CA R.J. Donovan Correctional Facility.
Chiavello, Donald C. '59 (CAM) Minotola, NJ St. Michael's Church.
Chichetto, James W. *c.s.c.* '68 (FR) [A] North Easton, MA Stonehill College; [A] North Easton, MA Holy Cross Fathers Religious.
Chicoine, Msgr. George D. '41 (MAN) Retired.
Chidiac, Bakhos '91 (OLL) St. Paul, MN Holy Family Church.
Chieffo, Ralph J. '75 (PH) [84] Philadelphia, PA King of Peace Church.
Chiesa, Robert *s.j.* '68 (FgM) Provinces.
Chiffriller, Edward J. *s.s.j.* '74 (BAL) [M] Baltimore, MD St. Joseph Society of the Sacred Heart House of Central Administration.
Chihak, Msgr. John P. '36 (DUB) Retired.
Child, John F. '59 (DET) [7] Dearborn, MI St. Martha Church.
Chilen, Michael D. '69 (CC) Military Chaplains.
Chiles, Richard P. *o.praem.* '87 (JKS) [2] Jackson, MS St. Mary Church; [7] Jackson, MS Christ the King Church; [E] Jackson, MS Priory of St. Moses the Black; [G] Jackson, MS Jackson State University Newman Center.
Chillog, Thomas A. '84 (STU) Lore City, OH SS. Peter and Paul Church.
Chilmark, Richard J. '60 (NEW) Roseland, NJ Our Lady of the Blessed Sacrament Church.
Chilson, Elbert V. '78 (DEN) [4] Fort Collins, CO St. Elizabeth Ann Seton Church.
Chilson, Richard W. *c.s.p.* '72 (P) [28] Portland, OR St. Philip Neri Church; [Q] Portland, OR Paulist Fathers Catholic Center for Evangelization.

Chilton, Michael '74 (HEL) Retired.
Chimera, Angelo M. '69 (BUF) [52] Buffalo, NY The Nativity of the Blessed Virgin Church.
Chimiak, Karl A. '80 (WDC) Ridge, MD St. Michael Church.
Chimiak, Mark '95 (WDC) Absent On Leave.
Chin, Donald J. *o.f.m.* '67 (FgM) Franciscan Foreign Missions.
Chinchar, Gerald T. *s.m.* '82 (CIN) [D] Dayton, OH The University of Dayton; [M] Dayton, OH Marianist Provincialate.
Ching, Herbert '47 (HON) Retired.
Chinh, Peter '50 (ORG) Retired.
Chinnappa, K. Francis '90 (CLV) [68] Cleveland, OH St. Rose Church.
Chinnici, Joseph P. *o.f.m.* '72 (OAK) [A] Berkeley, CA Franciscan School of Theology; [N] Oakland, CA Franciscan Friars Provincial Office, Province of St. Barbara.
Chiodini, Msgr. Jasper J. '42 (STL) Retired.
Chiodo, Msgr. Frank E. '76 (DM) [8] Des Moines, IA Basilica of Saint John Church; [J] Des Moines, IA Society of St. John (Brothers of Saint Benedict).
Chiodo, Peter *c.pp.s.* '60 (Y) Niles, OH Our Lady of Mt. Carmel Church.
Chiola, Richard '72 (SFD) On Duty Outside the Diocese.
Chiosso, James *s.d.b.* '49 (NY) [DD] New Rochelle, NY Salesian Provincial House.
Chirapurathel, Felix *o.praem.* '72 (TYL) Trinity, TX Most Holy Trinity Church.
Chirayath, Chummar *o.s.j.* '78 (FRS) [1] Bakersfield, CA Our Lady of Guadalupe Church.
Chirayath, Koshy George (NY) [101] New York, NY Our Saviour Church.
Chircop, Joseph *s.s.p.* '58 (DET) [K] Dearborn, MI Society of St. Paul.
Chirdon, Howard *c.p.* '50 (ALT) [J] Bedford, PA St. Mary's House of Greater Solitude.
Chiriaco, William J. (PH) [51] Philadelphia, PA Good Shepherd Church.
Chiriaco, William J. '86 (PH) [D] Philadelphia, PA West Philadelphia Catholic High School.
Chiriboga, Emiliano *s.d.b.* '63 (NY) [3] Port Chester, NY Our Lady of the Rosary Church.
Chirico, Peter F. *s.s.* '56 (CAM) On Duty Outside the Diocese.
Chirico, Peter F. *s.s.* '56 (SEA) [1] Seattle, WA St. James Cathedral.
Chisek, Anthony S. '43 (CHI) Retired.
Chisholm, Gregory *s.j.* '93 (DET) [K] Detroit, MI Jesuit Community at the University of Detroit.
Chisholm, Gregory C. *s.j.* '93 (BO) [W] Boston, MA The Society of Jesus of New England-Provincial Offices.
Chisholm, Thomas *o.s.b.* '89 (JOL) [J] Lisle, IL St. Procopius Abbey.
Chitwood, Dennis '84 (STL) [W] St. Louis, MO St. Louis Catholic Charismatic Renewal.
Chiusano, Louis *o.f.m.cap.* '57 (FgM) Capuchin Foreign Missions.
Chizmar, Msgr. John G. '75 (ALN) Jim Thorpe, PA Immaculate Conception Church.
Chladek, Melchior *o.cist.* '55 (DAL) [M] Irving, TX Cistercian Abbey of Our Lady of Dallas.
Chlebo, John C. '80 (CLV) Rocky River, OH St. Christopher Church.
Chleborad, Gerald '60 (CHY) Saratoga, WY St. Ann's Church.
Chlopecki, Robert J. '74 (BEL) Leave of Absence.
Chmely, Edward V. '41 (CHR) Retired.
Chmiel, Bronislaus '69 (CHI) [75] Chicago, IL St. Helen Church.
Chmiel, Gerald J. '70 (TOL) [2] Fremont, OH St. Ann Church.
Chmielewski, Francis J. '73 (BUF) [13] Buffalo, NY St. Bernard Church; Buffalo, NY Veterans Hospital.
Chmielewski, Msgr. Joseph '37 (CAM) Retired.
Chmielewski, Philip J. *s.j.* '81 (CHI) [N] Chicago, IL Chicago Province of the Society of Jesus-Provincial Office.
Chmil, John J. '95 (SCR) [16] Wilkes-Barre, PA St. Nicholas Church.
Chmura, Gary D. '78 (CLV) [58] Cleveland, OH Our Lady of Peace Church.
Chmura, Julian '64 (DET) [4] Detroit, MI St. Andrew Church.
Chmura, Stanislaus '70 (RIC) Retired.
Chmurski, Marek '95 (FR) Centerville, MA Our Lady of Victory Church.
Chmylar, Gregory *o.s.b.m.* '44 (STF) Long Island City, NY Holy Cross Church.
Cho, Laurentius '88 (ORG) Special Assignment.
Cho, Laurentius '90 (ORG) [G] Anaheim, CA St. Thomas Korean Catholic Center.
Choate, Lawrence M. *o.s.m.* '78 (CHI) [N] Chicago, IL Servite Friars - Eastern Province.
Choate, Norman *c.r.* '63 (L) [30] Louisville, KY Guardian Angels Church; [68] Louisville, KY Resurrection D.N.J.C. Church.
Choby, David R. '74 (NSH) Gallatin, TN St. John Vianney Church.
Choc, Pedro *o.s.b.* '90 (SFS) [F] Marvin, SD Blue Cloud Abbey.
Chocarro, Antonio (CGS) Caguas, PR Government Regional Hospital.
Chochol, Ronald '64 (STL) [63] St. Louis, MO St. Stephen, Protomartyr Church.
Chodacki, Jeremy *o.f.m.conv.* '29 (SPR) [A] Granby, MA St. Hyacinth College and Seminary.
Choi, Joachim Ngo *c.m.c.* '83 (STP) [28] Minneapolis, MN St. Joseph Hien Church.
Choi, Jun Gui (Michael) '91 (WDC) College Park, MD St. Andrew Kim Church.
Choi, Mark '94 (LA) Lomita, CA St. Margaret Mary Alacoque Church.
Choiniere, Gean Marie *o.mar.* '95 (SAM) [C] Petersham, MA Most Holy Trinity Monastery.
Chojnacki, Anthony *o.f.m.* (CHI) [N] Chicago, IL Holy Name Friary.
Chojnacki, David '69 (CLV) Absent on Leave.
Cholette, John B. '36 (NY) Retired.
Cholewa, Gregory *o.m.i.* '76 (CHI) [174] Chicago, IL Precious Blood Church.
Chomko, Stephen '46 (PHU) Berwick, PA SS. Cyril and Methodius Church.
Chomko, Stephen '46 (STF) Retired.
Chonko, Michael J. '43 (Y) Retired.
Chontos, Joseph E. '82 (KCK) [5] Topeka, KS Our Lady of Guadalupe Church.
Choo, Mary Joseph '94 (OKL) [9] Oklahoma City, OK St. Paul, Apostle Church.
Choo, Thomas *ss.cc.* '69 (HON) [4] Honolulu, HI St. Augustine Church.
Choondassery, Yesudasan '90 (NEW) Lodi, NJ St. Francis de Sales Church.
Choong, Norbert '84 (AMA) Retired.
Choorackunnel, John Vianney *c.m.i.* '64 (LAF) Loreauville, LA Our Lady of Victory Church.
Choppesky, John C. *s.j.* '44 (STL) [O] St. Louis, MO Fusz Pavilion.
Chorikavunkal, Joseph Augustine '75 (LUB) Muleshoe, TX Immaculate Conception Church.
Chornyak, Joseph '53 (PBR) New Salem, PA St. Mary's Church.
Choromanski, Zbigniew '81 (NEW) [10] Newark, NJ St. Casimir's Church.
Chorpenning, Joseph *o.s.f.s.* '79 (PH) [C] Philadelphia, PA St. Joseph's University.
Chorpenning, Joseph F. *o.s.f.s.* (PH) [AA] Wyndmoor, PA Villa de Sales Oblate Residence.
Chorpenning, Joseph F. *o.s.f.s.* '79 (PH) [AA] Wyndmoor, PA Oblates of St. Francis de Sales (O.S.F.S.).
Chortos, Donald '66 (PIT) Tarentum, PA Holy Martyrs Church.
Chotin, Msgr. Joseph L. '64 (NO) Mandeville, LA Our Lady of the Lake Church.
Chouinard, Lionel G. '65 (PRT) Augusta, ME St. Augustine's Church.
Chouinard, Marcel G. '56 (PRT) Skowhegan, ME Notre Dame De Lourdes Church.
Chouter, Oleksa (STF) Kerhonkson, NY Holy Trinity Church.
Chovanec, Paul R. '72 (GAL) [22] Houston, TX St. Christopher Church.
Chow, Luke L. '54 (PH) Levittown, PA St. Michael the Archangel Church.
Chowning, Daniel *o.c.d.* '88 (MIL) [P] Milwaukee, WI Provincial Offices - Discalced Carmelites; [P] Holy Hill, WI Discalced Carmelite Monastery.
Chowning, Michael *o.f.m.* '68 (LEX) Hazard, KY Mother of Good Counsel Church; Jackson, KY Holy Cross Church; [K] Hazard, KY Father Farrell Spiritual Life Center.
Chrepta, Msgr. Stephen J. '45 (STF) Retired.
Chretien, Richard L. '67 (FR) Westport, MA Our Lady of Grace Church.
Christ, John P. *o.s.c.* '65 (DET) Royal Oak, MI St. Dennis Church; [K] Riverview, MI Crosier Community of Riverview.
Christ, Raymond J. *o.s.f.s.* '51 (HBG) Manheim, PA St. Richard Church.
Christancho, Jorge '78 (ATL) Gainesville, GA St. Michael's Church.
Christen, Charles L. '89 (PIT) [70] Pittsburgh, PA St. Cyril of Alexandria Church; Allegheny County, PA University of the Health Science - Allegheny General Campus.
Christensen, Donald L. '59 (SAG) [8] Saginaw, MI St. Andrew Church.
Christensen, Lawrence P. *c.m.* '84 (DEN) Longmont, CO St. John the Baptist Church.
Christensen, Michael R. '79 (LIN) [10] Lincoln, NE St. Peter Church.
Christensen, Peter F. '85 (STP) [A] St. Paul, MN St. John Vianney Seminary; [C] St. Paul, MN University of St. Thomas.
Christensen, William A. *s.m.* '73 (STL) [P] St. Louis, MO Provincialate of the Society of Mary, Province of St. Louis.
Christi, Frank *o.s.m.* '56 (ORG) [H] Buena Park, CA Servite Fathers And Brothers.
Christian, George G. *o.p.* '55 (L) [47] Louisville, KY St. Louis Bertrand Church.
Christian, John S. '84 (TR) Leave of Absence.
Christian, Lawrence *c.m.f.* '83 (SAT) [B] San Antonio, TX Immaculate Heart Claretian Seminary.
Christian, Norman H. '67 (STL) Absent on Sick Leave.
Christian, Robert *o.p.* (OAK) [N] Oakland, CA Western Dominican Province.
Christian, Robert F. *o.p.* '76 (SFR) [N] San Francisco, CA St. Dominic Priory.
Christiana, Nicholas M. '78 (ALT) Absent on Leave.
Christiansen, Andrew J. *s.j.* '72 (WDC) [M] Washington, DC Leonard Neale House.
Christie, Maria Joseph *s.j.* '88 (STL) [P] St. Louis, MO Jesuit Community Corporation at St. Louis University - Jesuit Hall.
Christman, Msgr. Bernard E. '59 (OG) Lyon Mountain, NY St. Bernard Church; Lyon Mountain, NY Lyon Mountain Correctional Facility.
Christman, Ralph '56 (HON) Waianae, HI Sacred Heart Church; [H] Honolulu, HI Maryknoll Fathers House.
Christman, Robert '79 (MIA) Absent on Leave.
Christof, Francis T. *o.s.f.s.* '82 (WIL) [I] Childs, MD Oblates of St. Francis De Sales.
Christofferson, Kevin Lane '97 (GF) Miles City, MT Sacred Heart Church.
Christopher, Charles A. *c.s.b.* '60 (GAL) [7] Houston, TX St. Anne Church.
Christopher, Mark '57 (PMB) Fort Pierce, FL St. Anastasia Church.
Christopher, Patrick J. '91 (STL) [2] St. Louis, MO Epiphany of Our Lord Church.
Christy, Timothy A. '92 (MET) Somerset, NJ St. Matthias Church.
Christy, William H. *c.s.sp.* '92 (FgM) Holy Ghost Foreign Missions.
Chriszt, Dennis *c.pp.s.* '81 (CIN) Wapakoneta, OH St. Joseph Church.
Chrobak, Lyle *o.f.m.* '62 (FgM) Franciscan Foreign Missions.
Chrobak, Lyle *o.f.m.* '62 (GB) [I] Pulaski, WI Assumption of B.V.M. Friary.
Chrobot, Leonard F. '64 (FTW) [8] South Bend, IN St. Hedwig Church.
Chrusciel, Bogumil '68 (NEW) [35] Newark, NJ St. Stanislaus Church.
Chrysostom, Francis X. '60 (LA) [K] Inglewood, CA Daniel Freeman Memorial Hospital.
Chrysostom, John *s.j.* '74 (CHI) [C] Chicago, IL Jesuit Community at Loyola University of Chicago.
Chryst, Robert D. '68 (SY) [12] Syracuse, NY St. Anthony of Padua Church; Special Assignment.
Chrzastek, Brian *o.p.* '92 (PRO) [P] Providence, RI St. Thomas Aquinas Priory at Providence College.
Chu, Bernard M.C. *s.j.* '60 (OAK) [N] Oakland, CA Murray Residence Community; [S] Berkeley, CA Inter-Friendship House Association, Friendship Center.
Chu, Peter (GAL) [N] Houston, TX Pope John XXIII Priest Residence.
Chu, Peter *s.j.* '68 (LA) [R] Los Angeles, CA Columbiere House.
Chu, Quang Vinh '91 (ORG) [2] Anaheim, CA St. Boniface Church.
Chubirko, Michael *s.d.b.* '60 (PSC) Elizabeth, NJ SS. Peter and Paul Church.
Chudy, Carl *s.x.* '86 (FgM) Xaverian Foreign Missions.
Chudzinski, Frederick V. *s.s.* '36 (BAL) [J] Baltimore, MD St. Charles Villa; [M] Baltimore, MD St. Charles Villa.
Chueca, Ubaldo '66 (LA) [39] Los Angeles, CA St. Aloysius Gonzaga Church.
Chukwu, Christopher N. '80 (DET) Walled Lake, MI St. William Church.
Chun, Emmanuel Shin *p.y.o.* (ARL) Fairfax, VA St. Paul Chung Church.
Chun, Francis '63 (P) Absent on Leave.
Chung, Alex '88 (LA) Paramount, CA Our Lady of the Rosary Church.
Chung, Anthony '83 (SFR) Redwood City, CA St. Pius Church; San Francisco, CA Kaiser Hospital Redwood City; San Francisco, CA Sequoia Hospital; Special Assignment.
Chuong, Matthias Nguyen H. (SB) [6] San Bernardino, CA St. Anne Church.
Chupela, Msgr. Andrew A. '55 (GBG) [3] Uniontown, PA Nativity of the Blessed Virgin Mary Church.
Chura, Andrew '58 (PBR) Toronto, OH St. Joseph Church.
Church, Msgr. James F. '58 (SAC) [20] Sacramento, CA St. Philomene Church.
Church, Tim '95 (DAL) Coppell, TX St. Ann Church.
Church, Wenceslaus *o.f.m.* (CHI) [167] Chicago, IL St. Peter's Church.
Church, Wenceslaus '59 (CHI) [N] Chicago, IL St. Peter's Friary.
Churchill, Raymond '54 (HON) Retired.
Churchwell, Stephen T. '76 (ATL) [8] Atlanta, GA Sacred Heart of Jesus Church.
Chwalek, John C. '48 (SPR) Adams, MA St. Stanislaus Kostka Church.

Chwalek, Kazimierz *m.i.c.* '87 (SPR) [I] Stockbridge, MA Congregation of Marians; [I] Stockbridge, MA Congregation of Marians.
Chwalinski, Stanley R. '67 (BUF) Attica, NY St. Vincent de Paul Church.
Chwaliszewski, Roman *o.f.m.conv.* '60 (FR) [7] New Bedford, MA Our Lady of Perpetual Help Church.
Chwieroth, Edward J. '50 (PH) [56] Philadelphia, PA Holy Angels Church; Cheltenham, PA St. Joseph Church.
Chycinski, Gregory A. '71 (MIL) [61] Milwaukee, WI Our Lady of Sorrows Church.
Chylewski, Msgr. Anthony '52 (SD) Retired.
Chylko, Gerard *c.ss.r.* '79 (BAL) [68] Baltimore, MD Our Lady of Fatima Church.
Ciaiola, Joseph A. '47 (E) [2] Farrell, PA Our Lady of Fatima Church.
Cialene, Donald '75 (NEW) Montclair, NJ Our Lady of Mt. Carmel Church.
Ciambella, Perry A. '92 (BUF) Blossom, NY St. Gabriel Church.
Ciambelli, Blase A. '64 (WOR) On Special or Other (Arch)Diocesan Assignment.
Ciampaglio, Msgr. Joseph A. '62 (PAT) Rockaway Township, NJ St. Clement, Pope and Martyr Church.
Ciancimino, David S. *s.j.* '88 (NY) [F] New York, NY Xavier High School.
Ciandella, Roch *o.f.m.* '72 (NY) [FF] Wappingers Falls, NY Mt. Alvernia Retreat House.
Ciani, Francis P. '39 (ALB) Retired.
Ciano, Kenneth J. '95 (IND) Greenwood, IN Our Lady of the Greenwood Church.
Ciaramitaro, Victor P. '72 (MEM) Paris, TN Holy Cross Church.
Ciaravolo, Ronald '58 (NY) Absent on Leave.
Ciardiello, Bruno *o.f.m.* '45 (BRK) [106] Brooklyn, NY Our Lady of Peace Church.
Ciavaglia, Julio M. *c.r.s.p.* (BUF) [B] Youngstown, NY The National Shrine Basilica of Our Lady of Fatima.
Ciavaglia, Julio M. *c.r.s.p.* '66 (BUF) [B] Youngstown, NY St. Anthony M. Zaccaria Seminary.
Ciba, Thomas J. '74 (NEW) Nutley, NJ Our Lady of Mount Carmel Church.
Cibulskis, Pete *m.i.c.* '53 (MIL) [9] Kenosha, WI St. Peter Church.
Cicale, Henry *f.m.s.i.* '70 (BO) [B] Framingham, MA Sylva Maria.
Ciccarino, Christopher '96 (NEW) [1] Newark, NJ Cathedral Basilica of the Sacred Heart Church.
Ciccolini, Samuel R. '69 (CLV) [8] Akron, OH Immaculate Conception Church; [V] Akron, OH Interval Brotherhood Home Alcohol-Drug Rehabilitation Center.
Ciccone, Joseph A. *c.s.p.* '89 (DEN) [4] Boulder, CO St. Thomas Aquinas University Parish; [P] Boulder, CO University of Colorado (Boulder).
Ciccone, Mark K. *s.j.* '85 (LA) [F] Los Angeles, CA Loyola High School.
Ciccone, Michael *o.p.* '75 (WDC) [B] Washington, DC Dominican House of Studies.
Ciccone, Nicholas '84 (BO) [43] Boston, MA St. Margaret Church.
Cicerale, Charles W. '75 (MET) Raritan, NJ St. Joseph Church.
Cichanowicz, Casimir *s.s.e.* '43 (VEN) [G] Englewood, FL Society of St. Edmund Residence.
Cichon, Michael W. '85 (NY) [202] Staten Island, NY St. Clare Church.
Cici, William '59 (E) Retired.
Cicinato, Michael '76 (MRY) San Luis Obispo, CA Nativity of Our Lady Church.
Cicola, Alfred C. '67 (PIT) Harwick, PA Our Lady of Victory Church.
Cid, Manuel *o.de.m.* '45 (SJN) [40] San Juan, PR Nuestra Senora de la Merced Church.
Cieciorka, Josef '30 (MAD) Retired.
Ciemiega, Ernest '57 (CHI) [33] Chicago, IL St. Bruno Church.
Cieniewicz, Donald W. '83 (ALN) [9] Reading, PA St. Mary Church; [C] Reading, PA Reading Central Catholic High School (Monsignor Bornemann Memorial).
Cienik, Kenneth *s.a.* '77 (R) Apex, NC St. Andrew the Apostle Church.
Cieri, Domenic L. '81 (BAL) Severn, MD St. Bernadette Church.
Ciesielski, Heinc '46 (PEO) Retired.
Ciesla, Fred *c.r.* '49 (CHI) [D] Chicago, IL Weber High School.
Ciesla, Walter '81 (GRY) [5] Michigan City, IN Sacred Heart Church.
Ciesla, Walter M. '81 (GRY) Westville, IN Westville Correctional Center.
Cieslak, William M. *o.f.m.cap.* '73 (OAK) [A] Berkeley, CA Franciscan School of Theology; [N] Oakland, CA Franciscan Friars Provincial Office, Province of St. Barbara.
Cieslik, Eugene (SFD) [11] Springfield, IL Sacred Heart of Jesus Church.
Cieslik, Robert Dale '82 (L) [59] Louisville, KY Our Lady of Lourdes Church.
Cieslikowski, Thomas J. '88 (HRT) Yalesville, CT Our Lady of Fatima Church.
Cieslinski, Robert '43 (P) Retired.
Ciesniewski, Richard P. '57 (DET) Retired.
Ciesniewski, Richard P. '57 (PHX) Sun City, AZ St. Elizabeth Seton Church.
Cieszkowski, Andrew M. '85 (NY) [99] New York, NY Our Lady of Victory Church.
Ciferni, Andrew D. *o.praem.* '66 (PH) [AA] Paoli, PA Daylesford Abbey.
Cigan, John J. '74 (PSC) Binghamton, NY Holy Spirit Church.
Cigolini, Santo *c.s.* '58 (VEN) Clewiston, FL St. Margaret Church.
Cikovic, Charles '86 (VEN) Absent on Leave.
Cilia, Francis V. '79 (SJ) [8] San Jose, CA Holy Family Church.
Cilia, Joseph *o.carm.* '68 (FgM) Carmelite Foreign Missions.
Cilia, Joseph *o.carm.* '68 (JOL) [J] Darien, IL Carmelite Provincial Office.
Ciliberti, Francis J. *o.praem.* '44 (WIL) [I] Claymont, DE Immaculate Conception Priory of the Canons Regular of Premontre.
Cilinski, Msgr. John T. '48 (ARL) Woodbridge, VA Our Lady of Angels Church.
Cilinski, Julius J. '45 (ARL) Clifton, VA St. Andrew the Apostle Church; Retired.
Cilinski, Robert '79 (ARL) [M] Fairfax, VA George Mason University, Catholic Campus Ministry House.
Cilinski, Robert C. '79 (ARL) Special Assignment; [M] Fairfax, VA George Mason University, Catholic Campus Ministry House.
Cillo, David '85 (PIT) Pleasant Hills, PA St. Elizabeth Church.
Cilwick, Theodore T. '43 (CHR) Retired.
Cima, Jose Maria '58 (SB) Redlands, CA St. Mary Church.
Cima, Thomas E. '67 (CHI) Calumet City, IL St. Victor Church.
Cimarrusti, Francis A. '64 (CHI) [134] Chicago, IL St. Matthias Church; [G] Chicago, IL Catholic Charities of the Archdiocese of Chicago-Archdiocesan Offices.
Cimbala, Edward G. '88 (PSC) Jessup, PA Holy Ghost Church.
Cimerman, Krizolog *o.f.m.* '73 (NY) [30] New York, NY St. Cyril Church.
Cimino, Michael '86 (SFE) [10] Albuquerque, NM Our Lady of the Assumption Church.
Cimmarrusti, Francis A. '64 (CHI) [59] Chicago, IL St. Fidelis Church.
Cimperman, Victor J. '43 (CLV) [4] Akron, OH Christ the King Church; Retired.
Cimpl, Charles L. '78 (SFS) [8] Sioux Falls, SD St. Therese Church.
Cincinnati, Anthony '87 (WH) Follansbee, WV St. Anthony's Church.
Cincoski, Edward E. *s.j.* '50 (DET) [P] Clarkston, MI Colombiere Center.
Cincotta, Anthony '74 (SY) On Duty Outside the Diocese.
Cindric, John R. '74 (GBG) Belle Vernon, PA St. Sebastian Church.
Cinesi, Joseph '80 (MIA) [8] Fort Lauderdale, FL St. Jerome Church.
Cingle, Martin A. '73 (ALT) [17] Johnstown, PA Visitation of the B.V.M. Church.
Cingolani, Gabriele *c.p.* '59 (MET) [H] South River, NJ Passionist Provincial Office.
Cini, Msgr. J. Thomas '68 (WIL) Liftwood, DE Immaculate Heart of Mary Church.
Cini, Robert *m.s.s.p.* '53 (DET) [3] Dearborn, MI St. Bernadette Church.
Cinque, Frank *o.m.v.* '88 (BO) [B] Boston, MA Oblate Provincialate.
Cinque, Stephen J. '81 (NEW) Maywood, NJ Our Lady Queen of Peace Church.
Cinque, Thomas *o.m.v.* '91 (BO) [B] Boston, MA Oblate Provincialate.
Cinquegrani, David *c.p.* '96 (HRT) [C] West Hartford, CT Saint Joseph College; [M] West Hartford, CT Holy Family Monastery/Retreat; [Q] Farmington, CT Holy Family Retreat House.
Cinquegrani, R. Bruce '79 (MEM) [2] Memphis, TN St. Ann Church.
Cinson, Victor, Jr. '74 (STU) Harriettsville, OH St. Henry Church; Lowell, OH Our Lady of Mercy Church.
Cintolo, Antonio A. '45 (BO) Retired.
Cintron, Angel Luis '91 (CGS) Aibonito, PR Church of St. Joseph.
Cintron, Freddy '87 (BRK) [39] Brooklyn, NY St. Fortunata Church; [39] Brooklyn, NY St. Fortunata Church.
Cintron, Segismundo '89 (PCE) Penuelas, PR St. Joseph Church; [B] Ponce, PR The Pontifical Catholic University of Puerto Rico.
Cintula, Francis M. '65 (CHL) North Wilkesboro, NC St. John Baptist de LaSalle Church.
Cio, Robert '74 (NEW) New Providence, NJ Our Lady of Peace Church.
Cioffi, Alfred '85 (MIA) [24] Miami, FL St. Kevin Church.
Cioffi, Paul L. *s.j.* '59 (WDC) [M] Washington, DC The Jesuit Community at Georgetown University; [V] Washington, DC Institute for Pastoral Renewal, Inc.
Cioffi, Phillip F. '81 (CHI) Forest Park, IL St. Bernardine Church.
Cioffi, Ronald J. '69 (TR) Keyport, NJ St. Joseph Church.
Ciolek, Msgr. Casimir S. '46 (CLV) [37] Cleveland, OH St. John Cantius Church; [2] Garfield Heights, OH SS. Peter and Paul Church; Cleveland, OH Airport, Cleveland Hopkins International; Retired; [V] Cleveland, OH Society of St. Vincent de Paul, Diocesan Central Council.
Ciolek, Joseph F. '47 (CLV) [L] Cleveland, OH Holy Family Home.
Cioppa, John A. *m.m.* '59 (FgM) Maryknoll Foreign Missions.
Cioppa, Philip M. '83 (ALB) Hoosick Falls, NY Immaculate Conception Church.
Cioppi, Martin T. '81 (PH) Upper Gwynedd, PA Corpus Christi Church; [F] Lansdale, PA Lansdale Catholic High School.
Ciordia, Pedro Ma. '61 (LA) El Monte, CA Our Lady of Guadalupe Church.
Ciorra, Anthony '73 (NEW) Livingston, NJ St. Raphael Church.
Ciorra, Anthony J. *o.f.m.cap.* '73 (PAT) [B] Morristown, NJ College of Saint Elizabeth; [O] Convent Station, NJ College of St. Elizabeth Newman Center.
Ciotola, Msgr. Romano '65 (COL) Grove City, OH Our Lady of Perpetual Help Church.
Ciotoli, Vincent J. '76 (ALB) Ravena, NY St. Patrick Church.
Cipar, Daniel *m.s.c.* '61 (Y) East Palestine, OH Our Lady of Lourdes Church; [A] Youngstown, OH Sacred Heart Retreat House & Renewal Center.
Cipolla, Richard G. '84 (BGP) [D] Fairfield, CT Fairfield College Preparatory School; [S] Darien, CT Convent of St. Birgitta.
Cippel, John A. '60 (SP) Spring Hill, FL St. Frances Xavier Cabrini Church.
Ciprian, Carl A. '76 (CLV) [3] Barberton, OH Holy Trinity Church.
Cipriano, Joseph F. '59 (SCR) [2] Old Forge, PA St. Mary's Church.
Cipriano, Robert '87 (SFR) [2] San Mateo, CA St. Gregory Church.
Ciranni, Salvatore *r.c.j.* '55 (FRS) Sanger, CA St. Mary Church.
Cirba, Richard J. '89 (SCR) Forest City, PA Sacred Heart of Jesus Church.
Cirignani, Anthony *o.f.m.* '83 (CHI) [111] Chicago, IL St. Joseph Church.
Cirilli, Matthew R. '64 (PIT) [2] Butler, PA St. Michael the Archangel Church.
Cirillo, Nicholas A. '95 (BGP) Huntington, CT St. Lawrence Church.
Cirino, Andre *o.f.m.* '67 (NY) [FF] Wappingers Falls, NY Mt. Alvernia Retreat House.
Ciriza, Jesus M. '59 (SJN) Rio Grande, PR Nuestra Senora del Carmen Church.
Cirone, John *c.m.f.* '96 (CHI) [80] Chicago, IL Holy Cross/Immaculate Heart of Mary Church.
Cirone, Theodore Salvatore *c.m.f.* '55 (CHI) [N] Chicago, IL Claretian Missionaries, St. Jude League, Inc.; [N] Oak Park, IL Claretian Fathers Headquarters of U.S.A. Eastern Province.
Cirrincione, Msgr. Joseph A. '34 (ROC) Retired.
Cis, James '38 (FTW) Retired.
Ciscar, Tomas *o.c.* '78 (SJN) [61] San Juan, PR Santa Teresita Del Nino Jesus Church.
Cisco, Bede *o.s.b.* '78 (IND) [B] St. Meinrad, IN St. Meinrad Seminary-College of Liberal Arts; [J] St. Meinrad, IN St. Meinrad Archabbey.
Cisco, Mariano *c.s.* '15 (NY) [HH] New York, NY Friends of RADIO MARIA, Inc.
Cisco, Mariano *c.s.* '82 (BRK) [U] Jamaica, NY Saint Charles House of Studies.
Cisdyn, Myroslaw '96 (SJP) Apopka, FL St. Mary's Church; St. Petersburg, FL Epiphany of Our Lord Church; Spring Hill, FL St. Andrew Church.
Cisek, Herman W. *m.m.* '65 (FgM) Maryknoll Foreign Missions.
Cisetti, Joseph '91 (KC) [39] Kansas City, MO St. Therese Parish.
Cisewski, John '71 (NO) [46] New Orleans, LA St. Matthias Church.
Cislo, Robert '65 (DET) [4] Taylor, MI St. Paschal Church.
Cisneros, Hilario *m.sp.s.* '92 (LA) Huntington Park, CA St. Martha Church.
Cisneros, Msgr. Octavio '71 (BRK) [B] Douglaston, NY Cathedral Residence of the Immaculate Conception.
Cisneros, Msgr. Octavio '71 (NY) [HH] New York, NY Felix Varela Foundation, Inc., The.
Cistone, Joseph R. '75 (PH) [11] Philadelphia, PA St. Anne Church.
Citero, Samuel *o.carm.* '84 (CHI) [68] Chicago, IL St. Gelasius Church.

Citino, Angelo R. '77 (PH) [109] Philadelphia, PA Mother of Divine Grace Church.
Citro, Anthony M. '94 (GAY) Roscommon, MI St. Michael Church.
Ciuba, Msgr. Edward J. '59 (NEW) North Caldwell, NJ Notre Dame Church.
Ciuffoletti, Angelo G. '64 (GBG) Youngwood, PA Holy Cross Church.
Ciulek, Joseph '43 (ALB) Retired.
Ciullo, Michael *o.c.d.* '75 (MIL) [P] Milwaukee, WI Provincial Offices - Discalced Carmelites.
Ciullo, Michael J. '75 (MAN) Claremont, NH St. Mary Church.
Ciullo, Salvator L. '60 (ARL) Fairfax Station, VA St. Raymond of Penafort Church.
Ciungu, John '42 (ROM) Retired.
Ciupek, James D. '97 (BUF) Williamsville, NY St. Gregory the Great Church.
Ciurej, Richard S. '54 (OM) Retired.
Ciurpita, John '89 (PHU) Cherry Hill, NJ St. Michael's Church.
Civiello, John D. '68 (PRT) [5] Portland, ME St. Patrick's Church.
Civille, John R. '66 (CIN) Middletown, OH Holy Family Church.
Civzelis, Victor *m.i.c.* '64 (CHI) [162] Chicago, IL Our Lady of Aglona Church.
Cizik, Ladis '87 (PIT) Washington County, PA Canon House; Washington County, PA Charles House Home for the Aged; Washington County, PA Greenery Nursing Home; Washington County, PA Horizon Senior Care; Washington County, PA Pine Lawn Home; Washington County, PA Rest Haven Personal Care Home I; Washington County, PA Rest Haven Personal Care Home II; Washington County, PA Rest Haven Personal Care Home V; Washington County, PA South Hills Convalescent Center; Washington County, PA New Life Treatment Center.
Cizik, Ladis J. '87 (PIT) Washington County, PA Western Center; Washington County, PA Canonsburg Hospital.
Cizur, Ignacio *o.f.m.cap.* '72 (DAL) [8] Dallas, TX Our Lady of Lourdes Church.
Claassen, Richard *o.c.d.* '93 (TUC) [21] Tucson, AZ Santa Cruz Church.
Claerr, Francis *c.m.m.* '48 (DET) [K] Dearborn Heights, MI Our Lady of Grace Monastery.
Claffey, James E. *c.m.* '72 (PH) [AA] Philadelphia, PA Congregation of the Mission.
Clagett, Carl P. '55 (COL) [33] Columbus, OH Our Lady of the Miraculous Medal Church.
Clair, John J. '82 (CHI) [A] Chicago, IL St. Joseph Seminary.
Clancey, Msgr. Thomas C. '45 (BRK) [19] Brooklyn, NY St. Bernard's Church.
Clancy, Bede *o.f.m.* '44 (FgM) Franciscan Foreign Missions.
Clancy, Bernard *o.m.i.* '41 (MIA) [2] Miami, FL Christ the King Church.
Clancy, Douglas P. '71 (HRT) [4] Manchester, CT St. James Church.
Clancy, Frank *s.c.j.* '74 (BWN) Harlingen, TX Valley Baptist Medical Center; [E] Harlingen, TX Priests of the Sacred Heart.
Clancy, Frederick J. '45 (TR) Retired.
Clancy, Patrick M.J. *o.p.* '39 (CHI) [N] Chicago, IL Dominicans (Provincial Office).
Clancy, Raphael J. '76 (AUS) Giddings, TX St. Margaret Church.
Clancy, Rian *c.p.* '53 (CHI) [N] Chicago, IL Immaculate Conception Monastery.
Clancy, Richard '91 (BO) [16] Boston, MA St. Brigid Church.
Clancy, Robert E. '74 (CLV) [16] Akron, OH Sacred Heart of Jesus Church; Akron, OH Akron General Hospital.
Clancy, Thomas *s.j.* '55 (NO) [C] New Orleans, LA Loyola University; [S] New Orleans, LA Jesuit Seminary and Mission Fund.
Clancy, Msgr. Thomas C. '45 (BRK) Retired; [V] Queens Village, NY St. Ann's Novitiate, Little Sisters of the Poor.
Clancy, Timothy R. *s.j.* (SPK) [C] Spokane, WA Gonzaga University.
Claney, Richard (BO) [C] Boston, MA Emmanuel College.
Clanton, Bruce *s.d.s.* '78 (MIL) [P] Milwaukee, WI Salvatorian Provincial Residence.
Clapham, Bruce '95 (CHY) Rock Springs, WY Our Lady of Sorrows Church; Rock Springs, WY Our Lady of Sorrows/Sts. Cyril & Methodius Church.
Clapp, Kenneth A. '90 (MIL) On Duty Outside the Archdiocese.
Clarahan, Eugene F. '52 (WIL) Retired.
Clarahan, Michael '58 (CHI) [N] Chicago, IL St. Peter's Friary.
Clark, Andrew '83 (NY) Absent on Leave.
Clark, Anthony *s.v.d.* '85 (IND) [34] Indianapolis, IN St. Rita Church.
Clark, Benjamin *o.c.s.o.* '50 (CHR) [D] Moncks Corner, SC Mepkin Abbey.
Clark, C. Thomas (L) Louisville, KY Alliant Medical Pavillion.
Clark, C. Thomas '49 (L) Retired.
Clark, Curtis L. '84 (PH) [A] Wynnewood, PA Theological Seminary of St. Charles Borromeo, Overbrook.
Clark, Curtis L., Jr. '84 (ARL) On Duty Outside the Diocese.
Clark, Daniel '54 (DM) Stuart, IA All Saints Church.
Clark, Daniel C. '80 (L) On Special Assignment.
Clark, David '84 (P) On Duty Outside the Archdiocese.
Clark, Msgr. Dennis R. '66 (SD) Rancho Santa Fe, CA Church of the Nativity.
Clark, Douglas K. '76 (SAV) [1] Savannah, GA Cathedral of St. John the Baptist.
Clark, Edward F. *s.j.* '45 (NY) [DD] New York, NY Jesuit Community at Fordham University.
Clark, Msgr. Edward Wm. '72 (LA) [A] Camarillo, CA St. John's Seminary College of the Archdiocese of Los Angeles.
Clark, Emmanuel W. *o.s.b.* '61 (P) Mt. Angel, OR St. Mary Church; [L] St. Benedict, OR Mt. Angel Abbey.
Clark, Msgr. Eugene V. '51 (NY) [2] New York, NY St. Agnes Church; [HH] New York, NY Friends of American Art in Religion, Inc.; [HH] New York, NY Patrons of the Arts in the Vatican Museums.
Clark, Francis X. *s.j.* '43 (FgM) Provinces.
Clark, Gerard J. '40 (MIL) Retired.
Clark, H. Robert '51 (CHI) [179] Chicago, IL Queen of All Saints Basilica Church; Retired.
Clark, Howard T. '57 (WIL) [5] Wilmington, DE St. Elizabeth Church; Special or Other Diocesan Assignment.
Clark, J. Donald *s.j.* '48 (SY) [S] Syracuse, NY Jesuits at LeMoyne, Inc.
Clark, J. Michael '95 (OWN) Fulton, KY St. Edward Church; Hickman, KY Sacred Heart Church.
Clark, James (ALB) Schoharie, NY St. Joseph Church.
Clark, James B. '95 (BO) [52] Boston, MA Most Precious Blood Church.
Clark, James E. '96 (ALB) Middleburgh, NY St. Catherine Church.
Clark, James M. '72 (TR) Lincroft, NJ St. Leo the Great Church.
Clark, James P. '52 (NY) [140] Bronx, NY St. Francis of Assisi Church.
Clark, James W. '56 (FR) Retired.
Clark, James W. '83 (GBG) New Kensington, PA St. Joseph Church.
Clark, John '66 (SEA) Unassigned.
Clark, John F. *c.m.* '70 (STL) [A] St. Louis, MO Kenrick-Glennon Seminary; [P] St. Louis, MO Vincentian-St. Lazare Residence.
Clark, Msgr. John J. (CAM) Retired.
Clark, John R. '96 (WDC) [8] Silver Spring, MD St. Michael Church.
Clark, John W. *s.j.* '59 (SFR) [C] San Francisco, CA University of San Francisco.
Clark, Joseph J. '96 (ARL) Annandale, VA Holy Spirit Church.
Clark, Joseph L. '76 (RIC) Fort Monroe, VA St. Mary Star of the Sea Church.
Clark, Kevin *o.s.b.* '76 (NO) Bogalusa, LA Annunciation B.V.M. Church; [P] St. Benedict, LA St. Joseph Abbey.
Clark, Msgr. Laurence E. '54 (LA) Retired.
Clark, Lucian *c.p.* '65 (FgM) Passionist Foreign Missions.
Clark, Lucian *c.p.* '65 (MET) [H] South River, NJ Passionist Provincial Office.
Clark, Matthew R. *o.s.b.* '87 (NO) [A] St. Benedict, LA St. Joseph's Seminary College; [P] St. Benedict, LA St. Joseph Abbey.
Clark, Mike '95 (OWN) Clinton, KY St. Jude Church.
Clark, Patrick S. '61 (SEA) Issaquah, WA St. Joseph Church.
Clark, Peter A. *s.j.* '92 (PH) [AA] Philadelphia, PA Jesuit Community at St. Joseph's University.
Clark, Ray '91 (OWN) Mayfield, KY St. Joseph Church.
Clark, Richard D. '63 (ALT) Conemaugh, PA Sacred Heart Church.
Clark, Richard D. '93 (MRY) Carmel, CA San Carlos Borromeo Basilica Church.
Clark, Msgr. Robert '53 (CC) Retired.
Clark, Robert *s.s.c.* '65 (OM) [K] St. Columbans, NE St. Columban's Foreign Mission Society.
Clark, Robert P., Jr. '84 (NU) Absent on Leave.
Clark, Steven E. '90 (NY) Peekskill, NY Assumption Church.
Clark, Thomas F. *s.j.* '81 (BO) [22] Boston, MA St. Francis de Sales-St. Philip Church; [W] Boston, MA Loyola House; [W] Boston, MA The Society of Jesus of New England-Provincial Offices.
Clark, Thomas R. '62 (L) [2] Valley Station, KY Our Lady Help of Christians Church; [4] Valley Station, KY St. Timothy Church.
Clark, Timothy *o.c.s.o.* '80 (P) [L] Lafayette, OR The Cistercian (Trappist) Abbey of Our Lady of Guadalupe.
Clark, Tom '55 (OWN) Cloverport, KY St. Rose Church.
Clark, Tony '79 (LSC) Lordsburg, NM St. Joseph Church.
Clark, Vernon F. '80 (CHY) Buffalo, WY St. John the Baptist Church.
Clark, William *o.m.i.* '55 (BEL) [F] Belleville, IL Missionary Oblates of Mary Immaculate - St. Henry's Oblate Residence.
Clark, William A. *s.j.* '93 (FgM) Provinces.
Clark, William P. *o.m.i.* '55 (STP) [N] St. Paul, MN Oblate Residence.
Clarke, Arthur A. *s.j.* '47 (FgM) Provinces.
Clarke, Arthur A. *s.j.* '50 (SJN) [22] San Juan, PR San Ignacio de Loyola Church.
Clarke, David M. *s.j.* '64 (DEN) [B] Denver, CO Regis University; [M] Denver, CO Regis Jesuit Community (The Jesuits at Regis University).
Clarke, Gerardo R. *o.s.f.s.* '57 (CHL) Kernersville, NC Holy Cross Church.
Clarke, Msgr. Hugh '50 (CC) Retired.
Clarke, Msgr. James A. '70 (Y) Salem, OH St. Paul's Church.
Clarke, Msgr. James T. '38 (SCR) Retired; [N] Dunmore, PA Villa St. Joseph.
Clarke, Jim '80 (LA) Redondo Beach, CA St. James Church.
Clarke, John A. '59 (CAM) Washington Township, NJ SS. Peter and Paul Church.
Clarke, John W. '45 (DM) Imogene, IA St. Patrick Church.
Clarke, Kevin T. *s.j.* '73 (HEL) [5] Missoula, MT St. Francis Xavier Church.
Clarke, Noel (PAT) Denville, NJ St. Clare Hospital; [J] Denville, NJ Northwest Covenant Medial Center.
Clarke, Peter '63 (CHR) Murphy Village, SC St. Edward Church.
Clarke, Robert J. '73 (PIT) [47] Pittsburgh, PA Guardian Angels Church.
Clarke, Thomas E. *s.j.* '50 (NY) [DD] New York, NY Xavier Jesuit Community; [EE] Highland Mills, NY Religious of Jesus and Mary; [FF] Highland Mills, NY Bethany Retreat House.
Clarke, Msgr. Thomas J. '34 (EVN) Retired.
Clarke, W. Norris *s.j.* '45 (NY) [DD] New York, NY Jesuit Community at Fordham University.
Clarkin, Herbert '45 (HRT) [K] West Hartford, CT Saint Mary Home.
Clarkson, John *o.m.i.* '55 (SAT) [K] San Antonio, TX Oblate Madonna Residence.
Clarkson, Theodore J. *s.j.* '44 (SY) [S] Syracuse, NY Jesuits at LeMoyne, Inc.
Claro, Mario R. '67 (WH) Morgantown, WV St. Theresa's Church.
Clary, Brian M. '96 (BO) Braintree, MA St. Clare Church.
Clary, Michael O. '77 (KC) Blue Springs, MO St. John La Lande Church.
Class, Michael D. *s.j.* '90 (MIL) [P] Milwaukee, WI Jesuit Community at Marquette University.
Classick, Bede E. *o.s.b.* '67 (PAT) [M] Newton, NJ St. Paul's Abbey.
Clauder, J. Gibbs '73 (MAD) Leave of Absence.
Clausen, Kenneth J. '53 (GF) Retired.
Clausen, William J. '62 (RCK) Maple Park, IL St. Mary Church.
Clauss, Joseph '56 (EVN) Retired.
Clavelle, Richard F. *o.s.b.* '60 (MAN) [K] Manchester, NH St. Anselm Abbey.
Clavenna, Msgr. Charles G. '56 (STL) Augusta, MO Immaculate Conception Church.
Claver, Karl '79 (SCR) [M] Elmhurst, PA Priestly Fraternity of St. Peter (F.S.S.P.), North American District Headquarters.
Clavero, Jose M. *sch.p.* '64 (NY) [12] New York, NY Annunciation Church; [DD] New York, NY Calasanzian Fathers (Piarists).
Clavin, M. Oliver '70 (SPC) Kelso, MO St. Augustine Church.
Clavin, Nicholas P. '73 (SD) [37] San Diego, CA St. Vincent de Paul Church.
Clay, David J. *s.s.c.* '62 (FgM) St. Columban's Foreign Mission.
Clay, Frederick L. *c.s.b.* '83 (GAL) Angleton, TX St. Basil Church.
Clay, John C. '51 (STP) [33] St. Paul, MN St. Stanislaus Church.
Clay, Michael G. '80 (R) Chapel Hill, NC St. Thomas More Church.
Clayton, Msgr. C. Murray '56 (SHP) [5] Shreveport, LA Sacred Heart of Jesus Church.
Clayton, Daniel J. '68 (DAL) Rowlett, TX Sacred Heart Church.
Cleare, Rudi '83 (ORL) Sabbatical.
Cleary, Christopher *c.p.* '86 (WOR) [N] Shrewsbury, MA Passionist Fathers of Shrewsbury, Inc., Calvary Retreat Center; [P] Shrewsbury, MA Calvary Retreat Center, Passionist Community.
Cleary, Donald M. '71 (OM) Wayne, NE St. Mary Church; [G] Wayne, NE Providence Medical Center.
Cleary, Donald R. '68 (KC) Retired.
Cleary, Edward '56 (SFR) [4] South San Francisco, CA St. Veronica Church.
Cleary, Edward J. '40 (MEM) Retired.
Cleary, Edward L. *o.p.* '57 (CHI) [N] River Forest, IL

St. Thomas Aquinas Priory.
Cleary, Edward L. *o.p.* '57 (PRO) [P] Providence, RI St. Thomas Aquinas Priory at Providence College.
Cleary, Edward M. '56 (SFR) Retired.
Cleary, Francis X. *s.j.* (STL) [C] St. Louis, MO Saint Louis University.
Cleary, Francis X. *s.j.* '63 (STL) [P] St. Louis, MO Jesuit Community Corporation at St. Louis University - Jesuit Hall.
Cleary, Gerard '61 (BLX) Pascagoula, MS Our Lady of Victories Church.
Cleary, Herbert J. *s.j.* (BO) [U] Boston, MA Marian Manor.
Cleary, Herbert J. *s.j.* '68 (BO) [W] Boston, MA Loyola House.
Cleary, Hugh W. *c.s.c.* '73 (ALB) [T] Albany, NY The Family Rosary Worldwide Office
Cleary, Hugh W. *c.s.c.* '73 (BGP) [O] Bridgeport, CT Provincial Offices of the Priests and Brothers of Holy Cross, Eastern Province.
Cleary, Hugh W. *c.s.c.* '73 (LA) [DD] Los Angeles, CA.
Cleary, James *o.f.m.* (LA) [K] Lynwood, CA St. Francis Medical Center.
Cleary, James *t.o.r.* '41 (ARL) [J] Winchester, VA Sacred Heart Friary.
Cleary, James L. *o.f.m.cap.* '70 (LA) [74] Los Angeles, CA St. Lawrence of Brindisi Church.
Cleary, Msgr. Kevin '48 (FRS) Ridgecrest, CA St. Ann Church.
Cleary, Michael J. '53 (SR) Napa, CA St. Apollinaris Church.
Cleary, Patrick J. '78 (BO) [70] Boston, MA St. Stephen Church; [W] Boston, MA The Society of St. James the Apostle, Inc.
Cleary, Paul '74 (SAT) [34] San Antonio, TX St. Dominic Church.
Cleary, Philip C. '79 (CHI) Missionary Work.
Cleary, Richard E. *o.s.f.s.* '59 (R) [2] Durham, NC Holy Infant Church.
Cleary, Richard J. *o.s.b.* '55 (KC) [J] Conception, MO Conception Abbey.
Cleary, Richard T. *s.j.* '66 (BO) [W] Chestnut Hill, MA The Jesuit Community at Boston College; [CC] Chestnut Hill, MA Boston College University Chaplaincy.
Cleary, William *c.ss.r.* '62 (CHI) [N] Chicago, IL Redemptorists:.
Cleary, William *c.ss.r.* '62 (DEN) [M] Denver, CO The Redemptorists/Denver Province.
Cleary, William D. '55 (IND) Retired.
Cleary, William M. *c.ss.r.* '62 (FgM) Redemptorist Foreign Missions.
Cleaton, C. Thomas '75 (CLV) Bay Village, OH St. Raphael Church.
Cleator, Gerard B. *o.p.* '65 (CHI) [N] Chicago, IL Dominicans (Provincial Office)
Clegg, Thomas '90 (IND) [3] Indianapolis, IN Good Shepherd Church; [6] Indianapolis, IN Holy Rosary Church.
Clegg, Timothy '71 (LFT) On Duty Outside the Diocese.
Clemens, John W. '72 (CHI) [73] Chicago, IL St. Gregory Church; [X] Chicago, IL The Aquin Guild.
Clemens, Norbert H. *c.s.b.* '41 (GAL) Retired; [Q] Houston, TX Dillon House.
Clement, James P. '45 (BR) Retired.
Clement, Richard H. '85 (ALN) [1] Bethlehem, PA St. Anne Church.
Clement, Thomas '79 (DEN) Akron, CO St. Joseph Church.
Clement, Thomas '95 (SFS) Aberdeen, SD Sacred Heart Church.
Clemente, Joseph J. '81 (SY) [1] Rome, NY St. John the Baptist Church.
Clemente, Michael '55 (ALB) Retired.
Clemente, Oscar '80 (FR) West Harwich, MA Holy Trinity Church.
Clemente, Vincent L. '76 (VEN) [3] Sarasota, FL St. Martha Church.
Clementi, Innocent *s.d.b.* '49 (MIA) [25] Miami, FL St. Kieran Church.
Clementi, Innocent *s.d.b.* '51 (PAT) [N] Haledon, NJ Institute of the Daughters of Mary Help of Christians.
Clementich, LeRoy E. *c.s.c.* '57 (FTW) [J] South Bend, IN Congregation of Holy Cross Indiana Province Provincial House.
Clements, Charles '62 (MIA) [2] Miami, FL Christ the King Church; Special Assignment.
Clements, Daniel A. '54 (NSH) Retired.
Clements, George H. '57 (CHI) On Duty Outside the Archdiocese.
Clements, Richard '46 (OWN) Retired.
Clements, Robert (PHX) Chandler, AZ St. Mary's Church.
Clements, Robert '90 (PHX) Special Assignment.
Clements, Seamus *c.s.sp.* '47 (NEW) [22] Jersey City, NJ Our Lady of Victories Church.
Clements, Thomas P. '55 (CHL) Salisbury, NC Sacred Heart Church.
Clemins, Msgr. Francis J. '50 (PH) Trooper, PA Visitation B.V.M. Church.
Clemo, Ronald M. *s.j.* '67 (SJ) [D] San Jose, CA Bellarmine College Preparatory.
Clemons, Delma '66 (OWN) Fancy Farm, KY St. Jerome Church.
Clenaghan, Gerard *o.m.i.* '47 (SEA) [4] Seattle, WA St. Benedict Church.
Clennon, Raymond J. *o.carm.* '67 (JOL) [I] Darien, IL Carmelite Carefree Retirement Village; [J] Darien, IL Carmelite Community; [M] Darien, IL Office of the Carmelite Midwest Commissary Provincial.
Clerkin, Robert J. (RVC) Patchogue, NY St. Francis de Sales Church.
Clerkin, Thomas *c.s.p.* '85 (AUS) [11] Austin, TX St. Austin's Church.
Clermont, John *o.f.m.cap.* '53 (NY) [57] New York, NY St. John the Baptist Church.
Clerx, Theodore *c.i.c.m.* '57 (SAT) [K] San Antonio, TX Padua Place.
Cletus, Sales T. (Ranjan) *i.m.s.* '84 (TYL) Crockett, TX St. Francis of the Tejas Church.
Cleu, Paul E. '74 (OAK) [3] Fremont, CA St. James The Apostle Church.
Cleveland, S. Gregory *o.m.v.* '95 (MET) Avenel, NJ St. Andrew Church.
Cleves, Simeon *o.f.m.* '55 (L) [43] Louisville, KY St. Joseph Church.
Cleves, William F. '78 (COV) [A] Covington, KY Thomas More College.
Click, Patrick R. '71 (LFT) West Lafayette, IN St. Thomas Aquinas Church; [H] West Lafayette, IN St. Thomas Aquinas Parish and Foundation for Catholic Students Attending Purdue University.
Cliff, Joseph '39 (MIA) Retired.
Clifford, David K. '91 (NY) [133] Bronx, NY St. Benedict Church.
Clifford, Donald G. '43 (BO) Retired.
Clifford, Donald G. *s.j.* '62 (PH) [C] Philadelphia, PA St. Joseph's University; [AA] Philadelphia, PA Jesuit Community at St. Joseph's University.
Clifford, Donald P. '61 (BO) Marshfield, MA Our Lady of the Assumption Church.
Clifford, James *o.s.a.* '72 (P) Central Point, OR Shepherd of the Valley Church; [L] Gold Hill, OR Augustinian Community.
Clifford, James J. '45 (WOR) Retired.
Clifford, Jerome *s.c.j.* '61 (MIL) [P] Hales Corners, WI Priests of the Sacred Heart.
Clifford, Jerome A. *s.j.* '49 (DET) [P] Clarkston, MI Colombiere Center.
Clifford, Joseph '89 (VEN) [1] Sarasota, FL Incarnation Church.
Clifford, Leo *o.f.m.* '45 (NY) [115] New York, NY St. Stephen of Hungary Church.
Clifford, Marc J. *o.s.f.s.* '69 (OKL) Duncan, OK Assumption Church.
Clifford, Michael J. '60 (GB) Special Assignment.
Clifford, Mike (GB) Suring, WI St. Michael Church.
Clifford, Paul J. *s.j.* '56 (CHI) [89] Chicago, IL St. Ignatius Church.
Clifford, Paul T. '92 (BO) Dracut, MA St. Therese Church.
Clifford, Peter C. '76 (ROC) Newark, NY St. Michael Church.
Clifford, Richard J. *s.j.* '66 (BO) [W] Cambridge, MA Weston Jesuit Community.
Clifford, Richard L. *m.m.* '53 (FgM) Maryknoll Foreign Missions.
Clifford, Thomas *s.j.* '81 (WDC) [E] Washington, DC Gonzaga College High School.
Clifford, Thomas A. *o.p.* '60 (NO) [25] New Orleans, LA St. Anthony Of Padua Church.
Clift, James C. '57 (OAK) Point Richmond, CA Our Lady of Mercy Church.
Clifton, James F. '88 (OM) [K] Omaha, NE Jesuit Community At Creighton University.
Clinch, Kevin '83 (TUC) Hayden, AZ St. Joseph's Church.
Clines, Paul J. '44 (CLV) [1] Barberton, OH St. Augustine Church; Retired.
Clinet, Mircea '51 (ROM) Retired.
Clinton, Donald E. '90 (MAN) Wilton, NH Sacred Heart Church.
Clinton, Kenneth J. '48 (WIN) Retired.
Clinton, Kevin I. '74 (STP) Mendota, MN St. Peter Church; [H] Eagan, MN Faithful Shepherd Catholic School.
Clisch, Norman A. '65 (MAR) Iron River, MI St. Agnes Church.
Clody, Msgr. Albert W. '65 (BUF) [5] Buffalo, NY All Saints Church.
Clogher, Msgr. John J. '31 (OAK) Retired.
Cloherty, Francis J. '62 (BO) [7] Brockton, MA St. Patrick Church.
Cloherty, John J. '60 (SFR) Colma, CA Holy Angels Church.
Cloherty, Thomas '74 (DAL) [2] Dallas, TX All Saints Church; [O] Irving, TX Diocese of Dallas Campus Ministry.
Cloherty, Thomas '82 (DAL) [B] Irving, TX University of Dallas.
Clohessy, Kevin P. '85 (JC) Taos, MO St. Francis Xavier Church.
Cloney, Michael '68 (SR) Eureka, CA St. Bernard Church.
Cloney, Robert D. *s.j.* '60 (NY) [DD] New York, NY Jesuit Community at Fordham University.
Cloonan, Joseph F. '44 (ROC) Retired.
Clooney, David '64 (PHU) [A] Washington, DC St. Josaphat Seminary.
Clooney, Francis X. *s.j.* '78 (BO) [W] Chestnut Hill, MA The Jesuit Community at Boston College.
Cloquet, Victor '50 (SEA) Retired.
Clore, Victor '65 (DET) [17] Detroit, MI Christ the King Church.
Close, James J. '63 (CHI) [H] Chicago, IL Mission of Our Lady of Mercy-Mercy Home for Boys and Girls.
Close, John A. '69 (PH) [A] Wynnewood, PA Theological Seminary of St. Charles Borromeo, Overbrook.
Close, John L. '82 (ALB) [16] Albany, NY St. Teresa of Avila Church; Special Assignment.
Cloud, Charles W. '89 (TUC) Florence, AZ Assumption of the Blessed Virgin Mary Church.
Clough, Wulfstan F. *o.s.b.* '96 (GBG) [H] Latrobe, PA Saint Vincent Archabbey.
Cloutier, Roland C. '66 (NOR) Hebron, CT The Church of the Holy Family.
Cloutier, Ronald F. '72 (GAL) [2] Houston, TX All Saints Church; Houston, TX Harris County Jail.
Cloutier, Timothy '80 (STP) Minnetonka, MN Immaculate Heart of Mary Church.
Cloutier, Wilbur G. '58 (ALX) Retired.
Clovis, Stephen M. '89 (P) Scappoose, OR St. Wenceslaus Church.
Clubb, Ronald E. '86 (STP) [7] Minneapolis, MN Holy Name Church.
Clunan, Msgr. Paul W. '43 (MEM) Retired.
Clune, Gerald F. '40 (ALB) Retired.
Clune, Gerald F. '40 (SB) [E] Morongo Valley, CA St. Michael's of Morongo Valley, Inc.
Clune, Malaky *o.p.* '60 (SJN) Catano, PR Nuestra Senora del Carmen Church.
Clyde, George A. '42 (NEW) Retired.
Clyne, Msgr. James B. '47 (LA) Retired.
Clyne, Msgr. Vincent F. '45 (NY) [195] Staten Island, NY St. Ann Church; Retired.
Cnackalackal, Antony '79 (TOL) Payne, OH St. John the Baptist Church.
Coady, Edward L. '58 (BAL) Retired.
Coady, Frank (SAL) [2] Salina, KS St. Elizabeth Ann Seton Church.
Coady, John '59 (GF) Retired.
Coakley, John P. *s.j.* '70 (CHI) [D] Chicago, IL St. Ignatius Jesuit Community; [J] Maywood, IL Foster G. McGaw Hospital of Loyola University of Chicago.
Coakley, Lawrence R. '76 (HBG) New Cumberland, PA St. Theresa of the Infant Jesus Church.
Coakley, Paul S. '83 (WCH) [6] Wichita, KS Church of the Resurrection.
Coakley, Richard J. *s.j.* '37 (BO) [W] Weston, MA Campion Health Center, Inc.
Coates, John T. '45 (PH) Center Square, PA St. Helena Church; Retired.
Coates, Roderick J.D. *s.s.j.* '89 (WDC) [8] Washington, DC St. Benedict the Moor Church.
Cobb, Daniel *o.s.b.* '44 (NO) Mandeville, LA St. Tammany Parish Prison; [P] St. Benedict, LA St. Joseph Abbey.
Cobb, Gerald T. *s.j.* '81 (SEA) [A] Seattle, WA Seattle University.
Cobb, Richard E. *s.j.* '62 (LA) [F] Los Angeles, CA Loyola High School.
Cobbe, Jos *c.i.c.m.* '67 (FgM) Missionhurst Foreign Missions.
Cobeaga, Msgr. Victorino '54 (ARE) [6] Vega-Baja, PR Our Lady of Lourdes Church.
Cobel, Lawrence F. '73 (BUF) [4] Lackawanna, NY St. Barbara Church.
Coble, Scott W. *s.j.* '79 (SPK) [C] Spokane, WA Gonzaga University.
Coble, Timothy *o.cist.* '86 (DAL) [M] Irving, TX Cistercian Abbey of Our Lady of Dallas.
Coburn, Albert J. *o.p.* '48 (NO) [30] New Orleans, LA St. Dominic Church.
Coburn, Msgr. Vincent P. '41 (NEW) Bloomfield, NJ Church of St. Thomas the Apostle; Short Hills, NJ St. Rose of Lima Church; Retired.
Coby, Thomas W. '73 (RVC) Greenlawn, NY St. Francis of Assisi Church.
Cocca, Stephen M. '96 (WDC) Landover Hills, MD St. Mary's Catholic Church.
Cochran, George L. *o.p.* '62 (PRO) [P] Providence, RI St. Thomas Aquinas Priory at Providence College.
Cochran, Paul *s.j.* (FBK) [E] St. Marys, AK Native Ministry Training Program.
Cochran, Paul *s.j.* '94 (FBK) Marshall, AK Immaculate Heart of Mary Church.
Cochran, Paul M. *s.j.* '94 (FBK) [E] St. Marys, AK Brother Joe Prince Jesuit Community.
Cochran, Paul W. '88 (LFT) Kokomo, IN St. Joan of Arc Church.
Cochrane, Richard J. *o.s.a.* '73 (PH) [G] Malvern, PA

Malvern Preparatory School for Boys.
Cocio, Carlos '83 (TUC) Absent on Leave; [F] Tucson, AZ Regina Cleri Center.
Cockayne, John E. '85 (HRT) Thomaston, CT St. Thomas Church.
Coco, Francis J. *s.j.* '51 (LAF) [J] Grand Coteau, LA Our Lady of the Oaks Retreat House.
Cocozza, Dennis '75 (NEW) Belleville, NJ St. Anthony's Church.
Cocucci, Joseph M.P.R. '96 (WIL) Middletown, DE St. Joseph Church.
Cocuzzi, Bruno *o.c.d.* '56 (MAN) [M] Manchester, NH.
Cocuzzi, Msgr. George A. '49 (NY) [185] Bronx, NY St. Raymond Church.
Cocuzzi, Msgr. George A. '49 (ROC) Retired.
Coda, Joseph '63 (NEW) [N] Rutherford, NJ St. John Vianney Residence for Priests.
Coda, Joseph F. '63 (NEW) Oradell, NJ St. Joseph's Church; Retired.
Codd, Kevin '79 (SPK) Oroville, WA Immaculate Conception Church; Tonasket, WA Holy Rosary Church.
Coddaire, Louis *o.s.b.cam.* '52 (SR) [K] Arcata, CA Newman Community, Humboldt State University.
Coddaire, Louis *o.s.b.cam.* '78 (MRY) [G] Big Sur, CA New Camaldoli Hermitage.
Code, Sean A. '93 (ALT) Somerset, PA St. Peter's Church.
Cody, Aelred *o.s.b.* '57 (IND) [J] St. Meinrad, IN St. Meinrad Archabbey.
Cody, Daniel '62 (STA) [16] Jacksonville, FL St. Joseph's Church.
Cody, Henry P. '58 (HRT) [7] West Hartford, CT St. Timothy's Church.
Cody, John *c.ss.r.* '81 (SAT) [M] San Antonio, TX Redemptorists of Texas- San Antonio #1.
Cody, John F. '49 (WIN) Retired.
Cody, Msgr. John K. '73 (COL) [15] Columbus, OH St. Francis of Assisi Church.
Cody, John R. *c.ss.r.* '81 (SAT) [19] San Antonio, TX Our Lady Of Perpetual Help Church.
Cody, Kevin W. '93 (MAN) Military Chaplains.
Cody, Michael '58 (SEA) Retired.
Cody, Michael F. *s.s.c.* '73 (BO) [W] Quincy, MA St. Columban's Foreign Mission Society.
Cody, Nicholas A. '54 (STP) Retired.
Cody, Thomas '68 (STA) [13] Jacksonville, FL Resurrection Church.
Coelho, Gabriel Prashant *o.f.m.cap.* (DET) [K] Detroit, MI St. Bonaventure Friary.
Coello, Demetrio *s.d.b.* '60 (SJN) Catano, PR San Francisco de Sales Church.
Coels, Andrew *c.i.c.m.* '48 (SAT) [K] San Antonio, TX Padua Place.
Coen, Charles P. '68 (NY) Red Hook, NY St. Christopher Church.
Coen, James *c.ss.r.* '53 (WDC) [M] Washington, DC Holy Redeemer College.
Coen, John *s.a.c.* '62 (RNO) Sparks, NV Immaculate Conception Church; [B] Reno, NV St. Mary's Regional Medical Center.
Coen, Mark '90 (DUL) Brainerd, MN St. Francis Church.
Coen, William R. (BO) Retired.
Coen, William R. '49 (BO) [2] Milton, MA St. Elizabeth Church.
Coenen, Thomas (DM) Bedford, IA Sacred Heart Church; Villisca, IA St. Joseph Church.
Coenen, Tom '77 (DM) Clarinda, IA St. Clare Church.
Coens, Frank *o.f.m.* '73 (MEM) [5] Memphis, TN St. Augustine Church; [J] Memphis, TN Franciscan Friars (Sacred Heart Prov.) of Memphis.
Coerber, Joseph H. '66 (MIL) Marytown, WI St. Mary Church.
Coerver, Richard V. '76 (STL) Pacific, MO St. Bridget Church.
Coerver, Robert F. *c.m.* '41 (STL) [A] St. Louis, MO Kenrick-Glennon Seminary.
Cofenas, Robert G. '73 (ALN) [3] Reading, PA St. Catharine of Siena Church.
Coffey, Msgr. Andrew V. '47 (SAC) Davis, CA St. James Church; Retired and in Senior Ministry.
Coffey, Charles J. *c.s.sp.* '50 (GAL) [1] Galveston, TX St. Mary's Cathedral Basilica Church.
Coffey, Edward N. '37 (CHI) [4] Cicero, IL Mary, Queen of Heaven Church; Retired.
Coffey, Msgr. James F. '31 (RVC) Bay Shore, NY St. Patrick's Church; Retired.
Coffey, James H. '45 (BO) [1] Brookline, MA St. Aidan Church; Retired.
Coffey, John P. '73 (CHR) Camden, SC Our Lady of Perpetual Help Church.
Coffey, Joseph L. '96 (PH) [83] Philadelphia, PA St. Katherine of Siena Church.
Coffey, Mark *m.s.c.* '67 (SAT) [M] San Antonio, TX Missionaries of the Sacred Heart.
Coffey, Michael '91 (CAM) Atco, NJ Assumption Church.
Coffey, Peter *s.d.s.* '68 (NSH) Cookeville, TN St. Thomas Aquinas Church; Sparta, TN St. Andrew Church.
Coffey, Msgr. Thomas A. '48 (TR) Retired; [M] Trenton, NJ Villa Vianney.
Coffey, William H. '45 (OG) Retired.
Coffield, Msgr. John V. '41 (ORG) Capistrano Beach, CA San Felipe de Jesus Church; Retired.
Cogan, Patrick *s.a.* '77 (WDC) [B] Washington, DC Atonement Seminary-Franciscan Friars of the Atonement.
Cogan, William B. *s.j.* '55 (ALB) [O] Auriesville, NY Jesuit Retreat House for Priests, Religious and Lay People.
Coghill, Elstan *o.f.m.* '48 (GAY) Indian River, MI Cross in the Woods Catholic Shrine Church.
Coghlan, Msgr. Brian '63 (ORG) Seal Beach, CA Holy Family Church.
Coghlan, John '74 (MOB) Citronelle, AL St. Thomas Church; Mount Vernon, AL St. Cecilia Church.
Coghlan, John A. '44 (STO) Retired.
Coghlan, John C. '43 (CIN) Retired.
Cogo, Joseph A. *c.s.* '59 (BO) [67] Boston, MA Sacred Heart Church.
Cohalan, Msgr. Florence '38 (NY) [2] New York, NY St. Agnes Church; Retired.
Cohan, Dennis '74 (NEW) Glen Rock, NJ St. Catharine Church.
Cohan, Francis J. '46 (P) Retired.
Cohan, Msgr. Robert W. '55 (E) [18] Erie, PA St. James Church.
Cohea, Victor H. '80 (NO) [33] New Orleans, LA St. Francis De Sales Church.
Cohelo, Gabriel *o.f.m.cap.* (DET) Detroit, MI Harper Hospital and Rehabilitation Center.
Cohen, Gerald P. *c.s.c.* '63 (NOR) [K] Willimantic, CT Campus Ministry.
Cohen, Harold F. *s.j.* '58 (NO) [C] New Orleans, LA Loyola University.
Coholan, John F. *m.m.* '46 (FgM) Maryknoll Foreign Missions.
Coine, Robert E. '76 (WIL) Ridgely, MD St. Benedict Church.
Coiro, Gregory *o.f.m.cap.* '82 (LA) [F] La Canada Flintridge, CA St. Francis High School.
Coiro, Mark J. '84 (BO) Billerica, MA St. Theresa of Lisieux Church.
Coke, James E. '53 (LC) Retired.
Cokus, Msgr. Joseph J. '58 (LA) Sierra Madre, CA St. Rita Church.
Colacicco, Frank '79 (SAN) Retired.
Colacicco, Frank L. '79 (OAK) Danville, CA St. Isidore's Church.
Colacicco, Gerardo J. '82 (NY) [4] Newburgh, NY Sacred Heart Church.
Colagreco, Michael A. '77 (PH) Newtown Square, PA St. Anastasia Church.
Colaiacovo, Arthur J. '92 (PAT) Stirling, NJ St. Vincent de Paul Church.
Colaj, Rene Otzoy *o.s.b.* '82 (RCK) [H] Aurora, IL Marmion Abbey-St. Augustine's Abbey.
Colamarino, Dennis '73 (PIT) Duquesne, PA Christ the Light of the World Church.
Colankin, Dimitrij '76 (AUS) Caldwell, TX St. Mary's Church.
Colapietro, Peter M. '76 (NY) [45] New York, NY Holy Cross Church.
Colaresi, Robert E. *o.carm.* '67 (JOL) [J] Darien, IL Carmelite Community; [L] Darien, IL Carmelite Spiritual Center; [M] Darien, IL Society of the Little Flower.
Colasito, Basil C. '59 (RVC) Hicksville, NY Our Lady of Mercy Church.
Colasurdo, Peter '77 (STA) [4] St. Augustine, FL San Sebastian Church.
Colautti, John *o.s.b.* '55 (DET) [K] Detroit, MI St. Sylvester Monastery.
Colavechio, Francis D. '50 (LR) Fairfield Bay, AR St. Francis Assisi Church.
Colavechio, Xavier G. *o.praem.* '55 (JKS) [E] Jackson, MS Priory of St. Moses the Black.
Colberg, Msgr. James P. '55 (LA) Santa Maria, CA St. Mary of the Assumption Church.
Colbert, John '96 (BEA) [8] Beaumont, TX St. Pius X Church.
Colbert, Joseph D. '59 (BRK) [222] Queens, NY St. Pancras Church.
Colbert, Richard *s.m.* '64 (SP) [7] Tampa, FL Our Lady of Perpetual Help Church; [B] Tampa, FL Tampa Catholic High School.
Colbert, Richard A. *c.pp.s.* '69 (JC) Fayette, MO St. Joseph Church; [F] Fayette, MO Central Methodist College.
Colborn, Francis R. '64 (LA) [12] Los Angeles, CA Holy Name of Jesus Church.
Colchin, Stephen E. '84 (FTW) Besancon, IN St. Louis Church.
Cole, Barry '82 (CHI) [W] Oak Park, IL Oak Park Study Center.
Cole, Basil B. *o.p.* '66 (OAK) [N] Oakland, CA Dominican Order (Western Province), St. Albert's Priory.
Cole, Edwin '64 (JC) Columbia, MO Sacred Heart Church.
Cole, Edwin J. '64 (JC) Columbia, MO University Hospital & Clinics; Columbia, MO Veterans' Administration Medical Center.
Cole, James J. '71 (BGP) Brookfield, CT St. Marguerite Bourgeoys Church.
Cole, Raymond L. '72 (MET) East Millstone, NJ St. Joseph Church.
Cole, Robert F. '72 (MAN) Plymouth, NH St. Matthew Church; [N] Plymouth, NH Plymouth State College Campus Ministry.
Cole, Robert J. '72 (CLV) Olmsted Falls, OH St. Mary of the Falls Church.
Cole, Russan *o.f.m.conv.* '51 (MIL) Brandon, WI St. Brendan Church; Springvale, WI St. Mary Church; Waupun, WI St. Joseph Church.
Cole, Vincent P. *m.m.* '71 (FgM) Maryknoll Foreign Missions.
Colella, David *o.ss.t.* (BAL) [M] Baltimore, MD Holy Trinity Monastery.
Colella, David L. *o.ss.t.* '57 (DAL) [28] Dallas, TX Santa Clara Church.
Coleman, Msgr. Brian P. '63 (GB) [1] De Pere, WI St. Francis Xavier Church; Special Assignment.
Coleman, C. Michael '67 (KC) Special Assignment.
Coleman, Christopher *m.s.c.* '65 (SAT) [M] San Antonio, TX Missionaries of the Sacred Heart.
Coleman, Christopher Lee '94 (BRK) [158] Queens, NY Blessed Virgin Mary, Help of Christians Church.
Coleman, Donald E. '74 (SD) Carlsbad, CA St. Elizabeth Seton Church.
Coleman, Ed *o.m.i.* '56 (PHX) Sun City, AZ St. Clement of Rome Church.
Coleman, Ed '83 (P) Silverton, OR St. Paul Church.
Coleman, Edward C. *o.m.i.* '56 (STP) [N] St. Paul, MN Oblate Residence.
Coleman, Edward W. '70 (ALN) Nesquehoning, PA Sacred Heart Church.
Coleman, Msgr. George W. '64 (FR) [16] Fall River, MA St. Joseph's Church.
Coleman, Gerald D. *s.s.* '68 (SFR) [A] Menlo Park, CA St. Patrick Seminary; [U] Mountain View, CA Hospital and Health Services Liaison.
Coleman, Gerald J. '78 (TLS) [17] Tulsa, OK St. Thomas More Church.
Coleman, James '46 (SAN) Retired.
Coleman, James '46 (SAT) [K] San Antonio, TX Padua Place.
Coleman, James '73 (FgM) Society of St. James the Apostle.
Coleman, James '73 (P) On Duty Outside the Archdiocese.
Coleman, James *p.i.m.e.* '76 (COL) [H] Newark, OH P.I.M.E. Mission & Prayer Center.
Coleman, James F. *s.j.* '56 (NY) [DD] New York, NY Murray-Weigel Hall.
Coleman, Msgr. James G. '62 (HRT) Guilford, CT St. George Church.
Coleman, James G. '77 (TUC) [19] Tucson, AZ St. Pius X Church.
Coleman, John '50 (SJ) Gilroy, CA St. Mary Church; Palo Alto, CA Veterans Administration Medical Center; Retired.
Coleman, John '54 (NY) Absent on Sick leave.
Coleman, John '71 (SFR) On Duty Outside the Archdiocese.
Coleman, John *o.carm.* '78 (LA) [F] Encino, CA Crespi Carmelite High School.
Coleman, John '88 (PHX) [2] Mesa, AZ Christ the King Church.
Coleman, John A. *s.j.* '67 (OAK) [N] Berkeley, CA Jesuit Community at Jesuit School of Theology at Berkeley.
Coleman, John P. '50 (KC) [7] Kansas City, MO St. Catherine of Siena Church; Retired.
Coleman, Joseph (BO) Brighton, MA St. John of God Hospital.
Coleman, Joseph K. '81 (BO) [58] Boston, MA Our Lady of the Presentation Church; [R] Brighton, MA St. John of God Hospital.
Coleman, Michael *ss.cc.* '58 (FR) [J] Fairhaven, MA Sacred Hearts Provincial House.
Coleman, Michael '81 (JC) Osage Bend, MO St. Margaret Church; Wardsville, MO St. Stanislaus Church.
Coleman, Msgr. Robert F. '78 (NEW) [A] South Orange, NJ Immaculate Conception Seminary; [B] South Orange, NJ Seton Hall University.
Coleman, Robert J. '87 (JOL) Beaverville, IL St. Mary Church; Martinton, IL St. Martin Church.
Coleman, Robert P. '78 (CHI) Other Assignments.
Coleman, Thomas '87 (GLP) Quemado, NM Sacred Heart Church.
Coleman, W. Philip '59 (BGP) Retired.
Coleman, William J. *m.m.* '39 (NY) [DD] Maryknoll, NY Maryknoll Fathers and Brothers.
Colendrino, J. Rudolpho '94 (CHK) San Antonio Village, District 6, MP San Antonio De Padua Parish.
Coles, Edward T. *s.j.* '59 (GAL) [F] Houston, TX Strake, Jesuit College Preparatory Inc.
Coless, Gabriel M. *o.s.b.* '57 (PAT) [M] Morristown, NJ St. Mary's Abbey.
Coletta, Carmen J. *o.s.a.* '38 (BO) [C] North Andover, MA Merrimack College.
Coletta, Ralph V. '61 (CLV) [9] Akron, OH St. John the Baptist Church.

Coletta, Msgr. Thomas J. '63 (PAT) [14] Paterson, NJ Our Lady of Victories Church.
Coletti, Arnold F. '62 (BO) Lexington, MA Sacred Heart Church.
Coley, James E. '47 (TR) Retired.
Colfer, Robert *o.m.i.* '40 (PMB) Riviera Beach, FL St. Francis of Assisi Church.
Colgan, Arthur J. *c.s.c.* '73 (FgM) Holy Cross Foreign Missions.
Colgan, John '48 (SP) Retired.
Colgan, Marvin '40 (PEO) Retired.
Colgan, Myles *o.carm.* '48 (JOL) [J] Darien, IL Carmelite Provincial Office.
Colgan, Richard *c.s.p.* '79 (BO) [W] Boston, MA Paulist Fathers Residence.
Colgan, Richard J. *s.j.* '55 (BAL) [Q] Baltimore, MD Jesuit Mission Bureau, Maryland Province, Inc.; [Q] Baltimore, MD Jesuit Seminary Guild, Maryland Province, Inc.
Colgan, Richard J. *s.j.* '55 (PH) [AA] Philadelphia, PA Jesuit Community at St. Joseph's University.
Colgan, Richard J. *c.s.p.* '79 (BO) [P] Boston, MA Paulist Center; [BB] Boston, MA Chapel of the Holy Spirit.
Colgan, Thomas A. *s.j.* '75 (SPK) [E] Spokane, WA Gonzaga Preparatory School.
Colgan, Thomas J. '49 (RVC) Northport, NY St. Philip Neri Church.
Colgan, Tobias *o.s.b.* '82 (IND) [J] St. Meinrad, IN St. Meinrad Archabbey.
Colhour, David *c.p.* (GAL) [S] Houston, TX Holy Name Retreat Center.
Colhour, David *c.p.* '94 (GAL) [S] Houston, TX Holy Name Retreat Center.
Colibraro, Daniel '56 (CHY) Casper, WY Our Lady of Fatima Church; Retired.
Colibraro, Philip '57 (CHY) Casper, WY Our Lady of Fatima Church.
Colicchio, Damian *o.f.m.cap.* '62 (NEW) [B] Lodi, NJ Felician College; [O] Lodi, NJ Immaculate Conception Convent.
Colicchio, Ralph M. '67 (HRT) [7] New Haven, CT St. Casimir's Church; New Haven, CT Yale-New Haven Hospital.
Coll, Eduardo '88 (BRK) [48] Brooklyn, NY St. Gabriel The Archangel Church.
Coll, Jerome B. *s.j.* '59 (PH) [C] Philadelphia, PA St. Joseph's University; [AA] Philadelphia, PA Jesuit Community at St. Joseph's University.
Coll, John J. *s.j.* '56 (WH) [A] Wheeling, WV Wheeling Jesuit University.
Coll, Msgr. Robert J. '59 (ALN) Retired.
Collard, Bruce W. '80 (MAN) [3] Nashua, NH St. Christopher Church; [N] Durham, NH Campus Ministries.
Colleoni, Xavier *m.c.c.j.* '52 (LA) [11] Los Angeles, CA Holy Cross Church.
Coller, Jerome *o.s.b.* '59 (SCL) [I] Collegeville, MN St. John's Abbey, of the Order of St. Benedict.
Colleran, Desmond '56 (ORG) Inactive Leave.
Colleran, James A. '63 (CHI) Missionary Work.
Colleran, Msgr. Kevin J. '72 (NY) [183] Bronx, NY St. Philip Neri Church.
Collet, John *o.m.i.* (AUS) [H] Austin, TX Brothers of the Congregation of the Holy Cross.
Collet, John '67 (DAL) [A] Irving, TX Holy Trinity Seminary.
Collette, Msgr. Richard E. '52 (WOR) [5] Fitchburg, MA Immaculate Conception Church.
Colletti, Joseph A. '71 (LFT) Unassigned.
Colletti, Peter '84 (CLV) [10] Akron, OH St. Martha Church.
Colletti, Richard M. '78 (WIN) [3] Mankato, MN St. John the Baptist's Church; [I] Mankato, MN Newman Center.
Collier, Joseph Mel '58 (SD) [33] San Diego, CA St. Michael Church.
Colligan, Flavian *o.f.m.* '39 (PAT) [M] Ringwood, NJ Holy Name Friary, Inc.
Colligan, Msgr. Joseph F. '50 (RVC) Centerport, NY Our Lady Queen of Martyrs Church; Retired.
Colligan, Owen *o.f.m.* '39 (NY) [DD] New York, NY Franciscan Friars, Order of Friars Minor, Holy Name Province.
Collignon, James A. *m.m.* '53 (FgM) Maryknoll Foreign Missions.
Collignon, James A. *m.m.* '53 (NY) [DD] Maryknoll, NY Maryknoll Fathers and Brothers.
Colling, Paul J. '87 (GI) Scottsbluff, NE Our Lady of Guadalupe Church.
Collini, Msgr. Celsus '47 (BRK) [231] Queens, NY Queen of Peace Church.
Collini, Msgr. Celsus O. '47 (BRK) Retired.
Collins, Austin I. *c.s.c.* '82 (FTW) [B] Notre Dame, IN University of Notre Dame Du Lac; [J] Notre Dame, IN Holy Cross Community, Corby Hall, University of Notre Dame.
Collins, Msgr. Bernard (PHX) [5] Mesa, AZ St. Bridget Church.
Collins, Msgr. Bernard G. '37 (DUB) Retired.
Collins, Carl P. '91 (HT) Theriot, LA St. Eloi Church.
Collins, Charles E. '72 (BO) [8] Cambridge, MA St. John the Evangelist Church.
Collins, Charles I. '82 (WIN) Byron, MN Christ the King Church; Kasson, MN Holy Family Church.
Collins, Corwin *o.s.b.* '57 (SCL) Albany, MN Seven Dolors Church.
Collins, Daniel J. '58 (CHI) [128] Chicago, IL St. Mary of the Lake Church; [J] Evanston, IL Saint Francis Hospital of Evanston.
Collins, Denis E. *s.j.* '69 (SFR) [N] San Francisco, CA Jesuit Community at University of San Francisco.
Collins, Edward A. '68 (PAT) Pequannock, NJ Holy Spirit Church.
Collins, Edward F. '35 (DAV) Retired.
Collins, Edward J. *o.m.i.* '46 (FgM) Oblates Foreign Missions.
Collins, Edwin '54 (RVC) Retired.
Collins, Edwin J. '54 (RVC) Malverne, NY Our Lady of Lourdes Church.
Collins, Msgr. Fachtna P. '50 (LA) Retired.
Collins, Francis W. *m.m.* '49 (FgM) Maryknoll Foreign Missions.
Collins, Frederick J. '55 (BO) Georgetown, MA St. Mary Church.
Collins, James *s.d.b.* '39 (SFR) [N] San Francisco, CA Salesian Provincial Residence.
Collins, James '98 (CHL) Mooresville, NC St. Therese Church.
Collins, Msgr. James E. '39 (RVC) Oyster Bay, NY St. Dominic's Church; Retired.
Collins, James J. '64 (PH) [C] Philadelphia, PA Holy Family College.
Collins, James M. *s.j.* '58 (BO) [W] Chestnut Hill, MA The Jesuit Community at Boston College; [W] Cohasset, MA Bellarmine House.
Collins, James P. '69 (BRK) [30] Brooklyn, NY St. Columba Church; [G] Brooklyn, NY Bishop Kearney.
Collins, James R. '68 (CIN) [25] Cincinnati, OH St. Dominic Church.
Collins, James R. '81 (PRO) [3] Pawtucket, RI St. Edward Church.
Collins, John E. *c.s.p.* '74 (NY) [104] New York, NY St. Paul the Apostle Church.
Collins, John J.L. *s.j.* '44 (BO) [W] Chestnut Hill, MA The Jesuit Community at Boston College.
Collins, John M. '69 (LA) Military and VA Chaplains.
Collins, John M. '79 (CHI) [200] Chicago, IL St. Thaddeus Church.
Collins, John P. '72 (PH) Upper Darby, PA St. Alice Church; [D] Springfield, PA Cardinal O'Hara High School.
Collins, Joseph I. '40 (BO) Retired.
Collins, Kevin *o.m.i.* '82 (SAT) [C] San Antonio, TX Oblate School of Theology; [O] San Antonio, TX Oblate Renewal Center.
Collins, Lawrence '77 (CHI) [J] Evergreen Park, IL Little Company of Mary Hospital and Health Care Centers.
Collins, Leonard J. *c.s.c.* '69 (AUS) [H] Austin, TX Congregation of Holy Cross - Southern Province.
Collins, Michael (ORL) Sabbatical.
Collins, Msgr. Michael '43 (ORG) Seal Beach, CA St. Anne's Church; Retired.
Collins, Michael G. *m.m.* '59 (FgM) Maryknoll Foreign Missions.
Collins, Michael J. *o.s.b.* '37 (PAT) [M] Morristown, NJ St. Mary's Abbey.
Collins, Michael J. '67 (BR) [15] Baton Rouge, LA Most Blessed Sacrament Church.
Collins, Michael J. '85 (JOL) Absent on Leave.
Collins, Michael T. *o.praem.* '78 (WIL) [B] Claymont, DE Archmere Academy; [I] Claymont, DE Immaculate Conception Priory of the Canons Regular of Premontre.
Collins, Neil J. '58 (NEW) Belleville, NJ St. Anthony's Church.
Collins, Patrick W. '64 (PEO) On Duty Outside the Diocese.
Collins, Raymond *c.ss.r.* '70 (RVC) Bethpage, NY St. Martin of Tours Church.
Collins, Raymond F. '59 (PRO) On Duty Outside the Diocese.
Collins, Raymond F. *s.t.d.* '59 (WDC) [C] Washington, DC Catholic University of America, The; [C] Washington, DC Catholic University of America, The.
Collins, Raymond G. *o.s.f.s.* '59 (ARL) Vienna, VA Our Lady of Good Counsel Church.
Collins, Robert '81 (AUS) Retired.
Collins, Robert C. *s.j.* '67 (NY) [DD] New York, NY "America;" Residence and publication office of the America Press; [HH] New York, NY America Press, Inc., The.
Collins, Robert L. '66 (ROC) Livonia, NY St. Joseph Church.
Collins, Robert M. '83 (CHL) Franklin, NC St. Francis of Assisi Church.
Collins, Msgr. Russell J. '37 (BO) Retired.
Collins, Seamus *o.p.* '58 (SP) Hudson, FL St. Michael Church.
Collins, Stephen L., III '83 (E) On Leave of Absence.
Collins, T. Byron *s.j.* '52 (WDC) [M] Washington, DC The Jesuit Community at Georgetown University.
Collins, Terrence '71 (R) Kill Devil Hills, NC Holy Redeemer Church.
Collins, Thomas *o.p.* (WDC) [11] Washington, DC St. Dominic Church & Priory Church.
Collins, Thomas E. '92 (NY) [E] White Plains, NY Archbishop Stepinac High School.
Collins, Thomas R. '72 (RIC) Richlands, VA St. Mary Church.
Collins, Thomas S. '92 (PT) [1] Tallahassee, FL Co-Cathedral of St. Thomas More.
Collins, Timothy '54 (BAK) Retired.
Collins, Msgr. Timothy S. '58 (NY) [96] New York, NY Our Lady of the Rosary Church.
Collins, William '33 (ALB) Retired.
Collins, William *c.ss.r.* '49 (TR) [Q] Long Branch, NJ San Alfonso Retreat House.
Collins, William A. '61 (BAL) Randallstown, MD Holy Family Church; Special Assignment.
Collins, William B. '74 (PAT) Hamburg, NJ St. Jude the Apostle Church.
Collins, William F. '65 (CAM) Franklinville, NJ Nativity Church.
Collins, Msgr. William J. '60 (NY) [5] Kingston, NY St. Peter Church.
Collins, William J. *m.s.c.* '67 (SAT) [28] San Antonio, TX St. Anthony of Padua Church.
Collins, William P. '56 (RCK) [8] Rockford, IL St. Patrick Church; [J] Rockford, IL Martin House.
Collins, Wm. Emmett *c.ss.r.* '52 (STL) [B] St. Louis, MO St. John Neumann House.
Collison, Craig A. '78 (SC) Willey, IA St. Mary's Church; [B] Carroll, IA Kuemper Catholic High School.
Collogan, Robert '82 (JOL) Oswego, IL St. Anne Church.
Collopy, John C. (BAL) [J] Timonium, MD Stella Maris Operating Corporation.
Collopy, John C. '56 (BAL) Special Assignment; Retired.
Colloton, Paul *o.p.* '90 (GR) [I] Grand Rapids, MI Motherhouse of the Dominican Sisters.
Colloton, Paul H. *o.p.* '90 (CHI) [N] Chicago, IL Dominicans (Provincial Office).
Collova, S. Joseph '76 (MIL) On Leave.
Collucci, Bennett '57 (SAL) Hays, KS St. Joseph's Church; [D] Hays, KS St. Joseph's Friary.
Collum, Patrick '92 (NO) [21] New Orleans, LA The Resurrection Of Our Lord Church.
Colnaghi, Andrew *o.s.b.cam.* '79 (MRY) [G] Big Sur, CA New Camaldoli Hermitage.
Colnaghi, Andrew '79 (OAK) [S] Berkeley, CA Incarnation Monastery, Camaldolese Benedictines.
Colohan, Edward A. '61 (BGP) [3] Trumbull, CT St. Stephen Church.
Colomb, Jackson '90 (CHI) Other Assignments.
Colombo, Ronald A. '72 (GB) Cooperstown, WI St. James Church; Kellnersville, WI St. Joseph Church.
Colon, Hector *c.ss.r.* '76 (PCE) Guayama, PR St. Anthony of Padua Church.
Colon, Jorge *c.ss.r.* '77 (PCE) Guayama, PR St. Anthony of Padua Church.
Colon, Msgr. Jose '61 (PCE) Retired.
Colon, Jose E. '63 (PCE) On Duty Outside the Diocese.
Colon, Jose E. '63 (SJN) [E] San Juan, PR VA Medical Center.
Colon, Juan Jose '95 (CGS) Naguabo, PR Nuestra Senora del Rosario Church.
Colon, Timothy *o.s.c.* '79 (NY) [W] New York, NY St. Vincent's Hospital and Medical Center of New York.
Colon, Vincent A. '50 (STP) Retired.
Colonnese, Louis M. '57 (DAV) On Duty Outside the Diocese; [P] Davenport, IA Commitment.
Colopy, James L. '86 (COL) Zaleski, OH St. Sylvester Church.
Colosimo, Eugene J. '43 (SJ) [M] Los Gatos, CA Sacred Heart Jesuit Center.
Colosimo, Felix R. '65 (SY) [6] Utica, NY St. Anthony of Padua Church.
Colpitts, Albert B. '73 (PRT) Westbrook, ME St. Edmund Church.
Colter, Dennis J. '66 (DUB) [A] Dubuque, IA Seminary of St. Pius X; [C] Dubuque, IA Loras College; [L] Dubuque, IA Mt. St. Francis.
Colton, Bernard '50 (PHX) Retired.
Colton, Bradford '45 (HRT) Wethersfield, CT Corpus Christi Church; Retired.
Colton, Cyril *s.a.* '52 (NY) [DD] Garrison, NY Generalate of the Franciscan Friars of the Atonement-St. James Friary.
Colton, Gary '68 (HON) Haiku, HI St. Rita Church; Paia, HI Holy Rosary Church.
Colucci, Gregory (PAT) [9] Paterson, NJ St. Joseph's Church.
Comandini, Glenn J. '86 (MET) South River, NJ St. Stephen Protomartyr Church.
Comas, Jorge *c.m.* (BRK) [116] Brooklyn, NY St. Peter-St. Paul-Our Lady of Pilar Church.
Comber, Thomas E. *c.s.p.* '55 (NY) [DD] Jamaica Estates, NY Paulist Fathers Generalate.
Comber, Thomas E. *c.s.p.* '55 (WDC) [B] Washington, DC St. Paul's College; [V] Washington, DC Paulist

National Catholic Evangelization Assoc.
Comboy, Richard J. *s.j.* '69 (SPK) [B] Spokane, WA St. Michael's Institute.
Combs, Derran (NSH) [H] Nashville, TN Franciscan Friars.
Combs, Gordon *o.f.m.cap.* '64 (AGN) [E] Agana Heights, GU St. Fidelis Friary.
Combs, Gordon *o.f.m.cap.* '64 (FgM) Capuchin Foreign Missions.
Combs, Gordon *o.f.m.cap.* '64 (HON) Aiea, HI St. Elizabeth Church; [F] Honolulu, HI St. Francis Healthcare System of Hawaii.
Combs, J. Derran *o.f.m.* '94 (NSH) [13] Nashville, TN St. Vincent de Paul Church.
Combs, Regis V. '46 (LA) Retired.
Comeau, Gerard *m.s.* '61 (FR) [J] Attleboro, MA La Salette Provincial House.
Comeau, Ronald R. '71 (LFT) On Duty Outside the Diocese.
Comer, John P. '64 (STL) [34] St. Louis, MO St. Francis de Sales Church; [O] St. Louis, MO Mary, Queen and Mother Nursing Center.
Comer, Michael E. '80 (COV) Dayton, KY St. Bernard Church.
Comerford, Aidan '81 (LA) [89] Los Angeles, CA St. Sebastian Church.
Comerford, Christopher '96 (SFD) [2] Springfield, IL Blessed Sacrament Church.
Comerford, John J. *o.carm.* '77 (CHI) [N] Mundelein, IL Carmelite Monastery.
Comerford, Patrick '69 (LA) [K] Santa Monica, CA Saint John's Health Center.
Comeskey, Edwin T. '55 (SY) Vernon, NY Holy Family Church.
Comeskey, John H. (SY) [O] Utica, NY St. Elizabeth Hospital.
Comesky, Clement J. *o.f.m.* '55 (FgM) Franciscan Foreign Missions.
Comey, John M. *s.j.* '44 (PH) [AA] Philadelphia, PA Jesuit Community at St. Joseph's University.
Comiskey, Msgr. James A. '50 (LUB) [1] Lubbock, TX Cathedral Christ the King Church.
Comiskey, John *s.s.c.* '68 (FgM) St. Columban's Foreign Mission.
Comiskey, John P. '60 (NY) [E] New York, NY Monsignor Farrell High School.
Comisky, Ben *o.s.b.* '90 (TYL) Jefferson, TX Immaculate Conception Church.
Commane, William J. (BO) Retired.
Commons, Patrick M. '51 (IND) Retired.
Commons, Thomas *s.v.d.* '47 (CHI) [B] Techny, IL Divine Word Residence.
Commyn, James E. '86 (DET) Richmond, MI St. Augustine Church.
Como, Denis R. *s.j.* '66 (BO) [W] Boston, MA Jesuit Urban Center & Immaculate Conception Community.
Compaired, Fernando '63 (MIA) [9] Miami, FL Mother of Our Redeemer Church.
Compentente, Virgilio '67 (NY) [9] Yonkers, NY Immaculate Conception Church.
Complo, Daniel C. '54 (DET) Harper Woods, MI Our Lady Queen of Peace Church.
Compobello, Mark A. (RCK) [B] Aurora, IL Aurora Central Catholic High School.
Comstock, Douglas G. '67 (OG) Sackets Harbor, NY St. Andrew Church.
Comstock, Eliot *o.f.m.conv.* '69 (IND) [I] Mount Saint Francis, IN Mount Saint Francis Friary and Retreat Center.
Comtois, Norman *o.m.i.* '73 (MAN) [K] Hudson, NH Missionary Oblates of Mary Immaculate.
Comtois, Robert *o.p.* '49 (PRT) [I] Lewiston, ME SS. Peter and Paul Priory.
Comtois, Roger M. '55 (NOR) Rockville, CT St. Bernard Church.
Conaboy, Conan *c.p.* '47 (MET) [H] South River, NJ Passionist Provincial Office.
Conaboy, Conan *c.p.* '47 (SCR) [15] Scranton, PA St. Joseph's Church; [M] Scranton, PA Saint Ann's Passionist Monastery.
Conahan, John J. '62 (PH) Jenkintown, PA Immaculate Conception Church.
Conan, Constantine J. *c.s.sp.* '48 (PIT) [Q] Bethel Park, PA Holy Ghost Animation Center.
Conan, Paul F. '57 (DET) [P] Clarkston, MI Colombiere Center.
Conard, James A. *m.m.* '56 (FgM) Maryknoll Foreign Missions.
Conard, Raymond J. '55 (GB) On Duty Outside the Diocese.
Conaty, Charles '88 (CAM) Wildwood, NJ St. Ann's Church; [B] Wildwood, NJ Wildwood Catholic High School.
Conboy, Joseph T. '53 (SCR) Retired; [N] Dunmore, PA Villa St. Joseph.
Conboy, Michael F. '74 (ROC) Corning, NY St. Mary Church; Corning, NY St. Patrick Church; Corning, NY St. Vincent de Paul Church; Painted Post, NY Immaculate Heart of Mary Church.
Conboy, Richard L. '60 (PIT) Allegheny County, PA Depaul Institution; Allegheny County, PA Kane Regional Center - Scott; [P] Coraopolis, PA Our Lady of the Sacred Heart Convent.
Concagh, John *c.m.* (NY) [GG] New York, NY University Apostolate.
Concagh, Thomas V. *c.m.* '52 (BRK) [U] Jamaica, NY Vincentian Residence.
Concannon, Stephen F. '64 (PRT) Brunswick, ME St. Charles Church.
Concepcion, Francisco '65 (ARE) Vega-Alta, PR Immaculate Conception of Blessed Virgin Mary Church.
Concha, Alfonso J. '76 (PH) Military Chaplains.
Concha, Antonio *s.j.* '63 (ELP) [21] El Paso, TX Sacred Heart Church.
Concha, Augusto *o.p.* (PH) [156] Philadelphia, PA Visitation B.V.M. Church.
Concha, Sergio E. *c.s.c.* '63 (FTW) [J] South Bend, IN Congregation of Holy Cross Indiana Province Provincial House.
Concordia, George Lawrence *o.p.* '58 (NY) [22] New York, NY St. Catherine of Siena Church; [DD] New York, NY St. Catherine of Siena Priory; [HH] New York, NY Dominican Shrine of St. Jude, Inc.
Conde, Jose Ma. *s.f.* '68 (WDC) [B] Silver Spring, MD Holy Family Seminary.
Conde, Jose Maria *s.f.* '68 (WDC) Takoma Park, MD Our Lady of Sorrows Church.
Conde, Norberto '89 (GAL) [60] Houston, TX Our Lady of Sorrows Church.
Conde, Thomas P. '87 (CHI) Sauk Village, IL St. James Church.
Condon, Daniel J. '81 (ROC) Mount Morris, NY St. Patrick Church; Nunda, NY Holy Angels Church.
Condon, Denis '78 (CHI) [2] Mt. Prospect, IL St. Emily Church.
Condon, Edwin D. '61 (BO) Military & VA Chaplains.
Condon, Eugene L. '56 (CHR) Absent On Leave.
Condon, Gerald A. '56 (DUB) Dumont, IA St. Francis Church; Hampton, IA St. Patrick's Church.
Condon, Gerald W. '55 (BAK) Heppner, OR St. Patrick's Church; Ione, OR St. William Church.
Condon, John F.X. *s.j.* '55 (NY) [DD] New York, NY Murray-Weigel Hall.
Condon, Msgr. John J. '56 (BRK) [155] Queens, NY St. Benedict Joseph Labre Church.
Condon, Liam (ALB) Cambridge, NY St. Patrick Church.
Condon, Liam '63 (ALB) Salem, NY Holy Cross Church.
Condon, Louis M. '48 (PEO) Retired.
Condon, Msgr. Michael J. '41 (LA) [1] Oxnard, CA St. Anthony Church; Retired.
Condon, Msgr. Robert F. '54 (LA) [70] Los Angeles, CA St. Joan of Arc Church; Retired.
Condon, Robert M. (SC) Retired.
Condon, Robert M. '56 (SC) [A] Sioux City, IA Briar Cliff College.
Condon, T. Mark '89 (PAT) [5] Clifton, NJ SS. Cyril and Methodius Church.
Condon, Thomas M. *o.p.* '88 (STL) [P] St. Louis, MO St. Dominic Priory.
Condon, William *c.s.c.* '61 (FR) [J] North Dartmouth, MA St. Joseph's Hall.
Condon, William F. '54 (RIC) Retired.
Condren, William '73 (PT) Gulf Breeze, FL St. Ann Church.
Condron, Patrick A. '76 (WH) [7] Wheeling, WV St. Alphonsus Church.
Condron, Robert F. '69 (HRT) [1] Ansonia, CT Assumption Church.
Condry, John T. *s.j.* '49 (LAF) [J] Grand Coteau, LA Our Lady of the Oaks Retreat House.
Conesa, Msgr. Diego '57 (SP) Sun City Center, FL Prince of Peace Church.
Conesa, Msgr. Diego '57 (STA) On Duty Outside the Diocese.
Confer, Bernard T. *o.p.* '73 (HRT) [14] New Haven, CT St. Mary's Priory Church.
Confer, Thomas B. *o.p.* (HRT) [N] North Guilford, CT Monastery of Our Lady of Grace; [N] North Guilford, CT Monastery of Our Lady of Grace.
Confroy, Mark W. *o.s.b.* '42 (PAT) [M] Morristown, NJ St. Mary's Abbey; [N] Convent Station, NJ St. Anne Villa.
Confroy, Thomas *o.s.b.* (TR) Pennington, NJ St. James Church.
Confroy, Thomas J. *o.s.b.* '58 (PAT) [M] Morristown, NJ St. Mary's Abbey.
Cong, Joseph Chu '48 (WOR) [A] Spencer, MA St. Joseph's Abbey School of Theology and Institute of Monastic Studies; [N] Spencer, MA St. Joseph's Abbey.
Congdon, Stephen H. '62 (MET) Cranbury, NJ Nativity of Our Lord Church.
Congro, Basil P. '78 (CHR) Florence, SC St. Anthony's All Souls Memorial Church.
Conheeney, Thomas P. '55 (NEW) [1] Bayonne, NJ St. Mary Star of the Sea Church.
Coning, Jeffrey J. '97 (COL) Lancaster, OH St. Mary Church.
Conkle, Francis '78 (SJN) [2] Canovanas, PR Resurreccion del Senior Church.
Conklin, Christopher J. '73 (SAL) Retired.
Conlan, Msgr. F. Allan '54 (SCR) Elmhurst, PA St. Eulalia Church.
Conlan, Msgr. James S. '53 (NY) Pine Bush, NY The Infant Saviour Church; Absent on Sick leave; [DD] Suffern, NY Parish Mission Team Res.
Conlan, Timothy *o.p.* '67 (SFR) [13] San Francisco, CA St. Dominic Church; [N] San Francisco, CA St. Dominic Priory.
Conlan, Walter *s.j.* '76 (BO) [W] Chestnut Hill, MA The Jesuit Community at Boston College.
Conlan, William J. *o.p.* '48 (WDC) [B] Washington, DC Dominican House of Studies; [C] Washington, DC Catholic University of America, The.
Conley, Charles E. '74 (MIL) Union Grove, WI St. Robert Bellarmine Church.
Conley, Edward W. *o.p.* '43 (NO) [30] New Orleans, LA St. Dominic Church.
Conley, James '85 (WCH) On Duty Outside the Diocese.
Conley, John *c.p.* (GAL) [S] Houston, TX Holy Name Retreat Center.
Conley, John '93 (SFR) Absent on Leave.
Conley, John E. *c.s.c.* '79 (FTW) [B] Notre Dame, IN University of Notre Dame Du Lac; [J] Notre Dame, IN Holy Cross Community, Corby Hall, University of Notre Dame.
Conley, John J. *s.j.* '83 (NY) [DD] New York, NY Jesuit Community at Fordham University.
Conley, John P. *c.p.* '76 (GAL) [S] Houston, TX Holy Name Retreat Center.
Conley, Lawrence J. '67 (PRT) Norway, ME St. Catherine of Sienna Church.
Conley, Martin P. '57 (OM) Tekamah, NE St. Patrick Church.
Conley, Martin R. '83 (PIT) Forest Hills, PA St. Maurice Church.
Conley, Peter V. '64 (BO) [2] Brookline, MA Infant Jesus Church; [P] Boston, MA Archdiocesan Information Center.
Conley, Philip P. '62 (Y) Poland, OH Holy Family Church.
Conley, Msgr. Raymond J. '36 (DM) Retired.
Conley, Rory T. '89 (WDC) [4] Silver Spring, MD St. Catherine Laboure Church.
Conley, Roy H. '61 (PIT) Pleasant Hills, PA St. Elizabeth Church.
Conley, Seraphin *t.o.r.* (FgM) T.O.R. Foreign Missions.
Conley, Seraphin *t.o.r.* '61 (ORL) [D] Winter Park, FL San Pedro Spiritual Development Center; [F] Winter Park, FL San Pedro Center, Third Order Regular of St. Francis; [F] Winter Park, FL Franciscan Friars, T.O.R., Provincial Residence, San Pedro Friary.
Conley, Thomas P. '47 (CHI) [4] Des Plaines, IL St. Zachary Church; Stickney, IL St. Pius X Church; Retired.
Conlin, Bernard J. '40 (WOR) [12] Worcester, MA Our Lady of Lourdes Church; Retired.
Conlin, Daniel C. '90 (STP) Graduate Studies.
Conlin, Edward '42 (NY) Retired.
Conlin, Edward F. *s.s.e.* '46 (MOB) [H] Selma, AL Edmundite Fathers.
Conlin, Edwin J. '42 (NY) [52] New York, NY Immaculate Conception Church; Manhattan, NY Beth Israel Medical Center.
Conlin, John A. *s.j.* '54 (WDC) [2] Washington, DC St. Aloysius Church; [E] Washington, DC Gonzaga College High School.
Conlin, Leo E. *c.s.p.* '46 (NY) [DD] Jamaica Estates, NY Paulist Fathers Generalate.
Conlin, Robert *t.o.r.* '73 (SP) [13] Tampa, FL St. Patrick Church.
Conlon, Anthony J. '62 (WH) Vienna, WV St. Michael's Church.
Conlon, Arthur F. '54 (TR) [24] Trenton, NJ St. Vincent de Paul Church.
Conlon, Christopher W. *s.m.* '66 (CIN) [D] Dayton, OH The University of Dayton; [M] Dayton, OH Marianist Provincialate; [Q] Dayton, OH University of Dayton Campus Ministry.
Conlon, Colm '59 (ORG) Irvine, CA St. John Neumann Church.
Conlon, Edward F. '54 (CIN) Retired.
Conlon, Edward F. '56 (CIN) On Duty Outside the Archdiocese.
Conlon, James '64 (OAK) [B] Oakland, CA Holy Names College.
Conlon, John J. *s.s.j.* '40 (BAL) [M] Baltimore, MD St. Joseph Society of the Sacred Heart House of Central Administration.
Conlon, Msgr. Joseph E. '47 (CAM) Retired.
Conlon, Matthew T. *o.f.m.* '45 (ALB) [B] Loudonville, NY Siena College.
Conlon, Philip J. '55 (MAD) Retired.
Conlon, R. Daniel '77 (CIN) New Bremen, OH Holy Redeemer Church.
Conlon, Richard W. '90 (BRK) [28] Brooklyn, NY St. Cecilia Church.
Conlon, Timothy C. *o.s.c.* '79 (NY) [4] New York, NY All Saints Church; [DD] New York, NY Crosier (Canons Regular of the Order of the Holy Cross).

Conmy, John J. *o.s.f.s.* '36 (WIL) [I] Childs, MD Oblates of St. Francis De Sales.
Conmy, Thomas M. *c.s.c.* '57 (SP) Dunedin, FL Our Lady of Lourdes Church.
Conn, Jame J. *s.j.* '74 (BAL) [A] Emmitsburg, MD Mount St. Mary's Seminary.
Conn, James J. *s.j.* '74 (BAL) [A] Baltimore, MD St. Mary's Seminary and University; [A] Baltimore, MD St. Mary's Seminary and University.
Conn, Thomas V. *s.j.* '61 (LA) [C] Santa Paula, CA Thomas Aquinas College.
Connaghan, Daniel H. '90 (HRT) [3] Bristol, CT St. Gregory's Church.
Connall, Darrin '92 (SPK) Colville, WA Immaculate Conception Church; Kettle Falls, WA Sacred Heart Church; Northport, WA Pure Heart of Mary Church.
Connaughton, James '50 (MIA) Deerfield Beach, FL St. Ambrose Church; Retired.
Connaughton, Msgr. Lawrence M. '70 (NY) [62] New York, NY St. Joseph Church.
Conneally, J. Philip *s.j.* '44 (LA) [F] Los Angeles, CA Loyola High School.
Connealy, Gerald A. '87 (OM) Petersburg, NE St. John the Baptist Church; Raeville, NE St. Bonaventure Church.
Conneely, Sean *s.s.c.* '69 (CHI) [N] Chicago, IL Columban Fathers Mission Center.
Conneen, Laurence J. *o.s.a.* '37 (PH) [AA] Villanova, PA St. Thomas Monastery.
Connell, Msgr. Andrew F. '51 (BO) [73] Boston, MA St. Vincent de Paul Church; [BB] Boston, MA St. Thomas More Chapel; [FF] Boston, MA Propagation of the Faith and Holy Childhood Association & Society of St. Peter the Apostle.
Connell, James C. '44 (SJ) [M] Los Altos, CA Maryknoll.
Connell, James E. '87 (MIL) [1] Milwaukee, WI St. John Cathedral; Special Assignment.
Connell, John Andrew '81 (PAT) Morris Plains, NJ St. Virgilius Church.
Connell, John F. '62 (WOR) Northbridge, MA St. Peter Church.
Connell, John M. '85 (LR) [13] Little Rock, AR St. Theresa's Church.
Connell, Loren *o.f.m.* (HT) Houma, LA Terrebonne Parish General Hospital.
Connell, Mark (NY) Shrub Oak, NY Saint Elizabeth Ann Seton Church.
Connell, Mark J. '86 (NY) [E] Somers, NY John F. Kennedy High School.
Connell, Martin T. *s.j.* (DET) [E] Detroit, MI University of Detroit Jesuit High School and Academy.
Connell, Patrick J. '92 (DET) Bloomfield Hills, MI St. Regis Church.
Connell, Stephen J. '62 (WIL) Greenville, DE St. Joseph on the Brandywine Church.
Connell, Msgr. William J. '76 (Y) [1] Youngstown, OH Cathedral of St. Columba.
Connell, William R. '75 (MAD) [2] Beloit, WI St. Jude Church.
Connellan, Thomas J. *c.s.p.* '56 (PMB) [G] Vero Beach, FL Paulist Fathers Retirement Home.
Connelly, Brennan *o.f.m.* '56 (NEW) Fair Lawn, NJ St. Anne's Church.
Connelly, Christian T. '96 (ARL) [1] Arlington, VA Cathedral of St. Thomas More.
Connelly, Christopher D. '93 (SPR) [6] Springfield, MA Holy Name Church.
Connelly, Donald F. '58 (WIN) Plainview, MN St. Joachim's Church.
Connelly, Edward C. '65 (BAL) Crofton, MD St. Elizabeth Ann Seton Church.
Connelly, George R. '45 (TUC) Retired.
Connelly, James *c.s.c.* '64 (P) [B] Portland, OR University of Portland; [L] Portland, OR Holy Cross Fathers & Brothers, C.S.C. - University of Portland.
Connelly, Msgr. James A. '47 (HRT) Retired.
Connelly, Msgr. James F. '55 (PH) [147] Philadelphia, PA Stella Maris Church.
Connelly, Msgr. James N. '49 (BUF) Retired; [O] Tonawanda, NY O'Hara Residence.
Connelly, John J. '50 (BO) [8] Newton, MA Sacred Heart Church.
Connelly, Laurence '59 (GAL) [50] Houston, TX St. Michael Church.
Connelly, Mark J. *s.j.* (PH) [C] Philadelphia, PA St. Joseph's University.
Connelly, Mark J. *s.j.* '75 (PH) [AA] Philadelphia, PA Jesuit Community at St. Joseph's University.
Connelly, Msgr. Michael J. '60 (BRK) [246] Queens, NY St. Thomas More-St. Edmund Church.
Connelly, Norbert '56 (STU) Martins Ferry, OH St. Mary Church.
Connelly, Msgr. Paul J. (DM) Retired.
Connelly, Peter *o.s.b.* '87 (WOR) [N] Still River, MA Benedictine Monks, St. Benedict Abbey.
Connelly, Robert J. '49 (SAC) Retired and in Senior Ministry.
Connelly, William P. '45 (RIC) Retired.
Connelly, Xavier *o.s.b.* '89 (WOR) [N] Still River, MA Benedictine Monks, St. Benedict Abbey.
Conner, Glenn T. '50 (PIT) [O] Pittsburgh, PA St. John Vianney Manor.
Conner, Glenn T. '52 (PIT) Retired.
Conner, Herbert K. *s.j.* '61 (CHR) Simpsonville, SC St. Mary Magdalene Church.
Conner, John *o.f.m.cap.* '84 (NY) [57] New York, NY St. John the Baptist Church.
Conner, Michael P. '85 (GAY) Onekama, MI St. Joseph Church.
Conner, Paul M. *o.p.* '67 (PRO) [P] Providence, RI St. Thomas Aquinas Priory at Providence College.
Conner, Robert J. '49 (PH) Penndel, PA Our Lady of Grace Church.
Conner, Steven '94 (NEW) Lyndhurst, NJ Sacred Heart Church.
Conner, Steven C. '94 (NEW) Clark, NJ St. Agnes Church.
Conners, Quinn *o.carm.* '71 (WDC) [B] Washington, DC Whitefriars Hall.
Connerton, Barry R.L. '70 (PRO) [7] Providence, RI St. Augustine Church.
Connery, J. Thomas '63 (ALB) Glenville, NY Immaculate Conception Church.
Connery, John P. *o.s.f.s.* '69 (WIL) Elsmere, DE Veteran's Hospital; [B] Wilmington, DE Salesianum School.
Connery, Thomas '83 (ORL) [A] Daytona Beach, FL Father Lopez High School.
Connery, Thomas J. '83 (ORL) Daytona Beach, FL Our Lady of Lourdes Church.
Connick, Alfred J. (BO) Retired.
Conniff, Msgr. John J. (BUF) [S] Angola, NY St. Vincent de Paul Camp; [T] Buffalo, NY Good Counsel Apartments; [T] Buffalo, NY Timon Towers Housing Development Fund Company, Inc.
Conniff, Msgr. John J. '49 (BUF) Retired.
Connole, Marlin '68 (SEA) Bellevue, WA Sacred Heart Church.
Connolly, Brian W. '55 (PIT) On Duty Outside the Diocese.
Connolly, Charles B. *s.j.* '74 (BO) [W] Boston, MA Jesuit Urban Center & Immaculate Conception Community.
Connolly, Charles B. *s.j.* '75 (BO) [30] Boston, MA Immaculate Conception Church.
Connolly, Msgr. Clement J. '64 (LA) South Pasadena, CA Holy Family Church.
Connolly, Edward B. '66 (ALN) Mount Carbon, PA St. Francis de Sales Church; [2] Pottsville, PA St. Joseph Church.
Connolly, Edward J. '49 (SB) [4] Riverside, CA Sacred Heart Church.
Connolly, Eugene G. '54 (NY) [1] New York, NY Cathedral of St. Patrick.
Connolly, Fidelis *c.p.* '50 (PH) [AA] Philadelphia, PA St. Michael's Passionist Residence.
Connolly, Francis T. '59 (CHL) [5] Greensboro, NC St. Pius X Church.
Connolly, Gerard M. *t.o.r.* '69 (ALT) [1] Barnesboro, PA St. John the Baptist Church; [3] Barnesboro, PA Our Lady of Mt. Carmel Church.
Connolly, Msgr. James '56 (NY) [A] Yonkers, NY St. Joseph's Seminary.
Connolly, James H. '48 (BO) Bellingham, MA St. Blaise Church.
Connolly, James M. '78 (ALN) Military Chaplains.
Connolly, James P. '54 (NY) [58] New York, NY St. John the Evangelist Church.
Connolly, Jerry P. '67 (GF) Plentywood, MT St. Joseph's Church.
Connolly, John '64 (ALB) Delanson, NY Our Lady of Fatima Church.
Connolly, John *s.d.b.* '81 (NEW) Bloomfield, NJ Church of St. Thomas the Apostle.
Connolly, John G. '63 (BO) Wrentham, MA St. Mary Church.
Connolly, John J. '75 (GAL) Port Bolivar, TX Our Mother of Mercy Church.
Connolly, John P. *o.s.f.s.* '57 (CAM) [M] Pittsgrove, NJ Villa St. Joseph.
Connolly, John T. '78 (PAT) [15] Paterson, NJ St. Stephen's Church.
Connolly, Joseph *s.v.d.* '60 (BO) [W] Boston, MA Divine Word Missionaries.
Connolly, Joseph *t.o.r.* '68 (VEN) [2] Sarasota, FL Our Lady Queen of Martyrs Church.
Connolly, Joseph A. *o.s.f.s.* '52 (CAM) [M] Pittsgrove, NJ Villa St. Joseph.
Connolly, Kevin '85 (WIN) Worthington, MN St. Mary's Church.
Connolly, Larkin '47 (PMB) Lake Worth, FL St. Luke Church; Retired.
Connolly, Leo L. '81 (COL) [38] Columbus, OH St. Philip The Apostle Church.
Connolly, Leon '58 (DUB) [1] Waterloo, IA St. Joseph's Church.
Connolly, Luke *c.p.* '52 (CHI) [N] Chicago, IL Passionist Provincial Office; [N] Chicago, IL Immaculate Conception Monastery.
Connolly, Luke *c.p.* '52 (FgM) Mission Procurators.
Connolly, Mark '57 (BGP) [2] Greenwich, CT St. Michael the Archangel Church; [W] Greenwich, CT Clemons Productions, Inc.
Connolly, Martin '45 (NY) [DD] New York, NY Pope John Paul II Residence.
Connolly, Martin '49 (PAT) [P] Chester, NJ Nazareth Village.
Connolly, Martin C. '49 (PAT) Retired.
Connolly, Martin J. '46 (NY) Retired.
Connolly, Matthew J. '53 (ORL) [2] Orlando, FL Blessed Trinity Church; Special Assignment.
Connolly, Maurice V. (BO) Retired.
Connolly, Maurice V. '62 (BO) [3] Salem, MA St. James Church.
Connolly, Michael *o.f.m.cap.* '78 (NY) Valhalla, NY Westchester County Medical Center; [DD] White Plains, NY St. Conrad Friary.
Connolly, Michael C. *o.s.f.s.* '74 (ARL) Reston, VA St. John Neumann Church.
Connolly, Michael J. *s.j.* '68 (BO) [W] Boston, MA The Society of Jesus of New England-Provincial Offices.
Connolly, Michael J. *s.j.* '68 (SPK) [C] Spokane, WA Gonzaga University.
Connolly, Msgr. Neil A. '58 (NY) [70] New York, NY St. Mary Church.
Connolly, Patrick *s.j.* '66 (LA) [R] Los Angeles, CA Columbiere House.
Connolly, Patrick Francis *o.p.* '52 (NY) [22] New York, NY St. Catherine of Siena Church; [DD] New York, NY St. Catherine of Siena Priory.
Connolly, Patrick J. '67 (GRY) Schererville, IN St. Michael Church.
Connolly, Paul E. '83 (DAV) East Pleasant Plain, IA St. Joseph's Church; Richland, IA St. Frances Xavier Cabrini Church.
Connolly, Peter *c.ss.r.* '77 (MIL) [S] Oconomowoc, WI Our Mother of Perpetual Help Retreat Center.
Connolly, Robert P. '79 (PIT) [A] Pittsburgh, PA Saint Paul Seminary.
Connolly, Robert V. '45 (LC) Retired; [I] La Crosse, WI Holy Cross (Seminary) Diocesan Center.
Connolly, Scott '95 (SEA) Aberdeen, WA St. Mary's Church; Aberdeen, WA SS. Peter and Paul Church; Hoquiam, WA Our Lady of Good Help Church; Ocean Shores, WA St. Jerome Church.
Connolly, T. Gerard *s.j.* '58 (NY) [DD] New York, NY Jesuit Community at Fordham University.
Connolly, Thomas '52 (SFS) Retired.
Connolly, Thomas *s.j.* '63 (B) DeSmet, ID Sacred Heart Church.
Connolly, Thomas J. *o.m.i.* '47 (P) [Q] Portland, OR Oregon Catholic Conference.
Connolly, Vincent F. *s.j.* '70 (FgM) Provinces.
Connolly, William A. *s.j.* '46 (FgM) Provinces.
Connoly, James '78 (RNO) Fallon, NV Fallon Naval Air Station Base Chapel Church.
Connor, Adrian J. *o.praem.* '95 (ORG) [D] Siverado, CA St. Michael's College Preparatory High School; [H] Silverado, CA Norbertine Fathers of Orange Inc.
Connor, Brian P. '89 (LIN) David City, NE St. Francis Church; [C] David City, NE Aquinas/St. Mary's Schools; [L] David City, NE Aquinas High School Endowment Fund.
Connor, Charles P. '90 (SCR) [21] Scranton, PA St. Patrick's Church.
Connor, Francis J. '40 (STU) Retired.
Connor, Gerald T. '54 (ROC) [52] Rochester, NY St. Pius Tenth Church.
Connor, J. Patrick '61 (NSH) Columbia, TN St. Catherine Church.
Connor, James *s.j.* '59 (WDC) [M] Washington, DC Woodstock Jesuit Community.
Connor, James '78 (HEL) Kalispell, MT Risen Christ Church.
Connor, James E. '60 (PRT) [J] Saco, ME Bay View Community.
Connor, James L. *s.j.* '59 (WDC) [V] Washington, DC Woodstock Theological Center.
Connor, John *c.s.c.* (SB) Thermal, CA San Felipe de Jesus Church.
Connor, John E. '32 (BO) Retired.
Connor, John P. '62 (CAM) Bridgeton, NJ Immaculate Conception Church.
Connor, John S. *c.s.c.* '70 (SB) Coachella, CA Our Lady of Soledad Church.
Connor, John V. '46 (WDC) Retired.
Connor, Joseph J. *s.j.* '42 (BO) [W] Chestnut Hill, MA The Jesuit Community at Boston College; [W] Weston, MA Campion Health Center, Inc.
Connor, Kevin (STP) [C] St. Paul, MN University of St. Thomas.
Connor, Kevin T. (STP) [A] St. Paul, MN St. John Vianney Seminary.
Connor, Kevin T. '87 (MAN) On Duty Outside the Diocese.
Connor, Martin P. '64 (BO) [A] Boston, MA St. John's Seminary School of Theology; [FF] Boston, MA League of Catholic Women of the Archdiocese of Boston.
Connor, Patrick *s.v.d.* '57 (TR) [M] Bordentown, NJ Society of the Divine Word.
Connor, Patrick L. '83 (ROC) [1] Elmira, NY Sts. Peter

and Paul of Eastside Catholic Parish; [4] Elmira, NY St. John the Baptist of Eastside Catholic Parish; [6] Elmira, NY St. Cecilia of Eastside Catholic Parish.
Connor, Paul *o.p.* '67 (SFR) [N] San Francisco, CA St. Dominic Priory.
Connor, Robert A. '64 (NY) [II] New Rochelle, NY Opus Dei (Prelature of the Holy Cross and Opus Dei).
Connor, Robert M. '58 (BO) Norfolk, MA St. Jude Church.
Connor, Stephen *c.s.p.* (AUS) [11] Austin, TX St. Austin's Church.
Connor, Vincent '71 (SB) Chino, CA California Youth Authority.
Connor, William *m.s.c.* '57 (OG) [2] Watertown, NY Our Lady of the Sacred Heart, Missionaries of the Sacred Heart Church; Watertown, NY Watertown Correctional Facility.
Connor, William J. '46 (COL) Retired.
Connor, William J. '66 (LA) [65] Los Angeles, CA St. Gerard Majella Church.
Connor, William K. '66 (PBL) Cortez, CO St. Margaret Mary Church; Mancos, CO St. Rita Church.
Connors, Albert *c.m.f.* '73 (LA) [R] Rancho Dominguez, CA Dominguez Seminary Inc.
Connors, Brocard *o.carm.* '57 (NY) [DD] Tappan, NY St. Eliseus Priory.
Connors, Canice *o.f.m.conv.* '61 (ALB) [A] Rensselaer, NY Conventual Franciscan Friars; [L] Rensselaer, NY Provincialate, Immaculate Conception Friary - Order of Friars Minor Conventual.
Connors, Canice *o.f.m.conv.* '61 (FgM) Conventual Franciscan Foreign Missions.
Connors, Cletus *o.s.b.* (SCL) [I] Collegeville, MN St. John's Abbey, of the Order of St. Benedict.
Connors, Cletus *o.s.b.* '72 (SCL) Cold Spring, MN St. Boniface Church.
Connors, Edmund P. (NY) [217] Staten Island, NY Our Lady Help of Christians Church.
Connors, Edmund P. '66 (NY) [E] New York, NY Moore Catholic High School.
Connors, Msgr. Edward M. '47 (NY) Retired; [E] White Plains, NY Archbishop Stepinac High School.
Connors, Edward P. '36 (CHI) Blue Island, IL St. Benedict Church; Retired.
Connors, Francis B. '50 (FR) Retired.
Connors, Francis E. '73 (BUR) Burlington, VT Fletcher Allen Health Care.
Connors, J. M. *o.p.* '51 (FgM) Dominican - Order of Preachers Foreign Missions.
Connors, James V. *c.m.* '40 (LA) [X] Montebello, CA DePaul Center.
Connors, Joseph *s.v.d.* '52 (CHI) [B] Techny, IL Divine Word Residence.
Connors, Michael *c.s.c.* '84 (FTW) [L] Notre Dame, IN Holy Cross Mission House.
Connors, Michael E. *c.s.c.* '84 (FTW) [M] Notre Dame, IN Our Lady of Fatima Retreat Center.
Connors, Paul *s.v.d.* '63 (CHI) [B] Techny, IL Divine Word Residence; [N] Techny, IL Society of the Divine Word, Provincial Headquarter-Chicago Prov.
Connors, Richard '69 (MAN) [E] Salem, NH St. Joseph Regional School.
Connors, Richard P. (PH) Warrington, PA St. Joseph Church.
Connors, Richard P. '79 (PH) Absent on Sick Leave.
Connors, Richard W. '69 (MAN) Salem, NH St. Joseph Church.
Connors, Robert A. '55 (NEW) Oakland, NJ Our Lady of Perpetual Help Church.
Connors, Robert L. '71 (BO) Newburyport, MA Immaculate Conception Church; Newburyport, MA St. Louis de Gonzague Church.
Connors, Terrence L. '75 (MAD) Jefferson, WI St. John the Baptist Church.
Conole, Robert W. '92 (BO) Hudson, MA St. Michael Church.
Conoscenti, Frederick M. '65 (BUF) On Duty Outside the Diocese.
Conover, James A. '78 (TR) Keyport, NJ St. Joseph Church.
Conover, Sylvan J. *o.f.m.cap.* '49 (NY) Wassaic, NY Wassaic Development Center; [DD] Yonkers, NY St. Clare Friary.
Conrad, Anthony J. '49 (DAV) Retired; [M] Davenport, IA St. Vincent Center.
Conrad, Arthur Dennis '77 (RIC) [3] Richmond, VA Holy Rosary Church.
Conrad, Brian '81 (HBG) [K] Harrisburg, PA Catholic Campus Ministry.
Conrad, Brian P. '76 (HBG) Bonneauville, PA St. Joseph Church.
Conrad, James H. '64 (ALT) [2] Windber, PA SS. Cyril and Methodius Church.
Conrad, John F. '63 (GB) Clarks Mills, WI Immaculate Conception Church.
Conrad, Robert '70 (SY) New Hartford, NY St. Thomas Church.
Conrad, Simon *o.f.m.* '62 (GLP) St. Michaels, AZ St. Michael Church.
Conrad, Simon R. *o.f.m.cap.* '46 (STL) [54] St. Louis, MO St. Patrick Church; [P] St. Louis, MO St. Patrick Friary.
Conrad, Stanley '38 (AUS) Retired.
Conrad, Sylvester A. '52 (DAV) Knoxville, IA Veteran's Administration Hospital; Retired.
Conro, Ronald J. '65 (RCK) Elizabeth, IL St. Mary Church; Scales Mound, IL Holy Trinity Church.
Conroy, Cyril J. (BO) Retired.
Conroy, Cyril J. '52 (BO) Beverly, MA St. Margaret Church.
Conroy, Donald B. '64 (GBG) On Duty Outside the Diocese.
Conroy, Donald B. '64 (WDC) [V] Washington, DC National Institute for the Family, Inc.
Conroy, Edward '49 (NY) Retired.
Conroy, Edward G. '45 (BRK) Retired.
Conroy, Edward M. '49 (NY) [185] Bronx, NY St. Raymond Church.
Conroy, Francis M. '64 (BO) [1] Newton, MA St. Bernard Church.
Conroy, Francis X. '72 (BEA) Orange, TX St. Francis of Assisi Church.
Conroy, Gerard D. '42 (PH) [AA] Philadelphia, PA Congregation of the Mission.
Conroy, J. Peter *s.j.* '71 (BUF) [O] Buffalo, NY Canisius Jesuit Community.
Conroy, James A. '53 (CLV) Retired.
Conroy, James P. '53 (DAV) [5] Davenport, IA St. Anthony's Church.
Conroy, James R. *s.j.* '78 (BAL) [M] Baltimore, MD Ferdinand Wheeler Jesuit Community; [Q] Baltimore, MD Ignatian Lay Volunteer Corps.
Conroy, James R. *s.j.* '78 (WDC) [E] Washington, DC Gonzaga College High School.
Conroy, Jerome *o.p.* (NY) Manhattan, NY Memorial Sloan Kettering Cancer Center.
Conroy, John Jerome *o.p.* '49 (NY) [22] New York, NY St. Catherine of Siena Church; [DD] New York, NY St. Catherine of Siena Priory.
Conroy, Kevin M. '82 (CLV) Wooster, OH St. Mary of the Immaculate Conception Church.
Conroy, Martin J. *c.s.sp.* '54 (DET) [47] Detroit, MI St. Mary Church.
Conroy, Michael F. *s.p.s.* '65 (CHI) Park Ridge, IL Mary, Seat of Wisdom Church.
Conroy, Patrick J. *s.j.* '83 (WDC) [M] Washington, DC The Jesuit Community at Georgetown University.
Conroy, Phillip M. (BO) Boston, MA St. Elizabeth's Medical Center.
Conroy, Thomas J. '48 (STP) Retired; [C] St. Paul, MN University of St. Thomas.
Conry, Austin '65 (MOB) [11] Mobile, AL Little Flower Church.
Conry, James A. '53 (CLV) Wadsworth, OH Sacred Heart Church.
Conry, Roy *o.carm.* '56 (TUC) [A] Tucson, AZ Salpointe Catholic High School; [F] Tucson, AZ Carmelite Priory.
Conry, Thomas P. *s.j.* '43 (DET) [P] Clarkston, MI Colombiere Center.
Consalvi, Mark *ss.cc.* '43 (HON) [5] Honolulu, HI Blessed Sacrament Church; [H] Kaneohe, HI Sacred Hearts Center.
Consani, Robert E. (KAL) Retired.
Consentine, Rocco *c.pp.s.* '54 (TOL) [M] Bellevue, OH Sorrowful Mother Shrine.
Conserva, Stephen *o.m.i.* '74 (SFD) [A] Godfrey, IL Immaculate Heart of Mary Novitiate.
Considine, Msgr. John J. '36 (NY) [132] Bronx, NY St. Barnabas Church; Retired; [E] New York, NY Cardinal Spellman High School.
Considine, Matthew J. *s.m.m.* '77 (BRK) [195] Queens, NY St. Mary Gate of Heaven Church; [U] Ozone Park, NY Montfort Missionaries Provincialate - for Nation Community.
Considine, William J. *s.m.m.* (BRK) [U] Ozone Park, NY Montfort Missionaries Provincialate - for Nation Community.
Consla, Federico J. *c.ss.r.* '70 (CGS) San Lorenzo, PR Nuestra Senora de la Mercedes Church.
Constance, Jogues *o.f.m.cap.* '53 (DET) [P] Washington, MI Capuchin Retreat.
Constance, Msgr. Samuel C. '55 (TR) Retired.
Constant, Van L. '93 (HT) Raceland, LA St. Mary's Nativity Church.
Constantine, Bennett '58 (LAN) Eaton Rapids, MI St. Peter Church.
Constantine, Cyprian G. *o.s.b.* '77 (GBG) [H] Latrobe, PA Saint Vincent Archabbey.
Constantinides, Gus *c.pp.s.* (Y) Niles, OH Our Lady of Mt. Carmel Church.
Contadino, Eugene J. *s.m.* '70 (CIN) [D] Dayton, OH The University of Dayton.
Contadino, J. Eugene *s.m.* '70 (CIN) [M] Dayton, OH Marianist Provincialate.
Contardi, Michael *o.de.m.* '60 (CLV) [67] Cleveland, OH St. Rocco Church.
Conte, Denis A. '75 (BO) Health Leave.
Conte, James W. '48 (NY) Retired.
Conte, John P. '58 (ALN) Unassigned.
Conte, John P. '64 (HRT) Special and other (Arch)Diocesan Assignment; [A] Bloomfield, CT St. Thomas Seminary.
Conterno, Austin *s.d.b.* '48 (SFR) [45] San Francisco, CA SS. Peter and Paul Church.
Conti, Cornelius *o.f.m.* '62 (HRT) [14] Hartford, CT St. Patrick-St. Anthony Church.
Conti, Hilary *o.s.b.* '50 (NY) [HH] Esopus, NY Holy Shroud Guild.
Conti, Hilary *o.s.b.* '50 (PAT) [M] Clifton, NJ Holy Face of Jesus Monastery.
Conti, John P. '46 (NY) Retired.
Conti, Joseph A. '65 (OG) [5] Plattsburgh, NY St. Peter Church; [C] Plattsburgh, NY Seton Catholic Central.
Conti, Msgr. Leo J. '50 (EVN) Retired.
Continillo, Msgr. Rocco A. '56 (CAM) Carneys Point, NJ Corpus Christi Church.
Contons, Albert J. '48 (BO) [63] Boston, MA St. Peter Church.
Contran, Sergio *m.c.c.j.* '50 (CIN) [M] Cincinnati, OH Comboni Missionaries (Verona Fathers)-Comboni Mission Center.
Contran, Sergio *m.c.c.j.* '50 (LA) [55] Los Angeles, CA St. Cecilia Church.
Contreras, David '93 (AMA) Stratford, TX St. Joseph's Church.
Conva, Matthias T. '62 (NEW) Union, NJ St. Michael's Church.
Converse, Brian J. '91 (NOR) North Grosvenordale, CT St. Joseph Church.
Converset, John *m.c.c.j.* '71 (CIN) [M] Cincinnati, OH Comboni Missionaries (Verona Fathers)-Comboni Mission Center.
Converset, John *m.c.c.j.* '71 (FgM) Comboni Foreign Missions.
Convertino, David I. *o.f.m.* '77 (PRO) [P] Providence, RI St. Francis Friary.
Convery, Paul C. '84 (PH) [47] Philadelphia, PA St. Francis Xavier Church; [AA] Philadelphia, PA Archdiocesan Oratory of St. Philip Neri (C.O.).
Convery, Thomas L. *s.s.c.* '40 (PRO) [P] Bristol, RI St. Columban's Retirement House.
Convey, Edwin H. *s.j.* '53 (BAL) [B] Baltimore, MD Loyola College; [M] Baltimore, MD Jesuit Community of Loyola College, Inc.
Conway, David '52 (WDC) [29] Washington, DC St. Mary, Mother of God Church.
Conway, Dennis *m.c.c.j.* '68 (FgM) Comboni Foreign Missions.
Conway, Edwin M. '60 (CHI) [G] Chicago, IL Catholic Charities of the Archdiocese of Chicago-Archdiocesan Offices.
Conway, Gerald W. '56 (WIN) Wabasha, MN St. Felix Church.
Conway, James '65 (SAT) Castroville, TX St. Louis Church.
Conway, Msgr. Jeffrey '73 (NY) [221] Staten Island, NY Our Lady Star of the Sea Church.
Conway, John '62 (FAR) Retired.
Conway, John E. *m.m.* '73 (NY) [DD] Maryknoll, NY Maryknoll Fathers and Brothers.
Conway, Msgr. John L. '56 (GBG) Irwin, PA Immaculate Conception Church.
Conway, John R. '69 (SFE) [27] Albuquerque, NM St. Jude Thaddeus Church.
Conway, John T. '77 (PH) [29] Philadelphia, PA St. Carthage Church.
Conway, Laurence J. '59 (MIA) [3] Miami Beach, FL St. Mary Magdalen Church.
Conway, Malachy '94 (SAC) [19] Sacramento, CA St. Peter Church.
Conway, Msgr. Michael (PAT) On Duty Outside the Diocese.
Conway, Msgr. Michael '60 (MIA) Davie, FL St. David Church.
Conway, Michael *s.d.b.* '92 (BO) [N] Boston, MA Salesian Boys & Girls Club.
Conway, Michael J. *o.ss.t.* '73 (NY) [20] New York, NY St. Brigid Church.
Conway, Neil '63 (CLV) Retired.
Conway, Patrick F. *c.s.sp.* '47 (SFR) [K] San Rafael, CA Nazareth House.
Conway, Pierre H. *o.p.* '41 (WDC) [B] Washington, DC Dominican House of Studies.
Conway, Richard C. '63 (BO) Randolph, MA St. Bernadette Church.
Conway, Richard J. '45 (BAK) Retired.
Conway, Richard T. '83 (BO) Reading, MA St. Athanasius Church.
Conway, Robert *c.pp.s.* '53 (CIN) [B] Carthagena, OH St. Charles.
Conway, Thomas '86 (BLX) Columbia, MS Industrial and Training School.
Conway, Thomas A. *c.pp.s.* '57 (KC) Kearney, MO Church of the Annunciation; [J] Liberty, MO Precious Blood Center.
Conway, Thomas D. '60 (BO) Reading, MA St. Athanasius Church.
Conway, Tommy '86 (BLX) Columbia, MS Most Holy Trinity Church.
Conway, Msgr. Walter J. '48 (PH) [157] Philadelphia, PA St. William Church; Retired.

Conway, William '77 (JOL) Bensenville, IL St. Alexis Church.
Conwell, Joseph F. *s.j.* '50 (SPK) [B] Spokane, WA St. Michael's Institute.
Conwill, Giles A. '73 (SD) Leave of Absence.
Conyard, James R. *s.j.* '62 (P) [L] Portland, OR Colombiere Community.
Conyard, Joseph W. *s.j.* '59 (SEA) [M] Seattle, WA Jesuit Community.
Conyers, Richard *c.s.c.* '69 (FTW) [9] South Bend, IN Holy Cross Church.
Coogan, Roch A. *o.f.m.* '54 (SP) [O] St. Petersburg, FL St. Anthony Friary.
Coogan, Thomas M. '97 (RVC) Bay Shore, NY St. Patrick's Church.
Cook, Adrian L. '72 (MOB) Brewton, AL St. Maurice Church.
Cook, Blaine '44 (BIS) Retired; [G] Bismarck, ND Emmaus Place.
Cook, Daniel '90 (GR) On Duty Outside the Diocese.
Cook, Daniel '90 (STU) [J] Steubenville, OH The Fraternity of Priests, Inc.
Cook, Douglas '94 (ORG) Costa Mesa, CA St. Joachim Church.
Cook, Edward J. '67 (MIL) [30] Milwaukee, WI Congregation of the Great Spirit Church.
Cook, Emil *o.f.m.conv.* (FgM) Conventual Franciscan Foreign Missions.
Cook, John B. '49 (TR) Retired.
Cook, John N. '56 (GI) Retired.
Cook, John P. '45 (HRT) Retired.
Cook, Joseph T. '86 (CHI) [126] Chicago, IL St. Mary Church.
Cook, Louis G. '58 (WIN) St. Charles, MN St. Charles Borromeo Church.
Cook, Michael J. '73 (WIL) Woodcrest, DE St. Matthew Church.
Cook, Michael L. *s.j.* '66 (SPK) [C] Spokane, WA Gonzaga University.
Cook, Millard S. *o.s.b.* '92 (GBG) [H] Latrobe, PA Saint Vincent Archabbey; [H] Latrobe, PA Saint Vincent Archabbey.
Cook, Msgr. Paul G. '59 (BAL) Cockeysville, MD St. Joseph Church.
Cook, Philip C. *o.s.a.* '97 (TLS) [B] Tulsa, OK Cascia Hall Preparatory School.
Cook, Robert J. '65 (LC) [1] La Crosse, WI St. Joseph the Workman Cathedral.
Cook, Ronald '93 (B) Buhl, ID Immaculate Conception Church.
Cook, Steven '97 (KC) On Educational Leave of Absence.
Cook, Thomas '88 (LA) Burbank, CA St. Finbar Church.
Cook, Thomas E. '97 (WIN) Graduate Studies.
Cook, Thomas R. *o.s.a.* '57 (MIA) [H] Miami, FL Casa San Lorenzo.
Cook, Timothy R. '83 (STL) [17] St. Louis, MO Visitation-St. Ann's Shrine Church.
Cook, Walter A. *s.j.* '52 (WDC) [M] Washington, DC The Jesuit Community at Georgetown University.
Cook, William G. '88 (NEW) [6] Bayonne, NJ Mt. Carmel Church.
Cook, William R. (CLV) Retired.
Cooke, Colman M. '65 (SP) [5] Clearwater, FL St. Michael The Archangel Church.
Cooke, Msgr. John F. '59 (CAM) Pitman, NJ Our Lady Queen of Peace Church.
Cooke, Kevin '78 (BIR) Gadsden, AL St. James Church.
Cooke, Patrick *c.s.sp.* (STA) [17] Jacksonville, FL St. Matthew's Church.
Cooke, Vincent M. *s.j.* '67 (BUF) [C] Buffalo, NY Canisius College; [O] Buffalo, NY Canisius Jesuit Community.
Cooke, Vincent M. *s.j.* '67 (NY) [HH] New York, NY Catholic Medical Mission Board, Inc.
Cookson, Edmund L. *m.m.* '65 (FgM) Maryknoll Foreign Missions.
Cool, Brian C. '93 (ROC) Canandaigua, NY St. Mary Church; [M] Rochester, NY Diocesan Office of Campus Ministry.
Cooley, Fred *s.j.* '54 (FgM) Provinces.
Cooley, John E. '48 (LA) Retired.
Cooley, Stephen V. *o.carm.* '67 (GAL) [50] Houston, TX St. Michael Church.
Coolong, Raymond *s.m.* '71 (FgM) Marist Foreign Missions.
Coombs, James R. *s.s.e.* '52 (BUR) [E] Colchester, VT Society of St. Edmund.
Coombs, William *s.t.* (WDC) [M] Adelphi, MD Missionary Servants of the Most Holy Trinity.
Coomes, J. Eugene *s.j.* '48 (STL) [P] St. Louis, MO Jesuit Community Corporation at St. Louis University - Jesuit Hall.
Coon, David N. '93 (SPC) [3] Springfield, MO Immaculate Conception Church.
Coonan, James J. (PH) [87] Philadelphia, PA St. Leo Church.
Coonan, Joseph A. '89 (WOR) [25] Worcester, MA St. John's Church.
Coonan, Robert J. '65 (SPR) Hatfield, MA St. Joseph's Church.
Cooney, Arthur *o.f.m.cap.* '76 (SAG) [14] Saginaw, MI St. Joseph Church.
Cooney, Camillus '56 (LR) [A] Subiaco, AR Subiaco Monastery.
Cooney, David *s.d.s.* '67 (PHX) [17] Phoenix, AZ St. Mark Church.
Cooney, Dennis '74 (VEN) Bradenton, FL SS. Peter and Paul the Apostles Church.
Cooney, Francis C. *m.s.* '69 (HRT) [5] Hartford, CT Our Lady of Sorrows Church; [M] Hartford, CT Missionaries of LaSalette Provincial Secretary.
Cooney, Gerald (FWT) Retired.
Cooney, Msgr. James '64 (BRK) [163] Queens, NY St. Clare Church.
Cooney, John M. '62 (HRT) Watertown, CT St. John the Evangelist Church.
Cooney, Msgr. Joseph P. '42 (PH) Wayne, PA St. Katharine of Siena Church; Retired.
Cooney, Michael N. '75 (DET) Mount Clemens, MI St. Peter Church.
Cooney, Patrick *o.s.b.* '91 (IND) [A] St. Meinrad, IN St. Meinrad Seminary; [B] St. Meinrad, IN St. Meinrad Seminary-College of Liberal Arts; [J] St. Meinrad, IN St. Meinrad Archabbey.
Cooney, Robert F. *c.s.v.* '57 (LAV) [D] Las Vegas, NV Clerics of St. Viator Retirement Home.
Cooney, Roger P. '70 (COL) [A] Columbus, OH Pontifical College Josephinum.
Cooney, Roger P. '70 (COV) On Duty Outside the Diocese.
Cooney, Romaeus *o.carm.* '58 (ALB) [4] Troy, NY Holy Trinity Church; [5] Troy, NY St. Joseph Church.
Cooney, Sean K. '59 (ORL) Winter Park, FL Saints Peter and Paul Church.
Cooney, Stephen A. '76 (LIN) Brainard, NE Holy Trinity Church.
Cooney, Theophane *c.p.* '52 (BRK) [180] Queens, NY Immaculate Conception Church; [U] Jamaica, NY Immaculate Conception Monastery.
Cooney, Xavier *s.v.d.* '83 (WH) Webster Springs, WV St. Anne's Church.
Coons, David F. '83 (IND) [33] Indianapolis, IN St. Pius X Church; [C] Indianapolis, IN Bishop Chatard High School.
Cooper, Angus *o.f.m.* '61 (OAK) [N] Oakland, CA Franciscan Friars Provincial Office, Province of St. Barbara.
Cooper, Angus C. *o.f.m.* '61 (LA) [72] Los Angeles, CA St. Joseph Church.
Cooper, Craig D. '88 (BAL) Absent on Leave.
Cooper, Damian L. '86 (RVC) Lindenhurst, NY Our Lady of Perpetual Help Church.
Cooper, David E. '70 (MIL) [3] West Allis, WI Holy Assumption Church.
Cooper, Donald A. '53 (NEW) Washington Township, NJ Our Lady of Good Counsel Church; Retired.
Cooper, Donald J. '63 (E) Force, PA St. Joseph Church.
Cooper, Harold V. '49 (SC) Retired.
Cooper, James W. '80 (LIN) Friend, NE St. Joseph's Church.
Cooper, Jeffrey A. *c.s.c.* '94 (FTW) [J] South Bend, IN Congregation of Holy Cross Indiana Province Provincial House.
Cooper, John A. '80 (LIN) Tecumseh, NE St. Andrew's Church.
Cooper, Joseph M. *o.f.m.cap.* (MAN) [5] Manchester, NH Blessed Sacrament Church.
Cooper, Leo '43 (KCK) Special Assignment.
Cooper, Mark A. *o.s.b.* '76 (MAN) [K] Manchester, NH St. Anselm Abbey.
Cooper, Michael W. *s.j.* '73 (GRY) [J] East Chicago, IN Roque Gonzalez Residence-Jesuit Fathers; [O] Hammond, IN Seimetz Center; [O] Hammond, IN Spiritual Life Center.
Cooper, Patrick E. '91 (CHR) Cheraw, SC St. Peter's Church.
Cooper, R. John '83 (CLV) Released from Diocesan Assignment.
Cooper, Ronald C. '83 (CIN) Greenfield, OH St. Benignus Church; New Vienna, OH St. Michael Church.
Cooper, Thomas T. '55 (STL) Retired.
Cooper, Warren L. '71 (NO) Chalmette, LA Our Lady of Prompt Succor Church.
Coopmans, Joseph R. *o.praem.* '81 (GB) [4] Green Bay, WI Annunciation of the Blessed Virgin Mary Church.
Coover, Thomas (OLL) Leave of Absence.
Copeland, Leonard R. *o.c.d.* '67 (MIL) [24] Milwaukee, WI St. Florian Church.
Copenhaver, John L. '88 (LIN) Shelby, NE Sacred Heart Church.
Copp, Rodney J. '73 (BO) [1] Waltham, MA St. Charles Borromeo Church.
Coppenrath, Leonard A. '53 (BO) [1] Brookline, MA St. Aidan Church.
Copper, Stephen G. '95 (WOR) [23] Worcester, MA St. George Church.
Coppinger, Edmund T. '59 (WIL) Easton, MD SS. Peter and Paul Church.
Coppinger, John *s.a.* '72 (NY) [4] Yonkers, NY St. Bartholomew Church.
Coppola, David L. '86 (PAT) Kinnelon, NJ Our Lady of the Magnificat Church; [C] Wayne, NJ De Paul High School.
Coppola, Paul R. '51 (BUF) Retired.
Cops, Augustine *o.f.m.cap.* '85 (DET) [15] Detroit, MI St. Charles Borromeo Church.
Cops, Augustine *o.f.m.cap.* '86 (DET) [57] Detroit, MI Our Lady of Sorrows Church.
Cops, Peter *s.s.s.* '52 (CLV) [P] Cleveland, OH Congregation of the Blessed Sacrament Provincial House.
Cops, Peter E. *s.s.s.* '52 (LIN) [F] Waverly, NE Our Lady of Good Counsel Retreat House.
Copsey, Robert *s.o.l.t.* '94 (CC) Robstown, TX St. Anthony Church; [H] Robstown, TX Society of Our Lady of the Most Holy Trinity.
Copsey, Robert A. '78 (SAC) [16] Sacramento, CA St. Joseph's Church.
Corali, Serafino A. '47 (RVC) Retired; [N] Uniondale, NY St. Pius X Residence.
Corapi, John *s.o.l.t.* '91 (CC) [H] Robstown, TX Society of Our Lady of the Most Holy Trinity.
Corbally, Christopher *s.j.* '76 (TUC) [F] Tucson, AZ Kino House.
Corbelli, Vincent F. *m.m.* '60 (FgM) Maryknoll Foreign Missions.
Corbellini, Peter *c.s.* '82 (CHI) [17] Chicago, IL St. Anthony Church.
Corbett, Carlos *c.ss.r.* '53 (CGS) Aguas Buenas, PR Church of Tres Santos Reyes.
Corbett, Eugene J. *s.j.* '62 (SJ) Santa Clara, CA Santa Clara Valley Medical Center; [D] San Jose, CA Bellarmine College Preparatory.
Corbett, George J. *c.ss.r.* '43 (STL) [P] Liguori, MO St. Clement Health Care Center.
Corbett, John '95 (NEW) Jersey City, NJ B.S. Pollak Hospital.
Corbett, John B. '56 (PIT) [50] Pittsburgh, PA Holy Innocents Church.
Corbett, John D. *o.p.* '80 (COL) [A] Columbus, OH Pontifical College Josephinum.
Corbett, John V. *c.ss.r.* '46 (SPR) [8] Springfield, MA Our Lady of Hope Church.
Corbett, Michael E. '54 (PBL) Retired.
Corbett, Richard '95 (NEW) Secaucus, NJ Immaculate Conception Church.
Corbett, Robert '51 (STL) Manchester, MO Christ, Prince of Peace Church.
Corbett, W. Joseph '95 (ATL) Dunwoody, GA All Saints Catholic Church.
Corbin, Don '70 (TOL) [H] Oregon, OH St. Charles Mercy Hospital.
Corbino, Thomas A. '72 (JOL) Warrenville, IL St. Irene Church.
Corbo, Alfred P. '56 (CHI) Franklin Park, IL St. Gertrude Church.
Corces, Pedro '88 (MIA) [14] Miami, FL Prince of Peace Church.
Corciulo, Msgr. Cosimo '56 (SB) Norco, CA California Rehabilitation Center.
Corcoran, Albert C. *s.j.* '36 (SFR) [N] San Francisco, CA Jesuit Community at University of San Francisco.
Corcoran, Anthony J. *s.j.* '96 (NO) [P] New Orleans, LA Jesuit Provincial Office.
Corcoran, Brian M. '72 (SD) [1] El Cajon, CA Holy Trinity Church.
Corcoran, Msgr. Clifton J. '54 (AMA) Retired; [D] Panhandle, TX St. Joseph's Home for Retired Priests.
Corcoran, D. Stanley '90 (DAL) Commerce, TX St. Joseph Church; [O] Irving, TX Diocese of Dallas Campus Ministry.
Corcoran, Edward *o.s.f.s.* '41 (ARL) Vienna, VA Our Lady of Good Counsel Church.
Corcoran, Edward G. '56 (CHI) Berwyn, IL St. Leonard Church.
Corcoran, Frank '54 (JKS) Crystal Springs, MS St. John Church.
Corcoran, Harry T. *s.j.* '43 (OAK) [A] Berkeley, CA The Jesuit School of Theology at Berkeley; [N] Berkeley, CA Jesuit Community at Jesuit School of Theology at Berkeley.
Corcoran, John J. '55 (RVC) Center Moriches, NY St. John the Evangelist Church.
Corcoran, John W. '53 (BO) East Bridgewater, MA St. John Church.
Corcoran, Kevin '88 (SY) [3] Syracuse, NY Blessed Sacrament Church.
Corcoran, Lawrence E. *s.j.* '63 (BO) [W] Weston, MA Campion Center.
Corcoran, Msgr. Lawrence J. '43 (COL) [18] Columbus, OH Holy Cross Church; Retired.
Corcoran, Mel M. *o.s.m.* '44 (ORG) [H] Anaheim, CA Servite Fathers and Brothers.
Corcoran, Michael P. *s.j.* '88 (NY) [DD] New York, NY Jesuit Community at Fordham University.
Corcoran, Sean *c.ss.p.* '55 (SFR) [49] San Francisco, CA St. Stephen Church.
Corcoran, William D. '86 (BUR) Hinesburg, VT St. Jude the Apostle Church.
Corcoran, William T. '81 (CHI) [121] Chicago, IL St.

Margaret Mary Church.
Corcuera, Manuel R. '76 (CHK) Songsong Village, MP San Francisco de Borja Parish.
Cordano, Virgil *o.f.m.* '45 (LA) [R] Santa Barbara, CA Franciscan Friary, Order of Friars Minor (Old Mission).
Cordaro, Frank '85 (DM) Lacona, IA Holy Trinity Church of Southeast Warren County.
Cordeiro, Anthony *o.p.* (OAK) [N] Oakland, CA Western Dominican Province.
Cordeiro, Anthony *o.p.* '67 (P) [18] Portland, OR Holy Rosary Parish & Dominican Priory Church.
Cordero, Faustino '71 (BRK) [125] Brooklyn, NY St. Rocco's Church.
Cordero, Mamerto '74 (NEW) [18] Jersey City, NJ St. Nicholas Church; Jersey City, NJ Christ Hospital.
Cordery, Robert J. '80 (BO) [E] Boston, MA Catholic Memorial High School and Lower School.
Cordes, Christopher '95 (JC) [1] Jefferson City, MO St. Joseph Cathedral.
Cordier, Leonard *c.ss.r.* '38 (ORL) [F] New Smyrna Beach, FL St. Alphonsus Villa-Redemptorist Fathers and Brothers.
Cordileone, Salvatore '82 (SD) On Duty Outside the Diocese.
Cordisco, Philip *o.ss.t.* '60 (NY) [218] Staten Island, NY Our Lady of Mt. Carmel-St. Benedicta Church.
Cordova, Hugo *o.f.m.* '91 (ELP) [B] El Paso, TX St. Anthony's School of Theology.
Coreas, Edwin '92 (GAL) [19] Houston, TX St. Charles Borromeo Church.
Corena, Pedro *o.ss.t.* '66 (SJN) [14] Bayamon, PR Espiritu Santo Church.
Coric, Christopher *o.f.m.conv.* '71 (BUF) [7] Lackawanna, NY Our Lady of Bistrica Church.
Coric, Doiminik '40 (CHI) [N] Chicago, IL Croatian Franciscan Custody of the Holy Family.
Coriden, James A. '57 (GRY) On Duty Outside the Diocese.
Corigliano, Anthony *c.s.s.* '55 (BO) [W] Waltham, MA Stigmatine Fathers & Brothers Provincial House.
Corkery, Daniel '55 (ALX) Cloutierville, LA St. John the Baptist Church.
Corkery, Raymond *o.carm.* '59 (JOL) [4] Joliet, IL Mount Carmel Church.
Corl, Ronald *c.p.* '66 (DET) [K] Detroit, MI St. Paul of the Cross Community, Congregation of the Passion; [P] Detroit, MI St. Paul of the Cross Retreat Center.
Corley, Joseph M. (PH) [D] Philadelphia, PA John W. Hallahan Catholic Girls High School.
Corley, Joseph M. '75 (PH) [107] Philadelphia, PA Most Blessed Sacrament Church.
Corley, Malachy *o.c.s.o.* '55 (ATL) [I] Conyers, GA The Monastery of the Holy Spirit.
Corley, Theodosius *o.f.m.cap.* '74 (PRT) [3] Portland, ME St. Joseph's Church; [J] Portland, ME Motherhouse of the Sisters of Mercy of the Americas; [M] Portland, ME Westbrook College.
Corley, Thomas (JOL) [I] Naperville, IL St. John Vianney Villa.
Corley, Thomas '85 (JOL) Retired.
Cormack, James B. *c.m.* '76 (STL) [66] St. Louis, MO St. Vincent de Paul Church.
Cormack, Michael J. '54 (SAC) Roseville, CA St. Rose of Lima Church; Retired and in Senior Ministry.
Cormier, Allen L. *c.s.c.* '46 (AUS) [H] Austin, TX Congregation of Holy Cross - Southern Province.
Cormier, Allen L. *c.s.c.* '46 (FTW) [J] South Bend, IN Congregation of Holy Cross Indiana Province Provincial House.
Cormier, Gregory P. '83 (LAF) Parks, LA St. Joseph Church.
Cormier, Julien *m.afr.* (CHI) [124] Chicago, IL St. Martin De Porres Church.
Cormier, Julien *m.afr.* '62 (CHI) [N] Chicago, IL Missionaries of Africa.
Cormier, Leo G. (BO) Retired.
Cormier, Norman R. '59 (PRT) Retired.
Cormier, Robert (NEW) Newark, NJ Northern State Prison.
Cormier, Roger C. '61 (BO) [4] Everett, MA St. Therese Church.
Cormier, William N. '71 (WOR) East Douglas, MA St. Denis Church.
Corneille, Cecil '95 (STV) [1] St. Thomas, VI Cathedral of Sts. Peter and Paul; [2] Estate Elizabeth, VI Our Lady of Perpetual Help Church.
Cornejo, Quirino H. '91 (SAN) Junction, TX St. Theresa of the Child Jesus Church; Menard, TX Sacred Heart Church.
Cornejo, Vincent C. '56 (MET) Woodbridge, NJ Our Lady of Mt. Carmel Church.
Cornelius, Leonard *o.f.m.* '69 (AUS) Old Washington-on-the Brazos, TX Blessed Virgin Mary Church; [H] Brenham, TX Order of Friars Minor; [I] Brenham, TX Monastery of St. Clare.
Cornelius, Msgr. William R. '58 (STU) [8] Steubenville, OH St. Pius X Church.
Cornell, Robert J. *o.praem.* (GB) [B] De Pere, WI St. Norbert College; [I] De Pere, WI St. Joseph Priory.
Cornelli, Leo *o.s.b.* '35 (DET) [K] Detroit, MI St. Sylvester Monastery.
Cornelli, Neil '37 (LAN) Retired.
Cornelli, Neil '37 (STA) Fernandina Beach, FL St. Michael's Church.
Cornely, Francis J. '48 (PH) Essington, PA St. Margaret Mary Alacoque Church; Retired.
Cornett, David *s.v.d.* '87 (FgM) Society of the Divine Word Foreign Missions.
Corniel, Rafael G. '75 (NY) [103] New York, NY St. Paul Church.
Cornish, Daryl G. *s.j.* '82 (STL) [O] St. Louis, MO Fusz Pavilion.
Cornish, Ronald '68 (KCK) Holton, KS St. Dominic's Church; Mayetta, KS St. Francis Xavier Church.
Cornwell, Malcolm *c.p.* '69 (RVC) Shelter Island, NY Our Lady of the Isle Church.
Corominas, John *c.m.f.* '49 (LA) [R] Rancho Dominguez, CA Dominguez Seminary Inc.
Corona, Andrew '93 (GRY) [2] Hammond, IN Our Lady of Perpetual Help Church; [B] Hammond, IN Bishop Noll Institute.
Corona, John J. '71 (RNO) Gardnerville, NV St. Gall Church.
Corona, Msgr. Michael J. '68 (MET) Phillipsburg, NJ SS. Philip and James Church.
Coronado, Genero '51 (LA) Retired.
Corpora, Joseph V. *c.s.c.* '84 (PHX) Goodyear, AZ Saint John Vianney Church; [J] Goodyear, AZ St. John Vianney School Development Fund.
Corr, Msgr. John F. (PAT) Retired; [C] Madison, NJ Bayley-Ellard High School.
Corr, John Raymond *o.p.* '56 (FgM) Dominican - Order of Preachers Foreign Missions.
Corr, John Raymond *o.p.* '56 (NO) [P] New Orleans, LA Dominican Fathers & Brothers, Southern Dominican Province; [S] Metairie, LA Southern Dominican Foundation.
Corr, John Raymond *o.p.* '56 (SAT) [B] San Antonio, TX Dominican Priory of Juan Macias.
Corradi, Frank *s.c.* '85 (LC) [5] Eau Claire, WI St. Olaf Church.
Corradin, Gina *c.s.* '58 (CHI) [N] Stone Park, IL Scalabrini Mission Center.
Corrado, Dennis M. *c.o.* '70 (BRK) [22] Brooklyn, NY St. Boniface Church; [U] Brooklyn, NY Oratory of Saint Philip Neri, Congregation Pontifical Rite.
Corral, Jose '79 (TOL) Fostoria, OH St. Wendelin Church.
Corral, Jose C. *s.j.* '66 (BO) [27] Boston, MA Holy Family Church; [E] Boston, MA Boston College High School & Jesuit Community.
Corral, Roberto *o.p.* '88 (SFR) [13] San Francisco, CA St. Dominic Church; [N] San Francisco, CA St. Dominic Priory.
Corrales, Alirio '78 (TYL) Diboll, TX Our Lady of Guadalupe Church.
Corrao, John A. *c.s.* '56 (PRO) [4] Johnston, RI St. Rocco Church.
Correa, Adrian R. '84 (BWN) On Leave.
Correa, Gino *o.f.m.* '76 (CHI) [N] Chicago, IL St. Joseph Interprovincial Post-Novitiate Formation House.
Correa, Gino *o.f.m.* '76 (SFE) Jemez Pueblo, NM San Diego Indian Missions Church.
Corredato, John *c.s.v.* '68 (SFD) Edwardsville, IL St. Boniface Church.
Correia, Edward E. '68 (FR) [14] New Bedford, MA St. James Church.
Correlo, Bruce '85 (LA) [81] Los Angeles, CA St. Michael Church.
Correnti, Joseph M. '72 (LR) Springdale, AR St. Raphael's Church; Tontitown, AR St. Joseph's Church.
Correveau, Kip '95 (ROC) Pittsford, NY St. Louis Church.
Corriere, Basil *e.c.* '87 (STU) [F] Bloomingdale, OH Holy Family Hermitage.
Corrigan, Allen F. '82 (CLV) Maple Heights, OH St. Martin of Tours Church.
Corrigan, Austin B. '43 (SUP) Retired.
Corrigan, Msgr. Bernard '47 (NY) Warwick, NY St. Stephen Church.
Corrigan, Msgr. Bernard J. '47 (NY) Retired.
Corrigan, Edward *s.m.* '43 (CLV) [N] Cleveland, OH Sts. Mary and Joseph Home for the Aged.
Corrigan, Edward C. *s.m.* '43 (WDC) [M] Washington, DC Marist Provincial House.
Corrigan, F. J. '38 (SFD) Retired.
Corrigan, Francis J. (SFD) [K] Springfield, IL Priests' Retirement Facility.
Corrigan, Gregory M. '86 (WIL) Claymont, DE Holy Rosary Church; [A] Wilmington, DE St. Mark's High School.
Corrigan, Msgr. Hugh J. '63 (NY) [9] Yonkers, NY Immaculate Conception Church.
Corrigan, J. David *s.j.* '65 (STL) [P] St. Louis, MO Hallahan House.
Corrigan, James B. *s.j.* '49 (MIL) [P] Wauwatosa, WI Jesuit Community at St. Camillus.
Corrigan, James J. '56 (NY) [E] New York, NY Cardinal Spellman High School.
Corrigan, James V. *o.s.a.* '66 (CHI) [N] Olympia Fields, IL The Augustinian Provincialate Tolentine Center.
Corrigan, James V. *o.s.a.* '66 (SD) San Diego, CA Sharp Memorial Hospital.
Corrigan, Kevin B. *c.s.sp.* '60 (SJ) Mountain View, CA St. Athanasius Church.
Corrigan, Michael T. '75 (CHR) Florence, SC St. Ann Church; [G] Florence, SC Francis Marion University Newman Center.
Corrigan, Michael T. '75 (GAL) On Duty Outside the Diocese.
Corrigan, Roy *o.f.m.* '55 (FgM) Franciscan Foreign Missions.
Corriveau, Ernest J. *m.s.* '64 (FR) [J] Attleboro, MA La Salette Shrine.
Corriveau, Raymond *o.p.* '55 (PRT) [G] Lewiston, ME St. Marguerite d'Youville Pavilion; [I] Lewiston, ME SS. Peter and Paul Priory.
Corriveau, Real *o.m.i.* '61 (FgM) Oblates Foreign Missions.
Corriveau, Roger R. *a.a.* '74 (WOR) [N] Worcester, MA Assumptionists of Assumption College.
Corriveau, Ronald E. '71 (MAN) Epping, NH St. Joseph Church.
Corry, Francis '74 (NY) [E] Somers, NY John F. Kennedy High School.
Corry, Francis J. '74 (NY) [E] New York, NY Cardinal Spellman High School.
Corry, James J. *c.s.sp.* '57 (STA) [19] Jacksonville, FL St. Paul's Church.
Corry, John J. '52 (RC) Retired.
Corso, Charles W. *c.s.c.* '75 (FTW) [J] South Bend, IN Congregation of Holy Cross Indiana Province Provincial House.
Cortes, Antonio '96 (MRY) [2] Salinas, CA Sacred Heart Church.
Cortes, Jesse '62 (LAV) [6] Las Vegas, NV St. Anne Church.
Cortes, Raul '62 (LA) Reseda, CA St. Catherine of Siena Church.
Cortese, Francis X. *o.praem.* '62 (PH) [48] Philadelphia, PA St. Gabriel Church.
Cortese, Patrick S. '48 (SCR) Retired.
Cortese, Richard '82 (MEM) [16] Memphis, TN St. Louis Church.
Cortesi, David J. '63 (CHI) [58] Chicago, IL St. Ferdinand Church.
Cortez, Ramiro *o.m.i.* '70 (SAT) Eagle Pass, TX Sacred Heart Church.
Corti, Claudio *p.i.m.e.* '92 (DET) [K] Detroit, MI P.I.M.E. College Community.
Corti, Claudio *p.i.m.e.* '92 (PAT) [M] Wayne, NJ P.I.M.E. Missionaries Residence.
Cortney, Edward P. '63 (GI) Chadron, NE St. Patrick's Church.
Cortney, Kevin J. '50 (GI) Retired.
Cortney, Louis M. *o.s.m.* '39 (CHI) [N] Chicago, IL Servite Friars - Eastern Province.
Coruna, Roberto D. '77 (MET) Piscataway, NJ Our Lady of Fatima Church.
Coryer, Francis J. '82 (OG) De Kalb Junction, NY St. Henry Church; Edwards, NY Sacred Heart Church.
Cosby, R. Roy '54 (ARL) Falls Church, VA St. James Church.
Coschignano, Joseph C. '69 (RVC) Rocky Point, NY St. Anthony of Padua Church.
Cosellas, Ramon J. (SJN) [C] Rio Piedras, PR Fraternidad Santa Maria de Los Angeles.
Cosentino, Jack A. '70 (FAR) On Duty Outside the Diocese.
Cosentino, Jack A. '70 (VEN) [2] Venice, FL Our Lady of Lourdes Church.
Cosgayon, Gerard *o.a.r.* '88 (ORG) Fullerton, CA St. Mary's Church.
Cosgrove, (ROC) [H] Rochester, NY Unity Health System.
Cosgrove, Edward C. *c.ss.r.* '55 (BLX) [E] Biloxi, MS St. John Neumann Residence.
Cosgrove, Francis J. *s.j.* '48 (NY) [DD] New York, NY St. Ignatius Loyola Residence.
Cosgrove, Francis J. '65 (JKS) Madison, MS St. Francis of Assisi Church.
Cosgrove, Msgr. Henry P. '41 (BRK) Retired.
Cosgrove, J. Kelly '43 (LC) Retired.
Cosgrove, J. Kelly '43 (ORL) Retired.
Cosgrove, James (ROC) Rochester, NY St. Mary's Hospital.
Cosgrove, James R. (ROC) [4] Rochester, NY St. Anne Church.
Cosgrove, Jerome P. '63 (SC) Le Mars, IA St. Joseph's Church.
Cosgrove, Joseph '60 (LA) Moorpark, CA Holy Cross Church.
Cosgrove, Joseph J. '92 (BAL) Severna Park, MD St. John the Evangelist Church.
Cosgrove, Thomas *c.ss.r.* '45 (STL) [P] Liguori, MO Liguori Mission House/Redemptorists.
Cosgrove, William B. '74 (NY) Hopewell Junction, NY St. Denis Church; [HH] Scarsdale, NY Catholic Charismatic Renewal Office.
Cosgrove, William J. '55 (ROC) Shortsville, NY St. Dominic Church.
Coskren, Thomas M. *o.p.* '54 (PRO) [P] Providence, RI

St. Thomas Aquinas Priory at Providence College.
Coslowsky, Marion '42 (SB) Retired.
Cosmic, John J. '90 (OG) Chaumont, NY All Saints Church.
Coss, John *f.m.s.i.* '56 (BO) [B] Framingham, MA Sylva Maria.
Cossavella, Anthony J. '81 (PH) [3] Norristown, PA Holy Saviour Church.
Cossette, Raymond '55 (DUL) Retired.
Costa, Anthony J. '90 (PH) Graduate Studies.
Costa, Caetano F.X. '64 (RVC) Ronkonkoma, NY St. Joseph's Church.
Costa, Carl A. *m.m.* '71 (FgM) Maryknoll Foreign Missions.
Costa, David A. '85 (FR) [11] Fall River, MA Sacred Heart Church.
Costa, Eugene *o.de.m.* '74 (BUF) [O] LeRoy, NY Order of the BVM of Mercy/Mercedarian Friars; [O] LeRoy, NY St. Raymond Nonnatus Novitiate.
Costa, Eugene E. '76 (SFD) Athens, IL Holy Family Church; Sherman, IL St. John Vianney Church.
Costa, Gabriel B. '79 (NEW) [B] South Orange, NJ Seton Hall University.
Costa, Joseph M. *s.j.* '54 (SJ) [M] Los Gatos, CA Sacred Heart Jesuit Center.
Costa, Joseph M. '77 (FR) [1] Fall River, MA Cathedral of St. Mary of the Assumption.
Costa, Mario '53 (RVC) Brookville, NY St. Paul the Apostle Church.
Costa, Salvatore *o.m.i.* '42 (BO) [Z] Tewksbury, MA Immaculate Heart of Mary Novitiate-Infirmary.
Costa, Thomas C. '78 (RVC) Westbury, NY St. Brigid Church.
Costabile, George '58 (FRS) Retired.
Costantino, Msgr. Anthony J. '44 (SAT) Retired; [K] San Antonio, TX Padua Place.
Costantino, Joseph S. *s.j.* '87 (NY) [DD] New York, NY Jesuit Provincial's Office; [DD] New York, NY St. Ignatius Loyola Residence.
Costanzo, John J. '64 (PBL) Fruita, CO Sacred Heart Church; Grand Junction, CO St. Joseph Church.
Costello, Andrew *c.ss.r.* '65 (TOL) [2] Lima, OH St. Gerard Church.
Costello, Aquinas *o.p.* '68 (LA) [59] Los Angeles, CA St. Dominic Church.
Costello, Bernard B. '63 (PIT) Monroeville, PA North American Martyrs Church.
Costello, Charles P. *s.j.* '60 (BAL) [M] Baltimore, MD Ferdinand Wheeler Jesuit Community; [Q] Baltimore, MD Ignatian Lay Volunteer Corps.
Costello, Coleman '67 (BRK) [237] Queens, NY Sacred Heart of Jesus Church.
Costello, Edward *o.f.m.conv.* '61 (MET) [I] Watchung, NJ McAuley Hall Inc.
Costello, Edward *o.f.m.conv.* '61 (TR) Point Pleasant Beach, NJ St. Peter Church.
Costello, Msgr. Francis M. '45 (NY) Retired.
Costello, Frank B. *s.j.* '52 (SPK) [C] Spokane, WA Gonzaga University.
Costello, James J. *s.j.* '66 (COS) [E] Sedalia, CO Sacred Heart Retreat House - Jesuit Community; [G] Sedalia, CO Sacred Heart Jesuit Retreat House.
Costello, James P. '60 (CLV) [6] Parma, OH Holy Family Church.
Costello, Jim *s.j.* '60 (COS) Parker, CO Ave Maria Church.
Costello, John '89 (BRK) [T] Brooklyn, NY Catholic Migration & Refugee Office, Catholic Migration Services, Inc.
Costello, John F. *s.j.* '83 (CHI) [N] Chicago, IL Chicago Province of the Society of Jesus-Provincial Office.
Costello, John F. '96 (VEN) [4] Naples, FL St. William Church.
Costello, John J. '53 (SY) Sherrill, NY St. Helena Church.
Costello, John J. '89 (BRK) [150] Queens, NY St. Andrew Avellino Church; [Y] Brooklyn, NY Pro Sanctity Movement.
Costello, John M. '72 (STL) Washington, MO St. Francis Borgia Church.
Costello, John M. *s.j.* '84 (ROC) [B] Rochester, NY McQuaid Jesuit High School.
Costello, Joseph J. '60 (CLV) Hudson, OH St. Mary Church.
Costello, Msgr. Lawrence D. '64 (RVC) Mineola, NY Corpus Christi Church; Retired.
Costello, Mark Joseph *o.f.m.cap.* '91 (CHI) [N] Chicago, IL St. Clare Friary.
Costello, Paul *o.m.i.* '77 (WDC) [B] Washington, DC Oblate College/Oblate Center for Mission Studies.
Costello, Raymond *m.s.c.* '45 (ALN) [A] Center Valley, PA Missionaries of the Sacred Heart.
Costello, Richard D. *s.j.* '53 (BGP) [O] Fairfield, CT The Fairfield Jesuit Community-Fairfield University.
Costello, Robert B. '53 (BO) Abington, MA St. Nicholas Church.
Costello, Robert T. *s.j.* '63 (FgM) Provinces.
Costello, Ted '85 (SP) [5] Clearwater, FL St. Michael The Archangel Church.
Costello, Thomas J. '54 (SY) Special Assignment; [W] Syracuse, NY David W. Barry Foundation.
Costello, Timon *o.f.m.cap.* '58 (GB) [M] Appleton, WI Monte Alverno Retreat Center.
Costello, Vincent F. '76 (CHI) Arlington Heights, IL Our Lady of the Wayside Church.
Costello, Msgr. William '52 (RVC) Franklin Square, NY St. Catherine of Sienna Church.
Costello, William J. '64 (CHI) Antioch, IL St. Peter Church.
Costello, William M. '74 (FR) [8] Taunton, MA St. Mary's Church.
Costelloe, M. Joseph *s.j.* '46 (MIL) [P] Wauwatosa, WI Jesuit Community at St. Camillus.
Costigan, George (PAT) Retired.
Costigan, P. James '68 (SAV) [3] Augusta, GA St. Mary on the Hill Church.
Costigan, Richard F. *s.j.* '64 (CHI) [C] Chicago, IL Jesuit Community at Loyola University of Chicago.
Costigan, Richard J. '50 (TUC) Retired.
Cotant, Charles *c.ss.r.* '41 (FgM) Redemptorist Foreign Missions.
Cote, David P. '68 (PRT) Military Chaplains.
Cote, Donald J. '49 (FAR) Retired.
Cote, Duaine M. '62 (FAR) Edgeley, ND Transfiguration Church.
Cote, E. Joseph '69 (BAL) [22] Baltimore, MD St. Charles Borromeo Church.
Cote, Gerald M. '56 (TUC) Retired.
Cote, Joseph A. *o.p.* (WDC) [11] Washington, DC St. Dominic Church & Priory Church.
Cote, Joseph A. '51 (MAN) [J] Berlin, NH St. Vincent de Paul Nursing Home.
Cote, Normand C. '58 (OG) Cooperville, NY St. Joseph Church.
Cote, Paul E. '71 (PRT) Oquossoc, ME Our Lady of the Lakes Church.
Cote, Richard G. *o.m.i.* '60 (FgM) Oblates Foreign Missions.
Cote, Roland P. '71 (MAN) [1] Nashua, NH St. Aloysius Church.
Cotone, Michael *o.s.c.* '74 (DUL) Cass Lake, MN St. Charles Church.
Cotone, Michael T. *o.s.c.* '74 (CR) Pennington, MN St. Charles Church.
Cotta, Myron '87 (FRS) Gustine, CA Our Lady of Miracles Church.
Cotter, Charles B. '50 (OG) Retired.
Cotter, David W. *o.s.b.* '79 (MAN) [K] Manchester, NH St. Anselm Abbey.
Cotter, Eugene J. '56 (NEW) [B] South Orange, NJ Seton Hall University.
Cotter, Francis Xavier *o.c.d.* '89 (MIL) [P] Holy Hill, WI Discalced Carmelite Monastery.
Cotter, George G. *m.m.* '60 (NY) [DD] Maryknoll, NY Maryknoll Fathers and Brothers.
Cotter, John F. '80 (SAG) Beal City, MI St. Joseph the Worker Church.
Cotter, Lawrence E. '52 (OG) Colton, NY St. Patrick Church; Madrid, NY St. John the Baptist Church; Retired.
Cotter, Patrick John '57 (LA) Retired.
Cotter, Pius *o.f.m.cap.* '88 (GB) Brussels, WI St. Francis and St. Mary Parish.
Cotter, Raymond C. '86 (GAY) Absent on Leave.
Cotter, Robert L. '47 (OG) Glenfield, NY St. Mary Church; Retired.
Cotter, Vince '83 (OAK) Antioch, CA St. Ignatius Church.
Cottingham, David T. *c.s.sp.* '75 (PIT) [B] Pittsburgh, PA Duquesne University of the Holy Ghost.
Cotto, Carlos N. (CGS) Ceiba, PR San Antonio de Padua Church.
Cotton, Charles E. '73 (COL) [30] Columbus, OH St. Mary Magdalene Church.
Cottone, Paul P. '49 (SCR) [16] Scranton, PA St. Lucy's Church.
Cottrell, Frank '50 (SJ) Retired.
Cottrell, James '68 (SP) Retired.
Cotugno, Joseph '64 (ALB) Rensselaer, NY St. John Church.
Coucelo, Andres '68 (MIA) Hollywood, FL Nativity Church.
Couch, Edward W. *o.m.i.* '61 (GAL) [S] Dickinson, TX Christian Renewal Center.
Coughlan, Msgr. Michael J. '52 (SD) Retired.
Coughlan, R. E. '90 (SFE) [4] Santa Fe, NM St. Anne's Church.
Coughlin, Bernard J. *s.j.* '55 (SPK) [C] Spokane, WA Gonzaga University.
Coughlin, Conall R. *o.s.b.* '58 (PAT) [M] Morristown, NJ St. Mary's Abbey.
Coughlin, Daniel C. *c.s.c.* '50 (FTW) [18] South Bend, IN St. Stanislaus Church.
Coughlin, Daniel P. '60 (CHI) [41] Chicago, IL St. Clement Church.
Coughlin, Howard L. '53 (CHR) Mauldin, SC St. Elizabeth Ann Seton Church.
Coughlin, John '83 (NY) [A] Yonkers, NY St. Joseph's Seminary; [DD] New York, NY Franciscan Friars, Order of Friars Minor, Holy Name Province.
Coughlin, Msgr. Joseph F. '44 (BUF) Retired.
Coughlin, Kenneth F. '90 (LAN) Pinckney, MI St. Mary Church.
Coughlin, Leo '56 (LAV) [2] Las Vegas, NV Christ the King Church.
Coughlin, Paul '91 (BO) [1] Medford, MA St. Francis of Assisi Church.
Coughlin, Paul E. '66 (PRT) South Portland, ME Church of the Holy Cross; South Portland, ME St. John the Evangelist Church.
Coughlin, Paul F. '66 (PRT) [M] South Portland, ME Southern Maine Technical College.
Coughlin, Richard '53 (ORG) Inactive Leave.
Coughlin, Roger J. '51 (CHI) Retired; [G] Chicago, IL Catholic Charities of the Archdiocese of Chicago-Archdiocesan Offices.
Coughlin, Thomas '77 (HON) On Duty Outside the Diocese.
Coughlin, William D. '66 (BO) Wakefield, MA Most Blessed Sacrament Church.
Coughlin, William E. *c.s.b.* '58 (GAL) Missouri City, TX Holy Family Church.
Couhig, Michael D. *c.s.c.* '80 (LA) Burbank, CA St. Francis Xavier Church.
Coulombe, Dale '79 (ORG) Inactive Leave.
Coulter, Lawrence W. '86 (GI) Farwell, NE St. Anthony of Padua Church.
Coulthard, Gregory *s.d.s.* '67 (BIR) [3] Huntsville, AL St. Joseph's Church.
Coulthardt, Gregory *s.d.s.* '67 (GB) [I] New Holstein, WI Salvatorian Center Residence.
Counce, Paul D. '79 (BR) Special Assignment.
Countie, Charles G. *o.carm.* '78 (STO) [5] Stockton, CA St. Gertrude Church.
Coupar, David A. (LAF) Absent on Leave.
Cour, Raymond *c.s.c.* '41 (FTW) [17] South Bend, IN Faith & Hope & Charity Chapel Church.
Cour, Raymond F. *c.s.c.* '41 (FTW) [B] Notre Dame, IN University of Notre Dame Du Lac; [J] Notre Dame, IN Holy Cross Community, Corby Hall, University of Notre Dame.
Courcy, Timothy *o.s.b.* '62 (ROC) [I] Pine City, NY Mount Saviour Monastery.
Courier, Rick L. '85 (MAR) Menominee, MI Holy Redeemer Church.
Cournoyer, Alfred '85 (SPR) Belchertown, MA St. Francis of Assisi Church.
Cournoyer, Napoleon '34 (PRT) Retired.
Courteau, Allen *o.m.i.* '76 (FgM) Oblates Foreign Missions.
Courtemanche, Normand L. '65 (PRO) [10] Pawtucket, RI Our Lady of Consolation Church.
Courtney, Edward '55 (HEL) [8] Butte, MT St. John the Evangelist Church.
Courtney, Humphrey J. '51 (HEL) Retired; [B] Helena, MT Carroll College.
Courtney, Joseph B. *c.s.b.* '56 (GAL) [Q] Houston, TX Dominican Fathers and Brothers, St. Mark Priory, Inc.; [Q] Houston, TX Dillon House.
Courtney, Patrick E. '87 (LFT) Unassigned.
Courtney, Thomas M. '51 (SPR) [18] Springfield, MA St. Patrick's Church.
Courtright, Lawrence P. '61 (TLS) [E] Tulsa, OK St. John Medical Center, Inc.
Courtright, Raymond P. '92 (FAR) [4] Grand Forks, ND St. Thomas Aquinas Parish, UND Church; [H] Grand Forks, ND Univ. of North Dakota Newman Center.
Courville, J. Douglas '76 (LAF) [12] Lafayette, LA St. Jules Church.
Courville, Robert W. '63 (LAF) Krotz Springs, LA St. Anthony Church.
Coury, Paul J. *c.ss.r.* '72 (STL) [P] St. Louis, MO Redemptorist Fathers.
Coury, Philip J. *c.m.* '71 (PBL) Las Animas, CO St. Mary Church.
Cousens, Dennis '77 (L) [51] Louisville, KY St. Martin Church.
Cousineau, Robert H. *s.j.* '60 (CHY) Guernsey, WY St. Anthony's Church.
Cousins, John P. *o.f.m.cap.* '76 (DEN) [3] Denver, CO Annunciation Church; [7] Denver, CO Cure D'Ars Church.
Coutinha, Paul *s.a.c.* '82 (MIL) [35] Milwaukee, WI Holy Cross Church; [P] Milwaukee, WI Pallotti House.
Coutinho, Absalom '72 (PAT) [1] Wayne, NJ Annunciation Church.
Couto, Robert '96 (MAN) [5] Nashua, NH Immaculate Conception Church.
Coutts, Virendra *s.d.b.* '79 (OAK) [N] Berkeley, CA Salesian Community.
Coutu, Joseph '81 (GLP) On Duty Outside of Diocese.
Couture, Bernard G. '50 (BUR) Retired.
Couture, Fernand '43 (STA) Retired.
Couture, Fernand '70 (SFE) [J] Jemez Springs, NM The Jemez Program, Our Lady of Lourdes Novitiate.
Couture, Paul E. *s.s.e.* '56 (BUR) [E] Colchester, VT Society of St. Edmund.
Couture, Roger *o.m.i.* (NOR) [F] Willimantic, CT Oblates of Mary Immaculate; [I] Willimantic, CT Immaculata Retreat House.
Couture, Roland '53 (BO) [W] Lowell, MA Missionary

Oblates of Mary Immaculate.
Couturier, Albert '88 (GAY) St. Helen, MI St. Helen Church.
Couturier, David *o.f.m.cap.* '79 (NY) [DD] Garrison, NY St. Francis Friary.
Covarrubias, Raul R. '83 (B) Mountain Home, ID Our Lady of Good Counsel Church.
Covarrubias, Salomon P. '91 (YAK) Royal City, WA St. Michael the Archangel Church.
Covarrubias, Solomon P. '91 (YAK) Mattawa, WA Our Lady of the Desert Church.
Covas, Peter '57 (SB) Alta Loma, CA St. Peter & St. Paul Church.
Coveney, James B. '64 (ALT) Colver, PA Holy Family Church.
Coveny, Richard C. '56 (BUF) Colden, NY Our Lady of the Sacred Heart Church.
Coverdale, Gerald D. *o.p.* '54 (BR) Hammond, LA Holy Ghost Church.
Covert, James A. '76 (L) St. Francis, KY St. Francis of Assisi Church.
Covert, James A. '96 (L) Holy Cross, KY Holy Cross Church.
Covert, Kevin *o.f.m.cap.* (CHI) [146] Chicago, IL Our Lady Gate of Heaven Church.
Covertino, David I. *o.f.m.* (PRO) [N] Providence, RI St. Francis Chapel & City Ministry Center.
Covington, Larry '85 (AUS) [17] Austin, TX St. Louis Church; Austin, TX School for the Blind.
Cowan, Anthony '95 (SAT) [52] San Antonio, TX St. Margaret Mary Church.
Cowan, George R. '65 (BRK) [200] Queens, NY St. Mel Church.
Cowan, Vincent '43 (MRY) Retired.
Coward, Robert *c.p.* '68 (CHI) [N] Chicago, IL Passionist Provincial Office.
Cowart, Conrad '96 (STA) [14] Jacksonville, FL Sacred Heart Church.
Cowden, David '82 (ANC) Palmer, AK St. Michael Church.
Cowden, David '82 (OKL) On Duty Outside the Archdiocese.
Cowell, Raymond '56 (CHI) Missionary Work.
Cowell, Raymond '56 (FgM) Society of St. James the Apostle.
Cower, D. Craig '54 (RC) Retired; [D] Rapid City, SD Priest Retirement and Aid Association.
Cowgill, Msgr. Francis A. '52 (ANC) [2] Anchorage, AK St. Anthony Church.
Cowhig, Edward D. '45 (BO) Danvers, MA St. Alphonsus Church; Retired.
Cowie, Donald *s.m.* '61 (SAT) [F] San Antonio, TX Central Catholic High School; [M] San Antonio, TX Central Catholic Marianist Community.
Cowles, James M. '86 (RIC) Blacksburg, VA St. Mary & Newman Community Church.
Cox, Alan B. '76 (LFT) Rochester, IN St. Joseph Church.
Cox, Bernard '91 (IND) Bedford, IN St. Vincent de Paul Church; Mitchell, IN St. Mary/Assumption Church.
Cox, Brian '68 (BAL) Absent on Leave.
Cox, Msgr. Craig A. '78 (LA) Encino, CA Our Lady of Grace Church.
Cox, David D. '81 (JC) Canton, MO St. Joseph Church; [A] Hannibal, MO St. Thomas Aquinas Seminary.
Cox, Francis '50 (WCH) Arkansas City, KS Sacred Heart Church.
Cox, Msgr. Gregory A. (LA) [Z] Los Angeles, CA Catholic Charities of Los Angeles, Inc.
Cox, Msgr. Gregory A. '76 (LA) [42] Los Angeles, CA St. Anastasia Church; [Z] Los Angeles, CA Catholic Charities of Los Angeles, Inc.
Cox, Msgr. Gregory A. '76 (SAC) [O] Sacramento, CA Catholic Charities of California, Inc.
Cox, Msgr. James F. '51 (NY) Washingtonville, NY St. Mary Church.
Cox, James W. *s.j.* '51 (FgM) Provinces.
Cox, Jesse *o.p.* '87 (DET) [20] Detroit, MI St. Dominic Church.
Cox, John *o.s.b.* '91 (IND) [J] St. Meinrad, IN St. Meinrad Archabbey.
Cox, Msgr. John F. '36 (PRO) [7] Warwick, RI St. Peter Church; Retired.
Cox, John J. '53 (PH) [36] Philadelphia, PA St. Clement Church.
Cox, Joseph C. '46 (MAD) Retired.
Cox, Michael J. *m.s.* '37 (HRT) [M] Hartford, CT Missionaries of LaSalette Provincial Secretary.
Cox, Noel *c.s.sp.* '55 (STA) High Springs, FL St. Madeleine Sophie Parish.
Cox, Paul '54 (ALB) Lake George, NY Sacred Heart Church.
Cox, Robert M. '80 (DAL) Greenville, TX St. William Church.
Cox, William E. '42 (MIL) Retired.
Cox, William J. '56 (PH) Honey Brook, PA St. Peter Church.
Coxen, Gervis J. *m.m.* '37 (NY) [DD] Maryknoll, NY Maryknoll Fathers and Brothers.
Coy, William J. *m.m.* '55 (FgM) Maryknoll Foreign Missions.
Coyle, Alcuin *o.f.m.* '54 (NY) [35] New York, NY St. Francis of Assisi Church.
Coyle, Arthur M. '77 (BO) [13] Lowell, MA St. Patrick Church.
Coyle, Charles G. *s.j.* '65 (FWT) [J] Lake Dallas, TX Montserrat Jesuit Retreat House.
Coyle, Dan '89 (FRS) [3] Bakersfield, CA Sacred Heart Church.
Coyle, Msgr. Edward J. (ALN) Bally, PA Most Blessed Sacrament Church.
Coyle, Eugene P. '54 (BRK) [18] Brooklyn, NY St. Bernadette Church.
Coyle, James '83 (ORL) Sabbatical.
Coyle, Msgr. James A. '32 (PH) Levittown, PA Queen of the Universe Church.
Coyle, Patrick *s.m.* '45 (SFR) [B] San Francisco, CA St. Peter Chanel Seminary.
Coyle, Patrick '60 (DUL) Aitkin, MN St. James Church.
Coyle, Patrick J. *s.m.* '45 (SFR) [N] San Francisco, CA Provincial Residence.
Coyle, Robert J. '91 (RVC) Glen Cove, NY St. Patrick's Church.
Coyle, T. William *c.ss.r.* '44 (CHI) [N] Chicago, IL Redemptorists:; [N] Bodija, Ibadan, Oyo State, Nigeria.
Coyle, Thomas J. '70 (MAD) Darlington, WI Holy Rosary Church.
Coyne, Edwin J. '62 (BGP) Retired.
Coyne, Emmett A.. '66 (MAN) On Duty Outside the Diocese.
Coyne, Msgr. George R. '59 (STU) Tiltonsville, OH St. Joseph Church.
Coyne, George V. *s.j.* '65 (BAL) [M] Baltimore, MD Jesuit Fathers and Brothers Maryland Provincial Curia.
Coyne, George V. *s.j.* '65 (TUC) [F] Tucson, AZ Jesuit Community of the Vatican Observatory.
Coyne, James F. '56 (NY) Absent on Sick leave.
Coyne, James P. '75 (SEA) [3] Tacoma, WA St. Frances Cabrini Church.
Coyne, John J. *o.s.f.s.* '71 (FgM) Oblates of St. Francis de Sales Foreign Missions.
Coyne, Joseph '72 (HT) On Leave.
Coyne, Msgr. Joseph B. '45 (WDC) [3] Bethesda, MD Little Flower Church; Retired.
Coyne, Joseph C. '69 (HBG) Quarryville, PA St. Catherine of Siena Church.
Coyne, Martin P. *s.j.* '66 (FgM) Provinces.
Coyne, Msgr. Michael J. '55 (CAM) Absecon, NJ St. Elizabeth Ann Seton Church.
Coyne, Patrick J. '51 (BAL) Retired.
Coyne, Robert F. *m.m.* '83 (FgM) Maryknoll Foreign Missions.
Coyne, Robert R. '76 (PIT) Franklin Park Borough, PA St. John Neumann Church.
Coyne, Ronald D. '73 (BO) [15] Boston, MA St. Brendan Church.
Coyte, Thomas '74 (DEN) [10] Denver, CO Holy Cross Church.
Coz, Richard T. *s.j.* '58 (PHX) [B] Phoenix, AZ Brophy College Preparatory.
Cozzens, Andrew H. '97 (STP) [1] St. Paul, MN Cathedral of St. Paul.
Cozzens, Donald B. '65 (CLV) [A] Wickliffe, OH St. Mary Seminary and Graduate School of Theology; [AA] Wickliffe, OH Center for Pastoral Leadership Services, Inc.
Cozzini, Robert P. '60 (NEW) Cliffside Park, NJ Epiphany Church.
Cozzubbo, Gregory P. *c.m.* '84 (PH) [155] Philadelphia, PA St. Vincent de Paul Church.
Crabb, John T. *s.j.* (BO) Methuen, MA Holy Family Hospital, Inc.
Crabb, John T. *s.j.* '79 (BO) [Q] Methuen, MA Holy Family Hospital and Medical Center; [W] Boston, MA Loyola House.
Crable, John M. '53 (OG) [2] Plattsburgh, NY St. John the Baptist Church; Plattsburgh, NY Champlain Valley Physicians Hospital Medical Center.
Crafts, George W. '65 (GAL) [P] Houston, TX Opus Dei.
Crager, Richard *s.d.b.* '85 (NY) [FF] West Haverstraw, NY Don Bosco Retreat Center and Marian Shrine; [FF] West Haverstraw, NY Marian Shrine.
Crahen, Daniel E. *o.m.i.* '71 (OAK) Brentwood, CA Immaculate Heart of Mary Church.
Craig, August Bruce *s.d.b.* '74 (SP) [E] Tampa, FL Mary Help of Christians School.
Craig, Christopher '93 (IND) Leave of Absence.
Craig, Christopher A. '93 (IND) [2] Indianapolis, IN Christ The King Church.
Craig, Donald '74 (CHI) [J] Chicago, IL St. Anthony Hospital.
Craig, John V. *s.j.* '77 (STL) [P] St. Louis, MO De Smet Jesuit High School Community.
Craig, Lawrence *ss.cc.* '41 (FR) [J] Fairhaven, MA Sacred Hearts Provincial House.
Craig, Lawrence J. '73 (CHI) [20] Chicago, IL Assumption Church; [X] Chicago, IL Kolbe House.
Craig, Paul *o.f.m.cap.* '66 (FgM) Capuchin Foreign Missions.
Craig, Richard J. '61 (BO) Chelmsford, MA St. John the Evangelist Church.
Craig, Richard T. '88 (MAR) Leave of Absence.
Craig, Robert *o.f.m.cap.* '67 (PIT) Allegheny County, PA St. Francis Medical Center; [J] Pittsburgh, PA St. Francis Medical Center; [O] Pittsburgh, PA St. Augustine Friary.
Craig, Robert G. '64 (E) Cambridge Springs, PA St. Anthony Church; Cambridge Springs, PA Cambridge Springs Correction Institution.
Craig, Rod '77 (FRS) On Special Assignment.
Craig, Roderick L. '77 (FRS) Easton, CA St. Jude Mission Church.
Craig, Samuel L. '76 (WDC) [1] Bowie, MD Ascension Church.
Craig, Tom '82 (FWT) Muenster, TX Sacred Heart Church.
Craig, William R. *o.praem.* '55 (PH) [U] Darby, PA Mercy Catholic Medical Center.
Crain, George L. *s.j.* '51 (SJ) [M] Los Gatos, CA Sacred Heart Jesuit Center.
Cramblitt, Richard E. '72 (BAL) [89] Baltimore, MD Shrine of the Sacred Heart Church.
Cramer, David W. '91 (SCR) Kingston, PA St. Ignatius Church.
Cramer, Harry N. '84 (WH) Bridgeport, WV All Saints Church.
Cramer, Joe '77 (KCK) Osawatomie, KS St. Philip Neri Church.
Cramer, John R. '89 (SY) Norwich, NY St. Bartholomew the Apostle Church.
Cramer, Joseph '77 (KCK) Mound City, KS Sacred Heart Shrine to St. Philippine Duchesne Church.
Cramer, William '77 (PAT) [J] Paterson, NJ St. Joseph's Hospital and Medical Center.
Cramer, William N. (PAT) Paterson, NJ St. Joseph Hospital.
Crandall, Thom A. '81 (PT) Port St. Joe, FL St. Joseph Church.
Crandall, William W. '48 (ALB) Worcester, NY St. Joseph Church.
Crane, Jeff '89 (SAT) On Leave.
Crane, Msgr. Thomas E. '57 (BUF) [3] North Tonawanda, NY St. Joseph Church.
Crane, William H. *m.s.* '41 (HRT) [M] Hartford, CT Missionaries of LaSalette Provincial Secretary.
Cranor, Bernard *o.s.b.* '62 (SFE) [J] Abiquiu, NM Monastery of Christ in the Desert.
Craven, Msgr. Thomas P. '56 (PH) West Chester, PA St. Agnes Church.
Crawford, Brian *o.s.j.* '92 (SAC) [A] Loomis, CA Mount St. Joseph Novitiate and Seminary.
Crawford, C. Slade '65 (PT) [2] Pensacola, FL Little Flower Church.
Crawford, Canice (PIT) [56] Pittsburgh, PA St. Mary of the Mount Church.
Crawford, Canice *t.o.r.* '55 (PIT) [O] Pittsburgh, PA Franciscan Friars, T.O.R.
Crawford, John G. '63 (CLV) South Euclid, OH St. Gregory the Great Church.
Crawford, Larry P. '66 (IND) [36] Indianapolis, IN St. Simon Church.
Crawford, Richard E. '75 (PEO) Retired.
Crawford, Robert F. *m.m.* '61 (FgM) Maryknoll Foreign Missions.
Crawford, Robert P. *c.m.* '47 (FgM) Vincentian Foreign Missions.
Crawford, Robert P. *c.m.* '47 (PH) [AA] Philadelphia, PA Congregation of the Mission.
Cray, David G. *s.s.e.* '72 (NO) [I] New Orleans, LA Bishop Perry Middle School.
Cray, Kevin *s.d.s.* (WDC) [B] Silver Spring, MD Salvatorian Community.
Cray, Kevin *s.d.s.* '49 (E) Retired.
Craycroft, B. Leo '57 (L) Radcliff, KY St. Christopher Church.
Craycroft, George P. '58 (L) Retired.
Creagan, Michael S. '97 (STP) Stillwater, MN St. Michael Church.
Creagan, Robert F. '88 (KAL) Coldwater, MI St. Charles Church; Coldwater, MI Florence Crane Correctional Facility for Women; Coldwater, MI Camp Branch; Coldwater, MI Lakeland Correctional Facility for Men.
Creager, Robert J. '54 (PEO) [4] Ottawa, IL St. Patrick's Church.
Creagh, Kevin *c.m.* '96 (BUF) [R] Williamsville, NY Campus Ministry.
Creagh, Kevin G. *c.m.* '96 (BUF) [C] Niagara University, NY Niagara University; [O] Niagara University, NY Vincentian Community at Niagara University.
Creagh, Richard C. '76 (CHI) [84] Chicago, IL Holy Rosary Church.
Creagh, Thomas P. '67 (L) [37] Louisville, KY St. Ignatius Church.
Crean, Hugh F. '62 (SPR) [6] Springfield, MA Holy Name Church.
Crean, Msgr. Timothy J. '33 (LA) Pasadena, CA Assumption of the Blessed Virgin Mary Church; Retired.
Creane, Anthony J. '56 (SPR) [4] Westfield, MA St. Mary's Church.

Creary, J. Edwin '73 (MEM) [28] Memphis, TN St. William Church.
Creason, Hubert E. '58 (STL) Catawissa, MO St. James Church.
Creason, Richard H. '67 (STL) [11] St. Louis, MO Most Holy Trinity Church.
Creaven, John *c.ss.r.* '49 (HBG) Lititz, PA St. James Church.
Creaven, John J. *c.ss.r.* '49 (HBG) [H] Ephrata, PA St. Clement's Mission House.
Creed, C. Patrick '96 (L) Retired.
Creed, Peter M. '67 (SY) [5] Syracuse, NY Most Holy Rosary Church.
Creed, William E. *s.j.* '71 (CHI) [C] Chicago, IL Jesuit Community at Loyola University of Chicago.
Creeden, Patrick D. *o.s.b.* '78 (CHI) [N] Chicago, IL Monastery of the Holy Cross.
Creedon, Gerard '68 (ARL) [4] Arlington, VA St. Charles Borromeo Church.
Creedon, James J. *m.ss.a.* '79 (WH) Franklin, WV St. Elizabeth Ann Seton Church; Petersburg, WV St. Mary's Church.
Creedon, Joseph D. '68 (PRO) South Kingstown, RI Christ the King Church; [S] South Kingstown, RI University of Rhode Island Catholic Center.
Creel, Jesse (R) Retired.
Cregan, Francis A. *o.a.r.* '95 (NY) [B] Suffern, NY Tagaste Monastery; [W] Suffern, NY Good Samaritan Hospital of Suffern.
Cregan, James F. '63 (PT) [2] Tallahassee, FL Blessed Sacrament Church; Lanark Village, FL Sacred Heart of Jesus Church.
Cregan, John C. '87 (ARL) [1] Alexandria, VA Blessed Sacrament Church.
Cregan, John J. '61 (CLV) [52] Cleveland, OH Our Lady of Angels Church.
Cregan, Mark T. *c.s.c.* '83 (NY) [188] Bronx, NY Sacred Heart Church.
Cregan, Robert G. *s.j.* '67 (NEW) [C] Jersey City, NJ St. Peter's Preparatory School.
Cregon, Frank *o.a.r.* (NY) Suffern, NY Good Samaritan Hospital.
Crehan, Joseph L. *s.s.c.* '54 (BO) [2] Everett, MA Immaculate Conception Church; [W] Quincy, MA St. Columban's Foreign Mission Society.
Crehan, Lawrence F. '74 (PH) [11] Philadelphia, PA St. Anne Church.
Creider, Philip B. '77 (OKL) Military Chaplains.
Creighton, Bernard R. *o.f.m.* '67 (PAT) [M] Butler, NJ St. Anthony Friary.
Creighton, Msgr. Edward '47 (SD) Retired.
Creighton, Gerard E. '51 (BO) Retired.
Creighton, Henry *ss.cc.* '49 (FR) [J] Fairhaven, MA Sacred Hearts Provincial House.
Creighton, James J. *s.j.* '60 (CHI) [D] Chicago, IL St. Ignatius Jesuit Community; [J] Maywood, IL Foster G. McGaw Hospital of Loyola University of Chicago.
Creighton, Matthew E. *s.j.* '57 (CHI) [C] Chicago, IL Jesuit Community at Loyola University of Chicago.
Cremaldi, Angelo '60 (LAF) [3] Opelousas, LA Our Lady Queen of Angels Church.
Cremer, Matthias P. *s.c.j.* '44 (MIL) [B] Hales Corners, WI Sacred Heart School of Theology.
Cremer, Patrick M. *s.c.j.* '44 (MIL) [P] Franklin, WI Villa Maria; [Q] Milwaukee, WI Ancilla Convent.
Cremins, John J. '69 (BRK) [12] Brooklyn, NY Assumption of the Blessed Virgin Mary Church; Released from Diocesan Assignment.
Cremonie, Louis D. '72 (HRT) [4] Manchester, CT St. James Church.
Crenner, William A. (KAL) Retired.
Crepaz, Ilario '56 (NEW) [4] Union City, NJ St. Anthony of Padua Church.
Crepeau, John J. '72 (DET) Absent on Leave.
Crerand, Raymond F. (SEA) [G] Everett, WA Providence General Medical Center.
Crescenzi, Rocco *f.d.p.* '43 (BO) [U] Boston, MA Don Orione Nursing Home.
Creson, Michael '87 (KNX) Dunlap, TN Shepherd of the Valley Church; South Pittsburg, TN Our Lady of Lourdes Church.
Crespin, George E. (OAK) [S] Berkeley, CA Multicultural Institute.
Crespin, George E. '62 (OAK) [3] Berkeley, CA St. Joseph The Worker Church.
Crespo, Isidoro *o.p.* '87 (PCE) Yauco, PR Holy Rossary Church.
Cressman, Richard *s.d.b.* '80 (BO) [N] Boston, MA Salesian Boys & Girls Club.
Cretella, Biagio '49 (HRT) Retired.
Crevani, Decimo *c.s.* '61 (NEW) [12] Newark, NJ St. Columba's Church.
Crewe, Ronald O. '63 (MIL) Whitewater, WI St. Patrick Church.
Crews, Clyde F. '73 (L) [A] Louisville, KY Bellarmine College.
Crews, John S. '71 (SR) [H] Sonoma, CA Hanna Boys Center.
Cribben, Andrew *o.praem.* '94 (JKS) [2] Jackson, MS St. Mary Church; [7] Jackson, MS Christ the King Church; [E] Jackson, MS Priory of St. Moses the Black; [G] Jackson, MS Jackson State University Newman Center.
Cribben, Msgr. Philip J. '62 (PH) [76] Philadelphia, PA St. Joan of Arc Church.
Cribbin, Austin J. '56 (BAK) Retired.
Cribbin, James '85 (FgM) Society of St. James the Apostle.
Cribbin, James '85 (SD) On Duty Outside the Diocese.
Cribbin, Msgr. Thomas F. (BRK) [12] Brooklyn, NY Assumption of the Blessed Virgin Mary Church.
Cribbin, Msgr. Thomas F. '42 (BRK) Retired; [L] Brooklyn, NY Catholic Charities; [U] Brooklyn, NY St. Joseph's Priest Residence.
Cribbs, James '90 (ALB) Hancock, NY St. Paul the Apostle Church.
Cricchio, Santo *o.f.m.conv.* '91 (BAL) [26] Baltimore, MD St. Clement Mary Hofbauer Church.
Crider, Robert E. '53 (KC) Plattsburg, MO St. Ann's Church.
Crifasi, Peter D. '49 (BR) Baton Rouge, LA Nursing Homes not under Catholic auspices.
Crilly, James *c.s.v.* '56 (LAV) [1] Las Vegas, NV Guardian Angel Cathedral.
Crilly, Marc *o.s.b.* '93 (WOR) [N] Still River, MA Benedictine Monks, St. Benedict Abbey.
Crilly, Patrick *o.s.a.* '50 (ORG) Buena Park, CA St. Pius V Church.
Crimmins, Michael C. '70 (NY) [68] New York, NY St. Malachy's Church; [D] New York, NY Department of Education; [GG] New York, NY University Apostolate.
Crimmins, Thomas *o.f.m.conv.* (ALB) [12] Albany, NY Our Lady of Angels Church.
Crino, Patrick M. '88 (TUC) [20] Tucson, AZ Saints Peter and Paul Church.
Criqui, Kenneth '63 (KC) Carrollton, MO St. Mary's Church.
Criscitelli, Anthony *t.o.r.* '80 (STP) Brooklyn Park, MN St. Gerard Church.
Criscuolo, Salvatore A. '78 (WDC) Fort Washington, MD St. Ignatius Church; Special Ministries.
Crisologo, Aurelio P. '59 (SD) San Marcos, CA St. Mark Church.
Crisostomo, Abraham *o.f.m.conv.* (CHI) [N] Chicago, IL Conventual Franciscans of St. Bonaventure Province.
Crisostomo, Michael C. '96 (AGN) Yigo, GU Our Lady of Lourdes Church.
Crisp, Michael L. '96 (SUP) Mercer, WI St. Isaac Jogues and Companions Church.
Crisp, Michael L. '97 (SUP) Manitowish Waters, WI Our Lady Queen of Peace Church.
Crisp, Robert '75 (DAL) [P] Dallas, TX Commission on Ecumenism.
Crisp, Robert R. '75 (DAL) [1] Garland, TX Good Shepherd Church.
Crispo, John R. '50 (BO) Burlington, MA St. Margaret Church.
Crispo, Roderick A. *o.f.m.* '55 (BRK) [106] Brooklyn, NY Our Lady of Peace Church.
Cristancho, Francisco '85 (ARL) [2] Alexandria, VA Good Shepherd Church.
Cristobal, Adrian F. '89 (AGN) Barrigada, GU San Vicente Ferrer Church.
Cristobal, Daniel *o.f.m.cap.* '59 (AGN) Chalan Pago, GU Nuestra Senora de la Paz y Buen Viaje Church; [G] Agana, GU Secular Franciscans.
Cristobal, Daniel *o.f.m.cap.* '59 (FgM) Capuchin Foreign Missions.
Critchlow, Donald E. '82 (CC) [16] Laredo, TX St. Peter the Apostle Church.
Crivello, Peter A. '93 (MRY) Aptos, CA Resurrection Church.
Crkva, Odilo *o.s.b.* '53 (JOL) [A] Lisle, IL Benedictine University; [J] Lisle, IL St. Procopius Abbey.
Croagan, Daniel *s.j.* '58 (GAL) [3] Spring, TX St. Ignatius of Loyola Church.
Croak, David P. '66 (DEN) [4] Aurora, CO St. Therese Church.
Croak, Thomas *c.m.* '65 (CHI) [N] Chicago, IL Vincentian Community, Congregation of the Mission, Midwest Province.
Croal, James Joseph '96 (ORG) Inactive Leave.
Croal, Thomas '58 (ORG) Absent on Sick Leave.
Croce, Albert J. *c.s.c.* '50 (FR) [A] North Easton, MA Holy Cross Fathers Religious.
Croce, Angelus '58 (PAT) Newton, NJ St. Joseph's Church.
Crocenzi, George *c.s.sp.* '49 (CIN) [16] Dayton, OH St. James Church.
Crochet, Barry '93 (LAF) Four Corners, LA St. Peter the Apostle Church.
Crocker, John R. *s.j.* '61 (CHI) [N] Chicago, IL Chicago Province of the Society of Jesus-Provincial Office.
Crofut, Robert J. '72 (BGP) Huntington, CT St. Lawrence Church.
Croghan, James P. *s.j.* '85 (FgM) Provinces.
Croghan, James P. *s.j.* '85 (MI) Ebeye, MH Queen of Peace Church.
Croghan, John P. '75 (SY) Clinton, NY St. Mary Church; Special Assignment; [V] Clinton, NY Hamilton College Newman Center.
Croghan, Joseph F. *m.m.* '62 (NY) [DD] Maryknoll, NY Maryknoll Fathers and Brothers.
Croglio, James (BUF) [D] Buffalo, NY St. Joseph's Collegiate Institute.
Crohan, Robert F. *m.m.* '62 (FgM) Maryknoll Foreign Missions.
Croisetiere, David N. '77 (SD) [24] San Diego, CA St. Charles Borromeo Church.
Croke, Alfred M. '63 (NY) Livingston Manor, NY St. Aloysius Church.
Crombie, Francis H. '68 (SPR) [19] Springfield, MA St. Paul Church.
Cron, Steven D. '78 (GR) [11] Grand Rapids, MI St. James Church.
Cron, Walter '59 (NEW) [O] Englewood Cliffs, NJ St. Michael Villa.
Cronauer, David W. '73 (ALT) Cresson, PA St. Francis Xavier Church.
Cronauer, Patrick T. *o.s.b.* '84 (GBG) [H] Latrobe, PA Saint Vincent Archabbey.
Crone, Patrick H. '71 (CIN) Bethel, OH St. Mary Church.
Cronin, Blaise *o.f.m.* '44 (PHX) [19] Phoenix, AZ St. Mary's Basilica Church; [A] Phoenix, AZ St. Mary's High School.
Cronin, Boniface D. *o.s.b.* '40 (PAT) [M] Newton, NJ St. Paul's Abbey.
Cronin, Daniel C. '55 (NOR) Columbia, CT St. Columba Church.
Cronin, Daniel F. '46 (BO) Westford, MA St. Catherine of Alexandria Church.
Cronin, Daniel V. '53 (PMB) Lake Worth, FL St. Luke Church.
Cronin, David '48 (VEN) Retired.
Cronin, Edward '50 (SB) Retired.
Cronin, Edward J. *o.m.i.* '54 (SAT) [K] San Antonio, TX Oblate Madonna Residence; [T] San Antonio, TX Oblate Missions.
Cronin, Edward J. '80 (CHI) Palos Heights, IL St. Alexander Church.
Cronin, Msgr. Edward T. '50 (SB) [8] Riverside, CA St. John the Evangelist Church.
Cronin, Frank C. '58 (STU) On Duty Outside the Diocese.
Cronin, Harry *c.s.c.* '62 (LA) Venice, CA St. Mark Church.
Cronin, James (SFE) [C] Santa Fe, NM College of Santa Fe.
Cronin, James *o.s.b.* '54 (ROC) [I] Pine City, NY Mount Saviour Monastery.
Cronin, James D. '76 (JUN) Retired.
Cronin, James E. '47 (SPR) Retired.
Cronin, Msgr. James J. '45 (BAL) [43] Baltimore, MD St. Isaac Jogues Church; Aberdeen, MD St. Joan of Arc Church; Retired.
Cronin, James J. '62 (HRT) [4] Milford, CT St. Mary's Church.
Cronin, John F. '47 (BRK) Retired; [U] Douglaston, NY Bishop Mugavero Residence.
Cronin, John P. '57 (FR) [J] Fall River, MA St. John Vianney House.
Cronin, Kean D. '63 (DET) [4] Livonia, MI St. Genevieve Church.
Cronin, Kevin *o.f.m.* '74 (NEW) [N] Hohokus, NJ St. Anthony of Padua.
Cronin, Michael J. '95 (WIN) [7] Rochester, MN St. Pius X Church.
Cronin, Patrick '67 (SAT) [21] San Antonio, TX Prince of Peace Church.
Cronin, Msgr. Paul T. '56 (BUF) Retired; [O] Buffalo, NY Sheehan Residence for Priests.
Cronin, Peadar *ss.cc.* '72 (LA) [D] La Verne, CA Damien Boys High School; [R] La Verne, CA Congregation of the Sacred Hearts.
Cronin, Peter C. '81 (WDC) [8] Silver Spring, MD St. Michael Church.
Cronin, Peter J. *s.s.c.* (BUF) [5] West Seneca, NY Queen of Heaven Church.
Cronin, Richard '60 (JC) Loose Creek, MO Immaculate Conception Church.
Cronin, Richard J. *o.s.b.* '66 (PAT) [M] Morristown, NJ St. Mary's Abbey.
Cronin, Robert *s.o.l.t.* '83 (CC) [H] Robstown, TX Society of Our Lady of the Most Holy Trinity.
Cronin, Robert J. *s.o.l.t.* (FAR) Turtle Mountain Reservation, ND (Chippewa Indians) Church.
Cronin, Robert J. *s.o.l.t.* '83 (FAR) Belcourt, ND St. Ann Church.
Cronin, Robert W. (NOR) On Duty Outside the Diocese.
Cronin, Sean '73 (LA) Lomita, CA St. Margaret Mary Alacoque Church; [C] Rancho Palos Verdes, CA Marymount College, Palos Verdes, California; [CC] Los Angeles, CA Archdiocesan Office for Campus Ministry.
Cronin, Sylvester J. '88 (MET) Highland Park, NJ St. Paul the Apostle Church.
Cronin, Terence *o.f.m.* '30 (SFR) [7] San Francisco, CA St. Boniface Church.
Cronin, Thomas '69 (KC) On Duty Outside the Diocese.
Cronin, Thomas J. *s.j.* '53 (BR) [J] Convent, LA

Manresa, House of Retreats.
Cronin, Timothy F. *s.j.* '62 (SPK) [C] Spokane, WA Gonzaga University.
Cronin, Timothy P. '85 (STL) Cottleville, MO St. Joseph Church.
Cronin, Tom '69 (RNO) [6] Reno, NV St. Therese Church of the Little Flower.
Cronin, Vincent I. '57 (ALN) Palmerton, PA Sacred Heart Church.
Cronin, W. Vincent '43 (HRT) Retired.
Cronin, William *o.s.cam.* '76 (MIL) [N] Wauwatosa, WI San Camillo, Inc.
Cronin, William F. *o.s.cam.* (WOR) [R] Whitinsville, MA St. Camillus Institute, Inc.
Cronin, William F. *o.s.cam.* '76 (MIL) [N] Wauwatosa, WI St. Camillus Health Center, Inc.; [P] Wauwatosa, WI St. Camillus Provincialate; [Y] Wauwatosa, WI St. Camillus Institute, Inc.; [Y] Wauwatosa, WI St. Camillus Communities, Inc.; [Y] Wauwatosa, WI St. Camillus Ministries, Inc.
Cronk, James F. '69 (DET) Novi, MI St. James Church.
Cronkleton, Thomas E., Jr. '86 (CHY) Pine Bluffs, WY St. Paul's Church.
Cronogue, Michael P. *s.s.e.* '77 (BUR) [A] Colchester, VT St. Michael's College; [E] Colchester, VT Society of St. Edmund.
Crook, David G. '81 (BEL) Leave of Absence.
Crooker, Robert W. *c.s.b.* '53 (GAL) [Q] Houston, TX Residence of the Basilian Fathers of the University of St. Thomas.
Crookes, Brian '53 (VIC) St. John, TX St. John the Baptist Church.
Crookston, James F. '71 (ALT) [12] Altoona, PA St. Rose of Lima Church.
Crookston, Michael J. '80 (GBG) North Huntingdon, PA St. Elizabeth Ann Seton Church.
Crosby, Msgr. Charles E. '56 (MAN) [1] Manchester, NH St. Joseph Cathedral.
Crosby, Daniel *o.f.m.cap.* '64 (GF) Lame Deer, MT Blessed Sacrament Church.
Crosby, Donald *s.j.* '68 (OAK) [1] Concord, CA St. Agnes Church.
Crosby, Donald F. *s.j.* '68 (OAK) [N] Berkeley, CA Jesuit Community at Jesuit School of Theology at Berkeley.
Crosby, Donald W. '89 (JC) Absent on Leave.
Crosby, John M. '52 (CHI) Retired.
Crosby, Michael *o.f.m.* '64 (STL) [P] St. Louis, MO Franciscan Friary of St. Anthony of Padua; [T] Dittmer, MO Il Ritiro-The Little Retreat.
Crosby, Michael *o.f.m.cap.* '66 (MIL) [11] Milwaukee, WI St. Benedict the Moor Church.
Crosby, Neil A. '81 (CLV) Wadsworth, OH Sacred Heart Church.
Crosby, Vincent de Paul *o.s.b.* '72 (GBG) [H] Latrobe, PA Saint Vincent Archabbey.
Crosier, Raymond '75 (AMA) Groom, TX Immaculate Heart of Mary Church.
Cross, Charles V. '60 (BIR) [5] Birmingham, AL Blessed Sacrament Church.
Cross, Michael L. '62 (MRY) Felton, CA St. John's Church.
Cross, Peter '60 (DAV) Retired.
Cross, Robert A. '52 (CHI) Retired.
Cross, Vern F. '31 (DUB) Retired.
Cross, William D. '85 (STU) Wintersville, OH Blessed Sacrament Church; Wintersville, OH Our Lady of Lourdes Church; Freeport, OH St. Matthias Mission Church.
Cross, William H. '74 (CIN) [47] Cincinnati, OH St. John Vianney Church.
Crosse, Charles '53 (SEA) Retired.
Crosser, Raymond G. (ALT) Retired.
Crossin, John W. *o.s.f.s.* '76 (ARL) [J] Alexandria, VA Oblates of St. Francis de Sales Residence.
Crossin, John W. *o.s.f.s.* '76 (WDC) [B] Washington, DC DeSales School of Theology.
Crossman, James '46 (DUL) [1] Duluth, MN Cathedral of Our Lady of the Rosary Church.
Crossmeyer, Robert *c.p.* '88 (BIR) [7] Birmingham, AL Holy Family Church.
Crosthwait, Msgr. Joseph H. (GAL) Retired.
Croston, John J. *c.s.c.* '62 (FTW) [A] Notre Dame, IN Moreau Seminary.
Croteau, Fernand A. '57 (MAN) Hooksett, NH Holy Rosary Church.
Croteau, Francois A. '42 (HRT) Retired.
Crotty, Columban *ss.cc.* '58 (FR) [J] Fairhaven, MA Sacred Hearts Provincial House.
Crotty, Desmond G. '72 (NO) [32] New Orleans, LA St. Francis Of Assisi Church.
Crotty, John C. *s.s.j.* '55 (BAL) [83] Baltimore, MD St. Pius V Church; [M] Baltimore, MD St. Joseph's Manor.
Crotty, John M. '47 (NY) Retired.
Crotty, Msgr. Matthew M. '44 (BAK) Special Assignment.
Crotty, Thomas M. *o.s.m.* '60 (CHI) [N] Chicago, IL Servite Friars - Eastern Province.
Crotty, Vincent *c.ss.r.* '49 (RVC) Bethpage, NY St. Martin of Tours Church; Bethpage, NY Mid-Island Hospital.
Crouse, William S. '59 (ALT) Penns Valley, PA Blessed Kateri Tekakwitha Church; Bellefonte, PA State Correctional Institution.
Crowe, Francis R. *o.p.* '47 (AMA) [9] Amarillo, TX St. Martin De Porres Mission Church.
Crowe, Francis R. *o.p.* '47 (CHI) [N] Chicago, IL Dominicans (Provincial Office).
Crowe, George W. '65 (PH) [121] Philadelphia, PA Our Lady of Lourdes Church.
Crowe, Hugh '58 (LA) [43] Los Angeles, CA St. Ann Church.
Crowe, Martin *c.ss.r.* '40 (BRK) [107] Brooklyn, NY Our Lady of Perpetual Help Basilica Church.
Crowe, Raymond *o.m.i.* '54 (MIA) [2] Miami, FL Christ the King Church.
Crowe, Msgr. William A. '47 (PT) Panama City, FL St. Dominic Church.
Crowley, Alan N. *o.carm.* '41 (BO) [P] Peabody, MA Catholic Information Center; [BB] Peabody, MA St. Theresa Carmelite Chapel.
Crowley, Cale J. *s.s.* '69 (BAL) [M] Baltimore, MD Sulpician Provincial House.
Crowley, Charles '77 (TOL) Retired.
Crowley, Charles G. *s.j.* '51 (BO) [W] Boston, MA Loyola House.
Crowley, Charles J. '53 (KAL) Retired.
Crowley, Daniel (BO) South Weymouth, MA South Shore Hospital.
Crowley, Daniel J. '68 (BO) Braintree, MA St. Francis of Assisi Church.
Crowley, Edmund G. '70 (MAN) Military Chaplains.
Crowley, Edward T. *c.s.sp.* '50 (LR) Conway, AR St. Joseph's Church.
Crowley, Francis *c.m.* '57 (KC) [J] Kansas City, MO Vincentian Parish Mission Center.
Crowley, Francis J. '53 (BO) Military & VA Chaplains.
Crowley, Francis J. '53 (PRO) Providence, RI Veterans Administration Hospital.
Crowley, J. David '54 (PIT) [49] Pittsburgh, PA Holy Angels Church.
Crowley, James M. *o.m.i.* '87 (CHR) Joanna, SC St. Boniface Church; Newberry, SC St. Mark Church; [G] Clinton, SC Presbyterian College Newman Center; [G] Newberry, SC Newberry College Newman Center.
Crowley, John A. '61 (PMB) Vero Beach, FL St. John of the Cross Church.
Crowley, John D. '70 (BO) [9] Cambridge, MA St. Mary of the Annunciation Church.
Crowley, Kenan *o.f.m.cap.* '44 (PIT) [29] Pittsburgh, PA Our Lady of the Angels Church; Allegheny County, PA Kane Regional Center - McKeesport.
Crowley, Kevin J. '64 (BO) Absent on Leave.
Crowley, Patrick J. *ss.cc.* '72 (OAK) [3] Alameda, CA St. Joseph Basilica Church.
Crowley, Paul G. *s.j.* '92 (SJ) [B] Santa Clara, CA Santa Clara University.
Crowley, R. Kevin '68 (MET) Edison, NJ Guardian Angels Church.
Crowley, Richard P. '64 (BO) Braintree, MA St. Francis of Assisi Church.
Crowley, Stephen L. '55 (HRT) Retired.
Crowley, Thomas (DM) [2] Council Bluffs, IA Our Lady, Queen of Apostles Church.
Crowley, Thomas F. '56 (LC) Cadott, WI St. Rose of Lima Church; Drywood, WI St. Anthony Church.
Crowley, Thomas F. '76 (WDC) Greenbelt, MD St. Hugh Church.
Crowley, Timothy '76 (ANC) [6] Anchorage, AK Our Lady of Guadalupe Church.
Crowley, Timothy '76 (LAN) On Duty Outside the Diocese.
Crowley, William *c.s.sp.* '50 (PIT) [B] Pittsburgh, PA Duquesne University of the Holy Ghost.
Crowley, William C. '74 (B) Lewiston, ID St. James Church.
Crowley, William P. *c.s.sp.* '60 (SFR) [8] San Francisco, CA St. Brendan Church.
Cruces, Angel (NY) [45] New York, NY Holy Cross Church.
Crum, Thomas J. '75 (Y) Boardman, OH St. Charles Borromeo's Church.
Crum, William '76 (NEW) [1] Elizabeth, NJ St. Mary of the Assumption Church.
Crumbley, Charles W. '67 (Y) [4] Warren, OH St. James Church.
Crumley, William *c.s.c.* '64 (LAF) Charenton, LA Immaculate Conception Church.
Crumlish, John C. '58 (OAK) Castro Valley, CA Transfiguration Church.
Crumlish, Msgr. Richard C. '45 (BUF) [63] Buffalo, NY St. Teresa Church; Retired.
Crummy, Michael E. '86 (MET) Milford, NJ St. Edward the Confessor Church.
Crunican, James '63 (P) Grand Ronde, OR St. Michael Church; Sheridan, OR Good Shepherd Church.
Crupi, Msgr. Francis J. '52 (MET) [7] New Brunswick, NJ St. Mary of Mount Virgin Church.
Cruz, Carlos Dionisio '80 (SJN) [14] San Juan, PR Nuestra Senora de la Esperanza Church.
Cruz, David '86 (LUB) On Duty Outside the Diocese.
Cruz, David R. '86 (SAT) [A] San Antonio, TX The Assumption-St. John's Seminary.
Cruz, Domingo '73 (HT) Kraemer, LA St. Lawrence the Martyr Church.
Cruz, Edwin *o.s.a.* (MGZ) Aguada, PR St. Francis of Assisi Church.
Cruz, Faustino *s.m.* '88 (BO) [W] Boston, MA Marist Fathers and Brothers Provincial House.
Cruz, Gilbert J. '81 (LA) [17] Los Angeles, CA Mother of Sorrows Church; [81] Los Angeles, CA St. Michael Church.
Cruz, Gilbert J. '81 (SJN) Retired.
Cruz, Gustavo '74 (LAV) Overton, NV St. John, the Evangelist Church.
Cruz, Hector J. *s.m.* '77 (ELP) [39] El Paso, TX Santa Lucia Church.
Cruz, Jose Antonio (SJN) [4] San Juan, PR San Antonio Church.
Cruz, Luciano '86 (PAT) [2] Paterson, NJ St. Agnes Church.
Cruz, Manuel '80 (NEW) [1] Newark, NJ Cathedral Basilica of the Sacred Heart Church; Newark, NJ St. Michael Medical Center.
Cruz, Manuel '93 (NEW) [G] Newark, NJ Saint Michael's Medical Center.
Cruz, Michael *o.f.m.cap.* (AGN) [E] Agana Heights, GU St. Fidelis Friary.
Cruz, Msgr. Remberto '50 (SJN) Retired.
Cruz, Renato B. '81 (NY) [204] Staten Island, NY Holy Child Church.
Cruz, Robert-Joel '96 (HT) [5] Houma, LA St. Bernadette Church.
Cryan, James F. *o.s.f.s.* '65 (TOL) [K] Toledo, OH Oblates of St. Francis de Sales.
Cryan, John J. '81 (NEW) [20] Jersey City, NJ Our Lady of Mercy Church.
Cryans, Andrew W. '75 (MAN) Milford, NH St. Patrick Church.
Crynes, J. Peter '67 (SCR) Shavertown, PA St. Therese Church.
Cser, Ladislaus *s.j.* '45 (RVC) St. James, NY SS. Philip and James Church; Retired.
Csizmar, Richard A. '68 (BUF) Albion, NY St. Mary Assumption Church; Albion, NY St. Joseph Church.
Csizmazia, Placid *o.cist.* '40 (DAL) [B] Irving, TX University of Dallas; [M] Irving, TX Cistercian Abbey of Our Lady of Dallas.
Csorba, Dominic *o.f.m.* '62 (NY) [115] New York, NY St. Stephen of Hungary Church.
Csorba, Dominic L. *o.f.m.* '35 (NY) [HH] New York, NY Hungarian Catholic League of America, Inc.
Cuadrado, Angel *o.de.m.* '86 (CGS) Cayey, PR Nuestra Senora de la Merced Church.
Cuadrado, Hector *c.m.f.* '91 (SJN) [9] Bayamon, PR San Jose Church.
Cuadros, Jesus '66 (BRK) [157] Queens, NY Blessed Sacrament Church.
Cubells, Joseph *s.f.* '26 (WDC) [B] Silver Spring, MD Holy Family Seminary.
Cuccaro, John '79 (PBR) Homer City, PA Holy Protection of Mary, The Mother of God Church.
Cuccia, Salvatore H. *o.praem.* '66 (BAL) [76] Baltimore, MD Our Lady, Queen of Peace Church.
Cuddigan, John *s.j.* '62 (SD) [36] San Diego, CA St. Therese Church.
Cuddihy, Msgr. William '56 (SD) [22] San Diego, CA St. Catherine Laboure Church.
Cuddy, John '53 (SAV) Macon, GA St. Joseph's Church.
Cuddy, William F. '79 (BO) Military & VA Chaplains.
Cudemo, Nicholas V. '63 (PH) Retired.
Cudinach, Salvador *sch.p.* '53 (LA) [92] Los Angeles, CA Santa Teresita Church.
Cudnik, Chester C. '48 (CLV) [10] Cleveland, OH St. Barbara Church.
Cuenin, Walter H. '70 (BO) [6] Newton, MA Our Lady Help of Christians Church.
Cuesta, Benedicto '51 (SFE) Retired.
Cuevas, Geronimo '86 (MRY) [3] Salinas, CA St. Mary of the Nativity Church.
Cuevas, Jose Luis '76 (LA) [R] Azusa, CA Casa Comboni Mission Seminary.
Cuevas, Randy M. '82 (BR) Donaldsonville, LA Ascension of Our Lord Jesus Christ Church.
Cuevas, Wilson '81 (ELP) [6] El Paso, TX Corpus Christi Church.
Cuff, John P. *m.m.* '69 (FgM) Maryknoll Foreign Missions.
Cuff, Thomas E. '83 (SPR) Absent on Leave.
Culhane, Alberic *o.s.b.* '57 (SCL) [B] Collegeville, MN St. John's University; [I] Collegeville, MN St. John's Abbey, of the Order of St. Benedict.
Culhane, Eugene J. *s.j.* '45 (NEW) [B] Jersey City, NJ Saint Peter's College.
Culhane, Eugene K. *s.j.* '45 (NY) [DD] New York, NY Murray-Weigel Hall.
Culhane, Msgr. Thomas (KCK) [2] Overland Park, KS Holy Cross Church; Retired.
Culkin, Msgr. Francis J. '44 (SY) Lee Center, NY St. Joseph Church; Retired.
Culkin, Harry M. '42 (BRK) [U] Douglaston, NY Bishop Mugavero Residence.
Culkin, Harry W. '42 (BRK) Retired.

Culkin, J. Stewart '71 (ARL) Vienna, VA St. Mark's Church.
Culkin, Michael '78 (WDC) On Duty Outside the Archdiocese.
Cull, Lawrence W. '69 (NEW) Cranford, NJ St. Michael's Church.
Cull, Paul J. '45 (CHI) [3] Waukegan, IL St. Dismas Church; Retired.
Cullen, Bernard J. *o.c.s.o.* '48 (DUB) [K] Peosta, IA New Melleray Abbey, Order of Cistercians of the Strict Observance.
Cullen, Christopher M. *s.j.* '94 (WDC) [M] Washington, DC Carroll House.
Cullen, Daniel *s.m.a.* '47 (NEW) [N] Tenafly, NJ Society of African Missions, Provincialate, S.M.A. Fathers.
Cullen, Donald '71 (KCK) Roeland Park, KS St. Agnes Church.
Cullen, Msgr. Edward P. '62 (PH) [N] Rosemont, PA St. Edmond's Home for Children.
Cullen, Francis J. '54 (LA) [73] Los Angeles, CA St. Kevin Church; Sick Leave.
Cullen, George H. '48 (CHI) Retired.
Cullen, Msgr. J. Peter '67 (BGP) New Canaan, CT St. Aloysius Church.
Cullen, John F. '41 (PH) Wyndmoor, PA Seven Dolors Church; Retired.
Cullen, Kevin L. *s.j.* '86 (FgM) Provinces.
Cullen, Martin T. '57 (FAR) Retired.
Cullen, Patrick P. '68 (BIR) [1] Birmingham, AL St. Paul's Cathedral.
Cullen, Paul M. *o.s.m.* '65 (CHI) [18] Chicago, IL Assumption of the Blessed Virgin Mary Church; [N] Chicago, IL Servite Friars - Eastern Province; [N] Chicago, IL Servite Friars - Eastern Province.
Cullen, Robert B. *s.j.* '58 (BAL) [C] Baltimore, MD Loyola High School.
Cullen, Robert B. *s.j.* '58 (PIT) [S] Pittsburgh, PA Jesuit Community of Pittsburgh.
Cullen, Sean '62 (CHI) [N] Chicago, IL St. Patrick's Missionary Society.
Cullen, Thomas F. '53 (CLV) Westlake, OH St. Ladislas Church; Retired.
Cullen, Msgr. Thomas J. '52 (GAL) Texas City, TX St. Mary Church.
Cullen, Msgr. Thomas J. '52 (MOB) On Leave from the Archdiocese.
Cullen, William '48 (JOL) Retired.
Cullen, William '83 (JKS) Pearl, MS St. Jude Church.
Cullen, William J. *s.j.* '65 (BO) [H] Boston, MA Nativity Preparatory School; [W] Boston, MA Loyola House.
Culleton, James P. '46 (PEO) Retired.
Culleton, Thomas L. '91 (SLC) Roosevelt, UT St. Helen's Church.
Culley, Brian *c.m.f.* '84 (AUS) San Marcos, TX St. John the Evangelist Church; Uhland, TX St. Michael's Church.
Culley, Thomas D. *s.j.* '65 (NO) [P] New Orleans, LA Ignatius Residence.
Culligan, Kevin *o.c.d.* (CHI) [N] Chicago, IL Edith Stein House of Studies.
Culligan, Martin J. *c.m.* '57 (CHI) [C] Chicago, IL Vincentian Community at DePaul University.
Culligan, Michael A. '59 (SR) Petaluma, CA St. James Church.
Cullinan, James L. '87 (CHI) Oak Forest, IL St. Damian Church.
Cullinan, John '46 (PHX) [14] Phoenix, AZ St. Joan of Arc Church.
Cullinan, John F. '46 (PHX) Retired.
Cullinane, Brian P. *o.f.m.* '71 (NEW) Elmwood Park, NJ St. Leo's Church.
Cullinane, Briant *o.f.m.conv.* '58 (R) Castle Hayne, NC St. Stanislaus Kostka Church.
Cullinane, Jeremiah J. (DAL) [O] Irving, TX Diocese of Dallas Campus Ministry.
Cullinane, Jeremiah J. '59 (WH) On Duty Outside the Diocese.
Cullinane, John '56 (BRK) [171] Queens, NY St. Genevieve Church.
Cullings, David Ronald '67 (P) [5] Eugene, OR St. Peter Church.
Culliton, Leo J. '50 (VEN) Lake Placid, FL St. James Church.
Culloty, John P. '72 (BO) [16] Boston, MA St. Brigid Church.
Culnane, William R. '60 (SCR) [5] Wilkes-Barre, PA St. Dominic Church.
Culotta, Joachim *o.p.* '64 (DAL) [M] Irving, TX Dominican Priory of St. Albert the Great.
Culotta, Joseph '83 (BIR) Decatur, AL St. Ann's Church.
Culotta, Msgr. Salvador J. '53 (BEA) [8] Beaumont, TX St. Pius X Church.
Culotta, Thomas C. '61 (HRT) East Berlin, CT Sacred Heart Church.
Culver, Garry (DM) West Des Moines, IA Sacred Heart Church.
Culver, James A. '55 (SY) [4] Rome, NY St. Peter Church.
Culver, Richard J. '85 (OAK) Pittsburg, CA Our Lady Queen of the World Church.
Culver, Msgr. T. Joseph '63 (GAL) La Marque, TX Our Lady Queen of Peace Church.
Cumberland, Matthew T. '92 (LA) La Puente, CA St. Joseph Church.
Cumella, Anthony N. '66 (ALX) Retired.
Cumiskey, Thomas M. *o.p.* '55 (DAL) [M] Irving, TX Dominican Priory of St. Albert the Great.
Cummings, Brian J. *s.s.e.* '96 (BUR) [E] Colchester, VT Society of St. Edmund.
Cummings, Carl '75 (BAL) Military Chaplains.
Cummings, Charles *o.c.s.o.* '71 (SLC) [F] Huntsville, UT Abbey of Our Lady of the Holy Trinity of the Order of Cistercians.
Cummings, Charles J. '68 (SCR) Lords Valley, PA St. John Neumann Church.
Cummings, Frederick F. '41 (SY) Retired.
Cummings, Gabriel '84 (SAV) [9] Savannah, GA St. Peter the Apostle Church.
Cummings, Msgr. George '43 (SP) Citrus Springs, FL St. Elizabeth Ann Seton Church; Retired.
Cummings, James M. *s.m.* '43 (ATL) [C] Atlanta, GA Marist School.
Cummings, Jerome '64 (LA) La Canada Flintridge, CA St. Bede the Venerable Church.
Cummings, John J. '88 (LFT) Leave of Absence.
Cummings, Jose *c.m.* '77 (PCE) [14] Ponce, PR San Vicente-Cantera Church.
Cummings, Juniper *o.f.m.conv.* (FgM) Conventual Franciscan Foreign Missions.
Cummings, Leo B. *m.s.* '66 (ATL) Calhoun, GA St. Clements Church.
Cummings, Leo P. '64 (SCR) [I] Carbondale, PA Marian Community Hospital.
Cummings, Maurice *o.carm.* '71 (SPR) [K] Williamstown, MA Mount Carmel Retreat Center.
Cummings, Patrick John '78 (GAL) [73] Houston, TX St. Rose of Lima Church.
Cummings, Paul '55 (LAN) Retired.
Cummings, Paul J. '55 (KAL) Battle Creek, MI St. Jerome Church.
Cummings, Thomas W. *s.j.* '69 (DEN) [M] Denver, CO Regis Jesuit Community (The Jesuits at Regis University); [M] Denver, CO Xavier Jesuit Center.
Cummins, Anthony O. '65 (SAT) Boerne, TX St. Peter the Apostle Church.
Cummins, Charles E. '68 (SLC) [3] Ogden, UT St. Joseph's Church.
Cummins, Charles T. '68 (SLC) Huntsville, UT St. Florence Catholic Community Church; [H] Ogden, UT Weber State University, Newman Center.
Cummins, Charles T. '69 (LA) On Duty Outside the Archdiocese.
Cummins, Joseph V. *c.m.* '72 (FgM) Vincentian Foreign Missions.
Cummins, Michael E. '95 (KNX) [2] Knoxville, TN All Saints Catholic Church.
Cummins, Michael J. *c.m.* '77 (BRK) [U] Queens Village, NY DePaul Residence.
Cummins, Robert '86 (RIC) [1] Virginia Beach, VA Church of the Ascension.
Cummins, Timothy '45 (FRS) Retired.
Cuneo, James J. '63 (DEN) Arvada, CO Spirit of Christ Parish.
Cuneo, Msgr. James J. '67 (BGP) [1] Stratford, CT Holy Name of Jesus Church.
Cunnane, Jarlath '77 (LA) On Duty Outside the Archdiocese.
Cunnane, Michael A. '61 (SD) Santee, CA Guardian Angels Church.
Cunneen, Sean (NEW) New Providence, NJ Our Lady of Peace Church.
Cunney, Henry H. '59 (BO) Nahant, MA St. Thomas Aquinas Church.
Cunniff, Charles E. *c.s.p.* '83 (BO) [P] Boston, MA Paulist Center; [W] Boston, MA Paulist Fathers Residence; [CC] Boston, MA Newman House Catholic Center at Boston University.
Cunniff, Declan J. '68 (NEW) [B] South Orange, NJ Seton Hall University; [N] Newark, NJ Newark Abbey.
Cunniff, Hubert F. *s.j.* '38 (BO) [W] Weston, MA Campion Health Center, Inc.
Cunniff, Vincent '53 (P) Retired.
Cunniffe, James A. *s.c.j.* '57 (JKS) Hernando, MS Holy Spirit Church; [E] Nesbit, MS St. Michael Community House.
Cunningham, Ambrose '50 (PEO) [2] Rock Island, IL Sacred Heart Church.
Cunningham, Augustine W. *o.s.b.* '61 (RIC) [L] Richmond, VA Mary Mother of the Church Abbey.
Cunningham, Christopher '90 (LA) Palmdale, CA St. Mary Church.
Cunningham, Donald D. '87 (SY) Oxford, NY St. Joseph Church.
Cunningham, Donald M. *s.j.* '64 (SFD) Pana, IL St. Patrick Church.
Cunningham, Douglas '87 (SY) Norwich, NY St. Paul Church.
Cunningham, Edward *o.m.i.* '58 (WIN) Minnesota City, MN St. Paul's Church.
Cunningham, Gerard M. '93 (WDC) Military Chaplains.
Cunningham, James *c.s.s.* '50 (BO) [Z] Waltham, MA Stigmatine Fathers and Brothers.
Cunningham, James '61 (NY) [164] Bronx, NY St. Mary Church.
Cunningham, James B. '87 (BUF) [9] Cheektowaga, NY St. Philip the Apostle Church.
Cunningham, James J. '61 (NY) Bronx, NY Bronx Psychiatric Center.
Cunningham, James K. '95 (BRK) [50] Brooklyn, NY Good Shepherd Church.
Cunningham, John '91 (PMB) [1] West Palm Beach, FL Holy Name of Jesus Church.
Cunningham, John E. '51 (DM) Retired.
Cunningham, John F. *o.p.* '53 (PRO) [P] Providence, RI St. Thomas Aquinas Priory at Providence College.
Cunningham, John F. '56 (LA) [70] Los Angeles, CA St. Joan of Arc Church; Retired.
Cunningham, John F. '74 (PHX) [5] Mesa, AZ St. Bridget Church.
Cunningham, John H. '65 (ALX) Jena, LA St. Mary Church.
Cunningham, John J. '56 (CHI) [176] Chicago, IL St. Priscilla Church.
Cunningham, John P. '79 (BAL) [92] Baltimore, MD St. Thomas More Church.
Cunningham, Msgr. Joseph C. '71 (PH) Wayne, PA St. Isaac Jogues Church.
Cunningham, Joseph L. '56 (MIL) [7] West Allis, WI St. Mary, Help of Christians Church.
Cunningham, Joseph L. '63 (BRK) [174] Queens, NY St. Gregory the Great Church.
Cunningham, Kieran P. *o.s.b.* '62 (SEA) [G] Olympia, WA Providence St. Peter Hospital; [M] Lacey, WA St. Martin's Abbey.
Cunningham, Leonard A. *o.c.s.o.* '50 (CHR) [D] Moncks Corner, SC Mepkin Abbey.
Cunningham, Lloyd *s.v.d.* '81 (CHI) [N] Techny, IL Society of the Divine Word, Provincial Headquarter-Chicago Prov.
Cunningham, Michael '86 (OAK) [4] Concord, CA Queen of All Saints Church.
Cunningham, Nicholas J. '79 (TOL) Kelley's Island, OH St. Michael Church; Put-In-Bay, OH Mother of Sorrows Church.
Cunningham, Msgr. Patrick '41 (PT) Retired.
Cunningham, Peter J. '56 (MOB) [12] Mobile, AL St. Mary Church.
Cunningham, Philip *c.s.p.* '56 (SFR) [31] San Francisco, CA Old St. Mary's Cathedral.
Cunningham, Phillip J. *c.s.p.* '56 (NY) [DD] Jamaica Estates, NY Paulist Fathers Generalate.
Cunningham, Richard G. '57 (BO) [A] Boston, MA St. John's Seminary School of Theology.
Cunningham, Robert *s.j.* '55 (FgM) Provinces.
Cunningham, Msgr. Robert J. '69 (BUF) [O] Buffalo, NY Bishop's Residence; [T] Buffalo, NY Monsignor Adamski Village Housing Development Fund Company, Inc.; [T] Buffalo, NY Good Counsel Apartments.
Cunningham, Sebastian *o.f.m.conv.* '60 (LSC) [D] Mesilla Park, NM Holy Cross Retreat and Friary.
Cunningham, Vianney *t.o.r.* '70 (ORL) [2] Lakeland, FL St. Anthony's Church; [E] Lakeland, FL Florida Southern College Newman Center.
Cunningham, Vincent P. *s.m.m.* '60 (RVC) West Islip, NY Good Samaritan Hospital Medical Center; [I] West Islip, NY Good Samaritan Hospital Medical Center; [N] Bay Shore, NY Montfort Missionaries.
Cunnion, Theodore J. *s.j.* '43 (NY) [DD] New York, NY Murray-Weigel Hall.
Cuny, W. Timothy *o.s.a.* '70 (CHI) [N] Olympia Fields, IL The Augustinian Provincialate Tolentine Center; [N] Olympia Fields, IL Tolentine Monastery at Tolentine Center.
Cuomo, Rocco A. '64 (TR) Bayville, NJ St. Barnabas Church.
Cupich, Msgr. Blase J. '75 (OM) [40] Omaha, NE St. Robert Bellarmine Church.
Cupp, Edwin '69 (WH) Absent on Sick Leave.
Cupple, Gerard J. '85 (DET) Lincoln Park, MI St. Henry Church.
Curalli, Joseph *c.ss.r.* (KC) [J] Kansas City, MO Redemptorists of Kansas City.
Curalli, Joseph *c.ss.r.* '78 (KC) [32] Kansas City, MO Our Lady of Perpetual Help Church.
Curci, Richard G. '72 (GBG) New Kensington, PA Mt. St. Peter Church.
Curcio, Ralph V. '61 (NY) [109] New York, NY St. Rose of Lima Church; [1] Port Chester, NY Our Lady of Mercy Church.
Curesky, Mark L. *o.f.m.conv.* '75 (BAL) [M] Ellicott City, MD Order of Friars Minor Conventual.
Curesky, Mark L. *o.f.m.conv.* '75 (FgM) Conventual Franciscan Foreign Missions.
Curiel, James A. *o.c.d.* '99 (SAT) [18] San Antonio, TX Our Lady of Mt. Carmel and St. Therese, Discalced Carmelite Fathers National Shrine of the Little Flower Church.
Curiel, James Anthony *o.c.d.* '95 (SAT) [M] San

Antonio, TX Discalced Carmelites (Prov. of St. Therese).
Curley, Augustine J. *o.s.b.* '88 (NEW) [N] Newark, NJ Newark Abbey.
Curley, John H. '66 (BO) Dedham, MA St. Mary Church.
Curley, Msgr. Joseph K. '62 (RVC) Centereach, NY Assumption of the Blessed Virgin Mary Church.
Curley, Martin W. '56 (RVC) Bayville, NY St. Gertrude's Church.
Curley, Patrick J. '53 (JKS) Retired.
Curley, Patrick J. '70 (JKS) Yazoo City, MS St. Mary Church; Yazoo City, MS St. Francis Church.
Curley, Robert '51 (RVC) Retired.
Curley, Terence P. '72 (BO) Dedham, MA St. Susanna Church.
Curley, Thomas J. '39 (CHI) [206] Chicago, IL St. Thomas More Church; Retired.
Curley, Thomas J. '70 (NY) Chester, NY St. Columba Church.
Curnutte, William G. '82 (SLC) Retired.
Curran, Anthony '72 (ALB) [9] Schenectady, NY St. John the Evangelist Church.
Curran, Anthony T. '67 (ATL) Lawrenceville, GA St. Lawrence Church.
Curran, Charles E. '58 (ROC) On Duty Outside the Diocese.
Curran, David *c.i.c.m.* '37 (SAT) [M] San Antonio, TX Missionhurst Community Residence.
Curran, David *c.i.c.m.* '71 (SAT) [36] San Antonio, TX St. Gabriel Church.
Curran, Francis D. '50 (CLV) Willoughby, OH Immaculate Conception Church.
Curran, Msgr. Francis L. '38 (MAN) Retired.
Curran, Francis T. '69 (GI) Kimball, NE St. Joseph's Church.
Curran, George A. *s.j.* '51 (DET) [P] Clarkston, MI Colombiere Center.
Curran, Gerald X. '48 (Y) Retired.
Curran, Msgr. Hugh D. '54 (NY) Pelham Manor, NY Our Lady of Perpetual Help Church.
Curran, Hugh J. *c.s.b.* '51 (GAL) Missouri City, TX Holy Family Church.
Curran, James *c.m.f.* '83 (CHI) [N] Oak Park, IL Claretian Fathers Headquarters of U.S.A. Eastern Province.
Curran, James B. *s.d.b.* '51 (MIA) [25] Miami, FL St. Kieran Church.
Curran, James P. '63 (CAM) Glassboro, NJ Our Lady of Lourdes Church.
Curran, John *o.f.m.conv.* (SAV) Jesup, GA St. Joseph Church.
Curran, John *o.m.i.* '78 (MIA) Opa Locka, FL St. Monica Church.
Curran, John *l.c.* '96 (HRT) [V] Orange, CT Legion of Christ, Inc.
Curran, John F. '46 (HRT) Retired.
Curran, John J. '54 (WCH) Aleppo, KS Immaculate Conception Church; Garden Plain, KS St. Anthony Church.
Curran, John J. *s.j.* '59 (FgM) Provinces.
Curran, John W. '57 (CHI) Other Assignments.
Curran, Joseph F. *s.j.* '56 (BAL) [M] Baltimore, MD Jesuit Fathers and Brothers Maryland Provincial Curia.
Curran, Joseph L. '76 (BO) Watertown, MA Sacred Heart Church.
Curran, Juan *o.m.i.* (SJN) [24] Bayamon, PR Santa Teresa de Avila Church.
Curran, Michael J. '81 (BRK) Released from Diocesan Assignment.
Curran, Oliver '76 (GLP) Pinetop, AZ St. Mary of the Angels Church.
Curran, Patrick J. '55 (HRT) [6] West Hartford, CT St. Thomas the Apostle Church.
Curran, Patrick J. '55 (SLC) On Duty Outside the Diocese.
Curran, Msgr. Paul F. '57 (PH) Huntingdon Valley, PA St. Albert the Great Church.
Curran, Paul F. '59 (BO) Canton, MA St. Gerard Majella Church.
Curran, Peter *o.m.i.* '71 (FgM) Oblates Foreign Missions.
Curran, Robert F. *s.j.* '74 (SFR) [C] San Francisco, CA University of San Francisco; [N] San Francisco, CA Jesuit Community at University of San Francisco.
Curran, Thomas B. '84 (WIL) [B] Wilmington, DE Salesianum School.
Curran, Thomas M. '70 (BO) Hudson, MA St. Michael Church.
Curran, William *m.afr.* '66 (FgM) Missionaries of Africa Foreign Missions.
Curran, William J. '69 (CHI) Berwyn, IL St. Leonard Church.
Currans, Clem '74 (SC) [B] Granville, IA Spalding Catholic High School.
Currans, Clem W. '74 (SC) Granville, IA St. Joseph Church.
Current, Maurice H. '80 (LIN) Beaver Crossing, NE Sacred Heart Church.
Currid, Joseph '71 (MIA) Absent on Leave.
Currie, Charles L. *s.j.* '63 (PH) [C] Philadelphia, PA St. Joseph's University.
Currie, Charles L. *s.j.* '63 (WDC) [M] Washington, DC Leonard Neale House.
Currie, Donald '79 (SAT) On Leave.
Currie, John A. '97 (BO) [28] Boston, MA Holy Name Church.
Currie, Joseph *s.j.* (NY) [GG] New York, NY University Apostolate.
Currie, Joseph A. *s.j.* '68 (NO) [C] New Orleans, LA Loyola University.
Currie, Joseph A. *s.j.* '68 (NY) [DD] New York, NY Jesuit Community at Fordham University.
Currie, Robert F. *s.j.* '71 (BAL) [M] Baltimore, MD Jesuit Fathers and Brothers Maryland Provincial Curia.
Currie, Robert F. *s.j.* '71 (FgM) Provinces.
Currie, William J. *s.j.* '67 (BAL) [M] Baltimore, MD Jesuit Fathers and Brothers Maryland Provincial Curia.
Currie, William J. *s.j.* '67 (FgM) Provinces.
Currier, Thomas F. '50 (DUB) Retired.
Curry, Edward V. '47 (GBG) Retired; [G] Greensburg, PA Neumann House.
Curry, Frederic F. '49 (TUC) [15] Tucson, AZ St. Joseph Church; Retired.
Curry, James '94 (CHI) Tinley Park, IL Saint Julie Billiart Church.
Curry, James J. *s.j.* '74 (NY) [F] New York, NY Loyola School; [DD] New York, NY St. Ignatius Loyola Residence.
Curry, Joseph M. '86 (MET) [1] New Brunswick, NJ St. Peter Apostle Church.
Curry, Robert *s.j.* '64 (R) [E] Raleigh, NC Jesuit Community.
Curry, Robert O. *c.ss.r.* '73 (BR) [H] Baton Rouge, LA Redemptorist Vice Province.
Curry, Robert S. *s.j.* '64 (R) [7] Raleigh, NC St. Raphael Church.
Curry, Terrence M. *s.j.* '94 (DET) [K] Detroit, MI Jesuit Community at the University of Detroit.
Curry, Terrence W. *s.j.* '77 (WOR) [N] Worcester, MA Jesuits of Holy Cross College, Inc.
Curry, Thomas P. '51 (RVC) Retired; [J] Huntington, NY St. Joseph's Guest Home for the Aged, Inc.; [N] Uniondale, NY St. Pius X Residence.
Curso, Manuel '72 (SFR) Daly City, CA Our Lady of Mercy Church.
Curtin, Clifford J. '51 (NOR) Retired.
Curtin, Cornelius L. *s.j.* '56 (FgM) Provinces.
Curtin, Eugene P. '56 (BO) Lexington, MA St. Brigid Church.
Curtin, Gregory F. *s.j.* '65 (NO) [C] New Orleans, LA Loyola University.
Curtin, James E. '52 (DET) Melvindale, MI St. Mary Magdalen Church.
Curtin, James F. '51 (BO) [7] Quincy, MA Our Lady of Good Counsel Church.
Curtin, Jim '69 (JOL) [2] Lockport, IL St. Dennis Church.
Curtin, L. Michael '61 (WDC) [V] Washington, DC Catholic Information Center.
Curtin, Martin *o.f.m.cap.* '90 (NY) [83] New York, NY Our Lady Queen of Angels Church.
Curtin, Paul J. *s.j.* '53 (NY) [DD] New York, NY Murray-Weigel Hall.
Curtin, Msgr. Richard B. '42 (NY) Retired.
Curtin, Timothy *s.j.* '52 (BGP) [Q] Bridgeport, CT The Society of Our Lady of the Way.
Curtin, Timothy A. *s.j.* '52 (RVC) [P] Manhasset, NY St. Ignatius Retreat House, Inisfada.
Curtin, Vincent C. *s.j.* '68 (BAL) [M] Baltimore, MD Jesuit Fathers and Brothers Maryland Provincial Curia.
Curtis, Howard *o.c.s.o.* '57 (P) [L] Lafayette, OR The Cistercian (Trappist) Abbey of Our Lady of Guadalupe.
Curtis, John C. '84 (LEX) Berea, KY St. Clare Church; Mt. Vernon, KY Our Lady of Mt. Vernon Church; [L] Berea, KY St. Clare Church-Berea College.
Curtis, Joseph C. '69 (CHI) Other Assignments.
Curtis, Martin *o.carm.* '75 (CHI) [68] Chicago, IL St. Gelasius Church.
Curtis, Patrick *o.f.m.* '51 (SFD) Montrose, IL St. Rose of Lima Church; Teutopolis, IL St. Francis of Assisi Church; [K] Teutopolis, IL St. Francis Assisi Friary.
Curtis, Robert J. '36 (TOL) Retired.
Curtis, Robert P. *c.s.p.* '71 (LA) [86] Los Angeles, CA St. Paul the Apostle Church.
Curtis, Robert P. *c.s.p.* '71 (NY) [DD] Jamaica Estates, NY Paulist Fathers Generalate.
Curtis, William D. '47 (WIN) Retired.
Curtiss, Donald J. '71 (ROC) Rochester, NY Strong Memorial Hospital; [J] Rochester, NY St. Joseph Convent Infirmary.
Curtiss, John B. '57 (LC) Retired.
Curtsinger, George (FWT) Retired.
Curzydlo, Mieczislaus I. (ROC) Canandaigua, NY Veteran's Hospital.
Curzydlo, Ignatius *s.a.c.* '39 (BUF) [O] North Tonawanda, NY Society of the Catholic Apostolate.
Cusack, Msgr. Andrew T. '60 (BGP) On Duty Outside the Diocese.
Cusack, Msgr. Andrew T. '60 (NEW) [A] South Orange, NJ Immaculate Conception Seminary; [B] South Orange, NJ Seton Hall University.
Cusack, Francis V. '54 (MOB) Orange Beach, AL St. Thomas by the Sea Church.
Cusack, Francis W. *c.p.* '58 (L) [L] Louisville, KY Sacred Heart Retreat.
Cusack, James C. '56 (GR) Retired.
Cusack, John J. *c.m.* '45 (PH) [AA] Philadelphia, PA Congregation of the Mission.
Cusack, John J. '71 (PAT) Military Chaplains.
Cusack, Paul *c.p.* '59 (MET) [H] South River, NJ Passionist Provincial Office.
Cusack, Thomas *s.s.c.* '62 (LA) [R] Los Angeles, CA Columban Fathers, Procure House.
Cusatis, Girard J. '63 (PH) [1] Drexel Hill, PA St. Andrew Church.
Cusato, Michael *o.f.m.* (STP) [10] St. Paul, MN Sacred Heart Church.
Cuschieri, Msgr. Albert A. '61 (DAL) [7] Dallas, TX Mary Immaculate Church.
Cushing, Alan '57 (SFE) Retired.
Cushing, Charles B. '54 (BRK) Retired.
Cushing, Robert A. '78 (SAV) Special Assignment.
Cushing, Vincent de P. *o.f.m.* '63 (WDC) [B] Washington, DC Washington Theological Union.
Cushing, Vincent de Paul *o.f.m.* '63 (WDC) [M] Silver Spring, MD Gemelli House.
Cushing, Walter F. '56 (ROC) [11] Rochester, NY St. Cecilia Church.
Cusick, Eugene G. '64 (PH) Holland, PA St. Bede the Venerable Church.
Cusick, John C. '70 (CHI) [165] Chicago, IL St. Patrick Church.
Cusick, Kevin M. '92 (WDC) Military Chaplains.
Cusick, Thomas H. '64 (DET) Belleville, MI St. Anthony Church.
Cusimano, Francis J. *s.j.* '68 (FgM) Provinces.
Cusimano, Salvatore J. '49 (BUF) [11] Niagara Falls, NY Prince of Peace Church; Retired.
Cusma, Joseph S. '53 (NY) Retired.
Cusmano, John '64 (DET) [8] Dearborn Heights, MI St. Sebastian Church.
Custer, Edward O. *m.m.* '72 (CHI) [N] Chicago, IL Maryknoll Fathers & Brothers.
Custer, John S. '83 (PBR) [A] Pittsburgh, PA Byzantine Catholic Seminary of SS. Cyril and Methodius.
Custer, John S. '83 (PSC) On Duty Outside Diocese.
Custer, Michael H. *o.s.b.* '41 (MAN) [K] Manchester, NH St. Anselm Abbey.
Custodio, Rinaldo B. '62 (STP) Savage, MN St. John the Baptist Church.
Cutajar, Alfred *s.j.* '69 (BAL) [H] Cumberland, MD Sacred Heart Hospital of the Western Maryland Health System.
Cutie, Albert R. '95 (MIA) [5] Fort Lauderdale, FL St. Clement Church.
Cutrara, Vincent *c.s.* '57 (CHI) Melrose Park, IL Our Lady of Mount Carmel Church.
Cutrone, Dominick F. '55 (BRK) [96] Brooklyn, NY Our Lady of Grace Church.
Cvelbar, Joseph '32 (PIT) Retired; [O] Pittsburgh, PA St. John Vianney Manor.
Cwalina, Msgr. John F. '38 (RVC) Retired.
Cwiekowski, Bruce '75 (P) [G] Portland, OR Catholic Charities of the Archdiocese of Portland in Oregon.
Cwiekowski, Bruce W. '79 (FR) Special Assignment.
Cwiekowski, Frederick J. *s.s.* '62 (HRT) On Duty Outside the Archdiocese.
Cwiekowski, Frederick J. *s.s.* '62 (SFR) [A] Menlo Park, CA St. Patrick Seminary.
Cwik, Patrick (LAN) Bellevue, MI St. Ann Church.
Cwik, Patrick '74 (LAN) [4] Lansing, MI Immaculate Heart of Mary Church.
Cwynar, Paul '87 (PIT) [2] Swissvale, PA Word of God Church.
Cybruch, Lucian '91 (NY) [99] New York, NY Our Lady of Victory Church.
Cylwicki, Albert W. *c.s.b.* '60 (ROC) [I] Rochester, NY Basilian Residence.
Cymbor, Msgr. John A. '50 (STU) Flushing, OH St. Paul's Church.
Cymbrowski, Martin *c.m.* '30 (HRT) [M] Manchester, CT DePaul Provincial Residence.
Cymerman, Alex B. *o.f.m.conv.* '65 (PAT) [6] Clifton, NJ St. John Kanty Church.
Cyprys, Ronald '69 (DET) [6] Dearborn Heights, MI Our Lady of Grace Church.
Cyr, Guy *s.m.* '39 (BO) [10] Cambridge, MA Our Lady of Pity Church.
Cyr, Joel R. '71 (PRT) Brewer, ME St. Joseph's Church; Brewer, ME St. Teresa's Church.
Cyr, L. Chanel '53 (PRT) Limestone, ME St. Louis Church; Retired.
Cyr, Lawrence S. *c.pp.s.* '44 (SAN) Coleman, TX Sacred Heart Church.
Cyr, Myles *o.m.i.* '54 (PRT) Brownville Junction, ME St. Francis Xavier Church.
Cyr, Philip '69 (PRT) Houlton, ME St. Mary's Church.

Cyr, Richard E. '60 (DET) [6] Sterling Heights, MI St. Matthias Church.
Cyr, Roger '59 (PRT) Lincoln, ME St. Mary Church.
Cyr, Terrence *o.carm.* '75 (KCK) [1] Leavenworth, KS Immaculate Conception Church; [4] Leavenworth, KS St. Joseph's Church.
Cyr, William F. '71 (SPR) Williamstown, MA SS. Patrick and Raphael Church.
Cyscon, Peter J. '73 (CHI) Berwyn, IL St. Odilo Church.
Cyscon, Philip E. '84 (CHI) [44] Chicago, IL St. Columbanus Church.
Cyvas, Matthew '41 (ALB) Retired.
Czachor, Christopher '51 (PSC) Absent on Sick Leave.
Czachor, Richard E. '77 (SCR) West Hazleton, PA Transfiguration Church.
Czachorowski, Richard S. '65 (NEW) Lyndhurst, NJ St. Michael's Church.
Czahur, John P. '77 (TR) Riverton, NJ Sacred Heart Church.
Czaja, Blaise *c.p.* (GAL) [S] Houston, TX Holy Name Retreat Center.
Czaja, Blaise *c.p.* '64 (CHI) [N] Chicago, IL Passionist Provincial Office.
Czaja, Joseph S. '46 (Y) Retired.
Czajka, Norman M. '61 (CHI) [36] Chicago, IL St. Camillus Church.
Czajkcwski, Richard *m.m.* '61 (FgM) Maryknoll Foreign Missions.
Czajkowski, Andrew A. '74 (LAN) Davison, MI St. John Church.
Czapiewski, Stanislaus *s.j.* '40 (DET) Hamtramck, MI St. Ladislaus Church; [P] Clarkston, MI Colombiere Center.
Czapinski, Richard J. '58 (PIT) Penn Hills, PA St. Gerard Majella Church.
Czapla, Bruce C. *o.f.m.* '89 (HRT) [6] New Britain, CT St. Francis of Assisi Church.
Czarcinski, Edward A. '88 (MET) Milltown, NJ Our Lady of Lourdes Church.
Czarkowski, Joseph R. '74 (E) Lucinda, PA St. Joseph Church.
Czarnecki, Anthony '66 (WOR) Webster, MA St. Joseph's Church.
Czarnecki, Edmund S. '64 (ORL) Cocoa, FL Blessed Sacrament Church.
Czarnecki, Edward R. '66 (BUF) Blasdell, NY Our Mother of Good Counsel Church.
Czarnecki, Ervin J. *s.j.* '52 (WIN) [1] Mankato, MN SS. Peter and Paul's Church.
Czarnota, Reynold A. '53 (PH) Retired.
Czarnota, Stanley '56 (LAN) [F] Lansing, MI St. Lawrence Hospital and Healthcare Services; [G] Dimondale, MI St. Lawrence Dimondale Center.
Czartorynski, David F. '84 (ALN) Military Chaplains.
Czaster, Herman *o.f.m.conv.* '65 (HRT) Kensington, CT St. Paul's Church.
Czaus, Joseph C. '89 (ALN) Unassigned.
Czech, Edmund *o.f.m.* '44 (MIL) [P] Burlington, WI Queen of Peace Friary.
Czech, Edward M. '73 (CLV) Military Chaplains.
Czechowicz, Bernard J. '54 (BUF) Retired.
Czechowicz, Walter '51 (ALB) [8] Amsterdam, NY St. Stanislaus Church.
Czekala, Henry *c.m.* '44 (HRT) [M] Manchester, CT DePaul Provincial Residence.
Czekala, Henry *c.m.* '44 (SY) [S] Utica, NY St. Vincent's Mission House.
Czelusniak, Donald '78 (ALB) Gloversville, NY St. Mary of Mt. Carmel Church.
Czerkies, Joseph '62 (PAT) [6] Passaic, NJ St. Joseph's Church.
Czerwien, Richard *ss.cc.* '83 (BWN) Edinburg, TX Sacred Heart Church.
Czerwinski, James W. *o.f.m.* '77 (NEW) Wood-Ridge, NJ Our Lady of the Assumption Church.
Czerwionka, Frank *c.s.v.* '59 (JOL) [I] Bourbonnais, IL Our Lady of Victory Nursing Home.
Czuba, Flavius *o.f.m.* '47 (GAY) Indian River, MI Cross in the Woods Catholic Shrine Church.
Czywil, Valerian *o.f.m.conv.* (BO) [7] Lawrence, MA Holy Trinity Church.
Czyzynski, John *s.c.j.* '63 (MIL) [P] Franklin, WI St. Francis Residence; [P] Hales Corners, WI Priests of the Sacred Heart.

D

D'Abele, Peter *s.m.m.* '75 (BRK) [U] Ozone Park, NY Montfort Missionaries Provincialate - for Nation Community.
D'Addezio, Msgr. Louis A. '61 (PH) [137] Philadelphia, PA St. Philip Neri Church.
D'Agostini, Mario *s.p.* '65 (STL) [P] St. Louis, MO Servants of the Paraclete.
D'Agostino, Angelo *s.j.* '66 (BAL) [M] Baltimore, MD Jesuit Fathers and Brothers Maryland Provincial Curia.
D'Agostino, Angelo *s.j.* '66 (FgM) Provinces.
D'Agostino, Carl L. '59 (CLV) Independence, OH St. Michael Church.
D'Agostino, Joseph '41 (ALB) Retired.
D'Agostino, Lorenzo *s.s.e.* '42 (BUR) [E] Colchester, VT Society of St. Edmund.
D'Agostino, Rodolfo *r.c.j.* '64 (LA) [R] North Hills, CA Rogationist Fathers.
D'Albro, Thomas G. '71 (BRK) Released from Diocesan Assignment.
D'Alessandro, Benedict *o.f.m.* '66 (NY) [4] Mt. Vernon, NY Our Lady of Mount Carmel Church.
D'Alessandro, Benedict J. *o.f.m.* '66 (NY) [DD] Mount Vernon, NY St. Bernardine of Siena Friary.
D'Alessandro, Francis X. *o.f.m.* '53 (NY) [DD] New York, NY Padua Friary.
D'Alessandro, Peter P. *s.j.* '66 (PH) [G] Philadelphia, PA St. Joseph's Preparatory School; [AA] Philadelphia, PA St. Joseph's Preparatory School Jesuit Community, Arrupe House.
D'Alessandro, Salvatore '39 (SY) [3] Endicott, NY St. Anthony of Padua Church; Retired.
D'Alonzo, Alfred F. *c.s.c.* '53 (FTW) [B] Notre Dame, IN University of Notre Dame Du Lac; [J] Notre Dame, IN Holy Cross Community, Corby Hall, University of Notre Dame.
D'Amato, James J. '49 (BRK) Retired.
D'Ambrosi, Girolamo *s.a.c.* '39 (NY) [91] New York, NY Our Lady of Mt. Carmel Church; [DD] New York, NY Pallottine Fathers.
D'Ambrosia, Peter *s.m.* '85 (BO) [Y] Framingham Centre, MA The Marist House.
D'Amico, Carducci S. '64 (BGP) [19] Bridgeport, CT St. Raphael's Church.
D'Amico, Carmen A. '82 (PIT) [6] Pittsburgh, PA St. Benedict the Moor Church.
D'Amico, Frank '87 (STL) Overland, MO All Souls Church.
D'Amico, Joseph A. '95 (NEW) Verona, NJ Our Lady of the Lake Church.
D'Amico, Michael H. '64 (CAM) [2] Atlantic City, NJ St. Michael's Church.
D'Anca, Msgr. Achille '45 (BRK) Retired.
D'Andrea, Edward R. (RVC) [A] Huntington, NY Diocesan Seminary of the Immaculate Conception.
D'Andrea, Stephen D. '97 (NEW) North Arlington, NJ Queen of Peace Church.
D'Angelis, Henry *o.f.m.cap.* '41 (NY) [B] Beacon, NY St. Lawrence of Brindisi Friary.
D'Angelo, Anthony *s.d.b.* '67 (BIR) [8] Birmingham, AL Holy Rosary Church.
D'Angelo, Benedict *c.pp.s.* '42 (CIN) [B] Carthagena, OH St. Charles.
D'Angelo, Donald S. '68 (SFR) [3] Menlo Park, CA The Church of the Nativity.
D'Angelo, Joseph J. (RVC) [2] Rockville Centre, NY Campus Parish of Long Island Church.
D'Angelo, Joseph J. '68 (RVC) East Meadow, NY Nassau County Police Department; [Q] Rockville Centre, NY The Campus Parish of Long Island; [Q] Rockville Centre, NY The Campus Parish of Long Island.
D'Angelo, Rocco '56 (SP) Retired.
D'Angelo, Thomas P. '84 (NY) [140] Bronx, NY St. Francis of Assisi Church; Bronx, NY Our Lady of Mercy Medical Center; [W] New York, NY Our Lady of Mercy Medical Center.
d'Anjou, Henry G. (NY) [4] Port Chester, NY Sacred Heart of Jesus Church.
d'Anjou, Henry G. '48 (NY) Retired; [E] White Plains, NY Archbishop Stepinac High School.
d'Anjou, John R. *s.j.* '72 (BO) [W] Boston, MA Jesuit Urban Center & Immaculate Conception Community.
D'Antonio, Anthony '39 (NY) [174] Bronx, NY Our Lady of Mt. Carmel Church; Retired.
D'Antonio, John A. *o.praem.* '73 (WIL) [I] Claymont, DE Immaculate Conception Priory of the Canons Regular of Premontre.
D'Antonio, Ronald M. '77 (BRK) [167] Queens, NY St. Fidelis Church.
D'Arcy, William *o.f.m.conv.* '37 (TR) Point Pleasant Beach, NJ St. Peter Church.
D'Arcy, William '73 (AGN) On Duty Outside the Archdiocese.
D'Artiaga, Jose '63 (SJN) [53] San Juan, PR Santa Rosa de Lima Church.
d'Auby, Phillip *s.m.* '61 (SFR) [37] San Francisco, CA Notre Dame des Victoires Church.
D'Auriol, Vincent '60 (NY) Retired.
D'Aurizio, Joseph F. '56 (ROC) [30] Rochester, NY St. John Evangelist Church.
D'Aurora, Joseph '73 (RIC) Military Chaplains.
D'Aversa, Robert J. *t.o.r.* (FgM) T.O.R. Foreign Missions.
D'Aversa, Robert J. *t.o.r.* '73 (ORL) [D] Winter Park, FL San Pedro Spiritual Development Center; [F] Winter Park, FL San Pedro Center, Third Order Regular of St. Francis; [F] Winter Park, FL Franciscan Friars, T.O.R., Provincial Residence, San Pedro Friary.
D'Cruz, Ferreolus '59 (ALX) [C] Alexandria, LA St. Frances Cabrini Hospital.
D'Cruz, Michael *o.f.m.* '57 (NY) [DD] New York, NY Franciscan Province of the Immaculate Conception.
D'Elia, Michael A. '54 (BGP) [19] Bridgeport, CT St. Raphael's Church; Bridgeport, CT Bridgeport Health Care.
D'Emma, Gregory J. '70 (NEW) Military Chaplains.
d'Entremont, Clarence J. '36 (FR) Retired.
D'Eon, Earl '89 (PHX) Sun City, AZ St. Clement of Rome Church.
D'heedene, Walter O. *c.i.c.m.* '67 (SAT) [23] San Antonio, TX Sacred Heart Church.
D'Incecco, Alfred '75 (NY) [E] New York, NY Cardinal Hayes High School.
D'Ippolito, Donald *o.f.m.* (BO) [57] Boston, MA Our Lady of Mt. Carmel Church.
D'Mello, Olympio '81 (LA) Canoga Park, CA Our Lady of the Valley Church.
D'Onofrio, Ernest *o.f.m.* '43 (NY) County, NY Dutchess County Jail; [FF] Wappingers Falls, NY Mt. Alvernia Retreat House.
D'Ostilio, Silvio *c.s.sp.* '54 (SB) Hemet, CA Holy Spirit Parish.
D'Silva, Aloysius J. '61 (CHL) Spruce Pine, NC St. Lucien Church.
D'Silva, Joseph (TR) Little Silver, NJ Fort Monmouth.
D'Silva, Percival L. '64 (WDC) [10] Washington, DC Blessed Sacrament, Shrine of the Most Church.
D'Sousa, Paul '83 (ROC) Ithaca, NY Immaculate Conception Church.
D'Souza, Claude J. '65 (RVC) Westbury, NY St. Brigid Church.
D'Souza, Gilbert P. '73 (BGP) [2] Norwalk, CT St. Joseph's Church.
D'Souza, Paul *s.d.b.* '86 (OAK) [N] Berkeley, CA Salesian Community.
D'Souza, Robert (FTW) Fort Wayne, IN Parkview Memorial Hospital.
D'Souza, Robert '73 (FTW) [9] Fort Wayne, IN St. Jude Church.
D'Souza, Wilfred *s.d.b.* '71 (SJ) [3] Sunnyvale, CA St. Cyprian Church.
Da Costa, Darrell A. '97 (BRK) [132] Brooklyn, NY St. Saviour Church.
Da Costa, Joseph Dinis *o.f.m.* '42 (FRS) Faculties Only.
da Cunha, Domingos M. '71 (PRO) [5] Cumberland, RI Our Lady of Fatima Church.
Da Cunha, Edgar *s.d.v.* '83 (PAT) [I] Florham Park, NJ Vocationist Fathers Retreat Center; [M] Florham Park, NJ Father Justin Vocationary.
Da Custa, Leonard '58 (NY) [5] Mt. Vernon, NY SS. Peter and Paul Church.
da Ponte, Robert '64 (HON) [10] Honolulu, HI Our Lady of the Mount Church.
Da Prato, Felix *o.c.d.* '40 (LR) [A] Little Rock, AR Marylake - Carmelite Novitiate.
Da Roza, George *s.s.c.* '85 (OM) [K] St. Columbans, NE St. Columban's Foreign Mission Society.
da Silva, Antonio L. *s.d.v.* '83 (NEW) Palisades Park, NJ St. Nicholas Church.
Da Silva, Gilberto *c.m.* '97 (ARE) [7] Arecibo, PR Nuestra Senora de Fatima Church.
da Silva, Jorge '71 (SJ) [M] Cupertino, CA Marianist Provincial Residence; [M] Los Gatos, CA Marianists.
da Silva, Joseph '72 (B) [5] Boise, ID Risen Christ Catholic Community Church.
Dabash, G. Adrian *o.p.* '71 (PRO) [P] Providence, RI St. Thomas Aquinas Priory at Providence College.
Dabbene, Bernard J. *s.d.b.* '66 (SFR) [12] San Francisco, CA Corpus Christi Church.
Dabcosky, Edward J. '56 (ALT) [5] Altoona, PA Holy Rosary Church; Altoona, PA Veterans Medical Center.
Dabney, Philip *c.ss.r.* '78 (WDC) [M] Washington, DC Holy Redeemer College.
Dabovich, Louis '46 (OAK) Pittsburg, CA Good Shepherd Church.
Dabria, Jerry J. '55 (NO) Retired.
Dabrowski, George J. *c.m.* '58 (HRT) [M] Manchester, CT DePaul Provincial Residence.
Dabrowski, Hyacinth M. *o.f.m.cap.* '32 (MET) Manville, NJ Sacred Heart of Jesus Church.
Dabrowski, Hyacinth M. *o.f.m.cap.* '32 (PAT) [M] Oak Ridge-Milton, NJ St. Stanislaus B. M. Friary.
Dabrowski, James O. '84 (CAM) Mount Ephraim, NJ Sacred Heart Church.
Dabruzzi, James S. '53 (SUP) Retired.
Daceehen, Mario *o.s.b.m.* '88 (STN) Detroit, MI St. John the Baptist Church.
Dacey, Donald '53 (DET) Retired.
Dacey, Martin J. '44 (SCR) Retired.
Dachauer, Andrew C. *s.j.* '64 (STO) Mammoth Lakes, CA St. Joseph Church.
Dachille, Arnold V. '59 (DET) [4] Dearborn, MI St. Clement Church.
DaCorte, Allan *o.f.m.* '77 (STL) [P] St. Louis, MO Franciscan Friary of St. Anthony of Padua.
DaCosta, Eriberto '81 (SC) Early, IA Sacred Heart Church.
DaCosta, Lee '73 (BWN) Escobares, TX Sacred Heart Church; Grulla, TX Holy Family Church; Rio Grande City, TX Immaculate Conception Church; San Isidro, TX St. Isidore Church.
Dadey, Neil (ALT) [H] Hollidaysburg, PA Campus Ministry.

Dadey, Neil R. '81 (ALT) Lock Haven, PA St. Agnes Church.
Dadson, Eric A. '90 (NY) [148] Bronx, NY Holy Rosary Church.
Daenen, Arsene *ss.cc.* '50 (HON) [H] Honolulu, HI St. Patrick's Monastery.
Dafonte, Gregorio '57 (CGS) Cayey, PR Nuestra Senora de la Merced Church.
Dagelen, Anthony L. *s.j.* '65 (MIL) [P] Wauwatosa, WI Jesuit Community at St. Camillus.
Dagher, George *b.s.o.* '43 (NTN) Retired.
Dagit, Rick D. '86 (DUB) Ackley, IA St. Mary's Church; Eldora, IA St. Mary's Church.
Dagle, Harold F. '59 (ALN) [3] Allentown, PA Immaculate Conception Church.
Dagnoli, Albert *ss.cc.* '68 (FR) [J] Fairhaven, MA Sacred Hearts Provincial House.
Daguplo, Genaro P. '84 (TR) Brick Town, NJ St. Dominic Church.
Dahl, Henry J. '96 (FR) Sandwich, MA Corpus Christi Church.
Dahlberg, Daniel J. '67 (SUP) Balsam Lake, WI Our Lady of the Pines Church; Centuria, WI St. Patrick Church; Georgetown, WI Our Lady of the Holy Rosary Church; Osceola, WI St. Joseph Church.
Dahlby, Charles G. '77 (SFD) Kincaid, IL St. Rita Church; Pawnee, IL St. Mary Church.
Dahlheimer, Cosmas *o.s.b.* '36 (SCL) [I] Collegeville, MN St. John's Abbey, of the Order of St. Benedict.
Dahlheimer, Ronald W. '59 (STP) Kilkenny, MN St. Canice Church.
Dahlinger, James H. *s.j.* '91 (NEW) [B] Jersey City, NJ Saint Peter's College; [N] Jersey City, NJ Jesuits of Saint Peter's College, Inc.
Dahlke, Robert *s.j.* (NY) Greenwood Lake, NY Holy Rosary Church.
Dahlke, Robert W. *s.j.* '65 (NY) [DD] New York, NY Jesuit Provincial's Office.
Dahlquist, Thomas S. '96 (YAK) White Salmon, WA St. Joseph Church.
Dahm, Charles W. *o.p.* '64 (CHI) [86] Chicago, IL Holy Trinity Church; [173] Chicago, IL St. Pius V Church; [N] Chicago, IL Dominicans (Provincial Office); [N] Chicago, IL Dominican Community.
Dahm, Paul '62 (RVC) [I] West Islip, NY Good Samaritan Hospital Medical Center.
Dahmen, Vernon '76 (MOB) On Leave from the Archdiocese.
Dahms, Paul G. '58 (RC) Deadwood, SD St. Ambrose Church.
Dahms, Williams *s.s.s.* '43 (NY) [55] New York, NY St. Jean Baptiste Church.
Dahn, Paul '62 (RVC) West Islip, NY Good Samaritan Hospital Medical Center.
Daiber, Msgr. Sean J. '67 (CAM) On Duty Outside the Diocese.
Daigle, Christopher P. '78 (TLS) [5] Tulsa, OK St. Catherine Church.
Daigle, Donald R. '68 (PRT) North Vassalboro, ME St. Bridget's Church.
Daigle, Eugene *c.ss.r.* '72 (ORL) New Smyrna Beach, FL Sacred Heart Church.
Daigle, Gregory J. '93 (BR) Gonzales, LA St. Theresa of Avila Church; St. Amant, LA Holy Rosary Church.
Daigle, H.C. Paul '46 (HT) Retired.
Daigle, Msgr. Jules O. '25 (LKC) Retired.
Daigle, Karl J. '97 (SHP) [8] Shreveport, LA St. Joseph Church.
Daigle, Robert E. '63 (GAL) Retired.
Daigle, Roland *o.f.m.cap.* '84 (FgM) Capuchin Foreign Missions.
Daigle, Steven '89 (DUL) Chisholm, MN St. Joseph's Church.
Daigler, Theodore E. *s.j.* '36 (FgM) Provinces.
Dailey, Gary M. '85 (SPR) Lee, MA St. Mary's Church.
Dailey, John '64 (Y) On Duty Outside the Diocese.
Dailey, Joseph E. '77 (DET) Orion Township, MI Christ the Redeemer Church.
Dailey, Joseph W. '49 (ROC) Retired.
Dailey, Ronald G. '41 (PRO) Retired.
Dailey, Thomas F. *o.s.f.s.* '87 (ALN) [B] Center Valley, PA Allentown College of St. Francis de Sales; [K] Center Valley, PA Oblates of St. Francis de Sales.
Dailey, William G. '59 (RVC) Dix Hills, NY St. Matthew Church.
Dailey, Msgr. William J. '57 (TR) [18] Trenton, NJ St. Joseph Church; Trenton, NJ Helene Fuld Hospital.
Daily, Leo J. '44 (HRT) Yalesville, CT Our Lady of Fatima Church; Retired.
Daily, Vincent E. '59 (BO) [3] Lawrence, MA Asuncion de la Virgen Maria Church.
Dair, Richard J. '80 (ARL) Retired.
Daisy, George R., II '97 (LAN) Grand Blanc, MI Holy Family Church.
Dajao, Firmochito *s.d.b.* '79 (OAK) [N] Berkeley, CA Salesian Community.
Dakes, John T. '87 (WDC) Gaithersburg, MD St. John Neumann Church.
Dakin, Kenneth M. '88 (SAT) Uvalde, TX Sacred Heart Church.
Dalack, Adam (DET) [A] Orchard Lake, MI SS. Cyril and Methodius Seminary.
Dalbec, John *s.c.j.* '41 (MIL) [P] Franklin, WI Villa Maria.
Dalbec, Paul *m.s.* '53 (FR) [J] Attleboro, MA La Salette Shrine.
Dalbelo, Americo *c.s.s.r.* '73 (CHI) [208] Chicago, IL Transfiguration of Our Lord Church.
Dalbon, Luis '47 (CGS) [C] Aibonito, PR Casa Salesiana de Retiros.
Dale, J. Douglas '88 (ORG) [3] Anaheim, CA St. Justin Martyr Church.
Dale, Williams J. '74 (RIC) [7] Norfolk, VA St. Pius X Church.
Daleiden, Francis *o.s.b.* '57 (RCK) Amboy, IL St. Patrick Church; [H] Aurora, IL Marmion Abbey-St. Augustine's Abbey.
Daleke, Don (DM) Retired.
Daleo, Msgr. P. Joseph '71 (BEA) Orange, TX St. Mary Church.
Daleo, Paul *o.f.m.cap.* '77 (NEW) [N] Union City, NJ Capuchin Friars - Province of the Sacred Stigmata of St. Francis.
Dalessandro, Dennis G. (HBG) [5] Harrisburg, PA Holy Name of Jesus Church.
Daley, Brian *s.j.* (FTW) [B] Notre Dame, IN University of Notre Dame Du Lac.
Daley, Daniel P. '70 (BUR) On Duty Outside the Diocese.
Daley, Daniel P. '70 (GLP) Blanco, NM St. Rose Church; Bloomfield, NM St. Mary Church.
Daley, Msgr. Ernest J. '55 (E) [10] Erie, PA Our Lady of Peace Church.
Daley, Francis E. '63 (BO) [3] Arlington, MA St. James the Apostle Church.
Daley, Frederick '74 (SY) Utica, NY Mohawk Valley Psychiatric Center.
Daley, Frederick D. '74 (SY) [7] Utica, NY St. Francis de Sales Church.
Daley, Jacques de Paul *o.s.b.* '71 (GBG) Greensburg, PA Westmoreland Hospital; [H] Latrobe, PA Saint Vincent Archabbey.
Daley, James D. '54 (ALB) Delmar, NY St. Thomas the Apostle Church.
Daley, James J. '93 (BO) Acton, MA St. Elizabeth of Hungary Church.
Daley, James M. '42 (BUF) Retired.
Daley, John A. '56 (BO) [2] Malden, MA St. Joseph Church.
Daley, John J. '46 (SY) Fulton, NY Holy Family Church; Retired.
Daley, John T. '43 (RVC) New Hyde Park, NY Holy Spirit Church; Retired.
Daley, Joseph A. '68 (CHY) Cody, WY St. Anthony Church.
Daley, Joseph D. '37 (BO) Retired.
Daley, Neil '55 (ANC) Retired.
Daley, Owen W. *s.j.* '60 (NY) [DD] New York, NY West Side Jesuit Community.
Daley, Raymond *o.p.* '52 (NY) Pleasantville, NY Holy Innocents Church.
Daley, Msgr. Thomas J. '38 (WOR) Retired; [M] Worcester, MA Vianney House.
Daley, Tim '87 (TLS) [7] Tulsa, OK St. Francis Xavier-Our Lady of Guadalupe Church.
Daley, Timothy J. '87 (TLS) Special Assignment.
Daley, Wallace '55 (ORG) On Duty Outside the Diocese.
Daley, William F. *m.m.* '56 (FgM) Maryknoll Foreign Missions.
Dall, Msgr. Norbert P. '45 (LC) Retired.
Dall'Agnese, Sergio *c.s.* '79 (MIA) Lighthouse Point, FL St. Paul the Apostle Church.
Dalla Villa, Msgr. Anthony '64 (NY) [1] New York, NY Cathedral of St. Patrick.
Dallen, James '69 (SAL) On Duty Outside the Diocese.
Dallen, James '69 (SPK) [7] Spokane, WA St. Ann Church.
Dallmeier, Michael *o.f.m.* '63 (RNO) Dayton, NV St. Ann Church.
Dally, Peter F. '85 (TLS) Skiatook, OK Sacred Heart Church.
Dalpiaz, Gino *c.s.* '51 (CHI) [N] Stone Park, IL Scalabrini Mission Center.
Dalseth, Gerald '64 (SCL) Morris, MN Assumption of the Blessed Virgin Mary Church.
Dalton, Brendan '69 (MIA) Hollywood, FL St. Bernadette Church.
Dalton, Donald T. '60 (STL) Special Assignment.
Dalton, Howard '68 (NY) Absent on Leave.
Dalton, J. Paul '78 (SEA) Issaquah, WA Mary, Queen of Peace Church.
Dalton, James '68 (SEA) Lynnwood, WA St. Thomas More Church.
Dalton, James E. *o.s.f.s.* '72 (PH) [AA] Philadelphia, PA Father Judge Faculty House.
Dalton, James P. '68 (SAV) Albany, GA St. Teresa Church.
Dalton, John '48 (CLV) Retired.
Dalton, John '81 (AMA) [J] Channing, TX Disciples of the Lord Jesus Christ.
Dalton, John A. '55 (L) [67] Louisville, KY St. Raphael the Archangel Church.
Dalton, John Bryan '70 (MIA) Deerfield Beach, FL St. Ambrose Church.
Dalton, John C. '48 (CLV) [28] Cleveland, OH Holy Name Church.
Dalton, Msgr. John W. '58 (DUB) Retired.
Dalton, Michel *o.f.m.cap.* '78 (FgM) Capuchin Foreign Missions.
Dalton, Michel *o.f.m.cap.* '78 (HON) Aiea, HI St. Elizabeth Church.
Dalton, Michel W. *o.f.m.cap.* '78 (AGN) [E] Agana Heights, GU St. Fidelis Friary.
Dalton, Peadar '70 (MOB) On Leave from the Archdiocese.
Dalton, Robert A. '62 (BIR) Russellville, AL Good Shepherd Church.
Dalton, William P. '56 (NY) Katonah, NY St. Mary of the Assumption Church.
Dalupang, Arturo O. '95 (CHR) [14] Charleston, SC St. Thomas The Apostle Church.
DaLuz, Marcelo *o.f.m.conv.* '94 (WDC) [B] Washington, DC St. Bonaventure Friary.
Daly, Albert *o.carm.* (NY) Montrose, NY Franklin D. Roosevelt Hospital.
Daly, Albert *o.carm.* '33 (NY) [DD] Middletown, NY St. Albert's Priory.
Daly, Anthony C. *s.j.* (STL) [C] St. Louis, MO Saint Louis University.
Daly, Anthony C. *s.j.* '72 (STL) [P] St. Louis, MO Jesuit Community Corporation at St. Louis University - Jesuit Hall.
Daly, Bartholomew *m.h.m.* '62 (NY) [93] New York, NY Our Lady of Peace Church.
Daly, Msgr. Charles W. '51 (HRT) [12] Hartford, CT St. Luke Church; Retired.
Daly, Christopher H. '60 (NY) [2] White Plains, NY St. John the Evangelist Church.
Daly, Claude *s.j.* '43 (FgM) Provinces.
Daly, Denis E. *s.j.* (STL) [C] St. Louis, MO Saint Louis University.
Daly, Denis E. *s.j.* '64 (STL) [P] St. Louis, MO Jesuit Community Corporation at St. Louis University - Jesuit Hall.
Daly, Desmond '66 (SP) Hudson, FL St. Michael Church.
Daly, Edwin J. *s.j.* '59 (FgM) Provinces.
Daly, Francis *s.j.* '72 (CIN) [F] Cincinnati, OH St. Xavier High School.
Daly, Francis J. *s.j.* '72 (CHI) [D] Chicago, IL St. Ignatius Jesuit Community.
Daly, Frederick T. *s.j.* '44 (STL) [O] St. Louis, MO Fusz Pavilion.
Daly, George '47 (OAK) Retired.
Daly, J. Daniel *s.j.* '92 (BO) [W] Chestnut Hill, MA The Jesuit Community at Boston College.
Daly, James A. *s.j.* '56 (NY) [DD] New York, NY Murray-Weigel Hall.
Daly, James F. *c.s.sp.* '63 (MIA) [9] Fort Lauderdale, FL St. John the Baptist Church.
Daly, James J. '44 (BO) Retired.
Daly, James P. '39 (PH) [132] Philadelphia, PA Our Mother of Sorrows Church; Retired.
Daly, Jerome R. '87 (ARL) McLean, VA St. John's Church.
Daly, Msgr. John '36 (NY) Retired.
Daly, John '59 (LA) [14] Los Angeles, CA Holy Trinity Church; Retired.
Daly, John J. '46 (PH) Retired.
Daly, John J. '58 (HRT) North Haven, CT St. Barnabas Church.
Daly, Msgr. John K. '36 (NY) [5] White Plains, NY Our Lady of Sorrows Church.
Daly, John P. *s.j.* '56 (LA) [C] Los Angeles, CA Loyola Marymount University.
Daly, John R. *s.j.* '63 (STL) [P] St. Louis, MO The Jesuits of the Missouri Province.
Daly, John V. *s.j.* '66 (FgM) Provinces.
Daly, Joseph F. '42 (BRK) [192] Queens, NY St. Margaret Church; Retired.
Daly, Joseph V. *c.m.* (BRK) [D] Staten Island, NY St. John's University, Staten Island Campus; [D] Jamaica, NY St. John's University.
Daly, Joseph V. *c.m.* '60 (BRK) [U] Jamaica, NY St. Vincent's House.
Daly, Kevin *o.f.m.* '80 (ALB) [S] Loudonville, NY Siena College.
Daly, Kevin J. *o.f.m.* (BO) [BB] Boston, MA St. Anthony Shrine.
Daly, Leo J. *s.j.* '61 (RVC) [P] Manhasset, NY St. Ignatius Retreat House, Inisfada.
Daly, Lowrie *s.j.* '45 (STL) [K] Creve Coeur, MO St. John's Mercy Medical Center.
Daly, Lowrie J. *s.j.* '45 (STL) [P] St. Louis, MO Jesuit Community Corporation at St. Louis University - Jesuit Hall.
Daly, M. Paul (PAT) Sabbatical.
Daly, Manus P. '65 (JC) Marceline, MO St. Bonaventure Church.
Daly, Michael '75 (DET) [L] Livonia, MI Provincial House and Novitiate of the Sisters of St. Felix.
Daly, Peter J. '86 (WDC) Prince Frederick, MD St. John

Vianney Church; [C] Washington, DC Catholic University of America, The.
Daly, Richard L. '58 (BEL) Du Quoin, IL Sacred Heart of Jesus Church.
Daly, Robert J. *s.j.* '63 (BO) [W] Chestnut Hill, MA The Jesuit Community at Boston College.
Daly, Robert L. '41 (NEW) Hillside, NJ St. Catherine of Siena Church; Retired.
Daly, Shawn T. '95 (HRT) Branford, CT St. Mary Church.
Daly, Simeon *o.s.b.* '48 (IND) [A] St. Meinrad, IN St. Meinrad Seminary; [B] St. Meinrad, IN St. Meinrad Seminary-College of Liberal Arts; [J] St. Meinrad, IN St. Meinrad Archabbey.
Daly, Thomas A. '87 (SFR) Lagunitas, CA St. Cecilia Church; San Francisco, CA San Francisco Police Department; Special Assignment; [D] Kentfield, CA Marin Catholic College Preparatory (Coed).
Daly, Timothy '96 (ORL) [9] Orlando, FL St. John Vianney Church.
Daly, Vincent M. '71 (BRK) [244] Queens, NY St. Teresa of Avila Church.
Daly, Msgr. William J. '46 (NEW) Livingston, NJ St. Philomena Church; West Orange, NJ St. Joseph's Church; Retired.
Dalzell, James P. '49 (FR) Retired.
Damazio, Pedro J. (BO) [1] Lowell, MA St. Anthony Church.
Dambrauskas, Stephen '48 (SP) Retired.
Damhorst, Joseph *s.j.* '68 (RC) Kyle, SD Our Lady of Sorrows Church; Wanblee, SD Ignatius Loyola Church; Pine Ridge, SD Holy Rosary Church; [B] Pine Ridge, SD Jesuit Community of Holy Rosary Mission.
Damian, Lawrence P. '71 (BUF) Collins Center, NY St. Frances Cabrini Church; Eden, NY St. Mary of Immaculate Conception Church; Langford, NY St. Martin Church.
Damian, Ronald '77 (WOR) Absent on Leave.
Damico, Rodney M. '92 (COL) Marion, OH St. Mary Church.
Damis, Frank J. '84 (NY) [3] Kingston, NY St. Joseph Church.
Damjanov, Zvonimir '37 (SFD) Retired.
Dammeir, James L. '79 (MIL) [52] Milwaukee, WI St. Matthew Church.
Damoah, Augustine Ansu '90 (NY) Cortlandt Manor, NY St. Columbanus Church.
Damond, Patrick J. '96 (E) [3] Sharon, PA St. Joseph Church.
Damron, Robert '83 (LEX) Jellico, KY St. Boniface Church; Williamsburg, KY Our Lady of Perpetual Help Church.
Damroth, William J. '93 (NY) [4] Newburgh, NY Sacred Heart Church.
Danagher, Edward F. *c.m.* '46 (LA) [R] Los Angeles, CA Vincentian Fathers and Brothers.
Danaher, Msgr. Mortimer '53 (STA) Retired.
Danaher, Peter *o.f.m.cap.* '84 (FgM) Capuchin Foreign Missions.
Danaher, Philip M. *s.v.d.* '83 (JOL) Addison, IL St. Philip The Apostle Church.
Danaher, Msgr. T. Leo '55 (STA) Ponte Vedra Beach, FL Our Lady Star of the Sea Church.
Danaher, Thomas E. *m.m.* '62 (FgM) Maryknoll Foreign Missions.
Danber, Bernard *o.s.a.* '86 (PRM) Akron, OH St. Michael the Archangel Church.
Danber, Bernard R. *o.s.a.* '86 (CHI) [N] Olympia Fields, IL The Augustinian Provincialate Tolentine Center.
Danczyk, Mark J. '92 (MIL) [6] Kenosha, WI St. Mary Church.
Dandelet, James D. '54 (WIN) Retired.
Dandry, Anthony M. '89 (MET) South Plainfield, NJ Sacred Heart Church.
Dandurand, Douglas E. (STP) [C] St. Paul, MN University of St. Thomas.
Dandurand, Douglas E. '82 (SC) On Duty Outside the Diocese.
Dandurand, Douglas E. '82 (STP) [A] St. Paul, MN The Saint Paul Seminary.
Dandurand, Michael G. '97 (TOL) [1] Lima, OH St. Charles Borromeo Church.
Dane, James E. '83 (MOB) Bay Minette, AL St. Agatha Church.
Dane, John '91 (LEX) Ashland, KY Holy Family Church.
Daneault, Paul W. '66 (MAN) Absent on Sick Leave.
Danek, Michael E. *c.r.* '86 (CHI) [74] Chicago, IL St. Hedwig Church.
Danel, Joseph B. *s.j.* '52 (FgM) Provinces.
Danel, Joseph B. *s.j.* '52 (P) [L] Portland, OR Jesuit Provincial Office (Society of Jesus, Oregon Prov.).
Danen, Lyle '85 (ORL) Sabbatical.
Danforth, Clarence E. '81 (GRY) Graduate Studies.
Dang, Chin Van '83 (ORG) El Toro, CA El Toro Marine Base.
Dang, Chin Van '83 (RIC) Military Chaplains.
Dang, Francis Hoang '95 (LA) El Monte, CA Nativity Church.
Dang, Joseph *s.v.d.* '93 (DUB) [B] Epworth, IA Divine Word College.
Dang, Thien *o.s.b.* '93 (P) [L] St. Benedict, OR Mt. Angel Abbey.
Dang, Vincent '95 (SCR) [14] Wilkes-Barre, PA St. Mary's Church of the Immaculate Conception.
Danhauer, Richard T. '57 (OWN) Princeton, KY St. Paul Church.
Daniel, Bruno *o.s.b.* '75 (PAT) [M] Clifton, NJ Holy Face of Jesus Monastery.
Daniel, John C. '92 (SFE) Tucumcari, NM St. Anne Church.
Daniel, Joseph A. '52 (PH) [2] Phoenixville, PA Holy Trinity Church.
Daniel, Michael *s.a.* '57 (MRY) Seaside, CA St. Francis Xavier Church.
Daniele, Anthony J. (BO) Retired.
Danielewicz, Noel *o.f.m.conv.* '76 (BIR) Bessemer, AL St. Francis of Assisi Church.
Daniels, Eugene '84 (NY) Milton, NY St. James Church.
Daniels, John W. '36 (GRY) Retired.
Daniels, Joseph E. '90 (PRT) Northeast Harbor, ME St. Ignatius Church.
Daniels, Joseph F. '90 (PRT) Bar Harbor, ME Holy Redeemer Church.
Daniels, Lawrence *o.c.d.* '65 (MIL) [P] Milwaukee, WI Provincial Offices - Discalced Carmelites.
Daniels, Leo Francis *c.o.* (BWN) [I] Harlingen, TX KMBH-TV 60/KHID-FM 88.1/KMBH-FM 88.9.
Daniels, Leo Francis *c.o.* '65 (BWN) Pharr, TX St. Jude Thaddeus Church; [E] Pharr, TX Oratory of St. Philip Neri, of Pontifical Right.
Daniels, Paul A. '57 (MIL) [2] Menomonee Falls, WI Good Shepherd Church.
Danielsen, Thomas *c.ss.r.* '64 (TUC) [H] Tucson, AZ Redemptorist Picture Rocks Retreat.
Danielson, Charles R. '92 (BUR) Montpelier, VT St. Augustine Church.
Danielson, Daniel E. '63 (OAK) Pleasanton, CA St. Augustine Church.
Danik, Daniel A. '48 (NEW) Retired.
Danilak, John '61 (PSC) Retired.
Daniszewski, Msgr. Alfred '45 (MAN) [10] Manchester, NH St. Hedwig Church.
Daniszewski, Msgr. John D. '43 (E) Retired.
Danko, Michael S. '52 (LIN) Retired.
Danks, Arthur J. '43 (GB) Retired.
Danna, Msgr. Anthony S. '67 (BRK) [38] Brooklyn, NY St. Finbar's Church.
Danneker, David L. '82 (HBG) Palmyra, PA Holy Spirit Church.
Danneker, Edward A. '64 (ATL) Dahlonega, GA St. Luke Catholic Church; [L] Atlanta, GA Campus Ministry.
Dannenfelser, Lambert R. *o.f.m.* '40 (CIN) [P] Cincinnati, OH Friarhurst Retreat Center.
Danner, Brian '95 (SC) Fort Dodge, IA Corpus Christi Church.
Danner, James L. '74 (MEM) Military Chaplains.
Danner, Michael A. '65 (GR) On Special Assignment; [A] Grand Rapids, MI Christopher House-College Department of St. Joseph's Seminary.
Danos, Dean F. '80 (HT) Larose, LA Our Lady of the Rosary Church.
Danowski, Alexander J. '59 (PBL) Retired.
Danowski, Daniel G. '80 (CHI) Other Assignments.
Danquah, Anankwah '86 (BRK) [54] Brooklyn, NY Holy Family Church.
Dansak, Thomas E. '73 (PIT) Military Chaplains.
Dant, Nicholas J. '77 (IND) Graduate Studies.
Dante, Neal F. '64 (CAM) Westville Grove, NJ Most Holy Redeemer Church.
Danter, Albert F. '43 (STL) [O] St. Charles, MO St. Joseph Carmelite Home.
Dantinne, Gary J. '68 (GB) Little Suamico, WI St. Pius Church; Suamico, WI St. Benedict Church.
Danylo, Bohdan '96 (STF) [A] Stamford, CT St. Basil College.
Danyluk, Richard *ss.cc.* '75 (LA) San Dimas, CA Holy Name of Mary Church.
Dao, Anthony Chinh Quang *o.p.* '82 (GAL) [57] Houston, TX Our Lady of Lavang Church.
Dao, Ngo Van *c.ss.r.* '86 (LA) [R] Baldwin Park, CA Vietnamese Redemptorist Mission.
Daoust, Joseph P. *s.j.* '69 (DET) [K] Detroit, MI Jesuit Community at the University of Detroit.
DaPonte, Paul J. '93 (PRO) [7] Cranston, RI St. Paul Church.
Daprile, James '76 (Y) On Duty Outside the Diocese.
Daprile, James M. '76 (CIN) [B] Cincinnati, OH Mt. St. Mary's Seminary of the West.
Darbouze, Gerard '55 (MIA) [10] Miami, FL Notre Dame d'Haiti Church.
Darbouze, Msgr. Rollin J. '69 (BRK) [53] Brooklyn, NY Holy Cross Church.
Darby, Bernard M. '49 (CAM) Retired.
Darby, Thomas J. '47 (NY) Retired; [DD] New York, NY Pope John Paul II Residence.
Darcy, Brendan *s.m.a.* '67 (WDC) [M] Takoma Park, MD Society of African Missions (S.M.A.).
Darcy, David (SPR) [4] North Adams, MA Our Lady of Mercy Church; [P] Amherst, MA University of Massachusetts and Amherst College, Newman Center.
Darcy, David '94 (SPR) [2] North Adams, MA Notre Dame Church; [5] North Adams, MA Our Lady of Mercy Shrine Church.
Darcy, David M. '94 (SPR) [7] North Adams, MA St. Francis Church.
Darcy, James F. '66 (BO) Emergency Response Group.
Darcy, John J. '79 (PRO) East Greenwich, RI Our Lady of Mercy Church.
Dardis, Hugh A. '49 (NY) Wurtsboro, NY St. Joseph Church.
Dare, Glenn '74 (P) On Duty Outside the Archdiocese.
Dare, Glenn '74 (SAC) Auburn, CA St. Joseph Church.
Dargan, Peter S. '61 (HRT) Orange, CT Holy Infant Church.
Dargis, Andre E. *a.a.* '67 (WOR) [N] Worcester, MA Assumptionists (Augustinians of the Assumption).
Daries, Joseph *c.m.f.* '56 (LA) [R] Rancho Dominguez, CA Dominguez Seminary Inc.
Darilek, Dennis '73 (SAT) [60] San Antonio, TX St. Paul Church.
Darin, David M. '91 (BEL) New Athens, IL St. Agatha Church.
Darkowski, Msgr. Leon S. '43 (PIT) Retired.
Darling, Franklin (SPR) Retired.
Darling, George E. '84 (GR) Belding, MI St. Joseph's Church; Miriam, MI St. Mary's Church; On Special Assignment.
Darling, William G. '73 (ROC) [55] Rochester, NY St. Salome Church.
Darling, Willis F. *c.m.* '32 (STL) [P] Perryville, MO Congregation of The Mission.
Darnall, Thomas W. '52 (OKL) [17] Oklahoma City, OK Sacred Heart Church; Retired.
Darnell, Lawrence T. *o.m.v.* '82 (LA) Hawaiian Gardens, CA St. Peter Chanel Church.
Darnieder, Donald A. '55 (MIL) Retired.
Darow, Robert G. '63 (CHI) [78] Chicago, IL St. Hilary Church.
Darragh, John '68 (HEL) [1] Helena, MT Cathedral of St. Helena.
Das Neves, Antonio '61 (SB) Adelanto, CA Christ the Good Shepherd Church.
Dascenzo, Joseph J. '58 (PIT) Baden, PA St. John the Baptist Church.
Daschbach, Edwin G. *s.v.d.* '66 (WH) Glenville, WV Good Shepherd Church.
Daschbach, Richard *s.v.d.* '64 (FgM) Society of the Divine Word Foreign Missions.
Dash, Alan J. '67 (R) [2] Raleigh, NC Catholic Student Center, North Carolina State University Church; [H] Raleigh, NC Catholic Student Center.
Dash, George *o.f.m.cap.* (NY) State, NY St. Clare's Secure Unit.
Dash, George *o.f.m.cap.* '92 (NY) State, NY Taconic Correctional Facility; City, NY Anna M. Kross Center; [DD] White Plains, NY St. Conrad Friary.
Dash, George J. *o.f.m.cap.* '92 (NY) State, NY Bayview Correctional Facility.
DaSilva, Anthony '85 (NEW) Harrison, NJ Holy Cross Church.
DaSilva, Joseph '72 (B) [E] Boise, ID Nazareth.
daSilva, Marcos *c.s.* '88 (BO) [2] Somerville, MA St. Anthony Church.
Dasseville, Armand *o.f.m.cap.* (NY) [HH] New York, NY La Casa Sollievo Della Sofferenza Opera Di Padre Pio.
Dasseville, Armand *o.f.m.cap.* '49 (NY) [57] New York, NY St. John the Baptist Church.
Datko, James L. *o.m.i.* '51 (STP) [N] St. Paul, MN Oblate Residence.
Datko, Jerome *o.m.i.* '56 (DUL) Sandstone, MN St. Luke's Church.
Dattilo, Anthony M. '84 (CIN) [21] Dayton, OH Our Lady of the Rosary Church; [28] Dayton, OH St. Stephen Church.
Dattilo, Theophane *o.f.m.* '44 (DET) [5] Southfield, MI St. Michael Church.
Dattilo, Tony '90 (STL) [6] St. Charles, MO St. Robert Bellarmine Church.
Datty, Edward *s.a.* '49 (NY) [207] Staten Island, NY Immaculate Conception Church.
Datty, Edward J. *s.a.* (NY) Staten Island, NY Bayley Seton Hospital.
Datty, Edward J. *s.a.* '49 (NY) [W] New York, NY Bayley Seton Hospital.
Datzman, Harold L. *o.s.b.* '65 (PEO) Ladd, IL St. Benedict's Church; [A] Peru, IL St. Bede Abbey and Academy.
Daues, Mark J. *s.j.* '94 (KC) [J] Kansas City, MO Rockhurst High School - Jesuit Community.
Daues, Mark J. *s.j.* '95 (KC) [D] Kansas City, MO Rockhurst High School; [D] Kansas City, MO Rockhurst High School.
Daues, Vincent F. *s.j.* '48 (STL) [O] St. Louis, MO Fusz Pavilion.
Daugherty, Daniel L. '94 (TYL) Whitehouse, TX Prince of Peace Church.
Daugherty, Scott '83 (FRS) Porterville, CA St. Anne Church.
Daum, John J. '45 (Y) [6] Canton, OH St. Joan of Arc

Church; Retired.
Dauphinais, Gerard V. '70 (MAN) On Duty Outside the Diocese.
Dauphinais, Henry *m.s.* '55 (TUC) Tucson, AZ U.S. Veterans Hospital.
Dauphinais, Louis Marie *o.mar.* '70 (SAM) [C] Bethlehem, SD Holy Nativity Monastery; [C] Petersham, MA Most Holy Trinity Monastery.
Dauses, Jeffrey (BAL) Bel Air, MD St. Margaret Church.
Dauss, Francis '48 (SP) Retired.
Dautremont, Charles R. '60 (GR) [14] Grand Rapids, MI St. Dominic Church.
Davadilla, Patrick Joel *s.v.d.* '88 (FRS) [7] Fresno, CA St. Anthony of Padua Church.
Davalos, Carlos '78 (SAT) Pleasanton, TX St. Andrew Church.
Davantes, Charles B. '79 (TR) [17] Trenton, NJ St. Joachim Church.
Davanzo, Joseph V. '97 (RVC) Huntington Station, NY St. Hugh of Lincoln Church.
Davenport, Bernard '74 (WOR) Webster, MA St. Louis Church.
Davenport, Christopher M. '61 (PRO) [7] Pawtucket, RI St. Leo the Great Church.
Davenport, Clement A. '48 (SFR) [3] Menlo Park, CA The Church of the Nativity.
Davenport, Thomas J. (SFD) [K] Springfield, IL Priests' Retirement Facility.
Davenport, Thomas J. '42 (SFD) Retired.
Davern, Raymond J. '58 (KCK) [3] Kansas City, KS Christ the King Church.
Davern, Msgr. Robert B. '51 (SY) Syracuse, NY Van Duyn Home & Hospital; Special Assignment; [S] Syracuse, NY St. Pius X Home, Inc.
Davern, Timothy '78 (PHX) [2] Tempe, AZ Our Lady of Mt. Carmel Church.
Davern, Timothy R. '78 (PHX) [2] Tempe, AZ Our Lady of Mt. Carmel Church.
Davey, Edward M. '53 (PAT) Newton, NJ St. Joseph's Church.
Davey, Philip *o.s.b.* '65 (PEO) [C] Peru, IL St. Bede Academy.
Davey, Philip D. *o.s.b.* '75 (PEO) [A] Peru, IL St. Bede Abbey and Academy.
Davey, Robert W. '62 (SAG) Bridgeport, MI St. Christopher Church.
Davia, Liam '67 (B) Leave of Absence.
Davich, George F. '62 (SLC) [10] Salt Lake City, UT St. Vincent de Paul Church.
David, Christopher J. '97 (DAV) [2] Davenport, IA Our Lady of Victory Church.
David, Craig '96 (ATL) Lilburn, GA St. John Neumann Church.
David, George '71 (ROM) Roebling, NJ St. Mary Church; Trenton, NJ St. Basil Church.
David, Jose '80 (CHK) Saipan, MP San Jude Parish.
David, Joseph '93 (SAM) New Castle, PA St. John the Baptist Church.
Davidowich, Glenn M. '89 (PSC) Trumbull, CT St. John the Baptist Church.
Davids, John J. '76 (PH) Doylestown, PA Our Lady of Mount Carmel Church.
Davidson, Carl J. '64 (NO) [A] New Orleans, LA Notre Dame Seminary Graduate School of Theology.
Davidson, John '64 (EVN) [13] Evansville, IN St. Anthony Church.
Davidson, William '51 (DET) Retired.
Davidson, William B. '51 (DET) [3] Troy, MI St. Anastasia Church.
Davied, Frank L. *o.f.m.* '76 (PBL) Aguilar, CO St. Anthony Church; Gardner, CO Sacred Heart Church; Walsenburg, CO St. Mary Church.
Davies, Brian *o.p.* '82 (NY) [DD] New York, NY Jesuit Community at Fordham University.
Davies, Daniel T. *o.p.* '58 (NY) Hawthorne, NY Holy Rosary Church.
Davies, Julian A. *o.f.m.* '60 (ALB) [B] Loudonville, NY Siena College.
Davies, Steven E. '77 (SFR) [52] San Francisco, CA St. Thomas More Church; San Francisco, CA Kaiser Hospital San Francisco; Special Assignment; [S] San Francisco, CA Newman Center, San Francisco State University.
Davignon, Charles P. '56 (BUR) Essex Junction, VT Holy Family Church.
Davignon, Philip A. '62 (FR) Raynham, MA St. Ann Church.
Davila, Andres (ARE) On Duty Outside the Diocese.
Davila, Johnny '84 (SAT) On Leave.
Davila, Rafael R. *m.m.* '58 (GAL) [Q] Houston, TX Maryknoll Fathers and Brothers.
Davila, Reinaldo *o.f.m.* '90 (SFE) Albuquerque, NM Presbyterian Hospital; Albuquerque, NM University Hospital.
Davin, Neil *c.p.* '52 (BRK) [U] Jamaica, NY Immaculate Conception Monastery.
Davin, Neil W. *c.p.* '52 (MET) Edison, NJ St. Matthew Church; [H] South River, NJ Passionist Provincial Office.
Davin, William *c.p.* '56 (WH) Kingwood, WV St. Sebastian's Church; Masontown, WV St. Zita's Church.
Davino, Louis *o.f.m.* '72 (JOL) [11] Joliet, IL St. John the Baptist Church; [J] Joliet, IL St. John the Baptist Friary.
Davino, Michael J. '86 (CHR) [4] Charleston, SC Sacred Heart Church; [16] Charleston, SC Christ the Divine Teacher Church; [G] Charleston, SC The Citadel.
Davis, Alexander *o.f.m.cap.* '64 (NEW) [4] Orange, NJ Mt. Carmel Church; East Orange, NJ Veterans Administration Hospital.
Davis, Augustine *o.s.b.* '59 (IND) [J] St. Meinrad, IN St. Meinrad Archabbey.
Davis, Charles '67 (AUS) Cyclone, TX St. Joseph's Church.
Davis, Charles J. (CAM) On Duty Outside the Diocese.
Davis, Christopher *o.s.b.* (FWT) [M] Wichita Falls, TX Catholic Campus Ministry.
Davis, Christopher *o.s.b.* '58 (PRO) [P] Portsmouth, RI Abbey of St. Gregory the Great.
Davis, Clement T. '70 (IND) Columbus, IN St. Bartholomew Church.
Davis, Clyde F. *m.m.* '63 (SJ) [M] Los Altos, CA Maryknoll.
Davis, Cyprian *o.s.b.* '56 (IND) [A] St. Meinrad, IN St. Meinrad Seminary; [J] St. Meinrad, IN St. Meinrad Archabbey.
Davis, Daniel *o.p.* (CHI) [N] Oak Park, IL Dominican Community of St. Martin de Porres.
Davis, Daniel C. *o.p.* '94 (CHI) [D] Oak Park, IL Fenwick High School.
Davis, David J. '97 (LIN) [1] Lincoln, NE Cathedral of the Risen Christ.
Davis, Edward J. '49 (NOR) Retired.
Davis, Edward V. *m.m.* '61 (NY) [DD] Maryknoll, NY Maryknoll Fathers and Brothers.
Davis, Eugene V. '35 (TR) Retired; [M] Trenton, NJ Villa Vianney.
Davis, F. Hampton '90 (NO) [A] New Orleans, LA Notre Dame Seminary Graduate School of Theology.
Davis, Francis R. '45 (ROC) Corning, NY St. Mary Church; Retired.
Davis, Gary G. '75 (L) [11] Louisville, KY St. Barnabas Church.
Davis, Henry J. *s.s.j.* '93 (NO) [57] New Orleans, LA St. Raymond Church.
Davis, James J. *o.p.* '53 (PRO) [P] Providence, RI St. Thomas Aquinas Priory at Providence College.
Davis, John E. '69 (FAR) On Duty Outside the Diocese.
Davis, John E. '69 (FgM) Society of St. James the Apostle.
Davis, John P. '63 (PRT) Retired.
Davis, Joseph E. '76 (PRO) [6] Cumberland, RI St. Patrick Church.
Davis, Joseph P. '72 (PAT) Succasunna, NJ St. Therese Church.
Davis, Kenneth *o.f.m.conv.* (CHI) [A] Mundelein, IL University of St. Mary of the Lake-Mundelein Seminary.
Davis, Leo Donald *s.j.* '64 (P) [L] Portland, OR Jesuit Provincial Office (Society of Jesus, Oregon Prov.).
Davis, Mark E. '96 (TOL) Sandusky, OH SS. Peter and Paul Church.
Davis, Michael '87 (PH) West Chester, PA SS. Simon and Jude Church.
Davis, Michael '90 (MIA) [A] Miami, FL St. John Vianney College Seminary.
Davis, Noel (CC) [6] Laredo, TX San Augustin Church.
Davis, Raymond '84 (JOL) Bensenville, IL St. Alexis Church; Retired.
Davis, Richard *t.o.r.* '80 (STU) [A] Steubenville, OH Franciscan University of Steubenville; [F] Steubenville, OH Holy Spirit Monastery.
Davis, Richard P. '63 (LR) Adona, AR St. Elizabeth's Church; Bigelow, AR St. Boniface's Church.
Davis, Robert '51 (ROC) Retired.
Davis, Robert '97 (FRS) [6] Bakersfield, CA St. Philip the Apostle Church.
Davis, Royden B. *s.j.* '59 (SCR) [C] Scranton, PA University of Scranton.
Davis, Terrence '69 (SJ) [3] Santa Clara, CA St. Justin Church.
Davis, Thomas A. '68 (CC) [15] Laredo, TX St. Patrick Church.
Davis, Thomas E. '49 (NEW) Retired.
Davis, Thomas R. '83 (R) Fayetteville, NC St. Ann Church.
Davis, W. E. *o.s.f.s.* '82 (PH) [AA] Philadelphia, PA Oblates of St. Francis De Sales.
Davis, Msgr. Wilbur '64 (ORG) [2] Anaheim, CA St. Boniface Church.
Davis, William *o.m.i.* (AUS) [H] Austin, TX Brothers of the Congregation of the Holy Cross.
Davis, William *ss.cc.* '44 (FR) [J] Fairhaven, MA Sacred Hearts Provincial House.
Davis, William *o.m.i.* '57 (GAL) [38] Houston, TX Immaculate Heart of Mary Church.
Davis, William E. *o.s.f.s.* '84 (PH) [D] Philadelphia, PA Northeast Catholic High School for Boys.
Davis, Msgr. William F. '56 (MEM) Retired.
Davis, William F. *o.s.f.s.* '61 (WDC) [B] Washington, DC Oblates of St. Francis de Sales.
Davis, William J. '43 (BRK) Retired.
Davis, William T. '43 (BRK) [215] Queens, NY Our Lady of the Miraculous Medal Church.
Davish, William M. *s.j.* '46 (BAL) [B] Baltimore, MD Loyola College; [M] Baltimore, MD Jesuit Community of Loyola College, Inc.
Davison, Timothy L. '85 (TLS) [7] Tulsa, OK St. Francis Xavier-Our Lady of Guadalupe Church.
Davitt, James P. '55 (CHI) [4] Lemont, IL St. James at Sag Bridge Church; Retired.
DaVola, F. Robert '67 (BWN) [4] Mission, TX St. Paul Church.
Davoren, Stephen V. '96 (LA) Downey, CA St. Raymond Church.
Daw, Timothy M. '91 (CLV) [33] Cleveland, OH St. Ignatius Church.
Dawber, Stephen F. *s.j.* '69 (BO) [E] Boston, MA Boston College High School & Jesuit Community.
Dawes, Timothy '86 (PIT) Coraopolis, PA St. Joseph Church.
Dawidziak, Stanley J. (BUF) Retired.
Dawis, Ralph '54 (NY) Staten Island, NY St. Vincent's Medical Center of Richmond; [W] New York, NY Saint Vincent's Medical Center of Richmond.
Daws, Dominic '55 (B) Retired.
Dawson, Cletus *c.p.* '43 (BRK) [U] Jamaica, NY Immaculate Conception Monastery.
Dawson, George *c.ss.r.* '50 (B) Coeur D'Alene, ID St. Thomas Church.
Dawson, Msgr. James D. '54 (LIN) [1] Lincoln, NE Cathedral of the Risen Christ.
Dawson, John H. '67 (LA) Sick Leave.
Dawson, Msgr. Joseph '51 (STA) Retired.
Dawson, Joseph I. '62 (L) Calvary, KY Holy Name of Mary Church.
Dawson, Richard E. '81 (PT) Cantonment, FL St. Jude Thaddeus Church.
Dawson, William F. '54 (DAV) [B] Davenport, IA St. Ambrose University.
Dawson-Amoah, Jude *o.p.* '87 (HBG) Chambersburg, PA Corpus Christi Church.
Day, Charles J. '81 (CHR) Greenville, SC Our Lady of the Rosary Church.
Day, Dennis '76 (B) Priest River, ID St. Catherine's Church.
Day, Dennis C. '76 (B) Sandpoint, ID St. Joseph's Church.
Day, Edward E. '52 (BWN) Raymondville, TX St. Anthony Church.
Day, James R. *o.ss.t.* '72 (PH) Bristol, PA St. Ann Church.
Day, James Richard '96 (NO) [13] Metairie, LA St. Philip Neri Church.
Day, Jerome J. *o.s.b.* '95 (MAN) [K] Manchester, NH St. Anselm Abbey.
Day, Msgr. John D. '39 (BO) [52] Boston, MA Most Precious Blood Church; Retired.
Day, John P. *c.p.* '72 (STL) Ste. Genevieve, MO Ste. Genevieve's Church.
Day, L. Dudley *o.s.a.* '53 (CHI) [X] Chicago, IL The Institute on Religious Life.
Day, Lenox C. *s.j.* '63 (SJ) Santa Clara, CA Santa Clara Valley Medical Center; [D] San Jose, CA Bellarmine College Preparatory.
Day, Martin *o.f.m.conv.* '91 (IND) [4] Terre Haute, IN St. Joseph Church.
Day, Rick (NO) [D] Metairie, LA Archbishop Chapelle High School.
Day, Wilfred E. '67 (IND) New Albany, IN Holy Family Church.
Day, William '86 (GLP) Milan, NM St. Vivian Church; San Mateo, NM San Mateo Church; San Rafael, NM San Rafael Church.
Daya, John *o.f.m.cap.* '78 (HBG) [2] York, PA St. Joseph Church.
Daz, Rudolph A. '54 (SLC) Bountiful, UT St. Olaf Church.
De Adder, James W. '55 (BO) [A] Weston, MA Pope John XXIII National Seminary.
De Agostini, Claudio *c.s.j.* '58 (LA) San Pedro, CA St. Peter Church.
De Angelis, Mark '88 (BO) [1] Revere, MA St. Anthony of Padua Church.
De Angelis, Sante *o.f.m.* '62 (MIL) [P] Burlington, WI Queen of Peace Friary; [Y] Waterford, WI General Secretariat of the Franciscan Missions, Inc.
de Armas, Alexio *o.c.d.* '58 (PCE) [12] Ponce, PR San Jose Church.
de Armas, Alexio Jose *o.c.d.* '58 (PCE) [B] Ponce, PR The Pontifical Catholic University of Puerto Rico.
de Avila, Raphael (SFR) [1] South San Francisco, CA All Souls Church.
de Azevedo, Antonio Carvalho '62 (BGP) [2] Danbury, CT Immaculate Heart of Mary Church.
de Blas, Alonso *o.f.m.* '64 (PHX) [G] Scottsdale, AZ Franciscan Renewal Center, Inc. (Casa de Paz Y Bien).
De Brito Alves, Joseph '67 (BGP) [15] Bridgeport, CT Our Lady of Fatima Church.
De Caprio, John '49 (ALB) Retired.

De Carlo, Philip J. '55 (PIT) Monaca, PA St. John the Baptist Church.
De Celles, John C. '96 (ARL) [1] Alexandria, VA Blessed Sacrament Church.
De Clercq, Victor .*c.i.c.m.* '37 (FgM) Missionhurst Foreign Missions.
De Clerk, Msgr. Rainer J. '34 (LR) Retired.
De Conciliis, Anthony (WDC) [B] Washington, DC Washington Theological Union.
De Costa, George '64 (HON) Keaukaha, Hilo, HI Malia Puka'O Kalani (Mary Gate of Heaven) Church.
de Cristobal, Fernando (GRY) [12] East Chicago, IN St. Patrick Church.
de Dios, Francisco Mendez '60 (ARL) [4] Arlington, VA St. Charles Borromeo Church.
De Dominici, Lorenzo '46 (LA) San Pedro, CA Mary, Star of the Sea Church.
De Folco, Joseph A. '85 (SEA) Bellingham, WA Assumption B.V.M. Church; Bellingham, WA Sacred Heart Church.
De Francisco, Joseph '75 (DAV) [B] Davenport, IA St. Ambrose University.
De Ganck, Roger *o.c.s.o.* '35 (SR) [N] Whitethorn, CA Our Lady of the Redwoods Abbey.
De Garis, Herbert P. '91 (NY) Garnerville, NY St. Gregory Barbarigo Church.
De Groot, Ambrose '45 (GB) [I] Appleton, WI St. Fidelis Friary.
De Guzman, Dennis (OM) [B] Hartington, NE Cedar Catholic High School.
de Herrera, Christopher *o.s.* '97 (PCE) [11] Ponce, PR San Jose Obrero Church.
De Hondt, Ronald '73 (DET) [A] Detroit, MI Sacred Heart Major Seminary, Inc.
de Jesus, Carmelo *o.c.d.* '47 (PCE) [B] Ponce, PR The Pontifical Catholic University of Puerto Rico.
de Jesus, Hector Bruno (WDC) Riverdale, MD St. Bernard Church.
de Jesus, Msgr. Herminio '69 (PCE) Juana Diaz, PR Nuestra Senora de Lourdes Church; [B] Ponce, PR The Pontifical Catholic University of Puerto Rico.
de Jesus, Rafael Alvarado '94 (PCE) Patillas, PR Inmaculado Corazon de Maria Church; [B] Ponce, PR The Pontifical Catholic University of Puerto Rico.
de la Calle, Juan '54 (PMB) Indiantown, FL Holy Cross Church.
de la Cruz, Carlos E. *s.j.* '75 (FgM) Provinces.
De La Cruz, Jenaro *o.c.d.* '66 (OKL) [14] Oklahoma City, OK Our Lady of Mount Carmel and St. Therese Little Flower Church.
de la Cruz, Juan '57 (ATL) [1] Marietta, GA Holy Family Church.
de la Cruz, Luis Maria *s.e.m.v.* '81 (ARE) Hatillo, PR Our Lady of Guadalupe Church.
de la Cruz, Ven *c.i.c.m.* '94 (FgM) Missionhurst Foreign Missions.
De La Garza, Joseph G. '51 (SAT) Stonewall, TX St. Francis Xavier Church.
de la Iglesia, Celestino *c.m.f.* '31 (LA) [R] Rancho Dominguez, CA Dominguez Seminary Inc.
De La Pena, Richard (NY) Castle Point, NY Veterans Administration Medical Center.
De La Pena, Rick (NY) Fishkill, NY Church of St. Mary, Mother of the Church.
De La Pinera, Fernando '51 (NO) Retired.
de la Puebla, Tomas *c.m.* '49 (MGZ) [8] Mayaquez, PR San Vicente Church.
De La Rosa, Jose Luis '84 (SAT) [68] San Antonio, TX St. Vincent de Paul Church.
De La Rosa, Vincent '55 (SAT) On Leave.
de la Rosa Peguero, Frank '78 (SJN) [21] Carolina, PR San Francisco de Asis Church.
de la Torre, Bartholomew *o.p.* '67 (LA) [C] Santa Paula, CA Thomas Aquinas College.
de la Vega, Francis *o.a.r.* '43 (LA) [4] Oxnard, CA Mary Star of the Sea Church.
de Laire, Georges F. '97 (MAN) [7] Nashua, NH St. Joseph Church.
De LaTorre, Oscar *s.x.* '87 (FgM) Xaverian Foreign Missions.
De Laura, Felice J. '63 (BRK) [245] Queens, NY St. Thomas Apostle Church.
De Lazzer, Dorino '59 (DEN) [2] Aurora, CO St. Michael the Archangel Church.
de Leis, Sean *c.s.sp.* '81 (PMB) Fort Pierce, FL St. Mark Church.
De Leon, Jose A. '81 (CGS) Las Piedras, PR Inmaculada Concepcion Church.
De Leon, Juancho '94 (NEW) Lyndhurst, NJ Sacred Heart Church.
De Leon, Michael *o.s.b.* '86 (CC) [G] Sandia, TX Benedictine Retreat Center.
De Leon, Michael *o.s.b.* '95 (CC) [H] Sandia, TX Corpus Christi Abbey.
de Leon, Robert E. *c.s.c* '85 (BGP) [O] Bridgeport, CT Provincial Offices of the Priests and Brothers of Holy Cross, Eastern Province.
De Leonardis, Gerard *o.f.m.cap.* '49 (NY) [B] Beacon, NY St. Lawrence of Brindisi Friary.
De Lillio, Richard R. *o.s.f.s.* '66 (WIL) [I] Wilmington, DE Oblates of St. Francis De Sales.
de Llano, Domingo '66 (CC) [9] Laredo, TX San Martin De Porres Church.
de los Reyes, Joel '75 (AGN) Barrigada, GU San Vicente Ferrer Church.
de Loza, Jose *s.s.p.* '87 (YAK) Toppenish, WA St. Aloysius Church.
De Lucia, Vincent *o.p.* '94 (PRO) [P] Providence, RI St. Thomas Aquinas Priory at Providence College.
de M. Pereira, Luciano J. '54 (FR) Somerset, MA St. John of God Church.
De Man, Thomas *o.p.* '62 (SEA) [P] Seattle, WA Office of Campus and Young Adult Ministry; [P] Seattle, WA Office of Campus and Young Adult Ministry.
De Martini, Rodney *s.m.* (SJ) [M] Cupertino, CA Marianist Provincial Residence.
De Mayo, John B. '61 (PH) Penn Valley, PA St. Justin Martyr Church.
De Meersman, Clement *c.i.c.m.* '52 (SAT) Devine, TX St. Joseph's Church.
de Mello, Arthur T. '34 (FR) Absent on Sick Leave.
de Mentque, Edouard *f.s.s.p.* '97 (SCR) [M] Elmhurst, PA Priestly Fraternity of St. Peter (F.S.S.P.), North American District Headquarters.
De Mesa, Juan Perez '94 (NEW) [3] Jersey City, NJ St. Anne's Church.
de Miguel, Juan Pascual '57 (VEN) Arcadia, FL St. Paul Church.
de Morchoven, Werner Papeians *o.s.b.* '38 (LA) [R] Valyermo, CA St. Andrew's Abbey.
De Nard, Silvio *s.c.* '79 (PH) [B] Springfield, PA Don Guanella House of Formation.
De Noble, Augustine *o.s.b.* '55 (P) [L] St. Benedict, OR Mt. Angel Abbey.
De Pasquale, Daniel '61 (ALB) Retired.
De Paula, Aderbal T. '83 (NY) [19] Yonkers, NY Our Lady of Fatima Church.
De Peaux, Rowland C. *o.praem.* '51 (GB) [I] De Pere, WI St. Joseph Priory.
de Ranitz, Richard *o.p.* '70 (CHI) [N] Chicago, IL Dominicans (Provincial Office).
de Rivera, Crescente *s.v.d.* '81 (CHI) [N] Techny, IL Society of the Divine Word, Provincial Headquarter-Chicago Prov.
De Rosa, Arnold P. '63 (NEW) [B] South Orange, NJ Seton Hall University.
de Rossi, G. B. '46 (CLV) [P] Cleveland, OH Congregation of the Blessed Sacrament Provincial House.
De Russy, Edward *s.j.* '57 (SP) Crystal River, FL St. Benedict Church.
De Sanctis, Peter '79 (BRK) [208] Queens, NY Our Lady of the Cenacle Church.
De Santi, Bruno *c.s.j.* '51 (LA) San Pedro, CA St. Peter Church.
De Santis, Linus *o.f.m.conv.* '71 (ATL) [L] Atlanta, GA Campus Ministry.
de Serpa, Roberto '46 (PRO) Retired.
de Silva, Lionel A. *c.s.p.* '59 (NY) [41] New York, NY Good Shepherd Church.
De Simonc, David A. (NY) Port Jervis, NY Most Sacred Heart Church.
De Simone, Bartholomew *o.f.m.* '44 (NY) [DD] New York, NY Franciscan Province of the Immaculate Conception.
De Souza, Carl '66 (RIC) Franklin, VA St. Jude Church.
de Souza, Owen '70 (LA) Carson, CA St. Philomena Church.
De Tomasi, Gerardo *m.c.c.j.* '68 (LA) [55] Los Angeles, CA St. Cecilia Church.
De Tommaso, Louis *o.f.m.* '54 (NY) [DD] New York, NY Franciscan Province of the Immaculate Conception.
De Uries, James (MET) [F] New Brunswick, NJ St. Peter's Medical Center.
de Verteuil, Jack '89 (FBK) Healy, AK Holy Mary of Guadalupe Church.
de Vianney Guerra, Jesus *o.p.* '57 (NO) [P] New Orleans, LA Dominican Fathers & Brothers, Southern Dominican Province.
De Vita, James C. '57 (RVC) Retired.
de Water, Joseph M. '67 (NO) [12] New Orleans, LA Immaculate Heart Of Mary Church.
Deaconson, James '85 (VIC) Vanderbilt, TX St. John Bosco Church.
DeAdder, James W. (BO) Retired.
DeAguilar, J. Arturo '97 (CHL) Asheville, NC Basilica of St. Lawrence Church.
DeAmato, Norbert *o.f.m.* '48 (BO) [3] Cambridge, MA St. Francis of Assisi Church.
Dean, Alfred A. *s.s.j.* (MOB) [18] Mobile, AL Prince of Peace Church.
Dean, Frederic D. '65 (PRO) [2] Woonsocket, RI St. Aloysius Church.
Dean, Harry, Jr. '96 (AUS) [14] Austin, TX St. John Neumann Church.
Dean, James N. '91 (MOB) Auburn, AL St. Michael Church; [K] Auburn, AL Auburn University Newman Center.
Dean, John T. '72 (SPR) [5] Westfield, MA St. Peter's Church; [P] Amherst, MA University of Massachusetts and Amherst College, Newman Center.
Dean, Joseph *glmy.* '45 (CIN) [M] Fairfield, OH Headquarters of Glenmary Home Missioners.
Dean, Joseph *glmy.* '45 (TLS) Idabel, OK St. Francis De Sales Church.
Dean, Joseph '74 (GAL) [K] Houston, TX The Catholic Chaplain Corps.
Dean, Joseph *s.c.j.* '84 (GB) [M] Baileys Harbor, WI St. Joseph Retreat Center.
Dean, Walter R. *o.s.f.s.* '49 (WIL) [I] Wilmington, DE Oblates of St. Francis De Sales.
Dean, William E. '76 (PH) [144] Philadelphia, PA Sacred Heart of Jesus Church.
DeAndrea, Msgr. Joseph A. '53 (GBG) On Duty Outside the Diocese.
Deane, Declan (OAK) Moraga, CA St. Monica Church.
Deane, Declan *s.j.* '72 (OAK) [N] Berkeley, CA Jesuit Community at Jesuit School of Theology at Berkeley.
Deane, Edwin *o.f.m.* '44 (HT) [4] Houma, LA Our Lady of the Most Holy Rosary Church.
Deane, Gregory S. '54 (CC) Port Aransas, TX St. Joseph Church.
Deane, J. Peter *s.j.* '66 (TOL) [K] Toledo, OH St. Mary's Jesuit Community.
Deane, Msgr. Joseph '59 (SAT) [32] San Antonio, TX St. Cecilia Church.
DeAngelis, Antonio *c.s.* '81 (SJ) [7] San Jose, CA Holy Cross Church.
DeAngelis, William *o.s.b.* '50 (CC) Retired; [H] Sandia, TX Corpus Christi Abbey.
DeAngelo, Jude *o.f.m.conv.* '84 (ALB) [L] Rensselaer, NY Provincialate, Immaculate Conception Friary - Order of Friars Minor Conventual.
DeAngelo, Jude *o.f.m.conv.* '84 (CHL) [L] Charlotte, NC Diocesan Office of Campus Ministry.
DeAnta, Carlos *o.m.i.* '50 (FgM) Oblates Foreign Missions.
DeAntoniis, Paul J. *o.praem.* '63 (WIL) [B] Claymont, DE Archmere Academy; [I] Claymont, DE Immaculate Conception Priory of the Canons Regular of Premontre.
DeAntonio, Michael R. '71 (CHR) Spartanburg, SC St. Paul the Apostle Church; Spartanburg, SC St. Joseph's Church; [G] Spartanburg, SC Converse College, Wofford College, Spartanburg Methodist College Newman Center.
Dear, John S. *s.j.* '93 (BAL) [M] Baltimore, MD Jesuit Fathers and Brothers Maryland Provincial Curia.
Deardorff, Joseph F. *c.pp.s.* '82 (CIN) [M] Dayton, OH Provincial House of the Cincinnati Province of the Society of the Precious Blood.
Dearhammer, John '91 (CHI) [A] Mundelein, IL University of St. Mary of the Lake-Mundelein Seminary.
Dearhammer, John W. '91 (CHI) Other Assignments.
Dearing, Arnold *o.f.m.conv.* '51 (IND) Clarksville, IN St. Anthony of Padua Church.
Deary, John F. *o.s.a.* '66 (VEN) Cape Coral, FL Blessed Katharine Drexel Church.
Deas, Msgr. George T. (BRK) [U] Douglaston, NY Bishop Mugavero Residence.
Deas, Msgr. George T. '51 (BRK) Retired.
Dease, Dennis J. '69 (STP) [C] St. Paul, MN University of St. Thomas.
Deasio, August J. '75 (STU) Retired.
Deasy, Edward '62 (ALX) Retired.
Deasy, Jerry '67 (BIR) [21] Birmingham, AL Prince of Peace Church.
Deasy, Ken '87 (LA) [37] Los Angeles, CA St. Agatha Church.
Deasy, Msgr. Timothy '58 (MOB) Daphne, AL Christ the King Church.
Deasy, Wayman P. *m.m.* '59 (NY) [DD] Maryknoll, NY Maryknoll Fathers and Brothers.
Deatrick, John D. '66 (L) [50] Louisville, KY St. Martha Church.
Deaver, Stephen F. '59 (GI) Mitchell, NE St. Theresa's Church.
DeBacker, Thomas '54 (OM) Pierce, NE St. Joseph Church.
Debaenst, Emmanuel '34 (SFE) Retired.
Debany, Edgar J. *s.j.* '84 (BAL) [M] Baltimore, MD Jesuit Fathers and Brothers Maryland Provincial Curia.
Debany, Edgar J. *s.j.* '84 (FgM) Provinces.
DeBellis, John A. '85 (NY) [219] Staten Island, NY Our Lady, Queen of Peace Church.
DeBellis, Peter M. '97 (ROC) Newark, NY St. Michael Church.
DeBenedetto, David J. '94 (BR) On Leave.
DeBenedictis, Salvatore *o.f.m.* '44 (NY) [DD] New York, NY Franciscan Province of the Immaculate Conception.
DeBiase, William *o.f.m.* '65 (FgM) Franciscan Foreign Missions.
DeBiase, William *o.f.m.* '66 (ALB) [B] Loudonville, NY Siena College.
Debicki, John P. '64 (CHI) [127] Chicago, IL St. Mary of the Angels Church.
DeBisschop, James P. '88 (PEO) Rapids City, IL St. John the Baptist Church.
Debitetto, Ronald E. '63 (WOR) Retired.
DeBlanc, Msgr. Irving A. '38 (LKC) [8] Lake Charles, LA Our Lady Queen of Heaven Church; Retired; [E] Lake Charles, LA Our Lady Queen of Heaven Manor.

DeBlanc, Jefferson J. '77 (LAF) Henderson, LA Our Lady of Mercy Church.
DeBlase, Dominic *s.d.b.* '61 (FgM) Salesians of Don Bosco Foreign Missions.
Deblasio, Dominck A. '40 (PIT) Retired.
Deblasio, Ernie '88 (MEM) [8] Memphis, TN St. Francis of Assisi Church.
Debo, Peter (PIT) [2] Swissvale, PA Word of God Church.
Debo, William D. '95 (JC) Columbia, MO Our Lady of Lourdes Church; Columbia, MO University Hospital & Clinics.
DeBock, William A. '49 (MAD) East Bristol, WI St. Joseph Church.
DeBoe, Stanley W. *o.ss.t.* '83 (BAL) Jessup, MD St. Lawrence Church.
Debold, Walter A. '42 (NEW) Retired; [B] South Orange, NJ Seton Hall University.
DeBona, Guerric *o.s.b.* '86 (IND) [B] St. Meinrad, IN St. Meinrad Seminary-College of Liberal Arts; [J] St. Meinrad, IN St. Meinrad Archabbey.
DeBruin, Edward *s.d.s.* '53 (MIL) [P] Milwaukee, WI Salvatorians - Jordan Hall.
DeBruycker, James '82 (STP) [30] Minneapolis, MN St. Leonard of Port Maurice Church.
DeBruycker, James R. '82 (STP) Minneapolis, MN Hennepin County Medical Center.
Debski, Joseph E. '64 (MIL) Delavan, WI St. Andrew Church.
Decal, Wilfredo G. '77 (HT) [6] Houma, LA St. Gregory Barbarigo Church.
DeCarlo, Thomas M. '69 (DM) [E] Johnston, IA Bishop Drumm Retirement Center.
DeCarolis, Joseph R. '59 (HRT) Prospect, CT St. Anthony's Church.
DeCarolis, Vito C. '54 (HRT) [4] Milford, CT St. Mary's Church.
Decell, Stephen '87 (HT) On Leave.
Decewicz, Michael W. '78 (PIT) Monroeville, PA St. Bernadette Church.
Dechant, Leo *c.s.j.* '80 (CLV) [D] Lorain, OH Lorain Catholic High School; [P] Avon, OH Congregation of St. Joseph.
Dechant, Paul *c.s.p.* '90 (MEM) [20] Memphis, TN St. Patrick's Church; [M] Memphis, TN St. Patrick's Center.
Dechant, Paul *c.s.p.* '91 (MEM) [J] Memphis, TN Paulist Fathers (New York).
Dechering, Anton '62 (SP) [2] St. Petersburg, FL Blessed Trinity Church.
DeChico, Philip '74 (HBG) [2] Harrisburg, PA St. Catherine Laboure Church.
DeCicco, Pascal A. *o.s.a.* '52 (PH) [18] Philadelphia, PA St. Augustine Church.
Deck, Alcuin *o.s.b.* '39 (RCK) [H] Aurora, IL Marmion Abbey-St. Augustine's Abbey.
Deck, Allan F. *s.j.* '76 (LA) [R] Los Angeles, CA Columbiere House.
Deck, Marion *t.o.r.* '69 (ARL) [J] Winchester, VA Sacred Heart Friary.
Decker, Douglas '78 (OG) Adams, NY St. Cecilia Church.
Decker, James D. '85 (MAN) Military Chaplains.
Decker, Lawrence J. '84 (ALB) [3] Amsterdam, NY St. Joseph-St. Michael-Our Lady of Mount Carmel Church.
Decker, Maurice C. '50 (DET) Retired.
Decker, Neil F. *s.j.* '58 (BO) [W] Chestnut Hill, MA The Jesuit Community at Boston College.
Decker, Raymond G. '58 (SFR) Retired.
Decker, Robert L. '83 (OG) Long Lake, NY St. Henry Church; Newcomb, NY St. Therese Church.
Decker, William Jonathan '76 (OLL) Portland, OR Saint Sharbel Church; Portland, OR Saint Sharbel Church.
Deckman, Peter '64 (ROC) Penn Yan, NY St. Michael Church; [M] Rochester, NY Diocesan Office of Campus Ministry; [M] Penn Yan, NY St. Michael's Church.
DeClerk, Msgr. Rainer '34 (LR) [H] Little Rock, AR St. John Manor.
DeClippel, Ludo *c.j.* '68 (LA) [1] Santa Barbara, CA Holy Cross Church.
DeCneudt, Msgr. Ferdinand '39 (DET) Retired.
Decock, Robert *isch.* (CC) [J] Corpus Christi, TX Secular Institute of the Schoenstatt Fathers aka Schoenstatt Fathers.
DeCock, Robert *i.s.s.s.* '96 (CC) [14] Corpus Christi, TX SS. Cyril and Methodius Church.
DeCock, Robert *c.c.* '96 (MIL) [T] Waukesha, WI Secular Institute of Schoenstatt Fathers.
DeCola, Vincent *s.j.* (FgM) Jesuit Volunteers: International(S.J.).
DeCola, Vincent P. *s.j.* '88 (FgM) Provinces.
DeCola, Vincent P., S.J. '88 (WDC) [M] Washington, DC K Street Jesuit Community.
DeConciliis, Anthony J. *c.s.c.* '67 (FR) [A] North Easton, MA Stonehill College.
DeCondorpusa, Alfonso '95 (NEW) [1] Hackensack, NJ Holy Trinity Church.
DeCosta, George D. '64 (HON) Papaaloa, HI St. Anthony Church.
DeCosta, Joseph '90 (NOR) New London, CT St. Joseph Church.
DeCosta, Joseph F. '90 (NOR) Rockville, CT St. Bernard Church.
Decoteau, Joseph A. *m.s.* '40 (LKC) [2] Sulphur, LA Our Lady of LaSalette Church.
Decoteau, Vernon '75 (SPR) Belchertown, MA St. Francis of Assisi Church.
Decowski, Frank J. '59 (STP) Retired.
DeCraemer, Willy *s.j.* '57 (BAL) [M] Baltimore, MD Jesuit Fathers and Brothers Maryland Provincial Curia.
DeCrans, Joseph '84 (CR) Frazee, MN Sacred Heart Church.
DeCrits, Albert *c.i.c.m.* '40 (FgM) Missionhurst Foreign Missions.
Deddens, Norbert J. '51 (BWN) San Benito, TX Our Lady, Queen of the Universe Church.
Deddens, Norbert J. '51 (L) Retired.
Dede, James R. '51 (IND) Retired.
Dede, John F. (IND) Retired.
Dede, John F. '47 (IND) [5] Terre Haute, IN St. Margaret Mary Church.
Dede, Paul M. '64 (IND) Spencer, IN St. Jude the Apostle Church.
Dedek, John F. '55 (CHI) Elk Grove Village, IL St. Julian Eymard Church.
Dedera, Philip '72 (JOL) [I] Naperville, IL St. Patrick's Residence.
DeDomenico, Msgr. Francis A. '56 (NEW) Hasbrouck Heights, NJ Corpus Christi Church.
DeDominici, Lorenzo '46 (LA) Retired.
Dee, Dacian '56 (SP) Indian Rocks Beach, FL St. Jerome Church.
Dee, Neal '64 (AMA) [8] Amarillo, TX St. Joseph's Church.
Deegan, James D. *o.m.i.* '70 (STP) [Q] Buffalo, MN Christ the King Retreat Center.
Deegan, John E. *o.s.a.* '61 (FgM) Foreign Missions.
Deegan, John E. *o.s.a.* '61 (PH) [C] Villanova, PA Villanova University; [AA] Villanova, PA Provincial Offices of the Order of St. Augustine, Province of St. Thomas of Villanova; [AA] Villanova, PA St. John Stone Friary.
Deegan, Ronan J. *t.o.r.* '58 (WH) Moundsville, WV St. Francis Xavier's Church.
Deehan, Robert J. '83 (BO) [2] Plymouth, MA St. Bonaventure Church.
Deehr, Anselm *s.t.* '90 (LA) Compton, CA Our Lady of Victory Church; Long Beach, CA Veterans Affairs Medical Center.
Deeker, Geoffrey J. *c.s.s.* '60 (SPR) [3] Pittsfield, MA Our Lady of Mt. Carmel Church.
Deeley, Kevin J. (BO) Military & VA Chaplains.
Deeley, Msgr. Robert P. '73 (BO) Lexington, MA St. Brigid Church; [X] Lexington, MA Grey Nuns Provincial Offices.
Deely, John *o.m.i.* '70 (FgM) Oblates Foreign Missions.
Deeman, Andrew J. *s.j.* '41 (STL) [O] St. Louis, MO Fusz Pavilion.
Deeney, Aloysius *o.c.d.* '74 (LR) [A] Little Rock, AR Marylake - Carmelite Novitiate.
Deeney, Charles J. *o.m.i.* '71 (ORL) Altamonte Springs, FL Annunciation Church.
Deeney, John J. *s.j.* '52 (BAL) [M] Baltimore, MD Jesuit Fathers and Brothers Maryland Provincial Curia.
Deeney, John J. *s.j.* '52 (FgM) Provinces.
Deere, Msgr. Gerald '38 (DM) Retired.
Deering, Msgr. Mark '53 (AUS) [6] Waco, TX St. Louis Church.
Deering, William '41 (EVN) St. Bernard, IN St. Bernard Church.
Deering, William '56 (EVN) Special Assignment.
Deery, James T. *o.s.a.* '51 (BO) [C] North Andover, MA Merrimack College.
Deeter, Timothy '81 (BEA) Absent On Leave.
Deeves, John F. *s.j.* '58 (DAL) [D] Dallas, TX Jesuit College Preparatory School.
Deevy, Edward '62 (ALX) Absent on Leave.
Defayette, Jeffrey M. '88 (WDC) Germantown, MD Mother Seton Parish.
DeFazio, Crescenzio (BIR) Retired.
DeFazio, Vincent '92 (SFE) Ribera, NM San Miguel Del Vado Church; Villanueva, NM Our Lady of Guadalupe Church.
DeFazio, Vincent G. '92 (SFE) Las Vegas, NM Our Lady of Sorrows Church.
DeFelice, Jonathan P. *o.s.b.* '74 (MAN) [A] Manchester, NH St. Anselm Abbey Seminary; [B] Manchester, NH Saint Anselm College; [K] Manchester, NH St. Anselm Abbey.
Deffenbaugh, Joseph T. '79 (Y) On Duty Outside the Diocese.
Deffenbaugh, Terry A. *o.s.a.* '75 (CHI) [N] Olympia Fields, IL Austin Friary.
DeFilippis, Anthony '60 (JOL) Absent on Sick Leave.
DeFillippes, Gerardo (NY) Suffern, NY Good Samaritan Hospital.
Defler, Herman J. *m.s.f.* '38 (BWN) Donna, TX St. Joseph Church.
DeForge, Michael W. '79 (BUR) [H] Burlington, VT University of Vermont-The Catholic Center at UVM; [H] Burlington, VT University of Vermont-The Catholic Center at UVM.
DeForke, John C. (GAL) [N] Houston, TX Pope John XXIII Priest Residence.
DeForke, John C. '59 (GAL) Hitchcock, TX Our Lady of Lourdes Church; Texas City, TX St. Mary Church.
DeFour, Reginald *c.s.sp.* '64 (PIT) [B] Pittsburgh, PA Duquesne University of the Holy Ghost.
DeFrancesco, Albert J. '43 (CIN) Retired.
DeFrancisco, Joseph '75 (BEA) On Duty Outside the Diocese.
DeFranco, Anthony '38 (ALB) [2] Schenectady, NY St. Anthony Church; [9] Schenectady, NY St. John the Evangelist Church; Retired.
DeFrange, Jonathan M. *o.s.b.* '78 (NO) Folsom, LA St. John the Baptist Church; [A] St. Benedict, LA St. Joseph's Seminary College; [P] St. Benedict, LA St. Joseph Abbey.
DeFronzo, Anthony R. '81 (PSC) On Duty Outside Diocese.
DeFronzo, Anthony R. '83 (HRT) Rocky Hill, CT St. James Church.
DeGaetano, Louis J. (BRK) [169] Queens, NY St. Francis de Sales Church.
Degagne, Richard E. '82 (FR) North Attleboro, MA Sacred Heart Church.
Degan, Bernard P. *c.m.* '43 (NO) [P] New Orleans, LA Vincentian Fathers.
Degan, Siro Dal *o.s.j.* '60 (MRY) Davenport, CA St. Vincent De Paul Church; [G] Santa Cruz, CA Oblates of St. Joseph Provincial House and Shrine.
DeGante, Adalberto '79 (DEN) Iliff, CO St. Catherine of Siena Church; Peetz, CO Sacred Heart Church; Sterling, CO St. Anthony Church.
DeGante, Adalberto '79 (GLP) On Duty Outside of Diocese.
Degen, Jerome A. '59 (SC) Manson, IA St. Thomas Church.
Degenhardt, Gervase *o.f.m.cap.* '58 (PIT) [29] Pittsburgh, PA Our Lady of the Angels Church.
DeGeorge, Salvatore *o.m.i.* '65 (SAT) [M] San Antonio, TX Oblate Benson Residence (Southern Prov.).
DeGeorge, Salvatore F. '65 (GAL) [64] Houston, TX St. Patrick Church.
DeGeorge, Salvatore F. *o.m.i.* '65 (SAT) [M] San Antonio, TX Provincial Administration Office, Oblates of Mary Immaculate (Southern Prov.).
DeGerolami, Michael '74 (SAT) [60] San Antonio, TX St. Paul Church.
Degeyter, Edward '70 (LAF) Jeanerette, LA St. John the Evangelist Church.
DeGiorgio, John M. (RIC) [11] Richmond, VA St. Gabriel Church.
DeGiovine, Christopher '77 (ALB) Special Assignment; [B] Albany, NY The College of Saint Rose; [M] Albany, NY Convent of the Sacred Heart.
Deglaire, Pierre *c.s.sp.* '70 (SB) Colton, CA San Salvador Church.
Degnan, Daniel A. *s.j.* '66 (NEW) [C] Jersey City, NJ St. Peter's Preparatory School.
Degnan, Henry B. '48 (PH) [5] Norristown, PA St. Paul Church; Retired.
Degnan, James F. '55 (BO) Hopkinton, MA St. John the Evangelist Church.
Degnan, John F. '51 (JC) St. Elizabeth, MO St. Lawrence Church.
DeGrand, Robert '80 (SFD) Absent on Leave.
DeGrandis, Robert *s.s.j.* '60 (GAL) [2] Galveston, TX Holy Rosary Church.
DeGrocco, Joseph '88 (RVC) Wantagh, NY St. Frances de Chantal Church.
DeGrood, Donald E. '97 (STP) Lakeville, MN All Saints Church.
DeGroot, Francis J. '93 (MAR) Rudyard, MI St. Joseph Church.
DeGroot, Ignatius *o.f.m.* '81 (FRS) [G] Three Rivers, CA St. Anthony's Retreat House.
DeGroot, Kenneth J. *o.praem.* '61 (GB) [17] Green Bay, WI St. Willebrord Church.
Degutis, George D. '38 (PH) [10] Philadelphia, PA St. Andrew Church; Retired.
DeGuzman, Dennis '91 (OM) Coleridge, NE St. Michael Church.
DeGuzman, Francis *o.mar.* '95 (SAM) [C] Petersham, MA Most Holy Trinity Monastery.
Dehetre, Mark '93 (LAN) Goodrich, MI St. Mark the Evangelist Church.
Dehler, William A. *s.j.* '44 (CHI) [C] Chicago, IL Jesuit Community at Loyola University of Chicago.
Dehner, Eugene *o.s.b.* '40 (KCK) [A] Atchison, KS Benedictine College; [H] Atchison, KS St. Benedict's Abbey.
Dehner, Philip R. *o.c.s.o.* '53 (ATL) [I] Conyers, GA The Monastery of the Holy Spirit.
DeHondt, Ronald J. '73 (DET) [28] Detroit, MI St. Gregory Church.
Deibel, David (OAK) [B] Moraga, CA St. Mary's College.

Deibel, David L. '83 (SR) [M] Napa, CA Provincialate Community.
Deichert, Joseph '84 (BIS) On Duty Outside the Diocese.
DeIelse, Salvatore L. '66 (CAM) [2] Vineland, NJ Sacred Heart Church.
Deig, Robert A. '50 (EVN) [17] Evansville, IN St. John the Evangelist Church.
Deikel, Jeffrey J. '76 (LA) Santa Clarita, CA Our Lady of Perpetual Help Church.
Deimeke, L. Edward '75 (ALB) [7] Schenectady, NY Immaculate Conception Church.
Deimel, George *c.ss.r.* '37 (BAL) [96] Baltimore, MD St. Wenceslaus Church.
Deis, Dennis *o.m.i.* '65 (SFS) Rosholt, SD St. John the Baptist Church.
Deis, Michael S. *o.m.i.* '47 (BEL) [F] Belleville, IL Missionary Oblates of Mary Immaculate - St. Henry's Oblate Residence.
Deisch, Raymond '62 (RC) [D] Rapid City, SD Priest Retirement and Aid Association.
Deisch, Raymond J. '62 (RC) Gregory, SD St. Joseph Church.
Deister, Charles C. '63 (STL) [3] Creve Coeur, MO St. Monica Church.
Deitch, Richard S. '86 (SFR) Sausalito, CA St. Mary Star of the Sea Church.
Deitchman, Carl '84 (HEL) Shelby, MT St. William Church.
Deitelhoff, Bernard H. '57 (MAD) Argyle, WI St. Joseph Church.
Deiters, James E. '91 (BEL) O'Fallon, IL St. Clare Church.
Deiters, Robert M. *s.j.* '58 (FgM) Provinces.
Deitzer, Gerald E. *c.m.* '55 (PH) [AA] Philadelphia, PA Congregation of the Mission.
DeJardin, Joseph R. *s.j.* '61 (P) [D] Portland, OR Jesuit High School.
DeJong, Iain *c.s.b.* (OAK) [C] Oakland, CA Bishop O'Dowd High School.
DeJonghe, Harold J. '57 (LA) Retired.
DeJulio, David T. '90 (SP) [1] St. Petersburg, FL Cathedral of St. Jude the Apostle.
DeJulio, Robert J. '72 (NY) Brewster, NY St. Lawrence O'Toole Church.
Deka, John S. '58 (CLV) [32] Cleveland, OH St. Hyacinth Church.
Dekat, Carl M. '53 (KCK) Emmett, KS Holy Cross Church; Rossville, KS St. Stanislaus Church; St. Marys, KS Immaculate Conception Church.
Dekat, Earl '66 (KCK) Paola, KS Holy Trinity Church.
Deken, John C. '72 (STL) Ste. Genevieve, MO Ste. Genevieve's Church.
Del, Curtis Van *s.j.* (SAL) [E] Concordia, KS Nazareth Motherhouse for the Sisters of St. Joseph, Concordia.
del Burgo, Lucio *o.c.d.* '73 (MIA) [L] Miami, FL Discalced Carmelite Friars of Miami, Inc.
del Cerro, Helios *c.m.* '61 (LA) [29] Los Angeles, CA Our Lady of the Rosary of Talpa Church.
Del Conte, Eugene *o.s.a.* '55 (PH) [AA] Philadelphia, PA Augustinian Community (O.S.A.).
del Cura, Felix Martinez *o.p.* '54 (PCE) Yauco, PR Holy Rossary Church.
Del Giudice, Carl '81 (CHL) Brevard, NC Sacred Heart Church.
Del Marmol, Alfonso *s.j.* '51 (FgM) Provinces.
Del Monaco, Marion '66 (P) [K] Mt. Angel, OR Benedictine Nursing Center.
del Nino Jesus, Rene A. Maria *s.e.m.v.* '83 (ARE) Hatillo, PR Our Lady of Guadalupe Church.
Del Prete, Msgr. Frank G. '77 (NEW) [4] Hoboken, NJ SS. Peter and Paul's Church.
Del Priore, Kenneth '83 (SD) [11] San Diego, CA Our Lady of Angels Church; [B] San Diego, CA University of San Diego.
del Riego, Rutilio J. '65 (WDC) [B] Washington, DC Diocesan Laborer Priests, House of Studies.
Del Rio, Oscar (LUB) Anson, TX St. Michael's Church.
Del Toro, Jose *t.o.r.* '95 (STU) [A] Steubenville, OH Franciscan University of Steubenville; [F] Steubenville, OH Holy Spirit Monastery.
del Val, Feliciano (GAL) [N] Houston, TX Pope John XXIII Priest Residence.
del Val, Feliciano '36 (GAL) Retired.
Del Val, Jose '96 (FR) [17] New Bedford, MA St. Kilian Church; [P] New Bedford, MA The Institute of the Incarnate Word, Inc.
Del Valle, Jorge *m.sp.s.* '73 (LA) [A] Camarillo, CA St. John's Seminary.
Del Valle, Tomas '79 (SJN) On Duty Outside the Archdiocese.
Del Vecchio, Joseph F. '72 (WDC) [44] Washington, DC St. Vincent De Paul Church.
Dela Cruz, Erwin *m.s.* '92 (HON) Waipahu, HI St. Joseph Church.
Dela Cruz, Vincente '90 (HT) [2] Houma, LA Annunziata Church.
deLadurantaye, Paul F. '88 (ARL) [1] Arlington, VA Cathedral of St. Thomas More.
Delaere, Paul *c.i.c.m.* '43 (FgM) Missionhurst Foreign Missions.
Delahanty, Patrick D. '69 (L) [64] Louisville, KY St. Peter Claver Church.
Delahunty, Richard A. '65 (ORG) Yorba Linda, CA St. Martin Church.
Delahunty, Thomas '54 (SEA) Retired.
Delahunty, Thomas P. '55 (SAC) Retired and in Senior Ministry.
DeLand, Robert J. '73 (SAG) [15] Saginaw, MI SS. Peter and Paul Church.
Delaney, Brian '75 (LA) Montebello, CA Our Lady of the Miraculous Medal Church.
Delaney, Charles A. *c.s.c.* '49 (FgM) Holy Cross Foreign Missions.
Delaney, Charles A. *c.s.c.* '49 (FTW) [J] South Bend, IN Congregation of Holy Cross Indiana Province Provincial House.
Delaney, David F. '61 (BO) Melrose, MA Incarnation Church.
Delaney, Msgr. Dennis M. '76 (STL) [7] St. Louis, MO Immaculate Heart of Mary Church.
Delaney, Francis H. (BO) Retired.
Delaney, Francis H. '52 (BO) [8] Salem, MA St. Thomas the Apostle Church.
Delaney, Msgr. Howard L. '40 (PBL) Retired.
Delaney, J. Joseph '48 (ALB) Clinton Heights, NY St. Mary Church.
Delaney, James *c.s.sp.* '54 (BRK) [U] Long Island City, NY Holy Ghost Fathers of Ireland.
Delaney, James P. *o.m.i.* '36 (SAT) [K] San Antonio, TX Oblate Madonna Residence.
Delaney, James T. '61 (BAL) [B] Emmitsburg, MD Mount Saint Mary's College.
Delaney, James T. '61 (WIL) On Duty Outside the Diocese.
Delaney, Msgr. John '64 (MIA) Sabbatical.
Delaney, John '81 (FTW) [15] Fort Wayne, IN St. Peter Church.
Delaney, John H. '81 (FTW) [2] Fort Wayne, IN St. Andrew Church.
Delaney, John J. '62 (NY) [52] New York, NY Immaculate Conception Church.
Delaney, John W. '95 (BO) Needham, MA St. Joseph Church.
Delaney, Larry '90 (CR) East Grand Forks, MN Sacred Heart Church.
Delaney, Lawrence '67 (LAN) [I] De Witt, MI St. Francis Retreat Center.
Delaney, Matthew S. '51 (LA) Retired.
Delaney, Michael J. '85 (SCR) [1] Hazleton, PA St. Gabriel's Church.
DeLaney, Michael M. *c.s.c.* '87 (P) [B] Portland, OR University of Portland; [L] Portland, OR Holy Cross Fathers & Brothers, C.S.C. - University of Portland.
Delaney, Michael V. *s.j.* '85 (DEN) [1] Fort Collins, CO St. Joseph Church.
Delaney, Ralph B. *s.j.* '43 (BO) [W] Weston, MA Campion Health Center, Inc.
Delaney, Richard F. '62 (RVC) Garden City, NY St. Joseph's Church.
Delaney, T. Timothy '79 (SCR) [3] Wilkes-Barre, PA St. Boniface Church.
Delaney, Thomas '57 (JKS) Greenwood, MS Immaculate Heart of Mary Church.
Delaney, Thomas *o.m.i.* '60 (FgM) Oblates Foreign Missions.
Delaney, Thomas P. *s.j.* '61 (LA) [2] Santa Barbara, CA Our Lady of Sorrows Church.
Delaney, William *s.j.* (LA) [DD] Redondo Beach, CA SCRC (Southern California Renewal Communities).
Delaney, Msgr. William '44 (CHY) [2] Cheyenne, WY Holy Trinity Church; Retired.
Delaney, William *c.pp.s.* '63 (LA) [38] Los Angeles, CA St. Agnes Church.
Delaney, Msgr. William B. '42 (NY) [2] White Plains, NY St. John the Evangelist Church; Retired.
Delaney, William I. '61 (RVC) Retired.
Delaney, William J. '54 (NY) [47] New York, NY Holy Innocents Church.
DeLange, Maurice '71 (COV) Leave of Absence.
Delano, Kenneth J. '60 (FR) [10] Fall River, MA Our Lady of the Immaculate Conception Church.
Delargy, Torlach C. '66 (SFR) [T] San Francisco, CA Opus Dei.
Delarm, Curtis R. '89 (HBG) Carlisle, PA St. Patrick Church.
Delarue, Louis '75 (BEA) [6] Port Arthur, TX St. John Church.
deLaunay, Herbert C. '75 (LAF) Bayou Vista, LA St. Bernadette Church.
DeLay, Dominic *o.p.* '93 (SAC) Benicia, CA St. Dominic Church.
Delay, Donald R. '83 (BO) Awaiting Assignment.
Delbel, James A. '81 (OG) Hopkinton, NY Church of the Holy Cross; Saint Regis Falls, NY St. Ann Church.
Delclos, John L. '71 (BAL) Special Assignment.
DelConti, Eugene *o.s.a.* '55 (PH) [111] Philadelphia, PA St. Nicholas of Tolentine Church.
DelDuca, John A. '68 (CAM) Hammonton, NJ St. Martin de Porres Church.
DeLeers, Stephen V. '84 (MIL) [A] Milwaukee, WI St. Francis Seminary.
DeLeers, Vincent J. *o.praem.* '46 (SFE) [J] Albuquerque, NM Santa Maria de la Vid Priory.
DeLeeuw, John '44 (LAF) Retired.
Delehanty, Thomas F. '41 (SPR) Retired.
DeLellis, Francis V. '49 (PRO) Retired.
Delendick, John '77 (BRK) [3] Brooklyn, NY St. Agnes Church.
DeLeo, Roy James '69 (NEW) [6] Elizabeth, NJ St. Genevieve's Church.
DeLeon, Benedict '80 (SAC) Vacaville, CA St. Mary Church.
DeLeon, Eddie *c.m.f.* '91 (SPC) [E] Springfield, MO Claretians Missionaries' Residence-Villa Claret; [I] Springfield, MO The Nancy McGregor House, Southwest MO State University, Drury College, Ozarks Technical Comm. College.
DeLeon, Esteban '85 (WDC) [M] Washington, DC Divine Word College.
DeLeon, Robert *c.s.c.* '85 (BGP) [I] Bridgeport, CT St. Vincent's Medical Center.
Delgado, Enrique '96 (MIA) Key Biscayne, FL St. Agnes Church.
Delgado, Joseph '95 (SJ) [12] San Jose, CA St. John Vianney Church.
Delgado, Julio *c.ss.r.* (CGS) Fajardo, PR Santiago Apostol Church.
Delgado, Leo *c.m.f.* '55 (PHX) [G] Phoenix, AZ Mt. Claret Retreat Center.
Delgado, Leslie N. '55 (LA) [96] Los Angeles, CA Sanctuary of Our Lady of Guadalupe Church.
Delgado, Rodolfo '96 (SAC) [5] Sacramento, CA Our Lady of Guadalupe Shrine Church.
Delgado, Ruben '90 (BWN) Weslaco, TX San Martin de Porres Church.
Delich, David L. *o.p.* '63 (CHI) [N] Chicago, IL Dominicans (Provincial Office).
Deliman, Msgr. Edward M. '73 (PH) [156] Philadelphia, PA Visitation B.V.M. Church.
Delis, Robert *s.d.b.* '79 (SFR) [N] San Francisco, CA Salesian Provincial Residence.
Delisi, Anthony *o.c.s.o.* '54 (ATL) [I] Conyers, GA The Monastery of the Holy Spirit.
DeLisle, Henri A. *o.m.i.* '58 (NOR) [F] Willimantic, CT Oblates of Mary Immaculate; [I] Willimantic, CT Immaculata Retreat House.
Delisle, Richard *m.s.* '59 (FR) [J] Attleboro, MA La Salette Shrine.
Dell, Robert *c.o.* '90 (SEA) [1] Vancouver, WA Our Lady of Lourdes Church; [Q] Vancouver, WA Vancouver Oratorian Community.
Dell, Robert S. *c.o.* '90 (CHR) [D] Rock Hill, SC Oratory of St. Philip Neri, Congregation of the Oratory of Pontifical Rite.
Dell'Anno, Anthony V. '69 (BRK) [147] Queens, NY St. Aloysius Church.
Dell'Oro, Italo *c.r.s.* '82 (GAL) [11] Houston, TX Assumption Church.
Della Neve, Louis F. '52 (BUF) [1] Lockport, NY St. Anthony Church.
Della Penta, Joseph C. *o.p.* '35 (CHI) [N] River Forest, IL St. Thomas Aquinas Priory.
della Picca, Angelo A. '45 (CIN) [D] Cincinnati, OH College of Mount St. Joseph.
della Picca, Msgr. Paul B. '59 (ALN) [9] Bethlehem, PA Our Lady of Pompeii Church.
Della Pietra, Douglas '96 (ROC) [12] Rochester, NY St. Charles Borromeo Church.
DellaBadia, Leonard *c.s.s.* '35 (NY) [4] White Plains, NY Our Lady of Mt. Carmel Church.
Dellaporte, Dominic (TR) Manasquan, NJ St. Denis Church.
Dellaporte, Dominick (TR) Point Pleasant, NJ St. Martha Church.
DelliCarpini, John J. '76 (PH) [A] Wynnewood, PA Theological Seminary of St. Charles Borromeo, Overbrook.
Dello Russo, John F. *o.s.a.* '87 (NY) [168] Bronx, NY St. Nicholas of Tolentine Church.
Dellos, Richard '68 (SY) Greene, NY Immaculate Conception Church.
Delmonte, Albert L. '64 (ROC) East Rochester, NY St. Jerome Church.
Delmore, Eugene *s.j.* '69 (FBK) Kotlik, AK St. Joseph Church; Mountain Village, AK St. Lawrence Church.
Delmore, Eugene P. *s.j.* '69 (FBK) [E] St. Marys, AK Brother Joe Prince Jesuit Community.
DeLong, Allen *s.m.* '33 (LA) [F] Chatsworth, CA Chaminade College Preparatory.
Delonnay, Lawrence '75 (DET) Waterford, MI Our Lady of the Lakes Church.
DeLora, John P. '94 (NY) [5] New Rochelle, NY Holy Name of Jesus Church.
DeLorenzo, Francis Solanus *o.f.m.* '47 (ALB) [A] Catskill, NY St. Anthony Friary.
DeLorenzo, John R. '76 (SY) [17] Syracuse, NY St. John the Baptist Church.
DeLorenzo, Vincent '65 (LAN) Burton, MI Holy Redeemer Church.
DeLorme, R. Daniel '57 (SY) Homer, NY St. Margaret Church.
Delort, Norbert E. *c.ss.r.* '62 (STL) [P] Liguori, MO St.

Clement Health Care Center.
Delos, Bernard M. '45 (ALB) Retired.
DeLuca, Albert J. '57 (NY) [111] New York, NY Sacred Hearts of Jesus and Mary Church; Manhattan, NY New York University Medical Center.
DeLuca, Anthony G. '53 (PIT) Monroeville, PA North American Martyrs Church.
DeLuca, David *m.s.c.* '66 (FgM) Missionaries of the Sacred Heart Foreign Missions.
DeLuca, David *m.s.c.* '66 (RCK) [H] Aurora, IL Missionaries of the Sacred Heart Community.
DeLuca, Francis G. '58 (WIL) Retired.
DeLuca, Paul F. '81 (CIN) [10] Dayton, OH St. Helen Church.
DeLuca, Stephen J. '65 (BGP) [5] Greenwich, CT St. Agnes Church.
DeLucia, Gerald M. '78 (Y) Lowellville, OH Our Lady of the Holy Rosary Church.
Deluney, Gerald C. '69 (SB) [1] Corona, CA Corpus Christi Church.
DelValle, Tomas '80 (NY) [110] New York, NY Sacred Heart of Jesus Church.
DelVecchio, Msgr. Michael E. '54 (BUF) [24] Buffalo, NY St. Francis of Assisi Church.
Delzell, David G. (TR) Retired.
Delzingaro, Dick M. *c.r.s.p., m.a.* '96 (ALN) [K] Bethlehem, PA The Barnabite Fathers Barnabite Spiritual Center.
DeMaio, Joseph *o.carm.* '65 (ROC) [B] Rochester, NY McQuaid Jesuit High School; [I] Rochester, NY Whitefriars Priory.
DeMan, Thomas *o.p.* (OAK) [N] Oakland, CA Western Dominican Province.
DeManuele, James *c.p.* '78 (L) [L] Louisville, KY Sacred Heart Retreat.
Demarais, Garvin '85 (OG) Altona, NY Altona Correctional Facility.
Demarais, Garvin J. '81 (OG) West Chazy, NY St. Joseph Church.
DeMarco, Nathan I. '79 (CAM) West Collingswood, NJ Transfiguration Church.
DeMarco, Peter A. '60 (BGP) [4] Trumbull, CT St. Theresa's Church.
DeMaria, Herculan F.X. *o.f.m.cap.* '50 (BR) Gonzales, LA St. Mark Church.
DeMaria, Lawrence '51 (NO) New Orleans, LA Veterans Affairs Medical Center.
deMaria, Lawrence A. '51 (NO) [11] Metairie, LA St. Louis King of France Church.
DeMarinis, Msgr. John H. '62 (Y) [8] Youngstown, OH St. Anthony's Church.
DeMartini, Rodney J. *s.m.* '75 (SR) [O] Sebastopol, CA National Catholic AIDS Network.
DeMartinis, Michael G. '97 (E) [10] Erie, PA Our Lady of Peace Church; Du Bois, PA St. Michael Church.
DeMartinis, O. Robert '86 (ALB) Glens Falls, NY St. Mary Church; Glens Falls, NY Glens Falls Hospital.
DeMartino, Robert J '92 (ARL) Clifton, VA St. Andrew the Apostle Church.
Demasi, Michael A. '43 (BUR) East Dorset, VT St. Jerome Church; Retired.
DeMattia, John '68 (PAT) Whippany, NJ Our Lady of Mercy Church.
Dembow, Leonard '65 (NEW) Nutley, NJ St. Mary's Church.
Demeck, Norman *c.p.* '52 (MET) [H] South River, NJ Passionist Provincial Office.
Demeck, Norman *c.p.* '52 (TR) [A] Lakewood, NJ Georgian Court College.
DeMeester, Peter '28 (WH) Retired.
Demek, Martin H. '75 (BAL) [97] Baltimore, MD St. William of York Church.
Demers, Bertrand '48 (KNX) [B] Knoxville, TN St. Mary's Medical Center, Inc.
Demers, Francis *o.m.i.* '55 (BO) [W] Lowell, MA Missionary Oblates of Mary Immaculate.
Demers, Gerard A. *s.m.* '59 (BO) [12] Lawrence, MA Sacred Heart Church.
Demers, Normand J. '58 (PRO) [4] East Providence, RI St. Martha Church.
Demers, Paul R. *s.c.* '81 (MAN) [B] Nashua, NH Rivier College.
Demers, Raymond A. '55 (MAN) [J] Laconia, NH St. Francis Home for the Aged.
Demers, Richard D. '83 (OG) Military Chaplains.
Demers, Thomas *o.p.* '39 (PRT) [I] Lewiston, ME SS. Peter and Paul Priory.
Demers, Wilfred G. '59 (MAN) Windham, NH St. Matthew Church.
Demetzky, Alex D. '53 (CLV) [7] Lorain, OH St. Ladislaus Church; Retired.
DeMeulemeester, Patrick '95 (PEO) Elkhart, IL St. Patrick Church.
DeMeulenaere, Martin *o.s.b.* (KC) [1] Kansas City, MO Cathedral of Immaculate Conception.
DeMeulenaere, Martin *o.s.b.* '73 (KC) [10] Kansas City, MO St. Elizabeth's Church; [J] Conception, MO Conception Abbey.
DeMeules, Donald H. '83 (JKS) Retired.
Deming, Robert N. '58 (KC) Unassigned.
Demko, Dennis *c.ss.r.* '80 (CGS) San Lorenzo, PR Nuestra Senora de la Mercedes Church.
Demko, James '82 (PSC) Freeland, PA St. Mary's Church.
Demkovich, Msgr. John J. '65 (PAT) [3] Passaic, NJ Assumption of the Blessed Virgin Mary Church.
Demkovich, Michael T. *o.p.* '81 (SFE) [29] Albuquerque, NM St. Thomas Aquinas University Parish; [N] Albuquerque, NM Dominican Ecclesial Institute.
Deml, Frank '57 (DEN) [1] Lakewood, CO St. Bernadette Church.
Demmer, Donald '73 (DET) Garden City, MI St. Dunstan Church.
Demo, John M. '88 (OG) [2] Ogdensburg, NY Notre Dame Church.
DeMoraes, Jonas V. '70 (BGP) [5] Danbury, CT St. Peter's Church.
DeMott, Lester *c.m.* '55 (STA) [E] Jacksonville, FL St. Vincent's Medical Center, Inc.
DeMott, Lester T. *c.m.* '49 (PH) [AA] Philadelphia, PA Congregation of the Mission.
DeMott, Stephen T. *m.m.* '76 (NY) [DD] Maryknoll, NY Maryknoll Fathers and Brothers.
Dempsey, Dennis K. '80 (STP) On Duty Outside the Archdiocese.
Dempsey, Edward M. (NOR) Absent on Leave.
Dempsey, J. Richard *s.j.* '51 (DET) [P] Clarkston, MI Colombiere Center.
Dempsey, James '56 (BEA) [C] Beaumont, TX St. Elizabeth Hospital of Beaumont.
Dempsey, John G. '64 (STL) [39] St. Louis, MO St. Joan of Arc Church.
Dempsey, Msgr. Michael J. '58 (BRK) [218] Queens, NY Our Lady, Queen of Martyrs Church.
Dempsey, Nicholas '71 (SD) [19] San Diego, CA St. Agnes Church.
Dempsey, Patrick E. '97 (WDC) Leonardtown, MD St. Aloysius Church.
Dempsey, Richard J. '58 (CHI) Evergreen Park, IL Most Holy Redeemer Church.
Dempsey, Robert J. '80 (CHI) On Duty Outside the Archdiocese.
Dempsey, Terrence E. *s.j.* (STL) [C] St. Louis, MO Saint Louis University.
Dempsey, Terrence E. *s.j.* '85 (STL) [P] St. Louis, MO Jesuit Community Corporation at St. Louis University - Jesuit Hall.
Dempsey, Thomas J. '39 (PH) Lansdowne, PA St. Philomena Church; Retired.
Dempsey, Thomas J. '61 (RCK) [3] Elgin, IL St. Mary Church.
Dempsey, Msgr. Thomas J. '62 (STL) Mattese, MO Assumption Church.
Dempski, Daniel G. *o.s.b.* '79 (MAN) [K] Manchester, NH St. Anselm Abbey.
Dempster, A. Patrick '51 (Y) Retired.
Dempster, Douglas W. '62 (WIL) Retired.
Dempsy, Thomas F. '65 (BO) Retired.
Demse, Thomas P. '76 (MIL) Hartland, WI St. Charles Church.
Demski, Msgr. Arthur A. '54 (BRK) Absent on Sick Leave.
DeMuro, S. Patrick '85 (HRT) Retired.
Demuth, Msgr. George R. '46 (SCR) Retired.
Demuth, Paul E. '68 (GB) [15] Green Bay, WI Resurrection Church.
DeNardi, Charles A. '36 (OWN) Retired.
Denault, Paul *o.carm.* '80 (NY) [DD] Middletown, NY St. Albert's Priory; [DD] Middletown, NY Brandsma Priory.
Denburger, John J. *o.c.s.o.* '63 (ROC) [I] Piffard, NY Abbey of the Genesee.
Dendinger, Robert L. '75 (TOL) New Washington, OH St. Bernard Church; North Auburn, OH Mother of Sorrows Church.
Dendinger, William J. '65 (OM) Military Chaplains.
Dene, Charles J. '58 (ALN) Lost Creek, PA St. Mary Magdalen Church; Minersville, PA FCI-Schuylkill, Federal Correctional Institute.
Dene, Joseph '62 (WH) Retired.
Deneault, Normand J. '45 (PRO) Retired; [P] Providence, RI St. John Vianney Residence.
Denehy, Msgr. John '45 (ORL) Retired.
Denehy, John F. '56 (FR) Retired.
Denemark, Emil J. *s.j.* '81 (FgM) Provinces.
Denesha, J. Everett '50 (OG) Raymondville, NY St. Raymond Church.
Dengl, Nicholas *o.f.m.* '56 (Y) [J] Youngstown, OH Mt. Alverna Friary.
Denha, Suleiman '59 (EST) Oak Park, MI Mar Addai Chaldean Parish.
Denham, Jim (AUS) [F] Austin, TX Seton Medical Center.
Denig, Philip '85 (DEN) On Duty Outside the Archdiocese.
Denig, Stephen J. *c.m.* '75 (BRK) [U] Jamaica, NY Vincentian Residence.
Deniger, Joseph *c.s.sp.* '58 (LR) Conway, AR St. Joseph's Church.
DeNinno, Dale E. '78 (PIT) [16] Pittsburgh, PA Immaculate Conception Church; [20] Pittsburgh, PA St. Joseph Church.
DeNinno, Louis '76 (PIT) [7] Pittsburgh, PA St. Catherine of Siena Church.
Denison, Frederick J. '73 (IND) Frenchtown, IN St. Bernard Church.
Denison, Fredrick J. '73 (IND) St. Joseph, IN St. Joseph Church.
Denman, Donald '42 (P) Retired.
Denn, James J. *c.s.c.* '61 (WDC) [K] Washington, DC Georgetown University Hospital.
Dennehy, John D. '81 (NEW) Verona, NJ Our Lady of the Lake Church; [Q] Newark, NJ Essex County College, Rutgers University/Newark, NJIT.
Dennehy, Mark M. *o.s.m.* '46 (CHI) [N] Chicago, IL Servite Friars - Eastern Province.
Dennehy, Mark M. *o.s.m.* '56 (CHI) [15] Chicago, IL Annunciata Church.
Dennehy, Martin J. '51 (BGP) Retired.
Dennehy, Thomas '58 (MIA) Retired.
Dennemann, Thomas J. '73 (CIN) Mount Repose, OH St. Elizabeth Ann Seton Church.
Dennen, Gerard F. '41 (BRK) Retired.
Dennerlein, Arno A. '69 (JOL) Lombard, IL Sacred Heart Church.
Dennerlein, John L. '74 (JOL) [3] Joliet, IL Holy Family Church.
Dennett, John A. '62 (GI) Retired.
Dennigan, Patrick J. '62 (BUR) Retired.
Denning, John *c.s.c.* '87 (FR) [B] Taunton, MA Coyle and Cassidy High School.
Denning, John F. *c.s.c.* (BO) [CC] Bridgewater, MA Bridgewater State College Catholic Center.
Denning, John F. *c.s.c.* '87 (FR) [A] North Easton, MA Holy Cross Fathers Religious.
Denning, Joseph B. '60 (DAV) [8] Davenport, IA St. Paul the Apostle Church.
Dennis, Allan J. *m.m.* '32 (NY) [DD] Maryknoll, NY Maryknoll Fathers and Brothers.
Dennis, Clay '52 (SFE) Retired.
Dennis, George T. *s.j.* '54 (WDC) [C] Washington, DC Catholic University of America, The; [M] Washington, DC Leonard Neale House.
Dennis, James J. '42 (BGP) Retired.
Dennis, John J. *o.s.f.s.* '45 (PH) [D] Philadelphia, PA Father Judge High School for Boys; [AA] Philadelphia, PA Father Judge Faculty House.
Dennis, John M. *s.j.* '86 (CHI) [D] Chicago, IL St. Ignatius Jesuit Community.
Dennis, Patrick '74 (TUC) Tucson, AZ Metropolitan Correctional Complex.
Dennis, Patrick '78 (B) On Duty Outside the Diocese.
Dennis, Samuel *o.s.b.* '57 (SFE) [L] Pecos, NM Our Lady of Guadalupe Benedictine Abbey.
Dennis, Thomas J. '92 (SFD) [1] Springfield, IL Cathedral of the Immaculate Conception.
Dennison, Arthur '73 (MIA) Coral Springs, FL St. Andrew Church.
Denniston, John '79 (RVC) Huntington, NY St. Patrick's Church.
Denny, Charles '27 (TOL) Bono, OH Our Lady of Mt. Carmel Church.
Denny, Charles '69 (TOL) Oregon, OH St. Charles Mercy Hospital; [H] Oregon, OH St. Charles Mercy Hospital.
Denny, David '80 (PBL) [I] Crestone, CO Spiritual Life Institute of America, Inc.
Denny, John T. *o.s.a.* '90 (PH) [D] Drexel Hill, PA Monsignor Bonner High School.
Denny, Joseph P. '67 (PH) [21] Philadelphia, PA St. Bartholomew Church.
Denny, Thomas F. *s.j.* '60 (FgM) Provinces.
Deno, Msgr. Lawrence M. '59 (OG) Hammond, NY St. Peter Church; [A] Ogdensburg, NY Wadhams Hall.
Denomme, Msgr. George E. '48 (WOR) [3] Leominster, MA St. Cecilia's Church.
Densmore, Robert J. '61 (MAN) [2] Manchester, NH St. Anne Church; Manchester, NH Elliott Hospital.
Dente, Thomas A. '93 (NEW) [1] Newark, NJ Cathedral Basilica of the Sacred Heart Church.
Denti, Msgr. Carl J. '42 (SY) Retired.
Dentici, Thomas '53 (DEN) Minturn, CO St. Patrick's Church.
Dentinger, Roy E. '50 (L) Retired.
Dentinger, Vincent P. '54 (L) Raywick, KY St. Francis Xavier Church; St. Mary, KY St. Charles Church.
Dentzman, Robert *o.f.m.* '48 (GAY) Petoskey, MI St. Francis Xavier Church.
Denys, Charles *c.i.c.m.* '44 (ARL) [J] Arlington, VA Missionhurst, C.I.C.M.-Central House and Provincialate.
Denzel, F. William *o.m.i.* '55 (BO) [Z] Tewksbury, MA Immaculate Heart of Mary Novitiate-Infirmary.
Denzer, Joseph W. '68 (BRK) [77] Brooklyn, NY St. Malachy's Church; Absent on Sick Leave.
Denzer, Thomas F. *s.j.* '61 (KC) [B] Kansas City, MO Rockhurst College; [J] Kansas City, MO Rockhurst College - Jesuit Community.
DeOtero, Roberto '77 (HON) Leave of Absence.
DePaoli, Edward M. '70 (PH) Absent on Leave.
DePascale, Albert *c.pp.s.* '62 (Y) Niles, OH Our Lady of Mt. Carmel Church.
DePasquale, Dominic '61 (SB) Retired.

Depatie, Donald L. '78 (PRO) [1] Cumberland, RI St. Aidan Church.
Depaul, Genska *o.f.m.* '58 (CHI) [B] Chicago, IL The Catholic Theological Union at Chicago.
Depeaux, Bernard F. '50 (BUR) Retired.
DePetris, Joseph J. '72 (BAL) Absent on Leave.
DePew, Daniel R. (GR) Alpine, MI Holy Trinity Church.
Depinet, Robert L. *m.m.* '61 (CLV) [P] Cleveland, OH Maryknoll Fathers.
Depinet, Robert L. *m.m.* '61 (FgM) Maryknoll Foreign Missions.
DePinto, Basil '58 (OAK) Piedmont, CA Corpus Christi Church; Oakland, CA Kaiser-Permanente Medical Center.
Depman, Francis J. '81 (PH) West Grove, PA Assumption B.V.M. Church.
Deponai, Joseph J. '83 (NY) Military Chaplains.
DePorres-Cox, Jesse *o.p.* '87 (DET) Special Assignment.
DePorter, Arnold W. (WDC) Suitland, MD St. Bernardine Church.
DePra, Italo '51 (P) Retired.
DePriest, Ellis L. *s.m.* '53 (NO) New Orleans, LA Byzantine Catholic Mission Church; [A] New Orleans, LA Notre Dame Seminary Graduate School of Theology.
DeProfio, Msgr. Louis A. '56 (BGP) [4] Trumbull, CT St. Theresa's Church.
DeProspero, Nicholas '70 (PSC) Pottstown, PA St. John the Baptist Church.
Deptula, Jan '81 (NY) [99] New York, NY Our Lady of Victory Church.
Deptula, Michael '84 (PHX) Lake Havasu City, AZ Our Lady of the Lake Church.
Deptula, Rick *o.f.m.conv.* (BAL) [M] Ellicott City, MD St. Joseph Cupertino Friary, Friars Minor Conventual of St. Francis of Assisi; [M] Ellicott City, MD Friary of St. Joseph Cupertino.
Deptula, Stanley L. '96 (PEO) Moline, IL Sacred Heart Church.
Derasmo, John M. '81 (RVC) Massapequa, NY St. Rose of Lima Church.
Derbes, Louis J. *c.m.* '51 (STL) [P] Perryville, MO Congregation of The Mission.
Derbish, Michael *o.f.m.* '62 (SJP) Aliquippa, PA Ss. Peter and Paul Church.
Derbyshire, Joseph V. '36 (NEW) Garwood, NJ Church of St. Anne.
Derbyshire, Joseph V. '46 (NEW) Retired.
DeRea, Philip *m.s.c.* '68 (ALN) [K] Reading, PA Missionaries of the Sacred Heart.
DeRea, Philip *m.s.c.* '68 (WDC) [V] Washington, DC Missionary Vehicle Association, Inc.
DeRego, Frank '87 (HON) On Duty Outside the Diocese.
DeRego, Frank '87 (LFT) [H] West Lafayette, IN St. Thomas Aquinas Parish and Foundation for Catholic Students Attending Purdue University.
Deresienski, Stanely M. *s.s.e.* '78 (NOR) [A] Enders Island, CT St. Edmund's Novitiate.
Deresienski, Stanley M. *s.s.e.* '78 (NOR) [F] Mystic, CT Society of St. Edmund; [I] Enders Island, CT St. Edmund's Retreat.
Derfus, Kenneth J. '56 (MIL) East Troy, WI St. Peter Church.
Dericks, Msgr. John H. '41 (PAT) Retired.
Derise, Mark Gerard '97 (LAF) Abbeville, LA St. Mary Magdalen Church.
DeRitis, Gilbert J. *m.m.* '54 (SJ) [M] Los Altos, CA Maryknoll.
Derivan, Thomas B. '72 (NY) [145] Bronx, NY St. Helena Church.
Derivaux, Donald F. '55 (JKS) Rosedale, MS Sacred Heart Church; Shaw, MS St. Francis of Assisi Church.
Derks, Joel *o.s.b.* '63 (SPC) [6] Springfield, MO St. Joseph's Church.
Dermody, Michael '76 (SAC) Absent on Leave.
Dermody, Ralph R. '43 (COL) Retired.
Dermody, Thomas '62 (SAC) On Duty Outside the Diocese.
Dermody, Thomas '62 (SD) San Diego, CA Calipatria State Prison.
Dermond, Msgr. John K. '68 (TR) [13] Trenton, NJ St. Francis of Assisium Church.
Dermott, William R. '82 (ALN) [1] Bethlehem, PA St. Anne Church.
Dernbach, Arthur P. '53 (P) Sublimity, OR St. Boniface Church.
Dernek, Daniel R. '62 (WIN) Chatfield, MN St. Mary's Church.
Dernek, Richard '70 (WIN) Hayfield, MN Sacred Heart Church.
Dernek, Richard J. '70 (WIN) Blooming Prairie, MN St. Columbanus Church.
DeRoche, Wilfred L. '65 (OG) Rouses Point, NY St. Patrick Church.
DeRoeck, Walter G. '71 (CHI) Elmwood Park, IL St. Celestine Church.
DeRosa, Francis '97 (ARL) Vienna, VA St. Mark's Church.
Derosier, Edmond '73 (BO) Shirley, MA St. Anthony Church.
Derouen, Keith '83 (LAF) [1] Lafayette, LA St. John the Evangelist Cathedral.
DeRouen, Robert R. *s.j.* '54 (DEN) [M] Denver, CO Xavier Jesuit Center.
Derrane, Mark G. '95 (BO) [4] Medford, MA St. Raphael Church.
Derrenbacher, James W. '45 (NY) Centerville, NY St. John the Evangelist Church; Retired.
Derrera, Ferdinand *s.j.* '61 (GAL) [42] Houston, TX St. Joseph Church.
Derrig, Joseph M. '63 (PH) [124] Philadelphia, PA Our Lady of Mt. Carmel Church.
Derrig, Philip T. *s.j.* '44 (STL) [P] St. Louis, MO Jesuit Community Corporation at St. Louis University - Jesuit Hall.
Derry, Daniel '63 (SJ) Gilroy, CA St. Mary Church.
Derwinski, Victor A. '44 (LIN) Retired.
Dery, Dominic '71 (PIT) [78] Pittsburgh, PA Most Holy Name of Jesus Church.
Dery, Henry R. '48 (HRT) Retired.
Derylo, Walter W. '68 (GAY) [4] Alpena, MI St. Mary Church.
Derzack, Thomas A. '76 (ALN) Lansford, PA St. Michael Church.
Des Lauriers, Matthias '60 (NY) Tarrytown, NY Transfiguration Church.
Des Roches, Robert *o.f.m.* '87 (PRT) [I] Kennebunkport, ME St. Anthony's Friary.
Des Rosiers, Denis A. '69 (OAK) [10] Oakland, CA St. Jarlath's Church.
DeSa, Walter *o.s.f.s.* (FgM) Oblates of St. Francis de Sales Foreign Missions.
DeSalvo, Donald D. '69 (RCK) Somonauk, IL St. John the Baptist Church.
DeSalvo, Raphael *o.s.b.* '45 (LR) Scranton, AR St. Ignatius Church.
DeSalvo, William '88 (JOL) Elmhurst, IL Visitation Church.
DeSanctis, Albert '80 (SAL) Tipton, KS St. Boniface's Church.
DeSandre, John G. '64 (TR) Deal, NJ St. Mary of the Assumption Church.
DeSante, Paul J. '59 (E) [B] Erie, PA Gannon University.
DeSantis, Joseph A. '75 (ALN) West Bangor, PA St. Roch Church; [C] Bangor, PA Pius X High School.
DeSantis, Linus *o.f.m.conv.* '71 (ATL) Lithia Springs, GA St. John Vianney Church; [L] Atlanta, GA Campus Ministry.
DeSanto, Joseph A. '54 (NY) Larchmont, NY St. Augustine Church.
Desaulniers, Richard P. '70 (PRO) Lincoln, RI St. James Church.
Desautels, Alfred R. *s.j.* '50 (WOR) [N] Worcester, MA Jesuits of Holy Cross College, Inc.
Desch, Paul *o.f.m.* '56 (HT) [4] Houma, LA Our Lady of the Most Holy Rosary Church.
Deschamps, Wilfred H. '90 (MAN) Gorham, NH Holy Family Church.
DeSciose, Michael C. '75 (PBL) [D] Pueblo, CO Centura Health-St. Mary-Corwin Hospital.
Deshaies, Richard A. *s.j.* '92 (FgM) Provinces.
Deshotel, J. Douglas '78 (DAL) Irving, TX St. Luke Church.
DeSiano, Francis P. *c.s.p.* '72 (NY) [DD] Jamaica Estates, NY Paulist Fathers Generalate.
Desiderio, Frank R. *c.s.p.* '82 (WDC) [B] Washington, DC St. Paul's College.
Desilets, Donald A. '52 (SPR) Retired.
Desilets, Viateur '46 (LAF) [1] Opelousas, LA St. Landry Church; Retired.
DeSilva, Gregory Bede '82 (FRS) Kerman, CA St. Patrick Church; Tranquillity, CA St. Paul Church.
DeSilva, Praxid '69 (NY) Manhattan, NY St. Vincent Hospital; [W] New York, NY St. Vincent's Hospital and Medical Center of New York.
DeSimone, Russell J. *o.s.a.* '51 (PH) [AA] Villanova, PA St. Thomas Monastery.
Desjardins, Msgr. Dominique '38 (SFR) Redwood City, CA Our Lady of Mount Carmel Church.
Desjardins, George A. '59 (MAN) [9] Manchester, NH St. George Church.
Desjardins, James M. *s.j.* '77 (BAL) [M] Baltimore, MD Jesuit Fathers and Brothers Maryland Provincial Curia.
Desjardins, James M. *s.j.* '77 (FgM) Provinces.
Desjardins, Lionel '46 (BO) [W] Lowell, MA Missionary Oblates of Mary Immaculate.
Desjardins, Raymond S. '42 (MAN) Retired.
Deskevich, Andrew J. '97 (PBR) Munhall, PA St. John the Baptist Cathedral.
DesLauriers, Matthias *o.carm.* '60 (NY) [DD] Middletown, NY St. Albert's Priory; [FF] Middletown, NY National Shrine of Our Lady of Mount Carmel.
DeSloover, A. Robert '74 (TOL) Miller City, OH St. Nicholas Church; New Cleveland, OH Holy Family Church.
Desmarais, Gerard R. '75 (MAN) [7] Nashua, NH St. Joseph Church.
Desmarais, Paul E. '79 (PRO) [11] Pawtucket, RI Sacred Heart of Jesus Church; [A] Providence, RI Seminary of Our Lady of Providence.
Desmarais, Rene '63 (DET) Port Huron, MI St. Joseph Church.
Desmarais, Rene L. '63 (DET) [S] Port Huron, MI John Courtney Murray Newman Center.
Desmond, Barry '59 (MOB) Retired.
Desmond, Donald J. '64 (RVC) East Hampton, NY Most Holy Trinity Church.
Desmond, Hubert E. '58 (BO) [1] Woburn, MA St. Anthony Church.
Desmond, Msgr. Joseph E. '47 (MAN) Hudson, NH St. John the Evangelist Church; Retired.
Desmond, Joseph L. '94 (MET) Monmouth Junction, NJ St. Cecilia Church.
Desmond, Michael Finbar '40 (MOB) [F] Mobile, AL Little Sisters of the Poor, Home For the Aged, Inc.
Desmond, Michael J. '71 (NEW) Kearny, NJ St. Stephen's Church.
Desmond, Nicholas R. '84 (CHI) [63] Chicago, IL St. Francis of Assisi/Our Lady of the Angels Church.
DeSocio, Benedict '97 (PSC) Special or Other Diocesan Assignment.
DeSocio, John A. '78 (ROC) [I] Rochester, NY Becket Hall.
Desormeaux, Roland *c.s.* '82 (PMB) [2] Delray Beach, FL Our Lady of Perpetual Help Mission Church.
DesOrmeaux, Scott '91 (LKC) [5] Lake Charles, LA St. Margaret Church; Lake Charles, LA Lake Charles Memorial Hospital.
Desrochers, Timothy H. '64 (MAR) [F] Garden, MI Marygrove Retreat Center.
Desrosiers, Alfred R. '61 (PRO) Retired.
DesRosiers, Denis '69 (SPR) On Duty Outside the Diocese.
DesRosiers, N. Wilfrid *s.s.j.* '55 (BAL) [M] Baltimore, MD St. Joseph Society of the Sacred Heart House of Central Administration.
Desrosiers, Paul H. '75 (NO) Lacombe, LA Sacred Heart Church.
DesRosiers, Philip J. '66 (BO) [3] Everett, MA St. Joseph Church.
DesRuisseaux, Charles E. '60 (MAN) [3] Manchester, NH St. Anthony of Padua Church.
Desruisseaux, G. Frantz '78 (BGP) [2] Norwalk, CT St. Joseph's Church.
Dessert, Msgr. James A. '34 (LA) Retired.
Desso, Leo C. '79 (ANC) Eagle River, AK St. Andrew Church.
DeStefano, Msgr. Richard '62 (BEA) [9] Beaumont, TX St. Jude Thaddeus Church.
DeStephano, Mark T. *s.j.* '88 (NEW) [B] Jersey City, NJ Saint Peter's College; [N] Jersey City, NJ Jesuits of Saint Peter's College, Inc.
DeSutter, Gilbert J. '54 (STP) Retired.
DeSutter, Mark '82 (PEO) [O] Macomb, IL St. Francis of Assisi Newman Center.
DeTemple, Michael *o.p.* '81 (PRO) [29] Providence, RI St. Pius V Church; [P] Providence, RI St. Pius Priory.
Determan, Joseph *o.p.* '51 (SAT) [B] San Antonio, TX Dominican Priory of Juan Macias.
Determan, Joseph H. *o.p.* '51 (TYL) [C] Lufkin, TX Monastery of the Infant Jesus.
Deters, Frederick J. *s.j.* '67 (IND) [D] Indianapolis, IN Brebeuf Jesuit Preparatory School, Inc.; [F] Beech Grove, IN St. Francis Hospital and Health Centers.
Deters, Gregory J. '87 (DET) Temperance, MI St. Anthony Church.
Detig, Joseph E. *s.v.d.* '62 (LAF) Jeanerette, LA Our Lady of the Rosary Church.
Detisch, John J. '88 (E) [2] Erie, PA Blessed Sacrament Church.
Detisch, Scott P. '87 (E) [B] Erie, PA Gannon University.
DeTommaso, Louis *o.f.m.* '54 (SP) Tarpon Springs, FL St. Ignatius Church.
DeTore, Richard *c.m.f.* '64 (SAT) [B] San Antonio, TX Immaculate Heart Claretian Seminary; [D] San Antonio, TX Antonian College Preparatory High School.
Detscher, Msgr. Alan F. '71 (BGP) Riverside, CT St. Catherine of Siena Church.
Dettenwanger, Dennis '64 (CIN) [1] Hamilton, OH St. Ann's Church; [2] Hamilton, OH St. Joseph's Church.
Dettling, William *o.p.* '59 (COL) [A] Columbus, OH Pontifical College Josephinum.
Dettmer, Alfred J. '56 (GRY) Dyer, IN St. Maria Goretti Church.
Dettmer, David J. '80 (BRK) [18] Brooklyn, NY St. Bernadette Church; [G] Brooklyn, NY Xaverian.
Deutsch, Bernard F. '51 (STL) Retired.
Deutsch, Daniel J. '94 (RCK) [2] Aurora, IL Holy Angels Church.
Deutsch, George E. '57 (TR) Forked River, NJ St. Pius X Church.
Deutsch, Paul *s.j.* (SP) [C] Tampa, FL Jesuit High School.
Deutsch, Timothy '94 (DUL) Virginia, MN Holy Spirit Church; Virginia, MN Sacred Heart Church; [F] Duluth, MN University of MN-Duluth.

Deutschmann, Msgr. Edward J. '52 (STL) [38] St. Louis, MO St. James the Greater Church.
Devan, Msgr. Clarence M. '37 (OG) Hogansburg, NY St. Patrick Church; Retired.
Devane, John F. *s.j.* '52 (BO) [W] Chestnut Hill, MA The Jesuit Community at Boston College.
Devaney, Michael J. *o.m.i.* '57 (COL) West Jefferson, OH SS. Simon and Jude Church; [H] West Jefferson, OH SS. Simon and Jude.
Devaney, Roy J. '52 (WOR) Retired.
Devany, John *c.p.* '45 (DET) [K] Detroit, MI St. Paul of the Cross Community, Congregation of the Passion.
Devaraj, Arulappa '86 (TYL) Center, TX St. Therese Church.
Deveau, Adhemar *o.m.i.* '52 (BO) [FF] Lowell, MA Oblate Ministry Development Service.
Deveau, Adhemar S. *o.m.i.* '52 (MAN) [K] Colebrook, NH Shrine of Our Lady of Grace.
Deveau, Daniel R. '75 (MAN) Groveton, NH St. Francis Xavier Church; North Stratford, NH Sacred Heart Church.
DeVenney, Timothy '93 (DUB) Unassigned.
Devenny, Joseph A. *s.j.* '37 (BO) [W] Weston, MA Campion Health Center, Inc.
Dever, Msgr. Daniel '52 (HON) Retired.
Dever, Msgr. Daniel J. (HON) [J] Kaneohe, HI Augustine Educational Foundation.
Dever, Msgr. Daniel J. '52 (HON) [A] Kaneohe, HI St. Stephen's Diocesan Center.
Dever, Dennis A. '60 (BO) [5] Somerville, MA St. Clement Church.
Dever, Gerard V. '71 (BO) [1] Quincy, MA St. Ann Church.
Dever, James *o.f.s.f.* (TR) [S] Princeton, NJ Campus Ministry for the Diocese of Trenton.
Dever, Msgr. William '65 (MIA) [7] Fort Lauderdale, FL St. Helen Church.
Devereaux, Martin C. '66 (PMB) Special Assignment.
Devereaux, Thomas W. '68 (SR) Healdsburg, CA St. John the Baptist Church.
Devereux, James A. *s.j.* '58 (CHL) [9] Charlotte, NC St. Peter Church; [J] Charlotte, NC Jesuit Community.
Devereux, Raymond P. '68 (CHI) [7] Chicago, IL All Saints-St. Anthony Church; [203] Chicago, IL St. Therese Catholic Chinese Church.
Devereux, Thomas W. *o.s.b.* '59 (GBG) [H] Latrobe, PA Saint Vincent Archabbey.
deVerteuil, Jack '89 (FBK) Nenana, AK St. Theresa Church.
Devery, Thomas P. '77 (NY) [DD] Suffern, NY Parish Mission Team Res.
DeVille, George T. (PIT) Allegheny County, PA Mayview State Hospital.
DeVille, George T. '57 (PIT) [2] Bridgeville, PA Holy Child Church.
DeVille, William H. '62 (COL) [41] Columbus, OH Sacred Heart Church.
Devillers, Arnaud J. *f.s.s.p.* '85 (SCR) [M] Scranton, PA St. Gregory's Priory (Priestly Fraternity of St. Peter); [M] Elmhurst, PA Priestly Fraternity of St. Peter (F.S.S.P.), North American District Headquarters.
Devin, John *c.ss.r.* '49 (BO) [13] Boston, MA Our Lady of Perpetual Help Church.
Devine, Arthur '57 (TUC) [20] Tucson, AZ Saints Peter and Paul Church.
Devine, Charles '65 (SB) Idyllwild, CA Queen of Angels Church; San Jacinto, CA St. Anthony Church.
Devine, Daniel P. '65 (PH) Feasterville, PA Assumption B.V.M. Church.
Devine, Donald G. *s.j.* '65 (PAT) [I] Morristown, NJ Loyola House of Retreats.
Devine, Finbarr *ss.cc.* '70 (LA) South Pasadena, CA Holy Family Church.
Devine, Frank J. *s.j.* '54 (BO) [W] Cambridge, MA Weston Jesuit Community.
Devine, J. Donald *s.s.c.* '54 (OM) [K] St. Columbans, NE St. Columban's Foreign Mission Society.
Devine, James T. '60 (BRK) [217] Queens, NY Our Lady of Perpetual Help Church; [219] Queens, NY Our Lady of the Skies Chapel Church; Queens, NY Veterans Affairs Extended Care Center, St. Albans, NY.
Devine, Msgr. Joseph A. '49 (HRT) [4] Waterbury, CT Our Lady of Loreto Church.
Devine, Kevin A. *c.s.p.* '56 (NY) [41] New York, NY Good Shepherd Church.
Devine, Michael '57 (SP) Port Richey, FL St. James the Apostle Church.
Devine, Patrick A. '69 (HBG) Bloomsburg, PA St. Columba Church.
Devine, Patrick T. '61 (LC) Retired; [I] La Crosse, WI Holy Cross (Seminary) Diocesan Center.
Devine, Richard J. *c.m.* '55 (BRK) [U] Queens Village, NY DePaul Residence.
Devine, Stephen M. '64 (FRS) Huron, CA St. Frances Cabrini Church.
Devine, Terry '85 (OWN) Henshaw, KY St. Ambrose Church; Marion, KY St. William Church; Sturgis, KY St. Francis Borgia Church.
Devine, Thomas '68 (ELP) [8] El Paso, TX Guardian Angel Church.
Devine, Msgr. Thomas F. '45 (SPR) Longmeadow, MA St. Mary's Church.
Devine, Msgr. W. J. '31 (DM) Retired.
Devine, William G. *s.j.* '57 (BO) [Y] Gloucester, MA Eastern Point Retreat House.
Devine, William J. (CHI) Retired.
Devine, William J. '73 (BO) Military & VA Chaplains.
Devine, Msgr. William P. '50 (NEW) Short Hills, NJ St. Rose of Lima Church.
Devine, William P. '52 (DUB) Retired.
Devine, Wm. Denis '45 (MIL) [P] Franklin, WI Villa Maria.
Deviney, Raymond L. '59 (SCR) Blakeslee, PA Christ the King Church.
Devino, Terrence P. *s.j.* '87 (BO) [W] Chestnut Hill, MA The Jesuit Community at Boston College.
Devino, Terrence P. *s.j.* '87 (SPR) On Duty Outside the Diocese.
DeVita, Thomas F. '78 (KAL) New Buffalo, MI St. Mary of the Lake Church.
DeVita, Thomas F. '78 (RVC) Priests Released from Diocesan Assignment.
Devito, Darius *o.f.m.cap.* '57 (NY) [DD] Yonkers, NY St. Clare Friary.
DeVliegher, Joseph *c.s.c.* '68 (AUS) Betram, TX Holy Cross Church; Burnet, TX Our Mother of Sorrows Church.
Devlin, Chester J. '71 (WOR) Northboro, MA St. Bernadette Church.
Devlin, David J. *o.s.f.s.* '77 (VEN) [3] Fort Myers, FL St. Cecilia Church.
Devlin, Eugene J. *s.j.* '51 (NEW) [B] Jersey City, NJ Saint Peter's College; [N] Jersey City, NJ Jesuits of Saint Peter's College, Inc.
Devlin, Francis X. *o.s.a.* '73 (PH) [D] Drexel Hill, PA Monsignor Bonner High School.
Devlin, James E. '72 (BRK) [167] Queens, NY St. Fidelis Church.
Devlin, Joseph D. *s.j.* '66 (BGP) [O] Fairfield, CT The Fairfield Jesuit Community-Fairfield University.
Devlin, Joseph D. *s.j.* '66 (BO) [W] Boston, MA The Society of Jesus of New England-Provincial Offices.
Devlin, Joseph F. '48 (PH) Retired.
Devlin, Msgr. Joseph M. '36 (NY) [141] Bronx, NY St. Frances de Chantal Church; Retired.
Devlin, Msgr. Joseph W. '56 (CAM) [M] Cherry Hill, NJ Vianney Villa.
Devlin, Kevin '54 (OKL) Perry, OK St. Rose of Lima Church.
Devlin, Mark T. '79 (TR) Bayville, NJ St. Barnabas Church.
Devlin, Michael H. '68 (SPR) [1] Chicopee, MA Assumption Church; Springfield, MA Baystate Medical Center, Springfield Hospital Unit; Springfield, MA Wesson-Women's Hospital Unit.
Devlin, Philip T. *c.s.c.* '56 (FgM) Holy Cross Foreign Missions.
Devlin, Philip T. *c.s.c.* '56 (FTW) [J] South Bend, IN Congregation of Holy Cross Indiana Province Provincial House.
Devlin, Raymond A. *s.j.* '55 (SJ) [M] Los Gatos, CA Sacred Heart Jesuit Center.
Devlin, Vianney M. *o.f.m.* '55 (NY) [115] New York, NY St. Stephen of Hungary Church.
Devoe, Richard M. *m.m.* '56 (FgM) Maryknoll Foreign Missions.
Devold, Cyprian '84 (NO) [21] New Orleans, LA The Resurrection Of Our Lord Church.
DeVolder, Philip '80 (FTW) Decatur, IN St. Mary Church.
Devorak, James W. '72 (NU) Hutchinson, MN Church of St. Anastasia.
Devorak, James W. '73 (NU) Stewart, MN Church of St. Boniface.
DeVore, David G. '88 (CIN) On Special and Diocesan Assignment.
Devore, Gerald T. '62 (BGP) [11] Stamford, CT St. Maurice Church.
Devot, Paul *s.j.* '72 (SJ) [2] Santa Clara, CA St. Clare Church.
DeVries, Gary '85 (DUB) [H] Cedar Rapids, IA Mercy Medical Center, Cedar Rapids, Iowa.
DeVries, Thomas D. '89 (MIL) On Duty Outside the Archdiocese.
DeVries, William J. '90 (MEM) Covington, TN St. Alphonsus Church.
Dewaele, Joseph *c.i.c.m.* '49 (ARL) [J] Arlington, VA Missionhurst, C.I.C.M.-Central House and Provincialate.
Dewan, Wilfred *c.s.p.* '53 (BRK) [150] Queens, NY St. Andrew Avellino Church.
Dewan, Wilfred *c.s.p.* '53 (NY) [DD] Jamaica Estates, NY Paulist Fathers Generalate.
Dewan, William '86 (JOL) Bloomingdale, IL St. Isidore Church.
Dewane, Daniel '71 (GB) Kewaunee, WI Holy Rosary Church.
Dewane, Msgr. Frank J. '88 (GB) On Duty Outside the Diocese.
Dewane, Msgr. John B. '54 (GB) [O] Green Bay, WI Sacred Heart Seminary, Inc.
Dewane, Msgr. John B. '62 (GB) Special Assignment.
deWasseige, Eric *o.p.* '65 (CHI) [N] Chicago, IL Dominicans (Provincial Office).
Dewes, John W. '65 (CHI) Barrington, IL St. Anne Church.
Dewig, Eugene '50 (EVN) [11] Evansville, IN Sacred Heart Church.
DeWitt, Robert A. '60 (L) [M] Nazareth, KY Generalate, Motherhouse and Novitiate of the Sisters of Charity of Nazareth.
DeWolf, Paul *c.i.c.m.* '50 (ARL) [J] Arlington, VA Missionhurst, C.I.C.M.-Central House and Provincialate.
Dewson, Msgr. John H. '47 (WIL) Liftwood, DE Immaculate Heart of Mary Church; Retired.
Deye, Anthony H. '37 (COV) Retired.
Deye, Walter C. *s.j.* '75 (IND) [D] Indianapolis, IN Brebeuf Jesuit Preparatory School, Inc.
Deyo, Paul *ss.cc.* '61 (MIA) Hallandale, FL St. Matthew Church.
Deyo, Paul A. '76 (DAV) [4] Iowa City, IA St. Wenceslaus Church; [F] Iowa City, IA The Regina Catholic Education Center.
DeYoung, Thomas J. '83 (GR) [2] Grand Rapids, MI Basilica of St. Adalbert Church.
Deziel, William '97 (STP) Anoka, MN St. Stephen Church; [N] Anoka, MN Crosier Community of Anoka.
Dharmaraj, Anthony *m.s.f.s.* '92 (ALX) Ferriday, LA St. Patrick Church; Vidalia, LA Our Lady of Lourdes Church.
Dhondt, Edward F. '69 (LFT) Anderson, IN St. Ambrose Church.
Di Cerbo, Almerico F. '46 (ALB) Retired.
Di Falco, Anthony F. *s.d.b.* '44 (SFR) [45] San Francisco, CA SS. Peter and Paul Church.
Di Giralamo, Gerald F. *s.a.* '81 (RVC) Central Islip, NY St. John of God Church.
Di Gregorio, Michael F. *o.s.a.* '73 (PH) [142] Philadelphia, PA St. Rita of Cascia Church.
Di Lella, Alexander A. *o.f.m.* '55 (WDC) [C] Washington, DC Catholic University of America, The.
Di Lella, Mario *o.f.m.* '53 (ATL) [L] Atlanta, GA Campus Ministry.
Di Marco, Abel A. '56 (PCE) [B] Ponce, PR The Pontifical Catholic University of Puerto Rico.
Di Maria, Matthew *c.m.f.* (LA) Woodland Hills, CA St. Mel Church.
Di Mauro, Joseph *s.a.* '78 (BO) [W] Brockton, MA Chapel of Our Saviour; [BB] Brockton, MA Chapel of Our Saviour.
di Miglio, Isidoro *o.f.m.* '47 (NY) [DD] New York, NY Franciscan Province of the Immaculate Conception.
Di Pasquale, Donald '62 (NEW) [7] Bayonne, NJ Our Lady of the Assumption Church.
Di Pasquale, Ralph *o.f.m.* '56 (NY) [DD] New York, NY Franciscan Province of the Immaculate Conception.
Di Senso, Gerard J. '53 (NY) Otisville, NY Holy Name Church.
Diab, Thomas (LUB) Military Chaplains.
Diab, Thomas '71 (SAN) Military Chaplains.
Diacetis, Anthony C. '69 (ALB) Ballston Lake, NY Our Lady of Grace Church.
Diachek, Robert M. '71 (PAT) [P] Morristown, NJ Priests Residence.
Diadia, Chester '58 (RVC) Floral Park, NY St. Hedwig's Church.
Diaferio, Vincent F. '58 (FR) [9] Fall River, MA Our Lady of the Holy Rosary Church.
Diamond, David E. '83 (PH) Center Square, PA St. Helena Church.
Diamond, Matthew J. '71 (BRK) [150] Queens, NY St. Andrew Avellino Church.
Dianda, Carl F. '59 (WDC) [13] Washington, DC St. Francis de Sales Church.
Dias, Frank '71 (NY) [A] New York, NY Cathedral Preparatory Seminary.
Dias, John *c.s.c.* (NY) Manhattan, NY Cabrini Medical Center.
Dias, John F. *c.s.c.* '63 (FR) [J] North Dartmouth, MA Holy Cross Mission House.
Dias, Orsete '94 (RVC) Levittown, NY St. Bernard Church.
Diaz, Alberto '85 (ARE) [3] Arecibo, PR Nuestra Senora del Carmen Church.
Diaz, Alvaro *o.f.m.* (CAM) [4] Vineland, NJ St. Isidore Church.
Diaz, Alvaro '45 (SJN) Retired.
Diaz, Alvaro '73 (CAM) [P] Vineland, NJ Spanish Catholic Center.
Diaz, Angel '76 (ARE) [2] Vega-Baja, PR N.S. de la Providencia Church.
Diaz, Angel R. '85 (ARE) Lares, PR St. Judas Tadeos Church.
Diaz, Erno B. '69 (NY) [34] New York, NY Epiphany Church.
Diaz, Francisco G. (YAK) Special Assignment.
Diaz, Francisco G. '77 (MIA) [14] Miami, FL Prince of Peace Church.
Diaz, Francisco Restrepo '88 (DET) [3] St. Clair Shores, MI St. Isaac Jogues Church.

Diaz, Gilbert '94 (KNX) Oak Ridge, TN St. Mary Church.
Diaz, Gonzalo '52 (SJN) [G] Guaynabo, PR Opus Dei.
Diaz, Gonzalo '63 (MGZ) On Special Assignment.
Diaz, Gumersindo *s.d.b.* '70 (MIA) [25] Miami, FL St. Kieran Church.
Diaz, Heberto M. '89 (BWN) [2] Harlingen, TX Immaculate Heart of Mary Church.
Diaz, Heberto M., Jr. '89 (BWN) [1] Harlingen, TX Our Lady of the Assumption Church.
Diaz, Hernando (SLC) [4] Salt Lake City, UT Sacred Heart Church.
Diaz, Hernando '71 (SLC) Tooele, UT St. Marguerite's Church.
Diaz, Jesus '54 (ARE) Vega-Alta, PR Santa Ana Church.
Diaz, Jose Matias '89 (NEW) [A] Kearny, NJ Redemptoris Mater.
Diaz, Kevin Hunt (PHX) Camp Verde, AZ St. Frances Cabrini Church.
Diaz, Kevin Hunt '84 (PHX) Prescott Valley, AZ St. Germaine Church.
Diaz, Lorenzo *m.c.c.j.* '77 (CHI) [N] Chicago, IL Comboni Missionaries Theologate (M.C.C.J.), Verona Fathers.
Diaz, Martin *o.p.* '78 (LA) [59] Los Angeles, CA St. Dominic Church; [CC] Los Angeles, CA Archdiocesan Office for Campus Ministry.
Diaz, Michael '73 (SD) Military Chaplains.
Diaz, Miguel Gil '86 (CGS) Cidra, PR Nuestra Senora del Carmen Church.
Diaz, Oscar '94 (SR) Saint Helena, CA St. Helena Church.
Diaz, Raul '97 (FRS) Porterville, CA St. Anne Church.
Diaz, Robert '79 (BWN) Retired.
Diaz, Thomas K. '81 (SR) Fort Bragg, CA Our Lady of Good Counsel Church.
Diaz Vilar, J. Juan *s.j.* '69 (NEW) [N] Jersey City, NJ Jesuits of Saint Peter's College, Inc.
Diaz Vilar, Juan '68 (NEW) [B] Jersey City, NJ Saint Peter's College.
DiBacco, John V., Jr. '67 (WH) Martinsburg, WV St. Joseph's Church.
DiBardino, Anthony '76 (CAM) Pennsauken, NJ St. Cecilia's Church.
Dibb, William C. *s.j.* '60 (FBK) [C] Fairbanks, AK Jesuit Residence.
Dibble, Michael B. '60 (NY) [105] New York, NY St. Peter Church.
Dibble, Romuald '47 (MIL) [P] Milwaukee, WI Salvatorians - Jordan Hall.
DiBlasi, Msgr. Augustine J. '45 (NY) Retired; [E] White Plains, NY Archbishop Stepinac High School.
DiBuo, Roger '89 (WIL) Dover, DE Holy Cross Church.
DiBuono, Msgr. Pasquale M. '44 (CAM) Hammonton, NJ St. Martin de Porres Church; Retired.
DiCesare, Giosue Scotto *s.d.v.* '52 (NEW) [25] Newark, NJ St. Michael's Church.
Dicharry, Harold E. *c.m.* '42 (NO) [61] New Orleans, LA St. Stephen Church.
Dicharry, Warren F. *c.m.* '45 (DAL) [6] Dallas, TX Holy Trinity Church.
DiCicco, Mario *o.f.m.* (OAK) [A] Berkeley, CA Franciscan School of Theology.
DiCicco, Mario *o.f.m.* '59 (OAK) [N] Oakland, CA Franciscan Friars Provincial Office, Province of St. Barbara.
Dick, Firmus '54 (EVN) Schnellville, IN Sacred Heart Church.
Dick, Gregory M. *o.praem* '96 (ORG) [A] Silverado, CA St. Michael's Norbertine Postulancy, Novitiate and Juniorate; [H] Silverado, CA Norbertine Fathers of Orange Inc.
Dick, John '96 (DAL) Ennis, TX St. John Nepomucene Church.
Dickes, Jerome H. '48 (OM) Retired.
Dickey, Merrell '94 (SP) Spring Hill, FL St. Frances Xavier Cabrini Church.
Dickie, Msgr. John A. '56 (SD) [31] San Diego, CA St. Mary Magdalene Church.
Dickinson, Stephen '58 (FAR) Retired.
Dickinson, William '89 (CLV) [15] Cleveland, OH St. Catherine Church.
Dickinson, William R. '89 (CLV) Brecksville, OH St. Basil the Great Church.
Dickman, John W. '48 (L) Pewee Valley, KY St. Aloysius Church; Retired.
Dickman, Richard C. '93 (LC) Alma, WI St. Lawrence Church.
Dickmann, Louis H. '59 (COV) Falmouth, KY St. Francis Xavier Church.
Dickrell, Cyril *s.d.s.* '53 (MIL) [P] Milwaukee, WI Salvatorian Provincial Residence.
Dicks, Thomas K. '87 (NY) [138] Bronx, NY St. Dominic Church.
Dickson, Henry E. *s.s.j.* '60 (MOB) Prichard, AL St. James Major Church.
Dickson, Norman *s.j.* '67 (DET) [27] Detroit, MI Gesu Church.
Dickson, Norman J. *s.j.* (DET) [B] Berkley, MI Loyola House.
Dickson, Norman J. *s.j.* '67 (DET) [K] Detroit, MI Jesuit Provincial Office-Detroit Province of the Society of Jesus; [T] Detroit, MI Jesuit Seminary Association.
DiCristina, Frank A. (PAT) On Duty Outside the Diocese.
Dicristina, Frank T. '86 (SB) Redlands, CA Sacred Heart Church.
Didas, James F. *s.s.j.* '33 (BAL) [M] Baltimore, MD St. Joseph's Manor.
Didgeon, John '87 (PH) [71] Philadelphia, PA Incarnation of Our Lord Church.
Didier, Jacques R. *m.e.p.* '53 (SFR) [N] San Francisco, CA Paris Foreign Mission Society Residence.
DiDone, Matthew *c.s.* '67 (PMB) [3] Delray Beach, FL Our Lady Queen of Peace Church.
Diebel, Thomas '79 (LUB) Special Assignment.
Dieckhaus, Anthony W. '62 (PH) [152] Philadelphia, PA St. Timothy Church.
Dieckhaus, Joseph C. '74 (PH) [BB] Philadelphia, PA Sister Servants of the Holy Spirit of Perpetual Adoration (S.Sp.S.A.P.).
Dieckman, Leonard E. *s.j.* '62 (FgM) Provinces.
Dieckman, Vincent A. *o.f.m.* '38 (CIN) [M] Cincinnati, OH St. Clement Friary.
Dieckmann, Michael E. '74 (STL) Hillsboro, MO Church of the Good Shepherd.
Diederich, Donald '58 (RVC) Setauket, NY St. James Church.
Diederich, Everett A. *s.j.* '52 (STL) [P] St. Louis, MO Jesuit Community Corporation at St. Louis University - Jesuit Hall.
Diederichs, Michael F. '42 (PHX) Retired.
Diedrick, Charles T. '78 (CLV) Northfield, OH St. Barnabas Church.
Diefenbach, Gabriel *o.f.m.cap.* '36 (GB) [M] Appleton, WI Monte Alverno Retreat Center.
Diegel, Ron '75 (TYL) Marshall, TX St. Joseph Church.
Diegelman, Clarence L. '43 (CIN) Retired; [B] Carthagena, OH St. Charles.
Diegelman, Robert '93 (R) Wendell, NC St. Eugene Church.
Diehl, Dennis P. '74 (BAL) Fulton, MD St. Francis of Assisi Church.
Diehl, Michael C. '55 (TUC) Retired.
Diehl, Thomas J. *s.j.* '50 (CIN) [P] Milford, OH Milford Spiritual Center.
DieKemper, Barnabas '65 (CHI) [N] Chicago, IL St. Peter's Friary.
Dieker, James P. '93 (DOD) Pratt, KS Sacred Heart Church.
Diekhoff, Bernard *c.pp.s.* '47 (KC) [3] St. Joseph, MO St. Francis Xavier Church.
Diekmann, Godfrey *o.s.b.* '31 (SCL) [I] Collegeville, MN St. John's Abbey, of the Order of St. Benedict.
Diele, Joseph '85 (BRK) [8] Brooklyn, NY St. Ann-St. George Church; Brooklyn, NY The Brooklyn Hospital.
Diels, Gaston *ss.cc.* '47 (HON) [H] Kaneohe, HI Sacred Hearts Center.
Diem, Joseph '85 (BO) Hopkinton, MA St. John the Evangelist Church.
Diemand, James E. '68 (SPR) Orange, MA St. Mary Church.
Diemer, Charles J. '38 (CHI) Retired.
Diemer, Joseph *o.s.b.cam.* '49 (MRY) [G] Big Sur, CA New Camaldoli Hermitage.
Diemer, Michael J. *m.j.* '96 (PCE) [7] Ponce, PR Santa Maria Church.
Dien, Vincent '46 (SB) Retired.
Dienert, Robert T. '62 (LR) Searcy, AR St. James Church.
Dieninis, Lionginas '38 (GAY) Retired.
Dieringer, James J. '58 (P) Retired.
Dierkes, Richard '81 (KC) [1] St. Joseph, MO St. Joseph's Co-Cathedral.
Diermeier, Joseph *o.f.m.cap.* '78 (LC) Cassel, WI Sacred Heart Church; Halder, WI St. Patrick Church; Marathon City, WI Nativity of the Blessed Virgin Mary Church.
Diersen, William M. '50 (L) Retired.
Diersing, Leo '39 (SAN) Retired.
Diesbourg, Raymond *m.s.c.* '74 (FgM) Missionaries of the Sacred Heart Foreign Missions.
Diesbourg, Raymond *m.s.c.* '74 (RCK) [H] Aurora, IL Missionaries of the Sacred Heart Community.
Dieter, Thomas '83 (JOL) On Duty Outside the Diocese.
Dieter, Thomas '83 (SP) Hudson, FL St. Michael Church.
Dieter, Xavier L. *o.c.s.o.* '58 (DUB) [K] Peosta, IA New Melleray Abbey, Order of Cistercians of the Strict Observance.
Dietlein, Damian *o.s.b.* '57 (BIS) [A] Richardton, ND Assumption Abbey.
Dietlein, Damian *o.s.b.* '57 (IND) [A] St. Meinrad, IN St. Meinrad Seminary.
Dietlein, Raymond *o.s.b.* '54 (BIS) [A] Richardton, ND Assumption Abbey.
Dietmer, Charles J. (CHI) Schaumburg, IL St. Marcelline Church.
Dietrich, Christopher *o.f.m.cap.* '59 (NY) [17] Yonkers, NY Sacred Heart Church.
Dietrich, Edward (SB) Retired.
Dietrich, John J. '93 (HRT) Special and other (Arch)Diocesan Assignment; [A] Bloomfield, CT St. Thomas Seminary.
Dietrich, Michael A. '65 (SY) Special Assignment.
Dietrich, Severin *o.f.m.conv.* (MET) [G] North Plainfield, NJ Villa Maria Sanitarium.
Dietrich, Severin *o.f.m.conv.* '53 (MET) [I] North Plainfield, NJ Congregation of the Holy Infancy of Jesus Regional House.
Dietsch, William '71 (EVN) Poseyville, IN St. Francis Xavier Church.
Dietz, Conrad R. '57 (BRK) [B] Douglaston, NY Cathedral Residence of the Immaculate Conception.
Dietz, Conrad R. '57 (RVC) Oceanside, NY St. Anthony Church.
Dietz, Donald *o.m.i.* (BIR) [H] Tuscaloosa, AL University of Alabama in Tuscaloosa.
Dietz, Donald *o.m.i.* '57 (BIR) Tuscaloosa, AL St. Francis of Assisi University Parish.
Dietz, Donald L. '57 (STP) [N] St. Paul, MN Oblate Residence.
Dietz, Francis '40 (DET) Retired.
Dietz, Joseph S. '87 (NY) Scarsdale, NY Immaculate Heart of Mary Church.
Dietz, Msgr. Norbert J. '49 (STL) [3] University City, MO Our Lady of Lourdes Church.
Dietz, Xavier Ortiz '77 (SAT) On Leave.
Dietzel, Elmer J. '51 (MAD) Brodhead, WI St. Rose Church.
Dietzen, John J. '54 (PEO) [1] Bloomington, IL Holy Trinity Church.
Dietzen, Vincent E. '53 (PEO) [3] Bloomington, IL St. Patrick's Church; Retired.
Dietzenbach, John '80 (BAL) Libertytown, MD St. Peter Church.
Dietzler, William J. '69 (MIL) [K] Racine, WI St. Mary's Medical Center, Inc.
Diez, A. Oscar '68 (DAL) [13] Dallas, TX St. Augustine Church.
Diez, Alvaro '68 (YAK) East Wenatchee, WA Holy Apostles Church.
Diez, Antonio '59 (SP) Riverview, FL Resurrection Church.
Diez, Toribio Pascual *o.s.b.* '40 (MGZ) [6] Mayaquez, PR Sacred Heart Church.
Diez Antonanzas, Jesus R. '57 (PCE) [B] Ponce, PR The Pontifical Catholic University of Puerto Rico.
Diezel, Joseph J. '62 (SB) Retired.
Diezeman, Andrew S. '45 (IND) Retired.
DiFabio, Mark '95 (SPR) Absent on Leave.
DiFede, Thomas V. *o.p.* '59 (COL) Zanesville, OH St. Thomas Aquinas Church.
DiFederico, Gabriel '78 (MEM) [10] Memphis, TN Holy Rosary Church.
Diffenbacher, Brian (ROC) Hornell, NY St. James Mercy Hospital.
Diffley, Francis A. *m.m.* '50 (HON) [13] Honolulu, HI Sacred Heart Church; [H] Honolulu, HI Maryknoll Fathers House.
Diffley, Jerome E. '45 (SP) [4] St. Petersburg, FL Holy Family Church; Retired.
Diffley, Patrick J. '63 (BRK) Released from Diocesan Assignment.
DiFilippo, John V. *o.s.f.s.* '45 (PH) [AA] Philadelphia, PA Oblates of St. Francis De Sales.
DiFiore, John '97 (NO) [D] Marrero, LA Archbishop Shaw High School.
DiFolco, Thomas (CIN) [2] Cincinnati, OH St. Agnes Church.
DiFolco, Thomas P. '83 (CIN) [59] Cincinnati, OH St. Martin De Porres Church.
DiFrancesco, Walter L. '59 (SAV) [4] Augusta, GA St. Teresa of Avila Church.
DiFruscio, John A. '69 (BO) Health Leave.
Digal, Danilo C. '78 (NO) [1] Kenner, LA Nativity of Our Lord Church.
DiGeronimo, Michael A. '76 (WOR) Leicester, MA St. Joseph's Church; Leicester, MA St. Pius X Church.
DiGeronimo, Richard '73 (LFT) Unassigned.
Diggins, John Martin *o.p.* '94 (PRO) [P] Providence, RI St. Thomas Aquinas Priory at Providence College.
DiGiacobbe, Albert C. '66 (PH) [54] Philadelphia, PA St. Helena Church.
DiGiacomo, James J. *s.j.* '56 (NY) [F] New York, NY Regis High School; [DD] New York, NY "America;" Residence and publication office of the America Press.
DiGiovanni, Alfonso '96 (NEW) On Duty Outside the Archdiocese.
DiGiovanni, Msgr. Stephen M. '77 (BGP) [18] Bridgeport, CT St. Peter's Church.
DiGiralamo, Gerald '45 (RVC) Northport, NY Veteran's Hospital.
DiGirolamo, Dante '48 (NEW) Retired.
DiGirolamo, Paul A. *j.c.d.* (PH) [46] Philadelphia, PA St. Francis de Sales Church.
DiGiulio, Anthony '55 (MAN) [L] West Franklin, NH Our Lady of the Sacred Heart Convent.
DiGiulio, Anthony F. '55 (MAN) Retired.

Dignan, Eamon '59 (WDC) Waldorf, MD Our Lady Help of Christians Church.
Dignan, Thomas '57 (BIS) Tioga, ND St. Thomas Church.
DiGregorio, Joseph L. '66 (PH) Military Chaplains.
DiGuardo, Domenic *s.d.b.* '37 (NY) [FF] West Haverstraw, NY Don Bosco Retreat Center and Marian Shrine; [FF] West Haverstraw, NY Marian Shrine.
DiIanni, Albert *s.m.* '60 (BO) [59] Boston, MA Our Lady of Victories Church; [W] Boston, MA Marist Fathers and Brothers Provincial House; [W] Boston, MA Marist Fathers of Our Lady of Victories (Boston Prov.).
DiIenno, Nicholas C. *o.s.f.s.* '43 (CAM) [M] Pittsgrove, NJ Villa St. Joseph.
DiIorio, Michael C. '77 (PH) [115] Philadelphia, PA Our Lady of Consolation Church.
DiLella, Christopher C. '79 (PAT) Madison, NJ St. Vincent Martyr Church.
DiLeo, Anthony M. '64 (SB) Temecula, CA St. Catherine Church.
DiLeo, Richard *s.c.j.* '81 (GAL) [27] Houston, TX St. Elizabeth Ann Seton Church.
DiLeonardi, Rocco *o.carm.* '56 (JOL) [J] Joliet, IL St. Elias Carmelites.
Dilettuso, Joseph (BLX) Biloxi, MS V.A. Center; Gulfport, MS V.A. Hospital.
Dilettuso, Joseph '72 (BLX) Special Assignment.
Dilg, Donald *c.s.c.* '75 (COS) [10] Colorado Springs, CO Sacred Heart Church.
Dilgen, William M. *s.m.m.* '47 (RVC) [N] Bay Shore, NY Montfort Missionaries.
Dilger, Basil *o.s.b.* '61 (FgM) American - Cassinese Congregation Foreign Missions.
Dilger, Basil *o.s.b.* '61 (SFS) [F] Marvin, SD Blue Cloud Abbey.
Dilger, Donald '59 (EVN) Retired.
Diliberto, Peter J. '43 (LA) [R] Los Angeles, CA Amat House; [X] Montebello, CA DePaul Center.
Dilion, Joseph A. '46 (HRT) Retired.
Dilipy, Basilio '94 (CI) Puluwat, FM Santiago Church.
Dill, Edwin *s.t.* '59 (BIR) Demopolis, AL St. Leo Church.
Dilla, Francis E. (CHI) Retired.
Dillabough, Msgr. Daniel J. '74 (SD) [8] San Diego, CA Immaculata Church.
Dillane, Maurice '63 (SAT) On Duty Outside the Archdiocese.
Dillard, Msgr. Russell L. '78 (WDC) [7] Washington, DC St. Augustine Church.
Dillard, Steven *s.j.* '86 (SPK) [E] Spokane, WA Gonzaga Preparatory School.
Dillemuth, Frederick J. *s.j.* '54 (NY) [DD] New York, NY Jesuit Community at Fordham University.
Dillenburg, Msgr. James (GB) [16] Green Bay, WI St. Elizabeth Ann Seton Church.
Diller, Harold *c.pp.s.* '34 (CIN) [B] Carthagena, OH St. Charles.
Dilley, Gary *f.s.s.p.* (SCR) [M] Elmhurst, PA Priestly Fraternity of St. Peter (F.S.S.P.), North American District Headquarters.
Dilley, Gary *f.s.s.p.* '72 (Y) Vienna, OH Queen of the Holy Rosary Church.
Dilley, Gary D. '72 (CHR) Absent On Leave.
Dillinger, Joseph A. '96 (SC) [2] Sioux City, IA Blessed Sacrament Church.
Dillingham, Charles C. '73 (WIL) [5] Wilmington, DE St. Elizabeth Church.
Dillmann, Alan M. '59 (ATL) [12] Atlanta, GA Shrine of the Immaculate Conception Church.
Dillon, Arthur J. '45 (CHI) Barrington, IL St. Anne Church; Retired.
Dillon, Charles P. *s.s.* '39 (BAL) [J] Baltimore, MD St. Charles Villa; [M] Baltimore, MD St. Charles Villa.
Dillon, Ciarian *o.m.i.* '54 (OAK) Crockett, CA St. Rose of Lima Church.
Dillon, David *o.carm.* '65 (JOL) Glendale Heights, IL St. Matthew Church.
Dillon, Msgr. David A. '42 (STP) Retired.
Dillon, Dennis *s.j.* '69 (CLV) [E] Cleveland, OH St. Ignatius High School; [U] Cleveland, OH Jesuit Retreat House.
Dillon, Msgr. Desmond P. '41 (YAK) Kennewick, WA St. Joseph's Church; Retired.
Dillon, Msgr. Edward J. (ATL) [M] Atlanta, GA Carlow College Bicentennial Fund, Inc.
Dillon, Edward J. *o.f.m.* '55 (FgM) Franciscan Foreign Missions.
Dillon, Edward J. *o.f.m.* '55 (NY) [DD] New York, NY Franciscan Friars, Order of Friars Minor, Holy Name Province.
Dillon, Edward J. '60 (ROC) Clifton Springs, NY St. Felix / St. Francis Parish Cluster Church.
Dillon, Msgr. Edward J. '67 (ATL) [3] Atlanta, GA Holy Spirit Church.
Dillon, Edward J. '88 (PAT) [C] Madison, NJ Bayley-Ellard High School.
Dillon, Geoffrey R. *s.j.* '83 (SFR) [N] San Francisco, CA Jesuit Community at University of San Francisco.
Dillon, Gerald F. *c.s.b.* '62 (GAL) Angleton, TX St. Basil Church.
Dillon, James P. '73 (BRK) Military Chaplains.
Dillon, Jeffry T. '81 (BRK) [U] Douglaston, NY Bishop Mugavero Residence.
Dillon, Jerome V. '77 (OM) Military Chaplains.
Dillon, John '85 (RVC) Absent on Leave.
Dillon, John D. '59 (ROC) Auburn, NY Auburn Correctional Facility.
Dillon, John T. *s.j.* '63 (CHI) [C] Chicago, IL Jesuit Community at Loyola University of Chicago.
Dillon, Michael *c.ss.r.* (ATL) Hapeville, GA St. John the Evangelist Church.
Dillon, Michael J. '61 (SAC) Rocklin, CA SS. Peter and Paul Church.
Dillon, Richard J. '61 (NY) On Duty Outside the Archdiocese.
Dillon, Robert '65 (RIC) Appomattox, VA Our Lady of Peace Church; Buckingham, VA Church of the Nativity.
Dillon, Robert '97 (NY) [206] Staten Island, NY Holy Rosary Church; Graduate Studies.
Dillon, Msgr. Robert E. '36 (SY) Retired; [S] Syracuse, NY St. Pius X Home, Inc.
Dillon, Thomas J. *o.s.a.* '57 (PH) [130] Philadelphia, PA Our Mother of Consolation Church.
Dillon, Thomas J. '59 (GI) Sutherland, NE Sacred Heart Church.
Dillon, William *s.a.* '69 (NY) [DD] Garrison, NY Generalate of the Franciscan Friars of the Atonement-St. James Friary.
DiLorenzo, Thomas '79 (BO) Winthrop, MA Holy Rosary Church.
DiLoreto, Anthony '54 (B) Salmon, ID St. Charles Church.
DiLuzio, James *c.s.p.* '93 (LA) [86] Los Angeles, CA St. Paul the Apostle Church.
Dilworth, Kevin *s.j.* '84 (PHX) [B] Phoenix, AZ Brophy College Preparatory.
DiMaggio, Joseph F. '55 (ALB) Johnstown, NY Immaculate Conception Church.
Dimapilis, Jose Rizal *o.p.* '67 (NOR) Middletown, CT Connecticut Valley Hospital.
DiMaria, Peter J. '93 (PH) Media, PA Nativity of the Blessed Virgin Mary Church.
DiMarzio, Nicholas A. '70 (NEW) [28] Newark, NJ Our Lady of Mt. Carmel Church.
Dimas, Miguel A. *o.r.c.* '89 (PCE) Castaner, PR Our Lady of the Miraculous Medal Church.
DiMascola, Charles J. '81 (SPR) Turners Falls, MA Our Lady of Czestochowa Church.
DiMattei, Robert A. '91 (BAL) Pasadena, MD St. Jane Frances de Chantal Church.
DiMatteo, John *o.ss.t.* '36 (PH) Bristol, PA St. Ann Church.
DiMauro, John C. *o.f.m.* '56 (BO) [P] Andover, MA Franciscan Center; [W] Andover, MA St. Francis Friary; [Y] Andover, MA Franciscan Center - Retreat House.
DiMauro, Joseph *s.a.* '78 (BO) [P] Brockton, MA Chapel of Our Savior-Catholic Pastoral and Information Center.
DiMauro, Joseph A. *o.s.f.s.* '73 (PH) [D] Philadelphia, PA Father Judge High School for Boys; [AA] Philadelphia, PA Oblates of St. Francis De Sales.
DiMauro, Msgr. Joseph V. '67 (CAM) Blackwood, NJ St. Agnes Church.
Dimengo, Michael G. '77 (CLV) [1] Cleveland, OH Cathedral of St. John the Evangelist.
Dimic, Milan *s.d.b.* '85 (BGP) [4] Fairfield, CT Holy Cross Church.
Dimler, G. Richard *s.j.* '63 (NY) [DD] New York, NY Jesuit Community at Fordham University.
Dimock, Giles *o.p.* '66 (STU) [A] Steubenville, OH Franciscan University of Steubenville; [F] Steubenville, OH Holy Spirit Monastery.
Dimond, Arthur '51 (COL) Retired.
Dimond, Arthur J. '51 (COL) [29] Columbus, OH St. Mary Church.
Dinan, Dennis M. '92 (NY) [229] Staten Island, NY St. Sylvester Church.
Dinan, John '58 (WCH) Retired.
DiNardo, Daniel A. '66 (CAM) Bridgeton, NJ St. Teresa of Avila Church.
DiNardo, Hector *c.r.m.* '56 (NEW) Lodi, NJ St. Joseph's Church.
DiNardo, Lawrence A. *m.ch.a.* '74 (PIT) [73] Pittsburgh, PA Holy Wisdom Church.
DiNardo, Mark A. '58 (CLV) [60] Cleveland, OH St. Patrick Church.
DiNardo, Msgr. Ramon A. '50 (WDC) Retired.
DiNardo, Salvatore *o.p.* '31 (SFR) [N] San Francisco, CA St. Dominic Priory.
DiNardo, Salvatore M. *o.p.* '54 (SJ) [D] Mountain View, CA St. Francis High School; [K] Mountain View, CA Villa Siena.
Dincher, Carl L. *s.j.* '57 (BAL) [M] Baltimore, MD Jesuit Fathers and Brothers Maryland Provincial Curia.
Dincher, Carl L. *s.j.* '57 (FgM) Provinces.
Dinda, John J. '62 (PH) Spring City, PA St. Joseph Church.
Dindorf, Meinrad *o.s.b.* '58 (SCL) [H] St. Cloud, MN St. Benedict's Center.
Dindorf, Meinrad *o.s.b.* '58 (STP) Minneapolis, MN University of Minnesota Hospitals.
Dineen, Michael P. '49 (MIL) Kenosha, WI Kenosha Hospital and Medical Center.
Dineen, William *c.pp.s.* '66 (KC) [A] Liberty, MO Society of the Precious Blood Provincial Offices; [J] Liberty, MO Precious Blood Society Provincial Office; [J] Liberty, MO Precious Blood Center.
Dinelli, William J. '56 (SAC) Sacramento, CA University of California, Davis Medical Center.
Dinello, John '85 (PIT) Scott Township, PA SS. Simon and Jude Church.
Dinga, William '75 (RIC) Retired.
Dinger, Clair M. '53 (LAN) Milan, MI Immaculate Conception Church.
Dinger, Clair M. '53 (STU) On Duty Outside the Diocese.
Dinges, Anthony '57 (RIC) Retired.
Dinh, Dominic (DAV) Retired.
Dinh, Dominic Do van '72 (SJ) [21] San Jose, CA Our Lady Queen of Martyrs, Vietnamese Mission Church.
Dinh, Hai *c.ss.r.* '91 (DAL) [2] Garland, TX Mother of Perpetual Help Church.
Dinh, Hao '93 (SJ) Milpitas, CA St. John the Baptist Church.
Dinh, Quang Duc *s.v.d.* '92 (DUB) [B] Epworth, IA Divine Word College.
Dinh, Thomas Tranh *i.c.m.* '65 (BR) [H] Baton Rouge, LA Incarnation Consecratio Mission.
Dinh, Tran Thuc '61 (OAK) [3] San Leandro, CA St. Felicitas Church.
Dinh Tuan Ngan, Joseph (SPC) [E] Carthage, MO Congregation of the Mother Co-Redemptrix, United States Assumption Province.
Dinh Viet Luan, Felix M. *c.m.c.* (SPC) [E] Carthage, MO Congregation of the Mother Co-Redemptrix, United States Assumption Province.
Dinh Vuong Can, Anselm M. *c.m.c.* (SPC) [E] Carthage, MO Congregation of the Mother Co-Redemptrix, United States Assumption Province.
Dinh-Van-Thiep, Philip '83 (GB) Wautoma, WI St. Joseph Church.
Dininni, Nicholas J. *o.s.j.* '93 (SCR) [8] Pittston, PA St. Rocco Church.
Dinio, Miguel *o.p.* '64 (SAN) [5] San Angelo, TX St. Joseph Church.
Dink, Nghia '86 (HT) Larose, LA Our Lady of the Rosary Church.
Dinkel, Emil *c.pp.s.* '52 (DOD) Hugoton, KS St. Helen Church; Satanta, KS St. Alphonsus Church.
Dinkel, Harvey P. *o.f.m.cap.* '61 (DEN) [M] Denver, CO St. Francis of Assisi Friary.
Dinkins, Msgr. Jack M. '63 (GAL) Katy, TX Epiphany of the Lord Church.
Dinneen, James J. *s.j.* '62 (RVC) [P] Manhasset, NY St. Ignatius Retreat House, Inisfada.
Dinneen, John A. *s.j.* '60 (BO) [W] Chestnut Hill, MA The Jesuit Community at Boston College.
Dinnico, Henry P. '58 (GBG) Retired.
Dino, Gerald *o.e.s.l.* '65 (PSC) Linden, NJ St. George's Church.
DiNoia, Joseph Augustine *o.p.* '70 (WDC) [B] Washington, DC Dominican House of Studies.
DiNola, Leonard J. '58 (NY) Buchanan, NY St. Christopher Church.
DiNorcia, Americo '59 (WDC) Retired.
Diogo, Louis M. '46 (PRO) Retired.
Diomartich, Msgr. Felix S. '37 (LA) [45] Los Angeles, CA St. Anthony Church; Retired.
Dion, Gerard J. '92 (MAN) Manchester, NH Nursing Homes; Goffstown, NH Hillsborough County Nursing Home.
Dion, Louis F. *a.a.* '40 (WOR) [B] Worcester, MA Assumption College; [N] Worcester, MA Assumptionists (Augustinians of the Assumption).
Dion, Maurice B. '44 (SAL) Retired.
Dionne, Adrian L. *o.p.* '49 (COL) Somerset, OH St. Joseph's Church; Somerset, OH Holy Trinity Church; [H] Somerset, OH St. Joseph's Rectory.
Dionne, Earl J. '58 (MIL) Retired.
Dionne, Leo *o.m.i.* '59 (MIA) [2] Miami, FL Christ the King Church.
Dionne, Martin *o.p.* '49 (PRT) [I] Lewiston, ME SS. Peter and Paul Priory.
Dionne, Rene *m.afr.* '61 (FgM) Missionaries of Africa Foreign Missions.
Dionne, Vincente *c.ss.r.* '80 (PCE) Guayama, PR St. Anthony of Padua Church.
DiOrio, Ralph A. '57 (WOR) On Special or Other (Arch)Diocesan Assignment.
Dios, Alfredo de *o.a.r.* '60 (ORG) [5] Santa Ana, CA Our Lady of the Pillar Church.
DiPaul, Lawrence M. '73 (PH) Absent on Leave.
DiPeri, Joseph B. '56 (NEW) Retired.
DiPerri, James H. '88 (BO) [17] Boston, MA St. Catherine of Siena Church.
Diphe, Juan '76 (HEL) Military Chaplains.
DiPietro, Leroy A. '70 (PIT) Brentwood, PA St. Sylvester Church.
DiPietro, Rodric J. '76 (COL) [16] Columbus, OH St. Elizabeth Church.

Dippre, Mark '92 (PHX) [6] Mesa, AZ St. Timothy Church.
Dipre, Gilio L. '55 (E) [B] Erie, PA Gannon University.
DiPucchio, Anthony F.X. '52 (WOR) Retired.
DiRenzo, Michael J. '70 (LA) San Pedro, CA Fort MacArthur Annex.
Direnzo, Michael J. '70 (STU) On Duty Outside the Diocese.
Dirig, Walter F. *c.m.* '39 (PH) [AA] Philadelphia, PA Congregation of the Mission.
Dirkx, Dennis '72 (MIL) [C] Milwaukee, WI Mount Mary College.
Dirscherl, Denis A. *s.j.* '67 (CHI) [N] Chicago, IL Chicago Province of the Society of Jesus-Provincial Office.
DiRuscio, Romano *s.c.* '51 (PH) [M] Springfield, PA Don Guanella School for Retarded Boys; [M] Springfield, PA Cardinal Krol Center; [AA] Springfield, PA Servants of Charity (S.C.).
DiRusso, Anthony '63 (MAN) North Walpole, NH St. Peter Church.
DiSano, Frank E. '84 (ROC) Absent on Leave.
Disch, Msgr. John H. '39 (LAF) [1] New Iberia, LA St. Peter Church; Retired.
Dischler, Raymond J. '73 (MAD) Poynette, WI St. Thomas Church.
DiSciacca, Joseph V. '73 (HRT) Bloomfield, CT Sacred Heart Church.
Dishaw, Conrad J. '48 (MAR) Retired.
Diskin, Francis X. *c.s.p.* '46 (NY) [104] New York, NY St. Paul the Apostle Church; [DD] Jamaica Estates, NY Paulist Fathers Generalate.
Diskin, John J. *s.j.* '63 (BO) [W] Weston, MA Campion Center.
Diskin, Michael L. '77 (PHX) [24] Phoenix, AZ St. Theresa Church; Special Assignment.
Diskin, Miles Eric '75 (PIT) [38] Pittsburgh, PA Sacred Heart Church.
Dismachek, Francis M. '34 (PIT) Retired; [O] Pittsburgh, PA St. John Vianney Manor.
Disney, James K. '66 (RIC) [14] Richmond, VA St. Patrick Church; Richmond, VA McGuire VA Medical Center.
DiSpigno, Francis *o.f.m.* '96 (TR) Brant Beach, NJ St. Francis of Assisi Church.
DiSpigno, Gennaro '81 (RVC) Baldwin, NY St. Christopher Church.
Dissek, Jerome M. '69 (BUF) Cuba, NY Our Lady of Angels Church; Friendship, NY Sacred Heart Church.
DiStefano, Msgr. John '52 (BEA) Retired.
DiStefano, Joseph '84 (ORG) Absent on Sick Leave.
Distefano, Simeon *o.f.m.* '63 (NY) [DD] New York, NY Franciscan Province of the Immaculate Conception.
Dister, John E. *s.j.* '62 (DET) [K] Detroit, MI Jesuit Provincial Office-Detroit Province of the Society of Jesus; [K] Detroit, MI Jesuit Community at the University of Detroit.
DiTaddeo, Alessandro '54 (CC) [11] Laredo, TX St. Frances Cabrini Church.
Ditenhafer, John A. '61 (STL) [2] University City, MO Christ the King Church.
Ditillo, James J. *s.j.* '74 (BAL) Glyndon, MD Sacred Heart Church.
DiTomasi, Francisco *o.s.m.* '53 (ELP) [24] El Paso, TX St. Ignatius of Loyola Church.
Ditta, Angelo '86 (RVC) Ronkonkoma, NY St. Joseph's Church.
Ditta, Angelo '96 (RVC) [B] Patchogue, NY St. Joseph's College.
Dittberner, Arnold *o.s.b.* '33 (SCL) [I] Collegeville, MN St. John's Abbey, of the Order of St. Benedict.
Dittberner, Jerome M. '64 (STP) [A] St. Paul, MN The Saint Paul Seminary; [C] St. Paul, MN University of St. Thomas.
Dittman, Bernard F. '55 (RCK) Menominee, IL Nativity of the Blessed Virgin Mary Church.
Dittman, Bernard F. '55 (VEN) Retired.
Dittman, Msgr. Harold J. '48 (WIN) Retired.
Dittmeier, Charles (NY) [HH] Maryknoll, NY Maryknoll Mission Association of the Faithful.
Dittmeier, Charles R. *m.m.* '70 (FgM) Maryknoll Foreign Missions.
Dittmeier, Charles R. '70 (L) On Duty Outside the Archdiocese.
Dittmer, Antonio (PEO) Graduate Studies.
Ditto, Anthony W. '90 (GBG) Harrison City, PA St. Barbara Church.
Dittoe, Msgr. John T. '45 (COL) Retired.
Ditty, James '89 (RIC) Retired.
DiTullio, Peter S. *s.c.* '68 (PRO) [6] East Providence, RI Sacred Heart Church.
DiUlio, Albert J. *s.j.* '74 (SJ) [B] Santa Clara, CA Santa Clara University.
Diurczak, Eugene '68 (NEW) [2] Linden, NJ Holy Family Church.
Divan, Anthony L. '65 (PEO) Retired.
Diver, Patrick *s.d.b.* '74 (NY) [72] New York, NY Mary Help of Christians Church.
Diver, Patrick *s.d.b.* '74 (PAT) [D] Paterson, NJ Don Bosco Technical High School.
Diviney, Andrew *s.j.* '61 (LA) Northridge, CA Our Lady of Lourdes Church.
Diviney, Msgr. Charles E. '31 (BRK) [29] Brooklyn, NY St. Charles Borromeo Church; Retired.
Divis, Daniel O. '79 (CLV) [8] Lorain, OH St. Mary Church.
Divis, James '76 (LIN) McCool Junction, NE St. Patrick's Church; York, NE St. Joseph's Church.
DiVito, John *c.s.* (CHI) [M] Northlake, IL Villa Scalabrini Home for the Aged.
Divizia, John *s.d.b.* '35 (NY) [FF] West Haverstraw, NY Don Bosco Retreat Center and Marian Shrine; [FF] West Haverstraw, NY Marian Shrine.
Dixey, Edward J. *o.s.a.* '57 (PH) [AA] Villanova, PA St. Thomas Monastery.
Dixon, Daniel B. '56 (PIT) Beaver, PA SS. Peter and Paul Church.
Dixon, David (PIT) [K] Pittsburgh, PA Vincentian Home Inc.
Dixon, David '57 (PIT) Allegheny County, PA Regency Hall Nursing Home; Allegheny County, PA Vincentian Home for the Chronically Ill.
Dixon, David C. '57 (PIT) [L] Allison Park, PA Regency Hall Nursing Home, Inc.; [O] Pittsburgh, PA St. John Vianney Manor.
Dixon, Francis *o.carm.* (PMB) [G] Boca Raton, FL St. Elias Priory-Order of Carmelites, NY.
Dixon, Francis *o.carm.* '76 (PMB) Special Assignment.
Dixon, Francis A. *s.v.d.* '69 (NO) [51] New Orleans, LA St. Paul the Apostle Church.
Dixon, J. Isidore '64 (WDC) Rosaryville, MD Church of the Most Holy Rosary.
Dixon, James *s.j.* '73 (LR) Jonesboro, AR Blessed Sacrament Church.
Dixon, James M. *s.j.* (LR) Weiner, AR St. Anthony's Church.
Dixon, James R. '70 (NO) Military Chaplains.
Dixon, Jerome '57 (PIT) Allegheny County, PA James P. Wall Home for the Aged.
Dixon, Jerome A. '57 (PIT) [L] Pittsburgh, PA Home for the Aged of the Little Sisters of the Poor.
Dlabal, Norbert F. '72 (SAL) On Duty Outside the Diocese.
Dluge, James A. '70 (SUP) Retired.
Dlugos, Raymond *o.s.a.* '83 (ALB) [10] Albany, NY St. Margaret Mary Church.
Dmoch, Paul '76 (NY) Rosendale, NY St. Peter Church.
Dnuh, William (ROC) Sonyea, NY Livingston Correctional Facility and Seneca Correctional Facility.
Do, Vien Van '90 (PEO) Bement, IL St. Michael Church; Monticello, IL St. Philomena Church.
Do Ba Cong, James (SPC) [E] Carthage, MO Congregation of the Mother Co-Redemptrix, United States Assumption Province.
Do Binh Dinh, Luke M. *c.m.c.* '77 (SB) [E] Corona, CA Congregation of the Mother Coredemptrix.
Do Cao Tung, Francis Xavier M. *c.m.c.* (SPC) [E] Carthage, MO Congregation of the Mother Co-Redemptrix, United States Assumption Province.
Do Quang Chinh, Michael M. *c.m.c.* '93 (SPC) [E] Carthage, MO Congregation of the Mother Co-Redemptrix, United States Assumption Province.
Dobbin, Edmund J. *o.s.a.* '62 (PH) [C] Villanova, PA Villanova University; [AA] Villanova, PA St. Thomas Monastery.
Dobbin, Jay D. '64 (GF) On Duty Outside of the Diocese.
Dobbins, Robert R. *s.j.* '67 (NY) [DD] New York, NY Jesuit Community at Fordham University.
Dober, Edward J. '76 (LA) Paramount, CA Our Lady of the Rosary Church.
Dobes, Msgr. George E. '68 (CHI) Military Chaplains.
Dobihal, Robert F. '50 (STP) Retired.
Dobitz, Roger '85 (SFS) On Leave of Absence.
Dobkiewicz, Stanley '43 (PH) [D] Philadelphia, PA Father Judge High School for Boys.
Dobkowski, Msgr. Paulin J. '54 (BEL) Johnston City, IL St. Paul Church; Johnston City, IL St. Paul Church.
Dobnikar, Ivan *o.s.b.* '49 (JOL) [J] Lisle, IL St. Procopius Abbey.
Dobo, Leo '46 (ORL) Lake Wales, FL Holy Spirit Church; Retired.
Dobosiewciz, Leon W. '46 (Y) Retired.
Dobosiewicz, Stephen J. '42 (E) Retired.
Dobosz, Emil J. '49 (WH) Retired.
Dobosz, Jerry '95 (TYL) Texarkana, TX Sacred Heart Church.
DoBranski, John '89 (BAL) Westminster, MD St. John Church.
Dobrosky, John M. '83 (TR) Highlands, NJ Our Lady of Perpetual Help Church.
Dobrowski, Peter P. '71 (PHX) Bullhead City, AZ St. Margaret Mary Church.
Dobry, Jerome *o.s.b.* '44 (JOL) [J] Lisle, IL St. Procopius Abbey.
Dobrzenski, Francis G. '77 (MAR) Ewen, MI Sacred Heart Church; Watersmeet, MI Immaculate Conception Church.
Dobrzynski, Martin J. '84 (GRY) New Chicago, IN Assumption of the Blessed Virgin Mary Church.
Dobson, Christopher *t.o.r.* '78 (ARL) Herndon, VA St. Joseph Church.
Dobson, Gregory J. '83 (BUF) Olean, NY St. Mary of the Angels Church.
Dochstader, Richard '75 (JOL) [4] Naperville, IL St. Margaret Mary Church.
Dockendorf, Ronald '82 (SCL) Buckman, MN St. Michael's Church.
Dockendorff, Carl J. '45 (LC) Retired.
Dockerill, Walter J. '60 (PMB) Wellington, FL St. Rita Church.
Doctor, John *o.f.m.* '76 (STL) [P] St. Louis, MO Franciscan Friary of St. Anthony of Padua.
Doda, Eugene J., Jr. '77 (MIL) [3] Menomonee Falls, WI St. James Church.
Dodaro, Robert J. *o.s.a.* '82 (CHI) [N] Olympia Fields, IL The Augustinian Provincialate Tolentine Center.
Dodd, Anthony J. '61 (CLV) Brook Park, OH Assumption of Mary Church; Retired.
Dodd, Michael *o.c.d.* '79 (BO) [W] Brighton, MA Carmelite Monastery.
Dodd, Msgr. Richard F. '48 (COL) Junction City, OH St. Patrick Church.
Dodds, Michael *o.p.* (OAK) [N] Oakland, CA Western Dominican Province.
Dodds, Michael *o.p.* '77 (OAK) [A] Berkeley, CA Dominican School of Philosophy and Theology; [N] Oakland, CA Dominican Order (Western Province), St. Albert's Priory.
Dodds, Perry W. '54 (B) Retired.
Dodge, David *o.f.m.* (CHI) [N] Chicago, IL St. Joseph Interprovincial Post-Novitiate Formation House.
Dodge, Erwin J. *o.s.a.* (CHI) [J] Chicago, IL Holy Cross Hospital.
Dodge, Linus '50 (L) [L] Trappist, KY Abbey of Our Lady of Gethsemani, of the Order of Cistercians of the Strict Observance.
Dodgson, William '50 (B) Retired.
Doerfler, Camillus *o.f.m.cap.* '45 (FgM) Capuchin Foreign Missions.
Doerfler, John (GB) [1] Green Bay, WI St. Francis Xavier Cathedral.
Doerfler, John '91 (WDC) [B] Washington, DC St. Joseph's Seminary.
Doerfler, Joseph '55 (GB) [I] Appleton, WI St. Fidelis Friary.
Doerfler, Msgr. Marvin G. '59 (SAT) [I] San Antonio, TX St. Peter & Joseph Childrens Home.
Doerger, Berard *o.f.m.* '61 (GLP) [A] Gallup, NM Diocesan Diaconate Formation Program.
Doerger, Stanley D. '58 (CIN) [16] Cincinnati, OH St. Bernard Church.
Doerhoff, Dennis (STL) [W] St. Louis, MO Archdiocesan Stewardship Education Committee.
Doerhoff, Dennis E. '76 (STL) [49] St. Louis, MO St. Mary Magdalen Church.
Doerner, David L. *s.a.* '60 (LA) [63] Los Angeles, CA Maryknoll Japanese Catholic Center Church; [R] Los Angeles, CA Atonement Friars.
Doerr, Richard J. '93 (LFT) Carmel, IN Our Lady of Mount Carmel Church.
Doerre, Edmund J. '63 (LC) Chippewa Falls, WI Holy Ghost Church; Springfield, WI St. Bridget Church.
Doersam, Carl G. '45 (NY) Retired.
Doersching, Lawrence *s.m.* '73 (SFR) [N] San Francisco, CA Marianist Community.
Doersching, Lawrence *s.m.* '73 (STL) [P] St. Louis, MO Provincialate of the Society of Mary, Province of St. Louis.
Doffing, Gordon M. '60 (STP) [4] St. Paul, MN Holy Childhood Church.
Doga, Msgr. Al R. '49 (GAL) [2] Spring, TX St. Edward Church.
Dogali, Michael F. '92 (BGP) [1] Greenwich, CT St. Mary's Church.
Dohar, William J. *c.s.c.* '73 (OAK) [N] Berkeley, CA Holy Cross Fathers-Holy Cross Center.
Doheny, Richard '48 (SAC) Fair Oaks, CA St. Mel Church.
Doheny, Thomas R. '58 (MAD) [4] Beloit, WI St. Thomas the Apostle Church.
Doherty, Charles '58 (CC) Aransas Pass, TX St. Mary, Star of the Sea Church.
Doherty, D. G. *o.p.* '57 (FgM) Dominican - Order of Preachers Foreign Missions.
Doherty, Daniel C. *s.j.* '76 (BAL) [M] Baltimore, MD Jesuit Fathers and Brothers Maryland Provincial Curia.
Doherty, Daniel J. '94 (SCR) Carbondale, PA St. Rose of Lima Church.
Doherty, Donald J. *m.m.* '62 (NY) [DD] Maryknoll, NY Maryknoll Fathers and Brothers.
Doherty, Duane *o.f.m.conv.* '63 (DET) Bloomfield Hills, MI St. Regis Church.
Doherty, Duane *o.f.m.conv.* '63 (IND) [J] Mount Saint Francis, IN Provincial Headquarters for the Conventual Franciscan Province.
Doherty, Edward C. *o.s.a.* '57 (BO) [C] North Andover, MA Merrimack College.
Doherty, Edward C. *m.ss.a.* '68 (BGP) [K] Bridgeport, CT Roncalli Apartments.
Doherty, Eugene '39 (JOL) Retired; [I] Naperville, IL St. John Vianney Villa.

Doherty, Msgr. Francis E. '41 (MAD) Retired.
Doherty, George E. '50 (NEW) Retired.
Doherty, Glennon '78 (STL) Grantwood, MO Our Lady of Providence Church.
Doherty, Glennon C. '78 (STL) [A] St. Louis, MO Kenrick-Glennon Seminary.
Doherty, Henry F. '56 (BO) Hanover, MA St. Mary of the Sacred Heart Church.
Doherty, Msgr. John B. '39 (LA) Retired.
Doherty, John B. '80 (NY) Absent on Leave.
Doherty, John E. *c.ss.r.* '38 (BO) [13] Boston, MA Our Lady of Perpetual Help Church; Boston, MA Dana Farber Cancer Institute.
Doherty, John R. '64 (NEW) [2] Bayonne, NJ St. Andrew's Church.
Doherty, Msgr. John T. '45 (NY) [144] Bronx, NY St. Gabriel Church; Retired; [E] White Plains, NY Archbishop Stepinac High School.
Doherty, Joseph M. *c.s.c.* '41 (FgM) Holy Cross Foreign Missions.
Doherty, Joseph M. *c.s.c.* '41 (FTW) [J] South Bend, IN Congregation of Holy Cross Indiana Province Provincial House.
Doherty, Louis *c.p.* '57 (CHI) [N] Chicago, IL Immaculate Conception Monastery.
Doherty, Michael *o.f.m.* '76 (LA) [X] Malibu, CA Serra Retreat.
Doherty, Neil '69 (MIA) Margate, FL St. Vincent Church.
Doherty, Patrick A. '56 (ORG) Newport Beach, CA Our Lady of Mount Carmel Church.
Doherty, Patrick D. *s.j.* '65 (SJ) [M] Los Gatos, CA Sacred Heart Jesuit Center.
Doherty, Msgr. Patrick G. '45 (FRS) Retired.
Doherty, Msgr. Patrick J. '55 (BWN) [6] Brownsville, TX Our Lady of Guadalupe Church; Ranchito, TX St. Ignatius Church.
Doherty, Patrick J. '59 (MAD) Absent on Sick Leave.
Doherty, Msgr. Patrick J. '81 (BWN) [5] Brownsville, TX Our Lady of Good Counsel Church.
Doherty, Paul '95 (WOR) Whitinsville, MA St. Patrick's Church.
Doherty, Raymond J. *s.s.e.* '58 (BUR) [E] Colchester, VT Society of St. Edmund.
Doherty, Robert G. *s.j.* '60 (BO) [W] Weston, MA Campion Center.
Doherty, Robert J. '70 (BO) [5] Medford, MA Sacred Heart Church.
Doherty, Terrance *s.m.a.* '70 (FgM) Society of African Missions.
Doherty, Timothy '76 (RCK) [1] Rockford, IL St. Peter Cathedral.
Doherty, William J. '55 (SPR) [4] Holyoke, MA Immaculate Conception Church; [F] Springfield, MA Mercy Hospital.
Dohle, Benedict *o.s.b.* '54 (OM) [K] Elkhorn, NE Mount Michael Abbey.
Dohman, William *j.c.l.* '73 (B) Grangeville, ID SS. Peter and Paul Church.
Dohner, Stephen J. '76 (CLV) Cleveland Heights, OH St. Louis Church.
Dohogne, David '92 (SPC) Poplar Bluff, MO Poplar Bluff Hospital Ministry.
Dohogne, David J. '92 (SPC) Doniphan, MO St. Benedict Church.
Doiron, David E. '69 (WOR) [1] Worcester, MA St. Paul's Cathedral; On Special or Other (Arch)Diocesan Assignment.
Dokupil, Edward J. '64 (AUS) Bastrop, TX Ascension Church.
Dolak, Mark J. '79 (MET) [J] Little York, NJ Bethany Ridge.
Dolan, Bernard M. '66 (BGP) [1] Trumbull, CT Christ the King Church.
Dolan, Charles *c.s.s.* '58 (BO) [W] Waltham, MA Stigmatine Fathers & Brothers Provincial House.
Dolan, Charles F.X. *s.j.* '46 (NEW) [C] Jersey City, NJ St. Peter's Preparatory School.
Dolan, Charles F.X. *s.j.* '46 (TR) Manasquan, NJ St. Denis Church.
Dolan, Daniel *m.m.* '54 (WDC) [B] Washington, DC Maryknoll Fathers and Brothers.
Dolan, Edward *s.s.c.* '58 (OM) [K] St. Columbans, NE St. Columban's Foreign Mission Society.
Dolan, Francis *o.m.i.* '73 (FgM) Oblates Foreign Missions.
Dolan, Francis C. *s.j.* '60 (FgM) Provinces.
Dolan, Frank *o.m.i.* '73 (BO) [U] Lowell, MA D'Youville Manor.
Dolan, Gerald M. *o.f.m.* '56 (NY) [DD] New York, NY Franciscan Friars, Order of Friars Minor, Holy Name Province.
Dolan, Gerald M. *o.f.m.* '56 (PH) [V] Aston, PA Assisi House.
Dolan, Hugh '57 (PT) Marianna, FL St. Anne Church.
Dolan, J. L. *o.p.* '60 (FgM) Dominican - Order of Preachers Foreign Missions.
Dolan, James '54 (NEW) [B] Jersey City, NJ Saint Peter's College.
Dolan, James F. *s.j.* '51 (NEW) [N] Jersey City, NJ Jesuits of Saint Peter's College, Inc.
Dolan, James J. '49 (RVC) Retired.
Dolan, James L. *o.p.* '60 (FgM) Dominican - Order of Preachers Foreign Missions.
Dolan, James Linus *o.p.* '60 (NO) [P] New Orleans, LA Dominican Fathers & Brothers, Southern Dominican Province.
Dolan, James R. *s.j.* '70 (ROC) [B] Rochester, NY McQuaid Jesuit High School.
Dolan, James W. '75 (PIT) [59] Pittsburgh, PA Our Lady of Loreto Church.
Dolan, Jarlath '74 (LA) Arcadia, CA Annunciation Church.
Dolan, John J. *o.s.f.s.* '95 (ARL) Vienna, VA Our Lady of Good Counsel Church.
Dolan, John P. '89 (SD) Oceanside, CA St. Mary Star of the Sea Church.
Dolan, John R. *m.s.* '68 (BO) [BB] Ipswich, MA National Shrine of Our Lady of La Salette.
Dolan, John R. *m.s.* '79 (WOR) [6] Fitchburg, MA St. Joseph's Church.
Dolan, Joseph K. '60 (BRK) [18] Brooklyn, NY St. Bernadette Church.
Dolan, Joseph M. '92 (WOR) [4] Leominster, MA St. Leo's Church.
Dolan, Joseph V. *s.j.* '52 (NY) [DD] New York, NY Jesuit Community at Fordham University.
Dolan, Laurence P. *o.f.m.* '65 (ORG) [3] Huntington Beach, CA SS. Simon and Jude Church.
Dolan, Lawrence *c.ss.r.* '42 (ORL) [F] New Smyrna Beach, FL St. Alphonsus Villa-Redemptorist Fathers and Brothers.
Dolan, Leo A. '52 (STP) Retired.
Dolan, Leo M. '60 (SAT) [39] San Antonio, TX St. Helena Church.
Dolan, Louis F. *c.s.sp.* '50 (VEN) [G] Sarasota, FL Congregation of the Holy Ghost.
Dolan, Luis M. *c.p.* '45 (NY) [33] New York, NY St. Emeric Church.
Dolan, Mark A. '76 (STL) Bissell Hills, MO St. Jerome Church.
Dolan, Michael J. '96 (HRT) Newington, CT St. Mary Church.
Dolan, Msgr. Neal T. '64 (SD) Lakeside, CA Our Lady of Perpetual Help Church.
Dolan, Patrick '95 (DEN) [4] Englewood, CO St. Thomas More Church.
Dolan, Patrick G. '71 (JC) Salisbury, MO St. Joseph Church.
Dolan, Patrick J. '68 (BO) Permanent Disability.
Dolan, Patrick J. '78 (L) [2] Springfield, KY Holy Rosary Church.
Dolan, Paul A. (OAK) [R] Berkeley, CA Opus Dei (Prelature of the Holy Cross and Opus Dei).
Dolan, Paul A. '84 (RVC) Kings Park, NY St. Joseph's Church.
Dolan, Paul F. '45 (BAL) Taneytown, MD St. Joseph Church; Retired; [J] Timonium, MD Stella Maris Operating Corporation.
Dolan, Peter C. '54 (PMB) Port St. Lucie, FL St. Lucie Church; Retired.
Dolan, Raymond '56 (B) On Duty Outside the Diocese.
Dolan, Robert *s.j.* '76 (LA) [10] Los Angeles, CA Dolores Mission Church.
Dolan, Robert L. *s.j.* '73 (FgM) Provinces.
Dolan, Thomas D. '51 (BRK) [166] Queens, NY St. Elizabeth's Church; Retired.
Dolan, Thomas P. '45 (RCK) Harmon, IL St. Flannen Church; Maytown, IL St. Patrick Church; Walton, IL St. Mary Church.
Dolan, Timothy '83 (STP) Long Lake, MN St. George Church.
Dolan, Msgr. Timothy M. '76 (STL) On Duty Outside the Archdiocese.
Dolan, Walter *o.f.m.* '60 (CLV) [P] Cleveland, OH Padua Franciscan Friary.
Dolan, Walter *o.f.m.* '61 (CLV) [E] Cleveland, OH Padua Franciscan High School.
Dolan, William '96 (DM) [2] Council Bluffs, IA Our Lady, Queen of Apostles Church.
Dolan, William S. *s.j.* '82 (SY) [S] Syracuse, NY Jesuits at LeMoyne, Inc.
Dolandson, Richard *o.f.m.cap.* (NOR) Middletown, CT Middlesex Memorial Hospital.
Dolbec, Jacques *s.o.l.t.* '95 (CC) [H] Robstown, TX Society of Our Lady of the Most Holy Trinity.
Dolciamore, John V. '52 (CHI) Retired; [A] Mundelein, IL University of St. Mary of the Lake-Mundelein Seminary.
Dold, John F. '73 (DEN) Absent on Leave.
Dolehide, John R. *o.p.* '47 (CHI) [1] Oak Lawn, IL St. Catherine of Alexandria Church; [N] Chicago, IL Dominicans (Provincial Office).
Dolezal, Richard R. '76 (MIL) On Duty Outside the Archdiocese.
Dolezal, Thomas H. '70 (KCK) Axtell, KS St. Michael's Church; Summerfield, KS Holy Family Church.
Dolinic, Louis S. '66 (BUF) [5] Depew, NY Our Lady of the Blessed Sacrament Church.
Doll, Donald A. *s.j.* '68 (OM) [K] Omaha, NE Jesuit Community At Creighton University.
Doll, William P. '50 (PBL) Holly, CO St. Frances of Rome Church.
Dollar, Robert J. '60 (BEL) Retired.
Dollard, John J. '45 (OAK) Retired.
Dollard, Mark E. '91 (MAN) Lisbon, NH St. Catherine of Siena Church; Woodsville, NH St. Joseph Church.
Dollard, Richard D. '58 (RIC) Tappahannock, VA St. Timothy Church.
Dollen, Bernard '53 (ROC) [M] Rochester, NY Diocesan Office of Campus Ministry.
Dollen, Bernard F. '53 (ROC) North Chili, NY St. Christopher Church.
Dollen, Msgr. Charles '54 (SD) Retired.
Dollinger, Cletus *o.c.s.o.* '50 (SLC) [F] Huntsville, UT Abbey of Our Lady of the Holy Trinity of the Order of Cistercians.
Dollinger, Msgr. John M. '57 (E) [17] Erie, PA St. Hedwig/St. Patrick Church; Erie, PA Erie County Prison.
Dollinger, Robert J. '54 (L) Retired.
Dols, Francisco *t.o.r.* '47 (NEW) [14] Elizabeth, NJ Immaculate Heart of Mary Church.
Dolsina, Stanley '46 (DUL) Retired.
Dolski, V. Anthony '59 (GB) [1] De Pere, WI St. Francis Xavier Church.
Domaica, Jose Luis *o.a.r.* '64 (NEW) [N] West Orange, NJ Augustinian Recollects.
Domandich, Anthony '58 (SEA) Retired.
Domas, John Robert '50 (SB) Beaumont, CA San Gorgonio Church.
Domaszewicz, Chester '78 (VEN) [1] Venice, FL Epiphany Cathedral.
Dombroski, Dean H. '64 (GB) Humboldt, WI Our Lady Queen of Peace Church.
Dombroski, Dean W. '64 (GB) Eaton, WI SS. Cyril and Methodius Church.
Dombrow, William A. '70 (PH) [68] Philadelphia, PA Immaculate Conception Church.
Dombrowski, Francis J. *o.f.m.cap.* '59 (MIL) [S] Milwaukee, WI The Dwelling Place.
Dombrowski, John *o.f.m.* '84 (STP) [10] St. Paul, MN Sacred Heart Church.
Dombrowski, Robert J. '60 (FTW) Bremen, IN St. Dominic Church.
Dombrowski, Ronald J. '72 (SAG) Port Sanilac, MI St. Mary Church.
Dombrowski, Stanley J. *o.s.f.s.* '83 (WIL) [I] Wilmington, DE Oblates of St. Francis De Sales.
Dombrowski, Steven '89 (CHI) [3] Mt. Prospect, IL St. Raymond de Penafort Church.
Dombrowski, Timothy '73 (LAN) [F] Ann Arbor, MI St. Joseph Mercy Hospital.
Domec, Msgr. Charles C. '56 (GAL) The Woodlands, TX Sts. Simon and Jude Church.
Domeck, Casimiro '73 (ARE) Florida, PR Our Lady of Mercy Church.
Domhoff, Ronald J. '72 (L) [B] Louisville, KY Trinity High School.
Domin, Edward '88 (ALN) [3] Easton, PA St. Jane Frances de Chantal Church.
Domin, John M. '50 (P) Retired; [K] Beaverton, OR Maryville Nursing Home.
Domingo, Albert *c.m.f.* '79 (LA) [28] Los Angeles, CA Our Lady Queen of the Angels Church.
Domingo, Santiago '65 (CC) [14] Laredo, TX St. Jude Church.
Domingue, Kenneth '91 (LAF) Basile, LA St. Augustine Church.
Dominguez, Gustavo '96 (FR) [17] New Bedford, MA St. Kilian Church; [P] New Bedford, MA The Institute of the Incarnate Word, Inc.
Dominguez, Julio Fernandez *o.m.* '48 (SJN) [16] San Juan, PR Ntra. Sra. de Fatima Church.
Dominguez, M. Marciano *c.s.b.* '90 (GAL) [Q] Sugar Land, TX Basilian Mission Center.
Dominguez, Patricio *o.m.i.* '60 (SAT) Eagle Pass, TX Our Lady of Refuge Church.
Dominiak, Gerald J. '59 (MIL) Thiensville, WI St. Cecilia Church.
Dominiak, Thomas M. '61 (GAY) Afton, MI St. Monica Church; Onaway, MI St. Paul Church.
Dominic, Abraham B. '87 (NY) [217] Staten Island, NY Our Lady Help of Christians Church.
Dominic, Francis J. '52 (MAD) Retired.
Dominic, Joseph A. '39 (SEA) Aberdeen, WA SS. Peter and Paul Church; Retired.
Dominicis, Severino *s.a.c.* '39 (NY) [91] New York, NY Our Lady of Mt. Carmel Church; [DD] New York, NY Pallottine Fathers.
Dominik, Kevin J. '88 (PIT) Bethel Park, PA St. Valentine Church.
Dominik, Stanley J. '58 (GRY) [5] Hammond, IN St. John Bosco Church.
Dominique, Todd '94 (TOL) [4] Lima, OH St. Rose Church.
Dommer, Ian *o.s.b.* '79 (SCL) [I] Collegeville, MN St. John's Abbey, of the Order of St. Benedict.
Domnick, Alphonsus *t.o.r.* '44 (SCR) Retired.
Domnick, Alphonsus M. *t.o.r.* '44 (SCR) [N] Dunmore, PA Villa St. Joseph.
Dompka, John A. '49 (PIT) Retired.
Dompke, Ramon *c.ss.r.* '64 (CHI) [152] Chicago, IL Our

Lady of Lourdes Church.
Domurat, Thomas '79 (FgM) Society of St. James the Apostle.
Domurat, Thomas S. '79 (BO) Society of St. James the Apostle.
Don, Sextus (FTW) Columbia City, IN St. Paul of the Cross Church.
Dona, Thomas M. '65 (DEN) Byers, CO Our Lady of the Plains Church.
Donachie, Joseph J. '45 (NY) Retired.
Donadio, Vincent '73 (TR) Brick Town, NJ Visitation Church.
Donaghey, Bernard '29 (SB) Patton, CA Patton State Hospital.
Donaghey, Bernard *s.v.d.* '57 (SB) [D] San Bernardino, CA St. Bernardine Medical Center.
Donaghey, John *s.v.d.* '54 (CHI) [B] Techny, IL Divine Word Residence; [N] Techny, IL Society of the Divine Word, Provincial Headquarter-Chicago Prov.
Donaghey, Patrick H. '85 (ATL) Lilburn, GA St. John Neumann Church.
Donaghy, Harry '67 (ALB) [7] Troy, NY St. Mary Church.
Donaghy, Thomas J. '79 (BAL) Ellicott City, MD St. Paul Church.
Donahoe, James H. *s.j.* '51 (BAL) [M] Baltimore, MD Jesuit Fathers and Brothers Maryland Provincial Curia.
Donahoe, Patrick *t.o.r.* '74 (ALT) [F] Loretto, PA St. Francis Friary, Third Order Regular of St. Francis of Penance.
Donahoe, Patrick *t.o.r.* '74 (PIT) [O] Pittsburgh, PA Franciscan Friars, T.O.R.
Donahoe, Msgr. Thomas M. '54 (SC) Graettinger, IA Immaculate Conception Church.
Donahue, Aidan N. '86 (HRT) [A] Bloomfield, CT St. Thomas Seminary; [A] Bloomfield, CT St. Thomas Seminary.
Donahue, Anthony *o.f.m.cap.* (NY) Wingdale, NY Harlem Valley Psychiatric Center.
Donahue, Anthony *o.f.m.cap.* '51 (MAN) [5] Manchester, NH Blessed Sacrament Church.
Donahue, Bernard F. *o.s.f.s.* '58 (ALN) [B] Center Valley, PA Allentown College of St. Francis de Sales; [K] Center Valley, PA Oblates of St. Francis de Sales.
Donahue, Brian G. '83 (FAR) Special Assignment; [A] Fargo, ND Cardinal Muench Seminary.
Donahue, Cecil J. *o.s.b.* '54 (MAN) [K] Manchester, NH St. Anselm Abbey; [N] Durham, NH Campus Ministries.
Donahue, Daniel J. '58 (BO) Awaiting Assignment.
Donahue, Dennis M. '90 (ARL) Falls Church, VA St. Anthony's Church.
Donahue, Edward J. *o.f.m.* '56 (NEW) East Rutherford, NJ St. Joseph's Church.
Donahue, Edward J. '80 (ALN) On Duty Outside the Diocese.
Donahue, Eugene L. *s.j.* '70 (DET) [K] Detroit, MI Jesuit Community at the University of Detroit.
Donahue, John *s.j.* '64 (OAK) [A] Berkeley, CA The Jesuit School of Theology at Berkeley.
Donahue, John '73 (NEW) Belleville, NJ Clara Maass Hospital.
Donahue, John G. '60 (STP) [7] St. Paul, MN Maternity of the Blessed Virgin Church.
Donahue, John J. *c.s.c.* '70 (NY) Manhattan, NY St. Clare's Hospital & Health Center; [W] New York, NY St. Clare's Hospital and Health Center.
Donahue, John P. *c.s.p.* '57 (NY) [DD] Jamaica Estates, NY Paulist Fathers Generalate.
Donahue, John P. *c.s.p.* '57 (WDC) [B] Washington, DC St. Paul's College.
Donahue, John R. *s.j.* '64 (OAK) [N] Berkeley, CA Jesuit Community at Jesuit School of Theology at Berkeley.
Donahue, John R. *s.j.* '79 (FgM) Provinces.
Donahue, Joseph '70 (NY) Absent on Leave.
Donahue, Joseph F. *s.v.d.* (BO) [3] Woburn, MA St. Charles Church.
Donahue, Joseph P. '45 (HRT) Naugatuck, CT St. Francis of Assisi Church; Retired.
Donahue, L. Scott '82 (CHI) [186] Chicago, IL St. Robert Bellarmine Church; [H] Chicago, IL Mission of Our Lady of Mercy-Mercy Home for Boys and Girls.
Donahue, Martin P. '61 (WOR) [22] Worcester, MA St. Christopher Church.
Donahue, Michael E. *s.j.* '80 (NY) [DD] New York, NY Jesuit Provincial's Office.
Donahue, Paul H. '49 (DAV) Retired; [M] Davenport, IA St. Vincent Center.
Donahue, Richard T. '68 (BO) On Duty Outside the Archdiocese.
Donahue, Stephen '86 (IND) Charlestown, IN St. Michael Church; Henryville, IN St. Francis Xavier Church.
Donahue, Thomas J. '62 (LR) Retired.
Donahue, Tom '62 (LR) [H] Little Rock, AR St. John Manor.
Donahue, William '86 (SR) On Leave.
Donahue, William H. *c.s.c.* '49 (AUS) Copperas Cove, TX Holy Family Church.
Donahue, William P. '70 (GBG) [4] Latrobe, PA St. Rose Church.
Donahugh, Donald E. '62 (BEA) [C] Port Arthur, TX St. Mary Hospital.
Donahugh, Donald E. '62 (RCK) Active Outside the Diocese.
Donajkowski, Charles G. '91 (GAY) Rogers City, MI St. Ignatius Church.
Donald, John *s.j.* '72 (FgM) Provinces.
Donald, Michael L. '72 (STL) Crystal City, MO Sacred Heart Church.
Donaldson, Richard *o.f.m.cap.* '57 (NOR) [4] Middletown, CT St. Pius X Church.
Donaldson, Richardson *o.f.m.cap.* (NY) Yonkers, NY St. Joseph Hospital.
Donaldson, Thomas *c.ss.r.* '77 (STP) Brooklyn Center, MN St. Alphonsus Church.
Donaldson, Thomas J. '68 (LC) Ellsworth, WI St. Francis of Assisi Church.
Donarski, Richard *o.c.s.o.* '86 (ATL) [I] Conyers, GA The Monastery of the Holy Spirit.
Donat, Robert J. '66 (SB) Montclair, CA Our Lady of Lourdes Church.
Donatelli, Gino *s.j.* '82 (LEX) [6] Lexington, KY St. Paul Church; [7] Lexington, KY St. Peter Church; [8] Lexington, KY St. Peter Claver Church.
Donatelli, Philip J. '67 (PIT) Peters Township, PA St. Benedict the Abbot Church.
Donato, Gaudelio '87 (HON) Kahului, HI Christ the King Church.
Donato, John *c.s.c.* '91 (MIA) [3] Fort Lauderdale, FL St. Anthony Church.
Donato, Msgr. Thomas A. '65 (NEW) Ramsey, NJ St. Paul Church.
Donavan, William T. (RVC) [A] Huntington, NY Diocesan Seminary of the Immaculate Conception.
Donazar, Javier Sebastian '58 (NY) [98] New York, NY Our Lady of Sorrows Church.
Dondanville, Joseph '95 (PEO) Mendota, IL Holy Cross Church.
Dondapati, John N. '88 (PRO) [7] Warwick, RI St. Peter Church.
Donders, Sjef *m.afr.* '57 (WDC) [M] Washington, DC Missionaries of Africa.
Dondzila, Henry J. '56 (GR) Lakewood Club, MI St. Mary of the Woods Church.
Donegan, Msgr. James F. '35 (BRK) [184] Queens, NY St. Joan of Arc Church; Retired.
Donegan, William *ss.cc.* '65 (FR) [J] Fairhaven, MA Sacred Hearts Provincial House.
Donehue, Ambrose *o.f.m.* (PRO) [P] Providence, RI St. Francis Friary.
Donelan, James F. *s.j.* '53 (FgM) Provinces.
Donelin, John M. '40 (BO) Retired.
Donellan, Msgr. Thomas J. '56 (BAL) Hunt Valley, MD St. Francis Xavier Church.
Doner, Roy R. '81 (SAC) Chico, CA Our Divine Savior Church.
Dong, Quang Minh '91 (OAK) Pinole, CA St. Joseph's Church.
Donini, Augustin *o.f.m.* '44 (NY) [DD] New York, NY Franciscan Province of the Immaculate Conception.
Donini, Leone '95 (NEW) [4] Union City, NJ St. Anthony of Padua Church.
Donio, Frank S. *s.a.c.* '94 (BAL) [51] Baltimore, MD St. Jude Shrine Church.
Donio, Thomas S. '95 (CAM) Absecon, NJ St. Elizabeth Ann Seton Church.
Donish, Peter '70 (PSC) Beaver Meadows, PA SS. Peter and Paul Church.
Donlan, Francis *c.ss.r.* '45 (ORL) [F] New Smyrna Beach, FL St. Alphonsus Villa-Redemptorist Fathers and Brothers.
Donlan, Robert R. '67 (SP) Brooksville, FL St. Anthony Church.
Donlan, Thomas *o.p.* '44 (NY) [2] New York, NY St. Agnes Church; [HH] New York, NY Catholic Actors Guild of America, Inc., The.
Donlan, Thomas C. *o.p.* '44 (CHI) River Forest, IL St. Vincent Ferrer Priory Church.
Donlon, Aidan *s.a.c.* '55 (FWT) Wichita Falls, TX State Hospital; [F] Wichita Falls, TX Bethania Regional Health Care Center.
Donlon, James I. '75 (ALB) Lake George, NY Sacred Heart Church; [4] Watervliet, NY St. Patrick Church; Special Assignment.
Donlon, James W. '65 (PH) Conshohocken, PA St. Matthew Church.
Donlon, William J. '37 (BO) Natick, MA Sacred Heart Church; Retired.
Donnay, Raymond N. '50 (SCL) Sobieski, MN St. Stanislaus Church.
Donnellan, Francis A. *s.s.e.* '45 (MOB) [H] Selma, AL Edmundite Fathers.
Donnelly, Brendan '52 (ORL) Retired.
Donnelly, Brendan P. *o.s.b.* '46 (MAN) [K] Manchester, NH St. Anselm Abbey.
Donnelly, Eamonn *s.v.d.* '70 (FgM) Society of the Divine Word Foreign Missions.
Donnelly, Eamonn *s.v.d.* '70 (LA) [25] Los Angeles, CA Our Lady of Loretto Church; [R] Los Angeles, CA Society of the Divine Word Western Province.
Donnelly, Msgr. Edward J. '54 (RVC) Hicksville, NY Holy Family Church.
Donnelly, Elmer '33 (ALB) Retired.
Donnelly, Eugene F. '48 (BRK) [210] Queens, NY Our Lady of Fatima Church; Retired.
Donnelly, Msgr. Felix G. '45 (SAV) [1] Savannah, GA Cathedral of St. John the Baptist; Retired.
Donnelly, Gerard J. *o.s.b.* '46 (MAN) [K] Manchester, NH St. Anselm Abbey.
Donnelly, James J. *s.j.* '59 (FgM) Provinces.
Donnelly, Jeffrey *o.f.m.* '39 (JOL) [J] Joliet, IL St. John the Baptist Friary.
Donnelly, Jerome A. *o.f.m.* '39 (FgM) Franciscan Foreign Missions.
Donnelly, Msgr. John '58 (SPK) [8] Spokane, WA St. Anthony Church.
Donnelly, John P. *s.j.* '65 (MIL) [P] Milwaukee, WI Jesuit Community at Marquette University.
Donnelly, Joseph T. '71 (HRT) [3] Manchester, CT St. Bridget's Church.
Donnelly, Joseph-Benedict *o.c.s.o.* '43 (P) [L] Lafayette, OR The Cistercian (Trappist) Abbey of Our Lady of Guadalupe.
Donnelly, Msgr. Lawrence E. '49 (LA) Retired.
Donnelly, Lucien R. *o.s.b.* '48 (NEW) [N] Newark, NJ Newark Abbey.
Donnelly, Michael *s.s.c.* '63 (OM) [K] St. Columbans, NE St. Columban's Foreign Mission Society.
Donnelly, P. Martin '64 (TOL) [31] Toledo, OH St. Martin de Porres Church.
Donnelly, Paul J. '58 (BIR) Retired.
Donnelly, Paul V. '88 (STA) [1] Gainesville, FL St. Patrick's Church.
Donnelly, Richard A. '62 (PRO) [4] Cranston, RI St. Mark Church.
Donnelly, Robert *m.m.* '59 (HON) Honaunau, HI St. Benedict Church.
Donnelly, Robert '91 (ALB) [5] Albany, NY St. Catherine of Siena Church.
Donnelly, Robert J. '91 (ALB) [J] Albany, NY Villa Mary Immaculate.
Donnelly, Robert W. '57 (TOL) [1] Toledo, OH Queen of the Most Holy Rosary Cathedral.
Donnelly, Robert W. *m.m.* '59 (HON) [H] Honolulu, HI Maryknoll Fathers House.
Donnelly, Russell J. '75 (PH) Absent on Leave.
Donnelly, Sean '54 (SPK) Retired.
Donnelly, Sean '82 (CLV) [5] Akron, OH St. Francis de Sales Church.
Donnelly, Stephen H. '97 (RVC) New Hyde Park, NY Notre Dame Church.
Donnelly, Thomas *m.m.* '57 (HON) Hawi, HI Sacred Heart Church.
Donnelly, Thomas '61 (RNO) [5] Reno, NV St. Rose of Lima Church.
Donnelly, Thomas F. *m.m.* '57 (NY) [DD] Maryknoll, NY Maryknoll Fathers and Brothers.
Donnelly, Timothy *o.s.b.* (LR) [C] Subiaco, AR Subiaco Academy.
Donnelly, Timothy *o.s.b.* '65 (LR) [A] Subiaco, AR Subiaco Monastery.
Donnelly, Timothy M. *s.v.d.* '88 (TR) [7] Trenton, NJ Our Lady of the Divine Shepherd Church.
Donnelly, William '64 (ROC) [45] Rochester, NY St. Mary Church.
Donnelly, William E. '71 (JOL) [3] Naperville, IL St. Raphael Church.
Donnelly, William F. *s.j.* '63 (SJ) [B] Santa Clara, CA Santa Clara University.
Donnelly, William J. *o.s.a.* '67 (PH) [AA] Villanova, PA St. John Stone Friary.
Donnelly, William P. '64 (PH) Upper Darby, PA St. Alice Church.
Donnelly, William S. *m.m.* '65 (NY) [DD] Maryknoll, NY Maryknoll Fathers and Brothers.
Donnely, Michael *s.s.c.* (ELP) Fabens, TX Our Lady of Guadalupe Church.
Donner, Jeffrey '78 (SAG) Mount Pleasant, MI St. Mary University Parish.
Donner, Randall '92 (OM) [27] Omaha, NE St. Margaret Mary Church.
Donnolly, Robert '88 (ALB) Special Assignment.
Dono, Abram E. *s.t.* '64 (TUC) [2] Tucson, AZ Blessed Kateri Tekakwitha Church; [J] Tucson, AZ St. Nicholas Indian Center.
Donofrio, Michael J. '76 (PH) On Duty Outside the Archdiocese.
Donoghue, Harry T. *o.p.* '57 (NY) Pleasantville, NY Holy Innocents Church.
Donoghue, Henry A. '64 (WOR) [23] Worcester, MA St. George Church.
Donoghue, John F. '54 (B) [2] Boise, ID St. Mark's Church.
Donoghue, Kelly C. '94 (OG) Absent on Leave.
Donoghue, Paul *s.m.* '68 (STL) [P] St. Louis, MO Provincialate of the Society of Mary, Province of St. Louis.
Donoher, Edward *c.s.b.* '49 (DET) [E] Redford, MI Catholic Central High School.
Donohie, John M. '65 (PH) [54] Philadelphia, PA St.

Helena Church.
Donohoe, Edward '50 (STO) Retired.
Donohoe, John P. '45 (SEA) Retired.
Donohoe, Patrick K. '82 (CC) Taft, TX Holy Family Church; Taft, TX Immaculate Conception Church.
Donohoe, Peter '50 (SFD) Retired.
Donohoe, Philip M. '53 (OKL) El Reno, OK Sacred Heart Church.
Donohoe, Richard E. '84 (BIR) Anniston, AL Sacred Heart of Jesus Church.
Donohoe, Msgr. Robert J. '37 (PHX) Retired.
Donohoe, Robert W. '50 (CLV) [3] Elyria, OH St. Jude Church; Peninsula, OH Mother of Sorrows Church.
Donohoe, Stephen S. '92 (BO) Military & VA Chaplains.
Donohoe, Thomas C. *s.j.* '41 (OM) [C] Omaha, NE Creighton Preparatory School.
Donohoe, Thomas E. '62 (RVC) Long Beach, NY St. Mary of the Isle Church.
Donohoe, Thomas M. *s.j.* '43 (SJ) [M] Los Gatos, CA Sacred Heart Jesuit Center.
Donohoe, Thomas P. '52 (BO) Carlisle, MA St. Irene Church.
Donohoe, William *c.pp.s.* '48 (CIN) [B] Carthagena, OH St. Charles.
Donohoo, Daniel B. '86 (IND) Bloomington, IN St. John the Apostle Church.
Donohoo, Lawrence J. *o.p.* '85 (WDC) [B] Washington, DC Dominican House of Studies.
Donohue, Aidan N. '86 (HRT) Special and other (Arch)Diocesan Assignment.
Donohue, Edward J. '36 (JC) Retired.
Donohue, James *c.r.* (BAL) [B] Emmitsburg, MD Mount Saint Mary's College.
Donohue, John F. *o.carm.* '48 (JOL) [J] Darien, IL Carmelite Provincial Office.
Donohue, John J. '48 (CHI) [52] Chicago, IL St. Edward Church; Retired.
Donohue, John J. *s.j.* '59 (FgM) Provinces.
Donohue, John J. '73 (NEW) Bloomfield, NJ St. Valentine Church.
Donohue, John W. *s.j.* '50 (NY) [DD] New York, NY "America;" Residence and publication office of the America Press.
Donohue, Michael T. '75 (NOR) East Lyme, CT St. Matthias Church.
Donohue, Patrick W. '75 (NEW) [34] Newark, NJ Sacred Heart Church.
Donohue, Paul *m.c.c.j.* '75 (CIN) [M] Cincinnati, OH Comboni Missionaries (Verona Fathers)-Comboni Mission Center.
Donohue, Peter *c.s.c.* '56 (ORL) Retired; [F] Cocoa Beach, FL Holy Cross Fathers, Eastern Priests Province.
Donohue, Peter M. *o.s.a.* '79 (PH) [C] Villanova, PA Villanova University.
Donohue, Raymond A.J. '85 (BUF) Mayville, NY St. Mary Church; Sherman, NY St. Isaac Jogues Church.
Donohue, Robert W. '50 (CLV) Retired.
Donohue, Stephen '59 (NEW) [N] Cliffside Park, NJ St. Patrick's Missionary Society.
Donohue, Thomas '41 (L) [1] Valley Station, KY St. Clement Church.
Donohue, Thomas E. '41 (L) Retired.
Donohue, Timothy C. *o.carm.* '51 (NY) [DD] Scarborough, NY Carmelite Fathers, NY Prov. of St. Elias.
Donoso, Fermin J. *c.s.c.* '67 (FTW) [J] South Bend, IN Congregation of Holy Cross Indiana Province Provincial House.
Donovan, Charles A. *c.s.p.* '40 (NY) [DD] Jamaica Estates, NY Paulist Fathers Generalate.
Donovan, Charles A. *c.s.p.* '40 (SFR) [31] San Francisco, CA Old St. Mary's Cathedral.
Donovan, Charles F. *s.j.* '43 (BO) [W] Chestnut Hill, MA The Jesuit Community at Boston College.
Donovan, Daniel E. *c.m.* '49 (ALN) Roseto, PA Our Lady of Mt. Carmel Church.
Donovan, David I. *s.j.* '68 (BO) [W] Boston, MA Jesuit Urban Center & Immaculate Conception Community.
Donovan, Dennis *s.d.b.* '83 (NY) [DD] New Rochelle, NY Salesian Provincial House.
Donovan, Donald F. *m.m.* '55 (FgM) Maryknoll Foreign Missions.
Donovan, Edmund J. '41 (E) Retired.
Donovan, Edward *c.s.p.* '59 (LA) Carpinteria, CA St. Joseph Church.
Donovan, Msgr. Edward J. '54 (NY) State, NY Green Haven Correctional Facility.
Donovan, Edward R. *c.s.p.* '59 (NY) [DD] Jamaica Estates, NY Paulist Fathers Generalate.
Donovan, J. Michael '65 (SY) Marcellus, NY St. Francis Xavier Church.
Donovan, J. Paul '58 (TLS) Owasso, OK St. Henry Church.
Donovan, James *o.m.i.* '51 (BEL) [H] Belleville, IL Retreat and Renewal Center.
Donovan, James *o.p.* '55 (PRT) [I] Lewiston, ME SS. Peter and Paul Priory.
Donovan, James J. '87 (CHI) Niles, IL Our Lady of Ransom Church.
Donovan, James W. *c.s.p.* '68 (CHI) [125] Chicago, IL Old St. Mary Church.
Donovan, John L. (BO) Retired.
Donovan, John P. '86 (SY) Special Assignment; [V] Hamilton, NY Catholic Newman Community of Colgate University.
Donovan, Msgr. John T. '44 (MIL) Retired.
Donovan, Joseph D. '40 (ROC) Retired.
Donovan, Joseph F. '53 (BO) [4] Brockton, MA St. Margaret Church.
Donovan, Msgr. Joseph J. '51 (NEW) Bergenfield, NJ St. John the Evangelist Church; Retired.
Donovan, Joseph J. *m.m.* '79 (FgM) Maryknoll Foreign Missions.
Donovan, Kevin G. '88 (HRT) Avon, CT St. Ann's Church.
Donovan, Michael A. '62 (DET) [3] Roseville, MI St. Donald Church.
Donovan, Michael B. *o.s.f.s.* '67 (WIL) [I] Childs, MD Oblates of St. Francis De Sales; [L] Childs, MD De Sales Centre.
Donovan, Patrick *o.s.m.* '55 (ORG) Fullerton, CA St. Philip Benizi Church.
Donovan, Patrick J. *m.m.* '57 (FgM) Maryknoll Foreign Missions.
Donovan, Paul A. *s.j.* '56 (SD) [B] San Diego, CA University of San Diego.
Donovan, Richard *o.f.m.* '87 (HRT) [6] New Britain, CT St. Francis of Assisi Church.
Donovan, Richard J. *o.f.m.* '87 (HRT) [R] New Britain, CT Central Connecticut State University Newman House.
Donovan, Richard R. '58 (RVC) Garden City, NY St. Anne Church.
Donovan, Robert '53 (ROC) [3] Rochester, NY St. Andrew Church.
Donovan, Robert '54 (ROC) Retired.
Donovan, Robert C. '70 (FR) Pocasset, MA St. John the Evangelist Church.
Donovan, Thomas A. (GAL) [N] Houston, TX Pope John XXIII Priest Residence.
Donovan, Msgr. Thomas A. '50 (GAL) Retired.
Donovan, Msgr. Thomas F. '57 (BRK) [237] Queens, NY Sacred Heart of Jesus Church.
Donovan, Thomas P. *s.j.* '44 (BO) [W] Weston, MA Campion Center.
Donovan, Victor *c.p.* '36 (HRT) [M] West Hartford, CT Holy Family Monastery/Retreat.
Donovan, Vincent J. *c.s.sp.* '52 (CHL) Monroe, NC Our Lady of Lourdes Church.
Donovan, Msgr. Walter J. '44 (ATL) [8] Atlanta, GA Sacred Heart of Jesus Church; Retired.
Donovan, Msgr. William (SY) [W] Utica, NY Calvary.
Donovan, William D. '61 (BGP) [5] Fairfield, CT Holy Family Church.
Donovan, William G. '94 (PH) Collingdale, PA St. Joseph Church; Willow Grove, PA St. David Church; [D] Warminster, PA Archbishop Wood Catholic High School.
Donovan, Msgr. William L. '43 (SCR) Retired; [N] Dunmore, PA Villa St. Joseph.
Donton, Joseph P. '91 (PEO) [1] Peoria, IL St. Mary's Cathedral.
Doocey, Michael F. (BO) Retired.
Doody, Cyril J. '56 (BRK) [79] Brooklyn, NY St. Mark's Church.
Doody, Michael J. *s.j.* (STL) [C] St. Louis, MO Saint Louis University.
Doody, Michael J. *s.j.* '78 (BO) [W] Boston, MA The Society of Jesus of New England-Provincial Offices.
Doody, Michael J. *s.j.* '78 (STL) [P] St. Louis, MO Jesuit Community Corporation at St. Louis University - Jesuit Hall.
Doody, Patrick *c.s.sp.* (STA) [1] St. Augustine, FL Cathedral of St. Augustine.
Doody, Peter J. '71 (PAT) [8] Clifton, NJ St. Philip the Apostle Church.
Doody, Msgr. Timothy F. '42 (GRY) Retired.
Doogan, Msgr. John P. '46 (SEA) Retired.
Doogan, Joseph H. '48 (SEA) [27] Seattle, WA Our Lady of Fatima Church; Retired.
Dooher, John A. '69 (BO) [BB] Boston, MA Our Lady of Good Voyage Chapel; [FF] Braintree, MA Our Lady of Kazan Russian Greek Catholic Mission.
Dooher, John J. '68 (BO) Dedham, MA St. Mary Church.
Doolan, Ailbe *o.c.d.* '53 (SJ) [M] San Jose, CA Carmelite Monastery, Novitiate.
Doolan, John M. *s.j.* '63 (ALB) [O] Auriesville, NY Shrine of Our Lady of Martyrs.
Doolan, Vincent P. '80 (BO) Marshfield, MA St. Christine Church.
Dooley, Bernard J. *s.j.* '55 (BAL) [M] Baltimore, MD Jesuit Fathers and Brothers Maryland Provincial Curia.
Dooley, Daniel M. '61 (PH) Norwood, PA St. Gabriel Church.
Dooley, Francis B. '45 (IND) Retired.
Dooley, Harry J. *c.s.p.* '58 (NY) [DD] Jamaica Estates, NY Paulist Fathers Generalate.
Dooley, Msgr. Joseph P. '56 (ALN) Martins Creek, PA St. Rocco Church.
Dooley, Joseph W. '44 (IND) Retired; [O] Indianapolis, IN International Catholic Deaf Association (Chapter No. 38).
Dooley, Kevin F. '84 (MAD) Platteville, WI St. Mary Church.
Dooley, Malachy R. *o.p.* '49 (CHI) [D] Oak Park, IL Fenwick High School; [N] River Forest, IL St. Thomas Aquinas Priory.
Dooley, Michael D. *s.j.* '85 (DAL) [D] Dallas, TX Jesuit College Preparatory School.
Dooley, Peter C. '76 (RVC) Bellmore, NY St. Barnabas the Apostle Church.
Dooley, Msgr. R. Joseph '69 (WDC) Retired.
Dooley, Thomas V. '91 (DM) Leon, IA St. Brendan Church; Maloy, IA Immaculate Conception Church.
Dooley, William E. *s.j.* '46 (MIL) [P] Milwaukee, WI Jesuit Community at Marquette University.
Doolin, William *c.s.sp.* '37 (SFR) Millbrae, CA St. Dunstan Church.
Doolin, Msgr. William A. '45 (PH) [13] Philadelphia, PA St. Anselm Church; Upper Darby, PA St. Alice Church; Retired.
Dooling, J. Stuart *o.s.f.s.* '40 (CAM) [M] Pittsgrove, NJ Villa St. Joseph.
Dooling, Patrick '82 (MRY) Capitola, CA St. Joseph Church.
Doonan, John A. '52 (BO) Retired.
Dooner, William B. '70 (PH) Oxford, PA Sacred Heart Church; [EE] Philadelphia, PA Newman Apostolate.
Dopierala, Rafal *s.chr.* '94 (LA) [22] Los Angeles, CA Our Lady of the Bright Mount Church.
Dora, Msgr. Peter P. '67 (BGP) [1] Stratford, CT Holy Name of Jesus Church.
Dorais, Gerald A. '55 (WOR) [4] Fitchburg, MA St. Francis of Assisi Church.
Doran, Austin '78 (LA) [A] Camarillo, CA St. John's Seminary; [A] Camarillo, CA St. John's Seminary.
Doran, Brian '71 (LA) Vernon, CA Holy Angels Parish of the Deaf Church.
Doran, Edward *o.s.a.* '61 (PH) [111] Philadelphia, PA St. Nicholas of Tolentine Church.
Doran, Edward P. '84 (BRK) [47] Brooklyn, NY St. Francis Xavier Church.
Doran, John E. '66 (WOR) [4] Leominster, MA St. Leo's Church.
Doran, Msgr. John E. '72 (NEW) South Orange, NJ Our Lady of Sorrows Church.
Doran, Joseph *s.d.b.* '66 (BO) [Y] Ipswich, MA Sacred Heart Retreat Center.
Doran, Matthew J. '44 (SY) Retired.
Doran, Msgr. Thomas M. '47 (SY) Whitesboro, NY St. Anne Church; Retired.
Doran, William '58 (VIC) Meyersville, TX SS. Peter & Paul Church.
Doran, William J. *s.j.* '55 (OM) [C] Omaha, NE Creighton Preparatory School.
Dorcey, Joseph *c.ss.r.* '79 (CHI) [9] Chicago, IL St. Alphonsus Church.
Dorcy, Roger P. '80 (PBL) [7] Pueblo, CO Our Lady of the Meadows Church.
Dore, Denis '44 (BRK) Retired.
Dore, Denis M. '44 (BRK) [228] Queens, NY St. Pius X Church.
Dore, James *o.s.m.* '58 (ORL) Palm Bay, FL Our Lady of Grace Church.
Dore, James M. *o.s.m.* '58 (CHI) [N] Chicago, IL Servite Friars - Eastern Province.
Dore, M.J. Bernard '82 (PRO) [K] North Providence, RI St. Joseph Health Services of Rhode Island - Our Lady of Fatima Hospital.
Dore, Robert '89 (JKS) Chatawa, MS St. Teresa Church.
Dore, Thomas M. '61 (CHI) [4] Oak Park, IL St. Giles Church.
Dore, Timothy *o.f.m.conv.* '92 (BRK) [61] Brooklyn, NY Most Holy Trinity Church.
Dorenbusch, Thomas A. '57 (CIN) Tipp City, OH St. John the Baptist Church.
Dorenkemper, Mark *c.pp.s.* '48 (CIN) [B] Carthagena, OH St. Charles.
Dorff, Francis *o.praem* '60 (SFE) [J] Albuquerque, NM Santa Maria de la Vid Priory.
Dorff, John J. *c.ss.r.* '69 (HBG) Ephrata, PA Mother of Perpetual Help Church; [H] Ephrata, PA St. Clement's Mission House.
Dorgan, Gerard L. '58 (BO) Danvers, MA St. Mary of the Annunciation Church.
Dorgan, John J. '65 (RIC) [4] Norfolk, VA Sacred Heart Church.
Dorgan, Joseph A. *s.j.* '56 (NY) [F] New York, NY Regis High School; [DD] New York, NY St. Ignatius Loyola Residence.
Dorhauer, C. Robert '63 (STL) [5] Creve Coeur, MO St. Richard Church.
Dorian, Brendan '58 (YAK) On Duty Outside the Diocese.
Dorian, L. Brendon '58 (PHX) [21] Phoenix, AZ St. Paul Church.
Dorich, John '61 (VNN) Retired.
Dorin, Robert R. *s.j.* '67 (BO) [W] Boston, MA The Society of Jesus of New England-Provincial Offices.

Dorin, Robert R. *s.j.* '67 (SPK) [C] Spokane, WA Gonzaga University.
Doriot, Thomas E. '49 (FTW) On Special Assignment.
Doris, Andrew T. '47 (SAV) Retired.
Doris, Andrew T. '57 (SAV) [1] Augusta, GA Church of the Most Holy Trinity.
Doris, John A. '75 (SCR) [5] Dunmore, PA St. Mary of Mount Carmel Church.
Dorley, Paul D. (TOL) Retired.
Dormer, David J. '77 (SCR) Military Chaplains.
Dorn, George *c.ss.r.* '50 (ORL) [F] New Smyrna Beach, FL St. Alphonsus Villa-Redemptorist Fathers and Brothers.
Dorn, Jerry *glmy.* '78 (CIN) [M] Fairfield, OH Headquarters of Glenmary Home Missioners.
Dorn, Jim Van *o.f.m.conv.* '67 (IND) [I] Mount Saint Francis, IN Mount Saint Francis Friary and Retreat Center.
Dorn, John *o.ss.t.* '81 (BAL) [M] Baltimore, MD Holy Trinity Monastery.
Dorn, Louis E. '72 (JC) Marshall, MO St. Peter Church; Marshall, MO Marshall State School-Hospital.
Dorn, Rupert *o.f.m.cap* '51 (MAD) [M] Madison, WI San Damiano Friary.
Dornak, Melvin '92 (AUS) West, TX Assumption Church.
Dornbos, William '68 (HEL) Special Assignments.
Dorner, Joseph E. '95 (GB) [13] Green Bay, WI SS. Peter and Paul Church.
Dorney, Msgr. Dennis C. '67 (TLS) [11] Tulsa, OK Church of St. Mary.
Dorney, Msgr. James J. '58 (NY) [224] Staten Island, NY St. Peter Church.
Dorniak, Joseph *o.f.m.conv.* '79 (PMB) [B] Fort Pierce, FL John Carroll High School.
Dornier, Russell L. *s.j.* '44 (NO) [P] New Orleans, LA Ignatius Residence.
Doro, Michael J. '72 (MAD) [2] Janesville, WI St. John Vianney Church.
Doroin, Elias E. '64 (GAL) [K] Houston, TX The Catholic Chaplain Corps.
Dorr, James *c.m.* '44 (BRK) [U] Jamaica, NY Vincentian Residence.
Dorr, Richard J. '55 (DET) Retired.
Dorrill, James F. '60 (MOB) [1] Mobile, AL Cathedral of the Immaculate Conception; [K] Mobile, AL University of South Alabama Newman Center.
Dorrler, Michael E. *s.j.* '83 (CHI) [N] Chicago, IL Chicago Province of the Society of Jesus-Provincial Office; [T] Barrington, IL Bellarmine Hall.
Dorrmann, William J. '55 (CIN) Shandon, OH St. Aloysius Church.
Dorsch, Henry L. '68 (SPR) [8] Pittsfield, MA St. Mark's Church.
Dorsch, Larry W. '75 (WH) [1] Wheeling, WV St. Joseph's Cathedral.
Dorsel, John F. (R) Absent on Leave.
Dorsey, Daniel *glmy.* '78 (LR) Monticello, AR St. Mark Church.
Dorsey, Garret D. '59 (PIT) Allison Park, PA St. Ursula Church.
Dorsey, Joseph A. *c.s.c.* '57 (FgM) Holy Cross Foreign Missions.
Dorsey, Joseph A. *c.s.c.* '57 (FTW) [J] South Bend, IN Congregation of Holy Cross Indiana Province Provincial House.
Dorsey, Lawrence J. '59 (OM) Ralston, NE St. Gerald Church.
Dorsey, Patrick J. *s.j.* '96 (MIL) [P] Milwaukee, WI Jesuit Community at Marquette University.
Dorson, James E. '77 (RIC) [12] Virginia Beach, VA Star of the Sea Church.
Dorsonville, Mario E. '85 (WDC) [4] Bethesda, MD Our Lady of Lourdes Church.
Dorta, Juan M. *s.j.* (MIA) [H] Miami, FL Villa Arrieta.
Dorta, Juan Manuel *s.j.* '55 (MIA) [D] Miami, FL Belen Jesuit Preparatory School; [H] Miami, FL Villa Arrieta.
Dorton, John '70 (DM) [11] Des Moines, IA St. Peter's Church.
Dorwart, William D. *c.s.c.* '80 (FTW) [J] South Bend, IN Congregation of Holy Cross Indiana Province Provincial House.
Dory, Michael '76 (GB) Military Chaplains.
Dos Reis, Jose Q. '64 (PRO) Providence, RI Rhode Island Hospital; [C] Warwick, RI Bishop Hendricken High School.
dos Remedios, Francis *o.s.b.* '82 (BIS) Hebron, ND St. Ann Church; [A] Richardton, ND Assumption Abbey.
Dos Santos, Jose '68 (ALN) [4] Bethlehem, PA Holy Infancy Church.
dos Santos, Jose A.F. '53 (FR) [8] Fall River, MA Our Lady of Health Church.
Doscher, Joseph *s.c.j.* '73 (SP) [O] Pinellas Park, FL Priests of the Sacred Heart.
Dosen, Anthony *c.m.* '82 (CHI) [C] Chicago, IL Vincentian Community at DePaul University.
Doser, A. Ed *c.s.b.* '55 (GAL) [K] Houston, TX The Catholic Chaplain Corps.
Doser, Edward A. *c.s.b.* '55 (GAL) [F] Houston, TX St. Thomas High School.
Dosh, Mark B. '58 (STP) Excelsior, Lake Minnetonka, MN St. John the Baptist Church.
Doskey, Msgr. Clinton J. '54 (NO) [55] New Orleans, LA St. Pius X Church.
Dostie, Benoit C. *m.s.c.* '40 (OG) [2] Watertown, NY Our Lady of the Sacred Heart, Missionaries of the Sacred Heart Church.
Dotson, Msgr. Paul T. '68 (LA) Woodland Hills, CA St. Bernardine of Siena Church.
Doty, Craig A. '97 (LIN) [10] Lincoln, NE St. Peter Church.
Doub, Nicholas *o.s.b.* '87 (SCL) [I] Collegeville, MN St. John's Abbey, of the Order of St. Benedict.
Doucet, Camille *m.s.* '68 (FR) [J] Attleboro, MA La Salette Provincial House.
Doucet, David A. '69 (BO) [3] Somerville, MA St. Benedict Church.
Doucet, Ovila T. '53 (PRO) Retired; [M] Pawtucket, RI Jeanne Jugan Residence.
Doucette, Michael L. '75 (PRT) Madawaska, ME St. Thomas Aquinas Church.
Doudican, James '48 (CHY) [2] Cheyenne, WY Holy Trinity Church; Retired.
Dougher, John L. '64 (PRT) Westbrook, ME St. Mary's Church.
Dougherty, C. Peter '61 (LAN) Special Assignment.
Dougherty, Charles *c.p.* '68 (RVC) Shelter Island, NY Our Lady of the Isle Church.
Dougherty, Charles F. '63 (SJ) Milpitas, CA St. John the Baptist Church.
Dougherty, Damien *o.f.m.* '75 (STL) [T] Dittmer, MO Il Ritiro-The Little Retreat.
Dougherty, Daniel J. '70 (PH) Kennett Square, PA St. Patrick Church.
Dougherty, David *c.pp.s.* '49 (KC) [J] Liberty, MO Precious Blood Center.
Dougherty, Denis *o.s.b.* '56 (KC) [13] Kansas City, MO St. Gabriel Archangel Church; [O] Kansas City, MO Benedictine Counseling and Consulting Institute.
Dougherty, Msgr. Denis R. '48 (WCH) Colwich, KS Sacred Heart Church.
Dougherty, Edward '53 (TR) [M] Trenton, NJ Villa Vianney.
Dougherty, Edward C.A. *s.j.* '72 (BAL) [M] Baltimore, MD Jesuit Fathers and Brothers Maryland Provincial Curia.
Dougherty, Edward C.A. *s.j.* '72 (FgM) Provinces.
Dougherty, Edward J. '53 (TR) Retired.
Dougherty, Edward J. *s.j.* '70 (FgM) Provinces.
Dougherty, Edward J. *s.j.* '70 (NO) [P] New Orleans, LA Jesuit Provincial Office.
Dougherty, Edward M. *m.m.* '79 (FgM) Maryknoll Foreign Missions.
Dougherty, Edward M. *m.m.* '79 (NY) [DD] Maryknoll, NY Maryknoll Fathers and Brothers.
Dougherty, Eugene J. '53 (PIT) [73] Pittsburgh, PA Holy Wisdom Church.
Dougherty, Francis D. *o.s.f.s.* '38 (FgM) Oblates of St. Francis de Sales Foreign Missions.
Dougherty, George Patrick '67 (GAL) Retired.
Dougherty, Henry E. '41 (PH) Levittown, PA Queen of the Universe Church; Retired.
Dougherty, Hugh J. '69 (PH) South Coventry, PA St. Thomas More Church.
Dougherty, James '67 (JOL) [18] Joliet, IL St. Paul the Apostle Church.
Dougherty, James J. *s.j.* '59 (STL) [P] St. Louis, MO Hallahan House.
Dougherty, James R. '68 (BEL) Centralia, IL St. Mary Church.
Dougherty, John C. '45 (PH) [21] Philadelphia, PA St. Bartholomew Church; Retired.
Dougherty, John J. *c.s.c.* '93 (PHX) [J] Phoenix, AZ Andre House of Arizona.
Dougherty, Joseph A. *o.s.f.s.* '61 (PH) [D] Philadelphia, PA Father Judge High School for Boys; [AA] Philadelphia, PA Father Judge Faculty House.
Dougherty, Joseph D. '48 (PH) Hatboro, PA St. John Bosco Church; [EE] Philadelphia, PA Newman Apostolate.
Dougherty, Luke *o.s.b.* '55 (SD) [H] Oceanside, CA Prince of Peace Abbey, Benet Hill.
Dougherty, Matthew C. '60 (MIL) Retired.
Dougherty, Paul V. '80 (PH) [A] Wynnewood, PA Theological Seminary of St. Charles Borromeo, Overbrook; [S] Philadelphia, PA Catholic Center for the Deaf and Hard of Hearing.
Dougherty, Peter C. '61 (LAN) East Lansing, MI St. John the Evangelist, Student Parish.
Dougherty, Robert G. *s.j.* '60 (BO) [Y] Weston, MA Campion Renewal Center.
Dougherty, Stephen J. '73 (PH) Narberth, PA St. Margaret Church; [A] Wynnewood, PA Theological Seminary of St. Charles Borromeo, Overbrook.
Dougherty, Terrence *o.c.d.* '63 (MAN) [M] Manchester, NH.
Dougherty, William *c.pp.s.* '46 (CIN) [B] Carthagena, OH St. Charles.
Dougherty, William J. *o.s.f.s.* '59 (WIL) Elsmere, DE Veteran's Hospital; [I] Wilmington, DE DeSales House.
Dougherty, William J. *c.s.p.* '63 (TUC) [11] Tucson, AZ St. Cyril of Alexandria Church.
Dougherty, William J. '69 (PH) Absent on Sick Leave.
Dougherty, William J. '80 (PH) King of Prussia, PA Mother of Divine Providence Church.
Dougherty, William N. *o.s.f.s.* '65 (ARL) Reston, VA St. John Neumann Church.
Doughty, Edward '95 (BO) Danvers, MA St. Richard Church.
Doughty, Edward F. '95 (BO) [2] Plymouth, MA St. Bonaventure Church.
Doughty, Rees W. '94 (NY) [132] Bronx, NY St. Barnabas Church.
Douglas, David M. '65 (LFT) West Lafayette, IN Blessed Sacrament Church.
Douglas, Gordon '68 (SEA) [16] Seattle, WA St. Matthew Church; [B] Seattle, WA Blanchet High School.
Douglas, Jack *c.p.* '81 (BRK) [180] Queens, NY Immaculate Conception Church.
Douglas, John *c.p.* '81 (BRK) [U] Jamaica, NY Immaculate Conception Monastery.
Douglas, Louis '58 (ALB) Retired.
Douglas, Marian *o.f.m.* '57 (MAR) Calumet, MI Sacred Heart Church.
Douglas, Michael W. '75 (WDC) [8] Silver Spring, MD St. Michael Church; Pastoral Center Special Ministries.
Douglas, Norman K. '74 (CLV) [10] Akron, OH St. Martha Church.
Douglass, Vincent J. *c.ss.r.* '66 (ATL) Hapeville, GA St. John the Evangelist Church.
Doussan, Msgr. Douglas A. '60 (NO) [34] New Orleans, LA St. Gabriel the Archangel Church.
Dove, Thomas J. *c.s.p.* '61 (SFR) [31] San Francisco, CA Old St. Mary's Cathedral.
Dover, Edward R. '85 (LA) Monterey Park, CA St. Thomas Aquinas Church.
Dover, Jack (TR) [B] Holmdel, NJ St. John Vianney High School.
Dovick, Robert E. '53 (CHI) [2] Oak Lawn, IL St. Gerald Church.
Dovick, Robert E. '54 (CHI) Palos Heights, IL Incarnation Church.
Dovick, Robert F. '53 (CHI) Retired.
Dowalgo, Mitchell G. *c.s.b.* '82 (LSC) [4] Las Cruces, NM St. Albert the Great Newman Parish; [B] Las Cruces, NM Basilian Fathers.
Dowbush, Yaroslaw '86 (STN) Tucson, AZ St. Michael Church.
Dowd, Barry '82 (ORL) [1] Orlando, FL Mary Queen of the Universe Shrine Church.
Dowd, Barry G. '84 (BUR) On Duty Outside the Diocese.
Dowd, Brian P. '91 (BRK) [34] Brooklyn, NY St. Edmund's Church.
Dowd, James '56 (P) Cottage Grove, OR Our Lady of Perpetual Help Church.
Dowd, John *c.ss.r.* (CHI) [9] Chicago, IL St. Alphonsus Church.
Dowd, John M. *o.s.m.* '69 (CHI) [18] Chicago, IL Assumption of the Blessed Virgin Mary Church; [N] Chicago, IL Servite Friars - Eastern Province.
Dowd, John R. '63 (MAD) Green Lake, WI Our Lady of the Lake Church.
Dowd, Karl E. '60 (MAN) [3] Nashua, NH St. Christopher Church.
Dowd, Robert A. *c.s.c* '94 (FTW) [J] South Bend, IN Congregation of Holy Cross Indiana Province Provincial House.
Dowd, Robert A. *c.s.c.* '94 (LA) Santa Monica, CA St. Monica Church.
Dowd, Thomas M. '54 (GI) Retired.
Dowd, William J. '67 (NEW) Hohokus, NJ St. Luke's Church.
Dowdel, Lawrence J., Jr. '91 (LA) Ventura, CA Our Lady of the Assumption Church.
Dowdell, Aaron M. *o.ss.t.* '74 (BAL) [M] Baltimore, MD Holy Trinity Monastery.
Dowdell, Aaron M. *o.ss.t.* '74 (NY) [20] New York, NY St. Brigid Church.
Dowdell, Msgr. Joseph M. '63 (BUF) Lakewood, NY Sacred Heart Church.
Dowdell, Thomas '63 (OKL) [K] Norman, OK Campus Ministry for the Archdiocese of Oklahoma City.
Dowdell, Thomas R. '71 (OKL) [8] Oklahoma City, OK St. Francis of Assisi Church.
Dowdle, David P. '79 (CHI) [67] Chicago, IL St. Gall Church.
Dowds, James *c.ss.r.* '85 (WDC) [M] Washington, DC Holy Redeemer College.
Dowdy, James H. '69 (BAL) Absent on Leave.
Dowell, William J. '45 (DET) Retired.
Dower, Douglas '87 (RVC) Elmont, NY St. Boniface Church.
Dowling, Edward T. *s.j.* '69 (NY) [DD] New York, NY Jesuit Community at Fordham University.
Dowling, Edwin A. '77 (CLV) Loudonville, OH St. Peter Church; [Y] Berea, OH Office of Newman Campus Ministry.
Dowling, Finbarr *o.s.b.* '68 (STL) Concord Hill, MO St. Ignatius Church.
Dowling, John *m.s.f.* '74 (SAT) [M] San Antonio, TX

MSF Center & Provincialate.
Dowling, John C. '51 (NEW) Retired.
Dowling, John J. *o.s.a.* (CHI) [67] Chicago, IL St. Gall Church.
Dowling, John J. *o.s.a.* '68 (CHI) [185] Chicago, IL St. Rita of Cascia Church.
Dowling, John R. '83 (KNX) [6] Knoxville, TN St. John Neumann Church.
Dowling, Joseph Kevin '80 (NSH) Centerville, TN Christ the Redeemer Church; Hohenwald, TN Holy Trinity Church; Waynesboro, TN St. Cecilia Church.
Dowling, Jude '54 (HRT) [M] West Hartford, CT Holy Family Monastery/Retreat.
Dowling, Lawrence R. '91 (CHI) [50] Chicago, IL St. Denis Church.
Dowling, Michael J. '56 (NEW) Retired.
Dowling, P. Finbarr *o.s.b.* '68 (STL) [P] St. Louis, MO The Abbey of St. Mary and St. Louis.
Dowling, Msgr. Philip J. '56 (PH) [133] Philadelphia, PA St. Patrick Church.
Dowling, Raymond '61 (DAL) Seagoville, TX Federal Correctional Institution.
Dowling, Raymond G. '61 (GB) On Duty Outside the Diocese.
Dowling, Msgr. Thomas C. '55 (NO) Retired.
Dowling, Timothy '92 (PAT) Kinnelon, NJ Our Lady of the Magnificat Church.
Dowling, William '94 (LA) El Monte, CA Nativity Church.
Dowling, William P. '54 (SAV) Retired.
Downes, Msgr. Stephen N. '66 (LA) Goleta, CA St. Raphael Church.
Downes, Thomas J. '51 (CHI) Retired.
Downey, Alvin T. *o.s.b.* '70 (GBG) [H] Latrobe, PA Saint Vincent Archabbey.
Downey, Donald '81 (CC) On Special Assignment.
Downey, James *o.s.b.* '46 (KCK) [H] Atchison, KS St. Benedict's Abbey.
Downey, Joseph F. *s.j.* (DET) [K] Detroit, MI Jesuit Provincial Office-Detroit Province of the Society of Jesus.
Downey, Joseph F. *s.j.* '48 (CHI) [N] Evanston, IL Canisius House.
Downey, Joseph J. '43 (BO) Retired; [U] Somerville, MA Jeanne Jugan Residence.
Downey, Kevin *o.f.m.* (PAT) Pompton Lakes, NJ Our Lady of the Assumption Church.
Downey, Michael '73 (SAC) Fairfield, CA Holy Spirit Church.
Downey, Richard E. *m.m.* '44 (FgM) Maryknoll Foreign Missions.
Downey, Robert '54 (SB) Retired.
Downey, Timothy M. '38 (TOL) Retired.
Downing, Brendan W. '79 (BRK) [173] Queens, NY St. Gertrude Church.
Downing, Charles H. '65 (PRO) [5] West Warwick, RI St. Joseph Church.
Downing, Msgr. Joseph C. '62 (CAM) Pennsauken, NJ St. Stephen Church.
Downs, Bruce '94 (PHX) [3] Tempe, AZ Resurrection Church.
Downs, Gregory '91 (LAF) Carencro, LA St. Peter Church.
Downs, James A. '70 (PIT) Bessemer, PA St. Anthony Church; Hillsville, PA St. Lawrence Church; Lawrence County, PA Lawrence County Jail.
Downs, John L. '55 (OG) Massena, NY St. Joseph Church.
Downs, L. James '66 (WDC) [3] Rockville, MD St. Mary Church.
Downs, Richard J. '45 (ALB) Retired.
Downs, Robert '51 (ROC) Retired.
Downs, Walter J. *m.s.c.* '58 (Y) [A] Youngstown, OH Sacred Heart Retreat House & Renewal Center; [N] Youngstown, OH Sacred Heart Retreat and Renewal Center.
Doyen, Mitchell '91 (STL) [14] St. Louis, MO Our Lady of Sorrows Church; [E] St. Louis, MO Saint Mary's High School.
Doyle, Alan T. *m.m.* '64 (FgM) Maryknoll Foreign Missions.
Doyle, Brendan '63 (JC) Linn, MO St. George Church; [B] Jefferson City, MO Helias High School.
Doyle, Brendan '89 (ATL) Lawrenceville, GA St. Marguerite D'Youville Church.
Doyle, Charles E. '53 (GRY) Beverly Shores, IN St. Ann Church.
Doyle, Dan F. *s.m.* '67 (MIA) Special Assignment.
Doyle, Daniel E. *o.s.a.* '86 (PH) [B] Villanova, PA St. Augustine Friary; [C] Villanova, PA Villanova University.
Doyle, Daniel J. '48 (BO) [2] Salem, MA Immaculate Conception Church.
Doyle, Denis '70 (SR) Ferndale, CA Church of the Assumption.
Doyle, Dennis J. '65 (STL) [4] St. Charles, MO Sts. Joachim and Ann Church.
Doyle, Dennis M. '92 (STL) [2] St. Charles, MO St. Cletus Church.
Doyle, Donald E. '53 (ALB) Windham, NY St. Theresa of Child Jesus Church.
Doyle, Donald L. *c.m.* '48 (MET) [H] Plainsboro, NJ Vincentian Residence.
Doyle, Edward A. '64 (JC) Absent on Leave.
Doyle, Eugene '76 (SCL) Sauk Rapids, MN Sacred Heart Church.
Doyle, Francis J. *o.s.a.* '70 (WDC) [B] Washington, DC Augustinian College, Order of St. Augustine.
Doyle, Gerald '73 (GLP) Retired.
Doyle, James '61 (LKC) [6] Lake Charles, LA St. Theodore's Church.
Doyle, James F. '49 (ROC) Lima, NY St. Rose Church.
Doyle, Msgr. James F. '59 (NY) Bronxville, NY St. Joseph Church.
Doyle, Msgr. James J. '35 (PAT) Netcong, NJ St. Michael's Church; Retired.
Doyle, James J. *c.s.c.* '50 (SCR) [C] Wilkes-Barre, PA Kings College.
Doyle, James Michael '57 (SFS) [6] Sioux Falls, SD St. Mary Church.
Doyle, James P. '57 (CHI) Volo, IL St. Peter Church.
Doyle, Msgr. Jerald A. '69 (BGP) [4] Stratford, CT Our Lady of Grace Church.
Doyle, John '52 (DUL) Floodwood, MN St. Louis Church.
Doyle, John '58 (JOL) Joliet, IL Joliet Correctional Depot.
Doyle, John A. *c.m.* '48 (ALB) [L] Albany, NY Vincentian Fathers Residence.
Doyle, John F. '59 (NEW) Retired.
Doyle, John J. '58 (JOL) [7] Joliet, IL St. Anne Church.
Doyle, Msgr. John J. '70 (CHI) Evergreen Park, IL Queen of Martyrs Church.
Doyle, John J. *o.f.m.* '75 (PAT) Butler, NJ St. Anthony Church.
Doyle, John L. '52 (BO) [62] Boston, MA St. Peter Church.
Doyle, John T. *o.s.f.s.* '52 (VEN) [3] Fort Myers, FL St. Cecilia Church.
Doyle, John V. '41 (PRO) Retired.
Doyle, Joseph *s.j.* '70 (SP) [C] Tampa, FL Jesuit High School.
Doyle, Joseph C. '72 (NEW) Ridgefield Park, NJ St. Francis of Assisi Church.
Doyle, Joseph M. '40 (NEW) Retired.
Doyle, Joseph M. *s.s.j.* '68 (NO) [6] New Orleans, LA Epiphany Church; [F] New Orleans, LA St. Augustine High School; [H] New Orleans, LA St. Augustine High School; [S] New Orleans, LA Pierre Toussaint Foundation of New Orleans, Inc.
Doyle, Joshua *o.f.m.* (FgM) Custody of St. Mary of the Angels. Byzantine-Slavonic.
Doyle, Kennth '66 (ALB) [5] Albany, NY St. Catherine of Siena Church.
Doyle, Lawrence J. '45 (BO) [10] Lawrence, MA St. Patrick Church; Retired.
Doyle, Lawrence Michael *o.s.m.* '65 (CHI) [N] Chicago, IL Servite Friars - Eastern Province.
Doyle, Mark A. '58 (LC) [1] Wisconsin Rapids, WI Our Lady, Queen of Heaven Church.
Doyle, Martin *s.j.* '91 (FgM) Provinces.
Doyle, Martin *s.j.* '91 (NY) [DD] New York, NY Jesuit Provincial's Office.
Doyle, Mathias F. *o.f.m.* (BUF) [C] St. Bonaventure, NY St. Bonaventure University.
Doyle, Mathias F. '62 (BUF) [O] St. Bonaventure, NY St. Bonaventure Friary.
Doyle, Michael '59 (CAM) [9] Camden, NJ Sacred Heart Church.
Doyle, Michael '67 (SPR) [2] Springfield, MA All Souls Church.
Doyle, Michael '94 (TYL) [1] Tyler, TX Cathedral of the Immaculate Conception; [D] Tyler, TX Tyler Junior College and The University of Texas at Tyler Newman Center.
Doyle, Michael J. '67 (SPR) [3] Springfield, MA Blessed Sacrament Church; [M] Springfield, MA Casa Cristo Rey.
Doyle, Michael J. '85 (BO) Scituate, MA St. Mary of the Nativity Church.
Doyle, Michael L. *o.s.m.* '65 (DEN) [22] Denver, CO Our Lady of Mt. Carmel Church.
Doyle, Michael M. '89 (NU) Lake Benton, MN St. Genevieve Church; Tyler, MN St. Dionysius Church.
Doyle, Patrick A. '75 (IND) [20] Indianapolis, IN St. Joan of Arc Church.
Doyle, Paul F. *c.s.c.* '77 (FTW) [B] Notre Dame, IN University of Notre Dame Du Lac; [J] Notre Dame, IN Holy Cross Community, Corby Hall, University of Notre Dame.
Doyle, Philip R. '48 (NY) Retired.
Doyle, Richard J. '54 (ALB) Athens, NY St. Patrick Church.
Doyle, Robert A. *s.j.* '62 (STL) [P] St. Louis, MO White House Retreat Jesuit Community; [T] St. Louis, MO White House Retreat.
Doyle, Robert M. '49 (BO) [7] Somerville, MA St. Polycarp Church.
Doyle, Seamus '56 (MIA) Miami Shores, FL St. Rose of Lima Church.
Doyle, Stephen *o.f.m.* '62 (BO) [BB] Boston, MA St. Anthony Shrine.
Doyle, Msgr. Thomas '54 (LA) La Crescenta, CA St. James the Less Church.
Doyle, Thomas *s.s.* '60 (BAL) [M] Baltimore, MD Sulpician Provincial House.
Doyle, Thomas '84 (BRK) [U] Brooklyn, NY Curial Residence.
Doyle, Thomas D. (BUF) North Tonawanda, NY Orleans Correction Facility.
Doyle, Thomas D. '82 (BUF) Oakfield, NY St. Cecilia Church.
Doyle, Thomas F. '66 (PH) Royersford, PA Sacred Heart Church.
Doyle, Thomas J. *s.j.* '46 (PH) [AA] Philadelphia, PA Jesuit Community at St. Joseph's University.
Doyle, Thomas M. *s.j.* '97 (MIL) [E] Milwaukee, WI Marquette University High School; [P] Milwaukee, WI Pere Marquette House Jesuit Community.
Doyle, Thomas R. '62 (DAV) Albia, IA St. Mary's Church.
Doyle, Thomas S. '52 (DAV) Lovilia, IA St. Peter's Church.
Doyle, Msgr. Timothy '48 (ORG) Retired.
Doyle, Msgr. Vincent J. '65 (NEW) Union, NJ Holy Spirit Church.
Doyle, Msgr. Walter H. '43 (STO) Retired.
Doyle, William *s.j.* (BO) Boston, MA Spaulding Rehabilitation Hospital.
Doyle, William F. *s.j.* '53 (BO) [W] Boston, MA Loyola House.
Doyne, David A. '56 (PH) Oreland, PA Holy Martyrs Church.
Doyon, Bernard *o.m.i.* '48 (GAL) [S] Dickinson, TX Christian Renewal Center.
Drab, John '46 (RVC) Retired.
Drab, Stephen J. '37 (GBG) Retired.
Drabek, Howard '91 (GAL) [78] Houston, TX St. Vincent de Paul Church.
Drabik, Richard J. *m.i.c.* '60 (SFE) [J] Bernalillo, NM Southwest Marian Divine Mercy Center.
Drabik, Richard J. *m.i.c.* '60 (SPR) [I] Stockbridge, MA Congregation of Marians.
Drabiska, Frank J. '76 (PIT) [2] Swissvale, PA Word of God Church.
Drag, Roderick *o.f.m.* '49 (PH) [AA] Philadelphia, PA St. Pius X Friary.
Dragga, Thomas '83 (CLV) [A] Wickliffe, OH St. Mary Seminary and Graduate School of Theology.
Dragga, Thomas M. '83 (CLV) [A] Wickliffe, OH Borromeo Seminary.
Dragon, Joseph W. '78 (PH) East Goshen, PA SS. Peter and Paul Church.
Draim, David *o.s.b.* '73 (SP) [O] St. Leo, FL St. Leo Abbey.
Drain, William A. '74 (CIN) [62] Cincinnati, OH St. Matthias Church.
Drake, Roy A. *s.j.* '63 (NY) [DD] New York, NY Murray-Weigel Hall.
Drake, Sebastian *o.f.m.* '45 (SPK) [11] Spokane, WA St. Francis of Assisi, Friars Church.
Drake, Timothy A. '71 (RIC) [10] Virginia Beach, VA St. Matthew Church.
Drance, George *s.j.* '95 (NY) [82] New York, NY Notre Dame Church.
Drance, George W. *s.j.* '95 (MIL) [P] Milwaukee, WI Jesuit Provincial Office, Wisconsin Province.
Drapeau, Benoit J. *c.j.m.* '59 (BUF) [1] West Seneca, NY St. Bonaventure Church; [O] West Seneca, NY St. Bonaventure.
Draper, Andrew *t.o.r.* '88 (ARL) Luray, VA Our Lady of the Valley Church.
Drapp, Alfred E. '55 (CIN) Retired.
Drass, Damian P. *t.o.r.* '60 (WH) Philippi, WV St. Elizabeth Parish and Newman Center Church; [Q] Philippi, WV Alderson-Broaddus College Newman Center.
Draude, Frank C. '49 (RCK) Retired.
Draugialis, Josef '63 (LA) Los Nietos, CA Our Lady of Perpetual Help Church.
Dravecky, Msgr. Michael A. '33 (PIT) Retired.
Draves-Arpaia, Neil '79 (PHX) On Duty Outside the Diocese.
Dreasen, Msgr. John R. '79 (RVC) Elmont, NY St. Boniface Church.
Dreckman, Philip *s.j.* '62 (STP) [6] St. Paul, MN The Immaculate Heart of Mary Church.
Dreese, John J. '59 (COL) New Lexington, OH St. Rose of Lima Church.
Dreffein, Larry *o.f.m.* '76 (JOL) [I] Oak Brook, IL Mayslake Village.
Dreger, Msgr. Francis X. '51 (PH) [32] Philadelphia, PA St. Cecilia Church.
Dreher, Ernest O. '48 (MIL) Retired.
Dreher, Jacob J. '43 (DOD) Retired.
Dreher, John D. '64 (PRO) Coventry, RI Our Lady of Czenstochowa Church.
Dreici, Pascal *c.ss.r.* (DEN) [M] Denver, CO The Redemptorists/Denver Province.
Dreici, Pascal *c.ss.r.* '44 (CHI) [N] Chicago, IL Redemptorists:; [N] Bodija, Ibadan, Oyo State, Nigeria.
Dreier, Bruce A. '78 (SFR) [17] San Francisco, CA Church of the Epiphany.

Dreiling, Augustine *o.s.b.* '58 (KC) Conception Junction, MO St. Columba Church.
Dreiling, Gerald G. *c.pp.s.* '58 (CIN) [M] Dayton, OH Provincial House of the Cincinnati Province of the Society of the Precious Blood.
Dreiling, Msgr. Raymond C. '75 (FRS) Clovis, CA Our Lady of Perpetual Help Church; [J] Clovis, CA Catholic Professional & Business Breakfast Club of the Fresno Diocese.
Dreisbach, Charles V. '59 (BAK) Klamath Falls, OR Sacred Heart Church.
Dreisoerner, Msgr. John H. '38 (JC) Retired.
Drendel, Ralph J. *s.j.* '53 (SJ) [D] San Jose, CA Bellarmine College Preparatory.
Drennan, Jimmy D. '96 (SAT) [60] San Antonio, TX St. Paul Church.
Drennan, Lawrence J. '61 (BO) Bridgewater, MA St. Thomas Aquinas Church.
Drennan, Msgr. William A. '55 (STL) [58] St. Louis, MO St. Raphael The Archangel Church.
Drennen, Christopher J. *o.s.a.* '83 (ALB) Mechanicville, NY Assumption-St. Paul Church.
Drenzek, Peter C. '69 (MIL) [3] Fond du Lac, WI St. Mary Church.
Dresen, Arthur G. '44 (COS) Retired.
Dressel, Willard J. *s.j.* '54 (OM) [C] Omaha, NE Creighton Preparatory School.
Dressell, Stephen G. *m.s.* '47 (HRT) [5] Hartford, CT Our Lady of Sorrows Church; [M] Hartford, CT Missionaries of LaSalette Provincial Secretary.
Dressen, Nicholas '79 (SCL) Big Lake, MN Our Lady of the Lake Church.
Dressler, Philip J. '61 (CHI) [112] Chicago, IL St. Juliana Church.
Dressler, Robert A. '59 (ALN) Kelayres, PA Immaculate Conception Church.
Dressman, James J. *s.j.* '61 (NOR) Storrs, CT St. Thomas Aquinas Church; [K] Willimantic, CT Campus Ministry.
Dressman, Richard E. '72 (CIN) [51] Cincinnati, OH St. Jude the Apostle Church; [V] Cincinnati, OH Catholic Charismatic Renewal Liaison.
Dressman, Robert *s.j.* '55 (CIN) [M] Cincinnati, OH Faber Jesuit Community.
Dreves, Mark D. '95 (LEX) [3] Lexington, KY Mary, Queen of the Holy Rosary Church.
Drew, Andrew *o.f.m.cap.* '61 (SPR) [L] Springfield, MA St. Francis of Assisi Chapel and Catholic Information Center.
Drew, George W. *c.ss.r.* '50 (BO) [13] Boston, MA Our Lady of Perpetual Help Church.
Drew, James F. '74 (HON) On Duty Outside the Diocese.
Drew, James F. '74 (RVC) North Merrick, NY Sacred Heart Church.
Drew, John J. *m.m.* '42 (SJ) [M] Los Altos, CA Maryknoll.
Drewelow, David C. '80 (SPC) On Duty Outside the Diocese.
Drewniak, Stanley '78 (CHI) [36] Chicago, IL St. Camillus Church.
Drexel, John *o.m.i.* '62 (FgM) Oblates Foreign Missions.
Drexler, Charles H. '69 (E) [B] Erie, PA Gannon University.
Drexler, George D. '39 (NEW) Retired.
Drexler, Harold J. '55 (DUB) [7] Dubuque, IA Sacred Heart Church; Retired.
Drieci, Pat *c.ss.r.* (FRS) Faculties Only.
Driesch, Albert *t.o.r.* '46 (WH) Moundsville, WV St. Francis Xavier's Church.
Driesch, David A. '82 (PIT) Neshannock, PA St. Camillus Church; [R] Slippery Rock, PA Office for Campus Ministry.
Drilling, Peter '67 (BUF) [A] East Aurora, NY Christ the King Seminary.
Drilling, Peter J. (BUF) [2] Lackawanna, NY St. Anthony Church.
Drinan, Daniel *c.m.f.* '77 (CHI) [149] Chicago, IL Our Lady of Guadalupe Church.
Drinan, Robert F. *s.j.* '53 (BO) [W] Boston, MA The Society of Jesus of New England-Provincial Offices.
Drinan, Robert F. *s.j.* '53 (WDC) [M] Washington, DC The Jesuit Community at Georgetown University.
Drinane, Gerald A. *s.j.* '62 (FgM) Provinces.
Drinkwater, Warren *c.ss.r.* '62 (BLX) [E] Biloxi, MS St. John Neumann Residence.
Driscoll, Arthur J. '52 (BO) Andover, MA St. Robert Bellarmine Church.
Driscoll, Daniel '76 (HEL) [4] Anaconda, MT Anaconda Catholic Community Church.
Driscoll, Donald D. *s.j.* '65 (OM) [K] Omaha, NE Jesuit Community At Creighton University.
Driscoll, Donald T. (NY) Orangeburg, NY Rockland Psychiatric Center.
Driscoll, Eugene '70 (LUB) [4] Lubbock, TX St. Elizabeth University Parish.
Driscoll, George F. *s.j.* '61 (NY) [DD] New York, NY Murray-Weigel Hall.
Driscoll, James '55 (OAK) Retired.
Driscoll, James A. *o.p.* '54 (PRO) [B] Providence, RI Providence College; [P] Providence, RI St. Thomas Aquinas Priory at Providence College.
Driscoll, James E. '55 (OAK) Danville, CA St. Isidore's Church.
Driscoll, James J. '43 (NEW) Retired.
Driscoll, Jeremy *o.s.b.* '81 (P) [L] St. Benedict, OR Mt. Angel Abbey.
Driscoll, John '54 (JOL) Retired.
Driscoll, John M. *o.s.a.* '51 (PH) [C] Villanova, PA Villanova University; [AA] Villanova, PA St. Thomas Monastery.
Driscoll, John P. '47 (FR) [18] New Bedford, MA St. Lawrence Martyr Church.
Driscoll, John P. *s.j.* '52 (NO) [P] New Orleans, LA Ignatius Residence.
Driscoll, Joseph J. '79 (BO) On Duty Outside the Archdiocese.
Driscoll, Joseph J. '79 (MIL) [Y] Milwaukee, WI National Association of Catholic Chaplains.
Driscoll, Msgr. Maurice F. '42 (BEL) Retired.
Driscoll, Michael *o.carm.* '67 (PMB) [5] Boca Raton, FL St. Jude Church.
Driscoll, Michael '76 (FTW) [B] Notre Dame, IN University of Notre Dame Du Lac.
Driscoll, Michael '77 (HEL) On Duty Outside the Diocese.
Driscoll, Michael '92 (PEO) Tiskilwa, IL St. Mary's Church.
Driscoll, Michael A. '68 (MET) Belvidere, NJ St. Patrick Church.
Driscoll, Michael J. '92 (PEO) Camp Grove, IL St. Patrick Church.
Driscoll, Nicholas J. '69 (BO) Awaiting Assignment.
Driscoll, Paul G. '64 (RVC) Levittown, NY St. Bernard Church.
Driscoll, Richard *s.d.s.* (PHX) Buckeye, AZ Saint Henry Church.
Driscoll, Richard *s.d.s.* '65 (MIL) [P] Milwaukee, WI Salvatorian Provincial Residence.
Driscoll, Richard A. '55 (BO) Topsfield, MA St. Rose of Lima Church.
Driscoll, Samuel *o.f.m.cap.* '59 (FgM) Capuchin Foreign Missions.
Driscoll, Thomas F. '60 (OG) Alexandria Bay, NY St. Cyril of Alexandria Church; Redwood, NY St. Francis Xavier Church.
Driscoll, Msgr. Thomas J. '61 (BGP) [5] Stratford, CT Our Lady of Peace Church.
Driscoll, Walter L. '57 (BO) Permanent Disability.
Driscoll, William J. *o.mar.* '63 (SAM) [C] Petersham, MA Most Holy Trinity Monastery.
Driscoll, William J. '65 (E) Linesville, PA St. Philip Church.
Driscoll, William M. *s.j.* '51 (BAL) [J] Timonium, MD Stella Maris Operating Corporation.
Drobach, William F. *s.a.* '88 (LA) [83] Los Angeles, CA St. Odilia Church.
Drobel, William F. '32 (PH) [83] Philadelphia, PA St. Katherine of Siena Church; Retired.
Drobin, Paul J. '66 (SY) New Hartford, NY St. John the Evangelist Church.
Drobinski, Joseph J. '75 (WIL) Newark, DE Parish of the Resurrection Church.
Droessler, Joseph '95 (ORG) San Juan Capistrano, CA (Old Mission) Church.
Droessler, Wayne J. '69 (DUB) Clarion, IA St. John's Church; Eagle Grove, IA Sacred Heart Church.
Drogon, Greg '82 (PAT) [11] Paterson, NJ St. Michael the Archangel Church.
Drogowski, Joseph '49 (DET) Retired; [H] Southfield, MI Providence Hospital.
Drohan, James J. *s.j.* '43 (WOR) [N] Worcester, MA Jesuits of Holy Cross College, Inc.
Drohan, Joseph W. (ATL) Retired.
Drolet, Francis K. *s.j.* '47 (NY) [DD] New York, NY St. Ignatius Loyola Residence.
Drolet, Roger C. *c.s.v.* '33 (CHI) [N] Arlington Heights, IL Viatorian Province Center-Clerics of St. Viator.
Droll, Msgr. Larry J. '73 (SAN) Wall, TX St. Ambrose Church.
Droll, Louis J. '68 (SAN) Retired.
Drone, Msgr. Raphael E. '43 (BEL) Retired.
Drongowski, Stanley *o.p.* (MAD) [3] Madison, WI Blessed Sacrament Church.
Drongowski, Stanley A. *o.p.* '79 (STL) [P] St. Louis, MO Dominican Community of St. Louis.
Droski, Norman P. '64 (GR) Muskegon Heights, MI Sacred Heart Church.
Drouin, Marc B. '90 (MAN) Belmont, NH St. Joseph Church.
Drouncheck, Anthony M. '89 (ALN) [3] Reading, PA St. Catharine of Siena Church.
Drozd, Henry J. '62 (DAL) On Duty Outside the Diocese.
Drozdzal, John S. (SY) [10] Utica, NY St. Joseph and St. Patrick Church.
Drozdzik, Roch T. '96 (R) Pinehurst, NC Sacred Heart Church.
Droze, D. Anthony '85 (CHR) Greenville, SC St. Mary's Church.
Drucker, James '78 (PSC) Leave of Absence.
Druding, John C. '76 (ATL) Roswell, GA St. Andrew Church.
Druggan, Dennis *o.f.m.cap.* '84 (MIL) [B] Mount Calvary, WI St. Lawrence Seminary; [P] Mount Calvary, WI St. Lawrence Friary.
Drummond, Alexander '94 (ARL) Chantilly, VA St. Timothy Church.
Drummond, Robert T. *o.s.a.* '67 (NY) [216] Staten Island, NY Our Lady of Good Counsel Church.
Drummy, John A. '71 (SUP) Amery, WI St. Joseph Church.
Drupieski, Stanley R. *o.s.f.s.* '64 (WIL) [B] Wilmington, DE Salesianum School.
Drury, Dennis G. '82 (GB) Rosiere, WI St. Peter and St. Hubert Church.
Drury, George L. *s.j.* '52 (BO) [W] Cambridge, MA Weston Jesuit Community.
Drury, Michael J. '71 (PAT) Long Valley, NJ St. Luke Church.
Drury, Michael P. *c.o.* '84 (MRY) [G] Monterey, CA Oratorian Community-Congregation of the Oratory of Pontifical Right.
Drury, Robert '79 (OWN) Curdsville, KY St. Elizabeth Church; St. Joseph, KY St. Alphonsus Church.
Drutowski, Robert J. '79 (MIL) Mukwonago, WI St. James Church.
Dryden, John D. *s.j.* '53 (LA) [R] Los Angeles, CA Columbiere House.
Dryden, John D. *s.j.* '53 (SJ) [M] Los Gatos, CA Sacred Heart Jesuit Center.
Drzaic, Francis *s.v.d.* '62 (CHI) [B] Techny, IL Divine Word Residence.
Drzaic, Frank *s.v.d.* (CHI) [32] Chicago, IL St. Bronislava Church.
Drzal, Stanislaw *s.ch.* '73 (PAT) [6] Passaic, NJ St. Joseph's Church.
Du, Luke Pham Anh '54 (BRK) [147] Queens, NY St. Aloysius Church; [T] Brooklyn, NY Catholic Migration & Refugee Office, Catholic Migration Services, Inc.
Du Buisson, William *o.m.i.* '55 (SAN) Sonora, TX St. Ann's Church.
Du Charme, Paul E. '55 (GB) [14] Green Bay, WI St. Philip the Apostle Church.
Duaime, Jeffrey T. *c.s.sp.* '86 (ARL) [7] Arlington, VA Our Lady, Queen of Peace Church.
Duane, James M. *c.s.c.* '74 (FR) [A] North Easton, MA Holy Cross Fathers Religious.
Duane, Robert J. '53 (NY) Ardsley, NY Our Lady of Perpetual Help Church; Retired.
Duane, Thomas J. '71 (PH) Roslyn, PA St. John of the Cross Church.
Dubay, Thomas E. *s.m.* '50 (WDC) [M] Washington, DC Marist Provincial House.
Dube, Andre R. '85 (BGP) [4] Stamford, CT St. Clement's Church.
Dube, Donald V. '61 (SPR) Absent on Leave.
Dube, George *m.s.* '48 (FR) [J] Attleboro, MA La Salette Provincial House.
Dube, Marcel *o.carm.* '54 (JOL) [J] Darien, IL Carmelite Provincial Office.
Dube, Stephen D. '78 (WH) Weirton, WV St. Joseph the Worker Church.
Dubel, Edward A. *c.r.* '57 (SB) Rialto, CA St. Thomas More Church.
Dubell, Msgr. James H. '65 (TR) Burlington, NJ St. Paul Church.
Dubi, Leonard A. '68 (CHI) Hazel Crest, IL St. Anne Church.
Dubitsky, Roman '65 (PHU) Perth Amboy, NJ Assumption of B.V.M. Church; Toms River, NJ St. Stephen's Church.
Dublinski, Steven L. '85 (SPK) [15] Spokane, WA St. Mary Church; Rockford, WA St. Joseph Church.
Dubois, Andrew '95 (PRT) [5] Lewiston, ME St. Patrick's Church; [6] Lewiston, ME SS. Peter and Paul Church.
Dubois, Msgr. Charles J. '64 (LKC) [6] Lake Charles, LA St. Theodore's Church.
DuBois, David J. '80 (GAL) Tomball, TX St. Anne Church.
DuBois, Francis J. '70 (ALB) Latham, NY St. Ambrose Church.
Dubois, Raymond J. *s.s.s.* '49 (CLV) [P] Cleveland, OH Blessed Sacrament Community.
DuBois, Msgr. William '48 (SP) Retired.
Dubois, Yvon *a.a.* '53 (BO) [W] Brighton, MA Assumptionist Center.
Dubovici, Mihail '93 (STF) Auburn, NY SS. Peter and Paul Church.
Dubowski, George *o.f.m.* '41 (FTW) [K] Mishawaka, IN St. Francis Provincialate.
Dubowski, George *o.f.m.* '42 (GRY) [J] Cedar Lake, IN Our Lady of Lourdes Friary.
Dubriske, Edward J. *s.s.e.* '64 (BUR) [E] Colchester, VT Society of St. Edmund.
Dubriske, Edward J. *s.s.e.* '64 (FgM) Edmundite Foreign Missions.
Dubrouillet, James N. '97 (CHR) [17] Charleston, SC Christ Our King Church.
Duc, Dominic Tran Minh (PH) Pottstown, PA St.

Aloysius Church.
Duc Hau, Joseph Nguyen *s.e.* '69 (P) [1] Portland, OR Southeast Asian Vicariate Church.
Duc Tien, Msgr. Peter '60 (ORG) Special Assignment.
Duc-Minh, Joseph '61 (LA) [A] Camarillo, CA St. John's Seminary College of the Archdiocese of Los Angeles.
Duca, Michael '78 (DAL) [A] Irving, TX Holy Trinity Seminary.
Ducaji, John '54 (JOL) Wheaton, IL St. Mark Church.
Ducate, Richard '67 (KC) Butler, MO St. Patrick's Church.
Ducci, Alex '61 (STA) Orange Park, FL St. Catherine's Church.
Ducette, Msgr. John I. '62 (BUF) [5] Tonawanda, NY St. Timothy Church.
Ducey, William *ss.cc.* '55 (FR) [J] Fairhaven, MA Sacred Hearts Provincial House.
Duch, Robert G. '64 (PIT) Aspinwall, PA St. Scholastica Church.
Duchaine, R. Mark '78 (SC) Holstein, IA Our Lady of Good Counsel Church.
Duchala, Francis S. *o.f.m.* '36 (ALN) [K] Easton, PA St. Francis Friary.
Duchene, Joseph A. *c.s.sp.* '52 (PIT) [B] Pittsburgh, PA Duquesne University of the Holy Ghost.
Duchensky, Jonathan *s.s.m.i.* (STF) [G] Sloatsburg, NY St. Mary's Villa Spiritual, Cultural & Educational Center.
Duchesneau, Gaston *s.j.* '44 (FgM) Provinces.
DuChez, Daniel B. *o.s.* '56 (PCE) On Duty Outside the Diocese.
DuChez, Daniel B. *o.s.* '86 (LC) Chippewa Falls, WI St. Charles Borromeo Church.
Duchschere, Paul '90 (FAR) [6] Fargo, ND St. Paul Newman Center, N.D.S.U. Church; [H] Fargo, ND St. Paul's Catholic Chapel.
Ducre, Kennon Y. *s.t.l.* '83 (ELP) [2] El Paso, TX All Saints Church.
Ducthuan, Polycarp *c.m.c.* '91 (AMA) [5] Amarillo, TX Our Lady of Vietnam Church.
Duda, Francis *m.i.c.* '43 (SPR) [I] Stockbridge, MA Congregation of Marians.
Duda, Robert '84 (JOL) Elmhurst, IL Immaculate Conception Church.
Dudack, William E. '55 (HRT) Simsbury, CT St. Mary's Church.
Dudak, Msgr. George A. '56 (PAT) Schooley's Mountain, NJ Our Lady of the Mountain Church.
Dudash, Derrick F. '74 (GRY) Hebron, IN St. Helen Church.
Duddy, Patrick A. '39 (PH) Stowe, PA St. Gabriel Church; Retired.
Dudek, Anthony *m.s.* '37 (MIL) [P] Milwaukee, WI La Salette Fathers.
Dudek, Berard *o.f.m.conv.* '54 (BGP) [1] Fairfield, CT St. Anthony of Padua Church.
Dudek, Ladislaus '40 (SFS) Salem, SD St. Mary Church; Retired.
Dudek, Ladislaus J. '66 (ALN) [8] Allentown, PA SS. Peter and Paul Church.
Dudek, Stanislaw '71 (SLC) [4] Salt Lake City, UT Sacred Heart Church.
Dudek, Stephen S. '84 (GR) Holland, MI St. Francis de Sales Church; On Special Assignment.
Dudink, Edward *s.v.d.* '46 (BO) [W] Duxbury, MA Society of the Divine Word.
Dudkiewicz, Stanley '52 (SY) [9] Syracuse, NY Sacred Heart Church.
Dudley, Francis R. '46 (STP) [7] St. Paul, MN Maternity of the Blessed Virgin Church; Retired.
Dudley, James Q. *m.s.c.* '56 (CC) [3] Beeville, TX St. James Church.
Dudziak, Paul M. '69 (WDC) Dunkirk, MD Jesus the Good Shepherd Church.
Dudzik, Dariusz K. '95 (NOR) Pawcatuck, CT St. Michael Church.
Dudzinski, Anthony J. '96 (FAR) [3] Grand Forks, ND St. Michael's Church.
Dudzinski, Brian A. '97 (LFT) Muncie, IN St. Mary Church.
Dudzinski, Paul L. '86 (ARL) Falls Church, VA St. James Church.
Dudzinski, Sylvester W. '39 (CHI) Blue Island, IL St. Isidore Church; Retired.
Dudzinski, Theodore C., II '97 (LFT) Kokomo, IN St. Patrick Church.
Duell, James S. '82 (CIN) Bradford, OH Immaculate Conception Church; Covington, OH St. Teresa Church.
Duellman, Virgil S. '60 (WIN) Austin, MN Queen of Angels Church.
Duenas, Jaime H. '50 (NY) [167] Bronx, NY Nativity of Our Blessed Lady Church.
Duenas, Jose Luis *o.a.r.* '59 (NY) [126] Bronx, NY St. Anselm Church.
Duerr, Gregory *o.s.b.* '64 (P) [A] St. Benedict, OR Mount Angel Seminary; [L] St. Benedict, OR Mt. Angel Abbey.
Duesdieker, Robert W. '80 (JC) Bourbon, MO St. Francis Church; Cuba, MO Holy Cross Church; Steelville, MO St. Michael Church.
Duesman, Msgr. Jerome P. '68 (DAL) Irving, TX Holy Family of Nazareth Church.
Duesman, Msgr. Leon '65 (DAL) [4] Garland, TX St. Michael the Archangel Church.
Duesterhaus, Michael R. '91 (ARL) Military Chaplains.
Duet, Wayne J. '75 (LAF) Erath, LA Our Lady of Lourdes Church.
Dueweke, Donald G. '66 (SAG) Maple Grove, MI St. Michael Church.
Dueweke, Robert F. *o.s.a.* '79 (CHI) [185] Chicago, IL St. Rita of Cascia Church.
Dufault, Andrew J. *m.afr.* '39 (LR) [F] Hot Springs National Park, AR Monastery of Our Lady of Charity of Refuge (Good Shepherd).
Dufault, Omer L. '42 (BUR) Retired; [D] Burlington, VT St. Joseph's Home for Aged.
Dufault, Wilfrid J. *a.a.* '34 (WOR) [B] Worcester, MA Assumption College; [N] Worcester, MA Assumptionists of Assumption College.
Duff, Bill '63 (LAV) [4] Las Vegas, NV Our Lady of Las Vegas Church.
Duff, Gerard M. *o.s.a.* '59 (PH) [V] Flourtown, PA St. Joseph Villa; [AA] Villanova, PA St. Thomas Monastery.
Duff, John J. '77 (NY) Pawling, NY St. John the Evangelist Church.
Duff, Thomas M. *o.s.m.* '49 (CHI) [N] Chicago, IL Servite Friars - Eastern Province.
Duff, William '63 (LAV) Retired.
Duffe, Stephen J. '96 (NEW) Washington Township, NJ Our Lady of Good Counsel Church.
Duffell, John P. '69 (NY) [14] New York, NY Ascension Church.
Duffey, Joseph A. *o.s.a.* '52 (PH) Flourtown, PA St. Genevieve Church; [AA] Flourtown, PA Augustinians (O.S.A.).
Duffey, Thomas J. '49 (DET) [60] Detroit, MI St. Patrick Church; [Q] Detroit, MI St. Patrick's Senior Center, Inc.
Duffey, William R. *s.j.* '51 (MIL) [P] Milwaukee, WI Jesuit Provincial Office, Wisconsin Province.
Dufficy, Edward C. '50 (CHI) [3] Oak Park, IL St. Edmund Church; Retired.
Duffin, Stephen '91 (ORG) Laguna Beach, CA St. Catherine of Siena Church.
Duffner, Paul *o.p.* (OAK) [N] Oakland, CA Western Dominican Province.
Duffner, Paul A. *o.p.* '40 (P) [18] Portland, OR Holy Rosary Parish & Dominican Priory Church.
Duffner, Ralph J. '56 (SPC) New Hamburg, MO St. Lawrence Church.
Dufford, Robert *s.j.* '73 (GB) [M] Oshkosh, WI Jesuit Retreat House.
Duffy, Aidan *o.f.m.* '56 (BO) [BB] Boston, MA St. Anthony Shrine.
Duffy, David J. *o.s.a.* '57 (PH) [G] Malvern, PA Malvern Preparatory School for Boys.
Duffy, Donald '59 (NO) Edgard, LA St. John the Baptist Church.
Duffy, Donald J. '43 (CHI) Buffalo Grove, IL St. Mary Church; Retired.
Duffy, Edward *o.carm.* '82 (NY) Middletown, NY Our Lady of Mt. Carmel Church.
Duffy, Edward V. '52 (NEW) Harrington Park, NJ Our Lady of Victories Church.
Duffy, Edwin '42 (NY) Retired.
Duffy, Edwin J. '61 (HON) Retired.
Duffy, Emmanuel *o.f.m.* '30 (PAT) [M] Butler, NJ St. Anthony Friary.
Duffy, Eugene J. '50 (LA) Retired.
Duffy, Francis C. *o.p.* '60 (WDC) [11] Washington, DC St. Dominic Church & Priory Church.
Duffy, Francis J. '70 (PAT) Morristown, NJ St. Margaret's Church.
Duffy, Francis L. *s.j.* '58 (BAL) [H] Baltimore, MD Mercy Medical Center, Inc.
Duffy, Francis R. *c.s.sp.* '41 (PH) [L] Philadelphia, PA St. Joseph's House for Boys; [AA] Philadelphia, PA Holy Ghost Fathers.
Duffy, Msgr. Francis X. '49 (NY) Retired; [HH] New York, NY St. Paul's Guild, Inc.
Duffy, G. Ralph '65 (WDC) [2] Rockville, MD Shrine of St. Jude Church; Retired.
Duffy, George '63 (MIA) [6] Pompano Beach, FL St. Henry Church.
Duffy, George A. *s.j.* '55 (BO) [E] Boston, MA Boston College High School & Jesuit Community.
Duffy, Hugh '66 (PMB) Okeechobee, FL Sacred Heart Church.
Duffy, Hugh E. *o.s.f.s.* '60 (WIL) [I] Childs, MD Oblates of St. Francis De Sales.
Duffy, James '55 (JOL) Villa Park, IL St. John the Apostle Church.
Duffy, James D. *s.m.* '79 (STP) [25] St. Paul, MN St. Louis King of France Church.
Duffy, James H. '56 (MIL) Special Assignment.
Duffy, Msgr. John F. '45 (ROC) Retired.
Duffy, John J. '52 (PH) [2] Bensalem, PA St. Elizabeth Ann Seton Church; Retired.
Duffy, Msgr. John R. '45 (SY) [S] Syracuse, NY St. Pius X Home, Inc.
Duffy, Joseph P. *s.j.* '57 (BO) [W] Chestnut Hill, MA The Jesuit Community at Boston College.
Duffy, Jude *o.f.m.cap.* '58 (SP) [6] Tampa, FL Most Holy Redeemer Church.
Duffy, Michael A. *o.f.m.* (PH) [W] Philadelphia, PA Holy Name Province.
Duffy, Michael A. *o.f.m.* '71 (PH) [AA] Philadelphia, PA Order of Friars Minor of the Province of the Most Holy Name aka Holy Name Province.
Duffy, Patrick *o.c.s.o.* (SFE) Vaughn, NM St. Mary Church.
Duffy, Patrick '46 (FAR) Retired.
Duffy, Patrick *o.c.s.o.* '81 (ATL) [I] Conyers, GA The Monastery of the Holy Spirit.
Duffy, Patrick P. '74 (CIN) [71] Cincinnati, OH Our Lady of Victory Church.
Duffy, Patrick S. *o.c.s.o.* '81 (SFE) Anton Chico, NM San Jose Church.
Duffy, Paul *o.m.i.* '62 (FgM) Oblates Foreign Missions.
Duffy, Paul J. *m.m.* '79 (NY) [DD] Maryknoll, NY Maryknoll Fathers and Brothers.
Duffy, Raymond J. '68 (FRS) Riverdale, CA St. Ann Church.
Duffy, Regis *o.f.m.* (BUF) [C] St. Bonaventure, NY St. Bonaventure University.
Duffy, Regis A. *o.f.m.* '61 (BUF) [O] St. Bonaventure, NY St. Bonaventure Friary.
Duffy, Msgr. Robert E. '48 (NEW) [25] Jersey City, NJ St. Paul of the Cross Church; Retired.
Duffy, Robert M. '42 (CHI) Tinley Park, IL Saint Julie Billiart Church; Retired.
Duffy, Robert P. '40 (OM) Retired.
Duffy, Stephen '57 (NO) Unassigned; [C] New Orleans, LA Loyola University.
Duffy, Stephen F. '65 (NEW) [D] Summit, NJ The Oratory Catholic Preparatory School.
Duffy, Stephen V. *s.j.* '43 (NY) [F] New York, NY Regis High School; [DD] New York, NY St. Ignatius Loyola Residence.
Duffy, Thomas J. '66 (PH) Linfield, PA St. Clare Church.
Duffy, Msgr. Thomas M. '53 (WDC) [10] Washington, DC Blessed Sacrament, Shrine of the Most Church.
Duffy, Msgr. Thomas R. '58 (CHR) Garden City, SC St. Michael Church.
Duffy, Vincent *s.d.b.* '48 (PAT) [3] Paterson, NJ St. Anthony's Church.
Duffy, William J. *s.j.* '31 (BO) [W] Weston, MA Campion Health Center, Inc.
Dufner, Andrew J. *s.j.* '67 (P) [N] Pacific City, OR Nestucca Sanctuary.
Dufner, Daniel G. '96 (YAK) Kennewick, WA St. Joseph's Church.
Dufner, Thomas W. '83 (STP) St. Louis Park, MN Holy Family Church.
Dufour, Clement E. '58 (FR) [8] New Bedford, MA Sacred Heart Church.
Dufour, David '94 (NO) [7] Metairie, LA St. Clement of Rome Church.
Dufour, George J. '70 (BO) [1] Salem, MA St. Anne Church.
Dufour, Louis C. (BO) Retired.
DuFour, Rene *o.m.i.* '54 (BEL) [F] Belleville, IL Missionary Oblates of Mary Immaculate - St. Henry's Oblate Residence.
DuFour, Rene P. *o.m.i.* '54 (STP) [N] St. Paul, MN Oblate Residence.
Dufresne, Oliver J. '45 (STP) Retired.
Dufresne, Vincent J. '83 (BR) Labadieville, LA St. Philomena Church.
Dugal, James H. *c.pp.s.* '56 (COL) [23] Columbus, OH St. James the Less Church.
Dugan, Msgr. Edward T. '45 (NY) Marlboro, NY St. Mary Church; Retired.
Dugan, J. Thomas '70 (E) Fairview, PA Holy Cross Church.
Dugan, James L. *s.j.* '73 (BUF) [O] Buffalo, NY Canisius Jesuit Community.
Dugan, James M. '89 (ALT) [23] Johnstown, PA St. Benedict's Church.
Dugan, John L. *c.s.b.* '90 (ROC) [I] Rochester, NY Basilian Residence.
Dugan, Paul J. *s.j.* '56 (BUF) [O] Buffalo, NY Canisius Jesuit Community.
Dugan, T. Michael '88 (DAL) [17] Dallas, TX St. Elizabeth Church.
Dugan, Thomas P. *c.s.b.* '60 (GAL) [Q] Sugar Land, TX Basilian Mission Center.
Dugan, William M. '49 (SPK) Retired.
Dugandzic, Nicholas *o.p.* '65 (CHI) [N] Chicago, IL Croatian Dominican Fathers.
Dugandzic, Peter '95 (RVC) Seaford, NY St. William, the Abbot Church.
Dugas, Jerome A. '62 (BR) Plaquemine, LA St. Clement of Rome Church.
Dugas, Laurence A. *m.m.* '54 (FgM) Maryknoll Foreign Missions.
Dugas, Scott '77 (HT) [3] Thibodaux, LA Christ The Redeemer Church; [5] Thibodaux, LA St. John The Evangelist Church.
Dugas, Willard (LAF) On Special Assignment.
Dugay, Anthony *s.v.d.* '62 (FgM) Society of the Divine

Word Foreign Missions.
Duggan, Brendan *c.s.s.p.* '75 (TR) Freehold, NJ St. Robert Bellarmine Church.
Duggan, Charles T. '44 (BO) [4] Medford, MA St. Raphael Church; Retired.
Duggan, Dennis D. '80 (DET) [52] Detroit, MI Our Lady Gate of Heaven Church; [72] Detroit, MI St. Suzanne Church.
Duggan, Eugene F. '46 (SFR) Sausalito, CA St. Mary Star of the Sea Church; Retired.
Duggan, J. Edward '50 (CHI) [23] Chicago, IL St. Bartholomew Church; Retired.
Duggan, Jeremiah C. '55 (CHI) [25] Chicago, IL St. Bede the Venerable Church.
Duggan, John H. *s.j.* '57 (SCR) [C] Scranton, PA University of Scranton.
Duggan, Msgr. John M. '43 (BUF) Retired.
Duggan, Joseph P. '64 (VEN) Retired.
Duggan, Kevin P. '87 (MET) South River, NJ Corpus Christi Church.
Duggan, Michael A. *m.m.* '59 (NY) [DD] Maryknoll, NY Maryknoll Fathers and Brothers.
Duggan, Nicholas '62 (SAC) [18] Sacramento, CA St. Paul Church.
Duggan, Oliver F. '71 (SEA) Bothell, WA St. Elizabeth Ann Seton Church.
Duggan, Paul '71 (PAT) New Vernon, NJ Christ the King Church.
Duggan, Paul E. '48 (SFR) Retired.
Duggan, Peter '55 (SEA) [7] Seattle, WA St. Catherine Church.
Duggan, Robert D. '69 (WDC) Gaithersburg, MD St. Rose of Lima Church.
Duggan, Robert J. *c.s.b.* '64 (DET) [6] Detroit, MI Ste. Anne Church.
Duggan, Sean B. *o.s.b.* '88 (NO) [A] St. Benedict, LA St. Joseph's Seminary College; [P] St. Benedict, LA St. Joseph Abbey.
Duggan, Thomas '47 (JC) Brookfield, MO Immaculate Conception Church.
Duggan, Thomas *c.ss.r.* '53 (STL) [P] Liguori, MO Liguori Mission House/Redemptorists.
Duggan, William '53 (SFR) Retired.
Duggan, William E. '53 (SFR) Mill Valley, CA Our Lady of Mt. Carmel Church.
Duggins, Dominic *glmy.* '74 (CIN) [M] Fairfield, OH Headquarters of Glenmary Home Missioners.
Dugue, Nerva W. '93 (NEW) [2] East Orange, NJ Holy Spirit-Our Lady Help of Christians Church.
Duhaime, John N. '71 (WH) Hinton, WV St. Patrick Church.
Duhart, Clarence *c.ss.r.* '37 (DEN) [M] Denver, CO The Redemptorists/Denver Province.
Duhart, Maurice J. *m.e.p.* '48 (SFR) [N] San Francisco, CA Paris Foreign Mission Society Residence.
Duhe, Thomas P. '78 (BR) Greenwell Springs, LA St. Alphonsus Liguori Church.
Duignan, Msgr. Andrew (CAM) Ocean City, NJ Our Lady of Good Counsel Church.
Dukart, George A. '59 (BIS) [3] Dickinson, ND St. Patrick Church.
Dukart, Norman J. '67 (BIS) Williston, ND St. Joseph Church.
Duke, Msgr. Charles J. '47 (NO) Retired.
Duke, Jerome J. '68 (CLV) [2] Lakewood, OH SS. Cyril and Methodius Church.
Duke, Joseph A. *s.j.* '46 (PH) [AA] Philadelphia, PA Jesuit Community at St. Joseph's University; [BB] Philadelphia, PA Monastery of the Visitation Nuns.
Dukehart, Claude H. *s.s.* '43 (BAL) [J] Baltimore, MD St. Charles Villa; [M] Baltimore, MD St. Charles Villa.
Duker, Msgr. Russell A. *s.e.o.d.* '70 (PBR) [1] Pittsburgh, PA Holy Spirit Church.
DuLac, Msgr. Henri J. '45 (STP) Retired.
Dulaney, William R. '73 (BRK) [192] Queens, NY St. Margaret Church; [B] Elmhurst, NY Cathedral Preparatory Seminary of the Immaculate Conception.
Dulanto, Angel *o.s.a.* '51 (NY) [49] New York, NY Holy Rosary Church.
Dulberg, Albert V. '36 (B) Retired.
Dulek, Lawrence V. (MIL) [A] Milwaukee, WI St. Francis Seminary.
Dulek, Lawrence V. '73 (MIL) [7] Milwaukee, WI St. Anthony Church.
Dullahan, Robert J. *s.j.* '57 (WDC) [M] Washington, DC The Jesuit Community at Georgetown University.
Dullea, Charles W. *s.j.* '47 (SFR) [C] San Francisco, CA University of San Francisco; [N] San Francisco, CA Jesuit Community at University of San Francisco.
Dullea, John F. *s.j.* '59 (SJ) [D] San Jose, CA Bellarmine College Preparatory.
Dulles, Avery *s.j.* '56 (NY) [DD] New York, NY Jesuit Community at Fordham University.
Dulock, Vincent *c.s.b.* '69 (GAL) Angleton, TX St. Basil Church.
Dulzer, Kenan '48 (CHI) [N] Chicago, IL St. Peter's Friary.
Duma, Gregory '64 (ROM) Canton, OH St. Theodore Church; Canton, OH St. George Cathedral.
Dumais, George J. *s.j.* '71 (HEL) Special Assignments.
Dumais, Steven *s.d.b.* '78 (NO) [D] Marrero, LA Archbishop Shaw High School; [G] Marrero, LA Archbishop Shaw Junior High School.
Duman, Charles J. '52 (SFS) Retired.
Dumas, Msgr. Edmund H. '36 (OG) Tupper Lake, NY St. Alphonsus Church; Retired.
Dumas, Emile E. *m.m.* '67 (NY) [DD] Maryknoll, NY Maryknoll Fathers and Brothers.
Dumas, Salvador '74 (CHK) San Jose Village, MP San Jose Church.
Dumas, Terrence J. '88 (LAN) [2] Ann Arbor, MI St. Patrick Church.
Duminiak, John J. '60 (ALN) Beaver Meadows, PA St. Mary Church.
Duminuco, Vincent J. *s.j.* '64 (NY) [DD] New York, NY "America;" Residence and publication office of the America Press.
Dumm, Demetrius R. *o.s.b.* '47 (GBG) [H] Latrobe, PA Saint Vincent Archabbey.
Dumm, Wilfred M. *o.s.b.* '45 (SAV) [B] Savannah, GA Benedictine Military School; [F] Savannah, GA The Benedictine Priory.
Dummer, Anthony *o.m.i.* (LA) San Fernando, CA St. Ferdinand Church.
Dummer, Donald *o.m.i.* '97 (STP) [28] St. Paul, MN St. Mary Church.
Dummer, Leo *o.m.i.* '59 (OAK) [N] Oakland, CA Oblate Provincial House & Procure.
Dumminger, Urban *c.pp.s.* '51 (CIN) [B] Carthagena, OH St. Charles.
Dumont, C. Peter '71 (MAN) Suncook, NH St. John the Baptist Church.
Dumont, Gerald '80 (BRK) [27] Brooklyn, NY St. Catherine of Genoa Church.
DuMouchel, Raymond E. '56 (CHR) Summerton, SC St. Mary's Church.
Dumoulin, Marcel L. '61 (PRT) Fairfield, ME Immaculate Heart of Mary Church.
Dumphrey, Joseph C. *o.s.f.s.* '64 (BUF) [2] Lockport, NY St. John the Baptist Church; [5] Lockport, NY St. Patrick Church.
Dumphy, Charles J. '55 (WOR) [3] Worcester, MA Blessed Sacrament Church.
Dumpson, Roland J. '83 (NY) Retired.
Dunbar, Francis '55 (ALB) Johnstown, NY St. Anthony Church.
Dunber, Bernard *o.s.a.* (PRM) Barberton, OH St. Nicholas Church.
Duncan, Andrew '93 (CHY) Gillette, WY St. Matthew's Church.
Duncan, Msgr. Arthur L. '47 (CHL) Retired.
Duncan, Msgr. John C. '60 (LFT) Carmel, IN Our Lady of Mount Carmel Church; [I] Carmel, IN Our Lady of Mount Carmel Parochial School.
Duncan, Joseph '89 (PH) Manoa, PA Sacred Heart Church.
Duncan, William H. '90 (GR) On Special Assignment.
Duncan, William H. '90 (GR) Holland, MI Our Lady of the Lake Church.
Duncanson, Msgr. Richard F. '71 (SD) [4] Chula Vista, CA St. Rose of Lima Church.
Dunckel, Michael G. '92 (SAG) [1] Bay City, MI Holy Trinity Church.
Duncklee, Lawrence '80 (RVC) Brentwood, NY St. Luke Church.
Dundon, Raymond J. '36 (BRK) [144] Brooklyn, NY St. Vincent Ferrer Church; Retired.
Dundon, Robert W. *s.j.* '69 (FgM) Provinces.
Dundon, Robert W. *s.j.* '69 (MIL) [P] Milwaukee, WI Jesuit Provincial Office, Wisconsin Province.
Dunfee, Dirk *s.j.* (STL) [52] St. Louis, MO St. Matthew, Apostle Church.
Dunfee, Dirk *s.j.* '97 (STL) [P] St. Louis, MO St. Matthew Jesuit Community.
Dunfee, James M. '84 (STU) Burkhart, OH St. Joseph's Church; Miltonsburg, OH St. John the Baptist Church; Woodsfield, OH St. Sylvester Church; Sardis, OH St. John Bosco Mission Church.
Dungan, Cormac *o.f.m.* '41 (BO) [Z] Boston, MA Saint Anthony Residence.
Dunghe, Adelmo P. *s.j.* '95 (BUF) [O] Buffalo, NY Canisius Jesuit Community.
Dunkel, Henry N. '45 (DUB) Retired.
Dunklee, Lawrence G. '78 (LC) Genoa, WI St. Charles Borromeo Church.
Dunkley, George (WOR) On Duty Outside the Diocese.
Dunkley, George A. '70 (SD) Vista, CA St. Francis of Assisi Church.
Dunlap, James (CHI) [J] Evanston, IL Saint Francis Hospital of Evanston.
Dunlap, William M. '74 (TR) Brick Town, NJ Visitation Church.
Dunleavy, Francis J. '40 (MIA) [1] Miami Beach, FL St. Francis de Sales Church; Retired.
Dunleavy, Steven '84 (SD) Leave of Absence.
Dunleavy, Thomas J. *m.m.* '75 (FgM) Maryknoll Foreign Missions.
Dunleavy, Thomas J. '75 (PH) [23] Philadelphia, PA St. Bernard Church.
Dunleavy, Thomas P. '34 (MAR) Retired.
Dunmyer, Raymond A. '76 (BIR) Tuscaloosa, AL St. Francis of Assisi University Parish; [H] Tuscaloosa, AL Diocesan Campus Ministry Office; [H] Tuscaloosa, AL University of Alabama in Tuscaloosa.
Dunn, Charles J. *s.j.* '55 (WOR) [N] Worcester, MA Jesuits of Holy Cross College, Inc.
Dunn, Christopher J. *o.f.m.* '82 (FgM) Franciscan Foreign Missions.
Dunn, Didacus Joseph *o.f.m.cap.* '56 (STL) [P] St. Louis, MO St. Crispin's Friary.
Dunn, Donald F. '61 (COS) [1] Colorado Springs, CO St. Mary's Cathedral; [8] Colorado Springs, CO Our Lady of Guadalupe Church.
Dunn, Edmond J. '72 (DAV) [A] Davenport, IA St. Ambrose University Seminary; [B] Davenport, IA St. Ambrose University.
Dunn, Msgr. Edward C. '43 (TOL) Tiffin, OH St. Joseph Church; Retired.
Dunn, Edward T. *s.j.* '56 (BUF) [O] Buffalo, NY Canisius Jesuit Community.
Dunn, Gerald R. '57 (MAN) Dover, NH St. Mary Church.
Dunn, Harold F. *m.s.a.* '78 (WH) Rainelle, WV Sacred Heart Church.
Dunn, Jerome *o.f.m.cap.* '68 (PIT) [O] Pittsburgh, PA St. Augustine Friary.
Dunn, John '54 (DET) Retired.
Dunn, John J. *s.j.* '49 (P) [L] Portland, OR Colombiere Community.
Dunn, John P. '49 (STP) Retired.
Dunn, Joseph T. *o.s.f.s.* '41 (WIL) [I] Childs, MD Oblates of St. Francis De Sales.
Dunn, Laurence J. '68 (CHI) Northfield, IL St. Philip the Apostle Church.
Dunn, Lawrence E. '61 (DET) Yale, MI Sacred Heart Church.
Dunn, Lawrence P. *m.i.c.* '87 (WDC) [B] Washington, DC Marian Fathers Scholasticate.
Dunn, Leo F. *c.ss.r.* '44 (ROC) [K] Canandaigua, NY Notre Dame Retreat House.
Dunn, Msgr. Louis W. '47 (PRO) Retired; [P] Providence, RI St. John Vianney Residence.
Dunn, Msgr. Meinrad M. '45 (BEL) Retired.
Dunn, Michael L. (BGP) [C] Fairfield, CT Notre Dame Catholic High School.
Dunn, Michael L. '94 (BGP) [1] Stratford, CT Holy Name of Jesus Church.
Dunn, Ralph F. *c.s.c.* '60 (FTW) [J] South Bend, IN Congregation of Holy Cross Indiana Province Provincial House.
Dunn, Raymond V. *s.j.* '57 (BO) [W] Boston, MA The Society of Jesus of New England-Provincial Offices.
Dunn, Richard '80 (SY) Military Chaplains.
Dunn, Richard C. '45 (TOL) Retired.
Dunn, Msgr. Richard F. '58 (BRK) [165] Queens, NY Corpus Christi Church.
Dunn, Richard R. '33 (BGP) Retired.
Dunn, Robert '85 (CC) Gregory, TX Immaculate Conception Church.
Dunn, Robert T. '44 (NY) Retired.
Dunn, Stephen *c.p.* '64 (MET) [H] South River, NJ Passionist Provincial Office.
Dunn, Stephen '69 (OWN) Absent on Leave.
Dunn, Stephen '71 (SD) Special Assignment; [B] San Diego, CA University of San Diego.
Dunn, William A. '65 (COL) [32] Columbus, OH St. Michael Church.
Dunn, William J. '51 (OAK) San Lorenzo, CA St. John the Baptist Church.
Dunne, Andrew J. *o.s.f.s.* '59 (LAN) Michigan Center, MI Our Lady of Fatima Church.
Dunne, Dennis T. (STP) [N] Minneapolis, MN Maryknoll Fathers and Brothers, Catholic Foreign Mission Society of America.
Dunne, Edward *c.ss.r.* '49 (BRK) [107] Brooklyn, NY Our Lady of Perpetual Help Basilica Church.
Dunne, George H. *s.j.* '36 (LA) [C] Los Angeles, CA Loyola Marymount University.
Dunne, Gerald M. *o.s.f.s.* '77 (PH) [D] Philadelphia, PA Father Judge High School for Boys; [AA] Philadelphia, PA Father Judge Faculty House.
Dunne, James J. *s.s.c.* '47 (STP) [J] Hastings, MN Regina Medical Center; [M] Hastings, MN Regina Convalescent and Nursing Care and Retirement Center.
Dunne, James M. '61 (BRK) [160] Queens, NY St. Camillus Church.
Dunne, James P. *s.j.* (FgM) Provinces.
Dunne, John S. *c.s.c.* '54 (FTW) [B] Notre Dame, IN University of Notre Dame Du Lac; [J] Notre Dame, IN Holy Cross Community, Corby Hall, University of Notre Dame.
Dunne, Msgr. Joseph A. '42 (NY) Retired.
Dunne, P. Gerard *s.s.c.* '69 (OM) [K] St. Columbans, NE St. Columban's Foreign Mission Society.
Dunne, Patrick J. '70 (NY) [5] White Plains, NY Our Lady of Sorrows Church; White Plains, NY Burke Rehabilitation Center.
Dunne, Peter '50 (OM) [M] Omaha, NE Institute of the Apostolic Oblates.
Dunne, Msgr. Peter F. '44 (OM) Boys Town, NE Immaculate Conception B.V.M. Church; Retired.

Dunne, Peter J. '54 (PH) Retired.
Dunne, Raymond A. *s.j.* '50 (CHI) Prospect Heights, IL St. Alphonsus Liguori Church; [D] Wilmette, IL Loyola Academy.
Dunne, Richard J. '60 (BRK) Released from Diocesan Assignment.
Dunne, Thomas *s.d.b.* '72 (BO) [E] Boston, MA Don Bosco Preparatory School.
Dunnigan, Daniel D. *s.j.* '63 (CLV) [E] Cuyahoga Falls, OH Walsh Jesuit High School.
Dunning, James P. '63 (ORG) Mission Viejo, CA St. Kilian Church.
Dunphy, James R. *m.s.* '57 (STL) [P] St. Louis, MO La Salette Missionaries.
Dunphy, Larry *o.f.m.* '60 (OAK) [P] Danville, CA San Damiano Retreat.
Dunphy, Richard W. *s.j.* '73 (DEN) [M] Denver, CO Regis Jesuit Community (The Jesuits at Regis University).
Dunphy, Robert J. '65 (CAM) Mount Ephraim, NJ Sacred Heart Church.
Dunphy, Thomas R. '58 (CLV) Valley City, OH St. Martin of Tours Church.
Dunson, Donald '82 (CLV) [A] Wickliffe, OH St. Mary Seminary and Graduate School of Theology.
Duoba, Jonas *m.i.c.* '46 (CHI) [N] Chicago, IL Congregation of Marian Fathers of the Immaculate Conception.
Duong, Cu Minh '87 (MOB) [14] Mobile, AL St. Monica Church.
Duong, Paul '74 (SJ) Saratoga, CA Church of the Ascension.
Duong Binh Minh, Thomas '90 (OAK) Pittsburg, CA Our Lady Queen of the World Church.
DuPerry, Irenee *s.m.* '69 (BO) [4] Methuen, MA St. Theresa Church.
Duplessis, Donald M. *o.s.m.* '61 (ORG) Fullerton, CA St. Juliana Falconieri Church.
Duplessis, Omer *o.m.i.* '43 (FgM) Oblates Foreign Missions.
DuPont, Arthur J. '54 (HRT) Plantsville, CT Mary Our Queen Church; [V] Hartford, CT Catholic Cemeteries Association of the Archdiocese of Hartford, Inc.
Dupont, George '43 (BO) [W] Lowell, MA Missionary Oblates of Mary Immaculate.
Dupont, Guy B. *o.p* '68 (WDC) [11] Washington, DC St. Dominic Church & Priory Church.
Duprey, Msgr. Dennis J. '70 (OG) Chasm Falls, NY St. Helen Church; Malone, NY Notre Dame Church.
Dupuis, George H. '50 (BUR) Arlington, VT St. Margaret Mary Church.
Dupuis, Laurent *o.m.i.* '36 (SAT) [K] San Antonio, TX Oblate Madonna Residence.
Dupuis, Philip '51 (LAN) Chelsea, MI St. Mary Church; [L] Lansing, MI Diocesan Service Committee.
Dupuis, Ronald *s.c.* (PRO) [P] Woonsocket, RI Brothers of the Sacred Heart.
Dupuis, Wayne *c.s.v.* '70 (LAV) [15] Las Vegas, NV St. Viator Church.
Duque, Luis (BO) [69] Boston, MA Sacred Heart Church.
Duquesnay, Damian *o.s.b.* '46 (SP) [O] St. Leo, FL St. Leo Abbey.
Duquet, Heribert *m.e.p.* '39 (SFR) [10] San Francisco, CA St. Cecilia Church; [N] San Francisco, CA Paris Foreign Mission Society Residence.
Duquette, Delphis O. '46 (BO) Retired.
Duquette, Don Bosco *o.f.m.cap.* '64 (PRT) [3] Portland, ME St. Joseph's Church; [M] Portland, ME Westbrook College.
Duquette, Lucien G. '56 (BUR) Retired.
Duquette, Roy H. '58 (SPR) [1] Northampton, MA Annunciation Church.
Dura, Eduardo '77 (SFR) [2] South San Francisco, CA Mater Dolorosa Church.
Durack, Jerome F. *s.j.* '60 (FgM) Provinces.
Duraczynski, Msgr. Jerome A. '42 (SFS) Retired.
Duraczynski, Msgr. Jerry '42 (PH) [2] Norristown, PA St. Francis of Assisi Church.
Duraczynski, Walter '57 (PH) [5] Norristown, PA St. Paul Church.
Duraczynski, Walter '57 (SFS) Retired.
Duran, Alfonso M. *m.j.* '56 (PCE) On Duty Outside the Diocese.
Duran, Ernesto '42 (BRK) Retired.
Duran, Msgr. George '52 (LA) Maywood, CA St. Rose of Lima Church.
Duran, Jorge '75 (SAT) On Leave.
Duran, Juan Carlos *o.p.* '96 (NO) [P] New Orleans, LA Dominican Fathers & Brothers, Southern Dominican Province.
Duran, Said '94 (TYL) [1] Tyler, TX Cathedral of the Immaculate Conception.
Durand, Donald A. '58 (P) [12] Portland, OR St. Clare Church.
Durand, Henri *m.s.* '42 (SPR) [4] Holyoke, MA Immaculate Conception Church.
Durant, Thomas P. '76 (SY) Morrisville, NY St. Joan of Arc Church; Munnsville, NY St. Therese of the Infant Jesus Church.
Durante, Charles '93 (RNO) Carson City, NV St. Teresa's of Avila Church.
Durbin, Clarence R. *c.s.c.* '45 (FTW) [B] Notre Dame, IN University of Notre Dame Du Lac; [J] Notre Dame, IN Holy Cross Community, Corby Hall, University of Notre Dame.
Durbin, Clement B. '54 (COL) Retired.
Durbin, John G. *s.t.l.* '79 (R) Fayetteville, NC St. Patrick Church.
Durchholz, Jack J. '95 (EVN) Ferdinand, IN St. Ferdinand Church.
Durcz, Michael S. '73 (CLV) [10] Cleveland, OH St. Barbara Church.
Durette, Constant H. *m.afr.* '43 (SP) [O] St. Petersburg, FL Missionaries of Africa.
Durette, Mathias D. *o.s.b.* '93 (MAN) [K] Manchester, NH St. Anselm Abbey.
Durham, J. Charles '90 (BUR) Castleton, VT St. John the Baptist Church; [H] Burlington, VT University of Vermont-The Catholic Center at UVM.
Durham, Neal *s.d.s.* '82 (MIL) [K] Milwaukee, WI St. Joseph's Hospital of Franciscan Sisters, Milwaukee, Inc.
Durham, Neil *s.d.s.* '82 (MIL) [P] Milwaukee, WI Salvatorian Provincial Residence.
Durig, D. Kent '93 (WH) Fort Ashby, WV Annunciation of the Lord Church; Ridgeley, WV St. Anthony Church.
Duris, Lawrence M. '69 (CHI) [156] Chicago, IL Our Lady of Peace Church; [171] Chicago, IL St. Philip Neri Church.
Duritsa, George M. '53 (Y) [15] Youngstown, OH St. Elizabeth's Church; Retired.
Durka, Michael (VNN) Portland, OR Byzantine Catholic Community of Portland, OR Church.
Durka, Michael '97 (VNN) Olympia, WA St. George Byzantine Church.
Durkee, David R. '80 (CLV) Chardon, OH St. Mary Church.
Durkee, John E. *c.s.v.* '43 (CHI) [N] Olympia Fields, IL Viatorian Residence.
Durken, Daniel *o.s.b.* '56 (SCL) [I] Collegeville, MN St. John's Abbey, of the Order of St. Benedict.
Durkin, Charles (BEL) Lawrenceville, IL St. Lawrence Church.
Durkin, Msgr. Charles (SFR) [U] San Francisco, CA Italian Catholic Federation.
Durkin, Msgr. Charles J. '55 (SFR) [48] San Francisco, CA Star of the Sea Church.
Durkin, Charles T. '79 (CHI) Other Assignments.
Durkin, Daniel '73 (FTW) Avilla, IN St. Mary of the Assumption Church.
Durkin, Edward J. *s.j.* '75 (NY) [5] New York, NY St. Aloysius Church.
Durkin, Eugene F. '49 (CHI) [1] Chicago, IL Cathedral of the Holy Name; Retired.
Durkin, James J. '68 (CAM) [1] Vineland, NJ Our Lady of Pompeii Church.
Durkin, John L. '67 (NY) Amenia, NY Immaculate Conception Church.
Durkin, John R. '42 (DAV) Retired.
Durkin, Joseph T. *s.j.* '33 (WDC) [M] Washington, DC The Jesuit Community at Georgetown University.
Durney, Charles W. '63 (PH) Absent on Sick Leave; Retired.
Durr, Edmund J. '65 (SY) [4] Syracuse, NY Holy Trinity Church.
Durrie, Robert L. '54 (DEN) Retired.
Durso, Michael H. *s.j.* '66 (STL) [P] St. Louis, MO De Smet Jesuit High School Community.
Durst, Msgr. Gerald F. '44 (SUP) On Duty Outside the Diocese.
DuRussel, Henry P. '45 (SAG) Midland, MI Assumption Blessed Virgin Mary Church.
Duscher, Romuald *o.s.b.cam.* '76 (MAN) [M] New Boston, NH Epiphany Monastery.
Duscher, Romuald *o.s.b.cam.* '76 (MRY) [G] Big Sur, CA New Camaldoli Hermitage.
Duschinsky, Vitus J. *o.f.m.* '42 (SFD) Teutopolis, IL St. Francis of Assisi Church; [K] Teutopolis, IL St. Francis Assisi Friary.
Duschl, Frederick J. '65 (TOL) Blakeslee, OH St. Joseph Church; Montpelier, OH Sacred Heart Church.
Dusecina, Regis '73 (PBR) Greensburg, PA St. Nicholas of Myra Church.
Dushack, Douglas L. '72 (MAD) [8] Madison, WI St. James Church.
Dusheck, Leo *s.v.d.* '61 (CHI) [B] Techny, IL Divine Word Residence.
Dussan, Louis *c.m.f.* '49 (LUB) Petersburg, TX Sacred Heart Church.
Dusseau, Martin *o.s.b.* '55 (IND) [J] St. Meinrad, IN St. Meinrad Archabbey.
Dusseault, Emile *m.s.* '54 (R) Swansboro, NC St. Mildred Church.
Duster, Charles *s.s.c.* '61 (FgM) St. Columban's Foreign Mission.
Duster, James J. '59 (DUB) Anamosa, IA St. Patrick's Church; Mount Vernon, IA St. John's the Baptist Church.
Duston, Allen *o.p.* (OAK) [N] Oakland, CA Western Dominican Province.
Duston, Thomas L. '92 (MAN) Marlborough, NH Sacred Heart Church.
Duston, Thomas Lierre '92 (MAN) Troy, NH Immaculate Conception Church.
Dusza, Donald W. '83 (ALT) [14] Johnstown, PA Our Mother of Sorrows Church.
Dutchoff, C. Robert '56 (MAD) Absent on Sick Leave.
Dutel, Gilbert J. '70 (LAF) Scott, LA SS. Peter and Paul Church; Ville Platte, LA Our Lady Queen of All Saints Church.
Duterte, Manuel (CHI) [151] Chicago, IL Our Lady of Lourdes Church.
Dutkiewicz, Eugene M. *s.j.* '61 (MIL) [P] Milwaukee, WI Arrupe House Jesuit Community; [P] Milwaukee, WI Jesuit Provincial Office, Wisconsin Province; [Y] Milwaukee, WI The Jesuit Partnership.
Dutkiewicz, Eugene M. *s.j.* '61 (NO) [P] New Orleans, LA Jesuit Provincial Office.
Dutkiewicz, Thomas A. '56 (PIT) [O] Pittsburgh, PA St. Francis Friary.
Dutra, Luiz C. '55 (LAF) On Special Assignment; [H] Lafayette, LA De La Salle Christian Brothers.
Dutram, Charles J. '58 (WOR) Retired.
Duvall, Justin *o.s.b.* '78 (IND) [A] St. Meinrad, IN St. Meinrad Seminary; [J] St. Meinrad, IN St. Meinrad Archabbey.
Duvelius, Dennis *f.s.s.p.* '96 (SCR) [19] Scranton, PA St. Michael's Church; [M] Elmhurst, PA Priestly Fraternity of St. Peter (F.S.S.P.), North American District Headquarters.
Duvelsdorf, Peter *s.d.b.* '58 (PMB) North Palm Beach, FL St. Paul of the Cross Church.
Duvelsdorf, Peter L. '58 (RVC) Priests Released from Diocesan Assignment.
Dux, James M. '48 (PH) Retired.
Dux, John H. '73 (STA) Military Chaplains.
Duyka, Stephen Joseph (TYL) Mount Pleasant, TX St. Michael Church.
Duyshart, Edwin C. '84 (LA) Azusa, CA St. Frances of Rome Church.
Duzinski, Paul *o.f.m.conv.* '81 (BAL) [M] Ellicott City, MD Order of Friars Minor Conventual.
Duzinski, Paul *o.f.m.conv.* '81 (CLV) [N] Cleveland, OH Sts. Mary and Joseph Home for the Aged.
Dvorak, Donald T. *o.p.* '63 (NO) [25] New Orleans, LA St. Anthony Of Padua Church.
Dvorak, Franklin A. '70 (OM) [48] Douglas Co., NE St. Wenceslaus Church.
Dvorak, Gerald L. '79 (STP) West St. Paul, MN St. Michael Church.
Dvorscak, James '76 (JOL) Lombard, IL Christ the King Church.
Dwomoh, Charles '86 (VIC) [1] Victoria, TX Our Lady of Victory Cathedral.
Dworak, Joseph J. '65 (ALB) Special Assignment; [H] Amsterdam, NY St. Mary's Hospital.
Dworak, Walter W. '72 (PIT) O'Hara Township, PA St. Joseph Church.
Dwulit, Andrij Taras '90 (STN) Houston, TX Protection of the Mother of God Church.
Dwyer, Msgr. Adrian I. '36 (STL) [59] St. Louis, MO St. Roch Church; Retired.
Dwyer, Albert '58 (SAL) Junction City, KS St. Francis Xavier's Church.
Dwyer, Arthur *m.m.* '49 (HON) [H] Honolulu, HI Maryknoll Fathers House.
Dwyer, Arthur J. *m.m.* '49 (HON) [13] Honolulu, HI Sacred Heart Church; [H] Honolulu, HI Maryknoll Fathers House.
Dwyer, Daniel P. *o.f.m.* '88 (ALB) [B] Loudonville, NY Siena College.
Dwyer, David F. '54 (GF) Retired.
Dwyer, Dennis E. (COS) Castle Rock, CO St. Francis of Assisi Church.
Dwyer, Dennis E. '66 (COS) Parker, CO Ave Maria Church.
Dwyer, Dermot '62 (SAC) Colfax, CA St. Dominic Church.
Dwyer, Donald M. '79 (NY) [170] Bronx, NY Our Lady of the Assumption Church.
Dwyer, Eugene F. *s.j.* '59 (CHI) [C] Chicago, IL Jesuit Community at Loyola University of Chicago.
Dwyer, J. Floyd '48 (LC) Retired; [I] La Crosse, WI Holy Cross (Seminary) Diocesan Center.
Dwyer, Jack '92 (TR) Keyport, NJ Jesus the Lord Church.
Dwyer, James D. *s.s.c.* '58 (BRK) [U] Kew Gardens, NY St. Columbans Foreign Mission Society.
Dwyer, John A. '74 (WOR) [8] Fitchburg, MA Sacred Heart of Jesus Church.
Dwyer, John F. '56 (NY) Tappan, NY Our Lady of the Sacred Heart Church; Bronx, NY U.S.V.A. Medical Center.
Dwyer, Msgr. John R. '67 (BRK) [206] Queens, NY Our Lady of the Angelus Church.
Dwyer, John T. '60 (NY) Piermont, NY St. John Church.
Dwyer, Kevin F. *o.s.a.* '62 (BO) [C] North Andover, MA Merrimack College.
Dwyer, Kevin F. *o.s.a.* '62 (PH) [C] Villanova, PA Villanova University.

Dwyer, Msgr. M. Shields '32 (SY) Retired.
Dwyer, Michael *m.s.c.* (SAN) Eldorado, TX Our Lady of Guadalupe Church.
Dwyer, Msgr. Michael F. '38 (NY) Retired.
Dwyer, Msgr. Morris L. (OG) Retired.
Dwyer, Msgr. Morris L. '38 (OG) [5] Plattsburgh, NY St. Peter Church.
Dwyer, Morris R. '55 (ALB) Morris, NY Holy Cross Church.
Dwyer, Robert D. '62 (SY) East Syracuse, NY St. Matthew Church.
Dwyer, Thomas P. *o.s.a.* '53 (FgM) Foreign Missions.
Dwyer, Timothy *s.m.* '68 (STL) [P] St. Louis, MO Provincialate of the Society of Mary, Province of St. Louis.
Dwyer, Vincent *o.c.s.o.* '61 (WOR) [N] Spencer, MA St. Joseph's Abbey.
Dwyer, William M. '38 (SY) Retired.
Dybas, Richard W. '59 (ALB) [5] Cohoes, NY St. Michael Church.
Dych, William *s.j.* '63 (BO) [W] Chestnut Hill, MA The Jesuit Community at Boston College.
Dye, David M. '92 (ATL) Dunwoody, GA All Saints Catholic Church.
Dye, Gerald B. '57 (B) New Plymouth, ID St. Aloysius Church; Payette, ID Holy Family Church.
Dye, Robert M. '91 (TLS) [6] Tulsa, OK Christ the King Church.
Dyer, Donald L. '57 (STL) [4] Florissant, MO St. Christopher Church.
Dyer, Edward J. '41 (WOR) Retired.
Dyer, Francis X. *o.p.* '69 (CHI) [N] Chicago, IL Dominicans (Provincial Office).
Dyer, Gene '85 (CHI) [1] Des Plaines, IL St. Mary Church.
Dyer, George *o.p.* '61 (KNX) Lenoir City, TN St. Thomas the Apostle Church.
Dyer, George A. '36 (HRT) Retired.
Dyer, George J. '53 (CHI) Wadsworth, IL St. Patrick Church; Retired; [X] Mundelein, IL Civitas Dei Foundation.
Dyer, James W. '97 (STL) [3] Florissant, MO St. Angela Merici Church.
Dyer, Joseph '74 (JKS) Oxford, MS St. John Church; [G] Oxford, MS University of Mississippi Newman Center.
Dyer, Ralph J. *s.m.* '47 (SAT) [K] San Antonio, TX Marianist Residence: Skilled Nursing.
Dyer, Raymond E. '46 (PRO) Retired.
Dyer, Thomas P. '69 (Y) [6] Canton, OH St. Joan of Arc Church.
Dyer, Msgr. Timothy J. '74 (LA) [18] Los Angeles, CA Nativity Church; [57] Los Angeles, CA St. Columbkille Church.
Dyer, William *m.afr.* (FgM) Missionaries of Africa Foreign Missions.
Dyjak, Luke *o.f.m.conv.* '48 (BAL) [M] Ellicott City, MD Order of Friars Minor Conventual.
Dykas, Benjamin (ALT) [5] Johnstown, PA St. Columba's Church.
Dylag, Msgr. Michael R. '65 (DET) [T] Detroit, MI Pope John Paul II Cultural Foundation, Inc.
Dylag, Msgr. Michael R. '65 (GBG) On Duty Outside the Diocese.
Dymowski, Thomas *o.ss.t.* '85 (VIC) [F] Victoria, TX Trinity House.
Dymski, Daniel '60 (E) [11] Erie, PA Sacred Heart Church.
Dynak, Waldemar '80 (CHI) [209] Chicago, IL St. Turibius Church.
Dynes, Leo J. '54 (STP) Retired.
Dysinger, Luke *o.s.b.* '86 (LA) [R] Valyermo, CA St. Andrew's Abbey.
Dytkowski, Louis M. '60 (BGP) [4] Fairfield, CT Holy Cross Church.
Dzermejko, David F. '74 (PIT) [3] Charleroi, PA Mary Mother of the Church.
Dziadosz, Edward T. '55 (PH) Retired.
Dziadosz, Msgr. Henry J. '49 (NOR) Moodus, CT St. Bridget Church.
Dziak, Theodore *s.j.* '83 (BO) [W] Chestnut Hill, MA The Jesuit Community at Boston College.
Dziedzic, Gerald H. '74 (HRT) Terryville, CT Immaculate Conception Church.
Dziedziech, Wiktor '82 (SP) [7] St. Petersburg, FL St. Paul Church.
Dziedziejko, Edwin F. *o.f.m.cap.* '79 (MIL) [B] Mount Calvary, WI St. Lawrence Seminary; [P] Mount Calvary, WI St. Lawrence Friary.
Dzieglewicz, John T. *s.j.* '83 (NY) [DD] New York, NY Jesuit Community at Fordham University.
Dziekan, Wayne H. '94 (GAY) North Port, MI St. Gertrude Church; Suttons Bay, MI St. Michael the Archangel Church.
Dzielak, Msgr. Thomas L. '63 (RCK) Rock Falls, IL St. Andrew Church.
Dzien, Joseph Duc '83 (NO) Chalmette, LA Our Lady of Prompt Succor Church.
Dzienkiewicz, Edwin '64 (PT) Retired.
Dzienkiewicz, Edwin '64 (TR) [L] Lawrenceville, NJ Morris Hall-Saint Lawrence, Inc.
Dzierzek, Zygmunt *o.m.i.* '42 (BEL) [F] Belleville, IL Shrine of Our Lady of the Snows.
Dzieszko, Thaddeus '88 (CHI) [3] Cicero, IL St. Mary of Czestochowa Church; [U] Chicago, IL Catholic League for Religious Assistance to Poland.
Dzikowicz, Justin *o.s.b.* '79 (ANC) [4] Anchorage, AK St. Elizabeth Ann Seton Church.
Dzikowski, Piotr *s.ch.* '87 (SEA) [10] Tacoma, WA SS. Peter & Paul Church.
Dziob, Msgr. Michael W. '42 (PRO) Retired; [P] Providence, RI St. John Vianney Residence.
Dziordz, Walter *m.i.c.* '84 (SPR) [I] Stockbridge, MA Congregation of Marians; [I] Stockbridge, MA Congregation of Marians.
Dziorek, Anthony *c.r.* '75 (CHI) [192] Chicago, IL St. Stanislaus, Bishop and Martyr Church.
Dzuban, Giles *o.c.d.* '44 (BO) [W] Brighton, MA Carmelite Monastery.
Dzurenda, Thomas J. '65 (MET) Watchung, NJ St. Mary-Stony Hill Church.

E

Eades, B. G. '73 (DAL) Special Assignment.
Eagan, Henry J. *o.s.a.* '42 (PH) [AA] Villanova, PA St. Thomas Monastery.
Eagan, Joseph *s.j.* '53 (SFR) Larkspur, CA St. Patrick Church.
Eagan, Joseph F. *s.j.* '53 (MIL) [P] Milwaukee, WI Jesuit Provincial Office, Wisconsin Province.
Eagan, William J. *s.j.* '75 (BGP) [D] Fairfield, CT Fairfield College Preparatory School.
Eagle, Raphael *t.o.r.* '67 (FWT) [12] Fort Worth, TX St. Mary of the Assumption Church.
Eagleson, Donald W. '85 (SR) Eureka, CA Sacred Heart Church.
Earl, John P. '42 (RCK) Sterling, IL St. Mary Church.
Earl, Marcellus R. *o.c.s.o.* '63 (ROC) [I] Piffard, NY Abbey of the Genesee.
Earl, Patrick F. *s.j.* '74 (BAL) [B] Baltimore, MD Loyola College; [B] Baltimore, MD Loyola College; [M] Baltimore, MD Jesuit Community of Loyola College, Inc.
Earley, Daniel J. *o.s.f.s.* '48 (TOL) [C] Toledo, OH St. Francis de Sales High School; [K] Toledo, OH Oblates of St. Francis de Sales.
Earley, Jerome *o.c.d.* '95 (NO) [B] New Orleans, LA St. John of the Cross, Discalced Carmelite House of Studies.
Earley, Kiernan *c.p.* '57 (HRT) [M] West Hartford, CT Holy Family Monastery/Retreat.
Earls, John Patrick *o.s.b.* '65 (SCL) [I] Collegeville, MN St. John's Abbey, of the Order of St. Benedict.
Early, Francis J. '85 (WDC) Bushwood, MD Sacred Heart Church.
Early, Joseph E. *m.m.* '39 (SJ) [M] Los Altos, CA Maryknoll.
Early, Msgr. Thomas C. '51 (ALX) Retired.
Early, William F. '68 (BRK) Absent on Sick Leave.
Earner, Thomas F. '62 (SP) New Port Richey, FL St. Thomas Aquinas Church; [F] New Port Richey, FL St. Thomas Aquinas Early Childhood Center.
Earps, James D. *s.j.* (SFR) [U] Los Angeles, CA Christian Live Communities (Sodalities).
East, Msgr. Raymond '81 (WDC) [41] Washington, DC St. Teresa of Avila Church.
Easterling, William T. '82 (LA) Valinda, CA St. Martha Church.
Eastman, Patrick W. '84 (TLS) [4] Tulsa, OK St. Bernard of Clairvaux Church.
Easton, Frederick C. '66 (IND) [19] Indianapolis, IN St. Gabriel the Archangel Church.
Easton, Msgr. William M. '70 (DET) Royal Oak, MI Shrine of the Little Flower Church.
Eatlin, Bernard (LA) [65] Los Angeles, CA St. Gerard Majella Church.
Eaton, John *o.f.m.* '78 (LR) McGehee, AR St. Mary Church.
Eaton, Vincent M. *s.s.* '41 (BAL) [J] Baltimore, MD St. Charles Villa; [M] Baltimore, MD St. Charles Villa.
Ebach, Aloys *c.pp.s.* '74 (SUP) Fifield, WI St. Francis of Assisi Church; Park Falls, WI St. Anthony Church.
Ebacher, Jerome *o.c.s.o.* '49 (P) [L] Lafayette, OR The Cistercian (Trappist) Abbey of Our Lady of Guadalupe.
Ebarb, Walter E. '62 (SAT) [59] San Antonio, TX St. Patrick Church.
Ebarb, Walter E. '62 (SHP) On Duty Outside the Diocese.
Ebbe, James E. *m.m.* '88 (SJ) [M] Los Altos, CA Maryknoll.
Ebben, Bertrand E. *o.p.* '59 (FgM) Dominican - Order of Preachers Foreign Missions.
Ebben, Bertrand E. *o.p.* '59 (NO) [P] New Orleans, LA Dominican Fathers & Brothers, Southern Dominican Province.
Ebbesmier, John '78 (PHX) [8] Phoenix, AZ St. Augustine Church; [1] Glendale, AZ Our Lady of Perpetual Help Church; [A] Phoenix, AZ Bourgade Catholic High School.
Ebejer, George '47 (BRK) [125] Brooklyn, NY St. Rocco's Church; Retired.
Ebejer, Lino P. '91 (WH) Thomas, WV St. Thomas Aquinas Church.
Ebel, Stephen P. '70 (DAV) Long Grove, IA St. Ann's Church.
Ebenhoeh, John *o.s.f.s.* '64 (TOL) [C] Toledo, OH St. Francis de Sales High School.
Ebenhoeh, John O. '64 (TOL) [K] Toledo, OH Oblates of St. Francis de Sales.
Eberhardt, Norbert C. *s.j.* '52 (MIL) [P] Wauwatosa, WI Jesuit Community at St. Camillus.
Eberhardy, William '77 (GB) Absent on Leave.
Eberle, Richard *o.s.f.s.* '82 (TOL) [27] Toledo, OH St. John the Baptist Church.
Eberly, Herbert *c.p.* '58 (FgM) Passionist Foreign Missions.
Ebert, Mark S. '76 (STL) [4] Lemay, MO St. Bernadette Church.
Eberz, Ambrose G. *o.s.b.* '40 (GBG) [H] Latrobe, PA Saint Vincent Archabbey.
Eblen, James '64 (SEA) [17] Seattle, WA St. Patrick Church; Special Assignment.
Ebner, Frank '47 (SCL) Retired.
Ebrom, Robert L. '71 (CHI) Elk Grove Village, IL Queen of the Rosary Church.
Ebuk, Lawrence A. *m.s.p.* '88 (GAL) McNair, TX Holy Family Church.
Eburn, Brian '66 (STA) Crescent City, FL St. John the Baptist Church.
Eccleston, John '55 (SCL) Special Assignment; [J] Little Falls, MN St. Francis Convent.
Echave, Ignacio '54 (ELP) [37] El Paso, TX San Juan Bautista Church.
Echert, John '87 (STP) [A] St. Paul, MN The Saint Paul Seminary; [C] St. Paul, MN University of St. Thomas.
Echevarria, Wilfredo *o.ss.t.* '81 (ARE) Isabela, PR St. Anthony Church.
Echeverri-Tobon, Raul '86 (SY) [12] Syracuse, NY St. Anthony of Padua Church.
Echeverria, Miguel *o.a.r.* (LSC) Anthony, NM St. Anthony's Church.
Echeverria, Pedro Faustino '84 (PCE) Coamo, PR St. Blase Church.
Echeverria, Ramon J. '96 (PMB) Vero Beach, FL St. Helen Church.
Echle, Msgr. Harry A. '42 (WDC) [35] Washington, DC Our Lady of Victory Church; Retired.
Eck, Ivan C. '51 (WCH) Mount Vernon, KS St. Rose Church; Ost, KS St. Joseph Church; Waterloo, KS St. Louis Church.
Eck, John E. *c.s.v.* '63 (SFD) [9] Springfield, IL St. Patrick Church; [11] Springfield, IL Sacred Heart of Jesus Church.
Eck, Reinhard C. '50 (WCH) Andale, KS St. Joseph Church.
Eckart, Frank '69 (TOL) [8] Toledo, OH Holy Rosary Church; [39] Toledo, OH St. Stephen Church.
Eckart, Frank E. '69 (TOL) [14] Toledo, OH Sacred Heart of Jesus Church.
Eckart, Placidus *o.s.b.* '49 (LR) Fort Smith, AR St. Boniface Church.
Eckelkamp, David *o.f.m.* '53 (STL) [P] St. Louis, MO Franciscan Friary of St. Anthony of Padua.
Eckelkamp, Ianatius *o.f.m.* '54 (SFD) [K] Sherman, IL Our Lady of Angels Friary.
Eckenrod, Edward L. (ALT) Altoona, PA Altoona Hospital.
Eckenrod, Edward L. '78 (ALT) [11] Altoona, PA Our Lady of Lourdes Church.
Ecker, Msgr. John A. '58 (YAK) [1] Yakima, WA St. Paul Cathedral.
Ecker, Msgr. Robert J. '51 (BRK) Released from Diocesan Assignment.
Eckerman, Felix *s.v.d.* '47 (FgM) Society of the Divine Word Foreign Missions.
Eckermann, Msgr. Charles H. '56 (SY) Manlius, NY St. Ann Church.
Eckert, Carl E. '54 (LFT) Retired.
Eckert, John C. '72 (PH) Morrisville, PA Holy Trinity Church.
Eckert, Sidney (DET) [13] Detroit, MI St. Brendan Church.
Eckert, Sidney J. '66 (DET) [29] Detroit, MI Guardian Angels Church.
Eckert, William '64 (SPR) [8] Pittsfield, MA St. Mark's Church.
Eckert, William F. '64 (CAM) Retired.
Eckhard, John L. '88 (STL) Riverview Gardens, MO St. Catherine of Alexandria Church.
Eckhoff, Evan *o.f.m.* '57 (KNX) [F] Mountain City, TN Franciscan Friars.
Eckinger, Joseph Ambrose *o.p.* '81 (COL) Zanesville, OH St. Thomas Aquinas Church.
Eckley, Michael P. '91 (OM) Battle Creek, NE St. Patrick's Church.
Eckman, Mark A. '85 (PIT) [54] Pittsburgh, PA St. John Vianney Church; [C] Mt. Lebanon, PA Seton-LaSalle Catholic High School.
Eckrich, James P. '53 (WIL) Retired.
Eckroth, Leonard A. '58 (BIS) Hague, ND St. Mary Church; Strasburg, ND Sts. Peter and Paul Church.

Eckroth, Richard *o.s.b.* '52 (SCL) [I] Collegeville, MN St. John's Abbey, of the Order of St. Benedict.
Eckstein, Francis '58 (IND) New Marion, IN St. Magdalen Church; Osgood, IN St. John Church.
Eckstein, Frank '58 (IND) Millhousen, IN Immaculate Conception Church.
Eco, Roy '80 (OAK) Union City, CA Our Lady of the Rosary Church.
Eco, Roy V. '80 (OAK) [K] Hayward, CA St. Rose Hospital.
Ecweariri, Joseph (LA) [K] Burbank, CA Providence Health System.
Edamattam, Thomas '66 (RVC) Huntington, NY St. Patrick's Church.
Edapaddy, Thomas *c.m.i.* '64 (LAF) Coteau Holmes, LA St. Elizabeth Church.
Edassery, Mathew (TYL) Athens, TX St. Edward Church.
Edassery, Mathew '74 (TYL) Canton, TX St. Theresa Church.
Edathiparampil, Simon '60 (CHI) [94] Chicago, IL Immaculate Heart of Mary Church; Chicago, IL Knanite Syro-Malabar Catholic Mission of the Archdiocese of Chicago Church.
Edayadiyil, Jose (SFS) Ramona, SD St. William of Vercelli Church.
Eddy, William A. '75 (CHI) Chicago Heights, IL St. Kieran Church.
Edelen, Luke A. *o.s.b.* '80 (NEW) [N] Newark, NJ Newark Abbey.
Edelen, Richard D. '75 (LEX) Beattyville, KY Queen of All Saints Church.
Eden, Timothy *s.m.* (SJ) [M] Cupertino, CA Marianist Provincial Residence.
Edens, William *c.s.p.* '81 (LA) [86] Los Angeles, CA St. Paul the Apostle Church.
Eder, Donald '54 (LAN) Retired.
Eder, Donald J. '60 (LFT) Fishers, IN St. Louis de Montfort Church.
Ederer, John F. '77 (SAG) Ithaca, MI St. Paul the Apostle Church.
Edgerly, Leo, Jr. '84 (OAK) Antioch, CA St. Ignatius Church.
Ediza, Manuel '79 (SD) [29] San Diego, CA St. John the Evangelist Church; San Diego, CA Children's Hospital; San Diego, CA Sharp Memorial Hospital.
Edmonds, Stephen B. *m.m.* '40 (FgM) Maryknoll Foreign Missions.
Edmunds, John *s.t.* '76 (NEW) [10] Jersey City, NJ Christ, the King Church.
Edogwo, Linus V. '86 (NEW) [23] Newark, NJ St. Mary's Church.
Edokwe, Hyacinth *c.s.sp.* '91 (MIA) [2] Pompano Beach, FL San Isidro Church.
Edomobi, Eustace '75 (NEW) [5] Newark, NJ St. Antoninus Church; Newark, NJ University of Medicine & Dentistry.
Edrich, Paul J. '54 (CIN) [47] Cincinnati, OH St. John Vianney Church.
Eduvala, Andre *o.f.m.cap.* (AGN) [E] Agana Heights, GU St. Fidelis Friary.
Edwards, Bill (OG) Malone, NY Franklin Correctional Facility.
Edwards, Bill '85 (OG) Burke, NY St. George Church.
Edwards, Brice *c.p.* '70 (HRT) [M] West Hartford, CT Holy Family Monastery/Retreat.
Edwards, Byron H. '87 (SPC) Retired.
Edwards, Charles A. '86 (SFD) [9] Quincy, IL St. Rose of Lima Church.
Edwards, Cyril D. '84 (SCR) [1] Freeland, PA St. Ann's Church; [Q] Scranton, PA Catholic Youth Center.
Edwards, Edward M. *o.s.m.* '83 (CHI) [N] Chicago, IL Servite Friars - Eastern Province.
Edwards, Edward M. *o.s.m.* '83 (MET) [I] Watchung, NJ Mount St. Mary.
Edwards, J. Daniel '94 (LAF) Richard, LA St. Edward Church.
Edwards, James F. '61 (ORL) Retired.
Edwards, James T. '76 (STL) Normandy, MO St. Ann Church.
Edwards, John *s.j.* '54 (PMB) [3] West Palm Beach, FL St. Ann Church.
Edwards, John F. '55 (HRT) Wethersfield, CT Incarnation Church.
Edwards, John J. *s.j.* '54 (PMB) [J] West Palm Beach, FL Emmaus Residence.
Edwards, Lawrence A. '39 (DET) Retired.
Edwards, Michael W. '79 (PMB) Jupiter, FL St. Peter Church.
Edwards, Paul '83 (MIA) [10] Fort Lauderdale, FL St. Mark Church.
Edwards, Philip *o.s.b.* '67 (LA) [R] Valyermo, CA St. Andrew's Abbey; [X] Valyermo, CA St. Andrew's Abbey Retreat House (All Groups).
Edwards, Robert '81 (Y) Lisbon, OH St. George Church.
Edwards, Roy D. '46 (LAF) Retired.
Edwards, Thomas *t.o.r.* '40 (ALT) [F] Loretto, PA Mount Assisi Friary.
Edwards, Thomas '90 (OAK) [2] Oakland, CA St. Andrew-St. Joseph Church.
Edwards, Thomas L. '58 (ALN) Retired; [J] Bethlehem, PA Holy Family Villa.
Edwards, Tom J. (OAK) [21] Oakland, CA Sacred Heart Church.
Edwin, Rex '95 (CI) Seinwar, FM Most Pure Heart of Mary Church.
Edyk, Msgr. Eugene '61 (DET) [3] Clinton Twp., MI St. Paul of Tarsus Church.
Edyvean, Msgr. Walter J. '64 (BO) On Duty Outside the Archdiocese.
Eeles, Justin *o.f.m.* '39 (PAT) [M] Ringwood, NJ Holy Name Friary, Inc.
Eelman, William C. '53 (TR) Retired.
Eftink, Msgr. Edward M. '66 (SPC) Jackson, MO Immaculate Conception Church.
Eftink, Glenn A. '93 (SPC) Glennonville, MO St. Teresa Church; Malden, MO St. Ann Church.
Egan, Arthur B. '57 (CLV) Avon, OH St. Mary of the Immaculate Conception Church.
Egan, Brennan *o.f.m.* '65 (NY) [DD] New York, NY Franciscan Province of the Immaculate Conception; [DD] New York, NY Franciscan Province of the Immaculate Conception.
Egan, Brian J. '87 (WCH) Hutchinson, KS Holy Cross Church.
Egan, Charles *c.s.s.* '46 (BO) [Z] Waltham, MA Stigmatine Fathers and Brothers.
Egan, Daniel *s.a.* '45 (NY) [O] Barryville, NY New Hope Manor; [DD] Garrison, NY Franciscan Friars of the Atonement; [HH] Barryville, NY New Hope Manor.
Egan, Msgr. Edward F. '41 (PRO) Retired; [P] Providence, RI St. John Vianney Residence.
Egan, Eugene E. '54 (WIN) Fulda, MN St. Gabriel's Church.
Egan, Francis M. '45 (PH) Retired.
Egan, George A. *m.m.* '55 (NY) [DD] Maryknoll, NY Maryknoll Fathers and Brothers.
Egan, Gerard P. '65 (CHI) Other Assignments.
Egan, Harvey D. *s.j.* '69 (BO) [W] Chestnut Hill, MA The Jesuit Community at Boston College.
Egan, Harvey F. '41 (STP) Retired.
Egan, James A. *s.j.* '65 (OM) [K] Omaha, NE Jesuit Community At Creighton University.
Egan, Msgr. John J. '43 (CHI) [1] Chicago, IL Cathedral of the Holy Name; Retired; [C] Chicago, IL De Paul University.
Egan, John J. '59 (NEW) Retired.
Egan, John Martin *o.p.* '56 (WDC) [B] Washington, DC Dominican House of Studies.
Egan, John P. *s.j.* '63 (MIL) [P] Milwaukee, WI Jesuit Provincial Office, Wisconsin Province.
Egan, Joseph *s.a.* '50 (NY) [DD] Garrison, NY Franciscan Friars of the Atonement.
Egan, Joseph M. '42 (ROC) Retired.
Egan, Philip '82 (KC) [2] Kansas City, MO St. Monica Parish; [23] Kansas City, MO St. Monica Church.
Egan, Richmond J. *s.m.* '67 (WDC) [M] Washington, DC Marist Provincial House.
Egan, Robert '51 (ROC) Retired.
Egan, Robert J. *s.j.* '62 (SEA) [M] Seattle, WA Jesuit House, Seattle.
Egan, Robert J. *s.j.* '73 (SPK) [C] Spokane, WA Gonzaga University.
Egan, Robert M. '54 (ROC) [1] Auburn, NY Holy Family Church.
Egan, Robert M. '78 (CHI) [N] Chicago, IL Viatorian Residence; [N] Arlington Heights, IL Clerics of St. Viator-Provincial Residence.
Egan, Msgr. Robert P. '43 (NEW) Retired.
Egan, Thomas F. '75 (WOR) [2] Leominster, MA Holy Family of Nazareth Church.
Egan, Thomas R. *m.m.* '64 (FgM) Maryknoll Foreign Missions.
Egbers, James '96 (COV) [B] Alexandria, KY Bishop Brossart High School.
Egbers, James B. '95 (COV) Cold Spring, KY St. Joseph Church.
Egbule, Joseph '88 (SY) Camillus, NY St. Joseph Church.
Egbulem, Christian Nwaka *o.p.* '76 (WDC) [13] Washington, DC St. Francis de Sales Church.
Egbulem, Nwaka Chris *o.p.* '97 (BAL) [Q] Baltimore, MD Catholic Community at Relay.
Egert, Clifford A. '38 (DAV) Retired; [M] Davenport, IA St. Vincent Center.
Eggerling, Milton '54 (BO) [70] Boston, MA St. Stephen Church; [W] Boston, MA The Society of St. James the Apostle, Inc.
Eggerling, Milton '54 (FgM) Society of St. James the Apostle.
Eggerling, Milton '54 (OAK) Retired.
Eggert, Charles M. '38 (STP) Retired.
Eggert, Francis X. '58 (SFE) [7] Albuquerque, NM Our Lady of Fatima Church.
Egging, Martin L. '93 (GI) [2] Grand Island, NE Blessed Sacrament Church; [A] Grand Island, NE Central Catholic Middle School-High School.
Eggleston, Earl Edward '96 (SD) [5] San Diego, CA Good Shepherd Church.
Eggleston, William J. *m.m.* '47 (NY) [DD] Maryknoll, NY Maryknoll Fathers and Brothers.
Eggleton, Chris *o.p.* '88 (DAL) [A] Irving, TX Holy Trinity Seminary.
Eggleton, Christopher T. *o.p.* '88 (DAL) [M] Irving, TX Dominican Priory of St. Albert the Great.
Egierd, Henry A. '80 (MET) Retired.
Egitto, Philip J. '88 (ORL) Daytona Beach, FL Our Lady of Lourdes Church.
Egloff, Adolph '40 (EVN) Retired.
Eglsaer, Harry *s.j.* '51 (OM) [C] Omaha, NE Creighton Preparatory School; [G] Omaha, NE Archbishop Bergan Mercy Medical Center.
Ego, Anthony M. '85 (PEO) Chillicothe, IL St. Edward's Church.
Eguiguren, Jose' Martin '67 (CGS) [5] Caguas, PR Santisimo Sacramento Church.
Eguino, Desiderio *o.p.* '78 (MIA) [18] Miami, FL St. Dominic Church.
Egurrola, Vicente (SJN) Retired.
Ehler, Gerard *o.p.* '63 (OAK) [N] Oakland, CA Dominican Order (Western Province), St. Albert's Priory.
Ehmann, Benedict A. '29 (ROC) Retired; [L] Rochester, NY Censores Librorum.
Ehmke, Lyle *o.s.c.* '70 (STP) [N] Anoka, MN Crosier Community of Anoka.
Ehr, Donald J. *s.v.d.* '55 (CHI) [53] Chicago, IL St. Elizabeth Church.
Ehrens, Richard J. '58 (CHI) Harwood Heights, IL St. Rosalie Church; [S] Chicago, IL Kolping Center.
Ehrhardt, Joseph B. *o.f.m.* '76 (FgM) Franciscan Foreign Missions.
Ehrhardt, Philip *o.m.i.* '27 (FgM) Oblates Foreign Missions.
Ehrhart, Charles (RVC) Priests Released from Diocesan Assignment.
Ehrman, Dale *o.s.c.* '90 (STP) [N] Shoreview, MN Crosier Community of Shoreview.
Ehrne, Robert *c.p.* '53 (HRT) [M] West Hartford, CT Holy Family Monastery/Retreat.
Ehwald, Joseph A. '62 (COL) Reynoldsburg, OH St. Pius X Church.
Eiardi, Anthony J. *s.j.* '41 (BGP) [O] Fairfield, CT The Fairfield Jesuit Community-Fairfield University.
Eichenberger, Thomas P. '76 (MIL) Cudahy, WI Holy Family Church.
Eichenseer, Donald W. '61 (BEL) [8] Belleville, IL St. Teresa of the Child Jesus Church.
Eichhoff, Paul E. '70 (TLS) Claremore, OK St. Cecilia Church.
Eichhorst, Franklin *o.f.m.cap.* '57 (LSC) Lovington, NM St. Thomas Aquinas Church.
Eichman, Dominic P. '43 (LC) Retired; [I] La Crosse, WI Holy Cross (Seminary) Diocesan Center.
Eichner, Philip K. *s.m.* '66 (RVC) [D] Uniondale, NY Kellenberg Memorial High School; [N] Mineola, NY Provincial Residence and Novitiate.
Eichor, Msgr. Edward C. '59 (STL) [A] St. Louis, MO Kenrick-Glennon Seminary.
Eichorn, Harry B. *c.s.c.* '57 (FR) [A] North Easton, MA Stonehill College; [A] North Easton, MA Holy Cross Fathers Religious.
Eickhoff, Jeffrey R. '95 (LIN) [4] Lincoln, NE North American Martyrs Church.
Eickhoff, Matthew F. '89 (LIN) Nebraska City, NE St. Mary's Church; [C] Nebraska City, NE Lourdes Junior-Senior High School; [L] Nebraska City, NE Lourdes Central High School Endowment Fund.
Eickholt, Henry C. '44 (SAG) Retired.
Eid, Frederick M. '47 (NEW) [1] Hoboken, NJ Our Lady of Grace Church; Retired.
Eidenschink, John *o.s.b.* '41 (SCL) [H] Albany, MN Mother of Mercy Nursing Home and Retirement Center.
Eifler, John G. '61 (L) [26] Louisville, KY St. Frances of Rome Church.
Eigo, Francis A. *o.s.a.* '64 (PH) [C] Villanova, PA Villanova University; [AA] Villanova, PA St. Thomas Monastery.
Eikens, Leroy F. '62 (WIN) Retired.
Eikmeier, Msgr. Bernard J. '51 (HON) Kailua, HI St. Anthony Church; Retired.
Eilerman, Craig R. '87 (COL) [9] Columbus, OH St. Cecilia Church.
Eilerman, William *c.pp.s.* '51 (CIN) [B] Carthagena, OH St. Charles.
Eilert, Msgr. Edward J. '64 (NEW) Livingston, NJ St. Philomena Church.
Eimer, Frank J. '58 (L) Jeffersontown, KY St. Edward Church.
Eimer, Robert *o.m.i.* '53 (BEL) [F] Belleville, IL Shrine of Our Lady of the Snows.
Einck, Gregory J. '44 (DUB) Retired.
Einhaus, Henry *m.s.c.* '60 (ALN) [A] Center Valley, PA Missionaries of the Sacred Heart.
Einhaus, Henry *m.s.c.* '60 (FgM) Missionaries of the Sacred Heart Foreign Missions.
Einhaus, Henry *m.s.c.* '60 (RCK) [H] Aurora, IL Missionaries of the Sacred Heart Community.
Eiroa, Andres '88 (PCE) [G] Alhambra, Ponce, PR Prelature of the Holy Cross and Opus Dei.
Eis, Charles '66 (SPK) Retired.
Eisel, Howard P. *s.s.c.* '54 (DUL) Crosby, MN St. Joseph's Church.

Eisele, Francis X. '66 (RVC) West Islip, NY Our Lady of Lourdes Church.
Eisele, James F. '88 (LAN) Deerfield, MI St. Alphonsus Church.
Eisele, Paul F. '68 (SC) St. Joseph, IA St. Joseph's Church.
Eisemann, Frederick F. '53 (ROC) [21] Rochester, NY Holy Cross Church.
Eisler, Rudolph '63 (NY) Pearl River, NY St. Margaret Church.
Eisweirth, Thomas '74 (Y) [7] Youngstown, OH Sacred Heart of Jesus Church.
Eivers, Michael '55 (MIA) Pembroke Pines, FL St. Edward Church.
Ejeu, Ambrose '90 (BRK) [205] Queens, NY St. Nicholas of Tolentine Church.
Ejifor, Pius (NY) Staten Island, NY Staten Island University Hospital South.
Ejimadu, Festus '93 (DET) Inkster, MI Holy Family Parish; Inkster, MI St. Kevin and St. Norbert Church.
Ekanem, Anthony *m.s.p.* '89 (GAL) Barrett Station, TX St. Martin de Porres Church.
Ekdahl, Kenneth W. '91 (TR) Maple Shade, NJ Our Lady of Perpetual Help Church; [B] Delran, NJ Holy Cross High School.
Ekman, Robert '57 (SCL) Retired.
Ekpo, Joseph '86 (CHI) Bellwood, IL St. Simeon Church; [D] Oak Park, IL Fenwick High School.
Ekriott, Timothy P. '82 (STL) Josephville, MO St. Joseph Church.
Eksterowicz, Francis C. '85 (BUR) Richford, VT All Saints Church.
Ekwuribe, Matthew '67 (PIT) [74] Pittsburgh, PA Incarnation of the Lord Church.
El-Bacha, Assaad *m.l.m.* '92 (OLL) San Antonio, TX St. George Maronite Church; [A] San Antonio, TX The Congregation of Maronite Lebanese Missionaries.
El-Hayek, Nehmatallah '52 (SP) Beverly Hills, FL Our Lady of Grace Church.
El-Hayek, Nehmatallah '62 (SAM) Retired.
El-Khalli, Georges '81 (SAM) Williamsville, NY St. John Maron Church.
Elam, Ray *o.s.a.* '70 (P) Roseburg, OR St. Joseph Church.
Elambassery, Xavier '66 (SJP) Latrobe, PA Assumption of B.V.M. Church.
Elanjileth, John M. '45 (ROM) McKeesport, PA St. Mary Church.
Elanjileth, John M. '50 (PIT) Allegheny County, PA McKeesport Hospital.
Elbert, William A. '73 (MIA) [5] Hialeah, FL St. John the Apostle Church.
Elder, Jerome C. '57 (LA) [4] Long Beach, CA St. Bartholomew Church.
Elder, John W. *s.j.* '65 (BGP) [A] Fairfield, CT Fairfield University; [O] Fairfield, CT The Fairfield Jesuit Community-Fairfield University.
Elder, Leonard *s.c.j.* '96 (GAL) [27] Houston, TX St. Elizabeth Ann Seton Church.
Elder, William S. '81 (NY) [62] New York, NY St. Joseph Church.
Eldridge, Francis '77 (LA) [K] Los Angeles, CA St. Vincent Medical Center.
Eldridge, Louis J. '85 (MET) Dunellen, NJ St. John the Evangelist Church.
Eldringhoff, John '68 (KC) Raytown, MO Our Lady of Lourdes Church.
Eleanya, Conleth '88 (CAM) Washington Township, NJ Holy Family Church.
Eles, Joseph '65 (PSC) Retired.
Elewaut, Thomas J. *c.j.* '86 (LA) [B] Santa Maria, CA St. Joseph Seminary (Josephite Fathers' Novitiate); [D] Santa Maria, CA St. Joseph High School.
Elford, Ricardo *c.ss.r.* '64 (CHI) [N] Chicago, IL Redemptorists:; [N] Bodija, Ibadan, Oyo State, Nigeria.
Elford, Ricardo *c.ss.r.* '64 (DEN) [M] Denver, CO The Redemptorists/Denver Province.
Eli, Jude *o.p.* '76 (OAK) [N] Oakland, CA Dominican Order (Western Province), St. Albert's Priory.
Elia, Faouzi Y. '77 (OLL) Peoria, IL St. Sharbel Church.
Elia, Victor *c.m.* '57 (NY) [44] New York, NY Holy Agony Church; [DD] New York, NY Vincentian Fathers.
Elias, Marco Antonio *o.s.m.* '93 (CHI) [15] Chicago, IL Annunciata Church; [N] Chicago, IL Servite Friars - Eastern Province.
Elias, Woodrow '43 (DM) Retired.
Elis, Patrick H. '69 (BUF) Cassadaga, NY Immaculate Conception Church; Sinclairville, NY St. John the Evangelist Church.
Elis, Tomas A. '70 (LA) South El Monte, CA Epiphany Church.
Elizondo, Virgil '63 (SAT) [64] San Antonio, TX St. Rose of Lima Church.
Elkin, Fredic F. '77 (SY) Military Chaplains.
Elko, Joseph M. '70 (HRT) [13] New Haven, CT Saint Martin de Porres Church.
Eller, Hugh *o.f.m.* '53 (PRO) [P] Providence, RI St. Francis Friary.
Ellerbrock, Timothy '80 (BWN) Absent.
Ellerman, Thomas *s.m.* '61 (NO) [C] New Orleans, LA Our Lady of Holy Cross College.
Ellias, John P. '64 (ALT) St. Michael, PA St. Michael's Church.
Ellifritz, R. Michael '67 (COL) [10] Columbus, OH Christ the King Church.
Ellinghausen, Jude T. '58 (DET) North Branch, MI SS. Peter and Paul Church.
Elliot, James *o.f.m.conv.* (BAL) [M] Ellicott City, MD Friary of St. Joseph Cupertino.
Elliott, Edward C. '44 (MEM) Retired.
Elliott, James *o.f.m.conv.* (BAL) [M] Ellicott City, MD St. Joseph Cupertino Friary, Friars Minor Conventual of St. Francis of Assisi.
Elliott, Joseph *c.ss.r.* '49 (LA) Whittier, CA St. Mary of the Assumption Church; [R] Whittier, CA Redemptorist Fathers Mission House.
Elliott, Joseph W. '71 (OG) Brownville, NY Immaculate Conception of the B.V.M. Church.
Elliott, Msgr. Peter J. '73 (WDC) [V] Silver Spring, MD Catholics Committed to Support the Pope.
Elliott, Roger *c.p.* '58 (SCR) [2] Scranton, PA St. Ann's Basilica Parish; [M] Scranton, PA Saint Ann's Passionist Monastery.
Elliott, Thomas *c.s.c.* '67 (BGP) [I] Bridgeport, CT St. Vincent's Medical Center.
Elliott, Thomas *c.s.c* '67 (FTW) [J] South Bend, IN Congregation of Holy Cross Indiana Province Provincial House.
Elliott, Trumie Culpepper '88 (L) Samuels, KY St. Gregory Church.
Elliott, William *o.m.i.* '61 (AUS) [7] Austin, TX Our Lady of Guadalupe Church.
Elliott, Msgr. William E. '60 (SD) [14] San Diego, CA Our Lady of Refuge Church.
Elliott, William J. *s.j.* '61 (WDC) [E] North Bethesda, MD Georgetown Preparatory School.
Ellis, Alfred J. *o.s.a.* '63 (BO) Andover, MA St. Augustine Church.
Ellis, Kail C. *o.s.a.* '67 (PH) [C] Villanova, PA Villanova University; [AA] Villanova, PA St. John Stone Friary.
Ellis, Matthew '88 (DET) Absent on Leave.
Ellison, Joseph *c.ss.r.* '39 (ORL) [F] New Smyrna Beach, FL St. Alphonsus Villa-Redemptorist Fathers and Brothers.
Ellos, William *s.j.* '68 (SAT) [C] San Antonio, TX St. Mary's University of San Antonio, Texas.
Ellos, William J. *s.j.* '68 (MIL) [P] Milwaukee, WI Jesuit Provincial Office, Wisconsin Province.
Ellspermann, Camillus *o.s.b.* '50 (EVN) St. Henry, IN St. Henry Church.
Ellspermann, Camillus *o.s.b.* '50 (IND) [J] St. Meinrad, IN St. Meinrad Archabbey.
Ellspermann, Gerard *o.s.b.* '39 (IND) [J] St. Meinrad, IN St. Meinrad Archabbey.
Elmer, Msgr. Charles '52 (AUS) On Duty Outside the Diocese.
Elmer, Gregory *o.s.b.* '76 (LA) [R] Valyermo, CA St. Andrew's Abbey.
Elmer, John *o.f.m.conv.* '73 (MIL) Brandon, WI St. Brendan Church; Springvale, WI St. Mary Church; Waupun, WI St. Joseph Church.
Elmer, Philip *s.c.j.* '66 (GAL) [35] Houston, TX Holy Name Church.
Elmer, Richard J. *c.s.b.* '57 (DET) [E] Redford, MI Catholic Central High School.
Elmer, Timothy '73 (SY) Chittenango, NY St. Patrick Church.
Elmlinger, Msgr. Herbert '42 (FRS) Retired.
Elmo, Francis E. '63 (NY) Absent on Leave.
Elo, Richard *c.pp.s.* '63 (CIN) [B] Carthagena, OH St. Charles.
Elorriaga, Javier *o.ss.t.* '68 (SJN) [13] Bayamon, PR Ascension Del Senor Church.
Elsasser, Thomas G. '88 (CLV) Middleburg Heights, OH St. Bartholomew Church.
Elsbernd, Elmer *s.v.d.* '65 (FgM) Society of the Divine Word Foreign Missions.
Elsemann, Frederick F. '53 (ROC) Retired.
Elsen, Vincent *o.f.m.* '47 (FWT) [G] Crowley, TX St. Francis Village, Inc.; [H] Crowley, TX St. Maximilian Kolbe Friary.
Elser, William '86 (LR) Barling, AR Sacred Heart of Mary Church.
Elshoff, Matthew *o.f.m.cap.* '82 (LA) [F] La Canada Flintridge, CA St. Francis High School.
Elsinghorst, Francis X. *s.j.* '54 (NY) [DD] New York, NY St. Ignatius Loyola Residence.
Elskamp, Frederick J. '62 (JC) Holts Summit, MO St. Andrew Church; Mokane, MO St. Jude Thaddeus Church.
Elsner, Martin L. *s.j.* '62 (SAT) [17] San Antonio, TX Our Lady of Guadalupe Church.
Elston, Joseph '85 (SCR) [1] Williamsport, PA Annunciation Church.
Elverman, Donald A. '54 (MIL) Retired.
Elworthy, Joseph *c.ss.r.* '39 (BLX) [E] Biloxi, MS St. John Neumann Residence.
Ely, Peter B. *s.j.* '69 (SEA) [A] Seattle, WA Seattle University.
Emanuel, John F. '92 (TUC) Clifton, AZ Sacred Heart Church.
Emanuel, Steven '93 (OM) [B] Columbus, NE Scotus Central Catholic High School.
Emanuel, Steven D. '93 (OM) Columbus, NE St. Bonaventure Church.
Emechete, Innocent '72 (SAC) Vacaville, CA California Medical Facility, Solano Co.
Emerick, David *s.c.j.* '86 (MIL) [P] Hales Corners, WI Priests of the Sacred Heart.
Emerick, Stephen J. '58 (CIN) [L] Cincinnati, OH Mercy St. Theresa Center.
Emerling, James R. '53 (HRT) New Hartford, CT Immaculate Conception Church.
Emerson, George F. '56 (BO) [4] Framingham, MA St. Stephen Church.
Emerson, Richard A. '78 (GRY) Munster, IN St. Thomas More Church.
Emerson, Robert F. '55 (JOL) Gilman, IL Immaculate Conception Church.
Emery, Robert E. '87 (NEW) Belleville, NJ St. Peter's Church.
Emezie, Charles '83 (SFS) [D] Aberdeen, SD St. Luke's Midland Regional Medical Center; [E] Aberdeen, SD Mother Joseph Manor, Nursing Care Facility.
Emge, John P. '50 (EVN) Retired.
Emling, Bertin L. *o.s.b.* '35 (GBG) [H] Latrobe, PA Saint Vincent Archabbey.
Emling, Marion J. *o.s.b.* '78 (GBG) [H] Latrobe, PA Saint Vincent Archabbey.
Emmenegger, Msgr. Joseph E. '42 (MIL) Retired.
Emmert, Stuart '60 (GAL) Sugar Land, TX St. Laurence Church.
Emmons, Rayford E. '74 (PH) [3] Philadelphia, PA St. Agatha-St. James Church.
Emo, Eugene '61 (ROC) Unassigned.
Emon, Neil *o.s.c.* '67 (DET) [1] Taylor, MI St. Alfred Church.
Emon, Neil J. *o.s.c.* '67 (DET) Riverview, MI St. Cyprian Church; [K] Riverview, MI Crosier Community of Riverview.
Empereur, James L. *s.j.* '65 (MIL) [P] Milwaukee, WI Jesuit Provincial Office, Wisconsin Province.
Emperur, James L. *s.j.* '65 (SAT) [1] San Antonio, TX Cathedral of San Fernando.
Emrisek, Gene J. *o.f.m.cap.* '68 (DEN) [3] Denver, CO Annunciation Church; [M] Denver, CO Annunciation Friary.
Emuwen, Victor (NY) [63] New York, NY St. Joseph of the Holy Family Church.
Encinas, Andrew G. '90 (LA) Culver City, CA St. Augustine Church.
Encisco, Jesus A. '75 (NEW) Lodi, NJ St. Francis de Sales Church.
Enciso, Herman '81 (MRY) Absent on Sick Leave.
Endebrock, Msgr. Donald M. '51 (MET) [1] Carteret, NJ St. Joseph Church; Retired.
Endebrock, Msgr. John J. '38 (TR) Avon, NJ St. Elizabeth Church; Retired.
Endejan, John H. '57 (MIL) [1] Milwaukee, WI St. John Cathedral; [H] Milwaukee, WI All Saints Catholic East School System, Inc.; [Y] Milwaukee, WI Cathedral Preservation, Inc.
Enderle, Gilbert A. *c.ss.r.* '62 (CHI) [N] Chicago, IL Redemptorist Theology Residence.
Enderle, Msgr. M.N. '46 (BEA) Groves, TX St. Peter the Apostle Church.
Enderle, Msgr. Martin N. '46 (BEA) Retired.
Enderlin, Joseph J. '46 (LR) Bella Vista, AR St. Bernard Church.
Enderlin, Ronald E. '69 (PEO) Lacon, IL Immaculate Conception Church.
Enders, Robert F. '39 (MIL) Retired.
Endres, Gilbert J. '52 (STP) Retired.
Endres, James F. '82 (PH) Warminster, PA Nativity of Our Lord Church; [D] Warminster, PA Archbishop Wood Catholic High School.
Endres, John C. *s.j.* '76 (OAK) [A] Berkeley, CA The Jesuit School of Theology at Berkeley; [N] Berkeley, CA Jesuit Community at Jesuit School of Theology at Berkeley.
Endres, William '82 (ROC) Rochester, NY Rochester General Hospital.
Endress, James R. '60 (EVN) Special Assignment.
Engbarth, David R. '76 (RCK) [5] Aurora, IL St. Nicholas Church.
Engbers, Thomas J. '67 (MIA) Miami Shores, FL St. Martha Church.
Engbers, William J. '39 (IND) St. Nicholas, IN St. Nicholas Church; Retired.
Engel, John '54 (P) Retired.
Engel, Paul (ALB) Retired.
Engel, Paul *o.f.m.cap.* '64 (NY) [DD] White Plains, NY St. Conrad Friary.
Engel, Ronald G. '77 (MIL) [3] South Milwaukee, WI St. Mary Church.
Engelbrecht, Henry H. '68 (NO) [36] New Orleans, LA St. Henry Church.
Engelen, R. J. '30 (ALX) Retired.
Engelhardt, Adam J. '42 (FAR) Retired.

Engelhardt, Charles F. *o.s.f.s.* '77 (PH) [D] Philadelphia, PA Father Judge High School for Boys; [AA] Philadelphia, PA Father Judge Faculty House.
Engelhart, Henry Ray '63 (BEL) Shawneetown, IL St. Mary Church.
Engelhart, William '70 (JKS) Retired.
Engels, Eugene R. '63 (BR) Plaquemine, LA St. John the Evangelist Church.
Engels, Francis C. '62 (PEO) Absent on Leave.
Engels, Richard J. '60 (WIN) Mazeppa, MN SS. Peter and Paul Church.
Engen, Bruce '89 (DUL) Walker, MN St. Agnes Church; Duluth, MN Indian Missions Church.
Engh, Michael *s.j.* '81 (LA) [C] Los Angeles, CA Loyola Marymount University.
Engh, Michael E. *s.j.* '81 (LA) [C] Los Angeles, CA Loyola Marymount University.
England, Barry '68 (FTW) [3] South Bend, IN St. Anthony de Padua Church.
Engle, James '63 (BEA) Port Arthur, TX Convalescent Home Ministry.
Engle, Richard F. '56 (COL) Retired.
Englehardt, Msgr. Herbert G. '40 (BUF) Retired.
Engler, Clarence A. *m.m.* '59 (FgM) Maryknoll Foreign Missions.
Engler, Ernest '51 (DUB) Mount Vernon, IA St. John's the Baptist Church.
Engler, Ernest J. '51 (DUB) Retired.
Engler, Msgr. Francis V. '46 (BUF) [5] Buffalo, NY All Saints Church; Retired.
Engler, Simon *t.o.r.* (ALT) [F] Loretto, PA Mount Assisi Friary.
Englert, Anthony A. '87 (CHI) [145] Chicago, IL Our Lady of Fatima Church.
Englert, Michael *o.f.m.conv.* '89 (BUF) Athol Springs, NY St. Francis of Assisi Church.
Englert, Wilfred '86 (EVN) [18] Evansville, IN St. Joseph Church.
Englert, William J. '53 (CLV) Fairport Harbor, OH St. Anthony of Padua Church; Retired.
English, James M. *s.j.* '74 (PH) [82] Philadelphia, PA Old St. Joseph's Church.
English, Joseph *o.f.m.cap.* '90 (AGN) Mangilao, GU Santa Teresita Church.
English, Joseph *o.f.m.cap.* '90 (FgM) Capuchin Foreign Missions.
English, Paul F. '85 (ROC) [I] Rochester, NY Basilian Residence; [M] Rochester, NY Diocesan Office of Campus Ministry.
English, Richard P. *s.j.* '51 (NY) [DD] New York, NY Murray-Weigel Hall.
English, Robert K. '88 (OM) Constance, NE St. Joseph Church; Crofton, NE St. Rose of Lima Church.
English, Msgr. Tobias P. '63 (LA) Pasadena, CA St. Andrew Church.
English, William J. '60 (BO) [6] Quincy, MA Most Blessed Sacrament Church.
English, Msgr. William J. '69 (WDC) Pastoral Center Special Ministries; [N] Kensington, MD St. John Vianney House.
Enke, Msgr. Paul P. '72 (COL) [35] Columbus, OH Our Lady of Victory Church.
Enlow, Leo J. '75 (SFD) Effingham, IL St. Anthony of Padua Church.
Enman, Frederick *s.j.* '88 (BO) [W] Chestnut Hill, MA The Jesuit Community at Boston College.
Enneking, Marvin '91 (SCL) On Duty Outside the Diocese.
Enneking, Thomas (CHI) [135] Chicago, IL St. Maurice Church.
Enneking, Thomas *o.s.c.* '84 (CHI) [N] Chicago, IL Crosier Community of Chicago.
Ennis, James E. '50 (LC) Hillsboro, WI St. Aloysius Church; [E] Hillsboro, WI St. Joseph's Memorial Hospital, Inc.
Ennis, William '64 (ORL) [5] Orlando, FL Holy Family Church.
Eno, Robert B. *s.s.* '63 (WDC) [C] Washington, DC Catholic University of America, The.
Enojo, Jesus P. '67 (NY) [54] New York, NY St. James Church.
Enright, Columba J. *t.o.r.* '56 (WDC) [C] Washington, DC Catholic University of America, The; [Q] Washington, DC Basilica of the National Shrine of the Immaculate Conception.
Enright, Edward J. *o.s.a.* '73 (PH) [B] Villanova, PA St. Augustine Friary; [C] Villanova, PA Villanova University.
Enright, Frank E. '43 (WIN) Retired; [F] Austin, MN Sacred Heart Hospice, Inc.
Enright, James C. '69 (BUF) On Duty Outside the Diocese.
Enright, James C. '69 (ROC) [3] Auburn, NY St. Mary Church; Auburn, NY Auburn Correctional Facility.
Enright, John P. '53 (CHI) Retired.
Enright, Michael P. '84 (CHI) [93] Chicago, IL Immaculate Conception of the Blessed Virgin Mary Church.
Enright, Thomas M. '66 (CHI) Wauconda, IL Transfiguration Church.
Enright, Timothy *c.s.sp.* (SFR) San Francisco, CA Laguna Honda Home.
Enright, Msgr. Vincent L. '47 (E) Retired.
Enriquez, Alex '85 (TR) Red Bank, NJ St. James Church.
Enriquez, Juan '80 (LA) Pacoima, CA Guardian Angel Church.
Ensey, Eric (SCR) On Special or Other Diocesan Assignment.
Enslow, Batholomew *s.s.j.* (BLX) Pass Christian, MS Our Mother of Mercy Church.
Ensman, Raymond '66 (TOL) Port Clinton, OH Immaculate Conception Church.
Enyan-Boadu, Peter '84 (ROC) [21] Rochester, NY Holy Cross Church.
Enzler, Msgr. John J. '73 (WDC) Potomac, MD Our Lady of Mercy Church.
Enzman, David '83 (CLV) Absent on Leave.
Enzweiler, Donald A. '87 (COV) [1] Newport, KY Holy Spirit Church.
Eppenbrock, Donald J. '60 (SAG) Lexington, MI St. Denis Church.
Epperley, Wayne *c.s.sp.* (SB) Hemet, CA Our Lady of the Valley Church.
Epping, Robert L. *c.s.c.* '70 (FTW) [J] South Bend, IN Congregation of Holy Cross Indiana Province Provincial House.
Erb, Charles *s.v.d.* '33 (TR) [M] Bordentown, NJ Society of the Divine Word.
Erb, Francis J. '54 (ROC) Retired.
Erb, Vincent I. '50 (CHL) Retired.
Erbacher, Joseph F. '72 (EVN) St. James, IN St. James Church.
Erbacher, William J. '87 (ARL) [5] Alexandria, VA St. Lawrence Church.
Erbe, Edward J. '51 (MAD) Evansville, WI St. Paul Church.
Erbland, Philip N. *m.m.* '66 (FgM) Maryknoll Foreign Missions.
Erbrick, Thomas J. *o.s.f.s.* (PH) [D] Philadelphia, PA Father Judge High School for Boys.
Erbrick, Thomas J. *o.s.f.s.* '62 (ARL) [D] Alexandria, VA Bishop Ireton High School; [J] Alexandria, VA Oblates of St. Francis de Sales Residence.
Ercolano, Anthony S. '73 (BRK) [148] Queens, NY American Martyrs Church; [G] Middle Village, NY Christ the King.
Erdei, Joseph J. *o.s.b.m.* '58 (PSC) [A] Matawan, NJ Basilian Fathers of Mariapoch.
Erdeljac, Frank '83 (PIT) [10] New Castle, PA St. Vincent de Paul Church; Lawrence County, PA St. Francis Hospital; [P] Villa Maria, PA Sisters of the Humility of Mary.
Erdeljac, Frank G. '83 (PIT) Lawrence County, PA Jameson Memorial Hospital; [J] New Castle, PA St. Francis Hospital of New Castle.
Erdle, Thomas M. '55 (ROC) [44] Rochester, NY St. Mark Church.
Erdlen, Harry J. *o.s.a.* '57 (PH) [G] Malvern, PA Malvern Preparatory School for Boys; [AA] Malvern, PA Augustinians (O.S.A.).
Eremito, Anthony '67 (NY) Absent on Leave.
Erhart, Charles M. '60 (RVC) Military Chaplains.
Erhart, Henry *s.j.* '55 (BAL) [C] Baltimore, MD Loyola High School.
Erhueh, Msgr. Anthony O. '66 (NY) [229] Staten Island, NY St. Sylvester Church.
Ericksen, William '95 (MIL) [31] Milwaukee, WI St. Gregory The Great Church.
Erickson, David J. '97 (PEO) [4] Champaign, IL St. Matthew Church.
Erickson, John '66 (KCK) [6] Topeka, KS Sacred Heart Church.
Erickson, John R. *o.s.b.* '50 (GBG) [H] Latrobe, PA Saint Vincent Archabbey.
Erickson, Matthew *o.p.* '90 (Y) [13] Youngstown, OH St. Dominic's Church.
Erickson, Philip L. '95 (L) [67] Louisville, KY St. Raphael the Archangel Church.
Erickson, Robert *s.j.* '74 (SPK) Keller, WA St. Rose of Lima Church; Nespelem, WA Sacred Heart Mission Church.
Erickson, Robert E. *c.s.v.* '67 (CHI) [N] Arlington Heights, IL Clerics of St. Viator-Provincial Residence; [N] Arlington Heights, IL Viatorian Province Center-Clerics of St. Viator.
Erikson, Richard M. '85 (BO) [A] Boston, MA St. John's Seminary.
Erlenheim, Adrian *o.f.m.* '37 (LA) [R] Santa Barbara, CA Franciscan Friary, Order of Friars Minor (Old Mission).
Ermer, James R. '78 (FAR) [5] Fargo, ND St. Anthony of Padua Church.
Ermis, Norman '83 (SAT) [A] San Antonio, TX The Assumption-St. John's Seminary.
Ernest, Bryan D. '82 (GI) Alliance, NE Holy Rosary Church.
Ernest, Stephen *s.v.d.* '67 (OAK) [6] Oakland, CA St. Bernard's Church; [A] Berkeley, CA Dominican School of Philosophy and Theology.
Ernst, Albert C. '53 (NO) Retired.
Ernst, Francis P. *s.j.* '57 (BAL) [39] Baltimore, MD St. Ignatius Church.
Ernst, Jeff *o.f.m.cap.* '96 (STL) [P] St. Louis, MO St. Crispin's Friary.
Ernst, Norbert A. '72 (STL) House Springs, MO Our Lady, Queen of Peace Church.
Ernst, Stephen *s.t.* '86 (WDC) [M] Adelphi, MD Father Thomas O'Keeffe Missionary Cenacle.
Ernst, William W. '64 (IND) New Albany, IN St. Mary Church.
Ernster, James M. '55 (MIL) Retired.
Ernster, Milo L. '55 (WIN) Dodge Center, MN St. John Baptist de La Salle Church.
Ernstmann, Mark C. '51 (SPC) Forsyth, MO Our Lady of the Ozarks Church.
Erpelding, Edward '66 (FTW) Syracuse, IN St. Martin de Porres Church.
Erpelding, Martin L. '42 (DET) Retired.
Erpelding, Michael J. '89 (SC) Storm Lake, IA St. Mary's Church.
Erpen, Msgr. B. A. '47 (AMA) Retired.
Erps, Jim *s.j.* '80 (LA) [CC] Los Angeles, CA Archdiocesan Office for Campus Ministry.
Errecalde, Javier *o.de.m.* '54 (PCE) [13] Ponce, PR Santuario San Judas Tadeo Church.
Erro, Sabino *o.f.m.* '54 (DAL) [9] Dallas, TX Our Lady of Perpetual Help Church.
Erstad, William D. '56 (SB) Perris, CA St. James Church.
Ertzbischoff, Edmond L. '76 (LAN) [2] Ypsilanti, MI St. John Church.
Ervin, Mark '90 (WDC) [1] Bethesda, MD St. Bartholomew Church.
Ervin, Mark W. '90 (WDC) Piscataway, MD St. Mary Church.
Ervin, Thomas '74 (SFR) Absent on Leave.
Erwin, James M. *o.p.* '45 (CHI) [N] River Forest, IL St. Thomas Aquinas Priory.
Erwin, Patrick O. (PAT) [5] Clifton, NJ SS. Cyril and Methodius Church; Unassigned.
Erwin, Timothy *c.pp.s* '97 (OAK) [2] Alameda, CA St. Barnabas Church.
Esbind, Jace '87 (LKC) Graduate Studies.
Escalante, Agustin '88 (SFR) [3] San Rafael, CA St. Raphael Church.
Escalante, Peter '78 (SD) [21] San Diego, CA St. Brigid Church.
Escalante, Ronald '95 (ARL) [5] Alexandria, VA St. Lawrence Church.
Esch, Eugene *o.s.b.* '54 (B) Glenns Ferry, ID Our Lady of Limerick Station Church; [C] Jerome, ID Ascension Priory.
Eschbach, Victor J. '72 (PH) Parkesburg, PA Our Lady of Consolation Church.
Eschbacher, Jerome J. '56 (SPC) Retired.
Eschweiler, Edward R. '48 (MIL) Retired.
Escobar, Agustin '87 (ORG) Westminster, CA Blessed Sacrament Church.
Escobar, Joseph A. *o.p.* '88 (PRO) [1] Pawtucket, RI St. Anthony Church.
Escobar, Octavio '67 (STO) Ceres, CA St. Jude Church.
Escobar, Onesimo *m.s.c.* '95 (LA) Cudahy, CA Cudahy Mission Church.
Escobedo, Armando (BWN) [D] San Juan, TX San Juan Nursing Home.
Escobedo, Armando '64 (BWN) Mercedes, TX Our Lady of Mercy Church; Mercedes, TX Sacred Heart Church.
Escobedo, Jaime '93 (SD) [A] San Diego, CA St. Francis Seminary.
Escribano, Peter E. '88 (MET) On Duty Outside the Diocese.
Esenther, Keith *s.j.* '71 (DET) [E] Detroit, MI University of Detroit Jesuit High School and Academy.
Esenther, Keith J. *s.j.* '71 (DET) [K] Detroit, MI Jesuit Provincial Office-Detroit Province of the Society of Jesus.
Esguerra, Bernardino C. '87 (TR) Atlantic Highlands, NJ St. Agnes Church.
Eshiowu, Evaristus M. '83 (LA) [67] Los Angeles, CA St. Ignatius of Loyola Church.
Esmilla, Efren V. '93 (PH) Wallingford, PA St. John Chrysostom Church.
Esmond, William '55 (ALB) Whitehall, NY Our Lady of Angels Church.
Esmurdoc, Christopher F. '96 (CLV) Absent on Leave.
Esparza, Javier *ss.cc.* '58 (SJN) [8] Guaynabo, PR Nuestra Senora de la Paz Church.
Espejel, Rene J. *c.s.b.* '87 (GAL) [Q] Sugar Land, TX Basilian Mission Center.
Espelage, Arthur *o.f.m.* '71 (PMB) [2] West Palm Beach, FL Mary Immaculate Church.
Espelage, Thomas '70 (CIN) [45] Cincinnati, OH St. John the Evangelist Church.
Espenshade, William T. '68 (CHY) Riverton, WY St. Margaret's Church.
Esper, Abraham L. '85 (SY) Whitesboro, NY St. Paul Church.
Esper, Jerome *c.s.c.* '61 (CHI) [D] Niles, IL Notre Dame High School.
Esper, John (DET) [T] Eastpointe, MI Detroit Catholic Charismatic Renewal.
Esper, John C. '83 (DET) [5] St. Clair Shores, MI St. Lucy Church.

Esper, Joseph M. '82 (DET) [3] Redford, MI Our Lady of Loretto Church.
Esper, Thomas '51 (DET) Retired.
Espin, Orlando O. '72 (VEN) Absent on Leave.
Espineda, Cesar Ching *s.v.d.* '84 (NY) [17] New York, NY St. Bernard Church.
Espinel, Luis *o.p.* (SJN) [A] Bayamon, PR Bayamon Central University.
Espinel, Marcos Luis *o.p.* '59 (SJN) [3] Bayamon, PR Catalina de Siena Church.
Espino, Alfonso (DAV) Muscatine, IA Our Lady of Guadalupe Catholic Mission Church.
Espino, Jose '83 (MIA) North Miami, FL Holy Family Church.
Espinosa, Anthony '96 (OM) Columbus, NE St. Bonaventure Church.
Espinosa, Boris '78 (CGS) Maunabo, PR San Isidor Labrador Church.
Espinosa, Donald B. *a.a.* '71 (WOR) Fiskdale, MA St. Anne's and St. Patrick's Church.
Espinosa, Jesus *o.a.r.* '64 (LSC) [6] Las Cruces, NM Santa Rosa de Lima Church.
Espinosa, Ricardo *m.g.* (ATL) Alpharetta, GA St. Thomas Aquinas Church.
Espinosa, Sergio Del Carmen *c.ss.r.* (MGZ) [2] Mayaquez, PR Our Lady of Mt. Carmel Church.
Espinoza, Galo *o.a.r.* '92 (ORG) [5] Santa Ana, CA Our Lady of the Pillar Church.
Espitia, David '94 (SAN) On Special or Other Diocesan Assignment.
Espona, Msgr. Juan '82 (PCE) Special Assignment.
Esposito, Anthony '56 (Y) Retired.
Esposito, Augustine M. *o.s.a.* '79 (PH) [A] Wynnewood, PA Theological Seminary of St. Charles Borromeo, Overbrook; [D] Drexel Hill, PA Monsignor Bonner High School.
Esposito, Ernest T. '67 (BGP) [2] Fairfield, CT Assumption Church; [G] Bridgeport, CT Catholic Charities of Fairfield County.
Esposito, Joseph J. '54 (BRK) Absent on Sick Leave.
Esposito, Lawrence J. '76 (WOR) Berlin, MA St. Joseph the Good Provider Church.
Esposito, Louis '64 (BAL) [74] Baltimore, MD Our Lady of Pompei Church.
Esposito, Mario *o.carm.* '77 (ALB) [M] Germantown, NY St. Teresa's Motherhouse.
Esposito, Mario *o.carm.* '77 (NY) Middletown, NY Our Lady of Mt. Carmel Church; [DD] Middletown, NY St. Albert's Priory.
Esposito, Ralph '67 (LR) Van Buren, AR St. Michael's Church.
Esposito, Samuel J. '78 (PIT) Allegheny County, PA UPMC University of Pittsburgh Medical Center.
Esposito, William C. '58 (SY) Cleveland, NY St. Mary of the Assumption Church.
Esquivel, Msgr. John '68 (FRS) Fowler, CA St. Lucy Church; Selma, CA St. Joseph Church.
Esquivel, Miguel '82 (CC) On Special Assignment.
Esquivez, Miguel '82 (SAN) On Duty Outside the Diocese.
Ess, Thomas '66 (CHI) [N] Chicago, IL St. Peter's Friary.
Esseff, Msgr. John A. '53 (SCR) [A] Dalton, PA Saint Pius X Seminary.
Esselman, Thomas *c.m.* '80 (STL) [B] St. Louis, MO Aquinas Institute of Theology.
Esselman, Thomas E. *c.m.* '80 (STL) [P] St. Louis, MO Vincentian-St. Lazare Residence.
Esser, James J. *o.f.m.* '67 (GB) Krakow, WI St. Casimir Church.
Esser, Paul M. '57 (MIL) [11] Racine, WI St. Paul the Apostle Church.
Essex, Msgr. Donald S. '73 (WDC) [2] Bethesda, MD St. Jane Frances de Chantal Church.
Essig, Edward J. '94 (ALN) [4] Pottsville, PA St. Patrick Church.
Essig, Herbert '74 (JOL) Lombard, IL St. Pius X Church.
Essling, Harold W. *c.s.c.* (AUS) [H] Austin, TX Steiner Lodge Retreat.
Essman, Charles P. '56 (COL) Retired.
Essman, Ronald J. '76 (DET) [4] Troy, MI St. Elizabeth Ann Seton Church.
Estabrook, Joseph '69 (ALB) Military Chaplains.
Esteban, Pedro Antonio '85 (LA) [23] Los Angeles, CA Our Lady of Guadalupe Church.
Estensoro, Jose '60 (ARE) Hatillo, PR Perpetual Help Church.
Estephan, Andre S. *m.l.m.* '90 (OLL) Lewisville, TX Our Lady of Lebanon Mission Church; [A] San Antonio, TX The Congregation of Maronite Lebanese Missionaries.
Esterka, Msgr. Peter '63 (ORG) [3] Orange, CA St. Norbert Church.
Esteve, Alfonso '47 (SJN) On Duty Outside the Archdiocese.
Estevez, Felipe '70 (MIA) [15] Miami, FL St. Agatha Church.
Esti, Giovanni *m.c.c.j.* '91 (LA) [R] Azusa, CA Casa Comboni Mission Seminary.
Estibalez, Inocencio '52 (SP) Retired.
Estilette, Grady J. '63 (LAF) Gueydan, LA St. Peter Church.
Estok, Edward T. '85 (CLV) Shaker Heights, OH St. Dominic Church.
Estrada, Domingo *o.m.i.* '72 (SAT) Eagle Pass, TX Sacred Heart Church.
Estrada, Enrique '93 (MIA) Higher Studies.
Estrada, Hector Diaz (SJN) [E] San Juan, PR VA Medical Center.
Estrada, Lawrence E. '80 (LA) Monterey Park, CA St. Stephen Church.
Estrada, Manuel '86 (SFR) [17] San Francisco, CA Church of the Epiphany.
Estrada, Miguel *c.m.f.* '60 (CHI) [80] Chicago, IL Holy Cross/Immaculate Heart of Mary Church.
Estrada, Sabino '72 (BRK) [240] Queens, NY St. Sebastian Church.
Estrem, John '86 (STP) [1] St. Paul, MN Cathedral of St. Paul.
Esty, Gregory L. '75 (STP) Richfield, MN St. Richard Church; [H] Richfield, MN Blessed Trinity Catholic School of Richfield, Minnesota.
Etchingham, Msgr. Lawrence '56 (CHY) [2] Cheyenne, WY Holy Trinity Church; Retired.
Ethen, Jeff '88 (SCL) Belle River, MN St. Nicholas Church; Parkers Prairie, MN Church of St. William; Urbank, MN Sacred Heart Church.
Etheredge, F. William '75 (RCK) [B] Rockford, IL Boylan Central Catholic High School.
Ethier, Raymond '85 (ALB) Philmont, NY Sacred Heart Church.
Ethier, Robert D. '45 (PRO) Retired.
Etienne, Bernard '93 (EVN) Princeton, IN St. Joseph Church.
Etienne, Clifton *s.v.d.* '79 (SB) [A] Riverside, CA Divine Word Seminary.
Etlinger, Peter J. *c.s.b.* '47 (ROC) [I] Rochester, NY Residence of Basilian Fathers-The Aquinas Institute.
Ettel, Dale *o.s.c.* (STP) Dayton, MN St. John the Baptist Church.
Ettel, Dale *o.s.c.* '82 (STP) Anoka, MN St. Stephen Church; [N] Anoka, MN Crosier Community of Anoka.
Ettensohn, John *o.m.i.* '89 (BEL) [F] Belleville, IL Missionary Oblates of Mary Immaculate - St. Henry's Oblate Residence; [J] Belleville, IL Oblate Preaching Team.
Ettlinger, Gerard H. *s.j.* '66 (NY) [DD] New York, NY Jesuit Provincial's Office.
Ettner, Wilhelm J. '93 (ARL) [2] Arlington, VA St. Agnes Church.
Ettorre, George P. '62 (PH) [2] Norristown, PA St. Francis of Assisi Church.
Etuale, Etuale '77 (HON) [10] Honolulu, HI Our Lady of the Mount Church.
Etuale, Viane '90 (SPP) [1] Pago Pago, AS Cathedral of the Holy Family.
Etzel, George A. '42 (MIL) Retired.
Etzel, Peter J. *s.j.* '94 (MIL) [P] Milwaukee, WI Arrupe House Jesuit Community.
Etzel, Raymond A. '50 (TOL) Retired.
Eugenio, Romarico (CHI) [134] Chicago, IL St. Matthias Church.
Euk, Vincent T. '86 (NY) [E] New York, NY Cardinal Spellman High School.
Euker, John T. '74 (GBG) Perryopolis, PA St. John the Baptist Church.
Euresti, Jesse '65 (AUS) Luling, TX St. John the Evangelist Church.
Euresti, Jesse '65 (VIC) On Duty Outside the Diocese.
Eustace, Alexander F. *o.f.m.* '50 (FgM) Franciscan Foreign Missions.
Euteneur, Thomas '88 (PMB) Indiantown, FL Holy Cross Church.
Euvrad, Scott '93 (BO) [7] Lynn, MA St. Pius Fifth Church.
Euvrard, Scott (BO) [CC] Salem, MA Salem State College, Catholic Campus Ministry.
Evancho, George '64 (PBR) East Pittsburgh, PA St. Mary's Church; Rankin, PA St. John's Church.
Evancho, Robert '79 (PSC) St. Petersburg, FL St. Therese Church.
Evangelista, Humberto *c.m.f.* '61 (CGS) [8] Barrio Rio Canas, PR Inmaculado Corazon de Maria Church.
Evangelista, Humberto *c.m.f.* '61 (SJN) [27] San Juan, PR San Jose Obrero Church.
Evangelisto, Louis Anthony '54 (HRT) [8] New Haven, CT St. Donato's Church; [R] Hamden, CT Catholic Community at Quinnipac College.
Evanick, Michael '60 (PRM) Merrillville, IN St. Michael Church.
Evanish, Robin S. '83 (PIT) Monaca, PA St. John the Baptist Church.
Evanko, Joseph J. '91 (SCR) Mountaintop, PA St. Jude's Church.
Evanofski, Bernard P. '86 (SCR) Larksville, PA St. Anthony of Padua Church.
Evans, Alan Augustine *o.p.* '61 (NY) [DD] New York, NY St. Vincent Ferrer Priory.
Evans, Alan S. (PIT) Allegheny County, PA Mercy Health System of Pittsburgh.
Evans, Albert *ss.cc.* '48 (FR) [J] Fairhaven, MA Sacred Hearts Provincial House.
Evans, Edward '80 (WDC) Cheverly, MD St. Ambrose Church; Retired.
Evans, Eldridge T. '65 (CAM) [1] Atlantic City, NJ Holy Spirit Church.
Evans, Msgr. Ferdinand A. '34 (CIN) Retired; Retired.
Evans, Msgr. Ferdinand A. '34 (VEN) Englewood, FL St. Raphael Church.
Evans, Msgr. Francis J. '57 (BRK) [211] Queens, NY Our Lady of Grace Church; Retired.
Evans, G. William '78 (TR) Beverly, NJ St. Joseph Church.
Evans, George *s.s.s.* '57 (CLV) [P] Cleveland, OH Congregation of the Blessed Sacrament Provincial House; [P] Cleveland, OH Blessed Sacrament Community.
Evans, George *o.c.s.o.* '61 (SAT) San Antonio, TX Audie Murphy VA Hospital.
Evans, George J. *o.c.s.o.* '61 (ATL) [I] Conyers, GA The Monastery of the Holy Spirit.
Evans, George P. '77 (BO) [A] Boston, MA St. John's Seminary School of Theology; [A] Boston, MA St. John's Seminary.
Evans, James L. '94 (AUS) Dripping Springs, TX St. Martin de Porres Church.
Evans, John L., II '80 (FAR) Lisbon, ND St. Aloysius Church; Lisbon, ND Soldier's Home.
Evans, John Whitney '57 (DUL) Special Assignment.
Evans, Ken '86 (NEW) Scotch Plains, NJ Immaculate Heart of Mary Church.
Evans, Michael A. *s.j.* '83 (DET) [E] Detroit, MI Loyola High School.
Evans, Michael J. '92 (LA) Manhattan Beach, CA American Martyrs Church.
Evans, Paul J. '42 (DUB) Retired.
Evans, Richard A. '82 (CLV) [3] Parma, OH St. Charles Borromeo Church.
Evans, Msgr. Robert C. '73 (PRO) [2] Cumberland, RI St. Joan of Arc Church.
Evans, Tim I. '93 (DEN) [3] Lakewood, CO Our Lady of Fatima Church.
Evans, Timothy '94 (MOB) Daphne, AL Christ the King Church.
Evans, Timothy G. '73 (PIT) Elizabeth, PA St. Michael Church.
Evans, Wilfred F. '68 (SY) Syracuse, NY Veterans Administration Hospital; Special Assignment.
Evans, William Morris '81 (CHL) Hamlet, NC St. James Church.
Evanstock, Matthew *c.s.sp.* (SB) [E] Hemet, CA Holy Ghost Fathers.
Evard, Paul A. *o.f.m.conv.* '61 (IND) St. Mary-of-the-Woods, IN St. Mary Church; West Terre Haute, IN St. Leonard of Port Maurice Church.
Evatt, Thomas A. '76 (CHR) Aiken, SC St. Mary, Help of Christians Church.
Evenson, Dennis D. '67 (STP) Hazelwood, MN Annunciation of the B.V.M. Church.
Evenson, Robert L. '91 (SEA) Castle Rock, WA St. Mary Church; Kelso, WA St. Mary Church.
Everding, Richard F. '66 (STL) Fenton, MO St. Paul Church.
Everett, William J. *s.j.* '53 (FgM) Provinces.
Everett, Willis E. '90 (COL) [32] Columbus, OH St. Michael Church.
Everitt, Edward *o.p.* '68 (MEM) [J] Memphis, TN Order of Preachers (Southern Dominican Prov.).
Everitt, Edward E. *o.p.* '68 (MEM) [23] Memphis, TN St. Peter's Church.
Everling, Robert M. (SCR) [N] Dunmore, PA Villa St. Joseph.
Everling, Robert M. '47 (SCR) Retired.
Evernden, Michael E. *c.s.p.* '74 (WH) Morgantown, WV St. John's University Parish, Newman Hall Church.
Evers, Gerard A. '40 (CIN) [62] Cincinnati, OH St. Matthias Church; Retired.
Evers, Leonard M. '68 (GB) Cecil, WI St. Martin Church; Shawano, WI Sacred Heart Church.
Evers, Linus *c.pp.s.* '71 (SUP) Butternut, WI Immaculate Conception Church; Clam Lake, WI St. George Church; Glidden, WI Most Precious Blood Church.
Evers, Paul '80 (HON) Military Chaplains.
Evers, Paul C. '54 (WIN) Currie, MN Immaculate Heart of Mary Church.
Evers, Paul K. '71 (KC) Leave of Absence.
Evers, Robert B. '60 (GRY) Lake Station, IN St. Francis Xavier Church.
Eversole, Paul M. '95 (ARL) Woodbridge, VA Our Lady of Angels Church.
Everts, Donald (GB) [2] Green Bay, WI Nativity of Our Lord Church.
Every, Robert L. *o.p.* '55 (NO) [25] New Orleans, LA St. Anthony Of Padua Church.
Evich, Paul J. *o.s.b.* '51 (BO) [W] Hingham, MA Glastonbury Abbey.
Evoy, John J. *s.j.* '43 (SPK) [C] Spokane, WA Gonzaga University.
Evrard, Donald J. '56 (IND) [F] Indianapolis, IN St. Vincent Hospital and Health Care Center, Inc.

Ewald, Daniel M.J. '86 (PCE) On Duty Outside the Diocese.
Ewen, Kurt '93 (ORL) Winter Park, FL St. Margaret Mary Church.
Ewen, Sharbel *o.s.b.* '88 (SD) [H] Oceanside, CA Prince of Peace Abbey, Benet Hill; [K] Oceanside, CA Prince of Peace Retreat Center.
Ewens, James M. *s.j.* '70 (MIL) [P] Milwaukee, WI Jesuit Community at Marquette University.
Ewers, Paul *m.c.c.j.* '65 (NEW) [N] Montclair, NJ Comboni Missionaries of the Heart of Jesus (Verona Fathers).
Ewert, J. Michael *o.f.m.* (SFD) Maryville, IL Mother of Perpetual Help Church.
Ewert, J. Michael *o.f.m.* '59 (CHI) [X] Chicago, IL S.F.V., Inc.
Ewert, J. Michael *o.f.m.* '59 (FWT) [G] Crowley, TX St. Francis Village, Inc.; [G] Crowley, TX St. Francis Village, Inc.
Ewherido, Anthony (RVC) Stony Brook, NY Stony Brook University Hospital.
Ewing, Mathias *o.carm.* '54 (LA) [F] Encino, CA Crespi Carmelite High School.
Ewing, Matt J. *o.carm.* '54 (LA) [R] Los Angeles, CA Mount Carmel Priory, Carmelite Fathers and Brothers.
Ewing, Richard A. '46 (MET) High Bridge, NJ St. Joseph Church; Retired.
Exley, Thomas G. '46 (NU) Retired.
Extejt, John I. *o.s.f.s.* '85 (TOL) [C] Toledo, OH St. Francis de Sales High School; [K] Toledo, OH Oblates of St. Francis de Sales.
Extejt, Thomas J. '73 (TOL) [20] Toledo, OH St. Charles Borromeo Church.
Eybel, John W. *m.m.* '70 (FgM) Maryknoll Foreign Missions.
Eyerman, Matthew S. '95 (CHI) [4] Chicago, IL St. Agatha Church.
Eylar, William D. '53 (CLV) [43] Cleveland, OH St. Leo the Great Church; Retired.
Eyman, Bryan R. '85 (PRM) Fairport Harbor, OH St. Michael Church; Mentor-on-the-Lake, OH St. Andrew the Apostle Church.
Eyrrick, John (NY) New Hampton, NY MID Hudson Psychiatric Center.
Ezaki, Bernard J. '88 (ALN) [7] Bethlehem, PA Notre Dame of Bethlehem Church; [C] Bethlehem, PA Bethlehem Catholic High School.
Eze, Cyprian '88 (LKC) Westlake, LA St. John Bosco Church.
Ezerskis, Charles '61 (CHI) Evergreen Park, IL Most Holy Redeemer Church.
Ezharath, Joseph '66 (WH) Paden City, WV Mater Dolorosa Church; Sistersville, WV Holy Rosary Church.
Ezop, Dwight '97 (LAN) [3] Ann Arbor, MI St. Thomas the Apostle Church.

F

Faber, Emmett N. '55 (AUS) Bastrop, TX Federal Correctional Institute.
Faber, Emmett N. '55 (LC) On Duty Outside the Diocese.
Faber, Msgr. William '36 (FTW) Retired.
Fabian, Cyril *o.p.* '56 (WIN) [1] Winona, MN Cathedral of the Sacred Heart.
Fabian, Jack '68 (DET) [T] Detroit, MI Clergy Health Plan; [T] Newport, MI Companions of Christ the Lamb.
Fabian, John C. *o.p.* '59 (CHI) [N] Chicago, IL Dominicans (Provincial Office).
Fabian, John L. '48 (SCR) Retired; [N] Dunmore, PA Villa St. Joseph.
Fabiano, Philip *o.f.m.cap.* '64 (NY) [DD] White Plains, NY St. Conrad Friary.
Fabing, Robert J. *s.j.* '74 (OAK) [N] Berkeley, CA Jesuit Community at Jesuit School of Theology at Berkeley.
Fabing, Robert J. *s.j.* '74 (SJ) [L] Los Altos, CA Jesuit Retreat House; [P] Los Altos, CA Jesuit Institute for Family Life.
Fabish, Rapael A. *o.p.* '53 (CHI) [N] Chicago, IL Dominicans (Provincial Office).
Fabish, Raphael '42 (PEO) [K] Rock Island, IL St. Anthony's Continuing Care Center; [N] Rock Island, IL St. Mary of the Angels Convent.
Fabj, Frank T. '84 (GAL) [6] Galveston, TX Sacred Heart Church.
Fabre, Richard '73 (LAF) [13] Lafayette, LA St. Leo Church.
Fabre, Shelton J. '89 (BR) Grosse Tete, LA St. Joseph Church; Maringouin, LA Immaculate Heart of Mary Church.
Fabrizio, Henry E. '50 (Y) Retired.
Fabula, Vincent J. *o.c.s.o.* '68 (DAV) [O] Wheatland, IA Our Lady of the Prairie Retreat.
Facci, John *s.a.c.* '71 (ALB) [6] Cohoes, NY St. Rita-Sacred Heart Church.
Facura, Joseph C. '68 (RIC) Norton, VA St. Anthony Church.
Fadallan, Elbert '80 (LUB) Plainview, TX Sacred Heart Church.
Fadden, Msgr. Joseph A. '54 (SCR) [11] Scranton, PA St. Clare Church.
Faddish, Alvin V. *o.f.m.* '63 (PAT) [5] Paterson, NJ St. Bonaventure Church.
Fador, Francis R. '96 (HRT) Madison, CT St. Margaret Church.
Fadrowski, Stanislaus '39 (SCL) Retired.
Fadrowski, William J. '87 (NEW) North Arlington, NJ Queen of Peace Church.
Faeh, Linus *o.f.m.cap.* (FgM) American Capuchin Missions (O.F.M.Cap.).
Faesser, Arthur A. '76 (GI) Kearney, NE Youth Development Center; [D] Kearney, NE University of Nebraska at Kearney Newman Apostolate.
Fafinski, Donald S. '66 (BUF) Jamestown, NY St. John Church.
Fagan, Arthur J. '67 (CHI) Elk Grove Village, IL Queen of the Rosary Church.
Fagan, Bernard D. *s.j.* '52 (RC) [4] Rapid City, SD St. Isaac Jogues Church; [B] Howes, SD Kino Jesuit Community.
Fagan, Msgr. Daniel E. '61 (RVC) Valley Stream, NY Holy Name of Mary Church.
Fagan, Edward J. *o.a.r.* '63 (NY) [154] Bronx, NY St. John's Church.
Fagan, Msgr. Emmet (BRK) [L] Brooklyn, NY Catholic Charities.
Fagan, George V., Jr. '69 (COS) [F] Colorado Springs, CO Mount St. Francis.
Fagan, Gerard F. *s.j.* '47 (NY) [DD] New York, NY Jesuit Community at Fordham University.
Fagan, John E. *s.j.* '83 (BO) [47] Boston, MA St. Mary of the Angels Church; [W] Boston, MA Loyola House; [W] Boston, MA The Society of Jesus of New England-Provincial Offices.
Fagan, Msgr. John T. '52 (BRK) Retired; [O] Brooklyn, NY Little Flower Children's Services.
Fagan, Msgr. John T. '52 (RVC) [G] Wading River, NY Little Flower Children's Services of New York.
Fagan, Joseph K. '67 (BO) Stoughton, MA Immaculate Conception Church.
Fagan, Joseph P. '37 (NEW) Retired.
Fagan, Kevin '81 (FWT) Knox City, TX Santa Rosa Church; Rhineland, TX St. Joseph Church.
Fagan, Paul *c.p.* '86 (MET) [H] South River, NJ Passionist Provincial Office.
Fagan, Paul *c.p.* '86 (NY) [HH] New York, NY Passionist Residence.
Fagan, Paul E. *m.m.* '60 (FgM) Maryknoll Foreign Missions.
Fagan, Msgr. Robert Emmet '55 (RVC) Bay Shore, NY St. Patrick's Church.
Fagan, Robert R. '58 (ALN) Tamaqua, PA St. Jerome Church.
Faggioni, Ernest *s.d.b.* '47 (NO) [2] Harvey, LA St. John Bosco Church.
Fagin, Gerald M. *s.j.* '69 (NO) [C] New Orleans, LA Loyola University.
Fagnani, Anthony G. '48 (NY) Retired.
Fagnant, Msgr. Donat J. '28 (PRO) Retired; [M] North Smithfield, RI St. Antoine Residence.
Fagone, Benedict *o.f.m.conv.* '67 (SPR) [5] Chicopee, MA St. Anthony's Church.
Fagot, Hacker J. *s.j.* '57 (BR) [J] Convent, LA Manresa, House of Retreats.
Faherty, William B. *s.j.* '44 (STL) [P] St. Louis, MO Jesuit Community Corporation at St. Louis University - Jesuit Hall; [P] St. Louis, MO The Jesuits of the Missouri Province; [W] St. Louis, MO The Museum of Western Jesuit Missions.
Fahey, Msgr. Charles J. '59 (BRK) [L] Brooklyn, NY Catholic Charities.
Fahey, Msgr. Charles J. '59 (NY) [DD] New York, NY Jesuit Community at Fordham University.
Fahey, Msgr. Charles J. '59 (SY) [19] Syracuse, NY St. Lucy Church; On Duty Outside the Diocese.
Fahey, Edward J. (TR) On Duty Outside the Diocese.
Fahey, Edward J., Jr. '89 (WIL) [5] Wilmington, DE St. Elizabeth Church.
Fahey, George *s.m.* '46 (MRY) [G] Santa Cruz, CA Society of Mary, Marists.
Fahey, Msgr. Gerard '51 (SR) [5] Santa Rosa, CA Star of the Valley Church.
Fahey, James *c.s.c.* '56 (FTW) [2] South Bend, IN St. Adalbert Church.
Fahey, James L. '59 (BO) Beverly, MA St. Margaret Church.
Fahey, James W. '70 (FR) [5] Attleboro, MA St. Theresa of the Child Jesus Church.
Fahey, John H. '61 (WH) Lubeck, WV St. Monica's Church; Ravenswood, WV St. Matthew Church.
Fahey, John K. *s.j.* '45 (NY) [DD] New York, NY Murray-Weigel Hall.
Fahey, John M. '54 (TUC) [3] Tucson, AZ Holy Family Church; Retired.
Fahey, John P. '84 (LA) Graduate Studies; [K] Los Angeles, CA St. Vincent Medical Center.
Fahey, John P. *c.ss.r.* '96 (DEN) [33] Denver, CO St. Joseph's Church.
Fahey, Joseph R. *s.j.* '68 (BO) [E] Boston, MA Boston College High School & Jesuit Community.
Fahey, Kevin '53 (R) Laurinburg, NC St. Mary Church.
Fahey, Michael A. *s.j.* '64 (BO) [W] Boston, MA The Society of Jesus of New England-Provincial Offices.
Fahey, Michael A. *s.j.* '64 (MIL) [P] Milwaukee, WI Arrupe House Jesuit Community.
Fahey, Michael A. *s.j.* '64 (WDC) [V] Washington, DC Theological Studies, Inc.
Fahey, Robert *s.m.* '53 (SP) [7] Tampa, FL Our Lady of Perpetual Help Church.
Fahey, Thomas C. *o.f.m.* '47 (CHY) Retired.
Fahey, Thomas C. '47 (FTW) [K] Huntington, IN Victory Noll—Motherhouse of Our Lady of Victory Missionary Sisters.
Fahnestock, John '71 (SB) Victorville, CA St. Joan of Arc Church.
Fahnlander, William J. '46 (BIS) Retired; [G] Bismarck, ND Emmaus Place.
Fahrbach, Paul '84 (TOL) Custar, OH St. Louis Church; Deshler, OH Immaculate Conception Church.
Fahy, Msgr. Francis J. '61 (BRK) [122] Brooklyn, NY Resurrection Church.
Fahy, Msgr. John J. '42 (NEW) [1] Orange, NJ St. John's Church; Retired; [N] Rutherford, NJ St. John Vianney Residence for Priests.
Fahy, Joseph A. *c.p.* '56 (ATL) [11] Atlanta, GA St. Paul of the Cross Church.
Fahy, Murty M. *o.s.f.s.* '58 (STO) Lodi, CA St. Anne Church.
Fahy, Thomas *o.s.b.* '57 (WDC) [M] Washington, DC St. Anselm's Abbey.
Faiella, William W. *c.s.c.* '79 (FTW) [J] South Bend, IN Congregation of Holy Cross Indiana Province Provincial House.
Failla, Anthony (BRK) Absent on Sick Leave.
Failla, Anthony J. '56 (BRK) [L] Brooklyn, NY Catholic Charities.
Faiola, Msgr. Samuel J. '49 (BUF) Retired.
Faiola, Thomas *o.f.m.cap.* '85 (MAN) [2] Manchester, NH St. Anne Church.
Fairbairn, Frank '69 (FgM) Society of St. James the Apostle.
Fairbairn, Frank E. '69 (BO) Society of St. James the Apostle.
Fairbanks, Florian *o.s.b.* '39 (BIS) [A] Richardton, ND Assumption Abbey.
Fairbanks, Gregory J. '90 (PH) [34] Philadelphia, PA Christ the King Church.
Fairchild, Msgr. Edward J. '59 (COL) Westerville, OH St. Paul the Apostle Church.
Fairfield, Jeffry L. *o.carm.* '46 (STO) [5] Stockton, CA St. Gertrude Church.
Fairman, Timothy J. '88 (CHI) Arlington Heights, IL St. James Church.
Faistl, Msgr. Clement '37 (COL) Retired.
Faistl, Msgr. Clement F. '37 (COL) [10] Columbus, OH Christ the King Church.
Fait, Thomas G. '74 (MIL) Paris, WI St. John the Baptist Church.
Faith, Rudolph '41 (DUL) Retired.
Fajardo, Ricardo (NY) [65] New York, NY St. Jude Church.
Fajella, Francis J. *m.ss.a.* '82 (NY) Scarsdale, NY St. Pius X Church.
Fala, John G. '65 (PH) Absent on Sick Leave; Retired.
Falaniko, Mikaele '86 (SPP) [6] Pago Pago, AS Church of the Holy Cross.
Falardeau, Ernest *s.s.s.* '56 (SFE) [23] Albuquerque, NM St. Charles Borromeo Church.
Falardeau, Normand R. *s.s.s.* '52 (SFE) [23] Albuquerque, NM St. Charles Borromeo Church.
Falbo, Samuel J. '60 (SFE) [D] Albuquerque, NM St. Pius X High School.
Falco, Frank M. *o.s.m.* '67 (CHI) Hillside, IL St. Domitilla Church; [N] Chicago, IL Servite Friars - Eastern Province.
Falco, Ronald G. '81 (WOR) [1] Leominster, MA St. Anna's Church.
Falcone, Emilio '57 (RCK) Active Outside the Diocese.
Falcone, Mark D. *o.praem.* '66 (WIL) [I] Claymont, DE Immaculate Conception Priory of the Canons Regular of Premontre.
Falduti, James *o.f.m.* (BUF) [C] St. Bonaventure, NY St. Bonaventure University; [R] Williamsville, NY Campus Ministry.
Falduti, James *o.f.m.* '94 (BUF) [Q] West Clarksville, NY Mount Irenaeus, Franciscan Mountain Retreat & Holy Peace Friary.
Faletoi, Konelio '92 (HON) Papaikou, HI Immaculate Heart of Mary Church.
Faletta, Joseph '72 (ALB) Stuyvesant Falls, NY St. Mary Church.
Faletti, Stephen L. '83 (JC) Absent on Leave.
Faley, Roland *t.o.r.* '56 (RVC) [A] Huntington, NY Diocesan Seminary of the Immaculate Conception.
Faliskie, Edmund *c.ss.r.* '89 (BRK) [C] Whitestone, NY St. Alphonsus Formation Residence.
Falk, Conrad *o.s.b.* '52 (KC) [J] Conception, MO Conception Abbey.
Falk, Msgr. Dennis G. '57 (B) On Special Assignment.
Falk, Gerald R. '59 (GB) [8] Appleton, WI St. Thomas More Church.

Falk, Robert *s.d.b.* '63 (FgM) Salesians of Don Bosco Foreign Missions.
Falkenhan, Pierce M. '80 (PIT) [2] Bridgeville, PA Holy Child Church.
Falkenthal, Thomas W. '75 (CHI) Military Chaplains.
Falla, Gustavo Adolfo '96 (BGP) [7] Bridgeport, CT St. Charles Church.
Faller, Henry E. '47 (KC) Retired.
Falletta, Frank J. '66 (ROC) [41] Rochester, NY St. Lawrence Church.
Fallon, Daniel R. '76 (CHI) [154] Chicago, IL Our Lady, Mother of the Church.
Fallon, David F. '70 (CLV) [70] Cleveland, OH San Juan Bautista Church; [X] Cleveland, OH Diocesan Hispanic Office.
Fallon, Francis H. *s.s.j.* '45 (BAL) [M] Baltimore, MD St. Joseph Society of the Sacred Heart House of Central Administration.
Fallon, Msgr. James (PAT) [C] Madison, NJ Bayley-Ellard High School.
Fallon, James J. '62 (SY) Johnson City, NY St. James Church; Absent on Sick Leave.
Fallon, Msgr. James L. '43 (PAT) Morris Plains, NJ St. Virgilius Church; Retired.
Fallon, James P. *s.s.j.* (MOB) Chastang, AL St. Peter the Apostle Church.
Fallon, John '55 (OG) Absent on Sick Leave.
Fallon, John '69 (BIR) Tuscaloosa, AL Holy Spirit Church.
Fallon, John '95 (FAR) Pisek, ND St. John Nepomucene Church.
Fallon, John C.K. '71 (ATL) [9] Atlanta, GA St. Anthony of Padua Church; Atlanta, GA U.S. Penitentiary.
Fallon, John F. '58 (BO) Awaiting Assignment.
Fallon, John J. '46 (BO) Retired.
Fallon, John J. '52 (LA) Retired.
Fallon, John P. *o.s.f.s.* '60 (STO) [A] Stockton, CA St. Mary's High School.
Fallon, Joseph P. '96 (NY) Middletown, NY St. Joseph Church.
Fallon, William J. '64 (CAM) Paulsboro, NJ St. John's Church.
Falls, Msgr. Thomas B. '32 (PH) Manoa, PA Sacred Heart Church; Retired.
Falotico, Ronald S. '69 (CAM) Pleasantville, NJ St. Peter's Church.
Falsetto, Francis J. *s.j.* '48 (SPK) [C] Spokane, WA Gonzaga University.
Falsey, James E. '70 (SAG) On Duty Outside the Diocese.
Falsey, James E. '72 (FBK) Koyukuk, AK St. Patrick Church; Nulato, AK Our Lady of the Snows Church.
Falteisek, Edwin F. *s.j.* '57 (MIL) [P] Wauwatosa, WI Jesuit Community at St. Camillus.
Falter, John F. *c.pp.s.* '61 (CIN) [M] Dayton, OH Provincial House of the Cincinnati Province of the Society of the Precious Blood.
Faluszak, James G. '96 (E) Ridgway, PA St. Leo the Great Church.
Faluszczak, James G. '96 (E) [C] Saint Marys, PA Elk County Christian High School.
Falvella, Richard J. '41 (BUR) Retired.
Falvey, Edmund F. '61 (WOR) [18] Worcester, MA St. Bernard Church.
Falvey, Jeremiah A. *c.s.sp.* '55 (PH) [AA] Bensalem, PA Congregation of the Holy Ghost.
Falvey, Msgr. Sinon '45 (ORG) Retired.
Falzon, Angelo *o.f.m.* '84 (FgM) Franciscan Foreign Missions.
Fama, Benjamin Joseph '83 (ORG) On Duty Outside the Diocese.
Fama, Lawrence J. '92 (NEW) Livingston, NJ St. Philomena Church.
Famania, Edison *c.m.* '94 (FgM) Vincentian Foreign Missions.
Fambrini, Robert A. *s.j.* '79 (LA) [R] Culver City, CA Ignatius House, The Novitiate of the California Province, Society of Jesus.
Famiglietti, Rocco *o.f.m.* '47 (FgM) Franciscan Foreign Missions.
Fanale, James *c.s.v.* '69 (JOL) St. Anne, IL St. Anne Church.
Fane, Kevin R. *o.p.* '69 (CHI) [N] Chicago, IL Dominicans (Provincial Office).
Fanelli, Charles V. '71 (CHI) Northlake, IL St. John Baptist Vianney, Cure of Ars Church; [X] Northlake, IL Italian Catholic Federation.
Fanelli, Msgr. Eugene A. '40 (NEW) [28] Newark, NJ Our Lady of Mt. Carmel Church; Retired.
Fanelli, James G. '56 (HRT) [3] East Hartford, CT St. Christopher Church.
Faneye, Benedict *o.p.* '94 (WDC) Washington, DC St. Elizabeth's Hospital (Government Operated).
Fangman, Frederick '63 (DUB) [H] Oelwein, IA Mercy Hospital of Franciscan Sisters.
Fangman, James E. '63 (SC) Kingsley, IA St. Michael's Church.
Fangman, Paul J. '49 (OM) Retired.
Fangman, Robert M. (SC) Retired.
Fangman, Thomas M. '92 (OM) Norfolk, NE Sacred Heart Church.
Fangman, Wilfred *o.s.b.* '49 (KCK) [9] Kansas City, KS SS. Cyril and Methodius Church; [13] Kansas City, KS St. Joseph and St. Benedict Church.
Fangmann, Frederick C. '63 (DUB) Oelwein, IA Sacred Heart Church.
Fangmeyer, Leroy J. (WDC) Garrett Park, MD Holy Cross Church.
Fangmeyer, Leroy J. '89 (WDC) Pastoral Center Special Ministries.
Fanning, Gerard F. '38 (LAV) Retired.
Fanning, Gerard F. '38 (RNO) Retired.
Fanning, John E. '68 (NY) [99] New York, NY Our Lady of Victory Church.
Fanning, Leo M. '54 (ORL) Retired.
Fanning, Leo M. '54 (PAT) Retired.
Fanning, Patrick F. *ss.cc.* '83 (FR) [J] Fairhaven, MA Sacred Hearts Provincial House.
Fannon, Noel '61 (BLX) Waveland, MS St. Clare Church.
Fannon, Msgr. Robert C. '46 (Y) Retired.
Fannon, Thomas '41 (BAL) [J] Timonium, MD Stella Maris Operating Corporation.
Fannon, Thomas J. '41 (BAL) Retired.
Fanrak, James M. '71 (LR) Berryville, AR St. Anne's Church; Eureka Springs, AR St. Elizabeth's Church.
Fanta, Thomas G. '88 (CLV) Rocky River, OH St. Christopher Church.
Fanti, Joseph J. '90 (ALN) On Duty Outside the Diocese.
Fanti, Joseph J. '90 (SCR) [2] Swoyersville, PA Holy Name/St. Mary's Church.
Fanucci, Santino J. '58 (SCR) Peckville, PA Sacred Heart of Jesus Church.
Faour, George '91 (NEW) [4] Hoboken, NJ SS. Peter and Paul's Church.
Farabaugh, Kenneth '68 (BAL) Hickory, MD St. Ignatius Church.
Farace, Frederick A. (HBG) [G] Danville, PA Maria Hall.
Farace, Frederick A. '55 (HBG) Retired; [I] Danville, PA Villa Sacred Heart.
Faraci, Douglas F. '69 (BUF) Buffalo, NY Buffalo General Hospital; Buffalo, NY Roswell Park Memorial Institute.
Faraci, Francis '59 (LAN) [10] Flint, MI St. Mary Church.
Faraj, John *b.s.o.* '78 (NTN) Brooklyn, NY Church of the Virgin Mary.
Farana, Mario P. '71 (SFR) [42] San Francisco, CA St. Paul Church.
Farana, Nicholas E. '44 (SJ) [5] Sunnyvale, CA Church of the Resurrection; Retired.
Farano, Michael A. '68 (ALB) Loudonville, NY St. Pius X Church; Special Assignment.
Farao, John *o.f.m.conv.* '88 (LA) Hermosa Beach, CA Our Lady of Guadalupe Church.
Faraone, David J. '85 (ROC) Sodus, NY Epiphany Church.
Faraone, Emmanuel *o.f.m.* '41 (NY) [DD] New York, NY Padua Friary.
Faraone, Joseph J. '72 (NY) Carmel, NY St. James the Apostle Church.
Fardellone, Emil *s.d.b.* '44 (BO) [E] Boston, MA Don Bosco Preparatory School.
Fares, Lawrence '50 (DET) Retired.
Faretra, Albert M. '86 (BO) Hingham, MA St. Paul Church.
Faria, Andre H., Jr. '93 (FR) Absent on Leave.
Faria, Carl M.D. '88 (MRY) Marina, CA St. Jude Parish Community Church.
Faria, Manuel T. '38 (FR) [18] Fall River, MA St. Michael's Church.
Farias, Jorge '81 (BWN) Absent.
Farias, Joseph A. *s.d.b.* '64 (SFE) [18] Albuquerque, NM San Jose Church.
Farias, Joseph G. '75 (PAT) Mount Hope, NJ St. Bernard's Church; [O] Madison, NJ Drew University Catholic Campus Ministry; [O] Madison, NJ Fairleigh Dickinson University and Drew University.
Faricy, Robert L. *s.j.* '62 (MIL) [P] Milwaukee, WI Jesuit Provincial Office, Wisconsin Province.
Farin, Paul '88 (BRK) [E] Brooklyn, NY Office of Religious Education: Evangelization and Catholic Formation.
Farin, Paul W. '88 (BRK) [47] Brooklyn, NY St. Francis Xavier Church.
Farina, Carlo A. *s.j.* '64 (SJ) [B] Santa Clara, CA Santa Clara University.
Farina, Msgr. Michael diTeccia '54 (WDC) [36] Washington, DC St. Patrick Church; [V] Washington, DC Paul VI Institute for the Arts.
Farina, Msgr. Michael F. '54 (WDC) Retired.
Farkas, Paul *o.f.m.cap.* '51 (PIT) [O] Pittsburgh, PA St. Augustine Friary.
Farke, Rodney '72 (SFS) Yankton, SD St. Benedict Church; [I] Yankton, SD The House of Mary Shrine, Inc.
Farland, David '74 (SPR) [Q] Springfield, MA Gate of Heaven.
Farland, George A. '68 (SPR) [12] Springfield, MA Sacred Heart Church.
Farland, Norman '66 (ORL) Bartow, FL St. Thomas Aquinas Church.
Farland, Roch *o.f.m.* '54 (DET) [5] Southfield, MI St. Michael Church.
Farleo, Brennan Joseph *o.f.m.conv.* '86 (TR) Seaside Park, NJ St. Catharine of Siena Church.
Farley, Bernard C. '68 (PH) Absent on Sick Leave.
Farley, David G. '52 (RVC) Wantagh, NY St. Frances de Chantal Church; Retired.
Farley, James V. '65 (PRO) Hopkinton, RI Our Lady of Victory Church; [4] Westerly, RI St. Vincent de Paul Church.
Farley, John B. '93 (PBL) Grand Junction, CO Immaculate Heart of Mary Church.
Farley, Msgr. John J. '62 (NY) [A] Yonkers, NY St. Joseph's Seminary.
Farley, Laurence F. '54 (RIC) Retired.
Farley, Leo O. (NEW) [N] Caldwell, NJ The Rev. Msgr. James F. Kelley Residence for Retired Priests.
Farley, Leo O. '54 (NEW) Livingston, NJ St. Barnabas Medical Center.
Farley, Leslie A. '92 (LR) Walnut Ridge, AR Immaculate Heart of Mary Church.
Farley, Leslie A. '93 (LR) Engelberg, AR St. John the Baptist Church.
Farley, Thomas '79 (P) [P] Portland, OR University of Portland.
Farley, Thomas B. '79 (P) McMinnville, OR St. James Church.
Farmer, Bruce '81 (TOL) Marygrove, OH Immaculate Conception Church.
Farmer, Bruce L. '81 (TOL) [20] Toledo, OH St. Charles Borromeo Church; Richfield Center, OH St. Elizabeth of Hungary Church.
Farmer, J. Kevin '93 (BAL) Frederick, MD St. John the Evangelist Church.
Farmer, James '79 (BAL) [91] Baltimore, MD St. Thomas Aquinas Church.
Farmer, Michael '95 (MOB) [3] Montgomery, AL St. Bede Church.
Farmer, Regis M. '73 (PIT) Wildwood, PA St. Catherine of Sweden Church.
Farmer, Richard R. *o.p.* '56 (CHI) [N] River Forest, IL St. Thomas Aquinas Priory.
Farnan, Donald '87 (KC) [24] Kansas City, MO St. Louis Church; [38] Kansas City, MO St. Therese Little Flower Church.
Farnik, John M. *c.ss.r.* '62 (GAL) [34] Houston, TX Holy Ghost Church.
Faroh, Paul *o.f.m.conv.* '85 (FTW) LaGrange, IN St. Joseph Church.
Farrand, John L. *s.j.* '53 (NY) [DD] New York, NY Murray-Weigel Hall.
Farrar, Charles P. '97 (DET) Pontiac, MI St. Joseph Church; Pontiac, MI St. Vincent de Paul Church.
Farre, Ramon '53 (LA) Ventura, CA Sacred Heart Church; [A] Camarillo, CA St. John's Seminary College of the Archdiocese of Los Angeles.
Farre, Raymond P. '41 (TR) Retired.
Farrel, Patrick J. *o.c.d.* '62 (MIL) [P] Holy Hill, WI Discalced Carmelite Monastery.
Farrell, Anthony '64 (STV) [1] St. Thomas, VI Cathedral of Sts. Peter and Paul.
Farrell, Anthony G. '64 (DAV) On Duty Outside the Diocese.
Farrell, Bernard '65 (BLX) Ocean Springs, MS St. Alphonsus Church.
Farrell, Charles D. *o.p.* '54 (DET) [20] Detroit, MI St. Dominic Church.
Farrell, David E. *c.s.c.* (FgM) Holy Cross Foreign Missions.
Farrell, Dennis J. '73 (BRK) [58] Brooklyn, NY Holy Name Church.
Farrell, Donald J. '54 (PH) East Lansdowne, PA St. Cyril of Alexandria Church; Retired.
Farrell, Edmund J. '43 (GR) Retired.
Farrell, Emmet L. '65 (SD) San Ysidro, CA Our Lady of Mt. Carmel Church.
Farrell, Emmett L. '65 (SC) On Duty Outside the Diocese.
Farrell, Msgr. Francis '55 (BLX) [2] Biloxi, MS Our Lady of Fatima Church.
Farrell, George A. '96 (MET) Edison, NJ St. Matthew Church.
Farrell, Gerald J. *m.m.* '57 (FgM) Maryknoll Foreign Missions.
Farrell, Gerard *o.s.b.* '46 (SCL) [I] Collegeville, MN St. John's Abbey, of the Order of St. Benedict.
Farrell, J. Aloysius *c.s.p.* '43 (NY) [DD] Jamaica Estates, NY Paulist Fathers Generalate.
Farrell, James (IND) [11] Indianapolis, IN Our Lady of Lourdes Church.
Farrell, James *s.j.* '46 (CLV) [E] Cleveland, OH St. Ignatius High School; [U] Cleveland, OH Jesuit Retreat House.
Farrell, James '56 (OAK) [N] Oakland, CA Redemptorists.
Farrell, James '75 (IND) [17] Indianapolis, IN St. Bernadette Church.
Farrell, Jeremiah '87 (HON) On Duty Outside the Diocese.

Farrell, Jeremiah *s.s.* '87 (SFR) [U] Menlo Park, CA Vatican II Institute for Clergy Formation.
Farrell, John *c.ss.r.* '48 (BAL) [87] Baltimore, MD Sacred Heart of Jesus Church.
Farrell, John E. '62 (BO) Lynnfield, MA Our Lady of the Assumption Church.
Farrell, John F. '47 (PRO) Retired.
Farrell, Msgr. John J. '34 (CHI) Berwyn, IL St. Leonard Church; Retired.
Farrell, John J. *o.s.a.* '59 (PH) [C] Villanova, PA Villanova University; [AA] Villanova, PA St. Thomas Monastery.
Farrell, John P. *o.p.* '39 (NY) [EE] Blauvelt, NY Congregation of St. Dominic General Motherhouse of the Sisters of St. Dominic of Blauvelt.
Farrell, Joseph '74 (TR) Tabernacle, NJ Holy Eucharist Church.
Farrell, Joseph A. *m.m.* '59 (FgM) Maryknoll Foreign Missions.
Farrell, Joseph L. *o.s.a.* '91 (BO) [C] North Andover, MA Merrimack College; [CC] North Andover, MA Merrimack College Campus Ministry Center.
Farrell, Joseph L. '95 (PH) Upper Gwynedd, PA Corpus Christi Church.
Farrell, Msgr. Kevin J. '78 (WDC) Pastoral Center Special Ministries.
Farrell, Kevin R. '65 (JOL) Wood Dale, IL Holy Ghost Church.
Farrell, Lawrence *o.p.* '71 (SB) [E] Riverside, CA St. Vincent Ferrer House.
Farrell, Martin *o.s.d.* '78 (OG) Bombay, NY St. Joseph Church; Fort Covington, NY St. Mary Church.
Farrell, Michael A. '70 (ORL) Palm Bay, FL St. Joseph Church.
Farrell, Michael J. *s.s.j.* '60 (FWT) [7] Fort Worth, TX Our Mother of Mercy Church.
Farrell, Patrick '60 (JKS) [1] Jackson, MS St. Peter Cathedral; Jackson, MS University of Mississippi Medical Center.
Farrell, Patrick E. '61 (VEN) Holmes Beach, FL St. Bernard's Church.
Farrell, Paul *c.ss.r.* '52 (STL) [P] Liguori, MO Liguori Mission House/Redemptorists.
Farrell, Philip N. '93 (PIT) Green Tree, PA St. Margaret Church.
Farrell, Richard (ROC) Pine City, NY Southport Correctional Facility.
Farrell, Richard '52 (PHX) Prescott, AZ Sacred Heart Church.
Farrell, Richard T. '84 (ROC) [3] Elmira, NY St. Mary Church.
Farrell, Robert *s.j.* '64 (BO) [W] Chestnut Hill, MA The Jesuit Community at Boston College.
Farrell, Robert J. '80 (CIN) [67] Cincinnati, OH Nativity of Our Lord Church.
Farrell, Seamus J. '67 (OAK) [2] Hayward, CA St. Bede Church.
Farrell, Thomas (GB) Casco, WI Holy Trinity Church.
Farrell, Thomas '82 (LEX) [2] Lexington, KY The Newman Center, Holy Spirit Church; [L] Lexington, KY The Newman Center Holy Spirit Parish University of Kentucky.
Farrell, Thomas F. '43 (HRT) Windsor Locks, CT St. Robert Bellarmine Church.
Farrell, Timothy '89 (GLP) Farmington, NM Sacred Heart Church.
Farrell, Walter L. *s.j.* '47 (DET) [K] Detroit, MI Jesuit Provincial Office-Detroit Province of the Society of Jesus.
Farrell, William '78 (CHL) On Duty Outside the Diocese.
Farrell, William J. '47 (MIL) Retired.
Farrell, William J. *s.j.* '52 (NY) [DD] New York, NY Murray-Weigel Hall.
Farrelly, John '46 (ATL) [L] Atlanta, GA Campus Ministry.
Farrelly, John *o.s.b.* '55 (WDC) [M] Washington, DC St. Anselm's Abbey.
Farrelly, John P. '84 (ATL) Carrollton, GA Church of Our Lady of Perpetual Help.
Farrelly, Matthew *c.s.sp.* '42 (NY) [2] New York, NY St. Agnes Church.
Farrelly, Peter T. *s.j.* '53 (BO) [W] Weston, MA Campion Health Center, Inc.
Farrelly, Msgr. Terence J. '50 (ORL) Rockledge, FL St. Mary's Church; Retired.
Farrelly, Thomas '61 (NY) [134] Bronx, NY Blessed Sacrament Church.
Farren, Edward J. *s.j.* '62 (PH) [AA] Philadelphia, PA Jesuit Community at St. Joseph's University.
Farren, John Aquinas *o.p.* '64 (NY) [DD] New York, NY St. Vincent Ferrer Priory.
Farren, Paul (WDC) Lanham, MD St. Matthias Church.
Farrera, Rafael *s.m.* '70 (ELP) [11] El Paso, TX La Purisima Church.
Farricker, William J. *s.j.* '43 (NY) [DD] New York, NY Murray-Weigel Hall.
Farris, Daniel L. '67 (SFE) [19] Albuquerque, NM Santuario San Martin de Porres Church.
Farris, James M. '76 (ORG) Inactive Leave.
Farris, John V. *c.m.* '49 (STL) [P] St. Louis, MO Vincentian Bellerive Residence.
Farris, Msgr. Semaan '54 (ORL) Retired.
Farris, William J. *o.f.m.* '77 (IND) Batesville, IN St. Louis Church; St. Peter, IN St. Peter Church.
Farrow, Raphael G. (FRS) Goshen, CA St. Thomas the Apostle Church.
Farrow, Raphael G. '85 (FRS) Visalia, CA Holy Family Church.
Farrugia, David *o.p.* (SB) Chino Hills, CA St. Paul the Apostle Church.
Farrugia, Edwin W. '60 (SFR) [15] San Francisco, CA St. Elizabeth Church.
Farry, John A. '65 (CHI) [204] Chicago, IL St. Thomas Apostle Church.
Farry, John J. '67 (PH) [87] Philadelphia, PA St. Leo Church.
Farsaci, Francis A. *o.s.a.* '64 (PH) [C] Villanova, PA Villanova University; [AA] Villanova, PA St. Thomas Monastery.
Farwell, Richard B. '81 (CHL) Lincolnton, NC St. Dorothy Church.
Fary, Francis Solanus *o.f.m.cap.* '67 (FgM) Capuchin Foreign Missions.
Fasano, Jerome W. '77 (ARL) Clifton, VA St. Andrew the Apostle Church.
Faschan, Matthew '46 (BR) Retired.
Fasching, Felix J. '45 (NU) Regal, MN St. Anthony (Mission) Church; Spicer, MN Our Lady of the Lakes Church.
Fasching, Jeffery A. '97 (WCH) [3] Wichita, KS Blessed Sacrament Church.
Fasciglione, Max S. '74 (CAM) Cape May Court House, NJ Our Lady of the Angels Church.
Fasline, Anthony '62 (Y) Retired.
Faso, Charles '67 (CHI) [N] Chicago, IL St. Peter's Friary.
Fassbender, Anthony D. *c.m.* '38 (NO) [P] New Orleans, LA Vincentian Fathers.
Fassbinder, Richard W. '53 (CHI) Lake Villa, IL Prince of Peace Church; Retired.
Fassero, Jonathan *o.s.b.* '78 (IND) [B] St. Meinrad, IN St. Meinrad Seminary-College of Liberal Arts; [J] St. Meinrad, IN St. Meinrad Archabbey.
Fassett, Edward S. *s.j.* '88 (SFR) [E] San Francisco, CA St. Ignatius College Preparatory (Coed); [N] San Francisco, CA Jesuit Community at St. Ignatius College Preparatory.
Fata, Joseph A. '68 (Y) Boardman, OH St. Luke Church.
Fater, Douglas '70 (SAT) [10] San Antonio, TX Holy Trinity Church.
Fath, Gerald *o.p.* '71 (NO) [P] New Orleans, LA Dominican Fathers & Brothers, Southern Dominican Province.
Fath, Howard *m.s.c.* '61 (FgM) Missionaries of the Sacred Heart Foreign Missions.
Fath, Howard *m.s.c.* '61 (RCK) [H] Aurora, IL Missionaries of the Sacred Heart Community.
Fath, Robert *c.m.f.* '79 (CHI) [N] Chicago, IL Claretian Missionaries, St. Jude League, Inc.; [N] Oak Park, IL Claretian Fathers Headquarters of U.S.A. Eastern Province.
Fatooh, Charles G. '85 (MRY) Seaside, CA St. Francis Xavier Church; Special Assignment.
Fatora, Joachim R. *o.s.b.* '54 (ALT) Hastings, PA St. Bernard Church.
Faucher, Eugene J. (CHI) Morton Grove, IL St. Martha Church.
Faucher, Eugene J. '51 (CHI) Arlington Heights, IL St. Edna Church; Retired.
Faucher, Henry L. '52 (SR) Cloverdale, CA St. Peter's Church.
Faucher, W. Thomas '71 (B) On Duty Outside the Diocese.
Faucher, W. Thomas '71 (BAK) Sisters, OR St. Edward Church.
Faugno, Valerian *o.f.m.* (BO) [W] Brighton, MA St. Bonaventure Friary, Franciscan Friars.
Faul, Charles '80 (RIC) [1] Virginia Beach, VA Church of the Ascension; [2] Virginia Beach, VA Church of the Holy Apostles.
Faulhaber, Gregory *s.t.d.* '79 (BUF) [A] East Aurora, NY Christ the King Seminary; [A] East Aurora, NY Christ the King Seminary.
Faulkner, Matthew *o.carm.* '89 (NY) [97] New York, NY Our Lady of the Scapular/St. Stephen Church.
Faulstich, Paul J. *s.j.* '68 (CHI) [D] Wilmette, IL Loyola Academy.
Fauser, Arthur W. '50 (DET) Farmington, MI Our Lady of Sorrows Church; Retired.
Faust, Gary J. '78 (STL) Richmond Heights, MO Immacolata Church.
Faust, Louis J. '74 (WDC) Baden, MD St. Michael Church.
Faust, William (RNO) [B] Reno, NV St. Mary's Regional Medical Center.
Faustina, John '47 (PHX) Prescott, AZ Sacred Heart Church.
Faustina, John M. '47 (PHX) Retired.
Faustner, William J. '76 (COL) Kenton, OH Immaculate Conception Church.
Fausz, Kevin P. *c.m.* '91 (STL) Perryville, MO St. Vincent De Paul Church; Silver Lake, MO St. Rose of Lima Church; [W] St. Louis, MO St. Vincent de Paul Educational Foundation.
Favara, Joseph F. '41 (SAG) Retired.
Favreau, Bruce T. '80 (OG) Essex, NY St. Joseph Church; Willsboro, NY St. Philip of Jesus Church.
Favret, J. Raymond '48 (CIN) West Chester, OH St. John Church; Retired.
Fawcett, Brian C. '97 (RC) [2] Rapid City, SD Blessed Sacrament Church.
Fawcett, Msgr. Henry F. '64 (SD) [13] San Diego, CA Our Lady of Mt. Carmel Church.
Fawls, Daniel J. '97 (BUF) Harris Hill, NY Nativity of the Blessed Virgin Mary Church.
Faxen, David *m.s.c.* '67 (RCK) [H] Aurora, IL Missionaries of the Sacred Heart Community.
Fay, David E. '64 (CIN) [29] Cincinnati, OH St. Gabriel Church.
Fay, Edmund Gregory *o.p.* '53 (MIA) [2] Miami Beach, FL St. Joseph Church.
Fay, Gregory J. '76 (STA) Switzerland, FL San Juan Del Rio Church.
Fay, John F. *m.m.* '52 (NY) [DD] Maryknoll, NY Maryknoll Fathers and Brothers.
Fay, Michael Jude '78 (BGP) Darien, CT St. John Church.
Fay, Robert D. '67 (BO) Health Leave.
Fay, William J. '64 (GBG) [A] Latrobe, PA St. Vincent Seminary.
Fay, William J. '64 (PIT) On Duty Outside the Diocese.
Fay, Msgr. William P. '74 (BO) On Duty Outside the Archdiocese.
Fayad, Samuel *c.s.s.* '48 (BO) [Z] Waltham, MA Stigmatine Fathers and Brothers.
Fayle, Vaughn *o.m.i.* '87 (SAT) [M] San Antonio, TX De Mazenod House.
Fayle, Vaughn J. *o.m.i.* '87 (SAT) [C] San Antonio, TX Oblate School of Theology.
Fazio, Carmine *o.f.m.cap.* '75 (NY) [B] Beacon, NY St. Lawrence of Brindisi Friary.
Fazio, Cosimo '48 (NY) [3] New Rochelle, NY St. Joseph Church.
Fazio, Paul *o.f.m.conv.* '74 (OAK) San Pablo, CA St. Paul Church; [N] San Pablo, CA Franciscans, Conventual of California.
Fazzalaro, Msgr. Francis J. '45 (MIA) [5] Pompano Beach, FL St. Gabriel Church.
Fealey, Edward J. '86 (CHI) Western Springs, IL St. John of the Cross Church.
Feccia, Augusto *c.s.* '62 (LA) [Q] Sun Valley, CA Villa Scalabrini.
Fecher, Msgr. Vincent '50 (SAT) Hondo, TX St. John the Evangelist Church.
Fechner, Erich A. '92 (STL) Cottleville, MO St. Joseph Church.
Fecht, Geoffrey *o.s.b.* '76 (SCL) [I] Collegeville, MN St. John's Abbey, of the Order of St. Benedict.
Fecko, Leonard '89 (CIN) [Q] Cincinnati, OH University of Cincinnati Newman Center.
Fecko, Leonard J. '89 (CIN) [65] Cincinnati, OH St. Monica-St. George Parish Newman Center Church.
Fecteau, Raymond L. '72 (WDC) Darnestown, MD Our Lady of the Visitation Church.
Fedders, Albert V. *m.m.* '37 (FgM) Maryknoll Foreign Missions.
Fedders, Albert V. *m.m.* '37 (NY) [DD] Maryknoll, NY Maryknoll Fathers and Brothers.
Fedders, William '68 (LEX) [L] Morehead, KY Catholic Student Center-Morehead State University.
Fedders, William J. '68 (LEX) Morehead, KY Church of Jesus Our Savior.
Feddish, Msgr. Basil '31 (STF) Retired.
Fedell, Anthony *o.f.m.* '66 (NY) [35] New York, NY St. Francis of Assisi Church.
Federici, Martin J. '66 (BGP) Leave of Absence.
Federico, Cesidio J. '57 (WH) Clarksburg, WV Immaculate Conception Church.
Federico, Ralph P. '52 (BUF) Retired.
Federline, Thomas A. '85 (GBG) Brady's Bend, PA St. Patrick Church; Parker, PA St. Mary, Our Lady of the Snows Church.
Fedewa, Eugene F. '36 (DET) Harper Woods, MI Our Lady Queen of Peace Church; Retired.
Fedewa, Matthew J. '58 (LAN) Morrice, MI St. Mary Church.
Fedewa, Sylvester L. '54 (LAN) [6] Lansing, MI St. Gerard Church.
Fedigan, F. Terrence '74 (PIT) South Park Township, PA Nativity Church.
Fedigan, James J. *s.j.* '65 (NY) [DD] New York, NY Murray-Weigel Hall.
Fedor, Gregory '83 (Y) Boardman, OH St. Luke Church; [C] Youngstown, OH Cardinal Mooney High School.
Fedor, Lawrence M. *o.s.b.* '76 (TUC) [F] St. David, AZ Holy Trinity Monastery.
Fedor, Mark Q. '72 (CLV) [13] Cleveland, OH St. Boniface Church.
Fedor, Robert P. '61 (E) Conneautville, PA St. Peter Church.

Fedora, Joseph *m.m.* '84 (FgM) Maryknoll Foreign Missions.
Fedora, Joseph *m.m.* '84 (NY) [DD] Maryknoll, NY Maryknoll Fathers and Brothers; [DD] Maryknoll, NY Maryknoll Fathers and Brothers.
Fedorek, Msgr. Joseph J. '53 (PHU) Elizabeth, NJ St. Vladimir's Church.
Fedorowich, Msgr. Michael '55 (PHU) Shamokin, PA Transfiguration of Our Lord Church.
Fedyk, Msgr. Jaroslaw (SJP) Retired.
Fee, Msgr. John B. '37 (PH) [23] Philadelphia, PA St. Bernard Church; Retired.
Fee, John M. *ss.cc.* '56 (DET) Harper Woods, MI Our Lady Queen of Peace Church.
Fee, Pat '61 (ORG) Absent on Sick Leave.
Fee, Msgr. Paul A. '40 (BEA) Retired.
Feehan, Kenneth *s.v.d.* '59 (FgM) Society of the Divine Word Foreign Missions.
Feehan, Stephen S. '62 (NEW) Bloomfield, NJ Church of St. Thomas the Apostle.
Feehily, John W. '73 (OKL) Moore, OK St. Andrew's Church.
Feela, Paul F. '78 (STP) [A] St. Paul, MN The Saint Paul Seminary; [C] St. Paul, MN University of St. Thomas.
Feeley, Michael J. *s.m.a.* '41 (BO) [W] Dedham, MA African Mission House.
Feeley, Sylvester E. *c.ss.r.* '48 (BRK) [107] Brooklyn, NY Our Lady of Perpetual Help Basilica Church.
Feeley, Thomas M. *c.s.c.* '55 (FR) [A] North Easton, MA Stonehill College; [A] North Easton, MA Holy Cross Fathers Religious; [O] Norton, MA Wheaton College Newman Center.
Feely, Msgr. James B. '58 (GB) [6] Green Bay, WI St. John Church.
Feely, Thomas H. *s.j.* '75 (NY) [F] New York, NY Regis High School; [DD] New York, NY St. Ignatius Loyola Residence.
Feenan, Msgr. J. Francis '53 (PAT) Convent Station, NJ St. Thomas More Church.
Feeney, Bernard (PAT) Retired.
Feeney, Edward '37 (E) [13] Erie, PA St. Ann Church.
Feeney, Francis M. '33 (ROC) Penfield, NY Holy Spirit Church; Retired.
Feeney, J. Edward '37 (E) Retired.
Feeney, John J. '54 (PRT) Retired.
Feeney, John J. '55 (LA) Retired.
Feeney, John P. '52 (GB) Retired.
Feeney, Joseph J. *s.j.* '65 (PH) [C] Philadelphia, PA St. Joseph's University; [AA] Philadelphia, PA Jesuit Community at St. Joseph's University; [AA] Philadelphia, PA St. Alphonsus House.
Feeney, Kevin J. '77 (CHI) [196] Chicago, IL St. Sylvester Church.
Feeney, Msgr. Leo J. '66 (DAV) [M] Davenport, IA St. Vincent Center.
Feeney, Michael *o.s.b.* '46 (SEA) [G] Tacoma, WA St. Joseph Medical Center; [M] Lacey, WA St. Martin's Abbey.
Feeney, Michael *o.f.m.* '48 (BO) [BB] Boston, MA St. Anthony Shrine.
Feeney, Robert E. '56 (BIS) Mandan, ND St. Joseph Church.
Feeney, Robert E. '56 (GBG) Ford City, PA Holy Trinity Church.
Feeney, Robert T. '86 (PH) [124] Philadelphia, PA Our Lady of Mt. Carmel Church.
Feeney, Thomas '79 (CC) Refugio, TX Our Lady of Refuge Church.
Feeney, Thomas M. '48 (PH) Retired.
Feeney, Thomas P. '79 (CC) Refugio, TX St. James the Apostle Church.
Feeney, William P. '72 (PIT) Monongahela, PA Transfiguration Church.
Feeser, William '77 (SAC) [7] Sacramento, CA Presentation of the Blessed Virgin Mary Church.
Fegan, William P. '75 (CHI) Berwyn, IL St. Odilo Church.
Fehlner, Peter Damian M. *f.f.i.* '57 (FR) [J] New Bedford, MA Marian Friary of Our Lady, Queen of the Seraphic Order.
Fehn, Jerome W. '78 (STP) Edina, MN Our Lady of Grace Church; Edina, MN Fairview-Southdale Hospital; St. Louis Park, MN Methodist Hospital.
Fehrenbach, Charles (ALB) [L] Saratoga Springs, NY St. John Neumann Residence.
Fehrenbach, Charles G. *c.ss.r.* '35 (PH) [135] Philadelphia, PA St. Peter the Apostle Church.
Fehrenbach, James *o.f.m.* '71 (CIN) [M] Cincinnati, OH St. Francis Seraph Friary.
Fehrenbach, James *o.f.m.* '71 (FgM) Franciscan Foreign Missions.
Fehring, Fabian *o.f.m.cap.* '53 (GF) Hardin, MT St. Joseph's Church.
Feicht, Donald L. '70 (Y) Alliance, OH St. Joseph's Church.
Feichter, Paul *o.f.m.* '47 (SP) [O] St. Petersburg, FL St. Anthony Friary.
Feierfeil, Gerald F. '67 (SC) Boone, IA Sacred Heart Church.
Feigh, Conan E. *o.s.b.* '57 (ALT) [I] University Park, PA Penn State Catholic Community.
Feil, Carl *o.s.m.* '61 (SFE) Tome, NM Immaculate Conception Church.
Feil, Carl M. *o.s.m.* '61 (CHI) [N] Chicago, IL Servite Friars - Eastern Province.
Feild, Martin Eugene '59 (BAL) Taneytown, MD St. Joseph Church.
Feiss, Hugh *o.s.b.* '66 (B) [C] Jerome, ID Ascension Priory.
Feiss, Hugh *o.s.b.* '66 (P) [L] St. Benedict, OR Mt. Angel Abbey.
Feit, Matthias '56 (PHX) Retired.
Feiten, Msgr. J. Richard '48 (WIN) [F] Winona, MN St. Anne Hospice, Inc.
Fekete, George J. '65 (GR) Lowell, MI St. Mary's Church; On Special Assignment.
Feketie, Michael J. '57 (NEW) Rahway, NJ St. Mary's Church.
Felago, John F. *m.m.* '68 (FgM) Maryknoll Foreign Missions.
Felczak, Leonard J. '44 (CHI) [198] Chicago, IL St. Tarcissus Church; Retired.
Feld, Norbert F. *s.s.c.* '49 (PRO) [P] Bristol, RI St. Columban's Retirement House.
Feldbrugge, Theo M. *m.h.m.* '54 (LA) [R] Los Angeles, CA Mill Hill Missionaries Procure.
Feldcamp, William J. '65 (SCR) Carbondale, PA St. Rose of Lima Church.
Feldhaus, Msgr. Eugene A. '46 (BRK) [172] Queens, NY St. Gerard Majella Church; Retired.
Feldhaus, Thomas F. '76 (CIN) Ripley, OH St. Michael Church.
Feldkamp, Angelo J. *o.praem.* '68 (GB) [I] De Pere, WI St. Norbert Abbey.
Feldman, George J. *o.praem.* '43 (GB) [I] De Pere, WI St. Joseph Priory.
Feldmann, Jerome W. '58 (BEL) Retired.
Feldmeier, Peter E. '87 (STP) [A] St. Paul, MN The Saint Paul Seminary; [C] St. Paul, MN University of St. Thomas.
Feldmeier, Russell J. *m.m.* '80 (FgM) Maryknoll Foreign Missions.
Felice, John M. *o.f.m.* '68 (NY) [35] New York, NY St. Francis of Assisi Church; [DD] New York, NY Franciscan Friars, Order of Friars Minor, Holy Name Province; [HH] New York, NY Shrine of St. Jude, Inc.
Felice-Pace, Albert *o.p.* '60 (TUC) [I] Tucson, AZ University of Arizona.
Felices, Fernando '82 (SJN) [C] San Juan, PR Seminario Mayor Regional San Juan Bautista.
Felion, Jerome '47 (BWN) [2] Harlingen, TX Immaculate Heart of Mary Church.
Felion, Jerome '47 (CR) Retired.
Felix, Bernard '37 (CIN) [L] Cincinnati, OH St. Margaret Hall.
Felix, Bernard J. '37 (CIN) Retired.
Felix, Paul G. '90 (GAL) Navasota, TX Christ Our Light Church.
Felix, William P. '81 (LC) Chippewa Falls, WI St. Charles Borromeo Church; Cooks Valley, WI St. John the Baptist Church; Tilden, WI St. Peter Church; [N] Tilden, WI Institute of St. Joseph.
Feliz, Normando '75 (VEN) LaBelle, FL Our Lady Queen of Heaven Church.
Felker, Joseph F. '73 (SB) Redlands, CA Sacred Heart Church.
Fell, Gall *o.s.b.* '33 (SCL) [I] Collegeville, MN St. John's Abbey, of the Order of St. Benedict.
Fell, John N. '88 (MET) Whitehouse Station, NJ Our Lady of Lourdes Church.
Fellenz, Ralph *o.f.m.cap.* '68 (FgM) Capuchin Foreign Missions.
Feller, Donald J. '46 (GB) Retired.
Feller, Richard J. '53 (CHI) South Holland, IL Holy Ghost Church; Retired.
Fellin, Joseph H. *c.s.s.* '45 (SPR) [3] Pittsfield, MA Our Lady of Mt. Carmel Church.
Fellner, Msgr. John V. '49 (BEL) Retired.
Fellrath, Frank W. '89 (MET) Fords, NJ Our Lady of Peace Church.
Felt, James W. *s.j.* '56 (SJ) [B] Santa Clara, CA Santa Clara University.
Felt, Richard '69 (PHX) [3] Scottsdale, AZ St. Bernadette Church.
Felten, John N. *s.j.* '52 (CIN) [M] Cincinnati, OH Faber Jesuit Community.
Felter, Francis J. *m.m.* '69 (FgM) Maryknoll Foreign Missions.
Feltis, Jerome '79 (FAR) Absent on Leave.
Feltman, Harold R. '55 (GR) Retired.
Feltman, Philip S. '66 (TOL) Sandusky, OH St. Mary Church.
Felton, Daniel J. '81 (GB) [7] Oshkosh, WI St. Raphael Church.
Feltz, John G. '73 (BUR) Fairfax, VT St. Luke Church.
Feltz, Joseph E. '79 (PIT) Monongahela, PA St. Anthony Church.
Feltz, Thomas F. '85 (LA) Bellflower, CA St. Bernard Church.
Femenia, Nicholas '25 (SAN) Retired.
Femenia, Nicholas '25 (SAT) Retired.
Feminelli, John '87 (CC) On Special Assignment.
Feminelli, John J. '87 (CC) Tivoli, TX Our Lady of Guadalupe Church.
Femmineo, Joseph P. '58 (DET) Retired.
Fenech, Francis '50 (PMB) Retired.
Fenech, Francis X. '50 (PMB) Lake Worth, FL Sacred Heart Church.
Fenelon, David (DM) Retired.
Fenger, Guy '77 (MIA) Sunrise, FL All Saints Church; [C] Fort Lauderdale, FL St. Thomas Aquinas High School.
Fenili, J. Robert *c.ss.r.* '62 (DEN) [M] Denver, CO The Redemptorists/Denver Province.
Fenlon, John (SY) [W] Cortland, NY St. Mary.
Fenlon, John P. '70 (SY) Cortland, NY St. Mary Church.
Fenlon, Thomas B. '61 (NY) [89] New York, NY Our Lady of Lourdes Church.
Fenlon, Thomas J. '42 (HEL) Retired.
Fennell, Joseph G. *s.j.* '45 (BO) [W] Weston, MA Campion Health Center, Inc.
Fennell, Patrick A. *o.s.b.* '89 (PEO) [A] Peru, IL St. Bede Abbey and Academy.
Fenner, Charles J. *c.s.sp.* '54 (PIT) [B] Pittsburgh, PA Duquesne University of the Holy Ghost.
Fenner, Eric *o.f.m.conv.* '46 (TR) Seaside Park, NJ St. Catharine of Siena Church.
Fennessey, Luke T. '42 (SPR) Retired.
Fennessy, James J. '68 (ATL) Lilburn, GA St. John Neumann Church.
Fennessy, Joseph H. '56 (HBG) Berwick, PA Immaculate Conception of the Blessed Virgin Mary Church.
Fennessy, Peter *s.j.* '70 (CLV) [C] Cleveland, OH John Carroll University.
Fennessy, Peter J. *s.j.* '70 (BO) [W] Boston, MA The Society of Jesus of New England-Provincial Offices.
Fennessy, Peter J. *s.j.* '70 (CLV) [C] Cleveland, OH John Carroll Jesuit Community.
Fenske, Donald J. '58 (CHI) Calumet City, IL Our Lady of Knock Church.
Fenton, Cornelius *c.pp.s.* '49 (CIN) [B] Carthagena, OH St. Charles.
Fenton, Joseph D. *s.m.* '72 (WDC) [M] Washington, DC Marist Provincial House.
Fenton, Lawrence E. '63 (GI) On Duty Outside the Diocese.
Fenton, Norman H. *o.p.* '62 (WDC) [B] Washington, DC Dominican House of Studies.
Fenton, Patrick J. *s.s.s.* '50 (CLV) [P] Cleveland, OH Blessed Sacrament Community.
Fenton, William *o.c.d.* '48 (LA) Alhambra, CA St. Therese Church.
Fenzl, Roderick R. *o.praem.* '55 (GB) [I] De Pere, WI St. Norbert Abbey.
Ferenczy, George *o.cist.* '44 (DAL) [M] Irving, TX Cistercian Abbey of Our Lady of Dallas.
Ferens, Boniface D. (BUF) [39] Buffalo, NY St. John Kanty Church.
Ferens, Joseph F. '53 (DET) Retired.
Feret, Francis S. '62 (PH) [2] Philadelphia, PA St. Adalbert Church.
Fergus, Edward L. *s.j.* '53 (DET) [P] Clarkston, MI Colombiere Center.
Fergus, Kieran *o.p.* '65 (MET) [H] New Brunswick, NJ De Porres House; [M] New Brunswick, NJ Catholic Center at Rutgers University.
Ferguson, Carlos '77 (GAL) Retired.
Ferguson, Gary M. '71 (TOL) Archbold, OH St. Peter Church; Stryker, OH St. John the Evangelist Church.
Ferguson, James A. '85 (ALX) Marksville, LA St. Joseph's Church.
Ferguson, James J. *c.s.c.* '65 (FgM) Holy Cross Foreign Missions.
Ferguson, John *s.j.* '54 (SLC) [4] Ogden, UT St. Mary's Church.
Ferguson, Peter A. (GAL) Hitchcock, TX Our Lady of Lourdes Church.
Ferguson, Ronald J. *s.j.* '65 (CHI) [C] Chicago, IL Jesuit Community at Loyola University of Chicago.
Ferguson, Thomas P. '94 (ARL) On Duty Outside the Diocese.
Ferhatian, Basil *c.m.vd.* '32 (ARM) Los Angeles, CA Our Lady Queen of Martyrs Church.
Ferhatian, Basil *c.m.vd.* '32 (LA) [30] Los Angeles, CA Our Lady Queen of Martyrs Church.
Ferland, Martin '95 (RC) [B] Bethlehem, SD Holy Nativity Monastery.
Ferland, Martin *o.mar.* '95 (SAM) [C] Petersham, MA Most Holy Trinity Monastery.
Ferland, Msgr. Oscar R. '44 (PRO) Retired.
Ferland, Thomas J. '87 (PRO) Bristol, RI St. Elizabeth Church.
Ferlisi, Paschal A. *o.s.b.* '71 (BIR) [16] Birmingham, AL Our Lady of Sorrows Church; [E] Cullman, AL St. Bernard Abbey.
Ferlita, Ernest *s.j.* '62 (NO) [C] New Orleans, LA Loyola University.
Fernan, Matthew '89 (NY) [E] New York, NY Cardinal Hayes High School.
Fernandes, Babasino '75 (FTW) Monroeville, IN St. Rose of Lima Church.
Fernandes, David A. '97 (PH) Collingdale, PA St.

Joseph Church.
Fernandes, Herondi *s.x.* '76 (FgM) Xaverian Foreign Missions.
Fernandes, Herondi *s.x.* '76 (PAT) [M] Wayne, NJ Xaverian Missionary Fathers.
Fernandes, John '77 (OAK) [8] Oakland, CA St. Cyril Church.
Fernandes, Jose Manuel '66 (NEW) [15] Elizabeth, NJ Our Lady of Fatima Church.
Fernandes, Lucian '67 (RVC) East Islip, NY St. Mary's Church.
Fernandes, Mauro de Souza *o.s.b.* '84 (GBG) [H] Latrobe, PA Saint Vincent Archabbey.
Fernandes, Patrick O. (BUF) Jamestown, NY St. James Church.
Fernandes, Rogue '69 (LA) Azusa, CA St. Frances of Rome Church.
Fernandes, Roque '64 (LSC) [5] Las Cruces, NM St. Genevieve Church.
Fernandes, Stephen A. '76 (FR) [20] Fall River, MA SS. Peter and Paul Church.
Fernandes, Sydney '79 (HON) Kahuku, HI St. Roch Church.
Fernandez, Cesar A. '95 (LA) Norwalk, CA St. John of God Church.
Fernandez, Daniel '95 (ARE) On Duty Outside the Diocese.
Fernandez, Edward P. '70 (DAL) Retired.
Fernandez, Elias *c.ss.t.* '69 (ARE) Isabela, PR Our Lady of Mount Carmel Church.
Fernandez, Emmanuel '79 (LAF) Lydia, LA St. Nicholas Church.
Fernandez, Epifanio *o.ss.t.* '59 (SJN) [13] Bayamon, PR Ascension Del Senor Church.
Fernandez, Fausto '61 (MIA) Absent on Leave.
Fernandez, Felipe *o.s.a.* '71 (SJN) [42] San Juan, PR Ntra. Sra. de la Monserrate Church.
Fernandez, Fernando '90 (NY) [53] New York, NY Incarnation Church.
Fernandez, Fidel *o.de.m.* (SJN) [40] San Juan, PR Nuestra Senora de la Merced Church.
Fernandez, Fidel *o.m.* '74 (CGS) Cayey, PR Nuestra Senora de la Asuncion Church.
Fernandez, Francisco X. *o.f.m.cap.* '58 (FWT) [5] Fort Worth, TX Immaculate Heart of Mary Church.
Fernandez, Frank '79 (PHX) [15] Phoenix, AZ St. Joseph Church.
Fernandez, Gustavo *s.j.* '67 (FgM) Provinces.
Fernandez, Isidro '40 (CGS) [C] Aibonito, PR Casa Salesiana de Retiros.
Fernandez, Joaquin *s.m.* '68 (FgM) Marist Foreign Missions.
Fernandez, Jose *o.p.* '53 (PCE) Yauco, PR Holy Rossary Church.
Fernandez, Jose A. '60 (BGP) Retired.
Fernandez, Jose Luis *o.ss.t.* '69 (PCE) [10] Ponce, PR La Santisima Trinidad Church.
Fernandez, Jose Maria '59 (GAL) [20] Houston, TX Christ the King Church.
Fernandez, Luis J. '71 (NO) On Duty Outside the Archdiocese.
Fernandez, Msgr. Manuel '59 (TR) [3] Long Branch, NJ St. John the Baptist Church.
Fernandez, Manuel *s.d.b.* '69 (LA) Bellflower, CA St. Dominic Savio Church.
Fernandez, Manuel A. '62 (ORL) Eustis, FL St. Mary of the Lakes Church.
Fernandez, Marcellus '68 (B) [2] Boise, ID St. Mark's Church.
Fernandez, Marcellus '68 (STA) On Duty Outside the Diocese.
Fernandez, Michael *c.m.f.* '53 (CHI) [149] Chicago, IL Our Lady of Guadalupe Church.
Fernandez, Miguel A. '50 (MIA) Retired.
Fernandez, Nelson '56 (MIA) Retired.
Fernandez, Nobincio '65 (HON) Kalaupapa, HI St. Francis Church; [G] Kalaupapa, Molokai, HI Kalaupapa Settlement; [H] Kaneohe, HI Sacred Hearts Center.
Fernandez, Msgr. Orlando '49 (MIA) Retired.
Fernandez, Rafael *o.f.m.* '87 (FgM) Franciscan Foreign Missions.
Fernandez, Serapio '50 (ARE) [5] Arecibo, PR Church of Christ the King.
Fernandez, Serapio *o.f.m.* '50 (PCE) [B] Ponce, PR The Pontifical Catholic University of Puerto Rico.
Fernandez, Severiano *o.s.a.* '64 (BEA) Vidor, TX Our Lady of Lourdes Church.
Fernandez, Vicente '82 (SJN) [5] Guaynabo, PR Maria Madre de la Misericordia Church.
Fernandez Cartagena, Elias '88 (PCE) On Duty Outside the Diocese.
Fernando, A. Thomas '62 (KAL) [D] Kalamazoo, MI Borgess Medical Center.
Fernando, A. Thomas '66 (KAL) [1] Kalamazoo, MI St. Augustine Cathedral.
Fernando, Augustine '64 (RVC) Elmont, NY St. Vincent de Paul Church.
Fernando, Bernard '65 (NEW) Hackensack, NJ Hackensack Medical Center.
Fernando, Calixtus (WDC) [B] Washington, DC Oblate College/Oblate Center for Mission Studies.
Fernando, Damian '70 (LA) San Pedro, CA Holy Trinity Church.
Fernando, Gamini E. '71 (NY) [3] Poughkeepsie, NY Holy Trinity Church.
Fernando, Gamini E. '72 (NY) State, NY Green Haven Correctional Facility.
Fernando, Joachim '62 (BRK) [228] Queens, NY St. Pius X Church.
Fernando, Polycarp '78 (FTW) [3] Fort Wayne, IN St. Charles Borromeo Church.
Fernando, Simon '60 (RVC) Commack, NY Christ the King Church.
Fernando, Stanley (CHI) [J] Des Plaines, IL Holy Family Medical Center.
Fernando, Susil (TYL) Athens, TX St. Edward Church.
Fernando, Venantius M. '61 (NEW) [4] Irvington, NJ St. Paul the Apostle Church.
Fernando, Walter '73 (LA) Pasadena, CA Assumption of the Blessed Virgin Mary Church.
Fernando, Wellington *s.j.* '89 (BO) [W] Chestnut Hill, MA The Jesuit Community at Boston College.
Fernz, John (BO) Wrentham, MA Wrentham State School.
Fernz, John E. '62 (BO) Wrentham, MA St. Mary Church.
Ferone, John M. *s.j.* '83 (CIN) [M] Cincinnati, OH Faber Jesuit Community.
Ferracino, Placido *o.m.v.* '86 (BO) [B] Boston, MA Oblate Provincialate.
Ferraioli, Msgr. Frank B. '61 (PAT) Parsippany, NJ St. Christopher Church.
Ferraioli, Joseph *o.m.i.* '77 (MIA) Opa Locka, FL St. Monica Church.
Ferran, Michael *i.c.* '43 (SP) Seminole, FL Blessed Sacrament Church.
Ferrante, Frank J. *c.m.f.* '70 (LA) [R] Los Angeles, CA Claretian Retreat Center Community; [X] Los Angeles, CA Claretian Retreat Center (All Groups).
Ferrante, Msgr. Joseph L. '74 (TR) [12] Trenton, NJ St. Anthony Church.
Ferrara, Angelus P. *o.s.p.p.e.* '90 (PH) [AA] Doylestown, PA Pauline Fathers Monastery, Shrine of Our Lady of Czestochowa.
Ferrara, Bede *o.f.m.* '50 (BO) [W] Lynn, MA Franciscan Community (Province of Immaculate Conception).
Ferrara, Charles F. *s.j.* '90 (STL) [P] St. Louis, MO De Smet Jesuit High School Community.
Ferrara, Francis '53 (SP) Spring Hill, FL St. Theresa Church.
Ferrara, John *o.m.v.* '82 (BO) [B] Boston, MA Oblate Provincialate.
Ferrara, Joseph J. '42 (SCR) [4] Hazleton, PA Holy Trinity Church; Retired.
Ferrara, Joseph R. '77 (CAM) Hammonton, NJ St. Martin de Porres Church; Woodstown, NJ St. Joseph's Church.
Ferrara, Pasquale '37 (DAV) [L] Davenport, IA Kahl Home for the Aged and Infirm.
Ferrara, Pasquale L. '37 (DAV) Retired.
Ferrarese, Fernando A. *m.div.* '77 (BRK) [13] Brooklyn, NY St. Athanasius Church.
Ferrari, Steven A. '80 (BRK) [73] Brooklyn, NY St. Laurence Church.
Ferraro, Joseph '90 (NEW) Maplewood, NJ St. Joseph's Church.
Ferraro, Michael M. '68 (BO) [4] Lynn, MA St. Mary Church.
Ferraro, Patrick B. '92 (Y) [11] Youngstown, OH St. Christine's Church.
Ferraro, Romano J. '60 (BRK) Absent on Leave; [U] Jamaica, NY Parsons Manor.
Ferraro, Ronald A. '60 (HRT) [5] Waterbury, CT Our Lady of Lourdes Church.
Ferraro, Vincent J. '70 (BUF) [1] Kenmore, NY St. Andrew Church; [K] Kenmore, NY Kenmore Mercy Hospital.
Ferrazoli, Henry R. '61 (NEW) Retired.
Ferre, Antonio '53 (PCE) [17] Ponce, PR Our Lady of Mt. Carmel Church.
Ferreira, Alfonse *o.f.m.* '72 (BO) [W] Lynn, MA Franciscan Community (Province of Immaculate Conception); [W] Lynn, MA Franciscan Community (Province of Immaculate Conception).
Ferreira, Jose S. (BO) [1] Cambridge, MA St. Anthony Church.
Ferreira, Manuel P. '60 (FR) [5] Taunton, MA St. Anthony's Church.
Ferrence, John J. *o.s.a.* '52 (PH) [D] Drexel Hill, PA Monsignor Bonner High School.
Ferrer, Anthony P. *t.o.r.* '56 (AUS) [2] Waco, TX St. Francis on the Brazos Church.
Ferrer, Charles M. '64 (CHI) [127] Chicago, IL St. Mary of the Angels Church; [W] Chicago, IL Midtown Center.
Ferrer, Gonzalo *t.o.r.* '81 (SHP) [B] Shreveport, LA Schumpert Medical Center.
Ferrer, Guillermo Casa *t.c.* '46 (BAL) Odenton, MD St. Joseph Church.
Ferrer, Jorge *s.j.* '77 (SJN) [22] San Juan, PR San Ignacio de Loyola Church.
Ferrer, Miguel '67 (SJN) [15] Carolina, PR Ntra. Sra. Reina de la Paz Church.
Ferrer, Miguel A. '67 (SJN) [16] Carolina, PR Ntra. Sra. Reina de los Angeles Church.
Ferrer, Peter C. '61 (LA) Encino, CA Our Lady of Grace Church.
Ferreras, Isidro Gonzales '64 (PCE) [B] Ponce, PR The Pontifical Catholic University of Puerto Rico.
Ferrero, Anthony T. '81 (SB) Chino, CA Our Lady of Guadalupe Church.
Ferrero, Bartolomeo Santino '60 (DET) [55] Detroit, MI Our Lady of Mt. Carmel Church.
Ferrett, Walter L. '66 (SCR) [24] Scranton, PA Sacred Hearts of Jesus and Mary Church.
Ferretti, Samuel J. '74 (SCR) Military Chaplains.
Ferrick, Mortimer A. *c.s.c.* '57 (FR) [J] North Dartmouth, MA Holy Cross Mission House.
Ferrick, Raymond J. '77 (PRO) [6] Cranston, RI St. Matthew Church.
Ferrick, Robert T. *s.j.* '57 (BO) [W] Weston, MA Campion Center.
Ferrie, Francis '65 (NO) [13] New Orleans, LA Incarnate Word Church.
Ferrier, Francis *s.j.* '61 (BR) [F] Baton Rouge, LA Our Lady of the Lake Regional Medical Center.
Ferrier, Francis V. *s.j.* '61 (BR) [20] Baton Rouge, LA Sacred Heart of Jesus Church.
Ferrier, Ronald J. '68 (PH) [BB] Philadelphia, PA Provincial House of the Sisters of the Holy Family of Nazareth.
Ferrigan, Robert E. '61 (CHI) Winnetka, IL Sacred Heart Church.
Ferrigno, Denis P. '50 (HRT) Retired.
Ferring, Msgr. Robert L. '50 (DUB) Retired.
Ferris, Carl A. '55 (GI) Retired.
Ferris, James *c.ss.r.* '35 (NY) [92] New York, NY Our Lady of Perpetual Help Church.
Ferris, James *c.s.s.r.* '50 (ALB) [L] Saratoga Springs, NY St. John Neumann Residence.
Ferris, Msgr. Norman J. '53 (SAM) Fall River, MA St. Anthony of the Desert Church.
Ferris, Thomas B. '63 (PIT) [70] Pittsburgh, PA St. Cyril of Alexandria Church.
Ferrito, Msgr. Joseph L. (PAT) Retired.
Ferro, Ralph '71 (RVC) Roosevelt, NY Queen of the Most Holy Rosary Church.
Ferro, Robert A. '73 (BRK) Absent on Leave.
Ferron, Joseph B. '45 (LC) Retired.
Ferruzzi, William *s.d.b.* (NEW) [N] South Orange, NJ The Salesian Community.
Ferruzzi, William '76 (NEW) [N] South Orange, NJ Salesian Residence.
Ferry, James '84 (FR) [3] Fall River, MA Espirito Santo Church.
Ferry, James T. *m.m.* '56 (FgM) Maryknoll Foreign Missions.
Fertal, Joseph *s.v.d.* '59 (SB) [A] Riverside, CA Divine Word Seminary.
Feser, Victor *o.s.b.* '64 (BIS) [A] Richardton, ND Assumption Abbey; [B] Bismarck, ND University of Mary.
Fessard, Gerald B. *j.c.l.* '72 (LA) On Special or Other (Arch)Diocesan Assignment.
Fessio, Joseph D. *s.j.* '72 (SFR) [N] San Francisco, CA Jesuit Community at University of San Francisco.
Fest, Donald M. *s.s.j.* '76 (BAL) [94] Baltimore, MD St. Veronica Church.
Festle, Robert H. (CHI) Retired.
Festle, Robert H. '55 (CHI) [X] Wilmette, IL Musica Pacis.
Fetcho, John E. '64 (SY) Lakeland, NY Our Lady of Peace Church.
Fete, Msgr. Joseph N. '74 (COL) [1] Columbus, OH St. Joseph Cathedral.
Fete, Kevin L. '85 (Y) Middlebranch, OH St. Therese Little Flower Church.
Fetscher, James F. '68 (MIA) [26] Miami, FL St. Louis Church.
Fetterer, Raymond A. '35 (MIL) Retired.
Fetters, Donald *c.s.c.* '76 (FgM) Holy Cross Foreign Missions.
Fetters, Donald G. *c.s.c.* '76 (OAK) [N] Berkeley, CA Holy Cross Fathers-Holy Cross Center.
Feucht, Urban *o.s.b.* '55 (SEA) [G] Olympia, WA Providence St. Peter Hospital; [M] Lacey, WA St. Martin's Abbey.
Feudjio, Jerome '90 (STV) [1] St. Thomas, VI Cathedral of Sts. Peter and Paul; [1] St. Thomas, VI Cathedral of Sts. Peter and Paul.
Feuerbacher, Edward F. '57 (STL) Affton, MO St. Dominic Savio Church.
Feusahrens, Frederick J. '72 (RIC) [15] Richmond, VA St. Paul Church.
Fewing, Ross '77 (SEA) Special Assignment; [Q] Seattle, WA Catholic Hospital Ministries.
Fey, Albert J. *c.pp.s.* '46 (KCK) Baileyville, KS Sacred Heart Church.
Fey, Christian *o.f.m.cap.* '45 (SAL) [D] Victoria, KS St. Fidelis Friary.
Fey, George *c.pp.s.* '43 (SAN) [4] San Angelo, TX St. Mary's Church.

Fey, Joseph *c.s.c.* (FTW) [G] Notre Dame, IN University Health Services; [J] Notre Dame, IN Holy Cross Community, Corby Hall, University of Notre Dame.
Fey, Thomas J. '70 (ALX) Military Chaplains.
Fey, William *o.f.m.cap.* '68 (FgM) Capuchin Foreign Missions.
Fiala, John *s.o.l.t.* (CC) [2] Beeville, TX Sacred Heart Mission Church.
Fiala, John *s.o.l.t.* '84 (CC) [1] Beeville, TX Our Lady of Victory Church.
Fiala, John M. '84 (OM) Absent on Leave.
Fiala, Tim '96 (CHI) La Grange, IL St. Cletus Church.
Fialkowski, Edward '78 (CHI) Niles, IL St. Isaac Jogues Church.
Fialkowski, Thomas M. '66 (E) [9] Erie, PA Our Lady of Mt. Carmel Church; Erie, PA Veterans Administration Hospital.
Fiano, Guy *o.carm.* '83 (PMB) [G] Boca Raton, FL St. Elias Priory-Order of Carmelites, NY.
Fiano, Guy *o.carm.* '85 (PMB) [B] Boca Raton, FL Pope John Paul II High School.
Fice, Joseph J. *s.j.* '72 (PHX) [B] Phoenix, AZ Brophy College Preparatory.
Ficenec, Leonard C. '57 (OM) Tarnov, NE St. Michael Church; Retired.
Fichteman, William L. '81 (L) [1] Louisville, KY Cathedral of the Assumption.
Fichtner, Joseph '43 (PHX) [25] Phoenix, AZ St. Thomas the Apostle Church.
Fichtner, Joseph A. *o.s.c.* '43 (PHX) [F] Phoenix, AZ Crosier Community of Phoenix (Canons Regular of the Order of the Holy Cross).
Fichtner, Robert C. '55 (BO) Watertown, MA St. Patrick Church.
Fick, David J. '88 (ALN) West Reading, PA Sacred Heart Church.
Fickel, William F. *s.s.s.* '81 (CLV) [P] Cleveland, OH Blessed Sacrament Community.
Fickes, Daniel R. '91 (CLV) Olmsted Falls, OH St. Mary of the Falls Church.
Ficko, Anthony D. '56 (GRY) [1] Whiting, IN Immaculate Conception Church.
Ficorilli, Chad R. *o.s.b.* '79 (E) St. Marys, PA Sacred Heart of Jesus Church.
Fictum, Robert *s.d.s.* '78 (MIL) [3] Wauwatosa, WI St. Joseph Congregation Church.
Fidalgo, Federico '63 (CC) Retired.
Fidalgo, Manuel Garcia '47 (MIA) [A] Miami, FL St. John Vianney College Seminary.
Fider, William P. '66 (DUL) [14] Duluth, MN St. Michael's Church.
Fidler, W. Larch, IV (PRT) Machias, ME Holy Name of Jesus Church; [M] Machias, ME University of Maine at Machias.
Fidler, W. Larch, IV '87 (STL) On Duty Outside the Archdiocese.
Fiebelkorn, Daniel F. '97 (BUF) [5] Depew, NY Our Lady of the Blessed Sacrament Church.
Fiedler, Donald J. '59 (DOD) On Duty Outside the Diocese.
Fiedler, Donald J. '59 (TUC) [20] Tucson, AZ Saints Peter and Paul Church.
Fiedler, Msgr. Ernest J. '52 (KC) [1] Kansas City, MO Cathedral of Immaculate Conception; [27] Kansas City, MO Old St. Patrick's Church.
Fiedler, Kenneth J. '71 (MAD) [6] Madison, WI Our Lady, Queen of Peace Church.
Fiedler, Lloyd *s.v.d.* '70 (FgM) Society of the Divine Word Foreign Missions.
Fiedorczyk, Henry P. '42 (HRT) [2] New Britain, CT Holy Cross Church; Retired.
Fiedorowicz, Joseph '75 (KNX) Athens, TN St. Mary Church.
Field, James A. '90 (BO) [4] Norwood, MA St. Timothy Church.
Field, Michael J. '82 (CAM) [3] Cherry Hill, NJ St. Peter Celestine Church.
Field, Raymund *c.s.v.* '48 (SJ) Saratoga, CA Church of the Ascension; Retired.
Field, Raymund J. *c.s.v.* '48 (SJ) [3] Sunnyvale, CA St. Cyprian Church.
Field, Thomas E. *glmy.* '78 (CHL) Bryson City, NC St. Joseph Church.
Field, Msgr. William N. '40 (NEW) [B] South Orange, NJ Seton Hall University.
Fields, John '86 (PHU) Lansdale, PA Presentation of Our Lord Church; Warrington, PA St. Anne's Church; [D] Philadelphia, PA Ascension Manor, Inc.
Fields, Robert H. '82 (JC) Centralia, MO Holy Spirit Church; Columbia, MO University Hospital & Clinics.
Fields, Stephen M. *s.j.* '52 (WDC) [M] Washington, DC The Jesuit Community at Georgetown University.
Fields, William F. '91 (MOB) [1] Mobile, AL Cathedral of the Immaculate Conception.
Fierro, Msgr. David G. '76 (ELP) [16] El Paso, TX Our Lady of the Light Church.
Fierros, Rick '78 (FRS) Delano, CA St. Mary's of the Miraculous Medal Church.
Fifagrowicz, Joseph G. '62 (BUF) Lyndonville, NY St. Joseph Church; Medina, NY Sacred Heart Church.
Figaro, Egbert J. *c.s.sp.* '51 (CHI) [129] Chicago, IL St. Mary Magdalene Church.
Figel, Terence J. *o.m.i.* '64 (STP) [N] St. Paul, MN Oblate Residence; [N] St. Paul, MN Oblate Residence.
Figge, Edwin H. '41 (STL) Retired.
Figge, Glennon E. *c.m.* '55 (EVN) [F] Evansville, IN Seton Residence.
Figge, Glennon E. *c.m.* '55 (STL) [P] St. Louis, MO Vincentian Residence.
Figge, Leo *o.m.i.* '76 (BEL) [F] Belleville, IL Shrine of Our Lady of the Snows.
Figge, Urban '57 (BEL) [F] Belleville, IL Missionary Oblates of Mary Immaculate - St. Henry's Oblate Residence.
Figge, Urban *o.m.i.* '67 (FgM) Oblates Foreign Missions.
Figlia, Sidney *s.d.b.* '68 (NO) [2] Harvey, LA St. John Bosco Church.
Figliola, Nicholas J. '64 (RVC) Coram, NY St. Frances Cabrini Church.
Figliozzi, Richard '79 (RVC) Freeport, NY Our Holy Redeemer Church.
Figol, Volodymyr '32 (STF) Retired.
Figueiredo, Anthony J. '94 (NEW) Higher Studies.
Figueiredo, Anthony Jesus '94 (NEW) On Duty Outside the Archdiocese.
Figueredo, Sergio *s.j.* '60 (MIA) [5] Miami, FL Gesu Church.
Figueroa, Alberto *o.f.m.,cap.* '90 (ARE) [1] Utuado, PR San Miquel Church.
Figueroa, Angel '86 (SJN) [2] Toa Alta, PR San Fernando Church.
Figueroa, Edward *o.m.i.* '60 (FgM) Oblates Foreign Missions.
Figueroa, Marco Antonio *o.f.m.* '93 (OAK) [9] Oakland, CA St. Elizabeth's Church; [N] Oakland, CA Franciscan Friars.
Figueroa, Ruben *o.f.m.* (TYL) Mount Pleasant, TX St. Michael Church.
Figuerola, Adrian '71 (IND) [H] Indianapolis, IN St. Augustine Home, Little Sisters of the Poor.
Figurelle, Elwood F. '63 (ALT) Mount Union, PA St. Catherine's Church.
Figurelli, Nicholas G. '82 (NEW) Westfield, NJ Holy Trinity Church.
Filacchione, Msgr. Marc (NY) New York, NY New York Fire Department.
Filacchione, Msgr. Marc A. '80 (NY) [74] New York, NY St. Michael Church.
Filardi, Edward J. '94 (WDC) Gaithersburg, MD St. Martin Church.
Filary, Richard M. '82 (SAG) [3] Bay City, MI St. Hedwig Church.
Filiatreau, Hilary *o.s.b.* '49 (LR) Altus, AR St. Mary Church.
Filice, Francis '79 (SFR) [51] San Francisco, CA St. Thomas, The Apostle Church.
Filice, Peter F. *s.j.* '71 (SJ) [B] Santa Clara, CA Santa Clara University.
Filice, Richard '76 (CC) [12] Corpus Christi, TX Saint Andrew By the Sea Parish.
Filip, Francis B. '36 (PIT) Retired.
Filip, John T. '44 (ROM) Retired.
Filipetto, Silvano '86 (CHI) On Duty Outside the Archdiocese.
Filipich, Nicholas '53 (BLX) Retired.
Filipkowski, Peter '86 (PAT) Parsippany, NJ St. Peter the Apostle Church.
Filipowicz, Stefan *s.j.* '61 (CHI) [N] Chicago, IL Sacred Heart Mission House.
Filippelli, John L.M. *s.s.j.* (WDC) [B] Washington, DC St. Joseph's Seminary.
Filippine, John E. '58 (CIN) [88] Cincinnati, OH St. Vivian Church.
Filips, Mark D. '89 (OM) [41] Omaha, NE St. Rose Church.
Filipski, Raymond R. '75 (NEW) Bergenfield, NJ St. John the Evangelist Church.
Fillion, Normand A. *o.m.i.* '50 (MAN) [3] Manchester, NH St. Anthony of Padua Church.
Fillion, Stephen J. '79 (SAG) Harrison, MI St. Athanasius Church.
Fillman, G. Allan '77 (TOL) Tiffin, OH St. Mary Church; [B] Tiffin, OH Calvert High School; [L] Tiffin, OH St. Francis Convent.
Filmanski, Francis E. '53 (RVC) Floral Park, NY St. Hedwig's Church.
Filmyer, Bernard G. *s.j.* '52 (BAL) [M] Baltimore, MD Jesuit Fathers and Brothers Maryland Provincial Curia.
Filteau, Jerome E. '41 (FAR) Retired; [E] Fargo, ND Riverview Place, Inc.
Filut, David C. '68 (MIL) [4] Waukesha, WI St. William Church.
Fimbel, Duane G. '57 (BUF) [2] North Tonawanda, NY St. Albert the Great Church; North Tonawanda, NY DeGraff Memorial Hospital.
Fimiani, Msgr. Louis F. '60 (NEW) Roseland, NJ Our Lady of the Blessed Sacrament Church.
Fin, Robert G. '43 (E) Retired; [B] Erie, PA Gannon University.
Finamore, Robert A. '70 (WDC) College Park, MD Holy Redeemer Church.
Finan, James '59 (WDC) Retired.
Finan, James A. '59 (BAL) [Q] Upper Marlboro, MD Knights of Columbus.
Finch, G. William '89 (WDC) Cheverly, MD St. Ambrose Church.
Finch, Joseph E. '58 (ALB) [M] Germantown, NY St. Teresa's Motherhouse.
Finch, Joseph E. '58 (OM) Absent on Sick Leave.
Finch, Raymond J. *m.m.* '76 (FgM) Maryknoll(M.M.).
Finch, Raymond J. *m.m.* '76 (NY) [DD] Maryknoll, NY Maryknoll Fathers and Brothers.
Fincutter, John F. *s.v.d.* '50 (MIL) [P] East Troy, WI Divine Word Seminary.
Fincutter, Patrick *s.v.d.* '55 (FgM) Society of the Divine Word Foreign Missions.
Finder, James L. '91 (JC) Rich Fountain, MO Sacred Heart Church.
Findlan, Msgr. Joseph G. '38 (PIT) Retired; [O] Pittsburgh, PA St. John Vianney Manor.
Findlay, David '67 (E) [11] Erie, PA Sacred Heart Church.
Finegan, Gerard '67 (VEN) [1] Sarasota, FL Incarnation Church.
Finegan, Lawrence '70 (SFR) [4] South San Francisco, CA St. Veronica Church.
Finegan, Paul J. '70 (BO) Chelmsford, MA St. Mary Church.
Finelli, Jay A. '92 (PRO) [2] East Providence, RI St. Francis Xavier Church.
Finelli, Victor F. '89 (ALN) Whitehall, PA St. Elizabeth Church.
Fineran, A. Gerard *s.j.* '50 (FgM) Provinces.
Fineran, A. Gerard *s.j.* '50 (NO) [P] New Orleans, LA Jesuit Provincial Office.
Finerty, Bernard *o.f.m.cap.* '61 (PIT) [O] Rochester, PA St. Cecilia Friary.
Finerty, D. Bryan '59 (PRO) [5] Woonsocket, RI St. Charles Church.
Finerty, Raymond *o.p.* (OAK) [N] Oakland, CA Western Dominican Province.
Finerty, Raymond *o.p.* '71 (P) Ashland, OR Our Lady of the Mountain Church; [P] Portland, OR University of Portland.
Fingerle, Fred G. '63 (BUF) Andover, NY Blessed Sacrament Church; Whitesville, NY St. John of the Cross Church.
Finis, John '40 (EVN) Retired.
Fink, Msgr. Charles R. '76 (RVC) Hewlett, NY St. Joseph's Church.
Fink, Daniel *o.f.m.conv.* (ATL) Lithia Springs, GA St. John Vianney Church.
Fink, Frederick T. '61 (NU) Darwin, MN St. John Church; Forest City, MN St. Gertrude Church.
Fink, John '71 (MIA) Special Assignment.
Fink, John L. '69 (IND) New Albany, IN Our Lady of Perpetual Help Church.
Fink, Joseph P. '83 (STP) [23] St. Paul, MN St. John of St. Paul Church.
Fink, Karel '91 (AUS) Llano, TX Holy Trinity Church.
Fink, Peter E. *s.j.* '69 (BO) [W] Cambridge, MA Weston Jesuit Community.
Fink, Philip *o.f.m.cap.* '77 (FgM) Capuchin Foreign Missions.
Fink, Philip *o.f.m.cap.* '77 (PIT) [O] Pittsburgh, PA St. Patrick Friary.
Finlan, Robert T. '94 (ALN) [C] Reading, PA Holy Name High School.
Finlan, Robert T., Jr. '94 (ALN) Shillington, PA St. John Baptist de la Salle Church.
Finlay, Joseph F. '57 (STA) Palatka, FL St. Monica's Church; Palatka, FL St. Monica's Church.
Finley, James F. '63 (BRK) Released from Diocesan Assignment.
Finley, James F. '63 (TR) Lakehurst, NJ U.S. Naval Air Warfare Center.
Finley, Msgr. James J. '49 (STL) Retired.
Finley, James J. *s.j.* '52 (NY) [DD] New York, NY Murray-Weigel Hall.
Finley, Jeffrey *c.pp.s.* '90 (OAK) Newark, CA St. Edward's Church; Fremont, CA Washington Hospital.
Finley, Thomas (LAF) [6] Lafayette, LA Our Lady of Wisdom, University of Southwestern Louisiana Church.
Finley, Thomas M. *c.m.* '54 (PH) [AA] Philadelphia, PA Congregation of the Mission.
Finley, William '81 (ORL) Sabbatical.
Finn, Alfred E. '55 (BO) Permanent Disability.
Finn, Arthur *c.ss.r.* '29 (ALB) [L] Saratoga Springs, NY St. John Neumann Residence.
Finn, Daniel J. '72 (BO) [44] Boston, MA St. Mark Church.
Finn, Dominick *o.s.f.s.* '56 (PH) Norristown, PA Norristown State Hospital.
Finn, Dominick F. *o.s.f.s.* '56 (PH) [2] Norristown, PA St. Francis of Assisi Church.
Finn, Edward S. '52 (SCR) On Special or Other

Diocesan Assignment.
Finn, Firmin *o.f.m.conv.* '55 (ALB) [J] Latham, NY Our Lady of Hope Residence.
Finn, Firmin *o.f.m.conv.* '55 (SY) Syracuse, NY St. Joseph's Hospital Health Center; [O] Syracuse, NY St. Joseph's Hospital Health Center.
Finn, Francis J. '39 (NEW) Retired.
Finn, Gregory *o.s.j.* (SCR) [M] Pittston, PA Eastern Province of the Oblates of St. Joseph.
Finn, Gregory T. *o.s.j.* '89 (SCR) Exeter, PA St. Anthony of Padua Church; [B] Pittston, PA St. Joseph's Oblate Seminary.
Finn, John *o.s.f.s.* '62 (WIL) Newark, DE Christiana Care Health System.
Finn, John *m.s.c.* '84 (SAT) [M] San Antonio, TX Missionaries of the Sacred Heart.
Finn, John A. *o.s.f.s.* '62 (WIL) [I] Wilmington, DE DeSales House.
Finn, John P. '81 (NO) Luling, LA Holy Family Church.
Finn, Michael E. '77 (SCR) Moscow, PA St. Catherine of Siena Church.
Finn, Msgr. Peter (NY) [I] New York, NY The Catholic Charities of the Archdiocese of New York.
Finn, Msgr. Peter G. '65 (NY) [211] Staten Island, NY St. Joseph, St. Thomas Church.
Finn, Raymond C. *o.p.* '70 (NO) [P] New Orleans, LA Dominican Fathers & Brothers, Southern Dominican Province.
Finn, Robert E. *s.j.* '91 (CHI) [N] Chicago, IL Chicago Province of the Society of Jesus-Provincial Office.
Finn, Seamus *o.m.i.* '76 (FgM) American Oblate Missions(O.M.I.).
Finn, Seamus *o.m.i.* '76 (WDC) [B] Washington, DC Oblate College/Oblate Center for Mission Studies; [V] Silver Spring, MD Oblate Conference.
Finn, Msgr. Thomas B. '37 (COV) Retired.
Finn, William '73 (JUN) On Duty Outside the Diocese.
Finn, William '73 (SEA) Bellevue, WA St. Louise Church.
Finn, William P. '48 (PH) [AA] Philadelphia, PA Congregation of the Mission.
Finnane, Daniel P. '63 (MAD) De Forest, WI St. Olaf Church.
Finnegan, Ambrose *o.f.m.conv.* '26 (STP) [Q] Prior Lake, MN Franciscan Retreat House.
Finnegan, Charles V. *o.f.m.* '58 (PH) [AA] Philadelphia, PA Order of Friars Minor of the Province of the Most Holy Name aka Holy Name Province.
Finnegan, Corentine J. *o.c.s.o.* '47 (ATL) [I] Conyers, GA The Monastery of the Holy Spirit.
Finnegan, Gerald F. *s.j.* '67 (BO) [W] Boston, MA The Society of Jesus of New England-Provincial Offices.
Finnegan, Gerald F. *s.j.* '67 (PH) [C] Philadelphia, PA St. Joseph's University; [AA] Philadelphia, PA Jesuit Community at St. Joseph's University.
Finnegan, J. Kevin '96 (STP) Bloomington, MN St. Edward Church.
Finnegan, James P. *o.s.f.s.* '58 (ALN) Colesville, PA Assumption B.V.M. Church; [B] Center Valley, PA Allentown College of St. Francis de Sales; [K] Center Valley, PA Oblates of St. Francis de Sales.
Finnegan, John P. '54 (CHI) Vernon Hills, IL St. Mary of Vernon Church.
Finnegan, John S. '56 (SY) Camillus, NY St. Joseph Church.
Finnegan, John T. (BO) Retired.
Finnegan, Joseph '65 (HEL) Special Assignments.
Finnegan, Kevin '90 (GLP) Absent on Leave.
Finnegan, Michael '45 (HT) Retired.
Finnegan, Michael J. '74 (SP) [1] Largo, FL St. Catherine of Siena Church.
Finnegan, Peter J. '42 (WCH) Retired.
Finnegan, Robert K. *o.praem.* '52 (GB) [A] De Pere, WI St. Norbert Abbey; [I] De Pere, WI St. Norbert Abbey; [O] De Pere, WI Canons Regular of Magnovarad, Ltd.; [O] De Pere, WI NORBERT & CO.; [O] De Pere, WI Norbertine Generalate, Inc.
Finnegan, Roscoe L. '47 (SCL) Retired.
Finnegan, Msgr. Thomas J. (BO) Retired.
Finnegan, William J. '57 (CHI) Orland Park, IL Our Lady of the Woods Church; Retired.
Finnell, Eugene L. '56 (PEO) Morton, IL Blessed Sacrament Church.
Finnell, John H. '78 (WH) Absent on Sick Leave; [F] Wheeling, WV Paul VI Pastoral Center.
Finnell, Terrell M. (KC) Lexington, MO Immaculate Conception Church.
Finneran, Michael '42 (BIR) Retired.
Finnerty, Msgr. D. Joseph '63 (BRK) [240] Queens, NY St. Sebastian Church.
Finnerty, Msgr. James J. '55 (NEW) [18] Newark, NJ St. John's Church.
Finnerty, Joseph G. '61 (NOR) [4] Norwich, CT St. Mary Church; [J] Uncasville, CT Emmaus-Diocesan Spiritual Life Center.
Finnerty, Msgr. Joseph L. '57 (SD) Poway, CA St. Michael Church.
Finnerty, Peter F. '71 (CAM) Pomona, NJ Assumption Church.
Finnerty, Vincent H. *c.m.* '79 (CHL) [3] Greensboro, NC St. Mary Church; [O] Charlotte, NC Centro Catolico Hispano.
Finnerty, William A. '55 (KCK) [3] Overland Park, KS Holy Spirit Church.
Finnestad, Jerald L.C. '80 (FAR) [2] Grand Forks, ND St. Mary's Church.
Finney, Donald *m.i.c.* '94 (NOR) [F] Thompson, CT Marian Fathers.
Finney, Donald *m.i.c.* '94 (PMB) [1] Palm Beach, FL Cathedral of St. Ignatius Loyola.
Finnigan, Francis *c.p.* '68 (PMB) [G] North Palm Beach, FL Our Lady of Florida Spiritual Center.
Finnigan, John B. '61 (MAN) Newmarket, NH St. Mary Church.
Finnigan, Msgr. John C. '59 (Y) [1] Canton, OH All Saints Church; [12] Canton, OH St. Peter's Church.
Finnigan, Msgr. Thomas J. '55 (DET) [14] Detroit, MI St. Cecilia Church.
Finno, James P. '72 (CHI) Matteson, IL St. Lawrence O'Toole Church.
Finochietto, Arnold '36 (ELP) Retired.
Finster, Paul V. *s.j.* '45 (FgM) Provinces.
Finsterbach, Thomas P. *s.j.* '76 (SJ) [M] Los Gatos, CA Sacred Heart Jesuit Center.
Finucan, J. Thomas '55 (LC) Fountain City, WI Immaculate Conception Church.
Finucan, Msgr. James P. '47 (LC) Retired; [I] La Crosse, WI Holy Cross (Seminary) Diocesan Center.
Finucane, Joseph F. '59 (E) Corry, PA St. Elizabeth Church.
Finucane, Robert '54 (B) Genesee, ID St. Mary Station Church.
Fior, Ubaldo M. *c.r.s.p.* '51 (BUF) Lewiston, NY Holy Family Church; [B] Youngstown, NY St. Anthony M. Zaccaria Seminary.
Fiore, Arthur B. '75 (WIL) New Castle, DE St. Peter Church.
Fiore, Benjamin *s.j.* '74 (BUF) [O] Buffalo, NY Canisius Jesuit Community.
Fiore, James '72 (PMB) Lantana, FL Holy Spirit Church.
Fiore, John J. *c.s.b.* '57 (GRY) [B] Merrillville, IN Andrean High School; [J] Merrillville, IN Basilian Fathers Residence.
Fiore, Joseph A. (BUF) Darien Center, NY Our Lady of Good Counsel Church.
Fiore, Joseph A. '70 (BUF) Bennington Center, NY Sacred Heart of Jesus Church.
Fiore, Peter A. *o.f.m.* '55 (ALB) [B] Loudonville, NY Siena College.
Fiore, Salvatore *s.j.* '45 (NY) North Tarrytown, NY Immaculate Conception Church.
Fiorelli, Lewis S. *o.s.f.s.* '70 (WDC) [B] Washington, DC Deshairs Community-Oblates of St. Francis de Sales Residence.
Fiorentin, Francis *c.s.* '51 (PRO) [8] Providence, RI St. Bartholomew Church.
Fioretti, Jerome '32 (PRO) Retired.
Fiorillo, Antimo '43 (NY) [180] Bronx, NY Santa Maria Church; Retired.
Fiorino, Alfred L. *s.j.* '60 (NY) [DD] New York, NY Jesuit Provincial's Office.
Fiorino, Joseph '61 (NEW) Retired.
Firestone, Thomas (LAN) [L] Ann Arbor, MI Alma Redemptoris Mater.
Firestone, Thomas '78 (LAN) [J] Ypsilanti, MI Holy Trinity Student Chapel.
Firestone, Thomas M. (LAN) [J] Ann Arbor, MI St. Mary Student Parish.
Firestone, Thomas M. '78 (LAN) [4] Ann Arbor, MI St. Mary Student Parish.
Firko, Frank A. *s.t.l.* '77 (PBR) Hermitage, PA St. Michael Church.
Firneno, Ralph *s.a.c.* '57 (CAM) [C] Pennsauken, NJ Bishop Eustace Prep School.
Firpo, John A. '77 (ROC) [19] Rochester, NY St. Helen Church.
Fisch, Gerald M. '57 (SC) Ida Grove, IA Sacred Heart Church.
Fischer, Adrian *o.f.m.* '75 (SHP) Grambling, LA St. Benedict the Black Church; West Monroe, LA St. Paschal Church; [G] Grambling, LA Student Center.
Fischer, Andrew C. '82 (PIT) Sharpsburg, PA St. John Cantius Church; Sharpsburg, PA Madonna of Jerusalem Church.
Fischer, Anthony W. '29 (LC) Retired.
Fischer, Barry J. *c.pp.s.* '73 (CIN) [M] Dayton, OH Provincial House of the Cincinnati Province of the Society of the Precious Blood.
Fischer, Brian J. '79 (CHI) [A] Mundelein, IL University of St. Mary of the Lake-Mundelein Seminary.
Fischer, Charles G. '50 (OWN) Clarkson, KY St. Elizabeth of Hungary Church; St. Paul, KY St. Paul Church.
Fischer, Charles H. '71 (KAL) Hastings, MI St. Rose of Lima Church.
Fischer, Msgr. Don L. '67 (DAL) Richardson, TX St. Joseph Church.
Fischer, Emil W. *o.f.m.cap.* '66 (PIT) Clairton, PA St. Clare of Assisi Church.
Fischer, Emil William '66 (PIT) [O] Pittsburgh, PA St. Francis Friary.
Fischer, Eugene '65 (SD) Retired.
Fischer, G. William *o.s.f.s.* '69 (E) Special or Diocesan Assignment.
Fischer, G. Wm. *o.s.f.s.* '69 (TOL) [K] Toledo, OH Oblates of St. Francis de Sales.
Fischer, Henry J. '71 (BEL) Freeburg, IL St. Joseph Church.
Fischer, Hilary *m.s.c.* '57 (FgM) Missionaries of the Sacred Heart Foreign Missions.
Fischer, Hilary *m.s.c.* '57 (RCK) [H] Aurora, IL Missionaries of the Sacred Heart Community.
Fischer, James A. *c.m.* '43 (STL) [P] Perryville, MO Congregation of The Mission.
Fiscner, James J. *s.j.* '55 (ROC) [B] Rochester, NY McQuaid Jesuit High School.
Fischer, John '86 (SFS) Redfield, SD St. Bernard Church.
Fischer, John M. '63 (E) Albion, PA St. Lawrence Church.
Fischer, John P. '76 (CIN) Withamsville, OH St. Thomas More Church.
Fischer, Kenneth J. '71 (CHI) [51] Chicago, IL St. Dorothy Church.
Fischer, Louis A. '63 (SLC) Retired.
Fischer, Lowell '54 (JOL) Retired; [K] Frankfort, IL Motherhouse, Novitiate, Sacred Heart Residence, Portiuncula, Center for Prayer.
Fischer, Mark *f.s.s.p.* '95 (SCR) [M] Elmhurst, PA Priestly Fraternity of St. Peter (F.S.S.P.), North American District Headquarters.
Fischer, Mark F. *f.s.s.p.* '95 (ATL) [M] Alpharetta, GA St. Francis de Sales Latin Mass Community - Pastoral Center.
Fischer, Philip C. *s.j.* '61 (STL) [P] St. Louis, MO Jesuit Community Corporation at St. Louis University - Jesuit Hall.
Fischer, Richard O. '76 (BAK) Arlington, OR St. Francis Church; Condon, OR St. John's Church.
Fischer, Tarsicius '46 (CHI) [N] Chicago, IL St. Peter's Friary.
Fischer, William '69 (E) [C] Erie, PA Cathedral Preparatory School.
Fischer, William J. *o.praem.* '78 (GB) [I] De Pere, WI St. Norbert Abbey.
Fischer, William J. *o.praem.* '78 (PH) [AA] Paoli, PA Daylesford Abbey.
Fisette, Kevin R. '81 (PRO) [17] Providence, RI Holy Name of Jesus Church; [3] West Warwick, RI St. James Church.
Fish, Alfred H. '77 (OG) Brushton, NY St. Mary Church.
Fish, Eugene '97 (FAR) Anamoose, ND St. Francis Xavier Church.
Fish, Eugene J. '97 (FAR) Esmond, ND St. Boniface Church.
Fishel, Gregory *s.d.b.* '89 (NO) [4] Harvey, LA St. Rosalie Church.
Fisher, A. J. '56 (BAK) Retired.
Fisher, Albert '81 (BIR) Jasper, AL St. Cecilia Church.
Fisher, Bernard *s.v.d.* '45 (MIL) [P] East Troy, WI Divine Word Seminary.
Fisher, Charles '74 (RIC) Williamsburg, VA St. Bede's Church.
Fisher, Charles '90 (FAR) Drayton, ND St. Edward's Church.
Fisher, Clarence L. '61 (HON) Wahiawa, HI Our Lady of Sorrows Church.
Fisher, Craig B. '79 (PH) Absent on Leave.
Fisher, D. Theodore *s.j.* '53 (LA) [C] Los Angeles, CA Loyola Marymount University.
Fisher, David '84 (OLL) Special Assignment.
Fisher, David E. '86 (LAN) Owosso, MI St. Joseph Church.
Fisher, Msgr. David L. '56 (GBG) Penn, PA St. Boniface Church.
Fisher, Donald (L) [K] Louisville, KY St. Joseph Home for the Aged.
Fisher, Donald C. '61 (PIT) Slippery Rock, PA St. Peter Church.
Fisher, Donald J. '54 (L) [73] Louisville, KY St. Thomas More Church.
Fisher, Edward K. '92 (MEM) [2] Memphis, TN St. Ann Church.
Fisher, Msgr. Edward T. '49 (BUF) [2] North Tonawanda, NY St. Albert the Great Church.
Fisher, Frederick J. '42 (CHI) Retired.
Fisher, Gerald E. '51 (LC) [4] Stevens Point, WI St. Peter Church.
Fisher, Harry W. '64 (FWT) Valley View, TX St. John Church.
Fisher, James *c.s.p.* '59 (MEM) [J] Memphis, TN Paulist Fathers (New York).
Fisher, James F. *c.s.p.* '59 (MEM) [20] Memphis, TN St. Patrick's Church.
Fisher, James F. *c.s.p.* '59 (NY) [DD] Jamaica Estates, NY Paulist Fathers Generalate.
Fisher, John J. *o.s.f.s.* '88 (WIL) [B] Wilmington, DE Salesianum School.
Fisher, Kyle *c.ss.r.* '63 (DEN) Greeley, CO Our Lady of Peace Church.

Fisher, Martin '51 (GF) Retired; [G] Billings, MT Saint Vincent Hospital and Health Center.
Fisher, Martin '86 (ALB) Glens Falls, NY St. Mary Church; [C] Glens Falls, NY St. Mary-St. Alphonsus Regional Catholic School.
Fisher, Michael W. '90 (WDC) Hillcrest Heights, MD Holy Family Church.
Fisher, Paul R. *o.praem.* '94 (WIL) [B] Claymont, DE Archmere Academy.
Fisher, Paul R. *o.praem.* '95 (WIL) [I] Claymont, DE Immaculate Conception Priory of the Canons Regular of Premontre.
Fisher, Raymond A. '71 (TOL) [21] Toledo, OH St. Clement Church.
Fisher, Robert '92 (DET) [5] St. Clair Shores, MI St. Lucy Church.
Fisher, Robert B. *s.v.d.* '65 (GAL) Prairie View, TX St. Martin de Porres Church; [T] Prairie View, TX Prairie View A & M University Catholic Center.
Fisher, Robert D. '80 (DEN) [21] Denver, CO Our Lady of Lourdes Church.
Fisher, Robert J. '80 (TOL) [33] Toledo, OH St. Michael Church.
Fisher, Robert J. '92 (DET) Special Assignment.
Fisher, Terry A. '85 (FTW) Warsaw, IN Sacred Heart Church.
Fisher, William F. *o.s.f.s.* '15 (DET) [1] Monroe, MI St. Anne Church.
Fisher, William F. *o.s.f.s.* '61 (DET) [3] Monroe, MI St. Joseph's Church.
Fisherkeller, William P. *c.s.v.* '60 (SFD) Granite City, IL Holy Family Church.
Fishwick, Joseph '75 (MIA) Special Assignment.
Fiske, Jack J. *c.ss.r.* '80 (ORL) [F] New Smyrna Beach, FL Redemptorist Fathers of the Vice Province of Richmond.
Fister, Anselm *o.s.b.* '82 (BAK) Dufur, OR St. Alphonsus Church; Wasco, OR St. Mary's Church.
Fister, Anselm *o.s.b.* '82 (SD) [H] Oceanside, CA Prince of Peace Abbey, Benet Hill.
Fitch, David *s.j.* '54 (SJ) [M] Los Gatos, CA Sacred Heart Jesuit Center.
Fitterer, L. Paul *s.j.* '63 (P) [L] Portland, OR Jesuit Provincial Office (Society of Jesus, Oregon Prov.).
Fitterer, L. Paul *s.j.* '63 (SEA) [M] Seattle, WA Jesuit Community.
Fittin, Edward Seton *o.s.b.* '93 (PAT) [D] Morristown, NJ Delbarton School.
Fittin, Edward Seton J. *o.s.b.* '93 (PAT) [M] Morristown, NJ St. Mary's Abbey.
Fitts, Robert L. *s.j.* '69 (SPK) [K] Spokane, WA Regis Community.
Fitz, James F. *s.m.* '74 (CIN) [M] Dayton, OH Marianist Provincialate.
Fitz Gerald, John W. '53 (SFE) [13] Albuquerque, NM Queen of Heaven Church.
Fitz-Henry, Edward '85 (MRY) San Juan Bautista, CA San Juan Bautista Church.
Fitz-Patrick, David M. '79 (WDC) Military Chaplains.
Fitzgerald, Alfred J. '66 (STL) Absent on Sick Leave.
Fitzgerald, Allan D. *o.s.a.* '67 (PH) [C] Villanova, PA Villanova University.
Fitzgerald, Brennan *o.f.m.* '61 (NY) [35] New York, NY St. Francis of Assisi Church.
Fitzgerald, Christopher *i.c.* '58 (SP) Seffner, FL St. Francis of Assisi Church.
Fitzgerald, Cornelius J. (ATL) Released from Archdiocesan Assignment.
Fitzgerald, Denis *s.t.* '45 (WDC) [M] Adelphi, MD Missionary Servants of the Most Holy Trinity.
Fitzgerald, Donald J. '55 (BUF) Retired.
Fitzgerald, Edmund H. '57 (PRO) [1] Westerly, RI St. Clare Church.
Fitzgerald, Edmund J. '68 (FR) Westport, MA St. John the Baptist Church.
Fitzgerald, Edward P. '40 (CHI) Retired.
Fitzgerald, Edward T. '59 (SPR) Ware, MA All Saints Church.
Fitzgerald, Edward W. '95 (CHR) Aiken, SC St. Mary, Help of Christians Church; [G] Aiken, SC University of South Carolina, Aiken Extension Newman Center.
Fitzgerald, Garret J. '75 (MET) Hampton, NJ St. Ann Church.
Fitzgerald, Garrett J. *s.j.* '55 (NY) [DD] New York, NY Jesuit Community at Fordham University.
Fitzgerald, George R. *c.s.p.* '65 (DEN) [4] Boulder, CO St. Thomas Aquinas University Parish; [P] Boulder, CO University of Colorado (Boulder).
Fitzgerald, Gerald J. '70 (BO) [4] Chelsea, MA Our Lady of Grace Church.
Fitzgerald, Howard '78 (DM) Dunlap, IA St. Patrick Church; Woodbine, IA Sacred Heart Church.
Fitzgerald, Hugh V. (NEW) [24] Jersey City, NJ Parish of the Resurrection Church.
Fitzgerald, James '64 (JOL) Mokena, IL St. Mary Church.
Fitzgerald, James E. *s.j.* '61 (MIL) [P] Milwaukee, WI Jesuit Community at Marquette University.
Fitzgerald, James E. '67 (BUF) Brant, NY Our Lady of Mt. Carmel Church.
Fitzgerald, James W. *m.m.* '50 (FgM) Maryknoll Foreign Missions.
Fitzgerald, John '58 (RVC) Setauket, NY St. James Church; [Q] Rockville Centre, NY The Campus Parish of Long Island.
Fitzgerald, John '63 (STO) Twain Harte, CA All Saints Church.
Fitzgerald, John '74 (PIT) Robinson Township, PA Holy Trinity Church.
Fitzgerald, John B. '55 (LA) [10] Long Beach, CA St. Maria Goretti Church.
Fitzgerald, John B. *c.m.* '61 (ALN) Bangor, PA Our Lady of Good Counsel Church.
Fitzgerald, John E. '57 (PH) Narberth, PA St. Margaret Church.
Fitzgerald, John F. *o.s.b.* '50 (PEO) [A] Peru, IL St. Bede Abbey and Academy.
Fitzgerald, John G. '62 (LA) Lompoc, CA Our Lady Queen of Angels Church.
Fitzgerald, John J. *o.s.a.* '41 (PH) [AA] Villanova, PA St. Thomas Monastery.
Fitzgerald, John L. '67 (BAL) Military Chaplains.
Fitzgerald, John W. '53 (SFE) Retired.
Fitzgerald, Joseph *o.carm.* '77 (LA) [F] Encino, CA Crespi Carmelite High School.
Fitzgerald, Msgr. Joseph M. '58 (BGP) Huntington, CT St. Lawrence Church.
FitzGerald, Kevin T. *s.j.* '88 (CHI) [C] Chicago, IL Jesuit Community at Loyola University of Chicago.
Fitzgerald, Kevin T. *s.j.* '88 (MIL) [P] Milwaukee, WI Jesuit Provincial Office, Wisconsin Province.
Fitzgerald, M. Durkin *c.ss.r* '49 (P) [17] Portland, OR Holy Redeemer Church.
Fitzgerald, Mark J. *c.s.c.* '40 (FTW) [B] Notre Dame, IN University of Notre Dame Du Lac; [J] Notre Dame, IN Holy Cross Community, Corby Hall, University of Notre Dame.
Fitzgerald, Matthew '68 (PMB) Port St. Lucie, FL St. Lucie Church.
Fitzgerald, Michael C. '78 (DUB) Marion, IA St. Joseph's Church; Springville, IA St. Isidore's Church.
Fitzgerald, Neil F. '54 (HRT) [3] Hamden, CT Our Lady of Mt. Carmel Church.
Fitzgerald, P. Timothy '75 (DM) On Duty Outside the Diocese.
Fitzgerald, Patrick (KCK) [G] Kansas City, KS St. Joseph Care Center, Inc.
Fitzgerald, Patrick '39 (KCK) Retired.
Fitzgerald, Patrick Timothy '75 (FTW) [B] Notre Dame, IN University of Notre Dame Du Lac.
Fitzgerald, Paul J. *s.j.* '92 (SJ) [B] Santa Clara, CA Santa Clara University.
Fitzgerald, Peter A. *c.m.* '46 (BUF) [C] Niagara University, NY Niagara University; [O] Niagara University, NY Vincentian Community at Niagara University.
Fitzgerald, R. Martin '89 (R) On Duty Outside the Diocese.
Fitzgerald, Raymond R. *s.j.* '91 (NO) [F] New Orleans, LA Jesuit High School; [F] New Orleans, LA Jesuit High School.
Fitzgerald, Richard J. '87 (BO) Wellesley, MA St. Paul Church.
Fitzgerald, Robert H. *s.j.* '66 (STP) [M] St. Paul, MN Holy Family Residence; [N] Minneapolis, MN La Storta Jesuit Community.
Fitzgerald, Msgr. Stephen J. '41 (NY) Pocantico Hills, NY The Magdalene Church; Retired.
Fitzgerald, Thomas '68 (MAD) Portage, WI St. Mary Church.
Fitzgerald, Thomas J. *s.s.j.* '31 (BAL) [M] Baltimore, MD St. Joseph's Manor.
Fitzgerald, Thomas J. '42 (CHI) [204] Chicago, IL St. Thomas Apostle Church; Retired.
Fitzgerald, Thomas J. *s.s.s.* '64 (SAT) [45] San Antonio, TX St. Joseph Church.
Fitzgerald, Thomas J. '75 (PAT) [4] Clifton, NJ St. Clare's Church.
Fitzgerald, Thomas P. '66 (STP) Cottage Grove, MN St. Rita Church.
Fitzgerald, Thomas R. *s.j.* '52 (BAL) [M] Baltimore, MD Jesuit Fathers and Brothers Maryland Provincial Curia.
Fitzgerald, Timothy *c.p.* '56 (PIT) [O] Pittsburgh, PA St. Paul of the Cross Monastery; [O] Pittsburgh, PA St. Paul of the Cross Monastery.
Fitzgerald, Timothy J. '90 (SC) Gilmore City, IA St. John's Church; Rolfe, IA St. Margaret's Church.
Fitzgerald, Timothy J. *c.s.b.* '97 (ROC) [13] Rochester, NY Christ the King Church.
Fitzgerald, Vincent *o.m.i.* '50 (BEL) [F] Belleville, IL Missionary Oblates of Mary Immaculate - St. Henry's Oblate Residence.
Fitzgerald, William *c.ss.r.* '43 (CHI) [N] Chicago, IL Redemptorists:; [N] Bodija, Ibadan, Oyo State, Nigeria.
Fitzgerald, William *c.ss.r.* '43 (DEN) [M] Denver, CO The Redemptorists/Denver Province.
FitzGerald, William '44 (BAL) Retired.
Fitzgerald, William F. (OM) Retired.
Fitzgerald, Msgr. William F. '50 (TR) [8] Trenton, NJ Our Lady of Good Counsel Church.
Fitzgerald, William H. *s.j.* '51 (WOR) [N] Worcester, MA Jesuits of Holy Cross College, Inc.
Fitzgerald, William J. '57 (KAL) Battle Creek, MI St. Philip Church.
Fitzgerald, William M. *o.praem* (NSH) [C] Nashville, TN St. Cecilia Academy.
Fitzgerald, Willliam *c.ss.r.* '43 (FgM) Redemptorist Foreign Missions.
Fitzgibbon, Edmond J. '59 (STL) Shrewsbury, MO St. Michael Church.
Fitzgibbons, Al L. '54 (RCK) On Disability Leave.
Fitzgibbons, John A. '68 (PH) Sharon Hill, PA Holy Spirit Church.
Fitzgibbons, John P. *s.j.* '85 (OM) [K] Omaha, NE Campion House.
Fitzgibbons, Peter L. '84 (CHL) Statesville, NC St. Philip the Apostle Church; Military Chaplains.
Fitzhenry, John Stephen *o.p.* '58 (BO) [W] Dover, MA St. Stephen Priory.
Fitzhugh, David '86 (STN) San Diego, CA Our Lady of Perpetual Help Church.
Fitzmaurice, Msgr. Francis J. '48 (PH) Retired.
Fitzmaurice, James *o.f.m.* (ALB) [10] Albany, NY St. Margaret Mary Church.
Fitzmaurice, James *o.f.m.* '84 (BO) [5] Newton, MA Mary Immaculate of Lourdes Church; [W] Boston, MA Ministry of the Word.
Fitzmaurice, Terence *o.s.b.* '63 (JOL) [J] Lisle, IL St. Procopius Abbey.
Fitzmaurice, Terence *o.s.b.* '63 (SUP) Phillips, WI Our Lady of the North Church.
Fitzmaurice, V. Paul '73 (GBG) Harrison City, PA St. Barbara Church.
Fitzmyer, Joseph A. *s.j.* '51 (WDC) [C] Washington, DC Catholic University of America, The; [M] Washington, DC The Jesuit Community at Georgetown University.
Fitzpatrick, Bede *o.f.m.* '55 (FgM) Franciscan Foreign Missions.
Fitzpatrick, Daniel J. *s.j.* '55 (NY) [DD] New York, NY Jesuit Community at Fordham University.
Fitzpatrick, Donnelly J. '63 (PEO) Atkinson, IL St. Anthony's Church.
Fitzpatrick, Edmund J. '42 (CHI) Retired.
Fitzpatrick, Edmund J. '47 (CHI) [164] Chicago, IL St. Pascal Church.
Fitzpatrick, Edward (ALB) Retired.
Fitzpatrick, Edward '68 (RVC) Uniondale, NY St. Martha Church.
Fitzpatrick, Edward C. (RVC) Davis Park, NY Most Precious Blood Church.
Fitzpatrick, Edward J. '70 (DAV) [H] Iowa City, IA Newman Catholic Student Center; [M] Iowa City, IA O'Keefe Hall.
Fitzpatrick, Edward T. *o.s.f.s.* '74 (WIL) [I] Wilmington, DE Oblates of St. Francis De Sales.
FitzPatrick, Emmett J. '58 (PHX) Sun Lakes, AZ St. Steven Church.
Fitzpatrick, Msgr. Franklin E. '47 (BRK) Retired.
Fitzpatrick, Gerald J. *s.j.* '71 (ALN) [A] Wernersville, PA Novitiate of St. Isaac Jogues; [N] Wernersville, PA Jesuit Center for Spiritual Growth.
Fitzpatrick, James F. '95 (BRK) [21] Brooklyn, NY Blessed Sacrament Church.
Fitzpatrick, James J. '84 (PH) [A] Wynnewood, PA Theological Seminary of St. Charles Borromeo, Overbrook.
Fitzpatrick, James M. '71 (SAG) Standish, MI Resurrection of the Lord Church.
Fitzpatrick, James M. '84 (FR) [19] Fall River, MA St. Patrick's Church.
Fitzpatrick, Jerold F. '62 (MAD) Gratiot, WI St. Joseph Church.
Fitzpatrick, Jerome B. *o.s.b.* '43 (PAT) [M] Morristown, NJ St. Mary's Abbey.
Fitzpatrick, John '64 (ALB) [10] Albany, NY St. Margaret Mary Church.
Fitzpatrick, Msgr. John E. '70 (PAT) Oak Ridge, NJ St. Thomas, the Apostle Church.
Fitzpatrick, John J. '60 (SAV) Tybee Island, GA St. Michael's Church.
Fitzpatrick, John P. '52 (STP) Retired.
Fitzpatrick, Kevin P. '83 (BGP) [8] Stamford, CT St. John's Church.
Fitzpatrick, Mallick J. *s.j.* '60 (NY) [F] New York, NY Fordham Preparatory School; [DD] New York, NY Jesuit Community at Fordham University.
Fitzpatrick, Michael J. *s.j.* '77 (BAK) Pendleton, OR St. Andrew's Indian Mission Church.
Fitzpatrick, Michael J. '83 (PH) Springfield, PA St. Kevin Church; [D] Drexel Hill, PA Archbishop Prendergast High School.
Fitzpatrick, Patrick F.X. '39 (NEW) Retired.
Fitzpatrick, Patrick G. '62 (TR) Union Beach, NJ Holy Family Church.
Fitzpatrick, Peter A. '45 (PH) [133] Philadelphia, PA St. Patrick Church; Retired.
Fitzpatrick, R. Michael '71 (OM) [1] Omaha, NE St. Cecilia's Cathedral.
Fitzpatrick, Robert *o.m.i.* '71 (FgM) Oblates Foreign Missions.

Fitzpatrick, Robert J. '54 (CHI) Ingleside, IL St. Bede Church; Round Lake, IL St. Joseph Church; Retired.
Fitzpatrick, Robert J. '73 (STP) Little Canada, MN St. John the Evangelist Church.
Fitzpatrick, Thomas J. *o.s.f.s.* '61 (CHL) Thomasville, NC Our Lady of the Highways Church.
Fitzpatrick, Thomas J. *s.j.* '68 (FgM) Provinces.
Fitzpatrick, Thomas P. '61 (SY) [6] Syracuse, NY Our Lady of Lourdes Church.
Fitzpatrick, Vincent *s.t.* '44 (PAT) [M] Stirling, NJ Holy Spirit Missionary Cenacle.
Fitzpatrick, Vincent J. '92 (FAR) Wales, ND St. Michael's Church.
Fitzsimmons, Donald J. *c.s.v.* '60 (CHI) [N] Arlington Heights, IL Clerics of St. Viator-Provincial Residence.
Fitzsimmons, Msgr. Eugene J. '60 (CAM) Gibbstown, NJ St. Michael's Church.
Fitzsimmons, Francis *m.s.* '68 (LKC) [4] Sulphur, LA St. Theresa Church.
Fitzsimmons, Gerald *s.s.m.* (HRT) [V] Litchfield, CT Lourdes Shrine Guild, Inc.
Fitzsimmons, Gerald J. *s.m.m.* '75 (BRK) [U] Ozone Park, NY Montfort Missionaries Provincialate - for Nation Community.
Fitzsimmons, J. Thomas '62 (CIN) Eaton, OH Visitation of the Blessed Virgin Mary Church; New Paris, OH St. John Church.
Fitzsimmons, Richard '56 (PEO) Peterstown, IL SS. Peter and Paul Church.
Fitzsimmons, Msgr. Richard G. '56 (PEO) Mendota, IL Holy Cross Church.
Fitzsimmons, Robert Philip *o.p.* '55 (NY) [22] New York, NY St. Catherine of Siena Church; Manhattan, NY New York Hospital; [DD] New York, NY St. Catherine of Siena Priory.
Fitzsimmons, Thomas B. '62 (CAM) Stratford, NJ St. Luke Church.
Fitzsimons, Philip '81 (SEA) Monroe, WA St. Mary of the Valley Church.
Fitzwilliam, Ivan '48 (SB) Retired.
Fives, Carl J. '42 (BAL) [B] Emmitsburg, MD Mount Saint Mary's College.
Fives, Carl J. '42 (SCR) On Duty Outside the Diocese.
Fix, Donald P. '80 (PIT) Military Chaplains.
Fix, Joseph J. '68 (GR) Baldwin, MI St. Ann's Church.
Fix, Robert H. '53 (CHR) [4] Columbia, SC Our Lady of the Hills Church.
Fizcaya, Natividad Acevedo *o.p.* (SJN) [C] Toa Alta, PR Santo Domingo de Guzman Priory.
Flaat, Bart A. *c.i.c.m.* '63 (BWN) [4] McAllen, TX St. Joseph the Worker Church.
Flach, Carl J. '58 (P) Hillsboro, OR St. Matthew Church.
Flach, James A. '86 (SFD) Grantfork, IL St. Gertrude Church; Marine, IL St. Elizabeth Church; St. Jacob, IL St. James Church.
Flach, Thomas D. '71 (BEL) Caseyville, IL St. Stephen Church.
Flack, Robert *s.j.* (STL) [C] St. Louis, MO Saint Louis University.
Flack, Robert S. *s.j.* (STL) [P] St. Louis, MO Jesuit Community Corporation at St. Louis University - Jesuit Hall.
Fladung, Charles J. '92 (DAV) Charlotte, IA Assumption and St. Patrick's Church; Sugar Creek, IA Ss. Mary and Joseph Church.
Flagg, Robert W. '65 (BO) [A] Boston, MA St. John's Seminary.
Flagg, Wayne N. '88 (VIC) Frelsburg, TX SS. Peter and Paul Church; Mentz, TX St. Roch Church.
Flagor, David A. '91 (DOD) Greensburg, KS St. Joseph Church; Leoti, KS St. Anthony of Padua Church; Marienthal, KS St. Mary Church; Tribune, KS St. Joseph Church.
Flahavan, Edward J. '57 (STP) St. Paul, MN Ramsey County Correctional Facilities; Special Assignment; Retired.
Flahavan, Robert J. *s.j.* '50 (MIL) [P] Wauwatosa, WI Jesuit Community at St. Camillus.
Flaherty, Charles B. *s.s.c.* '50 (BO) [34] Boston, MA St. John Chrysostom Church; [W] Quincy, MA St. Columban's Foreign Mission Society.
Flaherty, Daniel E. '70 (BO) Awaiting Assignment.
Flaherty, Daniel J. '54 (DEN) Retired.
Flaherty, Daniel L. *s.j.* '60 (CHI) [N] Chicago, IL Chicago Province of the Society of Jesus-Provincial Office; [N] Evanston, IL Canisius House.
Flaherty, Edward F. *s.j.* '65 (DEN) [M] Denver, CO Xavier Jesuit Center.
Flaherty, Francis T. '62 (WDC) Retired.
Flaherty, Frederick R. *m.s.* '57 (R) Havelock, NC Annunciation Church.
Flaherty, Msgr. J. Francis *p.a.* '55 (CAM) Somerdale, NJ Our Lady of Grace Church; Retired.
Flaherty, James J. '80 (PT) De Funiak Springs, FL St. Margaret Church; Freeport, FL Christ the King Mission Church.
Flaherty, James P. *s.j.* '92 (MIL) [P] Milwaukee, WI Jesuit Provincial Office, Wisconsin Province.
Flaherty, James P. *s.j.* '92 (NY) [28] New York, NY Corpus Christi Church.
Flaherty, Jay '85 (KNX) Gatlinburg, TN St. Mary Church.
Flaherty, Jay M. '85 (NSH) On Duty Outside the Diocese.
Flaherty, John '90 (DUB) [D] Gilbertville, IA Don Bosco High School.
Flaherty, John J. *o.s.a.* '55 (CHI) [N] Olympia Fields, IL Tolentine Monastery at Tolentine Center.
Flaherty, John R. '90 (DUB) Raymond, IA St. Joseph's Church.
Flaherty, Kenneth *t.o.r.* (ALT) [F] Loretto, PA Mount Assisi Friary.
Flaherty, Kevin H. *s.j.* '83 (CHI) [N] Chicago, IL Chicago Province of the Society of Jesus-Provincial Office.
Flaherty, Kevin H. *s.j.* '83 (FgM) Provinces.
Flaherty, Kevin S. '69 (RVC) Absent on Leave.
Flaherty, Leon *c.pp.s.* '61 (GRY) [4] Whiting, IN St. John the Baptist Church.
Flaherty, Malachy *o.f.m.cap.* (RVC) Retired.
Flaherty, Malachy *o.c.s.o.* '60 (SLC) [F] Huntsville, UT Abbey of Our Lady of the Holy Trinity of the Order of Cistercians.
Flaherty, Malachy C. *o.f.m.cap.* '42 (RVC) Greenlawn, NY St. Francis of Assisi Church; Melville, NY Long Island Developmental Center.
Flaherty, Michael T. '73 (CIN) [55] Cincinnati, OH St. Margaret of Cortona Church.
Flaherty, Richard *o.f.m.* (BUF) [C] St. Bonaventure, NY St. Bonaventure University.
Flaherty, Richard C. *o.f.m.* '82 (BUF) [O] St. Bonaventure, NY St. Bonaventure Friary.
Flaherty, Thomas *o.s.b.* '48 (KCK) [H] Atchison, KS St. Benedict's Abbey.
Flaherty, William '52 (CHI) Winnetka, IL SS. Faith, Hope and Charity Church.
Flaherty, William H. '33 (RVC) Retired.
Flaherty, William J. '52 (CHI) Flossmoor, IL Infant Jesus of Prague Church; Retired.
Flahive, James J. '48 (SPR) [2] Chicopee, MA Holy Name of Jesus Church.
Flajole, John *o.f.m.* '64 (LA) [R] Santa Barbara, CA Franciscan Friary, Order of Friars Minor (Old Mission).
Flak, Mirko *s.d.b.* '49 (LA) [X] Rosemead, CA St. Joseph's Salesian Youth Renewal Center.
Flammia, Paul '96 (BO) Saugus, MA Blessed Sacrament Church.
Flanagan, Austin E. '66 (SCR) [2] Hazleton, PA Church of the Most Precious Blood; [I] Hazleton, PA Hazleton-Saint Joseph Medical Center.
Flanagan, Bernard A. '82 (ALN) [C] Pottsville, PA Nativity B.V.M. High School.
Flanagan, Bernard F. '82 (ALN) [3] Pottsville, PA Mary Queen of Peace Church.
Flanagan, Brian '63 (PAT) [7] Clifton, NJ St. Paul Church.
Flanagan, Bruce G. '78 (BO) Hanover, MA St. Mary of the Sacred Heart Church.
Flanagan, Damian '91 (MIA) [6] Miami, FL Good Shepherd Church.
Flanagan, David J. '87 (MAD) Dickeyville, WI Holy Ghost Church.
Flanagan, Edward *o.f.m.* '64 (SP) [O] Belleair Bluffs, FL St. James Friary.
Flanagan, Edward R. '88 (MET) Spotswood, NJ Immaculate Conception Church.
Flanagan, Francis A. *c.ss.r.* '42 (STL) [P] Liguori, MO St. Clement Health Care Center.
Flanagan, Msgr. Francis B. '32 (BUR) Retired.
Flanagan, Francis D. *o.m.i.* '36 (BO) [Z] Tewksbury, MA Immaculate Heart of Mary Novitiate-Infirmary.
Flanagan, James *s.o.l.t.* '52 (CC) Robstown, TX St. Anthony Church; [H] Robstown, TX Society of Our Lady of the Most Holy Trinity.
Flanagan, James D. '71 (NY) [147] Bronx, NY Holy Family Church.
Flanagan, James E. *c.s.s.* '50 (SPR) [9] Springfield, MA Our Lady of Mt. Carmel Church.
Flanagan, James H. '52 (BO) On Duty Outside the Archdiocese.
Flanagan, James W. '61 (CLV) [Y] Berea, OH Office of Newman Campus Ministry.
Flanagan, James W. '61 (DUB) On Duty Outside the Archdiocese.
Flanagan, John '59 (SY) [4] Utica, NY Sacred Heart Church.
Flanagan, John *m.s.f.* '74 (SAT) Kenedy, TX Our Lady of Peace Church; Runge, TX St. Anthony's Church.
Flanagan, John B. '97 (PH) Lansdale, PA St. Stanislaus Church.
Flanagan, John D. '73 (NY) [96] New York, NY Our Lady of the Rosary Church.
Flanagan, Joseph F. X. *s.j.* '59 (BO) [W] Chestnut Hill, MA The Jesuit Community at Boston College.
Flanagan, Lawrence W. *s.j.* '52 (OM) [K] Omaha, NE Jesuit Community At Creighton University.
Flanagan, Michael J. *m.s.* '60 (ATL) Snellville, GA St. Oliver Plunkett Church.
Flanagan, Michael T. '65 (JC) Columbia, MO Our Lady of Lourdes Church.
Flanagan, Msgr. P. Kevin '59 (PAT) Chester, NJ St. Lawrence the Martyr Church.
Flanagan, Patrick *c.m.* (BUF) [R] Williamsville, NY Campus Ministry.
Flanagan, Msgr. Patrick J. '56 (SAT) Converse, TX St. Monica Church.
Flanagan, Patrick S. *c.m.* '92 (BUF) [C] Niagara University, NY Niagara University.
Flanagan, Patrick S.L. *c.m.* '92 (BUF) [O] Niagara University, NY Vincentian Community at Niagara University.
Flanagan, Sean B. '59 (LA) Reseda, CA St. Catherine of Siena Church.
Flanagan, Thomas '56 (SAT) [31] San Antonio, TX St. Brigid Church.
Flanagan, Msgr. Thomas J. '49 (BRK) Retired.
Flanagan, Thomas J. '74 (SC) On Duty Outside the Diocese.
Flanagan, William '64 (JC) Monroe City, MO Holy Rosary Church.
Flanagan, William J. '28 (SFR) Belmont, CA St. Mark Church.
Flanagan, William J. '46 (SFR) Retired.
Flanary, Michael '89 (GB) Algoma, WI St. Mary Church.
Flanery, Joseph-Mary *o.c.d.* '55 (MIL) [P] Holy Hill, WI Discalced Carmelite Monastery.
Flanigan, Edward J. *m.m.* '56 (FgM) Maryknoll Foreign Missions.
Flanigan, Msgr. Gerald A. '51 (DET) Retired.
Flanigan, James F. *c.s.c.* '62 (FTW) [B] Notre Dame, IN University of Notre Dame Du Lac; [J] South Bend, IN Congregation of Holy Cross Indiana Province Provincial House.
Flanigan, Thomas K. '50 (ALB) [12] Troy, NY St. Peter Church.
Flanigan, Thomas P. '69 (PH) Upper Gwynedd, PA Corpus Christi Church.
Flanik, Rudolph *o.carm.* '42 (JOL) [J] Darien, IL Carmelite Provincial Office.
Flannery, Edward H. '37 (PRO) Smithfield, RI St. Michael Church.
Flannery, Edward M. '35 (CHI) [182] Chicago, IL St. Rene Goupil Church; Retired.
Flannery, Gerald K. '59 (DET) [1] Livonia, MI St. Aidan Church.
Flannery, Joseph D. '53 (SCR) Taylor, PA Immaculate Conception Church.
Flannery, Kevin L. *s.j.* '87 (DET) [K] Detroit, MI Jesuit Provincial Office-Detroit Province of the Society of Jesus.
Flannery, Michael '50 (NY) Retired.
Flannery, Michael '64 (JKS) [1] Jackson, MS St. Peter Cathedral.
Flannery, Michael '97 (ALB) Glenville, NY Immaculate Conception Church.
Flannery, Patrick R. '97 (NEW) Paramus, NJ Our Lady of the Visitation Church.
Flannery, Robert B. '73 (BEL) Trenton, IL St. Mary Church.
Flannigan, John G. *s.j.* '43 (STL) [O] St. Louis, MO Fusz Pavilion.
Flannigan, Patrick *o.f.m.* '90 (WDC) [M] Washington, DC Commissariat of the Holy Land, Franciscan Monastery - Mount St. Sepulchre.
Flaska, John '68 (SFE) Military Chaplains.
Flaska, Michael J. (DEN) [18] Denver, CO Notre Dame Church.
Flatley, Brian M. '66 (BO) [1] Arlington, MA St. Agnes Church.
Flatley, Eugene T. '46 (GB) Retired.
Flattery, John J. '55 (PEO) Retired.
Flavin, James *o.m.i.* '63 (MIA) Miramar, FL St. Stephen Church.
Flavin, James A. '87 (BO) [2] Brockton, MA St. Colman of Cloyne Church.
Flavin, John E. '61 (CHI) Glenview, IL Our Lady of Perpetual Help Church; [M] Glenview, IL Maryhaven Inc.
Fleck, David '75 (EVN) St. Philip, IN St. Philip's Church.
Fleck, John '59 (TOL) Spencerville, OH St. Patrick Church.
Fleck, John W. '59 (TOL) Landeck, OH St. John Baptist Church.
Fleck, Kenneth J. '76 (CHI) [22] Chicago, IL St. Barnabas Church.
Fleck, Richard A. *o.p.* '55 (BO) [W] Dover, MA St. Stephen Priory; [Y] Dover, MA St. Stephen Priory Spiritual Life Center.
Flecky, Michael J. *s.j.* '77 (OM) [K] Omaha, NE Jesuit Community At Creighton University.
Flegge, William '60 (SLC) Provo, UT St. Francis of Assisi Church.
Fleischhacker, John J. *o.s.c.* '61 (DUL) McGregor, MN Holy Family Church.
Fleischhacker, John J. *o.s.c.* '61 (SCL) [I] Onamia, MN Crosier Monastery.
Fleischman, Richard J. '68 (MIL) [2] Sheboygan, WI SS. Cyril and Methodius Church; [Y] Sheboygan, WI

St. Thomas High School, Inc.
Fleischmann, George R. '56 (MIL) Retired.
Fleiter, Robert F. '61 (STL) Herculaneum, MO Church of the Assumption of B.V.M.
Flek, Msgr. Ladis Laus J. (PAT) Retired.
Fleming, Alfred J. *m.m.* '60 (FgM) Maryknoll Foreign Missions.
Fleming, Austin H. '73 (BO) Concord, MA Our Lady Help of Christians Church.
Fleming, Daniel J. '96 (ATL) Duluth, GA St. Benedict Church.
Fleming, David *o.f.m.* '43 (BO) [Z] Boston, MA Saint Anthony Residence.
Fleming, David *s.m.* '69 (STL) [P] St. Louis, MO Provincialate of the Society of Mary, Province of St. Louis.
Fleming, David '90 (DM) On Special Assignment.
Fleming, David L. '65 (STL) [P] St. Louis, MO Jesuit Community Corporation at St. Louis University - Jesuit Hall; [P] St. Louis, MO The Jesuits of the Missouri Province.
Fleming, Msgr. Edward J. '44 (NEW) Retired; [B] South Orange, NJ Seton Hall University.
Fleming, Msgr. Francis J. '39 (STP) [M] St. Paul, MN Franciscan Health Community.
Fleming, Msgr. Francis J. '42 (STP) Retired.
Fleming, George '94 (ALB) [9] Schenectady, NY St. John the Evangelist Church.
Fleming, J. Brendan '52 (P) Sutherlin, OR St. Francis Xavier Church.
Fleming, J.J. '85 (SAG) Carrollton, MI St. John the Baptist Church.
Fleming, James J. *s.j.* '95 (BO) [W] Boston, MA The Society of Jesus of New England-Provincial Offices.
Fleming, James J. *s.j.* '95 (SJ) [B] Santa Clara, CA Santa Clara University.
Fleming, Jeffrey '92 (HEL) Graduate Studies.
Fleming, John F. '49 (NY) Retired.
Fleming, John M. '61 (CAM) Hammonton, NJ St. Anthony of Padua Church.
Fleming, John R. '42 (NU) Retired.
Fleming, John R. '42 (STP) [M] St. Paul, MN Franciscan Health Community.
Fleming, John W. '96 (MAN) [3] Nashua, NH St. Christopher Church.
Fleming, Msgr. Joseph H. '43 (ALT) Retired.
Fleming, Joseph W. '74 (ALT) St. Augustine, PA St. Augustine Church.
Fleming, Martin M.P. '52 (STP) Retired; [M] St. Paul, MN Franciscan Health Community.
Fleming, Patrick J. *c.m.* '43 (PH) [AA] Philadelphia, PA Congregation of the Mission.
Fleming, Msgr. Patrick V. '48 (ALT) Retired.
Fleming, R. Maurus *o.s.b.* '53 (PRO) [P] Portsmouth, RI Abbey of St. Gregory the Great.
Fleming, Raymond H. '82 (ROC) [46] Rochester, NY Emmanuel Church of the Deaf of the Diocese of Rochester; [48] Rochester, NY St. Monica Church; [L] Rochester, NY St. Francis de Sales Deaf Assn.
Fleming, Terence K. '67 (ROC) On Duty Outside the Diocese.
Fleming, Thomas (JOL) [I] Naperville, IL St. John Vianney Villa.
Fleming, Thomas '55 (JOL) Retired.
Fleming, Thomas B. '76 (WOR) [7] Worcester, MA Notre Dame des Canadiens - St. Joseph Church.
Fleming, Thomas E. *s.j.* '50 (BUF) [O] Buffalo, NY Canisius Jesuit Community.
Fleming, Thomas F. *s.j.* '42 (BO) [W] Chestnut Hill, MA The Jesuit Community at Boston College.
Fleming, Thomas J. '59 (BO) [3] Gloucester, MA St. Peter Church.
Fleming, Thomas J. '85 (SAG) Zilwaukee, MI St. Matthew Church.
Fleming, Msgr. Vincent A. '44 (SR) Retired.
Fleming, Msgr. W. Stanley '52 (COV) Retired.
Fleming, Msgr. William J. '48 (SCR) [1] Williamsport, PA Annunciation Church.
Fleming, William J. '58 (NSH) [1] Nashville, TN Cathedral of the Incarnation.
Flemming, James '86 (VEN) Lehigh Acres, FL St. Raphael Church.
Flemming, Neil '58 (VEN) Cape Coral, FL St. Andrew Church.
Flemming, Terrence K. (SP) [K] St. Petersburg, FL St. Anthony's Hospital, Inc.
Flens, Daniel A. '89 (CHI) Chicago Heights, IL St. Kieran Church.
Flesey, Msgr. John W. '69 (NEW) [A] South Orange, NJ Immaculate Conception Seminary; [B] South Orange, NJ Seton Hall University; [B] South Orange, NJ Seton Hall University.
Fletcher, Emeric *o.s.b.* (KCK) Fidelity, KS St. Augustine's Church; Sabetha, KS Sacred Heart Church.
Fletcher, Emeric *o.s.b.* '60 (KCK) [H] Atchison, KS St. Benedict's Abbey.
Fletcher, Patrick '85 (PCE) On Duty Outside the Diocese.
Fleury, Joseph M. '84 (WDC) [M] Washington, DC Marist Provincial House.
Flickinger, Don '64 (SJ) [6] San Jose, CA St. Frances Cabrini Church.
Flickinger, Don D. '64 (FRS) On Duty Outside the Diocese.
Flickinger, Robert E. '75 (KAL) Paw Paw, MI St. Mary Church.
Flinn, Msgr. George B. '66 (ALT) [1] Johnstown, PA St. John Gualbert Cathedral.
Flint, Edward A. *s.j.* (DET) [E] Detroit, MI University of Detroit Jesuit High School and Academy.
Flint, James *o.s.b.* '83 (JOL) [A] Lisle, IL Benedictine University; [J] Lisle, IL St. Procopius Abbey.
Flint, Kenneth '42 (NOR) Retired.
Flis, Stanislaw '69 (DET) [A] Orchard Lake, MI SS. Cyril and Methodius Seminary.
Flisiak, Stefan '32 (OM) Retired.
Fliss, James W. '75 (BUF) [3] Buffalo, NY St. Agatha Church.
Fliss, Paul J. '92 (MIL) [6] Sheboygan, WI St. Peter Claver Church.
Fliss, Richard '66 (LC) Oxford, WI Federal Correctional Institute.
Fliss, Richard L. '66 (LC) Awaiting Assignment.
Floch, W. Roy '77 (SPK) Odessa, WA St. Joseph Church; Wilbur, WA Sacred Heart Church.
Flock, Robert H. '82 (LC) Foreign Missions.
Floersh, Philip M. *c.m.* '62 (STL) [P] St. Louis, MO Vincentian Residence.
Flohr, Gregory J. '64 (GBG) Saltsburg, PA St. Matthew Church.
Flood, Augustine '64 (GBG) Crabtree, PA St. Bartholomew Church.
Flood, Charles J. *o.ss.t.* '90 (BAL) [M] Baltimore, MD Holy Trinity Monastery.
Flood, Francis A. *o.s.b.* '93 (SP) [O] St. Leo, FL St. Leo Abbey.
Flood, J. Michael '68 (PH) Glenside, PA St. Luke the Evangelist Church; [EE] Philadelphia, PA Newman Apostolate.
Flood, James F. '62 (CLV) Stow, OH Holy Family Church.
Flood, Msgr. James J. '58 (PH) Narberth, PA St. Margaret Church.
Flood, Matthew C. *s.j.* '61 (NY) [F] New York, NY Fordham Preparatory School; [DD] New York, NY Jesuit Community at Fordham University.
Flood, Maurice *o.c.s.o.* '91 (ARL) [J] Berryville, VA Cistercian Abbey of Our Lady of the Holy Cross; [L] Berryville, VA Retreat House, Holy Cross Abbey.
Flood, Msgr. Patrick '45 (FRS) Retired.
Flood, Paul A. '90 (ATL) Lithonia, GA Christ Our Hope Church.
Flood, Peter J. '69 (TR) Military Chaplains.
Flood, Msgr. William '57 (BRK) [211] Queens, NY Our Lady of Grace Church.
Flor, Carlos (NEW) [3] Union City, NJ SS. Joseph and Michael Church.
Flora, Carmel *o.f.m.cap.* '53 (DET) [K] Detroit, MI St. Bonaventure Friary.
Flora, Carmel *o.f.m.cap.* '53 (FgM) Capuchin Foreign Missions.
Florczyk, Franciszek '81 (CHI) [60] Chicago, IL Five Holy Martyrs Church.
Florczyk, Walter '62 (SY) Absent on Sick Leave.
Florek, Msgr. Frederick J. '64 (SD) [36] San Diego, CA St. Therese Church.
Florek, Richard *o.f.m.conv.* '72 (BAL) [26] Baltimore, MD St. Clement Mary Hofbauer Church.
Florek, Thomas W. *s.j.* (NY) [B] Bronx, NY Ciszek Hall.
Florek, Thomas W. *s.j.* '86 (CHI) [N] Chicago, IL Chicago Province of the Society of Jesus-Provincial Office.
Flores, Cirilo (ORG) La Habra, CA Our Lady of Guadalupe Church.
Flores, Msgr. Daniel '88 (CC) On Special Assignment; On Duty Outside the Diocese.
Flores, Efrain *s.v.d.* '91 (LA) [71] Los Angeles, CA St. John, The Evangelist Church.
Flores, Gabriel R. *m.c.c.j.* '85 (SFR) [54] San Francisco, CA Visitacion, Church of the.
Flores, Hector '91 (SR) Arcata, CA St. Mary's Church; Fortuna, CA St. Joseph Church.
Flores, Jose '73 (CGS) Caguas, P.R. Hospital Hima; [F] Caguas, PR Movimiento Juan XXIII.
Flores, Jose A. (ARE) On Duty Outside the Diocese.
Flores, Lee '85 (GAL) [39] Houston, TX St. Jerome Church.
Flores, Manuel M. '89 (ARE) [2] Camuy, PR Our Lady of the Miraculous Medal Church.
Flores, Ramiro '95 (OAK) Pinole, CA St. Joseph's Church.
Flores, Richard '74 (FWT) [15] Fort Worth, TX St. Rita Church.
Flores, Roberto *s.v.d.* (OAK) [6] Oakland, CA St. Bernard's Church.
Flores, Samuel *o.f.m.cap.* '44 (LA) Santa Maria, CA St. Mary of the Assumption Church.
Flores, Virgilio M. (LSC) Hobbs, NM Our Lady of Guadalupe Church.
Floretta, Edward A. '60 (BRK) [133] Brooklyn, NY SS. Simon and Jude Church.
Florez, Laurence A. '59 (PHX) Retired.
Florez, Luis '59 (STA) [1] Jacksonville, FL Assumption Church.
Florez Gallo, Jhon Jaime '91 (CGS) Vieques, PR Inmaculada Concepcion Church.
Flori, David J. '86 (DAL) Richardson, TX St. Paul the Apostle Church.
Florido, Msgr. Raphael A. '45 (BRK) Retired.
Florido, Vicente '70 (NY) [163] Bronx, NY St. Martin of Tours Church.
Florio, Anselmo M. *o.cist.* '54 (TR) Mount Laurel, NJ St. John Neumann Church; [M] Mount Laurel, NJ Cistercian Monastery of Our Lady of Fatima.
Florival, Lys *c.s.sp.* (CHI) [172] Chicago, IL St. Philomena Church.
Flour, Anton '35 (SPK) Retired.
Flower, Thomas A. '65 (HRT) Tariffville, CT St. Bernard's Church.
Flowers, Thomas A. '77 (WIL) Middletown, DE St. Joseph Church.
Fluetsch, John '91 (FRS) Planada, CA Sacred Heart Church.
Flusche, David '46 (LR) [A] Subiaco, AR Subiaco Monastery.
Flusche, Ernest A. '54 (OKL) Norman, OK St. Joseph's Church.
Flusche, Vincent '90 (LR) [6] Little Rock, AR St. Edward Church.
Flusk, Msgr. Joseph F. '53 (NEW) Hohokus, NJ St. Luke's Church.
Flynn, Anthony G. '66 (PH) Chester Heights, PA St. Thomas the Apostle Church.
Flynn, Arthur C. '52 (BO) Reading, MA St. Agnes Church.
Flynn, Brian V. *o.f.m.* '60 (SPK) [11] Spokane, WA St. Francis of Assisi, Friars Church.
Flynn, Charles '69 (DUL) [8] West Duluth, MN St. James Church.
Flynn, Charles R. *o.s.a.* '43 (PH) [AA] Villanova, PA St. Thomas Monastery.
Flynn, Msgr. Daniel V. '48 (NY) Harrison, NY St. Gregory the Great Church.
Flynn, Dennis *s.v.d.* '61 (SB) San Bernardino, CA San Bernardino County Medical Center.
Flynn, Edmund *o.c.s.o.* '70 (ARL) [J] Berryville, VA Cistercian Abbey of Our Lady of the Holy Cross.
Flynn, Edward J. '44 (RVC) Retired; [N] Uniondale, NY St. Pius X Residence.
Flynn, Edward R. '54 (SD) On Duty Outside the Diocese.
Flynn, Francis '67 (PMB) Retired.
Flynn, Francis J. '37 (GR) Retired.
Flynn, Francis J. '37 (KAL) Retired.
Flynn, Francis J. '50 (BRK) Retired.
Flynn, Francis J. '53 (BRK) Absent on Sick Leave.
Flynn, Francis J. '69 (OG) Potsdam, NY St. Mary Church; Potsdam, NY St. Francis of Assisi Campus Parish (Newman Center) Church.
Flynn, Francis J. *m.m.* '76 (NY) [DD] Maryknoll, NY Maryknoll Fathers and Brothers.
Flynn, George '41 (JOL) Retired.
Flynn, George '56 (FgM) Society of St. James the Apostle.
Flynn, George R. '56 (BO) Society of St. James the Apostle.
Flynn, J. Francis *m.m.* '52 (FgM) Maryknoll Foreign Missions.
Flynn, J. Joseph *o.f.m.cap.* (NY) [GG] New York, NY University Apostolate.
Flynn, J. Michael *s.j.* '96 (R) [7] Raleigh, NC St. Raphael Church.
Flynn, James '55 (L) [52] Louisville, KY St. Martin de Porres Church.
Flynn, Msgr. James B. '48 (SFR) Redwood City, CA St. Matthias Church.
Flynn, James B. '64 (WOR) Southborough, MA St. Matthew Church; [C] Worcester, MA Holy Name Central Catholic Junior/Senior High School.
Flynn, James E. *s.j.* '73 (PHX) [B] Phoenix, AZ Brophy College Preparatory.
Flynn, James F. '67 (CHI) [83] Chicago, IL Holy Name of Mary Church.
Flynn, James P. '36 (BUF) Retired.
Flynn, James P. '47 (NY) Patterson, NY Sacred Heart Church; Retired.
Flynn, James R. *o.s.a.* '72 (PH) [G] Malvern, PA Malvern Preparatory School for Boys.
Flynn, John C. '55 (NY) [163] Bronx, NY St. Martin of Tours Church.
Flynn, John E. *o.s.a.* '53 (CHI) [40] Chicago, IL St. Clare of Montefalco Church.
Flynn, Msgr. John F. '52 (SAT) [57] San Antonio, TX St. Matthew's Church.
Flynn, John F. *s.m.a.* '56 (PMB) Vero Beach, FL St. Helen Church.
Flynn, John H. (BO) Retired.
Flynn, John J. *s.j.* '69 (LA) [C] Los Angeles, CA Loyola Marymount University.
Flynn, John L. *s.j.* '64 (SJ) [D] San Jose, CA Bellarmine College Preparatory.
Flynn, John R. *o.s.a.* '71 (ORL) Casselberry, FL St. Augustine Church; [E] Orlando, FL University of

Central Florida Newman Center.
Flynn, Joseph A. '47 (HRT) Retired.
Flynn, Joseph D. '62 (BO) Hingham, MA St. Paul Church; Walpole, MA Blessed Sacrament Church.
Flynn, Joseph Leo *c.p.* '33 (HRT) [M] West Hartford, CT Holy Family Monastery/Retreat.
Flynn, Joseph P. *c.s.p.* '44 (NY) [104] New York, NY St. Paul the Apostle Church; [DD] Jamaica Estates, NY Paulist Fathers Generalate.
Flynn, Lawrence W. *m.m.* '87 (FgM) Maryknoll Foreign Missions.
Flynn, Mark F. '72 (HRT) Southbury, CT Sacred Heart Church.
Flynn, Msgr. Martin J. '30 (RVC) Huntington, NY St. Patrick's Church; Retired.
Flynn, Matthew *o.c.s.o.* '58 (WOR) [N] Spencer, MA St. Joseph's Abbey.
Flynn, Michael *o.carm.* '60 (CHI) [142] Chicago, IL Nativity of Our Lord Church.
Flynn, Michael *o.carm.* '61 (JOL) [J] Darien, IL Carmelite Provincial Office.
Flynn, Michael '71 (RVC) Copiague, NY Our Lady of the Assumption Church.
Flynn, Michael E. '77 (CHI) Hickory Hills, IL St. Patricia Church.
Flynn, Michael F. '91 (BGP) [7] Norwalk, CT St. Thomas the Apostle Church.
Flynn, Michael J. '94 (PT) [4] Pensacola, FL Nativity of Our Lord Church.
Flynn, Michael J. *s.j.* '96 (R) [E] Raleigh, NC Jesuit Community.
Flynn, Patrick *c.ss.r.* '69 (BAL) Annapolis, MD St. Mary Church; [M] Annapolis, MD Saint Mary Rectory.
Flynn, Robert G. '53 (BO) Retired.
Flynn, Robert J. *s.j.* '50 (FgM) Provinces.
Flynn, Robert V. '56 (Y) Streetsboro, OH St. Joan of Arc Church.
Flynn, Msgr. Sean P. '75 (TR) [1] Toms River, NJ St. Joseph Church.
Flynn, Stephen F.X. '58 (ALN) Retired.
Flynn, Thomas '61 (HEL) On Duty Outside the Diocese.
Flynn, Thomas A. '49 (SCR) Retired.
Flynn, Thomas A. '57 (SCR) [N] Dunmore, PA Villa St. Joseph.
Flynn, Thomas A. '60 (CLV) North Olmsted, OH St. Clarence Church.
Flynn, Thomas J. *c.s.sp.* '53 (SHP) Rayville, LA Sacred Heart Church.
Flynn, Msgr. Thomas M. '58 (CAM) Oaklyn, NJ St. Aloysius Church.
Flynn, Thomas P. (NY) [132] Bronx, NY St. Barnabas Church.
Flynn, Thomas P. '60 (DET) Grosse Ile, MI Sacred Heart Church.
Flynn, Vincent J. '45 (HRT) Retired.
Flynn, William J. *s.s.* '59 (SCR) Montdale, PA Corpus Christi Church.
Flynn, William J. '64 (NOR) [E] Windham, CT St. Joseph Living Center.
Flynt, James M. '85 (MIL) [16] Milwaukee, WI St. Casimir Church; [50] Milwaukee, WI St. Mary of Czestochowa Church.
Fobare, Scott D. '87 (OG) [1] Watertown, NY Holy Family Church.
Fodor, Nicholas Vitez *sch.p.* '49 (BUF) [O] Derby, NY Piarist Fathers.
Foeckler, Christopher *m.j.* '86 (PCE) [7] Ponce, PR Santa Maria Church.
Foelker, James *o.m.i.* '55 (CC) [4] Kingsville, TX St. Martin Church.
Foeller, Msgr. Charles J. '50 (COL) Cardington, OH Sacred Hearts Church.
Foerch, Benjamin J. *o.f.m.* '65 (SCR) [12] Wilkes-Barre, PA St. Joseph Church; Wilkes-Barre, PA Veteran's Administration Hospital; [M] Wilkes-Barre, PA St. Joseph's Friary.
Foerstler, Vincent *o.p.* (OAK) [N] Oakland, CA Western Dominican Province.
Fogal, Joseph B. '75 (WIN) Fairmont, MN St. John Vianney Church.
Fogarty, Austin '81 (ATL) McDonough, GA St. James The Apostle Church.
Fogarty, Daniel '49 (NY) Retired.
Fogarty, Declan (Finbarr) *o.s.a.* '59 (ORG) Buena Park, CA St. Pius V Church.
Fogarty, Msgr. George V. '46 (BRK) [189] Queens, NY St. Kevin Church; Retired; [U] Douglaston, NY Bishop Mugavero Residence.
Fogarty, Gerald J. *o.m.i.* '59 (NO) [R] Marrero, LA Ave Maria Retreat House.
Fogarty, Gerald P. *s.j.* '70 (WDC) [M] Washington, DC The Jesuit Community at Georgetown University.
Fogarty, James '54 (SLC) Retired.
Fogarty, Joseph *o.p.* '59 (MAD) [J] Sinsinawa, WI Dominican Motherhouse.
Fogarty, Joseph *o.p.* '94 (DUB) [I] Dubuque, IA St. Dominic Villa.
Fogarty, Msgr. Noel '57 (MIA) Plantation, FL St. Gregory Church.
Fogarty, Paul '67 (ATL) [2] Atlanta, GA Holy Cross Church.
Fogarty, Thomas *s.s.p.* '57 (Y) [A] Canfield, OH Society of St. Paul.
Fogle, Bruce '83 (OWN) Axtel, KY St. Anthony Church; McQuady, KY St. Mary-of-the-Woods Church.
Foglio, John '61 (LAN) Retired.
Fohlin, Paul *o.c.d.* '81 (MIL) [P] Holy Hill, WI Discalced Carmelite Monastery.
Foiliard, Msgr. John P. '50 (LA) Retired.
Foisy, Leonard R. '57 (MAN) [11] Manchester, NH St. John the Baptist Church; Retired.
Foix, Evarist V. *o.c.d.* '28 (LR) [A] Little Rock, AR Marylake - Carmelite Novitiate.
Foken, Herman J. '43 (TLS) Retired.
Folbrecht, Robert '75 (LA) Chatsworth, CA St. John Eudes Church; Los Angeles, CA L.A. County Fire Dept.
Folchetti, John T. '74 (BRK) Released from Diocesan Assignment.
Folda, John T. '89 (LIN) [1] Lincoln, NE Cathedral of the Risen Christ.
Foley, Msgr. Andrew E. '54 (SFS) Retired.
Foley, Augustine E. *o.s.b.* '89 (NO) [A] St. Benedict, LA St. Joseph's Seminary College; [P] St. Benedict, LA St. Joseph Abbey.
Foley, B. Patrick *c.s.c.* (SAT) [F] San Antonio, TX Holy Cross High School.
Foley, Brendan P. (HT) Retired.
Foley, Daniel *s.j.* '54 (CIN) [M] Cincinnati, OH Faber Jesuit Community.
Foley, Msgr. Daniel J. '40 (BGP) Retired; [J] Danbury, CT The Pope John Paul II Center for Health Care, Inc.
Foley, Daniel R. '60 (SPR) [10] Holyoke, MA St. Jerome's Church.
Foley, David '72 (MEM) [H] Memphis, TN St. Peter Villa.
Foley, David E. '56 (BIR) [1] Birmingham, AL St. Paul's Cathedral.
Foley, David M. '72 (MEM) [27] Memphis, TN St. Therese of the Infant Jesus Church.
Foley, Dennis *c.ss.r.* '61 (TR) [Q] Long Branch, NJ San Alfonso Retreat House.
Foley, Edward *o.f.m.cap.* '75 (CHI) [B] Chicago, IL The Catholic Theological Union at Chicago.
Foley, Eugene *o.carm.* '86 (PMB) [5] Boca Raton, FL St. Jude Church.
Foley, Francis P. '84 (PH) Military Chaplains.
Foley, Gerald J. '48 (BO) Saugus, MA Blessed Sacrament Church.
Foley, Gerald J. '59 (GB) [2] Manitowoc, WI Holy Innocents Church.
Foley, Gerald K. '61 (CR) On Duty Outside the Diocese.
Foley, Gerald K. '61 (STP) St. Paul, MN HealthEast, Inc.
Foley, Gerard M. '56 (ALX) Tioga, LA Immaculate Heart of Mary Church.
Foley, Hugh *c.s.b.* (LSC) Truth or Consequences, NM Our Lady of Perpetual Help Church.
Foley, Ignatius L. *c.m.* '41 (NO) [P] New Orleans, LA Vincentian Fathers.
Foley, James D. '60 (BO) [6] Salem, MA St. Joseph Church.
Foley, James F. '36 (NEW) Retired.
Foley, James F. '49 (BUR) Retired.
Foley, James J. '66 (PH) East Goshen, PA SS. Peter and Paul Church.
Foley, James J. '78 (BO) On Duty Outside the Archdiocese; [Q] Brighton, MA St. Elizabeth's Hospital of Boston.
Foley, Msgr. James S. '32 (TR) Bordentown, NJ St. Mary Church; Retired.
Foley, James S. *s.j.* '52 (NEW) [C] Jersey City, NJ St. Peter's Preparatory School.
Foley, Jerome '84 (SFR) Special Assignment.
Foley, Jerome P. '80 (SFR) [S] San Francisco, CA Newman Center, San Francisco State University.
Foley, Jerome P. '84 (SFR) [52] San Francisco, CA St. Thomas More Church.
Foley, John *o.s.f.s.* '59 (STO) Sonora, CA St. Patrick Church.
Foley, John B. *s.j.* (STL) [C] St. Louis, MO Saint Louis University.
Foley, John B. *s.j.* '72 (STL) [P] St. Louis, MO Jesuit Community Corporation at St. Louis University - Jesuit Hall.
Foley, John E. '40 (BO) Retired.
Foley, John F. *s.j.* '58 (BO) [W] Boston, MA The Society of Jesus of New England-Provincial Offices; [W] Weston, MA Campion Center; [Y] Weston, MA Campion Renewal Center.
Foley, John Fenton *s.j.* (BO) [U] Framingham, MA St. Patrick's Manor, Inc.
Foley, John I. '41 (BO) Retired.
Foley, John J. *s.j.* '59 (CHI) [D] Wilmette, IL Loyola Academy.
Foley, John J. *c.s.p.* '67 (SFR) [31] San Francisco, CA Old St. Mary's Cathedral.
Foley, John J. '74 (WOR) [4] Worcester, MA Christ the King Church.
Foley, John K. '59 (LA) Montrose, CA Holy Redeemer Church.
Foley, John P. *s.j.* '67 (CHI) [177] Chicago, IL St. Procopius Church; [D] Chicago, IL Cristo Rey Jesuit High School, Inc.; [N] Chicago, IL Miguel Pro Jesuit Community.
Foley, John T. '58 (BO) Permanent Disability.
Foley, Joseph P. *c.m.* '68 (BRK) [U] Jamaica, NY St. Vincent's House.
Foley, Leo A. *s.m.* '43 (WDC) [M] Washington, DC Marist Provincial House.
Foley, Louis *o.f.m.* '41 (SP) [O] St. Petersburg, FL St. Anthony Friary.
Foley, Marc *o.c.d.* (CHI) [N] Chicago, IL Edith Stein House of Studies.
Foley, Matthew '89 (CHI) Missionary Work.
Foley, Msgr. Matthew F. '56 (BRK) [37] Brooklyn, NY Epiphany Church.
Foley, Msgr. Maurice D. '34 (LFT) Retired; Retired.
Foley, Michael '70 (PT) [3] Tallahassee, FL Good Shepherd Church.
Foley, Michael *s.p.* '73 (STL) [P] St. Louis, MO Servants of the Paraclete.
Foley, Michael '74 (JOL) Morris, IL Immaculate Conception of the Blessed Virgin Mary Church.
Foley, Michael G. '70 (WOR) Milford, MA St. Mary of the Assumption Church.
Foley, Michael G. '86 (CHI) [105] Chicago, IL St. John Berchmans Church; [A] Chicago, IL Archbishop Quigley Preparatory Seminary.
Foley, Msgr. Noel '63 (JKS) [3] Jackson, MS St. Richard Church; Jackson, MS Institute for the Blind, Institute for the Deaf and Speech Impaired; [G] Jackson, MS Belhaven College Newman Center; [G] Jackson, MS Millsaps College Newman Center; [G] Jackson, MS University of Mississippi Medical Center - Newman Center.
Foley, Patrick *c.s.c.* '56 (SAT) [M] San Antonio, TX Holy Cross Community.
Foley, Patrick H. '72 (STA) Special Assignment.
Foley, Patrick J. '73 (SD) Unassigned.
Foley, Paul T. '55 (WOR) Retired.
Foley, Peter J. '67 (PH) Darby, PA Blessed Virgin Mary Church.
Foley, Richard L. *o.s.a.* '60 (BO) Andover, MA St. Augustine Church.
Foley, Stephen C. '67 (HRT) [A] Bloomfield, CT St. Thomas Seminary.
Foley, Thomas C. '57 (BO) [3] Milton, MA St. Mary of the Hills Church.
Foley, Thomas F. *m.m.* '48 (SJ) [M] Los Altos, CA Maryknoll.
Foley, Thomas S. '86 (BO) Winchester, MA St. Mary Church.
Foley, Timothy M. '65 (STL) Ferguson, MO Sts. John and James Church.
Foley, Walter W. '20 (ATL) Hartwell, GA Sacred Heart of Jesus Church.
Foley, William *s.m.* '48 (BO) [W] Boston, MA Marist Fathers and Brothers Provincial House.
Foley, William A. *s.m.* '48 (ORL) Retired.
Foley, William B. *s.j.* '77 (BO) [W] Boston, MA The Society of Jesus of New England-Provincial Offices.
Foley, William B. '77 (STL) [P] St. Louis, MO Jesuit Community Corporation at St. Louis University - Jesuit Hall.
Foley, William E. '79 (WDC) [35] Washington, DC Our Lady of Victory Church.
Foley, Msgr. William J. '67 (NY) New City, NY St. Augustine Church.
Foley, William P. '74 (BAL) [9] Baltimore, MD Annunciation Church.
Folger, Ronald H. '67 (CHI) Libertyville, IL St. Joseph Church.
Follen, George R. *s.j.* '49 (DET) [61] Detroit, MI SS. Peter and Paul Jesuit Church.
Folliard, Msgr. John '50 (LA) [5] Long Beach, CA St. Cornelius Church.
Follmann, Roland F. *o.s.a.* '60 (JOL) [C] New Lenox, IL Providence Catholic High School; [J] New Lenox, IL Augustinian Friary.
Follmar, A. Joseph '59 (LC) Greenwood, WI St. Mary Help of Christians Church; Willard, WI Holy Family Church.
Folmer, John '68 (SAC) Rancho Cordova, CA St. John Vianney Church.
Folsey, William David *o.p.* '60 (PRO) [P] Providence, RI St. Thomas Aquinas Priory at Providence College.
Folsom, Cassian *o.s.b.* '84 (IND) [J] St. Meinrad, IN St. Meinrad Archabbey.
Folsom, Paul '65 (SCL) Battle Lake, MN Our Lady of the Lake Church; Maine, MN Church of Saint James at Maine.
Folsom, William P., Jr. '91 (MOB) [7] Montgomery, AL Our Lady, Queen of Mercy Church; [K] Montgomery, AL Huntington College Newman Center.
Foltyn, Msgr. Emilian '64 (AUS) Dime Box, TX St. Joseph's Church; Lexington, TX Holy Family Church.
Foltz, Charles '68 (B) [B] Nampa, ID Mercy Medical Center.
Foltz, Michael H. '89 (CR) Argyle, MN St. Rose Church.
Folzenlogan, Joseph D. *s.j.* '71 (IND) [D] Indianapolis, IN Brebeuf Jesuit Preparatory School, Inc.

Folzenlogen, John N. *s.j.* '65 (GAL) [F] Houston, TX Strake, Jesuit College Preparatory Inc.
Fonck, Benet A. *o.f.m.* '72 (STL) [25] St. Louis, MO St. Anthony of Padua Church; [P] St. Louis, MO Franciscan Friary of St. Anthony of Padua.
Fondevila, Perfecto '62 (SJN) [20] San Juan, PR San Francisco Javier Church.
Fondriest, James '72 (Y) Absent on Leave.
Fones, Michael *o.p.* '92 (P) [6] Eugene, OR St. Thomas More Church.
Fonseca, Erwin A. *c.s.c.* '91 (FTW) [J] South Bend, IN Congregation of Holy Cross Indiana Province Provincial House.
Fonseca, Harvey '92 (FRS) Livingston, CA St. Jude Thaddeus Church.
Fonseca, John '50 (BGP) Retired.
Fonseka, Matthew '69 (NEW) Saddle Brook, NJ St. Philip the Apostle Church.
Fonsela, Rolando '94 (SB) [A] Riverside, CA Blessed Junipero Serra House of Formation.
Fontaine, David *o.carm.* '79 (JOL) [J] Darien, IL Carmelite Provincial Office.
Fontaine, Edouard '43 (LAF) Retired.
Fontaine, John-Paul '52 (WOR) Retired.
Fontana, Alphonso R. '97 (HRT) East Haven, CT St. Vincent de Paul's Church.
Fontana, Charles S. '69 (DET) Trenton, MI St. Timothy Church.
Fontana, Glenn '92 (PEO) [11] Peoria, IL St. Martin de Porres Church.
Fontana, Glenn J. '92 (PEO) Carthage, IL Immaculate Conception Church.
Fontana, John *o.s.m.* '78 (STL) Affton, MO Seven Holy Founders Church.
Fontana, John M. *o.s.m.* '78 (CHI) [N] Chicago, IL Servite Friars - Eastern Province.
Fontanella, Andrew J. '56 (HBG) Carlisle, PA St. Patrick Church.
Fontanez, Msgr. Rafael '57 (SJN) [26] San Juan, PR San Jose Church.
Fontanini, Christopher '97 (DM) West Des Moines, IA St. Francis of Assisi Church.
Fonte, Martin M. *f.f.i.* '94 (FR) [J] New Bedford, MA Marian Friary of Our Lady, Queen of the Seraphic Order.
Fontenot, Bryan J. *o.p.* '81 (NO) [25] New Orleans, LA St. Anthony Of Padua Church; [C] New Orleans, LA Xavier University of Louisiana.
Fonti, Joseph '92 (BRK) Graduate Studies.
Fonti, Joseph G. '92 (BRK) [141] Brooklyn, NY St. Thomas Aquinas Church.
Foote, Job J. *o.s.b.* '89 (FgM) American - Cassinese Congregation Foreign Missions.
Foran, Edward R. '60 (HRT) Retired.
Foran, Martin J. (NEW) Retired.
Foran, MArtin J. '62 (NEW) [B] South Orange, NJ Seton Hall University; [C] West Orange, NJ Seton Hall Preparatory School.
Foran, Peter '22 (LA) [6] Long Beach, CA St. Cyprian Church.
Forand, Clarence W. '45 (SPR) Retired.
Forbes, Eric *o.f.m.cap.* '90 (AGN) Merizo, GU San Dimas and Our Lady of the Rosary Church; Umatac, GU San Dionisio Church.
Forbes, Eric *o.f.m.cap.* '90 (FgM) Capuchin Foreign Missions.
Forbes, Msgr. Eugene A. '41 (SAG) Fisherville, MI St. Anthony Church.
Forbes, John J. '91 (R) Sanford, NC St. Stephen Church.
Forbes, Richard L. '67 (CAM) North Cape May, NJ St. John of God Church.
Forbes, Wayne A. '61 (P) [21] Portland, OR St. John Fisher Church.
Forbidussi, John E. '94 (PIT) Peters Township, PA St. Benedict the Abbot Church.
Forcano, Benito *sch.p.* '66 (PCE) [C] Coto Laurel, PR Colegio Ponceno.
Forcelle, Joseph '80 (SFS) Britton, SD St. John de Britto Church.
Forcier, Richard-Jacob *o.f.m.conv.* '86 (NOR) Stafford Springs, CT St. Edward Church.
Ford, Christopher M. '87 (HRT) [10] Hartford, CT St. Justin Church.
Ford, David R. '86 (CHI) Graduate Studies.
Ford, Harold L. '49 (LA) [8] Long Beach, CA St. Joseph Church.
Ford, J. Joseph '67 (PRT) Wells, ME St. Mary Church.
Ford, James M. '66 (LA) [5] Santa Barbara, CA San Roque Church.
Ford, John *c.s.s.* '56 (BO) [W] Waltham, MA Stigmatine Fathers & Brothers Provincial House.
Ford, John *s.t.* '74 (CLV) [P] Cleveland, OH Missionary Servants of the Most Holy Trinity.
Ford, John, S.T. '74 (CLV) [3] Cleveland, OH St. Agnes - Our Lady of Fatima Church.
Ford, John T. *c.s.c.* '59 (FTW) [J] South Bend, IN Congregation of Holy Cross Indiana Province Provincial House.
Ford, John T. *c.s.c.* '59 (WDC) [C] Washington, DC Catholic University of America, The.
Ford, Lawrence D. *o.f.m.* '96 (BO) [BB] Boston, MA St. Anthony Shrine.
Ford, Mark *c.m.* '92 (GLP) Page, AZ Immaculate Heart of Mary Church; Tuba City, AZ St. Jude Church.
Ford, Matthew M. *o.s.m.* '48 (CHI) [N] Chicago, IL Servite Friars - Eastern Province.
Ford, Michael F. *s.j.* '75 (WOR) [N] Worcester, MA Jesuits of Holy Cross College, Inc.; [Q] Worcester, MA Campus Ministry.
Ford, Nevin *o.f.m.* '54 (LA) [R] Santa Barbara, CA Franciscan Friary, Order of Friars Minor (Old Mission); [R] Santa Barbara, CA St. Anthony's Seminary.
Ford, Patrick J. *s.j.* '74 (SPK) [C] Spokane, WA Gonzaga University.
Ford, Richard J. '60 (ALN) [5] Reading, PA Holy Guardian Angels Church.
Ford, Msgr. Robert A. '44 (NY) [E] White Plains, NY Archbishop Stepinac High School.
Ford, William A. '82 (STO) Retired.
Fording, John D. '42 (PIT) Retired; [O] Pittsburgh, PA St. John Vianney Manor.
Forest, Gerald *m.s.* '49 (FR) [J] Attleboro, MA La Salette Shrine.
Forester, Raymond L. '66 (WIL) Perryville, MD Church of the Good Shepherd.
Forgach, Carl J. '60 (Y) [5] Canton, OH St. Benedict Church.
Forge, Michael D. '97 (DAL) [25] Dallas, TX St. Pius X Church.
Forgit, Ambrose R. *ss.cc.* '55 (WDC) [B] Cheverly, MD Damien House.
Foriadori, V. David '86 (E) Tidioute, PA St. John Church.
Forintos, Bradley '91 (DET) Armada, MI St. Mary Mystical Rose Church.
Forish, Andrew '42 (DET) Retired.
Forish, Msgr. Stephen T. '72 (ALN) [J] Bethlehem, PA Holy Family Villa.
Foriska, John M. '70 (GBG) Calumet, PA St. Stanislaus Church; United, PA St. Florian Church.
Forkin, Gerald *o.m.i.* (BO) [16] Lowell, MA Sacred Heart Church.
Forkin, Gerald R. *o.m.i.* (BO) [16] Lowell, MA Sacred Heart Church.
Forliti, John E. '62 (STP) [31] Minneapolis, MN St. Olaf Church.
Forman, Bruce H. '74 (STL) [55] St. Louis, MO SS. Peter and Paul Church.
Forman, Patrick J. '89 (BUR) Barton, VT Conversion of St. Paul Church.
Formusa, Salvatore '35 (JOL) Retired.
Fornasari, Archimedes *m.c.c.j.* '50 (CHI) [B] Chicago, IL The Catholic Theological Union at Chicago.
Forner, Craig '75 (SFR) San Francisco, CA Serra Club of San Francisco (Downtown); Special Assignment.
Forni, John V. '77 (ROC) Wolcott, NY St. Mary Magdalene Church; Wolcott, NY St. Thomas the Apostle Church.
Forno, R. Adam '87 (ALB) Rensselaer, NY St. Joseph Church.
Forrest, Thomas *c.ss.r.* '54 (WDC) [M] Washington, DC Holy Redeemer College.
Forrester, Donal F. *c.s.p.* '34 (NY) [104] New York, NY St. Paul the Apostle Church; [DD] Jamaica Estates, NY Paulist Fathers Generalate.
Forrey, William C. (HBG) [K] Harrisburg, PA Catholic Campus Ministry.
Forrey, William C. '90 (HBG) [K] Harrisburg, PA Catholic Campus Ministry.
Forry, Thomas (BO) Concord, MA MCI-Concord.
Forsen, James R. '79 (LA) Baldwin Park, CA St. John the Baptist Church.
Forsmann, Leonard '76 (SPK) Clarkston, WA Holy Family Church.
Forst, Aloysius A. '49 (STL) Berkeley, MO Holy Ghost Church.
Forst, Msgr. Charles '45 (STL) [2] Lemay, MO Most Precious Blood Church.
Forst, Msgr. Robert M. '51 (ALN) [7] Allentown, PA St. Paul Church.
Forst, William '54 (JC) Retired.
Forster, Francis P. *o.s.b.* '64 (CHL) [J] Belmont, NC Belmont Abbey.
Forster, Msgr. William J. '54 (BO) [4] Everett, MA St. Therese Church.
Forsthoefel, Paulinus F. *s.j.* '47 (DET) [K] Detroit, MI Jesuit Community at the University of Detroit.
Forsyth, George W. '46 (BRK) Retired.
Forsyth, Kevin J. '86 (HRT) Watertown, CT St. John the Evangelist Church.
Forte, Anthony '91 (NEW) [22] Newark, NJ St. Lucy's Church.
Forte, Anthony J. *s.j.* '83 (BO) [W] Boston, MA The Society of Jesus of New England-Provincial Offices.
Forte, Job-John *o.s.b.* '89 (GBG) [H] Latrobe, PA Saint Vincent Archabbey.
Forte, John Paul *o.p.* '93 (SJ) Stanford, CA Catholic Community at Stanford Church.
Fortenbaugh, Msgr. Francis W. '47 (BAL) [3] Baltimore, MD St. Agnes Church; Retired.
Fortenberry, Jerome D. *c.m.* '55 (BEL) Cairo, IL St. Patrick Church.
Fortener, Kenneth R. '69 (L) [6] Louisville, KY St. Andrew Church.
Fortier, Msgr. Charles '45 (LA) [9] Los Angeles, CA Divine Saviour Church.
Fortier, Harvey J. '55 (ALX) Evergreen, LA Little Flower Church.
Fortier, Joel F. '69 (JOL) Bloomingdale, IL St. Isidore Church.
Fortier, Joseph C. *s.j.* '90 (WH) [A] Wheeling, WV Wheeling Jesuit University.
Fortier, Roger A. '80 (MAN) Farmington, NH St. Peter Church.
Fortier, Theodore *a.a.* (BO) Quincy, MA Quincy Hospital.
Fortier, Theodore L. *a.a.* '53 (BO) [3] Quincy, MA St. John the Baptist Church; [W] Brighton, MA Assumptionist Center.
Fortier, Theodore N. *s.j.* '87 (SEA) [A] Seattle, WA Seattle University.
Fortin, Ernest *a.a.* '49 (BO) [W] Brighton, MA Assumptionist Center.
Fortin, John R. *o.s.b.* '76 (MAN) [K] Manchester, NH St. Anselm Abbey.
Fortin, Richard A. '62 (WOR) Millbury, MA Assumption Church.
Fortin, Robert *a.a.* '58 (BO) [W] Brighton, MA Assumptionist Center.
Fortin, Roger M. '65 (PRO) [5] Warwick, RI St. Gregory the Great Church.
Fortner, Douglas F. '70 (COV) Edgewood, KY St. Pius X Church.
Fortney, Kenneth E. '79 (HEL) Drummond, MT St. Michael Church; Philipsburg, MT St. Philip Church.
Fortuna, George B. '57 (DET) Retired.
Fortuna, Joseph J. '80 (CLV) [8] Cleveland, OH Ascension Church.
Fortuna, Stanley *c.f.r.* '90 (NY) [DD] New York, NY St. Crispin Friary.
Fortunato, Antonio *o.de.m.* (PH) [AA] Philadelphia, PA Monastery of Our Lady of Mercy.
Fortunato, Vincent *o.f.m.cap.* '80 (NEW) [N] Union City, NJ Capuchin Friars - Province of the Sacred Stigmata of St. Francis.
Fortunato, Vincent *o.f.m.cap.* '80 (PIT) [O] Pittsburgh, PA St. Conrad Friary.
Fortunato, Vincent *o.f.m.cap.* '80 (WDC) [B] Washington, DC St. Francis Friary-Capuchin College.
Fortune, William J. (DEN) [B] Denver, CO Regis University.
Fortunio, Carlo *o.p.* '85 (NEW) West New York, NJ St. Mary Help of Christians Church.
Foshage, Nathanael *o.s.b.* '68 (OM) [K] Elkhorn, NE Mount Michael Abbey.
Foshage, Nathanael *o.s.b.* '68 (PBL) Ouray, CO St. Daniel the Prophet Church; Silverton, CO St. Patrick Church.
Foshage, Ronald *m.s.* '75 (BEA) Jasper, TX St. Michael Church; Kirbyville, TX Our Lady of La Salette Mission Church; Sam Rayburn, TX St. Raymond Mission Church.
Fosnot, James '94 (RIC) Clarksville, VA St. Catherine of Siena Church; South Hill, VA Good Shepherd Church.
Fosselman, Albert '60 (RNO) Retired.
Fosselman, David H. *c.s.c.* '83 (FTW) [J] South Bend, IN Congregation of Holy Cross Indiana Province Provincial House.
Fosselman, Msgr. John '42 (LA) Downey, CA St. Raymond Church.
Fosselman, Msgr. John A. '42 (LA) Downey, CA Rancho Los Amigos Medical Center; Retired.
Fosselman, Robert J. '42 (LFT) Retired.
Fossier, Msgr. Emile '43 (HT) [1] Houma, LA Cathedral of St. Francis De Sales; Retired.
Fossier, Ignatius *o.s.b.* '44 (NO) [P] St. Benedict, LA St. Joseph Abbey.
Foster, Clyde K. '75 (CLV) [11] Lorain, OH St. Stanislaus Church; Solon, OH St. Rita Church.
Foster, Msgr. Edward C. '51 (BUR) Retired.
Foster, Edward M. '51 (DUL) Pine River, MN Our Lady of Lourdes Church.
Foster, James A. '72 (ALX) Colfax, LA St. Joseph Church.
Foster, James J. '80 (STL) [1] Jennings, MO Corpus Christi/St.Lucy Church; [3] Jennings, MO St. Louise de Marillac Church.
Foster, James K. *c.s.c.* (FTW) [B] Notre Dame, IN University of Notre Dame Du Lac; [J] Notre Dame, IN Holy Cross Community, Corby Hall, University of Notre Dame.
Foster, James M. '85 (ALT) Bellefonte, PA St. John the Evangelist's Church.
Foster, John F. *s.j.* '68 (SEA) [A] Seattle, WA Seattle University.
Foster, John J. '51 (PH) Fallsington, PA St. Joseph the Worker Church.
Foster, John J.M. '91 (STO) [1] Stockton, CA Cathedral of the Annunciation.
Foster, Jonathan D. *o.f.m.* '60 (JOL) [L] Downers Grove, IL Mayslake Marmion Ministries, Inc.

Foster, Joseph R. '91 (BO) Marblehead, MA Our Lady, Star of the Sea Church.
Foster, Patrick '56 (EVN) Jasper, IN St. Joseph Church.
Foster, Raymond *o.carm.* '73 (JOL) [J] Joliet, IL St. Elias Carmelites.
Foster, Reginald *o.c.d.* '66 (MIL) [P] Milwaukee, WI Provincial Offices - Discalced Carmelites.
Foster, Robert L. '47 (GI) Retired.
Foster, Thomas '82 (DUL) [1] Duluth, MN Cathedral of Our Lady of the Rosary Church.
Foster, Thomas W. *s.j.* '72 (SJ) [M] Los Gatos, CA Sacred Heart Jesuit Center.
Foster, Tom *s.j.* '72 (MRY) Capitola, CA St. Joseph Church.
Foster, William '85 (TOL) [H] Toledo, OH St. Vincent Medical Center.
Fostner, Jay *o.praem.* '88 (CHI) [N] Chicago, IL Premonstratensian Fathers and Brothers (Norbertines).
Fostner, Jay *o.praem.* '88 (GB) [F] Green Bay, WI St. Vincent Hospital.
Fostner, Jay J. *o.praem.* '88 (GB) [I] De Pere, WI St. Norbert Abbey.
Foudy, Denis D. '46 (SFR) Retired.
Foudy, Msgr. John T. '40 (SFR) [10] San Francisco, CA St. Cecilia Church; Retired.
Foudy, Msgr. Robert E. '43 (SPR) [4] Springfield, MA Holy Cross Church; Retired.
Foudy, Thomas F. '67 (MIA) [3] Pompano Beach, FL St. Coleman Church.
Fountain, Dennis *o.f.m.* '81 (LSC) Roswell, NM St. Peter Church; Roswell, NM St. John the Baptist Church.
Fountain, Robert J. '55 (BO) [3] Medford, MA St. Joseph Church.
Fournier, Denis *o.s.b.* '60 (BIS) [A] Richardton, ND Assumption Abbey; [B] Bismarck, ND University of Mary.
Fournier, Raymond *s.m.* '49 (BO) [12] Lawrence, MA Sacred Heart Church.
Fournier, Raymond J. *o.c.s.o.* '81 (ROC) [I] Piffard, NY Abbey of the Genesee.
Fournier, W. Donald '53 (SPR) Retired.
Fournier, William '73 (DUL) [11] Duluth, MN St. Lawrence's Church.
Fouser, Otto *o.f.m.conv.* (MET) [I] Watchung, NJ McAuley Hall Inc.
Foutts, Patrick D. *o.praem.* '93 (ORG) [H] Silverado, CA Norbertine Fathers of Orange Inc.
Fowerbaugh, Msgr. F. Raymond '55 (GRY) [2] Whiting, IN Sacred Heart Church.
Fowler, Msgr. Eugene A. '48 (NY) Retired.
Fowler, John W. '53 (DAL) Irving, TX St. Luke Church; Retired.
Fowler, Joseph M. '73 (L) [36] Louisville, KY Holy Trinity Church.
Fowler, Richard A. '88 (BUR) Bethel, VT St. Anthony Church.
Fowler, Terence L. '88 (BWN) [2] Harlingen, TX Immaculate Heart of Mary Church.
Fowler, Terrence '88 (BWN) On Leave.
Fowlkes, Eric L. '89 (NSH) Clarksville, TN Immaculate Conception Church.
Fox, Arnold J. *o.s.b.* '34 (SEA) [M] Lacey, WA St. Martin's Abbey.
Fox, Brian *s.s.j.* '91 (GAL) [31] Houston, TX St. Francis Xavier Church.
Fox, Charles J. *s.j.* '44 (FgM) Provinces.
Fox, Daniel *o.f.m.cap.* '75 (DET) [K] Detroit, MI St. Bonaventure Friary; [K] Detroit, MI St. Bonaventure Friary.
Fox, Daniel *o.f.m.cap.* '75 (FgM) Capuchin Foreign Missions.
Fox, Daniel '82 (LA) Bellflower, CA St. Bernard Church.
Fox, Donal R. *o.s.b.* '66 (PAT) Cedar Knolls, NJ Notre Dame of Mt. Carmel Church; [M] Morristown, NJ St. Mary's Abbey.
Fox, Francis E. '58 (PH) [101] Philadelphia, PA Maternity B.V.M. Church.
Fox, Francis J. '42 (ALN) Retired.
Fox, Frederick *s.v.d.* '50 (FgM) Society of the Divine Word Foreign Missions.
Fox, Fredrick '52 (DUL) Retired.
Fox, Gabriel '74 (GAY) Manistee, MI St. Mary of Mt. Carmel Shrine Church.
Fox, George W. '61 (MAD) Doylestown, WI St. Patrick Church.
Fox, James E. '74 (DEN) Longmont, CO St. John the Baptist Church.
Fox, James F. *s.j.* '71 (WDC) [V] Washington, DC Jesuit Secondary Education Association.
Fox, James J. *s.j.* '71 (WDC) [M] Washington, DC The Jesuit Community at Georgetown University.
Fox, James R. '90 (DEN) Westminster, CO St. Mark Church.
Fox, John J. '60 (BUF) Retired.
Fox, Joseph F. '43 (SCR) Retired.
Fox, Leo '56 (SFS) Retired.
Fox, Leonard D. '55 (SFS) Vermillion, SD St. Agnes Church.
Fox, Msgr. M. Davitt (NOR) [M] Middletown, CT Assisted Living Services, Inc. - Diocese of Norwich; [M] Middletown, CT Marian Housing Corporation.
Fox, Martin '65 (GB) [6] Oshkosh, WI Sacred Heart Church.
Fox, Melvin E. '63 (GR) Ionia, MI SS. Peter and Paul Church.
Fox, Msgr. Michael D. '50 (NOR) [1] Middletown, CT St. Francis Church.
Fox, Msgr. Patrick '52 (SD) La Jolla, CA All Hallows Church.
Fox, Peter D. *s.j.* '66 (CHI) [C] Chicago, IL Jesuit Community at Loyola University of Chicago.
Fox, Richard *o.c.s.o.* '59 (SPC) [E] Ava, MO Assumption Abbey (Trappist).
Fox, Richard '85 (SFS) Mitchell, SD Holy Spirit Church.
Fox, Richard E. '92 (SCR) [10] Scranton, PA Immaculate Conception Church.
Fox, Robert J. '55 (SFS) Alexandria, SD St. Mary of Mercy Church; [I] Alexandria, SD Fatima Family Apostolate.
Fox, Robert J. '59 (GF) Retired.
Fox, Sean P. '53 (SEA) Mountlake Terrace, WA St. Pius X Church.
Fox, Thomas *o.f.m.* '62 (IND) [31] Indianapolis, IN St. Patrick Church.
Fox, Thomas E. '59 (BRK) [54] Brooklyn, NY Holy Family Church.
Fox, Thomas E. '60 (LFT) Remington, IN Sacred Heart Church.
Fox, Thomas J. *o.f.m.* '46 (FgM) Franciscan Foreign Missions.
Fox, Thomas P. *m.m.* '56 (FgM) Maryknoll Foreign Missions.
Foxen, Bertin *o.f.m.* '45 (LA) [R] Santa Barbara, CA Franciscan Friary, Order of Friars Minor (Old Mission).
Foxen, David *m.s.c.* '67 (FgM) Missionaries of the Sacred Heart Foreign Missions.
Foxhoven, Msgr. Omer V. '44 (DEN) Retired.
Foy, Edward J. '45 (ROC) [4] Auburn, NY St. Alphonsus Church; Retired.
Foy, Felican *o.f.m.* '47 (NEW) Fair Lawn, NJ St. Anne's Church.
Foy, Felician A. *o.f.m.* '47 (PAT) [P] Paterson, NJ St. Anthony's Guild.
Foye, Harold J. *c.s.p.* '46 (BO) [P] Boston, MA Paulist Center; [W] Boston, MA Paulist Fathers Residence.
Foye, Harold J. *c.s.p.* '46 (NY) [DD] Jamaica Estates, NY Paulist Fathers Generalate.
Foye, Thomas M. '55 (NEW) [3] Bayonne, NJ St. Henry's Church.
Foynes, Aiden '33 (SP) [F] Clearwater, FL Little Nazareth Early Childhood Center.
Foynes, Aiden '61 (SP) [4] Clearwater, FL St. Cecelia Church.
Foyo, Alexis *o.s.b.* '83 (SD) [H] Oceanside, CA Prince of Peace Abbey, Benet Hill.
Foys, Msgr. Roger J. '73 (STU) Toronto, OH St. Francis of Assisi Church; Toronto, OH St. Joseph's Church; Toronto, OH Servants of Christ the King Church; [B] Steubenville, OH Catholic Central High School; [J] Steubenville, OH Charismatic Renewal; [J] Steubenville, OH Diocesan Committee of Administrative Review; [J] Steubenville, OH Lay Employees Pension Plan; [J] Steubenville, OH Synod Committee.
Fraats, Ralph J. '60 (ROC) [59] Rochester, NY St. Thomas the Apostle Church.
Fracaro, Mark '67 (JOL) Manteno, IL St. Joseph Church.
Frade, Paulo dos Santos '97 (NEW) [8] Newark, NJ St. Benedict's Church.
Fradet, Msgr. W. John '50 (BUR) [2] Burlington, VT St. Anthony's Church; [3] Burlington, VT Christ the King Church.
Fraenzle, Wilfred J. '64 (LEX) [5] Lexington, KY St. Elizabeth Ann Seton Church.
Fraga, Bento R. *v.f.* '56 (FR) [9] Taunton, MA St. Paul's Church.
Fragomeni, Richard '75 (ALB) On Duty Outside the Diocese.
Fragomeni, Richard '75 (CHI) [B] Chicago, IL The Catholic Theological Union at Chicago.
Fraher, Joseph P. '50 (CHY) Retired.
Fraher, Kevin *c.ss.r.* (CHI) [T] Glenview, IL Villa Redeemer.
Fraher, Kevin *c.ss.r.* '73 (CHI) [N] Glenview, IL The Redemptorists of Glenview, Illinois.
Fraher, Leonard W. '56 (SUP) Retired.
Fraile, Mariano *o.c.d.* '47 (PCE) [12] Ponce, PR San Jose Church.
Fraile, Tomas *c.r.* '63 (DEN) [27] Denver, CO St. Cajetan's Church.
Frambes, John C. *o.f.m.* '79 (ALB) [B] Loudonville, NY Siena College; [B] Loudonville, NY Siena College.
Frana, Clarence L. '51 (DUB) Retired.
Francavilla, Joseph F. '68 (NTN) McLean, VA Holy Transfiguration Church.
France-Kelly, Kenneth A. *o.p.* '81 (COL) [36] Columbus, OH St. Patrick Church; [42] Columbus, OH Shrine of Blessed Margaret of Castello Church; [L] Columbus, OH Blessed Margaret Guild, Inc.
Franceschini, Mark *o.s.m.* '59 (DEN) Westminster, CO Holy Trinity Church.
Franceschini, Mark M. *o.s.m.* '59 (DEN) [4] Denver, CO Assumption Church.
Franceschini, Msgr. Philip J. '66 (NY) [220] Staten Island, NY Our Lady of Pity Church.
Francesco, Richard G. '87 (NEW) [8] Newark, NJ St. Benedict's Church.
Francez, James *m.c.c.j.* '57 (FgM) Comboni Foreign Missions.
Francik, Gerard '87 (BAL) Special Assignment; [B] Emmitsburg, MD Mount Saint Mary's College.
Francis, A. Edwin '45 (CIN) Retired.
Francis, Bernard C. '69 (NO) Hahnville, LA Our Lady of the Holy Rosary Church.
Francis, Daniel *c.ss.r.* '91 (NY) [23] New York, NY St. Cecilia Church; [150] Bronx, NY Immaculate Conception Church.
Francis, Msgr. Eugene G. '52 (GAL) [40] Houston, TX St. John Neumann Church.
Francis, Msgr. George J. '37 (OAK) [2] Hayward, CA St. Bede Church; Retired.
Francis, Isaac O. '97 (GAL) [24] Houston, TX St. Cyril of Alexandria Church.
Francis, Mark R. *c.s.v.* '82 (CHI) [B] Chicago, IL The Catholic Theological Union at Chicago; [N] Chicago, IL Viatorian Residence.
Francis, Paul R. '41 (BO) Retired.
Francis, Ray A. '63 (NEW) [37] Newark, NJ St. Thomas Aquinas Church.
Francis, William C. '58 (BO) [27] Boston, MA Holy Family Church.
Francisco, Alexander M. '79 (HT) Schriever, LA St. Bridget Church.
Franciscus, Thomas *c.ss.r.* '65 (CHI) [N] Chicago, IL Redemptorists:.
Francisko, Gary '82 (PRM) Absent on Leave.
Franck, James E. *c.pp.s.* '64 (OAK) [N] San Leandro, CA Society of the Precious Blood.
Franck, John *c.pp.s.* '67 (LA) [38] Los Angeles, CA St. Agnes Church.
Franck, John L. *a.a.* '77 (BO) [W] Brighton, MA Assumptionist Center.
Franck, Marc E. '53 (PRT) Retired.
Franck, Mark '53 (PRT) [I] Waterville, ME Mt. St. Joseph Priest Retirement Home.
Franco, David *o.s.f.s.* '76 (LAN) [6] Ypsilanti, MI Transfiguration Catholic Church.
Franco, Geraldo Ildeo (BO) [2] Marlboro, MA Immaculate Conception Church.
Franco, Msgr. Hilary (NY) Ossining, NY St. Augustine Church.
Franco, Juan B. '86 (ARE) [8] Arecibo, PR Inmaculado Corazon de Maria Church.
Franco, Robert J. '82 (CLV) [6] Euclid, OH St. William Church.
Franco, Robert M. *m.ch.a.* '73 (PIT) Forest Hills, PA St. Maurice Church.
Franco, Ronald A. *c.s.p.* '95 (NY) [DD] Jamaica Estates, NY Paulist Fathers Generalate.
Franco, Salvator '53 (BRK) Retired.
Franco, Victor *l.c.* '81 (MAN) [A] Center Harbor, NH Immaculate Conception Apostolic School.
Francois, Jean-Augustin '90 (BRK) [238] Queens, NY Sacred Heart Church.
Francois, Theodore V. *s.j.* '70 (NY) [DD] New York, NY Jesuit Provincial's Office; [DD] New York, NY West Side Jesuit Community.
Franczek, J. August '48 (GAY) Hale, MI St. Pius X Church.
Franczek, Walter '41 (ORL) Retired.
Franczek, Walter J. '41 (MAR) Retired.
Franer, Msgr. William J. (CIN) Retired.
Franey, John A. '63 (PH) Collegeville, PA St. Eleanor Church; [EE] Philadelphia, PA Newman Apostolate.
Frank, Alfred E. (PAT) Permanent Deacons.
Frank, Edward R. '57 (SAV) Moultrie, GA Immaculate Conception Church.
Frank, Eugene G. '57 (BIS) Retired.
Frank, Gerald W. '70 (BWN) [5] McAllen, TX Holy Spirit Church.
Frank, Joseph A. '49 (NEW) Retired.
Frank, Paul *o.m.i.* '50 (MIA) [2] Miami, FL Christ the King Church.
Frank, Richard C. *m.m.* '53 (FgM) Maryknoll Foreign Missions.
Frank, Richard W. '72 (JC) Freeburg, MO Holy Family Church.
Frank, Thomas R. *s.s.j.* '78 (NO) [B] New Orleans, LA Josephite House of Studies.
Frank, Tom '70 (AUS) Pflugerville, TX St. Elizabeth Church.
Franken, William F. '88 (BAL) [77] Baltimore, MD Our Lady of Victory Church.
Frankenberger, William J. *c.s.b.* '73 (GAL) [Q] Sugar Land, TX Basilian Mission Center.
Frankey, Charles M. '57 (STL) Ellisville, MO St. Clare

of Assisi Church.
Frankhauser, William E. *s.j.* '29 (BUF) [7] Buffalo, NY St. Ann Church.
Franklin, David W. '85 (BGP) [4] Stamford, CT St. Clement's Church.
Franklin, Edward L. '62 (OG) Absent on Sick Leave.
Frankman, Gregory '81 (SFS) Florence, SD Blessed Sacrament Church.
Franko, George M. '50 (Y) Retired.
Franko, Jack *o.m.i.* '67 (BWN) Port Isabel, TX Our Lady Star of the Sea Church.
Frankovich, Frank '68 (SB) On Duty Outside the Diocese.
Frankovich, Lawrence *o.f.m.* '66 (MIL) [2] West Allis, WI St. Augustine Church.
Franks, Becket *o.s.b.* '86 (JOL) [J] Lisle, IL St. Procopius Abbey.
Franks, Donald E. '79 (COL) Chillicothe, OH St. Mary Church.
Fransco, Peter J. '58 (SC) Mallard, IA St. Mary's Church.
Fransiscus, Thomas *c.ss.r.* '44 (DEN) [M] Denver, CO The Redemptorists/Denver Province.
Fransiscus, Thomas *c.ss.r.* '65 (CHI) [N] Bodija, Ibadan, Oyo State, Nigeria.
Fransiscus, Thomas J. '65 (RNO) Stead, NV St. Michael's Church.
Frantz, Henry L. *c.pp.s.* '54 (ORL) Longwood, FL Church of the Nativity.
Franxman, Thomas W. *s.j.* '64 (FgM) Provinces.
Franz, Louis *c.m.* '57 (GLP) Page, AZ Immaculate Heart of Mary Church.
Franz, Paul R. '54 (BO) [2] Medford, MA St. James Church.
Franz, S. Michael '69 (CLV) [72] Cleveland, OH St. Stephen Church.
Franzen, Robert B. '53 (SFD) Chatham, IL St. Joseph Church.
Franzinell, Benjamin '50 (LAV) Retired.
Franzman, Thomas R. '70 (CHI) [138] Chicago, IL St. Michael Church.
Frapaul, Sam *o.f.m.cap.* (PAT) [7] Passaic, NJ Mt. Carmel Church.
Frappier, Msgr. George L. '56 (PRO) [4] Woonsocket, RI St. Anthony's Church.
Fraraccio, Ugo *s.d.v.* (PAT) [M] Florham Park, NJ Father Justin Vocationary.
Frascadore, Henry C. '59 (HRT) Southington, CT St. Dominic Church.
Frascati, Marino *o.de.m.* '51 (SP) [1] St. Petersburg, FL Cathedral of St. Jude the Apostle.
Frascati, Marion *o.de.m.* '51 (SP) [O] St. Petersburg, FL St. Peter Nolasco Residence.
Fraser, Donald D. '74 (B) McCall, ID Our Lady of the Lake Church.
Fraser, Gerald C. '72 (BO) Health Leave.
Fraser, Gerald D. '38 (CHI) Retired.
Fraser, James F. '65 (BRK) [179] Queens, NY Holy Trinity Church.
Fraser, John F. '96 (NY) [1] Yonkers, NY St. Anthony Church.
Fraser, Michael B. '75 (NO) [5] Marrero, LA The Visitation of Our Lady Church.
Fratic, Joseph P. '64 (BO) Dover, MA Most Precious Blood Church.
Fratus, James F. '81 (BO) [1] Chelsea, MA Our Lady of the Assumption Church; [2] Chelsea, MA St. Rose of Lima Church.
Fratus, Thomas *o.f.m.* '52 (CHI) [167] Chicago, IL St. Peter's Church; [N] Chicago, IL St. Peter's Friary.
Frausto, Jorge *o.f.m.* '86 (ELP) [15] El Paso, TX Our Lady of Guadalupe Church.
Frawley, Brian *o.s.a.* '86 (WDC) [B] Washington, DC Augustinian College, Order of St. Augustine.
Frawley, Gerard *s.a.c.* '68 (DET) [3] Wyandotte, MI St. Joseph Church.
Frawley, John P. '44 (CHI) [206] Chicago, IL St. Thomas More Church; Retired.
Frawley, Patrick J. '78 (BRK) [210] Queens, NY Our Lady of Fatima Church.
Frayne, Thomas M. '88 (CHI) [97] Chicago, IL St. James Church.
Frazer, Edward J. *s.s.* '61 (BAL) [M] Baltimore, MD Sulpician Provincial House.
Frazer, Francis '75 (PIT) [R] Slippery Rock, PA Office for Campus Ministry.
Frazer, J. Francis '75 (PIT) Beaver Falls, PA St. Philomena Church.
Frazer, Joseph H. '84 (AUS) [18] Austin, TX St. Margaret of Scotland Church.
Frazier, Lawrence K. '71 (BAL) Buckeystown, MD St. Joseph-on-Carrollton Manor Church.
Frazier, Richard W. '96 (COV) Fort Thomas, KY St. Thomas Church.
Frazier, William B. *m.m.* '56 (NY) [DD] Maryknoll, NY Maryknoll Fathers and Brothers.
Frazzitta, Barry W. '59 (BRK) [96] Brooklyn, NY Our Lady of Grace Church.
Frechette, Leo L. '55 (MAN) Retired.
Frechette, Leonard A. '52 (PRT) Retired.
Frechette, Paul *s.m.* '76 (FgM) Marist Foreign Missions.
Frechette, Paul G. '78 (NTN) Worcester, MA Our Lady of Perpetual Help Church.
Frechette, Thomas A. '86 (FR) Attleboro Falls, MA St. Mark's Church.
Frecker, Msgr. A. Anthony '72 (COL) Chillicothe, OH St. Peter Church.
Fredeman, Felix '57 (LR) [A] Subiaco, AR Subiaco Monastery.
Frederick, Curt J. '75 (MIL) Brookfield, WI St. Dominic Church.
Frederick, Edwin J. '50 (GAY) Retired.
Frederick, Joseph B. '56 (MIL) [79] Milwaukee, WI St. Veronica Church.
Frederick, Lawrence A. '66 (LR) [11] Little Rock, AR Our Lady of the Holy Souls Church; [B] Little Rock, AR Catholic High School.
Frederick, Ronald P. '69 (ROC) Unassigned.
Fredericks, James L. '77 (SFR) On Duty Outside the Archdiocese.
Fredericks, Michael '87 (SB) [8] Riverside, CA St. John the Evangelist Church.
Fredette, Albert *m.s.* '52 (FR) [J] Attleboro, MA La Salette Shrine.
Fredette, Joseph *m.s.* '57 (FR) [J] Attleboro, MA La Salette Shrine.
Free, Daniel *c.p.* '52 (BAL) [H] Baltimore, MD St. Agnes HealthCare, Inc.; [M] Baltimore, MD St. Joseph's Passionist Community.
Free, Harold J. *s.j.* '53 (LA) [K] Burbank, CA Providence Saint Joseph Medical Center.
Free, Henry *c.p.* '58 (FgM) Passionist Foreign Missions.
Freed, Robert '83 (WCH) Retired.
Freel, Frank J. *c.ss.r.* '46 (NY) [92] New York, NY Our Lady of Perpetual Help Church.
Freeman, George J. '65 (STP) Faribault, MN Immaculate Conception Church.
Freeman, Hilary J. *o.p.* '52 (CHI) [N] River Forest, IL St. Thomas Aquinas Priory.
Freeman, James '65 (DM) On Duty Outside the Diocese.
Freeman, James A. '65 (TUC) [15] Tucson, AZ St. Joseph Church; [E] Tucson, AZ Carondelet Health Network.
Freeman, John A. '73 (PH) [77] Philadelphia, PA St. John the Baptist Church; [EE] Philadelphia, PA Newman Apostolate.
Freeman, Joseph M. *s.j.* '44 (KC) [B] Kansas City, MO Rockhurst College; [J] Kansas City, MO Rockhurst College - Jesuit Community.
Freeman, Lawrence '69 (DEN) [5] Denver, CO Blessed Sacrament Church.
Freeman, Lawrence M. '69 (DEN) [G] Denver, CO Religious Education-Pastoral Care of Developmentally Disabled Persons.
Freeman, Msgr. Robert E. '57 (CC) [17] Corpus Christi, TX St. Patrick Church.
Freeman, Roland (DEN) [Q] Denver, CO Blessed Sacrament Catholic Educational Foundation.
Freeman, Roland '67 (DEN) [5] Denver, CO Blessed Sacrament Church.
Freemesser, Paul J. '59 (ROC) [4] Auburn, NY St. Alphonsus Church.
Freeswick, William J. '69 (PAT) [K] Denville, NJ St. Francis Health Resort.
Freeze, J. Donald '63 (BAL) [M] Baltimore, MD Jesuit Fathers and Brothers Maryland Provincial Curia.
Frega, John *o.f.m.cap.* '56 (NY) [B] Beacon, NY St. Lawrence of Brindisi Friary.
Fregapane, Msgr. Mercurio A. '51 (HBG) [2] Lebanon, PA St. Benedict the Abbot Church.
Fregault, Roland A. *o.f.m.* '43 (NEW) Elmwood Park, NJ St. Leo's Church.
Fregeau, Guido Anthony '95 (GAL) [18] Houston, TX St. Cecilia Church.
Frego, Max '63 (SAG) Retired.
Freidel, John J. '86 (SPC) [I] Cape Girardeau, MO Southeast Missouri State University, Newman Center.
Freiermuth, Harry '59 (MRY) Retired.
Freire, Gerardo *s.j.* '56 (MIA) [H] Miami, FL Villa Arrieta.
Freishyn-Chirovsky, John M. '90 (SJP) [3] Parma, OH Pokrova Ukrainian Catholic Parish.
Freitag, Patrick '96 (SEA) Bellingham, WA Assumption B.V.M. Church; Bellingham, WA Sacred Heart Church.
Freitas, Daniel L. '49 (FR) Retired.
Freitas, Fernando P. '48 (PRO) Retired.
Freitas, Patrick '65 (HON) [12] Honolulu, HI St. Philomena Church.
Fremgen, Edward '92 (LA) Lakewood, CA St. Pancratius Church.
Fremont-Smith, Peter *s.o.l.t.* '92 (CC) [H] Robstown, TX Society of Our Lady of the Most Holy Trinity.
French, D. James *s.j.* '74 (NEW) [C] Jersey City, NJ St. Peter's Preparatory School.
French, Donald J. '76 (HRT) [6] New Haven, CT St. Brendan's Church.
French, James R. '78 (STL) Park Hills, MO Immaculate Conception Church.
French, John F. '54 (ALB) Ballston Spa, NY St. Mary Church.
French, Michael D. *s.j.* '75 (BAL) [B] Baltimore, MD Loyola College; [M] Baltimore, MD Jesuit Community of Loyola College, Inc.
French, Raymond *c.s.sp.* '91 (PIT) [B] Pittsburgh, PA Duquesne University of the Holy Ghost.
French, Raymond D. *c.s.sp.* (PIT) [R] Slippery Rock, PA Office for Campus Ministry.
French, Robert E. '63 (RIC) [1] Hampton, VA Immaculate Conception Church.
French, Msgr. Thomas A. '49 (SAT) [K] San Antonio, TX Incarnate Word Motherhouse and Retirement Center.
French, Thomas J. *s.m.* '97 (BAL) Sykesville, MD St. Joseph Church.
French, Walter V. '65 (NEW) Retired.
Frenier, Steven G. *o.f.m.conv.* '82 (BUF) Athol Springs, NY St. Francis of Assisi Church.
Frenoy, Fortune *s.m.* '55 (ORL) [1] Orlando, FL Mary Queen of the Universe Shrine Church.
Freret, Warren Joseph (GAL) Retired.
Frerker, John W. '63 (BEL) Cahokia, IL St. Catherine Laboure Church.
Frerkes, James J. '62 (MRY) Nipomo, CA St. Joseph Church.
Frese, Joseph R. *s.j.* '44 (NY) [DD] New York, NY Jesuit Community at Fordham University.
Fresno, Leonidas *o.s.a.* '64 (SAT) [47] San Antonio, TX St. Jude Church.
Freson, Kenan *o.f.m.* '67 (CIN) [C] Cincinnati, OH St. Anthony Shrine, Franciscan Candidacy; [M] Cincinnati, OH St. Francis Seraph Friary; [U] Cincinnati, OH Community Support Charitable Trust; [U] Cincinnati, OH Friars Club Foundation, Inc.
Freuh, Robert '63 (BRK) [14] Brooklyn, NY St. Augustine Church.
Freund, John B. *c.m.* '65 (BRK) [U] Jamaica, NY St. Vincent's House.
Freund, Joseph *c.ss.r.* '66 (BAL) [87] Baltimore, MD Sacred Heart of Jesus Church.
Freund, Melchior *o.s.b.* '57 (SCL) [I] Collegeville, MN St. John's Abbey, of the Order of St. Benedict.
Frey, Msgr. Andrew F. '48 (BR) Retired.
Frey, Francis '58 (SAN) [5] Odessa, TX St. Mary's Church.
Frey, Frank D. *o.f.m.* '43 (CIN) [M] Cincinnati, OH St. Clement Friary.
Frey, Jerome '50 (LAF) [M] Lafayette, LA Community of Jesus Crucified.
Frey, John T. '70 (CAM) [4] Vineland, NJ St. Isidore Church.
Freyaldenhoven, George P. '48 (LR) Retired.
Freyer, Timothy '89 (ORG) San Clemente, CA Our Lady of Fatima Church.
Freymuth, Michael '79 (STL) [3] St. Louis, MO Holy Family Church.
Freyne, Barry '60 (SJ) [1] Palo Alto, CA St. Thomas Aquinas Church.
Frias, Ramon *o.f.m.cap.* '72 (NY) [57] New York, NY St. John the Baptist Church.
Frias, Ray *o.f.m.cap.* (NY) [GG] New York, NY University Apostolate.
Frias, Msgr. Santiago C. '59 (RIC) [3] Norfolk, VA Holy Trinity Church.
Friberg, Daniel W. '62 (STP) Hugo, MN St. John the Baptist Church.
Friday, Robert M. '61 (PIT) On Duty Outside the Diocese.
Friday, Robert M. '61 (WDC) [C] Washington, DC Catholic University of America, The; [C] Washington, DC Catholic University of America, The.
Fride, Edward O. '86 (LAN) [L] Ann Arbor, MI Christ the King Catholic Center.
Fridgen, Joseph '50 (SCL) Retired.
Fridrich, Sylvester W. '51 (CLV) Gates Mills, OH St. Francis of Assisi Church.
Friebel, Rick *c.pp.s.* '78 (ORL) [6] Orlando, FL St. Andrew Church.
Fried, Francis L. '68 (STP) Northfield, MN St. Dominic Church.
Friedel, James *o.s.a.* '65 (CHI) [N] Olympia Fields, IL Tolentine Monastery at Tolentine Center.
Friedel, John (J.) F. '86 (SPC) Special Assignment.
Friedel, Robert E. '57 (CLV) Twinsburg, OH SS. Cosmas and Damian Church.
Friedell, John C. '54 (DUB) [C] Dubuque, IA Loras College.
Friedell, Ronald G. '66 (DUB) State Center, IA St. Joseph's Church; Marshalltown, IA Veterans' Home.
Friederick, John J. '65 (DUB) Colesburg, IA St. Patrick's Church; Edgewood, IA St. Mark's Church.
Friedl, Bernard *o.s.b.* '92 (CR) Lake Park, MN St. Francis Xavier's Church.
Friedl, Bernard *o.s.b.* '92 (SCL) [I] Collegeville, MN St. John's Abbey, of the Order of St. Benedict.
Friedl, Erwin J. '71 (CHI) [46] Chicago, IL St. Cornelius Church.
Friedl, Msgr. Francis P. '43 (DUB) Retired.
Friedman, Cecil H. '50 (SC) Retired.
Friedman, Daniel L. '72 (BEL) Aviston, IL St. Francis

of Assisi Church.
Friedman, Robert (Y) Hubbard, OH St. Patrick's Church.
Friedrich, Aloys *c.pp.s.* '36 (CIN) [B] Carthagena, OH St. Charles.
Friedrich, Jim D. '89 (SFS) Herreid, SD St. Michael Church.
Friedrich, Lawrence '47 (SFS) Retired.
Friedrich, Ralph '43 (Y) Retired.
Friedrichs, Paul L. '78 (CIN) [4] Cincinnati, OH St. Aloysius Gonzaga Church; On Special and Diocesan Assignment.
Friedrichs, Richard M. '70 (PRO) [R] Narragansett, RI Our Lady of Peace Spiritual Life Center.
Friedrichsen, Timothy A. (SC) [A] Sioux City, IA Briar Cliff College.
Friedrichsen, Timothy A. '84 (SC) Struble, IA St. Joseph's Church; Special Assignment.
Friel, Edward J. *o.s.f.s.* '41 (WIL) [I] Childs, MD Oblates of St. Francis De Sales.
Friel, Edward M. '89 (CAM) Berlin, NJ Our Lady of Mt. Carmel Church.
Friel, James E. '52 (PBL) [9] Pueblo, CO St. Anne Church.
Friel, John F. *o.s.f.s.* '70 (WIL) [I] Wilmington, DE Oblates of St. Francis De Sales.
Friel, Lee G. *o.f.m.cap.* '56 (FgM) Capuchin Foreign Missions.
Friel, Mark M. '63 (BUF) [7] Niagara Falls, NY St. Mary of the Cataract Church; Niagara Falls, NY Niagara Falls Memorial Medical Centers.
Friend, R. Scott '87 (LR) De Queen, AR St. Barbara's Church.
Frient, Lawrence '84 (Y) Andover, OH Our Lady of Victory Church.
Fries, Msgr. Francis A. '35 (HRT) Retired.
Fries, Richard R. *m.m.* '76 (LA) [R] Los Angeles, CA Maryknoll Fathers and Brothers.
Frigault, Edward F. '49 (NOR) Willimantic, CT St. Joseph Church.
Frigo, Martin A. *o.praem.* '49 (WIL) [I] Claymont, DE Immaculate Conception Priory of the Canons Regular of Premontre.
Frigo, William M. *o.f.m.cap.* (CHI) [A] Chicago, IL St. Joseph Seminary.
Frilot, Msgr. Eugene '55 (LA) Glendale, CA Church of the Incarnation.
Frimpong-Manso, Robert (PBL) [D] Pueblo, CO Centura Health-St. Mary-Corwin Hospital.
Frimtong-Manso, Robert (CC) [E] Corpus Christi, TX Spohn Hospital.
Frink, John A. '87 (ALN) Emmaus, PA St. Ann Church.
Frisbie, Kenneth J. '48 (HRT) Cheshire, CT St. Thomas Becket Church.
Frisch, Joseph C. '45 (WIN) Dakota, MN Holy Cross Church.
Frisch, Kenneth J. '78 (MAD) Highland, WI SS. Anthony and Philip Church.
Frisch, Michael F. *o.praem.* '97 (GB) [I] De Pere, WI St. Norbert Abbey.
Frisch, Ralph *s.t.* '59 (PAT) [M] Stirling, NJ Holy Spirit Missionary Cenacle.
Frische, Emile *m.h.m.* '70 (NY) [DD] Hartsdale, NY Mill Hill Fathers Residence.
Friske, Joseph P. '62 (SAG) On Duty Outside the Diocese.
Frison, Basil *c.m.f.* '36 (LA) [R] Rancho Dominguez, CA Dominguez Seminary Inc.
Frison, Ted '72 (P) Salem, OR Youth Correctional Facility; Woodburn, OR MacLaren Youth Correctional Facility.
Frister, Jerome '57 (JUN) Retired.
Fritsch, Albert J. *s.j.* '67 (LEX) [J] Mount Vernon, KY Appalachia Science in the Public Interest.
Fritsch, Michael C. '85 (IND) Greencastle, IN St. Paul the Apostle Church; Putnamville, IN Indiana State Farm; [N] Greencastle, IN DePauw Catholic Campus Ministry.
Fritz, Francis E. '45 (CIN) Withamsville, OH St. Thomas More Church; Retired.
Fritz, Germain L. *o.s.b.* '61 (PAT) [M] Morristown, NJ St. Mary's Abbey.
Fritz, Henry H. *o.s.b.* '52 (PEO) Peru, IL St. Joseph's Church; [A] Peru, IL St. Bede Abbey and Academy.
Fritz, Norbert '42 (P) Retired.
Fritz, Peter *o.f.m.* '50 (FWT) [G] Crowley, TX St. Francis Village, Inc.; [H] Crowley, TX St. Maximilian Kolbe Friary.
Fritz, Richard A. '75 (KAL) Bronson, MI St. Mary's Church.
Fritzen, James C. (SY) [W] Syracuse, NY St. Mary-St. Agnes.
Fritzen, James C. '69 (SY) Phoenix, NY St. Stephen Church.
Fritzen, Michael J. *s.v.d.* '69 (GAL) [47] Houston, TX St. Mary of the Purification Church.
Frizelle, Msgr. John D. '51 (AUS) Lampasas, TX St. Mary's Church; Lometa, TX Good Shepherd Church; Retired.
Frizzell, Edward *s.d.b.* '75 (NY) [72] New York, NY Mary Help of Christians Church.
Frizzell, Lawrence E. '62 (NEW) [B] South Orange, NJ Seton Hall University.
Froehle, Charles L. '63 (STP) Buffalo, MN St. Francis Xavier Church.
Froehlich, Canice *o.f.m.cap.* '47 (STL) [P] St. Louis, MO St. Patrick Friary.
Froehlich, James *o.f.m.cap.* '82 (WDC) [B] Washington, DC St. Francis Friary-Capuchin College.
Froehlich, Msgr. Mark J. '69 (STU) Bridgeport, OH St. Joseph Church; [J] Steubenville, OH Holy Name Society.
Froelich, Canice *o.f.m.cap.* '47 (STL) [54] St. Louis, MO St. Patrick Church.
Froelich, James E. *c.pp.s.* '55 (LFT) [A] Rensselaer, IN Saint Joseph's College.
Froeschl, Msgr. Martin H. '49 (KC) Retired.
Froidurot, Michel '78 (SD) [24] San Diego, CA St. Charles Borromeo Church.
Fromholzer, Francis J. '58 (ALN) [7] Allentown, PA St. Paul Church.
Frommeht, Robert M. *s.j.* '38 (MIL) [Y] Milwaukee, WI The Jesuit Partnership.
Frommelt, Robert M. *s.j.* '38 (MIL) [P] Wauwatosa, WI Jesuit Community at St. Camillus.
Frommeyer, James F. '45 (CIN) Retired.
Frommholz, Anthony F. *c.s.sp.* '44 (ALX) [F] Natchitoches, LA Holy Ghost Fathers Home, Maison Brothier.
Fron, Raymond S. '64 (SAG) [6] Bay City, MI St. Joseph Church.
Fronckewicz, Stephen *o.s.b.* '57 (NOR) [E] Willimantic, CT Holy Family Home and Shelter, Inc.
Fronckowiak, Dennis F. '77 (BUF) [4] North Tonawanda, NY Our Lady of Czestochowa Church.
Fronczak, Dennis A. '75 (BUF) Grand Island, NY St. Stephen Church.
Fronczek, Louis *o.f.m.* '59 (GB) [J] Manitowoc, WI Holy Family Convent of Franciscan Sisters of Christian Charity.
Fronk, Christopher S. *s.j.* '97 (PH) [AA] Philadelphia, PA Jesuit Community at St. Joseph's University.
Fronske, Edward *o.f.m.* '67 (GLP) Whiteriver, AZ St. Francis Apache Indian Church.
Frontiero, Anthony '91 (WDC) [36] Washington, DC St. Patrick Church.
Frontiero, Anthony R. (MAN) On Duty Outside the Diocese.
Frontiero, Anthony R. '91 (MAN) [6] Manchester, NH St. Catherine Church.
Frost, Arthur *c.ss.r.* '41 (WCH) [G] Wichita, KS Redemptorist Mission House.
Frost, Arthur W. *c.ss.r.* '41 (WCH) [14] Wichita, KS St. Joseph Church.
Frost, James (BRK) [165] Queens, NY Corpus Christi Church.
Frost, John M. '87 (DM) Grand River, IA St. Patrick Church; Osceola, IA St. Bernard Church.
Frost, Peter J. '70 (BO) Health Leave.
Frost, Stephen '84 (ORG) Inactive Leave.
Frost, Stephen '84 (SR) [K] Penngrove, CA Newman Hall, Sonoma State University, Intercollegiate Catholic Ministries.
Frost, Stephen A. '77 (FRS) On Special Assignment; [J] Fresno, CA Catholic Truth International.
Frost, Stephen A. '89 (FRS) Oildale, CA Christ the King Church.
Frost, Thomas *o.f.m.* '60 (TUC) Topawa, AZ San Solano Missions - Tohono O'odham Indian Reservation Church.
Frost, William P. '58 (CIN) [D] Dayton, OH The University of Dayton.
Frozena, Kenneth R. '60 (GB) Sherwood/St. John, WI St. John-Sacred Heart Church.
Frueh, Robert '63 (BRK) Brooklyn, NY Kingsboro Psychiatric Center; [U] Brooklyn, NY St. Joseph's Priest Residence.
Fruge, Msgr. Donald J. '72 (AUS) Special Assignments.
Fruge, Msgr. Donald J. '72 (GAL) On Duty Outside the Diocese.
Frugoli, A. Francis *s.j.* '45 (SFR) [E] San Francisco, CA St. Ignatius College Preparatory (Coed); [N] San Francisco, CA Jesuit Community at St. Ignatius College Preparatory.
Frundt, Oscar H. '56 (WIL) Brandywood, DE Church of the Holy Child; Retired.
Fruth, Paul '74 (DUL) Brainerd, MN St. Andrew's Church.
Fry, James Q. '79 (ORG) Military Chaplains.
Fry, Richard C. '58 (SJ) [13] San Jose, CA St. Julie Church.
Fry, Timothy *o.s.b.* '41 (KCK) [H] Atchison, KS St. Benedict's Abbey.
Fryar, Thomas S. '78 (DEN) [1] Englewood, CO All Souls Church.
Fryberger, Paul *c.s.c.* '36 (P) [B] Portland, OR University of Portland; [L] Portland, OR Holy Cross Fathers & Brothers, C.S.C. - University of Portland.
Fryberger, Paul E. *c.s.c.* '36 (FTW) [J] South Bend, IN Congregation of Holy Cross Indiana Province Provincial House.
Fryda, William *m.m.* '88 (FgM) Maryknoll Foreign Missions.
Frydrych, Jerzy *s.ch.* '85 (GAL) [55] Houston, TX Our Lady of Czestochowa Church.
Frye, Kenneth *c.p.m.* '90 (L) Glasgow, KY St. Helen Church.
Fryer, Patrick L. '73 (WH) On Duty Outside the Diocese.
Frysiak, Msgr. Chester S. '54 (BUF) [58] Buffalo, NY Queen of Peace Church.
Fu, Bartholomew Paul *o.p.* '46 (NY) [DD] New York, NY St. Catherine of Siena Priory.
Fu, John *s.v.d.* '30 (CHI) [B] Techny, IL Divine Word Residence.
Fu, Joseph '60 (NEW) [1] Garfield, NJ Our Lady of Mt. Virgin Church.
Fu, Paul B. *o.p.* '46 (NY) [22] New York, NY St. Catherine of Siena Church; Manhattan, NY New York Hospital.
Fuccile, Dominic G. '66 (NEW) Maplewood, NJ Immaculate Heart of Mary Church.
Fucheck, Robert '66 (ORL) Lady Lake, FL St. Timothy Church.
Fuchs, Athanase *o.s.b.* '41 (DUL) Ball Club, MN St. Joseph's Church; Duluth, MN Indian Missions Church; Duluth, MN Indian Missions Church.
Fuchs, John D. *s.j.* '75 (SEA) [7] Tacoma, WA St. Leo the Great Church.
Fuchs, Moritz A. '55 (SY) Hannibal, NY Our Lady of the Rosary Church.
Fuchs, Msgr. Robert A. '41 (AUS) Retired.
Fuchs, Msgr. Sylvester '49 (AUS) Retired.
Fuchs, Msgr. Sylvester '49 (GAL) Retired.
Fucinaro, Thomas J. '89 (LIN) On Duty Outside the Diocese.
Fuemmeler, James R. '58 (JC) Camdenton, MO St. Anthony Church.
Fuente, Maximo *o.m.i.* '31 (SAT) [K] San Antonio, TX Oblate Madonna Residence.
Fuentes, Roberto T. *m.m.* '92 (FgM) Maryknoll Foreign Missions.
Fuentes, Rodolfo Godinez '91 (STA) [21] Jacksonville, FL San Jose Church.
Fuentes, Theo *c.m.f.* '51 (PHX) [G] Phoenix, AZ Mt. Claret Retreat Center.
Fuentez, Trini '78 (ELP) [9] El Paso, TX Holy Family Church.
Fuentez, Trinidad '78 (ELP) [20] El Paso, TX Queen of Peace Church.
Fugee, Michael Charles '94 (NEW) Short Hills, NJ St. Rose of Lima Church.
Fugini, Francis *o.f.m.cap.* '54 (FgM) Capuchin Foreign Missions.
Fugini, Francis *o.f.m.cap.* '54 (PIT) [O] Pittsburgh, PA St. Augustine Friary.
Fuhrman, Nicholas *o.s.b.* '54 (LR) [E] Jonesboro, AR St. Bernard's Regional Medical Center; [I] Jonesboro, AR Holy Angels Convent-Motherhouse.
Fuhrman, Robert J. (NY) [HH] New York, NY Catholic Medical Mission Board, Inc.
Fuhrman, Msgr. Robert J. '81 (NEW) Saddle River Borough, NJ St. Gabriel the Archangel Church.
Fuhrmann, Bruno *o.s.b.* '54 (FgM) American - Cassinese Congregation Foreign Missions.
Fuino, Crispin *o.f.m.conv.* '48 (TR) Riverside, NJ St. Peter Church.
Fuino, Michael A. '42 (NEW) [15] Newark, NJ St. Francis Xavier Church; Retired.
Fujihara, Fidelis *s.a.* '65 (NY) [DD] Garrison, NY Generalate of the Franciscan Friars of the Atonement-St. James Friary.
Fukes, Gary M. '88 (SY) Dewitt, NY Holy Cross Church.
Fulcher, John M. '56 (COL) Crooksville, OH Church of the Atonement.
Fulco, William J. *s.j.* '66 (LA) [C] Los Angeles, CA Loyola Marymount University.
Fuld, Charles '86 (SD) Escondido, CA Church of the Resurrection.
Fulgenzi, Mario A. *o.s.b.* '68 (GBG) [2] Latrobe, PA St. Vincent Basilica Church; [H] Latrobe, PA Saint Vincent Archabbey.
Fullam, Matthew N. *s.j.* '42 (FgM) Provinces.
Fullam, Paul Joseph *c.p.* '53 (BRK) [U] Jamaica, NY Immaculate Conception Monastery.
Fullam, Todd Dominick '94 (BLX) [2] Gulfport, MS St. James Church.
Fullam, Msgr. Vincent F. *j.d.* '65 (RVC) [A] Huntington, NY Diocesan Seminary of the Immaculate Conception.
Fullen, John N. '95 (BAL) Hagerstown, MD St. Mary Church.
Fullenkamp, Leonard *c.pp.s.* '39 (CIN) [B] Carthagena, OH St. Charles.
Fuller, Donald F. '58 (GB) Darboy, WI Holy Angels Church.
Fuller, Gerald *o.m.i.* '55 (SPC) Mansfield, MO Immaculate Heart of Mary Church.
Fuller, Jon D. *s.j.* '90 (BO) [W] Boston, MA Jesuit Urban Center & Immaculate Conception Community.

Fuller, Mark '88 (NSH) Lafayette, TN Holy Family Church; Lebanon, TN St. Frances Cabrini Church.
Fuller, Mark L. '79 (STL) Kirkwood, MO St. Joseph Hospital; [K] Kirkwood, MO St. Joseph Hospital of Kirkwood.
Fuller, Michael J. '97 (RCK) Loves Park, IL St. Bridget Church.
Fuller, Neil D. *s.v.d.* '69 (SB) Frontera, CA California Institute for Women.
Fuller, Msgr. Robert D. '56 (TUC) [12] Tucson, AZ St. Frances Cabrini Church.
Fuller, Roger J. '84 (DEN) Absent on Leave.
Fuller, Timothy M. '93 (OKL) Sulphur, OK St. Francis Xavier Church.
Fullerton, Daniel (SCR) On Special or Other Diocesan Assignment.
Fullmer, Hugh '72 (JOL) [4] Lockport, IL St. Joseph Church.
Fullum, Dominick '94 (BLX) Moss Point, MS St. Joseph Church.
Fullum, John J. '67 (BRK) [239] Queens, NY Sacred Heart Church.
Fulmer, Jeffrey '97 (CIN) [E] Hamilton, OH Stephen T. Badin High School.
Fulmer, Jeffrey M. '97 (CIN) [13] Cincinnati, OH Assumption Church.
Fulton, David I. '67 (MET) Baptistown, NJ Our Lady of Victories Church.
Fulton, Eugene '67 (NY) [D] New York, NY Department of Education; [FF] Larchmont, NY Trinity Retreat.
Fulton, Eugene '67 (PSC) On Duty Outside Diocese.
Fulton, Joseph *o.p.* '42 (SEA) [22] Seattle, WA Blessed Sacrament Church.
Fulton, Kenneth S. '50 (TLS) Sand Springs, OK St. Patrick's Church.
Fulton, Malachy *o.s.b.* '43 (IND) [J] St. Meinrad, IN St. Meinrad Archabbey.
Fulton, Robert '62 (MOB) Greenville, AL St. Elizabeth Church.
Fulton, Robert W. '62 (MOB) Andalusia, AL Christ the King Church.
Fulton, Terry A. '94 (SAC) [20] Sacramento, CA St. Philomene Church.
Fumo, Harold '55 (ORG) San Juan Capistrano, CA (Old Mission) Church; Absent on Sick Leave.
Fumo, Michael '42 (NEW) [N] Rutherford, NJ St. John Vianney Residence for Priests.
Funaro, Msgr. Joseph (BRK) [L] Brooklyn, NY Catholic Charities.
Funaro, Msgr. Joseph A. '65 (BRK) [12] Brooklyn, NY Assumption of the Blessed Virgin Mary Church.
Funcheon, Gerald A. '65 (LFT) Retired.
Funesti, Peter K. '88 (NEW) Bloomfield, NJ Church of St. Thomas the Apostle.
Funk, C. Alan '91 (LFT) Marion, IN St. Paul Church.
Funk, David *o.f.m.cap.* (GB) [5] Appleton, WI St. Pius X Church.
Funk, Msgr. David R. '74 (COL) [2] Columbus, OH St. Agatha Church.
Funk, Peter C. '64 (PH) [44] Philadelphia, PA Epiphany of Our Lord Church.
Funk, Virgil C. '63 (RIC) On Duty Outside the Diocese.
Funk, Wayne G. '62 (BAL) Frederick, MD St. John the Evangelist Church.
Funk, Wiatt A. '68 (NSH) Murfreesboro, TN St. Rose of Lima Church.
Funke, Gerald J. '80 (B) Idaho Falls, ID Holy Rosary Church.
Funke, Msgr. Richard P. '60 (DUB) [3] Dubuque, IA St. Columbkille's Church.
Funke, Ronald R. *s.j.* '68 (SEA) [A] Seattle, WA Seattle University.
Funtila, Aloysius *c.i.c.m.* (CHI) [1] Waukegan, IL St. Anastasia Church.
Fuoco, Armando '43 (SHP) Retired.
Furdek, John M. '84 (JOL) Villa Park, IL St. Alexander Church.
Furey, Frederick *ss.cc.* '46 (COL) Marion, OH St. Mary Church.
Furey, Frederick G. *ss.cc.* '46 (COL) Marion, OH Marion Correctional Institution.
Furey, J. Barry '71 (BGP) [3] Bridgeport, CT St. Andrew Church.
Furey, John *c.ss.r.* '60 (BO) [13] Boston, MA Our Lady of Perpetual Help Church.
Furey, Thomas J. '73 (PH) Holland, PA St. Bede the Venerable Church.
Furfaro, Msgr. Francis J. '41 (SY) Oswego, NY Oswego County Jail; Retired.
Furfaro, Virgil '83 (SFE) Bernalillo, NM Our Lady of Sorrows Church.
Furlan, Gerard *s.x.* '58 (FgM) Xaverian Foreign Missions.
Furlan, Gerard *s.x.* '58 (PAT) [M] Wayne, NJ Xaverian Missionary Fathers.
Furlan, Michael J. '75 (CHI) [117] Chicago, IL St. Leo The Great Church.
Furlan, William '48 (SCL) Retired.
Furlong, Aidan M. *a.a.* '53 (WOR) Fiskdale, MA St. Anne's and St. Patrick's Church.
Furlong, J. Daryl '66 (MAD) [3] Janesville, WI St. Patrick Church.
Furlong, James '84 (LUB) Special Assignment; [B] Lubbock, TX St. Mary of the Plains Hospital.
Furlong, Jude *l.c.* '74 (PRO) [U] South Kingstown, RI "Mater Ecclesiae" International Formation Center.
Furlong, Thomas D. '60 (OM) [24] Omaha, NE St. John Vianney Church.
Furman, Walter L. *s.j.* '50 (MOB) [B] Mobile, AL Spring Hill College.
Furmanski, Leonard A. '59 (PH) [81] Philadelphia, PA St. Josaphat Church.
Furnari, Casper '68 (BRK) [220] Queens, NY Our Lady of the Snows Church.
Furrevig, Edward G. '67 (NEW) Union, NJ Holy Spirit Church.
Furtado, Jose A. *o.de. m.* '97 (SP) [O] St. Petersburg, FL St. Peter Nolasco Residence.
Furtado, Steven R. '73 (FR) [3] Fall River, MA Espirito Santo Church.
Furtmann, John A. '57 (MIL) Retired.
Fus, Msgr. Edward A. '43 (BRK) [177] Queens, NY Holy Cross Church; Retired.
Fusco, Albin *o.f.m.* '59 (NY) [79] New York, NY Most Precious Blood Church.
Fusco, Blaise J. *o.f.m.cap.* '41 (PIT) [O] Pittsburgh, PA St. Conrad Friary; [P] Pittsburgh, PA Motherhouse and Novitiate of the Vincentian Sisters of Charity.
Fusco, Christopher J. '97 (OG) [5] Plattsburgh, NY St. Peter Church.
Fusco, Frederick *o.f.m.* '42 (ALB) [A] Catskill, NY St. Anthony Friary.
Fusco, Philip N. '46 (GRY) Retired.
Fusco, Thomas M. '85 (RVC) West Hempstead, NY St. Thomas, the Apostle Church; [A] Huntington, NY Diocesan Seminary of the Immaculate Conception.
Fuselier, Karl '94 (LKC) [2] Lake Charles, LA Immaculate Heart of Mary Church.
Fushek, Dale J. '78 (PHX) [6] Mesa, AZ St. Timothy Church.
Fuss, Edward F. *s.m.* '89 (WDC) [M] Washington, DC Marist Provincial House.
Fussner, Donald T. '60 (NY) [105] New York, NY St. Peter Church.
Futie, Richard F. '82 (BGP) [10] Stamford, CT St. Mary's Church.
Futo, Ignatius *s.j.* (STL) [C] St. Louis, MO Saint Louis University.
Futo, Ignatius *s.j.* '81 (STL) [P] St. Louis, MO Jesuit Community Corporation at St. Louis University - Jesuit Hall.
Futrell, John C. *s.j.* '58 (DEN) [M] Denver, CO Xavier Jesuit Center.
Futter, Volker *o.s.b.* '69 (OM) [K] Schuyler, NE Benedictine Mission House.
Fuytinck, Albert A. *c.ss.r.* '42 (STL) [P] Liguori, MO St. Clement Health Care Center.
Fye, Lawrence C. '59 (Y) [1] Youngstown, OH Cathedral of St. Columba.

G

Gaalaas, Patrick J. '72 (TLS) Broken Arrow, OK St. Benedict Church; Coweta, OK St. Vincent de Paul Church.
Gabadian, Msgr. Sarkis '52 (ARM) Philadelphia, PA St. Mark's Armenian Catholic Church.
Gabalski, Msgr. John R. '48 (BUF) [61] Buffalo, NY St. Stanislaus Church; [T] Buffalo, NY Monsignor Adamski Village, Inc.
Gabel, Garold L. '79 (LIN) [4] Lincoln, NE North American Martyrs Church.
Gabel, Manuel '57 (DEN) [28] Denver, CO St. Catherine of Siena Church.
Gabel, Martin '68 (JOL) Wheaton, IL St. Michael Church.
Gabel, Robert *o.f.m.* '51 (PAT) [M] Ringwood, NJ Holy Name Friary, Inc.
Gabela, Jose Luis Diez *o.s.a.* '72 (MGZ) Aguada, PR St. Francis of Assisi Church.
Gaber, Francis '51 (DUL) Retired.
Gaberle, Jiri P. (MIL) Awaiting Assignment.
Gabet, George '97 (SCR) [M] Elmhurst, PA Priestly Fraternity of St. Peter (F.S.S.P.), North American District Headquarters.
Gabet, George *f.s.s.p.* '97 (TLS) [2] Tulsa, OK Community of Saint Peter Church.
Gabin, John D. '75 (PH) Richboro, PA St. Vincent de Paul Church.
Gabino, Pedro '91 (STO) Absent on Leave.
Gaborit, Mauricio *s.j.* '78 (FgM) Provinces.
Gabraciak, Dariusz *s.v.d.* '96 (CHI) [N] Chicago, IL Divine Word Theologate.
Gabrian, John '70 (DEN) [2] Lakewood, CO Christ on the Mountain Parish.
Gabriel, Astrik L. '31 (FTW) [B] Notre Dame, IN University of Notre Dame Du Lac.
Gabriel, Eduardo *o.p.* (AUS) [H] Austin, TX St. Joseph Hall.
Gabriel, Eduardo *o.p.* '92 (AUS) [H] Austin, TX Dominican Fathers.
Gabriel, Eduardo *o.p.* '92 (DAL) [M] Irving, TX Dominican Priory of St. Albert the Great.
Gabriel, John '87 (NEW) Summit, NJ St. Teresa's Church.
Gabriel, John *m.s.* '91 (MIL) [P] Twin Lakes, WI La Salette Missionaries Shrine.
Gabriel, Kitira *c.ss.p.* (SB) [E] Hemet, CA Holy Ghost Fathers.
Gabriel, Michael A. '84 (CHI) Lansing, IL St. Ann Church.
Gabriele, John J. '68 (RVC) Absent on Leave.
Gabuzda, Richard J. '81 (SCR) On Duty Outside the Diocese.
Gacki, Peter '51 (CHI) [48] Chicago, IL St. Daniel the Prophet Church.
Gacki, Peter *o.f.m.cap.* '51 (PAT) [M] Oak Ridge-Milton, NJ St. Stanislaus B. M. Friary.
Gadarowski, Msgr. Bronislaw A. '43 (NOR) Retired.
Gaddy, Msgr. James '65 (LKC) Kinder, LA St. Philip Neri Church.
Gaddy, Kenneth *c.ss.r.* '88 (STV) [3] Frederiksted, VI Church of St. Patrick; [B] St. Thomas, VI Miscellaneous Organizations.
Gadenz, Pablo '96 (TR) Keansburg, NJ St. Ann Church.
Gadient, Peter J. '45 (LIN) Retired.
Gadziala, Timothy A., . (ATL) Blairsville, GA St. Francis of Assisi Church.
Gadzinski, Mark '82 (STU) Absent on Leave.
Gaebelein, Claude '46 (CLV) [N] Cleveland, OH Sts. Mary and Joseph Home for the Aged.
Gaebelein, Claude J. '46 (CLV) [4] Barberton, OH St. Mary's Church; Retired.
Gaeke, Thomas M. '75 (CIN) [14] Dayton, OH Holy Family Church; [18] Dayton, OH St. Mary's Church.
Gaelens, Albert R. *c.s.b.* '60 (ROC) [B] Rochester, NY The Aquinas Institute; [I] Rochester, NY Residence of Basilian Fathers-The Aquinas Institute.
Gaertner, Robert *c.pp.s.* '43 (CIN) [B] Carthagena, OH St. Charles.
Gaesser, Ronald E. '61 (ROC) Ithaca, NY St. Catherine of Siena Church; Lansing, NY All Saints Church.
Gaeta, Bernard N. '73 (Y) Ashtabula, OH Mother of Sorrows Church.
Gaeta, David (TR) McGuire Air Force Base, NJ McGuire Air Force Base.
Gaeta, David R. '80 (SLC) On Duty Outside the Diocese.
Gaeta, Francis X. '63 (RVC) Westbury, NY St. Brigid Church.
Gaetano, Francis *s.a.c.* '48 (NEW) Fairview, NJ Our Lady of Grace Church.
Gaetano, Msgr. Lewis F. '73 (STU) Mingo Junction, OH Annunciation Church; Mingo Junction, OH St. Agnes Church.
Gaffey, Eugene F. '69 (PRT) Camden, ME Our Lady of Good Hope Church.
Gaffey, Msgr. James P. '60 (SR) [1] Santa Rosa, CA Cathedral of St. Eugene.
Gaffey, Kevin P. '57 (SFR) Novato, CA St. Anthony of Padua Church.
Gaffigan, Charles A. '62 (ALB) Lake Luzerne, NY Holy Infancy Church.
Gaffigan, William J. '64 (ALB) Canajoharie, NY St. Peter's and Paul's Church.
Gaffney, Edward M. *o.p.* '49 (BAL) [A] Emmitsburg, MD Mount St. Mary's Seminary; [A] Emmitsburg, MD Mount St. Mary's Seminary.
Gaffney, Francis P. '64 (CAM) Bellmawr, NJ Mary, Mother of the Church.
Gaffney, J. Michael '73 (OG) Lake Placid, NY St. Agnes Church.
Gaffney, J. Patrick *s.m.m.* '54 (RVC) [N] Bay Shore, NY Montfort Missionaries.
Gaffney, J. Patrick *s.m.m.* '54 (STL) [W] Arnold, MO AJT, Inc.
Gaffney, James '52 (MEM) Retired.
Gaffney, James F. '85 (ALN) [1] Shenandoah, PA Annunciation Church.
Gaffney, Msgr. James J. (CAM) Retired.
Gaffney, Msgr. James J. '50 (CAM) Glassboro, NJ Our Lady of Lourdes Church.
Gaffney, John H. *o.s.a.* '45 (TLS) [B] Tulsa, OK Cascia Hall Preparatory School.
Gaffney, Joseph '67 (LA) Thousand Oaks, CA St. Paschal Baylon Church.
Gaffney, Michael *o.f.m.cap.* (DET) [K] Detroit, MI St. Mary's Friary.
Gaffney, Patrick *c.s.c.* '74 (FTW) [B] Notre Dame, IN University of Notre Dame Du Lac; [J] Notre Dame, IN Holy Cross Community, Corby Hall, University of Notre Dame.
Gaffney, Patrick W. *c.ss.r.* '81 (WIL) Seaford, DE Our Lady of Lourdes Church.
Gaffney, Thomas F. '58 (HRT) [9] New Britain, CT St. Joseph's Church.
Gaffney, Msgr. Thomas J. '50 (NY) [200] Staten Island, NY St. Charles Church.
Gaffney, William *c.s.s.r.* (NY) [150] Bronx, NY Immaculate Conception Church.
Gafney, Thomas E. *s.j.* '65 (FgM) Provinces.
Gagala, John '58 (DET) [1] Southfield, MI St. Beatrice Church; [H] Southfield, MI Providence Hospital.
Gagan, Charles R. *s.j.* '68 (SFR) [24] San Francisco, CA

St. Ignatius Church; [N] San Francisco, CA Jesuit Community at University of San Francisco.
Gagan, Philip R. '79 (STA) Absent on Sick Leave.
Gage, George D. '79 (ROM) Youngstown, OH St. Mary Church; Sharon, PA St. John Church.
Gage, Gregory A. '67 (P) Newberg, OR St. Peter Church.
Gage, Philip S. *s.m.* '69 (WDC) [M] Washington, DC Marist Provincial House.
Gaggawala, Paul *a.j.* '80 (ARL) [2] Arlington, VA St. Agnes Church.
Gaggawala, Paul O. *a.p.* (ALN) [P] Shenandoah, PA Apostles of Jesus.
Gagliano, Philip J. '76 (NY) Harrison, NY St. Gregory the Great Church; [1] Yonkers, NY St. Anthony Church.
Gagliardi, Carmelo *o.f.m.cap.* '73 (BRK) [105] Brooklyn, NY Shrine of Our Lady of Mount Carmel Church.
Gagliardi, Richard '62 (OAK) El Sobrante, CA St. Callistus Church.
Gagliardo, Anthony F. '61 (BUF) Retired.
Gaglione, John R. '76 (BUF) [10] Niagara Falls, NY Our Lady of the Rosary Church.
Gaglione, Joseph *c.s.sp.* '64 (SAT) [O] New Braunfels, TX Spiritan Renewal Center.
Gagnard, Louis '52 (ALX) Retired.
Gagne, Mark R. '85 (MAN) [5] Nashua, NH Immaculate Conception Church.
Gagne, Rene E. '51 (PRO) Retired; [P] Providence, RI St. John Vianney Residence.
Gagne, Roger C. '75 (PRO) [22] Providence, RI St. Mary Church.
Gagne, Ron *m.s.* '71 (ORL) [2] Orlando, FL Blessed Trinity Church.
Gagne, Ronald '66 (DUL) Keewatin, MN St. Mary's Church; Nashwauk, MN St. Cecilia's Church.
Gagne, Walter *s.a.* '71 (NY) [DD] Garrison, NY Generalate of the Franciscan Friars of the Atonement-St. James Friary; [DD] Garrison, NY Franciscan Friars of the Atonement.
Gagnepain, John F. *c.m.* '62 (STL) [P] Perryville, MO Congregation of The Mission.
Gagnier, John F. (ROC) Scipio Center, NY St. Bernard Church.
Gagnier, John F. '78 (ROC) Moravia, NY St. Patrick Church.
Gagnon, Adelard J. '56 (BO) [53] Boston, MA Our Lady of the Assumption Church.
Gagnon, Andre J. '57 (MAN) [3] Manchester, NH St. Anthony of Padua Church; Manchester, NH Nursing Homes; [L] Manchester, NH St. George Manor.
Gagnon, Daniel *o.m.i.* '87 (FgM) Oblates Foreign Missions.
Gagnon, George C. '55 (ALB) Whitehall, NY Notre Dame des Victoires Church.
Gagnon, Henry W. '64 (BO) Bedford, MA St. Michael Church.
Gagnon, Herve *o.m.i.* '45 (BO) [W] Lowell, MA Missionary Oblates of Mary Immaculate; [W] Lowell, MA Missionary Oblates of Mary Immaculate.
Gagnon, Jean Paul '82 (WOR) Millville, MA St. Augustine's Church.
Gagnon, Joseph A. '61 (DET) Melvindale, MI St. Conrad Church.
Gagnon, Leo G. '72 (MAN) Portsmouth, NH Immaculate Conception Church.
Gagnon, Mariano *o.f.m.* '58 (FgM) Franciscan Foreign Missions.
Gagnon, Michel *o.f.m.* '57 (SD) San Luis Rey, CA Mission San Luis Rey de Francia Church; [H] San Luis Rey, CA Mission San Luis Rey.
Gagnon, Raymond E. '72 (MAN) [6] Nashua, NH Infant Jesus Church.
Gagnon, Richard *s.d.s.* '65 (NSH) Smyrna, TN St. Luke Church.
Gagnon, Roland *o.m.i.* '51 (FgM) Oblates Foreign Missions.
Gagnon, Ronald P. '56 (TUC) [5] Tucson, AZ Most Holy Trinity Church.
Gahagan, William H. '70 (KNX) Johnson City, TN St. Mary Church; [J] Johnson City, TN ETSU-Catholic Center; [K] Knoxville, TN Diocesan Council of Catholic Women.
Gahan, James L. '68 (STL) [4] St. Charles, MO Sts. Joachim and Ann Church; [E] St. Charles, MO Duchesne High School.
Gaiardo, Martin J. '70 (SCR) Retired.
Gailiusis, George S. *o.f.m.* '40 (PRT) [I] Kennebunkport, ME St. Anthony's Friary.
Gainer, Msgr. Ronald W. '73 (ALN) Whitehall, PA Holy Trinity Church.
Gainer, Msgr. Ronald W. *m.a., j.c.l.* '73 (PH) [A] Wynnewood, PA Theological Seminary of St. Charles Borromeo, Overbrook.
Gaines, G. Timothy '87 (DEN) Erie, CO St. Scholastica Church; Frederick, CO St. Theresa Church.
Gaines, Michael T. '87 (E) North East, PA St. Gregory Thaumaturgus Church.
Gaitan, Ramon *o.a.r.* '60 (KCK) [K] Kansas City, KS Casa Juan Diego Centro de Evangelization.
Gaiter, Chester E. *s.j.* '76 (STL) [P] St. Louis, MO Jesuit Community Corporation at St. Louis University - Jesuit Hall.
Gaj, Zygmut '41 (GAY) Retired.
Gajdos, Thomas '70 (MIL) Cedarburg, WI Divine Word Catholic Church.
Gajdzinski, Norman A. '63 (CLV) [3] Garfield Heights, OH St. Therese Church.
Gajere, James D. '88 (BRK) [181] Queens, NY Immaculate Conception Church.
Gajewski, Msgr. Chester A. '50 (SCR) Retired; [N] Dunmore, PA Villa St. Joseph.
Gal, Gedeon *o.f.m.* (BUF) [C] St. Bonaventure, NY St. Bonaventure University.
Gal, Gedeon *o.f.m.* '29 (BUF) [O] St. Bonaventure, NY St. Bonaventure Friary.
Galambos, Stephen L. *o.f.m.* '96 (MET) [6] New Brunswick, NJ St. Ladislaus Church.
Galan, Jose M. '65 (PCE) [15] Ponce, PR Church of the Sacred Heart.
Galan, Juan Cerro '88 (SP) On Duty Outside the Diocese.
Galanaugh, Joseph T. '79 (PH) Absent on Leave.
Galang, Agerico (OAK) Pittsburg, CA St. Peter Martyr of Verona Church.
Galang, Jose '78 (SJ) [3] Santa Clara, CA St. Justin Church.
Galarza, Tomas '86 (CGS) Las Piedras, PR San Juan Bautista Church.
Galas, Daniel E '57 (OM) Snyder, NE St. Leo Church.
Galas, Daniel E. '57 (OM) North Bend, NE St. Charles Borromeo Church.
Galasso, Michael S. '71 (HRT) [15] Hartford, CT St. Peter Church.
Galaz, Jesse C. '81 (LA) [40] Los Angeles, CA St. Alphonsus Church.
Galban, Antonio M. *o.s.b.* '63 (MGZ) [6] Mayaquez, PR Sacred Heart Church.
Galban, Timothy S. '97 (WDC) [2] Rockville, MD Shrine of St. Jude Church.
Galchus, Robert *o.m.* '49 (STA) [E] Jacksonville, FL St. Vincent's Medical Center, Inc.
Galchus, Robert P. *c.m.* '49 (PH) [AA] Philadelphia, PA Congregation of the Mission.
Galdon, Joseph A. *s.j.* '59 (FgM) Provinces.
Galdon, Peter P. '68 (NEW) [18] Jersey City, NJ St. Nicholas Church.
Galdon, Richard M. '59 (NEW) Retired.
Gale, Robert '68 (BO) Awaiting Assignment.
Galea, John '62 (STU) [5] Steubenville, OH Our Lady of North America Martyrs Church.
Galea, John M. '62 (STU) Jewett, OH Our Lady of Perpetual Help Mission Church.
Galea, Michael A. '80 (BR) Donaldsonville, LA St. Francis of Assisi Church.
Galek, Adam '71 (CHI) [201] Chicago, IL St. Thecla Church.
Galek, Peter (CHI) Calumet City, IL St. Victor Church.
Galens, Jeffrey '90 (NY) [E] New York, NY Cardinal Hayes High School.
Galeon, Arnelo A. '91 (NEW) [3] Jersey City, NJ St. Anne's Church.
Galeone, Msgr. Victor B. '60 (BAL) [3] Baltimore, MD St. Agnes Church; [Q] Baltimore, MD Ladies of Charity.
Galetto, Paul W. '82 (CAM) [C] Richland, NJ St. Augustine Preparatory School.
Galiardi, Roman *o.s.b.* '57 (JOL) [J] Lisle, IL St. Procopius Abbey.
Galiardi, Roman S. *o.s.b.* '57 (JOL) Lisle, IL St. Joan of Arc Church.
Galic, Bernard J. '70 (FTW) [10] South Bend, IN Holy Family Church.
Galic, Joseph N. *o.f.m.* '66 (ALN) [6] Bethlehem, PA St. Joseph Church.
Galinada, Michael *s.m.* '78 (ORG) Costa Mesa, CA St. Joachim Church.
Galindo, Msgr. Rudolph '54 (SD) Retired.
Galipeau, Roland J. '64 (SPR) [2] Holyoke, MA Holy Cross Church.
Galivan, James F. '81 (CHI) Lyons, IL St. Hugh Church.
Galko, Joseph '80 (ALN) Unassigned.
Gall, Florian J. '61 (MET) Whitehouse Station, NJ Our Lady of Lourdes Church.
Gall, Jacob M. '62 (FTW) Kendallville, IN Immaculate Conception Church.
Gall, Sylvester '38 (SCL) Retired.
Gall, Thomas S. '92 (OM) [44] Omaha, NE St. Stephen the Martyr Church.
Gallager, Edward L. (BO) Retired.
Gallagher, Adrian *ofm conv.* '92 (BUF) [D] Athol Springs, NY St. Francis High School; [O] Athol Springs, NY St. Francis of Assisi Friary.
Gallagher, Andrew J. '46 (RVC) Point Lookout, NY Our Lady of the Miraculous Medal Church; Retired.
Gallagher, Brian (NY) [DD] Wassaic, NY Guardian Angel Chapel.
Gallagher, Brian *s.s.c.* '52 (PRO) [P] Bristol, RI St. Columban's Retirement House.
Gallagher, Brian T. '60 (YAK) On Duty Outside the Diocese.
Gallagher, Cathal J. *s.s.c.* '74 (WIN) [F] Rochester, MN Madonna Towers of Rochester, Inc.
Gallagher, Charles '44 (CHI) La Grange, IL St. Cletus Church.
Gallagher, Charles A. *s.j.* '58 (NEW) [B] Jersey City, NJ Saint Peter's College; [N] Jersey City, NJ Jesuits of Saint Peter's College, Inc.
Gallagher, Charles G. '44 (CHI) Retired.
Gallagher, Chester G. '50 (WIN) Absent on Leave.
Gallagher, Cornelius F. '42 (STU) Retired.
Gallagher, Cyrus *o.f.m.cap.* '65 (DEN) [3] Denver, CO Annunciation Church; [M] Denver, CO Annunciation Friary.
Gallagher, Daniel '65 (JKS) [1] Jackson, MS St. Peter Cathedral; Jackson, MS Veterans Administration Hospital.
Gallagher, Daniel J. '51 (PH) Doylestown, PA Our Lady of Mount Carmel Church.
Gallagher, David F. *c.s.s.* '59 (BO) [W] Waltham, MA Stigmatine House.
Gallagher, Dennis J. *o.s.a.* '65 (PH) [C] Villanova, PA Villanova University; [AA] Villanova, PA St. Thomas Monastery.
Gallagher, E. Henry *o.p.* '36 (BO) [W] Dover, MA St. Stephen Priory.
Gallagher, Earl *o.f.m.cap.* '71 (FgM) Capuchin Foreign Missions.
Gallagher, Edward *c.m.* '78 (FgM) Vincentian Foreign Missions.
Gallagher, Edward F. '46 (SCR) Retired; [N] Dunmore, PA Villa St. Joseph.
Gallagher, Edward L. '53 (BO) Carver, MA Our Lady of Lourdes Church.
Gallagher, Msgr. Eugene A. '43 (SFR) Retired.
Gallagher, Eugene P. '38 (NY) Retired.
Gallagher, F. Anthony '61 (TOL) Providence, OH St. Patrick Church.
Gallagher, Francis J. *s.j.* '55 (SJ) [M] Los Gatos, CA Sacred Heart Jesuit Center.
Gallagher, Francis J. '73 (PH) Jenkintown, PA Immaculate Conception Church.
Gallagher, Francis L. '48 (BO) Billerica, MA St. Andrew Church; Retired.
Gallagher, Francis M. '64 (PH) Croydon, PA St. Thomas Aquinas Church.
Gallagher, Francis M. '87 (PEO) [4] Rock Island, IL St. Pius X Church.
Gallagher, Gary *o.m.i.* '92 (BEL) [F] Belleville, IL Shrine of Our Lady of the Snows.
Gallagher, J. Gerald '57 (CAM) Woodbury, NJ St. Patrick's Church.
Gallagher, Jack *c.s.b.* (GAL) [A] Houston, TX St. Mary's Seminary.
Gallagher, Jack *o.s.cam.* '81 (WOR) [K] Whitinsville, MA St. Camillus Nursing Home Inc.
Gallagher, Msgr. James '44 (PT) [3] Pensacola, FL Holy Spirit Church; Retired.
Gallagher, James E. '87 (RIC) Prince George County, VA Church of the Sacred Heart.
Gallagher, John (GB) Suring, WI St. Michael Church.
Gallagher, John *o.f.m.cap.* (NEW) [N] Orange, NJ St. Veronica Giuliani Friary, Capuchin Franciscan Friars.
Gallagher, John (PIT) [J] Cranberry Township, PA St. Francis Nursing Center-North.
Gallagher, John *o.s.cam.* '81 (WOR) [N] Whitinsville, MA St. Camillus Community.
Gallagher, Msgr. John A. '55 (NY) [15] Yonkers, NY St. Paul the Apostle Church.
Gallagher, John C. *c.s.b.* '60 (GAL) [Q] Houston, TX Residence of the Basilian Fathers of the University of St. Thomas.
Gallagher, John E. '59 (BO) [7] Lowell, MA St. Louis de France Church.
Gallagher, John J. *o.s.cam.* (WOR) [K] Whitinsville, MA St. Camillus Hospice, Inc.
Gallagher, John J. *o.s.a.* '45 (PH) [AA] Villanova, PA St. Thomas Monastery.
Gallagher, John M. '71 (GB) Gillett, WI St. John Church.
Gallagher, John M. *o.f.m.cap.* '78 (MAN) [2] Manchester, NH St. Anne Church.
Gallagher, Msgr. John P. '51 (SCR) Retired.
Gallagher, John P. '57 (PH) Gladwyne, PA St. John Baptist Vianney Church.
Gallagher, John P. '68 (PIT) Cranberry Township, PA St. Ferdinand Church.
Gallagher, John P. '80 (DAV) Riverside, IA St. Mary of the Assumption Church.
Gallagher, John P. *c.ss.r.* '95 (FgM) Redemptorist Foreign Missions.
Gallagher, John R. *v.g.* (WH) [J] Wheeling, WV Welty Home for the Aged, Inc.
Gallagher, John R. '55 (DUB) [H] Cedar Rapids, IA Mercy Medical Center, Cedar Rapids, Iowa.
Gallagher, John R. '93 (WH) [1] Wheeling, WV St. Joseph's Cathedral; [R] Wheeling, WV Retirement Trust Agreement of the Infirm Priests' Association of the Diocese of Wheeling-Charleston.

Gallagher, Joseph J. '55 (BAL) Retired.
Gallagher, Joseph J. '63 (PH) [141] Philadelphia, PA St. Richard Church.
Gallagher, Joseph T. '42 (PRO) Retired.
Gallagher, Joseph W. *c.s.p.* '61 (GR) Grand Rapids, MI Chapel of St. Paul-Catholic Information Center.
Gallagher, Kevin E. *s.j.* '61 (CHI) [N] Chicago, IL Chicago Province of the Society of Jesus-Provincial Office.
Gallagher, Kevin E. *s.j.* '61 (FgM) Provinces.
Gallagher, Kevin P. '83 (ALN) [5] Reading, PA Holy Guardian Angels Church.
Gallagher, Maurice O. '50 (PBL) Avondale, CO Sacred Heart Church.
Gallagher, Michael *s.j.* '84 (ELP) [21] El Paso, TX Sacred Heart Church.
Gallagher, Michael F. '68 (NY) Military Chaplains.
Gallagher, Msgr. Michael J. '66 (SD) [2] El Cajon, CA Our Lady of Grace Church.
Gallagher, Michael J. '69 (WIL) On Duty Outside the Diocese.
Gallagher, Otmar *o.f.m.cap.* '48 (VEN) [D] Port Charlotte, FL Bon Secours-St. Joseph Hospital.
Gallagher, Patrick *o.f.m.conv.* '65 (SY) [2] Syracuse, NY Assumption B.V.M. Church.
Gallagher, Msgr. Patrick J. '66 (LA) San Pedro, CA Mary, Star of the Sea Church; [DD] San Pedro, CA Apostleship of the Sea, Catholic Maritime Ministry.
Gallagher, Patrick J. '70 (MOB) Dothan, AL St. Columba Church; [K] Dothan, AL George C. Wallace Jr. Community College Newman Center.
Gallagher, Paul *o.f.m.* '82 (GAL) [T] Houston, TX University of Houston Central Campus Catholic Newman Association.
Gallagher, Paul V. '63 (RIC) Retired.
Gallagher, Peter (IND) [36] Indianapolis, IN St. Simon Church.
Gallagher, Peter '92 (IND) [7] Indianapolis, IN Holy Spirit Church; [C] Indianapolis, IN Father Thomas Scecina Memorial High School.
Gallagher, Philip (LAN) [I] De Witt, MI St. Francis Retreat Center.
Gallagher, Raymond '43 (SAN) Retired.
Gallagher, Richard (TR) Leave of Absence.
Gallagher, Richard '60 (SEA) Raymond, WA St. Lawrence Church.
Gallagher, Msgr. Richard J. '49 (STL) [39] St. Louis, MO St. Joan of Arc Church; [61] St. Louis, MO St. Sebastian Church.
Gallagher, Richard J. '60 (SEA) Seaview, WA St. Mary Church.
Gallagher, Robert '73 (LA) Norwalk, CA St. John of God Church.
Gallagher, Robert A. '77 (STU) On Duty Outside the Diocese.
Gallagher, Robert J. '73 (LA) [D] Santa Fe Springs, CA St. Paul High School.
Gallagher, Roger P. '54 (WDC) Retired; [L] Washington, DC Cardinal O'Boyle Residence for Priests.
Gallagher, Simeon *o.f.m.cap.* '71 (STL) [54] St. Louis, MO St. Patrick Church; [P] St. Louis, MO St. Patrick Friary.
Gallagher, Simon P. *o.s.b.* '73 (PAT) [M] Morristown, NJ St. Mary's Abbey.
Gallagher, Thomas *s.p.s.* '49 (NO) [4] Slidell, LA St. Margaret Mary Church; Slidell, LA Greenbriar Nursing & Convalescent Home; Slidell, LA Guest House of Slidell Nursing Home; Slidell, LA Greenery Neurologic Rehabilitation Center at Slidell.
Gallagher, Thomas *s.j.* '61 (ANC) [G] Anchorage, AK Jesuit Residence.
Gallagher, Thomas '61 (CLV) Cleveland, OH Cleveland Psychiatric; Cleveland, OH Veterans Administration Hospitals, Brecksville V.A.
Gallagher, Thomas *s.j.* '61 (FBK) McGrath, AK St. Michael Church.
Gallagher, Thomas B. '56 (OAK) Retired; [M] Oakland, CA Bishop Begin Villa.
Gallagher, Thomas G. '68 (RVC) North Merrick, NY Sacred Heart Church.
Gallagher, Thomas J. *s.j.* '70 (BO) [W] Boston, MA Jesuit Urban Center & Immaculate Conception Community.
Gallagher, Thomas M. *o.f.m.* '82 (PAT) Little Falls, NJ Our Lady of the Holy Angels Church.
Gallagher, Thomas N. *s.j.* '61 (FBK) [E] St. Marys, AK Brother Joe Prince Jesuit Community.
Gallagher, Thomas P. *o.s.f.s.* '67 (PH) [D] Philadelphia, PA Father Judge High School for Boys; [AA] Philadelphia, PA Father Judge Faculty House.
Gallagher, Msgr. Thomas V. '45 (NY) Retired; [DD] New York, NY Our Lady of Consolation Residence.
Gallagher, Timothy *o.m.v.* '79 (BO) [B] Boston, MA Oblate Provincialate; [W] Milton, MA Oblate Residence (St. Joseph House).
Gallagher, William E. '46 (SEA) Retired.
Gallagher, William G. '53 (RVC) Priests Released from Diocesan Assignment.
Gallagher, William J. '47 (WOR) Retired.
Gallagher, Msgr. William J. '69 (BUF) [4] Orchard Park, NY St. John Vianney Church.
Gallagher, William M. '53 (PRO) On Duty Outside the Diocese.
Gallagher, Msgr. William M. '53 (YAK) Moxee City, WA Holy Rosary Church.
Gallagher, William P. '65 (BUR) Woodstock, VT Our Lady of the Snows Church.
Gallaher, James '65 (CHI) [J] Evergreen Park, IL Little Company of Mary Hospital and Health Care Centers.
Gallahue, John J. *m.m.* '62 (FgM) Maryknoll Foreign Missions.
Gallant, Fernard J. *s.m.* '44 (BO) [Y] Framingham Centre, MA The Marist House.
Gallant, John P. '60 (NY) Sloatsburg, NY St. Joan of Arc Church.
Gallant, Jon-Paul '78 (FR) [4] Taunton, MA Sacred Heart Church.
Gallant, Rodrigue J. '47 (MAN) Retired.
Gallarelli, George A. *s.j.* '62 (BGP) [D] Fairfield, CT Fairfield College Preparatory School; [O] Fairfield, CT The Fairfield Jesuit Community-Fairfield University.
Gallaro, George D. '72 (NTN) Warren, MI Our Lady of Redemption Church.
Gallas, Msgr. Francis A. '52 (WIN) Retired.
Gallas, James R. *s.j.* '52 (LA) [6] Los Angeles, CA Blessed Sacrament Church.
Gallatin, Joseph G. '97 (STP) Chanhassen, MN St. Hubert Church.
Gallatin, Paul H. '58 (OKL) [3] Oklahoma City, OK St. Charles Borromeo Church.
Gallego, Eduardo '71 (SJN) [19] Carolina, PR Ntra. Sra. de Fatima Church.
Gallego, Jose M. *o.m.* '57 (SJN) [16] San Juan, PR Ntra. Sra. de Fatima Church.
Gallegos, Albert *o.s.m.* '64 (SFE) Peralta, NM Our Lady of Guadalupe Church.
Gallegos, Albert M. *o.s.m.* '64 (CHI) [N] Chicago, IL Servite Friars - Eastern Province.
Gallegos, David *o.s.m.* (SFE) Belen, NM Our Lady of Belen Church.
Gallegos, David M. *o.s.m.* '66 (CHI) [N] Chicago, IL Servite Friars - Eastern Province.
Gallegos, Joseph *c.r.* '69 (PBL) Durango, CO Sacred Heart Church.
Gallegos, Stephen *c.m.* '88 (FgM) Vincentian Foreign Missions.
Gallemore, Timothy A. '92 (FRS) Laton, CA Shrine of Our Lady of Fatima Church.
Gallen, Msgr. Charles V. '47 (PH) [V] Immaculata, PA Camilla Hall Nursing Home; [Y] Huntingdon Valley, PA Redeemer Long Term Care & Elder Services.
Gallen, Msgr. F. Thomas '47 (COL) [C] Columbus, OH St. Charles Preparatory School.
Gallen, Francis H. '47 (PH) Bridgeport, PA St. Augustine Church; Retired.
Gallen, John A. '69 (HT) Morgan City, LA Sacred Heart of Jesus Church.
Gallen, John J. *s.j.* '63 (NY) [DD] New York, NY "America;" Residence and publication office of the America Press.
Gallenbach, Thomas '58 (SFD) Military Chaplains.
Gallenbach, Thomas E. '58 (LAV) [12] Las Vegas, NV St. Joseph, Husband of Mary Church.
Gallenstein, Joseph '90 (COV) Florence, KY St. Paul Church.
Gallenstein, Stephen '76 (LEX) Pikeville, KY St. Francis of Assisi Church.
Gallerani, Philip G. '62 (SPR) Springfield, MA Wesson-Women's Hospital Unit.
Gallerini, Philip G. '62 (SPR) Retired.
Galli, Clarence '53 (SFE) Retired.
Galli, Clarence F. '53 (SFE) Corrales, NM San Ysidro Church.
Gallia, Andrew R. '62 (SCR) Jessup, PA St. Mary's Assumption Church.
Galligan, Charles H. '87 (PRO) [12] Pawtucket, RI St. Teresa of the Child Jesus Church.
Galligan, Eymard *s.s.e.* '47 (BUR) [E] Colchester, VT Society of St. Edmund.
Galligan, James L. *o.s.a.* '50 (PH) [142] Philadelphia, PA St. Rita of Cascia Church.
Galligan, Richard H. *s.j.* '70 (BUF) [O] Buffalo, NY Canisius Jesuit Community.
Galligan, Richard R. *s.j.* (BUF) [R] Williamsville, NY Campus Ministry.
Gallina, Leo J. '65 (E) [14] Erie, PA St. Boniface Church.
Gallinger, Carl J. '89 (CHY) Laramie, WY St. Paul's Newman Center Church.
Gallipoli, Mario *c.p.* '61 (BRK) [U] Jamaica, NY Immaculate Conception Monastery.
Gallivan, Msgr. David M. '66 (BUF) Williamsville, NY SS. Peter and Paul Church.
Gallo, David M. *a.a.* '88 (WOR) [N] Worcester, MA Assumptionists of Assumption College.
Gallo, Dennis *c.m.f.* '85 (LA) San Gabriel, CA San Gabriel Church; [R] San Gabriel, CA Claretian Missionaries (Missionary Sons of the Immaculate Heart of Mary).
Gallo, Msgr. Joseph J. '46 (PAT) Retired; [P] Chester, NJ Nazareth Village.
Gallo, Msgr. Louis J. '48 (PAT) Retired; [P] Chester, NJ Nazareth Village.
Gallo, Regis *o.f.m.* (FR) [J] Onset, MA St. Joseph Novitiate-Franciscan Friars.
Gallo, Regis *o.f.m.* '62 (BO) [W] Boston, MA St. Christopher Friary.
Gallo, Vincent J. '60 (BRK) [19] Brooklyn, NY St. Bernard's Church.
Galluppi, Louis M. '83 (NOR) Ellington, CT St. Luke Church.
Gallus, David E. *o.s.c.* '66 (FgM) Crosier Foreign Missions.
Gallus, David E. *o.s.c.* '66 (STP) Anoka, MN St. Stephen Church; [N] Anoka, MN Crosier Community of Anoka; [W] Shoreview, MN Crosier Missions.
Galluzzo, James '90 (P) Absent on Leave.
Galonek, David B. '96 (WOR) Milford, MA St. Mary of the Assumption Church.
Galour, Joseph L. '38 (GF) Retired.
Galovich, George '71 (STL) Potosi, MO St. James Church.
Galuszka, Thaddeus *m.s.* '51 (MIL) [P] Twin Lakes, WI La Salette Missionaries Shrine.
Galuszka, Msgr. Walter C. '38 (BRK) [67] Brooklyn, NY St. John Cantius Church; Retired.
Galvan, Alfred '65 (LSC) Deming, NM St. Ann's Church.
Galvan, P. Michael '77 (OAK) Pinole, CA St. Joseph's Church.
Galvez, Elias *o.f.m.* '56 (FgM) Franciscan Foreign Missions.
Galvez, Salvador '87 (NO) [42] New Orleans, LA St. Julian Eymard Church.
Galvin, Aloysius C. *s.j.* '57 (WDC) [E] North Bethesda, MD Georgetown Preparatory School.
Galvin, Bartholomew J. *m.m.* '53 (NY) [DD] Maryknoll, NY Maryknoll Fathers and Brothers.
Galvin, Bartholomew J. *m.m.* '53 (RVC) Bohemia, NY St. John Nepomucene Church.
Galvin, Edward *s.m.a.* '62 (WDC) [V] Washington, DC S.M.A. Social Concerns Department.
Galvin, Gregory P. '94 (NOR) [1] Norwich, CT St. Patrick Cathedral.
Galvin, James *c.m.* '51 (LA) [X] Santa Barbara, CA St. Mary's Seminary Center.
Galvin, James G. '93 (SAT) [57] San Antonio, TX St. Matthew's Church.
Galvin, James M. *c.m.* (LA) [DD] Santa Barbara, CA World Wide Marriage Encounter.
Galvin, John *s.m.* '63 (FgM) Marist Foreign Missions.
Galvin, John P. '68 (BO) On Duty Outside the Archdiocese.
Galvin, John P. '68 (WDC) [C] Washington, DC Catholic University of America, The.
Galvin, Richard *o.s.b.* '48 (P) [L] St. Benedict, OR Mt. Angel Abbey.
Galvin, Thomas J. '82 (PIT) [83] Pittsburgh, PA Risen Lord Church.
Galvin, William J. *m.m.* '56 (NY) [DD] Maryknoll, NY Maryknoll Fathers and Brothers.
Galyo, Msgr. John M. '54 (PH) [4] Phoenixville, PA Sacred Heart Church; Pottstown, PA Holy Trinity Church.
Gamache, Barry J. '81 (PRO) Bristol, RI St. Mary Church.
Gamache, Daniel '45 (FR) Retired.
Gamache, Roland L. '67 (WOR) Winchendon, MA Immaculate Heart of Mary Church.
Gamallo, Edito '75 (NEW) [1] Jersey City, NJ St. Aedan's Church.
Gamba, John J. '42 (COL) Retired.
Gamba, Jose '86 (NEW) [26] Jersey City, NJ St. Paul's Church.
Gambatese, Angelus P. *o.f.m.* '59 (PAT) [5] Paterson, NJ St. Bonaventure Church.
Gamber, Matthew *s.j.* '95 (CIN) [M] Cincinnati, OH Jesuit Community at Xavier Unversity.
Gamber, William K. '64 (STP) Minneapolis, MN Veterans Administration Medical Center; Special Assignment; Retired.
Gambet, Daniel G. *o.s.f.s.* '57 (ALN) [B] Center Valley, PA Allentown College of St. Francis de Sales; [K] Center Valley, PA Oblates of St. Francis de Sales.
Gambino, Msgr. Anthony J. '69 (MET) [6] Perth Amboy, NJ Most Holy Rosary Church.
Gamble, Anthony *c.pp.s.* '42 (CIN) [B] Carthagena, OH St. Charles.
Gamboa, Damian *o.f.m.* '64 (SJ) [18] San Jose, CA Our Lady of Guadalupe Church.
Gambon, John A. '49 (STL) Retired.
Gambone, Michael J. '56 (PH) [134] Philadelphia, PA St. Paul Church.
Gambro, John M. *o.p.* '57 (CHI) [D] Oak Park, IL Fenwick High School; [N] River Forest, IL St. Thomas Aquinas Priory.
Gamel, Robert E. '90 (FRS) Boron, CA St. Joseph Church.
Gameros, L. Ignacio '81 (TUC) Marana, AZ St. Christopher's Church.
Gamm, David B. '72 (COV) [7] Covington, KY St. John Church.

Gamm, Joseph M. *c.m.f.* '45 (LA) [28] Los Angeles, CA Our Lady Queen of the Angels Church.
Gamrot, Jaroslaw *m.i.c.* '91 (WDC) [B] Washington, DC Marian Fathers Scholasticate.
Gamulani, Abdon *m.afr.* '72 (CHI) [124] Chicago, IL St. Martin De Porres Church; [N] Chicago, IL Missionaries of Africa.
Ganahl, James '56 (SB) Retired.
Gancayco, Richard K. '92 (WDC) On Duty Outside the Archdiocese.
Gandolfi, Louis *c.s.* '63 (CHI) [122] Chicago, IL Santa Maria Addolorata Church.
Gandolfo, Kenneth '82 (BO) Dedham, MA St. Susanna Church.
Gandrau, James '58 (SEA) [2] Seattle, WA St. Alphonsus Church.
Ganiel, Joseph F. '83 (CAM) Salem, NJ St. Mary's Church.
Ganley, Charles '52 (SAG) Retired.
Ganley, Thomas P. '85 (MET) Piscataway, NJ Our Lady of Fatima Church.
Ganly, John C. *m.m.* '59 (STL) [P] St. Louis, MO Maryknoll House.
Gann, Sean J. '94 (RVC) Sayville, NY St. Lawrence the Martyr Church.
Gannon, Bernard J. '71 (CAM) Brigantine, NJ St. Thomas Church.
Gannon, Brian P. '97 (BGP) Brookfield, CT St. Marguerite Bourgeoys Church.
Gannon, Charles E. '43 (DAV) Retired; [M] Davenport, IA St. Vincent Center.
Gannon, Clair F. *o.s.b.* '41 (GBG) [H] Latrobe, PA Saint Vincent Archabbey.
Gannon, Daniel J. *s.j.* '68 (CHY) St. Stephens, WY St. Stephen's Church; [C] St. Stephens, WY St. Stephens Mission - Jesuit Community.
Gannon, Dismas *o.c.s.o.* '50 (P) [L] Lafayette, OR The Cistercian (Trappist) Abbey of Our Lady of Guadalupe.
Gannon, Donald C. *s.j.* '76 (NY) [DD] New York, NY Xavier Jesuit Community.
Gannon, Earl A. '45 (TR) Retired; [L] Lawrenceville, NJ Morris Hall-Saint Lawrence, Inc.
Gannon, Gerard M. '56 (SCR) Archbald, PA St. Thomas Aquinas Church.
Gannon, James G. *o.f.m.* (PH) [92] Philadelphia, PA Saint Martha Church.
Gannon, Msgr. James J. '42 (E) Retired.
Gannon, Msgr. John M. '41 (E) [20] Erie, PA St. Joseph Church; Retired.
Gannon, Joseph T. '75 (STP) Retired.
Gannon, Michael F. '65 (NY) [I] New York, NY The Catholic Charities of the Archdiocese of New York; [R] Nanuet, NY St. Agatha Home of the New York Foundling Hospital.
Gannon, Patrick '76 (NO) Luling, LA St. Anthony of Padua Church.
Gannon, Patrick J. '60 (LA) La Mirada, CA St. Paul of the Cross Church.
Gannon, Robert I. '60 (NY) [219] Staten Island, NY Our Lady, Queen of Peace Church; [E] New York, NY Moore Catholic High School.
Gannon, Roger *c.p.* '47 (PMB) [G] North Palm Beach, FL Our Lady of Florida Spiritual Center.
Gannon, Msgr. Rowland '42 (STL) [2] Creve Coeur, MO St. John Bosco Church.
Gannon, Msgr. Rowland E. '41 (STL) Retired.
Gannon, Thomas M. *s.j.* '67 (GRY) [J] East Chicago, IN Roque Gonzalez Residence-Jesuit Fathers; [O] Hammond, IN Heartland Center.
Gannon, William Robert *o.p.* '53 (NY) Manhattan, NY Memorial Sloan Kettering Cancer Center; [DD] New York, NY St. Vincent Ferrer Priory.
Ganshert, Daniel T. '74 (MAD) [11] Madison, WI St. Patrick Church.
Ganss, George E. *s.j.* '37 (STL) [O] St. Louis, MO Fusz Pavilion.
Ganss, Karl P. '68 (RCK) DeKalb, IL St. Mary Church.
Ganssle, Joseph *o.f.m.* '58 (NY) [DD] New York, NY Franciscan Friars, Order of Friars Minor, Holy Name Province.
Gantley, Donald M. *o.s.m.* '59 (CHI) [N] Chicago, IL Servite Friars - Eastern Province.
Gantley, Mark J. '91 (SY) [15] Syracuse, NY St. Daniel Church.
Ganucheau, William R. (LAF) Absent on Leave.
Ganuza, Felix *sch.p.* '20 (NY) [DD] New York, NY Calasanzian Fathers (Piarists).
Ganuza, Felix '76 (NY) [12] New York, NY Annunciation Church.
Ganz, Richard H. *s.j.* '84 (P) [D] Portland, OR Jesuit High School.
Ganzy, F. Alexander '91 (SJP) Ambridge, PA Ss. Peter and Paul Church.
Gappa, Herbert T. *m.m.* '68 (FgM) Maryknoll Foreign Missions.
Gara, Msgr. Robert '45 (LA) Sierra Madre, CA St. Rita Church; Retired.
Garamendi, Martin *o.m.* '52 (SJN) [16] San Juan, PR Ntra. Sra. de Fatima Church.
Garanzini, Michael J. *s.j.* (STL) [C] St. Louis, MO Saint Louis University.
Garanzini, Michael J. *s.j.* '80 (STL) [C] St. Louis, MO Saint Louis University; [P] St. Louis, MO Jesuit Community Corporation at St. Louis University - Jesuit Hall.
Garatea, Juan Maria '59 (B) Burley, ID St. Theresa Church.
Garavel, Andrew J. *s.j.* '92 (BGP) [O] Fairfield, CT The Fairfield Jesuit Community-Fairfield University.
Garaventa, Louis T. *s.j.* '76 (BUF) [D] Buffalo, NY Canisius High School; [O] Buffalo, NY Canisius Jesuit Community.
Garay, Edward W. '66 (CAM) Cape May, NJ Our Lady Star of the Sea Church.
Garay, Jesus '91 (LA) Wilmington, CA Holy Family Church.
Garbacik, Louis S. '54 (SCR) [10] Hazleton, PA St. Stanislaus Church.
Garbacz, Kazimerz *s.v.d.* '69 (CHI) [B] Techny, IL Divine Word Residence.
Garbacz, Kazimerz *s.v.d.* '70 (CHI) [N] Techny, IL Society of the Divine Word, Provincial Headquarter-Chicago Prov.; [N] Techny, IL Society of the Divine Word, Provincial Headquarter-Chicago Prov.
Garbarino, Joseph J. '83 (PAT) Montville, NJ St. Pius X Church.
Garber, Andrew V. *o.s.b.* '56 (MIL) Bristol, WI St. Scholastica Church.
Garber, Stephen A. *s.j.* '54 (PH) [G] Philadelphia, PA St. Joseph's Preparatory School; [AA] Philadelphia, PA Jesuit Community at St. Joseph's University.
Garbin, Arthur L. '41 (PIT) [P] Coraopolis, PA Our Lady of the Sacred Heart Convent.
Garbin, Raymond P. '63 (JOL) Addison, IL St. Philip The Apostle Church.
Garceau, James G. *c.r.i.c.* '84 (LA) [64] Los Angeles, CA St. Francis of Assisi Church; [B] Los Angeles, CA Canons Regular of the Immaculate Conception-Novitiate; [R] Los Angeles, CA Canons Regular of the Immaculate Conception.
Garced, Wilberto Reyes '30 (NY) [HH] New York, NY Lumen Dei.
Garces, Francis *o.f.m.cap.* '66 (FWT) [6] Fort Worth, TX Our Lady of Guadalupe Church.
Garces-Henao, Carlos '95 (HRT) [2] Ansonia, CT Holy Rosary Church.
Garcia, Abraham R. *m.g.* '80 (LA) [R] Los Angeles, CA Guadalupe Missioners Procure.
Garcia, Albert *ss.cc.* '69 (HON) Waialua, HI St. Michael Church.
Garcia, Alfredo *ss.cc.* '63 (BWN) Santa Rosa, TX St. Mary Church.
Garcia, Antonio '55 (LA) [34] Los Angeles, CA Presentation of the B.V.M. Church.
Garcia, Antonio *o.dem.* '67 (PCE) [9] Ponce, PR La Merced Church.
Garcia, Antonio '81 (SJN) [14] Carolina, PR Ntra. Sra. Del Carmen Church.
Garcia, Avelino '68 (SP) On Duty Outside the Diocese.
Garcia, Avelino R. (BO) Boston, MA Veterans Administration Hospital.
Garcia, Daniel E. '88 (AUS) [24] Austin, TX St. Vincent de Paul Church.
Garcia, David *c.o.* (BWN) [E] Pharr, TX Oratory of St. Philip Neri, of Pontifical Right.
Garcia, David '75 (SAT) [1] San Antonio, TX Cathedral of San Fernando.
Garcia, E. Roberto '82 (PCE) On Duty Outside the Diocese.
Garcia, Edgar *o.m.i.* '85 (LA) San Fernando, CA Santa Rosa Church.
Garcia, Eduardo '93 (PCE) Arroyo, PR Our Lady of Mt. Carmel Church.
Garcia, Eduardo H. '90 (CC) Alice, TX St. Joseph Church.
Garcia, Eliseo *o.s.a.* '59 (SJN) [1] Bayamon, PR San Agustin Church.
Garcia, Emilio G. '57 (ORL) Dunnellon, FL St. John the Baptist Church.
Garcia, Esau N. *c.p.* '87 (ORL) Deltona, FL Our Lady of the Lakes Church.
Garcia, Francisco *o.f.m.cap.* '78 (PCE) [5] Ponce, PR Santa Teresita Church; [E] Ponce, PR Residencia Asis; [H] Ponce, PR Albergue La Providencia, Inc.
Garcia, Francisco *o.p.* '87 (SJN) [3] Bayamon, PR Catalina de Siena Church.
Garcia, George '73 (MIA) Coconut Grove, FL St. Hugh Church.
Garcia, Gerrardo M. *o.s.a.* '69 (CHI) [40] Chicago, IL St. Clare of Montefalco Church.
Garcia, Gildardo '85 (NEW) Fairview, NJ St. John the Baptist Church.
Garcia, Guillermo *c.s.* '88 (SD) Imperial, CA St. Anthony of Padua Church.
Garcia, Guillermo C. *c.j.* '75 (LA) [3] Santa Barbara, CA Our Lady of Guadalupe Church.
Garcia, Hector *c.ss.r.* (CGS) Fajardo, PR Santiago Apostol Church.
Garcia, Isidore *c.m.f.* (PHX) Seligman, AZ St. Francis Church.
Garcia, James L. '70 (SFR) [1] Menlo Park, CA St. Anthony Church.
Garcia, Javier (SAC) Absent on Leave.
Garcia, Jesus Alberto '94 (SJN) [2] Toa Alta, PR San Fernando Church.
Garcia, John G. '47 (OAK) Brentwood, CA Immaculate Heart of Mary Church.
Garcia, Jose '52 (MIA) [24] Miami, FL St. Kevin Church.
Garcia, Jose Isidore *o.m.i.* '64 (GAL) [16] Houston, TX Church of the Blessed Sacrament.
Garcia, Jose L. (ARE) On Duty Outside the Diocese.
Garcia, Jose L. *o.m.* '63 (CGS) Cayey, PR Nuestra Senora de la Asuncion Church.
Garcia, Jose Ma. *ss.cc.* '63 (SJN) [9] Guaynabo, PR Sagrados Corazones Church.
Garcia, Juan '67 (SPR) [2] Springfield, MA All Souls Church.
Garcia, Juan '70 (ELP) [A] El Paso, TX St. Charles Seminary College Program.
Garcia, Juan F. *c.r.i.c.* '67 (SPR) [3] Springfield, MA Blessed Sacrament Church; [M] Springfield, MA Casa Cristo Rey.
Garcia, Juan F. '96 (SHP) [1] Shreveport, LA St. John Berchmans Cathedral.
Garcia, Lorenzo '97 (SAV) Moultrie, GA Immaculate Conception Church.
Garcia, Louis (STO) Oakdale, CA St. Mary of the Annunciation Church.
Garcia, Louis '93 (STO) Absent on Leave.
Garcia, Luis '50 (LA) Lynwood, CA St. Emydius Church.
Garcia, Luis G. '97 (MIA) [3] Miami, FL Corpus Christi Church.
Garcia, Luis J. *j.c.l.* '76 (GLP) Aztec, NM St. Joseph Church; Flora Vista, NM Holy Trinity Church.
Garcia, Manuel (SJN) [E] San Juan, PR Centro Medico de P.R.
Garcia, Manuel '75 (SJN) Dorado, PR Ntra. Sra. de La Salud Church.
Garcia, Marcelino *s.j.* '70 (MIA) [D] Miami, FL Belen Jesuit Preparatory School; [H] Miami, FL Villa Javier.
Garcia, Michael A. *o.p.* '81 (CHI) [N] Chicago, IL Dominicans (Provincial Office).
Garcia, Miguel A. *c.ss.r.* '72 (SJN) [2] San Juan, PR San Agustin Church.
Garcia, Millan J. '62 (SFE) Albuquerque, NM University Hospital.
Garcia, Msgr. Otto L. *j.c.d.* '73 (BRK) [1] Brooklyn, NY The Cathedral-Basilica of St. James Church.
Garcia, Patrick Kenny Q. '68 (AGN) Mongmong, GU Nuestra Senora de Las Aquas Church.
Garcia, Paul '93 (ELP) [31] El Paso, TX St. Raphael Church.
Garcia, Pedro '64 (MIA) Naranja, FL St. Ann Mission Church.
Garcia, Pedro '92 (AUS) Taylor, TX Our Lady of Guadalupe Church; On Duty Outside the Diocese.
Garcia, Pedro V. '65 (GR) [13] Grand Rapids, MI St. Joseph The Worker Church.
Garcia, Pedro Valdemar *l.c.* '97 (HRT) [B] Cheshire, CT Novitiate of the Legion of Christ.
Garcia, Rafael *s.j.* '93 (ELP) [21] El Paso, TX Sacred Heart Church.
Garcia, Msgr. Raymond '55 (SAT) Retired.
Garcia, Reynaldo *s.j.* '76 (NO) [P] New Orleans, LA Jesuit Provincial Office.
Garcia, Ricardo '92 (BWN) [3] Mission, TX Our Lady of St. John of the Fields Church.
Garcia, Richard '73 (SJ) [4] Sunnyvale, CA St. Martin Church.
Garcia, Richard J. '73 (SJ) Special Assignment.
Garcia, Roberto *o.s.a.* '48 (MGZ) San German, PR St. Rose of Lima Church.
Garcia, Roberto *o.f.m.cap.* '59 (DAL) [8] Dallas, TX Our Lady of Lourdes Church.
Garcia, Roberto '82 (SJN) [3] Toa Baja, PR Espiritu Santo Church.
Garcia, Msgr. Roberto '86 (PCE) [B] Ponce, PR The Pontifical Catholic University of Puerto Rico.
Garcia, Rolando '86 (MIA) Leisure City, FL St. Martin de Porres Church.
Garcia, Ruben '97 (OKL) [14] Oklahoma City, OK Our Lady of Mount Carmel and St. Therese Little Flower Church.
Garcia, Salvador '52 (PCE) On Duty Outside the Diocese.
Garcia, Sergio *c.r.i.c.* '94 (LA) [B] Los Angeles, CA Canons Regular of the Immaculate Conception-Novitiate; [R] Los Angeles, CA Canons Regular of the Immaculate Conception.
Garcia, Sergio E. *c.r.i.c.* '94 (LA) [64] Los Angeles, CA St. Francis of Assisi Church.
Garcia, Severiano *c.m.f.* '50 (CGS) [8] Barrio Rio Canas, PR Inmaculado Corazon de Maria Church.
Garcia-Cardona, Carlos '92 (LKC) Iowa, LA St. Raphael Church.
Garcia-Fidalgo, Manuel '47 (MIA) Retired.
Garcia-Miro, Sergio '78 (MIA) North Miami Beach, FL St. Lawrence Church.

Gard, Charles '87 (LA) Glendale, CA Holy Family Church.
Gardella, Robert *o.s.a.* '66 (DET) Grosse Pointe Park, MI St. Clare of Montefalco Church.
Gardin, Msgr. Vernon E. '71 (STL) [5] Creve Coeur, MO St. Richard Church; [H] St. Louis, MO Catholic Guidance Center; [H] St. Louis, MO St. Mary's Special Services.
Gardiner, Christopher B. '68 (MAR) Gladstone, MI Holy Family Church.
Gardiner, James J. *s.a.* '69 (NY) [DD] New York, NY Atonement Friars.
Gardiner, James K. '69 (GAY) Traverse City, MI St. Francis of Assisi Church.
Gardiner, Richard E. '67 (WDC) Solomons, MD Our Lady Star of the Sea Church.
Garding, William '82 (SCL) Special Assignment.
Gardner, Clarence W. '42 (ROC) [4] Auburn, NY St. Alphonsus Church; Retired.
Gardner, Clement '67 (ALT) Hollidaysburg, PA St. Michael's Church.
Gardner, Daniel L. '78 (KCK) [5] Topeka, KS Our Lady of Guadalupe Church.
Gardner, George C. *c.ss.r.* '47 (BO) [13] Boston, MA Our Lady of Perpetual Help Church.
Gardner, Harold B. *c.s.b.* '59 (DET) [E] Redford, MI Catholic Central High School.
Gardner, Jerome J. '79 (CIN) Fayetteville, OH St. Patrick's Church.
Gardner, Msgr. Laurence R. '36 (MAN) [1] Manchester, NH St. Joseph Cathedral; Retired.
Gardner, Louis C. '54 (OG) Chazy, NY Sacred Heart Church.
Gardner, Maurice '52 (KCK) Retired.
Gardner, Royal J. '51 (SPR) [4] Pittsfield, MA Sacred Heart Church.
Gardner, Simeon '54 (SP) Retired.
Gardner, Thomas *o.f.m.* '79 (FgM) Franciscan Foreign Missions.
Gardner, Thomas *o.f.m.* '79 (STL) [P] St. Louis, MO Franciscan Friary of St. Anthony of Padua.
Gardner, William M. '92 (PEO) Lostant, IL St. John the Baptist's Church; Wenona, IL St. Mary's Church.
Gardner, William P. '62 (TR) [1] Toms River, NJ St. Joseph Church.
Gardocki, Thomas F. '65 (WIL) Retired.
Gardon, Emmanuel H. *c.p.* '50 (OAK) [1] Hayward, CA All Saints Church.
Gardzalla, Leo M. '45 (SCR) [4] Nanticoke, PA St. Joseph's Church.
Gareau, Timothy W. '88 (CLV) Fairview Park, OH St. Angela Merici Church.
Gargani, Francis J. *c.ss.r.* '71 (NY) [DD] Esopus, NY Redemptorist Priests and Brothers C.Ss.R. (Province of Baltimore); [FF] Esopus, NY Mount St. Alphonsus Redemptorist Retreat Center.
Gargantiel, Isidro T. '68 (GR) Free Soil, MI St. John Cantius Church; Scottville, MI St. Jerome Church; [K] Edmore, MI Montcalm Community College Newman Center.
Gariboldi, Ronald J. '61 (BO) Rockport, MA St. Joachim Church.
Gariepy, Andre M. '58 (WOR) [1] Gardner, MA Holy Spirit Church.
Gariepy, Robert E. '63 (WOR) Retired.
Gariepy, Thomas P. *c.s.c.* '74 (FR) [A] North Easton, MA Stonehill College; [A] North Easton, MA Holy Cross Fathers Religious.
Garinger, Grant S. *s.j.* '97 (MIL) [P] Milwaukee, WI Jesuit Community at Marquette University.
Gariolo, Joseph M. *c.r.s.p.* '50 (BUF) [B] Youngstown, NY St. Anthony M. Zaccaria Seminary.
Garisto, James '77 (NY) [219] Staten Island, NY Our Lady, Queen of Peace Church; [F] New York, NY St. Joseph by the Sea, High School.
Garity, Linus J. '33 (BEL) [E] Belleville, IL Our Lady of the Snows Apartment Community Retirement Home.
Garity, Linus J. '33 (MIL) Retired.
Garkowski, John G. '66 (BRK) [217] Queens, NY Our Lady of Perpetual Help Church.
Garland, Reynolds *o.f.m.* '61 (BR) Carville, LA National Hansen's Disease Center.
Garland, Msgr. Robert P. '53 (PIT) Cecil, PA St. Mary Church.
Garland, William T. *o.s.a.* '62 (FR) [O] Fall River, MA Diocesan Education Center.
Garlick, Thomas B. '84 (WOR) Sterling, MA St. Richard of Chichester Church.
Garneau, James F. (R) Graduate Studies.
Garner, Joel *o.praem.* '65 (SFE) [N] Albuquerque, NM Norbertine Community of New Mexico, Inc.
Garner, Joel P. *o.praem.* '65 (SFE) [11] Albuquerque, NM Our Lady of Most Holy Rosary Church; [J] Albuquerque, NM Santa Maria de la Vid Priory.
Garner, Kirby D. '77 (AUS) [26] Austin, TX San Jose Church.
Garofalo, Kenneth *o.f.m.* '55 (BO) [57] Boston, MA Our Lady of Mt. Carmel Church.
Garoffolo, Vincent '41 (NEW) Retired.
Garone, Thomas *o.f.m.* '73 (MAN) Derry, NH St. Thomas Aquinas Church.
Garrahy, Michael '51 (WCH) Retired.
Garramone, Dominic M. *o.s.b.* '92 (PEO) [A] Peru, IL St. Bede Abbey and Academy; [C] Peru, IL St. Bede Academy.
Garred, Msgr. John L. '52 (GBG) Retired; [G] Greensburg, PA Neumann House.
Garret, Sean '64 (SAT) On Duty Outside the Archdiocese.
Garrett, Mark A. *o.s.a.* '70 (SAT) Spring Branch, TX St. Joseph Church; [C] San Antonio, TX Oblate School of Theology.
Garrett, Sean '64 (PT) Fort Walton Beach, FL St. Mary Church.
Garrett, Thomas P. *o.s.a.* '39 (SD) [H] San Diego, CA Augustinian Community.
Garrick, David A. *c.s.c.* '76 (FTW) [B] Notre Dame, IN University of Notre Dame Du Lac; [J] Notre Dame, IN Holy Cross Community, Corby Hall, University of Notre Dame.
Garrido, Alejandro '92 (CHI) [2] Chicago, IL St. Adalbert Church.
Garrigan, Gerard *o.s.b.* '89 (STL) [1] Creve Coeur, MO St. Anselm Church; [P] St. Louis, MO The Abbey of St. Mary and St. Louis.
Garrity, Bernard R. *m.m.* '47 (FgM) Maryknoll Foreign Missions.
Garrity, Francis A. '41 (CHI) Park Forest, IL St. Irenaeus Church; Retired.
Garrity, Francis D. '56 (BO) Needham, MA St. Bartholomew Church.
Garrity, G. Patrick (KNX) Jefferson City, TN Holy Trinity Catholic Church.
Garrity, G. Patrick '76 (KNX) Morristown, TN St. Patrick Church.
Garrity, John M. '58 (CLV) Berea, OH St. Mary's Church.
Garrity, Paul V. '73 (BO) [4] Lynn, MA St. Mary Church.
Garrity, Robert M. '81 (RCK) Huntley, IL St. Mary Church.
Garrity, Stephen M. *s.j.* '63 (WDC) [P] Faulkner, MD Loyola on the Potomac Retreat House.
Garrity, Thomas F. *m.m.* '46 (FgM) Maryknoll Foreign Missions.
Garrote, Sancho E. '76 (NY) [143] Bronx, NY St. Francis Xavier Church.
Garrote, Sancho G. '76 (NY) Bronx, NY Bronx Municipal Hospital Center, Abraham Jacobi Hospital, Nathan B. VanEtten Hospital.
Garrott, William P. *o.p.* '94 (COL) Zanesville, OH St. Thomas Aquinas Church.
Garrow, Mark *m.i.c.* '84 (SPR) [I] Stockbridge, MA Congregation of Marians.
Garry, Gerald *s.v.d.* '59 (CHI) [B] Techny, IL Divine Word Residence.
Garry, Peter J. '68 (RVC) Northport, NY St. Philip Neri Church.
Garry, Ronald B. '83 (RC) Lemmon, SD St. Mary's Church.
Garst, Charles C. *o.s.f.s.* '83 (PH) [D] Philadelphia, PA Father Judge High School for Boys.
Garst, Charles C. *o.s.f.s.* '83 (WIL) [3] Wilmington, DE St. Anthony of Padua Church.
Garthwaite, Thomas F. '55 (LC) Retired.
Gartland, Daniel B. '82 (LFT) [4] Lafayette, IN St. Lawrence Church.
Gartland, James G. *s.j.* '93 (CHI) [177] Chicago, IL St. Procopius Church; [N] Chicago, IL Miguel Pro Jesuit Community.
Gartland, R. Vincent '81 (TR) Lawrenceville, NJ St. Ann Church.
Gartland, Msgr. Thomas A. '49 (NY) Bedford, NY St. Patrick Church.
Gartner, Charles A. '58 (RVC) Hicksville, NY Our Lady of Mercy Church; Retired.
Gartner, Edward J. *s.s.j.* '49 (BAL) [M] Baltimore, MD St. Joseph Society of the Sacred Heart House of Central Administration.
Gartner, John *s.s.s.* '53 (CLV) [P] Cleveland, OH Congregation of the Blessed Sacrament Provincial House; [P] Cleveland, OH Blessed Sacrament Community.
Gartner, Joseph *glmy.* '40 (CIN) [M] Fairfield, OH Headquarters of Glenmary Home Missioners.
Gartska, Joseph A. '39 (GB) Retired.
Garvey, Charles J. '47 (COV) [6] Covington, KY Holy Cross Church; Retired.
Garvey, Francis J. '59 (NU) Manannah, MN Church of Our Lady; Willmar, MN Regional Treatment Center; [G] Willmar, MN Willmar Regional Treatment Center.
Garvey, James W. '76 (PIT) Penn Hills, PA St. Bartholomew Church.
Garvey, John *glmy.* '57 (CIN) [M] Fairfield, OH Headquarters of Glenmary Home Missioners.
Garvey, John F. *s.j.* '74 (NY) [F] New York, NY Xavier High School.
Garvey, John J. *s.j.* '50 (BUF) [O] Buffalo, NY Canisius Jesuit Community.
Garvey, John M. *m.s.* '53 (HRT) [M] Hartford, CT Missionaries of LaSalette Provincial Secretary.
Garvey, John M. *m.s.* '53 (STL) [P] St. Louis, MO La Salette Missionaries.
Garvey, John M. '58 (SFS) Webster, SD Christ the King Church.
Garvey, Michael '71 (Y) Military Chaplains.
Garvey, Roderick *c.ss.r.* '49 (DEN) [M] Denver, CO The Redemptorists/Denver Province.
Garvey, Thomas *s.c.j.* '58 (MIL) [P] Hales Corners, WI Sacred Heart Monastery.
Garvey, Thomas J. '57 (STP) Retired.
Garvin, Msgr. Joseph P. '73 (PH) [35] Philadelphia, PA St. Christopher Church.
Garvin, Thomas R. *s.j.* '58 (P) [L] Portland, OR Colombiere Community.
Garvy, John '83 (ORL) Retired.
Gary, Paul Q. '84 (CHL) [1] Charlotte, NC St. Patrick Cathedral.
Garza, Amador '85 (BWN) On Assignment Outside the Diocese.
Garza, Amador '85 (IND) [A] St. Meinrad, IN St. Meinrad Seminary.
Garza, Carlos '90 (BWN) San Juan, TX Santuario de Nuestra Senora de San Juan del Valle Church; [I] San Juan, TX Virgen de San Juan del Valle Shrine.
Garza, Jesus P. '79 (CHI) [183] Chicago, IL Resurrection Church.
Garza, Raul *c.m.* '86 (DAL) Ferris, TX Corpus Christi Church.
Garza, Roberto '96 (MIA) Key West, FL St. Mary, Star of the Sea Church.
Garzarelli, Santo R. '61 (PH) On Duty Outside the Archdiocese.
Garzon, Ignatio *m.j.* '68 (GAL) [75] Houston, TX St. Stephen Church.
Garzon-Blanco, Armando '95 (TUC) Absent on Leave; [F] Tucson, AZ Regina Cleri Center.
Gasbarre, Msgr. Francis E. '41 (CLV) Bedford, OH St. Mary Church; Bedford Heights, OH Holy Trinity Church; Retired.
Gasbarri, Italo *o.ss.t.* '48 (BAL) [M] Baltimore, MD Holy Trinity Monastery.
Gasiunas, John '28 (BEL) Retired.
Gaska, Henry *s.v.d.* '88 (WDC) [M] Washington, DC Divine Word College.
Gaske, Bartholomew *o.f.m.conv.* '40 (SY) [2] Syracuse, NY Assumption B.V.M. Church.
Gaskin, Matthew L. *o.f.m.* '50 (PAT) [M] Butler, NJ St. Anthony Friary.
Gasnick, Roy *o.f.m.* '60 (SP) [O] St. Petersburg, FL St. Anthony Friary.
Gaspar, Joseph W. *m.s.c.* '41 (ALN) [K] Reading, PA Missionaries of the Sacred Heart.
Gasparik, Francis *o.f.m.cap.* '86 (NY) [57] New York, NY St. John the Baptist Church.
Gasparin, Giampietro *c.s.j.* '79 (CLV) [D] Lorain, OH Lorain Catholic High School; [P] Avon, OH Congregation of St. Joseph.
Gasparin, Giampietro *c.s.j.* '79 (LA) [R] Los Angeles, CA Congregation of St. Joseph Casa Nazareth.
Gasparini, Louis *m.c.c.j.* '65 (FgM) Comboni Foreign Missions.
Gasparro, Anthony *o.s.a.* '41 (PH) [111] Philadelphia, PA St. Nicholas of Tolentine Church.
Gaspeny, Peter J. '83 (SAG) [5] Bay City, MI St. James Church.
Gass, Michael W. '77 (DEN) [4] Lakewood, CO St. Jude Church.
Gass, Robert J. '53 (OM) [12] Omaha, NE Christ the King Church; [L] Omaha, NE Sisters of the Annunciation of the Archdiocese of Omaha.
Gass, Msgr. Sylvester F. '39 (MIL) Retired.
Gassert, Adelbert '48 (CLV) Northfield, OH Western Reserve Psychiatric Habilitation Center; Retired.
Gassert, Adelbert J. '48 (CLV) Independence, OH St. Michael Church.
Gastalver, Alfredo '76 (SJN) [G] Guaynabo, PR Opus Dei.
Gaston, James T. '70 (GBG) [3] Greensburg, PA Our Lady of Grace Church.
Gaston, Juan Cruz *o.f.m.cap.* '67 (DAL) [9] Dallas, TX Our Lady of Perpetual Help Church; [M] Dallas, TX Capuchin Franciscan Friars, Vice Province of Texas.
Gately, Alfred *o.p.* (WDC) [11] Washington, DC St. Dominic Church & Priory Church.
Gately, R. Troy '89 (GAL) [1] Houston, TX Sacred Heart Co-Cathedral; On Special Assignment.
Gately, Robert E. '52 (COL) Retired.
Gates, Martin *o.f.m.* '63 (FgM) Franciscan Foreign Missions.
Gathen, Anthony *c.m.m.* '71 (DET) [K] Dearborn Heights, MI Our Lady of Grace Monastery.
Gatlin, Larry B. '67 (OKL) [12] Oklahoma City, OK St. James Church.
Gatman, Ronald P. *o.s.b.* '79 (SAV) [B] Savannah, GA Benedictine Military School; [F] Savannah, GA The Benedictine Priory.
Gatschet, Fred '93 (SAL) [1] Salina, KS Cathedral of the Sacred Heart.
Gattari, Valentine A. '54 (DET) [7] Detroit, MI Annunciation Church.

Gatti, Daniel J. *s.j.* '72 (NY) [F] New York, NY Xavier High School.
Gatto, Dennis J. *s.m.* '81 (CIN) [M] Dayton, OH Marianist Provincialate.
Gatto, Joseph '83 (BUF) [A] East Aurora, NY Christ the King Seminary.
Gatto, Joseph C. (BUF) [A] Buffalo, NY Pope John II Residence.
Gatto, Joseph C. *s.t.d.* '83 (BUF) [A] East Aurora, NY Christ the King Seminary.
Gatto, Reynold J. *s.j.* '68 (SAC) [C] Sacramento, CA Jesuit High School; [G] Carmichael, CA Jesuit High School Community of Sacramento.
Gatto, Msgr. Vincent S. '55 (WDC) Garrett Park, MD Holy Cross Church.
Gatzak, John P. '75 (HRT) [1] Hartford, CT Cathedral of St. Joseph; Special and other (Arch)Diocesan Assignment.
Gau, David *s.j.* '62 (RC) Rosebud, SD St. Bridget Church; St. Francis, SD St. Charles Church; St. Francis, SD Rosebud Reservation Church.
Gau, Guy *o.s.b.* '62 (SFS) [F] Marvin, SD Blue Cloud Abbey.
Gaucci, Juan A. *c.ss.r.* '59 (SJN) [2] San Juan, PR San Agustin Church.
Gauchat, Eric *cap. o.f.m.* '92 (CLV) [N] Cleveland, OH Mount Alverna Home, Inc. & Mount Alverna Home Annex, Inc.; [P] Cleveland, OH St. Paul Friary.
Gauchet, Eric *o.f.m.cap.* '92 (CLV) [18] Cleveland, OH Conversion of St. Paul Church.
Gauci, Albert *o.f.m.* '71 (FgM) Franciscan Foreign Missions.
Gaudet, Joseph A. '52 (BO) [7] Brockton, MA St. Patrick Church.
Gaudet, Roger B. '89 (IND) Fortville, IN St. Thomas Church.
Gaudette, Edward J. '52 (BO) [6] Revere, MA St. Theresa Church.
Gaudin, Rene *ss.cc.* '57 (FR) [J] Fairhaven, MA Sacred Hearts Provincial House.
Gaudio, Robert '74 (ROC) Palmyra, NY St. Anne Church.
Gaudio, Robert '93 (ROC) Marion, NY St. Gregory Church.
Gaudreau, Bernard E. '75 (BUR) Stowe, VT Blessed Sacrament Church.
Gaudreau, James E. '69 (BO) [3] Lynn, MA St. Joseph Church.
Gaudreau, Walter *s.m.* '68 (PRT) Brunswick, ME St. John the Baptist Church.
Gaughan, James '74 (MIA) [B] Opa Locka, FL St. Thomas University.
Gaughan, James M. '74 (OM) Absent on Leave.
Gaughan, Joseph '94 (FTW) [3] South Bend, IN St. Anthony de Padua Church.
Gaughan, Msgr. Patrick E. '68 (STU) Athens, OH St. Paul's Church.
Gaughan, Paul '52 (RIC) [7] Virginia Beach, VA St. John the Apostle Church; Retired.
Gaughan, Thomas E. *c.s.c.* '87 (FTW) [B] Notre Dame, IN University of Notre Dame Du Lac; [J] Notre Dame, IN Holy Cross Community, Corby Hall, University of Notre Dame.
Gaughan, William T. *c.m.* '42 (CHI) [N] Chicago, IL Vincentian Community, Congregation of the Mission, Midwest Province.
Gaughran, John '53 (PEO) Retired.
Gaugler, Robert *c.ss.r.* '39 (SJN) [2] San Juan, PR San Agustin Church.
Gaul, Cornelius '45 (DM) Retired.
Gaul, Richard G. '68 (DUB) Garber, IA St. Michael's Church; Garnavillo, IA St. Joseph's Church.
Gaul, Thomas J. '73 (R) Hope Mills, NC Good Shepherd Church.
Gaulin, Frederick J. *c.m.* '50 (PH) [AA] Philadelphia, PA Congregation of the Mission.
Gaulin, Roger M. '65 (NOR) Absent on Leave.
Gaulrapp, Leo *c.pp.s.* '46 (CIN) [B] Carthagena, OH St. Charles.
Gaumond, Normand R. '73 (WOR) Harvard, MA St. Theresa's Church.
Gaumond, Paul J. '74 (NOR) Wauregan, CT Sacred Heart Church.
Gaunt, James J. *c.s.b.* '64 (GAL) Manvel, TX Sacred Heart of Jesus Church; [Q] Manvel, TX The Basilian Fathers' Monastery of Citeaux.
Gaunt, Thomas P. *s.j.* '81 (BAL) [M] Baltimore, MD Jesuit Fathers and Brothers Maryland Provincial Curia; [M] Baltimore, MD Ferdinand Wheeler Jesuit Community.
Gaunt, Thomas P. *s.j.* '81 (NY) [DD] New York, NY Jesuit Provincial's Office.
Gaus, Msgr. Arnold L. '59 (ALT) Ebensburg, PA Holy Name Church.
Gausch, Joseph P. '45 (PH) [51] Philadelphia, PA Good Shepherd Church; Retired.
Gauthier, Donald F., Jr. '75 (MAN) Goffstown, NH St. Lawrence Church.
Gauthier, Ernest L. '62 (KC) Holden, MO St. Patrick's Church.
Gauthier, John '65 (PHX) On Leave.
Gauthier, Lawrence T. '55 (MAR) Retired.
Gauthreaux, Msgr. L. Earl '56 (NO) [44] New Orleans, LA St. Maria Goretti Church.
Gautreau, Evan B. *c.ss.r.* '38 (STL) [P] Liguori, MO St. Clement Health Care Center.
Gautreau, Henry W. '79 (BR) [14] Baton Rouge, LA St. Louis, King of France Church.
Gautreaux, Francis *c.ss.r.* '50 (FgM) Redemptorist Foreign Missions.
Gauvin, Leo *o.m.i.* '51 (SAT) [K] San Antonio, TX Oblate Madonna Residence.
Gauvin, Maurice O. '86 (FR) [5] Taunton, MA St. Anthony's Church.
Gauvreau, Thomas H. '48 (SPR) Retired.
Gavaler, Campion P. *o.s.b.* '59 (GBG) [H] Latrobe, PA Saint Vincent Archabbey.
Gavigan, P. Patrick '53 (CHL) Retired.
Gavigan, Peter '62 (NY) [178] Bronx, NY Our Lady of Victory Church.
Gavigan, Thomas J. *c.ss.r.* '60 (PCE) Guayama, PR St. Anthony of Padua Church.
Gavin, Carney E. '65 (BO) [21] Boston, MA St. Columbkille Church.
Gavin, Emmett *o.carm.* '87 (CHI) [N] Chicago, IL Carmelite Fathers Residence.
Gavin, Francis T. '47 (NEW) Retired; [B] South Orange, NJ Seton Hall University.
Gavin, Harold E. '51 (WIN) Kellogg, MN St. Agnes Church.
Gavin, James *o.f.m.cap.* '65 (NY) [17] Yonkers, NY Sacred Heart Church.
Gavin, James M. '51 (LA) [R] Los Angeles, CA Amat House.
Gavin, John *o.s.a.* '48 (STL) [6] St. Louis, MO Immaculate Conception-St. Henry Church.
Gavin, John T. *o.s.f.s.* '60 (ARL) Reston, VA St. John Neumann Church.
Gavin, Kenneth J. *s.j.* '75 (FgM) Provinces.
Gavin, Kenneth J. *s.j.* '75 (NY) [DD] New York, NY Jesuit Provincial's Office; [DD] New York, NY St. Ignatius Loyola Residence.
Gavin, Patrick *o.carm.* '82 (PHX) [6] Phoenix, AZ St. Agnes Church.
Gavin, Robert A. *o.f.m.* '59 (NY) [35] New York, NY St. Francis of Assisi Church.
Gavin, Robert V. *s.s.* '61 (SFR) [A] Menlo Park, CA St. Patrick Seminary.
Gavin, Russell *o.carm.* '47 (JOL) Darien, IL Our Lady of Mount Carmel Church.
Gavin, Thomas M. *s.j.* '75 (BAL) [M] Baltimore, MD Jesuit Fathers and Brothers Maryland Provincial Curia.
Gavin, Thomas M. *s.j.* '75 (FgM) Provinces.
Gavin, William F. *s.j.* '62 (ALN) [A] Wernersville, PA Novitiate of St. Isaac Jogues.
Gavit, James F. '54 (SAG) [7] Bay City, MI St. Maria Goretti Church.
Gavit, Steven M. '97 (SAG) Midland, MI Blessed Sacrament Church.
Gavitt, J. Duane '84 (SCR) [17] Wilkes-Barre, PA St. Patrick's Church.
Gavotto, Robert W. *o.s.a.* '64 (OAK) Castro Valley, CA Our Lady of Grace Church.
Gawinek, Walter '35 (MIL) [N] Wauwatosa, WI St. Camillus Health Center, Inc.
Gawlik, Gilbert *s.v.d.* '54 (CHI) [B] Techny, IL Divine Word Residence; [N] Techny, IL Society of the Divine Word, Provincial Headquarter-Chicago Prov.
Gawronski, Chester J. '76 (E) [13] Erie, PA St. Ann Church.
Gawronski, Mark '91 (DET) [71] Detroit, MI St. Stephen-Mary Mother of the Church.
Gawronski, Raymond T. *s.j.* '86 (MIL) [P] Milwaukee, WI Jesuit Community at Marquette University.
Gawrylewski, Patrick *o.f.m.cap.* (GB) Institute, WI SS. Peter and Paul Church.
Gay, James A. '59 (BGP) Military Chaplains.
Gay, John Curry '56 (HRT) [2] Waterbury, CT Immaculate Conception Church.
Gayarre, Domingo *s.s.s.* '52 (CGS) [5] Caguas, PR Santisimo Sacramento Church.
Gayarre, Eugenio '61 (ARE) Corozal, PR Holy Family Church.
Gaydos, Anthony M. *o.s.m.* '48 (CHI) [N] Chicago, IL Servite Friars - Eastern Province.
Gaydos, Anthony M. *o.s.m.* '48 (SPC) Ironton, MO Ste. Marie Du Lac Church; [C] Pilot Knob, MO Arcadia Valley Hospital.
Gaydos, Francis A. *c.m.* '47 (FgM) Vincentian Foreign Missions.
Gaydos, Robert M. *c.ss.r.* '44 (STL) [P] Liguori, MO St. Clement Health Care Center.
Gaydosik, David L. '87 (STU) Carrollton, OH Our Lady of Mercy Church; Morges, OH St. Mary Church.
Gaynard, Thomas P. '65 (PH) King of Prussia, PA Mother of Divine Providence Church.
Gaynor, James E. *c.pp.s.* '67 (CIN) [M] Dayton, OH Provincial House of the Cincinnati Province of the Society of the Precious Blood.
Gaynor, Joseph T. '45 (ROC) [4] Auburn, NY St. Alphonsus Church; Retired.
Gayso, Edward V. '50 (IND) Retired.
Gaytan, Alfredo *s.o.l.t.* (CC) Robstown, TX St. Anthony Church.
Gaytan, Alfredo *s.o.l.t.* '82 (CC) [H] Robstown, TX Society of Our Lady of the Most Holy Trinity.
Gayton, John J. *m.i.c.* '86 (SPR) [I] Stockbridge, MA Congregation of Marians.
Gaza, J. Patrick '68 (GRY) [16] Gary, IN SS. Monica-St. Luke Church.
Gazarkiewicz, Joseph F. '85 (GRY) Schererville, IN St. Michael Church.
Gazin, Mark *c.s.b.* '75 (GAL) [C] Houston, TX University of St. Thomas.
Gazin, Mark R. *c.s.b.* '90 (GAL) [Q] Houston, TX Residence of the Basilian Fathers of the University of St. Thomas; [T] Houston, TX University of St. Thomas Campus Ministry.
Gaztelu, Msgr. Angel '38 (MIA) [22] Miami, FL St. John Bosco Church.
Geaney, Gregory *o.carm.* '59 (JOL) [J] Darien, IL Carmelite Provincial Office.
Geaney, James *o.carm.* '59 (FgM) Carmelite Foreign Missions.
Geaney, John *c.s.p.* '64 (WDC) [V] Washington, DC Paulist Media Works.
Geaney, John J. *c.s.p.* '64 (WDC) [B] Washington, DC St. Paul's College.
Geany, Nash P. (NY) West Point, NY Stewart Field.
Gearhart, Edwin F. '73 (CIN) [53] Cincinnati, OH St. Leo the Great Church.
Gearing, Msgr. Daniel A. '38 (PIT) Baldwin Boro, PA St. Albert the Great Church; Retired.
Gearing, Edward P. '44 (GBG) Retired.
Geary, Edward A. *s.j.* '62 (PH) [AA] Philadelphia, PA Jesuit Community at St. Joseph's University.
Geary, John C. *s.j.* '47 (SJ) [M] Los Gatos, CA Sacred Heart Jesuit Center.
Geary, Patrick G. '56 (DUB) [6] Waterloo, IA Blessed Sacrament Church.
Gebelein, Gary '74 (STL) [6] Florissant, MO St. Ferdinand Church.
Gebhard, Robert L. '87 (BUF) [35] Buffalo, NY St. James Church.
Gebhardt, Joseph M. '50 (B) Retired.
Gebhardt, Paul L. '91 (CIN) Middletown, OH Holy Family Church; [E] Middletown, OH Bishop Fenwick High School.
Gedeon, Thomas *s.j.* (FTW) [B] Notre Dame, IN University of Notre Dame Du Lac.
Gedeon, Thomas W. *s.j.* '56 (DET) [K] Detroit, MI Jesuit Provincial Office-Detroit Province of the Society of Jesus.
Geders, Joseph C. *c.m.* '84 (CHI) [N] Chicago, IL Vincentian Community, Congregation of the Mission, Midwest Province.
Geditz, Roger '69 (SFS) Watertown, SD Immaculate Conception Church.
Gedvila, Izidorius '48 (GF) Retired.
Gee, Daniel N. '95 (ARL) Manassas, VA All Saints Church.
Gee, John F. '53 (WOR) Auburn, MA North American Martyrs Church.
Gee, Peter *f.s.s.p.* '95 (KCK) [D] Maple Hill, KS Our Lady of Compassion.
Gee, Peter J. *f.s.s.p.* '95 (SCR) [M] Elmhurst, PA Priestly Fraternity of St. Peter (F.S.S.P.), North American District Headquarters.
Geelan, Thomas E. '62 (SC) [2] Sioux City, IA Blessed Sacrament Church.
Geenen, Roy J. '68 (GB) Menasha, WI St. Patrick Church.
Geers, Carl J. '43 (CIN) [1] Cincinnati, OH St. Peter in Chains Cathedral; Retired.
Geers, Frank *o.f.m.* '58 (CIN) [C] Cincinnati, OH St. Anthony Shrine, Francisan Candidacy.
Geers, Harold *o.f.m.* '60 (FgM) Franciscan Foreign Missions.
Gefell, Msgr. Gerard J. '41 (OG) Retired.
Gefell, Msgr. Gerard J. '41 (ROC) Retired.
Gefell, Msgr. Joseph G. '41 (OG) Retired.
Gefell, Msgr. Joseph G. '41 (ROC) Retired.
Gegotek, Tadeusz '91 (BEL) Military Chaplains.
Gehant, Rembert *o.s.b.* '44 (IND) [J] St. Meinrad, IN St. Meinrad Archabbey.
Gehl, James C. '74 (LA) Canoga Park, CA St. Joseph the Worker Church.
Gehl, James E. '69 (SY) Dewitt, NY Holy Cross Church.
Gehl, Walter N. '44 (MIL) Retired.
Gehlen, Elzear *s.v.d.* '44 (CHI) [1] Mt. Prospect, IL St. Cecilia Church; [B] Techny, IL Divine Word Residence.
Gehling, Kenneth B. '62 (DUB) [H] Mason City, IA North Iowa Mercy Health Center.
Gehring, Fredric P. *c.m.* '30 (PH) [AA] Philadelphia, PA Congregation of the Mission.
Gehring, Robert P. '66 (GRY) [1] Gary, IN Cathedral of Holy Angels.
Geib, David *o.p.* (SB) [10] Riverside, CA St. Andrew's Newman Center Church; [H] Riverside, CA St. Andrews Newman Center.
Geib, Harry F. *s.j.* '92 (WDC) [E] Washington, DC

Gonzaga College High School.
Geigel, Francis '38 (GB) Retired.
Geiger, Angelo Mary (NOR) [F] Baltic, CT Marian Friary of Our Lady of Guadalupe.
Geiger, Damon *o.ss.t.* '71 (BAL) [M] Baltimore, MD Holy Trinity Monastery.
Geiger, Damon *o.ss.t.* '71 (NTN) West Paterson, NJ St. Ann's Church.
Geiger, Eugene E. '47 (NEW) [2] Irvington, NJ St. Leo's Church; Retired.
Geiger, James A. '50 (COL) Sugar Grove, OH St. Joseph Church.
Geiger, James H. *c.ss.r.* '37 (SP) [9] Tampa, FL St. Joseph Church.
Geiger, William *c.ss.r.* '54 (HBG) [2] Lancaster, PA St. Anthony of Padua Church.
Geilenkirchen, Inde (DEN) [4] Aurora, CO St. Therese Church.
Geinzer, Eugene M. *s.j.* '74 (CHI) [C] Chicago, IL Jesuit Community at Loyola University of Chicago.
Geinzer, John A. '67 (PIT) Turtle Creek, PA St. Colman Church.
Geinzer, Patrick *c.p.* '95 (SCR) [2] Scranton, PA St. Ann's Basilica Parish; [M] Scranton, PA Saint Ann's Passionist Monastery.
Geis, John F. '64 (IND) St. Mary-of-the-Knobs, IN St. Mary-of-the-Knobs Church.
Geiser, Allen '90 (GB) Askeaton, WI St. Patrick Church.
Geiser, Xavier *o.f.m.* '55 (FgM) Custody of St. Mary of the Angels. Byzantine-Slavonic.
Geisinger, Robert J. *s.j.* '91 (CHI) [89] Chicago, IL St. Ignatius Church.
Geisser, Raymond E. *o.s.a.* '60 (MIA) [B] Opa Locka, FL St. Thomas University; [H] Miami, FL Casa San Lorenzo.
Geissler, Lloyd F. '42 (LC) Retired.
Geissler, Ralph J. '38 (LC) Retired.
Geissler, Msgr. Robert '47 (NY) Retired.
Geiszel, John I. *s.j.* '57 (LA) [F] Los Angeles, CA Loyola High School.
Geitner, John E. *m.m.* '53 (FgM) Maryknoll Foreign Missions.
Gelati, Dario '53 (PIT) Retired.
Gelencser, Paul L. *o.praem.* '41 (ORG) [H] Silverado, CA Norbertine Fathers of Orange Inc.
Gelfenbien, Gary Paul '71 (ALB) Chatham, NY St. James Church.
Gelin, Henry C. *s.j.* '51 (DET) [P] Clarkston, MI Colombiere Center.
Gelinas, Rene *m.s.* '60 (FR) [J] Attleboro, MA La Salette Shrine.
Gelinas, Rene '60 (STL) [P] St. Louis, MO La Salette Missionaries.
Gelineau, Msgr. Edward J. '42 (BUR) Retired; [D] Burlington, VT St. Joseph's Home for Aged.
Gelineau, H. Raymond '69 (WOR) Absent on Leave.
Gelis, Mark *m.j.* '94 (PCE) On Duty Outside the Diocese.
Gellel, Lawrence *s.j.* '54 (BRK) [221] Queens, NY Our Lady of Sorrows Church.
Geller, Charles '73 (SAN) Fort Stockton, TX St. Agnes Church.
Geller, Charles H. '73 (BEL) Special Assignment.
Gelpi, Donald L. *s.j.* '64 (OAK) [A] Berkeley, CA The Jesuit School of Theology at Berkeley; [N] Berkeley, CA Jesuit Community at Jesuit School of Theology at Berkeley.
Gelthaus, Harry J. '85 (L) [1] Valley Station, KY St. Clement Church.
Gelthaus, Lawrence J. '88 (L) Albany, KY Emmanuel Catholic Church.
Gembala, Joseph J. '87 (DET) [5] Sterling Heights, MI St. Malachy Church.
Gemperline, Joachim *c.p.* '53 (L) [L] Louisville, KY Sacred Heart Retreat.
Gemskie, Charles A. '77 (JOL) Carol Stream, IL Corpus Christi Church.
Gemuend, Msgr. David W. '65 (GAY) Frankfort, MI St. Ann Church.
Gemza, Richard J. '95 (BGP) Bethel, CT St. Mary's Church.
Gendelmann, Clemens J. '85 (PH) [EE] Philadelphia, PA Newman Apostolate.
Gendreau, Claude R. '93 (PRT) St. Francis, ME St. Charles Church; St. John, ME St. John Church.
Gendreau, Michael P. '90 (PRT) St. Agatha, ME St. Agatha's Church; Sinclair, ME St. Joseph Church.
Gendreau, Richard R. '69 (FR) [3] Swansea, MA St. Michael's Church.
Gendron, Charles A. *m.s.* '44 (LKC) [3] Sulphur, LA Our Lady of Prompt Succor Church.
Gendron, Michael E. '95 (MAN) [12] Manchester, NH St. Marie Church; [17] Manchester, NH Sacred Heart of Jesus Church.
Gendusa, Anthony *m.s.c.* '40 (FgM) Missionaries of the Sacred Heart Foreign Missions.
Gendusa, Anthony *m.s.c.* '40 (RCK) [H] Aurora, IL Missionaries of the Sacred Heart Community.
Genello, Patrick J. '83 (SCR) [3] Hazleton, PA Holy Rosary Church.
Genereux, Wayne C. *o.de.m.* '97 (BUF) [O] LeRoy, NY Order of the BVM of Mercy/Mercedarian Friars.
Genest, Giles *m.s.* '62 (MAN) Lebanon, NH Sacred Heart Church.
Geng, Dennis *o.c.d.* '89 (MIL) [P] Milwaukee, WI Provincial Offices - Discalced Carmelites.
Gengaro, Nicholas S. '81 (NEW) [B] South Orange, NJ Seton Hall University.
Gengras, Joseph C. '49 (HRT) Bloomfield, CT Sacred Heart Church; Retired.
Geniesse, Joseph '57 (AUS) [F] Austin, TX Seton Medical Center.
Genito, Joseph A. *o.s.a.* '75 (ORL) Casselberry, FL St. Augustine Church.
Gennardo, Vincent *c.s.* (CHI) [137] Chicago, IL St. Michael Archangel Church.
Genovese, Anthony M. *o.s.a.* '73 (PH) Villanova, PA St. Thomas of Villanova Parish Community Church.
Genovese, Seamus D. '75 (OAK) [18] Oakland, CA Our Lady of Lourdes Church.
Genovesi, James W. (LC) Norwalk, WI St. Augustine of Hippo Church.
Genovesi, James W. '71 (MAR) On Duty Outside the Diocese.
Genovesi, Vincent J. *s.j.* '69 (PH) [C] Philadelphia, PA St. Joseph's University; [AA] Philadelphia, PA Jesuit Community at St. Joseph's University.
Gensert, Bernon *o.f.m.* '47 (STL) [P] St. Louis, MO Franciscan Friary of St. Anthony of Padua.
Genska, Depaul A. *o.f.m.* '58 (NY) [DD] New York, NY Franciscan Friars, Order of Friars Minor, Holy Name Province.
Gensler, Harry J. *s.j.* '74 (SCR) [C] Scranton, PA University of Scranton.
Gensler, Thomas W. *s.j.* (DET) [K] Detroit, MI Jesuit Provincial Office-Detroit Province of the Society of Jesus.
Gentile, Carl J. '60 (PIT) Churchill Borough, PA St. John Fisher Church.
Gentile, Emile A. *t.o.r.* '64 (ORL) Mount Dora, FL St. Patrick's Church; Special Assignment.
Gentile, Gennaro L. '71 (NY) Croton-on-Hudson, NY Holy Name of Mary Church.
Gentile, Gilbert J. *s.j.* '78 (SD) [4] San Diego, CA Christ the King Church.
Gentile, Henry *c.s.* (NY) [205] Staten Island, NY Holy Family Church.
Gentile, Henry S. *c.s.* '59 (NY) [205] Staten Island, NY Holy Family Church; [DD] Staten Island, NY Scalabrinian Missionaries.
Gentile, Thomas E. '73 (L) [31] Louisville, KY St. Helen Church.
Gentili, Joseph P. '87 (PH) [1] Norristown, PA Epiphany of Our Lord Church; Graduate Studies.
Gentleman, Gerard J., Jr. '97 (RVC) Farmingdale, NY St. Kilian Church.
Gentleman, John W. '87 (BO) Chelmsford, MA St. John the Evangelist Church.
Genua, Ronald L. '65 (HRT) [2] Ansonia, CT Holy Rosary Church.
Genuardi, Gasper A. '68 (PH) Conshohocken, PA SS. Cosmas and Damian Church.
Genuario, Msgr. William A. '56 (BGP) Riverside, CT St. Catherine of Siena Church.
Genzlinger, Walter L. '49 (NEW) [17] Jersey City, NJ Mt. Carmel Church; Retired.
Geogan, Philip J. '79 (NOR) Stonington, CT St. Mary Church.
Geoghan, John J. (BO) Retired.
Geoghegan, Msgr. Arthur T. '41 (PRO) Retired.
Geoghegan, James *o.c.d.* '60 (SR) [M] Oakville, CA Carmelite House of Prayer.
Geohegan, James *o.c.d.* '60 (SR) [L] Oakville, CA Carmelite House of Prayer.
Geokge, Msgr. David M. '76 (SAM) Waterbury, CT Our Lady of Lebanon Church.
George, Alexander '65 (LA) [7] Los Angeles, CA Christ the King Church.
George, Dale '58 (SC) Rock Valley, IA St. Mary's Church. Midwest Patrons of the Arts in the Vatican Museums.
George, Francis M. '87 (LAN) Fowlerville, MI St. Agnes Church.
George, George C. '86 (AUS) McGregor, TX St. Eugene Church; Moody, TX Our Lady of San Juan Church.
George, J. Clark (ALT) Retired.
George, Jose '77 (BRK) [43] Brooklyn, NY St. Frances de Chantal Church.
George, Msgr. Joseph S. '62 (LA) Thousand Oaks, CA St. Paschal Baylon Church.
George, Lloyd D. *s.j.* '73 (BAL) [C] Baltimore, MD Loyola High School.
George, Patrick *t.o.r.* (PIT) Allegheny County, PA UPMC University of Pittsburgh Medical Center.
George, Patrick *t.o.r.* '55 (PIT) [O] Pittsburgh, PA Franciscan Friars, T.O.R.
George, Richard '95 (PMB) [B] West Palm Beach, FL Cardinal Newman High School.
George, Robert J. '76 (PIT) [P] Pittsburgh, PA Convent of Mercy.
George, Robert J. '95 (ALN) [1] Allentown, PA Cathedral of St. Catharine of Siena.
George, W. Frederick *o.s.b.* '75 (CHL) [J] Belmont, NC Belmont Abbey.
George, Walter *c.ss.r.* (CHI) [9] Chicago, IL St. Alphonsus Church.
George, William L. *s.j.* '73 (WDC) [M] Washington, DC The Jesuit Community at Georgetown University.
Georgia, John J. '75 (HRT) North Haven, CT St. Frances Cabrini Church.
Gephart, John B. '46 (L) Louisville, KY Jewish Hospital; Louisville, KY Kosair-Children's Hospital; Louisville, KY Norton Hospital; Retired; [L] Louisville, KY Bishop David Apartments.
Gera, Francis '64 (PSC) Ormond Beach, FL Holy Dormition Church.
Geracci, John R. *c.s.c.* '92 (SCR) [C] Wilkes-Barre, PA Kings College; [C] Wilkes-Barre, PA Kings College.
Geraci, Anthony J. '75 (CIN) Russells Point, OH St. Mary of the Woods Church.
Geraets, Chrysostom *o.p.* '56 (FgM) Dominican - Order of Preachers Foreign Missions.
Geraghty, James '68 (NY) Absent on Leave.
Geraghty, Msgr. Martin T. '64 (BRK) [169] Queens, NY St. Francis de Sales Church.
Gerardo, John A. '76 (WOR) On Duty Outside the Diocese.
Gerathy, Msgr. Kenneth A. '54 (NY) [201] Staten Island, NY St. Christopher Church.
Geraughty, Michael '84 (ORG) Inactive Leave.
Gerber, Francis J., Jr. '84 (DEN) Grand Lake, CO St. Anne Church.
Gerbino, A. Richard '52 (CAM) On Sick Leave; [M] Cherry Hill, NJ Vianney Villa.
Gerbus, Berard *o.f.m.* (CIN) [L] Cincinnati, OH Archbishop Leibold Home for the Aged.
Gerdelman, Clemens J. '85 (PH) [2] Chester, PA Blessed Katharine Drexel Church.
Gerdes, Harry J. '62 (CIN) [50] Cincinnati, OH St. Joseph Church.
Gerena, Luis Ricardo '85 (SJN) [25] San Juan, PR San Jorge Church.
Gerend, Lawrence '76 (GB) Retired.
Gerety, Msgr. John L. '57 (MET) South Amboy, NJ St. Mary Church; Retired.
Gerg, Joseph *o.s.b.* '65 (ALT) Patton, PA Our Lady of Perpetual Help Church; Patton, PA Queen of Peace Church.
Gergel, Stephen J. '62 (ALT) Military Chaplains.
Gergen, Charles L. '48 (LIN) York, NE St. Joseph's Church.
Gergen, Michael *s.d.b.* '79 (LA) [C] Rosemead, CA Don Bosco Technical Institute.
Gerhard, John J. *s.j.* '49 (NY) [DD] New York, NY Jesuit Provincial's Office.
Gerhard, John P. *o.p.* '53 (FgM) Dominican - Order of Preachers Foreign Missions.
Gerhard, John P. *o.p.* '53 (NY) [121] New York, NY St. Vincent Ferrer Church.
Gerhard, John Peter *o.p.* '53 (NY) [DD] New York, NY St. Vincent Ferrer Priory.
Gerhardt, Msgr. Bernard C. '53 (WDC) [1] Washington, DC St. Matthew Cathedral; Pastoral Center Special Ministries.
Gericke, Timothy F. '65 (MAD) Markesan, WI St. Joseph Church.
Gering, Kenneth *o.f.m.conv.* '58 (IND) [I] Mount Saint Francis, IN Mount Saint Francis Friary and Retreat Center.
Gerken, Theodore '57 (ALB) Germantown, NY Resurrection Church.
Gerl, Robert (GR) [E] Grand Rapids, MI St. Mary's Health Services.
Gerl, Robert '79 (KAL) [5] Kalamazoo, MI St. Thomas More Student Parish; [H] Kalamazoo, MI Western Michigan University, Kalamazoo College-Kalamazoo Valley Community College.
Gerl, Robert '79 (LAN) On Duty Outside the Diocese.
Gerlach, Dominic B. *c.pp.s.* '50 (LFT) [A] Rensselaer, IN Saint Joseph's College.
Gerlach, John H. *o.p.* '63 (SFD) [L] Springfield, IL Convent of Our Lady of the Sacred Heart.
Gerlach, Matthew J. '96 (TLS) [1] Tulsa, OK Holy Family Cathedral.
Gerlach, Michael J. '82 (PH) Chalfont, PA St. Jude Church; [EE] Philadelphia, PA Newman Apostolate.
Gerlich, Robert S. *s.j.* '73 (NO) [C] New Orleans, LA Loyola University.
Gerlock, Stanley '60 (SY) Binghamton, NY Broome County Jail.
Gerlock, Stanley J. '60 (SY) Chenango Forks, NY St. Rita Church.
Gerloff, Charles W. '45 (ARL) Retired.
Germain, Jean M. '47 (SHP) Retired.
Germaine, Kenneth *s.d.b.* '67 (SP) [E] Tampa, FL Mary Help of Christians School.
German, Ambrose *o.f.m.* '53 (JC) Hermann, MO St. George Church.
German, Gary *o.f.m.* (GLP) Acoma, NM San Esteban, Acoma Catholic Indian Mission Church.
German, Gary *o.f.m.* '88 (GLP) Laguna, NM St. Joseph Church.
German, Gary *o.f.m.* '88 (STL) [P] St. Louis, MO

Franciscan Friary of St. Anthony of Padua.
German, Kenneth N. '81 (BO) [10] Lawrence, MA St. Patrick Church; Awaiting Assignment.
German, Michael J. '68 (NEW) River Edge, NJ St. Peter the Apostle Church.
German, Timothy J. '73 (ORG) Inactive Leave.
Germann, Daniel V. *s.j.* '63 (SJ) [B] Santa Clara, CA Santa Clara University.
Germann, Lauren A. '78 (SCL) Staples, MN Sacred Heart Church.
Germovnik, Francis *c.m.* '41 (STL) [P] Perryville, MO Congregation of The Mission.
Gernatt, Msgr. David A. '47 (BUF) Retired.
Gerosa, Giuliano *c.r.s.* '78 (MAN) [H] Allenstown, NH Pine Haven Boys Center.
Gerres, Daniel W. '66 (WIL) Liftwood, DE Immaculate Heart of Mary Church; Wilmington, DE Delaware Army National Guard; Wilmington, DE Gander Hill Correctional Center.
Gerrety, James P. '57 (COV) Erlanger, KY Mary, Queen of Heaven Church; Retired.
Gerritts, John R. '63 (SUP) Rhinelander, WI St. Joseph's Church.
Gerrity, John J. '35 (CLV) Maple Heights, OH St. Martin of Tours Church; Retired.
Gerrity, John J. '58 (CLV) [N] Cleveland, OH Sts. Mary and Joseph Home for the Aged.
Gerrity, Raymond J. '45 (CHI) [145] Chicago, IL Our Lady of Fatima Church; Retired.
Gersbach, Karl A. *o.s.a.* '61 (CHI) [N] Olympia Fields, IL The Augustinian Provincialate Tolentine Center.
Gersbach, Karl A. *o.s.a.* '61 (PH) [AA] Villanova, PA St. Thomas Monastery.
Gerst, Lawrence G. '87 (STL) Retired.
Gerstenkorn, Msgr. Joseph J. '34 (WCH) Retired.
Gerstle, Fabian *o.f.m.* '48 (CIN) [M] Cincinnati, OH St. Clement Friary.
Gerth, John '93 (SP) [9] St. Petersburg, FL Transfiguration Church.
Gerth, Kenneth *m.c.c.j.* (SP) [K] Tampa, FL St. Joseph's Hospital, Inc.
Gerth, Kenneth *m.c.c.j.* '65 (CIN) [M] Cincinnati, OH Comboni Missionaries (Verona Fathers)-Comboni Mission Center.
Gerum, Jerome G. '50 (LC) Retired.
Gerut, William F. *s.j.* '67 (LC) Prairie du Chien, WI St. Gabriel Church; Prairie du Chien, WI St. John Nepomucene Church.
Gervacio, Adrian R. '67 (HON) Military Chaplains.
Gervais, Bernard *o.s.b.* (PBL) [E] Florence, CO Centura Health-St. Joseph Manor.
Gervais, Bernard P. *o.s.b.* '44 (PBL) [F] Canon City, CO Holy Cross Abbey.
Gervasio, Msgr. Thomas N. '82 (TR) [17] Trenton, NJ St. Joachim Church.
Gese, David '78 (SEA) [16] Tacoma, WA Visitation Church.
Gessler, James *s.m.a.* '63 (FgM) Society of African Missions.
Gessner, Glenn *o.f.m.cap.* '60 (FgM) Capuchin Foreign Missions.
Gessner, Henry E. '47 (STP) Retired.
Gessner, Kurt *o.f.m.cap.* '57 (GB) [3] Appleton, WI St. Joseph Church; [I] Appleton, WI St. Joseph Friary.
Gesy, Lawrence '75 (BAL) Brunswick, MD St. Francis of Assisi Church.
Getchel, Richard '76 (GB) [3] Green Bay, WI St. Agnes Church.
Getreu, David E. '94 (COL) Gahanna, OH St. Matthew Church.
Getsinger, Ronald A. '68 (WH) New Cumberland, WV Immaculate Conception Church.
Getsy, John *o.f.m.cap.* '66 (PIT) [29] Pittsburgh, PA Our Lady of the Angels Church.
Gettig, Diego J. *c.pp.s.* '71 (GRY) [5] East Chicago, IN Our Lady of Guadalupe Church.
Gettinger, Robert J. '64 (STL) [27] St. Louis, MO St. Augustine Church.
Gettlefinger, Robert (CHL) [5] Charlotte, NC St. Gabriel Church.
Getty, Roy G. '39 (PIT) Retired.
Getz, Joseph *o.s.a.* '51 (ALB) Mechanicville, NY Assumption-St. Paul Church.
Getz, Msgr. Robert '61 (LSC) Roswell, NM Assumption of the Blessed Virgin Mary Church.
Geurtz, Gary '81 (FWT) [9] Fort Worth, TX St. Bartholomew Church.
Geusic, Stephen *m.s.c.* '43 (ALN) [A] Center Valley, PA Missionaries of the Sacred Heart.
Geyer, Kenneth A. *o.s.b.* '53 (CHL) [J] Belmont, NC Belmont Abbey.
Geyer, Raymond J. *o.s.b.* '49 (CHL) [J] Belmont, NC Belmont Abbey.
Geyman, Donald R. '96 (GAY) Cheboygan, MI St. Mary-St. Charles Church.
Geysen, Clement *ss.cc.* '49 (HON) [H] Honolulu, HI St. Patrick's Monastery.
Gfroerer, Gerard J. '51 (RVC) Retired; [N] Uniondale, NY St. Pius X Residence.
Ghaby, John (NTN) Boston, MA Annunciation Cathedral.
Ghali, Adel (SJ) [H] San Jose, CA Alexian Brothers Hospital.
Ghanoum, Gabriel *b.s.o.* '93 (NTN) Miami, FL St. Jude Church; Delray Beach, FL St. Nicholas Church.
Ghavy, John (BO) [10] Boston, MA Annunciation Cathedral.
Ghazal, Edmond J. *b.c.o.* '58 (NTN) Plymouth, MI St. Michael Church; Warren, MI Our Lady of Redemption Church.
Ghebreyohannes, Kesete '92 (WDC) [5] Washington, DC St. Anthony Church.
Ghezzi, Giancarlo *p.i.m.e.* (CHI) [42] Chicago, IL St. Clotilde Church.
Ghezzi, Luciano *p.i.m.e.* '74 (PAT) [M] Wayne, NJ P.I.M.E. Missionaries Residence.
Ghezzi, Richard G. '86 (SCR) Bentley Creek, PA St. Ann's Church.
Ghiloni, Mark '83 (COL) Portsmouth, OH Holy Redeemer Church.
Ghio, John J. '80 (STL) [41] St. Louis, MO St. John the Baptist Church.
Ghiorso, David A. '81 (SFR) Special Assignment; [R] San Rafael, CA Catholic Youth Organization of the Archdiocese of San Francisco; [U] San Rafael, CA Catholic Scouting.
Ghirlando, Gabriel *s.j.* '66 (BO) [W] Weston, MA Campion Center.
Ghisalberti, Giacomo G. '51 (R) Retired.
Ghys, Philip *o.s.b.* (RIC) [6] Virginia Beach, VA St. Gregory the Great Church.
Ghyselinck, Mark R. *c.s.c.* '88 (FTW) [B] Notre Dame, IN University of Notre Dame Du Lac; [J] Notre Dame, IN Holy Cross Community, Corby Hall, University of Notre Dame.
Giachino, Valeriano *s.s.p.* '57 (LA) [R] Los Angeles, CA Society of St. Paul.
Giacomini, Antonio *o.f.m.cap.* (R) Retired.
Giacomini, Salvatore *s.d.b.* '51 (SFR) [45] San Francisco, CA SS. Peter and Paul Church.
Giacopelli, John A. '59 (KC) Retired.
Giacosa, Charley '62 (NSH) Dickson, TN St. Christopher Church.
Giambrone, Charles S. *c.s.sp.* '60 (FgM) Holy Ghost Foreign Missions.
Giammarino, George '41 (NY) Retired.
Giammarino, Msgr. Vincent J. '43 (CAM) Retired.
Giammona, Msgr. John J. '59 (GR) Retired.
Giampietro, Anthony *c.s.b.* '93 (NY) [174] Bronx, NY Our Lady of Mt. Carmel Church.
Giandurco, Joseph R. '87 (NY) [A] Yonkers, NY St. Joseph's Seminary.
Gianelli, Gene '70 (HRT) Woodbridge, CT Church of the Assumption.
Giangiacomo, Tosello *c.s.sp.* '48 (ARE) Orocovis, PR Our Lady of Fatima Church.
Giangiacomo, Tosello *c.s.sp.* '48 (PCE) [B] Ponce, PR The Pontifical Catholic University of Puerto Rico.
Giannamore, Msgr. Anthony J. '56 (CIN) [V] Centerville, OH St. Leonard Faith Community.
Giannamore, Msgr. Anthony J. '56 (STU) Retired.
Giannamore, Peter A. '95 (WH) Clarksburg, WV Immaculate Conception Church.
Gianni, Vincent J. '70 (BO) [5] Revere, MA Our Lady of Lourdes Church.
Giannini, Stephen '93 (IND) [1] Terre Haute, IN Sacred Heart of Jesus Church; [2] Terre Haute, IN St. Ann Church.
Giannini, Steve '93 (IND) [C] Indianapolis, IN Roncalli High School.
Giannitelli, Michael C. '91 (NOR) Colchester, CT St. Andrew Church.
Giannone, Ronald *o.f.m.cap.* '90 (WIL) [F] Wilmington, DE Ministry of Caring, Inc.; [I] Wilmington, DE St. Felix Friary; [J] Wilmington, DE Monastery of St. Veronica Giuliani.
Gianola, William '62 (CHY) Retired.
Giaquinto, Albert C. '48 (NOR) On Duty Outside the Diocese; Retired.
Giaquinto, Albert C. *s.s.* '48 (WDC) [A] Washington, DC Theological College of the Catholic University of America; [C] Washington, DC Catholic University of America, The.
Giardina, Robert J. '76 (PRO) [9] West Warwick, RI Sacred Heart Church.
Giardino, Andrew *o.f.m.* '62 (HRT) [14] Hartford, CT St. Patrick-St. Anthony Church.
Giardino, Louis '75 (BIR) [4] Huntsville, AL Holy Spirit Church.
Gibas, John J. '43 (PH) Retired.
Gibas, Robert G. '62 (Y) Navarre, OH St. Clement's Church.
Gibault, Damian '92 (PSC) [C] Miami, FL Holy Cross Community.
Gibbeaut, Wayne *o.f.m.* '83 (SFE) [1] Santa Fe, NM The Cathedral of San Francisco de Asis.
Gibbons, Christopher W. *m.m.* '45 (NY) [DD] Maryknoll, NY Maryknoll Fathers and Brothers.
Gibbons, D. Patrick '96 (SFD) Edwardsville, IL St. Mary Church.
Gibbons, Edward F. '97 (VEN) Bradenton, FL St. Joseph Church.
Gibbons, Francis X. '83 (ORG) Inactive Leave.
Gibbons, George J. '45 (MIL) Retired.
Gibbons, James *o.m.i.* '69 (FgM) Oblates Foreign Missions.
Gibbons, John '56 (DEN) [15] Denver, CO Montbello Catholic Parish-Church of the Ascension; Retired.
Gibbons, John J. '58 (NEW) Fairview, NJ St. John the Baptist Church.
Gibbons, Msgr. John J. '60 (TR) Brick Town, NJ St. Dominic Church.
Gibbons, John M. '89 (ALN) [5] Allentown, PA Our Lady Help of Christians Church.
Gibbons, Robert C. '81 (SP) [7] St. Petersburg, FL St. Paul Church.
Gibbons, Thomas F. *m.m.* '48 (PH) [59] Philadelphia, PA Holy Family Church.
Gibbons, Thomas J. *s.j.* '60 (BO) [W] Boston, MA The Society of Jesus of New England-Provincial Offices; [W] Boston, MA The Society of Jesus of New England-Provincial Offices.
Gibbons, William F. '57 (CLV) Independence, OH St. Michael Church; Retired.
Gibbons, Williams F. '57 (CLV) [6] Lorain, OH St. Joseph Church.
Gibbs, Philip G. '94 (DUB) [7] Cedar Rapids, IA St. Pius X Church.
Gibino, Joseph R. '81 (BRK) [1] Brooklyn, NY The Cathedral-Basilica of St. James Church; [E] Brooklyn, NY Office of Religious Education: Evangelization and Catholic Formation.
Gibino, Joseph R. '81 (RVC) [A] Huntington, NY Diocesan Seminary of the Immaculate Conception.
Giblin, Berard A. *o.f.m.* '43 (ALB) [B] Loudonville, NY Siena College.
Giblin, C. Homer *s.j.* '58 (NY) [DD] New York, NY Jesuit Community at Fordham University.
Giblin, Msgr. Lawrence E. '44 (SY) [12] Binghamton, NY St. Thomas Aquinas Church; Retired.
Giblin, Richard J. '66 (SY) [1] Endicott, NY Our Lady of Good Counsel Church.
Giblin, William M. '59 (NEW) [3] East Orange, NJ St. Joseph's Church.
Gibney, Laurence H. '54 (NY) New Windsor, NY St. Joseph Church.
Gibney, Robert G. '54 (NEW) Ridgewood, NJ Our Lady of Mount Carmel Church.
Gibney, Robert G. '69 (NEW) Washington Township, NJ Our Lady of Good Counsel Church; Retired; [N] Caldwell, NJ The Rev. Msgr. James F. Kelley Residence for Retired Priests.
Gibowski, Boguslaw T. '69 (PRO) [12] Woonsocket, RI St. Stanislaus Church.
Gibson, Beryl '96 (SAL) Hays, KS Immaculate Heart of Mary Church.
Gibson, Bruno *o.p.* '60 (OAK) [4] Berkeley, CA St. Mary Magdalen Church.
Gibson, Christopher *c.p.* '75 (CHI) [N] Chicago, IL Immaculate Conception Monastery.
Gibson, James *c.r.* '79 (CHI) [N] Chicago, IL Provincial Office of the Congregation of the Resurrection.
Gibson, Jay L. *c.m.* '93 (COS) Burlington, CO St. Catherine of Siena Church; Stratton, CO St. Charles Borromeo Church.
Gibson, John '88 (NY) [52] New York, NY Immaculate Conception Church; Manhattan, NY New York University Medical Center.
Gibson, John W. '45 (PIT) Retired.
Gibson, Msgr. Lawrence J. '55 (LA) San Marino, CA Saints Felicitas and Perpetua Church.
Gibson, Michael P. '48 (STL) Retired.
Gibson, Robert J. '58 (SCR) Unassigned or Leave of Absence.
Gibson, Stephen C. *c.s.c.* '70 (FTW) [L] Notre Dame, IN Holy Cross Mission House; [M] Notre Dame, IN Our Lady of Fatima Retreat Center.
Gibson, Stephen G. '81 (GRY) [11] East Chicago, IN St. Mary Church.
Gibson, Thomas '93 (PEO) [2] Champaign, IL St. John's Catholic Chapel Church; [O] Champaign, IL St. John's Catholic Student Chapel and Newman Foundation, University of Illinois.
Gicewicz, Edward *c.m.* '38 (HRT) [M] Manchester, CT DePaul Provincial Residence.
Gick, Francois *s.j.* '80 (BO) [W] Boston, MA The Society of Jesus of New England-Provincial Offices.
Gidaro, Joseph C. *o.ss.t.* '87 (BAL) [M] Baltimore, MD Holy Trinity Monastery.
Gidaro, Joseph C. *o.ss.t.* '87 (NY) [20] New York, NY St. Brigid Church.
Gideon, Peter M. '76 (COL) New Boston, OH St. Monica Church; Wheelersburg, OH St. Peter Church.
Gideon, Stephen G. '97 (NSH) [6] Nashville, TN St. Henry Church.
Gidley, Lawrence *o.s.b.* '40 (KC) [J] Conception, MO Conception Abbey.
Giebel, Alfred W. '72 (ANC) [3] Anchorage, AK St. Benedict Church.
Giedgaudas, Francis *o.f.m.* '47 (BRK) [U] Brooklyn, NY St. Casimir's Monastery, Printing Plant and Cultural Center.

Giel, John C. '78 (ORL) Leesburg, FL St. Paul's Church.
Gielow, Richard *c.m.* '70 (KC) [J] Kansas City, MO Vincentian Parish Mission Center.
Gienko, Marion *c.r.* '48 (CHI) [D] Chicago, IL Gordon Technical High School.
Gier, Thomas P. *s.o.l.t.* '62 (CC) [H] Robstown, TX Society of Our Lady of the Most Holy Trinity.
Gieranowski, William '49 (FTW) Retired.
Giermek, Joachin *o.f.m.conv.* '69 (BAL) [M] Ellicott City, MD Order of Friars Minor Conventual.
Gierut, Casimir '49 (SFD) Retired.
Gierut, Joseph A. '32 (DET) Retired.
Gies, Norman J. '49 (BAL) Retired.
Gies, William *m.s.c.* '53 (ALN) [K] Reading, PA Missionaries of the Sacred Heart.
Giese, Samuel C. '85 (WDC) [2] Silver Spring, MD St. Bernadette Church.
Giese, Vincent J. '65 (CHI) Retired.
Giesen, Cal *o.f.m.* '47 (SFD) [K] Teutopolis, IL St. Francis Assisi Friary.
Giesen, Donald '95 (MAR) Vulcan, MI St. Barbara Church.
Giesing, Msgr. Anthony A. '55 (SD) [29] San Diego, CA St. John the Evangelist Church.
Giesler, Linus T. '41 (L) Retired; [K] Louisville, KY Nazareth Home.
Giesler, Michael E. '79 (STL) [Q] Kirkwood, MO Opus Dei.
Gietl, Joseph A. '73 (GAL) [5] Houston, TX St. Ambrose Church.
Gietzen, Albin J. '56 (GAY) Hannah, MI St. Mary Church.
Gigante, Louis R. '59 (NY) [130] Bronx, NY St. Athanasius Church.
Gigantiello, Jamie J. '95 (BRK) [115] Brooklyn, NY St. Patrick Church.
Giganto, Jose A. *o.s.a.* '65 (SAT) [47] San Antonio, TX St. Jude Church.
Giggi, J. Robert '53 (BO) Natick, MA St. Linus Church.
Giglio, Msgr. Charles J. '58 (CAM) [1] Camden, NJ Immaculate Conception Cathedral.
Giglio, Michael E. '94 (ORL) [5] Orlando, FL Holy Family Church.
Gigliotti, James *t.o.r.* '80 (FWT) [4] Arlington, TX St. Maria Goretti Church.
Gigliotti, Vincent J. '76 (GBG) Brownsville, PA St. Peter Church.
Gignac, Francis T. *s.j.* (DET) [K] Detroit, MI Jesuit Provincial Office-Detroit Province of the Society of Jesus.
Gignac, Francis T. *s.j.* '67 (WDC) [C] Washington, DC Catholic University of America, The; [M] Washington, DC Carroll House.
Gil, Fernando '88 (ORL) Poinciana, FL St. Rose of Lima Church.
Gil, Rudi '78 (SB) On Leave.
Gilardi, Ronald *o.f.m.cap.* '88 (SAL) Catharine, KS St. Catherine's Church; [D] Victoria, KS St. Fidelis Friary; [F] Victoria, KS Capuchin Center for Spiritual Life.
Gilb, Msgr. Eugene A. '57 (LA) Rancho Palos Verdes, CA St. John Fisher Church.
Gilbert, Dennis '71 (MRY) Cambria, CA Santa Rosa Church.
Gilbert, Msgr. Donald J. '68 (MAN) Candia, NH St. Paul Church.
Gilbert, Douglas B. *s.m.a.* '83 (FgM) Society of African Missions.
Gilbert, Douglas B. *s.m.a.* '83 (NEW) [N] Tenafly, NJ Society of African Missions, Provincialate, S.M.A. Fathers.
Gilbert, John R. '56 (STP) Marystown, MN St. Mary of the Purification Church.
Gilbert, Joseph T. '79 (SCR) [18] Wilkes-Barre, PA Sacred Heart of Jesus Church.
Gilbert, Maurice L. '66 (WOR) [2] Southbridge, MA Notre Dame Church.
Gilbert, Philip F. *c.pp.s.* '60 (LFT) [A] Rensselaer, IN Saint Joseph's College.
Gilbert, Valmont R. '57 (PRT) Rockland, ME St. Bernard's Church.
Gilbertson, C. Lee '86 (SPR) [1] Holyoke, MA Blessed Sacrament Church.
Gilbertson, Lee '86 (SPR) [P] Amherst, MA University of Massachusetts and Amherst College, Newman Center.
Gilbo, Robert *c.s.c.* '67 (FgM) Holy Cross Foreign Missions.
Gilbo, Roberto M. *c.s.c.* '67 (FTW) [J] South Bend, IN Congregation of Holy Cross Indiana Province Provincial House.
Gilborges, Tony '89 (CHL) [4] Greensboro, NC St. Paul the Apostle Church.
Gilbride, Thomas '57 (NO) Unassigned.
Gilchrest, Francis J. '45 (ALB) [J] Albany, NY Villa Mary Immaculate.
Gilchrist, Frank '45 (ALB) [4] Albany, NY St. Casimir Church.
Gilchrist, Msgr. John J. '57 (NEW) Harrison, NJ Holy Cross Church.
Gilday, Francis J. *s.j.* '38 (BO) [W] Weston, MA Campion Health Center, Inc.
Gilday, Robert J. '75 (IND) [18] Indianapolis, IN St. Christopher Church.
Gildea, Arthur P. *c.ss.r.* '67 (HBG) Ephrata, PA Mother of Perpetual Help Church; [H] Ephrata, PA St. Clement's Mission House.
Gildea, Joseph J. *o.s.a.* '39 (PH) [AA] Villanova, PA St. Thomas Monastery.
Gildner, Leo H. '53 (PEO) [2] Ottawa, IL St. Francis of Assisi Church.
Gile, Joseph '88 (WCH) [6] Wichita, KS Church of the Resurrection.
Gile, Joseph M. '88 (WCH) [1] Wichita, KS Cathedral of the Immaculate Conception; [I] Wichita, KS Spiritual Life Center.
Giles, Dominic *s.d.s.* '46 (BIR) [2] Huntsville, AL St. Mary of the Visitation Church.
Giles, Gabriel *o.f.m.cap.* '35 (GBG) Export, PA St. Mary Church.
Giles, John H., Jr. '87 (LKC) [8] Lake Charles, LA Our Lady Queen of Heaven Church; [A] Lake Charles, LA St. Louis High School.
Gilette, Randall *c.p.* '71 (HRT) [M] West Hartford, CT Holy Family Monastery/Retreat.
Gilfether, Francis *s.m.a.* '60 (NEW) [N] Tenafly, NJ Society of African Missions, Provincialate, S.M.A. Fathers.
Gilfillan, Msgr. James M. '47 (SD) La Jolla, CA Mary, Star of the Sea Church; Retired.
Gilg, James E. '66 (OM) [48] Douglas Co., NE St. Wenceslaus Church; [B] Omaha, NE V.J. & Angela Skutt Catholic High School of Omaha.
Gilgun, Bernard E. '54 (WOR) Retired.
Gilhooley, James '55 (NY) Absent on Sick leave; [C] Newburgh, NY Mt. St. Mary College; [GG] New York, NY University Apostolate.
Gilhooley, Msgr. John P. '57 (BRK) Military Chaplains.
Giliberti, Francis A. '70 (PH) Media, PA Nativity of the Blessed Virgin Mary Church.
Gill, David H. *s.j.* '67 (BO) [W] Chestnut Hill, MA The Jesuit Community at Boston College.
Gill, Desmond '46 (SP) Inverness, FL Our Lady of Fatima Church; Retired.
Gill, Edward B. '41 (OM) St. Edward, NE St. Edward Church.
Gill, G. Dennis '83 (PH) Graduate Studies.
Gill, James J. *s.j.* (WDC) [V] Washington, DC The Christian Institute for the Study of Human Sexuality; [V] Washington, DC The Jesuit Educational Center for Human Development.
Gill, Joseph *s.j.* '59 (RC) St. Francis, SD Rosebud Reservation Church.
Gill, Joseph C. *s.j.* '59 (RC) Norris, SD Sacred Heart Church; Parmelee, SD St. Agnes Church.
Gill, Michael J. '66 (NOR) Oakdale, CT Our Lady of the Lakes Church.
Gill, Nicolas *c.p.* '40 (SCR) [M] Scranton, PA Saint Ann's Passionist Monastery.
Gill, Paul R. '66 (SB) Loma Linda, CA St. Joseph the Worker Church.
Gill, Richard *l.c.* '91 (WDC) [M] Potomac, MD Legionaries of Christ; [V] Bethesda, MD Alpha Omega, Inc. The Legion of Christ Inc.
Gill, Msgr. Richard J. '56 (BUF) Silver Creek, NY Our Lady of Mt. Carmel Church.
Gill, William J. '55 (RVC) Hampton Bays, NY St. Rosalie's Church.
Gillece, Alfred F. (GAL) Retired.
Gillece, Eugene E. (GAL) [N] Houston, TX Pope John XXIII Priest Residence.
Gilleece, Msgr. Thomas E. '68 (NY) Congers, NY St. Paul Church.
Gillelan, Robert M., Jr. '89 (HBG) Hanover, PA St. Joseph Church.
Gillen, C. H. '85 (BAK) Milton Freewater, OR St. Francis of Assisi Church.
Gillen, Edward B. *s.j.* '51 (NEW) [B] Jersey City, NJ Saint Peter's College; [N] Jersey City, NJ Jesuits of Saint Peter's College, Inc.
Gillen, George D. '71 (NEW) Roselle, NJ Church of St. Joseph the Carpenter.
Gillen, Msgr. James G. '52 (WDC) On Duty Outside the Archdiocese.
Gillen, Msgr. John J. '45 (NY) Retired; [A] Bronx, NY St. John Neumann Residence.
Gillen, Niles J. *o.carm.* '56 (L) [60] Louisville, KY Our Lady of Mount Carmel Church.
Gillen, Paul T. *c.ss.r.* '46 (ORL) [F] New Smyrna Beach, FL St. Alphonsus Villa-Redemptorist Fathers and Brothers.
Gillen, Peter D. '78 (BRK) [236] Queens, NY St. Rose of Lima Church.
Gillen, Timothy L. (PRO) [6] Pawtucket, RI St. Joseph Church.
Gillen, Timothy L. '42 (PRO) Retired.
Giller, Roderic *o.s.b.* '62 (KCK) Seneca, KS SS. Peter and Paul's Church.
Gilles, Charles W. *o.m.i.* '38 (WDC) [B] Washington, DC Oblate College/Oblate Center for Mission Studies.
Gilles, Eugene *s.a.c.* '58 (FAR) Lidgerwood, ND St. Boniface's Church.
Gilles, Richard W. '94 (LC) Graduate Studies.
Gilles, Robert F. '57 (PEO) Minonk, IL St. Patrick's Church.
Gilles, Thomas C. '67 (CLV) Chardon, OH St. Mary Church.
Gillespie, Anthony (FTW) Plymouth, IN St. Michael Church.
Gillespie, Barnabas *o.s.b.* (CIN) [32] Cincinnati, OH Guardian Angels Church.
Gillespie, Barnabas *o.s.b.* '80 (IND) [J] St. Meinrad, IN St. Meinrad Archabbey.
Gillespie, C. Kevin *s.j.* '86 (BAL) [B] Baltimore, MD Loyola College; [M] Baltimore, MD Jesuit Community of Loyola College, Inc.
Gillespie, Edward F. '57 (RCK) [6] Aurora, IL Our Lady of Good Counsel Church.
Gillespie, Francis J. *s.j.* '72 (CHL) [2] Charlotte, NC Our Lady of the Assumption Church; [J] Charlotte, NC Jesuit Community.
Gillespie, Francis T. '59 (ALN) Catasauqua, PA Annunciation B.V.M. - St. Mary's Church.
Gillespie, Jerome F. '82 (BO) [8] Lynn, MA Sacred Heart Church.
Gillespie, John D. '72 (STA) [4] Gainesville, FL St. Augustine Church; [L] Gainesville, FL University of Florida-St. Augustine Parish and Student Center.
Gillespie, Msgr. John E. '53 (PH) [114] Philadelphia, PA Our Lady of Calvary Church.
Gillespie, John L. '95 (R) Elizabeth City, NC Holy Family Church.
Gillespie, Joseph '50 (PHX) Sun City, AZ St. Elizabeth Seton Church.
Gillespie, Joseph P. *o.p.* '70 (STL) [B] St. Louis, MO Aquinas Institute of Theology; [P] St. Louis, MO Dominican Community of St. Louis.
Gillespie, Paul G. *o.s.f.s.* '56 (TOL) [C] Toledo, OH St. Francis de Sales High School; [K] Toledo, OH Oblates of St. Francis de Sales.
Gillespie, Robert B. '43 (GR) Retired.
Gillespie, Thomas E. '72 (MAD) Jefferson, WI St. Lawrence Church; [K] Jefferson, WI St. Coletta of Wisconsin, Inc.
Gillespie, Thomas F. '61 (SB) Chino, CA St. Margaret Mary Church.
Gillespie, Thomas M. *o.s.f.s.* '56 (PH) [AA] Philadelphia, PA Oblates of St. Francis De Sales.
Gillespie, Thomas M. '68 (BO) North Reading, MA St. Theresa Church.
Gillespie, Victor *o.s.b.* '56 (LR) Clarksville, AR Holy Redeemer Church; Morrison Bluff, AR SS. Peter and Paul Church.
Gillette, Theodore M. '78 (OG) Black River, NY St. Paul Church.
Gilley, Charles F. *s.j.* '96 (NY) [F] New York, NY Regis High School; [DD] New York, NY St. Ignatius Loyola Residence.
Gillgannon, Francis G. '54 (JC) California, MO Annunciation Church.
Gillgannon, Michael '58 (KC) Mission Duty.
Gillick, Lawrence E. *s.j.* '72 (OM) [K] Omaha, NE Campion House.
Gillig, John '57 (FTW) Retired.
Gillig, Russell F. '36 (TOL) Retired; [J] Tiffin, OH St. Francis Home Inc.
Gilligan, Adrian *o.s.a.* '29 (PH) [AA] Bryn Mawr, PA Augustinians Brothers (O.S.A.).
Gilligan, Adrian *o.s.a.* '68 (PH) Bryn Mawr, PA Our Mother of Good Counsel Church.
Gilligan, James M. *m.m.* '55 (FgM) Maryknoll Foreign Missions.
Gilligan, Michael J. '69 (CHI) Other Assignments.
Gillin, Joseph F. *o.s.a.* '75 (BO) [C] North Andover, MA Merrimack College.
Gillin, Thomas M. *s.j.* '52 (CHR) Aiken, SC St. Gerard's Church.
Gillin, Thomas P. '74 (PH) Absent on Leave; [G] Bryn Mawr, PA Country Day School of the Sacred Heart.
Gillis, David C. '79 (ALN) Shillington, PA St. John Baptist de la Salle Church.
Gillis, Edward F. '46 (BO) Retired.
Gillis, Francis B. *s.m.a.* '52 (BO) [W] Dedham, MA African Mission House.
Gillis, James *c.s.c.* '56 (LA) [S] Ventura, CA Sisters of the Holy Cross.
Gillis, Ralph J. '59 (GB) Argonne, WI St. Mary Church; Crandon, WI St. Joseph Church.
Gillis, Roger S. *s.j.* '78 (SEA) [A] Seattle, WA Seattle University.
Gillis, Ronald '67 (WDC) [T] Washington, DC Opus Dei.
Gillon, James A. *s.j.* '74 (BO) [W] Boston, MA Arrupe House.
Gillooly, Patrick J. '53 (WH) Retired.
Gills, Thomas '86 (BAL) Millersville, MD Our Lady of the Fields Church.
Gillum, William *o.f.m.cap.* '76 (PIT) Rochester, PA St. Cecilia Church; [O] Rochester, PA St. Cecilia Friary.
Gilmartin, Daniel J. (BO) Retired.
Gilmartin, Daniel J. '47 (BO) Bellingham, MA Assumption Church.
Gilmartin, Gregory J. *m.m.* '48 (NY) [DD] Maryknoll,

NY Maryknoll Fathers and Brothers.
Gilmartin, Msgr. John D. '72 (RVC) Wyandanch, NY Our Lady of the Miraculous Medal Church; [H] Hicksville, NY Catholic Charities Central Administration.
Gilmartin, Msgr. John E. '56 (BGP) [5] Stratford, CT Our Lady of Peace Church.
Gilmartin, Paul P. *s.j.* '62 (BO) [A] Weston, MA Pope John XXIII National Seminary; [W] Chestnut Hill, MA The Jesuit Community at Boston College.
Gilmore, Alan *o.c.s.o.* '70 (L) [L] Trappist, KY Abbey of Our Lady of Gethsemani, of the Order of Cistercians of the Strict Observance.
Gilmore, Brendan *o.carm.* '35 (NEW) Englewood, NJ St. Cecilia's Church.
Gilmore, Lawrence *s.d.b.* '84 (FgM) Salesians of Don Bosco Foreign Missions.
Gilmore, Raymond '62 (HEL) Hamilton, MT St. Francis Church.
Gilmore, Ronald M. '69 (WCH) [F] Wichita, KS Catholic Care Center, Inc.
Gilmore, Vincent M. *o.praem.* '90 (ORG) [D] Siverado, CA St. Michael's College Preparatory High School; [H] Silverado, CA Norbertine Fathers of Orange Inc.
Gilmour, James W. *c.ss.r.* '72 (PH) [25] Philadelphia, PA St. Boniface Church.
Gilmour, Robert G. *c.s.c.* '68 (FgM) Holy Cross Foreign Missions.
Gilroy, Gregory *o.f.m.conv.* (MRY) [G] Arroyo Grande, CA St. Joseph Cupertino Province, Provincial Center.
Gilroy, Gregory *o.f.m.conv.* '88 (ORG) [1] Orange, CA Cathedral of the Holy Family.
Gilroy, Robert G. *s.j.* '97 (BO) [W] Boston, MA The Society of Jesus of New England-Provincial Offices.
Gilroy, Robert G. *s.j.* '97 (RC) St. Francis, SD Rosebud Reservation Church.
Gilroy, Thomas *s.m.* '41 (ATL) [C] Atlanta, GA Marist School.
Gilsdorf, Daniel C. '60 (GB) [7] Appleton, WI St. Therese Church.
Gilsdorf, Gordon J. '49 (GB) Special Assignment.
Gilsdorf, Richard W. '56 (GB) Special Assignment.
Gilsenan, John P. '56 (WCH) [3] Wichita, KS Blessed Sacrament Church.
Gilsoul, James M. '86 (GB) [F] Appleton, WI St. Elizabeth Hospital.
Gilvary, Paul J. *s.j.* '51 (PH) [AA] Philadelphia, PA Jesuit Community at St. Joseph's University.
Gilvey, John A. *o.s.f.s.* '79 (CHL) [4] Greensboro, NC St. Paul the Apostle Church; [L] Charlotte, NC Diocesan Office of Campus Ministry.
Gimbrone, Richard J. '85 (BUF) Retired.
Gimeno, Fabian G. '60 (ORL) St. Cloud, FL St. Thomas Aquinas Church.
Gimpl, Carl '55 (P) Salem, OR St. Joseph Church; [P] Portland, OR University of Portland.
Ginart, Arthur J. '66 (NO) [49] New Orleans, LA St. Nicholas Of Myra Church.
Ginchereau, Dolor *s.m.* '38 (BO) [Y] Framingham Centre, MA The Marist House.
Ginel, Robert J. '78 (NY) Ellenville, NY St. Mary and St. Andrew Church.
Ging, Regis B. *m.m.* '66 (FgM) Maryknoll Foreign Missions.
Gingras, Dennis C. '90 (HRT) [1] Bristol, CT St. Ann Church.
Gingras, Jerome R. '78 (ALB) Clinton Heights, NY St. Mary Church.
Gini, John E. *o.f.m.* '63 (MRY) Jolon, CA San Antonio Mission Church.
Gini, John E. '63 (PBL) On Duty Outside the Diocese.
Ginn, Roman *o.c.s.o.* '53 (L) [L] Trappist, KY Abbey of Our Lady of Gethsemani, of the Order of Cistercians of the Strict Observance.
Gins, Paul E. *o.s.m.* '75 (ORG) Fullerton, CA St. Philip Benizi Church.
Gins, Paul M. *o.s.m.* '75 (CHI) [N] Chicago, IL Servite Friars - Eastern Province.
Ginsterblum, John M. *s.j.* '53 (STP) [N] Minneapolis, MN La Storta Jesuit Community.
Ginter, Michael '79 (JOL) Peotone, IL St. Paul the Apostle Church.
Ginther, Benjamin H. '41 (KAL) Retired.
Ginther, Lawrence P. '46 (WIN) Retired.
Ginther, Richard M. '83 (IND) [1] Indianapolis, IN SS. Peter and Paul Cathedral.
Gintoli, Msgr. Blase M. '69 (BGP) [2] Fairfield, CT Assumption Church.
Ginty, Msgr. Thomas M. '85 (HRT) Special and other (Arch)Diocesan Assignment.
Gionet, Urbain J. '51 (WOR) Retired.
Giordani, Msgr. Mark J. '69 (PAT) [1] Paterson, NJ Cathedral of St. John the Baptist; Paterson, NJ Passaic County Jail.
Giordano, John C. '67 (MET) North Plainfield, NJ St. Luke Church.
Giordano, Joseph *c.i.c.m.* '72 (BRK) [36] Brooklyn, NY St. Ephrem's Church.
Giordano, Pasquale T. *s.j.* '72 (FgM) Provinces.
Giorgi, Daniel *o.ss.t.* '41 (VIC) Cuero, TX Our Lady of Guadalupe Church.
Giorono, Stephen *s.t.* (CHI) [A] Mundelein, IL University of St. Mary of the Lake-Mundelein Seminary.
Gipson, Msgr. Robert W. '62 (LA) Downey, CA St. Raymond Church.
Gira, Stephen *c.r.* '77 (STL) Spanish Lake, MO Our Lady of Loretto Church.
Girard, Msgr. Armand '45 (SAL) Retired.
Girard, Charles A. '66 (WDC) [M] Washington, DC Marist Provincial House.
Girard, Cosmas *o.f.m.* '35 (PAT) [M] Ringwood, NJ Holy Name Friary, Inc.
Girard, Peter M. *o.p.* '92 (HRT) [14] New Haven, CT St. Mary's Priory Church.
Girard, Steven P. '74 (BAL) [25] Baltimore, MD St. Clement Church.
Girardeau, Robert A. '93 (SAV) [8] Savannah, GA St. James Church.
Girardin, Peter T. '60 (BO) Military & VA Chaplains.
Girdis, Joseph C. (PIT) [5] Munhall, PA St. Theresa of Lisieux Church.
Girdis, Joseph C. '44 (PIT) Retired.
Girnius, Charles F. *m.m.* '44 (NY) [DD] Maryknoll, NY Maryknoll Fathers and Brothers.
Giroir, Frank J. '81 (NO) Harahan, LA St. Rita Church.
Girolami, Dante L. *o.s.a.* '41 (PH) [AA] Villanova, PA St. Thomas Monastery.
Girone, Joseph D. '83 (NEW) Belleville, NJ St. Peter's Church.
Girone, Joseph F. *o.s.a.* '81 (FgM) Foreign Missions.
Girouard, Robert J. '59 (PRT) Sabbatical.
Giroux, Armand *m.s.* '58 (FR) [J] Attleboro, MA La Salette Shrine.
Giroux, Garry B. '76 (OG) Constable, NY St. Francis of Assisi Church; Trout River, NY St. Bridget Church.
Giroux, Harry E. '76 (OG) Canton, NY St. Thomas More Church.
Giroux, Raymond A. '63 (BUR) South Burlington, VT St. John Vianney Church.
Giroux, Regis '70 (SPR) [6] Holyoke, MA Our Lady of Perpetual Help Church; [9] Holyoke, MA Sacred Heart Church; [M] Holyoke, MA Casa Maria.
Giroux, Richard M. '69 (MAN) Keene, NH St. Margaret Mary Church.
Giroux, Msgr. Robert J. '50 (OG) [2] Ogdensburg, NY Notre Dame Church; Retired.
Giroux, William P. '80 (BUR) Essex Center, VT St. Pius X Church.
Girres, Edward M. '79 (SC) [1] Sioux City, IA Cathedral of the Epiphany.
Girse, Milton *c.ss.r.* '40 (CHI) [136] Chicago, IL St. Michael Church.
Girzone, Joseph '55 (ALB) Retired.
Gits, Douglas J. '53 (WIN) Retired.
Gitter, Aloysius A. '28 (GB) Retired.
Gitter, Aloysius A. '28 (SAT) Retired.
Gitter, Paul R. '93 (LC) Augusta, WI St. Anthony de Padua Church; Brackett, WI Holy Guardian Angels Church; Fall Creek, WI St. John the Apostle Church.
Gittins, Anthony *c.s.sp.* '67 (CHI) [B] Chicago, IL The Catholic Theological Union at Chicago.
Gittins, Gordon '68 (DM) Harlan, IA St. Michael Church.
Gitzen, Blase *o.f.m.cap.* '46 (DET) [K] Detroit, MI St. Bonaventure Friary.
Gitzen, Patrick *o.m.i.* '75 (FgM) Oblates Foreign Missions.
Gitzen, Patrick *o.m.i.* '75 (SAT) [F] San Antonio, TX St. Anthony Catholic High School; [M] San Antonio, TX St. Anthony Catholic High School House.
Giudice, Anthony *o.f.m.cap.* (CAM) Villas, NJ St. Raymond Church.
Giudice, Francis J. '56 (PRO) [1] Providence, RI Cathedral of SS. Peter and Paul.
Giuffre, Frank A. '97 (PH) [70] Philadelphia, PA Immaculate Heart of Mary Church.
Giuliani, John B. '60 (BGP) [N] West Redding, CT The Benedictine Grange.
Giuliani, John P. *c.o.* '80 (CHR) Rock Hill, SC St. Anne's Church; [D] Rock Hill, SC Oratory of St. Philip Neri, Congregation of the Oratory of Pontifical Rite.
Giuliano, Anthony J. '84 (NY) [140] Bronx, NY St. Francis of Assisi Church.
Giuliano, Carmen *s.a.* '61 (NY) [14] Yonkers, NY Our Lady of the Rosary Church.
Giuliano, Carmen *s.a.* '61 (WDC) [B] Washington, DC Atonement Seminary-Franciscan Friars of the Atonement.
Giuliano, Louis A. '44 (BRK) Retired.
Giuliano, Steven B. '80 (WIL) Elsmere, DE Corpus Christi Church.
Giulietti, Julio *s.j.* '72 (BO) [W] Boston, MA The Society of Jesus of New England-Provincial Offices.
Giulietti, Julio *s.j.* '72 (WDC) [M] Washington, DC The Jesuit Community at Georgetown University.
Giunta, S. C. '54 (JOL) Wilton Center, IL St. Patrick Church.
Giuntini, Robert '76 (RVC) Bay Shore, NY St. Patrick's Church.
Giusani, Augustine H. '47 (HRT) [1] New Britain, CT All Saints Church; [5] New Britain, CT St. Ann Church.
Giusta, Frank '63 (ATL) [7] Atlanta, GA Our Lady of Lourdes Church.
Givey, David W. '71 (PH) Milmont Park, PA Our Lady of Peace Church.
Glab, Joseph *c.r.* '75 (CHI) [D] Chicago, IL Gordon Technical High School.
Glab, Stephen *c.r.* '82 (CHI) [N] Chicago, IL Provincial Office of the Congregation of the Resurrection.
Glackin, Thomas J. '68 (VEN) [2] Naples, FL St. John the Evangelist Church.
Glade, Albert G. *o.p.* '72 (STL) [B] St. Louis, MO Aquinas Institute of Theology; [P] St. Louis, MO St. Dominic Priory.
Gladstone, James J. *s.j.* '66 (OM) [K] Omaha, NE Jesuit Community At Creighton University; [K] Omaha, NE Jesuit Community At Creighton University.
Glahn, Carl '52 (OWN) Retired.
Glancy, Alfred '55 (NY) [3] Kingston, NY St. Joseph Church.
Glancy, Christopher J. *c.s.v.* '93 (CHI) [N] Arlington Heights, IL Viatorian Province Center-Clerics of St. Viator.
Glancy, Joseph *t.o.r.* '59 (SFS) Wagner, SD St. John the Baptist Church.
Glanzmann, Edward J. *o.s.b.* (CHI) [J] Blue Island, IL St. Francis Hospital and Health Center.
Glanzmann, Edward J. *o.s.b.* '79 (CHI) [N] Chicago, IL Monastery of the Holy Cross.
Glapiak, Edward '61 (WIL) Newark, DE Christiana Care Health System; Special or Other Diocesan Assignment.
Glaser, Lawrence A. *o.c.s.o.* '58 (SAC) [A] Vina, CA Abbey of New Clairvaux, Trappist Seminary; [G] Vina, CA Abbey of New Clairvaux, Trappist.
Glasgow, Dennis T. *s.j.* '84 (CLV) University Heights, OH Gesu Church.
Glasgow, Mark W. '62 (PIT) [2] Munhall, PA St. Maximilian Kolbe Church; Allegheny County, PA Department of Veterans Affairs Medical Center Oakland.
Glasgow, Robert K. '85 (MAN) Military Chaplains.
Glasgow, Thomas G. '69 (NO) [27] New Orleans, LA St. Brigid Church.
Glasnovic, Serafin '45 (ALX) Retired.
Glass, Gerald J. '56 (PHX) Retired.
Glass, Robert H. *c.s.b.* '74 (OAK) [C] Oakland, CA Bishop O'Dowd High School.
Glass, Rolland T. '43 (MIL) Retired.
Glass, Senan *o.f.m.cap.* '57 (CLV) [31] Cleveland, OH Holy Trinity - St. Edward Church; [P] Cleveland, OH St. Paul Friary.
Glass, Senan *o.f.m.cap.* '66 (CLV) [18] Cleveland, OH Conversion of St. Paul Church.
Glassman, Douglas R. *o.f.m.* '89 (NY) [DD] New York, NY Franciscan Friars, Order of Friars Minor, Holy Name Province.
Glassmire, David R. '94 (BUF) Lancaster, NY St. Mary of the Assumption Church.
Glastetter, Donald A. '65 (STL) Wentzville, MO St. Patrick Church.
Glatt, Eugene '59 (SPK) Oakesdale, WA St. Catherine of Alexandria Church; Rosalia, WA Holy Rosary Church; St. John, WA Our Lady of Perpetual Help Church; Tekoa, WA Sacred Heart Church.
Glatts, Joseph M. '66 (PH) Military Chaplains.
Glaub, Eugene *o.m.i.* '55 (BEL) [F] Belleville, IL Missionary Oblates of Mary Immaculate - St. Henry's Oblate Residence.
Glaves, John J. '56 (LIN) Exeter, NE St. Stephen's Church.
Glavin, Joseph A. *s.j.* '48 (BO) [W] Chestnut Hill, MA The Jesuit Community at Boston College.
Glavin, Leonard *o.f.m.cap.* '54 (NY) [57] New York, NY St. John the Baptist Church.
Glavin, Patrick *o.f.m.cap.* '59 (PRT) [3] Portland, ME St. Joseph's Church; Portland, ME Maine Medical Center; [M] Portland, ME Westbrook College.
Glavina, Carmelo '54 (NY) Dobbs Ferry, NY Our Lady of Pompeii Church.
Gleason, Carl *s.d.s.* '56 (FgM) Salvatorian Foreign Missions.
Gleason, Jack A. '95 (TLS) [11] Tulsa, OK Church of St. Mary.
Gleason, James '50 (STL) [P] Liguori, MO Liguori Mission House/Redemptorists.
Gleason, James '67 (LA) Palmdale, CA St. Mary Church.
Gleason, John L. '46 (NU) Retired.
Gleason, Joseph F. '87 (PH) [19] Philadelphia, PA St. Barbara Church; [D] Philadelphia, PA Roman Catholic High School for Boys.
Gleason, Laurence J. '96 (PH) [126] Philadelphia, PA Our Lady of Ransom Church.
Gleason, Msgr. Paul D. '47 (PRT) Retired.
Gleason, Terence *c.o.* '80 (BRK) [22] Brooklyn, NY St. Boniface Church.
Gleason, William J. *s.j.* '36 (NY) [DD] New York, NY Murray-Weigel Hall.
Gleba, Peter W. '53 (SY) [9] Syracuse, NY Sacred Heart Church; [22] Syracuse, NY St. Stephen Church.
Glebe, Edward *c.ss.r.* '57 (GAL) [34] Houston, TX Holy

Ghost Church.
Gleeson, Donald P. '97 (NEW) Montclair, NJ Immaculate Conception Church.
Gleeson, Edward D. '69 (CHI) Other Assignments.
Gleeson, Emmet *o.carm.* '44 (JOL) [J] Joliet, IL St. Elias Carmelites.
Gleeson, Joseph '65 (BRK) Queens, NY Veterans Affairs Extended Care Center, St. Albans, NY.
Gleeson, Michael '75 (LA) San Gabriel, CA St. Anthony Church.
Gleeson, Patrick '52 (JOL) [I] Joliet, IL Our Lady of Angels Retirement Home.
Gleeson, Stephen J. '63 (BGP) [3] Trumbull, CT St. Stephen Church.
Gleeson, Terence P. *c.o.* '80 (BRK) [U] Brooklyn, NY Oratory of Saint Philip Neri, Congregation Pontifical Rite.
Gleeson, Thomas F. *s.j.* '68 (WDC) [M] Washington, DC Leonard Neale House.
Gleeson, William T. '66 (PBL) Capulin, CO St. Joseph Church.
Gleixner, Joseph *m.s.c.* '65 (FgM) Missionaries of the Sacred Heart Foreign Missions.
Gleixner, Joseph *m.s.c.* '65 (RCK) [H] Aurora, IL Missionaries of the Sacred Heart Community.
Glenn, Msgr. Francis A. '38 (PIT) [26] Pittsburgh, PA St. Mary of Mercy Church; Retired.
Glenn, Michael '90 (DEN) Wheat Ridge, CO SS. Peter and Paul Church.
Glennon, James G. *o.s.a.* '52 (MIA) Dania, FL Church of the Resurrection.
Glennon, Thomas G. *s.s.c.* '79 (CHI) [N] Chicago, IL Columban Fathers Mission Center.
Glennon, William P. '54 (PAT) Morristown, NJ Assumption of the Blessed Virgin Mary Church.
Glentzer, Harold M. *o.s.b.* '35 (PBL) [F] Canon City, CO Holy Cross Abbey.
Glepko, Robert J. '76 (CLV) Cleveland Heights, OH St. Ann Church.
Gliatta, Ronald *o.f.m.* '77 (HRT) [15] Waterbury, CT St. Michael Church.
Glick, George W. '63 (BAL) Hancock, MD St. Peter's Church.
Glimm, Msgr. Francis X. '35 (RVC) Retired.
Glinkowski, Raphael *o.s.p.p.e.* '62 (GBG) Kittanning, PA Armstrong County Hospital.
Glinkowski, Raphael K. *o.s.p.p.e.* '62 (GBG) [H] Kittanning, PA Pauline Fathers Monastery.
Glisson, Nicholas J. '79 (STA) Graduate Studies.
Glockner, David *glmy.* '66 (CIN) Manchester, OH St. Mary Church; Peebles, OH St. Mary Queen of Heaven Church; West Union, OH Holy Trinity Church.
Glogowski, John F. '71 (SFR) Daly City, CA Our Lady of Mercy Church.
Glogowski, John J. '62 (ROC) Hilton, NY St. Leo Church.
Gloisten, Robert '54 (RIC) [1] Virginia Beach, VA Church of the Ascension.
Gloninger, Hugh M. '56 (PIT) [3] Butler, PA St. Paul Church; Butler County, PA Butler County Jail.
Gloria de la Inmaculada, Alberto Jesus *s.e.m.v.* '94 (ARE) Hatillo, PR Our Lady of Guadalupe Church.
Glorie, Msgr. John W. '60 (MIA) [4] Pompano Beach, FL St. Elizabeth of Hungary Catholic Church.
Glorioso, Charles '95 (SHP) [1] Shreveport, LA St. John Berchmans Cathedral.
Glosser, William F. '84 (ALN) Schuylkill Haven, PA St. Ambrose Church; [M] Orwigsburg, PA St. Francis Center.
Gloudeman, Francis M. *o.praem.* '91 (ORG) [H] Silverado, CA Norbertine Fathers of Orange Inc.
Gloudeman, Robert J. '64 (MIL) Wauwatosa, WI Froedtert Memorial Lutheran Hospital.
Glover, Donald F. *m.m.* '70 (FgM) Maryknoll Foreign Missions.
Glover, Francis N. *s.j.* '58 (FgM) Provinces.
Glover, George *o.s.b.* '88 (RCK) [H] Aurora, IL Marmion Abbey-St. Augustine's Abbey.
Glovik, Karl L. '61 (DUB) [1] Cedar Rapids, IA Immaculate Conception Church; [8] Cedar Rapids, IA St. Wenceslaus Church.
Gluc, Vincent *o.f.m.conv.* '79 (BAL) [20] Baltimore, MD St. Casimir Church.
Glueckert, Leopold *o.carm.* '68 (JOL) [J] Joliet, IL St. Elias Carmelites.
Gluszek, Msgr. Joseph '35 (GF) [2] Great Falls, MT Eastside Catholic Communities Church; Retired.
Glynn, Edward *s.j.* (BO) [W] Cambridge, MA Weston Jesuit Community.
Glynn, Msgr. Francis J. '37 (NY) [205] Staten Island, NY Holy Family Church; Retired.
Glynn, Francis M. '51 (WIN) Retired.
Glynn, Francis M. '70 (BO) [1] Lowell, MA St. Anthony Church.
Glynn, Msgr. Gerard N. '41 (STL) Retired.
Glynn, John F. *o.s.a.* '39 (LA) [F] Ojai, CA Villanova Preparatory School.
Glynn, John P. '48 (PH) Retired.
Glynn, Martin G. '78 (PAT) Franklin, NJ Immaculate Conception Church.
Glynn, Msgr. Michael '46 (JKS) [3] Jackson, MS St. Richard Church; Retired.
Glynn, Seamus A. '58 (ORG) [4] Anaheim, CA San Antonio Church.
Glynn, Thomas J. '54 (LA) San Pedro, CA Holy Trinity Church.
Glynn, Thomas L. '64 (STN) [2] Chicago, IL St. Joseph Church.
Glynn, Msgr. William F. '47 (BO) Duxbury, MA Holy Family Church.
Gmache, Barry J. (PRO) [S] Bristol, RI Roger Williams University.
Gmerek, Ronald E. '71 (E) [B] Erie, PA Gannon University.
Gnall, Julian M. *o.s.b.* '55 (PBR) Retired.
Gnarackatt, Joseph '67 (TR) [10] Trenton, NJ Our Lady of Sorrows Church.
Gnat, Zdzislaw '88 (DET) [1] Roseville, MI St. Angela Church.
Gniewyk, Eugene G. '90 (NEW) Upper Montclair, NJ St. Cassian Church.
Gnirk, Lloyd A. '78 (OM) [38] Omaha, NE St. Pius X Church.
Gobitas, Msgr. Gerald '75 (ALN) [3] Easton, PA St. Jane Frances de Chantal Church.
Goblirsch, Robert P. '60 (NU) Dawson, MN St. James Church; Madison, MN St. Michael Church.
Goce, Lauro '37 (SD) Retired.
Goda, Paul J. *s.j.* '66 (SJ) [B] Santa Clara, CA Santa Clara University.
Godecker, Jeffery H. '69 (IND) [9] Indianapolis, IN Immaculate Heart of Mary Church.
Godenciuc, Vasile '81 (STF) Rochester, NY Epiphany of Our Lord Church.
Godfrey, Joseph J. *s.j.* '69 (PH) [C] Philadelphia, PA St. Joseph's University; [AA] Philadelphia, PA Jesuit Community at St. Joseph's University.
Godfrey, Kevin *o.f.m.conv.* '84 (IND) [I] Mount Saint Francis, IN Mount Saint Francis Friary and Retreat Center.
Godfrey, Timothy S. *s.j.* '85 (STL) [P] St. Louis, MO Bellarmine House of Studies.
Godic, Frank G. '73 (CLV) [42] Cleveland, OH St. Lawrence Church.
Godin, James M. '79 (MIL) Whitewater, WI St. Patrick Church; [X] Milwaukee, WI Milwaukee Archdiocesan Campus Ministry.
Godin, Norman J. '73 (PRO) [3] Providence, RI St. Agnes Church.
Godley, Msgr. James '40 (CHY) Retired.
Godley, Patrick '53 (SEA) Bainbridge Island, WA St. Cecilia's Church.
Goebel, Bernard M. '29 (SAT) Retired; [N] San Antonio, TX Our Lady of Czestochowa.
Goebel, Joseph A. '50 (CLV) Twinsburg, OH SS. Cosmas and Damian Church; Retired.
Goebel, Nicholas L. (MIL) Retired.
Goebel, Nicholas L. '58 (MIL) [Q] Campbellsport, WI St. Joseph Convent.
Goebel, Robert A. *s.j.* '63 (SPK) [E] Spokane, WA Gonzaga Preparatory School.
Goebel, Robert W. '74 (CIN) [81] Cincinnati, OH St. Saviour Church.
Goeckner, Jeffrey W. '95 (SFD) [2] Decatur, IL Our Lady of Lourdes Church.
Goedde, Bernard C., Jr. '72 (BEL) Millstadt, IL St. James Church.
Goedert, Robert A. *o.p.* '51 (CHI) [N] Chicago, IL Dominicans (Provincial Office).
Goedert, William O. '55 (CHI) [3] Oak Lawn, IL St. Germaine Church; Retired.
Goedken, James J. '66 (DUB) Key West, IA St. Joseph's Church.
Goedken, Nestor B. '43 (DUB) Retired.
Goehring, Raymond '64 (LAN) [4] Lansing, MI Immaculate Heart of Mary Church.
Goeke, James F. *s.j.* '88 (KC) [12] Kansas City, MO St. Francis Xavier Church.
Goeke, John W. '59 (COV) Leave of Absence.
Goekler, Thomas F. *m.m.* '67 (FgM) Maryknoll Foreign Missions.
Goekler, Thomas F. '67 (HRT) On Duty Outside the Archdiocese.
Goellner, Glennon '50 (STL) [6] Florissant, MO St. Ferdinand Church.
Goentges, Charles J. '40 (DET) Retired.
Goergan, Michael A. '62 (CHI) [186] Chicago, IL St. Robert Bellarmine Church.
Goergen, David J. *m.afr.* '69 (WDC) [M] Washington, DC Missionaries of Africa.
Goergen, Donald *o.p.* '75 (STL) [B] St. Louis, MO Aquinas Institute of Theology.
Goerner, Basil S. (MAR) Retired.
Goerner, James E. '93 (PH) Horsham, PA St. Catherine of Siena Church.
Goertz, Msgr. Alois J. '48 (SAT) Retired; [K] San Antonio, TX Casa De Padres.
Goertz, Bernard C. '52 (AUS) [10] Austin, TX Santa Barbara Church; Special Assignments.
Goertz, Howard '77 (AUS) Kyle, TX St. Anthony Marie De Claret Church; Stony Point, TX Blessed Juan Diego Church.
Goertz, Victor '52 (AUS) Special Assignments.
Goethals, Gregory M. *s.j.* '88 (SFR) [E] San Francisco, CA St. Ignatius College Preparatory (Coed); [N] San Francisco, CA Jesuit Community at St. Ignatius College Preparatory.
Goettemoeller, Leonard *c.pp.s.* '49 (KC) [J] Liberty, MO Precious Blood Center.
Goetz, Donald R. '68 (L) [17] Louisville, KY St. Brigid Church; [40] Louisville, KY St. James Church.
Goetz, Donatus *o.f.m.cap.* '45 (NY) [DD] Yonkers, NY St. Clare Friary.
Goetz, Gerald E. *s.j.* '73 (STP) [Q] Lake Elmo, MN Jesuit Retreat House.
Goetz, J. Raymond '81 (OWN) [I] Murray, KY Murray State University Newman House.
Goetz, Joseph W. '60 (CIN) Yellow Springs, OH St. Paul Church; [Q] Yellow Springs, OH Antioch College Campus Ministry.
Goetz, Martin G. '92 (DAV) Clinton, IA Jesus Christ, Prince of Peace Church.
Goetz, Ray '81 (OWN) Murray, KY St. Leo Church.
Goff, William P. *c.m.* '66 (BAL) Emmitsburg, MD St. Joseph Church; [M] Emmitsburg, MD Vincentian House.
Gogel, Odo *o.s.b.* '50 (SFS) [F] Marvin, SD Blue Cloud Abbey.
Goggin, Cornelius J. '56 (MAN) Bedford, NH St. Elizabeth Seton Church.
Goggin, Gerald *c.s.s.* '46 (BO) [Z] Waltham, MA Stigmatine Fathers and Brothers.
Goggin, John T. '64 (NU) On Duty Outside the Diocese.
Goggin, Msgr. Leo J. '39 (RVC) Dix Hills, NY St. Matthew Church; Retired.
Goggin, Thomas J. '57 (VEN) Fort Myers Beach, FL Ascension Church.
Goggins, James K. '94 (DEN) [1] Denver, CO Cathedral of the Immaculate Conception.
Goguen, Francis T. '66 (WOR) [3] Leominster, MA St. Cecilia's Church.
Gohm, Robert S. '75 (SAG) Hemlock, MI St. Mary Church.
Gohmann, Myron *c.p.* '55 (CHI) [N] Chicago, IL Immaculate Conception Monastery.
Gohring, William '84 (ORL) De Land, FL St. Peter's Church.
Goiburu, Ignacio *c.p.* '43 (ARE) Lares, PR St. Joseph Church.
Goicoechea, Greg *o.f.m.* (FWT) [5] Fort Worth, TX Immaculate Heart of Mary Church.
Goicoechea, Javier *sch.p.* '54 (SJN) [58] San Juan, PR Santisimo Salvador Church.
Going, Joseph G. *o.p.* '49 (PT) [9] Pensacola, FL St. John the Evangelist Church.
Goins, James A. '92 (OKL) [12] Oklahoma City, OK St. James Church.
Gojuk, Peter P. *o.m.v.* '81 (BO) [B] Boston, MA Our Lady of Grace Seminary.
Golas, Eugene S. '55 (GR) On Special Assignment.
Golas, John S. '81 (HRT) [1] Manchester, CT Assumption Church.
Golasinski, Donald J. '62 (BEA) Groves, TX Immaculate Conception Church.
Golasinski, Msgr. James L. '58 (GAL) [9] Houston, TX Annunciation Church.
Gold, William F. '65 (SD) Oceanside, CA St. Margaret Church.
Goldasich, Mark '81 (KCK) Tonganoxie, KS Sacred Heart Church.
Goldbach, Edmund *o.f.m.conv.* '64 (GR) [4] Grand Rapids, MI St. Anthony of Padua Church.
Goldbach, Peter D. *c.m.* '44 (BRK) [U] Jamaica, NY Vincentian Residence.
Goldberg, James M. '76 (GBG) Lucernemines, PA St. Louis Church.
Golden, Edward '61 (ROC) Fairport, NY Assumption of the Blessed Virgin Mary Church.
Golden, Frank *s.j.* '71 (SJN) [22] San Juan, PR San Ignacio de Loyola Church.
Golden, George E. '76 (WDC) Forestville, MD Mt. Calvary Church.
Golden, James '48 (DUL) Retired.
Golden, Patrick '96 (RIC) Williamsburg, VA St. Bede's Church.
Golden, Paul L. *c.m.* '65 (BUF) [C] Niagara University, NY Niagara University; [O] Niagara University, NY Vincentian Community at Niagara University.
Golden, Paul L. *c.m.* '65 (CHI) [N] Chicago, IL Vincentian Community, Congregation of the Mission, Midwest Province.
Golden, R. Thomas '63 (GB) Menasha, WI St. John Church.
Golden, Thomas P. *m.m.* '51 (FgM) Maryknoll Foreign Missions.
Goldian, Edward R. *s.j.* '69 (STL) [41] St. Louis, MO St. John the Baptist Church.
Goldikovskis, Msgr. Alexander I. '41 (CLV) [39] Cleveland, OH St. Josaphat Church; Retired.
Golding, Edward '88 (ALB) Summit, NY St. Anna Church; [S] Cobleskill, NY State University of New

York College of Agricultural & Technology at Cobleskill.
Goldrick, Timothy J. '72 (FR) Assonet, MA St. Bernard's Church.
Gole, Joseph '43 (MIL) [B] Hales Corners, WI Sacred Heart School of Theology; [P] Hales Corners, WI Sacred Heart Monastery.
Golemba, Msgr. Roman '75 (STF) Fall River, MA St. John-the-Baptist Church; Woonsocket, RI St. Michael Church.
Golias, Andrew J. '70 (PH) [A] Wynnewood, PA Theological Seminary of St. Charles Borromeo, Overbrook.
Golik, Stanislaus '39 (OM) [46] Omaha, NE St. Thomas More Church; Retired.
Golini, Ronald '68 (NTN) Leave of Absence.
Golino, Arthur A. '80 (NY) [229] Staten Island, NY St. Sylvester Church.
Golka, James R. '94 (GI) Kearney, NE St. James Church.
Gollatz, Ronald J. '72 (CHI) Lake Zurich, IL St. Francis de Sales Church.
Gollinge, Donald '58 (NY) Absent on Leave.
Gollob, Timothy A. '58 (DAL) [5] Dallas, TX Holy Cross Church; Dallas, TX Veterans Administration Hospital.
Golobich, John '48 (DUL) Retired.
Golombek, Msgr. Robert K. '65 (BUF) [2] Kenmore, NY Blessed Sacrament Church.
Goltz, William '50 (DUB) Unassigned.
Golueke, Thomas J. '77 (BAL) [84] Baltimore, MD St. Pius X Church.
Goman, Ralph J. '64 (STP) Hopkins, MN St. John the Evangelist Church.
Gomes, Benjamin '69 (BRK) [58] Brooklyn, NY Holy Name Church.
Gomes, Herman *ss.cc.* (HON) [H] Kaneohe, HI Sacred Hearts Center.
Gomes, Herman *ss.cc.* '78 (HON) [B] Honolulu, HI Chaminade University of Honolulu.
Gomes, Ignatius *s.f.x.* '70 (LR) [E] Little Rock, AR St. Vincent Infirmary Medical Center.
Gomes, John (CHI) [J] Chicago, IL St. Joseph Hospital.
Gomes, John A. '69 (FR) [3] Taunton, MA Our Lady of Lourdes Church.
Gomes, John Stanley '95 (NEW) [4] Elizabeth, NJ Blessed Sacrament Church.
Gomes, Martin *ss.cc.* '69 (FR) [J] Fairhaven, MA Sacred Hearts Provincial House.
Gomes, Martin *ss.cc.* '69 (WDC) Seat Pleasant, MD St. Margaret Church.
Gomes, Robert (CAM) On Duty Outside the Diocese.
Gomes, Ronald A. (BO) Absent on Leave.
Gomes, William '69 (RVC) Point Lookout, NY Our Lady of the Miraculous Medal Church.
Gomes-Kelly, John R. '62 (SD) Unassigned.
Gomez, Msgr. Antonio '51 (SJN) [13] San Juan, PR Cristo Rey Church.
Gomez, Arturo S. *c.m.f.* '80 (FRS) [8] Fresno, CA St. Anthony Claret Church.
Gomez, Daniel *o.f.m.cap.* '61 (FgM) Capuchin Foreign Missions.
Gomez, Daniel A. '84 (MET) Iselin, NJ St. Cecelia Church.
Gomez, Dario (BGP) [10] Stamford, CT St. Mary's Church.
Gomez, Edmund '93 (SB) [4] San Bernardino, CA Our Lady of Fatima Church; [8] San Bernardino, CA St. Bernardine Church.
Gomez, Edmundo '69 (NY) [145] Bronx, NY St. Helena Church.
Gomez, Emerito *o.f.m.* '82 (FRS) Delano, CA Our Lady of Guadalupe Church.
Gomez, Enrique '77 (CGS) Naranjito, PR San Miguel Arcangel Church.
Gomez, Eusebio *o.c.d.* '70 (MIA) [L] Miami, FL Discalced Carmelite Friars of Miami, Inc.
Gomez, Francisco (SJN) [23] Bayamon, PR Santa Maria Church.
Gomez, Francisco '50 (SLC) [2] Kearns, UT St. Francis Xavier Church; [C] Kearns, UT St. Francis Xavier Regional School.
Gomez, Francisco *o.f.m.conv.* '76 (STP) [Q] Prior Lake, MN Franciscan Retreat House.
Gomez, Francisco *s.t.* '83 (FgM) Trinity Missions.
Gomez, Frank '61 (BWN) Retired.
Gomez, Msgr. Henry '58 (LA) Bell Gardens, CA St. Gertrude Church.
Gomez, Jose '78 (GAL) [P] Houston, TX Opus Dei.
Gomez, Jose '78 (SAT) [R] San Antonio, TX Opus Dei (Prelature of the Holy Cross and Opus Dei).
Gomez, Jose '95 (AMA) Clarendon, TX St. Mary's Church; Memphis, TX Sacred Heart Church.
Gomez, Msgr. Jose A. '58 (ELP) [37] El Paso, TX San Juan Bautista Church.
Gomez, Jose H. '72 (GAL) [U] Houston, TX Asociacion Nacional de Sacerdotes Hispanos.
Gomez, Jose L. *s.d.b.* '61 (ARE) Orocovis, PR San Juan Bautista Church.
Gomez, Msgr. Leo '63 (GLP) [1] Gallup, NM Cathedral of the Sacred Heart.
Gomez, Lorenzo (DET) [T] Bloomfield Hills, MI The Legion of Christ, Inc.; [T] Bloomfield Hills, MI Opdyke, Inc.; [T] Bloomfield Hills, MI Logos, Inc. (Michigan).
Gomez, Miguel '81 (MIA) [6] Miami, FL Good Shepherd Church.
Gomez, Orlando De Jesus '86 (CGS) [7] Caguas, PR El Salvador Church.
Gomez, Ramon J. '85 (OAK) Union City, CA St. Anne Church.
Gomez, Raul *s.d.s.* '87 (MIL) [B] Hales Corners, WI Sacred Heart School of Theology.
Gomez, Rene J. '63 (SFR) San Bruno, CA St. Bruno Church.
Gomez, Walter (ARE) On Duty Outside the Diocese.
Gomez, Walter *o.f.m.* '80 (OAK) [A] Berkeley, CA Franciscan School of Theology Student Residence.
Gomide, Tomaz '71 (RVC) Mineola, NY Corpus Christi Church.
Gomolski, Joseph T. '81 (ORL) Haines City, FL St. Ann Church.
Gomolski, Joseph T. '81 (WIL) Retired.
Gomulka, Eugene T. '74 (ALT) Military Chaplains.
Gomulka, Henry J. '42 (GB) Retired.
Gonda, Andrew (GI) Retired.
Gonda, Gerard *o.s.b.* '80 (CLV) [E] Cleveland, OH Benedictine High School; [P] Cleveland, OH Benedictine Order of Cleveland.
Gondek, Albert *o.s.f.s.* '66 (R) Whiteville, NC Sacred Heart Church.
Gondek, Joseph A. '37 (MAR) Retired.
Gonder, David *s.d.b.* '81 (NY) [DD] New Rochelle, NY Salesian Provincial House.
Gonderinger, Gerald E. '74 (OM) [44] Omaha, NE St. Stephen the Martyr Church.
Gondra, Tomas '58 (SJN) [52] San Juan, PR Resurreccion del Senor Church.
Gonet, Charles F. '58 (SPR) [14] Springfield, MA St. Catherine of Siena Church.
Gongora, Luis '65 (DAL) [7] Dallas, TX Mary Immaculate Church.
Goni, Joachim *o.a.r.* '40 (ORG) [5] Santa Ana, CA Our Lady of the Pillar Church.
Goni, Paul *o.a.r.* '51 (LA) [4] Oxnard, CA Mary Star of the Sea Church.
Gonia, Raymond L. '90 (SUP) Military Chaplains.
Gonnelly, Theophane *o.s.b.* '47 (SFS) [F] Marvin, SD Blue Cloud Abbey.
Gonsalves, Lino S. (RVC) Manorhaven, NY Our Lady of Fatima Church.
Gonsalves, Valerian *o.s.b.* (DUB) [1] Cedar Rapids, IA Immaculate Conception Church.
Gonser, Richard A. '62 (CLV) North Ridgeville, OH St. Julie Billiart Church.
Gonsorcik, Joseph S. '38 (MET) Retired.
Gonsorcik, Pat *s.c.j.* '70 (MIL) [P] Hales Corners, WI Priests of the Sacred Heart.
Gonter, Louis J. '49 (BUF) Retired.
Gonter, Louis J. '49 (ORL) Lady Lake, FL St. Timothy Church; Retired.
Gonthier, Armand *m.s.* '40 (FR) [J] Attleboro, MA La Salette Shrine.
Gonyo, Lance M. '93 (ROC) [52] Rochester, NY St. Pius Tenth Church.
Gonyo, Roland G. '73 (OG) Absent on Sick Leave.
Gonzales, Antonio (FRS) Retired.
Gonzales, Emilio '88 (SEA) Unassigned.
Gonzales, Gabriel '39 (NO) Retired.
Gonzales, Gabriel '84 (LA) [36] Los Angeles, CA Sacred Heart Church.
Gonzales, George '79 (ORG) Absent on Sick Leave.
Gonzales, Hily *c.s.* '96 (LA) Sun Valley, CA Our Lady of the Holy Rosary Church.
Gonzales, Ignacio (BWN) [1] Harlingen, TX Our Lady of the Assumption Church.
Gonzales, Juan J. *s.m.* '82 (DET) [D] Pontiac, MI Notre Dame Preparatory High School and Marist Academy.
Gonzales, Loreto '78 (LA) Artesia, CA Holy Family Church; [DD] Los Angeles, CA Filipino Pastoral Ministry.
Gonzales, Orestes '86 (NY) [II] New Rochelle, NY Opus Dei (Prelature of the Holy Cross and Opus Dei).
Gonzales, Robert A. '78 (COL) [A] Columbus, OH Pontifical College Josephinum.
Gonzales, Robert A. '78 (TUC) On Duty Outside the Diocese.
Gonzales, Roberto Solivan '81 (CGS) [9] Barrio Rio Canas, PR San Pablo Apostol Church.
Gonzalez, Angel *s.p.* '52 (FRS) Reedley, CA St. Anthony Church.
Gonzalez, Anthoney '92 (LA) [5] Los Angeles, CA Assumption Church.
Gonzalez, Msgr. Antonio '62 (LUB) [2] Lubbock, TX Our Lady of Grace Church; Shallowater, TX St. Phillip Benizi Church; [A] Lubbock, TX Christian Renewal Center.
Gonzalez, Aquilino D. *o.s.a.* '72 (FgM) Foreign Missions.
Gonzalez, Arnold *c.m.f.* '58 (LA) [20] Los Angeles, CA Our Lady of Solitude Church.
Gonzalez, Charles G. *s.j.* '67 (CAM) [9] Camden, NJ Sacred Heart Church.
Gonzalez, Daniel '92 (TYL) Sulphur Springs, TX St. James Church.
Gonzalez, Domingo '64 (ORL) Bartow, FL St. Thomas Aquinas Church.
Gonzalez, Eduardo *s.d.b.* '81 (DAL) [16] Dallas, TX St. Edward Church.
Gonzalez, Felix J. '81 (NY) [172] Bronx, NY Our Lady of Grace Church.
Gonzalez, Flavio '77 (CHI) [1] Des Plaines, IL St. Mary Church.
Gonzalez, Francisco *s.f.* '64 (WDC) [B] Silver Spring, MD Holy Family Seminary.
Gonzalez, George '67 (SAV) [2] Columbus, GA Our Lady of Lourdes Church.
Gonzalez, George '71 (SB) Lake Elsinore, CA St. Frances of Rome Church.
Gonzalez, George G. '67 (SAT) Military Chaplains.
Gonzalez, Gonzalo *o.s.a.* '49 (SJN) [1] Bayamon, PR San Agustin Church.
Gonzalez, Hilario Rivera '74 (SJN) [9] San Juan, PR Santa Catalina Laboure Church.
Gonzalez, Hugo '89 (PHX) Peoria, AZ St. Charles Borromeo Church.
Gonzalez, Isaias *o.s.a.* '76 (SJN) [42] San Juan, PR Ntra. Sra. de la Monserrate Church.
Gonzalez, Jorge (SP) Beverly Hills, FL Our Lady of Grace Church.
Gonzalez, Jorge A. '87 (BWN) San Benito, TX Our Lady, Queen of the Universe Church.
Gonzalez, Jose (VEN) [L] Lake Placid, FL.
Gonzalez, Jose '54 (SP) [8] St. Petersburg, FL St. Raphael Church.
Gonzalez, Jose '69 (SR) Healdsburg, CA St. John the Baptist Church.
Gonzalez, Jose '91 (VEN) Lake Placid, FL Comunidad Catolica Hispana Santiago Apostol Church.
Gonzalez, Juan *c.pp.s.* '76 (GRY) [5] East Chicago, IN Our Lady of Guadalupe Church.
Gonzalez, Luis P. '94 (NEW) [A] Kearny, NJ Redemptoris Mater.
Gonzalez, Marcos '94 (LA) Camarillo, CA St. Mary Magdalen Church.
Gonzalez, Mario '55 (VEN) Retired.
Gonzalez, Mario *o.s.a.* '58 (SJN) [18] Bayamon, PR Santa Rita de Casia Church.
Gonzalez, Primitivo '62 (STO) Modesto, CA St. Stanislaus Church.
Gonzalez, Rafael J. *c.r.l.* '93 (ARE) Corozal-Palmarito, PR La Milagrosa Church.
Gonzalez, Msgr. Ricardo (NEW) [1] Orange, NJ St. John's Church.
Gonzalez, Ridolfo (TR) [1] Trenton, NJ St. Mary Cathedral.
Gonzalez, Romualdo M. *sch.p.* '71 (LA) [75] Los Angeles, CA St. Lucy Church.
Gonzalez, Ruben *c.m.f.* (SJN) [27] San Juan, PR San Jose Obrero Church.
Gonzalez, Rudolph F. '87 (NY) [31] New York, NY St. Elizabeth Church; Spring Valley, NY St. Joseph Church.
Gonzalez-Abreu, Hector '79 (MIA) [34] Miami, FL St. Vincent De Paul Church.
Gonzalez-Buelta, Benjamin '70 (MIA) [D] Miami, FL Belen Jesuit Preparatory School.
Gonzalez-Chao, Luis '58 (SJN) [3] Toa Baja, PR Espiritu Santo Church.
Gonzalez-Florez, Jose D. '96 (ATL) [4] Atlanta, GA Immaculate Heart of Mary Church.
Gonzalez-Montenegro, Julian *o.f.m.cap.* '84 (SFR) [B] San Francisco, CA Capuchin House of Studies.
Good, Clarence P. '46 (STL) Shrewsbury, MO Cure' of Ars Church.
Goodbout, George E. '63 (BR) [F] Baton Rouge, LA Our Lady of the Lake Regional Medical Center.
Goodbout, George E. '63 (STU) On Duty Outside the Diocese.
Goode, Frances *o.p.* (SB) [H] Riverside, CA St. Andrews Newman Center.
Goode, Francis '87 (SB) [10] Riverside, CA St. Andrew's Newman Center Church; [E] Riverside, CA St. Vincent Ferrer House.
Goode, James E. *o.f.m.* '72 (NY) [DD] New York, NY St. Clare Friary.
Goode, Joseph J. '73 (PAT) Rockaway, NJ Sacred Heart Church.
Goode, Lawrence C. '64 (SFR) [18] San Francisco, CA St. Finn Barr Church; [U] San Francisco, CA Legion of Mary.
Goode, Michael *c.pp.s.* '79 (SAN) Sweetwater, TX Holy Family Church; Sweetwater, TX Immaculate Heart of Mary Church.
Goode, William F. '60 (WDC) Indian Head, MD St. Mary Star of the Sea Church.
Goodill, Msgr. Robert D. '38 (E) [23] Erie, PA St. Luke Church; Retired.
Goodly, Timothy '93 (LKC) [4] Lake Charles, LA St. Henry Church.
Goodman, Fidelis C. *m.m.* '49 (NY) [DD] Maryknoll, NY Maryknoll Fathers and Brothers.
Goodman, Frank '59 (ORL) Retired.

Goodman, Frank '59 (SP) Retired.
Goodman, Julian B. '66 (RIC) [1] Norfolk, VA Blessed Sacrament Church.
Goodman, Leo M., III '91 (HBG) Mechanicsburg, PA St. Elizabeth Ann Seton Church.
Goodrow, Robert A. (DET) Retired.
Goodrum, James R. '57 (LFT) Monticello, IN Our Lady of the Lakes Church.
Goodwin, Calvin M. *s.j.* '79 (PRT) [C] Portland, ME Cheverus High School; [I] Portland, ME St. Ignatius Residence.
Goodwin, James P. *s.j.* '43 (SPK) [K] Spokane, WA Regis Community.
Goodwin, James S. '97 (FAR) Jamestown, ND The Basilica of St. James Church.
Goodwin, Owen *ss.cc.* '54 (FR) [J] Fairhaven, MA Sacred Hearts Provincial House.
Goodwin, Owen F. *ss.cc.* '54 (PRO) [P] Narragansett, RI Christian Brothers' Center.
Goodwin, Patrick A. '69 (OAK) Dublin, CA St. Raymond Church.
Goodwin, Raymond M., Jr. '69 (WOR) Hopedale, MA Sacred Heart of Jesus Church.
Goodwin, Robert T. '57 (MAN) Retired.
Goodwin, Thomas L. '86 (CC) Alice, TX Our Lady of Guadalupe Church.
Goodwine, Msgr. Joseph G. '39 (NY) Retired.
Goodyear, Robert *s.t.* '75 (JKS) Magee, MS St. Stephen Church; Sanatorium, MS Boswell Retardation Center.
Goolsby, Gregory D. '93 (ATL) Duluth, GA St. Benedict Church.
Goossens, Anthony *o.m.i.* '39 (SAT) [K] San Antonio, TX Oblate Madonna Residence.
Goossens, Hippolyte L. *c.j.* '56 (LA) Camarillo, CA Camarillo State Hospital-Development Center.
Goossens, Ludo *c.i.c.m.* '69 (FgM) Missionhurst Foreign Missions.
Gootee, Paul *s.v.d.* '55 (FgM) Society of the Divine Word Foreign Missions.
Gootee, Stanley J. *s.v.d.* '44 (GAL) [47] Houston, TX St. Mary of the Purification Church.
Gopaul, Antonius P. '97 (BRK) [65] Brooklyn, NY St. Jerome's Church.
Goraieb, Charles '91 (PHX) [9] Phoenix, AZ St. Catherine of Siena Church.
Gorak, Stanley C. '38 (GI) Retired.
Goralka, Albert A. '45 (PIT) Retired.
Gorczyca, Andrzej '74 (BRK) [241] Queens, NY St. Stanislaus Bishop and Martyr Church.
Gordan, Msgr. John '38 (NY) [212] Staten Island, NY St. Margaret Mary Church.
Gordinier, William '58 (ROC) Geneseo, NY St. Mary Church.
Gordon, Charles *s.t.* '67 (FgM) Trinity Missions.
Gordon, Charles B. *c.s.c.* '87 (FTW) [A] Notre Dame, IN Moreau Seminary; [J] South Bend, IN Congregation of Holy Cross Indiana Province Provincial House.
Gordon, Emmanuel *c.p.* '50 (MET) [H] South River, NJ Passionist Provincial Office.
Gordon, Gerald R. *s.j.* '60 (SPK) [C] Spokane, WA Gonzaga University; [G] Spokane, WA Sacred Heart Medical Center.
Gordon, Gerard A. '88 (RVC) Hicksville, NY St. Ignatius Loyola Church.
Gordon, Gregory *s.s.c.* '51 (LAV) [13] Las Vegas, NV St. Mary the Virgin Church.
Gordon, Gregory '88 (LAV) North Las Vegas, NV St. Christopher Church.
Gordon, James *i.c.* '69 (SP) Seminole, FL Blessed Sacrament Church.
Gordon, James E. '81 (RIC) [3] Chesapeake, VA St. Stephen Martyr Church.
Gordon, Msgr. John '39 (NY) Retired.
Gordon, John '85 (FgM) Society of St. James the Apostle.
Gordon, John '88 (NEW) Rutherford, NJ St. Mary's Church.
Gordon, John B. '85 (MET) On Duty Outside the Diocese.
Gordon, Msgr. John J. '39 (NY) [211] Staten Island, NY St. Joseph, St. Thomas Church.
Gordon, John T. '47 (DET) Harper Woods, MI Our Lady Queen of Peace Church.
Gordon, Joseph A. '71 (SFR) East Palo Alto, CA St. Francis of Assisi Church.
Gordon, Kevin M. '83 (SUP) Rice Lake, WI St. Joseph Church.
Gordon, L. William '65 (OG) Champlain, NY St. Mary Church.
Gordon, M. Gerald *t.o.r.* '69 (PH) [AA] Fairless Hills, PA St. Anthony Friary.
Gordon, Robert J. '73 (PAT) [8] Clifton, NJ St. Philip the Apostle Church.
Gore, Robert D. '65 (BEL) [8] Belleville, IL St. Teresa of the Child Jesus Church.
Gore, William R. *o.s.f.s.* '69 (PHU) Wilmington, DE St. Nicholas Church.
Gore, William R. *o.s.f.s.* '69 (WIL) [I] Wilmington, DE DeSales House.
Gorena, Pedro '66 (SJN) [13] Bayamon, PR Ascension Del Senor Church.
Gorges, Bernard X. '95 (WCH) [1] Wichita, KS Cathedral of the Immaculate Conception.
Gorges, Peter '68 (JUN) [1] Juneau, AK Cathedral of the Nativity of The Blessed Virgin Mary.
Gorgis, Noel '89 (EST) Scottsdale, AZ Mar Auraha Chaldean Catholic Parish.
Gorham, Francis X. *o.m.i.* '58 (BO) Lowell, MA Saints Memorial Medical Center.
Gorham, Peter P. '53 (PRT) Retired.
Gori, Peter G. *o.s.a.* '79 (BO) [4] Lawrence, MA St. Augustine Church.
Gorinas, Vytautas '70 (RCK) Retired.
Gorman, Charles L. '54 (GF) Retired.
Gorman, Cyril *o.s.b.* '90 (SCL) [I] Collegeville, MN St. John's Abbey, of the Order of St. Benedict.
Gorman, Edward *o.p.* '92 (FgM) Dominican - Order of Preachers Foreign Missions.
Gorman, Francis A. *o.f.m.* '39 (CHR) Greenville, SC St. Anthony of Padua Church.
Gorman, Francis P. '59 (NY) North Tarrytown, NY St. Teresa of Avila Church; North Tarrytown, NY Holy Cross Church.
Gorman, George F. '36 (PRO) Retired; [P] Providence, RI St. John Vianney Residence.
Gorman, James '81 (STP) Burnsville, MN Church of the Risen Savior.
Gorman, James H. *m.m.* '52 (FgM) Maryknoll Foreign Missions.
Gorman, James P. '73 (PH) [36] Philadelphia, PA St. Clement Church.
Gorman, Msgr. James T. (NY) [1] Port Chester, NY Our Lady of Mercy Church.
Gorman, Msgr. John '34 (DM) Retired.
Gorman, John '58 (SB) San Bernardino, CA San Bernardino Community Hospital.
Gorman, John E. *s.d.s.* '69 (WDC) Landover Hills, MD St. Mary's Catholic Church; [B] Silver Spring, MD Salvatorian Community.
Gorman, John F. '29 (CHI) Riverdale, IL Queen of Apostles Church; Retired.
Gorman, John J. '45 (RVC) Babylon, NY St. Joseph's Church; Retired.
Gorman, Joseph F. '55 (HRT) [12] Waterbury, CT St. Leo the Great Church; [D] Waterbury, CT Sacred Heart High School.
Gorman, Joseph P. '56 (NY) [38] New York, NY St. Frances Xavier Cabrini Church.
Gorman, Kevin *o.s.b.* '51 (PEO) Arlington, IL St. Patrick's Church; Cherry, IL Holy Trinity Church.
Gorman, Kevin D. *o.s.b.* '51 (PEO) [A] Peru, IL St. Bede Abbey and Academy.
Gorman, Lawrence J. (CHI) Retired.
Gorman, Leo J. *c.p.* '57 (NY) [DD] Pelham Manor, NY St. Vincent's Residence; [HH] Pelham, NY Passionist Communications, Inc.
Gorman, Michael (LC) [K] La Crosse, WI Catholic Charities of the Diocese of La Crosse, Inc.
Gorman, Michael J. '80 (LC) Special Assignment; [A] La Crosse, WI Holy Cross Seminary House of Formation; [I] La Crosse, WI Holy Cross (Seminary) Diocesan Center.
Gorman, Patrick J. '59 (LA) [48] Los Angeles, CA St. Bernadette Church.
Gorman, Paul J. '40 (NU) Retired.
Gorman, Richard F. '82 (NY) [E] New York, NY Cardinal Spellman High School; [I] New York, NY The Catholic Charities of the Archdiocese of New York.
Gorman, Robert G. '80 (MET) [7] Perth Amboy, NJ Holy Spirit Church.
Gorman, Rody I. '55 (LA) Huntington Park, CA St. Matthias Church.
Gorman, Thomas '59 (TOL) Delphos, OH St. John the Evangelist Church.
Gorman, William A. '73 (ALB) Fort Ann, NY St. Ann Church.
Gorman, William N. '76 (MOB) Heron Bay, AL St. Michael the Archangel Church.
Gormley, Charles E. '51 (PH) Bala Cynwyd, PA St. Matthias Church.
Gormley, Eugene *l.c.* '83 (DAL) [D] Irving, TX Highland School; [G] Irving, TX The Highland School; [M] Irving, TX Legionaries of Christ.
Gormley, George J. '45 (RIC) Retired.
Gormley, Gerard '85 (SR) [3] Santa Rosa, CA St. Rose of Lima Church.
Gormley, James J. *s.j.* '54 (PH) [AA] Philadelphia, PA Jesuit Community at St. Joseph's University.
Gormley, James W. '54 (PH) Stowe, PA St. Gabriel Church.
Gormley, Kevin '64 (JC) Absent on Leave.
Gormley, Michael *s.a.c.* '41 (DET) Allen Park, MI St. Frances Cabrini Church; Detroit, MI Oakwood Hospital.
Gormley, Raymond P. '92 (CAM) [2] Vineland, NJ Sacred Heart Church.
Gormley, William J. *c.m.* '49 (PH) [AA] Philadelphia, PA Congregation of the Mission.
Gorney, Joseph *c.ss.r.* '51 (SP) [9] Tampa, FL St. Joseph Church.
Gornick, Thomas '58 (WH) Retired.
Gorny, Edward V. *glmy.* '68 (SAV) Sylvania, GA Our Lady of the Assumption Church; [I] Sylvania, GA Catholic Cemetery.
Gorospe, Paterno '66 (NEW) [G] Teaneck, NJ Holy Name Hospital.
Gorowski, Roman *c.m.* '72 (BRK) [134] Brooklyn, NY St. Stanislaus Kostka Church.
Gorr, Benjamin '79 (VEN) Retired.
Gorra, Edward M. '55 (LAN) [11] Flint, MI St. Matthew Church.
Gorrell, Paul '91 (PAT) Absent on Leave.
Gorsic, Gregor '97 (JOL) [2] Naperville, IL Sts. Peter and Paul Church.
Gorski, Alex F. '43 (WIL) Retired.
Gorski, Donald '59 (FgM) Society of St. James the Apostle.
Gorski, Eugene F. *c.s.c.* '60 (SCR) [C] Wilkes-Barre, PA Kings College; [C] Wilkes-Barre, PA Kings College.
Gorski, Msgr. J. Donald '59 (CHR) On Duty Outside the Diocese.
Gorski, John F. *m.m.* '63 (FgM) Maryknoll Foreign Missions.
Gorski, John J. '64 (CLV) Avon, OH Holy Trinity Church.
Gorski, Lawrence E. '75 (CHI) [148] Chicago, IL Our Lady of Grace Church.
Gorski, Robert E. '80 (MAN) Merrimack, NH St. John Neumann Church.
Gorski, Terrence *o.f.m.* '75 (BWN) Rio Hondo, TX St. Helen Church.
Gorski, Msgr. Walter J. '53 (NEW) Wallington, NJ Most Sacred Heart of Jesus Church.
Gorsuch, Joseph G. '62 (TUC) Eloy, AZ St. Helen Church.
Gorton, Timothy J. '82 (PRO) [4] Warwick, RI St. Francis of Assisi Church.
Gosche, Msgr. Joseph E. '55 (SPC) Retired.
Goscinak, Darius '92 (HRT) [2] New Britain, CT Holy Cross Church.
Gosma, Robert D. '59 (MIL) Genesee Depot, WI St. Paul Church.
Gosnell, David H. (GRY) Valparaiso, IN St. Elizabeth Seton Church.
Gosnell, Stephen D. '78 (BAL) Edgewood, MD Prince of Peace Church.
Goss, Francis G. '47 (BO) [5] Brockton, MA Our Lady of Lourdes Church; Retired.
Goss, Joseph *o.p.* '55 (BR) Donaldsonville, LA Ascension of Our Lord Jesus Christ Church.
Gosselin, Andre *s.m.* '64 (BO) [3] Methuen, MA Our Lady of Mount Carmel Church.
Gosselin, Fernand L. *m.m.* '70 (BO) [W] East Walpole, MA Maryknoll Department of Development.
Gosselin, Gerard G. '85 (PRT) Bangor, ME St. John's Church.
Gosselin, Homer P. '69 (SPR) [3] Ludlow, MA St. John the Baptist Church.
Gosselin, Joseph *m.s.* '65 (FR) [J] Attleboro, MA La Salette Provincial House.
Gosselin, Lawrence '76 (NTN) Military Chaplains.
Gosselin, Michael H. '73 (HRT) [12] New Britain, CT St. Peter's Church.
Gosselin, Richard '58 (BO) Ayer, MA St. Mary Church.
Gosselin, Robert H. '56 (BO) Groveland, MA St. Patrick Church.
Gossman, John A. '71 (DUB) Hiawatha, IA St. Elizabeth Ann Seton Parish.
Goswitz, Leonard '90 (LA) Artesia, CA Holy Family Church.
Gosz, Isadore M. *o.praem.* '46 (GB) [I] De Pere, WI St. Norbert Abbey.
Gotay, Tarcisio *o.c.* '73 (SJN) [61] San Juan, PR Santa Teresita Del Nino Jesus Church.
Goth, Dennis J. '84 (LFT) Union City, IN St. Mary Church.
Gothe, Marcus '59 (P) Retired.
Gothie, George J. '67 (PAT) Hopatcong, NJ St. Jude's Church.
Gothing, Donald B. '65 (WOR) On Special or Other (Arch)Diocesan Assignment.
Gothman, August '93 (CR) Moorhead, MN St. Joseph's Church; [F] Moorhead, MN St. Thomas Aquinas Newman Center.
Gotimer, Msgr. James E. '53 (BRK) [154] Queens, NY St. Bartholomew's Church.
Gottemoeller, Mark '76 (IND) Martinsville, IN St. Martin of Tours Church.
Gottemoller, Bartholomew *o.c.s.o.* '42 (SLC) [F] Huntsville, UT Abbey of Our Lady of the Holy Trinity of the Order of Cistercians.
Gottin, Pio *o.f.m.cap.* '48 (BO) [60] Boston, MA St. Patrick Church.
Gottschalk, David *o.f.m.cap.* '69 (DEN) [M] Denver, CO St. Francis of Assisi Friary.
Gottschalk, Matthew *o.f.m.cap.* '53 (MIL) [Y] Milwaukee, WI House of Peace.
Gotwalt, Joseph F. '65 (HBG) [1] Harrisburg, PA Cathedral Parish of St. Patrick Church; [K] Harrisburg, PA Catholic Campus Ministry.
Goudreau, George W. '48 (PRT) Retired.

Goudreau, Joseph L. '63 (PRT) Military Chaplains.
Goudreau, Paul '60 (SP) Holiday, FL St. Vincent De Paul Church.
Goudreau, Remy A. *o.f.m.* '39 (BO) [Z] Boston, MA Saint Anthony Residence.
Goudreau, William G. *s.j.* '52 (FgM) Provinces.
Gouger, John *c.ss.r.* '65 (FgM) Redemptorist Foreign Missions.
Gough, James F. '40 (PH) [102] Philadelphia, PA St. Matthew Church; Retired.
Gough, Joseph E. *s.j.* '43 (KC) [B] Kansas City, MO Rockhurst College; [J] Kansas City, MO Rockhurst College - Jesuit Community.
Gouin, Joseph O. '65 (MAR) Kingsford, MI American Martyrs Church.
Gould, Clayton '81 (LR) Batesville, AR St. Mary's Church; Newport, AR St. Cecilia's Church.
Gould, Eugene '44 (PEO) Retired.
Gould, James C. *s.j.* '74 (FgM) Provinces.
Gould, Msgr. James C. *s.j.* '74 (MI) Majuro, MH Cathedral of the Assumption; Ebeye, MH Queen of Peace Church; MH Outer Island Parish.
Gould, James R. '81 (ARL) [2] Arlington, VA St. Agnes Church.
Gould, Lawrence *s.a.c.* '76 (FWT) Glen Rose, TX St. Rose of Lima Church; Granbury, TX St. Frances Cabrini Church.
Gould, Louis J. '62 (WOR) [10] Worcester, MA Our Lady of Fatima Church.
Gould, Michael A. *m.m.* '54 (FgM) Maryknoll Foreign Missions.
Gould, William R. '65 (B) Post Falls, ID St. George's Church.
Goulding, Laurence B. *glmy.* '62 (SAV) Claxton, GA St. Christopher Church.
Gouldrick, John W. *c.m.* '69 (PH) [69] Philadelphia, PA Immaculate Conception Church; [B] Philadelphia, PA St. Vincent's Seminary; [AA] Philadelphia, PA Congregation of the Mission.
Goulet, Raymond O. (BO) Retired.
Goulet, Wayne F. '74 (PHX) Special Assignment.
Gouthier, Nolan '84 (BEA) Absent On Leave.
Gouthro, Arthur *s.a.* '69 (NY) [DD] Garrison, NY Generalate of the Franciscan Friars of the Atonement-St. James Friary.
Goveas, Benedict *o.f.m.* '53 (NY) [DD] New York, NY Franciscan Province of the Immaculate Conception.
Govern, William H. '34 (RVC) Retired.
Governale, Russell *o.f.m.conv.* '88 (BRK) [61] Brooklyn, NY Most Holy Trinity Church.
Govorchin, Vincent '55 (SLC) On Duty Outside the Diocese.
Gowen, Daniel F. '89 (TR) [1] Toms River, NJ St. Joseph Church.
Gower, James M. '53 (PRT) Retired.
Gower, Peter J. '84 (PRO) [30] Providence, RI St. Raymond Church; Providence, RI Miriam Hospital.
Gowin, Wladyslaw *s.chr.* '54 (CHI) [87] Chicago, IL Holy Trinity Mission Church.
Gowing, Thomas '69 (SR) Garberville, CA Our Lady of the Redwoods Church.
Goyette, Giles R. *o.mar.* '82 (SAM) [C] Petersham, MA Most Holy Trinity Monastery.
Gozaloff, Msgr. Paul J. '56 (WDC) Mechanicsville, MD Immaculate Conception Church.
Graap, Augustine *o.carm.* '66 (NY) State, NY Mid-Orange Correctional Facility; State, NY Otisville Correctional Facility; [DD] Middletown, NY St. Albert's Priory.
Grab, Michael J. '77 (HBG) [6] Lancaster, PA Sacred Heart of Jesus Church.
Grabarz, Casimir *c.s.c.* '39 (FTW) [L] Notre Dame, IN Holy Cross Mission House.
Grabert, Colman *o.s.b.* '65 (IND) [J] St. Meinrad, IN St. Meinrad Archabbey.
Grabish, John J. '72 (ALN) [2] Easton, PA St. Bernard Church; [5] Easton, PA St. Michael Church.
Grabner, Donald *o.s.b.* '54 (KC) [A] Conception, MO Conception Seminary College; [J] Conception, MO Conception Abbey.
Grabner, Eugene '59 (WCH) [E] Fort Scott, KS Mercy Health System of Kansas, Inc.
Grabner, Kenneth *c.s.c.* (FTW) [J] Notre Dame, IN Congregation of Holy Cross, Midwest Province.
Grabowski, Dennis '76 (Y) Absent on Leave.
Grabowski, Eugene M. '89 (R) Edenton, NC St. Anne Church.
Grabowski, Fidelis *m.i.c.* '45 (SPR) [I] Stockbridge, MA Congregation of Marians.
Grabowski, Francis E. '44 (MET) Piscataway, NJ St. Frances Cabrini Church; Retired; [H] Somerset, NJ Maria Regina Residence.
Grabowski, Walter '81 (BUF) [10] Cheektowaga, NY Queen of Martyrs Church.
Grabowsky, Msgr. Myron '67 (PHU) Bristol, PA St. Mary's Church.
Grabrian, Dennis '70 (COS) On Duty Outside Diocese.
Grabys, Joseph J. '49 (ALB) [1] Amsterdam, NY St. Casimir Church.
Grace, Edward D. '67 (CHI) Skokie, IL St. Peter Church.
Grace, Edward G. *o.s.a.* '41 (CHI) [N] Olympia Fields, IL The Augustinian Provincialate Tolentine Center.
Grace, Gerald '65 (PMB) Highland Beach, FL St. Lucy Church.
Grace, Gerald P. *s.j.* '54 (CHI) [N] Chicago, IL Chicago Province of the Society of Jesus-Provincial Office; [N] Chicago, IL Chicago Province of the Society of Jesus-Provincial Office; [X] Chicago, IL Jesuit International Missions, Inc.
Grace, Gerald P. *s.j.* '54 (FgM) Provinces.
Grace, Gerard *s.s.e.* '55 (VEN) [G] Englewood, FL Society of St. Edmund Residence.
Grace, Hugh R. '64 (NY) Saugerties, NY St. Mary of the Snow Church.
Grace, James N. '59 (CHI) Other Assignments.
Grace, Msgr. James P. '61 (BRK) [150] Queens, NY St. Andrew Avellino Church.
Grace, John '88 (MAN) [12] Manchester, NH St. Marie Church.
Grace, John A. '79 (RIC) Harrisonburg, VA Blessed Sacrament Church.
Grace, John J. '48 (SAC) South Lake Tahoe, CA St. Theresa Church; Retired and in Senior Ministry.
Grace, John J. '50 (CHI) [198] Chicago, IL St. Tarcissus Church.
Grace, Joseph W. '53 (LFT) Portland, IN Immaculate Conception Church; Marion, IN U.S. Veteran's Hospital.
Grace, Patrick J. '49 (ROC) Retired.
Grace, Peter A. *c.p.* '72 (SCR) [M] Scranton, PA Saint Ann's Passionist Monastery; [R] Scranton, PA Saint Ann's Media, Inc.
Grace, Robert S. '55 (WDC) North Beach, MD St. Anthony Church.
Grace, Thomas A. *c.m.* '64 (CHI) [G] Chicago, IL Catholic Charities of the Archdiocese of Chicago-Archdiocesan Offices; [N] Chicago, IL Vincentian Community, Congregation of the Mission, Midwest Province.
Gracey, John '93 (FRS) Fowler, CA St. Lucy Church; Selma, CA St. Joseph Church.
Gracias, Urbano '52 (NO) [47] New Orleans, LA St. Maurice Church.
Gracz, Msgr. Henry C. '65 (ATL) McDonough, GA St. James The Apostle Church.
Graczyk, Carl *o.f.m.* '73 (PH) [D] Philadelphia, PA Archbishop Ryan High School; [AA] Philadelphia, PA St. Pius X Friary.
Graczyk, Glen G. (MIL) [H] Waukesha, WI Waukesha Catholic School System, Inc.
Graczyk, Glen G. '81 (MIL) [3] Waukesha, WI St. John Neumann Church.
Graczyk, Randolph *o.f.m.cap.* '68 (GF) Pryor, MT St. Charles Borromeo Mission Church.
Grad, Malcolm '58 (CIN) On Special and Diocesan Assignment.
Graden, John L. *o.s.f.s.* '76 (TOL) [37] Toledo, OH St. Pius X Church; [K] Toledo, OH Oblates of St. Francis de Sales.
Gradillas, Arnulfo *c.s.sp.* '78 (AMA) [2] Amarillo, TX St. Laurence Cathedral; [L] Amarillo, TX Marriage Encounter.
Gradilone, Msgr. Thomas J. '50 (BRK) [218] Queens, NY Our Lady, Queen of Martyrs Church.
Grady, Bernard C. '68 (DUB) On Duty Outside the Archdiocese.
Grady, Charles *c.s.s.* '48 (BO) [Z] Waltham, MA Stigmatine Fathers and Brothers.
Grady, Donald F. *s.j.* '44 (BO) [W] Boston, MA The Society of Jesus of New England-Provincial Offices.
Grady, Donald F. *s.j.* '44 (CHR) Hilton Head Island, SC St. Francis By the Sea Church.
Grady, Francis J. *s.s.c.* '63 (CHI) Forest Park, IL St. Bernardine Church.
Grady, James P. '77 (STL) Elsberry, MO Sacred Heart Church.
Grady, John P. *m.m.* '55 (FgM) Maryknoll Foreign Missions.
Grady, L. Augustine *s.j.* '46 (NY) [DD] New York, NY Jesuit Community at Fordham University.
Grady, Michael '94 (MIA) [1] Miami, FL St. Mary's Cathedral; [C] Miami, FL Msgr. Edward Pace High School.
Grady, Peter W. '53 (FAR) Retired; [E] Fargo, ND Riverview Place, Inc.
Grady, William R. '55 (LFT) Muncie, IN St. Mary Church.
Graeber, Msgr. Richard A. '53 (BUF) [1] Kenmore, NY St. Andrew Church.
Graef, Msgr. Franz '57 (NO) [A] New Orleans, LA Notre Dame Seminary Graduate School of Theology.
Graef, Msgr. Franz '57 (SHP) On Duty Outside the Diocese.
Graehler, Kenneth '63 (EVN) Sullivan, IN St. Mary Church.
Graf, Gary M. '84 (CHI) [4] Waukegan, IL Holy Family Church.
Graf, Harold '68 (PHX) Sun City West, AZ Our Lady of Lourdes Church.
Graf, Henry C. '49 (PH) Quakertown, PA St. Isidore Church.
Graf, Herbert *o.f.m.conv.* '59 (SAV) Hazlehurst, GA Good Shepherd Church.
Graf, James W. '72 (L) [62] Louisville, KY St. Patrick Church; Louisville, KY Central State Hospital.
Graf, John H. '46 (COL) Retired.
Graf, John W. '74 (PH) West Grove, PA Assumption B.V.M. Church.
Graf, Paul '82 (LFT) [C] Lafayette, IN St. Elizabeth Medical Center.
Graf, William E. '60 (ROC) [54] Rochester, NY Most Precious Blood Church; [L] Rochester, NY Archivist; [L] Rochester, NY Censores Librorum.
Graff, Ed '55 (AMA) Tulia, TX Church of the Holy Spirit.
Graff, Edward R. '55 (ALN) Retired.
Graff, Francis C. '65 (PIT) Neshannock, PA St. Camillus Church; Lawrence County, PA Almira Home; Lawrence County, PA Belvedere Residence, Inc.; Lawrence County, PA Golden Hill Nursing, Inc.; Lawrence County, PA Haven Convalescent Home; Lawrence County, PA Highland Hall Care Center; Lawrence County, PA Hill View Manor; Lawrence County, PA Indian Creek Nursing Center; Lawrence County, PA Jack Rees Nursing and Rehabilitation Services; Lawrence County, PA Overlook Nursing Home; Lawrence County, PA Castle Manor; Lawrence County, PA Cedar Manor; Lawrence County, PA Majors Manor; Lawrence County, PA Shenango United Presbyterian Home; Lawrence County, PA Silver Oak Nursing.
Graff, J. Austin '36 (CHI) Retired.
Graff, Joseph P. '76 (GAY) [1] Alpena, MI St. Anne Church; [2] Alpena, MI St. Bernard Church.
Graff, Robert L. '52 (TUC) Retired.
Graff, Timothy G. '85 (NEW) Saddle River Borough, NJ St. Gabriel the Archangel Church.
Graffis, Joseph T. '71 (L) [10] Louisville, KY St. Augustine Church.
Graffius, Peregrine *o.s.m.* '59 (ORG) [G] Orange, CA St. Vincent de Paul Society.
Graffius, Peregrine M. *o.s.m.* (ORG) [H] Anaheim, CA Servite Fathers and Brothers.
Graffius, Peregrine M. *o.s.m.* '59 (ORG) [H] Buena Park, CA Servite Fathers And Brothers.
Grafsky, George J. '71 (STP) Montgomery, MN Holy Redeemer Church; Shieldsville, MN St. Patrick Church.
Graham, Alfred '60 (MEM) [18] Memphis, TN St. Michael's Church.
Graham, D. Clifford *o.m.v.* '81 (BO) [W] Milton, MA Oblate Residence (St. Joseph House).
Graham, Daniel M. '70 (BO) [4] Quincy, MA St. Joseph Church.
Graham, Edgar B. *s.j.* '54 (BAL) [B] Baltimore, MD Loyola College; [B] Baltimore, MD Loyola College; [M] Baltimore, MD Jesuit Community of Loyola College, Inc.
Graham, Msgr. George P. '52 (RVC) Levittown, NY St. Bernard Church.
Graham, Gilbert J. *o.p.* '49 (CHI) [N] River Forest, IL St. Thomas Aquinas Priory.
Graham, Gilbert J. *o.p.* '49 (DAL) [19] Dallas, TX St. Jude Chapel and Information Center Church.
Graham, J. David '91 (MEM) [2] Memphis, TN St. Ann Church; [M] Memphis, TN Serra Club of Memphis.
Graham, James G. '66 (PIT) [22] Pittsburgh, PA St. Lawrence O'Toole Church.
Graham, Msgr. James J. '73 (PH) North Wales, PA St. Rose of Lima Church; [A] Wynnewood, PA Theological Seminary of St. Charles Borromeo, Overbrook.
Graham, James K. '93 (NTN) Fremont, CA St. Elias Church.
Graham, James P. *c.m.* '37 (STL) [P] Earth City, MO Congregation of the Mission Midwest Province (Vincentians); [P] Perryville, MO Congregation of The Mission.
Graham, John E. '44 (DAV) Retired.
Graham, John J. '90 (BO) [69] Boston, MA Sacred Heart Church.
Graham, Msgr. John K. *c.ss.r.* (NY) [23] New York, NY St. Cecilia Church.
Graham, Msgr. John K. '74 (NY) [E] New York, NY Cardinal Hayes High School.
Graham, Joseph B. '63 (PH) [74] Philadelphia, PA St. Jerome Church.
Graham, Michael *s.a.* '69 (NY) [DD] Garrison, NY Generalate of the Franciscan Friars of the Atonement-St. James Friary.
Graham, Michael J. *s.j.* '88 (CIN) [D] Cincinnati, OH Xavier University; [M] Cincinnati, OH Jesuit Community at Xavier Unversity.
Graham, Raymond *s.m.m.* '47 (RVC) [N] Eastport, NY Shrine of Our Lady of the Island.
Graham, Robert *s.m.* '50 (BO) [4] Haverhill, MA St. Joseph Church.
Graham, Thomas '60 (STL) [O] Mehlville, MO Nazareth Living Center.
Graham, Msgr. Thomas A. '62 (BRK) [228] Queens, NY St. Pius X Church.
Graham, Thomas D. '48 (PH) [102] Philadelphia, PA St. Matthew Church.

Graham, Walter F. *c.m.* '49 (MET) [H] Plainsboro, NJ Vincentian Residence.
Graham, William *o.f.m.cap.* '72 (PIT) [O] Pittsburgh, PA St. Patrick Friary.
Graham, William C. '76 (DUL) On Duty Outside the Diocese.
Graham, William C. '76 (NY) [4] New York, NY All Saints Church.
Graham, William F. *s.j.* '42 (ALN) [A] Wernersville, PA Novitiate of St. Isaac Jogues.
Graham, William P. '65 (CAM) Lindenwold, NJ St. Lawrence's Church.
Grailey, Joseph P. '80 (PH) Absent on Leave.
Grajeda, Miguel A. '97 (MRY) San Luis Obispo, CA San Luis Obispo Church.
Grajek, Lawrence F. '57 (SB) Big Bear Lake, CA St. Joseph Church.
Grala, Paul *s.o.l.t.* (CC) Robstown, TX St. Anthony Church; [H] Robstown, TX Society of Our Lady of the Most Holy Trinity.
Gralapp, Robert W. '64 (SC) Manilla, IA Sacred Heart Church.
Gralinski, Thomas J. '41 (HBG) [3] Lancaster, PA Assumption of the Blessed Virgin Mary Church.
Gramaje, Art *c.m.f.* (AUS) [M] San Marcos, TX Catholic Student Center.
Gramaje, Art *c.m.f.* '94 (AUS) San Marcos, TX St. John the Evangelist Church.
Gramajo, Rodolfo '92 (SR) Graduate Studies.
Gramata, Raymond '70 (E) Erie, PA St. Vincent's Health Center; [G] Erie, PA Saint Vincent Health Center.
Grambow, Arnold J. '69 (MAR) Gladstone, MI All Saints Church.
Gramigna, Francis J. '64 (CAM) Barrington, NJ St. Francis de Sales Church.
Gramkee, David (ROC) [L] Seneca Falls, NY Patrician Fund Trust.
Gramkee, David '66 (ROC) Seneca Falls, NY St. Patrick Church.
Grammond, Maurice '50 (P) Retired.
Grams, Douglas L. '87 (NU) Tracy, MN St. Mary Church; Walnut Grove, MN St. Paul Church.
Gramza, Ronald J. '73 (MIL) [1] Waukesha, WI St. Joseph Church.
Gran, Thomas '50 (PBR) Retired.
Granadino, David '81 (LA) Sepulveda, CA Our Lady of Peace Church.
Granados, Carlos E. '88 (ARE) On Duty Outside the Diocese.
Granahan, Gerard '66 (ORL) Sabbatical.
Granata, Joseph P. '75 (RVC) Central Islip, NY St. John of God Church.
Granato, Anthony F. '56 (NEW) East Newark, NJ St. Anthony's Church.
Granato, Msgr. Joseph J. '55 (NEW) [22] Newark, NJ St. Lucy's Church.
Granato, Marius *o.c.s.o.* '64 (WOR) [N] Spencer, MA St. Joseph's Abbey.
Grancini, Steven M. *c.r.s.p.* '57 (SD) [15] San Diego, CA Our Lady of the Rosary Church.
Grande, Alphonsus *c.p.* '42 (HRT) [M] West Hartford, CT Holy Family Monastery/Retreat.
Grande, Bernardine *c.p.* '45 (BRK) [U] Jamaica, NY Immaculate Conception Monastery.
Grande, Kenneth J. '78 (BRK) [240] Queens, NY St. Sebastian Church.
Grandi, Nelson '80 (WOR) Shrewsbury, MA St. Anne's Church.
Grandillo, James J. '54 (CLV) [1] Cleveland, OH Cathedral of St. John the Evangelist; [29] Cleveland, OH Holy Redeemer Church; Retired.
Grandpre, Louis E. '61 (DET) [3] Clinton Twp., MI St. Paul of Tarsus Church.
Graner, Thomas '94 (FAR) Rolette, ND Sacred Heart Church.
Graney, William F. '71 (WIL) Georgetown, DE St. Michael the Archangel Church.
Granfield, David *o.s.b.* '52 (WDC) [M] Washington, DC St. Anselm's Abbey.
Granfield, Patrick *o.s.b.* '57 (WDC) [C] Washington, DC Catholic University of America, The; [M] Washington, DC St. Anselm's Abbey.
Grange, John '66 (NY) [152] Bronx, NY St. Jerome's Church.
Granich, Msgr. Bernard '44 (STL) [O] Kirkwood, MO St. Agnes Home for the Elderly.
Granillo, Paul '97 (SB) Cathedral City, CA St. Louis Church.
Grankowski, Zbigniew W. '83 (DET) [2] Dearborn, MI St. Barbara Church.
Granstrand, Charles P. '66 (NEW) Park Ridge, NJ Our Lady of Mercy Church.
Grant, Douglas '80 (PRO) North Kingstown, RI St. Francis De Sales Church.
Grant, Frederick A. (BO) Retired.
Grant, James '56 (SPK) Retired.
Grant, James A. '66 (PH) Warrington, PA St. Joseph Church.
Grant, Jeffery A. '82 (SFD) Casey, IL St. Charles Borromeo Church; Greenup, IL Christ the King Church; Marshall, IL St. Mary Church.
Grant, Matthew M. '65 (BRK) Absent on Sick Leave.
Grant, Peter J. '95 (ALX) Winnfield, LA Our Lady of Lourdes Church.
Grant, Robert '84 (DM) On Duty Outside the Diocese.
Grant, Robert H. '49 (B) Retired.
Grant, Robert J. '93 (HRT) [17] Waterbury, CT SS. Peter and Paul Church; [I] Waterbury, CT St. Mary Hospital.
Grant, Robert L. '80 (DAV) [B] Davenport, IA St. Ambrose University.
Grant, William David '86 (LIN) Fairbury, NE St. Michael's Church.
Grant, Zachary *o.f.m.cap.* '56 (SPR) [L] Springfield, MA St. Francis of Assisi Chapel and Catholic Information Center.
Grantz, Leon *c.p.* '46 (CHI) [J] Chicago, IL Our Lady of the Resurrection Medical Center; [N] Chicago, IL Immaculate Conception Monastery.
Granville, Msgr. William (BO) Stoughton, MA New England Sinai Hospital.
Granville, Msgr. William A. '43 (BO) Retired.
Granzotto, Peter *s.d.b.* '57 (NY) [2] Port Chester, NY Corpus Christi Church.
Grappoli, Frank *s.x.* '63 (PAT) [M] Wayne, NJ Xaverian Missionary Fathers.
Grappoli, Frank B. *s.x.* '63 (FgM) Xaverian Foreign Missions.
Grasha, Donald F. '84 (LA) Torrance, CA St. Catherine Laboure Church.
Grasher, Albert, Jr. '86 (SPK) Chewelah, WA St. Mary of the Rosary Church; Springdale, WA Sacred Heart Church; Valley, WA Holy Ghost Church.
Grasing, John A. '88 (WIL) Newark, DE St. John the Baptist-Holy Angels Church.
Graskow, Paul '43 (STF) Retired.
Grass, Aloysius P. *c.m.* '51 (PH) [AA] Philadelphia, PA Congregation of the Mission.
Grass, Msgr. Don C. '61 (GRY) Crown Point, IN St. Mary Church.
Grass, Kenneth E. *c.m.* '56 (STL) [P] Perryville, MO Congregation of The Mission.
Grasselli, Renato '94 (NEW) [A] Kearny, NJ Redemptoris Mater.
Grassi, Dominic J. '73 (CHI) [109] Chicago, IL St. Josaphat Church.
Grassl, Joseph A. '50 (LC) Knowlton, WI St. Francis Xavier Church; Peplin, WI St. John the Baptist Church.
Grasso, Aldo *o.s.j.* '44 (MRY) [G] Santa Cruz, CA Oblates of St. Joseph Provincial House and Shrine.
Grasso, Anthony R. *c.s.c.* '78 (SCR) [C] Wilkes-Barre, PA Kings College.
Grasso, Philip A. '43 (MAD) Retired.
Grasso, Raymond (JOL) [I] Naperville, IL St. John Vianney Villa.
Grasso, Raymond '57 (JOL) Retired.
Grasso, Richard '63 (PAT) On Duty Outside the Diocese.
Grasso, Richard E. '63 (ORL) Retired.
Grathwohl, John M. '55 (KAL) Retired.
Gratkowski, Eugene W. '67 (CHI) [106] Chicago, IL St. John Bosco Church.
Gratsch, Edward J. '48 (CIN) Retired; [B] Cincinnati, OH Mt. St. Mary's Seminary of the West.
Grattan, Bernard V. (ALT) Johnstown, PA Memorial Hospital; Johnstown, PA Lee Hospital; [D] Johnstown, PA Good Samaritan Medical Center.
Grattaroti, Robert A. '62 (WOR) Charlton City, MA St. Joseph's Church.
Gratto, Stephen H. '73 (OG) Morrisonville, NY St. Alexander Church; [3] Plattsburgh, NY St. Joseph Church.
Grauel, Frank B. '84 (L) [35] Louisville, KY Holy Spirit Church; Retired.
Grauls, Paul *s.d.b.* '62 (NY) [117] New York, NY St. Thomas the Apostle Church.
Gravel, Claude *o.ss.t.* '81 (BAL) [M] Baltimore, MD Holy Trinity Monastery.
Graven, John P. '57 (FAR) On Duty Outside the Diocese.
Graven, John P. '57 (ORG) Stanton, CA St. Polycarp Church.
Graven, Thomas J. '68 (STU) Fairpoint, OH St. Joseph Church; Maynard, OH St. Stanislaus Church.
Graves, Alfred C. '67 (SPR) Absent on Leave.
Graves, C. Edwin, III '92 (LR) Helena, AR St. Mary's Church.
Graves, Joseph A. '56 (PEO) Retired.
Graves, W. Robert *c.s.sp.* '50 (VEN) [G] Sarasota, FL Congregation of the Holy Ghost.
Grawe, Michael *o.f.m.* '70 (FgM) Franciscan Foreign Missions.
Gray, Brian M. '86 (BGP) [5] Stamford, CT St. Gabriel Church; Stamford, CT Stamford Hospital.
Gray, Daniel J. '76 (PRO) Portsmouth, RI St. Anthony Church.
Gray, Edward J. *c.ss.r.* '58 (ORL) [F] New Smyrna Beach, FL Redemptorist Fathers of the Vice Province of Richmond.
Gray, Francis Jerome '49 (CHI) [N] Chicago, IL St. Peter's Friary.
Gray, Howard *s.j.* '61 (BO) [W] Chestnut Hill, MA The Jesuit Community at Boston College.
Gray, Howard J. *s.j.* (DET) [K] Detroit, MI Jesuit Provincial Office-Detroit Province of the Society of Jesus.
Gray, Jason '97 (PEO) Graduate Studies.
Gray, John F. '86 (PT) [6] Pensacola, FL St. Anne Church.
Gray, John H. *s.j.* '55 (BAL) [B] Baltimore, MD Loyola College; [B] Baltimore, MD Loyola College; [M] Baltimore, MD Jesuit Community of Loyola College, Inc.
Gray, John W. '58 (PRO) [11] Providence, RI St. Charles Borromeo Church.
Gray, Jude J. *o.s.b.* '68 (MAN) [K] Manchester, NH St. Anselm Abbey.
Gray, Kevin J. '84 (HRT) [14] Waterbury, CT St. Margaret's Church.
Gray, Paul '85 (DAL) [2] Dallas, TX All Saints Church.
Gray, Msgr. Philip A. '60 (SCR) [5] Scranton, PA St. Francis Church.
Gray, Robert '88 (SJ) [5] San Jose, CA Five Wounds Portuguese National Church; Special Assignment.
Gray, Robert B. '57 (L) [24] Louisville, KY St. Elizabeth of Hungary Church; [72] Louisville, KY St. Therese Church.
Gray, Ronald *o.carm.* '43 (NEW) Leonia, NJ St. John the Evangelist's Church.
Gray, Sherman W., Jr. '70 (BGP) [6] Stamford, CT Holy Name of Jesus Church.
Gray, Timothy *s.c.j.* '78 (GAL) [69] Houston, TX St. Philip of Jesus Church.
Graystone, Geoffrey *s.m.* '46 (NO) [A] New Orleans, LA Notre Dame Seminary Graduate School of Theology.
Graziadio, Msgr. Domenick T. '66 (RVC) Glen Cove, NY St. Rocco Church.
Graziani, Joseph A. '45 (HRT) Retired.
Graziano, Damien '67 (JOL) Oakbrook Terrace, IL Ascension of Our Lord Church.
Graziano, George R. *s.j.* '59 (FgM) Provinces.
Graziano, Gerard J. (NEW) [2] Hackensack, NJ Immaculate Conception Church.
Graziano, Peter N. '63 (FR) Attleboro Falls, MA St. Mark's Church.
Grealish, Msgr. James '69 (RIC) Radford, VA St. Jude Church.
Greaney, Francis M. (BO) Retired.
Greaney, John F. '55 (HBG) Marysville, PA Our Lady of Good Counsel Church.
Greaney, Thomas M. *o.s.m.* '70 (CHI) [N] Chicago, IL Servite Friars - Eastern Province.
Greany, Brendan *c.ss.r.* '63 (WIL) Chester, Kent Island, MD St. Christopher Church.
Greatorex, Robert W. '57 (LC) [E] Stevens Point, WI St. Michael's Hospital and School for Med. Technology; [J] Stevens Point, WI St. Joseph Congregational Home.
Greaves, Gerald F. '74 (NEW) Edgewater, NJ Holy Rosary Church.
Greaves, John G. '58 (PRO) [1] Cranston, RI St. Ann Church.
Greb, Michael *o.f.m.cap.* '89 (PIT) [5] Butler, PA St. Wendelin Church; [O] Herman, PA St. Mary's Friary.
Grebasch, Richard L. '58 (MIL) Lake Five, WI St. Columba Church; Monches, WI St. John Church.
Grecco, Robert J. '93 (PIT) Aliquippa, PA St. Titus Church.
Grech, Joseph '52 (MRY) Santa Margarita, CA Santa Margarita de Cortona Church.
Greco, Anthony F. '79 (WIL) Secretary, MD Our Lady of Good Counsel Church.
Greco, Evan J. *o.f.m.* '58 (NY) Yulan, NY St. Anthony of Padua Church.
Greco, Ray *o.s.b.* '63 (PHX) Litchfield Park, AZ St. Thomas Aquinas Church.
Greco, Raymond *o.s.b.* '63 (MRY) [G] San Luis Obispo, CA Monastery of the Risen Christ.
Greco, Robert *o.carm.* '55 (NY) [97] New York, NY Our Lady of the Scapular/St. Stephen Church; Manhattan, NY Bellevue Hospital.
Greeley, Andrew M. '54 (CHI) Other Assignments.
Green, Austin E. *o.p.* '53 (DAL) [M] Irving, TX Dominican Priory of St. Albert the Great.
Green, Bernard *s.d.s.* '73 (GLP) Cibecue, AZ St. Catherine Church.
Green, David E. '88 (PRO) [11] Warwick, RI St. Timothy Church.
Green, Francis J. *o.s.f.s.* '48 (PH) [AA] Philadelphia, PA Father Judge Faculty House.
Green, Fred *s.j.* '58 (FgM) Provinces.
Green, Msgr. Gerard A. '40 (NY) Retired.
Green, Msgr. Gerard L. '56 (BUF) Hamburg, NY SS. Peter and Paul Church.
Green, Gregory A. *c.s.c.* '62 (FTW) [B] Notre Dame, IN University of Notre Dame Du Lac; [J] Notre Dame, IN Holy Cross Community, Corby Hall, University of Notre Dame.
Green, Msgr. James P. '76 (PH) On Duty Outside the Archdiocese.
Green, Lacy '51 (JKS) Retired.

Green, Michael R. *o.s.b.* '70 (DET) [B] Oxford, MI St. Benedict Monastery.
Green, Ronald (NY) Manhattan, NY Terence Cardinal Cooke Health Care Center.
Green, Ronald '96 (MRY) Hollister, CA Sacred Heart Church.
Green, Ronald L. *m.m.* '85 (NY) [DD] Maryknoll, NY Maryknoll Fathers and Brothers.
Green, Thomas H. *s.j.* '63 (FgM) Provinces.
Green, Msgr. Thomas J. '63 (BGP) On Duty Outside the Diocese.
Green, Thomas J. '63 (WDC) [C] Washington, DC Catholic University of America, The.
Green, Thomas P. *s.j.* '61 (NY) [5] New York, NY St. Aloysius Church.
Green, William H. '63 (SUP) Cable, WI St. Ann Church; Hayward, WI St. Joseph's Church.
Green, William L. *c.m.* '55 (BUF) [C] Niagara University, NY Niagara University; [O] Niagara University, NY Vincentian Community at Niagara University.
Greenburg, Alcuin E. '55 (GAL) [K] Houston, TX The Catholic Chaplain Corps; [K] Houston, TX The Catholic Chaplain Corps.
Greene, Daniel P. '58 (YAK) Military Chaplains.
Greene, Edward *o.f.m.* '45 (NY) Jeffersonville, NY St. George Church; Youngsville, NY St. Francis of Assisi Church.
Greene, Frank '48 (PH) [D] Philadelphia, PA Father Judge High School for Boys.
Greene, Gordon L. '94 (KAL) Albion, MI St. John the Evangelist Church.
Greene, J. Gerard *m.m.* '43 (NY) [DD] Maryknoll, NY Maryknoll Fathers and Brothers.
Greene, James F. '61 (FR) [4] New Bedford, MA Our Lady of Fatima Church.
Greene, John C. '85 (GAY) Absent on Leave.
Greene, John L. '76 (SFR) [49] San Francisco, CA St. Stephen Church; San Francisco, CA San Francisco Fire Department.
Greene, Michael *c.p.* '82 (ATL) [11] Atlanta, GA St. Paul of the Cross Church.
Greene, Michael M. '79 (BRK) [229] Queens, NY Presentation of the Blessed Virgin Mary Church.
Greene, Richard '65 (LAF) Patterson, LA St. Joseph Church.
Greene, Robert W. *m.m.* '37 (CIN) [M] Cincinnati, OH The Catholic Foreign Mission Society of America, Inc.
Greene, Thomas S. '55 (SPR) Retired; [H] Springfield, MA St. Michael's Residence.
Greene, Msgr. William L. '50 (BR) St. Francisville, LA Our Lady of Mount Carmel Church.
Greenfield, James J. *o.s.f.s.* '90 (WDC) [B] Washington, DC Oblates of St. Francis de Sales; [S] Washington, DC Archdiocesan Campus Ministry.
Greenhalgh, Donald C. '84 (ARL) Fairfax, VA St. Mary of Sorrows Church.
Greenlaw, Martin F. '68 (SFR) Retired.
Greenleaf, Daniel P. '95 (PRT) Winslow, ME St. John the Baptist Church.
Greenough, Patrick *o.f.m.conv.* (CHI) [N] Libertyville, IL Marytown, Our Lady of Fatima Friary; [Q] Libertyville, IL Marytown, U.S. National Center of the Militia of the Immaculata Movement.
Greenslade, Robert J. '54 (DEN) [11] Denver, CO Holy Family Church; [35] Denver, CO St. Mary Magdalene's Church.
Greenwald, Alfred F. '58 (GAL) Retired.
Greenway, George '87 (SPR) [15] Springfield, MA St. Joseph's Church.
Greenwell, Charles C. '82 (SAN) [2] San Angelo, TX Holy Angels Church.
Greenwell, Joseph *c.ss.r.* '48 (LAF) Crowley, LA Immaculate Heart of Mary Church.
Greenwood, Kevin L. (STU) [J] Worthington, OH Seminary Review Board Vocations.
Greenwood, Kevin L. '90 (STU) On Duty Outside the Diocese.
Greer, G. Michael '81 (COV) Erlanger, KY St. Barbara Church.
Greer, Michael '75 (MIA) [6] Miami, FL Good Shepherd Church.
Greff, Francis A. *c.s.sp.* '47 (FgM) Holy Ghost Foreign Missions.
Grega, Bernard F. '62 (ALT) Conemaugh, PA Assumption of B.V.M. Church.
Gregoire, Jocelyn *c.s.sp.* (PIT) [R] Slippery Rock, PA Office for Campus Ministry.
Gregoire, Paul L. '55 (MAN) Dover, NH St. Charles Church.
Gregoire, Wilfrid G. '56 (PRO) [2] Westerly, RI Immaculate Conception Church.
Gregorek, Joseph C. *v.f.* '65 (E) [B] Erie, PA Gannon University.
Gregorek, Stan M. '66 (PIT) Natrona Heights, PA Our Lady of the Most Blessed Sacrament Church.
Gregori, Anthony F. '53 (GF) Retired.
Gregori, Emidio O. '58 (BGP) Retired.
Gregorie, Jocelyn *c.s.sp.* '86 (PIT) [B] Pittsburgh, PA Duquesne University of the Holy Ghost.
Gregorio, Robert J. '68 (CAM) Blue Anchor, NJ St. Lucy's Church.
Gregoris, Nicholas L. '97 (SCR) [M] Mount Pocono, PA Diocesan Oratory of Saint Philip Neri - Newman House.
Gregory, Joseph F. *s.j.* '47 (FAR) Retired.
Gregory, Joseph F. *s.j.* '47 (MIL) [P] Wauwatosa, WI Jesuit Community at St. Camillus.
Gregory, Kenneth (ALB) Berlin, NY Sacred Heart Church.
Gregory, Kenneth '73 (ALB) Grafton, NY St. John Francis Regis Church; Albany, NY Albany Medical Center Hospital; Special Assignment.
Gregory, Peter A. '73 (SPR) [5] Pittsfield, MA St. Charles Church.
Gregory, Robert S. '69 (KC) [10] Kansas City, MO St. Elizabeth's Church.
Gregovich, Lawrence B. '72 (SPC) Leave of Absence.
Grehl, Paul F. *o.s.f.s.* '60 (LAN) [B] Jackson, MI Lumen Christi High School.
Greig, Msgr. Harry D., II '76 (LKC) [1] Lake Charles, LA Immaculate Conception Cathedral.
Greig, Msgr. Kenneth R. '67 (BEA) Groves, TX St. Peter the Apostle Church.
Grein, Blane *o.f.m.* '62 (GLP) Chinle, AZ Our Lady of Fatima, Indian Mission Church; [A] Chinle, AZ Native American Lay Ministry and Diaconate Program.
Greiner, James A. '63 (OKL) Mustang, OK Church of the Holy Spirit.
Greiner, Kenneth A. '53 (ALT) Retired.
Greiner, Lawrence (SB) Retired.
Greiner, Lawrence '37 (SAG) Retired.
Greiner, Robert M. '93 (BAK) Nyssa, OR St. Bridget of Kildare Church.
Greisen, Thomas '82 (KC) [A] Conception, MO Conception Seminary College.
Greisen, Thomas A. '82 (OM) On Duty Outside the Archdiocese.
Greiten, Gregory J. '92 (MIL) Hales Corners, WI St. Mary Church.
Greiwe, Edward *o.s.c.* '64 (STP) Anoka, MN St. Stephen Church.
Greiwe, Edward *o.s.c.* '70 (STP) [N] Anoka, MN Crosier Community of Anoka.
Grek, Richard *c.r.* '67 (RCK) [A] Woodstock, IL Resurrection Center Retreat House.
Greka, David '62 (AMA) On Duty Outside the Diocese.
Grelak, Andrezj '71 (BO) [3] Chelsea, MA St. Stanislaus Church.
Grell, Loras K. '96 (LIN) [12] Lincoln, NE St. Thomas Aquinas Church; [I] Lincoln, NE University of Nebraska, Newman Club.
Grellinger, R. Michael '62 (MIL) [1] Pewaukee, WI Queen of Apostles Church.
Grembla, Joseph P. '57 (CHI) [33] Chicago, IL St. Bruno Church.
Grembocki, Joseph L. '71 (ALN) [1] McAdoo, PA St. Kunegunda Church.
Gremmels, John '91 (FWT) Keller, TX St. Elizabeth Ann Seton Church.
Grenache, Claude *a.a.* '66 (BO) [W] Brighton, MA Assumptionist Center.
Grendler, Albert O. '59 (SC) Spirit Lake, IA St. Mary's Church.
Grenham, John P. '80 (NO) St. Bernard, LA St. Bernard Church.
Grenham, John Patrick '80 (NO) Florissant, LA San Pedro Pescador Church.
Grenham, Thomas *s.p.s.* (BO) [18] Boston, MA St. Cecilia Church; Boston, MA St. Elizabeth's Medical Center.
Grenier, Carlton *s.m.* '54 (FgM) Marist Foreign Missions.
Grenier, Louis L. *s.j.* '49 (FgM) Provinces.
Grennan, James P. '51 (SAL) Logan, KS St. John's Church; Stockton, KS St. Thomas Church.
Grennan, Lawrence E. '66 (SAL) Manhattan, KS Seven Dolors Church.
Grennan, Thomas J. '48 (NO) Retired.
Grennan, Tom (GAL) [N] Houston, TX Pope John XXIII Priest Residence.
Grennon, John *o.c.d.* '97 (MIL) [P] Holy Hill, WI Discalced Carmelite Monastery.
Grenon, Paul R. '78 (PRO) [9] Woonsocket, RI Our Lady, Queen of Martyrs Church.
Gres-Gayer, Jacques '69 (WDC) [C] Washington, DC Catholic University of America, The.
Greskiewicz, Joseph A. '69 (SCR) Plains, PA SS. Peter and Paul Church.
Greskoviak, Neri *o.f.m.* '63 (PEO) Benson, IL St. John Church; Roanoke, IL St. Joseph Church.
Greskowiak, Stephen '89 (VNN) Anchorage, AK Saint Nicholas of Myra Church.
Gresock, Thomas G. '85 (BUF) Absent on Leave.
Gress, Armand E. *o.s.b.* '37 (CLV) [P] Cleveland, OH Benedictine Order of Cleveland.
Gress, Warren '83 (RVC) Absent on Leave.
Gretchko, A. Edward '72 (PBR) Ashtabula, OH St. Nicholas Church.
Gretchko, Andrew Edward '72 (Y) Conneaut, OH St. Frances Cabrini Church.
Gretz, James R. '94 (PIT) Glenshaw, PA St. Bonaventure Church.
Grevatch, William N. '64 (LC) [6] Wausau, WI St. Michael Church.
Grevencamp, Raymond *c.pp.s.* '49 (CIN) [B] Carthagena, OH St. Charles.
Greving, Daniel M. '97 (SC) [4] Sioux City, IA St. Casimir Church; [5] Sioux City, IA St. Francis of Assisi Church; [6] Sioux City, IA Immaculate Conception Church.
Greving, Louis H. '46 (SC) Retired.
Grewe, Michael W. '79 (OM) [21] Omaha, NE St. James Church.
Grey, Michael *c.s.sp.* '79 (PIT) [B] Pittsburgh, PA Duquesne University of the Holy Ghost.
Greytak, William '56 (HEL) Boulder, MT St. Catherine Church; Boulder, MT Boulder River School and Hospital; [A] Helena, MT Carroll College; [B] Helena, MT Carroll College.
Grib, Philip J. *s.j.* '72 (CHI) [45] Chicago, IL St. Constance Church.
Grib, Phillip J. *s.j.* '72 (CHI) [D] Chicago, IL St. Ignatius Jesuit Community.
Grib, Robert I. *s.j.* '72 (CHI) [89] Chicago, IL St. Ignatius Church.
Gribbin, Msgr. Robert C. '47 (HBG) Hanover, PA St. Joseph Church.
Gribble, G. Michael '81 (COL) Granville, OH St. Edward the Confessor Church.
Gribble, Richard E. *c.s.c.* '89 (FR) [A] North Easton, MA Stonehill College; [A] North Easton, MA Holy Cross Fathers Religious.
Gribbon, John J. '50 (BRK) [149] Queens, NY St. Anastasia Church.
Gribbon, Joseph *c.ss.r.* (ATL) Hapeville, GA St. John the Evangelist Church.
Gribbon, Michael C. '81 (BRK) [238] Queens, NY Sacred Heart Church.
Gribik, John '89 (SJP) Absent on Leave.
Grice, Edward M. '80 (NO) Arabi, LA St. Louise De Marillac Church.
Grieco, Charles '68 (PAT) Retired; [P] Chester, NJ Nazareth Village.
Grieco, Michael '83 (LA) [97] Los Angeles, CA Transfiguration Church.
Grieco, Msgr. Nicholas V. '59 (BGP) Weston, CT St. Francis of Assisi Church.
Grieman, Gerald G. (STP) [W] St. Paul, MN The Highland Catholic Community.
Grieman, Gerald G. '79 (STP) [21] St. Paul, MN St. Gregory the Great (Highland Catholic Community) Church; [24] St. Paul, MN St. Leo (Highland Catholic Community) Church; [34] St. Paul, MN St. Therese (Highland Catholic Community) Church.
Griener, George E. *s.j.* '73 (OAK) [A] Berkeley, CA The Jesuit School of Theology at Berkeley; [A] Berkeley, CA The Jesuit School of Theology at Berkeley; [N] Berkeley, CA Jesuit Community at Jesuit School of Theology at Berkeley.
Grier, Gregory A. '67 (TLS) [1] Tulsa, OK Holy Family Cathedral.
Grier, Matthew *m.h.m.* '69 (NY) Shrub Oak, NY Saint Elizabeth Ann Seton Church.
Gries, Andrew *o.c.s.o.* '59 (ARL) [J] Berryville, VA Cistercian Abbey of Our Lady of the Holy Cross.
Gries, Eugene E. *o.praem.* '68 (GB) [I] De Pere, WI St. Norbert Abbey.
Griesbach, John '76 (FRS) Kerman, CA St. Patrick Church; Tranquillity, CA St. Paul Church.
Griesedieck, Msgr. Edmund O. '65 (STL) Glencoe, MO St. Alban Roe Church.
Griesemer, Edward *s.c.j.* '57 (MIL) [7] Milwaukee, WI St. Anthony Church; [P] Hales Corners, WI Sacred Heart Monastery.
Griffey, Brendan M. '74 (JC) Missionary Assignment in Peru.
Griffin, Barry *s.d.s.* '64 (MIL) [P] Milwaukee, WI Salvatorian Provincial Residence.
Griffin, Bertram F. '57 (P) [24] Portland, OR Church of St. Michael, the Archangel.
Griffin, Charles R. '56 (COL) Chillicothe, OH St. Peter Church; Chillicothe, OH Chillicothe Correctional Institution; Chillicothe, OH Ross Correctional Institution and Honor Camp.
Griffin, Msgr. Charles T. '58 (BUF) [32] Buffalo, NY Holy Spirit Church.
Griffin, David G. '66 (BUF) [6] Niagara Falls, NY St. Leo Church.
Griffin, David R. *o.s.b.* '76 (GBG) [H] Latrobe, PA Saint Vincent Archabbey.
Griffin, Devin *o.carm.* '64 (JOL) [J] Darien, IL Carmelite Provincial Office.
Griffin, Edward J. *o.s.a.* '49 (PH) [142] Philadelphia, PA St. Rita of Cascia Church.
Griffin, Francis J. *s.j.* '39 (BO) [W] Weston, MA Campion Center.
Griffin, George J. '73 (ARL) [2] Alexandria, VA Good Shepherd Church.
Griffin, James '48 (PHX) Prescott, AZ Sacred Heart Church.
Griffin, James C. '82 (RIC) [4] Chesapeake, VA St.

Therese of Lisieux Church.
Griffin, James P. '49 (NY) [8] Yonkers, NY St. Eugene Church.
Griffin, John '72 (SR) Rohnert Park, CA St. Elizabeth Seton Church.
Griffin, John A. '38 (PH) [4] Bensalem, PA Our Lady of Fatima Church; Retired.
Griffin, John Cullen '77 (MRY) Corralitos, CA Holy Eucharist Church.
Griffin, Joseph F. '47 (DUB) Retired.
Griffin, Joseph J. *o.s.f.s.* '56 (PH) [AA] Philadelphia, PA Oblates of St. Francis De Sales.
Griffin, Joseph M. '82 (SAG) Chesaning, MI Our Lady of Perpetual Help Church.
Griffin, Joseph T. *c.s.p.* '46 (BO) [P] Boston, MA Paulist Center; [W] Boston, MA Paulist Fathers Residence.
Griffin, Joseph T. *c.s.p.* '46 (NY) [DD] Jamaica Estates, NY Paulist Fathers Generalate.
Griffin, Michael *o.c.d.* '50 (MIL) [P] Holy Hill, WI Discalced Carmelite Monastery.
Griffin, Michael '90 (SFS) White, SD St. Paul Attended Church; [H] Brookings, SD Pius XII Student Center.
Griffin, Michael J. '49 (MAN) Hampton, NH Our Lady of the Miraculous Medal Church.
Griffin, Noel '64 (LA) Sick Leave.
Griffin, Msgr. Patrick '45 (COL) Retired.
Griffin, Patrick E. '67 (STP) [33] Minneapolis, MN St. Stephen Church.
Griffin, Patrick J. *c.m.* '79 (FgM) Vincentian Foreign Missions.
Griffin, Patrick J. *c.m.* '79 (PH) [AA] Philadelphia, PA Congregation of the Mission.
Griffin, Paul D. '95 (BGP) [7] Fairfield, CT St. Thomas Aquinas Church.
Griffin, Richard J. '42 (PH) [4] Bensalem, PA Our Lady of Fatima Church; Retired.
Griffin, Robert *c.s.c.* (FTW) [B] Notre Dame, IN University of Notre Dame Du Lac; [J] Notre Dame, IN Holy Cross Community, Corby Hall, University of Notre Dame.
Griffin, Robert *s.j.* '61 (LA) [K] Duarte, CA Santa Teresita Hospital.
Griffin, Robert E. *s.j.* '61 (LA) [R] Los Angeles, CA Columbiere House.
Griffin, Robert E. *s.j.* '61 (SJ) [M] Los Gatos, CA Sacred Heart Jesuit Center.
Griffin, Robert F. '49 (MAN) Retired.
Griffin, Thomas *o.s.a.* (CHI) [J] Chicago, IL Holy Cross Hospital.
Griffin, Thomas A. *s.j.* '58 (MIA) [5] Miami, FL Gesu Church.
Griffith, Darragh W. '97 (ATL) [3] Atlanta, GA Holy Spirit Church.
Griffith, Edwin '64 (LSC) Retired.
Griffith, Gavin *o.f.m.* '65 (STL) [T] Dittmer, MO Il Ritiro-The Little Retreat.
Griffith, John O. '39 (PIT) Retired.
Griffith, Sidney H. *s.t.* '65 (WDC) [C] Washington, DC Catholic University of America, The; [M] Riverdale, MD Holy Spirit Missionary Cenacle.
Griffith, Thomas *s.v.d.* '69 (CHI) [B] Techny, IL Divine Word Residence; [N] Techny, IL Society of the Divine Word, Provincial Headquarter-Chicago Prov.; [N] Techny, IL Society of the Divine Word, Provincial Headquarter-Chicago Prov.; [N] Techny, IL Society of the Divine Word, Provincial Headquarter-Chicago Prov.; [X] Techny, IL Blessed Arnold Religious Charitable Trust.
Griffiths, James '56 (SJP) Retired.
Griffiths, John M. '76 (CHI) Graduate Studies.
Griffiths, Thomas *c.p.* '57 (BRK) [U] Jamaica, NY Immaculate Conception Monastery.
Grifone, Fabian *o.f.m.* '54 (NY) [79] New York, NY Most Precious Blood Church.
Grigassy, Daniel P. *o.f.m.* '77 (WDC) [B] Silver Spring, MD Holy Name College.
Grile, Harry A. *c.ss.r.* '68 (CHI) [N] Chicago, IL Redemptorist Theology Residence.
Grile, Patrick *c.ss.r.* '73 (GR) [3] Grand Rapids, MI St. Alphonsus Church.
Grill, Msgr. Philip '43 (LA) [5] Santa Barbara, CA San Roque Church.
Grill, Msgr. Philip L. '43 (LA) Retired.
Grilliot, Thomas J. '76 (CIN) West Milton, OH Transfiguration Church.
Grillo, Anthony '38 (BRK) Retired; [U] Douglaston, NY Bishop Mugavero Residence.
Grimaldi, Joseph R. '83 (BRK) [212] Queens, NY Our Lady of Hope Church.
Grimaldi, Robert B. *s.j.* '68 (FgM) Provinces.
Grimalia, Msgr. Vincent J. '68 (SCR) [1] Plymouth, PA Nativity of the Blessed Virgin Mary Church.
Grimes, Donald J. *c.s.c.* '73 (SCR) [C] Wilkes-Barre, PA Kings College.
Grimes, Edwin T. *o.s.a.* '36 (PH) [AA] Villanova, PA St. Thomas Monastery.
Grimes, Msgr. J. Colby '78 (COL) [5] Columbus, OH St. Andrew Church.
Grimes, John '71 (FgM) Society of St. James the Apostle.
Grimes, John J. '71 (BO) Society of St. James the Apostle.
Grimes, Jordan K. *c.p.* '49 (ORL) [F] Orlando, FL Bethany House of Beutel.
Grimes, Msgr. Kenneth F. '57 (COL) [34] Columbus, OH Our Lady of Peace Church.
Grimes, Mark E. '64 (BGP) Georgetown, CT Sacred Heart Church.
Grimes, Price D., Jr. '88 (OKL) Absent on Sick Leave.
Grimes, Raymond P. '55 (PBL) Lamar, CO St. Francis De Sales-Our Lady of Guadalupe Church.
Grimes, Robert R. *s.j.* '84 (NY) [DD] New York, NY Jesuit Community at Fordham University.
Grimm, Robert B. *s.j.* '76 (FgM) Provinces.
Grimm, Robert B. *s.j.* '76 (P) [L] Portland, OR Jesuit Provincial Office (Society of Jesus, Oregon Prov.); [L] Portland, OR Colombiere Community.
Grimm, William J. *m.m.* '77 (FgM) Maryknoll Foreign Missions.
Grimme, D. Timothy '77 (ALT) Bellefonte, PA St. John the Evangelist's Church.
Grimmer, James A. '54 (BUF) East Eden, NY St. Mary Church.
Grimmond, Christopher J. '87 (OM) Columbus, NE St. Anthony Church.
Grinena, Agustin '46 (PCE) Penuelas, PR Sacred Heart Church.
Griner, William S. '61 (L) Jeffersontown, KY St. Michael Church.
Grinis, Bruno B. '40 (CHI) [169] Chicago, IL SS. Peter and Paul Church; Retired.
Grinis, Julian G. '39 (CHI) [1] Lemont, IL St. Alphonsus Church; Retired.
Grinko, Frank *o.f.m.cap.* '81 (SAL) [C] Victoria, KS St. John's Rest Home.
Grinko, Frank X. *o.f.m.cap.* '81 (SAL) Victoria, KS St. Fidelis Church; Vincent, KS St. Boniface Church; [D] Victoria, KS St. Fidelis Friary.
Grinnell, Horace H. '74 (ARL) Falls Church, VA St. Anthony's Church.
Grinnen, John *t.o.r.* '72 (PH) [AA] Fairless Hills, PA St. Anthony Friary.
Grinsell, John *s.d.b.* '71 (NEW) [C] Ramsey, NJ Don Bosco Preparatory High School for Boys.
Grippe, Louis A. '69 (SCR) [2] Swoyersville, PA Holy Name/St. Mary's Church.
Grippo, Robert F. '72 (NY) [190] Bronx, NY St. Theresa of the Infant Jesus Church.
Gripshover, Ronald J., Jr. '96 (ARL) Lake Ridge, VA St. Elizabeth Seton Church.
Grisaitis, Joseph N. '64 (BRK) [151] Queens, NY St. Ann's Church.
Grise, J. Clifford '45 (BGP) Retired.
Grismer, Raymond J. '33 (CLV) Sheffield, OH St. Teresa Church; Retired.
Griswold, Edward J. '73 (TR) Colts Neck, NJ St. Mary Church.
Grix, Robert *o.f.m.cap.* (NY) [DD] New York, NY Immaculate Conception Friary.
Grix, Robert *o.f.m.cap.* '78 (NEW) [N] Union City, NJ Capuchin Friars - Province of the Sacred Stigmata of St. Francis.
Grizzelle-Reid, Paul *s.c.j.* '72 (MIL) [B] Hales Corners, WI Sacred Heart School of Theology.
Groarke, Francis P. '73 (PH) [41] Philadelphia, PA St. Edmond Church.
Grob, Jeffrey '92 (CHI) Winnetka, IL SS. Faith, Hope and Charity Church.
Grochowski, Bernard (LAV) Military Chaplains.
Grochowski, Bernard J. '63 (WOR) Military Chaplains.
Grochowski, Robert *s.v.d.* '96 (FgM) Society of the Divine Word Foreign Missions.
Grodavent, Msgr. Thomas J. '45 (WDC) Retired.
Grodecki, Henry W. *c.m.* '75 (DEN) [12] Denver, CO Holy Ghost Church.
Groden, Michael F. '65 (BO) [18] Boston, MA St. Cecilia Church.
Groeller, David J. '92 (IND) Jeffersonville, IN Sacred Heart Church.
Groenewold, Robert E. *s.j.* '62 (NY) [FF] Staten Island, NY Mount Manresa Jesuit Retreat House.
Groenewold, Thomas W. '87 (RVC) [1] Rockville Centre, NY St. Agnes Cathedral.
Groesch, Edward '51 (SFD) Greenfield, IL St. Michael Church; Hagaman, IL St. Catherine Church.
Groeschel, Benedict J. *c.f.r.* '59 (BRK) [O] Brooklyn, NY St. Francis Home for Boys.
Groeschel, Benedict J. *c.f.r.* '59 (NEW) [K] Hoboken, NJ Good Counsel, Inc. (St. Francis Home); [K] Hoboken, NJ Good Counsel, Inc. (St. Francis Home).
Groeschel, Benedict J. *c.f.r.* '59 (NY) [D] New York, NY Department of Education; [DD] New York, NY St. Crispin Friary; [FF] Larchmont, NY Trinity Retreat.
Grogan, Brendan '61 (MIA) Absent on Leave.
Grogan, Francis E. *c.s.c.* '55 (FR) [J] North Dartmouth, MA Holy Cross Mission House.
Grogan, Gerald P. '60 (VEN) Avon Park, FL Our Lady of Grace Church.
Grogan, James Clyde '68 (BEL) [4] East St. Louis, IL St. Patrick Church.
Grogan, James M. '95 (STP) New Brighton, MN St. John the Baptist Church.
Grogan, Richard P. *s.j.* '73 (NY) [DD] New York, NY Jesuit Provincial's Office; [FF] Staten Island, NY Mount Manresa Jesuit Retreat House.
Grogan, Thomas A. '68 (NEW) Scotch Plains, NJ St. Bartholomew Church.
Grogan, Todd '90 (CIN) Englewood, OH St. Paul's Church.
Grogan, Vincent B. *o.f.m.* '63 (NY) [35] New York, NY St. Francis of Assisi Church.
Grogan, William E. '83 (PH) Kimberton, PA St. Basil the Great Church.
Grogan, William P. '76 (CHI) [100] Chicago, IL St. Jerome Church.
Groh, Christopher '79 (JOL) [16] Joliet, IL St. Mary Nativity Church.
Grohe, Eugene J. *c.ss.r.* '42 (NY) Port Ewen, NY Presentation of the Virgin Mary Church.
Grohe, Eugene J. *c.ss.r.* '50 (NY) [DD] Esopus, NY Redemptorist Priests and Brothers C.Ss.R. (Province of Baltimore).
Groher, Robert C. '66 (GB) Special Assignment.
Grollig, Anthony J. *s.j.* '55 (FgM) Provinces.
Grollig, Francis X. *s.j.* '53 (DET) [P] Clarkston, MI Colombiere Center.
Grollmes, Eugene E. *s.j.* (STL) [C] St. Louis, MO Saint Louis University.
Grollmes, Eugene E. *s.j.* '64 (STL) [P] St. Louis, MO Jesuit Community Corporation at St. Louis University - Jesuit Hall.
Gromadzki, Stanley G. '89 (MET) Manville, NJ Sacred Heart of Jesus Church.
Gron, Stanislaw *s.j.* '86 (CHI) [N] Chicago, IL Sacred Heart Mission House.
Groncki, Msgr. Richard '66 (NEW) [1] Newark, NJ Cathedral Basilica of the Sacred Heart Church.
Grondalski, Thaddeus J. '41 (WH) Retired.
Groner, John W. '71 (JC) Hannibal, MO Holy Family Church.
Gronert, Stephen '86 (WCH) Marion, KS Holy Family Church.
Gronifillo, Alejandro A. '74 (TR) [2] Toms River, NJ St. Justin Church.
Gronin, Brian '74 (ALB) Rotterdam Junction, NY St. Margaret of Cortona Church.
Gronowski, Ronald V. '69 (GAY) Tawas City, MI Holy Family Church.
Gronski, Peter '71 (STF) Glen Spey, NY St. Volodymyr Church.
Groody, Daniel G. *c.s.c.* '92 (OAK) [N] Berkeley, CA Holy Cross Fathers-Holy Cross Center.
Groody, Daniel G. *c.s.c.* '93 (FTW) [J] South Bend, IN Congregation of Holy Cross Indiana Province Provincial House.
Groover, Henry B. *o.p.* '92 (MIA) [18] Miami, FL St. Dominic Church.
Groover, Henry B. *o.p.* '92 (NO) [P] New Orleans, LA Dominican Fathers & Brothers, Southern Dominican Province.
Gros, Edwin *s.j.* '80 (MIA) [5] Miami, FL Gesu Church.
Grosch, Robert D. '74 (GF) Havre, MT St. Jude Thaddeus Church.
Groschen, Ron *m.s.* (GAL) [B] Houston, TX Holy Ghost Fathers.
Groshek, Richard J. '62 (LAN) [13] Flint, MI St. Pius X Church.
Grosko, Joseph P. '59 (PIT) [64] Pittsburgh, PA Resurrection Church.
Gross, Barry '75 (LFT) On Duty Outside the Diocese.
Gross, Barry R. '75 (WDC) [E] Wheaton, MD Good Counsel High School.
Gross, Donald L. '59 (LFT) Logansport, IN All Saints Church; Lucerne, IN St. Elizabeth Church.
Gross, Francis *o.s.f.s.* '52 (BUF) [7] Niagara Falls, NY St. Mary of the Cataract Church.
Gross, Francis J. *o.s.f.s.* (FgM) Oblates of St. Francis de Sales Foreign Missions.
Gross, Gary L. '83 (LIN) Wahoo, NE St. Wenceslaus Church; [C] Wahoo, NE Neumann High School; [L] Wahoo, NE Bishop Neumann High School Endowment Fund.
Gross, Gerard *c.ss.r.* '78 (ATL) [I] Conyers, GA The Monastery of the Holy Spirit.
Gross, Joseph J. *o.ss.t.* '70 (TR) Asbury Park, NJ Our Lady of Mt. Carmel Church.
Gross, Justin *s.c.j.* '41 (MIL) [P] Franklin, WI Villa Maria.
Gross, Kenneth A. '71 (DM) [1] Council Bluffs, IA Holy Family Church.
Gross, Lawrence C. '53 (HBG) Danville, PA St. Joseph Church.
Gross, Lee W. '87 (ARL) On Duty Outside the Diocese.
Gross, Lee W. '87 (BAL) [A] Emmitsburg, MD Mount St. Mary's Seminary.
Gross, Matthew *o.f.m.cap.* '61 (DEN) [3] Denver, CO Annunciation Church; [M] Denver, CO Annunciation Friary.
Gross, Ralph C. '70 (MIL) [48] Milwaukee, WI St. Margaret Mary Church.
Gross, Richard C. '62 (NU) Watkins, MN Church of St. Anthony.

Gross, Richard J. '63 (FAR) Special Assignment.
Gross, Richard K. *s.j.* '76 (NOR) Storrs, CT St. Thomas Aquinas Church; [K] Willimantic, CT Campus Ministry.
Gross, Stephen *o.f.m.conv.* '69 (SFR) [43] San Francisco, CA St. Paul of the Shipwreck Church.
Gross, Stephen F. '66 (LC) [3] Wausau, WI St. James the Greater Church; [4] Wausau, WI St. Mary (Immaculate Conception) Church.
Gross, Thomas L. '75 (HON) Kailua, HI St. John Vianney Church.
Gross, Val '63 (FAR) [4] Fargo, ND SS. Anne & Joachim Church.
Grosser, Msgr. Elmer J. '46 (COV) Southgate, KY St. Therese of the Infant Jesus Church; Retired.
Grosskopf, Albert A. *s.j.* '83 (SFR) [24] San Francisco, CA St. Ignatius Church; [N] San Francisco, CA Jesuit Community at University of San Francisco.
Grosso, James D. '79 (BGP) [4] Danbury, CT St. Joseph's Church.
Grosso, Lucius *o.f.m.* '64 (PHX) [19] Phoenix, AZ St. Mary's Basilica Church.
Grote, Alan W. '82 (GBG) [1] Latrobe, PA Holy Family Church.
Groth, Msgr. Ronald C. '69 (LKC) [2] Lake Charles, LA Immaculate Heart of Mary Church.
Grothjan, James K. *c.pp.s.* '51 (CIN) [M] Dayton, OH Provincial House of the Cincinnati Province of the Society of the Precious Blood.
Grotovsky, Edward '94 (JOL) Downers Grove, IL St. Joseph Church.
Grotzinger, Alfred L. *o.s.b.* '41 (GBG) [H] Latrobe, PA Saint Vincent Archabbey.
Groucutt, George L. '46 (E) Retired.
Grous, Albin J. '87 (DET) [A] Orchard Lake, MI SS. Cyril and Methodius Seminary.
Grous, Albin J. '87 (PH) On Duty Outside the Archdiocese.
Grovenburg, Gregg '87 (BGP) [A] Fairfield, CT Fairfield University.
Grovenburg, Gregg *s.j.* '88 (BGP) [O] Fairfield, CT The Fairfield Jesuit Community-Fairfield University.
Grover, David A. '83 (CAM) [1] Cherry Hill, NJ St. Mary's Church.
Grover, Peter *o.m.v.* (BO) Cambridge, MA Mount Auburn Hospital; [BB] Boston, MA St. Clement's Archdiocesan Eucharistic Shrine.
Grover, Peter *o.m.v.* '90 (BO) [B] Boston, MA Our Lady of Grace Seminary.
Groves, Edmund '49 (PHX) Retired.
Groves, William '80 (PBL) Absent on Leave.
Grozio, Stephen M. *c.m.* '78 (BRK) [66] Brooklyn, NY St. John the Baptist Church; [U] Brooklyn, NY St. John the Baptist Rectory.
Grubb, James E. '55 (DAV) Retired.
Grubba, Dale W. '66 (MAD) Princeton, WI St. John the Baptist Church.
Gruben, John *o.a.r.* '74 (LA) [R] Oxnard, CA St. Augustine Priory O.A.R.
Gruben, John A. '74 (NY) [B] Suffern, NY Tagaste Monastery.
Gruber, Aloys Conrad '67 (STO) Oakdale, CA St. Mary of the Annunciation Church.
Gruber, Anthony '70 (NOR) Moosup, CT All-Hallows Church.
Gruber, Eric J. '91 (ALN) Schuylkill Haven, PA St. Ambrose Church; [O] Kutztown, PA Christopher House.
Gruber, J. Paul '45 (CIN) [38] Cincinnati, OH St. Ignatius Loyola Church; Retired.
Gruber, Kevin W. '80 (RVC) Center Moriches, NY St. John the Evangelist Church.
Gruber, Mark F.X. *o.s.b.* '83 (GBG) [H] Latrobe, PA Saint Vincent Archabbey.
Gruber, Robert L. '53 (COV) Florence, KY St. Paul Church; Retired.
Grubisch, Donald W. '53 (WIN) La Crescent, MN The Crucifixion Church.
Grubisic, Jozo *o.f.m.* '66 (CHI) [101] Chicago, IL St. Jerome Church.
Gruchot, Stanley J. '45 (CHI) Retired.
Gruden, William J. '79 (SAG) Argyle, MI St. Joseph Church.
Grudowski, Msgr. Robert J. '61 (PH) Conshohocken, PA St. Mary Church.
Gruenbauer, Hans H. '76 (CIN) Amelia, OH St. Bernadette's Church.
Gruhn, Raymond C. '66 (BRK) [137] Brooklyn, NY St. Sylvester Church.
Grumm, Thomas J. '75 (PH) [77] Philadelphia, PA St. John the Baptist Church.
Grummer, James E. *s.j.* '82 (FgM) Provinces.
Grummer, James E. *s.j.* '82 (MIL) [P] Milwaukee, WI Jesuit Provincial Office, Wisconsin Province; [P] Milwaukee, WI Jesuit Community at Marquette University.
Grumsey, David *o.f.m.conv.* '86 (HBG) [5] Shamokin, PA Mother Cabrini Church.
Grundhaus, Msgr. Roger L. '66 (CR) [1] Crookston, MN Cathedral of the Immaculate Conception; [E] Crookston, MN Marywood Residential Community.
Grundman, David P. '97 (SCL) [4] St. Cloud, MN St. Anthony of Padua Church.
Grundowski, Francis M. '71 (ALN) Brockton, PA St. Bartholomew Church; Tuscarora, PA St. Bertha Church.
Grunebach, Paul '76 (PIT) Glenshaw, PA St. Mary Church.
Grunewald, Bernard *er. o.l.s.* '77 (OLL) [D] Philippi, WV Our Lady of Solitude Hermitage.
Grunloh, Donatus *o.f.m.* '49 (SHP) West Monroe, LA St. Paschal Church.
Grunow, Stephen E. '97 (CHI) Northfield, IL St. Philip the Apostle Church.
Grupa, Henry '54 (FRS) Retired.
Grupczynski, Gerald *s.ch.* '88 (DET) [K] Sterling Heights, MI Society of Christ Provincial Home.
Grupczynski, Gerald R. *s.ch.* '88 (TOL) [15] Toledo, OH St. Adalbert Church.
Gruss, Robert D. '92 (DAV) Melcher, IA Sacred Heart Church.
Gruss, Robert D. '94 (DAV) Knoxville, IA St. Anthony's Church; Pella, IA St. Mary's Church.
Gruszczyk, Jerome H. '47 (NEW) [B] Jersey City, NJ Saint Peter's College; [N] Jersey City, NJ Jesuits of Saint Peter's College, Inc.
Gruver, David '85 (ORG) Yorba Linda, CA St. Martin Church.
Gryga, Theodore '64 (SY) Military Chaplains.
Grzankowski, Ted *o.f.m.conv.* (BAL) [M] Ellicott City, MD St. Joseph Cupertino Friary, Friars Minor Conventual of St. Francis of Assisi.
Grzechowiak, Francis *c.r.* '46 (CHI) [192] Chicago, IL St. Stanislaus, Bishop and Martyr Church.
Grzela, Andrew '63 (ROC) [60] Rochester, NY St. Thomas More Church.
Grzela, Andrew S. '91 (CHI) [184] Chicago, IL St. Richard Church.
Grzela, Marek '92 (CHI) Tinley Park, IL St. George Church.
Grzela, Wieslaw '89 (RCK) Algonquin, IL St. Margaret Mary Church.
Grzelak, Thaddeus A. '69 (BRK) [29] Brooklyn, NY St. Charles Borromeo Church.
Grzeskowiak, Edward S. '36 (STP) Retired.
Grzybowski, Joseph *o.f.m.conv.* '49 (FR) [1] Taunton, MA Our Lady of the Holy Rosary Church.
Grzybowski, Robert M. *o.f.m.conv.* '53 (ROC) [6] Auburn, NY St. Hyacinth Church.
Grzymski, Donald *o.f.m.conv.* '80 (BAL) [C] Baltimore, MD Archbishop Curley High School; [M] Baltimore, MD Immaculate Heart of Mary Friary.
Gschwend, James P. *s.j.* '65 (CHI) [N] Chicago, IL Chicago Province of the Society of Jesus-Provincial Office; [N] Chicago, IL Chicago Province of the Society of Jesus-Provincial Office.
Gschwind, Fred H. '52 (LFT) Tipton, IN St. John the Baptist Church.
Gsell, John W. '36 (PH) [59] Philadelphia, PA Holy Family Church; Retired.
Guadagnoli, Michael A. '97 (DAL) [22] Dallas, TX St. Patrick Church.
Guagliardo, Salvatore J. '59 (RCK) Lena, IL St. Joseph Church.
Guajardo, Hilario '89 (AUS) Gatesville, TX Our Lady of Lourdes Church.
Gualderon, Msgr. Ernest J. '45 (LA) [1] Long Beach, CA St. Anthony Church; Retired.
Gualtieri, Ray A. '64 (PIT) Scott Township, PA Our Lady of Grace Church.
Guandalini, Julius S. '44 (HRT) Retired.
Guarcello, Russell V. '43 (BO) Retired.
Guarino, Msgr. Charles A. '67 (RVC) St. James, NY SS. Philip and James Church.
Guarino, Michael J. '68 (BO) Bridgewater, MA St. Thomas Aquinas Church.
Guarino, Thomas G. '77 (NEW) [A] South Orange, NJ Immaculate Conception Seminary; [B] South Orange, NJ Seton Hall University.
Guarnieri, Lee (RIC) Special Assignment.
Guarnieri, Richard '71 (NY) [136] Bronx, NY St. Clare of Assisi Church.
Guarracino, Ralph '54 (BRK) [Y] Middle Village, NY St. John's.
Guastella, Luke *o.f.m.cap.* '41 (PAT) Passaic, NJ St. Mary Hospital.
Guastella, Msgr. Richard J. '72 (NY) [206] Staten Island, NY Holy Rosary Church.
Guay, Robert '73 (PIT) Conway, PA Our Lady of Peace Church.
Guba, Michael '65 (NEW) [3] Garfield, NJ Church of Our Lady of Sorrows.
Gubanich, Michael T. '47 (PIT) Retired.
Gubbels, Wayne '71 (DM) Neola, IA St. Patrick Church; Weston, IA St. Columbanus Church.
Gubbins, John '70 (MIA) Military Chaplains.
Gubbins, William B. '55 (CHI) [105] Chicago, IL St. John Berchmans Church.
Gubernat, Michael E. '77 (NEW) [6] Jersey City, NJ St. Anthony of Padua Church.
Gubser, John H. '62 (Y) Niles, OH St. Stephen's Church.
Gubser, Paul L. '67 (Y) Dungannon, OH St. Philip Neri Church; Salineville, OH St. Patrick's Church; Summitville, OH St. John's Church.
Guckert, William T. '66 (SY) Brewerton, NY St. Agnes Church.
Gudalefsky, Adam B. *m.m.* '59 (FgM) Maryknoll Foreign Missions.
Gude, George W. '32 (CIN) Retired.
Gude, Thomas A. '66 (WDC) Lexington Park, MD Immaculate Heart of Mary Church.
Gudewicz, John '70 (PIT) Finleyville, PA St. Francis of Assisi Church.
Gudime, Devasahayam '90 (CHI) Northlake, IL St. John Baptist Vianney, Cure of Ars Church.
Gudino, Eduardo '94 (SD) El Centro, CA Our Lady of Guadalupe Church.
Guenette, J. Andre '69 (WOR) [3] Gardner, MA Our Lady of the Holy Rosary Church.
Guenter, Frank '66 (GAL) New Caney, TX St. John of the Cross Church.
Guenther, Bernard *c.ss.r.* '31 (CHI) [9] Chicago, IL St. Alphonsus Church.
Guenther, Daniel C. '82 (SC) Grand Junction, IA St. Brigid's Church; Jefferson, IA St. Joseph's Church.
Guenther, Msgr. Donald E. '62 (NEW) Secaucus, NJ Immaculate Conception Church.
Guenther, George J. *s.j.* '45 (MIL) [P] Wauwatosa, WI Jesuit Community at St. Camillus.
Guenther, Msgr. Thomas A. '64 (CAM) West Collingswood, NJ Transfiguration Church.
Guentner, Francis J. *s.j.* '47 (STL) [P] St. Louis, MO Jesuit Community Corporation at St. Louis University - Jesuit Hall.
Guentner, Hugh *o.s.m.* '91 (DEN) [4] Denver, CO Assumption Church.
Guentner, Hugh M. *o.s.m.* '91 (DEN) Westminster, CO Holy Trinity Church.
Guerdet, Randy J. '89 (SC) [1] Sioux City, IA Cathedral of the Epiphany.
Guerette, William J. (BO) Retired.
Guerin, Msgr. Eugene '25 (SPR) [H] Holyoke, MA Mont Marie Health Care Center, Inc.
Guerin, Msgr. Eugene E. '25 (SPR) Retired.
Guerin, Louis T. '87 (PMB) Highland Beach, FL St. Lucy Church.
Guerin, Peter J. *o.s.b.* '63 (MAN) [K] Manchester, NH St. Anselm Abbey.
Guerin, Philip X. '42 (CHI) [11] Chicago, IL St. Andrew Church; Retired.
Guerini, Ademir *c.s.* '89 (WDC) [33] Washington, DC Our Lady Queen of the Americas Church; [38] Washington, DC Portuguese Catholic Community Church.
Guerra, Alcibiades *c.m.* '90 (FgM) Vincentian Foreign Missions.
Guerra, Aroldo (NY) [53] New York, NY Incarnation Church.
Guerra, Aroldo *sch.p.* '54 (NY) [12] New York, NY Annunciation Church.
Guerra, Jesus *o.p.* '57 (FgM) Dominican - Order of Preachers Foreign Missions.
Guerra, Juan Gabriel *l.c.* '91 (MAD) [I] Edgerton, WI Legion of Christ, Inc.; [M] Edgerton, WI Oaklawn Incorporated.
Guerra, Richard *o.m.i.* '78 (BWN) San Benito, TX St. Benedict Church.
Guerra-Mayaudon, Gerardo *o.p.* '69 (AUS) [H] Austin, TX Dominican Fathers.
Guerreiro, Clarence L. *ss.cc.* '70 (HON) Kaneohe, HI St. Ann Church.
Guerreiro, Clyde *ss.cc.* '76 (HON) [H] Kaneohe, HI Congregation of the Sacred Hearts of Jesus and Mary (Hawaii Province SS.CC.); [H] Kaneohe, HI Sacred Hearts Center.
Guerrera, Richard P. *s.j.* '73 (FgM) Provinces.
Guerrera, Vittorio '91 (HRT) Wolcott, CT St. Pius X Church.
Guerrero, Msgr. Andres '57 (PCE) Coamo, PR St. Blase Church.
Guerrero, Felix Leon *o.f.m.cap.* '86 (AGN) [E] Agana Heights, GU St. Fidelis Friary.
Guerrero, Felixberto Leon *o.f.m.cap.* '86 (AGN) Sinajana, GU Saint Jude Thaddeus Church.
Guerrero, Jose '72 (ELP) [14] El Paso, TX Our Lady of Assumption Church.
Guerrero, Jose Ma. (ARE) On Duty Outside the Diocese.
Guerrero, Joseph R. *c.i.c.m.* '85 (FgM) Missionhurst Foreign Missions.
Guerrero, Juan Manuel '81 (OKL) Ardmore, OK St. Mary Church.
Guerrero, Lawrence M. '83 (STO) [6] Stockton, CA St. Linus Church.
Guerrero, Pablo *s.j.* '94 (SJ) [B] Santa Clara, CA Santa Clara University.
Guerrero, Robert '92 (HON) On Duty Outside the Diocese.
Guerrero, Robert '92 (SB) Hesperia, CA Holy Family Church.
Guerrero, Toby '96 (SAT) [30] San Antonio, TX St. Bonaventure Church.

Guerrini, Roderic M. '63 (LA) Venice, CA St. Mark Church.
Guertin, Donald *c.s.c.* '61 (FTW) [20] South Bend, IN St. Therese, Little Flower Church.
Guesnier, Rene *o.s.b.* '61 (DOD) St. John, KS St. John the Apostle Church; Seward, KS St. Francis Xavier Church.
Guessetto, Robert J. *o.s.a.* '79 (WDC) [B] Washington, DC Augustinian College, Order of St. Augustine.
Guest, Francis *o.f.m.* '41 (LA) [R] Santa Barbara, CA Franciscan Friary, Order of Friars Minor (Old Mission).
Guest, Richard '94 (ARL) Stafford, VA St. William of York Church.
Guetter, Michael A. '41 (NU) Retired.
Guevara, Alfonso M. '77 (BWN) [2] Brownsville, TX Christ the King Church.
Guevara, Msgr. Jose Maria '68 (SAT) Crystal City, TX Sacred Heart Church.
Guevara, Miguel H. '67 (GI) Retired.
Guevera, Miguel Blanco *o.f.m.* '37 (FgM) Franciscan Foreign Missions.
Guevin, Benedict M. *o.s.b.* '85 (MAN) [K] Manchester, NH St. Anselm Abbey.
Guffey, David L. *c.s.c.* '91 (FTW) [A] Notre Dame, IN Moreau Seminary; [J] South Bend, IN Congregation of Holy Cross Indiana Province Provincial House.
Guggenbiller, Michael J. '95 (CLV) Concord Twp., OH St. Gabriel Church.
Gugino, Msgr. Henry J., '68 (BUF) [H] Buffalo, NY The Catholic Charities of the Diocese of Buffalo; [T] Buffalo, NY Good Counsel Apartments; [T] Buffalo, NY Monsignor Kirby Apartments Housing Development Fund Company, Inc.; [T] Buffalo, NY St. Timothy's Park Villa Housing Development Fund Company, Inc.; [T] Buffalo, NY La Casa Del Tainos Housing Development Fund Company, Inc. [M] Williamsville, NY St. Francis Home of Williamsville.
Guglielmelli, Michael V. *o.f.m.conv.* '70 (NEW) [3] Hoboken, NJ St. Francis Church.
Guglielmi, Donald A. '84 (BGP) Graduate Studies.
Guglielmo, Alan (NEW) Lyndhurst, NJ Sacred Heart Church.
Guglielmo, Alan '68 (NEW) Belleville, NJ Clara Maass Hospital; Montclair, NJ Mountainside Hospital.
Guglielmo, Allen '68 (NEW) [S] Jersey City, NJ Franciscan Health System of New Jersey, Inc.
Guglielmone, Msgr. Robert E. '78 (RVC) Wantagh, NY St. Frances de Chantal Church.
Gugliemelli, Michael *o.f.m.conv.* '70 (NEW) [2] Hoboken, NJ St. Joseph's Church.
Gugliemelli, Neil O. '54 (SCR) [7] Hazleton, PA Our Lady of Grace Church.
Gugliotta, Francis *s.x.* '52 (FgM) Xaverian Foreign Missions.
Gugliotta, Francis *s.x.* '52 (PAT) [M] Wayne, NJ Xaverian Missionary Fathers.
Gugliotta, Kevin A. '96 (NEW) Short Hills, NJ St. Rose of Lima Church.
Guichard, Alvaro '69 (MIA) [1] Miami Beach, FL St. Francis de Sales Church.
Guidera, John F. *s.j.* '56 (BAL) [M] Baltimore, MD Jesuit Fathers and Brothers Maryland Provincial Curia.
Guidera, John F. *s.j.* '56 (FgM) Provinces.
Guidice, Anthony *o.f.m.cap.* '54 (NY) [B] Beacon, NY St. Lawrence of Brindisi Friary.
Guido, Msgr. John L. '42 (NY) [190] Bronx, NY St. Theresa of the Infant Jesus Church.
Guido, Joseph J. *o.p.* '81 (PRO) [P] Providence, RI St. Thomas Aquinas Priory at Providence College.
Guido, Paul R. *o.f.m.* '66 (ALB) Palenville, NY Sacred Heart Church.
Guido, Thomas '87 (PT) [3] Tallahassee, FL Good Shepherd Church.
Guido, Msgr. William F. '44 (NY) Retired.
Guidon, Patrick '50 (SAT) [B] San Antonio, TX Joseph Gerard House of Studies.
Guidry, Dale '82 (AMA) Dalhart, TX St. Anthony's Church.
Guidry, Joseph I. *s.v.d.* '57 (BR) [18] Baton Rouge, LA St. Paul the Apostle Church.
Guidry, Michael '71 (LAF) [3] New Iberia, LA Our Lady of Perpetual Help Church.
Guidry, Mitchell Gregory '97 (LAF) Eunice, LA St. Anthony of Padua Church.
Guidry, Raymond *s.v.d.* '57 (LAF) [4] Opelousas, LA Holy Ghost Church.
Guijarro de Corzo, Mario A. '78 (SJN) [6] Guaynabo, PR San Pedro Martir de Verona Church.
Guilbault, Msgr. Oscar A. '31 (PRO) Retired; [M] North Kingstown, RI Scalabrini Villa.
Guilbeau, Aubrey V. '82 (LKC) [8] Lake Charles, LA Our Lady Queen of Heaven Church.
Guilbert, Norman J., Jr. '97 (BGP) [4] Bridgeport, CT St. Ann's Church.
Guillaume, Lionel A. '46 (ALB) Retired.
Guillemette, Arthur T. '39 (NU) Retired.
Guillemette, Joseph H. '23 (STP) Retired.
Guillemette, Marc '90 (MAN) Bedford, NH St. Elizabeth Seton Church.
Guillen, Arthur '78 (LA) La Puente, CA St. Louis of France Church.
Guillen, Juan '74 (TUC) Yuma, AZ Immaculate Conception Church.
Guillen, Manuel R. '62 (SB) Retired.
Guillen, Patricio '57 (SB) Retired.
Guillen, Randy A. '96 (NEW) [4] Union City, NJ St. Anthony of Padua Church.
Guillen, Robert T. '70 (WDC) [13] Washington, DC St. Francis de Sales Church.
Guillermo, Rodrigo J. (GAL) Retired.
Guillot, Msgr. Leo '56 (BR) Albany, LA St. Margaret Queen of Scotland Church.
Guilmain, Roland O. *a.a.* (WOR) [B] Worcester, MA Assumption College; [Q] Worcester, MA Campus Ministry.
Guilmain, Roland O. *a.a.* '53 (WOR) [N] Worcester, MA Assumptionists (Augustinians of the Assumption).
Guilmette, Emile *s.m.* '57 (BO) [4] Haverhill, MA St. Joseph Church.
Guiltnane, Justin *s.c.j.* '53 (MIL) [P] Hales Corners, WI Sacred Heart Monastery; [Y] Franklin, WI Congregation of the Priests of the Sacred Heart Support and Maintenance Trust.
Guimon, Michael M. *o.s.m.* '70 (CHI) Hillside, IL St. Domitilla Church; [N] Chicago, IL Servite Friars - Eastern Province; [N] Chicago, IL Servite Friars - Eastern Province.
Guimond, John *o.f.m.cap.* '82 (LC) [I] Marathon City, WI St. Anthony Retreat Center.
Guinan, Frank '66 (PMB) Juno Beach, FL St. Patrick Church.
Guinan, Michael '53 (GF) Retired.
Guinan, Michael D. *o.f.m.* '63 (OAK) [A] Berkeley, CA Franciscan School of Theology.
Guinan, Msgr. Thomas P. '45 (BGP) Retired.
Guindon, William G. *s.j.* '50 (BO) [W] Boston, MA Loyola House.
Guiney, John *s.m.a.* '61 (JOL) Roselle, IL St. Walter Church.
Guiney, John E. '47 (BO) Retired.
Guiniven, John *c.ss.r.* '37 (ALB) [L] Saratoga Springs, NY St. John Neumann Residence.
Guirsch, Bernard G. '40 (CHI) Chicago Heights, IL St. Paul Church; Retired.
Guischard, John A. '68 (BUR) Rutland, VT St. Peter Church; Retired.
Guise, Cyril *o.c.d.* '59 (MIL) [P] Holy Hill, WI Discalced Carmelite Monastery.
Guitierrez, Jeronimo '81 (SJ) Gilroy, CA St. Mary Church.
Guitron, Steven J. '94 (LA) Alhambra, CA All Souls Church.
Guixa, Jaime '82 (SJN) [G] Guaynabo, PR Opus Dei.
Gula, Richard *s.s.* '73 (OAK) [A] Berkeley, CA Franciscan School of Theology.
Gulas, William E. *o.f.m.* '61 (CLV) [71] Cleveland, OH St. Stanislaus Church; [P] Cleveland, OH St. Stanislaus Friary.
Gulash, George M. '92 (ALT) [1] Altoona, PA Cathedral of the Blessed Sacrament.
Gulczynski, Msgr. John T. '36 (DAL) [27] Dallas, TX St. Thomas Aquinas Church.
Gulig, Msgr. Robert (GB) New Denmark, WI Holy Trinity Church.
Gulig, Msgr. Robert F. '61 (GB) Denmark, WI All Saints Church.
Gulino, Stephen S. '97 (NOR) [1] Norwich, CT St. Patrick Cathedral.
Guljas, Andrew *c.s.c.* '68 (FTW) [L] Notre Dame, IN Holy Cross Mission House.
Gulley, Anthony D. '56 (ALB) [3] Albany, NY Blessed Sacrament Church; Special Assignment; [B] Albany, NY The College of Saint Rose.
Gulley, James '81 (ALB) [7] Amsterdam, NY St. Mary Church.
Gullickson, Msgr. Thomas E. '76 (SFS) On Duty Outside the Diocese.
Gullo, Joseph A. '85 (BUF) [1] Orchard Park, NY Nativity Church.
Gully, Bernard L. '62 (SAN) Andrews, TX Our Lady of Lourdes Church.
Gumapo, Polycarpo '70 (SAC) [2] Sacramento, CA All Hallows Church.
Gumataotao, Agustin *o.f.m.cap.* '73 (FgM) Capuchin Foreign Missions.
Gumataotao, Agustin *o.f.m.cap.* '82 (AGN) Talofofo, GU San Miguel Church; [E] Agana Heights, GU St. Fidelis Friary.
Gumbert, Kenneth R. *o.p.* '85 (PRO) [P] Providence, RI St. Thomas Aquinas Priory at Providence College.
Guminga, Theodore C. '59 (STP) [25] Minneapolis, MN St. Hedwig Church.
Gummersheimer, Gary P. '79 (BEL) Murphysboro, IL St. Andrew Church.
Gumpal, Domingo B. '80 (SFE) Socorro, NM San Miguel Church.
Gumprecht, Thomas *s.a.* '68 (NY) [DD] Garrison, NY Generalate of the Franciscan Friars of the Atonement-St. James Friary.
Gunderman, Richard J. *s.a.c.* '50 (MIL) [D] Milwaukee, WI Pius XI High School; [P] Milwaukee, WI St. Vincent Community.
Gunderson, Gerald T. '76 (CHI) Riverside, IL St. Mary Church.
Gundrum, Alfredo *o.f.m.cap.* (CHI) [113] Chicago, IL St. Kevin Church.
Gunia, Edward S. '49 (CHI) Retired.
Gunn, Andrew '97 (AUS) Round Rock, TX St. William's Church.
Gunn, Francis X. *o.f.m.* '81 (ALB) [B] Loudonville, NY Siena College; [B] Loudonville, NY Siena College; [S] Loudonville, NY Siena College.
Gunn, James L. '77 (MAD) Edgerton, WI St. Joseph Church.
Gunning, Eugene L. '55 (SCR) [26] Scranton, PA St. Vincent de Paul Church.
Gunning, Joseph *s.v.d.* '47 (TR) [M] Bordentown, NJ Society of the Divine Word.
Gunnoud, James B. '59 (HRT) Cheshire, CT St. Bridget's Church.
Gunther, William '60 (MIA) Retired.
Gunti, Charles E. *o.f.m.* '68 (STL) [P] St. Louis, MO Franciscan Friary of St. Anthony of Padua.
Gunti, Frederick W. '64 (LR) On Duty Outside the Diocese.
Gunti, Frederick W. '64 (MOB) [B] Mobile, AL Spring Hill College.
Guntzelman, Louis J. '57 (CIN) On Special and Diocesan Assignment.
Gunzel, Ray *s.p.* '69 (SFE) [J] Jemez Springs, NM The Jemez Program, Our Lady of Lourdes Novitiate.
Guppenberger, August *glmy.* '61 (CIN) [M] Fairfield, OH Headquarters of Glenmary Home Missioners.
Gurath, Guy G. '64 (MIL) Juneau, WI Immaculate Conception Church.
Gurath, Guy J. '64 (MIL) Clyman, WI St. John Church.
Gurdak, Joseph *o.f.m.cap.* '70 (NY) [98] New York, NY Our Lady of Sorrows Church.
Gurdak, Joseph R. *o.f.m.cap* '70 (ORL) Lake Wales, FL Holy Spirit Church.
Guredet, Randy J. '89 (SC) Special Assignment.
Gurka, Gerald J. '80 (SCR) Wanamie, PA St. Mary's Church.
Gurkis, Albin *m.i.c.* '43 (NOR) [C] Thompson, CT Marianapolis Preparatory School; [F] Thompson, CT Marian Fathers.
Gurnell, Anthony '64 (SAC) Retired and in Senior Ministry.
Gurnell, Anthony '69 (MRY) Cayucos, CA St. Joseph Church.
Gurovich, Daniel '74 (PHU) Bethlehem, PA St. Josaphat's Church.
Gurrieri, John A. '67 (BRK) [67] Brooklyn, NY St. John Cantius Church.
Gurski, John K. '64 (NEW) [3] Garfield, NJ Church of Our Lady of Sorrows.
Gurtler, Gary *s.j.* '79 (BO) [W] Chestnut Hill, MA The Jesuit Community at Boston College.
Gurtner, Mark Allen '96 (FTW) [19] Fort Wayne, IN St. Vincent de Paul Church.
Guschwan, George M. '72 (CLV) [5] Elyria, OH Sacred Heart of Jesus Church.
Gusiora, Alphonsus '83 (PCE) On Duty Outside the Diocese.
Gusmer, Msgr. Charles W. *v.e.* '66 (NEW) Cedar Grove, NJ St. Catherine of Siena Church.
Gussoni, Lino '44 (NY) Retired.
Gustafson, Christopher E. '95 (CHI) [39] Chicago, IL St. Christina Church.
Gustafson, George C. '76 (MAR) Manistique, MI St. Francis de Sales Church.
Gustafson, Gilbert J. '77 (STP) Mendota, MN St. Peter Church.
Gustas, Bernard J. '60 (ALB) [10] Schenectady, NY St. Joseph Church.
Guste, Placid *s.m.p.* '61 (SPC) [E] Marionville, MO The Society of Our Mother of Peace, Sons of Our Mother of Peace.
Guste, Placid *s.m.p.* '61 (STL) [P] High Ridge, MO Society of Our Mother of Peace; [T] High Ridge, MO Society of Our Mother of Peace-Maria Fonte Solitude.
Guste, Msgr. Robert I. '50 (NO) [18] New Orleans, LA Our Lady Of Lourdes Church.
Gustin, Clement *o.s.c.* '55 (DUL) Chisholm, MN St. Joseph's Church.
Gustin, Clement N. *o.s.c.* '55 (SCL) [I] Onamia, MN Crosier Monastery.
Gustin, Theodore F. '57 (BIS) Wilton, ND Sacred Heart Church.
Gutauskas, Vaclovas *s.j.* '45 (CHI) [N] Chicago, IL Lithuanian American Jesuits.
Gutekunst, John P. '80 (PH) [151] Philadelphia, PA St. Thomas Aquinas Church; [U] Philadelphia, PA St. Agnes Medical Center.
Guter, Lawrence '45 (DUB) Retired.
Gutgsell, Michael F. '74 (OM) [40] Omaha, NE St. Robert Bellarmine Church.
Gutgsell, Stephen J. '84 (OM) Aloys, NE St. Aloysius Church; Monterey, NE St. Boniface Church; St. Charles, NE St. Anthony Church.
Guth, Edward L. *s.j.* '60 (BUF) [50] Buffalo, NY St.

Michael Church.
Guthman, William (KCK) Topeka, KS Kansas Neurological Institute and Kansas Reception and Diagnostic Center.
Guthneck, Peter E. '71 (GF) Big Sandy, MT St. Margaret Mary Church.
Guthridge, Timothy *c.pp.s.* '97 (SAN) Sweetwater, TX Holy Family Church; Sweetwater, TX Immaculate Heart of Mary Church.
Guthrie, Alfred R. '55 (BRK) [57] Brooklyn, NY Holy Innocents Church.
Guthrie, Eric D. *o.s.b.* '81 (BIR) [E] Cullman, AL St. Bernard Abbey.
Guthrie, Frederick '62 (BO) [1] Gloucester, MA St. Ann Church.
Guthrie, John G. '90 (BIS) Belfield, ND St. Bernard Church; South Heart, ND St. Mary Church.
Guthrie, Milton J. '57 (MEM) [22] Memphis, TN Our Lady Of Perpetual Help Church.
Guthrie, Paul *o.f.m.* '53 (PSC) [A] Sybertsville, PA Holy Dormition Monastery.
Guthrie, Raymond (JOL) Bloomingdale, IL St. Isidore Church.
Guthrie, Raymond P. '84 (PEO) On Duty Outside the Diocese.
Gutierrez, Alvin '61 (PIT) Bobtown, PA St. Ignatius of Antioch Church.
Gutierrez, Celestino '64 (VEN) [3] Sarasota, FL St. Martha Church.
Gutierrez, Dionisio *o.a.r.* '63 (NY) [126] Bronx, NY St. Anselm Church.
Gutierrez, Msgr. Fernando '66 (SD) [22] San Diego, CA St. Catherine Laboure Church.
Gutierrez, Franco '65 (SJN) [3] San Juan, PR Nuestra Senora de la Altagracia Church.
Gutierrez, Gilberto '73 (PAT) [1] Paterson, NJ Cathedral of St. John the Baptist.
Gutierrez, Javier *o.m.* '71 (SJN) [16] San Juan, PR Ntra. Sra. de Fatima Church.
Gutierrez, Javier '83 (JUN) On Duty Outside the Diocese.
Gutierrez, Jose '73 (STP) [16] St. Paul, MN St. Bernard Church.
Gutierrez, Jose M. '76 (CC) [11] Corpus Christi, TX Sacred Heart Church; On Special Assignment; [E] Corpus Christi, TX Spohn Hospital.
Gutierrez, Julio '49 (CGS) Retired.
Gutierrez, Larry A. *s.s.j.* '85 (GAL) [67] Houston, TX St. Peter Claver Church.
Gutierrez, Michael (LA) [57] Los Angeles, CA St. Columbkille Church.
Gutierrez, Michael D. '91 (LA) [18] Los Angeles, CA Nativity Church.
Gutierrez, Vicente *m.sp.s.* '73 (LA) Huntington Park, CA St. Martha Church.
Gutman, Msgr. Gordon G. '33 (Y) Retired.
Gutmann, David '83 (P) Forest Grove, OR St. Anthony Church; Yamhill, OR St. John Church; [P] Portland, OR University of Portland.
Gutmann, Don '91 (P) Reedsport, OR St. John the Apostle Church.
Gutmann, Donald K. '91 (P) Florence, OR St. Mary, Our Lady of the Dunes Church.
Gutowski, Edmund *c.m.* '60 (BRK) [134] Brooklyn, NY St. Stanislaus Kostka Church.
Gutowski, Matthew J. '88 (OM) [L] Omaha, NE Sisters of the Annunciation of the Archdiocese of Omaha.
Guttenberger, Xavier '35 (AUS) Retired.
Guttendorf, James R. '65 (RIC) Highland Springs, VA St. John Church.
Gutting, James G. '75 (E) Titusville, PA St. Titus Church.
Gutting, John C. '54 (LA) Retired.
Guyder, Thomas F. '40 (SY) Retired; [S] Syracuse, NY St. Pius X Home, Inc.
Guyer, James B. *s.j.* '72 (DEN) [M] Denver, CO Regis Jesuit Community (The Jesuits at Regis University).
Guyon, Guy E. *o.praem* '40 (GB) [I] De Pere, WI St. Norbert Abbey.
Guyot, Gilmore H. *c.m.* '34 (STL) [P] Perryville, MO Congregation of The Mission.
Guz, Edmund F. '55 (CHI) Burnham, IL Mother of God Church.
Guz, Leonard '55 (JOL) Downers Grove, IL Divine Savior Church.
Guzik, Stanley *o.m.i.* '46 (GAL) Alvin, TX St. John the Baptist Church.
Guzikowski, Msgr. Gerard '43 (GAY) Manistee, MI Guardian Angels Church.
Guzinski, Joseph D. *c.p.* '51 (BRK) [U] Jamaica, NY Immaculate Conception Monastery.
Guzman, Agustin *s.m.* (GAL) [Q] Houston, TX Marianist Community.
Guzman, Alfonso *o.f.m.* '71 (SJN) [4] Toa Baja, PR Jose Obrero Church.
Guzman, Alfonso D. *o.f.m.* '71 (FgM) Franciscan Foreign Missions.
Guzman, Alfonso D. *o.f.m.* '71 (NY) [DD] New York, NY Franciscan Friars, Order of Friars Minor, Holy Name Province.
Guzman, Alfredo *s.j.* (SJN) [22] San Juan, PR San Ignacio de Loyola Church.
Guzman, Alfredo *s.j.* '83 (ARE) Special Assignment; [A] Arecibo, PR Pontificia Universidad Catholica de Puerto Rico, Recinto de Arecibo.
Guzman, Alfredo E. *s.j.* '83 (PCE) [B] Ponce, PR The Pontifical Catholic University of Puerto Rico.
Guzman, Armando '86 (SEA) [26] Seattle, WA Immaculate Conception Church.
Guzman, Baudilio *s.j.* '91 (SJN) [22] San Juan, PR San Ignacio de Loyola Church; [D] Rio Piedras, PR Centro Universitario Catolico.
Guzman, Julian *s.d.s.* (WDC) [B] Silver Spring, MD Salvatorian Community.
Guzman, Julian *s.d.s.* '68 (MIL) [P] Milwaukee, WI Salvatorian Provincial Residence.
Guzman, Mariano *o.f.m.* '57 (FgM) Franciscan Foreign Missions.
Guzman, Msgr. Raul '62 (PAT) [8] Passaic, NJ Our Lady of Fatima Church.
Gwiazda, Francis A. '69 (PH) [86] Philadelphia, PA St. Laurentius Church.
Gwinner, David M. '84 (COL) [1] Columbus, OH St. Joseph Cathedral.
Gwozdz, John P. '86 (HRT) Glastonbury, CT St. Paul's Church.
Gwozdz, Thomas *o.f.m.conv.* '53 (BAL) [M] Ellicott City, MD Order of Friars Minor Conventual.
Gwozdz, Thomas L. *s.d.b.* '75 (COL) [A] Columbus, OH Pontifical College Josephinum; [H] Columbus, OH Salesian Center.
Gwudz, John S. '72 (NOR) Military Chaplains.
Gyamfi, Paul Miki (NY) [183] Bronx, NY St. Philip Neri Church.
Gyan, Eric V. '86 (BR) Brusly, LA St. John the Baptist Church.
Gyhra, Lawrence J. '66 (LIN) Wahoo, NE St. Wenceslaus Church.
Gyure, William (NEW) Newark, NJ Northern State Prison; Elizabeth, NJ Union County Jail; Elizabeth, NJ Elizabeth Detention Center.
Gyure, William L. '91 (NEW) [4] Newark, NJ St. Aloysius Church.
Gyure, William Louis (NEW) Newark, NJ Office of Prison Ministry.

H

Ha, Alex H. '93 (ORG) Irvine, CA St. Elizabeth Ann Seton Church.
Ha, Louis M. *c.m.c.* '94 (DEN) Wheat Ridge, CO Queen of Vietnamese Martyrs Church.
Ha, Thomas '63 (ORG) Stanton, CA St. Polycarp Church.
Ha, Vinh '93 (CHI) [96] Chicago, IL Saint Ita Church.
Haag, Msgr. Christian D. '38 (PAT) Morristown, NJ St. Margaret's Church; Retired.
Haake, Christopher G. '97 (PEO) [13] Peoria, IL St. Philomena's Church.
Haake, Thomas *o.m.v.* '81 (BO) [B] Boston, MA Oblate Provincialate.
Haaland, Byron *s.c.j.* '77 (GB) [M] Baileys Harbor, WI St. Joseph Retreat Center.
Haar, George B. '51 (STL) Retired.
Haas, Dietrich A. '67 (MIL) [T] Waukesha, WI Secular Institute of Schoenstatt Fathers.
Haas, John '47 (SEA) Gig Harbor, WA Washington Corrections Center for Women.
Haas, Joseph H. '59 (MIL) Port Washington, WI St. Peter of Alcantara Church.
Haas, Julian '65 (STL) [P] St. Louis, MO St. Patrick Friary.
Haas, Lawrence '63 (FAR) Carrington, ND Sacred Heart Church.
Haas, Melvin B. '54 (BEL) Breese, IL St. Augustine Church.
Haas, Msgr. Murray V. '37 (PEO) Retired.
Haas, Ralph L. '55 (BEL) Hecker, IL St. Augustine of Canterbury Church; Chester, IL Chester Mental Health Center.
Haas, Robert '62 (TOL) New London, OH Our Lady of Lourdes Church.
Haas, Roger *ofm conv.* '69 (BUF) [D] Athol Springs, NY St. Francis High School; [O] Athol Springs, NY St. Francis of Assisi Friary.
Haas, Roger M. *o.f.m.conv.* '69 (BAL) [M] Ellicott City, MD Order of Friars Minor Conventual.
Haas, Roger M. *o.f.m. conv.* '69 (BUF) [A] East Aurora, NY Christ the King Seminary.
Haas, Theodore A. '44 (COS) [1] Colorado Springs, CO St. Mary's Cathedral.
Haase, Albert *o.f.m.* '83 (FgM) Franciscan Foreign Missions.
Haase, Albert '83 (STL) [P] St. Louis, MO Franciscan Friary of St. Anthony of Padua.
Haase, Howard G. '83 (MIL) [6] Kenosha, WI St. Mary Church.
Haasl, Edgar '58 (OAK) [13] Oakland, CA St. Louis Bertrand Church.
Hababag, Jimmy B. '82 (GAL) Kingwood, TX St. Martha Church.
Habe, Robert W. '62 (PIT) Russellton, PA Transfiguration Church.
Habenicht, James F. *m.m.* '50 (SJ) [M] Los Altos, CA Maryknoll.
Haber, Edward (NEW) [G] Elizabeth, NJ St. Elizabeth Hospital.
Haber, Edward '58 (NEW) Elizabeth, NJ St. Elizabeth Hospital.
Haber, Robert '58 (NEW) [1] Elizabeth, NJ St. Mary of the Assumption Church.
Haberek, Jerome A. '77 (PRO) On Duty Outside the Diocese.
Haberkern, Thomas A. '93 (STL) Absent on Sick Leave.
Haberkorn, Timothy '92 (KCK) [2] Overland Park, KS Holy Cross Church.
Haberman, C. Robert '75 (PBL) On Duty Outside the Diocese.
Haberman, Clayton J. '50 (WIN) Retired.
Haberman, Lawrence R. '68 (DAL) Retired.
Haberman, Robert '75 (SFR) Special Assignment.
Haberthier, John A. '48 (DOD) Retired.
Habiger, Msgr. James D. '51 (WIN) Retired.
Habiger, Matthew *o.s.b.* '68 (KCK) [H] Atchison, KS St. Benedict's Abbey.
Habing, Paul '80 (SFD) On Duty Outside the Diocese.
Hablewitz, James A. '67 (GB) [2] Green Bay, WI Nativity of Our Lord Church.
Habling, William J. (NEW) [3] Union City, NJ SS. Joseph and Michael Church.
Haby, Gerald *s.m.* '69 (FWT) [12] Fort Worth, TX St. Mary of the Assumption Church.
Hacala, Joseph R. *s.j.* '75 (WDC) [M] Washington, DC K Street Jesuit Community.
Hachey, Paul J. *s.m.* '84 (ATL) [C] Atlanta, GA Marist School.
Hack, Michael A. '70 (CHI) Flossmoor, IL Infant Jesus of Prague Church.
Hack, Thomas J. '55 (GR) [6] Muskegon, MI St. Michael's Church.
Hackel, Robert E. *s.m.* (GAL) [Q] Houston, TX Marianist Community.
Hackenmueller, Jerome B. '69 (STP) [31] St. Paul, MN St. Patrick Church.
Hacker, George *s.d.b.* '38 (SFR) [N] San Francisco, CA Salesian Provincial Residence.
Hacker, Jack *c.ss.r.* '59 (STL) [B] St. Louis, MO St. John Neumann House.
Hacker, Leonard G. *s.j.* '47 (FgM) Provinces.
Hacker, Leonard G. *s.j.* '47 (MI) Majuro, MH Cathedral of the Assumption.
Hackert, Eugene C. '51 (NU) Clements, MN St. Joseph Church; Morgan, MN St. Michael Church.
Hackett, Denis *o.f.m.conv.* '74 (R) Jacksonville, NC Shrine of the Infant of Prague, Church of the Holy Spirit.
Hackett, James F. '68 (L) [46] Louisville, KY St. Leonard Church.
Hackett, John P. '46 (BUR) Retired.
Hackman, Marvin R. '71 (CIN) [K] Springfield, OH Mercy Medical Center; [Q] Springfield, OH Mercy Medical Center, Wittenberg University Campus Ministry.
Hackman, Paul W. '52 (CLV) West Salem, OH St. Stephen Church; Retired.
Hadad, Gerard A. (DET) Retired.
Hadalski, Andrew *s.v.d.* '59 (TR) Yardville, NJ Garden State Correctional Center.
Haddad, Msgr. Edmond G. '46 (WOR) Retired; [M] Worcester, MA Vianney House.
Haddad, James J. '58 (BO) Needham, MA St. Joseph Church.
Haddad, John W. *b.s.o.* '43 (NTN) Miami, FL St. Jude Church.
Haddad, Norman A. *o.p.* '61 (NY) [HH] New York, NY St. Thomas Aquinas Foundation.
Haddad, Norman Alfred *o.p.* '61 (NY) [DD] New York, NY St. Vincent Ferrer Priory.
Haddad, Wayne M. '97 (MET) Iselin, NJ St. Cecelia Church.
Haddad, William F. *b.s.o.* '42 (NTN) Atlanta, GA St. John Church.
Hadden, Thomas P. '58 (R) Wilmington, NC St. Mary Church.
Haddid, Norman Alfred *o.p.* '61 (FgM) Dominican - Order of Preachers Foreign Missions.
Hadel, Richard E. *s.j.* '65 (STL) [F] St. Louis, MO St. Louis University High School, George H. Backer Memorial; [P] St. Louis, MO St. Louis University High School Jesuit Community.
Haden, Kyle '97 (KCK) [4] Topeka, KS Most Pure Heart of Mary Church; [B] Topeka, KS Hayden High School.
Hadgkiss, Joseph *s.o.l.t.* '93 (CC) [H] Robstown, TX Society of Our Lady of the Most Holy Trinity.
Hadnagy, John Raphael *o.f.m. conv.* '90 (GR) [4] Grand Rapids, MI St. Anthony of Padua Church.
Hadusek, Paul J. '69 (NU) Appleton, MN St. John Church.
Hadyka, Richard J. '67 (CAM) Salem, NJ St. Mary's Church.
Haefeli, Joaquin (LA) Wilmington, CA SS. Peter and Paul's Church.
Haefling, Maurice *o.s.b.* '94 (KCK) [H] Atchison, KS St.

Benedict's Abbey.
Haefner, Charles '32 (SUP) Retired.
Haefner, Douglas J. '83 (MET) Somerset, NJ St. Matthias Church.
Haegelin, William M. '76 (KCK) Prairie Village, KS St. Ann's Church.
Haemmerle, Gerald R. '67 (CIN) [B] Cincinnati, OH Mt. St. Mary's Seminary of the West; [B] Cincinnati, OH Mt. St. Mary's Seminary of the West.
Haemmmerle, Gerald R. '67 (CIN) [A] Cincinnati, OH The Athenaeum of Ohio.
Haener, Robert W. '57 (DET) Retired.
Haenke, Roger '91 (FAR) Absent on Leave.
Haesaert, William *c.s.v.* '80 (LAV) [15] Las Vegas, NV St. Viator Church.
Hafeman, Harry G. '76 (GB) Gresham, WI St. Francis Solanus Church; Leopolis, WI St. Mary Church.
Haffey, Thomas P. '69 (HEL) [6] Butte, MT St. Ann Church.
Hafner, M. Gerard '62 (ROC) Spencerport, NY St. John the Evangelist Church.
Hafner, Walter *s.v.d.* '37 (CHI) [B] Techny, IL Divine Word Residence.
Hagan, Aelred *o.c.s.o.* '89 (CHR) [D] Moncks Corner, SC Mepkin Abbey.
Hagan, Barry J. *c.s.c.* '60 (P) [B] Portland, OR University of Portland; [L] Portland, OR Holy Cross Fathers & Brothers, C.S.C. - University of Portland.
Hagan, Charles H. '70 (PH) Southampton, PA Our Lady of Good Counsel Church.
Hagan, David I. *o.s.f.s.* '66 (PH) [AA] Philadelphia, PA Inner City House.
Hagan, Harry *o.s.b.* '86 (IND) [A] St. Meinrad, IN St. Meinrad Seminary; [J] St. Meinrad, IN St. Meinrad Archabbey.
Hagan, James '69 (SFR) On Duty Outside the Archdiocese.
Hagan, Martin *s.j.* '50 (STL) [F] St. Louis, MO St. Louis University High School, George H. Backer Memorial; [P] St. Louis, MO Jesuit Community Corporation at St. Louis University - Jesuit Hall.
Hagan, Paul '82 (LFT) Unassigned.
Hagan, Robert A. *s.j.* '72 (PBL) Trinidad, CO Most Holy Trinity, Trinidad Area Catholic Community (Trinidad Cluster) Church; Trinidad, CO Our Lady of Mt. Carmel, Trinidad Area Catholic Community (Trinidad Cluster) Church; Trinidad, CO St. Joseph, Trinidad Area Catholic Community (Trinidad Cluster) Church; [F] Trinidad, CO Trinidad Area Catholic Community.
Hagan, Thomas C. '61 (PH) [32] Philadelphia, PA St. Cecilia Church.
Hagan, Vincent (RVC) Sick Leave.
Hagarman, Vincent A. *s.j.* '54 (CLV) [U] Akron, OH Loyola of the Lakes Jesuit Retreat House, Inc.
Hage, Simon '39 (NTN) Retired.
Hageder, James S. '94 (GBG) [1] Greensburg, PA Blessed Sacrament Cathedral.
Hagedorn, Robert L. '44 (CIN) Retired.
Hagedorn, Thomas J. '71 (CLV) [61] Cleveland, OH St. Patrick Church.
Hagee, Robert J. *s.j.* '61 (CIN) [M] Cincinnati, OH Faber Jesuit Community.
Hagemann, John *o.s.b.* '75 (OM) [C] Elkhorn, NE Mount Michael High School; [K] Elkhorn, NE Mount Michael Abbey.
Hagen, Gerald '91 (SUP) Highbridge, WI St. Anthony Church; Mellen, WI Holy Rosary Church.
Hagen, Gerald A. '91 (SUP) Sanborn, WI St. Anne Church.
Hagen, John J. *o.s.a.* '57 (PH) [C] Villanova, PA Villanova University; [AA] Villanova, PA St. Thomas Monastery.
Hagen, Joseph B. *o.f.m.* '46 (SHP) Hodge, LA St. Lucy Church.
Hagen, William E. *o.m.i.* '61 (STP) [N] St. Paul, MN Oblate Residence.
Hagenbach, George G. '54 (PH) Berwyn, PA St. Monica Church.
Hagendorf, Thomas A. *o.praem.* '63 (BAL) [76] Baltimore, MD Our Lady, Queen of Peace Church.
Hager, Carl G. *c.s.c.* '39 (FTW) [B] Notre Dame, IN University of Notre Dame Du Lac; [J] Notre Dame, IN Holy Cross Community, Corby Hall, University of Notre Dame.
Hager, Raymond D. '97 (STL) [3] Creve Coeur, MO St. Monica Church.
Hagerman, James W. '86 (MET) Bridgewater, NJ St. Bernard Church.
Hagerty, Msgr. John B. '55 (E) Hermitage, PA Church of Notre Dame.
Haggarty, Msgr. James J. '45 (BRK) Retired.
Haggarty, Msgr. James J. '45 (SFR) Redwood City, CA St. Pius Church.
Haggerty, Charles J. *o.carm.* '56 (NY) [DD] Middletown, NY St. Albert's Priory.
Haggerty, Colman *c.p.* '46 (BRK) [U] Jamaica, NY Immaculate Conception Monastery.
Haggerty, Donald '89 (NY) On Duty Outside the Archdiocese.
Haggerty, Donald F. '89 (BAL) [A] Emmitsburg, MD Mount St. Mary's Seminary.
Haggerty, Edward '57 (CIN) [14] Dayton, OH Holy Family Church; [M] Fairfield, OH Headquarters of Glenmary Home Missioners.
Haggerty, Msgr. James J. '50 (BRK) Retired.
Haggerty, John J. '61 (NY) [145] Bronx, NY St. Helena Church.
Haggerty, Thomas J. '79 (RVC) East Meadow, NY St. Raphael Church.
Haggerty, Thomas M. '64 (BRK) [137] Brooklyn, NY St. Sylvester Church.
Haggins, Martin *o.f.m.cap.* (BAK) Bend, OR St. Francis of Assisi Church.
Haglof, Anthony *o.c.d.* '71 (BO) [W] Brighton, MA Carmelite Monastery.
Hagman, William J. '55 (OWN) Retired.
Hagstrom, Thomas '93 (SFD) Jacksonville, IL Our Saviour Church; [M] Jacksonville, IL Illinois College Newman Center; [M] Jacksonville, IL MacMurray College Newman Center.
Hahn, Bernadine *o.f.m.* '43 (STL) [P] St. Louis, MO Franciscan Friary of St. Anthony of Padua.
Hahn, Bernardine *o.f.m.* '43 (OM) [46] Omaha, NE St. Thomas More Church.
Hahn, Dominic D. *o.s.b.* '80 (SEA) Shelton, WA St. Edward's Church; [M] Lacey, WA St. Martin's Abbey.
Hahn, Francis *o.m.i.* '72 (FgM) Oblates Foreign Missions.
Hahn, Gerald '79 (NEW) Upper Saddle River, NJ Church of the Presentation.
Hahn, James Cornelius *o.p.* (MAD) [3] Madison, WI Blessed Sacrament Church.
Hahn, James David '61 (SCL) Cambridge, MN Christ the King Church.
Hahn, Raymond W. '74 (E) [14] Erie, PA St. Boniface Church; [C] Erie, PA Cathedral Preparatory School.
Hai, Dinh Minh *c.ss.r.* '96 (LA) [R] Baldwin Park, CA Vietnamese Redemptorist Mission.
Haig, Frank R. *s.j.* '60 (BAL) [B] Baltimore, MD Loyola College; [M] Baltimore, MD Jesuit Community of Loyola College, Inc.
Haigerty, Leo J. '57 (LFT) Logansport, IN All Saints Church.
Haight, Roger D. *s.j.* '67 (BO) [W] Cambridge, MA Weston Jesuit Community.
Haikhana, Hilary Nguyen (BO) [62] Boston, MA St. Peter Church.
Hain, Msgr. Raymond B. '48 (LIN) Manley, NE St. Patrick's Church.
Hainen, Philip *o.f.m.cap.* '93 (WH) [N] Charleston, WV Capuchins-St. Anthony Friary.
Haines, Jeffrey R. '85 (MIL) West Bend, WI St. Frances Cabrini Church.
Haines, Kevin J. '87 (LFT) Carmel, IN Our Lady of Mount Carmel Church.
Haiss, Maurice '56 (MOB) Holy Trinity, AL St. Joseph Church.
Hajduch, Joseph *c.pp.s.* '47 (CIN) [B] Carthagena, OH St. Charles.
Hajduk, Msgr. Edward J. '53 (NEW) [3] Bayonne, NJ St. Henry's Church.
Hajduk, Kent *o.f.m.* '62 (DET) [H] Southfield, MI Providence Hospital.
Hajkowski, Stanislaw *s.ch.* '82 (WDC) [V] Silver Spring, MD Friends of John Paul II Foundation.
Hajtas, Francis '46 (NO) Retired.
Hakala, Thomas *o.carm.* '78 (JOL) [J] Darien, IL Carmelite Provincial Office.
Hake, Msgr. James E. '60 (SAL) [1] Salina, KS Cathedral of the Sacred Heart; Aurora, KS St. Peter's Church; [H] Salina, KS Marymount Diocesan Activities Center, Inc.
Hakewerth, Quentin *s.m.* '60 (STL) [P] St. Louis, MO Provincialate of the Society of Mary, Province of St. Louis.
Halabura, Stephen J. '61 (ALN) Lansford, PA St. Ann Church; Lansford, PA SS. Peter and Paul Church.
Halaburda, Walter A. '59 (HBG) [1] Lebanon, PA Assumption of the Blessed Virgin Mary Church.
Haladus, Victorian *o.f.m.* '61 (CHI) Oak Forest, IL Oak Forest Hospital; [N] Oak Forest, IL St. Roch Friary-Franciscan Fathers.
Halaiko, David J. '67 (CLV) [13] Akron, OH Nativity Of the Lord Jesus Church.
Halata, William '53 (VIC) Retired.
Halbach, Msgr. A. A. '32 (DUB) Retired.
Halbert, John K. *m.m.* '59 (NY) [DD] Maryknoll, NY Maryknoll Fathers and Brothers.
Halborg, John E. '80 (NY) [118] New York, NY St. Thomas More Church; [HH] New York, NY St. Ansgar Scandinavian Catholic League.
Haldane, Richard S. '92 (B) Salmon, ID St. Charles Church.
Hale, Msgr. Harry L. '52 (BGP) Retired.
Hale, Robert *o.s.b.cam.* '66 (MRY) [G] Big Sur, CA New Camaldoli Hermitage; [I] Big Sur, CA New Camaldoli Hermitage.
Hale, Robert B. *c.s.b.* '70 (ROC) [13] Rochester, NY Christ the King Church.
Haley, James A. *c.s.p.* '68 (WH) Morgantown, WV St. John's University Parish, Newman Hall Church.
Haley, James R. '87 (ARL) Manassas, VA All Saints Church.
Haley, Joseph '60 (GAL) [K] Houston, TX The Catholic Chaplain Corps.
Haley, Joseph V. *c.m.* '54 (SJ) [N] Los Altos Hills, CA Daughters of Charity of St. Vincent de Paul (Laboure Residence), Seton Provincialate.
Haley, Thomas J. '78 (STL) Crestwood, MO St. Elizabeth of Hungary Church.
Haley, William J. '52 (BO) Holliston, MA St. Mary Church.
Halfacre, Philip '91 (PEO) [B] Ottawa, IL Marquette High School.
Halfacre, Philip D. '91 (PEO) Utica, IL St. Mary Church.
Halfmann, Msgr. Curtis T. '59 (LUB) [5] Lubbock, TX St. John Neumann Church.
Halfpenny, Patrick F. '75 (DET) [A] Detroit, MI Sacred Heart Major Seminary, Inc.
Halkovic, Thomas M. *c.s.c.* '71 (FR) [A] North Easton, MA Stonehill College; [A] North Easton, MA Holy Cross Fathers Religious.
Hall, Adrian B. '64 (NO) Gretna, LA St. Cletus Church.
Hall, Alan *o.m.v.* '88 (LA) Hawaiian Gardens, CA St. Peter Chanel Church.
Hall, Bernard '77 (GR) Retired.
Hall, Charles D. (GR) Portland, MI St. Patrick's Church.
Hall, Daniel *c.s.v.* '88 (CHI) [N] Arlington Heights, IL Viatorian Province Center-Clerics of St. Viator.
Hall, Douglas C. '79 (OM) Military Chaplains.
Hall, Eric *o.f.m.cap.* '96 (NY) [DD] New York, NY Immaculate Conception Friary.
Hall, Henry '48 (MRY) Retired.
Hall, Howard *o.f.m.* '53 (LA) [4] Santa Barbara, CA St. Barbara Church; [R] Santa Barbara, CA Franciscan Friary, Order of Friars Minor (Old Mission).
Hall, Howard B. '62 (BR) St. James, LA St. James Church.
Hall, James W. '70 (ELP) [33] El Paso, TX St. Thomas Aquinas Church.
Hall, Jerome M. *s.j.* '77 (WDC) [M] Washington, DC Carroll House.
Hall, John '82 (PHX) Special Assignment.
Hall, John F. '55 (DET) [4] Westland, MI St. Richard Church.
Hall, John M. '80 (IND) French Lick, IN Our Lady of the Springs Church; Paoli, IN Our Lord Jesus Christ the King Church.
Hall, John R. '80 (CHI) Niles, IL Our Lady of Ransom Church.
Hall, Joseph S. '85 (L) Clementsville, KY St. Bernard Church.
Hall, Martin '52 (RVC) Retired.
Hall, Martin J. '52 (RVC) Levittown, NY St. Bernard Church.
Hall, Michael *o.s.b.* '65 (WDC) [M] Washington, DC St. Anselm's Abbey.
Hall, Ralph T. *o.p.* '55 (PRO) [P] Providence, RI St. Thomas Aquinas Priory at Providence College.
Hall, Randall C. *s.j.* '58 (DEN) [M] Denver, CO Loyola Parish - Jesuit Community.
Hall, Randel C. *s.j.* (DEN) [31] Denver, CO St. Ignatius Loyola Church.
Hall, Richard *o.m.i.* '93 (SAT) [F] San Antonio, TX St. Anthony Catholic High School; [M] San Antonio, TX St. Anthony Catholic High School House.
Hall, Robert '85 (HEL) Bozeman, MT Resurrection Church; [H] Bozeman, MT Montana State University.
Hall, Robert C. '79 (ALT) [11] Altoona, PA Our Lady of Lourdes Church.
Hall, Robert E. '42 (SY) Retired.
Hall, Rodger '94 (AUS) [18] Austin, TX St. Margaret of Scotland Church.
Hall, Rodney L. '91 (SAC) Alturas, CA Sacred Heart Church.
Hall, Sidney Peter '57 (SAC) [19] Sacramento, CA St. Peter Church.
Hall, Thomas P. *c.s.p.* '77 (NY) [DD] Jamaica Estates, NY Paulist Fathers Generalate.
Hall, Thomas P. *c.s.p.* '77 (ORG) El Toro, CA El Toro Marine Base.
Hall, Walter J. '49 (ALN) Heckscherville, PA St. Kieran Church.
Hallahan, Kenneth P. '75 (CAM) [7] Camden, NJ St. Joseph's Pro-Cathedral.
Hallahan, Timothy J. '57 (SPR) Southwick, MA Our Lady of the Lake Church.
Hallahan, William *o.m.i.* '59 (SEA) [28] Seattle, WA Our Lady of Guadalupe Church.
Hallee, Roger *o.m.i.* '63 (FgM) Oblates Foreign Missions.
Hallemann, John L. '55 (STL) Oakville, MO Queen of All Saints Church.
Haller, James W. '62 (MAN) Auburn, NH St. Peter Church.
Haller, Joseph A. *s.j.* '55 (WDC) [M] Washington, DC The Jesuit Community at Georgetown University.
Haller, Robert R. *o.p.* '69 (WDC) [11] Washington, DC St. Dominic Church & Priory Church.

Halleran, Thomas P. *s.v.d.* '44 (BO) [6] Somerville, MA Patronage of St. Joseph Church.
Halleron, James E. '97 (TOL) Mansfield, OH St. Peter Church.
Hallett, Garth L. *s.j.* (STL) [C] St. Louis, MO Saint Louis University.
Hallett, Garth L. *s.j.* '59 (STL) [P] St. Louis, MO Jesuit Community Corporation at St. Louis University - Jesuit Hall.
Halley, Kirino B. '92 (CI) Moen, FM Holy Family Church; [C] Tunnuk, Chuuk, FM Vicariate Residence.
Halley, Thomas A. *s.j.* '48 (OM) [23] Omaha, NE St. John Church; [K] Omaha, NE Jesuit Community At Creighton University.
Halligan, James '43 (LIN) Retired.
Halligan, James J. '51 (NY) [105] New York, NY St. Peter Church.
Halligan, John J. *s.j.* '61 (FgM) Provinces.
Halligan, John J. *s.j.* '61 (NY) [DD] New York, NY Jesuit Provincial's Office.
Halligan, Raymond F. *o.p.* '60 (NY) [HH] New York, NY Dominican Friars' Guilds.
Halligan, Raymond Ferrer *o.p.* '60 (NY) [DD] New York, NY St. Vincent Ferrer Priory.
Hallin, Msgr. Albert W. '61 (PEO) [1] Champaign, IL Holy Cross Church.
Hallinan, Edward J. '83 (PH) [93] Philadelphia, PA St. Martin De Porres Church.
Hallinan, Mark *s.j.* '95 (NY) [DD] New York, NY St. Ignatius Loyola Residence.
Hallinan, Mark C. *s.j.* '95 (NY) [51] New York, NY St. Ignatius Loyola Church.
Hallissey, Msgr. James T. '40 (B) Retired.
Hallissey, LaSalle *o.p.* '79 (ANC) [1] Anchorage, AK Holy Family Cathedral.
Hallisy, Peter *c.p.* '51 (HRT) [M] West Hartford, CT Holy Family Monastery/Retreat.
Halliwell, Raymond *m.ss.a.* '93 (NOR) [A] Cromwell, CT Holy Apostles College and Seminary; [F] Cromwell, CT Missionaries of the Holy Apostles.
Halliwell, Robert J. '57 (NEW) Northvale, NJ St. Anthony's Church.
Hallock, Addison *m.ss.a.* '74 (NOR) [A] Cromwell, CT Holy Apostles College and Seminary; [F] Cromwell, CT Missionaries of the Holy Apostles.
Halloran, Msgr. Edward D. '35 (BGP) Retired; [O] Stamford, CT Our Lady Queen of the Clergy Home.
Halloran, Emmet '50 (ROC) Retired.
Halloran, James F. '43 (COS) Calhan, CO St. Michael's Church.
Halloran, Jerome D. '54 (WIN) Retired.
Halloran, John '48 (HON) Retired.
Halloran, John C. '62 (PRO) Narragansett, RI St. Thomas More Church.
Halloran, John M. '87 (PH) [71] Philadelphia, PA Incarnation of Our Lord Church.
Halloran, Joseph '53 (ALB) New Lebanon, NY Immaculate Conception Church.
Halloran, Joseph H. '47 (COS) Retired.
Halloran, Paul F. '53 (WIN) Retired.
Halls, Jerome M. *s.j.* '77 (BAL) [M] Baltimore, MD Jesuit Fathers and Brothers Maryland Provincial Curia.
Hallsten, Thomas J. *o.s.b.* '90 (STP) Lake St. Croix Beach, MN St. Francis Of Assisi Church.
Halphen, Jude A. '93 (LAF) Cankton, LA St. John Berchmans Church.
Halphen, Marshall J. *o.s.a.* '63 (ALB) Waterford, NY St. Mary of the Assumption Church.
Halpin, John P. '54 (RVC) Central Islip, NY St. John of God Church; West Brentwood, NY Pilgrim Psychiatric Center.
Halpin, Joseph '79 (TR) [2] Toms River, NJ St. Justin Church.
Halpin, Joseph W. *m.m.* '52 (FgM) Maryknoll Foreign Missions.
Halpin, Leo F. '42 (NY) Retired.
Halpin, Raymond J. '32 (ALB) Retired.
Halpine, Msgr. James F. '37 (TLS) Retired.
Halpine, Msgr. James F. '52 (TLS) [1] Tulsa, OK Holy Family Cathedral.
Halstead, James R. *o.s.a.* '76 (CHI) Evanston, IL St. Nicholas Church.
Halstead, Philip '62 (PT) Retired.
Halter, Robert *o.s.b.* '60 (OM) [C] Elkhorn, NE Mount Michael High School; [K] Elkhorn, NE Mount Michael Abbey.
Halter, Robert *c.ss.r.* '70 (DET) [33] Detroit, MI Holy Redeemer Church.
Halton, Thomas P. '50 (WDC) [C] Washington, DC Catholic University of America, The.
Halus, Robert '82 (PBR) Pleasant City, OH St. Michael Church.
Haluska, Charles A. '51 (COL) Retired.
Halvey, William *s.v.d.* '76 (BLX) [A] Bay St. Louis, MS St. Augustine's.
Ham, George E. '67 (MAN) Hampton, NH Our Lady of the Miraculous Medal Church.
Ham, Jerome '68 (PEO) [2] Streator, IL St. Anthony of Padua Church.
Hamaday, Ronald *o.s.a.* '78 (CAM) [C] Richland, NJ St. Augustine Preparatory School.
Hamaday, Ronald A. *o.s.a.* '78 (PH) [G] Malvern, PA Malvern Preparatory School for Boys.
Hamak, William '92 (SFS) Armour, SD St. Paul the Apostle Church.
Hamame, Jaime '90 (SB) Alta Loma, CA St. Peter & St. Paul Church.
Hambach, Lawrence *s.v.d.* '61 (FgM) Society of the Divine Word Foreign Missions.
Hambrough, Patrick K. '85 (STL) [15] St. Louis, MO Our Lady of the Holy Cross Church.
Hamburger, Msgr. Donald C. '46 (CHR) Retired.
Hamel, Edward L. *o.s.a.* (PH) [AA] Willowburn, PA Order of St. Augustine.
Hamel, Edward L. *o.s.a.* '54 (KAL) Douglas, MI St. Peter Church; [E] Douglas, MI Order of St. Augustine.
Hamel, J. Thomas *s.j.* '58 (WOR) [N] Worcester, MA Jesuits of Holy Cross College, Inc.
Hamel, James A. '92 (NEW) Maywood, NJ Our Lady Queen of Peace Church.
Hamel, Joseph *o.m.i.* '32 (SAT) [K] San Antonio, TX Oblate Madonna Residence.
Hamel, Joseph L. *m.m.* '85 (FgM) Maryknoll Foreign Missions.
Hamel, Philip N. '85 (FR) Absent on Leave.
Hamel, Robert F. '83 (STP) Retired.
Hamel, Roland M. *o.m.i.* '53 (MAN) [K] Colebrook, NH Shrine of Our Lady of Grace.
Hamernick, Joseph M. *s.j.* '62 (SCR) [C] Scranton, PA University of Scranton.
Hamill, Francis J. *s.j.* '61 (NEW) [C] Jersey City, NJ St. Peter's Preparatory School.
Hamill, Gregory J. '94 (PH) [102] Philadelphia, PA St. Matthew Church.
Hamilton, Daniel E. '72 (ARL) Lake Ridge, VA St. Elizabeth Seton Church.
Hamilton, Msgr. Daniel S. '58 (RVC) Lindenhurst, NY Our Lady of Perpetual Help Church.
Hamilton, Donald Joseph *o.c.s.o.* '46 (SPC) [E] Ava, MO Assumption Abbey (Trappist).
Hamilton, Edward A. '59 (ORL) Retired.
Hamilton, James '36 (SEA) Retired.
Hamilton, James '58 (CC) Aransas Pass, TX St. Mary, Star of the Sea Church; On Special Assignment.
Hamilton, James J. '53 (PRO) [11] Warwick, RI St. Timothy Church.
Hamilton, John W. '70 (BUR) Shelburne, VT St. Catherine of Siena Church.
Hamilton, Joseph K. '54 (L) Retired.
Hamilton, Kenneth *s.v.d.* '95 (IND) [34] Indianapolis, IN St. Rita Church.
Hamilton, Lamont R. '79 (NY) [148] Bronx, NY Holy Rosary Church.
Hamilton, Mark M. '94 (L) [11] Louisville, KY St. Barnabas Church.
Hamilton, Philip A. '44 (DUB) Retired.
Hamilton, Terence J. '73 (CIN) [86] Cincinnati, OH St. Vincent Ferrer Church.
Hamilton, Thomas M. *s.m.* '88 (OAK) [N] Berkeley, CA Marist Fathers and Brothers.
Hamilton, William J. *s.j.* '63 (BO) [E] Boston, MA Boston College High School & Jesuit Community; [W] Boston, MA The Society of Jesus of New England-Provincial Offices.
Hamilton, William J. '80 (SPR) [2] Holyoke, MA Holy Cross Church.
Hamisi, Protus '93 (ROC) Pittsford, NY St. Louis Church.
Hamlet, Ralph '62 (RIC) Scottsville, VA St. George Church.
Hamlett, Christopher '82 (E) [B] Erie, PA Gannon University.
Hamlin, Raymond G. '91 (CLV) Cuyahoga Falls, OH St. Joseph Church.
Hamm, David A. *s.t.* '75 (JKS) Philadelphia, MS Holy Rosary Church.
Hamm, M. Dennis *s.j.* '70 (OM) [K] Omaha, NE Jesuit Community At Creighton University.
Hamm, Robert E. *s.j.* '68 (BAL) [M] Baltimore, MD Jesuit Fathers and Brothers Maryland Provincial Curia.
Hamm, Robert E. *s.j.* '68 (FgM) Provinces.
Hammel, Gerald *s.m.* '78 (SAT) Helotes, TX Our Lady of Guadalupe Church.
Hammelman, William *o.s.b.* '71 (P) [A] St. Benedict, OR Mount Angel Seminary; [L] St. Benedict, OR Mt. Angel Abbey.
Hammer, Msgr. Edmond '42 (NY) Retired.
Hammer, James *o.f.m.cap.* '65 (NOR) [4] Middletown, CT St. Pius X Church.
Hammer, Jefferson '60 (NY) Manhattan, NY St. Vincent Hospital; [W] New York, NY St. Vincent's Hospital and Medical Center of New York.
Hammer, John E. '79 (SAG) St. Louis, MI St. Joseph Church.
Hammer, Michael J. '69 (MIL) Special Assignment.
Hammer, William D. '80 (L) [28] Louisville, KY St. Gabriel the Archangel Church.
Hammerl, Msgr. Leo E. '44 (BUF) Retired; [O] Tonawanda, NY O'Hara Residence.
Hammerschmitt, Clemens '73 (PMB) Lake Worth, FL St. Matthew Church.
Hammerschmitt, Clemens '77 (PMB) [J] Palm Beach Gardens, FL Diocesan Council of Catholic Women.
Hammerstein, Harold *o.s.b.* '48 (IND) [J] St. Meinrad, IN St. Meinrad Archabbey.
Hammett, Peter *o.s.b.* '72 (NO) [P] St. Benedict, LA St. Joseph Abbey.
Hammett, Peter E. *o.s.b.* '72 (NO) [A] St. Benedict, LA St. Joseph's Seminary College.
Hammond, Charles *o.m.i.* '76 (LUB) Lamesa, TX St. Margaret Mary Church.
Hammond, Gerard E. *m.m.* '60 (FgM) Maryknoll Foreign Missions.
Hammond, H. Martin '73 (BAL) [43] Baltimore, MD St. Isaac Jogues Church.
Hammond, John *o.s.b.* '50 (BUR) [E] Weston, VT Priory of Benedictine Monks.
Hammond, Mark '89 (COL) [5] Columbus, OH St. Andrew Church.
Hammond, Robert W. '67 (ROC) Bath, NY St. Mary Church.
Hampe, Ray '54 (STL) [K] St. Charles, MO St. Joseph Health Center.
Hampe, Msgr. Raymond A. '54 (STL) [5] St. Charles, MO St. Peter Church; St. Charles, MO St. Joseph Health Center.
Hamperzonian, Jerry '70 (PSC) On Duty Outside Diocese.
Hamperzonian, Jerry '70 (SD) [3] San Diego, CA Blessed Sacrament Church; La Jolla, CA Veterans Administration Hospital.
Hampsch, John *c.m.f.* '52 (LA) [R] Los Angeles, CA Claretian Retreat Center Community.
Hampton, James J. '88 (MIA) [12] Fort Lauderdale, FL St. Pius X Church.
Hamrogue, John M. *c.ss.r.* '63 (FgM) Redemptorist Foreign Missions.
Han, Andrew '48 (LA) Retired.
Han Kim, Andrew Sung (P) [11] Portland, OR Church of Korean Martyrs.
Hanacsek, John '49 (TOL) Retired.
Hanauska, Joseph F. '40 (MIL) Retired.
Hanbury, Kevin M. '72 (NEW) [B] South Orange, NJ Seton Hall University.
Hanchak, Augustine *c.pp.s.* '52 (CIN) [B] Carthagena, OH St. Charles.
Hanchon, Donald F. '74 (DET) [24] Detroit, MI St. Gabriel Church.
Hancock, Msgr. George H. '47 (OWN) Grand Rivers, KY St. Anthony of Padua Church.
Hancock, Walter '47 (OWN) Retired.
Hand, Chester, Jr. '86 (AUS) Retired.
Hand, Dennis M. '75 (GRY) On Duty Outside the Diocese.
Hand, Kenneth J. '72 (BRK) [237] Queens, NY Sacred Heart of Jesus Church.
Hand, Msgr. Kevin '52 (AMA) White Deer, TX Sacred Heart Church.
Hand, Raymond *o.f.m.cap.* '62 (SPR) [L] Springfield, MA St. Francis of Assisi Chapel and Catholic Information Center.
Hand, Robert T. '97 (SAV) [4] Savannah, GA Most Blessed Sacrament Church.
Handges, Msgr. William E. '64 (ALN) [1] Easton, PA St. Anthony of Padua Church.
Handley, Robert '47 (LAN) Retired.
Handrahan, John *s.j.* '58 (MIA) [1] Pompano Beach, FL Assumption Church.
Handrahan, John B. *s.j.* '58 (BO) [W] Boston, MA The Society of Jesus of New England-Provincial Offices.
Hands, Michael '93 (RVC) West Islip, NY Our Lady of Lourdes Church.
Handwerker, Valentine '74 (MEM) Lexington, TN St. Andrew Church.
Hane, Howard S. (BO) Retired.
Hanefeldt, Joseph G. '84 (OM) [13] Omaha, NE St. Elizabeth Ann Church.
Hanel, Charles T. '83 (MIL) Hubertus, WI St. Hubert Church.
Haney, John R. '61 (PIT) Whitehall, PA St. Gabriel of the Sorrowful Virgin Church.
Haney, Michael *o.f.m.* '74 (SAT) [46] San Antonio, TX St. Joseph Church; [50] San Antonio, TX St. Leonard's Church.
Haney, Richard M. '35 (DET) Retired.
Haney, Thomas R. '58 (HBG) New Cumberland, PA St. Theresa of the Infant Jesus Church.
Haney, William *o.f.m.* '84 (SD) [H] San Luis Rey, CA Mission San Luis Rey; [K] San Luis Rey, CA Mission San Luis Rey Retreat.
Hanh, Joseph Phan Trong '70 (KC) [17] Kansas City, MO Church of the Holy Martyrs.
Hanhauser, Martin A. '42 (SP) [O] St. Petersburg, FL St. Anthony Friary.
Hanic, John D. '83 (CHL) [4] Charlotte, NC St. Ann Church.
Hanicak, Msgr. Robert A. '36 (GBG) Retired; [G] Greensburg, PA Neumann House.
Hanifin, Michael P. '87 (ORG) Garden Grove, CA St.

Columban Church.
Hankiewicz, Edward '79 (GR) On Special Assignment.
Hankiewicz, Edward A. '79 (GR) [21] Grand Rapids, MI Sacred Heart Church.
Hankinson, Aloysius *t.o.r.* '50 (ALT) [F] Hollidaysburg, PA St. Joseph Friary.
Hankomoone, Cornelius (BAL) [M] Baltimore, MD Sulpician Provincial House.
Hanks, Joseph H. '81 (NOR) Old Saybrook, CT St. John Church.
Hankus, David '84 (JOL) Bolingbrook, IL St. Francis of Assisi Church.
Hanley, Msgr. Andrew W. '40 (SD) Retired.
Hanley, Boniface F. *o.f.m.* '50 (PAT) West Milford Township, NJ St. Joseph Church.
Hanley, Charles *o.f.m.cap.* '80 (FgM) Capuchin Foreign Missions.
Hanley, Dennis '81 (CHY) Cheyenne, WY U.S. Veterans Administration Hospital 1.
Hanley, Dennis P. '81 (HRT) Military Chaplains.
Hanley, Foster *o.carm.* '63 (TUC) [A] Tucson, AZ Salpointe Catholic High School; [F] Tucson, AZ Carmelite Priory.
Hanley, Francis X. *c.s.sp.* '59 (PIT) [Q] Bethel Park, PA Holy Ghost Animation Center.
Hanley, Gerald T. '73 (RNO) Carson City, NV St. Teresa's of Avila Church.
Hanley, James F. *s.j.* '47 (MIL) [P] Milwaukee, WI Jesuit Provincial Office, Wisconsin Province.
Hanley, Msgr. James P. '51 (COL) Retired.
Hanley, James R. *s.j.* '58 (SJ) [L] Los Altos, CA Jesuit Retreat House.
Hanley, James T. '62 (PAT) Retired.
Hanley, John '56 (PHX) [1] Tempe, AZ Holy Spirit Church.
Hanley, John *o.m.i.* '70 (BO) [9] Lowell, MA St. Marie Church.
Hanley, John *o.s.f.s.* '86 (ALN) [B] Center Valley, PA Allentown College of St. Francis de Sales; [O] Kutztown, PA Christopher House.
Hanley, John A. *o.s.f.s.* '86 (ALN) [K] Center Valley, PA Oblates of St. Francis de Sales.
Hanley, John G. '50 (NEW) Retired.
Hanley, John P. '51 (MIL) Retired.
Hanley, John P. '94 (PAT) [8] Paterson, NJ St. Gerard Majella Church.
Hanley, John W. *o.m.i.* '70 (BO) [16] Lowell, MA Sacred Heart Church.
Hanley, Joseph F. '68 (CHR) [7] Charleston, SC Blessed Sacrament Church.
Hanley, Lawrence F. '52 (CHI) Retired.
Hanley, Thomas E. '65 (WIL) Dover, DE Holy Cross Church.
Hanley, William '45 (SPK) Retired.
Hanlon, Andrew J. '68 (PH) Brookhaven, PA Our Lady of Charity Church.
Hanlon, Berard J. *o.f.m.* '63 (FgM) Franciscan Foreign Missions.
Hanlon, Capistran J. *o.f.m.* '60 (ALB) [B] Loudonville, NY Siena College.
Hanlon, Edward J. '86 (WOR) [2] Southbridge, MA Notre Dame Church.
Hanlon, Francis J. *o.s.f.s.* '76 (WIL) [I] Wilmington, DE Oblates of St. Francis De Sales.
Hanlon, Gavin P. *o.f.m.* '56 (FgM) Franciscan Foreign Missions.
Hanlon, Msgr. James J. '38 (NY) Retired; [Z] New York, NY Kateri Residence.
Hanlon, John R. '55 (BO) Retired.
Hanlon, Kevin J. *m.m.* '89 (FgM) Maryknoll Foreign Missions.
Hanlon, Louis J. *s.j.* '39 (STL) [O] St. Louis, MO Fusz Pavilion.
Hanlon, Morgan *c.p.* '52 (NEW) [N] Union City, NJ Congregation of the Passion (Passionists)-St. Michael's Residence.
Hanlon, Robert M. *s.j.* '64 (BO) [E] Boston, MA Boston College High School & Jesuit Community; [W] Boston, MA The Society of Jesus of New England-Provincial Offices.
Hanlon, Robert P. *o.s.f.s.* '57 (PH) [AA] Philadelphia, PA Oblates of St. Francis De Sales.
Hanlon, Thomas C. '38 (CHI) Retired.
Hanly, Denis J. *m.m.* '59 (FgM) Maryknoll Foreign Missions.
Hanly, John J. '50 (LA) Retired.
Hanly, Joseph M. *c.s.p.* '53 (NY) [DD] Jamaica Estates, NY Paulist Fathers Generalate.
Hanly, Joseph M. *c.s.p.* '53 (SFR) [31] San Francisco, CA Old St. Mary's Cathedral.
Hanly, Michael A. '67 (NEW) Verona, NJ Our Lady of the Lake Church.
Hanly, Thomas '62 (MIA) Hollywood, FL Little Flower Church; Retired.
Hann, Michael *c.i.c.m.* '73 (FgM) Missionhurst Foreign Missions.
Hanna, Austin B. '36 (ROC) Retired.
Hanna, Don Michael '64 (RIC) Yorktown, VA St. Joan of Arc Church.
Hanna, George *s.d.b.* '66 (NY) [117] New York, NY St. Thomas the Apostle Church; [HH] New York, NY Don Bosco Harlem Association, Inc.
Hanna, Jack H. *c.s.b.* '74 (GAL) [F] Houston, TX St. Thomas High School.
Hanna, Jirjis '67 (EST) Troy, MI St. Joseph Chaldean Parish.
Hannafey, Francis T. *s.j.* '93 (BGP) [O] Fairfield, CT The Fairfield Jesuit Community-Fairfield University.
Hannah, Raymond *s.v.d.* (LAF) Leonville, LA St. Catherine Church.
Hannahs, Norman G. *c.s.sp.* '56 (DET) [47] Detroit, MI St. Mary Church.
Hannan, Gabriel *s.t.* '55 (WDC) [M] Adelphi, MD Missionary Servants of the Most Holy Trinity.
Hannan, Msgr. Herbert J. '37 (OG) Retired.
Hannan, Msgr. Herbert J. '39 (OG) Brasher Falls, NY St. Patrick Church.
Hannan, James E. *o.s.a.* '44 (SD) [H] San Diego, CA Augustinian Community.
Hannan, James G. '81 (BRK) [14] Brooklyn, NY St. Augustine Church.
Hannan, John '55 (SAC) Weed, CA Holy Family Church.
Hannan, Msgr. John P. '47 (ARL) Retired.
Hannappel, Joseph A. '84 (GI) Chappell, NE St. Joseph's Church.
Hannaway, Arthur W. '85 (VEN) [5] Sarasota, FL St. Patrick Church.
Hanneke, Richard E. '76 (STL) Ellisville, MO St. Clare of Assisi Church; [W] St. Louis, MO Archdiocesan Charitable Bequest Council.
Hanneman, Dennis A. '72 (OM) [47] Omaha, NE St. Vincent de Paul Church.
Hannes, David A. '83 (PRM) Flushing, MI St. Michael Church.
Hannick, Anthony S. '58 (OAK) [1] Walnut Creek, CA St. Anne Church; Military Chaplains.
Hannick, Anthony S. '58 (YAK) Retired.
Hannifin, Francis M. '45 (L) Retired.
Hannigan, John T. '76 (CHI) Other Assignments.
Hannigan, John T. '76 (SFD) Morrisonville, IL St. Maurice Church.
Hannigan, Raymond J. '91 (HEL) Libby, MT St. Joseph Church.
Hannigan, Msgr. Richard '59 (WOR) [M] Worcester, MA Vianney House.
Hannigan, Msgr. Richard F. (WOR) Retired.
Hannigan, Thomas J. '49 (MAN) [6] Manchester, NH St. Catherine Church.
Hannon, Msgr. James J. '45 (BLX) Retired.
Hannon, James J. '57 (RVC) Brentwood, NY St. Anne's Church.
Hannon, James W. '88 (BAL) Westernport, MD St. Peter Church.
Hannon, John Mark '60 (BO) Hanson, MA St. Joseph the Worker Church.
Hannon, John P. '76 (HRT) Retired.
Hannon, Ken *o.m.i.* '72 (SAT) [C] San Antonio, TX Oblate School of Theology; [M] San Antonio, TX De Mazenod House.
Hannon, Kevin E. '75 (SY) Mattydale, NY St. Margaret Church.
Hannon, Michael '47 (ORL) Retired.
Hannon, Patrick '89 (OAK) [3] San Leandro, CA St. Felicitas Church.
Hannon, Richard T. '93 (GAY) Elmira, MI St. Thomas Aquinas Church; Vanderbilt, MI Holy Redeemer Church.
Hannon, Robert E. '54 (HON) Retired.
Hannon, Robert J. '79 (Y) Masury, OH St. Bernadette Church.
Hannon, Timothy G. '62 (MIA) [3] Fort Lauderdale, FL St. Anthony Church.
Hanowsky, Andrew '88 (SJP) [1] Parma, OH St. Josaphat Cathedral.
Hanrahan, Denis G. '59 (OKL) Guthrie, OK St. Mary's Church.
Hanrahan, Edward J. *s.j.* '61 (BO) [W] Chestnut Hill, MA The Jesuit Community at Boston College.
Hanrahan, John A. '46 (GF) Retired.
Hanrahan, John A. *s.j.* '66 (RCK) [5] Rockford, IL Holy Family Church.
Hanrahan, John W. '55 (L) [61] Louisville, KY Our Mother of Sorrows Church.
Hanrahan, Michael '59 (ORL) Deltona, FL Our Lady of the Lakes Church.
Hanrahan, Michael F. '71 (COL) Leave of Absence.
Hanrahan, William (LAV) Military Chaplains.
Hanrahan, William P. '69 (NEW) Military Chaplains.
Hanratty, Brendan '45 (SR) Retired.
Hanratty, Brendan *o.c.s.o.* '58 (SLC) [F] Huntsville, UT Abbey of Our Lady of the Holy Trinity of the Order of Cistercians.
Hansen, Albert M. '65 (BUF) West Falls, NY St. George Church.
Hansen, Howard *o.f.m.conv.* '57 (DUB) Ames, IA St. Cecilia Church.
Hansen, John R. *s.m.p.* '81 (SPC) [E] Marionville, MO The Society of Our Mother of Peace, Sons of Our Mother of Peace.
Hansen, Lawrence H. '68 (NU) On Duty Outside the Diocese.
Hansen, Lawrence H. '68 (PH) [U] Philadelphia, PA Mercy Hospital of Philadelphia; [U] Darby, PA Mercy Catholic Medical Center.
Hansen, Michael H. '67 (NEW) West Orange, NJ Our Lady of Lourdes Church.
Hansen, Norbert P. *o.carm.* '54 (NY) [DD] Middletown, NY St. Albert's Priory.
Hansen, Robert H. '40 (LC) Retired.
Hansen, Thomas J. *s.j.* '96 (MIL) [P] Milwaukee, WI Jesuit Provincial Office, Wisconsin Province.
Hansen, Thomas J. *s.j.* '96 (OM) [K] Omaha, NE Jesuit Community At Creighton University.
Hanser, David J. '58 (MIL) [K] Milwaukee, WI St. Joseph's Hospital of Franciscan Sisters, Milwaukee, Inc.
Hanser, F. Patrick *c.m.* '70 (DAL) [I] Dallas, TX St. Paul Medical Center.
Hansmann, Joseph D. '62 (BEL) Paderborn, IL St. Michael Church.
Hanson, Christopher *o.s.b.* '96 (STL) [F] Creve Coeur, MO St. Louis Priory School; [P] St. Louis, MO The Abbey of St. Mary and St. Louis.
Hanson, Donald (RVC) Selden, NY St. Margaret of Scotland Church.
Hanson, Donald M. '71 (RVC) Priests Released from Diocesan Assignment.
Hanson, Howard *o.f.m.conv.* '57 (DUB) Gilbert, IA SS. Peter and Paul Church.
Hanson, Msgr. James E. '61 (STL) Zell, MO St. Joseph Church.
Hanson, Kirby C. '70 (SFR) [51] San Francisco, CA St. Thomas, The Apostle Church.
Hanson, Richard N. '75 (CHL) [11] Charlotte, NC St. Vincent de Paul Church.
Hanson, William A. '72 (RVC) Port Jefferson, NY St. Gerard Majella Church.
Hanudel, Francis *o.f.m.* '72 (NY) [DD] New York, NY Franciscan Province of the Immaculate Conception.
Hanudel, Francis *o.f.m.* '72 (PAT) Paterson, NJ St. Joseph Hospital; [J] Paterson, NJ St. Joseph's Hospital and Medical Center.
Hanus, Thomas J. '66 (AUS) Cameron, TX St. Monica's Church.
Hanwell, John J. *s.j.* '91 (BO) [E] Boston, MA Boston College High School & Jesuit Community.
Hanzely, Joseph B. *s.j.* '48 (ALN) [A] Wernersville, PA Novitiate of St. Isaac Jogues.
Hanzo, Robert '56 (CLV) Retired.
Hanzo, Robert G. '56 (CLV) Painesville, OH St. Mary Church.
Hapanowicz, Arthur R. '56 (SY) [2] Utica, NY Holy Trinity Church; [W] Utica, NY Holy Trinity.
Hapka, Jerome A. *s.a.c.* '55 (MIL) [P] Milwaukee, WI Pallotti House.
Happel, Stephen P. '70 (IND) On Duty Outside the Archdiocese.
Happel, Stephen W. '70 (WDC) [C] Washington, DC Catholic University of America, The.
Harahan, Msgr. Robert E. '74 (NEW) Summit, NJ St. Teresa's Church.
Harak, G. Simon *s.j.* '79 (BGP) [A] Fairfield, CT Fairfield University; [O] Fairfield, CT The Fairfield Jesuit Community-Fairfield University.
Haran, Ignatius '59 (SAC) Folsom, CA St. John the Baptist Church.
Haran, James E. '44 (BUF) Retired.
Harasim, Edward A. '78 (CHI) [77] Chicago, IL St. Henry Church.
Harbaugh, James M. *s.j.* '78 (SEA) [A] Seattle, WA Seattle University.
Harbaugh, Paul E. '74 (BEL) Leave of Absence.
Harbert, William S. '62 (PEO) Absent on Leave.
Harbison, William *c.ss.r.* '66 (BAL) [87] Baltimore, MD Sacred Heart of Jesus Church.
Harbour, Gerald G. '73 (PRO) Providence, RI Rhode Island Hospital.
Harbour, Linn S. '86 (OM) Military Chaplains.
Harcarik, Bernard M. '63 (PIT) [63] Pittsburgh, PA Prince of Peace Church.
Hardebeck, Donald E. '45 (LFT) Retired.
Harder, Ken '96 (TLS) [6] Tulsa, OK Christ the King Church.
Harder, William '86 (NY) [214] Staten Island, NY St. Mary of the Assumption Church.
Hardesty, Ernest '75 (LR) [J] Little Rock, AR Catholic Campus Ministries.
Hardesty, Ernest L. *v.f.* '75 (LR) Russellville, AR St. John's Church.
Hardesty, Lawrence A. '51 (L) [M] St. Catharine, KY Sansbury Memorial Infirmary.
Hardesty, Leo '31 (OKL) Retired.
Hardiman, Msgr. James C. '39 (CHI) Retired.
Hardiman, John J. '49 (ALB) Latham, NY Our Lady of the Assumption Church.
Hardiman, Michael J. '78 (BRK) [A] Douglaston, NY Immaculate Conception Pastoral Center; [U] Douglaston, NY Institutional Services Residence.
Hardin, Boniface *o.s.b.* '59 (IND) [J] St. Meinrad, IN St. Meinrad Archabbey.
Hardin, John *o.f.m.* '82 (OAK) [N] Oakland, CA

Franciscan Friars Provincial Office, Province of St. Barbara.
Hardin, John S. *o.f.m.* '86 (OAK) [N] Oakland, CA Franciscan Friars Provincial Office, Province of St. Barbara.
Hardin, Roy '64 (CAM) On Sick Leave.
Harding, Ignatius *o.f.m.* '65 (FgM) Franciscan Foreign Missions.
Harding, Pius X *o.s.b.* '93 (P) [L] St. Benedict, OR Mt. Angel Abbey.
Hardman, John E. *s.s.j.* '44 (GAL) [62] Houston, TX Our Mother of Mercy Church.
Hardman, John E. *s.s.j.* '44 (NO) [29] New Orleans, LA St. David Church.
Hardon, John *s.j.* '47 (WDC) [V] Kensington, MD Inter Mirifica.
Hardon, John A. *s.j.* '47 (DET) [27] Detroit, MI Gesu Church.
Hardy, John J. '38 (DET) Retired.
Hardy, Laurence A. *o.f.m.* '46 (SP) [O] St. Petersburg, FL St. Anthony Friary.
Hare, John B. '53 (PMB) Retired.
Hare, Robert '70 (NSH) [H] Nashville, TN Glenmary Home Missioners; [L] Nashville, TN Glenmary Department of Pastoral Services.
Haren, Donald J. *m.m.* '47 (SJ) [M] Los Altos, CA Maryknoll.
Haren, Thomas A. '73 (CLV) [36] Cleveland, OH St. Jerome Church.
Harer, Eric K. '84 (SY) [5] Oswego, NY St. Paul Church.
Harfmann, John G. *s.s.j.* '62 (WDC) [B] Washington, DC Josephite Pastoral Center; [B] Washington, DC St. Joseph's Seminary.
Hargadon, James E. '55 (L) Mount Washington, KY St. Francis Xavier Church.
Hargarten, Joseph F. '41 (GI) Retired.
Hargesheimer, Thomas J. '68 (WIN) Owatonna, MN St. Joseph's Church.
Hargreaves, Henry *s.j.* '47 (FBK) Nightmute, AK Our Lady of Perpetual Help Church; Tununak, AK St. Joseph Church.
Hargreaves, Henry G. *s.j.* '47 (FBK) [E] St. Marys, AK Brother Joe Prince Jesuit Community.
Hargrove, Gerard (WDC) [S] Washington, DC Archdiocesan Campus Ministry.
Hargrove, Jerry E. '76 (WDC) Special Ministries.
Harguindeguy, Msgr. John '67 (FRS) [1] Fresno, CA St. John Cathedral.
Harhager, John H. *s.m.* '79 (WDC) [M] Washington, DC Marist Provincial House.
Harkabus, Donald W. *o.s.a.* '58 (CHI) [N] Olympia Fields, IL The Augustinian Provincialate Tolentine Center.
Harkins, Bernard K. *o.p.* '67 (WDC) [C] Washington, DC Catholic University of America, The.
Harkins, Conrad *o.f.m.* '61 (STU) [A] Steubenville, OH Franciscan University of Steubenville; [F] Steubenville, OH Holy Spirit Monastery.
Harkins, Frederick A. *s.j.* '39 (BO) [W] Weston, MA Campion Health Center, Inc.
Harkins, John M. '65 (PH) [103] Philadelphia, PA St. Michael Church.
Harkins, Kenneth *o.p.* '67 (WDC) [B] Washington, DC Dominican House of Studies.
Harkins, Michael J. '79 (BO) Chelmsford, MA St. Mary Church.
Harkins, Msgr. Thaddeus '55 (JKS) Port Gibson, MS St. Joseph Church.
Harkins, Thomas A. '71 (CAM) [1] Camden, NJ Immaculate Conception Cathedral.
Harkrader, Edward O. '69 (PEO) Princeton, IL St. Louis Church.
Harlan, Anthony Vern (SAC) Absent on Leave.
Harlan, Michael J. *o.f.m.* (ALB) [S] Loudonville, NY Siena College.
Harland, Norman E. *s.j.* '67 (CHI) [D] Wilmette, IL Loyola Academy.
Harley, Ronald P. '67 (ROC) Geneva, NY St. Francis de Sales Church.
Harlow, Denis '58 (BLX) [4] Biloxi, MS Sacred Heart Church; Biloxi, MS Biloxi Regional Hospital, Gulf Coast Community Hospital.
Harlow, Francis '88 (B) Leave of Absence.
Harlow, Lance W. '93 (BUR) Rutland, VT Christ the King Church.
Harman, Charles W. '54 (LA) Retired.
Harman, Paul F. *s.j.* '68 (BO) [W] Boston, MA The Society of Jesus of New England-Provincial Offices.
Harman, Paul F. *s.j.* '68 (CHI) [C] Chicago, IL Jesuit Community at Loyola University of Chicago.
Harmening, Adrian W. *o.s.b.* '55 (RIC) [7] Richmond, VA St. Benedict Church; [B] Richmond, VA Benedictine High School; [L] Richmond, VA Mary Mother of the Church Abbey.
Harmless, J. William *s.j.* '87 (MOB) [B] Mobile, AL Spring Hill College.
Harmless, William J. *s.j.* '87 (CHI) [C] Chicago, IL Jesuit Community at Loyola University of Chicago.
Harmon, Alban *c.p.* '58 (R) Greenville, NC St. Peter's Church.
Harmon, Barry J. '90 (SFD) Carrollton, IL St. John the Evangelist Church; White Hall, IL All Saints Church.
Harmon, John '93 (DM) Logan, IA St. Anne Church.
Harmon, Philip Gregory (STN) On Duty Outside the Diocese.
Harms, Msgr. William C. '65 (NEW) [B] South Orange, NJ Seton Hall University; [B] South Orange, NJ Seton Hall University.
Harnan, James *m.s.c.* (AUS) [H] Blanco, TX Missionaries of the Sacred Heart, M.S.C.
Harnan, James *m.s.c.* '64 (AUS) Blanco, TX St. Ferdinand's Church.
Harness, H. Robert '82 (DAV) DeWitt, IA St. Joseph's Church.
Harnett, Brendan '73 (PRT) Brewer, ME St. Joseph's Church; Brewer, ME St. Teresa's Church.
Harnett, Edward F. '58 (CHI) Wilmette, IL St. Francis Xavier Church.
Harnett, Msgr. Timothy '56 (SD) Encinitas, CA St. John the Evangelist Church.
Harney, Kenneth '89 (NO) [6] Metairie, LA St. Christopher the Martyr Church.
Harney, Peter '53 (WIL) Retired.
Harney, Thomas C. '62 (GF) Laurel, MT St. Anthony's Church.
Harnischfeger, William '93 (PHX) Sun City, AZ St. Elizabeth Seton Church.
Harnish, Lionel '54 (GAY) Retired.
Harold, Thomas J. '91 (RVC) Williston Park, NY St. Aidan's Church.
Harpel, John *s.v.d.* '44 (DUB) [H] New Hampton, IA St. Joseph Community Hospital.
Harper, Henry *s.s.j.* '50 (BAL) [81] Baltimore, MD St. Peter Claver Church.
Harper, John '47 (R) Retired.
Harper, John H. '87 (GB) [2] De Pere, WI St. Mary Church.
Harr, Gerald J. '62 (GI) Gering, NE Christ the King Church.
Harr, Richard *o.m.i.* '52 (FgM) Oblates Foreign Missions.
Harren, Robert C. '66 (SCL) [4] St. Cloud, MN St. Anthony of Padua Church.
Harrer, Frederic J. '45 (RVC) Hicksville, NY St. Ignatius Loyola Church; Retired.
Harrer, Robert R. *o.m.i.* '70 (STP) Albertville, MN St. Albert Church.
Harrigan, Philip K. *s.j.* '56 (BO) [E] Boston, MA Boston College High School & Jesuit Community.
Harriman, Michael D. '68 (SFR) [10] San Francisco, CA St. Cecilia Church.
Harrington, Ashley *o.carm.* '67 (NEW) Tenafly, NJ Our Lady of Mount Carmel Church.
Harrington, Brian J. '67 (FR) North Dartmouth, MA St. Julie Billiart Church.
Harrington, Cornelius '41 (SEA) Retired.
Harrington, Msgr. D. B. '32 (HEL) Retired.
Harrington, Daniel J. *s.j.* '71 (BO) [W] Cambridge, MA Weston Jesuit Community.
Harrington, Donald J. *c.m.* (BRK) [D] Staten Island, NY St. John's University, Staten Island Campus; [D] Jamaica, NY St. John's University.
Harrington, Donald J. *c.m.* '73 (BRK) [U] Jamaica, NY St. Vincent's House.
Harrington, Donald J. *c.m.* '73 (NY) [C] Staten Island, NY St. John's University Staten Island Campus.
Harrington, Ignatius '82 (NTN) Columbus, OH Holy Resurrection Church; Zanesville, OH Holy Trinity Church.
Harrington, James J. '53 (BO) Manchester by the Sea, MA Sacred Heart Church.
Harrington, Jay M. *o.p.* '85 (STP) [15] Minneapolis, MN St. Albert the Great Church; [C] St. Paul, MN University of St. Thomas.
Harrington, Jeremy *o.f.m.* '59 (CIN) [24] Cincinnati, OH Corpus Christi Church.
Harrington, John D. '56 (BO) [E] Reading, MA Austin Preparatory School.
Harrington, Msgr. John F. '35 (SPR) [2] Holyoke, MA Holy Cross Church; Retired.
Harrington, Msgr. John M. '45 (NY) Retired.
Harrington, John P. (BRK) [234] Queens, NY St. Rita Church.
Harrington, Joseph D. '56 (HEL) [B] Helena, MT Carroll College.
Harrington, Kevin J. '75 (FR) [2] Attleboro, MA St. Joseph's Church.
Harrington, Mark E. '79 (SC) Auburn, IA St. Mary's Church; Sac City, IA St. Mary's Church.
Harrington, Maurice D. '96 (LA) Norwalk, CA St. John of God Church.
Harrington, Richard L. '66 (BO) Randolph, MA St. Mary Church.
Harrington, Msgr. Robert J. '71 (NEW) [1] Elizabeth, NJ St. Mary of the Assumption Church.
Harrington, Russel J. '79 (LAF) [1] Lafayette, LA St. John the Evangelist Cathedral.
Harrington, Msgr. Thomas J. '64 (FR) [1] New Bedford, MA Holy Name Church.
Harris, Alfred J. '94 (WDC) Norbeck, MD St. Patrick Church.
Harris, Andrew *o.m.i.* '53 (P) Sweet Home, OR St. Helen Church.
Harris, Anton T. *s.j.* '75 (P) [D] Portland, OR Jesuit High School.
Harris, Daniel *c.m.* '74 (LA) [A] Camarillo, CA St. John's Seminary.
Harris, Daniel E. *c.m.* '74 (STL) [P] St. Louis, MO Vincentian Residence.
Harris, David T. '47 (MAR) Retired.
Harris, Edward *s.j.* '45 (FRS) Faculties Only.
Harris, Edwin B. *s.j.* '75 (SAC) [C] Sacramento, CA Jesuit High School; [G] Carmichael, CA Jesuit High School Community of Sacramento.
Harris, George E. '65 (BWN) Los Fresnos, TX St. Cecilia Church.
Harris, George G. *c.s.v.* '63 (CHI) [D] Arlington Heights, IL St. Viator High School.
Harris, Gerald P. '79 (SUP) River Falls, WI St. Bridget Church.
Harris, Glenn H. '92 (PEO) [3] Bloomington, IL St. Patrick's Church.
Harris, Jack D. '74 (LR) Jonesboro, AR Blessed Sacrament Church; [J] Little Rock, AR Catholic Campus Ministries.
Harris, Msgr. James E. (CC) [6] Laredo, TX San Augustin Church; [J] Laredo, TX San Agustin Historical Preservation & Restoration Society, Inc.
Harris, James M. '48 (P) Retired.
Harris, John F. '84 (PRT) Sabattus, ME Our Lady of the Rosary Church.
Harris, Julian '91 (PMB) Wellington, FL St. Rita Church.
Harris, Msgr. Martin P. '55 (WDC) Hollywood, MD St. John Church.
Harris, Msgr. Michael '72 (ORG) Inactive Leave.
Harris, Michael B. '92 (SCR) [5] Dunmore, PA St. Mary of Mount Carmel Church.
Harris, Raymond L., Jr. '79 (BAL) [41] Baltimore, MD Immaculate Conception Church.
Harris, Richard D. '93 (CHR) [3] Charleston, SC St. Patrick's Church; [5] Charleston, SC Our Lady of Mercy Church.
Harris, Robert (DM) [5] Des Moines, IA St. Anthony's Church.
Harris, Msgr. Robert M. '59 (BRK) [O] Brooklyn, NY St. Vincent's Services, Inc.
Harris, Scott T. *m.m.* '78 (FgM) Maryknoll Foreign Missions.
Harris, Scott T. *m.m.* '78 (NY) [DD] Maryknoll, NY Maryknoll Fathers and Brothers.
Harris, Steven J. '80 (PH) [150] Philadelphia, PA St. Therese of the Child Jesus Church.
Harris, Msgr. Wallace A. '72 (NY) [24] New York, NY St. Charles Borromeo Church; [Q] New York, NY Society of St. Vincent De Paul, Archdiocesan Central Council of New York.
Harris, Whitney G. '80 (LKC) On Special Assignment.
Harris, William R. '78 (SEA) Anacortes, WA St. Mary's Church.
Harris, Xavier J. *o.f.m.* '48 (OAK) [A] Berkeley, CA Franciscan School of Theology.
Harrison, Arthur '56 (SJ) Retired.
Harrison, Brian *o.s.* '85 (PCE) [11] Ponce, PR San Jose Obrero Church.
Harrison, Brian W. *o.s.* '85 (PCE) [B] Ponce, PR The Pontifical Catholic University of Puerto Rico; [H] Ponce, PR Oblates of Wisdom.
Harrison, Craig F. '87 (FRS) Firebaugh, CA St. Joseph Church.
Harrison, Cyprian *o.c.s.o.* '57 (SPC) [A] Ava, MO Assumption Novitiate (Trappists).
Harrison, George E. '68 (FR) Seekonk, MA Our Lady of Mt. Carmel Church.
Harrison, James '55 (ATL) Kennesaw, GA St. Catherine of Siena Church.
Harrison, Jeffrey D. *s.j.* '82 (STL) [52] St. Louis, MO St. Matthew, Apostle Church.
Harrison, Jeffrey D. '87 (STL) [F] St. Louis, MO St. Louis University High School, George H. Backer Memorial; [P] St. Louis, MO St. Matthew Jesuit Community.
Harrison, John B. *c.ss.r.* '67 (BAL) Odenton, MD St. Joseph Church.
Harrison, Michael *s.s.c.* '48 (PRO) [P] Bristol, RI St. Columban's Retirement House.
Harrison, Patrick '91 (OM) On Duty Outside the Archdiocese.
Harrison, Robert '64 (NY) [E] New York, NY Cardinal Hayes High School.
Harrison, Timothy '75 (ALB) [1] Watervliet, NY St. Brigid Church; [H] Troy, NY Seton Health System, Inc.
Harrison, Timothy A. '91 (BO) Belmont, MA St. Joseph Church.
Harrison, Todd W. *s.j.* '96 (OM) [C] Omaha, NE Creighton Preparatory School.
Harrison, William S. '72 (PH) [45] Philadelphia, PA St. Francis of Assisi Church.
Harrity, Msgr. Dennis '60 (DET) Grosse Pointe, MI Our Lady Star of the Sea Church.
Harrity, Francis P. '33 (WOR) Retired.

Harrity, Patrick *c.m.* '68 (EVN) [H] Evansville, IN Daughters of Charity of St. Vincent de Paul of Indiana, Inc.
Harrold, John '73 (SY) On Duty Outside the Diocese.
Harrold, John J. '92 (GBG) [1] Uniontown, PA St. John The Evangelist Church.
Harrold, Michael '50 (VIC) [1] Victoria, TX Our Lady of Victory Cathedral.
Harry, Alwyn C. *s.j.* '54 (FgM) Provinces.
Harry, Bill *o.carm.* '83 (GAL) [58] Houston, TX Our Lady of Mt. Carmel Church.
Harry, William *o.carm.* (GAL) [Q] Houston, TX Carmelite Priory.
Harry, William J. *o.carm.* '83 (CHI) [N] Mundelein, IL Carmelite Monastery.
Harshaw, Albert E. '73 (CAM) Blue Anchor, NJ St. Lucy's Church; Ancora, NJ New Jersey State Mental Hospital.
Hart, Brian '63 (SEA) Special Assignment.
Hart, Charles *o.f.m.* (DET) Detroit, MI Henry Ford Hospital; [K] Detroit, MI St. Bonaventure Friary.
Hart, E. James '96 (FWT) Bedford, TX St. Michael Church.
Hart, Edward J. '55 (BUR) Retired; [D] Burlington, VT St. Joseph's Home for Aged.
Hart, Edward James '96 (FWT) [17] Fort Worth, TX St. Thomas More Church.
Hart, Gene *s.o.l.t.* '90 (CC) [H] Robstown, TX Society of Our Lady of the Most Holy Trinity.
Hart, Gregory G. '84 (LR) Mountain Home, AR St. Peter the Fisherman Church.
Hart, Harry J. '44 (SAG) Retired.
Hart, J. Joseph, Jr. '84 (BAL) Absent on Leave.
Hart, Msgr. James '40 (ALB) [8] Albany, NY St. James Church; Retired.
Hart, James '65 (KC) [39] Kansas City, MO St. Therese Parish.
Hart, James '74 (RVC) Absent on Leave.
Hart, James P. '41 (BO) Retired.
Hart, John B. '60 (SLC) [8] West Jordan, UT St. Joseph the Worker Church.
Hart, John E. '81 (PAT) Rockaway, NJ St. Cecilia's Church.
Hart, Joseph A. '73 (ROC) [38] Rochester, NY Our Lady Queen of Peace Church; [L] Rochester, NY Censores Librorum.
Hart, Joseph L. *s.s.e.* '55 (BUR) [E] Colchester, VT Society of St. Edmund.
Hart, Joseph L. *s.s.e.* '55 (FgM) Edmundite Foreign Missions.
Hart, Joseph L. *s.s.e.* '55 (NOR) [A] Mystic, CT Edmundite Seminary Guild.
Hart, Kevin '74 (WDC) Piscataway, MD St. Mary Church.
Hart, Msgr. Peter F. '36 (BO) [7] Lynn, MA St. Pius Fifth Church; Retired.
Hart, Philip *c.s.p.* '73 (ORG) Fountain Valley, CA Holy Spirit Church.
Hart, Philip W. *c.s.p.* '83 (NY) [DD] Jamaica Estates, NY Paulist Fathers Generalate.
Hart, Richard *o.f.m.cap.* '55 (MIL) [P] Milwaukee, WI St. Conrad House.
Hart, Robert A. '75 (GR) North Muskegon, MI Prince of Peace Church.
Hart, Robert P. *s.j.* '62 (OM) [K] Omaha, NE Jesuit Community At Creighton University.
Hart, Rolland A. '64 (OG) Heuvelton, NY St. Raphael's Church; Gouverneur, NY Gouverneur Correctional Facility.
Hart, Ronald (JOL) Herscher, IL St. Margaret Mary Church; Irwin, IL St. James The Apostle Church.
Hart, Thomas '80 (NEW) New Providence, NJ Our Lady of Peace Church.
Hart, Thomas B. '44 (PRO) Retired.
Hart, Thomas J. '74 (SC) Remsen, IA St. Mary's Church.
Hart, Thomas M. *o.s.b.* '88 (GBG) [H] Latrobe, PA Saint Vincent Archabbey.
Hart, William (GLP) Retired.
Hart, William C. '58 (CAM) [5] Cherry Hill, NJ St. Thomas More Church; [A] Cherry Hill, NJ Camden Catholic High School.
Hart, William M. '47 (ROC) Webster, NY Holy Trinity Church; Retired.
Hart, William T. '80 (NEW) Berkeley Heights, NJ Runnells County Hospital.
Harte, Msgr. Al F. '64 (RCK) [I] Rockford, IL The Poor Clares of Rockford.
Harte, F. Joseph '61 (ORL) [1] Orlando, FL Mary Queen of the Universe Shrine Church.
Harte, Paul D. '76 (CAM) Haddonfield, NJ Christ the King Regional School Church.
Hartel, Edward T. '62 (WDC) Retired.
Harten, Dennis J. *o.s.a.* '75 (PH) Villanova, PA St. Thomas of Villanova Parish Community Church.
Hartenbach, William E. *c.m.* '64 (FgM) Vincentian Foreign Missions.
Hartenbach, William E. *c.m.* '64 (STL) [66] St. Louis, MO St. Vincent de Paul Church; [P] Earth City, MO Congregation of the Mission Midwest Province (Vincentians).
Harter, Benedict W. '46 (SPC) Joplin, MO Joplin Hospital Ministry; Retired; [C] Joplin, MO St. John's Regional Medical Center; Mercy Lifecare Systems, Inc.
Harter, Leon A. *m.m.* '39 (SJ) [M] Los Altos, CA Maryknoll.
Harter, Michael G. *s.j.* '74 (STP) [B] St. Paul, MN Jesuit Novitiate.
Hartford, Msgr. A. Dixon '61 (ELP) [28] El Paso, TX St. Matthew Church.
Hartgen, Dennis T. '73 (ALN) Mohnton, PA St. Benedict's Church.
Hartgen, William E. *s.s.* '76 (BAL) [M] Baltimore, MD Sulpician Provincial House.
Harth, '36 (BRK) [R] Queens Village, NY Queen of Peace Residence.
Harth, Charles F. '36 (BRK) [39] Brooklyn, NY St. Fortunata Church; Retired.
Harth, John M. '87 (SPC) Neosho, MO St. Canera Church; Seneca, MO St. Mary Church.
Hartigan, Daniel J. *o.s.a.* '45 (CHI) [40] Chicago, IL St. Clare of Montefalco Church.
Hartigan, Dennis P. '80 (TOL) [4] Fremont, OH St. Joseph Church; [B] Fremont, OH St. Joseph Central Catholic High School.
Hartigan, Robert R. *s.j.* '83 (DET) [61] Detroit, MI SS. Peter and Paul Jesuit Church; [T] Detroit, MI SS. Peter & Paul Jesuit Church Historical Fund.
Hartke, Florian *c.pp.s.* '35 (CIN) [B] Carthagena, OH St. Charles.
Hartlage, Albert J. '56 (L) Fairfield, KY St. Michael Church.
Hartlage, William C. '41 (L) Retired; [L] Louisville, KY Bishop David Apartments.
Hartle, Thomas *o.f.m.* (PAT) Pompton Lakes, NJ Our Lady of the Assumption Church.
Hartlein, Jerome D. '58 (BEL) Mascoutah, IL Holy Childhood of Jesus Church.
Hartley, Christopher (NY) [77] New York, NY Most Holy Crucifix Church.
Hartley, George C. *s.j.* '86 (BAL) [M] Baltimore, MD Jesuit Fathers and Brothers Maryland Provincial Curia.
Hartley, Paul M. '81 (JC) Belle, MO St. Alexander Church; Owensville, MO Immaculate Conception Church.
Hartling, Charles W. '79 (NEW) Wyckoff, NJ St. Elizabeth Church.
Hartlove, Walter J. *o.s.f.s.* '48 (FgM) Oblates of St. Francis de Sales Foreign Missions.
Hartman, Augustine *o.p.* '66 (SEA) [G] Seattle, WA Providence Seattle Medical Center.
Hartman, Donald '50 (MAR) Retired.
Hartman, Glenn R. '76 (CAM) Merchantville, NJ St. Peter's Church.
Hartman, Joseph F. *o.s.a.* '47 (DET) Grosse Pointe Park, MI St. Clare of Montefalco Church.
Hartman, Msgr. Joseph W. '52 (WDC) [8] Silver Spring, MD St. Michael Church; Retired; [L] Washington, DC Cardinal O'Boyle Residence for Priests.
Hartman, Paul B. '94 (MIL) Graduate Studies.
Hartman, Ralph C. '59 (COV) Alexandria, KY St. Mary of the Assumption Church.
Hartman, Raymond S. '68 (COV) Crescent Springs, KY St. Joseph Church.
Hartman, Msgr. Thomas J. '71 (RVC) [C] Hicksville, NY Holy Trinity.
Hartmann, Cletus F. *s.j.* '46 (DET) [P] Clarkston, MI Colombiere Center.
Hartmann, Edward '76 (NY) On Duty Outside the Archdiocese.
Hartmann, Edward J. '76 (FBK) [1] Fairbanks, AK Sacred Heart Cathedral.
Hartmann, Msgr. John F. '53 (BRK) [239] Queens, NY Sacred Heart Church.
Hartmann, Joseph A. '78 (DEN) Lafayette, CO Immaculate Conception Church.
Hartmann, Richard A. '73 (DET) [18] Detroit, MI St. Christopher Church.
Hartmann, Robert J. '85 (WCH) Harper, KS St. Joan of Arc Church.
Hartmayer, Gregory J. *o.f.m.conv.* '79 (ATL) Jonesboro, GA St. Philip Benizi Church.
Hartmire, Chris (SAC) [O] Sacramento, CA Loaves & Fishes.
Hartnett, Daniel F. *s.j.* '74 (CHI) [C] Chicago, IL Jesuit Community at Loyola University of Chicago; [N] Chicago, IL Chicago Province of the Society of Jesus-Provincial Office.
Hartnett, Msgr. Donald '39 (FWT) Retired.
Hartnett, George '74 (SY) Syracuse, NY Crouse Irving Memorial Hospital.
Hartnett, George F. '74 (SY) Mattydale, NY St. Margaret Church; Special Assignment.
Hartnett, James '72 (ORG) Westminster, CA Blessed Sacrament Church.
Hartnett, James L. *s.m.* '55 (ATL) [C] Atlanta, GA Marist School.
Hartnett, Msgr. James R. '38 (STL) Retired.
Hartnett, Richard G. *s.j.* '43 (SP) [C] Tampa, FL Jesuit High School.
Hartnett, Robert L. '79 (BAL) [72] Baltimore, MD Our Lady of Mount Carmel Church.
Hartnett, Walter J. '45 (PH) Retired.
Hartrich, Kurt *o.f.m.* '66 (FgM) Franciscan Foreign Missions.
Hartrich, Kurt *o.f.m.* '66 (STL) [P] St. Louis, MO Franciscan Friary of St. Anthony of Padua.
Hartshorn, Christopher '94 (DM) Adair, IA St. John Church; Anita, IA St. Mary Church; Casey, IA St. Joseph Church.
Hartway, Alan *c.pp.s.* '76 (KC) [A] Kansas City, MO Precious Blood Mission House.
Hartwig, Lawrence N. '67 (GR) On Duty Outside the Diocese.
Hartz, Gerald '59 (SC) [F] Sioux City, IA Monastery of the Discalced Carmelite Nuns.
Hartzer, John '54 (IND) Lawrenceburg, IN St. Lawrence Church.
Harvan, Msgr. Michael S. '33 (SCR) Retired.
Harvey, Arthur S. *c.s.c.* '51 (FTW) [J] South Bend, IN Congregation of Holy Cross Indiana Province Provincial House.
Harvey, Charles K. '52 (WCH) Retired.
Harvey, David W. '68 (LAN) Fenton, MI St. John Church.
Harvey, George F. '55 (MAN) Tilton, NH St. Mary of the Assumption Church.
Harvey, James '86 (ORG) Inactive Leave.
Harvey, Msgr. James M. '75 (MIL) On Duty Outside the Archdiocese.
Harvey, James P., III '96 (KNX) [2] Chattanooga, TN Our Lady of Perpetual Help Church.
Harvey, Jeff *c.m.* '93 (FRS) [3] Fresno, CA The Catholic Community of Mt. Carmel & St. Alphonsus Church.
Harvey, John A. '66 (PIT) Bethel Park, PA St. Valentine Church.
Harvey, John D. '72 (BAL) [48] Baltimore, MD St. Jerome Church; [58] Baltimore, MD St. Martin Church; [80] Baltimore, MD St. Peter the Apostle Church.
Harvey, John F. *o.s.f.s.* '44 (ALN) [B] Center Valley, PA Allentown College of St. Francis de Sales; [K] Center Valley, PA Oblates of St. Francis de Sales.
Harvey, John F. *o.s.f.s.* '44 (NY) [74] New York, NY St. Michael Church; [HH] New York, NY Courage.
Harvey, John L. '86 (CHI) [27] Chicago, IL St. Benedict the African (West) Church.
Harvey, L. Warren '88 (LR) [3] Little Rock, AR St. Augustine Church; [10] Little Rock, AR Our Lady of Good Counsel Church.
Harvey, Peter J. *o.s.f.s.* '60 (FgM) Oblates of St. Francis de Sales Foreign Missions.
Harvey, Richard R. '51 (PRT) Retired.
Harvey, Wilfred *o.m.i.* '63 (MAN) [K] Hudson, NH Missionary Oblates of Mary Immaculate.
Harvey, Msgr. William R. '41 (ORG) Newport Beach, CA Our Lady Queen of Angels Church; Retired.
Hary, Melvin J. '54 (OAK) Rodeo, CA St. Patrick's Church.
Haryasz, Francis S. '58 (STA) Retired.
Hasbrouck, John-Baptist *o.c.s.o.* '54 (P) [L] Lafayette, OR The Cistercian (Trappist) Abbey of Our Lady of Guadalupe.
Hascall, John S. *o.f.m.cap.* '67 (MAR) Assinins, MI The Most Holy Name of Jesus-Blessed Kateri Tekakwitha Church; Assinins, MI The Most Holy Name of Jesus-Blessed Kateri Tekakwitha Church.
Haschka, David J. *s.j.* '75 (STP) [6] St. Paul, MN The Immaculate Heart of Mary Church; [26] St. Paul, MN St. Luke Church.
Haschka, Jonathan *s.j.* '75 (FgM) Provinces.
Haschka, Jonathan *s.j.* '75 (MIL) [P] Milwaukee, WI Jesuit Provincial Office, Wisconsin Province.
Haselbauer, Joseph *s.c.j.* '55 (SFS) [B] Chamberlain, SD St. Joseph Indian School; [F] Chamberlain, SD Priests of the Sacred Heart.
Haselhorst, Vincent A. '57 (BEL) Germantown, IL St. Boniface Church.
Hasenberg, Aloysius J. (MAR) Retired.
Hasenfuss, Louis B. *o.s.b.* '61 (TUC) [F] St. David, AZ Holy Trinity Monastery.
Hasenkamp, Robert '63 (KCK) Mission, KS St. Pius X Church.
Hasenoehrl, Daniel *o.s.b.* '60 (P) [L] St. Benedict, OR Mt. Angel Abbey.
Hasey, Adam J. '50 (FAR) Oakes, ND St. Charles Borromeo Church.
Hasieber, Joseph S. (ALX) On Duty Outside the Diocese.
Haskamp, Edward F. '50 (CIN) [37] Cincinnati, OH Holy Trinity Church; Retired.
Haskamp, Greg '93 (KC) [41] Kansas City, MO Visitation of the Blessed Virgin Church.
Haske, Henry B. *s.j.* '57 (WDC) [E] North Bethesda, MD Georgetown Preparatory School.
Haskin, Jay C. '67 (BUR) Winooski, VT St. Stephen Church.
Haskins, Robert J. *s.j.* '54 (NY) [DD] New York, NY Murray-Weigel Hall.
Haslach, Stephen *c.p.* '54 (NY) [DD] Pelham Manor, NY St. Vincent's Residence; [HH] Pelham, NY Passionist

Communications, Inc.
Haslam, Richard *o.m.i.* '50 (OAK) [N] Oakland, CA Oblate Provincial House & Procure.
Hasler, Clifford *m.s.* '71 (ATL) Snellville, GA St. Oliver Plunkett Church.
Haslinger, Philip S. '72 (LFT) Alexandria, IN St. Mary Church.
Haspedis, George '56 (SPK) [5] Spokane, WA Sacred Heart Church.
Hasse, James W. *s.j.* '69 (COL) [25] Columbus, OH Community of Holy Rosary and St. John Church.
Hasselhoff, Robert W. '59 (CIN) [14] Cincinnati, OH St. Bartholomew Church.
Hassett, Anthony *s.s.c.* '53 (BUF) [M] Silver Creek, NY St. Columbans on the Lake, Home for the Aged.
Hassett, James F. '75 (BUF) Barker, NY St. Patrick Church; Olcott, NY St. Charles Borromeo Church.
Hassey, Athanase '50 (NTN) Waterford, CT St. Ann Church; Retired.
Hasso, Bede J. *o.s.b.* '57 (GBG) [H] Latrobe, PA Saint Vincent Archabbey.
Hast, James *o.f.m.cap.* '77 (DET) [K] Detroit, MI St. Bonaventure Friary.
Hastillo, Stanley E. '42 (HRT) Retired.
Hastings, Edward T. *o.s.a.* '83 (PH) [C] Villanova, PA Villanova University; [AA] Villanova, PA Fray de Leon Community.
Hastings, James J. *s.s.c.* '72 (FgM) St. Columban's Foreign Mission Society(S.S.C.)(THE COLUMBAN FATHERS).
Hastings, James J. *s.s.c.* '72 (OM) [K] St. Columbans, NE St. Columban's Foreign Mission Society.
Hastings, William J. '73 (CHI) [214] Chicago, IL St. William Church.
Hastrich, George M. '50 (MAD) Argyle, WI St. Joseph Church; [K] Madison, WI Saint Martin House.
Hastrich, George M. '50 (RCK) [N] St. Charles, IL Queen of Americas Guild.
Hatcher, John E. *s.j.* '74 (RC) [B] Howes, SD Kino Jesuit Community; [D] Howes, SD The Diocese of Rapid City Mahpiya na Maka Okoigna.
Hatcher, Msgr. William C. '71 (NEW) Bloomfield, NJ Church of St. Thomas the Apostle.
Hater, Robert J. '59 (CIN) [22] Cincinnati, OH St. Clare Church; [D] Dayton, OH The University of Dayton.
Hatfield, Placid W. *o.s.b.* '58 (PEO) Dalzell, IL St. Thomas More Church; [A] Peru, IL St. Bede Abbey and Academy.
Hathaway, Edward C. '91 (ARL) Clifton, VA St. Andrew the Apostle Church.
Hatrick, Brian M. '79 (BUF) North Evans, NY St. Vincent Church.
Hattie, Eugene F. *s.j.* '53 (FgM) Provinces.
Hatton, Ronald '95 (PSC) Williamsburg, VA Ascension of Our Lord Church.
Hatton, Seamus *c.ss.r.* '62 (SP) Plant City, FL St. Clement Church.
Hattrick, Edward V. *o.s.a.* '56 (FgM) Foreign Missions.
Hattrup, Theobald *o.f.m.* '56 (CIN) [M] Cincinnati, OH St. Francis Seraph Friary.
Hauber, Douglas '89 (JOL) Bradley, IL St. Joseph Church.
Hauck, Bolivar *m.s.* '58 (STL) [P] St. Louis, MO La Salette Missionaries.
Hauck, Herbert C. '64 (STL) Kirkwood, MO St. Gerard Majella Church.
Hauer, Joseph L. '81 (DUB) Placid, IA St. John's Church.
Hauer, Maurus *o.f.m. conv.* '45 (LSC) Carlsbad, NM St. Edward Church.
Hauf, Edward *o.m.i.* '66 (PT) Perry, FL Immaculate Conception Church.
Haugen, John S. '84 (DUB) [N] Cedar Falls, IA St. Stephen the Witness Catholic Student Center, University of Northern Iowa.
Haughey, John C. *s.j.* '61 (CHI) [C] Chicago, IL Jesuit Community at Loyola University of Chicago.
Haughney, Msgr. William J. '47 (MET) Cranbury, NJ Nativity of Our Lord Church; Retired.
Haungs, Edwin C. *s.j.* '39 (NY) [DD] New York, NY Murray-Weigel Hall.
Haupt, Lloyd '54 (SCL) Retired.
Haus, Robert A. *s.j.* '55 (BUF) [O] Buffalo, NY Canisius Jesuit Community.
Hausen, C. William '65 (PIT) Bairdford, PA St. Victor Church.
Hauser, Albert *o.s.b.* '60 (KCK) [3] Overland Park, KS Holy Spirit Church.
Hauser, Albert J. '81 (OG) [A] Ogdensburg, NY Wadhams Hall.
Hauser, Gerald B. '45 (MIL) Retired.
Hauser, John G. '71 (BRK) [91] Brooklyn, NY Our Lady of Angels Church.
Hauser, Nathanael *o.s.b.* '83 (SCL) [I] Collegeville, MN St. John's Abbey, of the Order of St. Benedict.
Hauser, Richard J. *s.j.* '68 (OM) [K] Omaha, NE Jesuit Community At Creighton University.
Hausfeld, Bruce *o.f.m.* '62 (LSC) Alamogordo, NM Immaculate Conception Church.
Hausfeld, Bryant *o.f.m.* '65 (LSC) Alamogordo, NM Immaculate Conception Church.
Hausmann, Bill C. *s.j.* '66 (P) Tillamook, OR Sacred Heart Church.
Hausmann, Leo '92 (RC) Bison, SD Blessed Sacrament Church; Buffalo, SD St. Anthony Church; [D] Rapid City, SD Priest Retirement and Aid Association.
Haut, Msgr. Vincent J. '68 (STA) Orange Park, FL St. Catherine's Church.
Hauth, Msgr. Arthur W. '56 (NO) [53] New Orleans, LA SS. Peter and Paul Church; Retired.
Hautz, Roland *glmy.* '53 (CHL) Jefferson, NC St. Francis of Assisi Church.
Hauver, James H. '97 (DUL) Grand Rapids, MN St. Joseph's Church.
Havel, Elias '95 (RC) [B] Bethlehem, SD Holy Nativity Monastery.
Havel, Elias *o.mar.* '95 (SAM) [C] Petersham, MA Most Holy Trinity Monastery.
Havel, Gregory '90 (WIN) [4] Rochester, MN St. Bridget's Church.
Havel, Gregory G. '90 (WIN) Stewartville, MN St. Bernard's Church.
Havel, Thomas *s.m.* (SJ) [M] Cupertino, CA Marianist Provincial Residence.
Havener, J. Riley *o.s.a.* '55 (ALB) Waterford, NY St. Mary of the Assumption Church.
Havens, James '79 (MOB) Grove Hill, AL Sacred Heart Church.
Haviland, William T. '62 (HBG) Sunbury, PA St. Monica Church.
Havron, Daniel *o.f.m.* '77 (DET) Special Assignment; [B] Detroit, MI Duns Scotus.
Hawes, Msgr. Cletus J. '52 (DUB) Evansdale, IA St. Nicholas Church.
Hawes, Donald J. (DUB) Spillville, IA St. Wenceslaus Church.
Hawes, Donald J. '53 (DUB) Calmar, IA St. Aloysius Church; [F] Calmar, IA Calmar-Festina-Spillville (CFS) Catholic Elementary School.
Hawk, Pat *c.ss.r.* '69 (AMA) [H] Amarillo, TX Bishop DeFalco Retreat Center.
Hawken, Michael '94 (KCK) Leawood, KS Church of the Nativity.
Hawker, James '63 (CHL) [4] Charlotte, NC St. Ann Church.
Hawker, James F. '63 (BO) [8] Quincy, MA Sacred Heart Church; On Duty Outside the Archdiocese.
Hawkes-Teeples, Steven *s.j.* '93 (BUF) [O] Buffalo, NY Canisius Jesuit Community.
Hawkins, Allan R.G. '94 (FWT) [1] Arlington, TX Church of St. Mary the Virgin.
Hawkins, Charles E. '78 (PMB) [5] West Palm Beach, FL St. Juliana Church.
Hawkins, Donald A. *s.j.* '76 (NO) [F] New Orleans, LA Jesuit High School.
Hawkins, Douglas W. *c.s.c.* '57 (BUR) Brandon, VT St. Mary's Church.
Hawkins, John *o.s.c.* '66 (LIN) Kenesaw, NE Sacred Heart Church.
Hawkins, John G. *o.s.c.* '66 (LIN) Doniphan, NE St. Ann's Church; [A] Hastings, NE Crosier Monastery.
Hawkins, Ray (PBL) [E] Pueblo, CO Villa Pueblo.
Hawkins, Robert '65 (BAL) Special Assignment.
Hawkins, Robert '95 (BAL) [N] Baltimore, MD Little Sisters of the Poor-Provincial Residence.
Hawkins, Robert F. '75 (PRO) [6] Warwick, RI St. Kevin Church.
Hawkins, Robert G. '65 (BAL) [J] Baltimore, MD St. Martin's Home for Aged, Little Sisters of the Poor.
Hawkins, Stephen B. '75 (COL) Pickerington, OH Seton Parish.
Hawkins, Thomas '70 (KC) Weston, MO Holy Trinity Church.
Hawley, Gerard L. '92 (SCR) [4] Pittston, PA St. John the Evangelist Church.
Haworth, Marcus A. *s.j.* '46 (STL) [P] St. Louis, MO Jesuit Community Corporation at St. Louis University - Jesuit Hall.
Hawthorne, Patrick J. '82 (WOR) [26] Worcester, MA St. Margaret Mary Church.
Hay, Francis J. '42 (WCH) Retired.
Hay, Theodore H. '55 (MOB) Retired.
Hayatsu, Richard '65 (SEA) Renton, WA St. Anthony's Church.
Hayburn, Edmund L. '45 (OAK) Retired; [M] Oakland, CA Bishop Begin Villa.
Haycock, Anthony J. '72 (SEA) [15] Seattle, WA St. Mary Church; [L] Seattle, WA Catholic Seamen's Club.
Haycock, Donald J. *c.s.c.* '58 (ROC) [41] Rochester, NY St. Lawrence Church.
Hayda, Pavlo '92 (STN) [2] Chicago, IL St. Joseph Church.
Hayde, Msgr. Ronald E. '81 (RVC) [1] Rockville Centre, NY St. Agnes Cathedral; Ocean Beach, NY Our Lady of the Magnificat Church.
Haydel, Chris M. '75 (BR) [5] Baton Rouge, LA St. Charles Borromeo Church.
Hayden, Msgr. Carl T. '45 (GI) Retired.
Hayden, Donald *o.ss.t.* '81 (BAL) [M] Baltimore, MD Holy Trinity Monastery.
Hayden, Donald C. '81 (RVC) Deer Park, NY SS. Cyril and Methodius Church.
Hayden, Eamonn *s.p.s.* '62 (SJ) [M] Saratoga, CA St. Patrick's Missionary Society.
Hayden, Hilary *o.s.b.* '56 (WDC) [M] Washington, DC St. Anselm's Abbey.
Hayden, James P. '91 (GAY) Traverse City, MI Immaculate Conception Church; Special Assignment.
Hayden, Johnrose H. '95 (LUB) Rotan, TX St. Joseph Church.
Hayden, Joseph F. '63 (L) On Special Assignment.
Hayden, Joseph J. *s.j.* '70 (WH) [A] Wheeling, WV Wheeling Jesuit University.
Hayden, Joseph M. '48 (CAM) Retired.
Hayden, Joseph M. '48 (ORL) [2] Lakeland, FL St. Anthony's Church.
Hayden, Joseph Mark '48 (ORL) Retired.
Hayden, Lucian P. '49 (OWN) Russellville, KY Sacred Heart Church.
Hayden, Michael '85 (JUN) On Duty Outside the Diocese.
Hayden, Michael M. *o.c.s.o.* '54 (ROC) [I] Piffard, NY Abbey of the Genesee.
Hayden, Michael T. '85 (SUP) Pelican Lake, WI St. John Church; Rhinelander, WI Immaculate Conception Church.
Hayden, Patrick T. '90 (STL) On Duty Outside the Archdiocese.
Hayden, Ralph W. '64 (NU) Retired.
Hayden, Robert L. '70 (RVC) Williston Park, NY St. Aidan's Church.
Hayden, Terence '77 (NO) Crown Point, LA St. Pius X Church.
Hayden, Thomas E. *s.m.a.* '58 (BO) [W] Dedham, MA African Mission House.
Haydinger, Christian '76 (RIC) [1] Chesapeake, VA Prince of Peace Church.
Haydock, Kenneth '80 (SEA) Edmonds, WA Holy Rosary Church.
Hayduk, Michael (PRM) On Special or Other Diocesan Assignment; [A] North Royalton, OH Motherhouse and Novitiate.
Hayek, Msgr. Sami '59 (SAM) Easton, PA Our Lady of Lebanon Church.
Hayek, Msgr. Stanley J. '59 (DUB) Charles City, IA Immaculate Conception Church.
Hayer, James '89 (PSC) East Brunswick, NJ Nativity of Our Lord Church.
Hayes, Bonaventure F. *o.f.m.* '67 (BUF) [A] East Aurora, NY Christ the King Seminary.
Hayes, Brian '92 (SD) [17] San Diego, CA Our Mother of Confidence Church.
Hayes, Canisius *s.t.* '46 (B) Ferdinand, ID Assumption Church; Greencreek, ID St. Anthony's Church.
Hayes, Charles V. *o.f.m.* '46 (PAT) [M] Butler, NJ St. Anthony Friary.
Hayes, Msgr. Denis A. '37 (PAT) Retired.
Hayes, Dennis J. '76 (SY) South Onondaga, NY Corpus Christi Church.
Hayes, Dennis J., III '86 (NO) Avondale, LA St. Bonaventure Church; [A] New Orleans, LA Notre Dame Seminary Graduate School of Theology.
Hayes, Donald J. *s.j.* '56 (CHI) [T] Barrington, IL Bellarmine Hall.
Hayes, Edward A. *m.m.* '59 (FgM) Maryknoll Foreign Missions.
Hayes, Edward A. *m.m.* '59 (NY) [DD] Maryknoll, NY Maryknoll Fathers and Brothers.
Hayes, Edward J. '41 (NEW) Retired.
Hayes, Edward J. '57 (SY) Chadwicks, NY St. Anthony of Padua Church.
Hayes, Edwin *o.m.i.* '52 (MIA) [2] Miami, FL Christ the King Church.
Hayes, Eugene J. *o.praem* (ORG) [N] Silverado, CA Norbertine Association of St. Joseph, Inc.
Hayes, Eugene J. *o.praem.* '77 (ORG) [D] Siverado, CA St. Michael's College Preparatory High School.
Hayes, Finbarr *o.p.* '59 (OAK) [N] Oakland, CA Dominican Order (Western Province), St. Albert's Priory.
Hayes, Francis R. '39 (STP) Retired.
Hayes, Gary '85 (OWN) Peonia, KY St. Anthony's Church.
Hayes, Gary '90 (OWN) Grayson Springs, KY St. Augustine Church; Wax, KY St. Benedict Church.
Hayes, Gerard C. '60 (HT) Bayou Black, LA St. Anthony Church.
Hayes, Giles P. *o.s.b.* '65 (PAT) [D] Morristown, NJ Delbarton School; [M] Morristown, NJ St. Mary's Abbey.
Hayes, Msgr. J. Wayne '59 (FRS) Los Banos, CA St. Joseph Church.
Hayes, James *s.m.a.* '55 (FgM) Society of African Missions.
Hayes, James '66 (ALB) Comstock, NY Great Meadows Correctional Institution; Special Assignment.
Hayes, James *s.s.s.* '77 (NY) [8] New York, NY St. Andrew Church.
Hayes, James A. *m.s.c.* '50 (CC) Agua Dulce, TX St. Frances of Rome Church.
Hayes, James A. *s.s.j.* '55 (WDC) [B] Washington, DC St. Joseph's Seminary.

Hayes, James C. '65 (SY) Onondaga Hill, NY St. Michael Church; Warners, NY Our Lady of Good Counsel Church; Syracuse, NY Community General Hospital; Special Assignment.
Hayes, James E. '89 (DUB) [1] Dubuque, IA St. Raphael's Cathedral; [D] Dubuque, IA Wahlert High School.
Hayes, James L. '38 (DET) Retired.
Hayes, James M. *s.j.* '85 (WOR) [N] Worcester, MA Jesuits of Holy Cross College, Inc.; [Q] Worcester, MA Campus Ministry.
Hayes, James P. (NY) [8] New York, NY St. Andrew Church.
Hayes, John E. '33 (CHI) Zion-Beach Park, IL Our Lady of Humility Church; Retired.
Hayes, John H. '87 (ROC) Dryden, NY Holy Cross Church.
Hayes, John J. '60 (CLV) [34] Cleveland, OH Immaculate Conception Church; Cleveland, OH University Hospitals.
Hayes, Msgr. John M. '30 (CHI) [54] Chicago, IL Epiphany Church; Retired.
Hayes, Joseph '79 (MIA) Absent on Leave.
Hayes, Lawrence J. *o.f.m.* '89 (WIL) [10] Wilmington, DE St. Paul's Church.
Hayes, Leo J. '61 (BEL) Ava, IL St. Elizabeth Church; Menard, IL Menard Correctional Center.
Hayes, Martin '84 (OWN) Knottsville, KY St. William Church.
Hayes, Martin E. '84 (OWN) Philpot, KY St. Lawrence Church.
Hayes, Maurice *o.f.m.conv.* '69 (IND) Terre Haute, IN Regional Hospital/Union Hospital.
Hayes, Maurice *o.f.m.conv.* '69 (L) Pleasure Ridge Park, KY St. Paul Church.
Hayes, Michael T. '60 (DUL) Moose Lake, MN Holy Angels Church; Moose Lake, MN Moose Lake State Hospital.
Hayes, Patrick '71 (BLX) Gautier, MS St. Mary Church.
Hayes, Patrick J. *c.s.v.* '43 (LAV) [D] Las Vegas, NV Clerics of St. Viator Retirement Home.
Hayes, Msgr. Paul J. '48 (NEW) New Providence, NJ Our Lady of Peace Church; Retired.
Hayes, Paul R. *s.j.* '62 (FgM) Provinces.
Hayes, Peter F. '38 (CHI) [154] Chicago, IL Our Lady, Mother of the Church; Retired.
Hayes, Robert '71 (SJ) Cupertino, CA St. Joseph of Cupertino Church.
Hayes, Sam '83 (CHY) Jackson, WY Our Lady of the Mountains Church.
Hayes, Stephen D. *o.p.* '88 (COL) [36] Columbus, OH St. Patrick Church.
Hayes, Terrence M. '72 (STP) [14] Minneapolis, MN Our Lady of Victory Church.
Hayes, Thomas (ALB) [9] Albany, NY St. Joseph Church.
Hayes, Thomas *o.p.* (OAK) [N] Oakland, CA Western Dominican Province.
Hayes, Msgr. Thomas G. '46 (LA) Retired.
Hayes, Msgr. Thomas J. '35 (SY) New Hartford, NY St. John the Evangelist Church; Retired.
Hayes, Thomas J. *o.p.* '59 (SFR) [13] San Francisco, CA St. Dominic Church; [N] San Francisco, CA St. Dominic Priory.
Hayes, Thomas J. *o.m.i.* '64 (SFR) [35] San Francisco, CA Most Holy Redeemer Church.
Hayes, Thomas J. *o.m.i.* '64 (STP) [N] St. Paul, MN Oblate Residence.
Hayes, Thomas J. '73 (ALB) [15] Albany, NY Sacred Heart of Jesus Church.
Hayes, Thomas P. '94 (STO) Lodi, CA St. Anne Church.
Hayes, Timothy M. '85 (COL) Newark, OH Church of the Blessed Sacrament.
Hayes, William E. *s.j.* '58 (P) [D] Portland, OR Jesuit High School.
Hayes, William J. '42 (HRT) Retired.
Hayes, William L. *s.j.* '44 (FgM) Provinces.
Hayes, Xavier *c.p.* '59 (WOR) [N] Shrewsbury, MA Passionist Fathers of Shrewsbury, Inc., Calvary Retreat Center; [P] Shrewsbury, MA Calvary Retreat Center, Passionist Community.
Hayes, Zachary *o.f.m.* '59 (CHI) [B] Chicago, IL The Catholic Theological Union at Chicago; [N] Chicago, IL St. Joseph Interprovincial Post-Novitiate Formation House.
Hayman, Robert W. '66 (PRO) [9] Providence, RI Blessed Sacrament Church.
Hayn, Carl H. *s.j.* '47 (SJ) [B] Santa Clara, CA Santa Clara University.
Haynes, Mark J. '85 (PH) Southampton, PA Our Lady of Good Counsel Church.
Haynes, Stephen S. *c.ss.r.* '88 (TOL) [2] Lima, OH St. Gerard Church.
Hays, Edward (KCK) Special Assignment.
Hays, Henry Bryan *o.s.b.* '62 (SCL) [I] Collegeville, MN St. John's Abbey, of the Order of St. Benedict.
Hays, John '93 (SP) Zephyrhills, FL St. Joseph Church.
Hays, Joseph C. '51 (BEL) Retired.
Hays, Kevin W. '77 (CHI) Missionary Work.
Hays, R. Rex *c.m.* '93 (LR) Huntsville, AR St. John's Church.
Hays, Timothy '96 (SPK) Walla Walla, WA St. Francis of Assisi Church; Walla Walla, WA St. Patrick Church.
Hayward, William *m.i.c.* '89 (JOL) Darien, IL Our Lady of Peace Church.
Hazard, Michael D. '72 (KAL) [2] Kalamazoo, MI St. Joseph Church.
Hazebrouck, Maurice L. '45 (PRO) Retired.
Hazel, Robert L. '66 (STP) [4] Minneapolis, MN Ascension Church.
Hazel, Terrence J. '75 (Y) Canfield, OH St. Michael's Church.
Hazelton, James '61 (HEL); On Duty Outside the Diocese.
Hazewski, Eugene J. '59 (NEW) Emerson, NJ Church of the Assumption.
Hazler, George '67 (DET) [H] Southfield, MI Providence Hospital.
Hazler, George F. '67 (DET) [T] Waterford, MI Voluntas Dei Institute.
Hazlett, Canisius W. *c.p.* '36 (BO) [W] Brighton, MA St. Gabriel's Residence.
Hazuka, Jeremy L. '97 (LIN) [7] Lincoln, NE St. Joseph Church.
Hazzard, William M. '63 (WIL) Woodcrest, DE St. Matthew Church.
Hazzouri, Alex J. '57 (SCR) [N] Dunmore, PA Villa St. Joseph.
Head, Bernard '53 (IND) [K] Saint Mary-of-the-Woods, IN Sisters of Providence General Administration.
Headley, Donald J. '58 (CHI) [153] Chicago, IL Our Lady of Mercy Church.
Headley, William *c.s.sp.* '64 (PIT) [R] Slippery Rock, PA Office for Campus Ministry.
Headley, William R. *c.s.sp.* '64 (PIT) [B] Pittsburgh, PA Duquesne University of the Holy Ghost.
Heagerty, John J. '54 (SY) [S] East Syracuse, NY Bishop Grimes Priests Residence.
Heagerty, Kevin *o.f.m.cap.* '61 (FgM) Capuchin Foreign Missions.
Heagle, John L. '65 (LC) On Duty Outside the Diocese.
Healey, Andrew *ss.cc.* '59 (FR) [J] Fairhaven, MA Sacred Hearts Provincial House.
Healey, Bernard A. '95 (PRO) [7] Providence, RI St. Augustine Church.
Healey, Charles J. *s.j.* '65 (BO) [A] Weston, MA Pope John XXIII National Seminary; [W] Boston, MA The Society of Jesus of New England-Provincial Offices; [W] Chestnut Hill, MA The Jesuit Community at Boston College.
Healey, Msgr. Edward '43 (COL) Retired.
Healey, Edward J. '87 (FR) Mashpee, MA Christ The King Church.
Healey, Fergus *o.f.m.* '54 (BO) [BB] Boston, MA St. Anthony Shrine.
Healey, John C. *s.s.c.* '39 (PRO) [P] Bristol, RI St. Columban's Retirement House.
Healey, John E. '70 (MAN) [6] Nashua, NH Infant Jesus Church; Nashua, NH Nursing Homes and Memorial Hospital.
Healey, Joseph G. *m.m.* '66 (FgM) Maryknoll Foreign Missions.
Healey, Msgr. Joseph T. '31 (RCK) Retired.
Healey, Kenneth *s.m.* '70 (BO) [E] Reading, MA Austin Preparatory School.
Healey, Patrick D. '51 (SCR) [17] Scranton, PA St. Mary of the Assumption Church.
Healey, Timothy A. *s.j.* '61 (NY) Manhattan, NY Goldwater Memorial Hospital; [DD] New York, NY St. Ignatius Loyola Residence.
Healey, William B. '55 (SCR) Hawley, PA Blessed Virgin Mary, Queen of Peace Church.
Healy, Clement '45 (SP) [O] St. Petersburg, FL St. Anthony Friary.
Healy, Cletus J. *s.j.* '51 (MIL) [P] Wauwatosa, WI Jesuit Community at St. Camillus.
Healy, Gabriel *ss.cc.* '57 (FR) [J] Fairhaven, MA Sacred Hearts Provincial House; [L] Wareham, MA Sacred Hearts Retreat Center.
Healy, George F. *c.ss.sp.* '53 (SAT) San Antonio, TX St. Luke's Baptist Hospital; University Hospital; [M] San Antonio, TX Harcar House.
Healy, Gerald W. *s.j.* '46 (FgM) Provinces.
Healy, Gerard M. '61 (MAD) Stoughton, WI St. Ann Church.
Healy, Jack *o.carm.* '70 (ROC) [B] Rochester, NY McQuaid Jesuit High School; [I] Rochester, NY Whitefriars Priory.
Healy, James E. '72 (KC) [3] Independence, MO St. Mark Church.
Healy, James F. '66 (NY) Mamaroneck, NY St. Vito Church.
Healy, James J. *s.s.* '46 (BAL) [J] Baltimore, MD St. Charles Villa; [M] Baltimore, MD St. Charles Villa.
Healy, John '41 (SR) Retired.
Healy, John *s.v.d.* '43 (FgM) Society of the Divine Word Foreign Missions.
Healy, John C. *s.s.c.* '39 (BUF) [P] Silver Creek, NY Missionary Sisters of St. Columbans, St. Columban's on the Lake.
Healy, John J. '66 (SAC) [F] Sacramento, CA Mercy General Hospital.
Healy, Kieran *o.p.* (OAK) [N] Oakland, CA Western Dominican Province.
Healy, Kieran J. *o.p.* '61 (FgM) Dominican - Order of Preachers Foreign Missions.
Healy, Kilian *o.carm.* '37 (BO) [P] Peabody, MA Catholic Information Center; [BB] Peabody, MA St. Theresa Carmelite Chapel.
Healy, Michael J. '70 (SFR) [46] San Francisco, CA St. Philip the Apostle Church.
Healy, Neal '66 (SFR) San Anselmo, CA St. Anselm Church.
Healy, Patrick F. *o.m.i.* '47 (BO) [Z] Tewksbury, MA Immaculate Heart of Mary Novitiate-Infirmary.
Healy, Patrick J. '66 (E) Du Bois, PA St. Catherine Church.
Healy, Patrick J. '66 (E) Mercer, PA State Correctional Facility.
Healy, Msgr. Peter '53 (LA) Burbank, CA St. Robert Bellarmine Church.
Healy, Robert *glmy.* '46 (CIN) [M] Fairfield, OH Headquarters of Glenmary Home Missioners.
Healy, Robert *glmy.* '46 (SAV) Claxton, GA St. Christopher Church.
Healy, Stephen M. '85 (BO) Marshfield, MA St. Ann by the Sea Church.
Healy, Terence P. '62 (ALB) West Winfield, NY St. Joseph Church.
Healy, Thomas '67 (SAV) On Duty Outside the Diocese.
Healy, Thomas C. '95 (BO) [3] Weymouth, MA Immaculate Conception Church.
Healy, Thomas F. *s.j.* '65 (HEL) [5] Missoula, MT St. Francis Xavier Church.
Healy, Thomas I. '52 (CHI) [155] Chicago, IL Our Lady of Mount Carmel Church.
Healy, Thomas J. '66 (BRK) [221] Queens, NY Our Lady of Sorrows Church.
Healy, Msgr. Thomas P. '59 (SD) San Marcos, CA St. Mark Church.
Healy, William *o.c.d.* '46 (MIL) [24] Milwaukee, WI St. Florian Church.
Healy, William P. '66 (PHX) [2] Scottsdale, AZ Our Lady of Perpetual Help Church.
Heaney, John F. '57 (PRO) Charlestown, RI St. Mary Church.
Heaney, John J. *s.j.* '52 (SFE) [6] Albuquerque, NM Immaculate Conception Church.
Heaney, Msgr. John P. '53 (SFR) San Francisco, CA San Francisco Police Department.
Heaney, Joseph P. '53 (PRO) [1] Woonsocket, RI St. Agatha Church; Retired.
Heanue, William *c.ss.r.* '47 (NY) [92] New York, NY Our Lady of Perpetual Help Church.
Hearn, Edward C. '31 (SY) Retired.
Hearn, Philip A. '66 (SY) [4] Rome, NY St. Peter Church.
Hearns, Joseph A. '40 (NEW) Retired.
Heath, Christopher '88 (ORG) Tustin, CA St. Cecilia Church.
Heath, Mark *o.p.* '47 (WDC) [B] Washington, DC Dominican House of Studies.
Heath, T. R. *o.p.* '50 (FgM) Dominican - Order of Preachers Foreign Missions.
Heavey, Edward (NEW) [1] East Orange, NJ Holy Name of Jesus Church.
Heavey, Edward J. *s.j.* '60 (NEW) [B] Jersey City, NJ Saint Peter's College; [N] Jersey City, NJ Jesuits of Saint Peter's College, Inc.
Hebda, Bernard A. '89 (PIT) On Duty Outside the Diocese.
Hebda, Martin J. '67 (CHI) [J] Chicago, IL Mercy Hospital and Medical Center.
Hebda, Michael '96 (SAC) Chico, CA St. John the Baptist Church.
Hebein, James M. '57 (MAR) Retired.
Heberle, Frederick L. '56 (SPR) Sheffield, MA Our Lady of the Valley Church.
Heberlein, Kenneth '71 (GAL) [77] Houston, TX St. Thomas More Church.
Heberlein, Msgr. Louis '51 (E) Brandy Camp, PA Holy Cross Church.
Heberlein, Msgr. Louis J. '51 (E) Brockway, PA St. Tobias Church.
Hebert, Albert *s.m.* '54 (BR) Convent, LA St. Michael the Archangel Church.
Hebert, Daniel '79 (ANC) [6] Anchorage, AK Our Lady of Guadalupe Church.
Hebert, Donald J. '68 (LAF) Mire, LA Assumption of the Blessed Virgin Mary Church.
Hebert, Donald J. '68 (SY) Utica, NY St. Luke; Special Assignment.
Hebert, Donald J. '81 (SY) [8] Utica, NY St. George Church; [10] Utica, NY St. Joseph and St. Patrick Church.
Hebert, Earl '52 (SPR) [2] Pittsfield, MA Notre Dame Church.
Hebert, Francis '60 (B) Retired.
Hebert, Gerard A. '81 (FR) Westport, MA St. George's Church.
Hebert, Msgr. J. Gaston '60 (LR) [5] Little Rock, AR Christ the King Church.

Hebert, John M. '51 (LIN) Retired.
Hebert, John M. '51 (OM) Retired.
Hebert, Joseph E. *m.afr.* '63 (SP) [O] St. Petersburg, FL Missionaries of Africa.
Hebert, Lloyd P. (LAF) Absent on Leave.
Hebert, Mark '92 (PHX) [25] Phoenix, AZ St. Thomas the Apostle Church.
Hebert, Marvin A. '51 (GAL) Retired.
Hebert, Oliver J. *t.o.r.* '71 (ALT) [A] Loretto, PA St. Francis College.
Hebert, Paul L. '59 (NOR) Pomfret, CT Most Holy Trinity Church.
Hebert, Msgr. Ray P. '52 (NO) [1] Marrero, LA Immaculate Conception Church.
Hebert, Raymond L. '44 (WOR) Retired.
Hebert, Roger '49 (PAT) [3] Wayne, NJ Immaculate Heart of Mary Church; Retired.
Hebert, Roland G. '47 (WOR) Retired.
Hebert, Ronald '65 (SD) [18] San Diego, CA Sacred Heart Church.
Hebert, T. J. '49 (LAF) Retired.
Hebl, John H. '61 (MAD) Sullivan, WI St. Mary Help of Christians Church.
Hechenberger, Gerald R. '96 (BEL) Fairfield, IL St. Edward Church.
Hecht, F. Torrens *s.j.* '46 (CHI) [C] Chicago, IL Jesuit Community at Loyola University of Chicago.
Heck, Roger C. '51 (MIL) [77] Milwaukee, WI St. Therese Church.
Heck, Theodore *o.s.b.* '29 (IND) [B] St. Meinrad, IN St. Meinrad Seminary-College of Liberal Arts; [J] St. Meinrad, IN St. Meinrad Archabbey.
Heck, Thomas A. '76 (SFS) Brookings, SD St. Thomas More Church.
Heck, Msgr. Thomas W. '57 (NEW) [2] Union City, NJ St. Augustine's Church.
Heckathorne, Brad *ofm conv.* '81 (BUF) [D] Athol Springs, NY St. Francis High School; [O] Athol Springs, NY St. Francis of Assisi Friary.
Heckel, Guerric Frederick A. '66 (CHR) [D] Moncks Corner, SC Mepkin Abbey.
Heckel, John F. *o.s.f.s.* '44 (WIL) [B] Wilmington, DE Salesianum School.
Hecker, Msgr. Adolph J. '40 (SAL) Retired.
Hecker, Lawrence A. '58 (NO) Terrytown, LA Christ the King Church.
Hedberg, Earl M. '62 (AUS) Goldthwaite, TX St. Peter's Church; San Saba, TX St. Mary's Church.
Hedderman, Augustine Mary *m.f.v.a.* '95 (BIR) [E] Birmingham, AL Franciscan Missionaries of the Eternal Word, A Public Association of the Christian Faithful.
Hedderman, Msgr. John J. '60 (SLC) [5] Salt Lake City, UT St. Ambrose Church.
Hedges, John P. '87 (DET) [6] Wyandotte, MI St. Stanislaus Kostka Church.
Hedges, L. John '43 (ROC) Penfield, NY St. Joseph Church; Retired.
Hedrick, John '70 (MAD) Hollandale, WI St. Patrick Church.
Hedrick, Msgr. Kenneth J. '73 (NO) [1] New Orleans, LA St. Louis Cathedral.
Heeg, Lawrence S. '57 (GRY) Chesterton, IN St. Patrick Church.
Heekin, John M. '63 (PAT) [2] Wayne, NJ Holy Cross Church.
Heelan, Patrick A. *s.j.* '58 (WDC) [M] Washington, DC The Jesuit Community at Georgetown University.
Heemrood, Jan *o.m.i.* '45 (SAT) [C] San Antonio, TX Oblate School of Theology; [M] San Antonio, TX De Mazenod House.
Heenan, Michael F. '55 (RVC) Absent on Leave.
Heenan, Patrick F. '55 (MEM) [13] Memphis, TN St. James Church.
Heeney, Walter *o.s.b.* '43 (KC) [I] Savannah, MO La Verna Village Apartments; [K] Savannah, MO La Verna Heights Provincial House.
Heerdink, Eugene '51 (EVN) Dale, IN St. Joseph Church.
Heerey, John J. '55 (BRK) Retired.
Heerey, John J. '55 (STA) Interlachen, FL St. John's Mission Church.
Heery, William *o.carm.* '42 (LA) [F] Encino, CA Crespi Carmelite High School.
Heese, Henry '61 (AUS) Kovar, TX Sts. Peter and Paul Church; Smithville, TX St. Paul the Apostle Church.
Heet, Alan *o.f.m.* (PEO) Metamora, IL St. Mary's Church.
Heet, Donald J. *o.s.f.s.* (WDC) [C] Washington, DC Catholic University of America, The.
Heet, Donald J. *o.s.f.s.* '76 (WDC) [B] Washington, DC Deshairs Community-Oblates of St. Francis de Sales Residence.
Hefferan, John E. '56 (CHI) Ingleside, IL St. Bede Church.
Heffern, Colman *o.s.b.* '76 (SFE) [L] Pecos, NM Our Lady of Guadalupe Benedictine Abbey.
Heffernan, A. Joseph '65 (FRS) [4] Bakersfield, CA St. Francis Church.
Heffernan, Enda *o.f.m.cap.* '57 (SFR) [N] Burlingame, CA Capuchin Provincial House.
Heffernan, Enda *o.f.m.cap.* '73 (MRY) [I] Soquel, CA St. Clare's Retreat House.
Heffernan, Henry G. *s.j.* '62 (WDC) [E] Washington, DC Gonzaga College High School.
Heffernan, James F. '50 (BRK) Released from Diocesan Assignment.
Heffernan, John J. *o.f.m.* '32 (R) [3] Durham, NC Immaculate Conception Church.
Heffernan, Raymond J. '57 (SEA) Port Townsend, WA St. Mary's, Star of the Sea Church.
Heffernan, Robert G. '63 (HRT) [5] Hamden, CT St. Joan of Arc Church.
Heffernan, Thomas A. '61 (BRK) Released from Diocesan Assignment.
Heffernan, Thomas A. '61 (PAT) Denville, NJ St. Clare Hospital; [J] Denville, NJ Northwest Covenant Medial Center.
Heffernan, William P. *m.m.* '55 (FgM) Maryknoll Foreign Missions.
Heffner, Carroll E. '61 (NO) [4] Metairie, LA St. Benilde Church.
Heffner, George *s.v.d.* '57 (LAF) Mowata, LA St. Lawrence Church.
Heffner, Msgr. Helmut '69 (LA) [A] Camarillo, CA St. John's Seminary.
Heffron, William *ss.cc.* '68 (FR) Fairhaven, MA St. Joseph's Church.
Heffron, William M. (MIL) Retired.
Heft, James L. *s.m.* '73 (CIN) [D] Dayton, OH The University of Dayton; M] Dayton, OH Marianist Provincialate.
Hegarty, Daniel P. '63 (BO) [11] Boston, MA St. Anthony Church.
Hegarty, Frederick J. *m.m.* '53 (FgM) Maryknoll Foreign Missions.
Hegarty, John C. *c.s.sp.* '53 (NO) Diamond, LA St. Jude Church.
Hegarty, William '67 (CHI) [16] Chicago, IL St. Anselm Church.
Hegenauer, Msgr. John V. '40 (COV) Retired.
Hegenbarth, Robert S. '56 (LC) Bangor, WI St. Mary Church; West Salem, WI St. Leo the Great Church.
Hegener, Wilbert *o.f.m.* '36 (GAY) Petoskey, MI St. Francis Xavier Church.
Heggarty, Michael '95 (CAM) Somerdale, NJ Our Lady of Grace Church.
Hegyi, Martin A. *s.j.* '63 (NY) [DD] New York, NY Jesuit Community at Fordham University.
Heher, Michael '78 (ORG) Cypress, CA St. Irenaeus Church.
Hehir, J. Bryan '66 (BAL) Ellicott City, MD Resurrection Church.
Hehir, J. Bryan '66 (BO) On Duty Outside the Archdiocese; [CC] Cambridge, MA Harvard-Radcliffe Catholic Student Center.
Hehman, Lawrence W. '65 (LEX) [4] Lexington, KY Pax Christi Catholic Church.
Hehn, Robert E. '63 (DEN) Rifle, CO St. Mary's Church.
Hehr, Horst '67 (DAV) [J] Clinton, IA Samaritan Health System, Inc.
Heiar, James *s.v.d.* '70 (DUB) [B] Epworth, IA Divine Word College.
Heid, Clement J. *o.s.b.* '44 (GBG) [H] Latrobe, PA Saint Vincent Archabbey.
Heid, Richard '47 (SCL) Retired.
Heid, Richard J. '47 (SCL) Brandon, MN Church of St. Ann.
Heid, Roland L. *o.s.b.* '41 (GBG) [H] Latrobe, PA Saint Vincent Archabbey.
Heidecke, Albert J. *c.p.m.* '93 (LAF) Iota, LA St. Joseph Church.
Heidelberger, Ronald '46 (DET) Retired; [H] Southfield, MI Providence Hospital.
Heidenreich, Robert A. '69 (CHI) [26] Chicago, IL St. Benedict Church.
Heidenrich, Peter '76 (CHI) [26] Chicago, IL St. Benedict Church.
Heidlage, Benno *o.f.m.* '48 (PEO) Metamora, IL St. Mary's Church; Washburn, IL St. Elizabeth Church.
Heidt, Charles A. '59 (BIS) [5] Bismarck, ND St. Mary Church.
Heidt, William G. *o.s.b.* '40 (SCL) [I] Collegeville, MN St. John's Abbey, of the Order of St. Benedict.
Heier, Thomas *c.m.m.* '58 (DET) [K] Dearborn Heights, MI Our Lady of Grace Monastery.
Heier, Vergil *c.m.m.* '63 (DET) [K] Dearborn Heights, MI Our Lady of Grace Monastery.
Heier, Vincent A. '77 (STL) [5] St. Louis, MO Holy Innocents Church.
Heigl, John *m.afr.* (BUF) [7] Buffalo, NY St. Ann Church; [7] Buffalo, NY St. Ann Church.
Heikkala, Gregory R. '91 (MAR) L'Anse, MI Sacred Heart Church.
Heil, John P. '74 (STL) Grantwood, MO Our Lady of Providence Church; [A] St. Louis, MO Kenrick-Glennon Seminary.
Heile, Edwin B. '60 (COV) Walton, KY All Saints Church.
Heille, Gregory J. *o.p.* '75 (STL) [B] St. Louis, MO Aquinas Institute of Theology; [P] St. Louis, MO St. Dominic Priory.
Heilman, Richard M. '88 (MAD) [2] Janesville, WI St. John Vianney Church.
Heilman, Thomas O. '39 (LFT) Retired.
Heim, Edward L. '71 (STL) Imperial, MO St. John Lateran Church.
Heim, Hilary *o.s.b.* '49 (KCK) [H] Atchison, KS St. Benedict's Abbey.
Heim, Howard J. *s.j.* '53 (PH) [C] Philadelphia, PA St. Joseph's University; [AA] Philadelphia, PA Jesuit Community at St. Joseph's University.
Heim, John P. *s.j.* '65 (CIN) [M] Cincinnati, OH Faber Jesuit Community.
Heim, John S. '51 (PH) [90] Philadelphia, PA St. Madeleine Sophie Church; [Y] Philadelphia, PA Sacred Heart Manor.
Heim, Joseph A. *m.m.* '61 (FgM) Maryknoll Foreign Missions.
Heim, Michael J. '82 (PH) [76] Philadelphia, PA St. Joan of Arc Church.
Heiman, Harold *o.s.b.* '39 (LR) Ratcliff, AR St. Anthony Church; [A] Subiaco, AR Subiaco Monastery.
Heiman, Lawrence F. *c.pp.s.* '43 (LFT) [A] Rensselaer, IN Saint Joseph's College.
Heimann, Ambrose *c.pp.s.* '40 (CIN) [B] Carthagena, OH St. Charles.
Heimer, Michael G. '71 (GRY) Fish Lake, IN St. Anthony Church; Kingsford Heights, IN Immaculate Heart of Mary Church.
Heimerman, Francis D. '44 (DUB) Retired.
Heimos, Robert L. '67 (STL) Washington, MO Our Lady of Lourdes Church.
Hein, John L. *s.j.* '51 (NO) [R] Metairie, LA Cenacle Retreat House.
Heina, Steven (SAL) Concordia, KS Our Lady of Perpetual Help Church.
Heindel, Harold J. '66 (RVC) Centerport, NY Our Lady Queen of Martyrs Church.
Heindl, Arthur W. '40 (MAD) Retired.
Heindl, Elmer W. '36 (ROC) [12] Rochester, NY St. Charles Borromeo Church; Retired.
Heine, Michael *o.f.m.conv.* '90 (BAL) [C] Baltimore, MD Archbishop Curley High School; [M] Baltimore, MD Immaculate Heart of Mary Friary.
Heine, Simeon *s.a.* '48 (NY) [DD] Garrison, NY Franciscan Friars of the Atonement.
Heineman, Msgr. Donald P. '47 (DUB) Retired.
Heinen, Francis A. '59 (NEW) Nutley, NJ Holy Family Church.
Heinen, Gerald *o.carm.* '50 (NEW) Teaneck, NJ St. Anastasia's Church.
Heinen, Miles *c.m.* '82 (LR) Huntsville, AR St. John's Church.
Heinen, Msgr. Paul '29 (SFD) Retired.
Heinen, Virgil O. '60 (SUP) Retired.
Heines, Timothy '94 (DAL) Duncanville, TX Holy Spirit Church.
Heiney, Lawrence W. '75 (CHL) Tryon, NC St. John the Baptist Church.
Heinl, David A. '57 (CIN) St. Marys, OH Holy Rosary Church.
Heinlein, Anthony J. '65 (RVC) Massapequa Park, NY Our Lady of Lourdes Church.
Heinlein, Egbert *c.m.m.* '38 (DET) [K] Dearborn Heights, MI Our Lady of Grace Monastery.
Heinlein, Msgr. John T. '61 (RVC) New Hyde Park, NY Holy Spirit Church.
Heinrich, Harold D. '56 (HRT) [8] New Britain, CT St. John the Evangelist Church.
Heinsch, James *o.f.m.* '67 (GB) [I] Pulaski, WI Assumption of B.V.M. Friary.
Heinsz, Vernon R. *s.j.* '73 (FgM) Provinces.
Heintschel, Msgr. Donald '51 (TOL) [L] Sylvania, OH Sisters of St. Francis of the Congregation of Our Lady of Lourdes.
Heintz, Daniel W. '54 (ROC) Canisteo, NY St. Joachim Church; Rexville, NY St. Mary Church.
Heintz, Daniel W. '54 (SY) On Duty Outside the Diocese.
Heintz, Michael '93 (FTW) [3] Fort Wayne, IN St. Charles Borromeo Church.
Heintz, Robert L. '49 (SFD) Retired.
Heintzelman, Edward F. '84 (CAM) Westmont, NJ Holy Saviour Church.
Heintzelman, Gerard '79 (SR) [G] Napa, CA Queen of the Valley Hospital of Napa.
Heinz, David C. '77 (PEO) [5] Peoria, IL St. Bernard's Church.
Heinz, James J. (CAM) [I] Cherry Hill, NJ St. Mary's Nursing Home.
Heinz, John *o.f.m. conv.* '93 (SFR) [43] San Francisco, CA St. Paul of the Shipwreck Church.
Heinz, Martin G. '94 (RCK) [1] Rockford, IL St. Peter Cathedral.
Heinz, Robert P. '80 (CHI) Prospect Heights, IL St. Alphonsus Liguori Church.
Heinz, Walter E. '62 (STU) Pomeroy, OH Sacred Heart Church.
Heinze, Arthur G. '68 (MIL) Hales Corners, WI St. Mary Church.
Heinzel, Thomas R. '75 (HON) Kula, HI Our Lady

Queen of the Angels Church.
Heis, Clarence G. '82 (CIN) Mechanicsburg, OH St. Michael's Church; North Lewisburg, OH Immaculate Conception Church.
Heise, Bert *o.f.m.* '57 (CIN) [M] Cincinnati, OH St. Francis Seraph Friary.
Heiser, Basil *o.f.m.conv.* '32 (IND) [J] Mount Saint Francis, IN Provincial Headquarters for the Conventual Franciscan Province.
Heiser, Charles *s.j.* (STL) [C] St. Louis, MO Saint Louis University.
Heiser, W. Charles *s.j.* '53 (STL) [P] St. Louis, MO Jesuit Community Corporation at St. Louis University - Jesuit Hall.
Heisig, James *s.v.d.* '69 (FgM) Society of the Divine Word Foreign Missions.
Heisig, Kazimierz '78 (HRT) [9] Hartford, CT SS. Cyril and Methodius Church.
Heisler, James M. *s.a.c.* '70 (MIL) [8] Milwaukee, WI St. Anthony of Padua Church.
Heisse, John R. *m.m.* '85 (CHI) [N] Chicago, IL Maryknoll Fathers & Brothers.
Heit, Bruce *o.m.i.* '64 (FgM) Oblates Foreign Missions.
Heithoff, James H. '77 (GI) North Platte, NE Holy Spirit Church.
Heiting, Paul '87 (WIN) Luverne, MN St. Catherine's Church.
Heitkamp, Samuel '67 (SAT) Poth, TX Blessed Sacrament Church.
Heitke, Lawrence R. '67 (MAD) Madison, WI Veterans' Administration Hospital.
Heitz, Louis S. '57 (LFT) Winchester, IN St. Joseph Church.
Heitz, Warren *o.s.b.* '66 (IND) [J] St. Meinrad, IN St. Meinrad Archabbey.
Heitzman, Clarence J. '56 (COV) Southgate, KY St. Therese of the Infant Jesus Church.
Heizman, Leo J. '69 (SY) East Syracuse, NY St. Matthew Church.
Hejna, Lewis E. '81 (SPC) Oran, MO Guardian Angel Church.
Helduser, Msgr. Frederick J. '60 (PH) [4] Drexel Hill, PA St. Dorothy Church.
Heles, Msgr. Frederic G. '44 (DUB) Retired.
Helfenstein, Maurice R. '27 (SPK) Retired.
Helfrey, Donald (KC) [E] Kansas City, MO St. Stephen's School.
Helfrey, Donald '68 (KC) [31] Kansas City, MO Our Lady of Peace Church.
Helfrich, Emil G. *o.m.i.* '49 (SFD) Green Creek, IL St. Mary Help of Christians Church; Lillyville, IL Sacred Heart of Jesus Church.
Helfrich, Frederick (ROC) [57] Rochester, NY St. Theodore Church.
Helfrich, George J. '54 (CHI) [56] Chicago, IL St. Eugene Church; Retired.
Helfrich, P. Jeremiah *s.j.* '68 (LA) [2] Santa Barbara, CA Our Lady of Sorrows Church.
Helfrich, Peter G. '76 (OG) [G] Saranac Lake, NY St. Joseph's Carmelite Monastery, Discalced Carmelite Nuns.
Helfrich, Thomas J. *o.s.f.s.* (LAN) Adrian, MI St. Mary of Good Counsel Church.
Helget, Venard *o.s.b.* '40 (KCK) [H] Atchison, KS St. Benedict's Abbey.
Helldorfen, Julian Nichols *c.ss.r.* '36 (ALB) [L] Saratoga Springs, NY St. John Neumann Residence.
Hellenberg, Anthony *o.s.b.* '66 (FgM) American - Cassinese Congregation Foreign Missions.
Hellenberg, Anthony *o.s.b.* '66 (SCL) [I] Collegeville, MN St. John's Abbey, of the Order of St. Benedict.
Heller, Christopher J. '79 (RVC) Port Jefferson, NY St. Gerard Majella Church.
Heller, James '68 (SAG) [8] Bay City, MI St. Mary Church.
Hellman, Michael P. '83 (CHY) Green River, WY Immaculate Conception Church.
Hellmann, David E. '73 (LFT) Kokomo, IN St. Joan of Arc Church.
Hellmann, Msgr. Donald F. '53 (COV) [2] Covington, KY St. Agnes Church.
Hellmann, Wayne *o.f.m.conv.* '67 (STL) [P] St. Louis, MO St. Bonaventure Friary (Province of Our Lady of Consolation).
Hellstrom, R. Christopher '88 (DEN) [37] Denver, CO St. Vincent De Paul Church.
Hellwig, Lee W. '86 (HRT) [3] Ansonia, CT St. Anthony's Church; Military Chaplains.
Helly, Victor J. *s.j.* '54 (FgM) Provinces.
Helm, Edward J. '66 (WDC) Special Ministries; [V] Landover Hills, MD Catholic Deaf Center.
Helm, John B. '77 (L) [8] Louisville, KY Ascension of Our Lord Church.
Helman, Bradford N. '68 (Y) [10] Canton, OH St. Michael the Archangel Church.
Helmich, George F. *c.s.p.* '57 (NY) [DD] Jamaica Estates, NY Paulist Fathers Generalate.
Helmich, George F. *c.s.p.* '57 (PMB) [G] Vero Beach, FL Paulist Fathers Retirement Home.
Helmick, Raymond F. *s.j.* '63 (BO) [71] Boston, MA St. Theresa Church.
Helmick, Raymond G. *s.j.* '63 (BO) [W] Chestnut Hill, MA The Jesuit Community at Boston College.
Helmick, William M. '62 (BO) [71] Boston, MA St. Theresa Church.
Helmin, Virgil A. '75 (SCL) [3] St. Cloud, MN Holy Spirit Church.
Helminski, Gregory *c.r.* '77 (CHI) [N] Chicago, IL Provincial Office of the Congregation of the Resurrection.
Helms, Michael '90 (DOD) Hanston, KS St. Anthony Church; Jetmore, KS St. Lawrence Church; Spearville, KS St. John the Baptist Church.
Helms, Walter B. '69 (DAV) Oxford, IA St. Mary's Church.
Helmueller, Lawrence C. *s.j.* '42 (OM) [K] Omaha, NE Jesuit Community At Creighton University.
Heltemes, Alfred J. '54 (SCL) Foley, MN St. John's Church.
Helwig, Alan R. '58 (WDC) [2] Bethesda, MD St. Jane Frances de Chantal Church.
Helwig, Paul C. '74 (HBG) [5] Steelton, PA Prince of Peace Church.
Heman, Richard J. '67 (STL) Affton, MO St. Dominic Savio Church.
Hemann, David A. '85 (SC) Sanborn, IA St. Cecilia's Church.
Hemann, Everett '71 (DUB) Ames, IA St. Thomas Aquinas Church (and Catholic Student Center) Church; [N] Ames, IA St. Thomas Aquinas Church and Catholic Student Center (Iowa State University).
Hemann, John W. '60 (DUB) Duncan, IA St. Wenceslaus Church; Garner, IA St. Boniface Church.
Hemann, Maurice *o.m.i.* '50 (FgM) Oblates Foreign Missions.
Hemann, Melvin D. '59 (DUB) Balltown, IA St. Francis of Assisi Church; Rickardsville, IA St. Joseph's Church; Sherrill, IA SS. Peter and Paul Church.
Hemauer, Gilbert *o.f.m.cap.* '64 (GF) Forsyth, MT Immaculate Conception Church.
Hemberger, Kent A. '88 (WCH) [10] Wichita, KS St. Anne Church.
Hemberger, Robert E. '70 (WCH) [H] Wichita, KS Mt. St. Mary Convent, Motherhouse and Novitiate of the Sisters of St. Joseph.
Hembrow, William '60 (SFD) Fieldon, IL St. Mary Church; Jerseyville, IL Holy Ghost Church.
Hemenway, Richard '87 (SPK) Absent on Leave.
Hemler, Edward B. '64 (BAL) Fallston, MD St. Mark Church.
Hemler, Lawrence (HBG) York, PA York Hospital.
Hemler, Lawrence J. '88 (HBG) [1] York, PA Immaculate Conception of the Blessed Virgin Mary Church.
Hemler, Thomas J. '56 (HBG) Waynesboro, PA St. Andrew Church.
Hemm, Thomas *c.pp.s.* '78 (TOL) Ottawa, OH SS. Peter and Paul Church.
Hemmelgarn, Larry J. *c.pp.s* '84 (COL) Delaware, OH St. Mary Church.
Hemmer, Joseph *o.f.m.* '54 (FBK) Kaltag, AK St. Teresas Church; Ruby, AK St. Peter-in-Chains Church.
Hemmer, Joseph *o.f.m.* '59 (FgM) Franciscan Foreign Missions.
Hemmerle, R. Joseph '67 (L) [12] Louisville, KY St. Bartholomew Church; [B] Louisville, KY Trinity High School.
Hemmerling, Henry L. '66 (MET) Old Bridge, NJ Most Holy Redeemer Church.
Hemmersbach, Alfred F. '45 (LC) Retired; [I] La Crosse, WI Holy Cross (Seminary) Diocesan Center.
Hemming, Philip M. '67 (P) Keizer, OR St. Edward Church.
Hemp, Lawrence A. '67 (LUB) Post, TX Holy Cross Church; Slaton, TX Our Lady of Guadalupe Church.
Hempel, John L. '54 (ROC) Retired.
Hemrick, Eugene (WDC) [C] Washington, DC Catholic University of America, The.
Hemrick, Eugene F. '63 (JOL) On Duty Outside the Diocese.
Hemsing, John D. '88 (MIL) Wind Lake, WI St. Clare Church.
Henahan, Msgr. Thomas '30 (BGP) [K] Trumbull, CT St. Joseph's Manor.
Henahan, Msgr. Thomas F. '30 (BGP) Retired.
Henandez, Baltazar Nunez '88 (CGS) Cidra, PR Nuestra Senora del Carmen Church.
Henao, Alfonso '79 (NY) [1] Newburgh, NY St. Patrick Church.
Henao, Luis '74 (NO) On Duty Outside the Archdiocese.
Henault, James A. *m.s.* '72 (HRT) [M] Hartford, CT Missionaries of LaSalette Provincial Secretary.
Henault, John *o.m.i.* '63 (FgM) Oblates Foreign Missions.
Henchal, Michael J. '73 (PRT) Cape Elizabeth, ME St. Bartholomew Church.
Hencier, Jack *c.m.f.* '72 (LA) San Gabriel, CA San Gabriel Church; [R] San Gabriel, CA Claretian Missionaries (Missionary Sons of the Immaculate Heart of Mary).
Hendel, Lawrence '77 (SJ) [12] San Jose, CA St. John Vianney Church; Military Chaplains.
Hendel, Msgr. Richard P. '48 (RVC) Bay Shore, NY St. Patrick's Church; Retired.
Hendel, Msgr. Thomas W. '45 (BRK) Retired.
Henden, Brian *o.carm.* '93 (TUC) [A] Tucson, AZ Salpointe Catholic High School; [F] Tucson, AZ Carmelite Priory.
Henderson, Christopher J. '94 (SAM) Uniontown, PA St. George Church.
Henderson, Donald R. '70 (PEO) [3] Spring Valley, IL St. Anthony's Church; [4] Spring Valley, IL SS. Peter and Paul's Church.
Henderson, James B. *o.c.s.o.* '60 (DUB) [K] Peosta, IA New Melleray Abbey, Order of Cistercians of the Strict Observance.
Henderson, John *o.f.m.conv.* '84 (P) Tillamook, OR Sacred Heart Church.
Henderson, John H. '87 (JC) Folk, MO St. Anthony of Padua Church; Jefferson City, MO Jefferson City Correctional Center; Boonville, MO Boonville Correctional Center.
Henderson, Paul *c.ss.r.* '50 (BO) [13] Boston, MA Our Lady of Perpetual Help Church.
Henderson, Robert J. '65 (COV) Cold Spring, KY St. Joseph Church.
Henderson, Roy N. '90 (BGP) Ridgefield, CT St. Mary's Church.
Hendren, Lucien '63 (SFE) Retired.
Hendrick, Msgr. Frank J. '54 (ARL) Retired.
Hendrick, Matthew D. '85 (R) Wilmington, NC St. Mark Church.
Hendricks, Clare '63 (GRY) On Duty Outside the Diocese.
Hendricks, Msgr. Donald W. '55 (NY) Buchanan, NY St. Christopher Church.
Hendricks, Edward S. '77 (BAL) Special Assignment; [O] Baltimore, MD Archdiocesan Office-Newman Center.
Hendricks, James P. '60 (L) [13] Louisville, KY St. Basil Church; [22] Louisville, KY St. Denis Church.
Hendricks, John '52 (FgM) Society of St. James the Apostle.
Hendricks, John J. '52 (TR) On Duty Outside the Diocese.
Hendricks, Joseph *ss.cc.* '48 (HON) Lahaina, HI Maria Lanakila Church.
Hendricks, Msgr. Joseph M. '72 (COL) Dublin, OH St. Brigid of Kildare Church.
Hendricks, Scott B. '86 (BO) Stoneham, MA St. Patrick Church.
Hendricks, Theodore J. '65 (GB) Francis Creek, WI St. Anne Church; Kossuth, WI St. Augustine Church.
Hendricks, William J. *s.j.* '64 (FgM) Provinces.
Hendricks, William J. *s.j.* '64 (SJN) [22] San Juan, PR San Ignacio de Loyola Church.
Hendrickson, W. Frederick '56 (L) [A] Louisville, KY Bellarmine College.
Hendriks, Boniface '45 (SFE) Retired.
Hendry, Gerald '85 (SP) [3] St. Petersburg, FL Holy Cross Church; [B] St. Petersburg, FL St. Petersburg Catholic High School.
Hendry, Msgr. Owen J. '60 (NEW) Franklin Lakes, NJ Most Blessed Sacrament Church.
Hendry, Simon J. *s.j.* '77 (OAK) [N] Berkeley, CA Jesuit Community at Jesuit School of Theology at Berkeley.
Heneghan, James P. '83 (CHI) [30] Chicago, IL St. Bonaventure Church.
Heneghan, Jarlath '55 (SEA) Retired.
Heneghan, John F. '55 (YAK) Retired.
Heneghan, Sean '53 (SEA) Retired.
Heneghan, Msgr. Thomas F. (NY) [174] Bronx, NY Our Lady of Mt. Carmel Church.
Henehan, Thomas P. *m.m.* '65 (FgM) Maryknoll(M.M.).
Henehan, Thomas P. *m.m.* '65 (NY) [DD] Maryknoll, NY Maryknoll Fathers and Brothers.
Henery, Ronald *o.p.* '78 (NY) [DD] New York, NY St. Vincent Ferrer Priory.
Henesy, William '51 (RVC) Freeport, NY Our Holy Redeemer Church; Retired.
Heney, David '78 (LA) Santa Monica, CA St. Monica Church.
Heney, Frederick J. *s.j.* '63 (LA) West Hollywood, CA St. Victor Church; [R] Los Angeles, CA Columbiere House.
Hengel, Warren, Jr. '92 (FRS) Tipton, CA St. John Church.
Henger, Alcuin J. *o.m.i.* '55 (CR) Blackduck, MN St. Ann's Church.
Henger, Alcuin J. *o.m.i* '55 (DUL) Northome, MN St. Michael's Church.
Hengesbach, Julius L. '53 (KAL) Retired.
Hengle, John R. '68 (CLV) Tallmadge, OH Our Lady of Victory Church.
Henke, Donald E. '93 (STL) [2] St. Charles, MO St. Cletus Church; [E] St. Charles, MO Duchesne High School.
Henke, Msgr. James '66 (SAT) [35] San Antonio, TX St. Francis of Assisi Church.
Henkel, William M. '55 (CHI) Westchester, IL Divine Infant Church; Retired.
Henkels, Edmund *o.s.b.* '59 (WDC) [M] Washington, DC St. Anselm's Abbey.

Henkes, Donald E. '66 (MEM) On Duty Outside the Diocese.
Henkes, Donald E. '66 (SAG) Mount Pleasant, MI Sacred Heart Church.
Henle, Robert J. *s.j.* '40 (STL) [O] St. Louis, MO Fusz Pavilion.
Henley, Earl *m.s.c.* '69 (Y) [A] Youngstown, OH Sacred Heart Retreat House & Renewal Center.
Henley, Fred M. *s.j.* '58 (DET) [K] Detroit, MI Jesuit Provincial Office-Detroit Province of the Society of Jesus; [P] Clarkston, MI Colombiere Center.
Henley, Fred M. *s.j.* '58 (OAK) [N] Berkeley, CA Jesuit Community at Jesuit School of Theology at Berkeley.
Henley, John R. '75 (ATL) Retired.
Henn, Joseph *s.d.s.* '78 (MIL) [P] Milwaukee, WI Salvatorian Provincial Residence.
Henne, Paul '56 (PIT) [2] Swissvale, PA Word of God Church.
Hennelly, Alfred T. *s.j.* '60 (NY) [DD] New York, NY Jesuit Community at Fordham University.
Hennelly, Michael F. '91 (PH) [1] Bensalem, PA St. Charles Borromeo Church.
Hennes, Paul R. '35 (DET) Retired.
Hennes, Paul R. '35 (ORL) Retired.
Hennesey, James J. *s.j.* '57 (SY) [S] Syracuse, NY Jesuits at LeMoyne, Inc.
Hennessey, John E. '67 (CHI) Libertyville, IL St. Joseph Church.
Hennessey, John P. '47 (BUF) Retired.
Hennessey, Joseph '91 (BO) [8] Boston, MA St. Ann Church.
Hennessey, Lawrence R. '71 (CHI) [A] Mundelein, IL University of St. Mary of the Lake-Mundelein Seminary.
Hennessey, Robert F. '78 (BO) [51] Boston, MA Most Holy Redeemer Church; [BB] East Boston, MA Our Lady of the Airways Chapel.
Hennessey, Robert J. *o.p.* '56 (PRO) [B] Providence, RI Providence College; [P] Providence, RI St. Thomas Aquinas Priory at Providence College.
Hennessey, Ronald W. *m.m.* '64 (FgM) Maryknoll Foreign Missions.
Hennessey, William *s.s.c.* '35 (FgM) St. Columban's Foreign Mission.
Hennessey, Msgr. William *v.g.* '61 (MIA) [B] Opa Locka, FL St. Thomas University.
Hennessy, Douglas J. '63 (PEO) Danville, IL St. Paul's Church.
Hennessy, James W. '61 (WIN) [2] Winona, MN St. Casimir's Church.
Hennessy, John '78 (FWT) Burleson, TX St. Ann Church.
Hennessy, John A. *s.j.* '52 (RC) St. Francis, SD Rosebud Reservation Church.
Hennessy, John J. *c.ss.r.* '53 (BO) [13] Boston, MA Our Lady of Perpetual Help Church.
Hennessy, John J. *s.j.* '69 (RC) Martin, SD Our Lady of the Sacred Heart Church.
Hennessy, John P. *o.s.a.* '44 (PH) Flourtown, PA St. Genevieve Church; [AA] Flourtown, PA Augustinians (O.S.A.).
Hennessy, John V. *s.j.* '72 (FgM) Provinces.
Hennessy, John V. *s.j.* '72 (P) [L] Portland, OR Jesuit Provincial Office (Society of Jesus, Oregon Prov.).
Hennessy, Joseph I. '63 (PHX) Chandler, AZ St. Andrew the Apostle Church.
Hennessy, Joseph P. '75 (PIT) Military Chaplains.
Hennessy, Patrick '71 (NY) [137] Bronx, NY Christ the King Church.
Hennessy, Thomas C. *s.j.* '47 (NY) [DD] New York, NY Jesuit Community at Fordham University.
Hennessy, Thomas J. '96 (ATL) [3] Marietta, GA St. Joseph Church.
Henning, Edward *o.f.m.cap.* '96 (NEW) [4] Orange, NJ Mt. Carmel Church.
Henning, James *o.f.m.conv.* '82 (DET) [58] Detroit, MI Our Lady Queen of Angels Church.
Henning, Michael L. '74 (STL) St. Peters, MO All Saints Church; [W] St. Louis, MO Archdiocesan Stewardship Education Committee.
Henning, Phillip D. '93 (SAT) Fredericksburg, TX St. Mary's Church.
Henninger, George '85 (VIC) On Duty Outside the Diocese.
Henninger, Mark G. *s.j.* '78 (DET) [K] Detroit, MI Jesuit Community at the University of Detroit.
Hennington, Bruce M. '68 (MAD) Waunakee, WI St. John the Baptist Church.
Henrich, Steven *o.s.c.* '74 (DET) [K] Riverview, MI Crosier Community of Riverview.
Henrick, Eugene '63 (WDC) [24] Washington, DC St. Joseph on Capitol Hill Church.
Henrick, John C. '62 (NSH) Antioch, TN St. Ignatius of Antioch Church.
Henricksen, Francis C. '55 (DAV) Bettendorf, IA St. John Vianney Church.
Henriot, Peter J. *s.j.* '70 (FgM) Provinces.
Henritzy, Curtis E. *o.p.* '92 (PRO) [P] Providence, RI St. Thomas Aquinas Priory at Providence College.
Henry, Carol Ann *r.s.m.* (TR) [T] Asbury Park, NJ Mercy Center, Inc.
Henry, Charles W. *o.s.b.* '53 (IND) [F] Indianapolis, IN St. Vincent Hospital and Health Care Center, Inc.; [J] Indianapolis, IN St. Maur Priory.
Henry, Charles W. *o.s.b.* '53 (NEW) [N] Newark, NJ Newark Abbey.
Henry, Donald H. '71 (ALN) On Duty Outside the Diocese.
Henry, Donald H. '71 (VEN) [2] Naples, FL St. John the Evangelist Church.
Henry, Earl J. *o.s.b.* '64 (GBG) [H] Latrobe, PA Saint Vincent Archabbey.
Henry, Msgr. Edward C. '37 (TR) Retired.
Henry, James *s.v.d.* '59 (LA) [D] Lakewood, CA Saint Joseph High School.
Henry, James '71 (MRY) Arroyo Grande, CA St. Patrick Church.
Henry, James T. '64 (PH) [34] Philadelphia, PA Christ the King Church.
Henry, John F. *s.j.* '55 (BAL) [M] Baltimore, MD Jesuit Fathers and Brothers Maryland Provincial Curia.
Henry, John F. *s.j.* '55 (FgM) Provinces.
Henry, John P. '52 (RVC) Cutchogue, NY Sacred Heart Church; Retired.
Henry, Joseph A. '43 (PH) Riegelsville, PA St. Lawrence Church; Retired.
Henry, Joseph L. '36 (MAD) Retired.
Henry, Joseph P. '58 (PRO) Coventry, RI SS. John and Paul Church.
Henry, Larry *c.s.c.* '61 (GRY) [F] Michigan City, IN St. Anthony Hospital and Health Centers.
Henry, Leo G. '55 (PIT) Retired; [O] Pittsburgh, PA St. John Vianney Manor.
Henry, Patrick '81 (CLV) [10] Lorain, OH St. Peter Church.
Henry, Patrick '92 (SAC) Tulelake, CA Holy Cross Church.
Henry, Patrick J. '81 (CHI) [39] Chicago, IL St. Christina Church.
Henry, Paul '70 (BAL) [38] Baltimore, MD Holy Rosary Church.
Henry, Paul J. '68 (ORL) [9] Orlando, FL St. John Vianney Church.
Henry, Perry F. *c.m.* '83 (NO) [41] New Orleans, LA St. Joseph Church; [61] New Orleans, LA St. Stephen Church.
Henry, Peter '68 (ORL) On Duty Outside the Diocese.
Henry, Robert P. '79 (NY) Nyack, NY St. Ann Church.
Henry, Terence *t.o.r.* (ALT) [F] Loretto, PA Mount Assisi Friary.
Henry, Thomas '44 (RIC) Retired.
Henry, Thomas J. (NEW) Retired; [N] Caldwell, NJ The Rev. Msgr. James F. Kelley Residence for Retired Priests.
Henry, William '84 (JKS) McComb, MS St. Alphonsus Church.
Henseler, J. Thomas '63 (PEO) On Duty Outside the Diocese.
Henseler, Joseph N. '52 (LC) Chili, WI St. Stephen Church; Neillsville, WI St. Mary Church.
Henseler, Michael *s.d.s.* '77 (MIL) [P] Milwaukee, WI Salvatorian Provincial Residence.
Henseler, Thomas '63 (SFD) Mount Sterling, IL Holy Family Church.
Hensell, Eugene *o.s.b.* '69 (IND) [A] St. Meinrad, IN St. Meinrad Seminary; [B] St. Meinrad, IN St. Meinrad Seminary-College of Liberal Arts; [J] St. Meinrad, IN St. Meinrad Archabbey.
Hensen, Paul *o.carm.* (FgM) Carmelite Foreign Missions.
Hensgen, John A. *c.ss.r.* '36 (BLX) [E] Biloxi, MS St. John Neumann Residence.
Henson, Jerome M. '77 (ORG) Costa Mesa, CA St. John the Baptist Church.
Henson, Joel '93 (LA) [1] Oxnard, CA St. Anthony Church.
Hensy, Patrick E. *c.s.p.* '78 (AUS) [11] Austin, TX St. Austin's Church; [M] Austin, TX University Catholic Center.
Hentschel, Cletus B. '51 (BEL) Retired.
Hentz, Otto H. *s.j.* '68 (WDC) [M] Washington, DC The Jesuit Community at Georgetown University.
Hentzner, John T. '45 (MIL) Retired.
Henz, Kenneth W. '51 (CIN) Retired.
Heon, Charles *o.m.i.* '64 (FgM) Oblates Foreign Missions.
Heon, Paul J. *m.afr.* '41 (SP) [O] St. Petersburg, FL Missionaries of Africa.
Hepburn, Timothy M. '93 (ATL) Fort Oglethorpe, GA St. Gerard's Church.
Hepburn, Timothy M. '94 (ATL) [M] Atlanta, GA The Catholic Charismatic Renewal in Atlanta.
Hephner, John (GB) Coleman, WI Ss. Francis/Wenceslaus Church.
Hepnar, Bede *o.f.m.* '57 (GRY) Shelby, IN St. Theresa Church; [J] Cedar Lake, IN Our Lady of Lourdes Friary.
Hepner, Ernest C. '61 (CLV) Bedford Heights, OH Holy Trinity Church.
Heppe, Patrick E. '77 (MIL) [1] Fond du Lac, WI St. Joseph Church.
Heppen, Michael J. *c.s.c.* '63 (DET) Birmingham, MI Our Lady Queen of Martyrs Church.
Heppner, Sylvester *o.f.m.* '59 (IND) Oldenburg, IN Holy Family Church; [K] Oldenburg, IN Motherhouse of the Congregation of the Sisters of the Third Order of St. Francis.
Hept, Wilfrid *o.f.m.* '44 (BO) [BB] Boston, MA St. Anthony Shrine.
Herald, Robert (TYL) Palestine, TX Beto I Unit and Louie C. Powledge Unit, Texas Department of Corrections.
Herald, Robert P. '89 (AUS) On Duty Outside the Diocese.
Heramb, James '68 (JOL) Paxton, IL St. Mary Church.
Herard, Msgr. Joseph P. '55 (DUB) [6] Dubuque, IA Church of the Resurrection.
Heras, Msgr. Michael '84 (CC) [8] Corpus Christi, TX Our Lady of Perpetual Help Church.
Heraty, John T. '67 (RCK) Mooseheart, IL School of the Loyal Order of Moose.
Herba, Stanislaw '64 (SLC) [4] Midvale, UT St. Therese of the Child Jesus Church.
Herbe, Donnan *o.f.m.* '45 (SFE) Cerrillos, NM St. Joseph Church.
Herbein, John J. '74 (E) Franklin, PA St. Patrick Church.
Herbek, Msgr. Adrian F. '59 (LIN) David City, NE St. Mary's Church.
Herber, Alvin L. *c.pp.s.* '50 (KC) Cameron, MO St. Munchin Church.
Herber, John *c.pp.s.* (HBG) [G] Columbia, PA St. Anne's Home.
Herber, Stanley J. '64 (IND) Connersville, IN St. Gabriel Church; Knightstown, IN St. Rose Church; New Castle, IN St. Anne Church.
Herberger, Edward *s.v.d.* '60 (FgM) Society of the Divine Word Foreign Missions.
Herberger, Roy T. (BUF) [T] Buffalo, NY Hope of Buffalo, Inc.
Herberger, Roy T. '68 (BUF) Darien Center, NY Our Lady of Good Counsel Church.
Herbers, Simon *c.p.* (GAL) [S] Houston, TX Holy Name Retreat Center.
Herbert, Eugene '81 (LA) Covina, CA St. Louise de Marillac Church.
Herbert, G. Paul '86 (WDC) [1] Washington, DC St. Matthew Cathedral; Pastoral Center Special Ministries.
Herbert, J. Marc '50 (FR) [J] North Dartmouth, MA Holy Cross Mission House.
Herbert, John J. '83 (BUR) Rutland, VT St. Peter Church.
Herbert, Joseph *s.j.* '47 (DEN) Retired.
Herbert, Joseph L. *s.j.* '47 (STL) [P] St. Louis, MO The Jesuits of the Missouri Province.
Herbert, Leo P. '67 (ATL) Newnan, GA St. George's Church.
Herbert, Michael '92 (LAF) Port Barre, LA Sacred Heart of Jesus Church.
Herbert, Oliver *t.o.r.* '71 (ALT) [F] Loretto, PA St. Francis Friary, Third Order Regular of St. Francis of Penance.
Herbert, Ray *s.c.* (BR) Special Assignment.
Herbst, Charles T. *c.m.* '50 (STL) [P] Perryville, MO Congregation of The Mission.
Herbst, Justin J. '58 (TR) [J] Lawrenceville, NJ Morris Hall/Saint Lawrence, Inc.; [L] Lawrenceville, NJ Morris Hall-Saint Lawrence, Inc.; [O] Lawrenceville, NJ Our Lady of the Rosary Chapel; [T] Lawrenceville, NJ Morris Hall/St. Lawrence, Inc.
Herbst, Robert M. *o.f.m.conv.* '91 (SB) [11] Riverside, CA St. Thomas the Apostle Church.
Herbst, Thomas *o.f.m.* '92 (OAK) [N] Oakland, CA Franciscan Friars Provincial Office, Province of St. Barbara.
Hercek, Joseph R. '72 (MRY) Atascadero, CA St. William's Church.
Hercik, Terry A. '80 (GBG) Ford City, PA St. Mary Church.
Herda, Jerome G. '90 (MIL) [E] Milwaukee, WI Divine Savior Holy Angels High School.
Herdegen, Msgr. Anthony '46 (FRS) Retired.
Heredia, Agnel Jose de '80 (SFR) Half Moon Bay, CA Our Lady of the Pillar Church.
Heredia, Juan Victor (BWN) [D] San Juan, TX San Juan Nursing Home.
Heredia, Juan Victor '91 (BWN) [9] Brownsville, TX St. Luke Church.
Hereford, Thomas D. '56 (JC) On Duty Outside the Diocese.
Herek, Daniel P. '71 (OM) [39] Omaha, NE St. Richard Church; Absent on Leave.
Hereley, Peter J. *o.p.* (CHI) [N] River Forest, IL St. Thomas Aquinas Priory.
Hereley, Peter J. *o.p.* '63 (CHI) [N] River Forest, IL St. Thomas Aquinas Priory; [U] River Forest, IL American Friends of the Ecole Biblique.
Heretick, Joseph S. '47 (GF) Retired.
Herff, Jerome *c.m.* (GLP) Kayenta, AZ Our Lady of Guadalupe Church.
Hergenrother, John C. '66 (CHI) Other Assignments.

Herhenreader, Peter V. '59 (SCR) Royal, PA St. Pius X Church.
Heria, Fernando '96 (MIA) [32] Miami, FL St. Thomas the Apostle Church.
Herian, Kenneth J. *s.j.* '55 (MIL) [29] Milwaukee, WI Gesu Parish.
Heric, William '81 (SEA) Kirkland, WA St. John Mary Vianney Church.
Herkowski, Arthur M. '54 (MIL) Retired.
Herkowski, Arthur M. '54 (RNO) Retired.
Herle, Clifford *o.f.m.* '55 (LA) [R] Santa Barbara, CA Franciscan Friary, Order of Friars Minor (Old Mission).
Herlihy, Charles E. '94 (BO) [1] Arlington, MA St. Agnes Church.
Herlihy, Daniel J. '67 (MET) South Bound Brook, NJ Our Lady of Mercy Church.
Herlihy, Jude M. *o.s.m.* '56 (ORG) Fullerton, CA St. Juliana Falconieri Church.
Herlong, T.L. '58 (LKC) [6] Lake Charles, LA St. Theodore's Church.
Herlong, Theophilus L. '58 (LKC) Retired.
Herman, Charles A. '97 (FTW) [7] Fort Wayne, IN St. John Baptist Church.
Herman, Gerard *o.f.m.conv.* '57 (SAV) Hinesville, GA St. Stephen, First Martyr Church.
Herman, Jerome A. '43 (DET) Retired.
Herman, John A. *c.s.c.* '95 (PHX) Goodyear, AZ Saint John Vianney Church.
Herman, Michael T. '89 (CHI) [144] Chicago, IL Notre Dame Church.
Herman, Robert D. '60 (WIN) Medford, MN Christ the King Church.
Hermann, Msgr. Carlton P. '35 (SFS) Retired.
Hermann, Robert J. '63 (STL) Chesterfield, MO Incarnate Word Church.
Hermanns, Harold T. '54 (NEW) Retired; [N] Rutherford, NJ St. John Vianney Residence for Priests.
Hermanns, Mel *o.f.m.cap* '64 (GB) [M] Appleton, WI Monte Alverno Retreat Center.
Hermansen, Douglas U. '79 (TR) Neptune, NJ Jersey Shore Medical Center.
Hermansen, Douglas V. '79 (TR) Avon, NJ St. Elizabeth Church.
Hermes, Msgr. Daniel J. '69 (RCK) [5] Rockford, IL Holy Family Church.
Hermes, Eustace A. '41 (VIC) Retired.
Hermes, Joseph H. *m.m.* '62 (FgM) Maryknoll Foreign Missions.
Hermes, Michael '91 (KCK) [13] Kansas City, KS St. Joseph and St. Benedict Church.
Hermes, Roger J. '53 (STP) Retired.
Hermes, Thomas W. '82 (KC) Clinton, MO Holy Rosary Church.
Hermoso, Joseph '57 (ELP) [25] El Paso, TX St. Joseph's Church.
Hermoso, Msgr. Seth '67 (GAL) [12] Houston, TX St. Augustine Church.
Hernadez, Enrico A. '96 (SJ) Morgan Hill, CA St. Catherine of Alexandria Church.
Hernady, Martin '48 (TOL) Retired.
Hernan Dez Plata, Jose L. *o.s.a.* '74 (FgM) Foreign Missions.
Hernandez, Alberto *o.f.m.* '70 (ELP) [B] El Paso, TX Roger Bacon College.
Hernandez, Msgr. Alfred '55 (LA) Retired.
Hernandez, Alfred '82 (LA) [26] Los Angeles, CA Our Lady of Lourdes Church.
Hernandez, Alfred Ricardo '66 (SAT) Military Chaplains.
Hernandez, Alfredo '92 (PMB) [A] Boynton Beach, FL St. Vincent de Paul Regional Seminary.
Hernandez, Angelo J. '93 (PH) [154] Philadelphia, PA St. Veronica Church.
Hernandez, Anthony M. '95 (BRK) [198] Queens, NY St. Mary Star of the Sea Church.
Hernandez, Antonio *c.ss.r.* '67 (PCE) Guayama, PR St. Anthony of Padua Church.
Hernandez, Antonio A. *c.ss.r.* '67 (PCE) [B] Ponce, PR The Pontifical Catholic University of Puerto Rico.
Hernandez, Apolinar '90 (SR) Fort Bragg, CA Our Lady of Good Counsel Church.
Hernandez, Bernardo '63 (SJN) [62] San Juan, PR San Vicente de Paul Church.
Hernandez, Blas Alberto '69 (LA) Fillmore, CA St. Francis of Assisi Church.
Hernandez, Edgardo Lopez '83 (MGZ) Rincon, PR St. Rose of Lima Church.
Hernandez, Eliseo '82 (SB) [5] Riverside, CA St. Anthony Church.
Hernandez, Enrique *m.g.* '96 (LA) [85] Los Angeles, CA St. Paul Church.
Hernandez, Esteban *m.s.f.* '87 (BWN) Edinburg, TX Holy Family Church.
Hernandez, Fernando A. '90 (NY) [191] Bronx, NY St. Thomas Aquinas Church.
Hernandez, Francis G. *s.j.* '63 (SAC) [C] Sacramento, CA Jesuit High School; [G] Carmichael, CA Jesuit High School Community of Sacramento.
Hernandez, Francisco '64 (YAK) [F] Cowiche, WA St. Peter the Apostle Retreat Center.
Hernandez, Francisco '94 (MIA) [28] Miami, FL SS. Peter and Paul Church.
Hernandez, Francisco J. '90 (YAK) Cowiche, WA St. Peter's Church.
Hernandez, George M. '97 (BRK) [230] Queens, NY Queen of Angels Church.
Hernandez, Msgr. Gonzalo Diaz '63 (MGZ) Hormigueros, PR Shrine of Our Lady of Monserrate Church.
Hernandez, Javier '74 (CGS) Yabucoa, PR Santos Angeles Cutodios Church.
Hernandez, Jesus Gomez '52 (SJN) [45] San Juan, PR Ntra. Sra. del Perpetuo Socorro Church.
Hernandez, Jimmy '83 (ARE) On Duty Outside the Diocese.
Hernandez, Jose '60 (SFE) [24] Albuquerque, NM St. Edwin Church.
Hernandez, Jose Guillermo '89 (SJN) [43] San Juan, PR San Pablo Church.
Hernandez, Joseph '69 (LA) Fillmore, CA St. Francis of Assisi Church.
Hernandez, Juan Ramon *c.ss.r.* '80 (CGS) [1] Caguas, PR Cathedral Dulce Nombre de Jesus Church.
Hernandez, Lawrence C. *o.ss.t.* '78 (BAL) [M] Baltimore, MD Holy Trinity Monastery.
Hernandez, Manuel, Jr. '96 (CC) [17] Corpus Christi, TX St. Patrick Church.
Hernandez, Marco A. *c.s.b.* '87 (GAL) [Q] Sugar Land, TX Basilian Mission Center.
Hernandez, Martin A. '81 (BR) Prairieville, LA St. John the Evangelist Church.
Hernandez, P. Bernardo *c.m.* '63 (SJN) [24] San Juan, PR Jesus Maestro Church.
Hernandez, Pedro '89 (ARE) [4] Utuado, PR Nuestra Senora del Monte Carmelo Church.
Hernandez, Ramon '73 (SP) [14] Tampa, FL St. Paul Church.
Hernandez, Rene Javier '95 (MGZ) Lajas, PR Our Lady of the Purification Church.
Hernandez, Stephen '82 (LA) Retired.
Hernandez, Stephen C. '53 (LA) [24] Los Angeles, CA Our Lady of Guadalupe Church.
Hernandez, Steven '82 (LA) Los Angeles, CA L.A. County/University of Southern California Hospital.
Hernandez, Victor M. *s.j.* '76 (MIA) [D] Miami, FL Belen Jesuit Preparatory School; [H] Miami, FL Villa Javier.
Hernandez Velez, Antonio *s.t.* '57 (FgM) Trinity Missions.
Hernandez Vidal, Jesus *s.s.p.* '94 (LA) [R] Los Angeles, CA Society of St. Paul.
Hernandez-Tovar, Francisco '80 (SAC) Truckee, CA Assumption of the Blessed Virgin Mary Church.
Hernando, Henry L. '67 (LA) [16] Los Angeles, CA Immaculate Heart of Mary Church.
Hernando, Jose L. '62 (MIA) Key Biscayne, FL St. Agnes Church.
Herne, Robert G. '47 (CHI) Northbrook, IL Our Lady of the Brook Church; Palos Hills, IL Sacred Heart Church; Retired.
Hernes, Thomas (KC) [O] Kansas City, MO Catholic Woman's Club.
Hernik, Jan *o.f.m.conv.* '69 (BO) [55] Boston, MA Our Lady of Czestochowa Church.
Herold, Anthony J. '79 (DAV) Ottumwa, IA St. Patrick's Church.
Herold, Carl A. '35 (IND) Retired.
Heron, J. Thomas '78 (PH) Absent on Leave.
Herp, Joseph T. '73 (L) [39] Louisville, KY Incarnation Church.
Herpin, Msgr. L. Michael '66 (LAF) Broussard, LA Sacred Heart of Jesus Church.
Herpin, Wayne *s.j.* '74 (PMB) [3] West Palm Beach, FL St. Ann Church.
Herr, Charles W.A. '48 (NEW) [4] Hoboken, NJ SS. Peter and Paul's Church.
Herr, Kenneth '68 (EVN) [16] Evansville, IN St. John Church; Special Assignment; [A] Evansville, IN Reitz Memorial High School.
Herrador, Blas P. '52 (GAL) [72] Houston, TX Resurrection Church.
Herrera, Anthony W. '91 (OAK) Pleasanton, CA St. Augustine Church.
Herrera, David Lee '89 (SAN) [2] Odessa, TX St. Anthony Church; [4] Odessa, TX St. Joseph Church.
Herrera, David S. '69 (LA) Carpinteria, CA St. Joseph Church.
Herrera, Edward '91 (LSC) Sunland Park, NM St. Martin de Porres Church.
Herrera, Emigdio '77 (LA) Santa Maria, CA St. John Neumann Church.
Herrera, Francisco '67 (ELP) [25] El Paso, TX St. Joseph's Church.
Herrera, Jesus Enrique '96 (MRY) Watsonville, CA St. Patrick Church.
Herrera, Lawrence *s.j.* '81 (LA) [A] Camarillo, CA St. John's Seminary College of the Archdiocese of Los Angeles.
Herrera, Pedro E. *c.s.v.* '80 (CHI) [N] Arlington Heights, IL Viatorian Province Center-Clerics of St. Viator.
Herrera, Rosendo '96 (AMA) Dalhart, TX St. Anthony's Church.
Herrero, Jose *o.s.a.* '51 (NY) [67] New York, NY St. Lucy Church.
Herrero, Jose M. '52 (PCE) [B] Ponce, PR The Pontifical Catholic University of Puerto Rico.
Herrero, Msgr. Nicolas '59 (FRS) Exeter, CA Sacred Heart Church.
Herres, Msgr. Joseph W. '72 (LA) [46] Los Angeles, CA San Antonio de Padua Church; La Puente, CA St. Joseph Church.
Herrgott, George V. *s.s.c.* '79 (BO) [W] Quincy, MA St. Columban's Foreign Mission Society.
Herrgott, George V. *s.s.c.* '79 (OM) [K] St. Columbans, NE St. Columban's Foreign Mission Society.
Herrick, Marion L. *o.f.m.* '67 (GBG) Uniontown, PA Uniontown Hospital.
Herrlich, Neale W. *s.j.* '52 (SLC) [4] Ogden, UT St. Mary's Church.
Herrman, Gilbert P. '49 (DOD) Lakin, KS St. Anthony Church; Syracuse, KS St. Raphael Church.
Herrmann, Austin C. *c.pp.s.* '48 (SAN) Coleman, TX Sacred Heart Church.
Herrmann, Frank R. *s.j.* '74 (BO) [W] Chestnut Hill, MA The Jesuit Community at Boston College.
Herrmann, Jim *o.s.c.* '70 (STP) [N] Anoka, MN Crosier Community of Anoka.
Herrmann, Richard J. '44 (LC) Retired.
Herrmann, Robert W. '58 (PIT) Robinson Township, PA Holy Trinity Church.
Herron, Bernard J. '54 (PH) [20] Philadelphia, PA St. Barnabas Church; [97] Philadelphia, PA St. Mary of Czestochowa Church.
Herron, Denis '73 (BRK) [213] Queens, NY Our Lady of Lourdes Church.
Herron, Francis X. '55 (PH) Trooper, PA Visitation B.V.M. Church.
Herron, Jack B. '74 (FAR) Military Chaplains.
Herron, Msgr. Joseph P. '62 (CAM) Longport, NJ Epiphany Church; [G] Camden, NJ The Frank J. and Rosina W. Suttill Catholic Foundation.
Herron, Msgr. Thomas J. '73 (PH) Highland Park, PA St. Laurence Church.
Hertel, Msgr. Herbert N. '42 (WCH) Retired.
Hertel, James R. '65 (PAT) [4] Wayne, NJ Our Lady of Consolation Church.
Hertel, John *o.carm.* '53 (FgM) Carmelite Foreign Missions.
Hertel, John *o.carm.* '53 (JOL) [J] Darien, IL Carmelite Provincial Office.
Hertel, Joseph M. *o.f.m.* '66 (NY) [35] New York, NY St. Francis of Assisi Church.
Hertel, Joseph M. *o.f.m.* '66 (PAT) [P] Paterson, NJ St. Anthony's Guild.
Herttna, Matthew M. '45 (Y) [2] Massillon, OH National Shrine of St. Dymphna Church; Retired.
Hertweck, Robert W. *s.m.* '64 (CIN) [M] Dayton, OH Marianist Provincialate.
Heruday, Msgr. Joseph C. '41 (CLV) [AA] Cleveland, OH Catholic Tours of Ohio, Inc.
Heruday, Msgr. Joseph C. '43 (CLV) Maple Heights, OH St. Wenceslas Church; Retired.
Hervey, Paul '95 (SP) [5] Tampa, FL Incarnation Church.
Herzing, James '95 (SCL) Sauk Rapids, MN Sacred Heart Church.
Herzog, John M. '56 (DUB) Colo, IA St. Mary's Church; Nevada, IA St. Patrick's Church.
Herzog, Lawrence A. '80 (STL) [59] St. Louis, MO St. Roch Church.
Herzog, Mark J. '79 (TOL) [1] Fremont, OH Sacred Heart Church.
Herzog, Msgr. Ronald P. '68 (BLX) Pass Christian, MS St. Paul Church.
Herzstein, Joseph M. *c.s.sp.* '63 (FgM) Holy Ghost Foreign Missions.
Hesburgh, Theodore M. *c.s.c.* '43 (FTW) [B] Notre Dame, IN University of Notre Dame Du Lac; [J] Notre Dame, IN Holy Cross Community, Corby Hall, University of Notre Dame.
Heskamp, Charles *s.v.d.* '58 (LAF) [4] Lafayette, LA Immaculate Heart of Mary Church.
Heskamp, Joseph C. '48 (CIN) [86] Cincinnati, OH St. Vincent Ferrer Church; Retired.
Hesketh, John E. *o.s.b.* '94 (PAT) [M] Morristown, NJ St. Mary's Abbey.
Heskin, Thomas M. *o.s.m.* '55 (CHI) [J] Maywood, IL Foster G. McGaw Hospital of Loyola University of Chicago; [N] Chicago, IL Servite Friars - Eastern Province.
Hesko, Daniel C. '84 (TR) Middletown, NJ St. Catherine Church.
Hesler, Raymond F. *s.s.* '35 (BAL) [J] Baltimore, MD St. Charles Villa; [M] Baltimore, MD St. Charles Villa.
Heslin, Msgr. James J. '54 (STA) [7] Jacksonville, FL Holy Spirit Church.
Heslin, Philip J. (SUP) [9] Superior, WI St. William Church.
Heslin, Philip J. '57 (SUP) On Special or Other (Arch)Diocesan Assignment.

Heslin, Sean '67 (ORL) [1] Orlando, FL St. James Cathedral.
Hess, Charles *o.p.* '47 (OAK) [N] Oakland, CA Dominican Order (Western Province), St. Albert's Priory.
Hess, George A. *s.j.* '50 (BAL) [M] Baltimore, MD Jesuit Fathers and Brothers Maryland Provincial Curia.
Hess, George A. *s.j.* '50 (FgM) Provinces.
Hess, James *o.carm.* (PMB) [G] Boca Raton, FL St. Elias Priory-Order of Carmelites, NY.
Hess, James *o.carm.* '76 (PMB) [B] Boca Raton, FL Pope John Paul II High School.
Hess, James W. '53 (MIL) Retired.
Hess, John Paul '83 (STL) [7] Florissant, MO Sacred Heart Church.
Hess, Larry J. '79 (ALN) [O] Kutztown, PA Christopher House; [O] Kutztown, PA Christopher House.
Hess, Msgr. Michael N. '71 (DM) [A] West Des Moines, IA St. Joseph Educational Center; [C] West Des Moines, IA Dowling High School; [J] Des Moines, IA Dowling-St. Joseph Alumni Foundation.
Hess, Norbert *c.s.c.* '53 (CHI) [D] Niles, IL Notre Dame High School.
Hess, Richard J. '60 (DUB) St. Anthony, IA Sacred Heart Church; St. Anthony, IA Sacred Heart Church; Zearing, IA St. Gabriel Church; Zearing, IA St. Gabriel Church.
Hess, Robert *s.c.j.* '67 (JKS) [E] Nesbit, MS St. Michael Community House; [H] Walls, MS Sacred Heart League.
Hess, Stephen M. *s.j.* '95 (P) [19] Portland, OR St. Ignatius Church.
Hesse, Paul A '91 (CC) Odem, TX Sacred Heart Church.
Hesse, Peter *o.f.m.cap.* '43 (LC) [I] Marathon City, WI St. Anthony Retreat Center.
Hesse, Robert T. *c.s.c.* '58 (FgM) Holy Cross Foreign Missions.
Hesse, Thomas N. '63 (KCK) Flush, KS St. Joseph's Church; Wamego, KS St. Bernard's Church.
Hessel, Gerald J. '67 (MIL) Caledonia, WI St. Louis Church.
Hesseldenz, Msgr. Clarence H. '44 (STL) Retired.
Hessian, Msgr. Patrick J. '53 (STP) Retired.
Hessian, Roger J. '61 (STP) Cannon Falls, MN St. Pius V Church.
Hession, Msgr. Edward I. '41 (FTW) [3] Fort Wayne, IN St. Charles Borromeo Church; Retired.
Hession, James J. '59 (BO) Health Leave.
Hession, Mark R. '84 (FR) [7] Taunton, MA St. Joseph's Church; [O] Fall River, MA Diocesan Education Center.
Hessling, Ambrose B. *o.s.b.* '57 (PEO) [A] Peru, IL St. Bede Abbey and Academy.
Hestasusilo, Anton *c.i.c.m.* '96 (BWN) [3] Mission, TX Our Lady of St. John of the Fields Church.
Hester, John '59 (SJ) Milpitas, CA Stanford Medical Center.
Heter, Bernard P. '74 (NY) Cornwall-on-Hudson, NY St. Thomas of Canterbury Church.
Hetteberg, Marcan *o.f.m.* '54 (CIN) [M] Cincinnati, OH St. Francis Center.
Hettinger, Msgr. Clarence J. '42 (PEO) [15] Peoria, IL St. Vincent De Paul Church; Special Assignment; Retired.
Hettinger, Paul W. '39 (PEO) Retired.
Hetzler, Leo A. *c.s.b.* '55 (ROC) [I] Rochester, NY Basilian Residence.
Heuberger, Joseph '70 (P) Verboort, OR Visitation B.V.M. Church.
Heuberger, Mark '80 (PMB) [A] Boynton Beach, FL St. Vincent de Paul Regional Seminary.
Heuberger, Mark '80 (VEN) On Duty Outside the Diocese.
Heuman, George P. '81 (ROC) Ithaca, NY Immaculate Conception Church.
Heumann, Carl J. *s.j.* '72 (FgM) Provinces.
Heuring, Msgr. Alvan P. '44 (DUB) Retired.
Heuring, Msgr. Alvan P. '44 (SFR) Retired.
Heuschkel, Robert R. '50 (Y) [13] Youngstown, OH St. Dominic's Church.
Heuser, Frederick A. '55 (MIL) [4] Kenosha, WI St. James Church.
Heuser, James *s.d.b.* (NEW) [N] South Orange, NJ The Salesian Community.
Heusser, John F. (PAT) Paterson, NJ Preakness Hospital.
Heusser, John F. '51 (PAT) [4] Paterson, NJ Blessed Sacrament Church.
Heuvel, Jeffrey Vanden '86 (GB) [N] Green Bay, WI University of Wisconsin G.B. Ecumenical Center.
Hever, John J. '52 (BO) Foxboro, MA St. Mary Church; Medfield, MA Medfield State Hospital.
Hever, Thomas F. '62 (PHX) [3] Tempe, AZ Resurrection Church.
Hevern, Vincent W. *s.j.* '76 (SY) [S] Syracuse, NY Jesuits at LeMoyne, Inc.
Hevia, Todd O. '67 (PT) Milton, FL St. Rose of Lima Church.
Hewes, James E. '74 (ROC) [M] Rochester, NY Diocesan Office of Campus Ministry.
Hewes, Robert S. '78 (RVC) Hicksville, NY Our Lady of Mercy Church.
Hewett, Alfred J. '56 (CAM) Haddon Heights, NJ St. Rose's Church; Retired.
Hewitt, Msgr. Bernard P. '47 (CAM) Retired.
Hewitt, Charles L. '31 (BGP) [K] Trumbull, CT St. Joseph's Manor.
Hewitt, Charles L. '31 (HRT) Retired.
Hewitt, Kenneth R. (PAT) Retired.
Hewitt, Thomas E. *c.s.c.* '39 (FTW) [J] South Bend, IN Congregation of Holy Cross Indiana Province Provincial House.
Hewitt, Thomas E. *c.s.c.* '39 (SAT) [M] San Antonio, TX Holy Cross Community.
Hewitt, William J. '57 (MET) Hampton, NJ St. Ann Church.
Hewson, William J. '40 (BR) Retired.
Heyburn, Msgr. Kevin J. '48 (SAN) Olfen, TX St. Boniface Church; Rowena, TX St. Joseph's Church.
Heyburn, Theodore *c.ss.r.* '60 (WIL) Chester, Kent Island, MD St. Christopher Church.
Heyd, James '89 (CHI) Evanston, IL St. Athanasius Church.
Heyd, Joseph J. *o.s.b.* '56 (PEO) Peru, IL St. Joseph's Church; [A] Peru, IL St. Bede Abbey and Academy.
Heydens, Donald J. '70 (GR) On Special Assignment.
Heyman, Jerome M. *o.s.a.* '61 (KAL) Allegan, MI Blessed Sacrament Church.
Heymen, Richard H. '56 (GB) Whitelaw, WI St. Michael Church.
Heymer, Msgr. Edward D. '45 (MEM) Retired.
Heyndricks, Eugene P. '81 (NEW) Park Ridge, NJ Our Lady of Mercy Church.
Hezel, Francis X. *s.j.* '66 (FgM) Provinces.
Hezel, Francis X. *s.j.* '69 (CI) [A] Pohnpei, FM Micronesia Seminar; [C] Kolonia, Pohnpei, FM Jesuit House.
Hezel, Kenneth J. *s.j.* '66 (AGN) [G] Mangilao, GU Campus Ministry, Newman Center, University of Guam.
Hezel, Kenneth J. *s.j.* '66 (FgM) Provinces.
Hibner, Cyprian *o.carm.* '61 (PHX) [5] Glendale, AZ St. Raphael Church.
Hibner, Jerome H. '64 (BEL) Radom, IL St. Michael Church.
Hicarte, Mateo '53 (LA) [16] Los Angeles, CA Immaculate Heart of Mary Church.
Hickel, Msgr. John J. '55 (STL) St. Paul, MO St. Paul Church.
Hickens, William F. *c.s.c.* '46 (FTW) [J] South Bend, IN Congregation of Holy Cross Indiana Province Provincial House.
Hickey, Christopher J. '94 (BO) Dedham, MA St. Mary Church.
Hickey, Daniel J. '59 (BO) [3] Malden, MA Sacred Hearts Church.
Hickey, Dennis W. *c.s.p.* '76 (NY) [DD] Jamaica Estates, NY Paulist Fathers Generalate.
Hickey, Msgr. Edward T. '45 (COV) Retired.
Hickey, George J. *i.m.c.* '80 (MET) [H] Somerset, NJ Consolata Society for Foreign Missions.
Hickey, George W. '73 (PRT) Hampden, ME St. Matthew Church; Winterport, ME St. Gabriel Church.
Hickey, Gerald J. '63 (BO) Awaiting Assignment.
Hickey, Gregory J. '79 (PH) [117] Philadelphia, PA Our Lady Help of Christians Church; [D] Norristown, PA Kennedy-Kenrick Catholic High School.
Hickey, James C. *s.m.a.* '46 (BO) [W] Dedham, MA African Mission House.
Hickey, James C. *s.m.a.* '46 (FgM) Society of African Missions.
Hickey, James F. '68 (BO) Rockland, MA Holy Family Church.
Hickey, James V. '64 (HRT) Farmington, CT St. Patrick's Church.
Hickey, Jerome J. *o.c.s.o.* '59 (ATL) [I] Conyers, GA The Monastery of the Holy Spirit.
Hickey, John *c.m.* '49 (CHI) [C] Chicago, IL Vincentian Community at DePaul University.
Hickey, John '96 (AMA) Happy, TX Holy Name of Jesus Church; Nazareth, TX Holy Family Church.
Hickey, John P. '86 (PIT) Bellevue, PA Assumption of the Blessed Virgin Mary on the Beautiful River Church.
Hickey, Joseph M. '68 (RVC) Elmont, NY St. Vincent de Paul Church.
Hickey, Joseph W. '56 (NY) [143] Bronx, NY St. Francis Xavier Church.
Hickey, Kieran *o.f.m.cap.* (GB) Kaukauna, WI St. Mary of the Annunciation Church.
Hickey, Meidon *o.f.m.* '43 (GLP) Fort Defiance, AZ Our Lady of Blessed Sacrament Church.
Hickey, Meldon *o.f.m.* '51 (GLP) [A] Gallup, NM Diocesan Diaconate Formation Program.
Hickey, Peter D. *s.j.* '76 (BO) [E] Boston, MA Boston College High School & Jesuit Community.
Hickey, Regis *o.s.b.* '50 (KCK) [H] Atchison, KS St. Benedict's Abbey.
Hickey, Msgr. Robert P. '65 (NY) Ellenville, NY St. Mary and St. Andrew Church.
Hickey, Robert P. *o.s.a.* '92 (WDC) [B] Silver Spring, MD Austin Friars Hall, Order of St. Augustine.
Hickey, Thomas D. '49 (MIL) Retired.
Hickey, Thomas E. '70 (CHI) [41] Chicago, IL St. Clement Church.
Hickey, Thomas F. *c.ss.r.* '54 (BRK) [107] Brooklyn, NY Our Lady of Perpetual Help Basilica Church.
Hickey, Msgr. William T. '47 (BRK) [206] Queens, NY Our Lady of the Angelus Church; Retired.
Hickie, J. Noel '67 (BAK) On Duty Outside the Diocese.
Hickie, J. Noel '67 (P) [J] Eugene, OR Sacred Heart Medical Center.
Hickin, Michael W. '97 (FAR) [1] Fargo, ND St. Mary's Cathedral; Argusville, ND St. William Church.
Hickl, Robert *o.m.i.* '79 (FgM) Oblates Foreign Missions.
Hickman, J. Stephen '82 (RIC) Military Chaplains.
Hicks, Alfred J. *s.j.* '66 (BO) [H] Boston, MA Nativity Preparatory School; [W] Boston, MA The Society of Jesus of New England-Provincial Offices.
Hicks, Ronald A. '94 (CHI) Orland Hills, IL St. Elizabeth Seton Church.
Hicks, Steven '82 (SAN) Military Chaplains.
Hidaka, Ronald E. *s.j.* '74 (FgM) Provinces.
Hidalgo, Juan Vincente *f.m.m.* '95 (WIL) [I] Seaford, DE Missionary Fraternity of Mary, USA, Ltd.
Hidding, Thomas J. *s.j.* '86 (NO) [11] New Orleans, LA Immaculate Conception Church.
Hiebl, Charles J. '62 (LC) Southeastern Portage County, WI St. Maximilian Maria Kolbe Church.
Hien, John '63 (RVC) Seaford, NY St. William, the Abbot Church.
Hien, Joseph '64 (NY) [27] New York, NY St. Columba Church.
Hietpas, Raymond '35 (GB) Retired.
Higdon, C. Paul '46 (DET) Retired; [H] Port Huron, MI Mercy Hospital of Port Huron.
Higdon, Francis *m.m.* '67 (WDC) [B] Washington, DC Maryknoll Fathers and Brothers.
Higdon, Frank *m.m.* (PH) [AA] Philadelphia, PA Maryknoll House.
Higginbotham, Robert '75 (BLX) Military Chaplains.
Higgins, Charles J. '75 (BO) Danvers, MA St. Richard Church; [2] Haverhill, MA St. James Church.
Higgins, Msgr. Cornelius P. '44 (SAC) [7] Sacramento, CA Presentation of the Blessed Virgin Mary Church; Knights Landing, CA St. Paul Church; Retired and in Senior Ministry.
Higgins, Donald *c.s.s.* '64 (BO) [W] Waltham, MA Stigmatine House.
Higgins, E. E. '57 (PEO) Pontiac, IL St. Mary's Church.
Higgins, Edward F. '54 (GBG) Retired.
Higgins, Edward J. '76 (PSC) Mahanoy City, PA St. Mary's Church.
Higgins, Eugene F. *m.m.* '30 (NY) [DD] Maryknoll, NY Maryknoll Fathers and Brothers.
Higgins, Francis '64 (SC) Schaller, IA St. Joseph's Church.
Higgins, Francis C. '68 (SAV) Thunderbolt, GA Nativity of Our Lord Church.
Higgins, Msgr. George C. '40 (CHI) Retired.
Higgins, Msgr. George G. '40 (WDC) [C] Washington, DC Catholic University of America, The.
Higgins, James J. *c.ss.r.* '37 (STL) [P] Liguori, MO Liguori Mission House/Redemptorists.
Higgins, James P. *s.j.* '85 (BUF) [C] Buffalo, NY Canisius College; [O] Buffalo, NY Canisius Jesuit Community.
Higgins, Jerome *o.f.m.cap.* '54 (MIL) [B] Hales Corners, WI Sacred Heart School of Theology; [P] Milwaukee, WI St. Conrad House.
Higgins, John '81 (LA) [70] Los Angeles, CA St. Joan of Arc Church.
Higgins, John F. *m.s.* '72 (HRT) [M] Hartford, CT Missionaries of LaSalette Provincial Secretary.
Higgins, John J. '52 (WDC) Retired.
Higgins, John J. *s.j.* '66 (WOR) [N] Worcester, MA Jesuits of Holy Cross College, Inc.
Higgins, John J. '96 (NY) [148] Bronx, NY Holy Rosary Church.
Higgins, Msgr. Joseph P. '57 (MAD) Middleton, WI St. Bernard Church.
Higgins, Msgr. Laurence E. '53 (SP) [10] Tampa, FL St. Lawrence Church.
Higgins, Leonard H. '82 (TLS) Pawhuska, OK Immaculate Conception Church.
Higgins, Michael *o.carm.* '68 (LA) [3] North Hollywood, CA St. Jane Frances de Chantal Church.
Higgins, Michael *c.p.* '70 (CHI) [N] Chicago, IL Passionist Provincial Office.
Higgins, Michael *c.p.* '70 (DET) [K] Detroit, MI St. Paul of the Cross Community, Congregation of the Passion; [P] Detroit, MI St. Paul of the Cross Retreat Center.
Higgins, Michael *t.o.r.* '85 (ALT) [A] Loretto, PA St. Francis College.
Higgins, Michael J. *t.o.r.* (ALT) [F] Loretto, PA St. Bonaventure Friary.
Higgins, Michael J. '62 (BO) Health Leave.
Higgins, Msgr. Michael K. '64 (SD) Unassigned.
Higgins, Msgr. Patrick '54 (CC) [3] Corpus Christi, TX Holy Cross Church.
Higgins, Patrick O. '47 (SFD) Retired.

Higgins, Peter '56 (VIC) Blessing, TX St. Peter's Church.
Higgins, Raymond '94 (DM) Perry, IA St. Patrick Church.
Higgins, Richard B. '68 (SAC) Military Chaplains.
Higgins, Suzanne (BO) [Q] Brockton, MA Good Samaritan Medical Center.
Higgins, Thomas C. *m.m.* '50 (NY) [DD] Maryknoll, NY Maryknoll Fathers and Brothers.
Higgins, Thomas M. '85 (PH) [129] Philadelphia, PA Our Lady of Victory Church.
Higgins, Thomas P. *s.j.* '64 (LA) [C] Los Angeles, CA Loyola Marymount University; [CC] Los Angeles, CA Archdiocesan Office for Campus Ministry.
Higgins, Msgr. William '43 (NY) Retired; [DD] New York, NY Our Lady of Consolation Residence.
Higgs, Donald X. '88 (WH) Farmington, WV St. Peters Church; Mannington, WV St. Patrick's Church.
Highberger, Donald E. *s.j.* '81 (SPK) [C] Spokane, WA Gonzaga University.
Highberger, George E. '61 (PHX) Chandler, AZ St. Mary's Church.
Highfill, H. Brian '74 (NO) Military Chaplains.
Highland, Msgr. Charles F. '50 (STU) Churchtown, OH St. John the Baptist Church; [I] Beverly, OH Washington Technical College; [J] Marietta, OH Search.
Highland, Terence *o.s.a.* (BO) Andover, MA St. Augustine Church.
Hight, Michael '82 (RC) Presho, SD Christ the King Church.
Hightower, O. Lee. '61 (HEL) Military Chaplains.
Higley, Gregory L. '81 (JC) Mexico, MO St. Brendan Church.
Higson, John '80 (LA) [2] Oxnard, CA Santa Clara Church; Santa Maria, CA St. John Neumann Church.
Higuera, Federico '82 (BEL) Cobden, IL St. Joseph Church.
Higuera, Julio '78 (PHX) Gilbert, AZ St. Anne Church.
Higuero, Francisco J. '68 (BRK) Absent on Leave.
Hiland, George '58 (PEO) Retired.
Hiland, Gerard '85 (CIN) [51] Cincinnati, OH St. Jude the Apostle Church.
Hilbert, J. Robert *s.j.* '56 (MIL) [P] Milwaukee, WI Arrupe House Jesuit Community; [P] Milwaukee, WI Jesuit Provincial Office, Wisconsin Province.
Hilbert, John J. '60 (E) [24] Erie, PA St. Mark the Evangelist Church.
Hilbert, Joseph C. '52 (HBG) Gettysburg, PA St. Francis Xavier's Church.
Hilbert, Michael P. *s.j.* '83 (FgM) Provinces.
Hilbert, Michael P. *s.j.* '83 (NY) [DD] New York, NY Jesuit Provincial's Office.
Hildebrand, Thomas M. '75 (TLS) [15] Tulsa, OK St. Pius X Church.
Hildebrandt, Henry F. '87 (DOD) Liberal, KS St. Anthony Church.
Hilden, Michael J. *o.s.a.* '73 (FgM) Foreign Missions.
Hilderbrand, H. Michael '76 (IND) Jeffersonville, IN Sacred Heart Church; [C] Clarksville, IN Our Lady of Providence.
Hile, Donald E. '60 (WH) Salem, WV Sacred Heart Church; West Union, WV St. Patrick's Church.
Hilferty, John G. '78 (ALN) Jim Thorpe, PA St. Joseph Church.
Hilferty, Msgr. Thomas J. '52 (PH) Ardsley, PA Queen of Peace Church.
Hilfiker, Robert G. '87 (NY) Goshen, NY St. John the Evangelist Church; Ossining, NY St. Augustine Church.
Hilgartner, Richard B., Jr. '95 (BAL) Severna Park, MD St. John the Evangelist Church.
Hilgeman, Edward J. '52 (STL) [3] Lemay, MO St. Andrew Church.
Hilgeman, James L. *m.m.* '65 (FgM) Maryknoll Foreign Missions.
Hilgendorf, Patrick J. '97 (DAV) [8] Davenport, IA St. Paul the Apostle Church.
Hilgert, E. John *c.p.* '75 (BIR) [7] Birmingham, AL Holy Family Church; Fairfield, AL St. Mary Church.
Hilinski, Joseph T. '76 (CLV) [55] Cleveland, OH Our Lady of Mercy Church.
Hilkert, John J. '43 (CLV) [11] Akron, OH St. Mary Church.
Hilkert, Robert C. '42 (CLV) Brunswick, OH St. Ambrose Church.
Hill, Allan J. '83 (HRT) Harwinton, CT Immaculate Heart of Mary Church.
Hill, Benet *o.s.b.* '85 (WDC) [M] Washington, DC St. Anselm's Abbey.
Hill, Msgr. Charles E. '64 (LA) Panorama City, CA St. Genevieve Church.
Hill, Donald '67 (BIS) On Duty Outside the Diocese.
Hill, Donald M. '94 (L) [27] Louisville, KY St. Francis of Assisi Church.
Hill, Edward T. '60 (BAL) Retired.
Hill, Frederick *o.f.m.cap.* '67 (RVC) Smithtown, NY St. John's Episcopal Hospital.
Hill, George '66 (NY) [17] New York, NY St. Bernard Church.
Hill, George H. '68 (WOR) On Duty Outside the Diocese.
Hill, J. Clifton *c.s.sp.* '65 (PIT) [B] Pittsburgh, PA Duquesne University of the Holy Ghost.
Hill, James B. *s.m.a.* '45 (BO) [W] Dedham, MA African Mission House.
Hill, John H. '49 (SY) Retired.
Hill, Lawrence B. *s.j.* '46 (NY) [DD] New York, NY Murray-Weigel Hall.
Hill, Lawrence H. *o.s.b.* '65 (GBG) [H] Latrobe, PA Saint Vincent Archabbey.
Hill, Michael *o.f.m.* '77 (STL) [P] St. Louis, MO Franciscan Friary of St. Anthony of Padua.
Hill, Michael W. *o.f.m.* '77 (HON) [2] Honolulu, HI Co-Cathedral of St. Theresa of the Child Jesus.
Hill, Patrick J. '68 (LA) [49] Los Angeles, CA St. Bernard Church.
Hill, Paul J. *m.s.c.* '50 (Y) [A] Youngstown, OH Sacred Heart Retreat House & Renewal Center.
Hill, Msgr. Peter J. '36 (SFE) Retired.
Hill, Philip '71 (NY) Military Chaplains.
Hill, R. Cary '66 (WDC) Pastoral Center Special Ministries.
Hill, Richard A. *s.j.* '58 (OAK) [A] Berkeley, CA The Jesuit School of Theology at Berkeley.
Hill, Richard A. *s.j.* '58 (SFR) [N] San Francisco, CA Jesuit Community at University of San Francisco.
Hill, Robert '57 (Y) Retired.
Hill, Robert Cary '66 (WDC) Beltsville, MD St. Joseph Church.
Hill, Scott *o.m.i.* (MRY) Special Assignment.
Hill, Scott F. *o.m.i.* '79 (OAK) Santa Cruz, CA Dominican Santa Cruz Hospital.
Hill, Thomas F. *o.f.m.cap.* '66 (STP) Rosemount, MN St. Joseph Church.
Hill, Timothy '59 (BIR) [23] Birmingham, AL St. Stanislaus Church.
Hill, W. Paul '64 (WDC) [4] Bowie, MD St. Pius X Church.
Hill, William B. *s.j.* '45 (SCR) [C] Scranton, PA University of Scranton.
Hill, William J. *o.p.* '50 (WDC) [B] Washington, DC Dominican House of Studies; [C] Washington, DC Catholic University of America, The.
Hillard, Matthew J. *o.s.f.s.* '91 (ARL) [J] Fairfax, VA Oblates of St. Francis de Sales Residence.
Hillebrand, Albert J. '53 (DET) Retired.
Hillen, Daniel P. '69 (HEL) [B] Helena, MT Carroll College.
Hillenbrand, John T. '70 (CHI) [168] Chicago, IL St. Peter Canisius Church.
Hillenbrand, Thomas '65 (FgM) American - Cassinese Congregation Foreign Missions.
Hiller, Everett J. '54 (RCK) Apple River, IL St. Joseph Church; Warren, IL St. Ann Church.
Hillesheim, Gerald A. '68 (NU) Ghent, MN St. Eloi Church; Minneota, MN St. Edward Church; Taunton, MN SS. Cyril and Methodius Church.
Hilley, Stephen '79 (MIA) Coconut Creek, FL St. Luke Church.
Hilliard, William J. '62 (HRT) Poquonock, CT St. Joseph's Church.
Hillier, David A. '76 (TR) Brick Town, NJ Epiphany Church.
Hillier, John G. '88 (WOR) [3] Leominster, MA St. Cecilia's Church.
Hills, Matthew '86 (OAK) [1] Hayward, CA All Saints Church.
Hills, Richard L. '32 (CHI) Flossmoor, IL Infant Jesus of Prague Church; Retired.
Hillyard, Matthew J. *o.s.f.s.* '91 (ARL) [D] Fairfax, VA Paul VI High School.
Hilmer, Robert E. '86 (DUB) [1] Waterloo, IA St. Joseph's Church; [2] Waterloo, IA St. Mary's Church.
Hils, Damian J. '95 (FAR) Veseleyville, ND St. Luke Church; Warsaw, ND St. Stanislaus Church.
Hilton, Francis G. *s.j.* '92 (BAL) [B] Baltimore, MD Loyola College; [M] Baltimore, MD Jesuit Community of Loyola College, Inc.
Hilton, John '82 (DEN) Wheat Ridge, CO SS. Peter and Paul Church.
Hiltz, John T. '59 (ORG) Yorba Linda, CA St. Martin Church.
Hiltz, John T. '59 (TOL) On Duty Outside the Diocese.
Hilz, Robert *t.o.r.* '70 (STU) [A] Steubenville, OH Franciscan University of Steubenville; [F] Steubenville, OH Holy Spirit Monastery.
Himes, Kenneth R. *o.f.m.* '76 (WDC) [M] Silver Spring, MD Gemelli House.
Himes, Michael J. '72 (BRK) Released from Diocesan Assignment.
Himes, Robert P. '58 (YAK) Grandview, WA Blessed Sacrament Church.
Himmelsbach, James R. '77 (STP) Military Chaplains.
Himsworth, Raymond J. '62 (PH) Elkins Park, PA St. James Church; [EE] Philadelphia, PA Newman Apostolate.
Hinch, Msgr. Lawrence E. '59 (BRK) [243] Queens, NY St. Teresa Church.
Hinckley, Christopher '39 (FTW) Retired.
Hinde, Peter *o.carm.* '52 (JOL) [J] Darien, IL Carmelite Provincial Office.
Hindel, Richard *o.s.b.* (IND) Columbus, IN St. Bartholomew Church.
Hindel, Richard *o.s.b.* '47 (IND) [J] St. Meinrad, IN St. Meinrad Archabbey.
Hindelang, Joseph *s.m.* '78 (BO) [W] Boston, MA Marist Fathers and Brothers Provincial House; [W] Boston, MA Marist Fathers of Our Lady of Victories (Boston Prov.).
Hindelang, Michael L. *s.j.* '38 (OM) [K] Omaha, NE Jesuit Community At Creighton University.
Hinderlang, Joseph *s.m.* (BO) [59] Boston, MA Our Lady of Victories Church.
Hindley, Robert J. *o.s.f.s.* '58 (FgM) Oblates of St. Francis de Sales Foreign Missions.
Hindman, Gerald *o.s.b.* '45 (NO) [P] St. Benedict, LA St. Joseph Abbey.
Hindman, John R. '75 (SB) Crestline, CA St. Frances Xavier Cabrini Church.
Hinds, Edward J. '74 (PAT) Boonton, NJ Our Lady of Mount Carmel Church.
Hinds, William H. '87 (COV) Maysville, KY St. Patrick Church; [B] Maysville, KY St. Patrick High School.
Hindsley, Leonard P. *o.p.* '84 (PRO) [P] Providence, RI St. Thomas Aquinas Priory at Providence College.
Hines, Bartholomew F. *s.s.j.* '48 (BAL) [M] Baltimore, MD St. Joseph's Manor.
Hines, Bede F. *t.o.r.* '47 (ALT) [A] Loretto, PA St. Francis College; [F] Loretto, PA St. Francis Friary, Third Order Regular of St. Francis of Penance.
Hines, Hugh *o.f.m.* '60 (BO) [BB] Boston, MA St. Anthony Shrine.
Hines, J. William '72 (WDC) Military Chaplains.
Hines, Msgr. Leo F. '50 (MAN) Retired.
Hines, Msgr. Leo J. (PRO) [1] Cranston, RI St. Ann Church.
Hines, William F. '47 (SCR) Retired.
Hiney, Thomas J. '56 (ALB) Rensselaer, NY St. John Church; Special Assignment.
Hinfey, Donald J. *s.j.* '63 (FgM) Provinces.
Hinken, Michael *s.o.l.t.* '96 (BEA) Winnie, TX St. Louis Church.
Hinkes, Gabriel A. *o.praem.* '37 (GB) [I] De Pere, WI St. Norbert Abbey.
Hinkle, Ignatius *o.f.m.conv.* '59 (OAK) San Pablo, CA St. Paul Church.
Hinkley, Michael F.X. '91 (HRT) Windsor, CT St. Gabriel's Church.
Hinnebusch, John Frederick *o.p.* '50 (WDC) [B] Washington, DC Dominican House of Studies; [C] Washington, DC Catholic University of America, The.
Hinnebusch, Paul G. *o.p.* '44 (DAL) [M] Irving, TX Dominican Priory of St. Albert the Great.
Hinnen, James W. '71 (MAD) Sun Prairie, WI Sacred Hearts of Jesus and Mary Church.
Hinni, Thomas R. *c.m.* '63 (PBL) La Junta, CO La Junta Catholic Parish.
Hinojal, Ricardo *o.a.r.* '62 (LSC) San Miguel, NM San Miguel Church; [B] Mesilla, NM Augustinian Recollects Fathers.
Hinojosa, Pedro Nolasco, Jr. '96 (CC) Encinal, TX Immaculate Heart of Mary Church; [1] Laredo, TX Blessed Sacrament Church.
Hinrichsen, Msgr. Carl D. '55 (NEW) Franklin Lakes, NJ Most Blessed Sacrament Church; Park Ridge, NJ Our Lady of Mercy Church; Retired.
Hinsvark, John '66 (FBK) Nome, AK St. Joseph Church; Teller, AK St. Ann Church.
Hinton, Frederick '70 (BUF) [4] Kenmore, NY St. Paul Church.
Hinton, John T. '73 (NO) [15] New Orleans, LA Mater Dolorosa Church.
Hintz, David R. '86 (LIN) [9] Lincoln, NE St. Patrick's Church; [L] Lincoln, NE Calvary Cemetery and Mausoleum Association.
Hipp, Brian D. '92 (DOD) Wright, KS St. Andrew Church.
Hippee, Michael E. '73 (MAD) [2] Madison, WI St. Bernard Church.
Hipsley, Milton A. '70 (BAL) Cumberland, MD St. Mary Church.
Hipwell, Patrick J. '77 (STP) Minnetonka, MN Immaculate Heart of Mary Church.
Hiramatsu, Joseph *s.a.* '82 (NY) [DD] Garrison, NY Generalate of the Franciscan Friars of the Atonement-St. James Friary.
Hire, Richard P. '70 (FTW) Elkhart, IN St. Thomas the Apostle Church.
Hirsch, Msgr. Clinton F. '45 (EVN) Retired.
Hirsch, Harold L. '53 (MET) Spotswood, NJ Immaculate Conception Church.
Hirsch, Joseph W. '86 (LC) Altdorf, WI St. Joseph Church; [2] Wisconsin Rapids, WI St. Lawrence Church; [C] Wisconsin Rapids, WI Assumption High School.
Hirsch, Robert *c.ss.r.* '46 (DET) [33] Detroit, MI Holy Redeemer Church.
Hirsch, Robert M. '47 (DUB) Retired.
Hirt, Alan *o.f.m.* '77 (CIN) [65] Cincinnati, OH St. Monica-St. George Parish Newman Center Church; [M] Cincinnati, OH St. Francis Seraph Friary; [Q] Cincinnati, OH University of Cincinnati Newman Center.

Hirt, Edwin H. '39 (GBG) Retired; [G] Greensburg, PA St. Anne Home.
Hirt, Raymond E. *o.f.m.* '62 (TR) Brant Beach, NJ St. Francis of Assisi Church.
Hirt, William '70 (BAL) Absent on Leave.
Hirten, Timothy J. '93 (BRK) [184] Queens, NY St. Joan of Arc Church.
Hirtz, Daniel J. '73 (SPC) Pierce City, MO St. Mary Church.
Hisky, William G. '59 (BAL) On Duty Outside the Archdiocese.
Hislop, Edward J. '73 (HEL) [2] Helena, MT St. Mary Church.
Hissey, L. Pierre '66 (PHX) [13] Phoenix, AZ St. Jerome Church.
Hissrich, John E. '86 (PIT) [54] Pittsburgh, PA St. John Vianney Church.
Hitch, David F. '68 (DAV) [3] Iowa City, IA St. Thomas More Church.
Hitchcock, Msgr. James R. '46 (NSH) Joelton, TN St. Lawrence's Church.
Hitchcock, Martin B. '51 (BGP) Retired.
Hitchens, Robert '94 (PHU) Shenandoah, PA St. Michael's Church.
Hitchko, Daniel D. *v.f.* '64 (SCR) Exeter, PA St. Cecilia Church.
Hite, Gregory R. '81 (TOL) Mansfield, OH St. Mary Church.
Hite, James C. '73 (OWN) Retired.
Hite, Jordan *t.o.r.* '70 (SFS) Wagner, SD St. John the Baptist Church.
Hite, Richard B. *m.s.a.* '70 (WH) [G] Old Fields, WV Holy Spirit Hermitage.
Hitpas, Joseph *o.m.i.* '65 (STP) [28] St. Paul, MN St. Mary Church.
Hitpas, William J. '67 (BEL) O'Fallon, IL St. Nicholas Church.
Hitti, Michael '38 (OLL) Retired.
Hitti, Michael '38 (SAM) Retired.
Hix, John L. (KC) [3] Kansas City, MO St. Aloysius Church.
Hladky, Sylvester '36 (PBR) Warren, OH SS. Peter and Paul's Church.
Hladni, Mirko '71 (CLV) [62] Cleveland, OH St. Paul Church.
Hlavacek, John F. '55 (LR) Retired; [H] Little Rock, AR St. John Manor.
Hlond, Waclaw *c.m.* '55 (HRT) [18] New Haven, CT St. Stanislaus Church.
Hlopko, John J. '36 (SCR) Retired.
Hlubik, Joseph '93 (ALT) [I] University Park, PA Penn State Catholic Community.
Hmircik, Donald A. '56 (MIL) Retired.
Hnatyshyn, Robert '64 (SJP) McKeesport, PA St. John the Baptist Church.
Ho, Khanh '90 (BEA) [5] Beaumont, TX St. Joseph Church.
Ho, Mathias '55 (ORG) Retired.
Hoa, Bartholomew Do Thai *c.m.c.* '94 (DEN) Wheat Ridge, CO Queen of Vietnamese Martyrs Church.
Hoa, Trinh Duc *c.ss.r.* '93 (LA) [R] Baldwin Park, CA Vietnamese Redemptorist Mission.
Hoag, Michael R. *s.j.* '71 (NEW) [C] Jersey City, NJ St. Peter's Preparatory School.
Hoag, Timothy '95 (RC) [1] Rapid City, SD Cathedral of Our Lady of Perpetual Help.
Hoagland, James N. '57 (WCH) Little River, KS Holy Trinity Church; Lyons, KS St. Paul Church.
Hoagland, Victor *c.p.* '59 (MET) [H] South River, NJ Passionist Provincial Office.
Hoagland, Victor *c.p.* '59 (NEW) [N] Union City, NJ Congregation of the Passion (Passionists)-St. Michael's Residence.
Hoak, Jack *o.f.m.* '75 (NY) [DD] New York, NY Franciscan Province of the Immaculate Conception.
Hoan, Basil P. (TYL) Hemphill, TX St. Pius I Church.
Hoan, Joseph Cong '73 (FRS) [1] Fresno, CA St. John Cathedral.
Hoan, Michael '72 (ORG) Westminster, CA Blessed Sacrament Church.
Hoang, Doan T. *s.j.* (SJ) [D] San Jose, CA Bellarmine College Preparatory.
Hoang, Dominic Hung '90 (OKL) [2] Oklahoma City, OK St. Andrew Dung-Lac Church.
Hoang, Joseph Vien *s.d.b.* '83 (NO) [D] Marrero, LA Archbishop Shaw High School.
Hoang, Joseph Viet '94 (SD) Spring Valley, CA Santa Sophia Church.
Hoang, Khanh San '94 (COS) [14] Colorado Springs, CO Saint Paul Church.
Hoang, Louis Trung. '95 (DOD) [1] Dodge City, KS Cathedral of the Sacred Heart.
Hoang, Petrus Binh '96 (P) Salem, OR St. Joseph Church.
Hoang, Phuong '89 (SEA) Auburn, WA Holy Family Church.
Hoang, Thuan Van '97 (SFR) [10] San Francisco, CA St. Cecilia Church.
Hoang-Anh-Thang, Francis *c.m.c.* '93 (SB) [E] Corona, CA Congregation of the Mother Coredemptrix.
Hoar, Leo James '66 (SPR) [5] Northampton, MA St. Mary of the Assumption Church; [P] Amherst, MA University of Massachusetts and Amherst College, Newman Center.
Hoar, Richard J. *s.j.* '56 (BUF) [O] Buffalo, NY Canisius Jesuit Community.
Hoar, Thomas F.X. *s.s.e.* '72 (NOR) [I] Enders Island, CT St. Edmund's Retreat.
Hoar, Thomas F.X. *s.s.e.* '78 (NOR) [A] Enders Island, CT St. Edmund's Novitiate; [A] Mystic, CT Edmundite Seminary Guild; [F] Mystic, CT Society of St. Edmund.
Hoare, Liam *s.p.* '68 (SFE) Jemez Springs, NM Our Lady of the Assumption Church; [J] Jemez Springs, NM The Jemez Program, Our Lady of Lourdes Novitiate.
Hoare, Richard '69 (BRK) [244] Queens, NY St. Teresa of Avila Church.
Hoat, Rochus Vu Dinh '60 (BAL) [59] Baltimore, MD St. Mary of the Assumption Church; Retired.
Hoatson, Robert M. '97 (NEW) [2] Bayonne, NJ St. Andrew's Church.
Hoban, Alphonsus *s.a.* '38 (NY) [DD] Garrison, NY Franciscan Friars of the Atonement.
Hoban, Michael *s.s.c.* '70 (FgM) St. Columban's Foreign Mission.
Hoban, Paul T. *o.carm.* '41 (NEW) Cresskill, NJ St. Therese of Lisieux Church.
Hoban, Robert L. '79 (CLV) [5] Parma, OH St. Francis de Sales Church.
Hoban, Msgr. Thomas E. '60 (ALN) Emmaus, PA St. Ann Church.
Hobbes, Thomas F. '56 (SY) Endwell, NY Christ the King Church.
Hobbs, Msgr. James V. '57 (BAL) [2] Baltimore, MD Basilica of the National Shrine of the Assumption of the Blessed Virgin Mary Church.
Hober, Raymond *s.v.d.* '60 (FgM) Society of the Divine Word Foreign Missions.
Hobert, James M., Jr. '85 (TUC) Douglas, AZ St. Luke Church; Pirtleville, AZ St. Bernard's Church; [I] Douglas, AZ Cochise Community College.
Hobson, J. Mark '86 (CLV) Solon, OH Resurrection of Our Lord Church.
Hobson, Michael A. '97 (BO) [1] Framingham, MA St. Bridget Church.
Hobt, Phillip '92 (DM) [A] Council Bluffs, IA Council Bluffs Area Catholic Education Systems, Inc.
Hoch, George B. *s.j.* '44 (NY) [DD] New York, NY Jesuit Community at Fordham University.
Hochhalter, Lester '91 (JOL) Lombard, IL St. Pius X Church.
Hochheim, William A. '60 (STA) Starke, FL St. Edward's Church.
Hochreiter, Robert S. '68 (BEL) [J] Belleville, IL Scott Air Force Base.
Hochreiter, Robert S. '68 (SCR) Military Chaplains.
Hochstatter, Theodore '80 (PEO) Absent on Leave.
Hochwalt, Richard A. *m.m.* '51 (FgM) Maryknoll Foreign Missions.
Hock, William T. '48 (CHI) [198] Chicago, IL St. Tarcissus Church; Franklin Park, IL St. Gertrude Church; Retired.
Hocking, Harold J. *s.j.* '52 (ALN) [A] Wernersville, PA Novitiate of St. Isaac Jogues.
Hockman, Richard C. *c.s.c.* '80 (FR) South Easton, MA Holy Cross Church.
Hoctor, Thomas D. '57 (ROC) Rochester, NY Rochester Psychiatric Center.
Hoctor, Thomas J. '57 (ROC) [4] Rochester, NY St. Anne Church.
Hodapp, Timothy L. '85 (WIN) Absent on Leave.
Hodde, William G. '52 (FTW) Yoder, IN St. Aloysius Church.
Hoderny, Thomas S. '79 (E) Crown, PA St. Mary Church.
Hodes, Bertrand *o.f.m.conv.* '39 (FgM) Conventual Franciscan Foreign Missions.
Hodge, William A. '74 (CAM) [4] Atlantic City, NJ St. Nicholas of Tolentine Church.
Hodges, Henry D. '56 (PHX) Retired.
Hodges, Leo '86 (ORL) Ormond Beach, FL Prince of Peace Church; [E] Daytona Beach, FL Embry-Riddle Aeronautical University.
Hodges, Robert S. *o.praem.* '74 (ORG) [C] Santa Ana, CA Mater Dei High School; [H] Silverado, CA Norbertine Fathers of Orange Inc.
Hodgson, William M. '79 (SPC) Special Assignment.
Hodnett, John J. *c.m.* '59 (PH) [AA] Philadelphia, PA Congregation of the Mission.
Hoeberechts, Dwight C. *o.m.i.* (BO) [12] Lowell, MA Nuestra Senora del Carmen Church.
Hoebing, Philibert *o.f.m.* '50 (SFD) [B] Quincy, IL Quincy University.
Hoedebeck, Paul *o.s.b.* '43 (LR) Shoal Creek, AR St. Scholastica's Church; [A] Subiaco, AR Subiaco Monastery.
Hoeffner, Robert '73 (ORL) [8] Orlando, FL St. Isaac Jogues Church.
Hoefgen, Francis *o.s.b.* '79 (SCL) [I] Collegeville, MN St. John's Abbey, of the Order of St. Benedict.
Hoefgen, Raymond J. '63 (MAR) Nadeau, MI St. Bruno Church; Stephenson, MI Precious Blood Church.
Hoefler, Alexander *s.v.d.* '50 (LA) Torrance, CA Nativity Church.
Hoefler, Robert A. '85 (DM) [12] Des Moines, IA St. Theresa of the Child Jesus Church.
Hoegerl, Carl W. *c.ss.r.* '50 (BRK) [U] Brooklyn, NY Our Lady of Good Counsel Residence.
Hoehmann, George '92 (NY) Absent on Leave.
Hoek, John F. *s.j.* '44 (NY) [DD] New York, NY Murray-Weigel Hall.
Hoelck, Frank '59 (GI) Spalding, NE St. Michael's Church.
Hoelle, Philip C. *s.m.* '42 (CIN) [M] Dayton, OH Marianist Provincialate.
Hoelscher, James '58 (SAT) Pleasanton, TX St. Luke-Loire Church.
Hoelsken, Mark *s.j.* '91 (FBK) Chefornak, AK St. Catherine Church; Newtok, AK Holy Family Church; Toksook Bay, AK St. Peter the Fisherman Church.
Hoelsken, Mark A. *s.j.* '91 (FBK) [E] St. Marys, AK Brother Joe Prince Jesuit Community.
Hoene, Robert E. *s.j.* '53 (OM) [K] Omaha, NE Jesuit Community At Creighton University.
Hoenig, George B. '65 (DAV) Muscatine, IA St. Mathias Church.
Hoenig, Gerald A. '52 (DAV) Montrose, IA St. Joseph's Church; Fort Madison, IA Iowa State Penitentiary.
Hoenisch, Richard '80 (SFR) Absent on Leave.
Hoeper, Robert J. *s.m.* '51 (CIN) [M] Huntsville, OH St. George Chapel of Marianist Community.
Hoeppner, Michael J. '75 (WIN) Lewiston, MN St. Rose of Lima Church.
Hoerburger, Henry R. '43 (LC) Elk Mound, WI St. Joseph Church.
Hoernig, Alphonse X. *c.m.* '56 (STL) [P] Perryville, MO Congregation of The Mission.
Hoerning, Richard P. '73 (RVC) East Northport, NY St. Anthony of Padua Church.
Hoeser, Jerome G. '63 (LC) Mosinee, WI St. Paul Church.
Hoesing, Kenneth F. '97 (LIN) [9] Lincoln, NE St. Patrick's Church.
Hoevel, Robert J. '42 (FTW) Retired.
Hoewischer, Harry E. *s.j.* '57 (DEN) [M] Denver, CO Xavier Jesuit Center.
Hoey, James F. '65 (WOR) Spencer, MA Mary, Queen of the Rosary Church.
Hoey, Robert F. *s.j.* '54 (BO) [W] Boston, MA Loyola House.
Hoff, Alphonse *o.f.m.* '44 (IND) Batesville, IN St. Louis Church.
Hoff, James E. *s.j.* '65 (CIN) [D] Cincinnati, OH Xavier University; [M] Cincinnati, OH Jesuit Community at Xavier Unversity.
Hoffay, Thomas '74 (NY) Absent on Leave.
Hoffen, Henry A. *s.j.* '53 (NY) [DD] New York, NY Murray-Weigel Hall.
Hoffenkamp, Robert A. '89 (JOL) Wood Dale, IL Holy Ghost Church.
Hoffer, Charles '46 (COV) [6] Covington, KY Holy Cross Church; Retired.
Hoffman, David '75 (BAL) On Duty Outside the Archdiocese.
Hoffman, David '96 (GB) Kaukauna, WI Holy Cross Church.
Hoffman, Dennis '70 (DUL) Crosslake, MN Immaculate Heart Church.
Hoffman, Dennis L. '90 (DAV) Keokuk, IA All Saints Church.
Hoffman, Dominic *o.p.* '41 (P) [18] Portland, OR Holy Rosary Parish & Dominican Priory Church.
Hoffman, Donald J. '54 (STL) Crestwood, MO St. Elizabeth of Hungary Church; St. Louis, MO St. Anthony Medical Center.
Hoffman, Edward '61 (PIT) [J] Pittsburgh, PA St. Francis Nursing Center-East.
Hoffman, Edward L. '61 (PIT) Allegheny County, PA UPMC Shadyside Hospital; Allegheny County, PA West Penn Hospital.
Hoffman, Emmett G. '53 (GF) Retired.
Hoffman, Francis J. '92 (PIT) [N] Pittsburgh, PA Opus Dei.
Hoffman, Gerard J. '73 (PH) [D] Philadelphia, PA Roman Catholic High School for Boys; [Y] Elverson, PA St. Mary of Providence Center.
Hoffman, James *o.f.m.* '67 (CHI) [N] Countryside, IL St. Gratian Friary, Franciscan Friars.
Hoffman, James A. '67 (SUP) Lake Tomahawk, WI St. John Vianney Church; Woodruff, WI Our Lady Queen of the Universe Church.
Hoffman, James R. '57 (TOL) [1] Toledo, OH Queen of the Most Holy Rosary Cathedral.
Hoffman, John R. '75 (CHI) [199] Chicago, IL St. Teresa Church.
Hoffman, Joseph M. '79 (BRK) [80] Brooklyn, NY St. Martin of Tours-Fourteen Holy Martyrs Church.
Hoffman, Mark A. '90 (E) Franklin, PA St. Patrick Church.
Hoffman, Matthias H. '40 (CHI) Flossmoor, IL Infant Jesus of Prague Church; Retired.
Hoffman, Michael *s.d.s.* '82 (MIL) [P] Milwaukee, WI

Salvatorian Provincial Residence.
Hoffman, Patrick '68 (AMA) [2] Amarillo, TX St. Laurence Cathedral.
Hoffman, Raniero *o.s.b.cam.* '75 (MRY) [G] Big Sur, CA New Camaldoli Hermitage.
Hoffman, Richard L. '50 (EVN) Retired.
Hoffman, Robert *c.s.c.* '47 (FTW) [L] Notre Dame, IN Holy Cross Mission House.
Hoffman, Robert B. '69 (RCK) St. Charles, IL St. John Neumann Church.
Hoffman, Robert E. *m.m.* '60 (FgM) Maryknoll Foreign Missions.
Hoffman, Robert G. (MET) Annandale, NJ Mountainview Youth Correctional Facility.
Hoffman, Thomas '80 (CHI) [214] Chicago, IL St. William Church.
Hoffman, Thomas A. *s.j.* '56 (OM) [K] Omaha, NE Jesuit Community At Creighton University.
Hoffman, Thomas W. *s.j.* '76 (NO) [F] New Orleans, LA Jesuit High School.
Hoffman, William G. '61 (ATL) Gainesville, GA St. Michael's Church; [L] Atlanta, GA Campus Ministry.
Hoffmann, Andrew W. '74 (SC) Denison, IA St. Rose of Lima Church.
Hoffmann, Charles G. '63 (GB) Antigo, WI St. John Church.
Hoffmann, Chris '87 (ORL) [E] De Land, FL Stetson University Catholic Campus Ministry.
Hoffmann, Christopher A. '87 (ORL) Deltona, FL St. Clare Church.
Hoffmann, Edward M. '72 (DEN) [24] Denver, CO Church of the Risen Christ.
Hoffmann, Emmett G. '53 (GF) [K] Ashland, MT St. Labre Indian School Educational Association.
Hoffmann, Francis T. '89 (BGP) Bethel, CT St. Mary's Church.
Hoffmann, Frank '71 (RNO) [3] Reno, NV Our Lady of Wisdom Church; [F] Reno, NV University of Nevada, Newman Club.
Hoffmann, Lawrence R. '71 (DM) [5] Des Moines, IA St. Anthony's Church.
Hoffmann, Philip A. '64 (GB) Special Assignment.
Hoffmann, Msgr. Ralph G. '37 (GRY) Retired.
Hoffmann, Robert G. '69 (PAT) Netcong, NJ St. Michael's Church; Morris Plains, NJ Morris County Youth Center; Newton, NJ Sussex County Jail.
Hoffmann, Robert H. '56 (PEO) Clinton, IL St. John the Baptist's Church; Wapella, IL St. Patrick's Church.
Hoffmann, William A. '80 (GB) On Duty Outside the Diocese.
Hoffmaster, Harry '70 (DET) Retired.
Hoffner, Carlos *m.s.* '92 (RCK) South Beloit, IL St. Peter Church.
Hofmann, Arthur '44 (SJ) Retired.
Hofmann, Charles A. *s.j.* '66 (CHI) [N] Chicago, IL Chicago Province of the Society of Jesus-Provincial Office.
Hofmann, Charles A. *s.j.* '66 (SFR) [E] San Francisco, CA St. Ignatius College Preparatory (Coed); [N] San Francisco, CA Jesuit Community at St. Ignatius College Preparatory.
Hofmann, Raymond *c.r.* '56 (L) [30] Louisville, KY Guardian Angels Church; [68] Louisville, KY Resurrection D.N.J.C. Church; [E] Louisville, KY Thomas Merton Academy.
Hofmann, Stephen *o.s.b.* '41 (P) [L] St. Benedict, OR Mt. Angel Abbey.
Hofmann, Thomas X. '77 (CHR) Moncks Corner, SC St. Philip Benizi Church.
Hofschulte, Charles *c.j.* '71 (LA) [D] Santa Barbara, CA Bishop Garcia Diego High School.
Hofstede, John M. '75 (STP) [5] Minneapolis, MN Christ the King Church.
Hofstee, Gerard *s.v.d.* '35 (CHI) [B] Techny, IL Divine Word Residence.
Hofstetter, Robert J. '54 (KNX) [3] Chattanooga, TN St. Jude Church; [K] Knoxville, TN Diocesan Council of Catholic Women.
Hogan, Benedict *o.carm.* '59 (JOL) [J] Darien, IL Carmelite Provincial Office.
Hogan, Cornelius J. '38 (BO) Retired.
Hogan, Daniel M. '53 (STL) O'Fallon, MO St. Barnabas Church.
Hogan, David '55 (SC) Anthon, IA St. Joseph's Church; Danbury, IA St. Mary's Church.
Hogan, Dennis J. '73 (PAT) Lincoln Park, NJ St. Joseph's Church.
Hogan, Edward P. '46 (BRK) Retired.
Hogan, Francis E. *s.j.* '47 (FgM) Provinces.
Hogan, Francis E. *s.j.* '47 (MIL) [P] Milwaukee, WI Jesuit Provincial Office, Wisconsin Province.
Hogan, Francis T. '46 (BUF) Retired.
Hogan, Francis X. *c.m.f.* '49 (LA) [R] Rancho Dominguez, CA Dominguez Seminary Inc.
Hogan, Gary *c.r.* '86 (CHI) [74] Chicago, IL St. Hedwig Church.
Hogan, George C. '73 (BO) North Andover, MA St. Michael Church.
Hogan, James J. '61 (HEL) [1] Missoula, MT Christ the King Church; [H] Missoula, MT University of Montana.
Hogan, John *s.s.c.* '62 (DAL) [11] Dallas, TX St. Andrew Kim Church.
Hogan, Msgr. John F. '63 (WDC) [2] Bowie, MD Sacred Heart Church.
Hogan, John F., Jr. '88 (SY) Lacona, NY St. Frances Xavier Cabrini Church; Pulaski, NY St. John the Evangelist Church.
Hogan, John J. *o.m.i.* '65 (BO) Lowell, MA Saints Memorial Medical Center.
Hogan, John P. '73 (LC) Rudolph, WI St. Philip Church; [2] Wisconsin Rapids, WI St. Lawrence Church.
Hogan, John P. *o.f.m.* '75 (BO) [BB] Boston, MA St. Anthony Shrine.
Hogan, Joseph F. '88 (MET) Hillsborough, NJ Mary, Mother of God Church.
Hogan, LeRoy '57 (GB) Retired.
Hogan, Michael *o.s.a.* (CHI) [J] Chicago, IL Holy Cross Hospital.
Hogan, Michael '65 (ALB) [3] Schenectady, NY Sacred Heart-St. Columba Church; [B] Albany, NY Maria College.
Hogan, Michael C. '51 (ROC) Fairport, NY St. John of Rochester Church; Retired.
Hogan, Peter E. *s.s.j.* '46 (BAL) [M] Baltimore, MD St. Joseph Society of the Sacred Heart House of Central Administration.
Hogan, Phil D. *o.f.m.* '62 (CHI) [D] Chicago, IL Hales Franciscan High School, Inc.
Hogan, Richard '86 (DET) Absent on Leave.
Hogan, Richard M. '81 (STP) [23] St. Paul, MN St. John of St. Paul Church.
Hogan, Robert C. *s.j.* '64 (FgM) Provinces.
Hogan, Robert E. *s.m.* '83 (CIN) [M] Dayton, OH Marianist Provincialate.
Hogan, Robert E. *s.m.* '83 (SAT) [C] San Antonio, TX St. Mary's University of San Antonio, Texas; [M] San Antonio, TX Casa San Juan Marianist Community.
Hogan, Msgr. Robert G. '59 (DUB) [5] Cedar Rapids, IA St. Matthew's Church; [D] Cedar Rapids, IA Regis LaSalle Foundation.
Hogan, Msgr. Robert J. '51 (BUF) [4] Niagara Falls, NY St. John de La Salle Church; Retired.
Hogan, Sean M. *c.s.sp.* '69 (PIT) [B] Pittsburgh, PA Duquesne University of the Holy Ghost.
Hogan, Terence '80 (MIA) Coral Gables, FL St. Augustine Church.
Hogan, Thomas *s.m.* '46 (HON) Wailuku, HI St. Anthony Church.
Hogan, Thomas B. *s.m.* '45 (WDC) [M] Washington, DC Marist Provincial House.
Hogan, Thomas J. *s.j.* '65 (STL) [P] St. Louis, MO Hallahan House.
Hogan, Thomas W. *s.m.* '46 (HON) [H] Wailuku, Maui, HI Wailuku Marianist Community.
Hogan, Timothy A. '66 (L) On Special Assignment.
Hogan, Timothy D. '82 (DET) Military Chaplains.
Hogan, Timothy J. '82 (SC) Ashton, IA Our Lady of Perpetual Help Church; Sibley, IA St. Andrew's Church.
Hogan, Verne F. '57 (COV) Flemingsburg, KY St. Charles Church; May's Lick, KY St. Rose of Lima Church.
Hogan, Msgr. Vincent (WCH) Retired.
Hogan, William *c.ss.r.* '48 (STL) [P] Liguori, MO Liguori Mission House/Redemptorists.
Hogan, William A. '66 (GF) [1] Great Falls, MT St. Ann's Cathedral.
Hogan, William D. *s.s.j.* '51 (LKC) Welsh, LA St. Joseph Church.
Hogan, William E. '38 (L) Retired.
Hogan, Msgr. William F. '46 (NEW) Retired; [N] Rutherford, NJ St. John Vianney Residence for Priests.
Hogan, William H. *s.j.* '60 (CHI) [C] Chicago, IL Jesuit Community at Loyola University of Chicago.
Hogan, William T. *s.j.* '54 (NY) [DD] New York, NY Jesuit Community at Fordham University.
Hogarty, Paul '48 (PT) Retired.
Hoge, James *o.s.b.* '43 (SP) [O] St. Leo, FL St. Leo Abbey.
Hogenkamp, Leon J. *s.j.* '70 (ROC) [B] Rochester, NY McQuaid Jesuit High School.
Hohenbrink, Michael G. '74 (TOL) [19] Toledo, OH St. Catherine of Siena Church.
Hohenstein, Robert J. '68 (ALB) [13] Albany, NY Our Lady Help of Christians Church.
Hohenwarter, Norman C., Jr. '96 (HBG) Hanover, PA St. Joseph Church.
Hohl, Alan *o.c.s.o.* '63 (SLC) [F] Huntsville, UT Abbey of Our Lady of the Holy Trinity of the Order of Cistercians.
Hohlfeld, Raymond C. *m.m.* '34 (NY) [DD] Maryknoll, NY Maryknoll Fathers and Brothers.
Hohlmayer, Louis R. '53 (CIN) Lebanon, OH St. Francis de Sales Church; [S] Cincinnati, OH Archdiocesan Central Council of Cincinnati.
Hohman, Andrew *o.f.m.cap.* '54 (CLV) [18] Cleveland, OH Conversion of St. Paul Church; [P] Cleveland, OH St. Paul Friary.
Hohman, George R. *s.j.* '58 (CHL) [J] Charlotte, NC Jesuit Community.
Hoi, Joseph '77 (JC) St. James, MO Missouri Veterans' Home.
Hoi, Joseph '84 (JC) Rosati, MO St. Anthony Church; St. James, MO Immaculate Conception Church.
Hoisington, Thomas '95 (WCH) [13] Wichita, KS St. Francis of Assisi Church.
Hokanson, Richard P. '74 (CHL) Belmont, NC Queen of the Apostles Church.
Hokanson, Richard P. '74 (WOR) On Duty Outside the Diocese.
Hoke, John D. '76 (HBG) Annville, PA St. Paul the Apostle Church; [K] Harrisburg, PA Catholic Campus Ministry.
Hoke, Thomas J. '75 (HBG) [4] York, PA St. Rose of Lima Church.
Holachek, Terence *o.p.* '57 (MEM) [J] Memphis, TN Order Of Preachers (Southern Dominican Prov.).
Holachek, Terence A. *o.p.* '57 (CC) [E] Corpus Christi, TX Spohn Hospital.
Holachek, Terence A. *o.p.* '57 (GAL) [Q] Houston, TX Dominican Fathers and Brothers, St. Mark Priory, Inc.
Holahan, Matthew *o.f.m.* '79 (GAL) [4] Galveston, TX St. Patrick Church.
Holahan, Thomas J. *c.s.p.* '77 (DEN) [4] Boulder, CO St. Thomas Aquinas University Parish; [P] Boulder, CO University of Colorado (Boulder).
Holanhaw, Thomas J. *c.s.p.* '77 (BO) [P] Boston, MA Paulist Center.
Holberton, William B. '61 (ROC) Retired.
Holbrook, Harold M. '57 (BGP) On Duty Outside the Diocese.
Holbrook, John G. *s.j.* '52 (OM) [K] Omaha, NE Jesuit Community At Creighton University.
Holbrook, William M. '70 (CHI) [58] Chicago, IL St. Ferdinand Church.
Holbrook, William M. '70 (LFT) On Duty Outside the Diocese.
Holbus, Brian T. '81 (MIL) [10] Kenosha, WI St. Therese Church.
Holcomb, Joseph T. '80 (BRK) [120] Brooklyn, NY Queen of All Saints Church; [W] Astoria, NY St. Paul Center.
Hold, William '77 (SAC) Yreka, CA St. Joseph Church.
Holden, Edgar *o.f.m.conv.* '45 (CHL) Winston-Salem, NC Our Lady of Mercy Church.
Holden, James '62 (MOB) [6] Montgomery, AL St. Jude Church.
Holden, Paul '57 (WDC) Retired.
Holden, Robert A. '62 (TOL) Wauseon, OH St. Caspar Church.
Holder, Thomas '95 (KC) [9] Kansas City, MO Christ the King Church.
Holdereid, Kurt *o.carm.* (NEW) Ridgewood, NJ Valley Hospital.
Holdereid, Kurt *o.carm.* '69 (NEW) Westwood, NJ Pascack Valley Hospital.
Holderied, Kurt *o.carm.* '59 (NEW) Midland Park, NJ Nativity Church.
Holdren, John C. '71 (RCK) On Health Leave.
Holguin, Jose R. '75 (LA) Burbank, CA St. Finbar Church.
Holhmann, George '92 (NY) Absent on Leave.
Holian, John P. '63 (NEW) Summit, NJ Overlook Hospital.
Holick, Robert *m.h.m.* '69 (NY) [143] Bronx, NY St. Francis Xavier Church; Bronx, NY Bronx Municipal Hospital Center, Abraham Jacobi Hospital, Nathan B. VanEtten Hospital.
Holicky, Gregory '72 (GRY) [F] Hammond, IN St. Margaret Mercy Healthcare Centers - North Campus.
Holihan, Daniel M. '57 (CHI) [G] Chicago, IL Catholic Charities of the Archdiocese of Chicago-Archdiocesan Offices.
Holihan, John W. '49 (NY) Retired.
Holinga, Thomas P. '74 (SFD) Petersburg, IL St. Peter Church.
Holko, Robert J. *s.c.j.* '71 (MEM) [14] Memphis, TN St. John's Church.
Holl, James E. '48 (STP) Coon Rapids, MN Church of the Epiphany; Retired.
Holl, Kermit *o.s.c.* '90 (STP) [N] Shoreview, MN Crosier Community of Shoreview.
Holland, Cajetan *c.s.c.* (ORL) Retired.
Holland, Cajetan *c.s.c.* '79 (ORL) [F] Cocoa Beach, FL Holy Cross Fathers, Eastern Priests Province.
Holland, Daniel F. '65 (ROC) [57] Rochester, NY St. Theodore Church.
Holland, Edward T. '97 (CLV) North Royalton, OH St. Albert the Great Church.
Holland, Francis M. '52 (BUR) Retired.
Holland, George G. '55 (WOR) Retired.
Holland, Msgr. George T. '48 (PBL) Retired.
Holland, Msgr. Ian E. '58 (LA) Culver City, CA St. Augustine Church; Retired.
Holland, J. Michael '63 (SEA) Burlington, WA St. Charles Church.
Holland, Msgr. James J. '52 (STL) [14] St. Louis, MO Our Lady of Sorrows Church; Retired.
Holland, Jeremiah *ss.cc.* '67 (OAK) [3] Alameda, CA St.

Joseph Basilica Church.
Holland, Jerome *c.ss.r.* '56 (NY) [78] New York, NY Most Holy Redeemer Church.
Holland, Msgr. John P. '48 (STL) Warson Woods, MO Ste. Genevieve Du Bois Church; Retired.
Holland, Joseph I. *s.j.* (BO) [W] Weston, MA Campion Center.
Holland, Kilian '56 (SD) Retired.
Holland, Paul *s.j.* '80 (NOR) [K] Willimantic, CT Campus Ministry.
Holland, Paul D. *s.j.* '80 (NOR) Storrs, CT St. Thomas Aquinas Church.
Holland, Stanley *t.o.r.* '96 (STU) [A] Steubenville, OH Franciscan University of Steubenville; [F] Steubenville, OH Holy Spirit Monastery.
Holland, Thomas D. (SC) Retired.
Holland, Thomas D. '55 (SC) On Duty Outside the Diocese.
Hollas, Eric *o.s.b.* '75 (SCL) [B] Collegeville, MN St. John's University; [I] Collegeville, MN St. John's Abbey, of the Order of St. Benedict.
Hollenbach, David *s.j.* '71 (BO) [W] Chestnut Hill, MA The Jesuit Community at Boston College.
Hollenbach, Frank A. '49 (MAR) Retired.
Holler, Martin J. '66 (STU) Athens, OH Christ the King University Parish; [I] Athens, OH Christ the King University Parish - Ohio University.
Holleran, Msgr. J. Warren '52 (SFR) Special Assignment; [A] Menlo Park, CA St. Patrick Seminary.
Holleran, Leo C. *m.s.* '78 (ATL) Fairburn, GA St. Matthew's Church.
Holleran, Michael K. '79 (NY) [61] New York, NY St. Joseph Church.
Holley, Martin '87 (PT) [13] Pensacola, FL St. Paul Church.
Hollfelder, Eugene F. '68 (MAD) Ashton, WI St. Peter's Church.
Hollick, Leonard '61 (PSC) McAdoo, PA St. Michael Church.
Holliday, David D. (PAT) Absent on Leave.
Hollis, Mark L. '72 (CLV) Medina, OH St. Francis Xavier Church.
Holloran, Michael J. '82 (CIN) [1] Dayton, OH St. Adalbert's Church; [13] Dayton, OH Holy Cross Church.
Holloway, Alvin J. *s.j.* '56 (NO) [C] New Orleans, LA Loyola University.
Holloway, David L. '82 (KC) On Duty Outside the Diocese.
Holloway, James '70 (WDC) Chillum, MD St. John Baptist de la Salle Church.
Holly, Dennis '64 (NSH) [H] Nashville, TN Glenmary Home Missioners.
Holly, Dennis Leo '64 (NSH) [L] Nashville, TN Glenmary Department of Pastoral Services.
Holly, John *o.f.m.cap.* '80 (GB) [3] Appleton, WI St. Joseph Church; [I] Appleton, WI St. Joseph Friary.
Holly, Walter *o.f.m.* '51 (TUC) Topawa, AZ San Solano Missions - Tohono O'odham Indian Reservation Church.
Hollywood, Patrick J. *o.m.i.* (BO) [3] Lowell, MA Immaculate Conception Church.
Hollywood, Patrick J. *o.m.i.* '60 (BO) [W] Tewksbury, MA Oblate Fathers-Office of the Provincial Treasurer; [Z] Tewksbury, MA Immaculate Heart of Mary Novitiate-Infirmary.
Holm, Greg *s.x.* '87 (FgM) Xaverian Foreign Missions.
Holmer, James J. '76 (TOL) Fayette, OH Our Lady of Mercy Church; Lyons, OH Our Lady of Fatima Church.
Holmes, Albert '93 (SCL) Wadena, MN St. Ann's Church.
Holmes, Caedmon '96 (PRO) [P] Portsmouth, RI Abbey of St. Gregory the Great.
Holmes, Del *glmy.* '63 (CIN) [M] Fairfield, OH Headquarters of Glenmary Home Missioners.
Holmes, Dennis '72 (BAK) Absent on Leave.
Holmes, Emmett P. *s.j.* '59 (CLV) [E] Cuyahoga Falls, OH Walsh Jesuit High School.
Holmes, John '69 (STU) Absent on Leave.
Holmes, Kevin D. '84 (MAD) [4] Madison, WI Holy Redeemer Church.
Holmes, Paul A. '81 (NEW) [B] South Orange, NJ Seton Hall University.
Holmes, Raymond M. '65 (NEW) Hasbrouck Heights, NJ Corpus Christi Church.
Holmes, Msgr. Richard J. '44 (NEW) Glen Rock, NJ St. Catharine Church; Hohokus, NJ St. Luke's Church; Retired.
Holmes, Robert L. *s.j.* '70 (STL) [P] St. Louis, MO White House Retreat Jesuit Community; [T] St. Louis, MO White House Retreat.
Holmes, Thomas '91 (ALB) Glens Falls, NY St. Mary Church.
Holmgren, Raymond O. '53 (RCK) East Dubuque, IL St. Mary Church.
Holohan, Patrick *c.s.sp.* '56 (BRK) [U] Long Island City, NY Holy Ghost Fathers of Ireland.
Holoman, Msgr. Thomas L. '55 (LIN) Denton, NE St. Mary's Church; Denton, NE U.S. Veterans' Hospital.
Holoubek, K. William '97 (LIN) Hastings, NE St. Michael's Church.
Holoubek, Roger '69 (MIA) North Miami Beach, FL St. Lawrence Church.
Holpp, Lawrence V. '62 (PIT) Coraopolis, PA St. Joseph Church.
Holquin, Arthur '74 (ORG) [1] Orange, CA Cathedral of the Holy Family.
Holroyd, Patrick '74 (ARL) Reston, VA St. Thomas a Becket Church.
Holscher, Frank *c.i.c.m.* '56 (ARL) [J] Arlington, VA Missionhurst, C.I.C.M.-Central House and Provincialate.
Holscher, Raymond T. *s.j.* '72 (FgM) Provinces.
Holt, Paul '72 (DM) Des Moines, IA United States Veterans Hospital.
Holt, Paul-Stephen '72 (WDC) On Duty Outside the Archdiocese.
Holt, William A. *o.p.* '76 (CIN) [30] Cincinnati, OH St. Gertrude Church; [M] Cincinnati, OH St. Gertrude Priory.
Holtel, Melvin *o.f.m.* '60 (CIN) Centerville, OH St. Francis of Assisi Church.
Holterhoff, Edward G. '70 (PAT) On Duty Outside the Diocese.
Holterman, Herbert J. '51 (SPC) Retired.
Holtey, Gary (SD) Spring Valley, CA Santa Sophia Church.
Holtey, Gary M. '84 (SD) [26] San Diego, CA St. Didacus Church; San Diego, CA Alvarado, Grossmont and Kaiser Hospitals.
Holtgrewe, Don *o.f.m.* '63 (CIN) [24] Cincinnati, OH Corpus Christi Church.
Holthaus, Paul '70 (BAL) [93] Baltimore, MD St. Ursula Church.
Holtman, Msgr. Clyde '49 (AUS) Rockne, TX Sacred Heart Church; String Prairie, TX St. Mary's of the Assumption Church.
Holtman, Elmer E. '64 (AUS) [22] Austin, TX St. Thomas More Church.
Holtman, W. Jeffrey '85 (SFD) Neoga, IL St. Mary of the Assumption Church; Sigel, IL St. Michael the Archangel Church.
Holtschneider, Dennis *c.m.* '89 (BRK) [U] Jamaica, NY St. Vincent's House.
Holtz, Albert T. *o.s.b.* '69 (NEW) [N] Newark, NJ Newark Abbey.
Holtz, Arthur *o.s.b.* '54 (GBG) New Derry, PA St. Martin Church.
Holtz, Brian '95 (EVN) [7] Evansville, IN Holy Rosary Church.
Holtz, James A. (GAY) Special Assignment.
Holtz, James A. '74 (GAY) Fife Lake, MI St. Aloysius Church; Kalkaska, MI St. Mary of the Woods Church.
Holtz, Louis J. '58 (COV) Retired.
Holtz, Raymond C. '58 (COV) [8] Covington, KY Mother of God Church.
Holtz, Vernon A. *o.s.b.* '42 (GBG) [H] Latrobe, PA Saint Vincent Archabbey.
Holtzman, Jerome J. '57 (SFS) Watertown, SD Holy Name Church.
Holubowicz, Vincent B. '89 (MIL) Lomira, WI St. Mary Church.
Holubowicz, Vincent B.. (MIL) Theresa, WI St. Theresa Church.
Holup, James '59 (JOL) Ashkum, IL Assumption of the Blessed Virgin Mary Church.
Holup, Joseph M. '60 (MET) Warren, NJ Our Lady of the Mount Church.
Holwell, Harry '89 (P) Grants Pass, OR St. Anne Church.
Holzer, Ambrose W. '45 (MAD) Retired.
Holzer, Paul A. '41 (PIT) [16] Pittsburgh, PA Immaculate Conception Church; [20] Pittsburgh, PA St. Joseph Church; Retired.
Holzer, Wm. '51 (DUB) Retired.
Holzhauser, Joseph '82 (SFS) Hoven, SD St. Anthony of Padua Church.
Holzmann, Michael F. '88 (RVC) Medford, NY St. Sylvester Church.
Homa, Joseph '56 (PSC) New Brunswick, NJ St. Joseph Church.
Homa, Richard M. '73 (CHI) Tinley Park, IL Saint Julie Billiart Church.
Homa, Thomas D. '57 (PH) [4] Bensalem, PA Our Lady of Fatima Church.
Homan, Daniel J. *o.s.b.* '69 (DET) [B] Oxford, MI St. Benedict Monastery.
Homann, Frederick A. *s.j.* '62 (BAL) [M] Baltimore, MD Jesuit Fathers and Brothers Maryland Provincial Curia.
Homann, Frederick A. *s.j.* '62 (PH) [C] Philadelphia, PA St. Joseph's University; [AA] Philadelphia, PA Jesuit Community at St. Joseph's University.
Hombach, Leo J. *s.j.* '61 (SJ) [M] Los Gatos, CA Sacred Heart Jesuit Center.
Homco, Edward C. *c.pp.s.* '43 (GRY) [4] Whiting, IN St. John the Baptist Church.
Homer, P. Lawrence '59 (SCR) [18] Scranton, PA St. Mary's Church.
Homes, Ronald G. '93 (LIN) Prague, NE St. John's Church.
Homets, Frank S. '92 (SCR) [4] Pittston, PA St. John the Evangelist Church; [D] Pittston, PA Seton Catholic High School.
Hommel, George W. '66 (NY) West Hurley-Woodstock, NY St. John Church.
Hommrich, Thomas A. '64 (L) On Special Assignment.
Homola, Michael E. '49 (HBG) Millersville, PA St. Philip the Apostle Church.
Homola, William B. '50 (SFE) Retired.
Homolak, William J. '59 (GBG) Avonmore, PA St. Ambrose Church.
Homrich, Eugene E. *c.s.c.* '55 (FgM) Holy Cross Foreign Missions.
Homsey, Sam F. *c.pp.s.* '36 (SAN) Winters, TX Our Lady of Mt. Carmel Church.
Honan, Eugene D. '67 (SPR) [5] Northampton, MA St. Mary of the Assumption Church.
Honea, Lonnie '96 (DAL) [2] Dallas, TX All Saints Church.
Honeygosky, Stephen R. *o.s.b.* '75 (GBG) Marguerite, PA St. Benedict Church.
Hong-Phuc, John B. *c.s.s.r.* '48 (P) [1] Portland, OR Southeast Asian Vicariate Church.
Honhart, Mark A. '80 (KC) Richmond, MO Immaculate Conception Church.
Honma, Kenji *ss.cc.* '89 (FR) [J] Fairhaven, MA Sacred Hearts Provincial House.
Honner, Paschal D. *o.s.b.* '56 (JOL) [A] Lisle, IL Benedictine University; [J] Lisle, IL St. Procopius Abbey.
Honore, Lionel P. *s.j.* '68 (WOR) [N] Worcester, MA Jesuits of Holy Cross College, Inc.
Hont, Leon *o.s.b.* '80 (E) St. Marys, PA Queen of the World Church.
Hood, Carl J. '86 (MEM) Bolivar, TN St. Mary Church; Selmer, TN St. Jude Church; [M] Memphis, TN Society of St. Vincent DePaul.
Hood, Mervin J. '54 (SC) Early, IA Sacred Heart Church.
Hoog, Eric *c.ss.r.* '73 (BAL) Annapolis, MD St. Mary Church; [M] Annapolis, MD Saint Mary Rectory.
Hoogterp, John P. '49 (SAG) Retired.
Hoogterp, M. James '48 (GR) Retired.
Hoolahan, Michael J. *c.p.* '61 (CHI) [91] Chicago, IL Immaculate Conception Church; [N] Chicago, IL Immaculate Conception Monastery.
Hooper, J. Leon *s.j.* '75 (WDC) [M] Washington, DC Woodstock Jesuit Community; [V] Washington, DC Woodstock Theological Center.
Hooper, Robert K. '70 (PAT) [7] Clifton, NJ St. Paul Church.
Hoorman, Albert F.H. '67 (PHX) [2] Phoenix, AZ Corpus Christi Church.
Hoormann, Harry H. *s.j.* '58 (PBL) Trinidad, CO Most Holy Trinity, Trinidad Area Catholic Community (Trinidad Cluster) Church; Trinidad, CO Our Lady of Mt. Carmel, Trinidad Area Catholic Community (Trinidad Cluster) Church; Trinidad, CO St. Joseph, Trinidad Area Catholic Community (Trinidad Cluster) Church; [F] Trinidad, CO Trinidad Area Catholic Community.
Hoover, Brett *c.s.p.* '97 (NY) [104] New York, NY St. Paul the Apostle Church.
Hoover, Conrad '89 (CHL) Boone, NC St. Elizabeth Church.
Hoover, Edward F. '72 (CHI) Evanston, IL St. Mary Church.
Hoover, Gary *o.s.b.* '83 (CLV) [E] Cleveland, OH Benedictine High School; [P] Cleveland, OH Benedictine Order of Cleveland.
Hoover, James F. '60 (SAL) Oberlin, KS Sacred Heart Church; Selden, KS Sacred Heart Church.
Hoover, John P. '76 (CHL) Special Assignment.
Hoover, Matthew '95 (COL) [37] Columbus, OH St. Peter Church.
Hopcus, Daniel R. '64 (ORG) Los Alamitos, CA St. Hedwig Church.
Hope, Donald E. '76 (SLC) [2] Ogden, UT St. James Church.
Hopefl, Gregory J. '76 (SUP) New Post, WI St. Ignatius Church; Reserve, WI St. Francis of Solanus Church; Stone Lake, WI St. Philip Church.
Hopf, George S. '49 (MIL) Retired.
Hopkins, John *l.c.* (ATL) [I] Dunwoody, GA Legionaries of Christ; [M] Dunwoody, GA Legion of Christ, Inc.; [M] Dunwoody, GA Home and Family, Inc.
Hopkins, John P. '78 (WIL) Special or Other Diocesan Assignment.
Hopkins, Michael *c.ss.r.* '63 (STV) [3] Frederiksted, VI Church of St. Patrick.
Hopkins, Peter *l.c.* '91 (NY) [DD] Rye, NY Legionaries of Christ.
Hopkins, Richard J. '44 (GF) [1] Billings, MT St. Patrick's Co-Cathedral; Retired.
Hopkins, Robert '48 (BAL) Retired.
Hopmeir, Ronald J. '91 (STL) De Soto, MO St. Rose of Lima Church.
Hopp, Raymond '65 (BAK) Lakeview, OR St. Patrick's Church.

Hopp, Thomas R. '66 (CIN) [25] Dayton, OH Queen of Martyrs Church.
Hoppe, Arthur H. '47 (SCL) St. Rosa, MN St. Rose of Lima Church.
Hoppe, Lawrence L. '60 (GBG) Ford City, PA St. Francis of Paola Church.
Hoppe, Leslie J. *o.f.m.* '71 (CHI) [B] Chicago, IL The Catholic Theological Union at Chicago; [N] Chicago, IL Holy Name Friary.
Hoppe, Msgr. Ronald C. '58 (ALX) [3] Alexandria, LA St. Frances Xavier Cabrini Church; Glenmora, LA St. Louis Church.
Hoppe, Sean *o.s.b.* '82 (IND) Leopold, IN St. Augustine Church; St. Mark, IN St. Mark Church; [J] St. Meinrad, IN St. Meinrad Archabbey.
Hoppe, Sylvester J. '46 (KC) Retired.
Hoppe, William M. '78 (BRK) [139] Brooklyn, NY St. Therese of Lisieux Church.
Hoppenjans, Terence E. '55 (LEX) Paintsville, KY St. Michael Catholic Church.
Hopping, John-Paul '85 (ORG) [3] Orange, CA St. Norbert Church.
Hoppough, Gregory J. *c.s.s.* '74 (BO) [6] Waltham, MA Sacred Heart Church.
Hopwood, Msgr. Frederick J. '51 (CHR) Retired.
Hopwood, Robert *c.ss.r.* '52 (FgM) Redemptorist Foreign Missions.
Hora, Robert J. '83 (BUF) [31] Buffalo, NY Holy Name of Jesus Church.
Horacek, Mark '43 (ALX) Retired.
Horacek, Mark '43 (GAL) Retired.
Horack, Francis *c.p.* '42 (FgM) Mission Procurators.
Horak, Msgr. Donald E. '63 (STU) Athens, OH Christ the King University Parish; [I] Athens, OH Christ the King University Parish - Ohio University.
Horak, Mark F. *s.j.* '94 (BAL) [M] Baltimore, MD Ferdinand Wheeler Jesuit Community.
Horan, Denis F. '48 (MAN) Retired.
Horan, Edward *s.o.l.t.* '87 (CC) [H] Robstown, TX Society of Our Lady of the Most Holy Trinity.
Horan, George '72 (LA) [36] Los Angeles, CA Sacred Heart Church; Los Angeles, CA Los Angeles County Jails in the City of Los Angeles, Adult Facilities.
Horan, Gerald M. *o.s.m.* '82 (ORG) [D] Anaheim, CA Servite High School; Servite High School Development Fund; [H] Anaheim, CA Servite Fathers and Brothers.
Horan, James *o.s.b.* '82 (PMB) Belle Glade, FL St. Philip Benizi Church.
Horan, John '46 (SEA) Mercer Island, WA St. Monica Church; Retired.
Horan, John *c.s.sp.* '65 (NY) [193] Bronx, NY Visitation Church.
Horan, John C. '51 (MAN) Hudson, NH St. John the Evangelist Church.
Horan, Joseph '58 (NOR) Retired.
Horan, Michael '80 (SAT) Special Assignment.
Horan, Raymond F. '68 (ATL) [5] Atlanta, GA Most Blessed Sacrament Church.
Horan, Terence J. '68 (SFR) [3] San Mateo, CA St. Matthew Church.
Horan, Thomas *o.m.i.* '94 (MAN) [M] Hudson, NH Oblates of Mary Immaculate Retreat House.
Horan, Thomas A. '62 (ALN) Retired.
Horan, Msgr. Thomas C. '35 (SCR) Retired.
Horan, Timothy (ROC) [53] Rochester, NY St. Philip Neri Church.
Horan, Timothy E. '79 (ROC) [3] Rochester, NY St. Andrew Church.
Horanzy, Joseph M. '59 (SCR) [19] Wilkes-Barre, PA St. Stanislaus Kostka Church.
Horath, George B. '63 (MAD) Fennimore, WI St. Mary Church.
Horath, James R. '73 (SUP) Merrill, WI St. Francis Xavier Church.
Horath, William G. '75 (SUP) Three Lakes, WI St. Theresa Church.
Horejsi, Jeffrey P. '91 (NU) Willmar, MN St. Mary Church.
Horgan, Gerald B. '48 (BO) Georgetown, MA St. Mary Church; Retired.
Horgan, John A. '36 (HRT) Retired.
Horgan, John E. '72 (WOR) Sutton, MA St. Mark Church.
Horgan, Msgr. John V. '40 (BGP) Retired; [O] Stamford, CT Our Lady Queen of the Clergy Home.
Horgan, Joseph C. '41 (WIL) Retired.
Horgan, Joseph E. '53 (PRO) Retired.
Horgan, Joseph J. *m.s.* '44 (HRT) [M] Hartford, CT Missionaries of LaSalette Provincial Secretary.
Horgan, Paul J. *s.j.* '68 (FgM) Provinces.
Horgan, Paul L. *s.j.* '68 (CI) [B] Pohnpei, FM PATS (Pohnpei Agriculture and Trade School).
Horgan, Sean *c.ss.r.* '53 (MOB) Monroeville, AL Annunciation Church; [K] Monroeville, AL Alabama Southern Community College Newman Center.
Horgan, Timothy J. '55 (NEW) Ridgefield, NJ St. Matthew's Church.
Horgan, Msgr. William '38 (SAC) Fair Oaks, CA St. Mel Church; Retired and in Senior Ministry.
Horgas, Robert '91 (E) Ridgway, PA St. Leo the Great Church.
Horkan, Msgr. Vincent J. '41 (DET) Retired; [L] Livonia, MI Provincial House and Novitiate of the Sisters of St. Felix.
Horley, Ray J. '58 (CLV) [49] Cleveland, OH St. Mel Church.
Horn, Augustine S. *o.s.b.* '45 (OKL) [I] Shawnee, OK St. Gregory Abbey.
Horn, Francis J. *o.s.a.* '75 (WDC) [B] Washington, DC Augustinian College, Order of St. Augustine.
Horn, John *s.j.* '85 (OM) [23] Omaha, NE St. John Church.
Horn, John P. *s.j.* '85 (OM) [K] Omaha, NE Jesuit Community At Creighton University.
Horn, Joseph K. *o.praem.* '81 (ORG) [C] Santa Ana, CA Mater Dei High School; [H] Silverado, CA Norbertine Fathers of Orange Inc.
Horn, Joseph R. '97 (DET) Royal Oak, MI Shrine of the Little Flower Church.
Horn, Stephen R. '73 (GAL) [45] Houston, TX St. Luke the Evangelist Church.
Hornacek, Joseph F. '66 (MIL) [14] Racine, WI Sacred Heart Church.
Hornat, Stephen W. *s.s.e.* '76 (MOB) [A] Selma, AL Edmundite House of Formation; [H] Selma, AL Edmundite Fathers.
Horner, Arnold *c.p.* '34 (BRK) [U] Jamaica, NY Immaculate Conception Monastery.
Horner, Thomas J. '43 (PIT) Retired.
Horner, Timothy *o.s.b.* '53 (STL) [P] St. Louis, MO The Abbey of St. Mary and St. Louis.
Hornick, J. Michael '69 (ANC) [G] Anchorage, AK Holy Spirit Retreat House.
Hornstein, Eugene *o.s.b.* '46 (BIS) [A] Richardton, ND Assumption Abbey.
Horoshko, Michael '37 (PHU) Retired.
Horrigan, Msgr. Alfred F. '40 (L) [40] Louisville, KY St. James Church; Retired.
Horrigan, Finnbar *c.s.sp.* '55 (SFR) Millbrae, CA St. Dunstan Church.
Horrigan, J. P. *s.j.* '69 (FgM) Jesuit Foreign Missions.
Horrigan, Kevin D. '53 (STL) [R] Ladue, MO Carmel of St. Joseph.
Horrigan, Kevin P. '70 (BO) Newburyport, MA Immaculate Conception Church.
Horrigan, Leo R. '59 (DEN) [18] Denver, CO Notre Dame Church.
Horrigan, Sean *c.s.sp.* '49 (NY) [183] Bronx, NY St. Philip Neri Church.
Horst, Bernard L. *s.m.* '45 (KAL) [E] Portage, MI Society of Mary.
Horst, Kenneth '95 (NY) [6] Poughkeepsie, NY St. Martin de Porres Church; Absent on Leave.
Horstman, Keith L. '95 (LAN) Brighton, MI St. Patrick Church.
Hortiguela, Fernando *o.f.m.* '75 (SJN) [3] Carolina, PR Santa Clara de Asis Church.
Horton, John C. '66 (PEO) Mahomet, IL Our Lady of the Lake Church.
Horton, Joseph *o.m.i.* '69 (MAN) [K] Hudson, NH Missionary Oblates of Mary Immaculate.
Horton, W. Peter '79 (PIT) Allegheny County, PA UPMC Passavant Hospital; [B] Pittsburgh, PA La Roche College; [R] Slippery Rock, PA Office for Campus Ministry.
Horvat, Francis '58 (KCK) [10] Kansas City, KS St. John the Baptist Church.
Horvat, Matt J. '65 (KCK) [8] Kansas City, KS St. Mary-St. Anthony Church.
Horvath, Andrew B. '42 (GBG) Retired.
Horvath, Benedict A. *o.praem.* '40 (ORG) [H] Silverado, CA Norbertine Fathers of Orange Inc.
Horvath, Bert '70 (AMA) [7] Amarillo, TX St. Hyacinth's Church; Vega, TX Immaculate Conception Church; [J] Amarillo, TX St. Francis Convent, Novitiate and U.S. Provincial House.
Horvath, Gerlac A. *o.praem.* '46 (ORG) [H] Silverado, CA Norbertine Fathers of Orange Inc.
Horvath, Joseph P. '37 (FTW) Retired.
Horvath, Martin A. '43 (FTW) Goshen, IN St. John the Evangelist Church; Retired.
Horvath, Pius L. *o.s.b.* '53 (SFR) [N] Portola Valley, CA Woodside Priory.
Horvath, Richard E. '57 (PEO) [4] Peoria, IL St. Ann Church.
Horvath, Stephen '50 (Y) Retired.
Horvath, Stephen G. '40 (TR) Retired.
Horzen, Bernard A. *o.s.b.* '53 (PEO) [A] Peru, IL St. Bede Abbey and Academy.
Hosak, Peter J. '83 (ALN) [C] Allentown, PA Allentown Central Catholic High School.
Hosak, Peter J. '83 (PSC) Allentown, PA St. Michael Church.
Hose, Sam '91 (AUS) [15] Austin, TX St. John Vianney Church.
Hosey, Keith P. '56 (LFT) [G] Hartford City, IN John XXIII Center.
Hoshock, Richard '40 (TOL) Retired.
Hosie, James J. *s.j.* '65 (BO) [E] Boston, MA Boston College High School & Jesuit Community.
Hosie, Stanley W. *s.m.* '46 (WDC) [M] Washington, DC Marist Provincial House.
Hosinski, Albin L. *c.s.c.* '43 (FTW) [J] South Bend, IN Congregation of Holy Cross Indiana Province Provincial House.
Hosinski, Thomas *c.s.c.* '73 (P) [B] Portland, OR University of Portland; [L] Portland, OR Holy Cross Fathers & Brothers, C.S.C. - University of Portland.
Hosko, George H. *c.s.b.* '68 (GAL) Retired; [Q] Houston, TX Dillon House; [Q] Houston, TX Residence of the Basilian Fathers of the University of St. Thomas.
Hosler, Paul (KCK) Sabbatical.
Hospodar, Robert J. *j.c.l.* '78 (PSC) White Plains, NY St. Nicholas of Myra Church; Yonkers, NY St. Nicholas of Myra Church.
Hossan, John B. '53 (BGP) Redding, CT St. Patrick Church.
Host, Dick '74 (GR) [16] Grand Rapids, MI St. Mary's Church.
Hostetter, Laurence '87 (OWN) Studying Outside the Diocese.
Hostettler, Paul A. '50 (KNX) Copperhill, TN St. Catherine Church; Retired; [K] Knoxville, TN Diocesan Council of Catholic Women.
Hostia de la Purisima, Anibal Jesus *s.e.m.v.* '91 (ARE) Hatillo, PR Our Lady of Guadalupe Church.
Hosty, Thomas J. '35 (CHI) Retired.
Hotard, Msgr. Howard H. '55 (NO) [1] Slidell, LA Our Lady of Lourdes Church.
Hotchkin, John F. '60 (CHI) On Duty Outside the Archdiocese.
Hotchkiss, Msgr. Eugene '48 (GB) Retired.
Hotovy, Dennis W. '57 (LIN) Wymore, NE St. Mary's Church.
Hottinger, Paul (JOL) Downers Grove, IL St. Joseph Church.
Hottinger, Theodore *s.j.* '63 (WIN) [1] Mankato, MN SS. Peter and Paul's Church.
Hottle, Maximilian *o.f.m.* '61 (TUC) Topawa, AZ San Solano Missions - Tohono O'odham Indian Reservation Church.
Hotz, Ernest *c.p.* '45 (BRK) [U] Jamaica, NY Immaculate Conception Monastery.
Hotz, Robert V. *s.j.* '86 (OM) [C] Omaha, NE Creighton Preparatory School.
Hotze, Clement *s.v.d.* '47 (FgM) Society of the Divine Word Foreign Missions.
Hotze, John V. '93 (WCH) Newton, KS Our Lady of Guadalupe Church.
Hotze, Leo *s.v.d.* '43 (CHI) [B] Techny, IL Divine Word Residence.
Houck, Gregory *o.carm.* '92 (WDC) [B] Washington, DC Whitefriars Hall.
Houck, Peter '46 (ANC) Retired.
Houck, Richard '65 (SD) Retired.
Houde, Arthur O. '48 (MAN) Retired.
Houde, Daniel *o.s.s.t.* '87 (PH) Bristol, PA St. Ann Church.
Houde, Paul C. '96 (BUR) [5] Burlington, VT St. Mark's Church.
Houdek, Francis J. *s.j.* '65 (DET) [K] Detroit, MI Jesuit Provincial Office-Detroit Province of the Society of Jesus.
Houdek, Francis J. *s.j.* '65 (OAK) Lafayette, CA St. Perpetua Church; [A] Oakland, CA Graduate School of Theology, School of Applied Theology; [A] Berkeley, CA The Jesuit School of Theology at Berkeley; [N] Berkeley, CA Jesuit Community at Jesuit School of Theology at Berkeley.
Hough, Roger W. '64 (SAL) Osborne, KS St. Aloysius Church.
Houghton, Msgr. Francis J. '51 (NEW) Retired.
Houghton, Timothy '91 (RVC) Absent on Leave.
Houlahan, Richard A. *o.m.i.* '58 (SAT) [K] San Antonio, TX Oblate Madonna Residence; [T] San Antonio, TX Oblate Missions; [T] San Antonio, TX Oblate Lourdes Grotto Shrine of the Southwest.
Houle, Andre L. *o.m.i.* '52 (PRT) Howland, ME St. Leo Church.
Houle, Carroll B. *m.m.* '62 (FgM) Maryknoll Foreign Missions.
Houle, Cecil T. '38 (STP) Retired.
Houle, John A. *s.j.* '45 (LA) [R] Los Angeles, CA Columbiere House.
Houle, Michael R. '79 (STA) [A] Jacksonville, FL Bishop Kenny High School.
Houle, Norman H. *s.j.* '76 (BO) [W] Boston, MA Loyola House.
Houle, Roger A. '77 (PRO) [3] Woonsocket, RI St. Ann Church; [8] Woonsocket, RI Our Lady of Victories Church.
Houle, Thomas *o.f.m.cap.* '78 (NY) [57] New York, NY St. John the Baptist Church; City, NY James A. Thomas Center.
Houle, Thomas *o.f.m.cap.* '81 (NY) City, NY Anna M. Kross Center.
Houle, Wilfred Andre '74 (BUR) Rutland, VT St. Peter Church.
Houlihan, John J. '64 (GF) [1] Billings, MT St. Patrick's Co-Cathedral; [2] Billings, MT Holy Rosary Church.
Houlihan, Michael K. '79 (LIN) [2] Lincoln, NE Blessed

Sacrament Church.
Houlihan, Ralph D. *s.j.* '65 (STL) [F] St. Louis, MO St. Louis University High School, George H. Backer Memorial; [P] St. Louis, MO St. Louis University High School Jesuit Community.
Houlihan, Robert F. *s.j.* '57 (COS) [E] Sedalia, CO Sacred Heart Retreat House - Jesuit Community; [G] Sedalia, CO Sacred Heart Jesuit Retreat House.
Houndjame, Felicien K. '85 (STA) Orange Park, FL St. Catherine's Church.
Houran, J. William '52 (SFD) Retired.
Houran, William '52 (MIA) [G] Fort Lauderdale, FL Holy Cross Hospital.
Hourigan, Michael '66 (MIA) Sunrise, FL St. Bernard Church.
Hourihan, Brendan *o.carm.* '39 (NY) [DD] Middletown, NY St. Albert's Priory.
Hourihan, Raymond B. '87 (CHL) Waynesville, NC St. John the Evangelist Church.
Hourihane, Francis '51 (RVC) Retired.
House, Richard Mel '92 (YAK) Ephrata, WA St. Rose of Lima Church.
Householder, Paul C. '73 (PIT) [3] McKees Rocks, PA St. John of God Church.
Houseknecht, Eric '95 (CHL) Maggie Valley, NC St. Margaret Church.
Houser, Charles *c.s.c.* '46 (FgM) Holy Cross Foreign Missions.
Houser, Samuel E. '76 (HBG) [5] Steelton, PA Prince of Peace Church.
Housey, Walter *c.m.* '56 (LA) [X] Santa Barbara, CA St. Mary's Seminary Center.
Houston, James A. '68 (WOR) Northboro, MA St. Rose of Lima Church.
Houston, Joseph F. '64 (SCR) [4] Plymouth, PA St. Vincent de Paul Church.
Hovald, Regis R. *o.p.* '64 (CHI) [N] Chicago, IL Dominicans (Provincial Office).
Hovey, Adrian *o.s.b.* '91 (NO) [P] St. Benedict, LA St. Joseph Abbey.
Hovley, Vincent E. *s.j.* '69 (COS) [E] Sedalia, CO Sacred Heart Retreat House - Jesuit Community; [G] Sedalia, CO Sacred Heart Jesuit Retreat House.
Howaniec, Henry *o.f.m.* '56 (FgM) Franciscan Foreign Missions.
Howaniec, Henry *o.f.m.* '56 (GB) [I] Pulaski, WI Assumption of B.V.M. Friary.
Howard, Anthony '37 (L) Retired.
Howard, Anthony *o.f.m.conv.* '84 (SB) [3] Riverside, CA Queen of Angels Church.
Howard, C. Donald *s.a.* '72 (ARL) Sterling, VA Christ the Redeemer Church.
Howard, Clarence J. '61 (L) New Haven, KY St. Catherine Church; New Hope, KY St. Vincent de Paul Church.
Howard, Donald E. *c.s.p.* '58 (NY) [DD] Jamaica Estates, NY Paulist Fathers Generalate.
Howard, Evan *o.f.m.* '55 (PHX) [19] Phoenix, AZ St. Mary's Basilica Church.
Howard, Msgr. James J. '52 (PH) [1] Philadelphia, PA Cathedral Basilica of SS. Peter and Paul Church.
Howard, John *c.j.m.* '67 (SD) Solana Beach, CA St. James Church.
Howard, John W. *s.j.* '68 (BO) [W] Chestnut Hill, MA The Jesuit Community at Boston College.
Howard, Joseph '89 (GAL) La Marque, TX Our Lady Queen of Peace Church; [D] Galveston, TX O'Connell Catholic High School.
Howard, Joseph, Jr. '89 (SHP) On Duty Outside the Diocese.
Howard, Kenneth *s.s.j.* '87 (GAL) [8] Houston, TX St. Anne de Beaupre Church.
Howard, Kenneth J. *s.s.j.* '87 (GAL) [62] Houston, TX Our Mother of Mercy Church.
Howard, Philip *c.s.sp.* '79 (CHI) [129] Chicago, IL St. Mary Magdalene Church.
Howard, Msgr. Robert E. '62 (LA) [97] Los Angeles, CA Transfiguration Church.
Howard, T. Cyril '49 (SAG) Retired.
Howard, Theodore J. '65 (RVC) Shoreham, NY St. Mark Church.
Howard, Timothy J. *s.j.* '63 (MIL) [P] Milwaukee, WI Jesuit Provincial Office, Wisconsin Province.
Howard, Timothy J. *s.j.* '63 (TUC) [23] Tucson, AZ St. Thomas the Apostle Church.
Howard, Msgr. Vincent '47 (LAN) Retired.
Howarth, Joseph A. '90 (PRO) [7] Providence, RI St. Augustine Church.
Howarth, Joseph E. '80 (PH) [3] Bensalem, PA Saint Ephrem Church.
Howarth, Theodore J. *o.s.b.* '49 (NEW) [N] Newark, NJ Newark Abbey.
Howe, Christopher *o.s.a.* '86 (JOL) [B] Kankakee, IL Bishop McNamara High School.
Howe, J. Norbert '56 (TOL) [4] Lima, OH St. Rose Church.
Howe, Robert J. '94 (SAG) Shepherd, MI St. Vincent De Paul Church.
Howell, David '78 (LAN) Brighton, MI St. Mary Magdalen Church.
Howell, David W. '65 (BGP) [2] Norwalk, CT St. Joseph's Church.
Howell, F. Scott *s.j.* '77 (BAL) [M] Baltimore, MD Jesuit Fathers and Brothers Maryland Provincial Curia.
Howell, F. Scott *s.j.* '77 (FgM) Provinces.
Howell, Joseph W. '53 (TLS) [E] Tulsa, OK Saint Francis Hospital, Inc.
Howell, Michael '74 (CC) [1] Corpus Christi, TX Corpus Christi Cathedral.
Howell, Michael J. '69 (KAL) [G] Nazareth, MI Motherhouse and Novitiate of the Sisters of St. Joseph.
Howell, Patrick J. *s.j.* '72 (SEA) [A] Seattle, WA Seattle University.
Howell, Stephen H. '74 (SFR) Special Assignment; [D] San Mateo, CA Junipero Serra High School (Boys).
Hower, William J. '64 (MAD) Columbus, WI St. Jerome Church.
Howley, Msgr. Edward J. '47 (BGP) Darien, CT St. Thomas More Church.
Howley, Leo W. '36 (STP) Retired.
Howley, Vincent '97 (NY) Carmel, NY St. James the Apostle Church.
Howlin, Carroll '61 (JOL) On Duty Outside the Diocese.
Howlin, Carroll '61 (LEX) Whitley City, KY Good Shepherd Chapel Church.
Howren, John T. '96 (ATL) McDonough, GA St. James The Apostle Church.
Howscher, Franz *c.i.c.m.* '56 (ARL) [3] Alexandria, VA Queen of Apostles Church.
Howze, Joseph Lawson '59 (BLX) [H] Biloxi, MS Gabriel Manor II, Inc.
Hoy, Daniel J. '48 (PH) Strafford, PA Our Lady of the Assumption Church.
Hoye, Msgr. Daniel F. '72 (FR) [1] Attleboro, MA St. John the Evangelist Church.
Hoye, Ronald J. *c.m.* '91 (KC) [J] Kansas City, MO Vincentian Parish Mission Center.
Hoyer, Michael '80 (MIA) [2] Fort Lauderdale, FL Our Lady Queen of Martyrs Church.
Hoying, David A. *c.pp.s.* '83 (CIN) Carthagena, OH St. Aloysius Church; Cranberry Prairie, OH St. Francis Church.
Hoying, John *c.pp.s.* '62 (TOL) Cuba, OH St. Isidore Church; Kalida, OH St. Michael Church.
Hoying, Leo A. '56 (CIN) Frenchtown, OH Holy Family Church; Versailles, OH St. Denis Church.
Hoying, Mark *c.pp.s.* '85 (CIN) [23] Dayton, OH Precious Blood Church.
Hoying, Vincent *c.pp.s.* '58 (TOL) Lima, OH St. Rita Hospital and Medical Center; [H] Lima, OH St. Rita's Medical Center.
Hoynes, Richard '88 (LA) San Pedro, CA Holy Trinity Church.
Hoyng, William *c.pp.s.* '54 (TOL) Bismark, OH St. Sebastian Church; Marywood, OH St. Michael's Church; Reed, OH Assumption Church.
Hoyos, Franz *o.m.i.* '86 (FgM) Oblates Foreign Missions.
Hoyos, Jose E. '84 (ARL) Falls Church, VA St. Anthony's Church.
Hoyt, Stephen *o.f.m. cap.* '92 (CHL) [8] Charlotte, NC St. Matthew Church; [D] Charlotte, NC Mecklenburg Area Catholic Schools (M.A.C.S.).
Hoza, Rudolph *s.s.c.* '42 (PRO) [P] Bristol, RI St. Columban's Retirement House.
Hratz, Joseph A. '42 (DAV) Retired; [L] Davenport, IA Kahl Home for the Aged and Infirm.
Hrboka, Romildo *t.o.r.* '45 (PIT) [5] Millvale, PA St. Nicholas Church; [O] Pittsburgh, PA Croatian Commissariate, T.O.R.
Hrdlicka, Lambert A. '50 (STL) Retired.
Hrebic, Alban *o.s.b.* '52 (FgM) American - Cassinese Congregation Foreign Missions.
Hrebic, Alban *o.s.b.* '52 (JOL) [J] Lisle, IL St. Procopius Abbey.
Hreha, James D. '87 (WIL) New Castle, DE St. Peter Church.
Hren, Joseph I. *o.p.* '47 (CHI) [N] River Forest, IL St. Thomas Aquinas Priory.
Hren, Joseph I. *o.p.* '51 (CHI) [D] Oak Park, IL Fenwick High School.
Hribsek, Aloysius J. '49 (BGP) Retired.
Hricko, Michael A. *s.j.* '73 (PH) [C] Philadelphia, PA St. Joseph's University.
Hricko, Michael A. *s.j.* '73 (SCR) [C] Scranton, PA University of Scranton; [E] Scranton, PA Scranton Preparatory School.
Hrisko, Zachary *o.s.b.* '57 (JOL) [J] Lisle, IL St. Procopius Abbey.
Hritz, Paul '53 (CLV) [A] Wickliffe, OH St. Mary Seminary and Graduate School of Theology.
Hritz, Paul J. '53 (CLV) [44] Cleveland, OH Community of St. Malachi Church; [45] Cleveland, OH St. Malachi Church; Retired.
Hritzko, John '89 (STN) Munster, IN St. Josaphat Church.
Hrubiak, Dennis M. '70 (PRM) Parma, OH Holy Spirit Church.
Hruby, Paul '82 (LA) [57] Los Angeles, CA St. Columbkille Church.
Hruska, Eugene P. '58 (GF) Fort Shaw, MT St. Ann Church.
Hruska, Timothy W. '96 (MAR) [5] Marquette, MI St. Michael Church.
Hrydziuszko, Michael '95 (DET) [5] Clinton Twp., MI St. Thecla Church.
Hrynkiw, Wasyl '91 (STF) Lackawanna, NY Our Lady of Perpetual Help Church.
Hrynuck, Stephen '38 (PHU) Olyphant, PA SS. Cyril and Methodius Church.
Hsu, Peter '57 (BEL) Royalton, IL St. Aloysius Church.
Huan, Joseph Van Tran '73 (RIC) Military Chaplains.
Huar, Ralph F. '81 (STP) Rush City, MN Sacred Heart Church.
Huard, Leo *o.carm.* '65 (JOL) [J] Darien, IL Carmelite Provincial Office.
Hubba, David C. '74 (NEW) Palisades Park, NJ St. Michael's Church.
Hubbard, J. Randall '90 (L) [35] Louisville, KY Holy Spirit Church.
Hubbard, Lawrence E. '68 (STP) [4] Minneapolis, MN Ascension Church; [33] Minneapolis, MN St. Stephen Church; Special Assignment.
Hubbert, Joseph G. *c.m.* '77 (BUF) [C] Niagara University, NY Niagara University; [O] Niagara University, NY Vincentian Community at Niagara University.
Hubble, Karl D. '39 (DET) Retired.
Hubbs, Timothy '84 (CAM) [A] Haddonfield, NJ Paul VI High School.
Hubbs, Timothy L. '84 (CAM) Gloucester, NJ St. Mary's Church.
Huber, Clarence W. '69 (LUB) Littlefield, TX Sacred Heart Church.
Huber, Daniel R. '50 (PBL) Montrose, CO St. Mary Church.
Huber, David '86 (RCK) Crystal Lake, IL St. Thomas the Apostle Church.
Huber, George L. '48 (MIL) Retired.
Huber, J. William '59 (PBL) [16] Pueblo, CO St. Pius X Church.
Huber, John *c.s.b.* '92 (OAK) [C] Oakland, CA Bishop O'Dowd High School.
Huber, John R. '68 (PIT) Wireton, PA St. Catherine of Siena Church.
Huber, Justin *o.f.m.* '70 (KNX) [F] Mountain City, TN Franciscan Friars.
Huber, Kevin R. '91 (GRY) Saint John, IN St. John Evangelist Church.
Huber, Larry T., Jr. '95 (STL) House Springs, MO Our Lady, Queen of Peace Church.
Huber, Leo R. '67 (STP) Retired.
Huber, Mark D. (LIN) Graduate Studies.
Huber, Matthew '87 (HEL) [2] Missoula, MT Holy Family Church.
Huber, Paul A. *s.j.* '45 (CIN) [28] Cincinnati, OH St. Francis Xavier Church; [V] Cincinnati, OH Apostleship of Prayer.
Huber, Richard *m.s.c.* '59 (OG) [2] Watertown, NY Our Lady of the Sacred Heart, Missionaries of the Sacred Heart Church.
Huber, Richard J. '89 (STP) Golden Valley, MN St. Margaret Mary Church.
Huber, Robert L. '56 (L) [9] Louisville, KY St. Athanasius Church.
Huber, Vincent J. '64 (STU) Toronto, OH St. Francis of Assisi Church; Toronto, OH St. Joseph's Church.
Huber, Walter *s.m.b.* '46 (DEN) [18] Denver, CO Notre Dame Church.
Huber, William D. '55 (COL) [26] Columbus, OH St. Ladislas Church.
Hubert, James *c.i.c.m.* '51 (SAT) [G] San Antonio, TX Mount Sacred Heart School.
Hubert, Raymond '58 (PMB) [1] Delray Beach, FL Emmanuel Church.
Hubertus, Albert '50 (SAT) [27] San Antonio, TX St. Anthony Mary Claret Church.
Hubertus, Gerald '64 (SAT) Seguin, TX St. James Church.
Huberty, Mark A. '96 (STP) [21] Minneapolis, MN St. Charles Borromeo Church.
Huberty, Ronald V. '90 (NU) Benson, MN St. Francis Church; Clontarf, MN St. Malachy Church; Danvers, MN Church of the Visitation; De Graff, MN St. Bridget Church; De Graff, MN St. Bridget Church; Murdock, MN Church of the Sacred Heart.
Hubler, Tony '92 (IND) Navilleton, IN St. Mary Church.
Hubmann, William *c.pp.s.* '79 (KC) [20] Kansas City, MO St. James Church.
Huck, Joseph '69 (MIA) North Lauderdale, FL Our Lady Queen of Heaven Church.
Hudak, Cyril '53 (MIA) Retired.
Hudak, Msgr. Francis J. '55 (HBG) New Oxford, PA Immaculate Conception of the Blessed Virgin Mary Church.
Hudak, Ralph '77 (CLV) [35] Cleveland, OH Immaculate Heart of Mary Church.
Hudak, Richard E. '68 (CLV) Fairview Park, OH St. Angela Merici Church.
Hudak, Thomas R. '73 (SCR) Lake Silkworth, PA Our Lady of Mount Carmel Church.
Hudepohl, Al *o.f.m.* '56 (IND) Batesville, IN St. Louis Church.

Hudepohl, Howard *o.f.m.* '54 (FgM) Franciscan Foreign Missions.
Hudert, John P. *m.m.* '62 (NY) [DD] Maryknoll, NY Maryknoll Fathers and Brothers.
Hudgin, Christopher J. *o.s.f.s.* '81 (VEN) [A] Fort Myers, FL Bishop Verot High School; [K] Fort Myers, FL The Bishop Verot High School Foundation.
Hudson, Dan (LA) [K] Burbank, CA Providence Saint Joseph Medical Center.
Hudson, Francis X. '74 (CAM) Millville, NJ St. John Bosco Church.
Hudson, Frank X. '74 (CAM) [Q] Newfield, NJ Catholic Social Services Regional Counseling Center.
Hudson, Gerald F. *s.j.* '81 (SFR) [E] San Francisco, CA St. Ignatius College Preparatory (Coed); [N] San Francisco, CA Jesuit Community at St. Ignatius College Preparatory.
Hudson, Richard '96 (AUS) Round Rock, TX St. William's Church.
Hudziak, Jerome M. '64 (MIL) [3] Wauwatosa, WI St. Joseph Congregation Church.
Hudzik, Msgr. Leo A. '34 (CAM) Retired.
Huebner, Donald C. '54 (CIN) [1] Springfield, OH St. Bernard Church.
Huebner, Terrance J. '74 (MIL) Elkhorn, WI St. Patrick Church.
Huebsch, Joseph R. '50 (FAR) Retired.
Huegelmeyer, Charles T. *m.m.* '51 (FgM) Maryknoll Foreign Missions.
Huegelmeyer, Charles T. *m.m.* '51 (NY) [DD] Maryknoll, NY Maryknoll Fathers and Brothers.
Huehlefeld, Matthew '96 (VIC) Port Lavaca, TX Our Lady of the Gulf Church.
Hueller, Francis *s.a.c.* '48 (MIL) [P] Milwaukee, WI St. Vincent Community.
Huels, John M. *o.s.m.* '76 (CHI) [N] Chicago, IL Servite Friars - Eastern Province.
Huelsing, Justin *o.m.i.* '54 (SPC) Mountain Grove, MO Sacred Heart Church.
Huerga, Alvaro *o.p.* '50 (PCE) [B] Ponce, PR The Pontifical Catholic University of Puerto Rico.
Huerta, Enrique *s.v.d.* '86 (LA) [76] Los Angeles, CA St. Malachy Church.
Huerta, Orestes (DOD) Garden City, KS St. Mary Church.
Huesca, Omar A. '81 (MIA) [31] Miami, FL St. Robert Bellarmine Church.
Huesing, Paul D. *c.s.p.* '82 (WDC) [B] Washington, DC St. Paul's College.
Huesman, E. Gerard '41 (BAL) Baltimore, MD Franklin Square Hospital.
Huesman, John E. *s.j.* '49 (OAK) [A] Berkeley, CA The Jesuit School of Theology at Berkeley; [N] Berkeley, CA Jesuit Community at Jesuit School of Theology at Berkeley.
Huete, Francis W. *s.j.* '82 (LAF) [A] Grand Coteau, LA St. Charles College.
Huff, Thomas Mary (NOR) [F] Baltic, CT Marian Friary of Our Lady of Guadalupe.
Huffman, David L. '72 (STU) Belpre, OH St. Ambrose Church; [J] Belpre, OH Boy Scouts; [J] Steubenville, OH Ohio Conference Advisory Council.
Huffman, Timothy '93 (RIC) Bedford, VA Holy Name of Mary Church.
Huffman, Timothy J. '93 (STU) Absent on Leave.
Huffstetter, Stephen *s.c.j.* '89 (SAT) [B] San Antonio, TX Priests of the Sacred Heart- House of Formation.
Hug, Frederick (TOL) [J] Oregon, OH Sacred Heart Home.
Hug, Frederick I. '48 (TOL) Retired.
Hug, James E. *s.j.* '72 (MIL) [P] Milwaukee, WI Jesuit Provincial Office, Wisconsin Province.
Hug, James E. *s.j.* '72 (WDC) [M] Washington, DC K Street Jesuit Community; [V] Washington, DC Center of Concern.
Huggins, Michael L. '89 (L) [33] Louisville, KY Holy Family Church.
Huggins, Michael L. '89 (SD) Leave of Absence.
Huggins, Williams A. '67 (SPC) Leopold, MO St. John Church.
Hughes, Albert C. '57 (BO) [2] Framingham, MA St. George Church.
Hughes, Brian C. '81 (SC) [A] Sioux City, IA Briar Cliff College.
Hughes, Charles *glmy.* '54 (CIN) [M] Fairfield, OH Headquarters of Glenmary Home Missioners.
Hughes, Charles '54 (SAV) Dublin, GA Immaculate Conception Church.
Hughes, Charles J. '74 (BO) Beverly, MA St. Mary Star of the Sea Church.
Hughes, Dennis E. '75 (SP) San Antonio, FL St. Anthony of Padua Church.
Hughes, Derek '86 (MRY) Paso Robles, CA St. Rose Church.
Hughes, Donald R. '52 (BUF) Retired.
Hughes, Edward J. '51 (CHI) Schaumburg, IL St. Matthew Church; Retired.
Hughes, Edward R. '58 (RCK) Sublette, IL Our Lady of Perpetual Help Church; West Brooklyn, IL St. Mary Church.
Hughes, Eugene *s.m.* '57 (ATL) [6] Atlanta, GA Our Lady of the Assumption Church.
Hughes, F. Rodger '64 (WH) Chester, WV Sacred Heart Church.
Hughes, Francis *s.v.d.* '52 (CHI) [B] Techny, IL Divine Word Residence.
Hughes, Francis J. '45 (Y) Retired.
Hughes, Francis J. '80 (BRK) [175] Queens, NY St. Helen Church.
Hughes, Msgr. Gerald '58 (DAL) Retired.
Hughes, Gerald *s.j.* '85 (DAL) [26] Dallas, TX St. Rita Church.
Hughes, James A. '80 (BRK) [88] Brooklyn, NY St. Michael Archangel and St. Edward Church.
Hughes, James F. '52 (PH) Media, PA St. Mary Magdalen Church.
Hughes, John *m.s.* '53 (WOR) [6] Fitchburg, MA St. Joseph's Church.
Hughes, John '94 (BEA) Winnie, TX St. Louis Church.
Hughes, Msgr. John C. '49 (LA) Camarillo, CA St. Mary Magdalen Church.
Hughes, John F. '37 (BRK) Retired; [R] Queens Village, NY Queen of Peace Residence.
Hughes, John J. '54 (ARL) Springfield, VA St. Bernadette's Church.
Hughes, John Jay '54 (STL) [2] University City, MO Christ the King Church.
Hughes, Joseph '96 (KC) [10] Kansas City, MO St. Elizabeth's Church.
Hughes, Joseph A. '32 (DUL) [9] Duluth, MN St. John's Church; Retired.
Hughes, Joseph B. '67 (BAL) Retired.
Hughes, Joseph W. '70 (TR) Rumson, NJ Holy Cross Church.
Hughes, Kenneth J. *s.j.* '66 (BO) [W] Cambridge, MA Faber House; [W] Cambridge, MA Weston Jesuit Community.
Hughes, Lawrence J. '64 (MAN) Retired.
Hughes, M. Curtis '45 (ALB) South Glens Falls, NY St. Michael the Archangel Church; Retired.
Hughes, Mark F. '82 (WDC) Fort Washington, MD St. Ignatius Church.
Hughes, Martin F. '44 (B) Retired.
Hughes, Matthew '96 (JOL) Hinsdale, IL St. Isaac Jogues Church.
Hughes, Msgr. Michael '45 (LA) Ventura, CA San Buenaventura Mission Church.
Hughes, Msgr. Michael '45 (ORG) Retired.
Hughes, Michael '54 (OKL) Medford, OK St. Mary's Church.
Hughes, Michael J. *o.s.a.* '75 (MIA) Dania, FL Church of the Resurrection.
Hughes, Msgr. Nicholas V. '44 (B) Retired.
Hughes, Pablo *o.m.i.* '73 (SJN) [7] San Juan, PR Ntr. Sra. de la Caridad del Cobre Church.
Hughes, Patrick M. '56 (LA) Irwindale, CA Our Lady of Guadalupe Church.
Hughes, Pete '81 (OWN) Hardinsburg, KY St. Romuald Church; Irvington, KY Holy Guardian Angels Church.
Hughes, Peter *c.s.sp.* '61 (FAR) [1] Fargo, ND St. Mary's Cathedral.
Hughes, Msgr. Richard A. '52 (WDC) Upper Marlboro, MD Saint Mary of the Assumption Church.
Hughes, Robert *s.m.* '59 (SJ) [20] San Jose, CA Queen of Apostles Church.
Hughes, Robert E. '90 (CAM) Barrington, NJ St. Francis de Sales Church; [A] Haddonfield, NJ Paul VI High School.
Hughes, Robert T. '54 (PEO) Retired.
Hughes, Robert W. '68 (MAD) Military Chaplains.
Hughes, Ronald J. '82 (SCR) Towanda, PA SS. Peter and Paul Church.
Hughes, Royce '64 (GAL) On Duty Outside the Diocese.
Hughes, Vincent *o.f.m.* '85 (SD) San Luis Rey, CA Mission San Luis Rey de Francia Church; [H] San Luis Rey, CA Mission San Luis Rey.
Hughes, William C. '47 (STO) Retired.
Hughson, D. Thomas *s.j.* '71 (MIL) [P] Milwaukee, WI Arrupe House Jesuit Community.
Hughson, Robert S. '79 (BUF) [9] Niagara Falls, NY Our Lady of Mount Carmel Church; [D] Niagara Falls, NY Niagara Catholic Junior-Senior School.
Hugli, Richard *o.s.b.* '95 (SP) [O] St. Leo, FL St. Leo Abbey.
Hugo, William *o.f.m.cap.* '80 (BRK) [U] Brooklyn, NY St. Michael's Friary.
Hugo, William *o.f.m.cap.* '81 (BRK) [87] Brooklyn, NY St. Michael's Church.
Huguet, Dean M. '85 (PEO) Westville, IL St. Mary's Church.
Huguley, Vernon '93 (BIR) [18] Birmingham, AL Our Lady Queen of the Universe Church; [22] Birmingham, AL Sacred Heart Church.
Huh, Joseph (LA) [3] North Hollywood, CA St. Jane Frances de Chantal Church.
Huhmann, Msgr. John F. '50 (KC) Retired.
Huhn, Bernard F. '52 (STL) [O] St. Louis, MO Mother of Good Counsel Home.
Huhn, Donald W. '49 (STL) Retired.
Huhn, Thomas J. *m.s.* '69 (TYL) Lufkin, TX St. Patrick Church.
Huhtanen, Andrew *o.m.v.* '83 (MET) [H] Asbury, NJ Lanteri House.
Huitrado, Juan J. '80 (CHI) [187] Chicago, IL St. Roman Church.
Hulko, Joseph D. '67 (ALN) [1] Easton, PA St. Anthony of Padua Church.
Hull, Francis M. *s.s.j.* '57 (NO) [29] New Orleans, LA St. David Church.
Hull, Michael '93 (NY) Graduate Studies.
Huller, Karl '54 (SPR) [1] Springfield, MA St. Michael's Cathedral.
Hullings, Clifford '61 (SPK) Retired.
Hulscher, Alfred J. *o.s.b.* '60 (SEA) [M] Lacey, WA St. Martin's Abbey; [M] Lacey, WA St. Martin's Abbey.
Hulshof, David F. '82 (SPC) [1] Springfield, MO Cathedral of St. Agnes; Special Assignment.
Hultberg, William J. *o.s.f.s.* '62 (WIL) [I] Wilmington, DE Oblates of St. Francis De Sales.
Hultquist, Thomas H. '76 (WOR) Barre, MA St. Joseph's Church.
Humanitzki, Theodore '60 (STF) Retired.
Humbert, Robert G. *s.j.* '53 (CHI) [D] Wilmette, IL Loyola Academy.
Humbrecht, T. Allen '72 (KNX) [1] Knoxville, TN Cathedral of the Sacred Heart of Jesus.
Hume, Jorge '93 (SR) Graduate Studies.
Hume, Kenneth '63 (P) Retired.
Hume, Robert B. '43 (BRK) [57] Brooklyn, NY Holy Innocents Church; Retired.
Humenay, Robert '69 (E) On Duty Outside Diocese.
Huminski, Gregory J. '80 (BGP) [5] Norwalk, CT St. Matthew Church.
Humitz, Msgr. Robert S. '60 (DET) Clarkston, MI St. Daniel Church.
Hummel, Donald K. '78 (NEW) Westfield, NJ St. Helen Church.
Hummel, John D. *c.m.* '44 (PH) [AA] Philadelphia, PA Congregation of the Mission.
Hummell, John F. '65 (PH) [28] Philadelphia, PA St. Callistus Church.
Hummer, Lawrence L. '73 (COL) Military Chaplains.
Humphrey, Arthur Frank *s.t.m., m.a.* '75 (NEW) [15] Newark, NJ St. Francis Xavier Church.
Humphrey, Delos A. *m.m.* '54 (FgM) Maryknoll Foreign Missions.
Humphrey, Stephen J. '67 (BEL) Columbia, IL Immaculate Conception of the B.V.M. Church.
Humphrys, Richard '57 (SB) Bloomington, CA St. Charles Borromeo Church.
Hund, Francis '82 (KCK) Meriden, KS St. Aloysius Church; Perry, KS St. Theresa's Church.
Hund, Joseph *o.f.m.* '89 (FgM) Franciscan Foreign Missions.
Hund, William *c.s.c.* '60 (P) [B] Portland, OR University of Portland; [L] Portland, OR Holy Cross Fathers & Brothers, C.S.C. - University of Portland.
Hundt, George F. '81 (PAT) [8] Paterson, NJ St. Gerard Majella Church.
Hundt, Robert P. '61 (LC) Middle Ridge, WI St. Peter Church; Saint Joseph Ridge, WI St. Joseph Church.
Huneger, Richard J. '73 (P) [32] Portland, OR St. Rose of Lima Church.
Huneke, Robert D. '69 (RVC) Absent on Leave.
Hung, Joseph '70 (SFR) [3] San Rafael, CA St. Raphael Church.
Hung, Joseph K. '68 (ORG) On Duty Outside the Diocese.
Hung, Pham Quoc *c.ss.r.* '94 (LA) [R] Baldwin Park, CA Vietnamese Redemptorist Mission.
Hung, Trinh Peter '79 (CHI) [205] Chicago, IL St. Thomas of Canterbury Church; [V] Chicago, IL Ministry in Higher Education.
Hunke, Norman F. '73 (OM) [1] Omaha, NE St. Cecilia's Cathedral.
Hunkeler, Edward J. '44 (OM) Retired.
Hunkins, Richard C. '56 (JC) Special Assignments; [D] Stoutsville, MO Columbia Nursing Home Ministry.
Hunkler, Carl '83 (HEL) On Leave of Absence.
Hunkler, Jerome '83 (FAR) New Rockford, ND St. John's Church.
Hunko, Gerard A. '91 (GAY) Gills Pier, MI St. Wenceslaus Church; Lake Leelanau, MI St. Mary Church.
Hunstiger, Thomas P. '63 (STP) [21] St. Paul, MN St. Gregory the Great (Highland Catholic Community) Church; [24] St. Paul, MN St. Leo (Highland Catholic Community) Church; [34] St. Paul, MN St. Therese (Highland Catholic Community) Church.
Hunt, Daniel *c.p.* '38 (BO) [W] Brighton, MA St. Gabriel's Passionist Community.
Hunt, Daniel J. *c.p.* '38 (BO) [W] Brighton, MA St. Gabriel's Residence.
Hunt, Dennis '81 (LIN) Lawrence, NE Sacred Heart Church.
Hunt, Doug *c.r.* '92 (PBL) Conejos, CO Our Lady of Guadalupe Church.
Hunt, George W. *s.j.* '67 (NY) [DD] New York, NY "America;" Residence and publication office of the America Press; [HH] New York, NY America Press, Inc., The.
Hunt, Msgr. James A. '55 (BRK) [99] Brooklyn, NY Our Lady of Loreto Church; [108] Brooklyn, NY Our Lady of the Presentation Church.

Hunt, James M. '83 (GI) Ainsworth, NE St. Pius X Church.
Hunt, John M. '69 (OG) [2] Ogdensburg, NY Notre Dame Church.
Hunt, John W. '68 (PRO) [4] Cumberland, RI St. Joseph Church.
Hunt, Kevin *o.c.s.o.* '79 (WOR) [N] Spencer, MA St. Joseph's Abbey.
Hunt, Lawrence J. *s.j.* '57 (CHL) Winston-Salem, NC St. Benedict the Moor Church; [J] Charlotte, NC Jesuit Community.
Hunt, Msgr. Luke '67 (PT) Gulf Breeze, FL St. Ann Church.
Hunt, Mark J. '85 (PH) Yardley, PA St. Ignatius of Antioch Church; Graduate Studies.
Hunt, Michael J. '41 (BRK) [43] Brooklyn, NY St. Frances de Chantal Church; Retired.
Hunt, Michael J. *c.s.p.* '67 (BO) [CC] Medford, MA Tufts University Catholic Center.
Hunt, Michael J. *c.s.p.* '67 (NY) [104] New York, NY St. Paul the Apostle Church.
Hunt, Patrick J. '39 (PRO) Retired.
Hunt, Richard *s.j.* '71 (SY) Vestal, NY St. Vincent de Paul Church.
Hunt, Robert W. *c.pp.s.* '54 (CIN) [M] Dayton, OH Provincial House of the Cincinnati Province of the Society of the Precious Blood.
Hunt, Ted '54 (SFE) Retired.
Hunt, Ted J. '54 (SFE) [7] Albuquerque, NM Our Lady of Fatima Church.
Hunt, Thomas *s.c.j.* '55 (MIL) [P] Franklin, WI Villa Maria.
Hunter, Alan '77 (SFD) Assumption, IL Assumption B.V.M. Church; Macon, IL St. Stanislaus Church; Moweaqua, IL St. Frances de Sales Church.
Hunter, Charles T. *s.j.* '45 (FgM) Provinces.
Hunter, Eric '72 (SP) [5] Tampa, FL Incarnation Church.
Hunter, John J. '86 (NY) [2] Poughkeepsie, NY St. Mary Church.
Hunthausen, John F. '52 (HEL) Retired.
Hunthausen, John M. *s.j.* '70 (FgM) Provinces.
Huntimer, Donald W. *c.s.v.* '59 (CHI) [N] Arlington Heights, IL Viatorian Province Center-Clerics of St. Viator.
Huntington, Msgr. Christopher '52 (RVC) East Hampton, NY Most Holy Trinity Church; Retired.
Huntzinger, Msgr. Ralph '50 (COL) Retired.
Huon, Phan Phat *c.ss.r.* '53 (LA) [R] Baldwin Park, CA Vietnamese Redemptorist Mission.
Huot, Leopold J. '45 (PRT) Retired.
Hupp, Msgr. Robert P. '40 (OM) Retired.
Huppenbauer, Walter '57 (CHI) [M] Chicago, IL Little Sisters of the Poor Center for the Aging.
Hurd, Robert *s.j.* (STL) [C] St. Louis, MO Saint Louis University.
Hurd, Steven F. *s.j.* '80 (CHI) [D] Wilmette, IL Loyola Academy.
Hurd, Timothy C. '92 (SHP) [1] Monroe, LA Jesus the Good Shepherd Church.
Hurkes, Charles F. *o.m.i.* '58 (SFD) Beltrees, IL St. Michael Church; Grafton, IL St. Patrick Church.
Hurlbert, James F. '90 (CHI) Barrington, IL St. Anne Church.
Hurley, Brendan *s.j.* '93 (WDC) [M] Washington, DC The Jesuit Community at Georgetown University.
Hurley, Daniel *o.f.m.* '45 (BUF) [Q] West Clarksville, NY Mount Irenaeus, Franciscan Mountain Retreat & Holy Peace Friary; [R] Williamsville, NY Campus Ministry.
Hurley, Daniel A. *o.f.m.* (BUF) [C] St. Bonaventure, NY St. Bonaventure University.
Hurley, Msgr. Daniel J. '59 (RVC) Massapequa, NY St. Rose of Lima Church.
Hurley, Francis J. *c.s.c.* '53 (FR) [A] North Easton, MA Stonehill College; [A] North Easton, MA Holy Cross Fathers Religious.
Hurley, George '55 (JOL) Retired.
Hurley, Gerard '76 (JKS) Columbus, MS Annunciation Church; [G] Columbus, MS Mississippi State University for Women Student Center.
Hurley, J. Patrick *s.j.* '57 (P) [L] Portland, OR Colombiere Community.
Hurley, James *s.d.b.* '76 (COL) [H] Columbus, OH Salesian Center.
Hurley, James P. *s.j.* '40 (SPK) [K] Spokane, WA Regis Community.
Hurley, James P. *m.s.* '48 (ATL) [2] Marietta, GA Church of St. Ann.
Hurley, Jerome M. *o.s.m.* '38 (CHI) [N] Chicago, IL Servite Friars - Eastern Province.
Hurley, John F. *s.j.* (SPK) [C] Spokane, WA Gonzaga University.
Hurley, John J. '56 (CHI) Arlington Heights, IL St. Edna Church.
Hurley, John J. *o.s.f.s.* '68 (FgM) Oblates of St. Francis de Sales Foreign Missions.
Hurley, John J. *o.s.f.s.* '68 (WIL) [I] Wilmington, DE DeSales House.
Hurley, John J. '82 (WDC) [6] Silver Spring, MD St. John the Baptist Church.
Hurley, John W. '74 (CHI) Other Assignments.
Hurley, Joseph T. *c.ss.r.* '54 (CHI) [N] Glenview, IL The Redemptorists of Glenview, Illinois.
Hurley, Msgr. Leonard F. (WDC) [V] Washington, DC Carroll Manor Nursing & Rehabilitation Center.
Hurley, Msgr. Leonard F. '58 (WDC) Hospital & Nursing Home Ministries; [L] Washington, DC Cardinal O'Boyle Residence for Priests.
Hurley, Mark J. (SFR) Retired.
Hurley, Michael F. '43 (PHX) Cottonwood, AZ Immaculate Conception Church.
Hurley, Patrick M. *o.s.b.* '76 (NEW) [1] Linden, NJ St. Elizabeth's Church.
Hurley, Patrick M. *o.s.b.* '76 (PAT) [M] Morristown, NJ St. Mary's Abbey.
Hurley, Paul Kevin '95 (BO) Hanson, MA St. Joseph the Worker Church.
Hurley, Paul T. '82 (PRO) Burrillville, RI St. Theresa of the Child Jesus Church.
Hurley, Paul W. '70 (BO) [2] Cambridge, MA Blessed Sacrament Church.
Hurley, Stephen *s.j.* (PHX) [B] Phoenix, AZ Brophy College Preparatory.
Hurley, Thomas J. '93 (CHI) [A] Chicago, IL St. Joseph Seminary.
Hurley, Msgr. Walter A. '65 (DET) Farmington, MI Our Lady of Sorrows Church.
Hurst, H. David *o.s.b.* '46 (PRO) [P] Portsmouth, RI Abbey of St. Gregory the Great.
Hurst, Mark *o.f.m.* '80 (WDC) [M] Washington, DC Commissariat of the Holy Land, Franciscan Monastery - Mount St. Sepulchre.
Hurst, Maynard E. '79 (BR) [14] Baton Rouge, LA St. Louis, King of France Church.
Hurst, Paul F. '77 (CIN) Germantown, OH St. Augustine Church.
Hurst, Thomas R. *s.s.* '73 (WDC) [A] Washington, DC Theological College of the Catholic University of America; [C] Washington, DC Catholic University of America, The.
Hurtado-Badillo, Domingo '93 (CHI) [123] Chicago, IL St. Mark Church.
Hurteau, Robert A. *m.m.* '89 (FgM) Maryknoll Foreign Missions.
Hurteau, Robert A. *m.m.* '89 (LA) [R] Los Angeles, CA Maryknoll Fathers and Brothers.
Hurtuk, Joseph C. *s.m.* '74 (WDC) [B] Washington, DC Marist College, The Scholasticate.
Husain, Nicholas F. '85 (NO) New Orleans, LA Memorial Medical Center; New Orleans, LA Memorial Medical Center.
Huse, Ralph G. *s.j.* '75 (STL) [P] St. Louis, MO Bellarmine House of Studies.
Huse, Robert *o.a.r.* '56 (NY) [154] Bronx, NY St. John's Church.
Huse, Robert *o.a.r.* '56 (ORG) [5] Santa Ana, CA Our Lady of the Pillar Church.
Hushen, Mark A. *o.s.f.s.* '91 (WIL) [3] Wilmington, DE St. Anthony of Padua Church.
Huske, Leonard G. (CHI) Retired.
Hussack, Emil M. '49 (SCR) [24] Scranton, PA Sacred Hearts of Jesus and Mary Church.
Husselbeck, Francis E. '58 (ALB) Richfield Springs, NY St. Joseph Church.
Hussey, Daniel '85 (GLP) On Duty Outside of Diocese.
Hussey, Dennis R. '45 (HRT) East Haven, CT Our Lady of Pompeii Church.
Hussey, Gerald W. '78 (PRO) Little Compton, RI St. Catherine of Siena Church.
Hussey, M. Edmund '58 (CIN) [4] Springfield, OH St. Raphael Church.
Hussey, Michael J. *o.m.i.* '60 (CHR) Ridgeland, SC St. Anthony's Church.
Hussey, Michael J. *o.m.i.* '60 (STP) [N] St. Paul, MN Oblate Residence.
Hussli, Edward J. '67 (MIL) Elba, WI St. Columbkille Church; Reeseville, WI Holy Family Church.
Hussmann, John R. '54 (DUB) Retired.
Husted, Richard S. *o.f.m.* '66 (NEW) East Rutherford, NJ St. Joseph's Church.
Hustedde, Edwin H. '56 (BEL) Valmeyer, IL Seven Dolors of the B.V.M. Church; [A] Waterloo, IL Gibault Catholic High School.
Huston, Richard '95 (SD) [A] San Diego, CA St. Francis Seminary.
Huszti, Michael J. '76 (PRM) Burton, OH Church of Weeping Madonna; Solon, OH St. John the Baptist Church; [B] Burton, OH Shrine of the Weeping Madonna of Mariapoch.
Hut, Clemens '36 (EVN) Retired.
Hutcherson, Bartholomew *o.p.* '97 (SLC) [7] Salt Lake City, UT St. Catherine of Siena Church; [H] Salt Lake City, UT University of Utah, Newman Center.
Hutchins, H. James '67 (PH) [58] Philadelphia, PA Holy Cross Church.
Hutchins, Michael *s.v.d.* '75 (DUB) [B] Epworth, IA Divine Word College.
Hutchinson, Ronald '94 (GR) [8] Grand Rapids, MI Holy Spirit Church.
Huth, James *o.praem.* '88 (SFE) Albuquerque, NM St. Joseph Medical Center; [J] Albuquerque, NM Santa Maria de la Vid Priory.
Hutmacher, Robert '79 (CHI) [N] Chicago, IL St. Peter's Friary.
Hutnik, William J. '44 (PIT) Retired.
Hutsko, Basil J. '79 (PRM) Sterling Heights, MI St. Basil Church.
Hutsko, Joseph (DEN) [13] Denver, CO Holy Protection of the Mother of God Church.
Hutsko, Joseph '79 (VNN) Denver, CO Holy Protection of the Mother of God Church.
Hutsko, Michael '84 (PHU) Middleport, PA Nativity of B.V.M. Church; Minersville, PA St. Nicholas Church; [D] Philadelphia, PA Ascension Manor, Inc.
Hutter, Eugene M. '88 (PSC) Philadelphia, PA Holy Ghost Church.
Hutter, John P. '92 (PH) [114] Philadelphia, PA Our Lady of Calvary Church.
Hutton, Leon '80 (LA) [A] Camarillo, CA St. John's Seminary; [A] Camarillo, CA St. John's Seminary.
Hutzler, James '80 (AMA) Umbarger, TX St. Mary's Church.
Huu Du Nguyen, Vincent *o.p.* '46 (FgM) Dominican - Order of Preachers Foreign Missions.
Huvane, James H. *m.m.* '70 (CLV) [P] Cleveland, OH Maryknoll Fathers.
Huy, Dominic Trinh The *o.p.* '75 (GAL) [74] Houston, TX Our Lady of Lourdes Church.
Huy Quyen, Nguyen '73 (JOL) Glen Ellyn, IL Queenship of Mary Church; Glen Ellyn, IL St. Petronille Church.
Huyett, Gerald T. *s.j.* '73 (NY) [DD] New York, NY West Side Jesuit Community.
Huynh, Joseph Dinh C. '67 (PH) [151] Philadelphia, PA St. Thomas Aquinas Church.
Huynh, Viet '93 (PT) [2] Pensacola, FL Little Flower Church.
Huynh Ngoc Tran, J. B. '90 (GAL) [79] Houston, TX Vietnamese Martyrs Church.
Huynh Tan Cong, Simon (SPC) [E] Carthage, MO Congregation of the Mother Co-Redemptrix, United States Assumption Province.
Hvozdovic, Andrew S. '87 (SCR) Jersey Shore, PA St. Luke's Church.
Hwang, Bernard *o.s.b.* (P) Retired.
Hwang, Dominic Hwain '87 (RIC) [12] Richmond, VA St. Kim Taegon Church.
Hy, Hilary Tran-Khac '57 (WDC) [5] Bethesda, MD Our Lady of Vietnam Church.
Hyatt, Donald F. *c.s.b.* '68 (SFE) [D] Albuquerque, NM St. Pius X High School.
Hyatt, J.P. Martin A. *b.s.o.* '84 (NTN) [B] Methuen, MA Basilian Salvatorian Order.
Hyatt, John R. *s.j.* '77 (BRK) [62] Brooklyn, NY St. Ignatius Church.
Hyatt, Robert A. '63 (RVC) Amityville, NY Brunswick Hospital; Amityville, NY South Oaks Psychiatric Hospital; West Islip, NY Consolation Nursing Home; [J] West Islip, NY Our Lady of Consolation Geriatric Care Center.
Hybner, Joseph '63 (VIC) [5] Victoria, TX St. Mary's Church.
Hyclak, Walter J. '69 (CLV) [U] Cleveland, OH St. Joseph Christian Life Center.
Hyde, Mark *s.d.b.* '81 (BO) [N] Boston, MA Salesian Boys & Girls Club.
Hyde, Robert L. *o.praem.* '43 (GB) [I] De Pere, WI St. Norbert Abbey.
Hyde, Robert P. '88 (SY) Whitney Point, NY St. Patrick Church.
Hydo, Emerick J. *c.m.* '50 (ALN) Bangor, PA Our Lady of Good Counsel Church.
Hying, Donald J. '89 (MIL) Awaiting Assignment.
Hykawy, Roman *o.s.b.m.* '94 (STN) Warren, MI St. Josaphat Church.
Hyl, Robert J. '63 (BGP) Easton, CT Notre Dame of Easton Church.
Hyland, Edward F. '67 (HRT) [17] Waterbury, CT SS. Peter and Paul Church.
Hyland, James M. '81 (CHI) [147] Chicago, IL Our Lady of Good Counsel Church.
Hyland, John M. '68 (DAV) Burlington, IA St. John's Church; Burlington, IA St. Paul's Church.
Hyland, Sean J. '84 (MIA) [12] Miami, FL Our Lady of the Holy Rosary Church.
Hyland, Thomas J. '63 (CLV) North Ridgeville, OH St. Peter Church.
Hyman, David L. *o.f.m.* '60 (CHR) Anderson, SC St. Mary of the Angels Church.
Hyman, Robert A. '69 (TUC) Nogales, AZ Sacred Heart Church.
Hymel, Ray '87 (NO) Destrehan, LA St. Charles Borromeo Church.
Hymel, Stephen J. '90 (BR) Greenwell Springs, LA St. Alphonsus Liguori Church.
Hyndman, Ernest R., Jr. '96 (MOB) [6] Mobile, AL Holy Family Church.
Hynes, Aidan '81 (PMB) Hobe Sound, FL St. Christopher Church.
Hynes, Christopher J. '92 (NEW) [B] South Orange, NJ Seton Hall University.
Hynes, Francis S. *s.m.a.* '45 (BO) [W] Dedham, MA

African Mission House.
Hynes, Gerald *c.p.* '51 (BAL) [93] Baltimore, MD St. Ursula Church.
Hynes, Gerald *c.p.* '51 (MET) [H] South River, NJ Passionist Provincial Office.
Hynes, James B. '94 (NY) New City, NY St. Augustine Church.
Hynes, James F. *o.f.m.* '80 (NY) [48] New York, NY Holy Name of Jesus Church.
Hynes, James M. '73 (SAT) [43] San Antonio, TX St. John Berchmans Church.
Hynes, James P. '49 (PRO) [3] West Warwick, RI St. James Church.
Hynes, John F. '55 (DAV) Le Claire-Princeton, IA Our Lady of the River Church.
Hynes, John J. '54 (NY) [194] Staten Island, NY St. Adalbert Church.
Hynes, John M. '65 (WIL) Wilmington, DE St. Catherine of Siena Church.
Hynes, Joseph P. '55 (PRO) [12] Pawtucket, RI St. Teresa of the Child Jesus Church.
Hynes, Patrick '85 (PIT) Canonsburg, PA St. Patrick Church; Conway, PA Our Lady of Peace Church.
Hynes, Richard P. '72 (CHI) Western Springs, IL St. John of the Cross Church.
Hynes, Thomas *c.m.* '59 (FgM) Vincentian Foreign Missions.
Hynes, Thomas J. *c.m.* '59 (PH) [AA] Philadelphia, PA Congregation of the Mission.
Hynes, Msgr. William '49 (SR) Sebastopol, CA St. Sebastian Church.
Hynous, David M. *o.p.* '59 (CHI) [N] River Forest, IL St. Thomas Aquinas Priory.
Hypolite, Douglas J. *s.j.* '80 (GAL) [F] Houston, TX Strake, Jesuit College Preparatory Inc.

I

Iaconis, Anthony '97 (RVC) Mastic Beach, NY St. Jude Church.
Iacovacci, Nicholas J. '51 (PRO) [22] Providence, RI St. Mary Church; Retired.
Iacovone, Angelo *c.p.* '46 (BRK) [U] Jamaica, NY Immaculate Conception Monastery.
Iaia, Paul P. '56 (BAL) Frederick, MD St. John the Evangelist Church.
Ianieri, Stanley A. '89 (WIL) Sherwood Park, DE St. John the Beloved Church.
Iannarella, James M. '96 (PH) Aston, PA St. Joseph Church.
Iannone, Raphael *o.f.m.cap.* '64 (BRK) [87] Brooklyn, NY St. Michael's Church; [U] Brooklyn, NY St. Michael's Friary.
Iannotti, Pascal A. '61 (ALB) St. Johnsville, NY St. Patrick Church.
Iannuzzi, Joseph L. *o.s.j.* '97 (NOR) [5] Middletown, CT St. Sebastian Church.
Iannuzzi, Joseph L. *o.s.j.* '97 (SCR) [M] Pittston, PA Eastern Province of the Oblates of St. Joseph.
Iannuzzi, William (CAM) [3] Cherry Hill, NJ St. Peter Celestine Church.
Iantosca, August J. '77 (BRK) Queens, NY Creedmoor Psychiatric Center.
Ianucci, Thomas A. '94 (RIC) Bristol, VA St. Anne Church.
Iaquinta, Patsy '70 (WH) Bluefield, WV Sacred Heart Church.
Iaquinto, Richard *o.s.b.* '68 (BUR) [E] Weston, VT Priory of Benedictine Monks.
Iaquinto, Robert M. '81 (NEW) [11] Jersey City, NJ Holy Rosary Church.
Iasiello, Louis V. *o.f.m.* '78 (NY) [DD] New York, NY Franciscan Friars, Order of Friars Minor, Holy Name Province.
Iavarone, Armand *o.ss.t.* '43 (BAL) [M] Baltimore, MD Holy Trinity Monastery.
Iavarone, Armand *o.ss.t.* '43 (NY) Spring Valley, NY St. Joseph Church.
Iazzetta, Athanasius *o.f.m.* '54 (FgM) Franciscan Foreign Missions.
Iazzetta, Frank J. (TR) Leave of Absence.
Ibach, Michael J. '73 (YAK) Selah, WA Our Lady of Lourdes Church.
Ibach, William *s.j.* (BO) [W] Cambridge, MA Weston Jesuit Community.
Ibanez, Armando *o.p.* '93 (LA) [S] Los Angeles, CA Monastery of the Angels (Contemplative).
Ibanez, Rodolfo '51 (BR) Retired.
Ibarra, Genaro (BWN) Rio Hondo, TX St. Helen Church.
Ibeas, Emilio (WDC) [B] Washington, DC St. Francis Friary-Capuchin College.
Ibrahim, Ibrahim *b.s.o.* '87 (NTN) Brooklyn, OH St. Elias Church.
Ide, Harold J. '52 (MIL) Retired.
Idler, Peter M. (CAM) On Educational Leave of Absence.
Idranyi, Edmund M. '54 (VNN) San Luis Obispo, CA Saint Anne Church.
Idsert, Beltran '51 (SJN) [8] Bayamon, PR Invencion de la Santa Cruz Church.
Idzik, George '74 (NEW) [5] Jersey City, NJ St. Ann's Church.
Iffert, John C. '97 (BEL) [1] Belleville, IL Cathedral of St. Peter.
Iffert, Wilbert J. '52 (BEL) Retired.
Ifkovits, Edward M. *s.j.* '86 (CHL) Mars Hill, NC St. Andrew the Apostle Church; [J] Charlotte, NC Jesuit Community.
Igboanusi, Edmund C. *c.m.f.* '90 (STL) O'Fallon, MO Assumption Church.
Igle, Edward A. '74 (CAM) Newfield, NJ St. Rose of Lima Church.
Iglesias, Clement '58 (BEA) Cheek, TX St. Martin de Porres Mission Church.
Iglesias, Clement M. '58 (BEA) Fannett, TX St. Mary Church.
Iglesias, Etelvino *o.a.r.* '61 (ORG) [3] Santa Ana, CA Our Lady of Guadalupe Church.
Iglesias, Fernando '56 (LA) Pico Rivera, CA St. Marianne de Paredes Church.
Iglesias, Luis Fernando '53 (CC) Retired.
Ignacio, Alex C. '74 (FRS) Lindsay, CA Sacred Heart Church.
Ignacio, Roberto '74 (TR) [1] Toms River, NJ St. Joseph Church.
Ignacio, Vimencio '89 (SB) Apple Valley, CA Our Lady of the Desert Church.
Ignaszak, Michael A. '84 (MIL) [33] Milwaukee, WI St. Helen Church.
Igo, James P. '54 (OG) Retired.
Igoe, John T. '56 (BIR) [10] Birmingham, AL St. Joseph's Church.
Igoe, Martin S. '62 (BGP) [6] Greenwich, CT Sacred Heart Church.
Iheaka, Emmanuel '90 (LR) Mena, AR St. Agnes Church.
Iheanacho, Kenneth '90 (TLS) Stillwater, OK St. John University Parish and Catholic Student Center Church; [H] Stillwater, OK St. John's University Parish and Catholic Student Center.
Iheoha, Bernard (NY) [142] Bronx, NY St. Frances of Rome Church; Bronx, NY Our Lady of Mercy Medical Center; [W] New York, NY Our Lady of Mercy Medical Center.
Iheonunekwa, Alexander '77 (NY) [159] Bronx, NY St. Lucy Church.
Ihnatowicz, Janusz '62 (GAL) [Q] Houston, TX Residence of the Basilian Fathers of the University of St. Thomas.
Ihrie, Bernard R. '55 (WDC) Retired.
Ihrie, Bernard R., Jr. '55 (WDC) Camp Springs, MD St. Philip the Apostle Church.
Ikemeh, JohnBosco *o.p.* '96 (HBG) [3] York, PA St. Patrick Church.
Ilano, J. Ven '96 (RIC) Wytheville, VA St. Mary's Church.
Ilicki, Theodosius *o.s.b.m.* '88 (STF) [B] Glen Cove, NY Basilian Fathers Novitiate of the Order of St. Basil the Great.
Ililau, John Paul '90 (CI) Koror, FM Sacred Heart Church; Babeldaob, FM Catholic Churches Church.
Illies, Wilfred '50 (SCL) Retired.
Illig, A. Mark '85 (BUF) [R] Williamsville, NY Campus Ministry.
Illikattil, Mathew K. '71 (KAL) Three Rivers, MI Immaculate Conception Church.
Illo, Joseph P. '91 (STO) [1] Stockton, CA Cathedral of the Annunciation.
Ilmberger, Clement F. '46 (SPC) Retired.
Ilnicki, Theodosius *o.s.b.m.* '88 (RVC) [N] Glen Cove, NY St. Josaphatis Monastery, Novitiate and Retreat House.
Im, Andrew Yong Min '89 (SAT) San Antonio, TX Korean Catholic Community Church.
Imbelli, Robert '66 (NY) On Duty Outside the Archdiocese.
Imfeld, Thomas '59 (LEX) Corbin, KY Sacred Heart Church.
Imfield, Thomas J. '59 (LEX) Retired.
Imgrund, Norman P. '64 (ALT) Tyrone, PA St. Matthew's Church.
Imhof, James A. *s.m.* '51 (PCE) Villalba, PR Our Lady Mother of Divine Providence Church.
Imholte, Otto *s.s.c.* '63 (OM) [K] St. Columbans, NE St. Columban's Foreign Mission Society.
Immegart, Placid *o.s.b.* '41 (KC) [J] Conception, MO Conception Abbey.
Immel, Joseph '49 (LAN) Retired.
Immel, William A. '53 (DET) Retired.
Imming, David B. '65 (OKL) Alva, OK Sacred Heart Church; Cherokee, OK St. Cornelius Church; [K] Norman, OK Campus Ministry for the Archdiocese of Oklahoma City.
Imming, Donald R. '60 (SFS) Platte, SD St. Peter the Apostle Church.
Imokhai, Charles '68 (NY) [1] New Rochelle, NY Blessed Sacrament Church.
Imperial, Francisco '59 (NY) [177] Bronx, NY Our Lady of Solace Church.
Imse, James L. '75 (WOR) On Duty Outside the Diocese.
Inametti, Vincent (FWT) Cisco, TX Holy Rosary Church.
Inametti, Vincent '83 (FWT) Eastland, TX St. Francis Xavier Church; Strawn, TX St. John Church.
Inametti, Vincent B. '83 (FWT) Ranger, TX St. Rita Church.
Ince, Michael W. '64 (STP) Elysian, MN St. Andrew Holy Trinity, Waterville, MN Church; Waterville, MN Holy Trinity Church.
India, Stephen J. *c.m.* '49 (ALB) [L] Albany, NY Vincentian Fathers Residence.
Infante, Richard '92 (PIT) [R] Slippery Rock, PA Office for Campus Ministry.
Infante, Richard A. '92 (PIT) Monroeville, PA St. Bernadette Church.
Infuhr, Frank J. '49 (LA) Retired.
Ingalls, Fred D. '74 (BUF) Alden, NY St. John the Baptist Church.
Ingebretsen, Edward J. *s.j.* '81 (WDC) [M] Washington, DC The Jesuit Community at Georgetown University.
Ingels, Gregory '74 (SFR) Special Assignment.
Ingemie, Dominic '67 (ALB) [8] Albany, NY St. James Church.
Ingham, G. Nicholas *o.p.* '81 (PRO) [P] Providence, RI St. Thomas Aquinas Priory at Providence College.
Ingham, Jeffrey A. '75 (R) [3] Raleigh, NC Our Lady of Lourdes Church.
Inghilterra, Vincent J. '72 (TR) Military Chaplains.
Inglot, Mark '81 (LAN) [4] Jackson, MI Queen of the Miraculous Medal Church.
Ingold, Michael (GB) Montpelier, WI St. Joseph/St. John Church; Stangelville, WI St. Lawrence Church; West Kewaunee, WI St. Hedwig Church.
Ingram, Brian '90 (RVC) Bellmore, NY St. Barnabas the Apostle Church.
Ingram, James A. '85 (ORL) On Duty Outside the Diocese.
Ingram, James A. '85 (SR) Petaluma, CA U.S. Coast Guard Training Center.
Inigo, Javier *c.m.* '61 (PCE) [8] Ponce, PR La Milagrosa Church.
Inkel, Roland '47 (BIR) Retired.
Inman, Leonard T. '61 (ALT) Retired.
Innes, Ben *o.f.m.* '84 (SD) [K] San Luis Rey, CA Mission San Luis Rey Retreat.
Innes, Ben R. *o.f.m.* '84 (SD) [H] San Luis Rey, CA Mission San Luis Rey.
Innocenzi, Msgr. James G. '76 (TR) [19] Trenton, NJ St. Michael Church.
Inoue, Jun *s.v.d.* '88 (WDC) [M] Washington, DC Divine Word College.
Inserra, Ceaser *o.f.m.conv.* '47 (LA) [R] Torrance, CA Franciscan Friars, St. Bonaventure Friary.
Intranuovo, Ralph *s.c.j.* '83 (SAT) [B] San Antonio, TX Priests of the Sacred Heart- House of Formation.
Introini, Msgr. Elso C. (PAT) Hawthorne, NJ St. Anthony's Church.
Introvigne, Raymond D. '64 (NOR) Taftville, CT Sacred Heart Church.
Inveraradi, Luigi *i.m.c.* '70 (SB) [7] Riverside, CA St. Francis de Sales Church.
Inverso, Leon J '85 (TR) Atlantic Highlands, NJ St. Agnes Church.
Inwanyanwu, Linus '83 (NY) [28] New York, NY Corpus Christi Church.
Inzeo, Lawrence C. '78 (NY) [1] White Plains, NY St. Anthony Church.
Inzina, Joseph Robert '60 (SHP) Bastrop, LA St. Joseph Church; Monroe, LA Swanson Correctional Center for Youth.
Iorio, Peter '93 (KNX) [4] Chattanooga, TN St. Stephen Church.
Iott, Martin J. *o.p.* '70 (R) [E] Raleigh, NC Dominican Community; [E] Raleigh, NC De Porres House.
Iovino, Paul '61 (PAT) Totowa Borough, NJ St. James of the Marches Church.
Ipolito, Pascal D. '70 (BUF) [2] West Seneca, NY St. Catherine of Siena Church.
Irace, Dominic P. '75 (ARL) [1] Arlington, VA Cathedral of St. Thomas More.
Iraly, Matthew '75 (NY) [195] Staten Island, NY St. Ann Church.
Ireland, Dave R. '83 (CLV) Wickliffe, OH Our Lady of Mount Carmel Church.
Ireland, Donald '63 (MIA) Retired.
Iriondo, Josu '62 (NY) [129] Bronx, NY St. Anthony of Padua Church; [HH] New York, NY Centro Carismatico Catolico Hispano De La Arquidiocesis De Nueva York; [HH] New York, NY Hispanic Catholic Charismatic Center of the Archdiocese of New York.
Irish, Robert L. '92 (LAN) [5] Ypsilanti, MI Holy Trinity Student Chapel Church.
Irizarry, Alan '83 (ARE) On Duty Outside the Diocese.
Irizarry, Elvin '97 (ARE) [2] Arecibo, PR Church of Sagrado Corazon de Jesus.
Irizarry, Rafael (ARE) On Duty Outside the Diocese.
Irizarry, Msgr. Raul '41 (PCE) Retired.
Iroz, Anthony *o.a.r.* '36 (LA) [8] Los Angeles, CA Cristo Rey Church.
Irrgang, Kenneth E. '68 (NU) Retired.

Irvin, Charles E. '67 (LAN) Manchester, MI St. Mary Church.
Irving, Peter '83 (LA) Wilmington, CA SS. Peter and Paul's Church.
Irwin, James W. *c.s.c.* (FgM) Holy Cross Foreign Missions.
Irwin, James W. *c.s.c.* '65 (FTW) [J] South Bend, IN Congregation of Holy Cross Indiana Province Provincial House.
Irwin, Joseph F. '62 (NY) Mamaroneck, NY Holy Trinity Church.
Irwin, Kevin W. '71 (NY) On Duty Outside the Archdiocese.
Irwin, Kevin W. '71 (WDC) [C] Washington, DC Catholic University of America, The.
Irwin, Michael F. *f.s.s.p.* '64 (RC) [1] Rapid City, SD Cathedral of Our Lady of Perpetual Help.
Irwin, Michael T. *f.s.s.p.* '64 (SCR) [M] Elmhurst, PA Priestly Fraternity of St. Peter (F.S.S.P.), North American District Headquarters.
Irwin, Patrick '69 (SP) Valrico, FL St. Stephen Church.
Irwin, Patrick F. (MAN) Wolfeboro, NH St. Cecilia Church.
Irwin, Robert '44 (FAR) Special Assignment.
Irwin, Robert C. '95 (BAK) Pendleton, OR St. Mary's Church.
Irwin, William E. '64 (WIL) Ogletown, DE Holy Family Church.
Isacsson, Alfred J. *o.carm.* '58 (NY) Tarrytown, NY Transfiguration Church.
Ischay, Matthew A. '75 (CLV) [12] Cleveland, OH Blessed Sacrament Church.
Ischler, Paul *o.m.i.* '39 (STP) [N] St. Paul, MN Oblate Residence.
Isenecker, Lawrence E. *s.j.* '57 (DET) [P] Clarkston, MI Colombiere Center.
Isern, Fernando '93 (MIA) [4] Pompano Beach, FL St. Elizabeth of Hungary Catholic Church.
Isho, Emanuel Hana '84 (EST) North Hollywood, CA St. Paul Assyrian-Chaldean Catholic Parish.
Iskander, Sabri '68 (EST) Southfield, MI Our Lady of Chaldeans Cathedral, Mother of God Chaldean Parish.
Isla, Elias *sch.p.* (NY) [65] New York, NY St. Jude Church.
Isopo, Dominic '80 (ALB) [11] Schenectady, NY St. Luke Church.
Issac, Jose '75 (RNO) Hawthorne, NV Our Lady of Perpetual Help Church.
Issing, Daniel J. *c.s.c.* '90 (FR) [A] North Easton, MA Stonehill College; [A] North Easton, MA Holy Cross Fathers Religious.
Istok, Adolph *c.r.* '44 (CHI) [D] Chicago, IL Weber High School.
Isvanca, Alois '89 (ROM) Astoria, NY St. Mary Romanian Catholic Mission Church.
Iszczuk, Cyril *o.s.b.m.* '89 (STF) Long Island City, NY Holy Cross Church.
Itodo, Pius '90 (LA) [65] Los Angeles, CA St. Gerard Majella Church.
Ittiyappara, Mathew '67 (SR) Yountville, CA St. Joan of Arc Church.
Iturbe, Rene *s.m.* '74 (MRY) Santa Cruz, CA Star of the Sea Church; [G] Santa Cruz, CA Society of Mary, Marists.
Iturraran, Jose Luis *o.de.m.* '63 (PCE) [9] Ponce, PR La Merced Church.
Itzaina, John *s.d.b.* '74 (MRY) [D] Watsonville, CA St. Francis Youth Center.
Itzaina, John *s.d.b.* '74 (OAK) [E] Richmond, CA Salesian High School.
Ivan, Nicholas '56 (PRM) Livonia, MI Sacred Heart Church.
Ivanauskas, Balys C. '39 (CLV) [25] Cleveland, OH St. George Church; Retired.
Ivans, Joseph *o.c.d.* '53 (GRY) [J] Munster, IN Discalced Carmelite Fathers Monastery.
Ivers, Msgr. Leslie J. '79 (NY) [141] Bronx, NY St. Frances de Chantal Church.
Ivers, Michael T. '74 (CHI) [4] Chicago, IL St. Agatha Church.
Ivers, Victor J. '45 (CHI) Libertyville, IL St. Joseph Church; Retired.
Iverson, Msgr. Stanley J. '49 (NO) Retired.
Ivory, Msgr. Thomas P. '64 (NEW) New Milford, NJ Ascension Church.
Iwan, Januscz '76 (DET) Eastpointe, MI St. Veronica Church.
Iwaniec, Wieslaw '86 (SAT) Stockdale, TX St. Mary Church.
Iwanowski, Thomas B. '75 (NEW) [19] Jersey City, NJ Our Lady of Czestochowa Church.
Iwasiw, Nestor '93 (PHU) [1] Philadelphia, PA Immaculate Conception of Blessed Virgin Mary, Cathedral.
Iweh, Emmanuel '84 (SEA) [1] Tacoma, WA St. Ann Church; [5] Tacoma, WA St. John of the Woods Church; [15] Tacoma, WA Sacred Heart Church; [G] Tacoma, WA St. Joseph Medical Center.
Iwele, Gode *o.m.i.* '88 (WDC) [B] Washington, DC Oblate College/Oblate Center for Mission Studies.
Iwuanyanwu, Linus (NY) Manhattan, NY Columbia Presbyterian Medical Center.
Iwuc, Anthony D. '53 (PRO) [3] Central Falls, RI St. Joseph Church.
Iwuji, Matthew C. (GRY) [7] Hammond, IN St. Margaret Mary Church.
Izac, Andre C. '64 (R) Buxton, NC Our Lady of the Seas Church.
Izac, Andre C. '64 (WDC) On Duty Outside the Archdiocese.
Izer, Wesley W. *s.d.b.* '77 (VNN) [A] Phoenix, AZ Salesians of Don Bosco.
Izquierdo, William *l.c.* '58 (WDC) [M] Potomac, MD Legionaries of Christ.
Izral, John '56 (BLX) Retired.
Izyk, Andrew (CHI) [45] Chicago, IL St. Constance Church.
Izzo, David D. *o.p.* '94 (FgM) Dominican - Order of Preachers Foreign Missions.
Izzo, John *s.j.* '80 (BO) [W] Chestnut Hill, MA The Jesuit Community at Boston College.

J

Jaballa, Angelo '79 (LA) Artesia, CA Holy Family Church.
Jablinske, Raymond D. '68 (WH) [5] Wheeling, WV Our Lady of Peace Church.
Jablonovsky, John Cyril *c.p.* '40 (CHI) [N] Chicago, IL Immaculate Conception Monastery.
Jablonowski, Anthony *c.m.m.i.* '70 (CHY) On Duty Outside the Diocese.
Jablonowski, James N. '68 (MIL) [32] Milwaukee, WI St. Hedwig Church.
Jablonske, William J. '61 (LC) Weston, WI St. Agnes Church.
Jablonski, Edward J. (PH) Pottstown, PA St. Aloysius Church.
Jablonski, Joseph *m.s.c.* (SB) Upland, CA St. Joseph Church.
Jablonski, Msgr. Stanislaus '41 (NY) [192] Bronx, NY St. Valentine Church; Retired.
Jablonski, Msgr. William W. '63 (RVC) East Rockaway, NY St. Raymond's Church.
Jabo, Scott W. '90 (E) St. Marys, PA Sacred Heart of Jesus Church; [C] Saint Marys, PA Elk County Christian High School.
Jabusch, Willard F. '56 (CHI) [V] Chicago, IL Ministry in Higher Education; [X] Wilmette, IL Musica Pacis.
Jach, Edward M. *s.m.* '64 (CIN) [27] Cincinnati, OH St. Francis de Sales Church.
Jach, Edward M. *s.m.* '64 (STL) [P] St. Louis, MO Provincialate of the Society of Mary, Province of St. Louis.
Jack, Cuthbert A. *o.s.b.* '90 (GBG) [H] Latrobe, PA Saint Vincent Archabbey.
Jack, Duane C. '67 (PEO) Kewanee, IL St. Mary's Catholic Church.
Jack, Edward M. *s.m.* '64 (CIN) [M] Cincinnati, OH Marianist Community.
Jackanich, Msgr. Joseph '26 (PSC) Retired.
Jackels, Msgr. Michael O. '81 (LIN) On Duty Outside the Diocese.
Jackiewicz, F. W. (TR) [S] Princeton, NJ Campus Ministry for the Diocese of Trenton.
Jackiewicz, Frederick W. '71 (TR) West Long Branch, NJ St. Jerome Church.
Jackovic, George V. '46 (PIT) Retired.
Jackson, Charles '55 (MIA) Retired.
Jackson, Charles A. '60 (COL) [A] Columbus, OH Pontifical College Josephinum.
Jackson, David *s.c.j.* '66 (BWN) Lyford, TX Prince of Peace Church.
Jackson, Donald F. '59 (TUC) San Manuel, AZ St. Bartholomew Church.
Jackson, Edward W. *c.ss.r.* '49 (HBG) Ephrata, PA Mother of Perpetual Help Church; [H] Ephrata, PA St. Clement's Mission House.
Jackson, James '60 (STP) Minneapolis, MN Hennepin County Courts; Special Assignment.
Jackson, James '85 (WCH) On Duty Outside the Diocese.
Jackson, James J. '72 (SUP) Sarona, WI St. Catherine Church; Shell Lake, WI St. Joseph Church; Spooner, WI St. Francis De Sales Church.
Jackson, James M. '75 (WIL) Absent on Sick Leave.
Jackson, James R. *m.m.* '58 (FgM) Maryknoll Foreign Missions.
Jackson, James W. '60 (STP) [K] St. Paul, MN Our Lady of Good Counsel Home.
Jackson, James W. *f.s.s.p.* '85 (SCR) [M] Elmhurst, PA Priestly Fraternity of St. Peter (F.S.S.P.), North American District Headquarters.
Jackson, James W. *f.s.s.p.* '85 (TLS) [2] Tulsa, OK Community of Saint Peter Church.
Jackson, Joseph M. '74 (CHI) Palatine, IL St. Thomas of Villanova Church.
Jackson, Lawrence J. '60 (DET) [7] Sterling Heights, MI St. Michael Church.
Jackson, Owen R. *o.s.a.* '65 (PH) [C] Villanova, PA Villanova University.
Jackson, Pio (STL) [P] St. Louis, MO Franciscan Friary of St. Anthony of Padua; [R] St. Louis, MO Franciscan Sisters of Mary Administration.
Jackson, Pio *o.f.m.* '91 (FgM) Custody of St. Mary of the Angels. Byzantine-Slavonic.
Jackson, Raymond A. *c.s.b.* '58 (VIC) Wharton, TX Our Lady of Mt. Carmel Church.
Jackson, Robert '54 (RCK) [D] Belvidere, IL Saint Joseph Hospital.
Jackson, Robert H. '84 (CLV) Brunswick, OH St. Ambrose Church.
Jackson, Thomas *o.p.* '92 (CHI) [24] Chicago, IL St. Basil/Visitation Church.
Jackson, William J. *c.s.sp.* '58 (VEN) [G] Sarasota, FL Congregation of the Holy Ghost.
Jacmierski, Jan '60 (NY) [5] Poughkeepsie, NY St. Joseph Church.
Jacob, Anthony J. *o.s.b.* '65 (JOL) [C] Lisle, IL Benet Academy; [J] Lisle, IL St. Procopius Abbey.
Jacob, William *c.ss.r.* '46 (NY) [23] New York, NY St. Cecilia Church.
Jacobberger, Joseph '65 (P) [1] Portland, OR Cathedral of the Immaculate Conception.
Jacobi, Arthur H. '89 (DET) [2] Livonia, MI St. Colette Church.
Jacobi, Joseph A., '91 (OKL) Altus, OK Prince of Peace Church.
Jacobs, Allen A. '66 (R) Retired.
Jacobs, Charles E. *c.m.* '43 (BAL) Emmitsburg, MD St. Joseph Church; [M] Emmitsburg, MD Vincentian House.
Jacobs, Charles E. '86 (HRT) [8] Hartford, CT St. Augustine Church.
Jacobs, David E. '75 (LR) Texarkana, AR St. Edward's Church.
Jacobs, Eugene S. '46 (WH) Retired.
Jacobs, Gilbert *o.praem.* (GB) Osman, WI St. Isidore Church.
Jacobs, Gilbert H. *o.praem.* '55 (GB) Cleveland, WI St. Wendel Church.
Jacobs, Harry W. '73 (WDC) [42] Washington, DC St. Thomas Apostle Church.
Jacobs, James J. '74 (SCR) Unassigned or Leave of Absence.
Jacobs, James T. '43 (GB) Retired.
Jacobs, Joseph A. '40 (FTW) Retired.
Jacobs, Peter '55 (WDC) On Duty Outside the Archdiocese.
Jacobs, Pierre P. *s.j.* '44 (SJ) [M] Los Gatos, CA Sacred Heart Jesuit Center.
Jacobs, Richard A. (PAT) Retired.
Jacobs, Richard M. '83 (BO) [C] North Andover, MA Merrimack College.
Jacobs, Richard M. *o.s.a.* '83 (CHI) [N] Olympia Fields, IL The Augustinian Provincialate Tolentine Center.
Jacobs, Timothy *ss.cc.* '35 (HON) [H] Honolulu, HI St. Patrick's Monastery.
Jacobsen, James E. *s.j.* '59 (P) [L] Portland, OR Colombiere Community.
Jacobsmeyer, Gregory H. *s.j.* '46 (STL) [P] St. Louis, MO Hallahan House.
Jacobson, Clifford '96 (CHY) Casper, WY St. Anthony of Padua Church.
Jacobson, Gary '65 (P) Retired.
Jacobson, James *s.j.* '59 (P) Salem, OR Oregon State Penitentiary; Salem, OR Santiam Correctional Institution; Salem, OR Mill Creek Correctional Facility.
Jacolino, Dominic '41 (NY) Retired; [DD] New York, NY Pope John Paul II Residence.
Jacquel, John B. '83 (E) Edinboro, PA Our Lady of the Lake Church.
Jacques, Alfred '60 (PRT) Rumford, ME St. Athanasius-St. John Church.
Jacques, Donald W. '53 (PRT) Retired.
Jacques, E. J. *s.j.* '66 (MOB) [9] Mobile, AL St. Joseph Church.
Jacques, Eugene F. '80 (NO) [20] New Orleans, LA Our Lady Star Of The Sea Church.
Jacques, Kenneth *o.s.b.* '67 (P) Gervais, OR Sacred Heart-St. Louis Church; [L] St. Benedict, OR Mt. Angel Abbey.
Jacques, Michael P. *s.s.e.* '82 (NO) [52] New Orleans, LA St. Peter Claver Church; [54] New Orleans, LA St. Philip the Apostle Church.
Jacques, Roger N. '78 (BO) [2] Waltham, MA St. Joseph Church.
Jacubco, Bernard *m.s.c.* '64 (OG) Glenfield, NY St. Mary Church.
Jacunski, Robert D. '56 (NEW) Caldwell, NJ St. Aloysius Church.
Jadaa, John '46 (NTN) Retired.
Jadgchew, John *c.pp.s.* '75 (CIN) [B] Carthagena, OH St. Charles.
Jadin, Samuel D. *o.praem.* '55 (GB) [J] Manitowoc, WI Holy Family Convent of Franciscan Sisters of Christian Charity.
Jadwisiak, Edmund '79 (PRM) Parma, OH Saint John the Baptist, Cathedral; Retired.
Jaeb, Maurus P. *o.s.b.* '95 (LA) Montebello, CA St. Benedict Church.
Jaeb, Maurus P. *o.s.b.* '95 (OKL) [I] Shawnee, OK St. Gregory Abbey.

Jaeger, David '69 (SEA) Special Assignment.
Jaeger, David '86 (AUS) [17] Austin, TX St. Louis Church.
Jaeger, James P. '86 (ROC) Hornell, NY St. Ann Church.
Jaeger, Louis M. '73 (DUB) Epworth, IA St. Patrick's Church.
Jaeger, Robert E. '90 (COS) Monument, CO St. Peter Church.
Jaekle, Lawrence E. '38 (CIN) Retired.
Jaenicke, Alfred J. '54 (HRT) [13] Hartford, CT St. Michael Church.
Jagde, Bede *o.p.* '60 (FgM) Dominican - Order of Preachers Foreign Missions.
Jagdfeld, Lawrence '75 (CHI) [N] Chicago, IL The Holy Evangelists Friary.
Jagielski, James '77 (DET) Military Chaplains.
Jagodensky, Joe *s.d.s.* '80 (MIL) [N] Milwaukee, WI Alexian Village of Milwaukee, Inc.
Jagodzinski, Charles *ofm conv.* '68 (BUF) [D] Athol Springs, NY St. Francis High School; [O] Athol Springs, NY St. Francis of Assisi Friary.
Jagodzinski, Msgr. Jan '54 (DET) [A] Orchard Lake, MI SS. Cyril and Methodius Seminary.
Jagodzinski, Msgr. John J. '62 (PH) Wayne, PA St. Katharine of Siena Church.
Jagoe, Bede R. *o.p.* (CHI) [N] River Forest, IL St. Thomas Aquinas Priory.
Jagoe, Bede R. *o.p.* '60 (CHI) [N] Chicago, IL Dominicans (Provincial Office).
Jagosz, Mitchell '86 (ORG) Inactive Leave.
Jahner, Anton P. *s.j.* '67 (SPK) [K] Spokane, WA Regis Community.
Jakanovich, Roberto *o.m.v.* '87 (BO) [B] Boston, MA Oblate Provincialate.
Jakel, Pat G. '85 (SFD) Nokomis, IL St. Louis Church; Witt, IL St. Barbara Church.
Jakobiak, Arthur '56 (SFE) Santa Fe, NM St. Vincent's Hospital.
Jakows, Ronald M. '90 (PH) [58] Philadelphia, PA Holy Cross Church; [D] Philadelphia, PA Roman Catholic High School for Boys.
Jaksina, Edward S. '55 (HRT) Seymour, CT Good Shepherd Church.
Jakubco, Bernard '64 (OG) Houseville, NY St. Hedwig Church; Lowville, NY St. Peter Church.
Jakubek, Eugene J. *s.j.* '54 (OM) [K] Omaha, NE Jesuit Community At Creighton University.
Jakubik, Emil (SY) Retired.
Jakubik, Richard J. '93 (CHI) Glenview, IL Our Lady of Perpetual Help Church.
Jakubowski, Allen F. '75 (LC) Abbotsford, WI St. Bernard Church; Owen, WI Holy Rosary Church.
Jakubowski, Joseph J. '40 (KC) Retired.
Jakubowski, Kenneth J. '91 (CLV) [5] Lakewood, OH St. Luke Church.
Jalbert, Edward *c.j.* '87 (LA) [B] Santa Maria, CA St. Joseph Seminary (Josephite Fathers' Novitiate); [D] Santa Maria, CA St. Joseph High School.
Jalbert, Marcel '38 (SB) Retired.
Jalbert, Robert A. *m.m.* '79 (FgM) Maryknoll Foreign Missions.
Jallas, Robert J. '84 (SFD) [4] Alton, IL St. Matthew Church.
Jamail, Msgr. James A. '68 (GAL) [78] Houston, TX St. Vincent de Paul Church.
Jamail, Msgr. Michael '60 (BEA) [2] Beaumont, TX St. Anne Church.
James, Albert *s.m.a.* '73 (NEW) [N] Tenafly, NJ Society of African Missions, Provincialate, S.M.A. Fathers.
James, David J. '91 (SY) Cicero, NY Sacred Heart Church.
James, David L. '96 (ALN) [1] Allentown, PA Cathedral of St. Catharine of Siena.
James, Jamels (CHI) [97] Chicago, IL St. James Church.
James, Joseph '94 (Y) Absent on Leave.
James, Msgr. Joseph W. '57 (LUB) Idalou, TX St. Philip Benizi Church; [C] Slaton, TX Our Lady of Mercy Retreat Center.
James, Melvin P. *s.v.d.* '75 (LA) [71] Los Angeles, CA St. John, The Evangelist Church.
James, Peter Paul *o.f.m.* '51 (CIN) [M] Cincinnati, OH St. Francis Seraph Friary.
James, Msgr. R. Joseph '61 (STA) [9] Jacksonville, FL Mary Queen of Heaven Church.
James, Thomas *s.v.d.* '69 (LAF) [4] New Iberia, LA St. Edward Church.
James, Thomas *s.v.d.* '96 (BLX) [E] Bay St. Louis, MS Southern Province of St. Augustine - Provincial Residence.
James, V. Warwick '80 (SJ) [4] Santa Clara, CA St. Lawrence the Martyr Church.
James, Msgr. William R. '54 (MOB) Robertsdale, AL St. Patrick Church.
Jameson, Msgr. W. Ronald '68 (WDC) [1] Washington, DC St. Matthew Cathedral.
Jamieson, Andrew *o.f.m.cap.* '88 (NEW) [5] Hoboken, NJ St. Ann's Church.
Jamison, Dale *o.f.m.* '74 (GLP) Zuni, NM St. Anthony Indian Mission, Our Lady of Guadalupe Church.
Jamme, Albert *m.afr.* '41 (WDC) [M] Washington, DC Missionaries of Africa.
Jammes, Jean Marie (LAF) Retired.
Jammes, Jean Marie '43 (LAF) St. Martinville, LA St. Martin of Tours Church.
Jammo, Sarhad '64 (EST) Troy, MI St. Joseph Chaldean Parish.
Jamnicky, John A. '72 (CHI) Chicago, IL Chicago O'Hare International Airport; [X] Chicago, IL Catholic Chaplaincy at O'Hare.
Jamros, Daniel P. *s.j.* '76 (BO) [W] Boston, MA The Society of Jesus of New England-Provincial Offices.
Jamros, Daniel P. *s.j.* '76 (BUF) [O] Buffalo, NY Canisius Jesuit Community.
Jamroz, Sigmund S. *m.m.* '66 (FgM) Maryknoll Foreign Missions.
Jamroz, Waclaw *s.d.s.* (CHI) [36] Chicago, IL St. Camillus Church.
Janacek, Msgr. Balthasar '50 (SAT) [T] San Antonio, TX Pillars of San Fernando Cathedral.
Janacek, Msgr. Balthasar J. '50 (SAT) [1] San Antonio, TX Cathedral of San Fernando; San Antonio, TX Old Spanish Missions Church; [S] San Antonio, TX National Foundation for Mexican-American Vocations.
Janaczek, Joseph J. '71 (BUF) [1] Dunkirk, NY St. Hedwig Church.
Janaites, Stanley '55 (BAL) Sykesville, MD Springfield Hospital Center; Special Assignment.
Janak, Gary W. *j.c.l.* '88 (VIC) Yoakum, TX St. Joseph Church.
Janas, Camillus *o.f.m.* (GB) [5] Manitowoc, WI St. Andrew Church.
Janasik, Basil *o.f.m.* '45 (MIL) [P] Burlington, WI Queen of Peace Friary.
Jancarz, Janusz '83 (VEN) Parrish, FL St. Francis Xavier Cabrini Church.
Jancius, John *m.i.c.* '34 (CHI) [N] Chicago, IL Congregation of Marian Fathers of the Immaculate Conception.
Janda, James '72 (SLC) [6] Sandy, UT Blessed Sacrament Church.
Jandernoa, Ronald J. '94 (MET) [A] South Amboy, NJ St. Mary Regional High School.
Jandernoa, Ronald L. '94 (MET) Sayreville, NJ Our Lady of Victories Church.
Janecek, James E. '95 (CC) [4] Corpus Christi, TX Holy Family Church.
Janeck, Thomas More *o.f.m.cap.* '46 (DEN) [M] Denver, CO St. Francis of Assisi Friary; [N] Denver, CO Monastery of Our Lady of Light (Capuchin Poor Clares).
Janeczek, Vladimir '59 (GRY) [3] Hammond, IN St. Casimir Church.
Janelli, Msgr. Anthony '64 (FRS) Dinuba, CA St. Catherine Church.
Janer, Walter *s.j.* (SJN) [22] San Juan, PR San Ignacio de Loyola Church.
Janes, David A. '83 (SFS) De Smet, SD St. Thomas Aquinas Church.
Janesko, Francis J. '46 (LR) Retired.
Janesko, John A. '52 (LR) Slovak, AR SS. Cyril and Methodius Church; Stuttgart, AR Holy Rosary Church; [L] Stuttgart, AR Holy Rosary Catholic School "Vision 2000" Educational Trust Fund.
Janette, Paul '63 (MIL) [17] Milwaukee, WI St. Catherine Church.
Janette, Paul D. '63 (MIL) Special Assignment.
Janezic, Lawrence *o.f.m.* '78 (SAT) [69] San Antonio, TX San Francisco de la Espada Church.
Jangam, John (TLS) [H] Tulsa, OK University of Tulsa Newman Center.
Jangam, John '80 (TLS) [1] Tulsa, OK Holy Family Cathedral.
Janiak, Anthony J. '42 (CHI) Retired.
Janicki, Carl F. '94 (PH) [21] Philadelphia, PA St. Bartholomew Church.
Janicki, Joseph A. '64 (MIL) [4] Menomonee Falls, WI St. Mary Church.
Janicki, Laurian *o.f.m.* '64 (JOL) Wayne, IL Resurrection Church.
Janiga, Bruce G. '83 (NEW) [C] West Orange, NJ Seton Hall Preparatory School.
Janiga, Joseph '45 (DET) Retired.
Janik, Anthony F. *o.f.m.* '70 (GRY) [F] Crown Point, IN St. Anthony Medical Center, Inc.; [J] Cedar Lake, IN Our Lady of Lourdes Friary.
Janik, Bruno '66 (CHI) Burbank, IL St. Albert the Great Church.
Janik, Leszek T. '92 (NOR) Old Lyme, CT Christ the King Church.
Janish, James '69 (SAT) Spring Branch, TX St. Joseph Church.
Janiszeski, Joseph *t.o.r.* '78 (FWT) [8] Fort Worth, TX St. Andrew Church.
Janiunas, Albin F. (BO) Retired.
Jankaitis, Ronald V. '79 (ALN) [2] Saint Clair, PA St. Casimir Church; [C] Pottsville, PA Nativity B.V.M. High School.
Jankevicius, Daniel (BRK) [9] Brooklyn, NY Annunciation of the Blessed Virgin Mary Church.
Janko, Jack *s.d.b.* '78 (BO) [N] Boston, MA Salesian Boys & Girls Club.
Jankowiak, Patrick '92 (SAG) [17] Saginaw, MI St. Stephen Church.
Jankowiak, Valentine A. '38 (ROC) [56] Rochester, NY St. Stanislaus Church; Retired.
Jankowski, Daniel C. '73 (CHI) [G] Chicago, IL Catholic Charities of the Archdiocese of Chicago-Archdiocesan Offices.
Jankowski, Marcellus A. '57 (KC) Special Assignment.
Jankowski, Peter '96 (JOL) Absent on Leave.
Jankowski, Richard '92 (SP) [4] Largo, FL St. Patrick Church.
Jankowski, Valentine *o.f.m. conv.* '61 (LSC) Carlsbad, NM San Jose Church; Jal, NM St. Cecilia Church.
Jann, Francis J. '47 (BUF) Belfast, NY St. Patrick Church; Rushford, NY St. Mark Church.
Jannetta, Alfred L. '67 (MAN) Absent on Sick Leave.
Jannetta, Frank *o.f.m.* '79 (NY) [DD] New York, NY Franciscan Province of the Immaculate Conception; [DD] New York, NY Franciscan Province of the Immaculate Conception.
Janning, Timothy J. '82 (CIN) Military Chaplains.
Janning, Timothy J. '82 (ORG) Tustin, CA Marine Corps Air Station.
Janocha, Carl W. '91 (OKL) Frederick, OK St. Helen Church.
Janoski, Steven A. '88 (SFD) Troy, IL St. Jerome Church.
Janovec, James J. '64 (GI) Valentine, NE St. Nicholas Church.
Janowiak, Paul A. *s.j.* '84 (SEA) [A] Seattle, WA Seattle University.
Janowicz, Barney J. '57 (SAG) Retired.
Janowicz, Richard '80 (STN) Springfield, OR Nativity of the Mother of God Church.
Janowski, Lawrence *o.f.m.* (CHI) [N] Chicago, IL Holy Name Friary.
Janowski, Rock '64 (LA) Simi Valley, CA St. Peter Claver Church.
Janowski, Stanley *o.f.m.* '66 (CHI) [N] Chicago, IL Holy Name Friary.
Janowski, Wieslaw *c.r.* '93 (CHI) [88] Chicago, IL St. Hyacinth Church.
Jansch, Ronald *o.f.m.cap.* '50 (MIL) [P] Mount Calvary, WI St. Lawrence Friary.
Jansen, James H. '55 (BEL) Fairview Heights, IL Our Lady of the Assumption Church.
Jansen, William *m.c.c.j.* '66 (FgM) Comboni Foreign Missions.
Janski, Jerome J. '50 (STP) Retired.
Janson, Chris *s.m.* '73 (SAT) [C] San Antonio, TX St. Mary's University of San Antonio, Texas; [M] San Antonio, TX Casa Maria Marianist Community.
Janson, Eugene '76 (SAT) [K] San Antonio, TX Padua Place.
Janson, Eugene '76 (VIC) Retired.
Janson, John J. *o.f.m.* '41 (FgM) Franciscan Foreign Missions.
Janson, Leo F. '45 (GF) Retired.
Janson, Richard J. *c.m.* '77 (STL) Sappington, MO St. Catherine Laboure Church.
Jansonis, Alphonse B. '45 (BO) Permanent Disability.
Janssen, Henry *o.m.i.* '43 (BWN) [3] McAllen, TX Sacred Heart Church.
Janssen, James M. '48 (DAV) Retired; [M] Davenport, IA St. Vincent Center.
Janssen, Orville '52 (GB) Retired.
Jansze, Neville '86 (STO) Modesto, CA St. Joseph Church.
Janton, Anthony W. '77 (PH) [46] Philadelphia, PA St. Francis de Sales Church.
Janus, Mark-David *c.s.p.* '79 (NY) [DD] Jamaica Estates, NY Paulist Fathers Generalate.
Januszkiewicz, Henry '62 (WDC) Retired.
Janze, John E. '75 (ORG) Irvine, CA St. Thomas More Church.
Jaramillo, Cesar *c.ss.r.* '41 (MGZ) Aguadilla, PR St. Charles Borromeo Church.
Jaramillo, Fabio E. '81 (NY) [89] New York, NY Our Lady of Lourdes Church.
Jaramillo, Guillermo *o.f.m.* '94 (FgM) Custody of St. Mary of the Angels. Byzantine-Slavonic.
Jaramillo, Leonardo '92 (NEW) West New York, NJ St. Joseph of the Palisades Church.
Jaramillo, Luis D. '60 (SFE) [10] Albuquerque, NM Our Lady of the Assumption Church.
Jaramillo, Luis M. '95 (HRT) Wallingford, CT Holy Trinity Church.
Jaramillo, Oscar '90 (B) Homedale, ID St. Hubert Church; Parma, ID Sacred Hearts of Jesus and Mary Church.
Jaramillo, Peter '93 (KCK) Leawood, KS Cure of Ars Church.
Jaramillo, Roberto '95 (SAC) [5] Sacramento, CA Our Lady of Guadalupe Shrine Church.
Jaranilla, Roberto F., Jr. '96 (LA) [7] Los Angeles, CA Christ the King Church.
Jarboe, J. Bruce '86 (BAL) Special Assignment.
Jarboe, W. Raymond '89 (BAK) Ontario, OR Blessed Sacrament Church.

Jarco, Emil *s.d.s.* '74 (GRY) [J] Merrillville, IN Salvatorian Fathers (Society of the Divine Savior).
Jarcynski, Eugene T. *c.s.c.* '55 (RVC) Northport, NY Veteran's Hospital.
Jardiniano, Rolly '84 (LA) Whittier, CA St. Gregory the Great Church.
Jarecki, Michael S. '44 (OG) Retired.
Jarecki, Reynold *o.f.m.* '55 (MIL) [P] Burlington, WI Queen of Peace Friary.
Jarema, William '83 (COS) [3] Colorado Springs, CO Divine Redeemer Church.
Jarema, William '88 (COS) [H] Colorado Springs, CO Catholic Charismatic Renewal Services.
Jarka, Thomas H. '59 (CAM) [6] Cherry Hill, NJ Queen of Heaven Church.
Jarmak, Claude *o.f.m.conv.* '54 (SPR) [A] Granby, MA St. Hyacinth College and Seminary.
Jarmoluk, Joseph F. '84 (RCK) Geneva, IL St. Peter Church.
Jarnot, Clement *o.f.m.conv.* '65 (BAL) [M] Ellicott City, MD Order of Friars Minor Conventual.
Jarnot, Clement *o.f.m.conv.* '65 (NOR) [3] Middletown, CT St. Mary of Czestochowa Church.
Jaros, Joseph P. (TOL) Retired.
Jarosch, Eugene H. *s.a.c.* '51 (MIL) [P] Milwaukee, WI Pallotti House.
Jarosewic, Daniel F. '71 (CHI) [1] Oak Lawn, IL St. Catherine of Alexandria Church.
Jarosz, Joseph B. '62 (PH) [146] Philadelphia, PA St. Stanislaus Church.
Jarosz, Peter '89 (JOL) Roselle, IL St. Walter Church.
Jarosz, Stanley '65 (MET) Helmetta, NJ Holy Trinity Church.
Jaroszeski, Paul A. '76 (STP) [18] St. Paul, MN St. Cecilia Church.
Jarreau, Martin V. *s.j.* '36 (NO) [F] New Orleans, LA Jesuit High School.
Jarreau, Martin V. *s.j.* '49 (NO) [S] New Orleans, LA Jesuit Seminary and Mission Fund.
Jarreau, Niel J. *s.j.* '56 (FWT) [J] Lake Dallas, TX Montserrat Jesuit Retreat House.
Jarrell, Stephen '73 (IND) Greenwood, IN SS. Francis and Clare of Assisi Church.
Jarret, Peter A. *c.s.c.* '92 (FTW) Granger, IN St. Pius X Church; [J] South Bend, IN Congregation of Holy Cross Indiana Province Provincial House.
Jarumbo, James J. '66 (MIL) [3] Sheboygan, WI St. Dominic Church.
Jarvais, Msgr. Walter G. '30 (NEW) Retired; [N] Rutherford, NJ St. John Vianney Residence for Priests.
Jarvis, Edward A. *s.j.* '54 (PH) [82] Philadelphia, PA Old St. Joseph's Church.
Jarzabek, Mieczyslaw '76 (MET) Bound Brook, NJ St. Mary of Czestochowa Church.
Jarzombek, Casey '60 (VIC) Palacios, TX St. Anthony's Church.
Jarzombek, Dennis A. '79 (SAT) [56] San Antonio, TX St. Mary Magdalen Church.
Jarzynski, Edward '48 (CHI) [M] Niles, IL St. Benedict Home for the Aged.
Jarzynski, Edward M. '48 (CHI) Retired.
Jasaitis, Raymond J. '62 (PAT) Retired; [P] Chester, NJ Nazareth Village.
Jasany, Robert J. '79 (CLV) [1] Lakewood, OH St. Clement Church.
Jasinski, Msgr. Anthony J. '49 (BUF) [9] Cheektowaga, NY St. Philip the Apostle Church; Retired.
Jasinski, John B. (SB) Military Chaplains.
Jasinski, Kazimierz '78 (DET) [H] Livonia, MI St. Mary Hospital.
Jasinski, Paul F. *c.s.v.* '46 (JOL) Goodrich, IL Sacred Heart Church.
Jasinski, Raymond J. (CHI) Retired.
Jaskula, Edward J. *c.r.* '55 (CHI) [D] Chicago, IL Gordon Technical High School.
Jaskulski, Bronislaus *o.f.m.* '46 (GRY) [J] Cedar Lake, IN Our Lady of Lourdes Friary.
Jaskulski, George *o.f.m.* '55 (CLV) [P] Cleveland, OH St. Stanislaus Friary; [Q] Cleveland, OH Marymount Congregational Home.
Jasper, Frank *o.f.m.* '73 (IND) [12] Indianapolis, IN Sacred Heart of Jesus Church.
Jasper, Louis H. '51 (COV) Retired.
Jaspers, J. Dennis '66 (CIN) [3] Cincinnati, OH All Saints Church.
Jaspers, Louis *c.i.c.m.* '52 (SAT) [36] San Antonio, TX St. Gabriel Church.
Jasso, Stephen *t.o.r.* '65 (FWT) [2] Fort Worth, TX All Saints Church.
Jastrab, David J. '75 (PIT) Perrysville, PA St. Teresa of Avila Church.
Jaszovsky, Joseph '31 (SFR) Retired; [K] San Francisco, CA Home for the Aged of the Little Sisters of the Poor.
Jatsiv, Miroslaw '94 (STF) West Islip, NY Holy Family Church.
Jaume, John *c.r.* '66 (NY) Plattekill, NY Our Lady of Fatima Church.
Jautz, Martin L. '44 (MIL) Retired.
Java, Michael '73 (LA) Baldwin Park, CA St. John the Baptist Church.
Javor, Egon J. *o.s.b.* '41 (SFR) San Francisco, CA Knights of Malta; [N] Portola Valley, CA Woodside Priory.
Jawidzik, Edward M. '81 (TR) Belmar, NJ St. Rose Church.
Jaworowski, Msgr. Anthony E. '44 (PH) [2] Philadelphia, PA St. Adalbert Church; Swedesburg, PA Sacred Heart Church; Retired.
Jaworowski, Leon E. '43 (PH) Retired.
Jayachandra, Hermanagild '68 (DEN) [3] Boulder, CO St. Martin de Porres Church.
Jayaraj, M. Jones '83 (SCR) [17] Scranton, PA St. Mary of the Assumption Church.
Jayme, Eduardo *o.f.m.* '81 (CC) Hebbronville, TX Our Lady of Guadalupe Church.
Jazbec, Stanley '44 (SB) Retired.
Jazmines, Vicente '79 (OG) Gouverneur, NY St. James Church.
Jazowski, John F. '48 (BGP) Retired; [U] North Stamford, CT Villa Maria Retreat House.
Jazwiecki, John *s.m.* (SP) [7] Tampa, FL Our Lady of Perpetual Help Church.
Jean, Agapit H., Jr. '95 (MAN) Exeter, NH St. Michael Church.
Jean, Franky '93 (MIA) [10] Miami, FL Notre Dame d'Haiti Church.
Jean, Lesly '83 (MIA) [10] Miami, FL Notre Dame d'Haiti Church.
Jean, Raymond J. '57 (NOR) Absent on Leave.
Jeanfreau, James J., Jr. '92 (NO) [5] Metairie, LA St. Catherine of Siena Church.
Jeannot, Leandre '70 (BO) [41] Boston, MA St. Leo Church; [49] Boston, MA St. Matthew Church.
Jecewiz, Jerome T. '75 (BRK) [60] Brooklyn, NY Holy Spirit Church.
Jedrychowski, Janus '95 (STF) Rochester, NY St. Josaphat Church.
Jedrzejewski, Richard '74 (BUF) [10] Buffalo, NY Assumption Church.
Jeffers, Brian E. '92 (ROC) Geneva, NY St. Stephen Church.
Jeffers, Robert A. '54 (NY) [162] Bronx, NY St. Margaret Mary Church; Bronx, NY Bronx-Lebanon Hospital Center.
Jeffers, Msgr. Vincent W. '31 (NY) Retired; [E] White Plains, NY Archbishop Stepinac High School.
Jeffrey, C. James '59 (FAR) Cavalier, ND St. Bridget's Church.
Jeffrey, Donald *m.s.* '64 (MAN) West Lebanon, NH Holy Redeemer Church.
Jeffrey, George A. '65 (SCR) [20] Wilkes-Barre, PA St. Therese's Church.
Jeffries, Brian E. '73 (HRT) Seymour, CT St. Augustine's Church.
Jelenek, Matthew M. '96 (NY) Beacon, NY St. John Evangelist Church.
Jelinek, John P. *s.j.* '47 (OM) [K] Omaha, NE Jesuit Community At Creighton University.
Jelly, Frederick M. *o.p.* '56 (BAL) [A] Emmitsburg, MD Mount St. Mary's Seminary.
Jendersyk, Mark '85 (JOL) Coal City, IL Assumption Church.
Jendrek, Michael J. '87 (BAL) [42] Baltimore, MD Immaculate Heart of Mary Church.
Jendzura, John M. '47 (PIT) [Q] Bethel Park, PA Holy Ghost Animation Center.
Jenemann, Albert H. *s.j.* '60 (PH) [C] Philadelphia, PA St. Joseph's University; [AA] Philadelphia, PA Jesuit Community at St. Joseph's University.
Jenik, Msgr. John J. '70 (NY) [176] Bronx, NY Our Lady of Refuge Church.
Jenkins, Alan *s.v.d.* '73 (FgM) Society of the Divine Word Foreign Missions.
Jenkins, Floyd A. *s.j.* '48 (LA) [C] Los Angeles, CA Loyola Marymount University.
Jenkins, J. Michael '79 (SFD) Collinsville, IL SS. Peter and Paul Church.
Jenkins, J. Wayne '72 (L) [35] Louisville, KY Holy Spirit Church; [36] Louisville, KY Holy Trinity Church.
Jenkins, John I. *c.s.c.* (FTW) [J] Notre Dame, IN Holy Cross Community, Corby Hall, University of Notre Dame.
Jenkins, John I. *c.s.c.* '83 (FTW) [B] Notre Dame, IN University of Notre Dame Du Lac.
Jenkins, John M. '60 (CLV) [14] Akron, OH St. Paul Church.
Jenkins, Joseph A. '86 (WDC) Upper Marlboro, MD Saint Mary of the Assumption Church.
Jenkins, Kenneth '80 (SB) Yucaipa, CA St. Frances Xavier Cabrini Church.
Jenkins, Ronnie '89 (AUS) [17] Austin, TX St. Louis Church.
Jenkins, Wayne *s.c.j.* '77 (MIL) [P] Hales Corners, WI Sacred Heart Monastery.
Jenkinson, William R. '57 (PRO) Barrington, RI St. Luke Church.
Jenko, Aloysius '35 (NY) Retired.
Jenks, Francis C. '70 (CHI) [1] Oak Park, IL Ascension Church.
Jenky, Daniel R. *c.s.c.* '74 (FTW) [B] Notre Dame, IN University of Notre Dame Du Lac; [J] Notre Dame, IN Holy Cross Community, Corby Hall, University of Notre Dame.
Jenne, Walter H. '70 (CLV) [15] Cleveland, OH St. Catherine Church; Brecksville, OH St. Basil the Great Church.
Jenner, David C. '66 (MAR) Gwinn, MI St. Anthony Church.
Jenner, James S. *o.p.* '51 (SFR) [N] San Francisco, CA St. Dominic Priory.
Jennett, Michael '74 (LA) Ventura, CA Our Lady of the Assumption Church.
Jenniges, Leonard J. '48 (NU) Retired.
Jenniges, Leonard J. '48 (STP) Retired.
Jennings, Bernard J. '41 (LA) Altadena, CA St. Elizabeth of Hungary Church; Retired.
Jennings, Francis *c.ss.r.* '48 (ORL) Retired.
Jennings, Henry J. '62 (BO) [6] Somerville, MA Patronage of St. Joseph Church.
Jennings, John A. '50 (SEA) Retired; [N] Seattle, WA St. Joseph's Residence.
Jennings, John J. '49 (BO) [44] Boston, MA St. Mark Church; Retired; [U] Boston, MA St. Joseph Nursing Care Center.
Jennings, John P. '41 (CIN) Retired.
Jennings, Msgr. Joseph '43 (MOB) Retired.
Jennings, Kenneth E. '93 (NEW) [2] Jersey City, NJ St. Aloysius Church.
Jennings, Michael T. '69 (KNX) Rogersville, TN St. Henry Church.
Jennings, Mike '69 (KNX) Sneedville, TN St. James the Apostle Church.
Jennings, Oliver '72 (CHI) [104] Chicago, IL St. John de la Salle Church.
Jennings, Paul F., Jr. '74 (WIL) Easton, MD SS. Peter and Paul Church.
Jennings, Thomas J. '69 (WIN) Owatonna, MN Sacred Heart Church.
Jennings, Tommie '88 (SD) Military Chaplains.
Jennings, William E. '40 (WIL) Retired.
Jenniskens, Thomas J. *s.j.* '56 (LAF) [J] Grand Coteau, LA Jesuit Spirituality Center.
Jennrich, Michael J. *o.f.m.* '87 (NO) [P] New Orleans, LA Franciscan Fraternity.
Jensen, Benjamin E. '88 (SC) Charter Oak, IA St. Boniface Church; Dow City, IA St. Mary's Church.
Jensen, Daniel P. *m.m.* '62 (NY) [DD] Maryknoll, NY Maryknoll Fathers and Brothers.
Jensen, John A. *m.m.* '44 (FgM) Maryknoll Foreign Missions.
Jensen, Joseph *o.s.b.* '54 (WDC) [C] Washington, DC Catholic University of America, The; [M] Washington, DC St. Anselm's Abbey; [V] Washington, DC Catholic Biblical Association.
Jensen, Larry '88 (SAM) Fayetteville, NC Archangel Michael Church.
Jenson, Glen T. '95 (STP) Cleveland, MN Church of the Nativity of the Blessed Virgin Mary; Marysburg, MN Immaculate Conception Church; Montgomery, MN Holy Redeemer Church.
Jeon, Simon '92 (PHX) [5] Scottsdale, AZ St. Daniel the Prophet Church.
Jeong, John Hee-Wan (SAC) [15] Sacramento, CA St. Jeong-Hae Elizabeth Church.
Jerabeck, Joseph F. '48 (COL) Retired.
Jerabek, Joseph F. '48 (COL) [40] Columbus, OH St. Timothy Church.
Jerek, John M. '88 (Y) Kent, OH Immaculate Heart of Mary Church; [O] Kent, OH Kent State University Newman Center.
Jerge, Joseph W. '51 (E) Retired.
Jerge, Lawrence A. *c.s.c.* '68 (FR) [A] North Easton, MA Holy Cross Fathers Religious.
Jernejcic, Timothy '92 (SB) [2] Corona, CA St. Edward Church.
Jerome, Albert L. '59 (BEL) Nashville, IL St. Ann Church.
Jerome, Louis '88 (NY) Yorktown Heights, NY St. Patrick Church.
Jerome, Marc-Arthur '90 (PRO) [17] Providence, RI Holy Name of Jesus Church.
Jerome, Patrick '91 (KCK) Bonner Springs, KS Sacred Heart Church.
Jerse, William M. '80 (CLV) [4] Euclid, OH St. Paul Church.
Jerus, Manuel '73 (AGN) Dededo, GU Santa Barbara Church.
Jeruzal, Joseph *o.f.m.cap.* '88 (LC) Halder, WI St. Patrick Church.
Jeruzal, Joseph B. *o.f.m.cap.* '88 (LC) Cassel, WI Sacred Heart Church; Marathon City, WI Nativity of the Blessed Virgin Mary Church.
Jervis, Paul W. '83 (BRK) [225] Queens, NY St. Paul the Apostle Church.
Jeselnick, Stephen '77 (E) On Duty Outside Diocese.
Jeselnick, Stephen E. '77 (WIL) Perry Point, MD Veterans Admin.
Jesiolowski, Sylvester E. '41 (PEO) Retired.
Jesionowski, Richard A. '68 (BUF) Sardinia, NY St. Jude Church.

Jeske, Richard M. *o.f.m.* '59 (SFD) Quincy, IL Illinois Veterans' Home; [B] Quincy, IL Quincy University.
Jesselli, Kenneth A. '84 (NY) [143] Bronx, NY St. Francis Xavier Church.
Jette, Donald *s.s.s.* '53 (CLV) Highland Heights, OH St. Paschal Baylon Church.
Jette, Donald J. *s.s.s.* '53 (CLV) [P] Cleveland, OH Blessed Sacrament Community.
Jette, Donald J. *s.s.s.* '53 (GAL) [25] Houston, TX Corpus Christi Church.
Jette, Mark R. '72 (HRT) [2] Meriden, CT St. Joseph Church; [4] Meriden, CT St. Mary Church.
Jeub, Richard H. '66 (STP) Special Assignment.
Jewison, Harry P. '54 (WIN) Retired.
Jewitt, Bernard C. '59 (TLS) [4] Tulsa, OK St. Bernard of Clairvaux Church.
Jezak, Thomas M. '66 (ALX) [2] Alexandria, LA Our Lady of Prompt Succor Chruch; Glenmora, LA St. Louis Church.
Jezeski, Henry '51 (CLV) Retired.
Jezierski, Zbigniew J. '61 (CAM) Lindenwold, NJ St. Lawrence's Church.
Jezowski, Anthony C. '74 (BO) Awaiting Assignment.
Jicha, John '95 (BAL) Cockeysville, MD St. Joseph Church.
Jillisky, William F. '56 (ALB) Menands, NY St. Joan of Arc Church.
Jimenez, Adrian '87 (ARE) [1] Camuy, PR St. Joseph Church.
Jimenez, Msgr. Armando '46 (WDC) Retired; [L] Washington, DC Cardinal O'Boyle Residence for Priests.
Jimenez, David '96 (YAK) Wenatchee, WA St. Joseph's Church.
Jimenez, Edgar '75 (FRS) [1] Fresno, CA St. John Cathedral.
Jimenez, Eduardo '82 (MIA) [12] Miami, FL Our Lady of the Holy Rosary Church.
Jimenez, Felix *sch.p.* '26 (NY) [DD] New York, NY Calasanzian Fathers (Piarists).
Jimenez, Felix '70 (NY) [12] New York, NY Annunciation Church.
Jimenez, Francisco '65 (SJN) [2] Guaynabo, PR El Buen Pastor Church.
Jimenez, Francisco '88 (ARE) Vega-Alta, PR Perpetuo Socorro Church.
Jimenez, Jorge '73 (LUB) [2] Lubbock, TX Our Lady of Grace Church.
Jimenez, Jose Luis *o.a.r.* '59 (LA) [8] Los Angeles, CA Cristo Rey Church.
Jimenez, Jose Pio *c.m.* '68 (FgM) Vincentian Foreign Missions.
Jimenez, Rafael '74 (DET) [71] Detroit, MI St. Stephen-Mary Mother of the Church.
Jiminez, P. Victorino (ARE) On Duty Outside the Diocese.
Jindra, Frank E. '84 (OM) Spencer, NE St. Mary Church.
Jirik, Charles C. '35 (STP) Retired.
Jiru, Richard A. '65 (MAD) Cuba City, WI St. Rose of Lima Church.
Joaquin, M. Joseph '81 (BGP) Georgetown, CT Sacred Heart Church.
Jobst, Frank *o.m.i.* '72 (FgM) Oblates Foreign Missions.
Jocco, Joseph P. *o.s.f.s.* '84 (WDC) [B] Washington, DC Oblates of St. Francis de Sales.
Jocco, Joseph P. *o.s.f.s.* '84 (WIL) [I] Wilmington, DE Oblates of St. Francis De Sales.
Jocson, Salvador '57 (SFR) On Duty Outside the Archdiocese.
Jocys, Leonard '51 (GAY) Mackinaw City, MI St. Anthony of Padua Church; Riggsville, MI Sacred Heart Church.
Joda, Robert J. *s.j.* '58 (MIL) [P] Milwaukee, WI Jesuit Community at Marquette University.
Joeger, Louis '73 (DUB) [F] Epworth, IA Seton Catholic Elementary School.
Joensen, William '89 (DUB) Graduate Studies.
Joerger, Jacob *o.p.* '48 (CHI) [N] River Forest, IL St. Thomas Aquinas Priory.
Joerger, Jacob *o.p.* '48 (RCK) [N] St. Charles, IL Queen of Americas Guild.
Joerger, Robert *c.p.* '77 (FgM) Passionist Foreign Missions.
Joerger, Robert *c.p.* '77 (MET) [H] South River, NJ Passionist Provincial Office.
Joffe, William I. '57 (RCK) On Disability Leave.
Johanek, John '43 (GB) Retired.
Johannes, Nicholas A. '70 (GB) Maple Grove, WI St. Patrick Church.
John, Andrew Peter '64 (LAF) Lawtell, LA Holy Family Church; Mallet, LA St. Ann Church.
John, Francis Reginald (NY) [129] Bronx, NY St. Anthony of Padua Church.
John, Reginaldo '60 (NY) City, NY Bronx House of Detention.
John, Richard *o.s.c.* '46 (SCL) Milaca, MN St. Mary's Church.
John, Richard T. *o.s.c.* '41 (SCL) [I] Onamia, MN Crosier Monastery.
John, T. A. *s.j.* '89 (NY) [DD] New York, NY "America;" Residence and publication office of the America Press.
Johns, Thomas W. '78 (CLV) Mentor, OH St. John Vianney Church.
Johnson, Andrew *o.c.s.o.* '91 (WOR) [N] Spencer, MA St. Joseph's Abbey.
Johnson, Arte *s.a.* (NY) [HH] Barryville, NY New Hope Manor.
Johnson, Arte *s.p.* '77 (NY) [O] Barryville, NY New Hope Manor.
Johnson, Arthur M. *s.a.* '77 (OG) [E] Saranac Lake, NY St. Joseph's Rehabilitation Center, Inc.; [F] Saranac Lake, NY Atonement Friars.
Johnson, Bede L. *c.j.* '39 (LA) [B] Santa Maria, CA St. Joseph Seminary (Josephite Fathers' Novitiate).
Johnson, Bernard M. *o.praem.* '81 (ORG) [H] Silverado, CA Norbertine Fathers of Orange Inc.
Johnson, Brian *c.ss.r.* '86 (OM) [19] Omaha, NE Holy Name Church.
Johnson, Brian Anthony '97 (OWN) [1] Paducah, KY St. Francis de Sales Church; [2] Paducah, KY Rosary Chapel Church.
Johnson, Carl '77 (LEX) Special Assignment.
Johnson, Carl D. '78 (NY) Monroe, NY Sacred Heart Church.
Johnson, Msgr. Charles B. '60 (HRT) [1] West Hartford, CT St. Brigid's Church; Special and other (Arch)Diocesan Assignment.
Johnson, Christopher *o.p.* '60 (NY) [22] New York, NY St. Catherine of Siena Church; [DD] New York, NY St. Catherine of Siena Priory; [HH] New York, NY Dominican Shrine of St. Jude, Inc.
Johnson, Daniel '54 (ORG) [2] Huntington Beach, CA St. Mary's by the Sea Church.
Johnson, Daniel E. '51 (HRT) Wallingford, CT Resurrection Church.
Johnson, Dave '89 (OWN) Leitchfield, KY St. Joseph's Church; Sunfish, KY St. John the Evangelist Church.
Johnson, David *o.f.m.* '84 (FRS) [G] Three Rivers, CA St. Anthony's Retreat House.
Johnson, David R. '80 (BR) Denham Springs, LA Immaculate Conception Church.
Johnson, David R. '80 (PIT) On Duty Outside the Diocese.
Johnson, David W. *s.j.* '69 (WDC) [C] Washington, DC Catholic University of America, The.
Johnson, Donald '55 (NY) Manhattan, NY Columbia Presbyterian Medical Center.
Johnson, Douglas '83 (SFS) On Leave of Absence.
Johnson, Earl *s.j.* '58 (SHP) [1] Shreveport, LA St. John Berchmans Cathedral.
Johnson, Edward A. '55 (PRO) Retired.
Johnson, Edward J. '58 (LA) [66] Los Angeles, CA St. Gregory Nazianzen Church.
Johnson, Msgr. Edwin '42 (DAL) Retired.
Johnson, Edwin '62 (LA) [F] Chatsworth, CA Chaminade College Preparatory.
Johnson, Francis '76 (BUF) Grand Island, NY St. Stephen Church.
Johnson, Francis D. *s.j.* '53 (CIN) [M] Cincinnati, OH Jesuit Community at Xavier Unversity.
Johnson, Francis P. '60 (HRT) [2] West Hartford, CT St. Helena Church.
Johnson, Msgr. Gregory '47 (BLX) Retired.
Johnson, H. Thomas '78 (DET) Shelby Twp., MI St. Kieran Church.
Johnson, Harold J. '49 (BO) Retired.
Johnson, Henry J. '57 (LA) Retired.
Johnson, Howard '60 (JKS) On Duty Outside the Diocese.
Johnson, Howard '60 (WDC) [B] Washington, DC St. Joseph's Seminary.
Johnson, Howard J. '54 (MIL) Retired.
Johnson, J. Raymond '65 (NY) [DD] New York, NY Jesuit Community at Fordham University; [DD] New York, NY Jesuit Provincial's Office.
Johnson, Jacob *c.m.* '47 (FgM) Vincentian Foreign Missions.
Johnson, Msgr. James '42 (NEW) Ridgefield, NJ St. Matthew's Church; Retired.
Johnson, James '68 (LA) [B] Santa Ynez, CA San Lorenzo Novitiate and Seminary.
Johnson, James '80 (SP) [R] St. Petersburg, FL Our Lady of Good Counsel Camp.
Johnson, James B. '80 (SP) Inverness, FL Our Lady of Fatima Church.
Johnson, James R. *s.p.* '60 (Y) Hubbard, OH St. Patrick's Church.
Johnson, Jef '86 (JUN) [2] Juneau, AK St. Paul The Apostle Church.
Johnson, Jeff '92 (MAR) Sugar Island, MI Sacred Heart Church.
Johnson, Jeff G. '92 (MAR) Brimley, MI St. Francis Xavier Church; Bay Mills, MI Blessed Kateri Tekakwitha Church; Sault Sainte Marie, MI St. Isaac Jogues Church.
Johnson, Jeffrey *s.o.l.t.* '91 (CC) [H] Robstown, TX Society of Our Lady of the Most Holy Trinity.
Johnson, Jerome A. '86 (MET) [5] New Brunswick, NJ Sacred Heart Church.
Johnson, John A. '88 (GR) [4] Muskegon, MI St. Joseph's Church; [5] Muskegon, MI St. Mary's Church.
Johnson, Msgr. John G. '74 (COL) [37] Columbus, OH St. Peter Church.
Johnson, John J. '48 (SPR) West Springfield, MA Immaculate Conception Church; [G] Springfield, MA Marriage Counseling Service.
Johnson, John J. '66 (STL) [40] St. Louis, MO St. John the Apostle and Evangelist Church; Ste. Genevieve, MO Ste. Genevieve's Church.
Johnson, John R. '72 (SAG) Midland, MI Blessed Sacrament Church.
Johnson, Msgr. Joseph I. '32 (SPR) [8] Pittsfield, MA St. Mark's Church; Retired.
Johnson, Joseph P. *s.j.* '60 (LSC) Artesia, NM St. Anthony Church.
Johnson, Kevin '87 (PT) [2] Tallahassee, FL Blessed Sacrament Church.
Johnson, L. Bede *c.j.* '39 (LA) Santa Maria, CA St. Louis de Montfort Church.
Johnson, Lawrence C. *o.praem.* '94 (ORG) [H] Silverado, CA Norbertine Fathers of Orange Inc.
Johnson, Lawrence M. '83 (BAL) Special Assignment; [J] Timonium, MD Stella Maris Operating Corporation.
Johnson, Lawrence P. '76 (DUL) On Duty Outside the Diocese.
Johnson, Lawrence R. '75 (STP) Hassan Township, MN St. Walburga Church; Rogers, MN St. Martin Church.
Johnson, Lyle M. '76 (LIN) On Duty Outside the Diocese.
Johnson, Malcolm D. *c.s.c.* '59 (FgM) Holy Cross Foreign Missions.
Johnson, Malcolm D. *c.s.c.* '59 (FTW) [J] South Bend, IN Congregation of Holy Cross Indiana Province Provincial House.
Johnson, O. Kenneth '92 (FgM) Provinces.
Johnson, O. Kenneth *s.j.* '92 (NO) [P] New Orleans, LA Jesuit Provincial Office.
Johnson, Oliver F. '62 (AUS) [12] Austin, TX St. Catherine of Siena Church.
Johnson, Patrick *c.s.p.* '74 (AUS) [11] Austin, TX St. Austin's Church; Austin, TX State School.
Johnson, Paul *o.p.* '59 (SFE) [26] Albuquerque, NM St. John the Apostle Church.
Johnson, Paul J. *o.p.* '59 (SFE) [29] Albuquerque, NM St. Thomas Aquinas University Parish.
Johnson, Paul T. '63 (GR) Retired.
Johnson, Peter '91 (CHY) Greybull, WY Sacred Heart Church; Lovell, WY St. Joseph's Church.
Johnson, Philip L. '64 (FWT) [6] Arlington, TX St. Vincent de Paul Church.
Johnson, Richard *c.p.* '51 (CHI) [N] Chicago, IL Passionist Provincial Office.
Johnson, Msgr. Richard E. '60 (DAL) [22] Dallas, TX St. Patrick Church.
Johnson, Richard G. (BO) Retired.
Johnson, Richard G. '47 (BO) [3] Gloucester, MA St. Peter Church.
Johnson, Msgr. Robert (DAL) [P] Commerce, TX Apostleship of Prayer.
Johnson, Robert *s.v.d.* '92 (FgM) Society of the Divine Word Foreign Missions.
Johnson, Robert E. '76 (STP) Bloomington, MN Nativity of the Blessed Virgin Mary Church.
Johnson, Robert K. '90 (WOR) [1] Worcester, MA St. Paul's Cathedral.
Johnson, Stephen D. '72 (WOR) Athol, MA Our Lady Immaculate Church.
Johnson, Terrence M. '94 (CHI) Midlothian, IL St. Christopher Church.
Johnson, Tim '91 (SC) [B] Granville, IA Spalding Catholic High School.
Johnson, Timothy *o.carm.* '83 (PMB) [5] Boca Raton, FL St. Jude Church.
Johnson, Timothy K. '71 (OAK) [12] Oakland, CA St. Leo's Church.
Johnson, Walter (SJ) San Jose, CA St. Louise Hospital; [H] Morgan Hill, CA O'Connor Hospital dba Saint Louise Hospital & Health Center.
Johnson, Walter W. '53 (SJ) [M] Los Altos, CA Maryknoll.
Johnson, William J. '50 (CLV) Newbury, OH St. Helen Church; Retired.
Johnson, William T. *s.j.* '91 (MIL) [G] Milwaukee, WI Nativity Jesuit Middle School, Inc.; [P] Milwaukee, WI Jesuit Community at Marquette University.
Johnston, Donald '55 (NY) [95] New York, NY Our Lady Queen of Martyrs Church.
Johnston, Henry P. '76 (STO) Angels Camp, CA St. Patrick Church.
Johnston, J. Vann, Jr. *j.c.l.* '90 (KNX) [5] Knoxville, TN Holy Ghost Church.
Johnston, Jeffrey W. '86 (RVC) Hicksville, NY Holy Family Church.
Johnston, John F. '64 (BRK) Released from Diocesan Assignment.
Johnston, John F. '64 (NEW) [D] Summit, NJ The Oratory Catholic Preparatory School.
Johnston, Joseph A. *s.j.* '52 (FgM) Provinces.
Johnston, Kenneth J. '68 (CAM) Deptford, NJ St. John

Vianney Church; [B] Gloucester, NJ Gloucester Catholic High School.
Johnston, Michael O. '70 (NSH) [6] Nashville, TN St. Henry Church.
Johnston, Michael P. '96 (P) Woodburn, OR St. Luke Church.
Johnston, Richard *s.c.j.* '58 (GAL) [48] Houston, TX St. Matthew the Evangelist Church.
Johnston, Richard *s.c.j.* '58 (MIL) [P] Hales Corners, WI Priests of the Sacred Heart.
Johnston, Robert F. '62 (STL) Grantwood, MO Our Lady of Providence Church.
Johnston, Robert F. '71 (SAT) Retired.
Johnston, Thomas J. *o.p.* '86 (DET) [2] St. Clair Shores, MI St. Gertrude Church.
Jolicoeur, Fabian A. *o.praem.* '39 (GB) [I] De Pere, WI St. Norbert Abbey.
Jollet, Robert *m.s.c.* '49 (OG) Retired; [A] Ogdensburg, NY Wadhams Hall.
Jolley, Msgr. Edward W. '38 (BRK) Retired; [U] Douglaston, NY Bishop Mugavero Residence.
Joly, Henry L. (ALT) Retired.
Joly, Michael D. '94 (PAT) [1] Clifton, NJ Sacred Heart Church.
Jonaitis, Peter '44 (ALB) Retired.
Jonas, Lawrence A. *s.j.* '59 (MIL) [P] Milwaukee, WI Jesuit Provincial Office, Wisconsin Province.
Jonas, Lawrence A. *s.j.* '59 (SFS) Canton, SD St. Dominic Church.
Joncas, Jan Michael '69 (STP) [C] St. Paul, MN University of St. Thomas.
Jonczyk, Dariusz G. '97 (PRO) Coventry, RI SS. John and Paul Church.
Jones, Augustine *o.s.b.* '53 (RCK) [H] Aurora, IL Marmion Abbey-St. Augustine's Abbey.
Jones, Bernard P. '45 (COL) Retired.
Jones, Bob *c.m.* '69 (LA) [53] Los Angeles, CA St. Camillus De Lellis Church.
Jones, C. Gregory *c.s.v.* '96 (CHI) [210] Chicago, IL St. Viator Church.
Jones, Carleton Parker '87 (HRT) [14] New Haven, CT St. Mary's Priory Church.
Jones, Charles '45 (DEN) Retired.
Jones, Charles F. '63 (KC) [4] Independence, MO St. Mary's Church.
Jones, Clarence *c.o.* '94 (SEA) [1] Vancouver, WA Our Lady of Lourdes Church; [Q] Vancouver, WA Vancouver Oratorian Community.
Jones, Clarence Edward *c.o.* '94 (CHR) [D] Rock Hill, SC Oratory of St. Philip Neri, Congregation of the Oratory of Pontifical Rite.
Jones, Daniel J. '97 (DET) Awaiting Assignment.
Jones, David A. '89 (CHI) [10] Chicago, IL St. Ambrose Church.
Jones, David J. *m.m.* '62 (NY) [DD] Maryknoll, NY Maryknoll Fathers and Brothers.
Jones, Dunstan *o.f.m.cap.* '61 (FgM) Capuchin Foreign Missions.
Jones, Frank W. '67 (GAL) Magnolia, TX St. Matthias the Apostle Church.
Jones, Herbert *o.carm.* '60 (FgM) Carmelite Foreign Missions.
Jones, Herbert *o.carm.* '60 (JOL) [J] Darien, IL Carmelite Provincial Office.
Jones, Herbert *o.f.m.* '77 (SAT) [70] San Antonio, TX San Jose y San Miguel Church; [B] San Antonio, TX Franciscan Formation Program in San Jose Friary (Casa Juan Diego).
Jones, J. Overton '64 (CAM) [3] Atlantic City, NJ St. Monica's Church.
Jones, Jack B. (GAL) [N] Houston, TX Pope John XXIII Priest Residence.
Jones, James *o.s.b.* '48 (KC) [A] Conception, MO Conception Seminary College.
Jones, Msgr. James '57 (R) Retired.
Jones, James *o.f.m.* '76 (SP) [O] St. Petersburg, FL St. Anthony Friary.
Jones, James *o.f.m.cap.* '77 (NY) [DD] White Plains, NY St. Conrad Friary.
Jones, James W. '69 (COL) [41] Columbus, OH Sacred Heart Church.
Jones, Jim *o.f.m.* '76 (SP) [K] St. Petersburg, FL St. Anthony's Hospital, Inc.
Jones, Msgr. John B. '48 (GAL) Retired.
Jones, John E. '59 (L) On Special Assignment.
Jones, John L. '45 (ALB) [16] Albany, NY St. Teresa of Avila Church; Retired.
Jones, Joseph R. *c.p.* '65 (R) Greenville, NC St. Peter's Church.
Jones, Kenneth '69 (NEW) Plainfield, NJ St. Mary Church.
Jones, Mark R. '92 (MIL) Brookfield, WI St. Dominic Church.
Jones, Martin J. '94 (NOR) New London, CT St. Joseph Church.
Jones, Michael K. '92 (BGP) [7] Fairfield, CT St. Thomas Aquinas Church.
Jones, Michael T. '85 (WDC) Kensington, MD Holy Redeemer Church; Special Ministries; [E] Wheaton, MD Good Counsel High School.
Jones, Neil G. *m.s.* '72 (ATL) Canton, GA Our Lady of LaSalette Church.
Jones, Patrick F. '56 (PIT) Retired.
Jones, R. Donald (PIT) Elizabeth, PA St. Michael Church.
Jones, Raymond '36 (DET) Retired.
Jones, Raymond '36 (VEN) Lake Placid, FL St. James Church; Lake Placid, FL St. James Church.
Jones, Raymond A. *s.v.d.* '67 (LKC) [3] Lake Charles, LA Sacred Heart of Jesus Church.
Jones, Msgr. Raymond N. '59 (DEN) [1] Denver, CO Cathedral of the Immaculate Conception.
Jones, Richard S. '88 (PIT) Allegheny County, PA Mercy Health System of Pittsburgh.
Jones, Richard T. *s.j.* '46 (RC) St. Francis, SD Rosebud Reservation Church.
Jones, Rick L. (SPC) [I] Webb City, MO Newman Club, Missouri Southern College.
Jones, Rick L. '90 (SPC) Webb City, MO Sacred Heart Church.
Jones, Robert *s.v.d.* '68 (BO) [W] Duxbury, MA Society of the Divine Word.
Jones, Robert C. *c.ss.r.* '78 (BAL) [93] Baltimore, MD St. Ursula Church.
Jones, Robert J. '69 (LA) [R] Los Angeles, CA Amat House; [X] Montebello, CA DePaul Center.
Jones, Robert J. *s.j.* '70 (P) [L] Portland, OR Colombiere Community.
Jones, Robert M. '68 (BO) [Y] Duxbury, MA Miramar Retreat Center.
Jones, Robert W. '92 (RCK) St. Charles, IL St. John Neumann Church.
Jones, Ronald A. '73 (RCK) Special Assignment.
Jones, Thomas *o.f.m.* '59 (NY) Narrowsburg, NY St. Francis Xavier Church.
Jones, Thomas '70 (RVC) Port Jefferson, NY Mather Memorial Hospital; Port Jefferson, NY St. Charles Hospital, Port Jefferson, New York.
Jones, Thomas J. *c.s.c.* '72 (FTW) [6] South Bend, IN Christ the King Church.
Jones, Thomas W. *c.s.p.* '82 (NY) [DD] Jamaica Estates, NY Paulist Fathers Generalate.
Jones, Tony '89 (OWN) Brown's Valley, KY St. Anthony Church; [B] Owensboro, KY Owensboro Catholic High School.
Jones, W. Thomas *s.m.* '47 (P) Jordan, OR Our Lady of Lourdes Church.
Jones, Msgr. William E. '60 (ALN) [4] Pottsville, PA St. Patrick Church.
Jones, Msgr. William H. '47 (DEN) Retired.
Jones, William P. '69 (ALN) Retired; [J] Bethlehem, PA Holy Family Villa.
Jones, William R. '67 (SY) [8] Syracuse, NY Our Lady of Solace Church.
Jonientz, Bernard '63 (SEA) Unassigned.
Jooji, Innocent '85 (PIT) South Park Township, PA Nativity Church.
Joos, Justin *o.f.m.cap.* '36 (NY) [B] Beacon, NY St. Lawrence of Brindisi Friary.
Joppe, Stan N. *o.praem.* '55 (SFE) [J] Albuquerque, NM Santa Maria de la Vid Priory.
Joppe, Stanislaus N. *o.praem* '55 (GB) [I] De Pere, WI St. Norbert Abbey.
Jordan, Collins P. '85 (RC) Retired.
Jordan, Msgr. Edward F. '62 (AUS) [21] Austin, TX St. Theresa Church.
Jordan, Francis W. '50 (MIL) Retired.
Jordan, Msgr. Harold F. '49 (STA) [1] St. Augustine, FL Cathedral of St. Augustine; [2] St. Augustine, FL Mission of Nombre de Dios and Shrine of Our Lady of La Leche Church.
Jordan, Harry J. '61 (CAM) Gloucester, NJ St. Mary's Church.
Jordan, James J. '83 (PT) Retired.
Jordan, John M. '83 (PIT) Allegheny County, PA West Penn Hospital.
Jordan, Msgr. John W. '69 (SCR) [3] Nanticoke, PA St. Francis of Assisi Church.
Jordan, Joseph A. *o.s.a.* '58 (PH) [AA] Villanova, PA Provincial Offices of the Order of St. Augustine, Province of St. Thomas of Villanova; [AA] Villanova, PA St. Thomas Monastery.
Jordan, Lawrence E. *s.m.* '34 (STL) [P] St. Louis, MO Provincialate of the Society of Mary, Province of St. Louis.
Jordan, Maryon *o.s.b.* '83 (CC) [H] Sandia, TX Corpus Christi Abbey.
Jordan, Maryon C. *o.s.b.* '83 (LC) Coon Valley, WI St. Mary Church.
Jordan, Michael *s.o.l.t.* '83 (CC) [H] Robstown, TX Society of Our Lady of the Most Holy Trinity.
Jordan, Michael H. *s.j.* '55 (R) [E] Raleigh, NC Jesuit Community.
Jordan, Milton E. '72 (WDC) Germantown, MD Mother Seton Parish.
Jordan, Patrick (ORL) Retired.
Jordan, Patrick J. '78 (NY) Absent on Sick leave.
Jordan, Phelim *s.v.d.* '81 (CHI) [N] Techny, IL Society of the Divine Word, Provincial Headquarter-Chicago Prov.
Jordan, Phelin '81 (WDC) [M] Washington, DC Divine Word College.
Jordan, Regis *o.c.d.* '64 (WDC) [V] Washington, DC Institute of Carmelite Studies and ICS Publications.
Jordan, Regis *o.c.d.* '64 (WH) [N] Hinton, WV Monastery of Christ on the Mountain.
Jordan, Salvador *s.j.* (WDC) Chapel Point, MD St. Ignatius Church.
Jordan, Thomas *o.carm.* '70 (FgM) Carmelite Foreign Missions.
Jordon, Thomas *o.carm.* '70 (JOL) [J] Darien, IL Carmelite Provincial Office.
Jorge, Francisco '56 (NY) [19] Yonkers, NY Our Lady of Fatima Church.
Jorgensen, Kenneth J. *s.j.* '79 (BGP) [O] Fairfield, CT The Fairfield Jesuit Community-Fairfield University.
Jorgenson, James '69 (DET) [A] Detroit, MI Sacred Heart Major Seminary, Inc.
Joseph, Aaron *o.p.* (WDC) [2] Bethesda, MD St. Jane Frances de Chantal Church.
Joseph, Aloysius *s.n.b.* '91 (PIT) [7] Pittsburgh, PA St. Catherine of Siena Church.
Joseph, Augustine *s.d.b.* '90 (OAK) Rodeo, CA St. Patrick's Church.
Joseph, Benedict *o.p.* (COL) [I] Columbus, OH St. Mary of the Springs.
Joseph, Eappen (LKC) Raymond, LA St. Lawrence Church.
Joseph, John K. *c.m.i.* '77 (TOL) Leipsic, OH St. Mary Church.
Joseph, Jose A. *c.m.i.* '77 (GAL) [K] Houston, TX The Catholic Chaplain Corps.
Joseph, Msgr. Joseph D. '47 (BUF) Retired.
Joseph, Msgr. Joseph D. '47 (SAM) Retired.
Joseph, Louis '55 (CC) Retired.
Joseph, Louis '60 (FR) Retired.
Joseph, Msgr. Milam '64 (DAL) [B] Irving, TX University of Dallas.
Joseph, Msgr. Milam '64 (TYL) Special Assignment.
Joseph, Moussa '83 (SAM) Danbury, CT St. Anthony Church.
Joseph, Ramon A. '65 (RVC) Sick Leave.
Joseph, William '62 (PT) Retired.
Joseph, William T. '66 (PH) [2] Bensalem, PA St. Elizabeth Ann Seton Church.
Joslin, James R. '74 (ALB) Albany, NY Capital District Psychiatric Center; Special Assignment.
Joslyn, James W. '73 (CHI) Military Chaplains.
Josoma, Stephen S. '81 (BO) [15] Boston, MA St. Brendan Church.
Josson, Marcel *c.i.c.m.* '36 (FgM) Missionhurst Foreign Missions.
Jost, Aloys *o.f.m.* '80 (STL) Oakville, MO St. Francis of Assisi Church; [P] Oakville, MO St. Francis Friary.
Jost, C. Thomas *s.j.* '68 (DEN) [M] Denver, CO Loyola Parish - Jesuit Community.
Jost, Edward F., Jr. '96 (BUF) [2] Tonawanda, NY St. Christopher Church.
Jost, Thomas '68 (DEN) [31] Denver, CO St. Ignatius Loyola Church.
Josten, Paul T. '87 (SFS) Bowdle, SD St. Augustine Church; Roscoe, SD St. Thomas Apostle Church.
Joubert, Gerard *o.p.* (GAL) Retired.
Jovanovic, Msgr. Robert P. '61 (STL) Oakville, MO Queen of All Saints Church.
Jowdy, Albert W. '84 (ATL) Alpharetta, GA St. Thomas Aquinas Church.
Joy, James B., Jr. '61 (WDC) Retired.
Joy, Laurence '60 (LA) On Duty Outside the Archdiocese.
Joy, William '72 (BO) [6] Boston, MA St. Angela Church.
Joyal, Gerald F. '45 (MAN) Retired.
Joyal, Rene J (BO) Retired.
Joyce, Brian T. '63 (OAK) Pleasant Hill, CA Christ the King Church.
Joyce, David J. '68 (SPR) [8] Springfield, MA Our Lady of Hope Church.
Joyce, Donald *o.m.i.* '58 (WDC) [B] Washington, DC Oblate College/Oblate Center for Mission Studies.
Joyce, Edmund P. *c.s.c.* '49 (FTW) [B] Notre Dame, IN University of Notre Dame Du Lac; [J] Notre Dame, IN Holy Cross Community, Corby Hall, University of Notre Dame.
Joyce, Edwin '58 (JOL) Absent on Sick Leave.
Joyce, Fabian *o.f.m.* '43 (BO) [Z] Boston, MA Saint Anthony Residence.
Joyce, George V. '43 (SPR) [8] Springfield, MA Our Lady of Hope Church.
Joyce, George V. '43 (WDC) Retired.
Joyce, Gerald P. '61 (CHI) Westchester, IL Divine Infant Church.
Joyce, Jack *o.m.i.* '61 (FgM) Oblates Foreign Missions.
Joyce, James F. *s.j.* '75 (NY) [80] New York, NY Nativity Church; [DD] New York, NY Jesuit Provincial's Office.
Joyce, James K. '72 (SPR) [4] Pittsfield, MA Sacred Heart Church.
Joyce, James M. '48 (SFS) Brandon, SD Risen Savior Church.
Joyce, John *o.m.i.* '61 (SAT) [C] San Antonio, TX Oblate School of Theology; [O] San Antonio, TX Oblate Renewal Center.

Joyce, John E. '44 (STP) Retired.
Joyce, John J. '89 (BEL) Modoc, IL St. Leo Church; Ruma, IL St. Patrick Church; [G] Ruma, IL Province Center, Adorers of the Blood of Christ, Province of Ruma.
Joyce, John M. '54 (ORG) [3] Orange, CA St. Norbert Church.
Joyce, Joseph *o.carm.* '71 (GAL) [14] Houston, TX St. Bernadette Soubirous Church.
Joyce, Kevin '80 (SJ) [15] San Jose, CA St. Maria Goretti Church.
Joyce, Michael '67 (OAK) Livermore, CA St. Michael's Church.
Joyce, Michael *o.f.m.cap.* '85 (PIT) [29] Pittsburgh, PA Our Lady of the Angels Church.
Joyce, Michael P. *c.m.* '76 (STL) [P] Earth City, MO Congregation of the Mission Midwest Province (Vincentians); [P] St. Louis, MO Vincentian Residence.
Joyce, Michael S. *o.f.m.* '76 (FgM) Franciscan Foreign Missions.
Joyce, Peter (CAM) Williamstown, NJ St. Mary's Church.
Joyce, Peter J. '83 (WOR) [4] Southbridge, MA St. Mary's Church.
Joyce, Pierce J. '34 (CHI) La Grange, IL St. Francis Xavier Church; Retired.
Joyce, Randal *c.p.* '50 (DET) [K] Detroit, MI St. Paul of the Cross Community, Congregation of the Passion.
Joyce, Raymond '62 (WCH) On Duty Outside the Diocese.
Joyce, Stephen G. '78 (STL) Normandy, MO Ascension-St. Paul Church.
Joyce, Thomas *c.m.f.* '59 (CHI) [N] Oak Park, IL Claretian Fathers Headquarters of U.S.A. Eastern Province.
Joyce, Thomas *c.p.* '69 (BRK) [180] Queens, NY Immaculate Conception Church; [U] Jamaica, NY Immaculate Conception Monastery.
Joyce, Thomas J. '68 (DOD) On Duty Outside the Diocese.
Joyce, Thomas J. '91 (NY) [2] White Plains, NY St. John the Evangelist Church.
Joyce, Timothy J. '59 (BO) [W] Hingham, MA Glastonbury Abbey.
Joyce, Tom *c.m.f.* '59 (CHI) [80] Chicago, IL Holy Cross/Immaculate Heart of Mary Church.
Joyce, William F. '60 (BO) [9] Boston, MA St. Anne Church.
Joynes, Msgr. Joseph P. '64 (CAM) Washington Township, NJ Holy Family Church.
Jozefiak, Gregory J. '92 (PEO) Delavan, IL St. Mary's Church.
Jozefiak, Matthew W. *c.pp.s.* '87 (GRY) [4] Whiting, IN St. John the Baptist Church.
Jozwiak, Lawrence '87 (GAL) On Special Assignment.
Jozwiak, Richard E. '59 (SAG) Carrollton, MI St. Josaphat Church.
Jozwiak, Richard M. (CHI) Retired.
Jozwiak, Richard M. '48 (CHI) [3] Lemont, IL SS. Cyril and Methodius Church.
Jozwiak, Ronald J. '79 (DET) [39] Detroit, MI St. Josaphat Church; Special Assignment.
Jozwiak, Stanislaus J. '45 (PIT) Retired.
Jozwiak, Zygmunt '53 (SP) Retired.
Jozwicki, Stephen J. '53 (BRK) [94] Brooklyn, NY Our Lady of Czestochowa-St. Casimir Church; Retired.
Juaire, Joseph *o.m.i.* '49 (MAN) [K] Hudson, NH Missionary Oblates of Mary Immaculate.
Juan, Francisco *s.d.b.* '63 (ARE) Orocovis, PR San Juan Bautista Church.
Juan, Marcial D. '66 (LA) [2] Los Angeles, CA Cathedral Chapel Church.
Juango, Jose Maria *o.a.r.* (NEW) [1] Union City, NJ Holy Family Church.
Juarez, Alejandro *o.f.m.* '88 (ELP) [B] El Paso, TX St. Anthony's School of Theology.
Juarez, Lucio '91 (LA) Huntington Park, CA St. Matthias Church.
Juarez, Rene *o.f.m.* '70 (LA) Santa Paula, CA Our Lady of Guadalupe Church.
Juarez, Robert '80 (LA) [23] Los Angeles, CA Our Lady of Guadalupe Church.
Juarez, Rudolph T. '80 (DAV) [7] Davenport, IA St. Mary's Church.
Juarez, Thomas *s.d.b.* '66 (CC) [7] Laredo, TX San Luis Rey Church.
Juchcinski, Clarence J. '48 (CHI) Harvey, IL St. John the Baptist Church; Retired.
Juchniewicz, Leon '80 (SAC) Marysville, CA St. Joseph Church.
Juchnowski, Msgr. Francis B. '56 (BUF) [13] Buffalo, NY St. Bernard Church.
Juda, Stephen *c.r.* '42 (CHI) [D] Chicago, IL Gordon Technical High School.
Judd, P. Augustine *o.p.* '96 (PRO) [P] Providence, RI St. Thomas Aquinas Priory at Providence College.
Judd, Stephen P. *m.m.* '78 (FgM) Maryknoll Foreign Missions.
Judd, Stephen P. *m.m.* '78 (NY) [DD] Maryknoll, NY Maryknoll Fathers and Brothers.
Jude, Robert J. '49 (STP) Retired.
Jude, Msgr. Walter F. '45 (GR) Retired.
Judge, Anthony *c.ss.r.* '79 (DEN) [33] Denver, CO St. Joseph's Church.
Judge, James G. '72 (BUF) [8] Buffalo, NY Annunciation Church.
Judge, John G. '69 (NEW) Upper Montclair, NJ St. Cassian Church.
Judge, Michael *o.f.m.* '61 (NY) [35] New York, NY St. Francis of Assisi Church.
Judge, Philip G. *s.j.* '93 (NY) [DD] New York, NY Jesuit Community at Fordham University.
Judge, Robert K. *s.j.* '65 (BAL) [B] Baltimore, MD Loyola College; [M] Baltimore, MD Jesuit Community of Loyola College, Inc.
Judge, Russell R. '78 (JC) Macon, MO Immaculate Conception Church.
Judge, Timothy M. '79 (PH) [U] Meadowbrook, PA Holy Redeemer Hospital and Medical Center; [BB] Huntingdon Valley, PA Sisters of the Holy Redeemer Provincialate.
Judie, John T. '87 (L) [57] Louisville, KY Mother of Good Counsel Church.
Judy, Albert *o.p.* '59 (CHI) [176] Chicago, IL St. Priscilla Church.
Judy, Albert *o.p.* '62 (CHI) [N] River Forest, IL St. Thomas Aquinas Priory.
Judy, Edward *o.f.m.cap.* '68 (DEN) [3] Denver, CO Annunciation Church; [M] Denver, CO Annunciation Friary.
Judy, Myron *o.carm.* '63 (JOL) [J] Darien, IL Carmelite Provincial Office.
Juelfs, Daniel '73 (RC) [3] Rapid City, SD St. Therese the Little Flower Church.
Juenker, Msgr. Paul R. '45 (BUF) Retired; [O] Tonawanda, NY O'Hara Residence.
Juergens, William H. *o.s.f.s.* '57 (WIL) [I] Wilmington, DE DeSales House.
Juettner, Mark R. '79 (STP) Crystal, MN St. Raphael Church.
Jugan, Joseph '58 (PBR) Canonsburg, PA St. Michael Church.
Jugenheimer, James R. '87 (PH) [D] Wyncote, PA Bishop McDevitt High School.
Juhas, John S. '75 (CLV) Brooklyn, OH St. Thomas More Church.
Juhasz, Ladislaus F. *s.j.* '54 (BUF) [O] Buffalo, NY Canisius Jesuit Community.
Juhl, Dennis '73 (DUB) Hazleton, IA St. Mary's Church; Lamont, IA St. Mary's Church; Strawberry Point, IA St. Mary's Church.
Juknialis, Joseph J. '69 (MIL) [A] Milwaukee, WI St. Francis Seminary; [A] Milwaukee, WI St. Francis Seminary.
Juleen, Stuart '77 (SAT) Karnes City, TX St. Cornelius Church.
Julian, Mario F. *o.f.m.* '81 (HRT) New Milford, CT St. Francis Xavier's Church.
Julien, Roland M. '65 (STA) [1] Gainesville, FL St. Patrick's Church.
Julius, James A. '65 (STL) Retired.
Julius, Joseph W. '45 (KNX) Alcoa, TN Our Lady of Fatima Church; Townsend, TN St. Francis of Assisi Church.
Julius, Joseph W. '45 (NSH) Retired.
Jung, Dennet *o.f.m.* '63 (LAF) [2] Lafayette, LA St. Paul The Apostle Church.
Jung, Eugene *m.s.c.* '50 (ALN) [K] Reading, PA Missionaries of the Sacred Heart.
Jung, Jay *c.m.* '77 (CHI) [C] Chicago, IL Vincentian Community at DePaul University.
Jung, Jerome (PEO) [P] Urbana, IL Opus Dei.
Jung, Joseph B. '56 (PH) West Chester, PA St. Agnes Church.
Jung, Michael *o.s.b.* '63 (BR) Plaquemine, LA St. Clement of Rome Church; Baton Rouge, LA Baton Rouge General Medical Center.
Jung, Michael *o.s.b.* '63 (NO) [P] St. Benedict, LA St. Joseph Abbey.
Jung, Pius-Bio '89 (ALB) [11] Albany, NY St. Mary Church.
Jungbluth, Henry *s.v.d.* '30 (CHI) [B] Techny, IL Divine Word Residence.
Junge, Heiko T. '96 (P) [29] Portland, OR St. Pius X Church.
Jungwirth, Alphonse *c.pp.s.* '43 (CIN) [B] Carthagena, OH St. Charles.
Juniet, Paul *o.f.m.* '66 (SFE) [12] Albuquerque, NM Queen of Angels Native American Center and Archdiocesan Shrine to Kateri Tekakwitha Church.
Junio, Joven '86 (HON) [3] Honolulu, HI St. Anthony Church.
Junius, Richard *o.m.i.* '56 (FgM) Oblates Foreign Missions.
Junod, Louis J. '65 (KNX) Retired; [B] Chattanooga, TN Memorial Hospital.
Jupin, Alan D. '62 (ALB) [14] Schenectady, NY Our Lady of Fatima Church.
Juracek, Joseph *o.f.m.* '83 (NY) [35] New York, NY St. Francis of Assisi Church.
Juran, Michael P. '76 (BUF) Salamanca, NY St. Patrick Church.
Juras, Callistus *o.f.m.conv.* '54 (ROC) [6] Auburn, NY St. Hyacinth Church.
Jurasko, Joseph J. *o.p.* '40 (WDC) [11] Washington, DC St. Dominic Church & Priory Church.
Jurcak, Lawrence '81 (CLV) [1] Cleveland, OH Cathedral of St. John the Evangelist.
Jurcik, Peter '93 (ALN) Fountain Hill, PA St. Ursula Church.
Jurek, Daniel J. '73 (BEL) Dubois, IL St. Charles Borromeo Church; Tamaroa, IL Immaculate Conception Church.
Jurewich, Henry A. *s.j.* '54 (BO) [W] Weston, MA Campion Health Center, Inc.
Jurewicz, Francis Z. '59 (PIT) Richeyville, PA St. Agnes Church.
Jurgelaitis, Anthony A. *o.p.* '44 (PRO) [P] Providence, RI St. Thomas Aquinas Priory at Providence College.
Jurgelonis, Joseph J. '73 (WOR) Ashburnham, MA St. Denis Church; South Ashburnham, MA St. Anne Church.
Jurgensen, John J. '51 (BRK) [155] Queens, NY St. Benedict Joseph Labre Church.
Jurgensen, John W. '51 (BRK) Retired.
Jurgensmeier, Charles L. *s.j.* '88 (LA) [C] Los Angeles, CA Loyola Marymount University.
Jurich, James P. *s.j.* '67 (NY) [DD] New York, NY Xavier Jesuit Community; [HH] New York, NY Xavier Society for the Blind.
Jurisich, Melvin A. *o.f.m.* '70 (OAK) [N] Oakland, CA Franciscan Friars Provincial Office, Province of St. Barbara; [N] Oakland, CA Franciscan Friars Provincial Office, Province of St. Barbara.
Jurkiewicz, Benedict (STA) [J] Bunnell, FL Discalced Carmelite Fathers of Florida.
Jurkowski, Victor J. *o.f.m.cap.* '58 (CAM) Gibbstown, NJ St. Michael's Church.
Jurkus, Alan F. '70 (MIL) Whitefish Bay, WI St. Monica Church.
Jurzyk, Marek (CHI) [115] Chicago, IL St. Ladislaus Church.
Jussaume, Andre P. '52 (FR) Retired.
Jussaume, Lucien '41 (FR) Retired.
Jusseaume, John E. (BO) Retired.
Jusseaume, John J. '46 (BO) Newburyport, MA Immaculate Conception Church.
Justavino, Teodoro *c.m.* '90 (FgM) Vincentian Foreign Missions.
Justen, Bernard *s.d.b.* '48 (SP) [E] Tampa, FL Mary Help of Christians School.
Justi, Marvin *o.f.m.cap.* '58 (PIT) Rochester, PA St. Cecilia Church; Beaver County, PA The Medical Center Beaver; [O] Rochester, PA St. Cecilia Friary.
Justice, Joseph C. '75 (ORG) [6] Santa Ana, CA St. Anne's Church.
Justice, William J. '68 (SFR) [1] South San Francisco, CA All Souls Church.
Juszczak, Walter *c.ss.r.* (CHI) [58] Chicago, IL St. Ferdinand Church.
Jutt, Anthony J. '51 (SPR) Housatonic, MA Corpus Christi Church; Housatonic, MA All Saints Church.
Jutt, Julius A. '51 (SPR) South Deerfield, MA St. James Church.
Jutte, Edgar *c.pp.s.* '62 (CIN) [B] Carthagena, OH St. Charles.
Jutton, David J. '66 (SY) Truxton, NY St. Patrick Church.
Juya, Filemon '81 (CHR) Batesburg, SC St. John of the Cross Church.
Juza, Philip J. '95 (SUP) Flambeau, WI St. Francis of Assisi Church; Jump River, WI St. Michael Church; Sheldon, WI St. John the Apostle Church.
Juzix, Richard *o.f.m.* '75 (SAC) [13] Sacramento, CA St. Francis of Assisi Church.

K

Kaack, John *s.j.* '74 (SP) [C] Tampa, FL Jesuit High School.
Kabat, Daniel *o.f.m.cap.* (LA) Solvang, CA Old Mission Santa Ines Church.
Kabat, Robert J. '79 (GB) Greenleaf, WI St. Mary Church.
Kabel, Michael C. '90 (SJP) Jeannette, PA St. Demetrius Church.
Kabura, Paschal '87 (PIT) South Park Township, PA Nativity Church.
Kacena, T. Edward '97 (LFT) Fishers, IN Holy Spirit Church.
Kacerguis, Edward '71 (ALB) Special Assignment; [S] Troy, NY Rensselaer Polytechnic Institute.
Kachel, C. Leon '57 (PRO) [K] Providence, RI St. Joseph Health Services of Rhode Island - St. Joseph Hospital for Specialty Care.
Kachel, Steven J. '95 (LC) Custer, WI Immaculate Conception Church; [C] Stevens Point, WI Pacelli High School; [D] Stevens Point, WI Stevens Point Area Catholic Schools.
Kachmar, Msgr. Walter '43 (SJP) Retired.
Kachuba, John S. *m.a.* '74 (PRM) Euclid, OH St. Stephen Church.
Kachurka, Edward M. '90 (BRK) [141] Brooklyn, NY St. Thomas Aquinas Church.

Kacinko, Elmer A. '61 (GBG) Coral, PA St. Francis Church.
Kacir, Marian '89 (NY) [59] New York, NY St. John Nepomucene Church.
Kacirk, Raymond J. *s.m.* '59 (CIN) [M] Dayton, OH Marianist Provincialate.
Kacprowicz, Joseph A. '36 (E) Retired.
Kacprzak, Stanley G. '85 (ROC) [35] Rochester, NY Our Lady of Mercy Church.
Kaczkowski, Conrad J. *s.m.* '68 (SAT) [C] San Antonio, TX St. Mary's University of San Antonio, Texas; [M] San Antonio, TX Chaminade Community House.
Kaczkowski, Leon '34 (BAL) Retired; [J] Timonium, MD Stella Maris Operating Corporation.
Kaczmarck, Thaddeus J. '71 (GBG) North Huntingdon, PA St. Agnes Church.
Kaczmarek, James '69 (MAR) Military Chaplains.
Kaczmarek, Peter '69 (RVC) Bayville, NY St. Gertrude's Church.
Kaczorek, Placid *o.f.m.conv.* '64 (FgM) Conventual Franciscan Foreign Missions.
Kaczorek, Placid *o.f.m.conv.* '64 (SPR) [10] Chicopee, MA St. Stanislaus Basilica Church.
Kaczorowski, Edward J. '58 (WIL) [12] Wilmington, DE St. Stanislaus Kostka Church.
Kaczorowski, James '73 (CHI) [2] Chicago, IL St. Adalbert Church.
Kaczowka, Julian '88 (DET) Hamtramck, MI St. Florian Church.
Kadankavil, Jose *s.j.* (NEW) [N] Jersey City, NJ Jesuits of Saint Peter's College, Inc.
Kadankevil, Jose *s.j.* (NEW) [B] Jersey City, NJ Saint Peter's College.
Kaddo, Msgr. Joseph F. (SAM) [D] Brooklyn, NY Bishop's Residence.
Kadera, Thomas R. (CHY) Lander, WY Holy Rosary Church.
Kadlec, Jared C. '97 (FAR) [5] Fargo, ND St. Anthony of Padua Church.
Kadlec, Josef *s.j.* '77 (WDC) [M] Washington, DC The Jesuit Community at Georgetown University.
Kadzielawski, Edwin J. *c.s.c.* '49 (AUS) Marble Falls, TX St. John the Evangelist Church.
Kaeding, Robert F. '73 (TR) Wayside, NJ St. Anselm Church; Monmouth, NJ Monmouth County Jail.
Kaelin, Dennis (NEW) Hoboken, NJ St. Mary's Hospital.
Kaelin, Walter *c.p.* '42 (CHI) [N] Chicago, IL Passionist Provincial Office.
Kaelin, Walter *c.p.* '42 (FgM) Mission Procurators.
Kaelin, Walter *c.p.* '42 (L) [L] Louisville, KY Sacred Heart Retreat.
Kafara, Andrew *s.j.* '71 (SAT) Pearsall, TX Immaculate Heart of Mary Church.
Kafer, Gerald *o.f.m.cap.* (LC) [H] Marathon City, WI St. Anthony Retreat Center.
Kafer, Jerry *o.f.m.cap.* '76 (LC) [I] Marathon City, WI St. Anthony Retreat Center.
Kafka, Matthew S. '65 (FTW) [13] Fort Wayne, IN St. Patrick Church; [F] Fort Wayne, IN St. Joseph Medical Center.
Kagan, Msgr. David D. '75 (RCK) Special Assignment.
Kahle, George G. *c.s.c.* '53 (FTW) [J] South Bend, IN Congregation of Holy Cross Indiana Province Provincial House.
Kahlhamer, Bernard '59 (SCL) Sauk Centre, MN Our Lady of the Angels Church.
Kahlich, Daniel P. '66 (VIC) Columbus, TX St. Anthony's Church.
Kahn, Eric *o.f.m.* '55 (SPC) [G] Republic, MO Cordis House.
Kahn, Eric *o.f.m.* '55 (STL) [P] St. Louis, MO Franciscan Friary of St. Anthony of Padua.
Kahrs, Lee J. (GB) Glenmore, WI Immaculate Conception Church; Stark, WI St. Mary Church.
Kaicher, Edward '80 (SD) Fallbrook, CA St. Peter Church.
Kaifer, William J. *s.j.* '53 (WDC) [M] Washington, DC The Jesuit Community at Georgetown University.
Kaija, Peter '80 (FTW) [1] Fort Wayne, IN Cathedral of the Immaculate Conception.
Kail, Msgr. Michael J. '74 (OLL) Columbus, OH Maronite Catholic Community Church; Fairlawn, OH Our Lady of the Cedars of Mt. Lebanon Church.
Kaimann, Gerald J. '70 (JC) Jonesburg, MO St. Patrick Church; Montgomery City, MO Immaculate Conception Church.
Kain, Msgr. Peter V. (BRK) [36] Brooklyn, NY St. Ephrem's Church.
Kain, Stephan *o.f.m.* '74 (SFR) [7] San Francisco, CA St. Boniface Church.
Kaiser, Msgr. Charles '32 (EVN) Fort Branch, IN Holy Cross Church; Retired.
Kaiser, Cletus H. '56 (MIL) Retired.
Kaiser, Joseph '71 (BAL) [J] Timonium, MD Stella Maris Operating Corporation.
Kaiser, Joseph A. '71 (BAL) Retired.
Kaiser, Joseph W. '55 (RCK) Richmond, IL St. Joseph Church.
Kaiser, Lawrence '64 (DET) [1] Dearborn Heights, MI St. Albert the Great Church.
Kaiser, Lawrence B. '73 (DEN) Fort Morgan, CO St. Helena Church.
Kaiser, Leonard G. '58 (LC) Independence, WI SS. Peter and Paul Church; North Creek, WI St. Michael Church.
Kaiser, Ralph L. '54 (KC) Buckner, MO Church of the Santa Fe.
Kaiser, Roman F. '58 (LC) Loyal, WI St. Anthony of Padua Church.
Kaiser, Thomas J. '49 (SLC) [10] Salt Lake City, UT St. Vincent de Paul Church; Retired.
Kaising, John J. '62 (CIN) Military Chaplains.
Kaithackal, Sebastian *c.m.i.* '81 (MET) [I] Flemington, NJ The Carmel of Mary Immaculate and St. Mary Magdalen.
Kakalec, Joseph M. *s.j.* '67 (PH) [C] Philadelphia, PA St. Joseph's University; [AA] Philadelphia, PA Jesuit Community at St. Joseph's University; [AA] Philadelphia, PA St. Alphonsus House.
Kakareka, Joseph R. '72 (SCR) [6] Nanticoke, PA St. Stanislaus Church.
Kakascik, Msgr. Edward '55 (STU) Marietta, OH St. Mary's Church; [I] Marietta, OH Marietta College.
Kakaty, Edward G. '72 (BO) [10] Boston, MA Annunciation Cathedral.
Kakizaki, John T. '42 (BRK) Retired.
Kalabat, Frank Y. '95 (EST) Southfield, MI Our Lady of Chaldeans Cathedral, Mother of God Chaldean Parish.
Kalafsky, Andrew J. '43 (ROC) Bradford, NY St. Stanislaus Church; Retired.
Kalajian, Msgr. Joseph '31 (ARM) Detroit, MI St. Vartan's Church.
Kalamaja, Theodore M. *s.j.* '67 (MIL) [P] Milwaukee, WI Jesuit Provincial Office, Wisconsin Province.
Kalamaja, Theodore M. *s.j.* '67 (NO) New Orleans, LA Orleans Parish Correctional Center; [C] New Orleans, LA Loyola University.
Kalapura, Antony (PIT) [56] Pittsburgh, PA St. Mary of the Mount Church.
Kalapurra, George *c.m.i.* '60 (BEA) [8] Port Arthur, TX St. Mary Church.
Kalarickal, Thomas *c.m.i.* '55 (NY) [2] White Plains, NY St. John the Evangelist Church.
Kalariparampil, Joseph '53 (MIA) [7] Fort Lauderdale, FL St. Helen Church.
Kalas, Ronald N. '59 (CHI) Park Ridge, IL Mary, Seat of Wisdom Church.
Kalata, Dominik P. '65 (ALN) Frackville, PA St. Ann Church; Frackville, PA Annunciation B.V.M. Church.
Kalb, Bertram J. '44 (DUB) Retired.
Kalb, Howard E. *s.j.* '54 (OM) [K] Omaha, NE Jesuit Community At Creighton University.
Kalchthaler, James C. *m.m.* '56 (FgM) Maryknoll Foreign Missions.
Kalcic, Dismas *o.s.b.* '61 (JOL) [J] Lisle, IL St. Procopius Abbey.
Kalcic, Dismas B. *o.s.b.* '61 (SUP) Catawba, WI St. Paul the Apostle Church; Prentice, WI St. John Church.
Kalck, Michael V. '74 (CHI) [170] Chicago, IL SS. Peter and Paul Church.
Kaleikoa, Charles '81 (HON) Leave of Absence.
Kalema, Josephat Kato *o.c.s.o.* (NEW) [32] Newark, NJ St. Rocco's Church.
Kalema, Mark (CHI) [175] Chicago, IL Presentation Church.
Kalemeera, Augustine '85 (LA) El Segundo, CA St. Anthony Church.
Kalenty, Adalbert *o.f.m.* '53 (GB) [I] Pulaski, WI Assumption of B.V.M. Friary.
Kaler, Adolph *o.m.i.* '57 (GAL) [38] Houston, TX Immaculate Heart of Mary Church.
Kalert, David *o.m.i.* '64 (FgM) Oblates Foreign Missions.
Kalert, David A. *o.m.i.* '64 (STP) [N] St. Paul, MN Oblate Provincial Offices; [N] St. Paul, MN Oblate Residence; [W] St. Paul, MN Oblate Media and Communication Corporation.
Kaley, Richard *o.f.m.conv.* '75 (IND) St. Joseph Hill, IN St. Joseph Church; [I] Mount Saint Francis, IN Mount Saint Francis Friary and Retreat Center; [J] Mount Saint Francis, IN Provincial Headquarters for the Conventual Franciscan Province.
Kalich, Patrick J. '94 (GRY) Portage, IN Nativity of Our Savior Church.
Kalick, Quentin F. *s.s.c.* '42 (FgM) St. Columban's Foreign Mission.
Kalicky, John E. *c.pp.s.* '61 (GRY) [4] Whiting, IN St. John the Baptist Church.
Kalil, Gordon *o.p.* '94 (SR) Special Assignment.
Kalin, Msgr. Leonard I. '56 (LIN) [12] Lincoln, NE St. Thomas Aquinas Church; [I] Lincoln, NE University of Nebraska, Newman Club.
Kalin, William A. '59 (LIN) On Duty Outside the Diocese.
Kalina, Isaac *o.s.b.* '89 (LA) [R] Valyermo, CA St. Andrew's Abbey.
Kaliner, Frederick '59 (NEW) [N] Rutherford, NJ St. John Vianney Residence for Priests.
Kalinowski, Joseph J. '79 (E) East Brady, PA St. Eusebius Church.
Kalinowski, Loren M. '75 (SAG) [13] Saginaw, MI St. John Vianney Church.
Kalinowski, Ryszard *s.v.d.* '74 (LAF) [4] New Iberia, LA St. Edward Church.
Kalinowski, Stainslaus J. '45 (SCR) Retired.
Kalinski, Eugene E. '60 (GB) [I] Oshkosh, WI Community of Our Lady.
Kalita, Thomas M. '74 (WDC) Olney, MD St. Peter Church.
Kalkman, Richard '56 (SCL) On Duty Outside the Diocese.
Kalkman, Richard '56 (SFR) [4] South San Francisco, CA St. Veronica Church.
Kall, Anthony *o.f.m.conv.* '71 (ALB) [T] Rensselaer, NY Order of Friars Minor Conventual Immaculate Conception Province Charitable Trust.
Kall, Anthony *o.f.m.conv.* '71 (TR) [5] Trenton, NJ Immaculate Conception Church.
Kallabat, Stephen '66 (EST) Oak Park, MI Mar Addai Chaldean Parish.
Kalladan, Joseph K. '69 (GAL) New Waverly, TX St. Joseph Church.
Kallaher, Timothy S. '72 (CIN) [19] Dayton, OH Our Lady of the Immaculate Conception Church.
Kallanchira, Joseph *s.v.d.* '87 (MIL) [P] East Troy, WI Divine Word Seminary.
Kallarackal, Abraham *c.m.i.* '83 (ALX) Dupont, LA Immaculate Conception Church.
Kallarackal, Sebastian *c.m.i.* '77 (TYL) Jacksonville, TX Our Lady of Sorrows Church; Rusk, TX Rusk State Hospital and Skyview Unit, Texas Dept. of Corrections.
Kallattil, John '79 (BGP) Wilton, CT Our Lady of Fatima Church.
Kallepallil, Joseph *s.j.* (NEW) [B] Jersey City, NJ Saint Peter's College.
Kallepallil, Joseph *s.j.* '76 (NEW) [12] Jersey City, NJ St. John the Baptist Church.
Kallipollil, Joseph *s.j.* (NEW) [N] Jersey City, NJ Jesuits of Saint Peter's College, Inc.
Kallock, Michael J. *c.s.p.* '73 (BO) [P] Boston, MA Paulist Center; [W] Boston, MA Paulist Fathers Residence; [BB] Boston, MA Chapel of the Holy Spirit.
Kallookalam, Joseph *c.m.i.* '71 (TYL) Gun Barrel City, TX St. Jude Church.
Kallor, John '73 (PH) [71] Philadelphia, PA Incarnation of Our Lord Church.
Kallumady, Thomas '73 (NY) [227] Staten Island, NY Sacred Heart Church.
Kalonga, Simon '84 (DEN) [3] Englewood, CO St. Louis Church.
Kalousieh, Georges '81 (ARM) Paterson, NJ Sacred Heart Church.
Kalscheuer, Henry N. '59 (MAD) Dodgeville, WI St. Joseph Church; Ridgeway, WI St. Bridget Church.
Kalscheuer, Roger *s.j.* '85 (OM) [14] Omaha, NE St. Frances Cabrini Church.
Kaltenbach, Victor J. '94 (SFD) Greenville, IL St. Lawrence Church.
Kaltreider, Carl E. '79 (CHL) Shelby, NC St. Mary's Church.
Kalu, Clement '84 (LR) [2] Little Rock, AR St. Anne Church; [7] Little Rock, AR Immaculate Conception Church.
Kalu, Martin Ralph '89 (ATL) [1] Atlanta, GA Cathedral of Christ the King.
Kamas, John *s.s.s.* '75 (NY) [55] New York, NY St. Jean Baptiste Church.
Kambitsch, Lawrence J. '69 (MRY) King City, CA St. John the Baptist Church.
Kamenski, Thomas *o.f.m.* '82 (LAF) [F] Lafayette, LA Our Lady of Lourdes Regional Medical Center, Inc.
Kamide, Paul T. '63 (ORL) Port Orange, FL Epiphany Church.
Kamienski, Luciano *s.d.b.* '66 (LA) Inglewood, CA St. John Chrysostom Church.
Kamiensky, Joseph J. *s.j.* '77 (BUF) [D] Buffalo, NY Canisius High School; [O] Buffalo, NY Canisius Jesuit Community.
Kaminouchi, Alberto de Mingo *c.ss.r.* '93 (OAK) [10] Oakland, CA St. Jarlath's Church.
Kaminski, Frank T. *s.j.* '76 (CAM) [4] Camden, NJ Holy Name Church.
Kaminski, George '85 (FTW) [19] Fort Wayne, IN St. Vincent de Paul Church.
Kaminski, Henry T. '53 (NEW) Plainfield, NJ St. Mary Church; Plainfield, NJ St. Stanislaus Kostka Church.
Kaminski, Joseph M. '51 (GF) Retired.
Kaminski, Kevin A. '78 (MET) Raritan, NJ St. Joseph Church.
Kaminski, Louis T. '77 (SCR) Mansfield, PA Holy Child Church.
Kaminski, Neal *o.f.m.* (CHI) [N] Chicago, IL Holy Name Friary.
Kaminski, Stephen '91 (CLV) Medina, OH St. Francis Xavier Church.
Kaminski, Sy '53 (Y) [10] Youngstown, OH St. Casimir's Church.
Kaminski, Thomas J. '66 (CHI) [76] Chicago, IL St. Helena Church.

Kaminski, Walter '54 (HRT) [6] Meriden, CT St. Stanislaus Church.

Kaminsky, Joseph T. '60 (HRT) Oakville, CT St. Mary Magdalen Church.

Kamla, Jerome J. '42 (LC) Retired.

Kamlage, Herman '57 (COV) Retired.

Kammer, Fred *s.j.* '76 (WDC) [M] Washington, DC K Street Jesuit Community.

Kammerer, James '97 (SAT) [49] San Antonio, TX St. Leo Church.

Kammerer, Raymond '64 (CIN) Waynesville, OH St. Augustine Church.

Kammerer, Richard F. '80 (RVC) Lindenhurst, NY Our Lady of Perpetual Help Church.

Kamp, Francis J. *s.v.d.* '47 (CHI) [B] Techny, IL Divine Word Residence; [N] Techny, IL Society of the Divine Word, Provincial Headquarter-Chicago Prov.; [U] Techny, IL S.V.D., Catholic Universities, Inc.; [U] Techny, IL Divine Word Missionaries, Inc., Divine Word Funds, Inc.

Kampa, Dennis C. '68 (STP) Kenyon, MN St. Michael Church; Pine Island, MN St. Michael Church.

Kampfer, Gerald D. '67 (ALB) Wilton, NY Wilton Developmental Center.

Kampher, Gerald D. '67 (ALB) Special Assignment.

Kampschneider, Daniel J. '79 (OM) [37] Omaha, NE St. Philip Neri Church.

Kana, Steven '95 (AUS) Bryan, TX St. Anthony's Church.

Kanar, Richard '94 (PSC) Absent on Sick Leave.

Kanat, Kurian '58 (LAF) [1] Lafayette, LA St. John the Evangelist Cathedral.

Kanda, Francis P. *c.s.sp.* '53 (PRO) [1] Tiverton, RI St. Christopher Church.

Kanda, John R. *c.s.sp.* '42 (VEN) [G] Sarasota, FL Congregation of the Holy Ghost.

Kandathiduky, Joseph (CHI) Northlake, IL Syro-Malabar Catholic Mission of the Archdiocese of Chicago Church.

Kandathinkara, John J. *v.c.* '84 (BAL) Bradshaw, MD St. Stephen Church.

Kandathiparampil, Joseph '63 (WIL) Salisbury, MD St. Francis De Sales Church.

Kandel, Timothy '81 (ORL) On Duty Outside the Diocese.

Kandrac, Antone *o.f.m.conv.* (ALB) [L] Rensselaer, NY Franciscan Mission House.

Kandrac, Antone *o.f.m.conv.* '57 (ALB) Nassau, NY St. Mary Church.

Kandt, Gregory '90 (RIC) Salem, VA Our Lady of Perpetual Help Church.

Kandula, Charles R. '76 (TR) [12] Trenton, NJ St. Anthony Church.

Kane, Aloysius T. '38 (PH) Retired.

Kane, Msgr. Arthur J. (RVC) [N] Uniondale, NY St. Pius X Residence.

Kane, Msgr. Arthur J. '36 (RVC) Retired.

Kane, Brian E. '60 (LA) On Duty Outside the Archdiocese.

Kane, Cornelius T. *o.p.* '52 (WDC) [11] Washington, DC St. Dominic Church & Priory Church.

Kane, Edward *c.ss.r.* '47 (KC) [32] Kansas City, MO Our Lady of Perpetual Help Church; [J] Kansas City, MO Redemptorists of Kansas City.

Kane, Edward R. '78 (BRK) [55] Brooklyn, NY Holy Family Church.

Kane, Eugene '54 (PEO) Urbana, IL St. Patrick's Church; Retired.

Kane, Farrell J. *o.carm.* '65 (CHI) Gurnee, IL St. Paul the Apostle Church.

Kane, Msgr. Francis A. '35 (SCR) Retired.

Kane, Francis J. '53 (PRT) Retired.

Kane, Francis J. '69 (CHI) Wilmette, IL St. Joseph Church.

Kane, George J. '51 (CHI) Inverness, IL Holy Family Church; Schaumburg, IL Church of the Holy Spirit; Retired.

Kane, Herbert T. *s.j.* '52 (NY) [DD] Cornwall, NY Jogues Retreat.

Kane, Ignatius B. *o.s.b.* '61 (BIR) [E] Cullman, AL St. Bernard Abbey.

Kane, Msgr. James D. '58 (SY) Johnson City, NY Blessed Sacrament Church.

Kane, James E. '51 (DEN) Retired.

Kane, James J. '71 (ALB) [5] Schenectady, NY St. Helen Church; Special Assignment.

Kane, John E. *c.m.* '70 (FgM) Vincentian Foreign Missions.

Kane, John J. '66 (PH) Springfield, PA St. Kevin Church.

Kane, Msgr. John T. '63 (LA) Hacienda Heights, CA St. John Vianney Church.

Kane, John W. *c.ss.r.* '44 (TUC) [F] Cortaro, AZ Desert House of Prayer.

Kane, Joseph E. '67 (EVN) Jasper, IN Precious Blood Church.

Kane, Msgr. Joseph F. '38 (PBL) Retired.

Kane, Joseph F. '46 (SY) [S] Syracuse, NY St. Pius X Home, Inc.

Kane, Joseph M. '70 (BO) [U] Boston, MA Marian Manor.

Kane, Joseph P. *s.j.* '68 (NY) City, NY George M. Motchan Detention Center; City, NY George Viero Center; City, NY Rose M. Singer Center; [DD] New York, NY Jesuit Provincial's Office.

Kane, Joseph T. '62 (PH) Warrington, PA St. Robert Bellarmine Church.

Kane, Justin J. '44 (DUB) Retired.

Kane, Justin T. '44 (DUB) [4] Waterloo, IA St. Edward's Church.

Kane, Michael N. '80 (PSC) Coconut Creek, FL Our Lady of the Sign Church.

Kane, Mortimer F. *c.s.sp.* '56 (FgM) Holy Ghost Foreign Missions.

Kane, Paul '96 (MIA) Hollywood, FL Little Flower Church.

Kane, Philip M. '88 (JC) Glasgow, MO St. Mary Church; Slater, MO St. Joseph Church.

Kane, Thomas '69 (WOR) Absent on Leave.

Kane, Thomas A. '44 (PH) Bala Cynwyd, PA St. Matthias Church; Retired.

Kane, Msgr. Thomas A. '52 (WDC) Norbeck, MD St. Patrick Church.

Kane, Thomas A. *c.s.p.* '75 (NY) [DD] Jamaica Estates, NY Paulist Fathers Generalate.

Kane, Thomas C. *o.p.* '52 (WDC) [C] Washington, DC Catholic University of America, The.

Kane, Thomas S. '67 (RVC) Riverhead, NY St. John the Evangelist Church.

Kane, Timothy '82 (DET) [67] Detroit, MI St. Rita Church.

Kane, Walter J. *s.j.* '68 (BO) [W] Boston, MA The Society of Jesus of New England-Provincial Offices.

Kane, William *s.v.d.* '47 (BO) [W] Boston, MA Divine Word Missionaries.

Kane, William J. *s.j.* '48 (BEL) [D] Red Bud, IL St. Clement Health Services.

Kane, William J. *s.j.* '48 (STL) [P] St. Louis, MO The Jesuits of the Missouri Province.

Kane, Msgr. William J. '60 (WDC) [3] Bethesda, MD Little Flower Church; Pastoral Center Special Ministries.

Kang, John '59 (HON) [13] Honolulu, HI Sacred Heart Church.

Kang, Paul '91 (NEW) [6] Orange, NJ St. Andrew Kim Church.

Kang, Paul '91 (NY) On Duty Outside the Archdiocese.

Kangley, Bernard *o.carm.* '44 (LA) [R] Los Angeles, CA Mount Carmel Priory, Carmelite Fathers and Brothers.

Kania, Wojciech M. *s.chr.* '41 (LA) [22] Los Angeles, CA Our Lady of the Bright Mount Church.

Kanicki, Philip A. '85 (RIC) Military Chaplains.

Kanka, Robert (ROC) Hornell, NY St. Ann Church.

Kanka, Robert '56 (ROC) Retired.

Kannampuzha, Jose '92 (TYL) Longview, TX St. Mary Church.

Kannanaickal, Raphael *c.m.i.* '71 (PH) [9] Philadelphia, PA St. Ambrose Church.

Kannitzer, Columbian '50 (LR) [A] Subiaco, AR Subiaco Monastery.

Kanonik, Stephen F. '82 (CHI) [115] Chicago, IL St. Ladislaus Church.

Kanono, Joseph *m.s.c.* '76 (MI) Ebeye, MH Queen of Peace Church.

Kantner, William R. '75 (MEM) [12] Memphis, TN Incarnation Church.

Kantor, Msgr. Adolph A. '43 (SY) Retired.

Kanzic, Gerald B. '92 (PAT) Ringwood, NJ St. Catherine of Bologna Church.

Kao, Paulus '59 (LSC) Bayard, NM Our Lady of Fatima Church.

Kapalczynski, Msgr. Eugene J. '40 (MIL) Retired.

Kaparich, Albert N. '45 (HEL) Retired.

Kapfer, Lee *s.j.* '53 (SEA) [11] Seattle, WA St. Joseph Church.

Kapinus, Augustine *o.f.m.conv.* '58 (ALB) Northville, NY St. Francis of Assisi Church.

Kapitan, John *o.f.m.* '95 (PSC) [A] Sybertsville, PA Holy Dormition Monastery.

Kapitan, John *o.f.m.* '95 (VNN) Sacramento, CA St. Philip the Apostle Church.

Kapitz, Donald '73 (SFE) Retired.

Kaplinski, Peter '72 (VIC) [2] Victoria, TX Holy Family of Joseph, Mary & Jesus Church.

Kapoun, Robert E. '64 (STP) Special Assignment.

Kappalumakkel, Mathew '89 (HRT) [1] West Haven, CT Our Lady of Victory Church.

Kappe, John H. '71 (GAL) [23] Houston, TX St. Clare of Assisi Church.

Kappes, Joseph B. *s.j.* '77 (CLV) University Heights, OH Gesu Church.

Kapphahn, Leo W. *o.s.c.* '39 (PHX) [F] Phoenix, AZ Crosier Community of Phoenix (Canons Regular of the Order of the Holy Cross).

Kappler, Stephan (OAK) Richmond, CA St. Cornelius Church.

Kapral, Richard J. '70 (SY) Waterville, NY St. Bernard Church.

Kapron, Alan '94 (PSC) New Britain, CT Holy Trinity Church.

Kapushion, Marvin J. '56 (PBL) [3] Pueblo, CO Holy Family Church.

Kapusnak, Joseph '66 (PBR) Leisenring, PA St. Stephen Church; Perryopolis, PA St. Nicholas Church.

Kapustka, Gerald *o.m.i.* '65 (FgM) Oblates Foreign Missions.

Karabin, Joseph D. '74 (PIT) Braddock, PA Good Shepherd Church; Allegheny County, PA UPMC Braddock.

Karachira, Thomas '90 (WH) Harrisville, WV Christ Our Hope Church; St. Marys, WV St. John Church.

Karaffa, James G. *c.s.c.* '80 (FTW) Granger, IN St. Pius X Church.

Karal, John W. '53 (DUB) Retired.

Karalus, Peter J. '97 (BUF) Albion, NY St. Joseph Church.

Karamitis, Dennis R. *s.j.* '75 (STP) [N] Minneapolis, MN La Storta Jesuit Community.

Karas, Blase *o.f.m.* '59 (FgM) Franciscan Foreign Missions.

Karas, Bohdan (STF) Brooklyn, NY St. Nicholas Church.

Karas, Stephen C. '65 (Y) Struthers, OH Holy Trinity Church.

Karasek, Edward '87 (AUS) West, TX Assumption Church.

Karath, William E. '71 (P) Bandon, OR Holy Trinity Church.

Karatta, Charles (PIT) [J] Pittsburgh, PA St. Francis Medical Center.

Karava, Norbert '80 (TLS) Durant, OK St. William Church.

Karban, Roger R. '64 (BEL) Renault, IL Our Lady of Good Counsel Church; [A] Waterloo, IL Gibault Catholic High School.

Karcher, Jerome T. '83 (ORG) [4] Huntington Beach, CA St. Vincent de Paul Church.

Karcsinski, Joseph J. '79 (BGP) [13] Bridgeport, CT St. Mary's Church.

Karcz, Lawrence *o.f.m.* '41 (GB) [I] Green Bay, WI St. Mary of the Angels Friary.

Karczewski, Julian K. '74 (CAM) [5] Vineland, NJ St. Mary's Church.

Kardas, Thaddeus '70 (WOR) Absent on Leave.

Kardian, Richard S. *m.m.* '56 (CLV) [P] Cleveland, OH Maryknoll Fathers.

Kardian, Richard S. *m.m.* '56 (NY) [DD] Maryknoll, NY Maryknoll Fathers and Brothers.

Kardong, Terrence *o.s.b.* '63 (BIS) [A] Richardton, ND Assumption Abbey.

Kardos, Blase *o.f.m.conv.* '43 (NY) [B] New York, NY St. Francis Novitiate.

Kardos, Blase B. *o.f.m.conv.* (NY) Staten Island, NY Seaview Hospital and Home.

Kardzis, Krzysztof '84 (TOL) Norwalk, OH St. Paul Church.

Karekatt, Raphael *m.s.f.s.* '86 (ALX) Echo, LA St. Francis de Sales Church.

Karels, Agdus S. '44 (NU) Retired.

Karels, Agdus S. '44 (STP) Retired.

Karels, Ambrose G. '59 (KC) [33] Kansas City, MO Our Lady of Sorrows Church; Special Assignment.

Karem, Peter '88 (OLL) Leave of Absence.

Karenbauer, Richard P. '70 (GBG) New Kensington, PA St. Mary of Czestochowa Church.

Karepin, James M. *o.p.* '90 (CHI) [N] Chicago, IL Dominicans (Provincial Office).

Kareta, Gregory *o.f.m. con.* '56 (FRS) Avenal, CA St. Joseph Church.

Karg, Msgr. Andrew H. '64 (E) [10] Erie, PA Our Lady of Peace Church.

Karg, Msgr. William C. '57 (E) [3] Sharon, PA St. Joseph Church.

Karg, William D. '64 (CLV) [17] Akron, OH St. Sebastian Church.

Kari, Arnold A. '77 (RC) Philip, SD Sacred Heart Church.

Kariamadam, Joseph *c.m.i.* '74 (LKC) [4] Lake Charles, LA St. Henry Church.

Karikattil, Jose (SAC) Citrus Heights, CA Holy Family Church.

Karinki, Alphonsus Murariri *i.m.c.* '86 (MET) [H] Somerset, NJ Consolata Society for Foreign Missions.

Karisa, Nathaniel '87 (ROC) [I] Rochester, NY Basilian Residence.

Karl, Charles '57 (PEO) Retired.

Karl, Msgr. Edward B. '57 (BGP) Bethel, CT St. Mary's Church.

Karl, Kevin '80 (OWN) Providence, KY Holy Cross Church; Sebree, KY St. Michael Church.

Karle, William J. '72 (SCR) Sayre, PA Church of the Epiphany.

Karlen, Donald H. '64 (SY) [3] Utica, NY Our Lady of Lourdes Church; [W] Whitesboro, NY Mount Olivet.

Karlin, Paulinus I. *o.f.m.cap.* '43 (SAL) Hays, KS St. Joseph's Church; [D] Hays, KS St. Joseph's Friary.

Karlowicz, Edwin *c.r.* (CHI) [107] Chicago, IL St. John Cantius Church.

Karls, Victor *c.ss.r.* '70 (STL) [P] Liguori, MO Liguori Mission House/Redemptorists.

Karmanocky, Bernard *o.f.m.* '73 (ALT) [18] Johnstown,

PA St. Therese of the Child Jesus Church.
Karnik, George W. '58 (DUB) [5] Waterloo, IA St. John's Church.
Karnish, Robert A. '66 (GI) Gordon, NE St. Leo's Church.
Karns, David W. '74 (ALN) [1] Easton, PA St. Anthony of Padua Church.
Karoblis, Andrew K. '54 (LC) [4] Wisconsin Rapids, WI SS. Peter and Paul Church.
Karol, Msgr. Bernard A. '36 (MAR) Retired.
Karoor, Isaac (BAL) Ellicott City, MD Our Lady of Perpetual Help Church.
Karp, Joseph A. '67 (ORG) Special Assignment; [G] Yorba Linda, CA Polish Center.
Karpiel, Peter '86 (RVC) Copiague, NY Our Lady of the Assumption Church.
Karpiey, Daniel J. '59 (HRT) Terryville, CT St. Casimir Church.
Karpinski, Robert D. '93 (BGP) [2] Trumbull, CT St. Catherine of Siena Church; [C] Trumbull, CT St. Joseph High School.
Karpowicz, Jan *s.ch.* '94 (STP) [6] Minneapolis, MN Holy Cross Church.
Karpyn, Gregory '87 (ALN) [7] Bethlehem, PA Notre Dame of Bethlehem Church.
Karr, Raymond E. '59 (ALT) Absent on Leave.
Karrer, Walter *c.ss.r.* '47 (WCH) [G] Wichita, KS Redemptorist Mission House.
Karrer, Walter C. *c.ss.r.* '47 (WCH) [14] Wichita, KS St. Joseph Church.
Karris, Robert '65 (CHI) [N] Chicago, IL St. Peter's Friary.
Karssen, John H. *c.m.* '46 (DEN) [M] Denver, CO Congregation of the Mission Midwest Province: De Paul House.
Karuhn, Robert J. '65 (GB) Sturgeon Bay, WI St. Joseph Church.
Karvelis, Msgr. Bryan J. '56 (BRK) [142] Brooklyn, NY Transfiguration Church.
Karvelis, Francis V. '49 (HRT) [11] Waterbury, CT St. Joseph Church.
Karwacki, Bart *o.f.m.conv.* (BAL) [M] Ellicott City, MD St. Joseph Cupertino Friary, Friars Minor Conventual of St. Francis of Assisi; [M] Ellicott City, MD Friary of St. Joseph Cupertino.
Karwacki, Francis J. '83 (HBG) Lykens, PA Our Lady Help of Christians Church; Williamstown, PA Sacred Heart of Jesus Church.
Karwacki, Marion T. '36 (ORL) Retired.
Karwel, Henry *o.f.m.conv.* '57 (BAL) [M] Ellicott City, MD Order of Friars Minor Conventual.
Karwel, Henry *o.f.m.conv.* '57 (SPR) Ware, MA St. Mary's Church.
Karwin, John J. *s.j.* '67 (BO) [W] Boston, MA The Society of Jesus of New England-Provincial Offices.
Karwin, John J. *s.j.* '67 (WH) [A] Wheeling, WV Wheeling Jesuit University.
Karwowski, Edmund K '87 (HRT) Plainville, CT Our Lady of Mercy Church.
Karwowski, Ephram *o.f.m.cap.* '88 (NY) [DD] White Plains, NY St. Conrad Friary.
Karwowski, Ephrem *o.f.m.cap.* (RCK) Algonquin, IL St. Margaret Mary Church.
Kasak, Andrew *o.f.m.conv.* '45 (BAL) [90] Baltimore, MD St. Stanislaus Kostka Church.
Kasanda, Leonard *c.i.c.m.* '64 (FgM) Missionhurst Foreign Missions.
Kasarda, John '61 (PBR) Newton Falls, OH St. Michael Church.
Kaschenbach, Msgr. Arthur J. '51 (SCR) Mount Pocono, PA St. Mary of the Mount Church.
Kasel, Joseph M. '48 (NU) Retired.
Kaserow, John M. *m.m.* '69 (CHI) [B] Chicago, IL The Catholic Theological Union at Chicago.
Kaserow, John M. *m.m.* '69 (NY) [DD] Maryknoll, NY Maryknoll Fathers and Brothers.
Kaseta, Peter *o.f.m.cap.* '67 (FgM) Capuchin Foreign Missions.
Kaseta, Peter *o.f.m.cap.* '67 (NY) [57] New York, NY St. John the Baptist Church.
Kash, Robert J. '52 (CHI) Retired.
Kashmer, George B. '58 (GRY) Retired.
Kasinskas, Clement *c.p.* '54 (BO) [W] Brighton, MA St. Gabriel's Passionist Community.
Kasinskas, Clement *c.p.* '57 (BO) [6] Cambridge, MA Immaculate Conception Church.
Kasinski, James J. '66 (BUF) [12] Niagara Falls, NY Sacred Heart Church.
Kaska, E. William '69 (DAV) [2] Davenport, IA Our Lady of Victory Church.
Kaskie, Brian '92 (JKS) [4] Jackson, MS St. Therese Church.
Kaslyn, Robert *s.j.* '85 (BO) [W] Cambridge, MA Faber House; [W] Cambridge, MA Weston Jesuit Community.
Kasny, Jiri *s.d.b.* '87 (COL) [A] Columbus, OH Pontifical College Josephinum; [H] Columbus, OH Salesian Center.
Kasparek, John *s.c.j.* '69 (MIL) [P] Hales Corners, WI Priests of the Sacred Heart.
Kasparek, John '69 (PMB) Stuart, FL St. Joseph Church.
Kasper, Eugene J. '59 (NEW) Rahway, NJ St. Mark's Church.
Kasper, John *o.s.f.s.* '79 (OAK) Lafayette, CA St. Perpetua Church.
Kasper, Larry '97 (TUC) [8] Tucson, AZ Our Mother of Sorrows Church.
Kasperek, David D. '63 (GB) Flintville, WI SS. Edward and Isidore Church.
Kasprick, Roger *o.s.b.* '59 (SCL) [I] Collegeville, MN St. John's Abbey, of the Order of St. Benedict.
Kasprzak, John F. '75 (BUF) Woodlawn, NY Our Lady of Grace Church.
Kasprzak, Roman A. *m.m.* '51 (FgM) Maryknoll Foreign Missions.
Kasprzyk, James H. '65 (BUF) [8] Cheektowaga, NY Our Lady of Czestochowa Church; Retired.
Kasprzyk, Leon J. '61 (MET) Lambertville, NJ St. John the Evangelist Church.
Kasputis, Thomas R. '76 (CHI) Riverside, IL St. Mary Church.
Kass, George P. '43 (LA) Retired.
Kass, Thomas G. *c.s.v.* '77 (CHI) [N] Arlington Heights, IL Viatorian Province Center-Clerics of St. Viator.
Kassis, Daniel '81 (GLP) Absent on Leave.
Kasteel, Ben '64 (LUB) Plainview, TX Our Lady of Guadalupe Church.
Kasten, Edward F. '54 (MIL) Retired.
Kastenholz, John *o.praem.* (GB) Stephensville, WI St. Patrick Church.
Kastenholz, John P. *o.praem.* '65 (GB) [B] De Pere, WI St. Norbert College; [I] De Pere, WI St. Norbert Abbey.
Kaster, Alfred D. '60 (DUL) On Duty Outside the Diocese.
Kaster, Alfred D. '60 (SAC) Grass Valley, CA St. Patrick Church.
Kastigar, James J. '82 (CHI) [1] Cicero, IL St. Anthony Church.
Kastigar, John J. '52 (CHI) Military Chaplains.
Kastner, Edwin H. '51 (BEL) Retired.
Kastner, James A. '59 (OKL) [4] Oklahoma City, OK Christ the King Church.
Kasuboski, Walter *o.f.m.cap.* '74 (FgM) Capuchin Foreign Missions.
Kasun, Stanley L. '94 (OM) [32] Omaha, NE Our Lady of Guadalupe Church.
Kasza, John '93 (DET) Graduate Studies.
Kaszak, Edward '55 (DET) [12] Detroit, MI St. Bartholomew Church.
Kaszczak, Ivan '85 (STF) [A] Stamford, CT St. Basil College.
Kasznel, Richard C. '65 (STL) St. Mary's, MO Immaculate Conception Church.
Kaszynski, Robert S. '60 (FR) [21] Fall River, MA St. Stanislaus Church.
Katcher, Eugene T. '93 (DET) [5] Warren, MI St. Edmund Church.
Kathol, Quentin *o.s.b.* '63 (KC) Tarkio, MO St. Paul the Apostle Church; [A] Conception, MO Conception Seminary College; [J] Conception, MO Conception Abbey.
Kato, Stephen M. '48 (PIT) Retired.
Katorski, Robert H. '63 (MIL) [13] Milwaukee, WI Blessed Sacrament Church.
Katoski, Eugene *o.f.m.* '45 (CLV) [P] Cleveland, OH Padua Franciscan Friary; [Q] Cleveland, OH Monastery of the Poor Clares.
Katren, Scott E. '92 (E) [4] Oil City, PA St. Stephen Church.
Katricak, Kenneth J. *o.s.b.* '83 (CLV) [N] Beachwood, OH Villa Sancta Anna Home for the Aged, Inc.; [P] Cleveland, OH Benedictine Order of Cleveland.
Katrij, Julian *o.s.b.m.* '40 (RVC) [N] Glen Cove, NY St. Josaphatis Monastery, Novitiate and Retreat House.
Katrij, Julian *o.s.b.m.* '40 (STF) [B] Glen Cove, NY Basilian Fathers Novitiate of the Order of St. Basil the Great.
Katsuno, Peter *s.a.* '40 (NY) [DD] Garrison, NY Generalate of the Franciscan Friars of the Atonement-St. James Friary.
Kattady, Augustine '71 (TUC) Superior, AZ St. Francis of Assisi Parish.
Katz, Jerome A. '71 (SY) Cortland, NY St. Anthony Church.
Katz, Roger L. '89 (DUB) Rockford, IA Holy Name Church.
Katziner, Stephen F. '74 (PH) Warminster, PA Nativity of Our Lord Church.
Kauchak, Justin R. *o.p.* '66 (BR) Hammond, LA Holy Ghost Church.
Kaucheck, Kenneth R. '76 (DET) [3] Troy, MI St. Anastasia Church.
Kaucky, Francis '59 (CHI) Oak Forest, IL St. Damian Church.
Kauffman, Dennis J. *c.s.b.* '79 (ROC) [B] Rochester, NY The Aquinas Institute; [I] Rochester, NY Residence of Basilian Fathers-The Aquinas Institute.
Kauffman, John '75 (DEN) Kremmling, CO St. Peter Church.
Kauffman, Niles *o.f.m.cap.* '58 (MIL) [25] Milwaukee, WI St. Francis of Assisi Church.
Kauffman, William B. '90 (WIL) [1] Wilmington, DE Cathedral of St. Peter; Apostleship of the Sea.
Kauffmann, James F. '75 (RIC) Caroline County, VA St. Mary of the Annunciation Church.
Kaufman, Kent (TOL) Fostoria, OH St. Wendelin Church.
Kaufman, Philip *o.s.b.* '45 (SCL) [I] Collegeville, MN St. John's Abbey, of the Order of St. Benedict.
Kaufman, William C. '74 (PH) [140] Philadelphia, PA Resurrection of Our Lord Church.
Kaufmann, Leo B. *s.j.* '51 (SPK) [K] Spokane, WA Regis Community.
Kaukus, Edwin J. '57 (BUF) Retired.
Kaul, John '75 (DET) Military Chaplains.
Kaunas, Bronius *o.s.j.* '42 (MRY) [G] Santa Cruz, CA Oblates of St. Joseph Provincial House and Shrine.
Kaut, Msgr. Bernd (WDC) [V] Washington, DC Nativity of the Blessed Virgin (German Mission).
Kauta, John B. '67 (NY) Bedford, NY St. Patrick Church.
Kautzky, Jon '62 (DM) Red Oak, IA St. Mary Church.
Kautzman, Jerome G. '59 (BIS) [1] Dickinson, ND Queen of Peace Church.
Kauzlarich, John R. '55 (CHI) Glenwood, IL St. John Church.
Kavanagh, Aelred *o.s.b.* '94 (NO) [P] St. Benedict, LA St. Joseph Abbey.
Kavanagh, Aelred M. *o.s.b.* '93 (NO) [A] St. Benedict, LA St. Joseph's Seminary College.
Kavanagh, Aidan *o.s.b.* '57 (IND) [J] St. Meinrad, IN St. Meinrad Archabbey.
Kavanagh, Charles J. *s.j.* '44 (LA) [C] Los Angeles, CA Loyola Marymount University.
Kavanagh, Msgr. Charles M. '63 (NY) [185] Bronx, NY St. Raymond Church; [HH] New York, NY Alfred E. Smith Memorial Foundation, Inc., The.
Kavanagh, Dermon *c.s.sp.* '65 (SFR) Millbrae, CA St. Dunstan Church.
Kavanagh, Donald '72 (BRK) [213] Queens, NY Our Lady of Lourdes Church.
Kavanagh, Msgr. Edward J. '48 (SAC) [22] Sacramento, CA St. Rose Church; [D] Sacramento, CA St. Patrick Children's Home, Inc.
Kavanagh, Francis X. *o.c.s.o.* '38 (ATL) [I] Conyers, GA The Monastery of the Holy Spirit.
Kavanagh, Henry *c.p.* '75 (BRK) [U] Jamaica, NY Immaculate Conception Monastery.
Kavanagh, James F. '64 (LA) [69] Los Angeles, CA St. Jerome Church.
Kavanagh, Msgr. John C. '42 (PH) Wynnewood, PA Presentation B.V.M. Church.
Kavanagh, Joseph J. *s.j.* '46 (NY) [80] New York, NY Nativity Church.
Kavanagh, Kevin J. '83 (COL) Delaware, OH St. Mary Church.
Kavanagh, Morgan '55 (BLX) Retired.
Kavanagh, Msgr. Richard T. '36 (IND) Retired.
Kavanaugh, Msgr. Charles M. '63 (NY) [HH] New York, NY Partnership for Quality Education, Inc.
Kavanaugh, John '48 (SFR) [34] San Francisco, CA St. Monica Church.
Kavanaugh, Msgr. John C. '42 (PH) Retired.
Kavanaugh, John F. *s.j.* '71 (STL) [P] St. Louis, MO Jesuit Community Corporation at St. Louis University - Jesuit Hall.
Kavanaugh, John J. *s.j.* (STL) [C] St. Louis, MO Saint Louis University.
Kavanaugh, John J. '57 (WIL) Sherwood Park, DE St. John the Beloved Church.
Kavanaugh, John P. '48 (SFR) San Francisco, CA Knights of Malta.
Kavanaugh, Kieran *o.c.d.* '55 (WDC) [B] Washington, DC Monastery of Our Lady of Mount Carmel; [V] Washington, DC Institute of Carmelite Studies and ICS Publications.
Kavanaugh, Michael J. '85 (SAV) Port Wentworth, GA Our Lady of Lourdes Church.
Kavanaugh, Philip M. '73 (LA) [33] Los Angeles, CA Precious Blood Church.
Kavanaugh, Thomas *c.m.* '41 (SAT) [16] San Antonio, TX Our Lady of Grace Church.
Kavaney, C. Robert '85 (BIS) [2] Dickinson, ND St. Joseph Church.
Kavcak, John *m.s.c.* '73 (SB) Upland, CA St. Joseph Church.
Kaveney, Thomas J. '47 (CHI) Berwyn, IL St. Odilo Church; Retired.
Kavin, Msgr. Edward F. '56 (NEW) [N] Rutherford, NJ St. John Vianney Residence for Priests.
Kavookjian, Perry '87 (FRS) [12] Fresno, CA St. Paul Church; [H] Fresno, CA St. Paul Newman Center.
Kavumkal, Sebastian '79 (MAR) Trenary, MI St. Rita Church.
Kawa, Edward *s.d.s.* '64 (GRY) [J] Merrillville, IN Salvatorian Fathers (Society of the Divine Savior).
Kawa, Msgr. Robert J. '69 (STU) Beverly, OH St. Bernard Church; [J] Beverly, OH Marriage Encounter.
Kawamata, Louis *ss.cc.* '74 (FR) [J] Fairhaven, MA

Sacred Hearts Provincial House.
Kawamura, Peter *o.s.b.* '88 (SCL) [I] Collegeville, MN St. John's Abbey, of the Order of St. Benedict.
Kawanguzi, Emmanuel (AUS) [H] Austin, TX Brothers of the Congregation of the Holy Cross.
Kawczynski, Ronald '90 (FAR) Military Chaplains.
Kawecki, Andrew M. '80 (GBG) Leckrone, PA Our Lady of Perpetual Help (St. Mary) Church.
Kawiak, Matthew A. '77 (ROC) Rochester, NY Strong Memorial Hospital.
Kawka, Frederick J. '64 (SAG) Frankenmuth, MI Blessed Trinity Church.
Kawlak, Matthew '77 (ROC) [J] Rochester, NY Sisters of Mercy of the Americas Regional Community of Rochester.
Kawola, Marion *o.f.m.* '45 (PSC) [A] Sybertsville, PA Holy Dormition Monastery.
Kay, Joseph '48 (LR) Paragould, AR St. Mary's Church.
Kay, Kieran M. *o.f.m.* '55 (Y) [K] Canton, OH Sancta Clara Monastery.
Kayajan, Daniel *c.s.c.* '97 (FR) South Easton, MA Holy Cross Church.
Kayatta, Francis P. '80 (PRO) [4] Woonsocket, RI St. Anthony's Church.
Kayler, Gary W. '75 (OKL) Jones, OK St. Robert Bellarmine Church; [E] Oklahoma City, OK Mercy Memorial Health Center.
Kaylor, Lee '81 (SFR) [1] San Francisco, CA Cathedral of St. Mary (Assumption).
Kaylor, Robert W. '62 (Y) [C] Canton, OH Central Catholic High.
Kayranga, Jean Marie *c.i.c.m.* '53 (FgM) Missionhurst Foreign Missions.
Kayrouz, Victor '64 (OLL) Hillside, IL Our Lady of Lebanon Church; Louisville, KY Maronite Catholic Community Church.
Kayser, Leonard '59 (SFS) Mayfield, SD St. Columba Church; Sigel, SD St. Agnes Church; Yankton, SD State Hospital.
Kayser, Robert '52 (RVC) Dix Hills, NY St. Matthew Church; Retired.
Kaywell, Jerome P. '91 (VEN) Cape Coral, FL St. Andrew Church.
Kaza, Msgr. Charles A. '72 (E) Brockway, PA St. Tobias Church.
Kazanchy, Cordius P. *o.f.m.* '60 (PAT) [M] Butler, NJ St. Anthony Friary.
Kazanecki, Thaddeus J. *c.o.* '77 (BRK) [13] Brooklyn, NY St. Athanasius Church.
Kazarnowicz, Anthony S. '75 (WOR) [9] Worcester, MA Our Lady of Czestochowa Church.
Kazer, Michael '80 (DET) [1] Warren, MI St. Anne's Church.
Kazista, Francis G. '66 (WDC) [6] Silver Spring, MD St. John the Baptist Church.
Kazmierczak, Carl M. '55 (MIL) [43] Milwaukee, WI St. John Kanty Church.
Kazmierczak, Msgr. Edward L. '51 (BUF) Retired.
Kazmierczak, Eugene J. '51 (FTW) New Carlisle, IN St. Stanislaus Kostka Church.
Kaznowski, Valentine J. '41 (DET) Retired.
Kcira, Anton '67 (DET) [10] Warren, MI St. Paul Albanian Catholic Community Church.
Keady, John *s.m.* '47 (FgM) Marist Foreign Missions.
Keahi, Christopher '65 (HON) [11] Honolulu, HI St. Patrick Church; [H] Honolulu, HI St. Patrick's Monastery.
Kealey, Edward J. '89 (RVC) Medford, NY St. Sylvester Church.
Kealy, Francis de Paul *o.f.m.* '50 (NY) [35] New York, NY St. Francis of Assisi Church.
Kealy, Hubert J. '64 (GAL) [54] Houston, TX Notre Dame Church.
Kealy, Robert L. '72 (CHI) Highland Park, IL Immaculate Conception Church; [X] Chicago, IL Court of Appeals-Province of Chicago.
Kealy, Sean *c.s.sp.* '65 (PIT) [B] Pittsburgh, PA Duquesne University of the Holy Ghost.
Kean, Cary *o.f.m.* '55 (PAT) [M] Butler, NJ St. Anthony Friary.
Kean, James F. '97 (DET) Northville, MI Our Lady of Victory Church.
Kean, John '40 (BRK) [R] Queens Village, NY Queen of Peace Residence.
Kean, Msgr. John J. '40 (BRK) Retired.
Kean, Joseph H. '64 (ALN) Unassigned; [J] Bethlehem, PA Holy Family Villa.
Keane, Alfred *m.m.* '58 (BO) [W] East Walpole, MA Maryknoll Department of Development.
Keane, Aquinas *o.c.s.o.* '73 (WOR) [N] Spencer, MA St. Joseph's Abbey.
Keane, Brendan '50 (SFD) Retired.
Keane, Denis J. '63 (GF) Fort Benton, MT Immaculate Conception Church.
Keane, Dennis P. '71 (NY) [85] New York, NY Our Lady of Good Counsel Church.
Keane, Edward M. '39 (BRK) [178] Queens, NY Holy Family Church; Retired.
Keane, Eugene '55 (NY) Highland, NY St. Augustine Church.
Keane, James '47 (OAK) Retired.
Keane, Msgr. James P. '45 (SFR) Retired.
Keane, James T. '55 (LFT) Muncie, IN St. Mary Church.
Keane, John F. '57 (SAT) On Duty Outside the Archdiocese.
Keane, John F. '65 (BO) Emergency Response Group.
Keane, John J. '62 (HRT) [10] New Haven, CT St. John the Baptist Church.
Keane, John J. *s.a.* '62 (MRY) Seaside, CA St. Francis Xavier Church.
Keane, John J. '62 (PIT) [6] McKeesport, PA St. Pius V Church; [R] Pittsburgh, PA Office of Chaplaincies.
Keane, Joseph P. '49 (BRK) Retired.
Keane, Martin T. '43 (HRT) Retired.
Keane, Michael J. '57 (SFR) [2] San Rafael, CA St. Isabella Church.
Keane, Patrick '73 (NO) Absent on Leave.
Keane, Patrick J. '51 (SFR) Retired.
Keane, Patrick J. *o.s.a.* '52 (LA) Ojai, CA St. Thomas Aquinas Church.
Keane, Philip S. *s.s.* '67 (BAL) [A] Baltimore, MD St. Mary's Seminary and University.
Keane, Philip S. *s.s.* '67 (SY) On Duty Outside the Diocese.
Keane, Robert E. '78 (STP) Retired.
Keane, Robert L. *s.j.* '78 (BO) [W] Boston, MA The Society of Jesus of New England-Provincial Offices.
Keane, Thomas F. '56 (BO) [1] Quincy, MA St. Ann Church.
Keane, Thomas S. *m.m.* '56 (SJ) [M] Los Altos, CA Maryknoll.
Keane, Msgr. Vincent A. '58 (BRK) [207] Queens, NY Our Lady of the Blessed Sacrament Church.
Keane, Vincent E. '83 (TR) Eatontown, NJ St. Dorothea Church.
Keane, William F. *s.d.b.* '74 (SP) [E] Tampa, FL Mary Help of Christians School.
Keaney, Francis J. *s.s.c.* '66 (BO) [W] Quincy, MA St. Columban's Foreign Mission Society.
Keaney, James P. '54 (R) Retired.
Keaney, John B. *m.m.* '55 (FgM) Maryknoll Foreign Missions.
Kearney, A. Damian *o.s.b.* '56 (PRO) [P] Portsmouth, RI Abbey of St. Gregory the Great.
Kearney, Brendan *s.j.* (LA) Redondo Beach, CA St. James Church.
Kearney, Christopher '68 (LA) [B] Santa Ynez, CA San Lorenzo Novitiate and Seminary.
Kearney, Daniel S. '87 (NY) [95] New York, NY Our Lady Queen of Martyrs Church.
Kearney, Edward J. '51 (NEW) [23] Jersey City, NJ St. Patrick's Church; Woodcliff Lake, NJ Our Lady Mother of the Church.
Kearney, George W. '53 (DEN) Retired.
Kearney, John T. '83 (NY) Lake Katrine, NY St. Catherine Laboure Church.
Kearney, Joseph A. '67 (SCR) [2] Wilkes-Barre, PA Blessed Sacrament Church; Wilkes-Barre, PA Geisinger Wyoming Valley Hospital.
Kearney, Msgr. Joseph V. '46 (LA) Carpinteria, CA St. Joseph Church; Retired.
Kearney, Lawrence '50 (BAK) Jordan Valley, OR St. Bernard's Church.
Kearney, Michael J. '82 (BO) [2] Quincy, MA St. Boniface Church.
Kearney, Msgr. Patrick J. '53 (SD) Retired.
Kearney, Msgr. Philip J. '36 (BO) Retired.
Kearney, Thomas L. *o.p.* '50 (CHI) [N] Chicago, IL Dominicans (Provincial Office).
Kearney, Timothy '96 (BO) [4] Lynn, MA St. Mary Church.
Kearney, Msgr. Vincent L. '43 (KC) Retired.
Kearney, William '83 (SP) Retired.
Kearns, Adam '54 (TR) Marlton, NJ St. Joan of Arc Church.
Kearns, Daniel J. '86 (PH) Glenside, PA St. Luke the Evangelist Church.
Kearns, Daniel P. *c.m.* '69 (STL) [P] St. Louis, MO Vincentian Henrietta Residence.
Kearns, David *o.carm.* '61 (NY) Middletown, NY Our Lady of Mt. Carmel Church.
Kearns, Edward A. '63 (MET) Retired.
Kearns, Edward T. '77 (PH) Newtown, PA St. Andrew Church.
Kearns, Harold M. '61 (HRT) Thomaston, CT St. Thomas Church.
Kearns, John P. '88 (BO) Absent on Leave.
Kearns, Joseph J. '48 (SAG) St. Charles, MI Immaculate Conception Church.
Kearns, Owen *l.c.* '83 (HRT) [B] Cheshire, CT Novitiate of the Legion of Christ.
Kearns, Robert M. *s.s.j.* '63 (BAL) [M] Baltimore, MD St. Joseph Society of the Sacred Heart House of Central Administration.
Kearns, Thomas (KCK) Sabbatical.
Keating, Msgr. Bernard A. '47 (BAK) Retired.
Keating, C. Patrick '69 (SY) [6] Binghamton, NY St. John the Evangelist Church.
Keating, Carroll *s.j.* '61 (SAC) Fair Oaks, CA St. Mel Church.
Keating, David '54 (SFS) Retired.
Keating, Douglas '61 (MRY) Retired.
Keating, Earl *c.p.* '58 (HRT) [M] West Hartford, CT Holy Family Monastery/Retreat.
Keating, Earl *c.p.* '59 (HRT) [Q] Farmington, CT Holy Family Retreat House.
Keating, Edward C. *o.f.m.* '58 (SP) [10] Tampa, FL St. Lawrence Church.
Keating, Edward J. '94 (HBG) Coal Township, PA Our Lady of Hope Church; Trevorton, PA St. Patrick Church.
Keating, George M. '54 (NEW) Kenilworth, NJ St. Theresa's Church; Union, NJ Union Hospital.
Keating, James (COL) [A] Columbus, OH Pontifical College Josephinum.
Keating, James D. *o.p.* '56 (TR) New Monmouth, NJ St. Mary Church.
Keating, James P. '51 (CHI) [65] Chicago, IL St. Francis de Sales Church.
Keating, Msgr. James V. '43 (NY) [3] Kingston, NY St. Joseph Church; Retired.
Keating, James W. '34 (CHI) Lyons, IL St. Hugh Church; Retired.
Keating, John R. *s.j.* '61 (WDC) [M] Washington, DC The Jesuit Community at Georgetown University; [V] Washington, DC Theological Studies, Inc.
Keating, Joseph H. '77 (HRT) [3] Bristol, CT St. Gregory's Church.
Keating, Joseph R. '57 (LC) Retired.
Keating, Michael P. '97 (OM) Bellevue, NE St. Mary Church.
Keating, Pius F. *s.a.* '46 (NY) [DD] Garrison, NY Generalate of the Franciscan Friars of the Atonement-St. James Friary; [DD] Garrison, NY Franciscan Friars of the Atonement.
Keating, Thomas *o.c.s.o.* '49 (DEN) [M] Snowmass, CO St. Benedict's Monastery.
Keating, Thomas F. '66 (SY) Maine, NY Holy Rosary Church.
Keating, Timothy F. *c.ss.r.* '66 (ROC) [K] Canandaigua, NY Notre Dame Retreat House.
Keating, Timothy G. *s.m.* '85 (WDC) [M] Washington, DC Marist Provincial House.
Keaty, Jerome R. '62 (STL) Ladue, MO Church of the Annunziata.
Keaveney, George J. *c.ss.r.* '66 (BRK) [U] Brooklyn, NY Our Lady of Good Counsel Residence.
Keaveney, George J. *c.ss.r.* '66 (FgM) Redemptorist Foreign Missions.
Keaveney, John '59 (NY) Wesley Hills, NY St. Boniface Church.
Keblesh, John W. '93 (PRM) Brunswick, OH St. Emilian Church.
Keck, Barnabas *o.f.m.cap.* '51 (NY) New Paltz, NY St. Joseph Church; [DD] New Paltz, NY St. Joseph Friary.
Keck, Edward L. '73 (COL) Newcomerstown, OH St. Francis de Sales Church.
Keck, Robert J. *s.j.* '60 (NY) [DD] New York, NY West Side Jesuit Community.
Kedzierski, Casimir '60 (PIT) Glassport, PA Queen of the Rosary Church.
Kee, James S. '95 (MOB) [19] Mobile, AL St. Pius X Church.
Keebler, Paul J. '66 (SY) [2] Binghamton, NY St. Ann Church; Binghamton, NY Broome Developmental Center.
Keebler, William C., Jr. '91 (PEO) Alexis, IL St. Theresa's Church.
Keech, William J. *o.s.f.s.* '57 (WIL) [I] Wilmington, DE DeSales House.
Keefe, Bernard A. '63 (BGP) [11] Stamford, CT St. Maurice Church.
Keefe, Charles R. '76 (MIL) [N] Milwaukee, WI Milwaukee Catholic Home.
Keefe, Danel T. '54 (OG) [4] Plattsburgh, NY St. Mary of the Lake Church.
Keefe, Daniel G. '83 (HRT) [2] Meriden, CT St. Joseph Church; Cheshire, CT Connecticut Correctional Institution.
Keefe, Dennis A. '89 (BO) Awaiting Assignment.
Keefe, Donald J. *s.j.* '62 (NY) [A] Yonkers, NY St. Joseph's Seminary.
Keefe, Francis J. '58 (PRO) Scituate, RI St. Joseph Church.
Keefe, Francis L. *c.s.s.* '55 (BO) [W] Waltham, MA Stigmatine House.
Keefe, Gerald E. '47 (STP) Retired.
Keefe, James *ss.cc.* '42 (FR) [J] Fairhaven, MA Sacred Hearts Provincial House.
Keefe, Jeffrey *o.f.m.conv.* '52 (SY) [2] Syracuse, NY Assumption B.V.M. Church.
Keefe, John *c.s.c.* '59 (RNO) Battle Mountain, NV St. John Bosco Church.
Keefe, John A. '49 (ALB) [5] Albany, NY St. Catherine of Siena Church; Retired.
Keefe, John J. '68 (LIN) Aurora, NE St. Mary's Church.
Keefe, John P. *c.s.c.* '59 (FTW) [J] South Bend, IN Congregation of Holy Cross Indiana Province Provincial House.
Keefe, John W. '32 (ALB) Retired.
Keefe, Joseph L. '71 (WIN) [4] Winona, MN St. Mary's

Church; [J] Winona, MN St. Mary's Parish of Winona Endowment Fund, Inc.
Keefe, Thomas H. *m.m.* '55 (NY) [DD] Maryknoll, NY Maryknoll Fathers and Brothers; [DD] Maryknoll, NY Maryknoll Fathers and Brothers.
Keefe, William '36 (CR) Retired.
Keefer, Hugh *o.s.b.* '67 (KCK) [H] Atchison, KS St. Benedict's Abbey.
Keefer, John *o.p.* '56 (DEN) [29] Denver, CO St. Dominic's Parish.
Keefer, Msgr. Oliver D. '28 (PIT) Retired.
Keeffe, Anthony J. (SY) Parish, NY St. Ann Church.
Keefner, James *o.f.m.* '54 (SFD) Madison, IL Our Lady of Czestochowa Church.
Keegan, A. Peter '62 (SFR) Absent on Leave.
Keegan, Fintan *s.s.c.* '33 (PRO) [P] Bristol, RI St. Columban's Retirement House.
Keegan, Gregory J. *m.m.* '43 (NY) [DD] Maryknoll, NY Maryknoll Fathers and Brothers.
Keegan, James M. *s.j.* '71 (BO) [W] Boston, MA The Society of Jesus of New England-Provincial Offices.
Keegan, John *m.m.* (RVC) Stony Brook, NY Stony Brook University Hospital.
Keegan, John E. *m.m.* '60 (NY) [DD] Maryknoll, NY Maryknoll Fathers and Brothers.
Keegan, John W. *s.j.* '69 (PRT) [9] Portland, ME St. Pius X Church; [C] Portland, ME Cheverus High School; [C] Portland, ME Cheverus High School.
Keegan, Martin P. *m.m.* '65 (FgM) Maryknoll Foreign Missions.
Keegan, Terence J. *o.p.* '68 (PRO) [B] Providence, RI Providence College.
Keegan, Terence S. *o.p.* '68 (PRO) [P] Providence, RI St. Thomas Aquinas Priory at Providence College.
Keegstra, Garrett *o.f.m.cap.* '86 (MAD) [G] Madison, WI St. Marys Hospital Medical Center.
Keegstra, Gary *o.f.m.cap.* '86 (MAD) [M] Madison, WI San Damiano Friary.
Keehan, Msgr. Daniel J. (NY) [205] Staten Island, NY Holy Family Church.
Keehan, Edward J. '57 (NY) [16] Yonkers, NY St. Peter Church.
Keehan, John J. '60 (CHI) [14] Chicago, IL St. Ann Church.
Keehan, Terence M. '86 (CHI) [180] Chicago, IL Queen of Angels Church.
Keel, Edwin L. *s.m.* '70 (WDC) [B] Washington, DC Marist College, The Scholasticate.
Keelen, Kevin J. *o.s.a.* '91 (PH) [C] Villanova, PA Villanova University.
Keeley, Alban F. '38 (HRT) Retired.
Keeley, Isaac *o.c.s.o.* '92 (WOR) [N] Spencer, MA St. Joseph's Abbey.
Keeley, John A. '40 (BO) Retired.
Keeley, Patrick J. *c.m.* '58 (STL) Sappington, MO St. Catherine Laboure Church.
Keeley, Patrick P. '54 (NY) Military Chaplains.
Keeling, Paul M. *c.r.s.p.* (BUF) [B] Youngstown, NY The National Shrine Basilica of Our Lady of Fatima.
Keeling, Paul M. *c.r.s.p.* '75 (BUF) [B] Youngstown, NY St. Anthony M. Zaccaria Seminary.
Keen, William '89 (ATL) Roswell, GA St. Andrew Church.
Keena, James *c.ss.r.* '57 (CHI) [136] Chicago, IL St. Michael Church.
Keenan, Alexander J. '76 (BO) [25] Boston, MA Gate of Heaven Church.
Keenan, Basil *o.s.b.* '67 (OKL) Seminole, OK Immaculate Conception Church; [I] Shawnee, OK St. Gregory Abbey.
Keenan, Msgr. Charles J. '42 (LIN) Retired; [E] Lincoln, NE Bonacum House.
Keenan, Christopher *o.f.m.* '71 (NY) [35] New York, NY St. Francis of Assisi Church.
Keenan, Eugene T. '71 (TR) Lavallette, NJ St. Bonaventure Church.
Keenan, Francis T. *s.m.* '63 (RVC) [N] Mineola, NY Provincial Residence and Novitiate.
Keenan, Francis X. *c.p.* '61 (CHI) [N] Chicago, IL Immaculate Conception Monastery.
Keenan, James *s.j.* '61 (BO) [W] Cambridge, MA Weston Jesuit Community.
Keenan, James D. *o.s.f.s.* '49 (PH) [AA] Philadelphia, PA Father Judge Faculty House.
Keenan, James F. *s.j.* '69 (NEW) [C] Jersey City, NJ St. Peter's Preparatory School.
Keenan, John *s.s.s.* '69 (CHI) [U] Chicago, IL Trinity House.
Keenan, John *s.s.s.* '69 (CLV) [P] Cleveland, OH Congregation of the Blessed Sacrament Provincial House.
Keenan, Msgr. John C. '51 (ORG) Retired.
Keenan, John J. '43 (SD) Retired.
Keenan, John J. *s.j.* '55 (ALN) [A] Wernersville, PA Novitiate of St. Isaac Jogues.
Keenan, Joseph A. *c.ss.r.* '47 (BRK) [107] Brooklyn, NY Our Lady of Perpetual Help Basilica Church.
Keenan, Joseph F. '84 (PIT) [74] Pittsburgh, PA Incarnation of the Lord Church.
Keenan, Joseph P. *s.t.* '79 (JKS) Camden, MS Immaculate Conception Church.
Keenan, Msgr. Patrick J. '69 (NY) Cortlandt Manor, NY St. Columbanus Church.
Keenan, Paul *s.t.* '50 (WDC) [M] Adelphi, MD Missionary Servants of the Most Holy Trinity.
Keenan, Paul A. '77 (NY) [93] New York, NY Our Lady of Peace Church.
Keenan, Terence '65 (FR) South Dartmouth, MA St. Mary's Church.
Keenan, Thomas E. '55 (MAN) Retired.
Keenan, Thomas L. '63 (PRO) [3] East Providence, RI St. Margaret Church.
Keenan, Vincent *s.s.j.* '52 (NO) [P] New Orleans, LA Josephite Fathers and Brothers.
Keenan, William R. *o.f.m.* '56 (FgM) Franciscan Foreign Missions.
Keene, David A. '97 (BO) [2] Methuen, MA St. Monica Church.
Keene, James H. *s.j.* '73 (LA) [C] Los Angeles, CA Loyola Marymount University.
Keene, Kenneth R. '95 (PIT) Crafton, PA St. Philip Church.
Keene, Mark '84 (COV) [B] Covington, KY Covington Latin School.
Keene, Mark A. '84 (COV) [5] Covington, KY St. Benedict Church.
Keene, Michael *o.s.b.* '37 (IND) [J] St. Meinrad, IN St. Meinrad Archabbey.
Keene, Warren '81 (STA) [8] Jacksonville, FL Immaculate Conception Church.
Keener, Michael '92 (MIA) Absent on Leave.
Keener, Robert J. '95 (CHI) Chicago Ridge, IL Our Lady of the Ridge Church.
Keeney, Charles P. '78 (BRK) [190] Queens, NY St. Leo Church.
Keeney, Edward *ss.cc.* '61 (FR) [J] Fairhaven, MA Sacred Hearts Provincial House.
Keeney, Timothy '96 (RIC) [2] Newport News, VA Our Lady of Mount Carmel Church.
Keenoy, John A. '87 (STL) [4] St. Charles, MO Sts. Joachim and Ann Church.
Keese, John '74 (LA) Sepulveda, CA Our Lady of Peace Church.
Keesler, Robert L. '36 (WDC) Laurel, MD St. Mary Church; Retired.
Keferl, Francis J. '73 (CIN) Piqua, OH St. Mary Church.
Keffer, Joseph D. *o.s.a.* '47 (ALB) [2] Troy, NY St. Augustine Church.
Keffer, Robert *o.cist.* (LC) [I] Sparta, WI Our Lady of Spring Bank, Cistercian Abbey.
Keffer, Robert F. '68 (WDC) Special Ministries; [S] Washington, DC Archdiocesan Campus Ministry.
Keffer, Thomas '77 (SFR) [K] San Rafael, CA Nazareth House.
Keffer, Thomas '77 (SR) Retired.
Keffler, Leopold *o.f.m.conv.* '63 (IND) [B] Indianapolis, IN Marian College.
Kegel, William *s.j.* '42 (OAK) [1] Walnut Creek, CA St. Anne Church.
Kegel, William M. *s.j.* '42 (MIL) [P] Milwaukee, WI Jesuit Provincial Office, Wisconsin Province.
Kegel, William M. *s.j.* '42 (OAK) [N] Berkeley, CA Jesuit Community at Jesuit School of Theology at Berkeley.
Kegler, Maynard C. *o.m.i.* '51 (STP) [N] St. Paul, MN Oblate Residence.
Kegley, Jeffrey J. '96 (TR) New Monmouth, NJ St. Mary Church.
Kehew, Donal R. '63 (PRO) New Shoreham, RI St. Andrew Church.
Kehoe, Charles B. '73 (BRK) [189] Queens, NY St. Kevin Church.
Kehoe, Daniel J. '39 (PH) Sharon Hill, PA Holy Spirit Church; Retired.
Kehoe, James P. '70 (CHI) [142] Chicago, IL Nativity of Our Lord Church.
Kehoe, Joel *o.s.b.* '78 (B) [C] Jerome, ID Ascension Priory.
Kehoe, Joseph A. *c.s.c.* '39 (FTW) [J] South Bend, IN Congregation of Holy Cross Indiana Province Provincial House.
Kehoe, Joseph F. '66 (SY) Durhamville, NY St. Francis Church; New London, NY Holy Cross Church.
Kehoe, Richard J. '51 (BRK) [U] Jamaica, NY Vincentian Residence.
Kehoe, Richard J. *c.m.* '57 (PH) [B] Philadelphia, PA St. Vincent's Seminary.
Kehoe, Thomas F. '75 (WDC) [3] Bowie, MD St. Edward Church.
Kehres, Franklin P. '68 (TOL) Sandusky, OH SS. Peter and Paul Church.
Kehres, John C. *s.j.* (DET) [27] Detroit, MI Gesu Church.
Kehres, Paul S. *s.j.* '51 (FgM) Provinces.
Keigher, Bernard J. '74 (TR) Maple Shade, NJ Our Lady of Perpetual Help Church.
Keilty, Msgr. John P. '41 (BO) Retired.
Keine, Joachim *o.f.m.conv.* (IND) Indianapolis, IN Veterans' Administration Hospital.
Keiser, Jerome F. '71 (STP) [27] St. Paul, MN St. Mark Church.
Keiser, Ray W. '70 (BIR) Gardendale, AL St. Elizabeth Ann Seton Church.
Keith, Christopher R. '89 (GI) Bridgeport, NE All Souls Church.
Keith, John C. '56 (SD) Retired.
Keitz, Bernard L. *o.p.* '54 (NEW) Harrington Park, NJ Our Lady of Victories Church.
Keitz, Bernard L. *o.p.* '54 (NY) [GG] New York, NY University Apostolate.
Kekeisen, Robert E. '44 (COS) Retired.
Kekeisen, William E. '58 (SFD) Jerseyville, IL St. Francis Xavier Church.
Kekumano, Msgr. Charles A. '49 (JUN) Retired.
Kelaher, Msgr. Felix R. '48 (CHL) Retired.
Kelash, David '94 (PHX) [9] Phoenix, AZ St. Catherine of Siena Church.
Kelbel, Joseph '80 (BAK) Hood River, OR Immaculate Conception Church.
Kelchak, Joseph M. '50 (SUP) Retired.
Keleher, Msgr. J. Patrick '68 (BUF) [R] Williamsville, NY Campus Ministry.
Keliher, Michael *c.s.v.* '76 (LAV) Henderson, NV St. Thomas More Church.
Kelleher, Cornelius '56 (DUL) Beroun, MN St. Joseph's Church.
Kelleher, Cyril *o.f.m.cap.* '46 (LA) Solvang, CA Old Mission Santa Ines Church.
Kelleher, Denis *s.d.b.* '52 (NY) [72] New York, NY Mary Help of Christians Church.
Kelleher, Dennis (NY) Manhattan, NY New York University Medical Center.
Kelleher, Dennis *c.ss.r.* '63 (NY) [DD] Esopus, NY Redemptorist Priests and Brothers C.Ss.R. (Province of Baltimore).
Kelleher, James L. '54 (PRO) [1] Johnston, RI St. Brigid Church.
Kelleher, James P. '40 (DAV) Retired.
Kelleher, James R. *s.o.l.t.* '96 (CC) Skidmore, TX Immaculate Conception Church.
Kelleher, John *o.f.m.* '89 (NEW) [N] Hohokus, NJ St. Anthony of Padua.
Kelleher, Lawrence A. '93 (GAY) Black River, MI St. Gabriel Church; Ossineke, MI St. Catherine Church.
Kelleher, M. Joseph '53 (CHL) Lexington, NC Our Lady of the Rosary Church.
Kelleher, Mark A. '96 (WIL) Fairfax, DE St. Mary Magdalen Church.
Kelleher, Matthew H. *m.m.* '67 (FgM) Maryknoll Foreign Missions.
Kelleher, Michael '65 (BLX) Pascagoula, MS Sacred Heart Church.
Kelleher, Robert N. '59 (BO) [3] Brockton, MA St. Edward Church.
Kelleher, Msgr. Stephen '40 (NY) Retired; [Z] New York, NY Kateri Residence.
Kelleher, Timothy J. '71 (BO) Walpole, MA Blessed Sacrament Church.
Kelleher, Walter T. *m.m.* '56 (FgM) Maryknoll Foreign Missions.
Kelleher, William A. '91 (NY) Bronxville, NY St. Joseph Church.
Kelleher, William J. '52 (ALB) [17] Schenectady, NY St. Thomas the Apostle Church.
Kellen, Elmer W. '50 (WIN) Retired.
Keller, Bernard C. *s.v.d.* '55 (LR) Pine Bluff, AR St. Peter's Church.
Keller, Brendan J. '60 (MOB) Ozark, AL St. John Church.
Keller, Brian M. '73 (BRK) [192] Queens, NY St. Margaret Church.
Keller, Daniel E. '82 (OM) Columbus, NE St. Bonaventure Church.
Keller, Gary W. '71 (HEL) Ronan, MT Sacred Heart Church.
Keller, Gerald J. '65 (CLV) Berea, OH St. Adalbert Church.
Keller, Harvey M. '45 (TOL) Norwalk, OH St. Paul Church; Retired.
Keller, Herbert B. *s.j.* (SCR) [E] Scranton, PA Scranton Preparatory School.
Keller, Herbert B. *s.j.* '81 (PH) [AA] Philadelphia, PA St. Joseph's Preparatory School Jesuit Community, Arrupe House.
Keller, Herbert B. *s.j.* '81 (SCR) [C] Scranton, PA University of Scranton.
Keller, John D. *o.s.a.* '64 (SD) [B] San Diego, CA University of San Diego; [H] San Diego, CA Augustinian Community.
Keller, John F. *s.j.* '47 (NO) [C] New Orleans, LA Loyola University.
Keller, John R. '54 (ORG) [1] Huntington Beach, CA St. Bonaventure Church.
Keller, John T. '74 (GAL) [43] Houston, TX St. Justin Martyr Church.
Keller, Ken '69 (AMA) [10] Amarillo, TX St. Mary's Church.
Keller, Lawrence E. '47 (STP) Retired.
Keller, Lawrence W. '53 (COV) Bellevue, KY Sacred Heart Church; Retired.
Keller, Neil J. '55 (CIN) Retired.
Keller, Paul *c.m.f.* '96 (AUS) San Marcos, TX St. John

the Evangelist Church.
Keller, Paul J. *o.p.* '93 (HRT) [14] New Haven, CT St. Mary's Priory Church.
Keller, Robb '84 (B) Twin Falls, ID St. Edward's Church.
Keller, Robert *o.p.* '83 (SFE) [M] Albuquerque, NM St. Thomas Aquinas.
Keller, Robert E. '67 (CIN) [77] Cincinnati, OH Resurrection of Our Lord Church.
Keller, Robert J. '74 (DET) Harper Woods, MI St. Peter the Apostle Church.
Keller, Robert J. *o.p.* '83 (SFE) [29] Albuquerque, NM St. Thomas Aquinas University Parish.
Keller, Theodore '46 (LEX) [7] Lexington, KY St. Peter Church; Retired.
Keller, Thomas F. '84 (B) Hailey, ID St. Charles Borromeo Church.
Keller, Thomas G. '97 (STL) Mehlville, MO St. Margaret Mary Alacoque Church.
Keller, Thomas J. *m.s.c.* '55 (ORG) Los Alamitos, CA St. Hedwig Church.
Keller, Thomas W. '58 (LR) [10] Little Rock, AR Our Lady of Good Counsel Church.
Kellerman, Raymond C. '73 (CIN) [14] Cincinnati, OH St. Bartholomew Church.
Kellermann, Leonard P. *s.m.* '46 (WDC) [M] Washington, DC Marist Provincial House.
Kelley, Aloysius P. *s.j.* '62 (BGP) [A] Fairfield, CT Fairfield University; [D] Fairfield, CT Fairfield College Preparatory School; [O] Fairfield, CT The Fairfield Jesuit Community-Fairfield University.
Kelley, Arnold E. '56 (BO) Awaiting Assignment.
Kelley, Bennet *c.p.* '49 (HRT) [M] West Hartford, CT Holy Family Monastery/Retreat.
Kelley, Charles F. *s.j.* '84 (BO) [W] Boston, MA The Society of Jesus of New England-Provincial Offices.
Kelley, Charles F. *s.j.* '84 (BUF) [D] Buffalo, NY Canisius High School; [O] Buffalo, NY Canisius Jesuit Community.
Kelley, Clark T. *o.s.f.s.* '64 (STO) [A] Stockton, CA St. Mary's High School.
Kelley, Danny '95 (FWT) [11] Fort Worth, TX St. John the Apostle Church.
Kelley, David F. '88 (WIL) Newark, DE St. Thomas More Oratory Church; Newark, DE University of Delaware.
Kelley, David J. '74 (CIN) [K] Cincinnati, OH Mercy Hospital Anderson.
Kelley, Edward J. '66 (BO) On Duty Outside the Archdiocese.
Kelley, Edward J. '66 (MAN) North Conway, NH Our Lady of the Mountains Church.
Kelley, Edward J. '68 (PRO) On Duty Outside the Diocese.
Kelley, Francis H. '68 (BO) [69] Boston, MA Sacred Heart Church.
Kelley, J. Ralph '34 (NOR) Retired.
Kelley, James *c.pp.s.* '43 (CIN) [B] Carthagena, OH St. Charles.
Kelley, James F. '61 (ANC) Dillingham, AK Holy Rosary Church.
Kelley, John E. '61 (WOR) Baldwinville, MA St. Vincent De Paul Church; Otter River, MA Walter E. Fernald State School.
Kelley, John J. '45 (SCR) Retired.
Kelley, John J. *s.m.* '53 (CIN) [M] Dayton, OH Marianist Provincialate.
Kelley, John W. '59 (STP) [8] St. Paul, MN The Nativity of Our Lord Church.
Kelley, Joseph '46 (SPK) Retired.
Kelley, Joseph J. '87 (PH) [41] Philadelphia, PA St. Edmond Church; [D] Philadelphia, PA Little Flower Catholic High School for Girls.
Kelley, Laurence E. '60 (BO) West Newbury, MA St. Ann Church.
Kelley, Michael J. '75 (WDC) [28] Washington, DC St. Martin of Tours Church.
Kelley, Micheal (IND) Universal, IN St. Joseph Church.
Kelley, Micheal '85 (IND) Clinton, IN Sacred Heart Church.
Kelley, N. F. '62 (SPK) Retired.
Kelley, Omer (GB) White Lake, WI Ss. James & Stanislaus Church.
Kelley, Omer '49 (GB) [F] Antigo, WI Langlade Memorial Hospital.
Kelley, Omer C. '49 (GB) Retired.
Kelley, Paul G. '49 (BO) Winchester, MA St. Mary Church; Retired.
Kelley, Raymond H. *m.m.* '58 (FgM) Maryknoll Foreign Missions.
Kelley, Richard J. '72 (MAN) Jaffrey, NH St. Patrick Church.
Kelley, Robert E. '79 (WOR) Millbury, MA St. Brigid Church.
Kelley, Thomas (SAN) [3] Midland, TX Our Lady of San Juan de Los Lagos Church.
Kelley, Thomas '67 (E) On Duty Outside Diocese.
Kelley, Thomas J. '51 (PH) [11] Philadelphia, PA St. Anne Church.
Kelley, Thomas L. '88 (MAD) [6] Madison, WI Our Lady, Queen of Peace Church.
Kelley, Msgr. Thomas P. '67 (WDC) [1] Silver Spring, MD St. Andrew Apostle Church.
Kelley, William *s.v.d.* (BLX) [E] Bay St. Louis, MS Southern Province of St. Augustine - Provincial Residence.
Kelley, William *s.v.d.* '67 (BLX) [A] Bay St. Louis, MS St. Augustine's; [A] Bay St. Louis, MS St. Augustine's.
Kelley, William F. *s.j.* '44 (OM) [K] Omaha, NE Jesuit Community At Creighton University.
Kelley, William H. *c.s.c.* '70 (BUR) Bennington, VT Sacred Heart/St. Francis de Sales Church.
Kelley, William J. '54 (MAN) Peterborough, NH St. Peter Church.
Kelley, William J. *s.j.* '85 (R) [7] Raleigh, NC St. Raphael Church; [E] Raleigh, NC Jesuit Community.
Kellick, John W. (GAL) Retired.
Kelligar, William L. '53 (OM) [29] Omaha, NE St. Mary Magdalene Church.
Kelliher, Alexander *s.a.* '77 (NY) [DD] Garrison, NY Franciscan Friars of the Atonement.
Kelliher, Arthur J. '56 (MAN) Hanover, NH St. Denis Church.
Kelliher, Daniel *o.c.s.o.* '48 (DEN) [M] Snowmass, CO St. Benedict's Monastery.
Kelliher, Msgr. John J. '58 (WOR) [14] Worcester, MA Our Lady of the Rosary Church.
Kelliher, Michael M. *s.j.* '67 (SEA) [A] Seattle, WA Seattle University.
Kellner, Winfried M. '63 (ROC) [39] Rochester, NY Our Lady of Victory-St. Joseph Church.
Kelly, William A. '59 (STA) Jacksonville Beach, FL St. Paul's Church.
Kelly, Albert P. '72 (MOB) Millbrook, AL St. Elizabeth Ann Seton Church.
Kelly, Alfred '50 (SJ) Retired.
Kelly, Andrew E. '70 (DAV) Iowa City, IA Veteran's Administration Hospital; [J] Iowa City, IA Mercy Hospital.
Kelly, Anthony *s.a.c.* '59 (NY) [91] New York, NY Our Lady of Mt. Carmel Church.
Kelly, Anthony *s.c.j.* '73 (SFS) Chamberlain, SD St. James Church.
Kelly, Arnold E. '56 (BO) Dracut, MA St. Mary of the Assumption Church.
Kelly, Augustine G. *o.s.b.* '88 (MAN) [K] Manchester, NH St. Anselm Abbey.
Kelly, Bernard *c.sp.* '73 (NY) [DD] New York, NY Apostolic Society of the Crusade of the Holy Spirit.
Kelly, Bernard R. '61 (FR) Woods Hole, MA St. Joseph's Church.
Kelly, Bernard T. '41 (LC) Retired.
Kelly, Brian F. '77 (SCR) Military Chaplains.
Kelly, C. Richard '70 (DET) Canton, MI St. Thomas a Becket Church.
Kelly, Charles *s.c.j.* '71 (GAL) [35] Houston, TX Holy Name Church.
Kelly, Msgr. Charles A. '67 (RIC) [1] Richmond, VA Cathedral of the Sacred Heart.
Kelly, Charles F. '48 (CHI) [48] Chicago, IL St. Daniel the Prophet Church; Retired; [X] Chicago, IL Apostolate of the Handicapped.
Kelly, Charles F. '64 (MET) Old Bridge, NJ St. Ambrose Church.
Kelly, Charles H. '54 (PEO) [1] Spring Valley, IL Immaculate Conception Church.
Kelly, Charles S. '69 (NY) Haverstraw, NY St. Peter Church.
Kelly, Columba *o.s.b.* '58 (IND) [B] St. Meinrad, IN St. Meinrad Seminary-College of Liberal Arts; [J] St. Meinrad, IN St. Meinrad Archabbey.
Kelly, Cornelius F. *o.f.m.* '39 (BO) [Z] Boston, MA Saint Anthony Residence.
Kelly, Daniel A. '87 (PAT) [1] Passaic, NJ St. Nicholas Church.
Kelly, Daniel J. '59 (DAV) Retired.
Kelly, Daniel L. '72 (RIC) Onley, VA St. Peter's the Apostle Church.
Kelly, David *o.s.a.* '73 (ALB) Mechanicville, NY Assumption-St. Paul Church.
Kelly, David A. *c.pp.s.* '83 (CHI) [20] Chicago, IL Assumption Church; [X] Chicago, IL Kolbe House.
Kelly, David C. *m.m.* '57 (FgM) Maryknoll Foreign Missions.
Kelly, David F. '66 (PIT) [B] Pittsburgh, PA Duquesne University of the Holy Ghost.
Kelly, David F. '66 (WOR) On Duty Outside the Diocese.
Kelly, David F. '88 (WIL) [O] Newark, DE Univ. of Delaware Newman Center.
Kelly, Donald '63 (ALB) Green Island, NY St. Joseph Church; Retired.
Kelly, E. Francis '67 (SCR) [8] Wilkes-Barre, PA Holy Saviour Church.
Kelly, Edgar M. '43 (MEM) Retired.
Kelly, Msgr. Edward '56 (DM) [3] Council Bluffs, IA St. Patrick Church.
Kelly, Edward '65 (MEM) On Duty Outside the Diocese.
Kelly, Edward '80 (SAT) [42] San Antonio, TX St. John, The Evangelist Church.
Kelly, Edward C. '90 (PH) [70] Philadelphia, PA Immaculate Heart of Mary Church.
Kelly, Edward J. *c.s.sp.* '49 (ARL) [7] Arlington, VA Our Lady, Queen of Peace Church.
Kelly, Edward J. '68 (PH) Lafayette Hill, PA St. Philip Neri Church.
Kelly, Edward M. '68 (MIA) Coral Springs, FL St. Elizabeth Ann Seton Church.
Kelly, Emmett '55 (HEL) Retired.
Kelly, Ernest *o.p.* '43 (Y) [13] Youngstown, OH St. Dominic's Church.
Kelly, Eugene A. '38 (OG) Rosiere, NY St. Vincent de Paul Church; Retired.
Kelly, Eugene D. *s.j.* '53 (PBL) [8] Pueblo, CO Our Lady of Mt. Carmel Church.
Kelly, Eugene L. *o.s.f.s.* '65 (PH) [D] Philadelphia, PA Father Judge High School for Boys; [AA] Philadelphia, PA Father Judge Faculty House.
Kelly, Evangelist *o.f.m.cap.* '49 (SFR) Burlingame, CA Our Lady of Angels Church.
Kelly, Francis '57 (LA) West Los Angeles, CA Veterans Administration Wadsworth Hospital Center; Military and VA Chaplains.
Kelly, Francis *o.f.m.* '89 (PH) [D] Philadelphia, PA Archbishop Ryan High School.
Kelly, Msgr. Francis D. '63 (BO) [A] Weston, MA Pope John XXIII National Seminary.
Kelly, Msgr. Francis D. '80 (WOR) On Duty Outside the Diocese.
Kelly, Francis E. '55 (PH) Valley Forge, PA St. Teresa of Avila Church.
Kelly, Francis X. *o.f.m.* '88 (PH) [AA] Philadelphia, PA St. Pius X Friary.
Kelly, Frank F. '77 (GF) Retired.
Kelly, George *c.ss.r.* '59 (NEW) [2] East Orange, NJ Holy Spirit-Our Lady Help of Christians Church.
Kelly, George *c.ss.r.* '59 (ORL) [F] New Smyrna Beach, FL Redemptorist Fathers of the Vice Province of Richmond.
Kelly, Msgr. George A. '42 (NY) [58] New York, NY St. John the Evangelist Church; Retired.
Kelly, George F. *c.ss.r.* '59 (MET) Lyons, NJ U.S. Veterans Medical Center.
Kelly, Gerald E. *m.m.* '67 (BO) [W] East Walpole, MA Maryknoll Department of Development.
Kelly, Gerald G. '34 (ROC) Retired.
Kelly, Gerard D. '49 (PIT) Jefferson Boro, PA St. Thomas A'Becket Church.
Kelly, Gerard P. *c.m.* '82 (STL) Perryville, MO St. Vincent De Paul Church.
Kelly, Gregory '82 (DAL) McKinney, TX St. Gabriel the Archangel Church.
Kelly, Msgr. J. Morgan '45 (MET) East Brunswick, NJ St. Bartholomew Church; Retired.
Kelly, J. Patrick *o.f.m.* '71 (NY) [DD] New York, NY Franciscan Friars, Order of Friars Minor, Holy Name Province.
Kelly, James (ALB) Retired.
Kelly, James '44 (DOD) Retired.
Kelly, James '47 (MRY) Retired.
Kelly, James *glmy.* '48 (CIN) [M] Fairfield, OH Headquarters of Glenmary Home Missioners.
Kelly, James *c.m.* '53 (BRK) [U] Jamaica, NY Vincentian Residence.
Kelly, James *o.s.b.* '59 (ROC) [I] Pine City, NY Mount Saviour Monastery.
Kelly, James '60 (PHX) Camp Verde, AZ St. Frances Cabrini Church.
Kelly, Msgr. James A. '82 (NY) [II] New Rochelle, NY Opus Dei (Prelature of the Holy Cross and Opus Dei).
Kelly, James B. *o.p.* '62 (CHI) River Forest, IL St. Vincent Ferrer Priory Church.
Kelly, James E. *c.s.c.* '58 (SCR) [C] Wilkes-Barre, PA Kings College.
Kelly, Msgr. James G. '62 (BUF) [44] Buffalo, NY St. Margaret Church.
Kelly, James J. '50 (PH) Brookhaven, PA Our Lady of Charity Church; Broomall, PA St. Pius X Church; Retired.
Kelly, Msgr. James J. '60 (BRK) [24] Brooklyn, NY St. Brigid Church.
Kelly, James J. '83 (LA) Diamond Bar, CA St. Denis Church.
Kelly, Msgr. James P. '62 (RVC) [1] Rockville Centre, NY St. Agnes Cathedral.
Kelly, James Patrick *o.s.f.s.* '63 (SCR) [I] Williamsport, PA Divine Providence Hospital of the Sisters of Christian Charity.
Kelly, James S. *c.ss.r.* '37 (STL) [P] Liguori, MO St. Clement Health Care Center.
Kelly, James T. '92 (BO) [7] Haverhill, MA Sacred Hearts Church.
Kelly, James W. *o.p.* '63 (CHI) [J] Elk Grove Village, IL Alexian Brothers Medical Center, Inc.
Kelly, Joel *o.s.b.* '66 (SCL) St. Cloud, MN Minnesota State Reformatory for Men; [I] Collegeville, MN St. John's Abbey, of the Order of St. Benedict.
Kelly, John *o.m.i.* '47 (OAK) [N] Oakland, CA Oblate Provincial House & Procure.
Kelly, John D. '86 (ARL) McLean, VA St. Luke's Church.

Kelly, John E. '73 (BO) Stoughton, MA St. James Church.
Kelly, John E. '87 (BUF) Amherst, NY St. Leo Church; Angelica, NY Sacred Heart Church; Belmont, NY St. Mary Church.
Kelly, John F. '84 (PT) Bonifay, FL Blessed Trinity Church; Chipley, FL St. Joseph the Worker Church.
Kelly, Msgr. John J. '28 (CAM) Retired.
Kelly, John J. *o.s.a.* '42 (MIA) [H] Miami, FL Casa San Lorenzo.
Kelly, Msgr. John J. '44 (CAM) Wildwood Crest, NJ Assumption B.V.M. Church.
Kelly, John J. '64 (BLX) Clermont Harbor, MS St. Ann Church.
Kelly, John J. *o.s.f.s.* '71 (HBG) [K] Harrisburg, PA Catholic Campus Ministry.
Kelly, John J. '87 (PH) Huntingdon Valley, PA St. Albert the Great Church.
Kelly, John L. '54 (BAL) Glen Burnie, MD Church of the Good Shepherd.
Kelly, John P. '45 (BO) [6] Somerville, MA Patronage of St. Joseph Church; Retired.
Kelly, John R. '68 (NY) Military Chaplains.
Kelly, John R. '68 (R) Hope Mills, NC Good Shepherd Church.
Kelly, John T. '61 (ALB) Albany, NY Memorial Hospital; Special Assignment.
Kelly, John T. *s.j.* '74 (WDC) [M] Washington, DC The Jesuit Community at Georgetown University.
Kelly, John W. '44 (LIN) Retired; [E] Lincoln, NE Bonacum House.
Kelly, John W. *c.ss.r.* '51 (HBG) [H] Ephrata, PA St. Clement's Mission House.
Kelly, Joseph A. *o.praem.* '47 (HBG) Millersburg, PA Queen of Peace Church.
Kelly, Joseph A. '63 (NEW) [B] Jersey City, NJ Saint Peter's College; [N] Jersey City, NJ Jesuits of Saint Peter's College, Inc.
Kelly, Joseph A. *s.j.* '63 (NY) [68] New York, NY St. Malachy's Church.
Kelly, Joseph Anthony '31 (ALB) Retired.
Kelly, Joseph J. '57 (PEO) Brimfield, IL St. Joseph's Church.
Kelly, Joseph J. '78 (NY) [127] Bronx, NY St. Anthony Church.
Kelly, Joseph L. *c.s.sp.* '50 (FgM) Holy Ghost Foreign Missions.
Kelly, Msgr. Joseph P. '66 (SCR) [9] Scranton, PA Holy Rosary Church; [Q] Tunkhannock, PA Camp St. Andrew.
Kelly, Kenneth W. '79 (KCK) Burlington, KS St. Francis Xavier's Church; Emerald, KS St. Patrick's Church; Waverly, KS St. Joseph's Church; Westphalia, KS St. Teresa's Church.
Kelly, Msgr. Laurence F. '36 (PH) West Chester, PA St. Agnes Church; Retired.
Kelly, Lawrence D. *s.j.* '46 (MIL) [P] Milwaukee, WI Arrupe House Jesuit Community.
Kelly, Leonard A. *o.f.m.* '43 (PAT) [M] Butler, NJ St. Anthony Friary.
Kelly, Msgr. Martin '47 (NEW) [2] Jersey City, NJ St. Aloysius Church.
Kelly, Martin C. '48 (PHX) Retired.
Kelly, Martin T. '89 (MAN) [8] Nashua, NH St. Patrick Church.
Kelly, Msgr. Matthew H. '42 (LA) Retired.
Kelly, Maurus *o.f.m.* '56 (LA) [R] Santa Barbara, CA Franciscan Friary, Order of Friars Minor (Old Mission).
Kelly, Michael *ss.cc.* '65 (FR) [J] Fairhaven, MA Sacred Hearts Provincial House.
Kelly, Michael D. '71 (MOB) [19] Mobile, AL St. Pius X Church.
Kelly, Michael D. '76 (SFS) Huron, SD St. Martin Church.
Kelly, Michael D. '95 (ARL) Falls Church, VA St. James Church.
Kelly, Michael E. (STO) [10] Stockton, CA Presentation of B.V.M. Church.
Kelly, Msgr. Michael E. '66 (NEW) [C] West Orange, NJ Seton Hall Preparatory School.
Kelly, Michael E. '71 (SR) Graduate Studies.
Kelly, Michael J. '53 (OM) Retired.
Kelly, Michael J. '82 (PH) [A] Wynnewood, PA Theological Seminary of St. Charles Borromeo, Overbrook.
Kelly, Michael M. '81 (SR) Arcata, CA St. Mary's Church.
Kelly, Neil '91 (NY) [159] Bronx, NY St. Lucy Church.
Kelly, Pat '58 (IND) [13] Indianapolis, IN St. Andrew the Apostle Church.
Kelly, Patrick J. '48 (BO) Wayland, MA St. Ann Church.
Kelly, Patrick J. '58 (IND) [28] Indianapolis, IN St. Matthew Church; [D] Indianapolis, IN Cathedral High School (Cathedral Trustees, Inc.).
Kelly, Paul *s.c.j.* '77 (MIL) [B] Hales Corners, WI Sacred Heart School of Theology; [P] Milwaukee, WI St. Joseph House of Formation.
Kelly, Paul '83 (SC) Coon Rapids, IA Annunciation Church.
Kelly, Paul J. '74 (OG) Lake Pleasant, NY St. James, Major Church; Wells, NY St. Anne Church.
Kelly, Paul M. '47 (LA) Retired.
Kelly, Philip C.M. *c.s.c.* '42 (ORL) [F] Cocoa Beach, FL Holy Cross Fathers, Eastern Priests Province.
Kelly, Philip J. '93 (NY) [63] New York, NY St. Joseph of the Holy Family Church.
Kelly, Randy '94 (SAG) Ubly, MI St. Columbkille Church; Ubly, MI St. John the Evangelist Church.
Kelly, Raymond J. '61 (BRK) [77] Brooklyn, NY St. Malachy's Church; [L] Brooklyn, NY Catholic Charities.
Kelly, Raymond M. '49 (PRO) [28] Providence, RI St. Patrick's Church.
Kelly, Richard J. '88 (NEW) Ramsey, NJ St. Paul Church.
Kelly, Robert *s.v.d.* (BLX) [E] Bay St. Louis, MS Southern Province of St. Augustine - Provincial Residence.
Kelly, Robert '68 (WOR) Absent on Leave.
Kelly, Robert *s.v.d.* '86 (BLX) [A] Bay St. Louis, MS St. Augustine's.
Kelly, Robert F. *o.praem.* '53 (WIL) [B] Claymont, DE Archmere Academy; [I] Claymont, DE Immaculate Conception Priory of the Canons Regular of Premontre; [I] Claymont, DE Norbertine Fathers of Delaware, Inc.
Kelly, Robert G. *s.j.* '57 (NY) [A] Yonkers, NY St. Joseph's Seminary; [DD] New York, NY Jesuit Community at Fordham University.
Kelly, Msgr. Robert J. '34 (NY) [200] Staten Island, NY St. Charles Church; Retired.
Kelly, Robert J. *s.j.* '52 (FgM) Provinces.
Kelly, Msgr. Robert J. '53 (CHR) [11] Charleston, SC Church of the Nativity.
Kelly, Robert J. '74 (ALT) [12] Altoona, PA St. Rose of Lima Church.
Kelly, Robert L. '77 (SY) [1] Utica, NY Blessed Sacrament Church.
Kelly, Robert M. '68 (SAN) Retired.
Kelly, Robert M. *o.p.* '89 (STP) [15] Minneapolis, MN St. Albert the Great Church.
Kelly, Thomas *o.f.m.* '62 (NEW) Wood-Ridge, NJ Our Lady of the Assumption Church.
Kelly, Thomas D. '77 (DEN) On Duty Outside the Archdiocese.
Kelly, Thomas D. '77 (LA) Lompoc, CA Vandenberg Air Force Base.
Kelly, Thomas E.J. *s.j.* (STL) [C] St. Louis, MO Saint Louis University.
Kelly, Thomas E.J. *s.j.* '79 (STL) [P] St. Louis, MO Leo Brown Jesuit Community.
Kelly, Thomas F. (BRK) [91] Brooklyn, NY Our Lady of Angels Church.
Kelly, Thomas F. '41 (BRK) Retired.
Kelly, Msgr. Thomas F. '47 (Y) Retired.
Kelly, Thomas F. '56 (PEO) Bartonville, IL St. Anthony Church.
Kelly, Msgr. Thomas J. '36 (CLV) Peninsula, OH Mother of Sorrows Church; Retired.
Kelly, Thomas J. '43 (PH) Maple Glen, PA St. Alphonsus Church; Retired.
Kelly, Thomas J. '68 (ALB) [10] Troy, NY St. Patrick Church.
Kelly, Thomas J.C. *s.j.* '48 (BO) [E] Boston, MA Boston College High School & Jesuit Community.
Kelly, Thomas M. '90 (BIR) Guntersville, AL St. William's Church.
Kelly, Thomas P. '70 (BO) Watertown, MA St. Patrick Church.
Kelly, Thomas R. '67 (NY) [144] Bronx, NY St. Gabriel Church.
Kelly, Thomas W. *o.s.f.s.* '50 (CAM) [M] Pittsgrove, NJ Villa St. Joseph.
Kelly, Timothy *o.s.b.* '61 (SCL) [B] Collegeville, MN St. John's University.
Kelly, Tony *s.a.c.* '55 (NY) [DD] New York, NY Pallottine Fathers.
Kelly, Vincent J. *c.ss.r.* '39 (BO) [13] Boston, MA Our Lady of Perpetual Help Church.
Kelly, Vincent J. '57 (SY) Oriskany Falls, NY St. Joseph Church.
Kelly, Vincent T. '56 (MIA) [9] Fort Lauderdale, FL St. John the Baptist Church; [C] Fort Lauderdale, FL St. Thomas Aquinas High School.
Kelly, William *s.v.d.* '49 (TR) [M] Bordentown, NJ Society of the Divine Word.
Kelly, William E. '40 (NY) Retired; [DD] New York, NY Our Lady of Consolation Residence.
Kelly, William J. '48 (CHI) Retired.
Kelly, William J. *s.j.* '54 (MIL) [P] Milwaukee, WI Jesuit Community at Marquette University.
Kelly, Msgr. William M. '47 (SY) [3] Rome, NY St. Paul Church.
Kelly, William M. *s.d.s.* '79 (BIR) [2] Huntsville, AL St. Mary of the Visitation Church.
Kelly, William T. '78 (CIN) On Duty Outside the Archdiocese.
Kelmartin, John '49 (BAL) [77] Baltimore, MD Our Lady of Victory Church.
Kelmartin, John J. '49 (BAL) Retired.
Kelpinski, Donald *o.m.v.* (BO) Boston, MA Children's Hospital.
Kelpinski, Donald *o.m.v.* '89 (BO) [W] Milton, MA Oblate Residence (St. Joseph House).
Kelpsas, Anthony *m.i.c.* '53 (JOL) Darien, IL Our Lady of Peace Church.
Kelpsas, Francis J. '50 (CHI) [141] Chicago, IL Nativity of the Blessed Virgin Mary Church; Retired.
Kelsch, Dennis J. *o.s.f.s.* '72 (TOL) [37] Toledo, OH St. Pius X Church.
Kelsch, Emmanuel *o.s.b.* '38 (SCL) [I] Collegeville, MN St. John's Abbey, of the Order of St. Benedict.
Kelso, Francis E. '61 (MAN) Rochester, NH St. Mary Church.
Kelso, Ronald *s.s.c.* '73 (FgM) St. Columban's Foreign Mission.
Kelty, Charles J. '40 (L) Retired.
Kelty, Edward *o.s.* '89 (PCE) On Duty Outside the Diocese.
Kelty, Msgr. Leo A. '60 (TR) Howell Township, NJ St. William the Abbot Church.
Kelty, Matthew *o.c.s.o.* '46 (L) [L] Trappist, KY Abbey of Our Lady of Gethsemani, of the Order of Cistercians of the Strict Observance.
Kemberling, Andrew J. *o.s.b.* '88 (DEN) [2] Boulder, CO Sacred Heart of Mary Church.
Kemberling, Andrew J. *o.s.b.* '88 (PBL) [F] Canon City, CO Holy Cross Abbey.
Kemeter, Robert '72 (PSC) Pittston, PA St. Michael Church.
Kemme, Allen '91 (SFD) [4] Springfield, IL Little Flower Church.
Kemme, Carl A. '86 (SFD) [1] Decatur, IL Holy Family Church.
Kemme, Joseph A. *s.j.* '64 (WDC) [P] Faulkner, MD Loyola on the Potomac Retreat House.
Kemmer, Victor A. '43 (MIL) St. Kilian, WI St. Kilian Church; Retired.
Kemmery, Robert J. '54 (MAN) Retired.
Kemner, Gregory *o.f.m.* '55 (FgM) Franciscan Foreign Missions.
Kemner, Kieran *o.f.m.* '53 (CHI) [N] Countryside, IL St. Gratian Friary, Franciscan Friars.
Kemo, Kurt H. '83 (STU) Toronto, OH St. Francis of Assisi Church; Toronto, OH St. Joseph's Church; [J] Steubenville, OH RCIA.
Kemp, Dennis '73 (SEA) [14] Seattle, WA St. Mark Church.
Kemp, Patrick W. '55 (WDC) Retired.
Kemp, Raymond B. '67 (WDC) [40] Washington, DC St. Stephen Martyr Church; Special Ministries; [V] Washington, DC Woodstock Theological Center.
Kemp, Thomas L. '52 (BUF) East Bethany, NY Immaculate Conception Church.
Kempa, Stanislaus '73 (BO) [2] Lowell, MA Holy Trinity Church.
Kempczynski, Msgr. John '51 (BUF) Retired.
Kempczynski, Msgr. John '57 (BUF) [5] Tonawanda, NY St. Timothy Church.
Kempen, Gerald *o.praem.* (GB) Norman, WI St. Joseph Church.
Kempen, Gerald B. *o.praem.* (GB) Tisch Mills, WI Nativity of the Blessed Virgin Mary Church.
Kemper, Jeffrey M. '79 (CIN) [B] Cincinnati, OH Mt. St. Mary's Seminary of the West.
Kemper, John *s.s.* '83 (SAT) [A] San Antonio, TX The Assumption-St. John's Seminary; [C] San Antonio, TX Oblate School of Theology.
Kemper, John C. *s.s.* '83 (HBG) On Duty Outside the Diocese.
Kempf, Joseph G. '80 (STL) Ballwin, MO Holy Infant Church.
Kempf, William G. '84 (STL) Richmond Heights, MO St. Luke the Evangelist Church.
Kempfer, James T. '69 (JOL) Addison, IL St. Joseph Church.
Kempfirl, Fred '65 (NY) Milton, NY St. James Church.
Kemphues, Carl *o.f.m.* '56 (FgM) Franciscan Foreign Missions.
Kempkes, Lambert *c.m.m.* '50 (CHI) [J] Evergreen Park, IL Little Company of Mary Hospital and Health Care Centers.
Kempski, Leonard J. '66 (WIL) [4] Wilmington, DE Christ Our King Church.
Kencik, Marion M. '62 (KAL) Niles, MI St. Mary Church.
Kendall, Jeffrey A. '97 (CHR) [2] Columbia, SC St. Joseph Church.
Kendall, Michael *s.d.s.* '61 (FRS) [C] Fresno, CA Saint Agnes' Medical Center.
Kendall, Philip *c.s.v.* '62 (KCK) [1] Kansas City, KS Cathedral of St. Peter the Apostle; [I] Kansas City, KS Convent of the Sisters, Servants of Mary.
Kendall, R. Daniel *s.j.* '70 (SFR) [N] San Francisco, CA Jesuit Community at University of San Francisco.
Kendzierski, James *o.f.m.* '81 (MIL) Sturtevant, WI St. Sebastian Church.
Kendzierski, Norbert V. '64 (DET) Farmington, MI St. Colman Church.
Kenealy, John J. *s.j.* '58 (FgM) Provinces.
Kenealy, Thomas L. *s.j.* '58 (CHI) [N] Evanston, IL Canisius House.
Kenefick, Paul F. '56 (HRT) [11] Hartford, CT St.

Lawrence O'Toole Church; [3] West Hartford, CT St. John the Evangelist Church.
Kenehan, David A. *o.s.f.s.* '74 (TOL) [K] Toledo, OH Oblates of St. Francis de Sales.
Kenkel, Benedict J. '53 (DM) Guthrie Center, IA St. Mary Church.
Kenkel, Leonard A. '60 (DM) Creston, IA Holy Spirit Church.
Kenlon, Joseph *o.f.m.cap.* '58 (NY) State, NY Shawangunk Correctional Facility; State, NY Wallkill Correctional Facility.
Kenlon, Knute *o.f.m.cap.* '58 (NY) New Paltz, NY St. Joseph Church; [DD] New Paltz, NY St. Joseph Friary.
Kenna, Daniel *o.f.m.* '73 (R) [4] Raleigh, NC St. Francis of Assisi Church.
Kenna, Donald J. '64 (BRK) [4] Brooklyn, NY All Saints Church.
Kenna, John A. '39 (DET) Retired.
Kenna, John Thomas '88 (CC) On Special Assignment; [F] Corpus Christi, TX Mount Carmel Home.
Kenna, Joseph J. '67 (YAK) On Duty Outside the Diocese.
Kenna, Richard A. *s.j.* '57 (BAL) [M] Baltimore, MD Jesuit Fathers and Brothers Maryland Provincial Curia.
Kenna, Richard A. *s.j.* '57 (FgM) Provinces.
Kenna, Thomas J. '63 (NEW) Lyndhurst, NJ Our Lady of Mount Carmel Church.
Kennard, George V. *s.j.* '50 (STL) [P] St. Louis, MO Jesuit Community Corporation at St. Louis University - Jesuit Hall.
Kenneally, James P. '62 (DET) [8] Dearborn, MI Sacred Heart Church.
Kenneally, John A. '69 (SAV) [8] Savannah, GA St. James Church.
Kenneally, William F. (BO) Retired.
Kenneally, William G. '61 (CHI) [71] Chicago, IL St. Gertrude Church.
Kennealy, Thomas P. *s.j.* '62 (CIN) [D] Cincinnati, OH Xavier University; [M] Cincinnati, OH Jesuit Community at Xavier Unversity.
Kennedy, Alan '52 (P) Retired.
Kennedy, Alex '90 (TLS) Grove, OK St. Elizabeth Church; Langley, OK St. Frances of Rome Church; Vinita, OK Holy Ghost Church.
Kennedy, Andrew '63 (BIR) [15] Birmingham, AL Our Lady of Lourdes Church.
Kennedy, Arthur L. '67 (STP) [C] St. Paul, MN University of St. Thomas.
Kennedy, Bernard *o.f.m.* (CHI) [D] River Grove, IL Holy Cross High School.
Kennedy, Charles J. '66 (PH) Bridgeport, PA St. Augustine Church.
Kennedy, Charles T. '57 (BGP) [K] Trumbull, CT St. Joseph's Manor.
Kennedy, Charles T. '57 (HRT) Retired.
Kennedy, Msgr. Christopher J. '44 (LA) [3] Long Beach, CA St. Barnabas Church; Retired.
Kennedy, Daniel J. *o.p.* '60 (L) [47] Louisville, KY St. Louis Bertrand Church.
Kennedy, David G. '55 (BUR) Retired.
Kennedy, Msgr. David W. '53 (GAL) Conroe, TX Sacred Heart Church.
Kennedy, David William '97 (OWN) [1] Owensboro, KY St. Stephen Cathedral.
Kennedy, Donal P. '60 (YAK) Prosser, WA Sacred Heart Church.
Kennedy, Msgr. Edward J. (CAM) Retired.
Kennedy, Edward J. '68 (PH) [53] Philadelphia, PA St. Hedwig Church; [X] Darby, PA St. Francis Country House.
Kennedy, Edward J. '93 (GRY) Highland, IN Our Lady of Grace Church.
Kennedy, Edward M. '59 (SPR) [J] Holyoke, MA Sisters of Providence Infirmary.
Kennedy, Msgr. Edwin J. (SFR) [K] San Francisco, CA Home for the Aged of the Little Sisters of the Poor.
Kennedy, Msgr. Edwin J. '32 (SFR) Retired.
Kennedy, Ernest E. '56 (CHR) Special Assignment.
Kennedy, Msgr. Francis B. '39 (CIN) [89] Cincinnati, OH St. William Church; Retired; Retired.
Kennedy, Francis M. '64 (SPR) [7] Chicopee, MA St. Mary's Church.
Kennedy, Francis P. '46 (RCK) Rochelle, IL St. Patrick Church.
Kennedy, Gary L. '68 (PBL) Alamosa, CO Sacred Heart Church.
Kennedy, George *o.carm.* '78 (WDC) [B] Washington, DC Whitefriars Hall.
Kennedy, Hugh A. *s.j.* '48 (BAL) [M] Baltimore, MD Jesuit Fathers and Brothers Maryland Provincial Curia.
Kennedy, Msgr. J. Nevin '58 (MET) Somerville, NJ Immaculate Conception Church.
Kennedy, James '94 (SD) Leave of Absence.
Kennedy, James M. '54 (SY) North Syracuse, NY St. Rose of Lima Church.
Kennedy, Jeremiah *c.p.* '47 (HRT) [M] West Hartford, CT Holy Family Monastery/Retreat.
Kennedy, Jerrold F. '66 (OAK) [4] Alameda, CA St. Philip Neri Church.
Kennedy, Msgr. John '50 (MRY) Retired.
Kennedy, John '56 (SFD) Retired.
Kennedy, John A. '50 (LA) Retired.
Kennedy, John D. '93 (SHP) [3] Monroe, LA Our Lady of Fatima Church; [A] Monroe, LA St. Frederick High School; [G] Monroe, LA Catholic Campus Ministry at Northeast Louisiana University.
Kennedy, John F. *m.m.* '55 (FgM) Maryknoll Foreign Missions.
Kennedy, John F. '63 (NEW) Scotch Plains, NJ Immaculate Heart of Mary Church.
Kennedy, Msgr. John J. '49 (STL) Richmond Heights, MO St. Luke the Evangelist Church; Retired.
Kennedy, Msgr. John S. '35 (HRT) Retired.
Kennedy, John V. *c.m.* '49 (PH) [AA] Philadelphia, PA Congregation of the Mission.
Kennedy, Joseph J. '48 (PH) Media, PA Nativity of the Blessed Virgin Mary Church; Retired.
Kennedy, Joseph M. *s.j.* '55 (BAL) [B] Baltimore, MD Loyola College; [M] Baltimore, MD Jesuit Community of Loyola College, Inc.; [Q] Baltimore, MD Jesuit Jamshedpur Mission Society, Inc.
Kennedy, Joseph P. '56 (SY) Camden, NY St. John Church.
Kennedy, Joseph P. '73 (WDC) Landover Hills, MD St. Mary's Catholic Church.
Kennedy, Kevin C. '95 (WDC) Kensington, MD Holy Redeemer Church.
Kennedy, Laurence W. '57 (SY) [13] Syracuse, NY St. Brigid and St. Joseph Church.
Kennedy, Leo *o.f.m.conv.* '90 (L) [7] Louisville, KY St. Anthony Church.
Kennedy, Leo R. *m.m.* '59 (FgM) Maryknoll Foreign Missions.
Kennedy, Leonard A. *c.s.b.* '47 (GAL) [Q] Sugar Land, TX Basilian Mission Center.
Kennedy, Malcolm M. '61 (WDC) [T] Washington, DC Opus Dei.
Kennedy, Michael E. *s.j.* '77 (LA) [10] Los Angeles, CA Dolores Mission Church.
Kennedy, Michael J. *c.m.* '67 (BAL) Emmitsburg, MD St. Joseph Church; [M] Emmitsburg, MD Vincentian House.
Kennedy, Michael J. '67 (STP) Cedar, MN St. Patrick Church.
Kennedy, Oliver *s.s.c.* '47 (OM) [K] St. Columbans, NE St. Columban's Foreign Mission Society.
Kennedy, Patrick '53 (DEN) [19] Denver, CO Our Lady of Grace Church.
Kennedy, Patrick A. '77 (STP) Fridley, MN St. William Church.
Kennedy, Patrick J. R. '70 (NO) Luling, LA St. Anthony of Padua Church.
Kennedy, Patrick J.R. '70 (NO) Retired.
Kennedy, Paul M. '77 (PH) Rydal, PA St. Hilary of Poitiers Church; [D] Philadelphia, PA Cardinal Dougherty High School.
Kennedy, Richard '67 (TOL) Mansfield, OH St. Peter Church.
Kennedy, Richard C. '73 (ORG) [7] Santa Ana, CA St. Barbara's Church.
Kennedy, Robert (ROC) [A] Rochester, NY St. Bernard's Institute.
Kennedy, Robert E. *s.j.* '65 (NEW) [B] Jersey City, NJ Saint Peter's College; [N] Jersey City, NJ Jesuits of Saint Peter's College, Inc.
Kennedy, Robert J. *o.f.m.* '90 (NY) [48] New York, NY Holy Name of Jesus Church.
Kennedy, Robert R. '66 (BO) [48] Boston, MA St. Mary, Star of the Sea Church.
Kennedy, Robert T. '59 (NY) On Duty Outside the Archdiocese.
Kennedy, Robert T. '59 (WDC) [C] Washington, DC Catholic University of America, The.
Kennedy, Russell F. '75 (NOR) [4] Norwich, CT St. Mary Church.
Kennedy, Russell P. '75 (NOR) New London, CT St. Mary, Star of the Sea Church.
Kennedy, Stanley T. *m.s.* '70 (HRT) [M] Hartford, CT Missionaries of LaSalette Provincial Secretary.
Kennedy, T. Frank *s.j.* '76 (BO) [W] Chestnut Hill, MA The Jesuit Community at Boston College.
Kennedy, Thaddeus J. *o.c.s.o.* '58 (DUB) [K] Peosta, IA New Melleray Abbey, Order of Cistercians of the Strict Observance.
Kennedy, Msgr. Thomas I. '41 (SFR) Retired; [K] San Rafael, CA Nazareth House.
Kennedy, Thomas R. *c.m.* '64 (PH) [AA] Philadelphia, PA Congregation of the Mission.
Kennedy, Victor P. '77 (NEW) [3] Jersey City, NJ St. Anne's Church.
Kennedy, Vincent A. '44 (RVC) East Meadow, NY Nassau County, Fire Chiefs, Council of; Retired.
Kennedy, William H. '65 (ALB) Stottville, NY Holy Family Church; West Coxsackie, NY Coxsackie Correctional Facility.
Kennedy, William J. *s.j.* '65 (BGP) [2] Greenwich, CT St. Michael the Archangel Church; [O] Fairfield, CT The Fairfield Jesuit Community-Fairfield University.
Kennedy, William J. *s.j.* '65 (BO) [W] Boston, MA The Society of Jesus of New England-Provincial Offices.
Kennedy, William J. '69 (NY) Retired; [DD] New York, NY Pope John Paul II Residence.
Kennedy, William M. '71 (BO) Military & VA Chaplains.
Kennedy, William M. '71 (CIN) [8] Cincinnati, OH St. Ann Church.
Kennedy, Msgr. William P. '33 (STO) Modesto, CA Our Lady of Fatima Church; Retired.
Kennehan, John P. '62 (OG) Potsdam, NY St. Mary Church.
Kennelley, James J. '70 (E) Du Bois, PA St. Joseph Church.
Kennelly, Daniel '77 (BGP) [2] Stratford, CT St. James Church; [I] Bridgeport, CT St. Vincent's Medical Center.
Kennelly, Michael F. *s.j.* '46 (SP) [8] Tampa, FL Sacred Heart Church.
Kennelly, Stephen '69 (SAN) Miles, TX St. Thomas Church; Olfen, TX St. Boniface Church; Rowena, TX St. Joseph's Church.
Kennerk, T. Daniel *c.s.c.* '53 (FgM) Holy Cross Foreign Missions.
Kenney, Albert A. (PRO) [E] Providence, RI La Salle Academy.
Kenney, Albert A. '94 (PRO) [9] Pawtucket, RI St. Mary of the Immaculate Conception Church.
Kenney, Daniel J. *s.j.* '63 (FgM) Provinces.
Kenney, Daniel J. *s.j.* '63 (MIL) [P] Milwaukee, WI Jesuit Provincial Office, Wisconsin Province.
Kenney, Francis J. *s.m.* '49 (CIN) [9] Dayton, OH Emmanuel Church; [M] Dayton, OH Marianist Provincialate.
Kenney, Francis P. '87 (WIL) Brandywood, DE Church of the Holy Child.
Kenney, Gerard '97 (LUB) [1] Lubbock, TX Cathedral Christ the King Church.
Kenney, Henry *s.j.* '52 (LEX) Special Assignment.
Kenney, James J. *s.j.* '57 (FgM) Provinces.
Kenney, Msgr. Jeremiah '72 (BAL) [Q] Baltimore, MD Holy Name Society (Union).
Kenney, Msgr. Jeremiah F. (BAL) [41] Baltimore, MD Immaculate Conception Church.
Kenney, Msgr. Jeremiah F. '72 (BAL) Special Assignment.
Kenney, John B. '57 (BUR) Retired.
Kenney, Joseph A. '43 (BAL) [25] Baltimore, MD St. Clement Church; Retired; [J] Timonium, MD Stella Maris Operating Corporation.
Kenney, Kevin T. '94 (STP) [31] Minneapolis, MN St. Olaf Church.
Kenney, Mark G. *s.m.* '79 (WDC) [M] Washington, DC Marist Provincial House.
Kenney, Martin F. *s.s.j.* '54 (BAL) [M] Baltimore, MD St. Joseph's Manor.
Kenney, Paul C. *s.j.* '72 (BO) [W] Boston, MA The Society of Jesus of New England-Provincial Offices.
Kenney, Peter J. *s.s.j.* '46 (BAL) [M] Baltimore, MD St. Joseph Society of the Sacred Heart House of Central Administration.
Kenney, Msgr. Philip J. '39 (MAN) Retired.
Kenney, Robert D. *o.s.f.s.* '52 (WIL) [B] Wilmington, DE Salesianum School.
Kenney, Sean W. '91 (MET) Woodbridge, NJ St. James Church.
Kenney, Timothy '58 (Y) Kent, OH St. Patrick's Church.
Kenney, Timothy M. *s.m.* '82 (SFR) [D] San Francisco, CA Archbishop Riordan High School (Boys); [N] San Francisco, CA Marianist Community.
Kenney, William J. *c.s.p.* '51 (NY) [DD] Jamaica Estates, NY Paulist Fathers Generalate.
Kenney, William J. '56 (STP) [11] Minneapolis, MN Our Lady of Mount Carmel Church.
Kenney, William T. *c.s.p.* '51 (LA) [86] Los Angeles, CA St. Paul the Apostle Church.
Kenning, Herman H. '43 (CIN) Retired; [N] Cincinnati, OH St. Clare Convent, Franciscan Sisters of the Poor.
Kennington, John *c.ss.r.* '59 (NY) [DD] Esopus, NY Redemptorist Priests and Brothers C.Ss.R. (Province of Baltimore); [HH] Esopus, NY Holy Shroud Guild.
Kenny, Albert N. '54 (BRK) Retired.
Kenny, Donald '66 (JOL) [5] Naperville, IL St. Thomas the Apostle Church.
Kenny, Msgr. Donald A. (ATL) Special or Other (Arch)Diocesan Assignment.
Kenny, Msgr. Donald A. '84 (ATL) [3] Marietta, GA St. Joseph Church.
Kenny, Eugene P. '53 (DOD) McCracken, KS St. Mary Church.
Kenny, Gregory D. *c.m.f.* '59 (ATL) Stone Mountain, GA Corpus Christi Church; [L] Atlanta, GA Campus Ministry.
Kenny, Gregory D. *c.m.f.* '59 (CHI) [N] Oak Park, IL Claretian Fathers Headquarters of U.S.A. Eastern Province.
Kenny, James E. '49 (OM) Retired.
Kenny, Msgr. James T. '45 (SLC) Retired.
Kenny, John F. *o.s.f.s.* '69 (HBG) Manheim, PA St. Richard Church.

Kenny, Msgr. John J. '29 (SFR) Belmont, CA Immaculate Heart of Mary Church; Retired.
Kenny, John R. '51 (OAK) [3] Walnut Creek, CA St. Mary's Church.
Kenny, Johns J. *c.s.p.* '58 (CHR) Clemson, SC St. Andrew Church.
Kenny, Joseph H. *o.p.* '50 (FgM) Dominican - Order of Preachers Foreign Missions.
Kenny, Joseph P. *o.p.* '63 (CHI) [N] Chicago, IL Dominicans (Provincial Office).
Kenny, Kevin *o.f.m.conv.* '66 (ALB) Fonda, NY St. Cecilia Church; [O] Fonda, NY Blessed Kateri Retreat House; [R] Fonda, NY The National Shrine of Blessed Kateri Tekakwitha and Friary.
Kenny, Michael '73 (SAT) [52] San Antonio, TX St. Margaret Mary Church.
Kenny, Michael J. '35 (BRK) Retired.
Kenny, P. Edward, Jr. '74 (BAL) [18] Baltimore, MD Blessed Sacrament Church; [59] Baltimore, MD St. Mary of the Assumption Church.
Kenny, Patrick J. *o.s.a.* '35 (PH) [AA] Villanova, PA St. Thomas Monastery.
Kenny, Pierce *c.ss.r.* '69 (ALB) Saratoga Springs, NY St. Clement Church.
Kenny, Raymond G. '63 (SJ) [23] San Jose, CA Santa Teresa Church.
Kenny, Simon *o.carm.* '64 (TUC) [A] Tucson, AZ Salpointe Catholic High School; [F] Tucson, AZ Carmelite Priory.
Kenny, Msgr. Simon E. '38 (BAL) Retired.
Kenny, Stephen *c.p.* (HRT) [M] West Hartford, CT Holy Family Monastery/Retreat.
Kenny, Stephen K. '91 (MEM) Camden, TN St. Mary Church.
Kenny, Msgr. Thomas '65 (ATL) [1] Atlanta, GA Cathedral of Christ the King.
Kenny, Thomas A. '46 (NEW) Retired.
Kenny, Thomas C. *o.s.a.* '56 (BO) [C] North Andover, MA Merrimack College.
Kenny, Msgr. Walter F. '54 (NY) Larchmont, NY St. Augustine Church.
Kenny, William J.M. '71 (LAV) [2] Las Vegas, NV Christ the King Church.
Kenshol, Joseph W. '73 (GR) Sand Lake, MI Mary Queen of Apostles Church.
Kent, Daniel '63 (MIA) [B] Opa Locka, FL St. Thomas University.
Kent, James *o.f.m.conv.* (IND) [J] Mount Saint Francis, IN Provincial Headquarters for the Conventual Franciscan Province.
Kent, James *o.f.m.conv.* '91 (L) Pleasure Ridge Park, KY St. Paul Church.
Kent, Joseph E. '48 (SY) Retired.
Kent, Thomas J. *s.j.* '47 (SY) [S] Syracuse, NY Jesuits at LeMoyne, Inc.
Keogh, James P. *s.j.* '52 (CHL) [J] Charlotte, NC Jesuit Community.
Keogh, James V. *s.j.* '52 (CHL) Mooresville, NC St. Therese Church.
Keogh, Simeon '49 (GB) [I] Appleton, WI St. Fidelis Friary.
Keogh, Stephen *s.a.c.* '53 (DET) [K] Wyandotte, MI Pallottine Fathers.
Keogh, Thomas '45 (SR) Retired.
Keogh, Msgr. Thomas J. '33 (NY) [70] New York, NY St. Mary Church; Retired.
Keogh, William '78 (JC) Absent on Leave.
Keohan, Edward M. (BO) Salem, MA North Shore Medical Center.
Keohan, Edward M. '59 (BO) [7] Salem, MA St. Mary Church.
Keohane, Daniel C. '52 (TLS) Retired.
Keohane, Daniel G. '78 (BRK) [153] Queens, NY Ascension Church.
Keohane, Daniel T. '78 (SFR) [1] San Mateo, CA St. Bartholomew Church.
Keohane, Donal '68 (LA) [78] Los Angeles, CA St. Martin of Tours Church.
Keohane, Donal '68 (SAV) On Duty Outside the Diocese.
Keohane, Msgr. Mark H. '29 (BO) Retired.
Keohane, William *o.m.i.* '36 (BO) [Z] Tewksbury, MA Immaculate Heart of Mary Novitiate-Infirmary.
Keolker, Richard F. '63 (YAK) On Duty Outside the Diocese.
Keon, James J. *c.s.b.* '52 (GAL) [Q] Houston, TX Residence of the Basilian Fathers of the University of St. Thomas.
Keonig, Paul *o.c.d.* '93 (LA) Alhambra, CA St. Therese Church.
Keough, Joseph F. '96 (HRT) Southington, CT St. Thomas Church.
Keppel, Timothy F. *c.r.* '77 (SB) Lake Arrowhead, CA Our Lady of the Lake Church.
Keppeler, Richard J. '54 (BUF) Bergen, NY St. Brigid Church.
Keppens, Gustaaf M. *s.j.* '61 (WDC) [K] Washington, DC Georgetown University Hospital; [M] Washington, DC The Jesuit Community at Georgetown University.
Kepple, Robert '74 (LR) Retired.
Keppler, Daniel J. '58 (DUB) Monona, IA St. Patrick's Church.
Keppler, John F. '60 (BRK) [148] Queens, NY American Martyrs Church.
Kerbawy, Kevin '76 (SAG) Kinde, MI St. Mary-St. Edward Church.
Kerber, John V. '58 (STL) Festus, MO Our Lady Church.
Kerber, Joseph P. '88 (SFD) Alexander, IL Visitation B.V.M. Church; Franklin, IL Sacred Heart of Jesus Church; New Berlin, IL Sacred Heart of Mary Church.
Kerber, Justin *c.p.* '72 (BRK) [U] Jamaica, NY Immaculate Conception Monastery.
Kerby, Robert L. '70 (NTN) South Bend, IN St. John of Damascus Church.
Kerch, Rudolph S. '40 (GB) Retired.
Kerdiejus, John B. *s.j.* '58 (BO) [Y] Gloucester, MA Eastern Point Retreat House.
Kerestes, Michael '89 (PSC) Beltsville, MD St. Gregory of Nyssa Church.
Kerestus, Thomas J. '69 (ALN) Unassigned; [J] Bethlehem, PA Holy Family Villa.
Kereszty, Rochus *o.cist.* '60 (DAL) [M] Irving, TX Cistercian Abbey of Our Lady of Dallas.
Kerin, Msgr. Joseph A. '57 (CHL) Huntersville, NC St. Mark Church.
Kerkof, Loren *o.f.m.* '60 (P) [6] Portland, OR Ascension Church.
Kern, Charles '77 (NEW) Kenilworth, NJ St. Theresa's Church.
Kern, Charles P. '77 (NEW) Retired.
Kern, Msgr. Crosby W. '65 (NO) [2] Metairie, LA St. Angela Merici Church.
Kern, Jerome C. '66 (STP) Forest Lake, MN St. Peter Church.
Kern, John R. '68 (MIL) [66] Milwaukee, WI SS. Peter and Paul Church.
Kern, Joseph R. '57 (IND) Montezuma, IN Immaculate Conception Church; Rockville, IN St. Joseph Church.
Kern, Martin F. '94 (ALN) [9] Allentown, PA Sacred Heart of Jesus Church.
Kern, Msgr. Walter O. '58 (BUF) Bowmansville, NY Sacred Heart Church; [T] Bowmansville, NY International Institute of the Heart of Jesus.
Kern, Msgr. Walter O. '58 (MIL) [Y] Milwaukee, WI International Institute of the Heart of Jesus.
Kernan, Eugene J. '49 (CAM) Stone Harbor, NJ St. Paul's Church.
Kernan, James *o.m.i.* '59 (SD) Calipatria, CA St. Patrick Church.
Kernan, Michael H. '54 (PIT) Retired.
Kernan, Timothy J. '65 (STP) [11] St. Paul, MN St. Adalbert Church.
Kernan, William A. '93 (SD) [1] El Cajon, CA Holy Trinity Church.
Kerner, Terrence D. '72 (DET) [2] Monroe, MI St. John The Baptist Church.
Kerner, Timothy *c.ss.r.* '81 (BR) [10] Baton Rouge, LA St. Gerard Majella Church.
Kerns, John '85 (P) [3] Portland, OR All Saints Church.
Kerns, Paul R. '71 (PRT) Augusta, ME St. Mary's Church.
Kerper, Michael '85 (MAN) Franklin, NH St. Paul Church.
Kerper, Michael '85 (PH) [U] Philadelphia, PA Nazareth Hospital.
Kerr, Charles L. *s.j.* '50 (WIN) [1] Mankato, MN SS. Peter and Paul's Church.
Kerr, Cherubin *o.s.a.* '44 (CAM) [C] Richland, NJ St. Augustine Preparatory School.
Kerr, Joseph L. *s.m.* '46 (CIN) [M] Cincinnati, OH Marianist Community.
Kerr, Robert '95 (KC) Hamilton, MO Sacred Heart Church.
Kerr, Robert T. '64 (LAN) [3] Ypsilanti, MI St. Joseph Church.
Kerr, Seamus '60 (YAK) East Wenatchee, WA Holy Apostles Church.
Kerr, Msgr. William A. '66 (PIT) [B] Pittsburgh, PA La Roche College.
Kerr, Msgr. William A. '66 (PT) On Duty Outside the Diocese.
Kerrigan, Bernard '48 (WIN) Retired.
Kerrigan, James P. '70 (WOR) Rutland, MA St. Patrick's Church.
Kerrigan, Joe '90 (MEM) [H] Memphis, TN St. Peter Manor.
Kerrigan, Joseph '90 (MEM) [1] Memphis, TN Cathedral of the Immaculate Conception.
Kerrigan, Joseph P. '45 (PH) [2] Bensalem, PA St. Elizabeth Ann Seton Church; Retired.
Kerrigan, Michael F. '64 (DEN) Idaho Springs, CO St. Paul's Church.
Kerrigan, Michael P. *c.s.p.* '87 (NY) [DD] Jamaica Estates, NY Paulist Fathers Generalate.
Kerrigan, Neal *o.f.m.cap.* '52 (NY) Yonkers, NY St. John Hospital; [DD] Yonkers, NY St. Clare Friary.
Kerschen, Leo A. '62 (WCH) Coffeyville, KS Holy Name Church.
Kerschen, Leon J. '62 (WCH) Iola, KS St. John Church.
Kerschen, Matthew J. *c.ss.r.* '48 (BLX) [E] Biloxi, MS St. John Neumann Residence.
Kerscher, Charles J. '79 (ATL) Conyers, GA St. Pius X Catholic Church; Retired.
Kerscher, Francis R. '55 (GB) Seymour, WI St. John Church.
Kersey, Walter (SD) Oceanside, CA Tri City Hospital.
Kersey, Walter L. '81 (BR) Retired.
Kersgieter, Paul J. '45 (STL) Retired.
Kershner, Joseph J. *sch.p.* '64 (MIA) [C] Fort Lauderdale, FL Cardinal Gibbons High School.
Kerst, Pat '90 (SPK) Brewster, WA Sacred Heart Church; Twisp, WA St. Genevieve Church.
Kerstein, Thomas F. '70 (MIL) Special Assignment.
Kersten, Edward J. *o.s.a.* '56 (CHI) [185] Chicago, IL St. Rita of Cascia Church.
Kersten, John *s.v.d.* '40 (BLX) [A] Bay St. Louis, MS St. Augustine's.
Kersten, Kevin *s.j.* '72 (BO) [W] Chestnut Hill, MA The Jesuit Community at Boston College.
Kertz, Leo *o.m.i.* '63 (FgM) Oblates Foreign Missions.
Kertz, Raymond N. '67 (MAD) [1] Janesville, WI Nativity of St. Mary Church.
Kerwan, Francis T. '43 (HRT) [1] Enfield, CT Holy Family Church.
Kerwick, Robert J. '48 (PH) Retired.
Kerwin, Joseph *o.f.m.conv.* '93 (BRK) [61] Brooklyn, NY Most Holy Trinity Church.
Kerwin, Joseph A. '62 (SC) Retired.
Kerwin, Kilian *o.s.b.* '68 (IND) [J] St. Meinrad, IN St. Meinrad Archabbey.
Kerze, William F. '69 (LA) Malibu, CA Our Lady of Malibu Church.
Kesicki, Michael '88 (E) [B] Erie, PA Gannon University.
Kesicki, Michael T. '88 (E) [A] Erie, PA St. Mark's Seminary.
Kessel, Gerald *o.f.m.cap.* '82 (DET) [P] Washington, MI Capuchin Retreat.
Kessing, Bernadine *o.f.m.* (BUF) Vandalia, NY St. John the Baptist Church.
Kessing, Bernardine *o.f.m.* '60 (BUF) Allegany, NY St. Bonaventure Church.
Kessinger, David R. *o.s.b.* '58 (CHL) [J] Belmont, NC Belmont Abbey.
Kessler, Edward L. '48 (COL) Lancaster, OH Southeastern Correctional Institution; Retired.
Kessler, Matthew *c.ss.r.* '91 (CHI) [9] Chicago, IL St. Alphonsus Church.
Kessler, Thomas '74 (COL) Special Assignment.
Kessler, Thomas '75 (EVN) St. Joseph, IN St. Joseph's Church; St. Martin, IN St. Martin's Church.
Kessler, Thomas J. '84 (ALN) Miller Heights, PA Sacred Heart of Jesus Church; [C] Easton, PA Notre Dame High School.
Kester, William J. '70 (STL) [6] Lemay, MO St. Matthias Church.
Kestermeier, Charles T. *s.j.* '75 (OM) [K] Omaha, NE Jesuit Community At Creighton University.
Kesting, Philip A. '41 (CIN) Retired.
Kestler, Theodore E. *s.j.* '75 (FBK) St. Marys, AK Church of the Nativity; [C] Fairbanks, AK Jesuit Residence; [E] St. Marys, AK Native Ministry Training Program; [E] St. Marys, AK Brother Joe Prince Jesuit Community.
Ketcham, Gregory K. '94 (PEO) Monmouth, IL Immaculate Conception Church; Nauvoo, IL SS. Peter and Paul's Church.
Ketchersid, Corbin W. (R) Retired.
Kettelberger, John *c.m.* '78 (BUF) [C] Niagara University, NY Niagara University.
Kettelberger, John A. *c.m.* '78 (BUF) [O] Niagara University, NY Vincentian Community at Niagara University.
Ketteler, Aloys *s.v.d.* '40 (LSC) Deming, NM St. Ann's Church.
Ketteler, Ronald M. '61 (COV) Crescent Springs, KY St. Joseph Church.
Kettler, Msgr. Donald '70 (SFS) [5] Sioux Falls, SD St. Lambert Church.
Kettner, Joseph *m.s.* '50 (ORL) [3] Orlando, FL Good Shepherd Church.
Kettron, W. Michael '57 (LFT) Cicero, IN Sacred Heart Church.
Keu Sin, Peter Young (CLV) [6] Cleveland, OH St. Andrew Kim Church.
Keul, Msgr. Francis X. '48 (PH) Retired.
Keulman, Kenneth P. '69 (NO) [C] New Orleans, LA Loyola University.
Keulman, Kenneth P. '69 (SJ) On Duty Outside the Diocese.
Keusal, Eugene L. '61 (CHI) On Duty Outside the Archdiocese.
Keveney, William J. '56 (DET) Eastpointe, MI St. Barnabas Church.
Keveny, M. Valentine '73 (WDC) [40] Washington, DC St. Stephen Martyr Church.
Keville, Joseph '96 (BO) Beverly, MA St. John the Evangelist Church.
Kew, Larry J. '66 (GRY) [1] East Chicago, IN Assumption Church.

Key, Oren W. *s.j.* '53 (FWT) Crowell, TX St. Joseph Church; Quanah, TX St. Mary Church; Vernon, TX Holy Family Church.
Key, William '75 (MIL) [W] Milwaukee, WI Cursillos in Christianity.
Key, William W. '75 (MIL) [46] Milwaukee, WI St. Lawrence Church.
Keyes, Jeffrey R. *c.pp.s.* '91 (OAK) [2] Alameda, CA St. Barnabas Church.
Keyes, Patrick *c.ss.r.* '89 (FgM) Redemptorist Foreign Missions.
Keyes, Paul T. '63 (BO) North Andover, MA St. Michael Church.
Keyes, Raphael '64 (JC) Missionary Assignment in Peru.
Keyes, Thomas E. '73 (BO) [1] Methuen, MA St. Lucy Church.
Keymont, Walter F. '80 (BO) [8] Boston, MA St. Ann Church.
Keyrouze, Joseph E. '50 (ALB) [14] Troy, NY St. Williams Church.
Keys, Gordon L. *s.j.* '55 (P) [D] Portland, OR Jesuit High School.
Keys, Msgr. Thomas J. '70 (SFR) [U] San Francisco, CA The Ordinary Mutual, RRG.
Keys, Msgr. Thomas J. '70 (SR) [3] Santa Rosa, CA St. Rose of Lima Church; [F] Rohnert Park, CA Society of St. Vincent de Paul, District Council of Sonoma County; [O] Santa Rosa, CA Apostolic Endowment Trust.
Kezmarsky, Kenneth E. '97 (PIT) [P] Baden, PA St. Joseph Convent.
Khachan, Bernard C. '60 (OLL) Cleveland, OH St. Maron Church.
Kharuk, Vasyl '91 (PHU) Washington, DC Ukrainian Catholic National Shrine of the Holy Family Church.
Khoa, Nguyen *o.f.m.* '95 (WDC) [B] Silver Spring, MD Holy Name College.
Khoai, Huynh Huu (OAK) [3] Oakland, CA St. Anthony's Church.
Khoury, Ghattas '90 (OLL) Cincinnati, OH St. Anthony of Padua Church.
Khoury, Msgr. James T. '75 (BO) [2] Lawrence, MA St. Anthony Church.
Khoury, Msgr. James T. '75 (SAM) Lawrence, MA St. Anthony Church.
Khve, Thomas L.T. '91 (SPK) [17] Spokane, WA St. Patrick Church.
Kibby, Patrick J. '84 (NSH) Old Hickory, TN St. Stephen Church.
Kibler, Gary R. (BUF) Farnham, NY St. Anthony's Church.
Kibuka, Matthias W. '58 (BUF) [2] Batavia, NY St. Joseph Church.
Kichak, Joseph A. '43 (MAR) Retired.
Kicia, Chester *o.f.m.conv.* '36 (BGP) [14] Bridgeport, CT St. Michael The Archangel Church.
Kickham, Robert T. '97 (BO) [44] Boston, MA St. Mark Church.
Kicmal, Casimir C. *c.s.v.* '57 (CHI) [N] Arlington Heights, IL Viatorian Province Center-Clerics of St. Viator.
Kiczuk, Casimir *c.m.* '34 (HRT) [M] Manchester, CT DePaul Provincial Residence.
Kiczuk, Casimir *c.m.* '34 (SY) [S] Utica, NY St. Vincent's Mission House.
Kidd, Colin *o.f.m.* '48 (ORL) Merritt Island, FL Divine Mercy Church; Retired.
Kidd, Michael C. '54 (WDC) Mitchellville, MD Holy Family Church.
Kidd, Wayne R. '73 (LC) Richland Center, WI St. Mary (Assumption of B.V.M.) Church.
Kidd, William J. *s.j.* '63 (MIL) [P] Milwaukee, WI Jesuit Community at Marquette University.
Kidder, Msgr. James C. '67 (SAC) El Dorado Hills, CA Holy Trinity Church.
Kidder, Lawrence *o.f.m.* '32 (BO) [Z] Boston, MA Saint Anthony Residence.
Kiddy, Curtis '92 (MIA) [33] Miami, FL St. Timothy Church.
Kidner, M. Paul *o.s.b.* '58 (STL) [F] Creve Coeur, MO St. Louis Priory School; [P] St. Louis, MO The Abbey of St. Mary and St. Louis.
Kidney, Liam J. '68 (LA) Camarillo, CA Blessed Junipero Serra Church.
Kidney, Timothy '71 (SJ) [2] San Jose, CA St. Patrick Proto-Cathedral.
Kidwell, William *s.j.* '55 (MIA) [5] Miami, FL Gesu Church.
Kidykas, Jonas *s.j.* '35 (CHI) [N] Chicago, IL Lithuanian American Jesuits.
Kiedinger, Daniel J. '91 (LC) Cazenovia, WI St. Anthony de Padua Church; Keyesville, WI Nativity of the Blessed Virgin Mary Church; Lone Rock, WI Sacred Heart Church.
Kiefer, John D. '70 (LFT) Muncie, IN St. Francis of Assisi Church.
Kiefer, R. David '62 (GB) Mattoon, WI Holy Family Church; Neopit, WI St. Anthony Church; Phlox, WI St. Joseph Church.
Kiefer, Robert '91 (SJ) [6] San Jose, CA St. Frances Cabrini Church.
Kiefer, Msgr. Thomas '46 (LA) [2] North Hollywood, CA St. Charles Borromeo Church.
Kiefer, Thomas P. '81 (SPC) [1] Springfield, MO Cathedral of St. Agnes.
Kiefer, William J. '58 (SB) Trona, CA St. Madeleine Sophie Barat Church; Retired.
Kieffer, Charles G. '80 (PHX) [24] Phoenix, AZ St. Theresa Church.
Kieffer, Henry '40 (SAL) [C] Concordia, KS Mount Joseph Senior Community.
Kieffer, Henry '54 (SAL) Aurora, KS St. Peter's Church.
Kieffer, John *s.j.* '68 (LEX) Monticello, KY St. Peter Church.
Kieffer, John L. *s.j.* (DET) [K] Detroit, MI Jesuit Provincial Office-Detroit Province of the Society of Jesus.
Kieffer, John L. *s.j.* '68 (LEX) [J] Mount Vernon, KY Appalachia Science in the Public Interest.
Kieffer, Kenneth *o.f.m.* '55 (STL) [P] St. Louis, MO Franciscan Friary of St. Anthony of Padua.
Kieffer, Lawrence J. '50 (MAD) [4] Madison, WI Holy Redeemer Church; Madison, WI University Hospitals.
Kieffer, Merlin '60 (SAL) Hoxie, KS St. Frances Xavier Cabrini Church.
Kieffer, Robert J. '69 (SCL) Elk River, MN The Church of St. Andrew.
Kieffer, Thomas A. *c.o.* '65 (MRY) [G] Monterey, CA Oratorian Community-Congregation of the Oratory of Pontifical Right; [L] Monterey, CA Newman Institute for Historical and Religious Studies.
Kiel, William J. '93 (GBG) Kittanning, PA St. Mary, Our Lady of Guadalupe Church.
Kielb, John T. '75 (TR) Monmouth Beach, NJ Church of the Precious Blood.
Kielbasa, Richard '59 (SC) Rockwell City, IA St. Francis of Assisi Church.
Kieliszewski, Jan M. '73 (MIL) Cudahy, WI St. Frederick Church.
Kielkowski, Andrzej *s.d.s.* '81 (NEW) [N] Verona, NJ The Salvatorian Fathers.
Kielty, Henry *c.p.* '50 (L) [L] Louisville, KY Sacred Heart Retreat.
Kieltyka, Robert '58 (MOB) Butler, AL St. John Church.
Kiely, Brian P. '78 (BO) Dracut, MA St. Francis Church.
Kiely, Cornelius '67 (BAK) On Duty Outside the Diocese.
Kiely, Cornelius '67 (FgM) Society of St. James the Apostle.
Kiely, Thomas P. '88 (NY) Briarcliff Manor, NY St. Theresa Church.
Kiem, Anthony '46 (PT) Retired.
Kiemen, Mathias *o.f.m.* '43 (FWT) [G] Crowley, TX St. Francis Village, Inc.; [H] Crowley, TX St. Maximilian Kolbe Friary.
Kiener, Hugolinus *o.f.m.* '37 (SFD) [K] Sherman, IL Our Lady of Angels Friary.
Kienzle, Jerome C. '72 (MIL) Military Chaplains.
Kienzle, Jerry (BLX) Gulfport, MS Naval Const. Bn. Center.
Kiepura, Kenneth G. '69 (CHI) Buffalo Grove, IL St. Mary Church.
Kieran, Benet *c.p.* '39 (LA) [R] Pasadena, CA Passionist Community.
Kieran, Ed '59 (AMA) Bovina, TX St. Ann's Church.
Kieran, John C. '67 (ATL) Conyers, GA St. Pius X Catholic Church.
Kieran, Richard A. '65 (ATL) Monroe, GA St. Anna's Church.
Kierce, J. Joseph '43 (BO) Retired.
Kierce, J. Joseph '45 (BO) [4] Boston, MA St. Ambrose Church.
Kiernan, Arthur C. *m.m.* '32 (NY) [DD] Maryknoll, NY Maryknoll Fathers and Brothers.
Kiernan, Msgr. Donald (ATL) [M] Doraville, GA Korean Martyrs Pastoral Center.
Kiernan, Edward J. '54 (BRK) [30] Brooklyn, NY St. Columba Church.
Kiernan, James F. *c.m.* (BRK) [D] Staten Island, NY St. John's University, Staten Island Campus; [D] Jamaica, NY St. John's University.
Kiernan, James F. *c.m.* '70 (NY) [C] Staten Island, NY St. John's University Staten Island Campus.
Kiernan, James O. *c.m.* '70 (BRK) [U] Jamaica, NY St. Vincent's House.
Kiernan, James W. '62 (DM) [1] Des Moines, IA St. Ambrose Cathedral.
Kiernan, John G. '55 (PBL) Retired.
Kiernan, John L. '48 (BRK) [U] Jamaica, NY Parsons Manor.
Kiernan, Joseph V. *o.f.m.* '69 (ARL) Triangle, VA St. Francis of Assisi Church.
Kiernan, Michael F. '73 (SAC) Anderson, CA Sacred Heart Church.
Kiernan, Msgr. R. Donald '49 (ATL) Dunwoody, GA All Saints Catholic Church.
Kiernan, Robert J. *o.s.b.* '60 (BUR) [E] Weston, VT Priory of Benedictine Monks.
Kiernan, Thomas '48 (SY) Retired.
Kies, Emil '44 (P) Retired.
Kiesel, James '95 (BAL) Annapolis, MD St. Andrew by the Bay Church.
Kiesel, Leo C. '63 (EVN) Loogootee, IN St. John Church; [J] Loogootee, IN American-Innsbruck Alumni Association.
Kieselbach, Joseph '61 (CR) Dilworth, MN St. Elizabeth Church.
Kieser, Ellwood E. *c.s.p.* '56 (LA) [86] Los Angeles, CA St. Paul the Apostle Church; [DD] Pacific Palisades, CA Paulist Productions.
Kiesling, John *s.a.* '68 (NY) [DD] Garrison, NY Generalate of the Franciscan Friars of the Atonement-St. James Friary.
Kieton, Dennis J. '85 (PRO) [5] Cumberland, RI Our Lady of Fatima Church; [11] Woonsocket, RI Sacred Heart Church.
Kiff, Herbert J., Jr. '95 (NO) Covington, LA St. Peter Church.
Kiffmeyer, James G. '85 (CIN) [E] Cincinnati, OH Elder High School.
Kiggins, Roy J. '64 (ROC) Brockport, NY Nativity of the Blessed Virgin Mary Church.
Kigozi, Dennis S. '91 (COL) Pickerington, OH Seton Parish.
Kihm, Frederick C. '93 (STU) [1] Steubenville, OH Holy Name Cathedral; [6] Steubenville, OH St. Anthony of Padua Church.
Kihm, Peter J. '81 (NY) Nyack, NY St. Ann Church.
Kihneman, Msgr. Louis F. '77 (CC) Rockport, TX Sacred Heart Church.
Kijauskas, Gediminas *s.j.* '60 (CLV) [59] Cleveland, OH Our Lady of Perpetual Help Church.
Kikowski, Zdzislaw *o.s.p.p.e.* '61 (PH) [AA] Doylestown, PA Pauline Fathers Monastery, Shrine of Our Lady of Czestochowa.
Kilarecki, George W. '46 (PIT) Retired.
Kilas, Joseph F. '54 (JOL) [6] Joliet, IL St. Ambrose Church; Joliet, IL Joliet Correctional Depot.
Kilbride, Eugene M. '59 (HRT) [2] West Hartford, CT St. Helena Church.
Kilbridge, Robert A. *o.p.* '47 (CHI) [131] Chicago, IL St. Mary, Star of the Sea Church; [N] River Forest, IL St. Thomas Aquinas Priory.
Kilburn, Clayton F. *c.m.* (GLP) Keams Canyon, AZ St. Joseph's Indian Mission Church.
Kilcarr, Stephen M. '56 (NEW) [C] West Orange, NJ Seton Hall Preparatory School.
Kilcline, Francis I. '81 (LFT) Kokomo, IN St. Patrick Church.
Kilcourse, George A. '76 (L) [A] Louisville, KY Bellarmine College.
Kilcoyne, John '45 (CLV) Retired.
Kilcoyne, Patrick '75 (SJ) [6] San Jose, CA St. Frances Cabrini Church; San Jose, CA Santa Clara County Jail; Milpitas, CA Elmwood Rehabilitation Center.
Kilcoyne, Terence T. '76 (WOR) On Special or Other (Arch)Diocesan Assignment.
Kilcullen, John M. '55 (STL) Crestwood, MO St. Elizabeth of Hungary Church.
Kiley, Bonaventure *t.o.r.* '42 (ARL) [J] Winchester, VA Sacred Heart Friary.
Kiley, Francis *o.f.m.conv.* (CHI) [N] Chicago, IL Conventual Franciscans of St. Bonaventure Province.
Kiley, J. Cletus '74 (CHI) On Duty Outside the Archdiocese.
Kiley, John A. '66 (PRO) [7] Pawtucket, RI St. Leo the Great Church.
Kiley, John G. '70 (BO) Lincoln, MA St. Joseph Church.
Kiley, Philip *s.j.* (NOR) [A] Cromwell, CT Holy Apostles College and Seminary.
Kiley, Philip S. *s.j.* '71 (BO) [W] Boston, MA The Society of Jesus of New England-Provincial Offices; [W] Weston, MA Campion Center.
Kiley, Phillip C. '78 (CHI) [183] Chicago, IL Resurrection Church.
Kiley, Raymond P. '96 (BO) Canton, MA St. John the Evangelist Church.
Kilfoil, Msgr. Patrick '37 (EVN) Retired.
Kilgallen, John J. *s.j.* '65 (CHI) [C] Chicago, IL Jesuit Community at Loyola University of Chicago.
Kilgallon, John J. '69 (PH) Roslyn, PA St. John of the Cross Church.
Kilian, John '68 (BUF) Attica, NY Attica Correctional Facility.
Kilian, Sabbas J. *o.f.m.* '43 (NY) [6] Mt. Vernon, NY St. Ursula Church.
Kilian, Waldemar '87 (CHI) River Grove, IL St. Cyprian Church.
Kilian, William T. '53 (SAL) Retired.
Kilianski, Edward *s.c.j.* '83 (MIL) [P] Franklin, WI Dehon House.
Kilkelly, Timothy *m.m.* '90 (FgM) Maryknoll Foreign Missions.
Kill, Donald *s.s.c.* '72 (FgM) St. Columban's Foreign Mission.
Kill, Robert J. '71 (TOL) Hamler, OH St. Paul Church; Holgate, OH St. Mary Church.
Killackey, Cyprian *o.c.d.* '52 (TUC) [21] Tucson, AZ Santa Cruz Church.
Killackey, Edward R. *m.m.* '57 (NY) [DD] Maryknoll,

NY Maryknoll Fathers and Brothers.
Killackey, Thomas B. *m.m.* '56 (HON) Mililani Town, HI St. John Apostle and Evangelist Church; [H] Honolulu, HI Maryknoll Fathers House.
Killeen, Bernard D. '49 (HRT) Orange, CT Holy Infant Church.
Killeen, John C. '59 (CAM) [1] Cherry Hill, NJ St. Mary's Church.
Killeen, John F. *s.j.* '56 (LA) [C] Los Angeles, CA Loyola Marymount University.
Killeen, John J. '47 (HRT) Retired.
Killeen, John P. '57 (CC) George West, TX St. George Church; George West, TX St. George Church.
Killeen, Joseph P. '62 (DET) Holly, MI St. Rita Church.
Killeen, Msgr. Michael F. '59 (LA) Rowland Heights, CA St. Elizabeth Ann Seton Church.
Killeen, Thomas M. *o.m.i.* '58 (COS) Leadville, CO Catholic Community of Leadville, Annunciation(1879) & St. Joseph(1899) Church.
Killeen, Thomas M. *o.m.i.* '58 (FgM) Oblates Foreign Missions.
Killeen, Thomas M. *o.m.i.* '58 (STP) [N] St. Paul, MN Oblate Residence.
Killeen, William E. '75 (CHI) Midlothian, IL St. Christopher Church.
Killeen, William J. '59 (HRT) Derby, CT St. Jude Church.
Killian, Wayne E. '84 (ALN) Pen Argyl, PA St. Elizabeth of Hungary Church; [C] Bangor, PA Pius X High School.
Killilea, Patrick *ss.cc.* '69 (FR) [J] Fairhaven, MA Sacred Hearts Provincial House.
Killingsworth, Bradley '70 (P) On Duty Outside the Archdiocese.
Killion, Dennis W. *o.s.f.s.* '80 (PH) [D] Philadelphia, PA Father Judge High School for Boys; [AA] Philadelphia, PA Father Judge Faculty House.
Killion, Robert L. '53 (WOR) Bolton, MA St. Francis Xavier Church.
Killoren, John J. '45 (STL) [P] St. Louis, MO Jesuit Community Corporation at St. Louis University - Jesuit Hall.
Kilmartin, John *f.d.p.* (BO) Shirley, MA MCI-Shirley.
Kilmartin, John *f.d.p.* '86 (BO) [U] Boston, MA Don Orione Nursing Home; [BB] Boston, MA Madonna Queen Shrine.
Kilmurray, Fintan J. '77 (BLX) [1] Gulfport, MS St. Ann Church.
Kilpatrick, Andrew W. '96 (SCR) [1] Scranton, PA St. Peter's Cathedral.
Kilpatrick, John J. '61 (SCR) [8] Scranton, PA Holy Name Church.
Kilroy, Brendan K. *s.p.s.* '62 (NEW) [C] Ramsey, NJ Don Bosco Preparatory High School for Boys; [N] Cliffside Park, NJ St. Patrick's Missionary Society.
Kilroy, C. A. *o.p.* '61 (STP) [15] Minneapolis, MN St. Albert the Great Church.
Kilroy, Paul E. '70 (BO) [7] Boston, MA St. Ann Church; [6] Newton, MA Our Lady Help of Christians Church; [CC] Boston, MA St. Ann's University Parish.
Kilroy, Robert F. *o.m.i.* '40 (BO) [Z] Tewksbury, MA Immaculate Heart of Mary Novitiate-Infirmary.
Kilsdonk, Edward '37 (GB) Retired.
Kilty, Cornelius F. *o.s.f.s.* '69 (PH) [AA] Philadelphia, PA Oblates of St. Francis De Sales.
Kim, Alapaki K. *c.s.p.* '82 (HON) Pahoa, HI Sacred Heart Church.
Kim, Albert K.H. *c.s.p.* '82 (NY) [DD] Jamaica Estates, NY Paulist Fathers Generalate.
Kim, Alex K. '91 (ORG) Rancho Santa Margarita, CA San Francisco Solano Church.
Kim, Alfonso *m.m.* '97 (FgM) Maryknoll Foreign Missions.
Kim, Anthony (RVC) New Hyde Park, NY Notre Dame Church.
Kim, Augustine *m.s.c.* '95 (SAT) [M] San Antonio, TX Missionaries of the Sacred Heart.
Kim, Barthasar '77 (WDC) [5] Washington, DC St. Anthony Church.
Kim, Benedict '64 (ORG) Special Assignment; [G] Anaheim, CA St. Thomas Korean Catholic Center.
Kim, Carlos C. '93 (BO) Ashland, MA St. Cecilia Church.
Kim, Chrysostom *o.s.b.* '60 (SCL) [I] Collegeville, MN St. John's Abbey, of the Order of St. Benedict.
Kim, Dong Chun John '91 (STP) [15] St. Paul, MN St. Andrew Kim Church.
Kim, Francis *o.f.m.* '96 (NY) [35] New York, NY St. Francis of Assisi Church.
Kim, Insungt (BRK) [226] Queens, NY St. Paul Chong Ha-Sang Roman Catholic Chapel Church.
Kim, Jeong Uk '92 (IND) [24] Indianapolis, IN St. Lawrence Church.
Kim, John Sung Kyu '83 (BIR) [11] Birmingham, AL Korean Catholic Community, St. Luke Hwang Church.
Kim, Joseph Nam '90 (ELP) Clint, TX San Lorenzo Church.
Kim, Joseph Sy '90 (LAN) [5] Lansing, MI Resurrection Church.
Kim, Joseph Y. (BAL) [37] Baltimore, MD Holy Korean Martyrs Church.
Kim, Luis '61 (NEW) [6] Orange, NJ St. Andrew Kim Church.
Kim, Mary Joseph *o.cart* '92 (BUR) [E] Arlington, VT Carthusian Foundation, Charterhouse of the Transfiguration.
Kim, Michael '87 (CAM) Pleasantville, NJ St. Peter's Church.
Kim, Paul Chun Ho (GAL) [R] Houston, TX Handmaids of the Sacred Heart of Pohang (H.S.H.).
Kim, Paul Chun-Ho '71 (GAL) [6] Houston, TX St. Andrew Kim Church.
Kim, Roy '94 (ORG) Cypress, CA St. Irenaeus Church.
Kim, Sae Eul '84 (LA) [38] Los Angeles, CA St. Agnes Church.
Kim, Thomas '84 (CHI) [2] Des Plaines, IL St. Paul Chong Hasang Church.
Kim, Youchul Philip '70 (ANC) [2] Anchorage, AK St. Anthony Church.
Kim Thien, Joseph Tran '81 (PH) Upper Darby, PA St. Alice Church.
Kimathy, Alphonce *c.s.sp.* '80 (NO) [7] New Orleans, LA Holy Ghost Church.
Kimbrough, Conrad '78 (CHL) Retired.
Kimbrough, Conrad L. '78 (CHL) [Q] Charlotte, NC Room at the Inn, Inc.
Kime, Dave W. '97 (GRY) [11] East Chicago, IN St. Mary Church.
Kimecz, Aloysius *o.cist.* '53 (DAL) [M] Irving, TX Cistercian Abbey of Our Lady of Dallas.
Kimla, James E. '76 (MIL) [10] Milwaukee, WI St. Barbara Church.
Kimm, Gregory '87 (SJ) [8] San Jose, CA Holy Family Church.
Kimminau, Bernard F. '94 (LIN) Morse Bluff, NE St. George Church.
Kimminau, Irenaeus *o.f.m.* (SFD) [1] Quincy, IL St. Anthony of Padua Church.
Kimminau, Irenaeus *o.f.m.* '49 (SFD) [6] Quincy, IL St. Joseph Church.
Kimminu, Irenaeus *o.f.m.* (SFD) [B] Quincy, IL Quincy University.
Kimmons, Steven *s.j.* '94 (CHI) [C] Chicago, IL Jesuit Community at Loyola University of Chicago.
Kimpel, Edward J. *o.praem.* '49 (PH) [48] Philadelphia, PA St. Gabriel Church; [AA] Paoli, PA Daylesford Abbey.
Kin, Bohdan '77 (PHU) Great Meadows, NJ St. Nicholas Church; West Easton, PA Holy Ghost Church.
Kinane, Gerard P. '73 (NO) [28] New Orleans, LA St. Cecilia Church.
Kinane, James G. '84 (MOB) On Leave from the Archdiocese.
Kinane, Joseph J. '52 (CHI) Park Ridge, IL St. Paul of the Cross Church; Retired.
Kinane, William P. '57 (SAC) Vallejo, CA St. Catherine of Siena Church.
Kinast, Robert L. '68 (ATL) On Duty Outside the Archdiocese.
Kinast, Timothy J. '90 (CC) [4] Beeville, TX St. Joseph Church.
Kinch, Edwin M. *o.s.b.* '45 (CHI) [N] Chicago, IL Servite Friars - Eastern Province.
Kincl, Robert L. . '67 (AUS) [6] Waco, TX St. Louis Church.
Kindall, John J. *s.j.* '57 (P) Yamhill, OR St. John Church; [A] Portland, OR Jesuit Novitiate of St. Francis Xavier.
Kinderman, Dennis J. *c.pp.s.* '67 (LFT) [A] Rensselaer, IN Saint Joseph's College.
Kindon, W. Fred '74 (PH) [137] Philadelphia, PA St. Philip Neri Church.
Kinel, Robert *s.s.j.* '67 (WDC) [B] Washington, DC St. Joseph's Seminary.
Kinerk, E. Edward *s.j.* '72 (KC) [B] Kansas City, MO Rockhurst College; [J] Kansas City, MO Rockhurst College - Jesuit Community.
Kinerk, E. Edward *s.j.* '72 (STL) [P] St. Louis, MO Jesuit Community Corporation at St. Louis University - Jesuit Hall.
Kines, G. Jerome *o.s.a.* '62 (CHI) [N] Olympia Fields, IL Austin Friary.
King, Andrew '96 (NY) [202] Staten Island, NY St. Clare Church.
King, Anthony S. '59 (YAK) Retired.
King, Brian M. (LKC) [B] Lake Charles, LA St. Patrick Hospital of Lake Charles.
King, Msgr. Charles B. '56 (FWT) [11] Fort Worth, TX St. John the Apostle Church.
King, David G. *s.j.* '49 (P) [L] Portland, OR Colombiere Community.
King, Donald E. '74 (Y) [1] Warren, OH Blessed Sacrament Church.
King, Donald J. '37 (PRO) Retired; [P] Providence, RI St. John Vianney Residence.
King, Edward L. '42 (BO) [2] Haverhill, MA St. James Church.
King, Francis *o.c.s.o.* '58 (P) [L] Lafayette, OR The Cistercian (Trappist) Abbey of Our Lady of Guadalupe.
King, Francis E. *s.j.* '62 (SFR) [N] San Francisco, CA Jesuit Community at University of San Francisco.
King, Frederick Bruce *i.c.* '85 (PEO) Galesburg, IL St. Patrick's Church.
King, Geoffrey *s.j.* '73 (BO) [W] Chestnut Hill, MA The Jesuit Community at Boston College.
King, George L. '53 (B) Kamiah, ID St. Catherine's of Siena Church; Orofino, ID St. Theresa's Church.
King, Gerald J. *t.o.r.* '71 (FgM) T.O.R. Foreign Missions.
King, Gregory C. '76 (LA) [4] North Hollywood, CA St. Patrick Church.
King, Howard J. '63 (E) Bradford, PA St. Francis of Assisi Church; Lewis Run, PA Our Mother of Perpetual Help Church.
King, Hugh *o.f.m.* '44 (PAT) [M] Ringwood, NJ Holy Name Friary, Inc.
King, James '90 (BRK) [10] Brooklyn, NY St. Anselm's Church.
King, James B. *c.s.c.* '88 (FTW) [A] Notre Dame, IN Moreau Seminary.
King, James E. '71 (NTN) Retired.
King, James E. '71 (PBL) Canon City, CO St. Michael Church.
King, James E. '71 (PH) Philadelphia, PA Veterans Administration Medical Center.
King, James E. '92 (PEO) Creve Coeur, IL Sacre Coeur Church.
King, James J. *s.j.* '63 (CLV) [E] Cuyahoga Falls, OH Walsh Jesuit High School.
King, Msgr. James P. '46 (BRK) [200] Queens, NY St. Mel Church; Retired.
King, Jeffrey '87 (GLP) Chichiltah, NM St. Patrick Navajo Mission Church; Pinehaven, NM Good Shepherd Catholic Mission Church.
King, Jeremy *o.s.b.* (IND) Fulda, IN St. Boniface Church; Siberia, IN St. Martin of Tours Church.
King, Jeremy *o.s.b.* '75 (IND) St. Meinrad, IN St. Meinrad Church; [A] St. Meinrad, IN St. Meinrad Seminary; [B] St. Meinrad, IN St. Meinrad Seminary-College of Liberal Arts; [J] St. Meinrad, IN St. Meinrad Archabbey.
King, John '48 (PEO) Retired.
King, John *m.m.* '53 (STA) [H] Jacksonville, FL Maryknoll Fathers & Brothers.
King, John D. '88 (CLV) El Salvador, C.A., OH Parroquial de Nuestra Senora de Guadalupe.
King, John F. *c.m.* '42 (PH) [AA] Philadelphia, PA Congregation of the Mission.
King, John J. *s.j.* '53 (NY) [FF] Staten Island, NY Mount Manresa Jesuit Retreat House.
King, John J. *s.j.* '63 (NY) [DD] New York, NY Jesuit Community at Fordham University.
King, John R. *m.m.* '53 (NY) [DD] Maryknoll, NY Maryknoll Fathers and Brothers.
King, Kenneth A. (TLS) Retired.
King, Kenneth A. '57 (TLS) Grove, OK St. Elizabeth Church.
King, Larry '89 (GR) [12] Grand Rapids, MI St. John Vianney Church.
King, Leo *ss.cc.* '45 (FR) Fairhaven, MA St. Joseph's Church.
King, Martin L. '96 (P) Corvallis, OR St. Mary Church.
King, Michael J. '77 (WDC) Largo, MD St. Joseph Church.
King, Nicholas '66 (ORL) Rockledge, FL St. Mary's Church.
King, Norbert E. '33 (LC) Retired.
King, Norman '88 (RNO) Elko, NV St. Joseph's Church.
King, Stephen *o.f.m.conv.* '96 (TR) Riverside, NJ St. Casimir Church.
King, Stephen D. '50 (FAR) Retired.
King, Thomas '64 (LA) Temple City, CA St. Luke the Evangelist Church.
King, Thomas J. '60 (ALN) Miller Heights, PA Sacred Heart of Jesus Church.
King, Thomas M. *s.j.* '64 (WDC) [M] Washington, DC The Jesuit Community at Georgetown University.
King, Thomas M. '73 (CIN) [85] Cincinnati, OH St. Therese, The Little Flower Church.
King, Thomas P. *c.s.c.* '69 (FTW) [B] Notre Dame, IN University of Notre Dame Du Lac; [J] Notre Dame, IN Holy Cross Community, Corby Hall, University of Notre Dame.
King, Tommy *o.f.m.* '93 (OAK) [9] Oakland, CA St. Elizabeth's Church; [A] Berkeley, CA Franciscan School of Theology Student Residence.
King, William *s.j.* '61 (SFE) [6] Albuquerque, NM Immaculate Conception Church.
King, William F. *s.j.* '57 (CIN) [M] Cincinnati, OH Jesuit Community at Xavier Unversity.
King, William F. *s.j.* '57 (DET) [K] Detroit, MI Jesuit Provincial Office-Detroit Province of the Society of Jesus.
King, William J. '83 (HBG) Camp Hill, PA Good Shepherd Church.
Kingery, Patrick J. '93 (ATL) Woodstock, GA St. Michael the Archangel Church.
Kingery, Victor *o.f.m.* '49 (SFD) [B] Quincy, IL Quincy University.
Kingsbury, John G. *c.ss.r.* '80 (NY) [DD] Esopus, NY Redemptorist Priests and Brothers C.Ss.R. (Province of Baltimore); [FF] Esopus, NY Mount St. Alphonsus

Redemptorist Retreat Center.
Kingsley, Richard '83 (TUC) [19] Tucson, AZ St. Pius X Church.
Kiniry, Msgr. Joseph R. '50 (ALT) [23] Johnstown, PA St. Benedict's Church.
Kiniry, Lawrence R. '65 (GBG) [3] Greensburg, PA Our Lady of Grace Church.
Kinkead, Cormac *c.p.* '51 (HRT) [M] West Hartford, CT Holy Family Monastery/Retreat.
Kinkead, James A. '55 (BR) French Settlement, LA St. Joseph Church.
Kinkel, Robert J. '70 (DEN) Arvada, CO Spirit of Christ Parish.
Kinkopf, John J. '57 (CLV) Chagrin Falls, OH St. Joan of Arc Church; Kirtland, OH Divine Word Church; Retired.
Kinlough, Msgr. William C. '43 (AUS) Lampasas, TX St. Mary's Church; Lometa, TX Good Shepherd Church.
Kinlough, Msgr. William C. '43 (CC) Retired.
Kinn, James W. '57 (CHI) Mundelein, IL Santa Maria Del Popolo Church.
Kinnaman, Leroy G. '73 (LFT) Covington, IN St. Joseph Church; [H] Crawfordsville, IN Newman Center at Wabash College.
Kinnane, James F. '63 (HRT) Newington, CT Holy Spirit Church; Special and other (Arch)Diocesan Assignment.
Kinney, David *o.c.s.o.* '37 (SLC) [F] Huntsville, UT Abbey of Our Lady of the Holy Trinity of the Order of Cistercians.
Kinney, Donald *o.c.d.* '88 (SJ) [M] San Jose, CA Carmelite Monastery, Novitiate.
Kinney, Francis L. *c.pp.s.* '47 (STU) Pine Grove, OH St. Mary Church.
Kinney, George R. '63 (STP) Corcoran, MN St. Thomas the Apostle Church.
Kinney, John M. '76 (LFT) Military Chaplains.
Kinney, Leo '92 (FAR) Anamoose, ND St. Francis Xavier Church.
Kinney, M. Eugene '84 (MIL) Horicon, WI St. Malachy Church; [W] Horicon, WI Legion of Mary.
Kinney, Thomas '77 (NO) [9] Metairie, LA St. Francis Xavier Church.
Kinney, William G. '96 (CHR) Yonges Island, SC St. Mary Church.
Kinney, William J. *m.s.* '42 (HRT) [M] Hartford, CT Missionaries of LaSalette Provincial Secretary.
Kinross, Knute *o.f.m.* '51 (CIN) Centerville, OH St. Francis of Assisi Church.
Kinsella, Arthur L. *o.p.* '46 (STL) [P] St. Louis, MO St. Dominic Priory.
Kinsella, Charles R. '65 (BO) Health Leave.
Kinsella, Gerald A. *s.j.* '46 (BO) [W] Weston, MA Campion Health Center, Inc.
Kinsella, Msgr. John '64 (BAL) Absent on Leave.
Kinsella, John J. *s.j.* '59 (CHI) [C] Chicago, IL Jesuit Community at Loyola University of Chicago.
Kinsky, Richard *c.s.b.* (ROC) [E] Rochester, NY St. Ann's Home for the Aged.
Kinter, John P. '67 (WDC) [43] Washington, DC St. Thomas More Church; Hospital & Nursing Home Ministries.
Kintiba, George *s.v.d.* '69 (CHI) [53] Chicago, IL St. Elizabeth Church.
Kinzer, Gary '70 (ORG) Absent on Sick Leave.
Kinzer, Victor '49 (SCL) Osakis, MN Immaculate Conception Church.
Kinzig, James J. '53 (JOL) Retired.
Kinzig, James J. '53 (SD) [3] Chula Vista, CA St. Pius X Church.
Kinzler, Dale '74 (FAR) [3] Fargo, ND Nativity Church.
Kipfer, David '88 (PEO) [1] Ottawa, IL St. Columba Church.
Kippley, Robert H. '83 (BIS) [2] Minot, ND Our Lady of Grace Church.
Kirby, Daniel J. '94 (DM) Elkhart, IA St. Mary/Holy Cross Church.
Kirby, Donald J. *s.j.* '72 (SY) [S] Syracuse, NY Jesuits at LeMoyne, Inc.
Kirby, Edward A. '61 (PT) Mary Esther, FL St. Peter Church.
Kirby, Gerald S. '84 (NOR) On Duty Outside the Diocese.
Kirby, James '96 (DM) [12] Des Moines, IA St. Theresa of the Child Jesus Church.
Kirby, Jon *s.v.d.* '71 (FgM) Society of the Divine Word Foreign Missions.
Kirby, Larry Joseph '81 (BAK) Absent on Leave.
Kirby, Louis M. *o.s.b.* '44 (PBL) [F] Canon City, CO Holy Cross Abbey.
Kirby, Louis M. *o.s.b.* '48 (PBL) Westcliffe, CO Our Lady of the Assumption Church.
Kirby, Marc Daniel *o.cist.* (NOR) [A] Cromwell, CT Holy Apostles College and Seminary.
Kirby, Martin F. '67 (BRK) [B] Douglaston, NY Cathedral Residence of the Immaculate Conception.
Kirby, Martin F. '67 (RVC) Oceanside, NY St. Anthony Church.
Kirby, Robert F. '59 (FR) Retired.
Kirby, Thomas '57 (PIT) Allegheny County, PA Health-sound Harmarville Rehabilitation Hospital.
Kirby, Thomas M. '57 (PIT) Blawnox, PA St. Edward Church; Allegheny County, PA UPMC St. Margaret Hospital.
Kircher, August R. *m.m.* '41 (NY) [DD] Maryknoll, NY Maryknoll Fathers and Brothers.
Kircher, Edward '57 (CC) Retired.
Kirchgessner, Christopher A. *o.s.b.* '80 (CHL) [J] Belmont, NC Belmont Abbey.
Kirchmeyer, Robert W. '52 (BO) Danvers, MA St. Alphonsus Church.
Kirchmyer, Thomas B. *m.m.* '59 (NY) [DD] Maryknoll, NY Maryknoll Fathers and Brothers; [DD] Maryknoll, NY Maryknoll Fathers and Brothers.
Kirchner, Donnell *c.ss.r.* '66 (FgM) Redemptorist Foreign Missions.
Kirchner, James A. '63 (NEW) On Duty Outside the Archdiocese.
Kirchner, James A. '63 (SAV) Tifton, GA Our Divine Saviour Church.
Kirchner, Paul *o.carm.* '40 (NEW) [P] Mahwah, NJ Carmel Retreat House.
Kirchner, Peter K., Jr. '93 (SCL) BlueGrass, MN St. Hubert's Church; Verndale, MN St. Frederick's Church.
Kireilis, Fabian P. (CHI) Retired.
Kireilis, Fabian V. '39 (CHI) [92] Chicago, IL Immaculate Conception Church.
Kirila, Michael '87 (ROM) Detroit, MI St. John the Baptist Church.
Kiriti, Daniel (SJ) [1] Palo Alto, CA St. Thomas Aquinas Church.
Kirk, Albert E. '68 (MEM) [11] Memphis, TN Holy Spirit Church.
Kirk, Allan F. *s.j.* '65 (CHI) [C] Chicago, IL Jesuit Community at Loyola University of Chicago; [J] Maywood, IL Foster G. McGaw Hospital of Loyola University of Chicago.
Kirk, Daniel *o.s.b.* '49 (WDC) [M] Washington, DC St. Anselm's Abbey.
Kirk, David '64 (NTN) On Special Projects; [D] New York, NY Emmaus House/Harlem.
Kirk, David R. '83 (TOL) Military Chaplains.
Kirk, James T., Jr. '86 (WIL) Brandywood, DE Church of the Holy Child.
Kirk, Msgr. John A. '47 (E) McKean, PA St. Francis Xavier Church.
Kirk, John L. '70 (NSH) Tullahoma, TN St. Paul the Apostle Church.
Kirk, Thomas '69 (MEM) [C] Memphis, TN Immaculate Conception Cathedral Middle and High School.
Kirk, Thomas D. '69 (MEM) [1] Memphis, TN Cathedral of the Immaculate Conception.
Kirk, Tom '69 (MEM) [H] Memphis, TN St. Peter Manor.
Kirk, William J. *o.s.b.* '46 (PEO) [A] Peru, IL St. Bede Abbey and Academy.
Kirk, William S. '72 (PH) Secane, PA Our Lady of Fatima Church.
Kirke, Eugene K. '62 (BO) Society of St. James the Apostle.
Kirke, Eugene K. '62 (FgM) Society of St. James the Apostle.
Kirkhoff, Gerald J. '69 (IND) [23] Indianapolis, IN St. Jude Church.
Kirkilas, Michael '36 (CHI) Retired.
Kirkness, Michael (LA) Lompoc, CA US Penitentiary.
Kirkness, Michael D. '77 (GF) On Duty Outside of the Diocese.
Kirkpatrick, Cletus '56 (BAK) [A] Ontario, OR The Dominican Sisters of Ontario, Inc. dba Holy Rosary Medical Center.
Kirkpatrick, Robert *c.ss.r.* '33 (OAK) [N] Oakland, CA Redemptorists.
Kirley, Kevin J. *c.s.b.* '52 (GAL) [Q] Sugar Land, TX Basilian Mission Center.
Kirlin, Msgr. Bernard '71 (MIA) Sabbatical.
Kirouac, Richard '85 (STN) [1] Chicago, IL St. Nicholas Ukrainian Catholic Cathedral.
Kirouac, Richard L. '85 (STN) Mishawaka, IN St. Michael Church.
Kirovac, Richard L. '85 (FTW) [5] Mishawaka, IN St. Michael Ukrainian Catholic Church.
Kirrane, James A. '46 (BRK) Retired.
Kirrane, James A. '46 (RVC) East Northport, NY St. Anthony of Padua Church.
Kirsch, Edmund D. '88 (CHL) Murphy, NC St. William Church.
Kirsch, Gerard D. *o.s.b.* '70 (SEA) [M] Lacey, WA St. Martin's Abbey.
Kirsch, Gregory A. '81 (E) [1] Erie, PA St. Peter Cathedral.
Kirsch, Gregory G. '88 (STL) [30] St. Louis, MO St. Cecilia Church; St. Louis, MO Saint Louis University Hospital; [K] St. Louis, MO Saint Louis University Hospital.
Kirsch, John B. '69 (HEL) Retired.
Kirsch, Myron M. *o.s.b.* '73 (GBG) [H] Latrobe, PA Saint Vincent Archabbey.
Kirsch, Patrick V. '81 (SB) Phelan, CA Blessed Junipero Serra Church; Wrightwood, CA Our Lady of the Snows Church.
Kirschner, Anthony *c.m.m.* '37 (DET) [K] Dearborn Heights, MI Our Lady of Grace Monastery.
Kirtz, Raymond R. *o.m.i.* '58 (STP) [Q] Buffalo, MN Christ the King Retreat Center.
Kirwan, Christopher J., Jr. '92 (BO) Walpole, MA Blessed Sacrament Church.
Kirwan, Thomas P. '69 (DET) [1] Sterling Heights, MI St. Blase Church.
Kirwen, Michael C. *m.m.* '63 (FgM) Maryknoll Foreign Missions.
Kirwin, Arthur R. *o.p.* '84 (R) [E] Raleigh, NC Dominican Community; [E] Raleigh, NC De Porres House.
Kirwin, George *o.m.i.* '58 (BUF) [27] Buffalo, NY Holy Angels Church.
Kirwin, John '66 (ALB) [2] Albany, NY St. John-St. Ann Church.
Kirwin, Michael J. '76 (SCR) [1] Old Forge, PA St. Lawrence O'Toole Church.
Kirwin, Peter *o.f.m.* '81 (P) [6] Portland, OR Ascension Church.
Kirwin, Msgr. Robert J. '45 (RVC) Williston Park, NY St. Aidan's Church; Retired.
Kirwin, William J. *o.m.i.* '38 (BO) [Z] Tewksbury, MA Immaculate Heart of Mary Novitiate-Infirmary.
Kis-Horvath, Pascal *o.cist.* '57 (DAL) [M] Irving, TX Cistercian Abbey of Our Lady of Dallas.
Kisala, Robert *s.v.d.* '85 (FgM) Society of the Divine Word Foreign Missions.
Kiselica, John *s.m.* '84 (DET) [E] Harper Woods, MI Notre Dame High School.
Kiser, Karl J. *s.j.* (DET) [K] Detroit, MI Jesuit Provincial Office-Detroit Province of the Society of Jesus.
Kish, Carl '62 (Y) Cortland, OH St. Robert Bellarmine Parish.
Kish, Leslie Paul '97 (B) Caldwell, ID St. Mary Church.
Kish, Matthew J. '43 (GRY) [8] East Chicago, IN St. John Cantius Church; Retired.
Kish, Michael A. '65 (MIA) [26] Miami, FL St. Louis Church.
Kisluk, Aloysius J. '57 (NOR) [3] Middletown, CT St. Mary of Czestochowa Church.
Kiss, Barnabas G. *o.f.m.* '78 (DET) [31] Detroit, MI Holy Cross Church.
Kiss, Gabriel *s.j.* '55 (NY) [12] Yonkers, NY St. Margaret of Hungary Church.
Kiss, Matthew J. *o.f.m.* '40 (Y) [J] Youngstown, OH Mt. Alverna Friary.
Kissane, James M. '92 (RVC) East Northport, NY St. Anthony of Padua Church.
Kissane, Maurice J. '64 (CHI) Brookfield, IL St. Barbara Church.
Kissane, Michael *o.carm.* '86 (NY) [DD] Middletown, NY St. Albert's Priory; [DD] Tappan, NY St. Eliseus Priory.
Kissane, Richard *c.s.sp.* '45 (SB) [E] Hemet, CA Holy Ghost Fathers.
Kissel, Anthony (SP) [A] St. Leo, FL Saint Leo College.
Kissel, Anthony '73 (EVN) On Duty Outside the Diocese.
Kissel, Francis J. *s.m.* '71 (ATL) [C] Atlanta, GA Marist School.
Kissel, Ignatius M. *o.s.m.* '65 (CHI) [N] Chicago, IL Servite Friars - Eastern Province.
Kissel, Ignatius M. *o.s.m.* '65 (ORG) Fullerton, CA St. Philip Benizi Church; [H] Buena Park, CA Servite Fathers And Brothers; [H] Buena Park, CA Servite Fathers And Brothers.
Kissell, Terrence T. '78 (DEN) Commerce City, CO Our Lady Mother of the Church.
Kissell, Wilbur '51 (MOB) [2] Montgomery, AL Church of St. Andrew the Apostle.
Kissinger, Rodney T. *s.j.* '53 (SP) [C] Tampa, FL Jesuit High School.
Kissling, John M. '53 (DUB) Retired.
Kist, Harold W. '74 (CIN) Greenville, OH St. Mary Church.
Kisting, Thomas J. '73 (DUL) Longville, MN St. Edward's Church.
Kistler, Leonard A. *c.pp.s.* '61 (TOL) Alvada, OH St. Peter Church; New Riegel, OH St. Boniface Church.
Kistner, Hilarion H. *o.f.m.* '55 (CIN) [P] Cincinnati, OH Friarhurst Retreat Center.
Kitchin, George '70 (BLX) Ocean Springs, MS St. Elizabeth Ann Seton Church.
Kitko, Joseph F. '55 (BAL) Laurel, MD Resurrection of Our Lord Church.
Kitt, Liam J. '43 (CLV) Elyria Township, OH St. Vincent de Paul Church.
Kitt, William J. '43 (CLV) Retired.
Kitten, Marvin C. *s.j.* '65 (NO) [C] New Orleans, LA Loyola University.
Kittock, Francis R. '55 (STP) [21] Minneapolis, MN St. Charles Borromeo Church.
Kitz, Raphael *o.c.d.* '59 (LR) [A] Little Rock, AR Marylake - Carmelite Novitiate.
Kitzke, Timothy L. '89 (MIL) Whitefish Bay, WI Holy Family Church; [Y] Whitefish Bay, WI Association of Ladies of Charity of Milwaukee, Wisconsin.
Kivel, Joseph (STP) [23] Minneapolis, MN SS. Cyril &

Methodius Church.
Kivel, Joseph G. '61 (STP) [17] Minneapolis, MN St. Anthony of Padua Church.
Kizis, Kenneth G. '59 (SCR) Olyphant, PA St. Michael the Archangel Church.
Klaas, Gregory '67 (SR) [H] Sonoma, CA Hanna Boys Center.
Klaas, Msgr. Raymond E. '50 (MAD) Marshall, WI St. Mary's of the Nativity Church.
Klaers, Marvin J. '50 (STP) Miesville, MN St. Joseph Church; New Trier, MN St. Mary Church.
Klaia, John J. *o.p.* '52 (SFR) [13] San Francisco, CA St. Dominic Church; [N] San Francisco, CA St. Dominic Priory.
Klaiber, Jeffrey L. *s.j.* '74 (CHI) [N] Chicago, IL Chicago Province of the Society of Jesus-Provincial Office.
Klaiber, Jeffrey L. *s.j.* '74 (FgM) Provinces.
Klajbor, Richard J. '79 (CHI) [82] Chicago, IL Holy Innocents Church.
Klak, Jan Piotr '79 (SAT) Falls City, TX Holy Trinity Church.
Klamet, Francis X. '78 (CLV) [30] Cleveland, OH Holy Rosary Church; Released from Diocesan Assignment.
Klapp, John S. '45 (PH) [97] Philadelphia, PA St. Mary of Czestochowa Church; Retired.
Klapperich, Giles *o.p.* '53 (CHI) River Forest, IL St. Vincent Ferrer Priory Church.
Klapps, William J. '58 (WIL) Woodcrest, DE St. Matthew Church; Retired.
Klarer, Michael E. '79 (MAD) Military Chaplains.
Klasek, Stephen A. '83 (NSH) [7] Nashville, TN Holy Rosary Church.
Klasinski, George '51 (KCK) Retired.
Klasinski, Stanley J. '61 (CLV) Lyndhurst, OH St. Clare Church.
Klassen, John *o.s.b.* '77 (SCL) [I] Collegeville, MN St. John's Abbey, of the Order of St. Benedict.
Klassen, Roger *o.s.b.* '66 (SCL) Freeport, MN Sacred Heart Church; New Munich, MN Immaculate Conception Church; [I] Collegeville, MN St. John's Abbey, of the Order of St. Benedict.
Klatka, Joseph S. '67 (MAN) Littleton, NH St. Rose of Lima Church.
Klauck, Michael '94 (BIR) On Duty Outside the Diocese.
Klauck, Msgr. Peter N. '55 (GB) [1] Green Bay, WI St. Francis Xavier Cathedral.
Klauck, Stanley B. '46 (MIL) Retired.
Klauder, Francis *s.d.b.* '47 (NEW) [N] South Orange, NJ The Salesian Community.
Klauer, Gary *o.f.m.conv.* '75 (LA) Hermosa Beach, CA Our Lady of Guadalupe Church; [R] Torrance, CA Franciscan Friars, St. Bonaventure Friary.
Klauke, Raymond '49 (LAN) Retired.
Klaus, Donald R. '42 (TOL) Retired.
Klaus, Joseph J. '54 (R) Absent on Leave.
Kleas, Msgr. Milam E. '51 (GAL) Dickinson, TX Shrine of the True Cross Church.
Kleba, Gerald J. '67 (STL) Clayton, MO St. Joseph Church.
Kleber, Cecil *o.f.m.* '50 (SFE) [1] Santa Fe, NM The Cathedral of San Francisco de Asis.
Klecha, Joseph A. *m.m.* '69 (LA) [R] Los Angeles, CA Maryknoll Fathers and Brothers.
Kleczewski, Kieran (PHX) Flagstaff, AZ San Francisco de Asis Church.
Klee, Robert A. '49 (COL) Retired.
Kleefisch, Charles A. '42 (MIL) [17] Milwaukee, WI St. Catherine Church; Retired.
Kleene, Regis *s.d.s.* '60 (CHI) [3] Waukegan, IL St. Dismas Church.
Klees, Raymond F. '73 (CHI) La Grange, IL St. Cletus Church.
Kleffman, James F. '60 (DM) Missouri Valley, IA St. Patrick Church.
Kleiber, Kenneth R. '68 (CHI) Retired.
Kleiber, Richard '47 (GB) Retired.
Klein, Albert J. '36 (Y) Retired.
Klein, Bernard C. '49 (STP) Retired.
Klein, Charles R. '54 (NY) [DD] New York, NY Our Lady of Consolation Residence.
Klein, Charles R. '59 (BAL) [88] Baltimore, MD Sacred Heart of Mary Church; Retired.
Klein, David *c.s.b.* '74 (SFE) Albuquerque, NM Presbyterian Hospital.
Klein, David F. *s.j.* '71 (SAC) [G] Carmichael, CA Jesuit High School Community of Sacramento.
Klein, David J. '90 (CAM) [1] Camden, NJ Immaculate Conception Cathedral.
Klein, Dennis D. '66 (BRK) [B] Douglaston, NY Cathedral Residence of the Immaculate Conception.
Klein, Donald L. '65 (DUB) [7] Cedar Rapids, IA St. Pius X Church.
Klein, Douglas Michael '96 (SC) Carroll, IA St. Lawrence Church.
Klein, Msgr. Edward '43 (WIN) Retired.
Klein, Eugene J. '45 (DM) Retired.
Klein, Msgr. Frank W. '45 (WIN) Retired.
Klein, George W. '54 (CIN) Trenton, OH Holy Name Church.
Klein, George W. '59 (CHI) Wilmette, IL St. Francis Xavier Church.
Klein, Gregory L. *o.carm.* '75 (BUF) [C] Niagara University, NY Niagara University.
Klein, Gregory L. *o.carm.* '75 (JOL) [J] Darien, IL Carmelite Provincial Office.
Klein, J. Leo *s.j.* '64 (CIN) [D] Cincinnati, OH Xavier University; [M] Cincinnati, OH Jesuit Community at Xavier Unversity.
Klein, James T. '78 (CLV) Westlake, OH St. Bernadette Church.
Klein, John G. '75 (CHI) [5] Chicago, IL St. Agnes of Bohemia Church.
Klein, John J. '70 (PAT) Dover, NJ St. Mary's Church.
Klein, John P. '62 (PIT) Retired.
Klein, John P. '78 (LAN) [1] Flint, MI St. Agnes Church.
Klein, John Paul *o.m.v.* '89 (SFD) [2] Alton, IL Immaculate Conception-St. Mary's Church; [3] Alton, IL St. Patrick Church.
Klein, Karl J. '43 (DUB) Retired.
Klein, Lawrence J. '84 (BWN) La Feria, TX St. Francis Xavier Church.
Klein, Louis S. (BUF) [K] Buffalo, NY Sisters of Charity Hospital of Buffalo, NY.
Klein, Martin '91 (RVC) Westbury, NY St. Brigid Church.
Klein, Peter J. '74 (WIN) Madelia, MN St. Mary Church.
Klein, Pius *o.s.b.* '74 (EVN) Huntingburg, IN Visitation of the Blessed Virgin Mary Church.
Klein, Pius *o.s.b.* '74 (IND) [J] St. Meinrad, IN St. Meinrad Archabbey.
Klein, Robert P. '53 (COV) Retired.
Klein, Robert W. '56 (DUL) On Leave Without Assignment.
Klein, Msgr. Stanley H. '44 (BUF) Retired.
Klein, Msgr. Sylvester P. '35 (LFT) Retired.
Klein, Terrance W. '84 (COL) Graduate Studies.
Klein, Theodore J. '69 (NOR) Groton, CT St. Mary Church.
Kleiner, James E. '67 (DEN) Arvada, CO St. Joan of Arc Church.
Kleiner, Robert *m.c.c.j.* '71 (CHI) Blue Island, IL St. Donatus Church.
Kleinfehn, Walter J. '60 (DUB) Norway, IA St. Michael's Church; Watkins, IA St. Patrick's Church.
Kleinhans, Msgr. Thomas G. '67 (FRS) Visalia, CA St. Mary Church.
Kleinheinz, Joseph L. '54 (SUP) Retired.
Kleinhenz, John H. *s.j.* '52 (CLV) [E] Cleveland, OH St. Ignatius High School.
Kleinmann, Dennis W. '93 (ARL) Winchester, VA Sacred Heart of Jesus Church.
Kleinschmidt, Msgr. Anthony '33 (SCL) Retired.
Kleinschmidt, Msgr. Anthony A. '43 (COL) [A] Columbus, OH Pontifical College Josephinum.
Kleinschmidt, Sylvester '50 (SCL) Retired.
Kleinstuber, Joseph J. '64 (WDC) [1] Silver Spring, MD St. Andrew Apostle Church; Special Ministries.
Kleinwachter, John '77 (CR) Akeley, MN St. John's Church.
Kleinweber, Dennis J. '78 (CLV) East Cleveland, OH St. Philomena Church.
Kleinworth, Robert (ELP) Absent on Leave.
Klejnowski, Arcadius '54 (TR) [15] Trenton, NJ St. Hedwig Church.
Klem, Daniel N. '83 (RIC) [9] Virginia Beach, VA St. Mark Church.
Klem, Leo J. *c.s.b.* '40 (ROC) [I] Rochester, NY Basilian Residence.
Klem, Robert J. *c.s.b.* '56 (GAL) [Q] Sugar Land, TX Basilian Mission Center.
Klemash, Dennis *o.f.m.cap.* '90 (PH) [79] Philadelphia, PA St. John the Evangelist Church.
Klementowicz, Chester '46 (ALB) Retired.
Klemme, Dennis C. '57 (MIL) Special Assignment; [Q] Pewaukee, WI Carmel of the Mother of God.
Klemme, Robert W. '91 (LFT) Carmel, IN St. Elizabeth Ann Seton Church.
Klemmer, Marvin J. '66 (BIS) [2] Bismarck, ND Ascension Church.
Klenke, Elmer A. '65 (DOD) Retired.
Klepac, Msgr. Kenneth J. '58 (MOB) [8] Mobile, AL St. Joan of Arc Church.
Klepacki, Michael S. '78 (CHL) Military Chaplains.
Klepec, George F. '71 (JOL) [12] Joliet, IL St. Joseph Church.
Kleppner, Joseph J. '71 (PIT) Center Township, PA St. Frances Cabrini Church.
Klettner, Frederick J. '65 (DET) Farmington Hills, MI St. Clare of Assisi Church.
Kletzel, Thomas P. '83 (PH) [119] Philadelphia, PA Our Lady of Hope Church.
Kleve, Arthur W. '57 (DUB) [3] Waterloo, IA Sacred Heart Church; Retired.
Klevence, John P. '85 (WIL) Ocean City, MD St. Mary, Star of the Sea Church.
Klich, Jan P. (MET) [2] Perth Amboy, NJ St. Stephen Church.
Kliche, Anthony S. *c.s.sp.* '44 (PH) [AA] Bensalem, PA Congregation of the Holy Ghost.
Klieber, Kenneth '68 (PHX) Phoenix, AZ United States Veterans Affairs Medical Center.
Klikunas, Bruce J. *o.s.m.* '72 (OAK) [K] Hayward, CA St. Rose Hospital; [N] Berkeley, CA Servite Community, Sarpi Priory.
Klim, Vincent M. '89 (PAT) Haskell, NJ St. Francis of Assisi Church.
Klima, James A. '76 (COL) Marion, OH St. Mary Church.
Klimanskis, Adolfo (NOR) On Duty Outside the Diocese.
Klimanskis, Adolph '53 (PRO) [10] Providence, RI St. Casimir Church.
Klimas, George H. '51 (SAG) Retired.
Klimczyk, John '81 (FTW) [2] South Bend, IN St. Adalbert Church.
Klimczyk, Leon F. *s.j.* '79 (STP) [31] Minneapolis, MN St. Olaf Church; [N] Minneapolis, MN La Storta Jesuit Community.
Klimek, Edmund J. '53 (LC) [2] Eau Claire, WI Newman Community Church; [E] Eau Claire, WI Sacred Heart Hospital; [L] Eau Claire, WI Newman Parish.
Klimek, Jan '71 (FAR) Mooreton, ND St. Anthony's Church.
Klimowicz, Sigmund M. *o.f.m.cap.* '45 (PAT) [M] Oak Ridge-Milton, NJ St. Stanislaus B. M. Friary.
Kline, Charles '62 (LFT) Attica, IN St. Francis Xavier Church.
Kline, Donald '95 (PHX) [2] Tempe, AZ Our Lady of Mt. Carmel Church.
Kline, John J. '47 (CLV) [8] Lorain, OH St. Mary Church; Retired.
Kline, Omer U. *o.s.b.* '49 (GBG) [H] Latrobe, PA Saint Vincent Archabbey.
Kline, Msgr. Robert R. '45 (BAL) [B] Emmitsburg, MD Mount Saint Mary's College.
Kline, Msgr. Robert R. '45 (SCR) On Duty Outside the Diocese.
Kline, Robert W. '48 (CLV) Mentor, OH St. John Vianney Church.
Kline, Msgr. Roy F. '51 (ALT) Duncansville, PA St. Catherine of Siena Church.
Klingeisen, Richard H. '72 (GB) [1] Manitowoc, WI St. Boniface Church; [F] Manitowoc, WI Holy Family Memorial, Inc.
Klinger, Attilio *s.d.b* '54 (PMB) Belle Glade, FL St. Philip Benizi Church.
Klinger, Charles F. '83 (COL) Zanesville, OH St. Nicholas Church.
Klinger, John *s.c.j.* '67 (RC) [B] Eagle Butte, SD Sacred Heart Community House.
Klinger, Msgr. Nevin J. *j.c.l.* '83 (ALN) Birdsboro, PA Immaculate Conception Church.
Klingler, Donald P. '61 (KAL) Otsego, MI St. Margaret Church.
Klingler, John *s.c.j.* '67 (RC) Eagle Butte, SD All Saints Church; Eagle Butte, SD Cheyenne River Reservation Church.
Klingler, Ronald M. '65 (Y) [7] Canton, OH St. John the Baptist Church.
Klink, Anthony G. '58 (MIL) [1] Menomonee Falls, WI St. Anthony Church.
Klink, Delbert D. '60 (MAD) [4] Janesville, WI St. William Church.
Klink, Eugene A. '63 (LC) [1] Eau Claire, WI Immaculate Conception Church.
Klink, Kenneth J. '66 (MAD) Belleville, WI St. Mary of Lourdes Church.
Klink, Peter J. *s.j.* '81 (RC) Pine Ridge, SD Holy Rosary Church; [B] Pine Ridge, SD Jesuit Community of Holy Rosary Mission.
Klintworth, William P. *s.j.* '61 (FgM) Provinces.
Klinzing, Msgr. Thomas '71 (PMB) [1] Palm Beach, FL Cathedral of St. Ignatius Loyola.
Klister, Msgr. Roy M. *j.c.l.* '69 (GB) [13] Green Bay, WI SS. Peter and Paul Church.
Klitsch, Anthony L. '49 (PH) Retired.
Klizek, Duane R. (BUF) [9] Niagara Falls, NY Our Lady of Mount Carmel Church.
Kloak, David G. '78 (CHI) Military Chaplains.
Klobuchar, John Mary *m.f.v.a.* '93 (BIR) [E] Birmingham, AL Franciscan Missionaries of the Eternal Word, A Public Association of the Christian Faithful.
Klobuka, John J. *s.m.* '78 (KAL) Portage, MI St. Catherine of Siena Church; [E] Portage, MI Society of Mary.
Kloc, Thaddeus '70 (VEN) Bonita Springs, FL St. Leo Church.
Klocker, Harry R. *s.j.* '51 (STL) [P] St. Louis, MO Jesuit Community Corporation at St. Louis University - Jesuit Hall.
Klocker, Msgr. Henry J. '43 (CIN) Retired.
Klocker, John G. '58 (STL) Webster Groves, MO Annunciation Church.
Kloda, Marshall J. '89 (PH) [83] Philadelphia, PA St. Katherine of Siena Church.
Kloeckner, William '43 (SCL) Retired.
Kloepfer, John S. '53 (JOL) Retired.
Kloepfer, John S. '53 (RIC) Retired.
Klohr, Paul '30 (BRK) [R] Queens Village, NY Queen of Peace Residence.

Klohr, Paul McC. '30 (BRK) Retired.
Klopke, John R. *c.pp.s.* '53 (OAK) [N] San Leandro, CA Society of the Precious Blood.
Kloppenborg, Thomas *c.m.* '91 (COS) Cheyenne Wells, CO Sacred Heart Church.
Klores, Stanley J. '82 (NO) [A] New Orleans, LA Notre Dame Seminary Graduate School of Theology.
Klos, Joseph '80 (BUF) [1] Lackawanna, NY Basilica of Our Lady of Victory Church.
Klos, Walter '40 (BUF) Retired.
Klose, Kenneth P. '39 (CHI) Skokie, IL St. Peter Church; Retired.
Kloskowski, Msgr. Stanley E. '58 (CAM) Bridgeton, NJ St. Teresa of Avila Church.
Kloss, Anthony *o.s.b.* '91 (WOR) [N] Still River, MA Benedictine Monks, St. Benedict Abbey.
Kloster, Carl G. *s.j.* '48 (DEN) [M] Denver, CO Xavier Jesuit Center.
Kloster, Donald L. '95 (BGP) [1] Bridgeport, CT St. Augustine Cathedral.
Kloster, George M. '68 (CHL) Gastonia, NC St. Michael Church.
Kloster, Robert J. '65 (SY) [14] Utica, NY St. Peter Church.
Kloton, Michael J. '87 (SCR) Plains, PA SS. Peter and Paul Church; [D] Kingston, PA Bishop O'Reilly High School.
Klotter, Frederick W. '96 (L) Pewee Valley, KY St. Aloysius Church.
Klotz, Claude *s.d.s.* '43 (MIL) [P] Milwaukee, WI Salvatorians - Jordan Hall.
Kluba, Zbigniew (PAT) Convent Station, NJ St. Thomas More Church.
Kluba, Zbigniew '73 (PAT) Morristown, NJ Morristown Memorial Hospital.
Klubertanz, Kenneth E. '66 (MAD) Spring Green, WI St. John the Evangelist Church.
Klucinec, Benedict *m.ss.a.* '87 (NOR) [A] Cromwell, CT Holy Apostles College and Seminary; [F] Cromwell, CT Missionaries of the Holy Apostles.
Kluckman, T. Anthony *s.c.j.* '73 (SFS) [B] Chamberlain, SD St. Joseph Indian School.
Kluczynski, Campion *o.f.m.* '59 (GB) [F] Green Bay, WI St. Vincent Hospital; [I] Green Bay, WI St. Mary of the Angels Friary.
Klug, Jerome G. '49 (CHI) Bartlett, IL St. Peter Damian Church; Retired.
Klug, Richard L. '51 (CIN) [9] Cincinnati, OH Annunciation of the Blessed Virgin Mary Church.
Klump, Emmanuel *o.f.m.conv.* '51 (IND) [I] Mount Saint Francis, IN Mount Saint Francis Friary and Retreat Center.
Klunk, Timothy B. '79 (BAL) [12] Baltimore, MD St. Athanasius Church.
Kluonius, Joseph V. '47 (GAY) Retired.
Kluthe, Paul E. *s.s.j.* '56 (GAL) [8] Houston, TX St. Anne de Beaupre Church.
Klyber, Arthur B. *c.ss.r.* '32 (STL) [P] Liguori, MO St. Clement Health Care Center.
Kmech, John '61 (STN) [4] Chicago, IL St. Michael's Church.
Kmiec, Roman *c.m.* '86 (HRT) [18] New Haven, CT St. Stanislaus Church.
Knab, George E. *o.m.i.* '67 (NO) [1] New Orleans, LA St. Louis Cathedral; [17] New Orleans, LA Our Lady of Guadalupe /International Shrine of St. Jude Church.
Knapek, John A. *s.j.* '57 (CLV) [C] Cleveland, OH John Carroll Jesuit Community.
Knapik, Andrew '78 (CLV) [37] Cleveland, OH St. John Cantius Church.
Knapik, Andrew G. (ALT) Retired.
Knapp, Charles D. '63 (TUC) [8] Tucson, AZ Our Mother of Sorrows Church.
Knapp, Gerard J. *c.ss.r.* '75 (BRK) [U] Brooklyn, NY Our Lady of Good Counsel Residence.
Knapp, James G. *s.j.* '81 (STL) [F] St. Louis, MO St. Louis University High School, George H. Backer Memorial; [P] St. Louis, MO St. Louis University High School Jesuit Community.
Knapp, John M. '86 (NY) [177] Bronx, NY Our Lady of Solace Church.
Knapp, Joseph G. *o.c.s.o.* '48 (DUB) [K] Peosta, IA New Melleray Abbey, Order of Cistercians of the Strict Observance.
Knapp, Msgr. Kenneth R. '63 (EVN) [3] Evansville, IN Christ the King Church; Special Assignment.
Knapp, Msgr. Richard (SFR) [U] San Rafael, CA Third Order of St. Dominic Support and Charitable Trust Fund.
Knapp, Msgr. Richard K. '55 (SFR) Novato, CA Our Lady of Loretto Church.
Knapp, Roger A. '85 (DET) Gibraltar, MI St. Victor Church.
Knapp, Stephen V. '32 (STN) Retired.
Knapp, William L. '48 (SFR) [2] San Rafael, CA St. Isabella Church; Retired.
Knappik, Richard *c.ss.r.* '58 (ALB) [L] Saratoga Springs, NY St. John Neumann Residence.
Knaresborough, Francis J. '89 (TYL) Retired.
Knauer, Msgr. Paul F. '64 (PAT) Sparta, NJ Our Lady of the Lake Church.
Knauf, Edwin L. '33 (LC) Retired.
Knauf, Randall *o.f.m.cap.* '91 (MIL) [B] Mount Calvary, WI St. Lawrence Seminary; [P] Mount Calvary, WI St. Lawrence Friary.
Knaup, Alan J. '77 (STL) Mehlville, MO St. Margaret Mary Alacoque Church.
Kneafsey, Msgr. Cornelius T. '58 (BRK) [208] Queens, NY Our Lady of the Cenacle Church.
Kneal, Msgr. Ellsworth '44 (STP) Retired.
Knecht, Joseph *s.j.* '60 (FgM) Provinces.
Knees, Anton M. *s.j.* '51 (NY) [DD] New York, NY Murray-Weigel Hall.
Kneifl, Rodney V. '85 (OM) [6] Omaha, NE Assumption, B.V.M. Church.
Kneip, Paschal *o.s.b.* '51 (RIC) [6] Virginia Beach, VA St. Gregory the Great Church.
Kneipp, August J. '41 (CIN) Retired.
Kneis, G. Jerome *o.s.a.* '62 (CHI) [N] Olympia Fields, IL The Augustinian Provincialate Tolentine Center.
Knepper, Daniel J. '70 (DUB) Bellevue, IA St. Joseph's Church.
Knerr, Joseph '80 (ORG) Fountain Valley, CA Holy Spirit Church.
Knestout, Barry '89 (WDC) Pastoral Center Special Ministries.
Kniepp, August J. '41 (CIN) [L] Cincinnati, OH Archbishop Leibold Home for the Aged.
Knier, Aloysius M. '42 (GB) Retired.
Kniewel, Edward J. '38 (CHI) Melrose Park, IL Sacred Heart Church; Retired.
Knight, David B. '61 (MEM) [25] Memphis, TN Sacred Heart Church.
Knight, Jeffrey N. '88 (STL) [41] St. Louis, MO St. John the Baptist Church.
Knight, Robert D. '83 (STL) Absent on Sick Leave.
Knighton, Marvin T. '76 (MIL) Awaiting Assignment.
Knipe, Michael J. '88 (TLS) [16] Tulsa, OK Resurrection Church.
Knipe, William T. *m.m.* '58 (FgM) Maryknoll Foreign Missions.
Knippel, Kenneth P. '76 (MIL) Fox Point, WI St. Eugene Church.
Knipper, Daniel J. '67 (DUB) [2] Waterloo, IA St. Mary's Church.
Knittel, Kilian M. '60 (CHI) [43] Chicago, IL St. Columba Church.
Knoblach, Thomas '87 (SCL) On Duty Outside the Diocese.
Knoebel, Thomas L. '69 (MIL) Special Assignment; [B] Hales Corners, WI Sacred Heart School of Theology.
Knoeber, Joseph *o.m.i.* '59 (BEL) [F] Belleville, IL Missionary Oblates of Mary Immaculate - St. Henry's Oblate Residence.
Knoernschild, John *o.carm.* '70 (CHI) [D] Chicago, IL Mt. Carmel High School.
Knoernschild, William F. '47 (MIL) Retired.
Knoerschild, John *o.carm.* '70 (CHI) [N] Chicago, IL Carmelite Priory of St. Cyril.
Knoke, Kenneth F. '55 (FAR) Reynolds, ND Our Lady of Perpetual Help Church.
Knoll, Charles '54 (PIT) [O] Pittsburgh, PA St. Francis Friary.
Knoll, Jerome E. *c.s.c.* '60 (FTW) [B] Notre Dame, IN University of Notre Dame Du Lac; [J] Notre Dame, IN Holy Cross Community, Corby Hall, University of Notre Dame.
Knoll, Lester *o.f.m.cap.* '64 (PIT) [O] Herman, PA St. Mary's Friary.
Knoll, Mark *c.ss.r.* '36 (ORL) Retired; [F] New Smyrna Beach, FL St. Alphonsus Villa-Redemptorist Fathers and Brothers.
Knoll, Urban H. '69 (STL) Retired.
Knop, Andrew *o.m.i.* '89 (DUL) [3] Duluth, MN Holy Family, Church.
Knopik, Andrew J. '83 (BEL) [4] Belleville, IL St. Augustine of Canterbury Church.
Knopke, Roch *o.f.m.* '31 (PAT) [M] Ringwood, NJ Holy Name Friary, Inc.
Knopp, Benjamin *o.f.m.conv.* (TOL) Salem Twp., OH St. Joseph Church.
Knopp, Benjamin *o.f.m.conv.* '55 (TOL) Carey, OH Our Lady of Consolation, Basilica-National Shrine Church.
Knopp, John '78 (ELP) Absent on Leave.
Knotek, John T. '38 (MIL) Retired.
Knotek, Marcel '92 (PH) Absent on Leave.
Knotek, Michael P. '96 (CHI) Oak Forest, IL St. Damian Church.
Knotek, Wenceslaus F. *m.m.* '41 (SJ) [M] Los Altos, CA Maryknoll.
Knoth, Bernard P. *s.j.* '77 (NO) [C] New Orleans, LA Loyola University.
Knott, Edward J. '45 (MAN) Retired.
Knott, Francis X. *s.j.* '45 (BAL) [M] Baltimore, MD Jesuit Fathers and Brothers Maryland Provincial Curia.
Knott, J. Ronald '70 (IND) [A] St. Meinrad, IN St. Meinrad Seminary.
Knott, William P. '59 (RCK) Retired.
Knox, Bruce (IND) [31] Indianapolis, IN St. Patrick Church.
Knox, James '51 (PRT) Retired.
Knox, Stephen J. '89 (RCK) DeKalb, IL Christ the Teacher, University Parish of Northern Illinois University Church; [M] DeKalb, IL Newman Foundation for Catholic Students of Northern Illinois University.
Knudsen, Ronald '72 (SEA) Puyallup, WA All Saints Church.
Knueven, Gerald E. '68 (TOL) [7] Toledo, OH Good Shepherd Church; [18] Toledo, OH St. Anthony Church; [38] Toledo, OH St. Stanislaus Church.
Knueven, Harold L. '58 (IND) Greenwood, IN Our Lady of the Greenwood Church.
Knuffman, Donald '65 (SFD) [3] Quincy, IL St. Dominic Church.
Knuge, Richard K. *s.m.* '56 (CIN) [M] Dayton, OH Marianist Provincialate.
Knurek, Dennis A. '77 (BGP) Retired.
Knusel, Frank '73 (P) [26] Portland, OR St. Patrick Church.
Kobak, Cantius J. *o.f.m.* '57 (MIL) [P] Milwaukee, WI Francis and Clare House.
Kobasuk, Maxim *o.s.b.m.* '77 (STF) Kenmore, NY St. John the Baptist Church.
Kobayashi, Augustine *ss.cc.* '64 (FR) [J] Fairhaven, MA Sacred Hearts Provincial House.
Kobbeman, Gerald P. '66 (RCK) [2] Aurora, IL Holy Angels Church.
Kobe, Robert S. '79 (ELP) [5] El Paso, TX Christ The Savior Church.
Kobel, Stanley *o.f.m.cap.* '96 (NY) [B] Beacon, NY St. Lawrence of Brindisi Friary.
Kobida, Vincent F. '80 (MIL) On Duty Outside the Archdiocese.
Kobler, John F. *c.p.* '54 (CHI) [N] Chicago, IL Immaculate Conception Monastery.
Kobos, Martin *o.f.m.conv.* '76 (BAL) [M] Ellicott City, MD Order of Friars Minor Conventual.
Kobos, Martin *o.f.m.conv.* '76 (FgM) Conventual Franciscan Foreign Missions.
Kobs, Allan Von *o.f.m.* '82 (PAT) [P] Paterson, NJ St. Anthony's Guild.
Kobti, Labib '74 (SFR) [4] San Francisco, CA St. Anne Church.
Kobti, Labib '75 (LA) Pomona, CA St. Joseph Church.
Kobularik, Robert J. '73 (HBG) New Freedom, PA St. John the Baptist Church.
Kobus, Damian M. *o.s.m.* '49 (CHI) [N] Chicago, IL Servite Friars - Eastern Province.
Kobus, Damian M. *o.s.m.* '49 (TUC) Yuma, AZ St. John Neumann Church.
Kobus, John '77 (CHI) [J] Chicago, IL St. Mary of Nazareth Hospital Center.
Kobuszewski, Thomas P. '64 (SY) [2] Liverpool, NY Immaculate Heart of Mary Church.
Kobza, John *m.i.c.* '54 (WDC) [B] Washington, DC Marian Fathers Scholasticate.
Koch, Andrew *o.s.b.* '97 (WOR) [N] Still River, MA Benedictine Monks, St. Benedict Abbey.
Koch, Msgr. Charles J. '63 (EVN) Special Assignment.
Koch, David J. '69 (GB) Neenah, WI St. Margaret Mary Church.
Koch, Donald J. '60 (VEN) [1] Venice, FL Epiphany Cathedral.
Koch, Eugene R. '59 (DM) Granger, IA Assumption of the Blessed Virgin Mary Church.
Koch, Msgr. Frederick A. '43 (R) Retired.
Koch, George J. *s.j.* '59 (SJ) [M] Los Gatos, CA Sacred Heart Jesuit Center.
Koch, Ivor '84 (FWT) Wichita Falls, TX Sacred Heart Church.
Koch, Joseph '82 (SLC) [5] Salt Lake City, UT St. Ambrose Church; Salt Lake City, UT Oxbow Correctional Facility.
Koch, Kevin A. '85 (CHY) Torrington, WY St. Rose Church.
Koch, Michael R. '53 (GB) Special Assignment; [J] Oshkosh, WI SSM Franciscan Courts.
Koch, Patrick H. *s.j.* (DAL) [26] Dallas, TX St. Rita Church.
Koch, Paul M. '61 (DM) On Duty Outside the Diocese.
Koch, Paul M. '61 (FgM) Society of St. James the Apostle.
Koch, Terence E. *s.j.* '60 (SJ) [L] Los Altos, CA Jesuit Retreat House.
Kochaba, Myron E. *o.s.b.* '55 (PBR) Portage, PA SS. Peter and Paul Church; South Fork, PA St. Michael's Church.
Kochan, Frederick '55 (WIL) Sherwood Park, DE St. John the Beloved Church.
Kochery, Peter '70 (DAL) [1] Garland, TX Good Shepherd Church; [3] Garland, TX St. Mary Malankara Church.
Kochon, Michael A. '81 (MET) Washington, NJ St. Joseph Church.
Kochuparackal, Sebastian *c.m.i.* '75 (BRK) [56] Brooklyn, NY Holy Family Church; [U] Brooklyn, NY Carmelites of Mary Immaculate, Inc.
Kocik, Franc W. '76 (CAM) On Duty Outside the Diocese.
Kocik, Thomas M. '97 (FR) Seekonk, MA Our Lady of Mt. Carmel Church.

Kociolek, Charles *c.s.c.* '79 (SCR) [M] Wilkes-Barre, PA Moreau House.
Kociolek, Charles J. *c.s.c.* '79 (SCR) [C] Wilkes-Barre, PA Kings College.
Kocour, Robert F. '43 (WCH) Retired.
Kodakal, Berchmans '78 (MEM) [25] Memphis, TN Sacred Heart Church.
Kodekkanel, Mathew Jayanth *s.j.* '86 (OAK) [N] Berkeley, CA Jesuit Community at Jesuit School of Theology at Berkeley.
Koebel, Joseph A. '54 (VIC) Nada, TX Nativity of the Blessed Virgin Mary Church.
Koegel, Victor C. '43 (CIN) Retired.
Koehl, Keith '97 (AUS) [22] Austin, TX St. Thomas More Church.
Koehler, John E. '65 (SEA) [6] Tacoma, WA St. Joseph's Church; [13] Tacoma, WA Holy Rosary Church.
Koehler, Jon C. '74 (BR) [19] Baton Rouge, LA St. Pius X Church.
Koehler, Kenneth '72 (DEN) [16] Denver, CO Most Precious Blood Church.
Koehler, Paul G. *o.s.b.* '36 (BIR) [E] Cullman, AL St. Bernard Abbey.
Koehler, Paul L. '38 (FAR) Retired; [E] Hankinson, ND St. Gerard Community Nursing Home.
Koehler, Ralph C. *c.s.b.* '40 (GRY) [B] Merrillville, IN Andrean High School; [J] Merrillville, IN Basilian Fathers Residence.
Koehler, Steven C. '82 (DET) Madison Heights, MI St. Vincent Ferrer Church.
Koehler, Theodore A. *s.m.* '41 (CIN) [D] Dayton, OH The University of Dayton; [M] Dayton, OH Marianist Provincialate.
Koehne, David '49 (GB) Retired.
Koehr, Louis A. '87 (BEL) Sesser, IL St. Mary Church.
Koelker, Harry A. '68 (DUB) [4] Cedar Rapids, IA St. Ludmila's Church; [F] Cedar Rapids, IA Holy Family Catholic Consolidated School.
Koelsch, John W. '56 (B) [6] Boise, ID Sacred Heart Church.
Koelzer, Bonaventure *s.a.* '38 (NY) [DD] Garrison, NY Franciscan Friars of the Atonement.
Koen, Stephen E. '58 (BO) [5] Newton, MA Mary Immaculate of Lourdes Church.
Koenig, Msgr. Harry C. '32 (CHI) Retired.
Koenig, Msgr. John H. '42 (NEW) Summit, NJ St. Teresa's Church; Union, NJ Holy Spirit Church; Retired.
Koenig, Paul *o.f.m.cap.* '96 (MIL) [B] Mount Calvary, WI St. Felix Friary.
Koenig, Robert B. '45 (DET) Retired.
Koenig, Msgr. William A. '32 (PH) [T] Philadelphia, PA St. Vincent's Day Care Center.
Koenig, William E. '83 (RVC) [1] Rockville Centre, NY St. Agnes Cathedral.
Koenigsfeld, James F. '68 (PBL) Crested Butte, CO Queen of All Saints Church; Gunnison, CO St. Peter Church.
Koenigsknecht, William J. '68 (LAN) [5] Lansing, MI Resurrection Church; Retired.
Koeninger, Francis F.. '79 (STL) Mattese, MO Assumption Church.
Koeplin, John P. *s.j.* '91 (FWT) [J] Lake Dallas, TX Montserrat Jesuit Retreat House.
Koepling, John P. *s.j.* '91 (SFR) [N] San Francisco, CA Jesuit Community at University of San Francisco.
Koerber, George M. '60 (TOL) Retired; [H] Oregon, OH St. Charles Mercy Hospital.
Koerner, Frederick C. '59 (NEW) [2] Irvington, NJ St. Leo's Church; Retired.
Koerner, Robert *o.m.i.* '37 (SAT) [K] San Antonio, TX Oblate Madonna Residence.
Koerner, Robert H. (GF) [G] Billings, MT Saint Vincent Hospital and Health Center.
Koers, Eugene A. '62 (FTW) Arcola, IN St. Patrick Church.
Koesel, Douglas H. '78 (CLV) [46] Cleveland, OH St. Mark Church.
Koester, Timothy J. '83 (BUF) Military Chaplains.
Koesterer, David W. *s.j.* '64 (STL) [P] St. Louis, MO White House Retreat Jesuit Community; [T] St. Louis, MO White House Retreat.
Koestner, Alfred G. *o.s.b.* '39 (KCK) Wetmore, KS St. James Church.
Koetter, Paul D. '77 (IND) [30] Indianapolis, IN St. Monica Church.
Koeune, August '84 (CHY) Evanston, WY St. Mary Magdalen Church.
Koeune, George '95 (CHI) Niles, IL St. Isaac Jogues Church.
Kofski, James W. *m.m.* '91 (FgM) Maryknoll Foreign Missions.
Koh, Joseph *o.c.d.* '92 (WDC) [B] Washington, DC Monastery of Our Lady of Mount Carmel.
Koharchik, George D. '74 (ALT) [1] Portage, PA St. Joseph's Church.
Kohler, Edward '77 (HEL) Browning, MT Church of the Little Flower.
Kohler, Girard J. '63 (PIT) [O] Bethel Park, PA Holy Ghost Fathers and Brothers Provincialate; [Q] Bethel Park, PA Holy Ghost Animation Center.
Kohler, Joseph M. '54 (STL) [W] St. Louis, MO Dismas House of St. Louis.
Kohler, Lawrence A. *m.s.* '61 (LKC) [2] Sulphur, LA Our Lady of LaSalette Church.
Kohler, Peter D. '68 (STL) Maplewood, MO Immaculate Conception Church.
Kohler, Russell E. '73 (DET) [50] Detroit, MI Most Holy Trinity Church; [Q] Detroit, MI Pope John XXIII Hospitality House; [Q] Onsted, MI St. Patrick's Retreat.
Kohler, Thomas M. '68 (PH) [1] Bensalem, PA St. Charles Borromeo Church; Absent on Sick Leave.
Kohler, William *c.ss.r.* '83 (TUC) Tucson, AZ Tucson Medical Center.
Kohler, William E. '67 (MIL) [6] West Allis, WI Mary, Queen of Heaven Church.
Kohler, William F. '55 (PIT) [4] Bridgeville, PA St. Barbara Church.
Kohlerman, Charles W. *c.s.c.* '63 (FTW) [L] Notre Dame, IN Holy Cross Mission House; [M] Notre Dame, IN Our Lady of Fatima Retreat Center.
Kohli, Charles F. '61 (RVC) Stony Brook, NY L.I. State Veterans' Home.
Kohls, Msgr. Eugene C. '57 (STA) [1] Jacksonville, FL Assumption Church.
Kohls, Henry H. *s.j.* '42 (P) [L] Portland, OR Colombiere Community.
Kohmescher, Matthew F. *s.m.* '48 (CIN) [D] Dayton, OH The University of Dayton; [M] Dayton, OH Marianist Provincialate.
Kohmetscher, James *o.m.i.* '55 (FgM) Oblates Foreign Missions.
Kohner, David W. '90 (STP) Faribault, MN Sacred Heart - St. Lawrence of Fairbault Church.
Kohrman, Glenn '92 (FTW) [14] Fort Wayne, IN St. Paul Church; [17] Fort Wayne, IN Sacred Heart Church; [C] Fort Wayne, IN Bishop Luers High School.
Kohuch, Robert (PIT) Allegheny County, PA Jefferson Hospital.
Kohuch, Robert Andrew '66 (PIT) Elrama, PA St. Isaac Jogues Church.
Kohut, Msgr. Joseph J. '62 (BGP) Darien, CT St. John Church.
Koilparampil, Augustine '64 (OAK) Livermore, CA St. Michael's Church; Livermore, CA Veterans Administration Hospital; Military Chaplains.
Kok, Bede *o.c.s.o.* '41 (L) [L] Trappist, KY Abbey of Our Lady of Gethsemani, of the Order of Cistercians of the Strict Observance.
Kokjohn, Joseph '54 (DAV) [B] Davenport, IA St. Ambrose University.
Kokocinski, Bernard A. '66 (TOL) [29] Toledo, OH St. Jude Church.
Kolaczek, John Baptista *o.c.d.* '45 (GRY) [J] Munster, IN Discalced Carmelite Fathers Monastery.
Kolakowski, Marcel *o.f.m.* (PH) [92] Philadelphia, PA Saint Martha Church.
Kolanda, George A. '44 (MIL) Retired.
Kolanda, George A. '45 (MIL) [N] Wauwatosa, WI St. Camillus Health Center, Inc.
Kolanko, John R. '40 (MIL) [58] Milwaukee, WI Our Lady of Good Hope Church; Retired.
Kolano, Stanislaw '80 (PH) [78] Philadelphia, PA St. John Cantius Church.
Kolar, Thomas F. '60 (STP) Retired.
Kolarec, William T. *s.j.* '69 (OM) [K] Omaha, NE Jesuit Community At Creighton University.
Kolasa, Stanley *ss.cc.* '70 (FR) [J] Fairhaven, MA Sacred Hearts Provincial House.
Kolasinski, Daniel '57 (P) Retired.
Kolath, George (STP) North St. Paul, MN St. Peter Church.
Kolb, James *c.s.p.* '76 (NY) [DD] Jamaica Estates, NY Paulist Fathers Generalate.
Kolb, James M. '76 (FBK) [4] Fairbanks, AK St. Raphael's Church.
Kolb, Joseph C. '53 (OKL) Mangum, OK Sacred Heart Church.
Kolb, Joseph E. *s.j.* '63 (WH) [A] Wheeling, WV Wheeling Jesuit University.
Kolb, Michael R. *s.j.* '82 (MIL) [E] Milwaukee, WI Marquette University High School; [P] Milwaukee, WI Arrupe House Jesuit Community.
Kolberg, Lawrence R. '68 (ORG) Absent on Sick Leave.
Kolbusz, Stanley F. '55 (GB) [3] Oshkosh, WI St. Josaphat Church.
Kolcun, Stephen '46 (PBR) Beaverdale, PA St. Mary's Church.
Kolczaski, Richard '55 (PEO) Peru, IL St. Mary's Church.
Kolda, Donald *s.j.* '55 (ORG) Laguna Niguel, CA St. Timothy Church; [H] Laguna Niguel, CA Jesuits.
Kole, Eugene R. *o.f.m.conv.* '75 (SFD) [B] Quincy, IL Quincy University.
Kolenkiewicz, Louis J. '93 (PH) Hatboro, PA St. John Bosco Church.
Kolenski, Robert D. '62 (LAN) Owosso, MI St. Paul Church.
Kolesar, Casimir *o.f.m.* '61 (PEO) [3] Peoria, IL Sacred Heart Church.
Kolesar, Msgr. John C. '64 (STU) Adena, OH St. Casimir's Church.
Kolf, Gerry '94 (FTW) [I] South Bend, IN Prelature of the Holy Cross and Opus Dei.
Kolibas, Kenneth R. '94 (MET) Middlesex, NJ Our Lady of Mount Virgin Church.
Kolinovsky, Sebastian *c.p.* '51 (FgM) Mission Procurators.
Kolinovsky, Sebastian *c.p.* '51 (NEW) [N] Union City, NJ Congregation of the Passion (Passionists)-St. Michael's Residence.
Kolinsky, Arthur J. *c.m.* '71 (FgM) Vincentian Foreign Missions.
Koll, Jude *o.s.b.* '40 (SCL) [I] Collegeville, MN St. John's Abbey, of the Order of St. Benedict.
Kollar, Anton *o.carm.* '51 (JOL) [J] Darien, IL Carmelite Provincial Office.
Kollar, Edmund '46 (ARL) Retired.
Kollar, Rene M. *o.s.b.* '74 (GBG) [H] Latrobe, PA Saint Vincent Archabbey.
Kollasch, Eugene C. *s.j.* '59 (FgM) Provinces.
Kollasch, Eugene C. *s.j.* '59 (MIL) [P] Milwaukee, WI Jesuit Provincial Office, Wisconsin Province.
Kollasch, Msgr. Louis H. '58 (SC) Madrid, IA St. Malachy's Church; Woodward, IA St. John of God Church; Woodward, IA Woodward State Hospital and School.
Kollasch, Merle F. '64 (SC) Pocahontas, IA Church of the Resurrection; [G] Pocahontas, IA Opus Spiritus Sancti.
Kollath, Robert (GB) Shawano, WI Sacred Heart Church.
Koller, Gerold *c.pp.s.* '49 (CIN) [B] Carthagena, OH St. Charles.
Koller, Thomas *o.c.d.* (SB) [H] Redlands, CA University of Redlands Newman Community.
Koller, Thomas '90 (SB) [G] Redlands, CA El Carmelo Retreat House.
Kolling, James L. '65 (LA) [DD] Los Angeles, CA Rosary Hour Inc., The.
Kollithanath, Philip '84 (CHL) High Point, NC Christ the King Church.
Kollman, Paul *c.s.c.* (FgM) Holy Cross Foreign Missions.
Kollman, Paul V. *c.s.c* '91 (FTW) [J] South Bend, IN Congregation of Holy Cross Indiana Province Provincial House.
Kollross, Dennis D. '81 (SFD) [5] Decatur, IL St. Thomas the Apostle Church; [M] Decatur, IL Millikin University Newman Catholic Community.
Kolmaga, Bogdan *o.s.p.* '92 (NY) [113] New York, NY St. Stanislaus Church.
Kolmaga, Jan *o.s.p.p.e.* '82 (PH) [AA] Doylestown, PA Pauline Fathers Monastery, Shrine of Our Lady of Czestochowa.
Kolo, Vincent F. '95 (PIT) Penn Hills, PA St. Bartholomew Church.
Kolodziej, Maynard *o.f.m.* '53 (FTW) [K] Mishawaka, IN Our Lady of the Angels Convent.
Kolodziej, Maynard *o.f.m.* '53 (GRY) [J] Cedar Lake, IN Our Lady of Lourdes Friary.
Kolodziej, Michael *o.f.m.conv.* '70 (SPR) [10] Chicopee, MA St. Stanislaus Basilica Church.
Kolodziej, Ryszand '96 (R) Fayetteville, NC St. Patrick Church.
Kolodziejski, Karl *o.f.m.conv.* '78 (BUF) [21] Buffalo, NY Corpus Christi Church.
Kolofo'ou, Alatini *s.m.* '89 (WDC) [M] Washington, DC Marist Provincial House.
Kolp, James R. '50 (Y) [4] Massillon, OH St. Mary's Church.
Kolson, Lawrence F. '74 (BAL) Bradshaw, MD St. Stephen Church.
Kolton, Stanislaus J. '46 (CAM) Retired.
Koltuniak, Michael P. '39 (DET) Retired.
Koltzenburg, Otto '81 (SPK) Walla Walla, WA Assumption of the Blessed Virgin Mary Church.
Kolumber, Denis *m.s.* '67 (ATL) Canton, GA Our Lady of LaSalette Church.
Kolzow, Andrew K. *o.p.* '58 (DAL) [M] Irving, TX Dominican Priory of St. Albert the Great.
Koma, Joseph W. *c.s.c.* '61 (KAL) Niles, MI St. Mark Church.
Komar, John E. '64 (NEW) Ridgefield, NJ St. Matthew's Church; Englewood, NJ Englewood Hospital.
Komar, Msgr. Michael A. '36 (NEW) [2] Linden, NJ Holy Family Church; Retired.
Komatz, David M. *o.praem.* '75 (GB) [B] De Pere, WI St. Norbert College; [I] De Pere, WI St. Joseph Priory.
Komechak, Michael E. *o.s.b.* '59 (JOL) [A] Lisle, IL Benedictine University; [J] Lisle, IL St. Procopius Abbey.
Kommer, Jason *o.f.m.* '43 (JOL) [J] Joliet, IL St. John the Baptist Friary.
Kommer, Venard *o.f.m.* '46 (JOL) Clarendon Hills, IL Notre Dame Church; [J] Joliet, IL St. John the Baptist Friary.
Kommers, Thomas M. '80 (STP) Eagan, MN St. Thomas Becket Church.

Komonchak, Joseph A. '64 (NY) On Duty Outside the Archdiocese.
Komonchak, Joseph A. '64 (WDC) [C] Washington, DC Catholic University of America, The.
Komorowski, Louis A. *o.s.f.s.* '56 (LAN) Adrian, MI St. Mary of Good Counsel Church.
Komosinski, Msgr. Martin M. '51 (TR) Burlington, NJ All Saints Church.
Konarzewski, Bogdan *c.m.* '94 (BRK) [134] Brooklyn, NY St. Stanislaus Kostka Church.
Konath, Jacob '95 (BIS) Glenburn, ND St. Philomena Church.
Koncik, Michael *c.ss.r.* '82 (VEN) Wauchula, FL St. Michael Church.
Konda, Bernard A. *j.c.d.* '67 (JUN) Ketchikan, AK Holy Name Church.
Kondeja, Stanley '62 (RVC) Southampton, NY Our Lady of Poland Church.
Konderla, David A. '95 (AUS) College Station, TX St. Mary's Church; [M] College Station, TX St. Mary's Catholic Center.
Kondik, David M. *o.s.m.* '48 (CHI) [N] Chicago, IL Servite Friars - Eastern Province.
Kondik, David M. *o.s.m.* '48 (ORG) Fullerton, CA St. Juliana Falconieri Church.
Kondrath, James A. '50 (SFD) Retired.
Kondzielski, Thaddeus T. '67 (E) Crossingsville, PA St. Philip Church.
Kondziolka, Ronald L. '76 (CHI) [84] Chicago, IL Holy Rosary Church; [J] Chicago Heights, IL St. James Hospital and Health Centers.
Konechne, Louis D. '82 (GLP) [D] Gallup, NM Carmelite Monastery.
Konen, Lyle *c.ss.r.* '61 (SEA) [32] Seattle, WA Sacred Heart of Jesus Church.
Konerman, Gregory J. '93 (CIN) [25] Cincinnati, OH St. Dominic Church.
Kong, Denis *s.d.b* '90 (OAK) [N] Berkeley, CA Salesian Community.
Konicek, John J. *s.j.* '93 (NO) [C] New Orleans, LA Loyola University.
Konieczka, Edward J. '63 (SAG) Harbor Beach, MI Our Lady of Lake Huron Church.
Konieczny, Anthony M. *o.f.m.conv.* '43 (BUF) [21] Buffalo, NY Corpus Christi Church.
Koninkx, Msgr. William '46 (HT) Retired.
Konisky, Edward '38 (ALB) Retired.
Konkel, Eugene J. *s.s.* '57 (MIL) On Duty Outside the Archdiocese.
Konkel, Eugene J. *s.s.* '57 (SFR) [U] Menlo Park, CA Vatican II Institute for Clergy Formation.
Konkel, Joseph D. *o.p.* '70 (GAL) [36] Houston, TX Holy Rosary Church.
Konkler, Paul Jerome *o.c.s.o.* '68 (SAC) [A] Vina, CA Abbey of New Clairvaux, Trappist Seminary; [G] Vina, CA Abbey of New Clairvaux, Trappist.
Konkol, Robert *o.f.m.* '94 (MIL) [P] Burlington, WI Queen of Peace Friary.
Konnully, Berchmans '59 (BIS) Hazelton, ND St. Paul Church; Linton, ND St. Anthony Church.
Konobrocki, Marian '91 (VEN) [5] Fort Myers, FL St. Francis Xavier Church.
Konold, Lon *o.m.i.* '77 (BEL) [J] Belleville, IL Oblate Preaching Team.
Konold, Lon *o.m.i.* '77 (FgM) Oblates Foreign Missions.
Konopa, Robert *o.f.m.* '91 (SAG) [18] Saginaw, MI St. Thomas Aquinas Church.
Konopacky, Joseph R. '82 (LC) Rosholt, WI St. Adalbert Church.
Konopacky, Joseph R. '85 (LC) Polonia, WI Sacred Heart Church.
Konopka, Edward F. '45 (DET) [2] Troy, MI St. Alan Church; Retired.
Konopka, Edward M. '60 (NOR) Higganum, CT St. Peter Church.
Konopka, Thomas (ALB) Cambridge, NY St. Patrick Church.
Konopka, Thomas '90 (ALB) Greenwich, NY St. Joseph Church.
Konoske, Msgr. Paul M. '31 (LA) San Marino, CA Saints Felicitas and Perpetua Church; Retired.
Konowalek, Zenon '89 (CC) Three Rivers, TX Sacred Heart Church.
Konrad, Erwin R. '89 (JC) [2] Jefferson City, MO St. Peter Church; [C] Jefferson City, MO St. Marys Health Center.
Konrad, Msgr. Joseph G. '43 (BRK) [199] Queens, NY St. Matthias Church; Retired.
Kons, Alex *o.m.i.* '55 (FgM) Oblates Foreign Missions.
Konz, Gregory N. *s.j.* '90 (STL) [P] St. Louis, MO Jesuit Community Corporation at St. Louis University - Jesuit Hall.
Konz, Gregory N.P. *s.j.* '90 (CLV) [C] Cleveland, OH John Carroll Jesuit Community.
Koo, Matthew '88 (SJ) [14] San Jose, CA St. Leo the Great Church; [1] Santa Clara, CA Chinese Catholic Community Church.
Koob, Edward H. '45 (PH) Retired.
Kookoothe, Neil P. '95 (CLV) [5] Parma, OH St. Francis de Sales Church.
Koons, James W. '83 (FTW) [13] Fort Wayne, IN St. Patrick Church.
Koons, Thomas P. '97 (ALN) Emmaus, PA St. Ann Church.
Koonz, John A. '63 (SPR) Dalton, MA St. Agnes Church.
Koop, Cecil *o.f.m.* (SFD) [K] Sherman, IL Our Lady of Angels Friary.
Koopman, Dennis *o.f.m.* '70 (CHI) [N] Countryside, IL St. Gratian Friary, Franciscan Friars.
Koopmann, Robert *o.s.b.* '81 (SCL) [I] Collegeville, MN St. John's Abbey, of the Order of St. Benedict.
Koos, Gerald J. '66 (E) [13] Erie, PA St. Ann Church; Erie, PA Hamot Medical Center.
Kopacek, Jerry F. '88 (DUB) Marshalltown, IA St. Mary's Church.
Kopacz, Joseph R. '77 (SCR) [20] Scranton, PA Nativity of Our Lord Church.
Kopacz, Kazimierz '95 (FAR) Forman, ND St. Mary's Church.
Kopacz, Mark '92 (WIL) Newark, DE Christiana Care Health System.
Kopacz, Mark W. '92 (WIL) Special or Other Diocesan Assignment.
Kopacz, Msgr. Matthew S. '63 (BUF) [18] Buffalo, NY St. Casimir Church.
Kopacz, Stephen A. '72 (NEW) Livingston, NJ St. Philomena Church.
Kopaczynski, Germain *o.f.m. conv.* '74 (BO) [55] Boston, MA Our Lady of Czestochowa Church; [FF] Boston, MA Pope John Center.
Kopchik, Martin J. *m.s.f.s.* '86 (ATL) Norcross, GA Saint Patrick's Church.
Kopczewski, Linus E. *o.f.m.* '65 (PH) [AA] Philadelphia, PA St. Pius X Friary.
Kopczewski, Linus E. *o.f.m.* '65 (TR) Trenton, NJ St. Francis Medical Center; [I] Trenton, NJ St. Francis Medical Center.
Kopczynski, Michael R. '96 (BUF) [4] North Tonawanda, NY Our Lady of Czestochowa Church.
Kopec, Chester *o.p.* '63 (SB) Chino, CA California Institute for Men.
Kopec, Christopher A. '93 (WIL) Milford, DE St. John the Apostle Church.
Kopec, Edward S. '92 (PEO) Colfax, IL St. Joseph's Church.
Kopec, Jerome E. '79 (BUF) [4] Niagara Falls, NY St. John de La Salle Church.
Kopec, Rajmund '92 (NEW) Military Chaplains.
Kopecky, Joseph A. '45 (PIT) Retired.
Kopel, Jerry '77 (SFS) Tyndall, SD St. Leo Church.
Koper, Msgr. Francis B. '71 (DET) [A] Orchard Lake, MI SS. Cyril and Methodius Seminary; [C] Orchard Lake, MI Saint Mary's College.
Koper, Msgr. Francis B. '71 (WIL) On Duty Outside the Diocese.
Koper, Ryszard '78 (BRK) [177] Queens, NY Holy Cross Church.
Kopfensteiner, Thomas R. '81 (STL) On Duty Outside the Archdiocese.
Kopff, Herbert C. '38 (BEL) Retired.
Kopinski, Richard '64 (RVC) Glen Head, NY St. Hyacinth Church.
Koplik, Msgr. William J. '62 (NEW) Northvale, NJ St. Anthony's Church.
Koplinka, Quentin S. *o.s.b.* '79 (MIL) [P] Benet Lake, WI St. Benedict's Abbey.
Koplinka, Quentin S. *o.s.b.* '79 (PRM) Cleveland, OH Holy Ghost Church; Cleveland, OH St. Nicholas Church.
Kopp, Anthony Mary J. *o.praem.* '93 (ORG) [H] Silverado, CA Norbertine Fathers of Orange Inc.
Kopp, Richard M. '69 (SY) Baldwinsville, NY St. Mary Church; Special Assignment.
Kopp, Thomas A. '72 (BO) [8] Brockton, MA Sacred Heart Church.
Koppert, Elias *o.f.m.* '41 (IND) [12] Indianapolis, IN Sacred Heart of Jesus Church.
Koppes, Albert *o.carm.* '59 (JOL) [J] Darien, IL Carmelite Provincial Office.
Koprowski, Mitchell J. '41 (GI) Retired.
Kopystynski, Rafal *c.m.* '88 (MAN) [2] Concord, NH St. Peter Church.
Korabik, Joseph *c.r.* '38 (CHI) [D] Chicago, IL Weber High School.
Korah, James P. *s.i.o.l.* '92 (TYL) New Boston, TX St. Mary of the Cenacle Church.
Korba, Msgr. Frank '66 (PRM) Munster, IN Saint Nicholas Church.
Korban, Janusz '97 (RC) [1] Rapid City, SD Cathedral of Our Lady of Perpetual Help.
Korbelak, John J. '74 (NEW) North Bergen, NJ Our Lady of Fatima Church.
Korbic, Benno *o.f.m.* '40 (CHI) [N] Lemont, IL The Slovene Franciscan Fathers, Order of Friars Minor, Commissariat of the Holy Cross.
Korcsmar, John S. *c.s.c.* '74 (AUS) [8] Austin, TX Nuestra Senora De Dolores Church; [H] Austin, TX Congregation of Holy Cross - Southern Province.
Korda, Msgr. Edward L. '49 (CAM) Magnolia, NJ St. Gregory's Church.
Korda, J. James '79 (Y) [3] Youngstown, OH Immaculate Conception Church.
Kordas, Edward J. '68 (CLV) South Amherst, OH Nativity of Blessed Virgin Mary Church; [Y] Berea, OH Office of Newman Campus Ministry.
Kordek, Frank *o.f.m.* '72 (GAY) Harbor Springs, MI Holy Childhood of Jesus Church.
Kordsmeier, John W. '49 (LR) Harrison, AR Mary, Mother of God Church.
Korecki, Maximilian *o.f.m. conv.* '62 (IND) [I] Mount Saint Francis, IN Mount Saint Francis Friary and Retreat Center.
Koren, Henry J. *c.s.sp.* '37 (PIT) [O] Bethel Park, PA Holy Ghost Fathers and Brothers Provincialate; [Q] Bethel Park, PA Holy Ghost Animation Center.
Korenek, Gregory E. '93 (VIC) [2] Victoria, TX Holy Family of Joseph, Mary & Jesus Church.
Koressel, James '69 (EVN) Boonville, IN St. Clement Church.
Korf, Joseph '74 (SCL) Fergus Falls, MN Our Lady of Victory Church.
Korgie, Humbert *o.f.m.* '43 (SFD) [K] Sherman, IL Our Lady of Angels Friary.
Korinchock, Joseph '85 (PHU) Absent on Leave.
Kornacki, Matthew J. '73 (PH) [94] Philadelphia, PA St. Martin of Tours Church.
Kornacki, Thomas J. *o.f.m.* '88 (FgM) Franciscan Foreign Missions.
Kornath, Edwin M. '84 (MIL) Campbellsport, WI St. Matthew Church.
Kornbrust, Herman *o.s.b.* '62 (OM) [K] Schuyler, NE Benedictine Mission House.
Kornely, Benno G. *s.j.* '59 (DET) [P] Bloomfield Hills, MI Manresa Jesuit Retreat House.
Kornely, Benno G. *s.j.* '59 (MIL) [P] Milwaukee, WI Jesuit Provincial Office, Wisconsin Province.
Kornmeyer, Thomas E. '90 (OG) Malone, NY Notre Dame Church.
Kornoski, Joseph C. '88 (MET) South Plainfield, NJ Sacred Heart Church.
Korogi, Dale J. '83 (STP) [1] Minneapolis, MN The Basilica of St. Mary Co-Cathedral.
Koros, John J. '45 (OM) Retired.
Koros, John J. '50 (VEN) Lake Placid, FL St. James Church.
Korte, Ed (BIS) Crosby, ND St. Patrick Church.
Korte, Harry *c.ss.r.* '46 (STL) [P] Liguori, MO Liguori Mission House/Redemptorists.
Korte, Owen W. '81 (OM) Elgin, NE St. Boniface Church.
Korte, William L. '83 (JC) Mary's Home, MO Our Lady of the Snows Church.
Kortendick, Steven J. '85 (MAD) [1] Madison, WI St. Raphael Cathedral; [12] Madison, WI St. Paul University Parish.
Korth, David M. '92 (OM) Fremont, NE St. Patrick Church.
Korycki, Walter R. '49 (RVC) Retired.
Korytkowski, George J. *o.f.m.cap.* '70 (MET) [4] New Brunswick, NJ St. Joseph Church.
Korytkowski, George J. *o.f.m.cap.* '70 (PAT) [M] Oak Ridge-Milton, NJ St. Stanislaus B. M. Friary.
Korzinek, Richard *o.s.cam.* '53 (MAD) Durward's Glen, WI St. Camillus Church; [A] Durward's Glen, WI St. Camillus Monastery and Retreat Center.
Kos, Donald *o.f.m.conv.* '61 (BAL) [M] Ellicott City, MD Order of Friars Minor Conventual.
Kos, Joseph S. '66 (IND) Indianapolis, IN Wishard Memorial Hospital; Indianapolis, IN Larue D. Carter Hospital.
Kos, Stanislaw '96 (RCK) [4] Rockford, IL St. Edward Church.
Kosak, Msgr. Michael F. '70 (STV) [1] Barrenspot, VI Church St. Ann Church; [B] St. Thomas, VI Miscellaneous Organizations.
Kosaka, Paul *o.f.m.cap.* '84 (FgM) Capuchin Foreign Missions.
Kosaka, Paulo *o.f.m.cap.* '83 (AGN) [E] Agana Heights, GU St. Fidelis Friary.
Kosanke, Charles (DET) [T] Detroit, MI American Friends of the Vatican Library.
Kosanke, Charles '85 (DET) [A] Detroit, MI Sacred Heart Major Seminary, Inc.
Kosanke, Charles G. (DET) [45] Detroit, MI Madonna Church.
Kosatka, Leonard *c.p.* '59 (FgM) Mission Procurators.
Kosch, Leo D. '93 (LIN) Bellwood, NE Presentation Church.
Kosco, Arnold J. '60 (DET) West Bloomfield, MI Prince of Peace Church.
Kose, Robert *o.f.m.cap.* '92 (MIL) [25] Milwaukee, WI St. Francis of Assisi Church.
Kosem, Frank P. '70 (CLV) [3] Elyria, OH St. Jude Church.
Koser, Albert C. '59 (PIT) Boyers, PA St. Alphonsus Church.
Koser, Rudolph J., Jr. '74 (GBG) Military Chaplains.
Koshko, Dennis '75 (HON) Kailua, HI St. Anthony Church.
Kosicki, Bohdan (DET) Retired.
Kosicki, Bohdan W. '50 (DET) [T] St. Clair Shores, MI Catholic Kolping Society of America, Detroit Branch, Inc.

Kosicki, George *c.s.b.* '54 (ROC) [I] Rochester, NY Basilian Residence.
Kosicki, George *c.s.b.* '54 (SPR) [I] Stockbridge, MA Congregation of Marians; [I] Stockbridge, MA Congregation of Marians.
Kosik, Msgr. Edward J. '65 (E) Warren, PA Holy Redeemer Church.
Kosinski, Stephen D. '81 (GRY) [7] Gary, IN St. Ann Church.
Kosisko, Richard J. '85 (GBG) Slickville, PA St. Sylvester Church.
Kosler, Timothy '71 (VIC) Ammannsville, TX St. John The Baptist Church; Schulenburg, TX St. Rose of Lima Church.
Kosmicki, Raymond M. '68 (GI) Wood River, NE St. Mary's Church.
Kosmoski, David B. *o.m.v.* '81 (MET) Avenel, NJ St. Andrew Church.
Kosmowski, Gary J. '90 (MAN) Laconia, NH St. Joseph Church.
Kosnick, Eugene A. '60 (NY) Gardiner, NY St. Charles Borromeo Church.
Kosnik, Anthony '55 (DET) Special Assignment.
Kosowicz, Wojciech '65 (CC) Vattman, TX Our Lady of Consolation Church.
Kossak, Michael J. *s.j.* '87 (BO) [W] Boston, MA The Society of Jesus of New England-Provincial Offices.
Kossak, Michael J. *s.j.* '87 (MIA) [5] Miami, FL Gesu Church.
Kosse, Gerald C. '76 (WIN) Adrian, MN St. Adrian Church; Lismore, MN St. Anthony's Church.
Kosse, Theodore C. '71 (CIN) New Richmond, OH St. Peter Church.
Kossel, Clifford *s.j.* '48 (SPK) [C] Spokane, WA Gonzaga University.
Kost, Harold J. '45 (SCL) Belle Prairie, MN Holy Family Church.
Kostek, John '73 (ALB) [13] Schenectady, NY Our Lady of the Assumption Church.
Kostek, John Steven '73 (ALB) Waterford, NY St. Anne Church.
Kostelnick, Albert T. '54 (PH) Feasterville, PA Assumption B.V.M. Church.
Kostelz, Richard F. '52 (JOL) Cabery, IL St. Joseph Church.
Koster, Dale F. '54 (SC) Retired.
Koster, John *s.v.d.* '44 (CHI) [B] Techny, IL Divine Word Residence.
Koster, Kenneth '76 (SFS) Tea, SD St. Nicholas Church.
Koster, Theodore *o.c.s.o.* '59 (SPC) [E] Ava, MO Assumption Abbey (Trappist).
Kosterman, Richard A. '93 (GAY) Copemish, MI St. Raphael Church.
Kostic, Andrew (PAT) Permanent Deacons.
Kostick, Msgr. Adam J. '54 (WDC) [3] Rockville, MD St. Mary Church.
Kostiuk, Nick '80 (PHU) Nanticoke, PA Transfiguration of Our Lord Church; Plymouth, PA SS. Peter and Paul Church.
Kostka, Leonard J. *c.pp.s.* '40 (LFT) Rensselaer, IN St. Augustine Church; [A] Rensselaer, IN Saint Joseph's College.
Kostrzomb, Stanley '77 (NEW) [6] Jersey City, NJ St. Anthony of Padua Church.
Kosty, Robert J. '74 (WDC) Medley's Neck, MD Our Lady's Church.
Kostyk, Marian '90 (STF) Amsterdam, NY St. Nicholas Church; Little Falls, NY St. Nicholas Church.
Koszarek, Msgr. Paul P. '54 (GB) Antigo, WI St. Hyacinth Church.
Koszarek, Robert J. '74 (SUP) Eagle River, WI St. Peter the Fisherman Church.
Koszarek, Thaddeus J. '39 (GB) Retired; [H] Green Bay, WI The McCormick Memorial Home for the Aged.
Koszyk, Seweryn J. *s.a.c* '59 (BUF) [2] Niagara Falls, NY St. George Church; [O] North Tonawanda, NY Society of the Catholic Apostolate.
Kot, Christian *s.d.b.* '94 (FgM) Salesians of Don Bosco Foreign Missions.
Kot, Luke C. *o.c.s.o.* '48 (ATL) [I] Conyers, GA The Monastery of the Holy Spirit.
Kotara, James '76 (SAT) [5] San Antonio, TX Holy Family Church.
Kotecki, Ronald E. '72 (MIL) [40] Milwaukee, WI St. Hyacinth Church.
Koterski, Joseph W. *s.j.* '92 (NY) [DD] New York, NY Jesuit Community at Fordham University.
Koth, Arthur R. '57 (MAD) McFarland, WI Christ the King Church.
Kotheimer, Alex L. '42 (L) Retired.
Kothuis, Hans '81 (SD) Leave of Absence.
Kotkowski, Matthew *o.f.m.conv.* '45 (BAL) [90] Baltimore, MD St. Stanislaus Kostka Church.
Kotlanger, Michael J. *s.j.* '78 (SFR) [E] San Francisco, CA St. Ignatius College Preparatory (Coed); [N] San Francisco, CA Jesuit Community at St. Ignatius College Preparatory.
Kotlarczyk, Mark E. '88 (SB) Victorville, CA Holy Innocents Church.
Kotlarz, Robert '69 (DET) [44] Detroit, MI St. Luke Church.
Kotlinski, Bede *o.s.b.* (CLV) [E] Cleveland, OH Benedictine High School.
Kotlinski, Bede *o.s.b.* '84 (CLV) [P] Cleveland, OH Benedictine Order of Cleveland.
Kotnis, Gregory M. '56 (PHX) Retired.
Kottar, Michael T. '94 (MET) Kendall Park, NJ St. Augustine of Canterbury Church.
Kottaram, Mathew '63 (RVC) Elmont, NY St. Boniface Church.
Kottas, Charles '70 (DM) [4] Council Bluffs, IA St. Peter Church.
Kottayil, Joseph '79 (MIA) [23] Miami, FL St. John Neumann Church.
Kottenstette, William P. '73 (JC) Kirksville, MO Mary Immaculate Church; Memphis, MO St. John Church; [F] Kirksville, MO Catholic Newman Center, Truman State University.
Kottiry, Alphonsus '59 (DUL) On Duty Outside the Diocese.
Kottoor, Thomas '72 (NY) [133] Bronx, NY St. Benedict Church.
Kotula, Gerard *o.f.m.* '39 (GB) [I] Pulaski, WI Assumption of B.V.M. Friary.
Kotyuk, Stephen '47 (E) Retired.
Kotz, Anthony A. '50 (LIN) Retired.
Kotzbauer, Leonard '63 (SY) [16] Syracuse, NY St. James Church.
Kouba, Charles J. '51 (CHI) [191] Chicago, IL St. Simon the Apostle Church; Retired.
Kouba, John *s.d.s.* '52 (SAC) West Sacramento, CA Holy Cross Church.
Koury, James '92 (NTN) On Duty Outside the Eparchy.
Koury, Msgr. Joseph A. '50 (JKS) Retired.
Koury, Joseph J. '77 (PRT) Orono, ME St. Mary's Church; Orono, ME Our Lady of Wisdom Personal Campus Parish; [M] Orono, ME University of Maine.
Kovach, Blaise '55 (PBR) Braddock, PA SS. Peter and Paul Church.
Kovach, John '65 (PRM) Burton, OH Church of Weeping Madonna; [B] Burton, OH Shrine of the Weeping Madonna of Mariapoch.
Kovach, John '65 (VNN) On Special Assignment.
Kovach, Raymond J. '69 (NY) Absent on Leave.
Kovach, William J. '55 (ALT) Revloc, PA Most Holy Redeemer Church.
Kovacs, Msgr. John F. '41 (DM) Retired.
Kovacs, Louis D. '44 (PH) East Goshen, PA SS. Peter and Paul Church; Retired.
Kovacs, Matthew *o.cist.* '57 (DAL) [M] Irving, TX Cistercian Abbey of Our Lady of Dallas.
Kovacsik, Clement *s.t.* '44 (BLX) [3] Gulfport, MS St. John the Evangelist Church.
Kovalcin, John A. '81 (STL) Military Chaplains.
Kovalik, George J. '47 (STP) [2] Minneapolis, MN All Saints Church.
Kovanis, Joel M. '94 (SP) [1] St. Petersburg, FL Cathedral of St. Jude the Apostle.
Kovar, Vaclav '37 (OM) Retired.
Kovarik, James *o.s.cam.* '66 (MIL) Wood, WI Veterans Administration Medical Center.
Kovarik, James *o.s.cam.* '90 (MIL) [P] Wauwatosa, WI St. Camillus Provincialate; [P] Wauwatosa, WI St. Camillus Community House; [Y] Wauwatosa, WI St. Camillus Institute, Inc.
Kovarik, Peter '91 (RC) Piedmont-Black Hawk, SD Our Lady of the Black Hills Church.
Kovascik, Clement *s.t.* '44 (BLX) Gulfport, MS U.S. Naval Home.
Kovattiyil, Thomas *s.v.d.* '82 (CHI) [N] Chicago, IL Divine Word Theologate.
Kowal, John P. '57 (DOD) Johnson, KS St. Bernadette Church; Ulysses, KS Mary Queen of Peace Church.
Kowalczyk, Joseph A. *m.m.* '61 (FgM) Maryknoll Foreign Missions.
Kowalczyk, Sigismund '56 (DET) Anchorville, MI Immaculate Conception Church.
Kowalczyk, Thomas M. '67 (SAG) Linwood, MI St. Anne Church.
Kowaleski, Edward '53 (Y) Rock Creek, OH Sacred Heart Church.
Kowalewski, Francis P. '59 (BUF) Fillmore, NY St. Patrick Church.
Kowalewski, John A. '77 (WIL) [B] Wilmington, DE Salesianum School.
Kowalewski, Vincent J. *o.s.f.s.* '64 (WIL) [I] Childs, MD Oblates of St. Francis De Sales.
Kowalik, Jacek '79 (VEN) Military Chaplains.
Kowalkowski, Bruno H. *o.p.* '64 (CHI) Chicago, IL Hines V.A. Hospital; [N] Chicago, IL Dominicans (Provincial Office).
Kowalozyk, Adolph M. '88 (BUF) [2] Kenmore, NY Blessed Sacrament Church.
Kowalske, Kevin J. '95 (MIL) [9] West Allis, WI St. Rita Church.
Kowalski, Alfred J. '51 (NEW) [5] Elizabeth, NJ Immaculate Conception Church.
Kowalski, Edmund *c.m.* '44 (SY) [S] Utica, NY St. Vincent's Mission House.
Kowalski, Eric '93 (NEW) North Bergen, NJ Our Lady of Fatima Church.
Kowalski, Eugene S. '42 (NEW) [4] Garfield, NJ St. Stanislaus Kostka Church; Retired.
Kowalski, Francis *s.v.d.* '42 (CHI) [B] Techny, IL Divine Word Residence.
Kowalski, George '56 (DET) [2] Wyandotte, MI St. Helena Church; Detroit, MI Wyandotte General Hospital.
Kowalski, Isidore *o.f.m.conv.* '43 (FR) [7] New Bedford, MA Our Lady of Perpetual Help Church.
Kowalski, James C. '68 (GR) Ada, MI St. Robert Church.
Kowalski, Kasimierz A. '91 (NY) [2] New York, NY St. Agnes Church.
Kowalski, Lawrence T. '69 (OKL) Enid, OK St. Gregory the Great Church.
Kowalski, Leo S. '39 (MIL) Retired.
Kowalski, Matthew F. *o.s.b.* '87 (RCK) [H] Aurora, IL Marmion Abbey-St. Augustine's Abbey.
Kowalski, Ralph E. '42 (DET) Retired.
Kowalski, Ronald C. '81 (MIL) Twin Lakes, WI St. John Church.
Kowalski, Wladyslaw J. '51 (LC) Peplin, WI St. John the Baptist Church.
Kowalski, Wladyslaw J. '51 (SUP) Retired.
Kowalsky, Myron *o.f.m.cap* '58 (MIL) [P] Milwaukee, WI St. Conrad House.
Kowatch, Thomas P. '85 (CLV) [4] Lakewood, OH St. James Church; Cleveland, OH Lakewood Hospital.
Kownacki, Francis J. *s.j.* '60 (SCR) [C] Scranton, PA University of Scranton.
Kownacki, Raymond F. '60 (BEL) Leave of Absence.
Kownacki, Robert '63 (CHI) [J] Chicago, IL Resurrection Medical Center.
Kownacki, Robert '63 (SAT) On Duty Outside the Archdiocese.
Kowrach, Edward '38 (SPK) Retired.
Koys, Thomas R. '85 (CHI) Other Assignments.
Koza, John J., III '77 (PBR) Warren, OH SS. Peter and Paul's Church.
Kozacheson, Roman M. *o.f.m.cap.* '61 (PH) [79] Philadelphia, PA St. John the Evangelist Church.
Kozak, David J. '83 (ALN) Frackville, PA Annunciation B.V.M. Church; [C] Ashland, PA Cardinal Brennan Jr./Sr. High School.
Kozak, Eligius *o.f.m.conv.* '42 (BUF) [O] Athol Springs, NY Father Justin Rosary Hour Radio Apostolate.
Kozak, Remigius A. '54 (BLX) Retired.
Kozak, Richard J. '67 (CHI) Melrose Park, IL Sacred Heart Church.
Kozanecki, Charles *o.f.m.conv.* '53 (MRY) Pismo Beach, CA St. Paul the Apostle Church.
Kozar, John E. '71 (PIT) Aleppo Township, PA St. Mary Church.
Kozar, Joseph F. *s.m.* '77 (CIN) [D] Dayton, OH The University of Dayton; [M] Dayton, OH Marianist Provincialate.
Kozel, Msgr. Robert F. '61 (ALN) [1] Bethlehem, PA St. Anne Church.
Kozen, Bert S. '82 (SCR) Canton, PA St. Michael Church.
Koziczuk, Andrew '79 (SAC) [16] Sacramento, CA St. Joseph's Church.
Koziel, Piotr '97 (CC) [5] Kingsville, TX St. Thomas Aquinas, University Catholic Center Church.
Kozien, Casimir J. '50 (CHI) [23] Chicago, IL St. Bartholomew Church; Retired.
Kozikowski, Thad '75 (GF) Glasgow, MT St. Raphael's Church.
Kozina, Mark *o.f.m.* (CHI) [101] Chicago, IL St. Jerome Church; [N] Chicago, IL Croatian Franciscan Custody of the Holy Family.
Kozina, Vladimir '45 (OAK) Retired.
Koziol, John A. *o.f.m.conv.* '88 (ATL) Jonesboro, GA St. Philip Benizi Church.
Koziol, Stanley N. '58 (BGP) [3] Stratford, CT St. Mark's Church.
Kozlak, Stanley '74 (STP) Annandale, MN St. Ignatius Church.
Kozlowski, Daniel E. '72 (LC) Tomah, WI St. Mary (Immaculate Conception) Church; Warrens, WI St. Andrew Church.
Kozlowski, Edward A. '38 (NY) Bronx, NY Veterans Administration Hospital.
Kozlowski, Joseph F. '73 (BUF) Holley, NY St. Mary Church; Kendall, NY St. Mark Church.
Kozlowski, Joseph P. '49 (RVC) Glen Head, NY St. Hyacinth Church; Retired.
Kozlowski, Louis '38 (E) Retired.
Kozlowski, Theodore '58 (GR) [18] Grand Rapids, MI Our Lady of Sorrows Church.
Kozlowski, Wesley '85 (STL) [62] St. Louis, MO St. Stanislaus Kostka Church.
Kozma, Raymond M. '70 (BRK) Absent on Leave.
Kozminski, Msgr. Max M. '60 (BUF) [10] Cheektowaga, NY Queen of Martyrs Church.
Kozoil, Micah E. '76 (GBG) Clymer, PA Church of the Resurrection.
Kozon, John A. '32 (NOR) Retired.
Kozub, Tomasz *s.ch.* '92 (BAL) [38] Baltimore, MD Holy Rosary Church.

Kozuch, John L. *s.d.s.* '58 (NEW) [N] Verona, NJ The Salvatorian Fathers.
Kozyra, Oscar *o.de.m.* '73 (SP) Plant City, FL St. Clement Church; [O] St. Petersburg, FL St. Peter Nolasco Residence.
Krach, Joseph W. '57 (BAL) Retired.
Kraeger, David *t.o.r.* '68 (FWT) Scotland, TX St. Boniface Church; Windthorst, TX St. Mary Church.
Kraemer, Bartholomew *o.s.b.* '64 (DET) [K] Detroit, MI St. Sylvester Monastery.
Kraemer, Edwin J. '55 (SCL) [7] St. Cloud, MN St. Michael Church.
Kraemer, John A. '57 (RCK) Sandwich, IL St. Paul Church.
Kraeszig, Charles J. '52 (IND) Retired.
Krafchak, John S. '56 (SCR) [5] Nanticoke, PA St. Mary of Czestochowa Church.
Krafcik, Andrew W.P. '59 (ARL) Dale City, VA Holy Family Church; Retired.
Krafinski, Thomas S. *c.m.* '68 (BRK) [66] Brooklyn, NY St. John the Baptist Church; [U] Brooklyn, NY St. John the Baptist Rectory.
Krafl, Daniel A. '58 (DUB) [F] Cascade, IA Aquin Elementary School.
Kraft, Niles E. *o.f.m.* '55 (GLP) Navajo, NM St. Berard Church.
Kraft, Philip '62 (SFD) Special or Other Diocesan Assignment.
Kraft, Richard *s.v.d.* '55 (FgM) Society of the Divine Word Foreign Missions.
Kraft, Thomas *o.p.* (OAK) [N] Oakland, CA Western Dominican Province.
Kraft, Thomas K. *o.p.* '86 (FgM) Dominican - Order of Preachers Foreign Missions.
Kraft, William '86 (STO) Sonora, CA St. Patrick Church.
Kraft, Msgr. William A. '51 (SD) Retired.
Kraft, William L. '86 (STO) San Andreas, CA St. Andrew Church.
Krah, James B. '71 (PIT) Darlington, PA St. Rose of Lima Church.
Krah, Joseph '63 (SB) Ontario, CA St. George Church.
Krahel, David H. '86 (BGP) [13] Stamford, CT Our Lady Star of the Sea Church.
Krahenbuhl, Gary L. '84 (MAD) [1] Beloit, WI Our Lady of the Assumption Church.
Krahman, Philip G. '72 (STL) Richmond Heights, MO Little Flower, St. Teresa of the Infant Jesus Church; St. Louis, MO St. John's Mercy Medical Ctr.; [K] Creve Coeur, MO St. John's Mercy Medical Center.
Kraig, Dale *s.o.l.t.* (FAR) Belcourt, ND St. Ann Church; Turtle Mountain Reservation, ND (Chippewa Indians) Church.
Kraig, Robert J. '72 (CLV) Strongsville, OH St. John Neumann Church.
Krajci, Anthony *s.v.d.* '45 (CHI) [B] Techny, IL Divine Word Residence.
Krajcovic, Bernard '56 (STU) Yorkville, OH St. Lucy's Church.
Krajewski, Henry T. *o.f.m.cap.* '58 (PAT) [M] Oak Ridge-Milton, NJ St. Stanislaus B. M. Friary.
Krajewski, Henry T. *o.f.m.cap.* '58 (TR) [4] Trenton, NJ Holy Cross Church.
Krajewski, Joseph A. '73 (MET) South Amboy, NJ Sacred Heart Church.
Krajewski, Paul A. (PAT) Retired.
Krajewski, Msgr. Walter M. '54 (BUF) Retired.
Krajicek, Robert P. (OM) Retired.
Krajnik, Paul '50 (CLV) [2] Lorain, OH SS. Cyril and Methodius Church.
Kraker, James J. '65 (SUP) Erin, WI St. Patrick Church; Glenwood City, WI St. John the Baptist Church; Hammond, WI Immaculate Conception Church; Wilson, WI St. Bridget Church.
Kraker, John J. '59 (CLV) [2] Euclid, OH St. Felicitas Church.
Kraker, Joseph H. '64 (CLV) [18] Akron, OH St. Vincent Church.
Kraljic, John R. '69 (NY) [E] New York, NY Cardinal Spellman High School.
Krall, Jack '63 (P) [22] Portland, OR Church of St. Joseph the Worker.
Krall, Kenneth R. *s.j.* '71 (SPK) [C] Spokane, WA Gonzaga University.
Kralovich, Louis W. '60 (TR) [3] Toms River, NJ St. Luke Church; [S] Princeton, NJ Campus Ministry for the Diocese of Trenton.
Kram, Charles '75 (VIC) Yoakum, TX St. Joseph Church.
Kram, Thomas '49 (PIT) [P] Pittsburgh, PA Sisters of St. Francis of the Providence of God; [S] Pittsburgh, PA Priests' Benefit Plan of the Diocese of Pittsburgh.
Kramarz, Anthony M. '50 (MET) Retired.
Kramberg, Donald F. '74 (OG) Au Sable Forks, NY Holy Name Church; Black Brook, NY St. Matthew Church.
Kramer, Anthony '95 (RC) [B] Bethlehem, SD Holy Nativity Monastery.
Kramer, Anthony *o.mar.* '95 (SAM) [C] Petersham, MA Most Holy Trinity Monastery.
Kramer, Bernard *c.ss.r.* '36 (KC) [32] Kansas City, MO Our Lady of Perpetual Help Church; [J] Kansas City, MO Redemptorists of Kansas City.
Kramer, Carl (SAL) Retired.
Kramer, Daniel J. *c.m.* '47 (PH) [AA] Philadelphia, PA Congregation of the Mission.
Kramer, George C. '53 (BO) On Duty Outside the Archdiocese.
Kramer, George J. '62 (JC) Special Assignments.
Kramer, Herbert *s.m.* '34 (SAT) [K] San Antonio, TX Marianist Residence: Skilled Nursing.
Kramer, James F. '68 (CLV) Westlake, OH St. Bernadette Church.
Kramer, James G. '48 (MAD) Westport, WI St. Mary of the Lake Church.
Kramer, Lawrence A. '60 (FTW) Bluffton, IN St. Joseph Church.
Kramer, Noel R. *o.f.m.conv.* '58 (LSC) Carlsbad, NM St. Edward Church.
Kramer, Peter L. '79 (BIS) [5] Dickinson, ND St. Wenceslaus Church.
Kramer, Richard R. '66 (RCK) Harvard, IL St. Joseph Church.
Kramer, Robert L. *c.s.c.* '64 (PHX) [F] Phoenix, AZ Holy Cross Congregation of Casa Santa Cruz.
Kramer, Scott T. *c.pp.s.* '90 (CIN) [U] Dayton, OH Community Support Charitable Trust.
Kramer, Scott T. *c.pp.s.* '90 (COL) [23] Columbus, OH St. James the Less Church.
Kramer, Thomas '78 (DET) Absent on Leave.
Kramer, Thomas E. '58 (BIS) [1] Bismarck, ND Cathedral of the Holy Spirit.
Kramer, Urban J. *s.j.* '49 (STL) [P] St. Louis, MO The Jesuits of the Missouri Province.
Kramer, Urban J. *s.j.* '49 (TLS) [E] Tulsa, OK Saint Francis Hospital, Inc.
Kramer, William J. *c.pp.s.* '44 (LFT) [A] Rensselaer, IN Saint Joseph's College.
Kramer, William J. '73 (CIN) Beavercreek, OH St. Luke Church.
Kramis, Joseph '57 (SEA) Retired.
Kramlich, Lloyd P. *s.d.s.* '58 (PHX) [4] Mesa, AZ Queen of Peace Church.
Kramper, James P. *s.j.* '44 (OM) [K] Omaha, NE Jesuit Community At Creighton University.
Kramper, James V. '73 (OM) Emerson, NE Sacred Heart Church; Pender, NE St. John Church.
Kranch, Peter V. '51 (ALB) West Taghkanic, NY Holy Cross Church.
Krank, Michael T. (BIS) Retired.
Krantz, Ernest *c.pp.s.* '76 (GRY) [A] Whiting, IN Calumet College of St. Joseph.
Krantz, Robert V. '78 (SFS) Parkston, SD Sacred Heart Church.
Kranyc, Andrew G. '87 (WH) [3] Huntington, WV Sacred Heart Church; [4] Huntington, WV St. Peter Claver Church.
Kranz, Stephen *o.s.b.* '55 (BIS) Mandaree, ND St. Anthony Church; Fort Berthold Reservation, ND Sacred Heart Indian Mission Church; [A] Richardton, ND Assumption Abbey.
Krapfl, Daniel A. '58 (DUB) [E] Cascade, IA Aquin Religious Education Center.
Krapfl, Daniel J. '58 (DUB) Cascade, IA St. Matthias Church.
Krapfl, Gary '72 (DUB) Decorah, IA St. Benedict's Church.
Krasauskas, Rapolas (NOR) [G] Putnam, CT Matulaitis Nursing Home Inc.
Krasen, John W. '60 (CLV) Westlake, OH St. Bernadette Church.
Krasevac, Edward *o.p.* '77 (OAK) [A] Berkeley, CA Dominican School of Philosophy and Theology; [A] Berkeley, CA Dominican School of Philosophy and Theology.
Krasic, Ljubo *o.f.m.* (CHI) [N] Chicago, IL Croatian Franciscan Custody of the Holy Family.
Krasman, James *o.f.m.* '83 (DET) [T] Detroit, MI St. John Health System.
Krasman, James *o.f.m.* '86 (SAG) Helena, MI St. Anthony Church; Parisville, MI St. Mary Church.
Krason, Edward J. '58 (FTW) Goshen, IN St. John the Evangelist Church.
Krastel, Francis W. '54 (WDC) St. Mary's City, MD St. Cecilia Church; [S] Washington, DC Archdiocesan Campus Ministry.
Krastel, Joseph F. *c.ss.r.* '64 (FgM) Redemptorist Foreign Missions.
Kraszewski, Thomas J. '97 (Y) Struthers, OH St. Nicholas Church.
Kratz, Conrad J. *o. praem.* '73 (GB) [5] De Pere, WI Our Lady of Lourdes Church; [I] De Pere, WI St. Joseph Priory.
Kratz, Lawrence *o.s.b.* '52 (SFS) [F] Marvin, SD Blue Cloud Abbey.
Kraus, Charles A. '58 (BRK) [29] Brooklyn, NY St. Charles Borromeo Church.
Kraus, Conrad L. '67 (E) Girard, PA St. John the Evangelist Church.
Kraus, David *o.m.i.* '57 (BEL) [H] Belleville, IL Retreat and Renewal Center.
Kraus, David H. '67 (DOD) Elkhart, KS St. Joan of Arc Church.
Kraus, Msgr. Donald W. '54 (PIT) [73] Pittsburgh, PA Holy Wisdom Church.
Kraus, Leonard E. *s.j.* '72 (STL) [35] St. Louis, MO St. Francis Xavier Church; [P] St. Louis, MO Jesuit Community Corporation at St. Louis University - Jesuit Hall.
Kraus, Philip D. *s.j.* '75 (STL) [P] St. Louis, MO Jesuit Community Corporation at St. Louis University - Jesuit Hall.
Kraus, Robert J. '42 (STL) Retired.
Kraus, Stephen '75 (ROC) Dansville, NY St. Mary Church.
Kraus, Msgr. Theodore W. '63 (BUF) On Duty Outside the Diocese.
Kraus, William *o.f.m.cap.* '73 (DEN) [M] Denver, CO St. Francis of Assisi Friary.
Krause, Bruce *c.m.* '82 (MOB) Opelika, AL St. Mary of the Mission Church.
Krause, Bruce J. *c.m.* '82 (PH) [AA] Philadelphia, PA Congregation of the Mission.
Krause, Edward *c.s.c.* '70 (E) [6] Erie, PA Immaculate Conception Church.
Krause, Edward C. *c.s.c.* '66 (E) [B] Erie, PA Gannon University.
Krause, Edward C. *c.s.c.* '66 (FTW) [J] South Bend, IN Congregation of Holy Cross Indiana Province Provincial House.
Krause, Joseph A. '68 (TUC) Payson, AZ Saint Philip the Apostle Church.
Krause, Karl H. '92 (HON) [9] Honolulu, HI St. John the Baptist Church.
Krause, Kenneth J. '65 (ORG) Newport Beach, CA Our Lady of Mount Carmel Church.
Krauser, Karl *c.ss.r.* '85 (ORL) [F] New Smyrna Beach, FL Redemptorist Fathers of the Vice Province of Richmond.
Krauth, Lothar '73 (GF) [4] Great Falls, MT Our Lady of Lourdes Church.
Krautkremer, Leo D. '66 (STP) Golden Valley, MN North Memorial Hospital.
Krautsack, Blaise P. *o.praem.* '74 (WIL) [B] Claymont, DE Archmere Academy; [I] Claymont, DE Immaculate Conception Priory of the Canons Regular of Premontre.
Krawczyk, Henry R. '78 (PIT) [2] Munhall, PA St. Maximilian Kolbe Church.
Krawinkel, Msgr. Robert M. '58 (STL) Ladue, MO Church of the Annunziata.
Krawontka, Stephen '77 (SCR) [6] Hazleton, PA St. Joseph's Church.
Kraynak, Nicholas '59 (PSC) Old Forge, PA St. Nicholas Church.
Kraynak, William B. '81 (Y) Louisville, OH Sacred Heart of Mary Church; [I] Louisville, OH Emmaus House.
Kraynyak, Basil William '66 (PSC) New Port Richey, FL St. Anne's Church.
Krebs, Bruce '78 (BIS) Hettinger, ND Holy Trinity Church.
Krebs, Msgr. Donald H. '55 (CR) Moorhead, MN St. Joseph's Church.
Krebs, Gerard H. '63 (E) [20] Erie, PA St. Joseph Church.
Krebs, Msgr. Henry L. '60 (E) Du Bois, PA St. Michael Church.
Krebs, John F. '57 (CHI) Ingleside, IL St. Bede Church.
Krebs, John G. *s.j.* '65 (FgM) Provinces.
Krebs, Paul F. '57 (COV) Retired.
Krebs, Peter *s.t.* '69 (PAT) [M] Stirling, NJ Holy Spirit Missionary Cenacle; [M] Stirling, NJ Shrine of St. Joseph.
Kreckel, Robert G. '54 (ROC) Ontario, NY St. Mary of the Lake Church.
Kredel, Thomas E. '72 (PIT) [31] Pittsburgh, PA St. Louise de Marillac Church.
Kreder, Michael J. '85 (NEW) Rutherford, NJ St. Mary's Church.
Kreft, Henry S. '45 (DET) Retired.
Kreher, Albert E. '65 (BEL) Prairie du Rocher, IL St. Joseph Church.
Kreidler, Thomas W. '77 (CIN) Twenty Mile Stand, OH St. Margaret of York Church.
Kreig, Robert A. *c.s.c.* '73 (FTW) [A] Notre Dame, IN Moreau Seminary.
Kreikemeier, Leo A. '43 (OM) Retired.
Kreilein, Philip J. '74 (EVN) Ferdinand, IN St. Ferdinand Church.
Kreimer, Richard *glmy.* '79 (CIN) [M] Fairfield, OH Headquarters of Glenmary Home Missioners.
Kreimes, Paul '72 (DET) [A] Detroit, MI Sacred Heart Major Seminary, Inc.
Kreis, Peter '86 (CHI) [115] Chicago, IL St. Ladislaus Church.
Kreiser, Thomas L. '94 (NY) Monroe, NY Sacred Heart Church.
Krejci, Msgr. Albert L. '41 (OM) [8] Sarpy Co., NE St. Bernadette Church; Retired.
Krejci, Michael G. (MIL) [2] Pewaukee, WI St. Anthony Church.
Krekelberg, Richard G. '73 (LA) [33] Los Angeles, CA Precious Blood Church.

Krekelberg, William '70 (ORG) Irvine, CA St. Thomas More Church.
Krelovich, Michael A. '95 (SB) Beaumont, CA San Gorgonio Church.
Kremeier, James '55 (GI) Retired.
Kremen, Timothy M. *o.s.m.* '61 (CHI) [N] Chicago, IL Servite Friars - Eastern Province.
Kremen, Timothy M. *o.s.m.* '61 (STL) Affton, MO Seven Holy Founders Church.
Kremer, Barry *o.carm.* '46 (JOL) [J] Darien, IL Carmelite Provincial Office.
Kremer, John R. '59 (DUB) Delhi, IA St. John's Church; Hopkinton, IA St. Luke's Church.
Kremer, Leroy M. '68 (SCL) Little Falls, MN Our Lady of Lourdes Church.
Kremer, Philip *o.s.b.* '57 (RCK) [H] Aurora, IL Marmion Abbey-St. Augustine's Abbey.
Kremmell, William T. '66 (BO) [1] Plymouth, MA Blessed Kateri Tekakwitha Church.
Kremp, Bruno *o.f.m.* '65 (CIN) [M] Cincinnati, OH St. Francis Center.
Krempa, Adam J. '90 (BUR) Chittenden, VT St. Robert Church; Rutland, VT Immaculate Heart of Mary Church; Sherburne, VT Our Lady of the Mountains Church.
Krempa, Stanley J. '70 (ARL) [7] Alexandria, VA St. Mary's Church.
Krempel, Matthew *o.f.m.* '74 (BWN) Progreso, TX Holy Spirit Church.
Krenik, Michael J. '84 (STP) White Bear Lake, MN St. Pius X Church.
Krenik, Robert L. '84 (RIC) Abingdon, VA Christ the King Church; Marion, VA St. John the Evangelist Church.
Krenik, Thomas '77 (STP) [A] St. Paul, MN The Saint Paul Seminary; [C] St. Paul, MN University of St. Thomas.
Krenzke, John '57 (DEN) [6] Denver, CO Christ the King Church.
Krepp, Theodore '82 (PSC) Kingston, PA St. Mary's Church.
Kreps, Anthony L. '38 (CLV) Amherst, OH St. Joseph Church; Retired.
Kresinski, Daniel J. '70 (E) [1] Sharon, PA Sacred Heart Church.
Kresmer, Donald J. '56 (DET) Detroit, MI Bon Secours; Retired.
Kress, Msgr. Justin A. '39 (DUB) Retired.
Kress, Robert '58 (EVN) On Duty Outside the Diocese.
Kret, John A. '61 (CHI) [N] Chicago, IL St. Rita Monastery.
Kretschmer, Albert *s.v.d.* '47 (FgM) Society of the Divine Word Foreign Missions.
Krettek, Dan (DM) [D] Des Moines, IA Mercy Hospital Medical Center.
Krettek, G. Thomas *s.j.* '82 (BO) [W] Cambridge, MA Faber House.
Krettek, G. Thomas *s.j.* '82 (OM) [K] Omaha, NE Jesuit Community At Creighton University.
Kretz, Edward J. '56 (GBG) [G] Greensburg, PA St. Anne Home.
Kretz, James C. '91 (PEO) Rutland, IL Sacred Heart Church; Toluca, IL St. Ann's Church.
Kreutz, William H. *s.j.* '69 (FgM) Provinces.
Kreutzer, Isaac Daniel '97 (OWN) [2] Owensboro, KY Blessed Mother Church.
Kreuzer, Eugene T. '52 (MIL) Retired.
Kreuzer, Msgr. Gerald J. '38 (BUF) Retired.
Kreuzer, Msgr. Gerald J. '56 (BUF) Angola, NY Most Precious Blood Church.
Krewer, Edward M. '43 (PEO) Retired.
Kribs, Charles R. '51 (BEL) Retired.
Kricek, Henry C. '80 (CHI) Skokie, IL St. Peter Church; [A] Chicago, IL St. Joseph Seminary.
Krick, Howard K. '58 (PH) Retired.
Krieg, Charles F. *c.m.* '63 (MET) [H] Plainsboro, NJ Vincentian Residence; [J] Plainsboro, NJ Vincentian Renewal Center.
Krieg, Msgr. Gerard C. '53 (ROC) Geneva, NY St. Stephen Church; [M] Rochester, NY Diocesan Office of Campus Ministry.
Krieg, Jerome L. '38 (DET) Retired; [I] Waterford, MI Lourdes Nursing Home.
Krieg, Michael '82 (SPK) [N] Pullman, WA Washington State University - St. Thomas More Catholic Newman Center.
Krieg, Peter *o.f.m.* '40 (OAK) [9] Oakland, CA St. Elizabeth's Church.
Krieg, Peter *o.f.m.* '43 (OAK) [N] Oakland, CA Franciscan Friars.
Krieg, Thomas J. '92 (LC) [2] Eau Claire, WI Newman Community Church; [J] Eau Claire, WI St. Bede Priory; [L] Eau Claire, WI Newman Parish; [L] Menomonie, WI The Ministry to the University of Wisconsin-Stout.
Kriege, Roger L. '64 (COV) Williamstown, KY St. William Church.
Kriegel, Msgr. Henry A. '70 (E) [21] Erie, PA St. Jude the Apostle Church.
Krieger, Msgr. Wilfred L. '46 (STL) Retired.
Kriegshauser, J. Laurence *o.s.b.* '69 (STL) [F] Creve Coeur, MO St. Louis Priory School; [P] St. Louis, MO The Abbey of St. Mary and St. Louis.
Kriegsmann, William A. '44 (RCK) Retired.
Krier, John P. '69 (GF) On Duty Outside of the Diocese.
Krier, John P. '69 (SPK) Davenport, WA Immaculate Conception Church; Harrington, WA St. Francis of Assisi Church; Reardan, WA St. Michael Church.
Krigler, Bela *sch.p.* '50 (MIL) [22] Milwaukee, WI St. Emeric Church.
Krijnen, Joseph G. '46 (PHX) [3] Tempe, AZ Resurrection Church; Retired.
Krile, George F. '41 (FAR) Retired.
Krile, Stephen '83 (COL) Wellston, OH SS. Peter and Paul Church.
Kriley, Victor *o.f.m.cap.* '64 (HBG) [2] York, PA St. Joseph Church.
Krill, Jude Michael *o.f.m.conv.* '83 (PH) [C] Aston, PA Neumann College.
Krill, Jude Michael *o.f.m.conv.* '83 (TR) Riverside, NJ St. Casimir Church.
Kringe, Charles J. '64 (SCR) Unassigned or Leave of Absence.
Krings, James A. '71 (STL) [31] St. Louis, MO St. Cronan Church; St. Louis, MO St. Mary's Health Ctr.
Krinzner, William R. '79 (CLV) [D] Parma Heights, OH Holy Name High School.
Krisak, Anthony F. *s.s.* '75 (TR) On Duty Outside the Diocese.
Krisak, Anthony F. '75 (WDC) [V] Washington, DC Missionary Vehicle Association, Inc.
Krisanda, Stephen J. *m.s.* '60 (ORL) [3] Orlando, FL Good Shepherd Church.
Krische, Francis '57 (KCK) [4] Topeka, KS Most Pure Heart of Mary Church.
Krische, James '91 (BRK) [15] Brooklyn, NY St. Barbara Church.
Krische, Otto *o.f.m.* '37 (CIN) [M] Cincinnati, OH St. Clement Friary.
Krische, Vincent E. '64 (KCK) [J] Lawrence, KS St. Lawrence Catholic Campus Center at the University of Kansas and Residence.
Krisciunevicius, Victor '49 (DET) Retired.
Krisman, Ronald F. '73 (LUB) Levelland, TX St. Michael's Church.
Krispinsky, Msgr. Joseph A. '23 (Y) Retired.
Kriss, Aaron J. '91 (PIT) Natrona Heights, PA Our Lady of the Most Blessed Sacrament Church.
Kriss, David J. '79 (PIT) [4] Donora, PA Our Lady of the Valley Church.
Kriss, Zigford J. '58 (HRT) [2] West Hartford, CT St. Helena Church; Special and other (Arch)Diocesan Assignment.
Kristancic, Dennis '83 (CLV) Absent on Leave.
Kristancic, Dennis J. '83 (CLV) [11] Lorain, OH St. Stanislaus Church.
Kristofak, Terence *c.p.* '69 (HRT) [C] West Hartford, CT Saint Joseph College; [M] West Hartford, CT Holy Family Monastery/Retreat; [Q] Farmington, CT Holy Family Retreat House.
Kristofak, Terence *c.p.* '69 (MET) [H] South River, NJ Passionist Provincial Office.
Kristy, Mark *o.c.d.* '85 (SR) [M] Oakville, CA Carmelite House of Prayer.
Krivak, John A. '82 (ALN) [C] Allentown, PA Allentown Central Catholic High School; [O] Kutztown, PA Christopher House.
Krivanek, George E. *s.j.* '59 (LA) [R] Los Angeles, CA Columbiere House.
Kriz, Mark G. *s.j.* '95 (BUF) [O] Buffalo, NY Canisius Jesuit Community; [R] Williamsville, NY Campus Ministry.
Krizmanich, Germain *o.f.m.* '56 (CIN) [M] Cincinnati, OH St. Francis Center.
Krizner, William R. '79 (CLV) [2] Parma, OH St. Bridget Church.
Krlis, William F. '68 (BRK) [176] Queens, NY Holy Child Jesus Church.
Kroeger, Gerald C. *o.p.* '58 (CHI) Summit, IL St. Joseph Church; [N] Chicago, IL Dominicans (Provincial Office).
Kroeger, James H. *m.m.* '67 (FgM) Maryknoll Foreign Missions.
Kroeger, James H. *m.m.* '75 (NY) [DD] Maryknoll, NY Maryknoll Fathers and Brothers.
Kroeger, John '72 (CIN) Monroe, OH Our Lady of Sorrows Church.
Kroeger, Robert S. '94 (MIL) [1] Menomonee Falls, WI St. Anthony Church.
Kroeger, Timothy D. '90 (LFT) Kokomo, IN St. Joan of Arc Church.
Kroes, Ralph S. *m.m.* '58 (FgM) Maryknoll Foreign Missions.
Kroger, Daniel *o.f.m.* '73 (CIN) [M] Cincinnati, OH St. Francis Seraph Friary.
Kroger, Daniel *o.f.m.* '73 (FgM) Franciscan Foreign Missions.
Kroger, John H. '55 (COV) Bellevue, KY St. Anthony Church.
Krogman, David '81 (SFS) [5] Sioux Falls, SD St. Lambert Church.
Krogman, Philip J. '60 (MAD) Kieler, WI Immaculate Conception Church.
Krogol, Jude *o.s.b.* '65 (SP) [O] St. Leo, FL St. Leo Abbey.
Krol, Boleslaus '61 (DET) [12] Detroit, MI St. Bartholomew Church; [43] Detroit, MI St. Louis the King Church.
Krolczyk, David B. '72 (CHI) Posen, IL St. Stanislaus Bishop and Martyr Church.
Krolikowski, Lucian *o.f.m.conv.* '46 (BUF) [O] Athol Springs, NY Father Justin Rosary Hour Radio Apostolate.
Krolikowski, Walter P. *s.j.* '57 (CHI) [C] Chicago, IL Jesuit Community at Loyola University of Chicago.
Kroll, Anthony '61 (SCL) Flensburg, MN Sacred Heart Church.
Kroll, Lawrence W. '86 (KAL) [4] Kalamazoo, MI St. Monica Church.
Kromenaker, Joseph (CHI) [58] Chicago, IL St. Ferdinand Church.
Kromer, Stanley S. *o.carm.* '50 (VEN) Englewood, FL St. Raphael Church.
Kron, Kenneth M. '87 (YAK) Quincy, WA St. Pius X Church.
Kronewitter, Frank '62 (FTW) [H] Fort Wayne, IN Saint Anne Home & Retirement Community.
Kronkowski, Leonard J. (GRY) Retired.
Kropac, Robert J. '82 (CLV) [26] Cleveland, OH St. Henry Church.
Kropf, Richard '58 (GAY) [H] Johannesburg, MI Stella Maris Hermitage.
Kropf, Richard '58 (LAN) On Duty Outside the Diocese.
Kropiwnicki, Henry K. '58 (FR) [11] New Bedford, MA St. Casimir Church.
Kros, Donald M. '59 (OM) Lynch, NE Assumption B.V.M. Church; [O] Lynch, NE Niobrara Valley House of Renewal.
Krosfield, George '70 (ALX) Simmesport, LA Christ the King Church.
Krosnicki, Thomas A. *s.v.d.* '66 (CHI) [B] Techny, IL Divine Word Residence; [N] Techny, IL Society of the Divine Word, Provincial Headquarter-Chicago Prov.; [U] Techny, IL S.V.D., Catholic Universities, Inc.; [U] Techny, IL Divine Word Missionaries, Inc., Divine Word Funds, Inc.
Krosnicki, Thomas A. *s.v.d.* '66 (FgM) Society of the Divine Word Foreign Missions.
Krotec, Ivan '70 (STN) [3] Chicago, IL SS. Volodymyr and Olha Church.
Krotkiewicz, Luke '83 (DET) Detroit, MI Bi-County Osteopathic.
Krough, Jack (WIN) Brownsdale, MN Our Lady of Loretto Church.
Krouse, Dennis W. '68 (SD) [B] San Diego, CA University of San Diego.
Krozser, John J. *c.m.* '56 (MOB) [8] Montgomery, AL Resurrection Catholic Church.
Krozser, John J. *c.m.* '56 (NEW) On Duty Outside the Archdiocese.
Kruc, James '89 (RIC) Unassigned.
Krudwig, William C. '61 (SPC) El Dorado Springs, MO St. Elizabeth Church.
Krueger, Robert W. '56 (P) [4] Portland, OR St. Andrew Church.
Kruel, Ronald G. *o.p.* '78 (DEN) [29] Denver, CO St. Dominic's Parish.
Krugel, Stephen A. '88 (HRT) [4] New Haven, CT St. Bernadette's Church.
Kruger, Brent '97 (PHX) Tolleson, AZ Blessed Sacrament Church; [J] Phoenix, AZ Andre House of Arizona.
Kruger, Brent Allan *c.s.c.* '97 (FTW) On Duty Outside the Diocese.
Krukowski, Francis V. '58 (HRT) South Windsor, CT St. Margaret Mary Church.
Krul, Valentine C. '77 (SY) New York Mills, NY St. Mary Church.
Krulak, Michael '95 (PSC) Lansford, PA St. John the Baptist Church.
Krull, Michael G. '86 (MET) Port Reading, NJ St. Anthony of Padua Church.
Krumm, Gustave R. *o.f.m.* '82 (ORG) [3] Huntington Beach, CA SS. Simon and Jude Church.
Krumm, John E. '76 (CIN) [6] Dayton, OH Assumption Church; [20] Dayton, OH Our Lady of Mercy Church.
Krumpe, William F. '66 (CIN) [14] Cincinnati, OH St. Bartholomew Church.
Krupa, Sandor *o.f.m.* (Y) [J] Youngstown, OH Mt. Alverna Friary.
Krupa, Stephen T. *s.j.* '86 (CLV) [C] Cleveland, OH John Carroll Jesuit Community.
Krupa, Stephen T. *s.j.* '86 (OAK) [N] Berkeley, CA Jesuit Community at Jesuit School of Theology at Berkeley.
Krupa, Thomas J. '71 (ALB) Castleton-on-Hudson, NY Sacred Heart Church.
Krupa, William J. *o.s.a.* '44 (PH) [18] Philadelphia, PA St. Augustine Church.
Krupich, Thomas J. '88 (FAR) Tappen, ND St. Paul's Church.
Krupka, Michael '77 (SJP) [4] Akron, OH Holy Ghost Church.

Krupp, Albert '65 (CLV) El Salvador, C.A., OH Parroquial Inmaculada Concepcion.
Kruse, Clarence '57 (DUB) Retired.
Kruse, Msgr. Clement '41 (SAL) Retired.
Kruse, David B. '94 (BAL) [10] Baltimore, MD St. Anthony of Padua Church; [66] Baltimore, MD Most Precious Blood, Community of Church.
Kruse, James '96 (PEO) Pekin, IL St. Joseph's Church.
Kruse, Jay L. '91 (OM) St. James, NE SS. Philip and James Church; Wynot, NE Sacred Heart Church.
Kruse, Phillip (DM) West Des Moines, IA Sacred Heart Church.
Kruse, Robert J. *c.s.c.* '58 (FR) [A] North Easton, MA Stonehill College; [A] North Easton, MA Holy Cross Fathers Religious.
Krusinski, Andrew J. '45 (SCR) [4] Williamsport, PA Holy Rosary Church.
Krusling, Lawrence R. '51 (CIN) [79] Cincinnati, OH St. Rose of Lima Church.
Kruszynski, Joseph *o.f.m.conv.* (CHI) [N] Chicago, IL Conventual Franciscans of St. Bonaventure Province.
Krutcik, Stanley F. '80 (WOR) Manchaug, MA St. Anne's Church.
Krutzik, Norman '57 (GB) Special Assignment.
Kruzel, Leonard M. '83 (CHI) [60] Chicago, IL Five Holy Martyrs Church.
Krylowicz, Mark J. '91 (CHI) [160] Chicago, IL Our Lady of Tepeyac Church.
Krymski, Christopher *o.s.m.* '83 (CHI) Hillside, IL St. Domitilla Church.
Krymski, Christopher M. *o.s.m.* '83 (CHI) [N] Chicago, IL Servite Friars - Eastern Province.
Krynski, Leo '52 (SUP) Retired.
Krysa, Czeslaw M. '80 (BUF) On Duty Outside the Diocese.
Krysa, Czeslaw M. '80 (DET) [A] Orchard Lake, MI SS. Cyril and Methodius Seminary.
Kryston, Edward '74 (PIT) Baldwin Boro, PA St. Albert the Great Church.
Krystosek, Robert H. '56 (GI) Retired.
Krystosek, Robert H. '56 (NU) Retired.
Kryszak, Marian '56 (SAG) Retired.
Kryszkiewicz, Pawel '93 (CAM) Merchantville, NJ St. Peter's Church.
Krysztofik, Msgr. Joseph M. '50 (MET) Retired.
Kryzston, Stanley W. '88 (TR) [3] Trenton, NJ Holy Angels Church.
Krzewinski, Edwin *o.m.i.* '52 (FgM) Oblates Foreign Missions.
Krzysiak, Casimir J. '50 (SY) [15] Utica, NY St. Stanislaus Church.
Krzywda, Leonard *c.r.* '65 (SB) [1] Fontana, CA Church of the Resurrection.
Krzywicki, Lance P. '83 (PT) Military Chaplains.
Krzyzaniak, Timothy D. '91 (LAN) Hamburg, MI Holy Spirit Church.
Krzyzanowski, Casimir *m.i.c.* '56 (SPR) [I] Stockbridge, MA Congregation of Marians.
Krzyzanski, John P. *o.f.m.conv.* '82 (ATL) Jonesboro, GA St. Philip Benizi Church.
Krzyzopolski, Al '50 (SFS) Retired.
Kselman, John J. *s.s.* '67 (BAL) [M] Baltimore, MD Sulpician Provincial House.
Kselman, John J. *s.s.* '67 (TR) On Duty Outside the Diocese.
Kselman, Paul *s.d.b.* '77 (NY) [FF] West Haverstraw, NY Don Bosco Retreat Center and Marian Shrine; [FF] West Haverstraw, NY Marian Shrine.
Ku, Benedict (BRK) [226] Queens, NY St. Paul Chong Ha-Sang Roman Catholic Chapel Church.
Kub, Francis Q. '65 (CHI) [191] Chicago, IL St. Simon the Apostle Church.
Kuba, William M. '62 (E) Corry, PA St. Thomas The Apostle Church.
Kubacki, Anthony '80 (SJP) Johnstown, PA St. John the Baptist Church.
Kubacki, William J. '78 (TOL) [14] Toledo, OH Sacred Heart of Jesus Church.
Kubajak, James '77 (PRM) Northwood, OH St. Michael the Archangel Church.
Kubala, Daniel I. '76 (MIA) [32] Miami, FL St. Thomas the Apostle Church.
Kubart, Francis E. '49 (OM) Leigh, NE St. Mary Church.
Kubat, Alphonse M. '42 (STP) Retired.
Kubeck, John C. '65 (MIL) [O] Brookfield, WI Opus Dei-Prelature of the Holy Cross and Opus Dei.
Kuberski, Leonard '67 (PSC) Dunellen, NJ St. Nicholas Church.
Kubiak, Edward J. '34 (GR) Retired.
Kubiak, Joseph M. *o.f.m.cap.* '74 (MET) [4] New Brunswick, NJ St. Joseph Church; New Brunswick, NJ Robert Wood Johnson University Hospital.
Kubiak, Joseph M. *o.f.m.cap.* '74 (PAT) [M] Oak Ridge-Milton, NJ St. Stanislaus B. M. Friary.
Kubicki, James M. *s.j.* '83 (MIL) [P] Milwaukee, WI Jesuit Provincial Office, Wisconsin Province; [P] Milwaukee, WI Jesuit Community at Marquette University.
Kubik, John M. '49 (DET) [62] Detroit, MI SS. Peter and Paul Church; Retired.
Kubik, Thomas *c.r.* '72 (CHI) [D] Chicago, IL Gordon Technical High School.
Kubina, Eugene *t.o.r.* '53 (ALT) [F] Newry, PA St. Bernardine Monastery.
Kubinski, Scott M. '84 (ROC) Horseheads, NY St. Mary Our Mother Church.
Kubinyi, Julius '51 (PBR) Erie, PA SS. Peter and Paul Church.
Kubis, Alcuin *o.s.b.* (LR) [A] Subiaco, AR Subiaco Monastery.
Kucan, Jerome *o.f.m.* (CHI) [N] Chicago, IL Croatian Franciscan Custody of the Holy Family.
Kucera, Edward *o.s.b.* '53 (DEN) Aurora, CO Fitzsimons Army Medical Center.
Kucera, Edward *o.s.b.* '53 (JOL) [J] Lisle, IL St. Procopius Abbey.
Kucera, Edward C., Jr. *m.th.* '73 (GAL) Hempstead, TX Mary, Mother of God Church.
Kucera, Robert M. *o.s.m.* '53 (CHI) [N] Chicago, IL Servite Friars - Eastern Province.
Kuchar, Bryan M. '93 (STL) [1] St. Louis, MO Cathedral Basilica of St. Louis Church.
Kuchar, Michael W. '80 (LAN) [7] Lansing, MI St. Therese Church.
Kucharczyk, Dennis '80 (SAG) Caseville, MI St. Roch Church; Pinnebog, MI St. Felix Church.
Kucharski, Steven M. '77 (MAN) Rollinsford, NH St. Mary Church; Somersworth, NH Holy Trinity Church.
Kuchera, Michael J. *s.j.* '87 (BAL) [C] Baltimore, MD Loyola High School.
Kuchinsky, William Joseph '97 (WH) Weirton, WV St. Joseph the Worker Church.
Kuchta, Waldemar J. '89 (PRM) Dayton, OH St. Barbara Church.
Kucingis, Msgr. John A. '37 (LA) [54] Los Angeles, CA St. Casimir Church; Retired.
Kucyk, Msgr. Herman W. '57 (DET) [5] Dearborn, MI Divine Child Church.
Kuczaik, Stanislaw *s.ch.* '57 (DET) [K] Sterling Heights, MI Society of Christ Provincial Home.
Kuczborski, Joseph M. '82 (PEO) On Duty Outside the Diocese.
Kuczborski, Joseph M. '82 (PMB) [2] Boca Raton, FL Our Lady of Lourdes Church.
Kuczmanski, Gregory M. '75 (BWN) Edcouch, TX St. Theresa of the Infant Jesus Church.
Kuczynski, Edward P. '77 (PH) Pottstown, PA St. Peter Church.
Kuczynski, Edwin R. *o.s.a.* '47 (CHI) [N] Olympia Fields, IL Tolentine Monastery at Tolentine Center.
Kuczynski, Francis I. '43 (PIT) Retired.
Kuczynski, James H. *m.s.* '73 (HRT) [M] Hartford, CT Missionaries of LaSalette Provincial Secretary.
Kuczynski, John *c.m.* '44 (HRT) Derby, CT St. Michael Church.
Kuczynski, Kazimierz '76 (NEW) [6] Bayonne, NJ Mt. Carmel Church.
Kuder, Donald E. *c.s.b.* '63 (GAL) [K] Houston, TX The Catholic Chaplain Corps.
Kuder, Stephen R. *s.j.* '73 (SPK) [C] Spokane, WA Gonzaga University.
Kudilil, James '63 (FRS) Wofford Heights, CA St. Jude Church.
Kudlo, Frank '88 (MIA) Absent on Leave.
Kudrick, John '75 (PBR) McKees Rocks, PA Holy Ghost Church.
Kuebler, A.M. Seamus *o.a.s.* '75 (PRT) [L] Peaks Island, ME Mother of the Good Shepherd Monastery by the Sea.
Kuebler, A.M. Seamus '75 (WDC) On Duty Outside the Archdiocese.
Kuechmann, Theodore M. *m.m.* '53 (NY) [DD] Maryknoll, NY Maryknoll Fathers and Brothers.
Kuefer, Edward A. *o.s.f.s.* '55 (TOL) [K] Toledo, OH Oblates of St. Francis de Sales.
Kuehler, Msgr. Norbert '55 (AMA) Borger, TX St. John the Evangelist Church.
Kuehmeier, Carl L. '64 (BUF) West Valley, NY St. John the Baptist Church.
Kuehnemund, Thomas (DET) [7] Sterling Heights, MI St. Michael Church.
Kuenzig, Aloysius A. '43 (PIT) Retired.
Kuenzig, Peter A. '46 (PIT) Retired.
Kueter, David *o.m.v.* '84 (BO) [W] Milton, MA Oblate Residence (St. Joseph House).
Kuffel, Thomas P. *o.s.* '89 (LIN) Davey, NE St. Mary's Church.
Kuffel, Thomas P. *o.s.* '89 (PCE) On Duty Outside the Diocese.
Kugler, Michael '89 (GLP) Absent on Leave.
Kuhl, Charles E. (CAM) Retired.
Kuhl, Morgan J. '93 (NY) [204] Staten Island, NY Holy Child Church.
Kuhl, Msgr. Urban B. '45 (BEL) Retired; [J] Belleville, IL Catholic War Veterans.
Kuhlmann, John L. '68 (BUF) Bemus Point, NY Our Lady of Lourdes Church; Jamestown, NY Jamestown Women's Christian Association Hospital.
Kuhlmann, Steven F. *o.p.* '92 (CHI) [N] Chicago, IL Dominicans (Provincial Office).
Kuhlmann, Steven F. *o.p.* '92 (SFE) [29] Albuquerque, NM St. Thomas Aquinas University Parish.
Kuhn, Christopher A. *c.s.c.* '77 (CHI) [D] Niles, IL Notre Dame High School.
Kuhn, Christopher J. '97 (RCK) Woodstock, IL St. Mary Church.
Kuhn, Dennis R. '82 (CHL) Absent On Leave.
Kuhn, George J. '64 (NY) Rhinebeck, NY The Good Shepherd Church; [S] Rhinebeck, NY Astor Home for Children, The.
Kuhn, Herbert C. '57 (SAL) Retired.
Kuhn, James G. '71 (MAD) Roxbury, WI St. Norbert Church.
Kuhn, James J. *m.m.* '51 (FgM) Maryknoll Foreign Missions.
Kuhn, John C. *ss.cc.* '76 (HON) [11] Honolulu, HI St. Patrick Church.
Kuhn, John G. '58 (WDC) Special Ministries.
Kuhn, John H. '43 (BIS) Retired; [G] Bismarck, ND Emmaus Place.
Kuhn, Michael F. (FR) [B] Attleboro, MA Bishop Feehan High School.
Kuhn, Michael F. '97 (FR) Seekonk, MA St. Mary's Church.
Kuhn, Richard V. *s.m.* '58 (CAM) [P] Cape May Point, NJ Marianist Family Retreat Center.
Kuhn, Richard W. '53 (DUB) Festina, IA Our Lady of Seven Dolors Church; Ossian, IA St. Francis de Sales Church; [E] Calmar, IA Christian Family School.
Kuhn, Thomas A. '67 (CIN) Centerville, OH Incarnation Church.
Kuhns, Clement *c.pp.s.* (CIN) [B] Carthagena, OH St. Charles.
Kuhns, Howard *c.s.c.* '46 (PHX) Gila Bend, AZ St. Michael Church.
Kuhns, James '61 (SPK) [4] Spokane, WA Our Lady of Fatima Church.
Kuhr, William M. '67 (GB) [6] Appleton, WI Sacred Heart Church.
Kujawa, Patrick '94 (HT) Morgan City, LA Holy Cross Church.
Kujovsky, Msgr. Thomas (HBG) Retired.
Kujovsky, Thomas J. '57 (HBG) Elizabethtown, PA St. Peter Church.
Kujundzija, Zdravko (BO) [3] Cambridge, MA St. Francis of Assisi Church.
Kukla, Gerald F. '67 (SAG) [4] Bay City, MI St. Hyacinth Church.
Kuklich, Stepan (STF) Syracuse, NY St. John the Baptist Church.
Kukucka, Joseph G. '65 (PBL) Retired.
Kukulka, Janusz '85 (DET) [A] Orchard Lake, MI SS. Cyril and Methodius Seminary.
Kukulski, Stanislaus C. '55 (DET) Detroit, MI Northville State Hospital; [O] Northville, MI Our Lady of Providence Center.
Kukura, Joseph W. '67 (NEW) On Duty Outside the Archdiocese.
Kula, Frances *m.s.* '54 (MIL) [P] Milwaukee, WI La Salette Fathers.
Kula, Frank *m.s.* '54 (MIL) [65] Milwaukee, WI St. Paul Church.
Kula, Joseph '55 (BIR) Retired.
Kulak, Joseph F. '66 (RCK) [2] Elgin, IL St. Laurence Church.
Kulandai, Peter '69 (NY) Red Hook, NY St. Christopher Church.
Kulandairajan, S. '78 (NY) Shrub Oak, NY Saint Elizabeth Ann Seton Church.
Kulapurath, Mathew (BRK) [208] Queens, NY Our Lady of the Cenacle Church.
Kulapurath, Matthew *c.m.i.* (BRK) Queens, NY Jamaica Hospital - Trump Pavilion.
Kulas, John *o.s.b.* '57 (SCL) [I] Collegeville, MN St. John's Abbey, of the Order of St. Benedict.
Kulas, Robert A. '54 (WIN) Retired.
Kulas, William J. '74 (WIN) Rushford, MN St. Joseph's Church.
Kulathinal, Joseph *o.s.b.* '70 (PAT) [M] Clifton, NJ Holy Face of Jesus Monastery.
Kulavich, John J. '83 (SCR) Great Bend, PA St. Lawrence's Church.
Kulbicki, Timothy *o.f.m.conv.* '86 (BAL) [20] Baltimore, MD St. Casimir Church; [A] Baltimore, MD St. Mary's Seminary and University.
Kulbis, Augustine *o.s.m.* '58 (P) Milwaukie, OR Christ the King Church.
Kulbis, Augustine M. *o.s.m.* '58 (CHI) [N] Chicago, IL Servite Friars - Eastern Province.
Kulczynski, A. Jason '89 (PH) Highland Park, PA St. Laurence Church.
Kulesa, Daniel J. '62 (Y) McDonald, OH Our Lady of Perpetual Help Church.
Kulhawik, Frank '40 (CR) Retired.
Kulick, Larry J. '92 (GBG) Kent, PA Church of the Good Shepherd.
Kulig, Anthony J. '61 (NEW) [6] Bayonne, NJ Mt. Carmel Church.
Kulig, Francis G. '74 (SCR) [L] Dallas, PA Mercy Center Nursing Unit, Inc.; [O] Dallas, PA Mercy Center Convent.

Kuligowski, Peter Jacek '97 (ALT) [12] Altoona, PA St. Rose of Lima Church.
Kulik, Msgr. Alexander T. '54 (SCR) [15] Wilkes-Barre, PA Maternity of the Blessed Virgin Mary Church.
Kulik, Francis J. '69 (SCR) Unassigned or Leave of Absence.
Kulinski, Kenneth E. '72 (OKL) [9] Oklahoma City, OK St. Paul, Apostle Church.
Kull, Jack *o.f.m.* '66 (NEW) Fair Lawn, NJ St. Anne's Church.
Kull, Martin '76 (BRK) [83] Brooklyn, NY Mary Queen of Heaven Church.
Kulleck, Msgr. Donald R. '52 (SD) [3] Chula Vista, CA St. Pius X Church.
Kulleck, Thomas '74 (BWN) [5] McAllen, TX Holy Spirit Church; McCook, TX Immaculate Conception Church.
Kuller, Thomas *s.j.* '90 (ALN) [G] Reading, PA Saint Joseph Medical Center.
Kuller, Thomas J. *s.j.* '79 (ALN) [A] Wernersville, PA Novitiate of St. Isaac Jogues.
Kullmann, Charles *c.s.p.* '78 (NY) [104] New York, NY St. Paul the Apostle Church.
Kulovits, Fred A. '59 (LC) Retired.
Kulwicki, Raymond J. *c.s.sp.* '56 (VEN) [G] Sarasota, FL Congregation of the Holy Ghost.
Kulwiec, Richard *o.m.i.* '81 (NY) [FF] Newburgh, NY Our Lady of Hope Center.
Kumbalaparambil, Xavier '66 (SAV) [2] Savannah, GA St. Anthony's Church.
Kumle, Peter *c.p.* '52 (LA) [R] Pasadena, CA Passionist Community.
Kummer, John R. '72 (CIN) Fairborn, OH Mary Help of Christians Church.
Kummer, William '75 (FTW) [7] Fort Wayne, IN St. John Baptist Church.
Kummerer, Timothy '83 (TOL) On Duty Outside the Diocese; [O] Toledo, OH Office of Global Concerns.
Kumontis, Msgr. Francis M. '73 (HBG) Hershey, PA St. Joan of Arc Church.
Kumplamthanam, Chacko '80 (HRT) [I] New Haven, CT Hospital of St. Raphael.
Kumplamthanam, Chacko K. (HRT) [3] West Haven, CT St. Lawrence's Church.
Kumse, John M. '79 (CLV) [47] Cleveland, OH St. Mary Church.
Kuna, Lech '74 (HRT) [5] Bristol, CT St. Stanislaus Church.
Kunco, Edward J. '69 (PIT) [16] Pittsburgh, PA Immaculate Conception Church; [20] Pittsburgh, PA St. Joseph Church.
Kunda, Brendan J. '65 (SUP) Boulder Junction, WI St. Anne Church; Presque Isle, WI St. Rita Church; Sayner, WI St. Mary Church.
Kundert, Rudolph '82 (PHX) [6] Scottsdale, AZ St. Maria Goretti Church.
Kundrat, Michael J. '41 (DET) Retired.
Kunert, Kenneth M. *s.j.* (DET) [K] Detroit, MI Jesuit Provincial Office-Detroit Province of the Society of Jesus.
Kunert, Kenneth M. *s.j.* '57 (FgM) Provinces.
Kunes, James F. *s.m.* '60 (CIN) [M] Dayton, OH Marianist Provincialate.
Kunisch, Robert *c.pp.s.* '56 (TOL) Marywood, OH St. Michael's Church; [M] Bellevue, OH Sorrowful Mother Shrine; [O] Bellevue, OH Mary Lay Center.
Kunkel, A. Henry, III '70 (BAL) Pylesville, MD St. Mary Church.
Kunkel, Albert A. '57 (CLV) [5] Barberton, OH Sacred Heart Church.
Kunkel, Charles *o.s.c.* '67 (PHX) [F] Phoenix, AZ Crosier Community of Phoenix (Canons Regular of the Order of the Holy Cross).
Kunkel, George C. '77 (CIN) [58] Cincinnati, OH St. Martin of Tours Church.
Kunkel, James E. '73 (PIT) [1] McKeesport, PA St. Martin de Porres Church.
Kunkel, Raymond W. '60 (SPC) Joplin, MO St. Mary Church.
Kunnakkattuthara, Zacharias S. '75 (TYL) Palestine, TX Sacred Heart Church.
Kunnath, Matthew '60 (NEW) Nutley, NJ St. Mary's Church.
Kunnath, Sebastian '73 (NEW) Cranford, NJ St. Michael's Church.
Kunnath, Thomas '85 (NEW) [1] Jersey City, NJ St. Aedan's Church; Jersey City, NJ St. Francis Health Center; [S] Jersey City, NJ Franciscan Health System of New Jersey, Inc.
Kunnel, Lawrence '60 (TR) Neptune, NJ Holy Innocents Church.
Kunnumpuram, Paul *m.s.f.s.* '76 (ALX) Ferriday, LA St. Patrick Church; Vidalia, LA Our Lady of Lourdes Church.
Kuntoro Adi, Cyprianus *s.j.* '93 (MIL) [P] Milwaukee, WI Jesuit Community at Marquette University.
Kuntz, Aloysius G. '47 (BUF) Retired.
Kuntz, Aloysius G. '49 (BUF) [O] Buffalo, NY Sheehan Residence for Priests.
Kuntz, Donald B. '41 (DET) Retired.
Kuntz, Ildephonse *ss.cc.* '46 (HON) [H] Honolulu, HI St. Patrick's Monastery.
Kuntz, Kenneth E. '77 (DAV) [1] Iowa City, IA St. Mary of the Assumption Church.
Kunz, Alfred J. '56 (MAD) Dane, WI St. Michael Church.
Kunz, David C. '80 (WIN) [A] Winona, MN Immaculate Heart of Mary Seminary.
Kunz, Francis P. '49 (WIN) Retired.
Kunz, James '73 (WIN) [G] Rochester, MN Congregational Center of the Sisters of the Third Order Regular of St. Francis of the Congregation of Our.
Kunz, John M. '76 (WIN) Waseca, MN Sacred Heart Church.
Kunze, Robert W. '74 (NEW) On Duty Outside the Archdiocese.
Kunzman, Richard T. '63 (CAM) On Duty Outside the Diocese.
Kuolt, Benedict '47 (NY) Retired.
Kuolt, Benedict J. '47 (NY) [3] White Plains, NY St. Bernard Church; White Plains, NY White Plains Hospital.
Kuper, Raymond L. '64 (EVN) [12] Evansville, IN St. Agnes Church.
Kupisz, Julian F. '74 (FAR) Sykeston, ND St. Elizabeth's Church.
Kupke, Raymond J. '73 (PAT) Florham Park, NJ Holy Family Church.
Kuppe, Paul M. *o.f.m.cap.* '70 (PIT) [29] Pittsburgh, PA Our Lady of the Angels Church.
Kuragama, Cyril '64 (NY) Pleasant Valley, NY St. Stanislaus Kostka Church.
Kuras, Alexander A. '69 (DET) [3] Westland, MI Church of the Divine Savior.
Kuras, Felix '38 (DUL) Retired.
Kuras, Hippolite *o.f.m.conv.* '35 (RCK) [11] Rockford, IL St. Stanislaus Kostka Church.
Kurash, Stanley J. '71 (SCR) [2] Old Forge, PA St. Mary's Church.
Kurber, Robert '60 (ORL) [4] Orlando, FL Holy Cross Church.
Kurdziel, Dennis M. '75 (ALT) Williamsburg, PA St. Joseph Church; Smithfield, PA State Correctional Institution.
Kurek, Gerard '51 (BAL) [87] Baltimore, MD Sacred Heart of Jesus Church.
Kurera, Pius (STO) Stockton, CA O.H. Close School.
Kurgan, Charles *o.carm.* '65 (JOL) [J] Darien, IL Carmelite Provincial Office.
Kurian, Joseph '83 (TYL) Jefferson, TX Immaculate Conception Church.
Kurilec, Robert '68 (SB) On Duty Outside the Diocese.
Kurimay, Michael D. *s.j.* '73 (MIL) [P] Milwaukee, WI Jesuit Community at Marquette University.
Kurimsky, Francis M. '86 (PIT) [31] Pittsburgh, PA St. Louise de Marillac Church.
Kurimsky, Frank M. '86 (PIT) Washington, PA Immaculate Conception Church.
Kurkiewicz, Raymond J. '42 (MIL) Retired.
Kurkowski, Innocent *o.f.m.conv.* '56 (BGP) [1] Fairfield, CT St. Anthony of Padua Church.
Kurovsky, Andrew '85 (SCR) [6] Williamsport, PA St. Ann's Church; [D] Williamsport, PA Bishop Neumann Junior/Senior High School.
Kurowski, Andrzej *s.a.c.* '76 (BRK) [177] Queens, NY Holy Cross Church.
Kurowski, Andrzej *s.a.c.* '76 (BUF) [O] North Tonawanda, NY Society of the Catholic Apostolate.
Kurowski, Clement *o.f.m.* '53 (PH) [106] Philadelphia, PA St. Monica Church.
Kurps, Jack *s.c.j.* '77 (MIL) [P] Hales Corners, WI Priests of the Sacred Heart; [P] Milwaukee, WI St. Joseph House of Formation.
Kurt, Allan J. '55 (DUB) Retired.
Kurt, David L. '77 (PEO) Bushnell, IL St. Bernard Church.
Kurt, Msgr. Edgar J. '41 (DUB) Retired.
Kurtenbach, Harold '60 (GI) [1] Grand Island, NE Cathedral of the Nativity of the Blessed Virgin Mary.
Kurth, Earl J. *s.j.* '49 (RC) Pine Ridge, SD Holy Rosary Church; [B] Pine Ridge, SD Jesuit Community of Holy Rosary Mission.
Kurty, Msgr. John '42 (PRM) Allen Park, MI St. Stephen Church; Retired.
Kurtyka, Edward J. '71 (PAT) Prospect Park, NJ St. Paul's Church.
Kurtz, James *o.f.m.cap.* '87 (PIT) Herman, PA St. Mary of the Assumption Church; [O] Herman, PA St. Mary's Friary.
Kurtz, Jeffrey A. '90 (MAR) Leave of Absence.
Kurtz, Msgr. Joseph E. '72 (ALN) [7] Bethlehem, PA Notre Dame of Bethlehem Church; [F] Allentown, PA Catholic Social Agency-Catholic Charities Administrative Office.
Kurtz, R. James *s.j.* '77 (DET) [E] Detroit, MI University of Detroit Jesuit High School and Academy.
Kurtzke, John *c.s.c.* '85 (P) [B] Portland, OR University of Portland; [L] Portland, OR Holy Cross Fathers & Brothers, C.S.C. - University of Portland.
Kurutz, Gregory *o.f.m.* '54 (GAY) Lewiston, MI St. Francis of Assisi Church.
Kurutz, Joseph V. '59 (PIT) [35] Pittsburgh, PA St. Raphael Church.
Kuruvila, Jose P. *o.i.c.* '86 (SB) Lake Elsinore, CA St. Frances of Rome Church.
Kurwicki, Robert A. '85 (JC) Westphalia, MO St. Joseph Church.
Kurylo, Michael '34 (STN) San Diego, CA Our Lady of Perpetual Help Church; Retired.
Kurylowicz, Martin '79 (GR) On Duty Outside the Diocese.
Kuryvial, George *o.m.i.* (GB) Egg Harbor, WI St. John the Baptist Church; Fish Creek, WI St. Paul Church; Jacksonport, WI St. Michael Church.
Kurz, Michael (RCK) [10] Rockford, IL St. Rita Church.
Kurz, Michael A. '75 (PBL) On Duty Outside the Diocese.
Kurz, William S. *s.j.* '70 (MIL) [P] Milwaukee, WI Jesuit Community at Marquette University.
Kurzaj, Franciszek '76 (SAT) [6] San Antonio, TX Holy Name Church.
Kurzak, John '75 (SC) On Duty Outside the Diocese.
Kurzawa, Ronald W. '64 (DET) [6] St. Clair Shores, MI St. Margaret of Scotland Church.
Kurzawski, Casimir J. '58 (WOR) Retired.
Kurzendoerfer, Mark A. '81 (EVN) [4] Vincennes, IN St. Thomas Church; Special Assignment; [A] Evansville, IN Mater Dei High School.
Kurzyna, Andrew E. '74 (NY) Verplanck, NY St. Patrick Church.
Kus, Sebastian *o.f.m.* (NEW) [O] Lodi, NJ Immaculate Conception Convent.
Kuse, Michael '67 (SFD) [7] Quincy, IL St. Mary Church.
Kusevich, Nicholas '69 (PSC) Fort Pierce, FL SS. Cyril and Methodius Church; Lake Worth, FL Holy Apostles Church.
Kusevich, Nicholas '69 (ROM) Special Assignment.
Kusi, David (CHI) [51] Chicago, IL St. Dorothy Church.
Kusibab, Justin *o.f.m.conv.* '87 (CHI) [N] Chicago, IL Conventual Franciscans of St. Bonaventure Province; [O] Chicago, IL Mother of Good Counsel Provincialate.
Kuska, George *o.s.b.* '39 (JOL) [J] Lisle, IL St. Procopius Abbey.
Kusmirek, Mark (TYL) [D] Kilgore, TX Kilgore Junior College Newman Center.
Kusmirek, Mark '77 (TYL) Kilgore, TX Christ the King Church.
Kuss, Allen R. '84 (BIS) On Duty Outside the Diocese.
Kustanto, Johannes B. Hari *s.j.* '91 (BGP) [O] Fairfield, CT The Fairfield Jesuit Community-Fairfield University.
Kustanto, Johannes B. Hari *s.j.* '91 (HRT) [5] New Haven, CT St. Boniface's Church.
Kusunoki, Peter *ss.cc.* '79 (FR) [J] Fairhaven, MA Sacred Hearts Provincial House.
Kusy, George *j.c.l.* '86 (CLV) [14] Cleveland, OH St. Casimir Church.
Kuta, Frank J. '53 (CLV) Rittman, OH St. Anne Church; Retired.
Kutch, Joseph P. '88 (SCR) Elkland, PA St. Thomas the Apostle Church.
Kutch, Peter P. *o.f.m.cap.* '66 (MIL) Mount Calvary, WI Holy Cross Church; St. Cloud, WI St. Cloud Church; St. Joe, WI St. Joseph Church.
Kutil, Dale '73 (RC) Fort Pierre, SD St. John Church; [D] Rapid City, SD Priest Retirement and Aid Association.
Kutiuk, Casimir '57 (GB) Retired.
Kutner, Msgr. Raymond W. '64 (BRK) [157] Queens, NY Blessed Sacrament Church.
Kutsch, Eugene C. '51 (DUB) [2] Dubuque, IA St. Anthony's Church.
Kutsche, Javier F. '81 (OAK) [8] Oakland, CA St. Cyril Church.
Kuttikattukunnel, Francis *s.v.d.* '88 (DUB) [B] Epworth, IA Divine Word College.
Kutulas, Nicholas *s.m.* '55 (FgM) Marist Foreign Missions.
Kutys, Daniel J. '80 (PH) [2] Drexel Hill, PA St. Bernadette Church.
Kutz, Lawrence A. '65 (WDC) [T] Washington, DC Opus Dei.
Kutz, Msgr. Ralph G. '37 (JC) Argyle, MO St. Aloysius Church.
Kutzner, Roger '91 (CHI) [184] Chicago, IL St. Richard Church.
Kuveikis, Rufin *o.f.m.cap.* '42 (BGP) Norwalk, CT Norwalk Hospital.
Kuveikis, Rufin *o.f.m.cap.* '48 (BGP) [14] Stamford, CT Sacred Heart Church.
Kuykendall, Andy '78 (WCH) Haysville, KS St. Cecilia Church.
Kuykendall, Henry '86 (EVN) [9] Evansville, IN Nativity Church.
Kuykendall, Thomas S. '94 (YAK) [3] Yakima, WA Holy Redeemer Church.
Kuzara, George *c.pp.s.* '78 (CIN) Fort Recovery, OH St. Peter Church; St. Joseph, OH St. Joseph Church.
Kuzdal, Anthony P. '56 (NOR) Retired.
Kuzhippallil, George '67 (PAT) Budd Lake, NJ St. Jude Church.

Kuzia, Anthony F. *c.m.* '76 (PRT) Lisbon Falls, ME Holy Trinity Church.
Kuziemski, Ignatius H. '60 (MET) Great Meadows, NJ SS. Peter and Paul Church.
Kuzilla, John A. '55 (E) Kersey, PA St. Boniface Church.
Kuzinskas, John A. '52 (CHI) [141] Chicago, IL Nativity of the Blessed Virgin Mary Church; Retired.
Kuzma, Mykhailo '81 (STN) [6] Palatine, IL Immaculate Conception Church.
Kuzmann, Robert J. '85 (ALN) [2] Mahanoy City, PA St. Canicus Church; [4] Mahanoy City, PA St. Fidelis Church; [C] Tamaqua, PA Marian Catholic High School.
Kuzmeski, Charles H. '75 (SPR) Ware, MA St. Mary's Church.
Kuzmich, John M. '65 (FTW) [19] Fort Wayne, IN St. Vincent de Paul Church.
Kuzniewski, Anthony J. *s.j.* '79 (WOR) [N] Worcester, MA Jesuits of Holy Cross College, Inc.
Kvedas, Leonard J. '61 (HRT) Beacon Falls, CT St. Michael's Church.
Kvedrovicz, Richard J. '72 (SCR) Hudson, PA St. Joseph's Church.
Kwak, John A. '51 (PEO) Hennepin, IL St. Patrick's Church.
Kwak, Thaddeus '59 (FTW) [15] South Bend, IN Our Lady of Hungary Church.
Kwapisz, Gregory *o.f.m.conv.* (BUF) [21] Buffalo, NY Corpus Christi Church.
Kwatera, Michael *o.s.b.* '77 (SCL) St. Martin, MN St. Martin's Church; [I] Collegeville, MN St. John's Abbey, of the Order of St. Benedict.
Kweder, Joseph J. '85 (ALN) Whitehall, PA St. Elizabeth Church.
Kwiatkowski, Augustyn (STA) [J] Bunnell, FL Discalced Carmelite Fathers of Florida.
Kwiatkowski, Constantine '47 (BUF) Salamanca, NY Holy Cross Church.
Kwiatkowski, Michael '78 (SPK) Colbert, WA St. Joseph Church.
Kwiatkowski, Paul M. '64 (TOL) [9] Toledo, OH Immaculate Conception Church; [25] Toledo, OH St. James Church.
Kwiatkowski, Richard P. '72 (NEW) Bloomfield, NJ Sacred Heart Church.
Kwiatkowski, Robert M. '83 (HRT) [6] Hamden, CT St. Rita's Church.
Kwiecen, Wojiech '78 (CHI) [63] Chicago, IL St. Francis of Assisi/Our Lady of the Angels Church.
Kwiecien, John S. '76 (BUF) Perrysburg, NY St. Joan of Arc Church; South Dayton, NY St. John Fisher Church.
Kwiecien, Michael *o.carm.* (PHX) [I] Phoenix, AZ Kino Institute.
Kwiecien, Michael *o.carm.* '80 (PHX) [6] Phoenix, AZ St. Agnes Church.
Kwoka, Edward '78 (SY) [14] Utica, NY St. Peter Church.
Kwolek, Joseph '45 (BUF) Retired; [P] Buffalo, NY Immaculate Heart of Mary Provincial House and Convent.
Ky, Joseph *s.s.* '59 (HON) [3] Honolulu, HI St. Anthony Church; Retired.
Ky, Joseph Cao *s.s.* '59 (HON) [H] Honolulu, HI Society of the Priests of St. Sulpice (Sulpicians) S.S.
Kyfes, Robert J. '77 (CHI) [31] Chicago, IL St. Bride Church.
Kyle, Eric *o.f.m.* '52 (NY) [Z] Staten Island, NY Carmel Richmond Nursing Home, Inc.
Kyle, John M. '36 (CHI) Streamwood, IL St. John the Evangelist Church; Retired.
Kyne, John J. '50 (SAC) Dixon, CA St. Peter Church; Retired and in Senior Ministry.
Kyranon, Emil *o.f.m.* '43 (LA) [72] Los Angeles, CA St. Joseph Church.
Kyrie, James *o.f.m.* (MRY) San Miguel, CA San Miguel Church.
Kyrie, James *o.f.m.* '57 (MRY) [G] San Miguel, CA Franciscan Friars, O.F.M.
Kyrpczak, James A. '96 (MET) Alpha, NJ St. Mary Church.
Kyte, Michael G. *o.p.* '87 (DEN) [29] Denver, CO St. Dominic's Parish; [A] Denver, CO St. Dominic Priory.

L

L'Arche, Jeffrey *m.s.* (ALB) [A] Altamont, NY La Salette Shrine and Seminary.
L'Heureux, Ernest L. '62 (PRT) Gorham, ME St. Anne Church; [M] Portland, ME University of Southern Maine.
L'Heureux, William D. '91 (OM) Hooper, NE St. Rose of Lima Church.
La Belle, Ralph '78 (NY) Manhattan, NY Columbia Presbyterian Medical Center.
La Belle, Ralph W. '78 (NY) Patterson, NY Sacred Heart Church.
La Brake, John R. *s.s.e.* '57 (MOB) Belle Fontaine, AL St. Philip Neri Church.
La Casa, Vicente Paz en '66 (PBL) [17] Pueblo, CO Shrine of St. Therese Church.
La France, Val *o.p.* '58 (NEW) [28] Jersey City, NJ Sacred Heart Church.
La Fratta, William E. '63 (RIC) Charlottesville, VA Church of the Incarnation.
La Mazza, Carmen G. *m.m.* '55 (NY) [DD] Maryknoll, NY Maryknoll Fathers and Brothers.
La Monte, Richard A. '66 (NY) [4] Poughkeepsie, NY St. John the Baptist Church.
La Pan, Kenneth *t.o.r.* '52 (ALT) [F] Newry, PA St. Bernardine Monastery.
La Paz, Gabriel '78 (NY) [53] New York, NY Incarnation Church.
La Plante, Philip *s.m.* '48 (BO) [BB] Boston, MA Our Lady of Good Voyage Chapel.
La Porta, Gerald '57 (BAL) Retired.
La Puebla, Enrique *m.s.* '80 (SB) Moreno Valley, CA St. Christopher Church.
La Rocca, Jack '88 (SJ) [5] San Jose, CA Five Wounds Portuguese National Church.
La Rocca, Vincent '49 (BRK) [131] Brooklyn, NY Sacred Hearts of Jesus and Mary and St. Stephen Church.
La Rosa, Stephen J. *o.s.a.* '65 (CAM) [C] Richland, NJ St. Augustine Preparatory School.
La Rosa-Lopez, Manuel '96 (GAL) Conroe, TX Sacred Heart Church.
La-Xuan-Thuong, Msgr. Philippe '70 (GAL) [1] Houston, TX Sacred Heart Co-Cathedral.
Lab, Robert J. *s.j.* '60 (CHI) [T] Barrington, IL Bellarmine Hall.
Laba, Gerald *c.p.* '73 (PIT) [O] Pittsburgh, PA St. Paul of the Cross Monastery.
LaBaff, Arthur J. '66 (OG) [4] Watertown, NY St. Patrick Church.
LaBaire, Steven M. '87 (WOR) Westborough, MA St. Luke the Evangelist Church.
Labaj, Stephen V. '36 (MIL) Retired.
Labak, Joseph L. '77 (CLV) Wadsworth, OH Sacred Heart Church.
Labaka, Jose Francisco *o.f.m.* '68 (SJN) [3] Carolina, PR Santa Clara de Asis Church.
Labarda, Nathaniel C. '93 (HRT) [5] New Britain, CT St. Ann Church.
LaBarge, Charles F. '46 (DUB) Retired.
LaBarge, Christopher '85 (WIL) Marydel, MD Immaculate Conception Church.
Labat, Dennis '74 (NU) Faxon Township, MN St. John-Assumption Church.
Labat, Dennis C. '74 (NU) Green Isle, MN St. Brendan Church; On Special or Other Diocesan Assignment.
LaBau, Anthony F. *s.j.* '46 (NY) [DD] New York, NY St. Ignatius Loyola Residence; [HH] New York, NY Jesuit Seminary and Mission Bureau, Inc.
Labauve, J. Joel '70 (BR) Angola, LA Louisiana State Penitentiary.
LaBauve, John *s.v.d.* '51 (BLX) [A] Bay St. Louis, MS St. Augustine's.
Labbe, Clifton *s.v.d.* '69 (FgM) Society of the Divine Word Foreign Missions.
Labbe, Clifton *s.v.d.* '96 (BLX) [E] Bay St. Louis, MS Southern Province of St. Augustine - Provincial Residence.
Labbe, Donovan J. '97 (LAF) Kaplan, LA Our Lady of the Holy Rosary Church.
Labbe, Emil J. *c.pp.s.* '68 (CIN) Maria Stein, OH St. John the Baptist Church.
Labbe, Joseph P. '75 (CLV) Chagrin Falls, OH Holy Angels Church.
Labedis, Anthony *o.f.m.conv.* '60 (CHI) [N] Chicago, IL Conventual Franciscans of St. Bonaventure Province.
Labedis, Anthony *o.f.m.conv.* '60 (FgM) Conventual Franciscan Foreign Missions.
Labella, Robert '54 (CLV) [2] Akron, OH St. Anthony of Padua Church.
LaBelle, Jeffrey *s.j.* '88 (SJ) [17] San Jose, CA Most Holy Trinity Church.
LaBelle, Patrick *o.p.* (OAK) [N] Oakland, CA Western Dominican Province.
LaBelle, Patrick *o.p.* '65 (SJ) Stanford, CA Catholic Community at Stanford Church.
Labieniec, Alphonse S. '61 (HRT) [7] West Hartford, CT St. Timothy's Church; Cheshire, CT Manson Youth Institution.
Labinski, Jacek '83 (TR) Hightstown, NJ St. Anthony of Padua Church.
Labinsky, Paul '81 (PHU) Manville, NJ St. Michael's Church; New Brunswick, NJ Nativity of B.V.M. Church.
Labita, Francis J. '49 (BRK) [211] Queens, NY Our Lady of Grace Church; Retired.
Labonte, L. Roger '66 (MET) Edison, NJ St. Helena Church.
Labonte, Richard H. '70 (WOR) Blackstone, MA St. Theresa Church.
Labonte, Roger '94 (LA) Van Nuys, CA St. Elisabeth Church.
LaBonte, Roger A. *m.afr.* '62 (FgM) Missionaries of Africa Foreign Missions.
Laboon, Joseph D. '57 (NO) New Orleans, LA Veterans Affairs Medical Center.
Laboon, Joseph D. '57 (PIT) Military Chaplains.
Labosky, James M. '79 (R) Wilson, NC Church of St. Therese.
LaBran, Joseph J. *s.j.* '47 (WOR) [N] Worcester, MA Jesuits of Holy Cross College, Inc.; [Q] Worcester, MA Campus Ministry.
LaBranche, Raymond (NEW) [R] Kearny, NJ Eucharistic Shrine of the Adorable Face of Jesus.
LaBranche, Raymond '94 (NEW) [A] Kearny, NJ Redemptoris Mater.
LaBrecque, Frederick '67 (CHR) Conway, SC St. James Church.
Labrie, Jean Paul '82 (PRT) Daigle, ME Holy Family Church; Fort Kent, ME St. Louis Church.
Labrie, Robert (BO) Boston, MA St. Elizabeth's Medical Center.
Labrosse, Paul E. *m.s.c.* '42 (OG) [2] Watertown, NY Our Lady of the Sacred Heart, Missionaries of the Sacred Heart Church; Retired.
Labrun, Raymond A. *o.m.i.* '68 (NO) [17] New Orleans, LA Our Lady of Guadalupe /International Shrine of St. Jude Church.
LaBuda, David E. *m.m.* '71 (FgM) Maryknoll Foreign Missions.
LaBurt, Brian '86 (SAV) Waynesboro, GA Sacred Heart Church.
LaCanne, Stephen J. '76 (STP) Wayzata, MN St. Bartholomew Church.
Lacasse, Aime F. *m.afr.* '38 (SP) [O] St. Petersburg, FL Missionaries of Africa.
Lacasse, Andre-Joseph *o.p.* '92 (Y) [13] Youngstown, OH St. Dominic's Church.
Lacasse, Eugene *o.c.s.o.* '54 (WOR) [N] Spencer, MA St. Joseph's Abbey.
LaCasse, John P. '74 (DET) Ida, MI St. Joseph Church.
Lacasse, Raymond *o.m.i.* '58 (FgM) Oblates Foreign Missions.
Lacasse, Roger '53 (PRO) Retired.
Lacasse, Roland *s.m.* '60 (BO) [3] Methuen, MA Our Lady of Mount Carmel Church.
LaCaze, Msgr. J. Carson '57 (SHP) [4] Shreveport, LA Our Lady of the Holy Rosary Church.
Lacchin, Mario *i.m.c.* '63 (MET) [H] Somerset, NJ Consolata Society for Foreign Missions.
Lacerna, Rodolfo '68 (ELP) [31] El Paso, TX St. Raphael Church.
LaCerra, Msgr. Gerard T. '69 (MIA) [33] Miami, FL St. Timothy Church; [B] Opa Locka, FL St. Thomas University.
LaCerte, Henri *o.s.b.* (P) [P] Portland, OR University of Portland.
Lacerte, Henry W. *o.s.b.* '59 (PBL) [F] Canon City, CO Holy Cross Abbey.
Lacey, Msgr. Francis A. *p.a.* '51 (SFR) Tiburon, CA St. Hilary Church.
Lacey, George F. '45 (STO) [7] Stockton, CA St. Luke Church; Retired.
Lacey, James (ALB) [L] Saratoga Springs, NY St. John Neumann Residence.
Lacey, Joseph P. *s.j.* '71 (WDC) [20] Washington, DC Holy Trinity Church.
Lacey, Mark W. '95 (ATL) [L] Atlanta, GA Campus Ministry.
Lacey, Michael *m.s.c.* '78 (OAK) [4] Alameda, CA St. Philip Neri Church.
Lacey, Thomas E. '43 (SFR) Redwood City, CA St. Matthias Church; Retired.
LaChance, Charles P. '74 (CHI) Other Assignments.
Lachance, Marcel G. '56 (NOR) Putnam, CT St. Mary Church.
Lachance, Paul (CHI) [N] Chicago, IL St. Peter's Friary.
Lachance, Pierre E. *o.p.* '42 (FR) [12] Fall River, MA St. Anne's Church; [J] Fall River, MA Dominican House.
LaChance, Roger '67 (B) Coeur D'Alene, ID St. Pius X Church; [F] Coeur D'Alene, ID North Idaho College.
Lachapelle, Alphonsus *s.o.cist.* '82 (ALN) [K] New Ringgold, PA Cistercian Conventual Priory, St. Mary's Priory.
LaChapelle, Hector O. *m.s.* '68 (BO) [Y] Ipswich, MA LaSalette Retreat House at Newman Hall.
LaChapelle, Hector O. *m.s.* '68 (NY) Phoenicia, NY St. Francis de Sales Church.
LaCharite, Roger J. *s.s.e.* '55 (MOB) [H] Selma, AL Edmundite Fathers.
LaCharite, Roger J. *s.s.e.* '55 (NOR) [A] Mystic, CT Edmundite Seminary Guild.
Lache, Rodolfo '81 (LA) Sun Valley, CA Our Lady of the Holy Rosary Church.
Lachendro, Vincent *o.f.m.conv.* '63 (BAL) [M] Ellicott City, MD Order of Friars Minor Conventual.
Lachendro, Vincent *o.f.m.conv.* '63 (FgM) Conventual Franciscan Foreign Missions.
Lachowicz, Francis B. '60 (PIT) [4] McKeesport, PA St. Mary Czestochowa Church.
Lachowitzer, Charles V. '90 (STP) Maplewood, MN Presentation of the Blessed Virgin Mary Church.
Lachowski, Joseph *c.m.* '54 (BRK) [134] Brooklyn, NY St. Stanislaus Kostka Church.
Lachowsky, Clement *c.s.sp.* '47 (SB) Hemet, CA Our Lady of the Valley Church.
Lacienski, Michael *o.f.m.* '43 (PIT) [O] Ben Avon, PA St. Anthony Friary and Mission House.

Lack, Christopher '90 (CIN) [68] Cincinnati, OH Our Lady of Lourdes Church.
Lackamp, Franklin J. '58 (KC) Retired.
Lackenmier, James R. *c.s.c.* '64 (SCR) [C] Wilkes-Barre, PA Kings College.
Lackie, Dan *o.f.m.* (SFR) [U] San Francisco, CA St. Anthony Foundation.
Lackner, Bede *o.cist.* '52 (DAL) [M] Irving, TX Cistercian Abbey of Our Lady of Dallas.
Lackner, Francis J.X. '44 (PIT) Retired.
Lackner, Joseph H. *s.m.* (CIN) [M] Dayton, OH Marianist Provincialate.
Lackner, Joseph H. *s.m.* '72 (CIN) [D] Dayton, OH The University of Dayton; [M] Dayton, OH Marianist Provincialate.
Lackner, Msgr. Paul M. '42 (PIT) Retired.
Lackovic, Msgr. Stephen F. '39 (BUF) [7] Lackawanna, NY Our Lady of Bistrica Church; Retired.
Lacomara, Aelred *c.p.* '57 (FgM) Passionist Foreign Missions.
LaCombe, C. Terrence (GB) Oconto, WI Holy Trinity Church.
Lacombe, Robert E. '91 (PRO) Smithfield, RI St. Philip Church.
LaCorte, Richard P. '87 (FAR) On Duty Outside the Diocese.
LaCosse, Norbert R. '52 (MAR) Retired.
LaCoste, James P. *m.m.* '56 (FgM) Maryknoll Foreign Missions.
LaCount, Daniel E. '89 (SFD) Auburn, IL St. Benedict Church; Divernon, IL Sacred Heart Church; Waverly, IL St. Sebastian Church.
Lacovic, Lawrence L. '69 (ALT) [6] Johnstown, PA St. Stephen, First King of Hungary Church.
Lacroix, Daniel W. '88 (FR) Mansfield, MA St. Mary's Church.
Lacroix, Maurice R. '53 (MAN) [2] Berlin, NH St. Joseph Church.
LaCroix, Wilfred L. *s.j.* '69 (KC) [B] Kansas City, MO Rockhurst College; [J] Kansas City, MO Rockhurst College - Jesuit Community.
LaCrosse, James *s.m.* '67 (WH) [11] Wheeling, WV St. Vincent de Paul's Church.
Lacruz, Alfredo Alvarez '86 (PCE) [A] Ponce, PR Diocesan Seminary; [B] Ponce, PR The Pontifical Catholic University of Puerto Rico.
Lacruz, Cecilio *sch.p.* '59 (SJN) [58] San Juan, PR Santisimo Salvador Church.
Lacson, Tony '86 (RVC) Levittown, NY St. Bernard Church.
Lacy, Aidan '93 (PMB) [4] Delray Beach, FL St. Vincent Ferrer Church.
Laczko, T. Ansgar '60 (WDC) [6] Washington, DC Assumption Church.
Ladd, John O. '79 (GAY) Prudenville, MI Our Lady of the Lake Church.
Ladden, Timothy M. '53 (OG) [2] Watertown, NY Our Lady of the Sacred Heart, Missionaries of the Sacred Heart Church; Retired.
Ladewski, Roman *c.s.c.* (FTW) [J] Notre Dame, IN Congregation of Holy Cross, Midwest Province.
Ladewski, Roman S. *c.s.c.* '45 (FTW) [J] South Bend, IN Congregation of Holy Cross Indiana Province Provincial House.
Ladish, Robert W. '53 (HRT) [1] Torrington, CT St. Francis of Assisi Church; [3] Torrington, CT St. Mary's Church.
Ladkau, William D. '84 (CHR) [6] Columbia, SC Good Shepherd Church.
Ladra, Jose '82 (NO) Terrytown, LA Christ the King Church.
Ladzinski, Msgr. Casimir H. '62 (TR) Jackson, NJ St. Aloysius Gonzaga Church.
Laenen, Henry *o.m.i.* '52 (SAN) Ozona, TX Our Lady of Perpetual Help Church.
Laenen, Joseph C. *o.praem.* '51 (PH) [U] Darby, PA Mercy Catholic Medical Center; [AA] Paoli, PA Daylesford Abbey.
Laesch, Dennis C. '96 (DET) Rochester, MI St. Andrew Church.
LaFache, Anthony '68 (SY) [6] Utica, NY St. Anthony of Padua Church.
LaFavia, Louis M. *c.pp.s.* '47 (WDC) [C] Washington, DC Catholic University of America, The.
LaFay, Michael *o.carm.* '60 (FgM) Carmelite Foreign Missions.
LaFay, Michael *o.carm.* '60 (JOL) [J] Darien, IL Carmelite Provincial Office.
LaFemina, Msgr. Anthony A. '61 (VEN) Absent on Sick Leave.
Laferrera, John J. '73 (NEW) Caldwell, NJ St. Aloysius Church.
Laferrera, Robert G. '88 (NEW) [11] Jersey City, NJ Holy Rosary Church.
Laferriere, Raymond '60 (MAN) [3] Manchester, NH St. Anthony of Padua Church.
Laferty, Charles P. *o.s.a.* '53 (PH) [C] Villanova, PA Villanova University; [AA] Villanova, PA St. Thomas Monastery.
Lafey, Kevin *o.carm.* '72 (FgM) Carmelite Foreign Missions.
Lafey, Kevin *o.carm.* '72 (JOL) [J] Darien, IL Carmelite Provincial Office.
Lafferty, Charles L. '55 (BAL) [41] Baltimore, MD Immaculate Conception Church.
Lafferty, David '85 (OKL) Special Assignment; [I] Oklahoma City, OK House of Prayer for Priests.
Lafferty, David M. '85 (OKL) Chandler, OK Our Lady of Sorrows Church.
Lafferty, Msgr. James K. '54 (SC) Arcadia, IA St. John the Baptist Church.
Lafferty, Msgr. John J. (ALT) Retired.
Lafferty, Owen (NY) Manhattan, NY Mount Sinai Medical Center.
Lafferty, Owen J. '66 (NY) [1] Mt. Vernon, NY Sacred Heart Church.
LaFlamme, Julien J. '58 (BUR) Manchester Center, VT Conversion of St. Paul Church.
LaFleur, Alfred *o.s.a.* '44 (FWT) Hillsboro, TX Our Lady of Mercy Church.
LaFleur, Angelus *o.f.m.conv.* '35 (STL) [P] St. Louis, MO St. Bonaventure Friary (Province of Our Lady of Consolation).
LaFleur, Gerard A. '53 (SPR) [1] Chicopee, MA Assumption Church.
LaFleur, Paul J. '85 (LAF) Carencro, LA Our Lady of the Assumption Church.
Lafond, Donald E. (MAN) [4] Concord, NH Immaculate Heart of Mary Church.
LaFontaine, James F. *s.j.* '77 (WDC) [M] Washington, DC Leonard Neale House.
Lafontaine, James F. *s.j.* '87 (BO) [W] Boston, MA The Society of Jesus of New England-Provincial Offices.
LaFontaine, Paul A. '72 (STP) [19] St. Paul, MN St. Columba Church.
LaForest, Conrad V. '72 (MAN) Absent on Sick Leave.
LaForge, Joseph M. (TR) On Duty Outside the Diocese.
Laforge, Joseph M. '66 (WIL) Ogletown, DE Holy Family Church.
LaForge, Paul *s.v.d.* '58 (FgM) Society of the Divine Word Foreign Missions.
LaFosse, William D. *m.s.* '68 (SPR) [4] Holyoke, MA Immaculate Conception Church.
Laframboise, Ronald *o.m.i.* '67 (FgM) Oblates Foreign Missions.
Lafrenz, James '54 (ELP) Retired.
Lafrenz, James '54 (LSC) Retired.
Lagan, Hugh F. '54 (SP) Plant City, FL St. Clement Church.
Lagana, Frank A. (GAL) [N] Houston, TX Pope John XXIII Priest Residence.
Lagana, Msgr. Frank A. '39 (GAL) Retired; [U] Houston, TX St. Mary's Orphanage Board.
Lagasse, C. Brian '93 (PRO) [1] North Providence, RI St. Anthony Church.
Lagasse, Ronald J. (OAK) Military Chaplains.
Lager, John *o.f.m.cap.* '79 (DEN) [M] Denver, CO St. Francis of Assisi Friary.
Lagges, Patrick R. (CHI) [153] Chicago, IL Our Lady of Mercy Church.
Lagiovane, John M. '92 (NY) Pearl River, NY St. Aedan Church.
Laglera, Antonio '53 (ARE) [11] Arecibo, PR Church of San Martin de Porres.
Lago, Danilo *s.x.* '77 (FgM) Xaverian Foreign Missions.
Lago, Danilo *s.x.* '77 (PAT) [M] Wayne, NJ Xaverian Missionary Fathers.
Lagoa, Raul M. '79 (FR) Somerset, MA St. John of God Church.
Lagodinski, Dale '72 (FAR) Wahpeton, ND St. John's Church; Wahpeton, ND Newman Student Parish; [H] Wahpeton, ND State College of Science Newman Student Parish.
Lagomarsino, John *s.s.c.* '70 (SAC) Carmichael, CA St. John the Evangelist Church.
Lagomarsino, Vincent J. *s.j.* '56 (WH) [A] Wheeling, WV Wheeling Jesuit University.
Lagonegro, Msgr. Dominick J. '69 (NY) Hopewell Junction, NY St. Columba Church.
Lagor, Joseph '54 (BUR) [D] Rutland, VT Loretto Home for Aged.
Lagor, Joseph J. '54 (BUR) Retired.
Lagos, Benito M. *i.v.e.* '93 (FR) [17] New Bedford, MA St. Kilian Church; [P] New Bedford, MA The Institute of the Incarnate Word, Inc.
LaGuerre, Jean Gerard '95 (RVC) Brentwood, NY St. Anne's Church.
Lagueux, Maurice R. '61 (MAN) Absent on Sick Leave.
Laguna-Vargas, Enrique *o.carm.* '90 (JOL) [J] Darien, IL Carmelite Provincial Office.
Lahart, Daniel K. *s.j.* '94 (WDC) [E] Washington, DC Gonzaga College High School.
LaHart, Msgr. Richard T. '52 (PH) Lafayette Hill, PA St. Philip Neri Church.
Lahens, Alberto '95 (MIA) [1] Hialeah, FL Immaculate Conception Church.
Laheta, Andrew P. '43 (CLV) [55] Cleveland, OH Our Lady of Mercy Church; Retired.
Lahey, John '67 (SAL) Gypsum, KS St. Patrick's Church; Solomon, KS Immaculate Conception Church.
Lahey, John F. *c.s.c.* '70 (FTW) [A] Notre Dame, IN Moreau Seminary.
Lahey, Msgr. Maurice '50 (FRS) Retired.
Lahey, Piers M. '82 (SFR) Pacifica, CA Good Shepherd Church; Novato, CA Serra Club of Marin.
Lahiff, Bartholomew P. *s.j.* '55 (FgM) Provinces.
Lahoud, Joseph F. '59 (BO) [54] Boston, MA Our Lady of The Cedars of Lebanon Church.
Lahoud, Msgr. Joseph F. '59 (SAM) Jamaica Plain, MA Our Lady of the Cedars of Lebanon Church.
Lahout, Francis M. (HBG) [5] Harrisburg, PA Holy Name of Jesus Church.
Lahrs, Carey *s.d.s.* '72 (SAV) [A] Columbus, GA Pacelli Catholic High School.
Lai, Doan Van '73 (SD) [7] San Diego, CA Holy Spirit Church.
Laible, Jeffrey G. '88 (PEO) Rantoul, IL St. Malachy's Church.
Laicha, Michael M. '89 (HBG) [7] Harrisburg, PA St. Margaret Mary Alacoque Church.
Lainesca, Joseph '81 (RVC) Elmont, NY St. Boniface Church.
Laini, Valerian '69 (CHI) Evanston, IL St. Mary Church.
Lair, Gerald P. *o.s.b.* '60 (PAT) [M] Morristown, NJ St. Mary's Abbey.
Laird, Kenneth W. '75 (BR) Zachary, LA St. John the Baptist Church.
Laird, Martin S. *o.s.a.* '91 (CHI) [N] Olympia Fields, IL The Augustinian Provincialate Tolentine Center.
Laird, Peter A. '97 (STP) [31] Minneapolis, MN St. Olaf Church.
Laird, William F. '75 (ROC) Churchville, NY St. Vincent De Paul Church.
Laiton, Rafael '91 (MIL) [7] Milwaukee, WI St. Anthony Church.
Lajack, Edward F. '68 (CLV) [2] Barberton, OH SS. Cyril and Methodius Church.
Lajack, Jerome M. '66 (CLV) [77] Cleveland, OH St. Wendelin Church.
Lajo, Saturnino *o.m.i.* '63 (SAT) [T] San Antonio, TX Oblate Missions.
Lajoie, David *s.m.* '48 (PRT) Van Buren, ME St. Bruno - St. Remi Church.
Lajoie, Marcel *s.m.* '56 (PRT) Van Buren, ME St. Bruno - St. Remi Church.
Lajoie, Roland L. '88 (WOR) Warren, MA St. Paul's Church; West Warren, MA St. Thomas Aquinas Church.
Lajoie, Ronald A. *s.m.* '74 (BO) [10] Cambridge, MA Our Lady of Pity Church.
Lakers, John J. *o.f.m.* '58 (SFD) [B] Quincy, IL Quincy University.
Lal, Tej *i.m.s.* '68 (TYL) Crockett, TX St. Francis of the Tejas Church.
Laliberte, George G. '56 (HRT) Woodbury, CT St. Teresa's Church.
Laliberte, Robert L. '73 (FAR) Special Assignment; [A] Fargo, ND Cardinal Muench Seminary.
Laliberte, Stephen *o.f.m.cap.* '80 (PAT) [M] Oak Ridge-Milton, NJ St. Stanislaus B. M. Friary.
Laliberte, William F. '43 (BUR) Retired.
Lalic, Paul B. '58 (BGP) [10] Stamford, CT St. Mary's Church; [J] Stamford, CT St. Camillus Health Center.
Lalli, Tony *s.x.* '66 (BO) [W] Holliston, MA Xaverian Missionaries; [BB] Holliston, MA Our Lady of Fatima Shrine.
Lally, Brendan G. *s.j.* (SCR) [E] Scranton, PA Scranton Preparatory School.
Lally, Brendan G. *s.j.* '77 (SCR) [C] Scranton, PA University of Scranton.
Lally, Campion *o.f.m.* '53 (FgM) Franciscan Foreign Missions.
Lally, Msgr. Dennis '65 (GB) Lebanon Township, WI St. Patrick Church.
Lally, Edward J. (PAT) Permanent Deacons.
Lally, Joachim *c.s.p.* '65 (NY) [DD] Jamaica Estates, NY Paulist Fathers Generalate.
Lally, Martin '78 (DEN) Northglenn, CO Immaculate Heart of Mary Church.
Lally, Owen *c.p.* '59 (BRK) [U] Jamaica, NY Immaculate Conception Monastery.
Lally, Owen *c.p.* '59 (NY) [HH] Chelsea, NY The Fellowship of the Beloved Disciple.
LaLonde, Emile G. '41 (OG) Retired.
Lalonde, Venant *o.f.m.* '54 (NY) [DD] New York, NY Franciscan Friars, Order of Friars Minor, Holy Name Province.
Lalor, Thomas '66 (JKS) [4] Jackson, MS St. Therese Church.
Lam, John *s.d.b.* '71 (SFR) [45] San Francisco, CA SS. Peter and Paul Church.
Lama, Michael '84 (SB) Banning, CA Precious Blood Church.
Lamanna, Alfred '49 (ALB) Retired.
Lamanna, Thomas *s.j.* '97 (SPK) [E] Spokane, WA Gonzaga Preparatory School.
Lamantia, A. Robert '48 (TOL) Retired.
LaMar, Joseph P. *m.m.* '83 (NY) [DD] Maryknoll, NY Maryknoll Fathers and Brothers.
LaMarre, Theodore E. '45 (SAG) Retired.
LaMartina, Liborio J. *s.j.* '67 (BAL) [M] Baltimore, MD

Jesuit Fathers and Brothers Maryland Provincial Curia.
Lamas, Rodolfo '80 (SJN) [7] Guaynabo, PR Divino Nino Jesus Church.
Lamaute, Serges *s.d.b.* '50 (NO) [D] Marrero, LA Archbishop Shaw High School.
Lamb, Bruce '89 (SR) [1] Santa Rosa, CA Cathedral of St. Eugene.
Lamb, Gary E. '83 (MEM) Military Chaplains.
Lamb, Louis J. '61 (OKL) [13] Oklahoma City, OK St. Joseph Church.
Lamb, Matthew L. '62 (MIL) On Duty Outside the Archdiocese.
Lamb, Patrick H. *o.f.m.* '83 (ALN) [C] Reading, PA Reading Central Catholic High School (Monsignor Bornemann Memorial); [L] Reading, PA Sacred Heart Convent.
Lamb, Paul T. '96 (FR) Hyannis, MA St. Francis Xavier's Church.
Lamb, Thomas J. '71 (NEW) [M] South Orange, NJ Opus Dei.
Lamb, Weston J. *o.ss.t.* '81 (BAL) [M] Baltimore, MD Holy Trinity Monastery.
Lambe, Jeremiah F. *c.s.sp.* '52 (STA) [1] St. Augustine, FL Cathedral of St. Augustine Church.
Lambe, William '84 (VIC) Yoakum, TX St. Joseph Church.
Lambeck, Robert W. *s.j.* '49 (MIL) [P] Milwaukee, WI Jesuit Community at Marquette University.
Lambert, Andre *o.f.m.conv.* '57 (ALB) Fonda, NY St. Cecilia Church.
Lambert, Cornelius F. '83 (CAM) Blackwood, NJ St. Agnes Church.
Lambert, Curtis '74 (CHI) [151] Chicago, IL Our Lady of Lourdes Church.
Lambert, James J. '80 (PT) Panama City, FL St. Dominic Church.
Lambert, James L. *s.j.* '66 (SAT) [17] San Antonio, TX Our Lady of Guadalupe Church.
Lambert, John C. '69 (BWN) Retired.
Lambert, John C. '84 (SCR) Dallas, PA Gate of Heaven Church.
Lambert, Joseph J. '43 (PRO) Retired; [P] Providence, RI St. John Vianney Residence.
Lambert, Leo M. '45 (MIL) Retired.
Lambert, Louis J. *s.j.* '66 (ELP) [21] El Paso, TX Sacred Heart Church.
Lambert, Peter '72 (MIA) [5] Fort Lauderdale, FL St. Clement Church.
Lambert, Peter '79 (DUL) Military Chaplains.
Lambert, Raymond P. (BO) Retired.
Lambert, Richard '75 (PBR) [4] Pittsburgh, PA St. John Chrysostom Church.
Lambert, Richard D. '80 (CR) Mahnomen, MN St. Michael's Church.
Lambert, Richard T. *s.j.* '67 (FgM) Provinces.
Lambert, Rollins E. '49 (CHI) Retired.
Lambert, Theodore '76 (STO) Manteca, CA St. Anthony Church; Stockton, CA Karl Holton School.
Lambert, Timothy J. '92 (MET) [1] New Brunswick, NJ St. Peter Apostle Church.
Lambert, William '55 (RC) Retired.
Lamberty, Darrell V. '79 (SFS) Pierre, SD SS. Peter and Paul Church.
Lamberty, Philip J. *o.p.* '59 (STL) [P] St. Louis, MO St. Dominic Priory.
Lambertz, Wilfrid *o.s.b.* '58 (SFS) [F] Marvin, SD Blue Cloud Abbey.
Lambeth, K. Michael '94 (TR) Spring Lake, NJ St. Catharine Church.
Lambing, Gregory *o.c.s.o.* '59 (L) [L] Trappist, KY Abbey of Our Lady of Gethsemani, of the Order of Cistercians of the Strict Observance.
Lambino, Antonio *s.j.* '69 (SFR) [41] San Francisco, CA St. Patrick Church.
Lambino, Miguel B. *s.j.* '93 (NY) [DD] New York, NY Jesuit Community at Fordham University.
Lambour, Stephen *c.s.c.* (ORL) Retired.
Lambous, Stephen *c.s.c.* '55 (ORL) [F] Cocoa Beach, FL Holy Cross Fathers, Eastern Priests Province.
Lambro, Edward '74 (PAT) Unassigned.
Lamby, Robert J. *s.s.c.* '57 (CLV) Mentor, OH St. Mary of the Assumption Church.
Lamela, Juan *c.m.* '62 (MGZ) [8] Mayaquez, PR San Vicente Church.
Lamela, Juan *c.m.* '62 (PCE) [B] Ponce, PR The Pontifical Catholic University of Puerto Rico.
Lamendola, Francis S. '36 (NO) Retired.
Lamendola, Salvatore '90 (GBG) [3] Greensburg, PA Our Lady of Grace Church.
LaMer, Cletus (GB) Kiel, WI SS. Peter and Paul Church.
Lamica, Alan J. '78 (OG) Keene, NY St. Brendan Church.
Lamitie, James F. '53 (OG) Retired.
Lamitie, Robert O. '57 (OG) Malone, NY Barehill Correctional Facility.
Lamm, Timothy *o.s.b.* '56 (SD) [C] San Diego, CA St. Augustine High School.
Lamm, Timothy J. *o.s.b.* '54 (SEA) [M] Lacey, WA St. Martin's Abbey.
Lamm, William F. *s.j.* '57 (BAL) [M] Baltimore, MD Jesuit Fathers and Brothers Maryland Provincial Curia.
Lammeier, Francis G. '55 (CIN) [13] Cincinnati, OH Assumption Church.
Lammers, Donald W. '72 (JC) [2] Jefferson City, MO St. Peter Church.
Lammers, Ralph A. '63 (OM) Schuyler, NE St. Mary Church.
Lammert, Edward H. *o.f.m.* '58 (LEX) Cumberland, KY St. Stephen Church; Harlan, KY Holy Trinity Church; Lynch, KY Church of the Resurrection.
LaMoine, Gary W. '81 (CR) Red Lake Falls, MN St. Joseph's Church.
Lamonde, Joseph R. '74 (PIT) Military Chaplains.
LaMontagne, Bernard L. '63 (PRO) On Duty Outside the Diocese.
Lamore, Victor E. '80 (OG) West Leyden, NY St. Mary's Nativity Church.
LaMorte, Joseph P. '81 (NY) [3] Poughkeepsie, NY Holy Trinity Church.
LaMorte, Richard A. '66 (NY) [7] Poughkeepsie, NY Our Lady of Mt. Carmel Church.
Lamothe, C. Romero '48 (WOR) Retired.
Lamothe, Daniel O. '62 (MAN) Dover, NH St. Joseph Church.
Lamothe, Donat R. *a.a.* '62 (WOR) [N] Worcester, MA Assumptionists of Assumption College.
Lamothe, Philip R. '55 (BUR) Bradford, VT Our Lady of Perpetual Help Church.
LaMotte, Victor S. *o.p.* '56 (CHI) [N] River Forest, IL St. Thomas Aquinas Priory.
LaMountain, Michael V. '76 (PRO) Absent on Leave.
Lamoureaux, Richard L. *a.a.* '71 (WOR) [N] Worcester, MA Assumptionists of Assumption College.
Lamoureux, Roger '62 (SR) [2] Santa Rosa, CA Holy Spirit Church.
Lamoureux, Roger E. *o.m.i.* '83 (BO) [4] Lowell, MA Saint Jeanne d'Arc Church.
Lamoureux, Roger J. *o.m.i.* '59 (NOR) Willimantic, CT St. Mary Church.
Lamp, Edward '82 (SP) [15] Tampa, FL St. Peter Claver Church.
Lampe, Msgr. Irvin F. '43 (WCH) Retired.
Lampe, Stephen J. '82 (MIL) [80] Milwaukee, WI St. Vincent de Paul Church; [A] Milwaukee, WI St. Francis Seminary.
Lampert, Robert E. '65 (SAT) [C] San Antonio, TX Oblate School of Theology.
Lampert, Robert E. '65 (STL) On Duty Outside the Archdiocese.
Lampert, Vincent P. '91 (IND) Danville, IN Mary Queen of Peace Church.
Lamping, Thomas E. '84 (CHI) [180] Chicago, IL Queen of Angels Church.
Lamprich, Mark *m.i.c.* '90 (CHL) [1] Greensboro, NC Our Lady of Grace Church.
Lampron, Alfred J. '75 (PAT) Pequannock, NJ Holy Spirit Church.
Lampron, Maurice W. '63 (MAN) Retired.
Lamy, Raymond J. '81 (MAN) Military Chaplains.
Lamy, Robert E. *c.m.* '51 (NO) [P] New Orleans, LA Vincentian Fathers.
Lamy, Roland (MIA) [10] Miami, FL Notre Dame d'Haiti Church.
Lan Tran, Anthony '70 (SEA) Federal Way, WA St. Vincent De Paul Church.
Lanahan, Daniel *o.f.m.* '62 (NEW) [N] Hohokus, NJ St. Anthony of Padua.
Lanahan, William F. '55 (BRK) Released from Diocesan Assignment.
Lancaster, Leo '54 (WOR) Shrewsbury, MA St. Mary's Church.
Lancellotti, Vincent A. '68 (NY) Elmsford, NY Our Lady of Mt. Carmel Church.
Landa, Salvador '94 (ORG) [7] Santa Ana, CA St. Barbara's Church.
Landauer, Joseph '78 (PIT) [N] Pittsburgh, PA Opus Dei.
Landcraff, Thomas A. *o.s.f.s.* (TOL) [37] Toledo, OH St. Pius X Church.
Landewe, Robert A. '59 (SPC) Salem, MO Sacred Heart Church.
Landeza, Jayson J. '87 (OAK) [4] Fremont, CA St. Joseph Mission Church.
Landherr, Clayton R. '91 (DUB) [6] Dubuque, IA Church of the Resurrection.
Landi, Msgr. Andrew P. '34 (BRK) Retired.
Landi, Msgr. Andrew P. '34 (NY) [97] New York, NY Our Lady of the Scapular/St. Stephen Church.
Landi, L. Joseph (SFR) [U] San Francisco, CA Charismatic Movement.
Landi, Lodovico Joseph '90 (SFR) [10] San Francisco, CA St. Cecilia Church.
Landini, Lawrence *o.f.m.* '61 (FgM) Franciscan Foreign Missions.
Lando, Camillo *c.s.* (BO) [1] Everett, MA St. Anthony Church.
Landoll, Msgr. Gilbert J. '50 (SAL) Retired.
Landrau, Jose Antonio '90 (SJN) [34] San Juan, PR San Luis Gonzaga Church.
Landreau, Edward J. '57 (LA) Azusa, CA St. Frances of Rome Church.
Landreville, Norbert B. '58 (MAR) Ironwood, MI Our Lady of Peace Church.
Landry, Alduce '80 (HT) Permanent Deacons.
Landry, Alfred R. '32 (NOR) Retired.
Landry, Charles *c.ss.r.* '83 (BR) [16] Baton Rouge, LA Our Lady of Mercy Church.
Landry, Clyde B. '73 (BR) On Duty Outside the Diocese.
Landry, David J. '87 (FR) [2] Taunton, MA Our Lady of the Immaculate Conception Church.
Landry, Francis *c.p.* '76 (WOR) [N] Shrewsbury, MA Passionist Fathers of Shrewsbury, Inc., Calvary Retreat Center; [P] Shrewsbury, MA Calvary Retreat Center, Passionist Community.
Landry, Gary *c.m.* '73 (LA) [A] Camarillo, CA St. John's Seminary College of the Archdiocese of Los Angeles.
Landry, George *s.m.a.* '54 (NEW) [N] Tenafly, NJ Society of African Missions, Provincialate, S.M.A. Fathers.
Landry, George A. '43 (HT) Retired.
Landry, Ken Ramon '87 (BLX) Waynesboro, MS St. Bernadette Church.
Landry, Laval L. *m.s.* '25 (STL) [P] St. Louis, MO La Salette Missionaries.
Landry, Leroy *o.m.i.* '61 (FgM) Oblates Foreign Missions.
Landry, Maurice A. *s.m.m.* '41 (RVC) [N] Bay Shore, NY Montfort Missionaries.
Landry, Msgr. Michael '48 (NO) Retired.
Landry, Oneil A. '47 (LAF) Centerville, LA St. Joseph Church.
Landry, Philip '88 (NO) La Place, LA St. Joan of Arc Church.
Landry, Ralph J. '62 (LAF) Washington, LA Immaculate Conception Church.
Landry, Richard *m.s.* '69 (FR) [J] Attleboro, MA La Salette Shrine; [L] Attleboro, MA La Salette Center for Christian Living.
Landry, Thomas (WOR) [3] Worcester, MA Blessed Sacrament Church; Worcester, MA Memorial Hospital.
Landsberger, Nicholas '61 (SCL) Little Falls, MN St. Mary Church.
Landsberger, Robert '57 (SCL) Motley, MN St. Michael's Church.
Landwerlen, Paul '54 (IND) St. Vincent de Paul, IN St. Vincent de Paul Church.
Landwermeyer, Bart J. '56 (FWT) Megargel, TX St. Mary Church; Seymour, TX Sacred Heart Church.
Landwermeyer, Francis M. *s.j.* '66 (SAT) [31] San Antonio, TX St. Brigid Church.
Landy, Joseph V. *s.j.* '54 (NY) [DD] New York, NY Murray-Weigel Hall.
Lane, Brian '89 (RC) Winner, SD Immaculate Conception Church.
Lane, C. Vincent '61 (SY) Vestal, NY St. Vincent de Paul Church.
Lane, Edmund C. *s.s.p.* '64 (NY) [B] New York, NY Society of St. Paul.
Lane, Msgr. Frank P. '67 (COL) Dublin, OH St. Brigid of Kildare Church.
Lane, George A. *s.j.* '67 (CHI) [N] Chicago, IL Chicago Province of the Society of Jesus-Provincial Office; [X] Chicago, IL Loyola Press.
Lane, James H. '62 (BO) [12] Boston, MA St. Augustine Church.
Lane, John H. *s.j.* '38 (CHI) [D] Chicago, IL St. Ignatius Jesuit Community.
Lane, John Thomas *s.s.s.* '92 (CLV) [B] Cleveland, OH Blessed Sacrament Seminary, Congregation of the Blessed Sacrament; [P] Cleveland, OH Blessed Sacrament Community.
Lane, Mark '74 (RIC) Special Assignment.
Lane, Mark *c.o.* '83 (BRK) [22] Brooklyn, NY St. Boniface Church.
Lane, Mark J. *c.o.* '83 (BRK) [U] Brooklyn, NY Oratory of Saint Philip Neri, Congregation Pontifical Rite.
Lane, Michael '74 (JOL) Elmhurst, IL Visitation Church.
Lane, Robert C. '69 (STL) St. Peters, MO All Saints Church.
Lane, Thomas V. '64 (YAK) Goldendale, WA Holy Trinity Church.
Lane, Timothy R. *c.j.* '95 (LA) [3] Santa Barbara, CA Our Lady of Guadalupe Church.
Lane, Msgr. William '46 (MRY) Retired.
Lane, William '50 (SEA) Retired.
Lanergan, James F. (BO) Bridgewater, MA Bridgewater State Hospital & Treatment Center.
Lanergan, James F. '61 (BO) [3] Plymouth, MA St. Mary Church.
Lanese, John R. '73 (ALB) Clifton Park, NY St. Edward the Confessor Church.
Lanese, Pasquale *o.m.i.* '53 (BWN) [1] Brownsville, TX Immaculate Conception Cathedral.
Lang, B. Benedict *o.s.b.* '53 (PRO) [P] Portsmouth, RI Abbey of St. Gregory the Great.
Lang, Charles E. '65 (DUB) Anamosa, IA St. Patrick's Church; Belle Plaine, IA St. Michael Church; [2]

Cedar Rapids, IA All Saints Church; Chelsea, IA St. Joseph's Church.
Lang, Charles F. '75 (CIN) Fryburg, OH St. John Church; Glynwood, OH St. Patrick Church.
Lang, Msgr. Cordell J. '79 (MOB) [12] Mobile, AL St. Mary Church.
Lang, Henry A. '46 (BRK) Retired.
Lang, Hugh J. '56 (PIT) [5] Munhall, PA St. Theresa of Lisieux Church.
Lang, James P. '75 (SY) [V] Syracuse, NY Syracuse University, St. Thomas More Foundation, Inc.
Lang, James Paul '75 (SY) Special Assignment.
Lang, James Paul '75 (Y) Windham, OH St. Michael's Church.
Lang, Joseph J. '65 (CLV) Released from Diocesan Assignment.
Lang, Joseph R. *m.m.* '52 (NY) [DD] Maryknoll, NY Maryknoll Fathers and Brothers.
Lang, Jovian *o.f.m* '46 (FWT) [H] Crowley, TX St. Maximilian Kolbe Friary.
Lang, Julius '42 (FAR) Retired.
Lang, Julius '42 (VEN) [1] Naples, FL St. Ann Church.
Lang, Leonard P. '75 (TR) Asbury Park, NJ Holy Spirit Church.
Lang, Michael E. '92 (TR) [B] Trenton, NJ Notre Dame High School.
Lang, Michael P. '92 (TR) [21] Trenton, NJ St. Raphael Church.
Lang, Raymond '43 (SCL) Retired.
Langan, James J. '57 (SCR) Retired.
Langan, John P. *s.j.* (DET) [K] Detroit, MI Jesuit Provincial Office-Detroit Province of the Society of Jesus.
Langan, John P. *s.j.* '72 (WDC) [M] Washington, DC The Jesuit Community at Georgetown University; [V] Washington, DC Woodstock Theological Center.
Langan, Patrick *l.c.* '91 (HRT) [V] Orange, CT Legion of Christ, Inc.
Langan, Thomas F. '59 (HBG) Abbottstown, PA Immaculate Heart of Mary Church.
Langan, Vincent F. '60 (SCR) South Waverly, PA St. John the Evangelist Church.
Langan, William J.P. '77 (SCR) Friendsville, PA St. Francis Xavier's Church.
Langdon, Robert H. '56 (NEW) Fort Lee, NJ Madonna Church.
Lange, Donald F. '70 (MAD) Sinsinawa, WI St. Joseph Church.
Lange, George O. '57 (WOR) Westborough, MA St. Luke the Evangelist Church.
Lange, John J. *m.m.* '58 (FgM) Maryknoll Foreign Missions.
Lange, John W. *s.j.* '61 (SCR) [C] Scranton, PA University of Scranton.
Lange, Joseph '59 (PRT) Mexico, ME St. Theresa Church.
Lange, Lawrence P. '63 (TLS) Retired.
Lange, Matthew '38 (FTW) Retired.
Lange, Maurice *o.m.i.* '90 (GAL) [S] Dickinson, TX Christian Renewal Center.
Lange, Michael *o.f.m.* '46 (SUP) Odanah, WI St. Mary Church.
Lange, Raymond L. '50 (WOR) Retired.
Lange, Robert A. '86 (ARL) Culpeper, VA Precious Blood Church.
Lange, Ronald *s.v.d.* '71 (FgM) Society of the Divine Word Foreign Missions.
Lange, Timothy J. '61 (OM) Stanton, NE St. Peter Church.
Lange, William S. '92 (PH) [12] Philadelphia, PA Annunciation B.V.M. Church; Highland Park, PA St. Laurence Church.
Langelier, Msgr. Gerald J. '61 (BRK) [214] Queens, NY Our Lady of Mercy Church.
Langell, Michael '68 (SAV) Swainsboro, GA Holy Trinity Church.
Langenbrunner, Norman '70 (CIN) Fairfield, OH Sacred Heart of Jesus Church.
Langenderfer, Carl *o.f.m.* '71 (CIN) [23] Cincinnati, OH St. Clement Church.
Langenderfer, Carl J. *o.f.m.* '71 (CIN) [M] Cincinnati, OH St. Clement Friary.
Langenderfer, Max *o.f.m.* '73 (CIN) [M] Cincinnati, OH St. Francis Seraph Friary.
Langenderfer, Max *o.f.m.* '73 (FgM) Franciscan Foreign Missions.
Langenderfer, Norman *s.j.* '54 (FgM) Provinces.
Langenfeld, Thomas *c.s.v.* '60 (LAV) [15] Las Vegas, NV St. Viator Church.
Langenkamp, August *s.v.d.* '57 (JKS) Greenville, MS Sacred Heart Church.
Langer, Thomas E. '56 (LC) Bloomer, WI St. Paul Church; New Auburn, WI St. Jude Church.
Langerholz, Callistus F. *o.f.m.* '35 (CHI) [194] Chicago, IL St. Stephen Church.
Langevin, Fernand *m.s.* '48 (FR) [J] Attleboro, MA La Salette Provincial House.
Langford, Terry Lee '96 (L) Bardstown, KY St. Joseph Church.
Langguth, Laurence C. *s.j.* '40 (BO) [W] Weston, MA Campion Health Center, Inc.
Langhals, Henry *c.pp.s.* '37 (CIN) [B] Carthagena, OH St. Charles.
Langhans, Victor '84 (HEL) Frenchtown, MT St. John the Baptist Church.
Langheim, Albert *o.f.m.* '55 (GAY) Cross Village, MI Holy Cross Church; Good Hart, MI St. Ignatius Church; Larks Lake, MI St. Nicholas Church.
Langhirt, Carl J. *c.s.s.r.* '35 (ALB) [L] Saratoga Springs, NY St. John Neumann Residence.
Langhorst, Randall L. '92 (LIN) Weston, NE St. John Nepomucene Church.
Langille, Justin '80 (SD) Unassigned.
Langley, Barry *o.f.m.* '94 (WIL) [10] Wilmington, DE St. Paul's Church.
Langley, Barry J. *o.f.m.* '94 (WIL) [7] Wilmington, DE St. Joseph's R.C. Church of Wilmington, Inc.; [N] Wilmington, DE The Franciscan Center.
Langley, Joseph W. '42 (BO) Retired.
Langley, Terence *s.c.j.* '79 (BO) Carlisle, MA St. Irene Church.
Langley, Terence *s.c.j.* '79 (MIL) [P] Hales Corners, WI Priests of the Sacred Heart.
Langley, Wendell E. *s.j.* '53 (MIL) [P] Milwaukee, WI Jesuit Community at Marquette University.
Langlinais, J. Willis *s.m.* '52 (SAT) [C] San Antonio, TX St. Mary's University of San Antonio, Texas; [M] San Antonio, TX Casa Maria Marianist Community.
Langlois, Charles F. '96 (LAF) Henry, LA St. John Church.
Langlois, Frederick M. '91 (HRT) [4] Milford, CT St. Mary's Church.
Langlois, John A. *o.p.* '91 (PRO) [P] Providence, RI St. Thomas Aquinas Priory at Providence College.
Langlois, William A. '74 (GR) Grand Haven, MI St. Patrick's Church.
Langone, Robert E. *s.a.* '89 (ARL) Sterling, VA Christ the Redeemer Church.
Langsch, Gerold M. '72 (MIL) [T] Waukesha, WI Secular Institute of Schoenstatt Fathers.
Langsdorf, Karl '72 (CHI) [N] Chicago, IL St. Patrick's Missionary Society.
Langsdorf, Michael (CHL) Clemmons, NC Holy Family Church.
Langsfeld, Msgr. Paul J. '77 (WDC) On Duty Outside the Archdiocese.
Langston, Micheas *o.s.b.* '65 (EVN) New Boston, IN St. John Chrysostom Church.
Langston, Micheas *o.s.b.* '65 (IND) [B] St. Meinrad, IN St. Meinrad Seminary-College of Liberal Arts; [J] St. Meinrad, IN St. Meinrad Archabbey.
Langton, Bernard F. *o.p.* '69 (PRO) [P] Providence, RI St. Thomas Aquinas Priory at Providence College.
Langton, Edmund T. *c.ss.r.* '44 (STL) [P] Liguori, MO St. Clement Health Care Center.
Langweld, John *o.f.m.cap.* '46 (NY) [DD] Yonkers, NY St. Clare Friary.
LaNier, Michael L. '83 (LA) Sick Leave.
Lanigan, Leo *c.ss.r.* '44 (ORL) [F] New Smyrna Beach, FL St. Alphonsus Villa-Redemptorist Fathers and Brothers.
Lanigan, Patrick J. '51 (SAC) Retired and in Senior Ministry.
Lankford, Michael G. '92 (TR) [12] Trenton, NJ St. Anthony Church.
Lannan, Patrick D. '68 (STP) [8] St. Paul, MN The Nativity of Our Lord Church; [W] St. Paul, MN Nativity of Our Lord Endowment Fund.
Lannan, Paul A. '66 (LA) [86] Los Angeles, CA St. Paul the Apostle Church.
Lanning, Michael *o.f.m.* '78 (NY) [50] New York, NY Holy Trinity Church.
Lanning, Michael *o.f.m.* '78 (STL) [P] St. Louis, MO Franciscan Friary of St. Anthony of Padua.
Lannon, Timothy R. *s.j.* '86 (BO) [W] Cambridge, MA Faber House.
Lannon, Timothy R. *s.j.* '86 (MIL) [P] Milwaukee, WI Jesuit Provincial Office, Wisconsin Province.
LaNoue, Bertrand *o.s.b.* '52 (KCK) [A] Atchison, KS Benedictine College; [H] Atchison, KS St. Benedict's Abbey.
Lansang, Ferdinand *o.carm.* '96 (FgM) Carmelite Foreign Missions.
Lansang, Ferdinand *o.carm.* '96 (JOL) [J] Darien, IL Carmelite Provincial Office.
Lanser, Jerome E. '58 (MIL) On Leave.
Lanser, Wilbert *o.f.m.cap.* '59 (FgM) Capuchin Foreign Missions.
Lantry, Jerome *o.c.d.* '46 (LA) Alhambra, CA St. Therese Church.
Lantsberger, James *o.m.i.* '57 (SR) Imola, CA Napa State Hospital.
Lantsberger, John R. '76 (SFS) Aberdeen, SD Sacred Heart Church.
Lantz, David S. '78 (SFD) [3] Springfield, IL Christ The King Church; [C] Springfield, IL Springfield College in Illinois.
Lantz, Gary *s.c.j.* '80 (SFS) Pierre, SD SS. Peter and Paul Church.
Lanuevo, Victor '75 (HON) Military Chaplains.
Lanuza, Antonio G. '62 (TR) Eatontown, NJ St. Dorothea Church.
Lanwermeyer, Francis M. *s.j.* '66 (SAT) [D] San Antonio, TX Antonian College Preparatory High School.
Lanz, Mathias F. '94 (FAR) Leeds, ND St. Vincent de Paul Church.
Lanz, Placido *o.a.r.* '32 (NEW) [N] West Orange, NJ Augustinian Recollects.
Lanza, Daniel A. *m.m.* '59 (NY) [DD] Maryknoll, NY Maryknoll Fathers and Brothers.
Lanza, Steven M. '81 (CHI) [144] Chicago, IL Notre Dame Church.
Lanzaderas, Francisco H. '82 (NY) [211] Staten Island, NY St. Joseph, St. Thomas Church.
Lanzalaco, Joseph M. *c.s.b.* '87 (GRY) Michigan City, IN Indiana State Prison; [B] Merrillville, IN Andrean High School; [J] Merrillville, IN Basilian Fathers Residence.
Lanzrath, Curt C. *o.f.m.* '54 (CIN) [M] Cincinnati, OH St. Clement Friary.
Lanzrath, John *o.f.m.* '56 (LSC) Roswell, NM St. Peter Church.
Lanzrath, John P. '88 (WCH) Mulvane, KS St. Michael the Archangel Church.
Lao, Jonathan D. '75 (COL) Chillicothe, OH Veteran's Affairs Medical Center.
LaPalme, Paul M. '97 (ALX) Marksville, LA St. Joseph's Church.
Lapan, Robert '60 (BUR) Retired; [D] Burlington, VT St. Joseph's Home for Aged.
LaPastina, Cyprian P. '97 (BGP) [4] Danbury, CT St. Joseph's Church.
LaPata, Richard C. *o.p.* '59 (CHI) [J] Elk Grove Village, IL Alexian Brothers Medical Center, Inc.; [N] River Forest, IL St. Thomas Aquinas Priory.
Lapauw, Joseph *c.i.c.m.* '73 (ARL) [J] Arlington, VA Missionhurst, C.I.C.M.-Central House and Provincialate.
Lapauw, Joseph *c.i.c.m.* '73 (FgM) Missionhurst Foreign Missions.
Lape, Lydell T '90 (OM) Butte, NE SS. Peter and Paul Church.
Lapensky, John G. '77 (STP) Veseli, MN Most Holy Trinity Church.
LaPenta, Charles A. *o.s.f.s.* '54 (OKL) Duncan, OK Assumption Church.
LaPenta, Charles A. *o.s.f.s.* '54 (TOL) [K] Toledo, OH Oblates of St. Francis de Sales.
Lapera, John M. '84 (SCR) [15] Scranton, PA St. Joseph's Church.
Laperle, Theodore R. '54 (WOR) [2] Fitchburg, MA St. Bernard's Church; Retired.
LaPierre, David *o.f.m.cap.* '69 (FRS) Fresno, CA Community Hospital, Veterans' Hospital.
Lapierre, Msgr. Jean Gerard Yves '61 (PMB) [2] Delray Beach, FL Our Lady of Perpetual Help Mission Church.
Lapinski, Daniel A. '79 (BUF) Westfield, NY St. James Church.
LaPlante, David W. '78 (OM) Bancroft, NE Holy Cross Church; Lyons, NE St. Joseph Church.
Laplante, Jean-Paul '50 (BUR) Retired.
LaPlante, Joseph A. '54 (WIN) Retired; [A] Winona, MN Immaculate Heart of Mary Seminary.
Laplante, Laurant R. '57 (PRT) Kennebunk, ME St. Martha's Church.
LaPlante, Lawrence *s.v.d.* '67 (FgM) Society of the Divine Word Foreign Missions.
Laplante, Louis A. '87 (MET) Retired.
Laplante, Philip *s.m.* '48 (BO) [59] Boston, MA Our Lady of Victories Church; [W] Boston, MA Marist Fathers of Our Lady of Victories (Boston Prov.).
LaPlante, Robert J. '95 (CR) Thief River Falls, MN St. Bernards Church.
LaPlante, Roland M. '62 (HRT) South Meriden, CT Holy Angels Church.
Lapointe, J. Donald '67 (SPR) [8] Chicopee, MA St. Patrick's Church.
Lapointe, Jean Marie *o.p.* '39 (PRT) [I] Lewiston, ME SS. Peter and Paul Priory.
LaPointe, John G. '72 (PRO) [3] Johnston, RI St. Robert Bellarmine Church.
LaPointe, Laurence A.M. '70 (NOR) [K] Willimantic, CT Campus Ministry; [K] Willimantic, CT Campus Ministry.
Lapomarda, Vincent A. *s.j.* '64 (WOR) [N] Worcester, MA Jesuits of Holy Cross College, Inc.
LaPore, Arthur '76 (JOL) [8] Joliet, IL St. Anthony Church.
LaPorta, Ross A. '51 (BAL) [57] Baltimore, MD St. Mark Church.
LaPorte, Gerard *c.ss.r.* '83 (NO) [4] New Orleans, LA Chapel of the Vietnamese Martyrs Church.
LaPorte, Gerard B. *c.ss.r.* '65 (NO) [23] New Orleans, LA St. Alphonsus Church.
Laporte, Paul J. '65 (PRO) Coventry, RI St. Vincent de Paul Church.
Lappin, Peter *s.d.b.* '43 (NY) [FF] West Haverstraw, NY Don Bosco Retreat Center and Marian Shrine; [FF] West Haverstraw, NY Marian Shrine.
LaPrad, Steve '95 (KNX) Johnson City, TN St. Mary Church.

Laptuta, Demetrius *c.ss.r.* '45 (STF) Niagara Falls, NY Protection of B.V.M. Church.
Lara, Gustavo '49 (LA) [53] Los Angeles, CA St. Camillus De Lellis Church.
Lara, Gustavo '57 (LA) [24] Los Angeles, CA Our Lady of Guadalupe Church.
Lara, James C. '57 (SP) Brandon, FL Church of the Nativity.
Lara, Santiago G. '72 (LA) [R] Los Angeles, CA Guadalupe Missioners Procure.
Laraia, Joseph P. (BO) Retired.
Larche, James M. '91 (OG) Massena, NY Sacred Heart Church.
Lardner, Gerald V. *s.s.* '67 (BAL) [M] Baltimore, MD Sulpician Provincial House.
Laredo, Leopoldo *sch.p.* '40 (SJN) [58] San Juan, PR Santisimo Salvador Church.
Larena, Ismael '47 (PCE) Santa Isabel, PR St. James Church.
Large, John J. '75 (PH) Norwood, PA St. Gabriel Church.
Largent, Jeffery '84 (FTW) Culver, IN St. Mary of the Lake Church.
Largente, Laurent '59 (SJ) Retired.
Larger, Raymond E. '77 (CIN) [40] Cincinnati, OH St. James the Greater Church.
Larguier, Everett H. *s.j.* '41 (MOB) [B] Mobile, AL Spring Hill College.
Lariviere, Robert D. '78 (PRT) Kittery, ME St. Raphael's Church.
Larkin, Alexander C. '67 (SJ) Saratoga, CA Sacred Heart Church.
Larkin, Bartholomew *o.carm.* '58 (VEN) Grove City, FL St. Francis of Assisi Church.
Larkin, Donald L. *s.j.* '66 (FgM) Provinces.
Larkin, Edward A. *s.j.* '54 (OM) [K] Omaha, NE Jesuit Community At Creighton University.
Larkin, Ernest *o.carm.* '46 (PHX) [6] Phoenix, AZ St. Agnes Church.
Larkin, James *m.ss.a.* (NY) White Plains, NY St. Agnes Hospital.
Larkin, John *o.carm.* '51 (PHX) [6] Phoenix, AZ St. Agnes Church.
Larkin, John P. '44 (NY) Retired; [DD] New York, NY Pope John Paul II Residence.
Larkin, Joseph M. '57 (SY) Minetto, NY Our Lady of Perpetual Help Church.
Larkin, Kevin J. '59 (LA) Sherman Oaks, CA St. Francis de Sales Church.
Larkin, Michael J. '59 (STA) [12] Jacksonville, FL Prince of Peace Church.
Larkin, Michael T. (SC) On Duty Outside the Diocese.
Larkin, Patrick '57 (WCH) Caldwell, KS St. Martin of Tours Church.
Larkin, Richard '47 (STP) Retired.
Larkin, Msgr. Robert W. '73 (NY) [193] Bronx, NY Visitation Church.
Larkin, William J. *s.j.* '52 (BO) [W] Boston, MA Loyola House; [W] Chestnut Hill, MA The Jesuit Community at Boston College.
Larko, Ronald '82 (PBR) Irving, TX St. Basil the Great Church.
Larmann, Marian E. *o.s.b.* '47 (NO) St. Benedict, LA St. Benedict Church; [A] St. Benedict, LA St. Joseph's Seminary College; [P] St. Benedict, LA St. Joseph Abbey.
Larmore, Donald E. '63 (GI) [2] Grand Island, NE Blessed Sacrament Church.
Larner, James M. '57 (BO) [26] Boston, MA St. Gregory Church.
LaRocca, Christopher *o.c.d.* '97 (TUC) [21] Tucson, AZ Santa Cruz Church.
LaRocca, Jack '88 (SJ) San Jose, CA Detention Ministry for Juveniles.
LaRocca, John J. *s.j.* '75 (CIN) [M] Cincinnati, OH Jesuit Community at Xavier Unversity.
LaRocca, Msgr. Vincent R. '49 (BRK) Released from Diocesan Assignment.
LaRoche, Christopher J. '95 (PRT) Caribou, ME Holy Rosary Church.
Laroche, Leonidas B. '61 (BUR) St. Albans, VT Immaculate Conception Church.
Larochelle, Alphonse *m.s.* '59 (HON) Waipahu, HI St. Joseph Church.
Larochelle, Maurice R. '87 (MAN) Lancaster, NH All Saints Church.
LaRocque, Benedict J. *o.s.b.* '42 (KCK) [H] Atchison, KS St. Benedict's Abbey.
LaRocque, Benedict J. *o.s.b.* '42 (OM) Retired.
LaRocque, Leonard *a.a.* '56 (WOR) [N] Worcester, MA Assumptionists (Augustinians of the Assumption).
LaRocque, Msgr. Richard P. '63 (NOR) Old Lyme, CT Christ the King Church; Jewett City, CT St. Mary Church.
LaRoque, Paul M. '45 (TUC) Retired.
LaRosa, John J. '81 (PH) [152] Philadelphia, PA St. Timothy Church.
LaRose, Edward M. '66 (HRT) [7] New Britain, CT St. Jerome's Church.
LaRousse, William J. *m.m.* '80 (FgM) Maryknoll Foreign Missions.
Larran, Francisco *o.s.a.* '50 (MGZ) San German, PR St. Rose of Lima Church.
Larrea, Luis Eduardo *m.f.e.* '77 (LA) [68] Los Angeles, CA Santa Isabel Church.
Larreategui, Jose Luis *sch.p.* '53 (PCE) Jayuya, PR Our Lady of Monserrate Church; [B] Ponce, PR The Pontifical Catholic University of Puerto Rico.
Larrivee, Leo J. *s.s.* '77 (BAL) [67] Baltimore, MD Our Lady of the Angels Catholic Community Church.
Larrivee, Leo J. *s.s.* '77 (SEA) On Duty Outside the Archdiocese.
Larriviere, Marshall (LAF) Retired.
Larroque, Msgr. H. Alexandre '55 (LAF) On Special Assignment; [I] Lafayette, LA Discalced Carmelites.
Larry, Anthony J. *o.s.f.s.* '67 (HBG) New Bloomfield, PA St. Bernard Church.
Larsen, Kevin J. '93 (ARL) Burke, VA Church of the Nativity.
Larson, F. James '57 (RCK) Tampico, IL St. Mary Church.
Larson, F. James '62 (RCK) Special Assignment.
Larson, Jan '56 (SEA) Snoqualmie, WA Our Lady of Sorrows Church.
Larson, Jan '68 (SEA) Snoqualmie, WA Echo Glen School.
Larson, Lawrence A. '77 (BGP) Newtown, CT St. Rose of Lima Church.
Larson, Paul J. '79 (DUL) Coleraine, MN Mary Immaculate Church; Marble, MN St. Mary's Church.
Larue, Charles '93 (SAN) Retired.
Larue, Charles '93 (SAT) [K] San Antonio, TX Padua Place.
LaRusch, Msgr. Alton J. '41 (BUF) Retired.
Larussa, Raymond '74 (COL) [21] Columbus, OH Holy Spirit Church.
Las, Stefan '88 (PAT) [4] Passaic, NJ Holy Rosary Church.
Las, Wlodzimierz R. *s.d.s.* '86 (BRK) [93] Brooklyn, NY Our Lady of Consolation Church.
Las, Wlodzimierz R. *s.d.s.* '86 (NEW) [N] Verona, NJ The Salvatorian Fathers.
Lasalle, Donald *s.m.m.* '83 (HRT) [M] Litchfield, CT Montfort Missionaries; [M] Litchfield, CT Montfort Missionaries.
LaSalle, Donald G. *s.m.m.* '83 (WDC) [M] Washington, DC Missionaries of the Company of Mary-Montfort Missionaries.
Lascelle, Roger L. '77 (DEN) Meeker, CO Holy Family Church; Rangely, CO St. Ignatius Church; [P] Rangely, CO Colorado Northwestern Community College (Rangely).
Lasch, Msgr. Kenneth E. '62 (PAT) Mendham, NJ St. Joseph's Church.
Laschenski, Sigmund J. *s.j.* '55 (BAL) [M] Baltimore, MD Jesuit Fathers and Brothers Maryland Provincial Curia.
Laschenski, Sigmund J. *s.j.* '55 (FgM) Provinces.
Lasecki, Daniel J. '64 (MIL) Elkhart Lake, WI St. George Church; Glenbeulah, WI St. Fridolin Church.
Lash, Joseph J. '57 (CHL) Retired.
Lash, Theodore *o.f.m.conv.* '58 (SY) [10] Utica, NY St. Joseph and St. Patrick Church.
Lasheras, Antonio *o.a.r.* (NEW) [1] Union City, NJ Holy Family Church.
Lasheras, Antonio *o.a.r.* '62 (NY) [157] Bronx, NY St. John Vianney, Cure of Ars Church.
Lasic, Dionizije *o.f.m.* '37 (CHI) [N] Chicago, IL Croatian Franciscan Custody of the Holy Family.
Lasic, Miron '40 (CHI) [N] Chicago, IL Croatian Franciscan Custody of the Holy Family.
Laska, William M. '88 (E) [4] Erie, PA Holy Rosary Church.
Laske, Kenneth S. '58 (CHI) Berwyn, IL St. Leonard Church.
Laskey, Michael (BUF) [O] Athol Springs, NY St. Francis of Assisi Friary.
Lasko, Stephen J. *c.s.sp.* '47 (VEN) [G] Sarasota, FL Congregation of the Holy Ghost.
Laskowski, Norbert '71 (NEW) Kearny, NJ St. Cecilia's Church.
Lasky, Joseph J. '55 (SCR) Kingston, PA St. Mary's Annunciation Church.
Laslavich, Luke *o.praem.* '94 (ORG) [C] Santa Ana, CA Mater Dei High School.
Laslavich, Luke S. *o.praem.* '94 (ORG) [H] Silverado, CA Norbertine Fathers of Orange Inc.
Lasley, Jerry D. '92 (DAV) Iowa City, IA State University of Iowa Hospital.
Lasrado, Maxim *o.c.d.* (CHI) [58] Chicago, IL St. Ferdinand Church.
Lasseigne, John *o.m.i.* (BWN) [7] Brownsville, TX St. Eugene De Mazenod Church.
Lassuy, Raymond J. '39 (PEO) Retired.
Last, Carl A. '69 (MIL) [53] Milwaukee, WI St. Matthias Church.
Lastiri, Jean-Michael '85 (FRS) Merced, CA Our Lady of Mercy/St. Patricks Church.
Laszewski, Richard G. *m.m.* '51 (FgM) Maryknoll Foreign Missions.
Latcovich, Mark '81 (CLV) [A] Wickliffe, OH St. Mary Seminary and Graduate School of Theology.
Latella, Joseph A. *s.j.* '58 (NY) [DD] New York, NY St. Ignatius Loyola Residence; [HH] New York, NY Xavier Society for the Blind.
Later, Morse '55 (B) [4] Boise, ID Our Lady of the Rosary Church.
Later, Morse A. '55 (B) Idaho City, ID St. Joseph's Chapel Church; Retired; [B] Boise, ID St. Alphonsus Regional Medical Center, Inc.
Lathem, Msgr. E. Christopher '65 (CHR) Summerville, SC St. John the Beloved Church; [G] Charleston, SC Charleston Southern University.
Latimer, Msgr. Edward H. '39 (E) [1] Erie, PA St. Peter Cathedral; Retired.
Latino, Msgr. Joseph N. '63 (HT) [1] Houma, LA Cathedral of St. Francis De Sales.
Latka, John (CHI) [60] Chicago, IL Five Holy Martyrs Church.
Latona, Marcello J. '70 (BRK) [179] Queens, NY Holy Trinity Church.
LaTorre, Abraham '51 (SAT) [20] San Antonio, TX Our Lady of Sorrows Church.
LaTorre, Tony '97 (SFR) [2] San Rafael, CA St. Isabella Church.
Latosynski, Roger '84 (PT) Apalachicola, FL St. Patrick Church.
Latronico, P. '86 (NEW) [S] Rutherford, NJ The Community of God's Love.
Latsko, Andrew J. '92 (CHL) Swannanoa, NC St. Margaret Mary Church.
Lattis, Herbert L. '64 (L) Goshen, KY Transfiguration of Our Lord Church.
Latus, Charles J. '68 (ROC) Mendon, NY St. Catherine of Siena Church.
Latzko, Frank J. '84 (CHI) [155] Chicago, IL Our Lady of Mount Carmel Church.
Lau, Ignatius '58 (ORG) [1] Santa Ana, CA Immaculate Heart of Mary Church.
Lau, John Raymond *o.m.i.* '91 (MIA) [19] Miami, FL St. Francis Xavier Church.
Lau, Vincent '52 (FRS) [9] Fresno, CA St. Genevieve Church.
Lau, William '79 (SP) Absent on Leave.
Laubach, Barnabas *o.s.b.* '52 (SB) San Bernardino, CA San Bernardino Medical Center; [D] San Bernardino, CA St. Bernardine Medical Center.
Laubach, Barnabas *o.s.b.* '52 (SCL) [I] Collegeville, MN St. John's Abbey, of the Order of St. Benedict.
Laubacher, Carroll *s.j.* '56 (LA) [L] Ojai, CA St. Joseph's Health and Retirement Center.
Laubacker, Jerome P. *o.de.m.* '74 (BUF) [O] LeRoy, NY Order of the BVM of Mercy/Mercedarian Friars.
Laubenthal, Allan R. *s.t.d.* '61 (CLV) North Olmsted, OH St. Clarence Church.
Lauck, Anthony J. *c.s.c.* '46 (FTW) [A] Notre Dame, IN Moreau Seminary.
Laudati, Joseph J. '56 (NEW) Retired.
Lauder, Robert E. '60 (BRK) Released from Diocesan Assignment; [B] Douglaston, NY Cathedral Residence of the Immaculate Conception.
Laudick, John R. '64 (TOL) [H] Sandusky, OH Providence Hospital Inc.
Lauducci, V. James '57 (SY) Special Assignment; [V] Utica, NY SUNY Institute of Technology at Utica/Rome Newman Center; [V] Utica, NY Utica College of Syracuse University Newman Center.
Laudwein, James R. *s.j.* '62 (P) [L] Portland, OR Colombiere Community.
Laudwein, Joseph *s.j.* '62 (FBK) Tanana, AK St. Aloysius Church; [C] Fairbanks, AK Jesuit Residence.
Lauenstein, Gary *c.ss.r.* '71 (STL) [B] St. Louis, MO St. John Neumann House.
Lauer, Albert '77 (CIN) [76] Cincinnati, OH St. Pius Church.
Lauer, Albert E. '74 (CIN) On Special and Diocesan Assignment.
Lauer, Douglas J. '94 (COV) Crescent Springs, KY St. Joseph Church; [C] Covington, KY Villa Madonna High School.
Lauer, Eugene A. *o.s.b.* '43 (PEO) [A] Peru, IL St. Bede Abbey and Academy.
Lauer, Eugene F. '61 (FTW) [B] Notre Dame, IN University of Notre Dame Du Lac.
Lauer, Eugene F. '61 (PIT) On Duty Outside the Diocese.
Lauerman, James P. '70 (FAR) Napoleon, ND St. Philip Neri Church.
Laughery, Kevin M. '83 (SFD) Farmersville, IL St. Mary Church; Girard, IL St. Patrick Church.
Laughlin, James L. '91 (BO) Winchester, MA St. Eulalia Church.
Laughlin, Joseph R. *s.j.* '57 (BO) [E] Boston, MA Boston College High School & Jesuit Community.
Laughlin, Martin T. '52 (DUB) Retired.
Launderville, Dale *o.s.b.* '79 (SCL) [B] Collegeville, MN St. John's University; [I] Collegeville, MN St. John's Abbey, of the Order of St. Benedict.
Launtrie, Francis J. *c.s.b.* '56 (GAL) [Q] Sugar Land, TX Basilian Mission Center.
Laurance, John D. *s.j.* '70 (MIL) [P] Milwaukee, WI Jesuit Community at Marquette University.

Laurano, Anthony J. (BO) Retired.
Laurello, Msgr. Bartholomew J. '46 (BGP) Retired.
Laurent, Edward *o.f.m.cap.* '64 (PIT) [O] Pittsburgh, PA St. Patrick Friary.
Laurenzano, Roch M. '49 (NY) Retired.
Laurenzo, James M. '69 (DM) [A] West Des Moines, IA St. Joseph Educational Center.
Lauretti, George F. '56 (HRT) Southington, CT St. Thomas Church.
Lauri, John (NY) Graduate Studies.
Laurick, Richard A. *c.s.c.* '54 (FTW) [16] South Bend, IN St. Patrick Church.
Laurinaitis, Saulius P. '48 (COL) Retired.
Lauriola, Guglielmo *o.f.m.* '53 (SFR) [5] San Francisco, CA St. Anthony Church.
Lause, Richard *c.m.* '77 (SPC) Charleston, MO St. Henry Church.
Laushway, Aaron *o.p.* '80 (RIC) Charlottesville, VA St. Thomas Aquinas Church.
Lautermilch, David J. '62 (TOL) Awaiting Assignment.
Lautz, Boniface *o.s.b.* '60 (B) [C] Jerome, ID Ascension Priory.
Laux, Donald '48 (GB) Retired.
Lauze, Michael *o.m.i.* '75 (PRT) [I] Portland, ME.
Lauzon, Kris C. '91 (OG) [1] Ogdensburg, NY St. Mary's Cathedral.
Lauzon, Paul *s.d.s.* '71 (LC) [C] Marshfield, WI Columbus High School; [D] Marshfield, WI Holy Family Middle School.
Lauzon, Raymond J. '55 (PRT) Retired.
Lavagetto, Xavier M. *o.p.* '96 (SFR) [13] San Francisco, CA St. Dominic Church; [N] San Francisco, CA St. Dominic Priory.
Lavallee, Pierre A. '61 (BUR) [4] Burlington, VT St. Joseph's Church.
LaValley, Richard G. '64 (BUR) Winooski, VT St. Francis Xavier Church; [H] Burlington, VT University of Vermont-The Catholic Center at UVM.
LaVan, Kenneth G. '58 (STP) Lino Lakes, MN St. Joseph Church.
Lavaroni, Rino '67 (NEW) [11] Jersey City, NJ Holy Rosary Church.
Lavastida, Jose I. '87 (NO) [A] New Orleans, LA Notre Dame Seminary Graduate School of Theology.
Lavelle, Donald *c.m.f.* '46 (CHI) [N] Oak Park, IL Claretian Fathers Headquarters of U.S.A. Eastern Province.
Lavelle, Donald *c.m.f.* '46 (LA) [R] Rancho Dominguez, CA Dominguez Seminary Inc.
Lavelle, Edward R. '63 (HBG) [8] Harrisburg, PA Our Lady of the Blessed Sacrament Church.
Lavelle, Francis (SPR) [Q] Springfield, MA St. Michael's.
Lavelle, Francis P. '70 (SPR) [P] Amherst, MA University of Massachusetts and Amherst College, Newman Center.
Lavelle, Raymond E. '57 (COL) Powell, OH St. Joan of Arc Church.
Lavelle, Thomas E. *m.m.* '55 (FgM) Maryknoll Foreign Missions.
Lavely, Charles J. *c.s.c.* '65 (FTW) [16] South Bend, IN St. Patrick Church.
LaVerde, Calogero N. '68 (CAM) Egg Harbor City, NJ St. Nicholas Church.
LaVerde, Charles *c.s.* '65 (CHI) [17] Chicago, IL St. Anthony Church.
LaVerdiere, Eugene *s.s.s.* '64 (CLV) [B] Cleveland, OH Blessed Sacrament Seminary, Congregation of the Blessed Sacrament.
LaVerdiere, Eugene *s.s.s.* '64 (NY) [55] New York, NY St. Jean Baptiste Church.
LaVerdiere, Eugene A. *s.s.s.* '56 (CHI) [B] Chicago, IL The Catholic Theological Union at Chicago.
Lavere, Philip *o.f.m.* '47 (BO) [BB] Boston, MA St. Anthony Shrine.
LaVerghetta, Richard D. '86 (TR) [14] Trenton, NJ St. Gregory the Great Church.
Lavergne, Carlos J. *s.j.* '65 (SJN) [22] San Juan, PR San Ignacio de Loyola Church.
Laverone, Kenneth J. '79 (MRY) Special Assignment.
Laverty, Joseph F. *o.s.a.* '48 (PH) [AA] Villanova, PA St. Thomas Monastery.
Laverty, Seamus '68 (SEA) [9] Tacoma, WA St. Patrick's Church.
Laverty, Tod *o.f.m.* '72 (CHI) [N] Chicago, IL St. Joseph Interprovincial Post-Novitiate Formation House; [N] Chicago, IL St. Mary Magdalene Friary.
Lavery, Bruce '67 (ORG) Laguna Niguel, CA St. Timothy Church.
Laviano, Vincent A. *o.f.m.* '74 (NY) [35] New York, NY St. Francis of Assisi Church.
Lavigne, Lionel *s.s.s.* '41 (NY) [8] New York, NY St. Andrew Church.
Lavigne, Maurice D. '68 (MAN) [13] Manchester, NH Our Lady of Perpetual Help Church.
Lavigne, Richard R. '66 (SPR) Absent on Leave.
Lavin, Bernard C. '79 (PRO) Lincoln, RI St. Jude Church.
Lavin, Msgr. James M. '45 (STP) Retired; [C] St. Paul, MN University of St. Thomas.
Lavin, Msgr. John B. '64 (BRK) [235] Queens, NY St. Robert Bellarmine Church.
Lavin, John J. '64 (PRO) [3] Newport, RI St. Joseph Church.
Lavin, John P. *c.ss.r.* '66 (BAL) [62] Baltimore, MD St. Michael Church; [78] Baltimore, MD St. Patrick Church.
Lavin, Martin '67 (RIC) Martinsville, VA St. Joseph Church.
Lavin, Paul E. '69 (WDC) [24] Washington, DC St. Joseph on Capitol Hill Church.
Lavin, Msgr. Robert F. '56 (SY) East Syracuse, NY St. Matthew Church; Retired.
Lavin, Thomas *s.v.d.* '41 (MIL) [P] East Troy, WI Divine Word Seminary.
Lavin, Thomas *o.f.m.conv.* '87 (HRT) Kensington, CT St. Paul's Church.
Lavin, Wayne Patrick '71 (CAM) [3] Camden, NJ St. Bartholomew's Church.
LaViolette, Msgr. Matt H. '34 (MAR) Retired.
Laviste, Manuel J. '91 (HON) Kekaha, HI St. Theresa Church.
Lavitch, David *o.c.s.o.* '73 (WOR) [N] Spencer, MA St. Joseph's Abbey.
Lavoie, Merle L. '68 (SPR) [3] Northampton, MA Sacred Heart Church; [4] Northampton, MA St. John Cantius Church.
Lavoie, Michel J. *m.afr.* '70 (FgM) Missionaries of Africa Foreign Missions.
Lavoie, Rene G. '51 (PRT) [3] Lewiston, ME Holy Family Church; Retired.
Lavoie, Msgr. Robert G. '53 (PRT) Gray, ME St. Gregory Church.
Lavoie, Robert R. '40 (PRT) Retired; [I] Waterville, ME Mt. St. Joseph Priest Retirement Home.
Lavoie, Victor '71 (BO) Winchester, MA St. Eulalia Church.
Lavorin, Anthony F. *o.f.m.* (MRY) Jolon, CA San Antonio Mission Church.
Lavoy, Elwood '53 (LAV) Retired.
Lavrih, John '39 (DOD) Retired.
Law, Charles A. *s.j.* '64 (FgM) Provinces.
Law, Msgr. Joseph A. '49 (SCR) Retired.
Law, Michael '61 (P) Absent on Leave.
Lawie, Richard J. '69 (GR) On Special Assignment.
Lawler, Bruce A. '80 (SC) Salix, IA St. Joseph's Church.
Lawler, Daniel F. *s.j.* '48 (HBG) Chambersburg, PA Corpus Christi Church.
Lawler, David '62 (IND) Indianapolis, IN Methodist Hospital.
Lawler, Msgr. John F. (BO) Retired.
Lawler, John T. '43 (BO) Retired.
Lawler, Joseph A. '61 (BEL) Piopolis, IL St. John the Baptist Church.
Lawler, Msgr. Richard C. '59 (IND) [26] Indianapolis, IN St. Mark the Evangelist Church.
Lawler, Msgr. Robert L. '56 (OG) Waddington, NY St. Mary Church.
Lawler, Ronald '51 (PIT) [O] Pittsburgh, PA St. Francis Friary.
Lawler, Terrance M. '74 (MET) Sayreville, NJ Our Lady of Victories Church.
Lawler, William J. '72 (WIL) Centreville, MD Mother of Sorrows Church.
Lawless, Brendan '64 (JC) Richland, MO St. Jude Church; Waynesville, MO St. Robert Bellarmine Church.
Lawless, Joseph *m.s.f.* '71 (CC) [15] Corpus Christi, TX St. Joseph Church.
Lawless, Timothy J. *s.j.* '61 (DEN) [M] Denver, CO Xavier Jesuit Center.
Lawlor, Brendan '55 (SP) Temple Terrace, FL Corpus Christi Church.
Lawlor, Brendan W. '44 (BUR) Retired.
Lawlor, David T. *o.praem.* (HBG) Dauphin, PA St. Matthew, Apostle and Evangelist Church.
Lawlor, David T. *o.praem.* '71 (PH) [AA] Paoli, PA Daylesford Abbey.
Lawlor, Edward J. *s.s.j.* '40 (NO) [N] New Orleans, LA Chateau de Notre Dame.
Lawlor, Francis *o.s.a.* '45 (STL) [6] St. Louis, MO Immaculate Conception-St. Henry Church.
Lawlor, Francis '69 (SAC) [22] Sacramento, CA St. Rose Church.
Lawlor, J. Michael '73 (BO) Lynnfield, MA St. Maria Goretti Church.
Lawlor, John J. *c.m.* '44 (PH) [AA] Philadelphia, PA Congregation of the Mission.
Lawlor, John L. *c.m.* '44 (CHR) Gloverville, SC Our Lady of the Valley Church.
Lawlor, Joseph '62 (JC) Missionary Assignment in Peru.
Lawlor, Msgr. Joseph F. '35 (RVC) Baldwin, NY St. Christopher Church; Retired.
Lawlor, Mark '95 (CHL) Albemarle, NC Our Lady of the Annunciation Church.
Lawlor, Msgr. Timothy '43 (SB) Ontario, CA St. George Church; Retired.
Lawlor, William G. *s.j.* '49 (NY) [DD] New York, NY Murray-Weigel Hall.
Lawrence, David *s.j.* '74 (OAK) [2] Concord, CA St. Bonaventure Church.
Lawrence, David '97 (JOL) Woodridge, IL St. Scholastica Church.
Lawrence, David L. *s.j.* '74 (OAK) [N] Berkeley, CA Jesuit Community at Jesuit School of Theology at Berkeley.
Lawrence, Emeric *o.s.b.* '35 (SCL) [I] Collegeville, MN St. John's Abbey, of the Order of St. Benedict.
Lawrence, Francis '45 (JOL) [J] Lisle, IL St. Procopius Abbey.
Lawrence, James A. '70 (BUR) Ludlow, VT Annunciation Church.
Lawrence, James T. '61 (DAV) Retired; [M] Davenport, IA St. Vincent Center.
Lawrence, Jeffrey '90 (PEO) Danville, IL St. Paul's Church.
Lawrence, John '76 (SAC) Fort Jones, CA Sacred Heart Church.
Lawrence, Joseph '77 (FTW) Decatur, IN St. Mary Church.
Lawrence, Kenneth F. '60 (HBG) Columbia, PA Holy Trinity Church.
Lawrence, Kevin C. (PH) [S] Philadelphia, PA St. John Hospice for Men.
Lawrence, Kevin C. '87 (PH) [144] Philadelphia, PA Sacred Heart of Jesus Church.
Lawrence, Michael S. '73 (ALN) [7] Allentown, PA St. Paul Church; [L] Coopersburg, PA Carmelite Monastery.
Lawrence, Neal Henry *o.s.b.* '60 (FgM) American - Cassinese Congregation Foreign Missions.
Lawrence, Neal Henry *o.s.b.* '60 (SCL) [I] Collegeville, MN St. John's Abbey, of the Order of St. Benedict.
Lawrence, Ralph J. '53 (CIN) Retired.
Lawrence, Richard T. '68 (BAL) [95] Baltimore, MD St. Vincent de Paul Church.
Lawrence, Msgr. Robert E. '66 (HBG) New Cumberland, PA St. Theresa of the Infant Jesus Church.
Lawrence, Walter L. '73 (WDC) Kensington, MD Holy Redeemer Church.
Lawryniuk, Lawrence *o.s.b.m.* '64 (STF) New York, NY St. George Church.
Lawsine, Robert S. '81 (BRK) [84] Brooklyn, NY St. Mary, Star of the Sea Church.
Lawson, Harold F. '59 (BO) Permanent Disability.
Lawson, J. Douglas (R) Riegelwood, NC Christ the King Church.
Lawson, J. Douglas '62 (R) Southport, NC Sacred Heart Church.
Lawson, Meinrad J. *o.s.b.* '67 (SAV) [F] Savannah, GA The Benedictine Priory.
Lawson, Robert T. '62 (R) Pinehurst, NC Sacred Heart Church.
Lawson, Ronald (BO) Boston, MA Veterans Administration Hospital.
Lawson, Willaim T. '86 (SD) National City, CA St. Anthony of Padua Church.
Lawton, Robert B. *s.j.* '81 (WDC) [C] Washington, DC Georgetown University; [M] Washington, DC The Jesuit Community at Georgetown University.
Lawton, Thomas E. *c.s.c.* '36 (FR) [L] North Easton, MA Holy Cross Fathers Retreat House.
Lay, Thomas N. *s.j.* '66 (STL) [P] St. Louis, MO Jesuit Community Corporation at St. Louis University - Jesuit Hall.
Layton, Richard *o.c.s.o.* '82 (P) [L] Lafayette, OR The Cistercian (Trappist) Abbey of Our Lady of Guadalupe.
Laz, Medard P. '69 (CHI) [5] Cicero, IL Our Lady of Charity Church.
Lazar, Francis M. '60 (GRY) Highland, IN St. James the Less Church.
Lazar, John '42 (STN) Dearborn Heights, MI Our Lady of Perpetual Help Church; Flint, MI St. Vladimir's Church.
Lazar, John E. '80 (BRK) Absent on Leave.
Lazaro, Angel Millan *sch.p.* '55 (SJN) [58] San Juan, PR Santisimo Salvador Church.
Lazaro, Felix *sch.p.* '61 (PCE) Jayuya, PR Our Lady of Monserrate Church; [B] Ponce, PR The Pontifical Catholic University of Puerto Rico.
Lazaro, Lesmes Bernabe *o.s.a.* '49 (MGZ) Aguada, PR St. Francis of Assisi Church.
Lazarski, Marvin I. '62 (MIL) Awaiting Assignment.
Lazor, Bernard A. *o.s.a.* '51 (PH) [C] Villanova, PA Villanova University; [AA] Villanova, PA St. Thomas Monastery.
Lazor, Joseph '90 (STF) Manchester, NH Protection of B.V.M. Church.
Lazzaro, Nicholas A. '41 (PH) Conshohocken, PA SS. Cosmas and Damian Church; Retired.
Le, Hoang Viet '61 (TLS) [9] Tulsa, OK St. Joseph Church.
Le, James Vinh '87 (KAL) Dorr, MI St. Stanislaus Church.
Le, Joseph Ahn *s.d.b.* '95 (LA) [F] Bellflower, CA St. John Bosco High School.
Le, Paul Vung *s.v.d.* '85 (SB) [7] San Bernardino, CA St. Anthony Church.
Le, Tan Van '73 (CHL) [4] Charlotte, NC St. Ann Church.
Le Beau, Philip '93 (PAT) [2] Clifton, NJ St. Andrew the

Apostle Church.
Le Fevre, Francis J. '71 (BAL) Absent on Leave.
Le Frois, Christian G. *o.s.b.* '46 (GBG) [H] Latrobe, PA Saint Vincent Archabbey.
Le Jacq, Peter M. *m.m.* '87 (NY) [DD] Maryknoll, NY Maryknoll Fathers and Brothers.
Le Quang, Heini Joachim '74 (SPK) [10] Spokane, WA St. Charles Church.
Leach, Gregory '93 (DM) Ankeny, IA Our Lady's Immaculate Heart Church.
Leach, Jerome '76 (SFR) Absent on Leave.
Leach, Phillip M. '85 (R) Chapel Hill, NC Newman Catholic Student Center, University of North Carolina Church; [H] Chapel Hill, NC Newman Catholic Student Center.
Leach, Thomas F. '73 (BRK) [103] Brooklyn, NY Our Lady of Miracles Church.
Leach, William J. '58 (STL) Gildehaus, MO St. John the Baptist Church.
Leack, Lawrence J. '50 (MIL) Retired; [V] Milwaukee, WI Our Blessed Lady of Victory Mission, Inc.
Leahey, Patrick R. '77 (ALT) Dudley, PA Immaculate Conception Church.
Leahy, Anthony '55 (SB) Retired.
Leahy, Celestine *s.a.* '45 (NY) [DD] Garrison, NY Generalate of the Franciscan Friars of the Atonement-St. James Friary.
Leahy, Clement '50 (CHI) [N] Chicago, IL St. Peter's Friary.
Leahy, Edward W. *o.p.* '94 (STP) [8] Minneapolis, MN Holy Rosary Church; [15] Minneapolis, MN St. Albert the Great Church.
Leahy, Edwin D. *o.s.b.* '72 (NEW) [C] Newark, NJ St. Benedict's Preparatory School; [N] Newark, NJ Newark Abbey.
Leahy, John A. '57 (CLV) Middleburg Heights, OH St. Bartholomew Church.
Leahy, Juvenal F. *o.f.m.* '58 (FgM) Franciscan Foreign Missions.
Leahy, Liam '72 (TUC) [14] Tucson, AZ St. John the Evangelist Church.
Leahy, Msgr. Patrick J. '38 (DOD) Retired.
Leahy, Robert T. '60 (NEW) On Duty Outside the Archdiocese.
Leahy, Robert T. '60 (TR) Forked River, NJ St. Pius X Church.
Leahy, William *s.j.* '78 (BO) [W] Chestnut Hill, MA The Jesuit Community at Boston College.
Leahy, William J. '66 (SAV) St. Marys, GA Our Lady Star of the Sea Church.
Leahy, William P. *s.j.* '78 (BO) [C] Chestnut Hill, MA Boston College.
Leake, Jerome I. '68 (RCK) [3] Aurora, IL St. Joseph Church.
Lealofi, Msgr. Etuale '69 (SPP) [5] Pago Pago, AS Church of St. Peter and Paul.
Leannah, Scott R. '93 (MIL) [53] Milwaukee, WI St. Matthias Church.
Leary, Albert R. '54 (BIS) Mandan, ND Christ the King Church; Mandan, ND Christ the King Church; [G] Bismarck, ND Emmaus Place.
Leary, Daniel Paul '97 (WDC) Piscataway, MD St. Mary Church.
Leary, Donald G. '51 (WIN) Retired.
Leary, Edward *s.s.e.* '53 (VEN) [G] Englewood, FL Society of St. Edmund Residence.
Leary, James *o.f.m.cap.* '70 (DET) [K] Detroit, MI St. Bonaventure Friary; [T] St. Clair Shores, MI Catholic Kolping Society of America, Detroit Branch, Inc.
Leary, James *o.f.m.cap.* '80 (DET) [Q] Detroit, MI Capuchin Soup Kitchen.
Leary, James F. '68 (HRT) [4] Bristol, CT St. Joseph Church; [C] West Hartford, CT Saint Joseph College.
Leary, James V. '56 (PH) Retired.
Leary, Msgr. Joseph W. '53 (CAM) Retired.
Leary, Patrick *o.f.m.* '62 (BO) [BB] Boston, MA St. Anthony Shrine.
Leary, Patrick R. '76 (LAV) [14] Las Vegas, NV St. Paul Jung-Ha-Sang Church; [16] Las Vegas, NV Shrine of the Most Holy Redeemer Church.
Leary, Richard *c.p.* '46 (FgM) Passionist Foreign Missions.
Leason, Antoine *s.v.d.* (NO) [P] New Orleans, LA Society of the Divine Word Augustine Tolton House.
Leatham, Gerald '65 (LUB) Snyder, TX St. Elizabeth's Church.
Leavey, Msgr. Thomas G. '51 (RVC) Seaford, NY St. William, the Abbot Church.
Leavins, Brice A. *o.f.m.* '69 (BO) [BB] Boston, MA St. Anthony Shrine.
Leavitt, Robert F. *s.s.* '68 (BAL) [A] Baltimore, MD St. Mary's Seminary and University.
Leavitt, Robert F. *s.s.* '68 (HRT) On Duty Outside the Archdiocese.
Lebanowski, Gerald '59 (STL) [P] St. Louis, MO La Salette Missionaries.
Lebar, Ivan M. *t.o.r.* '58 (WH) Keyser, WV Assumption Church.
LeBar, James J. '62 (NY) Hyde Park, NY Regina Coeli Church; Poughkeepsie, NY Hudson River Psychiatric Center.
LeBarre, Renald D. '60 (PRT) Biddeford, ME St. Joseph's Church.
LeBauve, J. Joel '70 (BR) New Roads, LA St. Mary of False River Church.
Lebdowicz, Jan Krzysztof '80 (NEW) Wallington, NJ Most Sacred Heart of Jesus Church.
LeBeau, Cyril A. '48 (WOR) [M] Worcester, MA Vianney House.
LeBeau, Cyril A. '52 (WOR) Retired.
LeBeau, Joseph *s.v.d.* '49 (CHI) [B] Techny, IL Divine Word Residence.
Lebel, Charles E. *m.afr.* '39 (SP) [O] St. Petersburg, FL Missionaries of Africa.
Lebel, Maurice T. '67 (PRT) Auburn, ME Sacred Heart Church.
Lebiedz, Bernard *o.s.b.* '59 (SFE) [L] Pecos, NM Our Lady of Guadalupe Benedictine Abbey.
LeBlanc, Alvin J. '82 (HRT) [8] Waterbury, CT St. Anne Church; Special and other (Arch)Diocesan Assignment; [A] Bloomfield, CT St. Thomas Seminary.
LeBlanc, Charles R. '79 (NOR) Plainfield, CT St. John the Apostle Church.
LeBlanc, David E. (GR) Caledonia, MI Holy Family Church.
LeBlanc, Etienne '71 (HT) Morgan City, LA Holy Cross Church.
LeBlanc, Gregory '94 (DOD) Ingalls, KS St. Stanislaus Church.
LeBlanc, Gregory S. '94 (DOD) Garden City, KS St. Dominic Church.
LeBlanc, Harold E. '61 (BO) [4] Woburn, MA St. Joseph Church.
LeBlanc, J. Whitney '63 (LAF) Retired.
LeBlanc, James L. '96 (CHR) [3] Columbia, SC Saint Martin de Porres Church.
LeBlanc, Keith '96 (BO) [2] Everett, MA Immaculate Conception Church.
LeBlanc, Kenneth A. '76 (BO) [5] Waltham, MA Our Lady, Comforter of the Afflicted Church.
LeBlanc, Leo A. '74 (MAN) [11] Manchester, NH St. John the Baptist Church.
LeBlanc, Omer *c.j.m.* '61 (SD) [2] El Cajon, CA Our Lady of Grace Church.
LeBlanc, Paul '69 (NY) Absent on Leave.
LeBlanc, Steven C. '77 (LAF) [5] New Iberia, LA Sacred Heart of Jesus Church.
LeBleu, Wayne '95 (LKC) [8] Lake Charles, LA Our Lady Queen of Heaven Church.
LeBoeuf, Gerard J. '93 (DET) Allen Park, MI St. Frances Cabrini Church.
LeBouef, Raymond (HT) [4] Houma, LA Our Lady of the Most Holy Rosary Church.
LeBourgeois, Msgr. Louis P. '61 (NO) Jefferson, LA St. Agnes Church.
Lebranche, Raymond '94 (NEW) Special Assignment.
LeBrun, Paul *c.s.c.* '83 (FTW) [20] South Bend, IN St. Therese, Little Flower Church.
Lebrun, Raymond *o.m.i.* '68 (PRT) [I] Portland, ME.
Lebrun, Raymond A. *o.m.i.* '68 (NO) [1] New Orleans, LA St. Louis Cathedral.
LeCaptain, Douglas (GB) [7] Green Bay, WI St. Joseph Church.
Lech, Ferdinand F. '48 (PIT) Meadowlands, PA Our Lady of the Miraculous Medal Church.
Lech, Waclaw L. *o.c.d.* '74 (GRY) [J] Munster, IN Discalced Carmelite Fathers Monastery.
Lecheler, Anton L. '46 (LC) Rock Falls, WI St. Joseph Church.
Lechiara, Francis J. '59 (PMB) Palm Beach, FL St. Edward Church; [J] Palm Beach Gardens, FL Diocesan Health Plan Trust.
Lechnar, William J. '97 (GBG) Irwin, PA Immaculate Conception Church.
Lechner, Joel A. *o.s.m.* (CHI) [N] Chicago, IL Servite Friars - Eastern Province.
Lechner, Joel A. (ORG) [D] Anaheim, CA Servite High School; Servite High School Development Fund.
Lechner, Robert *c.pp.s.* '46 (CIN) [B] Carthagena, OH St. Charles.
Lechner, Msgr. Roger A. '66 (SD) [7] San Diego, CA Holy Spirit Church.
Lechtenberg, Msgr. Edward W. '51 (DUB) Lycurgus, IA St. Mary's Church; Waukon, IA St. Patrick's Church.
Leckie, Michael J. '76 (PRO) Hopkinton, RI St. Joseph Church.
LeClair, Lawrence J. '53 (HRT) Retired.
LeClair, Richard J. *c.s.sp.* '51 (FgM) Holy Ghost Foreign Missions.
LeClaire, Fred *c.m.f.* '87 (PHX) Prescott, AZ Sacred Heart Church.
LeClaire, Karl *s.d.s.* '87 (PHX) [4] Mesa, AZ Queen of Peace Church.
Leclerc, Gerard P. '60 (BUR) Enosburg Falls, VT St. John the Baptist Church.
Leclerc, Leo A. '61 (SPR) [9] Chicopee, MA St. Rose de Lima Church.
Leclercq, M. Duane '64 (PEO) [4] La Salle, IL St. Patrick's Church.
LeCompte, Glenn D. '86 (HT) Raceland, LA St. Hilary of Poitiers Church.
LeCompte, Glenn D. '86 (NO) [A] New Orleans, LA Notre Dame Seminary Graduate School of Theology.
LeCours, Sylva P. '47 (NOR) Ballouville, CT St. Anne Church.
Lecuivre, Joel A. '72 (PRO) [5] Pawtucket, RI St. John the Baptist Church.
Lecumberri, Rufino '54 (NY) [158] Bronx, NY St. Joseph Church.
Leddy, Aidan J. '56 (CC) Violet, TX St. Anthony Church.
Leddy, John J. *o.m.i.* '51 (WDC) [B] Washington, DC Oblate College/Oblate Center for Mission Studies; [Q] Washington, DC Basilica of the National Shrine of the Immaculate Conception.
Leddy, Seamus *s.s.c.* '42 (LA) [R] Los Angeles, CA Columban Fathers, Procure House.
Leder, Dennis M. *s.j.* '76 (FgM) Provinces.
Leder, Dennis M. *s.j.* '76 (NY) [DD] New York, NY Jesuit Provincial's Office.
Lederman, Paul '50 (DET) Retired.
Ledermann, Paul F. '63 (OG) On Duty Outside the Diocese.
Ledermann, Paul F. '63 (SR) Yountville, CA Veterans Administration Home.
Ledesma, Alberto '97 (LA) Goleta, CA St. Raphael Church.
Ledet, Msgr. Donald L. '63 (HT) Raceland, LA St. Mary's Nativity Church.
Ledford, John S. '75 (WH) Berkeley Springs, WV St. Vincent de Paul Church.
Ledoux, Albert H. '71 (ALT) On Duty Outside the Diocese.
Ledoux, Albert H. '87 (WDC) Beltsville, MD St. Joseph Church.
LeDoux, Jerome *s.v.d.* '57 (NO) [26] New Orleans, LA St. Augustine Church.
Ledoux, John C. '50 (BUR) Retired.
Ledoux, Louis V. '52 (LAF) Military Chaplains.
Ledoux, Michael Dominic *o.f.m.* '86 (PIT) [C] McKeesport, PA Serra Catholic High School.
Ledoux, Michael Dominic W. *o.f.m.* '86 (PIT) [O] McKeesport, PA Franciscan Friars.
Ledoux, William J. '93 (PRO) Coventry, RI SS. John and Paul Church.
LeDuc, Roger D. '60 (FR) [2] Swansea, MA St. Louis de France Church.
Leduff-Gutierrez, Larry *s.s.j.* '85 (BEA) [3] Port Arthur, TX Sacred Heart Church.
Ledwidge, Brendan K. '55 (LAN) Retired.
Ledwith, Harry '74 (TUC) [19] Tucson, AZ St. Pius X Church.
Ledwon, Jacob C. '72 (BUF) [40] Buffalo, NY St. Joseph Church; [R] Williamsville, NY Campus Ministry.
Ledwon, Josaphat *o.f.m.* '56 (GB) [I] Pulaski, WI Assumption of B.V.M. Friary.
Lee, Andrew '83 (RIC) [1] Newport News, VA Catholic Community of the Korean Martyrs Church.
Lee, Anthony '41 (SFR) [K] San Francisco, CA Home for the Aged of the Little Sisters of the Poor.
Lee, Anthony Sangwook '97 (LA) Claremont, CA Our Lady of the Assumption Church.
Lee, Arthur (BLX) Biloxi, MS Keesler Airforce Base.
Lee, Berchmans Yong-Woo *s.j.* '92 (COS) [7] Colorado Springs, CO St. Andrew Kim Quasi Parish.
Lee, Bernard J. *s.m.* '67 (NO) [C] New Orleans, LA Loyola University.
Lee, Blase '76 (DET) Northville, MI St. Andrew Kim Korean Catholic Church.
Lee, Msgr. David M. '68 (BUF) [R] Williamsville, NY Campus Ministry.
Lee, Dominic Savio '94 (SFR) [4] San Francisco, CA St. Anne Church.
Lee, Francis '42 (SFD) Retired.
Lee, Gabriel '97 (BRK) [206] Queens, NY Our Lady of the Angelus Church.
Lee, Gerard *o.f.m.* '50 (NY) [DD] New York, NY Franciscan Friars, Order of Friars Minor, Holy Name Province.
Lee, Gerard *o.f.m.* '71 (ALB) [J] Albany, NY Teresian House.
Lee, Henry H. '54 (LC) Retired.
Lee, Msgr. Howard T. '54 (FRS) Retired.
Lee, James '75 (SEA) Olympia, WA St. Michael's Church.
Lee, Jeffrey E. '92 (TR) Cinnaminson, NJ St. Charles Borromeo Church.
Lee, John '71 (SC) [D] Sioux City, IA Marian Health Center.
Lee, John M. *c.p.* '72 (MET) [H] South River, NJ Passionist Provincial Office.
Lee, John R. *c.s.b.* '56 (ROC) [I] Rochester, NY Basilian Residence.
Lee, Joseph '55 (CHI) [98] Chicago, IL St. James Church.
Lee, Joseph C. (DAL) Grand Prairie, TX St. Michael the Archangel Church.
Lee, Joseph Chun Yuan '58 (SFR) Retired.
Lee, Joseph P. '57 (LA) Sick Leave.
Lee, Joshua Peter '87 (LA) [40] Los Angeles, CA St. Alphonsus Church.
Lee, Keun-Soo '95 (BR) [12] Baton Rouge, LA St. Jean Vianney Church.

Lee, Lawrence (GAL) [N] Houston, TX Pope John XXIII Priest Residence.
Lee, Lawrence '49 (GAL) Retired.
Lee, Matthew (J.T.) '93 (WDC) Military Chaplains.
Lee, Michael (TR) Eatontown, NJ Immaculate Conception Church.
Lee, Michael G. '64 (WH) Absent on Sick Leave.
Lee, Michael G. *s.j.* '96 (MIL) [29] Milwaukee, WI Gesu Parish; [P] Milwaukee, WI Arrupe House Jesuit Community.
Lee, Michael J. *o.praem.* '70 (PH) [D] Philadelphia, PA St. John Neumann High School; [AA] Philadelphia, PA St. Norbert Priory.
Lee, O. William (MOB) [C] Mobile, AL McGill-Toolen High School.
Lee, Patrick J. '68 (SAC) [9] Sacramento, CA St. Anne Church.
Lee, Patrick J. '76 (CHI) [90] Chicago, IL Immaculate Conception of the Blessed Virgin Mary Church.
Lee, Patrick J. *s.j.* '78 (P) [A] Portland, OR Jesuit Novitiate of St. Francis Xavier.
Lee, Paul *o.f.m.* '90 (SD) [H] San Luis Rey, CA Mission San Luis Rey.
Lee, Paul D. '83 (WDC) Pastoral Center Special Ministries.
Lee, Peter '51 (LA) Retired.
Lee, R. Anthony '93 (PEO) Danville, IL St. Paul's Church; [B] Danville, IL Schlarman High School.
Lee, Robert E. *m.m.* '43 (NY) [DD] Maryknoll, NY Maryknoll Fathers and Brothers.
Lee, Robert E. *o.carm.* '55 (JOL) [J] Darien, IL Carmelite Community; [M] Darien, IL Provincial Office of Lay Carmelites and Scapular Confraternity.
Lee, Robert E. *o.carm.* '55 (PRT) [1] Portland, ME Cathedral of the Immaculate Conception; Portland, ME St. Joseph's Manor; Retired.
Lee, Robert E. '59 (PEO) Moline, IL Sacred Heart Church.
Lee, Roy A. '68 (MIL) Military Chaplains.
Lee, San Yil '92 (AUS) Leander, TX St. Yoo Peter Catholic Church.
Lee, Terence J. *m.h.m.* '57 (NY) [DD] Hartsdale, NY Mill Hill Fathers Residence.
Lee, Msgr. Thaddeus (PAT) Retired.
Lee, Thomas M. '53 (PRT) Lyman, ME St. Philip Church.
Lee, William '62 (HON) On Duty Outside the Diocese.
Lee, William J. *s.s.* '46 (BAL) [J] Baltimore, MD St. Charles Villa; [M] Baltimore, MD St. Charles Villa.
Leeber, Victor F. *s.j.* '53 (BGP) [A] Fairfield, CT Fairfield University; [O] Fairfield, CT The Fairfield Jesuit Community-Fairfield University.
Leech, George '56 (PIT) Allegheny County, PA Atrium I Nursing Research and Rehabilitation Center; Allegheny County, PA Shadyside Nursing and Rehabilitation Center; Allegheny County, PA St. Joseph Nursing and Health Care Center; [L] Pittsburgh, PA St. Joseph Nursing and Health Care Center, Inc.
Leech, George T. '56 (PIT) Allegheny County, PA Collins Nursing Center; Allegheny County, PA Heartland Health Care Center.
Leedale, Walter F. *s.j.* '59 (SPK) [C] Spokane, WA Gonzaga University.
Leehan, Patrick *c.ss.r.* '48 (OAK) [N] Oakland, CA Redemptorists.
Leehy, Stephen G. '73 (OG) On Duty Outside the Diocese.
Leek, Michael *o.s.b.* '93 (SFE) [L] Pecos, NM Our Lady of Guadalupe Benedictine Abbey.
Leeuw, Daniel '57 (FTW) Fort Wayne, IN Veterans Administration Hospital; [H] Avilla, IN Sacred Heart Home; [H] Avilla, IN LaVerna Terrace Apartments.
Lefebure, Leo D. '78 (CHI) [A] Mundelein, IL University of St. Mary of the Lake-Mundelein Seminary; [A] Mundelein, IL University of St. Mary of the Lake-Mundelein Seminary.
Lefebvre, Bruce A. '73 (SC) West Bend, IA SS. Peter and Paul Church.
Lefebvre, Msgr. Gerald M. '56 (BR) Maurepas, LA St. Stephen Martyr Church.
Lefebvre, James '59 (ALB) [11] Albany, NY St. Mary Church.
Lefebvre, Leo P. '55 (MAN) Penacook, NH Immaculate Conception Church.
Lefebvre, Simon *c.s.v.* '56 (SD) Borrego Springs, CA St. Richard Church.
LeFevre, Msgr. Michael C. '82 (DET) [1] Sterling Heights, MI St. Blase Church.
LeFevre, Robert J. '66 (ALB) Saratoga Springs, NY St. Peter Church.
Leffler, Richard J. '78 (MAD) Tennyson-Potosi, WI SS. Andrew-Thomas Church.
Lefko, John *c.pp.s.* '38 (CIN) [B] Carthagena, OH St. Charles.
Lefler, John '57 (EVN) Retired.
LeFleur, R.K. '61 (SAG) Bannister, MI St. Cyril Church.
Leflowitz, Christine (RVC) [I] Rockville Centre, NY Mercy Medical Center.
LeFrois, Christian *o.s.b* '46 (SAV) Lakeland, GA Queen of Peace Church.
LeFrois, Msgr. Marvin J. '49 (SAV) Retired.
Legarra, Francisco J. *o.a.r.* '74 (LA) [R] Oxnard, CA St. Augustine Priory O.A.R.
Legarski, Anthony J. '83 (ALT) Military Chaplains.
Legaspi, Alex L. '76 (SFR) [28] San Francisco, CA St. John of God Church; [S] San Francisco, CA Newman Center, University of California Medical Center.
Legendre, Msgr. Francis J. '61 (HT) Cut-Off, LA Sacred Heart Church.
Leger, Donald N. '68 (LAF) Church Point, LA Our Lady of the Sacred Heart Church.
Leger, Donald Nicholas '68 (LAF) Evangeline, LA St. Joseph Church.
Leger, G. Robert '71 (SJ) [6] San Jose, CA St. Frances Cabrini Church.
Leger, Jeffrey Patrick '97 (L) [28] Louisville, KY St. Gabriel the Archangel Church.
Leger, Laurie *m.s.* '54 (WOR) [3] Gardner, MA Our Lady of the Holy Rosary Church.
Leger, P. Austin '62 (LAF) St. Martinville, LA St. Martin of Tours Church.
Leger, Steven '86 (BEA) Absent On Leave.
Legere, Germain *c.p.* '42 (L) [K] Louisville, KY Nazareth Home; [L] Louisville, KY Sacred Heart Retreat.
Legerski, John '81 (B) On Duty Outside the Diocese.
Legerski, John '81 (SJ) [16] San Jose, CA St. Martin of Tours Church.
Lego, William E. *o.s.a.* '83 (CHI) [185] Chicago, IL St. Rita of Cascia Church.
Lehane, Brian J. *s.j.* (DET) [K] Detroit, MI Jesuit Provincial Office-Detroit Province of the Society of Jesus.
Lehane, Joseph *c.s.c.* '57 (FgM) Holy Cross Foreign Missions.
Lehane, Joseph E. '77 (CLV) Macedonia, OH Our Lady of Guadalupe Church.
Leheny, Msgr. Bernard M. '66 (LA) Norwalk, CA St. John of God Church.
Lehman, Darold R. '58 (NU) Springfield, MN St. Raphael Church.
Lehman, Joseph *t.o.r.* '96 (STU) [A] Steubenville, OH Franciscan University of Steubenville; [F] Steubenville, OH Holy Spirit Monastery.
Lehman, Joseph P. '80 (RIC) Roanoke, VA Our Lady of Nazareth Church.
Lehman, Mark A. '88 (PHX) Unassigned.
Lehman, Paul J. '54 (NEW) [5] Newark, NJ St. Antoninus Church.
Lehmann, Anthony *s.j.* '56 (SPK) [C] Spokane, WA Gonzaga University.
Lehmkuhl, Gerhardt B. *s.j.* '74 (STL) [P] St. Louis, MO Jesuit Community Corporation at St. Louis University - Jesuit Hall.
Lehmkuhl, John '45 (TOL) Retired.
Lehner, John *o.s.f.s.* '70 (DET) Inkster, MI Holy Family Parish; Inkster, MI St. Kevin and St. Norbert Church.
Lehnerd, Frank M. '58 (Y) [14] Youngstown, OH St. Edward's Church.
Lehning, Thomas J. '70 (ARL) Manassas, VA Sacred Heart Church.
Lehocky, Msgr. Leigh A. '68 (CHR) [1] Columbia, SC St. Peter's Church.
Lehr, Theodore F. *o.f.m.* '56 (NEW) Elmwood Park, NJ St. Leo's Church.
Lehrberger, James *o.cist.* '76 (DAL) [B] Irving, TX University of Dallas; [M] Irving, TX Cistercian Abbey of Our Lady of Dallas.
Leibenguth, Gerald T. *o.s.b.* '72 (BO) [W] Hingham, MA Glastonbury Abbey.
Leibham, David M. '87 (AUS) [1] Austin, TX St. Mary's Cathedral.
Leibold, Alcuin *o.s.b.* '56 (IND) [J] St. Meinrad, IN St. Meinrad Archabbey.
Leibold, James C. '80 (BRK) Military Chaplains.
Leibrecht, Robert G. '58 (STL) [3] St. Louis, MO Holy Family Church.
Leicht, Gerard *ss.cc.* '40 (HON) [11] Honolulu, HI St. Patrick Church.
Leicht, Gerard *ss.cc.* '45 (HON) [H] Honolulu, HI St. Patrick's Monastery.
Leidich, Kevin A. *s.j.* '82 (LA) [F] Los Angeles, CA Loyola High School.
Leies, John A. *s.m.* '56 (SAT) [C] San Antonio, TX St. Mary's University of San Antonio, Texas; [M] San Antonio, TX Marianist Residence.
Leies, John G. *s.m.* '38 (SAT) [K] San Antonio, TX Marianist Residence: Skilled Nursing.
Leif, Gregory P. '78 (WIN) Adams, MN Sacred Heart Church.
Leifeld, Msgr. Antony J. '38 (NU) [1] New Ulm, MN Cathedral of The Holy Trinity Church; Retired.
Leigh, David J. *s.j.* '68 (SEA) [A] Seattle, WA Seattle University.
Leighton, Donald E. '62 (PH) Collingdale, PA St. Joseph Church.
Leiker, Francis R. *s.j.* '54 (STL) [O] St. Louis, MO Fusz Pavilion.
Leiker, Perry D. '76 (LA) [17] Los Angeles, CA Mother of Sorrows Church.
Leikhim, Joel J. *o.s.b.* '61 (PAT) [M] Morristown, NJ St. Mary's Abbey.
Leinen, Ron *m.s.c.* (RCK) [D] Aurora, IL Mercy Health Corporation.
Leinen, Ronald *m.s.c.* '57 (RCK) [H] Aurora, IL Missionaries of the Sacred Heart Community.
Leinfelder, Philip '39 (LC) Retired; [I] La Crosse, WI Holy Cross (Seminary) Diocesan Center.
Leininger, Charles A. *s.j.* '53 (DAL) [D] Dallas, TX Jesuit College Preparatory School.
Leininger, Donald F. '58 (SP) Palm Harbor, FL St. Luke the Evangelist Church; [F] Palm Harbor, FL St. Luke Early Childhood Center.
Leininger, Joseph B. *s.j.* '53 (GAL) [F] Houston, TX Strake, Jesuit College Preparatory Inc.
Leininger, William '56 (SJ) Retired.
Leipert, Jack J. '75 (SAG) Bad Axe, MI Sacred Heart Church.
Leiphon, Donald A. '68 (FAR) Fairmount, ND St. Anthony's Church; [F] Wahpeton, ND Carmel of Mary.
Leise, Gerald A., Jr. '74 (OM) Ewing, NE St. Peter de Alcantara Church; St. John, NE St. John Church.
Leise, Leo V. *s.j.* '94 (FgM) Provinces.
Leise, Leo V. *s.j.* '94 (NO) [P] New Orleans, LA Jesuit Provincial Office.
Leisen, Leo '54 (SCL) Lake Henry, MN St. Margaret's Church; Roscoe, MN St. Agnes Church; Spring Hill, MN St. Michael's Church.
Leisen, Richard '56 (SCL) Paynesville, MN St. Louis Church.
Leising, Edmund *o.m.i.* '46 (FgM) Oblates Foreign Missions.
Leising, Msgr. Frederick D. '71 (BUF) Lancaster, NY St. Mary of the Assumption Church.
Leising, John J. '69 (BUF) Newfane, NY St. Bridget Church; Wilson, NY Our Lady of the Rosary Church.
Leisle, Charles E. '58 (LC) Retired.
Leissa, Eric B. '95 (CLV) Chesterland, OH St. Anselm Church.
Leissler, Joseph L. '32 (SB) Retired.
Leisy, Christian *o.s.b.* '88 (SFE) [J] Abiquiu, NM Monastery of Christ in the Desert.
Leitem, Leon *o.f.m.cap.* '57 (PIT) Freedom, PA St. Felix Church; [O] Rochester, PA St. Cecilia Friary.
Leith, James A. '81 (FAR) West Fargo, ND Holy Cross Church.
Leitheiser, Douglas '49 (FRS) Retired.
Leiting, Robert L. '67 (SC) Carroll, IA St. Anthony Regional Hospital; [E] Carroll, IA St. Anthony Nursing Home.
Leitner, John E. '55 (KC) [2] Independence, MO St. Joseph the Worker Church.
Leitner, Thomas Aquinas *o.s.b.* '92 (OM) [K] Schuyler, NE Benedictine Mission House.
Leiva, Emilio (ARE) On Duty Outside the Diocese.
Leiweke, Robert W. *s.j.* '58 (MIL) [P] Milwaukee, WI Jesuit Community at Marquette University.
Leja, Casimir '85 (CHI) Other Assignments.
LeJeune, Ronald J. '71 (TOL) [4] Fremont, OH St. Joseph Church.
Leketas, Peter J. '43 (LC) Retired.
Lekwot, Peter '89 (NY) [F] New York, NY All Hallows Institute.
Leliaert, Richard M. *o.s.c.* '67 (DET) Riverview, MI St. Cyprian Church; [K] Riverview, MI Crosier Community of Riverview.
Lelii, Raymond M. *s.j.* '61 (WDC) [E] North Bethesda, MD Georgetown Preparatory School.
Lelo-Luemba, Albert *c.i.c.m.* '96 (BWN) [4] McAllen, TX St. Joseph the Worker Church.
Leloczky, Julius *o.cist.* '61 (DAL) [M] Irving, TX Cistercian Abbey of Our Lady of Dallas.
LeLonde, Venant *o.f.m.* '54 (NY) [2] New York, NY St. Agnes Church.
Lelonis, Richard M. '71 (PIT) [3] McKees Rocks, PA St. John of God Church.
Lemanski, William E. *s.a.c.* '74 (MIL) [P] Milwaukee, WI Pallotti House.
Lemaster, Scott G. '85 (DAV) Richmond, IA Holy Trinity Church; Wellman, IA St. Joseph Church.
LeMay, Donald *o.s.b.* '57 (SCL) [I] Collegeville, MN St. John's Abbey, of the Order of St. Benedict.
Lemay, Donald H. '89 (RIC) Blacksburg, VA St. Mary & Newman Community Church.
Lemay, Jean '75 (MAN) [18] Manchester, NH St. Theresa Church.
LeMay, John M. *o.s.m.* '84 (CHI) [N] Chicago, IL Servite Friars - Eastern Province.
Lembo, Richard A. '75 (PRT) Lubec, ME Sacred Heart Church.
Lemen, William F. '36 (CR) Bemidji, MN St. Philip's Church; Retired.
LeMieux, Thomas A. '59 (MIL) [11] Kenosha, WI St. Thomas Aquinas Church.
Lemire, Paul W. '89 (WOR) [4] Southbridge, MA St. Mary's Church.
Lemke, Norbert *s.j.* (B) Cottonwood, ID Monastery of St. Gertrude; [B] Cottonwood, ID St. Mary's Hospital.
Lemke, Norbert J. *s.j.* '44 (OM) [K] Omaha, NE Jesuit Community At Creighton University.

Lemkuhl, David A. '79 (CIN) On Duty Outside the Archdiocese.
Lemkuhl, David A. '79 (FgM) Maryknoll Foreign Missions.
Lemlin, Timothy J. '78 (PRO) Burrillville, RI Our Lady of Good Help Church.
Lemm, Eugene '57 (SCL) Brandon, MN Church of St. Ann; Millerville, MN Seven Dolors Church.
Lemmens, Henry C. *c.s.sp.* '34 (VEN) [G] Sarasota, FL Congregation of the Holy Ghost.
Lemmert, Ronald J. '51 (NY) [HH] Peekskill, NY My Father's House, Inc.
Lemmert, Ronald J. '79 (NY) State, NY Sing Sing Correctional Facility.
Lemming, Patrick W. '81 (MOB) On Leave from the Archdiocese.
Lemoi, Paul R. '75 (PRO) [7] West Warwick, RI Our Lady of Good Counsel Church.
Lemoine, Daniel P. (BR) Baton Rouge, LA Earl K. Long Hospital.
Lemoine, Daniel P. '79 (BR) [F] Baton Rouge, LA Our Lady of the Lake Regional Medical Center.
Lemoine, Msgr. J. Guy '56 (LAF) [1] New Iberia, LA St. Peter Church.
Lemoine, Russell J. '70 (ALX) Mansura, LA St. Paul the Apostle Church.
Lemoine, Msgr. Vincent P. '51 (SAL) Retired.
Lemon, Msgr. Clement P. '64 (WIL) Hockessin, DE St. Mary of the Assumption Church.
Lemoncelli, Henry *o.m.i.* (WDC) [M] Washington, DC Missionary Oblates of Mary Immaculate.
Lemoncelli, Henry L. *o.m.i.* '79 (WDC) [B] Washington, DC Oblate College/Oblate Center for Mission Studies.
Lemos, Thomas F. *c.s.c.* '74 (FTW) [5] South Bend, IN St. Casimir Church; [19] South Bend, IN St. Stephen Church.
Lemoyne, William '49 (ALB) Retired.
Lemp, Joseph R. *s.t.l.* '56 (PIT) Koppel, PA Queen of Heaven Church.
Lempart, Ignatius *o.s.c.* '43 (LIN) [A] Hastings, NE Crosier Monastery.
Lemrise, Arthur *c.s.v.* '44 (JOL) [E] Momence, IL Good Shepherd Manor.
Lemrise, John-Marie *c.m.f.* '52 (CHI) [149] Chicago, IL Our Lady of Guadalupe Church.
Lemus, Francisco Arrivillaga *o.s.b.* '95 (SFS) [F] Marvin, SD Blue Cloud Abbey.
Lemus, Francisco J. *s.j.* '62 (MIA) [D] Miami, FL Belen Jesuit Preparatory School; [H] Miami, FL Villa Arrieta.
Lemus, Ovidio Ortega '83 (SJN) [41] San Juan, PR Ntra. Sra. de la Medalla Milagrosa Church.
Lenagham, James Jordan *o.p.* '95 (COL) [36] Columbus, OH St. Patrick Church.
Lenaghan, Charles G. *s.j.* '58 (CHI) [172] Chicago, IL St. Philomena Church.
Lenaghan, Jordan *o.p.* '96 (RIC) Charlottesville, VA St. Thomas Aquinas Church.
Lenahan, John B. '49 (L) Retired.
Lenane, William '50 (SJ) Retired.
Lenarz, Richard J. '56 (MAD) Benton, WI St. Patrick Church.
Lencewicz, Leonard E. '63 (SP) [O] St. Petersburg, FL St. Anthony Friary.
Lenchak, Timothy A. *s.v.d.* '75 (CHI) [B] Chicago, IL The Catholic Theological Union at Chicago; [B] Techny, IL Divine Word Residence; [N] Chicago, IL Divine Word Theologate; [N] Techny, IL Society of the Divine Word, Provincial Headquarter-Chicago Prov.
Lenczycki, Frederick '72 (STL) [K] Bridgeton, MO De Paul Health Center.
Lendacky, Francis G. '61 (PH) [4] Philadelphia, PA St. Agnes-St. John Nepomucene Church.
Lendvai, John B. '94 (PIT) [63] Pittsburgh, PA Prince of Peace Church.
Lenehan, Claude *o.f.m.* '55 (PAT) [M] Paterson, NJ St. Benedict the Moor Friary.
Lenehan, Vincent (SAC) [2] Sacramento, CA All Hallows Church.
Lenehan, Vincent '54 (SAC) Retired and in Senior Ministry.
Lengen, Msgr. James G. '29 (BGP) Retired; [O] Stamford, CT Our Lady Queen of the Clergy Home.
Lengerich, Ambrose R. *c.pp.s.* '42 (CIN) [B] Carthagena, OH St. Charles.
Lengerich, Msgr. Vincent L. '48 (GRY) Retired.
Lengwin, Ronald P. '66 (PIT) [26] Pittsburgh, PA St. Mary of Mercy Church.
Lenihan, Daniel F. *o.c.s.o.* '55 (DUB) [K] Peosta, IA New Melleray Abbey, Order of Cistercians of the Strict Observance.
Lenihan, James *m.m.* '55 (SPP) [1] Pago Pago, AS Cathedral of the Holy Family.
Lenihan, Msgr. John J. '53 (STA) [21] Jacksonville, FL San Jose Church.
Lenihan, John P. '69 (ORG) Dana Point, CA St. Edward Church.
Lenihan, Msgr. Michael '52 (LA) Redondo Beach, CA St. Lawrence Martyr Church.
Lenihan, Michael '71 (CC) [1] Kingsville, TX Our Lady of Good Counsel Church.
Lenk, Msgr. Charles (WOR) Retired.
Lenning, Terry '96 (RIC) Unassigned.
Lennon, Charles '80 (RVC) Absent on Leave.
Lennon, Francis P. '40 (PH) Collegeville, PA St. Eleanor Church; Retired.
Lennon, James M. '58 (JOL) [17] Joliet, IL St. Patrick Church.
Lennon, John '55 (NY) New York, NY New York Postal Service; New York, NY New York Sanitation Department; Yonkers, NY Yonkers Police Department; Yonkers, NY Yonkers Fire Department.
Lennon, John W. '55 (NY) [11] Yonkers, NY St. John the Baptist Church.
Lennon, Joseph L. *o.p.* '47 (PRO) [P] Providence, RI St. Thomas Aquinas Priory at Providence College.
Lennon, Peter F. '55 (NEW) [B] South Orange, NJ Seton Hall University.
Lennon, Raymond T. *s.v.d.* '64 (WDC) [M] Washington, DC Divine Word College.
Lennon, Richard G. '73 (BO) [4] Brookline, MA St. Mary of the Assumption Church.
Lennon, Robert *c.ss.r.* '57 (STV) [2] Christiansted, VI Church of the Holy Cross.
Lennon, Msgr. Robert T. '50 (NEW) Livingston, NJ St. Philomena Church.
Lenoch, Francis J. '44 (DAV) Retired.
Lenoci, Dominick '95 (NEW) Kenilworth, NJ St. Theresa's Church.
Lenoir, Jean (SB) Retired.
Lenti, Arthur *s.d.b.* '50 (OAK) [A] Berkeley, CA Dominican School of Philosophy and Theology; [N] Berkeley, CA Salesian Community.
Lentine, Peter S. '50 (DET) [63] Detroit, MI St. Philomena Church.
Lentz, Gerald J. *s.j.* '60 (SJ) [D] San Jose, CA Bellarmine College Preparatory.
Lentz, Lawrence D. *c.s.v.* '81 (JOL) Bourbonnais, IL Maternity of the Blessed Virgin Mary Church.
Lenz, Daniel *o.s.b.* '85 (OM) [C] Elkhorn, NE Mount Michael High School; [K] Elkhorn, NE Mount Michael Abbey.
Lenz, David *o.f.m.conv.* '86 (STL) [P] St. Louis, MO St. Bonaventure Friary (Province of Our Lady of Consolation).
Lenz, Frank B. '94 (VIC) Yorktown, TX Holy Cross Church.
Lenz, Frank M. '69 (MAR) Marquette, MI Marquette General Hospital.
Lenz, Henry J. *m.s.* '41 (TYL) Union Grove-Gladewater, TX St. Theresa of the Infant Jesus Church.
Lenz, Michael *o.f.m.* '76 (ALN) [K] Easton, PA St. Francis Friary.
Lenz, Msgr. Paul A. '49 (ALT) On Duty Outside the Diocese.
Lenzini, Donald J. (BEL) Ina, IL Big Muddy River Correctional Center.
Lenzini, Donald J. '51 (BEL) Benton, IL St. Joseph Church.
Lenzner, George G. '57 (GB) Oneida, WI St. Joseph Church.
Leo, Arthur R. '85 (NY) Peekskill, NY Assumption Church.
Leon, Antonio '57 (STA) [8] Jacksonville, FL Immaculate Conception Church.
Leon, Bartholomew *o.s.b.* '85 (CC) [H] Sandia, TX Corpus Christi Abbey.
Leon, J. Francisco *o.s.a.* '78 (GAL) Pasadena, TX Blessed Juan Diego Church.
Leon, Jose M. '81 (OAK) Union City, CA Our Lady of the Rosary Church.
Leon, Juan *o.f.m.* '57 (FRS) [G] Three Rivers, CA St. Anthony's Retreat House.
Leon, Mario Rodriguez *o.p.* (SJN) [A] Bayamon, PR Bayamon Central University.
Leon-Guerrero, Felixberto *o.f.m.cap.* '86 (FgM) Capuchin Foreign Missions.
Leonard, Clyde A. (BO) Retired.
Leonard, Edmond J. *c.s.sp.* '37 (SB) [E] Hemet, CA Holy Ghost Fathers.
Leonard, Edward '53 (COS) Retired.
Leonard, Edwin M. '84 (CLV) [6] Parma, OH Holy Family Church.
Leonard, Eugene A. '66 (CHR) Spartanburg, SC Jesus Our Risen Savior Church.
Leonard, Francis B. '50 (BO) [3] Revere, MA St. John Vianney Church.
Leonard, Gerald *s.v.d.* (SB) [6] San Bernardino, CA St. Anne Church.
Leonard, John '48 (JKS) Retired.
Leonard, John *o.f.m.* '96 (PAT) Little Falls, NJ Our Lady of the Holy Angels Church.
Leonard, John E. '65 (RIC) Glen Allen, VA St. Michael Church.
Leonard, John F. '55 (BO) [3] Salem, MA St. James Church.
Leonard, John J. *s.j.* '50 (NY) [F] New York, NY Fordham Preparatory School; [DD] New York, NY Jesuit Community at Fordham University.
Leonard, Joseph '45 (MRY) Retired.
Leonard, Lawrence J. *c.m.* (GAL) Retired.
Leonard, Patrick J. '63 (NEW) Mountainside, NJ Our Lady of Lourdes Church.
Leonard, Paul F. '89 (SCR) [21] Scranton, PA St. Patrick's Church.
Leonard, Peter *o.s.f.s.* '85 (ALN) [B] Center Valley, PA Allentown College of St. Francis de Sales.
Leonard, Peter J. *o.s.f.s.* '86 (ALN) [K] Center Valley, PA Oblates of St. Francis de Sales.
Leonard, Raymond J. '90 (MET) Iselin, NJ St. Cecelia Church; [A] Edison, NJ Bishop Ahr High School.
Leonard, Robert *s.j.* '49 (LA) [R] Los Angeles, CA Columbiere House.
Leonard, Robert R. *s.j.* '49 (SJ) [M] Los Gatos, CA Sacred Heart Jesuit Center.
Leonard, Sebastian *o.s.b.* '57 (HRT) [E] New Milford, CT Canterbury School.
Leonard, Sebastian *o.s.b.* '57 (IND) [J] St. Meinrad, IN St. Meinrad Archabbey.
Leonard, Msgr. Thomas P. '56 (NY) [50] New York, NY Holy Trinity Church.
Leonard, William F. '70 (MET) Colonia, NJ St. John Vianney Church.
Leonard, William J. *s.j.* '37 (BO) [W] Chestnut Hill, MA The Jesuit Community at Boston College.
Leonard, Msgr. William P. '43 (DUB) Retired.
Leonard, William T. (BO) Belmont, MA Fernald Developmental Center.
Leonardis, Charles F. '54 (ALT) [5] Windber, PA Holy Child Jesus Church.
Leonards, Martin C. '66 (LAF) Maurice, LA St. Alphonsus Church.
Leone, Arthur '56 (NY) [85] New York, NY Our Lady of Good Counsel Church.
Leone, James M. '60 (BRK) Military Chaplains.
Leone, Kenneth '67 (DEN) Littleton, CO St. Frances Cabrini Parish.
Leone, Mark *o.f.m.* '40 (NY) [DD] New York, NY Franciscan Province of the Immaculate Conception.
Leone, Richard D. *o.s.f.s.* '59 (WIL) [I] Wilmington, DE DeSales House.
Leone, William B. '74 (ROC) Cato, NY St. Patrick Church; Weedsport, NY St. John Church; Weedsport, NY St. Joseph Church.
Leong, Francis J. *m.m.* '87 (NY) [DD] Maryknoll, NY Maryknoll Fathers and Brothers.
Leong, Herman M. '91 (OAK) San Ramon, CA St. Joan of Arc Church.
Leonhardt, Douglas J. *s.j.* '69 (MIL) [E] Milwaukee, WI Marquette University High School; [P] Milwaukee, WI Pere Marquette House Jesuit Community.
Leonhardt, Louis J. '56 (DAV) Hills, IA St. Joseph's Church; Iowa City, IA Veteran's Administration Hospital.
Leonhardt, Robert *o.f.m.* '59 (SHP) West Monroe, LA St. Paschal Church.
Leopold, David C. '82 (BGP) Westport, CT Assumption Church.
Leotilo, Rocco *c.s.s.* '53 (BO) [Z] Waltham, MA Stigmatine Fathers and Brothers.
Leoz, Maximo '56 (BRK) [77] Brooklyn, NY St. Malachy's Church.
Lepak, Roy C. '62 (STP) Special Assignment.
LePine, Clement J. '46 (MAR) Retired.
Lepire, Roland M. '75 (PRO) Absent on Leave.
Lepleiter, Robert P. '63 (PH) Retired.
Lepping, George M. *s.m.* '38 (WDC) [M] Washington, DC Marist Provincial House.
Lequin, Thomas '77 (PRT) Mars Hill, ME St. Joseph Church; Presque Isle, ME Nativity of B.V.M. Church.
Lerch, Joseph R. *s.j.* '56 (BAL) Woodstock, MD St. Alphonsus Rodriguez Church.
Leroux, Edward N. '56 (ALB) Fort Edward, NY St. Joseph Church.
Leroux, Roger *m.s.* '52 (FR) Brewster, MA Our Lady of the Cape Church.
LeRoux, William F. *s.j.* '53 (SEA) [A] Seattle, WA Seattle University.
Lerox, Edward '56 (ALB) Retired.
Lery, Bruce *s.m.* '87 (HON) Kapaa, HI St. Catherine Church.
LeSage, Joseph '59 (PMB) Retired.
Lesak, William P. '75 (NEW) Military Chaplains.
Lesch, Howard J. *c.pp.s.* '44 (CIN) [M] Dayton, OH Provincial House of the Cincinnati Province of the Society of the Precious Blood.
Lescoe, Francis J. '42 (HRT) Retired.
Lesczynski, James J. '64 (LC) Necedah, WI St. Francis of Assisi Church.
Leser, Msgr. William J. *c.b.* '63 (LA) Westlake Village, CA St. Jude Church.
Leshney, Michael F. '73 (CIN) [E] Cincinnati, OH Moeller High School.
LeSieur, David '76 (LR) [11] Little Rock, AR Our Lady of the Holy Souls Church.
Leskiw, Peter '45 (STN) Retired.
Leskovar, Richard J. '68 (ALB) Special Assignment.
Leslie, Larry B. '80 (COV) Military Chaplains.
Leslie, Patrick J. '69 (SAC) On Duty Outside the Diocese.
Leslie, Patrick J. '69 (SR) [5] Santa Rosa, CA Star of

the Valley Church; Eldridge, CA Sonoma Developmental Center.
Lesniak, David '91 (DET) Port Huron, MI St. Stephen Church.
Lesniak, John E. '48 (CLV) [6] Euclid, OH St. William Church; Retired.
Lesniak, Marian J. '50 (LAN) [2] Jackson, MI St. Joseph Church.
Lesniak, Richard D. '66 (MAD) Berlin, WI St. Joseph Church; Berlin, WI St. Michael Church.
Lesnick, John F. '78 (BAL) [63] Baltimore, MD St. Michael Church.
Lesnick, Richard '67 (SEA) Unassigned.
Lesniewski, Stephen F. (CHI) [172] Chicago, IL St. Philomena Church.
Lesniowski, Francis A. '63 (GBG) [4] Connellsville, PA St. Rita Church.
Lesniowski, Stanley '70 (PAT) [4] Passaic, NJ Holy Rosary Church.
Lesousky, John *c.r.* '56 (L) [18] Louisville, KY St. Cecilia Church.
Lessard, Anatole *o.m.i.* '44 (BO) [4] Lowell, MA Saint Jeanne d'Arc Church.
Lessard, Eugene R. '59 (PRO) [1] Central Falls, RI The Holy Spirit Catholic Community Church.
Lessard, Gerard Arthur *o.p.* '84 (L) [4] Springfield, KY St. Rose Church.
Lessard, Joseph '80 (PHX) On Duty Outside the Diocese.
Lessard, Joseph M. '80 (RCK) [4] Aurora, IL St. Mary Church; [D] Aurora, IL Mercy Health Corporation.
Lessard, Joseph P. '52 (STL) Retired.
Lessard, Leo R. '60 (GB) Aurora, WI Sacred Heart Church; Florence, WI Immaculate Conception Church.
Lessard-Thibodeau, John G. '92 (SPR) [14] Springfield, MA St. Catherine of Siena Church.
Lesseps, Roland J. *s.j.* '65 (FgM) Provinces.
Lesseps, Roland J. *s.j.* '65 (NO) [P] New Orleans, LA Jesuit Provincial Office.
Lester, Msgr. J. William '45 (FTW) [1] Fort Wayne, IN Cathedral of the Immaculate Conception.
Lester, John E. '59 (TOL) Retired.
Lester, John J. '62 (NEW) Scotch Plains, NJ St. Bartholomew Church.
Lester, Thomas '57 (OAK) [4] San Leandro, CA St. Leander Church.
Lester, William F. *s.j.* '54 (SJ) [M] Los Gatos, CA Sacred Heart Jesuit Center.
LeStrange, Gregory C. '82 (SY) Fayetteville, NY Immaculate Conception Church.
Letendre, Theodore *f.i.c.* '97 (PRT) [I] Alfred, ME Notre Dame Institute; [J] Alfred, ME Sisters of Our Lady of the Holy Rosary.
Lethiez, Alphonse O. '55 (PRO) [4] West Warwick, RI St. John's Church.
Letko, Anthony '37 (FTW) Retired.
Leto, Nelo A. '54 (DM) Carlisle, IA St. Elizabeth Seton Church.
Letoile, Kenneth R. *o.p.* '74 (PRO) [29] Providence, RI St. Pius V Church; [P] Providence, RI St. Pius Priory.
Letourneau, F. E. (ORL) Retired.
Letourneau, Francis E. '36 (PRT) Retired.
Letourneau, Msgr. Paul R. '54 (BUF) [7] Cheektowaga, NY Our Lady Help of Christians Church; [T] Buffalo, NY Kolping Catholic Young Men's Association of Buffalo, NY dba Kolping Society of Buffalo.
Lettau, David '53 (Y) Retired.
Letteer, Michael C. '96 (HBG) [1] York, PA Immaculate Conception of the Blessed Virgin Mary Church.
Lettic, Edward P. '73 (WOR) Lancaster, MA Immaculate Conception Church.
Lettre, Msgr. Achille W. '33 (MAN) Retired.
Lettre, Raymond A. '88 (SP) New Port Richey, FL St. Thomas Aquinas Church.
LeTure, Theodore J. '49 (RVC) Valley Stream, NY Holy Name of Mary Church; Retired.
Leu, James E. '71 (DAV) Absent on Leave.
Leuer, Msgr. Anthony '61 (LA) [13] Los Angeles, CA Holy Spirit Church.
Leurck, Raymond J. '67 (CIN) Military Chaplains.
Leute, Charles J. *o.p.* '69 (FAR) Fort Totten, ND Seven Dolors Church; Fort Totten Reservation, ND (Sioux Indians) Church.
Leva, Stephen F. '88 (ARL) [3] Arlington, VA St. Ann Church.
Levan, Donald E. '89 (BUF) [P] Buffalo, NY Immaculate Heart of Mary Provincial House and Convent.
Levandusky, Edward '65 (PHU) Palmerton, PA St. Vladimir's Church.
Levario, Gilbert *o.c.d.* '83 (TUC) [16] Tucson, AZ St. Margaret's Church; [F] Tucson, AZ Discalced Carmelite Fathers of St. Margaret's.
LeVasseur, Angelo '83 (PRT) Frenchville, ME St. Luce's Church; [L] Upper Frenchville, ME Christian Life Center.
LeVasseur, Giles *o.s.b.* '84 (WDC) [M] Washington, DC St. Anselm's Abbey.
LeVasseur, Lawrence A. *c.s.c.* '51 (SAT) [B] San Antonio, TX Congregation of Holy Cross - Formation Community; [M] San Antonio, TX Holy Cross Community.
LeVay, R. Joseph '50 (SPR) Hinsdale, MA St. Patrick's Church.
LeVecke, John R. *s.j.* '84 (FgM) Provinces.
LeVecke, John R. *s.j.* '84 (SJ) [B] Santa Clara, CA Santa Clara University.
Leveille, Roger L. '79 (SPC) Portageville, MO St. Eustachius Church.
Leveille, Rudolph J. '57 (PRT) Retired.
Leveling, Carlos F. '59 (DAV) Retired.
Leven, Marvin F. '59 (OKL) Lawton, OK Holy Family Church; [K] Norman, OK Campus Ministry for the Archdiocese of Oklahoma City.
Levenhagen, Robert J. '57 (DUB) Cherry Mound, IA St. Pius Church; McGregor, IA St. Mary's Church.
Levens, Robert J. *s.j.* '81 (BO) [W] Boston, MA The Society of Jesus of New England-Provincial Offices; [W] Boston, MA The Society of Jesus of New England-Provincial Offices.
Levens, Robert J. *s.j.* '81 (FgM) Provinces.
Levernier, Donald *glmy.* '61 (CIN) [M] Fairfield, OH Headquarters of Glenmary Home Missioners.
Levesque, Edmond R. '55 (FR) [10] New Bedford, MA St. Anthony of Padua's Church.
Levesque, Gerald A. '64 (PRT) Farmington, ME St. Joseph's Church; [M] Farmington, ME University of Maine at Farmington.
Levesque, Joseph L. *c.m.* '67 (FgM) Vincentian Foreign Missions.
Levesque, Joseph L. *c.m.* '67 (PH) [B] Philadelphia, PA St. Vincent's Seminary; [B] Philadelphia, PA DePaul Novitiate; [AA] Philadelphia, PA Congregation of the Mission.
Levesque, Louis *c.j.m.* '50 (SD) [3] San Diego, CA Blessed Sacrament Church.
Levesque, Paul '89 (ORG) [1] Anaheim, CA St. Anthony Claret Church.
Levesque, Rene R. '55 (FR) Retired.
Levesque, Robert *o.m.i.* '60 (MAN) [K] Hudson, NH Missionary Oblates of Mary Immaculate.
Levesque, Roger J. '59 (FR) [16] New Bedford, MA St. Joseph's Church.
Levesque, Sylvio E. '46 (SPR) Three Rivers, MA St. Anne's Church.
Levesque, Sylvio J. '55 (PRT) Winthrop, ME St. Francis Xavier Church.
Levi, Anthony J. '93 (LFT) West Lafayette, IN St. Thomas Aquinas Church.
Levi, Tony '93 (LFT) [H] West Lafayette, IN St. Thomas Aquinas Parish and Foundation for Catholic Students Attending Purdue University.
Leville, Andre E. *c.s.c.* '78 (FTW) [J] South Bend, IN Congregation of Holy Cross Indiana Province Provincial House.
Levis, Robert J. '48 (E) Retired; [B] Erie, PA Gannon University.
Levitre, J. Albert, Jr. '80 (FBK) North Pole, AK St. Nicholas Church.
Levitt, Donald L. '79 (PEO) East Moline, IL St. Mary's Church.
Levko, John J. *s.j.* '78 (SCR) [C] Scranton, PA University of Scranton; [C] Scranton, PA University of Scranton.
Levkulic, Msgr. William '55 (PBR) Duquesne, PA SS. Peter and Paul Church.
LeVoir, John M. '81 (STP) South St. Paul, MN Holy Trinity Church.
LeVoy, Joseph T. '54 (CHI) [6] Cicero, IL Our Lady of the Mount Church.
Levri, Fidelis *glmy.* '67 (OWN) Beaver Dam, KY Holy Redeemer Church; Fordsville, KY St. John the Baptist Church; Morgantown, KY Holy Trinity Church.
Levy, Cyril '53 (GLP) McNary, AZ St. Anthony Church.
Levy, Michael *o.m.i.* '57 (SAT) [55] San Antonio, TX St. Mary Church.
Levytsky, Bohdan '32 (PHU) Retired.
Lewandowski, Andrew *o.f.m.* '76 (STL) [P] St. Louis, MO Franciscan Friary of St. Anthony of Padua.
Lewandowski, Andrzej *c.r.* '89 (CHI) [88] Chicago, IL St. Hyacinth Church.
Lewandowski, Bruce *c.ss.r.* '93 (NY) [23] New York, NY St. Cecilia Church.
Lewandowski, David J. '55 (HRT) Southington, CT Immaculate Conception Church.
Lewandowski, Dennis '85 (JOL) [3] Naperville, IL St. Raphael Church.
Lewandowski, Donald *o.s.a.* '69 (JOL) [5] Lockport, IL Our Mother of Good Counsel Church; [C] New Lenox, IL Providence Catholic High School.
Lewandowski, Glen *o.s.c.* '74 (FgM) Crosier Foreign Missions.
Lewandowski, John '96 (FAR) Zeeland, ND St. Andrew's Church.
Lewandowski, Leonard A. '77 (PH) [124] Philadelphia, PA Our Lady of Mt. Carmel Church.
Lewandowski, Michael *o.f.m.conv.* '75 (ALT) Davidsville, PA St. Anne Church.
Lewandowski, Raymond H. '85 (DET) [5] Wyandotte, MI St. Patrick Church.
Lewandowski, Richard P. '74 (WOR) [3] Fitchburg, MA St. Camillus de Lellis Church; [Q] Worcester, MA Campus Ministry.
Lewandowski, Robert M. *s.m.* '64 (FWT) Denton, TX Immaculate Conception Church; [M] Arlington, TX University of Texas at Arlington; [M] Denton, TX University of North Texas and Texas Woman's University.
Lewandowski, Ronald C. '95 (CHI) Arlington Heights, IL Our Lady of the Wayside Church.
Lewanski, Gary J. '82 (CHI) [161] Chicago, IL Our Lady of Victory Church.
Lewczak, Thomas J. '65 (NEW) [7] Elizabeth, NJ St. Hedwig's Church.
Lewett, George *o.f.m.* '88 (FgM) Custody of St. Mary of the Angels. Byzantine-Slavonic.
Lewicki, Roman B. *s.j.* '65 (FgM) Provinces.
Lewinski, Cassian *o.p.* '69 (SLC) [7] Salt Lake City, UT St. Catherine of Siena Church; [H] Salt Lake City, UT University of Utah, Newman Center.
Lewinski, Ronald J. '72 (CHI) Mundelein, IL St. Mary Church.
Lewinski, Stanislaus '86 (BRK) [140] Brooklyn, NY St. Thomas Aquinas Church.
Lewis, Alexander J. *o.f.m.conv.* '85 (LA) [R] Torrance, CA Franciscan Friars, St. Bonaventure Friary.
Lewis, Clyde A. '64 (OG) [1] Watertown, NY Holy Family Church.
Lewis, Daniel C. *s.j.* '62 (BO) [E] Boston, MA Boston College High School & Jesuit Community.
Lewis, David '90 (CI) Moen, FM Immaculate Heart of Mary Cathedral; [C] Tunnuk, Chuuk, FM Vicariate Residence.
Lewis, Dennis J. '75 (MIL) [54] Milwaukee, WI St. Michael Church; [71] Milwaukee, WI St. Rose Church.
Lewis, Edward J. '84 (SAC) Vallejo, CA St. Vincent Ferrer Church.
Lewis, Edward J. '92 (GBG) Herminie, PA St. Edward Church.
Lewis, Eric A. '69 (LA) West Covina, CA St. Christopher Church.
Lewis, Francis C. '68 (PH) [1] Coatesville, PA St. Cecilia Church.
Lewis, Francis W. *s.j.* '60 (BGP) [A] Fairfield, CT Fairfield University; [O] Fairfield, CT The Fairfield Jesuit Community-Fairfield University.
Lewis, Gerald (R) Special Assignment.
Lewis, Gerald *s.v.d.* '52 (GAL) [1] Galveston, TX St. Mary's Cathedral Basilica Church; [K] Houston, TX The Catholic Chaplain Corps.
Lewis, Gerald *s.v.d.* '52 (LAF) [4] New Iberia, LA St. Edward Church.
Lewis, Gerald F. '88 (PAT) Hainesville, NJ St. Thomas the Apostle Church; Montague, NJ St. James the Greater Church.
Lewis, Gerard *o.f.m.* '85 (PAT) [M] Ringwood, NJ Holy Name Friary, Inc.
Lewis, Harry J. '50 (SCR) Retired; [N] Dunmore, PA Villa St. Joseph.
Lewis, James *o.carm.* '83 (JOL) [J] Darien, IL Carmelite Provincial Office.
Lewis, James V. *s.j.* '69 (CLV) [E] Cleveland, OH St. Ignatius High School.
Lewis, Kenneth W. '91 (TLS) Fairfax, OK Sacred Heart Church.
Lewis, Lawrence J. *m.m.* '75 (NY) [DD] Maryknoll, NY Maryknoll Fathers and Brothers.
Lewis, Leo T. '60 (STL) Sunset Hills, MO St. Justin Martyr Church.
Lewis, Mark *o.s.b.* '68 (IND) [J] St. Meinrad, IN St. Meinrad Archabbey.
Lewis, Mark *s.j.* '91 (NO) [P] New Orleans, LA Jesuit Provincial Office.
Lewis, Sebastian C. *o.s.b.* '51 (CHI) [110] Chicago, IL St. Joseph Church.
Lewis, Sebastian C. *o.s.b.* '51 (PEO) [A] Peru, IL St. Bede Abbey and Academy.
Lewis, Walter G. '79 (RIC) [13] Richmond, VA St. Mary Church.
Lewkiewicz, Richard M. '68 (BRK) [50] Brooklyn, NY Good Shepherd Church.
Lex, Henry V. '51 (BUF) Retired.
Lex, Henry V. '57 (BUF) [O] Buffalo, NY Sheehan Residence for Priests.
Lex, James '50 (EVN) [13] Evansville, IN St. Anthony Church; Retired.
Lexa, Robert '70 (GB) Retired.
Ley, Richard J. '71 (ARL) [6] Alexandria, VA St. Louis Church.
Ley, Theodore *s.m.* (SJ) [M] Cupertino, CA Marianist Provincial Residence.
Ley, Theodore C. *s.m.* '71 (LA) Gardena, CA Maria Regina Church.
Leydon, William M. '86 (NY) [76] New York, NY St. Monica Church.
Leykam, John J. '72 (STL) St. Ann, MO St. Kevin Church.
Leykam, Lambert *o.f.m.* '56 (SFD) Teutopolis, IL St. Francis of Assisi Church; [K] Teutopolis, IL St. Francis Assisi Friary.
Leykem, Lambert *o.f.m.* '40 (SFD) Montrose, IL St. Rose of Lima Church.
Leyland, Thomas '65 (TOL) Bowling Green, OH St.

Aloysius Church.
Leyrita, Norbert L. '63 (GR) Saranac, MI St. Anthony Church; On Special Assignment.
Lezochowski, Walter '59 (DET) Detroit, MI Crittendon Hospital.
Li-Chung-Lun, Francis *o.f.m.* '46 (STL) [P] St. Louis, MO Franciscan Friary of St. Anthony of Padua.
Liable, Adrian *o.s.b.* '58 (OM) [K] Elkhorn, NE Mount Michael Abbey.
Liagas, Carlos *s.j.* (CHI) [151] Chicago, IL Our Lady of Lourdes Church.
Liana, Zbigniew (DET) [A] Detroit, MI Sacred Heart Major Seminary, Inc.
Libaire, Nathan *o.s.b.* '78 (SFE) [5] Santa Fe, NM St. John Baptist Church.
Libaire, Nathan *o.s.b.* '81 (SCL) [I] Collegeville, MN St. John's Abbey, of the Order of St. Benedict.
Libanati, Ciro '93 (SB) Rialto, CA St. Catherine of Siena Church.
Libasci, Peter A. '78 (RVC) Inwood, NY Our Lady of Good Counsel Church.
Libbey, Louis E. *s.j.* '91 (LA) [C] Los Angeles, CA Loyola Marymount University.
Libens, John F. *s.j.* '70 (DET) [E] Detroit, MI University of Detroit Jesuit High School and Academy; [K] Detroit, MI Jesuit Provincial Office-Detroit Province of the Society of Jesus.
Libens, John F. *s.j.* '70 (FgM) Provinces.
Libera, Angelo '57 (SY) Retired.
Libera, Thomas '69 (CHI) Orland Park, IL Our Lady of the Woods Church.
Liberatore, Albert M. '89 (SCR) Duryea, PA Sacred Heart of Jesus Church; [A] Dalton, PA Saint Pius X Seminary.
Liberatore, David D. '60 (CLV) Parma Heights, OH St. John Bosco Church.
Liberty, Donald *c.ss.r.* '61 (LA) Whittier, CA St. Mary of the Assumption Church; [R] Whittier, CA Redemptorist Fathers Mission House.
Liboroni-Pierozzi, Gilberto (BAL) [H] Baltimore, MD St. Joseph Medical Center, Inc.
Librandi, Michael A. '78 (RCK) Hanover, IL St. John the Evangelist Church.
Librea, Ralph (OM) [16] Omaha, NE Holy Cross Church.
Licari, Jonathan *o.s.b.* '76 (SCL) Collegeville, MN St. John the Baptist Church; [A] Collegeville, MN St. John's Seminary; [B] Collegeville, MN St. John's University; [I] Collegeville, MN St. John's Abbey, of the Order of St. Benedict.
LiCastro, Antonio (HRT) [3] New Haven, CT St. Anthony's Church.
Licata, Donald B. '59 (NY) Beacon, NY St. Joachim Church; State, NY Downstate Correction Facility; State, NY Fishkill Correctional Facility; Castle Point, NY Veterans Administration Medical Center.
Licciardi, Frederick T. *c.pp.s.* '82 (CIN) [M] Dayton, OH Provincial House of the Cincinnati Province of the Society of the Precious Blood.
Lichtefeld, James J. '59 (L) [71] Louisville, KY St. Stephen, Martyr Church.
Lichtenberger, Doug '88 (SFD) Absent on Leave.
Lichtenthal, Msgr. James J. '63 (BUF) Snyder, NY Christ the King Church.
Lichter, Mark '92 (SFS) Aberdeen, SD St. Mary Church.
Lichtle, Thomas A. '61 (LA) Retired.
Lickman, Peter '68 (PSC) Miami, FL St. Basil's Church.
Lickteig, Anthony J. '54 (KCK) Wea, KS Holy Rosary Church.
Lickteig, Bernard *o.carm.* '46 (KCK) Scipio, KS St. Boniface Church.
Lickteig, Fergus *o.carm.* (KCK) [4] Leavenworth, KS St. Joseph's Church.
Lickteig, Fergus *o.carm.* '75 (KCK) [1] Leavenworth, KS Immaculate Conception Church.
Lickteig, Norbert '61 (KCK) [2] Topeka, KS Christ the King Church.
Licznerski, Henryk *c.r.* '92 (MOB) [8] Montgomery, AL Resurrection Catholic Church.
Liddy, Msgr. Richard M. '63 (NEW) [B] South Orange, NJ Seton Hall University.
Liddy, Msgr. Richard M. '63 (WDC) [M] Washington, DC Woodstock Jesuit Community; [V] Washington, DC Woodstock Theological Center.
Liderbach, Daniel P. *s.j.* '73 (BUF) [O] Buffalo, NY Canisius Jesuit Community.
Liderbach, Daniel P. *s.j.* '73 (DET) [K] Detroit, MI Jesuit Provincial Office-Detroit Province of the Society of Jesus.
Lieb, Germain L. *o.s.b.* '45 (ALT) Hastings, PA St. Bernard Church.
Lieb, Germain L. *o.s.b.* '45 (GBG) [H] Latrobe, PA Saint Vincent Archabbey.
Lieb, Joel R. *o.s.b.* '46 (GBG) Trauger, PA Forty Martyrs Church; [H] Latrobe, PA Saint Vincent Archabbey.
Lieb, Marianus D. *t.o.r.* '44 (ALT) [F] Loretto, PA Mount Assisi Friary.
Liebert, William *s.v.d.* '57 (FgM) Society of the Divine Word Foreign Missions.
Lieberth, Joseph J. '68 (CLV) Stow, OH Holy Family Church.
Liebhardt, Kevin M. '74 (CLV) Eastlake, OH St. Justin Martyr Church.
Liebl, Harold J. *s.a.c.* '48 (MIL) [P] Milwaukee, WI St. Vincent Community; [Y] Milwaukee, WI Pallottine Fathers and Brothers, Inc., Disability Trust; [Y] Milwaukee, WI Pallottine Fathers and Brothers, Inc., Educational and Apostolic Ministry Trust.
Liebl, Michael *o.s.b.* '77 (OM) [C] Elkhorn, NE Mount Michael High School; [K] Elkhorn, NE Mount Michael Abbey.
Liebler, Thomas '81 (SFD) Granite City, IL St. Elizabeth Church.
Liebner, David C. (ALN) [1] Minersville, PA St. Barbara Church; [2] Minersville, PA St. Francis of Assisi Church.
Liebner, David M. '60 (ALN) Girardville, PA St. Vincent de Paul Church.
Liebner, James *s.v.d.* '85 (FgM) Society of the Divine Word Foreign Missions.
Liebscher, Arthur F. *s.j.* '84 (SJ) [B] Santa Clara, CA Santa Clara University.
Liekens, Ernest *o.m.i.* '61 (FgM) Oblates Foreign Missions.
Liem, Joseph Than Van *c.m.c.* '89 (SPC) Seneca, MO St. Mary Church.
Liem, Joseph Tran Van *c.m.c.* '89 (SPC) Neosho, MO St. Canera Church.
Lieneri, Charles '68 (P) [14] Portland, OR St. Francis of Assisi Church.
Lienert, Charles J. '68 (P) Gresham, OR St. Henry Church.
Lienhard, Joseph T. *s.j.* '71 (NY) [DD] New York, NY Jesuit Community at Fordham University.
Lies, Eric *o.s.b.* '45 (IND) [J] St. Meinrad, IN St. Meinrad Archabbey.
Lies, James Martin *c.s.c.* '97 (FTW) [B] Notre Dame, IN University of Notre Dame Du Lac.
Lies, Jim M. *c.s.c.* (FTW) [J] Notre Dame, IN Holy Cross Community, Corby Hall, University of Notre Dame.
Lies, William M. *c.s.c.* '94 (FTW) [J] South Bend, IN Congregation of Holy Cross Indiana Province Provincial House.
Lieser, Gregory '63 (SCL) [9] St. Cloud, MN St. Peter Church.
Lieser, Vincent '67 (SCL) Melrose, MN St. Mary's Church.
Liew, Richard (NY) White Plains, NY New York Hospital - Cornell Medical Center.
Liewer, David F. '74 (OM) South Sioux City, NE St. Michael Church.
Lifrak, Richard *ss.cc.* '95 (FR) [3] New Bedford, MA Our Lady of the Assumption Church.
Ligato, Anthony '95 (ALB) [3] Albany, NY Blessed Sacrament Church.
Ligeti, Angelus *o.f.m.* '79 (DET) [31] Detroit, MI Holy Cross Church.
Liggio, John R. *o.s.a.* '75 (PH) [G] Malvern, PA Malvern Preparatory School for Boys.
Ligonde, Jean-Marie Fritz '89 (NEW) [7] Jersey City, NJ Assumption/All Saints Church; [23] Jersey City, NJ St. Patrick's Church.
Ligory, Joseph '83 (NY) [145] Bronx, NY St. Helena Church.
Ligos, George A. '53 (NEW) [25] Jersey City, NJ St. Paul of the Cross Church.
Liguori, Henry A. '66 (TR) Military Chaplains.
Lihvar, Francis P. *s.j.* '61 (CLV) [C] Cleveland, OH John Carroll Jesuit Community.
Liistro, Frank J. '74 (WOR) [7] Fitchburg, MA Madonna of the Holy Rosary Church.
Lijewski, Thomas F. '70 (MIL) [6] Racine, WI St. John Nepomuk Church.
Lijewski, Timothy M. '93 (CHR) [2] Columbia, SC St. Joseph Church; [G] Columbia, SC University of South Carolina, St. Thomas More Center.
Lileart, Richard (DET) Detroit, MI Oakwood Hospital.
Lill, Kenneth J. '91 (TOL) Maumee, OH St. Joseph Church.
Lilly, Msgr. E. C. '29 (SC) Retired.
Lilly, Robert A. *m.m.* '62 (STL) [P] St. Louis, MO Maryknoll House.
Lilly, Robert M. *m.m.* '60 (FgM) Maryknoll Foreign Missions.
Lim, Candido O. *s.j.* '69 (SJ) [25] San Jose, CA St. Victor Church.
Lima, John H. '63 (LAV) Pahrump, NV Our Lady of the Valley Church.
Lima, Joseph *c.pp.s.* '44 (CIN) [B] Carthagena, OH St. Charles.
Lima, Vivian Ben '85 (LA) San Pedro, CA Mary, Star of the Sea Church.
Limanni, Joseph '87 (GAL) Sealy, TX Immaculate Conception Church.
Limanowski, Stanley C. '42 (CHI) Glenwood, IL St. John Church; Retired.
Limbani, George '94 (SEA) [2] Seattle, WA St. Alphonsus Church.
Limbert, William G. '51 (KAL) Retired.
Limmer, George A. '64 (BAL) Hagerstown, MD St. Mary Church.
Limon, Lidio *c.o.* '92 (MRY) [G] Monterey, CA Oratorian Community-Congregation of the Oratory of Pontifical Right.
Linakis, William *s.a.* '77 (NY) [DD] Garrison, NY Generalate of the Franciscan Friars of the Atonement-St. James Friary.
Linakis, William *s.a.* '77 (STO) Stockton, CA DeWitt Nelson Training Center.
Linares, Jose R. (PCE) [B] Ponce, PR The Pontifical Catholic University of Puerto Rico.
Linares, Jose R. '86 (MGZ) Cabo Rojo, PR St. Michael Church.
Linbeck, Augustine *o.s.b.* '32 (CC) [H] Sandia, TX Corpus Christi Abbey.
Linchan, Timothy (BO) [15] Boston, MA St. Brendan Church.
Linck, Joseph C. *c.o.* '94 (PIT) [O] Pittsburgh, PA Congregation of the Oratory of St. Philip Neri; [R] Slippery Rock, PA Office for Campus Ministry;
Lincoln, Daniel L. '84 (L) Jamestown, KY Holy Spirit Church.
Lincoln, Howard A. '93 (SB) Rialto, CA St. Catherine of Siena Church.
Lincon, J. Bruce '89 (BGP) On Duty Outside the Diocese.
Lincon, J. Bruce '89 (CC) [21] Corpus Christi, TX St. Pius X Church.
Lind, Joseph G. '65 (BO) Wellesley, MA St. Paul Church.
Lind, Thomas *s.c.j.* '58 (JKS) [E] Nesbit, MS St. Michael Community House.
Lindauer, Msgr. Clarence '37 (EVN) Retired.
Lindauer, Msgr. Clarence '38 (EVN) [F] Evansville, IN St. John's Home for the Aged.
Lindauer, Prosper *o.s.b.* '50 (IND) [J] St. Meinrad, IN St. Meinrad Archabbey.
Lindblad, Karl-Albert '87 (NY) Military Chaplains.
Lindbloom, Eric *o.f.m.* '67 (DEN) [M] Denver, CO St. Francis of Assisi Friary.
Lindemann, Gene E. '83 (BIS) St. Anthony, ND St. Anthony Church.
Linden, Emmet *c.p.* '51 (L) [69] Louisville, KY St. Rita Church; [L] Louisville, KY Sacred Heart Retreat.
Linden, Michael D. *s.j.* '80 (FgM) Provinces.
Lindenfelser, Timothy '94 (STA) [L] St. Augustine, FL Flagler College Newman Center.
Lindenfelser, Timothy M. '94 (STA) [1] St. Augustine, FL Cathedral of St. Augustine.
Lindenmeyer, Msgr. James '48 (GLP) Farmington, NM St. Mary's Church.
Linder, Msgr. William J. '63 (NEW) [33] Newark, NJ St. Rose of Lima Church.
Lindkugel, William *o.m.i.* '45 (FgM) Oblates Foreign Missions.
Lindle, Lawrence H. (L) [Q] New Haven, KY Archdiocesan Marian Committee.
Lindle, Lawrence H. '59 (L) Culvertown, KY Immaculate Conception Church; [Q] New Haven, KY World Apostolate of Fatima (Blue Army); [Q] New Haven, KY World Apostolate of Fatima (Blue Army).
Lindley, Phillip '83 (AMA) [3] Amarillo, TX Blessed Sacrament Church.
Lindner, Thomas F. '95 (LC) [1] Stevens Point, WI Newman University Parish; [L] Stevens Point, WI Newman University Parish.
Lindsay, John A. *o.s.f.s.* '70 (STO) [A] Stockton, CA St. Mary's High School.
Lindsay, Michael P. '87 (LSC) Santa Clara, NM Santa Clara Church.
Lindsay, Robert (TUC) Apache Junction, AZ St. George Church.
Lindsay, Robert E. *s.j.* '60 (BO) [W] Boston, MA The Society of Jesus of New England-Provincial Offices.
Lindsay, Stewart M. *o.s.f.s.* '74 (BUF) [11] Niagara Falls, NY Prince of Peace Church.
Lindsay, Stewart M. *o.s.f.s.* '74 (TOL) [K] Toledo, OH Oblates of St. Francis de Sales.
Lindstrom, Michael *s.v.d.* '82 (FgM) Society of the Divine Word Foreign Missions.
Linebach, Martin A. '87 (L) [1] Louisville, KY Cathedral of the Assumption.
Linehan, Brian *o.f.m.* '67 (NEW) East Rutherford, NJ St. Joseph's Church.
Linehan, Cornelius '43 (P) Retired.
Linehan, David '56 (SEA) Retired.
Linehan, Dennis *s.j.* '72 (NY) [DD] New York, NY "America;" Residence and publication office of the America Press.
Linehan, Eugene J. *s.j.* '53 (WDC) Bethesda, MD National Institutes of Health, Clinical Center; [E] North Bethesda, MD Georgetown Preparatory School.
Linehan, Jeremiah '48 (P) Retired.
Linehan, Maurice *m.s.* '52 (LKC) [1] Sulphur, LA Immaculate Conception of the B.V.M. Church.
Linehan, Patrick M. *o.m.i.* '34 (BO) [Z] Tewksbury, MA Immaculate Heart of Mary Novitiate-Infirmary.
Linehan, Stephen J. (BO) Military & VA Chaplains.
Ling, Peter '60 (LA) Montebello, CA Our Lady of the Miraculous Medal Church.

LIngan, Joseph E. *s.j.* '90 (SPK) [B] Spokane, WA St. Michael's Institute.
Lininger, Paul *o.f.m.conv.* (ALB) [A] Rensselaer, NY Conventual Franciscan Friars.
Link, David '91 (OAK) San Lorenzo, CA St. John the Baptist Church.
Link, Fred *o.f.m.* '70 (HT) [4] Houma, LA Our Lady of the Most Holy Rosary Church.
Link, Fred J. *o.f.m.* '70 (HT) [8] Houma, LA St. Lucy Church.
Link, Frederick G. '69 (CAM) Westville, NJ St. Anne's Church.
Link, Linus F. '45 (KC) Retired.
Link, Mark J. *s.j.* '60 (CHI) [C] Chicago, IL Jesuit Community at Loyola University of Chicago.
Link, Paul *c.pp.s.* '61 (STL) O'Fallon, MO Assumption Church.
Linkchorst, William J. '73 (ALN) Tamaqua, PA SS. Peter and Paul Church.
Linn, Matthew L. *s.j.* '73 (STP) [N] Minneapolis, MN La Storta Jesuit Community; [Q] Wayzata, MN Cenacle Retreat House.
Linnan, John E. *c.s.v.* '61 (CHI) [B] Chicago, IL The Catholic Theological Union at Chicago; [N] Chicago, IL Viatorian Residence.
Linnan, Roger '62 (SC) Spencer, IA Sacred Heart Church.
Linnan, Roger J. '62 (SC) Rockwell City, IA Calhoun County State Reformatory, Minimum Security for Men.
Linnane, Brian F. *s.j.* '86 (WOR) [N] Worcester, MA Jesuits of Holy Cross College, Inc.
Linnebur, David W. '82 (WCH) Conway Springs, KS St. Joseph Church.
Linnebur, Leroy '61 (WCH) Clonmel, KS St. John Church.
Linnebur, Vincent '60 (JC) Absent on Leave.
Linnemann, Eugene C. '80 (BEL) Leave of Absence.
Linnenbrink, Harry H. '57 (DAV) Retired.
Linowski, Eugene R. '57 (PRM) Columbus, OH St. John Chrysostom Church; Dayton, OH St. Barbara Church.
Lins, James R. '64 (MAD) Seymour, WI Our Lady of Hope Church; Shullsburg, WI St. Matthew Church.
Linse, Henry *c.s.s.* '48 (BO) [Z] Waltham, MA Stigmatine Fathers and Brothers.
Linsky, Gary S. '95 (CHR) Gaffney, SC Sacred Heart Church; Union, SC St. Augustine's Church; [G] Gaffney, SC Limestone College Newman Center.
Linsky, Thomas J. *s.j.* '52 (ALN) [A] Wernersville, PA Novitiate of St. Isaac Jogues.
Linsler, Christopher E. '77 (ROC) [5] Elmira, NY St. Casimir Church.
Linsler, Christopher E. '78 (ROC) Elmira Heights, NY St. Charles Borromeo Church.
Linster, Joseph B. '69 (RCK) St. Charles, IL St. Patrick Church.
Linton, Edward *o.s.b.* '91 (IND) [J] St. Meinrad, IN St. Meinrad Archabbey.
Linton, Terence H. *c.s.c.* '80 (OAK) [N] Berkeley, CA Holy Cross Fathers-Holy Cross Center.
Lintz, Charles *s.s.c.* '70 (FgM) St. Columban's Foreign Mission.
Lintz, Christoph (NEW) On Duty Outside the Archdiocese.
Lintzenich, Stephen P. '74 (EVN) [19] Evansville, IN St. Mary Church.
Linz, Lester A. *s.j.* '44 (CIN) [M] Cincinnati, OH Jesuit Community at St. Xavier High School.
Lioi, Frank E. '67 (ROC) [4] Rochester, NY St. Anne Church.
Lion, William J. '58 (CHI) [1] Oak Lawn, IL St. Catherine of Alexandria Church.
Liona, Kenneth J. '78 (BRK) Absent on Leave.
Lionelli, Anthony J. '72 (NEW) [21] Newark, NJ Immaculate Conception Church.
Lipareli, Michael '80 (NY) [125] Bronx, NY St. Ann Church.
Lipari, Anthony R. '89 (NEW) Ridgewood, NJ Our Lady of Mount Carmel Church.
Lipczewski, Boleslaus '58 (DET) [10] Detroit, MI Assumption Grotto Church; Absent on Sick Leave.
Lipiec, Bart (BUF) Silver Springs, NY St. Mary Church.
Lipiec, Bart '83 (BUF) Warsaw, NY St. Michael Church.
Lipinski, Alberic *s.o.cist.* '83 (CHI) [N] Willow Springs, IL Cistercian Fathers.
Lipinski, Edward '71 (CAM) Bellmawr, NJ Annunciation Church.
Lipinski, Edward J. '71 (CAM) Audubon, NJ Church of the Holy Maternity.
Lipinski, Paul M. '73 (RCK) [B] Woodstock, IL Marian Central Catholic High School.
Lipnicki, Thomas Paul '78 (NEW) [2] East Orange, NJ Holy Spirit-Our Lady Help of Christians Church.
Lipp, John F. *o.s.a.* '54 (PH) [U] Norristown, PA Sacred Heart Hospital and Rehabilitation Center; [AA] Villanova, PA St. Thomas Monastery.
Lippert, Donald *o.f.m.cap.* '85 (CLV) [A] Wickliffe, OH Borromeo Seminary.
Lippert, Paul R. '61 (MIL) Retired.
Lippold, John L. '57 (BAL) Linthicum Heights, MD St. Philip Neri Church.
Lipps, Frank J. '68 (NO) Violet, LA Our Lady of Lourdes Church.
Lipps, Louis *s.j.* '52 (LEX) [1] Lexington, KY Cathedral of Christ the King; Special Assignment.
Lippstock, Paul E. '78 (DUB) [6] Waterloo, IA Blessed Sacrament Church; [D] Waterloo, IA Columbus High School.
Lipscomb, N. Alan '94 (RIC) Lexington, VA St. Patrick Church.
Lipscomb, William W. '97 (GAY) Traverse City, MI St. Francis of Assisi Church.
Liptak, David Q. '53 (HRT) Broad Brook, CT St. Catherine's Church; Special and other (Arch)Diocesan Assignment.
Liptak, David Q. '53 (NOR) [A] Cromwell, CT Holy Apostles College and Seminary.
Liptak, Edward *s.d.b.* '59 (FgM) Salesians of Don Bosco Foreign Missions.
Liptock, Edward R. *v.f.* '55 (SCR) [1] Dunmore, PA All Saints Church.
LiPuma, David G. '87 (BUF) [O] Buffalo, NY Bishop's Residence.
Lira, Juan R. '85 (DAL) Sherman, TX St. Mary Church.
Lirette, Albert *o.m.i.* '45 (FgM) Oblates Foreign Missions.
Lirette, Msgr. Arthur J. '49 (LA) Glendale, CA Holy Family Church; Retired.
Lis, Albert *o.f.m.* (GB) Hofa Park, WI St. Stanislaus Church.
Lis, Albert *o.f.m.* '86 (GB) Pulaski, WI Assumption of the Blessed Virgin Mary Church.
Lis, John S. '73 (SPR) [1] Northampton, MA Annunciation Church.
Lisante, Msgr. James P. '81 (RVC) West Hempstead, NY St. Thomas, the Apostle Church.
Lisbeth, Michael L. *s.m.* '80 (CIN) [M] Cincinnati, OH Marianist Community.
Lischaa, Msgr. Sharbel '61 (SAM) Philadelphia, PA St. Maron Church.
Lischwe, Bruno V. *c.ss.r.* '52 (STL) [P] Liguori, MO St. Clement Health Care Center.
Lisik, Paul A. '81 (GBG) Monessen, PA The Epiphany of Our Lord Church.
Liska, Richard A. '70 (MIL) Butler, WI St. Agnes Church.
Lisowski, Brian A. '81 (CHI) Other Assignments.
Lisowski, Edward E. '64 (CHI) [3] Waukegan, IL St. Dismas Church.
Lisowski, Edward E. '64 (MIL) Wood, WI Veterans Administration Medical Center.
Lisowski, Jan '39 (SC) Retired.
Lisowski, Lawrence M. '84 (CHI) La Grange, IL St. Francis Xavier Church.
Lisowski, William J. '50 (CHI) [115] Chicago, IL St. Ladislaus Church; Retired.
Liss, Robert C. '62 (STL) Richwoods, MO St. Stephen's Church.
Liss, Valentine '40 (PEO) [4] Spring Valley, IL SS. Peter and Paul's Church; Retired.
Lisson, Edwin J. *s.j.* (STL) [C] St. Louis, MO Saint Louis University.
Lisson, Edwin L. *s.j.* '69 (STL) [P] St. Louis, MO Jesuit Community Corporation at St. Louis University - Jesuit Hall.
List, John E. '85 (LEX) Georgetown, KY St. John's Church.
Listecki, Jerome E. '75 (CHI) [A] Mundelein, IL University of St. Mary of the Lake-Mundelein Seminary.
Liston, Daniel P. '85 (SPR) [2] Northampton, MA Blessed Sacrament Church; [M] Northampton, MA Spanish Apostolate.
Liston, Paul F. '58 (WDC) [36] Washington, DC St. Patrick Church.
Liszewski, Francis A. '69 (NOR) Absent on Leave; Retired.
Liszewski, Peter B. '76 (NOR) Lebanon, CT St. Francis of Assisi Church.
Litavec, Edward S. '60 (PIT) Fredericktown, PA St. Oliver Plunkett Church.
Litcheck, Michael P. '71 (SCR) Carbondale, PA Our Lady of Mt. Carmel Church.
Literal, Peter '78 (MEM) Memphis, TN Federal Correctional Institute at Memphis.
Literski, Msgr. Roy E. '53 (WIN) Retired.
Litot, Msgr. Edward F. '47 (GRY) Retired.
Littelmann, Edward J. '69 (TOL) Huron, OH St. Peter Church.
Little, Msgr. Anthony B. '82 (ALT) [13] Altoona, PA St. Therese of the Child Jesus Church.
Little, Gregory (NY) Bronx, NY U.S.V.A. Medical Center.
Little, John '87 (OWN) [I] Bowling Green, KY Western Kentucky University Newman Center.
Little, Msgr. John J. '77 (ALT) Nanty-Glo, PA St. Mary's Church.
Little, John J. L. '88 (ALN) Northampton, PA Our Lady of Hungary Church.
Little, Richard P. '62 (BO) [2] Methuen, MA St. Monica Church.
Littlefield, Philaret '87 (NTN) Milwaukee, WI St. George Church.
Littleton, Gregory J. '90 (CHL) Maggie Valley, NC St. Margaret Church.
Littleton, Gregory J. '90 (MET) On Duty Outside the Diocese.
Litwin, Paul A. '79 (BUF) [O] Buffalo, NY Bishop's Residence.
Liu, Peter T. '60 (RVC) Ronkonkoma, NY St. Joseph's Church.
Liu, Vincent '54 (RVC) Smithtown, NY St. Patrick Church.
Liuima, Francis *s.j.* '45 (BO) [W] Chestnut Hill, MA The Jesuit Community at Boston College.
Liuzzi, Kenneth J. '75 (DEN) Arvada, CO Shrine of St. Anne Church.
Liuzzi, Peter J. *o.carm.* '65 (LA) [B] North Hills, CA Carmel West Community.
Liuzzo, Vincent *o.f.m.cap.* '49 (PAT) Passaic, NJ St. Mary Hospital; [J] Passaic, NJ St. Mary's Hospital.
Lively, Joseph A. '57 (BUR) Gilman, VT St. Theresa Church; St. Johnsbury, VT St. John the Evangelist Church.
Livigni, Salvatore J. '61 (BAL) [10] Baltimore, MD St. Anthony of Padua Church; [66] Baltimore, MD Most Precious Blood, Community of Church; Baltimore, MD Greater Baltimore Medical Center.
Livingston, Benedict *s.p.* '72 (SFE) [J] Jemez Springs, NM The Jemez Program, Our Lady of Lourdes Novitiate.
Livingston, James G. '91 (DET) [5] Dearborn Heights, MI St. Mel Church.
Livingston, James T. '90 (STP) Delano, MN St. Mary of Czestochowa Church; St. Bonifacius, MN St. Boniface Church.
Livingston, Morson Ravi *s.a.c.* '85 (ALX) Brouillette, LA St. Genevieve Church.
Livingston, Msgr. Robert C. '45 (PEO) Kickapoo, IL St. Mary's of Kickapoo Church; Retired.
Livingstone, Benedict *s.p.* '72 (SFE) [N] Jemez Springs, NM Fitzgerald Charitable Trust.
Livojevich, Ronald '70 (KCK) [4] Overland Park, KS Queen of the Holy Rosary Church.
Livolsi, Silvester J. '48 (PAT) [I] Branchville, NJ Sanctuary of Mary-Our Lady of the Holy Spirit.
Livolsi, Sylvester J. '48 (NEW) On Duty Outside the Archdiocese.
Lizarraga, Joaquin (ARE) Retired.
Lizarralde, Luis *o.f.m.* '51 (SJN) [4] Toa Baja, PR Jose Obrero Church.
Lizio, John R. '57 (BO) [4] Marlboro, MA St. Matthias Church.
Lizor, Joseph S., Jr. '58 (BAL) [56] Baltimore, MD St. Luke Church.
Llagas, Carlos *s.j.* '89 (CHI) [C] Chicago, IL Jesuit Community at Loyola University of Chicago.
Llamas, Rodolfo DLC *v.d.c.* '93 (SFR) [N] San Francisco, CA Verbum Dei Community.
Llambias, Martin '73 (SJN) [G] Guaynabo, PR Opus Dei.
Llano, Isidoro '51 (GLP) On Duty Outside of Diocese.
Llanos, Philip S. '78 (LA) Military and VA Chaplains.
Llanos, Philip S. '78 (TUC) Tucson, AZ Christ the King Chapel.
Llaria, Vincent '59 (VEN) Lake Placid, FL St. James Church.
Lleo, Pedro '76 (MIA) Miami Shores, FL St. Rose of Lima Church.
Llorente, Amando *s.j.* '48 (MIA) [J] Miami, FL John Paul II Retreat House.
Lloyd, James B. *c.s.p.* '48 (NY) [104] New York, NY St. Paul the Apostle Church; [A] Yonkers, NY St. Joseph's Seminary; [DD] Jamaica Estates, NY Paulist Fathers Generalate.
Lloyd, Patrick *s.c.j.* '69 (MIL) [P] Hales Corners, WI Sacred Heart Monastery; [Y] Franklin, WI Congregation of the Priests of the Sacred Heart Support and Maintenance Trust.
Lloyd, Msgr. Paul A. '37 (PRO) Retired; [M] Pawtucket, RI Jeanne Jugan Residence.
Lloyd, Robert J. *m.m.* '62 (FgM) Maryknoll Foreign Missions.
Lloyd, Robert J. *m.m.* '62 (NY) [DD] Maryknoll, NY Maryknoll Fathers and Brothers.
Lloyd, Ronald L. *s.m.m.* '43 (RVC) [N] Bay Shore, NY Montfort Missionaries.
Lloyd, Vincent A. '42 (TR) Retired.
Lloyd, Vincent A. '45 (ORL) Retired.
Lluch, Santiago *c.m.* '42 (NY) [44] New York, NY Holy Agony Church; [DD] New York, NY Vincentian Fathers.
Lo Bianco, Msgr. Francis R. '54 (NEW) Paramus, NJ Our Lady of the Visitation Church.
Lobacz, James E. '79 (MIL) [C] Milwaukee, WI Cardinal Stritch University.
Lobato, Nicanor '61 (VEN) Palmetto, FL Holy Cross Church.
Lobaton, Jose *o.f.m.* '73 (WDC) [1] Washington, DC St. Matthew Cathedral.
Lobby, Basil F. *o.f.m.* '46 (PAT) [M] Butler, NJ St. Anthony Friary.

Lobert, Richard C. '75 (BAL) Special Assignment.
Lobert, Richard C. '75 (LAN) [3] Ann Arbor, MI St. Thomas the Apostle Church.
LoBianco, Paschal *s.v.d.* '50 (CHI) [B] Techny, IL Divine Word Residence.
LoBianco, Richard J. '79 (CHI) [2] Oak Lawn, IL St. Gerald Church.
LoBiondo, Gasper F. *s.j.* '68 (WDC) [M] Washington, DC Woodstock Jesuit Community; [V] Washington, DC Woodstock Theological Center.
Lobo, Anthony *s.s.* '70 (SFR) [27] San Francisco, CA St. John the Evangelist Church.
Lobo, Benjamin '63 (GF) Culbertson, MT St. Anthony's Church.
Lobo, Stanley M. '65 (NEW) [25] Jersey City, NJ St. Paul of the Cross Church.
Lobo, Theodore '57 (TUC) Parker, AZ Sacred Heart Church.
Loc, Timothy Mai Vinh *c.m.c.* '77 (SPC) Carthage, MO St. Ann Church.
Locatelli, Paul L. *s.j.* '74 (SJ) [B] Santa Clara, CA Santa Clara University.
Loch, Richard J. '79 (SCR) [17] Scranton, PA St. Mary of the Assumption Church.
Lochner, Robert J. *c.s.c.* '46 (FTW) [J] South Bend, IN Congregation of Holy Cross Indiana Province Provincial House.
Lochner, Robert J. *c.s.c.* '46 (ORL) Retired; [F] Cocoa Beach, FL Holy Cross Fathers, Eastern Priests Province.
Lochs, Matthew *ss.cc.* '36 (HON) [11] Honolulu, HI St. Patrick Church.
Lock, Bertram *ss.cc.* '89 (HON) Kaneohe, HI St. Ann Church.
Lockard, Msgr. David A. '75 (ALT) Huntingdon, PA Most Holy Trinity Church.
Locke, James E. '61 (PH) Chadds Ford, PA St. Cornelius Church.
Locke, John K. *s.j.* '64 (FgM) Provinces.
Lockman, V. James '67 (WDC) Laurel, MD St. Mary Church.
Lockwood, Gregory J. '88 (STL) Hazelwood, MO Our Lady of Mercy Church; [A] St. Louis, MO Kenrick-Glennon Seminary.
Lodge, John G. '73 (CHI) [A] Mundelein, IL University of St. Mary of the Lake-Mundelein Seminary.
Lodge, Richard J. '69 (CAM) West Collingswood, NJ Transfiguration Church.
Lodi, George C. '74 (NY) [6] Yonkers, NY Christ the King Church.
Lody, John R. '62 (Y) Canal Fulton, OH SS. Philip and James Church.
Loeb, Karl E. '95 (BUF) Amherst, NY St. Leo Church.
Loeber, Germain *o.s.b* '55 (SCL) [I] Collegeville, MN St. John's Abbey, of the Order of St. Benedict.
Loebl, Jeffrey R. *s.j.* '82 (MIL) [P] Milwaukee, WI Jesuit Community at Marquette University.
Loecke, Douglas J. '89 (DUB) Grundy Center, IA Sacred Heart Church; Reinbeck, IA Queen of Heaven Church.
Loecker, Craig J. '92 (OM) [46] Omaha, NE St. Thomas More Church.
Loeffer, Earl '51 (TOL) [5] Toledo, OH Corpus Christi, University of Toledo Church.
Loeffler, Earl A. (TOL) Retired.
Loeffler, Richard A. *c.m.* '32 (PH) [AA] Philadelphia, PA Congregation of the Mission.
Loegering, Leonard '73 (FAR) [1] Grand Forks, ND Holy Family Church.
Loehr, Charles D. '47 (MIL) Retired.
Loehr, James P. '67 (MIL) Delafield, WI St. Joan of Arc Church.
Loehrlein, Richard A. *s.m.* '61 (CIN) [M] Dayton, OH Marianist Provincialate.
Loehrlein, Sylvester '56 (EVN) Red Brush, IN St. Rupert Church.
Loeper, David J. '83 (ALN) [10] Bethlehem, PA SS. Simon and Jude Church.
Loeper, Msgr. Richard J. '50 (ALN) [3] Bethlehem, PA Holy Ghost Church.
Loew, James H. *o.s.b.* '97 (GBG) Jeannette, PA Sacred Heart Church.
Lofgren, Eric D. '93 (SAC) Burney, CA St. Francis of Assisi Church.
LoFranco, Sofronio '60 (BRK) [B] Elmhurst, NY Cathedral Preparatory Seminary of the Immaculate Conception.
Loftin, Don '94 (AUS) Round Rock, TX St. William's Church.
Lofton, Msgr. Edward D. '82 (CHR) Summerville, SC St. Theresa the Little Flower Church.
Lofton, James J. '61 (ALN) New Philadelphia, PA Sacred Heart Church.
Loftus, Conrad W. *o.f.m.* '54 (NY) [DD] New York, NY Franciscan Friars, Order of Friars Minor, Holy Name Province.
Loftus, David '94 (LA) La Mirada, CA Beatitudes of Our Lord Church.
Loftus, J. Allan *s.j.* '74 (BAL) [M] Baltimore, MD Jesuit Fathers and Brothers Maryland Provincial Curia.
Loftus, Joseph J. '56 (ARL) Falls Church, VA St. Philip Church.
Loftus, Joseph V. *s.j.* '40 (DET) [P] Clarkston, MI Colombiere Center.
Loftus, Kenneth G. *s.j.* '91 (BO) [W] Boston, MA The Society of Jesus of New England-Provincial Offices.
Loftus, Kenneth G. *s.j.* '91 (SCR) [C] Scranton, PA University of Scranton.
Loftus, Msgr. Padraic '62 (LA) Woodland Hills, CA St. Mel Church.
Loftus, Msgr. Robert '43 (NY) Retired; [Z] New York, NY Kateri Residence.
Loftus, Robert A. '91 (BGP) Riverside, CT St. Catherine of Siena Church.
Loftus, Thomas B. *c.ss.r.* '57 (BAL) [87] Baltimore, MD Sacred Heart of Jesus Church.
Lofy, Guy *o.c.d.* '48 (MIL) [P] Milwaukee, WI Provincial Offices - Discalced Carmelites.
Lofy, Joseph M. *c.s.v.* '73 (CHI) [N] Arlington Heights, IL Viatorian Province Center-Clerics of St. Viator.
Logan, Aidan *o.c.s.o.* '85 (WOR) [N] Spencer, MA St. Joseph's Abbey.
Logan, Msgr. Daniel B. '63 (STA) [5] Jacksonville, FL Holy Family Church.
Logan, David '79 (VNN) Spokane, WA SS. Cyril & Methodius Church.
Logan, Francis A. *s.j.* '33 (SEA) [A] Seattle, WA Seattle University.
Logan, Gary W. '93 (SR) Willits, CA St. Anthony Church.
Logan, J. M. '79 (PEO) [3] Rock Island, IL St. Joseph's Church.
Logan, James J. '59 (LC) Marshfield, WI Our Lady of Peace Church.
Logan, James P. '86 (BAK) [1] Baker, OR Cathedral of St. Francis De Sales.
Logan, Msgr. James T. '54 (FRS) [2] Fresno, CA Holy Spirit Church; [J] Fresno, CA Apostolate of Christian Action.
Logan, John *o.carm.* '64 (NY) [97] New York, NY Our Lady of the Scapular/St. Stephen Church; Manhattan, NY Bellevue Hospital.
Logan, John D. *o.p.* '56 (TYL) [D] Nacogdoches, TX Stephen F. Austin University Catholic Student Center.
Logan, John W. *o.p.* (TYL) Nacogdoches, TX Sacred Heart Church.
Logan, Joseph P. *s.j.* '54 (SJ) [L] Los Altos, CA Jesuit Retreat House.
Logan, Michael *c.ss.r.* '57 (SEA) [32] Seattle, WA Sacred Heart of Jesus Church.
Logan, William R. '69 (RVC) Baldwin, NY St. Christopher Church.
LoGatto, Joseph J. '57 (PAT) Retired.
LoGatto, Rosario J. '42 (BRK) Retired.
LoGrasso, Pasquale '57 (DET) [2] Clinton Twp., MI St. Louis Church.
Logrip, Joseph L. '72 (PH) [100] Philadelphia, PA Mater Dolorosa Church; [A] Wynnewood, PA Theological Seminary of St. Charles Borromeo, Overbrook.
Logsdon, L. Peter *c.s.c.* '68 (FgM) Holy Cross Foreign Missions.
Logsdon, Wilfrid *o.f.m.conv.* '59 (SAV) Brunswick, GA St. Francis Xavier Church.
Logue, Charles D. (BO) Retired.
Logue, Charles D. '48 (BO) Halifax, MA Our Lady of the Lake Church.
Logue, Dennis *s.v.d.* '83 (PBR) Girard, PA SS. Cyril and Methodius Church.
Logue, Louis R. '53 (BUR) Waterbury, VT State Hospital.
Logue, Mark '73 (BAL) Owensville, MD Our Lady of Sorrows Church.
Lohan, James '73 (NO) [5] Metairie, LA St. Catherine of Siena Church.
Lohan, Louis '71 (BLX) Long Beach, MS St. Thomas the Apostle Church.
Lohkamp, Nicholas *o.f.m.* '52 (CIN) [M] Cincinnati, OH St. Ann Friary.
Lohr, Charles H. *s.j.* '61 (NY) [DD] New York, NY Jesuit Provincial's Office.
Lohrmeyer, Kenneth '70 (SAL) Minneapolis, KS Immaculate Conception of the Blessed Virgin Mary Church.
Lohse, Edward M. '89 (E) [A] Erie, PA St. Mark's Seminary.
Lohse, Walter H. '40 (E) Retired.
Loi, Nguyen '66 (OM) [4] Omaha, NE St. Ann Church.
Loiacono, James *o.m.i.* '71 (BO) [12] Lowell, MA Nuestra Senora del Carmen Church.
Loiselle, Joseph G. '57 (WOR) East Brookfield, MA St. John the Baptist Church.
Loiselle, Lucien H. '49 (BO) Dracut, MA St. Mary of the Assumption Church.
Lolio, John W. '70 (PRO) East Greenwich, RI Our Lady of Mercy Church.
Lomasiewicz, Donald E. '62 (GR) [10] Grand Rapids, MI St. Isidore's Church.
Lomasney, John P. *m.m.* '43 (FgM) Maryknoll Foreign Missions.
Lomax, Mark '80 (NO) Chalmette, LA St. Mark Church.
Lombard, Richard J. '53 (SHP) [8] Shreveport, LA St. Joseph Church.
Lombard, Roy A. '47 (WH) Retired.
Lombard, Samuel J. (BO) Retired.
Lombardi, Albert U. '47 (DET) Retired.
Lombardi, Gary '69 (SR) Petaluma, CA St. Vincent de Paul Church.
Lombardi, John J. '88 (BAL) Randallstown, MD Holy Family Church.
Lombardi, Joseph L. *s.j.* '75 (PH) [C] Philadelphia, PA St. Joseph's University; [AA] Philadelphia, PA Jesuit Community at St. Joseph's University.
Lombardi, Nicholas D. *s.j.* '72 (NY) [DD] New York, NY Jesuit Community at Fordham University.
Lombardi, Thomas '75 (FTW) Garrett, IN St. Joseph Church.
Lombardo, Msgr. Angelo J. '55 (BEL) Okawville, IL St. Barbara Church.
Lombardo, Francis *o.f.m.conv.* (BAL) [M] Ellicott City, MD St. Joseph Cupertino Friary, Friars Minor Conventual of St. Francis of Assisi; [M] Ellicott City, MD Friary of St. Joseph Cupertino.
Lombardo, Gerard M. '86 (NEW) [10] Elizabeth, NJ St. Patrick's Church.
Lombardo, Gregory J. *c.s.c.* '45 (FTW) [J] South Bend, IN Congregation of Holy Cross Indiana Province Provincial House.
Lombardo, Joseph A. '85 (TUC) Green Valley, AZ Our Lady of the Valley Church.
Lombardo, Michael J. '78 (PAT) Pompton Plains, NJ Our Lady of Good Counsel Church; Pompton Plains, NJ Chilton Memorial Hospital; Wayne, NJ Wayne General Hospital.
Lombardo, Robert *c.f.r.* '90 (NY) [DD] New York, NY St. Crispin Friary.
Lombardo, Msgr. Samuel L. '39 (BUF) Retired.
Lombo, German *o.s.a.* '53 (MGZ) Aguada, PR St. Francis of Assisi Church.
Lomello, Lucian *s.d.b.* '48 (LA) [R] Los Angeles, CA Dominic Savio Salesian Residence.
Lomello, Lucian B. *s.d.b.* (LA) [79] Los Angeles, CA St. Mary Church.
Lommel, George D. '46 (FAR) Retired.
Lonardo, Alfred C. '63 (PRO) [5] Cranston, RI St. Mary Church.
Loncar, Sebastian '37 (VEN) Retired.
Loncar, Stephen *o.f.m.conv.* '88 (GRY) [12] Gary, IN St. Joseph The Worker Church.
Loncarcic, Stanley J. '36 (KCK) Louisburg, KS Immaculate Conception Church.
Lonchyna, Taras '77 (PHU) [A] Washington, DC St. Josaphat Seminary.
Lonchyna, Taras R. '77 (PHU) Silver Spring, MD Holy Trinity Church; Manassas, VA Annunciation of the Blessed Virgin Mary Church; Richmond, VA St. John the Baptist Church.
London, Lawrence '53 (RCK) Retired.
Londono, Antonio '94 (SP) On Duty Outside the Diocese.
Londono, Antonio M. *s.p.* '94 (CHR) Greenville, SC St. Mary's Church.
Londono, Diego '96 (ORL) Daytona Beach, FL St. Paul's Church.
Londono, Heriberto '84 (SJN) [2] Toa Baja, PR Ntra. Sra. de la Candelaria Church.
Londono, Orlando '77 (SJN) [3] Canovanas, PR Sagrado Corazon de Jesus Church.
Lonek, Stephen C. '76 (NY) On Duty Outside the Archdiocese.
Lonek, Stephen C. '76 (WIL) Fairfax, DE St. Mary Magdalen Church.
Lonergan, David W. '61 (HRT) Wethersfield, CT Corpus Christi Church; Wethersfield, CT Sacred Heart Church.
Lonergan, James B. '66 (ALB) Hudson Falls, NY Church of St. Mary's/St. Paul's.
Lonergan, Michael J. '93 (PH) Collingdale, PA St. Joseph Church.
Long, Anthony Vu Khac *c.m.c.* '92 (RCK) DeKalb, IL St. Mary Church.
Long, Daniel *l.c.* '94 (WDC) [M] Potomac, MD Legionaries of Christ.
Long, Francis C. '47 (PHX) Retired.
Long, Galen '91 (SAL) Colby, KS Sacred Heart Church.
Long, Garrett J. *s.m.* (RVC) [D] Mineola, NY Chaminade High School (Boys).
Long, Garrett J. *s.m.* '76 (RVC) [N] Mineola, NY Provincial Residence and Novitiate.
Long, J. William '89 (R) Henderson, NC St. James the Greater Church.
Long, James T. '63 (BEL) Fairview Heights, IL St. Albert the Great Church.
Long, John *s.j.* (NY) [A] Yonkers, NY St. Joseph's Seminary.
Long, John '61 (JC) Lake Ozark, MO Our Lady of the Lake Church.
Long, John F. *s.j.* '56 (NY) [DD] New York, NY "America;" Residence and publication office of the America Press.
Long, John M. '78 (STP) Hopkins, MN St. Joseph's Church.
Long, John Paul '68 (BGP) [2] Bridgeport, CT St.

Ambrose Church.
Long, John R. '89 (SUP) Bruce, WI St. Mary Church; Strickland, WI Assumption of the Blessed Virgin Mary Church; Weyerhaeuser, WI SS. Peter and Paul Church.
Long, Joseph J. *c.s.c.* '59 (SCR) [C] Wilkes-Barre, PA Kings College.
Long, Melvin T. '66 (SAL) Manhattan, KS St. Thomas More Parish.
Long, Msgr. Michael J. '54 (PH) Sellersville, PA St. Agnes Church.
Long, Richard E. '89 (BRK) [23] Brooklyn, NY St. Brendan's Church.
Long, Thomas (GB) Brillion, WI St. Mary Church.
Long, Tran Phuc '48 (ORG) Costa Mesa, CA St. John the Baptist Church.
Long, Valentine *o.f.m.* '27 (PAT) [M] Ringwood, NJ Holy Name Friary, Inc.
Long, Vincent P. '69 (SY) Hinckley, NY St. Ann Church; Holland Patent, NY St. Leo Church.
Longanback, Carl *c.pp.s.* '34 (CIN) [B] Carthagena, OH St. Charles.
Longbucco, John L. '90 (MAR) Ontonagon, MI Holy Family Church; Rockland, MI St. Mary Church.
Longchamps, Adrien R. '75 (MAN) [4] Manchester, NH St. Augustin Church.
Longen, Louis *o.m.i.* '79 (BUF) [27] Buffalo, NY Holy Angels Church.
Longo, Robert M. *o.f.m.cap.* '85 (BRK) Released from Diocesan Assignment.
Longo, Roque *m.ss.cc.* '33 (CAM) [M] Linwood, NJ Villa Pieta.
Longres, Joaquin S. '62 (BRK) [191] Queens, NY St. Luke Church.
Longtin, Lucien F. *s.j.* '65 (WDC) [E] Washington, DC Gonzaga College High School.
Longua, Msgr. Paul '61 (PAT) Sabbatical.
Longweld, John *o.f.m.cap.* (NY) Wassaic, NY Wassaic Development Center.
Longwill, Cathal '54 (DEN) Craig, CO St. Michael Church.
Longworth, Kevin J. *s.p.s.* '53 (SFR) [2] San Mateo, CA St. Gregory Church.
Lonsdale, Richard G. '66 (PRT) Hallowell, ME Sacred Heart Church.
Lonteen, Daniel '94 (CLV) Absent on Leave.
Looby, John J. '66 (OG) Dannemora, NY St. Joseph Church.
Loomie, Albert J. *s.j.* '52 (NY) [DD] New York, NY Jesuit Community at Fordham University.
Loomis, Dennis J. *m.s.* (FR) [J] Attleboro, MA La Salette Provincial House; [J] Attleboro, MA La Salette Missionary Association.
Loomis, Msgr. Richard '76 (LA) [2] North Hollywood, CA St. Charles Borromeo Church.
Loomis, Richard P. '52 (WIN) Fairmont, MN St. John Vianney Church.
Loomis, Thomas A. '92 (WIN) Preston, MN St. Columban Church.
Looney, Daniel A. '71 (SAC) Davis, CA St. James Church.
Looney, Joseph E. '67 (HRT) [7] Waterbury, CT Sacred Heart Church.
Looney, Matthew D. '58 (NEW) Westfield, NJ Holy Trinity Church.
Looney, Thomas P. *c.s.c.* '87 (SCR) [C] Wilkes-Barre, PA Kings College; [M] Wilkes-Barre, PA Moreau House.
Loos, Francis *c.i.c.m.* '41 (ARL) [J] Arlington, VA Missionhurst, C.I.C.M.-Central House and Provincialate.
Loos, Frederick C. '63 (SAG) On Duty Outside the Diocese.
Loosbrock, Donald L. '51 (WIN) Retired.
Lopardo, Vito R. '55 (BEL) Retired.
Lopatesky, Raymond M. '75 (PAT) [P] Chester, NJ Nazareth Village.
Lopera, Rafael I. *c.s.b.* '94 (GAL) [Q] Sugar Land, TX Basilian Mission Center.
Lopes, Richard *o.f.m.cap.* '82 (SFR) [N] Burlingame, CA Capuchin Provincial House.
Lopes, Thomas C. '65 (FR) Nantucket, MA St. Mary's, Our Lady of the Isle Church.
Lopez, Abel '56 (SJ) [1] San Jose, CA Cathedral Basilica of St. Joseph Church.
Lopez, Adolfo '87 (GLP) Absent on Leave.
Lopez, Agustin *sch.p.* '57 (PCE) [4] Ponce, PR Our Lady of Mt. Carmel Church.
Lopez, Alberto '87 (SJN) [3] Guaynabo, PR Maria Madre de Mi Senor Church.
Lopez, Alfred *o.p.* (MAR) [1] Marquette, MI St. Peter Cathedral.
Lopez, Alvaro '95 (STO) Modesto, CA St. Stanislaus Church.
Lopez, Amador *o.m.i.* '58 (SD) Calipatria, CA St. Patrick Church.
Lopez, Antonio '95 (FR) [17] Fall River, MA St. Louis Church; [P] Fall River, MA Priestly Fraternity of the Missionaries of St. Charles Borromeo, Inc.
Lopez, Armando *o.f.m.* '88 (SD) San Luis Rey, CA Mission San Luis Rey de Francia Church; [H] San Luis Rey, CA Mission San Luis Rey.
Lopez, Benigno *o.de. m.* '62 (PCE) [13] Ponce, PR Santuario San Judas Tadeo Church.
Lopez, Bruce D. '88 (PEO) Galva, IL St. John's Church; Woodhull, IL St. John's Church.
Lopez, Calixto *c.m.* '80 (LA) [A] Camarillo, CA St. John's Seminary College of the Archdiocese of Los Angeles.
Lopez, Camilo L. '93 (NEW) Fort Lee, NJ Madonna Church.
Lopez, Msgr. Daniel M. '63 (FRS) Chowchilla, CA St. Columba Church.
Lopez, Domingo (NY) [1] Port Chester, NY Our Lady of Mercy Church.
Lopez, Edgardo (PCE) [B] Ponce, PR The Pontifical Catholic University of Puerto Rico.
Lopez, Edilberto '97 (ELP) Alpine, TX Our Lady of Peace Church.
Lopez, Edward *s.j.* (P) [D] Portland, OR Jesuit High School.
Lopez, Efrain '65 (CGS) Gurabo, PR San Jose Church.
Lopez, Enrique '94 (LSC) Special Assignment.
Lopez, Enrique A. *c.ss.r.* '64 (LA) Whittier, CA St. Mary of the Assumption Church; [R] Whittier, CA Redemptorist Fathers Mission House.
Lopez, Eugenio '84 (SAC) Vacaville, CA St. Mary Church.
Lopez, Fausto '60 (SJ) [1] San Jose, CA Cathedral Basilica of St. Joseph Church.
Lopez, Felipe '59 (NEW) [2] Union City, NJ St. Augustine's Church.
Lopez, Fernando *s.j.* '54 (MIA) [5] Miami, FL Gesu Church.
Lopez, Msgr. Francis R. '57 (MGZ) San German, PR San German de Auxerre Church.
Lopez, Francisco Javier *sch.p.* '78 (SJN) [58] San Juan, PR Santisimo Salvador Church.
Lopez, Frank '93 (ELP) [22] El Paso, TX St. Frances Xavier Cabrini Parish.
Lopez, G. *m.s.w.* (LA) [Z] Los Angeles, CA Catholic Charities of Los Angeles, Inc.
Lopez, Gerard '91 (SB) Barstow, CA St. Joseph Church.
Lopez, Guillermo Velez '88 (NY) [137] Bronx, NY Christ the King Church.
Lopez, Humberto '86 (MGZ) San German, PR San German de Auxerre Church.
Lopez, Jairo '94 (AUS) [26] Austin, TX San Jose Church.
Lopez, Jairo '94 (ELP) On Duty Outside of Diocese.
Lopez, Jesus Francisco '96 (CC) [4] Corpus Christi, TX Holy Family Church.
Lopez, Jose '91 (JKS) On Duty Outside the Diocese.
Lopez, Jose A. '71 (SAT) [A] San Antonio, TX The Assumption-St. John's Seminary; [C] San Antonio, TX Oblate School of Theology.
Lopez, Jose D. '91 (MIA) [24] Miami, FL St. Kevin Church.
Lopez, Jose Maria '90 (SJN) [F] Rio Piedras, PR Hogar Santa Teresa Jornet for the Aged.
Lopez, Joseph '59 (KCK) [1] Overland Park, KS Church of the Ascension.
Lopez, Juan '87 (SAV) Special Assignment.
Lopez, Juan J. '89 (ARE) On Duty Outside the Diocese.
Lopez, Juan M. '62 (MIA) [28] Miami, FL SS. Peter and Paul Church.
Lopez, Kharlosg '77 (CGS) Fajardo, PR Santisimo Redentor Church.
Lopez, Leo '85 (SLC) [H] St. George, UT Dixie College, Newman Center.
Lopez, Leonadis (SLC) St. George, UT St. George's Church.
Lopez, Lionel '96 (BWN) Escobares, TX Sacred Heart Church; Grulla, TX Holy Family Church; Rio Grande City, TX Immaculate Conception Church; San Isidro, TX St. Isidore Church.
Lopez, Luis E. *c.s.v.* '95 (CHI) [N] Arlington Heights, IL Viatorian Province Center-Clerics of St. Viator.
Lopez, Mauricio A. '92 (SAT) [13] San Antonio, TX Our Lady of the Angels Church.
Lopez, Pedro J. '81 (LA) El Monte, CA Nativity Church.
Lopez, Richard '73 (ATL) [H] Atlanta, GA Our Lady of Perpetual Help Home.
Lopez, Richard A. '82 (SFR) San Francisco, CA St. Mary's Medical Center.
Lopez, Serapio '82 (STV) [4] Mt. Pleasant, VI Church of St. Joseph.
Lopez, Severino *c.m.f.* '44 (ATL) Stone Mountain, GA Corpus Christi Church.
Lopez, Vicente *o.carm.* '68 (LA) [3] North Hollywood, CA St. Jane Frances de Chantal Church.
Lopez, Vincent *o.p.* '56 (P) [6] Eugene, OR St. Thomas More Church; [D] Eugene, OR Marist High School.
Lopez Aponte, Nelson '91 (CGS) Vieques, PR Inmaculada Concepcion Church.
Lopez Mairal, Jose Ma. '54 (SJN) [10] San Juan, PR Santa Cecilia Church.
Lopez Pedraz, Juan *s.j.* (SJN) [D] Rio Piedras, PR Centro Universitario Catolico.
Lopez Vega, Jose Antonio '92 (PCE) [17] Ponce, PR Our Lady of Mt. Carmel Church.
Lopez-Tovar, Ireneo '50 (CAM) Landisville, NJ Our Lady of Victories Church.
Lopez-Velez, Mauricio '92 (LKC) On Duty Outside the Diocese.
Lopilato, Art *s.j.* '80 (ANC) [6] Anchorage, AK Our Lady of Guadalupe Church; [G] Anchorage, AK Jesuit House.
LoPinto, Alfred (BRK) [160] Queens, NY St. Camillus Church.
LoPinto, Alfred P. '70 (BRK) Released from Diocesan Assignment.
LoPresti, Carl '97 (PEO) Monmouth, IL Immaculate Conception Church; Raritan, IL Church of St. Patrick.
Lorance, Douglas '84 (SJP) Lyndora, PA St. Michael Church.
Lord, Gary F. '92 (MAN) [1] Berlin, NH St. Anne Church.
Lord, John *o. carm.* '81 (NEW) Bogota, NJ St. Joseph's Church.
Lord, Laurence J. '64 (SY) [3] Binghamton, NY St. Catherine of Siena Church.
Lord, Robert J. '60 (HRT) Woodbridge, CT Church of the Assumption.
Lord, Ronald A. '64 (BUF) [53] Buffalo, NY Our Lady of Loretto Church.
Lordemann, Francis W. '72 (OM) Fremont, NE St. Patrick Church.
Lorden, Demetrio L. '70 (SP) Temple Terrace, FL Corpus Christi Church.
Loredo, Miguel A. *o.f.m.* '64 (NY) [35] New York, NY St. Francis of Assisi Church.
Lorenc, Henry '84 (TYL) Longview, TX St. Anthony Church.
Lorento, Anthony *s.a.c.* '72 (BRK) [110] Brooklyn, NY Our Lady of the Rosary of Pompeii Church.
Lorentsen, Michael *o.f.m.conv.* (R) [E] Burlington, NC Conventual Franciscans.
Lorentsen, Michael *o.f.m.conv.* '94 (R) Burlington, NC Blessed Sacrament Church; [H] Elon College, NC Elon College.
Lorenz, Bernard A. '85 (LIN) Harvard, NE St. Joseph's Church.
Lorenz, John F. '54 (DM) [6] Des Moines, IA St. Augustin's Church; [G] Des Moines, IA Institute of the Heart of Jesus.
Lorenz, Matthais E. '69 (CHI) On Duty Outside the Archdiocese.
Lorenz, Richard J. *s.a.c.* '60 (MIL) [P] Milwaukee, WI Pallotti House.
Lorenz, Msgr. Victor O. '31 (DET) Retired.
Lorenz, Vincent E. '53 (SD) Retired.
Lorenz, William A. '63 (SY) Oneida, NY St. Joseph Church.
Lorenzana, Elias *o.de.m.* '82 (CGS) Cayey, PR Nuestra Senora de la Merced Church.
Lorenzana, Mario '92 (CHI) [N] Chicago, IL Scalabrini House of Theology.
Lorenzetti, Msgr. Dino J. '53 (BUF) [5] Depew, NY Our Lady of the Blessed Sacrament Church; Retired.
Lorenzo, Avelino *s.d.b.* '60 (OAK) [N] Berkeley, CA Salesian Community.
Lorenzo, Eduardo '66 (LAN) [6] Flint, MI Our Lady of Guadalupe Church.
Lorenzo, Elias R. *o.s.b.* '89 (PAT) [M] Morristown, NJ St. Mary's Abbey.
Lorenzo, Joseph F. *o.f.m.* '76 (MAN) Derry, NH St. Thomas Aquinas Church.
Lorenzoni, Larry *s.d.b.* '51 (SFR) [N] San Francisco, CA Salesian Provincial Residence.
Lorfanfant, Ernest P. *s.m.* '68 (RVC) [N] Mineola, NY Provincial Residence and Novitiate.
Lorge, Felix P. '50 (SPK) Colfax, WA St. Patrick Church; Lacrosse, WA St. Joseph Church.
Lorig, Douglas E. '84 (PHX) Gilbert, AZ St. Anne Church.
Lorilla, Wilfredo '68 (AGN) Piti, GU Assumption of Our Lady Church.
Lorio, Msgr. Joseph O. '54 (NO) [11] Metairie, LA St. Louis King of France Church.
Lorio, Lloyd *s.j.* '56 (FgM) Provinces.
Lorkowski, Robert A. '77 (CLV) Solon, OH St. Rita Church.
Lorrain, Matthew P. '86 (BR) Lakeland, LA Immaculate Conception Church.
Losarcos, Javier '51 (NEW) [4] Newark, NJ St. Aloysius Church.
LoSchiavo, John J. *s.j.* '55 (SFR) [C] San Francisco, CA University of San Francisco; [N] San Francisco, CA Jesuit Community at University of San Francisco.
Loscocco, Angelo P. '53 (BO) [1] Methuen, MA St. Lucy Church.
Losemann, Heinrich J., Jr. '92 (BAL) Absent on Leave.
Losh, Joseph F. '64 (COL) La Rue, OH St. Joseph's Church.
Loshe, Norbert *c.pp.s.* '40 (CIN) Fort Recovery, OH Mary Help of Christians Church.
Losito, Msgr. Felix A. '58 (ALN) [6] Reading, PA Holy Rosary Church.
Loskarn, George '65 (BAL) [28] Baltimore, MD St. Dominic Church.
Loskot, Donald *s.d.s.* '76 (MIL) [P] Milwaukee, WI Salvatorian Formation Community.
Losoya, Jose Encarnacion *c.o.* '91 (BWN) Pharr, TX St.

Jude Thaddeus Church; [E] Pharr, TX Oratory of St. Philip Neri, of Pontifical Right.
Lossing, Larry '84 (ORL) [10] Orlando, FL St. Joseph Church; Special Assignment.
Lostritto, Paul *o.f.m.* '96 (NY) [48] New York, NY Holy Name of Jesus Church.
Loth, Alan J. '68 (OKL) Bison, OK St. Joseph's Church.
Lotha, Abraham '89 (NY) Stony Point, NY Immaculate Conception Church.
Lothamer, James W. *s.s.* '71 (LAN) Adrian, MI St. Joseph Church.
Lotito, Floyd A. *o.f.m.* '60 (SFR) [5] San Francisco, CA St. Anthony Church; [U] San Francisco, CA Franciscan Friars of California, Provincial Office of Communications.
Lott, Franklin '69 (SEA) Battle Ground, WA Sacred Heart Church.
Lott, Lawrence '90 (MOB) On Leave from the Archdiocese.
Lott, Michael D. '92 (L) LaGrange, KY Immaculate Conception Church.
Lott, Robert V. '65 (NY) [36] New York, NY St. Francis de Sales Church.
Lott, Roger R.S. *o.s.b.* '54 (BIR) [E] Cullman, AL St. Bernard Abbey.
Lotz, Joseph *o.f.m.conv.* '92 (PMB) Boynton Beach, FL St. Mark Church.
Lotz, Robert J. '73 (MIL) [X] Milwaukee, WI Milwaukee Archdiocesan Campus Ministry.
Lou, Aloysius '65 (HON) [15] Honolulu, HI Star of the Sea Church.
Louapre, Albert P. *s.j.* '60 (LAF) [J] Grand Coteau, LA Jesuit Spirituality Center.
Loucks, Thomas J. '77 (B) Twin Falls, ID Our Lady of Guadalupe Church; [F] Twin Falls, ID College of Southern Idaho.
Lougen, Louis *o.m.i.* '79 (FgM) Oblates Foreign Missions.
Loughery, Robert J. *c.s.c.* '89 (OAK) [3] Hayward, CA St. Clement Church; [Q] Hayward, CA California State University/Campus Ministry Center.
Loughlin, James F. '52 (NEW) Retired.
Loughlin, William J. '69 (BGP) [7] Fairfield, CT St. Thomas Aquinas Church.
Loughman, Kenneth M. '58 (NY) Walden, NY Most Precious Blood Church.
Loughnane, Msgr. James J. '61 (LA) Diamond Bar, CA St. Denis Church.
Loughnane, John B., Jr. '88 (BUR) Canaan, VT Assumption of the Blessed Virgin Mary Church.
Loughnane, John B., Jr. '88 (MAN) West Stewartstown, NH St. Albert Church.
Loughran, Francis J. '56 (PH) Upper Gwynedd, PA Corpus Christi Church; Retired.
Loughran, James N. *s.j.* '70 (NEW) [B] Jersey City, NJ Saint Peter's College; [N] Jersey City, NJ Jesuits of Saint Peter's College, Inc.
Loughran, John J. *o.s.f.s.* '80 (TOL) [K] Toledo, OH Oblates of St. Francis de Sales.
Loughran, Peter G. '48 (SPR) [1] Holyoke, MA Blessed Sacrament Church.
Loughren, James P. '91 (OG) Morrisonville, NY St. Alexander Church; [3] Plattsburgh, NY St. Joseph Church.
Loughrey, Thomas F. '45 (PH) [19] Philadelphia, PA St. Barbara Church; Retired.
Louis, A. J. *s.d.b.* '44 (PAT) [D] Paterson, NJ Don Bosco Technical High School.
Louis, A. Joseph *s.d.b.* '44 (NY) [FF] West Haverstraw, NY Don Bosco Retreat Center and Marian Shrine; [FF] West Haverstraw, NY Marian Shrine.
Louis, Anthony *s.d.b.* '49 (NY) West Haverstraw, NY Helen Hayes Hospital.
Louis, Conrad *o.s.b.* '40 (IND) [J] St. Meinrad, IN St. Meinrad Archabbey.
Louis, Jean Woady '91 (VEN) Immokalee, FL Our Lady of Guadalupe Church.
Louis, John F. *o.m.i.* '43 (STP) [N] St. Paul, MN Oblate Residence.
Louis, Msgr. John H. (SCR) [F] Clarks Green, PA Saint Gregory Early Childhood Center.
Louis, Msgr. John H. '62 (SCR) Clarks Green, PA St. Gregory Church.
Louis, Kevin C. '89 (LC) Cashton, WI Sacred Heart of Jesus Church; Norwalk, WI St. Augustine of Hippo Church; Saint Mary's Ridge, WI Nativity of the Blessed Virgin Mary Church; Summit, WI St. John the Baptist Church.
Lourdusamy, (NY) [230] Staten Island, NY St. Teresa Church.
Louwagie, Herman *c.i.c.m.* '58 (FgM) Missionhurst Foreign Missions.
Louwagie, Vincent *o.m.i.* '68 (FgM) Oblates Foreign Missions.
Louzon, Bede *o.f.m.cap.* '86 (MAR) South Range, MI Holy Family Church.
Louzon, Bede G. *o.f.m.cap.* '86 (MAR) Chassell, MI St. Anne Church.
Lovas, Donald J. '63 (WIN) [5] Rochester, MN St. Francis of Assisi Church.
Lovat, Rene *s.x.* '57 (FgM) Xaverian Foreign Missions.
Lovat, Rene *s.x.* '57 (PAT) [M] Wayne, NJ Xaverian Missionary Fathers.
Lovato, Charles *s.f.* (NY) Manhattan, NY U.S.V.A. Medical Center.
Lovato, Charles *s.a.* (PAT) Denville, NJ St. Clare Hospital; [J] Denville, NJ Northwest Covenant Medical Center.
Love, John '90 (LA) Moorpark, CA Holy Cross Church.
Love, Lester E. *s.j.* '91 (OAK) [N] Berkeley, CA Jesuit Community at Jesuit School of Theology at Berkeley.
Loveless, William J. '75 (Y) [7] Warren, OH St. Pius X Church.
Loveley, Arthur E. *s.j.* '44 (DET) [61] Detroit, MI SS. Peter and Paul Jesuit Church.
Loveley, Edward M. *s.j.* '47 (DET) [P] Clarkston, MI Colombiere Center.
Lover, Lawrence E. *c.ss.r.* '51 (BAL) [68] Baltimore, MD Our Lady of Fatima Church.
Lovett, Gerald F. '59 (SEA) Redmond, WA St. Jude Church.
Lovett, Msgr. John (RVC) Riverhead, NY St. John the Evangelist Church.
Lovisa, Eugene L. '49 (TOL) Retired.
Lovrencic, Athanasius *o.f.m.* '48 (CHI) [N] Lemont, IL The Slovene Franciscan Fathers, Order of Friars Minor, Commissariat of the Holy Cross.
Low, Msgr. Albert W. '47 (BO) Retired.
Lowe, Frank '85 (SB) On Duty Outside the Diocese.
Lowe, Philip J. '82 (PH) Collegeville, PA St. Eleanor Church; [D] Pottstown, PA St. Pius X High School.
Lowe, Russell P. '92 (CLV) North Royalton, OH St. Albert the Great Church.
Lowell, Ben '79 (TOL) [H] Lima, OH St. Rita's Medical Center.
Lower, Richard T. '71 (MAN) New London, NH Our Lady of Fatima Church; [N] Durham, NH Campus Ministries; [N] New London, NH Colby-Sawyer College Newman Center.
Lowery, Daniel L. *c.ss.r.* '55 (GR) [3] Grand Rapids, MI St. Alphonsus Church.
Lowery, James T. *m.s.* '55 (HRT) [M] Hartford, CT Missionaries of LaSalette Provincial Secretary.
Lowery, Martin J. *m.m.* '68 (NY) [DD] Maryknoll, NY Maryknoll Fathers and Brothers.
Lowery, Msgr. Philip A. '76 (TR) Red Bank, NJ St. James Church.
Lowery, Wilfred *c.ss.r.* '49 (CHI) [N] Glenview, IL The Redemptorists of Glenview, Illinois.
Lowery, Wilfred *c.ss.r.* '49 (FgM) Redemptorist Foreign Missions.
Lowery, William R. '53 (SFR) [1] San Mateo, CA St. Bartholomew Church; Retired.
Lowisz, Myron *o.f.m.* '60 (GRY) [J] Cedar Lake, IN Our Lady of Lourdes Friary.
Lowisz, Myron *o.f.m.* '95 (GRY) [H] Crown Point, IN St. Anthony Home, Inc.
Lowney, Edward *o.m.i.* '40 (BO) Tewksbury, MA St. William Church; Tewksbury, MA Tewksbury Hospital.
Lowney, Jeremiah '88 (HEL) [B] Helena, MT Carroll College.
Lowrey, Robert *o.m.v.* '78 (BO) [BB] Boston, MA St. Francis Chapel.
Lowry, Joseph K., Jr. '66 (BUF) Little Valley, NY St. Mary Church; Retired.
Lowry, Robert *o.m.v.* '78 (BO) [W] Milton, MA Oblate Residence (St. Joseph House).
Loy, Vincent P. '49 (RVC) Retired.
Loya, Daniel '66 (PBR) Windber, PA St. Mary (Dormition) Church.
Loya, John F. '74 (CLV) [A] Wickliffe, OH Borromeo Seminary; [A] Wickliffe, OH St. Mary Seminary and Graduate School of Theology.
Loya, Joseph *o.s.a.* '79 (PH) [C] Villanova, PA Villanova University.
Loya, Thomas '82 (PRM) Chicago, IL St. Mary Church; Joliet, IL St. Mary Assumption Church.
Loyacono, Charles '57 (JKS) Woodville, MS St. Joseph Church.
Loyd, Frederick A. '70 (COL) Powell, OH St. Joan of Arc Church; Leave of Absence.
Loyens, William J. *s.j.* '58 (FgM) Provinces.
Loyens, William J. *s.j.* '58 (P) [L] Portland, OR Jesuit Provincial Office (Society of Jesus, Oregon Prov.).
Loyson, Michael '92 (DET) Absent on Leave.
Lozano, Jose '65 (PCE) [16] Ponce, PR Church of the Good Shepherd.
Lozano, Roland *c.m.f.* '75 (LA) [R] Los Angeles, CA Missionary Sons of the Immaculate Heart of Mary; [R] Los Angeles, CA Claretian Retreat Center Community.
Lozier, Donald *o.m.i.* '60 (BO) [4] Lowell, MA Saint Jeanne d'Arc Church.
Lozier, Timothy R. '88 (STA) [4] Gainesville, FL St. Augustine Church; [L] Gainesville, FL University of Florida-St. Augustine Parish and Student Center.
Lozinski, Eugene L. '72 (NU) Glencoe, MN St. Pius X Church.
Lozinski, Robert W. *c.s.c.* '73 (PSC) Scranton, PA St. John the Baptist Church.
Lu, Matthias '42 (OAK) Retired.
Luat Nguyen, John *o.f.m.* '94 (SFR) [7] San Francisco, CA St. Boniface Church.
Lubanski, Armand *o.f.m* '47 (FWT) [H] Crowley, TX St. Maximilian Kolbe Friary.
Lubas, Feliks '57 (FAR) Minto, ND Sacred Heart Church.
Lubbers, John W. *c.s.c.* '57 (AUS) [H] Austin, TX St. Joseph Hall.
Lubbers, John W. *c.s.c.* '57 (FTW) [J] South Bend, IN Congregation of Holy Cross Indiana Province Provincial House.
Lubbers, Leland E. *s.j.* '59 (OM) [K] Omaha, NE Jesuit Community At Creighton University.
Lubeley, Msgr. Richard J. '49 (STL) Webster Groves, MO Mary, Queen of Peace Church.
Lubey, John A. '43 (WDC) Retired; [L] Washington, DC Cardinal O'Boyle Residence for Priests.
Lubic, Robert T. '96 (GBG) New Kensington, PA Mt. St. Peter Church.
Lubicky, Msgr. John R. '48 (CAM) Blackwood, NJ St. Agnes Church; Retired.
Lubinsky, Michael C. '78 (SAV) Warner Robins, GA Sacred Heart Church.
Lubrano, Joseph *s.d.s.* '74 (MIL) [P] Milwaukee, WI Salvatorian Provincial Residence.
Luca, Edward J. '54 (CLV) Sheffield, OH St. Teresa Church.
Luca, Msgr. Joseph L. '70 (BAL) Clarksville, MD St. Louis Church.
Lucal, John A. *s.j.* (DET) [K] Detroit, MI Jesuit Provincial Office-Detroit Province of the Society of Jesus.
Lucal, John A. *s.j.* '61 (WDC) [M] Washington, DC The Jesuit Community at Georgetown University.
Lucarelli, Gabriel M. *c.r.m.* '36 (NEW) Lodi, NJ St. Joseph's Church.
Lucas, Christopher *o.f.m.conv.* (MRY) [G] Arroyo Grande, CA St. Joseph Cupertino Province, Provincial Center.
Lucas, David '64 (CIN) [56] Cincinnati, OH St. Margaret Mary Church.
Lucas, Edward '61 (PBR) Weirton, WV St. Mary's Church.
Lucas, George *c.s.c.* '72 (FgM) Holy Cross Foreign Missions.
Lucas, Msgr. George J. '75 (STL) Special Assignment; [A] St. Louis, MO Kenrick-Glennon Seminary.
Lucas, Jeffery J. '81 (E) [20] Erie, PA St. Joseph Church.
Lucas, John '66 (STN) Sacramento, CA St. Andrew the Apostle Church.
Lucas, Msgr. John J. '65 (E) Conneaut Lake, PA Our Lady Queen of the Americas Church.
Lucas, John P. '69 (CHI) [3] Oak Park, IL St. Edmund Church; [X] Chicago, IL Court of Appeals-Province of Chicago.
Lucas, Lawrence E. '59 (NY) [89] New York, NY Our Lady of Lourdes Church; City, NY North Infirmary Command; City, NY Otis Bantum Correctional Center; Manhattan, NY North General Hospital.
Lucas, Neil '67 (TOL) [3] Toledo, OH Christ the King Church.
Lucas, Robert '59 (PSC) Doylestown, PA Christ the Saviour Byzantine Catholic Church at Our Lady of Czestochawa Shrine Church.
Lucas, Robert *c.m.* '74 (CHI) [J] Chicago, IL St. Joseph Hospital; [N] Chicago, IL Vincentian Community, Congregation of the Mission, Midwest Province.
Lucas, Theodore '84 (CLV) Willowick, OH St. Mary Magdalene Church.
Lucas, Thomas M. *s.j.* '85 (SFR) [N] San Francisco, CA Jesuit Community at University of San Francisco.
Lucas, William '90 (BIR) Jacksonville, AL St. Charles Church; [H] Jacksonville, AL Jacksonville State University.
Lucasinsky, Raymond *c.m.m.* '62 (DET) [K] Dearborn Heights, MI Our Lady of Grace Monastery.
Lucatero, Heliodoro '86 (SPK) Othello, WA Sacred Heart Church.
Lucavei, Tarcisio *o.s.b.m.* '91 (STN) Hamtramck, MI Immaculate Conception of B.V.M. Church.
Lucca, Augustine *s.d.s.* '51 (NSH) Smyrna, TN St. Luke Church.
Lucchesi, Joseph *o.carm.* '84 (FgM) Carmelite Foreign Missions.
Lucchesi, Joseph *o.carm.* '84 (JOL) [J] Darien, IL Carmelite Provincial Office.
Lucci, Fred *o.p.* '93 (TUC) [I] Tucson, AZ University of Arizona.
Lucci, Frederick *o.p.* (OAK) [N] Oakland, CA Western Dominican Province.
Lucero, Leo E. '60 (SFE) [3] Santa Fe, NM Cristo Rey Church.
Lucero, Lorenzo '56 (ELP) San Elizario, TX San Elceario Church.
Lucev, John '65 (SD) Retired.
Lucey, Beatus T. *o.s.b.* '59 (PAT) [I] Morristown, NJ St. Mary's Abbey Retreat Center; [M] Morristown, NJ St. Mary's Abbey.
Lucey, Gregory *s.j.* (MOB) [B] Mobile, AL Spring Hill College.
Lucey, Gregory F. *s.j.* '64 (WDC) [V] Washington, DC

Jesuit Conference, Inc.
Lucey, J. Roger *s.j.* '58 (MIL) [P] Milwaukee, WI Jesuit Provincial Office, Wisconsin Province.
Lucey, J. Roger *s.j.* '58 (OAK) Orinda, CA Santa Maria Church; [N] Berkeley, CA Jesuit Community at Jesuit School of Theology at Berkeley.
Lucey, John P. '32 (SPR) Retired.
Lucey, Paul T. *s.j.* '48 (BO) [W] Boston, MA Loyola House.
Lucey, William F. (BO) Retired.
Luchi, Robert J. *s.j.* '93 (BEL) [3] East St. Louis, IL St. Joseph Church.
Luchi, Robert J. *s.j.* '93 (STL) [52] St. Louis, MO St. Matthew, Apostle Church.
Lucia, Douglas J. '89 (OG) On Duty Outside the Diocese.
Luciana, Msgr. Lawrence (WH) [B] Huntington, WV St. Joseph Central Catholic High School.
Luciana, Msgr. Lawrence J. (WH) [1] Huntington, WV St. Joseph's Church.
Luciana, Msgr. Lawrence J. '63 (STU) Retired.
Luciani, Pompeo *s.a.c.* '36 (NEW) Fairview, NJ Our Lady of Grace Church.
Luciano, Angel *c.i.c.m.* '72 (FgM) Missionhurst Foreign Missions.
Luciano, William J. '83 (NY) [166] Bronx, NY St. Michael Church.
Lucid, Msgr. Michael '54 (OAK) [1] San Leandro, CA Assumption of the Blessed Virgin Mary Church.
Lucid, Philip J. *s.j.* '55 (SEA) [A] Seattle, WA Seattle University.
Lucid, Vincent F. '43 (BO) Retired.
Lucido, John (ELP) Kermit, TX St. Thomas & St. Joseph Church.
Lucido, John '73 (ELP) Monahans, TX St. John the Apostle and Evangelist Church.
Lucier, Charles V. *o.p.* '41 (WDC) [11] Washington, DC St. Dominic Church & Priory Church.
Lucier, Jude *o. praem* '74 (ORG) [3] Orange, CA St. Norbert Church.
Lucio, Justin '72 (DAL) Special Assignment.
Luck, Robert O. '62 (LA) Retired.
Lucking, Aloysius '50 (MIA) Retired.
Lucking, Aloysius A. '50 (SB) [E] Morongo Valley, CA St. Michael's of Morongo Valley, Inc.
Lucree, Lawrence A. '60 (SAV) Americus, GA St. Mary Church.
Luczak, Andrew E. '70 (CHI) Skokie, IL St. Lambert Church.
Luczak, Jay R. '92 (TUC) Miami, AZ Our Lady of the Blessed Sacrament Church.
Luczak, Thomas W. *o.f.m.* '70 (GB) [I] Pulaski, WI Assumption of B.V.M. Friary.
Luczak, Thomas W. *o.f.m.* '70 (GRY) [J] Cedar Lake, IN San Damiano Friary.
Luczycki, Msgr. Matthew C. '45 (SY) Oneida, NY St. Joseph Church; Retired.
Ludan, Vidal *c.i.c.m.* '76 (FgM) Missionhurst Foreign Missions.
Ludden, John J. '97 (VEN) [1] Sarasota, FL Incarnation Church.
Ludeman, Edward '95 (SFR) [23] San Francisco, CA Holy Name of Jesus Church.
Ludescher, Kenneth F. '61 (STP) Maplewood, MN St. Jerome Church.
Ludlum, William '46 (NEW) Retired.
Ludvik, John J. *s.j.* '71 (SEA) [M] Seattle, WA Jesuit Community.
Ludwick, Edmond '97 (CI) Tol, FM Assumption of the Blessed Virgin Mary Church.
Ludwig, Alexander P. '58 (SCL) Alexandria, MN St. Mary's Church.
Ludwig, Augustine W. *o.s.b.* '86 (RIC) [7] Richmond, VA St. Benedict Church; [L] Richmond, VA Mary Mother of the Church Abbey.
Ludwig, Eugene *o.f.m.cap.* '71 (SFR) Burlingame, CA Our Lady of Angels Church.
Ludwig, Eugene M. *o.f.m.cap.* '71 (NTN) Oakland, CA St. John The Theologian Church.
Ludwig, Eugene M. *o.f.m.cap.* '71 (OAK) [A] Berkeley, CA Dominican School of Philosophy and Theology.
Ludwig, John '74 (DM) [7] Des Moines, IA St. Catherine of Sienna Catholic Student Center Church; [I] Des Moines, IA St. Catherine of Siena Catholic Student Center.
Ludwig, Raphael A. '57 (DUB) St. Lucas, IA St. Luke's Church; Waucoma, IA St. Mary's Church.
Ludwig, Roman E. '43 (FAR) Larimore, ND St. Stephen's Church.
Ludwig, Thomas K. '87 (KC) Savannah, MO St. Rose of Lima Church; [C] St. Joseph, MO Bishop LeBlond High School.
Ludwikoski, James E. '73 (KCK) Military Chaplains.
Luebke, Martial *o.f.m.* '39 (FgM) Custody of St. Mary of the Angels. Byzantine-Slavonic.
Luebke, Martial *o.f.m.* '39 (LA) [72] Los Angeles, CA St. Joseph Church.
Luebking, Msgr. Thomas A. '71 (TR) Spring Lake, NJ St. Catharine Church.
Lueckenotte, Daniel I. '90 (JC) Ewing, MO Queen of Peace Church; Palmyra, MO St. Joseph Church.
Lueckenotto, Arthur A. *m.s.* '63 (STL) [P] St. Louis, MO La Salette Missionaries.
Luehrmann, Stanley E. '53 (CIN) Hillsboro, OH St. Mary's Church.
Luera, Ruben '86 (LUB) On Duty Outside the Diocese.
Lueras, Charles R. *c.r.i.c.* '81 (LA) [64] Los Angeles, CA St. Francis of Assisi Church; [B] Los Angeles, CA Canons Regular of the Immaculate Conception-Novitiate; [R] Los Angeles, CA Canons Regular of the Immaculate Conception.
Luerman, John H. '56 (IND) Cambridge City, IN St. Elizabeth of Hungary Church.
Luetkemeyer, Alexander *o.s.b.* '53 (KC) Bethany, MO Blessed Sacrament Church.
Luettgen, Lawrence J. *s.j.* '60 (NO) [P] New Orleans, LA Ignatius Residence.
Luevano, Rafael '81 (ORG) Los Alamitos, CA St. Hedwig Church.
Luft, Raymond P. '68 (PRO) [26] Providence, RI Our Lady of Mt. Carmel Church.
Luger, Paul P. *s.j.* '42 (SPK) [K] Spokane, WA Regis Community.
Lugger, William '89 (LAN) [2] Lansing, MI St. Casimir Church.
Lugo, Camilo '69 (RVC) Brentwood, NY St. Luke Church.
Lugo, Edward Acevedo '97 (MGZ) [1] Mayaquez, PR Cathedral of Our Lady of Purification.
Lugo, Joseph W. '62 (PAT) Retired.
Lugo, Martin *o.s.b.* '62 (OKL) [I] Shawnee, OK St. Gregory Abbey.
Lugue, Peter '63 (SB) [2] Corona, CA St. Edward Church.
Lui, Gabriel '79 (LA) Monterey Park, CA St. Thomas Aquinas Church.
Lui, Pius *o.f.m.* '53 (FgM) Franciscan Foreign Missions.
Luis, Anthony '50 (BRK) [U] Douglaston, NY Bishop Mugavero Residence.
Luisi, Joseph G. '83 (PIT) [66] Pittsburgh, PA St. Wendelin Church.
Luisini, Msgr. Anthony J. '56 (MET) Alpha, NJ St. Mary Church.
Luistro, Abelardo '50 (LA) [47] Los Angeles, CA St. Basil's Church.
Luiten, Gary '92 (FAR) Ellendale, ND St. Helena's Church.
Luiz, Gary M. *c.pp.s.* '77 (OAK) [N] Berkeley, CA Society of the Precious Blood.
Luka, Ronald *c.m.f.* '63 (CHI) [N] Oak Park, IL Claretian Fathers Headquarters of U.S.A. Eastern Province.
Lukac, Thomas M. '63 (GBG) [3] Latrobe, PA St. John the Evangelist Church.
Lukachinsky, Jerome A. '88 (CLV) [2] Parma, OH St. Bridget Church.
Lukaczyk, George '54 (STF) [9] Terryville, CT St. Michael Church.
Lukas, Andrew F. '58 (WH) Retired.
Lukas, Joseph S. (BO) Retired.
Lukas, Martin C. *o.s.f.s.* '80 (TOL) [C] Toledo, OH St. Francis de Sales High School; [K] Toledo, OH Oblates of St. Francis de Sales.
Lukas, Michael '36 (SEA) Retired.
Lukaschek, Ernest C. *m.m.* '64 (FgM) Maryknoll Foreign Missions.
Lukasik, Alexius *o.f.m.* '49 (MIL) [P] Burlington, WI Queen of Peace Friary.
Lukaszczyk, Josef '80 (STL) [P] Eureka, MO Our Lady of the Angels Monastery.
Lukaszewicz, John C. '55 (MIL) [1] Waukesha, WI St. Joseph Church.
Lukaszewski, Jerome *o.f.m.conv.* '43 (BAL) [M] Ellicott City, MD Order of Friars Minor Conventual.
Lukaszewski, Jerome *o.f.m.conv.* '48 (FgM) Conventual Franciscan Foreign Missions.
Lukaszewski, Joseph C. '79 (RVC) West Islip, NY Our Lady of Lourdes Church.
Lukaszewski, Leonard '54 (GRY) Retired.
Lukaszewski, Stanley P. '79 (TR) Willingboro, NJ Corpus Christi Church.
Luke, Eugene *o.s.b.* '61 (FWT) Lindsay, TX St. Peter Church.
Lukefahr, Oscar *c.m.* '66 (STL) [P] Perryville, MO Congregation of The Mission; [W] Perryville, MO Catholic Home Study Service.
Lukehart, Frederick '63 (Y) [16] Youngstown, OH St. Joseph Church.
Lukenda, Raymond T. '56 (NEW) Secaucus, NJ Immaculate Conception Church.
Lukes, Duane '57 (OM) [G] Norfolk, NE Faith Regional Health Services.
Lukianiuk, Andriej '86 (BRK) [43] Brooklyn, NY St. Frances de Chantal Church.
Lukoskie, Raymond M. '58 (PEO) Warsaw, IL Sacred Heart Church.
Luljak, Louis P. '61 (MIL) [4] Racine, WI Holy Trinity Church; [15] Racine, WI St. Stanislaus Church.
Lulko, Leo T. '65 (DET) Highland, MI Church of the Holy Spirit.
Lulloff, William '48 (GB) [I] Appleton, WI St. Fidelis Friary.
Lum, William '69 (ROC) Absent on Leave.
Luminais, Msgr. J. Anthony '54 (NO) Bridge City, LA Holy Guardian Angels Church.
Lumpkin, Thomas '64 (DET) Detroit, MI Southwest Detroit Hospital.
Lumsden, Patrick '96 (DAV) [3] Davenport, IA Holy Family Church.
Luna, Ezequiel Bas *o.s.b.* '84 (SFE) [J] Abiquiu, NM Monastery of Christ in the Desert.
Luna, Henry *c.m.f.* '55 (AUS) Martindale, TX Immaculate Heart of Mary Church; San Marcos, TX St. John the Evangelist Church.
Luna, Ignacio '65 (BWN) Escobares, TX Sacred Heart Church; Grulla, TX Holy Family Church; Rio Grande City, TX Immaculate Conception Church; San Isidro, TX St. Isidore Church.
Luna, Lambert Joseph '78 (SFE) [16] Albuquerque, NM San Felipe de Neri Church.
Luna, Miguel '89 (ELP) [28] El Paso, TX St. Matthew Church.
Luna, Roger *s.d.b.* (SFR) [N] San Francisco, CA Salesian Provincial Residence.
Lund, Donald F. *c.s.v.* '46 (JOL) Bourbonnais, IL Maternity of the Blessed Virgin Mary Church.
Lund, Donald J. '69 (CHI) [72] Chicago, IL Good Shepherd Church.
Lundberg, Jan *o.c.d.* '93 (SJ) [M] San Jose, CA Carmelite Monastery, Novitiate.
Lundberg, John W. '60 (TLS) Retired.
Lundergan, Barnabas *o.s.b.* '45 (RCK) [H] Aurora, IL Marmion Abbey-St. Augustine's Abbey.
Lundgren, Richard '96 (JOL) [5] Naperville, IL St. Thomas the Apostle Church.
Lundgren, Stephen A. '79 (DUB) [H] Dubuque, IA Mercy Health Center-St. Joseph's Unit.
Lundy, George F. *s.j.* '78 (DET) [K] Detroit, MI Jesuit Community at the University of Detroit.
Lungay, Jose Roel G. '84 (NO) [3] Metairie, LA St. Ann Church and Shrine Church.
Luniw, Paul '82 (STF) [8] New Haven, CT St. Michael Church.
Lunney, Msgr. John A. '56 (ANC) [6] Anchorage, AK Our Lady of Guadalupe Church; Retired.
Lunney, William '94 (SPR) Agawam, MA St. John the Evangelist Church.
Lunnon, William '82 (DET) [M] Detroit, MI St. Mary's Residence.
Lunsford, Keith '81 (KCK) Purcell, KS St. Mary's Church.
Lunsford, Keith '92 (KCK) Horton, KS St. Leo's Church.
Lunsford, Robert D. '60 (LAN) St. Johns, MI St. Joseph Church.
Lunzer, Matthew *s.v.d.* '45 (FgM) Society of the Divine Word Foreign Missions.
Luo, Matteo *o.f.m.conv.* '59 (BAL) [M] Ellicott City, MD Order of Friars Minor Conventual.
Luong, Dominic *s.s.s.* '67 (SAT) [74] San Antonio, TX Vietnamese Martyers Catholic Center Church.
Luong, Msgr. Dominic Mai Thanh '66 (NO) [14] New Orleans, LA Mary, Queen of Vietnam Church.
Luong Mihn Tuat, Francis M. *c.m.c.* (SPC) [E] Springfield, MO Congregation of Mother Co-Redemptrix, Our Lady of the Rosary House.
Luongo, Anthony '87 (NEW) [C] Ramsey, NJ Don Bosco Preparatory High School for Boys.
Luongo, John '78 (ORG) Absent on Sick Leave.
Lupa, Gerard '77 (SY) Absent on Leave.
Lupico, Samuel '70 (BAL) [H] Baltimore, MD St. Joseph Medical Center, Inc.
Lupico, Samuel J. '70 (BAL) Special Assignment.
Lupo, David *ss.cc.* '91 (FR) [J] Fairhaven, MA Sacred Hearts Provincial House; [L] Wareham, MA Sacred Hearts Retreat Center.
Lupo, Joseph F. *o.ss.t.* '45 (NY) [218] Staten Island, NY Our Lady of Mt. Carmel-St. Benedicta Church.
Lupo, William L. '65 (CHI) Bartlett, IL St. Peter Damian Church.
Lusch, Daniel J. *s.j.* '62 (BO) [W] Boston, MA The Society of Jesus of New England-Provincial Offices; [W] Chestnut Hill, MA The Jesuit Community at Boston College.
Lusch, Daniel J. *s.j.* '62 (BUF) [O] Buffalo, NY Canisius Jesuit Community.
Luschen, Timothy D. '88 (OKL) [17] Oklahoma City, OK Sacred Heart Church.
Lusik, William A. '97 (NEW) Little Ferry, NJ St. Margaret of Cortona Church.
Lusoski, Thomas J. '57 (CLV) South Euclid, OH St. Margaret Mary Church.
Lussier, Andre '55 (FR) [J] Attleboro, MA La Salette Provincial House.
Lussier, Bonaventure *o.c.d.* (CHI) [N] Chicago, IL Edith Stein House of Studies.
Lussier, Bonaventure *o.c.d.* '75 (WH) [N] Hinton, WV Monastery of Christ on the Mountain.
Lussier, Louis *o.s.cam.* '90 (MIL) [P] Wauwatosa, WI St. Camillus Provincialate; [P] St. Francis, WI St. Camillus Formation Community; [Y] Wauwatosa, WI St. Camillus Institute, Inc.

Lussier, Robert *s.s.s.* '56 (GB) Menasha, WI St. Mary Church.
Lussier, Robert *o.s.b.* '92 (SFE) [L] Pecos, NM Our Lady of Guadalupe Benedictine Abbey.
Lussier, Ronald P. '52 (SPR) [6] Chicopee, MA St. George's Church.
Lusson, David R. '80 (SUP) Frederic, WI St. Dominic Church; Grantsburg, WI Immaculate Conception Church.
Lustig, Victor Joseph '42 (B) Retired.
Luteri, Evaristo '30 (PIT) Retired; [O] Pittsburgh, PA St. John Vianney Manor.
Lutgen, Richard E. '62 (SAL) Chapman, KS St. Michael's Church.
Luther, Benjamin F. '64 (OWN) [3] Paducah, KY St. John the Evangelist Church.
Luther, Philip L. '87 (LIN) Trenton, NE St. James Church.
Lutjen, George J. '68 (BRK) [149] Queens, NY St. Anastasia Church.
Lutkenhoff, Bernard '71 (LFT) Unassigned.
Lutmer, Joseph H. '46 (CIN) Retired.
Lutostanski, Anthony '58 (BUF) [39] Buffalo, NY St. John Kanty Church.
Luttenberger, Gerard H. *c.m.* '65 (RVC) [A] Huntington, NY Diocesan Seminary of the Immaculate Conception; [N] Oyster Bay, NY Vincentian Community.
Lutz, Bernard A. '63 (EVN) Fort Branch, IN Holy Cross Church.
Lutz, Donald J. '70 (BUF) [13] Buffalo, NY St. Bernard Church.
Lutz, Frederick J. '73 (SPC) Advance, MO St. Joseph Church.
Lutz, George '62 (NEW) [17] Newark, NJ St. James Church.
Lutz, Gerald '56 (PIT) McKeesport, PA St. Patrick Church.
Lutz, Herman G. '58 (IND) [32] Indianapolis, IN St. Philip Neri Church.
Lutz, Joseph L. '87 (RCK) [3] Freeport, IL St. Mary Church; Shannon, IL St. Wendelin Church.
Lutz, Kevin F. '78 (COL) [19] Columbus, OH Holy Family Church.
Lutz, Robert J. '50 (CHI) Northbrook, IL St. Norbert Church; Retired.
Lutz, Thomas '93 (NY) Highland, NY St. Augustine Church.
Luu, John Khien *s.v.d.* '92 (FgM) Society of the Divine Word Foreign Missions.
Luu, Joseph (HT) Retired.
Lux, Joachim *o.f.m.* '61 (L) [43] Louisville, KY St. Joseph Church.
Lux, Joseph W. *s.j.* '71 (NEW) [B] Jersey City, NJ Saint Peter's College; [N] Jersey City, NJ Jesuits of Saint Peter's College, Inc.
Lux, Thomas J. '85 (LIN) Bruno, NE St. Anthony Church; [C] David City, NE Aquinas/St. Mary's Schools.
Luyet, Gregory T. '95 (LR) Hope, AR Our Lady of Good Hope Church.
Luzbetak, Louis *s.v.d.* '45 (CHI) [B] Techny, IL Divine Word Residence.
Luzetsky, Stephen '50 (PSC) Retired.
Luznicky, George *o.s.m.* '55 (CHI) [15] Chicago, IL Annunciata Church.
Luznicky, George M. *o.s.m.* '55 (CHI) [N] Chicago, IL Servite Friars - Eastern Province.
Luznicky, George M. *o.s.m.* '55 (DEN) Westminster, CO Holy Trinity Church.
Luzzi, Anthony *s.d.b.* '49 (NY) [FF] West Haverstraw, NY Don Bosco Retreat Center and Marian Shrine; [FF] West Haverstraw, NY Marian Shrine.
Lybarger, Curtis F. '77 (STP) Osseo, MN St. Vincent de Paul Church.
Lyddy, Daniel F. '34 (OG) Retired.
Lyden, Dennis P. '63 (STU) Retired.
Lydon, John J. *o.s.a.* '84 (FgM) Foreign Missions.
Lydon, Leo B. '50 (WH) Retired.
Lydon, Michael '74 (SP) [2] Largo, FL St. Justin Martyr Church.
Lydon, Michael J. '84 (STL) [57] St. Louis, MO St. Pius the Fifth Church.
Lyle, Dennis J. '91 (CHI) Graduate Studies; [C] Chicago, IL Loyola University-Chicago.
Lyle, John W. *o.s.f.s.* '85 (ARL) [D] Fairfax, VA Paul VI High School; [J] Fairfax, VA Oblates of St. Francis de Sales Residence.
Lyman, Edward P. '67 (SCR) Archbald, PA St. Thomas Aquinas Church.
Lynam, Gerald J. '50 (HEL) Retired; [B] Helena, MT Carroll College.
Lynam, Robert G. '84 (MET) Kendall Park, NJ St. Augustine of Canterbury Church.
Lynaugh, Msgr. Joseph E. '36 (PH) Ardsley, PA Queen of Peace Church; Retired.
Lynch, Antone J. '81 (BLX) [4] Gulfport, MS St. Joseph Catholic Church.
Lynch, Charles E. *c.s.b.* '58 (GAL) Rosenberg, TX Our Lady of Guadalupe Church.
Lynch, Charles M. '78 (NEW) Retired.
Lynch, Cletus J. '30 (CHI) La Grange Park, IL St. Louise de Marillac Church; Retired.
Lynch, Conall P. *o.f.m.* '51 (GLP) Houck, AZ St. John Church; [F] Gallup, NM Southwest Indian Foundation.
Lynch, Cornelius B. '54 (PRO) On Duty Outside the Diocese.
Lynch, Cornelois B. '54 (FgM) Society of St. James the Apostle.
Lynch, Cyprian *o.f.m.* '48 (PAT) [M] Ringwood, NJ Holy Name Friary, Inc.
Lynch, Damion J. '91 (CHL) [3] Charlotte, NC Our Lady of Consolation Church.
Lynch, Daniel C. '48 (SC) Retired.
Lynch, Daniel F. *o.carm.* '54 (NY) Montrose, NY Franklin D. Roosevelt Hospital; Montrose, NY FDR DVA Hospital; [DD] Middletown, NY St. Albert's Priory.
Lynch, Daniel G. '51 (BO) Retired.
Lynch, Denis '57 (GAL) Retired.
Lynch, Dennis J. '68 (LC) Mill Creek, WI St. Bartholomew Church; [6] Stevens Point, WI St. Stephen Church.
Lynch, Donald D. *s.j.* '59 (BGP) [A] Fairfield, CT Fairfield University; [O] Fairfield, CT The Fairfield Jesuit Community-Fairfield University.
Lynch, E. Patrick *c.ss.r.* '69 (BAL) Annapolis, MD St. Mary Church; [M] Annapolis, MD Saint Mary Rectory.
Lynch, Edward C. *s.j.* '64 (NY) [DD] New York, NY Murray-Weigel Hall.
Lynch, Msgr. Edward J. '57 (BAL) [41] Baltimore, MD Immaculate Conception Church.
Lynch, Eugene *s.m.m.* '54 (HRT) [M] Litchfield, CT Montfort Missionaries; [M] Litchfield, CT Montfort Missionaries.
Lynch, Francis A. *c.m.* '50 (MOB) Tallassee, AL St. Vincent De Paul Church.
Lynch, Frank '57 (BRK) [216] Queens, NY Our Lady of Mount Carmel Church.
Lynch, Gerald P. '73 (SLC) [8] Salt Lake City, UT St. Patrick's Church.
Lynch, Gerard F. *o.ss.t.* '74 (TR) Asbury Park, NJ Our Lady of Mt. Carmel Church.
Lynch, Ibar '52 (SEA) Retired.
Lynch, James *m.m.* '74 (FgM) Maryknoll Foreign Missions.
Lynch, James M. '74 (CLV) Released from Diocesan Assignment.
Lynch, John *m.afr.* '62 (FgM) Missionaries of Africa Foreign Missions.
Lynch, John A. '60 (ROC) [28] Rochester, NY St. James Church.
Lynch, John E. *c.s.p.* '51 (WDC) [B] Washington, DC St. Paul's College; [C] Washington, DC Catholic University of America, The; [C] Washington, DC Catholic University of America, The.
Lynch, John J. *s.j.* '66 (OM) [K] Omaha, NE Jesuit Community At Creighton University.
Lynch, John J. '96 (NY) Woodbourne, NY Immaculate Conception Church.
Lynch, John K. '56 (HRT) Cheshire, CT St. Bridget's Church.
Lynch, John R. '67 (CHI) [2] Oak Park, IL St. Catherine of Siena-St. Lucy Church.
Lynch, John S. '63 (E) Sharpsville, PA St. Bartholomew Church.
Lynch, Joseph P. '53 (CHI) Burbank, IL St. Albert the Great Church; Retired.
Lynch, Kenny *c.p.* '37 (CHI) [N] Chicago, IL Immaculate Conception Monastery.
Lynch, Kevin A. *c.s.p.* '53 (NEW) [S] Mahwah, NJ Paulist Press.
Lynch, Kevin A. *c.s.p.* '53 (NY) [104] New York, NY St. Paul the Apostle Church.
Lynch, Kevin A. *m.m.* '61 (FgM) Maryknoll Foreign Missions.
Lynch, Leo (ALT) [B] Altoona, PA Bishop Guilfoyle High School.
Lynch, Leo A. '93 (ALT) [4] Altoona, PA Sacred Heart Church.
Lynch, Leo X. '56 (BO) [1] Woburn, MA St. Anthony Church.
Lynch, M. Kevin '74 (PRO) [4] Cranston, RI St. Mark Church.
Lynch, Maurice J. '65 (DUB) On Leave of Absence.
Lynch, Michael '89 (MIA) Margate, FL St. Vincent Church.
Lynch, Michael J. '71 (LC) Wausau, WI Wausau Hospital Center.
Lynch, Michael J. '82 (TR) Marlboro, NJ St. Gabriel Church.
Lynch, Michael J. '88 (BRK) [55] Brooklyn, NY Holy Family Church.
Lynch, Michael J. *s.j.* '93 (BAL) [M] Baltimore, MD Jesuit Fathers and Brothers Maryland Provincial Curia.
Lynch, Michael J. *s.j.* '93 (FgM) Provinces.
Lynch, Myles *o.s.m.* '58 (ORG) [H] Buena Park, CA Servite Fathers And Brothers.
Lynch, Noel '62 (SAC) Susanville, CA Sacred Heart Church.
Lynch, Patrick J. '46 (ALB) Retired.
Lynch, Msgr. Patrick J. '50 (MEM) Retired.
Lynch, Patrick J. *s.j.* '72 (BUF) [O] Buffalo, NY Canisius Jesuit Community.
Lynch, Ralph *o.s.b.* (IND) [H] Beech Grove, IN St. Paul Hermitage.
Lynch, Ralph *o.s.b.* '46 (IND) [J] St. Meinrad, IN St. Meinrad Archabbey.
Lynch, Raymond J. *o.f.m.* '51 (SCR) [12] Wilkes-Barre, PA St. Joseph Church; [M] Wilkes-Barre, PA St. Joseph's Friary.
Lynch, Msgr. Richard '46 (LSC) Retired.
Lynch, Richard D. '63 (E) [4] Erie, PA Holy Rosary Church.
Lynch, Robert *o.f.m.* '43 (BO) [Z] Boston, MA Saint Anthony Residence.
Lynch, Robert B. '60 (NOR) [4] Norwich, CT St. Mary Church.
Lynch, Robert G. *s.j.* '56 (CHY) Pinedale, WY Our Lady of Peace Church.
Lynch, Stephen *o.f.m.* '55 (PRO) [P] Providence, RI St. Francis Friary.
Lynch, Stephen '77 (BRK) [229] Queens, NY Presentation of the Blessed Virgin Mary Church.
Lynch, T. Patrick '61 (NEW) [B] Jersey City, NJ Saint Peter's College; [N] Jersey City, NJ Jesuits of Saint Peter's College, Inc.
Lynch, Thomas *o.p.* '86 (FgM) Dominican - Order of Preachers Foreign Missions.
Lynch, Thomas '92 (NY) Graduate Studies.
Lynch, Thomas F. '48 (NEW) Retired.
Lynch, Thomas F. '71 (BGP) [2] Stratford, CT St. James Church.
Lynch, Thomas P. *o.p.* '86 (CHI) [N] Chicago, IL Dominicans (Provincial Office).
Lynch, Timothy J. '71 (PMB) [2] West Palm Beach, FL Mary Immaculate Church.
Lynch, William B. '35 (CHI) Palos Heights, IL Incarnation Church; Retired.
Lynch, William F. '57 (HRT) [4] Manchester, CT St. James Church.
Lynch, William J. *s.j.* '48 (CHL) Mooresville, NC St. Therese Church; [J] Charlotte, NC Jesuit Community.
Lynes, James F. '79 (GAL) Clute, TX St. Jerome Church.
Lynes, James F. '79 (SAN) On Duty Outside the Diocese.
Lynes, John '87 (MOB) Chickasaw, AL St. Thomas the Apostle Church.
Lynes, Thomas E. '43 (SPR) Retired.
Lynette, C. Franklyn *s.j.* '47 (NO) [C] New Orleans, LA Loyola University.
Lyng, Msgr. Eamonn F. '58 (SD) La Jolla, CA Mary, Star of the Sea Church.
Lyng, Matthew '57 (CC) Robstown, TX St. Thomas the Apostle Church.
Lynn, William D. *s.j.* '54 (COL) [A] Columbus, OH Pontifical College Josephinum.
Lynn, William J. '76 (PH) Ardsley, PA Queen of Peace Church.
Lyon, Msgr. E. Carl '46 (WDC) [6] Silver Spring, MD St. John the Baptist Church; Retired.
Lyon, George *o.s.b.* '50 (SFS) [F] Marvin, SD Blue Cloud Abbey.
Lyon, Msgr. Gerald F. '49 (SC) Le Mars, IA St. Joseph's Church; Retired.
Lyon, Joseph A. '50 (L) Retired.
Lyons, Denis '58 (ORG) Dana Point, CA St. Edward Church.
Lyons, Edward D. '62 (CAM) Ocean City, NJ St. Augustine's Church.
Lyons, Edward J. *c.s.p.* '53 (NY) [DD] Jamaica Estates, NY Paulist Fathers Generalate.
Lyons, Edward J. *c.s.p.* '53 (PMB) [G] Vero Beach, FL Paulist Fathers Retirement Home.
Lyons, Msgr. Eugene F. '42 (CHI) Winnetka, IL SS. Faith, Hope and Charity Church; Retired.
Lyons, Francis '59 (MIA) Retired.
Lyons, Francis A. '59 (MIA) North Lauderdale, FL Our Lady Queen of Heaven Church.
Lyons, Msgr. Frederick J. '52 (ALX) Retired.
Lyons, James *o.m.i.* (FgM) Oblates Foreign Missions.
Lyons, James A. '94 (PH) [13] Philadelphia, PA St. Anselm Church.
Lyons, James D. '60 (BO) Rowley, MA St. Mary Church.
Lyons, James F. '43 (FR) Retired.
Lyons, James H.C. '96 (CR) Bemidji, MN St. Philip's Church; [F] Bemidji, MN Holy Spirit Newman Center.
Lyons, James M. *v.g.* '88 (HBG) [2] Harrisburg, PA St. Catherine Laboure Church.
Lyons, James P. '45 (KC) Retired.
Lyons, James W. (CHI) Retired.
Lyons, John '80 (SAV) [6] Savannah, GA Sacred Heart of Jesus Church.
Lyons, John *o.m.v.* '84 (BO) [B] Boston, MA Oblate Provincialate.

Lyons, John *o.m.v.* '84 (MET) [H] Asbury, NJ Lanteri House.
Lyons, John F. '46 (Y) Retired.
Lyons, John F. '73 (CLV) Released from Diocesan Assignment.
Lyons, John J. *o.m.i.* '42 (BO) [3] Lowell, MA Immaculate Conception Church.
Lyons, John P. '55 (BO) Rochester, MA St. Rose of Lima Church.
Lyons, John P. '88 (TUC) [F] Tucson, AZ Regina Cleri Center.
Lyons, John T. '74 (PH) [19] Philadelphia, PA St. Barbara Church.
Lyons, Joseph *o.m.i.* '29 (SAT) [K] San Antonio, TX Oblate Madonna Residence.
Lyons, Lawrence '54 (MIA) Retired.
Lyons, Leo J. (CHI) Retired.
Lyons, Mark J. '38 (MIL) Retired.
Lyons, Michael '96 (VIC) El Campo, TX St. Philip the Apostle Church.
Lyons, Michael J. '70 (DUL) Pine City, MN Immaculate Conception Church.
Lyons, Michael Patrick '96 (BGP) [2] Stratford, CT St. James Church.
Lyons, Patrick J. '45 (LIN) Retired; [E] Lincoln, NE Bonacum House.
Lyons, Patrick M. '70 (CHI) Evergreen Park, IL Queen of Martyrs Church.
Lyons, Peter *t.o.r.* '66 (WDC) [M] Washington, DC St. Louis Friary.
Lyons, Peter A. *t.o.r.* '66 (BAL) [A] Baltimore, MD St. Mary's Seminary and University.
Lyons, Richard J. '74 (MET) Dunellen, NJ St. John the Evangelist Church.
Lyons, Robert *s.j.* '77 (SPK) [C] Spokane, WA Gonzaga University.
Lyons, Thomas J. '52 (BRK) [141] Brooklyn, NY St. Thomas Aquinas Church.
Lyons, Timothy *o.f.m.conv.* '42 (TR) Seaside Park, NJ St. Catharine of Siena Church.
Lyons, Timothy J. *c.m.* '86 (RVC) [N] Oyster Bay, NY Vincentian Community.
Lyons, Vincent '48 (SAC) Retired and in Senior Ministry.
Lyons, William J. '56 (CHI) Alsip, IL St. Terrence Church.
Lyons, Msgr. William J. '56 (STL) [A] St. Louis, MO Kenrick-Glennon Seminary; [V] St. Louis, MO Washington University Newman Centers.
Lyons, William P. '51 (CLV) [12] Akron, OH St. Matthew Church; Retired.
Lysaght, John *o.c.d.* '48 (SR) [M] Oakville, CA Carmelite House of Prayer.
Lysogorski, John '75 (ALB) [3] Troy, NY St. Francis de Sales Church; Albany, NY Albany Medical Center Hospital; Special Assignment.
Lysz, Robert J. '75 (HRT) Forestville, CT St. Matthew Church.
Lytle, Gerald A. '60 (HBG) [1] Lancaster, PA St. Anne Church.
Lyttle, Eugene '93 (DUL) Duluth, MN Indian Missions Church; Duluth, MN Indian Missions Church.
Lyttle, Eugene Francis '93 (DUL) Cloquet, MN Holy Family Church.
Lyttle, Gregory '75 (NY) [131] Bronx, NY St. Augustine Church.

M

Ma, Didacus '52 (SFR) [34] San Francisco, CA St. Monica Church.
Ma, Peter (NY) Manhattan, NY Beekman Downtown - New York Infirmary.
Ma, Peter '55 (NY) [70] New York, NY St. Mary Church.
Maag, Ronald E. '78 (BAK) The Dalles, OR St. Peter's Church.
Maas, Francis *m.s.f.* '35 (SAT) [K] San Antonio, TX Padua Place.
Maasen, Jeffrey A. '97 (STL) [3] St. Charles, MO St. Elizabeth Ann Seton Church.
Maat, William A. *o.s.b.* '33 (P) Rockaway, OR St. Mary by the Sea Church.
Maat, William A. *o.s.b.* '33 (SEA) [M] Lacey, WA St. Martin's Abbey.
Mabango, Ashiono Anthony '95 (PAT) Randolph, NJ Resurrection Church.
Mabarak, John R. *o.s.a.* '60 (CHI) [N] Olympia Fields, IL Tolentine Monastery at Tolentine Center.
Mabon, Msgr. Thomas K. '57 (ALT) [14] Johnstown, PA Our Mother of Sorrows Church.
MacAdam, Austin *m.afr.* '58 (CHI) [124] Chicago, IL St. Martin De Porres Church; [N] Chicago, IL Missionaries of Africa.
Macalintal, Dionisio '63 (SD) National City, CA St. Mary Church.
Macaranas, Rafael R. '64 (BRK) [206] Queens, NY Our Lady of the Angelus Church.
MacArthur, Bruce '53 (SFS) Retired.
Macartney, Ross J. '64 (PH) [101] Philadelphia, PA Maternity B.V.M. Church.
MacAulay, A. Gerard '59 (OKL) [11] Oklahoma City, OK Immaculate Conception Church.
MacAulay, Stephen A. '51 (TLS) Wagoner, OK Holy Cross Church.
Macauley, Thomas '91 (HBG) [4] York, PA St. Rose of Lima Church.
Macaya, Miguel '65 (LSC) Dona Ana, NM Our Lady of the Purification Church.
MacCandless, William J. *o.s.b.* '58 (NO) Abita Springs, LA St. Jane de Chantal Church; [A] St. Benedict, LA St. Joseph's Seminary College; [P] St. Benedict, LA St. Joseph Abbey.
Maccarone, Patrick C. '91 (MET) Flemington, NJ St. Magdalen de Pazzi Church.
MacCarthy, John P. *o.praem.* '69 (GB) [I] De Pere, WI St. Norbert Abbey.
MacCarthy, Joseph T. '97 (BO) [4] Brookline, MA St. Mary of the Assumption Church.
MacCarthy, Justin H. '64 (ORG) La Habra, CA Our Lady of Guadalupe Church.
MacCarthy, Liam '68 (SAC) Sutter Creek, CA Immaculate Conception Church.
MacCarthy, Peter T. '50 (BIR) Leeds, AL St. Theresa's Church.
MacCarthy, Timothy '60 (ORG) Tustin, CA St. Cecilia Church.
Macchi, William V. '64 (OAK) [3] Concord, CA St. Francis of Assisi Church.
Macchietto, Robert G. '71 (NY) [E] New York, NY Monsignor Farrell High School.
Macchler, Robert '62 (LA) Glendale, CA Church of the Incarnation.
MacCormack, James A. '97 (MAN) Salem, NH St. Joseph Church.
MacDonald, Msgr. Arthur F. '52 (GLP) Alpine, AZ St. Helena Church.
MacDonald, Charles J. '67 (HRT) Wallingford, CT Holy Trinity Church.
MacDonald, Colin '81 (SAC) Antelope, CA St. Clare Church.
MacDonald, Msgr. Colin A. '45 (MAN) [8] Manchester, NH St. Francis of Assisi Church; Retired.
MacDonald, David W. *s.j.* '61 (SAC) [14] Sacramento, CA St. Ignatius of Loyola Church.
MacDonald, Edward J. '42 (MAN) Retired.
MacDonald, Fabian '77 (SEA) Medical Leave.
MacDonald, Hugh J. '64 (HRT) North Haven, CT St. Barnabas Church.
MacDonald, James *s.a.c.* (CAM) [C] Pennsauken, NJ Bishop Eustace Prep School.
MacDonald, James H. '67 (SFR) Belmont, CA Immaculate Heart of Mary Church.
MacDonald, Kevin *c.ss.r.* '91 (RVC) Bethpage, NY St. Martin of Tours Church.
MacDonald, Paul V. '59 (BO) Scituate, MA St. Frances Xavier Cabrini Church.
MacDonald, Richard J. *s.c.j.* '65 (BWN) Lyford, TX Prince of Peace Church; Raymondville, TX Our Lady of Guadalupe Church.
MacDonald, Rupert A. *s.s.j.* '40 (BAL) [M] Baltimore, MD St. Joseph's Manor.
MacDonald, Sebastian *c.p.* '58 (DET) [K] Detroit, MI St. Paul of the Cross Community, Congregation of the Passion.
MacDonald, Sterling B. (BO) Retired.
MacDonald, Stirling '88 (BO) Groton, MA St. James Church.
MacDonald, Timothy *s.a.* '67 (NY) [DD] Garrison, NY Generalate of the Franciscan Friars of the Atonement-St. James Friary.
MacDonnell, John J. *s.j.* '58 (WOR) [N] Worcester, MA Jesuits of Holy Cross College, Inc.
MacDonnell, Joseph F. *s.j.* '61 (BGP) [A] Fairfield, CT Fairfield University; [O] Fairfield, CT The Fairfield Jesuit Community-Fairfield University.
MacDonnell, Martin *s.j.* '66 (BO) [W] Chestnut Hill, MA The Jesuit Community at Boston College.
MacDonough, Richard *s.s.* '60 (LA) [A] Camarillo, CA St. John's Seminary College of the Archdiocese of Los Angeles.
MacDougall, James L. *o.s.a.* '59 (MIA) [B] Opa Locka, FL St. Thomas University; [H] Miami, FL Casa San Lorenzo.
Mace, John D. *s.j.* '68 (FgM) Provinces.
Mace, John D. *s.j.* '68 (MIL) [P] Milwaukee, WI Jesuit Provincial Office, Wisconsin Province.
MacEachen, Bede *s.a.* '42 (NY) [DD] Garrison, NY Generalate of the Franciscan Friars of the Atonement-St. James Friary.
Maceda, Thomas *c.ss.r.* '63 (BRK) [107] Brooklyn, NY Our Lady of Perpetual Help Basilica Church.
Maceda, Thomas *c.ss.r.* '63 (NY) [23] New York, NY St. Cecilia Church.
Macedo, Charles '48 (SJ) [1] Palo Alto, CA St. Thomas Aquinas Church; Retired.
Macedo, Stephen A. '93 (HON) Naalehu, HI Sacred Heart Church; Pahala, HI Holy Rosary Church.
Macek, Joseph S. *s.s.j.* '87 (WDC) [23] Washington, DC Incarnation Church.
Maceli, Anthony J. '48 (BRK) Retired.
MacEntee, Francis J. *s.j.* '54 (SCR) [C] Scranton, PA University of Scranton.
MacEwen, Michael W. '85 (BO) [71] Boston, MA St. Theresa Church.
MacFarlane, John F. '66 (WDC) [1] Rockville, MD St. Elizabeth Church.
MacGabhann, Kevin (PMB) Lantana, FL Holy Spirit Church.
MacGee, James B. *o.m.i.* '57 (PT) Medart, FL St. Elizabeth Ann Seton Church.
MacGillivray, Arthur A. *s.j.* '44 (BO) [W] Chestnut Hill, MA The Jesuit Community at Boston College.
MacGillivray, John J. *c.m.* '76 (FgM) Vincentian Foreign Missions.
Macgregor, Donald '67 (HON) Makawao, HI St. Joseph Church.
Machado, Domingos *o.a.r.* '95 (NY) [154] Bronx, NY St. John's Church; [FF] Bronx, NY St. Joseph's Center.
Machado, Jose '93 (WCH) On Duty Outside the Diocese.
Machado, Manuel '64 (NY) [109] New York, NY St. Rose of Lima Church.
Machain, David '52 (PH) [23] Philadelphia, PA St. Bernard Church.
Machalski, Thomas C. '85 (BRK) [177] Queens, NY Holy Cross Church.
Machar, Jerome J. *o.c.s.o.* '75 (ROC) [I] Piffard, NY Abbey of the Genesee.
Machcinski, Anthony J. '50 (GAY) Retired.
Machesky, Peter I. *o.f.m.* '50 (JKS) Charleston, MS St. John Church.
Machlik, Jerome J. '71 (DET) Shelby Twp., MI St. John Vianney Church.
Machnik, Theodore F. '91 (COL) Reynoldsburg, OH St. Pius X Church.
Macho, George S. '53 (NEW) Retired.
Macho, Tomas *s.j.* '46 (MIA) [H] Miami, FL Villa Javier.
Machovec, Frank J. '59 (LIN) Superior, NE St. Joseph's Church.
Machovec, Martin F. *o.m.i.* '61 (CR) Ogema, MN Most Holy Redeemer Church; White Earth, MN St. Benedict Church.
Macias, Francisco A. '94 (SAT) Gonzales, TX St. James Church.
Macias, Jorge *c.s.s.r.* (SJN) [A] Bayamon, PR Bayamon Central University.
Macias, Salvador '82 (OAK) [2] Concord, CA St. Bonaventure Church.
Macias, Salvadore (OAK) Graduate Studies.
Maciej, David '80 (SCL) Rice, MN Immaculate Conception Church.
Maciejewski, Gerard *o.f.m.conv.* '59 (BRK) [146] Queens, NY St. Adalbert Church.
Maciejewski, Norbert '69 (DET) [2] Warren, MI Ascension Church.
Maciejewski, Richard J. '56 (STU) Retired.
Maciejewski, Tadeusz *c.m.* '88 (BRK) [32] Brooklyn, NY SS. Cyril and Methodius Church.
MacInnis, John E. '69 (BO) [A] Boston, MA St. John's Seminary School of Theology.
MacIntyre, Frederick H. '92 (WDC) Newport, MD St. Mary Church.
Macior, Lazarus *o.f.m.* '56 (CLV) [P] Cleveland, OH St. Stanislaus Friary.
Macior, Lazarus *o.f.m.* '56 (GB) [I] Pulaski, WI Assumption of B.V.M. Friary.
MacIssac, Charles S. *o.s.* '83 (PCE) On Duty Outside the Diocese.
Maciukiewicz, David J. '81 (E) [5] Erie, PA Holy Trinity Church.
Mack, Msgr. Ferdinand A. '31 (MAD) Retired.
Mack, Henry J. '49 (SFD) Retired.
Mack, John P. '85 (BUF) Lancaster, NY Our Lady of Pompeii Church; [D] Lancaster, NY St. Mary's High School.
Mack, Joseph W. '89 (CHL) Asheboro, NC St. Joseph Church.
Mack, Msgr. Robert A. '57 (BUF) [42] Buffalo, NY St. Louis Church.
Mack, Thomas '78 (PEO) Lincoln, IL Holy Family Church.
Macke, Paul B. *s.j.* '73 (ANC) [G] Anchorage, AK Jesuit House.
Macke, Richard J. '54 (SC) Pomeroy, IA St. Mary's Church.
Macken, Forrest *c.p.* '47 (L) [L] Louisville, KY Sacred Heart Retreat.
MacKenzie, William M. '66 (BO) Medway, MA St. Joseph Church.
Mackert, Albert J. '61 (CLV) [34] Cleveland, OH Immaculate Conception Church; Retired.
Mackesy, Robert L. *m.m.* '47 (NY) [DD] Maryknoll, NY Maryknoll Fathers and Brothers.
Mackey, James M. '61 (ALB) [8] Troy, NY St. Michael the Archangel Church.
Macki, Jacek *o.f.m.conv.* '95 (BUF) [O] Athol Springs, NY Father Justin Rosary Hour Radio Apostolate.
Mackiewicz, Richard E. '69 (GBG) Leechburg, PA St. Martha Church.
Mackin, Eamon *c.h.s.* '70 (ORG) [2] Huntington Beach, CA St. Mary's by the Sea Church.
Mackin, Francis C. *s.j.* '54 (BO) [W] Chestnut Hill, MA The Jesuit Community at Boston College.
Mackin, Gerard *m.s.f.* '66 (SAT) Seguin, TX Our Lady

of Guadalupe Church.
Mackin, John J. '38 (CHI) Arlington Heights, IL Our Lady of the Wayside Church; Hometown, IL Our Lady of Loretto Church; Retired.
Mackin, Kevin E. '64 (ALB) [B] Loudonville, NY Siena College; [B] Loudonville, NY Siena College.
Mackin, William H. '38 (MIL) Retired.
Mackinnon, Donald *c.ss.r.* '59 (OAK) [N] Oakland, CA Redemptorists.
MacKinnon, William *s.o.l.t.* '97 (STN) [1] Chicago, IL St. Nicholas Ukrainian Catholic Cathedral.
Mackle, Daniel E. '80 (PH) [1] Philadelphia, PA Cathedral Basilica of SS. Peter and Paul Church; [A] Wynnewood, PA Theological Seminary of St. Charles Borromeo, Overbrook.
Mackle, Liam *o.s.m.* '58 (ORG) [H] Buena Park, CA Servite Fathers And Brothers.
Macklin, Eckley *s.o.l.t.* '94 (CC) [H] Robstown, TX Society of Our Lady of the Most Holy Trinity.
Macklin, Eckley *s.o.l.t.* '94 (KC) [O] Kansas City, MO Society of Our Lady of the Most Holy Trinity.
Macko, Msgr. John '41 (PBR) Retired.
Mackowiak, Edward M. '55 (CHI) Burbank, IL St. Albert the Great Church.
Mackowski, Richard M. *s.j.* '61 (DET) [K] Detroit, MI Jesuit Provincial Office-Detroit Province of the Society of Jesus.
MacLeay, Richard Paul *o.p.* '57 (NO) [P] New Orleans, LA Dominican Fathers & Brothers, Southern Dominican Province.
MacLellan, Iain G. *o.s.b.* '87 (MAN) [K] Manchester, NH St. Anselm Abbey.
MacLellan, Richard H. '51 (CHY) Newcastle, WY Corpus Christi Church.
MacLennan, Donald '67 (DET) Absent on Sick Leave.
MacLeod, Thomas P. '56 (BO) Wakefield, MA Most Blessed Sacrament Church.
MacLoughlin, James '63 (ORL) Belleview, FL St. Theresa Church.
MacMahon, Craig *o.m.v.* '90 (SFD) [2] Alton, IL Immaculate Conception-St. Mary's Church; [3] Alton, IL St. Patrick Church; [H] Alton, IL Saint Anthony's Health Center; [N] Alton, IL Saint Anthony's Health System, Inc.; [N] Alton, IL Saint Clare's Hospital.
MacMahon, Msgr. Eamon '47 (MRY) Retired.
MacMahon, Michael '66 (BIR) [17] Birmingham, AL Our Lady of the Valley Church.
MacMahon, Patrick '69 (SPK) Colton, WA St. Gall Church; Uniontown, WA St. Boniface Church.
MacMaster, Thomas A. *o.c.s.o.* '57 (DUB) [K] Peosta, IA New Melleray Abbey, Order of Cistercians of the Strict Observance.
MacMillan, Donald A. *s.j.* '72 (BO) [W] Chestnut Hill, MA The Jesuit Community at Boston College.
MacMillan, Leonard '91 (B) Graduate Studies.
MacNamara, Robert C. '51 (ROC) Horseheads, NY St. Mary Our Mother Church; Retired.
MacNevin, Stanley F. *c.s.p.* '60 (BO) [P] Boston, MA Paulist Center; [W] Boston, MA Paulist Fathers Residence.
MacNevin, Stanley F. *c.s.p.* '60 (NY) [DD] Jamaica Estates, NY Paulist Fathers Generalate.
MacNew, James J. *o.s.f.s.* '80 (WIL) [I] Wilmington, DE Oblates of St. Francis De Sales.
Maco, Stephen L. '76 (ALN) [1] Bethlehem, PA St. Anne Church; [C] Bethlehem, PA Bethlehem Catholic High School.
Macora, Athanasius *o.f.m.* '92 (FgM) Custody of St. Mary of the Angels. Byzantine-Slavonic.
Macoskie, Melvin H. '55 (MIL) Retired.
MacPeck, Francis *s.j.* '67 (SFR) [44] San Francisco, CA St. Peter Church.
MacPeck, Francis D. *s.j.* '67 (SJ) [M] Los Gatos, CA Sacred Heart Jesuit Center.
MacPhaidin, Bartley J. *c.s.c.* '63 (FR) [A] North Easton, MA Stonehill College; [A] North Easton, MA Holy Cross Fathers Religious.
MacPherson, Albert P. *o.s.a.* '74 (BO) [C] North Andover, MA Merrimack College.
MacPherson, Damian *s.a.* '78 (NY) [DD] Garrison, NY Generalate of the Franciscan Friars of the Atonement-St. James Friary.
MacPherson, Stephen '86 (SR) McKinleyville, CA Christ the King Church.
MacPherson, Walter E. '55 (BEL) Retired.
MacPherson, Walter J. '86 (CIN) [15] Dayton, OH Holy Trinity Church.
MacQuarrie, John '78 (CIN) New Carlisle, OH Sacred Heart Church.
MacRae, Gordon J. '82 (MAN) Absent on Leave.
MacRory, Camillus *o.f.m.cap.* '51 (SFR) [N] Burlingame, CA Capuchin Provincial House.
Macunas, Theodore S. '64 (ALN) [10] Reading, PA St. Paul Church.
MacVeigh, Donal T. *s.j.* '72 (NEW) [B] Jersey City, NJ Saint Peter's College; [N] Jersey City, NJ Jesuits of Saint Peter's College, Inc.
MacVeigh, Michael C. '56 (PIT) Overbrook, PA St. Norbert Church.
MacWade, Joseph A. *s.j.* '61 (FgM) Provinces.
Madaj, John A. '39 (SCR) Retired.
Madariaga, Jesus M. *o.p.* '54 (CC) [13] Laredo, TX St. Joseph Church.
Madathiparampil, George (WDC) [36] Washington, DC St. Patrick Church.
Maday, Norbert J. '64 (CHI) Other Assignments.
Maddalena, Joseph P. '86 (GBG) Ligonier, PA Holy Trinity Church.
Madden, Benjamin *o.f.m.cap.* '58 (FgM) Capuchin Foreign Missions.
Madden, Msgr. Brendan P. '51 (PAT) [4] Clifton, NJ St. Clare's Church.
Madden, Daniel P. *o.p.* '60 (MIA) [B] Miami, FL Barry University; [H] Bal Harbour, FL Dominican Friars Residence.
Madden, Declan A. *o.f.m.conv.* '47 (DEN) [I] Denver, CO Francis Heights, Inc.; [K] Denver, CO Clare Gardens, Inc.
Madden, Denis (NY) [HH] New York, NY Catholic Near East Welfare Association.
Madden, Denis J. '67 (BAL) Special Assignment.
Madden, Edward T. '52 (DEN) [1] Boulder, CO Sacred Heart of Jesus Church.
Madden, Henry L. *o.f.m.* '46 (ALB) [B] Loudonville, NY Siena College.
Madden, J. Thomas '53 (SFR) [M] Menlo Park, CA Vallombrosa Center.
Madden, James J. *m.m.* (FgM) Maryknoll Foreign Missions.
Madden, James J. (GAL) [N] Houston, TX Pope John XXIII Priest Residence.
Madden, James J. (OG) Watertown, NY U.S. Army Headquarters Fort Drum.
Madden, Msgr. James J. '55 (GAL) Retired.
Madden, John '62 (NEW) [N] Rutherford, NJ St. John Vianney Residence for Priests.
Madden, John F. *c.s.b.* '47 (GAL) Retired; [Q] Houston, TX Dillon House.
Madden, John F. '84 (WOR) [27] Worcester, MA St. Peter Church; [C] Worcester, MA Holy Name Central Catholic Junior/Senior High School.
Madden, John J. '62 (NEW) Retired.
Madden, John J. *s.j.* '69 (FgM) Provinces.
Madden, John P. '86 (Y) Newton Falls, OH St. Joseph Church; Newton Falls, OH St. Mary Church.
Madden, Msgr. John R. '59 (SY) Hamilton, NY St. Mary Church.
Madden, Joseph *o.f.m.conv.* '62 (CHL) Winston-Salem, NC Our Lady of Mercy Church.
Madden, Lawrence J. *s.j.* '64 (WDC) [20] Washington, DC Holy Trinity Church.
Madden, Michael '75 (EVN) [8] Evansville, IN Holy Spirit Church.
Madden, Michael G. '62 (TOL) [4] Toledo, OH Community of the Risen Christ Church; [35] Toledo, OH St. Patrick of Heatherdowns Church.
Madden, Michael J. '95 (BGP) [2] Trumbull, CT St. Catherine of Siena Church.
Madden, Patrick '74 (SHP) On Duty Outside the Diocese.
Madden, Patrick '83 (MOB) Bayou LaBatre, AL St. Margaret Church.
Madden, Msgr. Patrick J. '45 (CAM) Retired.
Madden, Patrick J. '74 (BAL) [A] Baltimore, MD St. Mary's Seminary and University.
Madden, Msgr. Patrick M. '53 (STA) [14] Jacksonville, FL Sacred Heart Church.
Madden, Paul '70 (FgM) Society of St. James the Apostle.
Madden, Paul '70 (JKS) On Duty Outside the Diocese.
Madden, Ronald '70 (SAV) Military Chaplains.
Madden, Stephen J. '88 (BO) Foxboro, MA St. Mary Church.
Madden, Thomas '53 (SFR) Special Assignment.
Madden, Msgr. Thomas E. '32 (ALT) [1] Altoona, PA Cathedral of the Blessed Sacrament; Retired.
Madden, Thomas F. '76 (NY) [A] Bronx, NY St. John Neumann Residence; [HH] New York, NY The Center for Spirituality and Justice.
Madden, Msgr. Thomas G. '55 (NEW) North Arlington, NJ Queen of Peace Church.
Madden, Thomas J. *s.j.* '57 (MIA) [5] Miami, FL Gesu Church.
Madden, Thomas L. '81 (SP) Dunedin, FL Our Lady of Lourdes Church.
Madden, William O. *s.j.* '57 (CHI) Chicago, IL Cook County Hospital; [D] Chicago, IL St. Ignatius Jesuit Community; [N] Chicago, IL Chicago Province of the Society of Jesus-Provincial Office.
Madden, William T. *m.m.* '58 (NY) [DD] Maryknoll, NY Maryknoll Fathers and Brothers; [HH] Maryknoll, NY Friends of St. Maria Goretti, U.S.A., Inc.
Maddock, Andrew L. *s.j.* '85 (FBK) [2] Fairbanks, AK Immaculate Conception Church; [C] Fairbanks, AK Jesuit Residence.
Maddock, George *o.f.m.cap.* '64 (FgM) Capuchin Foreign Missions.
Maddock, George E.D. *o.f.m.cap.* (AGN) Agana Heights, GU Our Lady of the Blessed Sacrament Church.
Maddock, Jay '75 (FR) East Taunton, MA Holy Family Church.
Maddock, Jay T. '75 (FR) [N] Fall River, MA Diocesean Catholic Youth Organization.
Maddock, Laurence F. '56 (CHI) [96] Chicago, IL Saint Ita Church.
Maddox, Edward '96 (AUS) [9] Austin, TX Sacred Heart Church.
Maddox, Msgr. Edward C. '50 (LA) Inglewood, CA St. John Chrysostom Church.
Madej, Paul D. '90 (SY) Military Chaplains.
Madejczyk, Louis S. '36 (GRY) Retired.
Mader, George L. '59 (NEW) Oakland, NJ Our Lady of Perpetual Help Church; Retired; [N] Caldwell, NJ The Rev. Msgr. James F. Kelley Residence for Retired Priests.
Mader, Joseph '67 (IND) On Disability Leave.
Mader, Stan '92 (STP) [27] St. Paul, MN St. Mark Church.
Madey, Louis '68 (LAN) On Duty Outside the Diocese.
Madigan, Arthur R. *s.j.* '77 (BO) [W] Chestnut Hill, MA The Jesuit Community at Boston College.
Madigan, Daniel '64 (SAC) Clarksburg, CA St. Joseph Church.
Madigan, Francis C. *s.j.* '49 (FgM) Provinces.
Madigan, Henry *o.f.m.conv.* '56 (WDC) [B] Washington, DC St. Bonaventure Friary.
Madigan, Msgr. James '32 (MOB) Retired; [F] Mobile, AL Little Sisters of the Poor, Home For the Aged, Inc.
Madigan, John *o.m.i.* '77 (MIA) Opa Locka, FL St. Philip Church.
Madigan, John A. *o.p.* '66 (RVC) [B] Rockville Centre, NY Molloy College.
Madigan, John C. '74 (SEA) Renton, WA St. Stephen the Martyr Church.
Madigan, Msgr. John J. '54 (WDC) [9] Silver Spring, MD Our Lady of Grace Church.
Madigan, Kevin '92 (CHI) [B] Chicago, IL The Catholic Theological Union at Chicago.
Madigan, Kevin V. '71 (NY) [18] New York, NY Blessed Sacrament Church.
Madigan, Patrick S. *s.j.* '83 (FgM) Provinces.
Madigan, Patrick S. *s.j.* '83 (NO) [P] New Orleans, LA Jesuit Provincial Office.
Madison, Martan *s.a.* '62 (BRK) [113] Brooklyn, NY Our Lady of Victory Church.
Madley, Jeffrey J. '76 (RVC) Commack, NY Christ the King Church.
Madlon, Daniel *o.s.b.* '33 (SFS) [F] Marvin, SD Blue Cloud Abbey.
Madori, Peter J. '69 (NY) Warwick, NY St. Stephen Church.
Madrazo, Higinio *c.m.* '44 (SJN) [47] San Juan, PR Nuestra Senora del Pilar Church; [F] Rio Piedras, PR Asylum For Orphan Girls.
Madrid, J. Saul '85 (PHX) [7] Phoenix, AZ SS. Anthony and Pius X Church.
Madrid, Jaime '68 (ELP) Absent on Leave.
Madrigal, Hector '87 (AMA) [4] Amarillo, TX Our Lady of Guadalupe Church; Absent on Leave.
Madrigal, Idelfonso '57 (LA) Paramount, CA Our Lady of the Rosary Church.
Madrilejos, J. Rico '93 (NEW) Rahway, NJ St. Mary's Church.
Madsen, Msgr. Cletus P. '31 (DAV) Retired; [B] Davenport, IA St. Ambrose University; [M] Davenport, IA St. Vincent Center.
Madsen, Msgr. John W. '66 (BUF) [2] Depew, NY St. Barnabas Church.
Madu, Emmanuel '78 (NO) [5] New Orleans, LA Corpus Christi Church.
Madubuko, Michael N. *s.j.* '85 (CHI) [N] Chicago, IL Chicago Province of the Society of Jesus-Provincial Office.
Maduike, Basil '66 (SFS) Grenville, SD St. Joseph Church; Waubay, SD Immaculate Conception Church.
Maduri, John '87 (BRK) [126] Brooklyn, NY St. Rosalia-Regina Pacis Church.
Maduro, Gabriel '59 (ARE) [12] Arecibo, PR Church of Santa Teresita.
Madus, Msgr. Peter P. '68 (SCR) [14] Scranton, PA St. Joseph's Church.
Maduzia, Norbert '82 (GAL) [28] Houston, TX St. Frances Cabrini Church.
Maechler, Edmund F. '49 (LA) Retired.
Maechler, Gerald T. '55 (LA) Retired.
Maes, Allen *o.m.i.* '68 (STL) [W] St. Louis, MO Oblate House of Studies.
Maes, Clarence '87 (SFE) Chama, NM St. Patrick Church.
Maes, Clark B. '95 (STL) Brentwood, MO St. Mary Magdalen Church.
Maes, David *c.r.* '85 (ORG) [H] Orange, CA Theatine Fathers.
Maes, John J. '67 (DOD) Hoisington, KS St. John the Evangelist Church; Odin, KS Holy Family Church.
Maestri, William F. '77 (NO) [A] St. Benedict, LA St. Joseph's Seminary College.
Maestrini, Nicholas *p.i.m.e.* '30 (PMB) [G] Tequesta, FL P.I.M.E. Missionaries.
Mafezzini, Angel '54 (LA) [26] Los Angeles, CA Our Lady of Lourdes Church.
Maffei, Joseph *s.d.b.* '58 (NY) [DD] New Rochelle, NY Salesian Provincial House.

Maffei, Vincent R. '64 (BO) Plainville, MA St. Martha Church.
Maffeo, Michael '91 (RVC) Rocky Point, NY St. Anthony of Padua Church.
Magadia, Jose *s.j.* '91 (NY) [DD] New York, NY West Side Jesuit Community.
Magaldi, Phillip '60 (FWT) [11] Fort Worth, TX St. John the Apostle Church.
Magallanes, Alejandro *o.f.m.cap.* '69 (FRS) Fresno, CA Community Hospital, Veterans' Hospital.
Magallanes, Manuel J. *o.s.b.* '76 (LA) Montebello, CA St. Benedict Church.
Magary, Thomas A. '66 (STU) Martins Ferry, OH St. Mary Church.
Magdaleno, Richard D. '89 (FRS) Corcoran, CA Our Lady of Lourdes Church.
Magdaraog, Vincente '96 (TR) Barnegat, NJ St. Mary Church.
Magee, Andrew T. '45 (NY) Maybrook, NY Assumption Church; Retired; [DD] New York, NY Pope John Paul II Residence.
Magee, George P. *o.s.a.* '68 (PH) [D] Drexel Hill, PA Monsignor Bonner High School.
Magee, Michael K. '91 (PH) Graduate Studies.
Magee, Patrick F. '70 (TR) Point Pleasant, NJ St. Martha Church.
Magee, Paul L. '94 (STP) On Duty Outside the Archdiocese.
Magee, Robert L. '70 (PMB) Jensen Beach, FL St. Martin de Porres Church.
Magel, John E. '60 (L) Retired.
Mager, Martin J. *o.s.b.* '63 (SFR) [N] Portola Valley, CA Woodside Priory.
Mages, Mark C. *o.s.b.* '39 (BIR) [E] Cullman, AL St. Bernard Abbey.
Maggart, James M. '97 (CAM) Haddon Heights, NJ St. Rose's Church.
Maggio, J. Mark '90 (BR) On Leave.
Maggioni, Luigi *p.i.m.e.* '57 (DET) [K] Detroit, MI P.I.M.E. Missionaries of SS. Peter and Paul.
Maggs, William C. *c.ss.r.* '66 (PH) [135] Philadelphia, PA St. Peter the Apostle Church.
Maginnis, Andrew F. *s.j.* '52 (SFR) [N] San Francisco, CA Jesuit Community at University of San Francisco.
Maginnis, Edward L. *s.j.* '53 (DEN) [M] Denver, CO Regis Jesuit Community (The Jesuits at Regis University).
Maginnis, Robert P. '61 (PH) Ardmore, PA St. Colman Church.
Maginot, Michael '83 (GRY) [F] Dyer, IN St. Margaret Mercy Healthcare Centers, South Campus.
Maginot, Richard J. '50 (CHI) Prospect Heights, IL St. Alphonsus Liguori Church; Retired.
Maglione, Joseph J. '42 (BGP) Retired.
Magnan, Oscar G. '63 (NEW) [B] Jersey City, NJ Saint Peter's College; [N] Jersey City, NJ Jesuits of Saint Peter's College, Inc.
Magnano, Paul A. '67 (SEA) Burlington, WA St. Charles Church; LaConner, WA Sacred Heart Church; LaConner, WA St. Paul Church; Mount Vernon, WA Immaculate Conception Church; Sedro Woolley, WA Immaculate Heart of Mary Church; [Q] LaConner, WA Skagit Valley Regional Ministry.
Magni, Daniel M. '78 (BO) [15] Lowell, MA St. Rita Church.
Magni, Raffaele *p.i.m.e.* '56 (DET) [K] Detroit, MI P.I.M.E. Missionaries of SS. Peter and Paul.
Magnier, Patrick *c.ss.r.* '35 (BAL) [96] Baltimore, MD St. Wenceslaus Church; [Q] Baltimore, MD Legion of Mary.
Magoon, R. Dale '60 (GAY) Mancelona, MI St. Anthony Church.
Magraw, Msgr. Daniel E. '75 (E) [7] Erie, PA Mount Calvary Church.
Magri, Thomas '79 (RIC) Absent On Leave.
Magro, Emanuel '79 (WDC) [35] Washington, DC Our Lady of Victory Church.
Maguire, Alban *o.f.m.* '41 (WDC) [3] Silver Spring, MD St. Camillus Church.
Maguire, Connell J. '45 (PH) Retired.
Maguire, Daniel J. '69 (SFR) [44] San Francisco, CA St. Peter Church.
Maguire, Enda J. '59 (STO) Lockeford, CA St. Joachim Church.
Maguire, Eugene (PHX) Retired.
Maguire, Eugene '47 (PHX) [G] Phoenix, AZ Mt. Claret Retreat Center.
Maguire, Felix H. '50 (HRT) Retired.
Maguire, Francis *c.m.* '51 (FgM) Vincentian Foreign Missions.
Maguire, Francis *o.p.* '57 (DET) [20] Detroit, MI St. Dominic Church.
Maguire, Francis X. *c.m.* '78 (PH) [AA] Philadelphia, PA Congregation of the Mission.
Maguire, Hugh '57 (MOB) Enterprise, AL St. John Church.
Maguire, James F. *s.j.* '35 (CHI) [C] Chicago, IL Jesuit Community at Loyola University of Chicago.
Maguire, John J. '40 (BO) Retired.
Maguire, Msgr. John R. '50 (STL) Shrewsbury, MO Cure' of Ars Church.
Maguire, Joseph D. '70 (FR) Retired.
Maguire, Joseph T. '73 (MAN) Absent on Sick Leave.
Maguire, Paul J. '43 (CAM) Wildwood, NJ St. Ann's Church.
Maguire, Paul J. '48 (CAM) Retired.
Maguire, Robert *o.cist.* '76 (DAL) [B] Irving, TX University of Dallas; [M] Irving, TX Cistercian Abbey of Our Lady of Dallas.
Maguire, Robert E. *s.j.* '63 (BO) [W] Weston, MA Campion Center.
Maguire, Seamus J. '53 (WH) Retired.
Maguire, Thomas (SAC) Folsom, CA St. John the Baptist Church.
Maguire, Thomas '71 (SAC) Sacramento, CA Mule Creek State Prison.
Maguire, Vincent E. '55 (LR) [E] Fort Smith, AR St. Edward Mercy Medical Center.
Maguire, Msgr. William E. '50 (TR) Retired.
Maguire, William J. *c.s.sp.* '49 (PH) [FF] Philadelphia, PA Shrine of Our Lady of Victories at St. Peter Claver.
Magyar, Ladislaus *sch.p.* '38 (PH) [AA] Devon, PA Piarist Fathers (Order of the Pious Schools).
Mahalic, Philip A. '83 (LFT) Wheatfield, IN Sorrowful Mother Church.
Mahan, Daniel J. '88 (IND) [25] Indianapolis, IN St. Luke Church.
Mahan, George S. *s.j.* '40 (BO) [W] Boston, MA Loyola House.
Mahan, Paul J. '68 (BO) Health Leave.
Mahan, Terrance L. *s.j.* '54 (LA) [C] Los Angeles, CA Loyola Marymount University.
Mahaney, Hilary F. '69 (CHI) [127] Chicago, IL St. Mary of the Angels Church.
Mahar, Raymond '58 (BUF) [K] Lackawanna, NY Our Lady of Victory Hospital.
Mahedy, Brian *c.p.* '33 (CHI) [N] Chicago, IL Immaculate Conception Monastery.
Mahedy, Oliver '59 (WDC) [7] Silver Spring, MD St. John the Evangelist Church.
Maher, Arthur '54 (JOL) Retired.
Maher, Byron G. '50 (CHI) Wauconda, IL Transfiguration Church; Retired.
Maher, Charles E. '60 (PRO) [9] Providence, RI Blessed Sacrament Church.
Maher, Daniel J. '62 (ALB) [7] Albany, NY Church of the Holy Cross.
Maher, Daniel J. '91 (ARL) On Duty Outside the Diocese.
Maher, Daniel J. '91 (WDC) [Q] Washington, DC Basilica of the National Shrine of the Immaculate Conception.
Maher, Edmund J. '88 (PH) [147] Philadelphia, PA Stella Maris Church.
Maher, Edward A. *c.s.p.* '49 (NY) [DD] Jamaica Estates, NY Paulist Fathers Generalate.
Maher, Edward A. *c.s.p.* '49 (SFR) [31] San Francisco, CA Old St. Mary's Cathedral.
Maher, Edward J. '81 (CAM) Mays Landing, NJ St. Vincent de Paul Church.
Maher, Francis '54 (JOL) Wilmington, IL St. Rose Church.
Maher, Gerald John '94 (MRY) [1] Monterey, CA Cathedral of San Carlos Borromeo.
Maher, J. David '71 (JC) Kirksville, MO Mary Immaculate Church.
Maher, Msgr. James '43 (SJ) Retired.
Maher, James J. *c.m.* (BRK) [L] Brooklyn, NY Catholic Charities.
Maher, James J. *c.m.* '90 (BRK) [U] Jamaica, NY St. Vincent's House.
Maher, James J. '92 (LA) [AA] Los Angeles, CA Scouting and Camp Fire Ministry/Catholic Youth Camps.
Maher, James M. (LA) Sherman Oaks, CA St. Francis de Sales Church.
Maher, John *c.m.* '81 (PH) [155] Philadelphia, PA St. Vincent de Paul Church.
Maher, John J. '39 (NY) Retired.
Maher, John L. *s.j.* '74 (FgM) Provinces.
Maher, Joseph G. '55 (CHR) [11] Charleston, SC Church of the Nativity.
Maher, Michael *s.j.* (STL) [C] St. Louis, MO Saint Louis University.
Maher, Michael L. '48 (SAG) Retired.
Maher, Michael N. *ss.cc.* '63 (SB) Chino Hills, CA St. Paul the Apostle Church.
Maher, Michael W. *s.j.* '86 (STL) [P] St. Louis, MO Jesuit Community Corporation at St. Louis University - Jesuit Hall.
Maher, Patrick '53 (MOB) [16] Mobile, AL Our Lady of Lourdes Church.
Maher, Msgr. Patrick K. '47 (STU) Retired.
Maher, Patrick S. '71 (LUB) Snyder, TX Our Lady of Guadalupe Church.
Maher, Paul J. *s.j.* '64 (FgM) Provinces.
Maher, Paul P. *o.m.i.* '58 (P) Lebanon, OR St. Edward Church.
Maher, Raymond '44 (SJ) Retired.
Maher, Raymond V. *o.carm.* '97 (PMB) [B] Boca Raton, FL Pope John Paul II High School; [G] Boca Raton, FL St. Elias Priory-Order of Carmelites, NY.
Maher, Robert *o.f.m.cap.* '74 (HON) Aiea, HI St. Elizabeth Church.
Maher, Robert E. '71 (BWN) Edinburg, TX St. Joseph Church.
Maher, Robert G. '57 (WIN) On Duty Outside the Diocese.
Maher, Robert L. *o.f.m.cap.* '74 (FgM) Capuchin Foreign Missions.
Maher, Ryan J. *s.j.* (PH) [G] Philadelphia, PA St. Joseph's Preparatory School.
Maher, Thomas *o.m.i.* '57 (FgM) Oblates Foreign Missions.
Maher, Thomas *l.c.* '94 (LA) [R] Pasadena, CA Legionaries of Christ.
Maher, Thomas F. '47 (CHI) [69] Chicago, IL St. Genevieve Church; [132] Chicago, IL St. Mary of the Woods Church; Retired.
Maher, Thomas J. *c.ss.r.* '40 (BRK) [107] Brooklyn, NY Our Lady of Perpetual Help Basilica Church.
Maher, Thomas J. '62 (ALT) Loretto, PA Basilica of St. Michael the Archangel Church.
Maher, William *o.m.i.* '66 (FgM) Oblates Foreign Missions.
Maher, William F.X. *s.j.* '57 (NEW) [B] Jersey City, NJ Saint Peter's College; [N] Jersey City, NJ Jesuits of Saint Peter's College, Inc.
Mahfoud, Peter '55 (SAM) Retired.
Mahler, Msgr. Frank E. (ARL) Clifton, VA St. Claire of Assisi Church.
Mahler, Michael '73 (ROC) [M] Rochester, NY Diocesan Office of Campus Ministry.
Mahlmann, Raymond '85 (GLP) Farmington, NM St. Mary's Church.
Mahnke, Ronald *o.s.b.* '62 (CLV) [P] Cleveland, OH Benedictine Order of Cleveland.
Mahon, Ambrose J. '58 (STP) Edina, MN St. Patrick Church.
Mahon, Msgr. Dennis '70 (WDC) [C] Washington, DC Catholic University of America, The.
Mahon, Msgr. Dennis J. (NEW) [G] Newark, NJ Catholic Community Services (C.C.S.) Mt. Carmel Guild Hospital.
Mahon, Francis *s.v.d.* '40 (TR) [M] Bordentown, NJ Society of the Divine Word.
Mahon, Gerald A. '71 (WIN) [6] Rochester, MN St. John's Church.
Mahon, Joseph F. *c.s.p.* '56 (NY) [104] New York, NY St. Paul the Apostle Church.
Mahon, Leo '51 (CHI) [132] Chicago, IL St. Mary of the Woods Church.
Mahon, M. Shawn '88 (BAL) [43] Baltimore, MD St. Isaac Jogues Church.
Mahon, William A. '92 (NEW) Garwood, NJ Church of St. Anne.
Mahone, Casey B. '89 (WH) [2] Fairmont, WV Immaculate Conception Church.
Mahone, Michael Q. '80 (RNO) Incline Village, NV St. Francis of Assisi Church.
Mahoney, Arthur J. *c.ss.r.* '51 (HBG) [H] Ephrata, PA St. Clement's Mission House.
Mahoney, Bernard '53 (AUS) On Duty Outside the Diocese.
Mahoney, Bryan '95 (BO) Wellesley, MA St. John the Evangelist Church.
Mahoney, Charles J. *c.s.c.* '40 (FTW) [J] South Bend, IN Congregation of Holy Cross Indiana Province Provincial House.
Mahoney, Cornelius H. '78 (BRK) Special Assignment; [B] Douglaston, NY Cathedral Residence of the Immaculate Conception.
Mahoney, Daniel C. '70 (GBG) Murrysville, PA Mother of Sorrows Church.
Mahoney, Daniel F. '46 (NEW) Retired.
Mahoney, Daniel J. '52 (HBG) [5] Harrisburg, PA Holy Name of Jesus Church.
Mahoney, Daniel J. '56 (BO) [23] Boston, MA St. Francis de Sales Church.
Mahoney, Edward P. '86 (R) Chapel Hill, NC Newman Catholic Student Center, University of North Carolina Church; Special Assignment; [H] Chapel Hill, NC Newman Catholic Student Center.
Mahoney, Msgr. Francis '30 (NY) Retired.
Mahoney, Francis L. '60 (FR) [5] Fall River, MA Holy Name Church.
Mahoney, Gerard J. *o.s.f.s.* '71 (PH) [D] Philadelphia, PA Father Judge High School for Boys; [AA] Philadelphia, PA Father Judge Faculty House.
Mahoney, Gordon '56 (JOL) [2] Naperville, IL Sts. Peter and Paul Church.
Mahoney, Msgr. James '73 (PAT) Chatham Township, NJ Corpus Christi Church.
Mahoney, James F. (BO) Retired.
Mahoney, Jeremia W. '46 (KC) Retired.
Mahoney, John *o.m.i.* '54 (FgM) Oblates Foreign Missions.
Mahoney, John A. '56 (PEO) Geneseo, IL St. Malachy's Church; Retired.
Mahoney, John E. (BRK) [141] Brooklyn, NY St. Thomas Aquinas Church.

Mahoney, John E. *s.j.* '36 (DET) [P] Clarkston, MI Colombiere Center.
Mahoney, John F. '60 (RVC) Priests Released from Diocesan Assignment.
Mahoney, John J., Jr. '85 (MAN) [7] Manchester, NH St. Edmund Church.
Mahoney, John L. *s.j.* '51 (BO) [E] Boston, MA Boston College High School & Jesuit Community.
Mahoney, John P. '48 (BO) Hanover, MA St. Mary of the Sacred Heart Church; Retired.
Mahoney, Joseph P. '57 (WOR) [1] Worcester, MA St. Paul's Cathedral; [25] Worcester, MA St. John's Church.
Mahoney, Kevin J. '81 (STL) [3] St. Charles, MO St. Elizabeth Ann Seton Church.
Mahoney, Leo R. '53 (BO) Hudson, MA Christ the King Church.
Mahoney, Mark A. '86 (BO) Holliston, MA St. Mary Church.
Mahoney, Martin J. '94 (NY) Hopewell Junction, NY St. Columba Church.
Mahoney, Maurice J. *o.s.a.* '60 (FgM) Foreign Missions.
Mahoney, Michael *o.f.m.cap.* '74 (SFR) Burlingame, CA Our Lady of Angels Church.
Mahoney, Michael T. '75 (CIN) [22] Dayton, OH St. Peter Church.
Mahoney, Neil J. '70 (NEW) [2] Newark, NJ St. Patrick's Pro-Cathedral.
Mahoney, Peter (BRK) [L] Brooklyn, NY Catholic Charities.
Mahoney, Peter A. '61 (BRK) [15] Brooklyn, NY St. Barbara Church.
Mahoney, Richard J. '58 (STP) Retired.
Mahoney, Robert '59 (AUS) Manor, TX St. Joseph's Church.
Mahoney, Robert J. '55 (KC) Special Assignment.
Mahoney, Shaun L. '91 (PH) Graduate Studies.
Mahoney, Thomas D. '65 (CLV) [61] Cleveland, OH St. Patrick Church.
Mahoney, Thomas E. '68 (WOR) Mendon, MA St. Michael's Church.
Mahoney, Thomas M. *o.s.a.* '45 (PH) [D] Drexel Hill, PA Monsignor Bonner High School.
Mahony, John '58 (SP) Retired.
Mahony, Thomas J. *o.s.a.* '54 (PH) [C] Villanova, PA Villanova University; [AA] Villanova, PA St. Thomas Monastery.
Mahowald, Paul *s.j.* (DM) Cumberland, IA St. Timothy Church; Griswold, IA Our Lady Of Grace Church.
Mahowald, Paul A. *s.j.* '68 (OM) [K] Omaha, NE Jesuit Community At Creighton University.
Mahowald, Msgr. Richard '55 (SFS) [2] Sioux Falls, SD Christ the King Church.
Mai, Dai Viet *i.c.* '90 (SP) Seffner, FL St. Francis of Assisi Church.
Mai, Emmanuel K. '86 (MRY) Absent on Sick Leave.
Mai Chi Thanh, Joseph M. '58 (PEO) Pesotum, IL St. Mary Church; Pesotum, IL St. Joseph Church.
Mai Minh Luan, Dominic (SPC) [E] Carthage, MO Congregation of the Mother Co-Redemptrix, United States Assumption Province.
Maibusch, Henry B. *o.s.a.* '54 (MIL) [8] Kenosha, WI Our Lady of the Holy Rosary Church.
Maichen, Richard F. '54 (DUB) Retired.
Maichiki, Daniel '83 (NY) [6] Yonkers, NY Christ the King Church.
Maida, Thaddeus S. '58 (PIT) Perrysville, PA St. Teresa of Avila Church.
Maier, John C. '90 (DM) Audubon, IA St. Patrick Church.
Maier, Joseph *c.ss.r.* '65 (FgM) Redemptorist Foreign Missions.
Maier, Paul '70 (RIC) Lebanon, VA Good Shepherd Church; St. Paul, VA St. Therese Church.
Maierle, John P. '55 (DET) [5] Livonia, MI St. Maurice Church.
Maiers, Brennan *o.s.b.* '63 (SCL) [I] Collegeville, MN St. John's Abbey, of the Order of St. Benedict.
Maikowski, Thomas '76 (GLP) [2] Gallup, NM St. Francis of Assisi Church; Special Assignment.
Mailloux, Normand F. *m.s.* '55 (SPR) Bondsville, MA St. Adalbert's Church.
Mailloux, Orville C. *c.ss.r.* '42 (STL) [P] Liguori, MO St. Clement Health Care Center.
Mailloux, Thomas B. *c.s.b.* '50 (GAL) [7] Houston, TX St. Anne Church.
Maina, Wilson Mudha (BO) [18] Boston, MA St. Cecilia Church.
Mainardi, Donald G. '63 (ORL) [7] Orlando, FL St. Charles Borromeo Church.
Mainelli, Vincent P. '63 (HON) [8] Honolulu, HI Holy Trinity Church.
Mainelli, Vincent P. *c.o.* '63 (OM) Absent on Leave.
Mainzer, James S. '87 (WCH) Augusta, KS St. James Church.
Maio, Anthony V. '49 (SAC) Retired and in Senior Ministry.
Maione, Anthony '85 (ALB) Special Assignment.
Maione, Anthony J. '85 (ALB) Saratoga Springs, NY St. Peter Church.
Maione, Francis T. '65 (NEW) East Newark, NJ St. Anthony's Church; [K] Kearny, NJ New Jersey Boystown.
Mair, Henry *s.a.* '62 (LA) [R] Los Angeles, CA Atonement Friars.
Mair, Henry *s.a.* '62 (MRY) Seaside, CA St. Francis Xavier Church.
Mair, Henry G. *s.a.* '56 (LA) [63] Los Angeles, CA Maryknoll Japanese Catholic Center Church.
Mair, Robert G. '65 (CHI) [128] Chicago, IL St. Mary of the Lake Church.
Mairal, Jose Ma. Lopez '54 (SJN) Resident Chaplains.
Maisano, Richard J. '69 (PH) New Garden Township, PA St. Gabriel of the Sorrowful Mother Church.
Maiser, Raymond *c.ss.r.* (TUC) [J] Tucson, AZ Redemptorist Community Support Charity Trust.
Maiser, Raymond *c.s.sp.* '64 (SEA) [O] Federal Way, WA Palisades Retreat House.
Maison, Gabriel '78 (VIC) Moulton, TX St. Joseph's Church.
Maisonneuve, Joseph *o.carm.* '86 (JOL) [J] Joliet, IL St. Elias Carmelites.
Maivelett, Bruce A. *s.j.* '88 (SY) [A] Syracuse, NY Saint Andrew Hall.
Maiza, Felix *s.j.* '52 (LA) [K] Duarte, CA Santa Teresita Hospital.
Maiza, Felix A. *s.j.* '52 (LA) [R] Los Angeles, CA Columbiere House.
Maiza, Jesus Maria *s.s.s.* '67 (CGS) [5] Caguas, PR Santisimo Sacramento Church.
Maj, Msgr. George C. *s.a.c.* '58 (BUF) [O] North Tonawanda, NY Society of the Catholic Apostolate.
Maj, Msgr. George E. *s.a.c.* '58 (BUF) [11] Cheektowaga, NY Resurrection Church.
Maj, George J. *o.s.p.p.e.* '89 (PH) [AA] Doylestown, PA Pauline Fathers Monastery, Shrine of Our Lady of Czestochowa.
Majan, Ricardo '54 (ARE) [3] Vega-Baja, PR The Blessed Trinity Church.
Majarucon, Jon '84 (LA) Santa Monica, CA St. Monica Church.
Majcher, Tadeusz *s.d.s.* '87 (BRK) [93] Brooklyn, NY Our Lady of Consolation Church.
Majchrowski, Anthony P. '44 (LAN) [2] Flint, MI All Saints Church.
Majda, Francis A. '39 (PIT) Retired.
Majdanik, Albin J. '42 (SY) Retired.
Majerus, Daniel '57 (SCL) On Duty Outside the Diocese.
Majewicz, Frank *c.r.* '74 (CHI) [D] Chicago, IL Weber High School.
Majewski, Edmund W. *s.j.* '83 (NEW) [B] Jersey City, NJ Saint Peter's College; [N] Jersey City, NJ Jesuits of Saint Peter's College, Inc.
Majewski, Eugene *c.r.* '74 (RCK) Woodstock, IL Resurrection Church.
Majewski, Francis *o.f.m.cap.* '64 (PAT) [M] Oak Ridge-Milton, NJ St. Stanislaus B. M. Friary.
Majewski, John E. '53 (STL) Clover Bottom, MO St. Ann's Church.
Majewski, Joseph B. '66 (RIC) [3] Newport News, VA St. Jerome Church.
Majewski, Joseph J. *c.ss.r.* '67 (RIC) [2] Hampton, VA St. Joseph Church.
Majewski, Stephen *o.f.m.conv.* '34 (BO) [55] Boston, MA Our Lady of Czestochowa Church.
Majic, Timothy *o.f.m.* '39 (CHI) [N] Chicago, IL Croatian Franciscan Custody of the Holy Family.
Majikas, David J. '97 (CLV) Chagrin Falls, OH St. Joan of Arc Church.
Majka, Frank A. *s.j.* '74 (MIL) [P] Milwaukee, WI Jesuit Community at Marquette University.
Majka, George '72 (MAN) Pittsfield, NH Our Lady of Lourdes Church.
Majka, Philip S. '65 (ARL) Chancellorsville, VA St. Patrick's Church.
Majkut, Thaddeus '84 (TYL) Longview, TX St. Anthony Church.
Major, Charles M. '59 (SY) [4] Liverpool, NY St. Joseph the Worker Church.
Major, Stephen P. '87 (LIN) Nebraska City, NE St. Mary's Church.
Major, Thomas J. '91 (SCR) Clarks Summit, PA Our Lady of the Snows Church; Clarks Summit, PA Clarks Summit State Hospital.
Majoros, George A. '79 (PH) [33] Philadelphia, PA St. Charles Borromeo Church.
Majoros, Stephen '57 (TOL) [28] Toledo, OH St. Joseph Church.
Makacinas, Stanley *o.carm.* '70 (JOL) [J] Darien, IL Carmelite Provincial Office.
Makalla, Peter *a.l.c.p.* '86 (P) Tigard, OR St. Anthony Church.
Makanda, John Mary Vianney '57 (AUS) [H] Austin, TX St. Joseph Hall.
Makaras, Joseph V. '40 (CHI) Retired.
Makarewicz, Sylvester E. *o.f.m.* '48 (GB) [I] Pulaski, WI Assumption of B.V.M. Friary.
Makarewicz, Sylvester E. *o.f.m.* '48 (PIT) [O] Ben Avon, PA St. Anthony Friary and Mission House.
Makerewicz, Marion J. '87 (JC) [A] Hannibal, MO St. Thomas Aquinas Seminary.
Maki, George S. '88 (MAR) Newberry, MI St. Gregory Church.
Makothakat, John M. '62 (SAT) [66] San Antonio, TX St. Thomas More Church; [C] San Antonio, TX Oblate School of Theology.
Makowski, Douglas T. '66 (CLV) Parma Heights, OH St. John Bosco Church.
Makowski, Edward J. '32 (SCR) Retired.
Makowski, Lee J. *o.s.a.* '80 (PH) [2] Norristown, PA St. Francis of Assisi Church; [C] Villanova, PA Villanova University; [AA] Villanova, PA St. Thomas Monastery.
Makowski, Mariusz '87 (MAR) [1] Marquette, MI St. Peter Cathedral.
Makowski, Mark '87 (DUL) On Leave Without Assignment.
Makowski, Tomasz '93 (PMB) Sebastian, FL St. Sebastian Church.
Makranyi, Steven F. '69 (LAN) Flushing, MI St. Robert Church.
Maksimovich, Victor *o.f.m.* '54 (E) [4] Sharon, PA St. Stanislaus Kostka Church.
Maksvytis, Jerome J. '74 (MAD) Berlin, WI St. Stanislaus Church.
Maksymowicz, Msgr. John H. '70 (BRK) Released from Diocesan Assignment.
Makuch, Thaddeus J. '53 (CHI) Retired.
Malabad, Antonio R. '53 (RIC) Williamsburg, VA St. Bede's Church.
Malacaman, Pericles P. '72 (WH) Mullens, WV St. John the Evangelist Church.
Malachowski, Christopher *o.s.* '58 (PCE) On Duty Outside the Diocese.
Malagreca, Msgr. Joseph P. '76 (BRK) [183] Queens, NY SS. Joachim and Anne Church.
Malain, Dan '66 (BEA) Nederland, TX St. Charles Borromeo Church; [G] Beaumont, TX Rev. Herman Vincent Scholarship Fund.
Malanga, Salvatore T. '57 (NEW) Belleville, NJ St. Anthony's Church.
Malanowski, Msgr. Thaddeus F. '47 (NOR) Retired.
Malanyaon, Joven (TOL) [2] Toledo, OH Blessed Sacrament Church.
Malaric, Stephen L. '51 (DET) Retired.
Malarz, Andrew '92 (GRY) Hobart, IN St. Bridget Church.
Malatesta, Charles R. *o.p.* '44 (STL) [P] St. Louis, MO St. Dominic Priory.
Malatesta, Christopher '93 (SPR) [P] Amherst, MA University of Massachusetts and Amherst College, Newman Center.
Malatesta, Edward J. *s.j.* '61 (SFR) [N] San Francisco, CA Jesuit Community at University of San Francisco; [U] San Francisco, CA The Ricci Institute for Chinese-Western Cultural History at the Center for the Pacific Rim.
Malatesta, Vincent R. *s.j.* '61 (ATL) [K] Atlanta, GA Ignatius House.
Malave, Gervasio *c.ss.r.* '87 (STV) [1] St. Thomas, VI Cathedral of Sts. Peter and Paul.
Malave, Jason A. '97 (CHI) [26] Chicago, IL St. Benedict Church.
Malave, Will Roger '86 (WH) Camden, WV St. Boniface Church.
Malave, Will-Roger '86 (HRT) On Duty Outside the Archdiocese.
Malawy, Michael D. '81 (DET) Maybee, MI St. Joseph Church; Romulus, MI St. Aloysius Church.
Malayampuram, Joseph *c.m.i.* '68 (BEA) Liberty, TX Immaculate Conception Church.
Malboeuf, Gerald L. '54 (SPR) Retired.
Malcolm, Dennis E. '73 (NY) On Duty Outside the Archdiocese.
Malcolm, Lawrence J. '70 (CHI) [48] Chicago, IL St. Daniel the Prophet Church.
Malcom-Hollis, Raphael *o.ss.t.* '47 (TR) [16] Trenton, NJ St. James Church.
Malczyk, Joseph *c.r.* '69 (CHI) [D] Chicago, IL Gordon Technical High School.
Maldari, Donald C. *s.j.* '85 (BRK) [62] Brooklyn, NY St. Ignatius Church.
Maldari, Donald C. *s.j.* '85 (FgM) Provinces.
Maldonado, Edward *o.f.m.cap.* '83 (PCE) [5] Ponce, PR Santa Teresita Church; [E] Ponce, PR Residencia Asis.
Maldonado, Francisco '90 (TUC) [10] Tucson, AZ St. Ambrose Church.
Maldonado, Jorge Rivera *o.carm.* '96 (MGZ) Anasco, PR St. Anthony Abbot Church.
Maldonado, P. Jose A. Rivera '84 (CGS) Naguabo, PR Nuestra Senora del Rosario Church.
Maldonado, Santos Rene (WDC) [4] Silver Spring, MD St. Catherine Laboure Church.
Malec, Raymond S. '54 (BEL) Retired.
Malecki, John '48 (ALB) Special Assignment.
Malene, Robert '72 (E) On Duty Outside Diocese.
Males, Jake A. '76 (TLS) Sapulpa, OK Sacred Heart Church.
Malesic, Edward C. '87 (HBG) [7] Harrisburg, PA St. Margaret Mary Alacoque Church.
Maletta, Sammie L. '80 (GRY) [3] Merrillville, IN St.

Joan of Arc Church.
Maletz, Leo J. '73 (ALN) [4] Minersville, PA St. Stanislaus Kostka Church.
Malewitz, Joseph M. '55 (GR) Retired.
Maley, William A. '95 (CHR) Florence, SC St. Anthony's All Souls Memorial Church.
Malgeri, Albert '94 (NEW) Nutley, NJ Holy Family Church.
Malia, Thomas R. '84 (BAL) Bel Air, MD St. Margaret Church.
Maliakal, Varghese '85 (NY) [7] Yonkers, NY St. Denis Church.
Malicki, Jan '73 (MIA) [4] Miami, FL Epiphany Church.
Maliekal, Cyriac '71 (HRT) [2] New Haven, CT St. Aedan's Church.
Malik, John E. '53 (LC) Colby, WI St. Mary Help of Christians Church.
Malik, Joseph '52 (Y) Retired.
Malin, Delbert J. '58 (LC) Holmen, WI St. Elizabeth Ann Seton Church.
Malin, Gary J. '86 (CLV) [4] Elyria, OH St. Mary Church.
Malin, George '46 (SP) Retired.
Malin, Peter '37 (ALB) Retired.
Malinowski, Francis *c.s.sp.* '50 (PIT) [B] Pittsburgh, PA Duquesne University of the Holy Ghost.
Malinowski, Hilary L. '56 (SCR) Simpson, PA St. Michael's Church.
Malinowski, Msgr. John C. '63 (AUS) College Station, TX St. Thomas Aquinas Church; [F] Bryan, TX St. Joseph Regional Health Center.
Malinowski, Stanley '54 (PEO) Retired.
Malinowski, Stanley J. '54 (PEO) Rantoul, IL St. Malachy's Church.
Malinsky, Gregory J. '74 (PIT) Military Chaplains.
Maliszewski, Edward C. '45 (PIT) Retired.
Maliszewski, Francis '46 (PAT) [15] Paterson, NJ St. Stephen's Church; Retired.
Maliszewski, Francis S. '41 (DET) Retired.
Malitz, George Michael '97 (PSC) New York, NY St. Mary's Church.
Maliyekal, John *v.c.* '60 (SFS) Scotland, SD St. George Church.
Malkiewicz, Edward '71 (NEW) [2] Jersey City, NJ St. Aloysius Church.
Malkiewicz, Edward S. '71 (NEW) Retired.
Malkiewicz, Stephen *o.f.m.* '69 (MIL) [P] Milwaukee, WI Francis and Clare House.
Malkov, Leonid *c.ss.r.* '90 (PHU) Newark, NJ St. John the Baptist Church.
Mallaghan, Thomas P. *c.m.* '60 (BUF) [C] Niagara University, NY Niagara University; [O] Niagara University, NY Vincentian Community at Niagara University.
Mallahan, James '52 (SEA) Retired.
Mallak, Mark S. '88 (NU) Comfrey, MN St. Paul Church; Leavenworth, MN Church of the Japanese Martyrs.
Malleck, Joseph L. '56 (BRK) Retired.
Mallen, Charles *c.ss.r.* '44 (VEN) [G] Venice, FL St. Alphonsus Residence; [I] Venice, FL Our Lady of Perpetual Help Retreat and Spirituality Center.
Mallen, Santiago *c.ss.r.* '47 (CGS) San Lorenzo, PR Nuestra Senora de la Mercedes Church.
Mallet, W. Curtis '92 (LAF) [6] Lafayette, LA Our Lady of Wisdom, University of Southwestern Louisiana Church; [L] Lafayette, LA Our Lady of Wisdom Catholic Student Center.
Mallett, James K. '66 (NSH) [4] Nashville, TN Church of Christ the King.
Mallett, Raymond *o.f.m.conv.* (FgM) Conventual Franciscan Foreign Missions.
Mallett, Raymond *o.f.m.conv.* '76 (L) Pleasure Ridge Park, KY St. Paul Church.
Mallette, Daniel J. '57 (CHI) [120] Chicago, IL St. Margaret of Scotland Church.
Malley, James '56 (NY) [209] Staten Island, NY St. John Neumann Church.
Malley, James B. *s.j.* '64 (BO) [W] Chestnut Hill, MA The Jesuit Community at Boston College.
Malley, John *o.carm.* '56 (FgM) Carmelite Foreign Missions.
Malley, John *o.carm.* '56 (JOL) [J] Darien, IL Carmelite Community; [M] Darien, IL Carmelite Mission Office.
Malley, John *o.carm.* '56 (TUC) [A] Tucson, AZ Salpointe Catholic High School.
Malley, John *o.carm.* '97 (TUC) [F] Tucson, AZ Carmelite Priory.
Malley, Kenneth (SP) [8] St. Petersburg, FL St. Raphael Church.
Malley, Michael A. '34 (HRT) Canaan, CT St. Joseph's Church; Retired.
Malley, Raymond E. *s.m.* '68 (HON) Wailuku, HI St. Anthony Church; [H] Wailuku, Maui, HI Wailuku Marianist Community.
Malley, Vernon *o.carm.* '59 (TUC) [F] Tucson, AZ Carmelite Priory.
Malley, William J. *s.j.* '64 (FgM) Provinces.
Mallia, Joseph S. '92 (DET) Plymouth, MI St. Kenneth Church.
Mallick, Andrew '83 (ORL) [1] Lakeland, FL Church of the Resurrection.
Mallinson, Arthur D. '81 (DAL) Lancaster, TX St. Francis of Assisi Church.
Mallo, Walter '90 (SJ) [2] San Jose, CA St. Patrick Proto-Cathedral.
Mallon, Daniel *c.s.c.* (P) [B] Portland, OR University of Portland.
Mallon, Elias D. *s.a.* '71 (NY) [DD] New York, NY Atonement Friars; [DD] Garrison, NY Generalate of the Franciscan Friars of the Atonement-St. James Friary; [DD] Garrison, NY Franciscan Friars of the Atonement.
Mallon, John F. '40 (ALB) Cairo, NY Sacred Heart Church; Retired.
Mallon, John J. '50 (OAK) [3] Walnut Creek, CA St. Mary's Church.
Mallonee, Robert *s.v.d.* '67 (BO) [W] Duxbury, MA Society of the Divine Word.
Malloy, Brendan *o.f.m.cap.* '54 (PIT) [O] Pittsburgh, PA St. Augustine Friary.
Malloy, Msgr. David J. '83 (MIL) On Duty Outside the Archdiocese.
Malloy, Edward A. *c.s.c.* '70 (FTW) [B] Notre Dame, IN University of Notre Dame Du Lac; [J] Notre Dame, IN Holy Cross Community, Corby Hall, University of Notre Dame.
Malloy, Msgr. Faber J. '50 (ALT) Ebensburg, PA Holy Name Church; Retired.
Malloy, Francis X. '85 (MIL) Military Chaplains.
Malloy, Frank '86 (MIL) [D] Waukesha, WI Catholic Memorial High School.
Malloy, Joseph J. '70 (BGP) [4] Bridgeport, CT St. Ann's Church.
Malloy, Michael B. '76 (OM) Verdigre, NE St. Wenceslaus Church.
Malloy, Peter V. *s.d.b.* '74 (BIR) [8] Birmingham, AL Holy Rosary Church; [A] Birmingham, AL John Carroll High School.
Malloy, Richard G. *s.j.* '88 (CAM) [4] Camden, NJ Holy Name Church.
Malloy, Robert *o.f.m.cap.* '70 (SAG) [G] Saginaw, MI Queen of Angels Friary and Retreat House.
Malloy, Robert P. '83 (SFE) [13] Albuquerque, NM Queen of Heaven Church.
Malloy, Stephen J. '96 (BO) [1] Newton, MA St. Bernard Church.
Malloy, Thomas F. *o.s.f.s.* '67 (WIL) [I] Childs, MD Oblates of St. Francis De Sales.
Malloy, William E. '73 (CHI) [3] Oak Lawn, IL St. Germaine Church.
Mally, Edward J. *s.j.* '61 (NY) [DD] New York, NY Jesuit Provincial's Office.
Mallya, Gregory '83 (PIT) Glade Mills, PA Holy Sepulcher Church.
Malm, Raymond B. '76 (PRO) [23] Providence, RI St. Michael the Archangel Church.
Malnar, Matthew (NOR) [A] Cromwell, CT Holy Apostles College and Seminary.
Malnar, Matthew '66 (AMA) On Duty Outside the Diocese.
Malnar, Stan '72 (HEL) Special Assignments.
Malo, John B. *c.s.b.* '78 (OAK) [C] Oakland, CA Bishop O'Dowd High School.
Malo, Richard C. '87 (PRT) Jackman, ME St. Anthony Church.
Malonda, Anselme *c.i.c.m.* '92 (BWN) Alton, TX San Martin de Porres Church.
Malone, Alan '59 (PHX) [2] Scottsdale, AZ Our Lady of Perpetual Help Church; Special Assignment.
Malone, Bernard G. '50 (LR) [8] Little Rock, AR Immaculate Heart of Mary Church.
Malone, Donald '60 (NY) Absent on Leave.
Malone, Edward F. *m.m.* '52 (FgM) Maryknoll Foreign Missions.
Malone, Edward T. '72 (BO) [7] Lynn, MA St. Pius Fifth Church.
Malone, Francis I. '77 (LR) [2] Little Rock, AR St. Anne Church; [7] Little Rock, AR Immaculate Conception Church.
Malone, H. Patrick '69 (WCH) [7] Wichita, KS Holy Savior Church.
Malone, James P. *s.j.* '45 (ROC) [B] Rochester, NY McQuaid Jesuit High School.
Malone, John '65 (RVC) Seaford, NY Maria Regina Church.
Malone, John M. '67 (STP) [2] St. Paul, MN Assumption Church; [C] St. Paul, MN University of St. Thomas.
Malone, Michael T. *c.s.sp.* '65 (PRO) [B] Newport, RI Salve Regina University.
Malone, Msgr. Quintin J. '38 (WCH) Retired.
Malone, Msgr. Richard '62 (PH) [A] Wynnewood, PA Theological Seminary of St. Charles Borromeo, Overbrook.
Malone, Richard J. '72 (BO) [28] Boston, MA Holy Name Church.
Malone, Robert *c.s.c.* '61 (BGP) [I] Bridgeport, CT St. Vincent's Medical Center.
Malone, Robert J. *c.s.c.* '61 (BGP) [O] Bridgeport, CT Provincial Offices of the Priests and Brothers of Holy Cross, Eastern Province.
Malone, William P. '92 (CHI) Other Assignments.
Maloney, Andrew P. '34 (SCR) Retired.
Maloney, Bernard M. *o.f.m.cap.* '69 (NY) [17] Yonkers, NY Sacred Heart Church.
Maloney, Charles F. '57 (TUC) Apache Junction, AZ St. George Church.
Maloney, Msgr. Christopher '66 (NY) [82] New York, NY Notre Dame Church; [GG] New York, NY University Apostolate.
Maloney, Daniel *o.s.b.* '68 (BIS) [A] Richardton, ND Assumption Abbey; [B] Bismarck, ND University of Mary; [H] Bismarck, ND Annunciation Priory.
Maloney, Edward F. (NY) [DD] New York, NY Jesuit Community at Fordham University.
Maloney, Edward J. '55 (CHI) Palatine, IL Mision Juan Diego Church.
Maloney, Francis E. '59 (PMB) Lake Worth, FL St. Luke Church.
Maloney, Francis G. '56 (R) Fuquay-Varina, NC St. Bernadette Church; Garner, NC St. Mary, Mother of the Church.
Maloney, George A. *s.j.* '57 (MIL) [P] Milwaukee, WI Jesuit Provincial Office, Wisconsin Province.
Maloney, James *c.m.f.* '60 (CHI) [N] Oak Park, IL Claretian Fathers Headquarters of U.S.A. Eastern Province.
Maloney, James C. '37 (L) Retired; [J] Louisville, KY Boys' Haven.
Maloney, James G. '71 (CLV) Norton, OH St. Andrew the Apostle Church.
Maloney, John '75 (BRK) [196] Queens, NY St. Mary Magdalene Church.
Maloney, John '87 (MAR) Retired.
Maloney, John P. '64 (PIT) Glade Mills, PA Holy Sepulcher Church.
Maloney, John P. '66 (BRK) [189] Queens, NY St. Kevin Church.
Maloney, John W. '75 (BRK) [223] Queens, NY St. Pascal Baylon Church; [G] Brooklyn, NY Catherine McAuley.
Maloney, Joseph *o.f.m.cap.* '58 (DET) [K] Detroit, MI St. Bonaventure Friary.
Maloney, Joseph '91 (PH) [D] Springfield, PA Cardinal O'Hara High School.
Maloney, Joseph L. '91 (PH) Swarthmore, PA Notre Dame de Lourdes Church.
Maloney, Malcolm '55 (SAG) Pigeon, MI St. Francis Borgia Church.
Maloney, Patrick H. *c.s.c.* '54 (FTW) [B] Notre Dame, IN University of Notre Dame Du Lac; [J] Notre Dame, IN Holy Cross Community, Corby Hall, University of Notre Dame.
Maloney, Raymond G. '59 (BUR) Fair Haven, VT Our Lady of Seven Dolors Church.
Maloney, Richard *s.d.s.* '69 (WDC) [B] Silver Spring, MD Salvatorian Community.
Maloney, Richard E. '50 (DET) Retired.
Maloney, Robert L. *s.j.* '61 (SFR) [N] San Francisco, CA Jesuit Community at University of San Francisco.
Maloney, Robert P. *c.m.* '66 (FgM) Vincentian Foreign Missions.
Maloney, Robert P. *c.m.* '66 (PH) [AA] Philadelphia, PA Congregation of the Mission.
Maloney, Robert S. *s.x.* '57 (BO) [W] Holliston, MA Xaverian Missionaries.
Maloney, Rufino *o.f.m.conv.* '59 (ALB) [12] Albany, NY Our Lady of Angels Church.
Maloney, Msgr. Thomas F. '68 (BUF) [1] Tonawanda, NY St. Amelia Church.
Maloney, Thomas J. '65 (SCR) Pocono Pines, PA Our Lady of the Lake Church.
Maloney, Thomas J. *s.j.* '69 (LA) [C] Los Angeles, CA Loyola Marymount University.
Maloney, Thomas P. '70 (RVC) Babylon, NY St. Joseph's Church.
Maloney, Timothy P. *o.s.b.* '50 (LA) Montebello, CA St. Benedict Church.
Maloney, Tom '67 (PEO) Normal, IL Epiphany Church.
Maloney, Walter '47 (JKS) Retired.
Maloney, Wilfred F. '55 (PH) Maple Glen, PA St. Alphonsus Church.
Maloney, William '76 (CHI) [34] Chicago, IL St. Cajetan Church.
Maloney, William J. '48 (E) Retired.
Malooly, Msgr. Francis W. '70 (BAL) Special Assignment.
Malooly, Msgr. W. Francis '70 (BAL) [92] Baltimore, MD St. Thomas More Church.
Malorzo, Luigi *c.p.* '52 (MET) [H] South River, NJ Passionist Provincial Office.
Malovetz, Gregory E. S. '83 (MET) Skillman, NJ St. Charles Borromeo Church.
Maloy, Dale R. '54 (PEO) [1] La Salle, IL Queen of the Holy Rosary Church.
Maltese, James L. '65 (RVC) Valley Stream, NY Holy Name of Mary Church.
Malthaner, John P. '93 (E) [16] Erie, PA St. George Church.

Maluafiti, Soke *o.f.m.cap.* (AGN) [E] Agana Heights, GU St. Fidelis Friary.
Malvey, James '86 (PMB) Retired.
Malvey, Killian *o.s.b.* '73 (SEA) [M] Lacey, WA St. Martin's Abbey; [M] Lacey, WA St. Martin's Abbey.
Malvey, Sean R. *o.s.b.* '89 (SEA) [M] Lacey, WA St. Martin's Abbey.
Mamede, Carlos C. '69 (NEW) [26] Newark, NJ Our Lady of Fatima Church.
Mammarella, Dominick A. '53 (HBG) Berwick, PA St. Joseph's Church.
Mamo, Nathan '78 (HON) [1] Honolulu, HI Cathedral of Our Lady of Peace.
Mampaey, Lawrence *ss.cc.* '29 (HON) [H] Honolulu, HI St. Patrick's Monastery.
Mampara, Mathew '60 (PHX) Sun City, AZ St. Clement of Rome Church.
Mampilly, Joy *c.m.i.* '84 (NY) [206] Staten Island, NY Holy Rosary Church.
Man, Matthias Tinh An Tran '63 (FWT) [19] Fort Worth, TX Christ the King Church.
Man Tran, Joseph '95 (NO) Chalmette, LA St. Mark Church.
Manahan, Msgr. Emmanuel G. '84 (LA) Granada Hills, CA St. John Baptist de la Salle Church.
Manahan, John J. *s.m.* '68 (SAT) [8] San Antonio, TX Holy Rosary Church; [M] San Antonio, TX Holy Rosary Marianist Community.
Manahan, Martin J. '52 (WOR) Retired.
Manahan, Thomas *s.j.* '95 (OM) [K] Omaha, NE Jesuit Community At Creighton University.
Manalel, Matthew '72 (BRK) [58] Brooklyn, NY Holy Name Church.
Manalili, Feliciano *o.c.s.o.* '62 (CHR) [D] Moncks Corner, SC Mepkin Abbey.
Manalis, Edward W. '77 (BAL) Hagerstown, MD St. Ann Church.
Manalo, Pantaleon O. '63 (RIC) [E] Portsmouth, VA Maryview Medical Center.
Manarchuck, Joseph J.. '78 (SCR) Friendsville, PA St. Joseph's Church.
Mancha, George '88 (SJ) [10] San Jose, CA St. Anthony Church.
Manchapilly, George *c.m.i.* '71 (BRK) [3] Brooklyn, NY St. Agnes Church.
Manchas, Lawrence L. '79 (GBG) Herminie, PA St. Edward Church.
Manchino, John '65 (LR) Retired.
Mancilla, Pedro M. '58 (FRS) Riverdale, CA St. Ann Church.
Mancini, Anthony '78 (PRO) [15] Providence, RI Holy Cross Church.
Mancini, Domenic '76 (PIT) [35] Pittsburgh, PA St. Raphael Church.
Mancini, James E. '58 (LR) Cherokee Village, AR St. Michael's Church.
Mancini, John S. *o.s.f.s.* '80 (SAG) [4] Saginaw, MI SS. Simon and Jude Church.
Mancini, Marc (PAT) Rockaway, NJ Sacred Heart Church.
Mancini, Marc A. (PAT) On Duty Outside the Diocese.
Mancini, Nicholas J. (ALT) Beaverdale, PA Holy Spirit Church.
Mancini, Nicholas J. '75 (ALT) Dunlo, PA Corpus Christi Church.
Mancini, Robert A. *o.s.f.s.* '77 (WIL) [I] Wilmington, DE Oblates of St. Francis De Sales.
Mancuso, Anthony '83 (SJ) [8] San Jose, CA Holy Family Church; [10] San Jose, CA St. Anthony Church.
Mancuso, Dennis J. '96 (BUF) [3] West Seneca, NY Fourteen Holy Helpers Church.
Mancuso, Henry '75 (LKC) [5] Lake Charles, LA St. Margaret Church.
Mancuso, Joseph A. '64 (KC) [4] Kansas City, MO St. Anthony Church; [O] Kansas City, MO Diocesan Council of Catholic Women.
Mancuso, Joseph A. '70 (ALB) [15] Schenectady, NY Our Lady of Mt. Carmel Church.
Mancuso, Luke *o.s.b.* '83 (SCL) [I] Collegeville, MN St. John's Abbey, of the Order of St. Benedict.
Mandala, Michael J. *s.j.* '77 (LA) [R] Los Angeles, CA Columbiere House.
Mandarino, Constantino *o.m.* '65 (LA) [3] Los Angeles, CA All Saints Church; [R] Los Angeles, CA Minim Fathers.
Mandato, Kieran '87 (NY) Military Chaplains.
Mandel, Brian L. '94 (NU) Marshall, MN Holy Redeemer Church.
Manderfield, Paul G. '60 (MAR) Baraga, MI St. Ann Church.
Mandile, John J. *s.j.* '57 (BO) [W] Weston, MA Campion Center.
Manding, Benito O. '64 (SJ) [4] Sunnyvale, CA St. Martin Church.
Mandock, Patrick H. '72 (GBG) Military Chaplains.
Mandoli, Richard *o.c.d.* '92 (SB) [G] Redlands, CA El Carmelo Retreat House.
Mandry, Stephen A. *s.t.d.* '66 (GAL) Baytown, TX St. Joseph Church.
Mandziuk, Paul *m.s.* '80 (GAL) Friendswood, TX Mary, Queen Church.
Mandziuk, Paul *m.s.* '80 (STL) [K] St. Louis, MO Saint Louis University Hospital.
Manente, Vladimiro *o.m.i.* '46 (CC) [6] Laredo, TX San Augustin Church.
Manero, Ismael '37 (GLP) Retired.
Manerowski, Joseph '95 (ALB) Delhi, NY St. Peter Church; [S] Delhi, NY State University of New York College of Agricultural & Technology at Delhi.
Manetta, Andrew *o.f.m.cap.* '83 (HON) Ewa Beach, HI Our Lady of Perpetual Help Church.
Maney, Robert L. '51 (MIL) Retired.
Maney, Thomas J. *m.m.* '56 (NY) [DD] Maryknoll, NY Maryknoll Fathers and Brothers.
Manfred, Donald J. '67 (OG) Tupper Lake, NY St. Alphonsus Church.
Mangampo, Gil '91 (GLP) On Duty Outside of Diocese.
Mangampo, Gil '91 (ORG) [F] Fullerton, CA St. Jude Medical Center.
Mangan, Charles '89 (SFS) Gettysburg, SD Sacred Heart Church; Onida, SD St. Pius X Church.
Mangan, James '69 (SPK) Otis Orchards, WA St. Joseph Church.
Mangan, John J. '40 (PH) Retired.
Mangan, Martin '57 (SFD) [4] Decatur, IL St. James Church.
Mangan, Timothy *s.s.s.* '59 (ALB) Broadalbin, NY St. Joseph Church.
Manganello, Salvatore '82 (BUF) [14] Buffalo, NY Blessed Sacrament Church.
Mangano, Charles N. '90 (RVC) Bohemia, NY St. John Nepomucene Church.
Mangen, Daniel J. *c.pp.s.* '80 (CIN) [M] Dayton, OH Provincial House of the Cincinnati Province of the Society of the Precious Blood.
Manger, William '62 (BEA) [2] Beaumont, TX St. Anne Church.
Mangiafico, Paul '70 (HRT) [13] Waterbury, CT St. Lucy's Church.
Mangiaracina, Cayet *o.p.* '64 (SAT) [26] San Antonio, TX St. Ann Church; [B] San Antonio, TX Dominican Priory of Juan Macias.
Mangiaracina, George *o.c.d* '93 (MIL) [P] Milwaukee, WI Provincial Offices - Discalced Carmelites.
Mangini, Charles M. '56 (BRK) Absent on Sick Leave.
Mangini, Richard A. '67 (OAK) [2] Concord, CA St. Bonaventure Church.
Mangum, Peter '90 (SHP) Minden, LA St. Paul Church.
Manhard, Edward P. *s.j.* '32 (STL) [O] St. Louis, MO Fusz Pavilion.
Manhart, Paul *s.j.* '58 (RC) Pine Ridge, SD Holy Rosary Church; [B] Pine Ridge, SD Jesuit Community of Holy Rosary Mission.
Mani, L. David (PRT) Gardiner, ME St. Joseph's Church; Togus, ME Dept. of Veteran Affairs.
Maniangat, Joseph '64 (NO) [61] New Orleans, LA St. Stephen Church.
Maniangat, Joseph '64 (STA) Macclenny, FL St. Mary's Church.
Maniangatt, Joseph '72 (RVC) Roslyn, NY St. Francis Hospital.
Manickam, Selvaraj '73 (NY) [227] Staten Island, NY Sacred Heart Church.
Manieri, Msgr. Francis '60 (STU) Bridgeport, OH St. Anthony of Padua Church; [J] Bridgeport, OH Cursillo Moderator.
Manikowski, Stanislaus J. '38 (HT) Raceland, LA St. Mary's Nativity Church; Retired.
Maniola, Francis N. '38 (CHI) [197] Chicago, IL St. Symphorosa and Seven Sons Church; Retired.
Manion, Dominic *o.f.m.conv.* '68 (LSC) Loving, NM Our Lady of Grace Church.
Manion, Kevin '89 (SAT) [7] San Antonio, TX Holy Redeemer Church.
Manion, Thomas F. '57 (PIT) Sharpsburg, PA St. Mary Church.
Maniscalco, Msgr. Francis '71 (RVC) West Hempstead, NY St. Thomas, the Apostle Church; Priests Released from Diocesan Assignment.
Manista, Clemens D. '74 (WIL) Bear, DE St. Elizabeth Ann Seton Church.
Maniyangat, Jose '75 (STA) [1] Jacksonville, FL Assumption Church.
Manjadi, George (WH) Marlinton, WV St. John Neumann Church.
Mank, Virgil '65 (SFD) Godfrey, IL St. Ambrose Church.
Mankel, F. Xavier *s.t.l., v.g.* '61 (KNX) [5] Knoxville, TN Holy Ghost Church.
Mankel, Xavier '61 (KNX) [K] Knoxville, TN Diocesan Council of Catholic Women; [K] Knoxville, TN Ladies of Charity.
Manko, Rodney A. '78 (NO) Absent on Leave.
Mankowski, Edmund A. '46 (BRK) Retired.
Mankowski, Paul V. *s.j.* '65 (CHI) [N] Chicago, IL Chicago Province of the Society of Jesus-Provincial Office.
Manley, Bernard A. '87 (CHL) Retired.
Manly, Msgr. Alex F. '57 (RVC) Kings Park, NY St. Joseph's Church.
Mann, Francis J. '79 (BRK) [149] Queens, NY St. Anastasia Church.
Mann, Gordon '92 (EVN) Chrisney, IN St. Martin Church; Santa Claus, IN St. Nicholas Church.
Mann, Lawrence *s.m.* '53 (LA) [F] Chatsworth, CA Chaminade College Preparatory.
Mann, Peter '67 (RVC) Absent on Leave.
Mann, Raymond *o.f.m.* '59 (BO) [BB] Boston, MA St. Anthony Shrine.
Mann, Robert G. '59 (PEO) [J] Danville, IL United Samaritans Medical Center.
Manna, Louis *o.f.m.conv.* '73 (IND) Dover, IN St. John the Baptist Church; St. Leon, IN St. Joseph Church.
Mannara, Frederick R. '63 (SY) New Hartford, NY St. John the Evangelist Church.
Mannelli, David F. '80 (CHI) Niles, IL St. John Brebeuf Church.
Mannetta, Andrew *o.f.m.cap.* '83 (AGN) [E] Agana Heights, GU St. Fidelis Friary.
Mannetta, Andrew *o.f.m.cap.* '83 (FgM) Capuchin Foreign Missions.
Mannhardt, Daniel C. '57 (DAV) [2] Davenport, IA Our Lady of Victory Church.
Manning, Aedan *s.t.* (JKS) Carthage, MS St. Anne Church.
Manning, Aedan *s.t.* '63 (JKS) [3] Jackson, MS St. Richard Church.
Manning, Brian F. '74 (BO) [4] Somerville, MA St. Catherine of Genoa Church.
Manning, Charles Robert '97 (STL) Glencoe, MO St. Alban Roe Church.
Manning, Charles T. '75 (ROC) Cohocton, NY St. Pius V Church.
Manning, Daniel '91 (SFS) Kimball, SD St. Margaret Church.
Manning, Edward J. *m.m.* '47 (NY) [DD] Maryknoll, NY Maryknoll Fathers and Brothers; [DD] Maryknoll, NY Maryknoll Fathers and Brothers.
Manning, Francis J. '51 (SPR) [4] Ludlow, MA St. Mary Church.
Manning, Msgr. J. Leroy '40 (SAT) Retired; [K] San Antonio, TX Casa De Padres.
Manning, J. Patrick '78 (Y) Sabbatical.
Manning, James *s.m.m.* '58 (RVC) [N] Bay Shore, NY Montfort Missionaries.
Manning, James J. '75 (CIN) [3] Dayton, OH St. Albert the Great Church.
Manning, James T. *m.m.* '48 (FgM) Maryknoll Foreign Missions.
Manning, John '55 (OAK) Retired.
Manning, John E. '72 (CLV) [75] Cleveland, OH St. Vincent de Paul Church.
Manning, Joseph H. '61 (BO) [5] Brockton, MA Our Lady of Lourdes Church.
Manning, Justinian *c.p.* '54 (BO) [24] Boston, MA St. Gabriel Church; [W] Brighton, MA St. Gabriel's Passionist Community.
Manning, Martin B. '43 (DAV) Retired; [M] Davenport, IA St. Vincent Center.
Manning, Michael '69 (SB) [A] Riverside, CA Divine Word Seminary; [I] Riverside, CA Wordnet, Inc.
Manning, Michael '97 (TR) [14] Trenton, NJ St. Gregory the Great Church.
Manning, Paul F. '65 (BO) Awaiting Assignment.
Manning, Paul S. '85 (PAT) Rockaway, NJ St. Cecilia's Church; [C] Denville, NJ Morris Catholic High School.
Manning, Robert E. *s.j.* '67 (BO) [B] Cambridge, MA Weston Jesuit School of Theology; [W] Cambridge, MA Weston Jesuit Community.
Manning, Robert T. '54 (COL) New Philadelphia, OH Sacred Heart Church; Retired.
Manning, Roger M. *o.s.m.* (DEN) Westminster, CO Holy Trinity Church.
Manning, Thomas D. *o.m.i.* '35 (BO) [Z] Tewksbury, MA Immaculate Heart of Mary Novitiate-Infirmary.
Manning, Thomas J. '65 (SY) Retired.
Manning, Thomas R. *o.f.m.* (SPR) Stockbridge, MA St. Joseph's Church.
Manning, Thomas V. '84 (PIT) Mt. Lebanon, PA St. Bernard Church.
Manning, William F. *c.s.p.* '44 (NY) [DD] Jamaica Estates, NY Paulist Fathers Generalate.
Mannion, Bernard J. '50 (STO) Oakdale, CA St. Mary of the Annunciation Church.
Mannion, Edward C. *c.m.* '39 (PH) [AA] Philadelphia, PA Congregation of the Mission.
Mannion, Frank *s.s.c.* '52 (LA) Whittier, CA St. Bruno Church.
Mannion, James '81 (RVC) Wantagh, NY St. Frances de Chantal Church.
Mannion, John H. '68 (IND) [F] Beech Grove, IN St. Francis Hospital and Health Centers.
Mannion, John H. '68 (LFT) On Duty Outside the Diocese.
Mannion, John Patrick '55 (WCH) St. Mark's, KS St. Mark Church.
Mannion, Msgr. M. Francis '73 (SLC) [1] Salt Lake City, UT Cathedral of the Madeleine.
Mannion, Mark S. '95 (STL) [Q] Kirkwood, MO Opus Dei.
Mannion, Martin '66 (STL) [N] Normandy, MO St.

Vincent Home for Children.
Mannion, Msgr. Martin J. '62 (CAM) Collingswood, NJ St. John's Church.
Mannion, Martin K. '66 (STL) Special Assignment.
Mannion, Michael '71 (CAM) On Duty Outside the Diocese.
Mannion, Michael '71 (WDC) [C] Washington, DC Catholic University of America, The.
Mannion, P. John '66 (SAT) [4] San Antonio, TX Divine Providence Church.
Mannion, Thomas F. '46 (BRK) Retired.
Mannion, Thomas F. '46 (P) Brookings, OR Star of the Sea Church.
Mannion, Thomas Ignatius '65 (HBG) Roaring Creek, PA Our Lady of Mercy Church; Danville, PA State Hospital.
Mannion, Thomas J. '52 (LC) Prescott, WI St. Joseph Church.
Mannion, William D. '63 (CHI) Evanston, IL St. Athanasius Church.
Mannion, William M. '89 (BAL) [3] Baltimore, MD St. Agnes Church.
Mannis, James B. *c.s.c.* '55 (SCR) [4] Wilkes-Barre, PA St. Casimir's Church.
Manno, John K. '68 (SCR) Conyngham, PA St. John Bosco Church.
Manny, Msgr. Howard F. '44 (ALB) [11] Schenectady, NY St. Luke Church; Retired.
Mansell, C. Kirk *s.j.* '84 (SP) [8] Tampa, FL Sacred Heart Church.
Mansell, Kirk *s.j.* '86 (SP) [S] Tampa, FL University of Tampa.
Mansfield, John L. (BO) Retired.
Manship, D. Joseph '76 (PRT) Augusta, ME St. Mary's Church.
Manship, Paul E. '88 (SPR) [5] Springfield, MA Holy Family Church.
Mansilla, Joaquin '56 (SJN) [6] San Juan, PR Nuestra Senora de Belen Church.
Mansini, Guy *o.s.b.* '77 (IND) [A] St. Meinrad, IN St. Meinrad Seminary; [B] St. Meinrad, IN St. Meinrad Seminary-College of Liberal Arts; [J] St. Meinrad, IN St. Meinrad Archabbey.
Manske, James J. '62 (JUN) Retired.
Mansour, Gregory J. '82 (OLL) Los Angeles, CA Our Lady of Mt. Lebanon-St. Peter Cathedral.
Mansour, Yousif '75 (OLD) Toronto, St. Joseph Church.
Manternach, Msgr. Albert V. '52 (DUB) Retired.
Manternach, Carl J. '55 (DUB) New Melleray, IA Holy Family Church; Peosta, IA St. John the Baptist Church.
Manternach, Neil J. '85 (DUB) Fillmore, IA Sacred Heart Church.
Mantia, Armand '85 (NEW) Roselle Park, NJ The Assumption Church.
Mantica, A. Donald '60 (STU) Piney Fork, OH St. Therese Church; Smithfield, OH Our Lady, Queen of Peace Church.
Mantilla, Jorge I. *o.ss.t.* '89 (ARE) Isabela, PR St. Anthony Church.
Manton, Joseph E. *c.ss.r.* '29 (BO) [13] Boston, MA Our Lady of Perpetual Help Church.
Mantovani, Firmo *c.s.* '73 (SD) Imperial, CA St. Anthony of Padua Church.
Manuel, Albert William '87 (MIL) [P] Milwaukee, WI Jesuit Community at Marquette University.
Manuel, Armand J. *s.s.j.* (MOB) [5] Mobile, AL St. Francis Xavier Church.
Manuel, Gerdenio M. *s.j.* '79 (SJ) [M] Los Gatos, CA California Province of the Society of Jesus, Jesuit Provincial Office.
Manuel, Vincent *s.a.c.* '81 (ALX) [4] Alexandria, LA St. James Memorial Church; [5] Alexandria, LA St. Juliana Church.
Manuppella, Anthony J. '76 (CAM) Millville, NJ St. Mary Magdalen's Church.
Manville, Alexander *o.f.m.* '53 (PHX) [G] Scottsdale, AZ Franciscan Renewal Center, Inc. (Casa de Paz Y Bien).
Manwelo, Paulin *s.j.* '93 (BO) [W] Chestnut Hill, MA The Jesuit Community at Boston College.
Manz, John R. '71 (CHI) [144] Chicago, IL Notre Dame Church.
Manz, Msgr. Joseph C. '40 (NEW) [18] Jersey City, NJ St. Nicholas Church; Woodcliff Lake, NJ Our Lady Mother of the Church; Retired.
Manz, Michael J. '79 (PRO) [O] Providence, RI Opus Dei, Mathewson House.
Manzano, Paul L. '60 (FRS) Wasco, CA Prison Facility.
Manzelli, Michael '57 (RVC) Freeport, NY Our Holy Redeemer Church.
Manzi, Arcangelo *o.de.m.* (PH) [AA] Philadelphia, PA Monastery of Our Lady of Mercy.
Manzo, Fernando L. '83 (TUC) Somerton, AZ Immaculate Heart of Mary Church.
Manzo, Msgr. Francis J. '62 (BRK) Absent on Leave.
Manzo, Louis A. *c.s.c.* '65 (FR) [A] North Easton, MA Stonehill College; [A] North Easton, MA Holy Cross Fathers Religious.
Maples, Frederic A. *s.j.* '72 (BO) [W] Boston, MA The Society of Jesus of New England-Provincial Offices.
Maples, Frederic A. *s.j.* '72 (STP) [Q] St. Paul, MN Loyola.
Maples, Frederick *s.j.* (STP) [6] St. Paul, MN The Immaculate Heart of Mary Church.
Mappilamattel, Jose (NY) State, NY Eastern Correctional Facility.
Mara, John J. '48 (SPR) [6] Pittsfield, MA St. Francis Church.
Marable, Gerald C. '88 (CAM) Gibbsboro, NJ St. Andrew the Apostle Church.
Maraczewski, Edward S. '45 (CHI) [1] Waukegan, IL St. Anastasia Church; Retired.
Maraldo, Angelo F. *o.s.f.s.* '86 (VEN) [6] Fort Myers, FL Our Lady of Light Church.
Maramot, Faustino '71 (GAL) Galena Park, TX Our Lady of Fatima Church.
Marandu, Bede '82 (SJ) [5] Sunnyvale, CA Church of the Resurrection.
Marandu, Nicolaus '52 (P) [20] Portland, OR Immaculate Heart of Mary Church.
Marangone, Mark *s.x.* '84 (FgM) Xaverian Foreign Missions.
Marangone, Mark *s.x.* '84 (PAT) [M] Wayne, NJ Xaverian Missionary Fathers.
Marani, Philip *o.carm.* (NY) Manhattan, NY Bellevue Hospital.
Marani, Philip *o.carm.* '65 (NY) [97] New York, NY Our Lady of the Scapular/St. Stephen Church.
Marano, Fred '91 (BRK) [B] Elmhurst, NY Cathedral Preparatory Seminary of the Immaculate Conception.
Maranowski, Michael '87 (PIT) Scott Township, PA Our Lady of Grace Church.
Maranto, Charles L. *c.s.v.* '50 (CHI) [N] Arlington Heights, IL Viatorian Province Center-Clerics of St. Viator.
Maranto, Samuel C. *c.ss.r.* '72 (BR) [H] Baton Rouge, LA Redemptorist Vice Province.
Marasciulo, Msgr. John '45 (YAK) Cle Elum, WA St. John the Baptist Church.
Maravi, Raul *o.carm.* '97 (WDC) [B] Washington, DC Whitefriars Hall.
Maravic, Raul *o.carm.* '97 (JOL) [J] Darien, IL Carmelite Provincial Office.
Maravilla, Primitivo (MOB) Fairhope, AL St. Lawrence Church.
Maraya, Felipe '62 (ELP) Absent on Leave.
Marbach, Msgr. Joseph '43 (NY) Retired.
Marbach, Lawrence J. '52 (SFS) Retired.
Marbaugh, Meinrad '39 (LR) [A] Subiaco, AR Subiaco Monastery.
Marbury, Cabell '64 (ALB) Special Assignment.
Marbury, Cabell B. '64 (ALB) [C] Albany, NY Bishop Maginn High School.
Marcaccio, Anthony '91 (CHL) [6] Charlotte, NC St. John Neumann Church.
Marcaccio, Anthony J. '91 (CHL) Special Assignment.
Marcantonio, Clement '59 (PBL) Retired.
Marceau, Emmet L. '67 (SAG) [12] Saginaw, MI St. Helen Church.
Marceau, Timothy R. *o.s.b.* '52 (ALX) Belledeau, LA St. Martin of Tours Church.
Marceau, Timothy R. *o.s.b.* '52 (JOL) [J] Lisle, IL St. Procopius Abbey.
Marceau, William C. *c.s.b.* '57 (ROC) [I] Rochester, NY Basilian Residence.
Marceaux, Msgr. Sidney J. '70 (BEA) Military Chaplains.
Marceaux, Timothy *o.s.b.* '52 (ALX) Pineville, LA Central Louisiana State Hospital.
Marcell, Robert G. '56 (BR) St. Gabriel, LA St. Gabriel Church.
March, Ralph *o.cist.* '45 (DAL) [M] Irving, TX Cistercian Abbey of Our Lady of Dallas.
March, Thomas *o.f.m.cap.* '78 (RVC) East Patchogue, NY St. Joseph the Worker Church.
Marchand, Gerald A. '54 (NEW) West Orange, NJ Our Lady of Lourdes Church.
Marchand, Robert A. '52 (MAN) Retired.
Marchesani, Gino *f.d.p.* (BO) [Y] Bradford, MA Don Orione Center.
Marchesani, Gino *f.d.p.* '56 (BO) [B] Haverhill, MA Sons of Divine Providence School for Exceptional Boys; [U] Boston, MA Don Orione Nursing Home.
Marchese, Dominic A. *s.s.j.* '40 (BAL) [M] Baltimore, MD St. Joseph Society of the Sacred Heart House of Central Administration.
Marchese, Dominic A. *s.s.j.* '40 (TR) Bay Head, NJ Sacred Heart Church.
Marchese, Henry *s.a.* '64 (NY) [DD] Garrison, NY Generalate of the Franciscan Friars of the Atonement-St. James Friary; [DD] Garrison, NY Franciscan Friars of the Atonement.
Marchese, Joseph P. '69 (SPR) On Duty Outside the Diocese.
Marchese, Msgr. Richard E. '70 (BRK) [B] Elmhurst, NY Cathedral Preparatory Seminary of the Immaculate Conception.
Marchesin, Ivan *s.x.* '66 (BO) [W] Holliston, MA Xaverian Missionaries.
Marchessault, Edward T. *c.s.sp.* '64 (FgM) Holy Ghost Foreign Missions.
Marchetti, Carlo M. *o.s.m.* '59 (ORG) [H] Buena Park, CA Servite Fathers And Brothers.
Marchetti, Michael H. '82 (SCR) White Mills, PA St. Joseph's Church.
Marchetti, Peter E. *s.j.* '77 (FgM) Provinces.
Marchino, Louis H. '39 (IND) Retired.
Marchionda, James *o.p.* (CHI) [N] Oak Park, IL Dominican Community of St. Martin de Porres.
Marchitelli, Anthony (NY) Carmel, NY St. James the Apostle Church.
Marchitelli, Anthony D. '76 (NY) [E] Somers, NY John F. Kennedy High School; [P] New York, NY Catholic Youth Organization of the Archdiocese of New York Inc.
Marchlewski, Michael A. *s.j.* '67 (STL) [P] St. Louis, MO De Smet Jesuit High School Community.
Marchulones, Kenneth L. '65 (PEO) East Peoria, IL St. Monica's Church.
Marciano, Charles A. '72 (ALN) [11] Reading, PA St. Peter Church.
Marciano, Robert L. (PRO) [10] Warwick, RI St. Rose of Lima/St. Clement Church.
Marcil, Leo L. '47 (ALB) Hudson Falls, NY Church of St. Mary's/St. Paul's; Retired.
Marciniak, Bartholomew P. *o.s.p.* '84 (NOR) Rockville, CT St. Joseph Church.
Marciniak, Felix R. '79 (NEW) [4] Linden, NJ St. Theresa of the Child Jesus Church.
Marciniak, Henry P. '61 (NEW) Harrison, NJ Our Lady of Czestochowa Church.
Marciniak, John '56 (NOR) Retired.
Marciniak, Thomas R. *s.j.* '76 (SY) [S] Syracuse, NY Jesuits at LeMoyne, Inc.
Marcinkiewicz, Msgr. Eugene V. '36 (BUF) [18] Buffalo, NY St. Casimir Church; Retired.
Marciulonis, Benedict J. '43 (GAY) Retired.
Marco, Alfredo '60 (LKC) [3] Lake Charles, LA Sacred Heart of Jesus Church.
Marco, Michael J. *s.j.* '96 (OM) [C] Omaha, NE Creighton Preparatory School.
Marcone, Eugene F. '64 (NEW) Clark, NJ St. Agnes Church.
Marconi, John '87 (LR) Benton, AR Our Lady of Fatima Church.
Marconi, John E. '87 (LR) Malvern, AR St. John the Baptist Church.
Marconi, Paul *c.r.s.p.* '58 (SD) Pala, CA Mission San Antonio de Pala Church.
Marconi, Theodore B. '84 (E) Smethport, PA St. Elizabeth Church.
Marconyak, Albert J. '43 (PIT) Retired.
Marcotte, David P. *s.j.* '92 (NY) [DD] New York, NY Xavier Jesuit Community.
Marcotte, Joseph A. '69 (WOR) Webster, MA St. Louis Church.
Marcotte, Wayne E. '66 (MAR) Hancock, MI Resurrection Church.
Marcotte, William '60 (SB) Fontana, CA Kaiser Permanente Hospital.
Marcouiller, Douglas *s.j.* '86 (BO) [W] Chestnut Hill, MA The Jesuit Community at Boston College.
Marcoux, John *m.ss.a.* '87 (NOR) [F] Cromwell, CT Missionaries of the Holy Apostles.
Marcoux, Stephen '93 (MAN) Hampton, NH Our Lady of the Miraculous Medal Church.
Marcucci, John A. '68 (PIT) [3] Charleroi, PA Mary Mother of the Church.
Marcynski, Christopher '91 (BRK) [192] Queens, NY St. Margaret Church.
Marczewski, Robert '95 (PH) [35] Philadelphia, PA St. Christopher Church.
Marczewski, Ronald J. '74 (NEW) [2] Elizabeth, NJ St. Adalbert's Church.
Marczuk, Scott L. *j.c.l.* '81 (LR) [1] Little Rock, AR Cathedral of St. Andrew.
Mardelli, Maximos '38 (NTN) Retired.
Mardian, Joseph P. '45 (SFS) Retired.
Mardian, Pius '44 (SFS) Retired.
Marecki, Ronald (ROC) Bath, NY Soliders' Home and Veterans' Hospital.
Marecki, Ronald A. '83 (CHL) On Duty Outside the Diocese.
Marek, Dean V. '65 (MIL) On Duty Outside the Archdiocese.
Marek, Walter '46 (GAY) Retired.
Maresca, Ralph J. '78 (BRK) Special Assignment.
Maresh, Mark A. '94 (GI) Anselmo, NE St. Anselm's Church.
Marflak, Albert *o.s.b.* '75 (CLV) [E] Cleveland, OH Benedictine High School; [P] Cleveland, OH Benedictine Order of Cleveland.
Marfori, Antonio '78 (SCL) Zimmerman, MN St. Pius X Church.
Margason, James E. '71 (BEL) [6] Belleville, IL St. Luke Church; [9] Belleville, IL Chapel of St. John Children's Home Church; Lebanon, IL St. Joseph Church; [C] Belleville, IL St. John Children's Home.
Marggraf, Brian *ss.cc.* '55 (FR) [J] Fairhaven, MA Sacred Hearts Provincial House.
Margherio, Ronald L. *o.s.b.* '78 (PEO) [A] Peru, IL St.

Bede Abbey and Academy.
Margiotta, Msgr. Vincent S. '29 (RVC) Retired.
Margola, Joseph F. '84 (PCE) On Duty Outside the Diocese.
Marhafer, Maury *o.f.m.conv.* '54 (FgM) Conventual Franciscan Foreign Missions.
Maria Alabanza de la Trin, David A. *s.e.m.v.* '95 (ARE) Hatillo, PR Our Lady of Guadalupe Church.
Marian, Anthony S. '58 (NY) [2] Poughkeepsie, NY St. Mary Church; Poughkeepsie, NY Vassar Brothers Hospital.
Mariani, Charles J. '43 (BRK) [131] Brooklyn, NY Sacred Hearts of Jesus and Mary and St. Stephen Church; Retired.
Mariano, Angel *s.j.* '92 (SJ) [17] San Jose, CA Most Holy Trinity Church.
Mariano, John M. '58 (BRK) Released from Diocesan Assignment.
Mariano, Remigio Tupaz, Jr. '94 (TUC) [22] Tucson, AZ St. Elizabeth Ann Seton Church.
Marick, Thomas D. '97 (STN) On Duty Outside the Diocese.
Marickovic, Thomas C. (HBG) Mifflintown, PA St. Jude Church.
Marickovic, Thomas C. '81 (HBG) Lewistown, PA Sacred Heart of Jesus Church.
Marie, Adrien Ste. *c.s.c.* '50 (P) [B] Portland, OR University of Portland.
Marie, Louis '70 (RC) [B] Bethlehem, SD Holy Nativity Monastery.
Marien, Roy C. '85 (PT) Destin, FL Church of the Resurrection.
Marier, Edward '88 (SPK) Cusick, WA Our Lady of Sorrows Church; Ione, WA St. Bernard Church; Metaline Falls, WA St. Joseph Church; Newport, WA St. Anthony Church; Usk, WA St. Jude Church.
Marier, Euclid A. '72 (OG) Westport, NY St. Philip Neri Church; Moriah, NY Moriah Shock Incarceration Correctional Facility; Retired.
Marigliano, Michael *o.f.m.cap.* '84 (MIL) [B] Mount Calvary, WI St. Felix Friary.
Marin, James (SJN) [44] San Juan, PR Santos Pedro y Pablo los Apostoles Church.
Marin, John L. '83 (MET) On Duty Outside the Diocese.
Marin, Miguel '78 (ELP) Absent on Leave.
Marin, Moises M. '95 (CHI) [8] Chicago, IL St. Aloysius Church.
Marinacci, Msgr. Nicholas '38 (NY) [102] New York, NY St. Patrick Old Cathedral; Retired.
Marinak, Andrew P. '56 (HBG) Cornwall, PA Sacred Heart of Jesus Church.
Marincel, Frank '58 (DUL) Retired.
Marincioni, Raniero C. '90 (MET) Bernardsville, NJ Our Lady of Perpetual Help Church.
Marine, Robert A. '73 (CIN) [44] Cincinnati, OH St. John the Baptist Church.
Maring, William J. *s.j.* '45 (SJ) [M] Los Gatos, CA Sacred Heart Jesuit Center.
Marini, Francis J. '95 (SAM) [D] Staten Island, NY Pastoral Center.
Marini, John L. *c.s.sp.* '92 (PIT) [3] Millvale, PA Holy Spirit Church.
Marini, Joseph J. '52 (SFR) San Bruno, CA St. Robert Church; Retired.
Marini, Michael A. '72 (MRY) Santa Cruz, CA Holy Cross Church.
Marinko, John S. '55 (SCR) Olyphant, PA Holy Ghost Church.
Marino, Christopher '93 (MIA) [C] Miami, FL Archbishop Curley-Notre Dame High School.
Marino, Edward J. *c.s.* '57 (PRO) [M] North Kingstown, RI Scalabrini Villa.
Marino, Francis J. *s.m.* '57 (MET) [L] Phillipsburg, NJ The Anawim Community.
Marino, John J. *o.f.m.* '88 (PRO) [P] Providence, RI St. Francis Friary.
Marino, Msgr. Joseph '79 (BIR) On Duty Outside the Diocese.
Marino, Joseph *o.s.b.* '94 (STL) [F] Creve Coeur, MO St. Louis Priory School; [P] St. Louis, MO The Abbey of St. Mary and St. Louis.
Marino, Joseph T. '75 (PH) Havertown, PA St. Denis Church.
Marino, Ronald '73 (BRK) [T] Brooklyn, NY Catholic Migration & Refugee Office, Catholic Migration Services, Inc.
Marino, Ronald T. '73 (BRK) [126] Brooklyn, NY St. Rosalia-Regina Pacis Church; [T] Brooklyn, NY Catholic Migration & Refugee Office, Catholic Migration Services, Inc.; [T] Brooklyn, NY Catholic Migration & Refugee Office, Catholic Migration Services, Inc.; [T] Brooklyn, NY Catholic Migration & Refugee Office, Catholic Migration Services, Inc.
Marino, Umberto J. '54 (NY) On Duty Outside the Archdiocese.
Marinucci, Steven J. '74 (PH) [A] Wynnewood, PA Theological Seminary of St. Charles Borromeo, Overbrook.
Maristany, Edward '80 (NY) [II] New Rochelle, NY Opus Dei (Prelature of the Holy Cross and Opus Dei).
Maristela, Victor '86 (SD) Escondido, CA St. Mary Church.
Marjanczyk, Msgr. Joseph A. '45 (NEW) [6] Bayonne, NJ Mt. Carmel Church; Retired.
Markaitis, Bruno *s.j.* '48 (CHI) [N] Chicago, IL Lithuanian American Jesuits.
Markalonis, Joseph A. *t.o.r.* '66 (FgM) T.O.R. Foreign Missions.
Markell, John W. '84 (PIT) Turtle Creek, PA St. Colman Church.
Markelz, Carl *o.carm.* '91 (CHI) [N] Chicago, IL Carmelite Priory of St. Cyril.
Markelz, Carl J. *o.carm.* '91 (CHI) [D] Chicago, IL Mt. Carmel High School.
Markert, Leo F. '62 (ALB) Rotterdam, NY St. Gabriel the Archangel Church.
Market, John C. *o.f.m.* '45 (DET) [5] Southfield, MI St. Michael Church.
Markewuch, Uriy '65 (PHU) Whippany, NJ St. John the Baptist Church.
Markey, Earle L. *s.j.* '63 (WOR) [N] Worcester, MA Jesuits of Holy Cross College, Inc.
Markey, Francis '61 (MRY) Retired.
Markey, Gerard *s.s.c.* '71 (OM) [K] St. Columbans, NE St. Columban's Foreign Mission Society.
Markey, Gerard A. *s.s.c.* '71 (BRK) [U] Kew Gardens, NY St. Columbans Foreign Mission Society.
Markey, John *o.p.* '93 (OAK) [N] Oakland, CA Order of Preachers (Southern Province).
Markey, John J. *o.p.* '93 (BAL) [A] Baltimore, MD St. Mary's Seminary and University.
Markey, John J. *o.p.* '93 (DEN) Longmont, CO Spirit of Peace Parish.
Markey, Thomas J. '51 (WOR) Millbury, MA St. Brigid Church.
Markham, Msgr. James '51 (MAN) [11] Manchester, NH St. John the Baptist Church.
Markham, Msgr. James J. '51 (MAN) Retired.
Markham, John W. '54 (DET) [21] Detroit, MI St. Elizabeth Church.
Markiewicz, Stanley T. *o.s.b.* '61 (GBG) [2] Latrobe, PA St. Vincent Basilica Church; [H] Latrobe, PA Saint Vincent Archabbey.
Markley, Edward P. *o.s.b.* '66 (BIR) [E] Cullman, AL St. Bernard Abbey.
Markowicz, Joseph A. *m.s.* '43 (HRT) [M] Hartford, CT Missionaries of LaSalette Provincial Secretary.
Markowski, Clement A. '53 (SCR) Retired; [N] Dunmore, PA Villa St. Joseph.
Marks, Kenneth L. '77 (NY) [133] Bronx, NY St. Benedict Church.
Marks, Thomas (LR) Forrest City, AR St. Francis of Assisi Church.
Marks, Thomas C. '79 (LR) Wynne, AR St. Peter's Church.
Marks, William G. '92 (IND) [19] Indianapolis, IN St. Gabriel the Archangel Church.
Markunas, Robert *s.c.j.* '76 (MIL) [P] Hales Corners, WI Priests of the Sacred Heart.
Markunas, Robert '76 (ORL) Special Assignment.
Markus, Anthony L. '80 (CHI) Evergreen Park, IL Most Holy Redeemer Church.
Markwell, Benjamin *o.f.m.cap.* '66 (FgM) Capuchin Foreign Missions.
Markwell, George *m.afr.* '65 (WDC) [M] Washington, DC Missionaries of Africa.
Marley, Edward G. *c.s.sp.* '44 (LR) Center Ridge, AR St. Joseph's Church.
Marley, Edward G. *c.s.sp.* '45 (LR) Atkins, AR Assumption B.V.M. Church.
Marley, John *s.s.c.* '50 (FgM) St. Columban's Foreign Mission.
Marley, Msgr. Michael F. '40 (PH) [94] Philadelphia, PA St. Martin of Tours Church; Retired.
Marley, Thomas J. *c.s.p.* '49 (NY) [DD] Jamaica Estates, NY Paulist Fathers Generalate.
Marley, Thomas J. *c.s.p.* '49 (PMB) [G] Vero Beach, FL Paulist Fathers Retirement Home.
Marley, William F. *m.m.* '52 (FgM) Maryknoll Foreign Missions.
Marlow, Ransom *s.j.* '66 (NO) [C] New Orleans, LA Loyola University.
Marmentini, Alvadi *o.f.m.cap.* '73 (WDC) [B] Washington, DC St. Francis Friary-Capuchin College.
Marmion, Joseph '62 (GF) Chester, MT St. Mary's Church.
Marmion, Joseph B. (GF) Retired.
Marneni, Ignatius '69 (PH) [2] Chester, PA Blessed Katharine Drexel Church.
Marneni, M. Julian '67 (WH) [1] Huntington, WV St. Joseph's Church.
Maro, Wayne *c.p.p.s.* (LA) [CC] Los Angeles, CA Archdiocesan Office for Campus Ministry.
Maroney, Frank '92 (DEN) Basalt, CO St. Vincent Church.
Maroney, Maurice J. '67 (HRT) [3] Milford, CT St. Gabriel Church.
Maroon, Donald M. '67 (COL) London, OH St. Patrick Church.
Maroon, Msgr. William J. '67 (COL) Hilliard, OH St. Brendan Church.
Maroor, Joseph '63 (MIA) [3] Pompano Beach, FL St. Coleman Church.
Marot, Roger L. '50 (PRO) Retired; [N] Woonsocket, RI Fr. Marot CYO Center.
Marotta, Robert G. (NEW) [17] Jersey City, NJ Mt. Carmel Church.
Maroun, George F. '74 (OG) [A] Ogdensburg, NY Wadhams Hall.
Maroun, Sharbel G. '89 (OLL) Minneapolis, MN St. Maron Church.
Marpes, Thomas M. '50 (PIT) [62] Pittsburgh, PA St. Pius X Church; [L] Pittsburgh, PA St. Pius X Residence, Inc.
Marquard, Elmer E. '66 (CLV) North Olmsted, OH St. Richard Church.
Marquardt, Donald '51 (GB) Retired.
Marquardt, John J. '44 (TLS) Antlers, OK St. Agnes Church.
Marquart, Ernest J. '70 (SPC) Mountain View, MO St. John Vianney Church.
Marquart, Joseph M. '57 (SEA) Everett, WA St. Mary Magdalen Church.
Marquez, Esteban '95 (LA) Bell Gardens, CA St. Gertrude Church; Wilmington, CA Holy Family Church.
Marquina, Luis '64 (MIA) [G] Miami, FL Mercy Hospital.
Marquis, Clif *s.t.* (SB) [4] Fontana, CA St. Mary Church.
Marquis, J. Alphee '39 (PRT) Retired.
Marquis, John E. *s.m.* '78 (PRT) [M] Waterville, ME Colby College; [M] Waterville, ME Thomas College.
Marquis, John J. '62 (COL) Portsmouth, OH St. Mary Church.
Marquis, Paul R. '86 (PRT) Dover-Foxcroft, ME St. Thomas Church.
Marquis, Raymond *o.m.i.* '74 (FgM) Oblates Foreign Missions.
Marquis, William P. *o.p.* '83 (PRO) [P] Providence, RI St. Thomas Aquinas Priory at Providence College.
Marr, James G. '60 (STU) Retired.
Marr, Thomas P. '70 (MAD) Watertown, WI St. Bernard Church.
Marra, Msgr. Anthony C. '51 (SCR) [3] Dunmore, PA St. Anthony of Padua Church.
Marra, James *s.d.b.* '83 (FgM) Salesians of Don Bosco Foreign Missions.
Marrapese, Casto *p.i.m.e.* '44 (COL) [H] Newark, OH P.I.M.E. Mission & Prayer Center.
Marredan, Francisco J. *c.m.* '54 (ARE) [3] Manati, PR Sagrada Familia Church.
Marrell, Dennis P. '78 (LA) Military and VA Chaplains.
Marren, Hugh '76 (ATL) [9] Atlanta, GA St. Anthony of Padua Church.
Marren, Martin T. '84 (CHI) [2] Oak Lawn, IL St. Gerald Church.
Marrero, Adan L. '97 (SJN) [37] San Juan, PR Maria Auxiliadora Church.
Marrero, Francisco *s.j.* '70 (SJN) [22] San Juan, PR San Ignacio de Loyola Church.
Marrion, Malachy *o.c.s.o.* '54 (ARL) [J] Berryville, VA Cistercian Abbey of Our Lady of the Holy Cross.
Marro, Nicholas A. *c.s.* '63 (CHI) [118] Chicago, IL Santa Lucia-Santa Maria Incoronata Church.
Marro, Simeon D. *o.carm.* '55 (GBG) [H] New Florence, PA Mount Carmel Hermitage.
Marrokal, Donald '58 (Y) Retired.
Marron, Msgr. James '43 (MRY) Retired.
Marron, James F. '62 (BRK) [228] Queens, NY St. Pius X Church.
Marron, Joseph *c.ss.r.* '48 (BRK) [107] Brooklyn, NY Our Lady of Perpetual Help Basilica Church.
Marron, Leonard J. *m.m.* '57 (FgM) Maryknoll Foreign Missions.
Marron, Patrick L. '67 (SAT) Leon Springs, TX St. Elizabeth Ann Seton Church.
Marron, Peter J. *o.s.a.* '36 (SD) [H] San Diego, CA Augustinian Community.
Marrone, Robert J. '73 (CLV) [63] Cleveland, OH St. Peter Church.
Marroquin, Luis Antonio '86 (WDC) [5] Silver Spring, MD Christ the King Church.
Marrow, Stanley B. *s.j.* '61 (BO) [W] Cambridge, MA Weston Jesuit Community.
Marrufo, Manuel *c.m.f.* '70 (LA) [20] Los Angeles, CA Our Lady of Solitude Church.
Marrufo, Ramon R. '76 (SD) Vista, CA St. Francis of Assisi Church.
Marsar, Msgr. Joseph '44 (HFL) Retired.
Marsch, Dwaine J. *c.ss.r.* '49 (STL) [P] Liguori, MO St. Clement Health Care Center.
Marschner, Msgr. Aloysius J. '36 (STL) Retired.
Marse, John J. '81 (NO) Norco, LA Sacred Heart of Jesus Church.
Marsh, Ivan Cormac *o.carm.* '80 (NEW) [P] Mahwah, NJ Carmel Retreat House.
Marshall, David C. *c.s.sp.* '46 (VEN) [G] Sarasota, FL Congregation of the Holy Ghost.
Marshall, Eugene C. *o.s.b.* '50 (OKL) McLoud, OK St. Vincent de Paul Church; [I] Shawnee, OK St. Gregory Abbey.

Marshall, Hugh *s.t.* '56 (SAV) [E] Columbus, GA St. Francis Hospital.
Marshall, Msgr. James C. '57 (STU) [3] Steubenville, OH Holy Rosary Church.
Marshall, James C. '59 (STL) Glasgow Village, MO St. Pius X Church.
Marshall, John J. '59 (ALT) [4] Johnstown, PA SS. Casmir & Emerich Church; [12] Johnstown, PA Saints Casimir & Emerich Church.
Marshall, Oswald J. *s.j.* '46 (DET) [P] Clarkston, MI Colombiere Center.
Marshall, Patrick M. '79 (CHI) [V] Chicago, IL Ministry in Higher Education.
Marshall, Raymond '43 (DET) Retired.
Marshall, Robert A. '61 (STL) Valley Park, MO Sacred Heart Church.
Marshall, Thomas R. *c.s.p.* '59 (NY) [DD] Jamaica Estates, NY Paulist Fathers Generalate.
Marshall, William '63 (OAK) Retired.
Marsicek, Robert R. *s.d.s.* '68 (SAC) Orangevale, CA Divine Savior Church; [L] Orangevale, CA Catholic Committee on Scouting.
Marsick, James J. '72 (CLV) Cuyahoga Falls, OH St. Joseph Church.
Marszal, Theodore '68 (CLV) [1] Cleveland, OH Cathedral of St. John the Evangelist.
Marszalek, Francis G. '67 (PH) King of Prussia, PA Mother of Divine Providence Church.
Marszalek, Paul B. '52 (CHI) Retired.
Marta, Raul '72 (FRS) Tulare, CA St. Aloysius Church.
Marteja, Vincent '67 (RVC) East Islip, NY St. Mary's Church.
Marteka, Anthony T. '61 (WOR) Grafton, MA St. Philip's Church.
Martel, C. James '70 (PRT) Pittsfield, ME St. Agnes Church.
Martel, Leo E. '63 (BO) Chelmsford, MA St. Mary Church.
Martel, Luc *a.a.* '73 (BO) [W] Brighton, MA Assumptionist Center.
Martel, Marcel I. '79 (MAN) [4] Nashua, NH St. Francis Xavier Church.
Martel, Robert T. '49 (PRT) Retired; [I] Waterville, ME Mt. St. Joseph Priest Retirement Home.
Martell, James Joseph '88 (MEM) Savannah, TN St. Mary's Church; [M] Savannah, TN Charismatic Prayer Groups.
Martell, John J. *s.m.* '48 (WDC) [M] Washington, DC Marist Provincial House.
Martelli, Jose M. *c.s.c.* '73 (FTW) Notre Dame, IN Sacred Heart Church; [B] Notre Dame, IN University of Notre Dame Du Lac; [J] Notre Dame, IN Holy Cross Community, Corby Hall, University of Notre Dame.
Martello, Ernest *o.s.c.* '70 (FgM) Crosier Foreign Missions.
Martello, Lawrence N. '74 (CLV) Amherst, OH St. Joseph Church.
Martens, Francis E. *c.i.c.m.* '43 (HRT) Plainville, CT Our Lady of Mercy Church.
Martens, L. Gene *s.j.* '63 (STL) [P] St. Louis, MO Hallahan House; [P] St. Louis, MO The Jesuits of the Missouri Province; [W] St. Louis, MO The Jesuits of the Missouri Province.
Martensen, Carsten P. *s.j.* '77 (NEW) [B] Jersey City, NJ Saint Peter's College; [N] Jersey City, NJ Jesuits of Saint Peter's College, Inc.
Marth, Msgr. Loydell J. '56 (FRS) Buttonwillow, CA St. Mary Church; Taft, CA St. Mary Church.
Marthaler, Andrew '90 (SCL) Elbow Lake, MN St. Olaf Church; Tintah, MN St. Gall's Church.
Marthaler, Berard L. *o.f.m.conv.* '52 (WDC) [5] Washington, DC St. Anthony Church; [B] Washington, DC St. Bonaventure Friary; [C] Washington, DC Catholic University of America, The.
Marti, Julio *l.c.* '97 (HRT) [B] Cheshire, CT Novitiate of the Legion of Christ.
Marti, Ramon '55 (LA) Arcadia, CA Annunciation Church; Duarte, CA City of Hope Medical Center.
Marti, Thomas J. *m.m.* '65 (SEA) [M] Seattle, WA Maryknoll Fathers.
Marti, Tony *o.f.m.cap.* '96 (LA) [74] Los Angeles, CA St. Lawrence of Brindisi Church.
Martignon, John E. '84 (MAR) Cooks, MI St. Mary Magdalene Church; Garden, MI St. John the Baptist Church; Nahma, MI St. Andrew Church.
Martin, Andrew '67 (CAM) [7] Camden, NJ St. Joseph's Pro-Cathedral.
Martin, Andrew E. '67 (CAM) [A] Cherry Hill, NJ Camden Catholic High School.
Martin, Anselm *o.f.m.cap.* '45 (PH) [79] Philadelphia, PA St. John the Evangelist Church.
Martin, Benjamin (DOD) LaCrosse, KS St. Michael Church; Liebenthal, KS St. Joseph Church.
Martin, C. Lou '76 (BAL) [10] Baltimore, MD St. Anthony of Padua Church; [66] Baltimore, MD Most Precious Blood, Community of Church.
Martin, Charles A. *c.s.p.* '65 (STP) [29] Minneapolis, MN St. Lawrence Church; [N] Minneapolis, MN Paulist Fathers; [V] Minneapolis, MN University of Minnesota Newman Center and Chapel.
Martin, Clarence A. *s.j.* '46 (ALN) [A] Wernersville, PA Novitiate of St. Isaac Jogues.
Martin, Clifford '64 (SFR) [U] San Francisco, CA Spiritual Programs and Retreats.
Martin, Clifford A. '76 (SFR) [30] San Francisco, CA St. Kevin Church.
Martin, Msgr. Daniel J. '43 (E) Retired.
Martin, David A. '76 (EVN) Washington, IN St. Simon Church.
Martin, David L. '73 (ARL) Gordonsville, VA St. Mark's Church; Orange, VA St. John's Church.
Martin, Dean J. '88 (BR) Independence, LA Mater Dolorosa Church.
Martin, Dennis A. '75 (E) Erie, PA St. Vincent's Health Center; [G] Erie, PA Saint Vincent Health Center.
Martin, Dennis C. '67 (DAV) Washington, IA St. James Church.
Martin, Diosdado '66 (LA) [5] Los Angeles, CA Assumption Church.
Martin, Donald J. *s.j.* '62 (NO) [P] New Orleans, LA Jesuit Provincial Office.
Martin, Edward L. *o.p.* '59 (NEW) [28] Jersey City, NJ Sacred Heart Church.
Martin, Emilio '52 (MIA) [5] Hialeah, FL St. John the Apostle Church.
Martin, Msgr. F. Gerald '54 (DET) [Q] Detroit, MI St. Vincent de Paul Society.
Martin, Francis '43 (LAN) [F] Lansing, MI St. Lawrence Hospital and Healthcare Services.
Martin, Francis *o.s.m.* '48 (STL) Affton, MO Seven Holy Founders Church.
Martin, Francis M. *o.s.m.* '48 (CHI) [N] Chicago, IL Servite Friars - Eastern Province.
Martin, Francis T. '39 (LAN) Retired.
Martin, Francisco '53 (MIA) Miami Lakes, FL Our Lady of the Lakes Church.
Martin, Gerard R. '73 (BR) [21] Baton Rouge, LA St. Thomas More Church.
Martin, Gilmer J. '74 (NO) [8] Metairie, LA St. Edward the Confessor Church.
Martin, Msgr. Harrison A. '37 (NO) Retired.
Martin, Harry '66 (SAT) San Antonio, TX Audie Murphy VA Hospital.
Martin, Hilary *o.p.* '55 (OAK) [4] Berkeley, CA St. Mary Magdalen Church.
Martin, Msgr. Ignatius (LAF) Retired.
Martin, J. Dennis *c.m.* '61 (STL) [P] St. Louis, MO Vincentian-St. Lazare Residence.
Martin, James A. *s.j.* '34 (WDC) [M] Washington, DC The Jesuit Community at Georgetown University.
Martin, James J. '63 (PH) [59] Philadelphia, PA Holy Family Church.
Martin, James J. '68 (CHI) [27] Chicago, IL St. Benedict the African (West) Church.
Martin, James R. *c.s.c.* '93 (AUS) [25] Austin, TX San Francisco Church.
Martin, Joel W. *o.s.b.* '91 (BIR) [B] Cullman, AL St. Bernard Preparatory School, Inc.; [E] Cullman, AL St. Bernard Abbey.
Martin, John (NEW) [24] Jersey City, NJ Parish of the Resurrection Church.
Martin, John *c.ss.r.* (NY) [42] New York, NY Guardian Angel Church.
Martin, John *o.s.m.* '53 (ORL) Palm Bay, FL Our Lady of Grace Church.
Martin, John *a.a.* '57 (BO) [W] Brighton, MA Assumptionist Center.
Martin, John F. *s.j.* '74 (WDC) [M] Washington, DC The Jesuit Community at Georgetown University.
Martin, John H. *s.j.* '41 (SFR) [N] San Francisco, CA Jesuit Community at University of San Francisco.
Martin, John Hilary *o.p.* '55 (OAK) [A] Berkeley, CA Dominican School of Philosophy and Theology.
Martin, John J. *o.s.m.* '53 (CHI) [N] Chicago, IL Servite Friars - Eastern Province.
Martin, John J. '65 (SR) Mendocino, CA St. Anthony Church.
Martin, Msgr. John J. '72 (ALN) Colesville, PA Assumption B.V.M. Church.
Martin, John L. *m.m.* '65 (NY) [DD] Maryknoll, NY Maryknoll Fathers and Brothers.
Martin, John M. *s.j.* '84 (SJ) [2] Santa Clara, CA St. Clare Church.
Martin, Msgr. John P. '48 (WOR) Retired.
Martin, Msgr. John P. '61 (RVC) Farmingdale, NY St. Kilian Church.
Martin, John P. *m.m.* '66 (FgM) Maryknoll Foreign Missions.
Martin, John P. *m.m.* '66 (NY) [DD] Maryknoll, NY Maryknoll Fathers and Brothers.
Martin, Jon C. '65 (BO) Middleton, MA St. Agnes Church; Middleton, MA Essex County Correctional Facility.
Martin, Jose *o.p.* '62 (PCE) Yauco, PR Holy Rossary Church.
Martin, Msgr. Joseph A. '67 (NY) Fishkill, NY Church of St. Mary, Mother of the Church.
Martin, Joseph C. *s.s.* '48 (BAL) Special Assignment; [M] Baltimore, MD Sulpician Provincial House.
Martin, Joseph I. '56 (BO) Society of St. James the Apostle.
Martin, Joseph I. '56 (FgM) Society of St. James the Apostle.
Martin, Joseph L. *s.j.* '45 (SJ) [M] Los Gatos, CA Sacred Heart Jesuit Center.
Martin, Joseph P. '64 (Y) [11] Canton, OH St. Paul's Church.
Martin, Kenneth (NEW) Newark, NJ St. James Hospital; [G] Newark, NJ St. James Hospital.
Martin, Kenneth J. '89 (WIL) Ogletown, DE Holy Family Church.
Martin, Msgr. Kieran J. '50 (BRK) [141] Brooklyn, NY St. Thomas Aquinas Church; Retired.
Martin, Larok Obwano '80 (OKL) [5] Oklahoma City, OK Corpus Christi Church.
Martin, Leon J. *s.a.c.* '75 (MIL) [P] Milwaukee, WI Pallotti House.
Martin, Leonard A. *s.j.* '73 (SCR) [C] Scranton, PA University of Scranton; [E] Scranton, PA Scranton Preparatory School.
Martin, Luis '55 (ELP) [35] El Paso, TX San Antonio Church.
Martin, Malcolm *s.a.* '62 (BO) [P] Brockton, MA Chapel of Our Savior-Catholic Pastoral and Information Center; [W] Brockton, MA Chapel of Our Saviour; [BB] Brockton, MA Chapel of Our Saviour.
Martin, Manuel '45 (MIA) [1] Miami Beach, FL St. Francis de Sales Church.
Martin, Marciano G. *c.pp.s.* '64 (SP) [1] Tampa, FL Blessed Sacrament Church.
Martin, Michael *c.s.p.* '79 (GR) Grand Rapids, MI Chapel of St. Paul-Catholic Information Center.
Martin, Michael *o.f.m.conv.* '89 (BAL) [C] Baltimore, MD Archbishop Curley High School; [M] Baltimore, MD Immaculate Heart of Mary Friary.
Martin, Michael '94 (SFR) [1] San Francisco, CA Cathedral of St. Mary (Assumption).
Martin, Norman F. *s.j.* '47 (SJ) [B] Santa Clara, CA Santa Clara University.
Martin, Normand *s.m.* '59 (DET) [E] Harper Woods, MI Notre Dame High School.
Martin, Patrick '78 (NOR) [I] Wauregan, CT Ministry of His Able People.
Martin, Msgr. Paul M. '58 (ORG) San Juan Capistrano, CA (Old Mission) Church.
Martin, Ralph L. '65 (WIL) Smyrna, DE St. Polycarp Church; Smyrna, MD Delaware Home & Hospital for the Chronically Ill.
Martin, Raymond D. '94 (BAL) Ellicott City, MD Resurrection Church.
Martin, Reginald *o.p.* (OAK) [N] Oakland, CA Western Dominican Province.
Martin, Reginald *o.p.* (SFR) [13] San Francisco, CA St. Dominic Church.
Martin, Reginald E. *o.p.* '74 (SFR) [N] San Francisco, CA St. Dominic Priory; [U] San Francisco, CA Shrine of St. Jude Thaddeus.
Martin, Richard B. '66 (ARL) Burke, VA Church of the Nativity.
Martin, Richard J. '63 (CHI) Palos Heights, IL Incarnation Church.
Martin, Robert *c.ss.r.* '50 (FgM) Redemptorist Foreign Missions.
Martin, Robert A. (BUF) Elba, NY Our Lady of Fatima Church.
Martin, Robert A. '83 (BUF) [2] Batavia, NY St. Joseph Church; [D] Batavia, NY Notre Dame High School of Batavia.
Martin, Roger '51 (OG) Retired.
Martin, Roosevelt '88 (GAL) [46] Fort Bend Co., TX St. Mark the Evangelist Church.
Martin, Sean C. '81 (DAL) On Duty Outside the Diocese.
Martin, Sean C. '81 (GAL) [A] Houston, TX St. Mary's Seminary.
Martin, Shane P. *s.j.* '92 (LA) [C] Los Angeles, CA Loyola Marymount University.
Martin, Thomas *o.c.d.* '61 (MIL) [P] Milwaukee, WI Provincial Offices - Discalced Carmelites.
Martin, Thomas *o.s.a.* '69 (PH) [C] Villanova, PA Villanova University.
Martin, Thomas '70 (OAK) [3] Berkeley, CA St. Joseph The Worker Church.
Martin, Thomas '79 (COL) On Duty Outside the Diocese.
Martin, Thomas A. '79 (KAL) Mendon, MI St. Edward Church.
Martin, Thomas F. '56 (CLV) [24] Cleveland, OH St. Francis Church; [X] Cleveland, OH Diocesan Hispanic Office.
Martin, Thomas F. *o.s.a.* '69 (CHI) [N] Olympia Fields, IL The Augustinian Provincialate Tolentine Center.
Martin, Thomas F. *o.s.a.* '69 (PH) [B] Villanova, PA St. Augustine Friary.
Martin, Thomas P. *s.j.* '66 (BAL) [M] Baltimore, MD Jesuit Fathers and Brothers Maryland Provincial Curia.
Martin, Vicente M. '75 (VEN) Port Charlotte, FL St. Charles Borromeo Church.
Martin, Victor T. '80 (BGP) [7] Fairfield, CT St. Thomas Aquinas Church.
Martin, Vincent *o.s.b.* '36 (LA) [R] Valyermo, CA St.

Andrew's Abbey.
Martin, Vincente Moreno (CAM) On Duty Outside the Diocese.
Martin, Warren S. *s.j.* '32 (NO) [P] New Orleans, LA Ignatius Residence.
Martin, William *o.m.i.* '61 (PMB) [4] West Palm Beach, FL St. John Fisher Church; [C] West Palm Beach, FL Rosarian Academy.
Martin, William F. '78 (STP) Waverly, MN St. Mary Church.
Martin, William J. '50 (TOL) Marysdale, OH Immaculate Conception Church; The Bend, OH St. Stephen Church.
Martin, William J. '55 (CHI) Western Springs, IL St. John of the Cross Church.
Martin, William J. '71 (L) [69] Louisville, KY St. Rita Church.
Martin, Msgr. William L. '56 (GRY) Cedar Lake, IN Holy Name Church.
Martin, Zenaido '91 (ARE) [2] Camuy, PR Our Lady of the Miraculous Medal Church.
Martin-Calama, Florian (DEN) [A] Denver, CO Redemptoris Mater House of Formation.
Martina, Joseph '89 (SHP) Lake Providence, LA St. Patrick Church.
Martina, Joseph A., Jr. '89 (SHP) Oak Grove, LA Sacred Heart Church.
Martine, Michael '97 (NY) [142] Bronx, NY St. Frances of Rome Church.
Martineau, Laurier J. '59 (BO) [3] Marlboro, MA St. Mary Church.
Martineau, Maurice J. '63 (LKC) Lake Arthur, LA Our Lady of the Lake Church.
Martinek, John B. '73 (CHI) On Duty Outside the Archdiocese.
Martinek, John B. '73 (FBK) Kotzebue, AK St. Francis Xavier Church.
Martinez, Adam '85 (AUS) Lockhart, TX St. Mary's Church.
Martinez, Alberto (CGS) Gurabo, PR San Jose Church.
Martinez, Alfredo (CGS) Retired.
Martinez, Anthony L. '89 (SFE) Portales, NM St. Helen Church; [M] Portales, NM University Catholic Center - St. Thomas More Chapel.
Martinez, Antonio *o.a.r.* '48 (LSC) [3] Las Cruces, NM Our Lady of Health Church.
Martinez, Antonio Felipe '96 (TUC) Nogales, AZ Sacred Heart Church.
Martinez, Balduino *c.m.* (BRK) [W] Brooklyn, NY Centro Evangelizacion San Vicente de Paul.
Martinez, Balduino *c.m.* '89 (BRK) [Y] Brooklyn, NY Jornada Movement.
Martinez, Benjamin *c.m.f.* '58 (MET) [4] Perth Amboy, NJ Our Lady of Fatima Church.
Martinez, Benjamin '92 (CC) On Duty Outside the Diocese.
Martinez, Bulmaro Alvarado '88 (YAK) Prosser, WA Sacred Heart Church.
Martinez, Carlos '89 (ORG) [1] Anaheim, CA St. Anthony Claret Church.
Martinez, Celso '52 (SJN) [5] Carolina, PR Santo Cristo de los Milagros Church.
Martinez, Charles '80 (DEN) [1] Denver, CO Cathedral of the Immaculate Conception.
Martinez, Chas. *o.f.m.* '80 (DEN) [M] Denver, CO Holy Trinity Friary.
Martinez, Dario '87 (SJN) [21] Bayamon, PR Nuestra Sra. del Rosario Church.
Martinez, Felipe J. *c.m.* '55 (STL) Brewer, MO Christ the Savior Church.
Martinez, Francisco (ARE) Retired.
Martinez, Francisco *ss.cc.* '58 (SJN) [8] Guaynabo, PR Nuestra Senora de la Paz Church.
Martinez, Francisco X. '88 (CC) On Duty Outside the Diocese.
Martinez, Frank Perez *o.s.b.* '97 (MGZ) [6] Mayaquez, PR Sacred Heart Church.
Martinez, Frank R. '82 (DAV) Special Assignment; [M] Davenport, IA St. Vincent Center.
Martinez, German *o.s.b.* '67 (BGP) [1] Greenwich, CT St. Mary's Church.
Martinez, Gilbert *c.s.p.* '95 (MEM) [20] Memphis, TN St. Patrick's Church; [J] Memphis, TN Paulist Fathers (New York).
Martinez, Gilberto *s.s.p.* '75 (LA) [R] Los Angeles, CA Society of St. Paul.
Martinez, Ignacio (MRY) Santa Cruz, CA Holy Cross Church.
Martinez, James E. *o.s.a.* '57 (PH) Bryn Mawr, PA Our Mother of Good Counsel Church.
Martinez, Joachim *s.j.* '55 (BO) [3] Somerville, MA St. Benedict Church.
Martinez, John J. *s.j.* '62 (RIC) Dinwiddie County, VA St. John Church.
Martinez, Jose Luis *o.a.r.* '64 (LA) [R] Oxnard, CA St. Augustine Priory O.A.R.
Martinez, Juan *s.d.b.* '73 (SJN) [28] San Juan, PR San Juan Bosco Church.
Martinez, Julian *c.m.* '63 (SJN) [24] San Juan, PR Jesus Maestro Church.
Martinez, Msgr. Leo '63 (SAT) [11] San Antonio, TX Immaculate Conception Church.
Martinez, Leonel *o.s.a.* '34 (GAL) Pasadena, TX Blessed Juan Diego Church.
Martinez, Lorenzo '77 (NSH) Smyrna, TN St. Luke Church.
Martinez, Luis '96 (SR) Napa, CA St. John the Baptist Church.
Martinez, Manuel '66 (SAT) On Duty Outside the Archdiocese.
Martinez, Manuel C. *o.r.c.* '94 (PCE) Adjuntas, PR St. Joachim Church.
Martinez, Marcos '52 (CC) [9] Corpus Christi, TX Our Lady of the Pillar Church.
Martinez, Mariano '52 (CC) [10] Laredo, TX Santa Rita De Casia Independent Mission Church.
Martinez, Mark A. '96 (LA) Venice, CA St. Mark Church.
Martinez, Martin S. '93 (TUC) Yuma, AZ Immaculate Conception Church.
Martinez, Michael '89 (TUC) [17] Tucson, AZ St. Monica Church.
Martinez, Milton '97 (FgM) American - Cassinese Congregation Foreign Missions.
Martinez, Otto *s.j.* '63 (MIA) [H] Miami, FL Villa Arrieta.
Martinez, Ramon *o.s.a.* '78 (GAL) Baytown, TX Our Lady of Guadalupe Church.
Martinez, Ramon P. '89 (NO) Port Sulphur, LA St. Patrick Church.
Martinez, Raymond *c.m.f.* '41 (LA) [R] Rancho Dominguez, CA Dominguez Seminary Inc.
Martinez, Roberto *o.f.m.cap.* '96 (PCE) [5] Ponce, PR Santa Teresita Church; [E] Ponce, PR Residencia Asis.
Martinez, Rogelio '67 (SAT) Retired; [K] San Antonio, TX Casa De Padres.
Martinez, Roy *o.f.m.cap.* '84 (ARE) [1] Utuado, PR San Miquel Church.
Martinez, Ruben *o.m.i.* '68 (OAK) [N] Oakland, CA Oblate Provincial House & Procure.
Martinez, Timothy A. '90 (SFE) Mora, NM St. Gertrude Church.
Martinez, Tomas *s.s.p.* '75 (LA) [R] Los Angeles, CA Society of St. Paul.
Martinez, Vidal '70 (SFE) [7] Albuquerque, NM Our Lady of Fatima Church.
Martinez, Vidal *o.s.m.* '75 (CHI) [N] Chicago, IL Servite Friars - Eastern Province.
Martinez, Vidal *o.s.m.* '75 (ORL) Kissimmee, FL Holy Redeemer Church.
Martinez, Virgilio '65 (SJN) [35] San Juan, PR San Luis Rey Church.
Martinez y Alire, Jerome J. '76 (SFE) [7] Santa Fe, NM Santa Maria de La Paz Catholic Community Church; [N] Albuquerque, NM Fraternidad Piadosa de Nuestro Padre Jesus Nazareno.
Martinez-Mari, Joaquin *s.j.* '55 (BO) [E] Boston, MA Boston College High School & Jesuit Community.
Martinez-Mata, Jose '89 (ELP) [7] El Paso, TX Cristo Rey Church.
Martini, Alexis *o.f.m.conv.* '41 (L) [7] Louisville, KY St. Anthony Church.
Martini, Ivo '84 (SFS) Highmore, SD St. Mary Church.
Martini, Richard M. '80 (LA) Pacific Palisades, CA Corpus Christi Church.
Martinka, Stanley V. '61 (NU) On Duty Outside the Diocese.
Martinkovic, Joseph '54 (ALN) [2] McAdoo, PA St. Mary Church.
Martino, Joseph F. '70 (PH) [A] Wynnewood, PA Theological Seminary of St. Charles Borromeo, Overbrook.
Martinosky, Joseph A. '57 (STU) Retired.
Martins, John C. '55 (FR) [13] Fall River, MA St. Anthony of Padua Church.
Martinson, George G. *s.j.* '73 (FgM) Provinces.
Martinson, Keith Barry *s.j.* '75 (FgM) Provinces.
Martis, Albin A. '43 (WH) Retired.
Martis, Douglas '89 (JOL) Graduate Studies.
Martlock, Loville N. '63 (BUF) Retired.
Marto, Lawrence T. '88 (GB) [1] Marinette, WI Holy Family Church.
Martocchio, Peter T. '57 (BO) [3] Weymouth, MA Immaculate Conception Church.
Marton, Bernard *o.cist.* '67 (DAL) [M] Irving, TX Cistercian Abbey of Our Lady of Dallas.
Marton, Henry *o.cist.* '49 (DAL) [M] Irving, TX Cistercian Abbey of Our Lady of Dallas.
Martone, James '79 (BR) Darrow, LA St. Anthony of Padua Church; Sorrento, LA St. Anne Church.
Martorano, Nicholas *o.s.a.* '77 (PH) [111] Philadelphia, PA St. Nicholas of Tolentine Church.
Martus, Joseph A. *s.j.* '40 (BO) [W] Weston, MA Campion Health Center, Inc.
Martusciello, Msgr. Joseph A. '54 (BRK) [245] Queens, NY St. Thomas Apostle Church.
Martyn, George W. *o.s.f.s.* '71 (WIL) [I] Childs, MD Oblates of St. Francis De Sales.
Martyniuk, Joseph '58 (PHU) Pottstown, PA St. Michael's Church; Reading, PA Nativity of Blessed Virgin Mary Church.
Martyniuk, Pawlo '92 (STF) [10] Willimantic, CT Protection of B.V.M. Church.
Maruca, Michael J. *s.j.* '90 (BAL) [M] Baltimore, MD Jesuit Fathers and Brothers Maryland Provincial Curia.
Marucci, Msgr. Carl J. '83 (CAM) On Duty Outside the Diocese.
Marucci, Msgr. Carl J. '83 (NY) [2] New York, NY St. Agnes Church.
Marucci, Louis A. '87 (CAM) [O] Blackwood, NJ St. Pius X Spiritual Life Center.
Marullo, Lawrence *v.f.* '75 (OG) Inlet, NY St. Anthony of Padua Church; Old Forge, NY St. Bartholomew Church; Raquette Lake, NY St. William Church.
Marus, Msgr. Andrew G. '71 (BGP) [17] Bridgeport, CT St. Patrick Church.
Maruscak, Roland *o.f.m.* '41 (ALN) [K] Easton, PA St. Francis Friary.
Marusceac, Vladimir '88 (STF) Cohoes, NY SS. Peter and Paul Church; Troy, NY Protection of B.V.M. Church.
Marut, Paul *o.f.m.conv.* '72 (BAL) [M] Ellicott City, MD Order of Friars Minor Conventual.
Marut, Paul *o.f.m.conv.* '72 (FgM) Conventual Franciscan Foreign Missions.
Marut, Thomas '74 (STU) Malvern, OH St. Francis Xavier Church.
Marva, Robert *o.f.m.cap.* '97 (CLV) [A] Wickliffe, OH Borromeo Seminary.
Marvin, James J. '48 (ROC) Retired.
Marx, John '60 (ANC) Retired.
Marx, Lambert M. '44 (MAD) Retired.
Marx, Louis '66 (SB) Guasti, CA San Secondo d'Asti Church.
Marx, Paul *o.s.b.* '47 (SCL) [I] Collegeville, MN St. John's Abbey, of the Order of St. Benedict.
Marx, Paul *o.m.i.* '65 (FgM) Oblates Foreign Missions.
Marx, Paul B. *o.s.b.* '41 (WDC) [V] Front Royal, VA Human Life International.
Mary, Bernard (PEO) [O] Peoria, IL Newman Foundation at Bradley University & Illinois Central College.
Mary, Joseph '97 (PEO) [O] Peoria, IL Newman Foundation at Bradley University & Illinois Central College.
Maryanski, Fabian J. '71 (BUF) Absent on Leave.
Maryland, Joseph A. '40 (E) Retired.
Marzen, Msgr. Francis A. '51 (HON) Retired.
Marzheuser, Richard A. '77 (CIN) [B] Cincinnati, OH Mt. St. Mary's Seminary of the West.
Marzilli, Raphael '42 (GBG) On Duty Outside the Diocese.
Marzluf, George J. '46 (COL) Retired.
Marzocchi, Mario *s.s.s.* '84 (CLV) Highland Heights, OH St. Paschal Baylon Church.
Marzocchi, Mario T. '84 (CLV) [P] Cleveland, OH Blessed Sacrament Community.
Marzolf, John G. *s.j.* '66 (ALB) [O] Auriesville, NY Jesuit Retreat House for Priests, Religious and Lay People; [O] Auriesville, NY Shrine of Our Lady of Martyrs.
Masabakhwa, Raphael '95 (DM) [3] Council Bluffs, IA St. Patrick Church.
Masad, Frederick F. '60 (CHR) [5] Columbia, SC St. John Neumann Church.
Masakowski, Edward M. '57 (SCR) Inkerman, PA St. Mark's Church.
Masakowski, Msgr. John C. '49 (SCR) [2] Plymouth, PA St. John the Baptist Church.
Masar, Joseph G. '89 (SD) Brawley, CA Sacred Heart Church.
Mascardo, Editho '83 (STO) [4] Stockton, CA St. George Church.
Mascarella, Patrick J. '66 (BR) [6] Baton Rouge, LA Christ the King Church; [K] Baton Rouge, LA Christ the King Parish and Catholic Student Center.
Mascarenhas, Frazer *s.j.* '85 (CHI) [C] Chicago, IL Jesuit Community at Loyola University of Chicago.
Mascarenhas, Oswald A. *s.j.* '66 (DET) [K] Detroit, MI Jesuit Community at the University of Detroit.
Mascareno, Jose Ramon *o.s.b.* '81 (BIR) [E] Cullman, AL St. Bernard Abbey.
Mascari, Michael A. *o.p.* '87 (STL) [P] St. Louis, MO St. Dominic Priory.
Mascari, Peter '52 (SFD) Retired.
Mascherino, Alphonse '76 (ALT) Absent on Leave.
Maschmann, Elvan *o.f.m.* '46 (STL) [R] St. Louis, MO Villa Gesu.
Masciarelli, Rudolph '49 (BO) Retired.
Masciarelli, Rudolph '49 (FgM) Society of St. James the Apostle.
Masciocchi, Robert *c.s.s.* '54 (BO) [Y] Waltham, MA Espousal Retreat House and Conference Center; [Z] Waltham, MA Stigmatine Fathers and Brothers.
Mascioli, Joseph M. '57 (WH) Retired.
Mascolino, Charles E. '54 (STU) Barnesville, OH Assumption Church; Temperanceville, OH St. Mary's Church.
Mascolino, Robert A. '45 (STU) Retired.
Masek, James J. '74 (CLV) [54] Cleveland, OH Our Lady of Lourdes Church.
Masello, David W. '78 (PRO) Barrington, RI Holy

Angels Church; [1] Warren, RI St. Alexander Church.
Mash, Wesley M. '90 (PBR) Charleroi, PA Holy Ghost Church.
Masiar, Paul E. '69 (ALN) [3] Saint Clair, PA Immaculate Conception Church; Coaldale, PA Coaldale State Hospital.
Masich, Emil G. '45 (PRM) Retired.
Masich, Michael P. *o.f.m.cap.* (BAL) Cumberland, MD SS. Peter and Paul Church.
Masiello, Johon *s.d.b.* '58 (NEW) [3] Elizabeth, NJ St. Anthony's Church.
Masiello, Msgr. Joseph P. '69 (NEW) Westfield, NJ Holy Trinity Church.
Masin, Richard H. '85 (CC) On Duty Outside the Diocese.
Maskell, A. Joseph '65 (BAL) Absent on Leave.
Maslach, Paul *o.f.m.* '62 (CHI) [189] Chicago, IL Sacred Heart Church.
Maslak, Gregory '72 (PHU) Hazleton, PA St. Michael's Church; McAdoo, PA St. Mary's Church.
Maslanka, Andrzej '80 (FBK) Nome, AK St. Joseph Church; Teller, AK St. Ann Church.
Maslar, George *o.f.m.conv.* '63 (BAL) [M] Ellicott City, MD Order of Friars Minor Conventual.
Maslar, William J. '56 (ALN) [1] Mahanoy City, PA Assumption B.V.M. Church; [6] Mahanoy City, PA Sacred Heart Church.
Maslejak, Andrzej *s.ch.* '79 (DET) [K] Sterling Heights, MI Society of Christ Provincial Home.
Maslinski, Reginald *o.f.m.* '44 (MIL) [P] Burlington, WI Queen of Peace Friary.
Maslowski, Krzysztof '88 (NEW) Cranford, NJ St. Michael's Church.
Maslowski, Stanley '63 (STP) North St. Paul, MN St. Peter Church.
Maslowsky, Michael '86 (P) [5] Portland, OR St. Anthony Church.
Masluk, Alexander '79 (PH) [132] Philadelphia, PA Our Mother of Sorrows Church.
Masnicki, Marek '92 (NOR) [3] Middletown, CT St. Mary of Czestochowa Church.
Maso, Dario *s.x.* '82 (FgM) Xaverian Foreign Missions.
Maso, Dario *s.x.* '82 (PAT) [M] Wayne, NJ Xaverian Missionary Fathers.
Mason, Albert M. '48 (BO) Awaiting Assignment.
Mason, Brian G. '93 (MIL) [53] Milwaukee, WI St. Matthias Church.
Mason, Carl Louis *o.p.* '64 (L) [47] Louisville, KY St. Louis Bertrand Church.
Mason, Charlon O. '79 (GR) Pewamo, MI St. Joseph's Church.
Mason, Dennis *o.f.m.conv.* '78 (TR) Riverside, NJ St. Casimir Church.
Mason, Edward J. '87 (BRK) Absent on Leave.
Mason, James E. '67 (LC) On Duty Outside the Diocese.
Mason, James H. '80 (SD) Leave of Absence.
Mason, Mark (OKL) Special Assignment.
Mason, Mark '75 (OKL) Prison Ministry.
Mason, Mark E. '75 (OKL) Hennessey, OK St. Joseph's Church.
Mason, Robert E. '56 (RVC) Massapequa Park, NY Our Lady of Lourdes Church.
Mason, William *o.m.i.* '71 (CHI) [174] Chicago, IL Precious Blood Church.
Mass, Ronald J. '70 (CHI) Palos Heights, IL Incarnation Church.
Massa, James '86 (BO) [A] Weston, MA Pope John XXIII National Seminary.
Massa, Mark S. *s.j.* '80 (DET) [K] Detroit, MI Jesuit Provincial Office-Detroit Province of the Society of Jesus.
Massa, Mark S. *s.j.* '80 (NY) [DD] New York, NY Jesuit Community at Fordham University.
Massacavalo, Bruno '77 (JOL) Absent on Sick Leave.
Massacavolo, Bruno '77 (LA) [41] Los Angeles, CA St. Ambrose Church.
Massar, Richard A. '69 (BUF) [2] Cheektowaga, NY Infant of Prague Church.
Massarella, Francis A. '46 (CIN) Retired; [L] Dayton, OH Mercy Siena Woods.
Massaro, Gabriel *o.f.m.cap.* '66 (NOR) [4] Middletown, CT St. Pius X Church.
Massaro, Joseph *c.s.s.* '48 (SPR) [9] Springfield, MA Our Lady of Mt. Carmel Church.
Massaro, Thomas *s.j.* (BO) [W] Cambridge, MA Weston Jesuit Community.
Massart, James (GB) Reedsville/Maple Grove, WI St. Mary-St. Patrick Church.
Massengill, Damian *o.f.m.conv.* (TOL) Salem Twp., OH St. Joseph Church.
Massengill, Peter Damian *o.f.m.conv.* '76 (TOL) Carey, OH Our Lady of Consolation, Basilica-National Shrine Church.
Massett, Msgr. Robert D. '66 (NO) [12] Metairie, LA St. Mary Magdalen Church.
Massetti, Philip *o.s.j.* '76 (MRY) Santa Cruz, CA Shrine of St. Joseph Guardian of the Redeemer Church; [G] Santa Cruz, CA Oblates of St. Joseph Provincial House and Shrine.
Massetti, Philip *o.s.j.* '76 (SAC) [17] Sacramento, CA St. Mary Church.
Massey, Robert E. '73 (MIL) [1] Wauwatosa, WI St. Bernard Church; Special Assignment.
Massi, Anthony '84 (MIA) [13] Miami, FL Our Lady of Lourdes Church.
Massicotte, Bernard *o.s.b.cam.* '57 (MRY) [G] Big Sur, CA New Camaldoli Hermitage.
Massie, Daniel J. '80 (MIL) [1] West Allis, WI St. Aloysius Church.
Massie, Guy '83 (BRK) [98] Brooklyn, NY Our Lady Help of Christians Church; [E] Brooklyn, NY Office of Religious Education: Evangelization and Catholic Formation.
Massie, Guy A. '83 (BRK) Special Assignment.
Massimino, Jerome *o.f.m.* '77 (HRT) [14] Hartford, CT St. Patrick-St. Anthony Church.
Massingale, Bryan N. '83 (MIL) [A] Milwaukee, WI St. Francis Seminary.
Massion, John C. '56 (CHI) Wheeling, IL St. Joseph the Worker Church.
Massmann, Albert *o.s.b.* '54 (OM) [K] Elkhorn, NE Mount Michael Abbey.
Masson, Paul R. *m.m.* '72 (GAL) [Q] Houston, TX Maryknoll Fathers and Brothers.
Massoth, Charles *o.s.b.* '51 (OKL) Shawnee, OK St. Benedict Church.
Massucci, Joseph D. '70 (CIN) [D] Dayton, OH The University of Dayton.
Massucci, Joseph D. '70 (STU) On Duty Outside the Diocese.
Massung, Francis G. '40 (PIT) Retired; [O] Pittsburgh, PA St. John Vianney Manor.
Mast, Paul G. '72 (WIL) Hockessin, DE St. Mary of the Assumption Church.
Mastalir, Peter (GB) [2] Appleton, WI St. Bernard Church.
Masters, Andrew *s.v.d.* '34 (CHI) [B] Techny, IL Divine Word Residence.
Masters, Gerard G. '66 (HRT) [2] Torrington, CT Sacred Heart Church; [4] Torrington, CT St. Peter's Church.
Masters, Robert '95 (SJP) Pittsburgh, PA St. George Church.
Masterson, Clyde '85 (CC) On Duty Outside the Diocese.
Masterson, Clyde G. '85 (MAN) Absent on Sick Leave.
Masterson, Frank D. *s.j.* '53 (P) [D] Portland, OR Jesuit High School.
Masterson, Harold J. *c.s.p.* '37 (NY) [DD] Jamaica Estates, NY Paulist Fathers Generalate.
Masterson, John J. '57 (WIL) Bethany Beach, DE St. Ann Church.
Masterson, Thomas D. *s.j.* '64 (SCR) [C] Scranton, PA University of Scranton; [C] Scranton, PA University of Scranton.
Mastey, Gregory J. '95 (SCL) Alexandria, MN St. Mary's Church.
Mastrangelo, Joseph A. '40 (PIT) Retired.
Mastrangelo, Mario *o.f.m.cap.* '58 (FgM) Capuchin Foreign Missions.
Mastrangelo, Mario *o.f.m.cap.* '58 (SJN) [C] Rio Piedras, PR Fraternidad Santa Maria de Los Angeles.
Mastrangelo, Nicholas '64 (PIT) Holiday Park, PA Our Lady of Joy Church.
Mastria, Angelo *o.carm.* '58 (TUC) [D] Tucson, AZ Social Service Agencies: Pima County; [F] Tucson, AZ Carmelite Priory.
Mastrian, Mark J. '87 (E) [3] Oil City, PA St. Joseph Church; Polk, PA Polk Center.
Mastrobuono, Peter *s.c.j.* '66 (GAL) Sweeny, TX Our Lady of Perpetual Help Church.
Mastroeni, Anthony '72 (PAT) On Duty Outside the Diocese.
Mastrolia, Arthur (NY) [D] New York, NY Department of Education.
Mastrolia, Arthur '87 (NY) [A] New York, NY Cathedral Preparatory Seminary.
Mastrovito, Francis *t.o.r.* '51 (OWN) Central City, KY St. Joseph Church.
Maszkiewicz, Msgr. Mark '36 (TLS) Retired.
Mata, Antonio *o.c.d.* '46 (CGS) [2] Caguas, PR San Jose Church.
Matanic, George *o.p.* (OAK) [N] Oakland, CA Western Dominican Province.
Matanic, George M. *o.p.* '70 (OAK) [4] Berkeley, CA St. Mary Magdalen Church.
Matano, Msgr. Salvatore R. (PRO) [31] Providence, RI St. Sebastian Church.
Matar, Ghassan *m.l.m.* '96 (OLL) Houston, TX Our Lady of the Cedars Mission Church; [A] San Antonio, TX The Congregation of Maronite Lebanese Missionaries.
Matarazzo, Francis '67 (PAT) [3] Clifton, NJ St. Brendan Church; Passaic, NJ Passiac General Hospital.
Matarazzo, Salvatore *o.p.* '60 (NY) Valhalla, NY Holy Name of Jesus Church.
Matas, Msgr. Juan '65 (LA) Montebello, CA Our Lady of the Miraculous Medal Church.
Matash, Msgr. Edward M. '56 (NEW) [4] Bayonne, NJ St. Joseph's Church.
Matejune, Gerald *c.p.* '38 (HRT) [M] West Hartford, CT Holy Family Monastery/Retreat.
Mateljan, Roy A. '67 (MIL) [C] Fond du Lac, WI Marian College of Fond du Lac.
Mateo, Arturo *m.s.c.* '76 (SJ) San Jose, CA Alexian Brothers Hospital; [H] San Jose, CA Alexian Brothers Hospital.
Mateo, Jose *sch.p.* '49 (PCE) [4] Ponce, PR Our Lady of Mt. Carmel Church.
Mateo, Mateo *ss.cc.* '47 (SJN) [9] Guaynabo, PR Sagrados Corazones Church.
Mateo, Miguel *s.f.* '81 (SFE) Chimayo, NM Holy Family Church.
Mateo, P. Rafael *c.ss.r.* '89 (CGS) Yabucoa, PR Santos Angeles Cutodios Church.
Mateos, Francisco *c.m.* '58 (LA) [29] Los Angeles, CA Our Lady of the Rosary of Talpa Church.
Mateos, Tomas '45 (BWN) Retired; [I] McAllen, TX Secular Franciscan Order, Fraternity of Our Lady of Guadalupe.
Matera, Frank J. '68 (HRT) On Duty Outside the Archdiocese.
Matera, Frank J. '68 (WDC) [C] Washington, DC Catholic University of America, The.
Matera, Philip T. '51 (TR) Retired.
Maternoski, Robert (JOL) Kinsman, IL Sacred Heart Church.
Maternoski, Robert '55 (JOL) South Wilmington, IL St. Lawrence Church.
Mateus, Norberto '81 (ATL) [12] Atlanta, GA Shrine of the Immaculate Conception Church.
Mathai, Mani T. '80 (TYL) [1] Tyler, TX Cathedral of the Immaculate Conception.
Matheis, Joseph *m.m.* '56 (HON) [H] Honolulu, HI Maryknoll Fathers House.
Matheny, William K., Jr. '96 (WH) Beckley, WV St. Francis De Sales Church.
Mathers, Douglas J. (NY) [101] New York, NY Our Saviour Church.
Mathesius, William P. *d.min.* '76 (WIL) Greenville, DE St. Joseph on the Brandywine Church.
Mathew, Abraham P. '97 (BRK) [235] Queens, NY St. Robert Bellarmine Church.
Mathew, Hubby '86 (MAR) Ironwood, MI Our Lady of Peace Church.
Mathews, Abraham '79 (TYL) Atlanta, TX St. Catherine of Siena Church.
Mathews, James D. '62 (SY) [19] Syracuse, NY St. Lucy Church.
Mathews, Kenneth M. '78 (ALX) [1] Alexandria, LA St. Francis Xavier Cathedral.
Mathews, Paul *s.m.* '60 (B) Nampa, ID St. Paul's Church.
Mathews, Robert A. '64 (OAK) [10] Oakland, CA St. Jarlath's Church.
Mathewson, Dean '73 (COL) Newark, OH St. Francis de Sales Church.
Mathewson, Robert B. *s.j.* (SJ) [D] San Jose, CA Bellarmine College Preparatory.
Mathias, Edwin J. '67 (TR) Browns Mills, NJ St. Ann Church.
Mathias, Gregory A. '91 (FR) Norton, MA St. Mary's Church.
Mathias, Victor '71 (AUS) Rockdale, TX St. Joseph's Church; Temple, TX St. Mary's Church.
Mathie, D. Edward *s.j.* '68 (FgM) Provinces.
Mathie, D. Edward *s.j.* '68 (MIL) [P] Milwaukee, WI Jesuit Provincial Office, Wisconsin Province; [P] Milwaukee, WI Jesuit Community at Marquette University.
Mathieu, Rene T. '77 (PRT) [2] Lewiston, ME Holy Cross Church.
Mathieu, Robert '76 (GLP) Springerville, AZ St. Peter Church.
Mathis, George *glmy.* '55 (CIN) [M] Fairfield, OH Headquarters of Glenmary Home Missioners.
Mathis, R. Paul '72 (SY) Lee Center, NY St. Joseph Church.
Mathy, Francis H. *s.j.* '58 (FgM) Provinces.
Matienzo, Msgr. Rafael (SJN) [23] San Juan, PR Inmaculado Corazon de Maria Church.
Matlak, Marion A. '43 (CHI) [46] Chicago, IL St. Cornelius Church; Retired.
Matlenga, Joseph '40 (DET) Retired.
Matocha, Msgr. Edward C. '45 (AUS) [1] Austin, TX St. Mary's Cathedral; Special Assignments.
Matocha, Msgr. John L. '47 (SAT) Retired.
Matondo, Thomas *c.i.c.m.* '82 (FgM) Missionhurst Foreign Missions.
Matonti, Charles '60 (BRK) Released from Diocesan Assignment.
Matos, Angel '97 (WOR) [4] Fitchburg, MA St. Francis of Assisi Church; [1] Gardner, MA Holy Spirit Church.
Matos, David Diaz '79 (CGS) Humacao, PR Dulce Nombre de Jesus Church.
Matrishion, Joseph '82 (PSC) Leave of Absence.
Matro, Justin M. *o.s.b.* '89 (GBG) [A] Latrobe, PA St. Vincent Seminary; [H] Latrobe, PA Saint Vincent Archabbey.
Matsko, John M. '39 (PH) Bridgeport, PA Our Mother of Sorrows Church; Retired.

Matt, Erwin H. '56 (MIL) Retired.
Matt, J. Wilson '45 (LAF) Breaux Bridge, LA St. Bernard Church.
Matt, Joseph H. '74 (KC) Belton, MO St. Sabina's Church.
Matt, Thomas S. '86 (OM) Absent on Leave.
Matta, Pablo '90 (ELP) Horizon City, TX Holy Spirit Church.
Mattaliano, James *s.j.* '90 (BO) [3] Newton, MA St. Ignatius Church; [W] Chestnut Hill, MA The Jesuit Community at Boston College.
Mattas, Louis S. '60 (SAL) Abilene, KS St. Andrew's Church.
Mattath, Joseph *c.m.i.* '64 (SY) [2] Endicott, NY St. Ambrose Church.
Matte, Richard O. '64 (BO) Health Leave.
Mattei, Msgr. Saverio C. '55 (RVC) Dix Hills, NY St. Matthew Church.
Matteo, James P. '72 (PH) [76] Philadelphia, PA St. Joan of Arc Church.
Mattern, Joseph A. '59 (GB) Omro, WI St. Mary Church.
Matteucig, Joseph *s.x.* '84 (FgM) Xaverian Foreign Missions.
Matteucig, Joseph *s.x.* '84 (PAT) [M] Wayne, NJ Xaverian Missionary Fathers.
Mattey, Joseph J. '65 (SCR) Taylor, PA St. John the Baptist Church.
Matthew, Augustine *c.m.i.* '81 (NY) [5] Mt. Vernon, NY SS. Peter and Paul Church.
Matthew, Thomas '80 (SFR) San Bruno, CA St. Bruno Church.
Matthews, Andre '84 (ROM) Chesterland, OH Most Holy Trinity Church; Cleveland, OH St. Helena Church; Lorain, OH St. Basil Church.
Matthews, Donald C. *s.j.* '63 (NY) [DD] New York, NY Jesuit Community at Fordham University.
Matthews, Edward *o.m.i.* '84 (JUN) Wrangell, AK St. Rose of Lima Church.
Matthews, Edward R. *o.m.i.* '84 (FgM) Oblates Foreign Missions.
Matthews, Francis *o.f.m.* '88 (NY) [35] New York, NY St. Francis of Assisi Church.
Matthews, James '74 (OAK) [5] Oakland, CA St. Benedict Church.
Matthews, Ron '75 (ALX) On Duty Outside the Diocese.
Matthews, Ron '75 (SHP) Bossier City, LA Christ the King Church.
Matthiesen, Msgr. Monroe J. '43 (AMA) [D] Panhandle, TX St. Ann's Nursing Home; [D] Panhandle, TX St. Joseph's Home for Retired Priests.
Matthys, Donald R. *s.j.* '68 (MIL) [P] Milwaukee, WI Jesuit Community at Marquette University.
Mattice, George F. '64 (SY) Special Assignment.
Mattiello, Lucian C. '45 (ALT) Retired.
Mattimoe, Edward J. *s.j.* '65 (DET) [K] Detroit, MI Jesuit Provincial Office-Detroit Province of the Society of Jesus.
Mattimoe, Edward J. *s.j.* '65 (NY) [DD] New York, NY "America;" Residence and publication office of the America Press.
Mattimore, John J. *s.j.* '88 (BUF) [D] Buffalo, NY Canisius High School; [O] Buffalo, NY Canisius Jesuit Community.
Mattimore, John J. *s.j.* '88 (NY) [F] New York, NY Fordham Preparatory School.
Mattimore, William '51 (HON) Waimanalo, HI St. George Church.
Mattimore, William F. '51 (WOR) Retired.
Mattina, Louis A. '95 (MET) Bound Brook, NJ St. Joseph Church.
Mattingly, Allen J. *o.s.b.* '57 (PEO) [A] Peru, IL St. Bede Abbey and Academy.
Mattingly, Basil *o.s.b.* '46 (SD) [H] Oceanside, CA Prince of Peace Abbey, Benet Hill.
Mattingly, Jerry Alan '95 (JKS) Madison, MS St. Francis of Assisi Church.
Mattingly, John F. *s.s.* '48 (BAL) [J] Baltimore, MD St. Charles Villa; [M] Baltimore, MD St. Charles Villa.
Mattingly, John S. '72 (WDC) Newtowne, MD St. Francis Xavier Church.
Mattingly, Lawrence *o.f.m.conv.* (FgM) Conventual Franciscan Foreign Missions.
Mattingly, Lawrence *o.f.m.conv.* '64 (AUS) [3] Austin, TX Cristo Rey Church.
Mattingly, Martin '50 (OWN) Dawson Springs, KY Resurrection Church; Earlington, KY Immaculate Conception Church.
Mattingly, Robert '68 (VEN) Murdock, FL St. Maximilian Kolbe Church.
Mattingly, Thomas E. '97 (RIC) [5] Virginia Beach, VA Holy Spirit Church.
Mattioni, George *o.a.r.* '53 (NY) Suffern, NY Good Samaritan Hospital; [B] Suffern, NY Tagaste Monastery; [W] Suffern, NY Good Samaritan Hospital of Suffern.
Mattison, James H. '78 (BUR) Island Pond, VT St. James the Greater Church.
Mattison, Thomas V. '82 (BUR) Fairfield, VT St. Patrick Church.
Mattler, Albert A. '56 (STL) Flint Hill, MO St. Theodore Church.
Mattosha, Mansour (OLL) Hillside, IL Our Lady of Lebanon Church.
Mattscheck, John J. '53 (CIN) [38] Cincinnati, OH St. Ignatius Loyola Church; [V] Cincinnati, OH Priests Eucharistic League.
Mattucci, James J. '46 (MAD) Retired; [H] Janesville, WI St. Elizabeth Home.
Mattulke, Arthur J. '97 (BUF) Blossom, NY St. Gabriel Church.
Matty, Richard A. '83 (ELP) [1] El Paso, TX St. Patrick's Cathedral.
Matula, Lawrence *v.f.* '62 (VIC) El Campo, TX St. Robert Bellarmine Church.
Matula, Stanley '59 (SY) [9] Syracuse, NY Sacred Heart Church.
Matulenas, Raymond A. *o.s.b.* '40 (PEO) [A] Peru, IL St. Bede Abbey and Academy.
Matulewicz, Ronald '59 (ALB) Hagaman, NY St. Stephen Church.
Matulik, Martin '52 (Y) Retired.
Matulis, Albert J. '58 (NEW) [8] Bayonne, NJ St. Michael's Church.
Maturi, John Alexander Gregory *o.p.* (NY) Manhattan, NY Hospital for Special Surgery.
Maturi, John Gregory (NY) [GG] New York, NY University Apostolate.
Matus, Walter J. '70 (AUS) Killeen, TX St. Joseph Church.
Matusak, Michael W. '75 (GBG) Mount Pleasant, PA St. Pius X Church.
Matusz, Michael A. '89 (CLV) [4] Garfield Heights, OH St. Timothy Church.
Matuszak, Edward S. '55 (LFT) Retired.
Matuszak, Walter L. '58 (BUF) [11] Cheektowaga, NY Resurrection Church.
Matuszewski, Ramon '57 (SAG) Pinconning, MI St. Michael Church.
Matutis, Joseph J. '41 (HRT) Retired.
Maty, Robert J. '57 (BGP) [10] Bridgeport, CT Holy Rosary Church.
Matya, Robert A. '95 (LIN) [1] Lincoln, NE Cathedral of the Risen Christ.
Matyas, Francis B. '42 (STL) Retired.
Matyas, William *o.s.b.* '53 (CLV) [Q] Cleveland, OH Sisters of the Incarnate Word and Blessed Sacrament.
Matyas, William T. *o.s.b.* '53 (CLV) [P] Cleveland, OH Benedictine Order of Cleveland.
Matysik, Robert T. '84 (CAM) Somers Point, NJ St. Joseph's Church.
Matz, David *c.pp.s.* '95 (SAN) [3] Abilene, TX St. Francis of Assisi Church; [4] Abilene, TX St. Vincent Pallotti Church.
Matz, George A. '66 (KCK) Garnett, KS Holy Angels Church.
Matz, Joseph A. '64 (SCR) Jessup, PA St. James Church.
Matz, Leo '61 (MRY) Retired.
Matz, Michael J. '84 (PH) Bryn Mawr, PA St. John Neumann Church.
Matzek, William J. '63 (LC) Onalaska, WI St. Patrick Church.
Matzinger, Robert J. *c.s.b.* '57 (GAL) Sugar Land, TX St. Theresa Church.
Matzko, David *s.j.* '79 (CHY) [C] St. Stephens, WY St. Stephens Mission - Jesuit Community.
Matzko, David G. *s.j.* '79 (CHY) St. Stephens, WY St. Stephen's Church.
Matzko, David G. *s.j.* '79 (OM) [K] Omaha, NE Jesuit Community At Creighton University.
Mau, Joseph '39 (LAF) Retired.
Mau, Nguyen Duc *c.ss.r.* '70 (LA) [R] Baldwin Park, CA Vietnamese Redemptorist Mission.
Mauck, George A. '77 (BEL) Carlyle, IL St. Mary Church; Centralia, IL Centralia Correctional Center.
Maudlin, Stanislaus *o.s.b.* '42 (SFS) [F] Marvin, SD Blue Cloud Abbey.
Mauel, James E. *s.j.* '57 (MIL) [P] Milwaukee, WI Jesuit Community at Marquette University; [Q] Milwaukee, WI St. Joseph Convent, General Motherhouse of the School Sisters of St. Francis; [S] Milwaukee, WI Cardoner Retreat Center.
Mauel, John N. '50 (LC) Retired.
Mauer, Elmar *o.m.i.* '64 (BEL) Centreville, IL Immaculate Conception Church.
Maufort, Msgr. Richard A. '54 (GB) Special Assignment.
Maughan, Michael *s.m.a.* '43 (BEL) Retired.
Maughan, Richard N. '72 (NO) [10] Metairie, LA St. Lawrence the Martyr Church.
Maul, William '55 (SFD) Raymond, IL St Raymond Church.
Maullon, Alberto A., Jr. '82 (GAL) Katy, TX St. Bartholomew The Apostle Church.
Maung, Chrysostom Ah (WCH) Columbus, KS St. Rose Church; Scammon, KS St. Bridget's Church.
Maung, John S. '63 (IND) Shelbyville, IN St. Joseph Church.
Mauntel, Robert J. '49 (CIN) Retired.
Maurer, Daniel J. '97 (PIT) Graduate Studies.
Maurer, Edward L. '69 (BRK) [242] Queens, NY St. Stanislaus Kostka Church.
Maurer, Paul F. '43 (PH) [44] Philadelphia, PA Epiphany of Our Lord Church; Retired.
Maurer, Russell J. '60 (PIT) Blawnox, PA St. Edward Church.
Maurer, Thomas *s.d.s.* '64 (NSH) Dover, TN St. Francis of Assisi Church.
Mauricci, Bruno *o.p.* '90 (PHX) [5] Phoenix, AZ Most Holy Trinity Church.
Mauricio, Francisco S. *c.s.b.* '97 (GAL) [Q] Sugar Land, TX Basilian Mission Center.
Mauriello, Matthew R. '88 (BGP) [12] Stamford, CT Our Lady of Montserrat Church.
Maus, Christopher '93 (DET) [41] Detroit, MI St. Jude Church.
Maus, LeRoy '66 (SCL) Bertha, MN St. Joseph's Church; Henning, MN Church of St. Edward of Henning.
Maus, Marc T. '91 (STP) Monticello, MN St. Henry Church.
Maus, Omer *o.s.b.* '45 (SCL) [I] Collegeville, MN St. John's Abbey, of the Order of St. Benedict.
Maus, Msgr. Rudolph E. '39 (LR) Retired.
Mausolf, James H. '50 (GAY) Retired.
Mauss, Jasper *o.f.m.* '39 (SAT) [T] San Antonio, TX Pilgrim Center of Hope - Evangelization Center.
Mauthe, Richard '58 (GB) Dyckesville, WI St. Louis Church.
Mawhinney, John J. *s.j.* '65 (BAL) [M] Baltimore, MD Jesuit Fathers and Brothers Maryland Provincial Curia.
Mawhinney, John J. *s.j.* '65 (FgM) Provinces.
Mawicke, Joseph '63 (SB) Thousand Palms, CA St. Philip the Apostle Church.
Mawn, Benedict *c.p.* '45 (MET) [H] South River, NJ Passionist Provincial Office.
Mawn, Francis X. '82 (BO) [2] Chelsea, MA St. Rose of Lima Church.
Maxa, Edward J. '59 (CHI) [92] Chicago, IL Immaculate Conception Church.
Maxcy, Walter J. *m.m.* '47 (FgM) Maryknoll Foreign Missions.
Maxfield, Leo *m.s.* '55 (MAN) [M] Enfield, NH La Salette Shrine and Center of Enfield.
Maxim, Craig '91 (KC) On Duty Outside the Diocese.
Maxwell, Bruce C. *o.s.c.* '75 (DET) [K] Riverview, MI Crosier Community of Riverview.
Maxwell, Herbert (CHI) [J] Evanston, IL Saint Francis Hospital of Evanston.
Maxwell, John '59 (OAK) El Cerrito, CA St. John the Baptist Church.
Maxwell, Palmer *o.c.d.* '88 (SAT) [H] San Antonio, TX Santa Rosa Health Care System.
May, Anthony C. '75 (SD) Lakeside, CA Blessed Kateri Tekakwitha Church.
May, Douglas *m.m.* '86 (BUF) [O] Buffalo, NY Maryknoll House.
May, Gregory *c.ss.r.* '88 (DET) [33] Detroit, MI Holy Redeemer Church.
May, Herbert '75 (LKC) Welsh, LA Our Lady of the Seven Dolors Church.
May, James *c.ss.r.* '41 (NY) [92] New York, NY Our Lady of Perpetual Help Church.
May, Michael K. *s.j.* (STL) [C] St. Louis, MO Saint Louis University.
May, Michael K. *s.j.* '93 (STL) [P] St. Louis, MO Jesuit Community Corporation at St. Louis University - Jesuit Hall.
May, Raymond '93 (KCK) [J] Lawrence, KS St. Lawrence Catholic Campus Center at the University of Kansas and Residence.
May, Ronald P. '86 (HRT) Collinsville, CT St. Patrick's Church.
May, Thomas P. '83 (CHI) [108] Chicago, IL St. John Fisher Church.
Maya, Manuel *o.s.m.* '58 (ORG) Fullerton, CA St. Philip Benizi Church.
Maya, Tulio *s.d.s.* '56 (PHX) [17] Phoenix, AZ St. Mark Church; Phoenix, AZ Maricopa Medical Center.
Mayall, Daniel G. '77 (CHI) [64] Chicago, IL St. Francis Borgia Church.
Maybrier, Michael J. '86 (WCH) Chanute, KS St. Patrick Church; Humboldt, KS St. Joseph Church.
Mayefske, Thomas '62 (GB) On Duty Outside the Diocese.
Mayer, Charles P. '96 (LA) Northridge, CA Our Lady of Lourdes Church.
Mayer, David *s.v.d.* '66 (FgM) Society of the Divine Word Foreign Missions.
Mayer, Douglas J. '86 (GRY) Valparaiso, IN Our Lady of Sorrows Church.
Mayer, Francis X. *s.j.* '50 (FgM) Provinces.
Mayer, James *o.de.m.* '91 (CLV) [57] Cleveland, OH Our Lady of Mount Carmel Church.
Mayer, James '93 (CLV) Cleveland, OH Lutheran Medical Center; [P] Cleveland, OH Mercedarians.
Mayer, John L. '64 (STL) Millwood, MO St. Alphonsus Church.
Mayer, Jules A. '64 (LA) [77] Los Angeles, CA St. Marcellinus Church.

Mayer, Kenneth H. *o.s.b.* '42 (PAT) [M] Morristown, NJ St. Mary's Abbey.
Mayer, Laurence A. *o.praem.* '65 (GB) [I] De Pere, WI St. Norbert Abbey.
Mayer, Lawrence A. *o.praem.* '65 (GB) [A] De Pere, WI St. Norbert Abbey.
Mayer, Msgr. Richard G. '61 (E) West Middlesex, PA Good Shepherd Church.
Mayer, Robert *o.m.i.* '67 (FgM) Oblates Foreign Missions.
Mayer, Robert J. *s.j.* '57 (FgM) Provinces.
Mayer, Walter W. '59 (OAK) Livermore, CA St. Michael's Church.
Mayer, William J. *s.j.* '74 (PMB) [3] West Palm Beach, FL St. Ann Church.
Mayers, Gregory *c.ss.r.* '70 (AMA) [H] Amarillo, TX Bishop DeFalco Retreat Center.
Mayfield, Leo *m.s.* '55 (MAN) [K] Enfield, NH Shrine of Our Lady of La Salette.
Mayfield, Olin W. '96 (LA) Diamond Bar, CA St. Denis Church.
Mayhew, John A. *c.j.* '65 (LA) Santa Maria, CA St. Louis de Montfort Church; [B] Santa Maria, CA St. Joseph Seminary (Josephite Fathers' Novitiate).
Maynard, George C. *s.j.* '61 (DET) [K] Detroit, MI Jesuit Provincial Office-Detroit Province of the Society of Jesus.
Maynard, George C. *s.j.* '61 (LEX) Lexington, KY Veterans Administration Hospital.
Maynard, Jack G. *s.f.o.* '78 (COL) Lancaster, OH St. Mary Church.
Maynard, Joseph V. *m.m.* '48 (FgM) Maryknoll Foreign Missions.
Maynard, Leo E. '47 (HRT) Retired.
Maynard, Leon C. '54 (PRO) Retired; [P] Providence, RI St. John Vianney Residence.
Maynard, Lewis H. '69 (BRK) [2] Brooklyn, NY St. Agatha's Church.
Maynard, Richard C. (PRO) [6] Pawtucket, RI St. Joseph Church.
Maynard, Richard C. '56 (PRO) Retired.
Maynard, Robert J. '48 (PRO) [7] Cranston, RI St. Paul Church; Retired.
Mayne, Kenneth '94 (LAF) Abbeville, LA St. Mary Magdalen Church.
Mayo, J. Aidan '76 (P) Sandy, OR St. Michael the Archangel Church.
Mayo, James M. '79 (SAV) [3] Savannah, GA St. Benedict the Moor Church.
Mayo, Joseph M. '73 (SLC) [2] Kearns, UT St. Francis Xavier Church; [C] Kearns, UT St. Francis Xavier Regional School.
Mayo, Reid C. '63 (BUR) Rutland, VT Christ the King Church.
Mayotte, Allan J. '60 (MAR) Wakefield, MI Immaculate Conception of the Blessed Virgin Mary Church.
Mayovsky, David '97 (SEA) Bremerton, WA Our Lady, Star of the Sea Church.
Mayovsky, Frederick P. *s.j.* '75 (SEA) [C] Tacoma, WA Bellarmine Preparatory School.
Mayovsky, Gerald L. '59 (SEA) [30] Seattle, WA Our Lady of Lourdes Church; Tukwila, WA St. Thomas Church.
Mayworm, James A. '66 (DET) Auburn Hills, MI Sacred Heart Church.
Mayzik, James J. *s.j.* '85 (BGP) [A] Fairfield, CT Fairfield University; [O] Fairfield, CT The Fairfield Jesuit Community-Fairfield University.
Mazaika, Joseph J. '53 (TLS) Retired.
Mazanec, James '81 (CLV) Bedford, OH St. Pius X Church.
Mazon, Diego *o.f.m.* '60 (GLP) [2] Gallup, NM St. Francis of Assisi Church.
Mazouch, Charles J. '73 (DOD) Great Bend, KS St. Rose of Lima Church.
Mazuchowski, Hyacinth '63 (BEL) Flora, IL St. Stephen Church.
Mazuelas, Paulino *o.s.b.* '54 (MGZ) [6] Mayaquez, PR Sacred Heart Church.
Mazur, Clarence *o.f.m.* '42 (GRY) [J] Cedar Lake, IN Our Lady of Lourdes Friary.
Mazur, Francis X. (BUF) [26] Buffalo, NY St. Gerard Church.
Mazur, Robert C. '76 (ALT) [1] Altoona, PA Cathedral of the Blessed Sacrament.
Mazur, Timothy '95 (DET) [9] Warren, MI St. Martin de Porres Church.
Mazurchuk, Michael *c.m.* '86 (PH) [69] Philadelphia, PA Immaculate Conception Church.
Mazurek, James K. '73 (DET) [A] Orchard Lake, MI SS. Cyril and Methodius Seminary; [C] Orchard Lake, MI Saint Mary's College.
Mazurek, James K. '73 (PIT) On Duty Outside the Diocese.
Mazurkiewicz, Msgr. Benedict J. '55 (AUS) Fayetteville, TX St. John's Church.
Mazurkiewicz, Msgr. Harry C. '51 (AUS) La Grange, TX Sacred Heart of Jesus Church.
Mazurkiewicz, Joseph '84 (ALT) Somerset, PA St. Peter's Church; Somerset, PA State Correctional Institution.
Mazuryk, Ivan '97 (STF) Pittsfield, MA St. John the Baptist Church.
Mazuyk, Ivan '97 (STF) Hudson, NY St. Nicholas Church.
Mazza, Louis J. '53 (NY) North Tarrytown, NY Immaculate Conception Church.
Mazza, Mark G. '80 (GRY) North Judson, IN Ss. Cyril and Methodius Church.
Mazza, Victor J. '70 (PAT) [7] Clifton, NJ St. Paul Church.
Mazzarella, Cadmus D. '85 (CAM) Clayton, NJ St. Catherine's Church; [R] Glassboro, NJ Rowan University.
Mazzarella, Frederick *o.f.m.* '61 (NY) [DD] New York, NY Franciscan Province of the Immaculate Conception.
Mazziotta, Msgr. Robert R. '41 (NY) [220] Staten Island, NY Our Lady of Pity Church; Retired.
Mazzitello, John A. *s.j.* '69 (STP) [N] Minneapolis, MN La Storta Jesuit Community.
Mazzocchia, George *o.f.m.* '40 (NY) [DD] New York, NY Padua Friary.
Mazzola, Robert E. *s.t.b.* '63 (IND) Greenfield, IN St. Michael Church.
Mazzuchelli, Matthew C. *o.s.b.* '58 (PEO) [A] Peru, IL St. Bede Abbey and Academy.
Mbah, Jonathan U. *c.s.sp.* (PH) Media, PA St. Mary Magdalen Church.
Mbarikatta, Cletus *c.s.sp.* (PIT) Scott Township, PA Our Lady of Grace Church.
Mbemba, Jean Claude *c.s.sp.* '86 (PIT) [40] Pittsburgh, PA St. Patrick-St. Stanislaus Kostka Church.
Mbogo, Lawrence (SY) Vestal, NY Our Lady of Sorrows Church.
Mbogu, Christopher '83 (PIT) [3] McKees Rocks, PA St. John of God Church.
Mc Cullough, Michael '74 (LA) Burbank, CA St. Finbar Church.
Mc G.A. Nugent, Frank *s.j.* '50 (ALN) [A] Wernersville, PA Novitiate of St. Isaac Jogues.
Mc Menemie, Msgr. James '53 (NEW) Lyndhurst, NJ St. Michael's Church.
McAfee, Franklyn M. '71 (ARL) Great Falls, VA St. Catherine of Siena Church.
McAlear, Richard *o.m.i.* '70 (WDC) [B] Washington, DC Oblate College/Oblate Center for Mission Studies.
McAleer, Robert T. '71 (DAV) [3] Fort Madison, IA SS. Mary & Joseph Church.
McAlinden, Terence O. '67 (TR) Tuckerton, NJ St. Teresa Church.
McAlister, Msgr. Lawrence J. '44 (BRK) [150] Queens, NY St. Andrew Avellino Church.
McAlister, Msgr. Lawrence J. '59 (BRK) Retired.
McAlister, Richard A. *o.p.* '61 (PRO) [P] Providence, RI St. Thomas Aquinas Priory at Providence College.
McAllister, Alex '86 (SR) Retired.
McAllister, Donald '71 (PRT) Portland, ME Mercy Hospital; Portland, ME Maine Medical Center; [H] Portland, ME Mercy Hospital.
McAllister, Leo '54 (SAC) Carmichael, CA Our Lady of the Assumption Church.
McAllister, Robert J. *s.j.* '51 (ALN) [A] Wernersville, PA Novitiate of St. Isaac Jogues.
McAloon, Francis X. *s.j.* '92 (OAK) [N] Berkeley, CA Jesuit Community at Jesuit School of Theology at Berkeley.
McAlpin, James C. '64 (SC) Manning, IA Sacred Heart Church.
McAlpin, Leonard '69 (GBG) Fayette City, PA Holy Spirit Church.
McAlpine, Harry D. '87 (SC) Fort Dodge, IA Sacred Heart Church.
McAndrew, David T. '63 (HBG) [1] Lebanon, PA Assumption of the Blessed Virgin Mary Church; [G] Lebanon, PA Villa Vianney.
McAndrew, John '86 (ORG) Brea, CA St. Angela Merici Church.
McAndrew, John P. *c.s.sp.* '67 (PIT) [Q] Bethel Park, PA Holy Ghost Animation Center.
McAndrew, Joseph P. '85 (NY) [147] Bronx, NY Holy Family Church.
McAndrew, Michael *c.ss.r.* '73 (DEN) [33] Denver, CO St. Joseph's Church.
McAndrew, Stephen *o.m.v.* '91 (BO) [B] Boston, MA Oblate Provincialate.
McAndrew, Thomas F. '61 (DUB) Manly, IA Sacred Heart Church; Plymouth, IA St. Michael Church.
McAndrews, Msgr. Donald A. '54 (SCR) [1] Wilkes-Barre, PA St. Aloysius Church.
McAndrews, James F. *s.j.* '62 (BAL) [C] Baltimore, MD Loyola High School.
McAndrews, Richard J. '67 (PH) [110] Philadelphia, PA Nativity of the Blessed Virgin Mary Church.
McAnerney, Brendan *o.p.* '88 (P) Ashland, OR Our Lady of the Mountain Church.
McAnulty, John D. *s.j.* '57 (LA) [R] Los Angeles, CA Columbiere House.
McArdle, John F. '51 (MAR) Retired.
McArdle, Msgr. Joseph G. '38 (MOB) Retired; [F] Mobile, AL Little Sisters of the Poor, Home For the Aged, Inc.
McArdle, Kevin *o.c.d.* '43 (TUC) [16] Tucson, AZ St. Margaret's Church; [F] Tucson, AZ Discalced Carmelite Fathers of St. Margaret's.
McArdle, Sean '67 (CAM) Leesburg, NJ New Jersey State Medium Security Prison.
McAree, Msgr. Francis (NY) [D] New York, NY Department of Education.
McAree, Msgr. Francis J. '75 (NY) [A] Yonkers, NY St. Joseph's Seminary.
McArthur, John B. '74 (MEM) [21] Memphis, TN St. Paul The Apostle Church.
McArthur, Luke *s.d.s.* '57 (MIL) [P] Milwaukee, WI Salvatorian Provincial Residence.
McArtney, Robert J. '60 (BUF) [K] Lackawanna, NY Our Lady of Victory Hospital.
McAskill, Kenneth F. (BO) Retired.
McAskill, Kenneth F. '50 (BO) [3] Arlington, MA St. James the Apostle Church.
McAtavey, John J. '54 (PMB) Tequesta, FL St. Jude Church; Retired.
McAtee, John F. *o.s.a.* '66 (PH) [B] Villanova, PA St. Augustine Friary.
McAteer, James P. *i.c.* '64 (PEO) Galesburg, IL Corpus Christi Church.
McAteer, Kenneth P. '73 (PH) [119] Philadelphia, PA Our Lady of Hope Church.
McAteer, Patrick J. *s.j.* '73 (CHI) [89] Chicago, IL St. Ignatius Church.
McAuley, James D. *m.m.* '80 (FgM) Maryknoll Foreign Missions.
McAuley, John J. *m.m.* '81 (NY) [46] New York, NY Holy Family Church; [DD] Maryknoll, NY Maryknoll Fathers and Brothers.
McAuliff, Dennis (BRK) [E] Brooklyn, NY Office of Religious Education: Evangelization and Catholic Formation.
McAuliff, R. Richard *s.j.* '92 (MI) Majuro, MH Cathedral of the Assumption.
McAuliff, Richard R. *s.j.* '92 (FgM) Provinces.
McAuliffe, Dennis '73 (BRK) [13] Brooklyn, NY St. Athanasius Church.
McAuliffe, Kevin W. *j.c.l.* '90 (LAV) [8] Las Vegas, NV St. Elizabeth Ann Seton Church.
McAuliffe, Robert F. '57 (BO) [3] Arlington, MA St. James the Apostle Church.
McAuliffe, Robert J. (BO) Retired.
McAuliffe, Roger D. *s.j.* '49 (SJ) [M] Los Gatos, CA Sacred Heart Jesuit Center.
McAvey, James R. *o.p.* '39 (PRO) [P] Providence, RI St. Thomas Aquinas Priory at Providence College.
McAvoy, Msgr. Ambrose A. '39 (DUB) Retired.
McAvoy, Msgr. C. J. '63 (OG) [2] Plattsburgh, NY St. John the Baptist Church.
McBrady, Lawrence J. '71 (CHI) [90] Chicago, IL Immaculate Conception of the Blessed Virgin Mary Church.
McBrearity, Gerald *s.s.* '73 (SAT) [A] San Antonio, TX The Assumption-St. John's Seminary.
McBrearity, Gerald D. '84 (ATL) On Duty Outside the Archdiocese.
McBrearty, John J. *s.s.j.* '68 (ARL) [4] Alexandria, VA St. Joseph's Church.
McBrearty, William J. *s.j.* '47 (SY) [S] Syracuse, NY Jesuits at LeMoyne, Inc.
McBriar, David J. *o.f.m.* (R) [3] Durham, NC Immaculate Conception Church.
McBride, Alfred *o.praem.* '53 (BO) [A] Weston, MA Pope John XXIII National Seminary.
McBride, Alfred A. '53 (GB) [I] De Pere, WI St. Norbert Abbey.
McBride, Brendan '75 (SFR) [46] San Francisco, CA St. Philip the Apostle Church.
McBride, Daniel (PHX) Flagstaff, AZ San Francisco de Asis Church.
McBride, Daniel '51 (CLV) Northfield, OH St. Barnabas Church.
McBride, Eugene J. *o.s.f.s.* '89 (ARL) Vienna, VA Our Lady of Good Counsel Church.
McBride, Gerald E. '91 (TR) New Monmouth, NJ St. Mary Church.
McBride, Harold E. *s.m.m.* '47 (RVC) Bay Shore, NY Southside Hospital; [N] Bay Shore, NY Montfort Missionaries.
McBride, Henry '61 (CAM) Somerdale, NJ Our Lady of Grace Church.
McBride, Msgr. James P. '56 (PH) [83] Philadelphia, PA St. Katherine of Siena Church.
McBride, John *s.j.* '61 (P) [L] Portland, OR Colombiere Community.
McBride, John F. '62 (PH) Hilltown, PA Our Lady of the Sacred Heart Church.
McBride, Larry '87 (OWN) [6] Owensboro, KY St. Pius Tenth Church.
McBride, Malachy R. *o.f.m. cap.* '62 (DEN) [1] Aurora, CO Queen of Peace Church; [M] Denver, CO St. Francis of Assisi Friary.
McBride, Patrick *c.ss.r.* '85 (FgM) Redemptorist Foreign Missions.
McBride, Msgr. Peter A. (PAT) Unassigned.
McBride, Robert G. '72 (NEW) Saddle Brook, NJ St. Philip the Apostle Church.

McBride, Thomas A. *m.m.* '57 (FgM) Maryknoll Foreign Missions.
McBride, William F. '82 (MAD) Leave of Absence.
McBride, William T. '42 (PH) Richboro, PA St. Vincent de Paul Church; Retired.
McBrien, Kevin F. '86 (BRK) [174] Queens, NY St. Gregory the Great Church.
McBrien, Richard P. '62 (FTW) [B] Notre Dame, IN University of Notre Dame Du Lac.
McBrien, Richard P. '62 (HRT) On Duty Outside the Archdiocese.
McBurney, James D. *o.s.a.* '84 (PH) [B] Villanova, PA St. Augustine Friary.
McCaa, Msgr. Francis B. '48 (ALT) Retired.
McCabe, Brendan (NY) [16] Yonkers, NY St. Peter Church; County, NY Westchester County Jail; Bronx, NY Montefiore Medical Center.
McCabe, Charles J. '92 (MOB) [19] Mobile, AL St. Pius X Church.
McCabe, Edward D. '68 (BO) Awaiting Assignment.
McCabe, George V. *s.j.* '45 (BO) [W] Weston, MA Campion Health Center, Inc.
McCabe, George V. *s.j.* '45 (SPK) Retired.
McCabe, James F. *c.pp.s.* '58 (CIN) [M] Dayton, OH Provincial House of the Cincinnati Province of the Society of the Precious Blood.
McCabe, James F. *c.pp.s.* '58 (TOL) [M] Bellevue, OH Sorrowful Mother Shrine.
McCabe, James T. '71 (PH) Broomall, PA St. Pius X Church.
McCabe, John H. '55 (RVC) Uniondale, NY Holly Patterson Geriatric Center; [C] Hicksville, NY Holy Trinity.
McCabe, John J. *m.m.* '42 (SJ) [M] Los Altos, CA Maryknoll.
McCabe, John J. '59 (LIN) Hastings, NE St. Cecilia's Church.
McCabe, Joseph V. *m.m.* '77 (FgM) Maryknoll Foreign Missions.
McCabe, Kenneth O. *ss.cc.* '65 (LA) [K] Burbank, CA Providence Health System; [R] Mission Hills, CA Congregation of the Sacred Hearts.
McCabe, Michael G. '89 (LIN) Dawson, NE St. Mary's Church; [C] Falls City, NE Sacred Heart School.
McCabe, Msgr. Patrick A. '61 (CAM) Ocean City, NJ St. Frances Cabrini Church.
McCabe, Paul J. '59 (ROC) [8] Elmira, NY Our Lady of Lourdes Church.
McCabe, Peter '70 (AUS) Giddings, TX State School.
McCabe, Ramon J. *m.m.* '56 (FgM) Maryknoll Foreign Missions.
McCabe, Raymond M. *o.p.* (CAM) [M] Camden, NJ Dominican Sisters of the Perpetual Rosary Chaplain's Residence.
McCabe, Raymond M. *o.p.* '47 (CAM) [N] Camden, NJ Monastery of the Dominican Nuns of the Perpetual Rosary.
McCabe, Msgr. Richard '58 (AUS) [4] Austin, TX Emmaus Catholic Church.
McCabe, Msgr. Robert J. '64 (NY) Forestburgh, NY St. Thomas Aquinas Church.
McCabe, Robert J. '95 (DET) [8] Dearborn, MI Sacred Heart Church.
McCabe, Thomas '92 (STP) Belle Plaine, MN Our Lady of the Prairie Church.
McCabe, Msgr. Vincent '46 (LA) Retired.
McCabe, William J. '41 (SY) Retired.
McCafferty, David L. '64 (CLV) Wickliffe, OH Our Lady of Mount Carmel Church.
McCafferty, James B. *s.m.* '70 (WH) Buckhannon, WV Holy Rosary Church; [Q] Buckhannon, WV West Virginia Wesleyan College Newman Center.
McCafferty, Joseph F. '61 (PH) [Y] Lansdale, PA St. Mary Manor.
McCafferty, Michael F. . '87 (CHR) Hilton Head Island, SC St. Francis By the Sea Church.
McCafferty, Richard *s.j.* '62 (OAK) Livermore, CA St. Charles Borromeo Church.
McCafferty, Richard B. *s.j.* '62 (BO) [W] Boston, MA The Society of Jesus of New England-Provincial Offices.
McCaffrey, Daniel '58 (SAN) On Duty Outside the Diocese.
McCaffrey, Edmund *o.carm.* '53 (NY) [97] New York, NY Our Lady of the Scapular/St. Stephen Church; New York, NY New York City Veterans Administration Hospital; Manhattan, NY U.S.V.A. Medical Center.
McCaffrey, Edmund M. '59 (CHR) Hilton Head Island, SC Holy Family Church.
McCaffrey, Gerald T. *o.f.m.* '58 (BO) [BB] Boston, MA St. Anthony Shrine.
McCaffrey, Gerard D. '45 (PH) Retired.
McCaffrey, Howard A. *s.j.* '47 (NY) [DD] New York, NY Murray-Weigel Hall.
McCaffrey, James L. (SFR) Retired.
McCaffrey, James Leo '58 (STO) Retired.
McCaffrey, James P. *s.j.* '52 (BO) [W] Weston, MA Campion Center.
McCaffrey, Msgr. John '44 (CAM) Retired.
McCaffrey, John '76 (AUS) Bryan, TX St. Joseph's Church.
McCaffrey, John J. '48 (CLV) Sheffield Lake, OH St. Thomas the Apostle Church.
McCaffrey, Joseph (PIT) Lawrence County, PA Youth Development Center.
McCaffrey, Joseph J. '77 (ROC) [7] Elmira, NY St. Anthony Church.
McCaffrey, Joseph P. *c.m.* '54 (PH) [AA] Philadelphia, PA Congregation of the Mission.
McCaffrey, Joseph P. '77 (ROC) [2] Elmira, NY St. Patrick Church.
McCaffrey, Joseph R. '87 (PIT) New Bedford, PA St. James Church.
McCaffrey, Lawrence X. *s.j.* '51 (NY) Harriman, NY St. Anastasia Church; [EE] Harriman, NY St. Patrick's Villa.
McCaffrey, Patrick J. '59 (WDC) [15] Washington, DC St. Gabriel Church.
McCaffrey, Richard L. *s.j.* '73 (FBK) Bethel, AK Immaculate Conception Church; [E] St. Marys, AK Brother Joe Prince Jesuit Community.
McCaffrey, Msgr. Thomas F. '47 (NY) Retired.
McCaffrey, Thomas J. '47 (NY) Scarsdale, NY Our Lady of Fatima Church.
McCaffrey, Msgr. William J. '72 (PRO) [20] Providence, RI St. Joseph Church.
McCahill, Msgr. Patrick P. (NY) [O] New York, NY New York Catholic Deaf Center.
McCahill, Msgr. Patrick P. '68 (NY) [32] New York, NY St. Elizabeth of Hungary Church.
McCahill, Robert T. *m.m.* '64 (FgM) Maryknoll Foreign Missions.
McCahon, Joseph F.S. '75 (SP) Military Chaplains.
McCaig, John J. '58 (CHI) [5] Lemont, IL St. Patrick Church; Retired.
McCain, William '86 (SFR) Special Assignment.
McCall, James T. '60 (CAM) Delair, NJ St. Veronica's Church.
McCall, Msgr. John M. '58 (SP) [4] Largo, FL St. Patrick Church.
McCall, Peter *o.f.m.cap.* '62 (NY) [17] Yonkers, NY Sacred Heart Church; [HH] New York, NY House of Peace, Inc.
McCall, Robert E. *s.s.j.* '46 (BAL) [M] Baltimore, MD St. Joseph Society of the Sacred Heart House of Central Administration; [M] Baltimore, MD St. Joseph's Manor.
McCall, Stephen P. '79 (SD) Carlsbad, CA St. Patrick Church.
McCall, Thomas *s.j.* '52 (NY) State, NY St. Clare's Secure Unit.
McCall, Thomas D. *s.j.* '52 (NY) [DD] New York, NY St. Ignatius Loyola Residence.
McCallin, Frederick D. '42 (DEN) Retired.
McCallister, Charles E. '71 (WH) Absent on Sick Leave; [N] Wheeling, WV Webb Farm Residence.
McCallister, Richard '91 (SEA) Lynden, WA St. Joseph's Church.
McCallum, David C. *s.j.* (BUF) [O] Buffalo, NY Canisius Jesuit Community.
McCallum, Dougald J. '97 (HEL) [1] Helena, MT Cathedral of St. Helena.
McCallum, Gregory Paul '97 (GAY) [1] Alpena, MI St. Anne Church.
McCallum, Msgr. John V. '43 (DAL) Retired.
McCallum, Paul F. '62 (AUS) [19] Austin, TX St. Paul's Church.
McCamley, Martin Dugan '62 (ALT) State College, PA Our Lady of Victory Church.
McCandless, William T. *o.s.f.s.* '94 (PH) [D] Philadelphia, PA Northeast Catholic High School for Boys; [AA] Philadelphia, PA Oblates of St. Francis De Sales.
McCann, Arthur '62 (DM) Des Moines, IA City Chaplaincy Program; [J] Des Moines, IA City Hospital Chaplaincy Service.
McCann, Bill '94 (LSC) Hatch, NM Our Lord of Mercy Church.
McCann, Charles '69 (WDC) Camp Springs, MD St. Philip the Apostle Church.
McCann, James *s.j.* '79 (CIN) [M] Cincinnati, OH Jesuit Community at Xavier Unversity.
McCann, James M. *s.j.* '79 (CHI) [N] Chicago, IL Chicago Province of the Society of Jesus-Provincial Office.
McCann, Joachim *o.s.b.* '91 (P) [L] St. Benedict, OR Mt. Angel Abbey.
McCann, Msgr. John B. '85 (ALN) [3] Allentown, PA Immaculate Conception Church; [F] Allentown, PA Catholic Social Agency-Catholic Charities Administrative Office.
McCann, John H. *s.m.m.* '55 (HRT) Bantam, CT Our Lady of Grace Church.
McCann, Msgr. John J. '65 (RVC) Glen Cove, NY St. Patrick's Church.
McCann, Joseph H. '57 (HRT) [2] New Haven, CT St. Aedan's Church.
McCann, Luke (NY) [GG] New York, NY University Apostolate.
McCann, Robert J. '81 (OAK) [1] Hayward, CA All Saints Church.
McCann, Thomas *c.p.* '66 (R) Greenville, NC St. Gabriel Church.
McCann, Thomas A. '76 (PH) Levittown, PA Queen of the Universe Church.
McCann, Thomas E. '59 (SCR) Harding, PA Church of the Holy Redeemer.
McCann, Thomas W. '68 (CLV) Cuyahoga Falls, OH Immaculate Heart of Mary Church.
McCann, Vincent *o.f.m.* '41 (NY) [35] New York, NY St. Francis of Assisi Church.
McCarragher, Timothy '91 (Y) Absent on Leave.
McCarren, Charles K. '45 (RCK) Retired.
McCarren, Msgr. Edgar (SJ) Retired.
McCarren, Msgr. Edgar P. '43 (OAK) [B] Moraga, CA St. Mary's College.
McCarren, Msgr. Edgar P. '43 (RVC) Retired.
McCarren, Msgr. Edgar P. '43 (SJ) [5] Santa Clara, CA Our Lady of Peace Church.
McCarren, Gerald H. '91 (NEW) [B] South Orange, NJ Seton Hall University.
McCarren, Msgr. John C. '46 (PIT) Retired.
McCarren, Paul J. *s.j.* '74 (WDC) [20] Washington, DC Holy Trinity Church.
McCarren, Msgr. Stephen A. '55 (GBG) Retired.
McCarren, William J. '47 (BRK) Retired.
McCarron, Francis X. *o.m.i.* '45 (BO) [Z] Tewksbury, MA Immaculate Heart of Mary Novitiate-Infirmary.
McCarron, Gerard J. '70 (TR) Freehold, NJ St. Rose of Lima Church.
McCarron, Msgr. Michael D. '77 (RIC) [2] Newport News, VA Our Lady of Mount Carmel Church.
McCarthy, Anthony T. '71 (MIL) North Lake, WI St. Clare Church.
McCarthy, Bernard '47 (HEL) Retired.
McCarthy, Brian P. '75 (NY) [4] Yonkers, NY St. Bartholomew Church.
McCarthy, Brien R. '81 (WDC) [4] Washington, DC Annunciation Church; Special Ministries; [S] Washington, DC Archdiocesan Campus Ministry.
McCarthy, Carl '95 (OWN) Bowling Green, KY Holy Spirit Church.
McCarthy, Charles '81 (NTN) On Special Projects.
McCarthy, Charles A. *c.s.sp.* '51 (PEO) Eagle Township, IL Annunciation of Blessed Virgin Mary Church; Leonore, IL SS. Peter and Paul's Church.
McCarthy, Charles L. '50 (ROC) Retired.
McCarthy, Msgr. Charles W. '48 (BO) Retired; [Q] Brighton, MA St. Elizabeth's Hospital of Boston.
McCarthy, Cornelius Scott '74 (MRY) Carmel Valley, CA Our Lady of Mt. Carmel Church.
McCarthy, D. Joseph '78 (SAC) [J] Chico, CA Director of Campus Ministry.
McCarthy, Daniel *c.s.sp.* '66 (NY) [69] New York, NY St. Mark the Evangelist Church.
McCarthy, Daniel *o.s.b.* '91 (KCK) Wathena, KS St. Joseph's Church.
McCarthy, Daniel A. '37 (SCR) Retired.
McCarthy, Daniel J. *ss.cc.* '42 (BO) [31] Boston, MA St. James the Greater Church; Boston, MA New England Medical Center.
McCarthy, Daniel P. '43 (SR) [2] Santa Rosa, CA Holy Spirit Church; Retired.
McCarthy, Daniel P. '67 (CHI) [161] Chicago, IL Our Lady of Victory Church.
McCarthy, Daniel P. *o.s.b.* '91 (KCK) Bendena, KS St. Benedict's Church; Troy, KS St. Charles Church.
McCarthy, David F. *s.j.* '52 (DET) [P] Clarkston, MI Colombiere Center.
McCarthy, David J. '60 (CLV) Doylestown, OH SS. Peter and Paul Church.
McCarthy, Donal *ss.cc.* '65 (LA) [D] La Verne, CA Damien Boys High School; [R] La Verne, CA Congregation of the Sacred Hearts.
McCarthy, Donald E. *c.s.b.* '58 (ROC) Webster, NY St. Rita Church; [I] Rochester, NY Basilian Residence.
McCarthy, Donald G. '54 (CIN) [11] Cincinnati, OH St. Antoninus Church.
McCarthy, Donald P. '59 (SAL) Hill City, KS Immaculate Heart of Mary Church.
McCarthy, Edward '71 (ORL) Merritt Island, FL Divine Mercy Church.
McCarthy, Edward A. '43 (MIA) Retired.
McCarthy, Edward J. *s.j.* '49 (MIL) [P] Milwaukee, WI Jesuit Provincial Office, Wisconsin Province.
McCarthy, Edward P. *c.pp.s.* '40 (LFT) [A] Rensselaer, IN Saint Joseph's College.
McCarthy, Emmanuel Charles (NTN) [A] Newton, MA Seminary of St. Gregory the Theologian.
McCarthy, Msgr. Emmett '43 (ORG) Brea, CA St. Angela Merici Church; Retired.
McCarthy, Eugene J. '60 (VEN) Marco Island, FL San Marco Church.
McCarthy, Francis *s.s.j.* '51 (GAL) [62] Houston, TX Our Mother of Mercy Church.
McCarthy, Francis *o.carm.* '51 (JOL) [J] Darien, IL Carmelite Provincial Office.
McCarthy, Francis *o.carm.* '51 (TUC) [B] Nogales, AZ Our Lady of Lourdes High School.
McCarthy, Francis W. *c.pp.s.* '42 (CIN) [M] Dayton, OH Provincial House of the Cincinnati Province of the

Society of the Precious Blood.
McCarthy, Francis X. '54 (MIA) [8] Fort Lauderdale, FL St. Jerome Church.
McCarthy, George B. '56 (PRO) [4] Newport, RI St. Mary Church.
McCarthy, Gerald '57 (FAR) St. John, ND St. John the Baptist Church.
McCarthy, J. Joseph '66 (FgM) Society of St. James the Apostle.
McCarthy, James '45 (FR) Retired.
McCarthy, Msgr. James '68 (NY) [1] New York, NY Cathedral of St. Patrick.
McCarthy, James C. '62 (HEL) [E] Butte, MT St. James Community Hospital, Inc.
McCarthy, Msgr. James F. '68 (NY) Shrub Oak, NY Saint Elizabeth Ann Seton Church.
McCarthy, James H. '55 (CHI) Other Assignments.
McCarthy, Jeremiah *m.s.c.* '50 (SAN) Big Spring, TX Immaculate Heart of Mary Church.
McCarthy, Jeremiah '72 (LA) [A] Camarillo, CA St. John's Seminary.
McCarthy, Jeremiah J. '66 (BO) Society of St. James the Apostle.
McCarthy, Msgr. Jeremiah J. '72 (LA) [A] Camarillo, CA St. John's Seminary.
McCarthy, Jeremiah J. '72 (TUC) On Duty Outside the Diocese.
McCarthy, Jeremiah J. '78 (SAV) [4] Savannah, GA Most Blessed Sacrament Church.
McCarthy, Jerry '45 (TLS) Retired.
McCarthy, John *c.ss.r.* '62 (FgM) Redemptorist Foreign Missions.
McCarthy, John E. *c.s.c.* '58 (FR) [A] North Easton, MA Stonehill College; [A] North Easton, MA Holy Cross Fathers Religious.
McCarthy, Msgr. John F. '55 (HEL) On Duty Outside the Diocese.
McCarthy, John J. *m.s.* '69 (HRT) [M] Hartford, CT Missionaries of LaSalette Provincial Secretary.
McCarthy, John J. '84 (HRT) [1] Hartford, CT Cathedral of St. Joseph; Special and other (Arch)Diocesan Assignment.
McCarthy, John L. *s.j.* '62 (STL) [P] St. Louis, MO Jesuit Community Corporation at St. Louis University - Jesuit Hall.
McCarthy, Msgr. John M. '54 (NY) [222] Staten Island, NY St. Patrick Church.
McCarthy, John M. *m.s.* '69 (STL) [P] St. Louis, MO La Salette Missionaries.
McCarthy, John R. '55 (CLV) East Cleveland, OH St. Philomena Church.
McCarthy, John R. '55 (STU) On Duty Outside the Diocese.
McCarthy, Jose *o.f.m.cap.* '60 (ARE) [1] Utuado, PR San Miquel Church.
McCarthy, Jose *o.f.m.cap.* '60 (FgM) Capuchin Foreign Missions.
McCarthy, Jose *o.f.m.cap.* '60 (NY) [DD] White Plains, NY St. Conrad Friary.
McCarthy, Joseph F. '48 (SFD) Retired.
McCarthy, Joseph J. *o.carm.* '60 (GAL) [14] Houston, TX St. Bernadette Soubirous Church.
McCarthy, Joseph L. '69 (CHL) Retired.
McCarthy, Joseph S. '96 (BO) [16] Boston, MA St. Brigid Church.
McCarthy, Kevin P. '89 (GRY) [N] Valparaiso, IN Newman Apostolate-Valparaiso University.
McCarthy, Leo *o.carm.* '62 (FgM) Carmelite Foreign Missions.
McCarthy, Leo *o.carm.* '62 (JOL) [J] Darien, IL Carmelite Community; [J] Darien, IL Carmelite Provincial Office.
McCarthy, Leo F. *m.m.* '47 (NY) [DD] Maryknoll, NY Maryknoll Fathers and Brothers.
McCarthy, Msgr. Leo F. '59 (BUF) [2] Batavia, NY St. Joseph Church.
McCarthy, Martin F. *s.j.* '54 (BO) [W] Boston, MA The Society of Jesus of New England-Provincial Offices.
McCarthy, Martin F. *s.j.* '54 (TUC) [F] Tucson, AZ Jesuit Community of the Vatican Observatory.
McCarthy, Michael J. *c.s.sp.* '48 (BRK) [U] Long Island City, NY Holy Ghost Fathers of Ireland.
McCarthy, Michael J. '58 (BGP) [P] Ridgefield, CT Provincial House, Congregation de Notre Dame.
McCarthy, Michael J. '65 (PH) Absent on Sick Leave.
McCarthy, Patrick *m.s.* '78 (LKC) De Ridder, LA St. Joseph's Church.
McCarthy, Patrick P. '44 (SFR) Retired.
McCarthy, Paul (FRS) Corcoran, CA Prison Medical Facility.
McCarthy, Paul '84 (FTW) [14] South Bend, IN St. Mary of the Assumption Church.
McCarthy, Paul E. '80 (BO) [46] Boston, MA St. Mary Church.
McCarthy, Paul J. *s.j.* '57 (BUF) [O] Buffalo, NY Canisius Jesuit Community.
McCarthy, Raymond *c.ss.r.* '47 (NY) [92] New York, NY Our Lady of Perpetual Help Church.
McCarthy, Richard C. '69 (PRT) Retired.
McCarthy, Richard J. *c.m.* '58 (SAT) Losoya, TX El Carmen Catholic Church.
McCarthy, Msgr. Robert J. '46 (OG) Retired.
McCarthy, Msgr. Robert L. '58 (STL) [2] Jennings, MO St. Frances Xavier Cabrini Church.
McCarthy, Sean M. '91 (BO) [4] Norwood, MA St. Timothy Church.
McCarthy, Terrence A. '74 (CHI) [1] Waukegan, IL St. Anastasia Church.
McCarthy, Thomas '61 (Y) [L] Kent, OH Family and Community Services of Catholic Charities.
McCarthy, Thomas *s.j.* '62 (P) Sherwood, OR St. Francis Church.
McCarthy, Thomas *o.s.a.* '94 (CHI) [N] Chicago, IL St. Rita Monastery.
McCarthy, Msgr. Thomas A. '59 (NEW) Washington Township, NJ Our Lady of Good Counsel Church.
McCarthy, Thomas E. '49 (HRT) Avon, CT St. Ann's Church.
McCarthy, Thomas H. '43 (KC) Retired.
McCarthy, Thomas J. '51 (SPR) Retired.
McCarthy, Thomas J. '53 (RVC) Glen Cove, NY St. Patrick's Church.
McCarthy, Thomas J. '61 (Y) Mantua, OH St. Joseph's Church.
McCarthy, Thomas J. '80 (BUF) [3] Kenmore, NY St. John the Baptist Church.
McCarthy, Thomas P. *c.s.v.* '52 (CHI) [N] Arlington Heights, IL Viatorian Province Center-Clerics of St. Viator.
McCarthy, Vincent *s.s.c.* '64 (FgM) St. Columban's Foreign Mission.
McCarthy, Warren J. '52 (CHI) Schaumburg, IL St. Marcelline Church.
McCarthy, William *m.s.a.* '59 (NOR) [I] Moodus, CT My Father's House.
McCarthy, Msgr. William '63 (PAT) East Hanover, NJ St. Rose of Lima Church.
McCarthy, William D. *m.m.* '56 (NY) [B] Maryknoll, NY Center for Mission Research and Study at Maryknoll; [DD] Maryknoll, NY Maryknoll Fathers and Brothers.
McCarthy, William E. *m.m.* '58 (NY) [DD] Maryknoll, NY Maryknoll Fathers and Brothers.
McCarthy, William E. '58 (RVC) Shoreham, NY St. Mark Church.
McCarthy, William R. (BO) Retired.
McCarthy, William R. *m.m.* '40 (NY) [DD] Maryknoll, NY Maryknoll Fathers and Brothers.
McCarthy, William R. '52 (BO) [3] Quincy, MA St. John the Baptist Church.
McCartin, Francis P. *o.m.i.* '38 (BO) [Z] Tewksbury, MA Immaculate Heart of Mary Novitiate-Infirmary.
McCartney, James J. *o.s.a.* '70 (PH) [C] Villanova, PA Villanova University.
McCartney, Jim '84 (LUB) Slaton, TX St. Joseph's Church.
McCartney, Louis R. *o.s.f.s.* '52 (WIL) [I] Childs, MD Oblates of St. Francis De Sales.
McCartney, Marcellus A. *o.f.m.* '44 (NY) [35] New York, NY St. Francis of Assisi Church.
McCarty, Bruce '89 (OWN) Absent on Leave.
McCarty, Kieran *o.f.m.* '49 (TUC) [4] Tucson, AZ Mission San Xavier del Bac Church.
McCarty, Lawrence L. '63 (SC) [8] Sioux City, IA St. Michael Church.
McCarty, Paul T. *s.j.* '67 (BO) [W] Weston, MA Campion Center.
McCarty, Robert E. *s.j.* '67 (NEW) [B] Jersey City, NJ Saint Peter's College; [N] Jersey City, NJ Jesuits of Saint Peter's College, Inc.
McCarty, Shaun *s.t.* '56 (WDC) [M] Adelphi, MD Missionary Servants of the Most Holy Trinity.
McCarty, Thomas J. *o.c.s.o.* '56 (DUB) [K] Peosta, IA New Melleray Abbey, Order of Cistercians of the Strict Observance.
McCarver, Jim '91 (MEM) Union City, TN Immaculate Conception Church.
McCarville, John J. '65 (CHI) Bellwood, IL St. Simeon Church.
McCasland, Howard '44 (OG) Churubusco, NY Immaculate Heart of Mary Church; Retired.
McCaslin, James J. *s.s.c.* '54 (FgM) St. Columban's Foreign Mission.
McCaslin, John O. '55 (OM) [20] Omaha, NE Immaculate Conception, B.V.M. Church.
McCaslin, John T. *s.j.* '66 (ALN) [A] Wernersville, PA Novitiate of St. Isaac Jogues.
McCaslin, R. Patrick '61 (OM) [26] Omaha, NE St. Leo Church.
McCaslin, Richard F. *s.j.* '65 (GB) [M] Oshkosh, WI Jesuit Retreat House.
McCauley, Daniel *o.c.d.* '55 (MIL) [P] Milwaukee, WI Provincial Offices - Discalced Carmelites.
McCauley, David '63 (FAR) On Duty Outside the Diocese.
McCauley, David F. '63 (STP) [S] St. Paul, MN Minnesota Catholic Conference.
McCauley, George C. *s.j.* '61 (NY) [DD] New York, NY Jesuit Community at Fordham University.
McCauley, James P *s.j.* '56 (LAV) Tonopah, NV St. Patrick Church.
McCauley, James P. *s.j.* '56 (SJ) [M] Los Gatos, CA Sacred Heart Jesuit Center.
McCauley, James S. '56 (WIN) Lake City, MN St. Mary's of the Lake Church.
McCauley, Walter C. *s.j.* '56 (FWT) [J] Lake Dallas, TX Montserrat Jesuit Retreat House.
McCaulley, Cornelius W. '66 (PIT) [41] Pittsburgh, PA St. Stephen Church.
McCausland, Joseph E. '50 (CLV) Military Chaplains.
McCawley, Scott '93 (JOL) Downers Grove, IL St. Mary Church.
McCawley, William J. '60 (SCR) Brodheadsville, PA Our Lady Queen of Peace Church.
McClain, J. Thomas *s.j.* (DET) [K] Detroit, MI Jesuit Provincial Office-Detroit Province of the Society of Jesus.
McClain, J. Thomas *s.j.* '77 (NY) [F] New York, NY Regis High School; [DD] New York, NY St. Ignatius Loyola Residence.
McClain, Joseph P. *c.m.* '49 (MET) [H] Plainsboro, NJ Vincentian Residence.
McClanahan, Robert P. '84 (PT) Military Chaplains.
McClean, Msgr. John R. '57 (DUB) Guttenberg, IA St. Mary's Church; North Buena Vista, IA Immaculate Conception Church; [F] Guttenberg, IA Guttenberg-North Buena Vista Consolidated School.
McCleane, Michael J. (PH) [15] Philadelphia, PA Ascension of Our Lord Church.
McClear, J. Edmund *m.m.* '42 (NY) [DD] Maryknoll, NY Maryknoll Fathers and Brothers.
McCleary, Michael L. '78 (PBL) Durango, CO St. Columba Church; [D] Durango, CO Centura Health-Mercy Medical Center.
McClellan, Keith *o.s.b.* (CHI) Berwyn, IL St. Mary of Celle Church.
McClellan, Keith *o.s.b.* '79 (IND) [J] St. Meinrad, IN St. Meinrad Archabbey.
McClellan, Robert J. '81 (RCK) [3] Aurora, IL St. Joseph Church.
McClintock, James '86 (BEA) Bridge City, TX St. Henry Church.
McClory, Bernard J. '53 (COL) Retired.
McCloskey, C. John (TR) [R] Princeton, NJ Opus Dei.
McCloskey, Daniel J. '83 (WIL) Absent on Sick Leave.
McCloskey, Francis '63 (ALB) Special Assignment.
McCloskey, Gary N. *o.s.a.* '77 (MIA) [B] Opa Locka, FL St. Thomas University; [H] Miami, FL Casa San Lorenzo.
McCloskey, J. Terrence *c.ss.r.* '66 (WCH) [G] Wichita, KS Redemptorist Community; [I] Wichita, KS Spiritual Life Center.
McCloskey, Msgr. James A. '46 (SY) Retired.
McCloskey, James P. *c.s.sp.* '70 (PH) [G] Bensalem, PA Holy Ghost Preparatory School.
McCloskey, James P. *c.s.sp.* '80 (PH) [AA] Bensalem, PA Congregation of the Holy Ghost.
McCloskey, Joseph A. '39 (PH) [39] Philadelphia, PA St. Dominic Church; Retired.
McCloskey, Joseph M. *s.j.* '63 (WDC) [2] Washington, DC St. Aloysius Church; [E] Washington, DC Gonzaga College High School.
McCloskey, Joseph W. '61 (PH) [36] Philadelphia, PA St. Clement Church.
McCloskey, Lester '64 (SEA) Seahurst, WA St. Francis of Assisi Church.
McCloskey, Lester J. '64 (SEA) [17] Seattle, WA St. Patrick Church; [20] Seattle, WA St. Therese Church; [31] Seattle, WA Our Lady of Mount Virgin Church; Vashon, WA St. John Vianney Church.
McCloskey, Patrick *o.f.m.* '75 (CIN) [E] Cincinnati, OH Roger Bacon High School; [M] Cincinnati, OH St. Clare Friary.
McClosky, Adam S. '67 (GAL) [49] Houston, TX St. Maximilian Kolbe Church.
McClure, Jack *c.p.p.s.* (KC) [1] Kansas City, MO Cathedral of Immaculate Conception.
McClure, Jack *c.pp.s.* '76 (KC) [A] Kansas City, MO Precious Blood Mission House.
McClure, John A. '62 (TOL) [L] Sylvania, OH Sisters of St. Francis of the Congregation of Our Lady of Lourdes.
McCluskey, James F. '68 (OM) Duncan, NE St. Stanislaus Church.
McCluskey, John D. *s.j.* '45 (SEA) Bellevue, WA Sacred Heart Church.
McCluskey, John D. *s.j.* '71 (SEA) [M] Seattle, WA Jesuit Community.
McCluskey, Raymond E. *s.j.* '45 (BO) [W] Weston, MA Campion Health Center, Inc.
McCoart, Charles C., Jr. '90 (ARL) [2] Alexandria, VA Good Shepherd Church.
McCole, John F. '58 (PH) Pottstown, PA St. Aloysius Church.
McColl, Scott J. '80 (SD) [26] San Diego, CA St. Didacus Church.
McColligan, Raymond A. '43 (PIT) Retired.
McComiskey, Joseph C. '70 (RVC) Syosset, NY St. Edward Confessor Church.
McConaghy, R. Thomas '81 (NOR) Pawcatuck, CT St. Michael Church.
McConaghy, Robert J. '75 (ALN) Lehighton, PA SS. Peter and Paul Church.

McConnell, Bernard J. '36 (PH) [AA] Philadelphia, PA Jesuit Community at St. Joseph's University.
McConnell, James *s.m.a.* '72 (NEW) [N] Tenafly, NJ Society of African Missions, Provincialate, S.M.A. Fathers.
McConnell, James J. '54 (TR) Pennington, NJ St. James Church.
McConnell, James J. *s.m.a.* '72 (NEW) [14] Newark, NJ Queen of Angels Church.
McConnell, John *s.j.* '55 (NY) [DD] New York, NY Murray-Weigel Hall.
McConnell, William J. '53 (BO) [4] Brockton, MA St. Margaret Church.
McConnin, Robert J. '78 (BRK) [205] Queens, NY St. Nicholas of Tolentine Church.
McConvey, Michael '79 (GLP) Absent on Leave.
McConville, James P. '90 (STP) Shakopee, MN St. Mary Church; Special Assignment.
McConville, Philip G.J. '43 (BO) Retired.
McConville, William E. *o.f.m.* '73 (ALB) [B] Loudonville, NY Siena College.
McConway, Sean J. *o.p.* '87 (NY) Pleasantville, NY Holy Innocents Church.
McCoog, Thomas M. *s.j.* '71 (BAL) [M] Baltimore, MD Jesuit Fathers and Brothers Maryland Provincial Curia.
McCool, Gerald A. *s.j.* '52 (NY) [DD] New York, NY Jesuit Community at Fordham University.
McCool, Malachy '71 (HT) On Leave.
McCool, Patrick *o.s.b.* '63 (OKL) [I] Shawnee, OK St. Gregory Abbey.
McCord, Kent G. '81 (MET) On Duty Outside the Diocese.
McCorkell, Patrick M. *s.j.* '74 (RC) [4] Rapid City, SD St. Isaac Jogues Church; [B] Howes, SD Kino Jesuit Community.
McCorkle, Louis W. '53 (JC) [A] Hannibal, MO St. Thomas Aquinas Seminary.
McCormac, Michael P. '80 (PH) Glenolden, PA St. George Church.
McCormack, Brendan '60 (WDC) Retired.
McCormack, Daniel J. '94 (CHI) [A] Chicago, IL St. Joseph Seminary.
McCormack, Douglas '69 (LFT) Zionsville, IN St. Alphonsus Church.
McCormack, John '61 (KC) [39] Kansas City, MO St. Therese Parish.
McCormack, John B. '60 (BO) [2] Weymouth, MA St. Francis Xavier Church.
McCormack, Keith J. '76 (TOL) Columbus Grove, OH St. Anthony of Padua Church.
McCormack, Martin L. *o.f.m.* '48 (BO) [Z] Boston, MA Saint Anthony Residence.
McCormack, Michael *o.p.* (RIC) Charlottesville, VA St. Thomas Aquinas Church.
McCormack, Richard J. '61 (BRK) [143] Brooklyn, NY St. Vincent de Paul Church.
McCormack, Msgr. Robert '47 (NY) Retired.
McCormack, Thomas A. *s.s.c.* '35 (PRO) [P] Bristol, RI St. Columban's Retirement House.
McCormick, Andrew D. '82 (PH) [78] Philadelphia, PA St. John Cantius Church.
McCormick, Brian '66 (TR) [T] Trenton, NJ Martin House.
McCormick, Daniel J. '57 (ATL) Dunwoody, GA All Saints Catholic Church.
McCormick, Frank '68 (HEL) [3] Missoula, MT Pope John XXIII Church.
McCormick, George '84 (CAM) Retired.
McCormick, George '84 (PRT) Stonington, ME St. Mary Star of the Sea Church.
McCormick, Gerard *o.m.i.* '47 (NY) [FF] Newburgh, NY Our Lady of Hope Center.
McCormick, Gregory *s.p.* '49 (SB) [G] Cherry Valley, CA Servants of the Paraclete Guadalupe Retreat Center.
McCormick, Harold W. '63 (WCH) [1] Wichita, KS Cathedral of the Immaculate Conception.
McCormick, Howard W. '57 (SPR) Agawam, MA St. John the Evangelist Church.
McCormick, James '63 (SFS) On Leave of Absence.
McCormick, James '82 (E) [18] Erie, PA St. James Church; [C] Erie, PA Cathedral Preparatory School.
McCormick, James D. '62 (SC) Carroll, IA Holy Spirit Church.
McCormick, Msgr. James R. '39 (BEL) Retired.
McCormick, Jeffrey '96 (MIA) [26] Miami, FL St. Louis Church.
McCormick, Jerry '73 (MRY) Pacific Grove, CA St. Angela Church.
McCormick, John '75 (ORL) Kissimmee, FL Holy Redeemer Church.
McCormick, John D. '75 (DEN) Arvada, CO Shrine of St. Anne Church.
McCormick, John J. '56 (BO) Billerica, MA St. Theresa of Lisieux Church.
McCormick, Joseph E. *o.s.a.* '77 (DET) Grosse Pointe Park, MI St. Clare of Montefalco Church.
McCormick, Justin J. *c.s.p.* '61 (NY) [DD] Jamaica Estates, NY Paulist Fathers Generalate.
McCormick, Kieran J. '64 (SFR) [4] San Mateo, CA St. Timothy Church.
McCormick, Louis *o.f.m.* '65 (BUF) [Q] West Clarksville, NY Mount Irenaeus, Franciscan Mountain Retreat & Holy Peace Friary.
McCormick, Louis M. *o.f.m.* (BUF) [C] St. Bonaventure, NY St. Bonaventure University.
McCormick, Mark '91 (RC) Hot Springs, SD St. Anthony's Church.
McCormick, Martin F. *o.p.* '61 (DET) [L] Farmington Hills, MI Monastery of the Blessed Sacrament.
McCormick, Maurice M. '58 (SFR) [33] San Francisco, CA Mission Dolores Basilica Church; [U] Pacifica, CA Cursillo.
McCormick, Michael '85 (WH) Absent on Sick Leave.
McCormick, Myron *o.f.m.* '52 (BO) [BB] Boston, MA St. Anthony Shrine.
McCormick, Patrick G. '96 (PH) [1] Norristown, PA Epiphany of Our Lord Church.
McCormick, Patrick J. '57 (ATL) Military Chaplains.
McCormick, Patrick Joseph '75 (FRS) [11] Fresno, CA St. Mary Church.
McCormick, Paul *o.cist.* '97 (DAL) [M] Irving, TX Cistercian Abbey of Our Lady of Dallas.
McCormick, Peter *s.p.* '70 (SB) Palm Desert, CA Sacred Heart Church.
McCormick, Richard A. *s.j.* (DET) [K] Detroit, MI Jesuit Provincial Office-Detroit Province of the Society of Jesus.
McCormick, Richard A. *s.j.* '53 (FTW) [B] Notre Dame, IN University of Notre Dame Du Lac.
McCormick, Richard J. *s.d.b.* '70 (BO) [E] Boston, MA Don Bosco Preparatory School.
McCormick, Msgr. Robert F. '47 (NY) Ossining, NY St. Augustine Church.
McCormick, Robert J. '42 (MIL) Retired.
McCormick, Thomas F. *s.j.* '67 (LA) [F] Los Angeles, CA Loyola High School.
McCormick, Thomas G. '81 (RVC) Babylon, NY St. Joseph's Church.
McCormick, Thomas L. '59 (DEN) [1] Boulder, CO Sacred Heart of Jesus Church.
McCormley, Hugh J. '62 (PIT) Harmarville, PA St. Francis of Assisi Church.
McCorry, Msgr. Edward J. '56 (NY) Hastings-on-Hudson, NY St. Matthew Church; Hastings-on-Hudson, NY St. Stanislaus Kostka Church.
McCotter, Daniel E. *c.s.p.* '81 (SFR) [22] San Francisco, CA Holy Family Chinese Mission Church; [31] San Francisco, CA Old St. Mary's Cathedral.
McCouch, Richard S. *s.j.* '93 (SCR) [C] Scranton, PA University of Scranton; [E] Scranton, PA Scranton Preparatory School.
McCourt, Gerald P. *s.j.* '72 (SJ) [L] Los Altos, CA Jesuit Retreat House.
McCourt, Msgr. Robert R. '61 (BRK) [223] Queens, NY St. Pascal Baylon Church.
McCown, Robert M. *s.j.* '54 (MOB) Daphne, AL Shrine of the Holy Cross Church.
McCoy, Alan *o.f.m.* '38 (LA) [72] Los Angeles, CA St. Joseph Church.
McCoy, Alfred E. '54 (SC) Onawa, IA St. John's Church.
McCoy, Bernard *o.cist.* '95 (LC) [I] Sparta, WI Our Lady of Spring Bank, Cistercian Abbey.
McCoy, Charles J. '61 (BO) [7] Newton, MA St. Philip Neri Church.
McCoy, Daniel F. *s.j.* '45 (FgM) Provinces.
McCoy, Msgr. James P. '63 (PH) Chalfont, PA St. Jude Church.
McCoy, John '93 (STU) [3] Steubenville, OH Holy Rosary Church; [E] Steubenville, OH Trinity Health System.
McCoy, Kevin C. '81 (SC) [H] Sioux City, IA Diocese of Sioux City Priests' Welfare Foundation.
McCoy, Msgr. Patrick '60 (SR) [1] Santa Rosa, CA Cathedral of St. Eugene; [G] Santa Rosa, CA Santa Rosa Memorial Hospital.
McCoy, Perry *o.s.m.* '93 (TUC) Yuma, AZ St. Francis of Assisi Church.
McCracken, John E. (GAY) Special Assignment.
McCracken, John E. '79 (GAY) [1] Gaylord, MI St. Mary Cathedral.
McCracken, Msgr. John T. '44 (OAK) [1] Walnut Creek, CA St. Anne Church.
McCracken, Kevin *c.m.* '82 (LA) [A] Camarillo, CA St. John's Seminary.
McCrane, Gerard T. *m.m.* '59 (FgM) Maryknoll Foreign Missions.
McCrann, Peter J. *s.m.m.* '58 (RVC) Bay Shore, NY Southside Hospital; [N] Bay Shore, NY Montfort Missionaries.
McCrate, D. Stephen '89 (BEA) [7] Port Arthur, TX St. Joseph Church.
McCready, Daniel A. '47 (PHX) Retired.
McCready, James *s.j.* '63 (SPK) [K] Spokane, WA Regis Community.
McCreanor, David '75 (PT) [4] Tallahassee, FL St. Louis Church.
McCreanor, James '78 (MIA) Homestead, FL Sacred Heart Church.
McCreary, Glenn E. '95 (SCR) Sayre, PA Church of the Epiphany.
McCreary, Robert E. *o.f.m.cap.* '64 (BAL) Cresaptown, MD St. Ambrose Church.
McCreedy, Harry E. '72 (PH) [5] Norristown, PA St. Paul Church.
McCreedy, Justin D. *o.s.b.* '70 (SEA) [M] Lacey, WA St. Martin's Abbey.
McCreedy, Justin D. *o.s.b.* '70 (YAK) [B] Yakima, WA Providence Yakima Medical Center.
McCreesh, Eugene P. *s.j.* '54 (CHL) [9] Charlotte, NC St. Peter Church; [J] Charlotte, NC Jesuit Community.
McCreesh, Thomas P. *o.p.* '72 (WDC) [B] Washington, DC Dominican House of Studies.
McCreight, James H. '68 (CLV) [50] Cleveland, OH St. Michael Church.
McCrillis, Philip '61 (SJ) Special Assignment.
McCrone, John '82 (NEW) Paramus, NJ Bergen Pines County Hospital.
McCrone, John M. '82 (NEW) Paramus, NJ Annunciation Church.
McCue, Michael J. *o.s.f.s.* '90 (ARL) [D] Alexandria, VA Bishop Ireton High School; [J] Alexandria, VA Oblates of St. Francis de Sales Residence.
McCue, Richard T. '58 (CHL) Franklin, NC St. Francis of Assisi Church.
McCue, Will *s.c.* '74 (BR) Special Assignment.
McCulken, Michael T. '76 (PH) Brookline, PA Annunciation B.V.M. Church.
McCullagh, Msgr. John P. '55 (BRK) [143] Brooklyn, NY St. Vincent de Paul Church.
McCullen, John L. '44 (MIA) Deerfield Beach, FL St. Ambrose Church.
McCullen, John L. '44 (TOL) On Duty Outside the Diocese.
McCulloch, Lawrence F. *m.m.* '70 (FgM) Maryknoll Foreign Missions.
McCullough, Brian *s.c.j.* '73 (JKS) Southhaven, MS Christ the King Church.
McCullough, Hugh J. *s.j.b.* '79 (FR) South Yarmouth, MA St. Pius Tenth Church.
McCullough, J. Edward '67 (GBG) Dunbar, PA St. Aloysius Church.
McCullough, James '57 (E) [B] Erie, PA Gannon University.
McCullough, Michael P. '73 (LA) Los Angeles, CA L.A. Police Department.
McCumber, William M. '83 (STL) [1] Lemay, MO Mary Queen of the Universe Church.
McCune, James L. '58 (BO) Canton, MA St. John the Evangelist Church.
McCurdy, Richard L. *s.j.* '67 (SAC) [C] Sacramento, CA Jesuit High School; [G] Carmichael, CA Jesuit High School Community of Sacramento.
McCurdy, William J. *s.j.* '61 (ROC) [B] Rochester, NY McQuaid Jesuit High School.
McCurry, James E. *o.f.m.conv.* '77 (SPR) [A] Granby, MA St. Hyacinth College and Seminary; [Q] Granby, MA Knights of the Immaculata Movement (Militia Immaculatae, M.I.).
McCusker, William C. *s.j.* '51 (ROC) [B] Rochester, NY McQuaid Jesuit High School.
McDade, Robert *m.ss.cc.* '76 (CAM) [M] Linwood, NJ Villa Pieta.
McDade, Robert T. *m.ss.cc.* '76 (CAM) [I] Pleasantville, NJ Our Lady's Residence.
McDade, Msgr. Thomas J. '74 (NEW) On Duty Outside the Archdiocese.
McDaid, Msgr. Edward J. (CAM) Retired.
McDaid, Henry A. '63 (BIR) Talladega, AL St. Francis of Assisi Church; [H] Talladega, AL Talladega College Catholic Campus Ministry.
McDaid, J. Anthony '75 (DEN) On Duty Outside the Archdiocese.
McDaniel, George '70 (DAV) [B] Davenport, IA St. Ambrose University.
McDaniel, Isaac *o.s.b.* '82 (IND) St. Croix, IN Holy Cross Church; St. Croix, IN St. Isidore the Farmer Church; [B] St. Meinrad, IN St. Meinrad Seminary-College of Liberal Arts; [J] St. Meinrad, IN St. Meinrad Archabbey.
McDaniel, John W. *s.j.* '71 (PH) [AA] Philadelphia, PA Jesuit Community at St. Joseph's University.
McDaniel, Rodney '58 (CIN) [L] Cincinnati, OH St. Margaret Hall.
McDarby, J. Patrick *o.s.b.* '53 (SCL) [I] Collegeville, MN St. John's Abbey, of the Order of St. Benedict.
McDermott, Brian O. *s.j.* '68 (WDC) [M] Washington, DC The Jesuit Community at Georgetown University.
McDermott, Charles B. '63 (PRO) [6] Pawtucket, RI St. Joseph Church.
McDermott, Charles B. '73 (NEW) Union, NJ St. Michael's Church.
McDermott, Charles S. '60 (SAC) [22] Sacramento, CA St. Rose Church.
McDermott, Christopher H. *c.s.sp.* '81 (PH) [AA] Bensalem, PA Congregation of the Holy Ghost.
McDermott, Edwin J. *s.j.* '49 (SFR) [N] San Francisco, CA Jesuit Community at University of San Francisco.
McDermott, Eric *s.j.* '43 (PH) [AA] Philadelphia, PA Jesuit Community at St. Joseph's University.

McDermott, Francis A. '38 (PH) Retired.
McDermott, H. Thomas *c.s.c.* '79 (FgM) Holy Cross Foreign Missions.
McDermott, Msgr. Ignatius D. '36 (CHI) Retired.
McDermott, Msgr. James M. '48 (NY) [2] White Plains, NY St. John the Evangelist Church.
McDermott, James P. '42 (BRK) Retired.
McDermott, John '89 (BUR) [H] Burlington, VT University of Vermont-The Catholic Center at UVM.
McDermott, Msgr. John F. '57 (NEW) Upper Saddle River, NJ Church of the Presentation.
McDermott, John J. '86 (DUB) [C] Dubuque, IA Loras College.
McDermott, John J. '89 (BUR) Middlebury, VT Assumption of the Blessed Virgin Mary Church.
McDermott, John M. *s.j.* '71 (NY) [DD] New York, NY Jesuit Provincial's Office.
McDermott, Joseph *s.v.d.* '52 (DUB) [B] Epworth, IA Divine Word College.
McDermott, Joseph M. '95 (PH) Warrington, PA St. Robert Bellarmine Church.
McDermott, Joseph P. '62 (BO) Stoughton, MA Immaculate Conception Church.
McDermott, Martin F. *s.j.* '64 (FgM) Provinces.
McDermott, Michael '65 (SEA) [14] Tacoma, WA Our Lady, Queen of Heaven Church.
McDermott, Michael '66 (PIT) Allegheny County, PA UPMC University of Pittsburgh Medical Center.
McDermott, Michael F. '79 (GI) St. Paul, NE SS. Peter and Paul Church.
McDermott, Michael J. '75 (WIL) Special or Other Diocesan Assignment.
McDermott, Neal *o.p.* '61 (NO) [30] New Orleans, LA St. Dominic Church.
McDermott, Patrick '67 (SEA) Aberdeen, WA St. Mary's Church; Aberdeen, WA SS. Peter and Paul Church; Hoquiam, WA Our Lady of Good Help Church; Ocean Shores, WA St. Jerome Church.
McDermott, Patrick M. '64 (BLX) [4] Biloxi, MS Sacred Heart Church.
McDermott, Paul B. '59 (CHI) Wadsworth, IL St. Patrick Church.
McDermott, Paul B. '59 (PEO) Absent on Leave.
McDermott, Robert B. '90 (PH) West Chester, PA St. Agnes Church.
McDermott, Msgr. Robert T. '69 (CAM) [7] Camden, NJ St. Joseph's Pro-Cathedral.
McDermott, Robert T. '81 (MIL) [2] Kenosha, WI St. Casimir Church.
McDermott, Robert T. '81 (STA) [18] Jacksonville, FL St. Patrick Church.
McDermott, Thomas F. *s.j.* '38 (BO) [W] Weston, MA Campion Health Center, Inc.
McDermott, Thomas F. *m.m.* '44 (NY) [DD] Maryknoll, NY Maryknoll Fathers and Brothers.
McDermott, Msgr. Thomas J. '55 (SD) Retired.
McDermott, Thomas J. '56 (SCR) Wyalusing, PA St. Mary's Assumption Church.
McDermott, Thomas J. '97 (DUB) [4] Waterloo, IA St. Edward's Church.
McDermott, Thomas K. *o.p.* '83 (CHI) [N] Chicago, IL Dominicans (Provincial Office).
McDermott, Thomas K. *o.p.* '83 (FgM) Dominican - Order of Preachers Foreign Missions.
McDevitt, Msgr. Anthony '49 (MOB) [17] Mobile, AL Our Savior Church.
McDevitt, Edward P. *c.o.* '71 (CHR) York, SC Divine Saviour Church; [D] Rock Hill, SC Oratory of St. Philip Neri, Congregation of the Oratory of Pontifical Rite.
McDevitt, Edwin R. *m.m.* '49 (NY) [DD] Maryknoll, NY Maryknoll Fathers and Brothers.
McDevitt, Francis N. '41 (PH) Malvern, PA St. Patrick Church; Retired.
McDevitt, James '97 (ALB) Loudonville, NY St. Pius X Church.
McDevitt, James A. '90 (BGP) Danbury, CT Federal Correctional Institution.
McDevitt, James J. '35 (PBL) Retired.
McDevitt, John M. *o.s.f.s.* '66 (CAM) [M] Pittsgrove, NJ Villa St. Joseph.
McDevitt, Michael '71 (SPC) Poplar Bluff, MO Poplar Bluff Hospital Ministry.
McDevitt, Michael V. '71 (SPC) Poplar Bluff, MO Sacred Heart Church.
McDevitt, Patrick J. *c.m.* '86 (STL) [P] St. Louis, MO Vincentian Residence.
McDevitt, Robert *s.j.* '60 (LA) [2] Santa Barbara, CA Our Lady of Sorrows Church.
McDevitt, Thomas D. '58 (LAN) East Lansing, MI St. John the Evangelist, Student Parish.
McDonagh, Andrew J. '42 (CHI) [132] Chicago, IL St. Mary of the Woods Church; Retired.
McDonagh, Msgr. Charles (NY) [3] Kingston, NY St. Joseph Church.
McDonagh, Donald *s.p.s.* '55 (NEW) [N] Cliffside Park, NJ St. Patrick's Missionary Society.
McDonagh, Edward C. '62 (BO) West Bridgewater, MA St. Ann Church.
McDonagh, John P. '82 (SPR) [1] Springfield, MA St. Michael's Cathedral.
McDonagh, Michael *m.s.h.s.* '74 (DAL) [L] Dallas, TX Marian Servants of the Holy Spirit.
McDonald, A. John '56 (BR) Retired.
McDonald, Alexander F. *s.j.* '47 (SEA) [M] Seattle, WA Jesuit House, Seattle.
McDonald, Allan J. '80 (SAV) [1] Augusta, GA Church of the Most Holy Trinity; [I] Augusta, GA Catholic Cemetery.
McDonald, Bernard (NY) Port Jervis, NY Mercy Community Hospital.
McDonald, Bill '89 (STO) Modesto, CA St. Stanislaus Church.
McDonald, C. Alexander '91 (CHR) North Augusta, SC Our Lady of Peace Church.
McDonald, Charles *c.ss.r.* '71 (HBG) [2] Lancaster, PA St. Anthony of Padua Church.
McDonald, Charles J. '65 (LEX) Lawrenceburg, KY St. Lawrence Church.
McDonald, Daniel C. *s.j.* '81 (FgM) Jesuit Foreign Missions.
McDonald, Daniel C. *s.j.* '81 (MIL) [P] Milwaukee, WI Jesuit Provincial Office, Wisconsin Province.
McDonald, Daniel C. *s.j.* '81 (WDC) [M] Washington, DC Leonard Neale House; [V] Washington, DC Jesuit Conference, Inc.
McDonald, David M. '55 (HRT) [2] Hamden, CT Blessed Sacrament Church.
McDonald, Edward J. *c.s.p.* '41 (BO) [P] Boston, MA Paulist Center; [W] Boston, MA Paulist Fathers Residence.
McDonald, Edward J. *c.s.p.* '41 (NY) [DD] Jamaica Estates, NY Paulist Fathers Generalate.
McDonald, Elmer J. '49 (ROC) Retired.
McDonald, Eustace *c.p.* '45 (BAL) [M] Baltimore, MD St. Joseph's Passionist Community.
McDonald, Finian *o.s.b.* '62 (SCL) [I] Collegeville, MN St. John's Abbey, of the Order of St. Benedict.
McDonald, Francis B. '60 (JOL) Roselle, IL St. Walter Church.
McDonald, G. Malcolm '85 (PIT) [1] Pittsburgh, PA St. Paul Cathedral.
McDonald, Gerald R. *o.f.m.* '45 (PAT) [M] Butler, NJ St. Anthony Friary.
McDonald, J. Robert '37 (DUB) Retired.
McDonald, James E. *c.s.c.* (FTW) [B] Notre Dame, IN University of Notre Dame Du Lac; [J] Notre Dame, IN Holy Cross Community, Corby Hall, University of Notre Dame.
McDonald, Msgr. James M. '67 (RVC) Center Moriches, NY St. John the Evangelist Church.
McDonald, James T. (BO) Retired.
McDonald, John F. '47 (HRT) South Glastonbury, CT St. Augustine Church.
McDonald, John J. *s.j.* '57 (PAT) [I] Morristown, NJ Loyola House of Retreats.
McDonald, Joseph F., III '87 (B) Pocatello, ID St. John's Community Church; [F] Pocatello, ID Idaho State University, St. John's Community.
McDonald, Joseph S. *s.m.* '61 (CIN) [M] Dayton, OH Marianist Provincialate.
McDonald, Kenneth '57 (LAN) Mason, MI St. James Church.
McDonald, Lorne T. *o.m.i.* '57 (SFD) [A] Godfrey, IL Immaculate Heart of Mary Novitiate.
McDonald, Malcolm '85 (PIT) [R] Slippery Rock, PA Office for Campus Ministry.
McDonald, Mark *m.s.c.* '68 (OG) [2] Watertown, NY Our Lady of the Sacred Heart, Missionaries of the Sacred Heart Church.
McDonald, Martin '62 (MRY) Boulder Creek, CA St. Michael Church; Boulder Creek, CA Ben Lomond Youth Authority Camp.
McDonald, Matthew D. '40 (CHI) Skokie, IL St. Joan of Arc Church; Retired.
McDonald, Michael D. '85 (GI) Kearney, NE Prince of Peace Church.
McDonald, Paul *o.s.b.* '70 (PRO) [P] Portsmouth, RI Abbey of St. Gregory the Great.
McDonald, Paul F. '51 (DUB) Retired.
McDonald, Perry *o.f.m.cap.* '67 (DET) [K] Detroit, MI St. Bonaventure Friary; [K] Detroit, MI St. Bonaventure Friary.
McDonald, Peter '59 (SFR) San Anselmo, CA St. Anselm Church.
McDonald, Raphael *o.f.m.* '44 (PAT) [M] Ringwood, NJ Holy Name Friary, Inc.
McDonald, Robert *s.m.* '50 (PRT) Brunswick, ME St. John the Baptist Church.
McDonald, Thomas A. '52 (NY) Poughkeepsie, NY St. Francis Hospital; [W] Poughkeepsie, NY St. Francis Hospital.
McDonald, Thomas M. '56 (NY) On Duty Outside the Archdiocese.
McDonald, Vincent *o.carm.* (ALB) [5] Troy, NY St. Joseph Church.
McDonald, Vincent *s.c.j.* '58 (GAL) [35] Houston, TX Holy Name Church.
McDonnell, Anthony '70 (LA) Sick Leave.
McDonnell, Cyril '43 (CAM) Retired.
McDonnell, David '72 (PAT) Randolph, NJ St. Matthew the Apostle Church.
McDonnell, Donald C. '47 (SFR) Retired.
McDonnell, Francis P. '58 (HRT) Windsor Locks, CT St. Mary Church.
McDonnell, Francis R. *o.s.a.* '42 (DET) Grosse Pointe Park, MI St. Clare of Montefalco Church.
McDonnell, Francis W. '60 (SD) San Diego, CA Mercy Hospital; Retired; [F] San Diego, CA Mercy Hospital and Medical Center dba Mercy Healthcare San Diego.
McDonnell, Msgr. James T. '35 (NY) Retired.
McDonnell, John *c.m.* '43 (BRK) [U] Jamaica, NY Vincentian Residence.
McDonnell, John '73 (CHI) [38] Chicago, IL Christ the Redeemer Byzantine Bielarusian Church.
McDonnell, John H. '56 (WH) [3] Charleston, WV St. Agnes Church.
McDonnell, Msgr. John J. '44 (YAK) [2] Yakima, WA Holy Family Church.
McDonnell, John J. '73 (CHI) [1] Chicago, IL Cathedral of the Holy Name.
McDonnell, Msgr. Joseph '67 (DM) Urbandale, IA St. Pius X Church.
McDonnell, Joseph F. '55 (CHI) Western Springs, IL St. John of the Cross Church; Retired.
McDonnell, Joseph M. '30 (ROC) Newark, NY St. Michael Church; Retired.
McDonnell, Joseph T. '50 (SD) Retired.
McDonnell, Kilian *o.s.b.* '51 (SCL) [I] Collegeville, MN St. John's Abbey, of the Order of St. Benedict.
McDonnell, Martin '68 (PAT) Parsippany, NJ St. Ann Church.
McDonnell, Michael *o.f.m.* '65 (NY) [35] New York, NY St. Francis of Assisi Church.
McDonnell, P. William '64 (RCK) [4] Freeport, IL St. Thomas Aquinas Church.
McDonnell, Msgr. Patrick '57 (MIA) [13] Fort Lauderdale, FL St. Sebastian Church.
McDonnell, Patrick J. (TR) [10] Trenton, NJ Our Lady of Sorrows Church.
McDonnell, Patrick J. '73 (BWN) On Assignment Outside the Diocese.
McDonnell, Paul A. *o.s.j.* '91 (SCR) [1] Pittston, PA Our Lady of Mt. Carmel Church; [M] Pittston, PA Eastern Province of the Oblates of St. Joseph.
McDonnell, Robert *c.s.c.* '57 (ORL) Indialantic, FL Holy Name of Jesus Church.
McDonnell, Sean '88 (PAT) Parsippany, NJ St. Christopher Church.
McDonnell, Stephen '89 (RVC) Absent on Leave.
McDonnell, Thomas *s.j.* '68 (RIC) [4] Richmond, VA Our Lady of Lourdes Church.
McDonnell, Thomas J. '60 (BO) [12] Boston, MA St. Augustine Church.
McDonnell, Thomas J. '61 (BO) [50] Boston, MA St. Monica Church.
McDonnell, Thomas P. *m.m.* '65 (NY) [DD] Maryknoll, NY Maryknoll Fathers and Brothers.
McDonnell, Msgr. Timothy A. '63 (NY) Chappaqua, NY St. John and St. Mary Church.
McDonnell, Vincent '84 (MOB) Retired.
McDonnell, Msgr. William J. '54 (BUF) Amherst, NY St. Leo Church.
McDonough, Msgr. Charles (NY) Staten Island, NY St. Vincent's Medical Center of Richmond.
McDonough, Donat Michael '74 (SP) On Duty Outside the Diocese.
McDonough, Edward *c.ss.r.* '48 (BO) [13] Boston, MA Our Lady of Perpetual Help Church.
McDonough, James '42 (AGN) Dededo, GU Santa Barbara Church.
McDonough, James '84 (PIT) [2] Munhall, PA St. Maximilian Kolbe Church.
McDonough, James A. *s.j.* '41 (FgM) Provinces.
McDonough, James A. *o.p.* '62 (AUS) [H] Austin, TX Dominican Fathers.
McDonough, James A. *o.p.* '62 (NO) [P] New Orleans, LA Dominican Fathers & Brothers, Southern Dominican Province.
McDonough, James E. *ss.cc.* '68 (FR) [J] Fairhaven, MA Sacred Hearts Provincial House.
McDonough, James M. *s.j.* (SPK) [C] Spokane, WA Gonzaga University.
McDonough, Msgr. James T. '57 (PH) Strafford, PA Our Lady of the Assumption Church; [FF] Philadelphia, PA Ladies of Charity.
McDonough, John *o.p.* (OAK) [N] Moraga, CA Dominican Community.
McDonough, John '89 (OAK) [B] Moraga, CA St. Mary's College.
McDonough, Msgr. John P. '52 (BO) [3] Peabody, MA St. John the Baptist Church.
McDonough, John P. '95 (WH) [1] Charleston, WV Sacred Heart Co-Cathedral.
McDonough, John T. '50 (CLV) [17] Akron, OH St. Sebastian Church; Hinckley, OH Our Lady of Grace Church; Retired.
McDonough, Joseph F. *c.ss.sp.* '53 (PRO) [3] Tiverton, RI St. Madeleine Sophie Church.
McDonough, Kevin M. '80 (STP) [32] St. Paul, MN St. Peter Claver Church.
McDonough, Msgr. Martin J. '40 (PH) Doylestown, PA

Our Lady of Mount Carmel Church; Retired.
McDonough, Patrick M. '68 (WH) St. Albans, WV St. Francis of Assisi Church.
McDonough, Raymond *c.p.* '47 (SAC) [G] Citrus Heights, CA Christ the King Retreat; [I] Citrus Heights, CA Christ the King Retreat Center.
McDonough, Roger F. '76 (BGP) [3] Greenwich, CT St. Paul's Church.
McDonough, Msgr. T. Joseph '46 (MAN) Retired.
McDonough, Thomas R. '89 (STP) [3] St. Paul, MN Blessed Sacrament Church.
McDonough, Timothy T. *c.s.sp.* '56 (VEN) [G] Sarasota, FL Congregation of the Holy Ghost.
McDonough, Vincent *s.j.* '62 (ROC) [B] Elmira, NY Notre Dame High School.
McDonough, William C. '82 (STP) [A] St. Paul, MN The Saint Paul Seminary; [C] St. Paul, MN University of St. Thomas.
McDougal, Jon '79 (LR) Camden, AR St. Louis Church.
McDougall, James G. '75 (LAN) [1] Ann Arbor, MI St. Francis of Assisi Church.
McDougall, Jeffrey N. *s.j.* (P) [D] Portland, OR Jesuit High School.
McDougall, Russell *c.s.c.* '91 (FgM) Holy Cross Foreign Missions.
McDougall, Russell K. *c.s.c.* '91 (FTW) [J] South Bend, IN Congregation of Holy Cross Indiana Province Provincial House.
McDowell, John W. *o.f.m.* '77 (NY) [35] New York, NY St. Francis of Assisi Church.
McDowell, Leo George '94 (GF) [1] Billings, MT St. Patrick's Co-Cathedral; [2] Billings, MT Holy Rosary Church.
McDowell, Patrick '54 (DUL) [4] Duluth, MN Our Lady of Mercy Church; [13] Duluth, MN St. Mary Star of the Sea Church; [15] Duluth, MN St. Peter's Church.
McDowell, Patrick D. '68 (SCR) Meshoppen, PA St. Joachim's Church.
McDuffie, Paul A. '95 (BR) [3] Baton Rouge, LA St. Aloysius Church.
McDuffie, Paul A. '95 (CHR) Myrtle Beach, SC St. Andrew's Church; On Duty Outside the Diocese.
McDyre, Cajetan *s.t.* '45 (PAT) [M] Stirling, NJ Holy Spirit Missionary Cenacle.
McEachern, Bernard *c.p.* '64 (FgM) Passionist Foreign Missions.
McEachin, Cornelius '48 (SAG) Retired.
McEachin, Donald *c.s.sp.* (PIT) [B] Pittsburgh, PA Duquesne University of the Holy Ghost; [R] Slippery Rock, PA Office for Campus Ministry.
McElaney, Robert *o.s.b.* '82 (NEW) [N] Newark, NJ Newark Abbey.
McElduff, Edward W. '53 (ALN) Berlinsville, PA St. Nicholas Church.
McEleney, Neil J. *c.s.p.* '53 (NY) [DD] Jamaica Estates, NY Paulist Fathers Generalate.
McEleney, Neil J. *c.s.p.* '53 (WDC) [B] Washington, DC St. Paul's College.
McEleney, Robert J. '58 (RIC) Hurt, VA St. Victoria Church.
McElhinney, Thomas *glmy.* '62 (NSH) Fayetteville, TN St. Anthony Church; Pulaski, TN Immaculate Conception Church.
McElhinny, Michael *s.m.* '80 (BO) [W] Cambridge, MA Our Lady of Mercy Marist Novitiate.
McElligott, Msgr. Francis J. '38 (CHI) [108] Chicago, IL St. John Fisher Church; Retired.
McElligott, Thomas J. '69 (OAK) [3] Berkeley, CA St. Joseph The Worker Church.
McElligott, Thomas J. '69 (SFR) On Duty Outside the Archdiocese.
McElnee, Michael A. *s.j.* '95 (PH) [C] Philadelphia, PA St. Joseph's University.
McElroy, Charles J. '64 (PH) Delphi, PA St. Mary Church.
McElroy, Damian (TR) Point Pleasant, NJ St. Martha Church.
McElroy, Francis P. *c.ss.r.* '48 (BRK) [107] Brooklyn, NY Our Lady of Perpetual Help Basilica Church.
McElroy, Herbert '34 (BRK) Retired.
McElroy, James E. '56 (LA) [14] Los Angeles, CA Holy Trinity Church.
McElroy, John J. '45 (PRO) [6] Pawtucket, RI St. Joseph Church; Retired.
McElroy, John W. '56 (BO) Avon, MA St. Michael Church.
McElroy, Msgr. Robert W. '80 (SFR) [2] San Mateo, CA St. Gregory Church; Special Assignment.
McElroy, Thomas *ss.cc.* '67 (FR) [L] Wareham, MA Sacred Hearts Retreat Center.
McElwee, Michael A. *s.j.* '95 (PH) [AA] Philadelphia, PA Jesuit Community at St. Joseph's University.
McElwee, Robert W. '83 (WCH) Pittsburg, KS Our Lady of Lourdes Church.
McElynn, John D. *c.m.* '81 (BRK) [U] Queens Village, NY DePaul Residence.
McEneaney, Msgr. John P.A. '43 (SFS) Retired.
McEneany, Joseph *ss.cc.* '57 (ORG) [H] Costa Mesa, CA Fairview Developmental Center.
McEnery, Dennis '50 (DUL) Retired.
McEnery, James J. '53 (MAD) Milton, WI St. Mary Church.
McEnhill, Gerald A. '72 (DET) Farmington, MI St. Gerald Church.
McEnhill, John *s.m.* (SJ) [M] Cupertino, CA Marianist Provincial Residence.
McEnhill, John *s.m.* '56 (SFR) [B] San Francisco, CA Marianist Seminary.
McEniry, Robert F. *s.j.* '51 (OM) [K] Omaha, NE Jesuit Community At Creighton University.
McEnnis, Thomas '45 (SEA) Retired.
McEntee, John B. '61 (STL) Luebbering, MO St. Francis of Assisi Church.
McEntee, Paul H. '57 (BO) Watertown, MA Sacred Heart Church.
McEvilly, John W. '64 (BEL) [3] Belleville, IL Our Lady Queen of Peace Church.
McEvoy, David *o.carm.* '88 (NY) [DD] Middletown, NY Brandsma Priory.
McEvoy, John '52 (MRY) Retired.
McEvoy, William '87 (KCK) [2] Kansas City, KS Blessed Sacrament Church.
McFadden, Brian '88 (NEW) [3] Linden, NJ St. John the Apostle Church.
McFadden, Edward J. *s.j.* '54 (SJ) [D] San Jose, CA Bellarmine College Preparatory.
McFadden, Frank C. '83 (BAL) Havre de Grace, MD St. Patrick's Church.
McFadden, George B. '52 (SC) Retired.
McFadden, J. Michael '74 (HBG) [3] Lebanon, PA St. Cecilia Church.
McFadden, James J. *m.m.* '61 (HON) [9] Honolulu, HI St. John the Baptist Church; [H] Honolulu, HI Maryknoll Fathers House.
McFadden, John R. '62 (PH) Cheltenham, PA Presentation of Blessed Virgin Mary Church.
McFadden, Msgr. Joseph P. '81 (PH) Morton, PA Our Lady of Perpetual Help Church; [D] Springfield, PA Cardinal O'Hara High School.
McFadden, Msgr. Leo E. '53 (RNO) Retired.
McFadden, Michael '61 (SAC) [11] Sacramento, CA St. Charles Borromeo Church.
McFadden, Michael J. *o.s.a.* '67 (LA) [31] Los Angeles, CA Mother of Good Counsel Church.
McFadden, William C. *s.j.* '59 (WDC) [M] Washington, DC The Jesuit Community at Georgetown University.
McFadin, Marcus '92 (ELP) [30] El Paso, TX St. Pius X Church.
McFalls, Dean '95 (STO) [7] Stockton, CA St. Luke Church.
McFarland, Msgr. Edward J. '55 (COL) Gahanna, OH St. Matthew Church.
McFarland, Eugene H. '43 (ROC) Geneseo, NY St. Mary Church; Retired.
McFarland, Francis T. '57 (BO) [3] Medford, MA St. Joseph Church.
McFarland, Francis X. *s.j.* '50 (FgM) Provinces.
McFarland, James W. '47 (NEW) Retired.
McFarland, Michael C. *s.j.* '84 (BO) [W] Boston, MA The Society of Jesus of New England-Provincial Offices.
McFarland, Michael C. *s.j.* '84 (SPK) [C] Spokane, WA Gonzaga University.
McFarland, Timothy D. *c.pp.s.* '83 (LFT) [A] Rensselaer, IN Saint Joseph's College.
McGaffin, Joseph '96 (PHX) Chandler, AZ St. Mary's Church.
McGagh, Martin '54 (FRS) Retired.
McGagh, Martin A. '54 (FRS) Porterville, CA St. Anne Church.
McGahagan, James E. '68 (SCR) Buttonwood, PA Exaltation of the Holy Cross Church.
McGahee, Thomas *s.d.b.* '77 (PAT) [D] Paterson, NJ Don Bosco Technical High School.
McGahey, Charles R. '59 (BO) [9] Quincy, MA Star of the Sea Church.
McGahren, Joseph J. *m.m.* '97 (DEN) [M] Denver, CO Maryknoll Fathers, Catholic Foreign Mission Society of America (Legal Title).
McGann, Diarmuid F. '64 (RVC) Blue Point, NY Our Lady of the Snow Church.
McGann, Msgr. Francis J. (BO) Retired.
McGann, Msgr. Francis J. '48 (BO) Needham, MA St. Joseph Church.
McGann, Gerard J. '48 (BO) Retired.
McGann, Joseph F. '44 (NY) Retired.
McGann, L. Philip '71 (WIL) Retired.
McGann, Richard P. '70 (HRT) Plainville, CT Our Lady of Mercy Church.
McGann, Thomas F. *s.j.* '45 (NY) [DD] New York, NY Murray-Weigel Hall.
McGannon, Barry *s.j.* (STL) [C] St. Louis, MO Saint Louis University.
McGannon, J. Barry *s.j.* '55 (STL) [C] St. Louis, MO Saint Louis University; [P] St. Louis, MO Jesuit Community Corporation at St. Louis University - Jesuit Hall.
McGarr, Joseph '86 (ALN) [2] Allentown, PA St. Francis of Assisi Church.
McGarrigle, Michael '49 (PRT) Retired.
McGarrill, Colman *t.o.r.* '54 (SP) [13] Tampa, FL St. Patrick Church.
McGarrity, Patrick J. *c.ss.r.* '61 (HBG) New Holland, PA Our Lady of Lourdes Church; [H] Ephrata, PA St. Clement's Mission House.
McGarrity, Richard A. *s.j.* '70 (MIL) [P] Milwaukee, WI Jesuit Community at Marquette University.
McGarry, Gerard J. '34 (NEW) Mountainside, NJ Our Lady of Lourdes Church.
McGarry, James J. '70 (SCR) Clarks Summit, PA Our Lady of the Snows Church.
McGarry, John P. *s.j.* '93 (SAC) [C] Sacramento, CA Jesuit High School; [G] Carmichael, CA Jesuit High School Community of Sacramento.
McGarry, Joseph P. '55 (HRT) [5] West Hartford, CT St. Peter Claver Church.
McGarry, Michael B. *c.s.p.* '75 (OAK) [2] Berkeley, CA Holy Spirit Parish.
McGarry, Peter *o.carm.* '69 (CHI) [68] Chicago, IL St. Gelasius Church.
McGarry, Thomas (NY) Bronx, NY St. Barnabas Hospital.
McGarry, William C. '59 (BUF) [11] Niagara Falls, NY Prince of Peace Church.
McGarry, William J. '58 (CI) [C] Kolonia, Pohnpei, FM Jesuit House.
McGarry, William J. *s.j.* '58 (FgM) Provinces.
McGarty, Bernard O. '49 (LC) [2] La Crosse, WI Blessed Sacrament Church.
McGarvey, Joseph F. '50 (CAM) Retired.
McGaugh, Philip E. (BO) Boston, MA Massachusetts General Hospital.
McGaugh, Philip E. '78 (BO) [35] Boston, MA St. Joseph Church.
McGauley, Francis H. *s.j.* '55 (PH) [AA] Philadelphia, PA Jesuit Community at St. Joseph's University.
McGeady, Ignatius J. *o.f.m.* '48 (FgM) Franciscan Foreign Missions.
McGee, Dominic E. *o.f.m.conv.* '61 (SY) Minoa, NY St. Mary Church.
McGee, Francis J. '45 (BRK) [236] Queens, NY St. Rose of Lima Church; Retired.
McGee, Msgr. H. Desmond '71 (E) Warren, PA St. Joseph Church.
McGee, H. Desmond, Jr. '71 (E) [C] Bradford, PA Bradford Central Christian High School.
McGee, James J. *s.s.* '85 (SCR) On Duty Outside the Diocese.
McGee, Jim *s.s.* '85 (OAK) Pleasant Hill, CA Christ the King Church.
McGee, John E. *o.s.f.s.* '82 (R) [2] Durham, NC Holy Infant Church.
McGee, Leo J. '57 (PH) [117] Philadelphia, PA Our Lady Help of Christians Church.
McGee, Michael J. '77 (BRK) [188] Queens, NY St. Joseph Church.
McGee, Peter '53 (LA) Gardena, CA St. Anthony of Padua Church.
McGee, Richard F. *c.r.* '74 (SB) [3] Fontana, CA St. Joseph Church.
McGee, Thomas J. *o.s.f.s.* '71 (WIL) [B] Wilmington, DE Salesianum School.
McGee, Timothy H. '87 (CR) East Grand Forks, MN Sacred Heart Church.
McGeean, John T. '86 (JOL) Bradley, IL St. Joseph Church.
McGeory, Peter '76 (NY) Military Chaplains.
McGeough, Jude P. '58 (PRO) [4] East Providence, RI St. Martha Church.
McGeough, Martin *c.m.* '76 (BIR) Lanett, AL Holy Family Church.
McGeown, Joseph P. '65 (PH) Wallingford, PA St. John Chrysostom Church.
McGeown, William F. '70 (PH) [126] Philadelphia, PA Our Lady of Ransom Church.
McGerity, Francis X. '84 (CC) On Duty Outside the Diocese.
McGettigan, Msgr. D. James '67 (PH) [1] Drexel Hill, PA St. Andrew Church.
McGettigan, Neil J. *o.s.a.* '53 (PH) [C] Villanova, PA Villanova University; [AA] Villanova, PA St. Thomas Monastery.
McGettrick, Msgr. Thomas P. '56 (CC) [20] Corpus Christi, TX St. Philip The Apostle Church.
McGhee, James '95 (AMA) Canadian, TX Sacred Heart Church.
McGhee, William P. '82 (BEL) Mound City, IL Church of the Immaculate Conception-St. Mary.
McGill, Joseph F. '56 (NY) Absent on Leave.
McGill, Joseph P. *s.j.* '60 (LAF) [J] Grand Coteau, LA Our Lady of the Oaks Retreat House.
McGill, Malachy *c.p.* '46 (ALT) [J] Bedford, PA St. Mary's House of Greater Solitude.
McGilley, Michael J. '65 (CAM) Audubon, NJ Church of the Holy Maternity.
McGillicuddy, Sean J. *c.ss.r.* '86 (PH) [25] Philadelphia, PA St. Boniface Church.
McGilvary, A. Robert *o.s.f.s.* '62 (ALN) [B] Center Valley, PA Allentown College of St. Francis de Sales.
McGilvray, A. Robert *o.s.f.s.* '62 (ALN) [K] Center Valley, PA Oblates of St. Francis de Sales.

McGing, Thomas '71 (JKS) Vicksburg, MS St. Paul Church.
McGinley, Anthony J. '45 (HBG) Retired.
McGinley, Bernard P. *m.a.* '61 (HBG) [4] Harrisburg, PA Holy Family Church.
McGinley, James J. *s.j.* '40 (NY) [DD] New York, NY Murray-Weigel Hall.
McGinley, Jeremiah V. *o.f.m.* '55 (NEW) Fair Lawn, NJ St. Anne's Church.
McGinley, John F. *o.s.f.s.* '68 (ALN) [B] Center Valley, PA Allentown College of St. Francis de Sales; [K] Center Valley, PA Oblates of St. Francis de Sales.
McGinley, Kevin P. *s.j.* '91 (SPK) [E] Spokane, WA Gonzaga Preparatory School.
McGinley, Peter *m.c.c.j.* (LA) [11] Los Angeles, CA Holy Cross Church.
McGinn, Anthony F. *s.j.* '79 (NO) [F] New Orleans, LA Jesuit High School; [H] New Orleans, LA Jesuit High School.
McGinn, Charles T. '69 (KCK) Olathe, KS St. Paul's Church.
McGinn, Finian *o.f.m.prov.* (LA) [DD] Los Angeles, CA St. Francis Center.
McGinn, Finian *o.f.m.* (OAK) [S] Berkeley, CA Multicultural Institute.
McGinn, Finian *o.f.m.* '60 (OAK) [N] Oakland, CA Franciscan Friars Provincial Office, Province of St. Barbara.
McGinn, Finian *o.f.m.* '60 (SFR) [5] San Francisco, CA St. Anthony Church.
McGinn, John J. '52 (DEN) [4] Englewood, CO St. Thomas More Church.
McGinn, Msgr. Malachy M. '61 (SB) Palm Springs, CA St. Theresa Church.
McGinn, Sylvester P. '56 (NY) [195] Staten Island, NY St. Ann Church.
McGinness, Matthew C. '89 (WCH) [18] Wichita, KS St. Paul Parish; [K] Wichita, KS Wichita State University.
McGinnis, Albin C. '77 (PIT) Waynesburg, PA St. Ann Church; Green County, PA State Correctional Institution at Waynesburg (Women's Facility); Green County, PA Waynesburg County Jail; [R] Slippery Rock, PA Office for Campus Ministry.
McGinnis, Gary *s.d.s.* '62 (MIL) [P] Milwaukee, WI Salvatorians - Jordan Hall.
McGinnis, J. Donald *m.m.* '53 (FgM) Maryknoll Foreign Missions.
McGinnis, Jack P. (GAL) On Duty Outside the Diocese.
McGinnis, James '78 (PH) [93] Philadelphia, PA St. Martin De Porres Church.
McGinnis, Jay W. '76 (BUF) Lancaster, NY Our Lady of Pompeii Church.
McGinnis, Joseph '46 (WIN) [F] Wabasha, MN St. Elizabeth's Health Care Center.
McGinnis, Msgr. Joseph R. '46 (WIN) Retired; [D] Wabasha, MN St. Elizabeth's Hospital; [F] Wabasha, MN St. Elizabeth's Health Care Center.
McGinnis, N. Charles '41 (LR) Retired.
McGinnity, Ambrose T. '45 (GRY) Retired.
McGinnity, John C. '75 (WH) Ronceverte, WV St. Catherine of Siena Church.
McGinnity, Joseph P. '56 (CHI) [4] Des Plaines, IL St. Zachary Church.
McGinnity, P. J. '91 (KNX) [4] Chattanooga, TN St. Stephen Church.
McGinnity, Robert F. '55 (CHI) Palos Hills, IL Sacred Heart Church.
McGinty, John P. (BO) [A] Boston, MA St. John's Seminary School of Theology.
McGinty, John P. *s.j.* '58 (BAL) [M] Baltimore, MD Jesuit Fathers and Brothers Maryland Provincial Curia.
McGinty, John P. '83 (BO) [71] Boston, MA St. Theresa Church.
McGinty, Msgr. Michael J. '31 (OAK) Retired.
McGivern, John W. '91 (CHI) [41] Chicago, IL St. Clement Church.
McGivney, Thomas '91 (JOL) Addison, IL St. Joseph Church.
McGlade, Desmond *c.s.sp.* '41 (SJ) Mountain View, CA St. Athanasius Church.
McGlade, Thomas F. '43 (RVC) Setauket, NY St. James Church; Retired.
McGlauchlin, Michael J. '86 (STP) Maple Lake, MN St. Timothy Church.
McGlinchey, James J. '56 (TLS) Retired.
McGlinchy, Edward H. *s.j.* '49 (NY) [DD] Cornwall, NY Jogues Retreat.
McGlinn, Charles '67 (KCK) Leawood, KS Cure of Ars Church.
McGlinn, Msgr. Joseph J. '42 (PH) [126] Philadelphia, PA Our Lady of Ransom Church; Retired.
McGlinn, Robert J. '55 (CHI) Other Assignments.
McGlinn, Robert J. '55 (MIL) [2] Racine, WI Cristo Rey Church.
McGloin, James P. *s.j.* '74 (FgM) Provinces.
McGloin, Peter M. '56 (TUC) [6] Tucson, AZ Our Lady of Fatima Church.
McGloin, Richard D. *s.j.* '45 (OM) [K] Omaha, NE Jesuit Community At Creighton University.
McGlone, Gerald J. *s.j.* '87 (BAL) [M] Baltimore, MD Jesuit Fathers and Brothers Maryland Provincial Curia.
McGlone, Gerard M. '84 (SCR) Mocanaqua, PA St. Mary, Our Lady of Perpetual Help Church.
McGlone, Joseph F. '52 (BO) [2] Newton, MA Corpus Christi Church.
McGlothlin, Eugene J. *o.s.b.* '60 (STP) Hastings, MN St. Elizabeth Ann Seton Church.
McGlynn, Daniel J. '82 (WIL) Elkton, MD Immaculate Conception Church.
McGlynn, Francis '54 (KC) Retired.
McGlynn, Francis '54 (PRM) Sugar Creek, MO St. Luke, Byzantine Catholic Parish.
McGlynn, Philip M. *o.s.m.* '65 (CHI) [N] Chicago, IL Servite Friars - Eastern Province.
McGlynn, Thomas E. '84 (FR) Absent on Sick Leave.
McGoldrick, Albert W. '78 (BGP) Easton, CT Notre Dame of Easton Church.
McGoldrick, James F. *s.m.* (ATL) [L] Atlanta, GA Campus Ministry.
McGoldrick, James F. *s.m.* '67 (ATL) [6] Atlanta, GA Our Lady of the Assumption Church.
McGoldrick, John T. '38 (B) Retired.
McGoldrick, William J. '43 (DET) Retired.
McGonagle, James E. *c.ss.r.* '44 (ATL) Griffin, GA Sacred Heart Church.
McGonegal, James R. '71 (CLV) [33] Cleveland, OH St. Ignatius Church.
McGonigle, Thomas D. *o.p.* '68 (PRO) [P] Providence, RI St. Thomas Aquinas Priory at Providence College.
McGough, Msgr. James P. '57 (BLX) [2] Gulfport, MS St. James Church.
McGough, Stephen D. '68 (SCF) [3] Williamsport, PA St. Boniface's Church.
McGough, Msgr. Thomas J. '32 (HBG) Retired.
McGough, Timothy *o.c.d.* '49 (MIL) [24] Milwaukee, WI St. Florian Church.
McGough, William J. '47 (NO) Covington, LA St. Peter Church.
McGourn, Francis T. *m.m.* '64 (FgM) Maryknoll Foreign Missions.
McGourty, Thomas P. *c.m.* '53 (BUF) [C] Niagara University, NY Niagara University; [O] Niagara University, NY Vincentian Community at Niagara University.
McGovern, Arthur F. *s.j.* '62 (DET) [K] Detroit, MI Jesuit Community at the University of Detroit.
McGovern, Brian '69 (SEA) [I] Seattle, WA Providence Mount St. Vincent.
McGovern, Donan *o.f.m* '55 (BO) [BB] Boston, MA St. Anthony Shrine.
McGovern, Edward J. '51 (PRO) Retired; [P] Providence, RI St. John Vianney Residence.
McGovern, Eugene F. '56 (BRK) [147] Queens, NY St. Aloysius Church.
McGovern, Gerald *o.m.i.* '57 (FgM) Oblates Foreign Missions.
McGovern, Msgr. James J. '58 (TR) Moorestown, NJ Our Lady of Good Counsel Church.
McGovern, James O. '67 (BAL) Ellicott City, MD Resurrection Church.
McGovern, John J. *m.m.* '54 (FgM) Maryknoll Foreign Missions.
McGovern, John P. '65 (NEW) Berkeley Heights, NJ Church of the Little Flower.
McGovern, John Patrick *o.p.* '58 (WDC) [B] Washington, DC Dominican House of Studies.
McGovern, Joseph J. *s.j.* '48 (CHL) Mars Hill, NC St. Andrew the Apostle Church; [J] Charlotte, NC Jesuit Community; [M] Hot Springs, NC Jesuit House of Prayer.
McGovern, Lawrence J. '67 (STO) Manteca, CA St. Anthony Church.
McGovern, Mark J. '67 (DUB) Fairbank, IA Immaculate Conception Church; Independence, IA Mental Health Institute.
McGovern, Martin D. '46 (LA) Retired.
McGovern, Michael A. '45 (PHX) Retired.
McGovern, Michael G. '94 (CHI) [181] Chicago, IL Queen of the Universe Church.
McGovern, Thomas A. '58 (CLV) [12] Akron, OH St. Matthew Church.
McGovern, Walter J. '64 (BAL) Randallstown, MD Holy Family Church.
McGovern, William W. '55 (WOR) Retired; [M] Worcester, MA Vianney House.
McGowan, Msgr. Andrew J. (SCR) On Special or Other Diocesan Assignment.
McGowan, Msgr. Anthony '41 (ORG) San Clemente, CA Our Lady of Fatima Church; Retired.
McGowan, Denis *c.p.* '55 (FgM) Mission Procurators.
McGowan, Dennis M.. *o.s.a.* (BO) [6] Lawrence, MA Holy Rosary Church.
McGowan, Frederick R. '49 (BO) [2] Haverhill, MA St. James Church.
McGowan, James J. '62 (BO) Belmont, MA Our Lady of Mercy Church.
McGowan, Jeffrey A. '89 (STA) [3] Gainesville, FL Queen of Peace Church.
McGowan, John *c.ss.r.* '62 (TR) [Q] Long Branch, NJ San Alfonso Retreat House.
McGowan, John J. '52 (RCK) Retired.
McGowan, Msgr. Joseph '53 (PEO) [J] Bloomington, IL OSF St. Joseph Medical Center.
McGowan, Joseph F. *o.carm.* '62 (TUC) [9] Tucson, AZ Sacred Heart Church.
McGowan, Joseph O. *s.j.* '74 (SEA) [20] Seattle, WA St. Therese Church; [A] Seattle, WA Seattle University.
McGowan, Kenan *o.f.m.conv.* '52 (SY) [5] Binghamton, NY SS. Cyril and Method Church.
McGowan, Kilian *c.p.* '46 (NEW) [N] Union City, NJ Congregation of the Passion (Passionists)-St. Michael's Residence.
McGowan, Msgr. Myles '37 (BAL) [93] Baltimore, MD St. Ursula Church; Retired.
McGowan, Myles P. '45 (NU) Retired.
McGowan, Richard A. *s.j.* '83 (BO) [W] Chestnut Hill, MA The Jesuit Community at Boston College.
McGowan, Seamus '57 (CC) Retired.
McGowan, Seamus J. '57 (CC) Sinton, TX Sacred Heart Church.
McGowan, Thomas A. *o.s.a.* '45 (CHI) [N] Olympia Fields, IL Tolentine Monastery at Tolentine Center.
McGowan, Timothy '79 (LA) Woodland Hills, CA St. Bernardine of Siena Church.
McGowan, Wallace A. '62 (MIA) [26] Miami, FL St. Louis Church.
McGowan, William J. *s.j.* '62 (NY) [F] New York, NY Xavier High School.
McGrade, Kevin M. '85 (BO) Permanent Disability.
McGrade, William H. '49 (STP) Retired.
McGrail, Charles A. '80 (NOR) Mystic, CT St. Patrick Church.
McGrail, John A. *s.j.* '57 (DET) [P] Bloomfield Hills, MI Manresa Jesuit Retreat House.
McGrane, Msgr. Walter J. '33 (SPC) Retired.
McGrann, John '67 (SPK) On Duty Outside the Diocese.
McGrath, Andre *o.f.m.* '67 (SHP) [9] Shreveport, LA St. Mary of the Pines Church.
McGrath, Msgr. Andrew '38 (LA) Lompoc, CA La Purisima Concepcion Church; Retired.
McGrath, Brian F. '92 (SPR) Lee, MA St. Mary's Church.
McGrath, Conor '74 (SAT) Selma, TX Our Lady of Perpetual Help Church.
McGrath, Daniel F. '63 (NOR) Retired.
McGrath, E. Joseph '85 (LKC) Creole, LA Sacred Heart of Jesus Church.
McGrath, Msgr. Edmond G. '37 (YAK) Retired.
McGrath, Msgr. Edmund G. '37 (YAK) Moxee City, WA Holy Rosary Church.
McGrath, Edward F. '80 (WIN) Rollingstone, MN Holy Trinity Church.
McGrath, Edward H. *s.j.* '53 (BAL) [M] Baltimore, MD Jesuit Fathers and Brothers Maryland Provincial Curia.
McGrath, Edward H. *s.j.* '53 (FgM) Provinces.
McGrath, Felix P. *o.f.m.* '61 (NY) [35] New York, NY St. Francis of Assisi Church.
McGrath, Francis '78 (TR) Leave of Absence.
McGrath, Frank C. '70 (BGP) Westport, CT Assumption Church.
McGrath, Gerald F. '58 (MIA) Key West, FL St. Mary, Star of the Sea Church.
McGrath, Msgr. James '43 (PH) Manoa, PA Sacred Heart Church; Retired.
McGrath, James J. *c.s.c.* '59 (FTW) [B] Notre Dame, IN University of Notre Dame Du Lac; [J] Notre Dame, IN Holy Cross Community, Corby Hall, University of Notre Dame.
McGrath, James R. '54 (BUF) Retired.
McGrath, Jeremiah '80 (BEA) [1] Beaumont, TX St. Anthony Cathedral.
McGrath, John *o.m.i.* '53 (SAT) Eagle Pass, TX St. Joseph's Church.
McGrath, John '82 (BLX) Vancleave, MS Catholic Church of the Holy Spirit.
McGrath, John A. *s.m.* '66 (CIN) [D] Dayton, OH The University of Dayton; [M] Dayton, OH Marianist Provincialate.
McGrath, John D. '59 (MIA) Tavernier, FL San Pedro Church.
McGrath, John F. (CHI) Retired.
McGrath, John J. *s.j.* '51 (BO) [W] Weston, MA Campion Center.
McGrath, Jordan *o.p.* '59 (MAD) [3] Madison, WI Blessed Sacrament Church.
McGrath, Jordan A. *o.p.* (CHI) [N] River Forest, IL St. Thomas Aquinas Priory.
McGrath, Kevin *o.p.* '96 (WDC) [B] Washington, DC Dominican House of Studies.
McGrath, Kevin D. *o.s.b.* '74 (BIR) Cullman, AL Sacred Heart Church; [E] Cullman, AL St. Bernard Abbey.
McGrath, Laurence W. '57 (BO) [A] Boston, MA St. John's Seminary School of Theology.
McGrath, Leonard T. '53 (BO) [6] Lowell, MA St. Joseph Church.
McGrath, Mark G. *c.s.c.* '49 (FTW) [J] Notre Dame, IN Holy Cross Community, Corby Hall, University of Notre Dame.

McGrath, Patrick J. '65 (SAC) Rio Vista, CA St. Joseph Church.
McGrath, Peter *s.j.* '88 (OAK) [17] Oakland, CA St. Mary, Immaculate Conception-St. Francis de Sales Church.
McGrath, Peter R. *s.j.* '88 (BO) [W] Boston, MA The Society of Jesus of New England-Provincial Offices.
McGrath, Peter R. *s.j.* '88 (OAK) [N] Berkeley, CA Jesuit Community at Jesuit School of Theology at Berkeley.
McGrath, Philip J. '54 (LA) Bellflower, CA St. Bernard Church.
McGrath, Richard H. '50 (COV) Wilder, KY St. John Church; Retired; [M] Fort Thomas, KY Sisters of the Good Shepherd.
McGrath, Richard J. *o.s.a.* '73 (JOL) [C] New Lenox, IL Providence Catholic High School; [J] New Lenox, IL Augustinian Friary.
McGrath, Robert *o.m.i.* '55 (CC) [I] Corpus Christi, TX Incarnate Word Convent.
McGrath, Robert B. '71 (DET) Highland Park, MI St. Benedict Church.
McGrath, Robert D. '43 (HRT) Retired.
McGrath, Roger E. *s.s.* '71 (BAL) [A] Baltimore, MD St. Mary's Seminary and University; [A] Baltimore, MD St. Mary's Seminary and University.
McGrath, Roger E. *s.s.* '71 (CAM) On Duty Outside the Diocese.
McGrath, Sean '54 (LA) [56] Los Angeles, CA St. Columban Church.
McGrath, Sean *s.s.c.* '54 (OM) [K] St. Columbans, NE St. Columban's Foreign Mission Society.
McGrath, Sean J. '91 (DEN) [24] Denver, CO Church of the Risen Christ.
McGrath, Thomas '77 (JC) Rolla, MO St. Patrick Church.
McGrath, Thomas B. *s.j.* '64 (FgM) Provinces.
McGrath, Thomas J. '59 (SY) Skaneateles, NY St. Mary of the Lake Church.
McGrath, Thomas M. (PAT) Special Assignment.
McGrath, W. Aedan *s.s.c.* '29 (OM) [K] St. Columbans, NE St. Columban's Foreign Mission Society.
McGrath, William E. '47 (HRT) [3] East Hartford, CT St. Christopher Church; Retired.
McGrath, William J. *s.j.* '59 (SCR) [C] Scranton, PA University of Scranton; [E] Scranton, PA Scranton Preparatory School.
McGratty, John J. '71 (RVC) Manorville, NY St. Peter & Paul Church.
McGraw, John '81 (VEN) Absent on Leave.
McGraw, John T. '56 (SY) [7] Syracuse, NY Our Lady of Pompei Church; Syracuse, NY Hutchings Psychiatric Center.
McGraw, Rene *o.s.b.* '62 (SCL) [I] Collegeville, MN St. John's Abbey, of the Order of St. Benedict.
McGraw, Robert H. '76 (LAN) Grand Ledge, MI St. Michael Church.
McGraw, W. Howard *o.s.a.* '62 (ALB) Waterford, NY St. Mary of the Assumption Church.
McGraw, W. Howard *o.s.a.* '62 (PH) [18] Philadelphia, PA St. Augustine Church.
McGray, James W. '67 (SD) [B] San Diego, CA University of San Diego.
McGread, Thomas '53 (WCH) [13] Wichita, KS St. Francis of Assisi Church; [M] Wichita, KS Serra Club of Wichita - Metro.
McGready, Oliver '62 (WDC) [2] Rockville, MD Shrine of St. Jude Church.
McGreal, James '48 (SEA) Retired.
McGreal, Msgr. James R. '34 (MAN) Retired.
McGreevy, James V. '64 (SPK) Lind, WA St. Ambrose Church; Ritzville, WA St. Agnes Church; Sprague, WA Mary Queen of Heaven Church; Washtunca, WA Holy Trinity Church.
McGreevy, John G. *o.p.* '64 (CHI) River Forest, IL St. Vincent Ferrer Priory Church.
McGreevy, Thomas J. *o.p.* '64 (P) [18] Portland, OR Holy Rosary Parish & Dominican Priory Church.
McGregor, John F. *s.m.* '63 (SFR) [B] San Francisco, CA St. Peter Chanel Seminary; [N] San Francisco, CA Provincial Residence.
McGregor, Mark D. *s.j.* '96 (SEA) [M] Seattle, WA Jesuit Community.
McGrenra, Cornelius D. '51 (TUC) Retired.
McGroarty, Msgr. Charles E. '62 (PH) [102] Philadelphia, PA St. Matthew Church.
McGroarty, Hugh H. '45 (SCR) [4] Pittston, PA St. John the Evangelist Church.
McGroarty, Joseph *o.p.* '46 (TR) Holmdel, NJ St. Catharine Church.
McGroarty, William K. *s.j.* '55 (BAL) [B] Baltimore, MD Loyola College; [M] Baltimore, MD Jesuit Community of Loyola College, Inc.
McGrogan, James P. '64 (GRY) [1] Michigan City, IN St. Mary of the Immaculate Conception Church.
McGuffey, James W.. '95 (MET) Old Bridge, NJ St. Ambrose Church.
McGuigan, Francis W. *s.j.* '52 (FBK) [C] Fairbanks, AK Jesuit Residence; [E] Fairbanks, AK Monroe Foundation, Inc.
McGuigan, Hugh *o.s.f.s.* '97 (VEN) [A] Fort Myers, FL Bishop Verot High School.
McGuigan, John J. '68 (PAT) Hopatcong, NJ St. Jude's Church.
McGuigan, Patrick *o.carm.* '79 (NY) Middletown, NY Our Lady of Mt. Carmel Church; [DD] Middletown, NY St. Albert's Priory.
McGuigan, Robert '78 (WDC) Retired.
McGuigan, Steven '90 (SPR) [2] Springfield, MA All Souls Church; Springfield, MA Baystate Medical Center, Springfield Hospital Unit.
McGuill, Martin '64 (ARL) McLean, VA St. Luke's Church.
McGuine, Peter '90 (SD) Carlsbad, CA St. Thomas More Church.
McGuiness, Edward '61 (SB) Desert Hot Springs, CA St. Elizabeth of Hungary Church.
McGuinn, James T. '88 (PH) [4] Norristown, PA St. Patrick Church.
McGuinnerss, Fergal '86 (SR) [C] Napa, CA Justin-Siena High School.
McGuinness, Msgr. Brendan '47 (MRY) Retired.
McGuinness, David I. '73 (MOB) Troy, AL St. Martin Church; [K] Troy, AL Troy State University Newman Center.
McGuinness, Fergal '86 (SR) Napa, CA St. Apollinaris Church.
McGuinness, Gerard J. '60 (SB) Sun City, CA St. Vincent Ferrer Church.
McGuinness, J. Roger '65 (OG) [6] Plattsburgh, NY Newman Parish, John XXIII College Community Church.
McGuinness, Joseph P. '52 (PBL) Cortez, CO St. Margaret Mary Church; Mancos, CO St. Rita Church.
McGuinness, Lester A. '49 (NEW) Caldwell, NJ St. Aloysius Church; Retired.
McGuinness, Msgr. Michael '52 (MOB) Retired.
McGuinness, Msgr. Richard M. '51 (NEW) [3] Linden, NJ St. John the Apostle Church.
McGuire, Anthony *o.f.m.* '52 (PAT) [M] Butler, NJ St. Anthony Friary.
McGuire, Anthony '65 (SFR) [4] San Francisco, CA St. Anne Church.
McGuire, Msgr. Anthony W. '57 (PH) [101] Philadelphia, PA Maternity B.V.M. Church.
McGuire, Augustus S. *c.s.p.* '59 (CHR) Clemson, SC St. Andrew Church.
McGuire, David V. '88 (RIC) Danville, VA Sacred Heart Church.
McGuire, Donald J. *s.j.* '61 (CHI) [N] Evanston, IL Canisius House.
McGuire, Edward A. *o.f.m.* '40 (PAT) [M] Butler, NJ St. Anthony Friary.
McGuire, Francis X. *o.s.a.* '35 (PH) [AA] Villanova, PA St. Thomas Monastery.
McGuire, J. Frederick '81 (CIN) [2] Springfield, OH St. Joseph Church.
McGuire, James *o.a.r.* '54 (LA) [82] Los Angeles, CA San Miguel Church.
McGuire, James E. '70 (PH) [3] Bensalem, PA Saint Ephrem Church.
McGuire, James J. *o.s.f.s.* '50 (WIL) [I] Childs, MD Oblates of St. Francis De Sales.
McGuire, John *c.ss.r.* '44 (ALB) [L] Saratoga Springs, NY St. John Neumann Residence.
McGuire, John *c.ss.r.* '44 (BRK) [107] Brooklyn, NY Our Lady of Perpetual Help Basilica Church.
McGuire, John *o.p.* '79 (NY) [GG] New York, NY University Apostolate.
McGuire, Msgr. John A. '50 (RVC) Sound Beach, NY St. Louis de Montfort Church.
McGuire, John C. '79 (NY) East Kingston, NY St. Colman Church.
McGuire, John F. '76 (P) Coquille, OR Holy Name Church.
McGuire, John J. '60 (COV) Erlanger, KY Mary, Queen of Heaven Church; [S] Fort Thomas, KY Mission Share.
McGuire, John P. *o.p.* '73 (HRT) [V] New Haven, CT Angelicum Fund.
McGuire, John Patrick *o.p.* '73 (NY) [DD] New York, NY St. Vincent Ferrer Priory.
McGuire, John R. *m.m.* '43 (FgM) Maryknoll Foreign Missions.
McGuire, John V. *c.ss.r.* '41 (NY) [HH] Esopus, NY Holy Shroud Guild.
McGuire, Joseph E. '65 (DUB) Dysart, IA St. Joseph Church; Vinton, IA St. Mary's Church.
McGuire, Kenneth H. *c.s.p.* '68 (NY) [DD] Jamaica Estates, NY Paulist Fathers Generalate.
McGuire, Michael A. '58 (MET) South Plainfield, NJ Sacred Heart Church.
McGuire, Paul J. *s.c.j.* '68 (MIL) [P] Franklin, WI Dehon House.
McGuire, Richard '67 (SCL) Isanti, MN St. Elizabeth Ann Seton Church.
McGuire, Richard *o.s.c.* '73 (STP) Shoreview, MN St. Odilia Church; [N] Shoreview, MN Crosier Community of Shoreview.
McGuire, Richard G. *o.c.s.o.* '57 (CHR) [D] Moncks Corner, SC Mepkin Abbey.
McGuire, Msgr. Richard J. '60 (E) [22] Erie, PA St. Julia Church.
McGuire, Robert A. *s.j.* '58 (RVC) Plainview, NY St. Pius X Church.
McGuire, Thomas D. '81 (LIN) Osceola, NE St. Vincent's Church.
McGuire, Timothy P. '84 (STU) Neffs, OH Sacred Heart Church; Powhatan Point, OH St. John Vianney Church.
McGuire, William A. *o.s.a.* '65 (PH) [C] Villanova, PA Villanova University.
McGuirk, John (SC) Sheldon, IA St. Patrick's Church.
McGuirk, Raymond A. '47 (BRK) Retired.
McGuirk, William C. '82 (GBG) Delmont, PA St. John Baptist de La Salle Church.
McGuirl, John A. '72 (BRK) [184] Queens, NY St. Joan of Arc Church.
McGurk, Patrick '58 (HEL) Deer Lodge, MT Immaculate Conception Church.
McGurn, Richard H. *s.j.* '75 (CHI) [N] Chicago, IL Chicago Province of the Society of Jesus-Provincial Office.
McHale, Anthony I. *s.j.* '53 (WDC) [E] Washington, DC Gonzaga College High School.
McHale, Charles P. '50 (NY) Retired.
McHale, Damian *c.p.* '61 (LA) [R] Pasadena, CA Passionist Community.
McHenry, John *s.v.d.* '55 (SB) [A] Riverside, CA Divine Word Seminary.
McHenry, Stephen P. '73 (PH) Ambler, PA St. Anthony of Padua Church; [A] Wynnewood, PA Theological Seminary of St. Charles Borromeo, Overbrook.
McHenry, Vincent Ferrer *o.p.* (NY) Manhattan, NY New York Hospital.
McHenry, Vincent Ferrer *o.p.* '49 (NY) [22] New York, NY St. Catherine of Siena Church; [DD] New York, NY St. Catherine of Siena Priory.
McHugh, Alphonsus *ss.cc.* '69 (FR) Fairhaven, MA St. Mary's Church.
McHugh, Brian J. '88 (BO) [5] Weymouth, MA Sacred Heart Church.
McHugh, Conall *o.f.m.conv.* '56 (CHL) Winston-Salem, NC Our Lady of Mercy Church.
McHugh, Connell A. '72 (SCR) West Hazleton, PA St. Francis of Assisi Church.
McHugh, Dennis (PAT) Retired.
McHugh, Donald '57 (P) Absent on Leave.
McHugh, Edward T. *o.m.i.* '37 (SEA) [4] Seattle, WA St. Benedict Church.
McHugh, Francis B. *o.praem.* '40 (GB) [I] De Pere, WI St. Norbert Abbey.
McHugh, Frank *o.f.m.* '75 (PAT) Butler, NJ St. Anthony Church.
McHugh, James *c.p.* '61 (MET) [H] South River, NJ Passionist Provincial Office.
McHugh, James L. '60 (COV) Brooksville, KY St. James Church.
McHugh, James P. *o.s.f.s.* '77 (SLC) [B] Salt Lake City, UT Judge Memorial Catholic High School; [F] Salt Lake City, UT Oblate House.
McHugh, Jerome *o.f.m.cap.* '60 (NY) [DD] White Plains, NY St. Conrad Friary.
McHugh, John *s.o.l.t.* '52 (CC) [H] Robstown, TX Society of Our Lady of the Most Holy Trinity.
McHugh, John '54 (LA) Santa Fe Springs, CA St. Pius X Church.
McHugh, John *o.f.m.cap.* '69 (MAN) [N] Durham, NH Campus Ministries.
McHugh, John F. *o.m.i.* '73 (BO) [3] Lowell, MA Immaculate Conception Church.
McHugh, Msgr. John L. '31 (BUF) [1] Tonawanda, NY St. Amelia Church; Retired.
McHugh, John P. *o.f.m.cap.* '69 (MAN) [N] Hanover, NH The Catholic Student Center at Dartmouth, Aquinas House, Aquinas at Dartmouth, Inc.
McHugh, John T. '93 (LC) Special Assignment; [A] La Crosse, WI Holy Cross Seminary House of Formation; [C] La Crosse, WI Aquinas High School; [D] La Crosse, WI Aquinas Middle School; [I] La Crosse, WI Holy Cross (Seminary) Diocesan Center.
McHugh, John W. '76 (HRT) Guilford, CT St. George Church; [C] West Hartford, CT Saint Joseph College.
McHugh, Joseph B. *s.j.* '58 (BO) [Y] Gloucester, MA Eastern Point Retreat House.
McHugh, Joseph F. (TR) Leave of Absence.
McHugh, Joseph F. *s.j.* '83 (BO) [Y] Weston, MA Campion Renewal Center.
McHugh, Kieran A. '70 (PAT) [C] Sparta, NJ Pope John XXIII High School.
McHugh, Msgr. Martin '43 (FRS) Retired.
McHugh, Michael *s.j.* '51 (HEL) Browning, MT Church of the Little Flower.
McHugh, Michael J. '80 (BRK) [203] Queens, NY Most Precious Blood Church.
McHugh, Owen J. '50 (COS) [11] Colorado Springs, CO St. Francis of Assisi Church.
McHugh, Patrick J. '50 (LA) Torrance, CA Nativity Church.
McHugh, Patrick J. '54 (LA) Retired.
McHugh, Paul F. '53 (MAN) Retired.
McHugh, Msgr. Peter J. '65 (PAT) [2] Clifton, NJ St. Andrew the Apostle Church.

McHugh, Richard P. *s.j.* '60 (WDC) [20] Washington, DC Holy Trinity Church.
McHugh, Thomas J. '49 (CHI) [134] Chicago, IL St. Matthias Church; Retired.
McHugh, William *o.m.i.* '52 (P) Shady Cove, OR Our Lady of Fatima Church.
McIlhenny, Bernard R. *s.j.* '56 (SCR) [C] Scranton, PA University of Scranton.
McIlhon, Msgr. John J. '48 (DM) Retired.
McIlhone, James P. '74 (CHI) [A] Mundelein, IL University of St. Mary of the Lake-Mundelein Seminary.
McIlvane, Donald W. '52 (PIT) Retired.
McIlwain, Michael A. *o.s.b.* '94 (GBG) Latrobe, PA Latrobe Area Hospital; [H] Latrobe, PA Saint Vincent Archabbey; [I] Latrobe, PA Discalced Carmelite Nuns.
McInerey, Kieran *o.s.b.* '52 (FgM) American - Cassinese Congregation Foreign Missions.
McInerney, Blaise *o.carm.* '54 (JOL) [J] Darien, IL Carmelite Provincial Office.
McInerney, Henry '77 (BLX) Kiln, MS Annunciation Church.
McInerney, Maurice '59 (DEN) Absent on Leave.
McInerney, Walter L. *c.s.c.* '36 (FTW) [J] South Bend, IN Congregation of Holy Cross Indiana Province Provincial House.
McInerny, Msgr. Lawrence B. '79 (CHR) [10] Charleston, SC Stella Maris Church; [A] Charleston, SC Bishop England High School.
McInnes, Val A. *o.p.* '61 (NO) [30] New Orleans, LA St. Dominic Church; [P] New Orleans, LA Dominican Fathers & Brothers, Southern Dominican Province; [S] New Orleans, LA The Patrons of the Vatican Museums in the South, Inc.; [S] Metairie, LA Southern Dominican Foundation.
McInnes, William *s.j.* '57 (BO) [W] Chestnut Hill, MA The Jesuit Community at Boston College.
McInnis, Francis L. '56 (GF) Retired.
McInnis, Kevin *s.c.j.* '57 (MIL) [P] Hales Corners, WI Sacred Heart Monastery.
McInnis, Richard W. '69 (PRT) Retired.
McInnis, Thomas J. '57 (LC) Ettrick, WI St. Bridget Church; Melrose, WI St. Kevin Church.
McIntire, William J. *m.m.* '67 (FgM) Maryknoll Foreign Missions.
McIntosh, Alan R. *o.s.b.* '61 (IND) [J] St. Meinrad, IN St. Meinrad Archabbey.
McIntosh, Robert K. *s.j.* '72 (FgM) Provinces.
McIntosh, Thomas *c.ss.r.* '66 (FgM) Redemptorist Foreign Missions.
McIntrye, Allen J. '56 (STP) Hamel, MN St. Anne Church.
McIntyre, Gerald J. *s.j.* '74 (FgM) Provinces.
McIntyre, James *o.f.m.cap.* '53 (BGP) Greenwich, CT Greenwich Hospital.
McIntyre, James *o.f.m.cap.* '53 (NY) [DD] Yonkers, NY St. Clare Friary.
McIntyre, Msgr. James P. '38 (CLV) [33] Cleveland, OH St. Ignatius Church; Rocky River, OH St. Christopher Church; Retired.
McIntyre, Msgr. James P. '71 (CAM) Runnemede, NJ St. Maria Goretti Church.
McIntyre, John J. '92 (PH) Bristol, PA St. Mark Church.
McIntyre, John P. *s.j.* '63 (BO) [W] Chestnut Hill, MA The Jesuit Community at Boston College.
McIntyre, Justin '81 (SR) Retired.
McIntyre, Louis *t.o.r.* '53 (VEN) [2] Sarasota, FL Our Lady Queen of Martyrs Church.
McIntyre, Raymond T. '52 (RIC) Retired.
McIntyre, Thomas J. '50 (LA) [R] Los Angeles, CA Amat House; [X] Montebello, CA DePaul Center.
McIntyre, Msgr. Thomas J. '66 (CAM) Blackwood, NJ St. Jude's Church; [G] Camden, NJ The Tuition Assistance Fund, Inc.
McIntyre, William *o.f.m.* '95 (WIL) [10] Wilmington, DE St. Paul's Church.
McIsaac, Edward F. '48 (FR) Retired.
McKamy, Eldon J. '63 (OM) Absent on Leave.
McKane, Paul *o.s.b.* (WDC) Norbeck, MD St. Patrick Church.
McKane, Paul *o.s.b.* '88 (WDC) [M] Washington, DC St. Anselm's Abbey.
McKarns, James E. '62 (Y) North Canton, OH St. Paul's Church.
McKay, Alistair J. *c.ss.r.* '75 (CHR) Sumter, SC St. Anne's Church.
McKay, Anthony *c.s.sp.* '60 (LR) Conway, AR St. Joseph's Church.
McKay, Douglas M. '82 (PH) [Y] Philadelphia, PA Holy Family Home.
McKay, Frank '54 (NY) Absent on Sick leave.
McKay, Henry *m.s.* '48 (BEA) Orange, TX St. Therese Church.
McKay, Msgr. James '56 (SFR) [3] San Mateo, CA St. Matthew Church; San Mateo, CA Serra Club of San Mateo.
McKay, James R. *s.m.* '50 (PIT) [O] Pittsburgh, PA Marianist Community.
McKay, John F. '73 (WDC) Hospital & Nursing Home Ministries.
McKay, Joseph A. '84 (ALB) [16] Schenectady, NY St. Paul the Apostle Church.
McKay, Michael *o.s.b.* (BAL) [15] Baltimore, MD St. Benedict Church.
McKay, Michael *o.s.b.* '86 (GBG) [H] Latrobe, PA Saint Vincent Archabbey.
McKay, Robert J. '51 (SY) Retired; [S] Syracuse, NY St. Pius X Home, Inc.
McKay, William E. '49 (PHX) Retired.
McKean, Benedict B. *o.s.b.* '59 (PEO) [A] Peru, IL St. Bede Abbey and Academy.
McKean, Dan '87 (LAN) Williamston, MI St. Mary Church.
McKean, Louis '47 (P) Retired.
McKeaney, James J. '69 (PH) West Conshohocken, PA St. Gertrude Church.
McKearney, James L. '97 (HRT) [5] West Hartford, CT St. Peter Claver Church.
McKee, Msgr. Francis J. '39 (LR) Retired.
McKee, Francis X. '66 (PH) [59] Philadelphia, PA Holy Family Church.
McKee, Henry J. '72 (PH) [129] Philadelphia, PA Our Lady of Victory Church.
McKee, James C. *s.j.* '69 (E) Curwensville, PA St. Timothy Church.
McKee, John '46 (FRS) Retired.
McKee, Keith '54 (SP) [2] Clearwater, FL Light of Christ Church.
McKee, Roderick D. '66 (WDC) Beltsville, MD St. Joseph Church.
McKee, William *c.ss.r.* '48 (STL) [P] Liguori, MO Liguori Mission House/Redemptorists.
McKee, William A. '83 (SEA) [10] Seattle, WA St. John Church.
McKeefry, Brendan '67 (SAC) Paradise, CA St. Thomas More Church.
McKeever, Frederick *o.f.m.* '54 (PAT) [M] Butler, NJ St. Anthony Friary.
McKeever, Henry *c.ss.r.* '48 (STL) [P] Liguori, MO Liguori Mission House/Redemptorists.
McKeever, William '45 (MIA) Retired.
McKeever, Msgr. William F. '45 (MIA) [22] Miami, FL St. John Bosco Church.
McKeirnan, Michael J. *m.m.* '41 (FgM) Maryknoll Foreign Missions.
McKelvey, James P. '93 (PH) Collegeville, PA St. Eleanor Church.
McKelvey, Thomas P. '62 (PH) Linwood, PA Holy Saviour Church.
McKendrick, Norman G. *s.j.* '61 (DET) [K] Detroit, MI Jesuit Community at the University of Detroit.
McKenna, Brian *o.f.m.cap.* '65 (BAK) Bend, OR St. Francis of Assisi Church.
McKenna, Daniel *o.m.i.* '58 (GAL) Alvin, TX St. John the Baptist Church.
McKenna, Denis R. '47 (NEW) Retired.
McKenna, Dennis '47 (NEW) [2] Irvington, NJ St. Leo's Church.
McKenna, Edward J. '65 (CHI) Other Assignments.
McKenna, Edward T. *s.s.c.* '49 (FgM) St. Columban's Foreign Mission.
McKenna, Enda '64 (SAT) [49] San Antonio, TX St. Leo Church.
McKenna, Eugene F. *m.s.* '53 (LKC) Hackberry, LA St. Peter Apostle Church.
McKenna, Eugene J. *s.s.j.* '47 (BAL) [M] Baltimore, MD St. Joseph's Manor.
McKenna, Eugene J. '63 (PRO) Middletown, RI St. Lucy Church.
McKenna, F. Charles '60 (ALN) Retired; [J] Bethlehem, PA Holy Family Villa.
McKenna, Frank W. '94 (NOR) Colchester, CT St. Andrew Church.
McKenna, George P. '44 (CHI) [1] Oak Lawn, IL St. Catherine of Alexandria Church; Retired.
McKenna, Hugh J. *o.s.f.s.* '44 (WIL) [I] Childs, MD Oblates of St. Francis De Sales.
McKenna, James '50 (SPR) Retired.
McKenna, James *s.d.s.* '52 (MOB) Phenix City, AL Mother Mary Parish.
McKenna, James A. *s.d.b.* '80 (NY) [2] Port Chester, NY Corpus Christi Church.
McKenna, James D. '50 (SPR) [1] Holyoke, MA Blessed Sacrament Church.
McKenna, James George '61 (DAL) [5] Dallas, TX Holy Cross Church; On Duty Outside the Diocese.
McKenna, Msgr. James J. '42 (BRK) [198] Queens, NY St. Mary Star of the Sea Church; Retired.
McKenna, James T. '64 (NEW) Closter, NJ St. Mary's Church.
McKenna, Jerome *c.p.* '58 (WH) Kingwood, WV St. Sebastian's Church; Masontown, WV St. Zita's Church.
McKenna, John *c.m.* '64 (BRK) [U] Jamaica, NY St. Vincent's House.
McKenna, John '88 (PIT) Glenshaw, PA St. Mary Church.
McKenna, John J. '45 (WOR) Retired.
McKenna, John J. '47 (NY) Retired.
McKenna, Joseph C. *s.j.* '49 (NY) [DD] New York, NY Murray-Weigel Hall.
McKenna, Joseph J. *o.s.f.s.* '57 (WIL) Newark, DE Christiana Care Health System; [B] Wilmington, DE Salesianum School.
Mckenna, Joseph R. '57 (PRT) Bath, ME Immaculate Conception Church.
McKenna, Juan *c.ss.r.* '77 (CGS) San Lorenzo, PR Nuestra Senora de la Mercedes Church.
McKenna, Kenneth N. *o.s.f.s.* (TOL) [K] Toledo, OH Oblates of St. Francis de Sales.
McKenna, Kenneth N. *o.s.f.s.* '85 (DET) [Q] Warren, MI St. John's Deaf Center.
McKenna, Kevin '77 (ROC) Scottsville, NY St. Mary of the Assumption Church.
McKenna, Kevin E. (ROC) [19] Rochester, NY St. Helen Church.
McKenna, Michael G. '73 (GR) Big Rapids, MI St. Mary's Church.
McKenna, Peter '57 (SAT) La Vernia, TX St. Ann Church.
McKenna, Philip (FgM) Society of St. James the Apostle.
McKenna, Philip A. '62 (MOB) On Duty Outside the Archdiocese.
McKenna, Thomas F. *c.m.* '70 (PH) [B] Philadelphia, PA St. Vincent's Seminary; [B] Philadelphia, PA DePaul Novitiate; [AA] Philadelphia, PA Congregation of the Mission.
McKenna, Thomas J. '72 (PIT) Hopewell Township, PA Our Lady of Fatima Church.
McKenna, Timothy J. '79 (SEA) Military Chaplains.
McKenna, William *s.s.j.* '64 (MOB) [15] Mobile, AL Most Pure Heart of Mary Church.
McKenna, William A. *s.j.* '68 (NEW) [B] Jersey City, NJ Saint Peter's College; [N] Jersey City, NJ Jesuits of Saint Peter's College, Inc.
McKenney, Charles R. *s.j.* '44 (WOR) [N] Worcester, MA Jesuits of Holy Cross College, Inc.
McKenney, William G. *s.j.* '94 (RC) Pine Ridge, SD Holy Rosary Church; [B] Pine Ridge, SD Jesuit Community of Holy Rosary Mission.
McKenzie, John Harold *o.s.b.* '85 (CC) [H] Sandia, TX Corpus Christi Abbey.
McKenzie, John J. *o.s.a.* '65 (PH) [C] Villanova, PA Villanova University; [AA] Villanova, PA St. Thomas Monastery.
McKenzie, Mark D. *s.j.* '69 (PBL) Trinidad, CO Most Holy Trinity, Trinidad Area Catholic Community (Trinidad Cluster) Church; Trinidad, CO Our Lady of Mt. Carmel, Trinidad Area Catholic Community (Trinidad Cluster) Church; Trinidad, CO St. Joseph, Trinidad Area Catholic Community (Trinidad Cluster) Church; [F] Trinidad, CO Trinidad Area Catholic Community.
McKeon, Brian A. '77 (RVC) Garden City, NY St. Anne Church.
McKeon, Gerard R. *s.j.* '86 (FgM) Provinces.
McKeon, James F. '54 (LA) Retired.
McKeon, John Aedan *o.p.* '56 (NY) [DD] New York, NY St. Vincent Ferrer Priory.
McKeon, Michael '65 (SAC) [1] Sacramento, CA Cathedral of the Blessed Sacrament.
McKeon, Raymond '62 (NEW) [17] Newark, NJ St. James Church.
McKeon, Raymond T. '63 (NEW) Retired.
McKeon, Robert '59 (LAN) Retired.
McKeon, Robert '90 (NY) [A] Yonkers, NY St. Joseph's Seminary; [A] Bronx, NY St. John Neumann Residence.
McKeon, Robert F. '59 (LAN) Mount Morris, MI St. Mary Church.
McKeon, Thomas *s.s.s.* '50 (NY) [8] New York, NY St. Andrew Church; Manhattan, NY Beekman Downtown - New York Infirmary.
McKeon, William '57 (GAY) East Jordan, MI St. Joseph Church; Praga, MI St. John Nepomucene Church.
McKeon, William E. *c.m.* '49 (PH) [AA] Philadelphia, PA Congregation of the Mission.
McKeon, William J. '57 (LAN) Retired.
McKeone, William '72 (TR) On Duty Outside the Diocese.
McKeough, Brendan J. '53 (GB) [I] De Pere, WI St. Joseph Priory.
McKeough, James A. *s.j.* '54 (FgM) Provinces.
McKeown, Peter *m.s.* (ATL) Cartersville, GA St. Francis of Assisi Church.
McKeown, Peter '67 (NY) [11] Yonkers, NY St. John the Baptist Church.
McKeown, Timothy P. '97 (SAV) Macon, GA St. Joseph's Church.
McKercher, Mark J. '97 (OM) [48] Douglas Co., NE St. Wenceslaus Church.
McKernan, John P. *m.m.* '52 (FgM) Maryknoll Foreign Missions.
McKernan, Kenneth B. *c.s.b.* '66 (DET) [E] Redford, MI Catholic Central High School.
McKernan, Leo J. '83 (SCR) Avoca, PA St. Mary's Church.
McKernan, Louis F. *c.s.p.* '54 (NY) [DD] Jamaica Estates, NY Paulist Fathers Generalate.

McKevitt, Gerald L. *s.j.* '75 (SJ) [B] Santa Clara, CA Santa Clara University.
McKevitt, Msgr. Nolan B. '35 (MAR) Retired.
McKiernan, J. Michael '91 (ORG) [1] Orange, CA Cathedral of the Holy Family.
McKiernan, Joseph W. '51 (WOR) Sutton, MA St. Mark Church.
McKiernan, Raymond '56 (BRK) [58] Brooklyn, NY Holy Name Church.
McKiernan, Thomas M. '51 (CHI) Palos Heights, IL St. Alexander Church.
McKiernan, Vincent W. *c.s.p.* '57 (COL) [J] Columbus, OH Campus Ministry.
McKillin, David '76 (LR) [A] Subiaco, AR Subiaco Monastery.
McKillip, Dennis *s.v.d.* '47 (FgM) Society of the Divine Word Foreign Missions.
McKillop, Michael J. *m.m.* '35 (NY) [DD] Maryknoll, NY Maryknoll Fathers and Brothers.
McKinley, Joseph J. *s.s.j.* '85 (BAL) [M] Baltimore, MD St. Joseph Society of the Sacred Heart House of Central Administration.
McKinley, Michael J. '85 (LFT) [2] Lafayette, IN St. Ann Church.
McKinley, Steve *o.f.m.conv.* '94 (PEO) [2] Peoria, IL Holy Family Church.
McKinney, Floyd '80 (WCH) [9] Wichita, KS Our Lady of Perpetual Help Church.
McKinney, Francis *t.o.r.* '34 (ARL) [J] Winchester, VA Sacred Heart Friary.
McKinney, James F. '96 (FAR) Enderlin, ND St. Patrick's Church.
McKinney, Michael A. '93 (LFT) Muncie, IN St. Francis of Assisi Church; [H] Muncie, IN St. Francis of Assisi University Church.
McKinney, Ronald H. *s.j.* '83 (SCR) [C] Scranton, PA University of Scranton.
McKinney, Thomas A. '61 (GR) Greenville, MI St. Charles Church.
McKinney, Tom '96 (GAL) Humble, TX St. Mary Magdalene Church.
McKinnon, Eymard *o.f.m.cap.* '54 (AGN) [E] Agana Heights, GU St. Fidelis Friary.
McKinnon, Eymard *o.f.m.cap.* '54 (FgM) Capuchin Foreign Missions.
McKinstra, William M. '62 (RCK) Dundee, IL St. Catherine of Siena Church.
McKitrick, James V. '58 (RCK) McHenry, IL St. Patrick Church.
McKloskey, Msgr. James A. '46 (SY) Fayetteville, NY Immaculate Conception Church.
McKnight, James '59 (SAC) Nevada City, CA St. Canice Church.
McKnight, Kevin F. '94 (PIT) Washington, PA Immaculate Conception Church; [R] Slippery Rock, PA Office for Campus Ministry.
McKnight, Robert J. '73 (BUR) Orwell, VT St. Paul Church.
McKnight, W. Shawn '94 (WCH) On Duty Outside the Diocese.
McKnight, William F. '48 (GR) Custer, MI St. Mary's Church.
McLachlan, Frederick E. *s.s.e.* '64 (BUR) Putney, VT Our Lady of Mercy Church.
McLain, J. Clyde '57 (STL) Retired.
McLaughlin, Adrian T. *o.s.b.* '41 (PAT) [M] Morristown, NJ St. Mary's Abbey.
McLaughlin, Andrew '87 (DET) Absent on Leave.
McLaughlin, Anthony K.W. '97 (TYL) [1] Tyler, TX Cathedral of the Immaculate Conception.
McLaughlin, Bernard P. '59 (BO) Canton, MA St. Gerard Majella Church.
McLaughlin, Charles '62 (BRK) [10] Brooklyn, NY St. Anselm's Church.
McLaughlin, Charles J. (CHI) Retired.
McLaughlin, Daniel *o.s.a.* '83 (PH) [D] Drexel Hill, PA Monsignor Bonner High School.
McLaughlin, Daniel F. '61 (FgM) Maryknoll Foreign Missions.
McLaughlin, Daniel P. *s.t.* '63 (TUC) [2] Tucson, AZ Blessed Kateri Tekakwitha Church; [J] Tucson, AZ St. Nicholas Indian Center.
McLaughlin, David S. '96 (NEW) Kearny, NJ St. Stephen's Church.
McLaughlin, Don E. '81 (JOL) Bensenville, IL St. Charles Borromeo Church.
McLaughlin, Donald '67 (NEW) Dumont, NJ St. Mary's Church.
McLaughlin, Edward J. '52 (BO) Bridgewater, MA St. Thomas Aquinas Church.
McLaughlin, Edward J. '59 (CHI) Orland Park, IL St. Michael Church.
McLaughlin, Eugene '85 (STU) Absent on Leave.
McLaughlin, Farrell E. '71 (PRO) North Kingstown, RI St. Francis De Sales Church.
McLaughlin, Gerald L. *s.j.* '59 (FgM) Provinces.
McLaughlin, Gregory '85 (AUS) Calvert, TX St. Mary Church; Hearne, TX St. Mary's Church.
McLaughlin, Hugh J. '63 (HBG) Spring Grove, PA Sacred Heart Church.
McLaughlin, James '73 (SB) [9] Riverside, CA St. Patrick Church.
McLaughlin, James C., II '78 (GAY) Absent on Leave.
McLaughlin, James E. *m.m.* '40 (NY) [DD] Maryknoll, NY Maryknoll Fathers and Brothers.
McLaughlin, James J. '70 (PH) [20] Philadelphia, PA St. Barnabas Church.
McLaughlin, James W. '96 (MET) Old Bridge, NJ St. Ambrose Church.
McLaughlin, John '61 (SEA) Elma, WA St. Joseph's Church.
McLaughlin, John *c.ss.r.* '92 (BAL) [96] Baltimore, MD St. Wenceslaus Church.
McLaughlin, John E. '62 (BO) [3] Somerville, MA St. Benedict Church.
McLaughlin, John E. '95 (BO) [5] Somerville, MA St. Clement Church.
McLaughlin, John F. '56 (GB) Amberg, WI St. Agnes Church; Wausaukee, WI St. Augustine Church.
McLaughlin, John P. '66 (MIA) [1] Fort Lauderdale, FL Blessed Sacrament Church.
McLaughlin, Joseph (GLP) Retired.
McLaughlin, Joseph '55 (OKL) Retired.
McLaughlin, Joseph J. '66 (PH) Richboro, PA St. Vincent de Paul Church.
McLaughlin, Joseph J. *s.m.* '72 (WDC) [M] Washington, DC Marist Provincial House.
McLaughlin, Joseph M. *s.s.e.* '70 (BUR) [E] Colchester, VT Society of St. Edmund.
McLaughlin, Joseph P. '70 (PH) [AA] Paoli, PA Daylesford Abbey.
McLaughlin, Mike '82 (DM) [4] Des Moines, IA Holy Trinity Church.
McLaughlin, Neil P. *s.j.* '59 (SCR) [C] Scranton, PA University of Scranton.
McLaughlin, Owen F. '41 (MIL) Retired.
McLaughlin, Patrick J. '61 (BO) [3] Medford, MA St. Joseph Church.
McLaughlin, Patrick J. '74 (SCR) Dushore, PA St. Basil's Church.
McLaughlin, Paul E. '71 (VEN) Military Chaplains.
McLaughlin, Paul J. '55 (BO) [2] Marlboro, MA Immaculate Conception Church.
McLaughlin, Peter A. '78 (CAM) Military Chaplains.
McLaughlin, Richard '74 (PRT) [1] Lewiston, ME St. Joseph's Church.
McLaughlin, Richard P. '68 (BO) [37] Boston, MA St. Joseph-St. Lazarus Church.
McLaughlin, Robert A. '73 (PH) [91] Philadelphia, PA St. Malachy Church; [EE] Philadelphia, PA Newman Apostolate.
McLaughlin, Robert E. '66 (CHI) [1] Chicago, IL Cathedral of the Holy Name.
McLaughlin, Thomas *o.s.b.* '83 (RCK) [H] Aurora, IL Marmion Abbey-St. Augustine's Abbey.
McLaughlin, Thomas D. '76 (SCR) Stroudsburg, PA St. Luke's Church.
McLaughlin, Thomas J. *o.s.a.* '53 (SD) [34] San Diego, CA St. Patrick Church.
McLaughlin, Thomas R. '81 (NEW) Hillside, NJ St. Catherine of Siena Church; Newark, NJ Beth Israel Hospital.
McLaughlin, Thomas W. '49 (LA) [91] Los Angeles, CA St. Teresa of Avila Church; Retired.
McLaughlin, Msgr. William '58 (ORG) Newport Beach, CA Our Lady Queen of Angels Church.
McLaughlin, William A. '92 (BRK) [11] Brooklyn, NY St. Anthony of Padua-St. Alphonsus Church.
McLaughlin, William H. '68 (BO) [38] Boston, MA St. Joseph Church.
McLaughlin, William J. '70 (TR) [T] Trenton, NJ Martin House.
McLean, Barry *o.f.m.* '90 (SAN) Big Lake, TX St. Margaret of Cortona Church; Crane, TX Good Shepherd Church.
McLean, Barry L. '90 (SAN) McCamey, TX Sacred Heart Church.
McLean, Edward J. '52 (HRT) [1] West Hartford, CT St. Brigid's Church; Special and other (Arch)Diocesan Assignment.
McLean, George F. *o.m.i.* '55 (WDC) [B] Washington, DC Oblate College/Oblate Center for Mission Studies; [V] Washington, DC Council for Research in Values and Philosophy.
McLean, James F. *c.s.p.* '41 (NY) [DD] Jamaica Estates, NY Paulist Fathers Generalate.
McLean, William '69 (LA) [2] Long Beach, CA St. Athanasius Church.
McLearen, Daniel J. '92 (HRT) [6] Waterbury, CT Our Lady of Mt. Carmel Church.
McLellan, Alan J. *c.m.* '65 (FgM) Vincentian Foreign Missions.
McLellan, Daniel *o.f.m.* '76 (WDC) [B] Silver Spring, MD Holy Name College.
McLellan, James '70 (FR) North Dighton, MA St. Joseph's Church.
McLellan, Michael F. '76 (BO) [14] Boston, MA Blessed Sacrament Church; [56] Boston, MA Our Lady of Lourdes Church.
McLellan, Thomas J. *c.ss.r.* '56 (BRK) [107] Brooklyn, NY Our Lady of Perpetual Help Basilica Church.
McLeod, Daniel '42 (OAK) Retired.
McLeod, David (PAT) On Duty Outside the Diocese.
McLeod, Frederick G. *s.j.* (STL) [C] St. Louis, MO Saint Louis University.
McLeod, Frederick G. *s.j.* '62 (BO) [W] Boston, MA The Society of Jesus of New England-Provincial Offices.
McLeod, Frederick G. *s.j.* '62 (STL) [P] St. Louis, MO Jesuit Community Corporation at St. Louis University - Jesuit Hall.
McLeod, Malcolm C. *m.ss.cc.* '87 (CAM) Linwood, NJ Our Lady of Sorrows Church.
McLeod, Paul *ss.cc.* (HON) Lihue, HI Immaculate Conception Church.
McLeon, Robert (NY) [D] New York, NY Department of Education.
McLernan, Richard L. *o.s.f.s.* '57 (LAN) [B] Jackson, MI Lumen Christi High School.
McLernon, Thomas M. '57 (BGP) [V] Fairfield, CT Newman Centers - Campus Ministry.
McLernon, Thomas M. '57 (HBG) On Duty Outside the Diocese.
McLeroy, Jacob (SFE) Springer, NM St. Joseph Church.
McLinden, James E. *s.s.j.* '71 (WDC) [B] Washington, DC St. Joseph's Seminary.
McLoone, Joseph C. (PH) [1] Philadelphia, PA Cathedral Basilica of SS. Peter and Paul Church.
McLoraine, John A. '35 (CHI) [2] Mt. Prospect, IL St. Emily Church; Retired.
McLoud, Steven J. '93 (SC) Boone, IA Sacred Heart Church.
McLoughlin, Brendan '70 (PAT) Randolph, NJ Resurrection Church.
McLoughlin, Edward '78 (VEN) Absent on Leave.
McLoughlin, James W. '65 (RCK) Woodstock, IL St. Mary Church.
McLoughlin, John *c.ss.r.* (BAL) [96] Baltimore, MD St. Wenceslaus Church.
McLoughlin, John Francis *c.p.* '54 (HRT) [M] West Hartford, CT Holy Family Monastery/Retreat.
McLoughlin, John T. '73 (NY) [6] Mt. Vernon, NY St. Ursula Church; West Point, NY Catholic Chapel of the Most Holy Trinity Church; [GG] New York, NY University Apostolate.
McLoughlin, Luke '66 (STA) [17] Jacksonville, FL St. Matthew's Church.
McLoughlin, Michael P. '81 (NY) Highland Falls, NY Sacred Heart of Jesus Church.
McLoughlin, Nicholas '66 (VEN) Port Charlotte, FL St. Charles Borromeo Church.
McLoughlin, Paul J. '71 (SPC) Ozark, MO St. Joseph the Worker Church.
McLoughlin, Richard J. '69 (PH) Absent on Leave.
McLoughlin, William J. '57 (BRK) Retired; [U] Douglaston, NY Bishop Mugavero Residence.
McLoy, Alfred E. '54 (SC) [B] Sioux City, IA Bishop Heelan Catholic High School.
McLucas, James '79 (NY) Absent on Leave.
McLucas, James *f.s.s.p.* '79 (SCR) [M] Elmhurst, PA Priestly Fraternity of St. Peter (F.S.S.P.), North American District Headquarters.
McMackin, Thomas P. '63 (ORL) Ormond Beach, FL Prince of Peace Church.
McMahon, Aloysius J. '53 (OM) Boys Town, NE Immaculate Conception B.V.M. Church.
McMahon, Bartholomew *o.f.m.* '62 (FgM) Franciscan Foreign Missions.
McMahon, Bernard '48 (NY) [C] New Rochelle, NY College of New Rochelle.
McMahon, Brian F. '80 (BO) [Q] Brighton, MA St. Elizabeth's Hospital of Boston.
McMahon, Charles E. *s.s.j.* '58 (MOB) Plateau, AL Our Mother of Mercy Church.
McMahon, Desmond '60 (SEA) Medical Leave.
McMahon, Edward J. *s.j.* '60 (NY) [DD] New York, NY Xavier Jesuit Community.
McMahon, Edward M. '70 (BO) Billerica, MA St. Mary Church.
McMahon, Francis *c.ss.r.* '58 (OAK) [N] Oakland, CA Redemptorists.
McMahon, Francis X. *s.s.e.* '54 (NOR) Groton, CT Sacred Heart Church.
McMahon, George J. *s.j.* '53 (NY) [C] Bronx, NY Fordham University; [DD] New York, NY Jesuit Community at Fordham University.
McMahon, Gerald J. *s.j.* '62 (NY) [DD] New York, NY Murray-Weigel Hall.
McMahon, Gerard J. '59 (ROC) [39] Rochester, NY Our Lady of Victory-St. Joseph Church; Retired.
McMahon, Gerard T. '61 (BO) On Duty Outside the Archdiocese.
McMahon, Msgr. James B. '53 (BRK) [23] Brooklyn, NY St. Brendan's Church.
McMahon, Msgr. John '66 (PMB) [3] Boca Raton, FL St. Joan of Arc Church.
McMahon, John A. *o.p.* '68 (WDC) [11] Washington, DC St. Dominic Church & Priory Church.
McMahon, John B. '60 (WDC) Retired.
McMahon, John F. '76 (CLV) [64] Cleveland, OH SS. Philip and James Church; Retired.
McMahon, John J. '38 (CHI) Skokie, IL St. Joan of Arc Church; Retired.

McMahon, Msgr. John J. '48 (PHX) Special Assignment; [G] Phoenix, AZ Mt. Claret Retreat Center; [J] Phoenix, AZ St. Vincent De Paul Society.
McMahon, Joseph M. '43 (P) Retired.
McMahon, Joseph R. '71 (WIL) [2] Wilmington, DE St. Ann Church.
McMahon, Joseph S. '68 (P) Gresham, OR St. Henry Church.
McMahon, Joseph V. '84 (NSH) [6] Nashville, TN St. Henry Church; [B] Nashville, TN Father Ryan High School.
McMahon, Kevin T. '75 (PH) [A] Wynnewood, PA Theological Seminary of St. Charles Borromeo, Overbrook.
McMahon, Kevin T. '75 (WIL) On Duty Outside the Diocese.
McMahon, Kieran F. *o.f.m.* '47 (PAT) [M] Ringwood, NJ Holy Name Friary, Inc.
McMahon, Kieran M. '65 (SAC) [21] Sacramento, CA St. Robert Church.
McMahon, Msgr. Lawrence J. '55 (BGP) [3] Stratford, CT St. Mark's Church.
McMahon, Martin J. *o.m.i.* '56 (BUF) [27] Buffalo, NY Holy Angels Church.
McMahon, Marvin J. '51 (SFS) Retired.
McMahon, Michael F. '88 (CHI) Lake Forest, IL St. Mary Church.
McMahon, Patrick *o.carm.* (WDC) [B] Washington, DC Whitefriars Hall.
McMahon, Patrick *o.carm.* '76 (WDC) [B] Washington, DC Whitefriars Hall.
McMahon, Patrick Thomas *o.carm.* (WDC) [M] Washington, DC Carmelite Community.
McMahon, Sean '62 (ALB) Cairo, NY Sacred Heart Church.
McMahon, Msgr. Thomas '34 (NY) Rye, NY Resurrection Church; Retired.
McMahon, Thomas D. *s.j.* '51 (BUF) [50] Buffalo, NY St. Michael Church.
McMahon, Thomas F. *c.s.v.* '54 (CHI) [N] Chicago, IL Viatorian Residence.
McMahon, Msgr. Thomas V. '34 (NY) [E] White Plains, NY Archbishop Stepinac High School.
McMahon, Timothy M. *s.j.* '87 (KC) [12] Kansas City, MO St. Francis Xavier Church; [J] Kansas City, MO St. Francis Xavier - Jesuit Community.
McMahon, Walter M. '73 (SJ) [19] San Jose, CA St. Thomas of Canterbury Church.
McMahon, Msgr. William J. '45 (NY) Cortlandt Manor, NY Holy Spirit Church; Retired; [HH] New York, NY St. Anthony Welfare Center.
McMain, Msgr. Robert O. '49 (WDC) Special Ministries; Retired; [V] Washington, DC Catholic Historical Society of Washington.
McManamin, Francis G. *s.j.* '61 (BAL) [B] Baltimore, MD Loyola College; [M] Baltimore, MD Jesuit Community of Loyola College, Inc.
McManamon, James *o.f.m.* '49 (CLV) [6] Parma, OH Holy Family Church.
McManamon, John M. *s.j.* (DET) [K] Detroit, MI Jesuit Provincial Office-Detroit Province of the Society of Jesus.
McManimon, James P. '59 (TR) [3] Trenton, NJ Holy Angels Church; Leave of Absence.
McManus, Msgr. Charles '42 (NY) [144] Bronx, NY St. Gabriel Church.
McManus, Msgr. Charles J. '42 (NY) [4] Yonkers, NY St. Bartholomew Church; Retired.
McManus, Dennis *c.s.sp.* '58 (SFR) San Anselmo, CA St. Anselm Church; San Quentin, CA California State Prison.
McManus, Eamon '54 (WDC) Lanham, MD St. Matthias Church.
McManus, Eugene J. '57 (RVC) Hewlett, NY St. Joseph's Church; Retired.
McManus, Eugene P. *s.s.j.* '49 (BAL) [M] Baltimore, MD St. Joseph Society of the Sacred Heart House of Central Administration.
McManus, Fidelis *o.f.m.cap.* '45 (SAL) [D] Hays, KS St. Joseph's Friary.
McManus, Francis J. *s.j.* '73 (BGP) [O] Fairfield, CT The Fairfield Jesuit Community-Fairfield University.
McManus, Francis J. *s.j.* '73 (BO) [W] Boston, MA The Society of Jesus of New England-Provincial Offices.
McManus, Francis J. *s.j.* '73 (FR) [14] New Bedford, MA St. James Church.
McManus, Frederick R. (BO) Retired.
McManus, Msgr. Frederick R. '47 (WDC) [C] Washington, DC Catholic University of America, The.
McManus, Gerald D. '79 (PH) Military Chaplains.
McManus, Msgr. Hugh F. '61 (NY) Scarsdale, NY Our Lady of Fatima Church.
McManus, Msgr. J. Fleming '47 (CHR) Retired.
McManus, John E. *c.s.b.* '55 (GAL) [Q] Houston, TX Residence of the Basilian Fathers of the University of St. Thomas.
McManus, John H. *o.m.i.* '56 (SCL) [M] St. Cloud, MN St. Therese Center for Special Ministry.
McManus, John H. *o.m.i.* '56 (STP) [Q] Buffalo, MN Christ the King Retreat Center.
McManus, Joseph '56 (BAL) [42] Baltimore, MD Immaculate Heart of Mary Church.
McManus, Martin '59 (SD) Retired.
McManus, Msgr. Michael G. '48 (SAT) Bandera, TX St. Stanislaus Church.
McManus, Michael K. '85 (FR) Somerset, MA St. Thomas More Church.
McManus, Paul C. '65 (DUB) Blessing, IA Immaculate Conception Church; [H] Waterloo, IA Covenant Medical Center.
McManus, Paul G. '87 (BO) Awaiting Assignment.
McManus, Msgr. Paul J. '42 (BO) Retired.
McManus, Richard *o.f.m.* '83 (MRY) [I] San Juan Bautista, CA St. Francis Retreat Center.
McManus, Robert J. '78 (PRO) Barrington, RI St. Luke Church.
McManus, Msgr. Robert T. '52 (PH) Downingtown, PA St. Joseph Church.
McManus, Thomas *o.s.a.* '70 (ORG) Buena Park, CA St. Pius V Church.
McManus, Thomas F. *s.j.* '63 (ROC) [B] Rochester, NY McQuaid Jesuit High School.
McManus, Thomas J. *s.t.l.* '68 (PH) [157] Philadelphia, PA St. William Church.
McMenamin, John (OKL) Prison Ministry.
McMenamy, Alvin *s.m.* '67 (STL) [P] St. Louis, MO Provincialate of the Society of Mary, Province of St. Louis.
McMillan, Cliff J. '90 (DEN) Glenwood Springs, CO St. Stephen Church.
McMillan, John F. *c.p.* '56 (PIT) [O] Pittsburgh, PA St. Paul of the Cross Monastery.
McMillan, Keith P. *s.j.* '93 (KC) [J] Kansas City, MO Rockhurst College - Jesuit Community.
McMillan, Robert G. *s.j.* '62 (BO) [22] Boston, MA St. Francis de Sales-St. Philip Church; [W] Boston, MA Loyola House; [W] Boston, MA The Society of Jesus of New England-Provincial Offices.
McMillen, Michael *s.c.j.* '67 (CHI) [N] Chicago, IL Priests of the Sacred Heart.
McMonagle, Edward '47 (HON) [15] Honolulu, HI Star of the Sea Church.
McMorrow, Kevin *s.a.* '58 (NY) [A] Yonkers, NY St. Joseph's Seminary; [DD] Garrison, NY Franciscan Friars of the Atonement.
McMullan, John E. '61 (SEA) [16] Seattle, WA St. Matthew Church; [29] Seattle, WA Our Lady of the Lake Church.
McMullan, John E. '75 (SEA) [21] Seattle, WA Assumption Church.
McMullan, Msgr. Seamus O. '46 (FRS) Tehachapi, CA St. Malachy Church; Retired.
McMullen, Aidan C. '47 (NEW) [B] Jersey City, NJ Saint Peter's College; [N] Jersey City, NJ Jesuits of Saint Peter's College, Inc.
McMullen, Brendan J. *o.p.* '43 (STP) [15] Minneapolis, MN St. Albert the Great Church; Bloomington, MN Nativity of the Blessed Virgin Mary Church.
McMullen, Charles P. '34 (PH) Eddystone, PA St. Rose of Lima Church; Retired.
McMullen, Francis R. '51 (RVC) Priests Released from Diocesan Assignment.
McMullen, John *o.s.b.* '66 (SFS) Wilmot, SD St. Mary Church; [F] Marvin, SD Blue Cloud Abbey; [I] Marvin, SD Blue Cloud Abbey Retirement Trust.
McMullen, Roger '67 (SHP) Retired.
McMullin, Daniel '81 (ROC) [6] Rochester, NY St. Anthony of Padua Church; [15] Rochester, NY St. Francis Assisi Church; [20] Rochester, NY Holy Apostles Church; [51] Rochester, NY SS. Peter and Paul Church.
McMullin, Ernan '49 (FTW) [B] Notre Dame, IN University of Notre Dame Du Lac.
McMullin, Finian *o.f.m.* '46 (SFD) [H] Granite City, IL St. Elizabeth Medical Center.
McMurry, John E. *s.s.* '56 (BAL) [L] Baltimore, MD St. Mary's Spiritual Center.
McMurry, John E. *s.s.* '56 (NSH) On Duty Outside the Diocese.
McMurry, Vincent deP. *s.s.* '49 (NSH) On Duty Outside the Diocese.
McMurtrie, Msgr. James W. '62 (ARL) Ashburn, VA St. Theresa Church.
McNalis, John P. '76 (CHI) [66] Chicago, IL St. Gabriel Church.
McNally, Dennis E. *s.j.* '74 (PH) [C] Philadelphia, PA St. Joseph's University; [AA] Philadelphia, PA Jesuit Community at St. Joseph's University.
McNally, Donald *o.m.i.* (GAL) Richmond, TX Jester I Unit; Richmond, TX Jester II Unit; Richmond, TX Jester III Unit; Richmond, TX Jester IV Unit.
McNally, Donald *o.m.i.* '60 (SAT) [M] San Antonio, TX Provincial Administration Office, Oblates of Mary Immaculate (Southern Prov.).
McNally, Edward F. '95 (SY) Mattydale, NY St. Margaret Church.
McNally, James P. '80 (JC) Absent on Leave.
McNally, Joseph '58 (IND) [16] Indianapolis, IN St. Barnabas Church.
McNally, Lawrence R. '77 (CHI) [181] Chicago, IL Queen of the Universe Church.
McNally, Michael '73 (PMB) On Duty Outside the Diocese.
McNally, Michael J. '73 (PH) [A] Wynnewood, PA Theological Seminary of St. Charles Borromeo, Overbrook.
McNally, Michael R. '59 (SB) Colton, CA Immaculate Conception Church.
McNally, Nathan *o.f.m.* '57 (STL) [T] Dittmer, MO Il Ritiro-The Little Retreat.
McNally, Richard *ss.cc.* '75 (FR) [J] Fairhaven, MA Sacred Hearts Provincial House.
McNally, Stephen '86 (RIC) On Duty Outside the Diocese.
McNally, Theodore A. *o.f.m.* '55 (PAT) [M] Butler, NJ St. Anthony Friary.
McNally, Thomas *c.s.c.* '61 (OAK) [3] Hayward, CA St. Clement Church.
McNally, Thomas C. '46 (Y) Retired.
McNally, Vincent '84 (MIL) [B] Hales Corners, WI Sacred Heart School of Theology.
McNally, Vincent M. *s.j.* '48 (ALB) [O] Auriesville, NY Jesuit Retreat House for Priests, Religious and Lay People.
McNamara, Anthony *o.carm.* '67 (TUC) [9] Tucson, AZ Sacred Heart Church.
McNamara, Brian J. '84 (RVC) Plainview, NY St. Pius X Church.
McNamara, Daniel J. *s.j.* '80 (FgM) Provinces.
McNamara, Dennis L. *s.j.* '76 (WDC) [M] Washington, DC The Jesuit Community at Georgetown University.
McNamara, Donald P. '61 (FgM) Maryknoll Foreign Missions.
McNamara, Donald P. '61 (PH) On Duty Outside the Archdiocese.
McNamara, Elmer A. '33 (BUF) Kendall, NY St. Mark Church.
McNamara, Elmer A. '33 (ROC) Retired.
McNamara, Msgr. Eugene P. '53 (BO) Scituate, MA St. Mary of the Nativity Church.
McNamara, Francis J. *s.j.* '54 (ROC) [B] Rochester, NY McQuaid Jesuit High School.
McNamara, Msgr. James '71 (RVC) West Babylon, NY Our Lady of Grace Church.
McNamara, John '32 (ALB) Retired.
McNamara, John J. '53 (ALN) Port Carbon, PA St. Stephen Church.
McNamara, John P. '56 (CHI) Palatine, IL St. Theresa Church.
McNamara, Joseph '39 (SY) [S] Syracuse, NY St. Pius X Home, Inc.
McNamara, Joseph *s.p.* '56 (STL) [P] St. Louis, MO Servants of the Paraclete.
McNamara, Joseph F. *c.s.sp.* '42 (PRO) [3] Tiverton, RI St. Madeleine Sophie Church.
McNamara, Joseph M. '39 (ROC) Retired.
McNamara, Michael J. '79 (BO) Awaiting Assignment.
McNamara, Patrick M. *o.s.m.* '49 (P) [L] Portland, OR The Grotto, The National Sanctuary of Our Sorrowful Mother.
McNamara, Patrick V. '60 (NY) [2] New Rochelle, NY St. Gabriel Church.
McNamara, Peter J. '64 (CC) Zapata, TX Our Lady of Lourdes Church.
McNamara, Philip *s.a.c.* '58 (FWT) Stephenville, TX St. Brendan Church; Weatherford, TX St. Stephen Church.
McNamara, Philip D. '56 (WOR) Retired.
McNamara, Robert F. '36 (ROC) [59] Rochester, NY St. Thomas the Apostle Church; Retired; [L] Rochester, NY Archivist.
McNamara, Robert J. '69 (LA) Chatsworth, CA St. John Eudes Church.
McNamara, Stephen E. '67 (VEN) [2] Fort Myers, FL Church Of The Resurrection Of Our Lord.
McNamara, Thomas F. *m.s.* '47 (GAL) [J] Nassau Bay, TX St. John Hospital.
McNamara, Thomas J. '82 (SAG) Mount Pleasant, MI Sacred Heart Church; Rosebush, MI St. Henry Church.
McNamara, Thomas L. *o.s.f.s.* '52 (TOL) [C] Toledo, OH St. Francis de Sales High School; [K] Toledo, OH Oblates of St. Francis de Sales.
McNamara, Vincent P. '60 (NY) City, NY Bronx House of Detention.
McNamara, William *o.c.d.* '51 (MIL) [P] Milwaukee, WI Provincial Offices - Discalced Carmelites.
McNamara, William *o.c.d.* '51 (PBL) [I] Crestone, CO Spiritual Life Institute of America, Inc.
McNamara, William '65 (SAT) Elmendorf, TX St. Anthony Church.
McNamee, Msgr. Charles W. '50 (RCK) Special Assignment.
McNamee, Frank '95 (ATL) Kennesaw, GA St. Catherine of Siena Church.
McNamee, James P. '73 (LC) Kendall, WI St. Joseph Church; Wilton, WI St. John the Baptist Church.
McNamee, John C. '53 (LA) Rancho Palos Verdes, CA St. John Fisher Church.
McNamee, John P. '59 (PH) [91] Philadelphia, PA St. Malachy Church.

McNamee, Maurice *s.j.* (STL) [C] St. Louis, MO Saint Louis University.
McNamee, Maurice B. *s.j.* '40 (STL) [P] St. Louis, MO Jesuit Community Corporation at St. Louis University - Jesuit Hall.
McNamee, Patrick '70 (P) Salem, OR St. Vincent de Paul Church.
McNamee, Msgr. William J. '26 (FAR) Retired.
McNanna, Neal *o.carm.* '59 (SAC) Fairfield, CA Our Lady of Mount Carmel, Church.
McNearney, John *glmy.* '62 (CIN) [M] Fairfield, OH Headquarters of Glenmary Home Missioners.
McNeely, Maurice '58 (HON) [6] Honolulu, HI Holy Family Church.
McNeff, Thomas C. '77 (CHI) Schiller Park, IL St. Maria Goretti Church.
McNeice, Charles *s.s.e.* '62 (BIR) Marion, AL Marion Military Institute Church.
McNeice, Charles *s.s.e.* '62 (MOB) [K] Tuskegee Institute, AL Tuskegee University Newman Center.
McNeice, Charles E. *s.s.e.* '62 (MOB) Tuskegee Institute, AL St. Joseph Church.
McNeil, Aubrey *o.f.m.* '85 (NY) [146] Bronx, NY Holy Cross Church.
McNeil, Dennis M. '75 (CLV) Brook Park, OH Assumption of Mary Church.
McNeil, Frank J. '71 (SFS) On Leave of Absence.
McNeil, Joel (OM) Absent on Leave.
McNeil, Joel D. '87 (AUS) Frenstat, TX Holy Rosary Church; Somerville, TX St. Ann's Church.
McNeil, John (ORL) Retired.
McNeil, John R. '61 (BO) On Duty Outside the Archdiocese.
McNeil, Lawrence J. '73 (HBG) [K] Harrisburg, PA Catholic Campus Ministry.
McNeil, Nicholas J. *s.j.* '46 (BO) [W] Weston, MA Campion Health Center, Inc.
McNeill, Donald P. *c.s.c.* '65 (FTW) [B] Notre Dame, IN University of Notre Dame Du Lac; [J] Notre Dame, IN Holy Cross Community, Corby Hall, University of Notre Dame.
McNeill, Douglas '70 (GLP) Absent on Leave.
McNeill, John A. '46 (BRK) [213] Queens, NY Our Lady of Lourdes Church; Retired.
McNeill, Malachy '44 (B) Retired.
McNeilly, Dennis P. *s.j.* '85 (OM) [K] Omaha, NE Jesuit Community At Creighton University.
McNelis, Dennis M. *c.s.c.* '62 (FR) [H] Fall River, MA Rose Hawthorne Lathrop Home.
McNelis, Francis J. '65 (ALN) Sinking Spring, PA St. Ignatius Loyola Church.
McNelis, Patrick J. '62 (BRK) [64] Brooklyn, NY Immaculate Heart of Mary Church.
McNelis, Paul D. *s.j.* '77 (WDC) [M] Washington, DC The Jesuit Community at Georgetown University.
McNellis, Paul *s.j.* '87 (BO) [W] Chestnut Hill, MA The Jesuit Community at Boston College.
McNellis, Paul W. *s.j.* '87 (NY) [DD] New York, NY Jesuit Provincial's Office.
McNerney, James '81 (ALB) [11] Troy, NY St. Paul the Apostle Church.
McNew, Dwayne A. '95 (COL) Zanesville, OH St. Nicholas Church; [C] Zanesville, OH Bishop Rosecrans High School.
McNichol, Daniel J. '67 (HON) Pearl City, HI Our Lady of Good Counsel Church.
McNichol, Fabian *t.o.r.* '55 (ALT) [F] Loretto, PA St. Francis Friary, Third Order Regular of St. Francis of Penance.
McNicholas, Edward J. '54 (BRK) Released from Diocesan Assignment; [U] Douglaston, NY Bishop Mugavero Residence.
McNicholas, Raymond J. *s.s.c.* '49 (BUF) [2] Orchard Park, NY St. Bernadette Church.
McNicholas, Stephen '53 (ORL) Retired.
McNicholl, Michael P. '66 (BUF) Strykersville, NY St. Mary, Queen of the Rosary Church.
McNichols, William *s.j.* (NY) [DD] New York, NY West Side Jesuit Community.
McNichols, Msgr. William J. '38 (CHI) [2] Oak Lawn, IL St. Gerald Church; Retired.
McNiff, Msgr. James '36 (SFE) Retired.
McNiff, William T. *o.s.c.* '43 (SCL) Onamia, MN The Church of the Holy Cross of Onamia; [I] Onamia, MN Crosier Monastery.
McNulty, Charles L. '37 (ALN) Retired; [J] Bethlehem, PA Holy Family Villa.
McNulty, Edward P. '93 (SD) La Mesa, CA St. Martin of Tours Church.
McNulty, Edwin J. '44 (COL) Retired.
McNulty, Francis J. '52 (NEW) Retired.
McNulty, Frank '52 (NEW) Summit, NJ St. Teresa's Church.
McNulty, Gerard J. '67 (LA) Military and VA Chaplains.
McNulty, J. Brendan '74 (CLV) [64] Cleveland, OH SS. Philip and James Church.
McNulty, James '53 (LA) [86] Los Angeles, CA St. Paul the Apostle Church.
McNulty, James D. *c.s.p.* '53 (NY) [DD] Jamaica Estates, NY Paulist Fathers Generalate.
McNulty, Jerry (LAV) Military Chaplains.
McNulty, John '74 (PRO) [1] Newport, RI St. Augustin Church.
McNulty, John P. '73 (CLV) [3] Euclid, OH Holy Cross Church.
McNulty, Joseph D. '69 (CLV) [9] Cleveland, OH St. Augustine Church.
McNulty, Joseph P. '43 (BO) Retired.
McNulty, Msgr. Patrick '53 (LA) [49] Los Angeles, CA St. Bernard Church; Retired.
McNulty, Patrick J. '60 (FTW) On Special Assignment.
McNulty, Robert E. '56 (NOR) Retired.
McNulty, T. Michael *s.j.* '73 (MIL) [P] Milwaukee, WI Jesuit Community at Marquette University.
McNulty, Theodore '66 (CHI) [206] Chicago, IL St. Thomas More Church.
McNulty, William J. '61 (CHI) Lake Forest, IL St. Patrick Church.
McNulty, William J. '64 (NOR) Dayville, CT St. Joseph Church; Rogers, CT St. Ignatius Church.
McOwen, James F. '41 (LA) [R] Los Angeles, CA Amat House; [X] Santa Barbara, CA St. Mary's Seminary Center.
McPadden, Charles J. *m.m.* '69 (CHR) Greenville, SC St. Mary's Church.
McPadden, Malachy M. *o.s.b.* '57 (NEW) [N] Newark, NJ Newark Abbey.
McPartland, Aloysius M. *m.s.* '47 (NY) Phoenicia, NY St. Francis de Sales Church.
McPartland, Guy *o.carm.* '55 (JOL) [J] Darien, IL Carmelite Provincial Office.
McPartland, Guy I. *o.carm.* '55 (MET) [F] New Brunswick, NJ St. Peter's Medical Center.
McPartland, Paul G. '57 (BO) Halifax, MA Our Lady of the Lake Church.
McPartland, Thomas *c.ss.r.* '32 (NY) [92] New York, NY Our Lady of Perpetual Help Church.
McPeak, George *m.m.* '59 (NY) [DD] Maryknoll, NY Maryknoll Fathers and Brothers.
McPhail, J. Stuart *o.p.* '69 (PRO) [B] Providence, RI Providence College; [P] Providence, RI St. Thomas Aquinas Priory at Providence College.
McPhee, John *c.ss.r.* '46 (CHI) [N] Chicago, IL Redemptorists:.
McPhee, John *c.ss.r.* '46 (DEN) [M] Denver, CO The Redemptorists/Denver Province.
McPhee, Marvin E. '65 (SFS) Groton, SD St. Elizabeth Ann Seton Church.
McPhillips, James G. '83 (CLV) Newbury, OH St. Helen Church.
McPhillips, Thomas J. '44 (SFS) Retired; [E] Mitchell, SD Queen of Peace Hospital dba Brady Memorial Home.
McPolin, Patrick *c.m.f.* '43 (LA) [R] Rancho Dominguez, CA Dominguez Seminary Inc.
McQuade, Brian D. '94 (RVC) St. James, NY SS. Philip and James Church.
McQuade, Donald P. *m.m.* '65 (FgM) Maryknoll Foreign Missions.
McQuade, James F. *c.s.p.* '56 (NY) [104] New York, NY St. Paul the Apostle Church; Manhattan, NY St. Luke's-Roosevelt Hospital Center.
McQuade, Richard E. '57 (BO) Emergency Response Group.
McQuaid, Msgr. Eugene (PAT) Retired.
McQuaid, Thomas W. (CHI) [4] Waukegan, IL Holy Family Church.
McQueeney, Robert *m.ss.a.* '82 (NOR) [F] Cromwell, CT Missionaries of the Holy Apostles.
McQueeny, Thomas F. *s.j.* '56 (STL) [P] St. Louis, MO De Smet Jesuit High School Community.
McQuesten, Mark A. '87 (MAR) Norway, MI St. Mary Church.
McQuillan, Cornelius T. *c.s.sp.* (SJN) [C] Bayamon, PR Seminario Misionero del Espiritu Santo.
McQuillan, Edward *c.m.* '44 (STA) [E] Jacksonville, FL St. Vincent's Medical Center, Inc.
McQuillan, Edward F. *c.m.* '44 (PH) [AA] Philadelphia, PA Congregation of the Mission.
McQuillen, Paul G. *s.s.e.* (NO) [4] Marrero, LA St. Joseph the Worker Church.
McQuillen, Paul G. *s.s.e.* '77 (NO) [4] Marrero, LA St. Joseph the Worker Church.
McQuillen, Thomas '96 (TOL) Norwalk, OH St. Paul Church.
McQuinn, James '88 (PH) [D] Norristown, PA Kennedy-Kenrick Catholic High School.
McQuinn, Maurice '39 (KC) Retired.
McQuinn, Peter B. '91 (CHI) [54] Chicago, IL Epiphany Church.
McReavy, Thomas J. *c.s.b.* '59 (GAL) [7] Houston, TX St. Anne Church.
McReynolds, Eugene *o.s.b.* '70 (OM) Boys Town, NE Immaculate Conception B.V.M. Church; [I] Boys Town, NE Father Flanagan's Boys' Home; [K] Elkhorn, NE Mount Michael Abbey.
McShane, James J. '66 (BUR) Bellows Falls, VT St. Charles Church.
McShane, John '74 (LAV) [3] Las Vegas, NV Holy Family Church.
McShane, John A. '57 (BRK) [55] Brooklyn, NY Holy Family Church.
McShane, Joseph M. *s.j.* '77 (NY) [C] Bronx, NY Fordham University; [DD] New York, NY Jesuit Community at Fordham University.
McShane, Joseph Mary (NOR) [F] Baltic, CT Marian Friary of Our Lady of Guadalupe.
McShane, Patrick E. '79 (CLV) Retired.
McShane, Thomas S. *s.j.* '60 (OM) [K] Omaha, NE Jesuit Community At Creighton University.
McSheffery, Daniel F. '56 (HRT) North Branford, CT St. Augustine Church.
McSherry, John *s.v.d.* '61 (FgM) Society of the Divine Word Foreign Missions.
McSherry, John G. *s.j.* '72 (NY) [DD] New York, NY West Side Jesuit Community.
McSherry, Patrick *o.f.m.cap.* '78 (DET) [K] Detroit, MI St. Bonaventure Friary; [K] Detroit, MI St. Mary's Friary.
McSherry, Thomas '71 (OKL) Special Assignment.
McSherry, Tom '53 (TLS) On Duty Outside the Diocese.
McSorley, Aidan *o.s.b.* '69 (KC) [J] Conception, MO Conception Abbey.
McSorley, Gerald '64 (LA) [49] Los Angeles, CA St. Bernard Church.
McSorley, James P. *o.m.i.* '46 (OAK) [N] Oakland, CA Oblate Provincial House & Procure.
McSorley, Matthew T. *o.s.b.* '49 (CHL) [J] Belmont, NC Belmont Abbey.
McSorley, Richard T. *s.j.* '46 (WDC) [M] Washington, DC The Jesuit Community at Georgetown University.
McSpiritt, John *s.t.* '59 (ARL) [J] Arlington, VA Missionary Servants of the Most Holy Trinity, S.T.
McStravog, Patrick B. *o.s.a.* '89 (FgM) Foreign Missions.
McSweeney, Brian '86 (NY) [E] Somers, NY John F. Kennedy High School.
McSweeney, Edward F. '52 (PIT) West View, PA St. Athanasius Church; Retired.
McSweeney, Godfrey D. *o.f.m.* '42 (MRY) [I] San Juan Bautista, CA St. Francis Retreat Center.
McSweeney, James '47 (GI) Retired.
McSweeney, James '74 (SR) Sonoma, CA St. Francis Solano Church.
McSweeney, Msgr. James E. '50 (R) Retired.
McSweeney, Jeremiah F. '72 (WH) Cheat Lake, WV St. Luke Church.
McSweeney, John '48 (MRY) Retired.
McSweeney, Msgr. John J. '74 (CHL) Asheville, NC Basilica of St. Lawrence Church.
McSweeney, John R. *o.c.d.* '52 (SR) [M] Oakville, CA Carmelite House of Prayer.
McSweeney, Msgr. John R. '61 (BUR) [5] Burlington, VT St. Mark's Church.
McSweeney, Joseph *s.s.c.* '58 (PRO) [P] Bristol, RI St. Columban's Retirement House.
McSweeney, Liam P. '69 (SAC) Sacramento, CA California Youth Authority.
McSweeney, Noel *s.a.* '48 (NY) [DD] Garrison, NY Franciscan Friars of the Atonement.
McSweeney, Placid *o.s.c.o.* '59 (WOR) [N] Spencer, MA St. Joseph's Abbey; [P] Spencer, MA St. Joseph Abbey.
McSweeney, Thomas J. '71 (NY) [HH] New York, NY The Christophers.
McSweeney, William P. *o.m.i.* '52 (PMB) Riviera Beach, FL St. Francis of Assisi Church.
McSweeney, William P. '69 (SAC) [2] Sacramento, CA All Hallows Church.
McSweeny, Joseph *s.s.c.* '90 (FgM) St. Columban's Foreign Mission.
McSwigan, James *c.ss.r.* '55 (SJN) [2] San Juan, PR San Agustin Church.
McSwiggan, Thomas '67 (SAT) [59] San Antonio, TX St. Patrick Church.
McTaggart, Msgr. Edward P. '55 (SFR) [8] San Francisco, CA St. Brendan Church; San Francisco, CA Young Ladies' Institute; San Francisco, CA Serra Club of San Francisco (Golden Gate).
McTague, Charles H. '47 (NEW) [17] Newark, NJ St. James Church; Retired.
McTague, Thomas '57 (GF) Retired.
McTarsney, John F. '88 (DUB) Decorah, IA St. Benedict's Church; On Medical Leave.
McTavey, Lawrence G. '55 (ALB) [2] Cohoes, NY St. Bernard Church.
McTeigue, Robert J. *s.j.* '97 (SCR) [C] Scranton, PA University of Scranton.
McTighe, Edward P. *s.j.* '61 (P) [D] Portland, OR Jesuit High School; [J] Portland, OR Providence St. Vincent Medical Center.
McTighe, John *c.ss.r.* '94 (NY) [150] Bronx, NY Immaculate Conception Church.
McTighe, Simon *o.s.b.* '53 (IND) [J] St. Meinrad, IN St. Meinrad Archabbey.
McTigue, Norman P. (BUF) [20] Buffalo, NY Coronation of the Blessed Virgin Mary Church.
McTigue, Norman P. '70 (BUF) Buffalo, NY Buffalo Psychiatric Center.
McTommoney, Brian *o.f.m.* '53 (FgM) Custody of St. Mary of the Angels. Byzantine-Slavonic.

McTommoney, Brian *o.f.m.* '53 (WDC) [M] Washington, DC Commissariat of the Holy Land, Franciscan Monastery - Mount St. Sepulchre.
McVean, John J. *o.f.m.* '67 (NY) [35] New York, NY St. Francis of Assisi Church.
McVeigh, James E. '73 (PH) [1] Drexel Hill, PA St. Andrew Church.
McVeigh, John J. '58 (LAV) Retired.
McVernon, John J. '58 (BRK) [191] Queens, NY St. Luke Church; Released from Diocesan Assignment.
McVey, T. C. *o.p.* '60 (FgM) Dominican - Order of Preachers Foreign Missions.
McVinney, Paul *s.v.d.* '50 (TR) [M] Bordentown, NJ Society of the Divine Word.
McWeeney, Brian E. '73 (NY) [6] Poughkeepsie, NY St. Martin de Porres Church.
McWeeney, John W. *m.s.* '55 (NOR) Brooklyn, CT Our Lady of La Salette Church.
McWhorter, Michael L. (ATL) [L] Atlanta, GA Campus Ministry.
McWhorter, Michael L. '92 (ATL) Milledgeville, GA Sacred Heart of Jesus Church.
McWilliam, James J. '49 (CIN) Retired; [B] Cincinnati, OH Mt. St. Mary's Seminary of the West.
Mead, Brian E. '69 (BUR) Colchester, VT Our Lady of Grace Church.
Mead, Gary '97 (NY) [4] New Rochelle, NY Holy Family Church.
Mead, Leland C. '68 (NU) On Duty Outside the Diocese.
Meade, Denis *o.s.b.* '55 (KCK) [A] Atchison, KS Benedictine College.
Meade, Emilian *o.f.m.cap.* '46 (SFR) Burlingame, CA Our Lady of Angels Church.
Meade, Garvey C. (BUF) [C] Niagara University, NY Niagara University.
Meade, Garvey G. '65 (BRK) [50] Brooklyn, NY Good Shepherd Church.
Meade, Henry J. '57 (BO) Needham, MA St. Bartholomew Church; Retired.
Meade, James '52 (BRK) [R] Queens Village, NY Queen of Peace Residence.
Meade, James C. '52 (RVC) Retired.
Meade, James W. '81 (CIN) West Chester, OH St. John Church.
Meade, James W. '86 (GRY) Rolling Prairie, IN St. John Kanty Church.
Meade, John *s.m.* '53 (BO) [3] Methuen, MA Our Lady of Mount Carmel Church.
Meade, John F. '43 (NY) Retired.
Meade, John F. '43 (RVC) Malverne, NY Our Lady of Lourdes Church.
Meade, Maurice P. '48 (BO) Retired.
Meade, William *l.c.* '91 (HRT) [B] Cheshire, CT Novitiate of the Legion of Christ.
Meaden, Paul *o.s.b.* '84 (SFE) [L] Pecos, NM Our Lady of Guadalupe Benedictine Abbey.
Meagher, Msgr. Frank J. '60 (COL) Buckeye Lake, OH Our Lady of Mt. Carmel Church.
Meagher, John J. *s.s.e.* '66 (NOR) Groton, CT Sacred Heart Church.
Meagher, Joseph A. '92 (NEW) [3] Linden, NJ St. John the Apostle Church.
Meagher, Michael T. '65 (SY) [16] Syracuse, NY St. James Church.
Meagher, Patrick *o.s.b.* '35 (P) [L] St. Benedict, OR Mt. Angel Abbey.
Meagher, Msgr. Thomas '40 (SB) Retired.
Meagher, Thomas L. '64 (DET) White Lake, MI St. Patrick Church.
Mealey, Mark *o.s.f.s.* '78 (ARL) Vienna, VA Our Lady of Good Counsel Church.
Meaney, Brendan J. '65 (CAM) Sicklerville, NJ St. John Neumann Church.
Meaney, John *m.m.* '59 (HRT) [17] Waterbury, CT SS. Peter and Paul Church; [D] Waterbury, CT Sacred Heart High School.
Meaney, John J. *m.m.* '59 (NY) [DD] Maryknoll, NY Maryknoll Fathers and Brothers.
Meaney, Joseph P. *m.m.* '26 (NY) [DD] Maryknoll, NY Maryknoll Fathers and Brothers.
Meaney, M. Brendan *f.j.* '87 (CC) [H] Hebbronville, TX Catholic Solitudes.
Meaney, Peter J. *o.s.b.* '51 (PAT) [M] Morristown, NJ St. Mary's Abbey.
Means, David '81 (ANC) On Duty Outside Archdiocese.
Means, David A. '81 (STL) On Duty Outside the Archdiocese.
Meany, John J. *o.p.* '87 (CHI) [N] Chicago, IL Dominicans (Provincial Office).
Meany, Michael G. '80 (CHI) [42] Chicago, IL St. Clotilde Church.
Meany, Neill R. *s.j.* '54 (YAK) [4] Yakima, WA St. Joseph's Church.
Meany, Stephen J. *s.j.* '67 (NY) [DD] New York, NY Murray-Weigel Hall.
Meany, Msgr. Thomas '55 (CC) On Special Assignment; [I] Corpus Christi, TX Pax Christi Residence.
Mears, Charles T. '51 (GF) Retired.
Measer, Donald L. '63 (BUF) [2] Depew, NY St. Barnabas Church; Retired.
Meaux, Glenn *s.o.l.t.* '80 (CC) [H] Robstown, TX Society of Our Lady of the Most Holy Trinity.
Meaux, Glenn '80 (LAF) On Duty Outside the Diocese.
Mecca, Gregg D. '96 (BGP) [5] Danbury, CT St. Peter's Church.
Mecca, Msgr. Mark A. '36 (SCR) Retired.
Meccia, Francis S. *m.m.* '66 (NY) [DD] Maryknoll, NY Maryknoll Fathers and Brothers.
Mech, John J. '95 (DET) Grosse Pointe, MI Our Lady Star of the Sea Church.
Mecir, Joseph S. '80 (CLV) Painesville, OH St. Mary Church.
Mecwel, Pawel J. '90 (MAR) Sault Sainte Marie, MI St. Joseph Church.
Medairos, Anthony J. '70 (BO) [25] Boston, MA Gate of Heaven Church.
Medeiros, Antonio '54 (BO) [1] Lowell, MA St. Anthony Church.
Medeiros, Antonio S. (BO) Retired.
Medeiros, Arnold R. '75 (FR) Norton, MA St. Mary's Church.
Medeiros, Benjamin *t.o.r.* '77 (FWT) [8] Fort Worth, TX St. Andrew Church.
Medeiros, James S. '92 (FR) [15] New Bedford, MA St. John the Baptist Church; [B] North Dartmouth, MA Bishop Stang High School.
Medeiros, Paul *o.m.i.* '64 (FgM) Oblates Foreign Missions.
Meder, James R. '39 (L) Rhodelia, KY St. Theresa Church; Retired.
Meder, Stephen A. *s.j.* '43 (DET) [P] Clarkston, MI Colombiere Center.
Medina, Antonio *m.g.* '82 (SJ) [4] Sunnyvale, CA St. Martin Church; Los Gatos, CA Presentation Center.
Medina, Antonio *c.ss.r.* '89 (LA) Whittier, CA St. Mary of the Assumption Church.
Medina, Fabio '83 (SFR) Half Moon Bay, CA Our Lady of the Pillar Church.
Medina, Francisco (SJN) [11] Bayamon, PR San Miguel Arcangel Church.
Medina, George '87 (PCE) On Duty Outside the Diocese.
Medina, Hector '84 (FWT) Wichita Falls, TX Our Lady of Guadalupe Church.
Medina, Ignazio C. '77 (JC) Fulton, MO St. Peter Church.
Medina, Jose Angel *c.m.* '88 (FgM) Vincentian Foreign Missions.
Medina, Jose Felix *l.c.* '81 (HRT) [B] Cheshire, CT Novitiate of the Legion of Christ.
Medina, Juan B. '69 (CGS) Naranjito, PR San Miguel Arcangel Church.
Medina, Julian (SAC) Lincoln, CA St. Joseph Church.
Medina, Julian '73 (SAC) Gridley, CA Sacred Heart Church.
Medina, Mauricio '64 (B) Blackfoot, ID St. Bernard's Church.
Medina, Rolando '71 (MIA) Hialeah Gardens, FL Santa Barbara Church.
Medina, Tito *m.s.c.* '92 (RCK) [H] Aurora, IL Missionaries of the Sacred Heart Community.
Medinski, Francis J. '48 (BGP) Retired.
Medley, Robert W. '90 (MET) Warren, NJ Our Lady of the Mount Church.
Medley, William F. '82 (L) Bardstown, KY St. Joseph Church.
Medlock, Scott '96 (ANC) [4] Anchorage, AK St. Elizabeth Ann Seton Church.
Medrano, Marcus '86 (DEN) [25] Denver, CO Sacred Heart Church.
Medve, Kenneth A. '97 (ALN) Shillington, PA St. John Baptist de la Salle Church.
Medwid, John '90 (ALB) Catskill, NY St. Patrick Church.
Medwid, John M. '90 (ALB) [2] Schenectady, NY St. Anthony Church.
Mee, Michael *o.s.b.* '78 (FgM) American - Cassinese Congregation Foreign Missions.
Meegan, William H. '50 (BUF) Retired.
Meehan, Andrew M. '93 (MAN) Salem, NH Mary, Queen of Peace Church.
Meehan, Barry C. *s.j.* '86 (NOR) [5] Norwich, CT SS. Peter and Paul Church.
Meehan, Barry M. '78 (PRO) [4] West Warwick, RI St. John's Church.
Meehan, Daniel *o.m.i.* '61 (FgM) Oblates Foreign Missions.
Meehan, Francis X. '61 (PH) West Chester, PA SS. Simon and Jude Church.
Meehan, Gabriel '59 (CHL) Forest City, NC Immaculate Conception Church.
Meehan, Gery G. *o.praem.* '60 (GB) [6] De Pere, WI St. Norbert College Parish; [B] De Pere, WI St. Norbert College; [I] De Pere, WI St. Joseph Priory.
Meehan, James '59 (SEA) Friday Harbor, WA St. Francis Church.
Meehan, Msgr. James H. '50 (PH) Bryn Mawr, PA St. John Neumann Church.
Meehan, James L. '41 (OG) Redwood, NY St. Francis Xavier Church.
Meehan, James L. '51 (OG) Retired.
Meehan, James N. *s.j.* '59 (SEA) [A] Seattle, WA Seattle University.
Meehan, James T. *s.j.* '63 (FgM) Provinces.
Meehan, John P. *m.m.* '59 (FgM) Maryknoll Foreign Missions.
Meehan, John T. '64 (NY) [3] Mt. Vernon, NY St. Mary Church.
Meehan, Joseph '66 (STA) Atlantic Beach, FL St. John the Baptist Church.
Meehan, Joseph F. *s.j.* '49 (SJ) [M] Los Gatos, CA Sacred Heart Jesuit Center.
Meehan, Joseph J. '61 (PH) Primos, PA St. Eugene Church.
Meehan, Msgr. Joseph P. '54 (NY) Suffern, NY Sacred Heart Church.
Meehan, Kenneth E. *s.j.* '71 (WDC) [E] Washington, DC Gonzaga College High School.
Meehan, Kevin *l.c.* '91 (MAN) [A] Center Harbor, NH Immaculate Conception Apostolic School.
Meehan, Patrick *s.s.c.* '49 (BRK) [U] Kew Gardens, NY St. Columbans Foreign Mission Society.
Meehan, Peter K. '68 (NY) [33] New York, NY St. Emeric Church.
Meehan, Richard '69 (SPR) Absent on Leave.
Meehan, T.J. '72 (ATL) [12] Atlanta, GA Shrine of the Immaculate Conception Church.
Meehan, Terence A. '67 (CIN) [7] Cincinnati, OH St. Andrew Church; [34] Cincinnati, OH Holy Cross-Immaculata Church; [36] Cincinnati, OH Holy Name Church.
Meehan, Thomas '72 (CIN) [M] Fairfield, OH Headquarters of Glenmary Home Missioners.
Meehan, Thomas J. *o.s.a.* '80 (ALB) [2] Troy, NY St. Augustine Church.
Meehan, Timothy A. '59 (HRT) North Haven, CT St. Therese's Church.
Meehling, Donald '58 (SFD) [6] Springfield, IL St. Aloysius Church.
Meeks, Delphyn J. '83 (BEA) Mauriceville, TX St. Maurice Church.
Meemken, Eugene A. '59 (SCL) Clarissa, MN St. Joseph Church; Moran, MN St. Isidore Church.
Meenan, Francis P. *c.s.sp.* '44 (PIT) Emsworth, PA Sacred Heart Church.
Meenan, Msgr. Joseph S. '37 (PIT) Retired.
Meenihan, Regis J. (E) [C] Erie, PA Cathedral Preparatory School.
Meenihan, Regis J. '92 (E) North East, PA St. Gregory Thaumaturgus Church.
Meersman, Jerome *c.i.c.m.* '49 (ARL) [J] Arlington, VA Missionhurst, C.I.C.M.-Central House and Provincialate.
Meffan, Robert V. (BO) Retired.
Meger, Msgr. Thomas *v.g.* '62 (RNO) [2] Reno, NV Our Lady of the Snows Church.
Mehan, Joseph A., Jr. '96 (DAL) [21] Dallas, TX St. Monica Church.
Mehm, Richard J. '77 (BO) [5] Boston, MA St. Andrew Church.
Mehm, Msgr. Walter '46 (LAN) Retired.
Mehok, Charles J. *s.j.* '48 (MIL) [P] Milwaukee, WI Jesuit Community at Marquette University; [Y] Milwaukee, WI Catholic Information Center.
Mehok, William J. *s.j.* '43 (FAR) Retired; [E] Fargo, ND Riverview Place, Inc.
Mehok, William J. *s.j.* '43 (MIL) [P] Milwaukee, WI Jesuit Provincial Office, Wisconsin Province.
Mehrkens, Msgr. William '50 (CR) Red Lake, MN St. Mary's Mission Church; Retired.
Meidl, Gerald S. '74 (NU) Marshall, MN Holy Redeemer Church.
Meier, Msgr. Allen J. '51 (COV) Retired; [C] Covington, KY Academy of Notre Dame.
Meier, Alphonse H. *o.s.b.* '48 (GBG) [H] Latrobe, PA Saint Vincent Archabbey.
Meier, Cyprian T. '69 (BIS) Mandan, ND Spirit of Life Church.
Meier, David E. *s.j.* '53 (DET) [P] Clarkston, MI Colombiere Center.
Meier, Denis '63 (SFS) Beresford, SD St. Teresa of Avila Church.
Meier, Emeric *o.f.m.* '68 (BO) [BB] Boston, MA St. Anthony Shrine.
Meier, Gerald A. '66 (STL) Webster Groves, MO Mary, Queen of Peace Church.
Meier, Msgr. John P. '67 (NY) On Duty Outside the Archdiocese.
Meier, John P. '67 (WDC) [C] Washington, DC Catholic University of America, The.
Meier, Msgr. Joseph F. '39 (SCR) Retired.
Meier, Laverne G. '58 (MAD) Montfort, WI St. Thomas Church.
Meier, Msgr. Raymond '36 (E) [K] Hermitage, PA John XXIII Home.
Meier, Msgr. Raymond O. '36 (E) [3] Sharon, PA St. Joseph Church; Retired.
Meier, Timothy J. *s.j.* (DET) [K] Detroit, MI Jesuit Provincial Office-Detroit Province of the Society of Jesus.
Meier, Timothy J. *s.j.* '91 (SJ) [L] Los Altos, CA Jesuit Retreat House.

Meiergerd, Godfrey A. '42 (OM) Retired.
Meighan, Joseph F. '68 (SCR) [L] Scranton, PA Home for Aged of the Little Sisters of the Poor, Holy Family Residence; [N] Dunmore, PA Villa St. Joseph.
Meighan, Thomas A. '63 (WDC) [7] Silver Spring, MD St. John the Evangelist Church.
Meik, Thomas J. *c.m.* '48 (CHI) [C] Chicago, IL Vincentian Community at DePaul University.
Meiklejohn, Norman '54 (BO) [W] Brighton, MA Assumptionist Center.
Meilak, John '47 (LA) Retired.
Meilak, Peter Paul *o.f.m.* '49 (FgM) Franciscan Foreign Missions.
Meiluta, George J. *s.m.* '40 (WDC) [M] Washington, DC Marist Provincial House.
Meiman, Louis J. '87 (L) [38] Louisville, KY Immaculate Heart of Mary Church.
Meinen, Dennis W. '87 (SC) Churdan, IA St. Columbkille's Church; Scranton, IA St. Paul's Church.
Meiners, Andrew *c.ss.r.* '70 (KC) [32] Kansas City, MO Our Lady of Perpetual Help Church; [J] Kansas City, MO Redemptorists of Kansas City.
Meinhart, C. Joseph '91 (OKL) Norman, OK St. Thomas More University Parish; [K] Norman, OK Campus Ministry for the Archdiocese of Oklahoma City.
Meinhart, Joseph C. '91 (OKL) Special Assignment.
Meinholz, David J. '94 (MIL) Lake Geneva, WI St. Francis de Sales Church.
Meinholz, John M. '77 (MAD) [5] Madison, WI Immaculate Heart of Mary Church.
Meiring, Arnold *c.pp.s.* '40 (CIN) [B] Carthagena, OH St. Charles.
Meiring, Bernard *c.pp.s.* '55 (CIN) [B] Carthagena, OH St. Charles.
Meirose, Harold R. *s.j.* '62 (DET) [P] Clarkston, MI Colombiere Center.
Meisburger, Joseph '66 (KC) [4] Independence, MO St. Mary's Church.
Meisburger, Joseph C. '66 (KC) Retired.
Meisel, Charles '50 (BAL) [J] Timonium, MD Stella Maris Operating Corporation.
Meisel, Msgr. Charles F. '50 (BAL) Timonium, MD Church of the Nativity; Retired.
Meisel, Gerald '61 (LA) [11] Long Beach, CA St. Matthew Church.
Meismer, Paul J. '69 (PEO) Sheffield, IL St. Patrick's Church.
Meissner, Robert J. '69 (SAG) [10] Bay City, MI St. Vincent de Paul Church.
Meissner, William W. *s.j.* '61 (BO) [W] Chestnut Hill, MA The Jesuit Community at Boston College.
Meister, Andrew H. '44 (OM) Retired.
Meitl, Roger K. '59 (SAL) Grinnell, KS Immaculate Conception Church; Oakley, KS St. Joseph's Church.
Mejak, Msgr. Heliodore '35 (KCK) [4] Kansas City, KS Holy Family Church.
Mejia, Jose G. '91 (LA) Lynwood, CA St. Emydius Church.
Mejia, Leoncio *m.ss.cc.* '82 (SJN) [1] Trujillo Alto, PR San Bartolome Church.
Mejia, Manuel J. *m.m.* '63 (SFR) [N] San Francisco, CA Maryknoll Fathers and Brothers, Catholic Foreign Mission Society of America, Inc.
Mejia, Ricardo '76 (SD) San Ysidro, CA Our Lady of Mt. Carmel Church.
Melancon, Bill John '93 (LAF) Baldwin, LA Sacred Heart Church.
Melancon, Joseph Aaron '97 (LAF) [11] Lafayette, LA St. Genevieve Church.
Melancon, Msgr. Louis (LKC) On Duty Outside the Diocese.
Melancon, Msgr. Louis J. (LAF) Grand Prairie, LA St. Peter Church.
Melancon, Robert '62 (HT) On Leave.
Melaniuk, J. Maciej '86 (MET) South River, NJ St. Mary of Ostrabrama Church.
Melbourne, David '39 (JUN) Retired.
Melcher, Francis L. *o.s.a.* '53 (PH) [AA] Villanova, PA St. Thomas Monastery.
Melcher, Michael '92 (LUB) Stamford, TX St. Ann Church.
Melchior, Frank '59 (GB) Retired.
Melchior, Gerald P. '90 (OM) [9] Omaha, NE St. Bernard Church.
Melchior, Thomas '65 (KCK) [4] Topeka, KS Most Pure Heart of Mary Church.
Meldrum, James *o.c.d.* '42 (MIL) [P] Milwaukee, WI Provincial Offices - Discalced Carmelites.
Meldrum, James *o.c.d.* '42 (MOB) [F] Mobile, AL Little Sisters of the Poor, Home For the Aged, Inc.
Mele, Carmen *o.p.* '80 (FgM) Dominican - Order of Preachers Foreign Missions.
Mele, Carmen *o.p.* '80 (NO) [P] New Orleans, LA Dominican Fathers & Brothers, Southern Dominican Province.
Mele, Joseph M. '73 (PIT) Unity, PA St. John the Baptist Church.
Mele, Rudolph '77 (NO) Retired.
Mele, Tom '77 (SPK) Medical Lake, WA St. Anne Church.
Mele, Vincent *o.f.m.* '40 (NY) [Z] New York, NY Kateri Residence; [DD] New York, NY Franciscan Province of the Immaculate Conception.
Meledom, Joseph '68 (GAL) [77] Houston, TX St. Thomas More Church.
Melel, Andrew *o.i.c.* '51 (TYL) Gun Barrel City, TX St. Jude Church.
Melendez, Hector '80 (PAT) [8] Passaic, NJ Our Lady of Fatima Church.
Melendez, Jeronimo *o.s.m.* '72 (ELP) [24] El Paso, TX St. Ignatius of Loyola Church.
Melendez, Michael S. '89 (BRK) [166] Queens, NY St. Elizabeth's Church.
Melepuram, John '78 (DET) Melvindale, MI St. Mary Magdalen Church.
Melevage, Msgr. F. J. '42 (GRY) Retired.
Melican, Msgr. Francis J. '50 (NY) Scarsdale, NY St. Pius X Church.
Melican, Thomas J. '39 (NY) Port Jervis, NY Immaculate Conception Church.
Melicor, Celedonio G. '56 (DET) [2] Dearborn, MI St. Barbara Church.
Melillo, William J. '66 (NEW) [C] West Orange, NJ Seton Hall Preparatory School.
Melito, August A. '64 (DAL) [14] Dallas, TX St. Bernard of Clairvaux Church.
Melito, Joseph '75 (ORG) Inactive Leave.
Melka, John *o.c.d.* '64 (OAK) [N] Berkeley, CA Carmelite (Discalced) House of Studies.
Melki, Pierre '65 (OLD) Laval, St. Ephrem Church.
Mell, Darrell J. (NEW) [N] Union City, NJ Congregation of the Passion (Passionists)-St. Michael's Residence.
Melle, James J. '72 (PH) West Chester, PA SS. Simon and Jude Church; [D] West Chester, PA Bishop Shanahan High School.
Melley, James '77 (MIA) Military Chaplains.
Mellitt, John *o.f.m.cap.* '75 (NY) [98] New York, NY Our Lady of Sorrows Church.
Mello, Edward '46 (SAC) Nevada City, CA St. Canice Church; Walnut Grove, CA St. Anthony Church; Retired and in Senior Ministry.
Mello, Matthew '87 (ORL) Melbourne, FL Our Lady of Lourdes Church; [A] Melbourne, FL Central Catholic High School.
Melloh, John A. *s.m.* '73 (FTW) [B] Notre Dame, IN University of Notre Dame Du Lac.
Mellone, Michael J. '76 (WDC) Gaithersburg, MD St. Martin Church.
Mellone, Vincent P. '65 (BO) [2] Woburn, MA St. Barbara Church.
Mellott, Bob (PIT) [J] Pittsburgh, PA Mercy Providence Hospital.
Mellott, Robert '63 (PIT) Allegheny County, PA Mercy Providence Hospital.
Mellott, David *s.s.* '92 (BAL) [M] Baltimore, MD Sulpician Provincial House.
Mellott, David '92 (STU) On Duty Outside the Diocese.
Melmer, John H. '91 (ARL) Colonial Beach, VA St. Elizabeth Church.
Melnic, Msgr. James '78 (PHU) [4] Philadelphia, PA Annunciation of the B.V.M. Church; [6] Philadelphia, PA St. Josaphat's Church; [D] Philadelphia, PA Ascension Manor, Inc.
Melnick, Robert D. *o.f.m.conv.* '97 (RCK) [2] Rockford, IL St. Anthony of Padua Church.
Melnick, William D. '75 (WIL) [2] Wilmington, DE St. Ann Church.
Melo, Fidel '96 (CHL) Clemmons, NC Holy Family Church.
Melo, Nicholas P. '83 (HRT) [2] Bristol, CT St. Anthony's Church.
Meloch, Msgr. Chester A. '43 (BUF) Retired.
Melody, William P. *c.s.c.* '59 (FTW) [J] South Bend, IN Congregation of Holy Cross Indiana Province Provincial House.
Melone, Mark E. '78 (NTN) Sacramento, CA St. George Church.
Melovasich, Frank '50 (DUL) [14] Duluth, MN St. Michael's Church.
Meloy, Bernard F. '54 (MAD) Retired.
Melton, John H. *o.s.a.* '55 (PH) [G] Malvern, PA Malvern Preparatory School for Boys.
Melton, Thomas K. '59 (TLS) Bixby, OK St. Clement's Church.
Meluskey, Andre J. '59 (HBG) McSherrystown, PA Annunciation of the Blessed Virgin Mary Church.
Melvin, James M. '54 (CAM) Retired.
Melzer, Howard *s.c.j.* '58 (GAL) [21] Houston, TX Christ the Redeemer Church.
Memenas, Vytas '57 (JOL) Frankfort, IL St. Anthony Church.
Memolo, Rocco C. '76 (MAN) Absent on Leave.
Men, Vincent Mao '84 (LA) [DD] Granada Hills, CA Chinese Catholic Bishops Conference Vocations Center.
Mena, Antonio '81 (ELP) Pecos, TX Santa Rosa Church.
Mena, Jose '61 (ORL) Retired.
Menapace, James L. '63 (MAR) Retired.
Menard, Clarence C. *o.m.i.* '58 (NO) [A] New Orleans, LA Notre Dame Seminary Graduate School of Theology.
Menard, Francis A. '54 (OG) Retired.
Menard, Gilbert B. '55 (OG) Ellenburg, NY St. Edmund Church.
Menard, J. Godden *c.m.* '55 (GLP) Tuba City, AZ St. Jude Church.
Menard, James R. *s.j.* '54 (PHX) [B] Phoenix, AZ Brophy College Preparatory.
Menard, Msgr. Raymond '39 (SAL) [1] Salina, KS Cathedral of the Sacred Heart.
Menard, Robert *o.f.m.* '72 (ARL) Triangle, VA St. Francis of Assisi Church.
Menard, Roland V. '64 (OG) Malone, NY St. John Bosco Church.
Menard, Wilfrid A. *c.s.c.* '55 (KAL) Three Oaks, MI St. Mary of the Assumption Church.
Menasco, Edward '90 (OKL) Woodward, OK St. Peter's Church.
Menchaca, Gerardo '95 (SJ) [15] San Jose, CA St. Maria Goretti Church.
Mencsik, John *c.pp.s.* '74 (CIN) St. Anthony, OH St. Anthony Church.
Mende, Dennis W. '83 (BUF) [29] Buffalo, NY Holy Cross Church.
Mender, Lawrence *o.s.b.* '89 (SEA) Longview, WA St. Rose de Viterbo Church.
Mendes, Joseph *m.s.f.s.* (ATL) [J] Snellville, GA Monastery of the Visitation.
Mendez, Angel '90 (MGZ) [9] Mayaquez, PR Church of the Resurrection.
Mendez, David Perez '87 (MGZ) Moca, PR Our Lady of Monserrate Church.
Mendez, Edwin *o.f.m.conv.* '95 (BRK) [146] Queens, NY St. Adalbert Church.
Mendez, Enrique *s.d.b.* '52 (SJN) [28] San Juan, PR San Juan Bosco Church.
Mendez, Juan '73 (SFE) [5] Santa Fe, NM St. John Baptist Church.
Mendez, Oscar *s.j.* '64 (MIA) [A] Miami, FL St. John Vianney College Seminary.
Mendez, Oscar *o.f.m.* '89 (FgM) Franciscan Foreign Missions.
Mendez, Oscar *o.f.m.* '89 (OAK) [N] Oakland, CA Franciscan Friars Provincial Office, Province of St. Barbara.
Mendez, Rafael '93 (MGZ) Lajas, PR Our Lady of the Purification Church.
Mendez, Rafael '94 (PH) West Chester, PA St. Agnes Church.
Mendicoa, John J. '67 (BO) [69] Boston, MA Sacred Heart Church.
Mendis, Nimal '82 (NY) Beacon, NY St. John Evangelist Church; [DD] New York, NY Apostolic Society of the Crusade of the Holy Spirit.
Mendl, Michael *s.d.b.* '79 (NY) [DD] New Rochelle, NY Salesian Provincial House.
Mendonca, John '72 (BRK) [83] Brooklyn, NY Mary Queen of Heaven Church.
Mendonca, John '83 (BO) [5] Peabody, MA Our Lady of Fatima Church.
Mendonsa, August F. '42 (PRO) Retired.
Mendoza, Andres '95 (LUB) Denver City, TX St. William Church.
Mendoza, Armando Guerrero *m.n.m.* '90 (SAT) Del Rio, TX Our Lady of Guadalupe Church; Del Rio, TX Our Lady of Guadalupe Church.
Mendoza, Eduardo '84 (SFR) [1] Menlo Park, CA St. Anthony Church.
Mendoza, Fernando *o.f.m.* '74 (ELP) [B] El Paso, TX St. Anthony's School of Theology.
Mendoza, Gerardo '88 (SB) Victorville, CA St. Joan of Arc Church.
Mendoza, Msgr. Miguel A. '70 (CGS) Barranquitas, PR Church of St. Anthony of Padua.
Mendoza, Pablo Mora *s.j.* '91 (CHI) [N] Chicago, IL Chicago Province of the Society of Jesus-Provincial Office.
Mendoza, Wenceslao '87 (BWN) Mercedes, TX Our Lady of Mercy Church; Mercedes, TX Sacred Heart Church.
Mendrick, Paul P. '47 (PBL) Retired.
Menegatto, Gaetano *c.s.j.* '42 (CLV) [P] Avon, OH Congregation of St. Joseph.
Menegay, David C. '88 (PIT) Conway, PA Our Lady of Peace Church; [C] Baden, PA Quigley Catholic High School.
Meneghello, Serafino '49 (GRY) Retired.
Menei, Francis T. '67 (PH) On Duty Outside the Archdiocese.
Menendez, Adolph *s.x.* '68 (FgM) Xaverian Foreign Missions.
Menendez, Adolph *s.x.* '68 (PAT) [M] Wayne, NJ Xaverian Missionary Fathers.
Menendez, Jose L. '77 (MIA) [3] Miami, FL Corpus Christi Church.
Meneses, Miguel '61 (ELP) Horizon City, TX Holy Spirit Church.
Menezes, Mark '59 (JOL) Monee, IL St. Boniface Church.

Meng, David P. '89 (ARL) Ashburn, VA St. Theresa Church.
Meng, Robert A. '45 (ROC) Retired.
Menge, James Paul '62 (SPR) Greenfield, MA Holy Trinity Church.
Menge, Msgr. Kenneth M. '54 (BUF) [3] Kenmore, NY St. John the Baptist Church.
Mengel, Mark *s.s.c.* '71 (CHI) [N] Chicago, IL Columban Fathers Theologate.
Menghini, Peter D. '80 (SCR) [7] Wilkes-Barre, PA Holy Rosary Church.
Mengon, Albert *s.d.b.* '66 (FgM) Salesians of Don Bosco Foreign Missions.
Menig, Walter J. *c.m.* '47 (BAL) [M] Emmitsburg, MD Vincentian House.
Menihane, Daniel J. *o.s.a.* '57 (ALB) Pittstown, NY St. George Church; Waterford, NY St. Mary of the Assumption Church.
Meninger, William *o.c.s.o.* '58 (DEN) [M] Snowmass, CO St. Benedict's Monastery.
Menke, George R. *s.j.* '75 (CHI) [D] Chicago, IL St. Ignatius College Prep.
Menke, George R. *s.j.* '75 (IND) [D] Indianapolis, IN Brebeuf Jesuit Preparatory School, Inc.
Menke, Paul F. '66 (LA) [60] Los Angeles, CA St. Eugene Church.
Menke, Msgr. S. G. '38 (DAV) Retired.
Menke, Msgr. Sebastian J. '38 (DAV) [M] Davenport, IA St. Vincent Center.
Menker, Joseph *o.m.i.* '53 (STP) [28] St. Paul, MN St. Mary Church; St. Paul, MN St. Paul-Ramsey Hospital; St. Paul, MN Gillette Children's Hospital.
Menkhus, James *o.f.m.cap.* '73 (PH) [79] Philadelphia, PA St. John the Evangelist Church.
Menna, F. Dominic '58 (BO) [1] Revere, MA St. Anthony of Padua Church.
Menna, Msgr. Francis A. (PH) [V] Ventnor, PA Villa St. Joseph by the Sea.
Menna, Msgr. Francis A. '64 (PH) [V] Darby, PA Villa Saint Joseph.
Mennella, Luke *o.ss.t.* '56 (BAL) [M] Baltimore, MD Holy Trinity Monastery.
Menner, John H. *c.s.b.* '58 (DET) [E] Redford, MI Catholic Central High School.
Menner, Michael '93 (PEO) [K] Lacon, IL St. Joseph's Nursing Home.
Menner, Michael L. '93 (PEO) [Q] Moline, IL The Order of the Legion of Little Souls of the Merciful Heart of Jesus.
Menner, Robert J. '68 (STL) On Duty Outside the Archdiocese.
Mennis, James F. '62 (SAC) Military Chaplains.
Menniti, Daniel J. '53 (HBG) Carlisle, PA St. Patrick Church.
Mens, Theodore J. '67 (GRY) Griffith, IN St. Mary Church.
Mensah, Gabriel '83 (VIC) On Duty Outside the Diocese.
Mensah, Isaac '81 (RVC) Manhasset, NY North Shore Univ. Hospital.
Menster, William J. '38 (DUB) Retired.
Mentel, Joseph C. '40 (FAR) Retired.
Mentrup, Charles '88 (CIN) [8] Cincinnati, OH St. Ann Church.
Mentrup, Charles E. (CIN) [E] Middletown, OH Bishop Fenwick High School.
Menty, Ronald A. '69 (ALB) Scotia, NY St. Joseph Church.
Meny, Hilary G. '40 (IND) Retired.
Menz, Anthony (SB) Military Chaplains.
Menz, Anthony *o.c.s.o.* '68 (SPC) [E] Ava, MO Assumption Abbey (Trappist).
Menzel, Mark *s.s.c.* (CHI) [J] Chicago, IL Holy Cross Hospital.
Menzel, William G. '67 (LC) [3] Wisconsin Rapids, WI St. Vincent de Paul Church.
Menzies, Scott '85 (VEN) Graduate Studies.
Meograssi, Romuald *o.f.m.conv.* (BAL) [M] Ellicott City, MD St. Joseph Cupertino Friary, Friars Minor Conventual of St. Francis of Assisi; [M] Ellicott City, MD Friary of St. Joseph Cupertino.
Mercado, Edwin '86 (ARE) Special Assignment.
Mercado, Edwin '87 (ARE) [11] Arecibo, PR Church of San Martin de Porres.
Mercado, Miguel '83 (ARE) [14] Arecibo, PR Santisimo Sacramento Church.
Mercer, David '87 (SJ) [16] San Jose, CA St. Martin of Tours Church.
Mercer, James '97 (ARL) Chantilly, VA St. Timothy Church.
Mercer, John E. '70 (NY) [220] Staten Island, NY Our Lady of Pity Church.
Mercer, Robert *s.a.* '82 (NY) *[DD] Garrison,* NY Generalate of the Franciscan Friars of the Atonement-St. James Friary.
Mercer, Timmothy '90 (CC) On Duty Outside the Diocese.
Merchant, David M. *o.s.f.s.* '73 (PH) [D] Philadelphia, PA Father Judge High School for Boys; [AA] Philadelphia, PA Father Judge Faculty House.
Mercieca, Anthony '62 (MIA) Miami Springs, FL Blessed Trinity Church.
Mercier, J. Patrick '93 (IND) [16] Indianapolis, IN St. Barnabas Church.
Mercier, Msgr. Joseph '55 (BLX) Retired.
Mercier, Ronald A. *s.j.* '87 (BO) [W] Boston, MA The Society of Jesus of New England-Provincial Offices.
Mercure, Gary '74 (ALB) [13] Troy, NY Sacred Heart Church; [S] Glens Falls, NY Adirondack Community College.
Mercurio, Gregory J. '80 (BO) [1] Lynn, MA Holy Family Church.
Mercurio, Roger *c.p.* '44 (CHI) [N] Chicago, IL Immaculate Conception Monastery.
Mercy, Richard R. *s.j.* '71 (SPK) [E] Spokane, WA Gonzaga Preparatory School; [O] Spokane, WA Kateri Northwest Ministry Institute.
Merdian, Mark '91 (PEO) [12] Peoria, IL St. Peter's Church.
Merdinger, Philip E. '64 (NEW) On Duty Outside the Archdiocese.
Meredith, John '80 (OWN) [4] Owensboro, KY Our Lady of Lourdes Church.
Meredith, Philip S. '74 (DEN) [1] Fort Collins, CO St. Joseph Church.
Meredith, Richard '78 (OWN) Bowling Green, KY St. Joseph's Church.
Merfeld, Vincent C. '44 (DUB) Retired.
Mergenhagen, John J. (BUF) [Q] Derby, NY St. Columban's Center.
Mericantante, John J. '75 (PMB) Pahokee, FL St. Mary Church.
Meridier, Wilfred F. '69 (NO) [58] New Orleans, LA St. Rita Church; Jefferson, LA Ochsner Foundation Hospital.
Merino, Msgr. Baudilio '48 (SJN) [49] San Juan, PR Nuestra Senora de la Providencia Church.
Merino, Santiago '46 (LA) Retired.
Merino, Sean '94 (BIR) [16] Birmingham, AL Our Lady of Sorrows Church; [A] Birmingham, AL John Carroll High School.
Merity, John A. '49 (NEW) Glen Rock, NJ St. Catharine Church; Retired.
Meriwether, Stephen A. '83 (SFR) [2] South San Francisco, CA Mater Dolorosa Church; Special Assignment.
Merkatoris, Ralph C. '58 (GB) Pine Grove, WI Holy Trinity Church.
Merkel, James '73 (SP) Crystal River, FL St. Benedict Church.
Merkel, Mark K. '92 (OM) O'Neill, NE St. Patrick Church.
Merkel, Thomas *s.j.* '97 (RC) Pine Ridge, SD Holy Rosary Church.
Merkel, Tom *s.j.* (RC) [B] Pine Ridge, SD Jesuit Community of Holy Rosary Mission.
Merkelis, John *o.s.a.* '85 (JOL) [C] New Lenox, IL Providence Catholic High School.
Merkelis, John D. *o.s.a.* '85 (JOL) [J] New Lenox, IL Augustinian Friary.
Merkle, Charles W., III '88 (ARL) [1] Alexandria, VA Blessed Sacrament Church.
Merkovsky, Paul W. '90 (PIT) Bellevue, PA Assumption of the Blessed Virgin Mary on the Beautiful River Church.
Merkt, Joseph T. '66 (L) [27] Louisville, KY St. Francis of Assisi Church; [K] Louisville, KY Marian Home.
Merkt, Michael F. '81 (MIL) [6] West Allis, WI Mary, Queen of Heaven Church.
Merlino, James T. *o.f.m.* '87 (PIT) [60] Pittsburgh, PA St. Pamphilus Church.
Merlucci, Michael A. '75 (NEW) Scotch Plains, NJ St. Bartholomew Church.
Merman, Msgr. Raymond F. '60 (ALN) Hellertown, PA St. Theresa of the Child Jesus Church.
Merold, James E. '71 (CHI) North Chicago, IL Queen of Peace Church.
Merolla, George R. '87 (BRK) Absent on Leave.
Meronek, Andrew '43 (GRY) [J] Cedar Lake, IN Our Lady of Lourdes Friary.
Merrell, Arthur '70 (PIT) Butler County, PA The United Presbyterian Home for Children.
Merrell, Arthur R. '70 (PIT) [22] Pittsburgh, PA St. Lawrence O'Toole Church; Allegheny County, PA Allegheny County Jail; Allegheny County, PA Shuman Center.
Merrifield, Donald P. *s.j.* '65 (LA) [C] Los Angeles, CA Loyola Marymount University.
Merrill, Paul *c.s.s.* '61 (BO) [Z] Waltham, MA Stigmatine Fathers and Brothers.
Merrill, Thomas *o.f.m.conv.* (FgM) Conventual Franciscan Foreign Missions.
Merris, Christopher '82 (SD) Military Chaplains; Unassigned.
Merry, Christopher C. '92 (E) Bradford, PA St. Bernard Church.
Merry, Paul F. '71 (BGP) [6] Bridgeport, CT Blessed Sacrament Church.
Mersberger, Jerome '42 (MAD) Retired.
Mersinger, Arthur '42 (JC) Retired.
Mersinger, Arthur J. '42 (STL) Retired.
Mersinger, Norbert A. '55 (STL) Bel-Ridge, MO St. Thomas More Church.
Merson, Thomas S. '83 (SFR) [4] San Francisco, CA St. Anne Church; Special Assignment.
Mertens, Msgr. Arthur '49 (SPK) Retired.
Mertens, Michael G. '45 (LC) Retired; [I] La Crosse, WI Holy Cross (Seminary) Diocesan Center.
Mertensotto, Leon J. *c.s.c.* '56 (FTW) [B] Notre Dame, IN University of Notre Dame Du Lac; [J] Notre Dame, IN Holy Cross Community, Corby Hall, University of Notre Dame.
Mertes, Mark '87 (KCK) Hartford, KS St. Mary's Church; Olpe, KS St. Joseph's Church.
Mertes, Robert *s.v.d.* '78 (WDC) [L] Hyattsville, MD Sacred Heart Home Inc.; [M] Washington, DC Divine Word College.
Mertes, William H. '59 (COV) Retired.
Merth, Robert J. '44 (NU) Retired.
Mertz, Frederick A. '49 (STP) Retired.
Mertz, William H. '47 (STP) Retired.
Merwald, Melvin '71 (OM) [27] Omaha, NE St. Margaret Mary Church.
Merz, Albert *o.f.m.* '66 (CHI) [N] Countryside, IL St. Gratian Friary, Franciscan Friars.
Merz, Eugene F. *s.j.* '61 (MIL) [P] Milwaukee, WI Jesuit Community at Marquette University.
Merz, Fabiano *o.f.m.* (SFD) [K] Sherman, IL Our Lady of Angels Friary.
Merzena, Carl J. '41 (NEW) Retired; [N] Rutherford, NJ St. John Vianney Residence for Priests.
Merzweiler, David W. '77 (Y) Lake Milton, OH St. Catherine Church; North Jackson, OH St. James Parish Family Church.
Mesa, Jose *s.j.* (NY) [63] New York, NY St. Joseph of the Holy Family Church.
Mesa, Manuel *o.m.i.* '72 (SD) Westmorland, CA St. Joseph Church.
Mesa, Mario *o.f.m.cap.* '64 (SJN) [29] San Juan, PR San Juan de La Cruz Church.
Mescall, Msgr. John '52 (NY) [4] New Rochelle, NY Holy Family Church.
Mescall, John R. *c.p.* '59 (BRK) [U] Jamaica, NY Immaculate Conception Monastery.
Mescher, Michael '83 (DUB) [3] Waterloo, IA Sacred Heart Church.
Mesi, Vincent *o.f.m.* '72 (LA) [4] Santa Barbara, CA St. Barbara Church; [R] Santa Barbara, CA Franciscan Friary, Order of Friars Minor (Old Mission).
Mesiona, Erwin '95 (SAC) Vallejo, CA St. Vincent Ferrer Church.
Meskell, David B. '55 (BO) Health Leave.
Meskenas, Vincent A. '49 (BEL) Retired.
Meskenas, Vincent A. '49 (SAC) Yuba City, CA St. Isidore Church.
Meskill, M. Francis '58 (LA) [47] Los Angeles, CA St. Basil's Church.
Meskill, Patrick A. '53 (LA) Retired.
Meskill, Thomas A. '60 (LA) Sick Leave.
Mesko, Louis G. *sch.p.* '36 (PH) [G] Devon, PA Devon Preparatory School; [AA] Devon, PA Piarist Fathers (Order of the Pious Schools).
Mesley, Jerry '73 (GLP) Absent on Leave.
Mesmer, William A. '68 (SY) Oneida, NY St. Patrick Church.
Messaro, Michael A. *m.ss.cc.* '68 (HBG) Blue Ridge Summit, PA St. Rita Church; Fairfield, PA Immaculate Conception of the Blessed Virgin Mary Church.
Messaros, Msgr. Michael F. '36 (ALN) Retired.
Messenger, William '77 (LA) [32] Los Angeles, CA Our Saviour Catholic Center Church; [CC] Los Angeles, CA Archdiocesan Office for Campus Ministry.
Messer, Joseph V. '61 (BAL) Glen Burnie, MD Church of the Good Shepherd; Retired.
Messer, Paul A. *s.j.* '67 (BO) [W] Chestnut Hill, MA The Jesuit Community at Boston College.
Messer, Terry *c.f.r.* '94 (NY) [DD] New York, NY St. Crispin Friary.
Messerich, Valerius U. *o.f.m.* '46 (STP) Hampton, MN St. Mathias Church.
Messick, Severin *o.s.b.* '82 (IND) [37] Indianapolis, IN St. Therese of the Infant Jesus (Little Flower) Church; Cannelton, IN St. Michael Church; [J] St. Meinrad, IN St. Meinrad Archabbey.
Messier, Raymond P. '68 (WOR) Athol, MA St. Francis Church; Petersham, MA St. Peter Church.
Messina, Angelo '68 (ALX) Leesville, LA St. Michael Church.
Messina, John A. '96 (BAL) Bradshaw, MD St. Stephen Church.
Messina, Joseph M. '72 (CAM) [O] Blackwood, NJ St. Pius X Spiritual Life Center.
Messina, Richard C. '65 (BO) Winchester, MA St. Mary Church.
Messina, Samuel '65 (JKS) Belzoni, MS All Saints Church.
Messina, Victor G. '74 (BR) [16] Baton Rouge, LA Our Lady of Mercy Church.
Messing, Francis '59 (MOB) Grove Hill, AL Sacred Heart Church.
Messman, Gerald C. '31 (LIN) Retired.
Messner, Thomas *o.f.m.* '67 (MRY) [G] San Miguel, CA Franciscan Friars, O.F.M.; [G] San Miguel, CA

Novitiate House for the Franciscan Friars, O.F.M.
Mestas, Leonard '81 (SB) Loma Linda, CA Loma Linda Community Hospital; Loma Linda, CA Loma Linda University Medical Center.
Mestas, Leonard J. '81 (BWN) On Assignment Outside the Diocese.
Mestriparampil, Thomas '89 (NY) City, NY George M. Motchan Detention Center; City, NY Otis Bantum Correctional Center.
Meszaros, James J. '69 (BRK) [241] Queens, NY St. Stanislaus Bishop and Martyr Church.
Metcalf, Andrew '86 (SR) Middletown, CA St. Joseph Church.
Metcko, Leo E. '43 (WCH) Retired.
Meter, Msgr. Charles N. '36 (CHI) Wilmette, IL St. Joseph Church; Retired.
Methe, Msgr. Normand A. '58 (BGP) [7] Stamford, CT Holy Spirit Church.
Method, Fredrick '66 (DUL) Hibbing, MN St. Leo's Church.
Metrejean, Msgr. Paul '63 (LAF) Mermentau, LA St. John the Evangelist Church.
Metro, LeRoy '63 (SAL) Clyde, KS St. John the Baptist's Church.
Metsy, Msgr. Norman G. '47 (PRO) Retired.
Metts, Ralph E. *s.j.* '73 (WDC) [M] Washington, DC The Jesuit Community at Georgetown University; [V] Washington, DC Jesuit Secondary Education Association.
Metz, David '97 (SAL) Manhattan, KS Seven Dolors Church.
Metz, Earl O. '58 (CIN) Georgetown, OH St. George Church; Mount Orab, OH St. Michael Church.
Metz, Kenneth J. '65 (MIL) [5] Kenosha, WI St. Mark Church.
Metzbower, Francis X. *s.j.* '63 (BAL) [M] Baltimore, MD Jesuit Fathers and Brothers Maryland Provincial Curia.
Metzdorf, William C. '73 (WDC) Potomac, MD Our Lady of Mercy Church.
Metzer, Edwin '55 (FgM) Maryknoll Foreign Missions.
Metzger, Alvin P. *o.s.a.* '54 (MIL) [P] Racine, WI Augustinian Novitiate.
Metzger, Andrew *o.s.b.* '56 (SP) [O] St. Leo, FL St. Leo Abbey.
Metzger, Clement *s.j.* '65 (TOL) [6] Toledo, OH Gesu Church.
Metzger, Dennis M. '74 (TOL) [35] Toledo, OH St. Patrick of Heatherdowns Church.
Metzger, Edward C. *o.f.m.* '59 (BUF) [3] Kenmore, NY St. John the Baptist Church.
Metzger, Edward C. *o.f.m.* '59 (NY) [DD] New York, NY Franciscan Friars, Order of Friars Minor, Holy Name Province.
Metzger, Edwin B. '55 (ROC) On Duty Outside the Diocese.
Metzger, John L. '67 (COL) Corning, OH St. Bernard Church.
Metzger, Joseph H., III '91 (RIC) Farmville, VA St. Theresa Church.
Metzger, Paschal *o.f.m.conv.* (FgM) Conventual Franciscan Foreign Missions.
Metzger, Msgr. Paul E. '43 (STU) Retired.
Metzger, Richard L. '67 (COL) Johnstown, OH Church of the Ascension.
Metzger, Msgr. Robert E. '60 (COL) Jackson, OH Holy Trinity Church.
Metzger, Msgr. Samuel S. '59 (TYL) Athens, TX St. Edward Church.
Metzger, Stephen A. '70 (COL) Utica, OH Church of the Nativity.
Metzger, Thomas H. '82 (LFT) Lebanon, IN St. Joseph Church.
Metzger, William A. '78 (COL) [3] Columbus, OH St. Agnes Church.
Metzger, William J. '62 (COL) Waverly, OH St. Mary, Queen of the Missions Church.
Metzger, William J. *o.s.f.s.* '71 (ARL) [D] Alexandria, VA Bishop Ireton High School; [J] Alexandria, VA Oblates of St. Francis de Sales Residence.
Metzinger, John '82 (OKL) Norman, OK Church of St. Mark the Evangelist.
Metzinger, John R. '82 (OKL) Special Assignment.
Metzler, Warren W. '64 (PIT) Wilkinsburg, PA St. James Church.
Metzler, William R. '72 (HRT) Kent, CT Sacred Heart Church.
Meulemans, Carl *m.m.* '60 (GB) [1] Manitowoc, WI St. Boniface Church.
Meulemans, Dennis T. '61 (SUP) Medford, WI Our Lady of the Holy Rosary Church.
Meulemans, Edward G. '60 (SUP) [1] Superior, WI Cathedral of Christ the King.
Meulemans, Thomas O. *o.praem.* '59 (GB) [A] De Pere, WI St. Norbert Abbey; [I] De Pere, WI St. Norbert Abbey; [I] De Pere, WI St. Joseph Priory.
Meuree, James *c.i.c.m.* '47 (SAT) [M] San Antonio, TX Missionhurst Community Residence.
Meurer, David C. '51 (SAT) Harper, TX St. Anthony's Church.
Meuret, Donald L., Jr. '84 (WH) War, WV Christ the King Church; Welch, WV St. Peter Church.
Mevissen, Richard *c.ss.r.* '66 (DET) [33] Detroit, MI Holy Redeemer Church.
Meyer, Albert *o.s.b.* '56 (MRY) [G] San Luis Obispo, CA Monastery of the Risen Christ.
Meyer, Alfred *o.s.b.* '35 (KC) [J] Conception, MO Conception Abbey.
Meyer, Arthur D. '61 (PEO) Canton, IL St. Mary's Church.
Meyer, Ben *o.p.* '54 (GAL) [J] Houston, TX St. Joseph Hospital.
Meyer, Benedict *o.s.b.* '54 (IND) [J] St. Meinrad, IN St. Meinrad Archabbey.
Meyer, Benedict *o.s.b.* '54 (LR) Brinkley, AR St. John the Baptist Church.
Meyer, Bernard *s.m.* '51 (SAT) [8] San Antonio, TX Holy Rosary Church; [M] San Antonio, TX Marianist Residence.
Meyer, Bernard A. '59 (SFD) On Duty Outside the Diocese.
Meyer, Charles *c.pp.s.* '31 (CIN) [B] Carthagena, OH St. Charles.
Meyer, Charles R. '45 (CHI) Retired; [A] Mundelein, IL University of St. Mary of the Lake-Mundelein Seminary.
Meyer, Clayton '66 (SEA) [19] Seattle, WA St. Peter Church; Special Assignment.
Meyer, Cosmas A. *s.v.d.* '47 (SB) [A] Riverside, CA Divine Word Seminary.
Meyer, Daniel J. '82 (CIN) Centerville, OH Incarnation Church; [V] Centerville, OH Catholic Alumni Club (Dayton Chapter).
Meyer, Dennis J. *m.s.* '70 (STL) [P] St. Louis, MO La Salette Missionaries; [P] St. Louis, MO La Salette Missionaries.
Meyer, Earl R. *o.f.m.cap.* '60 (STL) Arnold, MO Immaculate Conception Church; [P] Arnold, MO Immaculate Conception Friary.
Meyer, Elmer J. *m.m.* '54 (FgM) Maryknoll Foreign Missions.
Meyer, Emmett F. '64 (OM) [22] Omaha, NE St. Joan of Arc Church.
Meyer, Eric *c.p.* '66 (CHI) [91] Chicago, IL Immaculate Conception Church; [N] Chicago, IL Immaculate Conception Monastery.
Meyer, Fred A. '65 (STL) [6] St. Charles, MO St. Robert Bellarmine Church.
Meyer, Frederick C. '56 (STP) St. Henry, MN Church of St. Henry.
Meyer, George R. '46 (SFR) [1] San Mateo, CA St. Bartholomew Church; Retired.
Meyer, Gerald J. '96 (PEO) [1] Ottawa, IL St. Columba Church.
Meyer, Msgr. Gilbert '42 (FRS) Retired.
Meyer, Harold K. *o.c.s.o.* '62 (SAC) [A] Vina, CA Abbey of New Clairvaux, Trappist Seminary; [G] Vina, CA Abbey of New Clairvaux, Trappist.
Meyer, Harry J. '64 (CIN) Mason, OH St. Susanna Church.
Meyer, Henry H. '35 (SC) Retired.
Meyer, James A. '94 (FAR) Wyndmere, ND St. John the Baptist Church.
Meyer, James L. '60 (DET) Detroit, MI Hutzel Hospital.
Meyer, Jerome P. '85 (MIL) [14] Milwaukee, WI Congregation of the Blessed Trinity Church.
Meyer, John A. '82 (IND) Madison, IN Prince of Peace Church; Vevay, IN Most Sorrowful Mother of God Church; [N] Madison, IN Hanover College Newman Center.
Meyer, John D. '73 (RVC) Absent on Leave.
Meyer, John R. '89 (CHI) [W] Chicago, IL Opus Dei.
Meyer, Joseph H. *s.j.* '46 (FgM) Provinces.
Meyer, Msgr. Joseph J. '45 (PAT) Retired.
Meyer, Leo A. '65 (NO) [38] New Orleans, LA St. James Major Church.
Meyer, Msgr. Louis F. '44 (STL) Retired; [W] St. Louis, MO Missionaries of the Kingship of Christ.
Meyer, Mark '97 (CIN) [5] Dayton, OH Ascension Church.
Meyer, Michael W. '93 (LA) [8] Long Beach, CA St. Joseph Church.
Meyer, Nicholas W. *o.f.m.* '52 (STP) [10] St. Paul, MN Sacred Heart Church.
Meyer, Msgr. Omer F. '49 (EVN) [11] Evansville, IN Sacred Heart Church; Special Assignment.
Meyer, P. Wayne '49 (COL) Mount Vernon, OH Mount Vernon State Institute.
Meyer, Pacian *o.f.m.* '46 (GLP) Tohatchi, NM St. Mary Church.
Meyer, Paul Wayne '49 (COL) Retired.
Meyer, Robert G. '74 (WIN) [5] Winona, MN St. Stanislaus Church.
Meyer, Robert J. '64 (PIT) [43] Pittsburgh, PA St. Basil Church.
Meyer, Robert L. '57 (SFD) Charleston, IL St. Charles Borromeo Church; [M] Charleston, IL Eastern Illinois University Newman Center.
Meyer, Robert S. '88 (NEW) [B] South Orange, NJ Seton Hall University; [B] South Orange, NJ Seton Hall University.
Meyer, Ronald J. *o.m.i.* '71 (CR) Waubun, MN St. Ann Church.
Meyer, Sebastian *o.carm.* (SAC) Fairfield, CA Our Lady of Mount Carmel, Church.
Meyer, Stephen *c.ss.r.* (TUC) [J] Tucson, AZ Redemptorist Community Support Charity Trust.
Meyer, Stephen *c.ss.r.* '76 (DEN) [M] Denver, CO The Redemptorists/Denver Province.
Meyer, Stephen *c.ss.r.* '76 (OAK) [N] Oakland, CA Redemptorists.
Meyer, Stephen L. '79 (DUB) Dougherty, IA St. Patrick's Church; Rockwell, IA Sacred Heart Church.
Meyer, Steven '90 (FAR) Hope, ND St. Agatha's Church.
Meyer, Theo (DET) Detroit, MI Bi-County Osteopathic.
Meyer, Thomas C. '55 (SCL) Swanville, MN St. John the Baptist Church.
Meyer, Thomas E. '70 (CIN) [12] Dayton, OH Holy Angels Church.
Meyer, Thomas G. *o.m.i.* '70 (SFD) [1] Alton, IL SS. Peter and Paul Church.
Meyer, Vernon (PHX) [I] Phoenix, AZ Kino Institute.
Meyer, William C. *c.s.v.* '56 (CHI) [N] Arlington Heights, IL Viatorian Province Center-Clerics of St. Viator.
Meyer, William J. *s.m.* '79 (SAT) [M] San Antonio, TX Marianist Woodlawn Community.
Meyer, William O. '49 (DAV) Mechanicsville, IA St. Mary's Church.
Meyers, Frederick *ss.cc.* '71 (FR) Fairhaven, MA St. Joseph's Church.
Meyers, James P. '70 (WDC) Leonardtown, MD St. Aloysius Church.
Meyers, John F. (PH) [39] Philadelphia, PA St. Dominic Church.
Meyers, John F. '56 (DAL) [21] Dallas, TX St. Monica Church.
Meyers, Joseph L. *c.s.b.* '43 (GAL) [Q] Houston, TX Residence of the Basilian Fathers of the University of St. Thomas.
Meyers, Louis E. *s.j.* '62 (NO) New Orleans, LA Delgado Community College, School of Nursing; New Orleans, LA Louisiana State University Medical Center.
Meyers, Msgr. Michael W. '77 (LA) [13] Los Angeles, CA Holy Spirit Church.
Meyers, Robert V. '87 (MET) Kendall Park, NJ St. Augustine of Canterbury Church.
Meyers, William *s.m.* '79 (SAT) [C] San Antonio, TX St. Mary's University of San Antonio, Texas.
Meyett, Irving C. '53 (SUP) Retired.
Meyr, Herbert J. '60 (CHI) Maywood, IL St. James Church.
Meysenberg, James '89 (LIN) [C] Hastings, NE St. Cecilia's Middle School/High School.
Meysenberg, James J. '89 (LIN) [L] Hastings, NE St. Cecilia High School Endowment Fund.
Meysenburg, James J. '89 (LIN) Hastings, NE St. Cecilia's Church.
Meystrik, Gregory C. '90 (JC) Baring, MO St. Aloysius Church; Edina, MO St. Joseph Church.
Meza, Arturo '88 (AMA) On Duty Outside the Diocese.
Meza, Arturo '88 (SFE) [A] Santa Fe, NM Immaculate Heart of Mary Seminary.
Meza, Fernando (FRS) Visalia, CA Holy Family Church.
Meza, Fernando '95 (FRS) Goshen, CA St. Thomas the Apostle Church.
Meznar, Joseph A. '58 (DEN) [14] Denver, CO Holy Rosary Church.
Meznar, Robert P. '60 (DEN) [28] Denver, CO St. Catherine of Siena Church.
Mezquida, Ramon '58 (PCE) On Duty Outside the Diocese.
Mezydlo, James A. '77 (CHI) [158] Chicago, IL Our Lady of the Snows Church.
Mezydlo, Leonard T. '50 (CHI) [3] Des Plaines, IL St. Stephen Protomartyr Church; Retired.
Mezyk, Wladek *o.f.m.conv.* '95 (BUF) [O] Athol Springs, NY Father Justin Rosary Hour Radio Apostolate.
Mezzanote, Joseph *o.f.m.cap.* '39 (NEW) [5] Hoboken, NJ St. Ann's Church.
Mezzomo, Charles '71 (STF) Hempstead, NY St. Vladimir Church.
Miah, Gabriel '77 (RVC) Roslyn, NY St. Francis Hospital.
Miani, Titian A. '55 (STO) [7] Stockton, CA St. Luke Church; Retired.
Mibach, Everett J. *s.j.* '51 (SFR) [N] San Francisco, CA Jesuit Community at University of San Francisco.
Micali, Cuthbert *s.a.* '48 (NY) [DD] Garrison, NY Franciscan Friars of the Atonement.
Micarelli, Edmond C. '59 (PRO) Retired.
Micca, Louis *s.a.c.* '66 (CAM) Hammonton, NJ St. Joseph's Church.
Micek, Joseph S. '42 (OM) Retired.
Micek, Sylvester *o.f.m.* '51 (GAY) Burt Lake, MI Assumption of St. Mary Church; Pellston, MI St. Clement Church.
Miceli, James A. '75 (ATL) Rome, GA St. Mary's Church; [L] Atlanta, GA Campus Ministry.

Miceli, John P. '94 (CLV) [7] Akron, OH St. Hilary Church.
Miceli, Matthew M. *c.s.c.* '52 (FTW) [B] Notre Dame, IN University of Notre Dame Du Lac; [J] Notre Dame, IN Holy Cross Community, Corby Hall, University of Notre Dame.
Miceli, Michael A. '97 (BR) [13] Baton Rouge, LA St. Jude the Apostle Church.
Miceli, Paul W. '72 (BO) [14] Cambridge, MA Sacred Heart of Jesus Church.
Miceli, Vincent F. '91 (BRK) [203] Queens, NY Most Precious Blood Church.
Mich, Kenneth A. '70 (MIL) West Bend, WI St. Frances Cabrini Church.
Mich, Mario *s.d.b.* '48 (LA) [F] Bellflower, CA St. John Bosco High School.
Michael, A. Maria '71 (TYL) Longview, TX St. Mary Church.
Michael, Msgr. Chester P. '42 (RIC) Retired.
Michael, David C. (BO) [4] Waltham, MA St. Mary Church.
Michael, David C. '86 (BO) [CC] Waltham, MA Brandeis University Campus Ministry.
Michael, David F. '96 (SAM) Worcester, MA Our Lady of Mercy Church.
Michael, Msgr. Kenneth A. '64 (OLL) Detroit, MI St. Maron/St. Sharbel Church.
Michael, Lawrence P. '75 (SAM) Torrington, CT St. Maron Church.
Michael, Matthew (PH) [U] Philadelphia, PA Mercy Hospital of Philadelphia.
Michael, Matthew '73 (PH) Upper Darby, PA St. Alice Church.
Michael, Peter *s.v.d.* '40 (FgM) Society of the Divine Word Foreign Missions.
Michael, Susainathan (SCL) Waite Park, MN St. Joseph's Church.
Michaels, Msgr. Anthony B. '43 (OM) Retired.
Michaels, Dana '82 (OAK) El Sobrante, CA St. Callistus Church.
Michaels, Emmett T. '38 (ALT) Retired.
Michaels, John L. '39 (PIT) Retired; [O] Pittsburgh, PA St. John Vianney Manor.
Michaels, Patrick T. '82 (SFR) [4] Menlo Park, CA St. Raymond Church.
Michalak, Jaromir '91 (CAM) North Cape May, NJ St. John of God Church.
Michalak, John *o.s.p.* (NY) [5] Yonkers, NY St. Casimir Church.
Michalek, George C. '78 (LAN) [1] Lansing, MI St. Mary Cathedral.
Michalek, Henry J. '43 (CHI) [214] Chicago, IL St. William Church; Retired.
Michalek, Stanislaw *s.ch.* '88 (DAL) [23] Dallas, TX St. Peter Church.
Michalenko, Alexei '68 (VNN) On Special Assignment.
Michalenko, Seraphim *m.i.c.* '56 (SPR) [I] Stockbridge, MA Congregation of Marians.
Michaletz, James *c.s.v.* (CHI) Park Ridge, IL Mary, Seat of Wisdom Church.
Michalicka, John J. '59 (OKL) Ponca City, OK Church of St. Mary; [H] Ponca City, OK St. Mary's Housing Foundation.
Michalik, Bernard *o.f.m.conv.* '47 (RNO) Virginia City, NV St. Mary in the Mountains Church.
Michalik, Gary M. '80 (DET) Hamtramck, MI Our Lady Queen of Apostles Church.
Michalik, Walter G. *c.s.c.* '56 (FTW) [J] South Bend, IN Congregation of Holy Cross Indiana Province Provincial House.
Michalisin, Gregory '92 (PBR) North Huntingdon, PA St. Stephen's Church.
Michalka, Msgr. Arthur '51 (AUS) Jarrell, TX Holy Trinity Church.
Michalowski, John W. *s.j.* '81 (PRT) [C] Portland, ME Cheverus High School; [I] Portland, ME St. Ignatius Residence.
Michalski, James L. *s.j.* '72 (OM) [F] Omaha, NE The Jesuit Middle School of Omaha; [K] Omaha, NE Jesuit Community At Creighton University.
Michalski, Melvin E. '70 (MIL) [A] Milwaukee, WI St. Francis Seminary.
Michalski, Michael F. '76 (MIL) [39] Milwaukee, WI Holy Trinity-Our Lady of Guadalupe Church.
Michalski, Thaddeus C. '43 (CLV) Retired.
Michand, Leo James '77 (PRT) Ellsworth, ME St. Joseph's Church.
Michatek, William C. '66 (ROC) Spencerport, NY St. John the Evangelist Church.
Michel, Delix '88 (SFD) East Alton, IL St. Kevin Church; Venice, IL St. Mark Church.
Michel, Engelbert G. '66 (PH) Secane, PA Our Lady of Fatima Church; [L] Philadelphia, PA St. Vincent's Orphanage Tacony; [FF] Philadelphia, PA Catholic Kolping Society.
Michel, Eugene *o.f.m.* '64 (SAT) [46] San Antonio, TX St. Joseph Church.
Michel, Richard *o.s.b.* '86 (GBG) [A] Latrobe, PA St. Vincent Seminary.
Michel, Richard B. *o.s.b.* '86 (GBG) [H] Latrobe, PA Saint Vincent Archabbey.
Michele, Robert *c.s.p.* '55 (AUS) [11] Austin, TX St. Austin's Church; Austin, TX St. David's Hospital.
Michele, Robert P. *c.s.p.* '55 (NY) [DD] Jamaica Estates, NY Paulist Fathers Generalate.
Michelini, Michael S. '71 (CHI) [8] Chicago, IL St. Aloysius Church.
Michell, George J. '64 (RVC) Southold, NY St. Patrick's Church.
Michell, Timothy *o.c.s.o.* '65 (P) [L] Lafayette, OR The Cistercian (Trappist) Abbey of Our Lady of Guadalupe.
Michels, Aloysius *o.s.b.* '39 (SCL) [I] Collegeville, MN St. John's Abbey, of the Order of St. Benedict.
Michels, Andrew J. '85 (NU) Nassau, MN St. James Church; Ortonville, MN St. John Church; Rosen, MN St. Joseph Church.
Michelson, Chris '80 (KNX) [2] Knoxville, TN All Saints Catholic Church.
Michet, John M. '78 (CHI) Other Assignments.
Michiels, Kenneth J. '91 (ALX) Marksville, LA Holy Ghost Church.
Michiels, Philip F. '69 (SHP) [9] Shreveport, LA St. Mary of the Pines Church; Shreveport, LA Overton Brooks Veteran's Administration Medical Center.
Michini, F. Joseph *s.j.* '80 (PH) [G] Philadelphia, PA St. Joseph's Preparatory School; [AA] Philadelphia, PA St. Joseph's Preparatory School Jesuit Community, Arrupe House.
Michler, James '87 (STL) On Duty Outside the Archdiocese.
Michlik, Michael '63 (PHU) Baltimore, MD St. Michael's Church.
Michniewicz, Martin E. '86 (CHI) Calumet City, IL St. Andrew the Apostle Church.
Michota, Piotr (NEW) Mountainside, NJ Our Lady of Lourdes Church.
Miciunas, Anthony *m.i.c.* '40 (CHI) [N] Chicago, IL Congregation of Marian Fathers of the Immaculate Conception.
Mick, Lawrence (CIN) [11] Cincinnati, OH St. Antoninus Church; Retired.
Mick, Lawrence E. '72 (CIN) On Special and Diocesan Assignment.
Mick, Robert '49 (CIN) [58] Cincinnati, OH St. Martin of Tours Church; Retired.
Micka, Alphonse *m.i.c.* '49 (JOL) Darien, IL Our Lady of Peace Church.
Micka, Ermin *o.f.m.* '38 (STL) Oakville, MO St. Francis of Assisi Church; [P] Oakville, MO St. Francis Friary.
Mickelson, Michael T. '76 (NEW) Fort Lee, NJ Holy Trinity Church.
Micketti, Gerald F. '83 (GAY) Traverse City, MI St. Patrick Church.
Mickey, Richard L. '88 (MEM) [4] Memphis, TN Church of the Ascension.
Mickiewicz, David '62 (ALB) Special Assignment.
Mickiewicz, David '84 (ALB) Albany, NY Albany Medical Center Hospital.
Mickiewicz, J. William '62 (MET) Califon, NJ St. John Neumann Church.
Mickler, Jeffrey *s.s.p.* '74 (Y) [A] Canfield, OH Society of St. Paul.
Mickus, James J. '72 (OKL) Enid, OK St. Francis Xavier Church.
Miclot, Brian *ph.d.* '74 (DAV) [B] Davenport, IA St. Ambrose University.
Middendorf, Cyril *s.m.* '53 (CIN) [M] Dayton, OH Marianist Provincialate.
Middendorf, Eugene *o.f.m.* '45 (SFD) [4] Quincy, IL St. Francis Solanus Church; [K] Quincy, IL St. Francis Solanus Friary.
Middendorf, Frederic G. *s.j.* '42 (CIN) [28] Cincinnati, OH St. Francis Xavier Church.
Middendorf, Raymar *o.f.m.* '50 (IND) Oldenburg, IN Holy Family Church; [K] Oldenburg, IN Motherhouse of the Congregation of the Sisters of the Third Order of St. Francis.
Middendorf, Raymond D. *s.m.* '57 (PCE) Villalba, PR Our Lady Mother of Divine Providence Church.
Middlecamp, Eric *s.d.s.* '52 (FgM) Salvatorian Foreign Missions.
Middlecamp, Eric *s.d.s.* '52 (MIL) [P] Milwaukee, WI Salvatorians - Jordan Hall.
Middleton, Charles '51 (WCH) Baxter Springs, KS St. Joseph Church; Galena, KS St. Patrick Church.
Midgley, James J. '90 (BGP) [C] Bridgeport, CT Kolbe-Cathedral High School.
Midile, Theodore *t.o.r.* '60 (WH) [F] Kearneysville, WV Priest Field Pastoral Center.
Midor, Adam *s.v.d.* '91 (TR) Neptune, NJ Our Lady of Providence Church.
Midowski, Leonard '51 (NEW) [N] Rutherford, NJ St. John Vianney Residence for Priests.
Midura, Msgr. Francis S. '70 (RVC) Carle Place, NY Church of Our Lady of Hope.
Midzak, Ihor '90 (STF) [5] Glastonbury, CT St. John The Baptist Church; [6] Hartford, CT St. Michael Church.
Miechielsen, Albert *ss.cc.* '46 (HON) [H] Honolulu, HI St. Patrick's Monastery.
Mieczchowski, Msgr. Chester J. '45 (BAL) [13] Baltimore, MD St. Augustine Church.
Mieczkowski, Msgr. Chester J. '45 (BAL) Retired.
Miekina, Stanislaw *c.m.* '59 (BRK) [134] Brooklyn, NY St. Stanislaus Kostka Church.
Miele, Joseph J. '56 (TR) Red Bank, NJ St. Anthony Church.
Mier, Cristian *d.l.p.* (SB) [2] Riverside, CA Our Lady of Perpetual Help Church.
Mierenfeld, Lawrence E. '73 (CIN) [11] Dayton, OH St. Henry Church.
Mierzwa, Ronald B. '76 (BUF) Ellicottville, NY Holy Name of Mary Church.
Mierzwiak, Liguori *o.f.m.* '59 (GB) [I] Pulaski, WI Assumption of B.V.M. Friary.
Mietelski, Joseph *c.m.* '59 (BRK) [32] Brooklyn, NY SS. Cyril and Methodius Church.
Mifsud, Carmelo '59 (OAK) Retired.
Mifsud, James J. *s.m.* '65 (SJ) [20] San Jose, CA Queen of Apostles Church.
Miglarese, Msgr. Sam R. '69 (CHR) [1] Charleston, SC Cathedral of St. John the Baptist.
Migliazzo, Felix '49 (MRY) Retired; [F] Monterey, CA Ave Maria Convalescent Hospital.
Migliazzo, Filex '49 (MRY) [H] Monterey, CA Ave Maria Convent.
Migliore, Angelus *t.o.r.* '64 (SP) [13] Tampa, FL St. Patrick Church.
Mignot, Msgr. John W. '54 (E) Reynoldsville, PA St. Mary Church.
Miguel, Eutiquiano *o.f.m.cap.* '51 (NO) [62] New Orleans, LA St. Theresa Of Avila Church; New Orleans, LA Charity Hospital.
Miguelez, Valeriano '66 (SJN) [15] San Juan, PR Espiritu Santo Church.
Migueli, Peter A. '91 (NY) [11] Yonkers, NY St. John the Baptist Church.
Mihalco, John J. '83 (PBR) Houston, TX St. John Chrysostom Church; San Antonio, TX Byzantine Catholic Mission Church.
Mihalec, Peter M. '76 (CLV) Fairport Harbor, OH St. Anthony of Padua Church.
Mihalic, Francis *s.v.d.* '44 (FgM) Society of the Divine Word Foreign Missions.
Mihalic, Peter M. '76 (CLV) [A] Wickliffe, OH St. Mary Seminary and Graduate School of Theology.
Mihalik, Msgr. Alexis E. '64 (PBR) Boardman, OH Infant Jesus of Prague Church.
Mihalyi, Gilbert E. *o.praem.* '43 (GB) [I] De Pere, WI St. Norbert Abbey.
Mihan, Msgr. John A. '59 (LA) Pacific Palisades, CA Corpus Christi Church.
Mihayli, Gilbert *o.praem.* '43 (GB) [I] De Pere, WI St. Joseph Priory.
Mihelich, Leopold '32 (DEN) Retired.
Mihelko, John J. *m.m.* '38 (NY) [DD] Maryknoll, NY Maryknoll Fathers and Brothers.
Mihovilovich, John B. '52 (SFR) Retired.
Mijas, Paul J. '85 (RVC) Centereach, NY Assumption of the Blessed Virgin Mary Church.
Mijatovic, Slaven *o.f.m.* (DET) [5] Troy, MI St. Lucy Church.
Mika, John M. '72 (LIN) Sick Leave.
Mika, Joseph *o.f.m.* (CHI) [M] Justice, IL Rosary Hill Home.
Mikalajunas, John '69 (SY) Binghamton, NY Binghamton General Hospital.
Mikalajunas, John E. '69 (SY) [7] Binghamton, NY St. Joseph Church; [11] Binghamton, NY St. Stanislaus Kostka Church.
Mikalofsky, Hilarion A. '75 (MIL) Military Chaplains.
Mikasauskas, Ronald *m.ss.a.* '77 (NOR) [F] Cromwell, CT Missionaries of the Holy Apostles.
Mikasauskas, Ronald H. *m.ss.a.* '77 (NOR) [A] Cromwell, CT Holy Apostles College and Seminary.
Mikes, Pavel '90 (GAL) [29] Houston, TX St. Francis de Sales Church.
Mikesch, Gregory R. '75 (STL) Ferguson, MO Good Shepherd Church.
Miketinac, Hilary '45 (SY) [5] Binghamton, NY SS. Cyril and Method Church.
Mikkelson, Scott '82 (AUS) Mexia, TX St. Mary's Church; Mexia, TX State School.
Miklas, Sebastian F. *o.f.m.cap.* '39 (WDC) [B] Washington, DC St. Francis Friary-Capuchin College.
Miklaszewski, Albin *o.f.m.* '46 (MIL) [P] Burlington, WI Queen of Peace Friary.
Mikolaitis, Vito E. '43 (CHI) [141] Chicago, IL Nativity of the Blessed Virgin Mary Church; Retired.
Mikolajczyk, Bruno '88 (CC) [18] Corpus Christi, TX St. Paul the Apostle Church.
Mikolajczyk, Edward M. '73 (CHI) [161] Chicago, IL Our Lady of Victory Church; [A] Chicago, IL Archbishop Quigley Preparatory Seminary.
Mikolajczyk, George *m.m.* '55 (NY) [201] Staten Island, NY St. Christopher Church.
Mikolajczyk, George M. *m.m.* '55 (NY) [DD] Maryknoll, NY Maryknoll Fathers and Brothers.
Mikonis, Gerald S. '74 (PIT) Port Vue, PA St. Mark Church.
Miksch, Joseph A. '66 (OM) Columbus, NE St. Isidore Church.

Mikschl, Luke *s.t.* '53 (STP) [4] Minneapolis, MN Ascension Church.
Mikstay, Michael '59 (Y) Military Chaplains.
Mikula, Gregory '87 (PEO) [3] Streator, IL St. Casimir Church.
Mikula, John J. *o.f.m.conv.* '56 (RCK) [11] Rockford, IL St. Stanislaus Kostka Church.
Mikulanis, Alcuin L. *o.f.m.* '55 (CLV) [71] Cleveland, OH St. Stanislaus Church; [P] Cleveland, OH St. Stanislaus Friary.
Mikulanis, Dennis '77 (SD) [23] San Diego, CA St. Charles Church.
Mikulich, Joseph *o.f.m.* '22 (SJ) [26] San Jose, CA St. Mary of the Assumption Church.
Mikulik, Kenneth E. '52 (GAL) Pattison/Brookshire, TX Sacred Heart Church.
Mikulski, Isadore J. '50 (GAY) Retired.
Mikulski, Michael '95 (LA) Norwalk, CA St. Linus Church.
Mikus, Elemir Joseph '57 (DET) [2] Sterling Heights, MI SS. Cyril and Methodius Church.
Mikus, Frank P. '41 (SCR) Retired; [N] Dunmore, PA Villa St. Joseph.
Milanese, John M. '74 (BUR) Randolph, VT SS. Donatian and Rogatian Church.
Milani, Joseph J. '50 (SJ) Cupertino, CA St. Joseph of Cupertino Church; Retired.
Milani, Vasco J. *s.x.* '67 (MIL) [B] Franklin, WI Xaverian Missionary Fathers College Seminary.
Milano, Cleo J. '83 (BR) Denham Springs, LA Immaculate Conception Church.
Milano, Msgr. James '40 (LSC) Retired.
Milanowski, Paul A. '65 (GR) Newaygo, MI St. Bartholomew's Church.
Milazzo, Nicholas F. '52 (NY) [128] Bronx, NY St. Anthony Church.
Milbauer, Robert '66 (LA) Van Nuys, CA St. Bridget of Sweden Church; [D] Mission Hills, CA Alemany High School.
Milby, Lawrence M. '65 (BUF) Gowanda, NY St. Joseph Church.
Milde, Robert F. '48 (BRK) Retired; [U] Douglaston, NY Bishop Mugavero Residence.
Milek, Richard '62 (CHI) River Forest, IL St. Luke Church.
Miles, Cassian *o.f.m.* '61 (NY) [35] New York, NY St. Francis of Assisi Church.
Miles, Cassian A. *o.f.m.* '61 (PAT) [P] Paterson, NJ St. Anthony's Guild.
Miles, Francis J. *s.j.* '60 (WDC) [P] Faulkner, MD Loyola on the Potomac Retreat House.
Miles, James '78 (LKC) On Duty Outside the Diocese.
Miles, John *c.r.* (L) [18] Louisville, KY St. Cecilia Church.
Miles, Michael (BAK) On Duty Outside the Diocese.
Miles, Richard M. '83 (NO) [2] Kenner, LA Our Lady of Perpetual Help Church.
Milewski, Casimir '69 (TR) Burlington, NJ All Saints Church.
Milewski, Douglas J. '89 (NEW) [B] South Orange, NJ Seton Hall University.
Milewski, John *k.h.s.* (KNX) Dayton, TN St. Bridget Church.
Milewski, Richard '83 (TR) Tabernacle, NJ Holy Eucharist Church; New Lisbon, NJ New Jersey State Colony.
Milewski, Robert '80 (E) On Duty Outside Diocese.
Milewski, Msgr. Stanley E. '55 (DET) [A] Orchard Lake, MI SS. Cyril and Methodius Seminary; [C] Orchard Lake, MI Saint Mary's College; [E] Orchard Lake, MI St. Mary's Preparatory.
Milewski, Stanley J. '44 (GRY) [3] Gary, IN Holy Family Church.
Miley, Eamon '73 (MOB) Dauphin Island, AL St. Edmund-by-the-Sea Church.
Miley, Edward *p.i.m.e.* '67 (DET) [K] Detroit, MI P.I.M.E. Missionaries of SS. Peter and Paul.
Milford, Joseph *o.m.i.* '46 (PMB) [4] West Palm Beach, FL St. John Fisher Church.
Milford, Kenneth F. *c.s.sp.* '33 (SB) [E] Hemet, CA Holy Ghost Fathers.
Mili, Jude J. *o.f.m.* '59 (WH) [G] Morgantown, WV Our Lady of Good Counsel Franciscan Friary.
Milia, Msgr. Anthony A. '50 (OG) [3] Watertown, NY St. Anthony Church.
Milienewicz, Frank J. '76 (NTN) Birmingham, AL St. George Church; [E] Birmingham, AL National Shrine of St. George.
Militello, Benedict P. '57 (NEW) [2] Garfield, NJ Holy Name Church.
Militello, Cosmo F. '60 (CHI) Melrose Park, IL Sacred Heart Church.
Millane, Thomas J. '63 (TUC) [22] Tucson, AZ St. Elizabeth Ann Seton Church.
Millar, Andrew L. '58 (RVC) Seaford, NY Maria Regina Church.
Millea, Thomas V. (CHI) Retired.
Millea, Msgr. William V. '80 (BGP) On Duty Outside the Diocese.
Millen, Edwin F. '56 (RCK) [7] Aurora, IL St. Peter Church.
Miller, A. Andrew '45 (MAN) Retired.
Miller, Abraham '79 (CHI) [J] Chicago, IL St. Mary of Nazareth Hospital Center.
Miller, Abraham '79 (STN) Chicago, IL St. Mary of Nazareth Hospital Center.
Miller, Alfred J. '64 (DET) Temperance, MI Our Lady of Mt. Carmel Church.
Miller, Bernard *m.s.c.* '59 (FgM) Missionaries of the Sacred Heart Foreign Missions.
Miller, Bernard *m.s.c.* '59 (RCK) [H] Aurora, IL Missionaries of the Sacred Heart Community.
Miller, Bert '91 (FAR) Grafton, ND St. John the Evangelist's Church.
Miller, Bertin *o.f.m.* '64 (STL) [T] Dittmer, MO Il Ritiro-The Little Retreat.
Miller, Brendan '83 (LR) [A] Subiaco, AR Subiaco Monastery.
Miller, Brendan '83 (NSH) On Duty Outside the Diocese.
Miller, Brian J. *t.o.r.* '53 (SP) [6] St. Petersburg, FL St. Mary Our Lady of Grace Church.
Miller, Bruce '77 (ALX) [6] Alexandria, LA St. Rita Church.
Miller, Burt '91 (FAR) Grafton, ND Grafton State School.
Miller, Byron *c.ss.r.* '90 (SAT) [B] San Antonio, TX Redemptorist Formation Program.
Miller, C. Anthony '80 (HBG) [3] York, PA St. Patrick Church.
Miller, Casper J. *s.j.* '64 (FgM) Provinces.
Miller, Charles *o.f.m.* '66 (NY) [48] New York, NY Holy Name of Jesus Church.
Miller, Charles B. *o.f.m.* '38 (PEO) Metamora, IL St. Mary's Church.
Miller, Charles E. *c.m.* '56 (LA) [A] Camarillo, CA St. John's Seminary.
Miller, Charles E. '91 (SB) Yucca Valley, CA St. Mary of the Valley Church.
Miller, Charles H. *s.m.* '64 (SAT) [C] San Antonio, TX St. Mary's University of San Antonio, Texas; [M] San Antonio, TX Chaminade Community House.
Miller, Charles J. *o.f.m.* '66 (NY) [DD] New York, NY Franciscan Friars, Order of Friars Minor, Holy Name Province.
Miller, Charles J. '72 (NEW) Lyndhurst, NJ Sacred Heart Church.
Miller, Christopher T. '93 (LFT) [4] Lafayette, IN St. Lawrence Church.
Miller, Cletus *o.s.b.* '44 (FgM) American - Cassinese Congregation Foreign Missions.
Miller, Cletus *o.s.b.* '44 (SFS) [F] Marvin, SD Blue Cloud Abbey.
Miller, Conrad *o.f.m.conv.* '38 (BAL) [C] Baltimore, MD Archbishop Curley High School; [M] Baltimore, MD Immaculate Heart of Mary Friary.
Miller, David L. '81 (SPC) Pulaskifield, MO SS. Peter and Paul Church.
Miller, Donald A. *o.f.m.* '72 (Y) [B] North Canton, OH Walsh University.
Miller, Donald S. '42 (KC) Maryville, MO St. Gregory Barbarigo Church; Retired.
Miller, Edward M. '71 (BAL) [17] Baltimore, MD St. Bernardine Church.
Miller, Elden J. '54 (FTW) [4] Mishawaka, IN Queen of Peace Church.
Miller, Ferdinand B. '46 (NEW) Retired.
Miller, Francis *o.c.d.* '49 (WDC) [B] Washington, DC Monastery of Our Lady of Mount Carmel.
Miller, Francis J. '50 (CIN) Retired.
Miller, Francis N. '37 (BUF) Retired; [K] Lackawanna, NY Our Lady of Victory Hospital.
Miller, Francis X. *s.j.* '59 (WOR) [N] Worcester, MA Jesuits of Holy Cross College, Inc.
Miller, Msgr. Frank '54 (AUS) Absent on Sick Leave.
Miller, Frank P. '54 (COL) Dresden, OH St. Ann's Church.
Miller, Franklin '89 (FAR) Special Assignment.
Miller, Frederick J. '41 (NY) Retired.
Miller, Frederick L. '72 (NEW) On Duty Outside the Archdiocese.
Miller, Frederick L. '72 (NY) [A] Yonkers, NY St. Joseph's Seminary.
Miller, Frederick L. '72 (PH) [A] Wynnewood, PA Theological Seminary of St. Charles Borromeo, Overbrook.
Miller, Gary A. '70 (COV) [K] Fort Thomas, KY Carmel Manor; [K] Fort Thomas, KY Regina Cleri Home for Retired Priests.
Miller, Gary M. '72 (CHI) [164] Chicago, IL St. Pascal Church.
Miller, Gary R. '83 (TOL) [21] Toledo, OH St. Clement Church.
Miller, George '78 (DET) Special Assignment.
Miller, George '79 (DET) [4] Dearborn Heights, MI St. Linus Church.
Miller, Gregory L. *s.j.* '85 (SFR) [E] San Francisco, CA St. Ignatius College Preparatory (Coed).
Miller, Harry *s.j.* '54 (FgM) Provinces.
Miller, Henry A. *o.s.c.* '43 (DUL) St. Mathias, MN St. Mathias Church.
Miller, Henry A. *o.s.c.* '43 (SCL) [I] Onamia, MN Crosier Monastery.
Miller, J. Michael *c.s.b.* (GAL) [C] Houston, TX University of St. Thomas.
Miller, J. Michael *c.s.b.* '75 (GAL) [Q] Houston, TX Residence of the Basilian Fathers of the University of St. Thomas.
Miller, James '54 (CIN) [B] Carthagena, OH St. Charles.
Miller, James *o.m.i.* '57 (GAL) [37] Houston, TX Immaculate Conception Church.
Miller, James '68 (FWT) [3] Arlington, TX St. Joseph's Church.
Miller, James C. (RVC) Graduate Studies.
Miller, James C. '83 (RVC) Garden City, NY St. Anne Church; [I] Port Jefferson, NY St. Charles Hospital, Port Jefferson, New York.
Miller, Msgr. James F. '61 (JUN) Haines, AK Sacred Heart Church; Retired.
Miller, James H. '68 (LC) Viroqua, WI Annunciation of the Blessed Virgin Mary Church.
Miller, James L. '76 (DUB) Waverly, IA St. Mary's Church.
Miller, James Norman '59 (NSH) [9] Nashville, TN St. Mary's of the Seven Sorrows Church.
Miller, James W. '67 (CHI) [160] Chicago, IL Our Lady of Tepeyac Church.
Miller, John '58 (SCL) St. Stephen, MN St. Stephen's Church.
Miller, John '82 (WCH) Cunningham, KS Sacred Heart Church; St. Leo, KS St. Leo the Great Church.
Miller, John C. '95 (BRK) [97] Brooklyn, NY Our Lady of Guadalupe Church.
Miller, John H. *c.s.c.* '51 (STL) [W] St. Louis, MO Central Bureau of the CCUA.
Miller, Msgr. John J. '64 (PH) Fairless Hills, PA St. Frances Cabrini Church.
Miller, John P. '78 (HEL) [4] Missoula, MT St. Anthony Church.
Miller, John P. '82 (WCH) Willowdale, KS St. Peter's Church; Zenda, KS St. John Church.
Miller, Joseph '36 (SFD) Retired.
Miller, Joseph *c.pp.s.* '77 (DAV) Centerville, IA St. Mary's Church.
Miller, Joseph A. '89 (BRK) Absent on Leave.
Miller, Joseph B. '36 (TR) Retired.
Miller, Joseph C. '49 (OWN) Retired.
Miller, Joseph K. '57 (SAG) Nine Mile, MI St. Mary Church; Pinconning, MI St. Agnes Church.
Miller, Joseph N. '48 (SUP) Minocqua, WI St. Patrick Church.
Miller, Joseph W. '59 (PIT) Retired.
Miller, Kenneth '77 (Y) Boardman, OH St. Luke Church.
Miller, Lawrence J. '69 (NEW) [1] Bayonne, NJ St. Mary Star of the Sea Church.
Miller, Leo *o.m.i.* '52 (LA) Lakewood, CA St. Pancratius Church.
Miller, Leo M. *o.m.i.* '52 (LA) Long Beach, CA Veterans Affairs Medical Center.
Miller, Leo M. *o.m.i.* '52 (STP) [N] St. Paul, MN Oblate Residence.
Miller, Loran *o.f.m.cap.* '64 (DET) [K] Detroit, MI St. Bonaventure Friary.
Miller, Loran *o.f.m. cap.* '64 (LC) [I] Marathon City, WI St. Anthony Retreat Center.
Miller, Louis '56 (L) [N] Louisville, KY Sacred Heart Home, Inc.
Miller, Mardean E. '94 (PH) [140] Philadelphia, PA Resurrection of Our Lord Church.
Miller, Mark *c.pp.s.* '71 (KC) [A] Kansas City, MO Precious Blood Mission House; [A] Liberty, MO Society of the Precious Blood Provincial Offices; [J] Liberty, MO Precious Blood Society Provincial Office.
Miller, Mark A. '69 (ROC) Stanley, NY St. Theresa Church.
Miller, Martin J. '94 (NY) [II] New Rochelle, NY Opus Dei (Prelature of the Holy Cross and Opus Dei).
Miller, Maurice R. '49 (LFT) [2] Lafayette, IN St. Ann Church.
Miller, Meinrad *o.s.b.* '94 (KCK) [A] Atchison, KS Benedictine College; [H] Atchison, KS St. Benedict's Abbey.
Miller, Michael (ALB) Albany, NY St. Peter's Hospital.
Miller, Michael '72 (MRY) [4] Salinas, CA Madonna Del Sasso Church; Special Assignment.
Miller, Michael *m.s.c.* '85 (FgM) Missionaries of the Sacred Heart Foreign Missions.
Miller, Michael *m.s.c.* '85 (RCK) [H] Aurora, IL Missionaries of the Sacred Heart Community.
Miller, Michael '86 (ALB) Colonie, NY St. Clare Church.
Miller, Michael J. '96 (STP) West St. Paul, MN St. Joseph Church.
Miller, Neil '61 (ROC) [37] Rochester, NY Our Lady of Perpetual Help Church.
Miller, Oscar J. *c.m.* '39 (SAT) Losoya, TX El Carmen Catholic Church.
Miller, Paul '44 (FTW) [10] South Bend, IN Holy Family Church.
Miller, Paul A. *c.ss.r.* '33 (NY) Port Ewen, NY Presentation of the Virgin Mary Church.

Miller, Paul A. *c.ss.r.* '62 (NY) [DD] Esopus, NY Redemptorist Priests and Brothers C.Ss.R. (Province of Baltimore).
Miller, Paul E. '67 (SCR) [1] Wilkes-Barre, PA St. Aloysius Church.
Miller, Paul N. '56 (HBG) Bonneauville, PA St. Joseph Church.
Miller, Paul W. '44 (KCK) Eudora, KS Holy Family Church.
Miller, Peter *s.c.j.* '45 (MIL) [P] Franklin, WI Villa Maria.
Miller, Philip '77 (Y) Ashtabula, OH St. Joseph's Church.
Miller, Randall J. '89 (LAN) Blissfield, MI St. Peter the Apostle Church.
Miller, Richard E. '76 (LFT) Reynolds, IN St. Joseph Church; Grissom, IN Grissom Air Force Base, St. Michael's Chapel; Special Assignment.
Miller, Richard G. '50 (TOL) [16] Toledo, OH St. Agnes Church.
Miller, Robert *o.p.* (CHI) [J] Des Plaines, IL Holy Family Medical Center.
Miller, Robert '70 (SB) [1] San Bernardino, CA Our Lady of the Rosary Cathedral.
Miller, Robert J. *o.p.* '56 (CHI) [N] River Forest, IL St. Thomas Aquinas Priory.
Miller, Robert J. '61 (MET) Edison, NJ Guardian Angels Church.
Miller, Robert J. '76 (CHI) [79] Chicago, IL Holy Angels Church.
Miller, Robert J. '80 (PIT) [43] Pittsburgh, PA St. Basil Church.
Miller, Robert M. '92 (PIT) [1] New Castle, PA Mary, Mother of Hope Church.
Miller, Roger F. '54 (KC) Lee's Summit, MO Holy Spirit Church.
Miller, Theodore '75 (TOL) [22] Toledo, OH St. Francis de Sales Church; [32] Toledo, OH St. Mary of the Assumption Church.
Miller, Thomas C. '93 (STL) [7] Florissant, MO Sacred Heart Church.
Miller, Msgr. Thomas G. '71 (RIC) [8] Richmond, VA St. Bridget Church.
Miller, Thomas J. *c.s.sp* '58 (NO) Pointe a la Hache, LA St. Thomas Church.
Miller, Thomas M. *c.s.b.* '45 (ROC) [I] Rochester, NY Residence of Basilian Fathers-The Aquinas Institute.
Miller, Thomas R. '77 (PIT) Clarksville, PA St. Thomas Church.
Miller, Thomas R. '79 (PEO) [15] Peoria, IL St. Vincent De Paul Church.
Miller, Thomas W. '77 (BEL) Anna, IL St. Mary Church; Anna, IL Anna State Hospital; Vienna, IL Vienna Correctional Center; Vienna, IL Dixon Springs Work Camp; Vienna, IL Shawnee Correctional Center.
Miller, Walt *s.v.d.* '69 (SB) [A] Riverside, CA Divine Word Seminary.
Miller, Whitney '80 (LKC) [7] Lake Charles, LA Our Lady of Good Counsel Church; [F] Lake Charles, LA Catholic Student Center.
Miller, William '61 (L) [59] Louisville, KY Our Lady of Lourdes Church.
Miller, William *c.pp.s.* '63 (JC) Sedalia, MO Sacred Heart Church.
Miller, William *s.j.* '72 (P) [A] St. Benedict, OR Mount Angel Seminary.
Miller, William C. '83 (E) [3] Oil City, PA St. Joseph Church.
Miller, William M. '56 (PIT) [26] Pittsburgh, PA St. Mary of Mercy Church.
Miller, William M. '91 (LKC) Big Lake, LA St. Mary of the Lake Church.
Miller, William T. *s.j.* '55 (DEN) [M] Denver, CO Xavier Jesuit Center.
Miller, William T. *s.j.* '72 (P) [L] Portland, OR Colombiere Community.
Miller, William T. *i.c.* '84 (PEO) [A] Peoria, IL Rosminian Novitiate.
Millerd, William H. *s.j.* '68 (WDC) [M] Washington, DC The Jesuit Community at Georgetown University.
Millet, John H. *s.j.* '47 (NO) [P] New Orleans, LA Ignatius Residence.
Millican, Ron '81 (P) [C] Portland, OR Central Catholic High School.
Millican, Ronald C. '81 (P) Vernonia, OR St. Mary Church.
Milligan, Richard A. '60 (PHX) [16] Phoenix, AZ St. Luke Church.
Milligan, Ronald '72 (DET) [3] Sterling Heights, MI St. Ephrem Church.
Milliken, Damian *o.s.b.* '58 (FgM) Ottilien Congregation Foreign Missions.
Milliken, Damian J. *o.s.b.* '58 (PAT) [M] Newton, NJ St. Paul's Abbey.
Milliken, David '77 (NEW) Berkeley Heights, NJ Church of the Little Flower.
Millisor, Daniel J. '86 (COL) Ada, OH Our Lady of Lourdes Church.
Millot, Andre '69 (WDC) [26] Washington, DC Church of St. Louis.
Millott, Thirburse F. '75 (WOR) Southborough, MA St. Anne Church.
Mills, Alexander '80 (TUC) Tucson, AZ Villa Maria.
Mills, Alexander *o.s.b.* '90 (TUC) [F] St. David, AZ Holy Trinity Monastery.
Mills, Brindley '64 (DAL) [21] Dallas, TX St. Monica Church.
Mills, Donald J. '82 (PH) Delphi, PA St. Mary Church.
Mills, James Leo '62 (NEW) Retired.
Mills, Joseph M. '53 (OWN) Rome, KY St. Martin Church.
Mills, Robert N. '55 (L) Retired.
Milon, Augustin *o.f.m.* '28 (CHI) [I] Chicago, IL Port Ministries.
Milosz, Bogdan '81 (DET) Capac, MI St. Nicholas Church.
Milota, Thomas '92 (JOL) [1] Joliet, IL The Cathedral of St. Raymond.
Milsted, Gordon '63 (MOB) Fairhope, AL St. Lawrence Church.
Milton, Hilary *o.carm.* '63 (NEW) Teaneck, NJ St. Anastasia's Church.
Milton, Kevin *c.ss.r.* '67 (NY) [DD] Esopus, NY Redemptorist Priests and Brothers C.Ss.R. (Province of Baltimore); [FF] Esopus, NY Mount St. Alphonsus Redemptorist Retreat Center.
Miltz, Karl J. '69 (IND) Leave of Absence.
Mimms, Wolfgang *o.ss.t.* '70 (VIC) [4] Victoria, TX Our Lady of Sorrows Church.
Mimnagh, Msgr. Peter F. '48 (SD) Retired.
Mina, John L. '89 (PBR) Clairton, PA Ascension of Our Lord Church.
Minamicki, George *s.j.* '54 (FTW) [B] Notre Dame, IN University of Notre Dame Du Lac.
Minassian, Raphael '73 (ARM) Los Angeles, CA Our Lady Queen of Martyrs Church.
Minassian, Raphael *p.i.a.* '73 (LA) [30] Los Angeles, CA Our Lady Queen of Martyrs Church.
Minch, Richard '69 (SAV) Military Chaplains.
Minchak, Paul *o.f.m.cap.* '69 (AGN) [E] Agana Heights, GU St. Fidelis Friary.
Minchak, Paul *o.f.m.cap.* '69 (FgM) Capuchin Foreign Missions.
Minchak, Paul *o.f.m. cap.* '69 (HON) Kailua, HI St. Anthony Church.
Minchiatti, Francis *c.s.* (PRO) [8] Providence, RI St. Bartholomew Church.
Minder, Kevin W. '89 (YAK) Wapato, WA St. Peter Claver Church.
Minder, Lawrence *o.s.b.* '89 (P) [L] St. Benedict, OR Mt. Angel Abbey.
Mindling, J. Daniel *o.f.m.cap.* '80 (BAL) [A] Emmitsburg, MD Mount St. Mary's Seminary.
Mindling, J. Daniel *o.f.m.cap.* '80 (WDC) [B] Washington, DC St. Francis Friary-Capuchin College.
Mindling, Joseph *o.f.m.cap.* '67 (WDC) [39] Washington, DC Shrine of the Sacred Heart Church.
Mindrup, Mark F. *o.f.m.conv.* '39 (STP) [Q] Prior Lake, MN Franciscan Retreat House.
Minehan, Michael P. (SY) [H] Syracuse, NY Bishop Joseph T. O'Keefe, Inc.
Minehan, Michael P. '80 (SY) Lafayette, NY St. Joseph Church; Special Assignment; [W] Syracuse, NY David W. Barry Foundation.
Minelli, Peter A. '63 (MAR) [1] Escanaba, MI St. Anne Church.
Minette, James '41 (SCL) Retired.
Minh, Joseph Duc '61 (LA) [A] Camarillo, CA St. John's Seminary.
Minh, Matthew T. '53 (COS) [1] Colorado Springs, CO St. Mary's Cathedral.
Minh, Vincent *c.ss.r.* '68 (P) [17] Portland, OR Holy Redeemer Church; [1] Portland, OR Southeast Asian Vicariate Church.
Minh, Vu Duc '80 (TLS) On Duty Outside the Diocese.
Minh Thanh Tran, Matthew '53 (COS) [15] Colorado Springs, CO The Vietnamese Holy Martyrs Quasi-Parish.
Minh Thu, Anthony Hoang '68 (ARL) [5] Arlington, VA Holy Martyrs of Vietnam Church.
Minhoto, Msgr. Walter '64 (FRS) [1] Fresno, CA St. John Cathedral.
Minhoto, Msgr. Walter F. '64 (FRS) Retired.
Minic, John F. '71 (CIN) Retired.
Minichello, Arthur '73 (BRK) [33] Brooklyn, NY St. Dominic Church.
Minielli, Anthony '45 (NY) Retired.
Minigan, William J. '86 (BO) [8] Cambridge, MA St. John the Evangelist Church.
Miniscalco, Donald C. *c.ss.r.* '68 (PH) [135] Philadelphia, PA St. Peter the Apostle Church.
Minj, Alexius *s.j.* '92 (MIL) [P] Milwaukee, WI Jesuit Community at Marquette University.
Mink, John J. '85 (WIL) Wilmington Manor, DE Our Lady of Fatima Church; Wilmington, DE Delaware Army National Guard.
Minkiel, Stephen J. *c.m.* '57 (BRK) [32] Brooklyn, NY SS. Cyril and Methodius Church.
Minkler, John '72 (ALB) Albany, NY Veterans' Administration Hospital; Military Chaplains.
Minnich, John F. (GRY) Retired.
Minniti, Anthony L. '70 (CAM) Elmer, NJ St. Ann's Church.
Minniti, David V. '72 (CAM) Millville, NJ St. Mary Magdalen's Church.
Minnoggio, Ferrando '47 (CLV) Retired.
Minogue, Austin F. *c.m.* '41 (CHI) [C] Chicago, IL Vincentian Community at DePaul University.
Minogue, John P. *c.m.* '72 (CHI) [C] Chicago, IL De Paul University; [C] Chicago, IL Vincentian Community at DePaul University.
Minogue, Liam A. '68 (MET) Hillsborough, NJ Mary, Mother of God Church.
Minogue, Michael '81 (PHX) Sun City West, AZ Our Lady of Lourdes Church.
Minson, Bartholomew *o.f.m.cap.* '64 (FgM) Capuchin Foreign Missions.
Minsterman, Joseph '61 (GBG) East Vandergrift, PA Our Lady, Queen of Peace Church.
Minta, John J. '50 (IND) Milan, IN St. Charles Borromeo Church; Retired.
Mintegui, Marc A. '68 (CHR) Military Chaplains.
Mintjal, Frank D. '59 (Y) Alliance, OH Regina Coeli Church.
Minturn, Joseph '57 (RVC) Manorhaven, NY Our Lady of Fatima Church.
Minvielle, John Q. *s.j.* '43 (NO) [P] New Orleans, LA Ignatius Residence.
Miodowski, Chester A. '46 (NEW) Retired.
Miodowski, Leonard A. '51 (NEW) Retired.
Miola, Luigi C. '77 (CLV) Madison, OH Immaculate Conception Church.
Miorin, Albert C. (TOL) Retired.
Miotke, Carmel *o.f.m.* '60 (BO) [BB] Boston, MA St. Anthony Shrine.
Mirabelli, Daniel J. *c.s.v.* '60 (PEO) [B] Rock Island, IL Alleman High School.
Miracky, James J. *s.j.* '88 (WOR) [N] Worcester, MA Jesuits of Holy Cross College, Inc.
Miraglia, Salvatore J. '75 (RVC) Priests Released from Diocesan Assignment.
Miralbes-Drago, Julio E. '72 (MIL) [81] Milwaukee, WI St. Wenceslaus Church.
Miranda, Daryl *s.j.* '97 (BO) [W] Chestnut Hill, MA The Jesuit Community at Boston College.
Miranda, Juan '51 (SJN) [21] San Juan, PR Nuestra Sra. de Guadalupe Church.
Miranda, Lorenzo '91 (LA) Compton, CA St. Albert the Great Church; Terminal Island, CA Federal Correctional Institution.
Miranda, Luis *o.carm.* '84 (ARE) Ciales, PR Holy Rosary Church.
Miranda, Luke '55 (FWT) Absent on Leave.
Miranda, R. Dario '92 (LA) Canoga Park, CA St. Joseph the Worker Church.
Miranda, Msgr. Rafael '56 (ELP) [38] El Paso, TX San Judas Tadeo Church.
Miranda, Victor '86 (CHI) South Holland, IL St. Jude the Apostle Church.
Miranne, Paul *o.s.b.* '47 (NO) [P] St. Benedict, LA St. Joseph Abbey.
Mirecki, Msgr. John '55 (RVC) Riverhead, NY St. Isidore's Church.
Mireles, Richard '74 (BWN) Absent.
Miriani, Gerald C. '62 (BEL) Shiloh, IL Corpus Christi Church.
Miroslaw, '77 (PIT) Wildwood, PA St. Catherine of Sweden Church.
Mirro, Joseph A. '76 (RVC) Mastic Beach, NY St. Jude Church.
Mirsberger, Richard E. '66 (MIL) [9] West Allis, WI St. Rita Church.
Mirto, Gregario L. '65 (DEN) Fort Lupton, CO St. William Church.
Misbrener, David M. '95 (PBR) North Hills-Gibsonia, PA St. Andrew the Apostle Church.
Miscamble, Wilson D. *c.s.c.* '88 (FTW) [B] Notre Dame, IN University of Notre Dame Du Lac; [J] South Bend, IN Congregation of Holy Cross Indiana Province Provincial House; [J] Notre Dame, IN Holy Cross Community, Corby Hall, University of Notre Dame.
Mischke, Bernard *o.s.c.* '51 (SCL) [I] Onamia, MN Crosier Monastery.
Mischke, Fridolin P. *o.s.c.* '42 (PHX) [F] Phoenix, AZ Crosier Community of Phoenix (Canons Regular of the Order of the Holy Cross).
Mischke, Gerald '64 (SCL) Holdingford, MN St. Hedwig's Church; Holdingford, MN St. Mary's Church; Opole, MN Our Lady of Mt. Carmel Church; St. Anna, MN Immaculate Conception Church; St. Wendel, MN St. Columbkille's Church.
Mischke, Walter *c.m.f.* (CHI) [N] Oak Park, IL Claretian Fathers Headquarters of U.S.A. Eastern Province.
Mischke, Walter *c.m.f.* '43 (CHI) [N] Oak Park, IL Claretian Fathers Headquarters of U.S.A. Eastern Province.
Mischke, Walter *c.m.f.* '43 (LA) [R] Rancho Dominguez, CA Dominguez Seminary Inc.
Mischkowiuski, Henry B. '65 (LR) Lake Village, AR Our Lady of the Lake Church.

Mischler, Thomas E. '81 (GRY) Lowell, IN St. Edward Church; Shelby, IN St. Theresa Church.
Misenko, John A. '78 (CLV) [4] Parma, OH St. Columbkille Church.
Misercola, Chester A. '64 (SY) [1] Oswego, NY St. John the Evangelist Church.
Misey, Leonard S. '63 (JC) Brunswick, MO St. Boniface Church; Indian Grove, MO St. Raphael Church.
Mish, Roy L. '60 (LC) Eau Galle, WI St. Henry Church.
Misho, Lloyd P. '58 (BEL) Retired.
Misiewicz, Chester J. '73 (WOR) Gilbertville, MA St. Aloysius Church.
Misiolek, Frederick '65 (DET) Flat Rock, MI St. Roch Church.
Miskella, Richard '64 (LA) Palmdale, CA St. Mary Church.
Miskiewicz, Paul *o.f.m.conv.* '82 (BRK) [146] Queens, NY St. Adalbert Church.
Miskolczy, Kalman *sch.p.* '45 (BUF) [3] Lackawanna, NY Assumption Church; [O] Derby, NY Piarist Fathers.
Missa, Msgr. John B. '32 (BO) [6] Brockton, MA Our Lady of Ostrobrama Church.
Missimi, Anthony N. '62 (COL) [22] Columbus, OH Immaculate Conception Church.
Missinne, William *c.i.c.m.* '54 (FgM) Missionhurst Foreign Missions.
Missler, John C. '78 (TOL) Shelby, OH Most Pure Heart of Mary Church.
Missler, Othmar *c.pp.s.* '37 (CIN) [B] Carthagena, OH St. Charles.
Mistretta, Msgr. Vito F. '42 (SAC) Citrus Heights, CA Holy Family Church; Retired and in Senior Ministry.
Misulich, Msgr. Raymond M. *j.c.l.* '56 (PSC) New York, NY St. Mary's Church.
Misurda, Matthew E. '77 (ALT) [B] Johnstown, PA Bishop McCort High School.
Miszkel, Ivot *o.f.m.cap.* '80 (PAT) [M] Oak Ridge-Milton, NJ St. Stanislaus B. M. Friary.
Mitas, Matthew M. '79 (STL) Kirkwood, MO St. Gerard Majella Church.
Mitchell, Charles I. '84 (ORL) Altamonte Springs, FL St. Mary Magdalen Church.
Mitchell, Conan *o.f.m.* '43 (SUP) Ashland, WI Our Lady of the Lake Catholic Community Church.
Mitchell, Edward J. '54 (DET) Rochester, MI St. Irenaeus Church.
Mitchell, Eugene *b.s.o.* '92 (NTN) Manchester, NH Our Lady of the Cedars Church; [B] Methuen, MA Basilian Salvatorian Order.
Mitchell, Francis *o.m.i.* '44 (FgM) Oblates Foreign Missions.
Mitchell, John C. '55 (BGP) On Duty Outside the Diocese.
Mitchell, John Dennis *c.s.p.* '38 (NY) [DD] Jamaica Estates, NY Paulist Fathers Generalate.
Mitchell, John E. '54 (STP) Retired.
Mitchell, Msgr. John J. '63 (RCK) Loves Park, IL St. Bridget Church.
Mitchell, John J. '96 (STP) Eagan, MN St. John Neumann Church.
Mitchell, John T. *s.j.* '72 (SJ) [M] Los Gatos, CA California Province of the Society of Jesus, Jesuit Provincial Office.
Mitchell, Joseph '56 (DAL) Frisco, TX St. Francis of Assisi Church.
Mitchell, Joseph O. *c.p.* '81 (SAC) [G] Citrus Heights, CA Christ the King Retreat; [I] Citrus Heights, CA Christ the King Retreat Center.
Mitchell, Joseph P. '79 (SEA) Bremerton, WA Our Lady, Star of the Sea Church.
Mitchell, Kenneth *s.c.j.* '48 (SP) [O] Pinellas Park, FL Priests of the Sacred Heart.
Mitchell, Lester *o.f.m.* '55 (PHX) [19] Phoenix, AZ St. Mary's Basilica Church.
Mitchell, Mark E. '76 (GR) On Special Assignment.
Mitchell, Michael J. '65 (SJ) Cupertino, CA St. Joseph of Cupertino Church; Special Assignment; [P] Santa Clara, CA St. Joseph Seminary Corporation; [P] Santa Clara, CA The Roman Catholic Welfare Corporation of San Jose.
Mitchell, Peter '78 (ORL) Port Orange, FL Epiphany Church.
Mitchell, Peter G. '51 (HRT) Derby, CT St. Mary's Church.
Mitchell, Robert (ORL) Rockledge, FL St. Mary's Church.
Mitchell, Robert A. *s.j.* '56 (SY) [B] Syracuse, NY Le Moyne College; [S] Syracuse, NY Jesuits at LeMoyne, Inc.
Mitchell, Robert J. (PAT) Budd Lake, NJ St. Jude Church.
Mitchell, Royce '74 (NO) Retired.
Mitchell, Msgr. Salvatore P. '42 (E) Retired.
Mitchell, Thomas R. '79 (HRT) On Duty Outside the Archdiocese.
Mitchell, Thomas R. '79 (MGZ) [4] Mayaquez, PR Church De El Buen Pastor Church.
Mitchell, Walter '61 (BRK) Brooklyn, NY Brooklyn House of Detention.
Mitchell, Walter '91 (MIA) Retired.
Mitchell, Walter A. '61 (BRK) [78] Brooklyn, NY St. Margaret Mary Church.
Mitchell, William *ss.cc.* '50 (FR) [J] Fairhaven, MA Sacred Hearts Provincial House.
Mitchell, William J. '49 (PHX) Retired.
Mitchko, James '77 (PSC) North Fort Myers, FL All Saints Byzantine Catholic Church.
Mitek, Josef '84 (DET) Lapeer, MI Immaculate Conception of the Blessed Virgin Mary Church.
Mitera, Stanislaus C. '41 (OM) Retired.
Mitka, John J. '66 (BUF) Jamestown, NY St. Peter and Paul Church.
Mitko, Joseph K. *o.ss.t.* '80 (TR) Asbury Park, NJ Our Lady of Mt. Carmel Church.
Mitolo, Frank A. '68 (PIT) Allegheny County, PA University of the Health Science - Allegheny General Campus.
Mitolo, Msgr. Nicholas A. '54 (GBG) Jeannette, PA Ascension Church.
Mitrano, Joseph *c.s.b.* '41 (AUS) Kingsland, TX St. Charles Borromeo Church.
Mitros, Joseph *s.j.* '47 (NY) [DD] New York, NY Jesuit Community at Fordham University.
Mittelstadt, John *o.f.m.* '62 (GLP) Tohatchi, NM St. Mary Church.
Mitten, Stephen F. *s.j.* '95 (RC) [B] Howes, SD Kino Jesuit Community; [D] Howes, SD The Diocese of Rapid City Mahpiya na Maka Okoigna.
Mitty, Msgr. Edward J. '50 (NY) [99] New York, NY Our Lady of Victory Church.
Mitulski, James M. '72 (STL) St. Peters, MO All Saints Church.
Mitzel, Daniel C. '81 (HBG) [3] Harrisburg, PA St. Francis of Assisi Church.
Mixtacki, Gene R. '79 (NEW) [4] Linden, NJ St. Theresa of the Child Jesus Church.
Miyares, Carlos '81 (MIA) Absent on Leave.
Miyares, Gustavo J. '73 (MIA) [1] Hialeah, FL Immaculate Conception Church; [B] Opa Locka, FL St. Thomas University; [C] Miami, FL Msgr. Edward Pace High School.
Mizener, Paul '64 (SP) [7] St. Petersburg, FL St. Paul Church.
Mizeur, Thomas '73 (PEO) [J] Peoria, IL St. Francis' Medical Center.
Mizicko, Carroll *o.f.m.* '68 (SHP) [2] Monroe, LA Little Flower of Jesus Church.
Mlapah, Bernard *o.ss.t.* '80 (CC) [2] Corpus Christi, TX Christ the King Church.
Mmassi, Gabriel '93 (WDC) [M] Washington, DC Carroll House.
Moala, Saimone (SFR) [4] San Mateo, CA St. Timothy Church.
Moan, Francis X. *s.j.* '57 (WDC) [E] Washington, DC Gonzaga College High School.
Moccia, Bonaventure *c.p.* '52 (FgM) Passionist Foreign Missions.
Mocco, Charles W. '57 (GB) Special Assignment; [N] Green Bay, WI University of Wisconsin G.B. Ecumenical Center.
Mocio, Stephen J. '76 (DAL) [24] Dallas, TX St. Philip Church.
Mociun, Casimir T. '42 (SFS) Retired.
Mock, Robert M. '84 (BUF) Canaseraga, NY St. Mary Church; Portageville, NY Assumption B.V.M. Church.
Mock, Timothy *c.m.m.* '52 (DET) [K] Dearborn Heights, MI Our Lady of Grace Monastery.
Mockaitis, Timothy '78 (P) [4] Eugene, OR St. Paul Church.
Mockel, George E. '75 (OAK) [1] Concord, CA St. Agnes Church.
Mockevicius, Charles '47 (ROC) [I] Rochester, NY St. George's Rectory.
Mockevicius, Charles L. '47 (ROC) [17] Rochester, NY St. George Church; Retired.
Mockevicius, Charles L. '47 (RVC) Northport, NY Veteran's Hospital; Retired.
Mockevicius, Dominic '48 (ROC) Retired; [I] Rochester, NY St. George's Rectory.
Mockler, Patrick J. '79 (BLX) Wiggins, MS St. Francis Xavier Church.
Mockler, Peter F. '73 (BLX) Bay St. Louis, MS Our Lady of the Gulf Church.
Mocry, Richard '75 (DET) [A] Detroit, MI Sacred Heart Major Seminary, Inc.
Moczarny, Chester B. '47 (LC) Retired; [I] La Crosse, WI Holy Cross (Seminary) Diocesan Center.
Moczydlowski, Chester M. '73 (CHR) Taylors, SC Prince of Peace Church.
Modde, Bradley E. '97 (STL) [39] St. Louis, MO St. Joan of Arc Church.
Mode, Daniel L. '92 (ARL) McLean, VA St. John's Church; [D] Arlington, VA Bishop Denis J. O'Connell High School.
Modeen, James '81 (TUC) [E] Tucson, AZ Carondelet Health Network; [F] Tucson, AZ Regina Cleri Center.
Moder, John *s.m.* '79 (SAT) [C] San Antonio, TX The United Colleges of San Antonio; [C] San Antonio, TX St. Mary's University of San Antonio, Texas; [M] San Antonio, TX Marianist Woodlawn Community.
Moder, John *s.m.* '79 (STL) [P] St. Louis, MO Provincialate of the Society of Mary, Province of St. Louis.
Moder, John J. *s.m.* '79 (SAT) [C] San Antonio, TX St. Mary's University of San Antonio, Texas.
Modica, John '45 (COV) [M] Melbourne, KY Holy Family Home.
Modino, Roman A. '86 (TR) [1] Trenton, NJ St. Mary Cathedral.
Modlin, William F. '96 (PRT) Augusta, ME St. Mary's Church; South Portland, ME Maine Youth Center; South Portland, ME Men's Correctional Center; Thomaston, ME Maine State Prison; Warren, ME Super Maximum Facility & Minimum Facility.
Modrys, Walter F. *s.j.* '78 (NY) [51] New York, NY St. Ignatius Loyola Church; [DD] New York, NY St. Ignatius Loyola Residence.
Modugno, Msgr. Thomas A. '66 (NY) [76] New York, NY St. Monica Church.
Moeder, August L. '53 (SAL) Retired.
Moeder, John A. '57 (SAL) Belleville, KS St. Edward's Church.
Moeggenberg, Raymond '56 (SAG) [E] Saginaw, MI St. Mary's Medical Center of Saginaw, Inc.
Moeglein, James G. *o.s.c.* '70 (LIN) [A] Hastings, NE Crosier Monastery.
Moell, Carl J. *s.j.* '53 (LEX) Danville, KY SS. Peter & Paul Church.
Moellenberndt, Duane R. '76 (MAD) Fort Atkinson, WI St. Joseph Church.
Moeller, Msgr. George B. '62 (BAL) [49] Baltimore, MD St. Joseph Church.
Moelter, Joel *o.carm.* '51 (FgM) Carmelite Foreign Missions.
Moelter, Joel *o.carm.* '51 (JOL) [J] Darien, IL Carmelite Provincial Office.
Moenkedrick, Leo '86 (SCL) Breckenridge, MN St. Mary of the Presentation Church.
Moerman, Stephen A. '94 (PH) Lansdale, PA St. Stanislaus Church.
Moert, Jerome S. '44 (L) Retired; [L] Louisville, KY Bishop David Apartments.
Moeschler, William H. *m.m.* '44 (NY) [DD] Maryknoll, NY Maryknoll Fathers and Brothers.
Moeslein, Francis R. '58 (R) Morehead City, NC St. Egbert Church.
Mofan, Feliciano '79 (SFR) San Carlos, CA St. Charles Church.
Moffat, Curtis *o.m.i.* (FgM) Oblates Foreign Missions.
Moffat, Gerald '56 (SEA) Langley, WA St. Hubert Church.
Moffat, Joseph *c.s.b.* '61 (CHI) [30] Chicago, IL St. Bonaventure Church.
Moffatt, Charles P. *s.s.j.* '57 (MOB) [15] Mobile, AL Most Pure Heart of Mary Church.
Moffatt, Timothy *t.o.r.* '66 (SP) [2] Tampa, FL Christ the King Church.
Moffitt, Joseph M. *s.j.* '44 (WDC) [M] Washington, DC The Jesuit Community at Georgetown University.
Moffo, James '77 (SD) Absent on Sick Leave.
Moffo, Joseph G. *c.s.* '59 (HRT) [3] New Haven, CT St. Anthony's Church.
Moga, Michael D. *s.j.* '64 (FgM) Provinces.
Mogilka, Erwin E. '49 (MIL) Retired.
Mohan, Bernard N. '61 (NEW) West Orange, NJ St. Joseph's Church.
Mohan, Msgr. Robert Paul '46 (WDC) Retired; [C] Washington, DC Catholic University of America, The.
Mohan, Msgr. Thomas J. '35 (CHI) [69] Chicago, IL St. Genevieve Church; Retired.
Mohl, Andrew '84 (BAL) Hagerstown, MD St. Ann Church.
Mohnickey, Ronald *t.o.r.* '71 (STU) [A] Steubenville, OH Franciscan University of Steubenville; [F] Steubenville, OH Holy Spirit Monastery.
Mohnickey, Ronald H. '71 (STU) [I] Steubenville, OH Jefferson County Technical Institute.
Moholy, John R. *s.j.* '44 (SJ) [M] Los Gatos, CA Sacred Heart Jesuit Center.
Moholy, Noel *o.f.m.* '41 (LA) [R] Santa Barbara, CA Franciscan Friary, Order of Friars Minor (Old Mission).
Mohr, J. Patrick *s.j.* '75 (SCR) [C] Scranton, PA University of Scranton.
Mohr, Richard G. '67 (BEL) Marion, IL St. Joseph Church.
Mohr, Simon *o.f.m.conv.* (ALB) [L] Rensselaer, NY Franciscan Mission House.
Mohr, Thomas H. '58 (DAV) [L] Clinton, IA The Alverno Health Care Facility; [N] Clinton, IA The Canticle.
Mohrbacher, Austin '57 (PSC) Philadelphia, PA Holy Trinity Church.
Mohrman, J. Gregory *o.s.b.* '86 (STL) [F] Creve Coeur, MO St. Louis Priory School; [G] Creve Coeur, MO St. Louis Priory School; [P] St. Louis, MO The Abbey of St. Mary and St. Louis.
Moineau, John A. '87 (GBG) Sutersville, PA St. Charles Borromeo Church.
Moisin, Michael '88 (ROM) Special Assignment.
Mokarzel, Galeb *o.m.i.* '51 (SAT) [K] San Antonio, TX Oblate Madonna Residence.
Mokluk, John M. *o.s.f.s.* '70 (WIL) [B] Wilmington, DE Salesianum School.

Mokris, Michael '61 (PBR) Retired.
Mokris, Michael '61 (PSC) Lopez, PA SS. Peter and Paul Church.
Mokrzycki, M. Joseph '65 (TR) [1] Long Branch, NJ Our Lady Star of the Sea Church.
Mol, Joseph '77 (CHI) [A] Mundelein, IL University of St. Mary of the Lake-Mundelein Seminary.
Mol, Joseph C. '77 (CHI) Hickory Hills, IL St. Patricia Church.
Molan, Msgr. John E. '53 (MAN) Auburn, NH St. Peter Church.
Molano, Ernesto '56 (MIA) Retired.
Molden, Rick (LA) [K] Burbank, CA Providence Saint Joseph Medical Center.
Moleski, Martin X. *s.j.* '81 (BUF) [O] Buffalo, NY Canisius Jesuit Community.
Molewski, Andrew '82 (WIL) [5] Wilmington, DE St. Elizabeth Church.
Moley, Kevin *c.ss.r.* '68 (BRK) [107] Brooklyn, NY Our Lady of Perpetual Help Basilica Church.
Molina, Angel '88 (DEN) [A] Denver, CO Redemptoris Mater House of Formation.
Molina, Angel '94 (CGS) [6] Caguas, PR Nuestra Senora del Perpetuo Socorro Church.
Molina, Arturo '83 (LEX) Manchester, KY St. Ann Church; Manchester, KY Federal Correctional Institution.
Molina, Jose F. '95 (ELP) [4] El Paso, TX Blessed Sacrament Church.
Molina, Seraphim '97 (WDC) Oxon Hill, MD St. Columba Church.
Molinari, Todd '95 (P) Grants Pass, OR St. Anne Church.
Molinaro, Kenneth *c.s.c.* '76 (CHI) [D] Niles, IL Notre Dame High School.
Molinaro, Matthew J. '49 (LC) Arkansaw, WI St. Joseph Church.
Molinelli, Louis *s.d.b.* '86 (NEW) [C] Ramsey, NJ Don Bosco Preparatory High School for Boys.
Molini, Thomas M. '85 (STL) [A] St. Louis, MO Kenrick-Glennon Seminary.
Molitor, Donald '63 (STL) [1] University City, MO All Saints Church.
Molitor, Donald F. '63 (STL) [A] St. Louis, MO Kenrick-Glennon Seminary.
Molka, Victor J., Jr. '78 (PIT) [1] New Castle, PA Mary, Mother of Hope Church.
Moll, Walter J. '85 (ALT) Ebensburg, PA Holy Name Church.
Mollan, Paul '54 (OKL) [1] Oklahoma City, OK Cathedral of Our Lady of Perpetual Help.
Mollan, Paul F. '54 (OKL) Special Assignment.
Mollan, Ralph R. '43 (CHI) [4] Mt. Prospect, IL St. Thomas a Becket Church; Retired.
Molling, Mark L. '80 (MIL) Wales, WI Ethan Allen School for Boys.
Mollison, Roger W. '64 (DEN) [3] Englewood, CO St. Louis Church.
Mollohan, J. Lester '51 (CHI) [23] Chicago, IL St. Bartholomew Church.
Mollohan, James L. '51 (CHI) Retired.
Molloy, Msgr. Cronan T. '44 (STU) Minerva, OH St. Gabriel the Archangel Church; Retired.
Molloy, Francis P. *s.j.* '50 (BO) [W] Chestnut Hill, MA The Jesuit Community at Boston College.
Molloy, Msgr. James E. '72 (PH) [A] Wynnewood, PA Theological Seminary of St. Charles Borromeo, Overbrook.
Molloy, John J. '46 (OWN) [F] South Union, KY Fathers of Mercy.
Molloy, Joseph '83 (SFD) Newton, IL St. Thomas Church.
Molloy, Msgr. Patrick J. '40 (STL) Retired.
Molloy, Msgr. Thomas E. *j.c.d.* '70 (RVC) Roosevelt, NY Queen of the Most Holy Rosary Church.
Molnar, Anthony '34 (FTW) [15] South Bend, IN Our Lady of Hungary Church; Retired.
Molnar, John J. *o.s.a.* '66 (MIL) [8] Kenosha, WI Our Lady of the Holy Rosary Church.
Molnar, Jude *t.o.r.* '65 (WH) [Q] Fairmont, WV Fairmont State College Newman Center.
Molnar, Michael A. '76 (DET) [6] Westland, MI St. Theodore of Canterbury Church.
Molnar, Richard L. '39 (PIT) Retired.
Molodowitz, Augustine '59 (PHU) Perth Amboy, NJ Assumption of B.V.M. Church.
Molokie, Jerome M. *o.praem.* '95 (ORG) [D] Siverado, CA St. Michael's College Preparatory High School; [H] Silverado, CA Norbertine Fathers of Orange Inc.
Moloney, Msgr. Alphonsus '63 (SD) [9] San Diego, CA Immaculate Conception Church.
Moloney, Msgr. James A. '56 (DET) [2] Dearborn Heights, MI St. Anselm Church.
Moloney, John '72 (LA) Downey, CA Our Lady of Perpetual Help Church.
Moloney, John C. '91 (PH) Ardsley, PA Queen of Peace Church.
Moloney, Patrick W. '77 (NTN) Leave of Absence.
Moloney, Sean '58 (SAC) Retired and in Senior Ministry.
Moloney, Msgr. Stephan J. '82 (COL) [39] Columbus, OH Saint Stephen the Martyr Church; Gahanna, OH St. Matthew Church.
Moloney, Thomas J. *s.a.c.* '73 (DET) [6] Sterling Heights, MI St. Matthias Church.
Molony, Francis J. '42 (NY) Retired; [DD] New York, NY Our Lady of Consolation Residence.
Molter, Richard J. '64 (MIL) [5] Racine, WI St. Edward Church.
Moltesz, Joseph E. *s.j.* '57 (NY) [FF] Staten Island, NY Mount Manresa Jesuit Retreat House.
Molumby, Donald J. '56 (SFS) Miller, SD St. Ann Church.
Molumby, Edward J. *s.t.* '61 (ORG) [H] Santa Ana, CA Trinitarian Missionaries/Missionary Servants of the Most Holy Trinity.
Molumby, John '77 (SAC) Auburn, CA St. Joseph Church.
Molyn, John A. '81 (ALB) Special Assignment; [G] Watervliet, NY St. Colman's Home; [M] Watervliet, NY St. Colman's Convent.
Molyneus, John *c.m.f.* '97 (CHI) [166] Chicago, IL St. Paul Church.
Monacell, Cornelius J. *s.j.* '59 (SJ) [M] Los Gatos, CA Sacred Heart Jesuit Center.
Monaco, James M. '85 (BUF) [4] Tonawanda, NY St. Francis of Assisi Church.
Monaco, Samuel '88 (NEW) North Arlington, NJ Queen of Peace Church.
Monaco, Vincent *c.s.* '57 (BO) [2] Somerville, MA St. Anthony Church.
Monaghan, Msgr. Charles J. '41 (PH) Retired.
Monaghan, Fergus '72 (SPC) [5] Springfield, MO St. Elizabeth Ann Seton Church.
Monaghan, Msgr. George '41 (SFR) [K] San Rafael, CA Nazareth House.
Monaghan, Msgr. George D. '41 (SR) Retired.
Monaghan, George P. '80 (DAL) Denison, TX St. Patrick Church.
Monaghan, James *s.j.* '46 (SJ) [M] Los Gatos, CA Sacred Heart Jesuit Center.
Monaghan, John T. '63 (NY) [E] New York, NY Cardinal Spellman High School.
Monaghan, Joseph F. *s.j.* '52 (BAL) [M] Baltimore, MD Jesuit Fathers and Brothers Maryland Provincial Curia.
Monaghan, Justin '66 (SPC) West Plains, MO St. Mary Church.
Monaghan, Robert '62 (STP) [9] Minneapolis, MN Incarnation Church.
Monaghan, Thomas E. *c.ss.r.* '44 (STL) [P] Liguori, MO St. Clement Health Care Center.
Monaghan, Thomas J. '70 (MAD) Mount Horeb, WI St. Ignatius Church.
Monagle, Robert J. '91 (BO) [4] Quincy, MA St. Joseph Church.
Monahan, David F. '53 (OKL) Pauls Valley, OK St. Catherine of Siena Church.
Monahan, George J. '97 (PH) [32] Philadelphia, PA St. Cecilia Church.
Monahan, Gregory *t.o.r.* '90 (WH) [H] Wheeling, WV Wheeling Hospital.
Monahan, Hugh F. '68 (KC) Leave of Absence.
Monahan, Msgr. Jeremiah P. '60 (NY) [E] New York, NY Cardinal Spellman High School.
Monahan, Joseph E. '77 (DEN) Golden, CO St. Joseph Church.
Monahan, Joseph R. '62 (STL) Ballwin, MO Holy Infant Church.
Monahan, Kieran *o.f.m.* '65 (PRT) [6] Portland, ME St. Peter's Church.
Monahan, Paul '60 (DM) Glenwood, IA Our Lady of the Holy Rosary Church.
Monahan, Richard J. '59 (BGP) Retired.
Monahan, Thomas J. '58 (RCK) Durand, IL St. Mary Church.
Monan, J. Donald *s.j.* '55 (BO) [W] Chestnut Hill, MA The Jesuit Community at Boston College.
Moncher, Raymond F. (MAR) Retired.
Monclova, Michael '97 (PEO) [4] Streator, IL St. Stephen's Church.
Mondello, Donald J. '60 (GBG) [1] Latrobe, PA Holy Family Church.
Mondik, Michael '73 (PSC) Minersville, PA SS. Peter and Paul Church.
Mondor, Christian *o.f.m.* '51 (ORG) [3] Huntington Beach, CA SS. Simon and Jude Church.
Mondragon, Anselmo *t.o.r.* '91 (AUS) [2] Waco, TX St. Francis on the Brazos Church.
Mondragon, Antonio '63 (SFE) [3] Albuquerque, NM Community of the Risen Saviour Church.
Mondragon, Ezequiel '62 (DET) Imlay City, MI Sacred Heart Church.
Mondzelewski, Dominic '69 (CLV) [E] Cleveland, OH Benedictine High School; [P] Cleveland, OH Benedictine Order of Cleveland.
Moneck, George '89 (PIT) Green County, PA State Correctional Institute at Green.
Moneck, George J. '89 (PIT) Roscoe, PA St. Joseph Church.
Monestero, John '75 (ORG) [3] Anaheim, CA St. Justin Martyr Church; Absent on Sick Leave.
Monestime, Perard C. *s.j.* '85 (BO) [E] Boston, MA Boston College High School & Jesuit Community.
Monet, Zachary *o.carm.* '60 (NEW) Paramus, NJ Carmelite Chapel of St. Therese Church.
Moneta, Msgr. Robert G. '51 (PSC) Newark, NJ St. George Church.
Monforton, Jeffrey '94 (DET) Graduate Studies.
Mongelluzzo, Msgr. James A. (WOR) On Duty Outside the Diocese.
Mongeon, Peter M. '83 (NO) On Duty Outside the Archdiocese.
Mongiano, Peter *i.m.c.* '38 (MET) [H] Somerset, NJ Consolata Society for Foreign Missions.
Mongiello, Anthony P. '80 (ALN) Girardville, PA St. Joseph Church; [C] Ashland, PA Cardinal Brennan Jr./Sr. High School.
Mongiello, Robert '87 (VEN) Punta Gorda, FL Sacred Heart Church.
Mongrain, Dennis P. '77 (LA) Sick Leave.
Moniuk, Evhen '92 (PHU) [5] Philadelphia, PA St. Nicholas Church.
Moniz, Hyacinth '40 (PRO) Retired.
Moniz, Joseph '64 (LA) Hawthorne, CA St. Joseph Church.
Monks, James L. *s.j.* '34 (BO) [W] Weston, MA Campion Health Center, Inc.
Monmonier, Hugh *o.s.b.* '45 (WDC) [M] Washington, DC St. Anselm's Abbey.
Monnens, Merle W. '56 (NU) Lucan, MN Our Lady of Victory Church; Milroy, MN St. Michael Church.
Monnerat, Brian W. '88 (HRT) [3] Enfield, CT St. Bernard's Church.
Monnig, Francis R. '60 (CIN) Camden, OH St. Mary's Church.
Monnin, Robert J. '55 (CIN) Vandalia, OH St. Christopher Church.
Monogue, Michael G. '85 (STP) [16] Minneapolis, MN St. Anne Church.
Monohan, Duncan W. '77 (SD) Winterhaven, CA St. Thomas Church.
Monostori, Benedict *o.cist.* '44 (DAL) [M] Irving, TX Cistercian Abbey of Our Lady of Dallas.
Monreal, Jesus *o.carm.* '69 (ARE) Morovis, PR Nuestra Senora del Carmen Church.
Monroe, Charles F. '75 (WOR) [8] Worcester, MA Our Lady of the Angels Church.
Monroe, Clement *c.ss.r.* '53 (NO) New Orleans, LA Memorial Medical Center.
Monroe, Edward *c.ss.r.* '61 (STP) Brooklyn Center, MN St. Alphonsus Church.
Monsalue, Alfred (BO) [9] Cambridge, MA St. Mary of the Annunciation Church.
Monsalve, German Barona *m.s.c.* '86 (FgM) Missionaries of the Sacred Heart Foreign Missions.
Monshau, Michael *o.p.* '88 (DET) [2] St. Clair Shores, MI St. Gertrude Church; [A] Orchard Lake, MI SS. Cyril and Methodius Seminary.
Monsour, Raymond G. '63 (STP) Le Center, MN St. Mary Church.
Montag, Bernard J. '32 (SC) Retired.
Montag, John F. *s.j.* '93 (MIL) [P] Milwaukee, WI Jesuit Provincial Office, Wisconsin Province.
Montague, George *s.m.* '51 (STL) [P] St. Louis, MO Provincialate of the Society of Mary, Province of St. Louis.
Montague, George *s.m.* '58 (SAT) [C] San Antonio, TX St. Mary's University of San Antonio, Texas.
Montague, George T. *s.m.* '58 (SAT) [M] San Antonio, TX Casa San Juan Marianist Community.
Montague, Hugh *s.o.cist.* '82 (ALN) [K] New Ringgold, PA Cistercian Conventual Priory, St. Mary's Priory.
Montague, James A. '90 (BO) Absent on Leave.
Montalbano, Frank *o.m.i.* '47 (NO) [1] New Orleans, LA St. Louis Cathedral; [A] New Orleans, LA Notre Dame Seminary Graduate School of Theology.
Montalbano, Joseph E. '55 (ALX) Moreauville, LA Our Lady of Sorrows Church; Moreauville, LA Sacred Heart Church.
Montanaro, Guido G. '69 (BGP) [10] Bridgeport, CT Holy Rosary Church.
Montano, Angel *m.j.* '92 (GAL) [75] Houston, TX St. Stephen Church.
Montano, Msgr. Edward J. '45 (NY) Retired.
Montavon, Thomas G. '61 (CLV) Brunswick, OH St. Colette Church.
Montcalm, Msgr. Rosario L.U. '36 (SPR) Retired.
Montealegre, Roy '93 (MIA) [22] Miami, FL St. John Bosco Church.
Montecalvo, Carlo F. '73 (PRO) On Duty Outside the Diocese.
Montecino, Henry R. *s.j.* '47 (LAF) [J] Grand Coteau, LA Jesuit Spirituality Center.
Monteiro, Alfredo '73 (NY) [116] New York, NY St. Teresa Church.
Monteiro, Galdino '65 (P) [37] Portland, OR St. Thomas More Church.
Monteiro, Ralph *o.s.a.* '66 (SR) Hoopa, CA Mission of Blessed Kateri Tekakwitha Church.
Montejano, John '94 (LA) Baldwin Park, CA St. John the Baptist Church.
Montelaro, Thomas (LAF) Leroy, LA Our Lady of

Perpetual Help Church; Absent on Sick Leave.
Monteleone, Jacob A. '75 (SP) Zephyrhills, FL St. Joseph Church.
Monteleone, Pascal A. '72 (PH) Wayne, PA St. Katharine of Siena Church; [D] Springfield, PA Cardinal O'Hara High School.
Monteleone, Raphael D. '30 (RVC) Retired.
Montella, Alban V. *o.f.m.* '55 (FgM) Franciscan Foreign Missions.
Montella, Alban V. *o.f.m.* '55 (NY) [DD] New York, NY Franciscan Province of the Immaculate Conception; [DD] Mount Vernon, NY St. Bernardine of Siena Friary.
Montemayor, Teodoro *s.d.b.* '83 (LA) [X] Rosemead, CA St. Joseph's Salesian Youth Renewal Center.
Montenegro, Blas *o.a.r.* '49 (NY) [126] Bronx, NY St. Anselm Church; [157] Bronx, NY St. John Vianney, Cure of Ars Church.
Montero, Eduardo G. '73 (PH) [L] Philadelphia, PA St. Vincent's Orphanage Tacony; [FF] Philadelphia, PA St. Vincent's Orphan Asylum-St. Vincent's Comprehensive Emergency Shelter Program.
Montero, Hugo L. '91 (STP) [9] St. Paul, MN Our Lady of Guadalupe Church.
Montes, Jesse *s.d.b.* '79 (MRY) [D] Watsonville, CA St. Francis Youth Center.
Montes de Oca, Jose '96 (NEW) On Duty Outside the Archdiocese.
Montesi, Eugenio *s.x.* '62 (CHI) [N] Chicago, IL Xaverian Missionaries (S.X.).
Montesino, Efrain '85 (ARE) [5] Vega-Baja, PR Parroquia de San Martin de Porres Church.
Montez, Paul *o.s.b.* '97 (DEN) [2] Boulder, CO Sacred Heart of Mary Church.
Montez, Paul J. *o.s.b.* (PBL) [F] Canon City, CO Holy Cross Abbey.
Montgomery, Msgr. James F. '56 (WDC) [4] Washington, DC Annunciation Church.
Montgomery, Matthias *o.c.d.* '62 (MIL) [P] Holy Hill, WI Discalced Carmelite Monastery.
Montgomery, William L. '79 (WDC) Special Ministries; [D] Washington, DC Archbishop Carroll High School.
Monti, Dominic V. *o.f.m.* '71 (WDC) [M] Silver Spring, MD Gemelli House; [U] West Bethesda, MD Missionaries of the Kingship of Christ.
Monti, Robert M. '61 (LC) On Duty Outside the Diocese.
Montiel, Jose M. '57 (FRS) Merced, CA Sacred Heart Church.
Montilla, Felix Abreu *c.s.sp.* (SJN) [C] Bayamon, PR Teologado Padre Liberman.
Montminy, Marc R. '77 (MAN) [12] Manchester, NH St. Marie Church; [17] Manchester, NH Sacred Heart of Jesus Church.
Montminy, Paul D. '78 (MAN) Gonic, NH St. Leo Church; Rochester, NH Holy Rosary Church.
Montondon, Walter '57 (BEA) Retired.
Montoro, Joseph J. '92 (GRY) [14] Gary, IN St. Mark Church; [F] Hobart, IN St. Mary Medical Center.
Montoya, Ernest (LA) [K] Torrance, CA Little Company of Mary Health Services.
Montoya, Ernest '89 (LA) [12] Long Beach, CA Our Lady of Refuge Church.
Montoya, Ernest '89 (SFE) Retired.
Montoya, Jose J. '57 (PBL) Retired.
Montoya, Juan '89 (MIA) Absent on Sick Leave.
Montoya, Luis F. '87 (PCE) [G] Alhambra, Ponce, PR Prelature of the Holy Cross and Opus Dei.
Montoya, Michael *c.i.c.m.* '94 (BWN) La Joya, TX Our Lady, Queen of Angels Church.
Montoya, Msgr. Paul '73 (LA) Inglewood, CA St. John Chrysostom Church.
Montplaisir, Roland A. '40 (MAN) Retired.
Montville, Edmund J. *s.j.* '45 (DET) [P] Clarkston, MI Colombiere Center.
Monzillo, Oneil '53 (NO) Retired.
Monzon-Tapia, Luis *m.c.c.j.* '95 (FgM) Comboni Foreign Missions.
Moodie, Michael R. *s.j.* '79 (SFR) [E] San Francisco, CA St. Ignatius College Preparatory (Coed).
Moody, Jerome *c.ss.r.* '73 (FgM) Redemptorist Foreign Missions.
Moody, Michael *s.v.d.* '64 (LAF) Plaisance, LA St. Joseph Church.
Moody, Quentin '85 (NO) [63] New Orleans, LA St. Theresa Of The Child Jesus Church.
Moody, Thomas A. '67 (OG) Louisville, NY St. Lawrence Church; Madrid, NY St. John the Baptist Church.
Moody, William '78 (BAL) Retired.
Moon, Msgr. Robert '59 (COL) Lancaster, OH St. Mark Church.
Mooney, Dennis M. '77 (PH) [66] Philadelphia, PA St. Hugh of Cluny Church.
Mooney, Msgr. George A. '48 (BRK) Retired.
Mooney, Harold T. '55 (PEO) Retired.
Mooney, Michael P. '63 (PT) [4] Pensacola, FL Nativity of Our Lord Church.
Mooney, Richard T. '79 (RIC) [4] Virginia Beach, VA Holy Family Church.
Mooney, Terence J. *c.m.* '48 (PH) [AA] Philadelphia, PA Congregation of the Mission.
Mooney, Thomas J. '47 (BO) Lakeville, MA Saints Martha and Mary Church; Retired.
Mooney, William '55 (SD) Poway, CA St. Michael Church.
Mooney, William C. '68 (STA) St. Augustine Shores, FL Corpus Christi Church.
Mooney, William J. '68 (PAT) Florham Park, NJ Holy Family Church.
Moons, Joseph *c.p.* '77 (CHI) [N] Chicago, IL Passionist Provincial Office.
Moons, Joseph *c.p.* '77 (FgM) Mission Procurators.
Mooradd, Paul '84 (SAM) Newtown Square, PA St. Sharbel Mission Church.
Moorby, William A. '82 (ROC) Newark Valley, NY St. John the Evangelist Church; [L] Rochester, NY Catholic Charismatic Renewal.
Moorby, William A. '97 (ROC) Owego, NY St. Patrick Church.
Moore, Andrew Robert '97 (BEA) Nederland, TX St. Charles Borromeo Church.
Moore, Anthony F. *o.f.m.* '51 (HRT) Winsted, CT St. Joseph's Church.
Moore, Augustine '60 (SFE) Espanola, NM Sacred Heart Church.
Moore, Brian R. '83 (COL) [A] Columbus, OH Pontifical College Josephinum.
Moore, Brian R. '83 (DOD) On Duty Outside the Diocese.
Moore, Charles E. '36 (CIN) [S] Cincinnati, OH Archdiocesan Central Council of Cincinnati.
Moore, Charles L. '36 (CIN) Retired.
Moore, Charles L. '38 (CIN) Middletown, OH Holy Family Church.
Moore, Christian *o.f.m.conv.* '65 (CLV) [1] Lorain, OH St. Anthony of Padua Church.
Moore, Christopher P. '77 (BAL) [30] Baltimore, MD St. Elizabeth of Hungary Church.
Moore, Clarke W. '64 (TUC) Tubac, AZ St. Ann Church.
Moore, Daniel F. '84 (MEM) [24] Memphis, TN Church of the Resurrection.
Moore, Donald C. '65 (OKL) [15] Oklahoma City, OK St. Patrick Church; Special Assignment; [F] Oklahoma City, OK St. Ann's Home Inc.
Moore, Donald J. *s.j.* '60 (NY) [DD] New York, NY West Side Jesuit Community.
Moore, Msgr. Edmund J. '59 (SHP) [1] Monroe, LA Jesus the Good Shepherd Church; Retired.
Moore, Edmund R. *o.f.m.* '45 (L) [16] Louisville, KY St. Boniface Church; [L] Louisville, KY St. Boniface Friary.
Moore, Edward F. *m.m.* '58 (SJ) [M] Los Altos, CA Maryknoll.
Moore, Edward F. '59 (BUR) Retired.
Moore, Elmer R. '54 (LEX) Retired.
Moore, Francis A. *s.j.* '47 (PHX) [B] Phoenix, AZ Brophy College Preparatory.
Moore, Francis M. *s.j.* '50 (DET) [P] Clarkston, MI Colombiere Center.
Moore, Frederick B. '80 (DET) [H] Pontiac, MI St. Joseph Mercy - Oakland.
Moore, Frederick Thomas '75 (STA) On Duty Outside the Diocese.
Moore, George B. '66 (PH) [22] Philadelphia, PA St. Benedict Church.
Moore, Gerald T. '39 (SEA) Retired.
Moore, Gregory *o.f.m.conv.* (BAL) [M] Ellicott City, MD St. Joseph Cupertino Friary, Friars Minor Conventual of St. Francis of Assisi; [M] Ellicott City, MD Friary of St. Joseph Cupertino.
Moore, Gregory *o.f.m.conv.* '82 (BAL) [M] Ellicott City, MD Order of Friars Minor Conventual.
Moore, Gregory J. *o.p.* (MAD) [3] Madison, WI Blessed Sacrament Church.
Moore, Harold W. '50 (WH) Oak Hill, WV SS. Peter and Paul Church.
Moore, J. Pat '89 (P) Aloha, OR St. Elizabeth Ann Seton Church.
Moore, Msgr. J. Raymond '56 (SD) Retired.
Moore, James P. '88 (SFE) [22] Albuquerque, NM St. Bernadette Church.
Moore, Msgr. James R. '67 (NY) Crestwood, NY Church of the Annunciation.
Moore, James T. '84 (GAL) [61] Houston, TX Our Lady of Walsingham Church.
Moore, James W. *s.j.* '59 (PH) [C] Philadelphia, PA St. Joseph's University; [AA] Philadelphia, PA Jesuit Community at St. Joseph's University.
Moore, John '45 (FAR) [E] Fargo, ND Riverview Place, Inc.
Moore, John Charles '78 (BAL) Middletown, MD Holy Family Catholic Community Church.
Moore, John E. '45 (FAR) Retired.
Moore, John F. '60 (FR) North Falmouth, MA St. Elizabeth Seton Church.
Moore, John J. *s.m.* '43 (WDC) [M] Washington, DC Marist Provincial House.
Moore, John J. '57 (FRS) Corcoran, CA Calif. State Prison.
Moore, John J. '57 (GF) On Duty Outside of the Diocese.
Moore, John P. *c.p.* '47 (BRK) [U] Jamaica, NY Immaculate Conception Monastery.
Moore, John P. '55 (NY) [52] New York, NY Immaculate Conception Church.
Moore, John Patrick *c.p.* '47 (BRK) [W] Jamaica, NY Bishop Molloy Retreat House for Laymen.
Moore, John R. '64 (RVC) Babylon, NY St. Joseph's Church.
Moore, Jon H. '81 (WIN) Absent on Leave.
Moore, Joseph P. '71 (BGP) Leave of Absence.
Moore, Lawrence *s.j.* '77 (NO) [C] New Orleans, LA Loyola University.
Moore, Manning C. *o.s.f.s.* '67 (ARL) [D] Alexandria, VA Bishop Ireton High School; [J] Alexandria, VA Oblates of St. Francis de Sales Residence.
Moore, Matthias *c.s.sp.* '52 (NO) [40] New Orleans, LA St. John The Baptist Church.
Moore, Michael *o.s.f.s.* (FgM) Oblates of St. Francis de Sales Foreign Missions.
Moore, Michael '77 (YAK) On Duty Outside the Diocese.
Moore, Michael *s.p.s.* '84 (NEW) [N] Cliffside Park, NJ St. Patrick's Missionary Society.
Moore, Neil J. '60 (P) [29] Portland, OR St. Pius X Church.
Moore, Raymond H. '81 (WDC) [4] Bowie, MD St. Pius X Church.
Moore, Robert A. '46 (BRK) [36] Brooklyn, NY St. Ephrem's Church; Retired.
Moore, Robert J. *o.c.s.o.* '49 (ROC) [I] Piffard, NY Abbey of the Genesee.
Moore, Robert J. '83 (NY) [165] Bronx, NY St. Mary Star of the Sea Church.
Moore, Steven C. '76 (ANC) [8] Anchorage, AK St. Patrick Church.
Moore, Terence M. '67 (SLC) [9] Salt Lake City, UT St. Thomas More Church.
Moore, Thomas *o.s.f.s.* '66 (SAG) [1] Saginaw, MI St. Mary Cathedral.
Moore, Thomas G. '88 (MET) Middlesex, NJ Our Lady of Mount Virgin Church.
Moore, Thomas M. *o.s.f.s.* '66 (SAG) [4] Saginaw, MI SS. Simon and Jude Church.
Moore, Timothy *o.carm.* '35 (JOL) [J] Darien, IL Carmelite Provincial Office.
Moore, Timothy *o.carm.* '35 (NEW) Englewood, NJ St. Cecilia's Church.
Moore, Ward P. '72 (NEW) Westwood, NJ St. Andrew's Church.
Moore, Wilbur E. '57 (OKL) Nicoma Park, OK Our Lady of Fatima Church.
Moore, William C. '68 (STO) [2] Stockton, CA St. Bernadette Church.
Moore, William F. '69 (CAM) Pennsville, NJ Queen of the Apostles Church.
Moorman, Marcellus *o.f.m.* '45 (BR) [H] Baton Rouge, LA Franciscan Residence.
Moorman, Raymond J. '46 (STP) Retired.
Moorman, William J. *o.ss.t.* '79 (BAL) [M] Baltimore, MD Holy Trinity Monastery.
Moorman, William J. *o.ss.t.* '79 (WDC) [A] Washington, DC Theological College of the Catholic University of America.
Moors, Clif *s.m.* (BO) Burlington, MA Lahey Hitchcock Medical Center.
Moors, Clifton W. *s.m.* '56 (BO) [12] Lawrence, MA Sacred Heart Church.
Moorse, Dustan *o.s.b.* '78 (SCL) [I] Collegeville, MN St. John's Abbey, of the Order of St. Benedict.
Moortgat, Luke *c.i.c.m.* '65 (FgM) Missionhurst Foreign Missions.
Moosbrugger, Robert F. *o.m.i.* '70 (STP) [N] St. Paul, MN Oblate Provincial Offices; [N] St. Paul, MN Oblate Residence.
Moozhihzhy, Antony *c.m.i.* '66 (BEA) [9] Port Arthur, TX St. Therese the Little Flower of Jesus Church.
Moquin, Raymond *m.s.* '54 (FR) [I] North Attleboro, MA Madonna Manor Inc.; [J] Attleboro, MA La Salette Shrine.
Mora, Pablo *s.j.* (CHI) [J] Chicago, IL Holy Cross Hospital.
Mora, Santiago A. *c.m.f.* '66 (CHR) Taylors, SC Prince of Peace Church.
Mora, Sergio '94 (OAK) [4] Hayward, CA St. Joachim Church.
Mora, Tito Medina *m.s.c.* '92 (FgM) Missionaries of the Sacred Heart Foreign Missions.
Morabito, Vincent R. '87 (PH) Royersford, PA Sacred Heart Church.
Moraczewski, Albert S. *o.p.* '54 (BO) [FF] Boston, MA Pope John Center.
Moraczewski, Albert S. *o.p.* '54 (STL) [P] St. Louis, MO St. Dominic Priory.
Moraes, Claudio *o.s.b.* '84 (GBG) [H] Latrobe, PA Saint Vincent Archabbey.
Moraga, Cecilio T. '84 (SD) Holtville, CA St. Joseph Church.
Moraghan, Vincent '65 (CLV) Cleveland, OH Cleveland Clinic Foundation.
Moraghan, Vincent J. '65 (CLV) [76] Cleveland, OH St. Vitus Church.
Moragne, Msgr. James C. '75 (NO) Paradis, LA St. John

the Baptist Church.
Morahan, Gerald B. *o.p.* '52 (DET) [2] St. Clair Shores, MI St. Gertrude Church.
Moral, Alejandro *o.c.d.* '60 (CGS) [2] Caguas, PR San Jose Church.
Morales, Angel '83 (ARE) On Duty Outside the Diocese.
Morales, Anibal '93 (MIA) [32] Miami, FL St. Thomas the Apostle Church.
Morales, Dan '90 (VIC) Port Lavaca, TX Our Lady of the Gulf Church.
Morales, Eduardo D. '96 (SAT) Fredericksburg, TX St. Mary's Church.
Morales, Elias '91 (PCE) Ensenada, PR Sacred Heart Church; Guanica, PR St. Anthony Abbot Church.
Morales, Eusebio Ramos '83 (CGS) Humacao, PR Dulce Nombre de Jesus Church.
Morales, Gonzalo '85 (FWT) Bridgeport, TX St. John the Baptizer Church; Decatur, TX Assumption of the Blessed Virgin Mary Church; Jacksboro, TX St. Mary Church.
Morales, Guillermo '88 (AMA) Dimmitt, TX Immaculate Conception Church.
Morales, Msgr. John F. '60 (GRY) Retired.
Morales, Jose '47 (ORG) Retired.
Morales, Juan Bautista '83 (MGZ) Moca, PR Our Lady of Monserrate Church.
Morales, Raul '75 (PHX) Retired.
Morales, Raymond '81 (LA) Van Nuys, CA St. Bridget of Sweden Church.
Morales, Robert P. '66 (BRK) [63] Brooklyn, NY Immaculate Conception of the Blessed Virgin Mary Church.
Morales, Romain G. *c.m.* '73 (STL) [P] St. Louis, MO Vincentian Henrietta Residence.
Morales, Salomon (ARE) On Duty Outside the Diocese.
Morales Berrios-Parroco, Raul '88 (CGS) Comerio, PR Santo Cristo de la Salud Church.
Moran, Msgr. Bernard J. '53 (OAK) [22] Oakland, CA St. Theresa of the Infant Jesus (The Little Flower) Church.
Moran, Charles *o.m.i.* '54 (BWN) [1] Brownsville, TX Immaculate Conception Cathedral.
Moran, Charles '67 (STU) Absent on Leave.
Moran, Daniel F. '47 (BO) Lakeville, MA Saints Martha and Mary Church.
Moran, Edward C. '89 (RIC) Military Chaplains.
Moran, Edward F. '34 (HEL) Retired.
Moran, Edward J. '62 (WOR) Shrewsbury, MA St. Anne's Church.
Moran, Edward M. '76 (HRT) [6] West Hartford, CT St. Thomas the Apostle Church.
Moran, Edwin *c.p.* '61 (PIT) [O] Pittsburgh, PA St. Paul of the Cross Monastery.
Moran, Faustinus *c.p.* '42 (CHI) [N] Chicago, IL Passionist Provincial Office.
Moran, Frank '59 (ORG) San Clemente, CA Our Lady of Fatima Church.
Moran, Gerard K. '71 (OAK) [2] Fremont, CA Holy Spirit Church.
Moran, Howard L. *s.j.* (SPK) [C] Spokane, WA Gonzaga University.
Moran, Msgr. J. Thomas '57 (BUF) Youngstown, NY St. Bernard's Church.
Moran, James *c.o.* '89 (ALX) Mansura, LA Our Lady of Prompt Succor Church.
Moran, James *c.o.* '89 (CHR) [D] Rock Hill, SC Oratory of St. Philip Neri, Congregation of the Oratory of Pontifical Rite.
Moran, James E. '59 (NU) Lafayette, MN St. Gregory the Great Church; West Newton Township, MN St. George Church.
Moran, James F. '71 (BO) On Duty Outside the Archdiocese.
Moran, James M. '74 (HRT) Newington, CT St. Mary Church.
Moran, Msgr. James P. (GR) [21] Grand Rapids, MI Sacred Heart Church.
Moran, Msgr. James P. '45 (GR) Retired.
Moran, Msgr. James P. '72 (MET) Iselin, NJ St. Cecelia Church.
Moran, James W. *c.s.p.* '64 (SD) [M] San Diego, CA University of California at San Diego (Campus Ministry).
Moran, John F. *s.j.* '57 (FgM) Provinces.
Moran, John J. *m.m.* '66 (FgM) Maryknoll Foreign Missions.
Moran, John P. *s.s.c.* '50 (FgM) St. Columban's Foreign Mission.
Moran, John V. '53 (MAN) Rye Beach, NH St. Theresa Church.
Moran, John W. '51 (DUB) Retired.
Moran, Joseph P. '56 (VEN) Retired.
Moran, Joseph P. '71 (HEL) [1] Butte, MT Butte Catholic Community North Church; [4] Butte, MT Immaculate Conception Church; [11] Butte, MT St. Patrick Church.
Moran, Kevin '65 (SEA) Federal Way, WA St. Theresa Church.
Moran, Lawrence '52 (IND) Seelyville, IN Holy Rosary Church.
Moran, Lawrence J. '52 (IND) [6] Terre Haute, IN St. Patrick Church.
Moran, Leonard J. *s.m.* '45 (WDC) [M] Washington, DC Marist Provincial House.
Moran, Martin O., III '88 (HBG) [4] York, PA St. Rose of Lima Church.
Moran, Michael '63 (VNN) Van Nuys, CA Cathedral of St. Mary.
Moran, Michael *s.m.a.* '81 (FgM) Society of African Missions.
Moran, Michael F. '82 (MIL) Sheboygan Falls, WI St. Mary Church.
Moran, Michael J. '58 (NEW) Hillsdale, NJ St. John the Baptist Church.
Moran, Owen '91 (PAT) Chatham, NJ St. Patrick's Church.
Moran, Patrick '43 (JOL) [I] Naperville, IL St. John Vianney Villa.
Moran, Patrick A. '43 (GF) Retired.
Moran, Patrick J. '58 (DUL) [7] Gary-New Duluth, MN St. Elizabeth's Church.
Moran, Msgr. Peter C. '65 (LA) Northridge, CA Our Lady of Lourdes Church.
Moran, Richard S. *c.ss.r.* '61 (BO) [13] Boston, MA Our Lady of Perpetual Help Church; [3] Quincy, MA St. John the Baptist Church.
Moran, Robert B. '64 (SJ) Mountain View, CA St. Joseph the Worker Church.
Moran, Robert E. *c.s.p.* '64 (KNX) [4] Knoxville, TN John XXIII Catholic Center Church; [J] Knoxville, TN UT-Knoxville, Newman Foundation, Inc.
Moran, Robert E. '69 (LFT) Hartford City, IN St. John the Evangelist Church.
Moran, Stephen P. '92 (CLV) [3] Parma, OH St. Charles Borromeo Church.
Moran, Terence J. '90 (BO) [1] Boston, MA Cathedral of the Holy Cross; [60] Boston, MA St. Patrick Church.
Moran, Terrance *c.ss.r.* '82 (NY) [78] New York, NY Most Holy Redeemer Church.
Moran, Thomas *c.m.f.* '55 (CHI) [N] Oak Park, IL Claretian Fathers Headquarters of U.S.A. Eastern Province.
Moran, Thomas '88 (SFR) [20] San Francisco, CA St. Gabriel Church.
Moran, Thomas A. '71 (CHI) Lyons, IL St. Hugh Church.
Moran, Thomas A. '77 (CLV) [58] Cleveland, OH Our Lady of Peace Church.
Moran, Thomas J. '48 (NY) Retired.
Moran, Msgr. Timothy J. '76 (BO) [A] Boston, MA St. John's Seminary School of Theology.
Moran, W. Lawrence *c.s.b.* '46 (GAL) [Q] Sugar Land, TX Basilian Mission Center.
Moran, William H. *s.j.* '55 (NO) [P] New Orleans, LA Ignatius Residence.
Morand, Robert '57 (DET) [56] Detroit, MI Our Lady of the Rosary Church.
Moratelli, Ronald J. '69 (HBG) Bloomsburg, PA St. Columba Church.
Moratiel, Felix *o.s.a.* '62 (SJN) [42] San Juan, PR Ntra. Sra. de la Monserrate Church; [18] Bayamon, PR Santa Rita de Casia Church.
Moraus, Govie '82 (SHP) [F] Shreveport, LA Motherhouse of the Daughters of the Cross in America.
Morawski, Stefan *o.f.m.conv.* '68 (BGP) [14] Bridgeport, CT St. Michael The Archangel Church.
Morbeck, George '52 (SPK) Curlew, WA St. Patrick Church.
Morbeck, George H. '52 (SPK) Republic, WA Immaculate Conception Church.
Morbito, Angelo L. '56 (SY) Solvay, NY St. Cecilia Church.
Morciniec, Peter J. '70 (SPC) Aurora, MO Holy Trinity Church; Verona, MO Sacred Heart Church.
Mordino, Robert F. '63 (WDC) Special Ministries; [P] Upper Marlboro, MD Our Lady of Mattaponi Youth Retreat and Conference Center.
Moreau, Charles *o.m.i.* '44 (MAN) [K] Colebrook, NH Shrine of Our Lady of Grace.
Moreau, Ernest P. '51 (SPR) Retired.
Moreau, George '51 (ORL) Retired.
Moreau, Raymond J. '85 (OG) North Bangor, NY St. Augustine Church.
Moreci, Francis A. '33 (OM) Retired.
Moredo, Wilfredo Pena '74 (SJN) [2] Carolina, PR Santa Bernardita Soubirous Church.
Moreeuw, Leroy *c.pp.s.* '68 (CLV) [53] Cleveland, OH Our Lady of Good Counsel Church.
Moreira, Nelson A. *s.s.j.* '72 (NO) [P] New Orleans, LA Josephite Fathers and Brothers.
Morel, Albert J. *s.c.* '72 (PRO) [P] Burrillville, RI Sacred Heart Brothers Provincial House.
Morel, John F. *c.i.c.m.* '39 (ARL) Madison, VA Our Lady of the Blue Ridge Church.
Morel, John J. '55 (NEW) Retired.
Morel, Patrice *o.m.i.* '54 (MAN) [K] Colebrook, NH Shrine of Our Lady of Grace.
Moreland, J. Gordon *s.j.* '64 (ORG) Special Assignment; [H] Orange, CA Jesuits; [K] Orange, CA House of Prayer for Priests.
Morell, Fernando '87 (ARE) Hatillo, PR Our Lady of Mt. Carmel Church.
Morell, J. William *o.m.i.* '70 (SAT) [C] San Antonio, TX Oblate School of Theology; [C] San Antonio, TX The United Colleges of San Antonio.
Morelle, Edmund J. '53 (SY) Verona, NY Our Lady of Good Counsel Church.
Morelli, Gary '81 (DET) [3] Taylor, MI St. Cyril of Jerusalem Church.
Morello, Carl '83 (CHI) Park Ridge, IL St. Paul of the Cross Church.
Morello, Peter '78 (GLP) On Duty Outside of Diocese.
Morello, Peter '78 (PHX) Phoenix, AZ United States Veterans Affairs Medical Center.
Morello, Sam Anthony *o.c.d.* '62 (DAL) [K] Dallas, TX Mount Carmel Center.
Morelock, George L. '65 (SFD) Hillsboro, IL St. Agnes Church; Hillsboro, IL Graham Correctional Center.
Morency, Raymond P. '87 (PRT) Military Chaplains.
Moreno, David *s.d.b.* '79 (NY) [DD] New Rochelle, NY Salesian Provincial House.
Moreno, James '76 (DEN) [11] Denver, CO Holy Family Church.
Moreno, Joaquin *o.f.m.* (SFR) [7] San Francisco, CA St. Boniface Church.
Moreno, Jorge (SAC) Absent on Leave.
Moreno, Jorge '63 (SD) Brawley, CA Our Lady of Perpetual Help Church.
Moreno, Jose (DAL) [1] Garland, TX Good Shepherd Church.
Moreno, Joseph '86 (BUF) [L] Buffalo, NY St. Francis Geriatric and Healthcare Services, Inc.
Moreno, Joseph F. '86 (BUF) [44] Buffalo, NY St. Margaret Church.
Moreno, Juan '60 (LSC) [5] Las Cruces, NM St. Genevieve Church.
Moreno, Luis (STL) [W] St. Louis, MO Hispanic Ministry of the Archdiocese of St. Louis.
Moreno, Maximilian A. *o.praem.* '92 (ORG) [H] Silverado, CA Norbertine Fathers of Orange Inc.
Moreno, Robert (BUF) Alden, NY Erie County Correctional Facility.
Moreno, Robert '93 (STF) Lancaster, NY St. Basil Church.
Moreschi, Alex *i.m.c.* '73 (PIT) [O] Pittsburgh, PA Consolata Fathers.
Moreshead, Harold D. '55 (PRT) Mechanic Falls, ME Our Lady of Ransom Church.
Moreton, Msgr. John '64 (FRS) [4] Fresno, CA Our Lady of Victory Church.
Moretta, Msgr. John T. '68 (LA) [35] Los Angeles, CA Resurrection Church.
Moretti, Msgr. August '54 (LA) Pasadena, CA Assumption of the Blessed Virgin Mary Church.
Moretti, Edward D. '60 (VEN) Bradenton, FL SS. Peter and Paul the Apostles Church.
Moretti, Mark E. '95 (ARL) Vienna, VA St. Mark's Church.
Morey, Charles W. '80 (SPC) Special Assignment.
Morey, Daniel *o.f.m.* (NY) [13] New York, NY St. Anthony of Padua Church.
Morey, Robert E. '96 (BAL) Westminster, MD St. John Church.
Morfeld, Msgr. Frank G. '51 (DEN) [30] Denver, CO St. Francis de Sales Church.
Morfin, Francois J. *c.s.b.* '77 (GAL) [Q] Sugar Land, TX Basilian Mission Center.
Morfin, John N. '67 (GAL) [41] Houston, TX St. John Vianney Church.
Morgan, Arthur '59 (LSC) Special Assignment.
Morgan, Brendan '64 (NO) River Ridge, LA St. Matthew the Apostle Church.
Morgan, Charles J. '79 (ALX) Winnsboro, LA St. Mary Church.
Morgan, Colum '51 (DET) Absent on Sick Leave.
Morgan, D. Terrence '76 (STA) Atlantic Beach, FL St. John the Baptist Church; On Duty Outside the Diocese.
Morgan, Dave J. *s.j.* '53 (SJ) [L] Los Altos, CA Jesuit Retreat House.
Morgan, Drew P. *c.o.* (PIT) [R] Slippery Rock, PA Office for Campus Ministry.
Morgan, Drew P. *c.o.* '85 (PIT) [O] Pittsburgh, PA Congregation of the Oratory of St. Philip Neri; [R] Slippery Rock, PA Office for Campus Ministry.
Morgan, Drew P. *c.o.* '94 (PIT) [R] Slippery Rock, PA Office for Campus Ministry.
Morgan, Edward *c.ss.r.* '64 (WCH) [G] Wichita, KS Redemptorist Mission House.
Morgan, Edward J. '37 (CHI) Retired.
Morgan, Edward T. *c.ss.r.* '64 (WCH) [14] Wichita, KS St. Joseph Church.
Morgan, Francis C. *ss.cc.* (NY) Manhattan, NY U.S.V.A. Medical Center.
Morgan, George *c.m.f.* '88 (CHI) [149] Chicago, IL Our Lady of Guadalupe Church.
Morgan, George R. *o.s.a.* '66 (BO) Andover, MA St. Augustine Church; [C] North Andover, MA Merrimack College.
Morgan, Guy *o.f.m.* (SP) [O] St. Petersburg, FL St. Anthony Friary.
Morgan, J.P. '91 (ORL) [1] Orlando, FL St. James Cathedral.

Morgan, James '60 (ALN) [G] Pottsville, PA Good Samaritan Regional Medical Center.
Morgan, James F. *s.j.* '54 (BO) [3] Newton, MA St. Ignatius Church; [W] Chestnut Hill, MA The Jesuit Community at Boston College.
Morgan, Jerome '62 (SAL) Dorrance, KS St. Joseph's Church; Wilson, KS St. Wenceslaus Church.
Morgan, John '58 (OAK) Retired.
Morgan, John A. '40 (ROC) Retired.
Morgan, John H. '51 (L) Retired.
Morgan, John W. '58 (B) Hailey, ID St. Charles Borromeo Church; Sun Valley, ID Our Lady of the Snows Church.
Morgan, Joseph A. '81 (OG) [2] Ogdensburg, NY Notre Dame Church; Ogdensburg, NY Riverview Correctional Facility.
Morgan, Jude *ss.cc.* '50 (FR) [J] Fairhaven, MA Sacred Hearts Provincial House.
Morgan, Julian *c.p.* '53 (HRT) [M] West Hartford, CT Holy Family Monastery/Retreat.
Morgan, Kirk '74 (GF) Miles City, MT Sacred Heart Church.
Morgan, Leo *o.f.m.cap.* '44 (FgM) Capuchin Foreign Missions.
Morgan, Maron '95 (RC) [B] Bethlehem, SD Holy Nativity Monastery.
Morgan, Maron *o.mar.* '95 (SAM) [C] Petersham, MA Most Holy Trinity Monastery.
Morgan, Martin '70 (TLS) [6] Tulsa, OK Christ the King Church.
Morgan, Matthew A. '51 (PMB) [1] Boca Raton, FL Ascension Church.
Morgan, Michael T. *o.s.b.* '40 (BIR) [E] Cullman, AL St. Bernard Abbey.
Morgan, Oliver J. *s.j.* '79 (SCR) [C] Scranton, PA University of Scranton.
Morgan, Raymond J. '42 (BRK) Retired; [U] Douglaston, NY Bishop Mugavero Residence.
Morgan, Msgr. Thomas '39 (MRY) Retired.
Morgan, Thomas '84 (SP) Lecanto, FL St. Scholastica Church.
Morgan, Thomas B. '55 (BO) Salisbury, MA Star of the Sea Church.
Morgan, Msgr. Thomas J. '65 (CAM) Haddonfield, NJ Christ the King Regional School Church.
Morgan, Walter N. '44 (MIL) Retired.
Morgan, William H. '50 (BO) Retired.
Morgan, William P. '57 (BUR) Washington, VT St. Cecilia Church.
Morgen, Paul '62 (SFS) Retired.
Morgenroth, Anton *c.s.sp.* '45 (GAL) [B] Houston, TX Holy Ghost Fathers.
Morgenthaler, John N. *o.p.* '41 (NO) [25] New Orleans, LA St. Anthony Of Padua Church.
Morgera, Michael A. '85 (MEM) [7] Memphis, TN Blessed Sacrament Church.
Morgia, Robustiano D. '76 (NO) Jefferson, LA St. Agnes Church.
Morhous, Robert *o.c.s.o.* '59 (WOR) [N] Spencer, MA St. Joseph's Abbey.
Moriarity, Daniel J. '64 (PH) Absent on Sick Leave.
Moriarity, William J. '66 (CHI) [1] Chicago, IL Cathedral of the Holy Name.
Moriarty, Francis *s.s.e.* '45 (VEN) [G] Englewood, FL Society of St. Edmund Residence.
Moriarty, Frederick L. *s.j.* '44 (BO) [W] Chestnut Hill, MA The Jesuit Community at Boston College.
Moriarty, James F. '51 (CHI) Skokie, IL St. Joan of Arc Church; Stickney, IL St. Pius X Church; Retired.
Moriarty, James J. '48 (NY) Pawling, NY St. John the Evangelist Church; Retired.
Moriarty, John '62 (JOL) On Duty Outside the Diocese.
Moriarty, John J. '62 (FgM) Society of St. James the Apostle.
Moriarty, John J. *s.j.* '78 (BO) [W] Boston, MA The Society of Jesus of New England-Provincial Offices.
Moriarty, John J. *s.j.* '78 (COL) [A] Columbus, OH Pontifical College Josephinum.
Moriarty, John P. '91 (LEX) Prestonsburg, KY St. Martha Church.
Moriarty, Joseph B. '93 (IND) [30] Indianapolis, IN St. Monica Church.
Moriarty, Msgr. Joseph T. '34 (CLV) Retired; [F] Cleveland, OH Incarnate Word Academy; [Q] Cleveland, OH Sisters of the Incarnate Word and Blessed Sacrament.
Moriarty, Philip M. '80 (JC) Wien, MO St. Mary of the Angels Church.
Moriarty, Quentin E. *o.p.* '59 (CHI) [N] River Forest, IL St. Thomas Aquinas Priory.
Moriarty, Thomas '92 (RVC) Floral Park, NY Our Lady of Victory Church.
Moriarty, Thomas W. '42 (BO) Retired.
Moriarty, W. Barry *c.m.* '67 (FgM) Vincentian Foreign Missions.
Morillo, Jose '49 (VEN) Absent on Sick Leave.
Morin, Benjamin R. *s.j.* '56 (FgM) Provinces.
Morin, Douglas J. '85 (LIN) Cheney, NE St. Michael Church.
Morin, Frank P. '73 (PRT) [7] Portland, ME Sacred Heart/St. Dominic Church.
Morin, George E. '70 (BO) Saugus, MA St. Margaret Church.
Morin, Henri D. '44 (PRO) [10] Woonsocket, RI Precious Blood Church; Retired.
Morin, John *o.m.i.* '51 (BO) [6] Boston, MA St. Angela Church.
Morin, Joseph *c.ss.r.* '64 (CHI) [9] Chicago, IL St. Alphonsus Church.
Morin, Michael J. '88 (LIN) Cortland, NE St. James Church; [C] Lincoln, NE Pius X Central High School; [L] Lincoln, NE Pius X Foundation and Pius X Endowment Fund.
Morin, Robert *o.m.i.* '69 (BEL) [F] Belleville, IL Missionary Oblates of Mary Immaculate - St. Henry's Oblate Residence; [J] Belleville, IL Oblate Preaching Team.
Morin, Msgr. Roger P. '71 (NO) [13] New Orleans, LA Incarnate Word Church.
Morin, Timothy '77 (STP) Lino Lakes, MN St. Joseph Church.
Moriones, Francis *o.a.r.* '34 (NY) [B] Suffern, NY Tagaste Monastery.
Morisco, Cyril *o.f.m.* '45 (NY) [DD] New York, NY Franciscan Province of the Immaculate Conception.
Morisette, Alfred *s.j.* '61 (SPK) [C] Spokane, WA Gonzaga University.
Morisette, Richard P. '61 (SY) Onondaga Hill, NY St. Michael Church.
Moritz, Msgr. Paul L. '41 (BO) [7] Brockton, MA St. Patrick Church; Retired.
Morlan, Lawrence A. '95 (PEO) [4] Bloomington, IL St. Patrick Church of Merna.
Morley, Edward T. *o.c.s.o.* '83 (ATL) [I] Conyers, GA The Monastery of the Holy Spirit.
Morley, Edward T. *o.c.s.o.* '83 (CHR) [D] Moncks Corner, SC Mepkin Abbey.
Morley, John F. '62 (NEW) [B] South Orange, NJ Seton Hall University.
Morley, John J. '32 (PH) [141] Philadelphia, PA St. Richard Church; Retired.
Morlino, Paschal A. *o.s.b.* '66 (BAL) [15] Baltimore, MD St. Benedict Church.
Morlino, Robert C. '74 (KAL) [1] Kalamazoo, MI St. Augustine Cathedral.
Morman, David '54 (BIS) [F] Sentinel Butte, ND Home On The Range.
Morman, David G. '89 (BIS) Beach, ND St. John the Baptist Church.
Morman, James *t.o.r.* '92 (WDC) [M] Washington, DC St. Louis Friary.
Morman, Kenneth '73 (TOL) [8] Toledo, OH Holy Rosary Church; [14] Toledo, OH Sacred Heart of Jesus Church; [39] Toledo, OH St. Stephen Church.
Morman, Wilbert *s.v.d.* '46 (CHI) [B] Techny, IL Divine Word Residence.
Mormando, Franco *s.j.* '93 (BO) [W] Chestnut Hill, MA The Jesuit Community at Boston College.
Moroney, Joseph E. '54 (CHY) [1] Cheyenne, WY St. Mary's Cathedral; Retired.
Moroney, Martin J. '67 (SAC) Rancho Cordova, CA St. John Vianney Church.
Moroney, Michael J. '71 (BR) [16] Baton Rouge, LA Our Lady of Mercy Church.
Moroney, William *m.afr.* '61 (FgM) Missionaries of Africa Foreign Missions.
Moroney, William F. *m.afr.* '61 (WDC) [M] Washington, DC Missionaries of Africa.
Morosini, Louis *s.m.* '56 (FgM) Marist Foreign Missions.
Morozowich, Mark '91 (SJP) Graduate Studies.
Morras, Ignacio '49 (MIA) [5] Hialeah, FL St. John the Apostle Church; Retired.
Morras, Msgr. Xavier '50 (MIA) Coral Gables, FL Little Flower Church.
Morrell, William *o.m.i.* '70 (SAT) [M] San Antonio, TX De Mazenod House.
Morrelly, Leonard '92 (RVC) Absent on Leave.
Morrier, David *t.o.r.* '97 (ARL) Herndon, VA St. Joseph Church.
Morrill, Bruce *s.j.* '92 (BO) [W] Chestnut Hill, MA The Jesuit Community at Boston College.
Morrill, Giles '50 (ALB) Retired.
Morris, Alan E. '92 (PIT) Whitehall, PA St. Gabriel of the Sorrowful Virgin Church.
Morris, Alexis P. '56 (SP) [O] St. Petersburg, FL St. Anthony Friary.
Morris, Anthony *c.ss.r.* (RIC) [2] Hampton, VA St. Joseph Church.
Morris, C. Eugene '96 (STL) [36] St. Louis, MO St. Gabriel the Archangel Church.
Morris, Charles M. '83 (DET) [1] Wyandotte, MI St. Elizabeth Church; [T] Roseville, MI Cursillos in Christianity Movement of the Archdiocese of Detroit.
Morris, George O. *s.j.* '68 (SPK) [C] Spokane, WA Gonzaga University.
Morris, Gerald R. '70 (MIA) Marathon, FL San Pablo Church.
Morris, James '63 (BO) [5] Salem, MA St. John the Baptist Church.
Morris, James '93 (STF) Salem, MA St. John the Baptist Church.
Morris, James A. '80 (BRK) [U] Jamaica, NY Vincentian Residence.
Morris, James A. '94 (KAL) St. Joseph, MI St. Joseph Church.
Morris, James H. '66 (SFR) San Bruno, CA St. Robert Church.
Morris, James J. '89 (BRK) Absent on Leave.
Morris, John *o.p.* '66 (OAK) [B] Moraga, CA St. Mary's College.
Morris, John *o.p.* '66 (SAC) Benicia, CA St. Dominic Church.
Morris, Msgr. John E. (PAT) Retired.
Morris, John J. '44 (CHI) Retired.
Morris, John J. '60 (NEW) Military Chaplains.
Morris, John J. *s.j.* '62 (P) [L] Portland, OR Jesuit Provincial Office (Society of Jesus, Oregon Prov.).
Morris, John S. '62 (BO) Health Leave.
Morris, Joseph E. '96 (ATL) [4] Marietta, GA Church of the Transfiguration.
Morris, Joseph W. *s.j.* '59 (SLC) East Carbon, UT Good Shepherd Church.
Morris, Ken *c.s.v.* '54 (LAV) Henderson, NV St. Thomas More Church.
Morris, Kenan *o.f.m.* '50 (BO) [Z] Boston, MA Saint Anthony Residence.
Morris, Kevin J. '97 (IND) Richmond, IN Holy Family Church; Richmond, IN St. Andrew Church; Richmond, IN St. Mary Church; [N] Richmond, IN Earlham College Newman Center.
Morris, Lester G. '91 (NOR) Middlefield, CT St. Colman Church.
Morris, Loyd '95 (DAL) Allen, TX St. Jude Church.
Morris, Michael *o.p.* (OAK) [N] Oakland, CA Dominican Order, Siena House.
Morris, Michael *o.p.* '77 (OAK) [B] Moraga, CA St. Mary's College.
Morris, Michael T. *o.p.* '77 (OAK) [A] Berkeley, CA Dominican School of Philosophy and Theology; [N] Moraga, CA Dominican Community.
Morris, Msgr. Philip D. *s.t.d., v.f.* '63 (NEW) Hillsdale, NJ St. John the Baptist Church.
Morris, Robert '49 (SFD) Collinsville, IL SS. Peter and Paul Church.
Morris, Robert '91 (SP) [12] Tampa, FL St. Mary Church.
Morris, Robert A. *o.p.* '50 (PRO) [P] Providence, RI St. Thomas Aquinas Priory at Providence College.
Morris, Robert F. '66 (PT) Destin, FL Corpus Christi Church.
Morris, Robert J. '53 (PAT) Retired; [P] Chester, NJ Nazareth Village.
Morris, Stephen P. (RVC) Priests Released from Diocesan Assignment.
Morris, Thomas A. *o.ss.t.* '81 (WDC) [M] Hyattsville, MD St. John de Matha Monastery, Order of Most Holy Trinity.
Morris, William J. *s.m.* '38 (STL) [P] St. Louis, MO Provincialate of the Society of Mary, Province of St. Louis.
Morris, William S. *s.s.* '31 (BAL) [J] Baltimore, MD St. Charles Villa; [M] Baltimore, MD St. Charles Villa.
Morris, William T. '69 (MET) [B] Watchung, NJ Mount St. Mary Academy.
Morris, William T. '69 (NEW) [Q] Mahwah, NJ Ramapo College.
Morrisette, Robert H. '75 (BO) Health Leave.
Morrisey, Michael E. '86 (RCK) [1] Elgin, IL St. Joseph Church.
Morrison, Anselm *a.a.* '48 (BO) [W] Brighton, MA Assumptionist Center.
Morrison, Anselm Harry *a.a.* '48 (SP) Dade City, FL St. Rita Church.
Morrison, Carl T. '69 (MIA) Miami Shores, FL St. Martha Church; [G] Miami, FL Mercy Hospital.
Morrison, Craig *o.carm.* '87 (JOL) [J] Darien, IL Carmelite Provincial Office.
Morrison, Craig *o.carm.* '87 (WDC) [B] Washington, DC Whitefriars Hall.
Morrison, Msgr. David J. '54 (ALN) [8] Bethlehem, PA Our Lady of Perpetual Help Church.
Morrison, Douglas A. '59 (HRT) On Duty Outside the Archdiocese.
Morrison, Francis X. '55 (PH) [152] Philadelphia, PA St. Timothy Church.
Morrison, Harry B. '76 (OAK) [4] Walnut Creek, CA St. Stephen Church.
Morrison, Howard L. *s.j.* '58 (FgM) Provinces.
Morrison, Howard L. *s.j.* '58 (P) [L] Portland, OR Jesuit Provincial Office (Society of Jesus, Oregon Prov.).
Morrison, James J. '74 (PRT) York Harbor, ME St. Christopher-by-the-Sea Church.
Morrison, James R. '87 (HT) [2] Houma, LA Annunziata Church.
Morrison, John A. *s.j.* '36 (NY) [DD] New York, NY Murray-Weigel Hall.
Morrison, John A. '92 (SAM) Troy, NY St. Ann Church.
Morrison, Larry '79 (RNO) Sun Valley, NV St. Peter Canisius Church.
Morrison, Michael G. *s.j.* '68 (OM) [A] Omaha, NE Creighton University; [K] Omaha, NE Jesuit Community At Creighton University.

Morrison, Raymond J. '39 (CHI) Northlake, IL St. John Baptist Vianney, Cure of Ars Church; Retired.
Morrison, Robert A. '49 (PH) Retired.
Morrison, Thomas A. *o.p.* '55 (CHI) [J] Chicago, IL Holy Cross Hospital; [N] Chicago, IL Dominicans (Provincial Office).
Morrison, Thomas F. '76 (CHR) Chester, SC St. Joseph's Church; Lancaster, SC St. Catherine's Church.
Morrisroe, Paschal *o.f.m.* '46 (LA) [R] Santa Barbara, CA Franciscan Friary, Order of Friars Minor (Old Mission).
Morrissette, Dominic '45 (JOL) Retired.
Morrissette, Joseph H. '53 (NOR) Retired.
Morrissey, Daniel W. *o.p.* '62 (CHI) [N] Chicago, IL Dominicans (Provincial Office).
Morrissey, Dunstan R. *o.s.b.* '53 (PEO) [A] Peru, IL St. Bede Abbey and Academy.
Morrissey, J. Michael '78 (P) Gresham, OR St. Anne Church.
Morrissey, James E. '38 (CHI) Mundelein, IL St. Mary Church; Retired.
Morrissey, Msgr. James L. '55 (PEO) [1] Streator, IL Immaculate Conception Church.
Morrissey, Jerome V. '47 (PEO) Wenona, IL St. Mary's Church; Retired.
Morrissey, John '63 (PMB) Stuart, FL St. Joseph Church.
Morrissey, John J. '37 (DAV) Retired; [M] Davenport, IA St. Vincent Center.
Morrissey, Joseph G. *o.s.f.s.* '77 (WIL) [I] Wilmington, DE Oblates of St. Francis De Sales.
Morrissey, Lawrence M. '54 (PEO) Retired.
Morrissey, Lawrence P. '57 (PEO) El Paso, IL St. Mary's Church.
Morrissey, Michael '51 (ORG) [G] Westminster, CA Korean Catholic Ministry; [H] Westminster, CA Columban Fathers.
Morrissey, Msgr. Michael J. '65 (DAV) [M] Davenport, IA St. Vincent Center; [P] Davenport, IA Kingdom Co.
Morrissey, Paul F. *s.m.* '75 (STP) [25] St. Paul, MN St. Louis King of France Church.
Morrissey, Philip T. '46 (BGP) Retired.
Morrissey, Robert '80 (RVC) Ocean Beach, NY Our Lady of the Magnificat Church.
Morrissey, Robert O. '83 (RVC) New Hyde Park, NY Holy Spirit Church.
Morrissey, Robert P. '76 (BGP) Ridgefield, CT St. Mary's Church.
Morrissey, Thomas E. '61 (FR) [6] Taunton, MA St. James Church.
Morrissey, William F. '52 (RCK) [4] Aurora, IL St. Mary Church.
Morrissy, Patrick *c.ss.r.* '55 (FgM) Redemptorist Foreign Missions.
Morrone, Louis S. *o.p.* '92 (CHI) River Forest, IL St. Vincent Ferrer Priory Church; [N] Chicago, IL Dominicans (Provincial Office).
Morrow, Brian S. '80 (DEN) [32] Denver, CO St. James Church.
Morrow, Dennis '75 (GR) [20] Grand Rapids, MI SS. Peter and Paul's Church; On Special Assignment.
Morrow, Lambert W. *o.s.b.* '42 (PBL) [F] Canon City, CO Holy Cross Abbey.
Morrow, Michael J. '86 (NY) [135] Bronx, NY St. Brendan Church.
Morrow, Richard B. '55 (ATL) [1] Atlanta, GA Cathedral of Christ the King; Retired.
Morrow, Thomas G. '82 (WDC) [42] Washington, DC St. Thomas Apostle Church.
Morrow, Thomas O. '71 (BRK) Absent on Leave.
Morry, Matthew F. *o.p.* '50 (PRO) [P] Providence, RI St. Thomas Aquinas Priory at Providence College.
Morsch, Msgr. Peter '31 (AMA) Retired; [D] Panhandle, TX St. Ann's Nursing Home.
Morse, Frederick H. '95 (PRT) South Portland, ME Church of the Holy Cross; South Portland, ME St. John the Evangelist Church.
Morse, Guy E. '81 (CHL) Retired.
Morse, James E. *s.j.* '50 (SJ) [D] San Jose, CA Bellarmine College Preparatory.
Morse, James H. '67 (FR) Special Assignment.
Morse, John *s.j.* '61 (YAK) Moses Lake, WA Our Lady of Fatima Church; Warden, WA Queen of All Saints Church.
Morse, John A. '52 (STL) Retired.
Morse, Jonathan '88 (STF) Special Assignment; [F] Stamford, CT Missionary Sisters of Mother of God.
Morse, Michael E. '84 (STA) Live Oak, FL St. Francis Xavier Church.
Morse, Richard *o.s.f.s.* '69 (TOL) [C] Toledo, OH St. Francis de Sales High School.
Morse, Richard D. '97 (FR) Special Assignment.
Morse, Richard E. *o.s.f.s.* '69 (TOL) [K] Toledo, OH Oblates of St. Francis de Sales.
Morslander, Edward '52 (SCL) Retired.
Mort, Ernest C. *c.s.p.* '59 (NY) [DD] Jamaica Estates, NY Paulist Fathers Generalate.
Mort, Ernest C. *c.s.p.* '59 (SD) Special Assignment.
Mortell, Anthony *s.s.c.* '60 (LA) [R] Los Angeles, CA Columban Fathers, Procure House.
Mortimer, Msgr. James E. '52 (PH) [157] Philadelphia, PA St. William Church.
Morton, Jake *s.j.* '75 (SPK) Ford, WA St. Philip Benizi Church; Inchelium, WA St. Michael's Mission Church; Wellpinit, WA Sacred Heart Church; Westend, WA Our Lady of Lourdes Church.
Morton, John *c.ss.r.* (DEN) [33] Denver, CO St. Joseph's Church.
Morton, John *c.ss.r.* '53 (DEN) Fort Lupton, CO St. William Church.
Morton, Vincent *o.s.b.* '86 (SP) [O] St. Leo, FL St. Leo Abbey.
Morton, Vincent R. '86 (SP) Inverness, FL Our Lady of Fatima Church.
Morvant, Kenneth '61 (OLL) Lafayette, LA Maronite Catholic Community Church.
Morvant, Kenneth R. (LAF) On Special Assignment.
Morvay, Andrew '60 (RC) Buffalo, SD St. Anthony Church; Retired.
Mosbrucker, Jacob '66 (P) [10] Portland, OR St. Charles Church.
Moscaritdo, Mario '64 (KC) Special Assignment.
Moscato, Angelo *c.s.* '62 (CHI) [N] Chicago, IL Scalabrini House of Theology.
Moschini, Christopher H. *o.p.* '52 (P) [18] Portland, OR Holy Rosary Parish & Dominican Priory Church.
Mosele, Victor *s.x.* '60 (FgM) Xaverian Foreign Missions.
Mosele, Victor *s.x.* '60 (PAT) [M] Wayne, NJ Xaverian Missionary Fathers.
Moseley, Stan *o.s.b.* '53 (NO) [P] St. Benedict, LA St. Joseph Abbey.
Moseley, Stanley '53 (NY) [118] New York, NY St. Thomas More Church.
Moser, Albert *c.s.p.* '60 (OAK) [2] Berkeley, CA Holy Spirit Parish.
Moser, Charles J. *s.m.a.* '32 (ORL) Retired.
Moser, Claudio *o.f.m.* '63 (NY) [DD] New York, NY Franciscan Province of the Immaculate Conception.
Moser, John A. '86 (DUB) Chester, IA St. Stephen's Church; New Haven, IA St. Peter's Church; Riceville, IA Immaculate Conception Church.
Moser, Tom '94 (KNX) Kingsport, TN St. Dominic Church.
Moser, Msgr. Victor G. '46 (KC) [5] St. Joseph, MO St. Mary's Church.
Mosey, Douglas L. *c.s.b.* (NOR) [M] Cromwell, CT Basilian Fathers of Connecticut, Inc.
Mosey, Douglas L. *c.s.b.* '74 (NOR) [A] Cromwell, CT Holy Apostles College and Seminary.
Mosher, Mark L. '88 (SAC) [4] Sacramento, CA Immaculate Conception Church.
Mosher, Robert E. *s.s.c.* '82 (FgM) St. Columban's Foreign Mission.
Mosher, Thomas '81 (BUR) [H] Burlington, VT University of Vermont-The Catholic Center at UVM.
Mosher, Thomas L. '81 (BUR) Lyndonville, VT St. Elizabeth Church.
Mosimann, John P. '97 (ARL) Fairfax, VA St. Leo's Church.
Moskal, Joseph E. '65 (SY) [10] Utica, NY St. Joseph and St. Patrick Church; Absent on Sick Leave.
Mosko, Msgr. Leon A. '56 (STF) Special Assignment.
Moskus, John T. '63 (HRT) [1] Milford, CT Christ the Redeemer Church.
Moslener, Robert E. '76 (GBG) Sagamore, PA Sacred Heart Church; Yatesboro, PA St. Mary Church.
Mosley, Charles A. '85 (GRY) Griffith, IN St. Mary Church.
Mosley, Daniel E. '77 (STL) Berger, MO St. Paul Church; New Haven, MO Assumption Church.
Mosley, Francis J. '39 (BO) Retired.
Mosley, Godfrey '79 (WDC) Oxon Hill, MD St. Columba Church.
Moslousky, Robert W. *c.s.b.* '74 (GAL) Sugar Land, TX St. Theresa Church.
Mosovsky, James J. '42 (CLV) Avon Lake, OH Holy Spirit Church; Retired.
Moss, Msgr. Charles T. '58 (ALN) West Bangor, PA St. Roch Church.
Moss, Darius G.C. '97 (HBG) Mechanicsburg, PA St. Joseph Church.
Moss, Donald G. '86 (AUS) Military Chaplains.
Moss, Donald Roy '86 (LA) Point Mugu, CA Naval Air Station.
Moss, James T. (PAT) Absent on Leave.
Moss, James T. '82 (STA) Williston, FL Holy Family Church.
Moss, Ray '86 (CHY) Laramie, WY St. Laurence O'Toole Church.
Moss, Robert D. '69 (BUF) Sloan, NY St. Andrew Church.
Moss, Robert H. *c.s.c.* '74 (FTW) [A] Notre Dame, IN Old College; [A] Notre Dame, IN Moreau Seminary; [B] Notre Dame, IN University of Notre Dame Du Lac; [J] Notre Dame, IN Holy Cross Community, Corby Hall, University of Notre Dame.
Mossett, Robert C. *o.s.f.s.* '65 (DET) [1] Monroe, MI St. Anne Church.
Mossi, John P. *s.j.* '73 (SPK) [C] Spokane, WA Gonzaga University.
Mossing, Msgr. Lawrence A. '40 (TOL) Retired.
Most, William G. '40 (DUB) Retired.
Mostardi, Joseph S. *o.s.a.* '75 (NY) [216] Staten Island, NY Our Lady of Good Counsel Church.
Moster, Humbert *o.s.b.* (IND) Oak Forest, IN St. Cecilia of Rome/Formerly St. Philomena Church.
Moster, Humbert *o.f.m.* '57 (IND) Oldenburg, IN Holy Family Church; St. Mary-of-the-Rock, IN St. Mary-of-the-Rock Church; St. Peter, IN St. Peter Church.
Moster, James *o.f.m.cap.* '76 (KCK) [H] Lawrence, KS St. Conrad's Friary.
Mostrangelo, David F. *s.j.* (DET) [E] Detroit, MI Loyola High School.
Moszur, Edward J. '71 (GRY) Highland, IN Our Lady of Grace Church.
Motherway, Thomas F. '69 (BO) Health Leave.
Motl, James R. *o.p.* '62 (STP) [15] Minneapolis, MN St. Albert the Great Church; [A] St. Paul, MN The Saint Paul Seminary; [C] St. Paul, MN University of St. Thomas.
Motolinia, Arturo *o.s.a.* '82 (NY) [40] New York, NY St. Gregory Church.
Motsay, Joseph '78 (RC) Ellsworth, SD Ellsworth AFB.
Motsay, Joseph R. '78 (SCR) Military Chaplains.
Motsay, Russell E. '72 (SCR) Carbondale, PA Our Lady of Mt. Carmel Church.
Motsett, Msgr. C. Bourke '34 (PEO) Retired.
Mott, James A. *o.s.a.* '65 (SD) [B] San Diego, CA Austin House - House of Formation; [H] San Diego, CA Augustinian Community.
Mott, Msgr. John D. '56 (RVC) Sick Leave.
Motta, Anthony '63 (ALB) Haines Falls, NY Immaculate Conception Church.
Motta, Michael J. '72 (HRT) Special and other (Arch-)Diocesan Assignment.
Mottau, Robert S. (BO) Retired.
Mottet, Marvin A. '56 (DAV) [1] Davenport, IA Sacred Heart Cathedral; [K] Davenport, IA Thomas Merton House, Inc.; [P] Davenport, IA Interfaith Housing, Ltd.
Mottin, Msgr. Charles A. '49 (STL) [S] St. Louis, MO Father Jim's Home; [S] St. Louis, MO Father Dempsey's Hotel, Inc.
Motycka, Robert R. '79 (CHI) Other Assignments.
Mouannes, Nabil '84 (OLL) San Diego, CA Saint Ephrem Mission Church; Phoenix, AZ Maronite Catholic Community Church.
Mouawad, Paul '69 (SAM) Pawtucket, RI Holy Trinity-St. George Church.
Mouch, Msgr. Frank (SP) [H] St. Petersburg, FL St. Petersburg Diocesan Library.
Mouch, Msgr. Frank M. '58 (VEN) Retired.
Moudry, Paul G. '87 (STP) Columbia Heights, MN Immaculate Conception Church.
Moudry, Richard P. '50 (STP) Retired.
Mould, Christopher J. '88 (ARL) Fredericksburg, VA St. Mary Church.
Moulder, John '90 (CHI) [1] Oak Park, IL Ascension Church.
Mountain, Edward C. '47 (WIN) Retired.
Mountain, Harold B. '42 (WIN) Retired.
Mountain, Joseph W. '52 (WIN) Mapleton, MN St. Teresa's Church; Retired.
Mounteer, Louis A. *s.j.* '56 (ALB) [O] Auriesville, NY Jesuit Retreat House for Priests, Religious and Lay People.
Mousbrugger, Edwin A. *s.j.* '36 (DET) [P] Clarkston, MI Colombiere Center.
Mouser, J. Irvin '65 (L) St. Thomas, KY St. Thomas Church; [M] Nerinx, KY Motherhouse and Novitiate of the Sisters of Loretto at the Foot of the Cross.
Mouser, Joseph Irvin '65 (L) Bardstown, KY St. Monica Church.
Moussier, Howard R. *o.s.b.* '65 (BIR) [E] Cullman, AL St. Bernard Abbey.
Moussier, Howard R. *o.s.b.* '65 (MOB) Elberta, AL St. Bartholomew Church.
Moutenot, Charles L. *s.j.* '84 (OAK) [N] Berkeley, CA Jesuit Community at Jesuit School of Theology at Berkeley.
Mouton, Msgr. C. Burton '49 (LAF) On Duty Outside the Diocese.
Mouton, Thomas Jason '92 (LAF) [7] Lafayette, LA Our Lady Queen of Peace Church.
Movelli, Gary '74 (SEA) Kirkland, WA Holy Family Church.
Mowatt, John J. (BO) Retired.
Mower, Scott '97 (PRT) Waterville, ME Holy Spirit Church.
Mowrer, Patrick '97 (PHX) [1] Phoenix, AZ SS. Simon and Jude Cathedral.
Mowry, Raymond G. '44 (SFS) Ipswich, SD Holy Cross Church; Retired.
Moy, Francis J. *s.j.* '69 (BGP) [1] Greenwich, CT St. Mary's Church; [O] Fairfield, CT The Fairfield Jesuit Community-Fairfield University.
Moy, Francis J. *s.j.* '69 (BO) [W] Boston, MA The Society of Jesus of New England-Provincial Offices.
Moya, Peter O. '85 (MET) On Duty Outside the Diocese.

Moyano, Felipe '48 (CAM) [1] Atlantic City, NJ Holy Spirit Church.
Moyer, Joseph *c.s.c.* '94 (FgM) Holy Cross Foreign Missions.
Moyer, Joseph M. *c.s.c.* '94 (NO) [22] New Orleans, LA Sacred Heart Of Jesus Church.
Moyer, Msgr. Richard '64 (PHX) Carefree, AZ Our Lady of Joy Church.
Moylan, Thomas *l.c.* '69 (MAD) [I] Edgerton, WI Legion of Christ, Inc.
Moyna, James Moneta *o.p.* '70 (NY) [DD] New York, NY St. Vincent Ferrer Priory.
Moyna, James P. '70 (RVC) East Rockaway, NY St. Raymond's Church.
Moyna, John L. '73 (ALB) Coxsackie, NY St. Mary Church; Coxsackie, NY Regional Medical Unit.
Moynahan, Joseph (SPR) [H] Holyoke, MA Sisters of Providence Care Centers, Inc.
Moynahan, Joseph A. '34 (WOR) Retired.
Moynahan, Kevin '54 (LSC) Retired.
Moynahan, Michael E. *s.j.* '73 (SPK) [C] Spokane, WA Gonzaga University.
Moynihan, Cornelius A. '47 (PHX) Retired.
Moynihan, Eugene J. *s.m.m.* '33 (RVC) [N] Bay Shore, NY Montfort Missionaries.
Moynihan, Eugene R. *s.s.j.* '57 (GAL) [62] Houston, TX Our Mother of Mercy Church.
Moynihan, George F. '74 (CHR) North Myrtle Beach, SC Our Lady Star of the Sea Church.
Moynihan, James M. '57 (SY) Special Assignment; [W] Syracuse, NY David W. Barry Foundation.
Moynihan, Jeremiah P. '74 (ROC) Hornell, NY St. Ignatius Loyola Church; Hornell, NY St. James Mercy Hospital.
Moynihan, John C. *m.m.* '67 (CHI) [N] Chicago, IL Maryknoll Fathers & Brothers.
Moynihan, Michael (NY) [GG] New York, NY University Apostolate.
Moynihan, Michael Robert '79 (BGP) [2] Greenwich, CT St. Michael the Archangel Church.
Moynihan, Noel '77 (BRK) [237] Queens, NY Sacred Heart of Jesus Church.
Moynihan, Paul V. (BO) Retired.
Moynihan, T. Joseph '57 (BO) Westwood, MA St. Margaret Mary Church.
Moynihan, Timothy '32 (SEA) [2] Seattle, WA St. Alphonsus Church; Retired.
Moys, Gregory '64 (P) [Q] Portland, OR Oregon Catholic Conference.
Moys, Gregory '65 (P) Grants Pass, OR St. Anne Church.
Mozer, Joseph F. '97 (BO) Duxbury, MA Holy Family Church.
Mozeris, Msgr. Damasus A. '39 (CHI) [92] Chicago, IL Immaculate Conception Church; Retired.
Mozos, Sebastian *o.m.i.* '33 (SAT) [K] San Antonio, TX Oblate Madonna Residence.
Mpeka, Rogatus L. (TR) [2] Trenton, NJ Blessed Sacrament Church.
Mrakuzic, Stephen A. '48 (CLV) [62] Cleveland, OH St. Paul Church; Retired.
Mraz, John S. '75 (ALN) [11] Allentown, PA St. Thomas More Church.
Mraz, Louis R. *o.s.c.* '59 (PHX) [2] Glendale, AZ St. Helen Church; [F] Phoenix, AZ Crosier Community of Phoenix (Canons Regular of the Order of the Holy Cross).
Mraz, Robert J. '74 (NU) Silver Lake, MN Church of the Holy Family.
Mrnarevic, Daniel Miho '84 (FAR) Rugby, ND St. Therese, Little Flower Church.
Mroczkowski, Msgr. Joseph '42 (CHI) [209] Chicago, IL St. Turibius Church.
Mroczkowski, Joseph A. '45 (LIN) Retired.
Mroczkowski, Msgr. Joseph J. '42 (CHI) Retired.
Mroczkowski, Leonard A. '46 (CAM) Retired.
Mroczynski, Edward *s.chr.* '57 (LA) [22] Los Angeles, CA Our Lady of the Bright Mount Church.
Mrowinski, Charles *c.r.* '55 (CHI) [D] Chicago, IL Weber High School; [M] Chicago, IL St. Joseph Home of Chicago, Inc.
Mrowka, Chester R. *c.m.* '59 (HRT) [M] Manchester, CT DePaul Provincial Residence.
Mroz, Richard J. '92 (NEW) Saddle Brook, NJ St. Philip the Apostle Church.
Mroziewski, Witold '91 (BRK) [94] Brooklyn, NY Our Lady of Czestochowa-St. Casimir Church.
Mrozinski, Ronald *o.f.m.conv.* (STP) [Q] Prior Lake, MN Franciscan Retreat House.
Mruk, Walter *o.f.m.conv.* '49 (HRT) [N] New Britain, CT Motherhouse of Daughters of Mary of the Immaculate Conception.
Mruk, Walter Leon *o.f.m.conv.* '49 (HRT) [M] New Britain, CT Conventual Franciscans.
Msaki, Joachim (PIT) [56] Pittsburgh, PA St. Mary of the Mount Church.
Msemwa, Severine (ROC) [M] Rochester, NY Diocesan Office of Campus Ministry.
Msongore, Josaphat *c.s.sp.* '63 (FgM) Holy Ghost Foreign Missions.
Muc, John *s.o.cist.* '90 (CHI) [N] Willow Springs, IL Cistercian Fathers.
Mucci, Flavian *o.f.m.* '63 (FgM) Franciscan Foreign Missions.
Muccilli, Sebastian L. '57 (MET) On Duty Outside the Diocese.
Muccino, Keith F. *s.j.* '96 (WDC) [M] Washington, DC The Jesuit Community at Georgetown University.
Muccitelli, Mario *s.d.v.* '48 (PAT) [M] Florham Park, NJ Father Justin Vocationary.
Mucha, Jan '54 (DEN) [34] Denver, CO St. Joseph's Church.
Mucha, John '53 (STU) [I] Nelsonville, OH Hocking Technical College.
Mucha, John '81 (STU) Glouster, OH Holy Cross Church; Nelsonville, OH St. Mary of the Hills Church.
Mucharski, Francis *o.f.m.cap.* '33 (PAT) [M] Oak Ridge-Milton, NJ St. Stanislaus B. M. Friary.
Muckenhaupt, Gregory F. *s.j.* (CI) [A] Pohnpei, FM Micronesia Seminar.
Muckenhaupt, Gregory F. *s.j.* '88 (CI) [C] Kolonia, Pohnpei, FM Jesuit House.
Muckenhaupt, Gregory F. *s.j.* '88 (FgM) Provinces.
Muckerman, Norman J. *c.ss.r.* '42 (STL) [P] Liguori, MO Liguori Mission House/Redemptorists.
Mucowski, Richard *o.f.m.* (KCK) [A] Leavenworth, KS Saint Mary College.
Mucowski, Richard *o.f.m.* '71 (NY) [DD] New York, NY Franciscan Friars, Order of Friars Minor, Holy Name Province.
Mudd, David A. '80 (WDC) Military Chaplains.
Mudd, Earl '60 (BEA) Retired.
Mudd, Gerald R. *o.f.m.* (BO) [BB] Boston, MA St. Anthony Shrine.
Mudd, James T. '64 (L) Hodgenville, KY Our Lady of Mercy Church; Howardstown, KY St. Ann Church.
Mudd, John '69 (WDC) Special Ministries; [D] Washington, DC Archbishop Carroll High School.
Mudrak, Lloyd '62 (DUL) Virginia, MN Holy Spirit Church; Virginia, MN Sacred Heart Church.
Mudry, Lubomyr '51 (STF) Staten Island, NY Holy Trinity Church.
Mueggenborg, Daniel H. '89 (TLS) [10] Tulsa, OK Church of the Madalene.
Muehlberger, Howard J. *s.s.e.* '71 (BUR) [E] Colchester, VT Society of St. Edmund.
Muehlberger, Howard J. *s.s.e.* '71 (FgM) Edmundite Foreign Missions.
Mueller, '36 (BRK) [R] Queens Village, NY Queen of Peace Residence.
Mueller, Anthony E. '36 (BRK) Retired.
Mueller, Charles L. '57 (NO) [6] Metairie, LA St. Christopher the Martyr Church; Metairie, LA East Jefferson General Hospital.
Mueller, Donald R. '61 (TOL) [I] Green Springs, OH St. Francis Health Care Center; [J] Green Springs, OH St. Francis Health Care Centre (ICF & Skilled).
Mueller, Eugene *s.t.* '55 (FgM) Trinity Missions.
Mueller, Eugene J. '56 (CIN) Retired.
Mueller, Francis E. *s.j.* '53 (FBK) Barrow, AK St. Patrick Church; [C] Fairbanks, AK Jesuit Residence.
Mueller, Gary A. *c.m.* '95 (DEN) [12] Denver, CO Holy Ghost Church; [P] Denver, CO Auraria Campus.
Mueller, George E. '59 (DOD) Fowler, KS St. Anthony Church; Meade, KS St. John the Baptist Church; Plains, KS St. Patrick Church.
Mueller, Glenn *s.j.* '73 (KC) [14] Kansas City, MO Guardian Angels Church.
Mueller, Glenn P. *s.j.* '73 (KC) [J] Kansas City, MO Rockhurst College - Jesuit Community.
Mueller, James *o.carm.* '69 (PHX) [5] Glendale, AZ St. Raphael Church.
Mueller, James J. '66 (BRK) [152] Queens, NY St. Anthony of Padua Church.
Mueller, John F. *s.m.* '41 (CIN) [M] Huntsville, OH St. George Chapel of Marianist Community.
Mueller, John J. *s.j.* (STL) [C] St. Louis, MO Saint Louis University.
Mueller, John J. '59 (CLV) Wooster, OH St. Mary of the Immaculate Conception Church.
Mueller, John J. *s.j.* '75 (STL) [P] St. Louis, MO Jesuit Community Corporation at St. Louis University - Jesuit Hall.
Mueller, Joseph G. *s.j.* (DET) [K] Detroit, MI Jesuit Provincial Office-Detroit Province of the Society of Jesus.
Mueller, Joseph J. '44 (MIL) Retired.
Mueller, Joseph P. '39 (BEL) Retired.
Mueller, Kevin '92 (BAL) [72] Baltimore, MD Our Lady of Mount Carmel Church.
Mueller, Matthias R. *o.p.* '49 (CHI) [173] Chicago, IL St. Pius V Church; [N] Chicago, IL Dominican Community.
Mueller, Maurice M. '48 (FAR) Retired; [E] Fargo, ND Riverview Place, Inc.; [F] Fargo, ND Presentation Center-Sacred Heart Convent.
Mueller, Michael '85 (ORL) On Duty Outside the Diocese.
Mueller, Noel *o.s.b.* '68 (IND) [B] St. Meinrad, IN St. Meinrad Seminary-College of Liberal Arts; [J] St. Meinrad, IN St. Meinrad Archabbey.
Mueller, Paul '49 (TOL) Bowling Green, OH St. Thomas More University Parish; Retired.
Mueller, Paul R. *s.j.* '93 (CHI) [N] Chicago, IL Chicago Province of the Society of Jesus-Provincial Office.
Mueller, Richard J. '44 (IND) Retired.
Mueller, Richard J. '63 (CHI) Northbrook, IL St. Norbert Church.
Mueller, Richard J. '66 (PIT) On Duty Outside the Diocese.
Mueller, Richard J. '66 (VEN) [1] Venice, FL Epiphany Cathedral.
Mueller, Robert F. '46 (MIL) [7] Milwaukee, WI St. Anthony Church; Retired.
Mueller, Roman *s.d.s.* (PHX) [17] Phoenix, AZ St. Mark Church.
Muellerleile, Ernest H. '44 (ANC) [5] Anchorage, AK Holy Cross Church.
Muench, Joseph '81 (LEX) Harrodsburg, KY St. Andrew Church.
Muench, R. Francis '81 (RIC) [3] Hampton, VA St. Rose of Lima Church.
Muench, William G. '59 (OG) Crown Point, NY Sacred Heart Church; Ticonderoga, NY St. Mary Church.
Muerder, Edward E. '58 (BUF) Bliss, NY St. Joseph Church; Java Center, NY St. Patrick Church; North Java, NY St. Nicholas Church.
Muesenfechter, Msgr. Robert J. '51 (STL) Fenton, MO St. Paul Church.
Muessiggang, Emmanuel *o.f.m.* (OAK) [P] Danville, CA San Damiano Retreat.
Mugan, William L. *s.j.* '55 (STL) [P] St. Louis, MO Jesuit Community Corporation at St. Louis University - Jesuit Hall.
Mugavero, Anthony P. '81 (ROC) [10] Rochester, NY St. Bridget Church; [37] Rochester, NY Our Lady of Perpetual Help Church.
Muggli, Boniface *o.s.b.* '90 (BIS) [A] Richardton, ND Assumption Abbey.
Muggli, Florian *o.s.b.* '51 (SCL) St. Joseph, MN St. Joseph's Church.
Muggli, Odo *o.s.b.* '66 (BIS) [A] Richardton, ND Assumption Abbey.
Muguerza, Octavio '92 (GAL) [18] Houston, TX St. Cecilia Church.
Muha, Edward J. '45 (HRT) Retired.
Muha, Joseph '60 (B) Cottonwood, ID St. Mary's Church.
Muha, Peter J. '88 (GRY) [5] Hammond, IN St. John Bosco Church.
Muheim, Martin *o.s.b.* '88 (PBL) [D] Canon City, CO Centura Health-St. Thomas More Hospital.
Muheim, Martin de Porres J. *o.s.b.* '88 (PBL) [F] Canon City, CO Holy Cross Abbey.
Muhich, Peter '89 (DUL) Proctor, MN St. Rose Catholic Church.
Muhiirwa, Robert *c.s.c.* '95 (FTW) [13] South Bend, IN St. Jude Church.
Muhlbaier, Howard E. '65 (CAM) Atco, NJ Assumption Church.
Muhlen, Micah *o.f.m.* '91 (PIT) Hopewell Township, PA Our Lady of Fatima Church.
Muhm, William (NY) [205] Staten Island, NY Holy Family Church.
Muhr, Michael '83 (SP) [2] Tampa, FL Christ the King Church.
Muhs, Edward J. '51 (RVC) Bellmore, NY St. Barnabas the Apostle Church; Retired.
Muir, Edmund D. '49 (DET) Retired.
Muir, Gavin W. (PH) Ridley Park, PA St. Madeline Church.
Muir, Gavin W. '65 (PH) [72] Philadelphia, PA Saint Irenaeus Church.
Muka, John R. *c.s.sp.* '39 (PH) [AA] Bensalem, PA Congregation of the Holy Ghost.
Mukalel, Joseph (NEW) Rahway, NJ St. Mary's Church.
Mukasa, Michael '96 (PIT) [62] Pittsburgh, PA St. Pius X Church.
Mula, Zarco *o.f.m.conv.* '85 (BUF) [7] Lackawanna, NY Our Lady of Bistrica Church.
Mulanjanany, Augustine '69 (LKC) Fenton, LA St. Charles Borromeo Church.
Mulcahy, Daniel R., Jr. '79 (WOR) Linwood, MA Good Shepherd Church.
Mulcahy, Msgr. Donal '51 (LA) Retired.
Mulcahy, Gerald F. '62 (CHI) Hickory Hills, IL St. Patricia Church.
Mulcahy, Howard J. '44 (ALB) Retired.
Mulcahy, Msgr. James R. '37 (LA) La Puente, CA St. Louis of France Church; Retired.
Mulcahy, John M. *c.s.c.* '65 (FTW) [J] South Bend, IN Congregation of Holy Cross Indiana Province Provincial House.
Mulcahy, Louis *o.s.b.* '89 (IND) [J] St. Meinrad, IN St. Meinrad Archabbey.
Mulcahy, Patrick J. '95 (SD) Calexico, CA Our Lady of Guadalupe Church.
Mulcahy, Richard E. *s.j.* '46 (SFR) [N] San Francisco, CA Jesuit Community at University of San Francisco.
Mulcahy, Sean C. '62 (MIA) [11] Fort Lauderdale, FL St. Maurice Church.

Mulcair, William W. *m.s.* '65 (HRT) [M] Hartford, CT Missionaries of LaSalette Provincial Secretary.
Mulchahey, Andrew *l.c.* '94 (DAL) [M] Irving, TX Legionaries of Christ.
Mulcrone, Charles '53 (SFD) Retired.
Mulcrone, Charles P. (SFD) [K] Springfield, IL Priests' Retirement Facility.
Mulcrone, Joseph '71 (CHI) [X] Chicago, IL Catholic Office of the Deaf.
Mulcrone, Joseph A. '71 (CHI) [64] Chicago, IL St. Francis Borgia Church.
Mulcrone, Thomas *s.j.* '46 (NO) [C] New Orleans, LA Loyola University.
Mulcrone, Thomas '77 (CHI) [144] Chicago, IL Notre Dame Church.
Mulderry, Anthony J. '67 (MIA) Sunrise, FL All Saints Church.
Muldoon, Brendan '64 (SP) Indian Rocks Beach, FL St. Jerome Church; [F] Largo, FL St. Jerome Early Childhood Center.
Muldoon, P. Christopher '71 (PAT) Lake Hopatcong, NJ Our Lady Star of the Sea Church.
Muldowney, James D. '52 (ARL) Middleburg, VA St. Stephen the Martyr Church.
Mulert, Donovan *m.s.c.* '54 (Y) [A] Youngstown, OH Sacred Heart Retreat House & Renewal Center.
Mulewski, Patrick M. '79 (NEW) Ridgewood, NJ Our Lady of Mount Carmel Church.
Mulgrew, John E. '56 (PH) [63] Philadelphia, PA Holy Spirit Church.
Mulhall, Emmanuel F. *o.praem.* '41 (GB) [I] De Pere, WI St. Norbert Abbey.
Mulhall, Msgr. Francis X. '47 (BRK) Retired; [U] Douglaston, NY Bishop Mugavero Residence.
Mulhall, J. Gregory '37 (ALB) Retired.
Mulhall, John W. *c.s.p.* '56 (LA) [86] Los Angeles, CA St. Paul the Apostle Church.
Mulhall, John W. *c.s.p.* '56 (NY) [DD] Jamaica Estates, NY Paulist Fathers Generalate.
Mulhall, Michael M. *o.carm.* '67 (NEW) Cresskill, NJ St. Therese of Lisieux Church.
Mulhauser, Daniel J. *s.j.* '60 (CI) Koror, FM Sacred Heart Church; [C] Koror, Palau, PW Manresa Jesuit House.
Mulhauser, Daniel J. *s.j.* '60 (FgM) Provinces.
Mulhearn, Michael *c.m.* '68 (KC) [J] Kansas City, MO Vincentian Parish Mission Center.
Mulhern, Bernard J. *s.j.* '51 (CHI) [T] Barrington, IL Bellarmine Hall.
Mulhern, James P. *o.f.m.* '44 (SP) [O] St. Petersburg, FL St. Anthony Friary.
Mulhern, Joseph Hugh *o.p.* '54 (NY) [DD] New York, NY St. Vincent Ferrer Priory.
Mulhern, Kevin P. '76 (SCR) Honesdale, PA St. John the Evangelist Church.
Mulhern, Lucian *o.f.m.* '50 (PAT) [M] Ringwood, NJ Holy Name Friary, Inc.
Mulhern, Lucian A. *o.f.m.* '62 (FgM) Franciscan Foreign Missions.
Mulhern, Patrick F. '64 (ATL) Decatur, GA St. Thomas More Church.
Mulhern, Raymond F. '52 (COV) Retired.
Mulholland, Charles H. (R) Retired.
Mulholland, John '65 (PH) Levittown, PA Immaculate Conception B.V.M. Church.
Mulica, James '67 (CLV) Retired.
Mulka, Arthur C. '51 (GAY) Retired.
Mulka, Raymond C. '49 (GAY) Retired.
Mulkerin, Terrence J. '61 (BRK) Military Chaplains.
Mulkern, Daniel *t.o.r.* (ALT) [F] Loretto, PA Mount Assisi Friary.
Mulkern, John F. '43 (BO) Retired.
Mulkern, Stephen M. '49 (PRT) Retired.
Mull, Thomas P. '76 (ROC) [1] Rochester, NY Sacred Heart Cathedral; [L] Rochester, NY Apostleship of Prayer.
Mullady, Brian T. *o.p.* '72 (NOR) [A] Cromwell, CT Holy Apostles College and Seminary.
Mullady, Brian T. *o.p.* '72 (SFR) [13] San Francisco, CA St. Dominic Church; [N] San Francisco, CA St. Dominic Priory.
Mullakkara, Joseph *m.s.f.s.* '75 (ATL) Norcross, GA Saint Patrick's Church.
Mullally, Gerald F. '76 (SCR) Milford, PA St. Patrick's Church.
Mullally, Thomas A. *s.v.d.* '70 (LAF) St. Martinville, LA Notre Dame de Perpetuel Secours Church.
Mullaly, Conor *o.f.m.* '51 (FgM) Franciscan Foreign Missions.
Mullan, Glen '94 (CC) On Special Assignment.
Mullan, Patrick '67 (PAT) Retired; [P] Chester, NJ Nazareth Village.
Mullan, Raymund A. '62 (FWT) Graham, TX St. Mary Church; Olney, TX St. Theresa of the Infant Jesus Church.
Mullan, William F. *m.m.* '62 (FgM) Maryknoll Foreign Missions.
Mullan, William F. *m.m.* '62 (NY) [DD] Maryknoll, NY Maryknoll Fathers and Brothers.
Mullane, Bernard J. '56 (RCK) Belvidere, IL St. James Church.
Mullane, Thomas '68 (MIA) Big Pine Key, FL St. Peter Church.
Mullaney, Aidan *t.o.r.* '52 (STU) [A] Steubenville, OH Franciscan University of Steubenville.
Mullaney, Aidan *t.o.r.* '54 (STU) [F] Steubenville, OH Holy Spirit Monastery.
Mullaney, Msgr. Bernard C. '58 (SAT) Retired; [K] San Antonio, TX Casa De Padres.
Mullaney, Cornelius J. '71 (BO) Braintree, MA St. Thomas More Church.
Mullaney, Edward John *o.c.s.o.* '73 (WOR) [A] Spencer, MA St. Joseph's Abbey School of Theology and Institute of Monastic Studies; [N] Spencer, MA St. Joseph's Abbey.
Mullaney, Gregory C. '90 (PBR) Tarentum, PA Sts. Peter and Paul Church.
Mullaney, Lawrence '88 (RIC) Clifton Forge, VA St. Joseph Church.
Mullaney, Leonard '62 (FR) East Falmouth, MA St. Anthony's Church.
Mullarkey, John T. '64 (GB) Kaukauna, WI Holy Cross Church.
Mullarkey, Msgr. Patrick J. '64 (SD) [25] San Diego, CA St. Columba Church.
Mullelly, Thomas J. '80 (TR) [S] Princeton, NJ Campus Ministry for the Diocese of Trenton.
Mullen, Anthony P. *c.s.sp.* '90 (BRK) [144] Brooklyn, NY St. Vincent Ferrer Church.
Mullen, Austin M. '65 (SP) [11] Tampa, FL St. Mark the Evangelist Church.
Mullen, Bernard *c.pp.s.* (KCK) Blue Rapids, KS St. Elizabeth Church; Frankfort, KS Annunciation Church; Waterville, KS St. Monica's Church.
Mullen, Bernard J. '61 (DET) Lake Orion, MI St. Joseph Church.
Mullen, Charles F. *s.j.* '43 (OM) [K] Omaha, NE Jesuit Community At Creighton University.
Mullen, Charles F. *c.pp.s.* '64 (FTW) Rome City, IN St. Gaspar del Bufalo Church.
Mullen, David J. '82 (BO) Bellingham, MA St. Brendan Church.
Mullen, Dennis M. '70 (SUP) Cumberland, WI St. Anthony The Abbot Church.
Mullen, Msgr. Edward F. '54 (CAM) Ocean City, NJ St. Augustine's Church.
Mullen, Edward F. '58 (CHR) Retired.
Mullen, Francis '36 (ALB) Retired.
Mullen, Godfrey *o.s.b.* '94 (IND) [J] St. Meinrad, IN St. Meinrad Archabbey.
Mullen, John '52 (WCH) Retired.
Mullen, John J. *s.j.* (BO) Boston, MA Nashua Street Jail.
Mullen, John J. '49 (RVC) Selden, NY St. Margaret of Scotland Church; Retired.
Mullen, John J. *s.j.* '62 (BO) [W] Boston, MA The Society of Jesus of New England-Provincial Offices; [W] Weston, MA Campion Center.
Mullen, Joseph *o.f.m.cap.* '47 (NY) [57] New York, NY St. John the Baptist Church.
Mullen, Joseph A. '48 (BRK) Retired.
Mullen, Joseph E. *s.j.* '50 (BO) [W] Boston, MA The Society of Jesus of New England-Provincial Offices.
Mullen, Joseph E. *s.j.* '50 (SD) Carlsbad, CA St. Patrick Church.
Mullen, Kevin J. *o.f.m.* '80 (BO) [BB] Boston, MA St. Anthony Shrine.
Mullen, L. James '53 (PH) [X] Philadelphia, PA St. John Neumann Nursing Home.
Mullen, Michael '62 (KCK) [14] Kansas City, KS St. Patrick's Church.
Mullen, Michael *i.c.* '75 (VEN) Bradenton, FL Sacred Heart Church.
Mullen, Michael F. *c.m.* '41 (BRK) [U] Jamaica, NY Vincentian Residence.
Mullen, Owen J. '64 (NY) West Point, NY Catholic Chapel of the Most Holy Trinity Church.
Mullen, Owen J. '64 (WIL) Military Chaplains.
Mullen, Patrick '85 (LA) Graduate Studies.
Mullen, Paul M. '73 (SCR) Mountaintop, PA St. Jude's Church.
Mullen, Peter P. *m.m.* '62 (NY) [DD] Maryknoll, NY Maryknoll Fathers and Brothers.
Mullen, Peter P. *m.m.* '62 (OG) Ray Brook, NY Federal Correctional Institution.
Mullen, Richard '55 (PEO) Retired.
Mullen, Richard *o.s.a.* '81 (FgM) Foreign Missions.
Mullen, Richard G. *o.s.a.* '81 (FgM) Foreign Missions.
Mullen, Thomas (BRK) Brooklyn, NY Veterans Administration Medical Center.
Mullen, Thomas '56 (LKC) On Duty Outside the Diocese.
Mullen, Timothy F. *o.praem.* '73 (WIL) [B] Claymont, DE Archmere Academy; [I] Claymont, DE Immaculate Conception Priory of the Canons Regular of Premontre.
Mullen, William *o.m.v.* '92 (SFD) [2] Alton, IL Immaculate Conception-St. Mary's Church; [3] Alton, IL St. Patrick Church.
Mullen, William E. '76 (ALT) Cresson, PA St. Aloysius Church.
Mullen, Msgr. William J. '47 (OAK) Retired.
Mullen, Msgr. William J. '51 (HRT) [4] West Hartford, CT St. Mark the Evangelist Church.
Muller, Anthony '68 (CIN) [73] Cincinnati, OH Our Lord, Christ the King Church.
Muller, Earl C. *s.j.* '77 (NO) [P] New Orleans, LA Jesuit Provincial Office.
Muller, Francis J. *o.f.m.* '42 (NY) [35] New York, NY St. Francis of Assisi Church.
Muller, Herman J. *s.j.* '41 (DET) [K] Detroit, MI Jesuit Community at the University of Detroit.
Muller, James B. *o.p.* '59 (NY) Hawthorne, NY Holy Rosary Church.
Muller, Joseph *m.s.c.* '58 (RCK) [H] Aurora, IL Missionaries of the Sacred Heart Community.
Muller, Joseph T. *m.s.c.* '58 (RCK) [10] Aurora, IL St. Therese of Jesus Church.
Muller, Kennard '66 (BAL) Retired.
Muller, Martin M. '57 (BIR) [16] Birmingham, AL Our Lady of Sorrows Church.
Muller, Myles '48 (BAL) Retired; [J] Timonium, MD Stella Maris Operating Corporation.
Muller, Noel *o.s.b.* '68 (IND) [A] St. Meinrad, IN St. Meinrad Seminary.
Muller, Peter D. *o.praem.* '93 (ORG) [H] Silverado, CA Norbertine Fathers of Orange Inc.
Muller, William H. *s.j.* '73 (SJ) [D] San Jose, CA Bellarmine College Preparatory.
Mullet, John W. '91 (SAG) Essexville, MI St. John the Evangelist Church.
Mullett, Msgr. Gene W. '76 (STU) Bellaire, OH St. John Church; Bellaire, OH St. Michael's Church.
Mulligan, Bede J.K. *o.carm.* '58 (GBG) [H] New Florence, PA Mount Carmel Hermitage.
Mulligan, Bernard *c.ss.r.* '42 (SEA) [32] Seattle, WA Sacred Heart of Jesus Church.
Mulligan, Bertram *o.f.m.cap.* '49 (SFR) [N] Burlingame, CA Capuchin Provincial House.
Mulligan, Charles '64 (ROC) [M] Rochester, NY Diocesan Office of Campus Ministry; [M] Penn Yan, NY St. Michael's Church.
Mulligan, Edward J. '56 (SP) [3] Clearwater, FL St. Brendan Church.
Mulligan, Emmett *o.f.m.* '52 (PMB) [D] West Palm Beach, FL St. Mary's Hospital, Inc.
Mulligan, George B. *c.s.c.* '82 (PRT) Saco, ME Most Holy Trinity Church.
Mulligan, James J. (PH) [39] Philadelphia, PA St. Dominic Church.
Mulligan, Msgr. James J. '61 (ALN) Northampton, PA Our Lady of Hungary Church.
Mulligan, John D. *s.m.* '57 (CIN) [M] Dayton, OH Marianist Provincialate.
Mulligan, John M. *v.g.* '64 (ROC) Henrietta, NY Church of the Good Shepherd; Rush, NY St. Joseph Church.
Mulligan, John T. '64 (NY) [101] New York, NY Our Saviour Church.
Mulligan, Joseph E. *s.j.* (DET) [K] Detroit, MI Jesuit Provincial Office-Detroit Province of the Society of Jesus.
Mulligan, Joseph E. *s.j.* '73 (FgM) Provinces.
Mulligan, Joseph V. '75 (CHL) [7] Charlotte, NC St Luke Church.
Mulligan, Louis J. '61 (DAV) Special Assignment.
Mulligan, Patrick Daniel Columba *m.s.c.* (CC) Zapata, TX Our Lady of Lourdes Church.
Mulligan, Paul F. '57 (BO) Ashland, MA St. Cecilia Church.
Mulligan, Robert G. *o.s.f.s.* '85 (PH) [AA] Philadelphia, PA Father Judge Faculty House.
Mulligan, Robert H. '90 (PH) South Coventry, PA St. Thomas More Church.
Mulligan, Robert W. *s.j.* '49 (CHI) [C] Chicago, IL Jesuit Community at Loyola University of Chicago.
Mulligan, William *s.s.* (BO) [W] Cambridge, MA Weston Jesuit Community.
Mulligan, William J. *s.j.* (BO) Brighton, MA Vencor Hospital Boston; Cambridge, MA Youville Lifecare, Inc.
Mulligan, William L. *s.j.* '65 (BO) [R] Cambridge, MA Youville Hospital & Rehabilitation Center, Inc.; [U] Cambridge, MA Youville Healthcare Center, Inc.; [W] Cambridge, MA Faber House; [FF] Cambridge, MA The Youville House, Inc.
Mulligan, William R. '45 (BUR) Retired.
Mullin, Douglas *o.s.b.* (SCL) [I] Collegeville, MN St. John's Abbey, of the Order of St. Benedict.
Mullin, Edward J. *c.m.* '54 (STL) [P] Perryville, MO Congregation of The Mission.
Mullin, Francis R. *o.p.* '71 (HBG) [I] Lancaster, PA Monastery of the Dominican Nuns of the Perpetual Rosary.
Mullin, Henry *c.s.sp.* '59 (MIA) [5] Fort Lauderdale, FL St. Clement Church.
Mullin, Hugh J. '46 (KC) Retired.
Mullin, Jay M. '69 (BO) Health Leave.
Mullin, John A. *s.j.* '75 (NY) [DD] New York, NY Jesuit Community at Fordham University; [GG] New York, NY University Apostolate.
Mullin, John F. *s.j.* '65 (BO) [W] Boston, MA The Society of Jesus of New England-Provincial Offices; [W] Chestnut Hill, MA The Jesuit Community at

Boston College.
Mullin, John F. *s.j.* '65 (MAN) Lebanon, NH Sacred Heart Church; Hanover, NH Mary Hitchcock Hospital.
Mullin, Patrick J. '75 (LA) [R] Los Angeles, CA Amat House; [X] Montebello, CA DePaul Center.
Mullin, Thomas '65 (NY) Military Chaplains.
Mullin, Thomas M. '75 (ALN) [A] Northampton, PA Mary Immaculate Seminary.
Mullin, Thomas M. '75 (PH) [A] Wynnewood, PA Theological Seminary of St. Charles Borromeo, Overbrook.
Mullin, William H. '64 (BO) Braintree, MA St. Francis of Assisi Church.
Mullink, Michael D. '88 (SFD) Arcola, IL St. John the Baptist Church; Tuscola, IL Forty Martyrs Church.
Mullins, Carlos A. '55 (NY) [102] New York, NY St. Patrick Old Cathedral; [124] Bronx, NY St. Angela Merici Church.
Mullins, Charles R. '50 (HRT) [3] Bristol, CT St. Gregory's Church.
Mullins, Kevin C. *o.s.a.* '90 (ORL) Casselberry, FL St. Augustine Church.
Mullins, Patrick *c.m.* '39 (CHI) [C] Chicago, IL Vincentian Community at DePaul University.
Mullins, Msgr. Raymond '52 (PT) Fort Walton Beach, FL St. Mary Church.
Mullins, Richard A. '95 (ARL) Annandale, VA St. Michael's Church.
Mullins, Robert J. '45 (FAR) Retired.
Mullowney, Edward J. *s.s.j.* '55 (BAL) [M] Baltimore, MD St. Joseph Society of the Sacred Heart House of Central Administration.
Mullowney, Thomas E. '55 (GI) Retired.
Mulloy, Francis *c.s.sp.* '52 (SFR) Millbrae, CA St. Dunstan Church.
Mulloy, James *s.d.b.* '85 (BO) [E] Boston, MA Don Bosco Preparatory School.
Mulloy, John F. '70 (BO) Saugus, MA Blessed Sacrament Church.
Mulloy, Matthew F. '53 (NY) Absent on Sick leave.
Mulloy, Michel '79 (RC) [2] Rapid City, SD Blessed Sacrament Church.
Mulloy, Sylvester '38 (JOL) Retired.
Mulloy, William '54 (NY) Absent on Leave.
Mulnix, John Gabriel R. *c.p.* '68 (CHI) [N] Chicago, IL Passionist Provincial Office.
Mulnix, John R. *c.p.* '68 (BEL) [J] Belleville, IL Scott Air Force Base.
Mulqueen, John C. '53 (BRK) Retired.
MulQueen, John D. '34 (Y) East Liverpool, OH St. Aloysius Church.
Mulqueen, Joseph C. '57 (BRK) Released from Diocesan Assignment.
Mulqueen, Martin B. '74 (PMB) [2] Boca Raton, FL Our Lady of Lourdes Church.
Mulranen, Francis J. '82 (PH) Trooper, PA Visitation B.V.M. Church.
Mulranen, John J. '50 (SY) Retired.
Mulrenan, Alexus J. *o.f.m.* '60 (PAT) [M] Butler, NJ St. Anthony Friary.
Mulrenan, Donald P. *s.v.d.* '60 (BO) [W] Boston, MA Divine Word Missionaries.
Mulroney, Joseph G. *j.c.l.* '93 (R) Smithfield, NC St. Ann Church.
Mulrooney, Charles F. '42 (SCR) Retired; [N] Dunmore, PA Villa St. Joseph.
Mulrooney, Conan P. *o.praem.* '67 (GB) [I] De Pere, WI St. Norbert Abbey.
Mulrooney, F. Harold '37 (SCR) Retired.
Mulroy, Richard D. *o.praem.* '40 (GB) [I] De Pere, WI St. Norbert Abbey.
Mulsoff, Donald J. '69 (CHI) [130] Chicago, IL St. Mary of Perpetual Help Church.
Mulvanerty, Thomas '65 (NY) Absent on Leave.
Mulvanerty, Thomas F. '79 (RVC) Farmingville, NY Church of the Resurrection.
Mulvanerty, Thomas M. '65 (OAK) Moraga, CA St. Monica Church.
Mulvaney, Andrew R. '68 (OG) Military Chaplains.
Mulvaney, James J. '53 (BIR) Retired.
Mulvanity, Francis C. '59 (CLV) [4] Euclid, OH St. Paul Church.
Mulvany, Michael '88 (KCK) Lapeer, KS St. Francis Church; Osage City, KS St. Patrick's Church; Scranton, KS St. Patrick's Church.
Mulvehill, John R. '57 (BO) Cohasset, MA St. Anthony Church.
Mulvehill, Louis J. '53 (ALT) South Fork, PA Most Holy Trinity Church.
Mulvey, Gerard *o.f.m.cap.* '91 (NY) [57] New York, NY St. John the Baptist Church; [X] New York, NY St. Rose's Home.
Mulvey, John J. '62 (NEW) On Duty Outside the Archdiocese.
Mulvey, John J. '62 (VEN) Port Charlotte, FL St. Charles Borromeo Church.
Mulvey, Michael '75 (AUS) On Duty Outside the Diocese.
Mulvihill, Daniel R. '53 (WCH) Retired.
Mulvihill, David J. '72 (CHI) Zion-Beach Park, IL Our Lady of Humility Church.
Mulvihill, John E. '65 (CHI) Graduate Studies.
Mulvihill, Martin J. '83 (STL) Hazelwood, MO St. Martin de Porres Church.
Mumper, Ed (JOL) Piper City, IL St. Peter Church.
Mun, Byung Hak, Joseph '83 (STL) Ellisville, MO St. Andrew Kim Korean Catholic Community Church.
Munari, Mario '50 (SR) Sonoma, CA St. Francis Solano Church.
Mundakal, Joseph A. *c.m.i.* '83 (JOL) Wheaton, IL St. Michael Church.
Mundell, Msgr. J. Joshua '47 (WDC) [22] Washington, DC Immaculate Conception Church.
Mundy, Joseph T. '81 (RVC) Wading River, NY St. John Baptist Church.
Mundy, Patrick W. '66 (OG) On Duty Outside the Diocese.
Mungari, Joseph *s.a.c.* '45 (CAM) [C] Pennsauken, NJ Bishop Eustace Prep School.
Munguia, Jorge *s.j.* '67 (MIA) [D] Miami, FL Belen Jesuit Preparatory School; [H] Miami, FL Villa Arrieta.
Muniz, Alberto '77 (PCE) Patillas, PR Inmaculado Corazon de Maria Church.
Muniz, Orlando Rosas '97 (MGZ) Moca, PR Our Lady of Monserrate Church.
Muniz, William '94 (MIA) [2] Fort Lauderdale, FL Our Lady Queen of Martyrs Church; [G] Fort Lauderdale, FL Holy Cross Hospital.
Munn, Daniel '80 (NTN) Augusta, GA St. Ignatios of Antioch Church.
Munn, Daniel '82 (SAV) [1] Augusta, GA Church of the Most Holy Trinity.
Munn, Daniel M. '82 (SAV) [E] Augusta, GA St. Joseph Hospital, Augusta, GA, Inc.
Munn, Thomas J. '51 (SC) Dayton, IA Christ the King Church; Ogden, IA St. John's Church.
Munoz, Antonio '60 (CGS) [10] Barrio Rio Canas, PR San Pedro Apostol Church.
Munoz, Arcadio '76 (NEW) [1] Hoboken, NJ Our Lady of Grace Church.
Munoz, Ariel '97 (LA) [15] Los Angeles, CA Immaculate Conception Church.
Munoz, Msgr. Ernesto '55 (ARE) Quebradillas, PR San Raphael Church.
Munoz, Eusiquio '64 (WOR) Milford, MA St. Mary of the Assumption Church.
Munoz, J. Francisco *s.d.b.* '73 (LA) [79] Los Angeles, CA St. Mary Church.
Munoz, Jose *c.m.* '90 (SJN) [27] San Juan, PR San Jose Obrero Church.
Munoz, Jose Antonio *c.m.f.* '90 (SJN) [9] Bayamon, PR San Jose Church.
Munoz, Jose F. '96 (ORL) Altamonte Springs, FL St. Mary Magdalen Church.
Munoz, Juan Francisco *s.d.b.* '73 (LA) [R] Los Angeles, CA Dominic Savio Salesian Residence.
Munoz, Rafael '60 (PCE) On Duty Outside the Diocese.
Munoz, Raul Saez '82 (SJN) [1] San Juan, PR Catedral De San Juan Bautista Church.
Munoz, Tomas G. '85 (TUC) Yuma, AZ Immaculate Conception Church.
Munro, Donald R. '87 (PMB) [1] Boca Raton, FL Ascension Church.
Munro, Hugh J. '57 (FR) [I] Taunton, MA Marian Manor Inc.
Munroe, Msgr. Henry T. *p.a.* '53 (FR) Centerville, MA Our Lady of Victory Church.
Munsch, Nathan *o.s.b.* (BO) [3] Brookline, MA St. Lawrence Church.
Munsch, Nathan *o.s.b.* '91 (GBG) [H] Latrobe, PA Saint Vincent Archabbey.
Munsell, Richard (BLX) Biloxi, MS Keesler Airforce Base.
Munsell, Richard F. '79 (GF) Military Chaplains.
Munshower, William G. '58 (IND) [38] Indianapolis, IN St. Thomas Aquinas Church.
Munson, Thomas N. (PBL) Retired.
Munster, Thomas P. *c.m.* '48 (CHI) [C] Chicago, IL Vincentian Community at DePaul University.
Muntone, Msgr. Anthony D. '64 (ALN) Whitehall, PA St. Elizabeth Church.
Muntz, James (NEW) [1] Garfield, NJ Our Lady of Mt. Virgin Church.
Munz, Theodore G. *s.j.* '83 (CHI) [D] Wilmette, IL Loyola Academy.
Munzing, Joel *o.f.m.* '47 (CAM) [M] Margate, NJ Franciscan Friars' Vacation Home.
Muodiaju, Samuel *c.s.sp.* '85 (MIA) [15] Miami, FL St. Agatha Church.
Muoneke, Romanus O. '74 (GAL) Kingwood, TX St. Martha Church.
Murasso, Jeremiah N. '79 (HRT) Naugatuck, CT St. Vincent Ferrer Church; Special and other (Arch)Diocesan Assignment; [G] New Haven, CT St. Francis Home for Children, Inc.; [V] New Haven, CT The Children's Foundation at St. Francis Home, Inc.
Murawski, Apolinary '34 (GBG) Retired; [G] Greensburg, PA Neumann House.
Murawski, Edward J. *s.j.* '66 (BO) [W] Boston, MA Loyola House.
Murcho, Charles S. '52 (E) Mercer, PA Immaculate Heart Church.
Murd, Francis A. '76 (TOL) Tiffin, OH St. Mary Church.
Murd, Frank A. '60 (TOL) Sycamore, OH St. Pius X Church.
Murdick, Msgr. Olin J. '45 (SAG) Retired.
Murdoch, Ian *s.d.b.* '69 (OAK) [N] Berkeley, CA Salesian Community.
Murdock, Paul J. '75 (NOR) Windham, CT Sagrado Corazon de Jesus Church.
Murhammer, Francis J. '88 (PIT) [38] Pittsburgh, PA Sacred Heart Church.
Murimi, Michael '88 (ROC) [I] Rochester, NY Basilian Residence.
Murnan, Sean *o.f.m.* '73 (SFE) Los Ojos, NM San Jose Church; Tierra Amarilla, NM Santo Nino Church.
Murnane, Patrick J. '60 (MIA) Hollywood, FL Nativity Church.
Murnane, Theodore *s.v.d.* '59 (FgM) Society of the Divine Word Foreign Missions.
Murnane, Thomas M. *o.s.a.* '65 (PH) [AA] Villanova, PA St. Thomas Monastery.
Murnion, Msgr. Philip J. '63 (NY) [88] New York, NY Our Lady of Loreto Church; On Duty Outside the Archdiocese.
Muro, Msgr. Victor S. '66 (CAM) [3] Vineland, NJ St. Francis of Assisi Church; [P] Vineland, NJ Spanish Catholic Center.
Murphy, Alfred E. *o.s.a.* '56 (PH) [B] Villanova, PA St. Augustine Friary; [AA] Villanova, PA Provincial Offices of the Order of St. Augustine, Province of St. Thomas of Villanova.
Murphy, Arthur J. '55 (HRT) [6] West Hartford, CT St. Thomas the Apostle Church.
Murphy, B. James '78 (CHI) [A] Mundelein, IL University of St. Mary of the Lake-Mundelein Seminary.
Murphy, Bartholomew J. *s.j.* '72 (FgM) Provinces.
Murphy, Bartholomew J. *s.j.* '72 (P) [L] Portland, OR Jesuit Provincial Office (Society of Jesus, Oregon Prov.).
Murphy, Brendan *s.v.d.* (LAF) Broussard, LA St. Joseph Church.
Murphy, Brian *o.carm.* '58 (ROC) [B] Rochester, NY McQuaid Jesuit High School; [I] Rochester, NY Whitefriars Priory.
Murphy, Campion *s.t.* '56 (PAT) [M] Stirling, NJ Holy Spirit Missionary Cenacle.
Murphy, Charles *s.a.* '61 (NY) [DD] Garrison, NY Franciscan Friars of the Atonement.
Murphy, Charles C. *s.j.* '62 (FgM) Provinces.
Murphy, Charles C. *s.j.* '62 (MIL) [P] Milwaukee, WI Jesuit Provincial Office, Wisconsin Province.
Murphy, Charles J. '60 (BO) [2] Weymouth, MA St. Francis Xavier Church.
Murphy, Charles J. '76 (SUP) On Leave.
Murphy, Msgr. Charles M. '61 (PRT) Falmouth, ME Holy Martyrs Church.
Murphy, Charles R. '91 (OKL) Guymon, OK St. Peter's Church; [K] Norman, OK Campus Ministry for the Archdiocese of Oklahoma City.
Murphy, Christopher '96 (ARL) [7] Alexandria, VA St. Mary's Church.
Murphy, Clarence '20 (FR) Retired.
Murphy, Columba *o.f.m.* '41 (SP) [O] St. Petersburg, FL St. Anthony Friary.
Murphy, Msgr. D. Declan '49 (MRY) Carmel, CA San Carlos Borromeo Basilica Church.
Murphy, Daniel A. '39 (NEW) Retired; [B] South Orange, NJ Seton Hall University.
Murphy, Daniel C. '51 (SB) [E] Hemet, CA Holy Ghost Fathers.
Murphy, Daniel G. '56 (SY) Windsor, NY Our Lady of Lourdes Church.
Murphy, Daniel J. '56 (DET) Bloomfield Hills, MI St. Regis Church.
Murphy, Daniel S. '70 (BRK) [7] Brooklyn, NY St. Andrew the Apostle Church.
Murphy, Daniel T. '62 (MIL) [N] Greenfield, WI Clement Manor Health Center.
Murphy, Daniel W. '73 (PAT) Sparta, NJ Blessed Kateri Tekakwitha Church.
Murphy, David *o.carm.* '42 (JOL) [J] Darien, IL Carmelite Provincial Office.
Murphy, David C. '63 (BO) [5] Brockton, MA Our Lady of Lourdes Church; Awaiting Assignment.
Murphy, David F. '87 (WIL) Claymont, DE Holy Rosary Church; Wilmington, DE Delaware Army National Guard.
Murphy, David M. (ROC) Retired.
Murphy, Denis J. '53 (LA) Retired.
Murphy, Dennis '74 (RIC) On Duty Outside the Diocese.
Murphy, Dennis *s.a.* '89 (WDC) [B] Washington, DC Atonement Seminary-Franciscan Friars of the Atonement.
Murphy, Dennis P. '75 (ALB) [1] Albany, NY Cathedral of the Immaculate Conception; Unassigned.
Murphy, Desmond P. '57 (WDC) Retired.
Murphy, Donald J. *s.j.* '61 (FgM) Provinces.
Murphy, Edward (ALB) [H] Troy, NY Seton Health System, Inc.

Murphy, Edward *s.j.* '43 (FgM) Provinces.
Murphy, Edward '93 (STA) Palm Coast, FL St. Elizabeth Ann Seton Church.
Murphy, Edward J. *s.j.* '68 (NY) [DD] New York, NY West Side Jesuit Community.
Murphy, Emmet *o.f.m.* '86 (NEW) [N] Hohokus, NJ St. Anthony of Padua.
Murphy, Eoin '64 (LAN) Clio, MI SS. Charles and Helena Church.
Murphy, Msgr. Eugene '34 (MAN) Retired.
Murphy, Msgr. Eugene F. '52 (RVC) Mineola, NY Corpus Christi Church; Mineola, NY Winthrop Hospital.
Murphy, F. Kevin '81 (NEW) [D] Summit, NJ The Oratory Catholic Preparatory School.
Murphy, Msgr. Francis '43 (R) Retired.
Murphy, Msgr. Francis '46 (MOB) Retired.
Murphy, Francis '58 (RNO) [6] Reno, NV St. Therese Church of the Little Flower.
Murphy, Msgr. Francis A. '57 (ANC) Retired.
Murphy, Msgr. Francis C. '46 (MOB) [4] Mobile, AL St. Dominic Church.
Murphy, Francis J. '51 (LIN) Ashland, NE St. Mary's Church.
Murphy, Francis J. *s.j.* '56 (KC) [B] Kansas City, MO Rockhurst College.
Murphy, Francis J. '58 (RNO) [2] Reno, NV Our Lady of the Snows Church.
Murphy, Francis J. '58 (WDC) On Duty Outside the Archdiocese.
Murphy, Francis J. '66 (GAY) Cadillac, MI St. Ann Church; Harietta, MI St. Edward Church.
Murphy, Francis J. *c.s.c.* '86 (FTW) [J] South Bend, IN Congregation of Holy Cross Indiana Province Provincial House.
Murphy, Francis W. '49 (NOR) Essex, CT Our Lady of Sorrows Church.
Murphy, Francis X. *c.ss.r.* '40 (BAL) Annapolis, MD St. Mary Church; [M] Annapolis, MD Saint Mary Rectory.
Murphy, Frank J. *s.j.* '56 (KC) [J] Kansas City, MO Rockhurst College - Jesuit Community.
Murphy, Frederick J. '57 (BO) [1] Boston, MA Cathedral of the Holy Cross.
Murphy, G. Ronald *s.j.* '69 (WDC) [M] Washington, DC The Jesuit Community at Georgetown University.
Murphy, George '66 (BLX) Hattiesburg, MS Sacred Heart Church.
Murphy, George R. *s.j.* '71 (BO) [W] Boston, MA The Society of Jesus of New England-Provincial Offices.
Murphy, George R. *s.j.* '71 (OAK) [A] Berkeley, CA The Jesuit School of Theology at Berkeley; [N] Berkeley, CA Jesuit Community at Jesuit School of Theology at Berkeley.
Murphy, Gerard '59 (SP) Brooksville, FL St. Anthony Church.
Murphy, Gerard '79 (SP) Ridge Manor, FL St. Anne Church.
Murphy, Gerasimos *b.s.o.* '67 (NTN) [A] Methuen, MA Seminary of St. Basil the Great.
Murphy, Gordon A. *o.f.m.* '55 (BO) [Z] Boston, MA Saint Anthony Residence.
Murphy, H. Joseph '61 (BO) Wakefield, MA St. Florence Church.
Murphy, Harold B. '68 (CHI) [207] Chicago, IL St. Timothy Church.
Murphy, Harry (SD) San Diego, CA Nazareth House.
Murphy, Harry '40 (SD) [G] San Diego, CA Nazareth House Retirement Home.
Murphy, Harry J. '40 (GBG) Retired.
Murphy, Henry *m.m.* '58 (STA) [H] Jacksonville, FL Maryknoll Fathers & Brothers.
Murphy, Henry J. *s.j.* '57 (BGP) [A] Fairfield, CT Fairfield University; [O] Fairfield, CT The Fairfield Jesuit Community-Fairfield University.
Murphy, Hugh J. '59 (NOR) Retired.
Murphy, Hugh P. '71 (PAT) [P] Morristown, NJ Priests Residence.
Murphy, Isaiah *o.s.b.* (CHI) [N] Chicago, IL Passionist Community-CTU.
Murphy, J. E. '60 (SFS) Huron, SD Church of the Resurrection.
Murphy, Msgr. J. Emmett '38 (ROC) Retired.
Murphy, J. Patrick *c.m.* '76 (CHI) [N] Chicago, IL Vincentian Community, Congregation of the Mission, Midwest Province.
Murphy, James (ORL) Retired.
Murphy, James *o.s.b.* '46 (OKL) Harrah, OK St. Teresa of Avila Church.
Murphy, James *c.s.c.* '58 (PRT) [J] Biddeford, ME Marie Joseph Spiritual Center.
Murphy, James '70 (MIA) Miami Lakes, FL Our Lady of the Lakes Church.
Murphy, James '78 (JOL) On Duty Outside the Diocese.
Murphy, James A. '39 (PH) Stowe, PA St. Gabriel Church; Retired.
Murphy, James D. *o.s.b.* '46 (OKL) [I] Shawnee, OK St. Gregory Abbey.
Murphy, James E. '52 (STL) Bridgeton, MO St. Lawrence the Martyr Church.
Murphy, James E. '55 (GI) Retired.
Murphy, James F. '47 (PH) Retired.
Murphy, James F. *c.s.c.* '58 (PRT) Saco, ME Most Holy Trinity Church; [L] Biddeford, ME Marie Joseph Spiritual Center.
Murphy, James F. '70 (PIT) [1] Butler, PA St. Fidelis of Sigmaringen Church.
Murphy, James H. '81 (MAD) Platteville, WI St. Augustine University Parish.
Murphy, James J. '45 (PH) Retired.
Murphy, James J. '52 (RCK) [4] Rockford, IL St. Edward Church.
Murphy, James J. '54 (WH) Weston, WV St. Patrick's Church.
Murphy, James P. '65 (CHI) Glenview, IL St. Catherine Laboure Church.
Murphy, James T. '68 (SAC) [11] Sacramento, CA St. Charles Borromeo Church.
Murphy, James W. '48 (MEM) Retired.
Murphy, James Wayne '65 (L) [73] Louisville, KY St. Thomas More Church.
Murphy, Jeremiah *m.s.c.* '46 (SAN) Big Spring, TX Immaculate Heart of Mary Church.
Murphy, Msgr. Jeremiah T. '63 (LA) [50] Los Angeles, CA St. Brendan Church.
Murphy, Jerome A. *c.ss.r.* '51 (SP) [9] Tampa, FL St. Joseph Church.
Murphy, Jerome J. '43 (NY) Retired.
Murphy, John (MRY) [H] Soquel, CA St. Clare's Retreat.
Murphy, John '50 (LA) On Duty Outside the Archdiocese.
Murphy, John *o.f.m.* '54 (HRT) [14] Hartford, CT St. Patrick-St. Anthony Church.
Murphy, John *f.m.s.i.* '72 (BO) [B] Framingham, MA Sylva Maria.
Murphy, John '79 (MRY) Retired.
Murphy, John B. *o.s.f.s.* '57 (CHL) [I] High Point, NC Maryfield Nursing Home.
Murphy, John C. '65 (SP) St. Pete Beach, FL St. John Church.
Murphy, John D. *s.j.* '77 (SJ) [D] San Jose, CA Bellarmine College Preparatory.
Murphy, John D. '79 (MET) Colonia, NJ St. John Vianney Church; Perth Amboy, NJ Raritan Bay Medical Center.
Murphy, Msgr. John F. '47 (COV) Retired.
Murphy, Msgr. John F. '47 (MIL) Retired.
Murphy, John F. '59 (CLV) [1] Cleveland, OH Cathedral of St. John the Evangelist.
Murphy, John J. '39 (FR) Somerset, MA St. Thomas More Church; Retired.
Murphy, John J. *c.s.c.* '49 (FR) [A] North Easton, MA Holy Cross Fathers Religious.
Murphy, Msgr. John J. '51 (SFR) Retired.
Murphy, John J. '57 (ALB) Catskill, NY St. Patrick Church.
Murphy, John J. '68 (DEN) Evergreen, CO Christ the King Church.
Murphy, John M. (ATL) [L] Atlanta, GA Campus Ministry.
Murphy, John M. '45 (MIL) Retired.
Murphy, John M. '51 (NU) Retired.
Murphy, John M. '65 (CHI) [52] Chicago, IL St. Edward Church.
Murphy, John M. '94 (ATL) LaGrange, GA St. Peter's Church.
Murphy, John P. *o.s.a.* '57 (JOL) New Lenox, IL St. Jude Church.
Murphy, Msgr. John P. '64 (ALN) [11] Allentown, PA St. Thomas More Church.
Murphy, John P. *s.j.* '69 (CHI) [C] Chicago, IL Jesuit Community at Loyola University of Chicago.
Murphy, John T. *o.p.* (NY) Manhattan, NY Rockefeller University.
Murphy, John T. '31 (LC) Retired; [I] La Crosse, WI Holy Cross (Seminary) Diocesan Center.
Murphy, John Thaddeus *o.p.* '54 (NY) [22] New York, NY St. Catherine of Siena Church; [DD] New York, NY St. Catherine of Siena Priory.
Murphy, John V. *s.j.* '52 (P) [L] Portland, OR Colombiere Community; [Q] Portland, OR Jesuit Development & Communications Office.
Murphy, Joseph *o.m.i.* '27 (BO) [Z] Tewksbury, MA Immaculate Heart of Mary Novitiate-Infirmary.
Murphy, Joseph '61 (PAT) Totowa Borough, NJ St. James of the Marches Church.
Murphy, Joseph A. *s.j.* '73 (FgM) Provinces.
Murphy, Joseph F. '49 (PRO) Retired; [P] Providence, RI St. John Vianney Residence.
Murphy, Joseph G. '44 (HRT) Retired.
Murphy, Joseph H. '61 (NEW) Old Tappan, NJ St. Pius X Church.
Murphy, Joseph J. '43 (CHR) Retired.
Murphy, Msgr. Joseph P. '54 (NY) [202] Staten Island, NY St. Clare Church.
Murphy, Joseph P. '88 (NOR) Warrenville, CT St. Philip Church.
Murphy, Joseph R. *s.s.j.* (GAL) Retired.
Murphy, Joseph R. *s.s.j.* '43 (BAL) [M] Baltimore, MD St. Joseph Society of the Sacred Heart House of Central Administration.
Murphy, Joseph T. '47 (PH) Glenside, PA St. Luke the Evangelist Church; Retired.
Murphy, Jude R. *o.f.m.* '61 (PRO) [P] Providence, RI St. Francis Friary.
Murphy, Kenneth *o.carm.* (PMB) [G] Boca Raton, FL St. Elias Priory-Order of Carmelites, NY.
Murphy, Kenneth *o.carm.* '81 (PMB) [B] Boca Raton, FL Pope John Paul II High School.
Murphy, Kenneth B. (BO) Retired.
Murphy, Kenneth J. '65 (IND) Military Chaplains.
Murphy, Kenneth R. '86 (MET) Spotswood, NJ Immaculate Conception Church.
Murphy, Kevin J. *o.s.b.* '62 (MIL) [P] Benet Lake, WI St. Benedict's Abbey.
Murphy, Kevin P. '68 (ROC) Penfield, NY St. Joseph Church.
Murphy, Laurence T. *m.m.* '54 (NY) [DD] Maryknoll, NY Maryknoll Fathers and Brothers.
Murphy, Lawrence B. *s.j.* '64 (LA) [F] Los Angeles, CA Loyola High School.
Murphy, Lawrence C. '50 (MIL) Retired.
Murphy, Lawrence F. '56 (BO) Retired.
Murphy, Lawrence J. '43 (PH) Retired.
Murphy, Lawrence V. '58 (ROC) [26] Rochester, NY Holy Rosary Church.
Murphy, Louis E. *s.t.* '60 (FgM) Trinity Missions.
Murphy, Martin F. *m.m.* '51 (FgM) Maryknoll Foreign Missions.
Murphy, Michael D. '66 (LAN) [1] Lansing, MI St. Mary Cathedral.
Murphy, Michael D. '77 (PH) [4] Drexel Hill, PA St. Dorothy Church.
Murphy, Michael F. '83 (SD) Coronado, CA Sacred Heart Church.
Murphy, Michael G. '87 (STL) [6] Florissant, MO St. Ferdinand Church.
Murphy, Michael J. *c.s.c.* '49 (FTW) [B] Notre Dame, IN University of Notre Dame Du Lac; [J] Notre Dame, IN Holy Cross Community, Corby Hall, University of Notre Dame.
Murphy, Michael P. '89 (JC) Kahoka, MO St. Michael the Archangel Church; St. Patrick, MO The Shrine of St. Patrick Church.
Murphy, Myles P. '90 (NY) [144] Bronx, NY St. Gabriel Church.
Murphy, Owen *s.a.* '52 (NY) [DD] Garrison, NY Franciscan Friars of the Atonement.
Murphy, Patrick *s.j.* (STA) Lake City, FL Epiphany Church.
Murphy, Patrick '53 (BIR) Madison, AL St. John the Baptist Church.
Murphy, Patrick '67 (LIN) [D] Lincoln, NE St. Elizabeth Community Health Center.
Murphy, Patrick E. '85 (MAR) Iron Mountain, MI Veterans Administration Hospital; [E] Iron Mountain, MI Monastery of the Holy Cross.
Murphy, Msgr. Patrick J. '50 (ALX) Tallulah, LA St. Edward Church.
Murphy, Patrick J. '53 (BIR) [I] Madison, AL St. John's Educational Foundation.
Murphy, Patrick Joseph '97 (SD) Carlsbad, CA St. Patrick Church.
Murphy, Patrick L. *s.j.* '67 (MIL) [P] Milwaukee, WI Jesuit Provincial Office, Wisconsin Province.
Murphy, Paul G. '94 (BGP) Shelton, CT St. Joseph's Church.
Murphy, Paul M. *c.m.* '60 (PH) [AA] Philadelphia, PA Congregation of the Mission.
Murphy, Peter J. '92 (BO) [1] Malden, MA Immaculate Conception Church.
Murphy, Peter P. '68 (PIT) Clairton, PA St. Clare of Assisi Church.
Murphy, Philip *ss.cc.* '70 (FR) [J] Fairhaven, MA Sacred Hearts Provincial House.
Murphy, Ralph J. *s.d.b.* '56 (OAK) [N] Berkeley, CA Salesian Community.
Murphy, Richard *o.p.* '35 (NO) [30] New Orleans, LA St. Dominic Church.
Murphy, Richard '57 (PMB) Fort Pierce, FL St. Mark Church.
Murphy, Richard '65 (PMB) Vero Beach, FL Holy Cross Church; [J] Palm Beach Gardens, FL Diocesan Property & Liability Insurance Committee.
Murphy, Richard '65 (ROC) [M] Rochester, NY Diocesan Office of Campus Ministry.
Murphy, Richard '80 (Y) Mineral Ridge, OH St. Mary's Church; [C] Youngstown, OH Ursuline High School.
Murphy, Richard Daniel '96 (BGP) [7] Norwalk, CT St. Thomas the Apostle Church.
Murphy, Richard J. *s.j.* '64 (TUC) [F] Tucson, AZ Jesuit Community of the Vatican Observatory.
Murphy, Richard J. '73 (BAL) Walkersville, MD St. Timothy Church.
Murphy, Robert '74 (KC) [2] St. Joseph, MO Our Lady of Guadalupe Church.
Murphy, Robert *m.ss.a.* '93 (NOR) [F] Cromwell, CT Missionaries of the Holy Apostles.
Murphy, Robert A. '93 (NOR) Old Saybrook, CT St. John Church.
Murphy, Msgr. Robert E. '42 (BUF) [1] Lackawanna,

NY Basilica of Our Lady of Victory Church; Retired.
Murphy, Robert J. *s.j.* '54 (LEX) [1] Lexington, KY Cathedral of Christ the King.
Murphy, Robert M. '93 (VEN) [3] Naples, FL St. Peter the Apostle Church.
Murphy, Roland *o.carm.* '42 (WDC) [B] Washington, DC Whitefriars Hall.
Murphy, Romeo J. *o.m.i.* (BO) Lowell, MA Saints Memorial Medical Center.
Murphy, Rory '88 (SFR) [2] San Rafael, CA St. Isabella Church.
Murphy, Msgr. Terrance J. '46 (STP) Retired.
Murphy, Msgr. Terrence J. '46 (STP) [C] St. Paul, MN University of St. Thomas.
Murphy, Theodore *s.m.m.* '58 (RVC) [N] Bay Shore, NY Montfort Missionaries.
Murphy, Thomas *o.f.m.cap.* (NY) Yonkers, NY St. Joseph Hospital.
Murphy, Thomas '36 (PIT) [K] Pittsburgh, PA Villa De Marillac Nursing Home.
Murphy, Thomas '43 (RVC) Mineola, NY Winthrop Hospital.
Murphy, Thomas *s.j.* '57 (NY) [161] Bronx, NY St. Margaret of Cortona Church.
Murphy, Thomas *m.s.c.* '65 (RCK) [H] Aurora, IL Missionaries of the Sacred Heart Community.
Murphy, Msgr. Thomas '66 (SAT) [61] San Antonio, TX St. Peter Prince of the Apostles Church.
Murphy, Thomas *o.f.m.cap.* '71 (NY) [17] Yonkers, NY Sacred Heart Church; [W] Yonkers, NY St. Joseph's Medical Center.
Murphy, Thomas '85 (IND) [21] Indianapolis, IN St. John the Evangelist Church.
Murphy, Thomas A. *s.j.* '39 (BGP) [O] Fairfield, CT The Fairfield Jesuit Community-Fairfield University.
Murphy, Thomas E. '73 (WDC) [B] Washington, DC Diocesan Laborer Priests, House of Studies.
Murphy, Thomas E. *o.s.f.s.* '76 (VEN) [3] Fort Myers, FL St. Cecilia Church.
Murphy, Thomas F. '51 (Y) Vienna, OH St. Vincent de Paul Church.
Murphy, Thomas F. '70 (RVC) Mineola, NY Corpus Christi Church.
Murphy, Thomas J. '87 (SAV) Perry, GA St. Patrick Church.
Murphy, Thomas K. *o.f.m.* '58 (SP) [O] St. Petersburg, FL St. Anthony Friary.
Murphy, Thomas M. '79 (PRT) Scarborough, ME St. Maximilian Kolbe Church.
Murphy, Thomas P. *c.s.p.* '62 (NY) [DD] Jamaica Estates, NY Paulist Fathers Generalate.
Murphy, Thomas R. '36 (PIT) Retired.
Murphy, Timothy *o.ss.t.* '67 (BAL) [L] Baltimore, MD Holy Trinity Spiritual Center; [M] Baltimore, MD Holy Trinity Monastery.
Murphy, Timothy '67 (P) [C] Portland, OR Central Catholic High School.
Murphy, Timothy *glmy.* '93 (JKS) Aberdeen, MS St. Francis of Assisi Church.
Murphy, Msgr. Timothy J. '62 (SAN) [1] Midland, TX St. Ann's Church.
Murphy, Timothy J. '63 (BO) [2] Salem, MA Immaculate Conception Church.
Murphy, Timothy J. '74 (SPR) Hampden, MA St. Mary's Church.
Murphy, Ultan P. '53 (DOD) Olmitz, KS St. Ann Church; Timken, KS Holy Trinity Church.
Murphy, Venard *o.f.m.* '61 (SP) [O] St. Petersburg, FL St. Anthony Friary.
Murphy, W. Maximus *c.s.b.* '44 (GAL) [Q] Sugar Land, TX Basilian Mission Center.
Murphy, Msgr. Walter C. '58 (BRK) [128] Brooklyn, NY Sacred Heart Church.
Murphy, Warren *t.o.r.* '60 (FWT) [8] Fort Worth, TX St. Andrew Church.
Murphy, William *s.a.* '40 (NY) [DD] Garrison, NY Franciscan Friars of the Atonement.
Murphy, William *c.p.* '73 (R) Tarboro, NC St. Catherine Church.
Murphy, William F. (BO) [28] Boston, MA Holy Name Church.
Murphy, William F. '56 (PRO) Retired; [P] Providence, RI St. John Vianney Residence.
Murphy, William F. '65 (BO) [DD] Boston, MA Chancery Office.
Murphy, William J. '57 (DET) Orchard Lake, MI Our Lady of Refuge Church.
Murphy, William J. '96 (SUP) Crescent Lake, WI Sacred Hearts of Jesus and Mary Church; Danbury, WI Our Lady of Perpetual Help Church; Webster, WI St. John the Baptist Church.
Murphy, William P. '43 (CHI) Evergreen Park, IL Queen of Martyrs Church; Retired.
Murphy, William P. '65 (DEN) [2] Englewood, CO Holy Name Church.
Murphy, William P. '86 (SPR) Hadley, MA Holy Rosary Church; Hadley, MA St. John's Church.
Murphy, William S. '90 (PH) [1] Philadelphia, PA Cathedral Basilica of SS. Peter and Paul Church; [123] Philadelphia, PA Chapel of Our Lady of the Miraculous Medal Church.
Murphy, William T. '50 (RVC) Retired.
Murr, Charles T. '77 (NY) [62] New York, NY St. Joseph Church.
Murray, Adrian '51 (OAK) Retired.
Murray, Adrian L. '43 (OAK) [M] Oakland, CA Bishop Begin Villa.
Murray, Msgr. Andrew '73 (BLX) [4] Biloxi, MS Sacred Heart Church.
Murray, Arthur *o.f.m.* '49 (SP) [O] St. Petersburg, FL St. Anthony Friary.
Murray, Bernard *o.c.s.o.* '50 (L) [L] Trappist, KY Abbey of Our Lady of Gethsemani, of the Order of Cistercians of the Strict Observance.
Murray, Bernard J. *o.s.a.* '83 (PH) [AA] Villanova, PA St. Thomas Monastery.
Murray, Brendan J. '68 (PAT) Rockaway, NJ St. Cecilia's Church.
Murray, Celestine '55 (CC) Woodsboro, TX St. Therese, The Little Flower Church.
Murray, Charles A. *m.m.* '51 (FgM) Maryknoll Foreign Missions.
Murray, Cornelius J. '63 (CLV) North Olmsted, OH St. Brendan Church.
Murray, Cyprian *o.f.m.cap.* '64 (NOR) [4] Middletown, CT St. Pius X Church.
Murray, D. Bradley *s.j.* '54 (BAL) [C] Baltimore, MD Loyola High School.
Murray, Daniel '86 (SD) [18] San Diego, CA Sacred Heart Church.
Murray, Msgr. Daniel A. '64 (PH) [3] Drexel Hill, PA St. Charles Borromeo Church.
Murray, Msgr. Daniel J. '73 (ORG) Garden Grove, CA St. Callistus Church.
Murray, Donald J. '61 (MAD) [14] Madison, WI St. Thomas Aquinas Church.
Murray, Donnan P. *o.f.m.* '56 (FgM) Franciscan Foreign Missions.
Murray, Edward (SFR) [J] San Francisco, CA St. Mary's Medical Center.
Murray, Edward *o.m.i.* '37 (SAT) San Antonio, TX Baptist Memorial Hospital; [M] San Antonio, TX Oblate Benson Residence (Southern Prov.); [M] San Antonio, TX Provincial Administration Office, Oblates of Mary Immaculate (Southern Prov.).
Murray, Edward G. '69 (SC) Whittemore, IA St. Michael's Church.
Murray, Edward J. *s.m.* '61 (WDC) [M] Washington, DC Marist Provincial House.
Murray, Edward K. '62 (SFR) Foster City, CA St. Luke Church; San Francisco, CA St. Mary's Medical Center.
Murray, Edward L. *c.s.sp.* '45 (PIT) [B] Pittsburgh, PA Duquesne University of the Holy Ghost.
Murray, Eugene L. '65 (SC) Emmetsburg, IA Holy Family Church.
Murray, Eugene M. *m.m.* '58 (FgM) Maryknoll Foreign Missions.
Murray, Msgr. Francis '49 (SAG) Retired.
Murray, Francis '53 (SFR) San Carlos, CA St. Charles Church; San Francisco, CA Kaiser Hospital Redwood City; San Francisco, CA Sequoia Hospital; Special Assignment.
Murray, Frank '51 (LAN) Retired.
Murray, Frank J. '81 (PRT) Bangor, ME St. Mary's Church.
Murray, Frederick J. '53 (BO) Westwood, MA St. Denis Church.
Murray, George B. *s.j.* (DET) [K] Detroit, MI Jesuit Provincial Office-Detroit Province of the Society of Jesus.
Murray, George B. *s.j.* '65 (BO) [W] Weston, MA Campion Center.
Murray, Msgr. Harold A. '49 (NEW) Retired.
Murray, Ignatius L. '57 (PH) Brookline, PA Annunciation B.V.M. Church.
Murray, J. Glenn *s.j.* '79 (CLV) [26] Cleveland, OH St. Henry Church.
Murray, James *o.p.* '50 (DET) [20] Detroit, MI St. Dominic Church.
Murray, James B. '57 (NSH) Retired.
Murray, Msgr. James H. '56 (PAT) Denville, NJ St. Mary's Church.
Murray, Msgr. James J. (NY) [I] New York, NY The Catholic Charities of the Archdiocese of New York.
Murray, Msgr. James J. '56 (NY) [I] New York, NY The Catholic Charities of the Archdiocese of New York; [Z] New York, NY Mary Manning Walsh Home; [HH] New York, NY The Housing Fund of the Archdiocese of New York.
Murray, James M. *o.s.b.* '93 (PEO) [A] Peru, IL St. Bede Abbey and Academy.
Murray, Msgr. Jerome E. '49 (LIN) Curtis, NE St. James Church.
Murray, John '54 (Y) Retired.
Murray, John *c.s.b.* '67 (ROC) [L] Rochester, NY Marriage Encounter Apostolate.
Murray, John '67 (RVC) New Hyde Park, NY Notre Dame Church.
Murray, John A. *c.m.* '49 (PH) [AA] Philadelphia, PA Congregation of the Mission.
Murray, John A. '54 (Y) Hubbard, OH St. Patrick's Church.
Murray, John A. '62 (BO) Concord, MA St. Bernard Church.
Murray, John B. *c.m.* '42 (BRK) [U] Jamaica, NY Vincentian Residence.
Murray, John C. *c.s.b.* '57 (ROC) [I] Rochester, NY Basilian Residence.
Murray, John D. (LA) Saugus, CA Pitchess Detention Center.
Murray, John E. '60 (CHY) Douglas, WY St. James Church.
Murray, John E. '63 (HEL) [4] Anaconda, MT Anaconda Catholic Community Church.
Murray, John E. '67 (RVC) Retired.
Murray, John F. *c.ss.r.* '73 (TR) [Q] Long Branch, NJ San Alfonso Retreat House.
Murray, John F. *c.ss.r.* '94 (FgM) Redemptorist Foreign Missions.
Murray, John Francis *s.m.a.* '57 (NEW) [N] Tenafly, NJ Society of African Missions, Provincialate, S.M.A. Fathers.
Murray, John I. '55 (SFS) Retired.
Murray, John J. '47 (PH) Retired.
Murray, John J. '61 (NY) Port Jervis, NY Immaculate Conception Church.
Murray, John J. '65 (BRK) [148] Queens, NY American Martyrs Church.
Murray, John L. '47 (E) Retired.
Murray, John P. *c.m.* '48 (PH) [AA] Philadelphia, PA Congregation of the Mission.
Murray, John P. '54 (RVC) Merrick, NY Cure of Ars Church; East Meadow, NY Nassau County Medical Center.
Murray, John P. *s.j.* '87 (BO) [W] Boston, MA The Society of Jesus of New England-Provincial Offices.
Murray, John S. '69 (ORL) Titusville, FL St. Teresa Church.
Murray, John W. '68 (CHI) Military Chaplains.
Murray, John William (SJ) Palo Alto, CA Veterans Administration Medical Center.
Murray, Joseph '55 (NEW) [5] Bayonne, NJ St. Vincent de Paul Church.
Murray, Msgr. Joseph '56 (RVC) Westhampton Beach, NY Immaculate Conception Church.
Murray, Msgr. Joseph W. '61 (PH) Lansdale, PA St. Stanislaus Church.
Murray, Kevin P. '77 (PH) [2] Chester, PA Blessed Katharine Drexel Church.
Murray, Kevin R. *c.ss.r.* '86 (PH) [25] Philadelphia, PA St. Boniface Church.
Murray, Leo A. *s.j.* '62 (PH) [82] Philadelphia, PA Old St. Joseph's Church.
Murray, Leonard M. *s.j.* '40 (STL) [O] St. Louis, MO Fusz Pavilion.
Murray, Maurice M. *s.j.* '66 (FgM) Provinces.
Murray, Maximillian '46 (SEA) Retired.
Murray, Michael *o.s.b.* '81 (PBL) Florence, CO St. Benedict Church.
Murray, Michael D. *o.s.b.* '56 (PBL) [F] Canon City, CO Holy Cross Abbey.
Murray, Michael J. '76 (WDC) Forestville, MD Church of the Holy Spirit.
Murray, Michael S. *o.s.f.s* '86 (PH) [D] Philadelphia, PA Northeast Catholic High School for Boys; [AA] Philadelphia, PA Oblates of St. Francis De Sales.
Murray, Nicholas *s.s.c.* '62 (FgM) St. Columban's Foreign Mission Society(S.S.C.)(THE COLUMBAN FATHERS).
Murray, Patrick '37 (MIA) Retired.
Murray, Patrick F. *s.j.* '45 (PH) [AA] Philadelphia, PA Jesuit Community at St. Joseph's University.
Murray, Paul E. '75 (WDC) [40] Washington, DC St. Stephen Martyr Church.
Murray, Peter *s.j.* '72 (NY) [DD] New York, NY West Side Jesuit Community.
Murray, Pius *c.s.s.* (BO) [A] Weston, MA Pope John XXIII National Seminary.
Murray, Pius C.W. *c.s.s.* '92 (BO) [W] Waltham, MA Stigmatine House.
Murray, Msgr. Richard H. '43 (LA) Woodland Hills, CA St. Bernardine of Siena Church; Retired.
Murray, Robert J. *o.s.a.* '83 (PH) [C] Villanova, PA Villanova University; [AA] Villanova, PA St. Thomas Monastery.
Murray, Robert P. '46 (TR) [L] Lawrenceville, NJ Morris Hall-Saint Lawrence, Inc.
Murray, Robert W. '88 (BO) [4] Somerville, MA St. Catherine of Genoa Church.
Murray, Msgr. Sean '52 (SD) [21] San Diego, CA St. Brigid Church; Retired.
Murray, Sean *c.ss.r.* '57 (SR) [L] Sebastopol, CA Diocesan House of Prayer.
Murray, Steven (OG) [C] Watertown, NY Immaculate Heart Central High School.
Murray, Steven M. '88 (OG) [3] Watertown, NY St. Anthony Church.
Murray, Thomas '44 (SJ) Los Altos, CA St. Simon Church; Retired.
Murray, Thomas A. '68 (PH) [94] Philadelphia, PA St. Martin of Tours Church.

Murray, Thomas F. '57 (BO) Natick, MA Sacred Heart Church.
Murray, Thomas P. '81 (RVC) Sound Beach, NY St. Louis de Montfort Church.
Murray, Timothy J. '77 (DET) [9] Warren, MI St. Martin de Porres Church.
Murray, Msgr. William F. '45 (PRO) Retired.
Murray, William F. '54 (MIL) Retired.
Murray, William J. *o.s.a.* '47 (PH) [AA] Villanova, PA St. Thomas Monastery.
Murrin, Donald *s.v.d.* '60 (LR) [4] Little Rock, AR St. Bartholomew's Church.
Murrin, Joseph *s.s.c.* '44 (PRO) [P] Bristol, RI St. Columban's Retirement House.
Murrin, Raymond '61 (BIR) [13] Birmingham, AL St. Mark's Church.
Murrin, Raymond J. '61 (BIR) [19] Birmingham, AL St. Patrick's Church.
Murrman, Jonathan J. *o.s.b.* '65 (GBG) [H] Latrobe, PA Saint Vincent Archabbey.
Murrman, Warren D. *o.s.b.* '65 (GBG) [H] Latrobe, PA Saint Vincent Archabbey.
Murtagh, George O. '50 (BUR) Retired.
Murtagh, James '66 (PMB) [1] West Palm Beach, FL Holy Name of Jesus Church.
Murtagh, John J. '69 (YAK) [2] Yakima, WA Holy Family Church.
Murtagh, Lawrence '53 (WIN) On Duty Outside the Diocese.
Murtagh, Thomas P. '81 (BRK) [218] Queens, NY Our Lady, Queen of Martyrs Church.
Murtaugh, Charles L. *s.j.* '69 (FgM) Provinces.
Murtaugh, James J. '48 (CHI) Skokie, IL St. Lambert Church; Retired.
Murtaugh, Lewis C. *s.j.* '69 (CHI) [N] Chicago, IL Chicago Province of the Society of Jesus-Provincial Office.
Murtaugh, William '72 (STP) New Brighton, MN St. John the Baptist Church.
Murtha, Chester '93 (SFS) [7] Sioux Falls, SD St. Michael Church.
Murtha, John *o.s.b.* '57 (SAV) [B] Savannah, GA Benedictine Military School; [F] Savannah, GA The Benedictine Priory.
Murtha, Michael G. '93 (PH) [1] Phoenixville, PA St. Ann Church.
Murugarren, Jesus *o.s.a.* '55 (SAT) [58] San Antonio, TX St. Michael Church.
Murzyn, John A. '59 (GRY) Absent on Leave.
Muscalino, Daniel C. '78 (SY) [18] Syracuse, NY St. John the Evangelist Church; Special Assignment.
Muscat, John '51 (NY) [2] New Rochelle, NY St. Gabriel Church; New Rochelle, NY South Shore Medical Center.
Muscat, John C. '84 (CAM) Collingswood, NJ St. John's Church.
Muschette, Emilian *o.s.b.* '58 (NEW) [N] Newark, NJ Newark Abbey.
Muscolino, Frank J. '68 (BIR) [24] Birmingham, AL St. Stephen University Parish; [H] Birmingham, AL St. Stephen University Parish.
Mushi, Peter A. *a.j.* '87 (ALN) [3] Shenandoah, PA St. George Church; [5] Shenandoah, PA Our Lady of Mt. Carmel Church.
Mushinsky, John E. (PAT) Retired.
Musholt, Silas *o.f.m.* '55 (STL) Oakville, MO St. Francis of Assisi Church; [P] Oakville, MO St. Francis Friary.
Musial, Msgr. Edward S. '46 (PH) [3] Bensalem, PA Saint Ephrem Church; Retired.
Musial, George '67 (CHI) [N] Chicago, IL St. Peter's Friary.
Musinski, Donald T. '62 (MIL) Johnsburg, WI St. John the Baptist Church.
Musinsky, John *s.v.d.* '44 (FgM) Society of the Divine Word Foreign Missions.
Musiol, Jozef '72 (AUS) Bremond, TX St. Mary's Church.
Musko, Andrew '34 (PSC) Retired.
Musngi, Efren *m.s.* '61 (SB) Moreno Valley, CA St. Christopher Church.
Musselman, Joseph G. *s.j.* '52 (NY) [DD] New York, NY Xavier Jesuit Community.
Mustaciuolo, Gregory '90 (NY) [1] New York, NY Cathedral of St. Patrick; Graduate Studies.
Musteikis, Leonard '38 (OM) Retired.
Mustos, Stephen N. *sch.p.* '58 (PAT) [9] Passaic, NJ St. Stephen's Church.
Musumbu, Gilberto Malu *m.s.p.* '88 (TUC) Yuma, AZ St. Francis of Assisi Church.
Musumeci, James S. '76 (BRK) [200] Queens, NY St. Mel Church.
Muszynski, Casimir '67 (RCK) [3] Rockford, IL St. Bernadette Church.
Mutefunya, Deo Gratias R. '63 (PEO) Moline, IL St. Mary's Church.
Muteru, Gabriel '87 (NY) Mamaroneck, NY Holy Trinity Church.
Muth, Joseph L. '74 (BAL) [61] Baltimore, MD St. Matthew Church.
Muthukattil, Thomas '66 (BRK) [152] Queens, NY St. Anthony of Padua Church.
Muthuplakel, James '67 (HBG) [5] Lancaster, PA St. Joseph Church; Lancaster, PA Lancaster General Hospital and Lancaster Community Hospital.
Muyombo, Gaston '83 (DEN) [N] Littleton, CO Carmel of Holy Spirit.
Muzdakis, John J. *o.s.f.s.* '65 (ARL) [D] Alexandria, VA Bishop Ireton High School; [J] Alexandria, VA Oblates of St. Francis de Sales Residence.
Muzic, Anthony J. '63 (CLV) [46] Cleveland, OH St. Mark Church; Retired.
Muzquiz, Lino *c.p.* '47 (MGZ) San Sebastian, PR San Sebastian Martir Church.
Muzzey, Charles H. '65 (PMB) [D] West Palm Beach, FL St. Mary's Hospital, Inc.
Muzzin, Victor *f.d.p.* '72 (NY) [11] New York, NY St. Ann Church.
Mwangi, Paul '88 (PIT) [64] Pittsburgh, PA Resurrection Church.
Mwariri, Alphonsus *i.m.c.* '86 (PIT) [O] Pittsburgh, PA Consolata Fathers.
Mwau, Julius '82 (NY) [153] Bronx, NY St. Joan of Arc Church.
Mychajlenko, Jaroslaw '78 (SJP) [10] Solon, OH Protection B.V.M. Church.
Mycue, Gordon E. '49 (STP) Retired.
Myer, Blase '68 (PHX) [6] Scottsdale, AZ St. Maria Goretti Church.
Myers, Albert J. '51 (CLV) North Olmsted, OH St. Brendan Church; Retired.
Myers, Christopher *s.o.l.t.* '90 (CC) [H] Robstown, TX Society of Our Lady of the Most Holy Trinity.
Myers, David A. *s.j.* '70 (P) [L] Portland, OR Jesuit Provincial Office (Society of Jesus, Oregon Prov.).
Myers, Edward J. '55 (NEW) Rahway, NJ St. Mary's Church.
Myers, Edward T. *o.p.* '50 (PRO) [P] Providence, RI St. Thomas Aquinas Priory at Providence College.
Myers, Gerald '94 (FAR) Walhalla, ND St. Boniface's Church.
Myers, James E. '80 (PEO) On Duty Outside the Diocese.
Myers, James E. *s.s.* '80 (SFR) [27] San Francisco, CA St. John the Evangelist Church.
Myers, James R. '57 (FTW) Elkhart, IN St. Vincent de Paul Church.
Myers, Jeremy '84 (DAL) Sherman, TX St. Mary Church.
Myers, John *o.f.m.cap.* '54 (DET) [K] Detroit, MI St. Bonaventure Friary.
Myers, Kenneth '80 (PIT) Beaver County, PA The Medical Center Beaver.
Myers, Kenneth C. '68 (CLV) Released from Diocesan Assignment; [AA] Cleveland, OH COAR Peace Mission, Inc.; [AA] San Antonio, TX.
Myers, Kenneth C. '68 (SAT) [T] San Antonio, TX Missionaries of Pastoral Charity Society.
Myers, Kenneth E. '80 (PIT) Beaver County, PA Beaver Valley Geriatric Center.
Myers, Rawley '49 (COS) Retired.
Myers, Regis F. '54 (ALT) Retired.
Myers, Robert *s.v.d.* '49 (CHI) [B] Techny, IL Divine Word Residence.
Myers, William (SFR) Novato, CA Our Lady of Loretto Church.
Myers, William F. '56 (RCK) Active Outside the Diocese.
Myers, Msgr. William R. '69 (STU) Gallipolis, OH St. Louis Church; [I] Rio Grande, OH Rio Grande University.
Myers, William S. '88 (STO) Absent on Leave.
Myett, Robert D. *o.p.* '60 (PRO) [P] Providence, RI St. Thomas Aquinas Priory at Providence College.
Myhalyk, Richard M. *s.s.e.* '71 (MOB) [A] Selma, AL Edmundite House of Formation; [H] Selma, AL Edmundite Fathers.
Mykyta, Andrew (SD) San Diego, CA Our Lady of Perpetual Help Church.
Mykyta, Andrew '48 (STN) [1] Chicago, IL St. Nicholas Ukrainian Catholic Cathedral; Retired.
Mykyta, Myron '97 (STN) [1] Chicago, IL St. Nicholas Ukrainian Catholic Cathedral.
Myladil, Thomas *o.c.d.* '78 (NY) [165] Bronx, NY St. Mary Star of the Sea Church.
Mylchreest, William F. '80 (MIA) [13] Fort Lauderdale, FL St. Sebastian Church.
Myler, John (BEL) [J] Ruma, IL World Apostolate of Fatima, The Blue Army, U.S.A.
Myler, John T. '82 (BEL) Cahokia, IL Holy Family Church.
Myles, A. James '62 (WH) [3] Wheeling, WV Corpus Christi Church.
Myles, John '64 (SAC) Maxwell, CA Sacred Heart Church.
Mylet, James J. *m.m.* '75 (FgM) Maryknoll Foreign Missions.
Mynaugh, Msgr. Charles B. '42 (PH) Retired.
Myshchuk, Mikhail '94 (STF) Watervliet, NY St. Nicholas Church.
Myslinski, John F. '80 (WDC) Great Mills, MD Holy Face Church.
Mysliwiec, Hal '70 (CHI) Mundelein, IL Santa Maria Del Popolo Church.
Mysliwiec, Jan J. *s.d.s.* '62 (NEW) [N] Verona, NJ The Salvatorian Fathers.
Mysliwiec, Jordan *s.d.s.* '62 (NEW) [3] Irvington, NJ Sacred Heart of Jesus Church.
Myszel, George G. '53 (MIL) Retired.
Myszka, Msgr. Daniel J. '58 (BUF) Retired.
Mytych, Joseph '39 (CHI) Argo, IL St. Blase Church.
Mytych, Joseph F. '39 (CHI) [170] Chicago, IL SS. Peter and Paul Church; Retired.
Myvett, Manuel *s.v.d.* '62 (TR) Lakewood, NJ St. Anthony Claret Church.

N

N'Zilamba, Norbert *o.praem.* '87 (JKS) [E] Jackson, MS Priory of St. Moses the Black.
Naaeke, Anthony '91 (PIT) [78] Pittsburgh, PA Most Holy Name of Jesus Church.
Naas, Stephen E. '78 (KAL) [3] Kalamazoo, MI St. Mary Church.
Naber, Herman J. '59 (L) [24] Louisville, KY St. Elizabeth of Hungary Church; [72] Louisville, KY St. Therese Church.
Naber, John T. '45 (BUF) Retired.
Nabozny, Peter J. '54 (ALB) Herkimer, NY St. Francis de Sales Church.
Nacarino, Raymond L. '85 (MET) [3] New Brunswick, NJ Our Lady of Mt. Carmel Church.
Nacca, John J. (ORL) Retired.
Nacca, John J. '41 (ROC) Retired.
Naccarato, Francis A. '79 (NY) [199] Staten Island, NY Blessed Sacrament Church.
Naccarato, Frank '79 (NY) State, NY Arthur Kill Correctional Facility.
Nacciarone, Ugo R. *s.j.* '64 (FgM) Provinces.
Nace, Msgr. Arthur J. '57 (PH) Absent on Sick Leave.
Nachajski, Richard E. '71 (ALN) [2] Reading, PA St. Anthony of Padua Church.
Nachef, Antoine *b.s.o.* '91 (NTN) [B] Methuen, MA Basilian Salvatorian Order.
Nachtigal, Fred '58 (Y) Retired.
Nacional, Perfecto '62 (SR) Ukiah, CA St. Mary of the Angels Church.
Nacius, Michael A. '89 (CHI) Rolling Meadows, IL St. Colette Church.
Nacke, Xavier *o.s.b.* '63 (KC) Maryville, MO St. Gregory Barbarigo Church; [A] Conception, MO Conception Seminary College; [N] Maryville, MO The Newman House at Northwest Missouri State University.
Nacu, Joseph *m.s.* '57 (SB) Barstow, CA St. Philip Neri Church.
Nadackal, Zacharias *c.m.i.* '64 (NY) Rye, NY Resurrection Church.
Nadal, Bart *c.r.* '47 (DEN) [A] Denver, CO St. Andrew's Theatine House.
Naddeo, Henry M. '56 (NEW) Kearny, NJ Our Lady of Sorrows Church.
Nadeau, J.H. Normand '68 (BUR) Brattleboro, VT St. Michael Church.
Nadeau, James A. '88 (PRT) [1] Portland, ME Cathedral of the Immaculate Conception.
Nadeau, Lance P. *m.m.* '90 (FgM) Maryknoll Foreign Missions.
Nadeau, Real J. '62 (PRT) [5] Lewiston, ME St. Patrick's Church; [6] Lewiston, ME SS. Peter and Paul Church.
Nadeau, Richard A. '80 (PRT) Limerick, ME St. Matthew Church.
Nadeau, Roland S. *m.s.* '69 (MAN) Hanover, NH Mary Hitchcock Hospital; [K] Enfield, NH Shrine of Our Lady of La Salette; [M] Enfield, NH La Salette Shrine and Center of Enfield.
Nadeau, Timothy J. '91 (PRT) Bradley, ME St. Ann Church; [4] Old Town, ME St. Ann Church, Indian Island Church.
Nadeau, William E. *o.m.i.* '68 (STP) [N] St. Paul, MN Oblate Residence.
Nadicksbernd, Elmer *s.v.d.* '64 (WH) Gassaway, WV St. Thomas; Maysel, WV Church of The Risen Lord.
Nadine, Jerome E. '58 (BRK) Released from Diocesan Assignment.
Nadine, Jerry '58 (LAV) [8] Las Vegas, NV St. Elizabeth Ann Seton Church.
Nadolny, Edmund S. '59 (HRT) [6] Meriden, CT St. Stanislaus Church.
Nadolny, Paul *s.v.d.* '89 (FgM) Society of the Divine Word Foreign Missions.
Nadolny, Stanley '68 (TUC) Bisbee, AZ St. Patrick Church.
Nadolski, Kevin M. '97 (WIL) [B] Wilmington, DE Salesianum School.
Nadon, Elgar *o.f.m.* '59 (FgM) Franciscan Foreign Missions.
Nadura, John '58 (NEW) [22] Jersey City, NJ Our Lady of Victories Church.
Naduvilekoot, Augustine '71 (NOR) Durham, CT Notre Dame Church.
Nadzam, John B. '50 (STU) Retired.

Naegele, Gary P. '79 (WH) [3] Fairmont, WV St. Anthony Church.
Naessens, Philip *o.f.m.cap.* '86 (DET) [K] Detroit, MI St. Bonaventure Friary.
Naffah, Msgr. John '39 (OLL) Hillside, IL Our Lady of Lebanon Church; Retired.
Naffah, Msgr. John '39 (SAM) Retired.
Nagai, Msgr. Alan '58 (HON) Kailua, HI St. John Vianney Church.
Nagaroor, Joseph '66 (MAR) [5] Escanaba, MI St. Thomas the Apostle Church.
Nagele, John *c.pp.s.* '52 (TOL) [M] Bellevue, OH Sorrowful Mother Shrine.
Nagengast, Maynard G. *o.s.b.* '62 (NEW) [N] Newark, NJ Newark Abbey.
Nagle, Austin *ss.cc.* '54 (BO) [U] Brockton, MA St. Joseph Manor Nursing & Extended Care Facility.
Nagle, Austin *ss.cc.* '54 (FR) [J] Fairhaven, MA Sacred Hearts Provincial House.
Nagle, Edmund W. *s.j.* '63 (PAT) [I] Morristown, NJ Loyola House of Retreats.
Nagle, Gerald J. *m.m.* '57 (SFR) [N] San Francisco, CA Maryknoll Fathers and Brothers, Catholic Foreign Mission Society of America, Inc.
Nagle, James B. *m.m.* '52 (NY) [DD] Maryknoll, NY Maryknoll Fathers and Brothers.
Nagle, John *s.a.c.* '47 (FWT) Mineral Wells, TX Our Lady of Lourdes Church.
Nagle, Msgr. Joseph P. '71 (BRK) [132] Brooklyn, NY St. Saviour Church.
Nagle, Kurt '97 (SEA) [2] Tacoma, WA St. Charles Borromeo Church.
Nagle, Michael R. '72 (FR) Edgartown, MA St. Elizabeth Church; Oak Bluffs, MA Sacred Heart Church; Vineyard Haven, MA St. Augustine Church.
Nagle, Richard *o.carm.* '37 (NY) [DD] Middletown, NY St. Albert's Priory.
Nagle, Vincent '92 (FR) [17] Fall River, MA St. Louis Church; [P] Fall River, MA Priestly Fraternity of the Missionaries of St. Charles Borromeo, Inc.
Nagle, William A. '49 (BGP) [8] Stamford, CT St. John's Church.
Nagler, Robert '56 (SB) Retired.
Nagler, Robert J. '56 (SD) [31] San Diego, CA St. Mary Magdalene Church.
Naglich, Robert T. *s.c.j.* '91 (GRY) Crown Point, IN St. Mary Church.
Naguszewski, Edward B. '30 (BO) Retired.
Nagy, Joseph '40 (LA) Retired.
Nahn, William J. '76 (ALN) [2] Easton, PA St. Bernard Church.
Nahoe, Francisco *o.f.m.conv.* '94 (LA) [R] Torrance, CA Franciscan Friars, St. Bonaventure Friary.
Naill, Joseph P. '97 (RCK) [1] Rockford, IL St. Peter Cathedral.
Nairn, Thomas *o.f.m.* (CHI) [D] Chicago, IL Hales Franciscan High School, Inc.
Nairn, Thomas *o.f.m.* '75 (CHI) [B] Chicago, IL The Catholic Theological Union at Chicago.
Najdowski, Msgr. John A. '51 (GR) Grandville, MI St. Pius X Church.
Najjar, Samuel A. '84 (SAM) Waterville, ME St. Joseph Church.
Najmowski, James J. *m.m.* '76 (FgM) Maryknoll Foreign Missions.
Nakagawa, Francis *s.m.* '57 (SJ) [M] Cupertino, CA Marianist Provincial Residence.
Nakowicz, Stanley T. '67 (PRO) [5] East Providence, RI Our Lady of Loreto Church.
Nalepa, Damien '70 (BAL) [35] Baltimore, MD St. Gregory the Great Church; Baltimore, MD Baltimore City Jail.
Nalepa, Richard *c.p.* '70 (SCR) [M] Scranton, PA Saint Ann's Passionist Monastery.
Nall, Brent '93 (SAC) Chico, CA St. John the Baptist Church.
Nall, James M. '87 (BEL) Special Assignment.
Nallen, James F. '66 (CHI) [55] Chicago, IL St. Ethelreda Church.
Nallen, Michael J. '58 (CHI) Markham, IL St. Gerard Majella Church.
Nalley, Robert W. '75 (GAY) Grayling, MI St. Mary Church; Special Assignment.
Nally, J. Brendan '56 (WOR) Clinton, MA Our Lady of the Rosary Church.
Nally, John J. *m.s.* '54 (WOR) [6] Fitchburg, MA St. Joseph's Church.
Nally, Joseph M. '72 (WOR) [24] Worcester, MA St. Joan of Arc Church.
Nalysnyk, Bohdan '68 (STN) Fairfield, ND St. Demetrius Church.
Nalysnyk, Bohdan '95 (STN) Belfield, ND St. John the Baptist Church.
Nalysnyk, Jaroslav (BO) [20] Boston, MA Christ The King Church.
Nalysnyk, Jaroslaw '91 (STF) Boston, MA Christ the King Church.
Nam, Heebong B. '97 (BRK) [207] Queens, NY Our Lady of the Blessed Sacrament Church.
Nam, Joseph M. Phan *c.m.c.* '89 (NO) [B] Metairie, LA Congregation of the Mother Coredemptrix Formation House.
Nam, Simon '52 (NY) [156] Bronx, NY St John Nam Church.
Nambiaparambil, Albert '59 (ALX) Moreauville, LA Our Lady of Sorrows Church.
Nami, Peter *o.m.i.* '76 (BUF) [35] Buffalo, NY St. James Church.
Namie, Msgr. James B. '54 (STP) On Duty Outside the Archdiocese.
Namiotka, Edward F. '87 (CAM) [5] Vineland, NJ St. Mary's Church; [A] Hammonton, NJ St. Joseph.
Namocatcat, Felix S. '62 (SFR) [3] South San Francisco, CA St. Augustine Church.
Nance, Gary Michael '97 (BLX) Ocean Springs, MS St. Alphonsus Church.
Nangle, C. Richard '45 (ROC) [7] Auburn, NY St. Francis of Assisi Church; Retired.
Nangle, Joseph *o.f.m.* '58 (WDC) [B] Washington, DC Franciscan Mission Service of North America.
Nangle, Thomas R. '70 (CHI) Other Assignments.
Nanley, William (ORL) Melbourne, FL Our Lady of Lourdes Church.
Nanthiyattu, Zacharias *o.i.c.* (CHI) Chicago, IL Syro-Malankara Catholic Mission of the Archdiocese of Chicago Church.
Nanthiyattu, Zacharias *o.i.c.* '79 (CHI) [73] Chicago, IL St. Gregory Church.
Nanz, Jack '71 (PIT) [4] Butler, PA St. Peter Church.
Napier, Robert L. '90 (STA) Jacksonville Beach, FL St. Paul's Church.
Napoli, Carlo *t.o.r.* (PIT) Allegheny County, PA UPMC University of Pittsburgh Medical Center; [O] Pittsburgh, PA Franciscan Friars, T.O.R.
Napoli, Felician *o.f.m.* '51 (NY) [DD] New York, NY Franciscan Province of the Immaculate Conception.
Napoli, Felician *o.f.m.* '51 (SP) [5] Tampa, FL Incarnation Church.
Napoli, Peter *o.f.m.cap.* '73 (PAT) [12] Paterson, NJ Our Lady of Lourdes Church.
Napolitano, Anthony M. '66 (NY) [3] Yonkers, NY St. Ann Church.
Napolitano, Joseph V. '76 (HRT) [11] New Britain, CT St. Maurice Church; [E] New Britain, CT St. Thomas Aquinas High School.
Nappo, Michael *o.f.m.* '90 (BO) [42] Boston, MA St. Leonard of Port Maurice Church.
Naquin, Roch (HT) Retired.
Naranjo, Francisco '95 (STO) Ceres, CA St. Jude Church.
Narcowich, Edward '53 (FTW) Geneva, IN St. Mary of the Presentation Church.
Nardo, Anthony J. '87 (NEW) Springfield, NJ St. James Church.
Nardoianni, Antonio *o.f.m.* ' 7 (NY) [DD] New York, NY Franciscan Province of the Immaculate Conception.
Nardone, Amadeo *o.f.m.* '68 (NY) [DD] New York, NY Franciscan Province of the Immaculate Conception.
Nardone, Richard M. '54 (NEW) [B] South Orange, NJ Seton Hall University.
Nardoni, Enrique *s.s.d.* '48 (DAL) [B] Irving, TX University of Dallas.
Narewski, Peter J. '47 (PRO) Retired; [P] Providence, RI St. John Vianney Residence.
Narez, Juan '93 (ELP) Pecos, TX Santa Rosa Church.
Nargaj, Andrew *o.f.m.* (NY) [171] Bronx, NY Our Lady of Good Counsel Church; [DD] New York, NY Franciscan Friars, Order of Friars Minor, Holy Name Province.
Narimattam, Joseph '64 (WIL) Claymont, DE Holy Rosary Church; Wilmington, DE St. Francis Hospital; [H] Wilmington, DE St. Francis Hospital, Inc.
Narita, Michael *ss.cc.* '68 (FR) [J] Fairhaven, MA Sacred Hearts Provincial House.
Narivelil, Victor Z. *c.m.i.* '64 (STA) [14] Jacksonville, FL Sacred Heart Church.
Narkun, Msgr. Peter P. '45 (NY) Retired; [E] New York, NY Cardinal Hayes High School.
Narlaly, Jose T. *o.ss.t.* '81 (BAL) [M] Baltimore, MD Holy Trinity Monastery.
Naro, Carl J. '52 (RIC) Retired.
Nartker, Michael *s.m.* '96 (CLV) [4] Cleveland, OH St. Aloysius - St. Agatha Church.
Naseman, Alfred *c.pp.s.* '67 (CIN) [B] Carthagena, OH St. Charles.
Nash, Denis P. '54 (GR) Jenison, MI Holy Redeemer Church.
Nash, Edward H. *s.j.* '46 (BAL) [M] Baltimore, MD Jesuit Fathers and Brothers Maryland Provincial Curia.
Nash, Edward H. *s.j.* '46 (FgM) Provinces.
Nash, Francis J. *s.j.* '69 (BAL) [B] Baltimore, MD Loyola College; [M] Baltimore, MD Jesuit Community of Loyola College, Inc.
Nash, Howard J. '61 (HRT) [4] New Haven, CT St. Bernadette's Church.
Nash, James '94 (WIL) [5] Wilmington, DE St. Elizabeth Church.
Nash, Msgr. James F. '34 (ORG) [1] Anaheim, CA St. Anthony Claret Church; Retired.
Nash, James R. '89 (SCR) Montrose, PA Holy Name of Mary Church.
Nash, John C. '75 (NOR) North Stonington, CT St. Thomas More Church.
Nash, Paul A. *s.j.* '52 (BO) [W] Chestnut Hill, MA The Jesuit Community at Boston College.
Nash, Robert C. '48 (WH) Retired.
Nash, Stephen F. '97 (WDC) [3] Bethesda, MD Little Flower Church.
Nash, Thomas C. (SC) Estherville, IA St. Patrick's Church.
Nash, Thomas C. '54 (SC) Armstrong, IA St. Mary's Church.
Nasini, Gino *s.x.* '65 (FgM) Xaverian Foreign Missions.
Nasini, Gino *s.x.* '65 (PAT) [M] Wayne, NJ Xaverian Missionary Fathers.
Nason, Dennis T. '66 (BO) [4] Medford, MA St. Raphael Church.
Nasr, Toufic '97 (OLL) Millbrae, CA Our Lady of Lebanon Church; Stockton, CA Maronite Catholic Community Church.
Nasre, Fouad *b.s.o.* '57 (NTN) [B] Methuen, MA Basilian Salvatorian Order.
Nasri, Youssef Bochra '85 (BRK) [86] Brooklyn, NY St. Michael's Church; [123] Brooklyn, NY Resurrection Catholic Coptic Chapel Church.
Nassal, Joseph F. *c.pp.s.* '82 (KCK) [K] Easton, KS Shantivanam Archdiocesan House of Prayer.
Nassaney, Daniel *o.m.i.* '74 (NOR) [F] Willimantic, CT Oblates of Mary Immaculate; [I] Willimantic, CT Immaculata Retreat House.
Nasser, Joseph M. *s.j.* '75 (GAL) [3] Spring, TX St. Ignatius of Loyola Church.
Nassetta, Peter W. '89 (ARL) Falls Church, VA St. James Church.
Nassr, Martin '67 (TOL) Findlay, OH St. Michael Church.
Nasta, Thomas A. '82 (PH) Abington, PA Our Lady Help of Christians Church.
Nastold, Donald O. *s.j.* '58 (CIN) [28] Cincinnati, OH St. Francis Xavier Church.
Natale, Samuel '79 (RIC) On Duty Outside the Diocese.
Natali, Alfred M. *o.s.a.* '43 (PH) [99] Philadelphia, PA St. Mary Magdalen de Pazzi Church.
Natalizia, Louis T. '80 (PRO) [4] North Providence, RI Presentation of the Blessed Virgin Mary Church.
Nathe, Joel '93 (SCL) Grey Eagle, MN St. Joseph's Church; Ward Springs, MN St. Bernard's Church.
Natho, Clifton J. '60 (GAL) Retired.
Nativo, Joseph S. '56 (NEW) [22] Newark, NJ St. Lucy's Church.
Natsuhara, Bruce K. '78 (OKL) Okeene, OK St. Anthony's Church.
Nau, Dale '78 (DUL) [F] Duluth, MN University of MN-Duluth; [G] Duluth, MN The Human Life and Development Fund of the Diocese of Duluth; [G] Duluth, MN Calvary Cemetery.
Nau, Thomas R. '78 (STU) Ironton, OH St. Joseph Church; Ironton, OH St. Lawrence Church.
Naucke, Alfred E. *s.j.* '65 (SAC) [C] Sacramento, CA Jesuit High School; [G] Carmichael, CA Jesuit High School Community of Sacramento.
Naughton, James *s.d.b.* '67 (BIR) [8] Birmingham, AL Holy Rosary Church; [9] Birmingham, AL St. John Bosco Church.
Naughton, Msgr. John T. '49 (LA) Woodland Hills, CA St. Mel Church; Retired.
Naughton, Msgr. Louis '71 (ATL) [1] Atlanta, GA Cathedral of Christ the King.
Naughton, Michael *o.s.b.* '66 (SCL) [I] Collegeville, MN St. John's Abbey, of the Order of St. Benedict.
Naughton, Patrick J. '91 (COL) On Duty Outside the Diocese.
Naughton, Patrick J. '91 (SCR) [2] Nanticoke, PA Holy Trinity Church.
Naughton, Thomas J. '61 (BO) Winchester, MA Immaculate Conception Church.
Naughton, William M. '72 (PAT) Randolph, NJ Resurrection Church.
Naumann, Joseph F. '75 (STL) Richmond Heights, MO Immacolata Church.
Naumann, Paul S. *s.j.* '63 (SY) [S] Syracuse, NY Jesuits at LeMoyne, Inc.
Naumes, Matthew '63 (SEA) Medical Leave.
Naus, John E. *s.j.* '55 (MIL) [P] Milwaukee, WI Jesuit Community at Marquette University.
Nav, Thomas '78 (STU) [I] St. Clairsville, OH Ohio University - Eastern.
Navarra, Peter '81 (SD) Escondido, CA St. Mary Church.
Navarre, Robert G. '45 (SAG) Retired.
Navarria, Antony '59 (TUC) [I] Thatcher, AZ Eastern Arizona Junior College.
Navarro, Jose Luis Duenas *o.a.r.* '59 (NY) [DD] New York, NY Augustinian Recollects Provincial Residence, Province of St. Nicholas of Tolentine.
Navarro, Modesto Martinez *t.c.* '37 (BAL) Odenton, MD St. Joseph Church.
Navarro, Nicolas '69 (SJN) [37] San Juan, PR Maria Auxiliadora Church.
Navarro, Msgr. Pablo A. '78 (MIA) On Duty Outside the Archdiocese.

Navarro, Msgr. Pablo A. '78 (PMB) [A] Boynton Beach, FL St. Vincent de Paul Regional Seminary.
Navarro, Pedro '63 (NEW) [2] Union City, NJ St. Augustine's Church.
Navarroli, Frederick '43 (RVC) Retired.
Navascues, Moises *sch.p.* '54 (PCE) Santa Isabel, PR St. James Church; [B] Ponce, PR The Pontifical Catholic University of Puerto Rico.
Nave, Francis A. '92 (ALN) Bath, PA Sacred Heart Church.
Nave, Francis R. '60 (ALN) Retired; [J] Bethlehem, PA Holy Family Villa.
Navien, Thomas A. '42 (BO) Retired.
Navin, Msgr. Cyril '45 (LA) Encino, CA St. Cyril Church; Retired.
Navin, Timothy M. '79 (VEN) [3] Naples, FL St. Peter the Apostle Church.
Navins, Robert J. '50 (NY) [212] Staten Island, NY St. Margaret Mary Church.
Navit, Zachary W. '94 (PH) Trooper, PA Visitation B.V.M. Church.
Navone, John J. *s.j.* '62 (P) [L] Portland, OR Jesuit Provincial Office (Society of Jesus, Oregon Prov.).
Navoy, Ronald E. '71 (CHI) River Grove, IL St. Cyprian Church.
Nawarskas, Msgr. Frederick '67 (SAN) [2] Abilene, TX Holy Family Church.
Nawrocki, Norman '82 (DET) [4] Redford, MI St. Valentine Church; Special Assignment.
Nawrocki, Robert W. '61 (MIL) [5] Milwaukee, WI St. Alexander Church.
Nawrocki, Xavier *o.f.m.* '57 (ROC) [6] Auburn, NY St. Hyacinth Church.
Nawrocki, Zdzislaw *s.ch.* '75 (PAT) Boonton, NJ SS. Cyril and Methodius Church.
Nayak, Christudas '68 (ALX) [C] Alexandria, LA St. Frances Cabrini Hospital.
Naylor, Ronald J. '60 (RIC) Retired.
Nazabal, Isidro '63 (CGS) Cidra, PR Nuestra Senora de Fatima Church.
Nazareth, George (BAK) Hermiston, OR Our Lady of Angels Church.
Nazareth, Longinus (NY) [1] Port Chester, NY Our Lady of Mercy Church.
Nazario, Herber *o.s.a.* '65 (SJN) [42] San Juan, PR Ntra. Sra. de la Monserrate Church.
Nazimek, David J. '93 (GBG) Monessen, PA The Epiphany of Our Lord Church.
Nazimek, Francis A. '48 (PIT) Carmichaels, PA St. Hugh Church.
Nazzaro, John *s.d.b.* '83 (SP) [E] Tampa, FL Mary Help of Christians School.
Nazzaro, Stanley J. '48 (HRT) Retired.
Ndagizimana, Isidore '85 (AUS) [5] Austin, TX Holy Cross Church.
Ndeukoya, Msgr. Augustine (SP) Ruskin, FL St. Anne Church.
Ndiokwere, Nathaniel '75 (HEL) [1] Butte, MT Butte Catholic Community North Church; [11] Butte, MT St. Patrick Church; [H] Butte, MT Montana College of Mineral Science and Technology.
Ndrevashay, Primus P. '61 (DET) Beverly Hills, MI Our Lady of Albanians Church.
Ndulaka, Matthias '78 (NY) [224] Staten Island, NY St. Peter Church.
Nealon, Msgr. Joseph A. '61 (STU) Retired.
Nealon, Joseph W. '40 (NEW) Haworth, NJ Sacred Heart Church; Retired.
Nealy, Francis D. *o.p.* '39 (PRO) [P] Providence, RI St. Thomas Aquinas Priory at Providence College.
Neary, Anthony *c.p.* '54 (PIT) [O] Pittsburgh, PA St. Paul of the Cross Monastery.
Neary, Mark J. '83 (SJ) [3] Sunnyvale, CA St. Cyprian Church.
Neary, Patrick *c.s.c.* '91 (FTW) [A] Notre Dame, IN Moreau Seminary.
Neary, Thomas E. '54 (SY) Retired.
Neault, Armand R. '52 (PRT) Springvale, ME Notre Dame Church.
Nebel, Msgr. Charles A. '38 (BEL) Retired.
Nebiolo, Emilio '52 (KCK) Retired.
Nebus, Vincent J. '51 (MET) Retired.
Necthi-nathan, Anthonysami '87 (MET) [H] Metuchen, NJ Libermann House.
Nedder, Edward T. '87 (SAM) Springfield, MA St. Anthony Church.
Nediakala, Kuriakose *m.c.b.s.* (BIS) [4] Bismarck, ND St. Anne Church.
Nee, Eugene O. '64 (SAT) Military Chaplains.
Nee, Kenneth T. '53 (RVC) Manorhaven, NY Our Lady of Fatima Church.
Nee, Robert *o.f.m.* '62 (NY) [35] New York, NY St. Francis of Assisi Church.
Nee, Thomas B. '66 (RIC) Smithfield, VA Good Shepherd Church; Suffolk, VA St. Mary of the Presentation Church.
Nee, Thomas M. '39 (PIT) Retired; [O] Pittsburgh, PA St. John Vianney Manor.
Needham, Msgr. Thomas J. '61 (WOR) [6] Worcester, MA Immaculate Conception Church.
Neeley, Peter G. *s.j.* '81 (STL) [P] St. Louis, MO Jesuit Community Corporation at St. Louis University - Jesuit Hall.
Neely, Harry M. *o.s.a.* '53 (SD) [C] San Diego, CA St. Augustine High School; [H] San Diego, CA Augustinian Community.
Neenan, Aidan *o.f.m.cap.* '44 (RVC) St. James, NY St. James Nursing Home.
Neenan, Benedict *o.s.b.* '88 (KC) [A] Conception, MO Conception Seminary College; [J] Conception, MO Conception Abbey.
Neenan, Robert P. *s.j.* '51 (STP) [N] Minneapolis, MN La Storta Jesuit Community.
Neenan, William B. *s.j.* '61 (BO) [C] Chestnut Hill, MA Boston College; [W] Chestnut Hill, MA The Jesuit Community at Boston College.
Nees, John '51 (PH) [D] Philadelphia, PA Father Judge High School for Boys.
Neethinathan, Anthonisamy (MET) Edison, NJ John F. Kennedy Medical Center.
Neff, Eugene J. '71 (BEL) Lebanon, IL St. Joseph Church.
Neff, Msgr. John F. '60 (SP) [14] Tampa, FL St. Paul Church; [F] Tampa, FL St. Paul Preschool.
Neff, John R. '86 (E) Brandy Camp, PA Holy Cross Church; Du Bois, PA Du Bois Regional Hospital.
Neffy, Arthur '47 (DET) Retired.
Negele, R. Philip *o.c.s.o.* '66 (DEN) [H] Denver, CO St. Joseph Hospital.
Negherbon, Vincent R. '46 (ALT) [F] Loretto, PA Mount Assisi Friary.
Negley, Phil M. *m.s.* '73 (BO) [Y] Ipswich, MA LaSalette Retreat House at Newman Hall.
Negley, Phil M. *m.s.* '73 (GAL) Friendswood, TX Mary, Queen Church.
Negrete, Wayne *s.j.* '91 (SD) [4] San Diego, CA Christ the King Church.
Negrillos, Ferdinand *sch.p.* '41 (PH) [G] Devon, PA Devon Preparatory School; [AA] Devon, PA Piarist Fathers (Order of the Pious Schools).
Negro, Carmelo *c.s.* '52 (WDC) [L] Mitchellville, MD Villa Rosa Nursing Home, Inc.
Negro, Sergio P. '53 (FRS) On Special Assignment; [C] Fresno, CA Saint Agnes' Medical Center.
Negron, Ramon H. (SJN) [4] San Juan, PR San Antonio Church.
Nehrig, Robert V. *m.m.* '54 (FgM) Maryknoll Foreign Missions.
Neidhart, William J. *c.s.c.* '56 (FTW) Granger, IN St. Pius X Church.
Neiheisel, Stanley H. '61 (CIN) [34] Cincinnati, OH Holy Cross-Immaculata Church.
Neilson, Joseph *o.c.d.* '62 (DAL) [K] Dallas, TX Mount Carmel Center.
Neilson, Kieran *o.s.b.* '60 (CHL) [L] Charlotte, NC Diocesan Office of Campus Ministry.
Neilson, Kieran A. *o.s.b.* '60 (CHL) [J] Belmont, NC Belmont Abbey.
Neilson, Richard J. '83 (NY) Retired.
Neiman, John W. '86 (LA) Redondo Beach, CA St. Lawrence Martyr Church.
Neis, Thomas A. '52 (GAY) Charlevoix, MI St. Mary Church.
Neiser, Francis '44 (SB) Soboba Indian Reservation, CA St. Joseph Church.
Neitzke, Ron '89 (JOL) Steger, IL St. Liborius Church.
Nejasmich, Stephen C. *s.j.* '78 (SFR) [E] San Francisco, CA St. Ignatius College Preparatory (Coed); [N] San Francisco, CA Jesuit Community at St. Ignatius College Preparatory.
Nekic, Simon J. '43 (CLV) [12] Lorain, OH St. Vitus Church.
Nekoliczak, Ted A. '59 (GI) Sidney, NE St. Patrick's Church.
Nelan, Francis *m.s.c.* '53 (SAT) [K] San Antonio, TX Padua Place.
Nelan, Kevin J. '77 (NY) [16] New York, NY St. Benedict the Moor Church; [110] New York, NY Sacred Heart of Jesus Church.
Nelipowitz, Charles *o.f.m.conv.* '54 (SY) [2] Syracuse, NY Assumption B.V.M. Church.
Nelke, Richard '51 (STL) Chesterfield, MO Ascension Church.
Nelligan, Paul J. *s.j.* '54 (WOR) [N] Worcester, MA Jesuits of Holy Cross College, Inc.
Nellis, Thomas F. '66 (ROC) Webster, NY Holy Trinity Church.
Nellissery, Joy (ATL) Athens, GA St. Joseph's Church.
Nelson, Andrew L. '57 (MIL) [A] Milwaukee, WI St. Francis Seminary.
Nelson, Bertram A. *c.s.c.* (FgM) Holy Cross Foreign Missions.
Nelson, Caye A. '88 (BR) Napoleonville, LA St. Anne Church; Plattenville, LA Assumption of the Blessed Virgin Mary Church.
Nelson, Charles T. '87 (SFD) Bluffs, IL St. Patrick Church; Murrayville, IL St. Bartholomew Church; Winchester, IL St. Mark Church.
Nelson, Daniel C. *o.f.m.* '77 (ALB) [B] Loudonville, NY Siena College.
Nelson, Francis J. '66 (SAV) [7] Savannah, GA St. Frances Xavier Cabrini Church.
Nelson, Francis P. *c.ss.r.* '64 (BRK) [U] Brooklyn, NY Our Lady of Good Counsel Residence.
Nelson, Francis X. (BRK) [84] Brooklyn, NY St. Mary, Star of the Sea Church.
Nelson, Frank M. '78 (RVC) Valley Stream, NY Blessed Sacrament Church.
Nelson, Glenn L. '93 (RCK) Special Assignment.
Nelson, Gregory '97 (PEO) [1] Bloomington, IL Holy Trinity Church.
Nelson, James (GAL) [N] Houston, TX Pope John XXIII Priest Residence.
Nelson, James D. *s.j.* '57 (SPK) [K] Spokane, WA Regis Community.
Nelson, Linden '81 (LC) [E] Marshfield, WI St. Joseph's Hospital.
Nelson, Martin Lester '97 (BEA) [A] Beaumont, TX Monsignor Kelly Catholic High School.
Nelson, Paul E. '61 (WIN) Austin, MN St. Augustine's Church; Austin, MN St. Edward's Church.
Nelson, Robert W. '77 (LC) Boyd, WI Sacred Heart of Jesus-St. Joseph Church; Stanley, WI Holy Family Church.
Nelson, Thomas J. (WDC) Garrett Park, MD Holy Cross Church.
Nelson, Thomas J. *c.m.* '75 (DEN) [M] Denver, CO Congregation of the Mission Midwest Province: De Paul House.
Nelson, Thomas M. *o.praem* (ORG) [N] Silverado, CA Norbertine Association of St. Joseph, Inc.
Nelson, Thomas W. *o.praem.* '81 (ORG) [A] Silverado, CA St. Michael's Norbertine Postulancy, Novitiate and Juniorate; [H] Silverado, CA Norbertine Fathers of Orange Inc.
Nelson, William R. '82 (PBL) Center, CO St. Francis Jerome Church; Del Norte, CO Holy Name of Mary Church; Monte Vista, CO St. Joseph Church.
Nemec, Joseph J. '84 (LIN) [11] Lincoln, NE St. Teresa's Church; [G] Lincoln, NE Adoration Convent and Church of Christ the King.
Nemecek, M. Cyril '60 (CHI) North Riverside, IL Mater Christi Church.
Nemeck, Francis Kelly *o.m.i.* '61 (CC) [G] Sarita, TX Lebh Shomea House of Prayer.
Nemeck, Francis Kelly *o.m.i.* '61 (SAT) [C] San Antonio, TX Oblate School of Theology.
Nemer, Lawrence *s.v.d.* '60 (FgM) Society of the Divine Word Foreign Missions.
Nemergut, Robert '77 (EVN) [1] Vincennes, IN Sacred Heart Church.
Nemeth, Edward M. *s.j.* '65 (CLV) University Heights, OH Gesu Church.
Nemeth, Maurus B. *o.s.b.* '72 (SFR) [N] Portola Valley, CA Woodside Priory.
Nemeth, Robert *o.f.m.* '67 (BGP) [3] Fairfield, CT St. Emery's Church.
Nemmers, Francis J. '57 (SC) Larchwood, IA St. Mary Church.
Nemmers, Mark R. '66 (DUB) St. Theresa, IA St. Theresa's Church; Sylvia, IA Assumption Church.
Nemmers, Reinhard E. '35 (SC) Retired.
Nenneau, Thomas D. '81 (LAN) Charlotte, MI St. Mary Church.
Nentwick, John '65 (Y) [2] Canton, OH Our Lady of Peace Church.
Nerino, Joseph C. *m.m.* '50 (FgM) Maryknoll Foreign Missions.
Nero, James *o.f.m.* '71 (NEW) Fair Lawn, NJ St. Anne's Church.
Neroda, Edward J. '57 (Y) [21] Youngstown, OH St. Stanislaus Kostka's Church.
Nesbit, Walter G. *s.j.* '59 (KC) [B] Kansas City, MO Rockhurst College; [J] Kansas City, MO Rockhurst College - Jesuit Community.
Nesbitt, James B. '53 (SUP) Retired.
Nesbitt, John B. '62 (SD) Retired.
Neske, Mark I. '83 (MOB) [11] Mobile, AL Little Flower Church.
Nespolo, Umberto *o.m.i.* '59 (FRS) [1] Fresno, CA St. John Cathedral; On Special Assignment.
Nesrsta, Steven '95 (AUS) Temple, TX St. Mary's Church.
Ness, Bernardine *o.s.b.* '64 (FgM) American - Cassinese Congregation Foreign Missions.
Ness, Bernardine *o.s.b.* '64 (SFS) [F] Marvin, SD Blue Cloud Abbey.
Ness, Scott C. *o.s.a.* '90 (BO) [C] North Andover, MA Merrimack College; [CC] North Andover, MA Merrimack College Campus Ministry Center.
Nessel, William J. *o.s.f.s.* '56 (HBG) Lewisburg, PA Sacred Heart of Jesus Church.
Nessinger, Philip *o.carm.* '50 (CHI) Gurnee, IL St. Paul the Apostle Church.
Nester, Edward J. '46 (MET) Baptistown, NJ Our Lady of Victories Church; Retired; [H] Somerset, NJ Maria Regina Residence.
Nesti, Donald S. *c.s.sp.* '63 (GAL) [Q] Houston, TX Western Province of the Congregation of the Holy Ghost.
Nestler, W. David *o.f.m.cap.* '89 (PIT) [O] Pittsburgh, PA St. Conrad Friary.

Nestor, Msgr. Michael (PHX) [5] Mesa, AZ St. Bridget Church.
Nestor, Msgr. Michael '65 (SJP) Retired.
Nestor, Robert P. '70 (NEW) [B] South Orange, NJ Seton Hall University.
Nestor, Thomas E. '81 (BO) [A] Boston, MA St. John's Seminary School of Theology.
Nestor, Thomas F. '80 (BO) [A] Boston, MA St. John's Seminary.
Nesvadba, Msgr. Reginald '66 (GAL) [A] Houston, TX St. Mary's Seminary.
Netta, John G. '57 (NEW) [6] Elizabeth, NJ St. Genevieve's Church.
Nettekoven, Joseph '75 (ORG) [3] Anaheim, CA St. Justin Martyr Church.
Netter, Msgr. Edmund '51 (NY) Nyack, NY St. Ann Church.
Netter, Msgr. Edmund W. '51 (NY) Retired.
Netzer, Angelus *o.f.m.conv.* (ALB) [L] Rensselaer, NY Franciscan Mission House.
Neu, Msgr. Hubert '51 (FWT) [1] Fort Worth, TX St. Patrick Cathedral.
Neu, Msgr. Leon M. '52 (BUF) Randolph, NY St. Patrick Church.
Neuberger, Michael T. '62 (MIL) On Leave.
Neubert, Germar '65 (OM) [K] Schuyler, NE Benedictine Mission House.
Neudecker, Urban '45 (WIN) Jackson, MN Good Shepherd Church.
Neudecker, Urban C. '45 (WIN) Retired.
Neufelder, Jerome '55 (IND) [A] St. Meinrad, IN St. Meinrad Seminary.
Neufelder, Msgr. Jerome M. '55 (EVN) On Duty Outside the Diocese.
Neugebauer, Robert G. '73 (ALT) [2] Altoona, PA Immaculate Conception Church.
Neugebaur, John (ALT) [3] Altoona, PA St. Mark's Church.
Neuhaus, Richard J. '91 (NY) [52] New York, NY Immaculate Conception Church; [A] Yonkers, NY St. Joseph's Seminary.
Neuhaus, William B. '83 (COV) Carrollton, KY St. John the Evangelist Church.
Neuman, Eugene C. '70 (MIL) [5] Fond du Lac, WI Sacred Heart Church.
Neuman, James L. '71 (SFD) Wood River, IL St. Bernard Church.
Neuman, Matthias *o.s.b.* '67 (EVN) [H] Ferdinand, IN Sisters of St. Benedict of Ferdinand, IN, Inc., Monastery Immaculate Conception.
Neuman, Matthias *o.s.b.* '67 (IND) [B] St. Meinrad, IN St. Meinrad Seminary-College of Liberal Arts; [J] St. Meinrad, IN St. Meinrad Archabbey.
Neuman, Peter *i.c.* '80 (NO) [14] New Orleans, LA Mary, Queen of Vietnam Church.
Neumann, Aloysius J. '60 (RCK) Stockton, IL Holy Cross Church.
Neumann, August '52 (MET) South River, NJ Corpus Christi Church; Retired.
Neumann, Don A. '72 (GAL) [K] Houston, TX The Catholic Chaplain Corps.
Neumann, Richard J. '65 (HRT) Windsor, CT St. Gabriel's Church.
Neumann, William J. '75 (ORL) [2] Ocala, FL Our Lady of the Springs Church.
Neumeier, Larry '95 (LA) Paramount, CA Our Lady of the Rosary Church.
Neuner, Donald L. '56 (STL) [3] St. Charles, MO St. Elizabeth Ann Seton Church.
Neurohr, Gilbert N. '54 (MAR) Retired; [D] Escanaba, MI Bishop Noa Home for Senior Citizens.
Neuroth, William C. '65 (COV) [R] Covington, KY Interfaith Commission of Northern Kentucky.
Neuser, John '62 (GB) Mishicot, WI Holy Cross Church.
Neuville, Joseph '46 (P) Retired.
Neuville, Joseph J. '47 (P) Milwaukie, OR St. John the Baptist Church.
Neuzil, Greg '67 (KNX) LaFollette, TN Our Lady of Perpetual Help Church; Tazewell, TN Christ the King Church.
Neva, Roman G. '35 (FAR) Retired.
Nevans, Robert '49 (DEN) Greeley, CO St. Mary Church.
Nevans, Robert V. '49 (DEN) Retired.
Nevares, Eduardo *m.s.* '81 (TYL) Lufkin, TX St. Patrick Church.
Neveu, Armand A. '45 (HRT) Retired.
Neville, Franklin A. '86 (WH) Weirton, WV St. Joseph the Worker Church.
Neville, Gary J. *o.praem.* '78 (GB) [I] De Pere, WI St. Norbert Abbey.
Neville, James J. *s.j.* '56 (WH) Monongah, WV Holy Spirit Church.
Neville, John *o.s.c.* '61 (FgM) Crosier Foreign Missions.
Neville, John J. *o.s.c.* '61 (STP) [N] Shoreview, MN Crosier Provincial House Province of St. Odilia.
Neville, Joseph B. *s.j.* '60 (SY) [S] Syracuse, NY Jesuits at LeMoyne, Inc.
Neville, Thomas W. '52 (RCK) Virgil, IL SS. Peter and Paul Church.
Nevin, Emmet R. '77 (NY) [E] New York, NY Monsignor Farrell High School.
Nevins, Albert J. *m.m.* '42 (NY) [DD] Maryknoll, NY Maryknoll Fathers and Brothers.
Nevins, Donald J. '75 (CHI) [62] Chicago, IL St. Francis of Assisi Church; [81] Chicago, IL Holy Family Church.
Nevins, Eugene J. *s.j.* '80 (CIN) [K] Cincinnati, OH Good Samaritan Hospital; [M] Cincinnati, OH Jesuit Community at St. Xavier High School.
Nevins, John J. '57 (PH) Essington, PA St. Margaret Mary Alacoque Church.
Nevins, Troy '96 (GR) Portland, MI St. Patrick's Church.
Nevlud, Gregory '82 (SAT) [C] San Antonio, TX University of the Incarnate Word.
New, Gary *s.d.s.* '91 (GB) Charlesburg, WI St. Charles Borromeo Church; Charlestown, WI St. Martin Church; Chilton, WI St. Augustine Church; Chilton, WI St. Mary Church; Jericho, WI Holy Trinity Church; Kloten, WI St. Elizabeth Church.
Newbold, Msgr. Robert C. '45 (PRO) [25] Providence, RI Our Lady of Lourdes Church.
Newbold, Ronan *c.p.* '69 (FgM) Mission Procurators.
Newbold, Thomas M. *c.p.* '42 (CHI) [N] Chicago, IL Passionist Provincial Office.
Newbold, Thomas More *c.p.* '42 (SAC) [G] Citrus Heights, CA Christ the King Retreat.
Newburn, Charles *sch.p.* '79 (MIA) [C] Fort Lauderdale, FL Cardinal Gibbons High School.
Newcomer, Joseph '71 (B) [B] Nampa, ID Mercy Medical Center.
Newell, John J. '58 (BRK) Absent on Sick Leave.
Newell, Joseph A. *s.j.* '66 (CAM) Somers Point, NJ St. Joseph's Church.
Newell, Joseph P. '45 (PIT) Cranberry Township, PA St. Ferdinand Church.
Newell, Matthias '87 (RIC) Brookneal, VA St. Elizabeth of Hungary Church; South Boston, VA St. Paschal Baylon Church.
Newfield, John L. '48 (HT) Retired.
Newhouse, Paul M. *c.i.c.m.* '54 (SAT) Somerset, TX St. Mary's Church.
Newland, Ronald A. '67 (NEW) Military Chaplains.
Newman, Aloysius T. '54 (WDC) Retired.
Newman, Brian *o.f.m.cap.* '61 (FgM) Capuchin Foreign Missions.
Newman, Charles *o.f.m.* '85 (PH) [D] Philadelphia, PA Archbishop Ryan High School; [AA] Philadelphia, PA St. Pius X Friary.
Newman, Earle A. *s.s.j.* '53 (BAL) [M] Baltimore, MD St. Joseph Society of the Sacred Heart House of Central Administration.
Newman, Francis M. '47 (NY) Verplanck, NY St. Patrick Church; Retired.
Newman, J. Scott '93 (CHR) [9] Charleston, SC Divine Redeemer Church.
Newman, Louis '58 (SD) [25] San Diego, CA St. Columba Church.
Newman, Louis I. '58 (RVC) Priests Released from Diocesan Assignment.
Newman, Mark L. *c.j.* '60 (LA) Santa Maria, CA St. Louis de Montfort Church.
Newman, Michael J. *s.d.s.* '67 (SAC) [J] Chico, CA Director of Campus Ministry; [J] Chico, CA Director of Campus Ministry.
Newman, Michael T. '69 (MIL) [2] Waukesha, WI St. Mary Church.
Newman, Nelson A. '54 (OM) Central City, NE St. Michael Church.
Newman, Paul *s.m.* '59 (FWT) [A] Fort Worth, TX Nolan Catholic High School.
Newman, Robert V. *s.c.* '81 (HRT) [1] New Haven, CT Sacred Heart Church.
Newman, William '54 (BAL) [Q] Joppa, MD Catholic Daughters of the Americas.
Newman, William A. *o.p.* '57 (WDC) [11] Washington, DC St. Dominic Church & Priory Church.
Newmeyer, George C. '68 (PIT) Glenshaw, PA St. Bonaventure Church.
Newns, John J. '74 (PH) [1] Phoenixville, PA St. Ann Church.
Newton, David J. '88 (LFT) Carmel, IN Our Lady of Mount Carmel Church.
Newton, John G. '53 (CAM) Military Chaplains.
Newton, Stephen *c.s.c.* '89 (FTW) [J] Notre Dame, IN Holy Cross Community, Corby Hall, University of Notre Dame.
Newton, Stephen P. *c.s.c.* '89 (FTW) [B] Notre Dame, IN University of Notre Dame Du Lac.
Newton, Thomas A. '88 (CAM) Mantua, NJ Incarnation Church; [R] Camden, NJ Rutgers College of South Jersey.
Ney, Charles '74 (NSH) On Duty Outside the Diocese.
Neyland, Quintin A. *o.f.m.* '46 (NY) [35] New York, NY St. Francis of Assisi Church.
Neylon, Bruce M. '75 (FR) Seekonk, MA St. Mary's Church.
Neyra, Hugo '84 (LA) Pico Rivera, CA St. Hilary Church.
Neyrey, Jerome H. *s.j.* '70 (FTW) [B] Notre Dame, IN University of Notre Dame Du Lac; [N] Granger, IN Jesuit Community.
Ng, Thomas '61 (OAK) [12] Oakland, CA St. Leo's Church.
Ngaway, Omer '91 (WDC) [M] Washington, DC Divine Word College.
Ngbatana, Tongele (SAC) Davis, CA St. James Church.
Ngbatara, Tongele (SAC) [J] Chico, CA Director of Campus Ministry.
Nghiem, Peter Hoan-Xuan '72 (GR) On Special Assignment.
Nghiem, Vu Minh *c.ss.r.* '51 (LA) [R] Baldwin Park, CA Vietnamese Redemptorist Mission; [DD] Baldwin Park, CA The Redemptorist Vietnamese Mission Corporation.
Ngo, Anthony '94 (RIC) [17] Richmond, VA Church of the Vietnamese Martyrs.
Ngo, Francis Huan Ton '89 (GAL) [40] Houston, TX St. John Neumann Church.
Ngo, Joseph Linh Duy '52 (NO) Retired.
Ngo Chau Minh, Peter M. *c.m.c.* (SPC) [E] Carthage, MO Congregation of the Mother Co-Redemptrix, United States Assumption Province.
Ngo Duc Vuong, John D.M. *c.m.c.* (SPC) [E] Carthage, MO Congregation of the Mother Co-Redemptrix, United States Assumption Province.
Ngoc Diep, Joseph M. Tran *c.m.c.* '82 (SPC) [A] Carthage, MO Congregation of the Mother Co-Redemptrix.
Ngugi, Joseph Njoroge '80 (WDC) [5] Washington, DC St. Anthony Church.
Nguyen, Am *s.d.b.* '94 (OAK) [N] Berkeley, CA Salesian Community.
Nguyen, Andrew *c.m.c.* (BO) [62] Boston, MA St. Peter Church.
Nguyen, Andrew Cuu (NY) Manhattan, NY Manhattan Psychiatric Center.
Nguyen, Anthony Giang '66 (BO) [2] Chelsea, MA St. Rose of Lima Church; [13] Lowell, MA St. Patrick Church.
Nguyen, Anthony Phuc *c.s.s.r.* '92 (P) [17] Portland, OR Holy Redeemer Church.
Nguyen, Augustine '70 (DAL) [2] Garland, TX Mother of Perpetual Help Church.
Nguyen, Charles D. '92 (SAC) Woodland, CA Holy Rosary Church.
Nguyen, Chau '86 (ORL) Palm Bay, FL St. Joseph Church.
Nguyen, Chinh '94 (SR) Petaluma, CA St. Vincent de Paul Church.
Nguyen, Cuong Scott '97 (WCH) [5] Wichita, KS Church of the Magdalen.
Nguyen, Dam '93 (PIT) Castle Shannon, PA St. Anne Church.
Nguyen, Dau '84 (NO) [A] New Orleans, LA Notre Dame Seminary Graduate School of Theology.
Nguyen, Doakim '93 (GAL) [41] Houston, TX St. John Vianney Church.
Nguyen, Doanh *s.j.* (PHX) [B] Phoenix, AZ Brophy College Preparatory.
Nguyen, Dominic H. *s.j.* '92 (P) [L] Portland, OR Jesuit Provincial Office (Society of Jesus, Oregon Prov.).
Nguyen, Dominic Hoa '95 (ORG) Garden Grove, CA St. Columban Church.
Nguyen, Dominic Huyen Duc '64 (NO) [14] New Orleans, LA Mary, Queen of Vietnam Church.
Nguyen, Dominic Khoai *i.c.m.* '96 (BR) [H] Baton Rouge, LA Incarnation Consecratio Mission.
Nguyen, Dominic Phu *s.s.s.* '68 (GAL) [25] Houston, TX Corpus Christi Church.
Nguyen, Dovan '93 (TLS) Broken Arrow, OK St. Anne Church.
Nguyen, Francis Khoi '90 (DOD) Dighton, KS St. Theresa Church.
Nguyen, Francis X. Khoi '90 (DOD) Scott City, KS St. Joseph Church.
Nguyen, Hien Minh '85 (SJ) Milpitas, CA St. Elizabeth Church.
Nguyen, Hieu '69 (SC) [1] Sioux City, IA Cathedral of the Epiphany.
Nguyen, Hoa '95 (OKL) [1] Oklahoma City, OK Cathedral of Our Lady of Perpetual Help.
Nguyen, Huan Tien '66 (CIN) On Special and Diocesan Assignment; [V] Cincinnati, OH Vietnamese-Catholic Community.
Nguyen, Hung '94 (SEA) Poulsbo, WA St. Olaf Church.
Nguyen, Hung Joseph *s.d.b.* (STO) [10] Stockton, CA Presentation of B.V.M. Church.
Nguyen, Hung Viet *i.c.m.* '69 (BR) [4] Baton Rouge, LA St. Anthony of Padua Church; [H] Baton Rouge, LA Incarnation Consecratio Mission; [L] Baton Rouge, LA St. Michael's Home.
Nguyen, Huy '95 (LA) Claremont, CA Our Lady of the Assumption Church.
Nguyen, Hy Khac '97 (OAK) [22] Oakland, CA St. Theresa of the Infant Jesus (The Little Flower) Church.
Nguyen, J. Kim-Dang '93 (LA) Torrance, CA St. Catherine Laboure Church.
Nguyen, Joachim Thamh '67 (PRT) Stockholm, ME St. Therese Church.
Nguyen, Joachim Thanh '67 (PRT) Caribou, ME Sacred

Heart Church.
Nguyen, Joe Van Anh '88 (AUS) [6] Austin, TX Holy Vietnamese Martyrs Church.
Nguyen, John Hoa '72 (LA) Burbank, CA St. Finbar Church.
Nguyen, Joseph '73 (FRS) [10] Fresno, CA St. Helen Church.
Nguyen, Joseph '80 (NOR) [B] Uncasville, CT St. Bernard High School.
Nguyen, Joseph An '92 (CAM) [7] Camden, NJ St. Joseph's Pro-Cathedral; [5] Atlantic City, NJ Our Lady Star of the Sea Church.
Nguyen, Joseph Chinh (BO) [74] Boston, MA St. William Church.
Nguyen, Joseph Chuan '78 (ORG) Inactive Leave.
Nguyen, Joseph Dau Van '84 (NO) [4] Metairie, LA St. Benilde Church.
Nguyen, Joseph Hoa '76 (HBG) [8] Harrisburg, PA Our Lady of the Blessed Sacrament Church.
Nguyen, Joseph Huong '85 (SAC) Yuba City, CA St. Isidore Church.
Nguyen, Joseph Kahn V. '63 (DAV) [M] Davenport, IA St. Vincent Center.
Nguyen, Joseph Luan '90 (ORG) [1] Huntington Beach, CA St. Bonaventure Church.
Nguyen, Joseph Ngoc Tu *o.p.* '64 (GAL) [Q] Houston, TX Dominican Fathers and Brothers, St. Mark Priory, Inc.
Nguyen, Joseph Phiet The '73 (GAL) Madisonville, TX St. Elizabeth Ann Seton Church.
Nguyen, Joseph Son '89 (ORG) Laguna Hills, CA St. Nicholas Church.
Nguyen, Joseph Son Van '82 (DAL) [7] Dallas, TX Mary Immaculate Church.
Nguyen, Joseph Tan Doan *o.f.m.* '86 (SFD) [B] Quincy, IL Quincy University.
Nguyen, Joseph Thai (CHI) [11] Chicago, IL St. Andrew Church.
Nguyen, Joseph Thai-Doan '88 (BR) Livonia, LA St. Frances Xavier Cabrini Church.
Nguyen, Joseph Thinh Duc '94 (MEM) [21] Memphis, TN St. Paul The Apostle Church.
Nguyen, Joseph Thuan *o.p.* '93 (OAK) [17] Oakland, CA St. Mary, Immaculate Conception-St. Francis de Sales Church.
Nguyen, Joseph Trong *s.v.d.* '91 (FgM) Society of the Divine Word Foreign Missions.
Nguyen, Jude Ban *c.m.c.* '73 (SAC) [23] Sacramento, CA Vietnamese Catholic Martyrs Church.
Nguyen, Khanh Pham '97 (COS) [1] Colorado Springs, CO St. Mary's Cathedral.
Nguyen, Khiet '96 (TLS) [1] Tulsa, OK Holy Family Cathedral.
Nguyen, Khiet T. '96 (TLS) Poteau, OK Immaculate Conception Church.
Nguyen, Kim Son (SAV) [1] Savannah, GA Cathedral of St. John the Baptist; [10] Savannah, GA Sts. Peter and Paul Church.
Nguyen, Lich Van '84 (NO) Arabi, LA St. Robert Bellarmine Church.
Nguyen, Liem *o.s.b.* '94 (P) [A] St. Benedict, OR Mount Angel Seminary; [L] St. Benedict, OR Mt. Angel Abbey.
Nguyen, Liep Van Joseph '63 (CC) On Special Assignment.
Nguyen, Linh '97 (LEX) Pikeville, KY St. Francis of Assisi Church.
Nguyen, Martin Lam *c.s.c.* '89 (FTW) [B] Notre Dame, IN University of Notre Dame Du Lac; [J] Notre Dame, IN Holy Cross Community, Corby Hall, University of Notre Dame.
Nguyen, Martin Thanh *i.c.m.* '97 (BR) [H] Baton Rouge, LA Incarnation Consecratio Mission.
Nguyen, Michael M. *c.m.* '95 (CHL) [3] Greensboro, NC St. Mary Church.
Nguyen, Michael Nam Hoang '93 (NO) On Duty Outside the Archdiocese.
Nguyen, Michael Joseph Vinh N. (NO) Graduate Studies.
Nguyen, Minh Hai '92 (NEW) West New York, NJ St. Joseph of the Palisades Church.
Nguyen, Nghiem Vinh '89 (NO) [12] Metairie, LA St. Mary Magdalen Church.
Nguyen, Nhuan D. *m.m.* '93 (FgM) Maryknoll Foreign Missions.
Nguyen, Pascal B. *o.praem.* '94 (ORG) [H] Silverado, CA Norbertine Fathers of Orange Inc.
Nguyen, Paul Chuong *s.d.b.* '88 (NEW) [C] Ramsey, NJ Don Bosco Preparatory High School for Boys.
Nguyen, Peter (SD) Vista, CA St. Francis of Assisi Church.
Nguyen, Peter Duc Hung '97 (SC) Carroll, IA Holy Spirit Church.
Nguyen, Peter Phong '46 (DAL) Grand Prairie, TX St. Joseph Vietnamese Catholic Community Church.
Nguyen, Peter Quang '90 (DEN) Greeley, CO St. Mary Church.
Nguyen, Peter Sam *s.v.d.* '86 (OAK) [6] Oakland, CA St. Bernard's Church.
Nguyen, Peter Sam Cao *s.v.d.* '86 (FgM) Society of the Divine Word Foreign Missions.
Nguyen, Peter T. (CHI) [205] Chicago, IL St. Thomas of Canterbury Church.
Nguyen, Peter Vinh Q. (NEW) Livingston, NJ St. Barnabas Medical Center.
Nguyen, Phillip D. '87 (GR) On Special Assignment; On Duty Outside the Diocese.
Nguyen, Quang '91 (NO) Gretna, LA St. Cletus Church.
Nguyen, Quang Dang '44 (CC) Rockport, TX St. Peter Indo-Chinese Parish; Retired.
Nguyen, Raphael Ho Xuan '96 (ORG) Garden Grove, CA St. Columban Church.
Nguyen, Stephen Tan (RIC) [4] Hampton, VA Our Lady of Viet Nam Chapel Church; [6] Norfolk, VA Our Lady of Lavang Church.
Nguyen, Stephen Tan *o.f.m.* '59 (SFR) [7] San Francisco, CA St. Boniface Church.
Nguyen, Sy Uy '91 (ORG) [4] Huntington Beach, CA St. Vincent de Paul Church.
Nguyen, Tam N. '82 (TLS) [14] Tulsa, OK SS. Peter and Paul Church.
Nguyen, Te Van '86 (SFR) [3] San Mateo, CA St. Matthew Church.
Nguyen, Thanh N. '94 (R) [5] Raleigh, NC St. Joseph Church.
Nguyen, Thanh T. '91 (STA) [3] Jacksonville, FL Christ the King Church.
Nguyen, Thanh Van *s.v.d.* (DUB) [B] Epworth, IA Divine Word College.
Nguyen, Thien (WIN) Geneva, MN St. Mary Church.
Nguyen, Thien Chi *s.o.l.t.* '91 (CC) [H] Robstown, TX Society of Our Lady of the Most Holy Trinity.
Nguyen, Thien Van '89 (WIN) New Richland, MN All Saints Church.
Nguyen, Thomas Thanh '69 (LAF) Louisa, LA St. Helen Church.
Nguyen, Thong *c.ss.r.* '56 (DAL) [2] Garland, TX Mother of Perpetual Help Church.
Nguyen, Thu Ngoc '93 (GAL) [45] Houston, TX St. Luke the Evangelist Church.
Nguyen, Thu Van '92 (VIC) El Campo, TX St. Philip the Apostle Church.
Nguyen, Thuong Hoai '91 (OAK) [3] Oakland, CA St. Anthony's Church.
Nguyen, Tien Tri '96 (SFE) Rio Rancho, NM St. Thomas Aquinas Church.
Nguyen, Toan '96 (SFR) Novato, CA St. Anthony of Padua Church.
Nguyen, Trong Duc '69 (SFR) [23] San Francisco, CA Holy Name of Jesus Church; Special Assignment.
Nguyen, Trung '94 (GAL) On Duty Outside the Diocese.
Nguyen, Trung John '95 (MOB) Bayou LaBatre, AL St. Margaret Church.
Nguyen, Tuan *s.d.b.* '88 (STO) [7] Stockton, CA St. Luke Church.
Nguyen, Tuan '92 (SEA) Centralia, WA St. Mary's Church; Chehalis, WA St. Joseph's Church; Chehalis, WA State Training School for Boys.
Nguyen, Tuan '95 (ORG) Westminster, CA Blessed Sacrament Church.
Nguyen, Tuan V. '86 (JOL) Villa Park, IL St. Alexander Church.
Nguyen, Tuyen '87 (ORG) Tustin, CA St. Cecilia Church.
Nguyen, Vandennis '89 (PEO) Pekin, IL St. Joseph's Church.
Nguyen, Vien The '89 (NO) [8] Metairie, LA St. Edward the Confessor Church; [A] New Orleans, LA Notre Dame Seminary Graduate School of Theology.
Nguyen, Vincent Kien (SJ) [21] San Jose, CA Our Lady Queen of Martyrs, Vietnamese Mission Church.
Nguyen, Vincent The' Quang '75 (CHR) Greenville, SC St. Mary's Church.
Nguyen Chau Dien, Raymond M. *c.m.c.* (SPC) [E] Carthage, MO Congregation of the Mother Co-Redemptrix, United States Assumption Province.
Nguyen Dan, Pius M. *c.m.c.* '83 (SB) [E] Corona, CA Congregation of the Mother Coredemptrix.
Nguyen Duc Kien, Barnabas M. *c.m.c.* (SPC) [E] Carthage, MO Congregation of the Mother Co-Redemptrix, United States Assumption Province.
Nguyen Huy Chuong, Matthias M. *c.m.c.* '81 (SB) [E] Corona, CA Congregation of the Mother Coredemptrix.
Nguyen Linh Uy, Athanasius M. *c.m.c.* (SPC) [E] Carthage, MO Congregation of the Mother Co-Redemptrix, United States Assumption Province.
Nguyen Mang Cach, Paul M. *c.m.c.* (SPC) [E] Carthage, MO Congregation of the Mother Co-Redemptrix, United States Assumption Province.
Nguyen Minh Tu, Andrew '69 (PT) Panama City, FL SS. Peter & Paul Mission Church.
Nguyen Minh Vu, Joseph *s.v.d.* '96 (FgM) Society of the Divine Word Foreign Missions.
Nguyen Ngoc Tu, Joseph *o.p.* '64 (GAL) [36] Houston, TX Holy Rosary Church.
Nguyen Phuoc, Joseph *s.d.b.* '95 (OAK) [N] Berkeley, CA Salesian Community.
Nguyen Quang Dan, Pius M. *c.m.c.* (SPC) [E] Carthage, MO Congregation of the Mother Co-Redemptrix, United States Assumption Province.
Nguyen Thanh Hue, Augustine '64 (PT) [5] Pensacola, FL Our Lady Queen of Martyrs, Mission Church.
Nguyen Trong Thuong, Bernard M. *c.m.c.* (SPC) [E] Carthage, MO Congregation of the Mother Co-Redemptrix, United States Assumption Province.
Nguyen-Thanh-Long, Peter '65 (WDC) [5] Bethesda, MD Our Lady of Vietnam Church.
Ngwatu, Anthony (PIT) [J] Pittsburgh, PA St. Francis Medical Center.
Nhan, Tran Tu *c.ss.r.* '47 (LA) [R] Baldwin Park, CA Vietnamese Redemptorist Mission.
Nhan Van Tran, John '92 (NO) [2] Metairie, LA St. Angela Merici Church.
Nhi, Tran Dinh '71 (ARL) [3] Alexandria, VA Queen of Apostles Church.
Nhien, Louis '95 (ROC) [6] Rochester, NY St. Anthony of Padua Church.
Nho, Do Duy '66 (LR) [12] Little Rock, AR St. Patrick's Church.
Nibberich, Msgr. Lawrence C. '50 (STL) Retired.
Nibler, James *o.m.v.* '87 (BO) [W] Milton, MA Oblate Residence (St. Joseph House); [BB] Boston, MA St. Francis Chapel.
Niblick, Charles W. '74 (GRY) [5] Whiting, IN Sts. Peter and Paul Church.
Nicastro, Thomas D. '90 (BGP) [4] Stratford, CT Our Lady of Grace Church.
Nicastro, Thomas More *o.f.m.* '42 (NY) [FF] Wappingers Falls, NY Mt. Alvernia Retreat House.
Niccoli, Andrew '42 (BRK) [203] Queens, NY Most Precious Blood Church; Retired.
Niccolls, Edward D. '74 (WOR) Lunenburg, MA St. Boniface Church.
Nicewicz, Edward '62 (WOR) Absent on Leave.
Nicgorski, David J. *o.m.v.* '91 (MET) Avenel, NJ St. Andrew Church.
Nicholas, Gerald A. *o.s.a.* '66 (JOL) [C] New Lenox, IL Providence Catholic High School; [J] New Lenox, IL Augustinian Friary.
Nicholl, Rex F. '67 (AMA) Perryton, TX Immaculate Conception Church.
Nicholls, Trevor '90 (NY) [E] Goshen, NY John S. Burke Catholic High School.
Nichols, Aquinas *o.s.b.* '80 (SD) [H] Oceanside, CA Prince of Peace Abbey, Benet Hill.
Nichols, Charles '48 (BRK) [131] Brooklyn, NY Sacred Hearts of Jesus and Mary and St. Stephen Church.
Nichols, Charles P. '48 (BRK) Retired.
Nichols, Earl W. '46 (OG) Retired.
Nichols, Edward '75 (SPC) On Duty Outside the Diocese.
Nichols, Edward P., Jr. '75 (SP) Brandon, FL Church of the Nativity.
Nichols, Harry E. '73 (PIT) Green Tree, PA St. Margaret Church.
Nichols, Henry P. '70 (BO) Boston, MA Veterans Administration Hospital; Military & VA Chaplains.
Nichols, Herbert T. '75 (FR) [12] Fall River, MA St. Anne's Church; [J] Fall River, MA Priests' Hostel.
Nichols, John J. '62 (BO) Watertown, MA St. Theresa of the Child Jesus Church.
Nichols, Joseph E. '62 (NOR) Retired.
Nichols, Louis J. '60 (SR) Clearlake, CA Our Lady, Queen of Peace Church.
Nichols, Louis J. '60 (SY) On Duty Outside the Diocese.
Nichols, Rodrick '89 (LSC) Silver City, NM St. Vincent de Paul Church.
Nichols, Stephen J. '86 (BUR) Troy, VT Sacred Heart of Jesus Church.
Nichols, Timothy '73 (LA) Redondo Beach, CA St. James Church.
Nichols, William H. *s.j.* '60 (CLV) [C] Cleveland, OH John Carroll Jesuit Community.
Nicholson, David *o.s.b.* '49 (P) [L] St. Benedict, OR Mt. Angel Abbey.
Nicholson, Francis J. *s.j.* '53 (BO) [W] Chestnut Hill, MA The Jesuit Community at Boston College.
Nicholson, John A. *s.j.* '46 (NY) [DD] New York, NY Murray-Weigel Hall.
Nicholson, Patrick '69 (MOB) On Leave from the Archdiocese.
Nickas, John P. '66 (NEW) Montclair, NJ St. Peter Claver Church.
Nickel, Leander F. '47 (GB) Stockbridge, WI St. Mary Church.
Nickels, Larry *o.f.m.* '86 (STL) [R] St. Louis, MO Franciscan Sisters of Our Lady of Perpetual Help.
Nickels, Peter *o.f.m. conv.* '60 (SAG) Oakley, MI St. Michael Church.
Nickerson, Oliver E. *s.j.* '54 (FgM) Provinces.
Nickerson, Russell *o.m.i.* '47 (MIA) Miramar, FL St. Stephen Church.
Nickle, Frederick *o.f.m.cap.* '65 (NOR) [4] Middletown, CT St. Pius X Church.
Nickless, R. Walker '73 (DEN) [3] Lakewood, CO Our Lady of Fatima Church.
Nicknair, Bernard L. '54 (PRT) Retired.
Nicknair, Harold '61 (PRT) [1] Portland, ME Cathedral of the Immaculate Conception; Retired.
Nicknair, Leopold G. '58 (PRT) Caribou, ME Holy Rosary Church.
Nickol, G. Eugene '73 (BAL) Glen Burnie, MD Holy

Trinity Church.
Nickolai, Arthur A. '43 (MIL) Retired.
Nickse, Jose P. '73 (MIA) [16] Miami, FL St. Brendan Church; [B] Opa Locka, FL St. Thomas University; [C] Miami, FL St. Brendan High School; [L] Key Largo, FL 1-800-Mass-Times Trust.
Nicola, John J. '55 (CHI) Other Assignments.
Nicolas, Jeffrey S. '93 (L) Elizabethtown, KY St. James Church; White Mills, KY St. Ignatius Church.
Nicolau, Bernardo *t.o.r.* '65 (FWT) [2] Fort Worth, TX All Saints Church.
Nicolau, Juan '60 (BWN) San Juan, TX Santuario de Nuestra Senora de San Juan del Valle Church; [I] San Juan, TX Virgen de San Juan del Valle Shrine.
Nicoletti, Maurizio *o.cist* '65 (TR) Mount Laurel, NJ St. John Neumann Church; [M] Mount Laurel, NJ Cistercian Monastery of Our Lady of Fatima.
Nicoletti, Robert *m.j.* '92 (PCE) On Duty Outside the Diocese.
Nicolicchia, James A. *o.p.* '65 (NY) Hawthorne, NY Holy Rosary Church.
Nicoll, Leo A. *s.j.* '61 (NO) [C] New Orleans, LA Loyola University.
Nicolo, Joseph J. '74 (PH) [127] Philadelphia, PA Our Lady of the Rosary Church.
Nicolosi, Joseph P. '97 (RCK) St. Charles, IL St. Patrick Church.
Nicolosi, Mark Ronald *o.s.b.* '67 (BUR) [E] Weston, VT Priory of Benedictine Monks.
Nicosia, Peter *o.f.m.cap.* '59 (NEW) [4] Hackensack, NJ St. Francis Church.
Nicosia, Vincent A. *s.o.l.t.* '92 (CC) [H] Robstown, TX Society of Our Lady of the Most Holy Trinity.
Nicosia, Vincent A. *s.o.l.t.* '92 (SFE) La Joya, NM Our Lady of Sorrows Church.
Nieberding, Richard *c.pp.s.* '80 (COL) [23] Columbus, OH St. James the Less Church.
Nieberding, Robert H. '56 (LEX) [3] Lexington, KY Mary, Queen of the Holy Rosary Church.
Nieblas, James *s.d.b.* '86 (LA) [79] Los Angeles, CA St. Mary Church; [R] Los Angeles, CA Dominic Savio Salesian Residence.
Niebrugge, Herman J. '56 (SFD) Mattoon, IL Immaculate Conception Church.
Niebrzydowski, Msgr. Walter J. '59 (NY) [34] New York, NY Epiphany Church.
Nieckarz, James P. *m.m.* '66 (NY) [DD] Maryknoll, NY Maryknoll Fathers and Brothers.
Niederberger, Vincent J. *c.s.sp.* '50 (PH) [AA] Bensalem, PA Congregation of the Holy Ghost.
Niedergeses, W. Bernard '50 (NSH) [3] Nashville, TN Assumption Church; [12] Nashville, TN St. Pius X Church.
Niedermier, Jerome G. '52 (TOL) Retired.
Niedzwicki, Thomas C. '53 (GR) Irons, MI St. Bernard's Church.
Niedzwiecki, Harold *o.f.m.* (NEW) [O] Lodi, NJ Immaculate Conception Convent.
Niehaus, Charles W. *s.p.* '74 (CHI) [177] Chicago, IL St. Procopius Church; [N] Chicago, IL Miguel Pro Jesuit Community.
Niehaus, Earl F. *s.m.* '51 (NO) [9] Metairie, LA St. Francis Xavier Church.
Niehaus, Francis H. '55 (CIN) Retired.
Niehaus, Jonathan J. '94 (MIL) [T] Waukesha, WI Secular Institute of Schoenstatt Fathers.
Niehaus, Theodore *o.f.m.cap.* '65 (FgM) Capuchin Foreign Missions.
Niehoff, Edmund A. '64 (SHP) Mansfield, LA St. Joseph Church.
Niehoff, Robert L. *s.j.* '82 (SFR) [N] San Francisco, CA Jesuit Community at University of San Francisco.
Nielsen, Eric '95 (MAD) Waunakee, WI St. John the Baptist Church.
Nielsen, Kenneth M. '80 (BUF) On Duty Outside the Diocese.
Nielsen, Philip W. *o.f.m.* '48 (PAT) [N] Parsippany, NJ St. Francis of Assisi Novitiate-Franciscan Sisters of St. Elizabeth.
Nielson, James P. *o.praem.* '93 (GB) [I] De Pere, WI St. Norbert Abbey.
Nielson, Thomas A. '59 (NY) [1] New York, NY Cathedral of St. Patrick; [HH] New York, NY St. Ansgar Scandinavian Catholic League.
Nieman, Raymond L. '54 (COV) Retired.
Niemann, Mark E. *s.j.* '50 (OM) [C] Omaha, NE Creighton Preparatory School.
Niemann, Paul '80 (PRM) St. Louis, MO St. Louis Mission Church.
Niemann, Paul J. '80 (STL) [1] St. Louis, MO Cathedral Basilica of St. Louis Church.
Niemczyk, Stefan J. '87 (SPR) [7] Springfield, MA Immaculate Conception Church.
Niemeier, Dennis '73 (CIN) Military Chaplains.
Niemeyer, James J. '74 (JC) Absent on Leave.
Niemeyer, John '55 (PEO) Retired.
Niemeyer, Roger *o.f.m.* '40 (SFD) [K] Sherman, IL Our Lady of Angels Friary.
Niemier, Roch *o.f.m.* '65 (MIL) [P] Milwaukee, WI Francis and Clare House; [Y] Milwaukee, WI Franciscan Pilgrimage Programs, Inc.
Niemira, Thomas '65 (JKS) On Duty Outside the Diocese.
Niemira, Thomas J. '53 (AUS) Waco, TX V.A. Hospital.
Nienaber, Msgr. Leonard B. '34 (LEX) Retired.
Nienaber, Robert H. '63 (OM) Genoa, NE St. Rose of Lima Church; Krakow, NE SS. Peter and Paul Church.
Nienhaus, Bernard '65 (STL) Hawk Point, MO St. Mary Church.
Nienhaus, Gerald T. '62 (STL) Spanish Lake, MO St. Aloysius Church.
Nienhaus, Ivan R. '89 (DUB) Masonville, IA Immaculate Conception Church; Winthrop, IA St. Patrick's Church.
Niese, Larry P. '95 (ATL) [2] Atlanta, GA Holy Cross Church.
Nieset, Frank E. '56 (TOL) Retired.
Niessen, John '51 (SB) Perris, CA St. James Church.
Nietfeld, Fred J. '46 (TOL) Retired.
Nietlong, Joseph (PIT) [4] Donora, PA Our Lady of the Valley Church.
Nietlong, Joseph '86 (NY) [W] New York, NY Saint Vincent's Medical Center of Richmond.
Nieto, Jose *c.m.f.* '66 (SJN) [9] Bayamon, PR San Jose Church.
Nieto-Ruiz, Jose de Jesus '94 (OAK) [2] Hayward, CA St. Bede Church.
Nieva, Constantino '55 (RVC) Bellport, NY Mary Immaculate Church.
Nieves, Encarnacion '83 (CGS) Aguas Buenas, PR Espiritu Santo Church.
Nieves, Jose Javier '95 (PAT) [7] Paterson, NJ St. George Church.
Niezgoda, Joseph R. (GRY) [8] East Chicago, IN St. John Cantius Church.
Niggemann, Bernard '31 (SUP) Retired.
Nightengale, Msgr. Francis '42 (SB) Retired.
Nigli, Francis A. '97 (OM) [47] Omaha, NE St. Vincent de Paul Church.
Niglis, Joseph C. '37 (MAD) Retired.
Nigro, Armand M. *s.j.* (SPK) [C] Spokane, WA Gonzaga University.
Nigro, Armond *s.j.* (SPK) [C] Spokane, WA Mater Dei Institute.
Nijem, Fred J. '68 (SAV) Warner Robins, GA Sacred Heart Church.
Niklas, Gerald R. '59 (CIN) [K] Cincinnati, OH Good Samaritan Hospital.
Nikliborc, Francis U. '47 (CHI) Retired.
Nikliborc, Robert D. '55 (SD) [20] San Diego, CA St. Anne Church.
Nikodem, Martin J. '67 (BGP) [16] Bridgeport, CT Our Lady of Good Counsel Church.
Nikodem, Ronald J. *s.m.* '94 (ATL) [C] Atlanta, GA Marist School.
Nikolai, William V. '48 (LC) Retired; [I] La Crosse, WI Holy Cross (Seminary) Diocesan Center.
Niland, Jack *o.f.m.cap.* '76 (AGN) Santa Rita, GU Our Lady of Guadalupe Church.
Niland, John *o.f.m.cap.* '76 (FgM) Capuchin Foreign Missions.
Nilema, Nicholas *a.l.c.p.* (P) Seaside, OR Our Lady of Victory Church.
Nilges, Harold L. '53 (RCK) Genoa, IL St. Catherine of Genoa Church.
Nilles, Msgr. Allan F. '49 (FAR) Park River, ND St. Mary's Church.
Nilles, Roger G. '59 (MAD) [13] Madison, WI St. Peter Church.
Nilsson, Richard A. '71 (RVC) Long Beach, NY St. Ignatius Martyr Church.
Nimal, George '76 (STO) Modesto, CA St. Stanislaus Church.
Nimerichter, Dean '92 (DM) Greenfield, IA St. John Church; Orient, IA St. Mark Church.
Nimocks, Michael F. '96 (COL) Bolivar, OH Holy Trinity Church.
Ninedorf, Robert W. '89 (CHR) Edgefield, SC St. Mary's Church; Ward, SC St. William's Church.
Ninemire, Kerry '75 (SAL) [3] Salina, KS St. Mary's Church.
Nino, Andres G. *o.s.a.* '62 (BO) [9] Cambridge, MA St. Mary of the Annunciation Church.
Nir, Roman '64 (DET) [A] Orchard Lake, MI SS. Cyril and Methodius Seminary.
Nirappel, Antony '63 (MAR) Perkins, MI St. Joseph Church.
Nirrengarten, Andrew (RVC) Port Jefferson, NY St. Charles Hospital, Port Jefferson, New York.
Nirschl, Nicholas E. *o.praem.* '56 (SFE) Isleta, NM St. Augustine Church; [J] Albuquerque, NM Santa Maria de la Vid Priory.
Nisbet, Jim '69 (MRY) Spreckels, CA St. Joseph Church.
Nischan, James R. '83 (PCE) On Duty Outside the Diocese.
Nishigaya, Msgr. Raymond J. '64 (HON) [14] Honolulu, HI St. Stephen Church.
Nishimura, Bryce T. *m.m.* '56 (FgM) Maryknoll Foreign Missions.
Nishimuta, James K. *m.m.* '54 (FgM) Maryknoll Foreign Missions.
Niskanen, Steven *c.m.f.* '90 (SAT) [B] San Antonio, TX St. Anthony Mary Claret Seminary.
Nissel, John J. *s.j.* '56 (BAL) [M] Baltimore, MD Jesuit Fathers and Brothers Maryland Provincial Curia.
Nissel, John J. *s.j.* '56 (FgM) Provinces.
Nist, Arthur '40 (Y) Retired.
Nistal, Alejandro *o.ss.t.* '66 (PCE) [10] Ponce, PR La Santisima Trinidad Church.
Nistler, Edward '54 (CR) Bemidji, MN St. Philip's Church; Retired.
Nitural, Leo (BRK) [54] Brooklyn, NY Holy Family Church.
Nitz, Eliot *s.d.s.* '68 (WDC) [B] Silver Spring, MD Salvatorian Community; [K] Silver Spring, MD Holy Cross Hospital of Silver Spring, Inc.
Nitzki, John *s.c.j.* '56 (MIL) Franklin, WI Sacred Hearts of Jesus and Mary Church.
Nix, Albert '73 (PAT) Stirling, NJ St. Vincent de Paul Church.
Nix, Julian *o.s.b.* '87 (BIS) [A] Richardton, ND Assumption Abbey.
Nixon, Edmond J. *c.ss.r.* '71 (NY) [34] New York, NY Epiphany Church.
Nixon, Joseph J. '85 (RVC) [C] Hicksville, NY Holy Trinity.
Niziolek, Terrence *m.s.* '66 (MIL) [P] Twin Lakes, WI La Salette Missionaries Shrine.
Njeim, Elias (OG) Retired.
Njoku, Gregory *c.s.sp.* '82 (MIA) Opa Locka, FL Our Lady of Perpetual Help Church.
Njoku, Hyacinth '86 (NY) [162] Bronx, NY St. Margaret Mary Church.
Njoku, Peter (STP) Bellechester, MN St. Mary Church; Zumbrota, MN St. Paul Church.
Nkackukwu, Michael '80 (DET) [8] Detroit, MI St. Anthony Church.
Nkedife, Peter '76 (LKC) Jennings, LA Our Lady of Perpetual Help Church.
Noah, Daniel '50 (CR) Retired.
Noah, Timothy T. '47 (CR) Hallock, MN St. Patrick's Church.
Nobile, Angelo '53 (MEM) On Duty Outside the Diocese.
Nobiletti, Raymond J. *m.m.* '69 (NY) [119] New York, NY Transfiguration Church; [DD] Maryknoll, NY Maryknoll Fathers and Brothers.
Noble, Bruce H. '87 (GAL) [K] Houston, TX The Catholic Chaplain Corps.
Noble, Charles F. '55 (NEW) Weehawken, NJ St. Lawrence's Church.
Noble, David H. '87 (GAL) [K] Houston, TX The Catholic Chaplain Corps.
Noble, Jeffrey J. '86 (E) [4] Oil City, PA St. Stephen Church.
Noble, Paul A. '81 (COL) [1] Columbus, OH St. Joseph Cathedral.
Nobleza, Dennis A., Jr. '70 (LA) Monrovia, CA Immaculate Conception Church.
Noboa, Origenes (VEN) LaBelle, FL Our Lady Queen of Heaven Church.
Nocero, Pascal F. '48 (LA) Retired.
Nochelski, Paul W. *s.j.* '71 (BUF) [O] Buffalo, NY Canisius Jesuit Community.
Nock, James J. '64 (HRT) [2] East Hartford, CT Our Lady of Peace Church.
Nockunas, Anthony N. *m.i.c.* '57 (WOR) [19] Worcester, MA St. Casimir's Church.
Noda, Jorge '84 (MIA) [1] Hialeah, FL Immaculate Conception Church.
Noe, John P. '74 (LEX) Ashland, KY Federal Correctional Institution; [D] Ashland, KY Our Lady of Bellefonte Hospital, Inc.
Noecker, Ronald J. '85 (OM) Beemer, NE Holy Cross Church.
Noel, Damian L. *t.o.r.* '53 (ALT) [F] Loretto, PA Mount Assisi Friary.
Noel, Donald C. *o.praem.* '59 (GB) [A] De Pere, WI St. Norbert Abbey; [I] De Pere, WI St. Norbert Abbey.
Noel, Guyma '97 (ATL) Peachtree City, GA Holy Trinity Catholic Church.
Noesen, Gerald L. '55 (CR) Fertile, MN St. Joseph Church; Fosston, MN St. Mary's Church; Mentor, MN St. Lawrence Church.
Noesen, Robert '93 (JOL) Mokena, IL St. Mary Church.
Noeson, Thomas *o.p.* '76 (DEN) [35] Denver, CO St. Mary Magdalene's Church.
Noetzel, Kenneth *s.j.* (DET) Detroit, MI Sinai Hospital.
Noetzel, Kenneth J. *s.j.* '51 (DET) [27] Detroit, MI Gesu Church.
Nofaley, Thomas Simon '92 (EST) Southfield, MI Our Lady of Chaldeans Cathedral, Mother of God Chaldean Parish; Leave of Absence.
Nofi, Michael A. *m.s.a.* '74 (WH) Moorefield, WV Epiphany of the Lord Church.
Noga, Edward P. '76 (Y) [18] Youngstown, OH St. Patrick's Church.
Noga, Gregory J. '79 (PSC) Coatesville, PA St. Mary's Church; Mont Clare, PA St. Michael Church.
Nogaro, Paul M. '71 (BUF) [4] Kenmore, NY St. Paul Church.

Nogosek, Bob '56 (SB) Thermal, CA San Felipe de Jesus Church.
Nogosek, Robert J. *c.s.c.* '56 (SB) Coachella, CA Our Lady of Soledad Church.
Noguera, Dagoberto '85 (BRK) [63] Brooklyn, NY Immaculate Conception of the Blessed Virgin Mary Church.
Noguera, Ronald '81 (MIA) [27] Miami, FL St. Michael the Archangel Church.
Nohava, Douglas (PHX) Flagstaff, AZ San Francisco de Asis Church.
Nohilly, Thomas B. '81 (BRK) [127] Brooklyn, NY St. Rose of Lima Church.
Nohs, Joseph E. '93 (RVC) East Meadow, NY St. Raphael Church.
Noia, Leonel C. '73 (SJ) [5] San Jose, CA Five Wounds Portuguese National Church.
Noiseux, Donald A. '84 (SPR) Huntington, MA St. Thomas Church.
Nojek, Mark *o.c.d.* '90 (GRY) [J] Munster, IN Discalced Carmelite Fathers Monastery.
Nolan, Brian J. '91 (MET) Somerville, NJ Immaculate Conception Church.
Nolan, Colman J. *s.t.* '56 (TUC) Sierra Vista, AZ St. Andrew Church.
Nolan, Dan *c.s.v.* '83 (LAV) Henderson, NV St. Thomas More Church.
Nolan, David F. '95 (NY) [135] Bronx, NY St. Brendan Church.
Nolan, Msgr. Edward J. '48 (BRK) [182] Queens, NY Incarnation Church; Retired.
Nolan, Emmet J. *c.m.* '92 (FgM) Vincentian Foreign Missions.
Nolan, Eugene A. *s.j.* '71 (WDC) [E] Washington, DC Gonzaga College High School.
Nolan, James L. *o.s.a.* '46 (PH) [AA] Villanova, PA St. Thomas Monastery.
Nolan, Jerome M. '74 (TR) Fair Haven, NJ Nativity Church.
Nolan, John '77 (SFD) Military Chaplains.
Nolan, Joseph *m.s.* '48 (ATL) [2] Marietta, GA Church of St. Ann.
Nolan, Joseph '56 (SR) Napa, CA St. John the Baptist Church.
Nolan, Joseph A. '60 (ORL) Melbourne Beach, FL Immaculate Conception Church.
Nolan, Joseph M. '47 (BRK) [238] Queens, NY Sacred Heart Church; Retired.
Nolan, Joseph T '53 (WCH) On Duty Outside the Diocese.
Nolan, Justin *o.s.b.* '55 (GBG) [H] Latrobe, PA Saint Vincent Archabbey.
Nolan, Kevin '90 (LA) Van Nuys, CA St. Elisabeth Church.
Nolan, Kieran *o.s.b.* '59 (FgM) American - Cassinese Congregation Foreign Missions.
Nolan, Kieran *o.s.b.* '59 (SCL) [I] Collegeville, MN St. John's Abbey, of the Order of St. Benedict.
Nolan, Larry '58 (COL) [G] Columbus, OH St. Raphael Home for the Aged, Inc.
Nolan, Michael E. '84 (WCH) Oxford, KS St. Mary Church; Winfield, KS Holy Name Church.
Nolan, Michael F. '87 (KNX) [2] Chattanooga, TN Our Lady of Perpetual Help Church.
Nolan, Niall '66 (GAL) The Woodlands, TX Sts. Simon and Jude Church.
Nolan, Norbert L. '51 (ROC) Retired.
Nolan, Msgr. Patrick '50 (SAC) Retired and in Senior Ministry.
Nolan, Msgr. Patrick M. '50 (SAC) [20] Sacramento, CA St. Philomene Church.
Nolan, Paul (NEW) Newark, NJ Essex County Jail; Caldwell, NJ Essex County Jail Annex.
Nolan, Paul '75 (NEW) Maywood, NJ Our Lady Queen of Peace Church.
Nolan, Paul J. '57 (NEW) [2] Union City, NJ St. Augustine's Church.
Nolan, Peter P. *c.s.sp.* (BO) [52] Boston, MA Most Precious Blood Church.
Nolan, Robert J. *s.a.c.* '70 (CAM) [C] Pennsauken, NJ Bishop Eustace Prep School.
Nolan, Shawn *o.f.m.conv.* '55 (NY) [B] New York, NY St. Francis Novitiate.
Nolan, Msgr. Terence '66 (SAT) [K] San Antonio, TX Casa De Padres.
Nolan, Timothy '92 (PEO) [13] Peoria, IL St. Philomena's Church.
Nolan, Timothy F. '67 (STP) Ham Lake, MN Saint Paul Church.
Nolan, Msgr. Walter E. '69 (TR) Princeton, NJ St. Paul Church.
Nolan, William A. '85 (MAD) Cambridge, WI St. Pius X Church.
Nolan, William J. '69 (TR) [2] Toms River, NJ St. Justin Church.
Nolan, Msgr. William L. '43 (MAN) Retired.
Nolan, William N '57 (NSH) Retired.
Nold, Joseph K. '45 (SY) Retired.
Nolen, Joseph *c.ss.r.* '76 (STL) [B] St. Louis, MO St. John Neumann House.
Nolette, Mark P. '87 (PRT) Ashland, ME St. Mark's Church.
Nolette, Roger '69 (BO) [W] Hingham, MA Glastonbury Abbey.
Nolin, John W. '60 (MAN) Sabbatical.
Nolin, Joseph A. '49 (ORL) Retired.
Nolker, Thomas C. '72 (CIN) [32] Cincinnati, OH Guardian Angels Church.
Noll, Daniel '76 (LEX) [6] Lexington, KY St. Paul Church; [7] Lexington, KY St. Peter Church; [8] Lexington, KY St. Peter Claver Church.
Noll, Donald T. '61 (CIN) Retired.
Noll, Joseph *c.s.s.r.* '33 (ALB) [L] Saratoga Springs, NY St. John Neumann Residence.
Noll, Joseph *c.ss.r.* '33 (NY) [92] New York, NY Our Lady of Perpetual Help Church.
Nollette, Louis A. '75 (GI) Mullen, NE St. Mary's Church.
Nollette, Neal P. '80 (GI) Elm Creek, NE Immaculate Conception Church.
Nolte, William J., Jr. '67 (WH) Retired.
Nombrado, Benjamin '79 (SFR) [15] San Francisco, CA St. Elizabeth Church.
Nomellini, Paul J. '77 (MAR) Kingsford, MI St. Mary Queen of Peace Church.
Nondorf, Aloysius J. '57 (GRY) Military Chaplains.
Noon, Msgr. Robert L. (COL) Lancaster, OH St. Mark Church.
Noon, Msgr. Robert L. '51 (COL) Retired.
Noonan, James P. *m.m.* '60 (FgM) Maryknoll Foreign Missions.
Noonan, John '83 (MIA) [A] Miami, FL St. John Vianney College Seminary.
Noonan, Joseph T. '95 (CHI) [64] Chicago, IL St. Francis Borgia Church.
Noonan, Mark L. '59 (BO) [A] Boston, MA St. John's Seminary.
Noonan, Patrick '63 (JKS) Canton, MS Sacred Heart Church; Canton, MS Holy Child Jesus Church; Carthage, MS St. Anne Church.
Noonan, Robert C. '64 (HEL) Choteau, MT St. Joseph Church; Fairfield, MT St. John Church.
Noonan, Msgr. Thomas F. '55 (BRK) [34] Brooklyn, NY St. Edmund's Church.
Noonan, William J. '39 (BO) Retired.
Noone, Charles J. '67 (PH) Feasterville, PA Assumption B.V.M. Church.
Noone, David E. '66 (ALB) Loudonville, NY St. Francis de Sales Church.
Noone, John '67 (BLX) Picayune, MS St. Charles Borromeo Church.
Noone, Msgr. Kevin B. '70 (BRK) [97] Brooklyn, NY Our Lady of Guadalupe Church.
Noone, Sean '52 (CC) Retired.
Nooney, P. Joseph '52 (SC) Fort Dodge, IA Trinity Regional Hospital.
Nooney, Patrick J. '52 (SC) Retired.
Norbeck, Ernest '84 (JOL) [1] Naperville, IL St. Elizabeth Seton Church.
Norcavage, Albert R. '50 (ALT) Absent on Leave.
Nord, Clarence C. '43 (L) Retired.
Norden, Emmett M. '62 (MAR) Bark River, MI St. Elizabeth Ann Seton Church; Perronville, MI St. Elizabeth Ann Seton Church; Schaffer, MI St. Elizabeth Ann Seton Church.
Nordenbrock, William A. *c.pp.s.* '83 (KCK) [K] Easton, KS Shantivanam Archdiocesan House of Prayer.
Norder, John '66 (MAD) Cassville, WI St. Charles Borromeo Church.
Nordhaus, Jeffrey J. '72 (TOL) Military Chaplains.
Nordick, Benedict *o.s.b.* '78 (SCL) [I] Collegeville, MN St. John's Abbey, of the Order of St. Benedict.
Nordick, Jerome G. '83 (SCL) Chokio, MN St. Mary's Church; Herman, MN St. Charles Church.
Nordick, John A. '90 (NU) Beardsley, MN St. Mary Church; Graceville, MN Holy Rosary Church.
Nordmeyer, Emeric *o.f.m.* '56 (GLP) Grants, NM St. Teresa Church.
Nordquist, Theodore A. '80 (GRY) La Porte, IN St. Joseph Church; [M] Gary, IN Catholic Charities.
Noreika, Michael *s.s.s.* '70 (GB) Menasha, WI St. Mary Church.
Norick, Daniel J. '97 (DEN) Loveland, CO St. John the Evangelist Church.
Noriega, Arnoldo '75 (TUC) Absent on Leave.
Norkett, Edward J. '36 (CHI) Retired.
Norkett, Michael '68 (OAK) [1] San Leandro, CA Assumption of the Blessed Virgin Mary Church.
Norkiewicz, Chester *c.r.* '44 (CHI) [D] Chicago, IL Gordon Technical High School.
Norkunas, Msgr. Anthony J. '44 (SCR) Retired.
Norman, Charles *o.s.f.s.* (ALN) [O] Kutztown, PA Christopher House; [O] Kutztown, PA Christopher House.
Norman, Clifford A. '60 (PBL) On Duty Outside the Diocese.
Norman, Gary '94 (YAK) Richland, WA Christ the King Church.
Norman, Gregory *o.cist.* '53 (LC) [I] Sparta, WI Our Lady of Spring Bank, Cistercian Abbey.
Norman, John (SLC) [B] Salt Lake City, UT Judge Memorial Catholic High School.
Norman, Richard W. *s.j.* '58 (ALN) [A] Wernersville, PA Novitiate of St. Isaac Jogues.
Normanly, Thomas *s.s.c.* '52 (OM) [K] St. Columbans, NE St. Columban's Foreign Mission Society.
Noronha, Valerian *o.c.d.* '91 (WDC) [B] Washington, DC Monastery of Our Lady of Mount Carmel.
Norrell, Msgr. Albert V. '88 (PH) [29] Philadelphia, PA St. Carthage Church.
Norris, David J. '74 (FRS) Hilmar, CA Holy Rosary Church.
Norris, Frank B. *s.s.* '50 (SFR) [A] Menlo Park, CA St. Patrick Seminary.
Norris, John P. '46 (ROC) Mendon, NY St. Catherine of Siena Church; Retired.
Norris, Mark *o.s.b.* '95 (SFE) [L] Pecos, NM Our Lady of Guadalupe Benedictine Abbey.
Norris, Patrick F. *o.p.* '89 (STL) [P] St. Louis, MO St. Dominic Priory.
Norris, Robert J. '80 (NY) [159] Bronx, NY St. Lucy Church.
Norris, Thomas P. *o.s.f.s.* (R) Goldsboro, NC St. Mary Church.
Norris, Timothy L. '94 (STP) Northfield, MN St. Dominic Church.
Norris, Walter J. '41 (WDC) Damascus, MD St. Paul Church; Retired.
Norsworthy, Richard '85 (SHP) Bossier City, LA St. Jude Church.
North, Robert G. *s.j.* '44 (MIL) [P] Milwaukee, WI Jesuit Provincial Office, Wisconsin Province.
Northrop, James '97 (SEA) Olympia, WA St. Michael's Church.
Northrop, John B. *m.m.* '74 (FgM) Maryknoll Foreign Missions.
Norton, Arthur E. '59 (BGP) Danbury, CT Danbury Area Mental Health Authority.
Norton, Claude B. '43 (DUB) Retired.
Norton, Daniel J. '65 (CAM) On Duty Outside the Diocese.
Norton, Edward *s.v.d.* '45 (CHI) [B] Techny, IL Divine Word Residence.
Norton, Emmet J. *s.j.* '48 (PAT) [I] Morristown, NJ Loyola House of Retreats.
Norton, George '83 (ROC) [8] Rochester, NY Blessed Sacrament Church; Rochester, NY Genesee Hospital.
Norton, John *o.p.* '56 (CHY) Sheridan, WY U.S. Veterans Administration Hospital.
Norton, Joseph E. '57 (WDC) Retired.
Norton, Michael *c.pp.s.* '70 (SAT) [H] San Antonio, TX Santa Rosa Health Care System.
Norton, Robert A. '72 (PIT) West View, PA St. Athanasius Church.
Norton, Robert J. *o.f.m.* '74 (NEW) Elmwood Park, NJ St. Leo's Church.
Norton, Thomas '63 (NEW) Northvale, NJ St. Anthony's Church; Westwood, NJ Pascack Valley Hospital.
Norton, William W. '67 (FR) Centerville, MA Our Lady of Victory Church.
Nortz, Alfred E. '55 (SY) [24] Syracuse, NY St. Vincent de Paul Church.
Norusis, Nicholas M. *o.s.m.* '44 (DEN) Westminster, CO Holy Trinity Church.
Norvel, William L. *s.s.j.* '65 (BAL) [33] Baltimore, MD St. Francis Xavier Church.
Nosbush, Peter C. '70 (NU) Litchfield, MN St. Philip Church.
Noser, J. Homer '43 (STL) Retired.
Nosoc, Ayub (GR) [E] Grand Rapids, MI St. Mary's Health Services.
Nosser, Msgr. Charles J. '53 (RVC) Floral Park, NY Our Lady of Victory Church.
Nosser, Msgr. John C. '64 (RVC) Montauk, NY St. Therese of Lisieux Church.
Notabartolo, Charles '77 (PMB) Jupiter, FL St. Peter Church.
Notaro, Carlo *o.s.cam.* '88 (MIL) [N] Wauwatosa, WI St. Camillus Health Center, Inc.; [N] Wauwatosa, WI San Camillo, Inc.; [P] Wauwatosa, WI St. Camillus Community House.
Notarpole, Joseph '49 (STA) [11] Jacksonville, FL Our Lady of the Angels Church.
Notebaart, James C. '71 (STP) Special Assignment.
Noto, James M. '63 (RIC) [11] Virginia Beach, VA St. Nicholas Church.
Nott, David L. '93 (RIC) Covington, VA Church of the Sacred Heart; Hot Springs, VA The Shrine of the Sacred Heart Church.
Notter, Richard E. '63 (TOL) [36] Toledo, OH SS. Peter and Paul Church; [O] Toledo, OH The Catholic Migrant Farmworker Network.
Noulaka, Matthias (NY) Ossining, NY St. Ann Church.
Nourie, Paul *o.m.i.* '64 (OAK) Pleasant Hill, CA Christ the King Church.
Nouws, Jacques J. '46 (LA) [R] Los Angeles, CA Amat House.
Nouws, James J. *c.m.* '46 (LA) [X] Montebello, CA DePaul Center.
Nouza, Frank M. *o.p.* '58 (CHI) [N] Chicago, IL Dominicans (Provincial Office).
Novack, Kevin F. *c.s.p.* '81 (NY) [DD] Jamaica Estates,

NY Paulist Fathers Generalate.
Novack, Kevin F. '81 (PBL) Telluride, CO St. Patrick Church.
Novacki, Michael *o.p.* (WDC) [11] Washington, DC St. Dominic Church & Priory Church.
Novak, Alfred *c.ss.r.* '56 (DEN) [M] Denver, CO The Redemptorists/Denver Province.
Novak, David A. '79 (CLV) [34] Cleveland, OH Immaculate Conception Church; [39] Cleveland, OH St. Josaphat Church.
Novak, David M. '77 (STL) Hazelwood, MO St. Bartholomew Church.
Novak, Francis *c.ss.r.* '49 (CHI) [136] Chicago, IL St. Michael Church.
Novak, Henry *c.ss.r.* (CHI) [N] Glenview, IL The Redemptorists of Glenview, Illinois.
Novak, James '57 (LAN) Retired.
Novak, John '42 (JOL) Retired.
Novak, Joseph A. *s.j.* '57 (NY) [DD] New York, NY Jesuit Community at Fordham University; [DD] New York, NY Jesuit Community at Fordham University.
Novak, Msgr. Leonard J. '56 (SCR) [24] Scranton, PA Sacred Hearts of Jesus and Mary Church.
Novak, Norbert *o.s.b.* '64 (P) [L] St. Benedict, OR Mt. Angel Abbey.
Novak, Paul M. *o.s.m.* '90 (CHI) [N] Chicago, IL Servite Friars - Eastern Province.
Novak, Robert J. '42 (CHI) Retired.
Novak, Thomas *s.d.s.* '59 (MIL) [P] Milwaukee, WI Salvatorian Provincial Residence.
Novak, Vincent M. *s.j.* '55 (NY) [C] Bronx, NY Fordham University; [DD] New York, NY Jesuit Community at Fordham University.
Novak, William '97 (OKL) [3] Oklahoma City, OK St. Charles Borromeo Church.
Novakowski, James E. '95 (GI) Stapleton, NE St. John the Evangelist Church.
Novello, Lawrence E. '84 (BO) [4] Waltham, MA St. Mary Church; Absent on Leave.
Novello, Msgr. Russell R. '53 (BO) Retired.
Novelly, Duane R. '79 (DET) [49] Detroit, MI St. Matthew Church.
Novicky, Msgr. William N. '46 (CLV) South Euclid, OH St. Gregory the Great Church.
Novielli, John J. *o.praem.* '74 (PH) [B] Paoli, PA Daylesford Abbey; [AA] Paoli, PA Daylesford Abbey.
Noviello, Anthony A. '43 (SCR) Retired.
Novoa, Dominic '83 (PMB) [D] West Palm Beach, FL St. Mary's Hospital, Inc.
Novoa, Dominic E. '83 (HRT) On Duty Outside the Archdiocese.
Novotney, Andrew J. *s.j.* '71 (BAL) [M] Baltimore, MD Jesuit Fathers and Brothers Maryland Provincial Curia.
Novotney, Jerome *o.m.i.* '68 (FgM) Oblates Foreign Missions.
Novotny, Allen P. *s.j.* '82 (BAL) [Q] Baltimore, MD Jesuit Educational Association of Maryland, Inc.
Novotny, Allen P. *s.j.* '82 (WDC) [E] Washington, DC Gonzaga College High School.
Novotny, James F. '64 (OM) Lindsay, NE Holy Family Church.
Novotny, Richard '81 (RC) On Duty Outside the Diocese.
Novotny, Robert J. '50 (MIL) Retired.
Nowacki, Jerome A. '93 (MAR) Rudyard, MI St. Joseph Church.
Nowacki, Peter *o.p.* '85 (CHI) [3] Lemont, IL SS. Cyril and Methodius Church.
Nowak, Bernard '52 (ROC) Retired.
Nowak, Bernard J. '52 (LC) Retired.
Nowak, Bernard U. (BUF) Angola, NY Most Precious Blood Church.
Nowak, Christopher *o.s.a.* '97 (NY) [168] Bronx, NY St. Nicholas of Tolentine Church.
Nowak, Daniel *o.f.m.* '59 (SAG) Bridgeport, MI Assumption of the Blessed Virgin Mary Church.
Nowak, David G. '85 (GRY) [5] Merrillville, IN St. Stephen, Martyr Church.
Nowak, Edward C. *c.s.p.* '89 (LA) Goleta, CA St. Mark University Parish; [CC] Los Angeles, CA Archdiocesan Office for Campus Ministry.
Nowak, Eugene J. '70 (CHI) Hoffman Estates, IL St. Hubert Church.
Nowak, Jacek *s.ch.* '92 (DET) [8] Sterling Heights, MI Our Lady of Czestochowa Church.
Nowak, James A. '67 (JOL) Westmont, IL Holy Trinity Church.
Nowak, John *c.f.* '71 (CHI) [D] Chicago, IL Weber High School.
Nowak, John H. *c.r.* '71 (CHI) [N] Chicago, IL Provincial Office of the Congregation of the Resurrection.
Nowak, Joseph G. '42 (CHI) [138] Chicago, IL St. Michael Church; Retired.
Nowak, Mark A. '75 (E) Cambridge Springs, PA St. Anthony Church; Meadville, PA St. Agatha Church; [P] Erie, PA Newman Centers and Campus Ministry.
Nowak, Michael E. '97 (MIL) [2] Wauwatosa, WI Christ King Church.
Nowak, Randolph *o.f.m.cap.* '52 (AGN) [E] Agana Heights, GU St. Fidelis Friary.
Nowak, Randolph *o.f.m.cap.* '52 (FgM) Capuchin Foreign Missions.
Nowak, Stanley F. '58 (BUF) [4] Depew, NY SS. Peter and Paul Church.
Nowak, Vincent A. '36 (ALB) Retired.
Nowakowski, Edward S. '48 (GB) Armstrong Creek, WI St. Stanislaus Kostka Church; Goodman, WI St. Joan of Arc Church.
Nowakowski, Francis M. '39 (ALB) Retired.
Nowakowski, Jerome '63 (TOL) [7] Toledo, OH Good Shepherd Church.
Nowakowski, Jerome F. '63 (TOL) [30] Toledo, OH St. Louis Church.
Nowakowski, Stanislaus A. '37 (KAL) Battle Creek, MI St. Joseph Church; Retired.
Nowel, Mark D. *o.p.* '86 (PRO) [P] Providence, RI St. Thomas Aquinas Priory at Providence College.
Nowery, C. Richard *c.s.c.* '68 (NO) [22] New Orleans, LA Sacred Heart Of Jesus Church.
Nowicki, Chester *s.v.d.* '46 (CHI) [B] Techny, IL Divine Word Residence; [N] Techny, IL Society of the Divine Word, Provincial Headquarter-Chicago Prov.
Nowicki, Gary D. '96 (MIL) [79] Milwaukee, WI St. Veronica Church.
Nowinski, Dennis '73 (DET) Memphis, MI All Saints Church.
Nowlan, Edward H. *s.j.* '41 (BO) [W] Chestnut Hill, MA The Jesuit Community at Boston College.
Nowlan, John T. '66 (DET) Redford Township, MI St. Hilary Church.
Nsionu, Patrick (RVC) Cedarhurst, NY St. Joachim Church.
Ntsiful-Amissah, Kofi '79 (ALB) Special Assignment.
Nuanez, Anthony '79 (LA) Sick Leave.
Nuelle, John R. *m.s.* '64 (HRT) [M] Hartford, CT Missionaries of LaSalette Provincial Secretary; [M] Hartford, CT Missionaries of LaSalette Provincial Secretary; [V] Hartford, CT North American La Salette Mission Center, Inc.
Nugent, Anthony A. '72 (JOL) Plainfield, IL St. Mary Immaculate Church.
Nugent, Msgr. Arthur W. '47 (PH) Retired.
Nugent, C. Robert *s.d.s.* '65 (MIL) [P] Milwaukee, WI Salvatorian Provincial Residence.
Nugent, Frank *s.d.b.* (NEW) [N] South Orange, NJ The Salesian Community.
Nugent, Frank '56 (NEW) [N] South Orange, NJ Salesian Residence.
Nugent, Msgr. Irvine '54 (PMB) Vero Beach, FL St. Helen Church.
Nugent, Irvine M. '97 (PMB) Lake Worth, FL Sacred Heart Church.
Nugent, James *c.ss.r.* '50 (CHI) [9] Chicago, IL St. Alphonsus Church.
Nugent, James *i.c.* '69 (PEO) [A] Peoria, IL Rosminian Novitiate.
Nugent, Msgr. James B. '56 (STU) Retired.
Nugent, John G. *c.m.* '49 (MET) [H] Plainsboro, NJ Vincentian Residence.
Nugent, Joseph '71 (BRK) [68] Brooklyn, NY St. John the Evangelist Church.
Nugent, Kevin *s.t.* '51 (FgM) Trinity Missions.
Nugent, Msgr. Michael A. '43 (COL) [40] Columbus, OH St. Timothy Church; Retired.
Nugent, Msgr. Peter D. '62 (LA) [2] Oxnard, CA Santa Clara Church.
Nugent, Raymond H. '58 (RVC) Ronkonkoma, NY St. Joseph's Church.
Nugent, Msgr. Richard T. '49 (BUF) [2] Orchard Park, NY St. Bernadette Church.
Nugent, Robert *s.d.s.* (WDC) [B] Silver Spring, MD Salvatorian Community.
Nugent, Robert '65 (ALB) South Glens Falls, NY St. Michael the Archangel Church.
Nugent, Vincent J. *c.m.* '42 (PH) [AA] Philadelphia, PA Congregation of the Mission.
Nunan, Jeremiah '63 (ALB) Cairo, NY Sacred Heart Church.
Nunes, James (RVC) [H] Hicksville, NY Catholic Charities Central Administration.
Nunes, Jose '68 (PH) [71] Philadelphia, PA Incarnation of Our Lord Church.
Nunes, Mario (NEW) [26] Newark, NJ Our Lady of Fatima Church.
Nunez, Albert G. '64 (LAF) Lyons Point, LA St. John the Baptist Church.
Nunez, Edgardo '96 (ARE) [1] Vega-Baja, PR Holy Rosary Church.
Nunez, Edward H. '76 (PBL) [6] Pueblo, CO Our Lady of Guadalupe Church; [13] Pueblo, CO St. Leander Church.
Nunez, Jose Felix *c.m.f.* '64 (SJN) [2] Bayamon, PR San Antonio Maria Claret Church.
Nunez, Mario '79 (SAC) Isleton, CA St. Therese's Church.
Nunez, Pedro F. '77 (NO) [35] New Orleans, LA St. Gerard Church; [66] New Orleans, LA St. Vincent De Paul Church.
Nunez, Philip '88 (ARE) On Duty Outside the Diocese.
Nunning, David H. '69 (EVN) St. Wendel, IN St. Wendel Church.
Nuno, Rafael '69 (ARE) [2] Utuado, PR San Pedro y San Pablo Church.
Nurre, Henry V. *o.s.b.* '56 (MIL) [P] Benet Lake, WI St. Benedict's Abbey.
Nusbaum, Daniel C. '61 (ALB) On Duty Outside the Diocese.
Nusbaum, Daniel C. '61 (BAL) [B] Emmitsburg, MD Mount Saint Mary's College.
Nuss, Francis B. '61 (RVC) Sayville, NY Good Samaritan Nursing Home.; [K] Sayville, NY Good Samaritan Nursing Home.
Nutt, Maurice *c.ss.r.* '89 (STL) [22] St. Louis, MO St. Alphonsus Liguori Church; [P] St. Louis, MO St. Alphonsus Rectory of the Redemptorist.
Nuttall, J. *o.p.* '69 (FgM) Dominican - Order of Preachers Foreign Missions.
Nuttall, William I. *s.j.* '41 (PH) [AA] Philadelphia, PA Jesuit Community at St. Joseph's University.
Nutter, N. John '89 (BR) Amite, LA St. Helena Church.
Nuttman, Joseph *c.ss.r.* '52 (RNO) Carlin, NV Sacred Heart Church; Eureka, NV St. Brendan's Church.
Nuttman, Joseph K. *c.s.s.r.* '52 (P) [17] Portland, OR Holy Redeemer Church.
Nuttmann, Joseph *c.ss.r.* '52 (CHI) [N] Chicago, IL Redemptorists:; [N] Bodija, Ibadan, Oyo State, Nigeria.
Nuttmann, Joseph *c.ss.r.* '52 (DEN) [M] Denver, CO The Redemptorists/Denver Province.
Nuwer, Herold M. '61 (BUF) Ransomville, NY Immaculate Conception Church.
Nuytten, Ralph *c.i.c.m.* '49 (SAT) [M] San Antonio, TX Missionhurst Community Residence.
Nuzzi, Ronald '84 (CIN) [5] Dayton, OH Ascension Church.
Nuzzi, Ronald '84 (Y) On Duty Outside the Diocese.
Nuzzo, Peter Damian *o.f.m.* '69 (NY) [175] Bronx, NY Our Lady of Pity Church.
Nwachukwu, Oliver (CHI) [121] Chicago, IL St. Margaret Mary Church.
Nwachukwu, Raphael '74 (NY) Rosendale, NY St. Peter Church.
Nwachukwu, Thomas Kizito '82 (SHP) [3] Monroe, LA Our Lady of Fatima Church.
Nwachukwu-Udaku, A. O. *s.s.j.* '93 (BAL) [33] Baltimore, MD St. Francis Xavier Church.
Nwalo, Msgr. Thoephilus '65 (NY) [133] Bronx, NY St. Benedict Church.
Nwamadi, Chima (CLV) [17] Akron, OH St. Sebastian Church.
Nwankwo, Nnamdi (CLV) Wickliffe, OH Our Lady of Mount Carmel Church.
Nwanze, John *o.p.* (SEA) [9] Seattle, WA St. George Church; [18] Seattle, WA St. Paul Church.
Nwanze, John *o.p.* '75 (SEA) [8] Seattle, WA St. Edward Church.
Nwaogu, Anthony '77 (DAL) [12] Dallas, TX St. Anthony Church.
Nwaorgu, Anselm I. '92 (NEW) Union, NJ St. Michael's Church.
Nwaru, Romanus '95 (MIL) Elm Grove, WI St. Mary Church.
Nwoga, Laserian I. '95 (CAM) Pleasantville, NJ St. Peter's Church.
Nwogwugwu, Emmanuel '86 (NY) [204] Staten Island, NY Holy Child Church.
Nwosuh, Cosmas *m.s.p.* '89 (WDC) [B] Washington, DC St. Joseph's Seminary.
Nyambo, Callist '69 (SP) [5] St. Petersburg, FL St. Joseph Church.
Nyambo, Callist N. (SP) [F] St. Petersburg, FL Immaculate Conception Pre-School.
Nyardy, Jeffrey S. *o.s.b.* '90 (SAV) [B] Savannah, GA Benedictine Military School; [F] Savannah, GA The Benedictine Priory.
Nycz, Mieczyslaw F. '94 (BUF) [3] Orchard Park, NY Our Lady of the Sacred Heart Church.
Nydegger, Thomas P. '92 (NEW) [B] South Orange, NJ Seton Hall University.
Nyein, Isidore Usit *s.o.l.t.* '73 (CC) Robstown, TX St. Anthony Church.
Nygaard, Robert C. '64 (STP) Roseville, MN Corpus Christi Church.
Nygren, David *c.m.* '77 (CHI) [N] Chicago, IL Vincentian Community, Congregation of the Mission, Midwest Province.
Nygren, David J. *c.m.* '77 (STL) [P] Earth City, MO Congregation of the Mission Midwest Province (Vincentians).
Nyhan, James '73 (BO) [D] Cambridge, MA Matignon High School.
Nyhan, W. James '73 (BO) [7] Cambridge, MA Immaculate Conception Church.
Nyquist, Raymond J. '54 (GF) Black Eagle, MT Most Blessed Sacrament Church.
Nys, Loren G. *s.d.s.* '67 (GB) Kiel, WI SS. Peter and Paul Church.
Nyssen, Jacques *s.v.d.* '59 (TR) [M] Bordentown, NJ Society of the Divine Word.
Nzekwe, Anselm (CLV) South Euclid, OH St. Margaret Mary Church.

O

O Shea, David T. '61 (PT) Panama City Beach, FL St. Bernadette Church.
O'Bell, John C. '91 (SCR) [1] Hazleton, PA St. Gabriel's Church.
O'Blaney, James *c.ss.r.* '58 (ALB) Saratoga Springs, NY St. Clement Church.
O'Boyle, Andrew F. '54 (CLV) Brooklyn, OH St. Thomas More Church; Newbury, OH St. Helen Church; Retired.
O'Boyle, Leo *c.p.* '96 (CHI) [N] Chicago, IL Passionist Community-CTU.
O'Brien, Anthony *ss.cc.* '34 (HON) [H] Honolulu, HI St. Patrick's Monastery.
O'Brien, Anthony '88 (MIA) Coral Gables, FL Little Flower Church.
O'Brien, Arthur '83 (HON) Retired.
O'Brien, Bartholomew J. '40 (ROC) Retired.
O'Brien, Bartholomew J. '65 (PH) [70] Philadelphia, PA Immaculate Heart of Mary Church.
O'Brien, Bernard P. '49 (PIT) Retired.
O'Brien, Charles H. *o.p.* '54 (L) [47] Louisville, KY St. Louis Bertrand Church.
O'Brien, Christian T. *o.praem.* '62 (SFE) Albuquerque, NM St. Joseph Medical Center; [J] Albuquerque, NM Santa Maria de la Vid Priory.
O'Brien, Christopher '54 (EVN) On Duty Outside the Diocese.
O'Brien, Msgr. Cornelius '36 (NY) [E] White Plains, NY Archbishop Stepinac High School.
O'Brien, Cornelius '55 (ARL) Chantilly, VA St. Timothy Church.
O'Brien, Msgr. Cornelius M. '36 (NY) [1] Port Chester, NY Our Lady of Mercy Church; Retired.
O'Brien, Daniel '75 (VIC) Shiner, TX SS. Cyril and Methodius Church; Retired.
O'Brien, Msgr. Daniel B. '39 (SY) Dewitt, NY Holy Cross Church; Retired.
O'Brien, Daniel J. *s.j.* '59 (NY) [DD] New York, NY Jesuit Community at Fordham University.
O'Brien, Daniel P. (HBG) Dallastown, PA St. Joseph Church.
O'Brien, David *o.m.i.* '59 (FgM) Oblates Foreign Missions.
O'Brien, David G. '62 (BRK) Absent on Sick Leave.
O'Brien, David W. *c.s.p.* '56 (COL) [J] Columbus, OH Campus Ministry.
O'Brien, Denis *m.m.* '53 (DAL) [25] Dallas, TX St. Pius X Church.
O'Brien, Denis J. '44 (RVC) Retired.
O'Brien, Dennis (PT) Santa Rosa Beach, FL St. Rita Church.
O'Brien, Dennis J. '77 (WOR) [N] Leicester, MA Father James Fitton House of Priestly Formation.
O'Brien, Donald *o.m.i.* '65 (BO) [3] Lowell, MA Immaculate Conception Church.
O'Brien, Donald J. '61 (GI) Cozad, NE Christ the King Church.
O'Brien, Donald J. '93 (TR) Howell Township, NJ St. Veronica Church.
O'Brien, Donald V. *s.j.* '55 (NY) [2] White Plains, NY St. John the Evangelist Church.
O'Brien, Edmund M. '57 (HRT) Lakeville, CT St. Mary's Church.
O'Brien, Edward C. *s.j.* '61 (STL) [P] St. Louis, MO Jesuit Community Corporation at St. Louis University - Jesuit Hall.
O'Brien, Edward J. '37 (PRT) Retired.
O'Brien, Edward P. '52 (CHI) [142] Chicago, IL Nativity of Our Lord Church; Retired.
O'Brien, Eugene C. '57 (MIL) Retired.
O'Brien, Eugene J. *s.j.* '56 (NY) [DD] New York, NY "America;" Residence and publication office of the America Press; [HH] New York, NY Gregorian University Foundation, The.
O'Brien, Forrest '55 (TLS) [7] Tulsa, OK St. Francis Xavier-Our Lady of Guadalupe Church.
O'Brien, Francis E. '66 (BO) [2] Framingham, MA St. George Church.
O'Brien, Francis E. '85 (BO) [4] Norwood, MA St. Timothy Church.
O'Brien, Frederick J. *s.j.* '62 (BO) [W] Boston, MA The Society of Jesus of New England-Provincial Offices.
O'Brien, Frederick J. *s.j.* '62 (NY) [DD] New York, NY "America;" Residence and publication office of the America Press; [DD] New York, NY Jesuit Provincial's Office.
O'Brien, Frederick W. (BO) Retired.
O'Brien, George '57 (LA) Beverly Hills, CA Good Shepherd Church.
O'Brien, George L. '58 (WOR) East Templeton, MA Holy Cross Church.
O'Brien, Gerard '95 (LA) La Crescenta, CA St. James the Less Church.
O'Brien, Gerard C. *s.j.* '59 (BO) [W] Chestnut Hill, MA The Jesuit Community at Boston College.
O'Brien, Gilbert L. *o.praem.* '90 (ORG) [H] Silverado, CA Norbertine Fathers of Orange Inc.
O'Brien, Howard E. *m.m.* '55 (FgM) Maryknoll Foreign Missions.
O'Brien, J. Paul *s.j.* '68 (CIN) [F] Cincinnati, OH St. Xavier High School; [M] Cincinnati, OH Jesuit Community at St. Xavier High School.
O'Brien, James '56 (BO) [W] Quincy, MA St. Columban's Foreign Mission Society.
O'Brien, James '60 (Y) Absent on Leave.
O'Brien, James A. *s.j.* '60 (WH) [A] Wheeling, WV Wheeling Jesuit University.
O'Brien, James C. *s.j.* '61 (BO) [W] Chestnut Hill, MA The Jesuit Community at Boston College.
O'Brien, James F. '49 (NEW) [21] Jersey City, NJ Church of Our Lady of Sorrows.
O'Brien, James F. *s.j.* '67 (NY) [DD] New York, NY St. Ignatius Loyola Residence; [HH] New York, NY Jesuit Seminary and Mission Bureau, Inc.
O'Brien, Msgr. James J. '40 (NOR) Retired.
O'Brien, James J. *s.j.* '59 (FgM) Provinces.
O'Brien, James J. '60 (CHI) [56] Chicago, IL St. Eugene Church.
O'Brien, James M. *m.m.* '49 (FgM) Maryknoll Foreign Missions.
O'Brien, James R. '66 (HBG) Mechanicsburg, PA Blessed Katharine Drexel Church.
O'Brien, James T. '63 (BRK) [122] Brooklyn, NY Resurrection Church.
O'Brien, James T. '70 (SY) [3] Syracuse, NY Blessed Sacrament Church.
O'Brien, John *c.p.* (BO) Burlington, MA St. Malachy Church.
O'Brien, John *o.s.b.* (IND) Liberty, IN St. Bridget Church.
O'Brien, John *s.j.* (MIL) [N] Wauwatosa, WI St. Camillus Health Center, Inc.
O'Brien, John '45 (BLX) Retired.
O'Brien, John *s.d.b.* '62 (SFR) [45] San Francisco, CA SS. Peter and Paul Church.
O'Brien, John '69 (SAV) Valdosta, GA St. John the Evangelist Church.
O'Brien, John '75 (PIT) Retired.
O'Brien, John A. '64 (MIL) North Fond du Lac, WI Presentation of the Blessed Virgin Church.
O'Brien, John E. '46 (NEW) Livingston, NJ St. Raphael Church; Retired.
O'Brien, John E. '50 (CHI) Highland Park, IL Immaculate Conception Church; Retired.
O'Brien, John E. '87 (BAL) [L] Sparks, MD Msgr. Clare J. O'Dwyer Retreat House.
O'Brien, John F. '55 (GB) [12] Green Bay, WI St. Patrick Church.
O'Brien, John F. '61 (PH) [139] Philadelphia, PA St. Raymond of Penafort Church.
O'Brien, John F. '62 (WIL) Fairfax, DE St. Mary Magdalen Church.
O'Brien, Msgr. John H. '62 (BRK) [155] Queens, NY St. Benedict Joseph Labre Church.
O'Brien, Msgr. John J. '38 (WOR) Retired.
O'Brien, John J. '40 (NEW) [B] Jersey City, NJ Saint Peter's College; [N] Jersey City, NJ Jesuits of Saint Peter's College, Inc.
O'Brien, Msgr. John J. '42 (SCR) Retired; [N] Dunmore, PA Villa St. Joseph.
O'Brien, John J. *s.j.* '49 (NEW) Saddle River Borough, NJ St. Gabriel the Archangel Church.
O'Brien, John J. *m.m.* '52 (NY) [DD] Maryknoll, NY Maryknoll Fathers and Brothers.
O'Brien, John J. *s.a.c.* '62 (RNO) Sparks, NV Immaculate Conception Church.
O'Brien, John M. *o.c.s.o.* '81 (ATL) [I] Conyers, GA The Monastery of the Holy Spirit.
O'Brien, John P. '49 (SPK) Retired.
O'Brien, John P. '90 (NY) [A] Bronx, NY St. John Neumann Residence.
O'Brien, John R. *c.p.m.* '52 (OWN) [F] South Union, KY Fathers of Mercy.
O'Brien, John T. '45 (BLX) Bay St. Louis, MS Our Lady of the Gulf Church.
O'Brien, John W. '67 (BO) [8] Quincy, MA Sacred Heart Church.
O'Brien, John W. '82 (PRO) [4] North Providence, RI Presentation of the Blessed Virgin Mary Church; Providence, RI Rhode Island Hospital.
O'Brien, Jon J. *s.j.* '63 (BAL) [M] Baltimore, MD Jesuit Fathers and Brothers Maryland Provincial Curia.
O'Brien, Joseph (BO) Roxbury, MA New England Baptist Hospital.
O'Brien, Joseph *o.carm.* '63 (NEW) Englewood, NJ St. Cecilia's Church.
O'Brien, Joseph *o.p.* '78 (PHX) [J] Phoenix, AZ The Malta Center.
O'Brien, Joseph '91 (ALB) Chestertown, NY St. John the Baptist Church; Hague, NY Blessed Sacrament Church; North Creek, NY St. James Church.
O'Brien, Joseph A. '56 (WDC) Special Ministries; [L] Washington, DC Cardinal O'Boyle Residence for Priests.
O'Brien, Joseph C. '84 (BO) [43] Boston, MA St. Margaret Church.
O'Brien, Joseph E. '51 (PH) [87] Philadelphia, PA St. Leo Church.
O'Brien, Joseph F. *s.j.* '44 (FgM) Provinces.
O'Brien, Joseph J. *o.m.i.* '54 (BWN) Port Isabel, TX Our Lady Star of the Sea Church.
O'Brien, Joseph J. '57 (CHI) Glenview, IL St. Catherine Laboure Church.
O'Brien, Joseph L. '55 (TOL) Retired.
O'Brien, Msgr. Joseph M. '57 (STL) Special Assignment.
O'Brien, Msgr. Joseph T. '46 (STL) Retired.
O'Brien, Joseph V. '57 (DUB) [1] Dubuque, IA St. Raphael's Cathedral; [5] Dubuque, IA St. Patrick's Church.
O'Brien, Msgr. Kenneth R. '40 (LA) Retired.
O'Brien, Kevin '79 (RIC) Lynchburg, VA St. Thomas More Church.
O'Brien, Kevin J. '81 (OG) Carthage, NY St. James Minor Church; Deferiet, NY St. Rita Church.
O'Brien, Kevin P. '54 (DET) [7] Livonia, MI St. Priscilla Church.
O'Brien, Msgr. Kevin P. '73 (NY) [10] New York, NY St. Ann's Roman Catholic Church; [52] New York, NY Immaculate Conception Church.
O'Brien, Msgr. Laurence '43 (LA) Glendale, CA Church of the Incarnation.
O'Brien, Leo P. '56 (ALB) [17] Albany, NY St. Vincent de Paul Church; Special Assignment.
O'Brien, Mark J. '84 (PH) Absent on Leave.
O'Brien, Martin F. '52 (NEW) [A] South Orange, NJ Immaculate Conception Seminary; [B] South Orange, NJ Seton Hall University.
O'Brien, Maurice '68 (SAC) Dixon, CA St. Peter Church.
O'Brien, Michael '72 (JKS) Starkville, MS St. Joseph Church; [G] Starkville, MS Mississippi State University Catholic Student Association.
O'Brien, Michael '79 (SP) [3] St. Petersburg, FL Holy Cross Church.
O'Brien, Michael C. '65 (SEA) [3] Vancouver, WA St. John Church.
O'Brien, Michael G. *c.s.c.* '42 (FTW) [J] South Bend, IN Congregation of Holy Cross Indiana Province Provincial House.
O'Brien, Michael J. *c.s.v.* '48 (CHI) [N] Arlington Heights, IL Viatorian Province Center-Clerics of St. Viator.
O'Brien, Michael J. '63 (NEW) Kearny, NJ Our Lady of Sorrows Church.
O'Brien, Nicholas J. '83 (ORL) Leesburg, FL St. Paul's Church.
O'Brien, Patrick *c.ss.r.* (TUC) [J] Tucson, AZ Retorno (Marriage Retorno).
O'Brien, Patrick *o.m.i.* '37 (SAT) [K] San Antonio, TX Oblate Madonna Residence.
O'Brien, Patrick '64 (PIT) [B] Pittsburgh, PA La Roche College.
O'Brien, Patrick *c.ss.r.* '64 (TUC) [H] Tucson, AZ Redemptorist Picture Rocks Retreat.
O'Brien, Patrick '69 (SAV) [9] Savannah, GA St. Peter the Apostle Church.
O'Brien, Patrick '74 (HT) [3] Thibodaux, LA Christ The Redeemer Church; [5] Thibodaux, LA St. John The Evangelist Church.
O'Brien, Patrick *c.ss.r.* '76 (TUC) [J] Tucson, AZ Redemptorist Community Support Charity Trust.
O'Brien, Msgr. Patrick J. '56 (LA) Ventura, CA San Buenaventura Mission Church.
O'Brien, Patrick K. '46 (SEA) [8] Tacoma, WA St. Martin of Tours Church.
O'Brien, Paul *s.j.* '38 (FgM) Provinces.
O'Brien, Paul A. *m.m.* '59 (FgM) Maryknoll Foreign Missions.
O'Brien, Paul B. '95 (BO) [3] Brookline, MA St. Lawrence Church.
O'Brien, Peter F. *s.j.* '71 (RVC) [P] Manhasset, NY St. Ignatius Retreat House, Inisfada.
O'Brien, Peter K. '83 (NEW) Westfield, NJ St. Helen Church.
O'Brien, Raymond C. '75 (WDC) Special Ministries; [C] Washington, DC Catholic University of America, The.
O'Brien, Richard *c.m.* '61 (KC) [J] Kansas City, MO Vincentian Parish Mission Center.
O'Brien, Richard '92 (PRT) Bangor, ME St. John's Church; Bangor, ME St. Mary's Church.
O'Brien, Richard J. *s.j.* '54 (CHI) [D] Chicago, IL St. Ignatius Jesuit Community.
O'Brien, Richard M. '92 (BO) On Duty Outside the Archdiocese.
O'Brien, Robert E. *s.j.* '54 (NY) [46] New York, NY Holy Family Church.
O'Brien, Roger '61 (SEA) [12] Seattle, WA St. Luke Church.
O'Brien, Msgr. Roger E. '42 (DUB) Retired.
O'Brien, Sean P. '93 (SY) [3] Utica, NY Our Lady of Lourdes Church.
O'Brien, Steven G. '86 (DUB) Belle Plaine, IA St. Michael Church; [1] Cedar Rapids, IA Immaculate Conception Church; Chelsea, IA St. Joseph's Church; [D] Cedar Rapids, IA Xavier High School dba Regis High School and LaSalle High School Center.
O'Brien, Terrance P. '81 (PEO) [4] Champaign, IL St. Matthew Church.
O'Brien, Msgr. Terrence '43 (ORG) Retired.
O'Brien, Thomas '47 (SAC) Retired and in Senior Ministry.

O'Brien, Msgr. Thomas *p.e.* '52 (BRK) [229] Queens, NY Presentation of the Blessed Virgin Mary Church; Retired.
O'Brien, Thomas *o.m.i.* '55 (FgM) Oblates Foreign Missions.
O'Brien, Thomas *o.s.c.* '74 (STP) [N] Shoreview, MN Crosier Community of Shoreview.
O'Brien, Thomas F. '55 (OM) [47] Omaha, NE St. Vincent de Paul Church.
O'Brien, Thomas F. '56 (WOR) Retired.
O'Brien, Thomas G. *c.s.v.* '47 (CHI) [N] Arlington Heights, IL Viatorian Province Center-Clerics of St. Viator.
O'Brien, Msgr. Thomas J. '50 (KC) Retired.
O'Brien, Thomas J. '55 (SAT) Martinez, TX St. Jerome Church.
O'Brien, Thomas J. *m.m.* '74 (FgM) Maryknoll Foreign Missions.
O'Brien, Msgr. Thomas L. '43 (LA) Retired.
O'Brien, Msgr. Thomas M. *p.e.* '52 (BRK) [205] Queens, NY St. Nicholas of Tolentine Church.
O'Brien, Msgr. Timothy '54 (SJ) Retired.
O'Brien, Timothy A. '94 (HRT) Suffield, CT Sacred Heart Church.
O'Brien, Timothy J. '69 (MIL) Special Assignment.
O'Brien, Vincent M. *s.j.* '55 (WDC) [E] North Bethesda, MD Georgetown Preparatory School.
O'Brien, Walter *o.f.m.cap.* '37 (SPR) [L] Springfield, MA St. Francis of Assisi Chapel and Catholic Information Center.
O'Brien, William (GB) [2] Two Rivers, WI Sacred Heart Church; [4] Two Rivers, WI Most Holy Redeemer Church.
O'Brien, William (NEW) Rochelle Park, NJ Sacred Heart Church.
O'Brien, William *m.s.* '49 (LKC) [3] Sulphur, LA Our Lady of Prompt Succor Church.
O'Brien, William '50 (DUB) Haverhill, IA Immaculate Conception Church.
O'Brien, William '78 (BAL) Awaiting Assignment.
O'Brien, William '88 (VNN) Los Gatos, CA St. Basil the Great Church.
O'Brien, Msgr. William B. '51 (NY) [135] Bronx, NY St. Brendan Church; On Duty Outside the Archdiocese.
O'Brien, William D. '50 (DUB) Haverhill, IA Immaculate Conception Church.
O'Brien, William G. (WOR) Retired.
O'Brien, William G. '51 (WOR) Otter River, MA St. Martin's Church.
O'Brien, William H. '77 (BAL) Baltimore, MD University of Maryland Hospital.
O'Brien, William J. (CHI) [180] Chicago, IL Queen of Angels Church.
O'Brien, William J. *c.m.* '67 (BUF) [T] Niagara University, NY Our Lady of Angels Association.
O'Brien, William J. *c.m.* '67 (PH) [69] Philadelphia, PA Immaculate Conception Church; [B] Philadelphia, PA St. Vincent's Seminary; [FF] Philadelphia, PA The Central Association of the Miraculous Medal.
O'Brien, William J. '80 (E) Bradford, PA St. Bernard Church.
O'Brien, William P. *s.j.* (IND) [D] Indianapolis, IN Brebeuf Jesuit Preparatory School, Inc.
O'Brien, William P. *m.s.* '49 (LKC) Sulphur, LA West Clacasieu Cameron Hospital.
O'Brien, William S. '69 (RIC) Waynesboro, VA St. John the Evangelist Church.
O'Bryan, Henry '41 (OWN) Retired.
O'Bryan, Msgr. J. A. '35 (L) Retired.
O'Byrne, Charles J. *s.j.* '97 (NY) [DD] New York, NY "America;" Residence and publication office of the America Press.
O'Byrne, John '61 (LA) Torrance, CA St. Catherine Laboure Church.
O'Byrne, Patrick J. '60 (LIN) Colon, NE St. Joseph's Church.
O'Byrne, Msgr. Sylvester '51 (LA) Montecito, CA Our Lady of Mount Carmel Church; Retired.
O'Callaghan, Dominic *o.c.d.* '44 (SB) [G] Redlands, CA El Carmelo Retreat House.
O'Callaghan, Msgr. Eugene '55 (SAT) New Braunfels, TX SS. Peter and Paul Church.
O'Callaghan, Msgr. James A. '43 (LA) Hacienda Heights, CA St. John Vianney Church; Retired.
O'Callaghan, John '65 (ORG) Inactive Leave.
O'Callaghan, John F. '45 (DET) Retired.
O'Callaghan, John J. *s.j.* '62 (CHI) [C] Chicago, IL Jesuit Community at Loyola University of Chicago.
O'Callaghan, Matthias J. '62 (SAC) Willows, CA St. Monica Church; Special Assignment.
O'Callaghan, Patrick '55 (SAT) Retired.
O'Callaghan, Msgr. Peter '52 (SAT) [24] San Antonio, TX St. Agnes Church.
O'Callaghan, Thomas '54 (SEA) Retired.
O'Callaghan, Tiernan *o.carm.* '56 (PHX) [6] Phoenix, AZ St. Agnes Church.
O'Campo, Arturo *o.f.m.* '85 (CHI) [D] Chicago, IL Hales Franciscan High School, Inc.
O'Carroll, Msgr. Donal '56 (STU) Lafferty, OH St. Mary Church.
O'Carroll, Eugene '62 (PHX) [21] Phoenix, AZ St. Paul Church.
O'Carroll, Philip A. '58 (SB) [2] Fontana, CA St. George Church.
O'Cinnsealaigh, Benedict '93 (CIN) Sidney, OH Holy Angels Church.
O'Connel, Walter *o.p.* '58 (DUL) Duluth, MN Indian Missions Church.
O'Connell, Anthony M. *o.s.m.* '67 (CHI) [18] Chicago, IL Assumption of the Blessed Virgin Mary Church; [A] Mundelein, IL University of St. Mary of the Lake-Mundelein Seminary; [N] Chicago, IL Servite Friars - Eastern Province.
O'Connell, Brendan M. *m.m.* '63 (FgM) Maryknoll Foreign Missions.
O'Connell, Brian J. *c.m.* '68 (PH) [AA] Philadelphia, PA Congregation of the Mission.
O'Connell, Brian J. *c.m.* '68 (WDC) [V] Washington, DC Carroll Manor Nursing & Rehabilitation Center.
O'Connell, Cuthbert '86 (BLX) Bassfield, MS St. Peter Church.
O'Connell, Damien A. *s.j.* '75 (SY) [A] Syracuse, NY Saint Andrew Hall.
O'Connell, Daniel '71 (SAV) Douglas, GA St. Paul's Church.
O'Connell, Daniel '83 (BO) [1] Newton, MA St. Bernard Church.
O'Connell, Daniel C. *s.j.* '58 (WDC) [M] Washington, DC The Jesuit Community at Georgetown University.
O'Connell, Daniel P. '71 (SAV) [I] Willacoochee, GA Catholic Cemetery.
O'Connell, David '79 (LA) [61] Los Angeles, CA St. Frances Xavier Cabrini Church.
O'Connell, David M. *c.m.* '82 (BRK) [U] Jamaica, NY Vincentian Residence.
O'Connell, George *o.m.i.* '41 (SAT) [K] San Antonio, TX Oblate Madonna Residence.
O'Connell, George M. *o.s.m.* '37 (CHI) [N] Chicago, IL Servite Friars - Eastern Province.
O'Connell, James (ROC) [E] Rochester, NY St. Ann's Home for the Aged.
O'Connell, Msgr. James E. '33 (LR) [L] Little Rock, AR St. John's Home Missions Seminary, Inc.
O'Connell, James F. '36 (ROC) Retired.
O'Connell, Msgr. James P. '53 (STL) Retired.
O'Connell, James R. *o.f.m.* '83 (NY) [35] New York, NY St. Francis of Assisi Church.
O'Connell, John '59 (SFD) Taylorville, IL St. Mary Church.
O'Connell, John B. '40 (HRT) [4] Enfield, CT St. Martha's Church.
O'Connell, John G. *o.p.* '44 (STP) [15] Minneapolis, MN St. Albert the Great Church.
O'Connell, John Q. *c.m.* '53 (DEN) [M] Denver, CO Congregation of the Mission Midwest Province: De Paul House; [Q] Denver, CO Kateri Catholic Indian Community of Colorado.
O'Connell, John R. '73 (NEW) Midland Park, NJ Nativity Church.
O'Connell, Joseph '51 (SFR) Mill Valley, CA Our Lady of Mt. Carmel Church.
O'Connell, Joseph *s.o.l.t.* '91 (CC) Robstown, TX St. John Nepomucene Church; [H] Robstown, TX Society of Our Lady of the Most Holy Trinity.
O'Connell, Msgr. Joseph F. '64 (CAM) Washington Township, NJ St. Charles Borromeo Church.
O'Connell, Joseph F. *s.j.* '73 (WDC) [M] Washington, DC The Jesuit Community at Georgetown University; [V] Washington, DC Jesuit Secondary Education Association.
O'Connell, Joseph P. *s.j.* '52 (SEA) [M] Seattle, WA Jesuit House, Seattle.
O'Connell, Kevin G. *s.j.* '69 (FgM) Provinces.
O'Connell, Luke A. *o.f.m.* '55 (ALB) [B] Loudonville, NY Siena College.
O'Connell, Mark '90 (BO) Graduate Studies.
O'Connell, Mark A. '79 (NEW) Belleville, NJ St. Peter's Church.
O'Connell, Marvin '56 (FTW) [B] Notre Dame, IN University of Notre Dame Du Lac.
O'Connell, Marvin R. '56 (STP) On Duty Outside the Archdiocese.
O'Connell, Maurice V. '72 (WDC) Riverdale, MD St. Bernard Church.
O'Connell, Michael '67 (STP) [1] Minneapolis, MN The Basilica of St. Mary Co-Cathedral.
O'Connell, Michael W. '83 (CHI) Orland Park, IL Our Lady of the Woods Church.
O'Connell, Neil J. *o.f.m.* '64 (NY) [115] New York, NY St. Stephen of Hungary Church; [HH] New York, NY Shrine of St. Jude, Inc.
O'Connell, Msgr. Patrick '55 (BEA) Retired.
O'Connell, Paul T. '60 (WOR) Shrewsbury, MA St. Mary's Church.
O'Connell, Richard C. '51 (ROC) [48] Rochester, NY St. Monica Church; Retired.
O'Connell, Robert '71 (SUP) Saxon, WI St. Ann's Church.
O'Connell, Robert E. '71 (SUP) Hurley, WI St. Mary of the Seven Dolors Church; Montreal, WI Sacred Heart of Jesus Church; Pence, WI Holy Redeemer Church.
O'Connell, Robert J. *s.s.j.* '41 (BAL) [M] Baltimore, MD St. Joseph's Manor.
O'Connell, Robert J. '70 (RVC) Patchogue, NY Our Lady of Mt. Carmel Church.
O'Connell, Robert Jerome *s.j.* '46 (NY) [DD] New York, NY Murray-Weigel Hall.
O'Connell, Robert John *s.j.* '57 (NY) [DD] New York, NY Murray-Weigel Hall.
O'Connell, Msgr. Robert M. '51 (NY) [105] New York, NY St. Peter Church.
O'Connell, Terrence E. *o.m.i.* '78 (BO) [12] Lowell, MA Nuestra Senora del Carmen Church.
O'Connell, Terry J. '92 (P) Coos Bay, OR St. Monica Church.
O'Connell, Msgr. Thomas '45 (LA) Westlake Village, CA St. Jude Church; Retired.
O'Connell, Thomas *c.ss.r.* '49 (NY) [92] New York, NY Our Lady of Perpetual Help Church.
O'Connell, Thomas C. '46 (PIT) Retired.
O'Connell, Thomas P. '63 (KNX) Seymour, TN Holy Family Church.
O'Connell, Msgr. Timothy '63 (LA) Lancaster, CA Sacred Heart Church.
O'Connell, Vincent *c.s.sp.* '59 (BRK) [U] Long Island City, NY Holy Ghost Fathers of Ireland.
O'Connell, Vincent J. *s.m.* '39 (WDC) [M] Washington, DC Marist Provincial House.
O'Connell, Walter *o.p.* '58 (DUL) Grand Marais, MN St. John's Church.
O'Connell, Walter T. *o.p.* '58 (CHI) [N] River Forest, IL St. Thomas Aquinas Priory.
O'Connell, William '54 (CHI) [4] Waukegan, IL Holy Family Church.
O'Connell, William *s.m.* '56 (HON) [D] Honolulu, HI St. Louis School; [H] Honolulu, HI Marianist Hall Community.
O'Connell, Msgr. William '57 (RC) McIntosh, SD St. Bonaventure's Church; McLaughlin, SD St. Bernard Church.
O'Connell, William '66 (VEN) Priests Released from Diocesan Assignment.
O'Connell, William A. '55 (SFR) Retired.
O'Connell, Msgr. William J. '57 (RC) Standing Rock, SD Standing Rock Reservation Church.
O'Connell, William M. (CHI) Retired.
O'Conner, Kevin *o.m.i.* '58 (P) Scio, OR St. Bernard Church.
O'Conner, William *o.m.i.* '43 (SAT) [M] San Antonio, TX Oblate Benson Residence (Southern Prov.).
O'Connor, Msgr. Albert G. '67 (SAC) Elk Grove, CA St. Joseph Church.
O'Connor, Msgr. Aloysius E. '40 (WDC) Avenue, MD Holy Angels Church; Retired.
O'Connor, Andrew '96 (NY) [70] New York, NY St. Mary Church.
O'Connor, Andrew J. '87 (STL) St. Ann, MO St. Kevin Church.
O'Connor, Bernard *c.m.f.* '50 (LA) Santa Monica, CA St. Monica Church.
O'Connor, Bernard F. *o.s.f.s.* '73 (ALN) [B] Center Valley, PA Allentown College of St. Francis de Sales; [K] Center Valley, PA Oblates of St. Francis de Sales.
O'Connor, Charles '58 (WCH) On Duty Outside the Diocese.
O'Connor, Charles *o.f.m., s.t.d.* '73 (BUF) [A] East Aurora, NY Christ the King Seminary.
O'Connor, Charles J. *c.m.* '34 (PH) [AA] Philadelphia, PA Congregation of the Mission.
O'Connor, Charles P. '50 (NEW) Fairfield, NJ St. Thomas More Church.
O'Connor, Charles T. '83 (MET) Bound Brook, NJ St. Joseph Church.
O'Connor, Msgr. Daniel J. '61 (ATL) [10] Atlanta, GA St. Jude Church.
O'Connor, Daniel P. '90 (ALX) Fifth Ward, LA Our Lady of Lourdes Church.
O'Connor, David *s.t.* '55 (WDC) [M] University Park, MD Holy Trinity Missionary Cenacle.
O'Connor, David '64 (JKS) On Duty Outside the Diocese.
O'Connor, David H. '86 (DUB) [A] Dubuque, IA Seminary of St. Pius X; [C] Dubuque, IA Loras College.
O'Connor, Desmond (NY) Warwick, NY St. Stephen Church.
O'Connor, Desmond *s.p.s.* '50 (PAT) Mount Arlington, NJ Our Lady of the Lake Church.
O'Connor, Donal P. '55 (LA) Lynwood, CA St. Emydius Church.
O'Connor, Donald *s.v.d.* '64 (FgM) Society of the Divine Word Foreign Missions.
O'Connor, Donald '64 (JOL) [9] Joliet, IL St. Bernard Church.
O'Connor, Edward '60 (ATL) Thomson, GA Queen of Angels Church.
O'Connor, Edward D. *c.s.c.* '48 (FTW) [B] Notre Dame, IN University of Notre Dame Du Lac; [J] Notre Dame, IN Holy Cross Community, Corby Hall, University of Notre Dame.
O'Connor, Msgr. Edward J. '39 (CAM) Retired.

O'Connor, Edward J. '81 (ALN) Lost Creek, PA St. Mary Magdalen Church; [1] Shenandoah, PA Annunciation Church.
O'Connor, Edward T. '44 (BRK) [64] Brooklyn, NY Immaculate Heart of Mary Church; Retired.
O'Connor, Eugene '54 (BIR) [3] Birmingham, AL St. Barnabas Church.
O'Connor, Msgr. Francis '46 (MOB) Retired.
O'Connor, Francis A. '28 (SPR) Retired.
O'Connor, Francis A. '62 (ALB) [4] Albany, NY St. Casimir Church; [14] Albany, NY St. Patrick Church.
O'Connor, Francis J. '53 (MAN) Retired.
O'Connor, Francis M. *s.j.* '58 (SY) [A] Syracuse, NY Saint Andrew Hall.
O'Connor, Francis M. *s.j.* '58 (WDC) [E] Washington, DC Gonzaga College High School.
O'Connor, Msgr. Fred P. '52 (GAL) Crosby, TX Sacred Heart Church.
O'Connor, Gerald P. *m.m.* '69 (FgM) Maryknoll Foreign Missions.
O'Connor, Gerald T. '66 (ROC) Addison, NY St. Catherine of Siena Church; Bradford, NY St. Stanislaus Church.
O'Connor, Gerald V. *s.j.* '76 (WDC) [E] Washington, DC Gonzaga College High School.
O'Connor, Glenn L. '80 (IND) [22] Indianapolis, IN St. Joseph Church; Indianapolis, IN Indianapolis International Airport.
O'Connor, Msgr. Hugh '39 (ORG) [3] Anaheim, CA St. Justin Martyr Church; Retired.
O'Connor, J. Kieran '45 (MAN) Retired; [J] Manchester, NH St. Teresas Manor & Bishop Primeau Apartments.
O'Connor, J. Paul *s.j.* '53 (STL) [O] St. Louis, MO Fusz Pavilion.
O'Connor, Msgr. James '40 (NY) Retired.
O'Connor, James '70 (LUB) [3] Lubbock, TX Our Lady of Guadalupe Church.
O'Connor, James C. '71 (BUF) Fredonia, NY St. Joseph Church.
O'Connor, James E. *o.c.s.o.* '57 (DUB) [K] Peosta, IA New Melleray Abbey, Order of Cistercians of the Strict Observance.
O'Connor, James E. '82 (WH) Madison, WV St. Mary, Queen of Heaven Church.
O'Connor, James J. '43 (FTW) Retired.
O'Connor, James J. '54 (CIN) Botkins, OH Immaculate Conception Church; Rhine, OH St. Lawrence Church.
O'Connor, James M. '52 (LIN) Minden, NE St. John's Church.
O'Connor, James T. '54 (CHI) Retired.
O'Connor, James T. '66 (NY) Millbrook, NY St. Joseph Church.
O'Connor, Jay '74 (BAL) Annapolis, MD St. Andrew by the Bay Church.
O'Connor, John *c.ss.r.* '55 (ALB) [L] Saratoga Springs, NY St. John Neumann Residence.
O'Connor, John C. '61 (LA) Lynwood, CA St. Emydius Church; Sick Leave.
O'Connor, John F. '44 (PEO) Retired.
O'Connor, John F. *s.t.b.* '64 (NEW) [21] Newark, NJ Immaculate Conception Church.
O'Connor, John F. *o.f.m.* '73 (ARL) Triangle, VA St. Francis of Assisi Church.
O'Connor, John F. '73 (R) [1] Raleigh, NC Cathedral of the Sacred Heart.
O'Connor, John H. (PAT) Absent on Leave.
O'Connor, John J. '58 (DUB) New Vienna, IA St. Boniface's Church; Petersburg, IA SS. Peter and Paul Church.
O'Connor, Msgr. John J. '60 (SFR) [1] San Francisco, CA Cathedral of St. Mary (Assumption).
O'Connor, John J. '68 (DUB) [F] New Vienna, IA Archbishop Hennessy Catholic School.
O'Connor, John J. *s.l.l.* '93 (BRK) [13] Brooklyn, NY St. Athanasius Church; [34] Brooklyn, NY St. Edmund's Church.
O'Connor, John L. '63 (ROC) [34] Rochester, NY Our Lady of Lourdes Church.
O'Connor, John P. '45 (PH) [83] Philadelphia, PA St. Katherine of Siena Church; Retired.
O'Connor, Msgr. John Philip '61 (NEW) Garwood, NJ Church of St. Anne.
O'Connor, John R. '33 (BGP) [K] Trumbull, CT St. Joseph's Manor.
O'Connor, John R. '33 (HRT) Retired.
O'Connor, John T. '46 (HRT) Newington, CT Holy Spirit Church; Retired.
O'Connor, John T. '52 (MIL) [B] Hales Corners, WI Sacred Heart School of Theology; [P] Hales Corners, WI Sacred Heart Monastery.
O'Connor, Msgr. Joseph A. '47 (TR) Retired; [M] Trenton, NJ Villa Vianney.
O'Connor, Joseph E. *s.j.* '59 (BO) [3] Newton, MA St. Ignatius Church.
O'Connor, Joseph X. *o.s.a.* '53 (BO) [C] North Andover, MA Merrimack College.
O'Connor, Mark *s.a.* '84 (NY) [DD] Garrison, NY Franciscan Friars of the Atonement.
O'Connor, Mathias *o.p.* (SFE) [K] Santa Fe, NM Discalced Carmelite Monastery.
O'Connor, Matthew '71 (MOB) Tillman's Corner, AL St. Vincent de Paul Church.
O'Connor, Matthew J. '56 (SPR) [8] Springfield, MA Our Lady of Hope Church; [O] Goshen, MA Holy Cross Camp Grounds.
O'Connor, Maurice '52 (NY) Absent on Sick leave.
O'Connor, Maurice J. '53 (BO) Stoughton, MA Our Lady of the Rosary Church.
O'Connor, Msgr. Michael '47 (FRS) Retired.
O'Connor, Michael F. '44 (NU) Retired.
O'Connor, Michael F. '44 (STP) Miesville, MN St. Joseph Church.
O'Connor, Msgr. Michael J. '34 (LA) Woodland Hills, CA St. Mel Church; Retired.
O'Connor, Michael J. '65 (SJ) [5] Sunnyvale, CA Church of The Resurrection.
O'Connor, Michael J. *o.s.a.* '71 (CHI) [D] Chicago, IL St. Rita High School; [N] Chicago, IL St. Rita Monastery.
O'Connor, Michael J. '72 (TR) Delran, NJ Holy Name Church.
O'Connor, Neil D. '69 (CLV) [4] Parma, OH St. Columbkille Church.
O'Connor, Norman J. *c.s.p.* '48 (NY) [DD] Jamaica Estates, NY Paulist Fathers Generalate.
O'Connor, Oliver J. *o.f.m.cap.* '42 (ROC) [I] Interlaken, NY St. Fidelis Friary.
O'Connor, Patrick *m.s.c.* '52 (CC) Bishop, TX St. James Church.
O'Connor, Patrick '55 (KC) Retired.
O'Connor, Patrick *o.s.f.s.* '97 (VEN) [A] Fort Myers, FL Bishop Verot High School.
O'Connor, Msgr. Patrick C. '54 (MOB) Gulf Shores, AL Our Lady of the Gulf Church.
O'Connor, Patrick C. '78 (SAG) [17] Saginaw, MI St. Stephen Church.
O'Connor, Patrick J. '58 (SAC) Tahoe City, CA Corpus Christi Church.
O'Connor, Patrick J. '64 (GBG) [G] Greensburg, PA Neumann House.
O'Connor, Patrick J. '85 (CLV) [3] Elyria, OH St. Jude Church.
O'Connor, Msgr. Paul '45 (CAM) Retired.
O'Connor, Pio *o.f.m.* '94 (GLP) Chinle, AZ Our Lady of Fatima, Indian Mission Church; [A] Chinle, AZ Native American Lay Ministry and Diaconate Program.
O'Connor, Raymond *c.m.f.* '64 (ATL) Stone Mountain, GA Corpus Christi Church.
O'Connor, Richard T. '37 (NU) Retired.
O'Connor, Robert B. '56 (NY) [18] New York, NY Blessed Sacrament Church.
O'Connor, Robert C. *s.j.* '64 (CIN) [28] Cincinnati, OH St. Francis Xavier Church.
O'Connor, Robert D. '55 (PEO) East Moline, IL St. Anne Church.
O'Connor, Robert F. *s.j.* '79 (STP) [6] St. Paul, MN The Immaculate Heart of Mary Church.
O'Connor, Robert W. '48 (PEO) Lewistown, IL St. Mary's Church.
O'Connor, Samuel *o.f.m.* '56 (BO) [BB] Boston, MA St. Anthony Shrine.
O'Connor, Shaun *m.i.c.* '82 (WDC) [B] Brookeville, MD Marian Novitiate; [B] Brookeville, MD Marian Spiritual Center.
O'Connor, Stephen '48 (ALB) Retired.
O'Connor, Steven J. '77 (PT) Tiger Point, FL St. Sylvester Church; [H] Navarre, FL Casa Stella Maris.
O'Connor, Thomas *c.ss.r.* '50 (GR) [3] Grand Rapids, MI St. Alphonsus Church.
O'Connor, Thomas *o.s.b.* '56 (BIR) Retired.
O'Connor, Thomas A. *s.j.* '62 (BUF) [O] Buffalo, NY Canisius Jesuit Community; [R] Williamsville, NY Campus Ministry.
O'Connor, Thomas J. '55 (TR) Freehold, NJ St. Robert Bellarmine Church.
O'Connor, Thomas J. *o.s.b.* '56 (BIR) [E] Cullman, AL St. Bernard Abbey.
O'Connor, Thomas J. '93 (BO) [W] Hingham, MA Glastonbury Abbey.
O'Connor, Thomas P. '56 (FTW) [10] Fort Wayne, IN St. Mary Church.
O'Connor, Thomas V. *s.j.* '63 (NEW) [C] Jersey City, NJ St. Peter's Preparatory School.
O'Connor, Timothy J. '75 (CLV) Avon Lake, OH St. Joseph's Church.
O'Connor, Timothy L. *c.s.c.* '91 (FTW) [12] South Bend, IN St. Joseph Church.
O'Connor, Vincent M. '48 (SPR) Leeds, MA St. Catherine's Church.
O'Connor, William '49 (SJ) Retired.
O'Connor, William B. (BO) Retired.
O'Connor, William C. *c.s.c.* '49 (LA) Burbank, CA St. Francis Xavier Church.
O'Connor, William F. *s.j.* '48 (BO) [W] Weston, MA Campion Health Center, Inc.
O'Connor, William J. '58 (BO) [3] Framingham, MA St. Jeremiah Church.
O'Connor, William T. '68 (CHI) Chicago Heights, IL St. Paul Church.
O'Curneen, Hugh '57 (SD) Retired.
O'Day, Msgr. Martin J. '47 (CHI) Oak Forest, IL St. Damian Church; Retired.
O'Day, Michael '38 (SB) Sun City, CA St. Vincent Ferrer Church; Retired.
O'Dea, James F. '38 (HRT) Beacon Falls, CT St. Michael's Church; Retired.
O'Dea, John W. '52 (SPK) Retired.
O'Dea, Msgr. Joseph J. '42 (PEO) Retired.
O'Dea, Loren F. '93 (DET) Farmington, MI Our Lady of Sorrows Church.
O'Dea, Sean '54 (MIA) Hollywood, FL St. Bernadette Church.
O'Dea, Thomas '58 (PHX) Fountain Hills, AZ Ascension Church.
O'Dea, Thomas E. '60 (FR) [18] New Bedford, MA St. Lawrence Martyr Church.
O'Dea, Vincent P. '36 (CLV) Hudson, OH St. Mary Church; Retired.
O'Dea, William (PMB) Lantana, FL Holy Spirit Church.
O'Dea, William '56 (PMB) Retired.
O'Dell, W. Paul '93 (SFR) Greenbrae, CA St. Sebastian Church.
O'Doherty, Edward '28 (CHL) Retired.
O'Doherty, Gerard *s.v.d.* '74 (LA) [25] Los Angeles, CA Our Lady of Loretto Church; [R] Los Angeles, CA Society of the Divine Word Western Province.
O'Doherty, John *s.s.c.* '39 (PRO) [P] Bristol, RI St. Columban's Retirement House.
O'Doherty, Msgr. Jude '65 (MIA) [4] Miami, FL Epiphany Church.
O'Doherty, Liam '65 (OG) Antwerp, NY St. Michael Church.
O'Doherty, Patrick J. '70 (ORL) [3] Ocala, FL Queen of Peace Church.
O'Donnell, Brian P. *s.j.* '86 (DET) [K] Detroit, MI Jesuit Community at the University of Detroit.
O'Donnell, Cornelius '55 (SAC) Dunsmuir, CA St. John the Evangelist Church; McCloud, CA St. Joseph Church.
O'Donnell, David P. '95 (BO) Lexington, MA St. Brigid Church.
O'Donnell, Dennis '83 (GR) Ludington, MI St. Stanislaus Church.
O'Donnell, Dennis J.W. '74 (PH) [CC] Malvern, PA St. Joseph's-in-the-Hills.
O'Donnell, Edmond G. '64 (SB) Upland, CA St. Anthony Church.
O'Donnell, Msgr. Edward C. '41 (OM) [16] Omaha, NE Holy Cross Church; Retired.
O'Donnell, Msgr. Edward D. '54 (NY) [110] New York, NY Sacred Heart of Jesus Church.
O'Donnell, Edward T. *s.j.* '74 (CIN) [M] Cincinnati, OH Jesuit Community at Xavier Unversity.
O'Donnell, Eugene P. '73 (SJ) Morgan Hill, CA St. Catherine of Alexandria Church.
O'Donnell, Francis P. *s.j.* '69 (CHI) [N] Chicago, IL Chicago Province of the Society of Jesus-Provincial Office.
O'Donnell, Francis T. *m.m.* '55 (FgM) Maryknoll Foreign Missions.
O'Donnell, Gabriel *o.p.* '70 (HRT) [14] New Haven, CT St. Mary's Priory Church.
O'Donnell, Gerard J. '81 (SFR) Novato, CA Our Lady of Loretto Church.
O'Donnell, Harold F. *s.j.* '64 (NY) [DD] New York, NY Xavier Jesuit Community.
O'Donnell, Harold F.X. *s.j.* (NY) Manhattan, NY Bird S. Coler Memorial Hospital and Home.
O'Donnell, Hugh '58 (SFR) [2] South San Francisco, CA Mater Dolorosa Church.
O'Donnell, Msgr. Hugh A. '54 (NEW) [6] Elizabeth, NJ St. Genevieve's Church.
O'Donnell, Hugh F. *c.m.* '61 (FgM) Vincentian Foreign Missions.
O'Donnell, James *o.s.b.* '42 (PAT) [M] Morristown, NJ St. Mary's Abbey.
O'Donnell, James '56 (CLV) Cleveland, OH Northeast Pre Release Center.
O'Donnell, James *s.j.* '61 (FgM) Provinces.
O'Donnell, James P. '56 (CLV) Cleveland, OH Cuyahoga County Detention Home.
O'Donnell, John '72 (DUL) Hibbing, MN Blessed Sacrament Church; Hibbing, MN Immaculate Conception Church; [F] Duluth, MN University of MN-Duluth.
O'Donnell, Msgr. John F. '54 (LR) Fort Smith, AR Immaculate Conception Church.
O'Donnell, John F. '63 (BO) [26] Boston, MA St. Gregory Church.
O'Donnell, John J. *s.j.* '74 (BO) [W] Cambridge, MA Weston Jesuit Community.
O'Donnell, Joseph '48 (CIN) [M] Fairfield, OH Headquarters of Glenmary Home Missioners.
O'Donnell, Joseph *glmy.* '48 (OWN) Fordsville, KY St. John the Baptist Church.
O'Donnell, Joseph '76 (CLV) [J] Cleveland, OH Marymount Hospital, Inc.
O'Donnell, Joseph F. *c.s.c.* (PHX) [F] Phoenix, AZ Holy Cross Congregation of Casa Santa Cruz.
O'Donnell, Joseph M. *c.m.* '43 (BRK) [U] Jamaica, NY Vincentian Residence.

O'Donnell, Luke *o.s.b.* '41 (P) Beaverton, OR St. Cecilia Church.
O'Donnell, Luke N. *o.s.b.* '41 (SEA) [M] Lacey, WA St. Martin's Abbey.
O'Donnell, Mark D. '85 (NOR) Montville, CT St. John Church.
O'Donnell, Matthew '95 (STO) Tracy, CA St. Bernard's Church.
O'Donnell, Patrick *glmy.* '49 (CIN) [M] Fairfield, OH Headquarters of Glenmary Home Missioners.
O'Donnell, Paul *m.c.c.j.* '93 (FgM) Comboni Foreign Missions.
O'Donnell, Msgr. Peter C. '58 (NY) [84] New York, NY Our Lady of Esperanza Church.
O'Donnell, Philip '58 (LAV) [11] Las Vegas, NV St. Joan of Arc Church.
O'Donnell, Ralph B. '97 (OM) [30] Omaha, NE Mary Our Queen Church.
O'Donnell, Raymond G. '72 (SD) [5] El Cajon, CA St. Luke Church.
O'Donnell, Richard '59 (PMB) Retired.
O'Donnell, Richard A. '55 (PRT) Yarmouth, ME Sacred Heart Church.
O'Donnell, Richard J. '35 (CHI) [147] Chicago, IL Our Lady of Good Counsel Church; Retired.
O'Donnell, Robert A. *c.s.p.* '51 (NY) [104] New York, NY St. Paul the Apostle Church; [DD] Jamaica Estates, NY Paulist Fathers Generalate.
O'Donnell, Robert E. *s.j.* '54 (PAT) [I] Morristown, NJ Loyola House of Retreats.
O'Donnell, Robert J. *c.s.p.* '74 (NY) [DD] Jamaica Estates, NY Paulist Fathers Generalate.
O'Donnell, Simon *o.s.b.* '68 (LA) [R] Valyermo, CA St. Andrew's Abbey.
O'Donnell, Terence *s.d.b.* '70 (BO) [N] Boston, MA Salesian Boys & Girls Club.
O'Donnell, Terence M. *c.m.* '55 (LA) [R] Los Angeles, CA Amat House.
O'Donnell, Thomas D. *s.m.* '44 (ATL) [C] Atlanta, GA Marist School.
O'Donnell, Thomas M. '60 (PIT) [66] Pittsburgh, PA St. Wendelin Church.
O'Donnell, Thomas M. '61 (HEL) East Helena, MT SS. Cyril and Methodius Church.
O'Donnell, Thomas P. '55 (RVC) Long Beach, NY St. Ignatius Martyr Church.
O'Donnell, Thomas V. '67 (CLV) [28] Cleveland, OH Holy Name Church; [50] Cleveland, OH St. Michael Church.
O'Donnell, Timothy R. '86 (MAN) Center Ossipee, NH St. Joseph Church.
O'Donnell, Walter *s.t.* '55 (BLX) DeLisle, MS The Catholic Church in DeLisle Church.
O'Donnell, William *o.m.i.* (BO) Tewksbury, MA St. William Church.
O'Donnell, William A. *c.pp.s.* '77 (CIN) Wapakoneta, OH St. Joseph Church; [M] Dayton, OH Provincial House of the Cincinnati Province of the Society of the Precious Blood.
O'Donnell, Msgr. William F '62 (WDC) [V] Washington, DC The Catholic Cemeteries of the Archdiocese of Washington, Inc.
O'Donnell, Msgr. William F. '62 (WDC) [42] Washington, DC St. Thomas Apostle Church; Special Ministries; [V] Capital Plaza, MD Archdiocese of Washington Division, The Blue Army.
O'Donnell, William J. (NY) Montrose, NY FDR DVA Hospital.
O'Donnell, William J. '52 (ALN) New Philadelphia, PA Holy Family Church.
O'Donnell, William J. '52 (PH) Warminster, PA Nativity of Our Lord Church.
O'Donnell, William J. '56 (OAK) [3] Berkeley, CA St. Joseph The Worker Church.
O'Donnell, William J. '58 (NY) Montrose, NY Franklin D. Roosevelt Hospital; On Duty Outside the Archdiocese.
O'Donnell, William J. '66 (NO) Des Allemands, LA St. Gertrude Church.
O'Donoghue, Brendon W. '50 (WOR) Retired.
O'Donoghue, Msgr. James P. '43 (SD) Retired.
O'Donoghue, John '64 (SAT) [2] San Antonio, TX Blessed Sacrament Church; [A] San Antonio, TX Diaconate Program.
O'Donoghue, Kevin J. '58 (BRK) [28] Brooklyn, NY St. Cecilia Church.
O'Donoghue, Patrick '61 (BIR) Trussville, AL Holy Infant of Prague Church.
O'Donoghue, Patrick F. *m.m.* '50 (FgM) Maryknoll Foreign Missions.
O'Donovan, Aidan *m.s.c.* (DAL) Irving, TX Holy Family of Nazareth Church.
O'Donovan, Dennis J. '69 (P) Beaverton, OR St. Cecilia Church.
O'Donovan, Donal '50 (WH) Retired.
O'Donovan, John '55 (SP) [1] Largo, FL St. Catherine of Siena Church.
O'Donovan, L. Aidan *m.s.c.* '80 (SAT) [M] San Antonio, TX Missionaries of the Sacred Heart.
O'Donovan, Leo J. *s.j.* '66 (WDC) [C] Washington, DC Georgetown University; [M] Washington, DC The Jesuit Community at Georgetown University.
O'Donovan, Martin E. '78 (CHI) [39] Chicago, IL St. Christina Church.
O'Donovan, Patrick G. '72 (PAT) New Vernon, NJ Christ the King Church.
O'Donovan, Rickard J. '49 (BO) Wilmington, MA St. Dorothy Church.
O'Donovan, Thomas P. '70 (CC) On Special Assignment; [E] Laredo, TX Mercy Regional Medical Center.
O'Donovan, Timothy John '49 (B) Retired.
O'Dowd, Bernard J. *o.s.a.* '58 (PH) [V] Flourtown, PA St. Joseph Villa; [AA] Villanova, PA St. Thomas Monastery.
O'Dowd, Brendan '49 (SAC) Retired and in Senior Ministry.
O'Dowd, Msgr. John '42 (VEN) Retired.
O'Driscoll, James J. '79 (BO) [1] Gloucester, MA St. Ann Church.
O'Driscoll, John C. '87 (PH) Graduate Studies.
O'Dwyer, Dominick '66 (MIA) Tamarac, FL St. Malachy Church.
O'Dwyer, Michael *s.a.c.* (LUB) [6] Lubbock, TX St. Joseph's Church.
O'Dwyer, Patrick '72 (LA) Whittier, CA St. Bruno Church.
O'Dwyer, Thomas '70 (MIA) Hollywood, FL Little Flower Church.
O'Farrell, Donal *s.s.c.* '53 (OM) [K] St. Columbans, NE St. Columban's Foreign Mission Society.
O'Farrell, Michael J. '43 (RVC) Northport, NY St. Philip Neri Church; Retired.
O'Farrell, William J. '39 (ORL) Retired.
O'Flaherty, Edward M. *s.j.* '65 (BO) [W] Chestnut Hill, MA The Jesuit Community at Boston College.
O'Flaherty, John '61 (STA) Flagler Beach, FL Santa Maria Del Mar Church; Korona, FL St. Mary's Church.
O'Flaherty, Michael '75 (PMB) [4] Boca Raton, FL St. John the Evangelist Church.
O'Flaherty, Thomas (PT) [6] Pensacola, FL St. Anne Church.
O'Flanagan, Thomas P. '95 (PMB) North Palm Beach, FL St. Clare Church.
O'Flannigan, Thomas L. '55 (TUC) Retired.
O'Flynn, John '61 (PBL) Florence, CO Federal Correctional Institute at Florence.
O'Flynn, Seamus '59 (STA) [3] St. Augustine, FL St. Anastasia Church.
O'Friel, Demetrius *o.f.m.* '50 (NY) [DD] New York, NY Franciscan Friars, Order of Friars Minor, Holy Name Province.
O'Friel, Msgr. John '45 (FRS) Lemoore, CA St. Peter Church.
O'Friel, LaSalle *o.f.m.* '54 (PAT) [M] Butler, NJ St. Anthony Friary.
O'Friel, Zachary *o.f.m.* '47 (BO) [BB] Boston, MA St. Anthony Shrine.
O'Gara, James *c.s.p.* '61 (CHI) [125] Chicago, IL Old St. Mary Church.
O'Gara, Stephen R. '71 (STP) [34] Minneapolis, MN St. Thomas the Apostle Church.
O'Gorman, Msgr. Charles F. '49 (LA) [2] Oxnard, CA Santa Clara Church.
O'Gorman, Eamon '67 (ORG) La Habra, CA Our Lady of Guadalupe Church.
O'Gorman, Msgr. George '37 (NEW) North Bergen, NJ Our Lady of Fatima Church; [N] Rutherford, NJ St. John Vianney Residence for Priests.
O'Gorman, Msgr. George A. '37 (NEW) Retired.
O'Gorman, Michael B. '64 (SAT) [38] San Antonio, TX St. Gregory's Church.
O'Gorman, Richard '57 (NY) Bangall, NY Immaculate Conception Church.
O'Gorman, Thomas H. *s.j.* '63 (FgM) Provinces.
O'Grady, Columkille *c.p.* (SPR) [3] Westfield, MA St. Casimir's Church.
O'Grady, Dennis R. '61 (CLV) [50] Cleveland, OH St. Michael Church; [X] Cleveland, OH Diocesan Hispanic Office.
O'Grady, Edward F. '46 (LAN) Retired; [E] Jackson, MI St. Joseph Home for Children, Inc.
O'Grady, Frank (PAT) Military Chaplains.
O'Grady, James (TOL) [J] Oregon, OH Sacred Heart Home.
O'Grady, James '50 (KCK) Retired.
O'Grady, James F. '54 (LA) El Segundo, CA St. Anthony Church.
O'Grady, James F. '58 (LA) [98] Los Angeles, CA Visitation Church.
O'Grady, James W. '42 (TOL) Retired.
O'Grady, John F. '66 (ALB) On Duty Outside the Diocese.
O'Grady, John F. '66 (MIA) [B] Miami, FL Barry University.
O'Grady, John G. '35 (ALB) Windham, NY St. Theresa of Child Jesus Church.
O'Grady, John G. '66 (ALB) Retired.
O'Grady, Michael '58 (PHX) [1] Phoenix, AZ SS. Simon and Jude Cathedral.
O'Grady, Michael J. '56 (NEW) [5] Bayonne, NJ St. Vincent de Paul Church.
O'Grady, Peter '63 (NO) Jefferson, LA St. Agnes Church.
O'Grady, Robert A. '72 (HRT) Windsor Locks, CT St. Mary Church.
O'Grady, Robert M. '78 (BO) Watertown, MA Sacred Heart Church; [P] Boston, MA Archdiocesan Information Center.
O'Grady, Vincent *c.s.sp.* '62 (GAL) [B] Houston, TX Holy Ghost Fathers.
O'Guinn, Jon '93 (BEL) Salem, IL St. Theresa of Avila Church.
O'Hagan, James P. '47 (DET) Waterford, MI St. Benedict Church.
O'Hagan, Patrick *ss.cc.* '65 (LA) Sepulveda, CA Veterans Administration Medical Center.
O'Haire, John A. '56 (SCR) Retired; [N] Dunmore, PA Villa St. Joseph.
O'Hala, Stephen '88 (MIA) On Duty Outside the Archdiocese.
O'Hala, Steven '88 (PMB) [A] Boynton Beach, FL St. Vincent de Paul Regional Seminary.
O'Hallaran, John E. *s.s.j.* '85 (NO) [4] New Orleans, LA Blessed Sacrament Church; [5] New Orleans, LA Corpus Christi Church.
O'Halloran, Edward '78 (NY) [7] Yonkers, NY St. Denis Church.
O'Halloran, Martin J. '47 (PH) Gladwyne, PA St. John Baptist Vianney Church; Retired.
O'Halloran, Michael *o.p.* '56 (SAC) Special Assignment.
O'Halloran, Richard '51 (MRY) Retired.
O'Halloran, Richard '59 (MRY) [H] Salinas, CA Congregation of the Sisters of the Holy Cross; [K] Salinas, CA Madonna Manor Retirement Home.
O'Halloran, William *s.s.s.* '50 (NY) [55] New York, NY St. Jean Baptiste Church.
O'Halloran, William J. *s.j.* '58 (WOR) [B] Worcester, MA College of the Holy Cross, Inc; [N] Worcester, MA Jesuits of Holy Cross College, Inc.
O'Hanlon, James J. '57 (SY) [2] Endicott, NY St. Ambrose Church; Retired.
O'Hanlon, Michael A. '57 (GF) Retired.
O'Hanlon, Thomas '83 (LA) Thousand Oaks, CA St. Paschal Baylon Church.
O'Hanlon, Msgr. William '49 (SHP) [2] Shreveport, LA Holy Trinity Church.
O'Hara, Arthur T. '78 (TLS) Pryor, OK St. Mark's Church.
O'Hara, Charles R. '70 (PH) [V] Downingtown, PA St. John Vianney Hospital.
O'Hara, Daniel J. '87 (SY) [16] Syracuse, NY St. James Church.
O'Hara, Edward '60 (SAC) West Sacramento, CA Our Lady of Grace Church.
O'Hara, Eugene *o.f.m. cap.* '61 (ROC) Trumansburg, NY St. James the Apostle Church; [I] Interlaken, NY St. Fidelis Friary.
O'Hara, Eugene P. '45 (NY) [DD] New York, NY Our Lady of Consolation Residence.
O'Hara, Eugene R. (NY) Retired.
O'Hara, Francis A. '56 (BO) [3] Plymouth, MA St. Mary Church.
O'Hara, Francis W. '59 (PRO) [6] Warwick, RI St. Kevin Church.
O'Hara, Frank J. '41 (SFD) [10] Springfield, IL SS. Peter and Paul Church.
O'Hara, Harold T. '30 (CHI) Arlington Heights, IL Our Lady of the Wayside Church; Retired.
O'Hara, James T. '66 (E) [3] Erie, PA Holy Family/St. Ann/St. Casimir Church; [13] Erie, PA St. Ann Church; [15] Erie, PA St. Casimir Church.
O'Hara, John F. '71 (PRT) Bucksport, ME St. Vincent de Paul Church; Stonington, ME St. Mary Star of the Sea Church; [M] Castine, ME Maine Maritime Academy.
O'Hara, John J. '84 (NY) [230] Staten Island, NY St. Teresa Church.
O'Hara, John T. '80 (ARL) Dale City, VA Holy Family Church.
O'Hara, Kieran *o.carm.* '37 (JOL) [J] Darien, IL Carmelite Provincial Office.
O'Hara, Kieran '37 (NO) Lacombe, LA St. John of the Cross Church.
O'Hara, Martin '41 (SFD) Stonington, IL Holy Trinity Church.
O'Hara, Martin F. '41 (PH) [74] Philadelphia, PA St. Jerome Church; Retired.
O'Hara, Michael '59 (NY) State, NY Beacon Correctional Facility; Federal, NY Federal Correctional Institution.
O'Hara, Michael '67 (SAC) [8] Sacramento, CA Sacred Heart of Jesus Church.
O'Hara, Michael D. '60 (BUF) Franklinville, NY St. Philomena Church.
O'Hara, Michael J. '47 (DET) Retired.
O'Hara, Peter J. '59 (BO) Awaiting Assignment.
O'Hara, Robert E. *m.s.f.* '65 (SAT) [M] San Antonio, TX MSF Center & Provincialate.
O'Hara, Msgr. Robert J. '46 (MAD) Retired.
O'Hara, Thomas J. *c.s.c.* '78 (SCR) [C] Wilkes-Barre, PA Kings College.
O'Hare, Daniel G. *s.j.* '79 (NY) [DD] New York, NY St.

Ignatius Loyola Residence.
O'Hare, Daniel M. '65 (NY) Maybrook, NY Assumption Church.
O'Hare, Dennis *c.s.c.* '73 (P) [B] Portland, OR University of Portland.
O'Hare, Dennis P. *c.s.c.* '73 (P) [L] Portland, OR Holy Cross Fathers & Brothers, C.S.C. - University of Portland.
O'Hare, Donal '54 (PMB) Vero Beach, FL St. John of the Cross Church.
O'Hare, Donald J. '54 (WCH) Retired.
O'Hare, Francis C. (BO) Retired.
O'Hare, Francis C. '51 (BO) Andover, MA St. Robert Bellarmine Church.
O'Hare, John B. (PMB) Vero Beach, FL Holy Cross Church.
O'Hare, Msgr. John J. '55 (SR) Boyes Hot Springs, CA St. Leo Church.
O'Hare, Joseph A. *s.j.* '61 (NY) [C] Bronx, NY Fordham University; [DD] New York, NY Jesuit Community at Fordham University.
O'Hare, Joseph P. '65 (STO) Modesto, CA St. Joseph Church.
O'Hare, Robert V. *s.j.* '95 (NY) [F] New York, NY Xavier High School.
O'Hear, Daniel J. '62 (SPR) [6] North Adams, MA St. Anthony of Padua Church.
O'Hearn, James E. *s.j.* '59 (MIL) [P] Milwaukee, WI Jesuit Provincial Office, Wisconsin Province.
O'Hearn, Michael '95 (FR) Edgartown, MA St. Elizabeth Church; Oak Bluffs, MA Sacred Heart Church; Vineyard Haven, MA St. Augustine Church.
O'Hearn, Paul V. '60 (BO) Permanent Disability.
O'Hern, Charles A. '46 (PHX) Retired.
O'Hern, Edward P. *c.s.p.* '32 (NY) [DD] Jamaica Estates, NY Paulist Fathers Generalate.
O'Hern, Edward Philip *c.s.p.* '32 (AUS) [11] Austin, TX St. Austin's Church.
O'Hern, Thomas G. *c.m.* '77 (FgM) Vincentian Foreign Missions.
O'Heron, Edward J. '57 (SY) Special Assignment; [V] Cortland, NY Newman Foundation of Cortland, Inc. at the State University College of New York.
O'Holohan, John *s.j.* '55 (ORL) [5] Orlando, FL Holy Family Church.
O'Hotto, Kenneth L. '80 (STP) Le Sueur, MN St. Anne Church.
O'Kane, James D. '65 (GI) Scottsbluff, NE St. Agnes Church.
O'Kane, Patrick J. (SC) On Duty Outside the Diocese.
O'Kane, Patrick J. '77 (SC) [F] Sioux City, IA Monastery of the Discalced Carmelite Nuns.
O'Keefe, Daniel Paul *o.s.b.* '93 (GBG) [H] Latrobe, PA Saint Vincent Archabbey.
O'Keefe, Edward *o.f.m.cap.* '65 (LA) [74] Los Angeles, CA St. Lawrence of Brindisi Church.
O'Keefe, Francis J. '60 (NOR) Putnam, CT St. Mary Church.
O'Keefe, George L. *o.carm.* '48 (CHI) [D] Chicago, IL Mt. Carmel High School; [N] Chicago, IL Carmelite Priory of St. Cyril.
O'Keefe, J. Kevin '95 (ARL) Falls Church, VA St. James Church.
O'Keefe, Msgr. John J. '72 (NY) [E] White Plains, NY Archbishop Stepinac High School.
O'Keefe, Joseph *s.j.* '86 (BO) [W] Chestnut Hill, MA The Jesuit Community at Boston College.
O'Keefe, Lawrence '70 (GLP) Holbrook, AZ Our Lady of Guadalupe Church; [A] Gallup, NM Diocesan Diaconate Formation Program.
O'Keefe, Mark *o.s.b.* '83 (IND) [A] St. Meinrad, IN St. Meinrad Seminary; [B] St. Meinrad, IN St. Meinrad Seminary-College of Liberal Arts; [J] St. Meinrad, IN St. Meinrad Archabbey.
O'Keefe, Martin D. *s.j.* '66 (STL) [P] St. Louis, MO Jesuit Community Corporation at St. Louis University - Jesuit Hall.
O'Keefe, Maurice L. '57 (NEW) Retired; [N] Rutherford, NJ St. John Vianney Residence for Priests.
O'Keefe, Michael *o.carm.* '75 (JOL) Darien, IL Our Lady of Mount Carmel Church.
O'Keefe, Michael A. '56 (JOL) Glen Ellyn, IL St. Petronille Church.
O'Keefe, Millard '65 (CHI) Other Assignments.
O'Keefe, Patrick T. '96 (BUF) Eggertsville, NY St. Benedict Church.
O'Keefe, Thomas E. '48 (NY) Retired; [E] White Plains, NY Archbishop Stepinac High School.
O'Keefe, Vincent T. *s.j.* '50 (NY) [DD] New York, NY "America;" Residence and publication office of the America Press; [HH] New York, NY John LaFarge Institute, The.
O'Keefe, William F. '60 (HRT) [3] Enfield, CT St. Bernard's Church.
O'Keeffe, Dennis J. '84 (LFT) Muncie, IN St. Lawrence Church.
O'Keeffe, Jeremiah '66 (LA) Temple City, CA St. Luke the Evangelist Church.
O'Keeffe, L. Joseph '66 (ALB) Military Chaplains.
O'Keeffe, Michael '68 (SAV) [5] Savannah, GA Most Pure Heart of Mary Church.
O'Keeffe, Patrick '59 (SB) Retired.
O'Keeffe, Msgr. Richard W. '59 (TUC) Yuma, AZ Immaculate Conception Church.
O'Keeffe, William J. '59 (LA) [12] Long Beach, CA Our Lady of Refuge Church.
O'Keeffe, William T. *s.s.* '45 (BAL) [J] Baltimore, MD St. Charles Villa; [M] Baltimore, MD St. Charles Villa.
O'Kelly, Colm '64 (SAC) Woodland, CA Holy Rosary Church.
O'Kelly, Fritz *o.f.m.conv.* (FgM) Conventual Franciscan Foreign Missions.
O'Kennedy, Philip N. '71 (BIR) [1] Huntsville, AL Good Shepherd Church.
O'Kere, Michael '90 (NY) [124] Bronx, NY St. Angela Merici Church.
O'Kielty, James '54 (PAT) Madison, NJ St. Vincent Martyr Church.
O'Konsky, Stanley J. *s.j.* '72 (NY) [F] New York, NY Fordham Preparatory School; [DD] New York, NY Jesuit Community at Fordham University.
O'Kruta, Francis A. '94 (WH) Cameron, WV St. Martin Church.
O'Kruta, Frank A. '94 (WH) St. Joseph Settlement, WV St. Joseph's Church.
O'Laughlin, Patrick J. '67 (STL) [2] Creve Coeur, MO St. John Bosco Church.
O'Leary, Adrian P. '47 (BO) Retired.
O'Leary, Arthur P. (BO) Retired.
O'Leary, Bartholomew J. '70 (HON) Retired.
O'Leary, Bernard C. *s.j.* '48 (WDC) La Plata, MD Sacred Heart Church.
O'Leary, Msgr. Cornelius '48 (CAM) On Duty Outside the Diocese.
O'Leary, Msgr. Cornelius '48 (SB) Retired.
O'Leary, Cornelius F. '56 (WOR) Otter River, MA St. Martin's Church.
O'Leary, Daniel F. *o.m.i.* '50 (BUF) [27] Buffalo, NY Holy Angels Church; [C] Niagara University, NY Niagara University; [O] Niagara University, NY Vincentian Community at Niagara University.
O'Leary, David A. '45 (WCH) Retired.
O'Leary, David M. '74 (BAL) [A] Baltimore, MD St. Mary's Seminary and University.
O'Leary, David M. '88 (BO) On Duty Outside the Archdiocese.
O'Leary, Donald J. '37 (HRT) Plantsville, CT St. Aloysius Church; Retired.
O'Leary, Harold V. *c.s.b.* '49 (GAL) [Q] Houston, TX Residence of the Basilian Fathers of the University of St. Thomas.
O'Leary, Hilary *o.s.b.* '68 (PAT) [M] Morristown, NJ St. Mary's Abbey.
O'Leary, James E. '68 (BO) [2] Arlington, MA St. Camillus Church.
O'Leary, James J. '56 (DET) Harrison Twp., MI St. Hubert Church.
O'Leary, James J. *s.j.* '65 (OM) [K] Omaha, NE Jesuit Community At Creighton University.
O'Leary, James M. *s.j.* '91 (CHI) [N] Chicago, IL Chicago Province of the Society of Jesus-Provincial Office.
O'Leary, James M. *s.j.* '91 (FgM) Provinces.
O'Leary, James S. '61 (KAL) Battle Creek, MI St. Joseph Church.
O'Leary, Jerome A. *o.p.* '57 (CHI) [N] River Forest, IL St. Thomas Aquinas Priory.
O'Leary, John '67 (FgM) Society of St. James the Apostle.
O'Leary, John '67 (MIA) On Duty Outside the Archdiocese.
O'Leary, John '78 (CAM) Washington Township, NJ St. Charles Borromeo Church.
O'Leary, John J. *s.j.* '60 (FgM) Provinces.
O'Leary, John P. '54 (BIS) New Town, ND St. Anthony Church.
O'Leary, Kevin J. '95 (BO) Lynnfield, MA Our Lady of the Assumption Church.
O'Leary, Msgr. Lawrence '53 (LA) [78] Los Angeles, CA St. Martin of Tours Church.
O'Leary, Lawrence J. '56 (RVC) West Brentwood, NY Pilgrim Psychiatric Center.
O'Leary, Malcolm *s.v.d.* '61 (LAF) [4] Opelousas, LA Holy Ghost Church.
O'Leary, Mark G. *o.p.* '84 (SR) [G] Santa Rosa, CA Santa Rosa Memorial Hospital.
O'Leary, Michael G. '43 (DET) Grosse Pointe Farms, MI St. Paul Catholic Church; Retired.
O'Leary, Niall F. '60 (LA) Retired.
O'Leary, Patrick B. *s.j.* '61 (SEA) [A] Seattle, WA Seattle University.
O'Leary, Patrick C. '76 (SY) Absent on Leave.
O'Leary, Patrick D. '51 (Y) Retired.
O'Leary, Raymond J. '62 (ORL) Port Orange, FL Our Lady of Hope Church.
O'Leary, Robert A. '53 (NEW) Retired.
O'Leary, Sean *o.carm.* '55 (NEW) Englewood, NJ St. Cecilia's Church.
O'Leary, Sean '61 (SAC) Red Bluff, CA Sacred Heart Church.
O'Leary, Msgr. Thomas M. '57 (NEW) Wyckoff, NJ St. Elizabeth Church.
O'Leary, Todd '58 (TUC) [23] Tucson, AZ St. Thomas the Apostle Church.
O'Leary, William A. '40 (BRK) Retired.
O'Leary, William F. *s.j.* '62 (OM) [C] Omaha, NE Creighton Preparatory School.
O'Leary, William R. *s.j.* '73 (PAT) [I] Morristown, NJ Loyola House of Retreats.
O'Leary, William T. *m.m.* '61 (FgM) Maryknoll Foreign Missions.
O'Lenny, Patrick J. '56 (LC) On Duty Outside the Diocese.
O'Liddy, Patrick H. *s.j.* '90 (DEN) [M] Denver, CO Regis Jesuit Community (The Jesuits at Regis University).
O'Loghlen, Martin P. *ss.cc.* '61 (LA) [R] La Verne, CA Congregation of the Sacred Hearts.
O'Looney, Martin J. *c.s.p.* '46 (NY) [DD] Jamaica Estates, NY Paulist Fathers Generalate.
O'Loughlin, Msgr. Eugene E. '44 (BUF) [64] Buffalo, NY St. Thomas Aquinas Church; Retired.
O'Loughlin, Eugene P. '43 (WH) Retired.
O'Loughlin, Francis A. '80 (PRO) [3] Newport, RI St. Joseph Church; Newport, RI Newport Hospital.
O'Loughlin, Frank '65 (PMB) Boynton Beach, FL St. Thomas More Church.
O'Loughlin, Michael *s.s.c.* '60 (FgM) St. Columban's Foreign Mission.
O'Loughlin, Padhraic *s.s.c.* '57 (FgM) St. Columban's Foreign Mission.
O'Loughlin, S. Raphael *c.s.b.* '42 (GAL) Retired; [Q] Houston, TX Dillon House.
O'Mahoney, Finbar P. *o.s.b.* '43 (MAN) [K] Manchester, NH St. Anselm Abbey.
O'Mahony, Donal *o.f.m.cap.* '66 (SFR) Burlingame, CA Our Lady of Angels Church.
O'Mahony, James '70 (HON) Retired.
O'Mahony, Jerome *m.s.c.* '50 (LA) Sherman Oaks, CA St. Francis de Sales Church.
O'Mahony, Maurice '67 (LA) Montecito, CA Our Lady of Mount Carmel Church.
O'Malley, Bartholomew J. *c.m.* '40 (PH) [AA] Philadelphia, PA Congregation of the Mission.
O'Malley, Dennis O. '90 (WOR) Auburn, MA St. Joseph's Church.
O'Malley, Edward J. '60 (JOL) Manhattan, IL St. Joseph Church.
O'Malley, Francis P. '73 (NY) [193] Bronx, NY Visitation Church; On Special or Other (Arch)Diocesan Assignment.
O'Malley, James *c.ss.r.* '55 (ORL) [F] New Smyrna Beach, FL St. Alphonsus Villa-Redemptorist Fathers and Brothers.
O'Malley, James '56 (CHI) Highwood, IL St. James Church.
O'Malley, James E. '46 (SFR) Novato, CA St. Anthony of Padua Church; Retired.
O'Malley, James J. '46 (SPK) Retired.
O'Malley, John A. '55 (BWN) [4] Brownsville, TX Holy Family Church.
O'Malley, John J. *o.p.* '59 (CHI) River Forest, IL St. Vincent Ferrer Priory Church.
O'Malley, John J. '65 (PIT) Wilmerding, PA St. Jude the Apostle Church.
O'Malley, John L. *s.j.* '63 (FgM) Provinces.
O'Malley, John W. *s.j.* (DET) [K] Detroit, MI Jesuit Provincial Office-Detroit Province of the Society of Jesus.
O'Malley, John W. *s.j.* '59 (BO) [W] Cambridge, MA Weston Jesuit Community.
O'Malley, Joseph M. '50 (DEN) Retired.
O'Malley, Joseph T. '54 (GAL) [77] Houston, TX St. Thomas More Church; [K] Houston, TX The Catholic Chaplain Corps.
O'Malley, Kenneth *c.p.* '64 (CHI) [B] Chicago, IL The Catholic Theological Union at Chicago; [N] Chicago, IL Passionist Community-CTU.
O'Malley, Leonard F. '74 (BO) Burlington, MA St. Malachy Church.
O'Malley, Mark Francis '95 (NEW) Caldwell, NJ St. Aloysius Church.
O'Malley, Michael P. (PH) Valley Forge, PA St. Teresa of Avila Church.
O'Malley, Michael W. '52 (WCH) Retired.
O'Malley, Patrick '57 (CHI) [A] Mundelein, IL University of St. Mary of the Lake-Mundelein Seminary.
O'Malley, Paul *s.s.c.* '57 (BO) [W] Quincy, MA St. Columban's Foreign Mission Society.
O'Malley, Thomas J. '66 (SCR) Ashley, PA St. Leo's Church.
O'Malley, Thomas P. *s.j.* '61 (BO) [W] Boston, MA The Society of Jesus of New England-Provincial Offices.
O'Malley, Thomas P. *s.j.* '61 (LA) [C] Los Angeles, CA Loyola Marymount University.
O'Malley, Timothy J. '97 (CHI) [5] Chicago, IL St. Agnes of Bohemia Church.
O'Malley, Vincent J. *c.m.* '73 (BUF) [C] Niagara University, NY Niagara University; [O] Niagara University, NY Vincentian Community at Niagara University.
O'Malley, William *o.carm.* '65 (NEW) Demarest, NJ St. Joseph's Church.

O'Malley, William J. *s.j.* '51 (NY) [DD] New York, NY Jesuit Community at Fordham University.
O'Malley, William J. *s.j.* '63 (NY) [F] New York, NY Fordham Preparatory School.
O'Malley, William M. *s.j.* '62 (P) Oakridge, OR St. Michael Church.
O'Malley, William P. '70 (PIT) Oakmont, PA St. Irenaeus Church.
O'Mara, Dennis *s.s.c.* '61 (DAL) Grand Prairie, TX Immaculate Conception Church.
O'Mara, Michael '88 (IND) Bloomington, IN St. Paul Catholic Center Church; [N] Bloomington, IN Indiana University, Bloomington Newman Center.
O'Mara, William T. '58 (CHI) Orland Hills, IL St. Elizabeth Seton Church.
O'Meara, Gerard '76 (FgM) Society of St. James the Apostle.
O'Meara, Gerard J. '56 (BO) Society of St. James the Apostle.
O'Meara, Henry *c.ss.r.* '43 (BAL) Annapolis, MD St. Mary Church; [M] Annapolis, MD Saint Mary Rectory.
O'Meara, James J. '49 (KAL) Retired.
O'Meara, Joseph M. '67 (BAL) [86] Baltimore, MD St. Rose of Lima Church.
O'Meara, Joseph P. '53 (NY) [155] Bronx, NY St. John Chrysostom's Church.
O'Meara, Marcian T. '59 (DEN) [8] Denver, CO Church of the Good Shepherd.
O'Meara, Thomas *o.p.* '62 (FTW) [B] Notre Dame, IN University of Notre Dame Du Lac.
O'Meara, Thomas Aquinas F. *o.p.* '62 (CHI) [N] River Forest, IL St. Thomas Aquinas Priory.
O'Mearain, Msgr. Ciaran P. '60 (CAM) Gibbsboro, NJ St. Andrew the Apostle Church.
O'Melia, Edward A. '77 (DAV) West Branch, IA St. Bernadette Church; West Liberty, IA St. Joseph's Church.
O'Neal, James E. *s.a.* '80 (STA) Interlachen, FL St. John's Mission Church.
O'Neal, Norman B. *s.j.* '59 (NO) [F] New Orleans, LA Jesuit High School.
O'Neal, Patrick K. '90 (PEO) Granville, IL Sacred Heart Of Jesus Church.
O'Neil, Dennis '66 (LA) [93] Los Angeles, CA St. Thomas the Apostle Church.
O'Neil, Edward '63 (NY) Mamaroneck, NY St. Vito Church.
O'Neil, Flann *o.f.m.* '52 (GLP) Ganado, AZ All Saints Church.
O'Neil, Francis J. *s.j.* '50 (BO) [FF] Framingham, MA Bethany Health Care Center, Inc.
O'Neil, James '85 (GF) [K] Malta, MT St. Mary's Catholic Education Trust.
O'Neil, James W. *s.j.* '57 (BO) [E] Boston, MA Boston College High School & Jesuit Community.
O'Neil, Jim '85 (GF) Malta, MT St. Mary's Church.
O'Neil, Joseph M. *m.s.* (HRT) [V] Hartford, CT Religious Trust of the Missionaries of Our Lady of LaSalette.
O'Neil, Joseph M. *m.s.* '93 (HRT) [5] Hartford, CT Our Lady of Sorrows Church; [M] Hartford, CT Missionaries of LaSalette Provincial Secretary; [M] Hartford, CT Missionaries of LaSalette Provincial Secretary.
O'Neil, Kevin *c.ss.r.* '81 (WDC) [M] Washington, DC Holy Redeemer College.
O'Neil, Lee '56 (MOB) Gulf Shores, AL Our Lady of the Gulf Church.
O'Neil, Lee E. '56 (TLS) Retired.
O'Neil, Leo J. '56 (WOR) [4] Leominster, MA St. Leo's Church; Boylston, MA Worcester County Sanitarium; Boylston, MA Worcester County Jail and House of Correction.
O'Neil, Lewis B. *s.j.* '63 (SFR) [53] San Francisco, CA St. Vincent de Paul Church.
O'Neil, Maurice *s.s.* '50 (TUC) Willcox, AZ Federal Prison Camp; Fort Grant Rural Station, AZ Fort Grant Training Center.
O'Neil, Maurice *s.s.* '57 (TUC) Willcox, AZ Sacred Heart Church.
O'Neil, Maurice L. '57 (OG) On Duty Outside the Diocese.
O'Neil, Michael '59 (SEA) Retired.
O'Neil, Patrick *o.p.* '95 (SEA) [22] Seattle, WA Blessed Sacrament Church.
O'Neil, Patrick J. '83 (WIL) Ocean City, MD St. Luke and St. Andrew Church.
O'Neil, Msgr. Philip E. '54 (RCK) Marengo, IL Sacred Heart Church.
O'Neil, Thomas D. '69 (PIT) Washington, PA St. Hilary Church.
O'Neil, W. Laurence *s.j.* '61 (BGP) [A] Fairfield, CT Fairfield University; [O] Fairfield, CT The Fairfield Jesuit Community-Fairfield University.
O'Neill, Blane *o.f.m.* '51 (STL) Oakville, MO St. Francis of Assisi Church; [P] Oakville, MO St. Francis Friary.
O'Neill, Brian E. '68 (CAM) Gloucester, NJ St. Mary's Church.
O'Neill, Charles '46 (DET) [6] Dearborn Heights, MI Our Lady of Grace Church.
O'Neill, Charles E. *s.j.* '57 (NO) [C] New Orleans, LA Loyola University.
O'Neill, Charles F. '46 (DET) Retired.
O'Neill, Cornelius J. '50 (FR) Retired.
O'Neill, Daniel *o.carm.* '69 (CHI) [N] Chicago, IL Carmelite Fathers Residence.
O'Neill, Daniel *o.carm.* '69 (JOL) [J] Darien, IL Carmelite Provincial Office.
O'Neill, Msgr. Daniel J. '76 (ALT) [21] Johnstown, PA St. Gregory's Church; [22] Johnstown, PA St. Barnabas Church; [H] Hollidaysburg, PA Campus Ministry.
O'Neill, Dennis B. '73 (CHI) [26] Chicago, IL St. Benedict Church.
O'Neill, Desmond (ROC) [57] Rochester, NY St. Theodore Church; Rochester, NY Monroe Community Hospital.
O'Neill, Edward M. '71 (MET) Colonia, NJ St. John Vianney Church.
O'Neill, Msgr. Felix M. '55 (CAM) Woodbury Heights, NJ St. Margaret's Church.
O'Neill, Francis J. *s.j.* '50 (BO) [E] Boston, MA Boston College High School & Jesuit Community; [W] Boston, MA The Society of Jesus of New England-Provincial Offices.
O'Neill, Francis S. '37 (HRT) Retired.
O'Neill, George F. '97 (BGP) Shelton, CT St. Joseph's Church.
O'Neill, George T. '41 (HRT) Retired.
O'Neill, Hugh (GLP) Gallup, NM Gallup Area Hospitals & Nursing Homes.
O'Neill, Msgr. James '54 (CHY) Casper, WY St. Anthony of Padua Church; [B] Casper, WY St. Anthony Manor.
O'Neill, James '57 (ALB) Stillwater, NY St. Peter the Apostle Church.
O'Neill, James A. '41 (CLV) Westlake, OH St. Bernadette Church; Retired.
O'Neill, James R. '40 (NEW) Ramsey, NJ St. Paul Church; Retired.
O'Neill, James V. *o.s.f.s.* '41 (WIL) [I] Childs, MD Oblates of St. Francis De Sales.
O'Neill, James W. *m.m.* '55 (FgM) Maryknoll Foreign Missions.
O'Neill, James W. *o.s.f.s.* '67 (CHL) [4] Greensboro, NC St. Paul the Apostle Church.
O'Neill, Jeremiah '59 (LA) Alhambra, CA St. Thomas More Church.
O'Neill, Jeremiah P. '57 (NY) [101] New York, NY Our Saviour Church.
O'Neill, John D. *s.j.* '60 (DET) [K] Detroit, MI Jesuit Community at the University of Detroit.
O'Neill, John J. *m.s.* '62 (NOR) Danielson, CT St. James Church.
O'Neill, John J. '67 (SFR) Novato, CA Our Lady of Loretto Church.
O'Neill, John M. *o.s.f.s.* '73 (ARL) Vienna, VA Our Lady of Good Counsel Church.
O'Neill, John P. *o.s.f.s.* '59 (STO) Turlock, CA Sacred Heart Church.
O'Neill, Joseph J. *m.m.* '49 (SJ) [M] Los Altos, CA Maryknoll.
O'Neill, Joseph P. *s.j.* '54 (BO) [E] Boston, MA Boston College High School & Jesuit Community.
O'Neill, Msgr. Kevin P. '77 (SCR) East Stroudsburg, PA St. John Church.
O'Neill, Kevin S. '77 (HEL) Kalispell, MT St. Matthew Church.
O'Neill, Msgr. Kevin T. '61 (BUF) East Aurora, NY Immaculate Conception Church.
O'Neill, Laurence M. *s.j.* '35 (NO) [P] New Orleans, LA Ignatius Residence.
O'Neill, Michael *i.c.* '70 (VEN) Bradenton, FL Sacred Heart Church.
O'Neill, Michael '81 (SP) Palm Harbor, FL St. Luke the Evangelist Church.
O'Neill, Michael F. '76 (NO) Military Chaplains.
O'Neill, Msgr. Patrick '45 (SD) La Mesa, CA St. Martin of Tours Church.
O'Neill, Patrick '53 (SEA) [1] Tacoma, WA St. Ann Church; [15] Tacoma, WA Sacred Heart Church; Retired.
O'Neill, Patrick G. '53 (SEA) [5] Tacoma, WA St. John of the Woods Church.
O'Neill, Patrick H. '67 (MIA) Special Assignment.
O'Neill, Msgr. Patrick J. '45 (SD) Retired.
O'Neill, Msgr. Patrick J. '47 (SAC) Retired and in Senior Ministry.
O'Neill, Patrick J. '90 (CHI) Alsip, IL St. Terrence Church.
O'Neill, Raymond '66 (SP) Gulfport, FL Most Holy Name of Jesus Church.
O'Neill, Richard '54 (SY) Marcy, NY Central New York Psychiatric Center.
O'Neill, Richard V. '54 (SY) [12] Utica, NY St. Mary Church.
O'Neill, Robert D. (STO) Hughson, CA St. Anthony Church.
O'Neill, Robert F. '62 (ROC) [5] Rochester, NY Church of the Annunciation.
O'Neill, Rory '55 (DOD) Retired.
O'Neill, Thomas '62 (FRS) Shafter, CA St. Therese Church.
O'Neill, Thomas D. '68 (PRO) On Duty Outside the Diocese.
O'Neill, Thomas H. *s.j.* '90 (LA) [F] Los Angeles, CA Loyola High School.
O'Neill, Thomas M. '78 (LC) [B] La Crosse, WI Viterbo College.
O'Neill, Thomas P. *o.s.f.s.* '57 (TOL) [C] Toledo, OH St. Francis de Sales High School; [K] Toledo, OH Oblates of St. Francis de Sales.
O'Neill, Timothy H. '67 (Y) Hubbard, OH St. Patrick's Church.
O'Neill, Vincent '71 (SR) On Sick Leave.
O'Neill, Virgil *o.s.b.* '46 (SCL) [I] Collegeville, MN St. John's Abbey, of the Order of St. Benedict.
O'Neill, William J. '65 (PRO) Jamestown, RI St. Mark Church.
O'Neill, William O. '67 (SAV) [1] Savannah, GA Cathedral of St. John the Baptist.
O'Neill, William P. '61 (CLV) Hinckley, OH Our Lady of Grace Church.
O'Neill, William R. *s.j.* '81 (OAK) [A] Berkeley, CA The Jesuit School of Theology at Berkeley; [N] Berkeley, CA Jesuit Community at Jesuit School of Theology at Berkeley.
O'Pira, Simon Peter '93 (STV) [1] Barrenspot, VI Church St. Ann Church.
O'Rafferty, Patrick '51 (SAC) Retired and in Senior Ministry.
O'Rafferty, Patrick '53 (SAC) Carmichael, CA St. John the Evangelist Church.
O'Regan, Denis '61 (STA) [2] Jacksonville, FL Blessed Trinity Church.
O'Regan, Hugh H. '57 (BO) [29] Boston, MA Holy Trinity Church; [31] Boston, MA St. James the Greater Church.
O'Reilly, Aidan '60 (SAC) Mount Shasta, CA St. Anthony Church.
O'Reilly, Msgr. Alvin J. '51 (NO) [3] New Orleans, LA St. Mary's Assumption Church; New Orleans, LA Shrine of St. Lazarus of Jerusalem Church; Retired.
O'Reilly, Andrew *c.pp.s.* '74 (ORL) Winter Garden, FL Resurrection Church.
O'Reilly, Msgr. Bernard '45 (LA) Paramount, CA Our Lady of the Rosary Church; Retired.
O'Reilly, Bernard M. '69 (PRO) Burrillville, RI St. Patrick Church.
O'Reilly, Edward M. '68 (NY) Military Chaplains.
O'Reilly, Francis J. '45 (PHX) Retired.
O'Reilly, Gabriel '67 (MIA) Davie, FL St. David Church.
O'Reilly, Gerald K. '85 (CHI) [116] Chicago, IL St. Laurence Church.
O'Reilly, James E. *s.j.* '57 (DET) [23] Detroit, MI St. Francis de Sales Church.
O'Reilly, James P. *m.s.* '37 (HRT) [M] Hartford, CT Missionaries of LaSalette Provincial Secretary.
O'Reilly, Msgr. John L. '40 (WH) Retired.
O'Reilly, Joseph '49 (SFD) Retired.
O'Reilly, Joseph F. '56 (WH) White Sulphur Springs, WV St. Charles Borromeo Church.
O'Reilly, Joseph P. '39 (SFR) [49] San Francisco, CA St. Stephen Church; Retired.
O'Reilly, Kevin '96 (NY) [169] Bronx, NY Our Lady of Angels Church.
O'Reilly, Kevin P. '84 (WDC) Laurel, MD St. Mary Church.
O'Reilly, Michael '96 (SAC) South Lake Tahoe, CA St. Theresa Church.
O'Reilly, Michael P. '61 (WH) Parkersburg, WV St. Francis Xavier's Church.
O'Reilly, P. J. '53 (ORL) Retired.
O'Reilly, Patrick J. '44 (GF) Retired.
O'Reilly, Patrick J. '65 (OG) [E] Lake Placid, NY Uihlein Mercy Center.
O'Reilly, Msgr. Peter A. '61 (LA) Oak Park, CA St. Maximilian Kolbe Church.
O'Reilly, Vincent '62 (SAC) Vacaville, CA St. Joseph Church.
O'Riley, Dennis H. '59 (PEO) Tolono, IL St. Patrick's Church.
O'Riley, James K. '67 (IND) Retired.
O'Riley, Robert F. *o.p.* '58 (CHI) [N] River Forest, IL St. Thomas Aquinas Priory.
O'Riordan, James '64 (JKS) Vicksburg, MS St. Michael Church.
O'Riordan, Jeremiah (PAT) Dover, NJ Dover General Hospital; [J] Denville, NJ Northwest Covenant Medial Center.
O'Riordan, William '85 (NO) [3] Harvey, LA St. Martha Church.
O'Rorke, Msgr. James H. '61 (PAT) [5] Wayne, NJ Our Lady of the Valley Church.
O'Rourke, Arthur G. *o.s.a.* '57 (BO) [9] Lawrence, MA St. Mary Immaculate Conception Church.
O'Rourke, Bryan A. '66 (STP) Plymouth, MN St. Mary of the Lake Church.
O'Rourke, Charles M. '58 (PH) Milmont Park, PA Our Lady of Peace Church.
O'Rourke, Colin *o.f.m.* '61 (BO) [BB] Boston, MA St. Anthony Shrine.
O'Rourke, Daniel J. '88 (GF) Scobey, MT St. Philip Bonitus Church.

O'Rourke, David *o.p.* '62 (OAK) [N] Oakland, CA Dominican Order, Siena House.
O'Rourke, Dennis J. '80 (PHX) [5] Scottsdale, AZ St. Daniel the Prophet Church; [H] Phoenix, AZ Office of Youth and Young Adult Ministries.
O'Rourke, Edmund F. *o.s.f.s.* (FgM) Oblates of St. Francis de Sales Foreign Missions.
O'Rourke, Edmund F. *o.s.f.s.* '56 (CAM) [M] Pittsgrove, NJ Villa St. Joseph.
O'Rourke, Francis J. '52 (MIL) Retired.
O'Rourke, Francis J. *c.ss.r.* '62 (BRK) [U] Brooklyn, NY Our Lady of Good Counsel Residence.
O'Rourke, Francis J. '75 (CHL) Clemmons, NC Holy Family Church.
O'Rourke, Gabriel A. '45 (SC) Retired.
O'Rourke, Hugh *s.s.c.* '52 (PRO) [12] Pawtucket, RI St. Teresa of the Child Jesus Church.
O'Rourke, James J. '58 (BO) [21] Boston, MA St. Columbkille Church.
O'Rourke, John F. *o.s.a.* '61 (PH) [142] Philadelphia, PA St. Rita of Cascia Church.
O'Rourke, Msgr. John G. '48 (DAL) Retired.
O'Rourke, John J. *s.s.j.* '66 (BLX) [5] Gulfport, MS St. Therese Church.
O'Rourke, Kevin David *o.p.* '54 (STL) [P] St. Louis, MO Dominican Community of St. Louis.
O'Rourke, Matthew J.. *s.s.j.* '47 (BAL) [M] Baltimore, MD St. Joseph's Manor.
O'Rourke, Michael J. *o.p.* '96 (NO) [P] New Orleans, LA Dominican Fathers & Brothers, Southern Dominican Province.
O'Rourke, Michael K. '69 (GB) [4] Appleton, WI St. Mary Church.
O'Rourke, P. Gerard '50 (SFR) [20] San Francisco, CA St. Gabriel Church; Special Assignment.
O'Rourke, Paul J. *s.s.c.* (PRO) [4] Warren, RI St. Mary of the Bay Church.
O'Rourke, Peter *c.p.* '64 (FgM) Passionist Foreign Missions.
O'Rourke, Richard *m.s.c.* (AUS) Harker Heights, TX St. Paul Chong Hasang Church.
O'Rourke, Robert *s.s.c.* '58 (OM) [K] St. Columbans, NE St. Columban's Foreign Mission Society.
O'Rourke, Terence *o.s.a.* '64 (NY) [195] Staten Island, NY St. Ann Church.
O'Rourke, Thomas J. '63 (BRK) [84] Brooklyn, NY St. Mary, Star of the Sea Church.
O'Rourke, Thomas J. '64 (HRT) [1] Hamden, CT Ascension Church.
O'Rourke, Thomas P. *m.m.* '41 (NY) [DD] Maryknoll, NY Maryknoll Fathers and Brothers.
O'Rourke, William '58 (RVC) Port Washington, NY St. Peter of Alcantara Church.
O'Rourke, William J. '56 (NOR) Quinebaug, CT St. Stephen Church.
O'Ryan, Colm '55 (LA) Beverly Hills, CA Good Shepherd Church.
O'Shaughnessy, Donald *s.j.* '55 (CIN) [M] Cincinnati, OH Faber Jesuit Community.
O'Shaughnessy, James J. '68 (NY) [E] New York, NY Cardinal Spellman High School.
O'Shaughnessy, Michael A. '50 (VIC) Edna, TX St. Agnes Church.
O'Shaughnessy, Patrick '68 (BLX) [8] Biloxi, MS St. Michael Church.
O'Shaughnessy, Thomas J. *s.j.* '44 (FgM) Provinces.
O'Shaughnessy, William J. *o.p.* '49 (PRO) [P] Providence, RI St. Thomas Aquinas Priory at Providence College.
O'Shea, Daniel *o.s.b.* '35 (KCK) [I] Leavenworth, KS Motherhouse of the Sisters of Charity of Leavenworth.
O'Shea, Daniel *s.a.* '64 (NY) [14] Yonkers, NY Our Lady of the Rosary Church.
O'Shea, Howard '58 (NY) [DD] New York, NY Franciscan Friars, Order of Friars Minor, Holy Name Province.
O'Shea, James *c.p.* '89 (BRK) [U] Jamaica, NY Immaculate Conception Monastery.
O'Shea, James B. '65 (WOR) [12] Worcester, MA Our Lady of Lourdes Church.
O'Shea, James D. '64 (SFD) Bethany, IL St. Isidore Church; Mt. Zion, IL Our Lady of the Holy Spirit Church.
O'Shea, James R. '56 (WCH) Halstead, KS Sacred Heart of Jesus Church.
O'Shea, Jeremiah T. '64 (PIT) Mt. Lebanon, PA St. Winifred Church.
O'Shea, John F. *s.j.* '52 (STL) [P] St. Louis, MO The Jesuits of the Missouri Province.
O'Shea, John G. '60 (YAK) Kennewick, WA Holy Spirit Church.
O'Shea, John J. '36 (CHI) [121] Chicago, IL St. Margaret Mary Church; Retired.
O'Shea, John J. '41 (ATL) Retired.
O'Shea, John J. '50 (WCH) [19] Wichita, KS St. Thomas Aquinas Church.
O'Shea, John T. '54 (BUF) Retired.
O'Shea, Joseph '61 (SEA) Woodland, WA St. Philip's Church.
O'Shea, Msgr. Joseph H. '47 (PMB) [2] Boca Raton, FL Our Lady of Lourdes Church; Retired.
O'Shea, Joseph J. '42 (NY) [145] Bronx, NY St. Helena Church; Retired.
O'Shea, Lawrence '56 (DUL) [17] Duluth, MN St. Raphael's Church.
O'Shea, Michael *o.f.m.cap.* '54 (FRS) [D] Fresno, CA Nazareth House.
O'Shea, Michael '61 (LA) Retired.
O'Shea, Michael '72 (NY) State, NY Bedford Hills Correctional Facility.
O'Shea, Patrick '61 (MIA) Hollywood, FL Little Flower Church.
O'Shea, Patrick '61 (LA) On Duty Outside the Archdiocese.
O'Shea, Patrick *m.s.c.* '73 (SAT) [M] San Antonio, TX Missionaries of the Sacred Heart.
O'Shea, Msgr. Patrick J. '58 (SFR) Absent on Leave.
O'Shea, Philip *o.f.m.* '75 (BO) [W] Boston, MA Ministry of the Word.
O'Shea, Philip A. '54 (WDC) [10] Washington, DC Blessed Sacrament, Shrine of the Most Church; Retired.
O'Shea, Robert J. '63 (BEL) Leave of Absence.
O'Shea, Vincent *o.s.m.* '38 (CHI) [N] Chicago, IL Servite Friars - Eastern Province.
O'Shea, Vincent M. *o.s.m.* '35 (CHI) Hillside, IL St. Domitilla Church.
O'Shea, William D. '62 (PMB) North Palm Beach, FL St. Clare Church.
O'Shea, William J. '63 (JOL) [4] Naperville, IL St. Margaret Mary Church.
O'Sullivan, Andrew C. *o.s.b.* '43 (PAT) [M] Newton, NJ St. Paul's Abbey.
O'Sullivan, Brendan '54 (SB) Retired.
O'Sullivan, Brendan *s.s.c.* '70 (FgM) St. Columban's Foreign Mission Society(S.S.C.)(THE COLUMBAN FATHERS).
O'Sullivan, Brendan *s.s.c.* '70 (OM) [K] St. Columbans, NE St. Columban's Foreign Mission Society.
O'Sullivan, Carrol '51 (LA) Montecito, CA Our Lady of Mount Carmel Church.
O'Sullivan, Cyril '80 (SFR) [18] San Francisco, CA St. Finn Barr Church.
O'Sullivan, Daniel '60 (DET) New Haven, MI St. Francis of Assisi Church; Detroit, MI Detroit Psychiatric Institute.
O'Sullivan, Daniel '63 (LA) Ventura, CA Sacred Heart Church.
O'Sullivan, Daniel A. *s.j.* '55 (SFR) [N] San Francisco, CA Jesuit Community at University of San Francisco.
O'Sullivan, Daniel J. '62 (CHI) Park Forest, IL St. Irenaeus Church.
O'Sullivan, Denis A. '72 (SR) [3] Santa Rosa, CA St. Rose of Lima Church.
O'Sullivan, Eugene M. (BO) Retired.
O'Sullivan, Msgr. Francis G. (BO) Retired.
O'Sullivan, Msgr. Francis G. '47 (BO) [3] Peabody, MA St. John the Baptist Church.
O'Sullivan, James '49 (CAM) On Sick Leave; [M] Cherry Hill, NJ Vianney Villa.
O'Sullivan, James J. '60 (JC) Eldon, MO Sacred Heart Church.
O'Sullivan, Msgr. Jeremiah '58 (SD) Coronado, CA Sacred Heart Church; Retired.
O'Sullivan, John '50 (B) Retired.
O'Sullivan, John C. '45 (PBL) Retired.
O'Sullivan, John J. '50 (BRK) Retired.
O'Sullivan, John V. '68 (PT) [2] Tallahassee, FL Blessed Sacrament Church.
O'Sullivan, Martin J. '53 (BRK) [R] Bayside, NY Ozanam Hall of Queens Nursing Home, Inc.
O'Sullivan, Michael '48 (MRY) Retired.
O'Sullivan, Michael '55 (SAT) On Leave.
O'Sullivan, Michael J. '55 (WDC) [37] Washington, DC St. Peter Church.
O'Sullivan, Msgr. Peter '34 (LA) Granada Hills, CA St. John Baptist de la Salle Church; Retired.
O'Sullivan, Peter '83 (KCK) Emporia, KS Sacred Heart Church.
O'Sullivan, Raymond '68 (FgM) Society of St. James the Apostle.
O'Sullivan, Raymond S. '68 (BO) Society of St. James the Apostle.
O'Sullivan, Robert '43 (BIR) Retired.
O'Sullivan, Sarsfield '51 (HEL) Retired.
O'Sullivan, Sean *i.c.* '47 (SP) Indian Rocks Beach, FL St. Jerome Church.
O'Sullivan, Sean '64 (MIA) Coral Gables, FL Little Flower Church; Retired.
O'Sullivan, T. Brendan '56 (SAC) [10] Sacramento, CA St. Anthony Church.
O'Sullivan, Thomas C. '51 (LA) Retired.
O'Sullivan, Msgr. Thomas Joseph '28 (LA) [98] Los Angeles, CA Visitation Church.
O'Sullivan, Thomas P. '71 (SR) Point Arena, CA St. Aloysius Church.
O'Sullivan, Timothy *o.f.m.cap.* '36 (LA) Solvang, CA Old Mission Santa Ines Church.
O'Sullivan, Timothy F. '94 (PH) Morton, PA Our Lady of Perpetual Help Church.
O'Sullivan, Timothy J. (WDC) [2] Rockville, MD Shrine of St. Jude Church.
O'Sullivan, Timothy J. '52 (BO) [44] Boston, MA St. Mark Church.
O'Sullivan, Timothy J. '71 (SR) Napa, CA St. John the Baptist Church.
O'Sullivan, Tracy *o.carm.* '62 (LA) [88] Los Angeles, CA St. Raphael Church.
O'Toole, Msgr. Anthony J. '44 (ALT) Retired.
O'Toole, Brian '86 (WOR) Shrewsbury, MA St. Mary's Church.
O'Toole, Charles '72 (SP) Retired.
O'Toole, Coleman P. '61 (PRT) [5] Portland, ME St. Patrick's Church.
O'Toole, Msgr. Fursey '60 (BRK) [115] Brooklyn, NY St. Patrick Church.
O'Toole, Henry *c.ss.r.* '44 (ORL) [F] New Smyrna Beach, FL St. Alphonsus Villa-Redemptorist Fathers and Brothers.
O'Toole, James '64 (FWT) Bedford, TX St. Michael Church.
O'Toole, John J. '52 (PEO) Retired.
O'Toole, John J. *c.ss.r.* '53 (FgM) Redemptorist Foreign Missions.
O'Toole, John M. '67 (PIT) [26] Pittsburgh, PA St. Mary of Mercy Church.
O'Toole, Msgr. Joseph M. '39 (ALT) Retired.
O'Toole, Kenneth '44 (NY) Chappaqua, NY St. John and St. Mary Church.
O'Toole, Kenneth E. '44 (NY) Retired.
O'Toole, Lawrence J. *s.j.* '58 (BO) Billerica, MA St. Mary Church; [W] Weston, MA Campion Center.
O'Toole, Lawrence J. *s.j.* '88 (BO) [W] Boston, MA The Society of Jesus of New England-Provincial Offices.
O'Toole, Matthew L. '95 (STL) [58] St. Louis, MO St. Raphael The Archangel Church.
O'Toole, Robert F. *s.j.* '67 (FgM) Provinces.
O'Toole, Terrence O. *o.f.m.cap.* '55 (SPR) [L] Springfield, MA St. Francis of Assisi Chapel and Catholic Information Center.
O'Toole, Thomas F. *c.ss.r.* '51 (ALB) [L] Saratoga Springs, NY St. John Neumann Residence.
O'Toole, Thomas L. '69 (OKL) Elk City, OK St. Matthew's Church.
O'Toole, Timothy L. '89 (B) Idaho Falls, ID Christ the King Church.
O'Toole, William F. '96 (GRY) [3] Michigan City, IN Queen of All Saints Church.
O'Toole, Msgr. William P. '61 (LA) Alhambra, CA All Souls Church.
Oakes, Edward T. *s.j.* '79 (DEN) [M] Denver, CO Regis Jesuit Community (The Jesuits at Regis University).
Oakham, Ronald *o.carm.* '77 (TUC) [F] Tucson, AZ Carmelite Priory.
Oates, Eugene *c.ss.r.* '44 (DEN) Greeley, CO Our Lady of Peace Church.
Oates, Thomas '63 (FgM) Society of St. James the Apostle.
Oates, Thomas F. '63 (BO) Society of St. James the Apostle.
Obaza, Theodore L. '61 (SCR) [9] Wilkes-Barre, PA Holy Trinity Church.
Obee, Gregory *o.s.b.* '56 (RCK) [H] Aurora, IL Marmion Abbey-St. Augustine's Abbey.
Obele, Oliver *m.s.p.* '95 (NO) [6] New Orleans, LA Epiphany Church.
Obeng-Kyeremeh, Simon '89 (BAL) [49] Baltimore, MD St. Joseph Church.
Obenrader, Paul F. '39 (E) Retired.
Ober, Anselm *o.s.b.* '42 (RIC) [6] Virginia Beach, VA St. Gregory the Great Church.
Ober, Lawrence M. *s.j.* '77 (CLV) [E] Cleveland, OH St. Ignatius High School.
Oberch, Msgr. Rick J. '85 (PEO) [N] East Peoria, IL Mt. Alverno Novitiate.
Oberg, Paul *s.s.j.* '85 (BIR) [14] Birmingham, AL Our Lady of Fatima Church.
Obergefell, Sylvan W. '58 (TOL) Ottoville, OH Immaculate Conception Church.
Oberkirch, Msgr. James W. '62 (MOB) [1] Mobile, AL Cathedral of the Immaculate Conception.
Oberle, James '87 (WDC) On Duty Outside the Archdiocese.
Oberle, James P. *s.s.* '87 (SFR) [A] Menlo Park, CA St. Patrick Seminary.
Oberle, Joseph *c.s.s.r.* '37 (ALB) [L] Saratoga Springs, NY St. John Neumann Residence.
Obermeyer, Robert A. '67 (CIN) [73] Cincinnati, OH Our Lord, Christ the King Church.
Obermiller, Edwin *c.s.c.* '96 (P) [B] Portland, OR University of Portland; [L] Portland, OR Holy Cross Fathers & Brothers, C.S.C. - University of Portland; [P] Portland, OR University of Portland.
Obersinner, Joseph L. *s.j.* '57 (B) DeSmet, ID Sacred Heart Church.
Oberstar, Richard *m.s.f.* '65 (SAT) New Braunfels, TX Our Lady of Perpetual Help Church.
Obersteiner, Ernest '77 (GLP) Absent on Leave.
Obert, Martin '56 (SP) Retired.
Oberto, Peter '78 (MAR) Ishpeming, MI St. John the Evangelist Church.

Oberts, David P. '69 (SUP) Birchwood, WI St. John Evangelist Church; Dobie, WI Our Lady of Lourdes Church; Haugen, WI Holy Trinity Church.
Oberwinder, Robert J. '35 (LC) Retired.
Obiajunwa, Chukwudi '82 (PAT) Sparta, NJ Our Lady of the Lake Church.
Obijiski, Herbert *o.f.m.conv.* '65 (HRT) Kensington, CT St. Paul's Church.
Obin, Arthur *o.m.i.* '64 (FgM) Oblates Foreign Missions.
Obin, Arthur T. *o.m.i.* '64 (MAN) [K] Hudson, NH Missionary Oblates of Mary Immaculate.
Obin, Gilbert *c.i.c.m.* '67 (SAT) [54] San Antonio, TX St. Martin de Porres Church; [73] San Antonio, TX Senyor Santo Nino de Cebu Church.
Oblinger, Joseph B. '46 (HEL) West Yellowstone, MT Our Lady of the Pines Church; Retired.
Obloj, Stanislaw J. '93 (DET) [11] Warren, MI St. Sylvester Church.
Obloy, Leonard G. '77 (BAL) [A] Emmitsburg, MD Mount St. Mary's Seminary.
Obloy, Leonard G. '77 (CLV) Released from Diocesan Assignment.
Obmann, Msgr. Russell J. '51 (STL) Retired.
Oborny, Paul J. '63 (WCH) Council Grove, KS St. Rose Church; Strong City, KS St. Anthony of Padua Church.
Oborny, Rudolf F. '71 (LIN) [6] Lincoln, NE St. John the Apostle Church.
Obregon, Miguel *o.f.m.* '81 (OAK) [N] Oakland, CA Franciscan Friars Provincial Office, Province of St. Barbara.
Obrimski, Paul G. '70 (BAL) On Duty Outside the Archdiocese.
Ocampo, Arturo *o.f.m.* '85 (CHI) [111] Chicago, IL St. Joseph Church.
Ocampo, Ramon Conde *o.de.m.* '59 (PCE) [13] Ponce, PR Santuario San Judas Tadeo Church.
Occhiuto, Joseph L. '79 (MRY) [1] Monterey, CA Cathedral of San Carlos Borromeo.
Ochiltree, Richard *c.ss.r.* '53 (SEA) [O] Federal Way, WA Palisades Retreat House.
Ochoa, Adrian *o.de.m.* '97 (SB) Ontario, CA Our Lady of Guadalupe Church.
Ochoa, David '72 (LA) Lynwood, CA St. Emydius Church.
Ochoa, Einer R. '85 (SAT) Sabinal, TX St. Patrick's Church.
Ochoa, Javier *m.s.c.* '79 (LA) Cudahy, CA Cudahy Mission Church.
Ochoa, Jose Luis '66 (LA) La Puente, CA St. Louis of France Church.
Ochoa, Rafael '78 (LA) [15] Los Angeles, CA Immaculate Conception Church.
Ochoa, Stephen '83 (SD) [H] San Diego, CA Augustinian Community.
Ochoa, Xavier '69 (SR) Special Assignment.
Ochs, Daniel L. '76 (COL) Reynoldsburg, OH St. Pius X Church.
Ochs, Robert J. *s.j.* '61 (CHI) [N] Chicago, IL Chicago Province of the Society of Jesus-Provincial Office.
Ochs, Robert J. *s.j.* '61 (OAK) [N] Berkeley, CA Jesuit Community at Jesuit School of Theology at Berkeley.
Ochu, Austin Charles *s.m.a.* '92 (FgM) Society of African Missions.
Ochu, Austin Charles *s.m.a.* '92 (WDC) [M] Takoma Park, MD Society of African Missions (S.M.A.).
Ochylski, Ronald S. *s.s.* '87 (BAL) [M] Baltimore, MD Sulpician Provincial House.
Ochylski, Ronald S. '87 (SFR) On Duty Outside the Archdiocese.
Ocilka, John A. '94 (CLV) [43] Cleveland, OH St. Leo the Great Church.
Odbert, Jerome K. *s.j.* (DET) [B] Berkley, MI Loyola House.
Oddo, Peter A. '61 (NEW) Military Chaplains.
Odenbrett, Stephen *o.s.b.* '46 (MRY) [G] San Luis Obispo, CA Monastery of the Risen Christ.
Odermann, John *o.s.b.* '55 (BIS) [A] Richardton, ND Assumption Abbey.
Odermann, John *o.s.b.* '55 (FAR) [F] Valley City, ND Sisters of Mary of the Presentation.
Odermann, Valerian *o.s.b.* '73 (BIS) [A] Richardton, ND Assumption Abbey; [B] Bismarck, ND University of Mary.
Odie, John P. '61 (BGP) Retired; [O] Stamford, CT Our Lady Queen of the Clergy Home.
Odien, Terry M. '73 (CAM) Westmont, NJ Holy Saviour Church.
Odoemela, Richard '92 (NEW) Nutley, NJ Our Lady of Mount Carmel Church.
Odom-Green, William '91 (OWN) Absent on Leave.
Odorizzi, Thomas A. '92 (MET) Monmouth Junction, NJ St. Cecilia Church.
Odozi, Anthony C., Jr. '97 (FAR) [1] Grand Forks, ND Holy Family Church.
Odufuye, Francis '79 (RVC) Elmont, NY St. Boniface Church; Valley Stream, NY Franklin Medical Center Hospital.
Oedy, Thomas E. '71 (TOL) Edgerton, OH St. Mary Church; Hicksville, OH St. Michael Church.
Oehmler, Gary W. '83 (PIT) [37] Pittsburgh, PA St. Rosalia Church.
Oehrlein, Felix G. '65 (MAD) Pine Bluff, WI St. Mary of Pine Bluff Church.
Oelerich, Robert *c.ss.r.* '49 (OM) [19] Omaha, NE Holy Name Church.
Oelrich, Anthony '92 (SCL) Holdingford, MN St. Hedwig's Church; Holdingford, MN St. Mary's Church; Opole, MN Our Lady of Mt. Carmel Church; St. Anna, MN Immaculate Conception Church; St. Wendel, MN St. Columbkille's Church.
Oen, Edward J. *c.pp.s.* '64 (SAL) Greenleaf, KS Sacred Heart Church; Hanover, KS St. John the Baptist Church.
Oesterle, John G. '67 (PIT) East McKeesport, PA St. Robert Bellarmine Church.
Oestreich, Brian W. '93 (NU) [1] New Ulm, MN Cathedral of the Holy Trinity.
Oestreich, Emil C. '45 (PH) [96] Philadelphia, PA St. Mary of the Assumption Church; [139] Philadelphia, PA St. Raymond of Penafort Church; Retired.
Oetgen, John A. *o.s.b.* '51 (CHL) [J] Belmont, NC Belmont Abbey.
Offer, Henry *s.s.j.* '44 (BEA) [7] Beaumont, TX Our Mother of Mercy Church.
Offerman, Paul '57 (SFS) Bridgewater, SD St. Stephen Church.
Offutt, Bradley S. '86 (KC) Harrisonville, MO Our Lady of Lourdes Church.
Offutt, J. James '62 (JC) [3] Jefferson City, MO Immaculate Conception Church.
Ofoa, Paul N. *m.s.p.* '89 (GAL) [66] Houston, TX St. Peter the Apostle Church.
Ofoegbu, Jerome '80 (NY) [145] Bronx, NY St. Helena Church.
Ofoha, Paul N. *m.s.p.* (GAL) [Q] Barrett Station, TX Missionary Society of St. Paul, Inc. - U.S. Region.
Ogbemure, Raymond '74 (OAK) El Cerrito, CA St. John the Baptist Church.
Ogbonna, Edmund '78 (MIA) Miramar, FL St. Bartholomew Church.
Ogbonna, Stanislaus '73 (NY) State, NY Sullivan Correctional Facility.
Ogden, Louis P. '85 (HBG) Middletown, PA Seven Sorrows of the Blessed Virgin Mary Church.
Oge, Raymond J. '67 (STL) Bloomsdale, MO St. Agnes Church; Lawrenceton, MO St. Lawrence's Church.
Ogg, Thomas '68 (CHY) Gillette, WY St. Matthew's Church.
Oggero, Roy J *c.s.b.* '61 (GAL) [Q] Sugar Land, TX Basilian Mission Center.
Ogle, Sean G. '77 (BRK) [198] Queens, NY St. Mary Star of the Sea Church.
Oglesby, J. Leonard '48 (MEM) Retired.
Ognibene, Joseph F. '52 (CHI) [154] Chicago, IL Our Lady, Mother of the Church; Rolling Meadows, IL St. Colette Church; Retired.
Ognibene, Salvatore J. '47 (CHI) [106] Chicago, IL St. John Bosco Church; Retired; [L] Chicago, IL St. Mary of Providence.
Ogorzaly, Adam (ROC) [56] Rochester, NY St. Stanislaus Church.
Ogrodowski, William M. '75 (PIT) On Duty Outside the Diocese.
Ogunnaike, Emmanuel *m.s.p.* '90 (STL) Dardenne, MO Immaculate Conception Church.
Ogurchock, John J. *m.m.* '54 (FgM) Maryknoll Foreign Missions.
Ohirko, Peter '55 (STF) Ozone Park, (1954) St. Mary Protectress Church.
Ohlemacher, Richard N. *o.s.c.* '55 (PHX) [F] Phoenix, AZ Crosier Community of Phoenix (Canons Regular of the Order of the Holy Cross).
Ohlig, John '95 (LUB) Floydada, TX St. Mary Magdalen Church.
Ohlinger, Vincent *s.v.d.* '68 (FgM) Society of the Divine Word Foreign Missions.
Ohm, Edward U. '92 (PEO) [4] Streator, IL St. Stephen's Church.
Ohmann, Daniel F. *m.m.* '55 (FgM) Maryknoll Foreign Missions.
Ohno, Ignatius *s.j.* '92 (SEA) [A] Seattle, WA Seattle University.
Ojeda, Filemon G. '46 (SFR) Retired.
Ojiako, Fortunate M. *o.p.* (PRO) [P] Providence, RI St. Thomas Aquinas Priory at Providence College.
Ojibway, Paul *s.a.* '78 (WDC) [B] Washington, DC Atonement Seminary-Franciscan Friars of the Atonement.
Ojimba, Felix (BO) Boston, MA Massachusetts General Hospital.
Okere, Remigius '94 (DM) [9] Des Moines, IA St. Joseph's Church.
Okochi, Cornelius (PIT) [8] Pittsburgh, PA St. Charles Lwanga Parish.
Okonmah, Emmanuel M. '97 (FAR) Devils Lake, ND St. Joseph's Church; Rutten, ND St. Benedict Church; Starkweather, ND Assumption of the Blessed Virgin Mary Church.
Okonski, Joseph F. '90 (PH) [110] Philadelphia, PA Nativity of the Blessed Virgin Mary Church.
Okopinski, Louis S. '51 (MIL) Retired.
Okorie, Joseph '81 (SJ) Milpitas, CA Elmwood Rehabilitation Center.
Okorn, Dusan A. '47 (HEL) Swan Valley, MT Swan Valley Catholic Community Church; Retired; [G] Swan Lake, MT The Sycamore Tree Contemplative Prayer Center.
Okoro, Joseph E. *c.m.f.* '90 (NO) [4] New Orleans, LA Blessed Sacrament Church.
Okorochukwu, Wilfred C. '75 (LR) Fordyce, AR Good Shepherd Church; Sheridan, AR Holy Cross Church.
Okoye, James C. *c.s.sp.* '70 (CHI) [B] Chicago, IL The Catholic Theological Union at Chicago.
Okpogba, Desmond '89 (TLS) Broken Arrow, OK St. Benedict Church.
Okroy, Francis *s.ch.* '48 (BAL) [38] Baltimore, MD Holy Rosary Church.
Okumu, Richard U.O. '81 (DAV) Victor, IA St. Bridget's Church.
Okuroski, Michael *o.c.d.* '44 (SAT) [18] San Antonio, TX Our Lady of Mt. Carmel and St. Therese, Discalced Carmelite Fathers National Shrine of the Little Flower Church; [M] San Antonio, TX Discalced Carmelites (Prov. of St. Therese).
Okwara, Hyacinth (STL) [57] St. Louis, MO St. Pius the Fifth Church.
Ola'aiga, Vitaliano '91 (P) [A] St. Benedict, OR Mount Angel Seminary.
Olczak, Joseph '65 (NOR) [A] Cromwell, CT Holy Apostles College and Seminary.
Olczak, Joseph M. *o.s.p.p.e.* '65 (NOR) Rockville, CT St. Joseph Church.
Oldani, Louis J. *s.j.* (KC) [B] Kansas City, MO Rockhurst College.
Oldani, Louis J. *s.j.* '64 (KC) [J] Kansas City, MO Rockhurst College - Jesuit Community.
Oldenski, Kenneth E. '66 (PIT) Richland Township, PA Saint Richard Church.
Oldershaw, Robert H. '62 (CHI) Evanston, IL St. Nicholas Church.
Oldfield, Albert E. '59 (SCR) [18] Scranton, PA St. Mary's Church.
Olds, Daryl *c.m.f.* '92 (AUS) San Marcos, TX St. John the Evangelist Church.
Olds, Daryld *c.m.f.* '92 (SAT) [B] San Antonio, TX St. Anthony Mary Claret Seminary.
Olds, Steve '88 (ORL) Sabbatical.
Olejniczak, Henry A. '51 (CHI) [43] Chicago, IL St. Columba Church; Retired.
Olek, Ralph F. *s.m.* '74 (ATL) [C] Atlanta, GA Marist School.
Oleksiak, Donald P. '89 (CLV) [1] Garfield Heights, OH St. Monica Church.
Oleksy, Stanislaus '82 (LR) [E] Rogers, AR St. Mary-Rogers Memorial Hospital.
Olendzki, Joaquim J. '58 (NY) Pine Island, NY St. Stanislaus Church.
Olenowski, Mark '85 (PAT) [5] Passaic, NJ Holy Trinity Church.
Olesh, Msgr. Bohdan '42 (PHU) Alden Station, PA St. Vladimir Church; Glen Lyon, PA St. Nicholas Church.
Oleshko, Myroslaw '40 (STN) Retired.
Olesik, William J. '72 (NOR) Bolton, CT St. Maurice Church.
Olges, H. Anthony '70 (L) [24] Louisville, KY St. Elizabeth of Hungary Church; [72] Louisville, KY St. Therese Church.
Olguin, Jacinto '74 (VIC) Bloomington, TX St. Patrick Church.
Olguin, Luis (SY) [9] Utica, NY St. John Church.
Olguin, Luis '92 (SY) [13] Utica, NY St. Mary of Mt. Carmel Church; Rome, NY Walsh Facility; Special Assignment.
Oligschlaeger, P. Gregory '93 (JC) [A] Hannibal, MO St. Thomas Aquinas Seminary.
Oliva, George M. *s.j.* '72 (SD) Special Assignment.
Oliva, Max *s.j.* '72 (SD) [12] San Diego, CA Our Lady of Guadalupe Church.
Olivares, Jesus *c.s.* (SJ) [7] San Jose, CA Holy Cross Church.
Olivares, Romo *c.i.c.m.* '74 (SAT) [23] San Antonio, TX Sacred Heart Church.
Olivas, J. Alfredo '81 (ELP) [40] El Paso, TX Santo Nino De Atocha Church.
Olivas, William V. *o.s.a.* '97 (LA) Ojai, CA St. Thomas Aquinas Church.
Olive, Louis A. *c.ss.r.* '64 (TOL) [2] Lima, OH St. Gerard Church.
Olive, Rodney J. *c.ss.r.* '86 (FgM) Redemptorist Foreign Missions.
Oliveira, Albano '55 (OAK) Piedmont, CA Corpus Christi Church; [S] Oakland, CA The Roman Catholic Cemeteries of the Diocese of Oakland.
Oliveira, Aventino *i.m.c.* '57 (MET) [H] Somerset, NJ Consolata Society for Foreign Missions.
Oliveira, Gastao A. '72 (FR) [23] Fall River, MA Santo Christo Church.
Oliveira, Humbert M. '77 (MAN) [1] Manchester, NH St. Joseph Cathedral.
Oliveira, Joel D. '54 (PRO) [5] Warren, RI St. Thomas the Apostle Church.

Oliveira, Joel D. '59 (BO) On Duty Outside the Archdiocese.
Oliveira, Msgr. John J. *p.a.* '67 (FR) [19] New Bedford, MA St. Mary's Church.
Oliveira, John J. '77 (FR) [15] New Bedford, MA St. John the Baptist Church.
Oliveira, Joseph '49 (FR) Retired.
Oliveira, Robert A. '77 (FR) North Attleboro, MA St. Mary's Church.
Oliveira, Vitor '73 (SPR) [2] Ludlow, MA Our Lady of Fatima Church.
Oliveira e.Costa, Virgilio *s.j.* '95 (BO) [W] Chestnut Hill, MA The Jesuit Community at Boston College.
Olivencia, Ramon '97 (ARE) Corozal, PR Holy Family Church.
Oliver, Harry T. *s.j.* '57 (PHX) [B] Phoenix, AZ Brophy College Preparatory.
Oliver, Homer G. '43 (Y) Louisville, OH St. Louis Church; Retired.
Oliver, James M. '88 (PH) Graduate Studies.
Oliver, Msgr. John A. '52 (TUC) Sunsites, AZ St. Jude Thaddius Church.
Oliver, Jorge *t.o.r.* '52 (NEW) [14] Elizabeth, NJ Immaculate Heart of Mary Church.
Oliver, Marc '89 (NY) [GG] New York, NY University Apostolate.
Oliver, R.B. Michael '91 (BUF) [6] Buffalo, NY St. Ambrose Church.
Oliver, William A. '77 (GAL) Baytown, TX St. John the Evangelist Church.
Oliver, William R. *s.v.d.* '58 (LAF) Maurice, LA St. Joseph Church.
Oliveras, Evaristo *c.m.* '88 (SJN) [62] San Juan, PR San Vicente de Paul Church.
Oliveras, Jose *o.carm.* '95 (ARE) Morovis, PR Nuestra Senora del Carmen Church.
Oliveras Villanueva, Felix '82 (CGS) [3] Caguas, PR Sagrado Corazon de Jesus Church.
Olivere, Michael S. '94 (PH) [15] Philadelphia, PA Ascension of Our Lord Church.
Oliveri, Armand *s.d.b.* '50 (SFR) [12] San Francisco, CA Corpus Christi Church.
Oliveri, Richard H. '66 (PAT) Dover, NJ St. Mary's Church.
Olivero, Michael A. '74 (CHI) [3] Des Plaines, IL St. Stephen Protomartyr Church.
Oliveros, Renato *s.j.* '96 (BGP) [O] Fairfield, CT The Fairfield Jesuit Community-Fairfield University.
Olivier, David S. *s.j.* '62 (P) [D] Portland, OR Jesuit High School.
Olivier, John H. *s.s.* '47 (MAR) Retired.
Olivier, Robert '57 (JKS) [C] Jackson, MS St. Dominic-Jackson Memorial Hospital.
Olivo, Stephen *s.j.* '69 (SFR) [N] San Francisco, CA Jesuit Community at University of San Francisco.
Olkovikas, Msgr. Albert W. '53 (MAN) [L] Manchester, NH Monastery of the Precious Blood.
Ollivier, John '50 (TOL) Retired.
Olmer, Vernon J. *o.f.m.* '62 (SUP) Ashland, WI Our Lady of the Lake Catholic Community Church.
Olmstead, Daryl '75 (SAL) Goodland, KS Our Lady of Perpetual Help Church.
Olmsted, Msgr. Thomas J. '73 (COL) [A] Columbus, OH Pontifical College Josephinum.
Olmsted, Msgr. Thomas J. '73 (LIN) On Duty Outside the Diocese.
Olowin, Msgr. Jan C. '68 (E) [16] Erie, PA St. George Church.
Ols, James R. '75 (CLV) Elyria Township, OH St. Vincent de Paul Church.
Olsaukas, Msgr. Algirdas '52 (LA) [54] Los Angeles, CA St. Casimir Church.
Olsavsky, John R. '62 (CLV) Chagrin Falls, OH St. Joan of Arc Church.
Olsem, Andrew D. '67 (WIN) Windom, MN St. Francis Xavier's Church.
Olsen, Charles R. *s.j.* '68 (SAC) [C] Sacramento, CA Jesuit High School; [G] Carmichael, CA Jesuit High School Community of Sacramento.
Olsen, Kenneth '73 (P) On Duty Outside the Archdiocese.
Olsen, Thomas F. '53 (NEW) Cliffside Park, NJ Epiphany Church.
Olson, Benedict *c.p.* '61 (LA) [R] Pasadena, CA Passionist Community; [X] Sierra Madre, CA Mater Dolorosa Retreat Center.
Olson, Eric E. '84 (MAR) Hubbell, MI St. Cecilia Church; Lake Linden, MI St. Joseph Church.
Olson, Hans '83 (SEA) [4] Vancouver, WA St. Joseph Church.
Olson, James P. '88 (PH) Hilltown, PA Our Lady of the Sacred Heart Church.
Olson, Michael P. '94 (GR) [1] Muskegon, MI Our Lady of Grace Church.
Olson, Randy E. '90 (LC) Athens, WI St. Anthony de Padua Church; Poniatowski, WI Holy Family Church.
Olson, Richard F. *s.j.* '59 (BO) [W] Weston, MA Campion Health Center, Inc.
Olson, Robert J. *o.m.i.* '65 (SPC) Mansfield, MO Immaculate Heart of Mary Church.
Olson, Ronald *o.f.m.conv.* '58 (RNO) [1] Reno, NV St. Thomas Aquinas Cathedral.
Olson, Theodore '72 (ORG) Brea, CA St. Angela Merici Church.
Olson, Theodore E. *j.v.* '79 (WIL) Elsmere, DE Corpus Christi Church.
Olson, Thomas F. '73 (SCL) Brennyville, MN St. Elizabeth Church; Morrill, MN St. Joseph's Church.
Olsovsky, George J. '56 (GAL) Huffman, TX St. Philip the Apostle Church.
Olszamowski, Leon M. *s.m.* '76 (DET) [D] Pontiac, MI Notre Dame Preparatory High School and Marist Academy.
Olszewski, Bernard *o.f.m.conv.* '79 (BUF) [C] Hamburg, NY Hilbert College; [D] Athol Springs, NY St. Francis High School; [O] Athol Springs, NY St. Francis of Assisi Friary; [R] Williamsville, NY Campus Ministry.
Olszewski, Clarence A. '57 (HBG) York Haven, PA Holy Infant Church.
Olszewski, Daniel D. '51 (SCR) Dupont, PA Sacred Heart of Jesus Church.
Olszewski, Edward '60 (MIA) Key Largo, FL St. Justin Martyr Church.
Olszewski, John S. '47 (NEW) Retired.
Olszewski, Laurence M. *c.s.c.* '64 (BUR) Bennington, VT Sacred Heart/St. Francis de Sales Church.
Olszewski, Paul A. '93 (CAM) Lindenwold, NJ St. Lawrence's Church.
Olszewski, Ronald W. *o.s.f.s.* '74 (TOL) [C] Toledo, OH St. Francis de Sales High School; [K] Toledo, OH Oblates of St. Francis de Sales.
Olszyk, Thomas P. '71 (MIL) Military Chaplains.
Olvida, Victor '82 (SEA) Sedro Woolley, WA Immaculate Heart of Mary Church.
Oman, Francis M. *i.c.* '57 (PEO) Abingdon, IL Sacred Heart Church; St. Augustine, IL St. Augustine Church.
Ombao, Manuel '70 (AGN) Tamuning, GU St. Anthony and St. Victor Church.
Omernick, Kenneth E. '74 (MIL) [31] Milwaukee, WI St. Gregory The Great Church.
Onaindia, Bernardo *c.p.* '46 (MGZ) San Sebastian, PR San Sebastian Martir Church.
Onderko, John M. '62 (PEO) [3] La Salle, IL Resurrection Church.
Ondic, John L. '65 (ALN) Tresckow, PA St. Bartholomew Church; Tresckow, PA St. Michael Church.
Ondo, Michael A. '54 (LFT) Carmel, IN Our Lady of Mount Carmel Church.
Ondrako, Edward J. '72 (ROC) [M] Rochester, NY Diocesan Office of Campus Ministry.
Ondreyka, Richard J. *m.s.* '54 (CLV) [2] Lakewood, OH SS. Cyril and Methodius Church.
Onesko, John '46 (PSC) Retired.
Ong, Walter J. *s.j.* '46 (STL) [P] St. Louis, MO Jesuit Community Corporation at St. Louis University - Jesuit Hall.
Ongaro, Mario *m.c.c.j.* '51 (CIN) [M] Cincinnati, OH Comboni Missionaries (Verona Fathers)-Comboni Mission Center.
Oniskiewicz, Mieczyslaw T. (MAR) Graduate Studies.
Onofrey, Robert *c.pp.s.* (CHI) [94] Chicago, IL Immaculate Heart of Mary Church.
Onofrey, Robert *c.pp.s.* '63 (CIN) [M] Dayton, OH Provincial House of the Cincinnati Province of the Society of the Precious Blood.
Ontiveros, Roy *o.carm.* '78 (GAL) [58] Houston, TX Our Lady of Mt. Carmel Church.
Onufer, Paul P. '59 (CAM) [5] Vineland, NJ St. Mary's Church.
Onuh, William I. '79 (ROC) [60] Rochester, NY St. Thomas More Church; Sonyea, NY Groveland Correctional Facility.
Onuoha, Anselm E. '83 (BRK) [21] Brooklyn, NY Blessed Sacrament Church.
Onuora, Felix *c.s.sp.* '79 (DM) [1] Des Moines, IA St. Ambrose Cathedral.
Onushco, William J. '76 (ALN) Weatherly, PA St. Nicholas Church.
Onwana, Jude '86 (CLV) [3] Akron, OH St. Bernard Church.
Onyebuchi, Martin (NY) [183] Bronx, NY St. Philip Neri Church.
Onyeihe, Cyprian I. '82 (NY) [132] Bronx, NY St. Barnabas Church.
Onze, Robert E. '64 (BGP) Retired.
Onze, Robert E. '64 (VEN) Sebring, FL St. Catherine Church.
Oonnoonny, George '91 (NY) Graduate Studies.
Oosdyke, Raymond *o.f.m.conv.* '37 (GR) [4] Grand Rapids, MI St. Anthony of Padua Church.
Opalenick, Msgr. John '61 (PSC) Hazleton, PA St. John the Baptist Church.
Opalewski, Walter '85 (GLP) [4] Gallup, NM St. John Vianney Church.
Opara, Ben M. '85 (ARL) Falls Church, VA St. Anthony's Church.
Opaski, Hilarion '91 (STN) Hamtramck, MI Immaculate Conception of B.V.M. Church.
Opat, Kenneth *o.s.c.* '69 (STP) Anoka, MN St. Stephen Church; [N] Anoka, MN Crosier Community of Anoka.
Opeil, Cyril *s.j.* '94 (BO) [W] Chestnut Hill, MA The Jesuit Community at Boston College.
Opem, Anthony '68 (SFS) Madison, SD St. Thomas Aquinas Church.
Ophals, Donald J. '61 (ALB) [3] Troy, NY St. Francis de Sales Church.
Opira, Simon Peter '93 (STV) [B] St. Thomas, VI Miscellaneous Organizations.
Opoka, Lloyd E. '68 (KC) Blue Springs, MO St. Robert Bellarmine Church.
Opondo-Owora, Charles '93 (SY) [9] Binghamton, NY St. Patrick Church.
Oppenheim, Frank M. *s.j.* '55 (CIN) [P] Milford, OH Milford Spiritual Center.
Oppenheimer, Daniel W. *f.s.s.p.* '91 (SCR) [M] Elmhurst, PA Priestly Fraternity of St. Peter (F.S.S.P.), North American District Headquarters.
Oppido, Harold J. *s.j.* '55 (NEW) [C] Jersey City, NJ St. Peter's Preparatory School.
Opps, Francis J. '58 (ALN) Tower City, PA SS. Peter and Paul Church.
Opris, Gheorghe (ROM) Leave of Absence.
Orandi, Nazareno '61 (NEW) Lyndhurst, NJ Our Lady of Mount Carmel Church.
Orapankal, Abraham '83 (NY) Blauvelt, NY St. Catharine Church.
Oravec, Christian R. *t.o.r.* '64 (ALT) [A] Loretto, PA St. Francis College; [F] Loretto, PA St. Francis Friary, Third Order Regular of St. Francis of Penance.
Oravec, Gregory *o.s.b.* '44 (CLV) [P] Cleveland, OH Benedictine Order of Cleveland.
Oravecz, John F. '35 (BRK) Retired; [U] Douglaston, NY Bishop Mugavero Residence.
Oravetz, Robert Franklin '97 (PBR) Awaiting Assignment.
Orbanek, Msgr. Gerald L. '66 (E) [B] Erie, PA Gannon University; [M] Erie, PA Villa Maria.
Orchik, Michael J. '73 (BAL) [55] Baltimore, MD Little Flower, Shrine of Church.
Ordax, Emiliano '48 (MIA) [4] Hialeah, FL St. Cecilia Church.
Ordenes, Guillermo *o.f.m.* '85 (ELP) [B] El Paso, TX Roger Bacon College.
Orel, Paul '84 (PHX) [6] Mesa, AZ St. Timothy Church; Special Assignment.
Orellana, Samuel '68 (LA) Gardena, CA St. Anthony of Padua Church.
Orengo, Juan Rodriguez '79 (PCE) [2] Ponce, PR Christ the King Church.
Oreshoski, Gary '88 (RC) Sturgis, SD St. Francis of Assisi Church.
Orf, Msgr. Raymond V. '55 (SPC) Lebanon, MO St. Francis De Sales Church.
Organ, Patrick C. '71 (VEN) North Port, FL San Pedro Church.
Ori, Kevin '81 (GB) [F] Manitowoc, WI Holy Family Memorial, Inc.
Oria, Enrique *o.carm.* (SJN) [A] Bayamon, PR Bayamon Central University.
Oria, Enrique *o.c.* '58 (SJN) [61] San Juan, PR Santa Teresita Del Nino Jesus Church.
Oria, Manuel '57 (PCE) Retired.
Orians, David '85 (RC) Belle Fourche, SD St. Paul Church.
Orians, Thomas *s.a.* '92 (FgM) Franciscan Friars Of The Atonement(S.A.).
Orians, Thomas *s.a.* '92 (NY) [DD] Garrison, NY Franciscan Friars of the Atonement.
Orimaco, Domingo '72 (SFR) Half Moon Bay, CA Our Lady of the Pillar Church.
Oriole, Philip M. '70 (E) [19] Erie, PA St. John the Baptist Church.
Oris, Fabian G. '42 (GBG) Retired.
Orlandi, Joseph J. '73 (PAT) [11] Paterson, NJ St. Michael the Archangel Church.
Orlando, Gerard *c.p.* '46 (NY) [Z] Bronx, NY St. Patrick's Home for the Aged and Infirm.
Orlando, Gerard A. *c.p.* '46 (MET) [H] South River, NJ Passionist Provincial Office.
Orlando, John V. (ALT) Retired.
Orlando, Richard J. '47 (ROC) [60] Rochester, NY St. Thomas More Church; Retired.
Orlando, Samuel '91 (CHL) Absent On Leave.
Orlando, Vincent A. *s.j.* '74 (GAL) [F] Houston, TX Strake, Jesuit College Preparatory Inc.
Orlett, Raymond *glmy.* '53 (CIN) [M] Fairfield, OH Headquarters of Glenmary Home Missioners.
Orlik, Dale A. '67 (SAG) [2] Bay City, MI St. Boniface Church.
Orlikiewicz, Stanley '53 (JOL) [1] Joliet, IL The Cathedral of St. Raymond.
Orlinski, Richard A. '73 (GRY) [4] Hammond, IN St. Catherine of Siena Church.
Orloski, Joseph F. '94 (SCR) [10] Scranton, PA Immaculate Conception Church.
Orloski, Raymond J. '62 (HBG) Kulpmont, PA Holy Angels Church.
Orlosky, Anselm *o.s.b.* '53 (PBR) Wall, PA Holy Trinity Church; [D] Butler, PA Holy Trinity Monastery.

Orlowski, Robert J. '97 (BUF) [2] Lockport, NY St. John the Baptist Church.
Orlowski, Walter C. '79 (BGP) [5] Norwalk, CT St. Matthew Church.
Orlowsky, Michael T. '93 (ARL) Manassas, VA Sacred Heart Church.
Ormaza, Antonio Liberman *s.c.s.* '95 (DAL) [28] Dallas, TX Santa Clara Church.
Ormechea, John Baptist *c.p.* '65 (L) [2] Louisville, KY St. Agnes Church; [L] Louisville, KY Sacred Heart Retreat.
Ormond, Henry *o.carm.* (OAK) [B] Oakland, CA Holy Names College.
Ormond, Henry *o.carm.* '77 (JOL) [J] Darien, IL Carmelite Provincial Office.
Ormsby, Owen J. *o.f.m.* '50 (PAT) [M] Ringwood, NJ Holy Name Friary, Inc.
Orndorff, Christopher '97 (TUC) [13] Tucson, AZ St. Francis de Sales Church.
Ornowski, Gerald *m.i.c.* '62 (FBK) [3] Fairbanks, AK St. Mark University Parish.
Orobiourritia, Juan J. *o.a.r.* '43 (LA) [8] Los Angeles, CA Cristo Rey Church.
Oroquieta, Jose Maria *o.f.m.* '53 (FWT) [5] Fort Worth, TX Immaculate Heart of Mary Church.
Orosco, James '81 (DAL) [A] Irving, TX Holy Trinity Seminary.
Orozco, Argemiro '92 (YAK) Toppenish, WA St. Aloysius Church.
Orozco, Raphael '50 (CHI) Palatine, IL Mision Juan Diego Church.
Orozco, Raphael R. (CHI) Retired.
Orozco, Rodolfo '48 (FRS) Parlier, CA Our Lady of Sorrows Church.
Orozco, Simon '73 (LA) [40] Los Angeles, CA St. Alphonsus Church.
Orr, Garrett D. *s.j.* '83 (WDC) [E] North Bethesda, MD Georgetown Preparatory School.
Orr, Joseph T. '82 (ALT) McConnellsburg, PA St. Stephen's Church.
Orr, Sherman A. '91 (WCH) [4] Wichita, KS Christ the King Church; [B] Wichita, KS Bishop Mark K. Carroll High School.
Orr, Msgr. Stephen (DM) [J] Des Moines, IA Roman Catholic Pastoral Center Foundation.
Orr, Msgr. Stephen '74 (DM) West Des Moines, IA St. Francis of Assisi Church.
Orrico, Msgr. Caesar G. '43 (NEW) Emerson, NJ Church of the Assumption.
Orrico, Msgr. Caeser G. '43 (NEW) Retired.
Orrigo, Mario '96 (BO) [10] Lowell, MA St. Michael Church.
Orru, Bruno *s.x.* '63 (FgM) Xaverian Foreign Missions.
Orru, Bruno *s.x.* '63 (PAT) [M] Wayne, NJ Xaverian Missionary Fathers.
Orsborn, Bruce '81 (SD) [6] San Diego, CA Holy Family Church.
Orsi, Michael P. '76 (CAM) Westmont, NJ Holy Saviour Church.
Orsini, James '74 (HON) Kaunakakai, HI Molokai Catholic Community Church.
Orsini, Joseph E. '64 (CAM) Retired.
Orsino, Gerald *o.m.i.* '66 (FgM) Oblates Foreign Missions.
Orsino, Gordon *o.m.i.* '84 (NY) [FF] Newburgh, NY Our Lady of Hope Center.
Orso, Claire Antonio *c.s.* '91 (CHI) Melrose Park, IL St. Charles Borromeo Church.
Orsolin, Vilmar *c.s.* '80 (VEN) Immokalee, FL Our Lady of Guadalupe Church.
Orsolits, Norbert F. '65 (BUF) [41] Buffalo, NY St. Lawrence Church; Buffalo, NY Buffalo General Hospital.
Orsulak, Thomas J. '90 (ALN) [11] Reading, PA St. Peter Church; [C] Reading, PA Holy Name High School.
Orsy, Ladislas *s.j.* '51 (NY) [DD] New York, NY Jesuit Community at Fordham University.
Orsy, Ladislas *s.j.* '51 (WDC) [M] Washington, DC The Jesuit Community at Georgetown University.
Orszulak, Henry A. '67 (BUF) [5] Lackawanna, NY St. Hyacinth Church.
Ortega, Agustin '93 (JOL) Bolingbrook, IL St. Dominic Church.
Ortega, Eduardo (BWN) [I] Harlingen, TX KMBH-TV 60/KHID-FM 88.1/KMBH-FM 88.9.
Ortega, Eduardo '77 (SFE) Absent on Leave.
Ortega, Efren '72 (DAL) [18] Dallas, TX St. James Church.
Ortega, Manuel '76 (MIA) [3] Miami Beach, FL St. Mary Magdalen Church.
Ortega, Ovidio (SJN) Resident Chaplains; [F] Puerta De Tierra, PR Asylum For The Aged and Infirm.
Ortega, Russell *o.s.a.* '86 (NY) [168] Bronx, NY St. Nicholas of Tolentine Church.
Ortega, Santos Leonel '96 (SB) Ontario, CA St. George Church.
Ortega, Vidal *o.s.a.* '65 (SJN) [42] San Juan, PR Ntra. Sra. de la Monserrate Church.
Ortega y Ortiz, Adam Lee (SFE) Dixon, NM St. Anthony Church.
Ortega y Ortiz, Adam Lee '92 (SFE) Penasco, NM San Antonio de Padua Church.
Ortez, Sofonias '96 (VEN) Bonita Springs, FL St. Leo Church.
Orth, Anthony F. '75 (PH) [3] Bensalem, PA Saint Ephrem Church.
Orthmann, James *o.c.s.o.* '94 (ARL) [J] Berryville, VA Cistercian Abbey of Our Lady of the Holy Cross.
Ortiz, Alexander F. *c.s.s.r.* '76 (PH) [25] Philadelphia, PA St. Boniface Church.
Ortiz, Alfredo (ORL) Mount Dora, FL St. Patrick's Church.
Ortiz, Angel '87 (MGZ) Cabo Rojo, PR St. Michael Church.
Ortiz, Arnold *o.s.j.* '72 (FRS) Madera, CA St. Joachim Church.
Ortiz, Benedicto '57 (BWN) Retired.
Ortiz, Carlos '97 (SJN) [5] Guaynabo, PR Maria Madre de la Misericordia Church.
Ortiz, Edwin Rafael Hernandez '83 (CGS) Cidra, PR Nuestra Senora del Carmen Church.
Ortiz, Emerito '96 (WOR) [24] Worcester, MA St. Joan of Arc Church.
Ortiz, Msgr. Hector '33 (MGZ) Moca, PR Our Lady of Monserrate Church.
Ortiz, J.C. '91 (PHX) Sedona, AZ St. John Vianney Church.
Ortiz, Jose '66 (LA) Pomona, CA Sacred Heart Church.
Ortiz, Jose Antonio '85 (CGS) Aibonito, PR Church of St. Joseph.
Ortiz, Maximo J. *o.s.a.* '74 (WDC) [B] Silver Spring, MD Austin Friars Hall, Order of St. Augustine.
Ortiz, Michael *s.c.j.* '56 (MIL) [P] Hales Corners, WI Priests of the Sacred Heart.
Ortiz, Michael G. '56 (SD) Encinitas, CA St. John the Evangelist Church.
Ortiz, Miguel *o.f.m.cap* '86 (LA) Solvang, CA Old Mission Santa Ines Church.
Ortiz, Rodrigo *o.f.m.* '73 (MRY) [G] San Miguel, CA Franciscan Friars, O.F.M.
Ortiz, Victor Raul '86 (CGS) Barranquitas, PR San Andres Apostol Church.
Ortmann, William '57 (SD) [1] San Diego, CA St. Joseph Cathedral.
Ortmeier, Paul '72 (OM) Bloomfield, NE St. Andrew Church.
Ortmeier, Richard J. '56 (SFS) Retired.
Ortner, John W. *s.j.* '44 (NY) [DD] New York, NY Jesuit Community at Fordham University.
Ortner, Paul *s.s.j.* '45 (VEN) [D] Port Charlotte, FL Bon Secours-St. Joseph Hospital.
Ortner, Paul A. *s.s.j.* '45 (BAL) [M] Baltimore, MD St. Joseph Society of the Sacred Heart House of Central Administration.
Ortyl, Stanley E. (NEW) Short Hills, NJ St. Rose of Lima Church.
Ortyl, Stanley E. '80 (NEW) Union, NJ Holy Spirit Church.
Oruche, Michael (BO) [5] Somerville, MA St. Clement Church.
Orumpakkat, James S. *c.m.i.* '64 (BEL) [5] Belleville, IL St. Henry Church; [G] Belleville, IL Poor Clare Monastery of Our Lady of Mercy.
Oryshkewych, Ostap '80 (PHU) [3] Philadelphia, PA St. Andrew Church; Retired.
Orzech, Eric S. '93 (CLV) Concord Twp., OH St. Gabriel Church.
Orzechowski, Aloysius M. *c.r.* '46 (CHI) [D] Chicago, IL Gordon Technical High School.
Orzechowski, Walter B. '49 (MIL) Retired.
Orzel, David J. '79 (SY) Boonville, NY St. Joseph Church.
Osbahr, Theodore '67 (NEW) Bloomfield, NJ Sacred Heart Church.
Osborn, Douglas '68 (LAN) [7] Flint, MI St. John Vianney Church.
Osborn, Michael A. '92 (KAL) Bangor, MI Sacred Heart of Jesus Church.
Osborn, William '66 (SFS) Lesterville, SD St. John the Baptist Church; Tabor, SD St. Wenceslaus Church.
Osborne, Francis J. *s.j.* '37 (BO) [W] Weston, MA Campion Health Center, Inc.
Osborne, Msgr. Francis M. '38 (LA) Encino, CA Our Lady of Grace Church; Retired.
Osborne, Kenan B. *o.f.m.* '55 (OAK) [A] Berkeley, CA Franciscan School of Theology; [S] Berkeley, CA Multicultural Institute.
Osborne, Martin J. '50 (RVC) Southold, NY St. Patrick's Church; Retired.
Osborne, Paul *o.f.m.* '64 (BUF) [59] Buffalo, NY SS. Rita & Patrick Church.
Osborne, Robert E. '54 (L) [59] Louisville, KY Our Lady of Lourdes Church; Louisville, KY Baptist Hospital East.
Osborne, Robert R. *s.m.* '66 (STL) [F] Kirkwood, MO Vianney High School.
Osborne, Ronald J. '83 (HRT) [6] East Hartford, CT St. Rose's Church.
Osborne, Stanley L. '59 (L) Cecilia, KY St. Ambrose Church; St. John, KY St. John the Baptist Church.
Osborne, Thomas *o.s.a.* '66 (JOL) [5] Lockport, IL Our Mother of Good Counsel Church.
Osborne, Msgr. William J. '24 (BRK) [167] Queens, NY St. Fidelis Church; Retired.
Osburg, Frank C. '60 (LEX) Versailles, KY St. Leo Church.
Osburg, Gregory E. '77 (COV) Kenton, KY St. Matthew Church.
Osebold, Richard A. '60 (DET) [2] Redford, MI St. John Bosco Church.
Osendorf, James *c.m.* '80 (STO) Patterson, CA Sacred Heart Church.
Oser, Donald '53 (Y) Retired.
Oser, Richard E. *s.j.* '92 (ORL) Eustis, FL St. Mary of the Lakes Church.
Osiander, Alfons M. (BUF) [A] East Aurora, NY Christ the King Seminary.
Osiander, Alfons M. '73 (BUF) Williamsville, NY SS. Peter and Paul Church.
Osigwe, Benneth '79 (ATL) Kennesaw, GA St. Catherine of Siena Church.
Osinski, Peter J. '69 (CAM) Pennsville, NJ Queen of the Apostles Church; [A] Carneys Point, NJ St. James High School.
Osinski, Ronald V. '72 (ALT) [2] Portage, PA Sacred Heart Church; [3] Portage, PA Assumption B.V.M. Church.
Oska, Krzysztof *s.ch.* '78 (WDC) [10] Silver Spring, MD Our Lady Queen of Poland and Saint Maximilian Kolbe Church.
Oslance, Michael E. '83 (STL) Washington, MO St. Francis Borgia Church.
Osle, Enrique *s.j.* '45 (MIA) [H] Miami, FL Villa Javier.
Osom, John *m.s.p.* '85 (BLX) Pass Christian, MS Our Mother of Mercy Church.
Osorio, Celimo '87 (ELP) [34] El Paso, TX Sts. Peter and Paul Church; San Elizario, TX San Felipe de Jesus Church.
Osorio, Rudolfo B. '55 (NEW) Retired.
Osowski, Chester J. '49 (LC) Arpin, WI St. Francis Church; Sigel, WI Holy Rosary Church; Vesper, WI St. James Church.
Ossa, Pedro Nel '63 (BRK) [90] Brooklyn, NY St. Nicholas Church.
Ossa Mora, Diego Alberto '96 (TYL) Kilgore, TX Christ the King Church.
Ossino, Angelo '57 (DEN) [3] Aurora, CO St. Pius X Church.
Ossola, John R. '64 (SFD) [1] Springfield, IL Cathedral of the Immaculate Conception.
Ostaszewski, George '58 (PH) [85] Philadelphia, PA St. Ladislaus Church.
Ostatek, Albert P. *o.s.p.p.e.* '45 (PH) [AA] Doylestown, PA Pauline Fathers Monastery, Shrine of Our Lady of Czestochowa.
Ostdick, Rupert *o.s.b.* '48 (IND) [J] St. Meinrad, IN St. Meinrad Archabbey.
Ostdiek, Gil *o.f.m.* '60 (CHI) [N] Chicago, IL St. Joseph Interprovincial Post-Novitiate Formation House.
Ostdiek, Gilbert *o.f.m.* '78 (CHI) [B] Chicago, IL The Catholic Theological Union at Chicago.
Ostdiek, Harold *o.p.* '60 (CHI) [D] Oak Park, IL Fenwick High School.
Ostdiek, John *o.f.m.* '49 (SFD) [K] Sherman, IL Our Lady of Angels Friary; [L] Springfield, IL St. Francis Convent.
Ostendorf, Mark G. '81 (SCL) Becker, MN Immaculate Conception Church.
Osterhage, Louis *c.pp.s.* '58 (CIN) [17] Dayton, OH St. Joseph Church.
Osterhaus, Mark '85 (DUB) Worthington, IA St. Paul's Church.
Osterhout, Conrad *c.f.r.* '83 (NY) [DD] Bronx, NY Our Lady of the Angels Friary.
Osterle, Paul V. *s.j.* '59 (SP) [8] Tampa, FL Sacred Heart Church.
Osterman, Gerald J. '67 (BO) [32] Boston, MA St. John-St. Hugh Church.
Osterman, Richard D. '69 (GF) Red Lodge, MT St. Agnes Church.
Ostertag, Robert C. *s.j.* '49 (MIL) [P] Wauwatosa, WI Jesuit Community at St. Camillus.
Ostidek, Harold D. *o.p.* '60 (CHI) River Forest, IL St. Vincent Ferrer Priory Church.
Ostini, Anthony *s.j.* '72 (BR) [J] Convent, LA Manresa, House of Retreats.
Ostrander, Gary L. '71 (OM) West Point, NE Assumption B.V.M. Church; [G] West Point, NE Franciscan Care Services, Inc., dba St. Francis Memorial Hospital.
Ostrowski, David T. *o.s.b.* '89 (STP) [6] Minneapolis, MN Holy Cross Church.
Ostrowski, Eugene S. '77 (WH) [1] Wheeling, WV St. Joseph's Cathedral.
Ostrowski, Joel *o.f.m.cap.* '51 (FgM) Capuchin Foreign Missions.
Ostrowski, Joseph C. '52 (SCR) [L] Elmhurst, PA St. Mary's Villa Nursing Home.
Ostrowski, Max J. '39 (GR) Retired.
Ostrowski, Theodore L. (CHI) [3] Chicago, IL St. Adrian Church.
Ostrowski, Walter *s.v.d.* '65 (PIT) [O] Pittsburgh, PA

Society of The Divine Word.
Osuagwu, Anthony (NY) [141] Bronx, NY St. Frances de Chantal Church.
Osuagwu, Denis A. *c.m.f.* '89 (GAL) [22] Houston, TX St. Christopher Church.
Osuagwu, Peter Chidi '89 (BRK) [153] Queens, NY Ascension Church.
Osuch, Michael *c.r.* '80 (CHI) [88] Chicago, IL St. Hyacinth Church.
Osuji, Boniface A.A. '66 (PH) Wayne, PA St. Isaac Jogues Church.
Osuji, Canice '79 (NY) [10] Yonkers, NY St. Joseph Church.
Osuji, Canice N. '79 (SY) [9] Utica, NY St. John Church.
Osuji, Cletus C. '74 (P) [36] Portland, OR St. Therese of the Child Jesus Church.
Osuji, Emmanuel '77 (LA) [65] Los Angeles, CA St. Gerard Majella Church.
Osuji, Ngozi '81 (NY) [82] New York, NY Notre Dame Church.
Osuji, Samuel '87 (LKC) [B] Lake Charles, LA St. Patrick Hospital of Lake Charles.
Osuna, E. Donald '63 (OAK) El Cerrito, CA St. Jerome's Church.
Oswald, John '61 (LR) Retired; [H] Little Rock, AR St. John Manor.
Oswald, Leo P. '78 (PH) Fairless Hills, PA St. Frances Cabrini Church.
Oswald, Norman R. '72 (MIL) Wood, WI Veterans Administration Medical Center.
Oswald, Randy *o.m.i.* '97 (BUF) [27] Buffalo, NY Holy Angels Church.
Oswald, Richard S. '65 (LR) Rogers, AR St. Vincent de Paul Church.
Oswald, Ted '84 (SR) Lakeport, CA St. Mary Church.
Oswalt, Matthew Price '96 (OKL) Norman, OK St. Joseph's Church.
Otellini, Msgr. Steven '78 (SFR) Special Assignment.
Otellini, Msgr. Steven D. '78 (SFR) [D] Kentfield, CA Marin Catholic College Preparatory (Coed).
Oter, Patrick *m.s.p.* '92 (GAL) [66] Houston, TX St. Peter the Apostle Church.
Oterino, Francis L. '87 (MET) On Duty Outside the Diocese.
Otero, Msgr. Henry '62 (WDC) [42] Washington, DC St. Thomas Apostle Church.
Otero, Jose (NY) [103] New York, NY St. Paul Church.
Otero, Manuel '62 (SJN) [48] San Juan, PR San Pio X Church.
Otero, Neil '49 (HRT) Retired.
Otillio, Peter *o.p.* '57 (CHI) [N] Chicago, IL Dominicans (Provincial Office).
Otillio, Peter *o.p.* '57 (FgM) Dominican - Order of Preachers Foreign Missions.
Ott, Msgr. Alfred R. '60 (ALN) [1] Allentown, PA Cathedral of St. Catharine of Siena.
Ott, Carlton A. '36 (TOL) Retired.
Ott, Francis M. '42 (GBG) Retired; [G] Greensburg, PA Neumann House.
Ott, Vincent *o.m.i.* '56 (DUL) Garrison, MN Our Lady of Fatima Church; Hillman, MN Holy Family Church.
Otten, Lammert B. *s.j.* '65 (SEA) [A] Seattle, WA Seattle University.
Ottensmeyer, Hilary *o.s.b.* '50 (IND) [J] St. Meinrad, IN St. Meinrad Archabbey; [K] Beech Grove, IN Our Lady of Grace Monastery for Sisters of St. Benedict of Beech Grove, IN, Inc.
Ottenweller, Albert '43 (TOL) [1] Toledo, OH Queen of the Most Holy Rosary Cathedral.
Otterbacher, John *glmy.* '56 (CIN) [M] Fairfield, OH Headquarters of Glenmary Home Missioners.
Otterbein, Adam *c.s.s.r.* '51 (ALB) [L] Saratoga Springs, NY St. John Neumann Residence.
Otterbein, Adam J. *c.ss.r.* '40 (NY) [HH] Esopus, NY Holy Shroud Guild.
Otting, Loras C. '62 (DUB) Retired.
Otting, Paul J. '66 (DUB) [8] Dubuque, IA Holy Ghost Church.
Ottman, Timothy *o.s.b.* '78 (HON) [H] Waialua, Oahu, HI Benedictine Monastery of Hawaii.
Otto, David C. '77 (KAL) Edwardsburg, MI Our Lady of the Lake Church.
Otto, James C. '97 (PH) Springfield, PA St. Francis of Assisi Church.
Otto, John A. '39 (DAV) On Duty Outside the Diocese.
Otto, Leo '56 (SCL) Dent, MN Sacred Heart Church; Rush Lake, MN St. Lawrence Church; Retired.
Otto, Peter B. '77 (AMA) Military Chaplains.
Otto, Ray *o.s.b.* '82 (SFS) Revillo, SD Annunciation Church; [D] Milbank, SD St. Bernard Providence Hospital; [E] Milbank, SD St. William Home for the Aged.
Otto, Raymond *o.s.b.* '82 (SFS) Big Stone City, SD St. Charles Church; [F] Marvin, SD Blue Cloud Abbey.
Otto, Thomas '73 (PMB) Port St. Lucie, FL Holy Family Church.
Ottoline, Robert A. '53 (STL) Retired.
Oubre, Carroll L. '91 (ARL) [7] Alexandria, VA St. Mary's Church.
Oubre, Louis T. '86 (BR) Morganza, LA St. Ann Church.
Oubre, Sinclair '86 (BEA) [5] Port Arthur, TX St. James Church.
Ouderkirk, Lloyd Paul '59 (DUB) Garwin, IA St. Boniface Church; Marshalltown, IA St. Mary's Church.
Ouelette, Francis *o.m.i.* (BO) [3] Lowell, MA Immaculate Conception Church.
Ouelette, Lionel P. (BO) Retired.
Ouellet, Maurice F. *s.s.e.* '52 (VEN) [G] Englewood, FL Society of St. Edmund Residence.
Ouellette, Donald C. '89 (WOR) [C] Fitchburg, MA St. Bernard's Central Catholic High School.
Ouellette, Donald C. '90 (WOR) Lunenburg, MA St. Boniface Church.
Ouellette, John C. '95 (CC) [21] Corpus Christi, TX St. Pius X Church.
Ouellette, Lionel P. '57 (BO) [3] Marlboro, MA St. Mary Church.
Ouellette, Paul *o.m.i.* '67 (LA) San Fernando, CA St. Ferdinand Church.
Ouellette, Raymond *s.m.* '52 (DET) [E] Harper Woods, MI Notre Dame High School.
Ouellette, Richard R. '75 (PRT) Grand Isle, ME St. Gerard-Mt. Carmel Church; Madawaska, ME St. David's Church.
Ouellette, Richard T. *m.m.* '63 (SFR) [N] San Francisco, CA Maryknoll Fathers and Brothers, Catholic Foreign Mission Society of America, Inc.
Ouellette, Roger J. '42 (PRT) Retired; [I] Waterville, ME Mt. St. Joseph Priest Retirement Home.
Ouellette, Vincent L. '63 (MAR) Ishpeming, MI St. Joseph Church.
Ouger, John '84 (JOL) Frankfort, IL St. Anthony Church.
Ouillette, Arthur A. (WOR) Retired.
Ouimet, J. Lawrence '74 (NOR) [2] Norwich, CT Sacred Heart Church.
Oulds, John V. '68 (PH) [3] Coatesville, PA St. Joseph Church; [4] Coatesville, PA St. Stanislaus Kostka Church.
Ouletta, James F. '60 (CHI) Lake Villa, IL Prince of Peace Church.
Oulvey, William T. *s.j.* '85 (STL) [P] St. Louis, MO Bellarmine House of Studies; [P] St. Louis, MO The Jesuits of the Missouri Province.
Ours, Donald *c.m.* '94 (CHI) [211] Chicago, IL St. Vincent de Paul Church; [C] Chicago, IL Vincentian Community at DePaul University.
Ours, Robert A. '80 (SY) [1] Endicott, NY Our Lady of Good Counsel Church; Special Assignment; [C] Binghamton, NY Seton Catholic Central High School of Broome County.
Oury, Dom Guy-Marie *o.s.b.* '54 (BUR) [F] Westfield, VT Monastery of the Immaculate Heart of Mary.
Ousepparampil, Sebastian '76 (NY) [99] New York, NY Our Lady of Victory Church.
Outlaw, S. Keith '89 (NY) [131] Bronx, NY St. Augustine Church.
Ovalle, Thomas *o.m.i.* (SAT) [Q] San Antonio, TX Catholic Campus Ministry.
Ovalle, Tom *o.m.i.* '77 (SAT) [72] San Antonio, TX San Juan De Los Lagos Church.
Overbaugh, Msgr. Hugh A. '61 (HBG) [2] Harrisburg, PA St. Catherine Laboure Church.
Overbaugh, Msgr. Lawrence R. '55 (HBG) [5] Mount Carmel, PA Our Lady of Mount Carmel Church.
Overbeck, Jerome T. *s.j.* '74 (CHI) [C] Chicago, IL Jesuit Community at Loyola University of Chicago.
Overbeck, Kenneth C. '96 (BO) [74] Boston, MA St. William Church.
Overberg, Kenneth *s.j.* '73 (CIN) [P] Milford, OH Milford Spiritual Center.
Overend, James *c.m.g.* '77 (LA) Covina, CA Sacred Heart Church.
Overman, Msgr. Robert F. '45 (STL) Retired.
Overmann, William J. '62 (SFD) North Arm, IL St. Aloysius Church; Paris, IL St. Mary Church.
Overmyer, John '97 (FTW) [4] Fort Wayne, IN St. Elizabeth Ann Seton Church.
Overstreet, Raymond J. '97 (PH) Downingtown, PA St. Joseph Church.
Oviedo, Francisco *o.a.r.* '25 (NY) [187] Bronx, NY St. Roch Church.
Owen, David (FWT) Absent on Leave.
Owen, John J. '48 (BIR) Retired.
Owens, Benjamin *c.ss.r.* '75 (OAK) [C] Oakland, CA Bishop O'Dowd High School.
Owens, Bernard J. *s.j.* '72 (DET) [P] Bloomfield Hills, MI Manresa Jesuit Retreat House.
Owens, Edward *o.ss.t.* '80 (LA) [A] Camarillo, CA St. John's Seminary.
Owens, J. Edward *o.ss.t.* (BAL) [M] Baltimore, MD Holy Trinity Monastery.
Owens, Jesse *c.s.b.* '67 (GAL) [Q] Sugar Land, TX Basilian Mission Center.
Owens, John '48 (BIR) Trussville, AL Holy Infant of Prague Church.
Owens, John J. '60 (BIS) Menoken, ND St. Hildegard Church.
Owens, Joseph P. *s.j.* '48 (CLV) Cleveland, OH Cleveland Clinic Foundation; [C] Cleveland, OH John Carroll Jesuit Community.
Owens, Joseph V. *s.j.* '71 (FgM) Provinces.
Owens, Leroy E. (BO) Medfield, MA St. Edward the Confessor Church.
Owens, Michael '84 (HON) [1] Honolulu, HI Cathedral of Our Lady of Peace.
Owens, Msgr. Peter J. '58 (SY) [9] Binghamton, NY St. Patrick Church.
Owens, S. Brian '95 (WH) [4] Fairmont, WV St. Joseph's Church.
Owens, Thomas J. '74 (PH) [A] Wynnewood, PA Theological Seminary of St. Charles Borromeo, Overbrook.
Owens-Howard, Robert J. '74 (CHR) Retired.
Owino, Felix *a.j.* '92 (PIT) [5] Pittsburgh, PA St. Bede Church.
Owlrich, Robert E. '89 (DEN) On Duty Outside the Archdiocese.
Owusu-Boateng, Johnson '85 (VIC) Cuero, TX St. Michael Church.
Oya, Msgr. Eufrasio (SJN) Retired.
Oyabu, Charles '70 (HON) Wailuku, HI St. Anthony Church; [H] Wailuku, Maui, HI Wailuku Marianist Community.
Oyanguren, Angel *c.m.* '53 (LA) [29] Los Angeles, CA Our Lady of the Rosary of Talpa Church.
Oyarbide, Pedro '62 (CGS) Humacao Playa, PR Nuestra Senora del Carmen Church.
Oyeyipo, Anthony (BO) [32] Boston, MA St. John-St. Hugh Church.
Oyler, George F. '57 (L) Retired.
Ozalas, Msgr. Michael C. '39 (SCR) Retired.
Ozanne, Thomas *c.pp.s.* '74 (KC) [J] Liberty, MO Precious Blood Center.
Ozbun, John W. '84 (WIN) Blue Earth, MN SS. Peter and Paul's Church.
Ozimek, Anthony *o.s.b.* '68 (CLV) [P] Cleveland, OH Benedictine Order of Cleveland.
Ozimek, Anthony J. *o.s.b.* '68 (GF) [G] Billings, MT Saint Vincent Hospital and Health Center.
Ozimek, Eugene '45 (SPR) [H] Holyoke, MA Sisters of Providence Care Centers, Inc.
Ozimek, Eugene F. '45 (SPR) Retired.
Ozminkowsi, Clyde R. *o.carm.* '54 (KCK) Richmond, KS St. Therese Church; Scipio, KS St. Boniface Church.
Ozug, John C. '77 (FR) [19] New Bedford, MA St. Mary's Church.

P

P., Msgr. Richard, LaRocque (NOR) Jewett City, CT St. Mary Church.
Paa, Donald R. '47 (KC) Retired.
Paa, Joseph F. '41 (BUF) Retired.
Paa, Msgr. Raymond F. '55 (BUF) Harris Hill, NY Nativity of the Blessed Virgin Mary Church.
Paala, Jonathan '75 (SFR) [34] San Francisco, CA St. Monica Church.
Pabayo, Antonio *s.j.* '96 (SFR) [N] San Francisco, CA Jesuit Community at University of San Francisco.
Pabin, Chester '92 (STU) Marietta, OH St. Mary's Church.
Pable, Martin *o.f.m.cap.* '58 (MIL) [Y] Milwaukee, WI House of Peace.
Pabst, Peter J. *s.j.* '86 (PHX) [B] Phoenix, AZ Brophy College Preparatory.
Pacacha, Joseph E. '45 (NY) Retired.
Pace, Paul J. '66 (HRT) [10] Waterbury, CT St. Francis Xavier's Church.
Pace, William J. '51 (SCR) Retired; [N] Dunmore, PA Villa St. Joseph.
Pace, Woodrow H. '95 (LC) [2] Wausau, WI St. Anne Church; [C] Wausau, WI Newman High School; [D] Wausau, WI Wausau Area Catholic Schools.
Pacheco, Agostinho S. '60 (BWN) [2] McAllen, TX Our Lady of Sorrows Church.
Pacheco, Alexandre '67 (STO) Manteca, CA St. Anthony Church.
Pacheco, Mario '76 (LA) Covina, CA Sacred Heart Church.
Pacheco, Norbert A. *m.m.* '79 (FgM) Maryknoll Foreign Missions.
Pacheco-Sanchez, Luis '79 (MIL) [N] West Allis, WI Villa Clement Health Center.
Pachence, Ronald A. '74 (SAV) On Duty Outside the Diocese.
Pachence, Ronald A. '74 (SD) [B] San Diego, CA University of San Diego.
Pachla, Stanley L., Jr. '83 (DET) Eastpointe, MI St. Veronica Church.
Pacho, Jesus '51 (PCE) Retired.
Pacho, Jesus '65 (PCE) [B] Ponce, PR The Pontifical Catholic University of Puerto Rico.
Pacholec, Daniel S. '96 (SPR) [4] Springfield, MA Holy Cross Church.
Pacini, Mario *s.a.c.* '66 (ALB) [T] Cohoes, NY Apostolate for the Suffering.
Paciorek, Joseph C. *c.m.* '35 (HRT) [6] Meriden, CT St. Stanislaus Church; [M] Manchester, CT DePaul Provincial Residence.
Pacitti, Gary '89 (PH) Holland, PA St. Bede the Venerable Church.

Packard, Nathan '87 (SCL) Hillman, MN St. Rita's Church; Wahkon, MN Sacred Heart Church.
Packard, Walter E. '71 (E) Warren, PA St. Joseph Church.
Pacocha, Edwin D. '62 (CHI) [46] Chicago, IL St. Cornelius Church.
Pacudan, Roland '83 (HON) Makakilo, HI St. Jude Church.
Pacwa, Mitchell *s.j.* '76 (DAL) [D] Dallas, TX Jesuit College Preparatory School.
Paczek, Valerian '34 (FAR) Retired.
Paczesny, John R. '61 (MIL) Whitefish Bay, WI St. Monica Church; [K] Milwaukee, WI St. Mary's Hospital of Milwaukee; [K] Mequon, WI St. Mary's Hospital Ozaukee, Inc.
Paczkowski, Vincent '86 (NEW) [3] Elizabeth, NJ St. Anthony's Church.
Padathuruthy, Charles (SCL) Pierz, MN St. Joseph's Church.
Padavick, William B. '63 (CLV) Oberlin, OH Sacred Heart Church.
Padazinski, C. Michael '88 (SFR) Special Assignment.
Padberg, John R. *s.j.* '41 (STL) [O] St. Louis, MO Fusz Pavilion.
Padberg, John W. *s.j.* '57 (STL) [P] St. Louis, MO Jesuit Community Corporation at St. Louis University - Jesuit Hall; [W] St. Louis, MO Institute of Jesuit Sources; [W] St. Louis, MO Seminar on Jesuit Spirituality.
Paddack, John N. '84 (NY) [53] New York, NY Incarnation Church; [E] New York, NY Cardinal Hayes High School.
Padden, Neil *o.f.m.* '55 (SP) [O] St. Petersburg, FL St. Anthony Friary.
Paddock, Richard W. '59 (RCK) Elburn, IL St. Gall Church.
Padelli, Emilio P. '62 (HRT) [4] East Hartford, CT St. Isaac Jogues Church.
Padilla, Aquino '60 (SFR) [3] San Mateo, CA St. Matthew Church.
Padilla, Gilbert '55 (TUC) Mammoth, AZ Blessed Sacrament Church.
Padilla, Rafael '89 (VEN) Cape Coral, FL St. Andrew Church.
Padilla, Steve '79 (DEN) Arvada, CO Spirit of Christ Parish.
Padin, Jose *m.m.* '97 (FgM) Maryknoll Foreign Missions.
Padinjarepeedika, Jose L.F. *c.m.i.* '72 (LAF) Melville, LA St. John the Evangelist Church.
Pado, Thomas '75 (ORG) Irvine, CA St. Elizabeth Ann Seton Church.
Padovani, Martin *s.v.d.* '60 (TR) [M] Bordentown, NJ Society of the Divine Word.
Padovano, Louis A. *s.j.* '69 (NY) [DD] New York, NY Jesuit Provincial's Office.
Padrez, Mark C. *o.p.* '95 (OAK) Antioch, CA Holy Rosary Church.
Padrnos, David *s.s.c.* '71 (FgM) St. Columban's Foreign Mission.
Padron, Julio Victor Garcia '89 (SJN) Catano, PR Santa Rosa de Lima Church.
Paduch, Frank '89 (BEA) Sour Lake, TX Our Lady of Victory Church.
Padula, Armand *o.f.m.* '56 (NY) [FF] Wappingers Falls, NY Mt. Alvernia Retreat House.
Pafchik, Lawrence F. *o.f.m.* '42 (PAT) [M] Ringwood, NJ Holy Name Friary, Inc.
Pagan, Alberto *o.p.* '93 (SJN) Catano, PR Nuestra Senora del Carmen Church.
Pagan, Angel '80 (ARE) [2] Manati, PR Our Savior Church.
Pagan, Tomas '83 (ARE) Morovis, PR St. Paul Apostle Church.
Pagano, Bernard T. '58 (WIL) On Duty Outside the Diocese.
Pagano, Peter E. '52 (SPR) Retired.
Page, Charles T. '91 (KAL) Buchanan, MI St. Anthony Church.
Page, David '58 (ORL) Indialantic, FL Holy Name of Jesus Church.
Page, Hugh H. '80 (FTW) [B] Notre Dame, IN University of Notre Dame Du Lac.
Page, Leon J. '56 (DET) [4] Sterling Heights, MI St. Jane Frances de Chantal Church.
Page, Msgr. Raymond J. '46 (WOR) Retired.
Page, Stephen C. '87 (DAV) Fairfield, IA St. Mary's Church.
Page, Thomas P. '79 (GR) Big Rapids, MI St. Paul's Campus Parish; On Special Assignment.
Pagel, John M. '80 (CHL) On Duty Outside the Diocese.
Pagel, John M. '80 (SAT) Rocksprings, TX Sacred Heart of Mary Church.
Pageot, Roger *s.s.s.* '53 (NY) [8] New York, NY St. Andrew Church.
Pagliara, Alfonso *o.f.m.cap.* '81 (CHL) Hendersonville, NC Immaculate Conception Church.
Pagliari, Robert M. *c.ss.r.* '75 (ORL) [F] New Smyrna Beach, FL Redemptorist Fathers of the Vice Province of Richmond.
Pagliuca, Joseph P. '43 (BUR) Retired.
Pagnotta, James V. '69 (NEW) [13] Jersey City, NJ St. Joseph's Church.
Pagone, Joseph '55 (WDC) Retired.
Pagones, Peter N. '68 (ALB) Averill Park, NY St. Henry Church.
Pahl, Norman *o.m.i.* '58 (DUL) Willow River, MN St. Mary's Church; Willow River, MN Youth Conservation Camp.
Pahler, Robert E. '57 (CLV) Green, OH Queen of Heaven Church.
Pai, Simon '52 (RVC) Retired.
Paider, Paul (GB) Black Creek, WI St. Mary Church; Navarino, WI St. Lawrence Church.
Paik, Francis M. '54 (CLV) [1] Euclid, OH St. Christine Church; Retired.
Paillacho, Jose Joffre '87 (MOB) Dothan, AL St. Columba Church.
Painter, Emmett B. *s.j.* '75 (P) Rainier, OR Nativity B.V.M. Church.
Painter, George F. *m.m.* '44 (FgM) Maryknoll Foreign Missions.
Painter, George F. *m.m.* '44 (NY) [DD] Maryknoll, NY Maryknoll Fathers and Brothers.
Paisley, James J. '85 (SCR) Laflin, PA St. Maria Goretti Church.
Paisley, John C. '62 (DUB) Belmond, IA St. Francis Xavier Church.
Paiva, Antonio M. '49 (PRO) [27] Providence, RI Our Lady of the Rosary Church.
Paiz, William *c.m.f.* '79 (ORG) [2] Orange, CA La Purisima Church.
Pajk, Thomas J. '87 (CLV) Gates Mills, OH St. Francis of Assisi Church.
Pakalniskis, John L. '39 (BRK) Retired; [U] Douglaston, NY Bishop Mugavero Residence.
Pakenham, Daniel J. '65 (MIL) Elm Grove, WI St. Mary Church.
Pakianather, Aloysius P. '78 (RVC) Valley Stream, NY Blessed Sacrament Church.
Pakiz, Rudolph '46 (DUL) Tower, MN St. Martin's Church.
Pakosta, Francis '52 (SUP) Retired.
Pakula, Michael G. '73 (PEO) Geneseo, IL St. Malachy's Church.
Pakulniewicz, Msgr. Raphael F. '50 (NY) [196] Staten Island, NY St. Anthony Church.
Pakutka, Msgr. William J. '43 (SCR) Retired; [N] Dunmore, PA Villa St. Joseph.
Pala, Francis *sch.p.* '55 (MIA) [C] Fort Lauderdale, FL Cardinal Gibbons High School.
Pala, Manuel Soler (SJN) [A] Bayamon, PR Bayamon Central University.
Pala, Manuel Soler *m.ss.cc.* '70 (SJN) [10] Bayamon, PR San Juan Bautista de la Salle Church.
Palacino, Joseph '82 (BGP) [1] Norwalk, CT St. Jerome Church.
Palacio, Fernando '79 (MGZ) [7] Mayaquez, PR Santa Teresita Church.
Palacio, Jorge *o.s.m.* '79 (ELP) [18] El Paso, TX Our Lady of Sorrows Church.
Palacios, Joseph M. '87 (LA) On Duty Outside the Archdiocese.
Palacios, Joseph M. *s.j.* '87 (OAK) [N] Berkeley, CA Jesuit Community at Jesuit School of Theology at Berkeley.
Palackal, Joseph *c.m.i.* (BRK) [242] Queens, NY St. Stanislaus Kostka Church.
Paladino, John (NEW) [D] Montvale, NJ St. Joseph Regional High School.
Paladino, John J. (NEW) Hillsdale, NJ St. John the Baptist Church.
Paladino, John J.F. '91 (NEW) [Q] Hoboken, NJ Stevens Institute of Technology; [Q] Jersey City, NJ Jersey City State College.
Palafox, Lorenzo J. *s.j.* '67 (SAC) [C] Sacramento, CA Jesuit High School; [G] Carmichael, CA Jesuit High School Community of Sacramento.
Palakovich, Michael G. '87 (DEN) Loveland, CO St. John the Evangelist Church.
Palamattathil, George '86 (OAK) [3] Walnut Creek, CA St. Mary's Church.
Palang, Mansueto P. '77 (BR) Belle Rose, LA St. Jules Church.
Palanga, Anthony J. *c.m.* '45 (SPC) [2] Cape Girardeau, MO St. Vincent de Paul Church.
Palardy, William B. '85 (BO) [A] Boston, MA St. John's Seminary School of Theology.
Palaroan, Moises '78 (STA) Keystone Heights, FL St. William Church.
Palasits, John A. '58 (NEW) South Orange, NJ Our Lady of Sorrows Church.
Palazzo, Michael L. '87 (NY) Hopewell Junction, NY St. Columba Church.
Palazzolo, Anthony P. '93 (STA) [21] Jacksonville, FL San Jose Church.
Palcheck, Gerald F. '67 (SD) Descanso, CA Our Lady of Light Church.
Palcisko, Raymond '58 (CR) Roseau, MN Sacred Heart Church.
Paleari, Giorgio *p.i.m.e.* '75 (DET) [K] Detroit, MI P.I.M.E. College Community; [K] Detroit, MI P.I.M.E. Missionaries of SS. Peter and Paul.
Palen, Robert L. '41 (DUB) Retired.
Palepale, Marisi *ss.cc.* '86 (HON) Lahaina, HI Maria Lanakila Church.
Palermo, Albert A. '63 (AUS) [2] Austin, TX St. Albert The Great Church.
Palermo, Albert A. '63 (MIL) On Duty Outside the Archdiocese.
Palermo, Angelo *s.a.c.* '60 (NY) [221] Staten Island, NY Our Lady Star of the Sea Church.
Palermo, Frank C. '55 (SPC) [2] Springfield, MO Holy Trinity Church; Springfield, MO Diocesan Hospital Ministry; Special Assignment.
Palermo, Joseph S., Jr. '94 (NO) [31] New Orleans, LA St. Frances Xavier Cabrini Church.
Paliathayil, Rubin Reynolds '79 (BR) [9] Baton Rouge, LA St. George Church.
Palica, Jacek *o.c.d.* '96 (GRY) [J] Munster, IN Discalced Carmelite Fathers Monastery.
Palick, George '58 (PIT) [1] Butler, PA St. Fidelis of Sigmaringen Church.
Paliokas, Algirdas *s.j.* '73 (CHI) [2] Lemont, IL Blessed Jurgis Matulaitis Church; [N] Chicago, IL Lithuanian American Jesuits.
Palis, Theo '45 (OAK) Pittsburg, CA Our Lady Queen of the World Church.
Paliwoda, Steven '94 (SJP) [8] Lorain, OH St. John the Baptist Church.
Palka, Bernard *s.a.* '72 (NY) [AA] Garrison, NY St. Christopher's Inn; [DD] Garrison, NY Generalate of the Franciscan Friars of the Atonement-St. James Friary; [DD] Garrison, NY Franciscan Friars of the Atonement.
Palka, Edwin '96 (SP) [2] Tampa, FL Christ the King Church.
Palko, John A. '54 (PIT) Retired.
Palko, John J. '67 (ALT) Hollidaysburg, PA St. Mary's Church.
Palko, Thomas J. *o.s.f.s.* '59 (VEN) [4] Fort Myers, FL St. Columbkille Church.
Palkowski, Jan '76 (PH) Clifton Heights, PA Sacred Heart Church.
Palladino, Msgr. Alfonso G. '43 (BO) Melrose, MA St. Mary of the Annunciation Church; Retired.
Palladino, Robert J. '58 (P) Estacada, OR St. Aloysius Church.
Pallard, Joseph *o.m.i.* '72 (PMB) [4] West Palm Beach, FL St. John Fisher Church.
Pallardy, James G. '87 (PEO) Andalusia, IL St. Patrick's Church.
Palliparambil, Jose Simon '62 (RVC) Plainview, NY St. Pius X Church; Plainview, NY North Shore Hospital at Plainview.
Pallivathuckal, Abraham Joseph '73 (MIA) Hollywood, FL Nativity Church.
Pallivathukkall, Jacob M. '65 (PT) Chattahoochee, FL Holy Cross Parish.
Pallo, Joseph L. '61 (LR) Blytheville, AR Immaculate Conception Church; Osceola, AR St. Matthew's Church; [L] Blytheville, AR Immaculate Conception Trust Fund.
Palluck, M. Charles '66 (SEA) Black Diamond, WA St. Barbara Church.
Palm, John B. *s.j.* '41 (FgM) Provinces.
Palma, Gregory *o.f.m.* '40 (ALB) [A] Catskill, NY St. Anthony Friary.
Palma, Raul *sch.p.* '58 (LA) [21] Los Angeles, CA Our Lady Help of Christians (Maria Auxiliadora) Church; [R] Los Angeles, CA Piarist Fathers.
Palmatier, David *o.s.b.* '57 (RCK) [H] Aurora, IL Marmion Abbey-St. Augustine's Abbey.
Palmeno, Alberto *o.s.a.* '68 (CC) [17] Laredo, TX St. Vincent de Paul Church.
Palmer, Frank S. '62 (DM) Indianola, IA St. Thomas Aquinas Church.
Palmer, Herbert *o.s.b.* '39 (SD) [H] Oceanside, CA Prince of Peace Abbey, Benet Hill.
Palmer, John *c.s.v.* '71 (JOL) [A] Lisle, IL Benedictine University.
Palmer, Michael C. '63 (BGP) Wilton, CT Our Lady of Fatima Church.
Palmer, Patrick J. '48 (SAT) Canyon Lake, TX St. Thomas the Apostle Church.
Palmer, Richard *o.s.a.* '87 (FgM) Foreign Missions.
Palmer, Richard D. *o.s.a.* '87 (CHI) [N] Olympia Fields, IL The Augustinian Provincialate Tolentine Center.
Palmer, Ronald L. '80 (PEO) [O] Normal, IL St. Robert Bellarmine Newman Center, Illinois State University.
Palmer, Samuel '57 (DM) Urbandale, IA St. Pius X Church.
Palmer, Msgr. Thomas M. '58 (SAT) LaCoste, TX Our Lady of Grace Church.
Palmese, Anthony '76 (ORL) [4] Ocala, FL St. Jude's Church.
Palmieri, Alexander J. '76 (PH) Conshohocken, PA SS. Cosmas and Damian Church; [A] Wynnewood, PA Theological Seminary of St. Charles Borromeo, Overbrook.
Palmieri, Frank *c.r.m.* '62 (CHR) Goose Creek, SC Immaculate Conception Church.

Palmieri, John A. '41 (BO) Retired.
Palmieri, Louis R. '93 (BO) Abington, MA St. Bridget Church.
Palmieri, Luigi '67 (ALN) [7] Allentown, PA St. Paul Church.
Palmieri, Luigi '67 (JC) On Duty Outside the Diocese.
Palmieri, Thaddeus *o.f.m.* '48 (NY) [DD] New York, NY Franciscan Province of the Immaculate Conception.
Palmigiano, James *o.c.s.o.* '88 (WOR) [N] Spencer, MA St. Joseph's Abbey.
Palmiotto, Paul '82 (BRK) [159] Queens, NY St. Bonaventure's Church.
Palmiotto, Paul C. '82 (BRK) [156] Queens, NY St. Benedict, the Moor Church.
Palmisano, Peter J. '93 (NEW) Oradell, NJ St. Joseph's Church.
Palmitessa, Paul '56 (SD) [13] San Diego, CA Our Lady of Mt. Carmel Church.
Palo, Anthony *o.carm.* '64 (NEW) Englewood, NJ St. Cecilia's Church.
Paloma, Victor E. '70 (NEW) [20] Jersey City, NJ Our Lady of Mercy Church.
Palombo, Albert B. '42 (PH) [100] Philadelphia, PA Mater Dolorosa Church; Retired.
Palomino, Esviardo '49 (NY) [67] New York, NY St. Lucy Church.
Palomino, Ignacio '85 (HBG) [3] Lancaster, PA Assumption of the Blessed Virgin Mary Church; [J] Lancaster, PA Iglesia de San Juan Bautista.
Palos, Anthony *o.a.r.* '60 (ORG) [3] Santa Ana, CA Our Lady of Guadalupe Church.
Palsa, Steven '79 (PIT) Wexford, PA St. Alexis Church.
Palubinskas, Vytautas A. '54 (BRK) [9] Brooklyn, NY Annunciation of the Blessed Virgin Mary Church.
Paluck, Casimir A. '61 (BIS) Fort Yates, ND St. Peter - Catholic Indian Mission Church; Selfridge, ND St. Philomena Church.
Palumbo, Joseph S. '93 (LA) Manhattan Beach, CA American Martyrs Church.
Palumbo, Richard W. '93 (MET) Somerville, NJ Immaculate Conception Church; [L] Phillipsburg, NJ The Anawim Community.
Palumbos, Edward L. '72 (ROC) [12] Rochester, NY St. Charles Borromeo Church.
Paluse, Richard V. '42 (PIT) Retired.
Palys, Daniel J. '69 (BUF) Blossom, NY St. Gabriel Church.
Pambello, Louis '81 (NEW) Montclair, NJ Immaculate Conception Church; Montclair, NJ Mountainside Hospital.
Pamment, Duaine H. '64 (LAN) Laingsburg, MI St. Isidore Church.
Pamment, Gary W. '63 (KAL) Wayland, MI St. Therese Church.
Pamplaniyil, Mathew '76 (FAR) [3] Grand Forks, ND St. Michael's Church.
Pan, Philip *o.p.* '84 (WDC) [B] Washington, DC Dominican House of Studies.
Panagia, Sal J. '73 (PAT) [13] Paterson, NJ Our Lady of Pompei Church.
Panagoplos, Christopher *t.o.r.* '76 (ALT) [13] Johnstown, PA SS. Peter and Paul's Church; Johnstown, PA Memorial Hospital; Johnstown, PA Lee Hospital.
Panakal, John Bosco (JOL) Winfield, IL St. John the Baptist Church.
Panakal, Thomson '60 (JOL) [2] Lockport, IL St. Dennis Church.
Panares, Auxentius '62 (WDC) Mount Rainier, MD St. James Church; Washington, DC Washington Hospital Center; Hospital & Nursing Home Ministries.
Panato, Pasquino *m.c.c.j.* '64 (NEW) [N] Montclair, NJ Comboni Missionaries of the Heart of Jesus (Verona Fathers).
Panchot, Daniel A. *c.s.c.* '65 (FgM) Holy Cross Foreign Missions.
Panchuk, Myron '82 (STN) [3] Chicago, IL SS. Volodymyr and Olha Church.
Pancorbo, Msgr. Marcos A. '58 (PCE) [1] Ponce, PR Cathedral of Our Lady of Guadalupe; [1] Ponce, PR Church Our Lady of Miraculous Medal Church; [H] Penuelas, PR Training School for the Lay Apostolate (Hermanos Cheos).
Panczuk, Bernard '63 (STF) New York, NY St. George Church.
Pandarathikudiyil, Sebastian *v.c.* '88 (NY) Highland Mills, NY St. Patrick Church.
Pandolfo, Anthony '60 (STU) Retired.
Pandolfo, Lawrence *o.p.* '39 (NO) Jefferson, LA Elmwood Medical Center.
Pane, Andrew '87 (NY) Absent on Leave.
Panek, Edward B. '91 (CHI) [A] Chicago, IL Archbishop Quigley Preparatory Seminary.
Panek, Robert M. '70 (NY) Military Chaplains.
Panepinto, Vincent '67 (ROC) Willard, NY Drug Treatment Center.
Panepinto, Vincent P. '67 (ROC) Geneva, NY St. Francis de Sales Church.
Paner, Robert (TR) Colts Neck, NJ Naval Weapons Station Earle.
Pangratz, Clement H. *o.s.b.* '47 (SEA) [M] Lacey, WA St. Martin's Abbey.
Paniagua, Jose L. '62 (MIA) [3] Hialeah, FL St. Benedict Church.
Paniagua, Pablo '49 (SAT) [K] San Antonio, TX Casa De Padres.
Paniagua, Pablo '59 (SAT) Retired.
Panickaurparampil, Thomas *t.o.r.* '62 (FWT) Carrollton, TX St. Catherine of Siena Church.
Paninski, John *m.s.* '61 (PEO) Georgetown, IL St. Isaac Jogues Church; [M] Georgetown, IL LaSalette Missionaries.
Pank, Julian F. '40 (L) Retired.
Panke, Robert '96 (WDC) Olney, MD St. Peter Church.
Pankiw, Roman '86 (PHU) [6] Philadelphia, PA St. Josaphat's Church.
Pankratz, Richard L. *s.s.c.* '74 (FgM) St. Columban's Foreign Mission.
Panos, Msgr. Patrick G. '68 (PAT) Ringwood, NJ St. Catherine of Bologna Church.
Pansini, Francis David *c.m.* '42 (LA) [R] Los Angeles, CA Vincentian Fathers and Brothers.
Pantaleo, Daniel C. (PH) [C] Philadelphia, PA LaSalle University.
Pantano, Salvatore *o.f.m.conv.* '51 (ALB) [12] Albany, NY Our Lady of Angels Church.
Panthalani, Thomas '64 (LKC) De Ridder, LA St. Joseph's Church.
Panthaplamthottiyil, Jose '75 (STA) Palm Coast, FL St. Elizabeth Ann Seton Church.
Pantle, G. Donald *s.j.* '60 (SCR) [C] Scranton, PA University of Scranton.
Pantyra, Anthony (RCK) Geneva, IL St. Peter Church.
Panula, Arne A. '73 (SFR) [T] San Francisco, CA Opus Dei.
Panuska, Joseph A. *s.j.* '60 (SCR) [C] Scranton, PA University of Scranton.
Panza, Msgr. Paul D. '54 (ALT) Retired.
Panza, Robert S. (HBG) Dallastown, PA St. Joseph Church.
Paoli, Livius *o.s.b.* '37 (DET) [70] Detroit, MI St. Scholastica Church; [K] Detroit, MI St. Sylvester Monastery.
Paolicelli, Lawrence M. '84 (NY) [E] New York, NY Cardinal Spellman High School; [HH] New York, NY Legion of Mary, Office.
Paolo, Francis de Sales *o.f.m.* '58 (BO) [57] Boston, MA Our Lady of Mt. Carmel Church.
Paolo, Francis DeSales *o.f.m.* '58 (BO) [W] Boston, MA St. Christopher Friary.
Paolozzi, Joseph L. '61 (MEM) Martin, TN St. Jude's Church; [L] Martin, TN Cooperative Ministries Interfaith Center.
Paone, Ernest C. '57 (PIT) On Duty Outside the Diocese.
Paonessa, Ralph *o.f.m.* '63 (NY) [DD] New York, NY Franciscan Province of the Immaculate Conception.
Papa, Charles E. '67 (RVC) Medford, NY St. Sylvester Church.
Papa, Christopher J. '89 (PH) [106] Philadelphia, PA St. Monica Church.
Papa, Dominic *c.p.* '60 (BRK) [U] Jamaica, NY Immaculate Conception Monastery.
Papa, Frank *s.o.l.t.* '89 (CC) [H] Robstown, TX Society of Our Lady of the Most Holy Trinity.
Papa, Frank E. *s.o.l.t.* '89 (HRT) [5] East Hartford, CT St. Mary's Church.
Papaj, Joseph J. *s.j.* '70 (NY) [F] New York, NY Loyola School; [DD] New York, NY St. Ignatius Loyola Residence.
Papalia, Pasquale A. '74 (NEW) On Duty Outside the Archdiocese.
Pape, William H. '70 (ALB) [1] Albany, NY Cathedral of the Immaculate Conception.
Papen, Gerald T. *c.s.c.* '63 (FgM) Holy Cross Foreign Missions.
Papen, Gerald T. *c.s.c.* '63 (FTW) [J] South Bend, IN Congregation of Holy Cross Indiana Province Provincial House.
Papera, Lewis V. '67 (NEW) Rochelle Park, NJ Sacred Heart Church.
Paperini, Richard '77 (P) [A] St. Benedict, OR Mount Angel Seminary.
Papes, Joseph T. '59 (GF) On Duty Outside of the Diocese.
Papes, Louis M. '88 (CLV) East Cleveland, OH Christ the King Church.
Papes, Rudy *c.ss.r.* '65 (GR) [3] Grand Rapids, MI St. Alphonsus Church.
Papesh, Michael L. '83 (STP) [5] St. Paul, MN Holy Spirit Church.
Papiernik, Roman J. '40 (LC) Retired.
Papineau, Andre *s.d.s.* '65 (MIL) [B] Hales Corners, WI Sacred Heart School of Theology.
Papp, Christopher '86 (WIL) Military Chaplains.
Papp, Edward E. '60 (OG) Potsdam, NY St. Mary Church.
Paprocki, John L. '59 (NEW) Fort Lee, NJ Madonna Church.
Paprocki, Thomas J. '78 (CHI) [1] Chicago, IL Cathedral of the Holy Name.
Paquet, Fernand *m.m.* '56 (FgM) Maryknoll Foreign Missions.
Paquet, Hubert J. '55 (PRT) Retired.
Paquet, Joseph A. *s.j.* '59 (BO) [W] Weston, MA Campion Health Center, Inc.
Paquet, Michael *o.s.c.* '78 (STP) Anoka, MN St. Stephen Church; [N] Anoka, MN Crosier Community of Anoka.
Paquet, Robert J. *s.j.* '45 (CHL) [9] Charlotte, NC St. Peter Church; [J] Charlotte, NC Jesuit Community.
Paquette, Francis '57 (DUL) Silver Bay, MN St. Mary's Church.
Paquette, Joseph R. '78 (PRO) [33] Providence, RI St. Thomas Church.
Paquette, Neil *o.c.s.o.* '94 (DUB) [K] Peosta, IA New Melleray Abbey, Order of Cistercians of the Strict Observance.
Paquin, Ronald H. '73 (BO) Health Leave.
Paraday, Mark *o.p.* '83 (FgM) Dominican - Order of Preachers Foreign Missions.
Paradis, Donald L. *m.s.* '58 (PRO) [B] Newport, RI Salve Regina University.
Paradis, Robert M. *o.m.i.* '37 (MAN) [K] Colebrook, NH Shrine of Our Lady of Grace.
Paradis, Roger *o.m.i.* '48 (FgM) Oblates Foreign Missions.
Paradis, Msgr. Wilfrid '49 (MAN) [11] Manchester, NH St. John the Baptist Church.
Paradis, Msgr. Wilfrid H. '49 (MAN) Retired.
Parambi, Thomas Seraphin *c.s.t.* '50 (NY) [177] Bronx, NY Our Lady of Solace Church.
Paramo, Raymond *c.s.b.* '66 (DET) [E] Redford, MI Catholic Central High School.
Paramo, Thomas *c.m.f.* '56 (CHI) [N] Oak Park, IL Claretian Fathers Headquarters of U.S.A. Eastern Province.
Parampath, Joseph K. '53 (BGP) Weston, CT St. Francis of Assisi Church.
Paraniuk, Michael '81 (CIN) [15] Cincinnati, OH St. Bernard Church; [K] Cincinnati, OH Franciscan Hospital, Mt. Airy Campus.
Parappally, James '59 (MIA) [5] Pompano Beach, FL St. Gabriel Church.
Parchem, Peter *o.f.m.conv.* '51 (MRY) Pismo Beach, CA St. Paul the Apostle Church.
Parcheski, Anthony *c.s.s.* '48 (BO) [Z] Waltham, MA Stigmatine Fathers and Brothers.
Pardee, Charles D. '84 (JC) Boonville, MO SS. Peter and Paul Church.
Pardue, John D. '88 (SHP) [10] Shreveport, LA St. Pius X Church.
Pare, Arthur H. *s.j.* '60 (BO) [W] Boston, MA The Society of Jesus of New England-Provincial Offices.
Pare, Arthur H. *s.j.* '60 (PRT) [9] Portland, ME St. Pius X Church.
Pare, Jean Dominique *o.p.* '41 (FR) [12] Fall River, MA St. Anne's Church.
Pare, Paul *o.f.m.* (CHI) [D] Chicago, IL Hales Franciscan High School, Inc.
Pare, Paul M. '53 (PRT) Richmond, ME St. Ambrose Church.
Pare, Paul U. '52 (PRT) Retired.
Paredes, Edmundo '85 (DAL) [15] Dallas, TX St. Cecilia Church.
Parekkat, Winson *c.m.i.* '72 (PH) [157] Philadelphia, PA St. William Church.
Parel, Joseph '57 (HRT) Northford, CT St. Monica's Church.
Parella, Francis *s.s.p.* (BUF) Eden, NY Immaculate Conception Church.
Parella, Francis J. *s.s.p.* '47 (Y) [A] Canfield, OH Society of St. Paul.
Parello, Joseph J. '74 (SJN) On Duty Outside the Archdiocese.
Parent, Basil R. '86 (NTN) Danbury, CT St. Ann Church.
Parent, J. Wilfrid '91 (WDC) Waldorf, MD St. Peter Church.
Parent, Norman *o.m.i.* (BO) [9] Lowell, MA St. Marie Church.
Parent, Philip *s.m.* '81 (BO) [W] Cambridge, MA Our Lady of Mercy Marist Novitiate.
Parent, Rene L. *m.s.* '76 (NOR) Jewett City, CT St. Mary Church.
Parent, Royal J. '56 (PRT) Boothbay Harbor, ME Our Lady, Queen of Peace Church.
Parente, Lino S. *o.cist.* '65 (TR) Mount Laurel, NJ St. John Neumann Church; [M] Mount Laurel, NJ Cistercian Monastery of Our Lady of Fatima.
Parente, Michael *s.a.c.* '47 (CAM) Hammonton, NJ St. Joseph's Church.
Parenteau, William J. '70 (TUC) Tombstone, AZ Sacred Heart Church.
Parenti, Robert J. '72 (TR) Manasquan, NJ St. Denis Church.
Parenti, Thomas M. '74 (SFR) Greenbrae, CA St. Sebastian Church.
Parenza, John Anthony '50 (DET) [H] Livonia, MI St. Mary Hospital; [K] Detroit, MI St. Paul of the Cross Community, Congregation of the Passion.
Paret, Joaquin '82 (MIA) Miami Springs, FL Blessed Trinity Church.
Paret, John J. *s.j.* '51 (ALB) [O] Auriesville, NY Shrine

of Our Lady of Martyrs.
Paretsky, Albert *o.p.* '81 (WDC) [B] Washington, DC Dominican House of Studies.
Parham, William J. '76 (MEM) Brownsville, TN St. John Church; Jackson, TN St. Mary's Church.
Pariante, Mario *s.m.* '90 (HON) [H] Honolulu, HI Center Marianist Community.
Pariante, Mario J. *s.m.* '90 (HON) [D] Honolulu, HI St. Louis School.
Parillo, Emery *o.f.m.* '55 (ALB) [3] Watervliet, NY Our Lady of Mt. Carmel Church.
Paris, Benedetto J. '95 (MAR) DeTour, MI Sacred Heart Church; Goetzville, MI St. Stanislaus Kostka Church.
Paris, Charles W. '55 (WIL) Retired.
Paris, Don Joseph *o.m.i.* '53 (STP) [Q] Buffalo, MN Christ the King Retreat Center.
Paris, John *s.j.* '69 (BO) [W] Chestnut Hill, MA The Jesuit Community at Boston College.
Paris, John U. '50 (BO) [4] Malden, MA St. Peter Church; [E] Needham, MA St. Sebastian's Country Day School, Inc.
Paris, Thomas *m.s.* '46 (FR) [J] Attleboro, MA La Salette Shrine.
Parise, Michael J. '79 (BO) Billerica, MA St. Andrew Church.
Parisi, Enrique *o.f.m.* '60 (LA) [72] Los Angeles, CA St. Joseph Church.
Parisi, Frank J. '85 (RVC) Smithtown, NY St. Patrick Church.
Parisi, Joseph L. '74 (STL) West Overland, MO St. Jude Church.
Parisi, Michael (PAT) Military Chaplains.
Parisi, Michael R. '55 (BRK) Special Assignment.
Parisi, Salvador *o.f.m.* '54 (SFR) [5] San Francisco, CA St. Anthony Church.
Parizek, Msgr. James F. '72 (DAV) [M] Davenport, IA St. Vincent Center; [P] Davenport, IA Quad Cities Catholic Deaf Ministry.
Park, Augustin C. '61 (NEW) [6] Orange, NJ St. Andrew Kim Church.
Park, Augustine '92 (MIL) [Y] Milwaukee, WI Korean Catholic Community.
Park, Austin *s.j.* '55 (LKC) Kinder, LA St. Philip Neri Church.
Park, Austin N. *s.j.* '55 (LAF) [J] Grand Coteau, LA Jesuit Spirituality Center.
Park, James (SJ) [2] Sunnyvale, CA Sts. Andrew and Paul Korean Catholic Mission of San Jose Church.
Park, John '82 (ORL) [1] Orlando, FL St. James Cathedral.
Park, Jung-Woo *s.j.* '91 (NY) [DD] New York, NY Jesuit Community at Fordham University.
Park, Morton '52 (P) [35] Portland, OR St. Stephen Church.
Park, Robert G. '57 (WH) [1] Wheeling, WV St. Joseph's Cathedral.
Park, Sung Wo (BRK) [226] Queens, NY St. Paul Chong Ha-Sang Roman Catholic Chapel Church.
Park, Thomas *o.s.b.* '65 (SEA) Seattle, WA Veterans Administration Medical Center.
Park, Thomas R. *o.s.b.* '65 (SEA) [M] Lacey, WA St. Martin's Abbey.
Parke, Frederick '75 (STA) Bunnell, FL St. Stephen Church; Palm Coast, FL St. Elizabeth Ann Seton Church.
Parke, James E. '65 (RIC) [1] Virginia Beach, VA Church of the Ascension.
Parker, Carroll *o.m.i.* '61 (FgM) Oblates Foreign Missions.
Parker, Charles '71 (PHX) On Leave.
Parker, Edmond L '56 (BO) Acton, MA St. Elizabeth of Hungary Church.
Parker, Frank J. *s.j.* '73 (BO) [W] Chestnut Hill, MA The Jesuit Community at Boston College.
Parker, Glenn D. *c.ss.r.* '85 (STA) [6] Jacksonville, FL Holy Rosary Church.
Parker, James '82 (CHR) [15] Charleston, SC Church of the Holy Spirit.
Parker, John W. '70 (CHI) [11] Chicago, IL St. Andrew Church.
Parker, Kenneth '65 (R) Retired.
Parker, Larry '84 (WCH) Chetopa, KS Sacred Heart Church; Oswego, KS Mother of God Church.
Parker, Michael J. '83 (BUF) [1] Tonawanda, NY St. Amelia Church.
Parker, Paul M. '82 (BO) [A] Weston, MA Pope John XXIII National Seminary.
Parker, Richard (SB) [B] Riverside, CA Notre Dame High School.
Parker, Rick '77 (OKL) On Duty Outside the Archdiocese.
Parker, Theodore K. *o.s.c.* '72 (NY) [4] New York, NY All Saints Church; [DD] New York, NY Crosier (Canons Regular of the Order of the Holy Cross).
Parker, Thomas P. *s.s.c.* '47 (LA) [R] Los Angeles, CA Columban Fathers, Procure House.
Parker, William C. '64 (TOL) Walbridge, OH St. Jerome Church.
Parkes, Joseph P. *s.j.* '76 (NY) [F] New York, NY Fordham Preparatory School; [DD] New York, NY Jesuit Community at Fordham University.
Parkinson, Forrest T. '94 (RVC) Deer Park, NY SS. Cyril and Methodius Church.
Parkos, John F. '64 (STP) Maple Grove, MN St. Joseph the Worker Church.
Parks, Jonathan *s.d.b.* '78 (NO) [4] Harvey, LA St. Rosalie Church.
Parks, Msgr. Joseph K. '39 (BRK) [115] Brooklyn, NY St. Patrick Church; Retired; [V] Brooklyn, NY Monastery of the Sisters Adorers of the Precious Blood.
Parks, Richard E. '59 (BAL) [88] Baltimore, MD Sacred Heart of Mary Church.
Parks, Richard L. *c.p.* '70 (L) [L] Louisville, KY Sacred Heart Retreat.
Parlante, Gregory (PH) Bridgeport, PA Our Mother of Sorrows Church.
Parle, Richard '56 (SEA) Lacey, WA Sacred Heart of Jesus Church.
Parlet, Steve '97 (COS) [13] Colorado Springs, CO St. Patrick's Church.
Parlette, Thomas L. '89 (DAV) Knoxville, IA St. Anthony's Church; Melcher, IA Sacred Heart Church; Pella, IA St. Mary's Church.
Parlsi, Michael '73 (BRK) [189] Queens, NY St. Kevin Church.
Parme, George J. '48 (PIT) Retired.
Parmisano, Fabian *o.p.* '53 (OAK) [N] Oakland, CA Dominican Order (Western Province), St. Albert's Priory.
Parnassus, Msgr. George J. '53 (LA) West Hollywood, CA St. Victor Church.
Parnell, Dennis R. *s.j.* '93 (SJ) [B] Santa Clara, CA Santa Clara University.
Parnisari, Eugene '68 (JOL) Retired.
Paron, William J. '69 (STP) New Prague, MN St. Wenceslaus Church.
Parr, John L. '78 (LC) Special Assignment; [I] La Crosse, WI Holy Cross (Seminary) Diocesan Center.
Parr, Norman B. '50 (OM) [36] Omaha, NE SS. Peter and Paul Church.
Parr, Raymond A. '39 (MIL) Retired.
Parra, Jesus A. '93 (LA) [36] Los Angeles, CA Sacred Heart Church.
Parrales, Napoleon J. '57 (SD) On Duty Outside the Diocese.
Parrini, Warren '53 (RVC) Retired.
Parrish, Bryan K. '88 (BO) Wellesley, MA St. Paul Church.
Parrish, Francis J. *s.j.* '42 (LA) [R] Los Angeles, CA Columbiere House.
Parrotta, Arthur J. '50 (MAR) Retired.
Parry, Charles '81 (WDC) Hyattsville, MD St. Mark Church; Pastoral Center Special Ministries.
Parsch, David '80 (SAG) Alma, MI St. Mary Church.
Parsieniczyk, Stanley '68 (BO) [4] Salem, MA St. John the Baptist Church.
Parson, Donald J. '90 (BAL) Ellicott City, MD Resurrection Church.
Parsons, Harold J. '29 (NY) Retired.
Parsons, Harry E. '56 (PIT) New Brighton, PA Holy Family Church.
Parsons, LaSalle *o.f.m.cap.* '57 (FgM) Capuchin Foreign Missions.
Parsons, Neil J. *c.p.* '37 (SAC) [G] Citrus Heights, CA Christ the King Retreat.
Parsons, Samuel R. *o.p.* '57 (SFR) [N] San Francisco, CA St. Dominic Priory.
Partee, Chrysostom *o.f.m.* '50 (SFE) Jemez Pueblo, NM San Diego Indian Missions Church.
Partensky, Leonard J. '42 (DET) Retired.
Parthie, Ralph R. *o.f.m.* '75 (NO) [P] New Orleans, LA Franciscan Fraternity.
Partida, Rafael A. '86 (SB) Indio, CA Our Lady of Perpetual Help Church.
Partika, Richard '51 (DUL) [12] Duluth, MN St. Margaret Mary Church.
Partridge, Bede *o.s.b.* '58 (P) [L] St. Benedict, OR Mt. Angel Abbey.
Partridge, Donald F. '90 (NY) [165] Bronx, NY St. Mary Star of the Sea Church.
Partridge, Francis C. '60 (GAY) Boyne City, MI St. Matthew Church; Boyne Falls, MI St. Augustine Church.
Partusch, Frank A. '72 (OM) [2] Omaha, NE St. Adalbert Church; [33] Omaha, NE Our Lady of Lourdes Church.
Parvensky, Msgr. Andrew D. '50 (PBR) Monessen, PA Assumption of the Blessed Virgin Church.
Parzymies, Joseph K. '77 (HRT) [6] Meriden, CT St. Stanislaus Church.
Pasadilla, Nicolas '72 (GAL) [13] Houston, TX St. Benedict the Abbot Church.
Pascale, Anthony '58 (HON) Retired.
Pascatore, Terence *o.f.m.conv.* '62 (R) Burlington, NC Blessed Sacrament Church.
Pascazi, Louis F. '80 (PIT) Sewickley, PA St. James Church.
Paschak, Patrick *o.s.b.m.* '47 (STF) New York, NY St. George Church.
Pasche, Fred *o.f.m.conv.* '64 (FTW) Angola, IN St. Anthony Church.
Pasciak, Marcel J. '74 (CHI) [197] Chicago, IL St. Symphorosa and Seven Sons Church.
Pasciuto, Joseph D. '91 (BRK) [98] Brooklyn, NY Our Lady Help of Christians Church.
Pascoe, Louis B. *s.j.* '64 (NY) [DD] New York, NY Jesuit Community at Fordham University.
Pascual, Antonio S. '60 (RVC) East Rockaway, NY St. Raymond's Church.
Pascual, Elias '51 (ARE) Ciales, PR Holy Rosary Church.
Pascual, Lope '82 (MET) [B] New Brunswick, NJ Shoreless Lake School; [H] New Village, NJ Society of Jesus Christ the Priest; [H] Raritan, NJ Clairvaux House.
Pascual, Manuel '46 (FRS) Retired.
Pascucci, Philip *s.d.b.* '51 (NY) [DD] New Rochelle, NY Salesian Provincial House.
Pasek, Timothy *o.f.m.conv.* '75 (BRK) [146] Queens, NY St. Adalbert Church.
Pash, Joseph '48 (SPK) Retired.
Pashak, Lawrence M. '63 (SAG) Freeland, MI St. Agnes Church.
Pashby, John J. '60 (BO) Society of St. James the Apostle.
Pashby, John J. '60 (FgM) Society of St. James the Apostle.
Pashley, Msgr. Wilfred J. '63 (PH) [143] Philadelphia, PA St. Rose of Lima Church.
Pasiecznik, Marcel M. *o.f.m.* '37 (PIT) [O] Ben Avon, PA St. Anthony Friary and Mission House.
Pasieczny, Roman '80 (DET) [4] St. Clair Shores, MI St. Joan of Arc Church.
Pasiewala, Jan *s.a.c.* '76 (BUF) [23] Buffalo, NY St. Florian Church.
Pasik, Mark A. '76 (SY) [4] Endicott, NY St. Casimir Church.
Paska, Walter '47 (PHU) Millville, NJ St. Nicholas Church.
Paskert, Leonard *o.f.m.* '36 (STL) [T] Dittmer, MO Il Ritiro-The Little Retreat.
Paskey, Robert V. *s.j.* '66 (BO) [W] Boston, MA The Society of Jesus of New England-Provincial Offices.
Paskey, Robert V. *s.j.* '66 (PRT) Bingham, ME St. Peter's Church.
Paskowicz, Marian '54 (ALN) Retired.
Pasley, Robert C. '82 (CAM) Collingswood, NJ St. John's Church; [A] Cherry Hill, NJ Camden Catholic High School.
Pasqualetto, Vicente *s.t.* '70 (SJN) [4] Canovanas, PR Santa Maria Madre de Dios Church.
Pasquinelli, Msgr. Frederick A. '52 (STU) [8] Steubenville, OH St. Pius X Church; Retired.
Passalacqua, Robert '83 (SJ) Retired.
Passalacqua, Robert '84 (SJ) Campbell, CA St. Lucy Church.
Passamonte, Philip B. '67 (RVC) Absent on Leave.
Passarella, Msgr. Anthony F. '42 (BRK) [11] Brooklyn, NY St. Anthony of Padua-St. Alphonsus Church; Retired.
Passarelli, Msgr. Robert S. '52 (BAL) Hagerstown, MD St. Mary Church; Retired.
Passauer, Gregory P. '86 (E) Grampian, PA St. Bonaventure Church.
Passaure, Gregory P. '86 (E) Curwensville, PA St. Timothy Church.
Passenant, Francis J. '79 (BRK) [210] Queens, NY Our Lady of Fatima Church; Released from Diocesan Assignment.
Passenant, Frank '79 (NY) City, NY Correctional Institution for Men; City, NY West Facility.
Passeri, Richard *o.f.m.* '47 (BO) [42] Boston, MA St. Leonard of Port Maurice Church.
Passero, Ernest *s.j.* '70 (BUR) Derby Line, VT St. Edward Church.
Passero, Ernest F. *s.j.* '70 (BO) [W] Boston, MA The Society of Jesus of New England-Provincial Offices.
Pastick, Joseph A. (CHI) Retired.
Pastirik, Joachim *o.s.b.* '69 (CLV) [E] Cleveland, OH Benedictine High School; [P] Cleveland, OH Benedictine Order of Cleveland.
Pastizzo, Michael H. *s.j.* '70 (BUF) [O] Buffalo, NY Canisius Jesuit Community.
Pastor, Eduardo '50 (MIA) [27] Miami, FL St. Michael the Archangel Church.
Pastore, Peter J. (CAM) Retired.
Pastorius, Vance *o.f.m.cap.* '60 (BAL) Cumberland, MD SS. Peter and Paul Church; [M] Cumberland, MD SS. Peter and Paul Friary.
Pastro, Vincent '78 (SEA) [1] Tacoma, WA St. Ann Church; [5] Tacoma, WA St. John of the Woods Church; [15] Tacoma, WA Sacred Heart Church.
Pastucci, Anthony '80 (VEN) Bradenton, FL SS. Peter and Paul the Apostles Church.
Paszko, John M. '74 (MIA) [3] Hialeah, FL St. Benedict Church.
Patala, William S. '56 (STU) Retired.
Patalano, Anthony M. *o.p.* '86 (LA) [59] Los Angeles, CA St. Dominic Church.
Patat, St. John E. '42 (CHR) Retired.
Patchala, Hrudaya Raj *m.s.f.s.* '93 (ATL) Norcross, GA Saint Patrick's Church.
Patella, Michael *o.s.b.* '90 (SCL) [I] Collegeville, MN St.

John's Abbey, of the Order of St. Benedict.
Patenaude, Andre *m.s.* '69 (FR) [J] Attleboro, MA La Salette Provincial House.
Patenaude, Gilbert A. '46 (PRT) Retired.
Patenaude, Laurent '43 (PRT) [I] Waterville, ME Mt. St. Joseph Priest Retirement Home.
Patenaude, Laurent O. '43 (PRT) Retired.
Pater, Aurel '90 (ROM) Chicago, IL Ss. Peter and Paul Mission Church; East Chicago, IN St. Nicholas Church.
Pater, Daniel R. '79 (CIN) On Duty Outside the Archdiocese.
Pater, Giles H. '58 (CIN) [46] Cincinnati, OH St. John Fisher Church.
Pater, Thomas '42 (WDC) [C] Washington, DC Catholic University of America, The.
Pater, Thomas G. '42 (CIN) Retired.
Paterno, Salvatore D. '64 (BRK) Released from Diocesan Assignment.
Paternoster, Alejandro '94 (LFT) [1] Lafayette, IN St. Mary Cathedral.
Paterson, Robert '58 (NEW) Scotch Plains, NJ Immaculate Heart of Mary Church.
Pates, Msgr. Richard E. '68 (STP) [12] Minneapolis, MN Our Lady of Peace Church.
Patete, Michael A. '62 (NEW) [5] Bayonne, NJ St. Vincent de Paul Church.
Pathe, Eugene W. '56 (PT) [11] Pensacola, FL St. Mary Church.
Pathilchirayil, Mathew *m.afr.* '87 (SP) [2] St. Petersburg, FL Blessed Trinity Church.
Pathiyamoola, Paul '70 (SFS) Eden, SD Sacred Heart Church.
Patik, Anthony *s.v.d.* '42 (FgM) Society of the Divine Word Foreign Missions.
Patil, Gabriel M. *c.r.s.p.* '72 (ALN) [K] Bethlehem, PA The Barnabite Fathers Barnabite Spiritual Center.
Patillo, Bennie J. '67 (BEA) Port Neches, TX St. Elizabeth Church.
Patin, Lawrence *c.ss.r.* '63 (FgM) Redemptorist Foreign Missions.
Patin, Paul *s.j.* '73 (NO) [8] New Orleans, LA Holy Name of Jesus Church.
Patino, Ruben M. *c.s.p.* '79 (LA) Goleta, CA St. Mark University Parish; [CC] Los Angeles, CA Archdiocesan Office for Campus Ministry.
Patnode, Msgr. Michael '72 (CR) Bemidji, MN St. Philip's Church; [F] Bemidji, MN Holy Spirit Newman Center.
Patnode, Ronald J. '61 (YAK) Wenatchee, WA St. Joseph's Church.
Patout, Rivers A. '67 (GAL) [4] Houston, TX St. Alphonsus Church.
Patragnoni, Ettore '42 (CLV) Retired.
Patras, Adam *o.s.b.* '94 (OM) [K] Schuyler, NE Benedictine Mission House.
Patricius, J. M. (NEW) Bayonne, NJ Bayonne Hospital.
Patricius, J. M. '57 (NEW) [8] Bayonne, NJ St. Michael's Church.
Patrick, Ernest '46 (PT) [2] Pensacola, FL Little Flower Church.
Patrick, Ernest E. '46 (PT) Retired.
Patrick, John E. '67 (MAR) [5] Marquette, MI St. Michael Church.
Patrick, Mary *s.c.m.c.* (NOR) [B] Uncasville, CT St. Bernard High School.
Patrick, Richard Martin *o.p.* '65 (GAL) [J] Houston, TX St. Joseph Hospital; [Q] Houston, TX Dominican Fathers and Brothers, St. Mark Priory, Inc.
Patrick, William '57 (ORG) [F] Fullerton, CA St. Jude Medical Center.
Patrick, William J. '58 (CLV) Released from Diocesan Assignment.
Patriquin, Garry D. '84 (PIT) Absent on Sick Leave.
Patrizi, Vincent '52 (CC) Retired.
Patrizi, Vincent M. '52 (CC) [10] Corpus Christi, TX Our Lady Star of the Sea Church.
Patrizio, Anthony *m.ss.cc.* '66 (CAM) [M] Linwood, NJ Villa Pieta.
Patron, Charles '62 (SB) Temecula, CA St. Catherine Church.
Patron, Juan '73 (SJN) [5] Toa Baja, PR San Pedro Apostol Church.
Patrylak, T. Frank '62 (PHU) [2] Philadelphia, PA Protection of Blessed Virgin Mary Church; Clifton Heights, PA SS. Peter and Paul Church.
Patte, Steven '69 (CHI) [A] Mundelein, IL University of St. Mary of the Lake-Mundelein Seminary.
Pattee, Daniel *t.o.r* '87 (STU) [A] Steubenville, OH Franciscan University of Steubenville; [F] Steubenville, OH Holy Spirit Monastery.
Patten, Patrick A. *c.s.sp.* '78 (FgM) Holy Ghost Foreign Missions.
Patterson, Alfred *o.s.b.* '90 (E) St. Marys, PA St. Mary Church.
Patterson, Bernard J. *o.s.b.* '44 (BIR) [E] Cullman, AL St. Bernard Abbey.
Patterson, Bernardin *o.s.b.* '53 (IND) [J] Indianapolis, IN St. Maur Priory.
Patterson, Bernardin J. *o.s.b.* '53 (NEW) [N] Newark, NJ Newark Abbey.
Patterson, Bruce A. '86 (ORG) Costa Mesa, CA St. John the Baptist Church.
Patterson, Msgr. Charles '51 (JC) [D] Jefferson City, MO St. Joseph's Home.
Patterson, David L. '68 (ATL) On Duty Outside the Archdiocese.
Patterson, Frank '67 (SAV) [1] Columbus, GA Holy Family Church.
Patterson, James *c.ss.r.* '54 (STL) [P] Liguori, MO Liguori Mission House/Redemptorists.
Patterson, Randall P. '70 (ALB) [9] Troy, NY Our Lady of Victory Church.
Patterson, Richard '89 (LA) [1] Long Beach, CA St. Anthony Church.
Patterson, Robert A. '71 (STP) Osseo, MN St. Vincent de Paul Church; Minneapolis, MN Abbott-Northwestern Hospital; Minneapolis, MN Minneapolis Children's Medical Center.
Patterson, Ronald '64 (LIN) [L] Lincoln, NE Calvary Cemetery and Mausoleum Association.
Patterson, Ronald E. '64 (LIN) [5] Lincoln, NE Sacred Heart Church.
Patterson, Terrence R. '66 (OG) Retired.
Patterson, William C. '51 (COL) Retired.
Patti, Angelo J. '82 (ALT) Everett, PA St. John the Evangelist Church.
Pattison, Msgr. Francis '58 (SD) [35] San Diego, CA St. Rita Church.
Patton, James J. '65 (CLV) Perry, OH St. Cyprian Church.
Patton, Mel *o.s.b.* '56 (IND) [J] St. Meinrad, IN St. Meinrad Archabbey.
Patton, Mel *o.s.b.* '56 (SFS) [G] Yankton, SD Sacred Heart Monastery.
Patton, Patrick G. '78 (HEL) Military Chaplains.
Pattussi, Roque R. *c.s.* '92 (BO) [5] Framingham, MA St. Tarcisius Church.
Paturzo, Louis S. '73 (HRT) [2] Bristol, CT St. Anthony's Church; [4] Bristol, CT St. Joseph Church.
Paul, Alexis *c.p.* '63 (PH) [AA] Philadelphia, PA St. Michael's Passionist Residence.
Paul, Bededict '78 (NY) [182] Bronx, NY SS. Philip and James Church.
Paul, David *s.m.* '70 (STL) [P] St. Louis, MO Provincialate of the Society of Mary, Province of St. Louis.
Paul, Dennis '93 (JOL) [18] Joliet, IL St. Paul the Apostle Church.
Paul, Gerald *m.s.c.* '60 (RCK) [9] Aurora, IL Sacred Heart Church; [H] Aurora, IL Missionaries of the Sacred Heart Community.
Paul, Gregory *c.p.* '58 (BAL) [50] Baltimore, MD St. Joseph Passionist Monastery Parish; [M] Baltimore, MD St. Joseph's Passionist Community.
Paul, John *s.j.* '92 (ELP) [21] El Paso, TX Sacred Heart Church.
Paul, John J. *m.s.c.* '58 (ALN) [K] Reading, PA Missionaries of the Sacred Heart.
Paul, John M. *s.j.* '80 (STP) [B] St. Paul, MN Jesuit Novitiate.
Paul, John P. '72 (PH) Newtown, PA St. Andrew Church; [D] Norristown, PA Kennedy-Kenrick Catholic High School; [D] Warminster, PA Archbishop Wood Catholic High School.
Paul, Leonard D. *c.s.c.* (FgM) Holy Cross Foreign Missions.
Paul, Raphael '87 (SFD) Brighton, IL St. Alphonsus Church; Medora, IL St. John the Evangelist Church.
Paul, Raymond F. '55 (HRT) [2] Ansonia, CT Holy Rosary Church; Retired.
Paul, Raymond L. '62 (Y) [3] Massillon, OH St. Joseph's Church.
Paul, Stanislaus (LA) Glendale, CA Holy Family Church.
Paul, Thomas '77 (JOL) Downers Grove, IL St. Mary Church.
Paul, Msgr. William J. '63 (PH) Lower Makefield, PA St. John the Evangelist Church.
Paulantonio, Joseph '45 (MAR) Retired.
Paulicek, Louis '71 (AUS) Rogers, TX St. Matthew Church; Temple, TX St. Luke's Church.
Paulin, George A. '70 (BUR) North Troy, VT St. Vincent de Paul Church.
Paulish, Jeffrey '88 (PHU) Nanticoke, PA St. Nicholas Church.
Paulish, W. Jeffrey '88 (SCR) [L] Wilkes-Barre, PA Little Flower Manor of the Diocese of Scranton.
Paulissen, Richard E. *m.m.* '63 (GAL) [Q] Houston, TX Maryknoll Fathers and Brothers; [U] Houston, TX Catholic Charismatic Center.
Paulissen, Richard E. *m.m.* '63 (NY) [DD] Maryknoll, NY Maryknoll Fathers and Brothers.
Paulits, Walter J. '72 (BAL) Retired.
Paulli, Kenneth *o.f.m.* (ALB) [B] Loudonville, NY Siena College.
Paulraj, Jude '68 (NY) [2] New Rochelle, NY St. Gabriel Church.
Paulsen, Harold P. '78 (TYL) Palestine, TX Sacred Heart Church.
Paulsen, Timothy *o.m.i.* (BWN) [1] Mission, TX Our Lady of Guadalupe Church.
Paulshock, Emil '65 (PSC) Leave of Absence.
Paulson, Brian G. *s.j.* (CHI) [N] Chicago, IL Chicago Province of the Society of Jesus-Provincial Office.
Paulson, Brian G. *s.j.* '92 (CHI) [C] Chicago, IL Jesuit Community at Loyola University of Chicago.
Paulson, Jerome E. '76 (NU) Montevideo, MN St. Joseph Church.
Paulson, Warren (LAN) Chelsea, MI Cassidy Lake Tech. School.
Paulus, Donard *o.f.m.* '48 (GAY) Indian River, MI Cross in the Woods Catholic Shrine Church.
Pauly, William *s.j.* '79 (RC) Pine Ridge, SD Holy Rosary Church; [B] Pine Ridge, SD Jesuit Community of Holy Rosary Mission.
Paur, Roman *o.s.b.* '66 (SCL) [B] Collegeville, MN St. John's University; [I] Collegeville, MN St. John's Abbey, of the Order of St. Benedict.
Paurazas, Peter P. '55 (CHI) [182] Chicago, IL St. Rene Goupil Church.
Pausche, Frederick F. '57 (CLV) Concord Twp., OH St. Gabriel Church.
Pauselli, Francis L. '75 (SCR) South Williamsport, PA St. Lawrence's Church.
Pautler, Mark '74 (SPK) [14] Spokane, WA St. Joseph Church.
Pavela, Wayne S. '79 (OM) Humphrey, NE St. Francis Church.
Pavelis, Harold '51 (SCL) Retired.
Pavignano, Steven J. *o.f.m.* '78 (ATL) [L] Atlanta, GA Campus Ministry.
Pavis, Raymond A. '45 (CHI) [1] Mt. Prospect, IL St. Cecilia Church; Retired.
Pavis, Msgr. Victor C. '42 (NY) Retired; [E] New York, NY Cardinal Hayes High School.
Pavlak, Robert P. *s.s.j.* '55 (NO) [P] New Orleans, LA Josephite Fathers and Brothers.
Pavlicek, Edward A., Jr. '83 (SAT) [29] San Antonio, TX St. Benedict Church.
Pavlick, Clement *c.p.* '42 (PIT) [O] Pittsburgh, PA St. Paul of the Cross Monastery.
Pavlick, Michael *s.m.* '53 (BO) [W] Boston, MA Marist Fathers Lourdes Residence; [BB] Boston, MA Chapel of Our Lady of Lourdes.
Pavlick, Raymond (NY) Castle Point, NY Veterans Administration Medical Center.
Pavlick, Raymond A. '71 (PAT) On Duty Outside the Diocese.
Pavlik, Albert *o.carm.* '61 (ALB) [5] Troy, NY St. Joseph Church.
Pavlik, David P. '78 (CHI) [A] Mundelein, IL University of St. Mary of the Lake-Mundelein Seminary.
Pavlik, James J. '63 (STL) Sullivan, MO Church of the Holy Martyrs of Japan.
Pavlik, John A. *o.f.m.cap.* '78 (WDC) [B] Washington, DC St. Francis Friary-Capuchin College.
Pavlik, Paul R. *t.o.r.* '59 (FgM) T.O.R. Foreign Missions.
Pavlina, Mark S. '75 (GRY) Dyer, IN St. Joseph Church.
Pavlock, Martin L. '66 (BUF) [7] Cheektowaga, NY Our Lady Help of Christians Church.
Pavlosky, John J. '71 (ALN) Northampton, PA St. Michael Church.
Pavlovsky, Wencil C. *c.s.b.* '91 (GAL) Richmond, TX St. John Fisher Church.
Pavone, Frank A. (NY) [HH] Port Chester, NY Priests for Life.
Pavone, Frank A. '88 (NY) On Duty Outside the Archdiocese.
Pavur, Claude N. *s.j.* (STL) [C] St. Louis, MO Saint Louis University.
Pavur, Claude N. *s.j.* '84 (STL) [P] St. Louis, MO Jesuit Community Corporation at St. Louis University - Jesuit Hall.
Pawelk, Steven P. *glmy.* '89 (JKS) New Albany, MS St. Francis of Assisi Church.
Pawell, Robert '66 (CHI) [N] Chicago, IL The Holy Evangelists Friary.
Pawelski, John '50 (GB) Absent on Leave.
Pawlak, Ed '68 (AMA) Retired.
Pawlak, Edwin F. '68 (ORL) Retired.
Pawlicki, James *s.v.d.* '73 (BLX) [A] Bay St. Louis, MS St. Augustine's; [A] Bay St. Louis, MS St. Augustine's; [E] Bay St. Louis, MS Media Production Center "In A Word".
Pawlicki, Joseph *c.s.c.* '50 (SB) Coachella, CA Our Lady of Soledad Church.
Pawlikowski, John M. *o.s.m.* '67 (CHI) [18] Chicago, IL Assumption of the Blessed Virgin Mary Church; [B] Chicago, IL The Catholic Theological Union at Chicago; [N] Chicago, IL Servite Friars - Eastern Province.
Pawlikowski, Matthew '97 (NEW) Bloomfield, NJ Church of St. Thomas the Apostle.
Pawlos, John D. *s.m.* '59 (CIN) [M] Dayton, OH Marianist Provincialate.
Pawloski, Gregory P. '74 (LIN) Imperial, NE St. Patrick's Church.
Pawlowski, Dariusz (TYL) Henderson, TX St. Jude Church.
Pawlowski, Joseph M. '73 (GRY) [15] Gary, IN St. Mary of the Lake Church.
Pawson, Msgr. Robert J. '66 (BRK) [213] Queens, NY

Our Lady of Lourdes Church.
Pax, Bart *o.f.m.* '68 (CIN) [U] Cincinnati, OH Community Support Charitable Trust.
Pax, Bart *o.f.m.* '68 (NO) [45] New Orleans, LA St. Mary Of The Angels Church.
Pax, Joseph *c.pp.s.* '47 (CIN) [N] Dayton, OH Sisters of the Precious Blood, Salem Heights Convent.
Pax, Maurus *o.f.m.* '50 (GLP) Grants, NM St. Teresa Church.
Pax, Raymond *m.c.c.j.* '65 (FgM) Comboni Foreign Missions.
Pax, Ulric *o.f.m.* '59 (GLP) [2] Gallup, NM St. Francis of Assisi Church.
Paxton, Philip *c.p.* '95 (LA) [R] Pasadena, CA Passionist Community; [X] Sierra Madre, CA Mater Dolorosa Retreat Center.
Payant, Remi J. '38 (STP) Retired.
Payant, Romain *o.c.s.o.* '53 (P) [L] Lafayette, OR The Cistercian (Trappist) Abbey of Our Lady of Guadalupe.
Payea, Gerald *o.carm.* '69 (JOL) [J] Darien, IL Carmelite Provincial Office.
Payea, Gerald *o.carm.* '70 (FgM) Carmelite Foreign Missions.
Payer, Emil S. '71 (GBG) Scottdale, PA St. John the Baptist Church.
Payikat, Zacharias *c.m.i.* '70 (NSH) Lafayette, TN Holy Family Church; Lebanon, TN St. Frances Cabrini Church.
Payne, Charles E. *o.f.m.* (CHI) [D] Chicago, IL Hales Franciscan High School, Inc.
Payne, Gary '85 (OWN) Absent on Leave.
Payne, John *o.s.a.* '89 (WDC) [7] Washington, DC St. Augustine Church.
Payne, John Michael *o.c.d.* '70 (DAL) [K] Dallas, TX Mount Carmel Center.
Payne, John R. *s.j.* '70 (MOB) [B] Mobile, AL Spring Hill College; [K] Mobile, AL Spring Hill College Newman Center.
Payne, John T. *c.s.c.* '46 (AUS) [13] Austin, TX St. Ignatius Martyr Church.
Payne, Joseph *o.p.* '63 (NY) Pleasantville, NY Holy Innocents Church.
Payne, Mark *o.praem.* (GB) [6] De Pere, WI St. Norbert College Parish.
Payne, Mark *o.praem.* '94 (GB) [I] De Pere, WI St. Joseph Priory.
Payne, Mark M. *o.s.b.* '81 (NEW) [N] Newark, NJ Newark Abbey.
Payne, Stephen J. '71 (GAL) Huntsville, TX St. Thomas the Apostle Church.
Payne, Steven *o.c.d.* '82 (WDC) [B] Washington, DC Monastery of Our Lady of Mount Carmel; [V] Washington, DC Institute of Carmelite Studies and ICS Publications.
Payne, Thomas H. '50 (SAV) Retired.
Paynter, Clement *c.p.* '52 (FgM) Mission Procurators.
Payo, Reuben '84 (DEN) Conifer, CO Our Lady of The Pines Church.
Paysse, Wayne C. '87 (NO) [2] Slidell, LA St. Genevieve Church.
Paz, Jose M. '52 (MIA) [27] Miami, FL St. Michael the Archangel Church.
Paz, Lorenzo '97 (SB) [1] San Bernardino, CA Our Lady of the Rosary Cathedral.
Pazmany, Geza *sch.p.* '61 (PH) [G] Devon, PA Devon Preparatory School; [AA] Devon, PA Piarist Fathers (Order of the Pious Schools).
Pazo, John T. '55 (RVC) Retired.
Pe're', Adrian C. '93 (BR) Prairieville, LA St. John the Evangelist Church.
Peace, John '36 (SJ) Retired.
Peacha, Thomas '59 (LA) [14] Los Angeles, CA Holy Trinity Church.
Peacock, Francis '53 (PHX) [1] Phoenix, AZ SS. Simon and Jude Cathedral.
Peacock, Francis A. '53 (PHX) [7] Phoenix, AZ SS. Anthony and Pius X Church.
Peake, Msgr. Daniel A. '49 (NY) Rye, NY Resurrection Church.
Peaker, James '48 (CIN) [42] Cincinnati, OH St. Jerome Church.
Peaker, James N. '48 (CIN) Retired; [S] Cincinnati, OH Archdiocesan Central Council of Cincinnati.
Pearce, Donald *s.j.* '59 (NO) [8] New Orleans, LA Holy Name of Jesus Church.
Pearce, John S. *c.m.* '57 (PH) [AA] Philadelphia, PA Congregation of the Mission.
Pearsall, Ernest P. '37 (BO) Retired.
Pearsall, William '53 (FgM) Society of St. James the Apostle.
Pearsall, William T. '53 (BO) Society of St. James the Apostle.
Pearson, Everett '91 (WDC) [6] Washington, DC Assumption Church.
Pearson, John A. '66 (NU) Cottonwood, MN St. Mary Church; Green Valley, MN St. Clotilde Church.
Pearson, John H. *c.s.c.* '73 (FTW) [B] Notre Dame, IN University of Notre Dame Du Lac; [J] Notre Dame, IN Holy Cross Community, Corby Hall, University of Notre Dame.
Pearson, Msgr. Robert A. '65 (SPK) [9] Spokane, WA St. Augustine Church.
Pearson, Robert L. *o.c.s.o.* '60 (ATL) [I] Conyers, GA The Monastery of the Holy Spirit.
Pease, Joseph M. '61 (HBG) [1] Mount Carmel, PA Divine Redeemer Church.
Pease, Raymond A. *s.j.* '68 (FgM) Provinces.
Peatee, Greg '92 (TOL) [3] Toledo, OH Christ the King Church.
Pecaric, Alfred F. '82 (BGP) [14] Stamford, CT Sacred Heart Church.
Pecchie, Paul '95 (SP) [4] St. Petersburg, FL Holy Family Church.
Pecci, Ronald *o.f.m.* '83 (BUF) [59] Buffalo, NY SS. Rita & Patrick Church.
Pecevich, Conrad S. '77 (WOR) [Q] Worcester, MA Campus Ministry.
Pecharich, Michael '73 (ORG) Rancho Santa Margarita, CA San Francisco Solano Church.
Pecharroman, Ovidio '87 (ARL) Falls Church, VA St. Philip Church.
Pecht, Gerard J. *c.ss.r.* '50 (WCH) [G] Wichita, KS Redemptorist Community; [I] Wichita, KS Spiritual Life Center.
Pechulis, John B. *c.p.* '47 (CHI) [N] Chicago, IL Immaculate Conception Monastery.
Pecinovsky, Albert '65 (KCK) Absent on Sick Leave.
Peck, David A. (RCK) St. Charles, IL St. Patrick Church.
Peck, David A. '94 (RCK) [B] Elgin, IL St. Edward Central Catholic High School.
Peck, John '89 (RIC) [6] Virginia Beach, VA St. Gregory the Great Church.
Peck, Msgr. Leon J. '42 (PH) Warrington, PA St. Joseph Church; Retired.
Pecklers, Keith F. *s.j.* '91 (NY) [DD] New York, NY Jesuit Provincial's Office.
Peckman, R. William '97 (JC) [2] Jefferson City, MO St. Peter Church; [B] Jefferson City, MO Helias High School.
Pecoraro, James A. '53 (KC) Retired.
Pecovnik, Karel '44 (SCL) Retired.
Pedata, Msgr. Armand A. '58 (TR) Marlton, NJ St. Joan of Arc Church.
Peddicord, Richard A. *o.p.* '86 (STL) [B] St. Louis, MO Aquinas Institute of Theology; [P] St. Louis, MO St. Dominic Priory.
Pedelesky, Nestor '67 (STN) Absent on Sick Leave.
Pedi, Mario *o.s.b.* '57 (RCK) [1] Aurora, IL Annunciation of the Blessed Virgin Mary Church; [H] Aurora, IL Marmion Abbey-St. Augustine's Abbey.
Pedigo, Jon '91 (SJ) [1] San Jose, CA Cathedral Basilica of St. Joseph Church.
Pedley, Christopher *s.j.* '86 (BO) [W] Cambridge, MA Faber House.
Pednekar, Joseph C. *m.s.f.s.* '62 (CLV) [61] Cleveland, OH St. Patrick Church.
Pedone, F. Stephen '78 (WOR) [23] Worcester, MA St. George Church.
Pedrano, Stephanos *o.s.b.* '91 (SD) [H] Oceanside, CA Prince of Peace Abbey, Benet Hill.
Pedraz, Juan Lopez *s.j.* '46 (SJN) [22] San Juan, PR San Ignacio de Loyola Church.
Pedretti, Raymond J. '56 (LC) Arcadia, WI Our Lady of Perpetual Help Church; Arcadia, WI St. Stanislaus Church.
Pedretti, Robert F. '64 (LC) Amherst, WI St. James Church; Fancher, WI St. Mary of Mount Carmel Church.
Pedrizetti, Raymond *o.s.b.* '58 (SCL) [I] Collegeville, MN St. John's Abbey, of the Order of St. Benedict.
Pedrosa, Agustin *s.m.* '59 (NEW) West New York, NJ St. Joseph of the Palisades Church.
Pedroso, Rafael '64 (MIA) Hialeah Gardens, FL Santa Barbara Church.
Pedrotti, Francis L. *s.j.* '70 (KC) [B] Kansas City, MO Rockhurst College; [J] Kansas City, MO Rockhurst College - Jesuit Community.
Pedroza, Salvador '81 (SAT) Dilley, TX St. Joseph's Church.
Pedulla, John G. '93 (NY) [222] Staten Island, NY St. Patrick Church.
Peduti, Douglas F. *s.j.* '96 (WDC) [20] Washington, DC Holy Trinity Church.
Pedzich, Henry J. '72 (SY) Cazenovia, NY St. James Church.
Pedzik, Vitalis B. '61 (RVC) Lindenhurst, NY Our Lady of Perpetual Help Church.
Peet, Msgr. Arthur V. '41 (STL) Retired.
Peeters, Ambrose J. *o.praem.* '53 (GB) [I] De Pere, WI St. Norbert Abbey.
Peeters, John N. *c.s.v.* '83 (JOL) Bourbonnais, IL Maternity of the Blessed Virgin Mary Church.
Peeters, R. Thomas '42 (GB) Retired.
Peffley, Francis J. '90 (ARL) Woodbridge, VA Our Lady of Angels Church.
Pegnan, William *o.f.m.cap.* '67 (SJ) [16] San Jose, CA St. Martin of Tours Church.
Pegoraro, Germano *s.c.* '52 (LAN) [L] Grass Lake, MI The Pious Union of St. Joseph.
Peguero, Lawrence (GAL) [N] Houston, TX Pope John XXIII Priest Residence.
Peguero, Msgr. Lawrence '47 (GAL) Retired.
Pehl, Jeffery '95 (SAT) [57] San Antonio, TX St. Matthew's Church.
Pehler, Gerald *o.f.m.cap.* '88 (DET) [P] Washington, MI Capuchin Retreat.
Pehrsson, Alfred *c.m.* '58 (GR) [J] Spring Lake, MI St. Lazare Retreat House.
Pehrsson, Alfred R. *c.m.* '58 (PH) [AA] Philadelphia, PA Congregation of the Mission.
Pei, Maurus *o.c.s.o.* '82 (SAC) [A] Vina, CA Abbey of New Clairvaux, Trappist Seminary; [G] Vina, CA Abbey of New Clairvaux, Trappist.
Peifer, Claude *o.s.b.* '50 (HRT) [N] Bethlehem, CT Abbey of Regina Laudis.
Peifer, Claude J. *o.s.b.* '52 (PEO) [A] Peru, IL St. Bede Abbey and Academy.
Peiffer, James E. '67 (TOL) Oak Harbor, OH St. Boniface Church.
Peil, William '49 (FTW) Retired.
Peil, William L. '49 (GRY) Retired.
Peinado, Louis A. *s.j.* '60 (LA) [F] Los Angeles, CA Loyola High School.
Peiris, Richard (OAK) Fremont, CA Washington Hospital.
Peiris, Richard '68 (NY) [Z] New York, NY Mary Manning Walsh Home.
Peixotto, Joseph S. *c.s.c.* '61 (FgM) Holy Cross Foreign Missions.
Pejza, John P. *o.s.a.* '61 (LA) [F] Ojai, CA Villanova Preparatory School.
Pekar, Atanasius B. *o.s.b.m.* '46 (RVC) [N] Glen Cove, NY St. Josaphatis Monastery, Novitiate and Retreat House.
Pekar, Athanasius B. *o.s.b.m.* '46 (STF) [B] Glen Cove, NY Basilian Fathers Novitiate of the Order of St. Basil the Great.
Pekar, Florian *c.p.* '40 (HRT) [M] West Hartford, CT Holy Family Monastery/Retreat.
Pekar, Msgr. Joseph W. '57 (BGP) [8] Bridgeport, CT SS. Cyril and Methodius Church.
Pekarske, Daniel T. *s.d.s.* '90 (MIL) [55] Milwaukee, WI Mother of Good Counsel Church.
Peklo, Edward *s.v.d.* '69 (CHI) [B] Techny, IL Divine Word Residence; [N] Techny, IL Society of the Divine Word, Provincial Headquarter-Chicago Prov.
Pekola, David J. '86 (MET) Hackettstown, NJ Assumption of the Blessed Virgin Mary Church.
Pelaez, Oscar A. '94 (STO) Turlock, CA Sacred Heart Church.
Pelant, William G. '94 (STP) Burnsville, MN Mary, Mother of the Church.
Pelc, Timothy R. '74 (DET) Grosse Pointe Park, MI St. Ambrose Church.
Pelczynski, Walter *m.i.c.* '42 (SPR) [I] Stockbridge, MA Congregation of Marians.
Pelensky, Ihor '43 (STF) Retired.
Pelep, Etwel '95 (CI) Sokehs, FM St. Peter's Church.
Peles, David S. '84 (ALT) [23] Johnstown, PA St. Benedict's Church.
Pelezar, Edward A. '62 (PH) [154] Philadelphia, PA St. Veronica Church.
Pelkey, Richard '84 (SY) On Duty Outside the Diocese.
Pelkington, Leo *o.p.* '68 (NY) Valhalla, NY Holy Name of Jesus Church.
Pelky, Theron E. '85 (GAY) Absent on Leave.
Pellegrini, Frederick J. *s.j.* '84 (RVC) Oceanside, NY St. Anthony Church.
Pellegrino, Francis B. '51 (SLC) [9] West Valley City, UT SS. Peter and Paul Church; Salt Lake City, UT Decker Lake Youth Center.
Pellegrino, Gerard *s.d.b.* '74 (BO) [Y] Ipswich, MA Sacred Heart Retreat Center.
Pellegrino, Joseph A. *v.f.* '77 (SP) Tarpon Springs, FL St. Ignatius Church; [F] Tarpon Springs, FL St. Ignatius Early Childhood Center.
Pelleteri, Manuel J. *c.m.* '53 (CHI) [C] Chicago, IL Vincentian Community at DePaul University.
Pelletier, Adrien O. *s.m.* '56 (BUR) White River Junction, VT St. Anthony Church; White River Junction, VT Veterans Administration Hospital.
Pelletier, Clement L. *s.j.* '62 (BO) [E] Boston, MA Boston College High School & Jesuit Community.
Pelletier, Edgar A. '47 (WOR) Retired.
Pelletier, Emile "Bud" '94 (PHX) Cottonwood, AZ Immaculate Conception Church.
Pelletier, Eugene J. '53 (MAN) Retired.
Pelletier, George C. '79 (PRT) Jay, ME St. Rose of Lima Church.
Pelletier, Gerard *s.m.* (HRT) Hartford, CT Hartford Hospital.
Pelletier, Gerard G. *s.m.* '51 (BRK) [45] Brooklyn, NY St. Francis of Assisi-St. Blaise Church.
Pelletier, Leonard E. '69 (BO) [7] Lowell, MA St. Louis de France Church.
Pelletier, Norman *s.s.s.* '69 (CLV) [P] Cleveland, OH Congregation of the Blessed Sacrament Provincial House.
Pelletier, Rosaire *o.p.* '50 (PRT) [I] Lewiston, ME SS. Peter and Paul Priory.
Pelletier, Walter R. *s.j.* '60 (BGP) [D] Fairfield, CT

Fairfield College Preparatory School; [O] Fairfield, CT The Fairfield Jesuit Community-Fairfield University.
Pellettieri, Joseph F. *c.ss.r.* (BR) [H] Baton Rouge, LA Redemptorist Vice Province.
Pellettieri, Joseph F. *c.ss.r.* '65 (ALX) Deville, LA St. John the Baptist Church.
Pellicane, Albert *c.p.* '56 (BRK) [U] Jamaica, NY Immaculate Conception Monastery.
Pellicane, Albert *c.p.* '56 (NY) [Z] Bronx, NY Franciscan Health System of New York, Inc.; [DD] New York, NY Pope Paul VI Residence.
Pellicore, Msgr. Edward M. (CHI) [12] Chicago, IL St. Angela Church.
Pellicore, Msgr. Edward M. '36 (CHI) Retired.
Pelligrin, Joseph (BRK) [139] Brooklyn, NY St. Therese of Lisieux Church.
Pellini, Robert R. *m.m.* '59 (FgM) Maryknoll Foreign Missions.
Pellissier, Francois '81 (JKS) Starkville, MS St. Joseph Church.
Peloso, Alex *c.s.* '39 (CHI) [122] Chicago, IL Santa Maria Addolorata Church.
Peloso, John '96 (MIA) Coral Springs, FL St. Andrew Church.
Pelous, Donald P. '77 (LAF) Breaux Bridge, LA St. Bernard Church.
Pelton, Robert S. *c.s.c.* '49 (FTW) [B] Notre Dame, IN University of Notre Dame Du Lac; [J] South Bend, IN Congregation of Holy Cross Indiana Province Provincial House.
Pelton, Robert S. *c.s.c.* '73 (FTW) [J] Notre Dame, IN Holy Cross Community, Corby Hall, University of Notre Dame.
Pelton, Thomas '66 (CHI) [133] Chicago, IL Maternity of the Blessed Virgin Mary Church.
Peltz, Carl F. '74 (KAL) St. Joseph, MI St. Joseph Church.
Peltzer, H. Michael '80 (WCH) Eureka, KS Sacred Heart Church; Hamilton, KS St. John Church; Madison, KS St. Teresa of Avila Church.
Peluse, Dominic A. *s.c.j.* '74 (GAL) [21] Houston, TX Christ the Redeemer Church.
Peluso, Francis E. *o.a.r.* '61 (NEW) [N] West Orange, NJ Augustinian Recollects.
Peluso, Francis E. *o.a.r.* '61 (NY) [154] Bronx, NY St. John's Church; [FF] Bronx, NY St. Joseph's Center; [HH] Bronx, NY St. Joseph's Center.
Peluso, Michael J. '58 (NY) Absent on Leave.
Pemberton, Joseph '77 (FWT) [3] Fort Worth, TX Holy Family Church.
Pena, Gustavo Aldolfo Tenorio '81 (SCR) [20] Scranton, PA Nativity of Our Lord Church.
Pena, Joseph '67 (SAT) Uvalde, TX Sacred Heart Church.
Pena, Raymundo J. '57 (BWN) [C] Brownsville, TX Catholic Charities; [D] San Juan, TX San Juan Nursing Home.
Pena, Richard '92 (SAT) [3] San Antonio, TX Christ the King Church; [T] San Antonio, TX Archdiocesan Union of Holy Name Societies.
Pena, Roberto *o.m.i.* '55 (SAT) Del Rio, TX St. Joseph's Church.
Pena, Vicente M. *o.p.* '36 (SAT) [B] San Antonio, TX Dominican Priory of Juan Macias.
Pena, Vincente M. *o.p.* '36 (SAT) [26] San Antonio, TX St. Ann Church.
Pena-Martinez, Gilberto '68 (SAC) Chico, CA St. John the Baptist Church.
Penafiel, Fausto '83 (PHX) [1] Glendale, AZ Our Lady of Perpetual Help Church.
Penalba, Vincente *c.m.f.* '69 (CGS) [8] Barrio Rio Canas, PR Inmaculado Corazon de Maria Church.
Penaloza, Jorge '60 (LA) Pico Rivera, CA St. Francis Xavier Church.
Penchi, Edward J. '56 (LC) Foreign Missions.
Penczynski, Richard M. '75 (GRY) [3] Hammond, IN St. Casimir Church.
Pendergast, Msgr. John F. '54 (OG) Massena, NY Sacred Heart Church.
Pendergast, Richard J. *s.j.* '63 (NY) [DD] New York, NY Murray-Weigel Hall.
Penderghest, William T. *ss.cc.* '67 (FR) [J] Fairhaven, MA Sacred Hearts Provincial House.
Pendergraft, Michael '81 (STA) Chiefland, FL St. John the Evangelist Church.
Pendleton, Arthur J. *o.s.b.* '64 (CHL) [J] Belmont, NC Belmont Abbey.
Pendolphi, Richard J. '76 (COL) Logan, OH St. John Church.
Pendzick, John S. '97 (ALN) [8] Reading, PA St. Margaret Church; Shillington, PA St. John Baptist de la Salle Church.
Penebsky, John P. (SFR) [U] San Francisco, CA Catholics for Truth & Justice.
Penebsky, John P. '65 (SFR) Redwood City, CA St. Pius Church.
Peng, John B. (CHI) Retired.
Penkala, Msgr. Edmund S. '45 (SCR) Retired; [N] Dunmore, PA Villa St. Joseph.
Penko, Francis G. '60 (SD) [3] El Cajon, CA St. Kieran Church.
Penn, Michael A. '54 (SCR) [3] Scranton, PA St. Anthony of Padua Church.
Penn, William '97 (VEN) Port Charlotte, FL St. Charles Borromeo Church.
Penna, Anthony *c.s.s.* '75 (BO) [W] Waltham, MA Stigmatine House.
Penna, Msgr. Joseph P. '67 (NY) Pearl River, NY St. Aedan Church.
Pennett, Frederick J. '71 (MAN) [J] Dover, NH St. Ann Home; [N] Durham, NH Campus Ministries; [N] Durham, NH Campus Ministries; [N] Durham, NH St. Thomas More Catholic Student Center at the University of New Hampshire.
Pennington, John *s.j.* (CHI) Chicago, IL Cook County Hospital.
Pennington, John F. *s.j.* '70 (CHI) [N] Chicago, IL Chicago Province of the Society of Jesus-Provincial Office.
Pennington, John R., III '79 (WDC) Burtonsville, MD Resurrection Parish.
Pennington, M. Basil *o.c.s.o.* '57 (WOR) [N] Spencer, MA St. Joseph's Abbey; [R] Spencer, MA Cistercian Publications, Inc.
Pennington, Matthew '88 (MRY) Scotts Valley, CA San Agustin Church.
Pennisi, Celestine *o.f.m.* '52 (NY) [DD] New York, NY Franciscan Province of the Immaculate Conception.
Pennisi, Ignatius F. *s.j.* '43 (BO) [E] Boston, MA Boston College High School & Jesuit Community.
Pennock, Michael '95 (JOL) Bolingbrook, IL St. Francis of Assisi Church.
Penonzek, Edward M. *o.s.m.* '58 (ORG) [D] Anaheim, CA Servite High School; Servite High School Development Fund; [H] Anaheim, CA Servite Fathers and Brothers.
Penta, Leo J. '78 (BRK) Released from Diocesan Assignment.
Pentecost, Denver B. '69 (NO) [1] Marrero, LA Immaculate Conception Church; Marrero, LA West Jefferson General Hospital; Marrero, LA Wynhoven Health Care Center.
Pentello, Richard J. '79 (Y) Garrettsville, OH St. Ambrose Church.
Pentis, William F. *c.o.* '66 (CHR) Rock Hill, SC St. Anne's Church; [D] Rock Hill, SC Oratory of St. Philip Neri, Congregation of the Oratory of Pontifical Rite.
Pentony, Liam '55 (JKS) Brookhaven, MS St. Francis Church; [G] Brookhaven, MS Lincoln Junior College Newman Center.
Penunuri, Umberto (SAC) Fairfield, CA Holy Spirit Church.
Penzes, Lawrence M. '78 (RVC) Lynbrook, NY Our Lady of Peace Church.
Penzimas, Joseph A. '40 (NU) Retired.
Peoples, J. Eugene '66 (HEL) [B] Helena, MT Carroll College.
Pepe, Msgr. Joseph A. '70 (PH) On Duty Outside the Archdiocese.
Pepe, Msgr. Joseph A. *j.c.d.* '70 (SFE) [1] Albuquerque, NM Annunciation Church.
Pepe, Mario P. '56 (HRT) Marlborough, CT St. John Fisher Church.
Pepe, Robert F. '50 (WCH) Retired.
Pepel, Clement '82 (MET) On Duty Outside the Diocese.
Pepel, Klemens (PHX) [4] Phoenix, AZ Immaculate Heart of Mary Church.
Pepel, Klemens '44 (PHX) Special Assignment.
Pepeu, Luis *o.f.m.cap.* '82 (WDC) [B] Washington, DC St. Francis Friary-Capuchin College.
Pepin, Darryl J. '78 (MAR) Iron Mountain, MI Immaculate Conception of the Blessed Virgin Mary Church.
Pepin, Normand A. *s.j.* '63 (FBK) [A] Fairbanks, AK Monroe Catholic Junior-Senior High School; [C] Fairbanks, AK Jesuit Residence; [E] Fairbanks, AK House of Prayer; (FgM) Provinces.
Pepin, Paul H. *s.m.* '39 (BO) [W] Boston, MA Marist Fathers Lourdes Residence; [BB] Boston, MA Chapel of Our Lady of Lourdes.
Pepka, Edward *a.a.* '77 (BO) [W] Brighton, MA Assumptionist Center.
Pepka, Edward '77 (SAC) Colusa, CA Our Lady of Lourdes Church.
Peplansky, Joseph *c.m.f.* '60 (SPC) [4] Springfield, MO Sacred Heart Church; [E] Springfield, MO Claretians Missionaries' Residence-Villa Claret.
Peplinski, Msgr. Raymond J. '42 (B) Retired.
Pepowski, Bert '61 (GRY) [J] Cedar Lake, IN Our Lady of Lourdes Friary.
Peppard, Patrick F. *s.j.* '73 (CLV) [E] Cuyahoga Falls, OH Walsh Jesuit High School.
Pepper, David J. '58 (DUB) Retired.
Pera, Sylvano *o.f.m.* '52 (SFD) Belleview, IL St. Agnes Church; Hardin, IL St. Norbert Church; Kampsville, IL St. Anselm Church; Michael, IL St. Michael Church.
Perales, Jorge '78 (MIA) On Duty Outside the Archdiocese.
Perata, Stephen F. '58 (SJ) [25] San Jose, CA St. Victor Church.
Perdue, John *m.ss.cc.* '90 (CAM) Linwood, NJ Our Lady of Sorrows Church.
Perea, Michael *o.praem.* '90 (LA) Wilmington, CA SS. Peter and Paul's Church.
Perea, Michael U. *o.praem.* '90 (ORG) [H] Silverado, CA Norbertine Fathers of Orange Inc.
Pereda, James F. (RVC) Graduate Studies.
Pereda, James F. '81 (RVC) Seaford, NY St. William, the Abbot Church.
Pereira, Albert F. '40 (RIC) Retired.
Pereira, Anthony '82 (SJ) Los Gatos, CA St. Mary of the Immaculate Conception Church.
Pereira, Cyril F. '54 (ALB) [10] Troy, NY St. Patrick Church; Special Assignment.
Pereira, Luciano J. '54 (FR) Retired.
Pereira, Manuel *m.s.* '95 (FR) [J] Attleboro, MA La Salette Shrine.
Pereira, Robert J. (STO) On Special or Other Diocesan Assignment.
Perera, Denzil M. '58 (NO) [19] New Orleans, LA Our Lady Of The Rosary Church; Retired.
Perera, Egerton *s.j.* '73 (CHI) [C] Chicago, IL Jesuit Community at Loyola University of Chicago.
Perera, Emile (FTW) Plymouth, IN St. Michael Church.
Perera, Leo Fredrick '79 (NY) Nyack, NY St. Ann Church.
Perera, Paul (ELP) Retired.
Perera, Raja '82 (FRS) [5] Fresno, CA Sacred Heart Church.
Perera, Romuald *o.s.b.* '71 (FRS) Avenal, CA California State Prison, Kings Co.
Peres, Mark R. *c.pp.s.* '85 (LFT) Rensselaer, IN St. Augustine Church.
Peretta, Andrew J. (PAT) Unassigned.
Peretti, Peter L. '73 (GBG) Leisenring, PA St. Vincent de Paul Church.
Perez, Anthony R. *s.s.* '77 (BAL) [A] Baltimore, MD St. Mary's Seminary and University.
Perez, Antonio '77 (AGN) On Duty Outside the Archdiocese.
Perez, Armando '62 (MIA) [2] Fort Lauderdale, FL Our Lady Queen of Martyrs Church.
Perez, Arturo (CHI) [J] Chicago, IL Holy Cross Hospital.
Perez, Arturo J. '72 (CHI) [62] Chicago, IL St. Francis of Assisi Church.
Perez, Aurelio '86 (MIL) Greendale, WI St. Alphonsus Church.
Perez, Carlos (NY) [31] New York, NY St. Elizabeth Church.
Perez, Carlos '60 (MIA) [2] Hialeah, FL San Lazaro Church.
Perez, Carlos '92 (B) Nampa, ID Our Lady of Guadalupe Chapel Church.
Perez, Enrique A. '71 (ARE) [6] Arecibo, PR Our Lady of Hope Church.
Perez, Francisco Javier '73 (LA) South Gate, CA St. Helen Church.
Perez, Gabino *o.a.r.* '51 (LA) [82] Los Angeles, CA San Miguel Church.
Perez, Gregory '86 (AUS) [17] Austin, TX St. Louis Church.
Perez, Gustavo '64 (SFR) [44] San Francisco, CA St. Peter Church.
Perez, Hector R.G. '81 (PT) [14] Pensacola, FL St. Stephen Church.
Perez, Henry '73 (ORG) Inactive Leave.
Perez, Isidro '81 (MIA) [4] Hialeah, FL St. Cecilia Church.
Perez, Javier H. '93 (TUC) [20] Tucson, AZ Saints Peter and Paul Church.
Perez, Jesse L. '74 (PBL) [3] Pueblo, CO Holy Family Church.
Perez, Jose '65 (LA) [93] Los Angeles, CA St. Thomas the Apostle Church.
Perez, Jose Caracoza *m.n.m.* '82 (SAT) Del Rio, TX Our Lady of Guadalupe Church.
Perez, Joseph '69 (GAL) On Duty Outside the Diocese.
Perez, Leo *o.m.i.* '84 (SAT) [M] San Antonio, TX St. Anthony Catholic High School House.
Perez, Leon '60 (ARE) Barceloneta, PR Our Lady of Victory Church.
Perez, Leopoldo *o.m.i.* '84 (SAT) [C] San Antonio, TX Oblate School of Theology.
Perez, Luis A. '95 (MIA) [2] Pompano Beach, FL San Isidro Church.
Perez, Maximiliano '49 (MIA) Retired.
Perez, Nelson J. '89 (PH) [66] Philadelphia, PA St. Hugh of Cluny Church.
Perez, Pedro Luis '52 (MIA) [2] Hialeah, FL San Lazaro Church.
Perez, Rafael '74 (GLP) On Duty Outside of Diocese.
Perez, Rafael *o.s.b.* '79 (CGS) Humacao, PR Maria Reina de la Paz Church.
Perez, Ramon '75 (CHI) Franklin Park, IL St. Gertrude Church.
Perez, Raul '86 (SAV) Cordele, GA St. Theresa Church.
Perez, Raymond *o.praem.* '88 (LA) San Pedro, CA Mary, Star of the Sea Church.

Perez, Raymond L. *o.praem.* '88 (ORG) [H] Silverado, CA Norbertine Fathers of Orange Inc.
Perez, Restituto *o.p.* '60 (MIA) [18] Miami, FL St. Dominic Church.
Perez, Robert (CHI) [J] Blue Island, IL St. Francis Hospital and Health Center.
Perez, Robert R. '86 (CHI) [178] Chicago, IL Providence of God Church.
Perez, Sacramento *o.de.m.* '72 (SB) Ontario, CA Our Lady of Guadalupe Church.
Perez, Salvador *o.s.a.* '61 (FWT) Clifton, TX Holy Angels Church; Morgan, TX Our Lady of Guadalupe Church.
Perez, Santos *o.f.m.* '85 (ELP) [15] El Paso, TX Our Lady of Guadalupe Church.
Perez, Victor *o.p.* '67 (SJN) [16] Bayamon, PR Nuestra Senora del Perpetuo Socorro Church.
Perez, Victor '75 (P) [P] Portland, OR University of Portland.
Perez, Victoriano '75 (P) Independence, OR St. Patrick Church.
Perez, Viktor *o.f.m.conv.* '89 (RNO) [1] Reno, NV St. Thomas Aquinas Cathedral.
Perez, William A. *o.s.a.* '62 (TLS) [B] Tulsa, OK Cascia Hall Preparatory School.
Perez Munoz, Jaime *o.f.m.cap.* '85 (SJN) [D] Rio Piedras, PR Centro Capuchino.
Perez Zapata, Urian J. '97 (MGZ) [A] San German, PR Hospital of the Immaculate Conception.
Perez-Castaneda, Daniel G. '96 (LA) Hawthorne, CA St. Joseph Church.
Perez-Diaz, German '97 (KAL) Paw Paw, MI St. Mary Church.
Perez-Lerena, Francisco *s.j.* '58 (MIA) [D] Miami, FL Belen Jesuit Preparatory School; [H] Miami, FL Villa Javier.
Perez-Pupo, Joaquin '76 (MIA) [8] Miami, FL Mother of Christ Church.
Perez-Recio, Jesus *o.a.r.* (LSC) La Mesa, NM San Jose Church; [B] Mesilla, NM Augustinian Recollects Fathers.
Perfetto, Anthony *s.m.* '66 (CIN) [L] Centerville, OH The Franciscan at St. Leonard.
Perfetto, Richard A. '66 (DET) Canton, MI Resurrection Church.
Pergl, James F. *c.s.sp.* '44 (PIT) [Q] Bethel Park, PA Holy Ghost Animation Center.
Perham, Arnold E. *c.s.v.* '56 (CHI) [D] Arlington Heights, IL St. Viator High School.
Peri, Paul '71 (P) Wilsonville, OR St. Cyril Church.
Perianayagam, Clement (FAR) Rugby, ND St. Therese, Little Flower Church.
Pericone, Nicholas '96 (NO) [1] Marrero, LA Immaculate Conception Church.
Peridans, Dominic *f.j.* (CC) [G] Laredo, TX Holy Spirit Retreat and Conference Center.
Peridans, Dominique F. *f.j.* '96 (CC) [H] Laredo, TX St. John's Priory, (F.J.).
Peries, Angelito *c.ss.r.* '74 (SR) Windsor, CA Our Lady of Guadalupe Church.
Peries, Ignatius *c.sp.* '79 (NY) [DD] New York, NY Apostolic Society of the Crusade of the Holy Spirit.
Perillo, Christopher G. '97 (BO) Walpole, MA Blessed Sacrament Church.
Perin, Glen W. '53 (CIN) Sidney, OH Holy Angels Church.
Perin, Isidro *m.s.* '67 (STL) [P] St. Louis, MO La Salette Missionaries.
Perini, Msgr. Armando J. '56 (MET) Edison, NJ St. Helena Church.
Perino, John M. '79 (NO) Ama, LA St. Mark Church.
Perjak, Edmond J. '67 (BEL) Retired.
Perkin, David R. '78 (NSH) [1] Nashville, TN Cathedral of the Incarnation.
Perkins, Bernard *o.c.d.* '82 (TUC) [16] Tucson, AZ St. Margaret's Church; [F] Tucson, AZ Discalced Carmelite Fathers of St. Margaret's.
Perkins, Charles J. '78 (HT) Amelia, LA St. Andrew Church.
Perkins, Dennis M. '95 (NOR) New London, CT St. Mary, Star of the Sea Church.
Perkins, Joseph F. '68 (WDC) [7] Silver Spring, MD St. John the Evangelist Church.
Perkins, Msgr. Robert M. '71 (RIC) Colonial Heights, VA St. Ann Church.
Perkins, Robert S. '72 (CHI) Other Assignments.
Perkins, Russell H. '58 (WIL) Retired.
Perkinton, John J. '85 (LIN) [2] Lincoln, NE Blessed Sacrament Church; [H] Lincoln, NE Villa Marie School and Home for the Educable Mentally Handicapped.
Perkl, James M. '84 (STP) Jordan, MN St. John the Baptist Church.
Perko, F. Michael *s.j.* '75 (CHI) [N] Evanston, IL Canisius House.
Perkovic, Anton '46 (NO) Retired.
Perkovich, Frank '54 (DUL) Biwabik, MN St. John's Church; Gilbert, MN St. Joseph's Church.
Perkowski, Joseph '46 (DET) Retired.
Perl, Richard D. *s.j.* '78 (FgM) Provinces.
Perlinski, Daniel A. '57 (TLS) Retired; [E] Tulsa, OK St. John Medical Center, Inc.
Perlite, John J. *s.j.* '49 (PHX) [B] Phoenix, AZ Brophy College Preparatory.
Perlite, Paul A. '46 (SFR) Fairfax, CA St. Rita Church; Retired.
Perluzzi, James *o.f.m.* '65 (FgM) Franciscan Foreign Missions.
Perluzzi, James *o.f.m.* '65 (STL) [P] St. Louis, MO Franciscan Friary of St. Anthony of Padua.
Pernia, Msgr. John R. '58 (SFR) Daly City, CA Our Lady of Perpetual Help Church.
Perno, Gerald '85 (BO) Winthrop, MA St. John the Evangelist Church.
Perozich, Richard L. '92 (SD) [16] San Diego, CA Our Lady of the Sacred Heart Church.
Perozzi, Julian '82 (FgM) Xaverian Foreign Missions.
Perozzi, Julian *s.x.* '82 (PAT) [M] Wayne, NJ Xaverian Missionary Fathers.
Perpete, Louis M. *m.s.* '45 (HRT) [M] Hartford, CT Missionaries of LaSalette Provincial Secretary.
Perreault, Aurele R. '53 (HRT) Retired.
Perreault, Joseph A. '75 (CAM) Brigantine, NJ St. Thomas Church; [A] Absecon, NJ Holy Spirit High School.
Perreault, Leonard '54 (SPR) Stockbridge, MA St. Joseph's Church; West Stockbridge, MA St. Patrick's Church.
Perreault, Louis G. *c.s.sp.* (SB) [E] Hemet, CA Holy Ghost Fathers.
Perrello, Blaise '77 (RIC) Richmond, VA MCV Hospital.
Perret, Gary *m.s.f.* '76 (SAT) [M] San Antonio, TX MSF Center & Provincialate.
Perretta, Andrew T. '75 (PAT) [1] Clifton, NJ Sacred Heart Church.
Perricone, Charles A. '74 (PAT) Sussex, NJ St. Monica Church.
Perricone, John A. '75 (NY) [2] New York, NY St. Agnes Church.
Perricone, John A. '76 (NEW) On Duty Outside the Archdiocese.
Perriello, Robert A. '76 (WH) Clarksburg, WV St. James Church.
Perrier, Martin '88 (RNO) Leave of Absence.
Perrier, Monroe G. *c.ss.r.* '58 (BR) [H] Baton Rouge, LA Redemptorist Vice Province.
Perrier, Thomas *o.s.b.* '80 (NO) [R] St. Benedict, LA Abbey Christian Life Center.
Perrier, Thomas E. *o.s.b.* '80 (NO) [A] St. Benedict, LA St. Joseph's Seminary College; [P] St. Benedict, LA St. Joseph Abbey.
Perrin, Thomas *s.d.s.* (BIR) [3] Huntsville, AL St. Joseph's Church.
Perrins, Samuel T. '86 (SCR) [1] Plymouth, PA Nativity of the Blessed Virgin Mary Church.
Perron, Gary *a.a.* '66 (BO) [W] Brighton, MA Assumptionist Center.
Perron, Richard J. '46 (BO) Retired.
Perron, Robert P. '81 (PRO) [1] Central Falls, RI The Holy Spirit Catholic Community Church.
Perrone, Eduard '78 (DET) [10] Detroit, MI Assumption Grotto Church.
Perry, Ashley J. *s.s.j.* '75 (NO) [6] New Orleans, LA Epiphany Church.
Perry, Carmen J. '77 (SCR) Stroudsburg, PA St. Luke's Church.
Perry, Daniel *ss.cc.* '49 (FR) [J] Fairhaven, MA Sacred Hearts Provincial House.
Perry, David T. '72 (PRO) [6] Cumberland, RI St. Patrick Church.
Perry, Francis J. '50 (DUB) Ionia, IA St. Boniface's Church; North Washington, IA Immaculate Conception Church.
Perry, Frederick J. '53 (LFT) Montpelier, IN St. Margaret of Scotland Church.
Perry, John A. '63 (FR) East Freetown, MA St. John Neumann Church.
Perry, John J. '83 (FR) [16] Fall River, MA St. Joseph's Church.
Perry, Joseph N. '75 (MIL) [63] Milwaukee, WI All Saints Church; [B] Hales Corners, WI Sacred Heart School of Theology; [Y] Milwaukee, WI St. Thomas More Lawyers Society.
Perry, Killian J. *t.o.r.* '74 (STP) [20] Minneapolis, MN St. Bridget Church.
Perry, Michael *o.f.m.* '84 (CHI) [47] Chicago, IL Corpus Christi Church.
Perry, Michael *o.f.m.* '84 (FgM) Franciscan Foreign Missions.
Perry, Michael *o.de.m.* '85 (CLV) [67] Cleveland, OH St. Rocco Church.
Perry, Michael *o.de.m.* '86 (CLV) Cleveland, OH Cuyahoga County Jail.
Perry, Michael A. '71 (BRK) [246] Queens, NY St. Thomas More-St. Edmund Church.
Perry, Michael V. *o.f.m.* '45 (PAT) [M] Butler, NJ St. Anthony Friary.
Perry, Paul '67 (SFR) Mill Valley, CA Our Lady of Mt. Carmel Church.
Perry, Paul E. '78 (TOL) Plymouth, OH St. Joseph Church; Willard, OH St. Francis Xavier Church.
Perry, Richard D. *s.j.* '70 (SEA) [M] Seattle, WA Jesuit Community.
Perry, Robert U. *o.p.* '59 (BR) Hammond, LA Holy Ghost Church.
Perry, Ronald V. *s.j.* '76 (BGP) [D] Fairfield, CT Fairfield College Preparatory School; [O] Fairfield, CT The Fairfield Jesuit Community-Fairfield University.
Perryman, John E. '45 (CIN) Retired.
Persac, Louis A. '47 (NO) Gretna, LA St. Anthony Church; Retired.
Persha, Gerald *m.m.* '78 (CHI) [B] Chicago, IL The Catholic Theological Union at Chicago.
Persha, Gerald J. *m.m.* '70 (FgM) Maryknoll Foreign Missions.
Pershe, Joseph N. *s.j.* '66 (NY) Manhattan, NY Bird S. Coler Memorial Hospital and Home.
Pershe, Joseph N. *s.j.* '66 (STP) [N] Minneapolis, MN La Storta Jesuit Community.
Persia, William *c.s.c.* '62 (FgM) Holy Cross Foreign Missions.
Persich, Nicholas E. *c.m.* '46 (STL) [P] Perryville, MO Congregation of The Mission.
Persich, Roy A. *c.m.* '60 (LA) [R] Los Angeles, CA Amat House; [X] Santa Barbara, CA St. Mary's Seminary Center.
Persico, Lawrence T. '77 (GBG) New Alexandria, PA St. James Church; [I] Greensburg, PA Benedictine Sisters (Eichstatt, Bavaria).
Persico, Pasquale *p.i.m.e.* '44 (PMB) [G] Tequesta, FL P.I.M.E. Missionaries.
Persinger, Patrick (FRS) Bakersfield, CA Kern Medical Center, Bakersfield Memorial Hospital & San Joaquin Community Hospital.
Persinger, Patrick '87 (FRS) [5] Bakersfield, CA St. Joseph Church.
Perumalil, Augustine *s.j.* '89 (CHI) [C] Chicago, IL Jesuit Community at Loyola University of Chicago.
Perumpuzha, Jose (WIN) [6] Rochester, MN St. John's Church.
Perunilam, Thomas V. '64 (MET) Milltown, NJ Our Lady of Lourdes Church.
Peruti, John J. '55 (HRT) [12] Hartford, CT St. Luke Church.
Perzan, Stephan B. '73 (GLP) Lumberton, NM St. Francis of Assisi Church.
Pesanka, Nicholas A. '75 (PIT) Bethel Park, PA St. Germaine Church.
Pesarchick, Robert A. '91 (PH) Graduate Studies.
Pesaresi, Constantine V. '35 (BRK) [221] Queens, NY Our Lady of Sorrows Church; Retired.
Pesaresi, Thomas E. *m.m.* '85 (FgM) Maryknoll Foreign Missions.
Pescatello, Joseph A. '89 (PRO) [5] Cranston, RI St. Mary Church.
Pescatore, Terence *o.f.m.conv.* (R) [E] Burlington, NC Conventual Franciscans.
Pesce, John Baptist *c.p.* '51 (HRT) [M] West Hartford, CT Holy Family Monastery/Retreat.
Pesch, Elroy *o.f.m.cap.* '63 (MIL) [B] Mount Calvary, WI St. Lawrence Seminary; [P] Mount Calvary, WI St. Lawrence Friary.
Peschel, Msgr. Anthony R. '35 (FAR) Retired.
Peschel, Roland A. '60 (OM) [8] Sarpy Co., NE St. Bernadette Church.
Pesci, Thomas A. *s.j.* '79 (KC) [D] Kansas City, MO Rockhurst High School; [J] Kansas City, MO Rockhurst College - Jesuit Community.
Pesek, Anthony '65 (SAT) [9] San Antonio, TX Holy Spirit Church.
Pesek, Fred C. '89 (CHI) Streamwood, IL St. John the Evangelist Church.
Pesenti, Paul *o.m.i.* '66 (NEW) [7] Bayonne, NJ Our Lady of the Assumption Church.
Pesola, Joseph G. '97 (IND) [33] Indianapolis, IN St. Pius X Church; [O] Indianapolis, IN International Catholic Deaf Association (Chapter No. 38).
Pestun, Aloysius *s.d.b.* '59 (SFR) [12] San Francisco, CA Corpus Christi Church.
Pesut, Louis J. '55 (RCK) Lee, IL St. James Church.
Peszkowski, Msgr. Zdzislaw '54 (DET) [A] Orchard Lake, MI SS. Cyril and Methodius Seminary.
Petcavage, Leonard *c.s.j.* '81 (CLV) Released from Diocesan Assignment.
Pete, Joseph P. '76 (WIN) Lake Crystal, MN Holy Family Church; [4] Mankato, MN St. Joseph the Worker Church.
Petekiewicz, Robert '91 (RVC) Bellmore, NY St. Barnabas the Apostle Church.
Peter, David J. '66 (BUF) Eden, NY Immaculate Conception Church.
Peter, Martin A. '67 (IND) [33] Indianapolis, IN St. Pius X Church.
Peter, Patrick N. '75 (BEL) Breese, IL St. Dominic Church.
Peter, Paul F. '52 (OM) Retired.
Peter, Valentine J. '59 (OM) Boys Town, NE Immaculate Conception B.V.M. Church; [C] Boys Town, NE Father Flanagan's Boys' Home; [E] Boys Town, NE Father Flanagan's Boys' Home; [I] Boys Town, NE Father Flanagan's Boys' Home.

Peterka, Dale '68 (CIN) [22] Cincinnati, OH St. Clare Church.
Peterka, Sylvester *c.m.* '76 (BAL) [21] Baltimore, MD St. Cecilia Church; [40] Baltimore, MD Immaculate Conception Church.
Peterka, Theodore '47 (SCL) Retired.
Peterlini, Luciano *s.x.* '63 (FgM) Xaverian Foreign Missions.
Peterlini, Luciano *s.x.* '63 (PAT) [M] Wayne, NJ Xaverian Missionary Fathers.
Peterman, Charles '58 (MIA) [16] Miami, FL St. Brendan Church.
Peterman, Thomas J. '57 (WIL) Galena, MD St. Dennis Church.
Petermeier, Virgil *o.s.c.* '77 (FgM) Crosier Foreign Missions.
Peternel, Warren *o.f.m.* '43 (SFD) [K] Sherman, IL Our Lady of Angels Friary.
Peters, Aaron *o.s.b.* '77 (KCK) [H] Atchison, KS St. Benedict's Abbey; [I] Paola, KS Our Lady of Lourdes Convent.
Peters, Daniel E. '89 (RCK) Prophetstown, IL St. Catherine Church; [B] Sterling, IL Newman Central Catholic High School.
Peters, David L. '58 (SFD) Highland, IL St. Paul Church.
Peters, Donald R. '50 (MIL) Retired.
Peters, Eric '80 (SP) [16] Tampa, FL St. Timothy Church.
Peters, Fred *s.d.s.* '56 (GB) Charlesburg, WI St. Charles Borromeo Church; Charlestown, WI St. Martin Church; Chilton, WI St. Augustine Church; Chilton, WI St. Mary Church; Jericho, WI Holy Trinity Church; Kloten, WI St. Elizabeth Church.
Peters, Herman B. '41 (CLV) [16] Cleveland, OH St. Cecilia Church; Shaker Heights, OH St. Dominic Church; Retired.
Peters, Msgr. John '60 (ELP) [26] El Paso, TX St. Luke Church.
Peters, John B. *c.i.c.m.* '53 (FgM) Missionhurst Foreign Missions.
Peters, John C. *v.f.* '74 (VIC) Hallettsville, TX Sacred Heart Church; Hallettsville, TX St. Mary Church.
Peters, Joseph J. *s.j.* '40 (DET) [P] Clarkston, MI Colombiere Center.
Peters, Jude *o.c.d.* '89 (MIL) [P] Holy Hill, WI Discalced Carmelite Monastery.
Peters, Julian *o.s.b.* '88 (IND) [J] St. Meinrad, IN St. Meinrad Archabbey.
Peters, Kenan *c.p.* '60 (BRK) [U] Jamaica, NY Immaculate Conception Monastery.
Peters, Kevin '90 (Y) [6] Canton, OH St. Joan of Arc Church.
Peters, Lyle '96 (DM) [C] West Des Moines, IA Dowling High School.
Peters, Mark M. *o.s.b.* '80 (GBG) Whitney, PA St. Cecilia Church.
Peters, Michael G. '88 (DM) Panama, IA St. Mary of the Assumption Church.
Peters, Noel *o.m.i.* '63 (FRS) Faculties Only.
Peters, Paul R. '62 (DUB) Elkader, IA St. Joseph's Church; Volga, IA Sacred Heart Church.
Peters, Raymond W. '47 (LC) Suspended.
Peters, Msgr. Roy V. '48 (HON) [17] Honolulu, HI Saints Peter and Paul Church.
Peters, Msgr. Roy V. '48 (SAC) Retired and in Senior Ministry.
Peters, Stephen '67 (ELP) [4] El Paso, TX Blessed Sacrament Church.
Petersen, Michael C. '92 (MIL) Burlington, WI Immaculate Conception Church.
Petersen, Vincent *o.f.m.conv.* (LSC) Artesia, NM Our Lady of Grace Church.
Peterson, Bradley *o.carm.* '92 (NEW) Leonia, NJ St. John the Evangelist's Church.
Peterson, Bruce '57 (STP) Belle Creek, MN St. Columbkill Church.
Peterson, C. Vincent '74 (SEA) [1] Tacoma, WA St. Ann Church; [5] Tacoma, WA St. John of the Woods Church; [15] Tacoma, WA Sacred Heart Church.
Peterson, Casimir M. '47 (BAL) Retired; [Q] Pasadena, MD Reparation Society of the Immaculate Heart of Mary.
Peterson, Charles *s.j.* (SPK) Omak, WA St. Joseph Church.
Peterson, Charles *s.j.* '74 (SPK) Omak, WA St. Mary Mission Church.
Peterson, Cyril P. '41 (DM) Retired.
Peterson, Cyril P. '41 (WIN) Retired.
Peterson, Dennis L. '73 (GAL) [76] Houston, TX St. Theresa Church.
Peterson, E. James (FRS) On Special Assignment.
Peterson, Francis '60 (HON) Retired.
Peterson, Francis A. '46 (B) Retired.
Peterson, Frederick *o.s.b.* '95 (RCK) [H] Aurora, IL Marmion Abbey-St. Augustine's Abbey.
Peterson, Frederick *o.s.b.* '95 (ROM) Aurora, IL St. George Church.
Peterson, G. Paul *s.j.* '61 (BGP) [O] Fairfield, CT The Fairfield Jesuit Community-Fairfield University.
Peterson, G. Paul *s.j.* '86 (BGP) [A] Fairfield, CT Fairfield University.
Peterson, Gerald *glmy.* '56 (BIR) Winfield, AL Holy Spirit Church.
Peterson, Harry *s.d.b.* '61 (FgM) Salesians of Don Bosco Foreign Missions.
Peterson, Msgr. James W. '47 (E) [O] Erie, PA Special Ministries.
Peterson, Jay H. '78 (GF) Lewistown, MT St. Leo's Church; [K] Lewistown, MT St. Leo's Catholic Education Trust.
Peterson, John '63 (FgM) Franciscan Foreign Missions.
Peterson, John P. '89 (ARL) Chancellorsville, VA St. Patrick's Church.
Peterson, John S. *o.p.* '62 (PRO) [P] Providence, RI St. Thomas Aquinas Priory at Providence College.
Peterson, Joseph L. '75 (WH) [2] Huntington, WV Our Lady of Fatima Church.
Peterson, Leonard N. (PH) [EE] Philadelphia, PA Newman Apostolate.
Peterson, Leonard N. '67 (PH) Hatfield, PA St. Maria Goretti Church.
Peterson, Louis P. '74 (BEL) Leave of Absence.
Peterson, Martin *c.m.* '47 (BRK) [U] Jamaica, NY Vincentian Residence.
Peterson, Maurice F. '87 (YAK) Cashmere, WA St. Francis Xavier Church; Leavenworth, WA Our Lady of the Snows Church.
Peterson, Paul *s.s.c.* '55 (LA) [Q] Los Angeles, CA Nazareth House; [S] Los Angeles, CA Congregation of the Poor Sisters of Nazareth Motherhouse, U.S.A. and Novitiate.
Peterson, Stephen J. '94 (WIN) Harmony, MN The Nativity of the Blessed Virgin Church.
Peterson, Steven J. '73 (RVC) East Islip, NY St. Mary's Church.
Peterson, Thomas R. *o.p.* '56 (NEW) [A] South Orange, NJ Immaculate Conception Seminary; [A] South Orange, NJ Seton Hall University College Seminary; [B] South Orange, NJ Seton Hall University; [B] South Orange, NJ Seton Hall University.
Peterson, William *c.ss.r.* '67 (CHI) [N] Chicago, IL Redemptorists:.
Peterson, William *c.ss.r.* '67 (DEN) [M] Denver, CO The Redemptorists/Denver Province.
Peterson, William A. *c.ss.r.* '67 (FgM) Redemptorist Foreign Missions.
Peterson, William F. '59 (RCK) Retired.
Petilla, Antonio '61 (SFR) Daly City, CA Our Lady of Perpetual Help Church.
Petinge, Roland *o.f.m.* '61 (BO) [P] Andover, MA Franciscan Center; [W] Andover, MA St. Francis Friary; [Y] Andover, MA Franciscan Center - Retreat House.
Petit, Edmund P. '46 (RCK) Retired.
Petit, Eliades '80 (MIA) [17] Miami, FL St. Catherine of Siena Church.
Petit, Leo *m.s.c.* '51 (RCK) [9] Aurora, IL Sacred Heart Church; [H] Aurora, IL Missionaries of the Sacred Heart Community.
Petit, Roland '38 (ALB) Retired.
Petit-Monsieur, Lamartine (BO) [4] Lynn, MA St. Mary Church.
Petkash, Donald J. *s.j.* '71 (CLV) [E] Cuyahoga Falls, OH Walsh Jesuit High School.
Petko, Paul *f.s.s.p.* '95 (SCR) [M] Elmhurst, PA Priestly Fraternity of St. Peter (F.S.S.P.), North American District Headquarters.
Petko, Paul S. *f.ss.p.* (IND) [26] Indianapolis, IN St. Mark the Evangelist Church; [31] Indianapolis, IN St. Patrick Church.
Petosa, Joseph '55 (SEA) Retired.
Petracca, Anthony '85 (ALT) State College, PA Our Lady of Victory Church.
Petraitis, David *o.s.a.* '79 (FWT) Gainesville, TX St. Mary Church.
Petraitis, Donald *m.i.c.* '64 (CHI) [N] Chicago, IL Congregation of Marian Fathers of the Immaculate Conception.
Petrarulo, John D. '53 (PIT) [4] New Castle, PA St. Vitus Church.
Petras, David M. '67 (PBR) [A] Pittsburgh, PA Byzantine Catholic Seminary of SS. Cyril and Methodius.
Petras, David M. '67 (PRM) On Duty Outside the Diocese.
Petrash, Reginald F. '84 (GAL) Freeport, TX St. Mary: Star of the Sea Church.
Petrasic, Martin J. '43 (OM) Retired.
Petrella, Robert '64 (WDC) Retired.
Petri, Gregg D. '61 (LSC) Alamogordo, NM Immaculate Conception Church.
Petri, John C. '45 (TR) Retired.
Petriano, Thomas '79 (RVC) Absent on Leave; [B] Patchogue, NY St. Joseph's College.
Petrich, John C. '83 (DUL) [4] Duluth, MN Our Lady of Mercy Church; Duluth, MN St. Luke's Hospital; Duluth, MN Miller Dwan Hospital; Saginaw, MN Northeast Regional Correctional Institution.
Petrie, Harry F. '45 (PIT) Wexford, PA St. Alexis Church; Retired.
Petrie, Michael J. '87 (MIL) Hartford, WI St. Kilian Church.
Petrie, Roderic *o.f.m.* '59 (SP) [O] Belleair Bluffs, FL St. James Friary.
Petrie, William *ss.cc.* '69 (FR) [J] Fairhaven, MA Sacred Hearts Provincial House.
Petrik, Clement J. *s.j.* '63 (BAL) [M] Baltimore, MD Jesuit Fathers and Brothers Maryland Provincial Curia.
Petrillo, Joseph A. '77 (NEW) [2] Jersey City, NJ St. Aloysius Church.
Petrillo, Thomas F. '83 (NY) [148] Bronx, NY Holy Rosary Church.
Petrillo, Thomas J. '59 (NEW) Montclair, NJ Our Lady of Mt. Carmel Church.
Petrimouix, Leo *o.f.m.cap.* '66 (MAD) [G] Madison, WI St. Marys Hospital Medical Center.
Petrimoulx, Leo *o.f.m.cap.* '66 (MAD) [M] Madison, WI San Damiano Friary.
Petringa, Gerard '88 (BO) [3] Quincy, MA St. John the Baptist Church.
Petro, John G. '68 (PBR) Beaver, PA Saint Nicholas Chapel Church; [A] Pittsburgh, PA Byzantine Catholic Seminary of SS. Cyril and Methodius.
Petro, William J. '68 (WH) [Q] Huntington, WV Marshall Newman Center.
Petrocelli, John '71 (PRO) [K] North Providence, RI St. Joseph Health Services of Rhode Island - Our Lady of Fatima Hospital.
Petronek, Msgr. Thomas C. (STU) [J] Cambridge, OH Propagation of the Faith Holy Childhood Association.
Petronek, Msgr. Thomas C. '65 (STU) Burkhart, OH St. Joseph's Church; Cambridge, OH St. Benedict Church; Miltonsburg, OH St. John the Baptist Church; Woodsfield, OH St. Sylvester Church; Sardis, OH St. John Bosco Mission Church.
Petronio, Rolando (CHK) Tanapag Village, District 8, MP Santa Remedios Church; San Roque Village, District 9, MP San Roque Parish.
Petroske, Peter '84 (DET) Southgate, MI St. Pius X Church.
Petrosky, Arnold *t.o.r.* '57 (SFS) White Lake, SD St. Peter Church.
Petrosky, Christopher *t.o.r.* (ARL) [J] Winchester, VA Sacred Heart Friary.
Petrovsky, Felix *o.f.m.cap.* '55 (SAL) [D] Victoria, KS St. Fidelis Friary.
Petrovsky, James F. '68 (GBG) Maxwell, PA St. James Church.
Petroy, Dominic J. *o.s.b.* '86 (GBG) Jeannette, PA Sacred Heart Church; Jeannette, PA Jeannette District Memorial Hospital; Jeannette, PA Monsour Medical Center; [F] Jeannette, PA Jeannette District Memorial Hospital.
Petru, Augustine *o.m.i.* '53 (FgM) Oblates Foreign Missions.
Petru, Msgr. Julius A. '37 (VIC) New Taiton, TX St. John Nepomucene Church.
Petru, Msgr. Stanley J. '48 (VIC) Cistern, TX SS. Cyril and Methodius Church; Hostyn, TX Holy Rosary Church.
Petruaskas, John C. *m.i.c.* '43 (WOR) [19] Worcester, MA St. Casimir's Church.
Petrucci, Dominic '82 (SFS) Retired.
Petrucci, Peter J. *m.m.* '49 (FgM) Maryknoll Foreign Missions.
Petrucci, Raymond '73 (BGP) [P] Monroe, CT Provincial House, Immaculate Heart of Mary Province, Sisters of the Holy Family of Nazareth, C.S.F.N.
Petruha, Louis J. *o.f.m.cap.* '65 (PIT) Cabot, PA St. Joseph Church; [O] Herman, PA St. Mary's Friary.
Petrunak, William '59 (Y) [C] Warren, OH John F. Kennedy High School.
Petrusic, Anthony A. '57 (OM) Retired.
Petruska, Christopher '59 (PSC) St. Clair, PA St. Mary's Church.
Petruska, William M. '73 (SCR) Military Chaplains.
Petry, Thomas G. '78 (COL) [14] Columbus, OH St. Dominic Church.
Petsch, Joseph P. '50 (SAT) Comfort, TX Sacred Heart Church.
Petsche, Daniel *o.s.b.* '67 (KC) Stanberry, MO St. Peter's Church; [A] Conception, MO Conception Seminary College; [J] Conception, MO Conception Abbey.
Petta, Gerard A. *m.s.a.* '84 (WH) Moorefield, WV Epiphany of the Lord Church.
Pettei, Thomas G. '86 (BRK) [232] Queens, NY St. Raphael Church.
Petter, Henry V. '76 (DAL) Plano, TX St. Elizabeth Ann Seton Church.
Pettingill, David M. (SFR) [16] San Francisco, CA St. Emydius Church.
Pettingill, David M. '62 (SFR) Special Assignment.
Pettit, Edward G. '51 (PBL) [5] Pueblo, CO Our Lady of the Assumption Church; [14] Pueblo, CO St. Mary Church; [15] Pueblo, CO St. Patrick Church.
Pettit, Joseph H. '56 (HRT) Retired.
Pettit, Joseph J. '55 (GR) [20] Grand Rapids, MI SS. Peter and Paul's Church; Retired.
Pettit, William J. (DET) Retired.
Pettit, William J. '54 (DET) [2] Westland, MI St. Damian Church.

Pettke, Lawrence A. '81 (DET) [2] Southfield, MI St. Bede Church.
Petty, Edward C. '77 (DUB) Dyersville, IA Basilica of St. Francis Xavier Church.
Petuskey, John A. '66 (OKL) Edmond, OK St. John the Baptist Church.
Peverada, Augustine J. *c.s.c.* '45 (FR) [A] North Easton, MA Holy Cross Fathers Religious.
Peyton, Msgr. John T. '61 (BRK) [124] Brooklyn, NY St. Rita's Church.
Peyton, Mark J. '77 (CLV) [66] Cleveland, OH St. Procop Church.
Peyton, Thomas '86 (BRK) Absent on Leave.
Peyton, Thomas A. *m.m.* '58 (FgM) Maryknoll Foreign Missions.
Pezzotti, Mario *s.x.* '59 (FgM) Xaverian Foreign Missions.
Pezzotti, Mario *s.x.* '59 (PAT) [M] Wayne, NJ Xaverian Missionary Fathers.
Pezzullo, Angelo B. '62 (BRK) [204] Queens, NY Nativity of the Blessed Virgin Mary Church.
Pfab, Charles *s.m.* '53 (ATL) [C] Atlanta, GA Marist School.
Pfab, Cletus H. *s.j.* '69 (MIL) [P] Milwaukee, WI Jesuit Provincial Office, Wisconsin Province.
Pfaff, Joseph A. '75 (BRK) [179] Queens, NY Holy Trinity Church.
Pfalzer, Juvenal *o.f.m.* '42 (CIN) [L] Centerville, OH The Franciscan at St. Leonard.
Pfalzer, Miles *o.f.m.* '47 (MAR) Ahmeek, MI Our Lady of Peace Church; Calumet, MI St. Paul the Apostle Church.
Pfannenstial, Celestine E. *s.t.* '41 (JKS) Camden, MS Immaculate Conception Church.
Pfannenstiel, Donald F. '75 (SAL) Herington, KS St. John the Evangelist Church.
Pfannenstiel, John *o.f.m.cap.* '82 (BAL) [6] Baltimore, MD St. Ambrose Church.
Pfau, Bernard A. '65 (FAR) Jamestown, ND The Basilica of St. James Church; [I] Jamestown, ND Jamestown College.
Pfeffer, Charles J. '77 (PH) [3] Philadelphia, PA St. Agatha-St. James Church; [EE] Philadelphia, PA Newman Apostolate.
Pfeffer, Msgr. Edward B. '56 (DM) Winterset, IA St. Joseph Church.
Pfeffer, Thomas '60 (DM) [13] Des Moines, IA Visitation Church.
Pfeifer, Francis *o.m.i.* (FgM) Oblates Foreign Missions.
Pfeifer, Frederick A. '93 (NEW) [15] Newark, NJ St. Francis Xavier Church.
Pfeifer, James *o.m.i.* '51 (BWN) [3] McAllen, TX Sacred Heart Church.
Pfeifer, John M. '65 (BIS) Watford City, ND Epiphany Church.
Pfeiffer, Carl *o.ss.t.* (BAL) [M] Baltimore, MD Holy Trinity Monastery.
Pfeiffer, Charles A. '54 (JC) Indian Creek, MO St. Stephen Church.
Pfeiffer, David L. *m.m.* '66 (FgM) Maryknoll Foreign Missions.
Pfeiffer, James S. '70 (NY) [DD] New York, NY Pope John Paul II Residence.
Pfeiffer, Msgr. Joseph C. '58 (BRK) [175] Queens, NY St. Helen Church.
Pfeiffer, Mark S. '82 (LIN) Benkelman, NE St. Joseph's Church.
Pfeiffer, Robert F. '61 (CLV) Medina, OH Holy Martyrs Church.
Pfender, Terrence *o.carm.* '77 (CHI) [68] Chicago, IL St. Gelasius Church.
Pfiester, Emeric J. *o.s.b.* '48 (GBG) [H] Latrobe, PA Saint Vincent Archabbey.
Pfister, Carl *o.carm.* '49 (NEW) Englewood, NJ St. Cecilia's Church.
Pfister, J. Emile *s.j.* '58 (NO) [11] New Orleans, LA Immaculate Conception Church; [A] New Orleans, LA Notre Dame Seminary Graduate School of Theology.
Pfister, John F. '66 (FTW) [16] Fort Wayne, IN Queen of Angels Church.
Pfister, Neal A. '90 (DEN) Holyoke, CO St. Patrick Church.
Pfisterer, Robert *o.f.m.* '51 (SFR) [5] San Francisco, CA St. Anthony Church.
Pfleger, Michael L. '75 (CHI) [188] Chicago, IL St. Sabina Church.
Pfleger, Phillip C. '79 (TR) Evesham Township, NJ St. Isaac Jogues Church.
Pflomm, Peter '70 (RVC) New Hyde Park, NY Notre Dame Church.
Pflumm, Robert '60 (KCK) [2] Overland Park, KS Holy Cross Church.
Pfnausch, Edward G. '68 (HRT) On Duty Outside the Archdiocese.
Pfnausch, Edward G. '68 (WDC) [C] Washington, DC Catholic University of America, The.
Pfotenhauer, Frederick W. '57 (FTW) [B] Notre Dame, IN University of Notre Dame Du Lac.
Pfundstein, George A. '63 (BRK) [151] Queens, NY St. Ann's Church.
Phalen, James *c.s.c.* (FgM) Holy Cross Foreign Missions.
Phalen, John L. '59 (DET) Lake Orion, MI St. Joseph Church.
Phalen, John P. *c.s.c.* '74 (ALB) [T] Albany, NY The Family Rosary Worldwide Office.
Phalen, John P. *c.s.c.* '74 (LA) [DD] Los Angeles, CA.
Pham, Chau *s.v.d.* '95 (STL) [65] St. Louis, MO St. Thomas of Aquin Church.
Pham, Francis *c.ss.r.* '93 (GAL) [43] Houston, TX St. Justin Martyr Church.
Pham, Hanh Van '93 (CC) [23] Corpus Christi, TX Collegiate Parish of St. Thomas More Church.
Pham, Hung Q. '89 (WCH) [11] Wichita, KS St. Anthony Church.
Pham, Huy P. '97 (ORG) Cypress, CA St. Irenaeus Church.
Pham, John '56 (SPR) [20] Springfield, MA St. Thomas Aquinas Church.
Pham, John H. '56 (SPR) Retired.
Pham, John-Peter '95 (PEO) [4] Champaign, IL St. Matthew Church.
Pham, Joseph '70 (BRK) [216] Queens, NY Our Lady of Mount Carmel Church.
Pham, Joseph Than Xuan '85 (RIC) [17] Richmond, VA Church of the Vietnamese Martyrs.
Pham, Joseph Tuan '88 (ORG) Garden Grove, CA St. Callistus Church.
Pham, Khoi '94 (STO) Modesto, CA Our Lady of Fatima Church.
Pham, Le-Minh '93 (AUS) [17] Austin, TX St. Louis Church.
Pham, Minh J. *c.m.* '91 (STO) Patterson, CA Sacred Heart Church.
Pham, Peter Chinh '71 (SJ) [21] San Jose, CA Our Lady Queen of Martyrs, Vietnamese Mission Church.
Pham, Phong Q. '91 (GR) Howard City, MI Christ the King Church; Lakeview, MI St. Francis de Sales Church.
Pham, Pierre '71 (SPR) On Duty Outside the Diocese.
Pham, Tan *s.o.l.t.* '91 (CC) [H] Robstown, TX Society of Our Lady of the Most Holy Trinity.
Pham, Tin Cosmas '95 (GAL) [4] Spring, TX St. James the Apostle Church.
Pham, Tuan '94 (ORG) Fountain Valley, CA Holy Spirit Church.
Pham, Vincent Hung '97 (ORG) Stanton, CA St. Polycarp Church.
Pham An Su, Bartholomew M. *c.m.c.* (SPC) [E] Carthage, MO Congregation of the Mother Co-Redemptrix, United States Assumption Province.
Pham duc Trin, Joseph '70 (VIC) Palacios, TX St. Anthony's Church.
Pham Minh Van, Bartholomew *c.m.c.* (SPC) [E] Carthage, MO Congregation of the Mother Co-Redemptrix, United States Assumption Province.
Pham Ngoc Bich, James M. *c.m.c.* (SPC) [E] Carthage, MO Congregation of the Mother Co-Redemptrix, United States Assumption Province.
Pham Tien Duc, John Bosco M. *c.m.c.* (SPC) [E] Carthage, MO Congregation of the Mother Co-Redemptrix, United States Assumption Province.
Pham Trung Thuc, John Bosco M. *c.m.c.* (SPC) [E] Carthage, MO Congregation of the Mother Co-Redemptrix, United States Assumption Province.
Pham Van Lan, Augustine '63 (CLV) [13] Cleveland, OH St. Boniface Church.
Pham Van Tue, Joseph '73 (NO) [2] Marrero, LA St. Agnes Le Thi Thanh Church.
Pham-Van-Ninh, James '67 (P) [1] Portland, OR Southeast Asian Vicariate Church.
Phan, Cho Dink Peter '72 (DAL) On Duty Outside the Diocese.
Phan, Dominic '70 (BLX) [8] Biloxi, MS St. Michael Church.
Phan, Joseph Duong '93 (OAK) [1] San Leandro, CA Assumption of the Blessed Virgin Mary Church.
Phan, Minh Cong '97 (NO) Harahan, LA St. Rita Church.
Phan, Nguyen Van *c.ss.r.* '93 (LA) [R] Baldwin Park, CA Vietnamese Redemptorist Mission.
Phan, Peter C. '72 (WDC) [C] Washington, DC Catholic University of America, The.
Phan, Peter Luc '90 (SJ) Cupertino, CA St. Joseph of Cupertino Church.
Phan, Philip '65 (NY) [42] New York, NY Guardian Angel Church.
Phan, Phu T. '92 (AMA) [11] Amarillo, TX St. Thomas the Apostle Church; Canyon, TX St. Ann's Church.
Phan, Vincent '95 (MOB) [11] Mobile, AL Little Flower Church.
Phan Cong Binh, John M. (SPC) [E] Carthage, MO Congregation of the Mother Co-Redemptrix, United States Assumption Province.
Phan Lam, Anthony '62 (OAK) [8] Oakland, CA St. Cyril Church.
Phan Sa, Dominic '88 (PT) Niceville, FL Holy Name of Jesus Church.
Pharr, Msgr. William N. '60 (CHL) [11] Charlotte, NC St. Vincent de Paul Church.
Phelan, Cornelius '59 (LA) Newbury Park, CA St. Julie Billiart Church.
Phelan, Edward '63 (SFR) [15] San Francisco, CA St. Elizabeth Church.
Phelan, Gerald J. *s.j.* '62 (SJ) [2] Santa Clara, CA St. Clare Church.
Phelan, John E. '74 (SY) Forestport, NY St. Patrick Church.
Phelan, Msgr. John F. '41 (BAK) Retired.
Phelan, John J. *s.j.* '58 (FgM) Provinces.
Phelan, John R. '46 (STL) Retired.
Phelan, Julian *o.f.m.cap.* '46 (ROC) [I] Interlaken, NY St. Fidelis Friary.
Phelan, Murray *o.carm.* '47 (JOL) [J] Darien, IL Carmelite Provincial Office.
Phelan, Nicholas '52 (SAC) Grass Valley, CA St. Patrick Church.
Phelan, Thomas '51 (ALB) [S] Troy, NY Rensselaer Polytechnic Institute.
Phelan, Thomas '53 (SEA) Retired.
Phelan, Thomas *m.s.w.* '76 (BEA) Eastgate, TX St. Anne Mission Church.
Phelan, Thomas E. '76 (BEA) Dayton, TX St. Joseph the Worker Church.
Phelan, Walter M. '49 (GI) Grand Island, NE U.S. Veterans' Hospital; Retired.
Phelps, John *c.ss.r.* '66 (CHI) [29] Chicago, IL Blessed Sacrament Church.
Phelps, Lawrence J. *o.s.b.* '63 (NO) [A] St. Benedict, LA St. Joseph's Seminary College; [P] St. Benedict, LA St. Joseph Abbey.
Phelps, Robert *o.f.m.cap.* '66 (AGN) [E] Agana Heights, GU St. Fidelis Friary.
Phelps, Robert *o.f.m.cap.* '66 (FgM) Capuchin Foreign Missions.
Phelps, Robert *o.f.m.cap.* '66 (HON) Ewa Beach, HI Our Lady of Perpetual Help Church.
Phen Van Pham, Joseph '78 (SD) [16] San Diego, CA Our Lady of the Sacred Heart Church.
Phifer, William *c.s.c.* '94 (OAK) [3] Hayward, CA St. Clement Church.
Philbin, John J. '44 (BO) Middleboro, MA Sacred Heart Church; Retired.
Philbin, Patrick *s.m.* '72 (ORG) [H] Orange, CA Marianists; [L] Irvine, CA Campus Ministry-Diocese of Orange; [L] Irvine, CA Campus Ministry-Diocese of Orange.
Philbin, Patrick B. *s.m.* '72 (ORG) [K] Orange, CA House of Prayer for Priests.
Philbin, William '37 (RC) Retired.
Philibert, Paul *o.p.* '63 (FTW) [B] Notre Dame, IN University of Notre Dame Du Lac.
Philion, Richard *o.m.i.* '61 (CC) [3] Kingsville, TX St. Joseph Church.
Philiposki, Richard G. *s.ch.* '79 (P) [34] Portland, OR St. Stanislaus Church.
Philipps, Clyde *m.m.* '78 (FgM) Maryknoll Foreign Missions.
Philipps, John J. '55 (ROC) East Bloomfield, NY St. Bridget Church.
Philips, Joseph H. '68 (SY) Special Assignment.
Philipsen, Martin *o.praem.* '42 (JKS) [E] Jackson, MS Priory of St. Moses the Black.
Philipsen, Todd K. '89 (GI) Crawford, NE St. John the Baptist Church.
Phillip, Alan *c.p.* (LA) [R] Pasadena, CA Passionist Community.
Phillipino, Lucio B. '60 (FR) North Easton, MA Immaculate Conception Church.
Phillippino, Michael L. '90 (NOR) [2] Norwich, CT Sacred Heart Church.
Phillips, A. Patrick *s.j.* '62 (BR) [J] Convent, LA Manresa, House of Retreats.
Phillips, Ambrose K. *t.o.r.* '71 (WDC) [B] Wheaton, MD St. Thomas More Friary, Third Order Regular of St. Francis.
Phillips, Benet C. *o.s.b.* '92 (MAN) [K] Manchester, NH St. Anselm Abbey; [N] Durham, NH Campus Ministries.
Phillips, C. Frank *c.r.* '77 (CHI) [107] Chicago, IL St. John Cantius Church; [N] Chicago, IL Provincial Office of the Congregation of the Resurrection.
Phillips, Christopher G. '83 (SAT) [14] San Antonio, TX Our Lady of the Atonement Catholic Church.
Phillips, Edward J. *m.m.* '74 (FgM) Maryknoll Foreign Missions.
Phillips, Gene D. *s.j.* '65 (CHI) [C] Chicago, IL Jesuit Community at Loyola University of Chicago.
Phillips, George '45 (ALB) Latham, NY St. Ambrose Church; Retired.
Phillips, George *c.ss.r.* '45 (SP) [9] Tampa, FL St. Joseph Church.
Phillips, Msgr. George M. '40 (OG) Retired.
Phillips, Glenn *o.f.m.* '66 (SUP) Bayfield, WI Holy Family Church; Cornucopia, WI St. Ann Church; LaPointe, WI St. Joseph Church; Red Cliff, WI St. Francis Church.
Phillips, Msgr. Hugh J. '35 (BAL) Retired; [B] Emmitsburg, MD Mount Saint Mary's College.
Phillips, John (ALB) [2] Cohoes, NY St. Bernard Church.
Phillips, John M. '87 (STA) [4] Gainesville, FL St.

Augustine Church; [L] Gainesville, FL University of Florida-St. Augustine Parish and Student Center.
Phillips, Joseph H. '68 (SY) [11] Syracuse, NY St. Ann Church; [N] Syracuse, NY Family Life Education.
Phillips, Joseph J. *s.p.* '66 (Y) [I] Canton, OH House of Loreto.
Phillips, Kenneth G. '91 (BIS) Carson, ND St. Theresa the Child Jesus Church; Flasher, ND St. Lawrence Church; Raleigh, ND St. Gertrude Church.
Phillips, Louis *f.a.c.* (NY) [GG] New York, NY University Apostolate.
Phillips, Msgr. Michael J. '60 (BRK) [10] Brooklyn, NY St. Anselm's Church.
Phillips, Michael T. '69 (DAV) [3] Davenport, IA Holy Family Church.
Phillips, Paschal *o.c.s.o.* '57 (L) [L] Trappist, KY Abbey of Our Lady of Gethsemani, of the Order of Cistercians of the Strict Observance.
Phillips, Randall R. '83 (DET) [4] Dearborn Heights, MI St. Linus Church.
Phillips, Randy '97 (SFS) Watertown, SD Immaculate Conception Church.
Phillips, Rene F. *o.f.m.* '56 (NY) [DD] New York, NY Franciscan Friars, Order of Friars Minor, Holy Name Province.
Phillips, Robert *s.j.* (STL) [C] St. Louis, MO Saint Louis University.
Phillips, Robert L. *s.j.* '72 (STL) [P] St. Louis, MO Jesuit Community Corporation at St. Louis University - Jesuit Hall.
Phillips, Steven '87 (ORL) [1] Ocala, FL Blessed Trinity Church.
Phillips, Thomas '42 (NY) Retired.
Phillips, Thomas L. '71 (BAL) [34] Baltimore, MD St. Gabriel Church; [98] Baltimore, MD Woodlawn Catholic Parish.
Phillips, Walter W. '55 (GI) Retired.
Philominsamy, Michaelraj *c.pp.s.* '91 (SR) Philo, CA St. Elizabeth Seton Church.
Phinn, Gilbert S. '53 (BO) [2] Milton, MA St. Elizabeth Church.
Phinn, Paul A. '57 (BO) [34] Boston, MA St. John Chrysostom Church.
Phipps, Charles T. *s.j.* '59 (SJ) [B] Santa Clara, CA Santa Clara University.
Phuc, Anthony *c.ss.r.* '56 (MRY) Pacific Grove, CA St. Angela Church.
Phuc, Hong *c.ss.r.* '48 (LA) [R] Baldwin Park, CA Vietnamese Redemptorist Mission.
Phuc, John '83 (NO) Destrehan, LA St. Charles Borromeo Church.
Phuc, Tran Dinh *c.ss.r.* '56 (LA) [R] Baldwin Park, CA Vietnamese Redemptorist Mission.
Phung, Chi Peter '90 (TLS) Krebs, OK St. Joseph's Church.
Phung, Le Quang *c.ss.r.* '69 (LA) [R] Baldwin Park, CA Vietnamese Redemptorist Mission.
Phung, Vincent '96 (DEN) Littleton, CO St. Mary Church.
Physician, Thomas R. '58 (DET) [2] Clinton Twp., MI St. Louis Church; Clinton Township, MI State Prisons; [T] Detroit, MI St. Mary Magdalen Catholic Community.
Piacentini, David '71 (PRO) [2] North Providence, RI St. Lawrence Church.
Piacitelli, Henry J. *c.m.* '45 (SLC) [1] Salt Lake City, UT Cathedral of the Madeleine.
Piano, Timothy '77 (MIA) Absent on Leave.
Piansay, Victor V. '64 (FRS) Hanford, CA Immaculate Heart Church.
Piasecki, Timothy (RCK) [9] Rockford, IL SS. Peter and Paul Church.
Piatek, Ignatius M. *o.f.m.conv.* '61 (BAL) [C] Baltimore, MD Archbishop Curley High School; [M] Baltimore, MD Immaculate Heart of Mary Friary.
Piatek, Joseph '69 (ORL) [10] Orlando, FL St. Joseph Church.
Piatkowski, Adalbert *o.f.m.conv.* '84 (SPR) [10] Chicopee, MA St. Stanislaus Basilica Church.
Piatkowski, Robert J. '53 (NEW) Springfield, NJ St. James Church.
Piazza, Msgr. Benjamin '49 (NEW) Caldwell, NJ St. Aloysius Church.
Piazza, Msgr. Benjamin A. '49 (NEW) Retired.
Piazza, Salvatore J. '48 (BUF) Ransomville, NY Immaculate Conception Church; Retired.
Picado, Rodrigo '71 (NO) On Duty Outside the Archdiocese.
Picard, Daniel '79 (LAF) Lawtell, LA St. Bridget Church.
Picard, Howard *c.i.c.m.* '56 (ARL) [J] Arlington, VA Missionhurst, C.I.C.M.-Central House and Provincialate.
Picard, Michael C. '66 (PH) Newtown, PA St. Andrew Church.
Picard, Raymond '65 (PRT) Newcastle, ME St. Patrick Church.
Picardi, Aubert Marie *o.f.m.* '62 (BO) [57] Boston, MA Our Lady of Mt. Carmel Church.
Picardi, John '83 (PHX) [6] Scottsdale, AZ St. Maria Goretti Church.
Picardi, John M. '83 (BO) On Duty Outside the Archdiocese.
Picarella, Dale M. '84 (BAL) [24] Baltimore, MD St. Clare Church.
Picariello, Anthony R. *s.j.* '80 (BO) [W] Boston, MA The Society of Jesus of New England-Provincial Offices; [W] Weston, MA Campion Center.
Picazo, Luis *s.f.* '72 (WDC) [B] Silver Spring, MD Holy Family Seminary.
Picciano, Daniel A. '71 (RVC) Seaford, NY St. James Church.
Piccinini, Claudio *c.p.* '72 (BRK) [U] Jamaica, NY Immaculate Conception Monastery.
Piccinino, Corey V. '86 (BGP) [5] Danbury, CT St. Peter's Church; [C] Danbury, CT Immaculate High School.
Piccioli, Giovanna (BRK) [103] Brooklyn, NY Our Lady of Miracles Church.
Piccione, John T. *o.f.m.* '95 (PAT) [5] Paterson, NJ St. Bonaventure Church.
Piccola, Michael J. *v.f.* '78 (SCR) Drums, PA Church of the Good Shepherd.
Piccoli, Gino L. *o.f.m.* '65 (TUC) San Carlos, AZ San Carlos Catholic Mission Church.
Piccolo, Bruno *p.i.m.e.* '65 (DET) [K] Detroit, MI P.I.M.E. College Community; [K] Detroit, MI P.I.M.E. Missionaries of SS. Peter and Paul; [T] Detroit, MI Foster Parents Mission Club.
Piccolomini, Rocco '85 (WOR) [13] Worcester, MA Our Lady of Mt. Carmel and St. Ann Church.
Pichard, Msgr. Lawrence '73 (DAL) [1] Dallas, TX Cathedral-Santuario de Guadalupe Church.
Piche, Donald J. '77 (STP) New Hope, MN St. Joseph Church.
Piche, Lee '84 (STP) [C] St. Paul, MN University of St. Thomas.
Piche, Marc A. '68 (BO) [7] Haverhill, MA Sacred Hearts Church.
Pichette, David '67 (SY) Absent on Leave.
Pichette, Msgr. Fernand L. '58 (MAN) Meredith, NH St. Charles Church.
Pick, Anthony P. '67 (SC) Royal, IA St. Louis Church.
Pick, Edward '60 (VEN) Longboat Key, FL St. Mary Star of the Sea Church.
Pick, Philip E. *s.j.* '50 (FgM) Provinces.
Pick, Philip E. *s.j.* '50 (MIL) [P] Milwaukee, WI Jesuit Provincial Office, Wisconsin Province.
Pickard, William B. '76 (SCR) [22] Scranton, PA St. Paul's Church; [J] Scranton, PA St. Joseph's Center.
Pickard, Msgr. William M. '54 (GAL) [29] Houston, TX St. Francis de Sales Church.
Pickarts, Bernard J. '55 (MAD) Footville, WI St. Augustine Church.
Pickert, Cecil *o.carm.* '58 (BEL) [I] Carbondale, IL The Newman Center.
Pickett, James '61 (COL) On Duty Outside the Diocese.
Pickett, James '61 (OAK) Pittsburg, CA Good Shepherd Church.
Pickett, Robert T. '55 (TLS) Retired.
Pico, Fernando *s.j.* (SJN) [F] Hato Rey, PR Jesuit Community - Casa Claver.
Picornell, Antonio *m.ss.cc.* '42 (SJN) [25] Bayamon, PR Santiago Apostol Church.
Picton, James '75 (SEA) Aberdeen, WA St. Mary's Church; Aberdeen, WA SS. Peter and Paul Church; Hoquiam, WA Our Lady of Good Help Church; Ocean Shores, WA St. Jerome Church; Special Assignment.
Picton, Thomas *c.ss.r.* '71 (SAT) [M] San Antonio, TX Redemptorists of Texas- San Antonio #1.
Piderit, John J. *s.j.* (CHI) [C] Chicago, IL Jesuit Community at Loyola University of Chicago.
Piderit, John J. *s.j.* '71 (CHI) [C] Chicago, IL Loyola University-Chicago.
Pidgeon, John J. '87 (PH) [D] Philadelphia, PA St. Hubert's Catholic High School for Girls.
Pieber, Carl L. *c.m.* '80 (PH) [AA] Philadelphia, PA Congregation of the Mission.
Pieber, Carl L. *c.m.* '80 (WH) [A] Wheeling, WV Wheeling Jesuit University.
Piechocki, Bruce '84 (FTW) [16] Fort Wayne, IN Queen of Angels Church; Pierceton, IN St. Francis Xavier Church; On Special Assignment.
Piechocki, Raymond S. '47 (ALB) [J] Amsterdam, NY Mt. Loretto Nursing Home.
Piechowski, Leonard E. '51 (MIL) Retired.
Pieczka, Walenty *c.m.* '43 (HRT) Derby, CT St. Michael Church.
Pied, Wilfred L. '51 (BO) Retired.
Piedrahita, Jose Gabriel *m.x.y.* (NY) [179] Bronx, NY Our Saviour Church.
Piedrahita-Tamayo, Msgr. Hernan A. '77 (SJN) [6] Carolina, PR Epifania Del Senor Church.
Piegl, Fred '70 (CHI) [W] Chicago, IL Northview University Center.
Piekarczyk, Marian *s.d.s.* '80 (SAT) [20] San Antonio, TX Our Lady of Sorrows Church; San Antonio, TX Methodist Hospital.
Piekarski, Joseph J. '86 (WIL) [6] Wilmington, DE St. Hedwig Church.
Pienciak, Daniel B. '87 (TR) Leave of Absence.
Pientek, Placid *o.s.b.* '44 (CLV) [P] Cleveland, OH Benedictine Order of Cleveland.
Pieper, George M. *s.j.* '48 (STL) [O] St. Louis, MO Fusz Pavilion.
Pieper, Msgr. James E. '57 (STL) Des Peres, MO St. Clement Church.
Pieper, Robert F. *o.p.* '54 (CHI) [M] Palatine, IL St. Joseph's Home for the Elderly; [N] Chicago, IL Dominicans (Provincial Office).
Pieper, Theodore X. '62 (STL) Old Mines, MO St. Joachim's Church; Tiff, MO St. Joseph's Church.
Piepmeyer, Ronald J. '97 (CIN) [58] Cincinnati, OH St. Martin of Tours Church.
Pier, Andrew *o.s.b.* '37 (CLV) [P] Cleveland, OH Benedictine Order of Cleveland.
Pier, Msgr. Joseph '38 (ALT) Retired.
Pierce, Blaine F. '46 (Y) Retired.
Pierce, Bradley *m.ss.a.* (NOR) [A] Cromwell, CT Holy Apostles College and Seminary; [F] Cromwell, CT Missionaries of the Holy Apostles.
Pierce, Bradley *m.ss.a.* '83 (NOR) Essex, CT Our Lady of Sorrows Church.
Pierce, Brian *o.p.* '88 (DAL) [M] Irving, TX Dominican Priory of St. Albert the Great.
Pierce, Brian J. *o.p.* '88 (NO) [P] New Orleans, LA Dominican Fathers & Brothers, Southern Dominican Province.
Pierce, Edward J. '72 (SFS) Mitchell, SD Holy Family Church.
Pierce, James L. *s.j.* '77 (BUF) [7] Buffalo, NY St. Ann Church.
Pierce, John *o.f.m.* '63 (NY) [DD] New York, NY Franciscan Friars, Order of Friars Minor, Holy Name Province.
Pierce, Joseph B. '92 (WDC) [3] Washington, DC St. Ann Church.
Pierce, Justin A. *s.d.s.* '48 (GB) [B] Manitowoc, WI Silver Lake College of the Holy Family.
Pierce, Larry E. '58 (SAL) Retired.
Pierce, Mark R. '81 (LC) [9] La Crosse, WI Roncalli Newman Parish; [L] La Crosse, WI Roncalli Newman Parish.
Pierce, Michael G. *s.j.* '40 (BO) [W] Weston, MA Campion Health Center, Inc.
Pierce, Msgr. Robert T. '54 (LA) Covina, CA St. Louise de Marillac Church.
Pierce, William C. '71 (CAM) [5] Camden, NJ St. Joan of Arc Church.
Pierceall, Patrick L. '69 (JC) Clarence, MO St. Patrick Church; Shelbina, MO St. Mary Church.
Pierick, Bernard E. '47 (MAD) Retired.
Pierini, Pascal *o.c.d.* '48 (SJ) [M] San Jose, CA Carmelite Monastery, Novitiate.
Pierini, Raymond G. *m.m.* '87 (NY) Manhattan, NY Cabrini Medical Center; [DD] Maryknoll, NY Maryknoll Fathers and Brothers.
Pieris, Timothy '46 (NO) Retired.
Pierjok, Harry A. '88 (PEO) Kickapoo, IL St. Mary's of Kickapoo Church.
Piermarini, Msgr. Louis R. '69 (WOR) Oxford, MA St. Roch's Church.
Pierog, Stanislaus '76 (VEN) [5] Fort Myers, FL St. Francis Xavier Church.
Pieroni, Edward L. '85 (PRO) [3] Woonsocket, RI St. Ann Church; [8] Woonsocket, RI Our Lady of Victories Church.
Pierre, Jean '88 (MIA) [20] Miami, FL St. James Church.
Pierre, Kenneth J. '63 (STP) [3] Minneapolis, MN Annunciation Church.
Pierre, Roger '93 (BRK) [139] Brooklyn, NY St. Therese of Lisieux Church.
Pierre, Roger P. '63 (STP) White Bear Lake, MN St. Mary of the Lake Church.
Pierre-Louis, Jean Marx '87 (BO) [8] Brockton, MA Sacred Heart Church.
Pierro, Sebastian C. '82 (BUF) [2] Dunkirk, NY Holy Trinity Church.
Pierse, Msgr. James J. '44 (ORG) Seal Beach, CA Holy Family Church; Retired.
Pierson, Robert *o.s.b.* '84 (SCL) [A] Collegeville, MN St. John's Seminary; [B] Collegeville, MN St. John's University; [I] Collegeville, MN St. John's Abbey, of the Order of St. Benedict.
Piesiur, Joseph '75 (PH) [2] Philadelphia, PA St. Adalbert Church.
Pietramale, John L. '92 (OM) [12] Omaha, NE Christ the King Church.
Pietrantonio, Thomas *o.f.m.cap.* '49 (WIL) [I] Wilmington, DE Capuchin Franciscan Friars, St. Francis Renewal Center; [L] Wilmington, DE St. Francis Renewal Center.
Pietras, Robert E. '62 (JOL) Downers Grove, IL Divine Savior Church.
Pietropaoli, David '84 (BAL) [A] Emmitsburg, MD Mount St. Mary's Seminary.
Pietropinto, Joseph P. '70 (NEW) Maywood, NJ Our Lady Queen of Peace Church.
Pietrowski, Stephen '92 (RVC) Williston Park, NY St. Aidan's Church.
Pietrucha, Edward S. *c.s.p.* '57 (TUC) [11] Tucson, AZ St. Cyril of Alexandria Church.

Pietrus, Henryk '70 (FAR) Absent on Leave.
Pietrzak, Bernard J. '81 (CHI) [3] Mt. Prospect, IL St. Raymond de Penafort Church.
Pietrzak, Daniel *o.f.m.conv.* '64 (BAL) [M] Ellicott City, MD Order of Friars Minor Conventual.
Pietrzynski, Boleslaus J. '42 (PIT) Retired.
Piette, Gilbert M. '79 (BWN) Graduate Studies.
Pifher, Cletus *o.f.m.conv.* '64 (SAV) Brunswick, GA St. Francis Xavier Church.
Pighini, Richard *c.s.v.* '85 (JOL) [2] Kankakee, IL St. Patrick Church.
Pignato, Salvatore A. '68 (PSC) Orlando, FL St. Nicholas of Myra Church.
Pigott, Edward L. *s.j.* '68 (CIN) [F] Cincinnati, OH St. Xavier High School; [M] Cincinnati, OH Jesuit Community at St. Xavier High School.
Piguet, Leo A. '51 (LFT) Carmel, IN St. Elizabeth Ann Seton Church.
Pijoan, L. Adrian M. Figuerola '71 (NO) Retired.
Pijunowski, Joseph J. '85 (WOR) [1] Southbridge, MA St. Hedwig's Church.
Pikturna, Vytautas '45 (BRK) Retired.
Pikula, Roman *s.d.s.* '94 (MIL) [P] Milwaukee, WI Salvatorian Provincial Residence.
Pikula, Zygmunt (NEW) Retired.
Pikulski, John F. '60 (BGP) [4] Danbury, CT St. Joseph's Church; Danbury, CT Danbury Hospital.
Pikus, Karl *f.s.s.p.* '94 (SCR) [M] Elmhurst, PA Priestly Fraternity of St. Peter (F.S.S.P.), North American District Headquarters.
Pilaczynski, John E. *o.m.i.* '58 (STP) [N] St. Paul, MN Oblate Residence.
Pilarski, Bernard '56 (DET) Detroit, MI Annapolis; Detroit, MI Garden City Osteopathic Hospital.
Pilarski, Chester J. '50 (SAG) Kawkawlin, MI Sacred Heart Church.
Pilarski, Raymond J. '55 (GAY) Atlanta, MI Jesus the Good Shepherd Church; Hillman, MI St. Augustine Church.
Pilarz, Scott R. *s.j.* '92 (PH) [C] Philadelphia, PA St. Joseph's University.
Pilarz, Scott R. *s.j.* '92 (WDC) [M] Washington, DC The Jesuit Community at Georgetown University.
Pilat, Edmund S. '56 (SY) Fulton, NY St. Michael Church.
Pilato, Sabato '92 (LA) Torrance, CA St. Catherine Laboure Church; [D] Gardena, CA Junipero Serra High School.
Pilatowski, Augustine *o.f.m.conv.* '59 (HRT) [M] New Britain, CT Conventual Franciscans.
Pilatowski, Eugene '60 (NOR) [3] Norwich, CT St. Joseph Church.
Pilcher, Gregory A. *o.s.b.* '78 (LR) El Dorado, AR Holy Redeemer Church.
Pilecki, Walter J. '43 (KC) Sugar Creek, MO St. Cyril Church.
Pileggi, Francis J. *o.s.f.s.* '61 (PH) [AA] Philadelphia, PA Oblates of St. Francis De Sales.
Piletic, William *c.m.* '77 (LA) [A] Camarillo, CA St. John's Seminary College of the Archdiocese of Los Angeles.
Pilger, G. Richard *i.c.* '79 (SP) Seminole, FL Blessed Sacrament Church.
Pilger, Joseph J. '55 (LEX) Retired.
Pilgram, Paul C. *s.j.* '70 (STL) [O] St. Louis, MO Fusz Pavilion.
Pili, Ignacio *c.m.* '84 (ARE) [7] Arecibo, PR Nuestra Senora de Fatima Church.
Pilipie, John P. '82 (PAT) Whippany, NJ Our Lady of Mercy Church.
Pilla, P. Carl '54 (SY) Retired; [S] Syracuse, NY St. Pius X Home, Inc.
Pillar, James J. *o.m.i.* '54 (STP) [N] St. Paul, MN Oblate Residence.
Pilliod, Francis B. '39 (CIN) [22] Dayton, OH St. Peter Church; Retired.
Pillon, Gordon '79 (CHL) Newton, NC St. Joseph Church.
Pillon, Gordon '79 (PEO) On Duty Outside the Diocese.
Pilola, Joseph S. '87 (HT) [4] Thibodaux, LA St. Genevieve Church.
Pilon, Daniel J. '76 (FAR) Wild Rice, ND St. Benedict's Church.
Pilon, James F. '30 (HRT) Cornwall Bridge, CT St. Bridget Church; Sharon, CT St. Bernard's Church.
Pilon, Jerome R. '89 (PEO) Hoopeston, IL St. Anthony's Church.
Pilon, Mark A. '75 (ARL) Annandale, VA St. Ambrose Church.
Pilones, Loji *r.c.j.* '75 (LA) [R] Camarillo, CA Rogationist Fathers.
Pilones, Loji *r.c.j.* '86 (FRS) Sanger, CA St. Mary Church.
Pilsner, Joseph E. *c.s.b.* '91 (GAL) [Q] Houston, TX Residence of the Basilian Fathers of the University of St. Thomas.
Pilsner, Peter R. '89 (NY) [E] New York, NY Cardinal Spellman High School.
Pimental, Francis M. *f.f.i.* '83 (FR) [J] New Bedford, MA Marian Friary of Our Lady, Queen of the Seraphic Order.
Pimentel, Jose *o.p.* '90 (OAK) [N] Oakland, CA Dominican Order (Western Province), St. Albert's Priory.
Pimentel, Jose *o.p.* '90 (P) [P] Portland, OR University of Portland.
Pina, Joseph D. '72 (LA) Ventura, CA San Buenaventura Mission Church.
Pina, Martin '93 (LUB) Hale Center, TX St. Theresa's Church.
Pina, Paolino *o.f.m.cap.* '73 (BO) [60] Boston, MA St. Patrick Church.
Pinard, Paul *s.s.e.* '59 (NOR) [A] Enders Island, CT St. Edmund's Novitiate; [F] Mystic, CT Society of St. Edmund.
Pincelli, Thomas L. '70 (BWN) [4] Harlingen, TX St. Anthony Church.
Pinchock, Joseph '72 (ORL) Winter Haven, FL St. Joseph's Church.
Pinci, August *o.ss.t.* '36 (BAL) [M] Baltimore, MD Holy Trinity Monastery.
Pinciaro, Albert G., III '84 (BGP) [6] Norwalk, CT St. Philip Church.
Pincince, Gerald P. '65 (PRO) On Duty Outside the Diocese.
Pincince, Marcel E. '83 (PRO) [A] Providence, RI Seminary of Our Lady of Providence.
Pinczewski, Phillip A. '87 (E) Kane, PA St. Callistus Church.
Pineau, Gerard J. '81 (BO) [4] Weymouth, MA St. Jerome Church.
Pineda, Juan *m.s.c.* '77 (LA) Cudahy, CA Cudahy Mission Church.
Pinette, Stuart H. '95 (HRT) [2] Hamden, CT Blessed Sacrament Church.
Pingatore, Thomas J. '44 (STP) [13] St. Paul, MN St. Ambrose Church.
Pinho, Antonio M. '66 (NEW) Military Chaplains.
Pinillos, Javier Bautista *m.s.c.* '95 (FgM) Missionaries of the Sacred Heart Foreign Missions.
Pinizotto, Anthony J. *o.s.f.s.* '78 (ARL) Stafford, VA St. William of York Church.
Pinizzotto, Anthony J. *o.s.f.s.* '78 (WIL) [I] Wilmington, DE Oblates of St. Francis De Sales.
Pinkerton, Samuel J. '95 (WCH) Pittsburg, KS Our Lady of Lourdes Church.
Pinkston, Robert L. *c.s.p.* '69 (GR) Grand Rapids, MI Chapel of St. Paul-Catholic Information Center.
Pinne, Christopher P. *s.j.* '87 (KC) [D] Kansas City, MO Rockhurst High School; [D] Kansas City, MO Rockhurst High School; [J] Kansas City, MO Rockhurst High School - Jesuit Community.
Pinon, Gilberto *o.m.i.* '71 (FgM) Oblates Foreign Missions.
Pins, Herbert '71 (HEL) [1] Helena, MT Cathedral of St. Helena.
Pins, Herbert '71 (SEA) On Duty Outside the Archdiocese.
Pins, Msgr. Joseph '70 (STL) Chesterfield, MO Ascension Church.
Pinterbone, John A. *k.h.s.* '79 (NY) [197] Staten Island, NY Assumption Church; [228] Staten Island, NY St. Stanislaus Kostka Church.
Pinti, Domenico C. '85 (TUC) Safford, AZ St. Rose of Lima Church.
Pinto, Agnelo '71 (BRK) [14] Brooklyn, NY St. Augustine Church.
Pinto, Danny '63 (FTW) Churubusco, IN St. John Bosco Church; Ege, IN Immaculate Conception Church.
Pinto, Edgar '80 (SJN) [2] Trujillo Alto, PR Santa Cruz Church.
Pinto, Peter J. '56 (HRT) [4] West Haven, CT St. Louis Church.
Pinto, Santan *s.o.l.t.* '77 (CC) [H] Robstown, TX Society of Our Lady of the Most Holy Trinity.
Pintye, Louis M. *o.f.m.* '90 (ALB) [1] Troy, NY St. Anthony of Padua Church.
Pinyan, Charles '92 (NEW) Paramus, NJ Annunciation Church.
Pinzon, Eduardo *s.j.* '60 (CHI) [128] Chicago, IL St. Mary of the Lake Church.
Piombini, Msgr. Mario G. '43 (BRK) Retired.
Piontkowski, Richard L., Jr. '82 (GI) North Platte, NE St. Patrick Church.
Piorkowski, Robert '76 (STN) [5] Madison, IL St. Mary's Church; St. Louis, MO Assumption B.V.M. Church.
Piorkowski, Msgr. Stanley W. '51 (SCR) Dickson City, PA Visitation of the Blessed Virgin Mary Church.
Piotrowicz, Maciej '95 (PMB) Wellington, FL St. Rita Church.
Piotrowski, Adrian C. *o.s.c.* '64 (NY) Katonah, NY St. Mary of the Assumption Church; [DD] New York, NY Crosier (Canons Regular of the Order of the Holy Cross).
Piotrowski, Leonard '93 (SP) Indian Rocks Beach, FL St. Jerome Church.
Piovan, Benjamin '64 (NO) La Place, LA Ascension of Our Lord Church.
Pipala, Edward A. '66 (NY) Absent on Leave.
Piper, Norbert G. *o.carm.* '32 (JOL) Glendale Heights, IL St. Matthew Church.
Pipp, Thomas J. *s.j.* '92 (TOL) [C] Toledo, OH St. John's Jesuit High School.
Pipta, Robert M. '94 (VNN) Las Vegas, NV St. Gabriel the Archangel Church.
Piquado, Thomas G. *s.j.* '72 (SFR) [24] San Francisco, CA St. Ignatius Church; [N] San Francisco, CA Jesuit Community at University of San Francisco.
Piran, Louis *c.s.* '71 (GAL) [44] Houston, TX St. Leo the Great Church.
Piraro, Don '67 (LKC) [C] Moss Bluff, LA St. Charles Center.
Pires, Francisco '84 (SLC) Brigham City, UT St. Henry Church.
Piro, Francis '54 (PH) [103] Philadelphia, PA St. Michael Church.
Piro, Frank R. '62 (SFR) Daly City, CA St. Andrew Church.
Piro, Gerald J. '79 (BRK) Absent on Leave.
Pirrera, Aaron *o.s.b.* '85 (LR) [A] Subiaco, AR Subiaco Monastery.
Pirrone, Roberto '88 (LA) Maywood, CA St. Rose of Lima Church.
Pirrung, George '54 (PHX) Retired.
Pirulli, Francis D. '45 (GBG) Retired; [G] Greensburg, PA Neumann House.
Pisanelli, Humbert D. '37 (NY) Retired; [DD] New York, NY Our Lady of Consolation Residence.
Pisanello, George M. '86 (MET) [7] Perth Amboy, NJ Holy Spirit Church.
Pisano, Andrew '42 (LA) Retired.
Pisarcik, John G. (PAT) Absent on Leave.
Piscilli, Constanzo J. '69 (PRT) Belfast, ME St. Francis of Assisi Church.
Piscitelli, Vincent J. '37 (BO) Retired.
Piscitello, Primo P. *o.f.m.* (BO) [W] Brighton, MA St. Bonaventure Friary, Franciscan Friars.
Piscitello, Primo P. *o.f.m.* '60 (BO) [W] Boston, MA St. Christopher Friary.
Pisegna, Cedric *c.p.* '91 (SAC) [G] Citrus Heights, CA Christ the King Retreat.
Pisik, Timothy E. '74 (CAM) On Sick Leave.
Piskula, Louis '75 (OWN) Non-Parochial Assignments; [G] Whitesville, KY St. Joseph's Monastery.
Piskura, Joseph H. '54 (CLV) Released from Diocesan Assignment.
Pisoni, Otto B. '41 (E) Retired.
Pisors, John A. *c.s.v.* '66 (CHI) [N] Arlington Heights, IL Viatorian Province Center-Clerics of St. Viator.
Pispeky, Steve '88 (GLP) Tinaja, NM San Lorenzo Church.
Pistacchio, Gene B. *o.f.m.* '89 (ARL) Triangle, VA St. Francis of Assisi Church.
Pistone, Bernardo '73 (HBG) [3] Lancaster, PA Assumption of the Blessed Virgin Mary Church; [J] Lancaster, PA Iglesia de San Juan Bautista.
Pistone, Dominic J., Jr. '78 (GAL) [65] Houston, TX St. Paul Church.
Pistorius, Francis X. *s.j.* '72 (GAL) [3] Spring, TX St. Ignatius of Loyola Church.
Pistulka, Celestine C. '56 (NU) Marshall, MN Holy Redeemer Church.
Piszczatowski, Maurice *o.f.m.conv.* (BGP) [6] Danbury, CT Sacred Heart Church.
Piszker, James E. '91 (E) Meadville, PA St. Brigid Church.
Pitlok, Andrew J. *s.d.s.* '52 (NEW) [N] Verona, NJ The Salvatorian Fathers.
Pitre, Eric J. '81 (GAL) Richmond, TX Sacred Heart Church.
Pitruzzello, Raymond '53 (HRT) [2] Waterbury, CT Immaculate Conception Church.
Pitstick, Rory '94 (SPK) Pasco, WA St. Patrick Church.
Pitt, Msgr. William L. '61 (RIC) [A] Virginia Beach, VA Catholic High School.
Pittappilly, Thomas '61 (BIS) Williston, ND St. Joseph Church.
Pittard, Wayne '83 (GF) Roundup, MT St. Benedict's Church.
Pittman, Robert S. *s.s.s.* '58 (CLV) [P] Cleveland, OH Congregation of the Blessed Sacrament Provincial House.
Pittman, Robert S. *s.s.s.* '58 (WDC) [V] Washington, DC Black Leadership and Christ's Kingdom Society; [V] Waldorf, MD Body of Christ Farm Community, Inc.
Pitts, Joseph A. *o.m.i.* '59 (CHI) [174] Chicago, IL Precious Blood Church; [V] Chicago, IL Ministry in Higher Education.
Pitts, William L. '70 (R) Wrightsville Beach, NC St. Therese Church; [H] Wilmington, NC Catholic Student Center.
Pitula, Zygmunt J. '39 (TOL) Retired.
Pitzen, John J. '45 (DUB) Retired.
Pius, Jung Bio '89 (ALB) Special Assignment.
Pivarnik, Gabriel *o.p.* '97 (WDC) [B] Washington, DC Dominican House of Studies.
Pivonka, David *t.o.r.* '96 (STU) [A] Steubenville, OH Franciscan University of Steubenville; [F] Steubenville, OH Holy Spirit Monastery.
Piwowar, Stanley J. '51 (MAN) Claremont, NH St. Joseph Church.
Piwowarczyk, Darius *s.v.d.* '90 (WDC) [M] Washington, DC Divine Word College.

Pizmoht, Louis A. '66 (CLV) Lyndhurst, OH St. Clare Church.
Pizzamiglio, Ernest E. '66 (PEO) Galesburg, IL Immaculate Heart of Mary Church.
Pizzarelli, Francis *s.m.m.* '79 (RVC) [N] Bay Shore, NY Montfort Missionaries.
Pizzarelli, Frank *s.m.m.* '80 (RVC) [B] Patchogue, NY St. Joseph's College.
Pizzo, Anthony B. *o.s.a.* '84 (CHI) [40] Chicago, IL St. Clare of Montefalco Church.
Pizzo, Philip '77 (BRK) [138] Brooklyn, NY St. Teresa of Avila Church.
Pizzuto, Alfred R. '55 (NY) Marlboro, NY St. Mary Church.
Placa, Msgr. Alan J. '70 (RVC) Deer Park, NY SS. Cyril and Methodius Church.
Placa, Stephen '95 (BRK) [47] Brooklyn, NY St. Francis Xavier Church.
Place, Michael D. '70 (CHI) Wilmette, IL St. Francis Xavier Church.
Place, Terry E. '72 (FTW) [11] South Bend, IN St. John the Baptist Church.
Plagens, James '65 (SAN) On Special or Other Diocesan Assignment.
Plagge, Robert J. '43 (CIN) Retired; [V] Cincinnati, OH Marian Center of Cincinnati.
Plaisted, Eugene D. *o.s.c.* '61 (STP) Anoka, MN St. Stephen Church; [N] Anoka, MN Crosier Community of Anoka.
Plakut, Peter *o.c.s.o.* '58 (P) [L] Lafayette, OR The Cistercian (Trappist) Abbey of Our Lady of Guadalupe.
Plamondon, Donald J. '72 (DUB) Holy Cross, IA Holy Cross Church; Luxemburg, IA Holy Trinity Church; [F] Holy Cross, IA Rickardsville-Holy Cross-Luxemburg (RHCL) Catholic School.
Planas, Salvador '54 (MIA) Retired.
Planea, John '82 (NO) On Duty Outside the Archdiocese.
Planinsek, Henry J. *c.s.sp.* '57 (ALX) [F] Natchitoches, LA Holy Ghost Fathers Home, Maison Brothier.
Plank, Stephen J. *o.s.b.* '94 (OM) [C] Elkhorn, NE Mount Michael High School; [K] Elkhorn, NE Mount Michael Abbey.
Plans, John *s.f.* (SFE) [28] Albuquerque, NM St. Therese of the Infant Jesus Shrine of the Little Flower Church.
Plante, Albert R. '48 (OG) [1] Watertown, NY Holy Family Church; Retired.
Plante, Georges J. '53 (PRT) Madison, ME St. Sebastian Church.
Plante, Msgr. Jacques L. '82 (PRO) [21] Providence, RI St. Maron Church; [T] Providence, RI Opus Spiritus Sancti-East Coast USA Region; [U] Providence, RI Miscellaneous Listings for the Diocese of Providence.
Plante, Paul A. '71 (PRT) Winslow, ME St. John the Baptist Church.
Plante, Pierre J. '78 (PRO) [1] Warwick, RI St. Benedict Church; [S] Smithfield, RI Bryant College.
Plante, Richard A. '53 (RC) Retired.
Plante, Roger J. *m.s.* '61 (MAN) [K] Enfield, NH Shrine of Our Lady of La Salette; [M] Enfield, NH La Salette Shrine and Center of Enfield.
Plantes, Francis P. '45 (PIT) Retired; [O] Pittsburgh, PA St. John Vianney Manor.
Planty, Donald J. '93 (ARL) On Duty Outside the Diocese.
Plappallil, Joseph A. '90 (MAR) Grand Marais, MI Holy Rosary Church.
Plascencia, Miguel '53 (LA) [9] Los Angeles, CA Divine Saviour Church.
Plasker, Alexander *o.s.b.* '62 (P) [L] St. Benedict, OR Mt. Angel Abbey.
Plasker, Robert *c.s.c.* '57 (FgM) Holy Cross Foreign Missions.
Plasker, Robert L. *c.s.c.* '57 (FTW) [J] South Bend, IN Congregation of Holy Cross Indiana Province Provincial House.
Plasse, Eugene J. '72 (SPR) Bondsville, MA St. Bartholomew's Church; Palmer, MA St. Thomas the Apostle Church.
Plaster, George '80 (LFT) On Duty Outside the Diocese.
Plaster, George F. '80 (IND) [F] Indianapolis, IN St. Vincent Hospital and Health Care Center, Inc.
Plastino, James L. '94 (MRY) [2] Salinas, CA Sacred Heart Church.
Plate, Brian G. '96 (NEW) Franklin Lakes, NJ Most Blessed Sacrament Church.
Plathanam, Ignatius J. '72 (STA) [2] Gainesville, FL Holy Faith Church.
Plathe, Anthony H. '63 (NU) On Duty Outside the Diocese.
Plathottam, Mathew '67 (PHX) [1] Scottsdale, AZ Blessed Sacrament Church.
Plathottam, Thomas '74 (NOR) Putnam, CT St. Mary Church.
Platt, Stewart '51 (Y) Retired.
Platt, W. Wallace *c.s.b.* '43 (GAL) [Q] Sugar Land, TX Basilian Mission Center.
Platt, William F. '88 (BGP) Riverside, CT St. Catherine of Siena Church.
Plaushin, Mark *o.s.f.s.* '89 (PH) [75] Philadelphia, PA St. Joachim Church.
Plavac, Timothy '86 (CLV) [A] Wickliffe, OH Borromeo Seminary.
Plavcan, Jon J. '94 (GRY) Munster, IN St. Thomas More Church.
Plawecki, Joseph '83 (DET) Erie, MI St. Joseph Church.
Plawny, Thaddeus *m.s.* '51 (PEO) [M] Georgetown, IL LaSalette Missionaries.
Playoust, Alfred G. *s.j.* '46 (SJ) [M] Los Gatos, CA Sacred Heart Jesuit Center.
Plazewski, Leonard J.M. '91 (SP) Temple Terrace, FL Corpus Christi Church.
Pleban, Alexander L. '57 (GBG) [2] Uniontown, PA St. Joseph Church.
Pleban, Leo J. '60 (Y) Campbell, OH St. Joseph the Provider Church.
Plechta, Sabin *o.f.m.* '43 (WDC) [M] Washington, DC Commissariat of the Holy Land, Franciscan Monastery - Mount St. Sepulchre.
Pleho, Anthony J. '79 (NY) [18] Yonkers, NY Most Holy Trinity Church.
Plei, Stephen *c.ss.r.* '56 (LAF) Crowley, LA Immaculate Heart of Mary Church.
Pleier, David (GB) [5] Green Bay, WI St. Bernard Church.
Pleiman, Kenneth F. *c.pp.s.* '70 (CIN) [M] Dayton, OH Provincial House of the Cincinnati Province of the Society of the Precious Blood.
Pleiness, Gregg '91 (LAN) [1] Jackson, MI St. John the Evangelist Church.
Plesa, Andrew J. '56 (RCK) Spring Grove, IL St. Peter Church.
Pleskac, Msgr. Myron J. '60 (LIN) [7] Lincoln, NE St. Joseph Church.
Pleva, Gerald *s.m.* '77 (SAT) Helotes, TX Our Lady of Guadalupe Church.
Plevyak, Valentine R. '44 (SCR) Retired; [N] Dunmore, PA Villa St. Joseph.
Plewka, Edwin J. '40 (GR) Retired.
Plewka, Mark A. '76 (PBL) [4] Pueblo, CO Holy Rosary Church.
Pliaplis, Christopher '87 (NY) Nanuet, NY St. Anthony Church.
Pliauplis, Christopher '87 (BRK) [133] Brooklyn, NY SS. Simon and Jude Church.
Pliauplis, Christopher '87 (STU) On Duty Outside the Diocese.
Plichta, Felician *o.f.m.conv.* '41 (BAL) [M] Ellicott City, MD Order of Friars Minor Conventual.
Plichta, Felician *o.f.m.conv.* '41 (FR) Sandwich, MA Corpus Christi Church.
Plo, John '61 (NY) Absent on Leave.
Ploch, Robert '96 (SAT) Panna Maria, TX Immaculate Conception of the Blessed Virgin Mary Church.
Plocharczyk, Msgr. Daniel J. '74 (HRT) [1] Hartford, CT Cathedral of St. Joseph.
Plock, Charles T. *c.m.* '73 (PH) [69] Philadelphia, PA Immaculate Conception Church.
Plocke, Donald J. *s.j.* '84 (BO) [W] Chestnut Hill, MA The Jesuit Community at Boston College.
Plocki, Msgr. Robert '45 (SFD) Retired.
Plocki, Msgr. Robert '45 (SFR) Retired.
Plocki, Msgr. Robert J. '54 (SFR) Tiburon, CA St. Hilary Church.
Ploeckl, Joseph M. '40 (SY) Retired.
Plokhooy, Christopher H. '59 (WIL) Retired; [G] Wilmington, DE Vianney House.
Plominski, Walter J. '68 (ROC) Caledonia, NY St. Columba Church.
Plominski, Walter J. '68 (SCR) On Duty Outside the Diocese.
Ploof, Gerald J. (LAN) Clio, MI SS. Charles and Helena Church.
Ploof, Msgr. Thomas M. '45 (WIN) Retired.
Ploplis, Theodore '77 (CHI) [J] Chicago, IL St. Anthony Hospital; [J] Chicago, IL Columbus Hospital; [J] Chicago, IL St. Joseph Hospital.
Plotka, Frank W. '68 (CHI) [6] Waukegan, IL Immaculate Conception B.V.M. Church.
Plotkowski, Jerome '65 (SFE) On Duty Outside the Archdiocese.
Plotkowski, Jerome '65 (WDC) Hyattsville, MD St. Jerome Church.
Plotkowski, John S. '74 (CHI) Buffalo Grove, IL St. Mary Church.
Ploude, Thomas E. '64 (CAM) Brooklawn, NJ St. Maurice's Church.
Plough, James H. '58 (PBL) Grand Junction, CO Immaculate Heart of Mary Church.
Plourde, Carroll W. *s.s.e.* (MOB) [H] Selma, AL Edmundite Fathers.
Plourde, Carroll W. *s.s.e.* '87 (MOB) Selma, AL Our Lady Queen of Peace Church; [K] Selma, AL Marion Institute Newman Center.
Plourde, James S. '82 (PRT) Waterville, ME Holy Spirit Church.
Plourde, John '84 (SP) Military Chaplains.
Plourde, Peter '83 (PMB) [A] Boynton Beach, FL St. Vincent de Paul Regional Seminary.
Plourde, Peter '83 (SP) On Duty Outside the Diocese.
Plummer, J. Bruce '40 (HEL) Retired.
Plummer, James R. '58 (CAM) Wildwood Crest, NJ Assumption B.V.M. Church.
Plunkett, Gregory J. '88 (PEO) Aledo, IL St. Catherine's Church.
Plunkett, Msgr. Joseph P. '60 (NEW) [4] Elizabeth, NJ Blessed Sacrament Church.
Plushkell, Robert B. *s.j.* '48 (SFR) [N] San Francisco, CA Jesuit Community at University of San Francisco.
Pluth, Paul *o.s.b.* '96 (LA) [R] Valyermo, CA St. Andrew's Abbey.
Pluth, Paul *o.s.b.* '96 (WDC) [B] Washington, DC Dominican House of Studies.
Plutz, Stanley *s.v.d.* '53 (FgM) Society of the Divine Word Foreign Missions.
Poage, Godfrey *c.p.* '46 (LA) [R] Pasadena, CA Passionist Community.
Poandl, Robert *glmy.* '68 (TYL) Pittsburg, TX Holy Cross Church.
Poblocki, Richard M. '83 (BUF) [3] Dunkirk, NY St. Hyacinth Church.
Pocernich, Eugene S. '74 (MIL) Awaiting Assignment.
Pocetto, Alexander T. *o.s.f.s.* '55 (ALN) [B] Center Valley, PA Allentown College of St. Francis de Sales; [K] Center Valley, PA Oblates of St. Francis de Sales.
Poche, Daniel M. '78 (HT) Gheens, LA Community of St. Anthony Church; Raceland, LA St. Hilary of Poitiers Church.
Poche, Msgr. Gerard W. '48 (NO) Gretna, LA St. Anthony Church.
Poche, Louis A. *s.j.* (LAF) [J] Grand Coteau, LA Our Lady of the Oaks Retreat House.
Pock, Donald P. '58 (JOL) Itasca, IL St. Peter the Apostle Church.
Pocovi, Juan *m.ss.cc.* '64 (SJN) Rio Grande, PR Nuestra Senora del Carmen Church.
Pocus, Msgr. Dominick A. '45 (NEW) Kearny, NJ Our Lady of Sorrows Church; Retired.
Poczworowski, Luke *o.f.m.conv.* '64 (RCK) [2] Rockford, IL St. Anthony of Padua Church.
Podesta, Msgr. John F. '35 (JOL) Retired.
Podgorny, Msgr. John '55 (PAT) [4] Passaic, NJ Holy Rosary Church.
Podgorski, Clarence '77 (PMB) Port St. Lucie, FL St. Elizabeth Ann Seton Church.
Podgorski, Francis (RVC) Glen Head, NY St. Hyacinth Church.
Podlesny, James *o.s.b.* '80 (GBG) [H] Latrobe, PA Saint Vincent Archabbey.
Podolak, William S. '50 (MIL) Retired.
Podrasky, Michael P. '43 (BEL) Retired.
Podraza, Timothy M. '97 (OM) [18] Omaha, NE Holy Ghost Church.
Podrosky, Alfred '52 (SCL) Retired.
Podskoch, Clement J. *c.s.c.* '56 (SCR) [C] Wilkes-Barre, PA Kings College.
Podson, Theodore E. *sch.p.* '76 (AMA) [6] Amarillo, TX St. Francis Church.
Podson, Theodore E. *sch.p.* '76 (WDC) [B] Washington, DC Queen of Pious Schools House of Studies-Piarist Fathers.
Podvin, Albert J. '62 (SFE) [20] Albuquerque, NM Sangre de Cristo Church.
Poecking, David G. '96 (PIT) Perrysville, PA St. Teresa of Avila Church.
Poehlmann, Edward J. '67 (DEN) Edwards, CO St. Clare of Assisi Church.
Poelker, Msgr. Gerard L. '42 (JC) Retired.
Poerio, John A. '59 (LKC) Bell City, LA St. John Vianney Church.
Poettgen, Edward '80 (ORG) Stanton, CA St. Polycarp Church.
Poetz, Lawrence *s.v.d.* '44 (CHI) [B] Techny, IL Divine Word Residence.
Poetzel, Richard K. *c.ss.r.* '63 (BAL) [68] Baltimore, MD Our Lady of Fatima Church.
Poff, Edward '57 (JOL) [G] Kankakee, IL St. Mary's Hospital.
Poff, Pius *o.f.m.conv.* '61 (LAN) [3] Lansing, MI Holy Cross Church.
Poggemeyer, Joseph T. '97 (TOL) Sandusky, OH St. Mary Church.
Pogorelc, Anthony '88 (LFT) [4] Lafayette, IN St. Lawrence Church.
Pogorelc, Anthony *s.m.* '88 (STL) [P] St. Louis, MO Provincialate of the Society of Mary, Province of St. Louis.
Pogorzelski, Eugeniusz '35 (GRY) Retired.
Pohl, Msgr. Daniel J. '53 (LIN) Indianola, NE St. Catherine's Church.
Pohl, Jerome H. '67 (PH) [2] Philadelphia, PA St. Adalbert Church.
Pohl, Leon H. '56 (KAL) Sturgis, MI Holy Angels Church.
Pohl, Stephen A. '85 (L) Bardstown, KY St. Monica Church; St. Thomas, KY St. Thomas Church.
Pohley, Robert G. '75 (BGP) [14] Stamford, CT Sacred Heart Church; [W] Shelton, CT Fr. McKenna St. Vincent de Paul Shoppe; [W] Stamford, CT Stamford

Catholic Library.
Pohlman, Stephen J. '84 (SFD) Glen Carbon, IL St. Cecilia Church.
Pohlmeier, Loren G. '82 (GI) Pleasanton, NE St. Mary's Church.
Pohorlak, Joseph '61 (PRM) Whiting, IN Assumption of the Blessed Virgin Church.
Pohto, J. Thomas *o.s.a.* '67 (VEN) Bokeelia, FL Our Lady of the Miraculous Medal Church.
Pointek, Msgr. Francis J. '40 (FRS) Tehachapi, CA St. Malachy Church; Retired.
Poirer, Robert *s.j.* (STL) [C] St. Louis, MO Saint Louis University.
Poirier, David *s.a.* '77 (NY) [DD] Garrison, NY Generalate of the Franciscan Friars of the Atonement-St. James Friary.
Poirier, J. Eugene *s.j.* '44 (WDC) [M] Washington, DC The Jesuit Community at Georgetown University.
Poirier, J. Eugene *s.j.* '57 (ARL) Annandale, VA St. Michael's Church.
Poirier, John '71 (MAN) Dover, NH St. Joseph Church.
Poirier, Joseph *s.c.j.* '73 (SP) [O] Pinellas Park, FL Priests of the Sacred Heart.
Poirier, Ralph *c.s.sp.* '63 (SD) [38] San Diego, CA San Rafael Church.
Poirier, Robert (STL) [P] St. Louis, MO Jesuit Community Corporation at St. Louis University - Jesuit Hall.
Poirier, Robert *s.m.* '54 (BO) [W] Boston, MA Marist Fathers and Brothers Provincial House.
Poirier, Ronald '88 (SP) [2] Clearwater, FL Light of Christ Church.
Poirier, Vincent H. '85 (BO) [2] Newton, MA Corpus Christi Church; [CC] Framingham, MA Framingham State College Campus Ministry; [CC] Wellesley, MA Wellesley College Campus Ministry.
Poissant, Msgr. Leeward J. '63 (OG) Morristown, NY St. John the Evangelist Church; [A] Ogdensburg, NY Wadhams Hall.
Poisson, Andre *o.cart.* '54 (BUR) [E] Arlington, VT Carthusian Foundation, Charterhouse of the Transfiguration.
Poisson, Thomas L. '78 (MAR) Houghton, MI St. Ignatius Loyola Church.
Poitras, Steven '93 (BO) [1] Somerville, MA St. Ann Church.
Pokladowski, Gregory F. (OAK) Military Chaplains.
Pokladowski, Gregory S. '73 (CHI) Other Assignments.
Pokornowski, Daniel A. '54 (BUF) [3] Cheektowaga, NY St. John Gualbert Church.
Pokorsky, Jerry '90 (ARL) Annandale, VA Holy Spirit Church.
Pokrzewinski, Justus *o.p.* '60 (FgM) Dominican - Order of Preachers Foreign Missions.
Pokrzewinski, Justus M. *o.p.* '60 (CHI) [N] Chicago, IL Dominicans (Provincial Office).
Pokusa, Msgr. Joseph W. '70 (CAM) Runnemede, NJ St. Teresa of the Infant Jesus Church.
Pol, Dom Te '70 (HT) Retired.
Polak, Michael J. '58 (PIT) [1] West Mifflin, PA St. Agnes Church.
Polakowski, Joseph '59 (MAR) Retired.
Polanco, Dennis *s.a.* '74 (NY) [DD] Garrison, NY Generalate of the Franciscan Friars of the Atonement-St. James Friary.
Polando, Msgr. Peter M. *j.c.l.* '80 (Y) [17] Youngstown, OH St. Matthias Church.
Polasek, Jeffrey S. '91 (TLS) Sallisaw, OK St. Francis Xavier Church.
Polc, Msgr. Jaroslav '55 (GB) On Duty Outside the Diocese.
Polcyn, Robert F. *o.f.m.cap.* '68 (LC) Pine Creek, WI Most Sacred Heart Church; [E] Arcadia, WI Franciscan Skemp Healthcare, Mayo Health System, Arcadia Campus Hospital; [G] Arcadia, WI Franciscan Skemp Healthcare, Mayo Health System, Arcadia Campus Nursing Home.
Polczyk, Stanislaus T. '82 (TR) Union Beach, NJ Holy Family Church.
Polednak, John V. '76 (SCR) Nicholson, PA St. Patrick's Church.
Polek, David *c.ss.r.* '62 (STL) [B] St. Louis, MO St. John Neumann House.
Polenz, Gordon '82 (ALB) Sidney, NY Sacred Heart Church.
Poletunow, Mark *o.f.m.cap.* '86 (WDC) [B] Washington, DC St. Francis Friary-Capuchin College.
Polewczak, Michael J. '73 (ALB) On Duty Outside the Diocese.
Polewczak, Michael J. '73 (CHR) Orangeburg, SC Holy Trinity Church.
Polgar, Capistran L. *o.f.m.* '67 (MET) [6] New Brunswick, NJ St. Ladislaus Church.
Poliafico, David A. '95 (COL) Westerville, OH St. Paul the Apostle Church.
Policetti, Sleeva R. '87 (CHI) [198] Chicago, IL St. Tarcissus Church.
Polich, James (DM) On Duty Outside the Diocese.
Polich, James '72 (KC) [A] Conception, MO Conception Seminary College.
Polichnowski, Nicholas *t.o.r.* '77 (BRK) [38] Brooklyn, NY St. Finbar's Church.
Policicchio, Luke *o.s.b.* '88 (RIC) [6] Virginia Beach, VA St. Gregory the Great Church.
Polidano, Carmel F. '81 (CAM) Blackwood, NJ St. Jude's Church.
Polifka, Charles *o.f.m.cap.* '71 (KCK) Lawrence, KS St. John the Evangelist Church; [H] Lawrence, KS St. Conrad's Friary.
Polimine, Alan *t.o.r.* '59 (ALT) [7] Altoona, PA Our Lady of Mt. Carmel Church.
Polinski, Casimir V. *c.r.* '44 (CHI) [74] Chicago, IL St. Hedwig Church.
Polinsky, John R. '60 (BGP) Retired; [O] Stamford, CT Our Lady Queen of the Clergy Home.
Polito, Martin F. '76 (CLV) [29] Cleveland, OH Holy Redeemer Church.
Polito, Victor J. '54 (MAN) Retired.
Polizzi, Daniel '69 (SD) Unassigned.
Polizzi, Msgr. Salvatore E. '56 (STL) [59] St. Louis, MO St. Roch Church.
Polizzi, Samuel J. '61 (ALX) Retired.
Poljicak, Vlatko '65 (LA) Panorama City, CA St. Genevieve Church.
Polk, Page E. *o.f.m.* '86 (GAL) [4] Galveston, TX St. Patrick Church.
Polk, Thomas '67 (BAL) Urbana, MD St. Ignatius Loyola Church.
Pollack, Anthony J. '55 (ALT) [6] Altoona, PA Our Lady of Fatima Church.
Pollack, Msgr. Joseph '49 (STU) Retired.
Pollak, Claude W. *o.s.b.* '57 (ALT) Nicktown, PA St. Nicholas Church.
Pollard, Daniel E. '53 (PRT) Retired.
Pollard, John E. '74 (CHI) On Duty Outside the Archdiocese.
Pollard, John L. '83 (STA) Absent on Sick Leave.
Pollard, Marcus A. '90 (ARL) [6] Alexandria, VA St. Louis Church.
Pollard, Patrick J. '72 (CHI) [50] Chicago, IL St. Denis Church; [Y] Chicago, IL Central Office.
Pollard, Msgr. Raymond J. '50 (NEW) Retired.
Pollard, Roy F. '66 (WIL) Hockessin, DE St. Mary of the Assumption Church.
Pollard, Thomas W. '66 (WDC) Clinton, MD Church of St. John the Evangelist.
Pollauf, Robert A. *s.j.* '46 (DET) [P] Clarkston, MI Colombiere Center.
Pollie, A. Frank '67 (DET) Ortonville, MI St. Anne Church.
Pollis, Robert '57 (BO) [31] Boston, MA St. James the Greater Church.
Pollis, Robert G. (BO) Retired.
Pollitt, Michael J. '83 (MAN) Absent on Leave.
Pollock, Paul *s.j.* '73 (FgM) Provinces.
Pollock, Msgr. Robert C. '48 (SLC) Retired.
Pollone, Ralph A. '83 (SPR) [9] Pittsfield, MA St. Mary the Morning Star Church.
Polmounter, Richard J. '78 (SCR) [6] Pittston, PA St. Mary, Help of Christians Church.
Polo, Antonio *s.d.b.* (SJN) [28] San Juan, PR San Juan Bosco Church.
Polo, Antonio *s.d.b.* '56 (SJN) [37] San Juan, PR Maria Auxiliadora Church.
Polo, Peter P. *c.s.* '68 (NY) [HH] New York, NY Scalabrini Pastoral Center; [HH] New York, NY American Committee on Italian Immigration, Inc.
Pologruto, C.S.P., Donald C. '82 (OAK) [Q] Oakland, CA Mills College Newman Center.
Polosky, Michael '91 (SJP) Ambridge, PA Ss. Peter and Paul Church.
Poloway, Michael '54 (SJP) Pittsburgh, PA St. John the Baptist Church.
Polselli, Leo *c.s.c.* '70 (BGP) [O] Bridgeport, CT Provincial Offices of the Priests and Brothers of Holy Cross, Eastern Province.
Polt, Albert *o.a.r.* '54 (LA) [R] Oxnard, CA St. Augustine Priory O.A.R.
Poltorak, George *s.a.c.* '90 (BUF) [O] North Tonawanda, NY Society of the Catholic Apostolate.
Poltorak, Stanley '82 (SAC) Truckee, CA Assumption of the Blessed Virgin Mary Church.
Poluikis, John A. *c.s.b.* '51 (ROC) [I] Rochester, NY Basilian Residence.
Polyak, Anthony V. *m.m.* '62 (FgM) Maryknoll Foreign Missions.
Polyak, John V. '69 (MET) North Brunswick, NJ Our Lady of Peace Church.
Polzer, Charles W. *s.j.* '64 (TUC) [F] Tucson, AZ Kino House.
Polzer, Daniel *l.c.* '94 (LIN) [F] Waverly, NE Our Lady of Good Counsel Retreat House.
Pomerlau, Claude *c.s.c.* '65 (P) [L] Portland, OR Holy Cross Fathers & Brothers, C.S.C. - University of Portland.
Pomerleau, Claude *c.s.c.* '65 (P) [B] Portland, OR University of Portland.
Pomerleau, William A. '79 (SPR) [20] Springfield, MA St. Thomas Aquinas Church.
Pomeroy, Joseph B. *s.j.* '62 (WOR) [N] Worcester, MA Jesuits of Holy Cross College, Inc.
Pomeroy, Thomas (GB) Hortonville, WI SS. Peter and Paul Church; Shiocton, WI St. Denis Church; Stephensville, WI St. Patrick Church.
Pomilio, Matthew J. '62 (BRK) Released from Diocesan Assignment.
Pommier, Richard *o.m.i.* '66 (FgM) Oblates Foreign Missions.
Pompei, Francis *o.f.m.* '74 (PH) [AA] Philadelphia, PA Order of Friars Minor of the Province of the Most Holy Name aka Holy Name Province.
Pompei, Frederick A. '66 (SY) [7] Syracuse, NY Our Lady of Pompei Church; Special Assignment.
Ponce, Demetrio '88 (ELP) Fort Davis, TX St. Joseph Church; Marfa, TX St. Mary's Church.
Ponce, Francisco R. '67 (NEW) Plainfield, NJ St. Mary Church.
Ponce, Gonzalo *s.s.p.* '76 (LA) [R] Los Angeles, CA Society of St. Paul.
Poncelet, Frank '87 (SCL) Sedan, MN Immaculate Conception Church.
Ponciroli, Robert '69 (OAK) [8] Oakland, CA St. Cyril Church.
Ponessa, Joseph '74 (GF) Glendive, MT Sacred Heart Church; [K] Glendive, MT Sacred Heart Educational Endowment Trust.
Pong, Peter *s.d.b.* '89 (NY) [DD] New Rochelle, NY Salesian Provincial House.
Ponnet, Chris '83 (LA) Los Angeles, CA L.A. County/ University of Southern California Hospital.
Ponnet, Christopher D. '83 (LA) [53] Los Angeles, CA St. Camillus De Lellis Church.
Pons, Antonio '60 (ORL) Haines City, FL St. Ann Church.
Pons, Miguel '53 (SJN) [5] Trujillo Alto, PR San Judas Tadeo Church.
Pons, Ramon *o.a.r.* '88 (SR) Petaluma, CA St. Vincent de Paul Church.
Ponso, Andres *o.s.m.* '50 (ELP) [18] El Paso, TX Our Lady of Sorrows Church.
Pontarelli, Michael M. *o.s.m.* '88 (ORG) [H] Anaheim, CA Servite Fathers and Brothers.
Pontarelli, Michael P. *o.s.m.* '82 (ORG) [D] Anaheim, CA Servite High School; Servite High School Development Fund.
Ponticello, Robert D. '81 (MEM) [19] Memphis, TN Church Of The Nativity.
Pontolillo, Dominic T. *o.f.m.cap.* '49 (FRS) Chowchilla, CA Department of Corrections, Central California Women's Facility.
Pontones, Manuel '58 (LA) Pico Rivera, CA St. Marianne de Paredes Church.
Ponzini, Thomas V. '96 (GAL) [70] Houston, TX Prince of Peace Church.
Pool, Jefferson *s.v.d.* '92 (FgM) Society of the Divine Word Foreign Missions.
Pool, Robert '55 (KCK) Retired.
Poole, James E. *s.j.* '53 (SEA) [C] Tacoma, WA Bellarmine Preparatory School; [G] Tacoma, WA St. Joseph Medical Center.
Poole, Richard '94 (SPK) Connell, WA St. Vincent Church; Eltopia, WA St. Paul Church.
Poole, Stafford *c.m.* '56 (LA) [R] Los Angeles, CA Vincentian Fathers and Brothers.
Poole, Steven F. '54 (BEL) Herrin, IL Our Lady of Mount Carmel Church.
Poole, William G. '63 (LEX) Ravenna, KY St. Elizabeth Church.
Pooler, Alfred *c.p.* '60 (CHI) [N] Chicago, IL Passionist Community-CTU.
Poore, Charles T. '89 (Y) [10] Canton, OH St. Michael the Archangel Church.
Poorman, James E. '71 (SJP) Ramey, PA Annunciation B.V.M. Church.
Poorman, Mark L. *c.s.c.* '82 (FTW) [B] Notre Dame, IN University of Notre Dame Du Lac; [J] Notre Dame, IN Holy Cross Community, Corby Hall, University of Notre Dame.
Poorten, William P. *s.j.* '63 (ALB) [O] Auriesville, NY Jesuit Retreat House for Priests, Religious and Lay People.
Poovakulam, Antony P. '63 (TR) Whiting, NJ St. Elizabeth Ann Seton Church.
Poovakulath, Jose *s.a.c.* '81 (VEN) [3] Sarasota, FL St. Martha Church.
Poovannal, Thomas '76 (WDC) Landover Hills, MD St. Mary's Catholic Church; Landover Hills, MD Syro-Malankara Mission Church; Washington, DC General Hospital.
Popadick, Msgr. Peter J. '70 (BUF) [1] Cheektowaga, NY St. Aloysius Gonzaga Church.
Popadiuk, Mauricio *o.s.b.m.* '84 (RVC) [N] Glen Cove, NY St. Josaphatis Monastery, Novitiate and Retreat House.
Popadiuk, Mauricio *o.s.b.m.* '84 (STF) Bronx, NY St. Mary Protectress Church; [B] Glen Cove, NY Basilian Fathers Novitiate of the Order of St. Basil the Great.
Pope, Charles '89 (WDC) [16] Washington, DC Holy Comforter—St. Cyprian Church.
Pope, George F. *c.s.c.* '58 (FgM) Holy Cross Foreign Missions.

Pope, L. Michael *s.j.* '81 (P) [L] Portland, OR Colombiere Community.
Pope, L. Michael *s.j.* '81 (STL) [P] St. Louis, MO Jesuit Community Corporation at St. Louis University - Jesuit Hall.
Pope, Nicholas F. *s.j.* '72 (STL) [P] St. Louis, MO Jesuit Community Corporation at St. Louis University - Jesuit Hall.
Popeleski, Frank '79 (BLX) Biloxi, MS V.A. Center; Gulfport, MS V.A. Hospital.
Popelka, Joseph '92 (SAL) Plainville, KS Sacred Heart Church; Zurich, KS St. Ann's Church.
Popesh, Msgr. Bernard '49 (DUL) Retired.
Popish, Edward *ss.cc.* '90 (HON) [F] Honolulu, HI St. Francis Healthcare System of Hawaii; [H] Kaneohe, HI Sacred Hearts Center.
Popivchak, Msgr. Ronald P. '67 (PHU) Bridgeport, PA SS. Peter and Paul Church; Phoenixville, PA SS. Peter and Paul Church.
Poplawski, John F. '73 (SCR) [2] Dunmore, PA Christ the King Church.
Popochock, James L. '68 (GBG) Footedale, PA St. Thomas Church; New Salem, PA St. Procopius Church.
Popovich, George '51 (Y) [5] Warren, OH St. Joseph Church; [G] Warren, OH St. Joseph Health Center.
Popovich, Josaphat '51 (PBR) Retired.
Popovich, Peter '85 (NY) [171] Bronx, NY Our Lady of Good Counsel Church; Greenburgh, NY Church of Our Lady of Shkodra.
Popovich, Stephen '81 (Y) [4] Youngstown, OH Immaculate Heart of Mary Church.
Popowski, Stanley '83 (HEL) Cut Bank, MT St. Margaret Church; Valier, MT St. Francis Church.
Popp, Kenneth J. '83 (SCL) Greenwald, MN St. Andrew's Church; Meire Grove, MN St. John's Church.
Popp, William *s.v.d.* '49 (FgM) Society of the Divine Word Foreign Missions.
Poppa, Chester *o.f.m.cap.* '53 (GF) Broadus, MT St. David's Church.
Popravak, Christopher *o.f.m.cap.* '74 (STL) [P] St. Louis, MO St. Crispin's Friary.
Popson, Michael George '87 (PSC) Danbury, CT St. Nicholas Church.
Porada, Casey *o.s.* '89 (LIN) David City, NE St. Mary's Church.
Porada, Casey *o.s.* '89 (PCE) On Duty Outside the Diocese.
Porada, Charles *o.f.m. conv.* (FR) [20] Fall River, MA SS. Peter and Paul Church.
Porazzo, Francis J. '44 (TR) Retired.
Porcari, Ernest M. '59 (DET) Northville, MI Our Lady of Victory Church.
Porpigilia, Joseph D. '85 (BUF) [1] Orchard Park, NY Nativity Church.
Porpora, Robert '90 (NY) [221] Staten Island, NY Our Lady Star of the Sea Church.
Porras-Gomez, Samuel E. '97 (ATL) Dalton, GA St. Joseph's Church.
Porrello, Joseph J. '51 (WOR) Retired.
Port, Dennis R. '74 (STL) Overland, MO Our Lady of the Presentation Church.
Portalatin, Antonio '91 (ARE) Special Assignment.
Portalatin, Antonio '91 (SJN) [C] San Juan, PR Seminario Mayor Regional San Juan Bautista.
Porten, Henry F. *c.ss.r.* '41 (BR) [10] Baton Rouge, LA St. Gerard Majella Church.
Porten, Henry F. *c.ss.r.* '41 (STL) [P] Liguori, MO St. Clement Health Care Center.
Porter, Daniel '75 (LSC) Hurley, NM Infant Jesus Church.
Porter, Jack W. '75 (IND) On Special or Other Archdiocesan Assignment.
Porter, John '56 (CIN) Princeton, OH St. Maximilian Kolbe Church.
Porter, John '57 (GR) On Special Assignment.
Porter, John Baptist *o.c.s.o.* '90 (SAC) [A] Vina, CA Abbey of New Clairvaux, Trappist Seminary; [G] Vina, CA Abbey of New Clairvaux, Trappist.
Porter, John E. '56 (CIN) [V] Cincinnati, OH St. Andrew Kim Korean Catholic Society.
Porter, John F. '57 (GR) Conklin, MI St. Francis Xavier Church; Ravenna, MI St. Catherine Church.
Porter, Lawrence B. '74 (NEW) [A] South Orange, NJ Immaculate Conception Seminary; [B] South Orange, NJ Seton Hall University.
Porter, Richard L. *s.j.* '47 (MIL) [P] Wauwatosa, WI Jesuit Community at St. Camillus.
Porter, Robert '81 (HEL) Dillon, MT St. Rose of Lima Church; [H] Dillon, MT Western Montana College.
Porter, Robert G. '81 (SFD) On Duty Outside the Diocese.
Porter, Robert N. '64 (SFD) Bunker Hill, IL St. Mary Church; Shipman, IL St. Denis Church; Wilsonville, IL Holy Cross Church.
Porter, Rocco S. '97 (DEN) [1] Aurora, CO Queen of Peace Church.
Porter, Stephen C. '81 (SB) Rancho Cucamonga, CA Sacred Heart Church.
Porter, Thomas *o.c.s.o.* '42 (SLC) [F] Huntsville, UT Abbey of Our Lady of the Holy Trinity of the Order of Cistercians.
Porter, William B. '80 (KCK) [J] Emporia, KS Didde Catholic Campus Center, Emporia State University.
Porter, William J. '75 (WIL) Ocean City, MD St. Luke and St. Andrew Church.
Porterfield, David J. *c.s.c.* '79 (FTW) [18] South Bend, IN St. Stanislaus Church.
Porterfield, Mark A. '94 (JC) Hannibal, MO Holy Family Church; [A] Hannibal, MO St. Thomas Aquinas Seminary.
Portland, Paul *s.d.s.* '76 (PHX) [4] Mesa, AZ Queen of Peace Church.
Portman, Msgr. John R. '56 (SD) Coronado, CA Sacred Heart Church; Retired.
Portmann, Frederick '79 (PHX) Retired.
Portrey, Msgr. Lawrence A. '39 (GI) Retired.
Portucheck, Joseph J. '49 (STL) [42] St. Louis, MO St. John Nepomuk Church.
Portz, Bernard J. *s.j.* '52 (OM) [K] Omaha, NE Jesuit Community At Creighton University.
Porunnolil, Abraham Z. '66 (RVC) Port Jefferson, NY Infant Jesus Church.
Posadas, Jose Antonio *o.f.m.* '95 (CLV) [P] Cleveland, OH Padua Franciscan Friary.
Posadas, Tony *o.f.m.* '95 (CLV) [E] Cleveland, OH Padua Franciscan High School.
Posanski, James B. '65 (MIL) [8] West Allis, WI Our Lady of Mt. Carmel Church.
Posch, Christopher *o.f.m.* '95 (CAM) [2] Camden, NJ St. Anthony of Padua Church.
Poschen, Msgr. Edward '53 (FRS) [13] Fresno, CA St. Therese Church.
Posco, Raphael A. '38 (SPR) Retired.
Poser, Gregory *o.s.c.* '75 (FgM) Crosier Foreign Missions.
Posey, Patrick L. '91 (ARL) Dominican Republic, VA San Jose, Pedro Santana Church; On Duty Outside the Diocese.
Posey, Thadeus J. *o.f.m.cap.* (STP) [C] St. Paul, MN University of St. Thomas.
Posiewala, Jan B. *s.a.c.* '76 (BUF) [O] North Tonawanda, NY Society of the Catholic Apostolate.
Poslusney, Venard *o.carm.* '42 (JOL) [J] Darien, IL Carmelite Provincial Office.
Posluszny, Francis '62 (BGP) On Duty Outside the Diocese.
Pospichal, Leo C. '56 (SFS) Epiphany, SD Church of the Epiphany.
Pospishil, Msgr. Victor J. '40 (PHU) Retired.
Post, Robert J. '82 (BGP) [14] Stamford, CT Sacred Heart Church.
Postell, Philip S. *s.j.* '70 (DAL) [D] Dallas, TX Jesuit College Preparatory School.
Poster, Richard J. '92 (DAV) Lost Nation, IA Sacred Heart Church; Toronto, IA St. James Church.
Poster, Richard J. '92 (DUB) Oxford Junction, IA Sacred Heart Church.
Postrano, Anastacio '84 (HON) Honokaa, HI Our Lady of Lourdes Church.
Poterucha, Michael '85 (SFD) Absent on Leave.
Poth, Thomas *s.m.m.* '83 (HRT) [M] Litchfield, CT Montfort Missionaries; [M] Litchfield, CT Montfort Missionaries.
Pothier, Glen K. '95 (PMB) [1] Palm Beach, FL Cathedral of St. Ignatius Loyola.
Potocek, Msgr. Cyril J. '36 (NY) North Tarrytown, NY Holy Cross Church; Retired.
Potter, Gerald (FAR) Retired.
Potter, Gerald L. '54 (FAR) Special Assignment.
Potter, Msgr. Joseph D. '54 (BGP) [7] Bridgeport, CT St. Charles Church; [U] Bridgeport, CT The Urban Center of St. Charles Parish.
Potter, Ronald J. *m.m.* '61 (FgM) Maryknoll Foreign Missions.
Potter, Stephen K. '78 (RCK) Crystal Lake, IL St. Elizabeth Ann Seton Church.
Potterton, Msgr. Daniel J. '37 (RVC) Bellmore, NY St. Barnabas the Apostle Church; Retired.
Potthast, Richard L. *c.s.c.* '67 (FgM) Holy Cross Foreign Missions.
Potthoff, Donald W. '49 (LA) Diamond Bar, CA St. Denis Church; Retired.
Potthoff, Msgr. Fred E. '44 (LFT) Retired.
Pottorff, Lisle J. '49 (DOD) Retired.
Potts, Donald G. '60 (KAL) Cassopolis, MI St. Ann Church.
Potts, Kenneth M. '68 (OM) Osmond, NE St. Mary of the Seven Dolors Church.
Potts, Richard *c.ss.r.* '91 (STL) [22] St. Louis, MO St. Alphonsus Liguori Church; [P] St. Louis, MO St. Alphonsus Rectory of the Redemptorist.
Potts, Robert J. '64 (ALN) [3] Shenandoah, PA St. George Church; [5] Shenandoah, PA Our Lady of Mt. Carmel Church.
Potts, Ronald A. '89 (WDC) [2] Bethesda, MD St. Jane Frances de Chantal Church.
Potts, Thomas *s.v.d.* '61 (FgM) Society of the Divine Word Foreign Missions.
Potvin, Leo F. '64 (ALB) Dolgeville, NY St. Joseph Church; Newport, NY St. John the Baptist Church.
Potvin, Raymond H. '48 (SPR) On Duty Outside the Diocese.
Potvin, Raymond H. '58 (WDC) [C] Washington, DC Catholic University of America, The.
Potvin, Raymond J. '80 (MAN) Hinsdale, NH St. Joseph Church.
Potvin, Thomas R. *o.p.* '62 (PRT) [I] Lewiston, ME SS. Peter and Paul Priory.
Poulin, Calvin H. *s.j.* '62 (FgM) Provinces.
Poulin, Donald J. '66 (NY) Beacon, NY St. Joachim Church.
Poulin, Edward C. '54 (NOR) Retired.
Poulin, Hector *s.d.b.* (BO) [Y] Ipswich, MA Sacred Heart Retreat Center.
Poulin, Neil C. *s.j.* '66 (CI) Gagil, FM St. Joseph Church; Tomil, FM St. Peter Chanel Church.
Poulin, Neil C. *s.j.* '66 (FgM) Provinces.
Poulin, Robert P. '48 (WOR) Retired.
Pouliot, Eugene A. '70 (STP) Farmington, MN St. Michael Church.
Pouliot, Francis A. '58 (STP) [35] Minneapolis, MN Visitation Church.
Poulsen, James N. '68 (SD) [27] San Diego, CA St. Gregory The Great Church.
Poulsen, Thomas R. *o.p.* '67 (STP) [15] Minneapolis, MN St. Albert the Great Church.
Poulson, David L. '79 (E) Clearfield, PA St. Francis Church.
Poupore, J. Gareth *c.s.b.* '53 (ROC) [I] Rochester, NY Basilian Residence.
Poupore, Norman E. '50 (OG) Retired.
Poussard, Bertrand R. '67 (PRT) [5] Lewiston, ME St. Patrick's Church; Lewiston, ME St. Mary's Regional Medical Center; [H] Lewiston, ME St. Mary's Regional Medical Center.
Pousson, Donald '66 (LAF) Morse, LA Immaculate Conception Church.
Poux, Francis A. *c.ss.r.* '62 (BAL) Odenton, MD St. Joseph Church.
Poveromo, Robert (NY) [122] New York, NY St. Vincent de Paul Church.
Poveromo, Robert '72 (NY) [E] New York, NY Cathedral High School.
Poveromo, Robert J. '72 (NY) [54] New York, NY St. James Church.
Povish, Robert W. '90 (PH) Jamison, PA St. Cyril of Jerusalem Church; [D] Warminster, PA Archbishop Wood Catholic High School.
Powderly, James J. '58 (WDC) [3] Rockville, MD St. Mary Church; Special Ministries.
Powell, Bernard F. '58 (PMB) Palm City, FL Holy Redeemer Church.
Powell, Daniel F. X. '92 (HBG) Mechanicsburg, PA St. Joseph Church.
Powell, Edward F. '54 (SUP) Retired.
Powell, Eric S. '90 (PEO) On Duty Outside the Diocese.
Powell, Harold W. '77 (KC) Retired.
Powell, John *o.s.b.cam.* '76 (MRY) [G] Big Sur, CA New Camaldoli Hermitage.
Powell, John J. *s.j.* '56 (CHI) [C] Chicago, IL Jesuit Community at Loyola University of Chicago.
Powell, Leon A. '71 (LC) Special Assignment; [I] La Crosse, WI Holy Cross (Seminary) Diocesan Center.
Powell, Matthew D. *o.p.* '75 (CHI) [N] Chicago, IL Dominicans (Provincial Office).
Powell, Matthew D. *o.p.* '75 (PRO) [P] Providence, RI St. Thomas Aquinas Priory at Providence College.
Powell, Michael '89 (JOL) [16] Joliet, IL St. Mary Nativity Church.
Powell, Paul P. '48 (OWN) Stanley, KY St. Peter of Alcantara Church.
Powell, Ralph A. *o.p.* '51 (STL) [P] St. Louis, MO Dominican Community of St. Louis.
Powell, Robert J. *d.m.a., m.a., m.div.* '74 (PH) Jamison, PA St. Cyril of Jerusalem Church.
Power, Bernard J. *c.ss.r.* '43 (RIC) [N] Hampton, VA Holy Family Retreat.
Power, David N. *o.m.i.* '56 (WDC) [B] Washington, DC Oblate College/Oblate Center for Mission Studies; [C] Washington, DC Catholic University of America, The.
Power, Eugene J. *s.j.* '51 (ALN) [A] Wernersville, PA Novitiate of St. Isaac Jogues.
Power, J. Timothy '66 (STP) Eden Prairie, MN Pax Christi Church.
Power, James E. *c.m.* '57 (PH) [AA] Philadelphia, PA Congregation of the Mission.
Power, James F. '62 (BO) Wellesley, MA St. James the Great Church.
Power, Joseph *o.s.f.s.* (BUF) [T] Stella Niagara, NY DeSales Resource Center.
Power, Patrick *c.ss.r.* '66 (KC) [32] Kansas City, MO Our Lady of Perpetual Help Church; [J] Kansas City, MO Redemptorists of Kansas City.
Power, Patrick A. '55 (LA) Santa Clarita, CA Our Lady of Perpetual Help Church.
Power, Robert E. *c.s.b.* '66 (LSC) Hatch, NM Our Lord of Mercy Church; [B] Las Cruces, NM Basilian Fathers.
Power, Thomas E. '44 (ANC) Retired.
Power, Virgil '39 (ORL) Retired.

Power, Virgil '39 (RVC) Retired.
Power, Walter D. '52 (WIL) Retired.
Power, William J. *s.j.* '41 (BO) [W] Weston, MA Campion Health Center, Inc.
Powers, Alfred J. '43 (CIN) Retired.
Powers, Aloysius '48 (OWN) Calvert City, KY St. Pius Tenth Church.
Powers, Anthony F. '42 (BRK) Retired.
Powers, Msgr. Bernard '52 (OWN) Reed, KY St. Augustine Church; [H] Maple Mount, KY Mt. St. Joseph Retreat Center.
Powers, Bruce J. '73 (RVC) Melville, NY St. Elizabeth Church.
Powers, Msgr. Charles (PAT) Retired.
Powers, Msgr. Charles F. '48 (PAT) Dover, NJ Sacred Heart Church.
Powers, Charles J., Jr. '97 (MIA) Coral Gables, FL St. Augustine Church.
Powers, Daniel *s.j.* '68 (HEL) Heart Butte, MT St. Anne Church.
Powers, Donald E. '36 (JC) Hermitage, MO St. Bernadette Church.
Powers, Donald E. '58 (JC) Camdenton, MO St. Anthony Church.
Powers, Donald E. '58 (KC) Retired.
Powers, Edward R. *s.j.* '45 (SCR) [C] Scranton, PA University of Scranton.
Powers, Gerard E. '69 (SP) New Port Richey, FL Our Lady Queen of Peace Church.
Powers, Glenn E. '87 (MIL) [5] Sheboygan, WI Immaculate Conception Church.
Powers, Harold J. *c.s.p.* '48 (LA) [86] Los Angeles, CA St. Paul the Apostle Church.
Powers, Harold J. *c.s.p.* '48 (NY) [DD] Jamaica Estates, NY Paulist Fathers Generalate.
Powers, Isaias *c.p.* '61 (PMB) [G] North Palm Beach, FL Our Lady of Florida Spiritual Center.
Powers, James E. *s.j.* '45 (BO) [W] Weston, MA Campion Health Center, Inc.
Powers, James G. *s.j.* '62 (SPK) [C] Spokane, WA Gonzaga University.
Powers, James P. '90 (SUP) Graduate Studies.
Powers, Jerome C. '47 (CHR) Retired.
Powers, Msgr. John '38 (SJ) Retired.
Powers, John *c.p.* '77 (NY) [DD] New York, NY Passionist Spiritual Center.
Powers, John A. *o.p.* '52 (NO) [25] New Orleans, LA St. Anthony Of Padua Church; [N] Metairie, LA Metairie Manor, Metairie II, and Metairie III.
Powers, John J. (CHI) Retired.
Powers, John J. '38 (ALB) Retired.
Powers, John J. '51 (CHI) South Holland, IL St. Jude the Apostle Church.
Powers, Joseph '50 (ORG) Retired.
Powers, Joseph B. '79 (KC) [15] Kansas City, MO Holy Cross Church.
Powers, Joseph L. '46 (FR) Retired.
Powers, Joseph M. *s.j.* '58 (OAK) [A] Berkeley, CA The Jesuit School of Theology at Berkeley; [N] Berkeley, CA Jesuit Community at Jesuit School of Theology at Berkeley.
Powers, Msgr. Raymond T. *s.t.d.* '51 (NY) Mahopac, NY St. John the Evangelist Church.
Powers, Richard '47 (BO) [13] Cambridge, MA St. Peter Church.
Powers, Richard E. *s.j.* '56 (E) [26] Erie, PA St. Matthew in the Woods Church; Waterford, PA St. Cyprian Church.
Powers, Richard E. *s.j.* '58 (STA) [8] Jacksonville, FL Immaculate Conception Church.
Powers, Richard J. (BO) Retired.
Powers, Richard M. '59 (OWN) Whitesville, KY St. Mary of the Woods Church.
Powers, Msgr. Richard T. '63 (PH) Levittown, PA St. Michael the Archangel Church.
Powers, Msgr. Robert J. '45 (BO) [1] Weymouth, MA St. Albert the Great Church.
Powers, Msgr. Robert J. '45 (BUR) Retired.
Powers, Robert M. '92 (BRK) [26] Brooklyn, NY St. Catharine of Alexandria Church.
Powers, Thomas '62 (ALB) Special Assignment.
Powers, Thomas F. '40 (GF) Retired.
Powers, Thomas F. '66 (BO) Wellesley, MA St. John the Evangelist Church.
Powers, Thomas J. *s.j.* '72 (TOL) [K] Toledo, OH St. Mary's Jesuit Community.
Powers, Thomas J. '95 (BO) Reading, MA St. Agnes Church.
Powers, Thomas J. *s.j.* '95 (SFR) [N] San Francisco, CA Jesuit Community at University of San Francisco.
Powers, Thomas M. '49 (CHI) River Grove, IL St. Cyprian Church; Retired.
Powers, Thomas M. '62 (ALB) Valatie, NY St. John the Baptist Church.
Powers, Thomas W. '97 (BGP) Graduate Studies.
Powers, Troy David '87 (SAC) Oroville, CA St. Thomas the Apostle Church.
Powers, Vincent J. '45 (RVC) Retired.
Powers, Msgr. William E. '36 (GR) Retired.
Powers, Msgr. William E. '36 (MIA) [7] Fort Lauderdale, FL St. Helen Church.
Powers, William V. '58 (PBL) Retired.
Powhida, Robert W. '78 (ALB) Glens Falls, NY St. Alphonsus Church; [C] Glens Falls, NY St. Mary-St. Alphonsus Regional Catholic School.
Powis, Msgr. John J. '59 (BRK) [15] Brooklyn, NY St. Barbara Church.
Poyatt, Msgr. William F. '49 (CAM) Barrington, NJ St. Francis de Sales Church.
Poynter, Gail A. '51 (CIN) Retired.
Pozanski, James B. '65 (MIL) [5] West Allis, WI St. Joseph Church.
Pozdol, Henry '50 (CHI) Summit, IL St. Joseph Church; Retired.
Pozza, Aldo *m.c.c.j.* '66 (CHI) Blue Island, IL St. Donatus Church; Calumet Park, IL Seven Holy Founders Church.
Pozzuoli, Dominic G. '55 (GBG) Leechburg, PA St. Catherine of Alexandria Church.
Prabell, Paul '72 (LEX) Danville, KY SS. Peter & Paul Church.
Prachar, Andrew '90 (NEW) Livingston, NJ St. Raphael Church.
Pracz, Ted '66 (PEO) Danville, IL Holy Family Church.
Prado, Alfred *o.m.i.* '57 (SAT) [K] San Antonio, TX Oblate Madonna Residence.
Prado, Cletus '58 (CHY) Retired.
Prado, Manuel *c.m.* (SJN) Loiza, PR Santiago Apostol, El Mayor Church.
Prado, Teodoro Tim Y. '77 (GAL) [K] Houston, TX The Catholic Chaplain Corps.
Prager, John P. *c.m.* '82 (FgM) Vincentian Foreign Missions.
Prakaiw, Basil (DEN) [38] Denver, CO Transfiguration of Our Lord Church.
Prakasam, John '88 (BRK) [52] Brooklyn, NY Guardian Angel Church.
Prakuzhy, Zacharias *c.m.i.* '68 (SHP) [B] Monroe, LA St. Francis Medical Center.
Prall, Arthur J. *m.m.* '52 (FgM) Maryknoll Foreign Missions.
Pralzer, Roman *o.f.m.* '47 (CIN) [L] Centerville, OH The Franciscan at St. Leonard.
Pramuk, Chris (DEN) [D] Aurora, CO Regis Jesuit High School.
Pranaitis, Mark *c.m.* '93 (DEN) [12] Denver, CO Holy Ghost Church.
Pranckus, Msgr. Francis J. '45 (BGP) Retired.
Pranzo, Joseph F. *c.s.* '71 (PRO) [8] Providence, RI St. Bartholomew Church.
Praski, Jacek '91 (CHI) [192] Chicago, IL St. Stanislaus, Bishop and Martyr Church.
Prass, Charles *o.m.i.* '45 (B) [D] Mesa, ID Marymount Hermitage, Inc., Hermit Sisters of Mary.
Prass, Charles *o.m.i.* '45 (FgM) Oblates Foreign Missions.
Prass, Charles *o.m.i.* '45 (STP) [N] St. Paul, MN Oblate Residence.
Prasser, Jeffery A. '89 (MIL) [18] Milwaukee, WI St. Catherine Church.
Prat, Camille *s.j.* '62 (PHX) Chandler, AZ St. Andrew the Apostle Church.
Pratico, Patrick J. '79 (SCR) Eynon, PA St. Mary's Czestochowa Church.
Prats, Charles V. '84 (MET) [H] Raritan, NJ Clairvaux House; [K] Raritan, NJ Shrine Chapel of the Blessed Sacrament.
Pratt, Burton W. *s.j.* '50 (LC) Prairie du Chien, WI St. Gabriel Church; Prairie du Chien, WI St. John Nepomucene Church.
Pratt, Dean '97 (DAL) Special Assignment.
Pratt, Edward C. '72 (ALB) Ushers, NY Corpus Christi Church.
Pratt, James F.X. *s.j.* '86 (BO) [W] Boston, MA The Society of Jesus of New England-Provincial Offices.
Pratt, James F.X. *s.j.* '96 (NSH) [1] Nashville, TN Cathedral of the Incarnation.
Pratt, James L. *s.m.* '46 (SFR) [B] San Francisco, CA St. Peter Chanel Seminary; [N] San Francisco, CA Provincial Residence.
Pratt, Lawrence E. '62 (BO) Melrose, MA Incarnation Church.
Pratt, Oscar J. '96 (BO) [8] Lynn, MA Sacred Heart Church.
Pravetz, Matthew A. *o.f.m.* '79 (NY) [146] Bronx, NY Holy Cross Church.
Pray, Joseph N '50 (BUR) Retired.
Prazan, Ceslaus R. *o.p.* '63 (BR) Tickfaw, LA Our Lady of Pompeii Church.
Prazan, Ceslaus R. *o.p.* '63 (CHI) [N] Chicago, IL Dominicans (Provincial Office).
Prebula, David W. *o.s.b.* '44 (SEA) Tacoma, WA Veterans Admin. Medical Center; [M] Lacey, WA St. Martin's Abbey.
Prechtl, Ronald G. '80 (WH) Grafton, WV St. Augustine Church.
Preciado, Rudolph J. '69 (ORG) Garden Grove, CA St. Callistus Church.
Precourt, Peter R. *a.a.* '76 (NY) [87] New York, NY Our Lady of Guadalupe Church.
Prefontaine, Roger C. *s.s.s.* '53 (GAL) [25] Houston, TX Corpus Christi Church.
Pregana, Craig A. '89 (FR) [11] Fall River, MA Sacred Heart Church.
Pregana, David A. '96 (FR) [1] Attleboro, MA St. John the Evangelist Church.
Preisinger, Robert F. '63 (OM) [8] Sarpy Co., NE St. Bernadette Church.
Preisner, Msgr. A. F. '40 (DOD) Retired.
Premoshis, Gregory F. '68 (GBG) Mount Pleasant, PA Visitation of the Blessed Virgin Mary Church; [C] Connellsville, PA Geibel Catholic High School.
Prempeh, John Duah *s.v.d.* '95 (GAL) [47] Houston, TX St. Mary of the Purification Church.
Prenatt, David E. '95 (E) [23] Erie, PA St. Luke Church.
Prendergast, Edmond '73 (MIA) [4] Fort Lauderdale, FL St. Bonaventure Church.
Prendergast, Edward F. '51 (CLV) Rocky River, OH St. Christopher Church; Retired.
Prendergast, Fergus '94 (MOB) [3] Montgomery, AL St. Bede Church.
Prendergast, Francis '54 (STO) Turlock, CA Sacred Heart Church; [G] Turlock, CA The McElligott Sacred Heart School Foundation.
Prendergast, John J. '76 (PEO) On Duty Outside the Diocese.
Prendergast, Joseph '54 (SJ) [3] Santa Clara, CA St. Justin Church.
Prendergast, Noel '58 (JKS) Clinton, MS Holy Savior Church; [G] Clinton, MS Mississippi College Newman Center; [G] Raymond, MS Hinds Community College Catholic Student Organization.
Prendergast, Richard J. '79 (CHI) Berwyn, IL St. Mary of Celle Church.
Prendergast, Robert E. '22 (PEO) Retired.
Prendergast, Msgr. Thomas '56 (SD) [10] San Diego, CA Mission Basilica San Diego De Alcala Church.
Prendeville, Eugene *o.m.i.* (PEO) Lincoln, IL Lincoln State School.
Prendiville, Edmond P. '63 (PRO) On Duty Outside the Diocese.
Prendiville, Kerry '84 (RC) Spearfish, SD St. Joseph Church.
Prendiville, Ned '85 (ORL) Special Assignment.
Prendiville, Thomas *s.d.b.* '56 (SFR) [N] San Francisco, CA Salesian Provincial Residence.
Preneta, Henry S. '67 (GBG) On Duty Outside the Diocese.
Preneta, Henry S. '67 (PIT) [3] Butler, PA St. Paul Church.
Prengaman, Leo Peter *s.j.* '93 (NY) [DD] New York, NY Xavier Jesuit Community.
Prengaman, Leo Peter *s.j.* '93 (RVC) Farmingdale, NY St. Kilian Church.
Prescott, Herbert W. '55 (KNX) Retired.
Prescott, Leslie T.H. '54 (LAF) Pine Prairie, LA St. Peter Church.
Presenti, Richard (LA) [DD] Bellflower, CA St. John Bosco High School Alumni.
Presenti, Richard R. *s.d.b.* '68 (LA) [F] Bellflower, CA St. John Bosco High School.
Preske, Venantius '52 (LR) Retired.
Preskenis, James T. *c.s.c.* '75 (FR) [A] North Easton, MA Holy Cross Fathers Religious.
Presley, William F. '56 (E) Sykesville, PA Assumption of Blessed Virgin Mary Church.
Presmanes, Jorge *o.p.* '91 (MIA) [18] Miami, FL St. Dominic Church.
Presta, James '86 (CHI) [A] Chicago, IL St. Joseph Seminary.
Prestera, Vincent J. (NEW) [N] Caldwell, NJ The Rev. Msgr. James F. Kelley Residence for Retired Priests.
Prestera, Vincent J. '47 (NEW) Retired.
Preston, Laurence *m.ss.a.* (NOR) [F] Cromwell, CT Missionaries of the Holy Apostles.
Preston, Richard '93 (LAN) East Lansing, MI St. John the Evangelist, Student Parish.
Presume, Marc '93 (MIA) [1] Miami, FL St. Mary's Cathedral.
Pretto, Franklin D. '72 (SFE) [6] Santa Fe, NM San Isidro Church.
Preuss, David *o.f.m.cap.* '79 (DET) [15] Detroit, MI St. Charles Borromeo Church; [57] Detroit, MI Our Lady of Sorrows Church.
Preuss, Richard *c.m.* '73 (FgM) Vincentian Foreign Missions.
Prevost, Frederick J. '48 (SY) Whitesboro, NY St. Anne Church.
Prevost, Normand *s.a.* '47 (NY) [DD] Garrison, NY Franciscan Friars of the Atonement.
Prevost, Robert F. *o.s.a.* '82 (CHI) [N] Olympia Fields, IL The Augustinian Provincialate Tolentine Center.
Prevost, Robert F. *o.s.a.* '82 (FgM) Foreign Missions.
Prevosto, Paul J. '96 (NEW) Mountainside, NJ Our Lady of Lourdes Church.
Prez, Daniel J. '74 (E) Union City, PA St. Teresa of Avila Church.
Pribonic, Phillip '67 (PIT) Library, PA St. Joan of Arc Church.
Pribula, Duane '70 (CR) Warroad, MN St. Mary's Church.
Pribyl, Francis T. '39 (CHI) [5] Chicago, IL St. Agnes of Bohemia Church; Retired.

Pricco, Richard A. '62 (PEO) Macomb, IL St. Paul's Church.
Price, Basil M. *s.j.* '54 (FgM) Provinces.
Price, Bede *o.s.b.* '96 (STL) [F] Creve Coeur, MO St. Louis Priory School; [P] St. Louis, MO The Abbey of St. Mary and St. Louis.
Price, Msgr. Edward G. '44 (NEW) [6] Elizabeth, NJ St. Genevieve's Church; Roselle Park, NJ The Assumption Church; Retired.
Price, Francis R. '44 (OM) Retired.
Price, James *c.p.* '94 (BRK) [U] Jamaica, NY Immaculate Conception Monastery.
Price, John R. '66 (CHI) [4] Cicero, IL Mary, Queen of Heaven Church.
Price, Rothell '88 (SHP) [1] Shreveport, LA St. John Berchmans Cathedral.
Price, Wayne '85 (STA) Jacksonville Beach, FL St. Paul's Church.
Price, William J. *m.m.* '56 (FgM) Maryknoll Foreign Missions.
Priebe, Msgr. Norman F. '67 (LA) Arcadia, CA Holy Angels Church.
Priest, Msgr. Gerald '68 (TYL) Texarkana, TX Sacred Heart Church.
Priester, Robert E. '59 (BUF) Retired.
Priestly, Keith '76 (DET) Eastpointe, MI St. Veronica Church.
Prieto, Frank '64 (SFE) [15] Albuquerque, NM Saint Joseph on the Rio Grande Church.
Prietto, Mario J. *s.j.* '73 (SJ) [B] Santa Clara, CA Santa Clara University; [B] Santa Clara, CA Santa Clara University.
Primeaux, Patrick D. *s.m.* '77 (WDC) [M] Washington, DC Marist Provincial House.
Primich, John F. '95 (MET) Basking Ridge, NJ St. James Church.
Primozic, Robert *o.carm.* '64 (JOL) [J] Darien, IL Carmelite Provincial Office.
Prince, Joseph A. '71 (BGP) Ridgefield, CT St. Elizabeth Seton Church.
Prince, Leo R. '86 (NY) [1] Poughkeepsie, NY St. Peter Church.
Principe, Francis J. '53 (NY) [E] New York, NY Cardinal Spellman High School.
Prindiville, Gerard T. '96 (NEW) [1] Bayonne, NJ St. Mary Star of the Sea Church.
Prindle, Richard G. '78 (LA) Altadena, CA St. Elizabeth of Hungary Church.
Prinelli, John A. '78 (RIC) Chincoteague, VA St. Andrew Church.
Pringle, Denis *s.a.* '89 (SEA) [4] Seattle, WA St. Benedict Church.
Pringle, John R. '72 (MET) Bridgewater, NJ Holy Trinity Church.
Printy, Michael G. '57 (OM) Jackson, NE St. Patrick Church.
Prinz, Gerald '68 (HT) On Leave.
Prior, Eugene J. *s.j.* '55 (NY) [F] New York, NY Loyola School; [DD] New York, NY St. Ignatius Loyola Residence.
Prior, Felix *o.carm.* '58 (JOL) [J] Darien, IL Carmelite Provincial Office.
Prior, Francis X. *c.m.* '51 (BUF) [C] Niagara University, NY Niagara University; [O] Niagara University, NY Vincentian Community at Niagara University.
Prior, James G. *c.m.* '53 (ALN) Roseto, PA Our Lady of Mt. Carmel Church.
Prior, Joseph G. '90 (PH) Graduate Studies.
Prior, Robert J. *c.m.* '94 (CHL) [3] Greensboro, NC St. Mary Church.
Prior, Thomas *c.m.* '59 (BRK) [U] Jamaica, NY Vincentian Residence.
Priscaro, Jerry S. '93 (E) [3] Sharon, PA St. Joseph Church.
Prist, Wayne F. '67 (CHI) [179] Chicago, IL Queen of All Saints Basilica Church.
Pritchard, Edward '74 (WDC) Retired.
Pritt, Phillip P. '62 (CLV) Rittman, OH St. Anne Church.
Pritzl, Kurt *o.p.* '91 (WDC) [B] Washington, DC Dominican House of Studies; [C] Washington, DC Catholic University of America, The.
Prive, Francis R. '69 (BUR) Underhill Center, VT St. Thomas Church.
Privett, John A. *s.j.* '72 (FgM) Provinces.
Privett, John A. *s.j.* '72 (OAK) [S] Oakland, CA Institute of Lay Theology.
Privett, John A. *s.j.* '72 (SJ) [M] Los Gatos, CA California Province of the Society of Jesus, Jesuit Provincial Office; [M] Los Gatos, CA Sacred Heart Jesuit Center.
Privett, Stephen A. *s.j.* '72 (SJ) [B] Santa Clara, CA Santa Clara University; [B] Santa Clara, CA Santa Clara University.
Privitera, Msgr. Santi J. (BRK) [18] Brooklyn, NY St. Bernadette Church.
Privitera, Msgr. Santi J. '27 (BRK) Retired.
Proback, Adrian *o.c.s.o.* '54 (WOR) [N] Spencer, MA St. Joseph's Abbey.
Probst, R. Dean '81 (SFD) Carlinville, IL SS. Mary & Joseph Church.
Probst, Msgr. Robert L. '45 (STP) Retired; [C] St. Paul, MN University of St. Thomas.
Probstfield, Edgar *o.s.b.* '52 (KC) Trenton, MO St. Joseph's Church.
Probstfield, Regis *o.s.b.* '57 (KC) [J] Conception, MO Conception Abbey.
Procaccini, David C. '93 (PRO) Barrington, RI St. Luke Church.
Procaccini, Joseph J. '58 (TR) Allentown, NJ St. John Church.
Procella, Paul '87 (GAL) Humble, TX St. Mary Magdalene Church.
Prochaska, John '93 (OAK) [4] San Leandro, CA St. Leander Church.
Prochaski, Adam F. '68 (BRK) Absent on Sick Leave.
Prochnow, Josef *o.f.m.* '63 (OAK) [N] Oakland, CA Franciscan Friars Provincial Office, Province of St. Barbara.
Procopio, Clement *o.f.m.* '44 (NY) [DD] New York, NY Franciscan Province of the Immaculate Conception.
Procter, John W. '85 (ORG) Dana Point, CA St. Edward Church.
Proctor, Burton *s.j.* '62 (ALN) [A] Wernersville, PA Novitiate of St. Isaac Jogues.
Proctor, John G., Jr. '72 (SD) Bonita, CA Corpus Christi Church.
Procyk, Marijan '80 (STF) Buffalo, NY St. Nicholas Church.
Prodehl, Richard B. '66 (JOL) [1] Lockport, IL St. Bernard Church.
Prodywus, Alexander (STN) Absent on Sick Leave.
Proehl, Douglas M. '74 (CLV) Fairview Park, OH St. Angela Merici Church.
Proeller, Ullric (FAR) Retired.
Proeller, Ullric J. '31 (SAT) [K] San Antonio, TX Padua Place.
Proenza, Rafael *o.p.* '96 (SAT) [B] San Antonio, TX Dominican Priory of Juan Macias.
Profeta, Salvatore '50 (PMB) Retired.
Proffit, James D. '91 (BAL) [41] Baltimore, MD Immaculate Conception Church.
Profota, James H. '75 (DET) Eastpointe, MI St. Basil Church.
Prohens, James *c.r.* '36 (DEN) [27] Denver, CO St. Cajetan's Church.
Prokes, Francis A. *s.j.* '57 (OM) [K] Omaha, NE Jesuit Community At Creighton University.
Prokop, Roger '87 (LAN) [3] Ann Arbor, MI St. Thomas the Apostle Church.
Prokopiw, Taras *o.s.b.m.* '58 (STF) New York, NY St. George Church.
Prokopiw, Wasyl '92 (STN) Denver, CO Transfiguration of Our Lord Church.
Promesso, William J. '89 (DET) [74] Detroit, MI St. Thomas Aquinas Church.
Promis, Christopher P. *c.s.sp.* '72 (FgM) Holy Ghost Foreign Missions.
Promis, Christopher P. *c.s.sp.* '72 (PIT) [O] Bethel Park, PA Holy Ghost Fathers and Brothers Provincialate.
Pronesti, Salvatore J. '67 (PH) Bridgeport, PA Our Lady of Mt. Carmel Church.
Proneza, Rafael *o.p.* '96 (SAT) [26] San Antonio, TX St. Ann Church.
Proodian, Paul C. *c.o.* '51 (CHR) [D] Rock Hill, SC Oratory of St. Philip Neri, Congregation of the Oratory of Pontifical Rite.
Proppe, John *o.f.m.cap.* '47 (NY) Hawthorne, NY Rosary Hill Home; [X] Hawthorne, NY Rosary Hill Home; [EE] Hawthorne, NY Motherhouse & Novitiate of the Sisters of St. Dominic, Congregation of St. Rose of Li.
Propst, Sergius R. *o.p.* '73 (OAK) [N] Oakland, CA Dominican Order (Western Province), St. Albert's Priory.
Prosen, Anthony J. '71 (LFT) Muncie, IN St. Mary Church; Pendleton, IN Indiana State Reformatory, St. Christopher Chapel; Pendleton, IN Correctional Industrial Complex Ecumenical Chapel; Special Assignment.
Prost, Charles *c.m.* '78 (KC) [J] Kansas City, MO Vincentian Parish Mission Center.
Protack, Thomas J. '96 (WIL) Wilmington Manor, DE Our Lady of Fatima Church.
Protano, Joseph, Jr. '63 (PRO) [5] Providence, RI St. Anthony Church.
Proterra, Michael *s.j.* '71 (OM) [A] Omaha, NE Creighton University; [K] Omaha, NE Jesuit Community At Creighton University.
Protomastro, Camillus *o.f.m.cap.* '59 (NY) [151] Bronx, NY Immaculate Conception Church.
Protopapas, George *o.m.i.* '43 (BO) [12] Lowell, MA Nuestra Senora del Carmen Church.
Protopapas, George *o.m.i.* '43 (FgM) Oblates Foreign Missions.
Proud, Albert J. '68 (SY) Jordan, NY St. Patrick Church.
Proulx, Donald R. '60 (PRT) Windham, ME Our Lady of Perpetual Help Church.
Proulx, Raymond G. '60 (HRT) Goshen, CT St. Thomas of Villanova Church.
Proulx, Roger F. '47 (PRT) Retired; [I] Waterville, ME Mt. St. Joseph Priest Retirement Home.
Prout, Thomas S. *s.j.* '92 (NY) [F] New York, NY Loyola School; [DD] New York, NY St. Ignatius Loyola Residence.
Provenza, Msgr. Earl V. '64 (SHP) Bossier City, LA Christ the King Church.
Provenza, John '90 (LA) [D] Santa Fe Springs, CA St. Paul High School.
Provinsal, Thomas G. *s.j.* '75 (FBK) Alakanuk, AK St. Ignatius Church; Emmonak, AK Sacred Heart Church; [E] St. Marys, AK Brother Joe Prince Jesuit Community.
Provinzano, Rocco F. '66 (NEW) Westwood, NJ St. Andrew's Church.
Provost, Armand J. '38 (MAN) Dover, NH St. Charles Church; Retired.
Provost, Msgr. Glen John '75 (LAF) [5] Lafayette, LA Our Lady of Fatima Church.
Provost, James H. '63 (HEL) On Duty Outside the Diocese.
Provost, James H. '63 (WDC) [C] Washington, DC Catholic University of America, The.
Provost, John T. '73 (ALB) [6] Schenectady, NY Holy Cross Church; [9] Schenectady, NY St. John the Evangelist Church; [12] Schenectady, NY St. Mary Church.
Provost, Raymond C. '36 (BUR) Retired.
Proxell, Leo '77 (HEL) Conrad, MT St. Michael Church; Dutton, MT St. William Church.
Proxell, Leo G. '77 (HEL) [B] Helena, MT Carroll College.
Prozny, Leopold V. '42 (SY) Retired.
Prucha, Francis Paul *s.j.* '57 (MIL) [P] Milwaukee, WI Jesuit Community at Marquette University.
Prudell, Msgr. Harold O. '39 (MIL) Retired.
Prudencio, Rodriguez *c.m.* '65 (PHX) Special Assignment.
Pruemer, Alexis *o.f.m.* (SFD) [H] Effingham, IL St. Anthony's Memorial Hospital.
Pruemer, Alexis *o.f.m.* '47 (SFD) Shumway, IL Church of the Annunciation; [K] Teutopolis, IL St. Francis Assisi Friary.
Pruett, Bill '79 (OKL) [7] Oklahoma City, OK St. Eugene's Church.
Pruett, John M. '55 (STO) Modesto, CA Our Lady of Fatima Church.
Prunier, Arthur J. '48 (WOR) Retired.
Prunty, Brian *o.praem.* '65 (CHI) [N] Chicago, IL Premonstratensian Fathers and Brothers (Norbertines).
Prus, Edward '61 (DET) Garden City, MI St. Raphael the Archangel Church.
Prus, Msgr. Eugene '64 (MET) Martinsville, NJ Blessed Sacrament Church.
Prusaitis, John P. '78 (BO) [1] Brockton, MA St. Casimir Church.
Prusakowski, Gerald *o.f.m.* '65 (GB) Abrams, WI St. Louis Church; Chase, WI St. Joseph Church; Sobieski, WI St. John Cantius Church.
Pruschowitz, Msgr. Walter '61 (PAT) [P] Chester, NJ Nazareth Village.
Prushinski, Carl T. '64 (SCR) Glen Lyon, PA St. Adalbert's Church.
Pruss, Rodney Lee A. '69 (GI) Ravenna, NE Our Lady of Lourdes Church.
Prussing, Charles *s.j.* '55 (LA) [R] Los Angeles, CA Columbiere House.
Prusynski, Chester *c.s.c.* '62 (P) [B] Portland, OR University of Portland; [L] Portland, OR Holy Cross Fathers & Brothers, C.S.C. - University of Portland.
Pruys, George L. '75 (STN) Wilton, ND SS. Peter and Paul Church.
Prybis, Raymond *o.m.i.* '67 (WDC) [B] Washington, DC Oblate College/Oblate Center for Mission Studies.
Pryor, Msgr. Donald J. '51 (NY) Pocantico Hills, NY The Magdalene Church.
Pryor, G. Robert '55 (CR) Retired.
Pryor, Msgr. Thomas P. '37 (PH) Retired.
Przechacki, Casimir J. '44 (MET) Retired.
Przepierski, Frank J. '62 (E) Clarion, PA Immaculate Conception Church.
Przewozny, Bernard *o.f.m.conv.* '69 (BAL) [M] Ellicott City, MD Order of Friars Minor Conventual.
Przyblski, Kevin *o.f.m.conv.* '89 (IND) [I] Mount Saint Francis, IN Mount Saint Francis Friary and Retreat Center.
Przybocki, Msgr. Bernard A. '58 (ALT) Gallitzin, PA St. Patrick's Church; Gallitzin, PA Our Lady of Czestochowa Church.
Przybyla, Kenneth '77 (COS) Salida, CO St. Joseph Church.
Przybyla, Kenneth '77 (PEO) On Duty Outside the Diocese.
Przybyla, Philip J. '70 (PIT) Canonsburg, PA St. Patrick Church.
Przybylo, William P. '68 (HRT) [9] Hartford, CT SS. Cyril and Methodius Church; [N] Hartford, CT SS. Cyril & Methodius Convent.
Przybylski, Donald L. '74 (LC) [5] Stevens Point, WI St. Stanislaus Church.
Przybysz, Joseph J. '75 (TOL) [23] Toledo, OH St.

Hedwig Church.
Przybysz, Mark C. '90 (GR) [22] Grand Rapids, MI St. Stephen's Church.
Przydzial, Frederick '56 (ALN) [11] Bethlehem, PA St. Stanislaus Church.
Przysucha, Joseph *c.r.* '53 (CHI) [D] Chicago, IL Weber High School.
Przywara, Gerald A. '67 (RIC) Columbia, VA St. Joseph Church; Palmyra, VA Ss. Peter & Paul Church.
Ptacek, Benedict *o.de.m.* '59 (SP) [O] St. Petersburg, FL St. Peter Nolasco Residence.
Ptacek, John P. '55 (DUB) Farley, IA St. Joseph's Church.
Ptak, Walter J. '87 (DET) [4] Wyandotte, MI Our Lady of Mt. Carmel Church.
Ptaszynski, Stephen F. '45 (HRT) Retired.
Ptaszynski, Thomas E. '73 (HRT) New Milford, CT Our Lady of the Lakes Church.
Pu, Matthew C. '43 (BAK) Burns, OR Holy Family Church.
Pu, Matthew C. '53 (B) On Duty Outside the Diocese.
Publicover, James L. '56 (BO) [4] Arlington, MA St. Jerome Church.
Pucar, August '63 (BEA) Liberty, TX Immaculate Conception Church.
Pucci, Alfred J. '54 (NY) [226] Staten Island, NY St. Roch Church.
Pucci, Francis L. '57 (PIT) Retired; [P] Elizabeth, PA Divine Redeemer Motherhouse.
Pucci, Joseph *o.m.i.* '41 (PMB) [4] West Palm Beach, FL St. John Fisher Church.
Pucciarelli, George W. '74 (BO) Military & VA Chaplains.
Puccinelli, Alfred H. *s.m.* '66 (B) Nampa, ID St. Paul's Church.
Puccini, Alfred V. '53 (BO) [4] Malden, MA St. Peter Church.
Puche, Patricio (DEN) [A] Denver, CO Redemptoris Mater House of Formation.
Puchenski, Anthony C. '71 (CHI) [92] Chicago, IL Immaculate Conception Church.
Puchner, Augustine R. *o.praem.* '97 (ORG) [A] Silverado, CA St. Michael's Norbertine Postulancy, Novitiate and Juniorate; [H] Silverado, CA Norbertine Fathers of Orange Inc.
Pucke, Michael U. '73 (CIN) [64] Cincinnati, OH St. Michael Church.
Pudenz, Anthony '48 (JKS) Retired.
Pudhota, J. Bosco '86 (OKL) Ponca City, OK Church of St. Mary.
Pudichery, Joseph '62 (PIT) [B] Pittsburgh, PA Duquesne University of the Holy Ghost.
Pudichery, Joseph P. '62 (PIT) Overbrook, PA St. Norbert Church.
Puentes, Jesus '86 (MAD) [4] Madison, WI Holy Redeemer Church.
Puerner, John W. '55 (LC) Thorp, WI St. Bernard-St. Hedwig Parish.
Puerta, Jorge '89 (MIA) Absent on Sick Leave.
Puetz, Richard W. '45 (LFT) Retired; [D] Delphi, IN St. Elizabeth Healthcare Center.
Pugevicues, Casimir A. '53 (BAL) Retired.
Pugh, Msgr. Charles '60 (SAT) Von Ormy, TX St. Peter the Fisherman Church.
Pugh, James L. '67 (MEM) [3] Memphis, TN St. Anne's Church.
Pugliese, Francis A. '68 (NY) Military Chaplains.
Pugliese, Steven *s.j.* '93 (BRK) [62] Brooklyn, NY St. Ignatius Church.
Puglisi, Msgr. Guy J. '71 (BRK) [3] Brooklyn, NY St. Agnes Church; [E] Brooklyn, NY Office of the Superintendent of Schools.
Puglisi, James *s.a.* '73 (NY) [DD] Garrison, NY Generalate of the Franciscan Friars of the Atonement-St. James Friary.
Puhak, Msgr. Nicholas I. '57 (PSC) Trenton, NJ St. Mary of the Assumption Church.
Puhl, Albert '44 (DEN) [35] Denver, CO St. Mary Magdalene's Church.
Puhl, Albert E. '44 (DEN) Retired.
Puhlman, Robert W.P. '84 (ORG) Newport Beach, CA Our Lady Queen of Angels Church.
Puisis, John C. *c.s.v.* '45 (CHI) [N] Arlington Heights, IL Viatorian Province Center-Clerics of St. Viator.
Puisis, Leonard '52 (MIA) Retired.
Pujdak, Steve *s.c.j.* '69 (BWN) Raymondville, TX Our Lady of Guadalupe Church.
Pulaski, Joseph S. *m.m.* '47 (NY) [DD] Maryknoll, NY Maryknoll Fathers and Brothers.
Puleo, Edward C. '88 (MET) [1] Carteret, NJ St. Joseph Church.
Pulicare, Michael J. '71 (SCR) Susquehanna, PA St. John the Evangelist Church.
Pulice, John J. '66 (MIL) [69] Milwaukee, WI St. Robert Church.
Pulickal, Sony George *c.m.f.* '83 (OG) Massena, NY Sacred Heart Church.
Pulikoottil, Abraham '56 (BUF) Clarence, NY Our Lady of Peace Church.
Pulikoottil, Abroham '65 (BUF) Retired.
Pulikoottil, Berard '62 (BUF) Lancaster, NY St. Mary of the Assumption Church.
Puljic, Marko *o.f.m.* '81 (NY) [29] New York, NY SS. Cyril and Methodius - St. Raphael Church.
Pullo, Francis S. '42 (BRK) Retired; [U] Douglaston, NY Bishop Mugavero Residence.
Pulskamp, Msgr. James E. '67 (SR) [2] Santa Rosa, CA Holy Spirit Church.
Pulvermacher, Claude *o.f.m.cap.* (MIL) [P] Wauwatosa, WI St. Camillus Community House.
Pulvermacher, Claude *o.f.m.cap.* '60 (MIL) [N] Wauwatosa, WI St. Camillus Health Center, Inc.; [P] Milwaukee, WI St. Conrad House.
Pulvermacher, Pius '48 (GB) [I] Appleton, WI St. Fidelis Friary.
Puma, Msgr. Vincent E. (PAT) Retired.
Punch, David '68 (MIA) Retired.
Punch, Nicholas W. *o.p.* '66 (SUP) [I] Webster, WI Thomas More Center for Preaching and Prayer, Inc.
Punderson, Msgr. Joseph R. '76 (TR) On Duty Outside the Diocese.
Pung, Karl L. '97 (LAN) East Lansing, MI St. Thomas Aquinas Church.
Pung, Robert *s.v.d.* '44 (FgM) Society of the Divine Word Foreign Missions.
Punke, Msgr. Robert H. '54 (STU) St. Clairsville, OH St. Mary's Church; [I] St. Clairsville, OH Ohio University - Eastern.
Punnakunnel, John '79 (BGP) [1] Bridgeport, CT St. Augustine Cathedral.
Puntal, Pedro C. '82 (ORL) Winter Park, FL Saints Peter and Paul Church.
Punti, George '55 (RVC) Elmont, NY St. Boniface Church.
Puodziunas, John *o.f.m.* '87 (GB) [3] Manitowoc, WI St. Mary Church; [I] Pulaski, WI Assumption of B.V.M. Friary.
Pupin, Vito A. '41 (BRK) Retired.
Pupius, George '63 (OKL) [K] Norman, OK Campus Ministry for the Archdiocese of Oklahoma City.
Pupius, George J. '63 (OKL) Ada, OK St. Joseph Church.
Pupius, George J. '63 (TLS) Coalgate, OK Blessed Sacrament Church.
Pupsys, Adam '52 (NOR) Retired.
Purcell, Arthur D. '79 (BRK) [43] Brooklyn, NY St. Frances de Chantal Church.
Purcell, Frank '78 (LA) Canyon Country, CA St. Clare Church.
Purcell, James '53 (PEO) Retired.
Purcell, Msgr. Lawrence M. '65 (SD) Solana Beach, CA St. James Church.
Purcell, Owen *o.s.b.* '57 (KCK) Kelly, KS St. Bede's Church.
Purcell, Msgr. Paul J. '54 (SCR) [22] Scranton, PA St. Paul's Church.
Purcell, Robert F. *s.j.* '67 (MIL) [P] Milwaukee, WI Jesuit Community at Marquette University.
Purcell, Robert H. '74 (ALB) Margaretville, NY Sacred Heart Church.
Purcell, Thomas P. *o.s.a.* '43 (FgM) Foreign Missions.
Purcell, William F. '47 (SCR) Retired; [N] Dunmore, PA Villa St. Joseph.
Purdy, David T. *s.d.b.* '70 (SFR) [45] San Francisco, CA SS. Peter and Paul Church.
Purdy, George *s.j.* '53 (YAK) Naches, WA St. John's Church.
Purdy, Robert M. '93 (BO) Awaiting Assignment.
Purfield, James R. '54 (DEN) [2] Denver, CO All Saints Church.
Puricell, Stephen G. '91 (STL) Maryland Heights, MO St. Blaise Church.
Purich, Michael *o.f.m.* (PRO) [P] Providence, RI St. Francis Friary.
Purnam, Richard *s.d.b.* '89 (MIA) [25] Miami, FL St. Kieran Church.
Purnell, Mark E. '85 (GBG) Republic, PA Holy Rosary Church.
Purta, Jerome J. '61 (SCR) On Duty Outside the Diocese.
Purtell, John *s.o.l.t.* '95 (CC) [H] Robstown, TX Society of Our Lady of the Most Holy Trinity.
Purtell, John J. '68 (DUB) Hawkeye, IA St. Francis Xavier Church; Sumner, IA Immaculate Conception Church.
Purtell, Thomas J. '61 (CHI) [108] Chicago, IL St. John Fisher Church.
Purtell, Thomas W. '53 (DUB) Retired.
Purvey, J. James '84 (BAL) [63] Baltimore, MD St. Michael Church.
Pusak, Ronald '61 (MIA) [30] Miami, FL St. Richard Church.
Pusateri, Christian *o.s.b.* '55 (RCK) [H] Aurora, IL Marmion Abbey-St. Augustine's Abbey.
Pusateri, Joseph *s.m.* '65 (FgM) Marist Foreign Missions.
Pusateri, Joseph E. '54 (GRY) Otis, IN St. Mary Church.
Pusateri, Philip A. *s.j.* '72 (BO) [E] Boston, MA Boston College High School & Jesuit Community.
Pusateri, Samuel D. *o.s.b.* '79 (PEO) [A] Peru, IL St. Bede Abbey and Academy.
Puscas, Louis *d.d.* '42 (ROM) Aurora, IL St. Michael Church.
Pusch, Richard K. '71 (SHP) [3] Shreveport, LA Our Lady of the Blessed Sacrament Church.
Pushporoj, Henry (NY) Yonkers, NY Yonkers General Hospital.
Putano, John '70 (SY) [1] Syracuse, NY The Cathedral of the Immaculate Conception.
Puthenparambil, Jose '78 (NEW) Teaneck, NJ Holy Name Hospital.
Puthiyadom, Thomas '94 (HRT) [I] Hartford, CT Saint Francis Hospital and Medical Center.
Puthoff, Chad C. *s.d.s.* '71 (SAC) West Sacramento, CA Holy Cross Church.
Puthota, Charles Isaac *s.j.* '89 (MIL) [P] Milwaukee, WI Jesuit Community at Marquette University.
Puthumayil, Chacko '71 (GAL) Sugar Land, TX St. Laurence Church.
Puthuppally, Joseph '66 (SHP) [5] Monroe, LA St. Matthew Church; [B] Monroe, LA St. Francis Medical Center.
Puthusseril, George '79 (MIA) [4] Miami Beach, FL St. Patrick Church.
Putka, John S. *s.m.* '69 (CIN) [D] Dayton, OH The University of Dayton; [M] Dayton, OH Marianist Provincialate.
Putnam, J.T. (WDC) [B] Washington, DC St. Joseph's Seminary.
Putnam, John T., Jr. '92 (CHL) Reidsville, NC Holy Infant Church.
Putnam, Richard *s.d.b.* '89 (MIA) [C] Miami, FL La Salle High School.
Putnick, Robert J. '45 (CIN) Retired.
Putz, Kenneth G. '73 (PH) Warminster, PA Nativity of Our Lord Church.
Putz, Louis J. *c.s.c.* (FTW) [J] Notre Dame, IN Holy Cross Community, Corby Hall, University of Notre Dame.
Putz, Louis J. *c.s.c.* '36 (FTW) [B] Notre Dame, IN University of Notre Dame Du Lac.
Puza, Paul G. '75 (ALN) Barnesville, PA St. Richard Church; [C] Tamaqua, PA Marian Catholic High School.
Puzio, Thomas '70 (DET) [4] Warren, MI St. Dorothy Church.
Puznakoski, Gilbert '75 (PIT) Allegheny County, PA UPMC Shadyside Hospital.
Pyka, Francis *c.m.f.* '46 (PHX) Prescott, AZ Sacred Heart Church.
Pyne, Donald E. '56 (SFR) Retired.
Pyo, Edward '85 (PBR) Ernest, PA St. Jude Thaddeus Church.
Pytel, Ronald '73 (BAL) [38] Baltimore, MD Holy Rosary Church.
Pytlik, Conrad E. '66 (LSC) Mesilla, NM St. Albino Church.

Q

Quach, Binh *c.s.sp.* '91 (OAK) [17] Oakland, CA St. Mary, Immaculate Conception-St. Francis de Sales Church.
Quach, Binh The '91 (WCH) On Duty Outside the Diocese.
Quackenbush, Daniel *o.f.m.conv.* (R) [E] Burlington, NC Conventual Franciscans.
Quackenbush, Daniel M. *o.f.m.conv.* '88 (R) Burlington, NC Blessed Sacrament Church; Siler City, NC St. Julia Church.
Quade, Alvin '54 (SCL) Randall, MN St. James Church.
Quadrini, Angelo '85 (EVN) [F] Jasper, IN Providence Home, Nursing Home for the Needy.
Quaine, Michael W. '85 (DET) [1] Dearborn, MI St. Alphonsus Church.
Quainoo, Clement '82 (VIC) Hillje, TX St. Andrew Church.
Qualizza, Franco *s.x.* '71 (FgM) Xaverian Foreign Missions.
Qualizza, Frank *s.x.* '71 (PAT) [M] Wayne, NJ Xaverian Missionary Fathers.
Quane, Joseph F. *s.j.* '38 (BO) [W] Chestnut Hill, MA The Jesuit Community at Boston College; [W] Weston, MA Campion Health Center, Inc.
Quane, Ralph L. '78 (DET) [4] Clinton Twp., MI St. Ronald Church.
Quang, John '70 (SAV) Military Chaplains.
Quang, Peter Le '97 (LR) [10] Little Rock, AR Our Lady of Good Counsel Church.
Quang Huy, John Vu *c.m.c.* '85 (FWT) Wichita Falls, TX Sacred Heart Church.
Quant, Roberto '91 (OKL) [10] Oklahoma City, OK Holy Angels Church.
Quante, Paul *o.s.a.* '84 (OAK) Castro Valley, CA Our Lady of Grace Church.
Quanz, Paul E. *c.s.b.* '84 (GRY) [B] Merrillville, IN Andrean High School; [J] Merrillville, IN Basilian Fathers Residence.
Quarato, Robert A. '92 (NY) [161] Bronx, NY St. Margaret of Cortona Church.
Quartana, Donald F. '53 (MIL) [1] Wauwatosa, WI St. Bernard Church; Retired.

Quartier, Neal E. '76 (SY) [1] Syracuse, NY The Cathedral of the Immaculate Conception; Special Assignment.
Quattropane, Joseph '72 (LA) Canyon Country, CA St. Clare Church.
Quaye-Foli, Anumu *s.v.d.* '85 (WDC) [M] Washington, DC Divine Word College.
Que, Dinh Ngoc *c.ss.r.* '56 (LA) [R] Baldwin Park, CA Vietnamese Redemptorist Mission.
Quealy, Philip J. '83 (NY) [E] White Plains, NY Archbishop Stepinac High School.
Queen, James T. '65 (SY) [C] Rome, NY Rome Catholic Junior-Senior High School.
Queen, James T. '66 (SY) Florence, NY St. Mary Church; [3] Rome, NY St. Paul Church.
Queenan, John M. (NY) [U] Ossining, NY The Cardinal McCloskey Emergency Residential School.
Queenan, William J. *s.s.* '60 (SFR) [3] Menlo Park, CA The Church of the Nativity.
Quesada, Manuel '53 (RVC) Sick Leave.
Quesada, Raul A. '80 (SJN) [1] Carolina, PR San Andres Church.
Quesada Gil, Raul (SJN) [5] Bayamon, PR Nuestra Sra. de los Dolores Church.
Quetchenbach, Raymond *s.v.d.* '57 (CHI) [B] Techny, IL Divine Word Residence; [N] Techny, IL Society of the Divine Word, Provincial Headquarter-Chicago Prov.
Quevedo, Alfredo S. *s.j.* '56 (BRK) [62] Brooklyn, NY St. Ignatius Church.
Quevedo-Rodriguez, Hernan '96 (ATL) [1] Atlanta, GA Cathedral of Christ the King.
Quezada, Francisco (GAL) [1] Spring, TX Christ the Good Shepherd Church.
Quezada, Sixto '81 (NY) [14] New York, NY Ascension Church.
Qui, Vincent '68 (NO) Retired.
Quiambo, Hermogenes '66 (AGN) Tamuning, GU St. Anthony and St. Victor Church.
Quic, Cristobal Coche '92 (RCK) [H] Aurora, IL Marmion Abbey-St. Augustine's Abbey.
Quiceno, Francisco Jose '72 (SJN) [20] Carolina, PR San Valentin Church.
Quiceno, Jose Francisco '72 (SJN) [57] San Juan, PR Santismo Sacramento Church.
Quickley, George W. *s.j.* '80 (BAL) [M] Baltimore, MD Jesuit Fathers and Brothers Maryland Provincial Curia.
Quickley, George W. *s.j.* '80 (FgM) Provinces.
Quigg, Harold '60 (SEA) [6] Seattle, WA St. Bridget Church.
Quigley, Brian *m.c.c.j.* '77 (FgM) Comboni Foreign Missions.
Quigley, Eugene J. *s.j.* '55 (NY) [DD] New York, NY Jesuit Community at Fordham University; [DD] New York, NY Murray-Weigel Hall.
Quigley, J. Joseph '56 (SPR) Retired; [P] Amherst, MA University of Massachusetts and Amherst College, Newman Center.
Quigley, James Ferrer *o.p.* '65 (PRO) [P] Providence, RI St. Thomas Aquinas Priory at Providence College.
Quigley, John *o.f.m.* '72 (CIN) [M] Cincinnati, OH St. Francis Seraph Friary.
Quigley, John *o.f.m.* '72 (FgM) Franciscan Foreign Missions.
Quigley, Joseph P. '60 (BRK) [79] Brooklyn, NY St. Mark's Church; Brooklyn, NY Coney Island Hospital.
Quigley, Martin J. '46 (BAK) Retired.
Quigley, Patrick '81 (NY) Absent on Leave.
Quigley, Robert L. '58 (NEW) [1] Jersey City, NJ St. Aedan's Church.
Quigley, William *c.i.c.m.* '74 (SAT) [B] San Antonio, TX Missionhurst Formation Community.
Quihuis, Luis H. *s.j.* '92 (SFR) [N] San Francisco, CA Jesuit Community at University of San Francisco.
Quijano, Antonio *m.s.* '92 (HON) Waipahu, HI St. Joseph Church.
Quijano, Jose Juan '73 (MIA) On Duty Outside the Archdiocese.
Quijano, Juan '73 (PMB) [A] Boynton Beach, FL St. Vincent de Paul Regional Seminary.
Quilan, Edward J., III (HBG) Middletown, PA Seven Sorrows of the Blessed Virgin Mary Church.
Quilici, Lawrence '68 (RNO) On Duty Outside the Diocese.
Quilici, Lawrence '68 (TUC) Florence, AZ Arizona State Prison.
Quill, J. Michael '82 (WDC) Pomfret, MD St. Joseph Church.
Quill, James E. '53 (COV) [2] Covington, KY St. Agnes Church; Retired.
Quill, John '74 (NEW) Summit, NJ Overlook Hospital.
Quillen, Andrew M. '91 (BO) [W] Hingham, MA Glastonbury Abbey.
Quilligan, Maurice '57 (SFD) Retired.
Quilligan, Michael '71 (MIA) West Hollywood, FL Annunciation Church.
Quilty, James B. '65 (HRT) Rocky Hill, CT Veterans' Home and Hospital; [M] Hartford, CT Missionaries of LaSalette Provincial Secretary.
Quinkert, Denis *o.s.b.* '76 (SFS) Milbank, SD St. Lawrence Church.
Quinlan, Eugene '62 (MIA) Retired.
Quinlan, Jack J. '97 (DET) Canton, MI Saint John Neumann Church.
Quinlan, James V. '76 (CHI) Maywood, IL St. Eulalia Church.
Quinlan, John J. '70 (PAT) Swartswood, NJ Our Lady of Mt. Carmel Church; Newton, NJ Newton Memorial Hospital.
Quinlan, Joseph M. '52 (NEW) Retired.
Quinlan, Leo F. *s.j.* '45 (FgM) Provinces.
Quinlan, Thomas J. '58 (RIC) Tabb, VA Blessed Kateri Tekawitha Church.
Quinlan, William J. '38 (CHI) Forest Park, IL St. Bernardine Church; Retired.
Quinlivan, Anthony *c.ss.r.* '71 (ORL) Melbourne, FL Ascension Church.
Quinlivan, Francis *c.s.c.* '70 (FgM) Holy Cross Foreign Missions.
Quinlivan, Thomas J. (BUF) [5] West Seneca, NY Queen of Heaven Church.
Quinlivan, William J. '75 (BUF) [4] Kenmore, NY St. Paul Church.
Quinn, Alban *o.carm.* '49 (FgM) Carmelite Foreign Missions.
Quinn, Msgr. Andrew F. '35 (NY) [227] Staten Island, NY Sacred Heart Church; Retired.
Quinn, Bernard '53 (HBG) Hanover, PA St. Vincent Church.
Quinn, Bernard J. '72 (LA) [R] Los Angeles, CA Amat House.
Quinn, Brendan H. '74 (NEW) Kearny, NJ St. Cecilia's Church.
Quinn, Bruce *o.f.m.cap.* '57 (NOR) [4] Middletown, CT St. Pius X Church.
Quinn, Carroll I. *m.m.* '45 (FgM) Maryknoll Foreign Missions.
Quinn, Charles '43 (BAL) [J] Timonium, MD Stella Maris Operating Corporation.
Quinn, Charles H. '43 (BAL) Retired.
Quinn, Charles J. '61 (WIN) Jackson, MN Good Shepherd Church.
Quinn, Charles P. '59 (NY) Pleasant Valley, NY St. Stanislaus Kostka Church.
Quinn, Charles P. '66 (PRO) Glocester, RI St. Eugene Church.
Quinn, Charles T. *o.p.* '55 (NEW) [28] Jersey City, NJ Sacred Heart Church.
Quinn, Desmond *s.s.c.* '54 (FgM) St. Columban's Foreign Mission.
Quinn, Don '83 (IND) [N] Indianapolis, IN Butler University Newman Center; [N] Indianapolis, IN Indiana University-Purdue University, Indianapolis Newman Center; [N] Indianapolis, IN University of Indianapolis Newman Center.
Quinn, Edward I. *s.s.c.* '55 (FgM) St. Columban's Foreign Mission.
Quinn, Edward J. *m.m.* '51 (FgM) Maryknoll Foreign Missions.
Quinn, Frank C. *o.p.* '59 (STL) [B] St. Louis, MO Aquinas Institute of Theology.
Quinn, Gavin *o.carm.* '65 (JOL) Darien, IL Our Lady of Mount Carmel Church.
Quinn, J. Gregory *s.j.* '85 (BAL) [C] Baltimore, MD Loyola High School.
Quinn, J. Patrick '65 (JC) St. Clement, MO St. Clement Church.
Quinn, J. Patrick *t.o.r.* '84 (STP) [20] Minneapolis, MN St. Bridget Church.
Quinn, Jack (ROC) [57] Rochester, NY St. Theodore Church.
Quinn, James '60 (NY) Absent on Leave.
Quinn, James A. '67 (MIA) Hallandale, FL St. Matthew Church.
Quinn, James A. '67 (SY) Absent on Leave.
Quinn, James E. '54 (MIA) Retired.
Quinn, James F. (SY) Special Assignment.
Quinn, James F. '58 (SY) [5] Syracuse, NY Most Holy Rosary Church.
Quinn, James J. *s.j.* '50 (OM) [K] Omaha, NE Jesuit Community At Creighton University.
Quinn, James P. '92 (TR) [21] Trenton, NJ St. Raphael Church.
Quinn, James Q. '67 (SY) [10] Utica, NY St. Joseph and St. Patrick Church.
Quinn, Jarlath '96 (NY) [170] Bronx, NY Our Lady of the Assumption Church.
Quinn, John (NY) White Plains, NY Burke Rehabilitation Center.
Quinn, John F. '71 (NY) Armonk, NY St. Patrick Church.
Quinn, Msgr. John J. '43 (NY) Retired; [A] Yonkers, NY St. Joseph's Seminary.
Quinn, John J. '50 (HRT) Retired.
Quinn, John J. *s.j.* '54 (SCR) [C] Scranton, PA University of Scranton.
Quinn, John J. '86 (TR) Moorestown, NJ Our Lady of Good Counsel Church.
Quinn, John M. *o.s.a.* '49 (PH) [AA] Villanova, PA St. Thomas Monastery.
Quinn, John M. '57 (SY) New Hartford, NY St. Thomas Church.
Quinn, Msgr. John M. '72 (DET) Special Assignment.
Quinn, Msgr. John P. '68 (MAN) [1] Manchester, NH St. Joseph Cathedral; [G] Manchester, NH Catholic Charities Administration.
Quinn, John R. (SFR) Retired.
Quinn, Msgr. John S. '40 (CHI) [11] Chicago, IL St. Andrew Church.
Quinn, Msgr. John S. '44 (CHI) Retired.
Quinn, John T. '67 (SD) Retired.
Quinn, John T. *s.j.* '92 (SAC) [C] Sacramento, CA Jesuit High School; [G] Carmichael, CA Jesuit High School Community of Sacramento.
Quinn, Joseph G. '85 (SCR) [1] Scranton, PA St. Peter's Cathedral.
Quinn, Msgr. Joseph J. '45 (NY) Retired; [DD] New York, NY Pope John Paul II Residence.
Quinn, Joseph L. *s.j.* '66 (SCR) [C] Scranton, PA University of Scranton.
Quinn, Joseph M. *c.s.c.* '50 (BUR) Wallingford, VT St. Patrick Church.
Quinn, Kenneth '71 (BO) Maynard, MA St. Bridget Church.
Quinn, Kevin P. *s.j.* '85 (WDC) [M] Washington, DC The Jesuit Community at Georgetown University.
Quinn, Kieran *o.f.m.cap.* '44 (WH) [2] Charleston, WV St. Anthony Church; [N] Charleston, WV Capuchins-St. Anthony Friary.
Quinn, Lawrence J. '71 (NY) [173] Bronx, NY Our Lady of Mercy Church; [P] New York, NY Catholic Youth Organization of the Archdiocese of New York Inc.
Quinn, Lawrence T. '67 (NY) [195] Staten Island, NY St. Ann Church.
Quinn, Liam '83 (MIA) [A] Miami, FL St. John Vianney College Seminary; [D] Miami, FL Christopher Columbus High School.
Quinn, Matthew *s.s.c.* '43 (LA) Montrose, CA Holy Redeemer Church.
Quinn, Michael F. '70 (JC) Columbia, MO Columbia Newman Center, University of Missouri Church; [F] Columbia, MO University of Missouri-Columbia, Campus Ministry.
Quinn, Peter '50 (ORL) Retired.
Quinn, Peter '62 (JKS) On Duty Outside the Diocese.
Quinn, Peter F. '72 (BO) [3] Quincy, MA St. John the Baptist Church.
Quinn, Peter N. '75 (PH) [51] Philadelphia, PA Good Shepherd Church.
Quinn, Peter O. '62 (BLX) [3] Biloxi, MS Our Mother of Sorrows Church.
Quinn, Richard *c.ss.r.* '62 (B) Coeur D'Alene, ID St. Thomas Church.
Quinn, Richard J. *m.m.* '54 (FgM) Maryknoll Foreign Missions.
Quinn, Msgr. Richard M. '40 (ROC) Retired.
Quinn, Robert C. '61 (ALN) Boyertown, PA St. Columbkill Church.
Quinn, Robert F. *c.s.p.* '53 (NY) [DD] Jamaica Estates, NY Paulist Fathers Generalate.
Quinn, Msgr. Robert J. '34 (SC) Retired.
Quinn, Seamus M. *c.ss.r.* '58 (PH) [135] Philadelphia, PA St. Peter the Apostle Church.
Quinn, Stephen *s.t.* '44 (PAT) [M] Stirling, NJ Holy Spirit Missionary Cenacle.
Quinn, Thomas '62 (SEA) [27] Seattle, WA Our Lady of Fatima Church.
Quinn, Thomas J. *s.j.* '68 (NY) [FF] Staten Island, NY Mount Manresa Jesuit Retreat House.
Quinn, Thomas J. '69 (PBL) Sabbatical.
Quinn, Thomas P. '48 (HRT) Farmington, CT St. Patrick's Church.
Quinn, Thomas S. '85 (TOL) Genoa, OH Our Lady of Lourdes Church.
Quinn, Vincent J. '54 (NEW) Palisades Park, NJ St. Michael's Church; Retired; [N] Caldwell, NJ The Rev. Msgr. James F. Kelley Residence for Retired Priests.
Quinn, Msgr. W. Louis '45 (WDC) [4] Bethesda, MD Our Lady of Lourdes Church; Retired.
Quinn, Walter J. *o.s.a.* '61 (PH) [18] Philadelphia, PA St. Augustine Church.
Quinn, Msgr. William '62 (CAM) Wildwood, NJ St. Ann's Church.
Quinn, Msgr. William J. '41 (CHI) Maywood, IL St. Eulalia Church; Retired.
Quinn, William J. '59 (CHI) [5] Oak Lawn, IL St. Louis De Montfort Church.
Quinn, William P. '55 (SFR) [23] San Francisco, CA Holy Name of Jesus Church.
Quinnan, Edward J. *s.j.* '87 (CHI) [C] Chicago, IL Jesuit Community at Loyola University of Chicago.
Quinnan, Michael F. '86 (SCR) Shohola, PA St. Ann's Church.
Quinones, Benjamin *c.r.l.* '85 (ARE) Corozal-Palmarito, PR La Milagrosa Church.
Quinones, Francisco (SJN) [B] Santurce, PR Academia Sagrado Corazon.
Quinones, Leoncio '46 (PCE) On Duty Outside the Diocese.
Quinones, Miguel P. '52 (WDC) Retired.
Quint, Dennis J. '96 (DUB) [3] Cedar Rapids, IA St. Jude Church.
Quintal, Gerald '65 (P) Dallas, OR St. Philip Church.

Quintana, Carlos *o.s.b.* '49 (FgM) American - Cassinese Congregation Foreign Missions.
Quintana, Carlos *o.s.b.* '49 (RCK) [H] Aurora, IL Marmion Abbey-St. Augustine's Abbey.
Quintana, Jose Luis '95 (GR) Holland, MI St. Francis de Sales Church.
Quinter, Paul S. '82 (PH) [A] Wynnewood, PA Theological Seminary of St. Charles Borromeo, Overbrook.
Quintero, Francisco (SJN) [5] Canovanas, PR San Jose Church.
Quintero, Gustavo '96 (STO) Lodi, CA St. Anne Church.
Quintero, Manuel '81 (LAV) North Las Vegas, NV St. Christopher Church.
Quinters, Msgr. Elmer T. '50 (GAL) Deer Park, TX St. Hyacinth Church.
Quinto, Armand *s.d.b.* '75 (NY) [2] Port Chester, NY Corpus Christi Church.
Quirk, Msgr. Edward J. '45 (NY) Pearl River, NY St. Aedan Church; Retired.
Quirk, Kevin M. '93 (WH) On Duty Outside the Diocese.
Quirk, Richard J. '78 (STL) [46] St. Louis, MO Basilica of St. Louis, the King Church; [W] St. Louis, MO Catholic Commission on Housing.
Quirk, William L. '54 (MAN) Bristol, NH St. Timothy Church.
Quiroz, Guido M. '44 (VIC) Retired.
Quitugua, David C. '83 (AGN) [1] Agana, GU Dulce Nombre de Maria Cathedral - Basilica Church.
Quitugua, David I.A. '64 (AGN) Ordot, GU San Juan Bautista Church.
Qunidlen, Joseph J. '73 (PH) Cheltenham, PA St. Joseph Church.
Quyet, Anthony '83 (JKS) Indianola, MS Immaculate Conception Church; Indianola, MS St. Benedict the Moor Church.

R

Raab, Alexander '36 (STU) Retired.
Raab, John *c.m.f.* '76 (LA) [R] Los Angeles, CA Claretian Retreat Center Community.
Raab, Ronald P. *c.s.c.* '83 (LA) Burbank, CA St. Francis Xavier Church.
Raaser, Eric P. '85 (NY) [E] White Plains, NY Archbishop Stepinac High School.
Raaz, Paul A. '70 (SAT) [22] San Antonio, TX Resurrection of the Lord Church.
Rabalais, Rusty P. '97 (ALX) [3] Alexandria, LA St. Frances Xavier Cabrini Church.
Rabaut, Francis D. *s.j.* '44 (DET) [P] Clarkston, MI Colombiere Center.
Rabay, Christopher *o.cist.* '44 (DAL) [M] Irving, TX Cistercian Abbey of Our Lady of Dallas.
Rabbat, Robert '94 (NTN) Hammond, IN St. Michael the Archangel Church.
Rabbitte, Martin '60 (AUS) [7] Waco, TX St. Mary of the Assumption Church.
Rabe, David (KCK) [5] Leavenworth, KS St. Joseph of the Valley Church.
Rabe, David '83 (KCK) Easton, KS St. Lawrence's Church; Mooney Creek, KS Corpus Christi Church.
Rabelo, William *o. de m.* '95 (PCE) [13] Ponce, PR Santuario San Judas Tadeo Church.
Rabenecker, David *o.s.b.* '91 (IND) [B] St. Meinrad, IN St. Meinrad Seminary-College of Liberal Arts; [J] St. Meinrad, IN St. Meinrad Archabbey.
Rabideau, Richard L. '46 (SAG) Retired.
Rabideau, Thomas R. *o.s.b.* '43 (OKL) [I] Shawnee, OK St. Gregory Abbey.
Rable, Cyril J. '56 (SCR) [4] Old Forge, PA St. Stanislaus Church.
Rabroker, Msgr. Edward '48 (AUS) Granger, TX SS. Cyril and Methodius Church.
Rabroker, Msgr. George F. '41 (BEA) [6] Beaumont, TX Our Lady of the Assumption Church; Retired.
Rabuck, Leo V. (STA) [G] Jacksonville, FL Housing Association of the Diocese of Saint Augustine.
Rabusa, Romeo '95 (HON) Waikane, HI Our Lady of Mt. Carmel Church.
Racco, Philip G. '77 (CLV) [30] Cleveland, OH Holy Rosary Church.
Racette, Norman *o.m.i.* '39 (BWN) [1] Mission, TX Our Lady of Guadalupe Church.
Rached, Jose *c.ss.r.* '70 (SJN) [2] San Juan, PR San Agustin Church.
Rachford, Nicholas (PRM) On Special or Other Diocesan Assignment.
Rachunek, Henry C. '62 (GAL) Beasley, TX St. Wenceslaus Mission Church.
Rachunek, Henry C. '62 (VIC) Hungerford, TX St. John the Baptist Church.
Racine, Michael S. '95 (FR) Awaiting Assignment.
Racivitch, Herve P. *s.j.* '62 (NO) [P] New Orleans, LA Ignatius Residence.
Racki, Leonard E. '62 (PBL) Retired.
Rackliffe, Donald O. (HRT) Bristol, CT Bristol Hospital.
Raczek, Kenneth T. '56 (LFT) Elwood, IN St. Joseph Church.
Raczka, Philip G. '80 (NTN) Cliffside Park, NJ St. Demetrius Church.
Raczynski, Paul L. '72 (MIL) [21] Milwaukee, WI SS. Cyril and Methodius Church.
Raczynski, Theodore T. '56 (HRT) Suffield, CT Sacred Heart Church.
Radaich, Thomas '70 (DUL) Grand Rapids, MN St. Joseph's Church.
Radano, Msgr. John A. '65 (NEW) On Duty Outside the Archdiocese.
Radasky, Robert (ALT) [19] Johnstown, PA St. Clement's Church.
Radchuk, Anthony '62 (PHU) Carteret, NJ St. Mary's Church.
Radde, James M. *s.j.* '72 (MIL) [P] Milwaukee, WI Jesuit Provincial Office, Wisconsin Province.
Radecki, Albin A. '49 (TOL) Retired.
Radecki, Dane *o.praem.* (GB) [I] De Pere, WI St. Joseph Priory.
Radecki, Dane *o.praem.* '77 (CHI) [N] Chicago, IL Premonstratensian Fathers and Brothers (Norbertines).
Radecky, Stephen F. '45 (CLV) [54] Cleveland, OH Our Lady of Lourdes Church; [4] Parma, OH St. Columbkille Church; Retired.
Radek, James '89 (JOL) [1] Naperville, IL St. Elizabeth Seton Church.
Rademacher, Germain P. '58 (NU) Morton, MN St. John Church; Redwood Falls, MN St. Catherine Church.
Rademacher, Msgr. Glen A. '44 (LA) Santa Fe Springs, CA St. Pius X Church; Retired.
Rademacher, John R. '70 (GI) [4] Grand Island, NE St. Leo Church.
Rademacher, Raymond M. '62 (LAN) Fowler, MI Most Holy Trinity Church.
Rademacher, Robert B. *glmy.* '55 (RIC) Clintwood, VA St. Joseph Church.
Rademacher, William '54 (LAN) Retired.
Rademaker, Jan *o.m.i.* '69 (BWN) [8] Brownsville, TX St. Joseph Church.
Rademaker, Martan *o.f.m.* '55 (GLP) Fort Defiance, AZ Our Lady of Blessed Sacrament Church.
Rader, John S. '91 (SFS) [4] Sioux Falls, SD Our Lady of Guadalupe Church.
Radetic, Branimir '52 (Y) [19] Youngstown, OH SS. Peter and Paul's Church.
Radetski, John J. '77 (MIL) Beaver Dam, WI St. Michael Church.
Radetski, Paul J. '82 (GB) Peshtigo, WI St. Mary Church.
Radice, Lawrence D. *m.m.* '85 (FgM) Maryknoll Foreign Missions.
Radloff, James A. '93 (BAK) La Pine, OR Holy Redeemer Church.
Radloff, Thomas H. *s.j.* '61 (DET) [K] Detroit, MI Jesuit Provincial Office-Detroit Province of the Society of Jesus.
Radocha, Stephen J. '77 (ALN) Catasauqua, PA St. Andrew Church; Northampton, PA Assumption of the Blessed Virgin Mary Church.
Radomski, Joseph A. '62 (TR) Avon, NJ St. Elizabeth Church.
Radon, Msgr. Eugene M. '47 (BUF) Retired.
Radosevich, Eugene A. '90 (PEO) Havana, IL St. Patrick's Church.
Radosevich, George '68 (SFD) Livingston, IL Sacred Heart Church; New Douglas, IL St. Ubaldus Church; Staunton, IL St. Michael Church.
Radtke, Fred '67 (CHI) [N] Chicago, IL St. Peter's Friary.
Radvansky, Joseph R. '65 (PRM) Marblehead, OH St. Mary Church.
Radvansky, Robert J. '55 (PSC) Edison, NJ St. Nicholas Church; Perth Amboy, NJ St. Nicholas Church.
Rae Cho, Andrew Myeong '85 (DEN) [5] Aurora, CO St. Lawrence Korean Catholic Community Church.
Raef, Scott '94 (AMA) Gruver, TX Cristo Redentor Church; Spearman, TX Sacred Heart Church.
Raeke, Joseph K. '80 (BO) Holbrook, MA St. Joseph Church.
Rafacz, Joseph J. *v.g.* '56 (LC) [8] La Crosse, WI St. Pius X Church; [10] La Crosse, WI St. Thomas More Church; Special Assignment; [I] La Crosse, WI Holy Cross (Seminary) Diocesan Center.
Rafalowski, Leonard '42 (SEA) Retired.
Raffaeta, George J. '56 (HRT) Woodmont, CT St. Agnes Church.
Raffel, Godfrey '53 (FRS) Tehachapi, CA St. Malachy Church; Retired.
Rafferty, Brian '94 (RIC) [2] Norfolk, VA Christ the King Church.
Rafferty, Brian M. '62 (BAL) Pasadena, MD Our Lady of the Chesapeake Church.
Rafferty, Colm '53 (LA) [56] Los Angeles, CA St. Columban Church.
Rafferty, Gerard F. '79 (NY) Scarsdale, NY Our Lady of Fatima Church; [A] Yonkers, NY St. Joseph's Seminary.
Rafferty, James A. '94 (SCR) Carbondale, PA St. Rose of Lima Church; [A] Dalton, PA Saint Pius X Seminary; [D] Carbondale, PA Sacred Heart Junior/Senior High School.
Rafferty, James E. '72 (SD) Escondido, CA Church of St. Timothy.
Rafferty, James F. '63 (BO) Hingham, MA St. Paul Church.
Rafferty, Joseph P. '83 (SCR) Harveys Lake, PA Our Lady of Victory Church.
Rafferty, Lawrence B. '67 (RVC) Seaford, NY Maria Regina Church.
Rafferty, Michael J. '57 (SCR) West Wyoming, PA Our Lady of Sorrows Church.
Rafferty, Raymond J. '54 (PRO) Retired.
Rafferty, Raymond M. '66 (NY) [40] New York, NY St. Gregory Church; On Duty Outside the Archdiocese.
Rafferty, Thomas A. '38 (WH) Retired.
Rafferty, Thomas F. '83 (GAL) La Porte, TX St. Mary of the Immaculate Conception Church.
Raffo-Rivasplata, Cesar '85 (LA) Carson, CA St. Philomena Church; Torrenace, CA L.A. County-Harbor-U.C.L.A. Medical Center.
Raftery, Paul *o.p.* '55 (SFR) [13] San Francisco, CA St. Dominic Church; [N] San Francisco, CA St. Dominic Priory.
Raftery, Thomas J. '44 (CHI) [37] Chicago, IL Christ the King Church; Winnetka, IL Sacred Heart Church; Retired.
Raftery, William J. '45 (WOR) Retired.
Raftery, William J. *s.j.* '57 (BO) [W] Boston, MA Loyola House; [W] Weston, MA Campion Health Center, Inc.
Raftis, J. Duane '47 (DUB) Retired.
Ragan, Gerald '79 (SAV) Dublin, GA Immaculate Conception Church.
Ragan, Gerald P. '79 (PH) On Duty Outside the Archdiocese.
Rager, Msgr. Charles D. '67 (ALT) Beans Cove, PA Seven Dolors B.V.M. Church; Retired.
Rager, Patrick F. '85 (PIT) Absent on Sick Leave.
Ragis, Gerald '63 (BUR) Charlotte, VT Our Lady of Mount Carmel Church.
Ragni, Richard R. '64 (PIT) Renton, PA St. Januarius Church.
Ragnoni, James V. '60 (CLV) [2] Akron, OH St. Anthony of Padua Church.
Ragsdale, Patrick J. '72 (SAT) [51] San Antonio, TX St. Luke Church.
Ragusa, Salvatore *s.d.s.* '88 (OAK) [B] Moraga, CA St. Mary's College; [Q] Moraga, CA St. Mary's College Campus Ministry.
Rahilly, James T. *c.s.c.* '64 (FgM) Holy Cross Mission Center(C.S.C.).
Rahilly, James T. *c.s.c.* '64 (FTW) [A] Notre Dame, IN Moreau Seminary.
Rahilly, Paul '81 (RVC) Cedarhurst, NY St. Joachim Church.
Rahm, Harold J. *s.j.* '50 (FgM) Provinces.
Rahn, David C. '94 (ARL) [6] Arlington, VA Our Lady of Lourdes Church.
Rahoy, Nicholas '77 (CI) Ulithi and Neighboring Islands, FM Queen of Heaven Church; Woleai and Neighboring Islands, FM St. Ignatius Church.
Rahrig, Gilbert O. '49 (LAN) Howell, MI St. Joseph Church.
Rai, Kevin '74 (AUS) Pflugerville, TX St. Elizabeth Church.
Raible, Daniel *c.pp.s.* '43 (CIN) [B] Carthagena, OH St. Charles.
Raible, Roland *o.f.m.cap.* '35 (PIT) [O] Pittsburgh, PA St. Augustine Friary.
Raica, Stephen '78 (LAN) Bellevue, MI St. Ann Church.
Raica, Steven J. '78 (LAN) [1] Lansing, MI St. Mary Cathedral.
Raich, Stephen *o.f.m.* '43 (NY) [29] New York, NY SS. Cyril and Methodius - St. Raphael Church.
Raiche, Brian '95 (ALB) Oneonta, NY St. Mary Church; [S] Oneonta, NY New York State University at Oneonta and Hartwick College.
Raila, Donald *o.s.b.* '83 (GBG) [H] Latrobe, PA Saint Vincent Archabbey.
Raila, Stanislaus '33 (BRK) Retired; [U] Douglaston, NY Bishop Mugavero Residence.
Raimer, Chester J. '74 (GBG) Blairsville, PA SS. Simon and Jude Church; Torrance, PA Torrance State Hospital.
Raimondi, Michele '50 (SFR) Retired.
Raimondo, Msgr. Joseph J. '40 (NY) Harrison, NY St. Gregory the Great Church; Retired.
Rainaldo, John H. *s.j.* '64 (MIL) [P] Milwaukee, WI Jesuit Provincial Office, Wisconsin Province.
Rainaldo, John H. *s.j.* '64 (NY) [DD] New York, NY Jesuit Provincial's Office.
Rainaldo, John H. *s.j.* '64 (RVC) [R] New Hyde Park, NY Apostleship of Prayer, National Office for the U.S.
Rainforth, Thomas G. (PAT) [7] Paterson, NJ St. George Church.
Rainone, John J. '70 (PRO) [20] Providence, RI St. Joseph Church; Providence, RI Rhode Island Hospital.
Rainville, Laurence P. *o.f.m.* '47 (ALB) [B] Loudonville, NY Siena College.
Rainville, Marcel *s.s.e.* '71 (BUR) [E] Colchester, VT Society of St. Edmund.

Rainville, Paul *m.s.* '65 (MAN) Enfield, NH St. Helena Church.
Raiser, Jerome K. '58 (COL) Washington Court House, OH St. Colman Church.
Raj, Percy Joseph *o.f.m.* '74 (NY) [206] Staten Island, NY Holy Rosary Church.
Rajanayagam, Thomas M. '66 (STO) Riverbank, CA St. Frances of Rome Church.
Rajter, Valentine *o.f.m.conv.* '48 (BUF) [21] Buffalo, NY Corpus Christi Church.
Raju, Anthony Prem (LA) Covina, CA St. Louise de Marillac Church.
Raju, Martin '85 (NY) [W] New York, NY St. Vincent's Hospital and Medical Center of New York.
Rakaczki, Andor '73 (PSC) Bridgeport, CT Holy Trinity Church.
Rakaczky, Basil M. *o.s.b.m.* '60 (PSC) Perth Amboy, NJ St. Michael Church; [A] Matawan, NJ Basilian Fathers of Mariapoch.
Rakatonocliarimanana, Raphael *m.s.* '65 (STL) [P] St. Louis, MO La Salette Missionaries.
Raker, Msgr. Clarence J. '39 (DUB) Retired.
Rakoczy, Richard S. '59 (DET) Waterford, MI St. Perpetua Church.
Rakoczy, Walter J. '78 (GRY) [3] Whiting, IN St. Adalbert Church.
Rakowicz, William J. *s.j.* '80 (FgM) Provinces.
Ralenkotter, Howard *c.p.* '38 (L) [L] Louisville, KY Sacred Heart Retreat.
Ralko, Martin J. '84 (COL) Dennison, OH Immaculate Conception Church.
Ralph, John '55 (WH) Retired.
Ralph, Msgr. Thomas J. '56 (DUB) Otter Creek, IA St. Lawrence Church.
Ramacciotti, Gabriel M. *o.s.m.* '51 (DEN) [4] Denver, CO Assumption Church.
Ramacciotti, James J. '85 (STL) [23] St. Louis, MO St. Ambrose Church; [A] St. Louis, MO Kenrick-Glennon Seminary.
Ramacher, Edward '45 (SCL) Spring Hill, MN St. Michael's Church; Retired.
Ramaeker, Victor F. '61 (SC) Vail, IA St. Ann's Church.
Ramaekers, Timothy '82 (ORG) Placentia, CA St. Joseph Church.
Ramellini, Msgr. P. Lino '47 (GBG) Retired.
Ramen, Paul F. '60 (NOR) Retired.
Ramenaden, Ronald (FTW) North Manchester, IN St. Robert Bellarmine Church.
Ramer, James K. '86 (PEO) [1] Rock Island, IL St. Mary Church.
Ramer, Leo '54 (LAN) Retired.
Ramirez, Adalberto *o.f.m.* '64 (CC) Hebbronville, TX Our Lady of Guadalupe Church; [H] Hebbronville, TX Franciscan Friars - O.F.M.
Ramirez, Allen A. *o.f.m.conv.* '72 (MRY) [G] Arroyo Grande, CA St. Joseph Cupertino Province, Provincial Center.
Ramirez, Cesar '96 (ARE) [1] Arecibo, PR Cathedral of San Felipe Apostol.
Ramirez, Charles J. '87 (LA) Monrovia, CA Immaculate Conception Church.
Ramirez, Cornelio C. *s.a.c.* '67 (LUB) [7] Lubbock, TX St. Patrick Church.
Ramirez, Enrique Espinosa *m.sp.s.* '79 (LA) [3] Oxnard, CA Our Lady of Guadalupe Parish.
Ramirez, Fernando '78 (SD) [5] San Diego, CA Good Shepherd Church.
Ramirez, Francisco X. '79 (LA) [84] Los Angeles, CA St. Patrick Church.
Ramirez, Gerardo '91 (PCE) Ensenada, PR Sacred Heart Church; Guanica, PR St. Anthony Abbot Church.
Ramirez, Hernando *s.j.* '75 (CC) On Special Assignment; [E] Laredo, TX Mercy Regional Medical Center.
Ramirez, J. Jesus '86 (YAK) Granger, WA Our Lady of Guadalupe Church.
Ramirez, Jairo H. '88 (STO) [8] Stockton, CA St. Mary of the Assumption Church.
Ramirez, Jose *s.m.* '69 (STL) [P] St. Louis, MO Marianist Community; [T] Eureka, MO Marianist Retreat & Conference Center.
Ramirez, Jose Nieves '79 (ELP) Absent on Leave.
Ramirez, Julio *m.x.y.* (NY) [179] Bronx, NY Our Saviour Church.
Ramirez, Oran de Jesus *c.ss.r.* '67 (MET) [8] Perth Amboy, NJ La Asuncion Church.
Ramirez, Pascual '92 (OAK) [6] Fremont, CA Santa Paula Church.
Ramirez, Renelmo '84 (CGS) Culebra, PR Nuestra Senora del Carmen Church.
Ramirez, Tulio *m.x.y.* (NY) [HH] Bronx, NY Yarumal Mission Society, Inc.
Ramirez-Alejos, Msgr. Pedro '74 (SPK) Pasco, WA St. Patrick Church.
Ramirez-Portugal, Daniel '91 (CC) [2] Laredo, TX Christ the King Church.
Ramler, Michael '74 (LEX) Frankfort, KY Good Shepherd Church.
Ramon, Gustavo '92 (LA) Montebello, CA St. Benedict Church.
Ramon, Robert C. '82 (GAL) Dickinson, TX Shrine of the True Cross Church.
Ramon, Valentin *c.m.f.* '64 (ORG) [2] Orange, CA La Purisima Church.
Ramon-Landry, Kenneth '87 (BLX) Laurel, MS Immaculate Conception Church; [G] Laurel, MS c/o Immaculate Conception Church.
Ramos, Andre '88 (SD) [4] Chula Vista, CA St. Rose of Lima Church.
Ramos, Angel Roman '90 (MGZ) Hormigueros, PR Shrine of Our Lady of Monserrate Church.
Ramos, Antonio W. '94 (SFS) Mellette, SD All Saints Church.
Ramos, Cipriano '52 (SAC) Retired and in Senior Ministry.
Ramos, Danilo G. *c.i.c.m.* '79 (DAL) Forney, TX St. Martin Church; Kaufman, TX St. Ann Church.
Ramos, Eleuterio '66 (ORG) Inactive Leave.
Ramos, Fausto '35 (PCE) Retired.
Ramos, Fausto '46 (PCE) Villalba, PR Our Lady of Mt. Carmel Church.
Ramos, Gregorio *o.m.i.* '50 (FgM) Oblates Foreign Missions.
Ramos, Justin S. *o.praem.* '95 (ORG) [D] Siverado, CA St. Michael's College Preparatory High School; [H] Silverado, CA Norbertine Fathers of Orange Inc.
Ramos, Ponciano M. '85 (SB) Murrietta, CA St. Martha's Church.
Ramos, Victoriano '54 (SJN) [33] San Juan, PR Santa Luisa de Marillac Church.
Ramoso, Irenio '89 (SFR) Foster City, CA St. Luke Church.
Ramsey, Boniface *o.p.* '73 (NEW) [A] South Orange, NJ Immaculate Conception Seminary.
Ramsey, James '84 (GAL) Damon, TX SS. Cyril and Methodius Church; Needville, TX St. Michael Church.
Ramsey, James Boniface *o.p.* '73 (NY) [121] New York, NY St. Vincent Ferrer Church; [DD] New York, NY St. Vincent Ferrer Priory.
Ramson, Ronald W. *c.m.* '59 (STL) [P] St. Louis, MO Vincentian Residence.
Ranalletti, Richard A. *c.s.b.* '73 (OAK) [C] Oakland, CA Bishop O'Dowd High School.
Ranalli, John '83 (R) Special Assignment.
Ranalli, John A. '83 (R) [I] Raleigh, NC Vocations Office.
Ranallo, John *o.s.a.* (OAK) Castro Valley, CA Eden Hospital.
Ranallo, John E. '75 (OAK) Castro Valley, CA Transfiguration Church.
Rancourt, Henry *s.m.* '57 (BO) [Y] Framingham Centre, MA The Marist House.
Rancourt, Mauril *o.m.i.* '60 (FgM) Oblates Foreign Missions.
Randall, Msgr. Edward '64 (GAL) [24] Houston, TX St. Cyril of Alexandria Church.
Randall, Edward L. *o.m.i.* '50 (LEX) Jenkins, KY St. George Church.
Randall, John F. '53 (PRO) [11] Providence, RI St. Charles Borromeo Church.
Randall, Jude *o.s.b.* '60 (JOL) [J] Lisle, IL St. Procopius Abbey.
Randall, Jude D. '60 (JOL) [C] Lisle, IL Benet Academy.
Randall, Robert J. '51 (PRO) Retired.
Randazzo, Anthony J. '86 (NEW) North Caldwell, NJ Notre Dame Church.
Randone, Michael C '95 (BO) North Andover, MA St. Michael Church.
Ranek, Jerome M. '91 (SFS) Mobridge, SD St. Joseph Church.
Raneri, Carmine B. '55 (HRT) [6] Waterbury, CT Our Lady of Mt. Carmel Church.
Raney, Isaac *m.ss.a.* '67 (DEN) Greeley, CO St. Peter Church.
Raney, Richard E. '38 (PEO) Retired.
Ranft, Paul J. '40 (TUC) San Manuel, AZ St. Bartholomew Church; Retired.
Ranges, Charles H. *s.s.e.* '72 (BUR) Highgate Center, VT St. Louis Church; Swanton, VT Nativity of the Blessed Virgin Mary Church.
Ranieri, John J. '82 (NEW) [B] South Orange, NJ Seton Hall University.
Ranieri, Msgr. Joseph A. '57 (WDC) Hyattsville, MD St. Jerome Church.
Rank, Robert *s.o.l.t.* '67 (CC) Robstown, TX St. Anthony Church; [B] Robstown, TX St. Anthony School; [H] Robstown, TX Society of Our Lady of the Most Holy Trinity.
Rank, Robert F. '68 (GB) On Duty Outside the Diocese.
Rank, Ronald G. '58 (MAD) Waterloo, WI St. Joseph Church.
Rankin, James '65 (SD) [37] San Diego, CA St. Vincent de Paul Church; Retired.
Rankin, Joseph M. '79 (L) [27] Louisville, KY St. Francis of Assisi Church.
Rankin, Paul B. *c.s.c.* '48 (AUS) [H] Austin, TX Congregation of Holy Cross - Southern Province.
Rankin, Paul B. *c.s.c.* '48 (FTW) [J] South Bend, IN Congregation of Holy Cross Indiana Province Provincial House.
Rankin, Robert '80 (LA) Montrose, CA Holy Redeemer Church.
Ranly, Ernest W. *c.pp.s.* '56 (CIN) [M] Dayton, OH Provincial House of the Cincinnati Province of the Society of the Precious Blood.
Rans, Norbert J. *m.m.* '64 (NY) [DD] Maryknoll, NY Maryknoll Fathers and Brothers.
Ransing, Bernard E. *c.s.c.* '35 (FTW) [J] South Bend, IN Congregation of Holy Cross Indiana Province Provincial House.
Ransom, Ralph R. *s.s.j.* '61 (BAL) [M] Baltimore, MD St. Joseph Society of the Sacred Heart House of Central Administration.
Ranzino, Thomas C. '78 (BR) [9] Baton Rouge, LA St. George Church.
Rapczynski, Joseph B. '34 (ALN) Retired; [J] Bethlehem, PA Holy Family Villa.
Raphael, John *s.s.j.* '95 (BEA) [7] Beaumont, TX Our Mother of Mercy Church.
Rapin, Cyril W. '46 (OG) Mooers, NY St. Joseph Church; Retired.
Raposo, John A. '77 (FR) Provincetown, MA St. Peter the Apostle Church.
Rapp, Bernard A. '77 (SD) Calexico, CA Our Lady of Guadalupe Church.
Rapp, Bertrand J. '50 (L) [3] Louisville, KY St. Albert the Great Church; [12] Louisville, KY St. Bartholomew Church; Retired.
Rapp, James F. *o.s.f.s.* '67 (OKL) Duncan, OK Assumption Church.
Rappl, Joseph P. '78 (BUF) Military Chaplains.
Rareshide, Msgr. Lanaux J. '61 (NO) [48] New Orleans, LA St. Monica Church.
Rarus, Boleslaus J. '40 (BGP) Retired.
Rasby, Msgr. James W. '52 (DEN) Retired.
Rasch, Richard *o.de.m.* '84 (CLV) [57] Cleveland, OH Our Lady of Mount Carmel Church; [P] Cleveland, OH Mercedarians.
Rascher, Joseph C. '81 (BEL) Evansville, IL St. Boniface Church.
Raschke, Bernard L. '58 (LC) Edgar, WI St. John the Baptist Church.
Raschko, Michael '75 (SEA) Special Assignment.
Rashford, John T. *s.j.* '71 (YAK) [4] Yakima, WA St. Joseph's Church; [B] Yakima, WA Providence Yakima Medical Center.
Rashford, Nicholas J. *s.j.* '71 (PH) [C] Philadelphia, PA St. Joseph's University; [AA] Philadelphia, PA Jesuit Community at St. Joseph's University.
Rasing, Linus E. '53 (DUB) Bankston, IA St. Clement's Church.
Rask, Phillip J. '72 (STP) [A] St. Paul, MN The Saint Paul Seminary; [C] St. Paul, MN University of St. Thomas.
Raskowski, Robert P. *s.j.* '46 (FgM) Provinces.
Rasky, Joseph G. *s.m.* '65 (SAT) [F] San Antonio, TX Central Catholic High School; [M] San Antonio, TX Central Catholic Marianist Community.
Rasmussen, Harry *s.d.b.* '62 (LA) [X] Rosemead, CA St. Joseph's Salesian Youth Renewal Center.
Rasmussen, John C. '69 (SFS) Elk Point, SD St. Joseph Church.
Rasner, David L. '72 (LFT) Special Assignment.
Rasner, David L. '82 (LFT) Otterbein, IN St. Charles Church.
Raso, Anthony '75 (BRK) [216] Queens, NY Our Lady of Mount Carmel Church.
Raspallo, Domenic (PRO) Retired.
Raspudic, Bruno *o.f.m.* '43 (PIT) [O] Beaver Falls, PA Our Lady of Peace Monastery.
Rasquinha, Ignatius '33 (SB) Joshua Tree, CA St. Christopher of the Desert Church.
Rassas, George J. '68 (CHI) Lake Forest, IL St. Mary Church.
Rassley, George *c.ss.r.* '53 (B) Coeur D'Alene, ID St. Thomas Church.
Rassmussen, Terrence *o.f.m.conv.* '79 (DUB) Ames, IA St. Cecilia Church; Gilbert, IA SS. Peter and Paul Church.
Rasura, James I. *s.j.* '56 (SD) [12] San Diego, CA Our Lady of Guadalupe Church; San Diego, CA Central Detention Facility and San Diego City Jail.
Raszeja, Norbert W. *c.r.* '72 (CHI) [N] Chicago, IL Provincial Office of the Congregation of the Resurrection.
Raszewski, Edward J. *c.s.sp.* '47 (FgM) Holy Ghost Foreign Missions.
Raszkowski, Robert P. *s.j.* '46 (FgM) Provinces.
Raszkowski, Robert P. *s.j.* '46 (MIL) [P] Milwaukee, WI Jesuit Provincial Office, Wisconsin Province.
Rataj, Stanley G. '79 (CHI) [143] Chicago, IL St. Nicholas of Tolentine Church.
Ratajczak, Justin *o.f.m.conv.* '77 (BAL) [26] Baltimore, MD St. Clement Mary Hofbauer Church.
Ratajczak, Michael '75 (SD) Spring Valley, CA Santa Sophia Church.
Ratajczak, Richard C. '58 (SAG) Beaver, MI St. Valentine Church.
Ratazak, Bernard A. '76 (RCK) Retired.
Ratchford, Robert J. *s.j.* '61 (NO) Gretna, LA Jefferson Parish Correctional Center; [C] New Orleans, LA

Loyola University; [P] New Orleans, LA Jesuit Provincial Office.
Raterman, Herbert J *s.j.* '55 (CIN) [M] Cincinnati, OH Faber Jesuit Community.
Raterman, Herbert J. *s.j.* '55 (CIN) [V] Cincinnati, OH Living Monuments of Reparation.
Ratermann, Msgr. David A. '51 (STL) On Duty Outside the Archdiocese.
Ratermann, George H. *m.m.* '47 (CLV) [P] Cleveland, OH Maryknoll Fathers.
Ratermann, Jerome B. '57 (BEL) Retired.
Rath, John G. '36 (Y) Retired.
Rath, Martin *o.s.b.* (NU) [B] Winsted, MN St. Mary's Care Center.
Rath, Martin *o.s.b.* '83 (NU) Winsted, MN St. Mary's Care Center.
Rath, Richard J. '88 (STL) Webster Groves, MO Holy Redeemer Church.
Rath, Thomas V. '49 (CLV) Amherst, OH St. Joseph Church; [5] Lorain, OH St. John Church; Retired.
Rathapilly, Emanuel '71 (SJP) Altoona, PA Immaculate Conception Church; Barnesboro, PA Immaculate Conception Church.
Rathfon, John R. '54 (CLV) Cuyahoga Falls, OH Immaculate Heart of Mary Church; Retired.
Rathgeb, William R. '67 (GBG) [E] Greensburg, PA Clelian Heights School for Exceptional Children; [I] Greensburg, PA Apostles of the Sacred Heart of Jesus.
Rathhinam, Belevendiram '74 (NY) [34] New York, NY Epiphany Church.
Rathschmidt, John *o.f.m.cap.* '69 (NY) [C] New Rochelle, NY College of New Rochelle; [DD] White Plains, NY St. Conrad Friary.
Ratigan, James '65 (JOL) Woodridge, IL Christ The Servant Parish.
Ratigan, Patrick A. '83 (OG) Military Chaplains.
Ratory, Paul *o.p.* '84 (P) [18] Portland, OR Holy Rosary Parish & Dominican Priory Church.
Ratterman, Kevin J. '94 (OKL) Edmond, OK St. John the Baptist Church; [K] Norman, OK Campus Ministry for the Archdiocese of Oklahoma City.
Ratzenberger, Raymond '85 (TUC) Benson, AZ Our Lady of Lourdes Church.
Ratzmann, George '87 (VEN) [1] Naples, FL St. Ann Church.
Rau, Msgr. Donald E. '56 (STL) [51] St. Louis, MO St. Mary of Victories Church.
Rau, Peter J. '85 (ATL) Cumming, GA Good Shepherd Church.
Rau, Msgr. Raymond '49 (BRK) [21] Brooklyn, NY Blessed Sacrament Church.
Rau, Raymond F. '49 (BRK) Retired; Retired.
Rau, Msgr. Raymond F. '49 (CC) [22] Corpus Christi, TX St. Theresa Church.
Raub, Jacob *o.c.s.o.* '62 (L) [L] Trappist, KY Abbey of Our Lady of Gethsemani, of the Order of Cistercians of the Strict Observance.
Rauch, David E. '70 (STL) [38] St. Louis, MO St. James the Greater Church.
Rauch, Edward L. *o.s.f.s.* '64 (PH) [D] Philadelphia, PA Father Judge High School for Boys; [AA] Philadelphia, PA Father Judge Faculty House.
Rauch, Laszlo F. '49 (TR) Normandy Beach, NJ Our Lady of Peace Church.
Raudabaugh, Joseph R. '62 (CIN) Fairborn, OH Mary Help of Christians Church.
Raudeliunas, Kazimieras *s.j.* '43 (CHI) [N] Chicago, IL Lithuanian American Jesuits.
Raught, Msgr. Horton '44 (NEW) [2] Newark, NJ St. Patrick's Pro-Cathedral.
Raulli, Enrico *s.j.* '65 (NEW) [C] Jersey City, NJ St. Peter's Preparatory School.
Raulli, Enrico *s.j.* '65 (NY) [DD] New York, NY West Side Jesuit Community.
Raum, Blair '71 (BAL) [91] Baltimore, MD St. Thomas Aquinas Church; Special Assignment.
Raun, Msgr. Douglas A. '82 (SFE) Rio Rancho, NM St. Thomas Aquinas Church.
Rausch, Clyde *o.m.i.* '68 (FgM) Oblates Foreign Missions.
Rausch, Dale J. '68 (DUB) Fayette, IA St. Francis of Assisi Church; West Union, IA Holy Name Church; [N] West Union, IA Upper Iowa University.
Rausch, Dennis '80 (MIA) [5] Fort Lauderdale, FL St. Clement Church.
Rausch, John '72 (CIN) [M] Fairfield, OH Headquarters of Glenmary Home Missioners.
Rausch, John *o.f.m.* '76 (STL) [P] St. Louis, MO Franciscan Friary of St. Anthony of Padua.
Rausch, John W. '47 (MIL) Retired.
Rausch, Leon S. *s.j.* '59 (LC) Gays Mills, WI St. Mary Church; Rolling Ground, WI St. Philip Church.
Rausch, Leon S. *s.j.* '59 (MIL) [P] Milwaukee, WI Jesuit Provincial Office, Wisconsin Province.
Rausch, Nicholas *o.s.b.* '56 (SEA) [M] Lacey, WA St. Martin's Abbey.
Rausch, Thomas P. *s.j.* '72 (LA) [C] Los Angeles, CA Loyola Marymount University.
Rauscher, Donald F. *s.j.* '68 (MIL) [P] Milwaukee, WI Jesuit Provincial Office, Wisconsin Province.
Rauscher, Msgr. Joseph G. '67 (SCR) [16] Wilkes-Barre, PA St. Nicholas Church.
Rauscher, Msgr. Martin F. '60 (PAT) Morristown, NJ Assumption of the Blessed Virgin Mary Church.
Rauscher, Russell G. '75 (CLV) [5] Parma, OH St. Francis de Sales Church.
Rauseo, Francis J. (PH) [88] Philadelphia, PA St. Lucy Church.
Rautenberg, Joseph F. '73 (IND) Beech Grove, IN Holy Name Church; Knightstown, IN St. Rose Church; New Castle, IN St. Anne Church; [F] Indianapolis, IN St. Vincent Hospital and Health Care Center, Inc.
Rauth, Philip J. '59 (LIN) Auburn, NE St. Joseph's Church.
Raux, Redmond (BO) Military & VA Chaplains.
Raux, Redmond '82 (PHX) Luke Air Force Base, AZ Luke Air Force Base.
Rauzi, Mario *c.s.* '45 (CIN) [80] Cincinnati, OH Sacred Heart Church.
Raveneau, Ricardo '90 (BRK) [86] Brooklyn, NY St. Michael's Church.
Ravey, Donald J. '61 (BUR) Williston, VT Immaculate Heart of Mary Church.
Ravlic, Msgr. Cornelius C. '37 (LA) Retired.
Rawa, Jerome D. *s.m.* '55 (WH) Richwood, WV Holy Family Church; Summersville, WV St. John The Evangelist Church.
Rawden, Msgr. John A. (LA) [K] Santa Barbara, CA St. Francis Medical Center of Santa Barbara.
Rawlins, John J. *s.s.j.* '45 (BAL) [M] Baltimore, MD St. Joseph's Manor.
Ray, James M. '75 (CHI) Other Assignments; [G] Chicago, IL Catholic Charities of the Archdiocese of Chicago-Archdiocesan Offices.
Ray, Robert E. '69 (L) Fairdale, KY St. Jerome Church.
Rayer, Thomas '93 (STP) Crystal, MN St. Raphael Church.
Rayes, Emanuel '54 (EST) Troy, MI St. Joseph Chaldean Parish.
Rayes, Joseph *o.f.m.* '57 (CIN) [M] Cincinnati, OH St. Ann Friary.
Raymaker, John *c.i.c.m.* (BO) [4] Boston, MA St. Ambrose Church.
Raymaker, John *c.i.c.m.* '64 (FgM) Missionhurst Foreign Missions.
Raymond, David R. '89 (SPR) South Hadley, MA St. Patrick's Church; [C] Springfield, MA Cathedral High School; [C] Holyoke, MA Holyoke Catholic High School.
Raymond, Maurice L. '62 (SCR) [2] Hazleton, PA Church of the Most Precious Blood.
Raymond, Wilfred J. '71 (BGP) [O] Bridgeport, CT Provincial Offices of the Priests and Brothers of Holy Cross, Eastern Province.
Raymundo, Gregorio G. '46 (LA) Retired.
Raynor, John P. *s.j.* '54 (MIL) [C] Milwaukee, WI Marquette University.
Re, Angelo '60 (SJ) Retired.
Rea, John W. '45 (ARL) Winchester, VA Sacred Heart of Jesus Church; Retired.
Read, Denis *o.c.d.* '52 (MIL) [P] Holy Hill, WI Discalced Carmelite Monastery; [W] Milwaukee, WI Cursillos in Christianity.
Read, Ignacio *o.c.d.* '56 (MIL) [P] Milwaukee, WI Provincial Offices - Discalced Carmelites.
Reading, Edward '72 (PAT) On Duty Outside the Diocese.
Ready, Francis P. '50 (BO) Retired.
Ready, Frank J. '59 (ARL) Annandale, VA Holy Spirit Church.
Reagan, Msgr. Donald '47 (Y) Retired.
Real, Fernando *m.id.* '81 (NY) [180] Bronx, NY Santa Maria Church; [DD] Bronx, NY Idente Missionaries - Santa Maria Residence.
Real, Gabriel D. *c.m.* '48 (BRK) [116] Brooklyn, NY St. Peter-St. Paul-Our Lady of Pilar Church.
Real, Jorge del (SFR) [4] San Mateo, CA St. Timothy Church.
Reale, Frank *s.j.* '81 (FgM) Provinces.
Reale, Frank *s.j.* '81 (STL) [P] St. Louis, MO The Jesuits of the Missouri Province.
Reale, Frank E. *s.j.* '81 (STL) [F] St. Louis, MO St. Louis University High School, George H. Backer Memorial; [P] St. Louis, MO St. Louis University High School Jesuit Community.
Reale, Sante *c.pp.s.* '60 (ORL) Kissimmee, FL Holy Redeemer Church.
Realmuto, George '87 (NOR) [F] Cromwell, CT Missionaries of the Holy Apostles.
Ream, Gerard J. (ALT) Retired.
Reamer, Mark *o.f.m.* '91 (R) [4] Raleigh, NC St. Francis of Assisi Church.
Reamer, William G. '87 (OG) Crown Point, NY Sacred Heart Church; Indian Lake, NY St. Mary's Church; Ticonderoga, NY St. Mary Church.
Reardon, Arthur L. '52 (BO) Permanent Disability.
Reardon, Daniel *c.s.v.* '61 (LAV) [1] Las Vegas, NV Guardian Angel Cathedral.
Reardon, Dennis A. '72 (PRO) [23] Providence, RI St. Michael the Archangel Church.
Reardon, Francis '78 (PMB) Vero Beach, FL Holy Cross Church.
Reardon, J. Daniel '97 (KC) [40] Kansas City, MO St. Thomas More Church.
Reardon, James E. '65 (BIS) Beulah, ND St. Joseph Church; Hazen, ND St. Martin Church.
Reardon, John D. '73 (PH) Wyndmoor, PA Seven Dolors Church.
Reardon, John F. '50 (NY) [225] Staten Island, NY St. Rita Church.
Reardon, John F. '76 (BO) [3] Brockton, MA St. Edward Church.
Reardon, John I. *o.p.* '49 (NO) [30] New Orleans, LA St. Dominic Church.
Reardon, John J. '39 (STU) Retired.
Reardon, Michael '74 (LA) [5] Long Beach, CA St. Cornelius Church.
Reardon, Patrick *o.p.* '60 (FgM) Dominican - Order of Preachers Foreign Missions.
Reardon, Robert *o.m.i.* '68 (FgM) Oblates Foreign Missions.
Reardon, Robert J. '59 (PIT) Upper St. Clair, PA St. John Capistran Church.
Reardon, Thomas J. '51 (LC) Mauston, WI St. Patrick Church.
Reasbeck, Msgr. David E. '56 (STU) Colerain, OH St. Frances Cabrini Church.
Reaume, Michael R. *s.m.* '69 (CIN) [M] Dayton, OH Marianist Provincialate.
Reaves, Phillip A. (LR) Fort Smith, AR Immaculate Conception Church.
Reaves, Phillip A. '94 (LR) Hartford, AR St. Leo's Church.
Rebaldo, Ronald '91 (RVC) Sayville, NY St. Lawrence the Martyr Church.
Rebamontan, Marito F. '70 (ORG) [1] Anaheim, CA St. Anthony Claret Church.
Rebanal, Jeremias R. '95 (NEW) [1] Jersey City, NJ St. Aedan's Church.
Rebaque, Jose *s.a.c.* '70 (BGP) [9] Bridgeport, CT St. George's Church; [18] Bridgeport, CT St. Peter's Church.
Rebatzki, George M. '64 (MIL) [49] Milwaukee, WI Old St. Mary Church.
Rebebes, Florencio B. '78 (HON) Lanai City, HI Sacred Hearts Church.
Rebeck, Eugene M. '65 (TR) Holmdel, NJ St. Catharine Church.
Rebeiro, Anthony J. '56 (BO) [1] Revere, MA St. Anthony of Padua Church.
Rebel, John W. '65 (PIT) Mars, PA St. Kilian Church.
Rebel, Patrick '85 (SP) Gulfport, FL Most Holy Name of Jesus Church.
Rebeyro, Lloyd '70 (ALB) [11] Albany, NY St. Mary Church.
Rebman, Msgr. Joseph F. '60 (WIL) [1] Wilmington, DE Cathedral of St. Peter.
Rebol, Anthony '56 (CLV) [42] Cleveland, OH St. Lawrence Church.
Rebol, Francis *m.m.* '53 (FgM) Maryknoll Foreign Missions.
Rebold, John '54 (SFE) Retired.
Reboli, John P. *s.j.* '70 (WOR) [N] Worcester, MA Jesuits of Holy Cross College, Inc.
Rebong, Nestor '86 (LA) Glendora, CA St. Dorothy Church.
Rebosura, II, Sabino B. '87 (HT) Cut-Off, LA Sacred Heart Church.
Rebovich, John '67 (PRM) Absent on Leave.
Rebuldelha, Alfred '72 (HON) Makawao, HI St. Joseph Church.
Recchuti, William A. *o.s.a.* '44 (PH) [AA] Flourtown, PA Augustinians (O.S.A.).
Recchuti, William A. *o.s.a.* '61 (PH) Flourtown, PA St. Genevieve Church.
Receconi, Edward R. *o.s.b.* '79 (SEA) [M] Lacey, WA St. Martin's Abbey.
Recera, Ricardo '89 (CHI) [208] Chicago, IL Transfiguration of Our Lord Church.
Rechenburg, Basil *o.s.b.* '68 (WOR) [N] Still River, MA Benedictine Monks, St. Benedict Abbey.
Rechtein, John *s.m.* '70 (SAT) [C] San Antonio, TX St. Mary's University of San Antonio, Texas.
Rechtien, John *s.m.* '70 (SAT) [M] San Antonio, TX Marianist Residence.
Recio, Jesus Perez *o.a.r.* '68 (NY) [186] Bronx, NY St. Rita of Cascia Shrine Church.
Reck, Donald W. *s.j.* (STL) [C] St. Louis, MO Saint Louis University.
Reck, Donald W. *s.j.* '65 (STL) [P] St. Louis, MO Leo Brown Jesuit Community.
Recker, Odo *o.s.b.* '78 (P) [A] St. Benedict, OR Mount Angel Seminary; [L] St. Benedict, OR Mt. Angel Abbey.
Recker, Philip F. '59 (DUB) Osage, IA Sacred Heart Church.
Reckinger, Robert A. '51 (DET) Retired.
Reckker, Stephen C. '63 (DET) Romeo, MI St. Clement of Rome Church.
Rector, Warren *o.f.m.* '68 (CAM) [H] Camden, NJ Our Lady of Lourdes Medical Center, Inc.

Rector, Warren *o.f.m.* '68 (PH) [AA] Philadelphia, PA St. Pius X Friary.
Reczek, Felix *o.f.m.* (PIT) [O] Ben Avon, PA St. Anthony Friary and Mission House.
Reczek, Felix J. *o.f.m.* '44 (BUR) Bellows Falls, VT Sacred Heart Church.
Reczek, Paul *o.f.m.* '72 (FgM) Franciscan Foreign Missions.
Reczek, Paul *o.f.m.* '72 (GB) [I] Pulaski, WI Assumption of B.V.M. Friary.
Redahan, Msgr. Patrick J. '33 (LA) Hawthorne, CA St. Joseph Church; Retired.
Reday, T. Christopher (PH) West Conshohocken, PA St. Gertrude Church.
Redcay, T. Christopher '89 (PH) [D] Radnor, PA Archbishop John Carroll High School.
Redden, Don '59 (PMB) Fellsmere, FL Our Lady of Guadalupe Mission Church.
Redden, Michael J. '72 (ATL) Covington, GA St. Augustine Church.
Reddick, E. Peter '72 (SY) [20] Syracuse, NY St. Patrick Church.
Reddington, Benjamin J. '43 (MAD) Retired.
Reddington, John A. '37 (ROC) Pittsford, NY St. Louis Church; Retired.
Reddy, Albert F. *s.j.* '51 (BGP) [A] Fairfield, CT Fairfield University.
Reddy, Albert F. *s.j.* '58 (BGP) [O] Fairfield, CT The Fairfield Jesuit Community-Fairfield University.
Reddy, Reginald J. *o.f.m.* '61 (ALB) [B] Loudonville, NY Siena College.
Reddy, Thomas J. *o.m.i.* '52 (BO) [W] Tewksbury, MA Oblate Fathers-Oblate World/Missionary Association of Mary Immaculate; [Z] Tewksbury, MA Immaculate Heart of Mary Novitiate-Infirmary.
Redinbo, Joseph *o.f.m.* '59 (SFE) Pena Blanca, NM Nuestra Senora De Guadalupe Church.
Reding, Aquinas *o.f.m.* '53 (BUF) Allegany, NY St. Bonaventure Church.
Reding, Michael A. '97 (STP) Oakdale, MN Transfiguration Church.
Redington, James D. *s.j.* '78 (BAL) [M] Baltimore, MD Jesuit Fathers and Brothers Maryland Provincial Curia.
Redington, James D. *s.j.* '78 (FgM) Provinces.
Redlon, Reginald A. *o.f.m.* '49 (NY) [115] New York, NY St. Stephen of Hungary Church.
Redmerski, Stanley '58 (LIN) [E] Lincoln, NE Madonna Rehabilitation Hospital.
Redmond, Arthur S. '55 (LC) Edson, WI Sacred Heart of Jesus Church; Rozellville, WI St. Andrew Church; Retired.
Redmond, Daniel P. '96 (CLV) [75] Cleveland, OH St. Vincent de Paul Church.
Redmond, Donald *o.s.b.* '57 (KCK) Atchison, KS St. Benedict's Church; Atchison, KS Sacred Heart Church.
Redmond, Lawrence '64 (ORL) Retired.
Redmond, Paul '54 (ALB) On Duty Outside the Diocese.
Redmond, Paul V. '54 (BAL) [B] Emmitsburg, MD Mount Saint Mary's College.
Redmond, Sean P. '90 (LIN) Paul, NE St. Joseph's Church.
Redstone, James J. '90 (NEW) [15] Newark, NJ St. Francis Xavier Church.
Redwanski, Dale H. *o.s.c.* '71 (DET) Riverview, MI St. Cyprian Church; [K] Riverview, MI Crosier Community of Riverview.
Redwick, Adolph '59 (DET) [6] Dearborn, MI St. Joseph Church.
Redwick, Stanislaus J. '54 (DET) Retired.
Reeb, Edward J. '45 (BEL) Retired.
Reece, Frederick W. '44 (DM) Retired.
Reece, Robert *o.s.f.s.* '65 (ALN) [L] Reading, PA St. Joseph Villa.
Reed, Albert A. *c.pp.s.* '54 (CIN) Burkettsville, OH St. Bernard Church; [U] Dayton, OH Community Support Charitable Trust.
Reed, Bruce '93 (RVC) Elmont, NY St. Vincent de Paul Church.
Reed, Daniel *o.f.m.* '84 (SAT) [70] San Antonio, TX San Jose y San Miguel Church.
Reed, David *s.j.* '64 (FgM) Provinces.
Reed, Dennis L. '69 (DOD) Garden City, KS St. Dominic Church; Ingalls, KS St. Stanislaus Church.
Reed, Douglas *o.f.m.conv.* '71 (R) [E] Wilmington, NC Conventual Franciscans O.F.M.Conv.
Reed, Douglas P. (R) [3] Raleigh, NC Our Lady of Lourdes Church.
Reed, H. William '62 (NO) [59] New Orleans, LA St. Rose Of Lima Church.
Reed, J. Philip *m.afr.* '88 (FgM) Missionaries of Africa Foreign Missions.
Reed, J. Philip *m.afr.* (FgM) Missionaries of Africa Foreign Missions.
Reed, John C. *s.j.* '50 (TOL) [K] Toledo, OH St. Mary's Jesuit Community.
Reed, Michael V. (PT) Crestview, FL Our Lady of Victory Church.
Reed, Robert A. '42 (BAL) [15] Baltimore, MD St. Benedict Church; Retired.
Reed, Robert E. '85 (BO) [71] Boston, MA St. Theresa Church.
Reed, Robert J. '61 (ALN) [10] Bethlehem, PA SS. Simon and Jude Church.
Reed, Thomas A. *s.j.* '47 (SFR) [N] San Francisco, CA Jesuit Community at University of San Francisco.
Reed, William C. '71 (NEW) [9] Elizabeth, NJ Our Lady of Most Holy Rosary/St. Michael Church; Elizabeth, NJ Elizabeth General Medical Center.
Reedy, Francis C. *o.s.b.* '58 (MIL) [P] Benet Lake, WI St. Benedict's Abbey.
Reedy, Gerard *s.j.* '70 (WOR) [B] Worcester, MA College of the Holy Cross, Inc.
Reedy, Gerard C. *s.j.* '70 (NY) [C] Bronx, NY Fordham University.
Reedy, Gerard C. *s.j.* '70 (WOR) [N] Worcester, MA Jesuits of Holy Cross College, Inc.
Reedy, John J. '35 (P) Retired.
Reehil, Philip J. '46 (RVC) Setauket, NY St. James Church; Retired.
Reemmer, A. Leonard '56 (LFT) Gas City, IN Holy Family Church; Marion, IN U.S. Veteran's Hospital.
Reen, Jeremiah *s.d.b.* '71 (PMB) Belle Glade, FL St. Philip Benizi Church.
Reese, Benjamin '91 (RC) [3] Rapid City, SD St. Therese the Little Flower Church.
Reese, Benjamin B. '97 (PEO) On Duty Outside the Diocese.
Reese, Charles T. '49 (CHL) Retired.
Reese, Donald B. '63 (CAM) On Duty Outside the Diocese.
Reese, Edward *s.j.* '73 (PHX) [B] Phoenix, AZ Brophy College Preparatory.
Reese, Francis X.D. *s.j.* '60 (BAL) [M] Baltimore, MD Jesuit Fathers and Brothers Maryland Provincial Curia.
Reese, Francis X.D. *s.j.* '60 (CHL) [J] Charlotte, NC Jesuit Community.
Reese, Robert P. '89 (ALT) [2] Altoona, PA Immaculate Conception Church.
Reese, Thomas J. *s.j.* '74 (WDC) [M] Washington, DC Woodstock Jesuit Community; [V] Washington, DC Woodstock Theological Center.
Reeson, David G. '80 (OM) Military Chaplains.
Reeves, Joseph '76 (BAK) On Duty Outside the Diocese.
Reeves, Joseph '76 (P) [J] Portland, OR Providence St. Vincent Medical Center.
Reeves, Nathaniel *o.s.b.* '78 (IND) [A] St. Meinrad, IN St. Meinrad Seminary; [J] St. Meinrad, IN St. Meinrad Archabbey.
Refalo, Anthony (RVC) Syosset, NY St. Edward Confessor Church.
Refalo, Anthony E. '89 (RVC) Manhasset, NY St. Mary's Church.
Refermat, Thomas '94 (CHI) Grayslake, IL St. Gilbert Church.
Regado, Justo Beltran '69 (BRK) Brooklyn, NY Woodhull Medical & Mental Health Center.
Regalado, Gonzalo E. '66 (NOR) Canterbury, CT St. Augustine Church.
Regalado, Luis *o.s.b.* '84 (SFE) [J] Abiquiu, NM Monastery of Christ in the Desert.
Regan, Charles (WCH) Retired.
Regan, Columkille *c.p.* '49 (PH) [AA] Philadelphia, PA St. Michael's Passionist Residence.
Regan, Msgr. Dennis M. '64 (RVC) Port Jefferson, NY Infant Jesus Church.
Regan, Desmond '46 (BIR) [1] Birmingham, AL St. Paul's Cathedral; Retired.
Regan, Francis A. '53 (BO) Marshfield, MA St. Christine Church.
Regan, Francis A. *s.s.c.* '66 (FgM) St. Columban's Foreign Mission.
Regan, Gerald T. *s.j.* '64 (MOB) [B] Mobile, AL Spring Hill College.
Regan, James *o.p.* '36 (CHI) [N] River Forest, IL St. Thomas Aquinas Priory.
Regan, James J. *s.j.* '67 (FgM) Provinces.
Regan, John '89 (JOL) Frankfort, IL St. Anthony Church.
Regan, John D. '53 (HRT) Middlebury, CT St. John of the Cross Church.
Regan, John J. '48 (BO) On Duty Outside the Archdiocese.
Regan, Msgr. John J. '53 (FR) Falmouth, MA St. Patrick's Church.
Regan, Matthew R.D. '70 (OAK) [4] San Leandro, CA St. Leander Church.
Regan, Msgr. Michael F. '38 (STL) Retired.
Regan, Msgr. Michael J. '46 (ATL) Carrollton, GA Church of Our Lady of Perpetual Help; Carrollton, GA Church of Our Lady of Perpetual Help; Retired.
Regan, Michael J. '62 (BO) Permanent Disability.
Regan, Michael J. '64 (BO) Abington, MA St. Bridget Church.
Regan, Richard '85 (SAN) On Duty Outside the Diocese.
Regan, Richard J. (CAM) Washington Township, NJ SS. Peter and Paul Church.
Regan, Richard J. *s.j.* '63 (NY) [DD] New York, NY Jesuit Community at Fordham University.
Regan, Robert F. *s.j.* '59 (BO) [W] Boston, MA The Society of Jesus of New England-Provincial Offices.
Regan, Robert F. *s.j.* '59 (PRT) [9] Portland, ME St. Pius X Church.
Regan, Terrence P. '68 (GF) Stanford, MT St. Rose of Lima Church.
Regan, Thomas J. *s.j.* '87 (BGP) [A] Fairfield, CT Fairfield University; [O] Fairfield, CT The Fairfield Jesuit Community-Fairfield University.
Regan, Timothy J. '91 (DAV) Keota, IA Holy Trinity Church.
Regan, William P. '56 (SY) Retired; [S] East Syracuse, NY Bishop Grimes Priests Residence.
Regensburger, Edmund *c.ss.r.* '46 (VEN) Wauchula, FL St. Michael Church.
Reger, George L. '69 (BUF) [15] Buffalo, NY Blessed Trinity Church.
Regh, John '53 (SUP) Retired.
Reginald, Edmund *o.m.i.* '92 (WDC) [B] Washington, DC Oblate College/Oblate Center for Mission Studies.
Reginato, Julian '64 (GR) [9] Grand Rapids, MI Immaculate Heart of Mary Church.
Regnier, William H. '48 (RCK) Retired.
Rego, Richard J. '83 (TUC) Ajo, AZ Immaculate Conception Church.
Regoli, John A. '61 (GBG) [4] Uniontown, PA St. Therese, the Little Flower of Jesus Church.
Regotti, Benjamin *o.f.m.cap.* '79 (PH) [79] Philadelphia, PA St. John the Evangelist Church.
Regula, Ronald R. '67 (NEW) Cedar Grove, NJ Essex County Hospital Center.
Regynski, Lawrence '95 (SFS) Yankton, SD Sacred Heart Church.
Rehage, Joseph W. *c.s.c.* '46 (AUS) [H] Austin, TX St. Joseph Hall; [H] Austin, TX Congregation of Holy Cross - Southern Province.
Rehkemper, Msgr. Robert '49 (DAL) Retired.
Rehling, Paul '56 (CIN) [4] Cincinnati, OH St. Aloysius Gonzaga Church.
Rehme, Albert A. '56 (STL) Retired.
Rehrauer, Matthew J. '92 (SPC) Piedmont, MO St. Catherine of Siena Church.
Reich, John C. '84 (WH) Elkview, WV Our Lady of the Hills Church.
Reich, Paul A. *s.m.* '57 (BAL) Sykesville, MD St. Joseph Church; [M] Baltimore, MD Marianist Community.
Reichel, William *o.f.m.* '61 (CIN) [M] Cincinnati, OH St. Clement Friary.
Reichenbacher, Charles *o.s.b.* '67 (RCK) [H] Aurora, IL Marmion Abbey-St. Augustine's Abbey.
Reicher, A. Paul '62 (CHI) River Forest, IL St. Luke Church.
Reichert, Eldon *s.m.* '52 (CLV) [4] Cleveland, OH St. Aloysius - St. Agatha Church.
Reichert, Henry J. '63 (JC) Tipton, MO St. Andrew Church; Tipton, MO State Correctional Pre-Release Center.
Reichert, J. Lawrence '71 (COL) Groveport, OH St. Mary's Church.
Reichert, James *o.s.b.* '59 (SCL) Avon, MN St. Benedict's Church.
Reichert, Msgr. James J. '71 (ALN) West Reading, PA Sacred Heart Church.
Reichert, Kenneth *o.s.b.* '59 (KC) [A] Conception, MO Conception Seminary College; [J] Conception, MO Conception Abbey.
Reichert, Ralph '49 (TOL) Retired.
Reichlin, Urban A. '39 (CLV) [75] Cleveland, OH St. Vincent de Paul Church; Retired.
Reichling, David *o.f.m.cap.* '67 (GF) [4] Billings, MT St. Bernard's Church.
Reichling, Paul *o.f.m.cap.* '65 (GF) [3] Billings, MT Little Flower Church; [5] Billings, MT Our Lady of Guadalupe Church.
Reichmann, James B. *s.j.* '53 (SEA) [A] Seattle, WA Seattle University.
Reicks, Allan '76 (SC) Odebolt, IA St. Martin's Church.
Reicks, Msgr. Leander H. '44 (DUB) Retired.
Reid, David P. *ss.cc.* '66 (FR) [3] New Bedford, MA Our Lady of the Assumption Church; [J] Fairhaven, MA Sacred Hearts Provincial House.
Reid, Francis R. '64 (CR) Retired.
Reid, George B. '53 (WDC) Barnesville, MD St. Mary Church and Shrine of Our Lady of Fatima Church.
Reid, Gerard E. '77 (OAK) [3] Berkeley, CA St. Joseph The Worker Church.
Reid, James H. *s.j.* '46 (NY) [DD] New York, NY Jesuit Community at Fordham University.
Reid, John J. *o.p.* '73 (PRO) [P] Providence, RI St. Thomas Aquinas Priory at Providence College.
Reid, Malcolm '57 (CHY) Rawlins, WY St. Joseph's Church; Rawlins, WY Wyoming State Penitentiary.
Reid, Michael '69 (RVC) Uniondale, NY Holly Patterson Geriatric Center; [C] Hicksville, NY Holy Trinity.
Reid, Michael R. (BRK) Special Assignment.
Reid, Paul *s.c.j.* '72 (MIL) [P] Hales Corners, WI Sacred Heart Monastery.
Reid, Sean *o.carm.* '33 (NY) [DD] Middletown, NY St. Albert's Priory.
Reidl, Msgr. Paul (SPR) [H] Holyoke, MA Mont Marie

Health Care Center, Inc.
Reidy, Edward J. *c.s.c.* '62 (FTW) [J] South Bend, IN Congregation of Holy Cross Indiana Province Provincial House.
Reidy, James '56 (STP) [C] St. Paul, MN University of St. Thomas.
Reidy, James E. '56 (STP) Retired.
Reidy, Martin F. '41 (RVC) Retired.
Reidy, Ned *c.s.c.* '62 (SB) Palm Desert, CA Christ of the Desert Church; [H] Palm Desert, CA Christ of the Desert Newman Center.
Reidy, Richard F. '94 (WOR) [1] Worcester, MA St. Paul's Cathedral.
Reidy, Msgr. Robert '62 (Y) On Duty Outside the Diocese.
Reidy, Robert J. '75 (CLV) [4] Lorain, OH Sacred Heart Chapel Church; [6] Lorain, OH St. Joseph Church; [X] Cleveland, OH Diocesan Hispanic Office.
Reidy, Msgr. Thomas E. '67 (SPC) [2] Springfield, MO Holy Trinity Church.
Reif, John T. '65 (ROC) Webster, NY St. Rita Church.
Reif, Marvin W. '89 (DOD) Ness City, KS Sacred Heart Church; Ransom, KS St. Aloysius Church.
Reifel, Mark *t.o.r.* '55 (ALT) [3] Windber, PA St. Anthony of Padua Church.
Reifenberg, Philip D. '79 (MIL) [62] Milwaukee, WI St. Martin de Porres Church.
Reiff, Dale E. '67 (SC) Barnum, IA St. Joseph's Church; Clare, IA St. Matthew's Church.
Reiff, Dennis E. '81 (NEW) [2] Orange, NJ Our Lady of the Valley Church.
Reifsnyder, John A. '41 (COV) Retired.
Reifsnyder, John A. '41 (PIT) [38] Pittsburgh, PA Sacred Heart Church.
Reigel, Joseph P. '97 (E) [1] Erie, PA St. Peter Cathedral.
Reiker, H. John '78 (STL) [7] St. Louis, MO Immaculate Heart of Mary Church.
Reiker, Robert J. '73 (STL) Dardenne, MO Immaculate Conception Church.
Reikowski, Miroslaw '96 (RCK) Cary, IL SS. Peter & Paul Church.
Reile, Louis *s.m.* '60 (SAT) [K] San Antonio, TX Marianist Residence: Skilled Nursing.
Reiley, Robert J. *m.m.* '59 (NY) [DD] Maryknoll, NY Maryknoll Fathers and Brothers.
Reilley, Thomas J. *s.j.* '95 (LA) [F] Los Angeles, CA Loyola High School.
Reilly, Bernard L. '73 (LAN) De Witt, MI St. Jude Church.
Reilly, Cristobal *s.t.* '55 (PCE) Coamo, PR St. Blase Church.
Reilly, David '75 (CIN) [17] Cincinnati, OH St. Bonaventure Church.
Reilly, Donald F. *o.s.a.* '74 (PH) [C] Villanova, PA Villanova University; [AA] Villanova, PA Order of St. Augustine.
Reilly, Msgr. Edward '54 (STL) Mattese, MO Mary, Mother of the Church.
Reilly, F. Joseph '58 (STL) Coffman, MO St. Catherine of Alexandria Church; River Aux Vases, MO SS. Phillip and James Church.
Reilly, Francis E. *s.j.* '53 (FgM) Provinces.
Reilly, Francis E. '80 (SPR) [6] Holyoke, MA Our Lady of Perpetual Help Church; [9] Holyoke, MA Sacred Heart Church; [M] Holyoke, MA Casa Maria.
Reilly, George M. '60 (NEW) Oradell, NJ St. Joseph's Church.
Reilly, James F. '68 (NEW) Palisades Park, NJ St. Michael's Church.
Reilly, James J. (NEW) [Q] Bloomfield, NJ Bloomfield College.
Reilly, Msgr. James J. '45 (FWT) Retired.
Reilly, James J. '68 (NEW) Harrison, NJ Holy Cross Church; [Q] Cranford, NJ Union County College.
Reilly, John '78 (SD) On Duty Outside the Diocese.
Reilly, John C. '39 (BRK) [231] Queens, NY Queen of Peace Church; Retired.
Reilly, John E. *s.j.* '59 (CHI) [C] Chicago, IL Jesuit Community at Loyola University of Chicago.
Reilly, John H. '63 (BRK) [11] Brooklyn, NY St. Anthony of Padua-St. Alphonsus Church.
Reilly, Msgr. John J. '48 (LA) [8] Long Beach, CA St. Joseph Church; Retired.
Reilly, John J. '48 (SFR) [3] Menlo Park, CA The Church of the Nativity; Special Assignment.
Reilly, Joseph L. '36 (BO) Retired.
Reilly, Joseph M. '84 (CAM) Marmora, NJ The Church of the Resurrection.
Reilly, Joseph R. '91 (NEW) [C] West Orange, NJ Seton Hall Preparatory School.
Reilly, Lawrence T. '64 (YAK) Grand Coulee, WA St. Henry's Church; Hartline, WA St. Patrick's Church.
Reilly, Mark Raymond '97 (OG) Lake Clear, NY St. John in the Wilderness Church; Saranac Lake, NY St. Bernard Church.
Reilly, Mathew V. *o.p.* '54 (NEW) [O] Summit, NJ Monastery of Our Lady of the Rosary.
Reilly, Michael P. '92 (NY) [F] New York, NY St. Joseph by the Sea, High School.
Reilly, Msgr. Patrick '58 (LA) Burbank, CA St. Robert Bellarmine Church.
Reilly, Msgr. Philip J. '60 (BRK) Special Assignment; [V] Brooklyn, NY Monastery of the Sisters Adorers of the Precious Blood.
Reilly, Rembert F. *o.s.b.* '59 (PAT) [M] Morristown, NJ St. Mary's Abbey.
Reilly, Robert E. '58 (L) [58] Louisville, KY Our Lady Church.
Reilly, Robert F. '55 (COL) Circleville, OH St. Joseph's Church.
Reilly, Msgr. Robert J. '45 (E) [25] Erie, PA St. Mary Church.
Reilly, Steven *l.c.* '94 (DAL) [D] Irving, TX Highland School; [G] Irving, TX The Highland School; [M] Irving, TX Legionaries of Christ.
Reilly, Terrence J. *o.p.* '59 (SFR) [13] San Francisco, CA St. Dominic Church; [N] San Francisco, CA St. Dominic Priory.
Reilly, Thomas *m.afr.* '78 (FgM) Missionaries of Africa Foreign Missions.
Reilly, Thomas J. '67 (BO) Foxboro, MA St. Mary Church.
Reilly, Msgr. William J. (NEW) [24] Jersey City, NJ Parish of the Resurrection Church.
Reilman, Thomas J. '61 (DAV) [L] Burlington, IA St. Francis Continuation Care and Nursing Home.
Reim, Daniel T. *s.j.* '95 (CLV) [C] Cleveland, OH John Carroll Jesuit Community.
Reiman, Frederick *o.s.m.* '45 (CHI) [N] Chicago, IL Servite Friars - Eastern Province.
Reimann, Oswald S. '53 (JOL) Bensenville, IL St. Alexis Church.
Reimer, Edward J. '67 (SY) [10] Syracuse, NY St. Andrew the Apostle Church; [23] Syracuse, NY St. Therese the Little Flower of Jesus Church; Jamesville, NY Jamesville Penitentiary.
Reimer, Elroy '57 (GB) Wrightstown, WI St. Paul Church.
Reimer, Ronald P. '62 (GB) [6] Manitowoc, WI St. Paul Church.
Reina, Nicholas J. *s.d.b.* '78 (FgM) Salesians of Don Bosco Foreign Missions.
Reina, Nicholas J. *s.d.b.* '78 (SFR) [N] San Francisco, CA Salesian Provincial Residence.
Reina, Richard A. '70 (BUF) [41] Buffalo, NY St. Lawrence Church.
Reinbold, Charles '56 (NEW) On Duty Outside the Archdiocese.
Reinbold, Msgr. Francis A. '40 (NEW) Scotch Plains, NJ St. Bartholomew Church; Retired.
Reinders, David '97 (TUC) Casa Grande, AZ St. Anthony Church.
Reiner, Charles J. *o.s.b.* '42 (BIR) [E] Cullman, AL St. Bernard Abbey.
Reiner, Charles J. *o.s.b.* '42 (MOB) Foley, AL St. Margaret Church.
Reinersman, Gerald L. '79 (COV) [M] Covington, KY St. Walburg Monastery.
Reinert, Duane F. *o.f.m.cap.* '76 (KC) [A] Conception, MO Conception Seminary College.
Reinert, Duane F. *o.f.m.cap.* '76 (KCK) Lawrence, KS Haskell Institute; [H] Lawrence, KS St. Conrad's Friary; [J] Lawrence, KS Haskell Catholic Campus Center.
Reinert, Ellis *o.carm.* '49 (NEW) Englewood, NJ St. Cecilia's Church.
Reinert, James M. '83 (LIN) On Duty Outside the Diocese.
Reinert, James M. '83 (NY) [2] New York, NY St. Agnes Church.
Reinert, Paul *s.j.* (STL) [C] St. Louis, MO Saint Louis University.
Reinert, Paul C. *s.j.* '40 (STL) [C] St. Louis, MO Saint Louis University; [P] St. Louis, MO Jesuit Community Corporation at St. Louis University - Jesuit Hall.
Reinhard, William *o.m.i.* '61 (FgM) Oblates Foreign Missions.
Reinhardt, Leo J. '78 (ROC) Clyde, NY St. John the Evangelist Church.
Reinhardt, Leo S. '55 (BEL) Albers, IL St. Bernard Church; Damiansville, IL St. Damian Church.
Reinhardt, Mark S. '96 (PRT) [2] Lewiston, ME Holy Cross Church.
Reinhart, Blaise R. *o.f.m.* '55 (ALB) [B] Loudonville, NY Siena College.
Reinhart, Joseph A. *m.m.* '50 (FgM) Maryknoll Foreign Missions.
Reinhart, Kenneth W. *o.f.m.cap.* '68 (LC) [I] Marathon City, WI St. Anthony Retreat Center.
Reinhart, Ralph W. (SC) Retired.
Reinhart, Robert '61 (TOL) [2] Toledo, OH Blessed Sacrament Church.
Reinhart, Robert C. *c.pp.s.* '53 (LFT) Bryant, IN Holy Trinity Church.
Reinke, Francis P. '57 (GB) Poy Sippi, WI Sacred Heart of Jesus Church; Redgranite, WI St. Mark Church.
Reinke, John H. *s.j.* '45 (CHI) [C] Chicago, IL Jesuit Community at Loyola University of Chicago.
Reinke, Robert J. '49 (COV) Retired.
Reinke, Robert J. '57 (COV) [4] Covington, KY St. Augustine Church.
Reinkemeyer, John C. '51 (WCH) Kingman, KS St. Patrick Church.
Reino, Joseph C. '93 (PH) Retired.
Reinsfelder, Msgr. John L. '49 (BAL) [36] Baltimore, MD Holy Cross Church; Retired.
Reiran, Eric A. *o.p.* '91 (STL) [P] St. Louis, MO Dominican Community of St. Louis.
Reis, Antonio (OAK) [4] San Leandro, CA St. Leander Church.
Reis, Daniel O. '75 (FR) [5] New Bedford, MA Our Lady of the Immaculate Conception Church.
Reis, John *o.f.m.* '25 (Y) [J] Youngstown, OH Mt. Alverna Friary.
Reis, Justin J. '69 (COL) Lancaster, OH St. Bernadette Church.
Reis, Lancelot '67 (PAT) Chester, NJ St. Lawrence the Martyr Church.
Reis, Michael J. '67 (COL) [11] Columbus, OH St. Christopher Church.
Reis, Raymond H. *s.j.* '37 (STL) [P] St. Louis, MO Jesuit Community Corporation at St. Louis University - Jesuit Hall.
Reis, Richard M. '61 (Y) Girard, OH St. Rose Church.
Reis, Timothy P. '86 (FR) Falmouth, MA St. Patrick's Church.
Reisch, Milton L. '60 (NO) [1] Metairie, LA Our Lady of Divine Providence Church.
Reischl, Fred P. '55 (DM) Avoca, IA St. Mary, Mediatrix of All Graces Church; Walnut, IA St. Patrick Church.
Reischman, Placidus G. *o.s.b.* '54 (SEA) [M] Lacey, WA St. Martin's Abbey.
Reischman, Virgil '69 (STU) Amsterdam, OH St. Joseph Church.
Reisdorff, Msgr. Clarence P. '46 (LIN) Retired; [E] Lincoln, NE Bonacum House.
Reiser, Bernard A. '49 (STP) Coon Rapids, MN Church of the Epiphany.
Reiser, John '56 (MIA) Absent on Sick Leave.
Reiser, Richard J. '80 (OM) O'Neill, NE St. Patrick Church.
Reiser, Robert *s.j.* '97 (BUF) [D] Buffalo, NY Canisius High School.
Reiser, Robert E. *s.j.* '97 (BUF) [O] Buffalo, NY Canisius Jesuit Community.
Reiser, William E. *s.j.* '72 (WOR) [N] Worcester, MA Jesuits of Holy Cross College, Inc.; [R] Worcester, MA Casa Santa Maria del Camino, Inc.
Reisert, Frederick J. *s.j.* '54 (BUF) [O] Buffalo, NY Canisius Jesuit Community.
Reisert, Gregory *o.f.m.cap.* '64 (NY) [DD] White Plains, NY St. Conrad Friary.
Reisig, Msgr. William E. '45 (NY) Retired.
Reising, Joseph H. '71 (NO) [F] New Orleans, LA Jesuit High School.
Reising, Raymond '45 (EVN) Retired.
Reisinger, Walter J. *c.m.* '55 (JC) Crocker, MO St. Cornelius Church; Dixon, MO St. Theresa Church.
Reiske, Steven '90 (FAR) Special Assignment.
Reiss, Francis R. '66 (DET) [62] Detroit, MI SS. Peter and Paul Church.
Reiss, John E. *o.f.m.* '69 (Y) [5] Youngstown, OH Our Lady of Hungary Church.
Reissmann, Richard A. '63 (WIL) Newark, DE St. John the Baptist-Holy Angels Church.
Reist, Thomas *o.f.m.conv.* '79 (WDC) [B] Washington, DC St. Bonaventure Friary.
Reisteter, William *o.f.m.* '71 (ALN) [K] Easton, PA St. Francis Friary; [M] Easton, PA St. Francis Retreat House.
Reisz, Adam '41 (DM) Retired.
Reisz, Leonard '50 (OWN) Non-Parochial Assignments.
Reiter, James E. '90 (ROM) McKeesport, PA St. Mary Church.
Reites, James W. *s.j.* '71 (SJ) [B] Santa Clara, CA Santa Clara University.
Reith, David H. '76 (MIL) Burlington, WI Immaculate Conception Church.
Reith, Herman R. *c.s.c.* '42 (FTW) [B] Notre Dame, IN University of Notre Dame Du Lac; [J] Notre Dame, IN Holy Cross Community, Corby Hall, University of Notre Dame.
Reitter, Frank *s.m.* '84 (DET) [E] Harper Woods, MI Notre Dame High School.
Reitz, Andrew J. *o.f.m.* '71 (TR) Brant Beach, NJ St. Francis of Assisi Church.
Reitz, Joseph A. '53 (GAY) Retired.
Reitz, Louis M. *s.s.* '55 (BAL) [84] Baltimore, MD St. Pius X Church; [M] Baltimore, MD Sulpician Provincial House.
Reitz, William J. '47 (GR) Carson City, MI St. Mary's Church; Hubbardston, MI St. John the Baptist Church.
Rejent, Michael *o.s.f.s.* '68 (LAN) [6] Lansing, MI St. Gerard Church.
Rejsek, J. Brian '86 (PEO) Princeville, IL St. Mary of the Woods Church.
Rekasi, Joseph '46 (GB) [I] De Pere, WI St. Joseph Priory.
Rekasi, Joseph S. *o.praem.* '46 (GB) [O] De Pere, WI Canons Regular of Magnovarad, Ltd.

Reker, Timothy T. '82 (WIN) On Duty Outside the Diocese.
Rekofke, Robert *s.j.* '59 (SEA) [12] Tacoma, WA Holy Cross Church.
Relihan, Thomas '47 (SAC) Ione, CA Sacred Heart Church.
Reller, Gary W. '71 (HEL) Polson, MT Immaculate Conception Church.
Remaklus, Charles W. '47 (LFT) Retired.
Rementeria, Alfonso *o.ss.t.* '76 (PCE) [10] Ponce, PR La Santisima Trinidad Church.
Remes, James A. '55 (STP) Retired.
Remigio, '69 (BRK) Brooklyn, NY Wyckoff Heights Hospital.
Remillard, Andre N. '70 (WOR) Jefferson, MA St. Mary's Church.
Remillard, Bernard M. *o.p.* '37 (PRT) [I] Lewiston, ME SS. Peter and Paul Priory.
Remke, Raymond J. '88 (BIR) Montevallo, AL St. Thomas the Apostle Church; [H] Montevallo, AL University of Montevallo.
Remm, George F. '60 (PEO) Urbana, IL St. Patrick's Church.
Remmel, William *s.d.s.* (WDC) [B] Silver Spring, MD Salvatorian Community.
Remmel, William J. *s.d.s.* '67 (BAL) [85] Baltimore, MD St. Rita Church.
Remmes, Richard R. '62 (SC) Marcus, IA Holy Name Church.
Remo, Zanatta *c.r.s.* (MAN) [H] Allenstown, NH Pine Haven Boys Center.
Rempe, Melvin L. '65 (LIN) Cambridge, NE St. John's Church.
Remy, Adrien T. '34 (SPR) Retired; [J] Holyoke, MA Mont Marie.
Remy, David P. '67 (DUB) Military Chaplains.
Renard, Eugene C. *s.j.* '60 (PBL) Trinidad, CO Most Holy Trinity, Trinidad Area Catholic Community (Trinidad Cluster) Church; Trinidad, CO Our Lady of Mt. Carmel, Trinidad Area Catholic Community (Trinidad Cluster) Church; Trinidad, CO St. Joseph, Trinidad Area Catholic Community (Trinidad Cluster) Church; [F] Trinidad, CO Trinidad Area Catholic Community.
Renard, John F. '65 (NEW) Guttenberg, NJ St. John Nepomucene Church.
Renard, Peter J. *o.praem.* '68 (GB) [I] De Pere, WI St. Norbert Abbey.
Renaud, Olivier *o.m.i.* '50 (NOR) [F] Willimantic, CT Oblates of Mary Immaculate; [I] Willimantic, CT Immaculata Retreat House.
Renaud, Ronald '60 (SPR) [1] Holyoke, MA Blessed Sacrament Church.
Render, Msgr. Bernard A. '40 (PEO) Retired; [L] Peoria, IL St. Augustine Manor.
Render, John T. *c.p.* '52 (CHI) [N] Chicago, IL Immaculate Conception Monastery.
Render, Patrick W. *c.s.v.* '68 (SFD) [8] Springfield, IL St. Joseph Church.
Rendon, Anthony *o.m.i.* '67 (FgM) Oblates Foreign Missions.
Rendon, Luis A. '73 (PAT) [1] Paterson, NJ Cathedral of St. John the Baptist.
Rendon, Matthias *o.f.m.* '92 (FgM) Custody of St. Mary of the Angels. Byzantine-Slavonic.
Rendon, Raul P. *o.ss.t.* '87 (VIC) [4] Victoria, TX Our Lady of Sorrows Church.
Rendon, Samuel '92 (LA) Canoga Park, CA Our Lady of the Valley Church.
Renehan, Edmond M. '58 (LA) Canyon Country, CA St. Clare Church.
Renfroe, Francis E. *s.j.* '68 (SFE) [6] Albuquerque, NM Immaculate Conception Church.
Rengers, Christopher *o.f.m.cap.* '42 (RCK) [N] St. Charles, IL Queen of Americas Guild.
Rengers, Christopher *o.f.m.cap.* '42 (WDC) [B] Washington, DC St. Francis Friary-Capuchin College.
Rengers, Joseph F. *c.s.sp.* '41 (PIT) [3] Millvale, PA Holy Spirit Church.
Renggli, John '68 (SEA) Bellevue, WA St. Madeleine Sophie Church.
Rengifo, J. Orlando '85 (NEW) [1] Hackensack, NJ Holy Trinity Church.
Renken, John A. '79 (SFD) Riverton, IL St. James Church.
Renkiewicz, Adolphe T. '56 (HRT) [N] Enfield, CT Felician Sisters - Our Lady of the Angels.
Renna, Anton J. *s.j.* '65 (PHX) [B] Phoenix, AZ Brophy College Preparatory.
Rennell, Albert F. '59 (RCK) Retired.
Renner, Christopher A. '91 (DEN) Julesburg, CO St. Anthony Church.
Renner, Frank G. '81 (EVN) Bicknell, IN St. Philip Neri Church.
Renner, Louis L. *s.j.* '57 (FBK) [C] Fairbanks, AK Jesuit Residence.
Renner, Ralph C. *s.j.* (STL) [C] St. Louis, MO Saint Louis University.
Renner, Ralph C. *s.j.* '70 (STL) [P] St. Louis, MO Jesuit Community Corporation at St. Louis University - Jesuit Hall.
Renninger, Michael A. '93 (RIC) [1] Richmond, VA Cathedral of the Sacred Heart.
Rensing, William F. '55 (BEL) Sparta, IL Our Lady of Lourdes Church.
Renteria, Rudy '79 (DAL) [I] Dallas, TX St. Paul Medical Center.
Renteria, Rudy '79 (FWT) On Duty Outside the Diocese.
Rentino, Pablo (NY) [173] Bronx, NY Our Lady of Mercy Church.
Rentko, Andrew *s.v.d.* '49 (FgM) Society of the Divine Word Foreign Missions.
Rentner, Randall *c.s.c.* '90 (CHI) [D] Niles, IL Notre Dame High School.
Rento, Richard G. '58 (PAT) [3] Clifton, NJ St. Brendan Church.
Renz, Christopher *o.p.* '97 (P) [6] Eugene, OR St. Thomas More Church.
Repchick, George *m.s.* '56 (LKC) [3] Sulphur, LA Our Lady of Prompt Succor Church.
Repenshek, Jerome V. '63 (MIL) West Bend, WI Holy Angels Church.
Repko, Cyril *o.f.m.cap.* '62 (FgM) Capuchin Foreign Missions.
Repko, Joseph '95 (PRM) Bedford, OH St. Eugene Church.
Replogle, Jack *s.j.* (NY) [DD] New Rochelle, NY Brothers of Holy Cross of the Eastern Province of the United States of America, Inc.
Repole, Celsus *o.f.m.cap.* '43 (NY) [DD] Yonkers, NY St. Clare Friary.
Repole, Charles *o.f.m.cap.* '43 (NY) [DD] Yonkers, NY St. Clare Friary.
Reppen, Robert B. *o.praem.* '46 (GB) [I] De Pere, WI St. Norbert Abbey.
Repschinski, Liborius *s.j.* '90 (CHI) [C] Chicago, IL Jesuit Community at Loyola University of Chicago.
Resch, Gerard F. *c.ss.r.* '44 (STL) [P] Liguori, MO St. Clement Health Care Center.
Resch, Julian C. *o.praem.* '38 (GB) [I] De Pere, WI St. Norbert Abbey.
Reschick, Joseph W. '77 (PIT) [37] Pittsburgh, PA St. Rosalia Church.
Resconich, Emil C. *t.o.r.* '54 (ALT) [A] Loretto, PA St. Francis College; [F] Loretto, PA St. Francis Friary, Third Order Regular of St. Francis of Penance.
Resheske, Florian '55 (GB) Absent on Leave.
Reskey, George '73 (MOB) On Leave from the Archdiocese.
Reskey, George A. '73 (SP) St. Pete Beach, FL St. John Church.
Resko, Blane L. *o.s.b.* (GBG) [2] Greensburg, PA St. Bruno Church.
Resma, Louis (DET) Farmington, MI Botsford General Hospital; Detroit, MI Saratoga General Hospital.
Resma, Luis (DET) [13] Detroit, MI St. Brendan Church.
Resop, Michael A. '79 (MAD) Plain, WI St. Luke Church.
Ressler, Clint C. '93 (GAL) On Duty Outside the Diocese.
Ressler, Mark A. '76 (DUB) [A] Dubuque, IA Seminary of St. Pius X; [C] Dubuque, IA Loras College.
Ressler, Wayne A. '64 (DUB) [10] Dubuque, IA Nativity Church.
Resta, Vincent A. '55 (NY) [181] Bronx, NY St. Peter and St. Paul Church.
Restivo, Maurice *c.s.b.* '86 (DET) [6] Detroit, MI Ste. Anne Church.
Restrepo, George *s.j.* '65 (BAL) [91] Baltimore, MD St. Thomas Aquinas Church.
Restrepo, Jairo '92 (B) Weiser, ID St. Agnes Church.
Restrepo-Restrepo, Rodrigo Archangel '86 (NEW) [3] Hoboken, NJ St. Francis Church.
Restrick, Jacob *o.p.* '89 (BUF) [P] Buffalo, NY Monastery of Our Lady of the Rosary.
Resultay, Angel V. '67 (RVC) Farmingdale, NY St. Kilian Church.
Reszel, Marc W. '88 (CHI) Glenview, IL Our Lady of Perpetual Help Church.
Reszkowski, Msgr. Joseph V. '54 (E) [9] Erie, PA Our Lady of Mt. Carmel Church.
Reteller, Charles E. '60 (L) [M] St. Catharine, KY Sansbury Memorial Infirmary.
Reteneller, Charles E. '60 (L) Elizabethtown, KY St. James Church; White Mills, KY St. Ignatius Church; [M] St. Catharine, KY St. Catharine of Siena Convent.
Rethamel, Roger R. '60 (DUB) Alta Vista, IA St. Bernard Church; Elma, IA Immaculate Conception Church; Lourdes, IA Our Lady of Lourdes Church.
Rethinger, Omer '53 (TOL) Kansas, OH St. James Church; Millersville, OH St. Mary Church.
Retortillo, Benito *o.p.* '62 (CC) San Diego, TX St. Francis de Paula Church; [H] San Diego, TX Vicariate of Holy Rosary.
Rettger, Emmeran A. *o.s.b.* '38 (GBG) [H] Latrobe, PA Saint Vincent Archabbey.
Rettger, Thaddeus E. *o.s.b.* '74 (GBG) Vandergrift, PA St. Gertrude Church.
Rettig, Donald R. '71 (CIN) [5] Cincinnati, OH St. Aloysius-on-the-Ohio Church; [E] Cincinnati, OH Elder High School.
Rettig, Hermann-Joseph K. *o.praem.* '84 (LA) [90] Los Angeles, CA St. Stephen Church.
Rettig, Hermann-Joseph K. *o.praem.* '84 (ORG) [H] Silverado, CA Norbertine Fathers of Orange Inc.
Retzel, Joseph R. *s.j.* '60 (GF) Hays, MT St. Paul's Indian Mission Church.
Retzner, James '95 (SD) [H] San Diego, CA Augustinian Community.
Retzner, James P. *o.s.a.* '95 (SD) [34] San Diego, CA St. Patrick Church.
Reudon, Nicholas (LUB) Shallowater, TX St. Phillip Benizi Church.
Reuse, Patrick J. *s.j.* '73 (PHX) [11] Phoenix, AZ St. Francis Xavier Church.
Reusing, James '94 (BAL) Pasadena, MD St. Jane Frances de Chantal Church.
Reuss, Louis L. '38 (RVC) Bohemia, NY St. John Nepomucene Church; Retired.
Reuss, Norbert C. *c.s.b.* '38 (GAL) [F] Houston, TX St. Thomas High School.
Reuter, Arnold F. '52 (LC) Retired; [I] La Crosse, WI Holy Cross (Seminary) Diocesan Center.
Reuter, Charles *o.f.m.* '49 (STL) Oakville, MO St. Francis of Assisi Church; [P] Oakville, MO St. Francis Friary.
Reuter, Christian *o.f.m.* '66 (CHI) [47] Chicago, IL Corpus Christi Church.
Reuter, James B. *s.j.* '46 (FgM) Provinces.
Reuter, John F. '67 (GB) On Duty Outside the Diocese.
Reuter, Lars *s.j.* (STL) [C] St. Louis, MO Saint Louis University.
Reuter, Lars '95 (STL) [P] St. Louis, MO Leo Brown Jesuit Community.
Reuter, Lawrence *s.j.* '71 (CHI) [C] Chicago, IL Loyola University-Chicago; [C] Chicago, IL Jesuit Community at Loyola University of Chicago; [V] Chicago, IL Ministry in Higher Education.
Reuter, Leon *o.f.m.* '62 (STL) [P] St. Louis, MO Franciscan Friary of St. Anthony of Padua.
Reuter, Lloyd '57 (DUB) Blessing, IA Immaculate Conception Church.
Reuter, Lloyd E. '57 (DUB) Eagle Center, IA St. Mary of Mt. Carmel Church; La Porte City, IA Sacred Heart Church.
Revak, Msgr. Francis C. '40 (ALN) Catasauqua, PA St. Lawrence Church; [C] Allentown, PA Allentown Central Catholic High School.
Revak, Msgr. Raymond '59 (PHU) Scranton, PA St. Vladimir's Church.
Revel, Peter '82 (TYL) Jacksonville, TX Our Lady of Sorrows Church.
Revello, James K.I. '73 (DEN) On Duty Outside the Archdiocese.
Revilla, Francisco '54 (STA) Special Assignment.
Revilla, Isaias *o.s.a.* '60 (MGZ) Aguada, PR St. Francis of Assisi Church.
Revilla, Teofilo '78 (NEW) [3] Elizabeth, NJ St. Anthony's Church.
Revuelto, Manuel '59 (NEW) [1] Orange, NJ St. John's Church.
Rewak, William J. *s.j.* '64 (OAK) [A] Berkeley, CA The Jesuit School of Theology at Berkeley.
Rewtiuk, Michael '69 (SJP) [1] Parma, OH St. Josaphat Cathedral.
Reycraft, Robert J. '75 (DEN) [9] Denver, CO Guardian Angels Church.
Reyes, Alejandro '97 (ELP) [9] El Paso, TX Holy Family Church; Van Horn, TX Our Lady of Fatima Church.
Reyes, Andres J. '70 (NEW) [25] Jersey City, NJ St. Paul of the Cross Church.
Reyes, Francisco *o.f.m.* '42 (SFR) [5] San Francisco, CA St. Anthony Church.
Reyes, Jaime *o.s.b.* '64 (CGS) [C] Humacao, PR San Antonio Abad Abbey of the Order of St. Benedict.
Reyes, Jorge A. *o.s.a.* (BO) [9] Lawrence, MA St. Mary Immaculate Conception Church.
Reyes, Jose *o.f.m.conv.* '84 (LSC) Hobbs, NM St. Helena Church.
Reyes, Jose L. '93 (MIA) Absent on Leave.
Reyes, Jose Maria *o.de.m.* (SJN) [40] San Juan, PR Nuestra Senora de la Merced Church.
Reyes, Msgr. Lonnie C. '69 (AUS) [16] Austin, TX St. Julia Church.
Reyes, Marco '85 (LA) San Gabriel, CA St. Anthony Church.
Reyes, Pedro Luis '90 (SJN) Graduate Studies.
Reyes, Ralph *o.c.d.* '69 (SAT) [18] San Antonio, TX Our Lady of Mt. Carmel and St. Therese, Discalced Carmelite Fathers National Shrine of the Little Flower Church; [M] San Antonio, TX Discalced Carmelites (Prov. of St. Therese).
Reyes, Raymund (SFR) [41] San Francisco, CA St. Patrick Church.
Reyes, Reynaldo '93 (LUB) [4] Lubbock, TX St. Elizabeth University Parish.
Reyes, Victor J. '94 (ATL) [10] Atlanta, GA St. Jude Church.
Reyes, Wilberto *l.d.* '83 (PCE) [18] Ponce, PR Church Santisimo Sacramento Church.

Reyes Lebron, Pedro Luis (SJN) [4] Trujillo Alto, PR Bienveturada Virgen Maria de Lourdes Church.
Reymann, Albert I. *m.m.* '47 (CLV) [3] Akron, OH St. Bernard Church.
Reymann, Albert I. *m.m.* '47 (NY) [DD] Maryknoll, NY Maryknoll Fathers and Brothers.
Reymann, James J. '58 (CLV) Wellington, OH St. Patrick Church.
Reyna, Cecilio C. '93 (LAN) [4] Ann Arbor, MI St. Mary Student Parish.
Reyna, Marcos *o.f.m.conv.* '86 (ELP) [17] El Paso, TX Our Lady of Mt. Carmel Church.
Reynierse, Peter J. '95 (WDC) Pastoral Center Special Ministries.
Reynolds, Brad R. *s.j.* '77 (P) [L] Portland, OR Jesuit Provincial Office (Society of Jesus, Oregon Prov.); [L] Portland, OR Colombiere Community.
Reynolds, Daniel '53 (P) [2] Eugene, OR St. Mark Church.
Reynolds, Msgr. Edward J. '45 (NY) Retired; [DD] New York, NY Pope John Paul II Residence.
Reynolds, Fred G. *s.j.* '78 (LAF) [J] Grand Coteau, LA Jesuit Spirituality Center.
Reynolds, George L., II '97 (LA) Ventura, CA Our Lady of the Assumption Church.
Reynolds, Ignatius C. '35 (PH) Gladwyne, PA St. John Baptist Vianney Church; Retired.
Reynolds, J. Patrick '80 (OWN) Sorgho, KY St. Mary Magdalene Church.
Reynolds, Msgr. James B. '50 (MIA) [6] Pompano Beach, FL St. Henry Church.
Reynolds, James J.M. '84 (BRK) [199] Queens, NY St. Matthias Church.
Reynolds, James L. '71 (SPC) Billings, MO St. Joseph Church.
Reynolds, Jeffrie S. '90 (BIR) On Duty Outside the Diocese.
Reynolds, Jeffrie S. '90 (WIL) Perry Point, MD Veterans Admin.
Reynolds, John C. *c.s.p.* '47 (NY) [104] New York, NY St. Paul the Apostle Church; [DD] Jamaica Estates, NY Paulist Fathers Generalate.
Reynolds, John C. '90 (KCK) Alma, KS Holy Family Church; Eskridge, KS St. John Vianney's Church; Paxico, KS Sacred Heart Church.
Reynolds, Msgr. John P. '49 (NO) [50] New Orleans, LA St. Patrick Church; [S] New Orleans, LA Stella Roman Foundation, Inc.
Reynolds, John R. '83 (STA) [17] Jacksonville, FL St. Matthew's Church.
Reynolds, Joseph F. '59 (NY) Harriman, NY St. Anastasia Church.
Reynolds, Kirk R. *s.j.* '79 (RVC) Oceanside, NY St. Anthony Church.
Reynolds, Paul A. *c.s.p.* '94 (BO) [W] Boston, MA Paulist Fathers Residence; [CC] Cambridge, MA Massachusetts Institute of Technology Catholic Community.
Reynolds, Paul F. '65 (PRO) [6] West Warwick, RI St. Mary Church.
Reynolds, Paul H. '63 (ATL) Roswell, GA St. Andrew Church.
Reynolds, Robert E. '52 (PEO) Rushville, IL St. Rose Church; Retired.
Reynolds, Msgr. Roger A. '43 (NEW) Harrington Park, NJ Our Lady of Victories Church; Retired.
Reynolds, Stephen B. '89 (GAL) [20] Houston, TX Christ the King Church.
Reynolds, Thomas D. '58 (BO) [4] Brockton, MA St. Margaret Church.
Reynolds, Thomas J. '54 (RVC) Massapequa Park, NY Our Lady of Lourdes Church.
Reynolds, Thomas P. *s.s.c.* '61 (CHI) [N] Chicago, IL Columban Fathers Mission Center.
Reynolds, William E. '81 (DAV) Grinnell, IA St. Mary's Church.
Reynolds, William V. '55 (NY) Nanuet, NY St. Anthony Church.
Rezabek, Msgr. William J. '31 (LIN) [E] Lincoln, NE Bonacum House.
Rezac, Keith D. '87 (OM) Creighton, NE St. Ludger Church.
Rezuła, Leon J. '69 (CHI) [201] Chicago, IL St. Thecla Church.
Rezza, Boniface *o.f.m.* '44 (NY) [DD] New York, NY Franciscan Province of the Immaculate Conception.
Rhatigan, Msgr. John '49 (SD) Retired.
Rheault, Francois *o.cart.* '93 (BUR) [E] Arlington, VT Carthusian Foundation, Charterhouse of the Transfiguration.
Rhein, George V. (GAL) [N] Houston, TX Pope John XXIII Priest Residence.
Rhein, Msgr. George V. '39 (GAL) Retired.
Rhinehart, R. William *c.m.* '79 (COS) Limon, CO Our Lady of Victory(1925) Church.
Rhoades, C. Michael '70 (MAR) St. Ignace, MI St. Ignatius Loyola Church.
Rhoades, Kevin '83 (BAL) [B] Emmitsburg, MD Mount Saint Mary's College.
Rhoades, Kevin C. '83 (BAL) [A] Emmitsburg, MD Mount St. Mary's Seminary; [A] Emmitsburg, MD Mount St. Mary's Seminary.
Rhoden, Raymond '76 (PIT) Sewickley, PA St. James Church.
Rhodes, C. Michael '70 (MAR) Moran, MI Immaculate Conception Church.
Rhodes, David W. '65 (Y) [11] Youngstown, OH St. Christine's Church.
Rhodes, Edmund L. *s.m.* '41 (CIN) [M] Dayton, OH Marianist Provincialate.
Rhodes, George V. '53 (WIL) Retired.
Rhodes, Joseph '41 (OWN) Retired; [E] Owensboro, KY Carmel Home.
Rhodes, Ronald E. '81 (R) Graduate Studies.
Rhodes, Terence *o.f.m.* '43 (GLP) Zuni, NM St. Anthony Indian Mission, Our Lady of Guadalupe Church.
Rhomberg, Thomas W. '53 (DUB) Retired.
Rhyner, Robert E. '59 (GB) [9] Green Bay, WI Holy Martyrs of Gorcum Church.
Ri, Paul (BO) [7] Newton, MA St. Philip Neri Church.
Riani, Peter R. '55 (OG) Peru, NY St. Augustine Church.
Ribando, William R. *c.s.c.* '64 (SCR) [C] Wilkes-Barre, PA Kings College.
Ribaudo, Msgr. Charles A. '67 (RVC) Oyster Bay, NY St. Dominic's Church.
Ribble, Msgr. James M. *ph.d.* '57 (SPK) [1] Spokane, WA Cathedral of Our Lady of Lourdes.
Ribeiro, Alvaro *s.j.* '87 (WDC) [M] Washington, DC The Jesuit Community at Georgetown University.
Ribeiro, George *s.a.* '67 (NY) [14] Yonkers, NY Our Lady of the Rosary Church; [DD] Garrison, NY Franciscan Friars of the Atonement.
Ribeiro, Nelson *c.m.* '54 (HRT) [3] Waterbury, CT Our Lady of Fatima Church.
Ribero, Arthur '50 (OAK) Retired.
Ribezzi, Rinaldo A. *c.s.s.* '39 (SPR) [3] Pittsfield, MA Our Lady of Mt. Carmel Church.
Ribits, Thomas A. *o.s.f.s.* '82 (TOL) [K] Toledo, OH Oblates of St. Francis de Sales.
Ribotta, Frank *s.d.b.* '47 (LA) [F] Bellflower, CA St. John Bosco High School.
Ribotta, Michael *s.d.b.* '49 (OAK) [A] Berkeley, CA Dominican School of Philosophy and Theology; [N] Berkeley, CA Salesian Community.
Ricafort, Juvencio D. '82 (SD) [35] San Diego, CA St. Rita Church.
Ricard, David F. '69 (PRO) [2] West Warwick, RI Christ the King Church; Warwick, RI Kent County Memorial Hospital.
Ricard, Joseph M. '64 (NOR) Retired.
Ricard, Rodney Anthony '95 (NO) [58] New Orleans, LA St. Rita Church.
Riccardi, Salvatore *c.p.* '62 (MET) [H] South River, NJ Passionist Provincial Office.
Riccardi, Salvatore *c.p.* '62 (NY) Crestwood, NY Church of the Annunciation.
Riccardo, John C. '96 (DET) [5] Dearborn, MI Divine Child Church.
Riccardo, Joseph J. '75 (E) Punxsutawney, PA SS. Cosmas and Damian Church.
Ricchini, Joseph *o.f.m.* '64 (CIN) [M] Cincinnati, OH St. Ann Friary.
Ricci, Alfred V. '80 (PRO) [5] Warwick, RI St. Gregory the Great Church.
Ricci, Andrew P. '97 (SUP) [1] Superior, WI Cathedral of Christ the King.
Ricci, Daniel A. *c.m.* '74 (STL) [P] St. Louis, MO Vincentian Residence.
Ricci, Philip C. '65 (PH) North Wales, PA Mary, Mother of the Redeemer Church.
Ricci, Roberto J. *s.j.* '37 (NY) [28] New York, NY Corpus Christi Church.
Ricciardelli, Albert '84 (TR) [2] Long Branch, NJ Holy Trinity Church.
Ricciardi, August A. '83 (SCR) Throop, PA St. Anthony's Church; Throop, PA St. Bridget's Church; Throop, PA St. John the Baptist Church.
Ricciardi, Robert P. '79 (HRT) [6] East Hartford, CT St. Rose's Church.
Riccio, Alexis D. '34 (HRT) Retired.
Riccio, Fred A. '77 (OAK) San Ramon, CA St. Joan of Arc Church.
Riccio, Salvatore M. '66 (PH) Springfield, PA St. Francis of Assisi Church.
Riccitelli, Dennis '85 (PHX) [3] Mesa, AZ Holy Cross Church.
Riccomini, Msgr. Dino F. '57 (FRS) Wasco, CA St. John the Evangelist Church.
Rice, Charles F. *c.m.* '43 (STL) [P] Perryville, MO Congregation of The Mission.
Rice, Msgr. Charles O. '34 (PIT) Castle Shannon, PA St. Anne Church; Retired.
Rice, Edward M. '87 (STL) [A] St. Louis, MO Kenrick-Glennon Seminary.
Rice, George N. '67 (L) On Special Assignment.
Rice, John A. '57 (SEA) Retired.
Rice, Joseph P. '77 (NEW) Paramus, NJ Bergen Pines County Hospital.
Rice, Lawrence *c.s.p.* (WDC) [V] Washington, DC Paulist Media Works.
Rice, Lawrence *c.s.p.* '89 (WDC) [B] Washington, DC St. Paul's College.
Rice, Michael D. '64 (KC) Lee's Summit, MO Our Lady of the Presentation Church.
Rice, Owen (ALB) [L] Saratoga Springs, NY St. John Neumann Residence.
Rice, Patrick '74 (PAT) Mountain Lakes, NJ St. Catherine of Siena Church.
Rice, Patrick J. *o.s.a.* '48 (PH) [C] Villanova, PA Villanova University; [AA] Villanova, PA St. Thomas Monastery.
Rice, Patrick J. *s.j.* '54 (DET) [E] Detroit, MI University of Detroit Jesuit High School and Academy.
Rice, Richard M. *s.j.* '72 (STP) [6] St. Paul, MN The Immaculate Heart of Mary Church; [Q] St. Paul, MN Loyola.
Rice, Richard P. '60 (PRT) Sanford, ME Holy Family Church.
Rice, Robert A. *s.j.* '53 (FgM) Provinces.
Rice, Thomas G. '77 (DET) [7] Warren, MI St. Louise Church.
Rice, William A. '63 (E) Houtzdale, PA Christ the King Church.
Rich, John A. *m.m.* '58 (NY) [DD] Maryknoll, NY Maryknoll Fathers and Brothers.
Rich, Joseph C. '74 (SJ) [5] Sunnyvale, CA Church of The Resurrection.
Rich, Orlando S. '43 (Y) Retired.
Rich, William W. '80 (BAL) [A] Baltimore, MD St. Mary's Seminary and University.
Richard, Alain *o.f.m.* (LAV) Special Assignment.
Richard, Antonio J. '38 (FAR) Retired.
Richard, Charles J. '46 (OG) Retired; [B] Ogdensburg, NY Mater Dei College.
Richard, Claude *o.p.* '73 (PRT) [I] Lewiston, ME SS. Peter and Paul Priory.
Richard, Edward '41 (TLS) Retired.
Richard, Edward *m.s.* '91 (STL) [P] St. Louis, MO La Salette Missionaries.
Richard, Edward D. '68 (MAN) Pelham, NH St. Patrick Church.
Richard, Edward J. '91 (STL) [A] St. Louis, MO Kenrick-Glennon Seminary.
Richard, Hudson R. '73 (HRT) Hartford, CT Hartford Hospital.
Richard, James S. *s.j.* '70 (DEN) [M] Denver, CO Regis Jesuit Community (The Jesuits at Regis University).
Richard, Joseph *a.a.* '46 (BO) [W] Brighton, MA Assumptionist Center.
Richard, Joseph E. '58 (RNO) Winnemucca, NV St. Paul Church.
Richard, Joseph E. '58 (SFR) On Duty Outside the Archdiocese.
Richard, Louis J. '81 (LAF) Crowley, LA St. Michael Archangel Church; Milton, LA St. Joseph Church.
Richard, Lucien *o.m.i.* '59 (BO) [W] Lowell, MA Missionary Oblates of Mary Immaculate.
Richard, Mark '96 (LAF) Rayne, LA St. Joseph Church.
Richard, Normand P. '72 (PRT) Millinocket, ME St. Martin of Tours Church.
Richard, Raymond *o.f.m.cap.* '72 (FgM) Capuchin Foreign Missions.
Richard, Rusty P. '97 (LAF) Crowley, LA St. Michael Archangel Church.
Richard, Theodule *m.s.* '51 (FR) [J] Attleboro, MA La Salette Provincial House.
Richard, Timothy '92 (LAF) Mamou, LA St. Ann Church.
Richard, Msgr. Wayne R. '40 (LAF) Retired.
Richard, William '81 (DAL) Rockwall, TX Our Lady of the Lake Church.
Richards, Damian '92 (SAL) Atwood, KS Sacred Heart Church; Herndon, KS Assumption Church.
Richards, Edward W. '59 (BRK) [217] Queens, NY Our Lady of Perpetual Help Church.
Richards, Fabian '80 (ORG) Brea, CA St. Angela Merici Church.
Richards, George J., Jr. '95 (NOR) Willimantic, CT St. Mary Church.
Richards, Harry G. '91 (PH) North Wales, PA Mary, Mother of the Redeemer Church.
Richards, John '85 (CLV) Painesville, OH Lake County Memorial Hospital-East; Willoughby, OH Lake County Memorial Hospital-West.
Richards, John M. (CLV) Wickliffe, OH Our Lady of Mount Carmel Church.
Richards, Joseph '96 (CR) Thief River Falls, MN St. Bernards Church.
Richards, Lawrence '89 (E) [23] Erie, PA St. Luke Church; [C] Erie, PA Cathedral Preparatory School.
Richards, Mark (SAC) Graduate Studies.
Richards, Richard E. *a.a.* '50 (BO) [W] Brighton, MA Assumptionist Center.
Richardson, Albert '83 (HT) Retired.
Richardson, Francis X. '93 (ATL) Lookout Mountain, GA Our Lady of the Mount Church.
Richardson, J.W. Albert '83 (SHP) Retired.
Richardson, James *s.c.* '92 (HRT) [1] New Haven, CT Sacred Heart Church.
Richardson, James E. '65 (WIL) Special or Other Diocesan Assignment.
Richardson, John L. '54 (R) Retired.

Richardson, John M. *o.f.m.* '56 (NY) Obernburg, NY St. Mary Church.
Richardson, John T. *c.m.* '49 (CHI) [C] Chicago, IL De Paul University.
Richardson, John T. *c.m.* '49 (FgM) Vincentian Foreign Missions.
Richardson, Matthew Paul '91 (ARL) [6] Alexandria, VA St. Louis Church.
Richardson, Paul *s.s.c.* '54 (FgM) St. Columban's Foreign Mission.
Richardson, Peter *glmy.* (LEX) West Liberty, KY Prince of Peace Church.
Richardson, Peter *glmy.* '86 (CIN) [M] Fairfield, OH Headquarters of Glenmary Home Missioners.
Richardson, Robert C. '71 (WDC) Chillum, MD St. John Baptist de la Salle Church.
Richardson, Robert C. '87 (BUR) Middletown Springs, VT St. Anne Church.
Richardson, Msgr. Ronald A. '61 (RVC) Babylon, NY St. Joseph's Church.
Richardson, William *s.s.j.* '66 (BEA) Beaumont, TX Baptist Hospital; Beaumont, TX Columbia Beaumont Hospital.
Richardson, William J. *s.j.* '53 (BO) [W] Chestnut Hill, MA The Jesuit Community at Boston College.
Richardson, Msgr. William M. '72 (HBG) [1] Harrisburg, PA Cathedral Parish of St. Patrick Church.
Richardson, William O. *s.j.* '52 (SFR) [N] San Francisco, CA Jesuit Community at University of San Francisco.
Richardt, J. Lawrence '62 (IND) [A] St. Meinrad, IN St. Meinrad Seminary.
Richart, Paul F. '61 (IND) Sellersburg, IN St. Paul Church.
Richel, Michael C. '87 (MAD) Lodi, WI St. Patrick Church.
Richers, David E. *s.s.c.* '52 (PRO) [P] Bristol, RI St. Columban's Retirement House.
Richert, Antoine *s.m.m.* '62 (PMB) Fort Pierce, FL Notre Dame Mission Church.
Richetta, John J. '55 (MIL) [7] Kenosha, WI Our Lady of Mount Carmel Church.
Richey, Msgr. Dennis A. '66 (ALN) [I] Pottsville, PA Queen of Peace Apartments.
Richey, Msgr. Terrence '64 (LA) [53] Los Angeles, CA St. Camillus De Lellis Church.
Richey, Msgr. Terry '64 (LA) Los Angeles, CA L.A. County/University of Southern California Hospital.
Richman, Bertrand N. '62 (PRO) [4] Tiverton, RI St. Theresa Church.
Richman, Randy (DM) Ankeny, IA Our Lady's Immaculate Heart Church.
Richmeier, Garry *c.pp.s.* '83 (KC) [8] Kansas City, MO St. Charles Borromeo Church.
Richmond, John A. *s.m.* '39 (WDC) [M] Washington, DC Marist Provincial House.
Richstatter, Thomas *o.f.m.* '66 (IND) [A] St. Meinrad, IN St. Meinrad Seminary.
Richter, David T. '86 (SHP) Zwolle, LA St. Joseph Church.
Richter, Helmut W. '94 (OAK) Pittsburg, CA Good Shepherd Church.
Richter, Msgr. James B. '51 (RVC) Huntington, NY St. Patrick's Church.
Richter, John A. '64 (NU) Sleepy Eye, MN St. Mary Church.
Richter, Kevin M. '88 (SC) Hawarden, IA St. Mary's Church.
Richter, Norbert M. '41 (RCK) Retired.
Richter, Raynor E. '47 (JOL) Lombard, IL Sacred Heart Church; Retired.
Richter, Robert J. '67 (MIL) Military Chaplains.
Richter, Thomas J. '96 (BIS) [1] Bismarck, ND Cathedral of the Holy Spirit.
Richter, William '58 (TOL) Retired.
Richter, William L. '58 (TOL) Sandusky, OH Holy Angels Church.
Richtsteig, Erik J. '94 (SLC) Helper, UT St. Anthony's Church.
Ricken, David L. *j.c.l.* '80 (PBL) On Duty Outside the Diocese.
Ricker, John Michael '55 (FgM) Society of St. James the Apostle.
Rickert, William '45 (GB) Retired.
Rickey, James E. '69 (PEO) Campus, IL Sacred Heart Church; Dwight, IL St. Patrick's Church; Dwight, IL Dwight Correctional Center.
Rickle, William C. *s.j.* '79 (PH) [82] Philadelphia, PA Old St. Joseph's Church.
Rickles, Gary A. '96 (GAL) Pearland, TX St. Helen Church.
Ricks, Paul C. '78 (SAC) Jackson, CA St. Patrick's Church.
Rickson, Stephen E. '90 (TUC) Absent on Leave.
Rico, Herminio *s.j.* '93 (BO) [W] Chestnut Hill, MA The Jesuit Community at Boston College.
Ridella, Joseph '52 (VNN) Retired.
Ridgell, John E. '67 (RIC) Gloucester, VA St. Therese, the Little Flower Church.
Ridgeway, Kenneth *s.m.* '69 (PRT) Brunswick, ME St. John the Baptist Church.
Ridgway, John K. *s.j.* '82 (DEN) [M] Denver, CO Regis Jesuit Community (The Jesuits at Regis University).
Ridi, Pio '47 (P) Retired.
Ridick, George J. '73 (WOR) [20] Worcester, MA St. Catherine of Sweden Church.
Riding, Raymond *s.t.* '75 (SJN) [2] Canovanas, PR Resurreccion del Senior Church.
Ridley, Harold E. *s.j.* '69 (BAL) [B] Baltimore, MD Loyola College; [M] Baltimore, MD Jesuit Community of Loyola College, Inc.
Ridore, Danis '67 (PMB) Palm Beach, FL St. Edward Church.
Ridyard, John J. *m.m.* '56 (SJ) [M] Los Altos, CA Maryknoll.
Riebe, Bruce '85 (PRM) Brecksville, OH St. Joseph Church.
Riebe, Todd M. *m.c.c.j.* '80 (IND) Richmond, IN Holy Family Church; Richmond, IN St. Andrew Church; Richmond, IN St. Mary Church; Richmond, IN Richmond State Hospital; [N] Richmond, IN Earlham College Newman Center.
Riebe-Estrella, Gary '71 (CHI) [B] Chicago, IL The Catholic Theological Union at Chicago; [B] Techny, IL Divine Word Residence; [N] Techny, IL Society of the Divine Word, Provincial Headquarter-Chicago Prov.
Riebe-Estrella, Gary L. *s.v.d.* '71 (CHI) [N] Chicago, IL Divine Word Theologate.
Rieboldt, Richard '75 (LAF) On Duty Outside the Diocese.
Rieck, Raymond '56 (SFD) Retired.
Riede, Clifford A. '52 (L) Retired.
Riedel, Richard R. *c.pp.s.* '52 (CIN) Celina, OH Immaculate Conception of the Blessed Virgin Mary Church.
Riedel, Robert B. '92 (WDC) Valley Lee, MD St. George Church.
Riedemann, Kenneth '64 (SCL) Kensington, MN Our Lady of the Runestone Church; Lake Reno, MN St. John Nepomuk Church.
Rieden, Thomas W. *o.s.f.s.* '68 (LAN) [B] Jackson, MI Lumen Christi High School.
Rieder, David J. '56 (SCL) Perham, MN St. Henry's Church; Perham, MN St. Stanislaus Church.
Rieder, Donald '55 (SCL) Retired.
Rieder, Michael J. '94 (RVC) Port Jefferson, NY Infant Jesus Church.
Rieder, Ronald *o.f.m.cap.* '63 (FTW) Huntington, IN SS. Peter and Paul Church.
Riedl, Paul D. '35 (SPR) Retired.
Riedman, John '62 (SFS) Garretson, SD St. Rose of Lima Church.
Riedman, Joseph G. '56 (IND) [7] Indianapolis, IN Holy Spirit Church.
Riedmann, Boniface *s.a.* '45 (BO) [P] Brockton, MA Chapel of Our Savior-Catholic Pastoral and Information Center; [W] Brockton, MA Chapel of Our Saviour; [BB] Brockton, MA Chapel of Our Saviour.
Riedmann, Boniface *s.a.* '45 (LUB) Anson, TX St. Michael's Church.
Riedmueller, Leo A. '48 (LR) Hot Springs National Park, AR St. Mary's of the Springs Church.
Riedy, Robert I. '39 (PH) Spring City, PA St. Joseph Church; Retired.
Rieger, Alan J. *o.c.d.* '61 (MIL) [P] Milwaukee, WI Provincial Offices - Discalced Carmelites.
Riegler, Frederick J. '67 (PH) [77] Philadelphia, PA St. John the Baptist Church.
Riehle, James L. *c.s.c.* '64 (FTW) [B] Notre Dame, IN University of Notre Dame Du Lac; [J] Notre Dame, IN Holy Cross Community, Corby Hall, University of Notre Dame.
Riel, James A. '83 (MAN) Derry, NH Holy Cross Church.
Riel, Joseph A. *s.j.* '49 (BO) [W] Boston, MA Loyola House.
Riel, Robert H. '80 (SPR) [3] Chicopee, MA Nativity of the Blessed Virgin Mary Church.
Rielly, John *s.m.* '53 (SJ) [M] Cupertino, CA Marianist Provincial Residence.
Rielly, Scott *l.c.* '97 (ATL) [I] Dunwoody, GA Legionaries of Christ.
Rieman, Richard W. '58 (BO) [V] Chestnut Hill, MA Opus Dei.
Riemer, Matthew *m.s.h.s.* '95 (DAL) [L] Dallas, TX Marian Servants of the Holy Spirit.
Riemer, Robert *s.v.d.* '60 (FgM) Society of the Divine Word Foreign Missions.
Rien, Robert K. '74 (OAK) [19] Oakland, CA St. Paschal Baylon Church.
Riendeau, Richard '57 (SPR) South Hadley, MA St. Theresa of the Infant Jesus Church.
Riendeau, Walter A. *s.s.s.* '50 (SLC) Eureka, UT St. Patrick's Church; Payson, UT San Andres Church.
Riepe, Charles K. '60 (BAL) Special Assignment; [O] Baltimore, MD Archdiocesan Office-Newman Center.
Riera, John *t.o.r.* '48 (NEW) [20] Newark, NJ Immaculate Heart of Mary Church.
Ries, Carl A. '70 (DUB) Mason City, IA St. Joseph's Church.
Ries, Donald C. '59 (SC) Fort Dodge, IA Corpus Christi Church.
Ries, James C. '93 (ORG) Placentia, CA St. Joseph Church.
Ries, Richard S. '63 (SC) Le Mars, IA St. James Church.
Ries, Victor F. '45 (CIN) Retired.
Riesberg, Leo L. '57 (SC) Wall Lake, IA St. Joseph's Church.
Riesenberg, John J. '60 (COV) Fort Thomas, KY St. Thomas Church.
Riesthuis, Henk *m.h.m.* '59 (LA) [R] Los Angeles, CA Mill Hill Missionaries Procure.
Rietti, John '57 (JKS) Lexington, MS St. Thomas Church.
Riffle, David '67 (B) Emmett, ID Sacred Heart Church.
Riffle, Donald J. '62 (B) [1] Boise, ID Cathedral of St. John the Evangelist.
Riffle, Douglas H. '57 (B) Retired.
Riffle, Henry J. '70 (SP) Beverly Hills, FL Our Lady of Grace Church.
Riffle, Raymond E. '79 (GBG) [4] Greensburg, PA St. Paul Church.
Rigali, Joseph L. *o.f.m.* '58 (CIN) [23] Cincinnati, OH St. Clement Church; [M] Cincinnati, OH St. Clement Friary.
Rigali, Norbert J. *s.j.* '59 (SD) [B] San Diego, CA University of San Diego.
Rigatuso, Leo '94 (OM) Papillion, NE St. Columbkille Church.
Rigdon, Vincent J. '77 (WDC) [1] Silver Spring, MD St. Andrew Apostle Church; Special Ministries.
Rigert, James A. *c.s.c.* '66 (FTW) [A] Notre Dame, IN Moreau Seminary; [B] Notre Dame, IN University of Notre Dame Du Lac; [J] Notre Dame, IN Holy Cross Community, Corby Hall, University of Notre Dame.
Rigney, Msgr. Dennis A. (ALN) [I] Saint Clair, PA Neumann Apartments.
Rigney, Msgr. Dennis A. '66 (ALN) [2] Allentown, PA St. Francis of Assisi Church; [H] Bethlehem, PA Holy Family Manor; [I] Bethlehem, PA Holy Family Apartments; [I] Bethlehem, PA Trexler Pavilion, Personal Care Residence of Holy Family Manor; [I] Easton, PA Antonian Towers; [I] New Philadelphia, PA Holy Family Apartments; [I] Orwigsburg, PA Holy Family Residence; [I] Orwigsburg, PA Holy Family Adult Day Care at St. Francis Center; [I] Reading, PA Queen of Angels Apartment; [I] Bethlehem, PA Grace Mansion Personal Care Residence of Holy Manor; [J] Bethlehem, PA Holy Family Villa.
Rigney, Msgr. James '47 (NY) Retired.
Rigney, Msgr. Philip '49 (CAM) Retired.
Rigney, Msgr. Raymond P. '42 (NY) Retired; [E] White Plains, NY Archbishop Stepinac High School.
Rigoli, Anthony *o.m.i.* '72 (BUF) [27] Buffalo, NY Holy Angels Church; [R] Williamsville, NY Campus Ministry.
Rigonan, Antonio R. '88 (SPC) Springfield, MO U.S. Medical Center.
Rigouts, Alphonse *c.i.c.m.* '48 (FgM) Missionhurst Foreign Missions.
Riha, Francis A. *m.m.* '68 (FgM) Maryknoll Foreign Missions.
Rihn, Msgr. Roy '42 (SAT) Retired; [K] San Antonio, TX Casa De Padres.
Rikteraitis, John E. '56 (HRT) [4] New Britain, CT St. Andrew's Church.
Riler, Robert '94 (SEA) Puyallup, WA All Saints Church.
Riley, Andrew '80 (PMB) [2] Boca Raton, FL Our Lady of Lourdes Church.
Riley, Daniel *o.f.m.* (BUF) [R] Williamsville, NY Campus Ministry.
Riley, Daniel *o.f.m.* '71 (BUF) [Q] West Clarksville, NY Mount Irenaeus, Franciscan Mountain Retreat & Holy Peace Friary.
Riley, Daniel J. '84 (BO) [74] Boston, MA St. William Church.
Riley, Daniel P. *o.f.m.* (BUF) [C] St. Bonaventure, NY St. Bonaventure University.
Riley, David J. '64 (BGP) Sherman, CT Holy Trinity Church.
Riley, Dennis S. (CHI) [12] Chicago, IL St. Angela Church.
Riley, Edward H. *o.p.* '60 (CHI) [N] Chicago, IL Dominicans (Provincial Office).
Riley, Edward H. *o.p.* '60 (FgM) Dominican - Order of Preachers Foreign Missions.
Riley, Finian A. *o.f.m.* '55 (FgM) Franciscan Foreign Missions.
Riley, George F. *o.s.a.* '62 (PH) [C] Villanova, PA Villanova University; [AA] Villanova, PA St. Thomas Monastery.
Riley, J. Norman '57 (CLV) Copley, OH Guardian Angels Church.
Riley, James *s.j.* '74 (CLV) [U] Cleveland, OH Jesuit Retreat House.
Riley, James H. (BO) Retired.
Riley, James L. '70 (SY) New Hartford, NY Our Lady of the Rosary Church.
Riley, John F. '55 (STP) Retired.
Riley, John F. '56 (ALB) Pittstown, NY St. George Church.

Riley, John J. '91 (ARL) Warrenton, VA St. John the Evangelist Church.
Riley, John P. *c.s.c.* '94 (FTW) [6] South Bend, IN Christ the King Church.
Riley, Kenneth A. '92 (KC) [5] Kansas City, MO St. Bernadette's Church.
Riley, Leo P. '82 (DUB) Clermont, IA St. Peter's Church; Postville, IA St. Bridget's Church.
Riley, Mark J. '90 (BO) Stoneham, MA St. Patrick Church.
Riley, Mark R. '95 (CLV) [4] Lakewood, OH St. James Church.
Riley, Miles O'Brien '63 (SFR) Belmont, CA St. Mark Church; Special Assignment.
Riley, Patric '84 (KCK) [8] Topeka, KS St. Matthew Church.
Riley, Patrick '48 (SCL) Retired.
Riley, Placidus H. *o.s.b.* '46 (MAN) [K] Manchester, NH St. Anselm Abbey.
Riley, Robert D. *o.p.* '60 (WDC) [11] Washington, DC St. Dominic Church & Priory Church.
Rilley, John F. '53 (PH) Retired.
Rimassa, Paul S. '83 (TR) [10] Trenton, NJ Our Lady of Sorrows Church; Trenton, NJ Donnelly Memorial Hospital of City of Trenton.
Rimelspach, Jeffrey J. '85 (COL) Powell, OH St. Joan of Arc Church.
Rimes, Robert B. *s.j.* '55 (MOB) [B] Mobile, AL Spring Hill College.
Rimes, William J. *s.j.* '49 (SEA) [M] Seattle, WA Jesuit House, Seattle.
Rimmele, Leo *o.s.b.* '55 (P) [L] St. Benedict, OR Mt. Angel Abbey.
Rimselis, Victor *m.i.c.* '43 (CHI) [N] Chicago, IL Congregation of Marian Fathers of the Immaculate Conception.
Rimshaw, Joseph J. *s.s.j.* '48 (BAL) [M] Baltimore, MD St. Joseph Society of the Sacred Heart House of Central Administration.
Rimshaw, Joseph J. *s.s.j.* '48 (ORL) Retired.
Rinaldi, Francis J. *o.s.f.s.* '69 (WIL) [C] Ridgely, MD The Benedictine School for Exceptional Children; [J] Ridgely, MD St. Gertrude's Monastery, Motherhouse and Novitiate of the Sisters of St. Benedict.
Rinaldo, Alexander '39 (SP) Retired.
Rinaldo, Joseph *s.c.* '67 (LAN) [E] Chelsea, MI St. Louis Center for Exceptional Children & Adults; [L] Grass Lake, MI The Pious Union of St. Joseph.
Rincon, Rafael *o.f.m.* (ELP) Presidio, TX Santa Teresa de Jesus Church.
Rindos, Paul T. '59 (HBG) Mount Joy, PA Mary, Mother of the Church.
Riney, C. Phil '48 (OWN) [2] Owensboro, KY Blessed Mother Church.
Riney, Maury '77 (OWN) Whitesville, KY St. Mary of the Woods Church.
Riney, W. Jerry '75 (OWN) Bowling Green, KY Holy Spirit Church.
Ring, Msgr. Arthur R. '37 (DM) Retired.
Ring, Daniel J. '68 (TOL) Fostoria, OH St. Wendelin Church.
Ring, Francis J. *s.j.* '47 (FgM) Provinces.
Ring, Francis J. *s.j.* '47 (MIL) [P] Milwaukee, WI Jesuit Provincial Office, Wisconsin Province.
Ring, James W. *s.j.* '41 (BO) [W] Chestnut Hill, MA The Jesuit Community at Boston College.
Ring, John K. '61 (SFR) [53] San Francisco, CA St. Vincent de Paul Church.
Ring, Joseph G. '88 (SFD) Charleston, IL St. Charles Borromeo Church.
Ring, Paul L. '95 (BO) North Reading, MA St. Theresa Church.
Ring, Vincent D. '64 (SFR) San Bruno, CA St. Robert Church.
Ringenback, Gerard A. '72 (RVC) Islip Terrace, NY St. Peter the Apostle Church.
Ringenberger, Harry '69 (MIA) [12] Fort Lauderdale, FL St. Pius X Church.
Ringholz, Benedict E. '45 (TOL) Retired.
Ringwood, Joseph D. *s.j.* '59 (SPK) [K] Spokane, WA Regis Community.
Rini, John '67 (ELP) [19] El Paso, TX Our Lady of the Valley Church.
Rink, George (SEA) Retired.
Rinkowski, George M. '41 (TOL) Retired.
Rinn, Richard A. *c.s.v.* '48 (CHI) [N] Arlington Heights, IL Viatorian Mission House.
Rinn, Richard A. *c.s.v.* '78 (CHI) [N] Arlington Heights, IL Clerics of St. Viator-Provincial Residence.
Rinn, Richard A. *c.s.v.* '81 (CHI) [N] Arlington Heights, IL Viatorian Province Center-Clerics of St. Viator.
Rinschler, Msgr. William J. '38 (NY) [111] New York, NY Sacred Hearts of Jesus and Mary Church; Retired.
Rinzel, Jerome A. '64 (MIL) Muskego, WI St. Leonard Congregation Church.
Riono, Camilo (SJN) [23] Bayamon, PR Santa Maria Church.
Riordan, Msgr. Brendan P. '70 (RVC) Deer Park, NY SS. Cyril and Methodius Church.
Riordan, Brice E. *o.carm.* '44 (NEW) Paramus, NJ Carmelite Chapel of St. Therese Church.
Riordan, Daniel F. '28 (BO) Retired.
Riordan, Eugene *s.m.a.* '53 (WDC) [M] Takoma Park, MD Society of African Missions (S.M.A.).
Riordan, Jerome F. '43 (CHI) Hanover Park, IL St. Ansgar Church; Retired.
Riordan, John B. *o.f.m.cap.* '71 (NY) [17] Yonkers, NY Sacred Heart Church.
Riordan, Patrick M. '90 (PEO) Silvis, IL Our Lady of Guadalupe Church.
Riordan, Richard J. '60 (WIN) Retired.
Rios, Angel L. *m.c.* '85 (MGZ) Maricao, PR St. John the Baptist Church.
Rios, Francisco *i.v.e.* '91 (SJ) [14] San Jose, CA St. Leo the Great Church; San Jose, CA Santa Clara County Jail; Milpitas, CA Elmwood Rehabilitation Center.
Rios, Juan Carlos '93 (MIA) Higher Studies.
Rios, Manuel D. '86 (NEW) [1] Elizabeth, NJ St. Mary of the Assumption Church.
Rios, Teodoro A. *c.m.* '76 (FgM) Vincentian Foreign Missions.
Riotte, Jules '51 (STN) On Duty Outside the Diocese.
Rioux, J. Robert *c.s.c.* '56 (FR) [J] North Dartmouth, MA St. Joseph's Hall.
Rioux, Raymond '94 (LAV) [8] Las Vegas, NV St. Elizabeth Ann Seton Church.
Rioux, Raymond '94 (SR) On Duty Outside the Diocese.
Ripko, DePaul *o.f.m.cap.* '53 (PIT) [O] Herman, PA St. Mary's Friary.
Riplog, Duane T. '84 (CHR) Summerville, SC St. John the Beloved Church.
Ripoli, Roland *o.s.b.* '64 (PIT) Bairdford, PA St. Victor Church.
Ripoli, Roland R. *o.s.b.* '64 (GBG) [H] Latrobe, PA Saint Vincent Archabbey.
Ripp, Anthony *m.s.c.* '67 (ALN) [A] Center Valley, PA Missionaries of the Sacred Heart.
Ripp, Joseph '64 (SFS) Salem, SD St. Mary Church.
Ripper, Thomas J. *m.s.* '68 (STL) Maplewood, MO Immaculate Conception Church.
Ripperger, Chad *f.s.s.p.* '97 (SCR) [M] Elmhurst, PA Priestly Fraternity of St. Peter (F.S.S.P.), North American District Headquarters.
Ripperger, Chad A. *f.ss.p.* '97 (OM) [34] Omaha, NE St. Patrick Church.
Ripperger, Edward J. '61 (IND) Mooresville, IN St. Thomas More Church.
Ripperger, Harold A. '58 (IND) Lanesville, IN St. Mary Church.
Ripperger, Mark *o.cist.* '93 (DAL) [M] Irving, TX Cistercian Abbey of Our Lady of Dallas.
Ripperger, William G. '41 (IND) Napoleon, IN St. Maurice Church.
Ripperger, William G. '55 (IND) Millhousen, IN Immaculate Conception Church.
Rippinger, Joel *o.s.b.* '74 (RCK) [H] Aurora, IL Marmion Abbey-St. Augustine's Abbey.
Rippy, Robert J. '84 (ARL) [6] Arlington, VA Our Lady of Lourdes Church.
Risacher, James E. '52 (TOL) Retired.
Rischmann, Edward '48 (NEW) Retired.
Rischmann, Robert J. '61 (NEW) [1] East Orange, NJ Holy Name of Jesus Church.
Risden, George '84 (SR) [H] Sonoma, CA Hanna Boys Center.
Rishel, Robert F. '55 (PIT) Creighton, PA Holy Family Church.
Risley, John C. *o.p.* '65 (DEN) [29] Denver, CO St. Dominic's Parish.
Risley, L. Thomas '64 (RCK) Carpentersville, IL St. Monica Church.
Riss, Dennis '84 (RC) Faith, SD St. Joseph Church.
Risse, Claire *s.v.d.* '47 (CHI) [B] Techny, IL Divine Word Residence.
Risse, James *s.v.d.* '61 (FgM) Society of the Divine Word Foreign Missions.
Risse, Roger *s.v.d.* '54 (FgM) Society of the Divine Word Foreign Missions.
Rissling, Ron *o.m.i.* (STO) Tracy, CA Deuel Vocational Institution.
Ristori, Michael *o.f.m.cap.* '53 (NY) [151] Bronx, NY Immaculate Conception Church.
Ristuccia, Leon *o.f.m.* '45 (HRT) Winsted, CT St. Joseph's Church.
Rita, Carmine J. '94 (NY) Bronxville, NY St. Joseph Church.
Rita, Thomas L. '70 (FR) Osterville, MA Our Lady of the Assumption Church.
Ritacco, Richard '76 (WOR) Absent on Leave.
Ritari, Raymond '83 (PHX) [18] Phoenix, AZ St. Martin de Porres Church; [20] Phoenix, AZ St. Matthew Church.
Ritchey, Samuel E. '73 (COL) [12] Columbus, OH Corpus Christi Church; Columbus, OH Regency Manor.
Ritchey, Scott '94 (PHX) [22] Phoenix, AZ Our Lady of the Valley Church.
Ritchey, Timothy '85 (B) Eagle, ID St. Matthew Church.
Ritchey, Timothy M. '85 (B) Meridian, ID Holy Spirit Church.
Ritchie, Donald E. '59 (BUR) Waitsfield, VT Our Lady of the Snows Church; Waterbury, VT St. Andrew Church.
Ritchie, Francis J. '58 (BO) [3] Salem, MA St. James Church.
Ritchie, Msgr. G. Carlton '32 (E) Retired.
Ritchie, Gerald T. '68 (E) [8] Erie, PA Our Lady of Mercy Church.
Ritchie, Robert T. '71 (NY) [21] New York, NY St. Catherine of Genoa Church; [Q] New York, NY Society of St. Vincent De Paul, Archdiocesan Central Council of New York.
Ritchie, Vincent J. *s.j.* '74 (RVC) [P] Manhasset, NY St. Ignatius Retreat House, Inisfada.
Riter, Dennis G. '71 (BUF) [55] Buffalo, NY Our Lady of Perpetual Help Church; [66] Buffalo, NY St. Valentine Church.
Ritt, Paul E. '81 (BO) [A] Boston, MA St. John's Seminary School of Theology.
Rittenhouse, Thomas R. '76 (TR) Matawan, NJ St. Clement Church; Retired.
Ritter, Charles F. '67 (TOL) Bryan, OH St. Patrick Church.
Ritter, Edward W. '51 (DET) St. Clair, MI St. Mary Church.
Ritter, J. Patrick *s.d.s.* '76 (SAC) Orangevale, CA Divine Savior Church.
Ritter, Patrick J. '74 (SEA) [2] Tacoma, WA St. Charles Borromeo Church.
Rittmeyer, Robert '80 (SP) Zephyrhills, FL St. Joseph Church; Retired.
Ritz, Robert G. *c.s.b.* '51 (GAL) Sugar Land, TX St. Theresa Church.
Ritzert, William J. '64 (PIT) Evans City, PA St. Matthias Church; Butler County, PA Department of Veterans Affairs- Deshon Hospital.
Riva, Gerald '68 (JOL) Elmhurst, IL Immaculate Conception Church.
Riva, Hugo *m.c.c.j.* '50 (CHI) Blue Island, IL St. Donatus Church.
Riva, Paolo *c.r.s.* '96 (MAN) [H] Allenstown, NH Pine Haven Boys Center.
Rivard, Robert *f.m.s.i.* (BO) Norfolk, MA MCI-Norfolk.
Rivard, Robert *f.m.s.i.* '77 (BO) [B] Framingham, MA Sylva Maria.
Rivard, Roland J. '56 (BUR) [2] Burlington, VT St. Anthony's Church; [D] Burlington, VT St. Joseph's Home for Aged; [D] Derby Line, VT Michaud Memorial Manor; [D] Rutland, VT Loretto Home for Aged.
Rivas, David '85 (ARE) [1] Camuy, PR St. Joseph Church.
Rivas, Jorge *o.f.m.* '48 (ELP) [B] El Paso, TX St. Anthony's School of Theology.
Rivas, Juan *l.c.* '82 (LA) [R] Pasadena, CA Legionaries of Christ; [DD] El Monte, CA Hombre Nuevo.
Rivas, Romeo '59 (MIA) Retired; [K] Miami, FL Shrine of Our Lady of Charity.
Rivas-Campiz, Eral Jose (SJN) [59] San Juan, PR Stella Maris Church.
Rive, Gino G. '57 (SB) [E] Morongo Valley, CA St. Michael's of Morongo Valley, Inc.
Rively, William E. *s.j.* '46 (NY) [DD] New York, NY Murray-Weigel Hall.
Rivera, Adalin '77 (PCE) Juana Diaz, PR Santa Teresita Church; [B] Ponce, PR The Pontifical Catholic University of Puerto Rico.
Rivera, Anastacio *s.j.* '74 (LA) [6] Los Angeles, CA Blessed Sacrament Church.
Rivera, Andres *s.d.b.* '74 (SJN) [37] San Juan, PR Maria Auxiliadora Church.
Rivera, Eddie '90 (SJN) [50] San Juan, PR Nuestra Senora de la Providencia Church.
Rivera, Felix *o.carm.* '91 (LA) [88] Los Angeles, CA St. Raphael Church.
Rivera, Felix '97 (ARE) Barceloneta, PR Church of Our Lady of Mt. Carmel.
Rivera, Guadalupe '49 (SFE) Retired.
Rivera, Hector E. '82 (MGZ) Sabana Grande, PR Church of San Isidro.
Rivera, Hilario '74 (CGS) [4] Caguas, PR Nuestra Senora de la Providencia Church.
Rivera, Jaime Velasco *o.s.b.* '93 (MIL) [P] Benet Lake, WI St. Benedict's Abbey.
Rivera, Jesus *s.t.* '81 (ARL) [J] Arlington, VA Missionary Servants of the Most Holy Trinity, S.T.
Rivera, Joaquin '79 (SJN) [8] Carolina, PR San Fernando Church.
Rivera, Luis '84 (MIA) [11] Miami, FL Our Lady of Divine Providence Church.
Rivera, Luis Antonio '83 (CGS) San Lorenzo, PR Sagrado Corazon de Jesus y 12 Apostoles Church.
Rivera, Msgr. Manuel '79 (SJN) [39] San Juan, PR San Mateo Church.
Rivera, Miguel '83 (ARE) Corozal-Padilla, PR Our Lady of the Seven Sorrows Church.
Rivera, Miguel A. '86 (SJN) [37] San Juan, PR Maria Auxiliadora Church.
Rivera, Narciso *o.a.r.* '77 (LSC) [3] Las Cruces, NM Our Lady of Health Church.
Rivera, Orlando '90 (PCE) Guayanilla, PR Immaculate Conception Church.

Rivera, Oscar *o.s.b.* '78 (CGS) [C] Humacao, PR San Antonio Abad Abbey of the Order of St. Benedict.
Rivera, Oscar '79 (CGS) [6] Caguas, PR Nuestra Senora del Perpetuo Socorro Church.
Rivera, Raymond L. '86 (PCE) Guayanilla, PR Immaculate Conception Church.
Rivera, Ricardo *o.f.m.* (CC) Hebbronville, TX Our Lady of Guadalupe Church.
Rivera, Ubladimiro *o.f.m.* '75 (FgM) Franciscan Foreign Missions.
Rivera-Martinez, Pius *o.s.c.o.* '53 (WOR) [N] Spencer, MA St. Joseph's Abbey.
Rivero, Andres *o.f.m.* '75 (LA) [R] Santa Barbara, CA Franciscan Friary, Order of Friars Minor (Old Mission).
Rivero, Jordi '88 (MIA) [27] Miami, FL St. Michael the Archangel Church.
Rivero, Jordi S. '82 (MIA) [K] Miami, FL Respect Life Office.
Rivero, Juan '72 (FWT) Denton, TX Immaculate Conception Church; Denton, TX State School.
Rivero, Julio B. *t.o.r.* '69 (SP) St. Pete Beach, FL St. John Church.
Rivero, Leonides '78 (ELP) [27] El Paso, TX St. Mark Church.
Rivero-Perez, Carlos Alfredo (SJN) Luquillo, PR Madre del Redentor Church.
Riveroll, Jesus R. *s.j.* '88 (FgM) Provinces.
Rivers, Clarence J. '56 (CIN) On Special and Diocesan Assignment.
Rivers, Clarence R.J. *ph.d.* '56 (CIN) [V] Cincinnati, OH Stimuli, Inc.
Rivers, Robert S. *c.s.p.* '68 (WDC) [B] Washington, DC St. Paul's College; [V] Washington, DC Paulist National Catholic Evangelization Assoc.
Rivet, Hilton L. *s.j.* '54 (BR) [11] Baton Rouge, LA Immaculate Conception Church.
Rivi, Geno G. '57 (GBG) Retired.
Rivituso, Mark (STL) [49] St. Louis, MO St. Mary Magdalen Church.
Rizo, Sergio '89 (FWT) Cleburne, TX St. Joseph Church.
Rizzi, Salvatore '41 (BRK) Retired.
Rizzo, John C. '56 (OM) [4] Omaha, NE St. Ann Church; [35] Omaha, NE St. Peter Church.
Rizzo, Mateo J. '73 (BRK) [72] Brooklyn, NY Shrine Church of St. Jude.
Rizzo, Robert C. '74 (CHI) Niles, IL Our Lady of Ransom Church; Park Ridge, IL St. Paul of the Cross Church.
Rizzotto, Msgr. Vincent M. '56 (GAL) [18] Houston, TX St. Cecilia Church.
Rizzuto, Mariano J. *s.m.* '59 (BR) Convent, LA St. Michael the Archangel Church.
Roach, Charles B. '45 (PIT) Retired.
Roach, Daniel *o.p.* '56 (FgM) Dominican - Order of Preachers Foreign Missions.
Roach, Francis J. '56 (STP) Retired.
Roach, Francis J. '73 (WOR) Worcester, MA Worcester State Hospital; [J] Worcester, MA Saint Vincent Hospital, Inc.
Roach, John A. '58 (SPR) Shelburne Falls, MA St. Joseph's Church.
Roach, John E. '43 (ROC) Retired.
Roach, Joseph W. *s.a.g.* '48 (SAG) Retired.
Roach, Joseph W. *s.a.g.* '48 (SB) Retired; [E] Morongo Valley, CA St. Michael's of Morongo Valley, Inc.
Roach, Michael G. '81 (KC) [34] Kansas City, MO St. Patrick Church.
Roach, Michael J. '71 (BAL) Manchester, MD St. Bartholomew Church; [A] Emmitsburg, MD Mount St. Mary's Seminary.
Roach, Richard *s.j.* '69 (SEA) Mountlake Terrace, WA St. Pius X Church.
Roach, Richard R. *s.j.* '69 (SEA) [A] Seattle, WA Seattle University.
Roach, Robert N. *c.s.sp.* '48 (PH) [AA] Bensalem, PA Congregation of the Holy Ghost.
Roach, Thomas E. *s.j.* '70 (WDC) [E] North Bethesda, MD Georgetown Preparatory School.
Roach, Virgil J. *s.j.* '43 (OM) [K] Omaha, NE Jesuit Community At Creighton University.
Roache, James P. '60 (CHI) [1] Chicago, IL Cathedral of the Holy Name.
Roark, John L. '56 (SY) [11] Syracuse, NY St. Ann Church.
Roark, Michael B. '70 (KNX) Crossville, TN St. Alphonsus Church.
Robak, Anthony G. '74 (NEW) North Bergen, NJ Sacred Heart Church.
Robak, Charles P. *m.m.* '70 (FgM) Maryknoll Foreign Missions.
Robards, Charles P. '76 (PEO) Thomasboro, IL St. Elizabeth's Church.
Robb, Dennis E. '74 (SEA) Everett, WA Immaculate Conception Church; Everett, WA Our Lady of Perpetual Help Church.
Robb, Kevin Dominic *o.p.* '77 (NY) [DD] New York, NY St. Vincent Ferrer Priory.
Robb, Paul V. *s.j.* '60 (CHI) [N] Chicago, IL Chicago Province of the Society of Jesus-Provincial Office; [N] Chicago, IL Chicago Province of the Society of Jesus-Provincial Office.
Robbins, Charles J. *c.pp.s.* '39 (LFT) [A] Rensselaer, IN Saint Joseph's College.
Robbins, John '72 (ROC) [I] Rochester, NY Basilian Residence.
Robbins, John F. *c.s.b.* '72 (ROC) [M] Rochester, NY Diocesan Office of Campus Ministry.
Robbins, Robert J. '74 (NY) [46] New York, NY Holy Family Church.
Robbins, Roger P. '63 (SAT) Schertz, TX Church of the Good Shepherd.
Robbins, Thomas P. '74 (COV) Taylor Mill, KY St. Anthony Church; [B] Covington, KY Holy Cross High School.
Robello, Louis J. '65 (SFR) Retired.
Roberge, Francis (WOR) West Boylston, MA Our Lady of Good Counsel Church.
Roberge, Francis A. '78 (WOR) [P] Worcester, MA Community of Teresian Carmelites; [Q] Worcester, MA Campus Ministry.
Roberge, Frederick *s.s.s.* '35 (CLV) [P] Cleveland, OH Blessed Sacrament Community.
Roberge, Richard A. '85 (MAN) [3] Berlin, NH St. Kieran Church.
Roberson, Henry '71 (OKL) Special Assignment.
Roberson, Michael '74 (NO) [53] New Orleans, LA SS. Peter and Paul Church.
Roberson, Ronald G. *c.s.p.* '77 (WDC) [B] Washington, DC St. Paul's College.
Robert, Darin '71 (LAN) Ann Arbor, MI University of Michigan Hospitals/Pastoral Care Dept.
Robert, Emile A. '50 (PRO) [3] Warren, RI St. Jean Baptiste Church.
Robert, Rene '89 (STA) [1] St. Augustine, FL Cathedral of St. Augustine; [D] St. Augustine, FL Religious Education for Catholic Deaf and Blind.
Roberts, Allan '80 (LA) [10] Long Beach, CA St. Maria Goretti Church.
Roberts, Anthony P. *s.j.* '56 (PH) [AA] Philadelphia, PA Jesuit Community at St. Joseph's University.
Roberts, Art *c.s.b.* '55 (LSC) Truth or Consequences, NM Our Lady of Perpetual Help Church.
Roberts, David *c.p.* '52 (FgM) Passionist Foreign Missions.
Roberts, David G. (BO) [5] Newton, MA Mary Immaculate of Lourdes Church.
Roberts, Don J. '78 (SFD) Oconee, IL Sacred Heart of Jesus Church; Ramsey, IL St. Joseph Church.
Roberts, Edward *s.s.s.* '60 (CLV) [P] Cleveland, OH Congregation of the Blessed Sacrament Provincial House.
Roberts, Edward A. *s.s.c.* '60 (BO) [W] Quincy, MA St. Columban's Foreign Mission Society.
Roberts, Edward J. '96 (PEO) Pontiac, IL St. Mary's Church.
Roberts, Eugene J. '75 (TR) Marlboro, NJ St. Gabriel Church.
Roberts, G. Richard '91 (LC) Elroy, WI St. Patrick Church; Wonewoc, WI St. Jerome Church.
Roberts, Kenneth J. '66 (DAL) On Duty Outside the Diocese.
Roberts, Mark '83 (LAV) Henderson, NV St. Peter the Apostle Church.
Roberts, Marshall (SCR) On Special or Other Diocesan Assignment.
Roberts, Ralph *s.s.s.* '75 (CLV) [P] Cleveland, OH Congregation of the Blessed Sacrament Provincial House.
Roberts, Randall *o.f.m.* '84 (GB) [I] Pulaski, WI Assumption of B.V.M. Friary.
Roberts, Thomas C. '84 (NEW) Plainfield, NJ St. Bernard's Church.
Roberts, Victor W. *o.s.b.* '69 (OKL) [I] Shawnee, OK St. Gregory Abbey.
Robertson, Douglas C. '96 (LC) Marshfield, WI St. John the Baptist Church; [C] Marshfield, WI Columbus High School; [D] Marshfield, WI Holy Family Middle School.
Robertson, Eugene '78 (STL) Farmington, MO St. Joseph Church.
Robertson, Msgr. Glendon E. '57 (CAM) Retired.
Robertson, Msgr. Harold J. '49 (NY) [1] Yonkers, NY St. Anthony Church.
Robertson, J. Felton *o.f.m.* '47 (PAT) [M] Butler, NJ St. Anthony Friary.
Robertson, James E. '77 (BO) Pembroke, MA St. Thecla Church.
Robertson, John W. '71 (HEL) Special Assignments.
Robertson, Thomas J. '41 (STP) Retired.
Robertson, Thomas M. '65 (STL) Riverview Gardens, MO St. Catherine of Alexandria Church.
Robertson, Vernon W. '67 (L) [10] Louisville, KY St. Augustine Church; Retired.
Robertson, Msgr. William P. '60 (GAL) [1] Spring, TX Christ the Good Shepherd Church.
Robeson, Steve '84 (STL) Mattese, MO Mary, Mother of the Church.
Robichand, Paul G. *c.s.p.* '75 (NY) [DD] Jamaica Estates, NY Paulist Fathers Generalate.
Robichaud, Armand *s.m.* '50 (BO) [W] Boston, MA Marist Fathers of Our Lady of Victories (Boston Prov.).
Robichaud, George H. '75 (MAN) Ashland, NH St. Agnes Church.
Robichaud, J. Armand *s.m.* '50 (BO) [W] Boston, MA Marist Fathers Lourdes Residence; [BB] Boston, MA Chapel of Our Lady of Lourdes.
Robichaud, J. Armand *s.m.* '50 (FgM) Marist Foreign Missions.
Robichaud, James P. *o.m.i.* '79 (BO) [11] Lowell, MA Notre Dame de Lourdes Church.
Robichaud, Paul G. *c.s.p.* '75 (WDC) [C] Washington, DC Catholic University of America, The.
Robichaux, Robie E. '76 (LAF) [15] Lafayette, LA St. Patrick Church; On Special Assignment.
Robicheau, Armand *s.m.* (BO) [59] Boston, MA Our Lady of Victories Church.
Robida, Raymond A. '48 (FR) Retired.
Robideau, Jeffery '97 (LAN) Burton, MI Holy Redeemer Church.
Robigue, Euan Garcia Jesus '97 (MIL) [B] Franklin, WI Xaverian Missionary Fathers College Seminary.
Robillard, Joseph R. '84 (ORG) Costa Mesa, CA St. Joachim Church.
Robillard, Raymond A. '66 (FR) Absent on Leave; [J] Fall River, MA Priests' Hostel.
Robillard, Msgr. Thomas J. '44 (OG) Norfolk, NY Visitation of the B.V.M. Church; Retired.
Robin, Richard A. *s.j.* '67 (LA) [C] Los Angeles, CA Loyola Marymount University; [C] Los Angeles, CA Loyola Marymount University.
Robine, Paul M. '59 (ALT) Mundys Corner, PA St. John Vianney's Church.
Robins, Dean '85 (NO) Mandeville, LA Our Lady of the Lake Church.
Robinson, Charles *o.f.m.cap.* '70 (GF) Crow Agency, MT St. Dennis Church.
Robinson, Christopher S. *c.m.* '89 (STL) [P] Earth City, MO Congregation of the Mission Midwest Province (Vincentians).
Robinson, David C. *s.j.* '92 (SFR) [N] San Francisco, CA Jesuit Community at University of San Francisco.
Robinson, David J. '90 (SFR) [N] San Francisco, CA Jesuit Community at St. Ignatius College Preparatory.
Robinson, Denis *o.s.b.* '93 (IND) [A] St. Meinrad, IN St. Meinrad Seminary; [B] St. Meinrad, IN St. Meinrad Seminary-College of Liberal Arts; [J] St. Meinrad, IN St. Meinrad Archabbey.
Robinson, Denis P. *c.s.sp.* '79 (PH) [AA] Bensalem, PA Congregation of the Holy Ghost.
Robinson, Donald '80 (OG) [A] Ogdensburg, NY Wadhams Hall.
Robinson, Edmund J. *s.j.* '55 (SPK) [K] Spokane, WA Regis Community.
Robinson, Edward M. *o.p.* '41 (DAL) [M] Irving, TX Dominican Priory of St. Albert the Great.
Robinson, Ernest E. '79 (RVC) Huntington, NY St. Patrick's Church.
Robinson, Fisher *s.v.d.* '56 (LA) [71] Los Angeles, CA St. John, The Evangelist Church.
Robinson, Gerald H. *s.j.* (SAC) [I] Applegate, CA Our Lady of the Oaks Villa.
Robinson, Gerald H. *s.j.* '77 (SAC) [14] Sacramento, CA St. Ignatius of Loyola Church.
Robinson, Gerald J. '64 (TOL) [29] Toledo, OH St. Jude Church.
Robinson, Jack Clark *o.f.m.* '86 (SFE) [4] Albuquerque, NM Holy Family Church.
Robinson, Msgr. James P. *s.s.e.* '57 (DET) [1] Detroit, MI Cathedral, Church of the Most Blessed Sacrament.
Robinson, Jerome (MOB) On Leave from the Archdiocese.
Robinson, John *o.s.b.* '61 (CHY) In Residence.
Robinson, John *o.s.b.* '61 (PBL) [F] Canon City, CO Holy Cross Abbey.
Robinson, John A. '71 (CHI) Elk Grove Village, IL Queen of the Rosary Church.
Robinson, John C. '54 (MOB) [6] Mobile, AL Holy Family Church.
Robinson, Joseph A. '64 (CIN) [18] Cincinnati, OH St. Boniface Church.
Robinson, Joseph P. '68 (BO) Bedford, MA St. Michael Church; Boston, MA Veterans Administration Hospital; Military & VA Chaplains.
Robinson, Ken '92 (FWT) Grapevine, TX St. Francis of Assisi Church.
Robinson, Lawrence F. *s.j.* '65 (P) [D] Portland, OR Jesuit High School.
Robinson, Michael Dean '96 (SD) [23] San Diego, CA St. Charles Church.
Robinson, Monte E. '75 (MAD) Belmont, WI St. Philomena Church.
Robinson, Patrick '91 (PHX) Chandler, AZ St. Benedict Church.
Robinson, Paul *o.carm.* '67 (JOL) [J] Darien, IL Carmelite Provincial Office.
Robinson, Perry L. *s.j.* '72 (OM) [K] Omaha, NE Jesuit Community At Creighton University.
Robinson, Richard J. (MIL) [76] Milwaukee, WI St.

Stephen, Martyr Church.
Robinson, Richard J. '63 (MIL) [56] Milwaukee, WI Mother of Perpetual Help Church.
Robinson, Robert M. '69 (BRK) [224] Queens, NY St. Patrick Church.
Robinson, Tyrone '79 (DET) [46] Detroit, MI Martyrs of Uganda Church.
Robisch, David C. '62 (CIN) [61] Cincinnati, OH St. Mary Church.
Robitaille, Henry J. '39 (PRO) Retired.
Robitaille, Jean C. *m.afr.* '73 (SP) [O] St. Petersburg, FL Missionaries of Africa.
Robitaille, Joseph S. '57 (ALB) [3] Cohoes, NY St. Joseph Church.
Robitaille, Marcel '64 (PRT) [I] Waterville, ME Mt. St. Joseph Priest Retirement Home.
Robitaille, Marcell L. '64 (PRT) Sabbatical.
Robitaille, Raymond '45 (LAF) [G] New Iberia, LA Consolata Home.
Robitaille, Raymond '47 (LAF) Retired.
Robitaille, Yves '53 (ALX) Retired.
Robl, Eugene J. '50 (JC) Retired.
Robles, Antonio '61 (CGS) [C] Aibonito, PR Casa Salesiana de Retiros.
Robles, Victor G. '86 (AUS) Bryan, TX Santa Teresa's Church.
Robles-Sanchez, Jose' A. '95 (ALX) Bordelonville, LA St. Peter Church; Kleinwood, LA St. Michael Church.
Robling, Landelin A. *o.s.b.* '52 (STP) Hastings, MN St. Elizabeth Ann Seton Church.
Robotnik, Lawrence R. '57 (COV) Bellevue, KY Sacred Heart Church.
Robouam, Thierry-Jean *s.j.* '92 (OAK) [N] Berkeley, CA Jesuit Community at Jesuit School of Theology at Berkeley.
Roby, Brian '96 (OWN) LaCenter, KY St. Mary Church; [4] Paducah, KY St. Thomas More Church.
Roca, Albert L. '77 (MET) Port Murray, NJ St. Theodore Church.
Roca, Casimiro *s.f.* '43 (SFE) Chimayo, NM Holy Family Church.
Roca, Jordi *l.d.* '97 (PCE) [18] Ponce, PR Church Santisimo Sacramento Church.
Roca, W. Wayne *s.j.* '70 (NO) [C] New Orleans, LA Loyola University.
Rocca, Gregory *o.p.* '77 (OAK) [A] Berkeley, CA Dominican School of Philosophy and Theology; [A] Berkeley, CA Dominican School of Philosophy and Theology; [N] Oakland, CA Dominican Order, Siena House.
Rocca, Peter D. *c.s.c.* '74 (FTW) [A] Notre Dame, IN Moreau Seminary; [B] Notre Dame, IN University of Notre Dame Du Lac.
Rocchi, Frank J. '82 (NEW) Maplewood, NJ Immaculate Heart of Mary Church.
Rocco, Daniel '90 (CAM) Haddonfield, NJ Christ the King Regional School Church.
Rocco, Msgr. Remigio G. '66 (PAT) Haskell, NJ St. Francis of Assisi Church.
Roccosalvo, Joseph *s.j.* (NY) [DD] New York, NY West Side Jesuit Community.
Rocha, Ivo D. '66 (STO) Tracy, CA St. Bernard's Church.
Rocha, Manuel '30 (SPR) Retired; [H] Springfield, MA St. Michael's Residence.
Rocha, Michael '88 (LA) Santa Monica, CA St. Monica Church.
Rocha, Victor J. '53 (PIT) [64] Pittsburgh, PA Resurrection Church.
Rocha-Sosa, Carlos '96 (ATL) [8] Atlanta, GA Sacred Heart of Jesus Church.
Roche, Christopher J. '31 (BUF) Retired; [O] Buffalo, NY Sheehan Residence for Priests.
Roche, David '58 (PEO) [J] Pontiac, IL Saint James Hospital.
Roche, David V. '42 (BUF) Retired; [O] Buffalo, NY Sheehan Residence for Priests.
Roche, Evan *o.f.m.* '43 (ALB) [12] Albany, NY Our Lady of Angels Church.
Roche, John *s.d.b.* '86 (LA) [X] Rosemead, CA St. Joseph's Salesian Youth Renewal Center.
Roche, John S. *s.s.c.* '59 (BO) [W] Quincy, MA St. Columban's Foreign Mission Society.
Roche, Joseph L. *s.j.* '58 (FgM) Provinces.
Roche, Msgr. M. Edward '36 (CHI) Chicago Ridge, IL Our Lady of the Ridge Church; Retired.
Roche, Matthew F. *s.j.* '81 (RVC) Oceanside, NY St. Anthony Church.
Roche, Randall H. *s.j.* '68 (HON) [7] Honolulu, HI Newman Center-Holy Spirit Parish; [H] Honolulu, HI Jesuit Fathers House.
Roche, Robert *o.s.b.* '62 (ALT) Patton, PA Our Lady of Perpetual Help Church; Patton, PA Queen of Peace Church.
Roche, Ronald '61 (PBL) [11] Pueblo, CO St. Francis Xavier Church.
Roche, Stanley *o.s.b.* '47 (SCL) [I] Collegeville, MN St. John's Abbey, of the Order of St. Benedict.
Roche, Msgr. William H. '50 (BO) [1] Boston, MA Cathedral of the Holy Cross; Retired.
Roche, William J. '59 (BUF) [M] Lancaster, NY St. Elizabeth's Home.
Roche, Msgr. William M. '55 (ROC) Retired.
Roche, Msgr. William M. '55 (SFR) Redwood City, CA Our Lady of Mount Carmel Church.
Rocheford, Dennis J. '77 (WOR) Military Chaplains.
Rochefort, Maurice J. '66 (MAN) Exeter, NH St. Michael Church.
Rochel, Anthony J. *s.j.* '51 (STL) [P] St. Louis, MO Jesuit Community Corporation at St. Louis University - Jesuit Hall.
Rocheleau, Raymond '52 (BR) Retired.
Rochford, E. Michael '62 (CHI) Missionary Work.
Rochford, Eugene *s.v.d.* '74 (FgM) Society of the Divine Word Foreign Missions.
Rochford, John J. '47 (CHI) Country Club Hills, IL St. Emeric Church; Retired.
Rochford, Jude *o.f.m.conv.* (FgM) Conventual Franciscan Foreign Missions.
Rochon, Bernard M. *s.m.* '58 (SAT) [67] San Antonio, TX St. Timothy's Church.
Rochon, Bernard M. *s.m.* '58 (STL) [P] St. Louis, MO Provincialate of the Society of Mary, Province of St. Louis.
Rochon, Robert A. '74 (FR) [G] Fall River, MA Saint Anne's Hospital.
Rochon, Robert A. '74 (PRO) On Duty Outside the Diocese.
Rock, John J. '54 (NEW) Retired.
Rock, John J. *s.j.* '87 (WH) [A] Wheeling, WV Wheeling Jesuit University.
Rock, Joseph A. '72 (ALN) [H] Bethlehem, PA Holy Family Manor; [J] Bethlehem, PA Holy Family Villa.
Rock, Leo P. *s.j.* '58 (SJ) [M] Los Gatos, CA Sacred Heart Jesuit Center.
Rock, Martin *s.j.* '59 (SLC) [4] Ogden, UT St. Mary's Church.
Rock, Michael *o.de.m.* '86 (BUF) [O] LeRoy, NY Order of the BVM of Mercy/Mercedarian Friars.
Rock, Michael R. *o.de.m.* '86 (BUF) [Q] LeRoy, NY St. Peter Nolasco Spiritual Center.
Rock, Richard J. *c.m.* '73 (PH) [69] Philadelphia, PA Immaculate Conception Church.
Rock, Russell L. '62 (CAM) Haddon Township, NJ St. Vincent Pallotti Church; [A] Haddonfield, NJ Paul VI High School.
Rock, Stephen B. '74 (BO) Military & VA Chaplains.
Rock, William J. *o.p.* '58 (Y) [13] Youngstown, OH St. Dominic's Church.
Rockensperger, Nobert *o.f.m.conv.* '54 (FRS) Coalinga, CA St. Paul The Apostle Church.
Rockenstein, James *o.f.m.* '57 (SAC) Lincoln, CA St. Joseph Church.
Rocker, Stephen R. '79 (OG) Ogdensburg, NY Ogdensburg Correctional Facility; [A] Ogdensburg, NY Wadhams Hall.
Rockers, Alfred '62 (KCK) Leawood, KS Church of the Nativity.
Rockford, Thomas M. *s.j.* '76 (WDC) [M] Washington, DC Leonard Neale House.
Rocky, Ronald *o.f.m.conv.* '84 (SB) [3] Riverside, CA Queen of Angels Church.
Rodak, Joseph V. *c.pp.s.* '62 (LFT) [A] Rensselaer, IN Saint Joseph's College.
Rodakowski, Louis '42 (P) Retired.
Rodas, Mauro G. '65 (IND) [27] Indianapolis, IN St. Mary/Immaculate Conception Church.
Rodda, Regis *o.f.m.conv.* '59 (SY) [2] Syracuse, NY Assumption B.V.M. Church.
Roddy, James *s.s.c.* '41 (PRO) [P] Bristol, RI St. Columban's Retirement House.
Roden, Raymond P. '81 (BRK) [216] Queens, NY Our Lady of Mount Carmel Church; [G] Astoria, NY St. John Preparatory School.
Roden-Lucero, Edward G. '82 (ELP) [3] El Paso, TX Blessed Juan Diego Parish.
Rodenfels, Jerome P. '74 (COL) New Albany, OH Church of the Resurrection.
Rodenspiel, James E. '64 (B) Chubbuck, ID St. Paul's Church.
Roder, Terry A. '88 (SC) Dedham, IA St. Joseph's Church; [B] Carroll, IA Kuemper Catholic High School.
Roderhero, Jeffrey A.G. (STF) Syracuse, NY St. John the Baptist Church.
Rodgers, Arthur E. '65 (PH) Bala Cynwyd, PA St. Matthias Church.
Rodgers, Dermut '91 (FR) [18] Fall River, MA St. Michael's Church.
Rodgers, Francis M. '41 (PIT) Retired; [O] Pittsburgh, PA St. John Vianney Manor.
Rodgers, Kenneth '43 (GB) Retired.
Rodgers, Kieran *o.s.b.* '46 (ALT) Carrolltown, PA St. Benedict's Church.
Rodgers, Philip F. '81 (ALN) Boyertown, PA St. Columbkill Church.
Rodgers, Thomas M. '44 (PIT) Retired; [S] Pittsburgh, PA Society of Saint Vincent de Paul.
Rodgers, Msgr. William J. '49 (BRK) Retired; [R] Queens Village, NY Queen of Peace Residence.
Rodi, Msgr. Thomas J. '78 (NO) On Special or Other Archiocesan Assignment.
Rodia, James C. *o.praem.* '72 (PH) [D] Philadelphia, PA St. John Neumann High School; [AA] Philadelphia, PA St. Norbert Priory.
Rodighiero, Dominic *c.s.* '61 (NY) [DD] Staten Island, NY Scalabrinian Missionaries.
Rodini, Rick '83 (SJ) [C] San Jose, CA Archbishop Mitty High School.
Rodino, Salvatore A. '80 (ALB) Speigletown, NY St. Bonaventure Church.
Rodis, James '60 (STL) [19] St. Louis, MO St. Agatha Church.
Rodis, Rodney '86 (RIC) Buckner, VA Immaculate Conception Church; Mineral, VA St. Jude Church.
Rodman, Hugh B. *s.j.* '42 (CHI) [C] Chicago, IL Jesuit Community at Loyola University of Chicago.
Rodney, John *s.v.d.* '60 (WDC) [5] Washington, DC St. Anthony Church; [M] Washington, DC Divine Word College.
Rodney, Joseph C. *s.s.j.* '68 (BR) Napoleonville, LA St. Benedict the Moor Church.
Rodo, Anthony C. '55 (PH) Ridley Park, PA St. Madeline Church.
Rodoni, Rick '91 (SJ) [1] San Jose, CA Cathedral Basilica of St. Joseph Church.
Rodrigo, Marcelo Blazquez '60 (NY) State, NY Woodbourne Correctional Facility.
Rodrigo, Salvador *o.carm.* '62 (ARE) Ciales, PR Holy Rosary Church.
Rodrigue, Raymond '97 (NEW) Lyndhurst, NJ Sacred Heart Church.
Rodrigues, Alberto *o.s.s.t.* '87 (PMB) [1] West Palm Beach, FL Holy Name of Jesus Church.
Rodrigues, Alberto Edgardo *o.ss.t.* '87 (BAL) [M] Baltimore, MD Holy Trinity Monastery.
Rodrigues, Amancio '66 (P) [30] Portland, OR Queen of Peace Church.
Rodrigues, Anthony '54 (RIC) Big Stone Gap, VA Sacred Heart Church; Pennington Gap, VA Church of the Holy Spirit.
Rodrigues, Antonio *isch.* (CC) [J] Corpus Christi, TX Secular Institute of the Schoenstatt Fathers aka Schoenstatt Fathers.
Rodrigues, Antonio '33 (MRY) Retired.
Rodrigues, Carlos '95 (BGP) [10] Stamford, CT St. Mary's Church.
Rodrigues, Ignatius '66 (SB) [2] Riverside, CA Our Lady of Perpetual Help Church.
Rodrigues, Januarius E. '59 (SAC) [9] Sacramento, CA St. Anne Church.
Rodrigues, Joseph *s.d.s.* '93 (MIL) [P] Milwaukee, WI Salvatorian Provincial Residence.
Rodriguez, Alberto *o.p.* '71 (FgM) Dominican - Order of Preachers Foreign Missions.
Rodriguez, Alberto *o.p.* '71 (NO) [25] New Orleans, LA St. Anthony Of Padua Church; [P] New Orleans, LA Dominican Fathers & Brothers, Southern Dominican Province; [S] Metairie, LA Southern Dominican Foundation.
Rodriguez, Aloysius M. (OG) Watertown, NY U.S. Army Headquarters Fort Drum.
Rodriguez, Aloysius M. '66 (BR) Military Chaplains.
Rodriguez, Ambiorix '97 (NY) [95] New York, NY Our Lady Queen of Martyrs Church.
Rodriguez, Anthony *l.c.* '83 (HRT) [B] Cheshire, CT Novitiate of the Legion of Christ.
Rodriguez, Antonio *i.sch.* (CC) On Special Assignment.
Rodriguez, Antonio *o.carm.* '79 (ARE) Morovis, PR Nuestra Senora del Carmen Church.
Rodriguez, Antonio *c.c.* '93 (MIL) [T] Waukesha, WI Secular Institute of Schoenstatt Fathers.
Rodriguez, Antonio '93 (PAT) [5] Passaic, NJ Holy Trinity Church.
Rodriguez, Antonio L. '49 (BUF) [33] Buffalo, NY Immaculate Conception Church.
Rodriguez, Armando J. '55 (GAL) [59] Houston, TX Our Lady of St. John Church.
Rodriguez, Arturo '84 (YAK) Bridgeport, WA St. Anne's Church.
Rodriguez, Benigno A. '89 (LA) [34] Los Angeles, CA Presentation of the B.V.M. Church.
Rodriguez, Bernardo C. '80 (BGP) Awaiting Assignment.
Rodriguez, Carlos *o.c.s.o.* '70 (L) [L] Trappist, KY Abbey of Our Lady of Gethsemani, of the Order of Cistercians of the Strict Observance.
Rodriguez, Carlos M. '87 (NY) [134] Bronx, NY Blessed Sacrament Church.
Rodriguez, D. Andres G. '36 (RIC) Retired.
Rodriguez, David *o.f.m.* '89 (CHI) [D] Chicago, IL Hales Franciscan High School, Inc.
Rodriguez, Delfin '86 (ARE) [3] Arecibo, PR Nuestra Senora del Carmen Church.
Rodriguez, Domingo *s.t.* '67 (ARL) [J] Arlington, VA Missionary Servants of the Most Holy Trinity, S.T.
Rodriguez, Domingo *s.t.* '67 (FgM) Trinity Missions.
Rodriguez, Edgar Antonio Carlo '97 (MGZ) San German, PR San German de Auxerre Church.
Rodriguez, Edmundo *s.j.* '66 (LAF) [J] Grand Coteau, LA Jesuit Spirituality Center.
Rodriguez, Eduardo (NY) [GG] New York, NY University Apostolate.
Rodriguez, Eduardo *o.c.s.o.* '69 (ATL) [I] Conyers, GA

The Monastery of the Holy Spirit.
Rodriguez, Eduardo *m.id.* '96 (NY) [180] Bronx, NY Santa Maria Church; [DD] Bronx, NY Idente Missionaries - Santa Maria Residence.
Rodriguez, Msgr. Efranin '74 (SJN) [31] San Juan, PR Nuestra Senora de Lourdes Church.
Rodriguez, Epifanio *o.p.* '54 (CC) Benavides, TX St. Rose of Lima Church; [H] San Diego, TX Vicariate of Holy Rosary.
Rodriguez, Estebon *o.carm.* '87 (NY) [189] Bronx, NY St. Simon Stock Church.
Rodriguez, Fabian *s.j.* '66 (SJN) [22] San Juan, PR San Ignacio de Loyola Church.
Rodriguez, Felix M. '97 (YAK) Moses Lake, WA Our Lady of Fatima Church; Warden, WA Queen of All Saints Church.
Rodriguez, Francis *o.c.s.o.* '55 (WOR) [N] Spencer, MA St. Joseph's Abbey.
Rodriguez, Gerardo Ibarra *o.s.b.* '97 (MGZ) [6] Mayaquez, PR Sacred Heart Church.
Rodriguez, Gilbert '74 (SAN) [2] Midland, TX Our Lady of Guadalupe Church.
Rodriguez, Guillermo (SAC) Colusa, CA Our Lady of Lourdes Church.
Rodriguez, Guillermo '56 (SFR) Retired.
Rodriguez, Guillermo '69 (LA) [11] Long Beach, CA St. Matthew Church.
Rodriguez, Henry '86 (SD) [30] San Diego, CA St. Jude Church.
Rodriguez, J. Rigoberto '89 (LA) [93] Los Angeles, CA St. Thomas the Apostle Church.
Rodriguez, Jesse *s.j.* '95 (BO) [W] Chestnut Hill, MA The Jesuit Community at Boston College.
Rodriguez, Jesus A. '93 (ARE) [4] Manati, PR Nuestra Senora del Mar Church.
Rodriguez, Joaquin '72 (MIA) [13] Miami, FL Our Lady of Lourdes Church.
Rodriguez, Msgr. John F. '59 (SFR) [2] Menlo Park, CA St. Denis Church.
Rodriguez, Jorge *o.f.m.conv.* (PAT) [10] Paterson, NJ St. Mary's Church.
Rodriguez, Jose '75 (GLP) Overgaard, AZ Our Lady of Assumption Church; Snowflake, AZ Our Lady of the Snows Church.
Rodriguez, Jose A. '34 (SFR) [11] San Francisco, CA St. Charles Borromeo Church.
Rodriguez, Jose A. '80 (ARE) [1] Vega-Baja, PR Holy Rosary Church.
Rodriguez, Jose Andres '95 (WOR) [27] Worcester, MA St. Peter Church.
Rodriguez, Jose Diego '81 (PCE) Villalba, PR Our Lady of Mt. Carmel Church.
Rodriguez, Jose Trinidad '92 (LA) [15] Los Angeles, CA Immaculate Conception Church.
Rodriguez, Juan '79 (PCE) [B] Ponce, PR The Pontifical Catholic University of Puerto Rico.
Rodriguez, Lawrence '52 (LA) Retired.
Rodriguez, Luis *s.j.* '65 (MIL) [P] Wauwatosa, WI Jesuit Community at St. Camillus.
Rodriguez, Luis Alberto (PCE) [B] Ponce, PR The Pontifical Catholic University of Puerto Rico.
Rodriguez, Luis R. '93 (HBG) New Cumberland, PA St. Theresa of the Infant Jesus Church.
Rodriguez, Manuel '62 (ATL) [I] Conyers, GA The Monastery of the Holy Spirit.
Rodriguez, Manuel J. *o.s.a.* '59 (BRK) [U] Forest Hills, NY Augustinian Fathers-Province of Castile, Spain.
Rodriguez, Martin S. *o.r.c.* '82 (SB) [5] San Bernardino, CA Our Lady of Guadalupe Church.
Rodriguez, Martin S. '92 (SB) [1] Riverside, CA Our Lady of Guadalupe Shrine Church; Riverside, CA Riverside Community Hospital.
Rodriguez, Michael '90 (SAN) Eden, TX St. Charles Church.
Rodriguez, Michael '96 (ELP) [19] El Paso, TX Our Lady of the Valley Church.
Rodriguez, Nestor '93 (PMB) [5] West Palm Beach, FL St. Juliana Church.
Rodriguez, Msgr. Pablo M. '61 (RVC) Hempstead, NY Our Lady of Loretto Church.
Rodriguez, Peter *c.m.f.* '57 (CHI) [80] Chicago, IL Holy Cross/Immaculate Heart of Mary Church.
Rodriguez, Plinio '70 (PCE) On Duty Outside the Diocese.
Rodriguez, Rafael A. '75 (CGS) Cayey, PR San Esteban Protomartir Church.
Rodriguez, Reyes G. '67 (SLC) [6] Salt Lake City, UT St. Ann Church; Salt Lake City, UT Salt Lake County Jail.
Rodriguez, Ricardo *o.f.m.* '82 (ELP) [15] El Paso, TX Our Lady of Guadalupe Church.
Rodriguez, Richard *s.j.* '74 (SFE) [6] Albuquerque, NM Immaculate Conception Church.
Rodriguez, Robert '53 (MIL) Retired.
Rodriguez, Roberto '96 (NY) [B] Suffern, NY Tagaste Monastery.
Rodriguez, Robin E. *c.m.* '93 (BRK) [116] Brooklyn, NY St. Peter-St. Paul-Our Lady of Pilar Church; [116] Brooklyn, NY St. Peter-St. Paul-Our Lady of Pilar Church.
Rodriguez, Roy '94 (CHY) [1] Cheyenne, WY St. Mary's Cathedral.
Rodriguez, Ruben *o.carm.* '89 (NY) [189] Bronx, NY St. Simon Stock Church.
Rodriguez, Sabbas (RVC) Freeport, NY Our Holy Redeemer Church.
Rodriguez, Salvador (ARE) On Duty Outside the Diocese.
Rodriguez, Santos '70 (SFR) [33] San Francisco, CA Mission Dolores Basilica Church.
Rodriguez, Sebastian Ortega *o.s.a.* '93 (FgM) Foreign Missions.
Rodriguez Cotton, Franklin '64 (CGS) Maunabo, PR San Isidor Labrador Church.
Rodriguez Gamboa, John E. '77 (NEW) [27] Newark, NJ Our Lady of Good Counsel Church.
Rodriguez Jimenez, Leonardo '90 (SJN) [38] San Juan, PR Santa Maria de Los Angeles Church.
Rodriguez-Hernandez, Edwin '95 (ALX) [2] Alexandria, LA Our Lady of Prompt Succor Church; [J] Alexandria, LA Louisiana State University at Alexandria.
Rodriquez, Arturo '84 (YAK) Chelan, WA St. Francis de Sales Church.
Rodriquez, Reyes '67 (SLC) Park City, UT St. Mary of the Assumption Church.
Rodulfa, Julius '85 (NY) [209] Staten Island, NY St. John Neumann Church.
Roebert, Michael '66 (LA) [9] Long Beach, CA St. Lucy Church.
Roebuck, John H. '76 (PH) [2] Drexel Hill, PA St. Bernadette Church.
Roedel, Richard P. '59 (STP) Heidelberg, MN St. Scholastica Church; Lexington, MN St. Joseph Church.
Roedel, Robert H. '56 (PH) Feasterville, PA Assumption B.V.M. Church; Absent on Sick Leave.
Roedig, Louis '53 (STL) Richmond Heights, MO Immacolata Church.
Roehrich, Andrew '50 (FAR) Windsor, ND St. Mathias Church.
Roehrich, David '84 (SFS) Colman, SD St. Peter Church; Flandreau, SD SS. Simon and Jude Church.
Roehrig, Matthew *s.s.p.* '84 (BUF) [O] Derby, NY Society of St. Paul.
Roelke, Joseph Paul *m.s.f.* '81 (STL) [67] St. Louis, MO St. Wenceslaus Church.
Roeltgen, Msgr. Kenneth W. '79 (WDC) [40] Washington, DC St. Stephen Martyr Church.
Roensch, Frederick J. '55 (MIL) Retired.
Roensch, Msgr. Roger '57 (WDC) On Duty Outside the Archdiocese.
Roensch, Msgr. Roger C. '57 (WDC) Special Ministries.
Roerig, Peter A. '64 (P) [1] Eugene, OR St. Jude Church.
Roesch, David H. '67 (ALT) Bellwood, PA St. Joseph's Church.
Roesch, Joseph *m.i.c.* (WDC) [B] Washington, DC Marian Fathers Scholasticate.
Roesch, Karl J. *o.s.b.* '60 (NEW) [1] Linden, NJ St. Elizabeth's Church.
Roesch, Karl J. *o.s.b.* '60 (PAT) [M] Morristown, NJ St. Mary's Abbey.
Roesslein, Charles *s.v.d.* '36 (CHI) [B] Techny, IL Divine Word Residence.
Roeten, Msgr. Winus '48 (NO) Retired.
Roets, Perry J. *s.j.* '52 (MIL) [P] Wauwatosa, WI Jesuit Community at St. Camillus.
Roetzel, Robert E. *c.s.c.* '87 (FTW) [J] South Bend, IN Congregation of Holy Cross Indiana Province Provincial House.
Roetzer, Russell G. '63 (MIL) [E] Racine, WI St. Catherine's High School.
Roetzer, Russell G. '64 (MIL) [1] Racine, WI St. Casimir Church; [13] Racine, WI St. Rose Church.
Rofrano, Peter J. *s.a.c.* '39 (NY) [91] New York, NY Our Lady of Mt. Carmel Church; [DD] New York, NY Pallottine Fathers.
Rog, Francis *c.r.* '55 (CHI) [88] Chicago, IL St. Hyacinth Church.
Rog, Theodore C. '64 (BUF) [60] Buffalo, NY St. Rose of Lima Church.
Rogala, Gerard E. '66 (CHI) [201] Chicago, IL St. Thecla Church.
Rogalla, William '96 (LAF) [1] New Iberia, LA St. Peter Church.
Rogalski, Christopher '80 (STF) [4] Colchester, CT St. Mary Dormition Church.
Rogawski, Ralph *o.p.* '59 (AUS) [H] Austin, TX Dominican Fathers.
Roger, Richard G. '64 (WOR) [7] Worcester, MA Notre Dame des Canadiens - St. Joseph Church.
Rogers, Daniel J. '53 (DUB) Retired.
Rogers, Foster P. '66 (ROC) [4] Auburn, NY St. Alphonsus Church.
Rogers, Francis J. '81 (WIL) Elsmere, DE Corpus Christi Church; Wilmington, DE Delaware Air National Guard.
Rogers, Francis P. '46 (PH) [152] Philadelphia, PA St. Timothy Church; Retired.
Rogers, Furman '78 (MOB) Retired.
Rogers, Gary P. '72 (BRK) [51] Brooklyn, NY St. Gregory the Great Church.
Rogers, Herbert W. *s.j.* '44 (NY) [DD] New York, NY Jesuit Community at Fordham University.
Rogers, James '39 (EVN) Retired.
Rogers, James M. '51 (BO) Retired.
Rogers, Jerry '76 (CR) Detroit Lakes, MN Holy Rosary Church.
Rogers, John S. (LA) [C] Los Angeles, CA Loyola Marymount University.
Rogers, Joseph '54 (DAV) Brooklyn, IA St. Patrick Church; [P] Brooklyn, IA St. Patrick Parish Foundation.
Rogers, Nicholas P. '55 (MAN) [14] Manchester, NH St. Patrick Church.
Rogers, Patrick W. '82 (COL) [38] Columbus, OH St. Philip The Apostle Church.
Rogers, Paul J. '77 (RVC) Holbrook, NY Good Shepherd Church.
Rogers, Peter S. *s.j.* '74 (NO) [C] New Orleans, LA Loyola University.
Rogers, Philip E. '80 (Y) Struthers, OH St. Nicholas Church.
Rogers, Robert C. '92 (HT) Montegut, LA Sacred Heart Church; Pointe-Aux-Chenes, LA St. Charles Borromeo Church.
Rogers, Stephen (TOL) [2] Toledo, OH Blessed Sacrament Church.
Rogers, Stephen G. '95 (TOL) [B] Toledo, OH Central Catholic High School.
Rogers, Thomas W. '52 (GBG) Rostraver, PA St. Anne Church.
Rogers, Vincent '93 (KC) [4] St. Joseph, MO St. James Church.
Rogerson, Daniel '77 (SEA) On Duty Outside the Archdiocese.
Rogerson, Dave *o.s.b.* '82 (P) [A] St. Benedict, OR Mount Angel Seminary.
Rogge, Louis *o.carm.* '54 (JOL) [J] Joliet, IL St. Elias Carmelites.
Rogge, Norman J. *s.j.* '56 (LAF) [J] Grand Coteau, LA Jesuit Spirituality Center.
Rogina, Walter, Jr. '85 (SR) [1] Santa Rosa, CA Cathedral of St. Eugene.
Rogliano, Joseph S. '85 (BUF) Williamsville, NY St. Gregory the Great Church.
Rogmans, Gerard *c.i.c.m.* '55 (FgM) Missionhurst Foreign Missions.
Rogusz, Joseph A. *c.s.c.* '46 (FTW) [J] South Bend, IN Congregation of Holy Cross Indiana Province Provincial House.
Roh, Raymond V. *o.s.b.* '59 (MRY) [G] San Luis Obispo, CA Monastery of the Risen Christ.
Roh, Robert A. '65 (LIN) Falls City, NE SS. Peter and Paul Church; [C] Falls City, NE Sacred Heart School; [L] Falls City, NE Sacred Heart High School Endowment Fund.
Rohan, John P. '72 (HRT) South Windsor, CT St. Francis of Assisi Church.
Rohen, Patrick '96 (TOL) [4] Fremont, OH St. Joseph Church.
Rohleder, Earl '63 (EVN) [13] Evansville, IN St. Anthony Church; New Harmony, IN Holy Angels Church.
Rohlfs, Msgr. Steven P. '76 (PEO) [13] Peoria, IL St. Philomena's Church.
Rohling, Msgr. George W. '39 (NSH) [8] Nashville, TN St. Mary Villa Parish Community Church; [E] Nashville, TN St. Mary Orphanage, Inc. dba St. Mary Villa; [L] Nashville, TN Ladies of Charity Welfare Agency, Inc.
Rohling, Paul '75 (BIR) [6] Birmingham, AL St. Francis Xavier Church; [I] Birmingham, AL Agape Institute of St. Teresa of Jesus.
Rohlinger, Joseph A. *o.praem* '43 (GB) [I] De Pere, WI St. Norbert Abbey.
Rohloff, Ivan *o.f.m.conv.* (FgM) Conventual Franciscan Foreign Missions.
Rohmiller, Christian A. '79 (CIN) [4] Dayton, OH St. Anthony of Padua Church; [Q] Fairborn, OH Campus Ministry Center.
Rohr, Jerome M. '94 (DEN) Littleton, CO Light of the World Parish.
Rohr, John J. *s.j.* '60 (NEW) [C] Jersey City, NJ St. Peter's Preparatory School.
Rohr, Richard *o.f.m.* '70 (SFE) [N] Albuquerque, NM Center for Action and Contemplation.
Rohrer, Jerome E. *s.j.* '54 (MIL) [P] Wauwatosa, WI Jesuit Community at St. Camillus.
Rohrer, Richard '94 (PSC) Cary, NC SS. Cyril & Methodius Byzantine Catholic Church.
Rohrkemper, Charles B. '43 (CIN) Troy, OH St. Patrick Church; Retired.
Roia, Martino *s.x.* '82 (PAT) [M] Wayne, NJ Xaverian Missionary Fathers.
Roide, Russell J. *s.j.* '70 (SFR) [2] San Francisco, CA St. Agnes Church.
Roig, Vicente Perez '58 (MGZ) Rosario, PR Rosary Church.
Rojas, Alberto '97 (CHI) [73] Chicago, IL St. Gregory Church.
Rojas, Jaime Vazquez '83 (SJN) [20] Bayamon, PR

Nuestra Senora del Rosario Church.
Rojas, Manuel I. '64 (NY) [203] Staten Island, NY St. Clement Church; [215] Staten Island, NY St. Michael Church.
Rojas, Melquiades '91 (ARE) [10] Arecibo, PR San Juan Bosco Church.
Rojas, Ramon '85 (LA) Baldwin Park, CA St. John the Baptist Church.
Rojas, Roberto P. *c.s.b.* '97 (GAL) [Q] Sugar Land, TX Basilian Mission Center.
Rojas, Tito '68 (ORL) [6] Orlando, FL St. Andrew Church; Apopka, FL St. Francis of Assisi Church.
Rojas, Victor '85 (ARE) Special Assignment; On Duty Outside the Diocese; [A] Arecibo, PR Seminario de Jesus Maestro.
Rokicinski, Stanley J. '39 (CHI) [148] Chicago, IL Our Lady of Grace Church; [209] Chicago, IL St. Turibius Church; Retired.
Rokos, Richard V. '56 (PRT) Bangor, ME St. Joseph's Hospital; [H] Bangor, ME St. Joseph Hospital.
Rokosz, Charles W. '70 (SCR) Duryea, PA Holy Rosary Church.
Rokusek, Robert J. (WDC) [E] Washington, DC Gonzaga College High School.
Rolak, Patrick *o.f.m.conv.* '56 (BAL) [M] Ellicott City, MD Order of Friars Minor Conventual.
Roland, Charles '67 (PT) On Duty Outside the Diocese.
Roland, Charles W. '67 (SAV) Waycross, GA St. Joseph's Church.
Roldan, Basilio '59 (SJN) [55] San Juan, PR Sagrado Corazon de Jesus Church.
Roldan, Juan '56 (SJN) On Duty Outside the Archdiocese.
Rolek, John A. '61 (CHI) [5] Cicero, IL Our Lady of Charity Church.
Roleke, H. James *s.j.* '62 (BUF) [50] Buffalo, NY St. Michael Church.
Rolewicz, Richard S. *m.m.* '65 (FgM) Maryknoll Foreign Missions.
Rolf, Msgr. John '57 (LEX) Mt. Sterling, KY St. Patrick Church.
Rolfes, Robert E. '77 (SCL) Rockville, MN Mary of the Immaculate Conception Church.
Rolfs, Richard W. *s.j.* '61 (LA) [C] Los Angeles, CA Loyola Marymount University.
Rolfson, Gunther *o.s.b.* '46 (SCL) Farming, MN St. Catherine's Church.
Roll, Bertin *o.f.m.cap.* '42 (PIT) [O] Pittsburgh, PA St. Augustine Friary.
Roll, David H. '70 (SD) Retired.
Roll, Robert J. '77 (CHI) [170] Chicago, IL SS. Peter and Paul Church.
Roll, Ron *o.f.m.conv.* '80 (FgM) Conventual Franciscan Foreign Missions.
Roll, Ronald *o.f.m.conv.* (FgM) Conventual Franciscan Foreign Missions.
Roll, Ronald *o.f.m.conv.* '80 (BAL) [M] Ellicott City, MD Order of Friars Minor Conventual.
Rolland, Daniel *o.p.* '93 (PHX) [F] Tempe, AZ Dominicans (Dominican Community-Jordan House); [H] Phoenix, AZ Office of Youth and Young Adult Ministries.
Rolland, Michael *o.p.* '58 (PHX) [5] Phoenix, AZ Most Holy Trinity Church.
Roller, John W. '60 (CHI) [4] Mt. Prospect, IL St. Thomas a Becket Church.
Rolwing, Msgr. Richard C. '53 (SPC) [1] Cape Girardeau, MO Cathedral of St. Mary.
Rom, Gregory A. '75 (CHI) Blue Island, IL St. Isidore Church.
Roma, Paul E. '88 (MAN) Military Chaplains.
Romage, George J. '95 (WH) [10] Wheeling, WV St. Michael's Church.
Romagosa, Edward J. *s.j.* '54 (BR) [J] Convent, LA Manresa, House of Retreats.
Romagosa, Msgr. Elmo L. '47 (NO) [1] Harvey, LA Infant Jesus of Prague Church.
Roman, Bede *o.s.b.* '66 (SFS) [F] Marvin, SD Blue Cloud Abbey.
Roman, Carlos '89 (PCE) [1] Ponce, PR Cathedral of Our Lady of Guadalupe.
Roman, Charles '70 (HEL) Whitefish, MT St. Charles Church.
Roman, Julio '73 (LA) Sylmar, CA St. Didacus Church.
Roman, Manuel R. '56 (BAL) [11] Baltimore, MD Ascension Church.
Roman, Paul A. '71 (ALB) Oneonta, NY St. Mary Church.
Roman, Stephen '57 (SEA) Aberdeen, WA St. Mary's Church; Aberdeen, WA St. Mary's Church; Hoquiam, WA Our Lady of Good Help Church; Ocean Shores, WA St. Jerome Church.
Roman, Victor '84 (DET) Ecorse, MI St. Francis Xavier Church.
Romanenko, Oleh '93 (LA) [19] Los Angeles, CA Nativity of Blessed Virgin Mary Church.
Romanenko, Oleh '93 (STN) Los Angeles, CA Nativity of B.V.M. Church.
Romani, Joseph '34 (PRT) Retired.
Romano, Blase *t.o.r.* '89 (ORL) Mount Dora, FL St. Patrick's Church.
Romano, Charles P. '79 (RVC) New Hyde Park, NY Holy Spirit Church.
Romano, Eugene L. '57 (PAT) [I] Chester, NJ Hermits of Bethlehem of the Heart of Jesus.
Romano, Harry A. '57 (PH) [2] Coatesville, PA Our Lady of the Rosary Church.
Romano, Joseph (ALB) West Coxsackie, NY Coxsackie Correctional Facility.
Romano, Joseph '66 (ALB) [5] Albany, NY St. Catherine of Siena Church; Coxsackie, NY Greene County Correctional Institution; Special Assignment.
Romano, Joseph E. '63 (BUR) Pittsford, VT St. Alphonsus Liguori Church.
Romano, Joseph L. '63 (DET) [7] Dearborn Heights, MI St. Sabina Church.
Romano, Philip *o.f.m.cap.* '94 (NY) [57] New York, NY St. John the Baptist Church.
Romano, Robert J. *m.div.* '77 (BRK) [18] Brooklyn, NY St. Bernadette Church.
Romanoski, Joseph V. '86 (MET) South Amboy, NJ Sacred Heart Church.
Romanowski, Francis C. '39 (BRK) [241] Queens, NY St. Stanislaus Bishop and Martyr Church; Retired.
Romanowski, Jerome C. (CAM) Malaga, NJ St. Mary's Church.
Romanski, Aloysius *o.f.m.conv.* '57 (CHI) [L] Lake Zurich, IL Mt. St. Joseph Home.
Romanski, Edward '75 (CHI) Harvey, IL St. John the Baptist Church.
Romanski, Gregory A. *c.s.p.* '77 (NY) [DD] Jamaica Estates, NY Paulist Fathers Generalate.
Romansky, Joseph A. '75 (CLV) [N] Cleveland, OH St. Augustine Manor.
Romeo, Peter '72 (LAV) Laughlin, NV St. John the Baptist Catholic Mission Church.
Romeo, Robert A. '87 (RVC) Merrick, NY Cure of Ars Church.
Romero, Anthony E. *o.p.* '70 (CHI) [N] Chicago, IL Dominicans (Provincial Office).
Romero, Antonio *o.p.* (CHI) [173] Chicago, IL St. Pius V Church.
Romero, Antonio *m.ss.cc.* (SJN) Rio Grande, PR Nuestra Senora del Carmen Church.
Romero, David H. *s.j.* '91 (FgM) Provinces.
Romero, Donald '91 (DEN) Longmont, CO Spirit of Peace Parish.
Romero, Gilbert '61 (LA) [CC] Los Angeles, CA Archdiocesan Office for Campus Ministry.
Romero, J. Robert '75 (LAF) Ville Platte, LA Sacred Heart of Jesus Church.
Romero, Jose *o.s.a.* '77 (CC) [4] Laredo, TX Holy Redeemer Church.
Romero, Joseph *c.r.* '81 (DEN) [2] Fort Collins, CO Holy Family Church.
Romero, Joseph J. '69 (BEA) [4] Port Arthur, TX St. Catherine of Siena Church.
Romero, Juan '64 (LA) Santa Monica, CA St. Clement Church.
Romero, Marcelino *c.m.f.* (SJN) [A] Bayamon, PR Bayamon Central University.
Romero, Marcelino *c.m.f.* '59 (SJN) [2] Bayamon, PR San Antonio Maria Claret Church.
Romero, Mario '90 (LAF) Delcambre, LA Our Lady of the Lake Church.
Romero, William '67 (VEN) Retired.
Romero-Rios, Adolfo '88 (NY) [184] Bronx, NY St. Pius V Church.
Romfh, Paul *o.s.b.* '63 (SP) [O] St. Leo, FL St. Leo Abbey.
Romito, Donald '74 (ORG) Garden Grove, CA St. Columban Church.
Romo, Eugenio *m.g.* '87 (LA) [85] Los Angeles, CA St. Paul Church.
Romo, Sergio '93 (CHI) [69] Chicago, IL St. Genevieve Church.
Rompa, John '51 (SPK) Retired.
Romza, Msgr. Victor G. '54 (PBR) Campbell, OH St. Michael Church.
Ronaghan, John J. '80 (BO) Melrose, MA St. Mary of the Annunciation Church.
Ronald, Robert *s.j.* '65 (FgM) Provinces.
Ronald, Msgr. Roy K. '60 (BUF) Retired.
Ronan, Charles E. *s.j.* '45 (CHI) [C] Chicago, IL Jesuit Community at Loyola University of Chicago.
Ronan, Edward X. *c.s.b.* '52 (GAL) [Q] Sugar Land, TX Basilian Mission Center.
Ronan, Eugene *m.s.f.* (STL) [67] St. Louis, MO St. Wenceslaus Church.
Ronan, Henry T. '55 (BO) [1] Malden, MA Immaculate Conception Church; Retired.
Ronan, Msgr. Hugh F. '61 (TR) [6] Trenton, NJ Incarnation Church.
Ronan, James J. '82 (BO) On Duty Outside the Archdiocese.
Ronayne, Michael *o.f.m.cap.* '97 (SFR) Burlingame, CA Our Lady of Angels Church.
Roncase, Robert A. '82 (PH) Penndel, PA Our Lady of Grace Church.
Ronchi, Vincenzo *c.s.* (BRK) [71] Brooklyn, NY St. Joseph Patron of the Universal Church.
Rondeau, John S. *c.s.sp.* '38 (PIT) [Q] Bethel Park, PA Holy Ghost Animation Center.
Rondeau, Julian *s.m.* '71 (BO) [4] Haverhill, MA St. Joseph Church.
Rondeau, Lawrence J. '58 (BO) [6] Salem, MA St. Joseph Church.
Rondon, Pedro Arturo *m.ss.c.* '94 (SJN) [25] Bayamon, PR Santiago Apostol Church.
Roney, David A. '45 (NU) Retired.
Roney, George '78 (LUB) Woodrow, TX San Ramon Church.
Ronik, Michael E. '57 (Y) [2] Youngstown, OH Holy Name Church.
Ronquest, Msgr. John T. '45 (STL) Concord Village, MO St. Simon the Apostle Church; Retired.
Roock, John D. '59 (SY) Endwell, NY Our Lady of Angels Church.
Roodbeen, Henry W. '75 (DET) [2] Livonia, MI St. Colette Church.
Roof, Francis '72 (OWN) Madisonville, KY Christ the King Church.
Rook, Paul '47 (TUC) Retired.
Rookey, Peter M. *o.s.m.* '41 (CHI) [N] Chicago, IL Servite Friars - Eastern Province.
Rooks, Charles W. '52 (COV) Retired; [M] Covington, KY St. Joseph Heights Provincialate and Novitiate of the Sisters of Notre Dame.
Rooney, Aidan R. *c.m.* '84 (PH) [155] Philadelphia, PA St. Vincent de Paul Church.
Rooney, Bernard *c.ss.r.* '59 (GR) [3] Grand Rapids, MI St. Alphonsus Church.
Rooney, Bill *o.f.m.* '81 (CHI) [N] Chicago, IL St. Peter's Friary.
Rooney, Donald A. '79 (CLV) Mentor, OH St. John Vianney Church.
Rooney, Donald J. '94 (ARL) Dominican Republic, VA San Francisco de Asis, Banica Church; On Duty Outside the Diocese.
Rooney, Edward '62 (STA) Middleburg, FL St. Luke's Church.
Rooney, Eugene M. *s.j.* '57 (BAL) [M] Baltimore, MD Jesuit Fathers and Brothers Maryland Provincial Curia.
Rooney, Eugene M. *s.j.* '57 (FgM) Provinces.
Rooney, Msgr. Francis J. '41 (PIT) Retired.
Rooney, Msgr. Hugh J. '45 (NY) Retired; [DD] New York, NY Our Lady of Consolation Residence.
Rooney, James T. '64 (BRK) [247] Queens, NY Transfiguration Church.
Rooney, John C. '89 (LIN) [A] Seward, NE St. Gregory the Great Seminary.
Rooney, John E. '37 (NY) Port Jervis, NY Immaculate Conception Church.
Rooney, John J. '62 (ALB) [5] Watervliet, NY Sacred Heart of Mary Church.
Rooney, Jordon *o.carm.* '54 (JOL) [J] Darien, IL Carmelite Provincial Office.
Rooney, Joseph S. *s.j.* '66 (NY) [F] New York, NY Fordham Preparatory School; [DD] New York, NY Jesuit Community at Fordham University.
Rooney, Kevin E. '62 (BUR) Northfield, VT St. John the Evangelist Church.
Rooney, Martin D. *m.ss.a.* (NOR) [F] Cromwell, CT Missionaries of the Holy Apostles.
Rooney, Michael F. *s.j.* '72 (FgM) Provinces.
Rooney, Michael J. *s.m.a.* '41 (BO) [W] Dedham, MA African Mission House.
Rooney, Michael R. '89 (TLS) Miami, OK Sacred Heart Church; [H] Miami, OK Northeastern Oklahoma A & M College Newman Center.
Rooney, Robert '63 (GI) Broken Bow, NE St. Joseph's Church.
Rooney, Sean *s.d.b.* '66 (BIR) [9] Birmingham, AL St. John Bosco Church.
Rooney, Stephen '85 (DET) [5] Monroe, MI St. Michael Church.
Rooney, Msgr. Thaddeus '47 (RVC) Retired.
Rooney, Thomas J. '91 (PH) [140] Philadelphia, PA Resurrection of Our Lord Church.
Rooney, William A. '51 (NY) Mamaroneck, NY Holy Trinity Church.
Rooney, William J. (CHI) Retired.
Rooney, William J. '40 (WDC) [C] Washington, DC Catholic University of America, The.
Roos, Edward M. '66 (NY) [3] White Plains, NY St. Bernard Church.
Roos, H. Jules '56 (PIT) On Duty Outside the Diocese.
Roos, John R. '55 (ALB) Cooperstown, NY St. Mary Church.
Roos, Jules '56 (FgM) Society of St. James the Apostle.
Roos, Lee R. '90 (ARL) McLean, VA St. Luke's Church.
Roos, Paul '61 (EVN) Mariah Hill, IN Mary, Help of Christians Church.
Roos, Richard H. *s.j.* (BO) [Y] Gloucester, MA Eastern Point Retreat House.
Roos, Robert E. '39 (ALB) Retired.
Roos, William A. '59 (MET) Retired.
Roost, Joseph F. '89 (DAV) Marengo, IA St. Patrick's Church; Williamsburg, IA St. Mary's Church.
Root, James A. '84 (SAM) Pittsburgh, PA Our Lady of Victory Church.

Root, Richard '90 (SPK) [A] Spokane, WA Bishop White Seminary.
Ropelski, Msgr. Stanley A. '58 (BUF) Hamburg, NY SS. Peter and Paul Church.
Ropke, John '78 (SJP) New Kensington, PA St. Vladimir Church.
Roppolo, Msgr. Ignatius M. '54 (NO) [A] New Orleans, LA Notre Dame Seminary Graduate School of Theology.
Roque, Alejandro '88 (MIA) Opa Locka, FL St. Monica Church.
Ros, Joseph *s.d.b.* '61 (NY) [DD] New Rochelle, NY Salesian Provincial House.
Ros, Manuel '60 (BRK) [221] Queens, NY Our Lady of Sorrows Church.
Rosa, Edward *c.ss.r.* '41 (ALB) [L] Saratoga Springs, NY St. John Neumann Residence.
Rosa, Joseph '76 (BRK) [119] Brooklyn, NY Most Precious Blood Church.
Rosa, Salvatore J. '68 (HRT) [10] New Britain, CT St. Mary's Church.
Rosack, Msgr. Edward V. '54 (PBR) Ambridge, PA St. Mary's Church.
Rosaforte, Msgr. Anthony S. '70 (NOR) [1] Norwich, CT St. Patrick Cathedral.
Rosage, Msgr. David E. '43 (SPK) Retired.
Rosales, Angelito *s.d.v.* '96 (NEW) [25] Newark, NJ St. Michael's Church.
Rosales, Cresencio *s.d.b.* '88 (LA) [R] Los Angeles, CA Dominic Savio Salesian Residence.
Rosales, Cris *s.d.b.* '88 (LA) [D] Los Angeles, CA Bishop Mora Salesian High School.
Rosales, Deo G. '82 (WDC) [T] Washington, DC Opus Dei.
Rosales, Fredi A. '92 (BRK) [99] Brooklyn, NY Our Lady of Loreto Church; [108] Brooklyn, NY Our Lady of the Presentation Church.
Rosales, Fruto '70 (RVC) Hempstead, NY Our Lady of Loretto Church.
Rosales, Ramon '81 (SB) [5] San Bernardino, CA Our Lady of Guadalupe Church.
Rosales, Raul H. '93 (TUC) Morenci, AZ Holy Cross Church.
Rosales, Samuel *s.j.* '73 (SAT) [17] San Antonio, TX Our Lady of Guadalupe Church.
Rosario, Jose Francisco *o.c.d.* '86 (MIA) [L] Miami, FL Discalced Carmelite Friars of Miami, Inc.
Rosario, Juan Edgardo *c.ss.r.* '79 (MGZ) Aguadilla, PR St. Charles Borromeo Church.
Rosario, Socorro do '86 (BEA) [5] Port Arthur, TX St. James Church.
Rosas, Francisco Manuel *s.s.p.* '94 (LA) [R] Los Angeles, CA Society of St. Paul.
Rosato, Philip J. *s.j.* '71 (BAL) [M] Baltimore, MD Jesuit Fathers and Brothers Maryland Provincial Curia.
Rosca, Paschal *o.de.m.* '63 (CLV) [67] Cleveland, OH St. Rocco Church.
Roscioli, Dominic J. '74 (MIL) Retired.
Rosczewski, Steven M. *o.de.m.* '89 (SP) [O] St. Petersburg, FL St. Peter Nolasco Residence.
Rose, Alphonse G. (BAL) [Q] Joppa, MD Catholic Daughters of the Americas.
Rose, Alphonse G. '56 (BAL) Baltimore, MD Johns Hopkins Medical Institutions; Special Assignment; [Q] Baltimore, MD Johns Hopkins Hospital Apostolate.
Rose, Msgr. Donald '53 (GB) Retired.
Rose, Frank '90 (NEW) West New York, NJ St. Joseph of the Palisades Church.
Rose, James '57 (FTW) Retired.
Rose, James '57 (LFT) Marion, IN U.S. Veteran's Hospital.
Rose, John '72 (SY) Baldwinsville, NY St. Augustine Church.
Rose, Justin '95 (NTN) Fullerton, CA Holy Cross Church; San Bernardino, CA St. Philip Church.
Rose, Michael F. '81 (WOR) South Grafton, MA St. James Church.
Rose, William J. '56 (TOL) Sycamore, OH St. Pius X Church.
Rose, William J. '96 (TOL) Tiffin, OH St. Mary Church.
Rosebrough, Robert T. '69 (STL) Valley Park, MO Sacred Heart Church.
Roselada, Eulogio '93 (CHI) [N] Chicago, IL The Holy Evangelists Friary.
Roselli, Marc J. *s.j.* '85 (NY) [F] New York, NY Xavier High School.
Rosemeyer, John C. '58 (CHI) Westchester, IL Divine Providence Church.
Rosemeyer, Paul F. '52 (CHI) [1] Des Plaines, IL St. Mary Church; Retired.
Rosen, Cyprian *o.f.m.cap.* '62 (NEW) [N] Union City, NJ Capuchin Friars - Province of the Sacred Stigmata of St. Francis.
Rosen, Cyprian *o.f.m.cap.* '62 (WIL) [I] Wilmington, DE Capuchin Franciscan Friars, St. Francis Renewal Center; [L] Wilmington, DE St. Francis Renewal Center.
Rosenau, Alan '88 (LR) Arkadelphia, AR St. Mary's Church; Malvern, AR St. John the Baptist Church; [E] Hot Springs National Park, AR St. Joseph's Regional Health Center.
Rosenbaum, William E. '76 (ALT) [19] Johnstown, PA St. Clement's Church.
Rosendale, Glenn (LUB) Spur, TX St. Mary Church.
Rosendale, Glenn '76 (LUB) Ralls, TX St. Michael Church.
Rosenfelder, Richard M. *s.j.* '51 (CLV) [E] Cuyahoga Falls, OH Walsh Jesuit High School.
Rosenkranz, George J. '62 (BO) Health Leave.
Rosensteel, William A. '69 (ALT) Newry, PA St. Patrick's Church.
Rosensweig, Walter F. '53 (TUC) Absent on Leave; [F] Tucson, AZ Regina Cleri Center.
Rosero, Leo V. '90 (BRK) [181] Queens, NY Immaculate Conception Church.
Roseto, James '90 (E) On Leave of Absence.
Rosette, Fabian Maria *h.o.carm.* '80 (SAN) [A] Christoval, TX Mount Carmel Hermitage.
Rosetti, Gabriel A. *o.f.m.* '59 (PH) [D] Philadelphia, PA Archbishop Ryan High School; [AA] Philadelphia, PA St. Pius X Friary.
Rosettie, Msgr. Frederick D. '45 (TUC) Retired.
Rosevear, Anthony *o.p.* '78 (P) Ashland, OR Our Lady of the Mountain Church.
Rosie, Joseph N. '90 (TR) Freehold, NJ St. Rose of Lima Church.
Rosielski, Eugene '54 (SY) [5] Rome, NY Transfiguration Church.
Rosin, Richard *s.d.b.* '95 (NY) [F] New Rochelle, NY Salesian High School.
Rosing, Paul J. '73 (CLV) [1] Akron, OH Annunciation Church.
Rosing, Robert '53 (COV) [H] Covington, KY St. Elizabeth Medical Center, North.
Rosing, Robert C. (COV) [P] Erlanger, KY Marydale Retreat Center.
Rosing, Robert C. '53 (COV) [9] Covington, KY Church of Our Savior; Retired.
Rosinski, Bernard *s.c.j.* '59 (MIL) [P] Hales Corners, WI Priests of the Sacred Heart.
Rosinski, Edward B. '63 (CAM) Sicklerville, NJ St. John Neumann Church.
Rosinski, Richard A. '91 (RCK) Dixon, IL St. Anne Church.
Rosko, Ladislaus '52 (CLV) Orange Village, OH St. Margaret of Hungary Church.
Rosloniec, Leo S. '54 (GR) Wright Township, MI St. Joseph's Church.
Roslovich, Peter J. *s.j.* '63 (NY) [DD] New York, NY Murray-Weigel Hall.
Roslowski, Romulus *o.f.m. conv.* '74 (ALT) Hooversville, PA Holy Family Church.
Rosner, William F. *c.ss.r.* '51 (HBG) Ephrata, PA Mother of Perpetual Help Church; [H] Ephrata, PA St. Clement's Mission House.
Rosoh, James '72 (ALB) Fort Edward, NY St. Joseph Church.
Rosolen, Emil '86 (AMA) Absent on Leave.
Rosonke, Steven J. '82 (DUB) [6] Cedar Rapids, IA St. Patrick's Church.
Rosonke, Vince G. '75 (DM) Altoona, IA SS. John and Paul Church.
Ross, Msgr. Charles E. '37 (IND) Retired.
Ross, Christopher M. *o.s.m.* '54 (ORG) [H] Buena Park, CA Servite Fathers And Brothers.
Ross, Daniel *s.j.* '66 (FgM) Provinces.
Ross, David M. '75 (TOL) [1] Lima, OH St. Charles Borromeo Church.
Ross, James H. '46 (OKL) Retired.
Ross, Joseph *m.s.* '55 (FR) [J] Attleboro, MA La Salette Shrine.
Ross, Joseph *c.s.c.* '89 (GRY) Michigan City, IN Indiana State Prison.
Ross, Joseph D. '69 (STL) [31] St. Louis, MO St. Cronan Church.
Ross, Joseph D. *c.s.c.* '89 (FTW) [B] Notre Dame, IN University of Notre Dame Du Lac.
Ross, Joseph R. '69 (OKL) [4] Oklahoma City, OK Christ the King Church.
Ross, Kenneth '92 (ORL) Retired.
Ross, Laurence *s.m.* '43 (BO) [12] Lawrence, MA Sacred Heart Church.
Ross, Lowery A. '97 (CC) [1] Corpus Christi, TX Corpus Christi Cathedral.
Ross, Mark J. '88 (SAV) Vidalia, GA Sacred Heart Church.
Ross, Raymond *c.m.* '48 (STL) Sappington, MO St. Catherine Laboure Church.
Ross, Richard G. '67 (JOL) [15] Joliet, IL St. Mary Magdalene Church.
Ross, Robert *s.d.s.* '58 (WDC) [B] Silver Spring, MD Salvatorian Community.
Ross, Robert J. *s.j.* '72 (CIN) [M] Cincinnati, OH Faber Jesuit Community.
Ross, Robert J. *s.j.* '72 (COV) [H] Covington, KY St. Elizabeth Medical Center, North; [H] Edgewood, KY St. Elizabeth Medical Center, South; [H] Williamstown, KY St. Elizabeth Medical Center, Grant County.
Ross, Stephen-Joseph *o.c.d.* '84 (BO) [W] Brighton, MA Carmelite Monastery.
Ross, Theodore C. *s.j.* '67 (CHI) [C] Chicago, IL Jesuit Community at Loyola University of Chicago.
Ross, William B. '54 (OKL) Purcell, OK Our Lady of Victory Church.
Rossbach, Msgr. George F. '36 (NY) Retired.
Rossbach, Robert *c.ss.r.* '47 (STL) [P] Liguori, MO Liguori Mission House/Redemptorists.
Rosse, John V. '54 (ROC) [24] Rochester, NY Holy Name of Jesus Church.
Rossell, Richard *o.f.m.conv.* '61 (TR) Point Pleasant Beach, NJ St. Peter Church.
Rosselli, Msgr. Charles '36 (NY) Retired.
Rossello, Nicholas A. '60 (BUF) [3] Lockport, NY St. Joseph Church.
Rosser, Aelred *o.s.b.* '67 (KC) [J] Conception, MO Conception Abbey.
Rossetti, Mark T. '85 (SCR) Unassigned or Leave of Absence.
Rossetti, Salvatore J. *o.p.* '42 (MET) Edison, NJ St. Helena Church.
Rossetti, Stephen '84 (SY) On Duty Outside the Diocese.
Rossetti, Stephen J. '13 (WDC) [V] Silver Spring, MD Saint Luke Institute, Inc.
Rossey, Stephen J. *o.praem.* '59 (GB) [I] De Pere, WI St. Norbert Abbey.
Rossi, Anthony M. '49 (PH) Retired.
Rossi, Desmond '92 (ALB) Guilderland, NY St. Madeleine Sophie Church.
Rossi, Domenic A. *o.praem.* '74 (PH) Paoli, PA St. Norbert Church.
Rossi, Dominic *p.i.m.e.* '38 (DET) [K] Detroit, MI P.I.M.E. Missionaries of SS. Peter and Paul.
Rossi, Frank H. '83 (GAL) On Special Assignment.
Rossi, Joseph M. '84 (BO) Braintree, MA St. Thomas More Church.
Rossi, Joseph S. *s.j.* '80 (BAL) [B] Baltimore, MD Loyola College; [M] Baltimore, MD Jesuit Community of Loyola College, Inc.
Rossi, Pat F. (NY) [182] Bronx, NY SS. Philip and James Church.
Rossi, Paul '74 (SFR) Marin, CA Serra Club of Marin.
Rossi, Paul J. '74 (SFR) [3] San Rafael, CA St. Raphael Church.
Rossi, Philip J. *s.j.* '71 (MIL) [P] Milwaukee, WI Arrupe House Jesuit Community.
Rossi, Raymond R. '58 (LR) Hot Springs Village, AR Sacred Heart of Jesus Church.
Rossi, Robert *o.s.c* '70 (FgM) Crosier Foreign Missions.
Rossi, Ronald J. *o.praem.* '70 (PH) [D] Philadelphia, PA St. John Neumann High School.
Rossi, Thomas J. *o.praem.* '73 (PH) [134] Philadelphia, PA St. Paul Church; [AA] Paoli, PA Daylesford Abbey.
Rossi, Walter R. '87 (SCR) On Duty Outside the Diocese.
Rossi, Walter R. '87 (WDC) [Q] Washington, DC Basilica of the National Shrine of the Immaculate Conception.
Rossie, Arthur *c.ss.r.* '57 (STP) Brooklyn Center, MN St. Alphonsus Church.
Rossiter, Msgr. Francis S. '42 (BO) Bilerica, MA Middlesex County House of Correction; Cambridge, MA Middlesex County Jail; Retired.
Rossiter, John F. '58 (KCK) [1] Topeka, KS Assumption Church.
Rossitto, Joseph V. '69 (BGP) [4] Danbury, CT St. Joseph's Church; Retired.
Rossman, George M. '66 (SFR) [T] San Francisco, CA Opus Dei.
Rossman, Richard '71 (P) Tualatin, OR Church of the Resurrection.
Rosso, Norbert *c.s.sp.* '54 (ALX) Natchitoches, LA St. Anthony Church.
Rosson, John Peter '75 (ALB) [8] Schenectady, NY St. John the Baptist Church.
Rosswog, Bernard L. *o.s.b.* '37 (CHL) [J] Belmont, NC Belmont Abbey.
Rosswog, Kenneth *o.f.m.* '57 (STL) [25] St. Louis, MO St. Anthony of Padua Church; [P] St. Louis, MO Franciscan Friary of St. Anthony of Padua.
Rosswurm, Michael J. '73 (FTW) [18] Fort Wayne, IN St. Therese Church.
Rost, Msgr. George W. '51 (HBG) Conewago Township, PA Basilica of the Sacred Heart of Jesus Church.
Rost, Louis B. *m.m.* '55 (FgM) Maryknoll Foreign Missions.
Rost, Robert A. (KC) [5] Independence, MO Nativity of the Blessed Virgin Church.
Roszel, Stephen A. '77 (ARL) Purcellville, VA St. Francis de Sales Church.
Roszko, Edward J. *o.s.f.s.* '70 (ARL) [D] Alexandria, VA Bishop Ireton High School; [J] Alexandria, VA Oblates of St. Francis de Sales Residence.
Roszko, Edward J. *o.s.f.s.* '70 (PH) [D] Philadelphia, PA Father Judge High School for Boys.
Roszkowski, Donald '97 (PEO) [13] Peoria, IL St. Philomena's Church.
Rotelle, John E. *o.s.a.* '65 (PH) [AA] Villanova, PA Provincial Offices of the Order of St. Augustine, Province of St. Thomas of Villanova; [AA] Villanova,

PA St. John Stone Friary.
Roten, Johann B.G. *s.m.* '69 (CIN) [D] Dayton, OH The University of Dayton; [D] Dayton, OH The University of Dayton; [M] Dayton, OH Marianist Provincialate.
Rotert, J. Martin '94 (KC) Lee's Summit, MO Our Lady of the Presentation Church.
Rotert, Norman '57 (KC) [41] Kansas City, MO Visitation of the Blessed Virgin Church.
Rotert, Msgr. Norman '57 (OAK) [S] Oakland, CA Pacific Institute for Community Organization.
Roth, Jacob P. '53 (DUB) Retired.
Roth, James H. *o.s.f.s.* '95 (TOL) [C] Toledo, OH St. Francis de Sales High School; [K] Toledo, OH Oblates of St. Francis de Sales.
Roth, James J. '46 (WCH) Bushton, KS Holy Name of Jesus Church.
Roth, James V. *m.m.* '54 (FgM) Maryknoll Foreign Missions.
Roth, Msgr. Joseph R. '79 (CHR) Myrtle Beach, SC St. Andrew's Church.
Roth, Robert J. *s.j.* '51 (NY) [DD] New York, NY Jesuit Community at Fordham University.
Roth, Timothy *m.i.c.* '74 (CHI) [N] Chicago, IL Congregation of Marian Fathers of the Immaculate Conception.
Roth, Timothy *m.i.c.* '74 (NOR) [C] Thompson, CT Marianapolis Preparatory School; [F] Thompson, CT Marian Fathers.
Roth, Wallace F. '47 (CLV) South Amherst, OH Nativity of Blessed Virgin Mary Church; Retired.
Rothbauer, Francis J. '66 (STU) Retired.
Rothe, James A. '56 (LA) Santa Paula, CA St. Sebastian Church.
Rothermel, Paul L. '94 (ALN) [7] Bethlehem, PA Notre Dame of Bethlehem Church.
Rothfuchs, Gregory '95 (JOL) [2] Naperville, IL Sts. Peter and Paul Church.
Rothrauff, Leo P. *o.s.b.* '56 (FgM) American - Cassinese Congregation Foreign Missions.
Rothrauff, Leo P. *o.s.b.* '56 (GBG) [H] Latrobe, PA Saint Vincent Archabbey.
Rothrauff, Noel H. *o.s.b.* '54 (FgM) American - Cassinese Congregation Foreign Missions.
Rothrauff, Noel H. *o.s.b.* '54 (GBG) [H] Latrobe, PA Saint Vincent Archabbey.
Rothrock, Theodore D. '83 (LFT) Oxford, IN St. Patrick Church; Special Assignment.
Rothschild, Paul J. '84 (STL) Overland, MO All Souls Church.
Rothwell, Joseph T. '52 (BO) Permanent Disability.
Rotola, Albert C. *s.j.* (STL) [C] St. Louis, MO Saint Louis University.
Rotola, Albert C. *s.j.* '68 (STL) [P] St. Louis, MO Jesuit Community Corporation at St. Louis University - Jesuit Hall.
Rotolo, Michael '51 (STU) Barton, OH Our Lady of Angels Church; Blaine, OH All Saints Church.
Rotondi, Paul *o.f.m.* '56 (MET) [6] New Brunswick, NJ St. Ladislaus Church.
Rotrige, Msgr. Henry J. '38 (STL) Retired.
Rott, Bernard E. '79 (MAD) Watertown, WI St. Henry Church.
Rottloff, Linus *c.p.* '51 (HRT) [M] West Hartford, CT Holy Family Monastery/Retreat.
Rotunno, Anthony '61 (PRT) Greenville, ME Holy Family Church.
Rotunno, Floyd '70 (NEW) [2] Orange, NJ Our Lady of the Valley Church.
Rotunno, Philip J. '66 (NEW) West New York, NJ Our Lady of Libera Church.
Rouch, Nicholas J. '89 (E) [B] Erie, PA Gannon University.
Rouech, Chris '96 (GR) [12] Grand Rapids, MI St. John Vianney Church.
Roueche, Msgr. John F. '33 (CHL) Retired.
Rouelle, Forrest '56 (STU) [J] Steubenville, OH The Fraternity of Priests, Inc.
Rouelle, Forrest W. '56 (BUR) Newport, VT St. Mary Star of the Sea Church.
Rougeau, Marc *s.d.b.* '77 (LA) [C] Rosemead, CA Don Bosco Technical Institute; [D] Rosemead, CA Don Bosco Technical Institute.
Roughan, Richard F. '63 (NOR) Waterford, CT St. Paul Church.
Rourke, John C. '63 (VEN) [4] Sarasota, FL St. Michael the Archangel Church.
Rouse, Charles '76 (BAL) Absent on Leave.
Rouse, John-Vincent (GAL) The Woodlands, TX St. Anthony of Padua Church.
Rouse, Paul (BO) [28] Boston, MA Holy Name Church.
Rouse, Silvan *c.p.* '49 (ALT) [J] Bedford, PA St. Mary's House of Greater Solitude.
Rouse, Warren *o.f.m.* '57 (LA) [X] Malibu, CA Serra Retreat.
Rousseau, Julian *s.s.s.* '50 (SFE) [23] Albuquerque, NM St. Charles Borromeo Church; Albuquerque, NM Veterans Administration Medical Center.
Rousseau, Peter A. '49 (BUR) Retired.
Rousseau, Richard W. *s.j.* '54 (BO) [W] Boston, MA The Society of Jesus of New England-Provincial Offices.
Rousseau, Richard W. *s.j.* '54 (SCR) [C] Scranton, PA University of Scranton.
Rousseau, Robert J. '67 (HRT) [1] Bristol, CT St. Ann Church.
Rousseau, Robert P. *s.s.s.* '76 (GAL) [25] Houston, TX Corpus Christi Church.
Rousseau, Sean K. '95 (ARL) Fairfax, VA St. Leo's Church.
Rousseau, Msgr. Stanley B. '56 (BGP) [1] Bridgeport, CT St. Augustine Cathedral.
Roussel, Joseph P. *c.s.b.* '52 (GAL) Retired; [Q] Houston, TX Residence of the Basilian Fathers of the University of St. Thomas.
Roussel, Matthew '96 (LAF) Ville Platte, LA Sacred Heart of Jesus Church.
Routhier, Peter A. '78 (BUR) Barre, VT St. Monica Church.
Roux, G. Albert (PRT) Special or Other Diocesan Assignment.
Roux, Gerard *o.m.i.* '64 (MAN) [M] Hudson, NH Oblates of Mary Immaculate Retreat House.
Roux, Philippe '73 (SPR) South Deerfield, MA St. Stanislaus B. and M. Church.
Rowan, Gerald F. '57 (WCH) Castleton, KS St. Agnes Church; Hutchinson, KS St. Teresa Church.
Rowan, Gerard J. '47 (STP) Carver, MN St. Nicholas Church.
Rowan, Msgr. John '61 (RVC) Sayville, NY St. Lawrence the Martyr Church.
Rowan, John M. '89 (BO) [5] Quincy, MA St. Mary Church.
Rowan, Joseph *c.ss.r.* '45 (ALB) [L] Saratoga Springs, NY St. John Neumann Residence.
Rowan, Mark P. '91 (RVC) Lynbrook, NY Our Lady of Peace Church.
Rowan, Stephen '70 (SEA) Special Assignment.
Rowe, Donald F. *s.j.* '72 (CHI) [C] Chicago, IL Jesuit Community at Loyola University of Chicago; [D] Chicago, IL St. Ignatius College Prep.
Rowe, Douglas L. '67 (OM) Absent on Leave.
Rowe, William J. '64 (BEL) Mount Carmel, IL St. Mary Church.
Rowgh, T. Matthew '75 (WH) Shepherdstown, WV St. Agnes Church.
Rowland, Msgr. Charles H. '70 (CHR) [2] Columbia, SC St. Joseph Church.
Rowland, Edward P. '53 (JOL) [19] Joliet, IL St. Thaddeus Church.
Rowland, Thomas '49 (ELP) On Duty Outside of Diocese.
Rowland, William F. *c.j.m.* '70 (SD) [3] San Diego, CA Blessed Sacrament Church.
Rowland, William F. *s.m.* '79 (WDC) [M] Washington, DC Marist Provincial House.
Rowley, James J. '37 (CHI) Palatine, IL St. Thomas of Villanova Church; Retired.
Rowntree, Stephen C. *s.j.* '75 (FgM) Provinces.
Rowntree, Stephen C. *s.j.* '75 (NO) [P] New Orleans, LA Jesuit Provincial Office.
Rowsome, Morgan '70 (CC) [19] Corpus Christi, TX St. Peter Prince of Apostles Church.
Roxas, Rodolfo P. '69 (SAV) [E] Savannah, GA St. Joseph's Hospital.
Roy, Msgr. Allen J. '54 (NO) [10] New Orleans, LA Holy Spirit Church.
Roy, Donald J. '70 (BUR) Milton, VT St. Ann Church.
Roy, Duane *o.s.b.* '67 (FgM) American - Cassinese Congregation Foreign Missions.
Roy, F. Gilles '57 (WOR) On Duty Outside the Diocese.
Roy, Gregory *s.j.* '46 (ALB) [L] Valatie, NY St. Joseph.
Roy, Gregory R. *s.j.* '46 (BO) [W] Boston, MA The Society of Jesus of New England-Provincial Offices.
Roy, J. Jean '56 (WDC) Retired.
Roy, James '61 (ALX) Hessmer, LA St. Alphonsus Church.
Roy, James R. *m.m.* '61 (FgM) Maryknoll Foreign Missions.
Roy, Joe *s.s.s.* '56 (SLC) [7] Taylorsville, UT St. Martin de Porres Church.
Roy, Kenneth J. '78 (ALX) Natchitoches, LA Immaculate Conception Church; Powhatan, LA St. Francis Church.
Roy, Maurice J. '73 (BUR) St. Albans, VT Holy Angels Church.
Roy, Michael J. '75 (WOR) Webster, MA Sacred Heart of Jesus Church.
Roy, Paul M. *m.s.* '58 (FR) [J] Attleboro, MA La Salette Provincial House.
Roy, Richard *m.afr.* '71 (FgM) Missionaries of Africa Foreign Missions.
Roy, Richard M. '75 (FR) Orleans, MA St. Joan of Arc Church.
Roy, Robert P. '94 (HRT) [2] Meriden, CT St. Joseph Church; [4] Meriden, CT St. Mary Church.
Roy, Roger *o.m.i.* '49 (FgM) Oblates Foreign Missions.
Roy, Sheldon L. '86 (ALX) Natchitoches, LA Holy Cross Church; [J] Natchitoches, LA Northwestern State University.
Royal, E. Peter (AUS) Marlin, TX V.A. Hospital.
Royal, E. Peter '53 (AUS) Lott, TX Sacred Heart Church; Marlin, TX St. Joseph's Church.
Royal, Kevin T. *s.t.l.* '85 (BGP) [O] Stamford, CT St. John Fisher Seminary Residence.
Royce, Thomas R. *s.j.* '56 (YAK) [4] Yakima, WA St. Joseph's Church.
Royer, Msgr. George C. '27 (MOB) Retired; [F] Mobile, AL Little Sisters of the Poor, Home For the Aged, Inc.
Royer, Msgr. Ronald E. '58 (LA) Lakewood, CA St. Pancratius Church.
Royer, Thomas J. '60 (PEO) [3] Champaign, IL St. Mary's Church; Ivesdale, IL St. Joseph's Church.
Royer, Yvon J. '90 (BUR) [4] Burlington, VT St. Joseph's Church.
Rozanski, Mitchell T. '84 (BAL) [36] Baltimore, MD Holy Cross Church; [60] Baltimore, MD St. Mary, Star of the Sea Church.
Rozansky, Joseph G. *o.f.m.* '76 (NY) [146] Bronx, NY Holy Cross Church.
Rozman, Thomas J. '86 (HBG) [1] Harrisburg, PA Cathedral Parish of St. Patrick Church.
Rozniak, Msgr. Ronald J. '71 (NEW) Ridgewood, NJ Our Lady of Mount Carmel Church.
Roznowski, Thomas *o.s.b.* '76 (SFS) [F] Marvin, SD Blue Cloud Abbey.
Rozum, George A. *c.s.c.* '68 (FTW) [B] Notre Dame, IN University of Notre Dame Du Lac; [J] Notre Dame, IN Holy Cross Community, Corby Hall, University of Notre Dame.
Rozycki, George '70 (HON) On Duty Outside the Diocese.
Rozycki, George '70 (SP) Brandon, FL Church of the Nativity.
Rozycki, Isidore '68 (AUS) Tours, TX St. Martin Church.
Rozycki, Julian S. *o.p.* (CAM) [N] Cherry Hill, NJ Little Servant Sisters of the Immaculate Conception.
Ruan, John Ming '97 (WDC) [4] Rockville, MD St. Raphael Church.
Ruane, Dennis *s.s.s.* '59 (SFE) [23] Albuquerque, NM St. Charles Borromeo Church.
Ruane, Edward M. *o.p.* '69 (CHI) [N] Chicago, IL Dominicans (Provincial Office); [N] Chicago, IL Dominicans (Provincial Office); [X] Chicago, IL St. Thomas Aquinas Foundation.
Ruane, Edward M. *o.p.* '69 (FgM) Dominican - Order of Preachers Foreign Missions.
Ruane, George '73 (NEW) Fairfield, NJ St. Thomas More Church.
Ruane, John P. *s.j.* '49 (NEW) [B] Jersey City, NJ Saint Peter's College; [N] Jersey City, NJ Jesuits of Saint Peter's College, Inc.
Ruane, Martin '63 (JKS) Pearl, MS St. Jude Church; Pearl, MS Rankin County Prison; Whitfield, MS Mississippi State Hospital.
Ruane, Michael '69 (BAL) Poplar Springs, MD St. Michael Church.
Ruba, Msgr. Nicholas J. '51 (SC) Retired.
Rubadue, Paul E. *o.s.b.* '86 (GBG) [1] Latrobe, PA Holy Family Church.
Rubaj, Leon '60 (SAT) On Duty Outside the Archdiocese.
Rubalcaba, Francisco '57 (SJN) [13] Carolina, PR Nuestra Senora de Lourdes Church.
Rubba, John C. *o.p.* '32 (PRO) [P] Providence, RI St. Thomas Aquinas Priory at Providence College.
Rubbelke, Ronald J. '64 (STL) O'Fallon, MO Assumption Church.
Rubey, Charles T. '66 (CHI) [G] Chicago, IL Catholic Charities of the Archdiocese of Chicago-Archdiocesan Offices; [L] Chicago, IL St. Joseph's Carondelet Child Center.
Rubiano, Cesar *c.j.m.* '96 (SD) [M] San Diego, CA San Diego State University Newman Center.
Rubino, Msgr. David A. '73 (E) [B] Erie, PA Gannon University.
Rubio, Gerardo '78 (SAC) Vallejo, CA St. Vincent Ferrer Church.
Rubio, Jose (SJ) [22] San Jose, CA Sacred Heart of Jesus Church.
Rubio, Jose '80 (SJ) Special Assignment; [O] San Jose, CA The Newman Center/Catholic Campus Ministry.
Rubio-Boitel, Fernando '75 (SFE) [A] Santa Fe, NM Immaculate Heart of Mary Seminary.
Rubsys, Anthony L. *f.s.c.a.* '38 (NY) [DD] New York, NY Brothers of the Christian Schools of Manhattan College, Inc.
Ruby, David C. '91 (GB) Little Chute, WI St. John Church.
Rucando, Anthony M. '70 (BRK) [98] Brooklyn, NY Our Lady Help of Christians Church.
Ruchgy, Wayne J. '66 (STN) Dearborn, MI St. Michael's Church.
Rucinski, Joseph S. '42 (TR) Retired.
Rucinski, Willard *o.s.f.s.* '65 (R) Fayetteville, NC St. Elizabeth Ann Seton Church.
Ruck, Michael J. *m.m.* '46 (SJ) [M] Los Altos, CA Maryknoll.
Rucker, G. Neville '46 (LA) Pacific Palisades, CA Corpus Christi Church.
Rucker, Lawrence *s.c.j.* '66 (JKS) Holly Springs, MS St. Joseph Church; [G] Holly Springs, MS Rust College Newman Center.

Rucker, Neville '46 (LA) Retired.
Rudcki, Stanley R. '53 (CHI) Retired.
Rudd, Richard (FAR) Retired.
Rudd, Thad B. '91 (ATL) Atlanta, GA Atlanta Veterans Administration Hospital.
Rudden, Matthew T. '59 (RCK) [3] Rockford, IL St. Bernadette Church.
Ruddick, James J. *s.j.* '55 (BUF) [O] Buffalo, NY Canisius Jesuit Community; [T] Amherst, NY St. Andrew Kim Roman Catholic Church Society of Amherst, NY, Diocese of Buffalo.
Ruddy, Msgr. Donald J. '55 (LA) Whittier, CA St. Gregory the Great Church.
Ruddy, Edward J. '40 (PAT) Retired.
Ruddy, H. Paul *o.s.f.s.* '64 (LAN) Hudson, MI Sacred Heart Church.
Rude, James A. *s.j.* '64 (LA) [6] Los Angeles, CA Blessed Sacrament Church.
Rudemiller, Edward L. '58 (CIN) [68] Cincinnati, OH Our Lady of Lourdes Church.
Rudisill, James A. '51 (NSH) Retired.
Rudnay, Clement A. *o.praem.* '38 (ORG) [H] Silverado, CA Norbertine Fathers of Orange Inc.
Rudnick, Kenneth J. *s.j.* '91 (SPK) [B] Spokane, WA St. Michael's Institute; [C] Spokane, WA Gonzaga University.
Rudnicki, Wladyslaw (RVC) Cutchogue, NY Our Lady of Ostrabrama Church.
Rudnik, John J. '61 (CHI) [208] Chicago, IL Transfiguration of Our Lord Church.
Rudnik, Tadeusz '55 (SY) [22] Syracuse, NY St. Stephen Church.
Rudolf, Roger G. '92 (IND) Rushville, IN Immaculate Conception/St. Mary Church.
Rudolph, Frederick *s.v.d.* '54 (CHI) [B] Techny, IL Divine Word Residence.
Rudolph, Patrick '88 (ORG) [1] Orange, CA Cathedral of the Holy Family.
Rudolph, Thomas J. '61 (LC) Rozellville, WI St. Andrew Church; Stratford, WI St. Joseph Church.
Rudolphi, Stephen A. '79 (BEL) Carmi, IL St. Polycarp Church; Enfield, IL St. Patrick Church.
Rudolphi, Timothy '89 (STP) Chaska, MN Guardian Angels Church.
Rudy, John W. *o.f.m.* '77 (HRT) Winsted, CT St. Joseph's Church.
Rudy, Noel T. '53 (SAG) AuGres, MI St. Mark Church.
Rudy, Richard E. '76 (PH) [102] Philadelphia, PA St. Matthew Church.
Rudy, Theodore '54 (PSC) Dunmore, PA St. Michael Church.
Rudzewicz, Jan *s.ch.* '83 (DET) [8] Sterling Heights, MI Our Lady of Czestochowa Church.
Rueda, John (NY) [173] Bronx, NY Our Lady of Mercy Church.
Rueda, Silverio '81 (SJN) [12] Carolina, PR San Juan de Dios Church.
Ruede, Ernest '66 (R) New Bern, NC St. Paul Church.
Ruedel, Richard P. '59 (STP) St. Thomas, MN St. Thomas Church.
Ruedisueli, Robert A. '69 (DET) [8] Warren, MI St. Mark Church.
Ruef, Msgr. James L.T. '78 (COL) [20] Columbus, OH Holy Name Church.
Ruef, John *c.ss.r.* '50 (TR) [Q] Long Branch, NJ San Alfonso Retreat House.
Rueger, William J. '75 (BRK) [207] Queens, NY Our Lady of the Blessed Sacrament Church.
Ruehl, William F. '58 (ARL) Front Royal, VA St. John the Baptist Church.
Ruekert, Thomas E. *s.d.b.* '73 (NO) [4] Harvey, LA St. Rosalie Church.
Ruelle, Gerald *o.s.b.* '50 (BIS) Halliday, ND St. Paul Church; Killdeer, ND St. Joseph Church.
Ruelle, Gerald *o.s.b.* '52 (BIS) [A] Richardton, ND Assumption Abbey.
Ruess, Charles W. '31 (TOL) Retired.
Ruessmann, John J. *m.m.* '79 (FgM) Maryknoll Foreign Missions.
Rueter, Joseph J. '46 (COV) Cold Spring, KY St. Joseph Church; Retired.
Ruetz, Edward J. '62 (FTW) Retired.
Rueve, Charles R. *c.pp.s.* '43 (LFT) [A] Rensselaer, IN Saint Joseph's College.
Ruff, Anthony *o.s.b.* '93 (SCL) [I] Collegeville, MN St. John's Abbey, of the Order of St. Benedict.
Ruff, Charles R. '46 (STL) Retired.
Ruff, Daniel M. *s.j.* '86 (BAL) [A] Baltimore, MD St. Mary's Seminary and University.
Ruff, Frank '63 (NSH) [L] Nashville, TN Glenmary Department of Pastoral Services.
Ruff, Frank *glmy.* '72 (OWN) Franklin, KY St. Mary of the Woods Church; Scottsville, KY Christ the King Church.
Ruffing, Joseph R. '55 (LFT) Retired.
Ruffing, Norman '63 (OAK) Retired.
Ruffo, John *o.f.m. conv.* '74 (R) Jacksonville, NC Shrine of the Infant of Prague, Church of the Holy Spirit.
Ruffolo, George *c.m.f.* '56 (CHI) [166] Chicago, IL St. Paul Church.
Ruge, Kenneth C. '63 (CHI) Other Assignments.
Rugel, Msgr. James J. (PAT) Retired.
Rugen, Patrick J. '76 (CHI) On Duty Outside the Archdiocese.
Ruggere, Peter *m.m.* '68 (WDC) [B] Washington, DC Maryknoll Fathers and Brothers.
Ruggeri, Joseph A. '65 (BO) [8] Lowell, MA St. Margaret Church.
Ruggieri, James T. '95 (PRO) [6] Cranston, RI St. Matthew Church.
Ruggieri, Joseph '95 (Y) Kent, OH St. Patrick's Church.
Ruggieri, Pasquale *f.d.p.* '52 (NY) [11] New York, NY St. Ann Church.
Ruggles, John J. '60 (BEL) Retired.
Ruglovsky, Robert '61 (PRM) Absent on Leave.
Ruhl, John '64 (ORG) Inactive Leave.
Ruhl, Matthew D. *s.j.* '92 (STL) [52] St. Louis, MO St. Matthew, Apostle Church; [P] St. Louis, MO St. Matthew Jesuit Community.
Ruhl, William J. *o.s.f.s.* (R) Goldsboro, NC St. Mary Church.
Ruhland, Carl J. '45 (DUB) Retired.
Ruhling, James '60 (E) [10] Erie, PA Our Lady of Peace Church; Erie, PA Soldiers and Sailors Home.
Ruhnke, Robert *c.ss.r.* '66 (SAT) [37] San Antonio, TX St. Gerard Majella Church.
Ruhnke, Robert A. *c.ss.r.* '66 (BR) [H] Baton Rouge, LA The Redemptorist Education and Formation.
Ruisanchez, Jose P. '86 (SFR) [T] San Francisco, CA Opus Dei.
Ruiz, Adolfo '29 (BR) Retired.
Ruiz, Msgr. Agustin '56 (BRK) [118] Brooklyn, NY SS. Peter and Paul's Church.
Ruiz, Albert '73 (AUS) Killeen, TX St. Joseph Church.
Ruiz, Alberto M. *c.m.f.* '84 (LA) [R] Rancho Dominguez, CA Dominguez Seminary Inc.
Ruiz, Antonio *c.m.* '65 (LA) [95] Los Angeles, CA St. Vincent De Paul Church.
Ruiz, Antonio A. '71 (TUC) Nogales, AZ San Felipe de Jesus Church.
Ruiz, Dominic *o.s.b.* '83 (SCL) Richmond, MN SS. Peter and Paul's Church; [I] Collegeville, MN St. John's Abbey, of the Order of St. Benedict.
Ruiz, Enrique '56 (SAT) On Leave.
Ruiz, Faustino C. '91 (MET) On Duty Outside the Diocese.
Ruiz, Gabriel *c.m.f.* '89 (LA) [R] Los Angeles, CA Claretian Retreat Center Community.
Ruiz, J. Antonio *c.m.* '65 (PHX) [26] Phoenix, AZ St. Vincent de Paul Church.
Ruiz, Jean-Pierre *s.t.d.* '82 (BRK) [224] Queens, NY St. Patrick Church; Released from Diocesan Assignment.
Ruiz, John '55 (HT) [1] Thibodaux, LA St. Joseph Co-Cathedral.
Ruiz, Jose Domingo (STO) [6] Stockton, CA St. Linus Church.
Ruiz, Jose H. '58 (VEN) Sebring, FL St. Catherine Church.
Ruiz, Jose Luis '89 (LA) Bell Gardens, CA St. Gertrude Church.
Ruiz, Joseph B. '66 (CHI) [3] Oak Park, IL St. Edmund Church.
Ruiz, Juan Carlos '95 (PAT) [16] Paterson, NJ St. Therese Church.
Ruiz, Lorenzo '63 (SJN) [28] San Juan, PR San Juan Bosco Church.
Ruiz, Lorenzo *o.f.m.* '66 (GLP) St. Michaels, AZ St. Michael Church.
Ruiz, Luis (CGS) Barranquitas, PR Church of St. Anthony of Padua.
Ruiz, Luis '68 (SAT) [65] San Antonio, TX St. Stephen Church.
Ruiz, Pedro *o.de.m.* '88 (PCE) [13] Ponce, PR Santuario San Judas Tadeo Church.
Ruiz, Ricardo '93 (ELP) Alpine, TX Our Lady of Peace Church.
Ruiz, Rudy '79 (MRY) Castroville, CA Our Lady of Refuge Church.
Rukavina, Steven '87 (B) Pocatello, ID St. Joseph's Church.
Ruland, Vernon J. *s.j.* '63 (SFR) [N] San Francisco, CA Jesuit Community at University of San Francisco.
Rule, Philip C. *s.j.* (DET) [K] Detroit, MI Jesuit Provincial Office-Detroit Province of the Society of Jesus.
Rule, Philip C. *s.j.* '62 (WOR) [N] Worcester, MA Jesuits of Holy Cross College, Inc.
Rule, Steven R. '75 (RIC) Roanoke, VA St. Andrew Church.
Rulli, Joseph A. '92 (FTW) Elkhart, IN St. Vincent de Paul Church.
Rumble, Clarence F. '86 (SY) [3] Endicott, NY St. Anthony of Padua Church.
Runde, David H. '57 (MAD) Cottage Grove, WI St. Patrick Church.
Runde, Raymond E. '56 (MAD) Absent on Sick Leave.
Runde, William H. *s.j.* '69 (STL) [P] St. Louis, MO White House Retreat Jesuit Community; [T] St. Louis, MO White House Retreat.
Rundzio, Mark A. '81 (MAN) Winchester, NH St. Stanislaus Church.
Runge, Msgr. Fenton J. '53 (STL) [50] St. Louis, MO SS. Mary and Joseph Church.
Runte, Richard M. '73 (SPR) Easthampton, MA Immaculate Conception Church.
Runtz, Anthony *c.j.* '58 (LA) [B] Santa Maria, CA St. Joseph Seminary (Josephite Fathers' Novitiate).
Ruoff, John C. *s.j.* '61 (STL) [P] St. Louis, MO Jesuit Community Corporation at St. Louis University - Jesuit Hall.
Ruoff, Lou '84 (RIC) [3] Norfolk, VA Holy Trinity Church.
Rupert, Msgr. Dale R. '77 (SCR) Lake Winola, PA St. Mary of the Lake Church; [A] Dalton, PA Saint Pius X Seminary.
Rupiper, Darrell *o.m.i.* '63 (SFD) [A] Godfrey, IL Immaculate Heart of Mary Novitiate.
Rupp, Daniel N. '66 (MAR) Leave of Absence.
Rupp, Edward F. '60 (CLV) Absent on Leave.
Ruppenkamp, Raymond '50 (DAV) Retired.
Ruppenthal, William J. *s.j.* '48 (PH) [AA] Philadelphia, PA Jesuit Community at St. Joseph's University.
Ruppert, Donald R. '78 (VIC) East Bernard, TX Holy Cross Church.
Ruppert, E. Alan '78 (BEL) Dahlgren, IL St. John Nepomucene Church; McLeansboro, IL St. Clement Church.
Ruppert, Nelson J. *o.f.m.cap.* '66 (ROC) Interlaken, NY St. Francis Solanus Church; Ovid, NY Holy Cross Church; [I] Interlaken, NY St. Fidelis Friary.
Rusay, Leonard F.A. '85 (MET) High Bridge, NJ St. Joseph Church.
Ruscetta, Dominic *c.s.s.* '38 (BO) [Z] Waltham, MA Stigmatine Fathers and Brothers.
Rusch, Donald P. '61 (LAN) Clinton, MI St. Dominic's Church.
Ruschau, Ambrose *c.pp.s.* '50 (CIN) [B] Carthagena, OH St. Charles.
Ruschman, Albert E. '53 (COV) Fort Mitchell, KY Blessed Sacrament Church.
Rusconi, Richard A. '71 (PAT) [4] Paterson, NJ Blessed Sacrament Church.
Ruse, Fred R. '76 (ORL) Winter Haven, FL St. Matthew Church.
Rusell, Benjamin J. *o.p.* '60 (CHI) [N] Chicago, IL Dominicans (Provincial Office).
Rush, Alfred C. *c.ss.r.* '36 (ALB) [L] Saratoga Springs, NY St. John Neumann Residence.
Rush, Gerald V. '89 (OM) Absent on Leave.
Rush, Msgr. J. Kenneth '71 (RIC) Lynchburg, VA Holy Cross Church.
Rush, James C. '68 (HRT) Windsor, CT St. Gabriel's Church; Retired.
Rush, James P. '72 (CAM) Bridgeton, NJ Immaculate Conception Church.
Rush, Joseph P. '62 (CAM) Pomona, NJ Assumption Church.
Rush, Michael P. '73 (CAM) Mullica Hill, NJ Holy Name of Jesus Church.
Rush, Patrick J. '69 (KC) [35] Kansas City, MO St. Peter's Church; Special Assignment.
Rush, Robert T. *s.j.* '59 (FgM) Provinces.
Rush, Thomas *o.m.i.* '73 (LA) Pacoima, CA Mary Immaculate Church.
Rush, Thomas *o.m.i.* '73 (OAK) [N] Oakland, CA Oblate Provincial House & Procure.
Rush, Msgr. Vincent '72 (RVC) Huntington Station, NY St. Hugh of Lincoln Church.
Rushford, William A. '55 (BIS) Retired; [G] Bismarck, ND Emmaus Place.
Rushman, John '55 (GAY) Retired.
Rushofsky, John R. '79 (PIT) [1] McKeesport, PA St. Martin de Porres Church.
Rusin, Joseph C. '46 (SCR) Retired.
Rusk, John '68 (SB) Blythe, CA Chuckawalla Valley State Prison.
Rusk, Richard '90 (ROC) [K] Corning, NY Anawim Community Center.
Rusk, Richard M. '90 (MET) Phillipsburg, NJ SS. Philip and James Church; [L] Phillipsburg, NJ The Anawim Community.
Ruskamp, Robert L. '85 (ARL) Woodstock, VA St. John Bosco Church.
Ruskoski, William '74 (LAF) Arnaudville, LA St. Francis Regis Church; Arnaudville, LA St. Catherine Church.
Ruskowski, Clifford '62 (DET) [3] Clinton Twp., MI St. Paul of Tarsus Church; [A] Detroit, MI Sacred Heart Major Seminary, Inc.
Rusnak, Mark E. '87 (E) Emlenton, PA St. Michael Church.
Rusnak, Melvin E. '70 (Y) [22] Youngstown, OH St. Stephen of Hungary Church.
Russ, Francis J. '51 (KC) Retired.
Russel, James *s.m.* '64 (MIA) Hollywood, FL Nativity Church.
Russel, William *s.j.* '65 (BO) [W] Cambridge, MA Faber House.
Russell, Alfred *o.s.f.s.* '66 (LAN) Brooklyn, MI St. Joseph's Shrine Church.
Russell, Anselm *o.s.b.* '97 (IND) [J] St. Meinrad, IN St. Meinrad Archabbey.

Russell, Benjamin J. *o.p.* '60 (CHI) [N] Chicago, IL Dominicans (Provincial Office).
Russell, David '64 (MIA) [23] Miami, FL St. John Neumann Church.
Russell, David P. '81 (WDC) [17] Washington, DC Holy Name Church.
Russell, Edward '83 (NY) [184] Bronx, NY St. Pius V Church.
Russell, J. Christopher '79 (STP) Retired.
Russell, James A. *s.m.* '64 (CIN) [M] Dayton, OH Marianist Provincialate.
Russell, James D. '60 (WIN) Madison Lake, MN All Saints Church.
Russell, Msgr. James M. '70 (BLX) [1] Biloxi, MS Cathedral of the Nativity of the Blessed Virgin Mary.
Russell, John F. *o.carm.* '60 (NEW) [A] South Orange, NJ Immaculate Conception Seminary; [B] South Orange, NJ Seton Hall University.
Russell, Kenneth '58 (OAK) Retired.
Russell, Patrick '86 (B) Boise, ID Chateau de Boise Retirement Center.
Russell, Paul F. '87 (BO) Graduate Studies.
Russell, Paul M. '32 (L) Retired; [K] Louisville, KY Nazareth Home.
Russell, Raymond R. '56 (BUF) Getzville, NY St. Pius X Church.
Russell, Richard '60 (LA) [W] Los Angeles, CA Catholic Kolping House.
Russell, Richard J. '60 (SD) Retired.
Russell, Richard R. '61 (HRT) West Simsbury, CT St. Catherine of Siena Church.
Russell, Samuel *o.s.b.* '94 (KC) [A] Conception, MO Conception Seminary College; [J] Conception, MO Conception Abbey.
Russell, Stanley J. '61 (WIL) Bellefonte, DE St. Helena Church.
Russell, Msgr. W. Joyce '30 (WDC) [4] Silver Spring, MD St. Catherine Laboure Church; Retired.
Russell, William C. *s.j.* '65 (BO) [W] Boston, MA The Society of Jesus of New England-Provincial Offices; [W] Cambridge, MA Weston Jesuit Community.
Russi, Fred F. '66 (LKC) Oakdale, LA Sacred Heart Church.
Russi, John *s.m.* (SJ) [M] Cupertino, CA Marianist Provincial Residence.
Russman, Thomas *o.f.m.cap.* '72 (WDC) [B] Washington, DC St. Francis Friary-Capuchin College.
Russo, Alfred E. '62 (BGP) [K] Trumbull, CT St. Joseph's Manor.
Russo, Anthony *s.c.j.* '66 (MIL) [P] Hales Corners, WI Priests of the Sacred Heart.
Russo, Anthony P. *s.c.j.* '66 (MIL) Franklin, WI Sacred Hearts of Jesus and Mary Church; St. Martins, WI Holy Assumption Church; [P] Franklin, WI St. Francis Residence; [P] Hales Corners, WI Priests of the Sacred Heart.
Russo, Anthony T. *c.ss.r.* '65 (PH) [25] Philadelphia, PA St. Boniface Church; [S] Philadelphia, PA Catholic Center for the Deaf and Hard of Hearing.
Russo, Armando C. '44 (SPR) Russell, MA Our Lady of the Rosary Church.
Russo, Caesar '74 (STA) On Duty Outside the Diocese.
Russo, Carmen *c.s.s.* '45 (BO) [W] Waltham, MA Stigmatine Fathers & Brothers Provincial House.
Russo, Cesar (NY) [GG] New York, NY University Apostolate.
Russo, Msgr. Charles J. (PAT) Retired.
Russo, Francis X. *o.f.m.cap.* '59 (WDC) [39] Washington, DC Shrine of the Sacred Heart Church.
Russo, Frank '81 (LA) Pico Rivera, CA St. Hilary Church.
Russo, John W. (TR) Leave of Absence.
Russo, Lawrence J. '80 (BO) Military & VA Chaplains.
Russo, Michael '88 (LAF) Franklin, LA Assumption B.V.M. Church.
Russo, Michael A. '71 (NEW) On Duty Outside the Archdiocese.
Russo, Michael A. '71 (OAK) [B] Moraga, CA St. Mary's College.
Russo, Nicodemus A. '48 (PEO) Retired.
Russo, Peter '76 (ALB) Copake Falls, NY St. Bridget Church.
Russo, Reginald *o.f.m.cap.* '67 (BAL) [M] Cumberland, MD SS. Peter and Paul Friary.
Russo, Reginald *o.f.m.cap.* '67 (HBG) [2] York, PA St. Joseph Church.
Russo, Ricardo *o.f.m.* '74 (SFE) Santa Fe, NM New Mexico State Penitentiary.
Russo, Richard M. '82 (RCK) [4] Elgin, IL St. Thomas More Church.
Russo, Robert T. '61 (HRT) East Windsor, CT St. Philip's Church.
Russo, Thomas *o.s.j.* '56 (MRY) [G] Santa Cruz, CA Oblates of St. Joseph Provincial House and Shrine.
Rusteika, John B. '45 (WCH) Retired.
Ruston, Robert L. '76 (ALT) Cassandra, PA St. Agnes Church; Wilmore, PA St. Bartholomew's Church.
Ruszel, Henry *c.r.* '54 (SB) [3] Fontana, CA St. Joseph Church.
Ruszel, Humphrey *c.r.* '46 (SB) [1] Fontana, CA Church of the Resurrection.
Rutan, Albert E. '57 (GF) Absent on Leave.
Ruth, A. John *c.s.b.* '42 (GAL) [Q] Sugar Land, TX Basilian Mission Center.
Ruth, John C. '85 (SCR) [20] Scranton, PA Nativity of Our Lord Church; [I] Scranton, PA Mercy Hospital.
Ruth, Robert F. '60 (RIC) Retired.
Ruth, Ronald A. '70 (RIC) [9] Richmond, VA St. Edward The Confessor Church.
Ruthenberg, Gari *o.m.i.* '95 (SFS) Sisseton, SD St. Catherine Church; Sisseton, SD St. Peter Church.
Ruthenberg, Michael C. *o.p.* (WIN) [1] Winona, MN Cathedral of the Sacred Heart Church.
Ruther, William E. '90 (LA) La Puente, CA St. Joseph Church.
Rutherford, Donald L. '81 (ALB) Military Chaplains.
Rutherford, Richard *c.s.c.* '64 (P) [B] Portland, OR University of Portland; [L] Portland, OR Holy Cross Fathers & Brothers, C.S.C. - University of Portland.
Rutkowski, George A. '60 (DET) [54] Detroit, MI Our Lady Help of Christians Church.
Rutkowski, James N. '77 (STL) St. Louis, MO St. Mary's Health Ctr.
Rutkowski, Nicholas J. (STL) [K] St. Louis, MO St. Mary's Health Center.
Rutkowski, Ronald J. '69 (GBG) Cardale, PA Madonna of Czestochowa Church; Palmer, PA St. Albert Church.
Rutkowski, Stephen C. '58 (NEW) Retired.
Rutkowski, Theodore A. '63 (PIT) Scott Township, PA Our Lady of Grace Church.
Rutledge, Arthur F. *s.j.* '51 (SJ) [M] Los Gatos, CA Sacred Heart Jesuit Center.
Rutledge, John D. *c.m.* '51 (FgM) Vincentian Foreign Missions.
Rutledge, Robert M. *o.s.f.s.* '89 (ALN) [B] Center Valley, PA Allentown College of St. Francis de Sales; [K] Center Valley, PA Oblates of St. Francis de Sales.
Rutledge, William G. '53 (PIT) Reserve Township, PA St. Aloysius Church.
Rutler, George W. (NY) [HH] New York, NY Guild of Catholic Lawyers, The.
Rutler, George W. '81 (NY) [2] New York, NY St. Agnes Church; On Duty Outside the Archdiocese.
Rutowski, William J. '87 (SAG) [9] Bay City, MI St. Stanislaus Church.
Ruttle, Paul *c.p.* '80 (FgM) Passionist Foreign Missions.
Ruttle, Paul *c.p.* '80 (MET) [H] South River, NJ Passionist Provincial Office.
Rutz, Gil (PHX) [14] Phoenix, AZ St. Joan of Arc Church.
Rutz, Gilbert J. (PHX) [I] Phoenix, AZ Kino Institute.
Rutz, Gilbert J. '66 (COV) On Duty Outside the Diocese.
Ruvalcaba, Victor J. '96 (LA) Pasadena, CA St. Andrew Church.
Ruvo, Msgr. John A. '54 (NY) [174] Bronx, NY Our Lady of Mt. Carmel Church.
Ruyechan, Matthew *o.f.m.* '80 (E) [2] Sharon, PA St. Anthony Church.
Ruygt, Hans '85 (SR) Ukiah, CA St. Mary of the Angels Church.
Ruzich, Boniface *o.ss.t.* '59 (TR) [16] Trenton, NJ St. James Church.
Ruzicka, Gary J. '76 (CHY) Casper, WY Saint Patrick's Church.
Ruzzo, Paul F. '83 (MAN) [8] Manchester, NH St. Francis of Assisi Church.
Rweyemamu, Justinian B. '93 (NOR) Gales Ferry, CT Our Lady of Lourdes Church.
Ryalt, Lawrence *c.p.* '92 (BRK) [W] Jamaica, NY Bishop Molloy Retreat House for Laymen.
Ryan, Adam *o.s.b.* '90 (KC) [J] Conception, MO Conception Abbey.
Ryan, Alan J. *m.m.* '60 (NY) [DD] Maryknoll, NY Maryknoll Fathers and Brothers; [DD] Maryknoll, NY Maryknoll Fathers and Brothers.
Ryan, Albert J. '58 (FR) [12] New Bedford, MA St. Francis of Assisi Church.
Ryan, Alphonsus '64 (SD) Retired.
Ryan, Barry '76 (BRK) Absent on Leave.
Ryan, Msgr. Bernard J. '55 (RVC) Bellport, NY Mary Immaculate Church.
Ryan, C. Duane '54 (KC) Retired.
Ryan, Clarence R. '56 (KC) Retired.
Ryan, Cornelius J. *c.s.c.* '66 (FgM) Holy Cross Foreign Missions.
Ryan, Daniel J. '89 (TR) Holmdel, NJ St. Benedict Church.
Ryan, David '79 (CHI) [X] Chicago, IL Catholic Youth, Archdiocese of Chicago.
Ryan, Dennis K. '66 (DEN) Broomfield, CO Nativity of Our Lord Church.
Ryan, Dennis M. '74 (GB) Freedom, WI St. Nicholas Church.
Ryan, Donald L. '63 (L) Fairfield, KY St. Michael Church; Fairfield, KY St. Michael Church.
Ryan, Edmund G. *s.j.* '59 (SY) [B] Syracuse, NY Le Moyne College; [S] Syracuse, NY Jesuits at LeMoyne, Inc.
Ryan, Edmund K. *o.p.* '65 (P) Brookings, OR Star of the Sea Church.
Ryan, Edward '47 (ALB) Retired.
Ryan, Edward A. '71 (BRK) [197] Queens, NY Mary's Nativity Church.
Ryan, Msgr. Edward J. '33 (SY) Fayetteville, NY Immaculate Conception Church; Retired.
Ryan, Edward M. '74 (WOR) [10] Worcester, MA Our Lady of Fatima Church; Worcester, MA University of Mass Medical Center.
Ryan, Eugene D. '69 (VEN) [6] Sarasota, FL St. Thomas More Church.
Ryan, F. Lee '68 (JOL) Watseka, IL St. Edmund Church.
Ryan, Francis J. *c.ss.r.* '44 (STL) [P] Liguori, MO St. Clement Health Care Center.
Ryan, Francis J. *s.j.* '56 (FgM) Provinces.
Ryan, Francis J. '58 (PEO) Odell, IL St. Paul's Church.
Ryan, Francis X. *s.j.* '84 (CLV) [C] Cleveland, OH John Carroll Jesuit Community.
Ryan, Frank *o.m.i.* '54 (CR) Baudette, MN Sacred Heart Church.
Ryan, Frederick J. '64 (BO) Kingston, MA St. Joseph Church.
Ryan, G. Philip '88 (ATL) Washington, GA St. Joseph's Church.
Ryan, George J. '62 (BRK) [188] Queens, NY St. Joseph Church.
Ryan, Gerald E. '55 (DM) [10] Des Moines, IA St. Mary of Nazareth Church.
Ryan, Msgr. Gerald J. '45 (NY) [160] Bronx, NY St. Luke Church; Retired.
Ryan, Herbert J. *s.j.* '62 (LA) [C] Los Angeles, CA Loyola Marymount University.
Ryan, J. Patrick '76 (PAT) Rockaway, NJ St. Cecilia's Church.
Ryan, Jack '76 (HON) Holualoa, HI St. Michael The Archangel Church.
Ryan, James '60 (JUN) Retired.
Ryan, James *s.j.* '69 (RC) Kyle, SD Our Lady of Sorrows Church; Manderson, SD St. Agnes Church.
Ryan, James *s.j.* '74 (RC) Pine Ridge, SD Holy Rosary Church.
Ryan, James F. *s.s.e.* '56 (MOB) [H] Selma, AL Edmundite Fathers.
Ryan, James G. *o.s.a.* '49 (FWT) Abbott, TX Immaculate Heart of Mary Church; Penelope, TX Nativity of the Blessed Virgin Mary Church.
Ryan, James H. *s.j.* '69 (RC) Porcupine, SD Church of Christ the King.
Ryan, James M. '75 (COV) Melbourne, KY St. Philip Church.
Ryan, James R. '66 (CAM) Pennsauken, NJ St. Cecilia's Church.
Ryan, James S. *s.j.* '69 (RC) [B] Pine Ridge, SD Jesuit Community of Holy Rosary Mission.
Ryan, Msgr. James W. '48 (BRK) [39] Brooklyn, NY St. Fortunata Church; Retired.
Ryan, James W. '70 (BIS) Underwood, ND St. Bonaventure Church.
Ryan, John '45 (MAR) Retired.
Ryan, John '50 (SB) Highland, CA St. Adelaide Church.
Ryan, John *c.ss.r.* '53 (BO) [13] Boston, MA Our Lady of Perpetual Help Church.
Ryan, John '53 (Y) Absent on Leave.
Ryan, John '54 (ALX) Retired.
Ryan, John '64 (JOL) Park Forest, IL St. Mary Church.
Ryan, John '74 (NO) Lafitte, LA St. Anthony Church.
Ryan, John A. '70 (SFR) San Carlos, CA St. Charles Church.
Ryan, John Chrysostom *c.p.* '48 (BRK) [U] Jamaica, NY Immaculate Conception Monastery.
Ryan, Msgr. John F.C. '50 (FRS) Retired.
Ryan, John J. *o.p.* '42 (WDC) [11] Washington, DC St. Dominic Church & Priory Church.
Ryan, John J. '51 (PEO) Absent on Leave.
Ryan, John J. '71 (ORL) Ormond Beach, FL St. Brendan Church.
Ryan, John J. *c.s.c.* '90 (SCR) [C] Wilkes-Barre, PA Kings College.
Ryan, Msgr. John M. '55 (BUF) Eggertsville, NY St. Benedict Church.
Ryan, John M. '64 (CHI) [3] Waukegan, IL St. Dismas Church.
Ryan, John P. '63 (NEW) Fort Lee, NJ Madonna Church.
Ryan, Msgr. John R. '46 (PAT) Retired.
Ryan, Msgr. John R. '47 (PAT) [P] Chester, NJ Nazareth Village.
Ryan, John R. '50 (DM) Retired.
Ryan, John T. '56 (IND) [15] Indianapolis, IN St. Anthony Church.
Ryan, John T. *s.j.* '76 (NY) [FF] Staten Island, NY Mount Manresa Jesuit Retreat House.
Ryan, Joseph (PAT) Mount Arlington, NJ Our Lady of the Lake Church.
Ryan, Joseph '58 (SAG) Clare, MI St. Cecilia Church.
Ryan, Joseph A. *o.m.i.* '42 (BO) [Z] Tewksbury, MA Immaculate Heart of Mary Novitiate-Infirmary.
Ryan, Joseph D. '43 (CHI) [212] Chicago, IL St. Walter Church; Flossmoor, IL Infant Jesus of Prague Church; Retired.
Ryan, Joseph D. *s.j.* '43 (NY) [DD] New York, NY Murray-Weigel Hall.

Ryan, Joseph E. '47 (BO) Retired.
Ryan, Joseph F. '46 (SCR) Retired.
Ryan, Joseph J. '51 (STL) Retired.
Ryan, Joseph L. *s.j.* '51 (BGP) [O] Fairfield, CT The Fairfield Jesuit Community-Fairfield University.
Ryan, Msgr. Joseph P. '38 (DM) Retired.
Ryan, Joseph T. *d.d.* '45 (ALB) Retired.
Ryan, Kenan *s.t.* '59 (JKS) Philadelphia, MS Holy Cross Church.
Ryan, Kevin *o.s.b.* (HEL) Helmville, MT St. Thomas Church.
Ryan, Kevin *o.s.b.* '42 (IND) [J] St. Meinrad, IN St. Meinrad Archabbey.
Ryan, Kevin E. '70 (SAT) [53] San Antonio, TX St. Mark the Evangelist Church.
Ryan, Laurence D. *s.j.* '77 (BGP) [O] Fairfield, CT The Fairfield Jesuit Community-Fairfield University.
Ryan, Lawrence A. '42 (SAC) Vacaville, CA St. Mary Church; Retired and in Senior Ministry.
Ryan, Lawrence D. *s.j.* '77 (BGP) [D] Fairfield, CT Fairfield College Preparatory School.
Ryan, Msgr. Leo P. '54 (PAT) Retired; [P] Chester, NJ Nazareth Village.
Ryan, LeRoy F. *s.j.* '56 (DET) [P] Clarkston, MI Colombiere Center.
Ryan, Martin E. *s.j.* '48 (BO) [W] Weston, MA Campion Health Center, Inc.
Ryan, Msgr. Martin P. '76 (BGP) New Fairfield, CT St. Edward the Confessor Church.
Ryan, Michael G. '66 (SEA) [1] Seattle, WA St. James Cathedral.
Ryan, Michael J. '68 (SEA) Kent, WA Holy Spirit Parish.
Ryan, Michael J. '72 (PH) Bristol, PA St. Mark Church.
Ryan, Milton Fleming *c.m.* (SPC) [2] Cape Girardeau, MO St. Vincent de Paul Church.
Ryan, Noel '63 (LA) [66] Los Angeles, CA St. Gregory Nazianzen Church.
Ryan, Noel S. *s.s.c.* '63 (SD) [25] San Diego, CA St. Columba Church.
Ryan, Patrick '62 (SJ) [16] San Jose, CA St. Martin of Tours Church.
Ryan, Patrick '85 (PMB) On Duty Outside the Diocese.
Ryan, Patrick D. '70 (STL) [2] Lemay, MO Most Precious Blood Church.
Ryan, Patrick J. '58 (STP) On Duty Outside the Archdiocese.
Ryan, Patrick J. *s.j.* '59 (BO) [W] Chestnut Hill, MA The Jesuit Community at Boston College.
Ryan, Patrick J. *s.j.* '68 (FgM) Provinces.
Ryan, Patrick J. *s.j.* '68 (NY) [DD] New York, NY Jesuit Community at Fordham University.
Ryan, Patrick J. *m.m.* '77 (NY) [DD] Maryknoll, NY Maryknoll Fathers and Brothers.
Ryan, Paul *s.m.* '45 (SAT) [M] San Antonio, TX Marianist Residence.
Ryan, Paul *o.p.* '58 (SCL) Melrose, MN St. Mary's Church.
Ryan, Paul J. '73 (ROC) Aurora, NY St. Patrick Church; Cayuga, NY St. Joseph Church; King Ferry, NY Our Lady of the Lake, King Ferry Church; Union Springs, NY St. Michael's Church; [M] Rochester, NY Diocesan Office of Campus Ministry.
Ryan, Paul T. '58 (BO) [26] Boston, MA St. Gregory Church.
Ryan, Peter F. *s.j.* '87 (BAL) [B] Baltimore, MD Loyola College; [M] Baltimore, MD Jesuit Community of Loyola College, Inc.
Ryan, Philip J. '57 (SR) Guerneville, CA St. Elizabeth Church.
Ryan, Philip R. '57 (DAV) Keswick, IA Our Lady of Lourdes Church.
Ryan, Philip V. '57 (DAV) Sigourney, IA St. Mary's Church.
Ryan, Raymond R. *o.s.a.* '57 (JOL) New Lenox, IL St. Jude Church.
Ryan, Regis J. '66 (PIT) [3] McKees Rocks, PA St. John of God Church; Allegheny County, PA Ohio Valley General Hospital.
Ryan, Msgr. Richard '73 (STO) [9] Stockton, CA St. Michael Church.
Ryan, Richard '77 (PHX) Sun City, AZ Church of St. Joachim & St. Anne.
Ryan, Richard R. *c.m.* '69 (DEN) [M] Denver, CO Congregation of the Mission Midwest Province: De Paul House.
Ryan, Robert F. '47 (PH) Retired.
Ryan, Robin *c.p.* '84 (BRK) [U] Jamaica, NY Immaculate Conception Monastery; [W] Jamaica, NY Bishop Molloy Retreat House for Laymen.
Ryan, Robin C. *c.p.* '84 (BO) [A] Boston, MA St. John's Seminary School of Theology.
Ryan, Stephen *s.d.b.* '92 (PAT) [D] Paterson, NJ Don Bosco Technical High School.
Ryan, Stephen '95 (NY) [183] Bronx, NY St. Philip Neri Church.
Ryan, Stephen D. *o.p.* '93 (BO) [W] Dover, MA St. Stephen Priory.
Ryan, Steve *o.s.m.* (LA) [K] Los Angeles, CA Queen of Angels-Hollywood Presbyterian Medical Center.
Ryan, Steven '86 (AUS) Temple, TX St. Luke's Church.
Ryan, Steven P. *s.j.* '82 (AUS) [H] Temple, TX Jesuit Fathers and Brothers.
Ryan, T. Kenneth '30 (STP) Retired.
Ryan, Msgr. T. Peter '62 (RVC) Centerport, NY Our Lady Queen of Martyrs Church.
Ryan, Terrence P. *c.s.p.* '77 (KNX) [4] Knoxville, TN John XXIII Catholic Center Church; [J] Knoxville, TN UT-Knoxville, Newman Foundation, Inc.
Ryan, Thomas *o.m.i.* '43 (SAT) [K] San Antonio, TX Oblate Madonna Residence.
Ryan, Thomas '68 (FTW) Elkhart, IN St. Thomas the Apostle Church.
Ryan, Thomas '73 (BAL) [1] Baltimore, MD Cathedral of Mary Our Queen.
Ryan, Thomas A. '64 (GI) [1] Grand Island, NE Cathedral of the Nativity of the Blessed Virgin Mary.
Ryan, Thomas F. '93 (MET) [2] New Brunswick, NJ St. John the Baptist Church.
Ryan, Thomas J. '54 (SFS) Retired.
Ryan, Thomas J. '69 (OAK) [1] Berkeley, CA St. Ambrose Church.
Ryan, Thomas J. '79 (SY) Johnson City, NY St. James Church.
Ryan, Thomas M. *s.j.* (DET) [E] Detroit, MI University of Detroit Jesuit High School and Academy.
Ryan, Msgr. Timothy A. '57 (CAM) Cape May, NJ Our Lady Star of the Sea Church.
Ryan, Timothy K. '62 (SAV) Special Assignment.
Ryan, Vincent B. *s.j.* '45 (SY) [S] Syracuse, NY Jesuits at LeMoyne, Inc.
Ryan, William '55 (JOL) Retired; [I] Naperville, IL St. John Vianney Villa.
Ryan, William A. *c.m.* '41 (CHI) [C] Chicago, IL Vincentian Community at DePaul University.
Ryan, William A. *s.j.* '45 (PH) [AA] Philadelphia, PA Jesuit Community at St. Joseph's University.
Ryan, William A. *o.s.a.* '66 (P) Myrtle Creek, OR All Souls Church.
Ryan, William A. '80 (WDC) Gaithersburg, MD St. Martin Church.
Ryan, William Arthur '59 (PEO) Ransom, IL St. Patrick's Church.
Ryan, William B. *o.p.* '47 (HRT) [14] New Haven, CT St. Mary's Priory Church.
Ryan, William F. '62 (CAM) Bellmawr, NJ Annunciation Church.
Ryan, William F. *s.j.* '62 (SPK) [C] Spokane, WA Gonzaga University.
Ryan, Msgr. William H. '48 (ELP) [10] El Paso, TX Immaculate Conception Church.
Ryan, William P. *s.j.* '94 (BAL) [M] Baltimore, MD Jesuit Fathers and Brothers Maryland Provincial Curia.
Ryba, Charles J. '69 (CLV) Columbia Station, OH St. Elizabeth Ann Seton Church.
Rybacki, Czeslaw *s.ch.* '92 (SFR) [36] San Francisco, CA Nativity Church.
Rybarczyk, Melvin *c.r.* '69 (VNN) San Diego, CA Holy Angels Church.
Ryberg, James C. '57 (OM) Platte Center, NE St. Joseph Church.
Rybicki, Daryl '79 (FTW) [2] South Bend, IN St. Adalbert Church; [4] South Bend, IN St. Augustine Church.
Rybicky, Walter *o.s.b.m.* '83 (STN) [7] Palos Park, IL Nativity of B. V. M. Church.
Rybinski, Marvin '59 (DET) Retired.
Rybka, Damien *o.f.m.* '52 (GB) [I] Pulaski, WI Assumption of B.V.M. Friary.
Rybolt, John E. *c.m.* '67 (STL) [P] St. Louis, MO Vincentian Residence.
Rydelek, Theodore '89 (TYL) Fairfield, TX St. Bernard of Clairvaux Church.
Ryder, Frederick *c.pp.s.* '63 (CIN) Cassella, OH Nativity of the Blessed Virgin Mary Church; St. Rose, OH St. Rose Church.
Ryder, Joseph F. '46 (DET) Retired.
Ryder, Matthais '62 (ORG) Inactive Leave.
Rydz, Zygmund S. '48 (LIN) Retired.
Rydzon, Walter C. '76 (PIT) [55] Pittsburgh, PA St. Justin Church.
Rye, Gary C. *o.s.a.* '65 (LA) [31] Los Angeles, CA Mother of Good Counsel Church.
Ryfinski, Gerald J. '90 (CHR) Hartsville, SC St. Mary the Virgin Mother Church; [G] Hartsville, SC Coker College Newman Center.
Rykowski, Jerome A. '55 (PBL) Retired.
Rykowski, Valerian J. '43 (GAY) [D] Traverse City, MI Infant Jesus of Prague Monastery.
Rykowski, Valerian J. '43 (MIL) Retired.
Rykwalder, David L. '85 (GI) St. Libory, NE St. Libory's Church.
Ryland, Raymond '83 (SD) Unassigned.
Ryle, Edward J. '56 (PHX) Special Assignment.
Ryle, Edward J. '56 (TUC) On Duty Outside the Diocese.
Ryle, Gerald '68 (SAC) North Highlands, CA St. Lawrence Church.
Rymdeika, Joseph (PH) [D] West Chester, PA Bishop Shanahan High School.
Rymdeika, Joseph F. '82 (PH) Newtown Square, PA St. Anastasia Church; [A] Wynnewood, PA Theological Seminary of St. Charles Borromeo, Overbrook.
Rynda, Reynold *o.f.m.cap.* '54 (MIL) [P] Milwaukee, WI St. Conrad House.
Rynes, Theodore J. *s.j.* '62 (SJ) [B] Santa Clara, CA Santa Clara University.
Rynish, Msgr. John F. '43 (SPC) Retired.
Rynne, Msgr. James J. '59 (CAM) Deptford, NJ St. John Vianney Church.
Rynne, Paul P. (BO) Retired.
Rynne, Thomas '56 (PMB) Retired.
Rynne, Thomas J. '56 (PMB) Jensen Beach, FL St. Martin de Porres Church.
Rys, Paschal *o.f.m.conv.* '51 (OG) Constableville, NY St. Mary Church.
Ryscavage, Richard J. *s.j.* '77 (FgM) Jesuit Foreign Missions.
Ryscavage, Richard J. *s.j.* '77 (WDC) [M] Washington, DC Leonard Neale House; [V] Washington, DC Jesuit Missions, Inc.; [V] Washington, DC Jesuit Refugee Service.
Ryu, Hae-Wuk *s.j.* '91 (BO) [W] Cambridge, MA Faber House.
Ryu, Joseph *s.j.* '90 (MAN) Salem, NH St. Joseph Church.
Rywalt, Lawrence *c.p.* '92 (BRK) [U] Jamaica, NY Immaculate Conception Monastery.
Rzeczkowski, Matthew *o.p.* '69 (WDC) [B] Washington, DC Dominican House of Studies.
Rzepiela, Thomas R. '72 (CHI) [45] Chicago, IL St. Constance Church.
Rzeszutek, Martin *m.i.c.* '51 (SPR) [I] Stockbridge, MA Congregation of Marians.
Rzonca, Michael W. '73 (PH) Spring City, PA St. Joseph Church; Graterford, PA Graterford State Correctional Institution.

S

Saad, Antoun '47 (OLL) Retired.
Saad, Antoun '47 (SAM) Retired.
Saad, Msgr. Richard '72 (OLL) New Orleans, LA Maronite Catholic Community Church.
Saad, Msgr. Richard D. '72 (OLL) Birmingham, AL St. Elias Church.
Saade, Bassam '92 (SAM) Utica, NY St. Louis Gonzaga Church.
Saah-Buckman, Michael K. *s.s.j.* '93 (BR) [8] Baton Rouge, LA St. Francis Xavier Church.
Saale, Richard T. '50 (KC) Retired.
Saalfeld, Lawrence '44 (P) Retired.
Saathoff, Alexis *o.s.b.* '59 (KC) [A] Conception, MO Conception Seminary College; [J] Conception, MO Conception Abbey.
Saato, Fred '67 (NTN) Yonkers, NY Christ the Savior Church.
Saavedra, Juan de Dios '89 (CC) [H] Laredo, TX St. John's Priory, (F.J.).
Saba, Joseph '74 (JUN) On Duty Outside the Diocese.
Saba, Joseph '74 (TUC) [E] Tucson, AZ Carondelet Health Network.
Saba, Joseph J. '70 (BGP) [3] Bridgeport, CT St. Andrew Church.
Sabadell, Juan *l.c.* (PRO) [U] South Kingston, RI Hombre Nueva (RI), Inc.; [U] South Kingstown, RI Mater Ecclesiae, Inc.; [U] South Kingstown, RI Overbrook, Incorporated; [U] South Kingstown, RI The Legion of Christ (RI) Incorporated.
Sabadish, Joseph F. '45 (PH) Retired; [U] Norristown, PA Sacred Heart Hospital and Rehabilitation Center.
Saban, Michael J. '89 (PH) [157] Philadelphia, PA St. William Church.
Sabatini, Francis J. '63 (PH) [88] Philadelphia, PA St. Lucy Church.
Sabatino, Robert A. '56 (Y) Ravenna, OH Immaculate Conception Church.
Sabatos, Daniel C. '62 (BRK) Absent on Sick Leave.
Sabatte, Frank *c.s.p.* '80 (OAK) [2] Berkeley, CA Holy Spirit Parish.
Sabbagh, Stephen F. *o.f.m.* '59 (WDC) [M] Washington, DC Commissariat of the Holy Land, Franciscan Monastery - Mount St. Sepulchre.
Sabella, Charles A. '94 (MET) [L] Phillipsburg, NJ The Anawim Community.
Sabia, Msgr. John B. '64 (BGP) Monroe, CT St. Jude Church.
Sable, Msgr. Robert M. '74 (DET) Special Assignment.
Sable, Thomas F. *s.j.* '75 (SCR) [C] Scranton, PA University of Scranton; [C] Scranton, PA University of Scranton.
Sabo, Edward *t.o.r.* '68 (WH) Stonewood, WV Our Lady of Perpetual Help Church.
Sabo, Gerald J. *s.j.* '80 (CLV) [C] Cleveland, OH John Carroll Jesuit Community.
Sabo, Paul P. '69 (BUF) [68] Buffalo, NY The Visitation of the B.V.M. Church.
Sabog, Henry '60 (HON) Retired.
Sabol, Casimir *o.f.m.conv.* '49 (R) Hampstead, NC St. Jude the Apostle Church; [E] Wilmington, NC Conventual Franciscans O.F.M.Conv.
Sabol, Sebastian *o.s.b.m.* '34 (STN) Warren, MI St. Josaphat Church.

Sabourin, Gerard O. '60 (PRO) North Kingstown, RI St. Bernard Church.
Sabourin, Leo F. '58 (DET) [2] Taylor, MI St. Constance Church.
Sabulis, Paul P. '43 (HRT) [11] Waterbury, CT St. Joseph Church; Retired.
Saburo, Rusk R. '93 (CI) Koror, FM Sacred Heart Church; Babeldaob, FM Catholic Churches Church.
Sacca, Raymond '79 (OAK) [2] San Leandro, CA St. Alphonsus Liguori Church.
Saccacio, Msgr. Robert J. '61 (RVC) Amityville, NY St. Martin's Church.
Sacco, Carmine J. *s.j.* '57 (SEA) [11] Tacoma, WA St. Rita Church.
Sachs, John R. *s.j.* '76 (BO) [W] Cambridge, MA Weston Jesuit Community.
Sackett, Frederick *o.m.i.* '41 (SAT) [C] San Antonio, TX Oblate School of Theology.
Sackett, Fredrick '41 (SAT) [M] San Antonio, TX De Mazenod House.
Sackevich, Paul E. '84 (BUR) Chester, VT St. Joseph Church.
Sacks, Msgr. Edward R. '64 (ALN) [8] Bethlehem, PA Our Lady of Perpetual Help Church.
Sacks, Francis W. *c.m.* '67 (BIR) Lineville, AL The Vincentian Mission of East Central Alabama Church.
Sacks, Randall *s.j.* (BO) [B] Cambridge, MA Weston Jesuit School of Theology.
Sacus, Samuel S. '66 (WH) Beckley, WV St. Francis De Sales Church.
Sadaba, Eugenio *c.m.* '62 (SJN) [62] San Juan, PR San Vicente de Paul Church.
Sadek, Msgr. Ignace '56 (SAM) Brooklyn, NY Cathedral of Our Lady of Lebanon.
Sadie, P. Edward '57 (WH) [1] Charleston, WV Sacred Heart Co-Cathedral.
Sadler, Alfred H. '34 (DET) Retired.
Sadlier, Richard T. *s.s.j.* '63 (NO) [57] New Orleans, LA St. Raymond Church.
Sadlowski, Ronald F. '72 (SPR) Easthampton, MA Sacred Heart Church.
Sadowski, Robert J. *c.s.p.* (BO) [P] Boston, MA Paulist Center.
Sadowski, Robert J. *c.s.p.* '85 (BO) [W] Boston, MA Paulist Fathers Residence.
Sadowsky, James A. *s.j.* '57 (NY) [DD] New York, NY Jesuit Community at Fordham University.
Sadusky, Msgr. Joseph F. '70 (WDC) [37] Washington, DC St. Peter Church; Pastoral Center Special Ministries.
Saelzler, Richard '76 (TOL) [N] Bowling Green, OH Bowling Green State University Campus Ministry.
Saelzler, Richard J. '76 (TOL) Bowling Green, OH St. Thomas More University Parish.
Saenz, Alonso '97 (PHX) [12] Phoenix, AZ St. Gregory Church.
Saenz, Francisco J. '89 (SAC) Woodland, CA Holy Rosary Church.
Saenz, Roberto B. *s.j.* '59 (YAK) [3] Yakima, WA Holy Redeemer Church.
Saenz, Urbano *o.s.a.* '70 (MGZ) San German, PR St. Rose of Lima Church.
Saenz, Urbano *o.s.a.* '70 (SJN) [42] San Juan, PR Ntra. Sra. de la Monserrate Church.
Saez, Jose '49 (ELP) Retired.
Saez, Raul (SJN) [D] San Juan, PR Santa Ana Chapel.
Safiejko, Edward M. '48 (MIL) [19] Milwaukee, WI St. Charles Borromeo Church.
Safko, Gerard F. '90 (SCR) [18] Wilkes-Barre, PA Sacred Heart of Jesus Church.
Safko, Stephen '73 (PSC) Phillipsburg, NJ SS. Peter and Paul Church.
Safranek, William '96 (OM) [13] Omaha, NE St. Elizabeth Ann Church.
Safraniec, Joseph '76 (STU) On Duty Outside the Diocese.
Sagala, James F. '61 (PIT) Military Chaplains.
Sagardia, Reinaldo '79 (SJN) [32] San Juan, PR San Lucas Church.
Sagardoy, Angel '60 (LA) [1] Oxnard, CA St. Anthony Church.
Sagayaraj, Sekar '88 (NY) [222] Staten Island, NY St. Patrick Church.
Saglimbeni, Bernardine (NY) Bronx, NY U.S.V.A. Medical Center.
Saglio, Charles A. '74 (RIC) [E] Newport News, VA Mary Immaculate Hospital.
Sagorski, Peter A. '95 (ORL) Daytona Beach, FL St. Paul's Church.
Sah, Sushil '87 (DET) [K] Detroit, MI Jesuit Community at the University of Detroit.
Saharic, Michael C. '88 (MET) [1] Metuchen, NJ Cathedral of St. Francis.
Sahlfeld, Francis J. '48 (CIN) Retired.
Sailstad, Kenton '88 (DUL) Cloquet, MN Queen of Peace Church.
Saja, Thaddeus A. '46 (BO) [2] Boston, MA St. Adalbert Church; Retired.
Sajda, Michael *o.f.m.conv.* '79 (PMB) [B] Fort Pierce, FL John Carroll High School.
Sajdak, John *s.m.* (DET) [E] Harper Woods, MI Notre Dame High School.
Sajdak, Ronald P. '96 (BUF) [2] Orchard Park, NY St. Bernadette Church.
Sakalys, Raphael J. *o.f.m.* '53 (PRT) [I] Kennebunkport, ME St. Anthony's Friary.
Sakano, Msgr. Donald '71 (NY) [47] New York, NY Holy Innocents Church; [HH] New York, NY The Housing Fund of the Archdiocese of New York.
Saksons, Richard *o. praem.* '92 (BAK) Enterprise, OR St. Katherine's Church.
Sakwoicz, Gregory '79 (CHI) [132] Chicago, IL St. Mary of the Woods Church.
Sala, Charles *p.i.m.e.* '38 (COL) [H] Newark, OH P.I.M.E. Mission & Prayer Center.
Sala, Michael J. *s.j.* (NY) Manhattan, NY Metropolitan Hospital.
Sala, Michael J. *s.j.* '77 (NY) [80] New York, NY Nativity Church.
Salach, Conrad *o.f.m.conv.* (BO) [7] Lawrence, MA Holy Trinity Church.
Salada, Urbano '59 (SD) Retired.
Saladna, George E. '58 (PIT) Springdale, PA St. Alphonsus Church.
Salah, Michael A. '91 (WDC) [14] Washington, DC St. Francis Xavier Church.
Salamon, John *c.ss.r.* '45 (ORL) [F] New Smyrna Beach, FL St. Alphonsus Villa-Redemptorist Fathers and Brothers.
Salanitro, Alfred J. '89 (OM) Laurel, NE St. Mary Church.
Salanitro, Carl A. '70 (OM) [30] Omaha, NE Mary Our Queen Church.
Salas, Raul *o.m.i.* '80 (SAT) [F] San Antonio, TX St. Anthony Catholic High School; [M] San Antonio, TX St. Anthony Catholic High School House.
Salas, Sipio '50 (SFE) Retired.
Salas, Vicente *o.m.* '66 (PCE) [B] Ponce, PR The Pontifical Catholic University of Puerto Rico.
Salata, Gregory '94 (MEM) [16] Memphis, TN St. Louis Church.
Salatino, John C. '94 (SPR) [4] Westfield, MA St. Mary's Church.
Salazar, Alejandro '91 (CC) [3] Laredo, TX Holy Family Church.
Salazar, Alexander '84 (LA) [91] Los Angeles, CA St. Teresa of Avila Church.
Salazar, Cesar M. '93 (ORG) [6] Santa Ana, CA St. Anne's Church.
Salazar, Donald *o.f.m.* '67 (FgM) Franciscan Foreign Missions.
Salazar, Felipe '86 (SEA) Unassigned.
Salazar, Franklin '75 (RVC) Mastic Beach, NY St. Jude Church.
Salazar, George V. '67 (SFE) Las Vegas, NM Immaculate Conception Church; [M] Las Vegas, NM Highlands University Newman Center.
Salazar, Jairo '91 (SJN) [3] Toa Alta, PR San Jose Church.
Salazar, Jose Angel '85 (CC) Mathis, TX Sacred Heart Church.
Salazar, Joseph A. *m.s.a.* '77 (WH) Romney, WV Our Lady of Grace Church.
Salazar, Mario A. '61 (YAK) Grandview, WA Blessed Sacrament Church.
Salazar, Mario P. '90 (YAK) Quincy, WA St. Pius X Church.
Salazar-Jimenez, John '84 (AMA) Tulia, TX Church of the Holy Spirit.
Salberg, James G. '69 (PIT) Center Township, PA St. Andrew Church.
Salca, Louis A. '65 (SD) [4] El Cajon, CA St. Louise de Marillac Church.
Salcedo, Crescenciano *s.d.b.* '59 (LA) [R] Los Angeles, CA Dominic Savio Salesian Residence.
Salcedo, Cresenciano *s.d.b.* '59 (LA) [79] Los Angeles, CA St. Mary Church.
Salcedo, Luis G. '89 (WDC) [1] Bethesda, MD St. Bartholomew Church; Retired.
Salciccia, Ralph '49 (STU) Bellaire, OH St. John Church; Retired.
Saldana, Ermeregildo *s.t.* '94 (LA) Compton, CA Our Lady of Victory Church.
Saldana, Jesus '82 (MIA) [21] Miami, FL St. Joachim Church.
Saldana, Jose '61 (DAL) Bonham, TX St. Elizabeth Church; Bonham, TX Veterans Administration Hospital.
Saldanha, Vincent S. *s.j.* '85 (WDC) [M] Washington, DC The Jesuit Community at Georgetown University.
Salditos, Ricardito P. '80 (LUB) Morton, TX St. Ann Church.
Salem, George J. *o.s.b.* '40 (BIR) [E] Cullman, AL St. Bernard Abbey.
Salemi, Msgr. Cajetan P. '61 (NEW) Allendale, NJ Guardian Angel Church.
Salemi, Vincent *i.m.c.* '68 (SB) [7] Riverside, CA St. Francis de Sales Church.
Salemi, Vincenzo *i.m.c.* '68 (MET) [H] Somerset, NJ Consolata Society for Foreign Missions.
Salera, Alfredo J. (CHI) Evergreen Park, IL St. Bernadette Church.
Salerno, Emilio J. '59 (BRK) [41] Brooklyn, NY St. Frances Cabrini Church.
Salerno, Joseph '80 (SY) [13] Utica, NY St. Mary of Mt. Carmel Church.
Salerno, Joseph A. (CAM) Mantua, NJ Incarnation Church.
Salerno, Joseph A. '65 (CAM) Rosenhayn, NJ St. Mary's Church.
Salerno, Michael *s.a.c.* '93 (BAL) [54] Baltimore, MD St. Leo Church.
Saletrik, E. George '96 (GBG) Belle Vernon, PA St. Sebastian Church.
Salgado, Jose' *f.s.s.p.* '93 (SCR) [M] Elmhurst, PA Priestly Fraternity of St. Peter (F.S.S.P.), North American District Headquarters.
Salgueiro da Costa, Jose *i.m.c.* '73 (MET) [H] Somerset, NJ Consolata Society for Foreign Missions.
Saliba, John A. *s.j.* '65 (DET) [K] Detroit, MI Jesuit Community at the University of Detroit.
Salicone, Aniello *s.x.* '66 (BO) [W] Holliston, MA Xaverian Missionaries.
Salim, Anthony J. '74 (OLL) Youngstown, OH St. Maron Church.
Salinas, Octavio Jose *o.f.m.* '83 (NY) [4] Mt. Vernon, NY Our Lady of Mount Carmel Church.
Salisbury, Paschal Donald *o.p.* '67 (P) White City, OR U.S. Veternan's Affiars Domiciliary.
Salisbury, Paschal (Donald) '67 (P) Ashland, OR Our Lady of the Mountain Church.
Salisbury, W. Dayton *s.s.j.* '59 (BAL) [M] Baltimore, MD St. Joseph Society of the Sacred Heart House of Central Administration.
Saliva, Juan J. '90 (PCE) Yauco, PR St. Martin de Porres Church.
Salko, John H. '60 (PBR) Scottdale, PA St. John the Baptist Church.
Salkovski, Basil *o.s.b.m.* '88 (STN) Warren, MI St. Josaphat Church.
Saller, Neil *t.o.r.* '56 (PH) [AA] Fairless Hills, PA St. Anthony Friary.
Sallese, Albert J. '66 (BO) [33] Boston, MA St. John Baptist Church; [68] Boston, MA Sacred Heart Church.
Sallis, Steven '80 (SEA) Bothell, WA St. Brendan Church.
Sallot, Steven '80 (ORG) [8] Santa Ana, CA St. Joseph's Church; [C] Santa Ana, CA Mater Dei High School.
Salmani, Frank S. '82 (PRO) [4] Providence, RI St. Ann Church.
Salmi, Richard P. *s.j.* '82 (CLV) [C] Cleveland, OH John Carroll University; [C] Cleveland, OH John Carroll Jesuit Community.
Salmon, Charles P. '44 (DEN) Retired; [I] Denver, CO Gardens at St. Elizabeth.
Salmon, Edward F. *s.j.* (NY) [B] Bronx, NY Ciszek Hall.
Salmon, Edward M. '59 (CHI) [4] Oak Park, IL St. Giles Church.
Salmon, James F. *s.j.* '64 (BAL) [B] Baltimore, MD Loyola College; [M] Baltimore, MD Jesuit Community of Loyola College, Inc.
Salmon, William F. '65 (BO) [58] Boston, MA Our Lady of the Presentation Church.
Salnicky, Michael J. '93 (PSC) Old Forge, PA St. Nicholas Church.
Salocks, Stephen E. '80 (BO) [A] Boston, MA St. John's Seminary School of Theology.
Salois, Phillip (BO) Boston, MA Veterans Administration Hospital.
Salomon, Jean Francois (NEW) Retired.
Salomone, Gregory *o.p.* '72 (RIC) Charlottesville, VA St. Thomas Aquinas Church.
Salomone, Ramon A. *s.j.* '65 (FgM) Provinces.
Saloy, Lee John '72 (NO) [13] Metairie, LA St. Philip Neri Church.
Saloy, Thomas '88 (RVC) West Babylon, NY Our Lady of Grace Church.
Saltarin, Jose '67 (NEW) [18] Jersey City, NJ St. Nicholas Church.
Salter, Bartholomew *c.s.c.* (WOR) Spencer, MA Mary, Queen of the Rosary Church.
Saltry, Joseph A. '44 (SCR) Retired.
Saltysiak, Paul M. '92 (WDC) Military Chaplains.
Salus, Jude S. *o.s.b.* '75 (PAT) Cedar Knolls, NJ Notre Dame of Mt. Carmel Church; [M] Morristown, NJ St. Mary's Abbey.
Salvador, John '54 (PHX) Prescott, AZ Sacred Heart Church.
Salvador, Stephen B. '74 (FR) [4] Attleboro, MA Holy Ghost Church.
Salvagna, Michael *c.p.* '69 (PIT) [O] Pittsburgh, PA St. Paul of the Cross Monastery; [Q] Pittsburgh, PA St. Paul of the Cross Retreat Center.
Salvana, Bonifacio '56 (YAK) Waterville, WA St. Joseph's Church.
Salvas, John V. *o.f.m.cap.* '88 (SP) [6] Tampa, FL Most Holy Redeemer Church.
Salvaturian, Stanley Oleksy '82 (LR) Huntsville, AR St. John's Church.
Salvi, Americo *c.r.m.* '55 (NEW) Lodi, NJ St. Joseph's Church.

Salwach, Jeffery *o.f.m.* '84 (SAT) [46] San Antonio, TX St. Joseph Church.
Salwach, Jeffery *o.f.m.* '88 (SAT) [33] San Antonio, TX St. Clare Church.
Salwowski, Francis J. *o.f.m.cap.* '45 (PAT) [M] Oak Ridge-Milton, NJ St. Stanislaus B. M. Friary.
Salwowski, John F. *o.f.m.cap.* '45 (MET) [4] New Brunswick, NJ St. Joseph Church.
Saly, Msgr. Robert J. '85 (ALT) [3] Altoona, PA St. Mark's Church; [E] Hollidaysburg, PA Dmitri Manor Priests' Residence.
Salz, Marvin C. '64 (DUB) Lawler, IA Our Lady of Mt. Carmel Church; New Hampton, IA St. Mary's Church; [E] New Hampton, IA St. John's School.
Salzbrunn, Tony '52 (SCL) Dumont, MN St. Peter's Church; Wheaton, MN Ave Maria Church.
Salzmann, George S. *o.s.f.s.* '77 (BO) [CC] Cambridge, MA Harvard-Radcliffe Catholic Student Center.
Salzmann, George S. *o.s.f.s.* '77 (WIL) [I] Wilmington, DE Oblates of St. Francis De Sales.
Salzmann, George S. *o.s.f.s.* '78 (BO) [12] Cambridge, MA St. Paul Church.
Samaha, Jeffrey F. '78 (WDC) Hospital & Nursing Home Ministries.
Samaniego, Eduardo A. *s.j.* '90 (SD) [4] San Diego, CA Christ the King Church.
Samaniego, Tarciscio *l.c.* (HRT) [B] Cheshire, CT Novitiate of the Legion of Christ.
Samay, Sebastian A. '59 (GBG) [H] Latrobe, PA Saint Vincent Archabbey.
Samayoa, Emmanuel G. '89 (ROM) Dearborn, MI St. Mary Church.
Sambor, David R. '78 (SY) Special Assignment; [S] East Syracuse, NY Bishop Grimes Priests Residence.
Samiano, Marvin '92 (HON) Hilo, HI St. Joseph Church.
Sammon, Msgr. John F. '42 (ORG) Special Assignment.
Sammon, Peter J. '47 (SFR) [50] San Francisco, CA St. Teresa Church.
Sammon, Richard J. *m.m.* '56 (FgM) Maryknoll Foreign Missions.
Sammons, Msgr. Francis L. '47 (SY) Retired.
Sammons, Msgr. Frank L. '47 (SY) [S] East Syracuse, NY Bishop Grimes Priests Residence.
Sammons, Joseph F. '49 (SCR) Retired.
Sammut, Tito '52 (GB) New London, WI Most Precious Blood Church.
Samonie, Jacob '56 (DET) Retired.
Samperi, Charles J. '96 (GAL) [54] Houston, TX Notre Dame Church.
Sampietro, Vincent *c.s.p.* '45 (P) [28] Portland, OR St. Philip Neri Church.
Sampietro, Vincent J. *c.s.p.* '45 (NY) [DD] Jamaica Estates, NY Paulist Fathers Generalate.
Sample, Alex K. (MAR) [1] Marquette, MI St. Peter Cathedral.
Sample, Alexander K. '90 (MAR) [2] Marquette, MI St. Christopher Church; Special Assignment.
Sampon, Robert G. '53 (MIL) Newburg, WI Holy Trinity Church.
Sampson, Elric '85 (CHI) [N] Chicago, IL St. Peter's Friary.
Sampson, J. Gregory *c.j.m.* '54 (BUF) [1] West Seneca, NY St. Bonaventure Church; [O] West Seneca, NY St. Bonaventure.
Sampson, James *s.p.* '65 (SFE) [J] Jemez Springs, NM The Jemez Program, Our Lady of Lourdes Novitiate.
Sampson, James G. *s.j.* '87 (DEN) [M] Denver, CO Regis Jesuit Community (The Jesuits at Regis University).
Sampson, Patrick '55 (GF) Retired.
Sampson, William P. *s.j.* '59 (WDC) [E] Washington, DC Gonzaga College High School.
Samra, Basil '86 (NTN) Phoenix, AZ St. John of the Desert Church.
Sams, Ronald W. *s.j.* '59 (BUF) [D] Buffalo, NY Canisius High School; [O] Buffalo, NY Canisius Jesuit Community.
Sams, Ronald W. *s.j.* '59 (FgM) Provinces.
Samsa, Bert *o.f.m.cap.* (GB) Manawa, WI Sacred Heart Church.
Samsa, Bertin L. *o.f.m.cap.* (GB) Weyauwega, WI SS. Peter and Paul Church.
Samsa, John Francis *o.f.m.cap.* '61 (FgM) Capuchin Foreign Missions.
Samson, John F. '61 (SCR) Ashley, PA Holy Rosary Church.
Samson, Robert J. '79 (STL) [9] Florissant, MO St. Sabina Church.
Samter, James '87 (GB) Special Assignment.
Samudio, Francisco *c.m.* '92 (FgM) Vincentian Foreign Missions.
Samuel, Francis '72 (RVC) Seaford, NY St. James Church.
Samway, Patrick H. *s.j.* '69 (NY) [DD] New York, NY "America;" Residence and publication office of the America Press.
Samy, Edward '67 (SJ) Milpitas, CA St. Elizabeth Church.
Samy, S. Anthony '85 (NY) [138] Bronx, NY St. Dominic Church.
San Andres, Vito B. '79 (AGN) Yigo, GU Our Lady of Lourdes Church.
San Fratello, Sennen C. *o.f.m.* '58 (ALB) [B] Loudonville, NY Siena College.
San Juan, Alfonso *c.p.* (GAL) [S] Houston, TX Holy Name Retreat Center.
San Llorente, Faustino '41 (ARE) Retired.
San Llorente, Ricardo '53 (ARE) Retired.
San Marco, Salvator J. *s.j.* '53 (MIA) [5] Miami, FL Gesu Church.
San Martin, Miguel Angel *c.p.* '63 (MGZ) San Sebastian, PR San Sebastian Martir Church.
San Nicasio, Julian *s.d.b.* '76 (ARE) Orocovis, PR San Juan Bautista Church.
Sana, Yoshia '84 (EST) San Jose, CA St. Mary Assyrian-Caldean Parish.
Sanahuja, Manuel *sch.p.* '67 (LA) [92] Los Angeles, CA Santa Teresita Church.
Sanches, Joseph A. '70 (ATL) On Duty Outside the Archdiocese.
Sanches, Joseph A. '70 (NSH) [10] Nashville, TN Church of the Most Holy Name; [11] Nashville, TN St. Patrick's Church.
Sanchez, Alejandro '93 (STV) [1] St. Thomas, VI Cathedral of Sts. Peter and Paul.
Sanchez, Angel '90 (PCE) Salinas, PR Our Lady of Monserrat Church.
Sanchez, Angelo G. *c.ss.r.* '91 (MGZ) Aguadilla, PR St. Charles Borromeo Church.
Sanchez, Antonio '90 (MRY) Special Assignment.
Sanchez, Castor G. '61 (TR) [13] Trenton, NJ St. Francis of Assisium Church.
Sanchez, Eliseo '57 (LA) Retired.
Sanchez, Enrique '55 (SAC) [9] Sacramento, CA St. Anne Church.
Sanchez, Esequiel '95 (CHI) [148] Chicago, IL Our Lady of Grace Church.
Sanchez, Felix '65 (SP) Dade City, FL St. Rita Church.
Sanchez, Frank *o.carm.* (FgM) Carmelite Foreign Missions.
Sanchez, Frank *o.carm.* '54 (JOL) [J] Darien, IL Carmelite Provincial Office.
Sanchez, Guadalupe *o.s.j.* '60 (FRS) Madera, CA St. Joachim Church.
Sanchez, J. Antonio '90 (MRY) Watsonville, CA Assumption Church.
Sanchez, Jose '61 (BRK) [225] Queens, NY St. Paul the Apostle Church.
Sanchez, Jose *c.m.* '62 (MIA) Homestead, FL Sacred Heart Church.
Sanchez, Jose *c.m.* '62 (PH) [AA] Philadelphia, PA Congregation of the Mission.
Sanchez, Jose *c.m.f.* '95 (LA) San Gabriel, CA San Gabriel Church; [R] San Gabriel, CA Claretian Missionaries (Missionary Sons of the Immaculate Heart of Mary).
Sanchez, Jose M. '58 (GAL) Freeport, TX St. Henry Church.
Sanchez, Joseph '60 (SFR) Special Assignment; [K] San Francisco, CA Home for the Aged of the Little Sisters of the Poor.
Sanchez, Joseph G. '83 (LA) Lynwood, CA St. Philip Neri Church.
Sanchez, Juan '93 (CHI) [100] Chicago, IL St. Jerome Church.
Sanchez, Juan Luis '84 (MIA) [28] Miami, FL SS. Peter and Paul Church.
Sanchez, Juan Pablo *o.s.b.* '94 (TUC) [14] Tucson, AZ St. John the Evangelist Church.
Sanchez, Julio (SLC) Monticello, UT St. Joseph Church.
Sanchez, Julio '92 (SLC) Moab, UT St. Pius X Church.
Sanchez, Luis C. (NEW) North Bergen, NJ St. Brigid Church.
Sanchez, Msgr. Manuel O. '54 (LA) Pomona, CA Sacred Heart Church.
Sanchez, Marco Antonio *s.t.* '92 (SJN) Loiza, PR San Patricio Church.
Sanchez, Msgr. Paul R. '71 (BRK) [2] Brooklyn, NY St. Agatha's Church.
Sanchez, Prudencio '59 (WDC) Waldorf, MD St. Peter Church.
Sanchez, Raul '74 (GLP) On Duty Outside of Diocese.
Sanchez, Raul '93 (FRS) Earlimart, CA St. Jude Church.
Sanchez, Stephen *o.c.d.* '92 (LR) [A] Little Rock, AR Marylake - Carmelite Novitiate.
Sanchez, Stephen A. '82 (SFE) [13] Albuquerque, NM Queen of Heaven Church.
Sanchez, Steve '82 (SFE) Albuquerque, NM Lovelace Hospital.
Sanchez, Victor '90 (ARE) Quebradillas, PR San Raphael Church.
Sanchez, Vincente '88 (BRK) [24] Brooklyn, NY St. Brigid Church.
Sanchez, William E. '83 (SFE) [2] Santa Fe, NM Our Lady of Guadalupe Church.
Sancho, Jesus *o.c.d.* '64 (DAL) [20] Dallas, TX St. Mary of Carmel Church.
Sancho Piquer, Enrique '50 (PCE) On Duty Outside the Diocese.
Sand, John P. '55 (SPK) Dayton, WA St. Joseph Church; Pomeroy, WA Holy Rosary Church; Waitsburg, WA St. Mark Church.
Sandberg, Stuart '68 (NY) [HH] White Plains, NY Company of St. Paul.
Sander, Bernard *o.s.b.* '44 (P) [L] St. Benedict, OR Mt. Angel Abbey.
Sander, Francis *o.s.b.* '49 (NO) [P] St. Benedict, LA St. Joseph Abbey.
Sander, Reginald *o.s.b.* '63 (KC) Chillicothe, MO St. Columban's Church.
Sander, Timothy *o.s.b.* '41 (P) [L] St. Benedict, OR Mt. Angel Abbey.
Sanders, Daniel J. '78 (MIL) [4] Sheboygan, WI Holy Name Church.
Sanders, Dennis *c.r.* '67 (CHI) [D] Chicago, IL Weber High School; [N] Chicago, IL Provincial Office of the Congregation of the Resurrection.
Sanders, Edwin J. *s.j.* '59 (ALN) [A] Wernersville, PA Novitiate of St. Isaac Jogues.
Sanders, Msgr. John C. '73 (BGP) [4] Norwalk, CT St. Mary's Church.
Sanders, John R. *o.s.a.* '74 (SD) [C] San Diego, CA St. Augustine High School; [H] San Diego, CA Augustinian Community.
Sanders, Joseph P. *s.j.* '61 (WH) [A] Wheeling, WV Wheeling Jesuit University.
Sanders, Lawrence *c.ss.r.* '93 (DET) [33] Detroit, MI Holy Redeemer Church.
Sanders, Patrick B. '90 (NO) Reserve, LA St. Peter Church.
Sanders, Peter C. *c.o.* '84 (MRY) [G] Monterey, CA Oratorian Community-Congregation of the Oratory of Pontifical Right.
Sanders, Raymond *s.v.d.* '45 (WDC) [M] Washington, DC Divine Word College.
Sanders, William F. '75 (WOR) [28] Worcester, MA St. Stephen's Church.
Sandersfeld, John '66 (SJ) [3] San Jose, CA St. Francis of Assisi Church.
Sanderson, William E. '83 (OM) Hartington, NE Holy Trinity Church.
Sandhage, Martin J. '86 (LFT) Noblesville, IN Our Lady of Grace Church.
Sandheinrich, Msgr. Bernard H. '60 (STL) [46] St. Louis, MO Basilica of St. Louis, the King Church.
Sandi, Thomas P. '73 (NY) Military Chaplains.
Sandman, Gregory '80 (MRY) Watsonville, CA St. Patrick Church.
Sandmann, Augustus C. *o.s.a.* '47 (NY) [216] Staten Island, NY Our Lady of Good Counsel Church.
Sandor, Albert *o.f.m.cap.* '82 (DET) [K] Detroit, MI St. Bonaventure Friary.
Sandor, George *o.f.m.conv.* '72 (SY) [5] Binghamton, NY SS. Cyril and Method Church.
Sandoval, Clarence J. '87 (SLC) Logan, UT St. Thomas Aquinas Church; [H] Logan, UT St. Thomas Aquinas, Newman Center.
Sandoval, Jose Luis '74 (SAT) [25] San Antonio, TX St. Alphonsus Church.
Sandoval, Victoriano F. *o.s.a.* '59 (TR) Mount Holly, NJ Christ the Redeemer Church.
Sandoz, Robert *o.f.m.* '86 (R) [4] Raleigh, NC St. Francis of Assisi Church.
Sandrick, Philip *o.s.b.m.* '84 (STF) Long Island City, NY Holy Cross Church.
Sands, Francis *c.ss.r.* '47 (CHL) Concord, NC St. James Church.
Sands, Joseph C. *s.j.* '92 (BAL) [M] Baltimore, MD Jesuit Fathers and Brothers Maryland Provincial Curia.
Sandstrom, Philip J. '62 (NY) Absent on Sick leave; [HH] New York, NY St. Ansgar Scandinavian Catholic League.
Sandweg, Michael J. '79 (STL) Portage Des Sioux, MO St. Francis Church.
Saner, Daniel J. '69 (COV) Augusta, KY St. Augustine Church.
Sanfelippo, Frank J. '58 (MIL) Retired.
Sanfilippo, David '94 (PHX) [8] Phoenix, AZ St. Augustine Church.
Sanford, Harry L. *s.j.* '75 (PBL) [8] Pueblo, CO Our Lady of Mt. Carmel Church.
Sanford, James R. '86 (TOL) [C] Toledo, OH St. Francis de Sales High School; [K] Toledo, OH Oblates of St. Francis de Sales.
Sanford, Mark *o.f.m.* (L) [K] Louisville, KY St. Joseph Home for the Aged.
Sang, Andrew Dolinh *c.m.c.* (STP) [28] Minneapolis, MN St. Joseph Hien Church.
Sang, Francis '73 (RVC) Amityville, NY St. Martin's Church.
Sanger, Charles P. '37 (DEN) Retired.
Sangermano, Charles L. '78 (PH) [106] Philadelphia, PA St. Monica Church.
Sangiovanni, William F. '77 (BGP) [4] Trumbull, CT St. Theresa's Church; [C] Fairfield, CT Notre Dame Catholic High School.
Sangl, Harry R. '54 (PIT) Chippewa Township, PA Christ the Divine Teacher Church.
Sankoorikal, George '71 (BGP) [6] Fairfield, CT St. Pius X Church.

Sankoorikal, Paul L. '59 (LC) Bangor, WI St. Mary Church; [E] La Crosse, WI Franciscan Skemp Healthcare, Mayo Health System, La Crosse Campus Medical Center.
Sankovitz, Msgr. John P. '47 (STP) Retired; [C] St. Paul, MN University of St. Thomas.
Sanks, T. Howland *s.j.* '65 (OAK) [A] Berkeley, CA The Jesuit School of Theology at Berkeley; [N] Berkeley, CA Jesuit Community at Jesuit School of Theology at Berkeley.
Sanner, Msgr. James E. '59 (E) On Duty Outside Diocese.
Sans, Pablo '53 (BRK) [208] Queens, NY Our Lady of the Cenacle Church.
Sans, Theodore R. '59 (L) [3] Louisville, KY St. Albert the Great Church.
Sansaricq, Carl '51 (NY) Spring Valley, NY St. Joseph Church.
Sansaricq, Guy '60 (BRK) [65] Brooklyn, NY St. Jerome's Church; [T] Brooklyn, NY Catholic Migration & Refugee Office, Catholic Migration Services, Inc.; [Y] Brooklyn, NY National Center of the Haitian Apostolate.
Sansom, Lawrence W. '41 (ROC) Retired.
Sanson, Robert J. '67 (CLV) Strongsville, OH St. Joseph Church.
Sansone, Anthony J. '80 (BRK) [188] Queens, NY St. Joseph Church.
Sansone, Simon *o.c.s.o.* '89 (WOR) [N] Spencer, MA St. Joseph's Abbey.
Santa, Michael *o.s.b.* '56 (KCK) [H] Atchison, KS St. Benedict's Abbey.
Santa, P. Juan '85 (SJN) [5] San Juan, PR Asuncion de La Virgen Church.
Santa, Thomas M. *c.ss.r.* '78 (STL) [P] St. Louis, MO Redemptorist Fathers; [W] Liguori, MO Redemptorists Fathers dba Liguori Publications.
Santa Barbara, Robert L. '90 (MET) [7] New Brunswick, NJ St. Mary of Mount Virgin Church.
Santa-Bibiana, Joseph *s.d.b.* '66 (PAT) [3] Paterson, NJ St. Anthony's Church.
Santa-Olaya, Aureliano '63 (VEN) [7] Fort Myers, FL Hispanic Missions of Fort Myers Church.
Santaella, Esteban '58 (PCE) [3] Ponce, PR Church of the Resurrection; Jayuya, PR Our Lady of Monserrate Church; [B] Ponce, PR The Pontifical Catholic University of Puerto Rico.
Santamaria, Max '56 (MRY) Retired.
Santana, Edward '86 (CGS) [B] San Lorenzo, PR Casa Charlie Rodriguez; [E] San Lorenzo, PR Diocesan Shrine Our Lady of Mount Carmel; [F] Caguas, PR Diocesan Tribunal of Caguas.
Santana, Francisco '68 (MIA) [K] Miami, FL Shrine of Our Lady of Charity.
Santana, Franklin *m.c.* '72 (MGZ) Aguadilla, PR San Jose Obrero Church.
Santana, Ramon '89 (CGS) Yabucoa, PR Santos Angeles Cutodios Church.
Santangelo, Michael A. '95 (TR) Marlton, NJ St. Joan of Arc Church.
Santen, Thomas J. '70 (STL) [23] St. Louis, MO St. Ambrose Church.
Santerre, Richard R. '82 (BO) Belmont, MA St. Joseph Church; Health Leave.
Santiago, Angelo '88 (ARE) On Duty Outside the Diocese.
Santiago, Felipe *c.ss.r.* '81 (MGZ) Aguadilla, PR St. Charles Borromeo Church.
Santiago, Florentino '78 (HT) Lockport, LA Holy Savior Church.
Santiago, Francisco *s.j.* '64 (SJN) [22] San Juan, PR San Ignacio de Loyola Church.
Santiago, Hiran '92 (MGZ) Aguadilla, PR San Jose Obrero Church.
Santiago, Jesse *c.s.b.* '96 (GAL) Missouri City, TX Holy Family Church.
Santiago, Jose M. *o.p.* '93 (DEN) [29] Denver, CO St. Dominic's Parish.
Santiago, Juan J. *s.j.* '66 (SJN) [22] San Juan, PR San Ignacio de Loyola Church.
Santiago, Leoncio S. '73 (CHI) [69] Chicago, IL St. Genevieve Church.
Santiago, Manuel '85 (PCE) Jayuya, PR Our Lady of Monserrate Church.
Santiago, Marciano, II '78 (OAK) [2] Hayward, CA St. Bede Church.
Santiago, Msgr. Rafael '69 (PCE) [6] Ponce, PR San Conrado Church.
Santiago, Samuel *c.ss.r.* '76 (CGS) San Lorenzo, PR Nuestra Senora de la Mercedes Church.
Santiago Mateo, Victor *s.t.* '82 (FgM) Trinity Missions.
Santich, Jan *o.s.b.* '90 (SCL) [I] Collegeville, MN St. John's Abbey, of the Order of St. Benedict.
Santich, Jan J. *o.s.b.* '90 (CHY) Riverton, WY St. Margaret's Church.
Santillan, Juan *sch.p.* '69 (LA) [21] Los Angeles, CA Our Lady Help of Christians (Maria Auxiliadora) Church.
Santillanes, Jose Flavio '65 (SFE) Pojoaque, NM N.S. de Guadalupe del Valle de Pojoaque Church.
Santilli, Francis C. '80 (PRO) [2] Pawtucket, RI St. Cecilia Church; [C] Pawtucket, RI St. Raphael Academy.
Santini, Camillo *c.s.s.* '42 (BO) [Z] Waltham, MA Stigmatine Fathers and Brothers.
Santitoro, Francis E. '66 (TR) [4] Toms River, NJ St. Maximilian Kolbe Church.
Santo, Mark C. (MIL) Special Assignment.
Santo, Vincent '45 (SCL) Retired.
Santoalla, Jesus '57 (SJN) [25] San Juan, PR San Jorge Church.
Santor, John E. '65 (E) [12] Erie, PA St. Andrew Church; [M] Erie, PA Congregation of the Divine Spirit.
Santora, Alexander M. '82 (NEW) [19] Jersey City, NJ Our Lady of Czestochowa Church; [Q] Union, NJ Kean College.
Santora, Msgr. Gerard M. '38 (NEW) [11] Jersey City, NJ Holy Rosary Church; Retired; [N] Rutherford, NJ St. John Vianney Residence for Priests.
Santoro, Charles M. *o.p.* '71 (STP) [8] Minneapolis, MN Holy Rosary Church; [15] Minneapolis, MN St. Albert the Great Church; [N] Minneapolis, MN St. Albert the Great Priory.
Santoro, David *o.p.* '77 (DM) [10] Des Moines, IA St. Mary of Nazareth Church.
Santoro, David J. *o.p.* '77 (CHI) [N] River Forest, IL St. Thomas Aquinas Priory.
Santoro, Michael C. '80 (NEW) Bloomfield, NJ St. Valentine Church.
Santorsola, Albert J. '86 (PH) [D] Wyncote, PA Bishop McDevitt High School.
Santorsola, Albert J. '87 (PH) Abington, PA Our Lady Help of Christians Church.
Santos, Andrew J., III '97 (CHI) Matteson, IL St. Lawrence O'Toole Church.
Santos, Angel M. '77 (ARE) [9] Arecibo, PR La Milagrosa Church.
Santos, Cesar '93 (ARE) Vega-Alta, PR Immaculate Conception of Blessed Virgin Mary Church.
Santos, Cesar E. '93 (PCE) [B] Ponce, PR The Pontifical Catholic University of Puerto Rico.
Santos, Frankie L. G. *c.s.sp.* '84 (GAL) [B] Houston, TX Holy Ghost Fathers.
Santos, Gregory *o.c.s.o.* '59 (SLC) [F] Huntsville, UT Abbey of Our Lady of the Holy Trinity of the Order of Cistercians.
Santos, Maximiano *c.m.* '66 (SJN) [47] San Juan, PR Nuestra Senora del Pilar Church.
Santos, Raul '63 (CGS) Barranquitas, PR San Andres Apostol Church.
Santos, Sergio '85 (SFR) [7] San Francisco, CA St. Boniface Church.
Santos, Tomas '95 (ARE) Quebradillas, PR San Raphael Church.
Santos, Ubaldo *c.m.f.* '87 (SAT) Gonzales, TX St. James Church.
Santos, Victor '49 (SJN) [62] San Juan, PR San Vicente de Paul Church.
Santre, William *t.o.r.* '61 (ALT) [3] Windber, PA St. Anthony of Padua Church.
Santry, Robert '86 (HON) Military Chaplains.
Santucci, Hugo *s.d.b.* '55 (SFR) [12] San Francisco, CA Corpus Christi Church.
Santucci, Louis '74 (Y) Absent on Leave.
Santulin, Msgr. Joseph M. '39 (NY) Retired; [DD] New York, NY Pope John Paul II Residence.
Santurri, Joseph '42 (PRO) Retired.
Sanz, Eleutherio '59 (MRY) Soledad, CA Our Lady of Solitude Church.
Sanz, Florentino '65 (SJN) [4] Guaynabo, PR San Juan M. Vianney Church.
Sanz, Jose '73 (SB) [A] Riverside, CA Blessed Junipero Serra House of Formation.
Sanz, Jose '73 (WDC) On Duty Outside the Archdiocese.
Sanz, Julian '77 (TUC) Somerton, AZ Immaculate Heart of Mary Church.
Sanz, Martin '30 (SAT) [12] San Antonio, TX Immaculate Heart of Mary Church.
Saoncella, Valentino *m.c.c.j.* '44 (CHI) [N] La Grange Park, IL Comboni Mission Center.
Sapeta, Joseph S. '47 (NEW) Retired.
Sapio, Thadeus M. *o.f.m.* '65 (NY) [146] Bronx, NY Holy Cross Church.
Saplak, Sergio *o.s.b.m.* '92 (STN) Hamtramck, MI Immaculate Conception of B.V.M. Church.
Saporito, Msgr. Cosmo G. '54 (BRK) [18] Brooklyn, NY St. Bernadette Church.
Saporito, Louis R. *s.s.j.* '60 (GAL) [63] Houston, TX Our Lady Star of the Sea Church.
Saporito, Michael A. '92 (NEW) River Edge, NJ St. Peter the Apostle Church.
Saporito, Peter M. '77 (CAM) Mullica Hill, NJ Holy Name of Jesus Church; [E] Penns Grove, NJ St. James.
Sapp, James '86 (FTW) [B] Fort Wayne, IN University of St. Francis.
Sapporito, Msgr. Cosmo G. '54 (BRK) Retired.
Saprano, Samuel '71 (STU) Carlisle, OH St. Michael Church; Fulda, OH Immaculate Conception Church.
Sapuay, Orlando '73 (STL) [P] St. Louis, MO La Salette Missionaries.
Sara, Solomon I. *s.j.* '63 (BO) [W] Boston, MA The Society of Jesus of New England-Provincial Offices.
Sara, Solomon I. *s.j.* '63 (WDC) [M] Washington, DC The Jesuit Community at Georgetown University.
Sarachaga, Felix *c.m.* '52 (LA) [29] Los Angeles, CA Our Lady of the Rosary of Talpa Church.
Sarauskas, Msgr. R. George '73 (CHI) On Duty Outside the Archdiocese.
Sardina, John J. '60 (BUF) [10] Cheektowaga, NY Queen of Martyrs Church; [M] Clarence, NY Brothers of Mercy Nursing & Rehabilitation Center; [M] Clarence, NY Brothers of Mercy Sacred Heart Home, Inc.; [O] Clarence, NY Provincial Motherhouse of Brothers of Mercy.
Sardina, Jorge *s.j.* '59 (MIA) [D] Miami, FL Belen Jesuit Preparatory School; [H] Miami, FL Villa Javier.
Sardinas, Jorge '77 (MIA) [B] Opa Locka, FL St. Thomas University.
Sarge, John S. '73 (SAG) [10] Saginaw, MI St. Casimir Church; [11] Saginaw, MI St. George Church.
Sargent, John '53 (Y) Retired.
Sargus, Edward T. '39 (BAL) Retired.
Sariego, Francis *o.f.m.cap.* '69 (NEW) [N] Union City, NJ Capuchin Friars - Province of the Sacred Stigmata of St. Francis.
Sariego, Francis '69 (NY) [151] Bronx, NY Immaculate Conception Church.
Sarjeant, Francis X. *s.j.* '61 (BO) [W] Boston, MA The Society of Jesus of New England-Provincial Offices.
Sarjeant, Francis X. *s.j.* '61 (SP) [4] Clearwater, FL St. Cecelia Church.
Sarjumanarsa, Thomas *s.j.* '75 (CHI) [C] Chicago, IL Jesuit Community at Loyola University of Chicago.
Sarkies, Jeffery L. '65 (SEA) [25] Seattle, WA Holy Rosary Church.
Sarmiento, Oscar '78 (MIA) [2] Miami Beach, FL St. Joseph Church.
Sarmiento, Oscar '82 (PT) On Duty Outside the Diocese.
Sarno, Msgr. Robert J. '73 (BRK) Released from Diocesan Assignment.
Sarosiek, John H. '93 (GAY) Retired.
Sarrazin, Victor J. *c.m.* '85 (LA) [X] Montebello, CA DePaul Center.
Sarrazin, Victor J. '90 (LA) [R] Los Angeles, CA Amat House.
Sarrazine, Kenneth '62 (FTW) [5] Fort Wayne, IN St. Henry Church.
Sarro, John A. '79 (WIL) Bellefonte, DE St. Helena Church.
Sarsfield, Emmett W. '97 (YAK) [1] Yakima, WA St. Paul Cathedral.
Sartain, J. Peter '78 (MEM) [16] Memphis, TN St. Louis Church.
Sartor, Alfred J. *o.f.m.conv.* '58 (TOL) Carey, OH Our Lady of Consolation, Basilica-National Shrine Church; Frenchtown, OH St. Nicholas Church.
Sartorelli, Otto J. '50 (MAR) Caspian, MI St. Cecilia Church.
Sartori, Hector *c.s.* '54 (PRO) [4] Johnston, RI St. Rocco Church; Johnston, RI Port of Providence Catholic Chaplain.
Sartori, Peter V. '40 (STU) Retired.
Sarzynski, Msgr. Edward W. '79 (ALN) [2] Shenandoah, PA St. Casimir Church; [6] Shenandoah, PA St. Stanislaus Church.
Sas, Thomas J. '76 (HRT) [4] West Hartford, CT St. Mark the Evangelist Church.
Sasin, Jan '77 (NEW) [9] Elizabeth, NJ Our Lady of Most Holy Rosary/St. Michael Church.
Sass, Donald E. '60 (MIL) Milwaukee, WI St. Luke's Medical Center.
Sassano, Rock '63 (P) Lake Oswego, OR Our Lady of the Lake Church.
Sasso, Frank M. '73 (CHI) [102] Chicago, IL St. Joachim Church.
Sasso, Joseph M. '58 (ROC) [4] Rochester, NY St. Anne Church; Retired.
Sassone, James '57 (SD) [2] San Diego, CA Ascension Church.
Sastre, Raphael '51 (MGZ) Hormigueros, PR El Salvador Church.
Sasway, Msgr. John R. '62 (ALT) Lilly, PA St. Brigid's Church; Lilly, PA Our Lady of the Alleghenies Church.
Satchell, Martin J. '93 (PH) Absent on Sick Leave.
Sato, Damian *s.a.* '45 (NY) [DD] Garrison, NY Generalate of the Franciscan Friars of the Atonement-St. James Friary.
Satterfield, Msgr. Carroll E. '54 (BAL) Retired.
Sattler, Fred F. '70 (ALN) [8] Bethlehem, PA Our Lady of Perpetual Help Church.
Sattler, Frederick F. '70 (ALN) [4] Pottsville, PA St. Patrick Church.
Sattler, Henry E. *c.ss.r.* '76 (BAL) [68] Baltimore, MD Our Lady of Fatima Church.
Sattler, Henry V. '43 (BAL) [87] Baltimore, MD Sacred Heart of Jesus Church.
Sattler, Paul E. *c.pp.s.* '58 (KC) [8] Kansas City, MO St.

Charles Borromeo Church.
Sattler, Wayne V. '97 (BIS) [2] Minot, ND Our Lady of Grace Church.
Sauber, A. Michael '69 (STP) Lonsdale, MN Immaculate Conception Church.
Saucci, Ronald R. *m.m.* '65 (FgM) Maryknoll Foreign Missions.
Sauchelli, James J. (TR) On Duty Outside the Diocese.
Saucier, Thomas *o.p.* (CHI) River Forest, IL St. Vincent Ferrer Priory Church.
Saudis, Richard B. '55 (CHI) Berwyn, IL St. Odilo Church.
Sauer, Alban '59 (SCL) Retired.
Sauer, Anthony P. *s.j.* '71 (SFR) [E] San Francisco, CA St. Ignatius College Preparatory (Coed); [N] San Francisco, CA Jesuit Community at St. Ignatius College Preparatory.
Sauer, James '77 (EVN) [7] Evansville, IN Holy Rosary Church.
Sauer, John M. '85 (WIN) [1] Winona, MN Cathedral of the Sacred Heart.
Sauer, Simon *o.f.m.conv.* (L) [K] Louisville, KY St. Joseph Home for the Aged.
Sauer, Simon *o.f.m.conv.* '57 (L) [7] Louisville, KY St. Anthony Church.
Sauer, Timothy J. '76 (SEA) Ferndale, WA St. Joseph Church.
Sauerbier, Paul W. *c.m.* '68 (DAL) [6] Dallas, TX Holy Trinity Church.
Sauerwein, Msgr. Anthony '48 (BAL) [J] Timonium, MD Stella Maris Operating Corporation.
Sauerwein, Msgr. Anthony L. '48 (BAL) Retired.
Saul, James *o.s.b.* '52 (JOL) [J] Lisle, IL St. Procopius Abbey; [J] Lisle, IL St. Procopius Abbey.
Saulaitis, Antanas V. *s.j.* '69 (CHI) [N] Chicago, IL Lithuanian American Jesuits.
Saulenas, Simeon W. '44 (BO) [6] Cambridge, MA Immaculate Conception Church.
Saulino, Joseph A. '67 (LEX) Winchester, KY St. Joseph Church.
Saulnier, Joseph *f.m.s.i.* '72 (BO) [B] Framingham, MA Sylva Maria.
Saumell, Amaro '92 (SB) Ontario, CA St. Elizabeth Ann Seton Church.
Saunders, Allan L. '86 (SPC) Chaffee, MO St. Ambrose Church.
Saunders, Charles D. *c.m.* '43 (STL) [P] Perryville, MO Congregation of The Mission.
Saunders, Donald E. *s.j.* '84 (SP) [C] Tampa, FL Jesuit High School.
Saunders, Msgr. Douglas W. '65 (LA) [8] Long Beach, CA St. Joseph Church.
Saunders, John A. '40 (BO) Retired.
Saunders, Robert J. '41 (DUB) Retired.
Saunders, Ronald *s.m.* '59 (BUR) White River Junction, VT St. Anthony Church.
Saunders, Thomas C. *m.m.* '65 (FgM) Maryknoll Foreign Missions.
Saunders, William P. '84 (ARL) [3] Alexandria, VA Queen of Apostles Church; [B] Arlington, VA Notre Dame Graduate School of Christendom College.
Sauppe, Timothy J. '92 (PEO) Annawan, IL Sacred Heart Church.
Saurimakel, Joseph '75 (BRK) [T] Brooklyn, NY Catholic Migration & Refugee Office, Catholic Migration Services, Inc.
Sauter, David A. *s.j.* '72 (PH) [G] Philadelphia, PA St. Joseph's Preparatory School; [AA] Philadelphia, PA St. Joseph's Preparatory School Jesuit Community, Arrupe House.
Sauter, John '85 (GLP) Shiprock, NM Christ the King Church.
Sauter, Thomas M. '47 (DET) Rockwood, MI St. Mary Church.
Savage, Charles H. '81 (WH) Retired.
Savage, James W. '70 (BO) [12] Cambridge, MA St. Paul Church.
Savage, Paul J. '57 (PIT) Beaver Falls, PA Divine Mercy Church; Beaver County, PA Beaver Valley Geriatric Center.
Savage, Peter M. '89 (KC) Odessa, MO St. George Church.
Savage, Robert *s.d.b.* '46 (NY) [DD] New Rochelle, NY Salesian Provincial House.
Savage, Roger A. '77 (MIL) Eldorado, WI St. Mary Church; Woodhull, WI St. John the Baptist Church.
Savage, Thomas J. '47 (MAN) Retired.
Savage, Thomas J. *s.j.* '47 (OAK) [N] Oakland, CA Murray Residence Community.
Savage, Thomas J. *s.j.* '79 (BO) [W] Boston, MA The Society of Jesus of New England-Provincial Offices.
Savage, Warren '95 (SPR) Absent on Leave.
Savard, John *s.j.* '91 (BO) [W] Chestnut Hill, MA The Jesuit Community at Boston College.
Savard, Wilfred '48 (SFE) Retired.
Savarimuthu, Simon (NY) Staten Island, NY Staten Island University Hospital North.
Savary, James '60 (LR) Retired.
Savastano, Msgr. Anthony J. '56 (RVC) Woodbury, NY Holy Name of Jesus Church.
Savela, Erwin M. *c.s.v.* '71 (SFD) Edwardsville, IL St. Boniface Church.
Savelesky, Michael '73 (SPK) Walla Walla, WA St. Francis of Assisi Church; Walla Walla, WA St. Patrick Church.
SavelKoul, Leonard '95 (BIS) Fort Yates, ND St. Peter - Catholic Indian Mission Church.
Savial, J. Clarence '70 (LAV) [5] Las Vegas, NV Prince of Peace Church.
Saviano, Frederick L. '68 (BGP) [3] Danbury, CT Our Lady of Guadalupe Church.
Savickas, Michael G. '74 (DET) Walled Lake, MI St. William Church.
Savilla, Edmund '77 (SFE) Taos, NM Nuestra Senora De Guadalupe Church.
Savino, Dominic *o.carm.* '65 (LA) [B] North Hills, CA Carmel West Community; [F] Encino, CA Crespi Carmelite High School.
Savino, Michael A. '82 (CIN) Blanchester, OH Holy Name Church; Saint Martin, OH Saint Martin Church; [B] Cincinnati, OH Mt. St. Mary's Seminary of the West.
Savinski, John M. *m.div.* '71 (ALN) [A] Northampton, PA Mary Immaculate Seminary.
Savinski, John M. '71 (PH) [A] Wynnewood, PA Theological Seminary of St. Charles Borromeo, Overbrook.
Savio, John '67 (CHY) Rock Springs, WY Our Lady of Sorrows Church; Rock Springs, WY Our Lady of Sorrows/Sts. Cyril & Methodius Church; [F] Rock Springs, WY Rock Springs Catholic School Foundation.
Savio, Michael G. '92 (MIL) [59] Milwaukee, WI Our Lady of Lourdes Church.
Savio, Samuel '83 (NY) [1] New Rochelle, NY Blessed Sacrament Church.
Savitt, Alan F. '73 (PAT) [3] Clifton, NJ St. Brendan Church.
Savoca, Americo '93 (NY) Carmel, NY St. James the Apostle Church.
Savoie, Johnny S. '95 (MOB) [4] Mobile, AL St. Dominic Church.
Savoree, John M. (SFD) Altamont, IL St. Clare Church; Edgewood, IL St. Anne Church; St. Elmo, IL St. Bonaventure Church; St. Elmo, IL St. Mary Church.
Savukynas, John *m.i.c.* '44 (JOL) Plano, IL St. Mary Church.
Saw, Paul Fatt Lean *f.m.s.* '81 (CHI) [N] Chicago, IL Passionist Community-CTU.
Sawdy, Wallace E. '51 (HBG) Retired.
Sawher, Msgr. Clifford F. '52 (DET) Retired.
Sawicki, Eugene A. '86 (NY) [100] New York, NY Our Lady of Vilna Church.
Sawicki, Gregory *s.d.s.* '86 (SAT) Cestohowa, TX Nativity of the Blessed Virgin Mary Church; Hobson, TX St. Boniface Church.
Sawicki, Henry *c.m.* '36 (HRT) [18] New Haven, CT St. Stanislaus Church.
Sawicki, John *c.s.s.p.* (BO) [1] Somerville, MA St. Ann Church.
Sawicki, John A. *c.s.sp.* '86 (PH) [AA] Bensalem, PA Congregation of the Holy Ghost.
Sawyer, Don (OLL) Tulsa, Maronite Catholic Community Church.
Sawyer, Don '74 (OLL) Baton Rouge, LA Maronite Catholic Community Church; Lake Charles, LA Maronite Catholic Community Church.
Sawyer, Donald '74 (OLL) Austin, TX Our Lady's Maronite Parish.
Sawyer, Lucien A. *o.m.i.* (BO) Dorchester, MA Daughters of Charity National Health System - Boston, Inc.
Sawyer, Lucien A. *o.m.i.* '49 (BO) [Q] Boston, MA Daughters of Charity National Health System - Boston, Inc.
Sawyer, Michael *o.s.b.* '74 (HON) [H] Waialua, Oahu, HI Benedictine Monastery of Hawaii.
Sax, John C. '73 (NO) [1] New Orleans, LA St. Louis Cathedral.
Saxon, JaVan J. (R) Rocky Mount, NC Our Lady of Perpetual Help Church.
Say, Celestino '58 (VIC) [3] Victoria, TX Our Lady of Lourdes Church.
Say, James K. '60 (TOL) Tiffin, OH St. Joseph Church.
Sayasaya, Fernando '95 (FAR) West Fargo, ND Blessed Sacrament Church.
Sayers, Gle n *s.d.s.* '97 (NSH) Cookeville, TN St. Thomas Aquinas Church.
Sayers, Glen '97 (NSH) Sparta, TN St. Andrew Church.
Sayers, James M. '58 (CHI) Homewood, IL St. Joseph Church.
Sayers, Monty '86 (E) Frenchtown, PA St. Hippolyte Church.
Sayers, Raymond J. '64 (DET) [41] Detroit, MI St. Jude Church.
Sayes, Ronald '57 (DET) [1] Westland, MI St. Bernardine Church.
Sayles, Bartholomew *o.s.b.* '48 (SCL) [I] Collegeville, MN St. John's Abbey, of the Order of St. Benedict.
Saylor, Msgr. Philip P. '55 (ALT) Philipsburg, PA SS. Peter and Paul Church.
Sazama, Warren J. *s.j.* '77 (MIL) [P] Milwaukee, WI Jesuit Provincial Office, Wisconsin Province; [P] Milwaukee, WI Pere Marquette House Jesuit Community; [Y] Milwaukee, WI The Jesuit Partnership.
Sbordone, Gaetano J. '83 (BRK) [212] Queens, NY Our Lady of Hope Church.
Scadron, Christopher '83 (RC) Retired.
Scafidi, William *m.ss.a.* '83 (NY) [1] New York, NY Cathedral of St. Patrick.
Scafidi, William A. '83 (NY) [3] Newburgh, NY St. Mary Church.
Scaglione, Paul A. '73 (TR) Manalapan, NJ St. Thomas More Church.
Scagnelli, Louis *o.c.d.* '42 (SAT) [18] San Antonio, TX Our Lady of Mt. Carmel and St. Therese, Discalced Carmelite Fathers National Shrine of the Little Flower Church; [M] San Antonio, TX Discalced Carmelites (Prov. of St. Therese).
Scagnelli, Peter J. '76 (PRO) Absent on Leave.
Scahill, James J. '74 (SPR) [16] Springfield, MA St. Mary's Church.
Scahill, John J. '46 (PRT) [1] Portland, ME Cathedral of the Immaculate Conception; Retired.
Scala, Thomas A. '73 (HBG) Milton, PA St. Joseph Church.
Scalco, Joseph *c.s.j.* '78 (LA) [D] Lancaster, CA Paraclete High School.
Scalco, Joseph *c.s.j.* '79 (LA) Lancaster, CA Blessed Junipero Serra Church.
Scales, Donald *o.s.b.* '55 (RIC) [7] Richmond, VA St. Benedict Church.
Scales, Donald F. *o.s.b.* '55 (RIC) [L] Richmond, VA Mary Mother of the Church Abbey.
Scales, George B. '88 (FR) Falmouth, MA St. Patrick's Church.
Scaletty, Thomas F. '63 (WCH) [15] Wichita, KS St. Jude Church.
Scalia, Paul D. '96 (ARL) Springfield, VA St. Bernadette's Church.
Scallon, Joseph D. *s.j.* '57 (MIL) [P] Wauwatosa, WI Jesuit Community at St. Camillus.
Scallon, Kevin *c.m.* '61 (SP) [T] Palm Harbor, FL St. Vincent Ministry to Priests, Inc.
Scalone, Jonathan '87 (FWT) Lewisville, TX St. Philip the Apostle Church.
Scanagatta, Joseph *s.d.b.* '47 (SFR) [N] San Francisco, CA Salesian Provincial Residence.
Scanlan, Charles V. '54 (NEW) Retired; [N] Rutherford, NJ St. John Vianney Residence for Priests.
Scanlan, Cornelius J. *o.m.i.* '59 (SAN) Big Spring, TX Sacred Heart Church; Big Spring, TX St. Thomas Church.
Scanlan, Msgr. Edward J. '53 (BUF) [13] Niagara Falls, NY St. Stanislaus Kostka Church; Retired.
Scanlan, Francis G. '61 (CHI) [25] Chicago, IL St. Bede the Venerable Church.
Scanlan, Msgr. John J. '59 (WDC) Lanham, MD St. Matthias Church.
Scanlan, Kevin *s.m.a.* '55 (NEW) [N] Tenafly, NJ Society of African Missions, Provincialate, S.M.A. Fathers.
Scanlan, Lambert '33 (GB) Retired.
Scanlan, Michael *t.o.r.* '64 (STU) [A] Steubenville, OH Franciscan University of Steubenville; [F] Steubenville, OH Holy Spirit Monastery.
Scanlan, Michael J. *o.s.a.* '64 (PH) [AA] Villanova, PA St. John Stone Friary.
Scanlan, Patrick J. '28 (SB) Retired.
Scanlan, William J. '72 (BO) Health Leave.
Scanlin, Joseph T. '89 (HBG) Carlisle, PA St. Patrick Church; [K] Harrisburg, PA Catholic Campus Ministry.
Scanlon, Msgr. Bernard S. '45 (BGP) Retired; [O] Stamford, CT Our Lady Queen of the Clergy Home.
Scanlon, Charles *s.v.d.* '54 (FgM) Society of the Divine Word Foreign Missions.
Scanlon, Frank '83 (NY) [27] New York, NY St. Columba Church.
Scanlon, James M. *m.m.* '52 (NY) [DD] Maryknoll, NY Maryknoll Fathers and Brothers.
Scanlon, John J. '42 (PIT) Retired.
Scanlon, Msgr. John J. '53 (NY) Scarsdale, NY Immaculate Heart of Mary Church.
Scanlon, Michael J. *o.s.a.* '64 (PH) [C] Villanova, PA Villanova University.
Scanlon, Michael M. *o.s.m.* '30 (CHI) [N] Chicago, IL Servite Friars - Eastern Province.
Scanlon, Paul E. *o.p.* '59 (P) [N] McKenzie Bridge, OR St. Benedict Lodge-Dominican Retreat & Conference Center.
Scanlon, Peter J. '57 (WOR) [16] Worcester, MA Sacred Heart Church; [Q] Worcester, MA Campus Ministry; [Q] Worcester, MA Campus Ministry; [Q] Worcester, MA Campus Ministry; [Q] Worcester, MA Campus Ministry.
Scanlon, Regis *o.f.m.cap.* '72 (DEN) [M] Denver, CO St. Francis of Assisi Friary.
Scanlon, Richard M. '28 (RVC) Blue Point, NY Our Lady of the Snow Church; Retired.
Scanlon, Msgr. Thomas F. '49 (NY) [2] Mt. Vernon, NY Our Lady of Victory Church.
Scanlon, Msgr. Thomas J. '59 (PH) [6] Norristown, PA St. Titus Church.

Scanlon, Thomas M. *t.o.r.* '53 (SP) [6] St. Petersburg, FL St. Mary Our Lady of Grace Church.
Scanlon, Thomas R. '57 (BAK) Retired.
Scanlon, Wilfred *c.p.* '45 (MET) [H] South River, NJ Passionist Provincial Office.
Scanlon, William J. *s.j.* '70 (NY) [DD] New York, NY St. Ignatius Loyola Residence; [HH] New York, NY Jesuit Seminary and Mission Bureau, Inc.
Scannel, Anthony *o.f.m.cap.* '55 (LA) [F] La Canada Flintridge, CA St. Francis High School.
Scannell, Anthony *o.f.m.cap.* '55 (MIL) [Y] Milwaukee, WI Santa Fe Communications, Inc.
Scannell, John W. '34 (DEN) Retired.
Scannell, Joseph S. *s.j.* '50 (WOR) [N] Worcester, MA Jesuits of Holy Cross College, Inc.
Scannell, Msgr. Peter '46 (ORG) Retired.
Scannell, Msgr. Thomas P. '37 (ARL) [2] Arlington, VA St. Agnes Church; Retired.
Scannell, Timothy J. '69 (NY) Irvington-on-the-Hudson, NY Immaculate Conception Church.
Scantlebury, Neil (STV) [1] Cruz Bay, VI Our Lady of Mt. Carmel Parish.
Scantlin, Joseph S. '59 (FWT) [2] Arlington, TX Most Blessed Sacrament Church.
Scaramella, Renzo L. '95 (NEW) Plainfield, NJ St. Mary Church.
Scaramuzzo, Peter C. '66 (NY) [1] White Plains, NY St. Anthony Church.
Scarangella, Joseph A. '92 (NEW) Cliffside Park, NJ Epiphany Church.
Scarangello, John R. *o.f.m.* '81 (NY) [DD] Mount Vernon, NY St. Bernardine of Siena Friary.
Scarborough, Henry *o.c.s.o.* '63 (WOR) [N] Spencer, MA St. Joseph's Abbey.
Scarcella, Philip J. '77 (MET) On Duty Outside the Diocese.
Scarcello, Michael S. '56 (B) Rathdrum, ID St. Stanislaus Church.
Scarcia, John J. '74 (PH) East Greenville, PA St. Philip Neri Church.
Scardella, Joseph E. '81 (SY) [7] Syracuse, NY Our Lady of Pompei Church.
Scarfia, Gabriel *o.f.m., s.t.d.* '64 (BUF) [A] East Aurora, NY Christ the King Seminary.
Scarmozzino, Steven P. '97 (RVC) Garden City, NY St. Joseph's Church.
Scepaniak, Russell G. '93 (WIN) Le Roy, MN St. Patrick's Church; Spring Valley, MN St. Ignatius Church.
Scerbo, Joseph *s.a.* '70 (NY) [DD] Garrison, NY Generalate of the Franciscan Friars of the Atonement-St. James Friary.
Sceski, Alfred P. '91 (HBG) Camp Hill, PA Good Shepherd Church.
Scesney, Everard S. *o.f.m.* '68 (GB) Aniwa, WI St. Boniface Church; Birnamwood, WI St. Philomena Church.
Scezney, Leonard J. '85 (DEN) Absent on Leave.
Schaab, Dennis *c.pp.s.* '68 (JC) Warsaw, MO St. Ann Church.
Schaab, Denny M. '76 (STL) Webster Groves, MO Annunciation Church.
Schaab, R. Michael '71 (PEO) Orion, IL Mary, Our Lady of Peace Church.
Schaab, Thomas J. '74 (STL) [2] Florissant, MO Our Lady of Fatima Church.
Schaad, Jerome *s.c.j.* '66 (MIL) [P] Hales Corners, WI Priests of the Sacred Heart; [P] Hales Corners, WI Sacred Heart Monastery.
Schaaf, Paul F. *c.pp.s.* '60 (CIN) [M] Dayton, OH Provincial House of the Cincinnati Province of the Society of the Precious Blood.
Schaal, John K. (SCR) La Plume, PA Keystone Junior College.
Schaal, John K. '96 (SCR) Clarks Summit, PA Our Lady of the Snows Church.
Schabel, Joseph A. '56 (SAG) Retired.
Schabowski, Henry F. '60 (TR) [15] Trenton, NJ St. Hedwig Church.
Schackmuth, William A. '47 (CHI) Norridge, IL Divine Savior Church; Retired.
Schad, Edward '48 (OM) [39] Omaha, NE St. Richard Church.
Schad, Edward '49 (OM) [H] Omaha, NE Mercy Villa.
Schad, Joseph J. *s.j.* '91 (BO) [W] Boston, MA The Society of Jesus of New England-Provincial Offices.
Schad, Sylvester *o.s.b.* '38 (CC) [H] Sandia, TX Corpus Christi Abbey.
Schade, Martin J. *s.j.* '88 (FgM) Provinces.
Schaden, J. Robert '62 (DET) [S] Livonia, MI Schoolcraft College, Newman House.
Schaedel, Joseph F. '82 (IND) [15] Indianapolis, IN St. Anthony Church; Brownsburg, IN St. Malachy Church.
Schaefer, Bernard *o.s.b.* '56 (RCK) [H] Aurora, IL Marmion Abbey-St. Augustine's Abbey.
Schaefer, Dennis R. '75 (BEL) Chester, IL St. Mary Help of Christians Church.
Schaefer, Edgar J. '54 (WIN) Retired.
Schaefer, Edward F. '75 (BEL) St. Rose, IL St. Rose Church.
Schaefer, Ferdinand T. *o.carm.* '48 (BO) [P] Peabody, MA Catholic Information Center; [BB] Peabody, MA St. Theresa Carmelite Chapel.
Schaefer, Francis R. '55 (COL) Retired.
Schaefer, James F. '61 (LC) Dorchester, WI St. Louis Church.
Schaefer, Joseph P. *o.s.f.s.* '56 (CAM) [M] Pittsgrove, NJ Villa St. Joseph.
Schaefer, Kenneth J. '74 (BEL) Herrin, IL Our Lady of Mount Carmel Church.
Schaefer, Les F. *c.s.b.* '61 (OAK) [C] Oakland, CA Bishop O'Dowd High School.
Schaefer, Martin T. '92 (WIN) Pipestone, MN St. Leo's Church.
Schaefer, Philip *c.p.* '58 (DET) [K] Detroit, MI St. Paul of the Cross Community, Congregation of the Passion.
Schaefer, Richard Allen '96 (PMB) Port St. Lucie, FL St. Lucie Church.
Schaefer, Richard L. '68 (DUB) [C] Dubuque, IA Loras College.
Schaefer, Roman J. '42 (MIA) [2] Fort Lauderdale, FL Our Lady Queen of Martyrs Church.
Schaefer, Roman J. '42 (NU) Retired.
Schaefer, Thomas '53 (WDC) Retired.
Schaefer, Thomas *c.s.sp.* '82 (PIT) [B] Pittsburgh, PA Duquesne University of the Holy Ghost.
Schaefer, Thomas G. *c.s.sp.* '82 (PIT) [40] Pittsburgh, PA St. Patrick-St. Stanislaus Kostka Church.
Schaefer, Verne B. '55 (MIL) Retired.
Schaefer, Vernon J. '45 (WIN) Retired.
Schaeffer, Bradley M. *s.j.* '77 (CHI) [D] Chicago, IL St. Ignatius Jesuit Community.
Schaeffer, Bradley M. *s.j.* '77 (FgM) Provinces.
Schaeffer, Bradley M. *s.j.* '77 (WDC) [M] Washington, DC Leonard Neale House.
Schaeffer, Bradley W. *s.j.* '77 (CHI) [N] Chicago, IL Chicago Province of the Society of Jesus-Provincial Office.
Schaeffer, Richard C. '83 (MAR) Wells, MI St. Anthony Church.
Schaeflein, Msgr. Charles J. '49 (PH) Retired; [V] Philadelphia, PA Mount Nazareth.
Schaeufele, Robert L. '75 (SP) [3] St. Petersburg, FL Holy Cross Church.
Schafer, Dennis *o.f.m.* '80 (SFD) [B] Quincy, IL Quincy University.
Schafer, Dennis R. '89 (BIS) Mott, ND St. Vincent de Paul Church.
Schafer, Raymond E. '89 (IND) Aurora, IN St. Mary of the Immaculate Conception Church.
Schafer, William *s.d.b.* '61 (LA) [R] Los Angeles, CA Dominic Savio Salesian Residence.
Schaff, Tyrone J. '73 (SPK) [13] Spokane, WA St. John Vianney Church.
Schaffer, Gregory J. '94 (STP) On Duty Outside the Archdiocese.
Schaffer, Msgr. Gregory T. '60 (NU) On Duty Outside the Diocese.
Schaffer, J. Darrell '90 (DEN) [6] Denver, CO Christ the King Church.
Schaffner, Mark J. *o.carm.* '89 (GAL) [3] Houston, TX St. Albert of Trapani Church.
Schaffner, William E. '48 (ALN) [A] Wernersville, PA Novitiate of St. Isaac Jogues.
Schaftlein, Stephen '78 (IND) Greensburg, IN St. Mary Church.
Schaible, Donald '89 (ALN) Orefield, PA St. Joseph The Worker Church.
Schaible, Donald J. '89 (ALN) [C] Allentown, PA Allentown Central Catholic High School.
Schak, John R. *s.j.* '61 (FgM) Provinces.
Schak, John R. *s.j.* '61 (MIL) [P] Milwaukee, WI Jesuit Provincial Office, Wisconsin Province.
Schalk, Sebastian R. *o.praem.* '60 (GB) [I] De Pere, WI St. Norbert Abbey.
Schall, James V. *s.j.* '63 (WDC) [M] Washington, DC The Jesuit Community at Georgetown University.
Schallberger, Meinrad *o.s.b.* '64 (B) [C] Jerome, ID Ascension Priory.
Schaller, Harvey B. *o.p.* '37 (CIN) [30] Cincinnati, OH St. Gertrude Church; [M] Cincinnati, OH St. Gertrude Priory.
Schaller, Pascal *o.f.m.cap.* '51 (PIT) [O] Pittsburgh, PA St. Augustine Friary.
Schaller, Robert A. '87 (LC) Bakerville, WI Corpus Christi Church; Marshfield, WI Sacred Heart of Jesus Church.
Schanberger, J. Lawrence *m.m.* '49 (FgM) Maryknoll Foreign Missions.
Schanz, John P. '50 (E) [B] Erie, PA Gannon University.
Schappert, James P. *s.s.j.* '49 (BAL) [M] Baltimore, MD St. Joseph Society of the Sacred Heart House of Central Administration.
Schappler, Norbert *o.s.b.* '52 (KC) [J] Conception, MO Conception Abbey.
Schardt, William B. '75 (ARL) [3] Arlington, VA St. Ann Church.
Scharf, David '85 (PIT) East McKeesport, PA St. Robert Bellarmine Church.
Scharf, Joseph *s.j.* '51 (CLV) [U] Cleveland, OH Jesuit Retreat House.
Scharf, Lawrence C. '65 (TOL) Monroeville, OH St. Joseph Church.
Scharf, T. Patrick (TOL) Napoleon, OH St. Augustine Church.
Scharfenberger, Msgr. Edward B. '73 (BRK) [214] Queens, NY Our Lady of Mercy Church.
Schario, D. Clayton *s.j.* '56 (DET) [K] Detroit, MI Jesuit Community at the University of Detroit.
Schartz, Kennneth '85 (CIN) Xenia, OH St. Brigid Church.
Schatteman, Rene J. '60 (LA) [Y] Los Angeles, CA Opus Dei. Prelature of the Holy Cross and Opus Dei.
Schatzel, John E. '61 (BO) [2] Brockton, MA St. Colman of Cloyne Church.
Schatzle, Michael J. *c.s.s.r.* '74 (BR) New Roads, LA St. Mary of False River Church.
Schauerman, Msgr. Henry J. '51 (E) Meadville, PA St. Agatha Church.
Schaukowitch, James V. *s.j.* '79 (LA) [F] Los Angeles, CA Loyola High School.
Schaut, Gregory F. '85 (CLV) Brooklyn, OH St. Thomas More Church.
Schaver, David '80 (SFD) Absent on Leave.
Schavitz, Peter *c.ss.r.* (CHI) [9] Chicago, IL St. Alphonsus Church.
Scheaffer, Msgr. Walter T. '66 (ALN) Kutztown, PA St. Mary Church.
Scheble, Carl J. '83 (STL) [33] St. Louis, MO St. Elizabeth, Mother of John the Baptist Church.
Scheck, Francis M. '36 (LFT) Retired.
Scheckel, Roger J. '84 (LC) [5] La Crosse, WI St. James the Less Church.
Scheckenback, Robert C. '89 (RVC) Holbrook, NY Good Shepherd Church.
Schecker, Robert J.W. '71 (TR) Mount Holly, NJ Sacred Heart Church; Burlington, NJ Burlington County Hospital & Extended Care Center; Burlington, NJ Burlington County Jail.
Scheel, Msgr. Daniel '69 (GAL) [39] Houston, TX St. Jerome Church.
Scheeler, Jeffrey *o.f.m.* '80 (CIN) [65] Cincinnati, OH St. Monica-St. George Parish Newman Center Church; [Q] Cincinnati, OH University of Cincinnati Newman Center.
Scheeler, Jeffrey *o.f.m.* '80 (GAL) [Q] Houston, TX Franciscan Friars.
Scheer, Allen '95 (SAL) Mankato, KS St. Theresa of Infant Jesus Church.
Scheer, Joseph O. '42 (STL) Retired.
Scheerer, Dominic T. *o.c.d.* '47 (MIL) [24] Milwaukee, WI St. Florian Church.
Scheets, Francis Kelly *o.s.c.* '51 (NY) [4] New York, NY All Saints Church; [DD] New York, NY Crosier (Canons Regular of the Order of the Holy Cross).
Scheetz, Daniel L. '65 (SAL) Ellsworth, KS St. Bernard's Church; Gorham, KS St. Mary's Church; Holyrood, KS St. Mary's Church; Kanopolis, KS St. Ignatius Loyola Church.
Scheetz, Joseph H. '54 (SAL) WaKeeney, KS Christ the King Church.
Schefers, Eberhard '64 (SCL) Sartell, MN St. Francis Xavier Church.
Scheffler, Mark *c.ss.r.* '70 (SAT) San Antonio, TX Santa Rosa Hospital System; [H] San Antonio, TX Santa Rosa Health Care System.
Schehr, Timothy P. '73 (CIN) [B] Cincinnati, OH Mt. St. Mary's Seminary of the West.
Scheib, Joseph C. '76 (PIT) [43] Pittsburgh, PA St. Basil Church.
Scheible, Alan *o.praem.* '69 (GB) [I] De Pere, WI St. Joseph Priory.
Scheible, Alan D. *o.praem.* (GB) [M] De Pere, WI Norbertine Center for Spirituality.
Scheible, Alan D. *o.praem.* '69 (CHI) [N] Chicago, IL Premonstratensian Fathers and Brothers (Norbertines).
Scheich, Gene '66 (L) [55] Louisville, KY St. Matthias Church.
Scheick, James C. '63 (DET) [3] Livonia, MI St. Edith Church.
Scheider, David J. '53 (BUF) East Pembroke, NY Holy Name of Mary Church.
Scheiding, Philip '81 (MIA) On Duty Outside the Archdiocese.
Scheidler, Alfred J. *o.s.b.* '52 (PEO) [A] Peru, IL St. Bede Abbey and Academy.
Scheidler, David J. *c.s.c.* '94 (FTW) [B] Notre Dame, IN University of Notre Dame Du Lac; [J] Notre Dame, IN Holy Cross Community, Corby Hall, University of Notre Dame.
Scheierl, LeRoy '91 (SCL) Belgrade, MN St. Francis De Sales Church; Elrosa, MN SS. Peter and Paul Church.
Scheiner, Richard *c.p.* '60 (NY) [DD] New York, NY Passionist Spiritual Center.
Scheinost, Douglas P. '92 (OM) Stuart, NE St. Boniface Church.
Scheip, Michael (NEW) On Duty Outside the Archdiocese.
Schelble, T. Michael '61 (LC) Auburndale, WI Nativity

of the Blessed Virgin Mary Church; Hewitt, WI St. Michael Church.
Schelble, Thomas M. *s.m.* '46 (SAT) [K] San Antonio, TX Marianist Residence: Skilled Nursing.
Schelich, Anthony T. *o.s.f.s.* '65 (WIL) [G] Newark, DE Jeanne Jugan Residence; [I] Childs, MD Oblates of St. Francis De Sales.
Schelich, Theodosius *o.f.m.* '59 (STL) [P] St. Louis, MO Franciscan Friary of St. Anthony of Padua.
Schelich, Theodosius A. *o.f.m.* '59 (SFD) [H] Litchfield, IL St. Francis Hospital.
Schell, Joseph O. *s.j.* '44 (CLV) [C] Cleveland, OH John Carroll Jesuit Community.
Schellberg, L. Eugene '60 (MET) Parlin, NJ St. Bernadette Church.
Schellemans, Francis *ss.cc.* '49 (HON) [H] Honolulu, HI St. Patrick's Monastery.
Schellenberg, James '77 (SAT) San Antonio, TX Brooke Army Medical Center.
Schellenberg, Milton A. '46 (WDC) Retired.
Scheller, Albert J. '61 (EVN) [5] Vincennes, IN St. Vincent de Paul Church.
Scheller, John '58 (OKL) Retired.
Scheller, Raymund B. '47 (FAR) Retired.
Schelling, Michael '74 (TOL) Fort Jennings, OH St. Joseph Church.
Schemel, Francis *s.j.* '58 (WDC) [M] Washington, DC The Jesuit Community at Georgetown University.
Schemel, George J. *s.j.* '64 (SCR) [C] Scranton, PA University of Scranton; [R] Scranton, PA ISECP, Inc.
Schemm, Michael J. '93 (WCH) Parsons, KS St. Patrick Church.
Schendt, Richard L. '63 (CHI) [W] Oak Park, IL Oak Park Study Center.
Schenick, Joseph D. '51 (PRO) Retired.
Schenk, Arthur J. *s.j.* '45 (SJ) [M] Los Gatos, CA Sacred Heart Jesuit Center.
Schenk, Francisco *glmy.* '55 (CIN) [M] Fairfield, OH Headquarters of Glenmary Home Missioners.
Schenk, Richard *o.p.* '78 (OAK) [A] Berkeley, CA Dominican School of Philosophy and Theology; [N] Oakland, CA Dominican Order (Western Province), St. Albert's Priory.
Schenkelberg, Edwin J. '51 (CLV) [49] Cleveland, OH St. Mel Church.
Schenning, Kevin T. '81 (BAL) Aberdeen, MD St. Joan of Arc Church.
Scheper, Msgr. John B. '30 (LR) Retired.
Schepers, Frank '55 (KCK) Greeley, KS St. John the Baptist's Church.
Schepers, M. B. *o.p.* '56 (FgM) Dominican - Order of Preachers Foreign Missions.
Scher, James *o.s.c.* (FgM) Crosier Foreign Missions.
Scherba, Raymond M. '82 (BGP) [1] Danbury, CT St. Gregory's Church.
Scherer, Albert *o.f.m.conv.* '85 (SPR) [10] Chicopee, MA St. Stanislaus Basilica Church.
Scherer, Donald R. '67 (NEW) Retired.
Scherer, Gary M. *c.pp.s.* '67 (CIN) [K] Dayton, OH Franciscan Medical Center - Dayton Campus.
Scherer, Gerald N. '54 (RC) Retired.
Scherer, James F. '64 (ATL) On Duty Outside the Archdiocese.
Scherer, Philip M. *o.s.m.* '55 (CHI) [N] Chicago, IL Servite Friars - Eastern Province.
Scherer, Richard '49 (MIA) Retired.
Scherer, Steven J. '79 (GB) Absent on Leave.
Scherf, Gerard H. '47 (PH) [92] Philadelphia, PA Saint Martha Church; Retired.
Scherger, Herman F. '58 (TOL) Antwerp, OH St. Mary Church; Cecil, OH Immaculate Conception Church.
Scherman, Charles J. *s.j.* '57 (LC) Chippewa Falls, WI Holy Ghost Church; Springfield, WI St. Bridget Church.
Scherman, Charles J. *s.j.* '57 (MIL) [P] Milwaukee, WI Jesuit Provincial Office, Wisconsin Province.
Schermer, Paul '82 (LAN) [5] Flint, MI Holy Rosary Church.
Scherpenberg, Sergius H. *o.f.m.* '51 (L) [16] Louisville, KY St. Boniface Church; [L] Louisville, KY St. Boniface Friary.
Scherrer, Carl E. '73 (BEL) Carbondale, IL St. Francis Xavier Church.
Scherrer, Ralph *o.f.m.* '41 (SFD) [K] Sherman, IL Our Lady of Angels Friary.
Scherrer, Steven *m.m.* '72 (NY) [DD] Maryknoll, NY Maryknoll Fathers and Brothers.
Scherzer, Edwin J. '50 (L) Retired; [L] Louisville, KY Bishop David Apartments; [Q] Louisville, KY Our Lady's Rosary Makers.
Schetelick, Paul D. (NEW) [11] Newark, NJ St. Charles Borromeo's Church.
Schetelick, Paul D. '76 (NEW) [3] Newark, NJ Blessed Sacrament Church.
Schetter, Albert E. '55 (CIN) Retired.
Schettler, Charles H. '54 (OKL) [8] Oklahoma City, OK St. Francis of Assisi Church.
Scheuer, James '59 (DUL) Babbitt, MN St. Pius X Church; Ely, MN St. Anthony's Church; [F] Duluth, MN University of MN-Duluth.
Scheuer, James W. '59 (DUL) Hinckley, MN St. Patrick's Church.
Scheuerell, Charles A. '57 (MIL) Beaver Dam, WI St. Patrick Church.
Scheuerman, Edward L. '50 (DET) Retired.
Schevers, Joel *o.carm.* '42 (VEN) [1] Venice, FL Epiphany Cathedral; [G] Venice, FL Carmel in Venice.
Schexnayder, Daniel '63 (LAF) Leonville, LA St. Leo the Great Church.
Schexnayder, Francis F. *m.m.* '64 (FgM) Maryknoll Foreign Missions.
Schexnayder, Gary '69 (LAF) [9] Lafayette, LA St. Edmond Church.
Schexnayder, James (OAK) [H] Oakland, CA Catholic Charities of the Diocese of Oakland, Inc.
Scheyd, Msgr. William J. '65 (BGP) [7] Norwalk, CT St. Thomas the Apostle Church.
Schiavi, Giulio *p.i.m.e.* (DET) [7] Clinton Twp., MI San Francesco Community Church.
Schiavone, Alphonse A. *m.m.* '46 (RVC) [N] West Hempstead, NY Maryknoll Residence.
Schiavone, Christopher F. '84 (BO) Absent on Leave.
Schiavone, Jeldo J. '52 (LFT) Retired.
Schiavone, John S. '73 (LA) Culver City, CA St. Augustine Church.
Schiavone, Robert '69 (MIL) [B] Hales Corners, WI Sacred Heart School of Theology.
Schiavone, Robert W. '69 (GB) On Duty Outside the Diocese.
Schiblin, Richard *c.s.s.r.* '61 (P) [17] Portland, OR Holy Redeemer Church.
Schichtel, Kenneth H. '62 (GR) Ludington, MI St. Simon's Church.
Schidel, George E. *c.s.c.* '41 (FTW) [J] South Bend, IN Congregation of Holy Cross Indiana Province Provincial House.
Schieber, Joachim *o.s.b.* (KC) [H] Blue Springs, MO St. Mary's Manor.
Schieber, Lawrence J. '49 (STL) Moselle, MO St. Mary's Church.
Schiefen, Richard J. *c.s.b.* '61 (GAL) [Q] Houston, TX Residence of the Basilian Fathers of the University of St. Thomas.
Schiefen, Msgr. Robert W. '46 (VEN) Sanibel, FL St. Isabel Church.
Schieffer, Stanley F. '56 (LIN) Red Cloud, NE Sacred Heart Church.
Schiel, Nicholas E. *s.j.* '55 (FgM) Provinces.
Schiel, Nicholas E. *s.j.* '55 (MIL) [P] Milwaukee, WI Jesuit Provincial Office, Wisconsin Province.
Schiele, John D. '93 (PH) Brookhaven, PA Our Lady of Charity Church.
Schierse, Msgr. Paul J. '55 (WIL) Special or Other Diocesan Assignment.
Schifalacqua, Ildebrando E. '43 (PH) [21] Philadelphia, PA St. Bartholomew Church; Retired.
Schifano, James *s.c.j.* '75 (JKS) Senatobia, MS St. Gregory the Great Church; Walls, MS Sacred Heart Church; [E] Nesbit, MS St. Michael Community House; [G] Senatobia, MS Northwest Mississippi Community College Newman Center.
Schiff, John S. '74 (OKL) Absent on Sick Leave.
Schiffbauer, Rory '91 (CHY) [1] Cheyenne, WY St. Mary's Cathedral.
Schiffer, James A. '71 (MET) [H] South River, NJ Passionist Provincial Office.
Schiffer, Thomas E. '63 (WH) Weirton, WV St. Paul's Church.
Schifferli, Jerome F. '45 (ROC) Retired.
Schik, Jerome *o.s.c.* '75 (STP) Shoreview, MN St. Odilia Church; [N] Shoreview, MN Crosier Community of Shoreview.
Schilder, David '68 (Y) Salem, OH St. Paul's Church.
Schilder, David M. '68 (COL) On Duty Outside the Diocese.
Schilken, Karl '80 (FWT) Mansfield, TX St. Jude Church.
Schill, Damien '87 (FAR) [2] Fargo, ND Holy Spirit Church.
Schill, Frederick J. '57 (TOL) Gibsonburg, OH St. Michael Church.
Schill, Paul '80 (E) Anita, PA St. Joseph Church.
Schill, Paul A. '63 (E) Walston, PA St. Anthony Church.
Schill, Paul A., Jr. '63 (E) Delancey, PA St. Adrian Church.
Schill, Victor J. '50 (FAR) Retired.
Schiller, Daniel (AUS) [M] Brenham, TX Blinn College Catholic Student Union.
Schiller, Davis J. '55 (CHR) Retired.
Schiller, Francis E. '65 (NEW) [7] Jersey City, NJ Assumption/All Saints Church; [23] Jersey City, NJ St. Patrick's Church.
Schiller, Thomas A. '55 (GR) Montague, MI St. James Church.
Schilli, Richard J. '77 (STL) Mattese, MO Assumption Church.
Schilling, Francis X. '57 (KNX) Gatlinburg, TN St. Mary Church.
Schillinger, James '84 (ATL) [L] Atlanta, GA Campus Ministry.
Schilly, Msgr. Adolph M. '44 (STL) Retired.
Schilly, Joseph '48 (SB) Retired.
Schiltz, Roger J. '68 (WIN) Retired.
Schimelpfening, James *s.m.* '80 (STL) [P] St. Louis, MO Provincialate of the Society of Mary, Province of St. Louis.
Schiml, Ronald J. *c.pp.s.* '55 (LFT) Star City, IN St. Joseph Church.
Schimmelman, Wayne *c.m.f.* (CHI) [166] Chicago, IL St. Paul Church.
Schimmer, Robert J. '68 (SC) [7] Sioux City, IA St. Joseph Church.
Schimscheiner, Francis *o.s.f.s.* '65 (BUF) [5] Lockport, NY St. Patrick Church.
Schindler, Carl *c.ss.r.* '63 (SAT) [37] San Antonio, TX St. Gerard Majella Church.
Schindler, Carl A. *c.ss.r.* '63 (BR) [H] Baton Rouge, LA Redemptorist Vice Province.
Schindler, Frederic *o.s.b.* '45 (OM) [K] Elkhorn, NE Mount Michael Abbey.
Schindler, John H. '49 (YAK) Retired.
Schindler, John L. '85 (L) [62] Louisville, KY St. Patrick Church.
Schindler, Paul E. '67 (CLV) [3] Akron, OH St. Bernard Church; [X] Cleveland, OH Diocesan Hispanic Office.
Schindler, Robert '54 (FRS) Faculties Only; Retired.
Schindler-McGraw, Kevin *o.f.m.conv.* '84 (SFR) [43] San Francisco, CA St. Paul of the Shipwreck Church.
Schineller, Peter *s.j.* '70 (FgM) Provinces.
Schinelli, Giles A. *t.o.r.* '70 (ALT) [7] Altoona, PA Our Lady of Mt. Carmel Church.
Schinn, Dom Bernard *o.s.b.* (DET) [K] Detroit, MI St. Sylvester Monastery.
Schinski, Msgr. Stanislaus E. '51 (PAT) [1] Wayne, NJ Annunciation Church.
Schipp, John H. '64 (EVN) [2] Vincennes, IN Basilica of St. Francis Xavier Church; [J] Vincennes, IN Old Cathedral Library & Museum, Inc.
Schipp, Ralph '65 (EVN) Special Assignment; [E] Evansville, IN St. Mary's Medical Center of Evansville, Inc.
Schipper, Carl A. '68 (SFR) Special Assignment; [A] Menlo Park, CA St. Patrick Seminary.
Schiro, Nicholas T. *s.j.* '57 (NO) [F] New Orleans, LA Jesuit High School.
Schirra, Peter M. '37 (PIT) Retired.
Schiska, Paul A. '57 (MAR) Retired.
Schissel, Gregory A. *s.j.* '79 (MIL) [P] Milwaukee, WI Jesuit Community at Marquette University.
Schissel, John G. '40 (SC) Retired.
Schlachter, Msgr. Clarence A. '46 (EVN) Special Assignment.
Schlachter, Eric A. '81 (JC) Pilot Grove, MO St. Joseph Church.
Schlade, Joseph F. '58 (RCK) Retired.
Schladen, Donald R. '56 (PEO) Marseilles, IL St. Joseph's Church.
Schladen, Robert G. '59 (PEO) [10] Peoria, IL St. Mark's Church.
Schlaefer, Joseph H. '58 (MAD) Neshkoro, WI St. James Church.
Schlaf, John E. '64 (GI) Ogallala, NE St. Luke's Church.
Schlafer, Joseph M. '75 (RVC) Nesconset, NY Church of the Holy Cross.
Schlaffer, James J. '45 (MIL) Retired.
Schlageter, Robert *o.f.m.conv.* '83 (BGP) [6] Danbury, CT Sacred Heart Church; [V] Fairfield, CT Newman Centers - Campus Ministry.
Schlagheck, Regis T. *o.f.m.conv.* '66 (CLV) [1] Lorain, OH St. Anthony of Padua Church.
Schlangen, Louis '57 (SFD) Mendon, IL St. Edward Church.
Schlarb, Gregory *c.m.* '97 (PHX) [26] Phoenix, AZ St. Vincent de Paul Church.
Schlatter, Fredric *s.j.* '56 (SPK) [C] Spokane, WA Gonzaga University.
Schlattmann, Edward B. '34 (STL) Retired.
Schlauer, David E. *c.s.c.* '71 (FTW) [J] South Bend, IN Congregation of Holy Cross Indiana Province Provincial House.
Schlautman, Wayne W. '65 (OM) Atkinson, NE St. Joseph Church.
Schlax, Charles M. '66 (CHI) Palatine, IL St. Theresa Church.
Schlegel, Daniel F. '88 (CLV) [3] Euclid, OH Holy Cross Church.
Schlegel, Msgr. George J. '66 (COL) New Philadelphia, OH Sacred Heart Church.
Schlegel, John P. *s.j.* '73 (SFR) [C] San Francisco, CA University of San Francisco; [N] San Francisco, CA Jesuit Community at University of San Francisco.
Schlegel, Lawrence *o.s.b.* '54 (MAN) [K] Manchester, NH St. Anselm Abbey.
Schleicher, Edward R. '83 (PIT) Muse, PA Holy Rosary Church.
Schleicher, James R. '54 (CLV) [5] Akron, OH St. Francis de Sales Church; [V] Cleveland, OH Society of St. Vincent de Paul, Diocesan Central Council.
Schlenker, Richard '56 (MIL) [B] Hales Corners, WI Sacred Heart School of Theology.
Schlenkler, Richard J. '56 (MIL) Special Assignment.

Schlert, Alfred A. '80 (ALN) Special Assignment.
Schlesselmann, Gregory '93 (FAR) Special Assignment.
Schleter, Edward J. '67 (TOL) Defiance, OH St. Mary Church.
Schlett, Francis J. '70 (PH) [1] Coatesville, PA St. Cecilia Church.
Schleupner, Msgr. G. Michael '72 (BAL) [89] Baltimore, MD Shrine of the Sacred Heart Church; Special Assignment.
Schlick, Regis *o.f.m.cap.* '65 (FgM) Capuchin Foreign Missions.
Schlick, Regis *o.f.m.cap.* '65 (WH) Point Pleasant, WV Sacred Heart Church.
Schlick, Regis *o.f.m.cap.* '69 (WH) [N] Charleston, WV Capuchins-St. Anthony Friary.
Schliessmann, Thomas '89 (IND) Scottsburg, IN American Martyrs Church.
Schliessmann, Thomas L. '89 (IND) Salem, IN St. Patrick Church.
Schlight, Harry J. *o.s.f.s.* '44 (FgM) Oblates of St. Francis de Sales Foreign Missions.
Schlim, Robert J. *s.j.* '62 (SPK) [K] Spokane, WA Regis Community.
Schlimm, Chrysostom V. *o.s.b.* '61 (GBG) [H] Latrobe, PA Saint Vincent Archabbey.
Schlinkmann, John W. '31 (MIA) Retired.
Schlitt, Dale M. *o.m.i.* '69 (STP) [N] St. Paul, MN Oblate Residence.
Schlitt, Harry G. '64 (SFR) [20] San Francisco, CA St. Gabriel Church; Special Assignment.
Schlitt, Robert T. '56 (TLS) Stillwater, OK St. Francis Xavier Church.
Schloeder, Paul (SAC) Ione, CA Sacred Heart Church.
Schloeder, Paul '60 (SAC) Preston, CA School of Industry.
Schloeder, Paul '87 (SAC) Vacaville, CA California Medical Facility, South.
Schloemer, Bernard J. '60 (STL) Sunset Hills, MO St. Justin Martyr Church.
Schloemer, Leo '56 (TYL) Daingerfield, TX Our Lady of Fatima Church.
Schloemer, Thomas N. *s.j.* (OM) [K] Omaha, NE Campion House.
Schloesser, Stephen R. *s.j.* '92 (MIL) [P] Milwaukee, WI Jesuit Provincial Office, Wisconsin Province.
Schloesser, Stephen R. *s.j.* '92 (SJ) [B] Santa Clara, CA Santa Clara University.
Schlosser, Richard '74 (GF) [2] Great Falls, MT Eastside Catholic Communities Church.
Schloth, Brian D. *m.s.* '89 (NOR) Danielson, CT St. James Church.
Schludecker, Andre *o.f.m.* '64 (GAY) Bay Shore, MI St. Francis Solanus Church; Petoskey, MI St. Francis Xavier Church.
Schlueter, Clemens M. '58 (TUC) Retired.
Schlut, Michael '86 (DEN) [8] Denver, CO Church of the Good Shepherd.
Schluter, O. Charles '78 (MAD) Mazomanie, WI St. Barnabas Church.
Schmainda, Robert D. '64 (SCL) St. Augusta, MN St. Mary Help of Christians Church.
Schmalhofer, John '74 (HBG) [1] Harrisburg, PA Cathedral Parish of St. Patrick Church.
Schmaltz, Albert F. '43 (STL) Retired.
Schmaltz, Bernard W. '73 (NO) [34] New Orleans, LA St. Gabriel the Archangel Church; Absent on Leave.
Schmalzried, Bernard R. '69 (Y) [6] Warren, OH St. Mary's Church.
Schmaus, James E. '92 (CHI) Lake Zurich, IL St. Francis de Sales Church.
Schmeer, John P. '64 (PH) New Hope, PA St. Martin of Tours Church.
Schmeidler, John *o.f.m.cap.* '97 (STL) [P] Arnold, MO Immaculate Conception Friary.
Schmeising, Julian *o.s.b.* '58 (SCL) [H] Cold Spring, MN Assumption Home; [H] Cold Spring, MN John Paul Apartments; [H] Cold Spring, MN Assumption Court.
Schmelz, Damian *o.s.b.* '58 (IND) [B] St. Meinrad, IN St. Meinrad Seminary-College of Liberal Arts; [J] St. Meinrad, IN St. Meinrad Archabbey.
Schmelzer, Delbert L. '56 (MAD) Verona, WI St. Andrew Church.
Schmelzer, Joseph M. '77 (TOL) Van Wert, OH St. Mary Church.
Schmelzer, Linus L. '45 (MIL) Retired.
Schmelzer, Paul '43 (SCL) Retired.
Schmenk, Cleo '53 (TOL) Paulding, OH St. Joseph Church.
Schmid, Wayne L. '68 (WCH) Military Chaplains.
Schmidberger, Richard M. '57 (DET) North Branch, MI St. Mary's Burnside Church.
Schmidlin, Donald L. '57 (IND) [28] Indianapolis, IN St. Matthew Church.
Schmidlkofer, Bruce J. *s.j.* '91 (P) [D] Portland, OR Jesuit High School.
Schmidt, Anthony '50 (SFD) Retired.
Schmidt, Bosco *s.a.* '49 (NY) [DD] Garrison, NY Franciscan Friars of the Atonement.
Schmidt, Carl '50 (SFD) Coffeen, IL St. John the Baptist Church; Panama, IL Sacred Heart Church.
Schmidt, Charles W. *m.m.* '48 (HON) [H] Honolulu, HI Maryknoll Fathers House.
Schmidt, David (GB) Kaukauna, WI St. Aloysius Church.
Schmidt, David L. '77 (SFD) Litchfield, IL Holy Family Church.
Schmidt, Dennis '80 (JC) Columbia, MO Columbia Newman Center, University of Missouri Church; [F] Columbia, MO University of Missouri-Columbia, Campus Ministry.
Schmidt, Dennis C. '80 (STL) On Duty Outside the Archdiocese.
Schmidt, Donald A. '73 (MIL) Belgium, WI St. Mary Church.
Schmidt, Edward *s.j.* '71 (FgM) Provinces.
Schmidt, Edward W. *s.j.* '73 (CHI) [N] Chicago, IL Chicago Province of the Society of Jesus-Provincial Office.
Schmidt, Edwin A. '63 (JC) St. Martins, MO St. Martin Church.
Schmidt, Elmer J. '56 (ROC) Retired.
Schmidt, Eugene '56 (GB) Retired.
Schmidt, Florian J. '61 (DUB) [4] Dubuque, IA St. Mary's Church.
Schmidt, Francis J. '58 (MAD) Martinsville, WI St. Martin Church.
Schmidt, Msgr. Francis X. '57 (PH) Bridgeport, PA St. Augustine Church.
Schmidt, Frederick A. *c.s.c.* '37 (FgM) Holy Cross Foreign Missions.
Schmidt, Frederick N. '42 (MIL) Retired.
Schmidt, George, Jr. '70 (KNX) [K] Chattanooga, TN Mount Olivet.
Schmidt, George E., Jr. '70 (KNX) [1] Chattanooga, TN SS. Peter and Paul Church.
Schmidt, Msgr. George N. '41 (WCH) Retired.
Schmidt, Gerald *o.f.m.cap.* '66 (GB) Lakewood, WI St. Mary of the Lake Church; Wabeno, WI St. Ambrose Church.
Schmidt, Gregory L. '61 (STL) Old Monroe, MO Immaculate Conception Church.
Schmidt, Gustav H. *s.j.* '66 (HEL) St. Ignatius, MT St. Ignatius Church.
Schmidt, Henry C. '57 (SFD) [4] Springfield, IL Little Flower Church.
Schmidt, Herbert (SPR) West Springfield, MA St. Thomas the Apostle Church.
Schmidt, Jan Kevin '90 (CIN) [39] Cincinnati, OH Immaculate Heart of Mary Church.
Schmidt, Jerome J. '49 (BRK) [122] Brooklyn, NY Resurrection Church; Retired.
Schmidt, John *c.s.s.r.* '89 (CHI) [136] Chicago, IL St. Michael Church.
Schmidt, John W. '56 (Y) Retired.
Schmidt, Joseph F. '66 (B) Moscow, ID St. Mary's Church.
Schmidt, Joseph L. *c.s.p.* (P) [Q] Portland, OR Paulist Fathers Catholic Center for Evangelization.
Schmidt, Kenneth W. '81 (KAL) [5] Kalamazoo, MI St. Thomas More Student Parish; [H] Kalamazoo, MI Western Michigan University, Kalamazoo College-Kalamazoo Valley Community College.
Schmidt, Leo C. '56 (COV) [4] Covington, KY St. Augustine Church.
Schmidt, Leslie *glmy.* '61 (RIC) Big Stone Gap, VA Sacred Heart Church.
Schmidt, Louis R. '54 (LEX) [3] Lexington, KY Mary, Queen of the Holy Rosary Church; Retired.
Schmidt, Lukas *o.carm.* '65 (WDC) [B] Washington, DC Whitefriars Hall.
Schmidt, Nicholas '67 (ORG) Inactive Leave.
Schmidt, Paul J. '64 (OAK) [14] Oakland, CA St. Margaret Mary Church.
Schmidt, Ralph G., Jr. '73 (GAL) Texas City, TX St. Mary Church.
Schmidt, Raymond F. '60 (BRK) [194] Queens, NY St. Mary Church.
Schmidt, Raymond F. '84 (WDC) [10] Washington, DC Blessed Sacrament, Shrine of the Most Church.
Schmidt, Richard C. *s.j.* '61 (WDC) [P] Faulkner, MD Loyola on the Potomac Retreat House.
Schmidt, Robert H. *s.j.* '69 (FgM) Provinces.
Schmidt, Msgr. Robert R. '43 (COL) Retired.
Schmidt, Robert W. *s.j.* '42 (CIN) [M] Cincinnati, OH Jesuit Community at Xavier Unversity.
Schmidt, Sebastian *o.s.b.* '60 (BIS) [A] Richardton, ND Assumption Abbey.
Schmidt, Sebastian *o.s.b.* '60 (FgM) American - Cassinese Congregation Foreign Missions.
Schmidt, Thomas *c.s.s.r.* '62 (RVC) Bethpage, NY St. Martin of Tours Church.
Schmidt, Thomas '76 (STL) Arnold, MO St. David Church.
Schmidt, Msgr. W. Robert (DAV) [5] Davenport, IA St. Anthony's Church.
Schmidt, Msgr. W. Robert '57 (DAV) [M] Davenport, IA St. Vincent Center.
Schmidt, Wilfred W. '50 (DUB) [4] Dubuque, IA St. Mary's Church; Retired.
Schmidt, William F. *s.a.* '59 (R) Apex, NC St. Andrew the Apostle Church.
Schmidt, William T. '76 (BO) Stoneham, MA St. Patrick Church.
Schmidtzinsky, Msgr. Victor '41 (SAT) [K] San Antonio, TX Padua Place.
Schmidtzinsky, Msgr. Victor '41 (VIC) Retired.
Schmied, Msgr. Michael S. '71 (RIC) [6] Richmond, VA St. Augustine Church.
Schmied, Thomas *o.f.m.cap.* '69 (MAR) Special Assignment.
Schmieg, Brennan *o.f.m.* '58 (SUP) Washburn, WI St. Louis Church.
Schmiesing, Julian *o.s.b.* '58 (SCL) Jacob's Prairie, MN St. James Church.
Schmit, Arthur G. *o.s.b.* '57 (PEO) [A] Peru, IL St. Bede Abbey and Academy.
Schmit, George V., Jr. '68 (NU) [1] New Ulm, MN Cathedral of the Holy Trinity; Searles, MN St. John the Baptist Church.
Schmit, Jerome L. '57 (LA) Altadena, CA Sacred Heart Church.
Schmit, Kenneth A. '79 (ORG) El Toro, CA Santiago de Compostela Church.
Schmit, Louis L. *c.pp.s.* '63 (CIN) [M] Dayton, OH Provincial House of the Cincinnati Province of the Society of the Precious Blood.
Schmit, Meyrl E. '65 (JKS) Grenada, MS St. Peter Church.
Schmit, Msgr. Ralph R. '46 (MIL) Retired.
Schmit, Roger W. *o.s.b.* '62 (CHY) Laramie, WY St. Paul's Newman Center Church; [E] Laramie, WY University of Wyoming.
Schmit, Ronald G. '85 (OAK) Byron, CA St. Anne Church.
Schmit, Stanley T. '94 (OM) Hartington, NE Holy Trinity Church.
Schmitmeyer, James M. '81 (CIN) North Star, OH St. Louis Church; Osgood, OH St. Nicholas Church.
Schmitt, Adam '57 (FTW) [8] Fort Wayne, IN St. Joseph Church.
Schmitt, Allen M. '71 (DUB) Fort Atkinson, IA St. John Nepomucene's Church; Little Turkey, IA Assumption of the B. V. M. Church; Protivin, IA Holy Trinity Church.
Schmitt, Bowan '97 (PEO) [14] Peoria, IL St. Thomas Church.
Schmitt, Carl L. '61 (DUB) New Hampton, IA St. Joseph's Church.
Schmitt, Charles R. '59 (E) Port Allegany, PA St. Gabriel the Archangel Church.
Schmitt, Christopher '60 (PMB) [F] Delray Beach, FL Opus Dei.
Schmitt, Conrad *s.t.* '55 (SAV) Blakely, GA Holy Family Church.
Schmitt, David J. '67 (WH) Logan, WV St. Francis of Assisi Church; Man, WV St. Edmund Church.
Schmitt, Donald P. '62 (DUB) Barclay, IA St. Francis Church; Jesup, IA St. Athanasius Church.
Schmitt, Ervin J. '58 (PBL) [5] Pueblo, CO Our Lady of the Assumption Church; [14] Pueblo, CO St. Mary Church; [15] Pueblo, CO St. Patrick Church.
Schmitt, Eugene A. '45 (WH) Retired.
Schmitt, Frank J. *s.j.* '83 (FgM) Provinces.
Schmitt, Gregory *c.s.s.r.* '69 (SEA) [32] Seattle, WA Sacred Heart of Jesus Church.
Schmitt, Harold F. '59 (PEO) [3] Ottawa, IL St. Mary's Church.
Schmitt, Msgr. J. Harley '40 (DEN) Retired; [I] Denver, CO Mullen Home.
Schmitt, James, J. '51 (LAN) Retired.
Schmitt, James C. '66 (GI) [3] Grand Island, NE Resurrection Church; Grand Island, NE Nebraska Veterans Home.
Schmitt, James J. '74 (PIT) Crafton, PA St. Philip Church.
Schmitt, John P. '44 (GB) Retired.
Schmitt, Msgr. Joseph J. '55 (AUS) Lago Vista, TX St. Mary, Our Lady of the Lake Church.
Schmitt, Kent A. '73 (MAD) [7] Madison, WI St. Dennis Church.
Schmitt, Michael T. '71 (ALB) Colonie, NY St. Clare Church.
Schmitt, Phillip E. '56 (DUB) Iowa Falls, IA St. Mark's Church.
Schmitt, Reinhold *c.m.m.* '52 (AUS) Westphalia, TX Visitation Church.
Schmitt, Reinhold *c.m.m.* '52 (DET) [K] Dearborn Heights, MI Our Lady of Grace Monastery.
Schmitt, Silverius J. '58 (SCL) Bowlus, MN St. Stanislaus Kostka Church; North Prairie, MN Holy Cross Church.
Schmitt, Thomas '91 (SPR) Graduate Studies.
Schmitt, Thomas G. '45 (DET) Retired.
Schmitt, Urban *o.s.c.* '49 (OM) Cedar Rapids, NE St. Anthony Church.
Schmitt, Urban J. *o.s.c.* '49 (LIN) [A] Hastings, NE Crosier Monastery.
Schmitt, Warren J. '42 (MIL) Retired.
Schmitt, William *s.s.c.* '68 (LSC) [2] Las Cruces, NM Holy Cross Church.
Schmitt, William *s.s.c.* '68 (OM) [K] St. Columbans, NE St. Columban's Foreign Mission Society.

Schmitt, William J. *s.j.* '58 (FgM) Provinces.
Schmitter, Phillip '71 (LAN) Special Assignment.
Schmittgens, Kevin V. '83 (STL) Union, MO Immaculate Conception Church.
Schmitz, Aloysius F. *s.j.* '59 (STP) [N] Minneapolis, MN La Storta Jesuit Community.
Schmitz, Bartley *s.v.d.* '44 (FgM) Society of the Divine Word Foreign Missions.
Schmitz, Msgr. Bernard (IND) St. Pius, IN St. Pius Church.
Schmitz, Bernard A. '74 (DEN) On Duty Outside the Archdiocese.
Schmitz, Msgr. Bernard R. '57 (IND) Milan, IN St. Charles Borromeo Church; Morris, IN St. Anthony of Padua Church; St. Nicholas, IN St. Nicholas Church.
Schmitz, Charles *s.j.* '72 (YAK) [4] Yakima, WA St. Joseph's Church.
Schmitz, Charles E. *s.j.* '72 (FgM) Provinces.
Schmitz, Charles E. *s.j.* '72 (P) [Q] Portland, OR Jesuit Development & Communications Office.
Schmitz, Donald J. '80 (WIN) Caledonia, MN St. Mary Church.
Schmitz, Donald P. '64 (WIN) [3] Rochester, MN Resurrection Church.
Schmitz, Eugene *s.v.d.* '67 (FgM) Society of the Divine Word Foreign Missions.
Schmitz, George '69 (CIN) [7] Dayton, OH St. Charles Borromeo Church.
Schmitz, Gerald P. '62 (MIL) [3] Kenosha, WI St. George Church.
Schmitz, Gerald T. '48 (MIL) Retired.
Schmitz, Gerard G. '68 (HRT) Madison, CT St. Margaret Church.
Schmitz, James P. '86 (CLV) Amherst, OH St. Joseph Church.
Schmitz, John A. '52 (MIL) Ripon, WI St. Patrick Church.
Schmitz, John J. '91 (JC) Brinktown, MO Guardian Angels Church; Vienna, MO Visitation Church.
Schmitz, Michael D '96 (OM) Columbus, NE St. Isidore Church.
Schmitz, Robert A. '55 (OM) Tilden, NE Our Lady of Mt. Carmel Church.
Schmitz, Robert E. '75 (CIN) [19] Cincinnati, OH St. Catharine Church.
Schmitzer, Richard C. '46 (STP) Retired.
Schmock, Hilarion *o.c.s.o.* '43 (L) [L] Trappist, KY Abbey of Our Lady of Gethsemani, of the Order of Cistercians of the Strict Observance.
Schmoldt, William F. *s.j.* '54 (DET) [P] Clarkston, MI Colombiere Center.
Schmoll, John '85 (FRS) Lamont, CA St. Augustine Church.
Schmuhl, Lawrence R. *s.m.* '47 (ATL) [C] Atlanta, GA Marist School.
Schnacky, Paul R. '53 (ROC) Wayland, NY St. Joseph's Church.
Schnaubelt, Joseph C. *o.s.a.* '57 (PH) [AA] Villanova, PA St. Thomas Monastery.
Schnaus, Urban *o.s.b.* '40 (WDC) [M] Washington, DC St. Anselm's Abbey.
Schneck, Richard *s.j.* '72 (FgM) Provinces.
Schneebeck, Paul Otto *c.m.* (CHI) [C] Chicago, IL Vincentian Community at DePaul University.
Schneibel, Jeffrey *c.s.c.* '85 (P) [B] Portland, OR University of Portland; [L] Portland, OR Holy Cross Fathers & Brothers, C.S.C. - University of Portland.
Schneible, Peter *o.f.m.* (BUF) [C] St. Bonaventure, NY St. Bonaventure University.
Schneible, Peter *o.f.m.* '89 (BUF) [O] St. Bonaventure, NY St. Bonaventure Friary.
Schneid, Michael '58 (CLV) Retired.
Schneider, Adrian *o.f.m.* '41 (CIN) [M] Cincinnati, OH St. Francis Center.
Schneider, Msgr. Alfred '38 (GB) Retired.
Schneider, Anthony *o.f.m.* '52 (NY) [146] Bronx, NY Holy Cross Church.
Schneider, Aquinas *o.f.m.* '54 (CIN) [K] Cincinnati, OH Franciscan Hospital, Western Hills Campus.
Schneider, Msgr. Arnold J. '51 (BUF) Bowmansville, NY Sacred Heart Church; Retired.
Schneider, Barry *o.f.m.* '56 (SUP) Dauby, WI St. Peter Church; Iron River, WI St. Michael Church.
Schneider, Bernard R. '67 (FAR) Mayville, ND Our Lady of Peace Church; [H] Mayville, ND Mayville State University Newman Center.
Schneider, Bernardin *o.f.m.* '44 (FgM) Franciscan Foreign Missions.
Schneider, Charles *s.v.d.* '46 (FgM) Society of the Divine Word Foreign Missions.
Schneider, Charles J. '63 (WH) New Martinsville, WV St. Vincent de Paul Church.
Schneider, Christopher *o.f.m.* '49 (CIN) [M] Cincinnati, OH St. Clement Friary.
Schneider, Conrad *o.f.m.* '51 (CHI) [N] Oak Forest, IL St. Roch Friary-Franciscan Fathers.
Schneider, Craig '89 (CIN) [K] Dayton, OH Franciscan Medical Center - Dayton Campus.
Schneider, Donald '50 (GB) Retired.
Schneider, Edward '64 (EVN) Petersburg, IN SS. Peter and Paul Church.
Schneider, Msgr. Ernest P. '77 (GR) Ada, MI St. Robert Church.
Schneider, Msgr. Francis J. '83 (RVC) Elmont, NY St. Vincent de Paul Church.
Schneider, Fredrick *o.f.m.* '49 (LR) Horseshoe Bend, AR St. Mary of the Mount Church.
Schneider, George D. '56 (FAR) Rolla, ND St. Joachim's Church.
Schneider, George E. '58 (COV) Florence, KY St. Paul Church.
Schneider, George P. '45 (PH) Parkesburg, PA Our Lady of Consolation Church; Retired.
Schneider, Gilbert *o.f.m.* '64 (SFE) [J] Albuquerque, NM San Antonio Provincial Friary Franciscan Friars.
Schneider, Harold '74 (KCK) [3] Topeka, KS Holy Name Church.
Schneider, Harold E. '62 (COL) Heath, OH St. Leonard Church.
Schneider, Henry W. '53 (BIS) [3] Minot, ND St. John the Apostle Church.
Schneider, Herbert *s.j.* '70 (FgM) Provinces.
Schneider, J. Daniel *m.m.* '77 (NY) [DD] Maryknoll, NY Maryknoll Fathers and Brothers.
Schneider, Jerzy *s.d.b.* '53 (NEW) [C] Ramsey, NJ Don Bosco Preparatory High School for Boys.
Schneider, John G. '48 (STL) Retired.
Schneider, John H. '68 (STL) Bonne Terre, MO St. Joseph's Church.
Schneider, John W. '83 (CHL) Arden, NC St. Barnabas Church.
Schneider, Joseph M. '74 (DUB) Meyer, IA Sacred Heart Church; St. Ansgar, IA St. Ansgar Church; Stacyville, IA Church of the Visitation.
Schneider, Juniper *o.f.m.conv.* (MRY) [G] Arroyo Grande, CA St. Joseph Cupertino Province, Provincial Center.
Schneider, Karl J. '59 (MIL) [4] West Allis, WI Immaculate Heart of Mary Church.
Schneider, Kevin C. *s.j.* '94 (RC) Pine Ridge, SD Holy Rosary Church; [B] Pine Ridge, SD Jesuit Community of Holy Rosary Mission.
Schneider, Leon J. '53 (MIL) [9] Racine, WI St. Mary by the Lake Church.
Schneider, Michael '81 (SFS) Howard, SD St. Agatha Church.
Schneider, Michael '94 (GF) Poplar, MT Our Lady of Lourdes Church.
Schneider, Msgr. Nicholas A. '56 (STL) [3] Creve Coeur, MO St. Monica Church.
Schneider, Paul *o.f.m.* '43 (SFE) [K] Rio Rancho, NM Felician Sisters.
Schneider, Philip *o.f.m.conv.* '61 (FTW) Angola, IN St. Anthony Church; Clear Lake, IN St. Paul Chapel Church.
Schneider, Ralph *c.pp.s.* '64 (TOL) Ottawa, OH SS. Peter and Paul Church.
Schneider, Ric *o.f.m.* '59 (PEO) [2] Bloomington, IL St. Mary's Church.
Schneider, Richard J. *s.m.* '83 (SAT) [K] San Antonio, TX Marianist Residence: Skilled Nursing.
Schneider, Msgr. Robert E. '57 (COL) Coshocton, OH Sacred Heart Church.
Schneider, Robert J. '78 (WIN) Albert Lea, MN St. Theodore's Church; [J] Albert Lea, MN St. Theodore Catholic School Endowment.
Schneider, Robert J. '81 (SP) [4] St. Petersburg, FL Holy Family Church.
Schneider, Ronald '75 (GB) Absent on Leave.
Schneider, Ronald F. '67 (GR) Hart, MI St. Gregory's Church.
Schneider, Stephen *o.f.m.* '38 (L) [L] Louisville, KY St. Boniface Friary.
Schneider, Stephen A. '72 (SPC) [3] Springfield, MO Immaculate Conception Church.
Schneider, Stephen V. *o.f.m.* '38 (L) [16] Louisville, KY St. Boniface Church.
Schneider, Terrance L. '79 (CIN) Oxford, OH St. Mary Church and Catholic Campus Ministry Church; [Q] Oxford, OH Miami University Catholic Campus Ministry.
Schneider, Thomas H. *s.j.* '79 (BO) [W] Boston, MA The Society of Jesus of New England-Provincial Offices; [W] Cambridge, MA Faber House.
Schneider, Thomas H. *s.j.* '79 (FgM) Provinces.
Schneider, Todd '85 (SCL) Elmdale, MN St. Edward's Church; Upsala, MN St. Mary Church.
Schneider, Vincent N. '38 (MIL) Retired.
Schneider, William F. '68 (NOR) Gales Ferry, CT Our Lady of Lourdes Church.
Schneider, William T. '63 (TR) Freehold, NJ St. Rose of Lima Church; Marlboro, NJ New Jersey State Hospital.
Schneller, Michael J. '72 (NO) Belle Chasse, LA Our Lady of Perpetual Help Church.
Schneweis, Emil F. *o.f.m.cap.* '39 (MIL) [P] Mount Calvary, WI St. Lawrence Friary.
Schnipke, Eugene '80 (SB) Military Chaplains.
Schnipke, Eugene H. *c.pp.s.* '80 (B) Mountain Home Air Force Base, ID St. Mary's Church.
Schnipke, Eugene H. *c.pp.s.* '80 (CIN) [M] Dayton, OH Provincial House of the Cincinnati Province of the Society of the Precious Blood.
Schnipke, Kenneth R. *c.pp.s.* '90 (ORL) Longwood, FL Church of the Nativity.
Schnitzius, Donald J. '48 (STP) Retired.
Schnoebelen, Kenneth F. '46 (LIN) Retired.
Schnupp, Luzerne A. '57 (NSH) Franklin, TN St. Matthew Church.
Schnur, Edward C. '91 (EVN) Rockport, IN St. Bernard Church.
Schnurr, Msgr. Dennis M. '74 (SC) On Duty Outside the Diocese.
Schnurr, Herman J. '39 (FTW) Avilla, IN St. Mary of the Assumption Church; Retired.
Schnurr, Thomas J. *o.s.b.* '32 (BIR) [E] Cullman, AL St. Bernard Abbey.
Schober, Robert J. (BUF) Bolivar, NY St. Mary Church; Portville, NY Sacred Heart Church.
Schober, Robert J. '77 (BUF) Williamsville, NY SS. Peter and Paul Church.
Schock, Ronald A. '96 (TOL) Findlay, OH St. Michael Church.
Schock, William A. *s.j.* '62 (FgM) Provinces.
Schoderbek, Charles *s.v.d.* '47 (CHI) [B] Techny, IL Divine Word Residence.
Schoeberle, John *o.m.i.* '61 (FgM) Oblates Foreign Missions.
Schoefer, James W. '56 (STL) Ozora, MO Sacred Heart Church.
Schoellmann, Edward R. *m.m.* '65 (NY) [DD] Maryknoll, NY Maryknoll Fathers and Brothers.
Schoemann, Robert L. '66 (DM) Waukee, IA St. Boniface Church.
Schoen, Thomas A. *s.m.* '87 (CIN) [D] Dayton, OH The University of Dayton; [M] Dayton, OH Marianist Provincialate.
Schoen, Timothy *o.s.b.* '64 (KC) [A] Conception, MO Conception Seminary College; [J] Conception, MO Conception Abbey.
Schoenauer, Francis P. '73 (ALN) [8] Reading, PA St. Margaret Church.
Schoenbachler, Charles *c.r.* '42 (L) [18] Louisville, KY St. Cecilia Church.
Schoenberg, Oscar C. *o.s.c.* '48 (LIN) [A] Hastings, NE Crosier Monastery.
Schoenberg, Wilfred P. *s.j.* '51 (P) [L] Portland, OR Colombiere Community.
Schoenberger, James T. '57 (STP) North Branch, MN St. Gregory Church; Shakopee, MN Women's State Reformatory.
Schoenfeldt, Arthur *c.s.c.* '59 (P) [B] Portland, OR University of Portland; [L] Portland, OR Holy Cross Fathers & Brothers, C.S.C. - University of Portland.
Schoenhofen, Darr '82 (SY) On Duty Outside the Diocese.
Schoenhofen, Darr F. '82 (SY) [1] Endicott, NY Our Lady of Good Counsel Church.
Schoenhofen, Roger *o.m.i.* '66 (BEL) [H] Belleville, IL Retreat and Renewal Center.
Schoening, Sylvester H. '58 (PBL) Retired.
Schoenstein, Raymond *o.m.i.* (FgM) Oblates Foreign Missions.
Schoenstene, Robert L. '75 (CHI) [A] Mundelein, IL University of St. Mary of the Lake-Mundelein Seminary.
Schoenstene, Robert L. '75 (JOL) On Duty Outside the Diocese.
Schoeppe, Charles K. (GAL) [N] Houston, TX Pope John XXIII Priest Residence.
Schoeppe, F. Warren *s.j.* '58 (SLC) Brigham City, UT St. Henry Church.
Schoettelkotte, Msgr. Charles T. '34 (EVN) Retired.
Schoettelkotte, John (IND) St. Anne, IN St. Anne Church.
Schoettelkotte, John B. '60 (IND) North Vernon, IN St. Mary/Nativity of the Blessed Virgin Mary Church; St. Joseph, IN St. Joseph Church.
Schoettelkotte, Lawrence A. *s.m.* '70 (KAL) Portage, MI St. Catherine of Siena Church; [E] Portage, MI Society of Mary.
Schoettmer, Kenneth J. '68 (CIN) Millville, OH Queen of Peace Church.
Schoffelmeer, Arnold L. '56 (SPK) Retired.
Scholl, William G. *o.s.f.s.* '61 (PH) [AA] Philadelphia, PA Oblates of St. Francis De Sales.
Scholla, Rob *s.j.* '86 (LA) [F] Los Angeles, CA Loyola High School.
Scholsky, Martin J. '56 (HRT) [5] East Hartford, CT St. Mary's Church.
Scholz, James P. '71 (OM) [42] Omaha, NE Sacred Heart Church; [F] Omaha, NE Christian Urban Education Service Foundation; [O] Omaha, NE Christian Urban Education Service.
Scholz, LeRoy '66 (SCL) Clear Lake, MN St. Marcus Church.
Scholz, William J. '52 (PIT) Robinson Township, PA Holy Trinity Church.
Schoming, Henry C. *c.s.sp.* '43 (VEN) [G] Sarasota, FL Congregation of the Holy Ghost.
Schommer, George '94 (CIN) [30] Cincinnati, OH St. Gertrude Church; [M] Cincinnati, OH St. Gertrude Priory.

Schommer, Msgr. Mark J. '63 (GB) Bear Creek, WI St. Mary Church; Clintonville, WI St. Rose Church.
Schommer, Michael '93 (FAR) Langdon, ND St. Alphonsus Church.
Schon, Randy L. '88 (SC) Oyens, IA St. Catherine's Church.
Schons, Msgr. Gerard '47 (SAC) Retired and in Senior Ministry.
Schoofs, Robert *o.s.b.* '58 (FgM) American - Cassinese Congregation Foreign Missions.
Schook, James R. '75 (L) Payneville, KY St. Mary Magdalen of Pazzi Church; Rhodelia, KY St. Theresa Church.
Schooler, William C. '74 (FTW) [9] Fort Wayne, IN St. Jude Church.
Schoone, Raymond L. '58 (SUP) Retired.
Schopfer, John C. '69 (SY) [1] Syracuse, NY The Cathedral of the Immaculate Conception; Special Assignment.
Schopman, Joop *s.j.* '66 (BO) [W] Chestnut Hill, MA The Jesuit Community at Boston College.
Schopp, George L. '74 (CHI) Blue Island, IL St. Benedict Church.
Schoppe, Msgr. Charles K. '49 (GAL) Retired.
Schopps, William J. '85 (ARL) Colonial Beach, VA St. Elizabeth Church; Colonial Beach, VA St. Elizabeth Church.
Schork, John *c.p.* (GAL) [S] Houston, TX Holy Name Retreat Center.
Schork, John *c.p.* '76 (GAL) [S] Houston, TX Holy Name Retreat Center.
Schorp, W. Franz *s.m.* '64 (SAT) [C] San Antonio, TX St. Mary's University of San Antonio, Texas; [M] San Antonio, TX Marianist Residence.
Schorr, James D. '68 (CLV) [2] Elyria, OH Holy Cross Church.
Schorr, W. David '73 (PIT) [78] Pittsburgh, PA Most Holy Name of Jesus Church.
Schott, Edward *s.j.* '63 (ELP) [21] El Paso, TX Sacred Heart Church.
Schott, Fred '88 (COV) Leave of Absence.
Schott, James '61 (NO) [61] New Orleans, LA St. Stephen Church.
Schott, Kevin J. '90 (NEW) Cedar Grove, NJ St. Catherine of Siena Church.
Schott, Paul *s.j.* '60 (NO) [8] New Orleans, LA Holy Name of Jesus Church.
Schott, Timothy R. '70 (SC) Cherokee, IA Immaculate Conception Church.
Schott, Valerian *o.f.m.* '32 (STL) Oakville, MO St. Francis of Assisi Church; [P] Oakville, MO St. Francis Friary.
Schott, Victor P. '56 (LFT) Retired.
Schotzko, Philip M. '73 (NU) Hector, MN Church of St. John.
Schotzko, Philip M. '77 (NU) Bird Island, MN St. Mary Church.
Schouten, Frank L. '58 (CHI) [56] Chicago, IL St. Eugene Church.
Schoutten, Francis *o.m.i.* '41 (SAT) [K] San Antonio, TX Oblate Madonna Residence.
Schrad, Merlin J. '77 (SC) [B] Carroll, IA Kuemper Catholic High School.
Schrader, James C., Jr. '76 (LIN) Campbell, NE St. Ann's Church.
Schrader, James H. *c.pp.s.* '56 (KC) Nevada, MO St. Mary's Church.
Schrader, Robert J. '78 (ROC) [3] Auburn, NY St. Mary Church.
Schrage, Frank (GB) Shiocton, WI St. Denis Church.
Schrage, Frank P. '68 (GB) [F] Green Bay, WI St. Mary's Hospital-Medical Center.
Schramel, Michael J. (ROC) [2] Rochester, NY St. Ambrose Church.
Schramel, Sebastian *o.s.b.* '45 (SCL) [I] Collegeville, MN St. John's Abbey, of the Order of St. Benedict.
Schramko, Stewart R. *c.s.v.* '64 (LAV) [1] Las Vegas, NV Guardian Angel Cathedral.
Schramm, Charles H. '71 (MIL) [73] Milwaukee, WI St. Sebastian Church.
Schramm, Donald C. '67 (STL) Troy, MO Sacred Heart Church.
Schramm, Edward J. '69 (STL) Kinloch, MO Holy Angels Church.
Schramm, Mark *s.v.d.* '75 (CHI) [N] Chicago, IL Divine Word Theologate.
Schramm, Robert *o.s.f.s.* '69 (SAG) [4] Saginaw, MI SS. Simon and Jude Church.
Schratz, Martin *o.f.m.cap.* '83 (CHL) [10] Charlotte, NC St. Thomas Aquinas Church.
Schray, Karl '65 (P) North Bend, OR Holy Redeemer Church.
Schreck, Christopher J. '77 (PH) [A] Wynnewood, PA Theological Seminary of St. Charles Borromeo, Overbrook.
Schreck, Christopher J. '77 (SAV) On Duty Outside the Diocese.
Schreck, J. Gerard '83 (SAV) [A] Columbus, GA Pacelli Catholic High School.
Schreck, Joseph *o.f.m.cap.* '55 (ARE) [1] Utuado, PR San Miquel Church.
Schreck, Joseph Gerard '83 (SAV) [3] Columbus, GA St. Anne Church.
Schreck, Paul C. '45 (BUF) [K] Lewiston, NY Mount St. Mary's Hospital of Niagara Falls.
Schreiber, Bernard G. '47 (LC) Retired.
Schreiber, Edmund J. '44 (CHI) Franklin Park, IL St. Gertrude Church; Retired.
Schreiber, Gerard H. *c.ss.r.* '54 (RIC) [N] Hampton, VA Holy Family Retreat.
Schreiber, Lawrence *o.f.m.* '60 (SFE) [J] Albuquerque, NM San Antonio Provincial Friary Franciscan Friars.
Schreiber, William A. '79 (SC) Le Mars, IA St. Joseph's Church; [B] Le Mars, IA Gehlen Catholic School.
Schreiner, Bernard P. '42 (NU) Retired.
Schreiner, John E. (TOL) Retired.
Schreiner, Robert C. *s.t.l.* '89 (CR) Stephen, MN St. Stephen's Church.
Schreiner, William M. *c.s.c.* '42 (FTW) [L] Notre Dame, IN Holy Cross Mission House.
Schreiter, Daniel A. '50 (GB) Retired.
Schreiter, John P. '69 (MIL) Dousman, WI St. Bruno Church.
Schreiter, Robert *c.pp.s.* '75 (CHI) [B] Chicago, IL The Catholic Theological Union at Chicago.
Schreitmueller, Henry J. '56 (NEW) [B] South Orange, NJ Seton Hall University.
Schremmer, Robert A. '76 (DOD) Belpre, KS St. Bernard Church; Larned, KS Sacred Heart Church.
Schrenger, Arthur C. '75 (MOB) [4] Montgomery, AL Church of the Holy Spirit.
Schriber, Robert T. '96 (R) Cary, NC St. Michael the Archangel Church.
Schriefer, Msgr. Robert F. '44 (E) Retired.
Schrimpf, Raymond *s.d.s.* '56 (MIL) [P] Milwaukee, WI Salvatorian Provincial Residence.
Schrimpf, Reginald '50 (MIL) [P] Milwaukee, WI Salvatorians - Jordan Hall.
Schriver, Ragan '95 (KNX) [6] Knoxville, TN St. John Neumann Church.
Schrod, Merlin '77 (SC) Lidderdale, IA Holy Family Church.
Schroder, John F. *s.j.* '53 (FgM) Provinces.
Schroder, John F. *s.j.* '53 (NO) [P] New Orleans, LA Jesuit Provincial Office.
Schroeder, Dennis A. '61 (TOL) Bucyrus, OH Holy Trinity Church.
Schroeder, Edward H. '58 (BUF) Clarence Center, NY St. Augustine Church.
Schroeder, Eugene '79 (EVN) [20] Evansville, IN St. Theresa Church.
Schroeder, Francis J. *s.s.j.* '45 (BR) [8] Baton Rouge, LA St. Francis Xavier Church.
Schroeder, Fred A. '42 (LFT) Carmel, IN St. Elizabeth Ann Seton Church.
Schroeder, George *o.f.m.conv.* '43 (SAV) St. Simons Island, GA St. Williams Church.
Schroeder, George J. '42 (PEO) [1] Rock Island, IL St. Mary Church; Retired.
Schroeder, George M. '62 (DEN) Steamboat Springs, CO Holy Name Church; [P] Steamboat Springs, CO Colorado Mountain College.
Schroeder, James *s.c.j.* '70 (MIL) [P] Franklin, WI Dehon House.
Schroeder, Jerome *o.f.m.cap.* '70 (MIL) [S] Milwaukee, WI The Dwelling Place.
Schroeder, Karl G. '34 (DUB) Retired; [C] Dubuque, IA Loras College.
Schroeder, Kenneth J. *c.pp.s.* '65 (CIN) [M] Dayton, OH Provincial House of the Cincinnati Province of the Society of the Precious Blood.
Schroeder, Richard F. '45 (CHI) Retired.
Schroeder, Roger P. *s.v.d.* '79 (CHI) [B] Chicago, IL The Catholic Theological Union at Chicago; [B] Techny, IL Divine Word Residence; [N] Chicago, IL Divine Word Theologate; [N] Techny, IL Society of the Divine Word, Provincial Headquarter-Chicago Prov.
Schroeder, Thomas H. '64 (MAD) Pardeeville, WI St. Mary Church.
Schroeder, Timothy C. '88 (FAR) [3] Fargo, ND Nativity Church.
Schroeder, Msgr. Walter L. '41 (NY) Armonk, NY St. Patrick Church; Retired.
Schroeder, William H. '55 (PIT) Wexford, PA St. Alphonsus Church.
Schroeder, William L. '45 (CIN) [32] Cincinnati, OH Guardian Angels Church; Retired.
Schroeppel, Stephen L. *m.m.* '58 (STL) [P] St. Louis, MO Maryknoll House.
Schroer, Joseph *o.c.s.o.* '52 (SLC) [F] Huntsville, UT Abbey of Our Lady of the Holy Trinity of the Order of Cistercians.
Schroer, Thomas A. *s.m.* '72 (CIN) [D] Dayton, OH The University of Dayton; [M] Dayton, OH Marianist Provincialate.
Schroering, Francis A. '59 (EVN) Haubstadt, IN SS. Peter and Paul Church.
Schroering, Raymond A. '49 (EVN) Retired.
Schroll, Bernard A. '69 (DET) Clawson, MI Guardian Angels Church; Retired.
Schroth, Raymond A. *s.j.* '67 (NO) [C] New Orleans, LA Loyola University.
Schroth, Raymond A. *s.j.* '67 (NY) [DD] New York, NY Jesuit Community at Fordham University.
Schubeck, Thomas L. *s.j.* '68 (CLV) [C] Cleveland, OH John Carroll Jesuit Community.
Schubert, Gerard H. *o.s.f.s.* '59 (ALN) [B] Center Valley, PA Allentown College of St. Francis de Sales; [K] Center Valley, PA Oblates of St. Francis de Sales.
Schubert, Gerold *o.f.m.* '54 (JOL) [J] Joliet, IL St. John the Baptist Friary.
Schubert, Herbert B. '56 (MIL) [1] South Milwaukee, WI St. Adalbert Church.
Schubiger, Albert B. '49 (MAD) Retired.
Schuck, Hugh *o.s.b.* '34 (RCK) [H] Aurora, IL Marmion Abbey-St. Augustine's Abbey.
Schuck, Joseph J. '53 (ALB) Sidney, NY Sacred Heart Church.
Schuck, Joseph J. '53 (BRK) Released from Diocesan Assignment.
Schuckenbrock, Harry *o.m.i.* '59 (BWN) [7] Brownsville, TX St. Eugene De Mazenod Church.
Schuckman, Kenneth J. '92 (WCH) Newton, KS St. Mary Church; [M] Wichita, KS Serra Club of Wichita - Downtown.
Schudde, Derk M. '89 (OG) Absent on Leave.
Schue, Dennis L. '57 (FAR) Retired; [D] Devils Lake, ND Mercy Hospital.
Schuele, Francis J. (KC) [I] Kansas City, MO Jeanne Jugan Center.
Schuele, Francis J. '68 (KC) Special Assignment.
Schuele, John C. '76 (KC) [7] Kansas City, MO St. Catherine of Siena Church.
Schueller, Anthony L. *s.s.s.* '77 (CLV) [B] Cleveland, OH Blessed Sacrament Seminary, Congregation of the Blessed Sacrament; [P] Cleveland, OH Congregation of the Blessed Sacrament Provincial House; [P] Cleveland, OH Blessed Sacrament Community.
Schueller, La Verne L. '66 (DUB) Military Chaplains.
Schueller, Michael G. '97 (DUB) Mason City, IA St. Joseph's Church.
Schuer, Robert J. '48 (COL) [2] Columbus, OH St. Agatha Church; Retired.
Schuerger, Anthony J. '77 (CLV) [44] Cleveland, OH Community of St. Malachi Church; [45] Cleveland, OH St. Malachi Church.
Schuerman, James T. '86 (MIL) Graduate Studies; [A] Milwaukee, WI St. Francis Seminary.
Schuessler, Peter *s.d.s.* '80 (MIL) [B] Hales Corners, WI Sacred Heart School of Theology; [P] Milwaukee, WI Salvatorian Provincial Residence.
Schuessler, William R. '67 (RCK) Special Assignment.
Schuett, John T. *s.j.* '58 (DET) [P] Bloomfield Hills, MI Manresa Jesuit Retreat House.
Schuetze, John (GB) [5] Green Bay, WI St. Bernard Church.
Schug, John *o.f.m.cap.* '54 (SPR) [L] Springfield, MA St. Francis of Assisi Chapel and Catholic Information Center.
Schuh, Earl '43 (GB) Retired.
Schuh, Earl J. '43 (GB) [13] Green Bay, WI SS. Peter and Paul Church.
Schuh, Msgr. John H. '65 (GB) Special Assignment.
Schuh, Walter *l.c.* '94 (HRT) [B] Cheshire, CT Novitiate of the Legion of Christ.
Schuhmacher, George J. '57 (COV) Warsaw, KY St. Joseph Church.
Schuler, A. John '74 (STL) Ferguson, MO Our Lady of Guadalupe Church.
Schuler, Emett '69 (PIT) [O] Pittsburgh, PA St. Francis Friary.
Schuler, Emitt *o.f.m.cap.* '69 (PIT) Allegheny County, PA Department of Veterans Affairs Medical Center Aspinwall; Allegheny County, PA Department of Veterans Affairs Medical Center Oakland.
Schuler, Gregory '77 (LEX) [1] Lexington, KY Cathedral of Christ the King.
Schuler, Msgr. Richard J. '45 (STP) [12] St. Paul, MN St. Agnes Church.
Schuler, Robert J. '89 (JOL) Clarendon Hills, IL Notre Dame Church.
Schuler, Stephen *s.v.d.* '79 (BLX) [A] Bay St. Louis, MS St. Augustine's.
Schuller, Frederick E. *s.j.* '52 (STL) [P] St. Louis, MO The Jesuits of the Missouri Province.
Schulmeister, Lawrence *o.f.m.* (BAL) Baltimore, MD University of Maryland Hospital.
Schulmeister, Lawrence *o.f.m.* '67 (NY) [DD] New York, NY Franciscan Friars, Order of Friars Minor, Holy Name Province.
Schulte, Bernard C. *s.j.* '47 (STL) [O] St. Louis, MO Fusz Pavilion.
Schulte, Carl G. *c.m.* '48 (KC) [J] Kansas City, MO Vincentian Parish Mission Center.
Schulte, Francisco *o.s.b.* '79 (FgM) American - Cassinese Congregation Foreign Missions.
Schulte, Francisco *o.s.b.* '79 (SCL) [I] Collegeville, MN St. John's Abbey, of the Order of St. Benedict.
Schulte, Gary '72 (DET) [11] Warren, MI St. Sylvester Church.
Schulte, John R. '77 (COV) [M] Erlanger, KY Monastery of the Sacred Passion.

Schulte, Msgr. Joseph M. '37 (DM) Retired.
Schulte, Lyle L. '60 (LC) Boyceville, WI St. Luke Church; Menomonie, WI St. Joseph Church.
Schulte, Mark A. '97 (SFD) [5] Springfield, IL St. Agnes Church.
Schulte, Oswald W. '45 (LC) Retired; [I] La Crosse, WI Holy Cross (Seminary) Diocesan Center.
Schulte, Robert '75 (FTW) [4] Fort Wayne, IN St. Elizabeth Ann Seton Church.
Schulte, William P. '52 (NEW) Retired.
Schultenover, David G. *s.j.* '69 (OM) [K] Omaha, NE Campion House.
Schulterbrandt, Henrique *c.ss.r.* '94 (FgM) Redemptorist Foreign Missions.
Schultheis, Michael J. *s.j.* '65 (FgM) Provinces.
Schultheis, Michael J. *s.j.* '65 (P) [L] Portland, OR Jesuit Provincial Office (Society of Jesus, Oregon Prov.).
Schultheis, Raymond *c.pp.s.* '56 (CLV) Cleveland, OH Deaconess Hospital.
Schultz, Blaine *o.s.b.* '60 (KCK) [A] Atchison, KS Benedictine College; [H] Atchison, KS St. Benedict's Abbey.
Schultz, Bruce *o.p.* '88 (NO) [25] New Orleans, LA St. Anthony Of Padua Church.
Schultz, Henry A. *c.ss.r.* '49 (STL) [P] Liguori, MO St. Clement Health Care Center.
Schultz, John (PEO) Danville, IL Veterans' Administration Hospital.
Schultz, John A. '65 (LC) [4] Eau Claire, WI St. James the Greater Church.
Schultz, John C. '57 (LFT) On Duty Outside the Diocese.
Schultz, John M. '82 (E) [2] Oil City, PA Our Lady Help of Christians Church; [C] Oil City, PA Venango Christian High School.
Schultz, Ray '91 (LAV) [4] Las Vegas, NV Our Lady of Las Vegas Church.
Schultz, Msgr. Raymond T. '47 (PIT) Beaver, PA SS. Peter and Paul Church; Beaver County, PA Beaver County Jail.
Schultz, Russell '66 (SAN) Retired.
Schultz, Russell '66 (SAT) [K] San Antonio, TX Padua Place.
Schultz, Msgr. William E. '70 (ALT) Roaring Spring, PA St. Thomas More Church.
Schultz, Msgr. William F. '64 (BGP) [4] Stratford, CT Our Lady of Grace Church.
Schultze, C. Ray '91 (BEL) Special Assignment.
Schultze, George E. *s.j.* '94 (LA) [R] Culver City, CA Ignatius House, The Novitiate of the California Province, Society of Jesus.
Schulz, Albert H. *s.j.* '44 (STL) [P] St. Louis, MO Jesuit Community Corporation at St. Louis University - Jesuit Hall.
Schulz, Msgr. Donald C. '53 (COL) [4] Columbus, OH St. Aloysius Church; Retired.
Schulz, James W. *s.j.* '77 (GRY) [J] East Chicago, IN Roque Gonzalez Residence-Jesuit Fathers; [O] Hammond, IN Heartland Center.
Schulz, Raymond B. '37 (LC) Retired.
Schulz, Ronald (PMB) On Duty Outside the Diocese.
Schulz, Wilfred *o.s.b.* '53 (NEW) [1] Linden, NJ St. Elizabeth's Church.
Schulz, Wilfred G. *o.s.b.* '53 (PAT) [M] Morristown, NJ St. Mary's Abbey.
Schulze, Paul *s.d.s.* (GB) [H] Kaukauna, WI St. Paul Home, Inc.
Schulze, Robert R. '69 (TR) New Egypt, NJ Assumption Church.
Schulzetenberg, Raymond A. '46 (SCL) Gilman, MN SS. Peter and Paul Church.
Schumacher, Andrew J. '59 (B) [3] Boise, ID St. Mary's Church.
Schumacher, Anthony J. '60 (MAD) Oregon, WI Holy Mother of Consolation Church.
Schumacher, Charles P. '48 (LC) Bakerville, WI Corpus Christi Church; Retired.
Schumacher, Ernest *c.r.* '41 (L) Raywick, KY St. Francis Xavier Church; St. Mary, KY St. Charles Church.
Schumacher, Eugene T. '56 (SC) Rock Rapids, IA Holy Name Church.
Schumacher, Gerard (CHL) Clemmons, NC Holy Family Church.
Schumacher, Jacob J. (BIS) Retired.
Schumacher, Jacob J. '52 (BIS) [G] Bismarck, ND Emmaus Place.
Schumacher, James A. '95 (CHY) Sheridan, WY Holy Name Church.
Schumacher, John N. *s.j.* '57 (FgM) Provinces.
Schumacher, Msgr. Joseph A. '57 (FWT) [5] Arlington, TX St. Matthew Church.
Schumacher, Leo C. '32 (SC) Retired.
Schumacher, Louis E. '47 (IND) Brookville, IN St. Michael Church; Cedar Grove, IN Holy Guardian Angels Church.
Schumacher, Mark R. '84 (B) Moscow, ID St. Augustine's Church; [F] Moscow, ID University of Idaho, St. Augustine Catholic Center.
Schumacher, Patrick A. '52 (BIS) Regent, ND St. Henry Church.
Schumacher, Patrick A. '93 (BIS) New England, ND St. Mary Church.
Schumacher, Paul '48 (GB) Retired.
Schumacher, Paul A. '62 (NU) Kandiyohi, MN St. Patrick Church; Lake Lillian, MN St. Thomas More Church.
Schumacher, Robert A. '49 (SPC) Sikeston, MO St. Francis Xavier's Church.
Schuster, Anthony J. '70 (GF) [5] Great Falls, MT St. Luke the Evangelist Church; [K] Great Falls, MT St. Joseph's Education Trust.
Schuster, Charles G. *c.m.* '55 (FgM) Vincentian Foreign Missions.
Schuster, Francis J. *k.h.s.* '63 (ALN) Whitehall, PA St. John the Baptist Church.
Schuster, Msgr. George J. '38 (LIN) Retired.
Schuster, Msgr. George M. '57 (BRK) [215] Queens, NY Our Lady of the Miraculous Medal Church.
Schuster, Paul '93 (FAR) Manvel, ND St. Timothy's Church.
Schuster, Peter L. '95 (WIN) Worthington, MN St. Mary's Church.
Schuster, Philip *o.s.b.* (KC) [G] Maryville, MO St. Francis Hospital & Health Services.
Schuster, Raymond '93 (SAT) [30] San Antonio, TX St. Bonaventure Church.
Schuster, Robert C. '95 (DET) Utica, MI St. Lawrence Church.
Schuster, Valery P. '41 (MIL) Retired.
Schuster, Vincent *c.pp.s.* '44 (CIN) [B] Carthagena, OH St. Charles.
Schuster, Wilfred J. '46 (MAD) [10] Madison, WI St. Maria Goretti Church; Retired.
Schute, Arthur B. (NEW) On Duty Outside the Archdiocese.
Schute, Arthur B. '67 (VEN) [D] Port Charlotte, FL Bon Secours-St. Joseph Hospital.
Schute, Bruce J. *s.a.c.* '60 (MIL) [P] Milwaukee, WI Pallotti House.
Schutte, James R. '79 (CIN) [2] Dayton, OH St. Agnes Church; [8] Dayton, OH Corpus Christi Church.
Schutte, Robert W. '43 (CIN) Retired.
Schutten, Msgr. Marion '45 (NO) Mandeville, LA Southeast Louisiana Hospital.
Schutter, Thomas '68 (JOL) Carol Stream, IL St. Luke Church.
Schutty, John J. '83 (JC) Meta, MO St. Cecilia Church.
Schuwey, Emil A. *c.pp.s.* '49 (CIN) [M] Dayton, OH Provincial House of the Cincinnati Province of the Society of the Precious Blood.
Schuyler, David *s.m.* '60 (SJ) Special Assignment.
Schuyler, Henry C. '45 (PH) Trooper, PA Visitation B.V.M. Church; Retired.
Schuyler, Joseph B. *s.j.* '51 (NY) [DD] New York, NY Murray-Weigel Hall.
Schwaab, Paul J. '54 (OM) [24] Omaha, NE St. John Vianney Church.
Schwab, Donald F. '73 (ROC) Absent on Leave.
Schwab, Elwin C. '60 (P) St. Helens, OR St. Frederic Church.
Schwab, James A. '81 (JOL) [13] Joliet, IL St. Jude Church.
Schwab, Jerome F. '92 (CHR) Lexington, SC Corpus Christi Church.
Schwab, Joseph '48 (OAK) Retired.
Schwab, Joseph C. *o.m.i.* '53 (PT) Madison, FL St. Vincent de Paul Church; Monticello, FL St. Margaret Church.
Schwab, Msgr. Robert C. '41 (BUF) Retired.
Schwab, Steven '90 (IND) [10] Indianapolis, IN Nativity of Our Lord Jesus Christ Church.
Schwab, Thomas E. '56 (CHI) Rosemont-Des Plaines, IL Our Lady of Hope Church.
Schwaegel, Msgr. Joseph R. '65 (BEL) Leave of Absence.
Schwaig, R. John '90 (STL) Chesterfield, MO Ascension Church.
Schwalenberg, Msgr. Martin '45 (BAL) Retired.
Schwalm, Donald '52 (KCK) On Duty Outside the Archdiocese.
Schwan, Paul Mark *o.c.s.o.* '88 (SAC) [A] Vina, CA Abbey of New Clairvaux, Trappist Seminary; [G] Vina, CA Abbey of New Clairvaux, Trappist.
Schwane, Robert A. *c.m.* '53 (DEN) [12] Denver, CO Holy Ghost Church.
Schwanger, Kenneth '90 (MIA) [2] Hialeah, FL San Lazaro Church.
Schwantes, John A. *s.j.* '69 (RC) [B] Howes, SD Kino Jesuit Community; [D] Howes, SD The Diocese of Rapid City Mahpiya na Maka Okoigna.
Schwantner, James *o.f.m.* '55 (SP) [O] St. Petersburg, FL St. Anthony Friary.
Schware, Richard A. '75 (ALN) Pen Argyl, PA St. Elizabeth of Hungary Church.
Schwarte, Michael '95 (JUN) Hoonah, AK Sacred Heart Church; Skagway, AK St. Therese of the Child Jesus Church; Yakutat, AK St. Ann Church.
Schwarte, Msgr. Michael W. '38 (DM) Retired.
Schwarting, J. Donald '66 (GAL) Military Chaplains.
Schwartz, Anthony '49 (PHX) Retired.
Schwartz, Christopher *o.s.b.* '74 (CLV) Broadview Heights, OH Assumption Church; [P] Cleveland, OH Benedictine Order of Cleveland.
Schwartz, David C. *s.j.* '54 (OAK) [N] Oakland, CA Murray Residence Community.
Schwartz, Edwin V. '60 (ALN) Northampton, PA Our Lady of Hungary Church.
Schwartz, Hugh F. '56 (OM) Blair, NE St. Francis Borgia Church.
Schwartz, James A. '68 (ROC) Pittsford, NY St. Louis Church.
Schwartz, John *s.j.* '64 (SEA) Mount Vernon, WA Immaculate Conception Church.
Schwartz, Kevin '93 (SCL) Bluffton, MN St. John the Baptist Church; Butler, MN Holy Cross Church; Menahga, MN The Church of the Assumption of Our Lady of Menahga.
Schwartz, Norman R. '69 (MIL) [K] Milwaukee, WI St. Joseph's Hospital of Franciscan Sisters, Milwaukee, Inc.
Schwartz, Paul E. '53 (CHI) Sauk Village, IL St. James Church; Retired.
Schwartz, Peter *o.s.b.* '62 (SFS) [F] Marvin, SD Blue Cloud Abbey.
Schwartz, Robert M. '67 (STP) Eagan, MN St. John Neumann Church; [H] Eagan, MN Faithful Shepherd Catholic School.
Schwartz, Rodney '92 (SFD) [6] Springfield, IL St. Aloysius Church.
Schwartz, Rodney A. '92 (SFD) [7] Springfield, IL St. Frances Cabrini Church.
Schwartz, William H. '53 (CIN) [4] Hamilton, OH St. Peter in Chains Church.
Schwartz, Msgr. William H. '68 (RCK) [1] Rockford, IL St. Peter Cathedral.
Schwartz, William J. '68 (PIT) Oakdale, PA St. Patrick Church.
Schwartz, William T. '58 (DUB) Retired.
Schwartzkopf, Gary W. *s.j.* '69 (NY) [DD] New York, NY Murray-Weigel Hall.
Schwarz, Bernard F. '66 (OKL) Retired.
Schwarz, Elmer C. '53 (OKL) Chickasha, OK Holy Name Church; [K] Norman, OK Campus Ministry for the Archdiocese of Oklahoma City.
Schwarz, Paul E. *c.ss.r.* '39 (STL) [P] Liguori, MO St. Clement Health Care Center.
Schwarz, Robert '65 (MRY) Retired.
Schwarzhaupt, Robert '86 (HON) Nanakuli, HI St. Rita Church.
Schwebs, Daniel L. *o.s.j.* '86 (NOR) [5] Middletown, CT St. Sebastian Church.
Schweda, Phillip '79 (LAN) [3] Jackson, MI St. Mary, Star of the Sea Church.
Schweder, Msgr. John (DET) [73] Detroit, MI Sweetest Heart of Mary Church.
Schweder, Msgr. John F. '60 (DET) [40] Detroit, MI St. Joseph Church.
Schweers, Gregory *o.cist.* '81 (DAL) [M] Irving, TX Cistercian Abbey of Our Lady of Dallas.
Schwehr, Charles '76 (LA) West Covina, CA St. Christopher Church.
Schweibold, Conrad L. *o.f.m.conv.* '47 (FTW) Angola, IN St. Anthony Church; Big Long Lake, IN St. Mary of the Angels Church.
Schweifler, Michael *o.s.a.* '84 (TLS) [B] Tulsa, OK Cascia Hall Preparatory School.
Schweigardt, Erwin H. '67 (ALB) [4] Watervliet, NY St. Patrick Church.
Schweiger, Troy '95 (LIN) Hastings, NE St. Cecilia's Church.
Schweihofer, Frederick J. '68 (DET) [9] Sterling Heights, MI St. Rene Goupil Church.
Schweihofer, Walter J. '38 (DET) Retired.
Schweikert, John *m.s.c.* '96 (ALN) Nazareth, PA Holy Family Church.
Schweiss, Kurt *o.f.m.* '85 (LA) [72] Los Angeles, CA St. Joseph Church.
Schweitzer, Msgr. Francis X. '45 (COL) Retired.
Schweitzer, Gerald H. '71 (GRY) Wanatah, IN Sacred Heart Church.
Schweitzer, Joachim B. *o.s.b.* '58 (PAT) [M] Morristown, NJ St. Mary's Abbey.
Schweitzer, Paul A. *s.j.* '70 (FgM) Provinces.
Schweitzer, Peter '93 (SP) Absent on Leave; [L] Clearwater, FL The Tepeyac Corporation dba/La Clinica Guadalupana.
Schweitzer, Robert '67 (PIT) [83] Pittsburgh, PA Risen Lord Church; Allegheny County, PA Allegheny County Jail.
Schweitzer, Tom '82 (LA) Vernon, CA Holy Angels Parish of the Deaf Church.
Schweizer, Paul *o.carm.* '62 (NEW) Bogota, NJ St. Joseph's Church.
Schweizer, Vincent J. '58 (L) Pewee Valley, KY St. Aloysius Church.
Schwellenbach, Aloysius '48 (SFD) Absent on Leave.
Schwemin, Ralph H. '41 (SPK) Retired.
Schwendeman, Msgr. Francis J. '31 (COL) Retired.
Schwenk, William M. '60 (EVN) [15] Evansville, IN St. Boniface Church.

Schwenzer, Ronald G. *c.s.b.* '68 (SFE) [D] Albuquerque, NM St. Pius X High School; [N] Albuquerque, NM St. Pius X High School Foundation, Inc.
Schwer, Albert *c.p.* (L) [2] Louisville, KY St. Agnes Church.
Schwer, Albert *c.p.* '55 (L) [L] Louisville, KY Sacred Heart Retreat.
Schwertley, James F. '61 (OM) Fort Calhoun, NE St. John the Baptist Church.
Schwet, Edward N. '82 (CLV) [18] Akron, OH St. Vincent Church.
Schwetner, Msgr. Timothy '65 (LUB) Plainview, TX St. Alice Church.
Schwider, John *o.m.i.* '40 (FgM) Oblates Foreign Missions.
Schwieters, Severin '50 (SCL) Retired.
Schwietz, Paul *o.s.b.* '82 (SCL) [I] Collegeville, MN St. John's Abbey, of the Order of St. Benedict.
Schwind, Donald F. '46 (BRK) Retired.
Schwinger, Msgr. William A. '58 (BUF) [1] Buffalo, NY St. Joseph's Cathedral; Retired.
Schwinghamer, David J. *m.m.* '73 (FgM) Maryknoll Foreign Missions.
Schwinghammer, Claude '35 (SCL) Retired.
Schwinn, Alexander L. '35 (NU) Retired.
Schwinn, Joseph F. '43 (MIL) Retired.
Schwinn, Thomas J. '58 (DUB) Fairfax, IA St. Patrick's Church; Walford, IA Holy Trinity Church.
Scianna, Bernard C. *o.s.a.* '84 (TLS) [B] Tulsa, OK Cascia Hall Preparatory School.
Sciarra, John N. '45 (IND) [16] Indianapolis, IN St. Barnabas Church; Retired.
Sciarrotta, Lee *s.m.* '67 (CIN) [9] Dayton, OH Emmanuel Church; [M] Dayton, OH Marianist Provincialate.
Sciarrotta, Paul J. '62 (CLV) [Q] Chardon, OH Provincial House of the Sisters of Notre Dame, Juniorate, Novitiate.
Sciberras, Michael J. '67 (GBG) [1] Connellsville, PA Immaculate Conception Church.
Sciera, Msgr. Ronald P. '61 (BUF) [56] Buffalo, NY Precious Blood Church.
Scillieri, Charles P. '73 (MET) Jamesburg, NJ St. James the Less Church.
Scioli, Joseph *c.o.* '97 (PIT) [R] Slippery Rock, PA Office for Campus Ministry.
Scioli, Richard A. *c.s.s.* '79 (SPR) [9] Springfield, MA Our Lady of Mt. Carmel Church.
Scioscia, Gerard *o.f.m.conv.* (FgM) Conventual Franciscan Foreign Missions.
Scirghi, Thomas J. *s.j.* '86 (NY) [DD] New York, NY Jesuit Community at Fordham University.
Sciumbato, Michael R. '94 (SLC) Richfield, UT St. Elizabeth's Church; [H] Ephraim, UT St. Jude Catholic Center.
Sciurba, Salvatore *o.c.d.* '71 (BO) [W] Brighton, MA Carmelite Monastery.
Scocco, Victor *o.ss.t.* '81 (VIC) [4] Victoria, TX Our Lady of Sorrows Church; [F] Victoria, TX Trinity House.
Scolamiero, Dominic A. '69 (PAT) Unassigned.
Scollen, Msgr. Francis J. '71 (WOR) [27] Worcester, MA St. Peter Church.
Scolozzi, Angelo *m.c.iii.o.* '65 (BEA) Cleveland, TX St. Mary Church.
Scopa, Joseph A. *c.s.* '48 (BO) [5] Framingham, MA St. Tarcisius Church.
Scopp, Andrew *s.j.* '63 (HRT) [K] Enfield, CT The Home for the Aged of the Little Sisters of the Poor.
Scopp, Andrew J. *s.j.* '63 (BO) [W] Boston, MA The Society of Jesus of New England-Provincial Offices.
Scordo, Joseph Anthony *o.p.* '69 (NY) [DD] New York, NY St. Vincent Ferrer Priory.
Scornaienchi, Frank *t.o.r.* '79 (ALT) [F] Newry, PA St. Bernardine Monastery.
Scorzello, Joseph F. '69 (BO) [1] Medford, MA St. Francis of Assisi Church.
Scotchie, David '93 (ORL) Indialantic, FL Holy Name of Jesus Church.
Scott, Alfonso '59 (LA) [12] Long Beach, CA Our Lady of Refuge Church; [D] Lakewood, CA Saint Joseph High School.
Scott, Brendan T. *s.j.* '78 (BUF) [O] Buffalo, NY Canisius Jesuit Community.
Scott, Charles '61 (DM) [D] Council Bluffs, IA Bergan Mercy-Alegant Health System: Mercy Hospital.
Scott, Daniel J. *m.s.* '73 (HRT) [10] New Haven, CT St. John the Baptist Church; [M] Hartford, CT Missionaries of LaSalette Provincial Secretary.
Scott, Daniel V. *m.s.* '73 (HRT) West Haven, CT V.A. CT Health Care System.
Scott, Delroy Thomas '86 (MGZ) Las Marias, PR Immaculate Heart of Mary Church.
Scott, Edward R. '56 (SCR) Lake Ariel, PA St. Thomas More Church.
Scott, Francis (BLX) Retired.
Scott, Hilary *o.f.m.* '49 (PAT) [M] Ringwood, NJ Holy Name Friary, Inc.
Scott, James C. (PAT) Unassigned.
Scott, John *o.s.b.* '72 (SEA) [M] Lacey, WA St. Martin's Abbey.
Scott, John M. *s.j.* '44 (OM) [K] Omaha, NE Jesuit Community At Creighton University.
Scott, John V. '69 (GRY) Portage, IN Nativity of Our Savior Church.
Scott, Joseph *s.v.d.* '75 (OAK) [6] Oakland, CA St. Bernard's Church.
Scott, Joseph J. *c.s.p.* '73 (P) [28] Portland, OR St. Philip Neri Church; [Q] Portland, OR Paulist Fathers Catholic Center for Evangelization.
Scott, Kenny *o.f.m.* '57 (OAK) [N] Oakland, CA Franciscan Friars.
Scott, Kenny *o.f.m.* '58 (OAK) [9] Oakland, CA St. Elizabeth's Church.
Scott, Msgr. Leonard G. '64 (CAM) [2] Cherry Hill, NJ Holy Rosary Church.
Scott, Mark A. *o.c.s.o.* '87 (SAC) [A] Vina, CA Abbey of New Clairvaux, Trappist Seminary; [G] Vina, CA Abbey of New Clairvaux, Trappist.
Scott, Michael Craig '96 (ALX) [2] Alexandria, LA Our Lady of Prompt Succor Church.
Scott, Michael P. '87 (MET) [1] Perth Amboy, NJ St. Mary Church.
Scott, Patrick J. '60 (PAT) Pompton Plains, NJ Our Lady of Good Counsel Church.
Scott, Philip '89 (SP) Spring Hill, FL Saint Joan of Arc Church.
Scott, Philip P. '79 (PSC) Roswell, GA Epiphany Byzantine Church.
Scott, Raymond J. '48 (DAL) Terrell, TX St. John Church; Terrell, TX State Hospital.
Scott, Richard A. (WDC) Clinton, MD Church of St. John the Evangelist.
Scott, Robert T. '49 (ALB) [L] Lake George, NY St. Mary of the Lake.
Scott, Robert T. *c.s.p.* '49 (AUS) Horseshoe Bay, TX St. Paul the Apostle Church.
Scott, Samuel V. '95 (BGP) Westport, CT St. Luke Church.
Scott, Vincent J. '75 (OAK) [2] Walnut Creek, CA St. John Vianney Church.
Scotti, P. Paschal *o.s.b.* '89 (PRO) [P] Portsmouth, RI Abbey of St. Gregory the Great.
Scotto, Dominic *t.o.r.* '67 (STU) [A] Steubenville, OH Franciscan University of Steubenville; [F] Steubenville, OH Holy Spirit Monastery.
Scrima, Claude *o.f.m.* '61 (NY) [DD] New York, NY Franciscan Province of the Immaculate Conception.
Scuderi, Carmen *o.f.m.* '83 (GRY) [F] Crown Point, IN St. Anthony Medical Center, Inc.; [J] Cedar Lake, IN Our Lady of Lourdes Friary.
Scuderi, Salvatore A. *m.ss.cc.* '88 (CAM) [8] Camden, NJ Our Lady of Fatima and Mount Carmel Church.
Scull, Msgr. Edward J. '51 (BGP) [6] Fairfield, CT St. Pius X Church.
Scull, James P. *s.j.* '58 (BGP) [O] Fairfield, CT The Fairfield Jesuit Community-Fairfield University.
Scull, James P. *s.j.* '58 (MIL) [P] Milwaukee, WI Jesuit Provincial Office, Wisconsin Province.
Scullin, Robert J. *s.j.* '76 (COL) [25] Columbus, OH Community of Holy Rosary and St. John Church.
Scullion, James P. *o.f.m.* '80 (WDC) [B] Silver Spring, MD Holy Name College.
Scully, Msgr. Donald J. '51 (E) [1] Sharon, PA Sacred Heart Church.
Scully, G. Michael *c.s.c.* '58 (FR) [A] North Easton, MA Holy Cross Fathers Religious.
Scully, Msgr. John '48 (SP) Spring Hill, FL St. Theresa Church.
Scully, John J. *s.j.* '57 (NY) [DD] New York, NY Jesuit Community at Fordham University.
Scully, John J. '72 (TR) Matawan, NJ St. Clement Church.
Scully, John T. *s.s.e.* '55 (BUR) Putney, VT Our Lady of Mercy Church.
Scully, Michael *o.f.m.cap.* '65 (SAL) Hays, KS St. Joseph's Church; [B] Hays, KS Thomas More Prep-Marian; [D] Hays, KS St. Joseph's Friary.
Scully, Michael G. *s.j.* '86 (SJ) [D] San Jose, CA Bellarmine College Preparatory.
Scully, Patrick A. '56 (SHP) Awaiting Assignment.
Scully, Philip A. '42 (PH) Springfield, PA St. Kevin Church; Retired.
Scully, Richard D. '78 (AMA) Dumas, TX SS. Peter and Paul Church.
Scully, Robert E. *s.j.* '96 (SY) [S] Syracuse, NY Jesuits at LeMoyne, Inc.
Scully, Timothy R. *c.s.c.* '81 (FTW) [B] Notre Dame, IN University of Notre Dame Du Lac; [B] Notre Dame, IN University of Notre Dame Du Lac; [J] Notre Dame, IN Holy Cross Community, Corby Hall, University of Notre Dame.
Scully, William *o.f.m.* '67 (PAT) Hewitt, NJ Our Lady Queen of Peace Church.
Scurti, Louis J. '73 (PAT) Totowa, NJ North Jersey Developmental Center; [O] Haledon, NJ William Paterson University of New Jersey Catholic Campus Ministry Center.
Se Mang, Peter Kim *s.j.* '78 (BO) [W] Chestnut Hill, MA The Jesuit Community at Boston College.
Seabold, John P. '88 (CLV) [1] Garfield Heights, OH St. Monica Church.
Seabridge, Thomas L. '88 (SAC) Corning, CA Immaculate Conception Church; Orland, CA St. Dominic Church; Special Assignment.
Seagrave, Thomas L. '68 (SFR) [54] San Francisco, CA Visitacion, Church of the.
Seagraves, Richard '91 (NY) Hartsdale, NY Sacred Heart Church.
Seagriff, Edward M. '81 (RVC) Lindenhurst, NY Our Lady of Perpetual Help Church.
Sealy, Robert J. *s.j.* '51 (NY) [DD] New York, NY Jesuit Community at Fordham University.
Seaman, Cyril *o.f.m.* '56 (BO) [BB] Boston, MA St. Anthony Shrine.
Seaman, Paul G. '85 (CHI) Country Club Hills, IL St. Emeric Church.
Searles, Thaddeus *s.t.* '56 (MOB) Holy Trinity, AL St. Joseph Church.
Searles, Wendell H. '55 (BUR) [F] Burlington, VT Mount St. Mary Convent.
Sears, Eugene A. '58 (KAL) St. Joseph, MI St. Joseph Church.
Sears, G. David '63 (NY) [226] Staten Island, NY St. Roch Church.
Sears, G. David '63 (SY) On Duty Outside the Diocese.
Sears, Gerald *o.c.s.o.* '73 (WOR) [N] Spencer, MA St. Joseph's Abbey; [P] Spencer, MA St. Joseph Abbey.
Sears, Michael J. '94 (LA) Encino, CA Our Lady of Grace Church.
Sears, Robert T. *s.j.* '66 (CHI) [C] Chicago, IL Jesuit Community at Loyola University of Chicago.
Sears, William F. '84 (PRO) [20] Providence, RI St. Joseph Church.
Sears, William J. '62 (BRK) Released from Diocesan Assignment.
Seasoltz, Kevin *o.s.b.* '56 (SCL) [I] Collegeville, MN St. John's Abbey, of the Order of St. Benedict.
Seaver, Paul E. *o.p.* '59 (PRO) [P] Providence, RI St. Thomas Aquinas Priory at Providence College.
Seavey, Michael J. (PRT) Sabbatical.
Seay, Robert C. *o.f.m.* '76 (NO) [45] New Orleans, LA St. Mary Of The Angels Church.
Sebaali, George M. '83 (SAM) Richmond, VA St. Anthony Church.
Sebahar, John M. '58 (JOL) Glen Ellyn, IL St. James the Apostle Church.
Sebastian, Gregory *o.s.b.* '83 (SCL) [I] Collegeville, MN St. John's Abbey, of the Order of St. Benedict.
Sebastian, Ignatius '91 (FAR) Jamestown, ND The Basilica of St. James Church; Jamestown, ND State Hospital.
Sebescak, Gary '94 (BEL) Leave of Absence.
Sebesta, James A. *s.j.* (STL) [C] St. Louis, MO Saint Louis University.
Sebesta, James A. *s.j.* '70 (STL) [P] St. Louis, MO Jesuit Community Corporation at St. Louis University - Jesuit Hall.
Sebra, Anthony G. '72 (STA) Lake City, FL Epiphany Church.
Secondo, Louis J. *t.o.r.* '46 (ALT) [7] Altoona, PA Our Lady of Mt. Carmel Church.
Secor, Gary '77 (HON) Mililani Town, HI St. John Apostle and Evangelist Church.
Secora, James L. '75 (DUB) Cedar Falls, IA St. Patrick Church.
Seculoff, James F. '62 (FTW) Bristol, IN St. Mary of the Annunciation Church.
Seda, Jon M. '88 (DUB) Ames, IA St. Thomas Aquinas Church (and Catholic Student Center) Church; [N] Ames, IA St. Thomas Aquinas Church and Catholic Student Center (Iowa State University).
Sederwall, Donald F. '85 (SFD) Barry, IL Holy Redeemer Church; Pittsfield, IL Immaculate Conception Church.
Sedita, Msgr. Vincent A. '72 (LKC) Jennings, LA Our Lady Help of Christians Church.
Sedlacek, Richard D. '79 (YAK) Benton City, WA St. Frances Xavier Cabrini Church; Kennewick, WA St. Joseph's Church.
Sedlacko, Louis S. *o.s.b.* '44 (GBG) [H] Latrobe, PA Saint Vincent Archabbey.
Sedlak, John A. '82 (GBG) Grindstone, PA St. Cecilia Church; Smock, PA St. Hedwig Church; [K] Smock, PA Ladies of Charity.
Sedlak, Kenneth *c.ss.r.* '72 (CHI) [136] Chicago, IL St. Michael Church.
Sedlak, Valentine G. '44 (PIT) Retired.
Sedley, Joseph *c.p.* '69 (WOR) [N] Shrewsbury, MA Passionist Fathers of Shrewsbury, Inc., Calvary Retreat Center; [P] Shrewsbury, MA Calvary Retreat Center, Passionist Community.
Sedlmayer, Lauro C. '85 (MET) [9] Perth Amboy, NJ Our Lady of the Rosary of Fatima Church.
Sedlock, David W. '91 (MAR) Rapid River, MI St. Charles Borromeo Church.
Sedlock, Stephen *c.s.c.* '66 (P) [L] Portland, OR Holy Cross Fathers & Brothers, C.S.C. - University of Portland.
Sedlock, Stephen J. *c.s.c.* '66 (P) [38] Portland, OR St. Vincent de Paul Church; [B] Portland, OR University of Portland.
Seeberger, Claude *o.s.b.* '49 (BIS) Glen Ullin, ND Sacred Heart of Jesus Church; [A] Richardton, ND Assumption Abbey.

Seed, Michael *s.a.* '86 (NY) [DD] Garrison, NY Generalate of the Franciscan Friars of the Atonement-St. James Friary.
Seedorf, Warren '49 (DEN) Greeley, CO St. Mary Church.
Seedorf, Warren H. *c.s.p.* '49 (NY) [DD] Jamaica Estates, NY Paulist Fathers Generalate.
Seefeldt, Wilbert T. '39 (STP) Retired.
Seegar, Kenneth M. '87 (SCR) Blossburg, PA St. Mary's Church.
Seeger, Francis J. '41 (BRK) Retired.
Seeger, James E. '85 (PIT) Canonsburg, PA St. Patrick Church.
Seeger, Peter J. '35 (BRK) [167] Queens, NY St. Fidelis Church; Retired.
Seekamp, Walter J. '79 (BGP) [4] Trumbull, CT St. Theresa's Church.
Seelaus, William O. *o.s.f.s.* '51 (PH) [D] Philadelphia, PA Father Judge High School for Boys; [AA] Philadelphia, PA Father Judge Faculty House.
Seelman, Patrick *t.o.r.* '63 (ALT) [10] Johnstown, PA St. Anthony's Church.
Seeman, Robert L. '79 (PIT) [R] Slippery Rock, PA Office for Campus Ministry; [R] Slippery Rock, PA Office for Campus Ministry.
Seery, William O. '95 (HRT) Naugatuck, CT St. Francis of Assisi Church; Oakville, CT St. Mary Magdalen Church.
Seetch, William D. *c.s.c.* '79 (FTW) [A] Notre Dame, IN Moreau Seminary; [B] Notre Dame, IN University of Notre Dame Du Lac; [J] Notre Dame, IN Holy Cross Community, Corby Hall, University of Notre Dame.
Seethaler, Scott *o.f.m.cap.* '69 (PIT) [O] Pittsburgh, PA St. Augustine Friary.
Seeton, Philip '91 (OKL) Special Assignment.
Seeton, Philip '95 (OKL) [B] Oklahoma City, OK Bishop McGuinness High School.
Seewald, Carl H. *s.v.d.* '68 (OAK) Martinez, CA St. Catherine of Siena Church.
Sefcik, Dennis L. '65 (SC) Lake City, IA St. Mary's Church; Lohrville, IA St. Joseph's Church.
Segaric, John '48 (LA) [45] Los Angeles, CA St. Anthony Church.
Segatta, Bruno '74 (B) On Duty Outside the Diocese.
Seger, Michael '88 (CIN) [B] Cincinnati, OH Mt. St. Mary's Seminary of the West.
Seger, Oscar H. '70 (CIN) Egypt, OH St. Joseph Church; On Special and Diocesan Assignment.
Segerson, Thomas M. '69 (MAD) Mineral Point, WI Congregation of St. Mary-St. Paul Church.
Seginak, Theodore J. *o.s.b.* '49 (PBR) Punxsutawney, PA SS. Peter and Paul Church.
Sego, Msgr. Arthur A. '46 (LFT) Retired.
Segotta, Vincent *c.p.* (WOR) [P] Shrewsbury, MA Calvary Retreat Center, Passionist Community.
Segotta, Vincent *c.p.* '77 (PIT) [O] Pittsburgh, PA St. Paul of the Cross Monastery.
Segotta, Vincent *c.p.* '77 (WOR) [N] Shrewsbury, MA Passionist Fathers of Shrewsbury, Inc., Calvary Retreat Center.
Segovia, Norman '67 (SJ) [4] San Jose, CA Christ the King Church.
Segreve, Richard J. *c.s.c.* '61 (FR) [A] North Easton, MA Holy Cross Fathers Religious.
Segrue, Joseph D. '53 (SY) Retired.
Seguin, Robert J. *c.s.b.* '69 (GAL) [Q] Sugar Land, TX Basilian Mission Center.
Segura, Leonicio '63 (ORG) [6] Santa Ana, CA St. Anne's Church.
Seher, Philip O. '65 (CIN) [49] Cincinnati, OH St. Joseph Church; [89] Cincinnati, OH St. William Church.
Sehler, Michael E. *s.j.* '73 (NY) [F] New York, NY Loyola School; [DD] New York, NY "America;" Residence and publication office of the America Press.
Seib, Herbert *o.c.s.o.* '37 (L) [L] Trappist, KY Abbey of Our Lady of Gethsemani, of the Order of Cistercians of the Strict Observance.
Seibert, Gary *s.j.* (NY) [45] New York, NY Holy Cross Church.
Seibert, Gary G. *s.j.* '73 (NY) [DD] New York, NY West Side Jesuit Community.
Seibert, Herman *o.f.m.conv.* '45 (SY) [2] Syracuse, NY Assumption B.V.M. Church.
Seibert, James C. *c.pp.s.* '77 (CIN) Celina, OH Immaculate Conception of the Blessed Virgin Mary Church; [M] Dayton, OH Provincial House of the Cincinnati Province of the Society of the Precious Blood.
Seibert, Thomas E. *i.c.* '75 (PEO) Elmwood, IL St. Patrick's Church; Farmington, IL St. Matthew's Church; [B] Peoria, IL Notre Dame High School.
Seichepine, Albert M. *c.s.sp.* '51 (PH) [AA] Bensalem, PA Congregation of the Holy Ghost.
Seidel, George J. *o.s.b.* '58 (SEA) [M] Lacey, WA St. Martin's Abbey.
Seidel, Michael L. '87 (STL) [46] St. Louis, MO Basilica of St. Louis, the King Church.
Seidel, Ricardo '65 (RIC) [6] Richmond, VA St. Augustine Church.
Seidel, Thomas *c.s.c.* '57 (KAL) [1] Kalamazoo, MI St. Augustine Cathedral.
Seidel, Victor *s.t.* '61 (SAV) Thomasville, GA St. Augustine's Church.
Seidenburg, Msgr. Augustine J. (CAM) Retired.
Seidl, Larry J. '75 (GB) [1] Two Rivers, WI St. Luke Church; [3] Two Rivers, WI St. Mark Church.
Seidl, Neil W. *s.d.s.* '54 (SAC) Orangevale, CA Divine Savior Church.
Seif, Magdi *s.j.* '97 (BO) [W] Chestnut Hill, MA The Jesuit Community at Boston College.
Seifert, Michael *s.m.* '85 (BWN) [11] Brownsville, TX San Felipe de Jesus Church.
Seifert, Michael D. '84 (Y) Waynesburg, OH St. James Church.
Seifert, Raymond *c.pp.s.* '44 (CIN) [B] Carthagena, OH St. Charles.
Seifert, William *s.v.d.* '67 (FgM) Society of the Divine Word Foreign Missions.
Seifert, William '81 (ALN) [C] Tamaqua, PA Marian Catholic High School.
Seifert, William N. '81 (ALN) Tamaqua, PA St. Jerome Church.
Seifferly, Richard R. '63 (GAY) Retired.
Seifner, Thomas J. '92 (JC) Chamois, MO Most Pure Heart of Mary Church; Morrison, MO Assumption Church; Rhineland, MO Church of the Risen Savior.
Seifried, Msgr. Kenneth A. (ATL) Atlanta, GA Fort McPherson.
Seifried, Kenneth A. '63 (SC) On Duty Outside the Diocese.
Seigel, Timothy J. '91 (RCK) Mount Carroll, IL SS. John and Catherine Church.
Seigle, Timothy J. '91 (RCK) Savanna, IL St. John the Baptist Church.
Seiker, Daniel J. '87 (LIN) [G] Lincoln, NE School Sisters of Christ the King, Villa Regina Motherhouse & Novitiate.
Seiker, Leo V. '91 (LIN) Bellwood, NE St. Peter's Church.
Seiker, Mark E. '84 (LIN) Beatrice, NE St. Joseph's Church.
Seil, Paul D. '89 (BUF) [32] Buffalo, NY Holy Spirit Church.
Seiler, Andrew J. '88 (WCH) Wellington, KS St. Anthony Church; Wellington, KS St. Rose of Lima Church.
Seiler, Gerald L. *j.c.l.* '90 (NO) Gretna, LA St. Anthony Church.
Seiler, Gerald L., Jr. '90 (NO) [A] New Orleans, LA Notre Dame Seminary Graduate School of Theology.
Seiler, John A. '59 (COV) Fort Thomas, KY St. Luke Hospital East.
Seipp, William J. '63 (MAD) Sauk City, WI St. Aloysius Church.
Seis, Michael '93 (GB) On Duty Outside the Diocese.
Seiter, George C. '83 (CAM) Gloucester, NJ St. Mary's Church.
Seiter, Joseph A. *c.s.sp.* '62 (LR) Morrilton, AR Sacred Heart Church.
Seitz, Cyprian *o.s.b.* '37 (SCL) [I] Collegeville, MN St. John's Abbey, of the Order of St. Benedict.
Seitz, Gilbert '82 (BAL) Abingdon, MD St. Francis de Sales Church.
Seitz, James J. '94 (WIN) [4] Mankato, MN St. Joseph the Worker Church; [C] Mankato, MN Mankato Area Catholic Schools.
Seitz, Joseph W. '58 (CHI) [37] Chicago, IL Christ the King Church.
Seitz, Mark Joseph '80 (DAL) Waxahachie, TX St. Joseph Church.
Seitz, Patrick K. '92 (BWN) San Benito, TX St. Theresa Church.
Seitz, Paul F.X. '58 (CHR) Walterboro, SC St. Anthony's Church.
Seitz, Thomas R. '52 (CHI) [204] Chicago, IL St. Thomas Apostle Church; Retired.
Seitzinger, Msgr. John P. '60 (ALN) Retired.
Sekellick, Msgr. John T. '69 (PSC) Wilkes-Barre, PA St. Mary's Church.
Seland, John *s.v.d.* '68 (FgM) Society of the Divine Word Foreign Missions.
Seleccion, Romeo *m.s.* '92 (SB) Moreno Valley, CA St. Christopher Church.
Seli, Msgr. John J. '46 (PIT) Retired.
Seli, William F. *s.m.* '58 (WH) Richwood, WV Holy Family Church; Summersville, WV St. John The Evangelist Church.
Sell, Robert L., III '78 (LFT) Special Assignment.
Sella, Donald '83 (PAT) [N] West Paterson, NJ Missionary Sisters of the Immaculate Conception, Convent of the Immaculate Conception.
Sella, Peter *s.d.b.* '68 (NEW) [C] Ramsey, NJ Don Bosco Preparatory High School for Boys.
Sellars, Charles *o.m.i.* '54 (BEA) Buna, TX St. Francis of Assisi Mission Church; Silsbee, TX St. Mark the Evangelist Church.
Selle, Paulinus J. *o.s.b.* '39 (GBG) [H] Latrobe, PA Saint Vincent Archabbey.
Selleck, John P. '57 (CAM) On Duty Outside the Diocese.
Selleck, John P. '57 (PT) Blountstown, FL St. Francis of Assisi Church.
Sellentin, Thomas J. '65 (OM) Howells, NE SS. Peter and Paul Church; Howells, NE St. John Nepomucene Church.
Sellers, Benedict *o.s.b.* '75 (CLV) [P] Cleveland, OH Benedictine Order of Cleveland.
Selvam, Xavier Panneer '81 (P) Lake Oswego, OR Our Lady of the Lake Church; [P] Portland, OR University of Portland.
Selvan, Mount Joseph *s.j.* '91 (MIL) [P] Milwaukee, WI Jesuit Community at Marquette University.
Selvaraj, Balappa '86 (ATL) Decatur, GA St. Thomas More Church.
Selvaraj, Bose Raja '63 (BGP) New Fairfield, CT St. Edward the Confessor Church.
Selvaraj, Peter '82 (NY) [213] Staten Island, NY St. Mary Church.
Selvester, Guy W. '97 (MET) [1] Metuchen, NJ Cathedral of St. Francis.
Selzer, Eugene '61 (PRM) St. Louis, MO St. Louis Mission Church.
Selzer, Eugene P. '61 (STL) Woodson Terrace, MO St. William Church.
Selzler, Norbert E. '38 (BUF) Retired.
Semaan, Charbel T. '89 (SAM) New Bedford, MA Our Lady of Purgatory Church.
Semancik, Msgr. Joseph F. '53 (GRY) [6] East Chicago, IN Sacred Heart Church; [M] Gary, IN Catholic Charities.
Semanych, Petro '91 (PHU) Elizabeth, NJ St. Vladimir's Church.
Seminack, Msgr. Richard '67 (SJP) Carnegie, PA Holy Trinity Church.
Seminara, Ron *s.j.* (RC) Mission, SD St. Thomas the Apostle Church.
Seminara, Ron *s.j.* '74 (RC) White River, SD St. Ignatius Church; St. Francis, SD Rosebud Reservation Church.
Seminara, Ronald *s.j.* '74 (RC) White River, SD Sacred Heart Church.
Seminara, Ronald S. *s.j.* '74 (RC) St. Francis, SD Rosebud Reservation Church.
Seminatore, Joseph J. '69 (CLV) [M] Parma, OH Parmadale.
Semko, Edward '69 (PSC) Carteret, NJ St. Elias Church.
Semler, Albert J. '67 (PIT) Franklin Park Borough, PA Saints John and Paul Church.
Semmer, Dean F. '79 (CHI) Westchester, IL Divine Infant Church.
Semonin, James R. '71 (CLV) Cleveland, OH Parma Community Hospital; [M] Parma, OH Parmadale.
Sempa, John J. '80 (SCR) [18] Wilkes-Barre, PA Sacred Heart of Jesus Church.
Sempko, Walter A. '50 (HBG) [G] Harrisburg, PA Villa Teresa Nursing Home.
Semple, James '61 (SLC) [3] Salt Lake City, UT Our Lady of Lourdes Church.
Sena, Charles A. '92 (PBL) Delta, CO St. Michael Church.
Sena, Sotero A. '81 (SFE) Fort Sumner, NM St. Anthony Church; Santa Rosa, NM St. Rose of Lima Church.
Senchur, Becket G. *o.s.b.* '73 (GBG) [H] Latrobe, PA Saint Vincent Archabbey.
Sendell, John (FAR) Retired.
Sendlein, Thomas A. *c.m.* '72 (FgM) Vincentian Foreign Missions.
Sendlein, Thomas A. *c.m.* '72 (PH) [AA] Philadelphia, PA Congregation of the Mission.
Sendra, Jesus '64 (ARE) [5] Utuado, PR Our Lady of Sorrows Church.
Senecal, Gerard *o.s.b.* '54 (KCK) Atchison, KS St. Joseph's Church; St. Patrick, KS St. Patrick's Church.
Seneschal, Theodore T. *o.s.b.* '70 (OKL) [I] Shawnee, OK St. Gregory Abbey.
Senetsky, Msgr. Robert *j.c.d.* '60 (PSC) Peekskill, NY SS. Peter and Paul Church.
Senger, Daniel *o.f.m.* '93 (CLV) [E] Cleveland, OH Padua Franciscan High School; [P] Cleveland, OH Padua Franciscan Friary.
Senger, Joseph P. '54 (FAR) Velva, ND St. Cecilia's Church.
Senger, William *m.m.* '73 (FgM) Maryknoll Foreign Missions.
Senior, Donald *c.p.* '67 (CHI) [B] Chicago, IL The Catholic Theological Union at Chicago; [B] Chicago, IL The Catholic Theological Union at Chicago; [N] Chicago, IL Passionist Community-CTU.
Senior, Timothy (PH) [M] Springfield, PA Divine Providence Village.
Senior, Timothy C. '85 (PH) [K] Philadelphia, PA The Catholic Social Services of the Archdiocese of Philadelphia.
Seniw, John '82 (PHU) Frackville, PA St. Michael's Church.
Senk, Christopher L. *o.s.b.* '76 (MAN) [K] Manchester, NH St. Anselm Abbey.
Senkewicz, Robert M. *s.j.* '76 (SJ) [B] Santa Clara, CA Santa Clara University.
Senko, Martin R. '56 (P) Cornelius, OR St. Alexander Church.

Senn, Edward R. '58 (SUP) Retired.
Sennik, Thomas W. '76 (NOR) West Willington, CT St. Jude Church.
Sennott, Msgr. Robert J. '40 (BO) Retired.
Sensening, Andrew *o.m.i.* '97 (LA) Pacoima, CA Mary Immaculate Church.
Senske, Joseph A. '48 (PH) Retired.
Seo, Matthias Ju Kob (TR) Browns Mills, NJ The Church of the Korean Martyrs.
Sepe, Kevin M. '86 (BO) Randolph, MA St. Mary Church.
Seper, John M. '83 (STL) Richmond Heights, MO Immacolata Church.
Sepich, Larry '74 (MIL) [70] Milwaukee, WI St. Roman Church.
Sepich, Lawrence '74 (PEO) On Duty Outside the Diocese.
Sepp, Michael P. (NY) [107] New York, NY Resurrection Church.
Sepulveda, Miguel A. *o.f.m.* '85 (NY) [35] New York, NY St. Francis of Assisi Church.
Sepulveda, Thomas W. *c.s.b.* '74 (GAL) [Q] Sugar Land, TX Basilian Mission Center.
Sequeira, Glenn N. '91 (LA) Glendale, CA Holy Family Church.
Sequeira, Lazarus '56 (NY) [76] New York, NY St. Monica Church.
Sequeira, Michael '66 (NOR) Clinton, CT St. Mary of the Visitation Church.
Sera, Enrique '78 (ORG) [1] Santa Ana, CA Immaculate Heart of Mary Church.
Serado, Msgr. William '40 (SR) Retired.
Serafin, Thomas J. '93 (MET) Edison, NJ St. Matthew Church.
Serafini, Augustine '62 (GB) [I] Oshkosh, WI Community of Our Lady.
Seramur, Leo J. '45 (MIL) Retired.
Serano, Joseph A. *o.praem.* '69 (PH) [B] Paoli, PA Daylesford Abbey; [AA] Paoli, PA Daylesford Abbey.
Serban, Ron '93 (SR) Military Chaplains.
Seremet, Hyacinth '51 (SY) [4] Utica, NY Sacred Heart Church; Special Assignment.
Serena, Edward T. '68 (BO) Marshfield, MA St. Ann by the Sea Church.
Sergi, Michael *c.ss.r.* '79 (BAL) [96] Baltimore, MD St. Wenceslaus Church.
Sergot, Stanley *o.m.i.* '35 (STP) [N] St. Paul, MN Oblate Residence.
Sergott, Joseph *o.p.* '96 (OAK) Antioch, CA Holy Rosary Church.
Serio, Anthony M. '67 (NO) Westwego, LA Our Lady of Prompt Succor Church.
Serio, John J. *s.d.b.* '82 (NY) [F] New Rochelle, NY Salesian High School.
Sermak, Jerzy *s.j.* '79 (CHI) [N] Chicago, IL Sacred Heart Mission House.
Sermak, Ronald *o.f.m.conv.* '60 (BAL) [M] Ellicott City, MD Order of Friars Minor Conventual.
Sermak, Ronald *o.f.m.conv.* '60 (BUF) [P] Hamburg, NY Immaculate Conception Convent.
Serna, F. Mark *o.s.b.* '86 (PRO) [E] Portsmouth, RI Portsmouth Abbey School.
Serna, Luis '96 (DAL) [16] Dallas, TX St. Edward Church.
Sernett, Msgr. Michael D. '70 (SC) [9] Sioux City, IA Nativity of Our Lord Jesus Christ Church.
Serour, George A. '59 (SAG) Gagetown, MI St. Agatha Church.
Serour, George J. '59 (SAG) Sebewaing, MI Holy Family Church.
Serowik, James P. '87 (SY) [5] Endicott, NY St. Joseph Church.
Serpa, Vincent *o.p.* (OAK) [N] Oakland, CA Western Dominican Province.
Serpa, Vincent A. *o.p.* '68 (OAK) [N] Oakland, CA Dominican Order (Western Province), St. Albert's Priory.
Serra, Dominic '72 (NY) On Duty Outside the Archdiocese.
Serra, Dominic '72 (STP) [A] St. Paul, MN The Saint Paul Seminary; [C] St. Paul, MN University of St. Thomas.
Serraglio, Mario '58 (COL) [24] Columbus, OH St. John the Baptist Church.
Serraino, Fred *c.s.c.* '68 (LA) [DD] Los Angeles, CA.
Serraino, Frederick *c.s.c.* (ORL) Retired.
Serrano, Dionisio '97 (PCE) On Duty Outside the Diocese.
Serrano, Edgar '87 (HON) [3] Honolulu, HI St. Anthony Church.
Serrano, Heriberto (SAC) Willows, CA St. Monica Church.
Serrano, Heriberto '70 (SAC) Maxwell, CA Sacred Heart Church.
Serrano, John J. '42 (RVC) Retired; [N] Uniondale, NY St. Pius X Residence.
Serrano, Jose '95 (NY) [31] New York, NY St. Elizabeth Church.
Serrano, Jose Orlando '96 (CGS) [1] Caguas, PR Cathedral Dulce Nombre de Jesus Church.
Serrano, Salvador V. '85 (SFR) [T] San Francisco, CA Opus Dei.
Serrano Rivera, Ivan *c.s.sp.* '87 (SJN) [F] Dorado, PR Santuario del Espiritu Santo.
Serratelli, Arthur '68 (NEW) [A] South Orange, NJ Seton Hall University College Seminary.
Serratelli, Msgr. Arthur J. (NEW) [B] South Orange, NJ Seton Hall University.
Serratelli, Arthur J. '68 (NEW) [A] South Orange, NJ Immaculate Conception Seminary; [B] South Orange, NJ Seton Hall University.
Serrick, James K. *s.j.* '62 (DET) [P] Bloomfield Hills, MI Manresa Jesuit Retreat House.
Serruys, Paul *c.i.c.m.* '36 (FgM) Missionhurst Foreign Missions.
Serva, Donald M. *s.j.* (DET) [K] Detroit, MI Jesuit Provincial Office-Detroit Province of the Society of Jesus.
Serva, Donald M. *s.j.* '78 (WH) [A] Wheeling, WV Wheeling Jesuit University.
Servatius, Msgr. Robert R. '64 (SLC) [6] Sandy, UT Blessed Sacrament Church.
Service, Msgr. Gerald H. '69 (OG) Canton, NY St. Mary Church.
Servinsky, Msgr. Michael E. '70 (ALT) Coupon, PA St. Joseph's Church.
Servis, Gregg *s.j.* '96 (SJ) [2] Santa Clara, CA St. Clare Church.
Servodidio, Msgr. John T. '54 (NY) [210] Staten Island, NY St. Joseph Church.
Serwa, Gregory P. *s.a.c.* '70 (MIL) [S] Elkhorn, WI St. Vincent Pallotti Center.
Sescon, Esteban '77 (ELP) [23] El Paso, TX St. Francis Xavier Church.
Sesek, Raphael A. *o.f.m.* '41 (CHI) [70] Chicago, IL St. George Church.
Sessa, Eugene *s.j.* '97 (DAL) [D] Dallas, TX Jesuit College Preparatory School.
Sestito, Joseph N. '59 (OG) On Duty Outside the Diocese.
Sesto, Gennaro *s.d.b.* '50 (NY) [FF] West Haverstraw, NY Don Bosco Retreat Center and Marian Shrine; [FF] West Haverstraw, NY Marian Shrine.
Setonga, Mansuetus '86 (DAV) [M] Iowa City, IA O'Keefe Hall.
Setter, H. Jay '88 (WCH) Derby, KS St. Mary's Church.
Settle, Anthony P. '90 (NY) [185] Bronx, NY St. Raymond Church.
Settles, Dennis F. '65 (JOL) [1] Kankakee, IL St. Martin of Tours Church.
Setzer, Frank *s.m.m.* '37 (BRK) [U] Ozone Park, NY Montfort Missionaries Provincialate - for Nation Community.
Setzer, Frank A. *s.s.m.* '37 (RVC) [N] Bay Shore, NY Montfort Missionaries.
Seubert, August *o.f.m.cap.* '57 (FgM) Capuchin Foreign Missions.
Seubert, Xavier *o.f.m.* (BUF) [C] St. Bonaventure, NY St. Bonaventure University.
Seubert, Xavier J. *o.f.m.* '71 (BUF) [O] St. Bonaventure, NY St. Bonaventure Friary.
Seuferling, George '56 (KCK) Shawnee, KS Good Shepherd Church.
Seung Chi Baek, John '81 (RVC) Great Neck, NY St. Aloysius Church.
Seuntjens, LeRoy L. '60 (SC) Special Assignment; [E] Sioux City, IA Holy Spirit Retirement Home.
Sevastian, M.R.P. *c.s.c.* (NOR) [C] Baltic, CT Academy and Boarding-School of the Holy Family.
Sevastian, M.R.P. '67 (NOR) [G] Baltic, CT Holy Family Motherhouse.
Sevcik, Lawrence *o.s.b.* '53 (CLV) [P] Cleveland, OH Benedictine Order of Cleveland.
Severson, Richard '82 (ALB) Wilton, NY Mount McGregor Correctional Facility; Special Assignment.
Severt, William (CLV) [J] Cleveland, OH Marymount Hospital, Inc.
Sevick, John M. '73 (CHI) [212] Chicago, IL St. Walter Church.
Sevigny, Michael E. *o.f.m.cap.* '78 (MAN) [5] Manchester, NH Blessed Sacrament Church.
Sevigny, Robert '53 (HT) Chauvin, LA St. Joseph Church.
Sevilla, Dennis C. '69 (SEA) Port Orchard, WA St. Gabriel's Church; Retsil, WA Washington Veterans Home Hospital.
Sevola, Frank *o.f.m.* (PHX) [18] Phoenix, AZ St. Martin de Porres Church; [20] Phoenix, AZ St. Matthew Church.
Sewall, Msgr. Charles H. '60 (SY) On Duty Outside the Diocese.
Sewar, Dennis R. '83 (ROC) Waterloo, NY St. Mary Church.
Sewell, Jack '78 (ORG) Westminster, CA Blessed Sacrament Church.
Sewvello, Robert '94 (YAK) Toppenish, WA St. Aloysius Church.
Sexstone, James H. '69 (ATL) [4] Atlanta, GA Immaculate Heart of Mary Church.
Sexton, Charles E. '38 (IND) Retired.
Sexton, Cornelius *s.s.j.* '43 (MOB) [10] Mobile, AL St. Joseph Church.
Sexton, John J. '36 (SPR) Retired; [H] Springfield, MA St. Michael's Residence.
Sexton, Msgr. Michael '61 (BIR) Florence, AL St. Joseph's Church; [H] Florence, AL University of North Alabama.
Sexton, Patrick D. '77 (BRK) Absent on Leave.
Sexton, Thomas *s.j.* '49 (SEA) [C] Tacoma, WA Bellarmine Preparatory School.
Seyer, Francis L. '52 (BEL) Waterloo, IL SS. Peter and Paul Church.
Seyer, James A. '50 (SPC) Retired.
Seyer, Lawrence '97 (LA) [3] Long Beach, CA St. Barnabas Church.
Seymour, Francis J. '61 (LA) Sick Leave.
Seymour, Msgr. Francis R. '63 (NEW) Kearny, NJ St. Cecilia's Church.
Seymour, James P. '97 (BO) [10] Lawrence, MA St. Patrick Church.
Seymour, James W. '87 (OG) On Duty Outside the Diocese.
Seymour, John T. *s.t.* '71 (ORG) [H] Santa Ana, CA Trinitarian Missionaries/Missionary Servants of the Most Holy Trinity.
Seynaeve, Jaak *m.afr.* '44 (BR) Special Assignment.
Sezzi, Michael J. '96 (LA) South Pasadena, CA Holy Family Church.
Sgarbossa, Lino *s.x.* '64 (CHI) [N] Chicago, IL Xaverian Missionaries (S.X.).
Sgarioto, Michael *o.carm.* '85 (FgM) Carmelite Foreign Missions.
Sgarioto, Michael *o.carm.* '85 (JOL) [J] Darien, IL Carmelite Provincial Office.
Sgueglia, Charles J.M. '52 (SPR) Retired.
Shackelford, Christopher '91 (TYL) Sulphur Springs, TX St. James Church.
Shad, Joseph J. *s.j.* '91 (BGP) [V] Fairfield, CT Newman Centers - Campus Ministry.
Shadeg, Norbert *s.v.d.* '49 (FgM) Society of the Divine Word Foreign Missions.
Shadeg, Werner *s.v.d.* '45 (FgM) Society of the Divine Word Foreign Missions.
Shadwell, Damian '90 (WDC) Olney, MD St. Peter Church.
Shadwell, Steven G. '89 (PAT) Prospect Park, NJ St. Paul's Church.
Shaefer, Konrad *o.s.b.* '80 (FgM) American - Cassinese Congregation Foreign Missions.
Shafer, Drake R. '73 (DAV) [B] Davenport, IA St. Ambrose University; [B] Davenport, IA St. Ambrose University.
Shafer, James A. '75 (FTW) [1] Mishawaka, IN St. Bavo Church.
Shafer, Richard '46 (GB) Retired.
Shafer, Wendelin *o.f.m.cap.* '46 (FgM) Capuchin Foreign Missions.
Shaffer, G. Scott '89 (TR) Neptune, NJ Holy Innocents Church.
Shafran, Steven *s.d.b.* '85 (COL) [H] Columbus, OH Salesian Center.
Shaheen, Joseph '59 (SAM) Unassigned.
Shaheen, Robert (OLL) Columbia, MO Maronite Catholic Community Church.
Shakalis, Peter A. (BO) Retired.
Shaleta, Emanuel Isho '84 (LA) [5] North Hollywood, CA St. Paul Assyrian-Chaldean Church.
Shallbetter, Martin B. '69 (STP) Bloomington, MN St. Edward Church.
Shallow, Edmund J. '81 (MET) [2] Carteret, NJ Holy Family Church.
Shamleffer, John B. '83 (STL) Warson Woods, MO Ste. Genevieve Du Bois Church.
Shamon, Albert J. '40 (ROC) Fleming, NY St. Isaac Jogues Church; Retired.
Shamsher, Paul '67 (HRT) Retired.
Shanahan, Daniel A. *o.p.* '62 (DAL) [M] Irving, TX Dominican Priory of St. Albert the Great.
Shanahan, Edward J. '52 (RVC) Retired.
Shanahan, John '48 (TOL) Retired.
Shanahan, John D. '50 (SFR) Larkspur, CA St. Patrick Church.
Shanahan, Michael *ss.cc.* '62 (FR) [J] Fairhaven, MA Sacred Hearts Provincial House.
Shanahan, Michael J. '92 (CHI) La Grange, IL St. Francis Xavier Church.
Shanahan, Robert J. *s.j.* '55 (OM) [K] Omaha, NE Jesuit Community At Creighton University.
Shanahan, Thomas J. *s.j.* '67 (OM) [K] Omaha, NE Jesuit Community At Creighton University; [K] Omaha, NE Jesuit Community At Creighton University.
Shane, Donald R. '54 (RVC) Ronkonkoma, NY St. Joseph's Church.
Shane, Donald W. '69 (OM) [36] Omaha, NE SS. Peter and Paul Church.
Shaner, Edward G. '96 (MET) Old Bridge, NJ St. Thomas the Apostle Church.
Shanfelt, Thomas G. '78 (ALN) [7] Reading, PA St. Joseph Church.
Shangraw, Philip A. (GR) On Special Assignment.

Shangraw, Philip A. '79 (GR) Sparta, MI Holy Family Church.
Shanks, Thomas E. *s.j.* '77 (SJ) [B] Santa Clara, CA Santa Clara University.
Shanley, Albert J. *m.s.* '38 (STP) Taylors Falls, MN St. Joseph's Church.
Shanley, Brian J. *o.p.* '87 (WDC) [B] Washington, DC Dominican House of Studies; [C] Washington, DC Catholic University of America, The.
Shanley, Charles M. *c.m.* '55 (PH) [B] Philadelphia, PA DePaul Novitiate.
Shanley, Gerry *ss.cc.* '61 (BWN) Pharr, TX St. Anne, Mother of Mary Church.
Shanley, James A. '80 (HRT) Rocky Hill, CT St. Elizabeth Seton Church.
Shanley, Joseph D. '43 (PRO) Retired; [M] Woonsocket, RI Saint Francis House.
Shanley, Kevin *o.carm.* '56 (JOL) [J] Darien, IL Carmelite Community; [L] Darien, IL Carmelite Spiritual Center.
Shanley, Matthew R. '55 (HRT) East Haven, CT Our Lady of Pompeii Church.
Shanley, Matthias *ss.cc.* '65 (BWN) [3] Harlingen, TX Queen of Peace Church.
Shanley, Owen F. '53 (ALB) Corinth, NY Immaculate Conception Church.
Shanley, Paul R. (BO) Retired.
Shanley, Thomas Q. *o.p.* '40 (HRT) [14] New Haven, CT St. Mary's Priory Church.
Shannon, Albert C. *o.s.a.* '44 (PH) [AA] Villanova, PA St. Thomas Monastery.
Shannon, Bernard E. *s.j.* '80 (RVC) [P] Manhasset, NY St. Ignatius Retreat House, Inisfada.
Shannon, Charles T. *o.p.* '77 (HRT) [14] New Haven, CT St. Mary's Priory Church.
Shannon, David *c.ss.r.* '48 (STP) Brooklyn Center, MN St. Alphonsus Church.
Shannon, Francis '87 (BRK) [76] Brooklyn, NY St. Lucy-St. Patrick Church; [104] Brooklyn, NY Our Lady of Monserrate-St. Ambrose Church.
Shannon, Joseph E. '64 (CAM) On Sick Leave.
Shannon, Joseph L. *o.s.a.* '37 (PH) [AA] Villanova, PA St. Thomas Monastery.
Shannon, Joseph P. *c.s.b.* '48 (GAL) [Q] Sugar Land, TX Basilian Mission Center.
Shannon, Michael T. *s.j.* '44 (SPK) [K] Spokane, WA Regis Community.
Shannon, Patrick J. '72 (HBG) Lewisburg, PA Sacred Heart of Jesus Church.
Shannon, Richard J. '59 (CHI) [5] Lemont, IL St. Patrick Church.
Shannon, Robert J. (CHI) Retired.
Shannon, Timothy '75 (STU) [1] Steubenville, OH Holy Name Cathedral; [6] Steubenville, OH St. Anthony of Padua Church.
Shannon, Timothy T. *s.j.* '88 (DET) [E] Detroit, MI University of Detroit Jesuit High School and Academy.
Shannon, William '71 (HON) Kahului, HI Christ the King Church.
Shannon, Msgr. William H. '43 (ROC) Retired; [J] Rochester, NY Sisters St. Joseph Motherhouse; [L] Rochester, NY Censores Librorum.
Shappard, Christopher *o.s.b.* '62 (IND) [B] St. Meinrad, IN St. Meinrad Seminary-College of Liberal Arts; [J] St. Meinrad, IN St. Meinrad Archabbey.
Shappelle, James '48 (CIN) [15] Cincinnati, OH St. Bernard Church; [66] Cincinnati, OH Mother of Christ Church.
Sharanevych, Emile '32 (STF) Retired.
Sharkey, Msgr. John A. '56 (PH) [95] Philadelphia, PA Old St. Mary's Church.
Sharkey, Owen *c.p.* '45 (HRT) [M] West Hartford, CT Holy Family Monastery/Retreat.
Sharkey, Peter G. *s.j.* '74 (CHI) [N] Chicago, IL Chicago Province of the Society of Jesus-Provincial Office.
Sharkey, Robert Urban *o.p.* '63 (NY) [DD] New York, NY St. Vincent Ferrer Priory.
Sharkey, Thomas *c.s.sp.* '51 (ARE) Barceloneta, PR Church of Our Lady of Mt. Carmel.
Sharkey, Msgr. Thomas H. '48 (CAM) Retired; [G] Ocean City, NJ The Sharkey Family Charitable Trust.
Sharkey, William *s.o.l.t.* '89 (CC) [H] Robstown, TX Society of Our Lady of the Most Holy Trinity.
Sharman, Robert F. '84 (HBG) [1] Lebanon, PA Assumption of the Blessed Virgin Mary Church.
Sharon, Charles *s.a.* '72 (NY) [DD] New York, NY Atonement Friars.
Sharon, Norbert *s.t.* '48 (LA) [27] Los Angeles, CA Our Lady of Victory Church.
Sharp, David L. *c.s.b.* '70 (PHX) Special Assignment; [H] Phoenix, AZ Office of Youth and Young Adult Ministries.
Sharp, Donald B. *s.j.* '71 (SFR) [N] San Francisco, CA Jesuit Community at University of San Francisco.
Sharp, Edward A. *s.j.* '53 (OM) [K] Omaha, NE Jesuit Community At Creighton University.
Sharp, George (NEW) Elizabeth, NJ Elizabeth Detention Center.
Sharp, George '89 (NEW) Nutley, NJ St. Mary's Church.
Sharp, James R. '84 (DAL) [27] Dallas, TX St. Thomas Aquinas Church.
Sharp, Kenneth W. '81 (PH) Havertown, PA St. Denis Church.
Sharpe, John O'M. *c.m.* '38 (PHX) [26] Phoenix, AZ St. Vincent de Paul Church.
Sharpe, Msgr. Joseph F. '43 (LA) Retired.
Sharpe, Patrick F. '42 (E) Retired.
Sharrett, Victor F. '65 (PH) Kennett Square, PA St. Patrick Church.
Sharrock, David J. *c.ss.r.* '55 (CHR) Sumter, SC St. Anne's Church.
Sharum, Peter *o.s.b.* '52 (LR) Charleston, AR Sacred Heart Church.
Shashy, Daniel '91 (STA) [13] Jacksonville, FL Resurrection Church.
Shatzel, Richard J. '69 (ROC) [40] Rochester, NY Our Mother of Sorrows Church.
Shaughnessy, James D. '40 (PEO) Retired.
Shaughnessy, James E. '73 (KCK) Lawrence, KS Corpus Christi Church.
Shaughnessy, James M. *s.j.* '79 (BO) [30] Boston, MA Immaculate Conception Church; Boston, MA New England Medical Center; [W] Boston, MA Jesuit Urban Center & Immaculate Conception Community.
Shaughnessy, John *c.ss.r.* '49 (OAK) [N] Oakland, CA Redemptorists.
Shaughnessy, John A. *c.m.* '49 (STL) [P] St. Louis, MO Vincentian Henrietta Residence.
Shaughnessy, Martin G. *s.j.* '63 (BGP) [D] Fairfield, CT Fairfield College Preparatory School; [O] Fairfield, CT The Fairfield Jesuit Community-Fairfield University.
Shaughnessy, Paul J. *s.j.* '87 (BAL) [M] Baltimore, MD Jesuit Fathers and Brothers Maryland Provincial Curia.
Shaughnessy, Thomas *o.f.m.* '60 (SAT) [70] San Antonio, TX San Jose y San Miguel Church.
Shaughnessy, Thomas *s.s.c.* '66 (FgM) St. Columban's Foreign Mission.
Shaughnessy, William *o.f.m.* (PHX) [G] Scottsdale, AZ Franciscan Renewal Center, Inc. (Casa de Paz Y Bien).
Shaughnessy, William G. '92 (WDC) [T] Washington, DC Opus Dei.
Shaules, Patrick R. *s.j.* '48 (PH) [AA] Philadelphia, PA Jesuit Community at St. Joseph's University.
Shaum, David '46 (BAL) Retired.
Shaum, David W. '46 (BAL) [B] Emmitsburg, MD Mount Saint Mary's College.
Shaunessy, Francis W. '45 (CHI) [56] Chicago, IL St. Eugene Church; Retired.
Shaver, James R. '89 (LAN) [1] Jackson, MI St. John the Evangelist Church.
Shaw, Brian A. '66 (HRT) [5] Bristol, CT St. Stanislaus Church.
Shaw, Charles E. '51 (HRT) Retired.
Shaw, David '68 (SR) [4] Santa Rosa, CA Resurrection Church.
Shaw, Dennis '74 (ROC) [25] Rochester, NY Holy Redeemer-St. Francis Xavier Church; [36] Rochester, NY Our Lady of Mount Carmel Church.
Shaw, Dennis J. '74 (ROC) [47] Rochester, NY St. Michael Church.
Shaw, Eugene F. *s.j.* '60 (MIL) [P] Milwaukee, WI Jesuit Provincial Office, Wisconsin Province.
Shaw, Eugene F. *s.j.* '60 (PH) [AA] Philadelphia, PA Jesuit Community at St. Joseph's University.
Shaw, John '57 (YAK) White Swan, WA St. Mary's Church.
Shaw, Kenneth *s.d.b.* (PAT) [D] North Haledon, NJ Mary Help of Christians Academy.
Shaw, Kenneth *s.d.b.* '78 (PAT) [3] Paterson, NJ St. Anthony's Church.
Shaw, Mario '56 (PEO) [Q] Peoria, IL St. Augustine Community.
Shaw, Mario W. '56 (PEO) [L] Peoria, IL St. Augustine Manor.
Shaw, Michael B. '96 (PT) [1] Pensacola, FL Cathedral of the Sacred Heart.
Shaw, Richard '68 (ALB) Albany, NY Albany County Jail; Special Assignment.
Shaw, William (CHL) [4] Greensboro, NC St. Paul the Apostle Church.
Shaw, William E. '57 (YAK) Zillah, WA Resurrection Church.
Shay, Michael *s.d.s.* '73 (MIL) [P] Milwaukee, WI Salvatorian Provincial Residence.
Shay, Robert M. *s.t.* (BLX) Pineville, MS Our Lady of Lourdes Church.
Shea, Arthur F. *s.j.* '38 (FgM) Provinces.
Shea, Baldwin *o.c.s.o.* '53 (SLC) [F] Huntsville, UT Abbey of Our Lady of the Holy Trinity of the Order of Cistercians.
Shea, Bernard J. *s.j.* (BO) Melrose, MA St. Mary of the Annunciation Church.
Shea, Daniel '69 (HEL) [3] Helena, MT Our Lady of the Valley Church.
Shea, Daniel B. '69 (HEL) [B] Helena, MT Carroll College.
Shea, Donald *c.pp.s.* '53 (TOL) [M] Bellevue, OH Sorrowful Mother Shrine.
Shea, Msgr. Donald W. '62 (HEL) Military Chaplains.
Shea, Edward *o.f.m.* '87 (JOL) [11] Joliet, IL St. John the Baptist Church; [J] Joliet, IL St. John the Baptist Friary.
Shea, Evan P. '86 (CHY) Lusk, WY St. Leo's Church.
Shea, James *c.ss.r.* (KC) [O] Kansas City, MO Our Lady of Perpetual Help Charitable Trust.
Shea, James *c.s.s.* '43 (BO) [Z] Waltham, MA Stigmatine Fathers and Brothers.
Shea, James *c.ss.r.* '65 (KC) [32] Kansas City, MO Our Lady of Perpetual Help Church; [J] Kansas City, MO Redemptorists of Kansas City.
Shea, James J. *sch.p.* '92 (PH) [AA] Devon, PA Piarist Fathers (Order of the Pious Schools).
Shea, James M. '65 (BUR) Springfield, VT Maternity of the Blessed Virgin Mary Church.
Shea, James M. *s.j.* '75 (BO) [W] Boston, MA The Society of Jesus of New England-Provincial Offices.
Shea, James M. *s.j.* '75 (WDC) [K] Washington, DC Georgetown University Hospital; [M] Washington, DC The Jesuit Community at Georgetown University.
Shea, James M. '85 (WOR) [14] Worcester, MA Our Lady of the Rosary Church.
Shea, James P. *sch.p.* '92 (PH) [G] Devon, PA Devon Preparatory School.
Shea, John J. '45 (SPR) Granby, MA Immaculate Heart of Mary Church.
Shea, John J. '61 (BO) [4] Plymouth, MA St. Peter Church.
Shea, John J. *s.j.* '75 (CLV) [C] Cleveland, OH John Carroll University; [C] Cleveland, OH John Carroll Jesuit Community.
Shea, John J. *s.j.* '75 (NY) [C] Bronx, NY Fordham University.
Shea, Joseph *o.f.m.cap.* '67 (RVC) East Patchogue, NY St. Joseph the Worker Church.
Shea, Joseph '78 (LA) Glendale, CA Holy Family Church.
Shea, Joseph C. *m.s.* '57 (STL) Maplewood, MO Immaculate Conception Church; [P] St. Louis, MO La Salette Missionaries.
Shea, L. M. *o.p.* '52 (FgM) Dominican - Order of Preachers Foreign Missions.
Shea, Leo A. '64 (MAN) Retired.
Shea, Leo B. *m.m.* '66 (FgM) Maryknoll Foreign Missions.
Shea, Leo B. *m.m.* '66 (NY) [DD] Maryknoll, NY Maryknoll Fathers and Brothers.
Shea, Lewis M. *o.p.* '52 (FgM) Dominican - Order of Preachers Foreign Missions.
Shea, Lewis M. *o.p.* '66 (CHI) [N] Chicago, IL Dominicans (Provincial Office).
Shea, Maurice F. '56 (SJ) [14] San Jose, CA St. Leo the Great Church; Special Assignment.
Shea, Michael *c.ss.r.* '64 (FgM) Redemptorist Foreign Missions.
Shea, Michael J. *c.m.* '70 (GR) [J] Spring Lake, MI St. Lazare Retreat House.
Shea, Michael J. '76 (SFE) Alameda, NM Nativity of the Blessed Virgin Mary Church.
Shea, Michael M. *c.m.* '70 (PH) [AA] Philadelphia, PA Congregation of the Mission.
Shea, Peter D. '75 (WOR) West Brookfield, MA Sacred Heart of Jesus Church.
Shea, Peter G. *c.s.p.* '56 (SFR) [31] San Francisco, CA Old St. Mary's Cathedral.
Shea, Msgr. Richard J. '61 (BGP) [2] Trumbull, CT St. Catherine of Siena Church.
Shea, Robert F. '55 (R) Roanoke Rapids, NC St. John the Baptist Church.
Shea, Roy *c.i.c.m.* '86 (FgM) Missionhurst Foreign Missions.
Shea, Thomas '49 (SJ) Retired.
Shea, Thomas *c.s.c.* '67 (FgM) Holy Cross Foreign Missions.
Shea, Thomas '73 (PEO) Absent on Leave.
Shea, Thomas F. '64 (PH) Retired.
Shea, Thomas J. *o.s.a.* '52 (PH) [AA] Villanova, PA St. Thomas Monastery.
Shea, Thomas J. *m.m.* '67 (FgM) Maryknoll Foreign Missions.
Shea, Thomas M. '66 (SPR) [4] Springfield, MA Holy Cross Church.
Shea, Thomas W. (NOR) On Duty Outside the Diocese.
Shea, Timothy J. '61 (BO) [3] Woburn, MA St. Charles Church.
Shea, Vincent *o.f.m.* '51 (PAT) [M] Ringwood, NJ Holy Name Friary, Inc.
Shea, William *s.v.d.* '64 (DUB) [B] Epworth, IA Divine Word College.
Shea, Msgr. William B. (BO) Retired.
Sheaffer, John K. '93 (SPR) Easthampton, MA Immaculate Conception Church.
Sheahan, Msgr. Donal C. '60 (SD) [17] San Diego, CA Our Mother of Confidence Church.
Sheahan, Donal J. '60 (CAM) [4] Atlantic City, NJ St.

Nicholas of Tolentine Church.
Sheahan, Gerald E. *s.j.* '51 (STL) [P] St. Louis, MO Jesuit Community Corporation at St. Louis University - Jesuit Hall.
Sheahan, John (SFD) [J] Alton, IL Marian Heights Apartments.
Sheahan, John A. '60 (ORG) Retired.
Sheahan, John F. '46 (SFD) Retired.
Sheahan, Kevin '88 (CHI) [34] Chicago, IL St. Cajetan Church.
Sheahan, Richard D. '69 (PRO) [2] Cranston, RI Holy Apostles Church.
Shean, William F. '73 (RVC) Centereach, NY Assumption of the Blessed Virgin Mary Church.
Shear, Michael P. '64 (PSC) Harrisburg, PA St. Ann Church.
Shearer, Thomas M. '78 (CIN) [4] Dayton, OH St. Anthony of Padua Church.
Shebuski, Charles '65 (GB) Absent on Leave.
Shecterle, Ross A. '86 (BAL) [A] Baltimore, MD St. Mary's Seminary and University.
Shecterle, Ross A. '86 (MIL) Graduate Studies.
Sheedlo, Walter J. '71 (MAR) Sabbatical.
Sheeds, Gerald E. '68 (KCK) Gardner, KS Sacred Heart Church.
Sheedy, Edward J. '72 (BUF) On Duty Outside the Diocese.
Sheedy, Edward J. '72 (OG) [A] Ogdensburg, NY Wadhams Hall.
Sheedy, Mateo E. '77 (SJ) [22] San Jose, CA Sacred Heart of Jesus Church.
Sheedy, Patrick J. '65 (ORL) [1] Ocala, FL Blessed Trinity Church.
Sheedy, Timothy J. '76 (DAV) [4] Fort Madison, IA Sacred Heart Church.
Sheedy, Val J. '55 (ORL) [1] Lakeland, FL Church of the Resurrection.
Sheehan, Augustine J. '55 (RVC) Central Islip, NY St. John of God Church; Northport, NY Veteran's Hospital.
Sheehan, Bernard *o.s.b.* '68 (OM) [K] Elkhorn, NE Mount Michael Abbey.
Sheehan, Daniel *c.p.m.* '46 (OWN) [F] South Union, KY Fathers of Mercy.
Sheehan, Daniel J. '53 (BO) [8] Salem, MA St. Thomas the Apostle Church.
Sheehan, Daniel J. '79 (BRK) [R] Bayside, NY Ozanam Hall of Queens Nursing Home, Inc.; [U] Jamaica, NY Parsons Manor.
Sheehan, David M. *s.s.c.* '53 (FgM) St. Columban's Foreign Mission.
Sheehan, Msgr. Dennis F. '63 (BO) [12] Cambridge, MA St. Paul Church.
Sheehan, Donald P. '68 (NEW) Dumont, NJ St. Mary's Church.
Sheehan, Edward *s.m.* '61 (PRT) Brunswick, ME St. John the Baptist Church.
Sheehan, George *s.d.s.* '53 (MIL) [P] Milwaukee, WI Salvatorians - Jordan Hall.
Sheehan, George F. '61 (SY) [S] East Syracuse, NY Bishop Grimes Priests Residence.
Sheehan, George F. '63 (SY) [C] East Syracuse, NY Bishop Grimes Jr./Sr. High School.
Sheehan, Gerald *s.o.l.t.* '85 (CC) [H] Robstown, TX Society of Our Lady of the Most Holy Trinity.
Sheehan, Gerald P. '64 (BUF) Forestville, NY St. Rose of Lima Church; Sheridan, NY St. John Bosco Church.
Sheehan, J. Peter '56 (BIR) Retired.
Sheehan, J. William *o.m.i.* '65 (WDC) [B] Washington, DC Oblate College/Oblate Center for Mission Studies; [M] Washington, DC Missionary Oblates of Mary Immaculate.
Sheehan, James '75 (PMB) Retired.
Sheehan, James F. *s.j.* '61 (BO) [W] Boston, MA The Society of Jesus of New England-Provincial Offices.
Sheehan, James F. *s.j.* '61 (FgM) Provinces.
Sheehan, James T. *s.j.* '59 (BO) [W] Boston, MA Loyola House.
Sheehan, John F.X. *s.j.* (STL) [C] St. Louis, MO Saint Louis University.
Sheehan, John F.X. *s.j.* '64 (BO) [W] Boston, MA The Society of Jesus of New England-Provincial Offices.
Sheehan, John F.X. *s.j.* '64 (STL) [P] St. Louis, MO Jesuit Community Corporation at St. Louis University - Jesuit Hall.
Sheehan, Msgr. John J. '37 (BO) Retired.
Sheehan, John J. '54 (NY) [219] Staten Island, NY Our Lady, Queen of Peace Church.
Sheehan, John P. '89 (NY) [155] Bronx, NY St. John Chrysostom's Church.
Sheehan, John R. *s.j.* '92 (FgM) Provinces.
Sheehan, Joseph (NEW) [3] Linden, NJ St. John the Apostle Church.
Sheehan, Joseph *o.carm.* '63 (SFS) [A] Aberdeen, SD Presentation College.
Sheehan, Joseph A. '59 (ALN) [4] Easton, PA St. Joseph Church.
Sheehan, Joseph D. *s.j.* '49 (MIL) [P] Wauwatosa, WI Jesuit Community at St. Camillus.
Sheehan, Joseph G. '48 (NEW) Retired.
Sheehan, Justin R. *o.c.s.o.* '91 (ROC) [I] Piffard, NY Abbey of the Genesee.
Sheehan, Lawrence A. *s.j.* '47 (RVC) Massapequa, NY St. Rose of Lima Church; Retired.
Sheehan, Lourdes *r.s.m.* (FTW) [B] Notre Dame, IN University of Notre Dame Du Lac.
Sheehan, Mark S. '63 (BO) Bedford, MA St. Michael Church.
Sheehan, Maurice *o.f.m.cap.* (NOR) [A] Cromwell, CT Holy Apostles College and Seminary.
Sheehan, Maurice '55 (PIT) [O] Pittsburgh, PA St. Francis Friary.
Sheehan, Michael J. '64 (PH) [144] Philadelphia, PA Sacred Heart of Jesus Church.
Sheehan, Michael J. '78 (NEW) Paramus, NJ Annunciation Church.
Sheehan, Myles N. *s.j.* '94 (BO) [W] Boston, MA The Society of Jesus of New England-Provincial Offices.
Sheehan, Myles N. *s.j.* '94 (CHI) [C] Chicago, IL Jesuit Community at Loyola University of Chicago.
Sheehan, Paul M. *s.j.* '52 (FgM) Provinces.
Sheehan, Richard J. *o.m.i.* '61 (BWN) San Juan, TX St. John the Baptist Church.
Sheehan, Thomas *o.f.m.* '60 (BUF) [A] East Aurora, NY Christ the King Seminary.
Sheehan, Thomas '70 (CLV) [6] Parma, OH Holy Family Church.
Sheehan, Thomas D. *o.p.* '45 (GAL) [Q] Houston, TX Dominican Fathers and Brothers, St. Mark Priory, Inc.
Sheehan, Thomas J. *s.j.* (NO) New Orleans, LA Memorial Medical Center.
Sheehan, Thomas J. '53 (WDC) [37] Washington, DC St. Peter Church; Retired.
Sheehan, Thomas J. *s.j.* '97 (BO) [W] Boston, MA The Society of Jesus of New England-Provincial Offices.
Sheehan, William *o.m.i.* '42 (FgM) Oblates Foreign Missions.
Sheehan, William *o.m.i.* '58 (BO) [DD] Tewksbury, MA The Society of Oblate Fathers for Missions Among the Poor Formation Charitable Trust.
Sheehan, William *o.m.i.* '58 (FgM) Oblates Foreign Missions.
Sheehan, William *o.m.i.* '65 (BO) [DD] Tewksbury, MA The Society of Oblate Fathers Continuing Support Fund.
Sheehan, William J. *s.j.* '65 (BO) [W] Weston, MA Campion Center; [Y] Weston, MA Campion Renewal Center.
Sheehan, William J. *c.s.b.* '66 (ROC) [I] Rochester, NY Basilian Residence.
Sheehey, Robert J. *s.s.e.* '47 (BUR) [E] Colchester, VT Society of St. Edmund.
Sheehey, Robert J. *s.s.e.* '47 (MOB) [H] Selma, AL Edmundite Fathers.
Sheehy, Charles I. '44 (BO) Braintree, MA St. Francis of Assisi Church.
Sheehy, Charles I. '64 (BO) Retired.
Sheehy, Dennis E. '68 (GBG) Yukon, PA Seven Dolors Church.
Sheehy, Joseph T. '53 (BO) Swampscott, MA St. John the Evangelist Church.
Sheehy, Paul E. '54 (LIN) Hebron, NE Sacred Heart Church.
Sheehy, Sean O. '70 (BR) [K] Hammond, LA St. Albert the Great Catholic Center.
Sheehy, Vincent J. '61 (VEN) [2] Venice, FL Our Lady of Lourdes Church.
Sheehy, Wilfred '60 (SR) Retired.
Sheehy, Yvon *s.c.j.* '78 (RC) Lower Brule, SD St. Mary's Church; Lower Brule, SD Lower Brule Reservation Church; [B] Lower Brule, SD SCJ Community House.
Sheehy, Yvon *s.c.j.* '78 (SFS) Fort Thompson, SD St. Joseph Church; Stephan, SD Immaculate Conception Church.
Sheekey, Philip P. '64 (WIL) Rehoboth, DE St. Edmond Church.
Sheeran, Kevin J. *o.s.b.* '65 (JOL) [A] Lisle, IL Benedictine University; [J] Lisle, IL St. Procopius Abbey.
Sheeran, Michael J. *s.j.* '70 (DEN) [M] Denver, CO Regis Jesuit Community (The Jesuits at Regis University).
Sheeran, Michael J. *s.j.* '93 (DEN) [B] Denver, CO Regis University.
Sheeran, Msgr. Robert '70 (NEW) [A] South Orange, NJ Immaculate Conception Seminary.
Sheeran, Msgr. Robert T. '70 (NEW) [A] South Orange, NJ Seton Hall University College Seminary; [B] South Orange, NJ Seton Hall University; [B] South Orange, NJ Seton Hall University.
Sheerin, James O. '56 (NEW) Little Ferry, NJ St. Margaret of Cortona Church.
Sheets, James P. (SAC) Sacramento, CA Sutter General Hospital; Sacramento, CA Sutter Memorial Hospital.
Sheets, John R. *s.j.* (OM) [K] Omaha, NE Jesuit Community At Creighton University.
Sheets, Joseph B. '57 (IND) Brownstown, IN Our Lady of Providence Church; Seymour, IN St. Ambrose Church.
Sheetz, Stephen A. '57 (HBG) Millersville, PA St. Philip the Apostle Church.
Sheffield, Walter N. '82 (GAL) [65] Houston, TX St. Paul Church.
Sheffler, Mark *c.ss.r.* '70 (SAT) [M] San Antonio, TX Redemptorists of Texas- San Antonio #1.
Sheganoski, Fabian '65 (ORL) Bushnell, FL St. Lawrence Church.
Sheherd, Eugene '78 (AUS) Chappell Hill, TX St. Stanislaus Church.
Sheil, James '66 (CLV) Military Chaplains.
Shelander, Donald E. '70 (CIN) Newport, OH SS. Peter and Paul Church.
Shelby, Charles F. *c.m.* '68 (STL) [P] Perryville, MO Congregation of The Mission; [W] Perryville, MO The Association of the Miraculous Medal.
Sheldon, Denis (FBK) Alakanuk, AK St. Ignatius Church.
Sheldon, William W. *c.m.* '52 (PH) [B] Philadelphia, PA St. Vincent's Seminary; [AA] Philadelphia, PA Congregation of the Mission; [AA] Philadelphia, PA Congregation of the Mission.
Sheley, John '73 (SPC) Dexter, MO Sacred Heart Church.
Shellem, John J. '52 (PH) Newtown Square, PA St. Anastasia Church.
Shelley, John J. '61 (PH) Cheltenham, PA Presentation of Blessed Virgin Mary Church.
Shelley, Jonathan P. '95 (STP) Bayport, MN St. Charles Church.
Shelley, Owen *o.f.m.cap.* '45 (RVC) Huntington, NY St. Patrick's Church; Huntington, NY Huntington Hospital.
Shelley, Thomas '62 (NY) [118] New York, NY St. Thomas More Church.
Shelley, William M. '50 (NY) [2] New York, NY St. Agnes Church.
Shellito, Edward D. *m.m.* '80 (FgM) Maryknoll Foreign Missions.
Shellman, Richard L. '86 (HRT) Bethlehem, CT Church of the Nativity.
Shelly, Otto *s.v.d.* '42 (FgM) Society of the Divine Word Foreign Missions.
Shelly, Roy J. *s.d.b.* '78 (NY) [FF] West Haverstraw, NY Don Bosco Retreat Center and Marian Shrine; [FF] West Haverstraw, NY Marian Shrine.
Shelly, Thomas J. '62 (NY) [A] Yonkers, NY St. Joseph's Seminary.
Shelton, Charles *o.f.m.conv.* '81 (RNO) [1] Reno, NV St. Thomas Aquinas Cathedral.
Shelton, Charles M. *s.j.* '82 (DEN) [M] Denver, CO Regis Jesuit Community (The Jesuits at Regis University).
Shelton, Henry '69 (JKS) Tupelo, MS St. James Church.
Shelton, Lawrence '66 (LA) [44] Los Angeles, CA St. Anselm Church.
Sheltz, Anton R. '76 (GAL) [26] Houston, TX St. Dominic Church.
Sheltz, George A. '71 (GAL) [70] Houston, TX Prince of Peace Church.
Shema, George T. '67 (PAT) [3] Wayne, NJ Immaculate Heart of Mary Church.
Shemuga, Kevin C. '83 (CLV) [43] Cleveland, OH St. Leo the Great Church.
Shen, Louis *s.j.* '83 (OAK) Union City, CA St. Anne Church.
Shen, Raphael *s.j.* '70 (DET) [K] Detroit, MI Jesuit Community at the University of Detroit.
Shenk, Bertrand J. '37 (TOL) Sandusky, OH Soldiers and Sailors Home; Retired.
Shenoy, Leslie F. '76 (FRS) Mojave, CA St. Mary's Church.
Shenrock, Msgr. Joseph C. '53 (TR) Whiting, NJ St. Elizabeth Ann Seton Church.
Shepanski, Don C. '62 (SAT) [57] San Antonio, TX St. Matthew's Church.
Shepard, Thomas B. '77 (HRT) Rocky Hill, CT St. James Church.
Shepard, Timothy J. *s.j.* '82 (DET) [B] Berkley, MI Loyola House; [K] Detroit, MI Jesuit Provincial Office-Detroit Province of the Society of Jesus.
Shepardson, Eleanor '90 (OAK) [S] Oakland, CA St. Mary's Center.
Sheperd, Raymond C. '57 (TOL) [13] Toledo, OH Regina Coeli Church; Special Assignment.
Shepherd, Maurice *s.o.l.t.* '88 (CC) [H] Robstown, TX Society of Our Lady of the Most Holy Trinity.
Shepherd, Thomas N. '45 (BUF) [46] Buffalo, NY St. Martin Church; Retired.
Shepler, Charles C. '43 (DAV) Retired.
Shepley, Brian J. '92 (DAV) [1] Iowa City, IA St. Mary of the Assumption Church.
Sheputa, Albin *m.i.c.* '43 (NOR) [F] Thompson, CT Marian Fathers.
Sherba, Girard M. '79 (R) Kinston, NC Holy Trinity-Our Lady of the Atonement Church.
Sherbno, John '49 (TOL) Retired.
Sherbo, Albert G. (DM) [3] Des Moines, IA Christ the King Church.
Sherburne, Richard F. *s.j.* '56 (MIL) [P] Milwaukee, WI

Jesuit Community at Marquette University.
Sherdel, Lawrence '81 (HBG) [K] Harrisburg, PA Catholic Campus Ministry.
Sherdel, Lawrence W. '81 (HBG) Shippensburg, PA Our Lady of the Visitation Church.
Sherer, Richard B. '58 (HRT) [1] West Hartford, CT St. Brigid's Church.
Sheridan, Brian *m.s.* '83 (ORL) [3] Orlando, FL Good Shepherd Church.
Sheridan, Daniel P. '79 (RVC) St. James, NY SS. Philip and James Church.
Sheridan, Denis J. '81 (RVC) Rockville Centre, NY Mercy Medical Center; [I] Rockville Centre, NY Mercy Medical Center.
Sheridan, Edward J. '63 (CHL) [5] Charlotte, NC St. Gabriel Church.
Sheridan, Eugene *c.m.* (BAL) [21] Baltimore, MD St. Cecilia Church; [40] Baltimore, MD Immaculate Conception Church.
Sheridan, Eugene '45 (NY) Retired.
Sheridan, James B. *o.p.* '35 (NY) Pleasantville, NY Holy Innocents Church.
Sheridan, James B. '50 (PH) Retired.
Sheridan, James J. *o.s.a.* '61 (TLS) [B] Tulsa, OK Cascia Hall Preparatory School.
Sheridan, John E. '91 (BO) [8] Boston, MA St. Ann Church.
Sheridan, John F. '87 (ALN) Retired.
Sheridan, John J. *o.s.a.* '85 (VEN) Cape Coral, FL Blessed Katharine Drexel Church.
Sheridan, Msgr. John V. '43 (LA) Malibu, CA Our Lady of Malibu Church; Retired.
Sheridan, Mark *o.s.b.* '65 (WDC) [M] Washington, DC St. Anselm's Abbey.
Sheridan, Matthew W. '54 (BRK) [230] Queens, NY Queen of Angels Church.
Sheridan, Michael '75 (PRT) Indian Township, ME St. Ann Church; Woodland, ME St. James the Greater Church.
Sheridan, Michael J. '71 (STL) [58] St. Louis, MO St. Raphael The Archangel Church.
Sheridan, Paul G. *s.j.* '65 (STL) [F] St. Louis, MO St. Louis University High School, George H. Backer Memorial.
Sheridan, Paul G. *s.j.* '75 (STL) [P] St. Louis, MO St. Louis University High School Jesuit Community.
Sheridan, Msgr. Paul W. '56 (SFD) Pierron, IL Immaculate Conception Church; Pocahontas, IL St. Nicholas Church.
Sheridan, Peter C. *o.f.m.* '41 (WDC) [B] Silver Spring, MD Holy Name College.
Sheridan, Philip A. '51 (HRT) Union City, CT St. Mary's Church.
Sheridan, Robert A. '43 (CHI) [120] Chicago, IL St. Margaret of Scotland Church; Retired.
Sheridan, Thomas '64 (CHY) Rock Springs, WY Our Lady of Sorrows Church; Rock Springs, WY Our Lady of Sorrows/Sts. Cyril & Methodius Church.
Sheridan, Thomas L. *s.j.* '57 (NEW) [B] Jersey City, NJ Saint Peter's College; [N] Jersey City, NJ Jesuits of Saint Peter's College, Inc.
Sheridan, William H. '54 (CHI) [171] Chicago, IL St. Philip Neri Church.
Sheridan, William J. '72 (CHI) [1] Chicago, IL Cathedral of the Holy Name.
Sheridan, William P. '89 (NEW) [A] South Orange, NJ Seton Hall University College Seminary; [B] South Orange, NJ Seton Hall University.
Sherlock, Alexander '66 (MOB) [1] Montgomery, AL St. Peter Church.
Sherlock, James C. '64 (PH) [121] Philadelphia, PA Our Lady of Lourdes Church.
Sherlock, John '69 (WCH) [19] Wichita, KS St. Thomas Aquinas Church; [B] Wichita, KS Kapaun Mt. Carmel High School.
Sherlock, R. Marc '79 (CIN) Wilmington, OH St. Columbkille Church; [Q] Wilmington, OH Wilmington College Campus Ministry.
Sherman, Msgr. Anthony F. '70 (BRK) [199] Queens, NY St. Matthias Church.
Sherman, Charles E. '51 (RCK) Retired.
Sherman, Daniel J. *m.m.* '47 (NY) [DD] Maryknoll, NY Maryknoll Fathers and Brothers.
Sherman, Daniel M. '77 (CAM) Pomona, NJ Assumption Church.
Sherman, Edward '56 (FAR) St. Michael, ND St. Michael's Church; St. Michael, ND St. Michael's Indian Mission Church.
Sherman, Gary '85 (TLS) [3] Tulsa, OK St. Augustine's Church; [12] Tulsa, OK St. Monica's Church.
Sherman, Kenneth '80 (NTN) Rochester, NY St. Nicholas Church.
Sherman, Thomas P. *s.j.* '87 (MIL) [P] Milwaukee, WI Jesuit Provincial Office, Wisconsin Province.
Sherman, William C. '55 (FAR) [3] Grand Forks, ND St. Michael's Church; Grand Forks, ND School for the Blind.
Sherrer, Charles D. *c.s.c.* '61 (P) [B] Portland, OR University of Portland; [L] Portland, OR Holy Cross Fathers & Brothers, C.S.C. - University of Portland.
Sherry, Brendan '52 (AMA) Absent on Leave.
Sherry, Bryan W. *j.c.l.* '62 (TUC) Special Assignment.
Sherry, Edward F. '68 (BO) Wilmington, MA St. Thomas of Villanova Church.
Sherry, Francis T. *c.p.m.* '89 (OWN) [F] South Union, KY Fathers of Mercy.
Sherry, Peter Thomas *o.carm.* '38 (BO) [P] Peabody, MA Catholic Information Center; [BB] Peabody, MA St. Theresa Carmelite Chapel.
Sherry, Robert N. '66 (RCK) McHenry, IL Church of Holy Apostles.
Shershanovich, Michael '74 (SPR) [7] Pittsfield, MA St. Joseph's Church.
Sherwood, Lan S. '75 (PHX) Unassigned.
Sherwood, Stephen K. *c.m.f.* '71 (SAT) [B] San Antonio, TX St. Anthony Mary Claret Seminary; [C] San Antonio, TX Oblate School of Theology.
Sherwood, Timothy '93 (SP) Safety Harbor, FL Espiritu Santo Church.
Sherzer, Msgr. William J. '46 (DET) Bloomfield Hills, MI St. Owen Church; Retired.
Sheslo, Charles '61 (SD) Retired.
Shetler, Msgr. Carl A. (EVN) Retired.
Shetler, John '92 (PHX) [13] Phoenix, AZ St. Jerome Church.
Shetler, John E. '57 (ORG) Irvine, CA St. John Neumann Church.
Shevlin, John *s.v.d.* '60 (SB) [A] Riverside, CA Divine Word Seminary.
Shevlin, Msgr. John G. '48 (NY) Bangall, NY Immaculate Conception Church; Retired.
Shevlin, Msgr. Raymond R. '44 (BRK) [122] Brooklyn, NY Resurrection Church; Retired.
Shibley, Amel '62 (SPC) Fredericktown, MO St. Michael Church.
Shibley, Amel A. '62 (SPC) Retired.
Shidler, Anthony *o.s.b.* '64 (SPC) [6] Springfield, MO St. Joseph's Church; [C] Joplin, MO St. John's Regional Health Center, Mercy LifeCare Systems, Inc.
Shields, David M. *s.j.* '73 (MIL) [64] Milwaukee, WI St. Patrick Church; [P] Milwaukee, WI Jesuit Community at Marquette University.
Shields, Hugh J. '72 (PH) On Duty Outside the Archdiocese.
Shields, Hugh Joseph '72 (FgM) Society of St. James the Apostle.
Shields, James J. '63 (PH) [13] Philadelphia, PA St. Anselm Church.
Shields, James P. '52 (CHI) Other Assignments; Retired.
Shields, Msgr. Joseph A. '49 (PH) Kimberton, PA St. Basil the Great Church.
Shields, Joseph E. '36 (MAN) Newmarket, NH St. Mary Church; Retired.
Shields, Lester O. *s.j.* '94 (FgM) Provinces.
Shields, Msgr. Maurice L. '57 (MOB) [11] Mobile, AL Little Flower Church.
Shields, Michael '79 (ANC) On Duty Outside Archdiocese.
Shields, Patrick J. '64 (CLV) [7] Lorain, OH St. Ladislaus Church.
Shields, Robert J. '64 (YAK) Retired.
Shields, Stephen L. '74 (CLV) Parma Heights, OH St. John Bosco Church; Sheffield Lake, OH St. Thomas the Apostle Church.
Shields, W. Bry '84 (MOB) [7] Mobile, AL St. Ignatius Church; [C] Mobile, AL McGill-Toolen High School.
Shields, William J. '52 (CHI) Mundelein, IL Santa Maria Del Popolo Church; Retired.
Shields, William J. '58 (ALN) [J] Bethlehem, PA Holy Family Villa.
Shiffer, Jim *s.s.c.* '65 (LA) [R] Los Angeles, CA Columban Fathers, Procure House.
Shiffler, John (TOL) [J] Oregon, OH Sacred Heart Home.
Shigo, Francis *s.v.d.* (LA) [K] Torrance, CA Little Company of Mary Health Services.
Shigo, Francis L. (LA) [K] Torrance, CA Little Company of Mary Health Services.
Shigo, Francis L. *s.v.d.* '60 (LA) [R] Los Angeles, CA Society of the Divine Word Western Province.
Shih, John '49 (NEW) [N] Rutherford, NJ St. John Vianney Residence for Priests.
Shih, John M. '49 (NEW) Retired.
Shikany, Paul M. '79 (IND) Edinburgh, IN Holy Trinity Church; Franklin, IN St. Rose of Lima Church; [N] Franklin, IN Franklin College Newman Center.
Shillcox, Timothy *o.praem.* '87 (GB) [I] De Pere, WI St. Joseph Priory.
Shillcox, Timothy D. *o.praem.* '87 (GB) Bay Settlement, WI Holy Cross Church.
Shillito, Edward D. '55 (RVC) [N] Uniondale, NY St. Pius X Residence.
Shimanek, Joseph '54 (JOL) Retired.
Shimizu, Kazuo Louis Ibar *s.m.* (CIN) [M] Dayton, OH Marianist Provincialate.
Shimmaly, Edward E. '61 (B) Retired.
Shimmaly, Edward F. '61 (LA) Retired.
Shimotsu, John '94 (ORG) Military Chaplains.
Shin, Jung Soon (Benedict) (WDC) College Park, MD St. Andrew Kim Church.
Shin, Simon Hyun-Man (ARL) Fairfax, VA St. Paul Chung Church.
Shindelar, Vincent J. '56 (RCK) [4] Rockford, IL St. Edward Church.
Shine, Con '60 (ORL) Silver Springs Shores, FL Immaculate Heart of Mary Church.
Shine, Daniel J. *s.j.* '51 (BO) [W] Weston, MA Campion Health Center, Inc.
Shine, Edward J. '57 (CIN) [44] Cincinnati, OH St. John the Baptist Church.
Shine, Francis J. *c.m.* '55 (STL) St. Louis, MO Regional Hospital; [P] St. Louis, MO Vincentian Henrietta Residence.
Shine, John V. *c.m.* '63 (PHX) [26] Phoenix, AZ St. Vincent de Paul Church.
Shine, Robert W. '55 (SAG) Port Austin, MI St. Michael Church.
Shine, Sean '52 (ORL) Silver Springs Shores, FL Immaculate Heart of Mary Church.
Shiner, Kenneth H. '71 (HRT) Branford, CT St. Elizabeth Church.
Shinners, Charles T. *s.j.* '50 (MIL) [P] Wauwatosa, WI Jesuit Community at St. Camillus.
Shinney, Robert J. *s.j.* '68 (SJ) [D] San Jose, CA Bellarmine College Preparatory.
Shinnick, Edward P. '56 (GF) Retired.
Shinnick, James F. '39 (B) Retired.
Shinos, Robert '63 (ALB) Herkimer, NY St. Anthony-St. Joseph Church.
Shipe, William '61 (Y) [3] Canton, OH Sacred Heart Church.
Shipley, Msgr. William L. '54 (SD) [B] San Diego, CA University of San Diego.
Shipp, Edmund M. '61 (SFR) [44] San Francisco, CA St. Peter Church; San Francisco, CA San Francisco General Hospital.
Shipps, Frank Bede *o.p.* '85 (NY) [22] New York, NY St. Catherine of Siena Church; [DD] New York, NY St. Catherine of Siena Priory.
Shiraki, Gabriel *s.a.* '89 (NY) [DD] Garrison, NY Generalate of the Franciscan Friars of the Atonement-St. James Friary.
Shiras, Natalie '82 (BGP) [I] Bridgeport, CT St. Vincent's Medical Center.
Shirey, John W. '43 (CHI) [114] Chicago, IL St. Kilian Church; Retired.
Shirey, Joseph E. *s.j.* '56 (P) White City, OR U.S. Veternan's Affiars Domiciliary; [J] Medford, OR Providence Medford Medical Center.
Shirilla, Gerald '68 (DET) Absent on Leave.
Shirima, Amadeus *s.j.* '92 (CHI) [C] Chicago, IL Jesuit Community at Loyola University of Chicago.
Shirley, John T. *o.s.a.* '65 (MIL) [12] Racine, WI St. Rita Church.
Shirley, Msgr. Richard '67 (CC) [21] Corpus Christi, TX St. Pius X Church.
Shirley, Ronald R. '73 (MRY) [4] Salinas, CA Madonna Del Sasso Church.
Shiroda, Daniel L. (MAR) Retired.
Shiverski, John J. '68 (MAR) Negaunee, MI St. Paul Church.
Shlesinger, Bernard E., III '96 (R) Wilmington, NC St. Mary Church.
Shmaruk, Richard J. '65 (BO) [21] Boston, MA St. Columbkille Church.
Shmauz, Donald A. '60 (MIL) On Duty Outside the Archdiocese.
Shnob, Alan D. '78 (OG) Massena, NY St. Mary Church.
Shoback, Edward J. '67 (SCR) [23] Scranton, PA SS. Peter and Paul Church.
Shoback, Thomas P. '77 (SCR) Montoursville, PA Our Lady of Lourdes Church.
Shockey, David P. '56 (COV) Retired; [M] Walton, KY St. William Convent.
Shocklee, Msgr. John A. '42 (STL) Retired.
Shoda, D. Brian '87 (WH) Inwood, WV St. Leo Church.
Shoda, Richard W. '78 (WH) [Q] Bethany, WV St. John Fisher Catholic Chapel; [Q] West Liberty, WV West Liberty State College, St. Thomas Aquinas Campus Ministry.
Shoemaker, Msgr. Samuel E. '66 (PH) Yardley, PA St. Ignatius of Antioch Church.
Shoemaker, Thomas R. '90 (FTW) [1] South Bend, IN St. Matthew Cathedral.
Sholander, Anthony E. *s.j.* '84 (SJ) [B] Santa Clara, CA Santa Clara University.
Shonebarger, Thomas '69 (COL) [40] Columbus, OH St. Timothy Church.
Shonis, Anthony J. '71 (OWN) Non-Parochial Assignments; [A] Owensboro, KY Brescia College; [G] Maple Mount, KY Mount St. Joseph.
Shoppe, Eric *o.f.m.* '45 (PAT) [M] Ringwood, NJ Holy Name Friary, Inc.
Shore, Zachary J. '81 (SFR) [35] San Francisco, CA Most Holy Redeemer Church.
Shori, Nicholas R. '74 (Y) New Middletown, OH St. Paul the Apostle Church.
Short, Anthony J. *s.j.* '71 (DEN) [M] Denver, CO Xavier Jesuit Center.
Short, James M. *s.j.* '61 (FgM) Provinces.

Short, Joseph '90 (SFS) Clear Lake, SD St. Mary Church.
Short, Redemptus *o.c.d.* '47 (MIL) [P] Holy Hill, WI Discalced Carmelite Monastery.
Shortall, Robert '74 (DAL) Plano, TX St. Elizabeth Ann Seton Church.
Shortall, Robert '74 (DAV) On Duty Outside the Diocese.
Shorter, Melvin *c.p.* '86 (ATL) [11] Atlanta, GA St. Paul of the Cross Church.
Shortt, David J. '89 (PBR) [2] Youngstown, OH St. Nicholas Church.
Shortt, Patrick J. '66 (JC) Moberly, MO St. Pius X Church; Moberly, MO Missouri Training Center For Men.
Shott, Stephen E. *o.s.f.s.* '95 (WIL) [B] Wilmington, DE Salesianum School.
Shoup, Steven L. '84 (CIN) [11] Dayton, OH St. Henry Church.
Shovelton, Gerald T. *v.f.* '56 (FR) West Harwich, MA Holy Trinity Church.
Shovelton, William J. '46 (FR) Retired.
Showalter, Paul E. '66 (PEO) [4] Rock Island, IL St. Pius X Church.
Showfety, Msgr. Joseph S. '55 (CHL) [2] Greensboro, NC St. Benedict Church.
Showutter, Joseph *s.j.* '75 (SPK) [E] Spokane, WA Gonzaga Preparatory School.
Shrader, Dwight E. '82 (RIC) [7] Virginia Beach, VA St. John the Apostle Church.
Shreenan, Timothy J. *o.f.m.* '84 (NY) [35] New York, NY St. Francis of Assisi Church.
Shreve, Msgr. Thomas F. '61 (RIC) [2] Richmond, VA Church of the Epiphany.
Shroeder, Danielmose *o.f.m.* '91 (FgM) Custody of St. Mary of the Angels. Byzantine-Slavonic.
Shubiak, Stephen '88 (STF) Special Assignment.
Shuda, Paul R. '60 (HBG) [8] Harrisburg, PA Our Lady of the Blessed Sacrament Church.
Shuda, Msgr. Robert J. '59 (GBG) [1] Greensburg, PA Blessed Sacrament Cathedral.
Shugrue, Michael P. '66 (R) [H] Durham, NC Catholic Student Center for Students at Duke University.
Shugrue, Paul S. '70 (BO) Braintree, MA St. Clare Church.
Shugrue, Msgr. Timothy J. '73 (NEW) Montclair, NJ Immaculate Conception Church.
Shuhler, Ralph V. *o.s.a.* '39 (PH) [AA] Villanova, PA St. Thomas Monastery.
Shuley, Keith '92 (CC) Military Chaplains.
Shuman, Killian E. *t.o.r.* '59 (E) Ramey, PA Holy Trinity Church.
Shuppert, William T.J. '71 (TUC) On Duty Outside the Diocese.
Shurer, Ralph C. *o.s.a.* '54 (PH) [C] Villanova, PA Villanova University; [AA] Villanova, PA St. Thomas Monastery.
Shurtleff, F. James '66 (OG) Malone, NY St. Joseph's Church.
Shurtleff, Robert M. '70 (OG) Tupper Lake, NY Holy Name of Jesus Church.
Shust, Yaroslav '30 (STF) Retired.
Shuster, Anthony J. '70 (GF) [3] Great Falls, MT St. Joseph's Church.
Shuttleworth, Edward J. '90 (LC) Durand, WI St. Mary's Assumption Church; Lima, WI Holy Rosary Church.
Shwe, Jerome Aung '73 (CHL) Morganton, NC St. Charles Borromeo Church.
Siani, Angelo *o.m.i.* '65 (FgM) Oblates Foreign Missions.
Sibel, John J. (PH) [96] Philadelphia, PA St. Mary of the Assumption Church.
Sibenik, Simeon B. '81 (PBR) Du Bois, PA Nativity of the Mother of God Church; Sykesville, PA Holy Trinity Church.
Sibilano, Joseph D. *o.s.j.* '65 (NOR) [5] Middletown, CT St. Sebastian Church.
Sibilano, Joseph D. *o.s.j.* '65 (SCR) [M] Pittston, PA Eastern Province of the Oblates of St. Joseph.
Sica, Joseph F. '82 (SCR) Tunkhannock, PA Nativity of Blessed Virgin Mary Church.
Sicard, Kenneth *o.p.* '90 (PRO) [P] Providence, RI St. Thomas Aquinas Priory at Providence College.
Sicari, Joseph J. '82 (BUF) [H] Buffalo, NY The Catholic Charities of the Diocese of Buffalo.
Sicilia, Msgr. Pablo A. '60 (SAT) Carrizo Springs, TX Our Lady of Guadalupe Church.
Siciliano, Donald E. '93 (JC) Vandalia, MO Sacred Heart Church.
Siciliano, John M. '82 (WOR) [1] Fitchburg, MA St. Anthony of Padua Church.
Siciliano, Jude *o.p.* (R) [E] Raleigh, NC De Porres House; [E] Raleigh, NC De Porres House.
Siciliano, Jude *o.p.* '69 (OAK) [N] Oakland, CA Order of Preachers (Southern Province).
Siciliano, Jude *o.p.* '69 (R) [E] Raleigh, NC Dominican Community.
Sickler, Robert *m.ss.a.* '87 (NOR) [A] Cromwell, CT Holy Apostles College and Seminary.
Sickler, Thomas G. *m.s.* '73 (NOR) Brooklyn, CT Our Lady of La Salette Church.
Sicoli, David C. '75 (PH) [14] Philadelphia, PA St. Anthony of Padua Church.
Siconolfi, Msgr. Constantine V. '59 (SCR) [7] Scranton, PA Holy Family Church; [R] Scranton, PA St. Francis of Assisi Kitchen.
Siconolfi, Michael *s.j.* '72 (SPK) [C] Spokane, WA Gonzaga University.
Siconolfi, Thomas *c.ss.r.* '70 (BAL) Annapolis, MD St. Mary Church; [M] Annapolis, MD Saint Mary Rectory.
Sidera, Joseph A. *c.s.c.* '68 (SCR) [C] Wilkes-Barre, PA Kings College; [C] Wilkes-Barre, PA Kings College.
Sides, Gary '73 (AMA) Panhandle, TX St. Theresa Church.
Sidler, Fred '92 (DAL) Ennis, TX St. John Nepomucene Church.
Sidler, Gordon L. '97 (ATL) Conyers, GA St. Pius X Catholic Church.
Sidler, Peter *o.s.b.* '46 (PRO) [P] Portsmouth, RI Abbey of St. Gregory the Great.
Sidney, Walter T. *s.j.* '78 (DEN) [D] Aurora, CO Regis Jesuit High School; [M] Aurora, CO Regis Jesuit High School - Jesuit Community.
Sidoti, Anthony '40 (ALB) [8] Albany, NY St. James Church; Retired.
Sidoti, James *o.carm.* '92 (BRK) [140] Brooklyn, NY St. Thomas Aquinas Church.
Siebenaler, John M. '61 (STP) Retired.
Siebenaler, Leonard '59 (STP) St. Michael, MN St. Michael Church.
Siebenaler, Martin J. '59 (STP) Waconia, MN St. Joseph Church.
Siebenand, Ambrose F. '41 (NU) Retired.
Siebenand, John N. '38 (NU) Retired.
Siebenand, Paul Alcuin '60 (LA) Avalon, CA St. Catherine of Alexandria Church.
Siebenand, Richard '67 (LA) [26] Los Angeles, CA Our Lady of Lourdes Church.
Siebeneck, Robert *c.pp.s.* '44 (CIN) [B] Carthagena, OH St. Charles.
Siebers, Glen F. *o.praem* '50 (GB) [I] De Pere, WI St. Norbert Abbey.
Siebert, Anthony G. '59 (STL) On Duty Outside the Archdiocese.
Siebert, Edward J. *s.j.* (DET) [K] Detroit, MI Jesuit Provincial Office-Detroit Province of the Society of Jesus.
Siebert, Paul S. '86 (E) Emporium, PA St. Mark Church.
Siebert, William P. '79 (DET) [2] Roseville, MI St. Athanasius Church.
Siebold, Gerard F. *c.ss.r.* '58 (SAT) [37] San Antonio, TX St. Gerard Majella Church.
Siebor, John '58 (RVC) Hempstead, NY St. Ladislaus Church.
Siebs, Robert L. '49 (OKL) Absent on Leave.
Siecienski, A. Edward '95 (TR) Medford, NJ St. Mary of the Lakes Church.
Siecker, James A. (TOL) Retired.
Siedlecki, Edmund J. (CHI) [60] Chicago, IL Five Holy Martyrs Church.
Siedlecki, Edmund J. '52 (CHI) Retired.
Siedlicki, Edmund J. '52 (CHI) [T] Mundelein, IL Cardinal Stritch Retreat House.
Siefer, Richard R. '75 (E) Du Bois, PA St. Catherine Church.
Siefert, Ralph A. *s.m.* '73 (STL) [F] Creve Coeur, MO Chaminade College Preparatory School Inc.; [G] Creve Coeur, MO Chaminade College Preparatory.
Sieffert, John S. '89 (STL) [9] Florissant, MO St. Sabina Church.
Sieg, Leslie M. *c.s.p.* '76 (NY) [DD] Jamaica Estates, NY Paulist Fathers Generalate.
Sieg, Leslie M. *c.s.p.* '76 (P) Tigard, OR St. Anthony Church.
Sieg, Robert *o.f.m.* '75 (IND) [12] Indianapolis, IN Sacred Heart of Jesus Church.
Sieg, Thomas H. '71 (STP) Burnsville, MN Church of the Risen Savior.
Siegel, Joseph '88 (JOL) Plainfield, IL St. Mary Immaculate Church.
Siegel, Kenan *o.f.m.cap.* '56 (MIL) [B] Mount Calvary, WI St. Lawrence Seminary; [P] Mount Calvary, WI St. Lawrence Friary.
Siegfried, Gerard *c.s.sp.* '37 (ARE) Barceloneta, PR Church of Our Lady of Mt. Carmel.
Siekaniec, Ladislas *o.f.m.* (SFD) [K] Sherman, IL Our Lady of Angels Friary.
Siekierski, Msgr. John J. '67 (GRY) [13] East Chicago, IN St. Stanislaus Church.
Siekierski, Matthew J. '77 (WDC) La Plata, MD Sacred Heart Church.
Sielski, Joseph *m.i.c.* '41 (BAL) [J] Baltimore, MD St. Joseph's Nursing Home; [N] Baltimore, MD Sisters Servants of Mary Immaculate, Inc.
Sielski, Joseph *m.i.c.* '41 (WDC) [B] Washington, DC Marian Fathers Scholasticate.
Siemanowski, John S. '89 (CHI) Chicago Heights, IL St. Agnes Church.
Siener, Albert '46 (NSH) Retired.
Siener, Msgr. Leo C. '48 (KNX) Retired.
Siepka, Richard W. '82 (BUF) [A] East Aurora, NY Christ the King Seminary.
Siepker, Dan '93 (DM) [D] Corning, IA Mercy Midlands: Mercy Hospital.
Siepker, Daniel E. '93 (DM) Corning, IA St. Patrick's Church.
Sierachi, Aloysius *o.carm.* (JOL) [M] Darien, IL Provincial Office of Lay Carmelites and Scapular Confraternity.
Sieracki, Aloysius A. *o.carm.* '59 (CHI) [N] Chicago, IL Brandsma House.
Sieradski, Alfred A. *c.ss.r.* '49 (STA) [6] Jacksonville, FL Holy Rosary Church.
Sierminski, Vernon '56 (SAG) Retired.
Sierocki, Paul E. '44 (DET) Retired.
Sierra, Angel (PEO) On Duty Outside the Diocese.
Sierra, Angel (SFD) Altamont, IL St. Clare Church; Edgewood, IL St. Anne Church; St. Elmo, IL St. Bonaventure Church; St. Elmo, IL St. Mary Church.
Sierra, Angel '80 (SFD) Effingham, IL St. Anthony of Padua Church.
Sierra, Francis A. '46 (SD) Retired.
Sierra, John A. *s.f.* '40 (WDC) [B] Silver Spring, MD Holy Family Seminary.
Sierra, Luis Alberto '73 (SJN) [4] Toa Alta, PR Nuestra Senora de la Medalla Milagrosa Church.
Sierra-Posada, Pedro J. '76 (ALX) [1] Alexandria, LA St. Francis Xavier Cathedral; Glenmora, LA St. Louis Church; [D] Forest Hill, LA Our Lady of Guadalupe Mission.
Sievel, Thomas A. '78 (HRT) [3] West Haven, CT St. Lawrence's Church.
Sieverding, Dale '89 (SFS) [1] Sioux Falls, SD St. Joseph Cathedral.
Siffert, Etienne *s.m.* '58 (SFR) [37] San Francisco, CA Notre Dame des Victoires Church.
Siffrin, Robert '79 (Y) [9] Youngstown, OH St. Brendan's Church.
Sigaran, Mamerto (SFR) [42] San Francisco, CA St. Paul Church.
Sigler, Gary L. '79 (FTW) Huntington, IN St. Mary Church.
Sigler, John W. '94 (LA) Simi Valley, CA St. Rose of Lima Church.
Sigman, Louis A. '67 (PHX) [2] Phoenix, AZ Corpus Christi Church.
Sigmund, Andrew J. '64 (STL) Kimmswick, MO St. Joseph's Church.
Signey, Lawrence '87 (LA) La Canada Flintridge, CA St. Bede the Venerable Church.
Signiski, Michael M. '66 (CAM) [2] Cherry Hill, NJ Holy Rosary Church.
Signorelli, Francis *s.x.* '59 (FgM) Xaverian Foreign Missions.
Signorelli, Francis *s.x.* '59 (PAT) [M] Wayne, NJ Xaverian Missionary Fathers.
Siguenza, Francisco *o.a.r.* '56 (ELP) [12] El Paso, TX Saint Therese of the Little Flower Parish.
Siguere, Robert *o.f.m.* '73 (FgM) Franciscan Foreign Missions.
Sigwarth, Reynold J. '41 (DUB) Retired.
Sihuay, Francis X. *o.f.m.* '51 (WDC) [M] Washington, DC Commissariat of the Holy Land, Franciscan Monastery - Mount St. Sepulchre.
Sikandar, Anthony '90 (BRK) [151] Queens, NY St. Ann's Church.
Sikander, Anthony '90 (BRK) [T] Brooklyn, NY Catholic Migration & Refugee Office, Catholic Migration Services, Inc.
Sikiric, Grgo *t.o.r.* '52 (PIT) [5] Millvale, PA St. Nicholas Church; [O] Pittsburgh, PA Croatian Commissariate, T.O.R.
Siklodi, Sandor '71 (CLV) [22] Cleveland, OH St. Emeric Church.
Sikon, Michael P. '96 (GBG) [1] Greensburg, PA Blessed Sacrament Cathedral.
Sikora, Eric L. (BUF) [1] Kenmore, NY St. Andrew Church.
Sikora, James (GF) [A] Great Falls, MT University of Great Falls.
Sikora, James R. '67 (GF) [A] Great Falls, MT University of Great Falls.
Sikora, Msgr. Joseph G. '49 (PH) Retired.
Sikora, Stanley J. '57 (HRT) [A] Bloomfield, CT St. Thomas Seminary.
Sikora, Thomas More *o.s.b.* '97 (GBG) [H] Latrobe, PA Saint Vincent Archabbey.
Sikorski, Harold R. '56 (SAG) On Duty Outside the Diocese; Retired.
Sikorski, Jeffery P. '73 (TOL) Maumee, OH St. Joseph Church.
Sikorski, Leszek M. '97 (VEN) Awaiting Assignment.
Sikorski, Louis S. '64 (GAL) Anderson, TX St. Stanislaus Church.
Silcox, John D., Jr. '95 (PH) Exton, PA SS. Philip and James Church.
Sileo, Joseph R. '71 (WDC) [30] Washington, DC Nativity Church; [37] Washington, DC St. Peter Church.
Siler, Francis A. '63 (PIT) [26] Pittsburgh, PA St. Mary

of Mercy Church.
Siler, Paschal *o.f.m.cap.* '60 (GF) Ashland, MT St. Labre's Church.
Siliako, Petelo '86 (SPP) [8] Pago Pago, AS Church of Sacred Heart.
Silio, Antonio R. '88 (MIA) Pembroke Pines, FL St. Boniface Church.
Silipigni, Stephan A. '81 (PRO) [3] North Providence, RI Mary, Mother of Mankind Church.
Silk, John D. '59 (BO) Amesbury, MA St. Joseph Church; Retired.
Silk, William J. '60 (WDC) [4] Bethesda, MD Our Lady of Lourdes Church.
Silko, Herbert *o.f.m.* '55 (MIL) [P] Burlington, WI Queen of Peace Friary.
Sill, Theodore K. '89 (COL) [30] Columbus, OH St. Mary Magdalene Church.
Silva, Alvaro '74 (BO) [V] Chestnut Hill, MA Opus Dei.
Silva, Alvaro '87 (SJN) [22] Bayamon, PR Sagrada Familia Church.
Silva, Caesar '74 (HT) [3] Houma, LA Maria Immacolata Church.
Silva, David E. '54 (CLV) Retired.
Silva, Edwin Lugo '89 (MGZ) [5] Mayaquez, PR Nuestra Senora De Fatima Church.
Silva, Francis J. *s.j.* '42 (SJ) [D] San Jose, CA Bellarmine College Preparatory.
Silva, Frank J. '76 (BO) [1] Malden, MA Immaculate Conception Church.
Silva, George '97 (SFE) Clayton, NM St. Francis Xavier Church.
Silva, Ismael '79 (ORG) [1] Santa Ana, CA Immaculate Heart of Mary Church.
Silva, James M. '67 (PRO) Retired.
Silva, John F. '34 (BO) Retired.
Silva, Jose D. '51 (HRT) [4] Hartford, CT Our Lady of Fatima Church.
Silva, Juan '92 (LA) [93] Los Angeles, CA St. Thomas the Apostle Church.
Silva, Langes L. (SLC) Layton, UT St. Rose of Lima Church.
Silva, Larry '75 (OAK) [2] Oakland, CA St. Andrew-St. Joseph Church.
Silva, Miguel '84 (SAC) Corning, CA Immaculate Conception Church; Orland, CA St. Dominic Church.
Silva, Robert J. '65 (STO) [1] Stockton, CA Cathedral of the Annunciation.
Silveira, Eduino '87 (SAC) [12] Sacramento, CA St. Elizabeth Church; Special Assignment.
Silver, Bertram *o.m.i.* '54 (FgM) Oblates Foreign Missions.
Silver, E. John '92 (OG) Rosiere, NY St. Vincent de Paul Church.
Silver, E. Thomas '93 (OG) Cape Vincent, NY St. Vincent of Paul Church.
Silver, Jeffrey P. '84 (CIN) [3] Hamilton, OH St. Julie Billiart Church.
Silver, Martin J. '54 (NEW) [3] Hackensack, NJ St. Joseph's Church.
Silveri, Donato P. '64 (PH) [99] Philadelphia, PA St. Mary Magdalen de Pazzi Church.
Silverio, Gilbert *o.f.m.* '59 (NY) [DD] New York, NY Franciscan Province of the Immaculate Conception.
Silverman, Robert '67 (SAT) [44] San Antonio, TX St. John Neumann Church; [T] San Antonio, TX The Blue Army.
Silvers, Rudolph M. '75 (PIT) Bulger, PA St. Ann Church.
Silvester, George E. *c.s.b.* '46 (GAL) Sugar Land, TX St. Theresa Church.
Silvester, Peter *s.v.d.* '78 (TR) [M] Bordentown, NJ Society of the Divine Word.
Silvestri, Luke A. '52 (SCR) On Duty Outside the Diocese.
Silvestri, Vincent A. '64 (MIL) Retired.
Silvestrini, Dino F. '85 (MAR) Menominee, MI Resurrection Church.
Silvestro, Dominic '60 (SPR) [L] Springfield, MA St. Francis of Assisi Chapel and Catholic Information Center.
Silvia, Kenneth *c.s.c.* '64 (SJ) Saratoga, CA Sacred Heart Church.
Sima, John *s.j.* '76 (FgM) Provinces.
Sima, John R. *s.j.* '71 (CHI) [N] Chicago, IL Chicago Province of the Society of Jesus-Provincial Office.
Simard, Robert E. '56 (BAK) Prineville, OR St. Joseph's Church.
Simas, Msgr. Manuel C. '61 (OAK) [4] Fremont, CA St. Joseph Mission Church.
Simboli, Ronald L. '75 (GBG) Apollo, PA St. James the Greater Church.
Simburger, R. Joseph '79 (SFD) Unassigned.
Simcox, Thomas *s.c.j.* '40 (SP) [O] Pinellas Park, FL Priests of the Sacred Heart.
Simeone, Francis P. *o.s.f.s.* '61 (R) Shallotte, NC St. Brendan the Navigator Church.
Simeone, Gary F. '75 (HRT) East Haven, CT St. Vincent de Paul's Church.
Simeone, Ronald P. '82 (PRO) [2] Johnston, RI Our Lady of Grace Church.
Simington, Ralph P. '62 (DUB) Manchester, IA St. Mary's Church; [E] Manchester, IA St. Paul's School of Religion.
Simko, James G. '91 (DEN) Estes Park, CO Our Lady of the Mountains Church.
Simko, Michael S. '44 (NEW) Retired.
Simlik, Frank P. '54 (PHX) Sun City, AZ Church of St. Joachim & St. Anne.
Simmons, Msgr. Donald W. '43 (B) Retired.
Simmons, Franklin '79 (GAL) [5] Houston, TX St. Ambrose Church; [K] Houston, TX The Catholic Chaplain Corps.
Simmons, Hilary F. '43 (LC) Retired.
Simmons, Jerome S. '68 (E) [11] Erie, PA Sacred Heart Church; [O] Erie, PA Ecclesia Center/Renewal Center.
Simmons, Joseph C. '61 (BAL) Joppa, MD Church of the Holy Spirit.
Simmons, Norman J. *c.ss.r.* '73 (PH) [25] Philadelphia, PA St. Boniface Church.
Simmons, Msgr. Walter E. '55 (RVC) Port Washington, NY St. Peter of Alcantara Church.
Simmons, William B. *c.s.c.* '52 (FTW) [L] Notre Dame, IN Holy Cross Mission House.
Simms, Robert A. *s.j.* '46 (FgM) Provinces.
Simms, William '62 (BAL) [91] Baltimore, MD St. Thomas Aquinas Church; Special Assignment.
Simoes, Gilbert '61 (FR) Absent on Leave.
Simon, Ambrose '50 (GB) [I] Appleton, WI St. Fidelis Friary.
Simon, Bernard '42 (SP) Retired.
Simon, Brian '96 (SFS) [2] Sioux Falls, SD Christ the King Church.
Simon, Carl A. '71 (LAN) Deerfield, MI St. Augustine Church.
Simon, David P. '67 (ROC) Apalachin, NY St. Margaret Mary Church.
Simon, Eugene P. *s.j.* '57 (DET) [P] Bloomfield Hills, MI Manresa Jesuit Retreat House.
Simon, George H. '57 (LAF) Scott, LA Saint Martin de Porres Church.
Simon, John L. '73 (MIL) Beaver Dam, WI St. Peter Church.
Simon, Joseph M. '71 (STL) Webster Groves, MO Holy Redeemer Church.
Simon, Julian *o.s.b.* '45 (CGS) [C] Humacao, PR San Antonio Abad Abbey of the Order of St. Benedict.
Simon, Martin M. '55 (MIL) Retired.
Simon, Raphael *o.c.s.o.* '47 (WOR) [N] Spencer, MA St. Joseph's Abbey.
Simon, Richard T. '75 (CHI) [205] Chicago, IL St. Thomas of Canterbury Church.
Simon, Robert *c.ss.r.* '48 (B) Coeur D'Alene, ID St. Thomas Church.
Simon, Robert G. *c.s.c.* '61 (FgM) Holy Cross Foreign Missions.
Simon, Robert G. *c.s.c.* '61 (FTW) [J] South Bend, IN Congregation of Holy Cross Indiana Province Provincial House.
Simon, Robert J. '90 (SCR) [4] Scranton, PA St. David's Church.
Simon, Thomas *m.ss.a* '79 (HRT) [2] Waterbury, CT Immaculate Conception Church.
Simon, Vincent J. '46 (DUB) Retired.
Simonar, Matthew (GB) [2] Manitowoc, WI Holy Innocents Church.
Simonds, Donald D. *m.s.* '63 (HRT) [M] Hartford, CT Missionaries of LaSalette Provincial Secretary.
Simone, Earl Francis '77 (CIN) [22] Dayton, OH St. Peter Church.
Simone, Michael A. *m.m.* '56 (NY) [DD] Maryknoll, NY Maryknoll Fathers and Brothers.
Simoneau, Norman J. '67 (MAN) On Duty Outside the Diocese.
Simoneau, Norman J. '67 (SR) Fortuna, CA St. Joseph Church.
Simoneau, Ronald L. '78 (PRO) Smithfield, RI St. Philip Church.
Simoneaux, Jody '82 (LAF) [11] Lafayette, LA St. Genevieve Church.
Simonelli, Gerald '90 (JOL) Glen Ellyn, IL St. Petronille Church.
Simonetti, Gennaro M. '38 (BRK) [103] Brooklyn, NY Our Lady of Miracles Church; Retired.
Simoni, Salvador '80 (CHI) Northlake, IL St. John Baptist Vianney, Cure of Ars Church.
Simonin, Msgr. John A. '47 (CHR) [2] Charleston, SC St. Mary's Church.
Simonini, Michael (GB) [2] Appleton, WI St. Bernard Church.
Simonini, Michael F. '75 (RCK) Active Outside the Diocese.
Simonnet, Philippe *s.s.e.* '52 (BUR) [E] Colchester, VT Society of St. Edmund.
Simonnet, Philippe *s.s.e.* '52 (FgM) Edmundite Foreign Missions.
Simons, Derek *s.v.d.* '70 (CHI) [B] Techny, IL Divine Word Residence; [N] Chicago, IL Divine Word Theologate; [N] Techny, IL Society of the Divine Word, Provincial Headquarter-Chicago Prov.
Simons, Edward J. *o.s.f.s.* '43 (PH) [AA] Philadelphia, PA Oblates of St. Francis De Sales.
Simons, Lawrence D. '48 (HEL) Retired.
Simons, Msgr. Richard J. '38 (PH) Newtown Square, PA St. Anastasia Church; Retired.
Simons, Thomas G. '77 (GR) [2] Muskegon, MI St. Francis de Sales Church.
Simonson, Earl C. '69 (STP) [22] Minneapolis, MN St. Clement Church.
Simpson, Brian L. '72 (CHI) Military Chaplains.
Simpson, David *o.carm.* '70 (NEW) [P] Mahwah, NJ Carmel Retreat House.
Simpson, Gerald T. '57 (STL) Neier, MO St. Joseph's Church.
Simpson, Kenneth C. '78 (CHI) [V] Chicago, IL Ministry in Higher Education.
Simpson, Mark '79 (CHI) Winnetka, IL Sacred Heart Church.
Simpson, Mauro *o.s.b.* '52 (CGS) Humacao, PR Maria Reina de la Paz Church.
Simpson, Robert A. '65 (RNO) [4] Reno, NV St. Albert the Great Church.
Simpson, Roger '52 (SFD) Retired.
Sims, Henry F.H. '51 (PRT) Retired.
Sims, Paul *c.r.* '86 (CHI) [D] Chicago, IL Gordon Technical High School.
Sims, Robert W. '71 (IND) Leave of Absence.
Sinasac, Alvin A. *c.s.b.* '78 (GAL) [B] Houston, TX Casa San Basilio.
Sinatra, Leonard '67 (PHU) Northampton, PA St. John the Baptist Church.
Sinatra, William D. '64 (DET) [4] Southfield, MI St. Ives Church.
Sinclair, Alexander B. '57 (KC) [36] Kansas City, MO St. Raphael the Archangel Church.
Sinclair, Calvin F. *s.s.j.* '79 (BAL) [M] Baltimore, MD St. Joseph's Manor.
Sinclair, Roger A. (BO) Boston, MA Veterans Administration Hospital.
Sinclair, Roger A. '74 (GBG) Military Chaplains.
Sindik, Msgr. George E. '59 (PT) [13] Pensacola, FL St. Paul Church.
Sindik, Matthew A. '62 (MOB) [6] Montgomery, AL St. Jude Church; [F] Montgomery, AL City of St. Jude, Inc., The; [L] Montgomery, AL The City of St. Jude, Inc.
Singarayar, Philip *o.m.i.* '64 (CHI) [N] Chicago, IL The Oblate House of Theology.
Singelyn, Robert K. '60 (DET) On Duty Outside the Archdiocese.
Singer, Jerome C. '63 (DET) [51] Detroit, MI Nativity of Our Lord Church.
Singer, Thomas J. *o.m.i.* '57 (STP) [N] St. Paul, MN Oblate Provincial Offices; [N] St. Paul, MN Oblate Residence.
Singler, Charles E. '84 (TOL) Perrysburg, OH St. Rose Church.
Singler, James E. '82 (CLV) Cleveland Heights, OH St. Ann Church.
Singler, John P. '82 (CLV) Willowick, OH St. Mary Magdalene Church.
Singleton, William '50 (RVC) Retired.
Singleton, William V. '50 (RVC) East Rockaway, NY St. Raymond's Church.
Sinibaldi, Daniel J. '96 (MAN) Merrimack, NH Our Lady of Mercy Church.
Sinisi, Daniel *t.o.r.* '66 (STU) [A] Steubenville, OH Franciscan University of Steubenville; [F] Steubenville, OH Holy Spirit Monastery.
Siniskey, Joseph M. '48 (ALB) East Greenbush, NY Holy Spirit Church.
Sinisky, Joseph '48 (ALB) Retired.
Sinkele, W. T. *o.p.* '73 (FgM) Dominican - Order of Preachers Foreign Missions.
Sinkler, Michael D. '81 (LR) Bentonville, AR St. Stephen Church; Rogers, AR St. Vincent de Paul Church.
Sinnema, Paul *o.f.m.* '63 (NEW) East Rutherford, NJ St. Joseph's Church; Wood-Ridge, NJ Our Lady of the Assumption Church.
Sinner, Msgr. Emil E. '42 (SAL) Retired.
Sinner, Richard W. '52 (FAR) Retired.
Sinnerud, James A. *s.j.* '72 (OM) [C] Omaha, NE Creighton Preparatory School.
Sinnott, James P. *m.m.* '60 (FgM) Maryknoll Foreign Missions.
Sinor, Michael J. '88 (SD) Ramona, CA Immaculate Heart of Mary Church.
Sinski, Norbert J. *c.s.c.* '77 (FTW) [J] South Bend, IN Congregation of Holy Cross Indiana Province Provincial House.
Sinz, Eugene R. '60 (STL) High Ridge, MO St. Anthony of Padua Church.
Siok, Slavomir *s.a.c.* '90 (BUF) Lewiston, NY St. Peter Church; [O] North Tonawanda, NY Society of the Catholic Apostolate.
Siola, Roman *o.f.m.conv.* (BUF) [21] Buffalo, NY Corpus Christi Church.
Sioleti, Andrew *o.f.m.* (NY) Manhattan, NY Cabrini Medical Center.
Sioli, Joseph *c.o.* '97 (PIT) [1] Pittsburgh, PA St. Paul Cathedral.
Sioli, Joseph E. *c.o.* '97 (PIT) [O] Pittsburgh, PA

Congregation of the Oratory of St. Philip Neri.
Sipaco, Cecilio E. '67 (MET) [F] New Brunswick, NJ St. Peter's Medical Center.
Sipe, Robert J. '59 (STP) Forest Lake, MN St. Peter Church.
Sipitkowski, James A. '74 (SPR) [4] Westfield, MA St. Mary's Church.
Siple, Donald M. *o.s.m.* '92 (CHI) [N] Chicago, IL Servite Friars - Eastern Province; [N] Chicago, IL Servite Friars - Eastern Province.
Siple, Donald M. *o.s.m.* '92 (ORG) [H] Buena Park, CA Servite Fathers And Brothers.
Siple, William R. '92 (PIT) [16] Pittsburgh, PA Immaculate Conception Church; [20] Pittsburgh, PA St. Joseph Church.
Sippel, Bernard S. '65 (MIL) Germantown, WI St. Boniface Church.
Sippel, David E. *s.j.* '61 (NY) [DD] New York, NY Murray-Weigel Hall.
Sippel, Edward F. '47 (MIL) Retired.
Sipperly, Edward '53 (ALB) [8] Amsterdam, NY St. Stanislaus Church.
Siracuse, Aloysius *o.f.m.* '47 (FgM) Franciscan Foreign Missions.
Siracuse, Guy F. '67 (BUF) [4] Buffalo, NY St. Agnes Church.
Sirba, Joseph '87 (DUL) Aurora, MN Holy Rosary Church; Hoyt Lakes, MN Queen of Peace Church.
Sirba, Paul D. '86 (STP) [A] St. Paul, MN St. John Vianney Seminary; [C] St. Paul, MN University of St. Thomas.
Siriani, Klaus-Werner J. '78 (WDC) Military Chaplains.
Sirianni, Anthony '89 (MET) [2] New Brunswick, NJ St. John the Baptist Church; New Brunswick, NJ Robert Wood Johnson University Hospital.
Sirianni, Jasper F. '46 (DET) Emmett, MI Our Lady of Mount Carmel Church; Retired.
Sirianni, Louis A. '74 (ROC) [22] Rochester, NY Holy Family Church.
Sirianni, Richard D. '78 (P) [23] Portland, OR St. Mary Magdalene Church.
Sirianni, Sam A. '84 (TR) [3] Trenton, NJ Holy Angels Church.
Sirico, Robert *c.s.p.* (LAN) St. Johns, MI St. Joseph Church.
Sirico, Robert *c.s.p.* '89 (GR) Grand Rapids, MI Chapel of St. Paul-Catholic Information Center.
Sirico, Robert A. *c.s.p.* '89 (NY) [DD] Jamaica Estates, NY Paulist Fathers Generalate.
Sirois, George *o.m.i.* '53 (PRT) Lincoln, ME St. Mary Church.
Sirois, Gerald *s.d.s.* (GB) School Hill, WI Holy Trinity Church.
Sirois, Gerald *s.d.s.* '61 (GB) St. Nazianz, WI St. Gregory Church.
Sirois, Msgr. Joseph V. '51 (WOR) [5] Worcester, MA Holy Name of Jesus Church.
Sirois, Lionel *c.ss.r.* '38 (LA) Whittier, CA St. Mary of the Assumption Church; [R] Whittier, CA Redemptorist Fathers Mission House.
Siroki, David '93 (PSC) Leave of Absence.
Sirolli, Francis A. *o.s.a.* '65 (PH) [130] Philadelphia, PA Our Mother of Consolation Church.
Siroskey, P. Larry '80 (DET) Allen Park, MI St. Frances Cabrini Church.
Sirvent-Dominguez, Francisco '87 (PCE) Penuelas, PR St. Joseph Church; [B] Ponce, PR The Pontifical Catholic University of Puerto Rico.
Siry, Philip L. '62 (WIL) Delaware City, DE St. Paul Church; Delaware City, DE Governor Bacon Health Center.
Sis, Michael J. '86 (AUS) College Station, TX St. Mary's Church; [M] College Station, TX St. Mary's Catholic Center.
Sisco, Michael A. '97 (PRO) [2] East Providence, RI St. Francis Xavier Church.
Sise, John '45 (ALB) Retired.
Sisk, Richard J. *s.j.* '51 (SPK) [K] Spokane, WA Regis Community.
Siska, Ernest (TR) Washington Crossing, NJ St. George Church.
Siska, Ernest '60 (TR) [M] Trenton, NJ Villa Vianney.
Siska, Ernest J. '60 (TR) Retired.
Sison, Alden J. '87 (LA) Canoga Park, CA Our Lady of the Valley Church.
Sison, Bernabe '65 (NY) [94] New York, NY Our Lady of Pompeii Church.
Sisul, Paul A. '72 (CHI) [N] Chicago, IL Vincentian Community, Congregation of the Mission, Midwest Province.
Sitar, Richard T. '79 (GAY) Retired.
Sitko, Joseph S. '68 (SCR) Mayfield, PA Sacred Heart of Jesus Church.
Sito, Joseph '62 (DET) Retired.
Sitter, Leonard F. *s.j.* '61 (SPK) [C] Spokane, WA Gonzaga University.
Sittinger, Edward J. *s.t.* '77 (LA) [27] Los Angeles, CA Our Lady of Victory Church.
Sitzmann, Eugene E. '62 (SC) Cherokee, IA St. Dymphna Church; Maryhill, IA Visitation of the B.V.M. Church; Cherokee, IA State Mental Health Institute.
Sitzmann, Richard A. '62 (SC) [3] Sioux City, IA St. Boniface Church; Sioux City, IA Marian Health Center; [D] Sioux City, IA Marian Health Center.
Siu, Peter K.C. *s.j.* '93 (SAC) [14] Sacramento, CA St. Ignatius of Loyola Church.
Siu, Robert K.C. '54 (CHY) Lander, WY Holy Rosary Church; In Residence.
Siu, Robert K.C. '54 (HON) Retired.
Sivalon, John C. *m.m.* '75 (FgM) Maryknoll Foreign Missions.
Sivan, Arul *s.j.* '80 (BO) [W] Chestnut Hill, MA The Jesuit Community at Boston College.
Sivillo, Msgr. Nicholas W. '64 (BRK) [212] Queens, NY Our Lady of Hope Church.
Sivinski, Vasyl '92 (PHU) [D] Philadelphia, PA Home of Divine Providence.
Sivinsky, Vasyl '92 (PHU) [F] Fox Chase Manor, PA Provincial Motherhouse of the Sisters of St. Basil the Great.
Sivinsky, Wasyl '92 (PHU) [5] Philadelphia, PA St. Nicholas Church.
Sivore, Victor J. '64 (CHI) [3] Lemont, IL SS. Cyril and Methodius Church.
Sivric, Ivo *o.f.m.* '41 (STL) [44] St. Louis, MO St. Joseph Church.
Siwek, Daniel S. '73 (CHI) [A] Mundelein, IL University of St. Mary of the Lake-Mundelein Seminary.
Siwek, Jerome S. '56 (CHI) [184] Chicago, IL St. Richard Church.
Sizelove, Dennis M. '90 (NO) Military Chaplains.
Sizemore, David W. '96 (COL) Dublin, OH St. Brigid of Kildare Church.
Sizing, Theodore '55 (SY) Retired.
Skach, Charles J. (CHI) Retired.
Skach, Charles J. '51 (CHI) [3] Mt. Prospect, IL St. Raymond de Penafort Church.
Skaff, Elias B. '36 (NTN) Retired.
Skagen, Robert '70 (PHX) [2] Glendale, AZ St. Helen Church.
Skaj, John P. *c.s.sp.* '63 (PIT) Emsworth, PA Sacred Heart Church.
Skalb, Antoni '81 (STL) [P] St. Louis, MO La Salette Missionaries.
Skalko, John Dominic *o.p.* '39 (PRO) [P] Providence, RI St. Thomas Aquinas Priory at Providence College.
Skalski, Francis S. '56 (DET) [34] Detroit, MI St. Hyacinth Church.
Skalsky, Ted A. '72 (DOD) [2] Dodge City, KS Our Lady of Guadalupe Church.
Skarbek, Richard *m.ss.a.* '86 (NOR) [F] Cromwell, CT Missionaries of the Holy Apostles.
Skarohlid, Robert F. '88 (FAR) Lakota, ND St. Mary's Church.
Skaskiw, Bohdan '80 (STN) Retired.
Skeabeck, Andrew *c.ss.r.* '47 (TR) [Q] Long Branch, NJ San Alfonso Retreat House.
Skechus, Francis E. *s.j.* '75 (PH) [G] Philadelphia, PA St. Joseph's Preparatory School; [AA] Philadelphia, PA Jesuit Community at St. Joseph's University.
Skeehan, William K. '60 (TLS) Bartlesville, OK The Community of St. James Church.
Skehan, James W. *s.j.* '54 (BO) [W] Chestnut Hill, MA The Jesuit Community at Boston College.
Skehan, John A. '52 (PMB) [4] Delray Beach, FL St. Vincent Ferrer Church.
Skehan, John R. '86 (PRT) Special or Other Diocesan Assignment.
Skehan, Msgr. Martin O. '44 (YAK) Moses Lake, WA Our Lady of Fatima Church; Retired.
Skelly, Francis *c.ss.r.* '72 (NY) [150] Bronx, NY Immaculate Conception Church.
Skelly, Msgr. John J. '53 (RVC) Manhasset, NY St. Mary's Church.
Skelly, Laurence J. *s.j.* '56 (BO) [W] Weston, MA Campion Health Center, Inc.
Skelly, Msgr. Richard J. '54 (PH) Morton, PA Our Lady of Perpetual Help Church.
Skelly, Stephen (SFE) Awaiting Assignment.
Skelskey, David A. *s.j.* '80 (FgM) Provinces.
Skelton, Paul H. '64 (SFD) Hume, IL St. Michael Church; Villa Grove, IL Sacred Heart Church.
Skenderovic, Ivan '76 (BUF) Alden, NY St. John the Baptist Church.
Skeris, Robert A. '61 (ARL) [A] Front Royal, VA Christendom College.
Skeris, Robert A. '61 (MIL) On Duty Outside the Archdiocese.
Skerl, Alphonse '55 (GRY) [3] East Chicago, IN Holy Trinity Church.
Skerry, Donald *s.v.d.* '62 (BO) [W] Boston, MA Divine Word Missionaries.
Skertich, Mark J. '77 (PIT) Ellsworth, PA Ave Maria Church.
Skiba, Andrew *o.f.m.conv.* '47 (SPR) [5] Holyoke, MA Mater Dolorosa Church.
Skiba, Walter F. '56 (SCR) Wyoming, PA St. Joseph's Church.
Skidmore, Harold G. *c.m.* '50 (FgM) Vincentian Foreign Missions.
Skillin, Harmon D. *j.c.d.* '60 (STO) [7] Stockton, CA St. Luke Church.
Skillingstad, M. Delmar '60 (SPK) [C] Spokane, WA Gonzaga University.
Skindeleski, Thomas J. '71 (PH) On Duty Outside the Archdiocese.
Skindeleski, Thomas J. '71 (PMB) [3] Boca Raton, FL St. Joan of Arc Church.
Skinner, Charles D. '53 (E) Retired.
Skinta, Stephen J. *o.s.b.m.* '59 (PSC) Trenton, NJ St. Nicholas Church; [A] Matawan, NJ Basilian Fathers of Mariapoch.
Skirkus, Joseph K. '28 (PEO) Retired.
Skirtich, John '90 (PIT) [6] Ambridge, PA Good Samaritan Church.
Skitzki, Francis P. '70 (SCR) [7] Hazleton, PA Our Lady of Grace Church.
Skluzacek, Michael C. '80 (STP) Stillwater, MN St. Michael Church; [H] Stillwater, MN St. Croix Catholic Educational Programs.
Skoczylas, Walter '75 (CR) On Duty Outside the Diocese.
Skok, Charles D. '52 (SPK) [13] Spokane, WA St. John Vianney Church.
Skoneki, William J. '87 (MOB) [4] Mobile, AL St. Dominic Church.
Skonezny, Ray '61 (ORG) Irvine, CA St. John Neumann Church.
Skonny, Thomas F. *o.c.s.o.* '51 (ATL) [I] Conyers, GA The Monastery of the Holy Spirit.
Skonseng, Dennis A. '82 (FAR) Special Assignment; [A] Fargo, ND Cardinal Muench Seminary.
Skornia, Bernard L. '57 (SAG) Retired.
Skorup, Ildephonse *o.f.m.* '59 (CHI) [65] Chicago, IL St. Francis de Sales Church; [N] Countryside, IL St. Gratian Friary, Franciscan Friars.
Skotek, Thomas D. '63 (SCR) [1] Wilkes-Barre, PA St. Aloysius Church.
Skotnicki, Andrew *o.carm.* (WDC) [M] Washington, DC Carmelite Community.
Skotnicki, Andrew *o.carm.* '77 (WDC) [B] Washington, DC Whitefriars Hall.
Skowronski, John P. '36 (SPR) [10] Springfield, MA Our Lady of the Rosary Church.
Skrapits, John '51 (BUF) [22] Buffalo, NY St. Elizabeth of Hungary Church.
Skriba, Raymond F. '57 (CHI) Round Lake, IL St. Joseph Church.
Skriba, Richard L. '49 (CHI) [181] Chicago, IL Queen of the Universe Church; Retired.
Skrincosky, Msgr. Peter '47 (STF) [A] Stamford, CT St. Basil College.
Skrypek, Gregory A. '70 (STP) Stillwater, MN Minnesota State Prison.
Skrzypiec, Andrzej '82 (SLC) [3] Magna, UT Our Lady of Lourdes Church.
Skudlarek, William *o.s.b.* '64 (FgM) American - Cassinese Congregation Foreign Missions.
Skudlarek, William *o.s.b.* '64 (SCL) [I] Collegeville, MN St. John's Abbey, of the Order of St. Benedict.
Skufca, Ronald J. '79 (MAR) [4] Escanaba, MI St. Joseph & St. Patrick Church.
Skupien, Edward D. '37 (CHI) Retired.
Skupien, Msgr. Francis M. '51 (BUF) Retired.
Skupien, Msgr. Joseph F. '47 (BUF) Retired.
Skura, Mark David *ofm conv.* '82 (BUF) [D] Athol Springs, NY St. Francis High School; [O] Athol Springs, NY St. Francis of Assisi Friary.
Skurla, Anthony *o.f.m.* '54 (PSC) [A] Sybertsville, PA Holy Dormition Monastery.
Skurla, Robert J. '56 (PSC) Jersey City, NJ St. Mary's Church.
Skurla, William '87 (VNN) Tucson, AZ St. Melany Church.
Skwara, John M. '59 (MET) South Plainfield, NJ Our Lady of Czestochowa Church.
Skwor, Donald *s.d.s.* (WDC) [B] Silver Spring, MD Salvatorian Community.
Skwor, Donald *s.d.s.* '53 (MIL) [P] Milwaukee, WI Salvatorian Provincial Residence.
Slaby, Joseph A. *m.m.* '66 (FgM) Maryknoll Foreign Missions.
Slacke, Varian *o.f.m.* '44 (CIN) [C] Cincinnati, OH St. Anthony Shrine, Francisan Candidacy.
Sladek, Robert '47 (GB) Retired.
Sladicka, Phillip J. '76 (SCR) Olyphant, PA St. Patrick's Church.
Slafkosky, Andrew L. '38 (ORL) Retired.
Slafkosky, Andrew L. '38 (PH) Pottstown, PA Holy Trinity Church; Retired.
Slampak, John A. '66 (RCK) Byron, IL St. Mary Church.
Slane, Anthony *c.ss.r.* '42 (SEA) [32] Seattle, WA Sacred Heart of Jesus Church.
Slate, William '55 (SEA) Retired.
Slater, Dennis W. '62 (SY) Special Assignment.
Slater, Msgr. John J. '52 (E) Retired.
Slater, William T. '77 (RVC) New Hyde Park, NY Notre Dame Church.
Slatterie, Leo '51 (LAV) Caliente, NV Holy Child Church.
Slatterie, Leo '51 (P) [Q] Beaverton, OR Our Lady of

Peace Institute in Catholic Teaching.
Slattery, Dennis J. *m.m.* '37 (NY) [DD] Maryknoll, NY Maryknoll Fathers and Brothers.
Slattery, Edmund *s.s.s.* '40 (NY) [55] New York, NY St. Jean Baptiste Church; Manhattan, NY Lenox Hill Hospital.
Slattery, James F. '41 (ROC) Pittsford, NY St. Louis Church; Retired.
Slattery, Msgr. John T. '54 (SB) Retired.
Slattery, Joseph A. '66 (RIC) On Duty Outside the Diocese.
Slattery, Kenneth '94 (SP) New Port Richey, FL Our Lady Queen of Peace Church.
Slattery, Kenneth F. *c.m.* '48 (BRK) [U] Jamaica, NY Vincentian Residence.
Slattery, Kevin '86 (JKS) Canton, MS Sacred Heart Church.
Slattery, Maurice C. '55 (NY) Absent on Sick leave; [DD] New York, NY Our Lady of Consolation Residence.
Slattery, Michael *o.m.i.* '41 (SAT) [K] San Antonio, TX Oblate Madonna Residence.
Slattery, Michael *o.s.a.* '77 (CHI) [J] Evergreen Park, IL Little Company of Mary Hospital and Health Care Centers; [N] Chicago, IL St. John Stone Friary.
Slattery, Michael J. '62 (LA) Granada Hills, CA St. John Baptist de la Salle Church.
Slattery, William *l.c.* '91 (NY) [DD] Rye, NY Legionaries of Christ.
Slaughter, Martin '85 (LA) Pico Rivera, CA St. Marianne de Paredes Church.
Slaven, Don (SC) [1] Sioux City, IA Cathedral of the Epiphany.
Slaven, Donald (SC) Ruthven, IA Sacred Heart Church.
Slaven, Frederick '59 (Y) Louisville, OH St. Louis Church.
Slavish, Richard '59 (PEO) Matherville, IL St. Anthony's Church.
Sleasman, Martin J. *c.m.* '42 (BUF) [C] Niagara University, NY Niagara University; [O] Niagara University, NY Vincentian Community at Niagara University.
Sledesky, Stephen M. '93 (HRT) [2] Torrington, CT Sacred Heart Church; [4] Torrington, CT St. Peter's Church.
Sledzaus, Alexander L. '50 (RVC) Patchogue, NY Our Lady of Mt. Carmel Church; Retired.
Sledziona, John S. *c.m.* '70 (HRT) [M] Manchester, CT DePaul Provincial Residence.
Slejzer, Ferdinand E. '53 (BO) Retired.
Slemba, Dominic *o.f.m.conv.* '51 (BAL) [M] Ellicott City, MD Order of Friars Minor Conventual.
Slemba, Dominic *o.f.m.conv.* '51 (FgM) Conventual Franciscan Foreign Missions.
Slepicka, Msgr. Joseph J. '55 (DUB) Clear Lake, IA St. Patrick's Church.
Slesinski, Robert '76 (PSC) Bethlehem, PA SS. Peter and Paul Church.
Slesinski, Sebastian *o.f.m.conv.* '51 (FR) [7] New Bedford, MA Our Lady of Perpetual Help Church.
Sleszynski, Darius '66 (BO) Ashland, MA St. Cecilia Church.
Slevin, Henry '62 (WDC) [13] Washington, DC St. Francis de Sales Church; On Duty Outside the Archdiocese.
Slevin, Patrick C. '57 (MIA) [12] Fort Lauderdale, FL St. Pius X Church.
Sleyman, Kenneth C. *m.m.* '90 (FgM) Maryknoll Foreign Missions.
Slezak, Raymond P. '74 (ALN) Sheppton, PA St. Joseph Church.
Slight, William *m.s.* '65 (FR) [J] Attleboro, MA La Salette Provincial House.
Slikas, William '86 (JOL) [2] Joliet, IL Holy Cross Church.
Slimak, Bernard *o.s.b.* '40 (CLV) [P] Cleveland, OH Benedictine Order of Cleveland.
Slinger, Msgr. Joseph T. '70 (NEW) [1] Newark, NJ Cathedral Basilica of the Sacred Heart Church.
Slipe, Robert H. '73 (NEW) River Edge, NJ St. Peter the Apostle Church.
Slipski, William P. '46 (Y) Retired.
Slisz, Charles E. '71 (BUF) [4] Cheektowaga, NY St. Josaphat Church.
Slivonik, Stanley '69 (ARL) Retired.
Sliwak, Msgr. Stanley A. '66 (CC) [1] Laredo, TX Blessed Sacrament Church.
Sliwinski, Phillip A. '97 (GR) [2] Muskegon, MI St. Francis de Sales Church.
Sloan, Daniel *i.c.* '41 (VEN) Bradenton, FL Sacred Heart Church.
Sloan, Daniel '82 (MET) Manville, NJ Christ the King Church.
Sloan, James *c.pp.s.* '62 (OAK) [N] Berkeley, CA Society of the Precious Blood.
Slobig, John '90 (PHX) [4] Glendale, AZ St. Louis The King Church.
Sloboda, Michael J. *m.m.* '85 (FgM) Maryknoll Foreign Missions.
Slobogin, Roland D. '73 (PH) [107] Philadelphia, PA Most Blessed Sacrament Church.
Slocum, Samuel B. '80 (E) Eldred, PA St. Raphael Church; Shinglehouse, PA St. Theresa Church.
Slodowski, Bronislaw '68 (MIL) [N] Kenosha, WI St. Joseph's Home for the Aged.
Slomba, Eugene S. '64 (BUF) [4] Batavia, NY Sacred Heart Church; Albion, NY Albion Correctional Facility.
Slominski, Fabian B. '48 (DET) Pontiac, MI St. Joseph Church; Retired.
Slominski, George A. '38 (CHI) Retired.
Slominski, Leon '58 (SCL) Luxemburg, MN St. Wendelin's Church.
Slomski, Joseph P. '53 (WCH) Chase, KS St. Mary Church.
Slon, Thomas R. *s.j.* '90 (SCR) [C] Scranton, PA University of Scranton.
Slonecki, Michael *o.f.m.conv.* '41 (SPR) [5] Chicopee, MA St. Anthony's Church.
Sloneker, Patrick L. '97 (CIN) [40] Cincinnati, OH St. James the Greater Church.
Slosarcik, Edward A. (CHI) Retired.
Slota, Frederick V. '53 (PRO) [2] Providence, RI St. Adalbert Church.
Slough, Charles R. '56 (HBG) Elysburg, PA Queen of the Most Holy Rosary Church.
Sloun, Russell J. *s.j.* '73 (NY) [F] New York, NY Xavier High School.
Sloup, Ernest O. '53 (LIN) Retired; [E] Lincoln, NE Bonacum House.
Slovacek, Emil C. (DAL) Retired.
Slovikovski, John J. '96 (ALT) [1] Altoona, PA Cathedral of the Blessed Sacrament.
Slowey, John P. '57 (SUP) Retired.
Slowiak, Allan L. '73 (LC) Rothschild, WI St. Mark Church.
Slowik, Joseph S. '72 (RIC) Portsmouth, VA St. Paul Church.
Slowinski, Jerome '90 (DET) [1] Warren, MI St. Anne's Church; Special Assignment.
Slowinski, Thomas F. '81 (DET) [1] Redford, MI St. Agatha Church.
Slubecky, Msgr. David S. '73 (BUF) [3] West Seneca, NY Fourteen Holy Helpers Church.
Slusser, Michael '66 (PIT) [B] Pittsburgh, PA Duquesne University of the Holy Ghost.
Slusser, Michael S. '66 (STP) On Duty Outside the Archdiocese.
Slydan, Gerard S. '44 (TR) Retired.
Slyva, Joseph '72 (BO) Randolph, MA St. Bernadette Church.
Smaistrla, Benjamin '72 (GAL) [76] Houston, TX St. Theresa Church.
Small, Edward *s.j.* '70 (BGP) Ridgefield, CT St. Mary's Church.
Small, Edward J. *s.j.* '70 (BGP) [O] Fairfield, CT The Fairfield Jesuit Community-Fairfield University.
Small, Edward J. *s.j.* '70 (BO) [W] Boston, MA The Society of Jesus of New England-Provincial Offices.
Small, James *c.ss.r.* '54 (HBG) [2] Lancaster, PA St. Anthony of Padua Church.
Small, Jeffery '93 (PEO) [4] Streator, IL St. Stephen's Church.
Small, Joseph H. *s.j.* '60 (FgM) Provinces.
Small, Joseph H. *s.j.* '60 (P) [L] Portland, OR Jesuit Provincial Office (Society of Jesus, Oregon Prov.).
Small, William T. '77 (PH) Broomall, PA St. Pius X Church.
Smalley, William R. '55 (NEW) [4] Irvington, NJ St. Paul the Apostle Church.
Smar, Michael J. '69 (Y) Champion, OH St. William Church.
Smarsh, Charles F. '64 (NY) On Duty Outside the Archdiocese.
Smart, Raymond W. '70 (PH) Absent on Sick Leave.
Smeenk, Karl *o.m.i.* '50 (FgM) Oblates Foreign Missions.
Smegal, John T. '77 (SPR) Lanesboro, MA North American Martyrs Church.
Smegelsky, John J. '66 (SY) Central Square, NY St. Michael Church.
Smeltzer, Stuart M. '96 (WCH) [12] Wichita, KS St. Elizabeth Ann Seton Church.
Smet, Joachim *o.carm.* '42 (JOL) [J] Darien, IL Carmelite Provincial Office.
Smet, Leroy R. '59 (GB) Winneconne, WI St. Mary Church.
Smetana, Brendan L. *o.s.b.* '40 (GBG) [H] Latrobe, PA Saint Vincent Archabbey.
Smetanka, Gary T. '82 (DET) [5] Clinton Twp., MI St. Thecla Church.
Smialowski, Raymond S. '82 (HRT) Newington, CT Holy Spirit Church; [R] Hartford, CT University of Hartford Newman Center; [R] Hartford, CT University of Hartford Newman Center.
Smiciklas, Msgr. Nicholas X. '56 (PBR) [6] Pittsburgh, PA St. Pius X Church.
Smidt-Jernstrom, Kurt '85 (P) [K] Mt. Angel, OR Benedictine Nursing Center.
Smiech, Charles *o.f.m.* '81 (DET) [3] Detroit, MI St. Aloysius Church.
Smiga, George '75 (CLV) Willoughby Hills, OH St. Noel Church.
Smigiel, Edgar *o.f.m.* '47 (RCK) [6] Rockford, IL St. James Church.
Smigiel, Walter J. '50 (PBL) Retired.
Smilanic, Daniel A. '73 (CHI) Park Ridge, IL St. Paul of the Cross Church.
Smilga, Zenon A. '50 (NOR) Fishers Island, NY Our Lady of Grace Church.
Smiroldo, Msgr. Onofrio R. '53 (BUF) [3] Tonawanda, NY St. Edmund Church.
Smit, Gerard C. '50 (LKC) Retired.
Smith, A. Philip *o.p.* '68 (PRO) [P] Providence, RI St. Thomas Aquinas Priory at Providence College.
Smith, Al '65 (PH) [D] Philadelphia, PA Father Judge High School for Boys.
Smith, Alberic *o.f.m.* '58 (TUC) [4] Tucson, AZ Mission San Xavier del Bac Church.
Smith, Albert J. *o.s.f.s.* '65 (PH) [C] Philadelphia, PA Holy Family College.
Smith, Alexei '87 (LA) El Segundo, CA St. Andrew Church.
Smith, Alexei R. '87 (NTN) El Segundo, CA St. Paul Church.
Smith, Msgr. Alfred D. '53 (TR) Belmar, NJ St. Rose Church.
Smith, Alfred E. '56 (BAL) Williamsport, MD St. Augustine Church.
Smith, Alphonsus M. '56 (WDC) Retired.
Smith, Andrew T. *o.s.b.* '64 (PAT) [M] Morristown, NJ St. Mary's Abbey.
Smith, Anthony *c.ss.r.* '84 (DEN) [M] Denver, CO The Redemptorists/Denver Province.
Smith, Aquinas '59 (SD) Retired.
Smith, Arthur F. *o.s.a.* '54 (PH) [AA] Villanova, PA St. Thomas Monastery.
Smith, Arthur J. '71 (BUF) [64] Buffalo, NY St. Thomas Aquinas Church.
Smith, Bernard *o.f.m.cap.* '64 (FgM) Capuchin Foreign Missions.
Smith, Bernard *o.f.m.cap.* '64 (NY) [DD] White Plains, NY St. Conrad Friary.
Smith, Msgr. Bernard E. '33 (TOL) Retired; [L] Toledo, OH Notre Dame Provincialate.
Smith, Bernardine J. *t.o.r.* '59 (SP) [6] St. Petersburg, FL St. Mary Our Lady of Grace Church.
Smith, Brendan *s.t.* '54 (ORG) Orange, CA Juvenile Hall; Orange, CA Theo Lacy Minimum Security Facility; [H] Santa Ana, CA Trinitarian Missionaries/Missionary Servants of the Most Holy Trinity.
Smith, Brian P. '86 (STL) [8] Florissant, MO St. Norbert Church.
Smith, Charles *s.v.d.* '95 (IND) [34] Indianapolis, IN St. Rita Church.
Smith, Msgr. Charles A. '45 (WCH) Retired.
Smith, Charles C. *c.s.b.* '60 (DET) [E] Redford, MI Catholic Central High School.
Smith, Charles Clyde (FBK) Alakanuk, AK St. Ignatius Church.
Smith, Charles D. '65 (PH) [94] Philadelphia, PA St. Martin of Tours Church.
Smith, Charles F. '76 (FRS) [5] Fresno, CA Sacred Heart Church.
Smith, Chester *s.v.d.* '95 (IND) [34] Indianapolis, IN St. Rita Church.
Smith, Christopher H. '78 (ORG) [8] Santa Ana, CA St. Joseph's Church.
Smith, Clifford G. '96 (DAL) Richardson, TX St. Joseph Church.
Smith, Cyril J. *o.s.a.* '55 (MIA) [C] Miami, FL Msgr. Edward Pace High School; [H] Miami, FL Casa San Lorenzo.
Smith, D. Stephen '73 (MAD) Cross Plains, WI St. Francis Xavier Church.
Smith, Daniel *o.carm.* '46 (NEW) Paramus, NJ Carmelite Chapel of St. Therese Church.
Smith, David *s.j.* (RC) [B] Pine Ridge, SD Jesuit Community of Holy Rosary Mission.
Smith, David '82 (MIA) Special Assignment.
Smith, David A. *m.m.* '85 (FgM) Maryknoll Foreign Missions.
Smith, David G. '73 (BAL) [69] Baltimore, MD Our Lady of Good Counsel Church.
Smith, David L. *c.ss.sp.* '58 (PIT) [B] Pittsburgh, PA Duquesne University of the Holy Ghost.
Smith, David L. *s.j.* '85 (RC) Pine Ridge, SD Holy Rosary Church.
Smith, David W. '64 (STP) [C] St. Paul, MN University of St. Thomas.
Smith, Dennis '75 (FWT) [1] Fort Worth, TX St. Patrick Cathedral.
Smith, Donald C. '61 (NEW) [B] South Orange, NJ Seton Hall University.
Smith, Donald R. '57 (SC) Retired.
Smith, Douglas '57 (GAL) [39] Houston, TX St. Jerome Church.
Smith, Edmund *o.s.b.* '65 (P) Mt. Angel, OR St. Mary Church; [L] St. Benedict, OR Mt. Angel Abbey.
Smith, Edward E. '82 (MOB) On Leave from the Archdiocese.
Smith, Edward J. *o.praem.* (GB) [O] Green Bay, WI

Green Bay Area Catholic High School Foundation, L.T.D.
Smith, Edward J. '65 (BRK) [85] Brooklyn, NY St. Matthew's Church; [92] Brooklyn, NY Our Lady of Charity Church.
Smith, Edward J. *o.praem.* '73 (WIL) [I] Claymont, DE Immaculate Conception Priory of the Canons Regular of Premontre; [I] Claymont, DE Norbertine Fathers of Delaware, Inc.
Smith, Edward J. *c.m.* '86 (PH) [AA] Philadelphia, PA Congregation of the Mission.
Smith, Edward P. '82 (CIN) On Duty Outside the Archdiocese.
Smith, Elmer W. '50 (CIN) [20] Cincinnati, OH St. Cecilia Church; [V] Cincinnati, OH Legion of Mary.
Smith, Ermin R. *o.s.b.* '45 (GBG) Latrobe, PA Latrobe Area Hospital; [H] Latrobe, PA Saint Vincent Archabbey.
Smith, Eugene D. '50 (LC) Retired.
Smith, Eugene M. *o.s.m.* '88 (ORG) [D] Anaheim, CA Servite High School; Servite High School Development Fund; [H] Anaheim, CA Servite Fathers and Brothers; [H] Buena Park, CA Servite Fathers And Brothers.
Smith, Eugene P. '50 (LC) Boyd, WI Sacred Heart of Jesus-St. Joseph Church.
Smith, F. Harold '50 (L) Retired.
Smith, Francis J. *s.j.* '52 (CLV) [C] Cleveland, OH John Carroll Jesuit Community.
Smith, Msgr. Francis J. '67 (ELP) [31] El Paso, TX St. Raphael Church.
Smith, Francis N. *o.f.m.* '86 (NEW) [N] Hohokus, NJ St. Anthony of Padua.
Smith, Francis R. *s.j.* '70 (SJ) [B] Santa Clara, CA Santa Clara University.
Smith, Francis X.J. '64 (ORL) Melbourne, FL Ascension Church.
Smith, Fred A. '47 (MIL) Retired.
Smith, Gabriel J. '82 (CHR) [12] Charleston, SC St. Joseph Church.
Smith, Gary N. *s.j.* '71 (P) [38] Portland, OR St. Vincent de Paul Church.
Smith, Gene F. '84 (CHI) [165] Chicago, IL St. Patrick Church.
Smith, Geoffrey '74 (HRT) [7] New Haven, CT St. Casimir's Church.
Smith, Geoffrey C. '74 (HRT) New Haven, CT Yale-New Haven Hospital.
Smith, Gerald S. '64 (PH) North Wales, PA St. Rose of Lima Church.
Smith, Gerard *c.ss.r.* '45 (ALB) [L] Saratoga Springs, NY St. John Neumann Residence.
Smith, Glen E. *s.j.* '63 (FgM) Provinces.
Smith, Gregory D. '92 (HEL) On Leave of Absence.
Smith, Gregory J. '74 (GB) Howard, WI St. John the Baptist Church.
Smith, Msgr. Gregory M. '67 (BGP) [16] Bridgeport, CT Our Lady of Good Counsel Church; Leave of Absence.
Smith, Herbert F. *s.j.* '62 (PH) [AA] Philadelphia, PA Jesuit Community at St. Joseph's University; [FF] Philadelphia, PA Apostleship of Prayer.
Smith, Howard C. *s.m.* '72 (WDC) [M] Washington, DC Marist Provincial House.
Smith, Ignatius E. *o.f.m.* '56 (NY) Callicoon, NY Holy Cross Church.
Smith, Ignatius J. *o.s.b.* '46 (PBL) [F] Canon City, CO Holy Cross Abbey.
Smith, Ivan E. '91 (GB) Special Assignment.
Smith, James A. '52 (CLV) Retired.
Smith, James A.D. '56 (PAT) Succasunna, NJ St. Therese Church.
Smith, James B. '85 (WIL) Salisbury, MD St. Francis De Sales Church.
Smith, James D. '87 (STP) Oakdale, MN Transfiguration Church.
Smith, James E. *c.m.* '61 (ALB) [L] Albany, NY Vincentian Fathers Residence; [M] Menands, NY De Paul Provincial House.
Smith, James F. *m.m.* '35 (NY) [DD] Maryknoll, NY Maryknoll Fathers and Brothers.
Smith, James F. *s.j.* '62 (SY) [S] Syracuse, NY Jesuits at LeMoyne, Inc.
Smith, James G. *o.praem.* '77 (ORG) [D] Siverado, CA St. Michael's College Preparatory High School; [H] Silverado, CA Norbertine Fathers of Orange Inc.
Smith, James H. '63 (HRT) Derby, CT St. Mary's Church.
Smith, James R. '67 (SC) Breda, IA St. Bernard's Church.
Smith, James T. '56 (BRK) [189] Queens, NY St. Kevin Church.
Smith, James T. '65 (COL) [31] Columbus, OH St. Matthias Church.
Smith, Jerome '96 (PEO) [2] Streator, IL St. Anthony of Padua Church.
Smith, Jerry A. '65 (AUS) [1] Austin, TX St. Mary's Cathedral.
Smith, John *s.s.c.* (CHI) [N] Chicago, IL Korean Catholic Center.
Smith, John B. '59 (STP) Military Chaplains.
Smith, John D. *s.j.* '59 (FgM) Provinces.
Smith, John F. '62 (HBG) Columbia, PA St. Peter Church.
Smith, John F.X. '61 (NY) Cornwall-on-Hudson, NY St. Thomas of Canterbury Church; Tuxedo, NY Our Lady of Mt. Carmel Church.
Smith, Msgr. John J. '59 (FR) South Yarmouth, MA St. Pius Tenth Church.
Smith, John P. '42 (DUB) Retired.
Smith, Joseph A. '96 (SAV) [3] Columbus, GA St. Anne Church.
Smith, Joseph F. '35 (PH) [35] Philadelphia, PA St. Christopher Church; Retired.
Smith, Joseph F.X. *c.s.p.* '74 (NY) [DD] Jamaica Estates, NY Paulist Fathers Generalate.
Smith, Joseph J. *s.j.* '57 (FgM) Provinces.
Smith, Msgr. Joseph P.T. '60 (ALN) [3] Reading, PA St. Catharine of Siena Church.
Smith, Joseph S. *m.m.* '51 (NY) [DD] Maryknoll, NY Maryknoll Fathers and Brothers.
Smith, Jude *o.f.m.* '53 (PAT) [M] Butler, NJ St. Anthony Friary.
Smith, Kenneth A. '63 (BR) [20] Baton Rouge, LA Sacred Heart of Jesus Church.
Smith, Kenneth G. '84 (HBG) Rohrerstown, PA St. Leo the Great Church.
Smith, Kenneth J. '64 (NY) [17] New York, NY St. Bernard Church; [120] New York, NY St. Veronica Church.
Smith, Kevin M. '88 (RVC) Manhasset, NY St. Mary's Church.
Smith, Laurence H. (MET) Edison, NJ John F. Kennedy Medical Center.
Smith, Laurence H.F. '68 (MET) [H] Metuchen, NJ Libermann House.
Smith, Lawrence '97 (DAV) [4] Iowa City, IA St. Wenceslaus Church.
Smith, Lawrence C. *s.j.* '82 (BO) [W] Boston, MA The Society of Jesus of New England-Provincial Offices.
Smith, Lawrence R. '76 (PIT) [3] McKees Rocks, PA St. John of God Church.
Smith, Leland J. '53 (WIN) Retired.
Smith, Leonard A. (WH) Wayne, WV Nativity of Our Lord Church.
Smith, Leonard A. '91 (WH) Williamson, WV Sacred Heart Church.
Smith, Leroy (SPR) Pittsfield, MA Berkshire Medical Center.
Smith, LeRoy J. '78 (BRK) Released from Diocesan Assignment.
Smith, Lester E. '75 (SY) Marathon, NY St. Stephen Church.
Smith, Malachy *o.carm.* '43 (JOL) [J] Darien, IL Carmelite Provincial Office.
Smith, Malcolm *m.afr.* '69 (ORG) [1] Orange, CA Cathedral of the Holy Family.
Smith, Mark C. '83 (JC) Absent on Leave.
Smith, Mark S. '96 (JC) [3] Jefferson City, MO Immaculate Conception Church; [B] Jefferson City, MO Helias High School.
Smith, Martin D. '79 (STU) On Duty Outside the Diocese.
Smith, Martin G. '36 (PH) Retired.
Smith, Martin L. *o.s.a.* '77 (WDC) [B] Washington, DC Augustinian College, Order of St. Augustine.
Smith, Matthew '95 (BAL) [28] Baltimore, MD St. Dominic Church.
Smith, Maury *o.f.m.* '66 (MEM) [17] Memphis, TN St. Mary's Church; [J] Memphis, TN Franciscan Friars (Sacred Heart Prov.) of Memphis.
Smith, Michael '73 (SD) Retired.
Smith, Michael '77 (HEL) Bonner, MT St. Ann Church.
Smith, Michael B. '74 (CLV) Brunswick, OH St. Ambrose Church.
Smith, Michael H. '66 (SAV) McRae, GA Holy Redeemer Church.
Smith, Michael N. *s.j.* '67 (PBL) Paonia, CO Sacred Heart Church.
Smith, Michael S. '92 (NOR) Portland, CT St. Mary Church; [B] Middletown, CT Mercy High School; [B] Middletown, CT Xavier High School.
Smith, Myles H. '70 (IND) Leave of Absence.
Smith, Neil B. '48 (MAR) Retired.
Smith, Nicholas '94 (STL) [5] Lemay, MO St. Martin of Tours Church.
Smith, Nicholas P. (PRO) South Kingstown, RI South County Hospital.
Smith, Nicholas P. '65 (PRO) South Kingstown, RI St. Francis of Assisi Church.
Smith, Norman (GLP) Retired.
Smith, Norman N. '70 (CLV) Kirtland, OH Divine Word Church.
Smith, Paschal *c.p.* '51 (NY) [DD] Pelham Manor, NY St. Vincent's Residence; [HH] Pelham, NY Passionist Communications, Inc.
Smith, Patrick '67 (PHX) [5] Scottsdale, AZ St. Daniel the Prophet Church; Scottsdale, AZ Scottsdale Memorial Hospital.
Smith, Patrick A. '90 (WDC) St. Inigoes, MD St. Peter Claver Church.
Smith, Paul '59 (ALB) Altamont, NY St. Lucy Church; Special Assignment; [D] Albany, NY Academy of the Holy Names Upper, Middle and Lower Schools.
Smith, Paul '62 (HON) Retired.
Smith, Paul B. '79 (CHI) [79] Chicago, IL Holy Angels Church.
Smith, Paul F. '73 (CLV) Thompson, OH St. Patrick Church.
Smith, Paul H. '62 (NEW) On Duty Outside the Archdiocese.
Smith, Paul O. '64 (COL) Leave of Absence.
Smith, Paul P. '46 (PHX) Retired.
Smith, Paul R. '59 (ALB) [B] Albany, NY Maria College.
Smith, Peter '51 (NY) [Z] Rhinebeck, NY Ferncliff Nursing Home.
Smith, Peter J. '51 (BWN) Retired.
Smith, Philip A. *o.p.* '68 (PRO) [B] Providence, RI Providence College.
Smith, Philip T. *o.praem.* (ORG) Fountain Valley, CA Holy Spirit Church.
Smith, Philip T. *o.praem.* '84 (ORG) [H] Silverado, CA Norbertine Fathers of Orange Inc.
Smith, R. Douglas *o.s.f.s.* '62 (WIL) [B] Wilmington, DE Salesianum School.
Smith, R. Leroy '54 (COV) Retired.
Smith, Ramon *o.f.m.* '53 (LSC) Roswell, NM St. Peter Church.
Smith, Raymond J. '50 (CLV) [11] Akron, OH St. Mary Church.
Smith, Raymond K. '56 (SFR) Special Assignment; On Duty Outside the Archdiocese; [M] Petaluma, CA Silver Penny Farm Retreat Center.
Smith, Raynard (MET) [F] New Brunswick, NJ St. Peter's Medical Center.
Smith, Richard '76 (JOL) Channahon, IL St. Ann Parish.
Smith, Richard '84 (JKS) Forest, MS St. Michael Church; Paulding, MS St. Michael Church; [G] Forest, MS East Central Community College Newman Center.
Smith, Richard '97 (NY) Haverstraw, NY St. Peter Church.
Smith, Richard A. '56 (MAN) Whitefield, NH St. Matthew Church.
Smith, Richard E. '66 (BAL) Ellicott City, MD Our Lady of Perpetual Help Church.
Smith, Richard J. '60 (BO) Norwell, MA St. Helen Church.
Smith, Richard P. *m.m.* '76 (FgM) Maryknoll Foreign Missions.
Smith, Robert '89 (ATL) Roswell, GA St. Andrew Church.
Smith, Robert D. '56 (BO) [2] Haverhill, MA St. James Church.
Smith, Robert F., Jr. (FAR) Starkweather, ND Assumption of the Blessed Virgin Mary Church.
Smith, Robert F., Jr. '97 (FAR) Devils Lake, ND St. Joseph's Church; Rutten, ND St. Benedict Church.
Smith, Robert G. '53 (ROC) Red Creek, NY Butler Correctional Facility.
Smith, Robert H. '56 (LIN) Retired.
Smith, Robert J. '55 (OM) Valley, NE St. John Church.
Smith, Msgr. Robert J. '70 (E) [J] Erie, PA Bishop Michael J. Murphy Residence for Retired Priests.
Smith, Robert J. '83 (RVC) [A] Huntington, NY Diocesan Seminary of the Immaculate Conception.
Smith, Robert V. '61 (CAM) Glassboro, NJ St. Bridget's Church.
Smith, Roger '76 (CC) [2] Kingsville, TX St. Gertrude Church.
Smith, Roger J. '73 (SEA) Morton, WA Sacred Heart Church.
Smith, Ronald T. '73 (HRT) [4] New Britain, CT St. Andrew's Church; New Britain, CT New Britain General Hospital.
Smith, S. Douglas *c.s.c.* '76 (FTW) [J] South Bend, IN Congregation of Holy Cross Indiana Province Provincial House.
Smith, Msgr. Sherill '55 (SAT) Retired.
Smith, Msgr. Sherrill '55 (SAT) [K] San Antonio, TX Casa De Padres.
Smith, Simon E. *s.j.* '61 (BO) [W] Boston, MA Jesuit Urban Center & Immaculate Conception Community.
Smith, Stanley C. *o.s.a.* '60 (PH) [B] Villanova, PA St. Augustine Friary.
Smith, Stephen K. *o.p.* '58 (KNX) Elizabethton, TN St. Elizabeth Church.
Smith, Terrance W. '73 (CIN) Loveland, OH St. Columban Church.
Smith, Terrence T. *t.o.r.* '73 (ALT) [7] Altoona, PA Our Lady of Mt. Carmel Church.
Smith, Terry *c.ss.p.* '80 (STA) [1] St. Augustine, FL Cathedral of St. Augustine.
Smith, Theodore R. *o.praem.* '91 (ORG) [H] Silverado, CA Norbertine Fathers of Orange Inc.
Smith, Thomas *o.f.m.conv.* (STP) [Q] Prior Lake, MN Franciscan Retreat House.
Smith, Thomas '51 (ORL) Altamonte Springs, FL St. Mary Magdalen Church.
Smith, Thomas A. '83 (L) Flaherty, KY St. Martin of Tours Church; Vine Grove, KY St. Brigid Church.
Smith, Thomas Bernard *o.p.* (L) [4] Springfield, KY St.

Rose Church.
Smith, Thomas E. '51 (PIT) Retired.
Smith, Thomas E. '67 (E) [27] Erie, PA St. Patrick/St. Hedwig Church.
Smith, Thomas E. *s.j.* '74 (NY) [DD] New York, NY Jesuit Provincial's Office; [DD] New York, NY St. Ignatius Loyola Residence.
Smith, Thomas F. *o.c.s.o.* '58 (ATL) [I] Conyers, GA The Monastery of the Holy Spirit.
Smith, Msgr. Thomas H. '57 (HBG) [5] Lancaster, PA St. Joseph Church.
Smith, Thomas J. *o.s.f.s.* '58 (LAN) Michigan Center, MI Our Lady of Fatima Church.
Smith, Thomas J. '60 (LC) [G] La Crosse, WI St. Joseph's Nursing Home; [G] La Crosse, WI Bethany-St. Joseph Care Center; [I] La Crosse, WI Holy Cross (Seminary) Diocesan Center.
Smith, Thomas J. '73 (PH) [51] Philadelphia, PA Good Shepherd Church.
Smith, Thomas J. '82 (NOR) New London, CT St. Mary, Star of the Sea Church.
Smith, Thomas R. '81 (CLV) [5] Lorain, OH St. John Church.
Smith, Thomas W. *c.s.c.* '72 (FgM) Holy Cross Foreign Missions.
Smith, Vernon '90 (FAR) Harvey, ND St. Cecilia's Church.
Smith, Msgr. Vincent J. '55 (HBG) Camp Hill, PA Good Shepherd Church.
Smith, Vincent Leo '66 (DEN) Breckenridge, CO St. Mary Church.
Smith, W. Andrew '80 (LR) Pine Bluff, AR St. Joseph's Church.
Smith, Walter J. *s.j.* '72 (BO) [W] Boston, MA The Society of Jesus of New England-Provincial Offices.
Smith, Walter J. *s.j.* '72 (NY) [DD] New York, NY "America;" Residence and publication office of the America Press.
Smith, Wilfred T. '56 (CLV) Mentor, OH St. Mary of the Assumption Church.
Smith, William *glmy.* '47 (CIN) [M] Fairfield, OH Headquarters of Glenmary Home Missioners.
Smith, William *o.carm.* '54 (FgM) Carmelite Foreign Missions.
Smith, William *o.carm.* '54 (JOL) [J] Darien, IL Carmelite Provincial Office.
Smith, William *c.s.sp.* '74 (PIT) [B] Pittsburgh, PA Duquesne University of the Holy Ghost.
Smith, William '78 (BRK) [59] Brooklyn, NY Holy Rosary Church.
Smith, William A. '73 (BRK) [215] Queens, NY Our Lady of the Miraculous Medal Church.
Smith, Msgr. William B. '66 (NY) [A] Yonkers, NY St. Joseph's Seminary.
Smith, William C. '45 (HRT) Retired.
Smith, William F. '52 (JOL) Gibson City, IL Our Lady of Lourdes Church.
Smith, William J. '47 (PH) Downingtown, PA St. Joseph Church; Retired.
Smith, Msgr. William J. '60 (NY) [130] Bronx, NY St. Athanasius Church.
Smith, William J. '81 (MET) Blairstown, NJ St. Jude Church.
Smith, William P. '67 (BO) Bedford, MA St. Michael Church.
Smith, Wilton S. '58 (SFR) [4] South San Francisco, CA St. Veronica Church.
Smithers, Stephen T. *o.p.* '53 (GAL) [Q] Houston, TX Dominican Fathers and Brothers, St. Mark Priory, Inc.
Smithes, Donald F. '79 (RCK) Polo, IL St. Mary's Church.
Smits, Joseph *c.i.c.m.* '56 (ARL) [J] Arlington, VA Missionhurst, C.I.C.M.-Central House and Provincialate.
Smits, Joseph B. *c.i.c.m.* '56 (PH) [C] Gwynedd Valley, PA Gwynedd-Mercy College.
Smits, Kenneth *o.f.m.cap.* (MAD) [4] Madison, WI Holy Redeemer Church.
Smits, Lambert H. (DET) Royal Oak, MI Shrine of the Little Flower Church.
Smits, Pete *s.v.d.* '41 (BLX) [A] Bay St. Louis, MS St. Augustine's.
Smochko, Msgr. Basil '46 (PRM) Lakewood, OH St. Gregory the Theologian Church.
Smolar, Joseph *c.pp.s.* '42 (CIN) [B] Carthagena, OH St. Charles.
Smolarski, Dennis C. *s.j.* '79 (SJ) [B] Santa Clara, CA Santa Clara University.
Smolenski, Stanley '68 (HRT) [4] Enfield, CT St. Martha's Church.
Smoley, Rudolph F. '69 (PIT) [1] Carnegie, PA St. Elizabeth Ann Seton Church.
Smolich, Thomas H. *s.j.* '86 (SJ) [2] Santa Clara, CA St. Clare Church.
Smolinski, Arcadius *o.f.m.* '47 (GB) [I] Pulaski, WI Assumption of B.V.M. Friary.
Smolinski, Clarence D. '53 (GAY) Retired.
Smolinski, Joseph J. '48 (NY) Retired.
Smolko, John F. '57 (BGP) On Duty Outside the Diocese.
Smolko, John F. '57 (WDC) [C] Washington, DC Catholic University of America, The.
Smolley, Robert '82 (STF) [A] Stamford, CT St. Basil College.
Smolley, Robert J. '82 (BR) On Duty Outside the Diocese.
Smoot, K. Robert '95 (STL) Dardenne, MO Immaculate Conception Church.
Smuda, Alfred J. *o.s.f.s.* '66 (FgM) Oblates of St. Francis de Sales Foreign Missions.
Smulders, Raphael M. *ss.cc.* '34 (HON) Lahaina, HI Maria Lanakila Church.
Smullen, Martin J. '82 (NO) [60] New Orleans, LA St. Simon Peter Church.
Smutelovic, Peter '95 (NEW) North Arlington, NJ Queen of Peace Church.
Smutko, Gregory *o.f.m.cap.* '58 (FgM) Capuchin Foreign Missions.
Smutny, Jan '42 (GI) Retired.
Smutny, Wenceslaus J. *c.ss.r.* '53 (PH) [25] Philadelphia, PA St. Boniface Church.
Smyer, Msgr. Francis A. '46 (AMA) [10] Amarillo, TX St. Mary's Church.
Smyka, James *o.f.m.conv.* '73 (BGP) [14] Bridgeport, CT St. Michael The Archangel Church.
Smylie, Benjamin '85 (TYL) Carthage, TX St. William of Vercelli Church.
Smyth, Henry J. '50 (PH) Horsham, PA St. Catherine of Siena Church.
Smyth, James '56 (NY) Hastings-on-Hudson, NY St. Matthew Church.
Smyth, James '57 (NY) Retired.
Smyth, John L. *c.ss.r.* '64 (ATL) Griffin, GA Sacred Heart Church.
Smyth, John P. '62 (CHI) [H] Des Plaines, IL Maryville Academy; [X] Chicago, IL Catholic Youth, Archdiocese of Chicago.
Smyth, Joseph P. '59 (BO) Emergency Response Group.
Sneck, William J. *s.j.* '71 (BAL) [B] Baltimore, MD Loyola College; [M] Baltimore, MD Jesuit Community of Loyola College, Inc.
Snedeker, Arthur A. '74 (CLV) [8] Akron, OH Immaculate Conception Church.
Snee, Msgr. Joseph T.V. '42 (NY) Retired.
Snell, Roger K. '72 (FAR) Retired.
Snella, Adolph A. '51 (ARL) Retired.
Sneyd, Derrick '70 (FTW) New Haven, IN St. John the Baptist Church.
Snider, Harold *o.f.m.cap.* '89 (OAK) [N] Berkeley, CA Capuchin Franciscan Order, House of Studies.
Sniechota, Gerard *o.m.i.* (SFD) [1] Alton, IL SS. Peter and Paul Church.
Snieg, Marion J. '55 (CHI) [M] Wheeling, IL Addolorata Villa.
Snieg, Peter '93 (CHI) [155] Chicago, IL Our Lady of Mount Carmel Church; [A] Chicago, IL Archbishop Quigley Preparatory Seminary.
Sniegowski, Msgr. Thaddeus R. '43 (GR) Retired.
Sniezyk, Msgr. Richard S. '62 (SPR) [16] Springfield, MA St. Mary's Church.
Snincak, Stephen A. '35 (WH) Retired.
Snipes, Roy Lee *o.m.i.* '80 (BWN) [1] Mission, TX Our Lady of Guadalupe Church.
Snock, Bernard C. '62 (GAL) Frydek, TX St. Mary's Church.
Snock, Francis '50 (Y) Retired.
Snodgrass, Thomas A. '76 (CIN) [6] Cincinnati, OH St. Aloysius Church; [21] Cincinnati, OH St. Charles Borromeo Church.
Snoeren, Cornelius M. *m.h.m.* '52 (NY) [DD] Hartsdale, NY Mill Hill Fathers Residence.
Snoha, Joseph J. *c.m.* '90 (PH) [AA] Philadelphia, PA Congregation of the Mission.
Snoich, Stephen *o.s.b.* '72 (IND) [J] St. Meinrad, IN St. Meinrad Archabbey.
Snoke, F. Richard '65 (COL) Danville, OH St. Luke Church.
Snopek, Charles J. '86 (CHR) Pawleys Island, SC Precious Blood of Christ Church.
Snouffer, Philip T. '62 (BAL) Special Assignment.
Snow, Glen *o.carm.* '89 (CHI) [D] Chicago, IL Mt. Carmel High School; [N] Chicago, IL Carmelite Priory of St. Cyril.
Snow, Msgr. Harry K. '77 (OG) [1] Ogdensburg, NY St. Mary's Cathedral.
Snow, J. Lee '55 (OG) Retired.
Snyder, Alexander N. '59 (OAK) [5] San Leandro, CA Our Lady of Good Counsel Church.
Snyder, Brian '79 (SEA) Special Assignment; [Q] Seattle, WA Catholic Hospital Ministries.
Snyder, Chester P. '77 (HBG) Mechanicsburg, PA St. Joseph Church.
Snyder, Clatus E. '34 (BUF) Retired.
Snyder, Daniel L. '84 (KAL) Absent on Leave.
Snyder, Donald E. (CLV) Westlake, OH St. Ladislas Church.
Snyder, Edward J. *s.j.* '52 (NEW) [C] Jersey City, NJ St. Peter's Preparatory School.
Snyder, Frederick '52 (GI) Retired.
Snyder, Frederick N. '52 (GI) Ashton, NE St. Francis Church.
Snyder, Gary B. '74 (SC) Halbur, IA St. Augustine's Church; Roselle, IA Holy Angels Church; Templeton, IA Sacred Heart Church.
Snyder, Joachim J. *o.carm.* '48 (NY) [DD] Scarborough, NY Carmelite Fathers, NY Prov. of St. Elias.
Snyder, John F. *s.j.* '55 (MIL) [P] Milwaukee, WI Jesuit Provincial Office, Wisconsin Province.
Snyder, John F. *s.j.* '55 (STL) [P] St. Louis, MO Jesuit Community Corporation at St. Louis University - Jesuit Hall; [W] St. Louis, MO Gregorian University Foundation.
Snyder, Msgr. John R. '54 (E) Retired.
Snyder, Larry J. '88 (STP) Special Assignment.
Snyder, Michael E. '97 (BLX) [1] Biloxi, MS Cathedral of the Nativity of the Blessed Virgin Maryh.
Snyder, Michael J. *m.m.* '78 (FgM) Maryknoll(M.M.).
Snyder, Michael J. *m.m.* '79 (NY) [DD] Maryknoll, NY Maryknoll Fathers and Brothers.
Snyders, William J. *s.j.* '66 (STL) [P] St. Louis, MO De Smet Jesuit High School Community.
Snyderwine, L. Thomas '68 (E) [23] Erie, PA St. Luke Church; Erie, PA Erie County Geriatric Center Annex.
Snyers, Peter '53 (SCL) [6] St. Cloud, MN St. John Cantius Church.
Soares, Bernardo '54 (MRY) Watsonville, CA Our Lady Help of Christians Church.
Soares, John P. '93 (PRO) [S] South Kingstown, RI University of Rhode Island Catholic Center.
Soares, Msgr. Nicholas J. '64 (NY) [203] Staten Island, NY St. Clement Church; [215] Staten Island, NY St. Michael Church.
Soares, Patrick *c.s.sp.* '73 (STA) [16] Jacksonville, FL St. Joseph's Church.
Soave, Msgr. Alfred '48 (RVC) Retired; [N] Uniondale, NY St. Pius X Residence.
Sobczak, Marek W. '81 (HRT) [4] Ansonia, CT St. Joseph's Church.
Sobejano, Jesus *o.a.r.* '51 (NY) [157] Bronx, NY St. John Vianney, Cure of Ars Church; [DD] New York, NY Augustinian Recollects Provincial Residence, Province of St. Nicholas of Tolentine.
Soberal, Jose '60 (ARE) Special Assignment.
Soberal, Jose Diman (SJN) [A] Bayamon, PR Bayamon Central University.
Soberick, George J. '62 (MAN) Lakeport, NH Our Lady of the Lakes Church.
Sobiech, Stanley *o.f.m.conv.* (BO) [7] Lawrence, MA Holy Trinity Church.
Sobieck, Elmer '46 (SCL) Retired.
Sobiecki, Peter S. '66 (HRT) [2] New Britain, CT Holy Cross Church.
Sobierajski, Msgr. Edward J. '61 (BUF) Retired; [O] Tonawanda, NY O'Hara Residence.
Sobierajski, Joseph A. *s.j.* '74 (BAL) [B] Baltimore, MD Loyola College; [M] Baltimore, MD Jesuit Community of Loyola College, Inc.
Sobiesiak, Msgr. Joseph R. '76 (ALN) [6] Allentown, PA Our Lady of Mt. Carmel Church; [9] Allentown, PA Sacred Heart of Jesus Church; [C] Allentown, PA Allentown Central Catholic High School.
Sobolewski, Edward F. '69 (CAM) National Park, NJ St. Matthew's Church.
Sobon, Walter A. '67 (PIT) Ingram, PA Ascension Church.
Sobosan, Jeffrey *c.s.c.* '73 (P) [B] Portland, OR University of Portland; [L] Portland, OR Holy Cross Fathers & Brothers, C.S.C. - University of Portland.
Sobotka, De Paul *o.f.m.* '63 (GB) [I] Pulaski, WI Assumption of B.V.M. Friary.
Sobr, Clement *o.s.b.* '51 (JOL) [J] Lisle, IL St. Procopius Abbey.
Sobr, Clement *o.s.b.* '51 (SUP) [C] Fifield, WI King of Martyrs Priory.
Sobus, James M. '86 (WH) [10] Wheeling, WV St. Michael's Church.
Soce, Jago *o.f.m.* '94 (CHI) [189] Chicago, IL Sacred Heart Church.
Socha, Bronislaw F. *o.c.d.* '89 (GRY) [J] Munster, IN Discalced Carmelite Fathers Monastery.
Sochacki, Walter L. '68 (STP) Roseville, MN St. Rose of Lima Church.
Socias, James '78 (CHI) [W] Chicago, IL Midtown Center.
Sockol, Timothy '77 (PMB) Sebastian, FL St. Sebastian Church.
Sodano, Ralph H. '67 (PAT) Military Chaplains.
Sodano, Ralph H. '67 (TUC) Yuma, AZ MCAS Chapel.
Sodano, Thomas M. '91 (PH) [101] Philadelphia, PA Maternity B.V.M. Church.
Soderlund, David '65 (ALN) Unassigned.
Sodini, Pierre G. '68 (PIT) Avella, PA St. Michael Church.
Sodja, Richard H. '65 (HEL) Bigfork, MT St. Catherine Church.
Sodomora, John *c.ss.r.* '78 (BAL) Annapolis, MD St. Mary Church; [M] Annapolis, MD Saint Mary Rectory.
Sodoro, Carl F. '77 (OM) [5] Omaha, NE St. Anthony Church; [L] Omaha, NE Sisters of the Annunciation of the Archdiocese of Omaha.

Soehner, Mark *o.f.m.* '87 (DET) [3] Detroit, MI St. Aloysius Church.
Soerries, Denis *o.s.b.* '56 (LR) Subiaco, AR St. Benedict Church.
Sofie, J. Frank, Jr. '94 (MOB) [7] Mobile, AL St. Ignatius Church.
Sogiuzzo, W. Gerard '79 (NEW) Union, NJ St. Michael's Church.
Sogliuzzo, Louis P. *s.j.* '80 (NY) [DD] New York, NY Xavier Jesuit Community.
Sogliuzzo, Louis S. *s.j.* '87 (NY) [37] New York, NY St. Francis Xavier Church.
Soha, Roderick *t.o.r.* '95 (ORL) [2] Lakeland, FL St. Anthony's Church.
Sohm, John E. '58 (SFD) Sullivan, IL St. Columcille Church.
Soileau, Charles L. '57 (LKC) Vinton, LA St. Joseph Church.
Soisson, Clifford F. '37 (PIT) Retired.
Soisson, F. Clifford '37 (PIT) [O] Pittsburgh, PA St. John Vianney Manor.
Sojka, Msgr. Ferdinand M. '44 (PIT) Retired; [O] Pittsburgh, PA St. John Vianney Manor.
Sojka, Louis *o.s.b.* '90 (OM) [C] Elkhorn, NE Mount Michael High School.
Sojka, Louis L. *o.s.b.* '90 (OM) [K] Elkhorn, NE Mount Michael Abbey.
Sojka, Remi '95 (RIC) [8] Richmond, VA St. Bridget Church.
Sokalski, Marcel *o.f.m.conv.* '50 (BGP) [C] Bridgeport, CT Kolbe-Cathedral High School.
Sokalski, Marcel '59 (BGP) [14] Bridgeport, CT St. Michael The Archangel Church.
Sokol, Alfred J. *s.d.b.* '47 (NEW) Mahwah, NJ Immaculate Heart of Mary Church.
Sokol, Stanley '85 (SPR) [10] Springfield, MA Our Lady of the Rosary Church.
Sokolowski, Bernard T. '45 (BUF) [4] Cheektowaga, NY St. Josaphat Church; Retired.
Sokolowski, Edward V. '44 (SCR) Retired.
Sokolowski, Robert S. '61 (WDC) [C] Washington, DC Catholic University of America, The.
Sokolowski, Msgr. Robert S. '65 (HRT) On Duty Outside the Archdiocese.
Sokolowski, Thomas J. '79 (SCR) East Stroudsburg, PA St. Matthew's Church.
Sokolowski, Waclaw *o.f.m.conv.* '84 (PAT) [6] Clifton, NJ St. John Kanty Church.
Sokolowski, William R. '65 (HRT) Wolcott, CT St. Maria Goretti Church.
Sokolski, John *o.m.i.* '55 (NO) [1] New Orleans, LA St. Louis Cathedral; [17] New Orleans, LA Our Lady of Guadalupe /International Shrine of St. Jude Church.
Solan, Lawrence T. '80 (DEN) Aspen, CO St. Mary Church.
Solana, Fermin '70 (MIA) [11] Miami, FL Our Lady of Divine Providence Church.
Solano, Julio '93 (MIA) [4] Miami Beach, FL St. Patrick Church.
Solari, James K. '55 (CHL) Winston-Salem, NC St. Leo's Church.
Solari, Placid D. *o.s.b.* '80 (CHL) [A] Belmont, NC Belmont Abbey College; [J] Belmont, NC Belmont Abbey.
Solarski, Jack '76 (DAL) [L] Irving, TX Opus Dei.
Solarzano, Miguel '93 (GAL) Pasadena, TX St. Pius the Fifth Church.
Solazzo, Michael J. '76 (CHI) Other Assignments.
Solcia, Louis M. *c.r.s.p.* '57 (SD) [15] San Diego, CA Our Lady of the Rosary Church.
Soldo, Slavko '72 (CHI) [N] Chicago, IL Croatian Franciscan Custody of the Holy Family.
Soler, Lawrence *t.o.r.* '51 (AUS) [1] Waco, TX Sacred Heart Church.
Soler, Luis Augusto '67 (CHR) North Augusta, SC Our Lady of Peace Church.
Soler, Roberto '62 (MGZ) Aguada, PR Santuario Protomartires de la Concepcion Church.
Soles, John '64 (BRK) [T] Brooklyn, NY Catholic Migration & Refugee Office, Catholic Migration Services, Inc.
Soles, John '64 (NY) [75] New York, NY St. Michael Chapel Church.
Soles, Juan '64 (NY) Federal, NY Metropolitan Correctional Center.
Soleta, Chester A. *c.s.c.* '42 (FTW) [J] South Bend, IN Congregation of Holy Cross Indiana Province Provincial House.
Soley, Roger A. '78 (WDC) Huntingtown, MD Jesus the Divine Word Parish.
Solier, Jess Eric '57 (NY) [3] New Rochelle, NY St. Joseph Church.
Solis, Marco T. '97 (LA) Lomita, CA St. Margaret Mary Alacoque Church.
Solis, Oscar A. '79 (HT) Golden Meadow, LA Our Lady of Prompt Succor Church.
Solis, Ralph, Jr. '93 (ELP) Van Horn, TX Our Lady of Fatima Church.
Solla, Santiago '53 (PCE) Juana Diaz, PR St. Raymond Nonato Church.
Solma, Martin A. *s.m.* '78 (CIN) [M] Dayton, OH Marianist Provincialate.
Soloman, Louis E. *s.j.* '64 (NY) [DD] New York, NY Murray-Weigel Hall.
Solomia, Paul '59 (DM) [D] Des Moines, IA Mercy Hospital Medical Center.
Solors, Stephen '91 (DUL) Bigfork, MN Our Lady of the Snows Church.
Solorzano, Marcelo *o.p.* '95 (MIA) [18] Miami, FL St. Dominic Church.
Soltis, John F. *m.m.* '62 (FgM) Maryknoll Foreign Missions.
Soltys, Daniel F. '68 (OM) Gretna, NE St. Patrick Church.
Soltys, Raymond A. '79 (SPR) [1] Ludlow, MA Christ the King Church.
Somarriba, Marcos '93 (MIA) [33] Miami, FL St. Timothy Church; [C] Miami, FL Our Lady of Lourdes Academy.
Somers, Eldon K. '51 (E) Retired.
Somers, Michael '82 (GB) Absent on Leave.
Somers, Richard '66 (JKS) Greenville, MS St. Joseph Church.
Somerville, Alvin *o.f.m.conv.* (R) [E] Burlington, NC Conventual Franciscans.
Somerville, Alvin *o.f.m.conv.* '58 (R) Burlington, NC Blessed Sacrament Church.
Somerville, Conrad *o.f.m.conv.* '54 (ALB) Tribes Hill, NY Sacred Heart Church.
Somerville, Walter F. (CHI) Retired.
Somma, James E. '59 (PIT) Pitcairn, PA St. Michael Church; Allegheny County, PA AUMC Forbes Regional.
Sommer, Allan J. '66 (MIL) Port Washington, WI St. Mary Church.
Sommer, Gerald J. *m.s.c.* '47 (Y) [9] Canton, OH St. Mary Church.
Sommer, Gerald R.J. *m.s.c.* '47 (Y) [A] Youngstown, OH Sacred Heart Retreat House & Renewal Center.
Sommer, Harold *s.j.* '65 (CIN) [M] Cincinnati, OH Faber Jesuit Community.
Sommer, Msgr. Jerome '40 (JC) Retired.
Sommer, Jerome '40 (STL) Retired; Retired.
Sommer, Kenneth J. *s.m.* '59 (CIN) [M] Dayton, OH Marianist Provincialate.
Sommer, Leo J. *m.m.* '48 (NY) [DD] Maryknoll, NY Maryknoll Fathers and Brothers.
Sommer, Paul J. *m.m.* '44 (NY) [DD] Maryknoll, NY Maryknoll Fathers and Brothers.
Sommer, Ralph '83 (RVC) Hauppauge, NY St. Thomas More Church.
Sommermeyer, Gary '91 (BRK) [197] Queens, NY Mary's Nativity Church.
Sommers, Edward P. '73 (CAM) [4] Vineland, NJ St. Isidore Church; [I] Vineland, NJ Bishop McCarthy Residence.
Sommerville, William P. '93 (GAL) Brazoria, TX St. Joseph Church.
Somngam, Prasert *s.d.b.* '93 (OAK) [N] Berkeley, CA Salesian Community.
Somos, Joseph '59 (CHI) [195] Chicago, IL St. Stephen, King of Hungary Church.
Somos, Joseph '59 (STL) On Duty Outside the Archdiocese.
Somoza, Jose I. *o.f.m.* '65 (WDC) [33] Washington, DC Our Lady Queen of the Americas Church.
Son, Kyungsu *m.m.* (GAL) [Q] Houston, TX Maryknoll Fathers and Brothers.
Son, Nguyen Thanh *c.ss.r.* '85 (LA) [R] Baldwin Park, CA Vietnamese Redemptorist Mission.
Son Le, Peter Ha '74 (LA) Santa Fe Springs, CA St. Pius X Church.
Sondej, Cyprian *o.f.m.conv.* '48 (SPR) [A] Granby, MA St. Hyacinth College and Seminary.
Sondergeld, Theodore '59 (SEA) Medical Leave.
Sonderman, Msgr. James W. '45 (AMA) Retired; [D] Panhandle, TX St. Joseph's Home for Retired Priests.
Sondgeroth, Louis *o.m.i.* '57 (DUL) International Falls, MN St. Thomas Aquinas Church; Littlefork, MN St. Columban Church.
Sonefeld, Raymond G. '48 (KAL) Retired.
Song, James '82 (OAK) [8] Oakland, CA St. Cyril Church.
Song, S. Jin-yeul *s.j.* '96 (BO) [W] Boston, MA Loyola House.
Songster, John *s.j.* '44 (WDC) [M] Washington, DC The Jesuit Community at Georgetown University.
Songy, David *o.f.m.cap.* '87 (DEN) [3] Denver, CO Annunciation Church; [M] Denver, CO Annunciation Friary.
Songy, Msgr. Donald J. '53 (BR) [20] Baton Rouge, LA Sacred Heart of Jesus Church; Retired.
Songy, Msgr. James B. '54 (HT) Special and other Diocesan Assignment.
Sonnberger, Albert W. '56 (LC) Chippewa Falls, WI Notre Dame Church.
Sonnier, Cedric '97 (LAF) [1] Lafayette, LA St. John the Evangelist Cathedral.
Sonnier, Charles '64 (VIC) Koerth, TX St. John the Baptist Church; Sweet Home, TX Queen of Peace Church.
Sonnier, T. Alcide '56 (LAF) Chataignier, LA Our Lady of Mount Carmel Church.
Sonntag, Luis *o.f.m.cap.* '42 (MIL) [P] Mount Calvary, WI St. Lawrence Friary.
Sontheimer, W. Wendell '47 (NO) [1] Metairie, LA Our Lady of Divine Providence Church; Retired.
Soper, Paul R. '90 (BO) [15] Lowell, MA St. Rita Church; [CC] Lowell, MA The Catholic Center U Mass, Lowell.
Sopiak, Donald A. '78 (DET) [59] Detroit, MI Our Lady Queen of Heaven Church.
Sopke, Philip *c.s.c.* '69 (P) [B] Portland, OR University of Portland.
Sopke, Philip *c.s.c.* '88 (P) [L] Portland, OR Holy Cross Fathers & Brothers, C.S.C. - University of Portland; [P] Portland, OR University of Portland.
Sopoliga, Michael '79 (PSC) Leave of Absence.
Sopp, Michael '75 (SJP) Ford City, PA St. Mary Church.
Soprano, Ernest R. '79 (CAM) Landisville, NJ Our Lady of Victories Church.
Soprych, Marion '75 (CHI) [25] Chicago, IL St. Bede the Venerable Church.
Soranno, Joseph M. '74 (SPR) Wilbraham, MA St. Cecilia's Church.
Sorce, John J. '61 (CHR) Absent On Leave.
Sorci, Msgr. Francis P. '42 (BUF) Retired.
Sordillo, Ronald '75 (PAT) Morris Plains, NJ St. Virgilius Church.
Sorensen, Bartley A. '76 (PIT) Chicora, PA Mater Dolorosa Church; North Oakland, PA St. Joseph Church.
Sorensen, Bryan '88 (RC) Custer, SD St. John the Baptist Church; Hill City, SD St. Rose of Lima Church.
Sorento, Armand *o.f.m.conv.* '42 (TR) Seaside Park, NJ St. Catharine of Siena Church.
Soreth, James F. '41 (PH) Retired.
Sorgie, Anthony D. (NY) [D] New York, NY Department of Education.
Sorgie, Anthony D. '82 (NY) [A] Yonkers, NY St. Joseph's Seminary.
Soria, Jorge A. '86 (SD) Lemon Grove, CA St. John of the Cross Church.
Soria, Manuel '81 (SAC) Yuba City, CA St. Isidore Church.
Soria, Santiago *o.c.d.* '59 (PCE) [12] Ponce, PR San Jose Church.
Soriano, Danilo C. '78 (CHI) Matteson, IL St. Lawrence O'Toole Church.
Soriano, Eugene '52 (BRK) [154] Queens, NY St. Bartholomew's Church; [T] Brooklyn, NY Catholic Migration & Refugee Office, Catholic Migration Services, Inc.
Soriano, Jesus '70 (SAC) Vallejo, CA St. Catherine of Siena Church.
Sorinson, Phil (PBL) [D] Pueblo, CO Centura Health-St. Mary-Corwin Hospital.
Sork, Msgr. David A. '70 (LA) La Puente, CA St. Louis of France Church.
Sorohan, Msgr. David V. '59 (COL) [8] Columbus, OH St. Catharine Church.
Sors, Vladimir '28 (PEO) Retired.
Sorvillo, Mark B. '78 (CHI) [121] Chicago, IL St. Margaret Mary Church.
Sosa, Carlos '89 (MIL) On Leave.
Sosa, Juan J. '72 (MIA) [17] Miami, FL St. Catherine of Siena Church.
Sosa, Philip *m.s.f.* '68 (BWN) Donna, TX St. Joseph Church.
Soseman, Richard '92 (PEO) [L] Peoria, IL St. Joseph's Home of Peoria.
Sosinski, Thomas P. '58 (MAD) Absent on Sick Leave.
Sosnowski, Msgr. Stanley T. '77 (ALN) Whitehall, PA Holy Trinity Church.
Sostrich, John L. '62 (SD) Retired.
Sota, Pascual *c.m.* '56 (SJN) [47] San Juan, PR Nuestra Senora del Pilar Church; [62] San Juan, PR San Vicente de Paul Church.
Sotak, Donald J. '62 (PIT) Natrona, PA St. Joseph Church.
Sotak, John *o.s.a.* '92 (JOL) [B] Kankakee, IL Bishop McNamara High School.
Sotelo, Andrew *s.j.* '82 (SB) [B] San Bernardino, CA Aquinas High School.
Sotelo, Angel L. '91 (FRS) Orange Cove, CA St. Isidore the Farmer Church.
Sotelo, Antonio '58 (PHX) [4] Phoenix, AZ Immaculate Heart of Mary Church.
Sotiroff, Stephen T. '81 (SFD) Vandalia, IL Mother of Dolors Church.
Soto, Angel Leonides '89 (MGZ) [1] Mayaquez, PR Cathedral of Our Lady of Purification.
Soto, Calixto '85 (SJN) Palmer, PR Cristo Rey Church.
Soto, Carmelo '89 (SJN) [1] Canovanas, PR Nuestra Senora del Pilar Church.
Soto, Charles *o.f.m.* '70 (NY) [DD] New York, NY Franciscan Province of the Immaculate Conception.
Soto, Edward '58 (LA) Maywood, CA St. Rose of Lima Church.
Soto, Msgr. Jaime '82 (ORG) [2] Santa Ana, CA Our Lady of Guadalupe Church.
Soto, Roberto Angel '95 (CGS) Comerio, PR Santo

Cristo de la Salud Church.
Soto, Ruben Albano *f.m.m.* '96 (WIL) [I] Seaford, DE Missionary Fraternity of Mary, USA, Ltd.
Sottek, James J. *o.s.f.s.* '57 (TOL) [K] Toledo, OH Oblates of St. Francis de Sales.
Soucey, Louis A. '74 (MAN) North Conway, NH Our Lady of the Mountains Church; Retired.
Soucie, Edward A. *s.j.* '62 (CI) [B] Pohnpei, FM PATS (Pohnpei Agriculture and Trade School).
Souckar, Michael '88 (MIA) Higher Studies.
Soucy, A. Francis *o.f.m.* '67 (PAT) [M] Ringwood, NJ Holy Name Friary, Inc.
Soucy, Bertrand *s.m.* '53 (FgM) Marist Foreign Missions.
Soucy, D. Wilfrid '30 (PRT) Retired.
Soucy, Maurice P. '49 (HRT) [3] Meriden, CT St. Laurent Church.
Soucy, Neil *s.m.* '62 (FgM) Marist Foreign Missions.
Soucy, Robert P. '62 (BO) Stow, MA St. Isidore Church.
Soucy, Timothy J. '73 (OG) Lake Clear, NY St. John in the Wilderness Church; Saranac Lake, NY St. Bernard Church.
Souffrant, Claude *s.j.* '65 (CHI) [120] Chicago, IL St. Margaret of Scotland Church.
Soukup, Gervase *o.s.b.* '45 (SCL) [I] Collegeville, MN St. John's Abbey, of the Order of St. Benedict.
Soukup, Gregory *o.s.b.* '41 (SCL) [I] Collegeville, MN St. John's Abbey, of the Order of St. Benedict.
Soukup, Paul *s.j.* '79 (SJ) San Jose, CA Catholic Scouting.
Soukup, Paul A. *s.j.* '79 (SJ) [B] Santa Clara, CA Santa Clara University.
Soule, W. Becket *o.p.* '93 (WDC) [11] Washington, DC St. Dominic Church & Priory Church.
Soulliere, John Richard '76 (MIA) Lighthouse Point, FL St. Paul the Apostle Church.
Sousa, Douglas H. '91 (FR) Absent on Leave.
Sousa, Eugene *o.p.* '31 (SAC) Benicia, CA St. Dominic Church.
Sousa, Jose M. '85 (FR) [1] Fall River, MA Cathedral of St. Mary of the Assumption.
Sousa, Kevin '82 (SPR) Absent on Leave.
Sousa, Manuel F. '80 (STO) Turlock, CA Our Lady of the Assumption of the Portuguese Church.
Sousa, Peter E. *c.ss.r.* '78 (BRK) [C] Whitestone, NY St. Alphonsus Formation Residence.
Souse, Stephen J. *o.s.b.* '40 (PEO) [C] Peru, IL St. Bede Academy.
Souse, Stephen J. *o.s.b.* '43 (PEO) [A] Peru, IL St. Bede Abbey and Academy.
Southerton, Gary '88 (SEA) Puyallup, WA Holy Disciples Church.
Soutiere, Ronald '74 (BUR) Military Chaplains.
Soutus, Hugo '94 (STN) Phoenix, AZ Assumption of B.V.M. Church.
Soutuyo, Raul '93 (MIA) [16] Miami, FL St. Brendan Church.
Souva, Eileen *o.p.* (LAN) [1] Jackson, MI St. John the Evangelist Church.
Souvenir, Jean Paul *s.m.* (BO) [10] Cambridge, MA Our Lady of Pity Church.
Sowada, Arlie '73 (SCL) Brown's Valley, MN St. Anthony's Church.
Sowada, Terrance '92 (SP) [14] Tampa, FL St. Paul Church.
Sowinski, Albin F. '51 (MIL) Retired.
Sowinski, Richard E. '74 (BUF) [4] Kenmore, NY St. Paul Church.
Soy, Esteban G. '52 (VEN) [1] Venice, FL Epiphany Cathedral.
Soyka, Giles '50 (GB) [I] Appleton, WI St. Fidelis Friary.
Spacek, Frank W. '97 (BRK) [204] Queens, NY Nativity of the Blessed Virgin Mary Church.
Spacht, Andres *c.ss.r.* '61 (CGS) Aguas Buenas, PR Church of Tres Santos Reyes.
Spadaro, Thomas L. '64 (RVC) Holbrook, NY Good Shepherd Church.
Spadini, Marian '62 (JKS) On Duty Outside the Diocese.
Spadini, Marian '62 (MEM) [22] Memphis, TN Our Lady Of Perpetual Help Church.
Spagnolia, D. George '64 (BO) Franklin, MA St. Mary Church.
Spagnolo, Nicholas *c.s.s.* '52 (BO) [W] Waltham, MA Stigmatine House.
Spahn, James *o.p.* '81 (FgM) Dominican - Order of Preachers Foreign Missions.
Spahn, James A. *o.p.* '81 (CHI) [N] Chicago, IL Dominicans (Provincial Office).
Spahr, Matthew D. '92 (SD) Alpine, CA Queen of Angels Church; [B] San Diego, CA University of San Diego.
Spaight, Msgr. Robert L. '56 (DUB) Nashua, IA St. Michael's Church.
Spain, John H. *m.m.* '70 (NY) [DD] Maryknoll, NY Maryknoll Fathers and Brothers.
Spain, P. Arnold '47 (BIS) Retired.
Spaits, George S. '43 (PH) Retired.
Spalatin, Christopher A. *s.j.* '71 (FgM) Provinces.
Spalding, J. Mark '91 (L) Lebanon, KY St. Augustine Church.
Spalding, Leon C. '59 (L) [1] Springfield, KY St. Dominic Church.
Spalding, William '45 (GB) Retired.
Spalding, William '48 (LEX) Retired.
Spalding, William A. '48 (L) [K] Louisville, KY Nazareth Home.
Spalthoff, Daniel J. '97 (NY) Congers, NY St. Paul Church.
Spanel, Hubert J. '59 (GI) Hemingford, NE St. Bridget Church.
Spangenberg, Robert E. *c.s.sp.* '74 (PIT) [11] Pittsburgh, PA Epiphany Church.
Spanier, Marian '81 (NEW) [4] Garfield, NJ St. Stanislaus Kostka Church.
Spanjers, John J. '59 (SUP) Almena, WI Sacred Heart of Jesus Church; Turtle Lake, WI St. Ann Church.
Spanley, Anthony L. '68 (GRY) Hamlet, IN Holy Cross Church.
Spano, Anthony *s.d.b.* '43 (NY) [DD] New Rochelle, NY Salesian Provincial House.
Spano, Philip F. '82 (BR) Gonzales, LA St. Theresa of Avila Church.
Sparklin, Paul '91 (BAL) [49] Baltimore, MD St. Joseph Church.
Sparks, Joseph R. '66 (DAV) Solon, IA St. Mary's Church.
Sparks, Kenneth A. '95 (PIT) Ross Township, PA St. Sebastian Church.
Sparks, Richard C. *c.s.p.* '78 (CHI) [125] Chicago, IL Old St. Mary Church.
Sparks, Thomas J. (MAN) [B] Warner, NH Magdalen College.
Sparks, Thomas J. '56 (LAN) Retired.
Sparks, Timothy H. *o.p.* '30 (CHI) [N] River Forest, IL St. Thomas Aquinas Priory.
Sparough, J. Michael *s.j.* '78 (CHI) [T] Barrington, IL Bellarmine Hall.
Spatorico, Joseph S. '66 (BUF) [1] Batavia, NY St. Anthony Church.
Spatt, John *c.pp.s.* '43 (CIN) [B] Carthagena, OH St. Charles.
Spaulding, Donald E. '57 (EVN) Dubois, IN St. Raphael Church.
Spaulding, John '71 (PHX) [25] Phoenix, AZ St. Thomas the Apostle Church.
Spear, Arthur J. *c.s.p.* '38 (NY) [DD] Jamaica Estates, NY Paulist Fathers Generalate.
Specht, Joseph *s.j.* (SFR) [2] San Francisco, CA St. Agnes Church.
Specht, Terry W. '96 (ARL) Fairfax, VA St. Mary of Sorrows Church.
Speck, Gregory M. *s.c.j.* '76 (BWN) Raymondville, TX Our Lady of Guadalupe Church.
Speck, James A. '50 (WIN) Retired.
Speckman, Harry *o.f.m.* '61 (SFD) [B] Quincy, IL Quincy University.
Speer, Patrick '41 (BGP) [K] Trumbull, CT St. Joseph's Manor.
Speer, Patrick J. '41 (HRT) Retired.
Speers, David B. '90 (TUC) Absent on Leave.
Speerstra, William F. '59 (SUP) Land-O'-Lakes, WI St. Albert Church; Phelps, WI St. Mary Church.
Spegele, Michael A. '41 (B) Retired.
Speice, Msgr. Lawrence T. '61 (E) [A] Erie, PA St. Mark's Seminary.
Speicher, Charles W. '75 (PIT) Baldwin Boro, PA St. Albert the Great Church.
Speicher, David '86 (LAN) Hartland, MI St. John The Baptist Church.
Speichinger, Lawrence '55 (KC) Retired.
Speier, Francis J. '75 (TOL) [27] Toledo, OH St. John the Baptist Church.
Speier, Thomas *o.f.m.* '58 (CIN) [24] Cincinnati, OH Corpus Christi Church.
Speiler, Joe *s.j.* '75 (SD) [4] San Diego, CA Christ the King Church.
Speiser, Allan '48 (SCL) Retired.
Speiser, Thomas M. '77 (DAL) Plano, TX St. Mark the Evangelist Church.
Speitel, Edmond J. '55 (PH) Brookhaven, PA Our Lady of Charity Church; East Greenville, PA St. Philip Neri Church.
Spekschate, John '42 (LAF) Retired.
Spelgatti, Msgr. David P. '41 (MAR) Retired.
Spellen, Lawrence M. '46 (SLC) Retired.
Spellerberg, Joseph R. *s.j.* '53 (BUF) [50] Buffalo, NY St. Michael Church.
Spellman, Francis J. '40 (CHI) [4] Cicero, IL Mary, Queen of Heaven Church; Retired.
Spellman, John P. *o.s.f.s.* '66 (WIL) [B] Wilmington, DE Salesianum School.
Spellman, Robert '74 (WOR) Shrewsbury, MA St. Anne's Church.
Speltz, Msgr. Richard '33 (WIN) Retired.
Spencer, F. Richard '88 (BAL) Oakland, MD St. Peter the Apostle Church.
Spencer, Francis M. *m.s.* '50 (MAN) [2] Nashua, NH St. Casimir Church.
Spencer, Gregory D. (R) Wilmington, NC St. Mark Church.
Spencer, Jeremiah L. '65 (KCK) [5] Kansas City, KS Holy Name Church; Kansas City, KS K.U. Medical Center and Chapel.
Spencer, John *s.j.* '79 (BO) [W] Chestnut Hill, MA The Jesuit Community at Boston College.
Spencer, Robert K. (BEA) Beaumont, TX Federal Correctional Complex-Penitentiary.
Spencer, William *o.f.m.* '74 (SHP) [6] Shreveport, LA St. Catherine of Siena Church.
Spendov, Vendelin *o.f.m.* '47 (CHI) [N] Lemont, IL The Slovene Franciscan Fathers, Order of Friars Minor, Commissariat of the Holy Cross.
Spener, Robert M. '82 (RIC) Petersburg, VA St. Joseph Church.
Spengler, Msgr. James F. '68 (BRK) [172] Queens, NY St. Gerard Majella Church.
Spenner, Jerome I. '64 (OM) [9] Omaha, NE St. Bernard Church.
Spenner, Wilfred J. '73 (OM) Albion, NE St. Michael Church.
Speno, Eugene '60 (SB) Palm Springs, CA Our Lady of Guadalupe Church.
Spera, James F. '77 (NEW) [B] South Orange, NJ Seton Hall University; [B] South Orange, NJ Seton Hall University.
Sperber, Timothy '78 (HBG) On Duty Outside the Diocese.
Sperber, Timothy '78 (MIA) Pembroke Pines, FL St. Boniface Church.
Sperger, Herbert J. '79 (PH) [9] Philadelphia, PA St. Ambrose Church.
Sperl, August '54 (SFD) Palmyra, IL Holy Rosary Church.
Sperl, August J. '54 (SFD) Virden, IL Sacred Heart Church.
Sperlak, Charles S. '64 (ALN) [4] Reading, PA SS. Cyril and Methodius Church.
Sperry, Msgr. James E. '41 (E) Retired.
Spexarth, Daniel J. '84 (WCH) Schulte, KS St. Peter's Church; Wichita, KS Sedgwick County Adult Local Detention Facility.
Spexarth, James '55 (WCH) Retired.
Spexarth, Joachim *o.s.b.* '65 (OKL) [I] Shawnee, OK St. Gregory Abbey.
Speyrer, Jules (LAF) Retired.
Spezia, Leo J. '76 (STL) Wentzville, MO St. Patrick Church.
Spezia, Robert R. '96 (DET) Clawson, MI Guardian Angels Church.
Spezzano, James '97 (YAK) Sunnyside, WA St. Joseph's Church.
Spicer, Kevin *c.s.c.* (BO) [6] Newton, MA Our Lady Help of Christians Church.
Spicer, Kevin P. *c.s.c.* '92 (FR) [A] North Easton, MA Holy Cross Fathers Religious.
Spicer, Leo M. *o.s.m.* '76 (ORG) [H] Buena Park, CA Servite Fathers And Brothers.
Spicer, Richard J. '86 (SEA) Arlington, WA Immaculate Conception Church.
Spicijaric, Anthony '33 (PH) Retired.
Spicuzza, Anthony P. '46 (IND) Brazil, IN Annunciation of the Blessed Virgin Mary Church.
Spiegel, John D. '76 (DAV) Houghton, IA St. John's Church; St. Paul, IA St. James Church.
Spiegel, Msgr. Robert H. '66 (DAV) Military Chaplains.
Spiegel, Thomas J. '67 (DAV) Bettendorf, IA Our Lady of Lourdes Church.
Spiekermeier, Michael J. '69 (DAV) Keokuk, IA All Saints Church.
Spielman, Paul J. '61 (STL) [3] Lemay, MO St. Andrew Church.
Spielmann, Henry V. *o.s.a.* '39 (TLS) [B] Tulsa, OK Cascia Hall Preparatory School.
Spier, Mathias *o.s.b.* '58 (STP) [19] Minneapolis, MN St. Boniface Church.
Spiers, Msgr. Edward F. '39 (COL) On Duty Outside the Diocese.
Spiess, Kevin J. '86 (CHI) [1] Lemont, IL St. Alphonsus Church.
Spika, Anthony '35 (SFR) [K] San Rafael, CA Nazareth House.
Spika, Anthony L. '35 (SJ) Retired.
Spilka, Anthony Francis *o.f.m.conv.* '69 (SPR) [10] Chicopee, MA St. Stanislaus Basilica Church.
Spillane, Emmanuel *o.c.s.o.* '44 (SLC) [F] Huntsville, UT Abbey of Our Lady of the Holy Trinity of the Order of Cistercians.
Spillane, Jeremiah '86 (VEN) [1] Sarasota, FL Incarnation Church.
Spillane, Michael '68 (BAL) Special Assignment.
Spillane, Thomas J. *s.j.* '53 (BO) [W] Weston, MA Campion Center.
Spillane, Walter J. '60 (KAL) Retired.
Spillett, Thomas '64 (SP) [3] Largo, FL St. Matthew Church.
Spilly, William V. '74 (ROC) [29] Rochester, NY St. John the Evangelist Church.
Spilman, Robert D. '96 (PEO) [1] Champaign, IL Holy Cross Church.
Spina, Douglas J. '76 (PRO) [2] Johnston, RI Our Lady of Grace Church.
Spine, William J. *s.j.* '73 (CHI) [C] Chicago, IL Jesuit

Community at Loyola University of Chicago.
Spinelli, Joseph A. *o.s.a.* '55 (VEN) Golden Gate, FL St. Elizabeth Seton Church.
Spinler, Ruben C. '94 (WIN) Rose Creek, MN St. Peter's Church.
Spinner, Hubert '50 (RVC) Retired; [N] Uniondale, NY St. Pius X Residence.
Spino, John '91 (NEW) Roselle, NJ Church of St. Joseph the Carpenter.
Spinos, Vincent J. *t.o.r.* '50 (STP) [20] Minneapolis, MN St. Bridget Church.
Spinosa, Anthony S. '83 (OLL) Flint, MI Our Lady of Lebanon Church.
Spirko, Nicholas A. '72 (PIT) Ellwood City, PA Purification of the Blessed Virgin Mary Church.
Spisak, Stephen M. '82 (CLV) North Olmsted, OH St. Brendan Church.
Spisak, Thomas M. '77 (Y) [2] Warren, OH Christ Our King Church; [3] Warren, OH SS. Cyril and Methodius Church.
Spishak, Carl A. '59 (ALT) [5] Altoona, PA Holy Rosary Church.
Spitale, John '26 (Y) Retired.
Spiteri, George '70 (NY) [3] White Plains, NY St. Bernard Church.
Spiteri, Laurence '78 (LA) [98] Los Angeles, CA Visitation Church.
Spittler, Ernest G. *s.j.* '62 (CLV) [C] Cleveland, OH John Carroll Jesuit Community.
Spitz, Gregory M. '67 (MIL) Mequon, WI St. James Church.
Spitzer, Robert J. *s.j.* '83 (SEA) [A] Seattle, WA Seattle University.
Spitzig, Msgr. Joseph '42 (CLV) Retired.
Spitzley, Denis R. '75 (LAN) Burton, MI Blessed Sacrament Church.
Splain, Thomas E. *s.j.* '71 (FgM) Provinces.
Splawski, Bernard J. *o.f.m.* '63 (PAT) West Milford Township, NJ St. Joseph Church.
Spleet, Julius A. '62 (SAG) Gladwin, MI Sacred Heart Church.
Splonskowski, Wilfrid J. *o.s.b.* '52 (BIS) New Hradec, ND SS. Peter and Paul Church; [A] Richardton, ND Assumption Abbey.
Spodnik, A. Leo '48 (HRT) Retired.
Spoletini, Pasquale M. *s.j.* '54 (SEA) [31] Seattle, WA Our Lady of Mount Virgin Church; [M] Seattle, WA Jesuit House, Seattle.
Spolny, Joseph R. '78 (CLV) [38] Cleveland, OH St. John Nepomucene Church.
Sponders, John '93 (JOL) Westmont, IL Holy Trinity Church.
Spong, William '79 (FWT) On Duty Outside the Diocese.
Spontak, James '75 (PBR) Morgantown, WV St. Mary's Holy Protection Church; [E] Mount St. Macrina, PA Motherhouse and Novitiate of the Sisters of St. Basil the Great.
Spors, Roman '58 (DUL) Emily, MN St. Emily's Church.
Spotswood, Cecil Reeves '97 (MOB) Dothan, AL St. Columba Church.
Sprague, George Raymond '34 (PEO) Retired; [L] Peoria, IL St. Augustine Manor.
Spraker, Msgr. Gerard W. '34 (BAL) [11] Baltimore, MD Ascension Church; Retired.
Spranger, William J. '56 (GRY) San Pierre, IN All Saints Church; [H] San Pierre, IN Holy Cross Care Services dba Little Company of Mary Health Facility, Inc.
Sprauer, Michael '72 (P) Salem, OR Oregon State Correctional Institution; Salem, OR Oregon Women's Correction Center.
Spreen, John W. '53 (SFD) Ashland, IL St. Augustine Church.
Sprenger, Alan M. '60 (COL) Special Assignment.
Spriet, Jules *c.i.c.m.* '44 (FgM) Missionhurst Foreign Missions.
Sprietsma, Leo *o.f.m.* '53 (LA) [R] Santa Barbara, CA Franciscan Friary, Order of Friars Minor (Old Mission); [R] Santa Barbara, CA St. Anthony's Seminary.
Spriggs, Robert W. '65 (SFD) Highland, IL St. Paul Church.
Sprigler, William A. '75 (NU) Clara City, MN St. Clara Church; Granite Falls, MN St. Andrew Church.
Spring, Mark P. '80 (DAV) Muscatine, IA St. Mary's Church.
Springer, Francis *s.m.* '55 (SFR) [B] San Francisco, CA St. Peter Chanel Seminary; [N] San Francisco, CA Provincial Residence.
Springer, James *c.ss.r.* '49 (KC) [32] Kansas City, MO Our Lady of Perpetual Help Church; [J] Kansas City, MO Redemptorists of Kansas City.
Springer, Lawrence F. '59 (CHI) [4] Des Plaines, IL St. Zachary Church.
Springer, Robert *s.j.* '48 (NY) [DD] New York, NY West Side Jesuit Community.
Springer, William A. '72 (SD) [10] San Diego, CA Mission Basilica San Diego De Alcala Church.
Springman, Donald W. '67 (L) [3] Valley Station, KY Our Lady of Consolation Church.
Sprinkle, R. Russell *m.m.* '35 (FgM) Maryknoll Foreign Missions.
Sprouffske, Matthew *o.carm.* '54 (JOL) [J] Darien, IL Carmelite Provincial Office.
Sproul, John M. '63 (SD) La Mesa, CA St. Martin of Tours Church.
Sproule, Robert N. *s.j.* '61 (BGP) [O] Fairfield, CT The Fairfield Jesuit Community-Fairfield University.
Sprute, Mel '69 (B) Kellogg, ID St. Rita's Church; Wallace, ID St. Alphonsus Church.
Spychala, Daniel S. '84 (ARL) Winchester, VA Sacred Heart of Jesus Church.
Spyrka, Edward C. *o.c.d.* '62 (GRY) [J] Munster, IN Discalced Carmelite Fathers Monastery.
Squeo, Eugene P. '71 (NEW) [7] Jersey City, NJ Assumption/All Saints Church; [23] Jersey City, NJ St. Patrick's Church.
Squiller, Msgr. John '56 (STF) Rochester, NY St. Josaphat Church.
Srebernak, Francis '37 (LAN) Retired.
Sreboth, Michael J. '86 (MOB) Atmore, AL St. Robert Bellarmine Church.
Sredzinski, Joseph L. '70 (GBG) Everson, PA St. Joseph Church.
Srenn, Thomas E. '77 (CHI) [99] Chicago, IL St. Jane de Chantal Church.
Srion, Charles N. '78 (RVC) Floral Park, NY Our Lady of Victory Church.
Srnec, Msgr. Stanley J. '42 (STP) Retired.
Sroba, Andrew '93 (ALN) [4] Allentown, PA St. John the Baptist Church.
Srode, John S. *c.pp.s.* '72 (CIN) [M] Dayton, OH Provincial House of the Cincinnati Province of the Society of the Precious Blood.
Sroka, Gerald A. '60 (GRY) La Porte, IN Sacred Heart Church; Valparaiso, IN St. Elizabeth Seton Church.
Srumpf, David *o.f.m.* '90 (CHI) [N] Lemont, IL The Slovene Franciscan Fathers, Order of Friars Minor, Commissariat of the Holy Cross.
Ssebadduka, George '78 (MIL) Mequon, WI St. James Church.
Ssekiwala, Maximus (CHI) [207] Chicago, IL St. Timothy Church.
Sserunjogi, Expedit '86 (LA) Culver City, CA St. Augustine Church.
St-Jean, Mary Kidney '92 (MIA) [10] Miami, FL Notre Dame d'Haiti Church.
St. Charles, Paul W. '66 (MEM) Retired.
St. Clair, Joseph A. '40 (PH) Ardmore, PA St. Colman Church; Retired.
St. Clair, Robert L. *s.j.* '58 (OAK) [S] Oakland, CA Institute of Lay Theology.
St. Clair, Robert L. *s.j.* '58 (SJ) [M] Los Gatos, CA California Province of the Society of Jesus, Jesuit Provincial Office.
St. Claire, Robert L. *s.j.* '58 (SJ) [B] Santa Clara, CA Santa Clara University.
St. Cyr, John *o.m.i.* '61 (FgM) Oblates Foreign Missions.
St. Cyr, Richard E. '66 (PRT) Saco, ME Notre Dame de Lourdes Church.
St. George, John A. *s.j.* '52 (FgM) Provinces.
St. George, John P. *s.j.* '66 (NEW) [B] Jersey City, NJ Saint Peter's College; [N] Jersey City, NJ Jesuits of Saint Peter's College, Inc.
St. George, Peter Thomas '95 (CIN) [71] Cincinnati, OH Our Lady of Victory Church.
St. Germain, Andre '96 (NTN) On Special Projects.
St. Germain, Antoine F. '76 (CAM) Pennsauken, NJ St. Stephen Church.
St. Germain, Brian '88 (PRM) Absent on Leave.
St. Godard, Edward G. '64 (PRO) [6] Woonsocket, RI Holy Family Church.
St. Jacques, Clement *s.a.* '45 (WDC) [B] Washington, DC Atonement Seminary-Franciscan Friars of the Atonement.
St. James, Paul F. '68 (BUR) Essex Junction, VT St. Lawrence, Martyr Church.
St. Jean, Marcel '96 (BGP) [7] Bridgeport, CT St. Charles Church.
St. John, George G. '52 (ALB) East Greenbush, NY Holy Spirit Church.
St. John, Norman R. *s.v.d.* '62 (MET) Belle Mead, NJ Carrier Clinic.
St. John, Norman R. *s.v.d.* '62 (TR) [M] Bordentown, NJ Society of the Divine Word.
St. Jules, Stephen '79 (RCK) Batavia, IL Holy Cross Church.
St. Laurent, Daniel A. '71 (MAN) Durham, NH St. Thomas More Church.
St. Marie, Denis L. '59 (CLV) Independence, OH St. Michael Church; El Salvador, C.A., OH The Catholic Center.
St. Marie, Michael '93 (B) Gooding, ID St. Elizabeth's Church; Shoshone, ID St. Peter's Church.
St. Martin, Robert *o.f.m.conv.* '77 (IND) [4] Terre Haute, IN St. Joseph Church.
St. Martin, Robert J. '56 (HRT) Unionville, CT St. Mary's Church.
St. Onge, Omer *s.m.* '46 (BRK) [45] Brooklyn, NY St. Francis of Assisi-St. Blaise Church.
St. Onge, Msgr. Paul J. '41 (NOR) New London, CT St. Joseph Church; Retired.
St. Peter, Lawrence '59 (DEN) Absent on Leave.
St. Pierre, Michel J. '57 (BUR) [2] Burlington, VT St. Anthony's Church.
St. Pierre, Roland *o.m.i.* '52 (MAN) [K] Colebrook, NH Shrine of Our Lady of Grace.
St. Pierre, Romeo A. '54 (PRT) Retired.
St. Pierre, Ronald L. '83 (BO) Tyngsboro, MA St. Mary Magdalen Church.
St. Pierre, Thomas J. '80 (RVC) Brentwood, NY St. Anne's Church.
St. Sure, Donald F. *s.j.* '39 (SJ) [M] Los Gatos, CA Sacred Heart Jesuit Center.
St.John, Norman *s.v.d.* (TR) Howell Township, NJ St. Veronica Church.
Sta. Maria, Nicanor *s.d.b.* '80 (SJN) [37] San Juan, PR Maria Auxiliadora Church.
Staak, John *o.m.i.* '95 (FgM) Oblates Foreign Missions.
Staal, David E. '90 (OAK) Livermore, CA St. Michael's Church; [S] Oakland, CA Adventus; [S] Oakland, CA The Roman Catholic Cemeteries of the Diocese of Oakland.
Staar, Robert J. '77 (NY) Stony Point, NY Immaculate Conception Church.
Stab, Herbert J. '59 (MET) Piscataway, NJ Our Lady of Fatima Church.
Stacer, John *s.j.* '63 (FgM) Provinces.
Stacer, John R. *s.j.* '63 (NO) [P] New Orleans, LA Jesuit Provincial Office.
Stacherczak, Idzi '75 (CHI) [33] Chicago, IL St. Bruno Church.
Stachewicz, Msgr. Henry J. '47 (BUF) [1] Depew, NY St. Augustine Church; Retired.
Stachnik, Kenneth R. '86 (GAY) [3] Alpena, MI St. John the Baptist Church.
Stachowiak, Conrad P. '74 (BUF) [1] Depew, NY St. Augustine Church.
Stachura, Thaddeus X. '64 (WOR) [9] Worcester, MA Our Lady of Czestochowa Church.
Stachurski, David *o.f.m.conv.* '80 (SAV) Statesboro, GA St. Matthew's Church.
Stack, Aquinas E. *o.carm.* '85 (PMB) [5] Boca Raton, FL St. Jude Church.
Stack, Christopher '66 (PMB) Retired.
Stack, Daniel '82 (ATL) Dalton, GA St. Joseph's Church; [L] Atlanta, GA Campus Ministry.
Stack, Gabriel D. *o.praem.* '82 (ORG) [D] Siverado, CA St. Michael's College Preparatory High School; [H] Silverado, CA Norbertine Fathers of Orange Inc.; [N] El Toro, CA Aid to the Church In Need, Inc.
Stack, George J. '59 (BRK) [220] Queens, NY Our Lady of the Snows Church.
Stack, Gilbert *o.s.b.* '39 (KC) [J] Conception, MO Conception Abbey.
Stack, James M. '86 (WDC) [4] Washington, DC Annunciation Church; Special Ministries.
Stack, Jerome *c.pp.s.* '72 (LA) Norwalk, CA Metropolitan State Hospital.
Stack, John G. *s.j.* '71 (DAL) [D] Dallas, TX Jesuit College Preparatory School.
Stack, John J. '53 (HRT) [6] West Hartford, CT St. Thomas the Apostle Church; [C] West Hartford, CT Saint Joseph College.
Stack, John J. '88 (DAV) Camanche, IA Church of the Visitation; [J] Clinton, IA Samaritan Health System, Inc.
Stack, John P. '55 (WDC) Chaptico, MD Our Lady of the Wayside Church.
Stack, John P. *o.s.a.* '74 (PH) [C] Villanova, PA Villanova University; [AA] Villanova, PA St. Thomas Monastery.
Stack, Joseph O. *o.m.i.* '34 (BO) [Z] Tewksbury, MA Immaculate Heart of Mary Novitiate-Infirmary.
Stack, Lambert *s.t.* '44 (WDC) [M] Adelphi, MD Missionary Servants of the Most Holy Trinity.
Stack, Philip Dan '48 (SUP) Sugar Camp, WI St. Kunegunda Church.
Stack, Msgr. Richard J. '56 (E) [28] Erie, PA St. Paul Church.
Stack, Thomas Mannix '73 (MIA) [10] Fort Lauderdale, FL St. Mark Church.
Stack, William E. '48 (MAD) Retired.
Stackpoole, Edward V. *s.j.* '56 (SFR) [N] San Francisco, CA Jesuit Community at University of San Francisco.
Stacy, Bernard *c.m.f.* '47 (LA) [R] Rancho Dominguez, CA Dominguez Seminary Inc.
Stacy, Ronald W. '72 (ROC) Absent on Leave.
Stadalnikas, Casimir J. '40 (MIA) Retired.
Stadmeyer, Raymond *o.f.m.cap.* '97 (DET) Hazel Park, MI St. Mary Magdalen Church.
Stadtmueller, Msgr. Fred '40 (SFE) Retired.
Stadtmueller, Roman *s.d.s.* '54 (WDC) [B] Silver Spring, MD Salvatorian Community.
Staebell, James A. (BUF) Angola, NY Most Precious Blood Church.
Staebell, James E. '57 (BUF) Retired.
Staehler, Adrian *o.f.m.cap.* '67 (MIL) [P] Milwaukee, WI St. Conrad House.
Staes, Robert *o.p.* '71 (DEN) [35] Denver, CO St. Mary

Magdalene's Church.
Staff, Stephen M. *c.m.* '90 (MOB) Auburn, AL St. Michael Church.
Stafford, Dennis '91 (CHI) [50] Chicago, IL St. Denis Church.
Stafford, James D.M. '61 (OKL) Lawton, OK Blessed Sacrament Church.
Stafford, Joseph E. *o.s.f.s.* '52 (WIL) [I] Childs, MD Oblates of St. Francis De Sales.
Stafford, Msgr. Joseph L. '57 (BRK) [178] Queens, NY Holy Family Church.
Stafford, Michael *o.s.b.* '58 (KAL) Battle Creek, MI Veteran's Administration Hospital.
Stafford, Michael *o.s.b.* '58 (PRO) [P] Portsmouth, RI Abbey of St. Gregory the Great.
Stafford, Raymond W. '59 (BRK) [203] Queens, NY Most Precious Blood Church.
Stagaman, David J. *s.j.* '66 (OAK) [A] Berkeley, CA The Jesuit School of Theology at Berkeley; [N] Berkeley, CA Jesuit Community at Jesuit School of Theology at Berkeley.
Stagg, Robert B. '75 (NEW) Springfield, NJ St. James Church.
Stagnaro, John J. '76 (BO) Holbrook, MA St. Joseph Church.
Stahel, Thomas H. *s.j.* '71 (NO) [P] New Orleans, LA Jesuit Provincial Office.
Stahl, Allen '75 (ORL) On Duty Outside the Diocese.
Stahl, David A. '91 (DEN) [23] Denver, CO Presentation of Our Lady Church.
Stahl, George '56 (IND) On Disability Leave.
Stahl, Robert J. *s.m.* '34 (WDC) [M] Washington, DC Marist Provincial House.
Stahura, Joseph L. '81 (HBG) Greencastle, PA St. Mark the Evangelist Church.
Staiger, Charles '56 (RVC) Sick Leave.
Staigers, P. Del '87 (CIN) Milford, OH St. Andrew Church; [B] Cincinnati, OH Mt. St. Mary's Seminary of the West.
Stajkowski, James '73 (MIL) [P] Twin Lakes, WI La Salette Missionaries Shrine.
Stajkowski, Leo S. '66 (ALN) [9] Reading, PA St. Mary Church.
Stake, Ronald P. '85 (CHI) Military Chaplains.
Stakem, Gary *o.f.m.cap.* '51 (CLV) [18] Cleveland, OH Conversion of St. Paul Church; [65] Cleveland, OH St. Philip Neri Church; [P] Cleveland, OH St. Paul Friary.
Stakem, Ward *o.f.m.cap.* '78 (PIT) Rochester, PA St. Cecilia Church; [O] Rochester, PA St. Cecilia Friary.
Stalavicz, George P. '51 (SCR) Retired.
Staley, Robert P. '95 (R) Roxboro, NC SS. Mary and Edward Church.
Stallings, John E. '50 (BEL) Harrisburg, IL St. Mary Church.
Stallings, Michael W. '74 (TUC) Patagonia, AZ St. Theresa Church.
Stalter, Cal '94 (AMA) Wellington, TX Our Mother of Mercy Church; Wellington, TX Our Mother of Mercy Church.
Stalzer, David '74 (JOL) [16] Joliet, IL St. Mary Nativity Church.
Stalzer, Joseph '59 (JOL) Itasca, IL St. Peter the Apostle Church.
Stammitti, Anthony '90 (LIN) Wahoo, NE St. Wenceslaus Church.
Stampiglia, Fausto *s.a.c.* '60 (VEN) [3] Sarasota, FL St. Martha Church; [F] Sarasota, FL St. Martha's Housing, Inc.; [F] Sarasota, FL St. Martha's Housing II, Inc.
Stamschror, Robert P. '61 (WIN) [J] Winona, MN Saint Mary's Press, Christian Brothers Publications.
Stanbery, Stephen '80 (TOL) New Bavaria, OH Sacred Heart of Jesus Church; North Creek, OH St. Joseph Church.
Stanchik, Dennis P. '59 (LC) Adams, WI St. Joseph Church; Brooks, WI St. Ann Church.
Stander, Charles J. *s.m.* '81 (CIN) [M] Dayton, OH Marianist Provincialate.
Stander, Edwin L. '63 (LIN) [5] Lincoln, NE Sacred Heart Church; Lincoln, NE Nebraska Penal Complex.
Stanek, Msgr. Wenceslaus '30 (CHI) Retired.
Stanfield, Francis E. '80 (GLP) Retired; [F] Gallup, NM Southwest Indian Foundation.
Stanfield, William L. '76 (MIL) Awaiting Assignment.
Stang, Charles L. *s.j.* '67 (MIL) [E] Milwaukee, WI Marquette University High School; [P] Milwaukee, WI Arrupe House Jesuit Community.
Stang, Mark '90 (SCL) Long Prairie, MN St. Mary of Mt. Carmel Church.
Stang, William J. *c.pp.s.* '77 (LFT) [A] Rensselaer, IN Saint Joseph's College.
Stanganelli, Anthony M. '79 (RVC) Northport, NY St. Philip Neri Church.
Stange, Henry '90 (ALT) [3] Altoona, PA St. Mark's Church.
Stange, James '95 (P) [3] Eugene, OR St. Mary Church.
Stangel, Mark J. '65 (MIL) Retired.
Stanger, Edward J. '91 (STL) Oakville, MO Queen of All Saints Church.
Stanger, Harold B. '77 (CHI) [1] Oak Park, IL Ascension Church; [A] Chicago, IL Institute of Vocation Awareness.
Stangl, Alfred '63 (SCL) St. Cloud, MN U.S. Veteran's Hospital.
Stangl, Alfred '67 (SCL) Special Assignment.
Stangl, Frank J. '53 (JC) Retired.
Stangl, Frank J. '53 (R) Chapel Hill, NC St. Thomas More Church.
Stanibula, Christopher '95 (FR) North Dartmouth, MA St. Julie Billiart Church.
Stanichar, Joseph '68 (VNN) Seattle, WA St. John Chrysostom Church.
Stanievich, J. Walter '46 (DET) Retired.
Stanion, Robert *c.f.r.* '92 (NY) [DD] Yonkers, NY St. Felix Friary.
Staniskis, Daniel '84 (PSC) Flanders, NJ Holy Wisdom Church.
Staniszewski, Ignatius *s.s.p.* '64 (NY) [B] New York, NY Society of St. Paul.
Staniszewski, Jerome B. *o.f.m.* '48 (PIT) [O] Ben Avon, PA St. Anthony Friary and Mission House.
Staniszewski, Stanley *c.m.* '63 (HRT) [M] Manchester, CT DePaul Provincial Residence.
Staniszewski, Stanley *c.m.* '64 (BGP) [6] Stamford, CT Holy Name of Jesus Church.
Staniszewski, Stanley T. '74 (KAL) Hartford, MI Immaculate Conception Church.
Stankard, Albert H. '59 (BO) [4] Framingham, MA St. Stephen Church.
Stankavage, Joseph G. '90 (WDC) Laurel, MD St. Mary Church.
Stankiewicz, John A. *s.s.e.* '41 (BUR) [E] Colchester, VT Society of St. Edmund.
Stanko, Andrew (ALT) Johnstown, PA Lee Hospital.
Stanko, Andrew C. (ALT) Johnstown, PA Memorial Hospital.
Stanko, Andrew C. '71 (ALT) [3] Johnstown, PA Immaculate Conception Church; [11] Johnstown, PA St. Michael's Church; [D] Johnstown, PA Good Samaritan Medical Center.
Stanko, Edward '56 (PSC) Forest City, PA St. John the Baptist Church.
Stankus, Gregory A. '78 (BRK) [81] Brooklyn, NY St. Mary Mother of Jesus Church.
Stanley, Brian L. '96 (KAL) [4] Kalamazoo, MI St. Monica Church.
Stanley, Charles '71 (FgM) Society of St. James the Apostle.
Stanley, Charles R. '71 (BO) Society of St. James the Apostle.
Stanley, Colm *s.s.c.* '69 (OM) [K] St. Columbans, NE St. Columban's Foreign Mission Society.
Stanley, Matthew '91 (SJ) [1] Palo Alto, CA St. Thomas Aquinas Church.
Stanley, Melvin *o.f.m.* '52 (FgM) Franciscan Foreign Missions.
Stanley, Melvin *o.f.m.* '52 (OAK) [N] Oakland, CA Franciscan Friars.
Stanley, Michael H. *o.s.a.* '81 (FgM) Foreign Missions.
Stanley, Richard J. *s.j.* '74 (BGP) [A] Fairfield, CT Fairfield University; [O] Fairfield, CT The Fairfield Jesuit Community-Fairfield University; [V] Fairfield, CT Newman Centers - Campus Ministry.
Stanley, Ronald A. *o.p.* '67 (MET) [H] New Brunswick, NJ De Porres House; [M] New Brunswick, NJ Catholic Center at Rutgers University.
Stanley, Thomas J. *s.m.* '50 (CIN) [M] Dayton, OH Marianist Provincialate.
Stanley, William S. *m.m.* '92 (FgM) Maryknoll Foreign Missions.
Stano, Luke *o.s.m.* '61 (DET) [37] Detroit, MI St. John Berchmans-St. Juliana Church.
Stano, Luke M. *o.s.m.* '61 (CHI) [N] Chicago, IL Servite Friars - Eastern Province.
Stanonik, Anthony '82 (SD) Unassigned.
Stanosz, Paul A. '84 (MIL) [58] Milwaukee, WI Our Lady of Good Hope Church.
Stansberry, Richard '92 (OKL) Graduate Studies.
Stansley, Ralph W. '73 (TR) Hopewell, NJ St. Alphonsus Church.
Stanton, Finbarr P. '67 (SAV) Albany, GA St. Teresa Church.
Stanton, Francis M. '59 (COL) [34] Columbus, OH Our Lady of Peace Church.
Stanton, Joseph '51 (COL) Retired.
Stanton, Joseph F. *o.c.s.o.* '84 (ROC) [I] Piffard, NY Abbey of the Genesee.
Stanton, Terence *o.s.b.* '43 (RCK) [H] Aurora, IL Marmion Abbey-St. Augustine's Abbey.
Stanton, Thomas J. '92 (BO) [68] Boston, MA Sacred Heart Church.
Stanton, Msgr. William G. '49 (BUF) [6] Buffalo, NY St. Ambrose Church.
Stanton, William J. '52 (PH) Wyndmoor, PA Seven Dolors Church.
Stanton, Msgr. William J. '56 (SPC) Sikeston, MO St. Francis Xavier's Church.
Stapenhorst, Verne P. '61 (SC) [1] Sioux City, IA Cathedral of the Epiphany; [B] Sioux City, IA Bishop Heelan Catholic High School.
Staples, Terrence R. '95 (ARL) Fairfax, VA St. Mary of Sorrows Church.
Stapleton, Edward J. *s.s.s.* '60 (CLV) [P] Cleveland, OH Congregation of the Blessed Sacrament Provincial House; [P] Cleveland, OH Blessed Sacrament Community.
Stapleton, Gerard '85 (NO) [11] Metairie, LA St. Louis King of France Church.
Stapleton, James *c.s.p.* '74 (BRK) [239] Queens, NY Sacred Heart Church.
Starbuck, James (OAK) Military Chaplains.
Starc, Martin '30 (STO) San Andreas, CA St. Andrew Church.
Staricek, Andrew '40 (RC) Retired.
Stark, John W. '57 (DUB) Retired.
Stark, Paul V. *s.j.* (STL) [C] St. Louis, MO Saint Louis University.
Stark, Paul V. *s.j.* '85 (STL) [P] St. Louis, MO Jesuit Community Corporation at St. Louis University - Jesuit Hall.
Stark, Robert *s.s.s.* '77 (SFE) [23] Albuquerque, NM St. Charles Borromeo Church.
Stark, Ronald P. *o.f.m.* '66 (NY) [35] New York, NY St. Francis of Assisi Church.
Starkloff, Carl F. *s.j.* '65 (FgM) Provinces.
Starks, R. Mansfield '42 (ALB) Glenville, NY Immaculate Conception Church; Retired.
Starmann, Joseph W. '63 (JC) Absent on Leave.
Staron, Stanley R. '74 (HRT) [I] Waterbury, CT St. Mary Hospital.
Starostka, John C. '61 (OM) [15] Omaha, NE St. Francis Assisi Church.
Starus, Ralph E. '60 (CHI) [119] Chicago, IL St. Malachy Church.
Starzynski, Stefan P. '96 (ARL) Annandale, VA St. Michael's Church.
Stasell, Dean *l.c.* (ATL) [I] Dunwoody, GA Legionnaries of Christ.
Stash, Robert '82 (PRM) Bay City, MI Saint George Church; Omer, MI St. John Church.
Stashek, Leonard C. '56 (LC) Milan, WI St. Thomas Church; Wuerzburg, WI St. John the Baptist Church.
Stasiak, Kurt *o.s.b.* '80 (IND) [A] St. Meinrad, IN St. Meinrad Seminary; [J] St. Meinrad, IN St. Meinrad Archabbey.
Stasik, Thaddeus '60 (NEW) [5] Jersey City, NJ St. Ann's Church.
Stasiowski, John S. '65 (FWT) Bowie, TX St. Jerome Church; Henrietta, TX St. Mary Church; Montague, TX St. William Church; Nocona, TX St. Joseph Church.
Stasker, R. Louis '65 (GR) [19] Grand Rapids, MI St. Paul the Apostle Church.
Stasyszen, Lawrence R. *o.s.b.* '94 (OKL) [I] Shawnee, OK St. Gregory Abbey.
Staszak, Bernard C. '65 (BUF) French Creek, NY St. Matthias Church.
Staszak, David J. *o.p.* '55 (CHI) [N] Chicago, IL Dominicans (Provincial Office).
Staszewski, Joseph P. '64 (E) Brookville, PA Immaculate Conception Church.
Staszewski, Robert M. '72 (PIT) [1] Carnegie, PA St. Elizabeth Ann Seton Church.
Statkus, Edward '38 (GR) Retired.
Statkus, Msgr. Francis J. '46 (PH) Ardmore, PA St. Colman Church; Retired.
Statnick, Roger A. '73 (GBG) Derry, PA St. Joseph Church.
Statt, Thomas R. '58 (ROC) [40] Rochester, NY Our Mother of Sorrows Church.
Statz, James '84 (SCL) Brooten, MN St. Donatus Church; Padua, MN Church of St. Anthony of Padua.
Staub, Msgr. Edward F. '61 (BAL) Severna Park, MD St. John the Evangelist Church.
Staub, Eugene J. *c.ss.r.* '52 (BR) [H] Baton Rouge, LA Redemptorist Vice Province.
Stauber, James '59 (SB) On Leave.
Staublin, Daniel J. '82 (IND) Brownsburg, IN St. Malachy Church.
Staud, Paul R. '70 (PIT) Kennedy Township, PA St. Malachy Church.
Staud, Msgr. Sylvester W. '42 (WH) Retired.
Staudenmaier, John M. *s.j.* '70 (DET) [K] Detroit, MI Jesuit Community at the University of Detroit.
Staudenmaier, Wilbert '43 (GB) Retired.
Stauder, Paul W. '48 (BEL) Retired.
Stauder, William V. *s.j.* (STL) [C] St. Louis, MO Saint Louis University.
Stauder, William V. *s.j.* '52 (STL) [P] St. Louis, MO Jesuit Community Corporation at St. Louis University - Jesuit Hall.
Staudinger, Greg '81 (GF) Sidney, MT St. Matthew Church.
Staudt, Joseph W. '78 (RVC) Commack, NY Christ the King Church.
Staunton, Patrick J. '60 (LA) La Puente, CA St. Joseph Church.
Stauter, Andrew '57 (MOB) On Leave from the Archdiocese.
Stavinoha, Donald *o.m.i.* '70 (SAT) [K] San Antonio, TX Oblate Madonna Residence.

Stavoy, Stephen J. '79 (SCR) White Haven, PA St. Patrick's Church.
Stawasz, James '53 (HON) Retired.
Stawasz, John B. '53 (HON) Holualoa, HI St. Michael The Archangel Church.
Stawowy, Norbert *s.d.s.* '58 (GRY) [J] Merrillville, IN Salvatorian Fathers (Society of the Divine Savior).
Staysniak, Dale W. '75 (CLV) [1] Parma, OH St. Anthony of Padua Church.
Ste. Marie, Adrien *c.s.c.* '50 (P) [L] Portland, OR Holy Cross Fathers & Brothers, C.S.C. - University of Portland.
Stead, Julian *o.s.b.* '52 (PRO) [P] Portsmouth, RI Abbey of St. Gregory the Great.
Stead, Mell '56 (P) Lincoln City, OR St. Augustine Church.
Steakem, John J. '60 (FR) Somerset, MA St. Thomas More Church.
Stearns, John '53 (FAR) [E] Fargo, ND Riverview Place, Inc.
Stearns, Msgr. John D. '53 (CR) Retired.
Stearns, Joseph E. '63 (VEN) [4] Naples, FL St. William Church.
Steber, Michael '86 (MAR) Channing, MI St. Rose Church.
Stec, Emil *c.r.* '48 (CHI) [193] Chicago, IL St. Stanislaus Kostka Church.
Stec, John P. '94 (MET) [2] Perth Amboy, NJ St. Stephen Church.
Stec, Joseph C. '57 (PH) [53] Philadelphia, PA St. Hedwig Church; [A] Wynnewood, PA Theological Seminary of St. Charles Borromeo, Overbrook.
Stec, Mark D. '88 (BEL) Equality, IL St. Joseph Church.
Stec, Mark D.. '88 (BEL) Ridgway, IL St. Joseph Church.
Stec, Michael S. '94 (LIN) Syracuse, NE St. Paulinus Church.
Stec, Robert '88 (CLV) [A] Wickliffe, OH Borromeo Seminary.
Stecher, John E. '72 (DAV) [H] Iowa City, IA Newman Catholic Student Center; [M] Iowa City, IA O'Keefe Hall.
Stecher, Kenneth C. '68 (DUB) Dike, IA St. Mary Church; Parkersburg, IA St. Patrick's Church.
Steck, Christopher W. *s.j.* '94 (BGP) [O] Fairfield, CT The Fairfield Jesuit Community-Fairfield University.
Steckbauer, Linus J. '42 (GB) Retired.
Steckel, Gregory A. '81 (DAV) On Duty Outside the Diocese.
Stecklein, Warren L. '90 (DOD) Great Bend, KS St. Patrick Church.
Steckler, Gerard *s.j.* '57 (AUS) [H] Temple, TX Jesuit Fathers and Brothers.
Steckler, Gerard *s.j.* '57 (P) Waldport, OR St. Anthony Church.
Steckler, Kenneth '96 (EVN) Jasper, IN St. Joseph Church.
Steed, Donald R. *m.m.* '54 (NY) [DD] Maryknoll, NY Maryknoll Fathers and Brothers.
Steele, John *c.s.c.* '97 (FTW) [19] South Bend, IN St. Stephen Church.
Steele, John Arthur *c.s.c.* '97 (FTW) [5] South Bend, IN St. Casimir Church.
Steele, Joseph S. '97 (LIN) [6] Lincoln, NE St. John the Apostle Church.
Steele, Michael J. '77 (BO) Wakefield, MA St. Joseph Church.
Steele, Peter *s.j.* '70 (CHI) [C] Chicago, IL Jesuit Community at Loyola University of Chicago.
Steele, Philip G. *s.j.* '80 (DEN) [M] Aurora, CO Regis Jesuit High School - Jesuit Community.
Steele, Philip G. *s.j.* '80 (STL) [F] St. Louis, MO St. Louis University High School, George H. Backer Memorial; [P] St. Louis, MO St. Louis University High School Jesuit Community; [P] St. Louis, MO The Jesuits of the Missouri Province.
Steele, Steven G. '90 (MAD) [1] Madison, WI St. Raphael Cathedral; [12] Madison, WI St. Paul University Parish.
Steen, Charles A. *o.f.m.* '64 (FgM) Franciscan Foreign Missions.
Steen, Raymond (TR) Fort Dix, NJ Fort Dix.
Steenken, George W. *s.j.* '54 (CHI) [T] Barrington, IL Bellarmine Hall.
Stefan, Bonaventure *o.f.m.cap.* '56 (PIT) [O] Pittsburgh, PA St. Patrick Friary.
Stefanelli, Joseph *s.m.* (SJ) [M] Cupertino, CA Marianist Provincial Residence.
Stefaniak, James J. *m.m.* '50 (FgM) Maryknoll Foreign Missions.
Stefaniuk, Msgr. Dmytro '58 (PHU) Retired.
Stefanko, Paul F. '76 (PRT) Special or Other Diocesan Assignment.
Stefanotti, Robert (TR) Washington Crossing, NJ St. George Church.
Stefanski, Gary W. '79 (CHI) [6] Cicero, IL Our Lady of the Mount Church.
Stefanski, Jacek (CAM) [6] Camden, NJ St. Joseph's Church.
Stefanski, Walter '40 (CHI) [163] Chicago, IL St. Pancratius Church; Retired.
Steffan, Paul *o.f.m.cap.* '57 (NY) [DD] White Plains, NY St. Conrad Friary.
Steffen, Arnold *s.v.d.* '57 (FgM) Society of the Divine Word Foreign Missions.
Steffen, Carl J. '58 (HBG) Buchanan Valley, PA St. Ignatius Loyola Church.
Steffen, Francis J. '57 (MAD) [1] Madison, WI St. Raphael Cathedral; [K] Madison, WI Society of St. Vincent de Paul.
Steffen, Kenneth C. '84 (SFD) Riverton, IL St. James Church.
Steffens, Terrence J. '82 (GRY) Crown Point, IN St. Matthias Church.
Steffensmeier, Ralph J. '59 (OM) [18] Omaha, NE Holy Ghost Church.
Steffes, James D. *s.c.j.* '63 (GAL) [56] Houston, TX Our Lady of Guadalupe Church.
Steffes, James P. '93 (WIN) [A] Winona, MN Immaculate Heart of Mary Seminary.
Steffes, Joseph X. *c.ss.r.* '40 (LAF) Crowley, LA Immaculate Heart of Mary Church.
Steffes, LuVerne W. '95 (OM) [37] Omaha, NE St. Philip Neri Church.
Steffes, Marvin J. *c.pp.s.* '58 (MRY) Los Gatos, CA Christ Child Church.
Steffes, Raymond *o.s.c.* '58 (SCL) Vineland, MN St. Therese, Little Flower Indian Mission Church.
Steffes, Raymond A. *o.s.c.* '58 (SCL) [I] Onamia, MN Crosier Monastery.
Steffey, John M. '53 (KAL) Parchment, MI St. Ambrose Church.
Steffy, David *l.c.* '94 (MAN) [A] Center Harbor, NH Immaculate Conception Apostolic School.
Stefula, Salvator *t.o.r.* '74 (FWT) [16] Fort Worth, TX St. Thomas Church.
Stefun, Bonaventure *o.f.m.cap.* '56 (PIT) Allegheny County, PA St. Francis Medical Center; [J] Pittsburgh, PA St. Francis Medical Center.
Steger, Francis R. *o.c.s.o.* '56 (ROC) [I] Piffard, NY Abbey of the Genesee.
Steger, John J. '51 (ROC) [32] Rochester, NY St. Jude the Apostle Church.
Steggert, Bruce A. *s.j.* '93 (WDC) [E] Washington, DC Gonzaga College High School.
Stegman, Leonard F. '40 (ELP) Retired.
Stegman, Thomas D. *s.j.* '95 (MIL) [P] Milwaukee, WI Jesuit Provincial Office, Wisconsin Province.
Stegman, Vincent G. *c.s.sp.* '62 (FgM) Holy Ghost Foreign Missions.
Stegmann, Msgr. Raymond V. '50 (RVC) Retired.
Stegmann, Robert (GB) Kimberly, WI Holy Name of Jesus Church.
Stehling, Larry '88 (AUS) [1] Austin, TX St. Mary's Cathedral.
Stehling, Lawrence J. '88 (AUS) [F] Austin, TX Seton Medical Center.
Stehly, Dennis '77 (STL) Mehlville, MO St. Margaret Mary Alacoque Church.
Stehly, James '85 (LA) [A] Camarillo, CA St. John's Seminary College of the Archdiocese of Los Angeles.
Stehly, Mark '66 (SEA) Special Assignment; [Q] Seattle, WA Catholic Hospital Ministries.
Stehly, Thomas J. '61 (LA) Retired.
Stehr, James P. *s.j.* '75 (NY) [DD] New York, NY "America;" Residence and publication office of the America Press.
Steibel, Gary R. '63 (MIA) Hallandale, FL St. Charles Borromeo Church.
Steichen, John A. '54 (OKL) Union City, OK St. Joseph's Church.
Steidle, Mark '93 (COV) [3] Covington, KY St. Ann Church.
Steier, Charles '73 (SAL) Russell, KS St. Mary's Church.
Steiger, Richard A. '67 (PAT) Andover, NJ Good Shepherd Church.
Steigmeyer, Bob *c.s.c.* '47 (FTW) [19] South Bend, IN St. Stephen Church.
Steigmeyer, Robert C. *c.s.c.* '47 (FTW) [5] South Bend, IN St. Casimir Church.
Steik, Dennis *s.m.* '69 (MRY) [G] Santa Cruz, CA Society of Mary, Marists; [J] Monterey, CA Department of Campus Ministry.
Steimel, Craig E. '89 (DUB) Buffalo Center, IA St. Patrick's Church; Forest City, IA St. James Church; Lake Mills, IA St. Patrick Church.
Steimel, Msgr. Paul T. '52 (DUB) Retired.
Stein, Benjamin *o.s.b.* '36 (SCL) [I] Collegeville, MN St. John's Abbey, of the Order of St. Benedict.
Stein, C. William *c.m.* '39 (STL) [P] Perryville, MO Congregation of The Mission.
Stein, E. John *o.f.m.* '85 (CIN) [26] Cincinnati, OH St. Francis Seraph Church.
Stein, James *o.praem.* '86 (CHI) [N] Chicago, IL Premonstratensian Fathers and Brothers (Norbertines).
Stein, Jerry '66 (AMA) Happy, TX Holy Name of Jesus Church; Nazareth, TX Holy Family Church.
Stein, John *o.f.m.* '85 (CIN) [M] Cincinnati, OH St. Francis Seraph Friary.
Stein, Norbert W. *s.s.j.* '61 (LAF) Cecilia, LA St. Rose of Lima Church.
Stein, Robert E. '81 (CLV) [14] Akron, OH St. Paul Church.
Stein, Timothy P. '84 (ALT) Chest Springs, PA St. Monica's Church.
Steinauer, Carl J. '76 (SAC) Absent on Leave.
Steinbacher, Will *glmy.* '62 (CIN) [M] Fairfield, OH Headquarters of Glenmary Home Missioners.
Steinbauer, Joseph '79 (TOL) Rossford, OH All Saints Church.
Steinbeisser, Joseph A. '86 (NU) Willmar, MN St. Mary Church.
Steinberger, Edward J. '45 (WCH) Caney, KS Sacred Heart Church; Moline, KS St. Mary's Church; Sedan, KS St. Robert Bellarmine Church.
Steinbicker, Carl R. '34 (CIN) Retired.
Steinbock, Leo E. '54 (LA) [73] Los Angeles, CA St. Kevin Church.
Steinbrunner, Jerome *c.pp.s.* '74 (CLV) [2] Cleveland, OH St. Adalbert Church.
Steinbugler, Thomas B. *s.j.* '61 (FgM) Provinces.
Steiner, Bernard J. '61 (NU) Lamberton, MN St. Joseph Church; Sanborn, MN St. Thomas Church; Wanda, MN St. Mathias Church.
Steiner, Msgr. Carl E. '55 (GB) Oconto Falls, WI St. Anthony Church; Stiles, WI St. Patrick Church.
Steiner, Msgr. Clarence J. '44 (STP) [8] St. Paul, MN The Nativity of Our Lord Church; Retired.
Steiner, Daniel R. '79 (CHI) Other Assignments.
Steiner, Edward F., III '82 (NSH) Madison, TN St. Joseph's Church.
Steiner, Msgr. John M. '69 (SPK) [19] Spokane, WA St. Thomas More Church.
Steiner, John W. '74 (LC) [3] Eau Claire, WI Sacred Heart of Jesus Church; [6] Eau Claire, WI St. Patrick Church.
Steiner, Kenneth '62 (P) [Q] Portland, OR Oregon Catholic Conference.
Steiner, Luke *o.s.b.* '56 (SCL) [I] Collegeville, MN St. John's Abbey, of the Order of St. Benedict.
Steiner, William *c.ss.r.* '54 (FgM) Redemptorist Foreign Missions.
Steingraeber, John *c.ss.r.* '74 (DEN) [M] Denver, CO The Redemptorists/Denver Province.
Steingreaber, Paul *o.s.b.* '65 (KCK) [H] Atchison, KS St. Benedict's Abbey.
Steinhauser, Kenneth B. '70 (BRK) Released from Diocesan Assignment.
Steinhauser, Michael G. '67 (BRK) Released from Diocesan Assignment.
Steinhauser, Raymond W. '54 (COV) Retired.
Steinhilber, Richard *s.s.c.* '51 (OM) [K] St. Columbans, NE St. Columban's Foreign Mission Society.
Steinhoff, Henry '67 (B) Retired.
Steinhoff, Henry '67 (HEL) Eureka, MT Our Lady of Mercy Church.
Steinkirchner, Edward E. '49 (ROC) Penfield, NY St. Joseph Church; Retired.
Steinle, David '79 (DAV) Blue Grass, IA St. Andrew Church.
Steinle, David G. '79 (DAV) [4] Davenport, IA St. Alphonsus Church.
Steinle, James '53 (TOL) Retired.
Steinman, Robert E. *o.s.a.* '50 (PH) [AA] Villanova, PA St. Thomas Monastery.
Steinmetz, Paul B. *s.j.* '59 (MIL) [P] Milwaukee, WI Jesuit Provincial Office, Wisconsin Province.
Steinmetz, Paul B. *s.j.* '59 (OAK) Orinda, CA Santa Maria Church.
Steinmetz, Ricardo *s.j.* '55 (FgM) Provinces.
Steinmiller, G. Alexander *c.p.* '70 (SAT) [M] San Antonio, TX Casa Pasionista Guadalupe.
Stella, Livio *c.s.* '75 (CHI) [N] Oak Park, IL Missionaries of Saint Charles.
Stella, Livio *c.s.* '75 (LA) Sun Valley, CA Our Lady of the Holy Rosary Church.
Stella, Thomas A. *c.s.c.* '72 (COS) [E] Cascade, CO Holy Cross Novitiate.
Stella, Tom '72 (COS) [B] Colorado Springs, CO Centura Health-Penrose-St. Francis Health Services.
Steller, Paul W. (BUF) [A] East Aurora, NY Christ the King Seminary.
Steller, Paul W. *episcopal* '65 (BUF) [R] Williamsville, NY Campus Ministry.
Stelling, William F. '64 (MEM) [15] Memphis, TN St. Joseph's Church.
Stelmach, Jerome J. '80 (BUF) Limestone, NY St. Patrick Church; Olean, NY Transfiguration Church.
Stelmach, Michael '70 (STN) Minneapolis, MN St. Constantine Church.
Stelten, Leo F. '50 (FAR) Retired.
Steltenkamp, Michael F. *s.j.* (DET) [K] Detroit, MI Jesuit Provincial Office-Detroit Province of the Society of Jesus.
Steltenkamp, Michael F. *s.j.* '76 (WH) [A] Wheeling, WV Wheeling Jesuit University.
Stelter, Richard T. '80 (RVC) Amityville, NY St. Martin's Church.
Stelzer, Mark (SPR) Indian Creek, MA St. Jude Church.

Stelzer, Mark S. '83 (SPR) [12] Springfield, MA Sacred Heart Church.
Stelzner, Barnabas W. *o.s.b.* '88 (PBL) [F] Canon City, CO Holy Cross Abbey.
Stemac, Msgr. Louis V. '42 (LR) Retired; [H] Little Rock, AR St. John Manor.
Stembler, James G. '89 (CC) Alice, TX St. Elizabeth Church.
Stempora, Daniel F. '60 (JOL) Oswego, IL St. Anne Church.
Stempsey, William E. *s.j.* '92 (WOR) [N] Worcester, MA Jesuits of Holy Cross College, Inc.
Stencil, Rallen H. '63 (GB) Hilbert, WI St. Mary Church.
Stencil, Steven G. '81 (TUC) Casa Grande, AZ St. Anthony Church; [I] Casa Grande, AZ Central Arizona College, Holy Family Newman Center.
Stengel, Msgr. Charles G. '56 (NEW) [12] Jersey City, NJ St. John the Baptist Church.
Stengel, Mark '72 (LR) [A] Subiaco, AR Subiaco Monastery.
Stengel, Michael J. *c.p.* '57 (CHI) [N] Chicago, IL Immaculate Conception Monastery.
Stengel, Michael Joseph *c.p.* '57 (CHI) [N] Chicago, IL Passionist Provincial Office.
Stengel, Michael Joseph *c.p.* '57 (FgM) Mission Procurators.
Stengel, Msgr. Paul F. '59 (BUF) Boston, NY St. John the Baptist Church.
Stengel, William J. '57 (GB) [F] Green Bay, WI St. Vincent Hospital.
Stenger, Msgr. Frederick R. '28 (JOL) Retired.
Stenger, James R. '81 (CLV) [4] Parma, OH St. Columbkille Church.
Stenger, Joseph *c.ss.r.* '57 (FgM) Redemptorist Foreign Missions.
Stenger, William J., Sr. '94 (WH) Glen Dale, WV St. Jude Church.
Stenson, Brian '74 (LAV) [5] Las Vegas, NV Prince of Peace Church.
Stenson, James F. '51 (Y) Streetsboro, OH St. Joan of Arc Church; Retired.
Stenson, Patrick *m.s.c.* '63 (SAT) [M] San Antonio, TX Missionaries of the Sacred Heart.
Stenzel, Duane R. *o.f.m.* '54 (HT) [C] Schriever, LA Lumen Christi Retreat Center.
Stenzel, Eugene F. '67 (WIN) Wells, MN St. Casimir's Church.
Stenzel, William J. '75 (CHI) La Grange, IL St. Francis Xavier Church.
Stepanich, Martin *o.f.m.* '41 (CHI) [N] Lemont, IL The Slovene Franciscan Fathers, Order of Friars Minor, Commissariat of the Holy Cross.
Stepanski, Thomas *s.t.* '62 (IND) [24] Indianapolis, IN St. Lawrence Church.
Stepek, Robert A. '81 (CHI) Homewood, IL St. Joseph Church.
Stephan, George *s.v.d.* '35 (LA) [71] Los Angeles, CA St. John, The Evangelist Church.
Stephan, George J. '62 (BUF) [25] Buffalo, NY St. Francis Xavier Church; [37] Buffalo, NY St. John the Baptist Church.
Stephan, Matthew J. '83 (CC) Falfurrias, TX Sacred Heart Church.
Stephen, John *c.r.* '38 (CHI) [D] Chicago, IL Gordon Technical High School.
Stephens, Gerald '63 (FWT) Retired.
Stephens, Rod '74 (ORG) Placentia, CA St. Joseph Church.
Stephenson, Alphonse J. '75 (PAT) On Duty Outside the Diocese.
Stephenson, Lloyd '80 (RIC) [4] Newport News, VA St. Vincent de Paul Church.
Stephenson, Lloyd F. '80 (RIC) Hampton, VA VA Medical Center.
Stephenson, Patrick '68 (SR) American Canyon, CA Holy Family Church.
Stephenson, Robert B. (SY) [H] Syracuse, NY Bishop Joseph T. O'Keefe, Inc.
Stephenson, Robert B. '78 (SY) [18] Syracuse, NY St. John the Evangelist Church; [H] Syracuse, NY Catholic Charities of the Roman Catholic Diocese of Syracuse.
Stepien, Allen F. '65 (PAT) Long Valley, NJ St. Mark the Evangelist Church.
Steriti, Edward *o.c.s.o.* '57 (WOR) [N] Spencer, MA St. Joseph's Abbey.
Sterk, Francis R. '65 (CLV) [1] Euclid, OH St. Christine Church.
Sterker, Msgr. Louis F. '46 (CHR) Retired.
Sterling, Donald A. '74 (BAL) [4] Baltimore, MD The New All Saints Church.
Sterling, John J. '96 (COV) [2] Covington, KY St. Agnes Church; [B] Covington, KY Covington Catholic High School.
Sterling, John K. '94 (DAV) Burlington, IA St. Patrick's Church; Dodgeville, IA St. Mary's Church; West Burlington, IA St. Mary's Church.
Stern, Jean *m.s.* '64 (STL) [P] St. Louis, MO La Salette Missionaries.
Stern, Jerome F. '63 (LEX) London, KY St. William/St. Sylvester Church.
Stern, Msgr. Robert L. '58 (NY) [HH] New York, NY Catholic Near East Welfare Association.
Sternemann, Richard *o.s.b.* '68 (FWT) Gainesville, TX St. Mary Church.
Sterner, James M. '70 (HBG) Littlestown, PA St. Aloysius Church.
Sterowski, Scott P. '91 (SCR) Olyphant, PA St. Patrick's Church; [D] Dunmore, PA Bishop O'Hara High School.
Sterrett, Brad '85 (SAL) Leave of Absence.
Stessman, Msgr. Gerald J. '59 (DM) [4] Des Moines, IA Holy Trinity Church.
Stets, Ihor '85 (STF) Johnson City, NY Sacred Heart Ukrainian Catholic Church.
Stetson, William H. '62 (CHI) [W] Chicago, IL Opus Dei.
Stetz, Allan '66 (DM) Chariton, IA Sacred Heart Church.
Stetz, Mark '90 (MRY) Los Osos, CA St. Elizabeth Ann Seton Church.
Steuer, James '63 (ALB) Mohawk, NY Blessed Sacrament Church.
Steuernol, E. Slider '96 (P) Gresham, OR St. Henry Church.
Steuterman, James M. '75 (WOR) North Oxford, MA St. Ann's Church.
Stevens, Clifford J. '56 (OM) Retired.
Stevens, Michael J. '80 (STP) [11] St. Paul, MN St. Adalbert Church; Special Assignment.
Stevensky, Msgr. John '63 (SJP) Miami, FL Assumption of B.V.M. Church.
Stevenson, Alden J. *s.j.* '46 (SFR) [N] San Francisco, CA Jesuit Community at University of San Francisco.
Stevenson, Anthony '81 (OWN) Bardwell, KY St. Charles Church; Fancy Farm, KY St. Denis Church.
Stevenson, Dennis E. *j.c.l.* '88 (COL) [4] Columbus, OH St. Aloysius Church.
Stevenson, Francis R. (SAC) Military Chaplains.
Stevenson, Msgr. Frederick J. '42 (PH) Wallingford, PA St. John Chrysostom Church; Retired.
Stevenson, William J. '82 (LAN) Saline, MI St. Andrew Church.
Stevenson, William P. '86 (SD) Santa Ysabel, CA Santa Ysabel Indian Mission Church.
Stevko, Victor *s.v.d.* '57 (FgM) Society of the Divine Word Foreign Missions.
Stewart, August '94 (COS) Castle Rock, CO St. Francis of Assisi Church.
Stewart, Columba *o.s.b.* '90 (SCL) [I] Collegeville, MN St. John's Abbey, of the Order of St. Benedict.
Stewart, Edward R. '89 (BRK) [36] Brooklyn, NY St. Ephrem's Church.
Stewart, George '94 (NY) Pearl River, NY St. Margaret Church.
Stewart, Msgr. George N. '35 (DOD) Retired.
Stewart, J. Keith '93 (MEM) Jackson, TN St. Mary's Church.
Stewart, J. Patrick *s.j.* '61 (SPK) [C] Spokane, WA Gonzaga University.
Stewart, James *o.f.m.cap.* (NY) Valhalla, NY Westchester County Medical Center.
Stewart, James *o.f.m.cap.* '85 (NY) [DD] White Plains, NY St. Conrad Friary.
Stewart, Jonathan '91 (IND) Enochsburg, IN St. John the Evangelist Church; Hamburg, IN St. Anne Church; St. Maurice, IN St. Maurice Church.
Stewart, Kenneth C. *o.f.m.cap.* '67 (DET) [65] Detroit, MI Presentation-Our Lady of Victory Church.
Stewart, Michael L. '75 (MEM) [6] Memphis, TN St. Brigid Church.
Stewart, Patrick F. '78 (LEX) Somerset, KY St. Mildred Church.
Stewart, Paul (BLX) Biloxi, MS Keesler Airforce Base.
Stewart, Robert *o.f.m.* (BUF) [C] St. Bonaventure, NY St. Bonaventure University.
Stewart, Robert *o.f.m.* '80 (BUF) [O] St. Bonaventure, NY St. Bonaventure Friary.
Stewart, Robert H. '82 (KC) [16] Kansas City, MO Holy Family Church.
Stewart, Msgr. Terrence L. '70 (GR) Marne, MI St. Mary's Church; On Special Assignment.
Sthokal, Edward S. *s.j.* '54 (STP) [Q] Lake Elmo, MN Jesuit Retreat House.
Sticco, Peter *s.a.c.* (BRK) [110] Brooklyn, NY Our Lady of the Rosary of Pompeii Church.
Sticco, Peter T. *s.a.c.* (BRK) [Y] Brooklyn, NY Bay Webster Corporation, Inc.
Sticco, Peter T. *s.a.c.* '69 (BAL) [M] Baltimore, MD Pallottine Center for Apostolic Causes.
Stickle, William '50 (RIC) Retired.
Stieferman, Lowell L. '63 (OKL) [6] Oklahoma City, OK Church of the Epiphany of the Lord.
Stiefvater, Robert X. '77 (MIL) Special Assignment.
Stiegeler, A. Francis *s.j.* '78 (SAC) [C] Sacramento, CA Jesuit High School; [G] Carmichael, CA Jesuit High School Community of Sacramento.
Stieger, Msgr. Joseph '50 (MRY) Retired.
Stier, Timothy '79 (OAK) [1] Fremont, CA Corpus Christi Church.
Stika, Msgr. Richard F. '85 (STL) Special Assignment.
Stikel, Roman S. '88 (MIL) [69] Milwaukee, WI St. Robert Church.
Stiles, J. Roy '63 (L) [42] Louisville, KY St. John Vianney Church; Fairdale, KY St. Jerome Church.
Stiles, Wallis '61 (SAT) D'Hanis, TX Holy Cross Church.
Stiller, Ludwig F. *s.j.* '62 (FgM) Provinces.
Stillmock, Martin *c.ss.r.* '58 (STP) Brooklyn Center, MN St. Alphonsus Church.
Stillmunks, Steven J. '77 (OM) Papillion, NE St. Columbkille Church.
Stillwell, Msgr. William J. '67 (BUF) [7] Niagara Falls, NY St. Mary of the Cataract Church.
Stilwell, Dennis R. '71 (GAY) Cheboygan, MI St. Mary-St. Charles Church.
Stimiman, Jeffrey '95 (PEO) [B] Rock Island, IL Alleman High School.
Stine, Jerome E. '48 (DET) Retired.
Stine, Robert F. '73 (BR) St. Amant, LA Holy Rosary Church.
Stinebrickner, Msgr. David W. '63 (OG) Retired.
Stineman, William F. '49 (IND) Retired.
Stingel, Louis F. '60 (MET) Jamesburg, NJ St. James the Less Church.
Stingle, Lawrence A. '41 (GB) Retired.
Stinson, James G. *s.j.* '94 (BO) [W] Boston, MA The Society of Jesus of New England-Provincial Offices.
Stipe, Jack H. '61 (P) Retired.
Stirniman, Jeffrey '95 (PEO) [4] Rock Island, IL St. Pius X Church.
Stirpe, Carlo (SY) Fulton, NY Immaculate Conception Church.
Stislow, Louis *o.f.m.* '61 (PH) [D] Philadelphia, PA Archbishop Ryan High School; [AA] Philadelphia, PA St. Pius X Friary.
Stites, John F. (TOL) [B] Oregon, OH Cardinal Stritch High School.
Stitz, John '53 (KCK) Retired.
Stivason, Paul R. '89 (GBG) Indiana, PA St. Bernard Church.
Stluka, Jerome D. '69 (COL) [11] Columbus, OH St. Christopher Church.
Stobba, Joseph G. *o.s.a.* '59 (MIL) [12] Racine, WI St. Rita Church.
Stober, William P. '73 (PAT) Branchville, NJ Our Lady Queen of Peace Church.
Stobie, Stephen (P) [K] Portland, OR Mt. St. Joseph Residence and Extended Care Center.
Stochl, John J. *s.j.* '54 (FgM) Provinces.
Stochmal, Marek P. '95 (DET) Lincoln Park, MI Christ the Good Shepherd Church.
Stock, Augustine *o.s.b.* '48 (KC) [J] Conception, MO Conception Abbey.
Stockelman, William R. '78 (CIN) Batavia, OH Holy Trinity Church; Williamsburg, OH St. Ann Church.
Stocker, Bede *o.s.b.* '42 (RCK) [H] Aurora, IL Marmion Abbey-St. Augustine's Abbey.
Stocker, Thomas '63 (GB) Absent on Leave.
Stockert, Donfred H. '58 (RIC) Retired.
Stockert, Harold '63 (PSC) Granville, NY SS. Peter and Paul Church.
Stockhausen, Gerard L. *s.j.* '79 (OM) [K] Omaha, NE Jesuit Community At Creighton University.
Stockhausen, Paul G. *s.j.* '40 (MIL) [P] Wauwatosa, WI Jesuit Community at St. Camillus.
Stocking, Joseph R. *s.j.* '67 (SEA) [23] Seattle, WA Christ the King Church; [A] Seattle, WA Seattle University.
Stockinger, Tony '63 (JOL) Retired.
Stockinger, Tony A. '63 (JOL) Winfield, IL St. John the Baptist Church.
Stocklosa, J. Walter '40 (BO) Retired.
Stockman, Gerald '64 (JC) On Duty Outside the Diocese.
Stockmeyer, Basil *c.p.* '40 (BAL) [11] Baltimore, MD Ascension Church.
Stockmeyer, Basil *c.p.* '42 (BAL) [M] Baltimore, MD St. Joseph's Passionist Community.
Stockus, Edward S. '91 (CHI) [3] Oak Lawn, IL St. Germaine Church.
Stockwell, C. Robert '53 (LAN) Retired.
Stodola, Francis '89 (CC) [8] Laredo, TX Santa Margarita De Escocia Independent Mission Church.
Stoeckig, Robert '94 (LAV) [2] Las Vegas, NV Christ the King Church.
Stoegbauer, Carlton C. '82 (CAM) [6] Cherry Hill, NJ Queen of Heaven Church.
Stoeger, James A. *s.j.* '74 (CHI) [C] Chicago, IL Jesuit Community at Loyola University of Chicago.
Stoeger, James A. *s.j.* '75 (CHI) [N] Chicago, IL Chicago Province of the Society of Jesus-Provincial Office.
Stoeger, John '72 (LA) [A] Camarillo, CA St. John's Seminary.
Stoeger, John D. '72 (LA) [A] Camarillo, CA St. John's Seminary.
Stoeger, William R. *s.j.* '72 (TUC) [F] Tucson, AZ Jesuit Community of the Vatican Observatory.
Stoerlein, Msgr. Joseph G. '49 (CAM) [2] Vineland, NJ Sacred Heart Church.
Stoetzel, Charles D. '80 (LC) Marshfield, WI St. John

the Baptist Church; Spencer, WI Christ the King Church.
Stofcik, John A. '40 (GBG) Retired.
Stoffel, Msgr. Jerome C. '36 (SLC) Retired.
Stoffel, Richard J. '79 (MIL) [7] Racine, WI St. Joseph Church.
Stoffer, Patrick *o.f.m.conv.* '97 (PEO) [2] Peoria, IL Holy Family Church.
Stofft, Kenneth '75 (RIC) [3] Richmond, VA Holy Rosary Church; Special Assignment.
Stoga, Stanley C. '30 (CHI) Retired.
Stohrer, Walter J. *s.j.* '60 (MIL) [P] Milwaukee, WI Jesuit Community at Marquette University.
Stokes, David *s.j.* '63 (RIC) [5] Richmond, VA Sacred Heart Church.
Stokes, Edward J. *s.j.* '51 (BEL) [1] Belleville, IL Cathedral of St. Peter.
Stokes, Thomas A. *s.m.* '63 (SP) [7] Tampa, FL Our Lady of Perpetual Help Church.
Stoklie, Eugene J. '60 (BRK) [83] Brooklyn, NY Mary Queen of Heaven Church.
Stokowski, Lucjan '77 (CLV) [2] Garfield Heights, OH SS. Peter and Paul Church.
Stolcis, Ronald A. '68 (CHY) Worland, WY St. Mary Magdalen Church.
Stoley, Lawrence J. '91 (LIN) Rulo, NE Immaculate Conception Church; [C] Falls City, NE Sacred Heart School.
Stolinksi, Dennis R. '69 (OM) Bellevue, NE St. Matthew The Evangelist Church of Bellevue.
Stolinski, Robert A. (BUF) [62] Buffalo, NY St. Stephen Church.
Stolinski, Robert A. '70 (BUF) Buffalo, NY Erie County Medical Center.
Stoll, Eugene '30 (CHI) [B] Techny, IL Divine Word Residence.
Stoll, Jerome L. '59 (MIL) Special Assignment.
Stoll, Kenneth *s.c.j.* '45 (JKS) [E] Nesbit, MS St. Michael Community House.
Stoll, Mark J. '92 (SC) Neptune, IA St. Joseph Church.
Stollenwerk, Charles J. '73 (CLV) North Olmsted, OH St. Richard Church.
Stolowski, Stephen '79 (NSH) [I] Nashville, TN Mercy Convent.
Stoltz, John J. '90 (L) Edmonton, KY Christ the Healer Church.
Stoltz, Joseph H. '73 (L) Louisville, KY Caritas Medical Center; [H] Louisville, KY Caritas Medical Center.
Stoltz, Richard L. '74 (STL) Richmond Heights, MO St. Luke the Evangelist Church.
Stolz, Paul L. '61 (CIN) [75] Cincinnati, OH Sts. Peter and Paul Church.
Stolz, William K. *s.j.* '62 (SAC) [C] Sacramento, CA Jesuit High School; [G] Carmichael, CA Jesuit High School Community of Sacramento.
Stolze, Edward B. '72 (CIN) [54] Cincinnati, OH St. Louis Church.
Stolzman, William F. '71 (STP) Shakopee, MN St. Mark Church.
Stommel, Russel J. '67 (MIL) Neosho, WI St. Matthew Church; Woodland, WI St. Mary Church.
Stommel, Russell J. '67 (MIL) Rubicon, WI St. John Church.
Stone, Carl '42 (ALB) Retired.
Stone, Colm *o.c.d.* '62 (SEA) Stanwood, WA St. Cecilia's Church.
Stone, Harold *s.t.* '59 (FgM) Trinity Missions.
Stone, Michael J. '68 (ALN) Schuylkill Haven, PA St. Ambrose Church.
Stone, Robert *c.m.* '77 (BIR) Ashland, AL St. Mark's Catholic Community Church.
Stone, Robert '90 (KC) Montrose, MO Immaculate Conception Church.
Stone, Robert J. *c.m.* '77 (BIR) Alexander City, AL St. John the Apostle Church.
Stone, Stanley R. '60 (SC) Special Assignment.
Stone, Theodore '52 (CHI) Park Ridge, IL Mary, Seat of Wisdom Church.
Stone, Msgr. William S. '43 (BAK) Retired.
Stoneberg, Jeff '90 (JOL) Glen Ellyn, IL St. James the Apostle Church.
Stonebridge, John '38 (BRK) [R] Queens Village, NY Queen of Peace Residence.
Stonebridge, John H. '38 (BRK) Retired.
Stoner, John Bosco *o.s.b.* '76 (LA) [R] Valyermo, CA St. Andrew's Abbey.
Stoner, Timothy L. '96 (GI) Alliance, NE Holy Rosary Church.
Stonich, Raymond '56 (JOL) Addison, IL St. Philip The Apostle Church.
Stookey, Gerald L. *o.p.* '78 (CHI) [N] Chicago, IL Dominicans (Provincial Office).
Stopponi, John (DET) [32] Detroit, MI Holy Family Church.
Stopponi, John *o.s.b.* '38 (DET) [K] Detroit, MI St. Sylvester Monastery.
Stopyra, David M. *o.f.m.conv.* '60 (FR) [1] Taunton, MA Our Lady of the Holy Rosary Church.
Storan, William P. '61 (SAC) Vallejo, CA St. Basil Church.
Storch, Richard F. *s.a.c.* '45 (MIL) [P] Milwaukee, WI Pallotti House.
Storck, Edward J. '52 (WIL) Nursing Homes.
Storey, Finan *c.p.* '39 (CHI) [N] Chicago, IL Immaculate Conception Monastery; [N] Chicago, IL Daneo Hall.
Storey, John R. '47 (CLV) Retired.
Stormes, James R. *s.j.* '79 (BAL) [M] Baltimore, MD Jesuit Fathers and Brothers Maryland Provincial Curia; [M] Baltimore, MD Ferdinand Wheeler Jesuit Community.
Stormes, James R. *s.j.* '79 (FgM) Provinces.
Storms, Francis *o.f.m.* (BUF) [C] St. Bonaventure, NY St. Bonaventure University.
Storms, Francis *o.f.m.* '75 (BUF) [C] St. Bonaventure, NY St. Bonaventure University; [O] St. Bonaventure, NY St. Bonaventure Friary.
Storms, Louis B. *c.m.* '40 (BAL) Emmitsburg, MD St. Joseph Church.
Storms, Louis B. *c.m.* '45 (BAL) [M] Emmitsburg, MD Vincentian House.
Stortz, Donald '64 (OM) [1] Omaha, NE St. Cecilia's Cathedral.
Stortz, Mario '49 (AMA) Retired.
Stotenbur, David M.. '68 (LAN) East Lansing, MI St. Thomas Aquinas Church.
Stott, Thomas D. '83 (CHL) Mt. Airy, NC Holy Angels Church.
Stout, O. Hugh '61 (CAM) On Duty Outside the Diocese.
Stout, O. Hugh '61 (NO) [7] New Orleans, LA Holy Ghost Church.
Stout, Richard E. *c.s.c.* '71 (FgM) Holy Cross Foreign Missions.
Stout, Thomas '77 (BEL) Red Bud, IL St. John the Baptist Church.
Stouvenel, Gerald E. '72 (DAV) Burlington, IA St. Patrick's Church; Dodgeville, IA St. Mary's Church; West Burlington, IA St. Mary's Church.
Stoviak, Leonard W. '73 (GBG) [4] Greensburg, PA St. Paul Church.
Stovik, Raphael *o.s.b.* '56 (BIS) [A] Richardton, ND Assumption Abbey.
Stowe, John *o.f.m.conv.* '95 (ELP) [17] El Paso, TX Our Lady of Mt. Carmel Church.
Stowell, Jerome G. *c.p.* '40 (CHI) [N] Chicago, IL Passionist Provincial Office.
Stowell, Jerome G. *c.p.* '40 (STL) [K] Lake St. Louis, MO St. Joseph Hospital West.
Stoyle, James (FTW) Lakeville, IN Sacred Heart Church.
Stoyle, James '91 (FTW) [13] South Bend, IN St. Jude Church.
Strachota, Dennis '67 (BAK) Pendleton, OR St. Mary's Church.
Strachota, Michael D. '79 (MIL) [20] Milwaukee, WI Corpus Christi Church.
Strader, Kenneth '84 (Y) Absent on Leave.
Strader, Mark '91 (LA) Santa Monica, CA St. Clement Church; [D] Playa Del Rey, CA St. Bernard High School.
Stradinger, Stephen J. '74 (MIL) Fontana, WI St. Benedict Church.
Strafalace, Francis *s.c.j.* '65 (GAL) [56] Houston, TX Our Lady of Guadalupe Church.
Stragisher, Raphael *o.f.m.* '39 (ALT) [18] Johnstown, PA St. Therese of the Child Jesus Church.
Strahan, Francis V. '59 (BO) [1] Framingham, MA St. Bridget Church.
Strahl, Ernest '45 (IND) Retired.
Strain, Eugene '53 (DET) Rochester Hills, MI St. Mary's of the Hills Church.
Straka, Francis P. '90 (ALN) Hellertown, PA St. Theresa of the Child Jesus Church.
Straley, Michael '83 (PHX) [12] Phoenix, AZ St. Gregory Church; Special Assignment.
Stram, Msgr. Gideon '38 (AUS) Retired.
Strancar, Ignatius '32 (SB) Retired.
Strand, Msgr. Edward (TR) Retired.
Strand, Ralph S. '64 (CHI) Other Assignments.
Strange, J. Michael *s.s.* '65 (BAL) [M] Baltimore, MD Sulpician Provincial House.
Strano, Antonio *o.m.i.* '51 (SAT) [K] San Antonio, TX Oblate Madonna Residence.
Stransky, Thomas F. *c.s.p.* '57 (NY) [DD] Jamaica Estates, NY Paulist Fathers Generalate.
Strass, Richard *c.ss.r.* '60 (ANC) Seward, AK Sacred Heart Church.
Strass, Richard *c.ss.r.* '60 (CHI) [N] Chicago, IL Redemptorists:.
Strass, Richard *c.ss.r.* '60 (DEN) [M] Denver, CO The Redemptorists/Denver Province.
Strassberger, H. Richard '42 (BUF) Retired.
Strassberger, Richard '50 (BUF) [12] Niagara Falls, NY Sacred Heart Church.
Strasser, John R. '76 (DOD) [1] Dodge City, KS Cathedral of the Sacred Heart.
Strassle, Paul '58 (LR) Retired.
Strassner, Henry E. '47 (ALN) Tamaqua, PA St. Jerome Church.
Strasz, James *s.m.* '80 (BO) [Y] Framingham Centre, MA The Marist House.
Stratman, Joseph '77 (BEA) China, TX Our Lady of Sorrows Church.
Stratman, Raymond '55 (LEX) Retired.
Stratman, Thomas F. '50 (DAV) [1] Davenport, IA Sacred Heart Cathedral.
Stratman, Thomas F. '56 (DAV) Retired.
Stratman, William J. (DAV) Retired.
Straub, David R. '94 (CHI) [140] Chicago, IL St. Monica Church.
Straub, Edward F. '65 (NY) Liberty, NY St. Peter Church.
Strausser, George '77 (PH) [3] Philadelphia, PA St. Agatha-St. James Church.
Stravinskas, Peter '77 (B) On Duty Outside the Diocese.
Stravinskas, Peter M.J. '77 (SCR) [M] Mount Pocono, PA Diocesan Oratory of Saint Philip Neri - Newman House.
Strawn, Nicholas *s.v.d.* '62 (FgM) Society of the Divine Word Foreign Missions.
Strebel, Milton C. *o.praem.* '54 (GB) [I] De Pere, WI St. Norbert Abbey.
Strebel, Roger '66 (GB) Wagner, WI St. Edward Church; Walsh, WI St. Joseph Church.
Strebig, John J. '52 (GRY) Retired.
Strebler, Charles F. '94 (CLV) Strongsville, OH St. Joseph Church.
Stredny, Anthony G. (GAL) Retired.
Streff, Joseph N. '42 (STP) Retired.
Streichardt, Wolfgang '82 (SAG) Croswell, MI St. Patrick Church.
Streicher, Bernard J. *s.j.* '60 (CLV) [E] Cleveland, OH St. Ignatius High School.
Streit, David *s.v.d.* '69 (FgM) Society of the Divine Word Foreign Missions.
Streit, Joseph C. '60 (SCR) [I] Wilkes-Barre, PA Mercy Hospital.
Streit, Thomas G. *c.s.c.* '86 (FTW) [B] Notre Dame, IN University of Notre Dame Du Lac; [J] Notre Dame, IN Holy Cross Community, Corby Hall, University of Notre Dame.
Strelick, Charles J. '56 (MAR) Retired.
Strelinski, Ernest '65 (PIT) Allison Park, PA St. Ursula Church.
Stremel, Adolph '36 (WCH) Retired.
Strempeck, Martin R. '55 (BAL) Hydes, MD St. John the Evangelist Church.
Stremski, John P. '60 (SUP) Lac du Flambeau, WI St. Anthony Catholic Church.
Streng, Msgr. James E. '51 (BUF) Gasport, NY St. Mary Church; Middleport, NY St. Stephen Church; Retired.
Strenski, David F. *o.praem.* '68 (GB) [A] De Pere, WI St. Norbert Abbey; [I] De Pere, WI St. Norbert Abbey; [O] De Pere, WI NORBERT & CO.
Strenski, Joseph A. '45 (MIL) Retired.
Stretch, Daniel P. '53 (STL) On Duty Outside the Archdiocese.
Stretton, Noel '59 (DUL) [10] Duluth, MN St. Joseph's Church; Duluth, MN Duluth Federal Prison.
Streveler, Robert A. '69 (LC) Rothschild, WI St. Therese of the Child Jesus Church.
Streza, Charles V. '43 (ROM) Retired.
Stricker, Robert A. '48 (CIN) [85] Cincinnati, OH St. Therese, The Little Flower Church; Retired.
Strickland, Msgr. Joseph E. '85 (TYL) [1] Tyler, TX Cathedral of the Immaculate Conception.
Strieder, Leon '76 (AUS) On Duty Outside the Diocese.
Strieder, Leon '76 (GAL) [A] Houston, TX St. Mary's Seminary.
Striedl, Max J., Jr. '96 (RCK) [5] Rockford, IL Holy Family Church.
Striegel, Robert M. '73 (DAV) Ottumwa, IA St. Mary of the Visitation Church.
Stringini, John L. '79 (RCK) Dixon, IL St. Patrick Church.
Stripe, Keith A. '96 (TOL) [35] Toledo, OH St. Patrick of Heatherdowns Church.
Strish, Andrew F. '67 (SCR) [3] Pittston, PA St. John the Baptist Church.
Stritch, Morris G. '42 (MEM) Retired; [C] Memphis, TN Christian Brothers High School.
Strittmatter, Andre *t.o.r.* '61 (ALT) [F] Loretto, PA St. Francis Friary, Third Order Regular of St. Francis of Penance.
Strittmatter, J. Joseph '56 (ALT) Retired.
Strittmatter, Lawrence R. '57 (CIN) [3] Dayton, OH St. Albert the Great Church.
Strittmatter, Robert '66 (FWT) [1] Fort Worth, TX St. Patrick Cathedral.
Stroba, Mark *o.m.i.* '85 (CHI) [174] Chicago, IL Precious Blood Church.
Strobel, Charles '70 (NSH) Absent on Leave.
Strock, Richard M. '65 (LR) Siloam Springs, AR St. Mary's Church.
Strohmeyer, George E. '64 (E) [F] Erie, PA L'Arche Community.
Stroike, Placid *o.f.m.* (NY) [DD] New York, NY St. Clare Friary.
Strollo, Charles P. *c.m.* '73 (MET) [H] Plainsboro, NJ Vincentian Residence; [J] Plainsboro, NJ Vincentian

Renewal Center.
Strom, Charles W. '72 (HEL) Retired.
Stromberg, Floyd G. '59 (TUC) [7] Tucson, AZ Our Lady, Queen of All Saints Church.
Stromberg, James S. '57 (STP) Retired; [C] St. Paul, MN University of St. Thomas.
Strommer, James G. *c.p.* '70 (SAC) [G] Citrus Heights, CA Christ the King Retreat.
Stromski, Adam F.X. '46 (MIA) [12] Miami, FL Our Lady of the Holy Rosary Church.
Stromski, Adam F.X. '46 (STU) Retired.
Stronkowski, John '85 (BGP) [1] Danbury, CT St. Gregory's Church.
Stroot, Ralph E. '60 (STL) [21] St. Louis, MO St. Aloysius Gonzaga Church.
Stroot, Thomas J. '70 (WCH) Pittsburg, KS Our Lady of Lourdes Church; [B] Pittsburg, KS St. Mary-Colgan High School.
Stroud, J. Francis *s.j.* '61 (NY) [DD] New York, NY Jesuit Community at Fordham University.
Stroup, Edmund F. '49 (BAL) Retired.
Stroupe, Scott T. '91 (E) [12] Erie, PA St. Andrew Church.
Strub, Herman A. '34 (DAV) Retired; [L] Davenport, IA Kahl Home for the Aged and Infirm.
Struc, Marian '69 (PHU) Jersey City, NJ SS. Peter and Paul Church.
Struck, Msgr. John W. '40 (PRO) Retired.
Struik, Felix *o.p.* '58 (SJN) Catano, PR Nuestra Senora del Carmen Church.
Struik, Felix A.P. *o.p.* (SJN) [A] Bayamon, PR Bayamon Central University.
Struminski, Robert *s.m.* '71 (HRT) [I] New Haven, CT Hospital of St. Raphael.
Strumski, Matthew J. '48 (PRO) [2] Warren, RI St. Casimir Church.
Strupp, James A. '67 (MIL) Retired.
Strupp, Joachim *o.f.m.cap.* '34 (MIL) [N] Fond du Lac, WI St. Francis Home for Aged.
Strupp, Joachim *o.f.m.cap.* '63 (MIL) [P] Mount Calvary, WI St. Lawrence Friary.
Strus, Walter A. '94 (CHI) Bridgeview, IL St. Fabian Church.
Struzik, Edward J. '85 (MET) Plainsboro, NJ Queenship of Mary Church.
Struzynski, Robert *o.f.m.* '63 (BUF) [59] Buffalo, NY SS. Rita & Patrick Church.
Struzzieri, Andrew L. '75 (BRK) [109] Brooklyn, NY Our Lady of Refuge Church.
Struzzo, John A. *c.s.c.* '65 (FTW) [J] South Bend, IN Congregation of Holy Cross Indiana Province Provincial House.
Strycharz, Stanislaw J. '91 (VEN) Marco Island, FL San Marco Church.
Stryjewski, John J. '66 (MOB) Grand Bay, AL St. John Baptist Church.
Stryk, Jerome J. '44 (VIC) Plum, TX SS. Peter and Paul Church.
Strynkowski, Msgr. John J. *s.t.d.* '63 (BRK) [177] Queens, NY Holy Cross Church.
Strzadala, Wieslaw P. *s.d.s.* '90 (BRK) [93] Brooklyn, NY Our Lady of Consolation Church.
Strzelec, Thaddeus B. '42 (HBG) Lewistown, PA Sacred Heart of Jesus Church.
Strzelinski, Ernest '65 (PIT) Allegheny County, PA Kane Regional Center - Ross.
Stua, Ronald *c.m.f.* '81 (ATL) Stone Mountain, GA Corpus Christi Church.
Stua, Ronald '81 (CHI) [N] Oak Park, IL Claretian Fathers Headquarters of U.S.A. Eastern Province.
Stuardi, Msgr. J. Edwin '41 (MOB) Retired; [F] Daphne, AL Mercy Medical; [L] Daphne, AL Apostleship of Prayer.
Stuart, Francis *o.s.b.* '61 (SAL) Sharon Springs, KS Holy Ghost Church.
Stuart, George '89 (WDC) [3] Bethesda, MD Little Flower Church.
Stubbs, Msgr. Charles W. '63 (BGP) Leave of Absence.
Stubbs, Michael C. '78 (KCK) Lansing, KS St. Francis de Sales Church.
Stubeda, Anthony J. '85 (NU) On Special or Other Diocesan Assignment.
Stubna, Kris D. '85 (PIT) Scott Township, PA SS. Simon and Jude Church.
Stuchlak, John *c.ss.r.* '58 (PHU) Newark, NJ St. John the Baptist Church.
Stuchlik, Richard '68 (WCH) Hutchinson, KS St. Teresa Church; [B] Hutchinson, KS Trinity High School.
Stucky-Abbott, Leona (SFE) [C] Santa Fe, NM College of Santa Fe.
Stuczko, Richard J. '54 (SY) Oriskany, NY Oneida County Jail; Retired.
Studeny, Colman *o.f.m.cap.* '61 (FgM) Capuchin Foreign Missions.
Studer, James *o.s.b.* '54 (SCL) [I] Collegeville, MN St. John's Abbey, of the Order of St. Benedict.
Studer, Louis *o.m.i.* '76 (BEL) [F] Belleville, IL Shrine of Our Lady of the Snows.
Studer, Louis B. *o.m.i.* '76 (BEL) [J] Belleville, IL Our Lady of the Snows Layman's Association; [J] Belleville, IL Missionary Association of Mary Immaculate-Missionary Oblates of Mary Immaculate.
Studerus, Gregory J. (NEW) [24] Jersey City, NJ Parish of the Resurrection Church.
Studney, J. Edward '87 (WDC) Retired; [L] Washington, DC Cardinal O'Boyle Residence for Priests.
Studniewski, Gary R. '95 (WDC) Hollywood, MD St. John Church.
Studwell, Joachim *o.f.m.* '87 (MIL) [P] Burlington, WI Queen of Peace Friary.
Studzinski, Lambert '40 (FAR) [E] Fargo, ND Riverview Place, Inc.
Studzinski, Lambert V. '40 (FAR) Retired.
Studzinski, Raymond *o.s.b.* '69 (IND) [J] St. Meinrad, IN St. Meinrad Archabbey.
Studzinski, Raymond *o.s.b.* '69 (WDC) [C] Washington, DC Catholic University of America, The.
Stuebben, Anthony A. *c.ss.r.* '48 (STL) [P] Liguori, MO St. Clement Health Care Center.
Stuebben, Msgr. George '54 (SAT) Retired.
Stuebben, Lawrence '55 (SAT) [24] San Antonio, TX St. Agnes Church.
Stueber, Edwin *o.s.b.* '46 (SCL) [I] Collegeville, MN St. John's Abbey, of the Order of St. Benedict.
Stuecker, Henry C. '38 (L) [61] Louisville, KY Our Mother of Sorrows Church; Retired.
Stuempel, Robert L. '75 (L) [44] Louisville, KY St. Lawrence Church.
Stueve, Bernard C. *s.m.* '38 (CIN) [M] Dayton, OH Marianist Provincialate.
Stulb, Joseph A. '61 (NEW) Ridgewood, NJ Our Lady of Mount Carmel Church; Ridgewood, NJ Valley Hospital.
Stulting, Robert J. *c.s.p.* '61 (NY) [DD] Jamaica Estates, NY Paulist Fathers Generalate.
Stulting, Robert J. *c.s.p.* '61 (TUC) [11] Tucson, AZ St. Cyril of Alexandria Church.
Stump, David X. *s.j.* '71 (NEW) [B] Jersey City, NJ Saint Peter's College; [N] Jersey City, NJ Jesuits of Saint Peter's College, Inc.
Stump, James *o.f.m.cap.* (SFR) [28] San Francisco, CA St. John of God Church.
Stump, James *o.f.m.cap* '88 (SFR) [B] San Francisco, CA Capuchin House of Studies; [S] San Francisco, CA Newman Center, University of California Medical Center.
Stumpf, Thomas W. *o.s.b.* '52 (RIC) [H] Richmond, VA St. Joseph's Home for the Aged; [L] Richmond, VA Mary Mother of the Church Abbey.
Stumpf, William F. '85 (IND) [1] Indianapolis, IN SS. Peter and Paul Cathedral.
Stumpf, WilliamPaul '85 (IND) Nashville, IN St. Agnes Church.
Stunek, Howard *o.f.m.* '57 (LAN) Milan, MI Federal Correctional Institution.
Stunek, Leonard *o.f.m.* '60 (SAG) [18] Saginaw, MI St. Thomas Aquinas Church.
Stuparitz, George P. '46 (PIT) Retired; [O] Pittsburgh, PA St. John Vianney Manor.
Stupca, Edward L. '61 (HEL) Madison, MT Madison County Catholic Community Church.
Sturm, Donald E. '58 (KC) Hamilton, MO Sacred Heart Church.
Sturm, George *c.m.f.* '37 (SAT) [12] San Antonio, TX Immaculate Heart of Mary Church.
Sturm, John G. *s.j.* '50 (BUF) [50] Buffalo, NY St. Michael Church.
Sturm, Michael O. '69 (MIL) [4] Fond du Lac, WI St. Patrick Church.
Sturmer, Jeffrey M. '94 (BUF) [1] Kenmore, NY St. Andrew Church; [D] Buffalo, NY Nardin Academy High School.
Sturn, Michael L. '77 (SB) [3] San Bernardino, CA Our Lady of the Assumption Church.
Sturtz, Richard S. '56 (OG) Olmstedville, NY St. Joseph Church; Schroon Lake, NY Our Lady of Lourdes Church.
Stutz, Edward J. '46 (E) Retired.
Styczen, Emil '55 (SP) Holiday, FL St. Vincent De Paul Church.
Styles, Kenneth A. *s.j.* '72 (DET) [E] Detroit, MI University of Detroit Jesuit High School and Academy.
Su, Stanislaus *c.s.j.b.* '69 (LA) [DD] Monterey Park, CA Congregation of St. John the Baptist.
Su, Msgr. Tomas '50 (SJN) [54] San Juan, PR Sagrada Familia Church.
Suan, Charito '85 (SFR) Redwood City, CA Our Lady of Mount Carmel Church.
Suarez, Carlos *o.s.b.* '86 (BIS) [A] Richardton, ND Assumption Abbey.
Suarez, Carlos *o.s.b.* '86 (FgM) American - Cassinese Congregation Foreign Missions.
Suarez, Jesus '86 (TYL) Fairfield, TX St. Bernard of Clairvaux Church.
Suarez, Jose '55 (SJ) Retired.
Suarez, Msgr. Jose V. '54 (SJ) [13] San Jose, CA St. Julie Church.
Suarez, Michael F. *s.j.* '94 (NY) [DD] New York, NY Jesuit Provincial's Office.
Suarez, Octavio '64 (TYL) Nacogdoches, TX Sacred Heart Church.
Suarez, Pedro A. *s.j.* '72 (MIA) [B] Miami, FL Barry University; [H] Miami, FL Villa Arrieta.
Suaybagio, Evangelio R. '75 (NY) [211] Staten Island, NY St. Joseph, St. Thomas Church.
Suazo, Rafael '64 (SJN) [7] Carolina, PR San Felipe Apostol Church.
Subb, Victor *glmy.* '87 (LR) Crossett, AR Holy Cross Church.
Suberlak, Donald *c.r.* '67 (PT) Panama City, FL St. John the Evangelist Church.
Subocz, Adam '86 (HRT) [2] Enfield, CT St. Adalbert's Church.
Suchan, Robert J. *s.j.* '56 (FgM) Provinces.
Suchan, William T. *s.j.* '58 (FgM) Provinces.
Sucharski, Michael *s.v.d.* '83 (BLX) [A] Bay St. Louis, MS St. Augustine's.
Sucher, Frederick *c.p.* '44 (CHI) [N] Chicago, IL Immaculate Conception Monastery.
Suchnicki, Michael *o.f.m.cap.* (SAL) Hays, FL St. Joseph's Church; [D] Hays, KS St. Joseph's Friary.
Suchocki, James '62 (MIA) Coral Gables, FL St. Augustine Church.
Suchocki, James A. '62 (GAY) Special Assignment.
Suchocki, Marek '86 (NY) [228] Staten Island, NY St. Stanislaus Kostka Church.
Sucholet, James Joseph '91 (NOR) Voluntown, CT St. Thomas Apostle Church.
Suchy, Theodore D. *o.s.b.* '67 (JOL) [A] Lisle, IL Benedictine University; [J] Lisle, IL St. Procopius Abbey.
Suda, Conrad P. '40 (MAR) Retired.
Sudano, Glenn *c.f.r.* (NY) [DD] New York, NY St. Joseph's Friary.
Sudario, Msgr. Antonio '69 (ORG) Cypress, CA St. Irenaeus Church.
Sudekum, Msgr. Edward J. '61 (STL) [3] University City, MO Our Lady of Lourdes Church.
Sudhoff, Leonard *c.pp.s.* '39 (CIN) [B] Carthagena, OH St. Charles.
Sudlik, Leonard '76 (GR) [8] Grand Rapids, MI Holy Spirit Church.
Sudlik, Richard *o.m.i.* '72 (MIA) [7] Miami, FL Holy Redeemer Church.
Sudol, Gerard J. '80 (NEW) [3] Jersey City, NJ St. Anne's Church; Jersey City, NJ St. Francis Health Center; [S] Jersey City, NJ Franciscan Health System of New Jersey, Inc.
Suellentrop, Anthony J. '73 (DOD) Kiowa, KS St. John the Apostle Church; Medicine Lodge, KS Holy Rosary Church; Sharon, KS St. Boniface Church.
Suellentrop, Bernard '45 (STL) Shrewsbury, MO St. Michael Church.
Suellentrop, Daniel M. *o.s.b.* '51 (OKL) [I] Shawnee, OK St. Gregory Abbey.
Suelzer, Msgr. John N. '65 (FTW) [3] Fort Wayne, IN St. Charles Borromeo Church.
Suen, Benito *o.a.r* '54 (LSC) [B] Mesilla, NM Augustinian Recollects Fathers.
Suenram, John Magdalene *o.c.d.* '87 (SAT) [18] San Antonio, TX Our Lady of Mt. Carmel and St. Therese, Discalced Carmelite Fathers National Shrine of the Little Flower Church; [M] San Antonio, TX Discalced Carmelites (Prov. of St. Therese).
Sueper, Alban *s.s.c.* '53 (OM) [K] St. Columbans, NE St. Columban's Foreign Mission Society.
Suess, Milton M. '63 (GB) Luxemburg, WI Immaculate Conception Church.
Suffredini, Louis M. '57 (MOB) [F] Mobile, AL Little Sisters of the Poor, Home For the Aged, Inc.
Suggs, Fred H. '46 (CHR) Retired.
Sughrue, Denis B. *c.s.c.* '39 (FR) [A] North Easton, MA Holy Cross Fathers Religious.
Sugrue, John F. '62 (CAM) Mays Landing, NJ St. Vincent de Paul Church.
Sugrue, Patrick *o.c.d.* '64 (SB) [G] Redlands, CA El Carmelo Retreat House.
Sugrue, Timothy F. *s.m.* '63 (WDC) [M] Washington, DC Marist Provincial House.
Suh, Daniel '95 (NEW) [6] Orange, NJ St. Andrew Kim Church.
Suhaka, Peter G. '86 (MET) Manville, NJ Sacred Heart of Jesus Church.
Suhoza, J. Edward '68 (PIT) Bethel Park, PA St. Thomas More Church.
Suibielski, Kenneth J. '77 (PRO) [8] Pawtucket, RI St. Maria Goretti Church.
Suing, Benedict *o.s.b.* '54 (P) [33] Portland, OR Sacred Heart Church.
Suit, Robert J. '74 (STL) De Soto, MO St. Rose of Lima Church.
Suitan, Martin '79 (NY) Pine Bush, NY The Infant Saviour Church.
Sujka, Andrew *o.f.m.conv.* '75 (BO) [55] Boston, MA Our Lady of Czestochowa Church.
Sukovaty, G. L. *o.p.* '51 (FgM) Dominican - Order of Preachers Foreign Missions.
Sukup, Joseph G. '56 (MIL) Oak Creek, WI St. Matthew Church.
Sulahian, Mesrop (ARM) [C] Glendale, CA Mekhitarian Educational Foundation.

Sularz, Thomas '71 (JOL) Woodridge, IL St. Scholastica Church.
Sulkowski, Anthony P. '86 (DET) [4] Monroe, MI St. Mary's Church.
Sullivan, Alan *o.f.m.* '56 (NY) [DD] New York, NY Franciscan Friars, Order of Friars Minor, Holy Name Province.
Sullivan, Andrew '94 (BIR) [6] Birmingham, AL St. Francis Xavier Church; [A] Birmingham, AL John Carroll High School.
Sullivan, Andrew J. '47 (WOR) Retired.
Sullivan, Msgr. Arthur A. '37 (PRO) Retired.
Sullivan, Athanasius *o.p.* (NY) Manhattan, NY New York Hospital.
Sullivan, Brendan J. '78 (BO) On Duty Outside the Archdiocese.
Sullivan, Brendan V. '60 (CAM) Ventnor, NJ St. James Church.
Sullivan, C. Otis (CHI) Retired.
Sullivan, Charles D. *s.j.* '72 (NY) [F] New York, NY Fordham Preparatory School; [DD] New York, NY Jesuit Community at Fordham University.
Sullivan, Charles J. '50 (SFR) [51] San Francisco, CA St. Thomas, The Apostle Church.
Sullivan, Charles J. '65 (SPR) Absent on Leave.
Sullivan, Charles J. '66 (PH) [23] Philadelphia, PA St. Bernard Church.
Sullivan, Charles K. '64 (VEN) [4] Fort Myers, FL St. Columbkille Church.
Sullivan, Cletus *o.carm.* '45 (CHI) [N] Mundelein, IL Carmelite Monastery.
Sullivan, D. Edward '42 (CHL) Retired.
Sullivan, Dan *c.p.* '68 (PIT) [O] Pittsburgh, PA St. Paul of the Cross Monastery.
Sullivan, Daniel '75 (TR) Hainesport, NJ Our Lady Queen of Peace Church.
Sullivan, Msgr. Daniel F. '38 (LA) Beverly Hills, CA Good Shepherd Church; Retired.
Sullivan, Daniel F. '57 (CHI) Arlington Heights, IL St. Edna Church.
Sullivan, Daniel J. *c.m.* '53 (BRK) [U] Jamaica, NY Vincentian Residence.
Sullivan, Daniel J. '53 (CHI) Retired.
Sullivan, Daniel J. *s.j.* '61 (NY) [DD] New York, NY Jesuit Community at Fordham University.
Sullivan, Daniel J. *s.j.* '72 (HON) [7] Honolulu, HI Newman Center-Holy Spirit Parish; [H] Honolulu, HI Jesuit Fathers House.
Sullivan, Daniel J. '77 (PH) [60] Philadelphia, PA Holy Innocents Church.
Sullivan, Daniel James '63 (HRT) [3] Hamden, CT Our Lady of Mt. Carmel Church.
Sullivan, Daniel Jeremiah '63 (HRT) South Windsor, CT St. Margaret Mary Church.
Sullivan, Msgr. Daniel L. '40 (NY) [199] Staten Island, NY Blessed Sacrament Church; Retired.
Sullivan, Msgr. Daniel L. '48 (NY) [229] Staten Island, NY St. Sylvester Church.
Sullivan, David D. '58 (STL) [K] Creve Coeur, MO St. John's Mercy Medical Center.
Sullivan, Dennis J. '71 (NY) [116] New York, NY St. Teresa Church; Manhattan, NY Gouverneur Hospital.
Sullivan, Dennis L. *t.o.r.* '54 (PH) Newtown Square, PA St. Anastasia Church.
Sullivan, Donal '64 (STA) Green Cove Springs, FL Sacred Heart Church.
Sullivan, Msgr. Donald E. '52 (STL) Retired.
Sullivan, E. Hartrick *c.m.* '46 (DEN) [M] Denver, CO Congregation of the Mission Midwest Province: De Paul House.
Sullivan, Edward *o.f.m.* (NY) Warwick, NY St. Anthony Community Hospital; [W] Warwick, NY St. Anthony Community Hospital, Inc.; [Z] Warwick, NY Villa Frances at the Knolls; [EE] Warwick, NY Franciscan Sisters of Poor Mt. Alverno Center, Inc. Franciscan Health Systems of Warwick, Inc.; [FF] Warwick, NY Mount Alverno Center and Convent.
Sullivan, Edward '55 (RVC) Copiague, NY Our Lady of the Assumption Church.
Sullivan, Edward P. *s.j.* '46 (BUF) [O] Buffalo, NY Canisius Jesuit Community.
Sullivan, Msgr. Edward T. '42 (SCR) Retired; [N] Dunmore, PA Villa St. Joseph.
Sullivan, Msgr. Edwin V. '46 (NEW) Retired; [B] South Orange, NJ Seton Hall University.
Sullivan, Emmanuel *o.c.d.* '52 (BO) [W] Brighton, MA Carmelite Monastery.
Sullivan, Emmanuel *o.c.d.* '52 (PRT) [A] Standish, ME Saint Joseph's College.
Sullivan, Emmanuel *s.a.* '55 (NY) [DD] Garrison, NY Generalate of the Franciscan Friars of the Atonement-St. James Friary.
Sullivan, Ernest L. '61 (LA) [R] Los Angeles, CA Columban Fathers, Procure House.
Sullivan, Eugene P. '59 (CHY) Sheridan, WY Holy Name Church.
Sullivan, Eugene P. '68 (BO) [2] Weymouth, MA St. Francis Xavier Church.
Sullivan, F. Norman '63 (BUF) [5] Cheektowaga, NY Most Holy Redeemer Church.
Sullivan, Francis *c.ss.r.* '59 (PH) [135] Philadelphia, PA St. Peter the Apostle Church.
Sullivan, Francis A. *s.j.* '51 (BO) [W] Chestnut Hill, MA The Jesuit Community at Boston College.
Sullivan, Francis D. *o.f.m.* '43 (BUF) [5] Cheektowaga, NY Most Holy Redeemer Church.
Sullivan, Francis E. '88 (BO) [3] Malden, MA Sacred Hearts Church.
Sullivan, Francis J. '30 (SPR) Retired; [H] Springfield, MA St. Michael's Residence.
Sullivan, Francis P. '37 (BO) Retired.
Sullivan, Francis X. '48 (SPR) [2] Westfield, MA Our Lady of the Blessed Sacrament Church.
Sullivan, Frederick '53 (NY) Cold Spring-on-Hudson, NY Our Lady of Loretto Church.
Sullivan, Gael *s.d.b.* '92 (LA) Bellflower, CA St. Dominic Savio Church.
Sullivan, George *o.f.m.conv.* '74 (CHL) Winston-Salem, NC Our Lady of Mercy Church.
Sullivan, George '76 (LA) [1] Oxnard, CA St. Anthony Church.
Sullivan, George D. '80 (OAK) [14] Oakland, CA St. Margaret Mary Church.
Sullivan, George D. '80 (STO) On Duty Outside the Diocese.
Sullivan, George R. *s.j.* '75 (LA) [R] Los Angeles, CA Columbiere House.
Sullivan, George R. *s.j.* '75 (MIL) [P] Milwaukee, WI Jesuit Provincial Office, Wisconsin Province.
Sullivan, Gerald A. '59 (CHY) [2] Cheyenne, WY Holy Trinity Church.
Sullivan, Gerald P. *s.j.* '62 (SJ) [B] Santa Clara, CA Santa Clara University.
Sullivan, J. Bernard '44 (HEL) Retired.
Sullivan, J. David *m.m.* '60 (FgM) Maryknoll Foreign Missions.
Sullivan, J. Richard '77 (L) Elizabethtown, KY St. James Church; White Mills, KY St. Ignatius Church.
Sullivan, James '47 (SFD) Retired.
Sullivan, James *o.m.i.* '53 (FgM) Oblates Foreign Missions.
Sullivan, James B. '58 (NEW) Fort Lee, NJ Holy Trinity Church.
Sullivan, James E. '46 (BRK) [179] Queens, NY Holy Trinity Church; Retired.
Sullivan, James E. *o.m.i.* '53 (WDC) [B] Washington, DC Oblate College/Oblate Center for Mission Studies.
Sullivan, James F. (PH) [39] Philadelphia, PA St. Dominic Church.
Sullivan, James H. *s.m.a.* '60 (NEW) [N] Tenafly, NJ Society of African Missions, Provincialate, S.M.A. Fathers.
Sullivan, James J. '40 (HRT) Retired.
Sullivan, James K. '65 (SAT) [C] San Antonio, TX Oblate School of Theology.
Sullivan, James L. '43 (BO) Permanent Disability.
Sullivan, James M. '60 (HEL) On Duty Outside the Diocese.
Sullivan, James M. '60 (OM) [24] Omaha, NE St. John Vianney Church.
Sullivan, James M. '66 (STL) Port Hudson, MO Holy Family Church.
Sullivan, James M. *o.p.* '95 (CIN) [M] Cincinnati, OH St. Gertrude Priory.
Sullivan, James M. *o.p.* '96 (CIN) [30] Cincinnati, OH St. Gertrude Church.
Sullivan, Msgr. James P. '70 (NY) [8] Yonkers, NY St. Eugene Church.
Sullivan, James T. *o.p.* '45 (PRO) [P] Providence, RI St. Thomas Aquinas Priory at Providence College.
Sullivan, Jan C. '91 (COL) [9] Columbus, OH St. Cecilia Church.
Sullivan, Jan C.P. '91 (COL) Columbus, OH Children's Hospital.
Sullivan, Jeremiah *c.s.p.* '59 (LA) [86] Los Angeles, CA St. Paul the Apostle Church.
Sullivan, Jeremiah T. '62 (HEL) [B] Helena, MT Carroll College.
Sullivan, John *o.p.* (NY) Orangeburg, NY Rockland Psychiatric Center.
Sullivan, John '54 (JOL) Glen Ellyn, IL St. Petronille Church.
Sullivan, John *o.f.m.* '59 (SFD) Batchtown, IL St. Barbara Church; Brussels, IL St. Mary Church; Meppen, IL St. Joseph Church.
Sullivan, John *s.m.* '65 (HON) [15] Honolulu, HI Star of the Sea Church.
Sullivan, John '72 (SAC) Placerville, CA St. Patrick's Church.
Sullivan, John A. (PAT) Retired.
Sullivan, John Andrew '78 (LAV) [9] Las Vegas, NV St. Francis de Sales Church.
Sullivan, John B. '61 (NY) [164] Bronx, NY St. Mary Church.
Sullivan, John E. '49 (TR) Retired.
Sullivan, John G. *m.m.* '60 (FgM) Maryknoll Foreign Missions.
Sullivan, John J. '41 (NOR) [3] Middletown, CT St. Mary of Czestochowa Church; Retired.
Sullivan, John J. *s.j.* '44 (FgM) Provinces.
Sullivan, Msgr. John J. '51 (SLC) [6] Salt Lake City, UT St. Ann Church.
Sullivan, John J. '66 (DET) Plymouth, MI Our Lady of Good Counsel Church.
Sullivan, John J. '67 (CLV) Mentor, OH St. Bede the Venerable Church.
Sullivan, John J. '77 (CHI) [206] Chicago, IL St. Thomas More Church.
Sullivan, John J. *o.s.f.s.* '81 (PH) [AA] Philadelphia, PA Oblates of St. Francis De Sales.
Sullivan, John James *o.p.* '39 (NY) [DD] New York, NY St. Vincent Ferrer Priory.
Sullivan, John L. '41 (HRT) Retired.
Sullivan, John L. '45 (PRT) Retired; [I] Waterville, ME Mt. St. Joseph Priest Retirement Home.
Sullivan, John L. *o.p.* '49 (NY) [EE] Blauvelt, NY Congregation of St. Dominic General Motherhouse of the Sisters of St. Dominic of Blauvelt.
Sullivan, John L. '52 (BO) Society of St. James the Apostle.
Sullivan, John L. '52 (FgM) Society of St. James the Apostle.
Sullivan, John L. '71 (SPR) Agawam, MA St. Theresa of the Child Jesus Church.
Sullivan, John L. '74 (BO) [A] Boston, MA St. John's Seminary School of Theology.
Sullivan, John M. '90 (FR) North Attleboro, MA St. Mary's Church.
Sullivan, John M. '91 (BO) [1] Malden, MA Immaculate Conception Church.
Sullivan, John P. *o.p.* '41 (NY) Pleasantville, NY Holy Innocents Church.
Sullivan, John P. '65 (HRT) [12] New Haven, CT St. Joseph's Church; [R] New Haven, CT Southern Connecticut State University Newman Center.
Sullivan, Msgr. John P. '65 (RVC) Greenport, NY St. Agnes Church.
Sullivan, John P. *m.s.* '70 (HRT) [M] Hartford, CT Missionaries of LaSalette Provincial Secretary.
Sullivan, John R. '94 (LIN) Ulysses, NE Immaculate Conception Church.
Sullivan, John T. '42 (PHX) Retired.
Sullivan, John W. *s.j.* '47 (BO) [W] Weston, MA Campion Health Center, Inc.
Sullivan, Joseph *o.f.m.* '55 (FgM) Franciscan Foreign Missions.
Sullivan, Msgr. Joseph A. '45 (DUB) Retired.
Sullivan, Joseph A. '58 (BGP) [3] Greenwich, CT St. Paul's Church.
Sullivan, Joseph C. '53 (DEN) [26] Denver, CO St. Anthony of Padua Church.
Sullivan, Joseph D. '56 (NY) Montgomery, NY Holy Name of Mary Church.
Sullivan, Msgr. Joseph J. '38 (ROC) Retired.
Sullivan, Joseph P. '58 (HEL) Columbia Falls, MT St. Richard Church.
Sullivan, Joseph T. '52 (BUR) Retired.
Sullivan, Kenneth J. *m.m.* '57 (FgM) Maryknoll Foreign Missions.
Sullivan, Kevin B. (SFD) Bethalto, IL Our Lady Queen of Peace Church.
Sullivan, Kevin L. (NY) [I] New York, NY The Catholic Charities of the Archdiocese of New York.
Sullivan, Kevin L. '76 (NY) [40] New York, NY St. Gregory Church; [I] New York, NY The Catholic Charities of the Archdiocese of New York; [HH] New York, NY Carmel Housing Development Fund Co., Inc.; [HH] New York, NY The Housing Fund of the Archdiocese of New York.
Sullivan, Lawrence F. (BO) Chelsea, MA Quigley Memorial Hospital.
Sullivan, Lawrence F. *o.c.d.* '60 (BO) [W] Brighton, MA Carmelite Monastery.
Sullivan, Lawrence J. '92 (CHI) Elmwood Park, IL St. Celestine Church.
Sullivan, Liam '72 (BIR) Bessemer, AL St. Aloysius Church.
Sullivan, Martin J. '53 (BRK) [186] Queens, NY St. Josaphat Church.
Sullivan, Matthew *ss.cc.* '55 (FR) New Bedford, MA Bristol Co. House of Correction & Eastern Massachusetts Correctional Alcohol Center; [J] Fairhaven, MA Sacred Hearts Provincial House.
Sullivan, Michael '66 (MIA) Deerfield Beach, FL Our Lady of Mercy Church.
Sullivan, Michael '81 (CR) Warren, MN SS. Peter and Paul Church.
Sullivan, Michael *o.f.m.cap.* '84 (MIL) [11] Milwaukee, WI St. Benedict the Moor Church; [25] Milwaukee, WI St. Francis of Assisi Church.
Sullivan, Michael B. *c.s.c.* '75 (FTW) [J] Notre Dame, IN Holy Cross Community, Corby Hall, University of Notre Dame.
Sullivan, Michael Bruce *c.s.c.* '75 (FTW) [B] Notre Dame, IN University of Notre Dame Du Lac.
Sullivan, Michael D. '45 (BO) Retired.
Sullivan, Michael J. '79 (SCR) Wellsboro, PA St. Peter's Church.
Sullivan, Michael P. *o.s.a.* '67 (PH) [AA] Villanova, PA St. Thomas Monastery.
Sullivan, Neil S. '82 (HBG) [4] Lancaster, PA St. John

Neumann Church.
Sullivan, Patrick '62 (DEN) Retired.
Sullivan, Patrick *o.f.m.cap.* '71 (FgM) Capuchin Foreign Missions.
Sullivan, Patrick A. *s.j.* '45 (BO) [W] Weston, MA Campion Center.
Sullivan, Patrick A. '82 (CR) Red Lake, MN St. Mary's Mission Church; [A] Red Lake, MN St. Mary's Mission School.
Sullivan, Patrick H. '55 (LA) [80] Los Angeles, CA St. Mary Magdalen Church.
Sullivan, Patrick J. *s.j.* '50 (NY) [DD] New York, NY Jesuit Community at Fordham University.
Sullivan, Patrick J. '63 (BIR) [20] Birmingham, AL St. Peter the Apostle Church.
Sullivan, Patrick J. *s.j.* '71 (CI) [B] Chuuk, FM Xavier High School.
Sullivan, Patrick J. '71 (FgM) Provinces.
Sullivan, Patrick M. *o.s.b.* '87 (MAN) [K] Manchester, NH St. Anselm Abbey.
Sullivan, Patrick T. *s.j.* '64 (BUF) [50] Buffalo, NY St. Michael Church.
Sullivan, Paul '63 (BO) Winthrop, MA St. John the Evangelist Church.
Sullivan, Paul M. *s.j.* '83 (BO) [W] Boston, MA The Society of Jesus of New England-Provincial Offices.
Sullivan, Paul M. *s.j.* '83 (PRT) Eastport, ME St. Joseph Church; Perry, ME St. Ann Church.
Sullivan, Paul V. (BO) Retired.
Sullivan, Paul V. '50 (NY) [10] Yonkers, NY St. Joseph Church; Retired.
Sullivan, Peter '70 (ALB) [7] Albany, NY Church of the Holy Cross.
Sullivan, Peter J., III '70 (ALB) [1] Albany, NY Cathedral of the Immaculate Conception; Special Assignment.
Sullivan, R. William *o.s.a.* '67 (CHI) [N] Chicago, IL St. John Stone Friary.
Sullivan, Raymond F. *m.m.* '54 (NY) [DD] Maryknoll, NY Maryknoll Fathers and Brothers.
Sullivan, Richard H. *c.s.c.* '50 (FR) [L] North Easton, MA Holy Cross Fathers Retreat House.
Sullivan, Richard J. '58 (E) [12] Erie, PA St. Andrew Church.
Sullivan, Robert (FTW) [A] Notre Dame, IN Moreau Seminary.
Sullivan, Robert *o.m.i.* '41 (FgM) Oblates Foreign Missions.
Sullivan, Robert *s.s.j.* '72 (BLX) Pascagoula, MS St. Peter the Apostle Church.
Sullivan, Robert E. '80 (BO) [A] Boston, MA St. John's Seminary School of Theology.
Sullivan, Robert J. *s.j.* '40 (BO) [W] Boston, MA The Society of Jesus of New England-Provincial Offices.
Sullivan, Robert J. *s.j.* '45 (PRT) Bangor, ME St. John's Church; Bangor, ME Eastern Maine Medical Center.
Sullivan, Robert J. '63 (SY) Special Assignment; [V] Vestal, NY Binghamton University Newman Center.
Sullivan, Robert J. '78 (BO) Pembroke, MA St. Thecla Church.
Sullivan, Robert J. '93 (BIR) [20] Birmingham, AL St. Peter the Apostle Church; [A] Birmingham, AL John Carroll High School.
Sullivan, Robert L. *s.j.* '67 (BEL) [3] East St. Louis, IL St. Joseph Church.
Sullivan, Sean *t.o.r.* '57 (VEN) [2] Sarasota, FL Our Lady Queen of Martyrs Church.
Sullivan, Terence *o.s.b.* '56 (KCK) Hiawatha, KS St. Ann's Church.
Sullivan, Terrence J. '64 (SJ) Campbell, CA St. Lucy Church.
Sullivan, Thomas D. *s.s.e.* '38 (VEN) [G] Englewood, FL Society of St. Edmund Residence.
Sullivan, Thomas F. '41 (CLV) Retired; [N] Akron, OH Francesca Residence; [Q] Akron, OH Provincial Motherhouse and Novitiate of the Daughters of Divine Charity.
Sullivan, Thomas G. *c.ss.r.* '72 (HRT) [5] Enfield, CT St. Patrick's Church.
Sullivan, Thomas K. '52 (STA) [19] Jacksonville, FL St. Paul's Church.
Sullivan, Thomas L. *c.s.v.* '32 (CHI) [N] Arlington Heights, IL Viatorian Province Center-Clerics of St. Viator.
Sullivan, Thomas P. '53 (BIS) Parshall, ND St. Bridget Church.
Sullivan, Timothy *s.a.* '90 (NY) [DD] Garrison, NY Franciscan Friars of the Atonement.
Sullivan, Msgr. Timothy E. '37 (BO) Retired.
Sullivan, Timothy F. *c.s.p.* '85 (NY) [DD] Jamaica Estates, NY Paulist Fathers Generalate.
Sullivan, Timothy J. '38 (PRO) Retired; [M] Newport, RI St. Clare Home.
Sullivan, Vincent *s.j.* (NEW) [24] Jersey City, NJ Parish of the Resurrection Church.
Sullivan, Msgr. W. Jerome '61 (BUF) Hamburg, NY St. Mary of the Lake Church.
Sullivan, Walter J. *c.s.p.* '35 (BO) [P] Boston, MA Paulist Center; [W] Boston, MA Paulist Fathers Residence.
Sullivan, Walter J. *c.s.p.* '35 (NY) [DD] Jamaica Estates, NY Paulist Fathers Generalate.
Sullivan, Wilfred '40 (WIN) Retired.
Sullivan, William *s.j.* '61 (BO) [W] Chestnut Hill, MA The Jesuit Community at Boston College.
Sullivan, William *s.j.* '66 (MI) Kwajalein, MH Blessed Sacrament Church.
Sullivan, William '72 (FTW) [3] Mishawaka, IN St. Monica Church.
Sullivan, William *o.ss.t.* '81 (BAL) [M] Baltimore, MD Holy Trinity Monastery.
Sullivan, William F. *s.s.c.* '56 (PRO) [P] Bristol, RI St. Columban's Retirement House.
Sullivan, William H. *o.s.a.* '52 (SD) [H] San Diego, CA Augustinian Community.
Sullivan, William J. '59 (HBG) Rohrerstown, PA St. Leo the Great Church.
Sullivan, William J. *s.j.* '61 (SEA) [A] Seattle, WA Seattle University.
Sullivan, William J. *o.s.b.* '71 (SFR) [N] Portola Valley, CA Woodside Priory.
Sullivan, William J. *o.ss.t.* '81 (WDC) [E] Hyattsville, MD De Matha Catholic High School.
Sullivan, William M. *s.j.* '66 (FgM) Provinces.
Sullivan, William M. '81 (BO) Westford, MA St. Catherine of Alexandria Church.
Sullivan, William P. '39 (BO) Retired.
Sullivan, Msgr. William V. '66 (RIC) Ashland, VA St. Ann Church.
Sullivant, Raymond L. *s.j.* '66 (FgM) Provinces.
Sumampong, Jed '84 (SFR) [3] South San Francisco, CA St. Augustine Church.
Sumler, Kevin '82 (BEA) Absent On Leave.
Sumler, Paul E. '80 (BEA) Kountze, TX Holy Spirit Mission Church; Lumberton, TX Infant Jesus Church.
Summerfield, Michael L. '86 (NU) [2] New Ulm, MN St. Mary Church.
Summers, Bryan F. *c.o.* '72 (PIT) [O] Pittsburgh, PA Congregation of the Oratory of St. Philip Neri; [R] Slippery Rock, PA Office for Campus Ministry.
Summers, John '54 (Y) Retired.
Summers, Msgr. R. Emmett '52 (KC) Retired.
Summitt, James A. '81 (BIR) Absent on Leave.
Sumpter, Gary '79 (SR) Napa, CA St. Thomas Aquinas Church.
Sun, Paul *s.j.* '95 (BAL) [B] Baltimore, MD Loyola College; [M] Baltimore, MD Jesuit Community of Loyola College, Inc.
Sunberg, David (CIN) Military Chaplains.
Sundararaj, Lazar (NY) [3] Yonkers, NY St. Ann Church.
Sundborg, Stephen V. *s.j.* '74 (SEA) [A] Seattle, WA Seattle University.
Sunderland, James C. *s.j.* '58 (DEN) [M] Denver, CO Xavier Jesuit Center.
Sundholm, Conrad J. '55 (ROC) [1] Auburn, NY Holy Family Church.
Sunds, Elvin '72 (JKS) Meridian, MS East Mississippi State Hospital.
Sunds, Elvin '73 (JKS) Meridian, MS St. Patrick Church; Meridian, MS St. Joseph Church.
Sung, Thomas '51 (BRK) [T] Brooklyn, NY Catholic Migration & Refugee Office, Catholic Migration Services, Inc.; [U] Elmhurst, NY Congregation of St. John the Baptist of China.
Sung, Thomas *c.s.j.b.* '69 (BRK) [209] Queens, NY Our Lady of China Chapel Church.
Suntum, James J. *s.f.* '84 (WDC) Takoma Park, MD Our Lady of Sorrows Church.
Sunturn, Jim *s.f.* '84 (WDC) [B] Silver Spring, MD Holy Family Seminary.
Supancheck, Norm '68 (LA) Santa Clarita, CA Our Lady of Perpetual Help Church.
Super, David J. '80 (CR) Moorhead, MN St. Francis de Sales Church.
Super, Msgr. Joseph J. '44 (SCR) [3] Pittston, PA St. John the Baptist Church; Retired.
Superiaso, Jose '85 (SFR) Belmont, CA Immaculate Heart of Mary Church.
Suppa, F. Thomas '78 (E) [1] Oil City, PA Assumption of the Blessed Virgin Mary Church; Rouseville, PA St. Venantius Church; [O] Du Bois, PA Nazareth In The Woods, Inc.
Suppe, Bernard A. *s.j.* '56 (BAL) [H] Baltimore, MD Mercy Medical Center, Inc.
Supple, Edmund R. *c.s.sp.* '38 (PIT) [B] Pittsburgh, PA Duquesne University of the Holy Ghost.
Supple, Msgr. James '36 (DUB) Ames, IA St. Thomas Aquinas Church (and Catholic Student Center) Church.
Supple, Msgr. James A. '36 (DUB) Retired; [N] Ames, IA St. Thomas Aquinas Church and Catholic Student Center (Iowa State University).
Suquilvide, Abel '55 (LA) Guadalupe, CA Our Lady of Guadalupe Church.
Surace, Robert J. '79 (NY) Absent on Leave.
Suran, Joachim '49 (BRK) Retired.
Suran, Joaquin '49 (BRK) [225] Queens, NY St. Paul the Apostle Church.
Surban, Edmundo A. '61 (NEW) Jersey City, NJ Jersey City Medical Center.
Suren, John '58 (STL) Weingarten, MO Our Lady Help of Christians Church.
Suren, Richard H. '53 (STL) High Ridge, MO St. Anthony of Padua Church.
Surette, John E. *s.j.* '67 (BO) [W] Boston, MA The Society of Jesus of New England-Provincial Offices.
Surges, Robert F. '64 (MIL) Big Bend, WI St. Joseph Church.
Suriani, Raymond N. '85 (PRO) [3] Westerly, RI St. Pius X Church.
Suriano, Thomas M. '64 (MIL) [59] Milwaukee, WI Our Lady of Lourdes Church.
Surman, Stanislaus '56 (SAG) Sandusky, MI St. Joseph Church.
Surmeier, William J. '65 (SAL) Hays, KS St. Nicholas of Myra Church; Munjor, KS St. Francis of Assisi Church.
Surowiec, Jude *o.f.m.conv.* '75 (SPR) [A] Granby, MA St. Hyacinth College and Seminary.
Surprenant, John L. '78 (NOR) Absent on Leave.
Surprenant, Paul W. '73 (WIN) [7] Rochester, MN St. Pius X Church.
Surufka, Michael *o.f.m.* '91 (PH) [D] Philadelphia, PA Archbishop Ryan High School; [AA] Philadelphia, PA St. Pius X Friary.
Survil, Bernard '67 (GBG) On Duty Outside the Diocese.
Surwilo, Msgr. Edward R. '63 (BGP) [13] Stamford, CT Our Lady Star of the Sea Church.
Susa, Robert P. '61 (E) [B] Erie, PA Gannon University.
Susann, Robert *m.s.* '74 (ATL) [2] Marietta, GA Church of St. Ann.
Susany, L. James '67 (PIT) Duquesne, PA St. Joseph Church.
Susi, Msgr. Joseph M. '50 (ALX) Special Assignment; Retired.
Susin, Angelo J. *c.s.* '38 (PRO) [16] Providence, RI Holy Ghost Church.
Suskey, Robert G. '90 (PH) Warrington, PA St. Joseph Church.
Susko, Msgr. Martin S. '61 (Y) Girard, OH St. Rose Church.
Suslenko, Mark S. '86 (HRT) [1] West Haven, CT Our Lady of Victory Church.
Suslowicz, Michael S. '80 (PIT) Nemacolin, PA Our Lady of Consolation Church.
Susnik, Bernardin *o.f.m.* '59 (CHI) [N] Lemont, IL The Slovene Franciscan Fathers, Order of Friars Minor, Commissariat of the Holy Cross.
Suss, Thomas '73 (SEA) McNeil Island, WA McNeil Island Correction Center.
Sustarsic, John '52 (DUL) Babbitt, MN St. Pius X Church.
Sustatya, Paul A. '91 (LA) Pasadena, CA St. Andrew Church.
Sustrick, Stephen J. *o.s.b.* '42 (PBL) [F] Canon City, CO Holy Cross Abbey.
Suszek, Eugene A. '87 (SPR) [1] Pittsfield, MA Holy Family Church.
Suszynski, Michael *o.f.m.conv.* '86 (FgM) Conventual Franciscan Foreign Missions.
Suszynski, Michale *o.f.m.conv.* '86 (CHI) [O] Chicago, IL Mother of Good Counsel Provincialate.
Sutherland, Thomas J. '60 (DET) Shelby Twp., MI St. Therese of Lisieux Church.
Sutherland, William E. '83 (E) [27] Erie, PA St. Patrick/St. Hedwig Church.
Sutherland, Msgr. William J. '33 (BUF) Retired.
Sutil, Florencio (SJN) On Duty Outside the Archdiocese.
Sutman, Frank I. *o.p.* '85 (FgM) Dominican - Order of Preachers Foreign Missions.
Sutschek, Francis C. '40 (MIL) Retired.
Sutter, Raymond A. '73 (CLV) [7] Parma, OH St. Matthias Church.
Suttmann, Donnul *o.f.m.* '53 (CIN) [M] Cincinnati, OH St. Clement Friary.
Sutton, Alphonsus M. *f.f.i.* (FR) [J] New Bedford, MA Marian Friary of Our Lady, Queen of the Seraphic Order.
Sutton, Donald '82 (COS) Parker, CO Ave Maria Church.
Sutton, Donald '82 (DEN) [6] Denver, CO Christ the King Church.
Sutton, John '56 (FAR) Cando, ND Sacred Heart Church.
Sutton, John '70 (PMB) [3] Boca Raton, FL St. Joan of Arc Church.
Sutton, John H. '56 (PBL) Retired.
Sutton, John V. '83 (BO) [D] Peabody, MA Bishop Fenwick High School.
Sutton, Stephen R. '84 (BAL) [49] Baltimore, MD St. Joseph Church.
Sutton, Thomas E. '73 (SAG) Auburn, MI St. Joseph Church.
Sutula, Leo S. '49 (NOR) Quaker Hill, CT Our Lady of Perpetual Help Church.
Suver, Robert J. '40 (CIN) Retired.
Suwalsky, David J. *s.j.* '95 (KC) [D] Kansas City, MO Rockhurst High School;[J] Kansas City, MO Rockhurst High School - Jesuit Community.
Suwinski, Leo S. '43 (BGP) Retired.

Suzy, Dennis *o.p.* '55 (DEN) [29] Denver, CO St. Dominic's Parish.
Svarczkopf, Mark A. '74 (IND) [13] Indianapolis, IN St. Andrew the Apostle Church; [24] Indianapolis, IN St. Lawrence Church.
Svea, Timothy E. '92 (LC) [I] St. Mary's Ridge, WI Immaculate Conception Priory; [O] Cashton, WI Institute of Christ the King-Sovereign Priest.
Sverchek, Michael P. '34 (ALN) Retired.
Sviokla, Edmond J. '51 (BO) [2] Everett, MA Immaculate Conception Church.
Svirskas, Joseph J. '51 (BO) Retired.
Svitan, Martin '79 (NY) Kingston, NY Benedictine Hospital; [W] Kingston, NY Benedictine Hospital.
Svobodny, Aloysius *o.m.i.* '49 (STP) [Q] Buffalo, MN Christ the King Retreat Center.
Swacha, Stanley J. '79 (E) Falls Creek, PA St. Bernard Church.
Swade, Thomas J. '61 (CHI) Other Assignments.
Swain, Kenneth J. '72 (ALB) Fort Plain, NY St. James Church.
Swain, Paul J. '88 (MAD) [I] Madison, WI Bishop O'Connor Catholic Pastoral Center.
Swain, Robert J. '59 (BRK) [U] Jamaica, NY Vincentian Residence.
Swalina, Msgr. Michael F. '70 (SPC) New Madrid, MO Immaculate Conception Church.
Swaner, James J. (PEO) [B] Peoria, IL Notre Dame High School.
Swaner, James J. '61 (PEO) Washington, IL St. Patrick's Church.
Swanson, Charles F. '66 (OM) [16] Omaha, NE Holy Cross Church.
Swanson, James *l.c.* '94 (WDC) [M] Potomac, MD Legionaries of Christ.
Swanson, Mark W. '81 (DAV) Georgetown, IA St. Patrick's Church; Melrose, IA St. Patrick's Church; Knoxville, IA Veteran's Administration Hospital.
Swarthout, James (CHI) Lake Zurich, IL St. Francis de Sales Church.
Swarthout, James E. '86 (RCK) Active Outside the Diocese.
Swartvagher, Marc '96 (BRK) [215] Queens, NY Our Lady of the Miraculous Medal Church.
Swartz, Joseph '75 (EVN) Mount Vernon, IN St. Matthew Church.
Swartz, Lawrence *o.c.s.o.* '34 (ATL) [I] Conyers, GA The Monastery of the Holy Spirit.
Swartz, Michael R. '87 (BUF) Absent on Leave.
Swast, George W. '80 (GBG) Arnold, PA All Saints Church; New Kensington, PA St. Joseph Church.
Sweany, Thomas M. '80 (CLV) Chesterland, OH St. Anselm Church.
Swearingen, Eric '87 (FRS) [10] Fresno, CA St. Helen Church.
Sweeney, Callistus *o.f.m.* (FgM) Franciscan Foreign Missions.
Sweeney, Charles J. *s.j.* '62 (TOL) [C] Toledo, OH St. John's Jesuit High School.
Sweeney, Msgr. Cornelius '50 (MRY) Morro Bay, CA St. Timothy Church.
Sweeney, D. Gilbert *s.j.* '54 (ALN) [A] Wernersville, PA Novitiate of St. Isaac Jogues.
Sweeney, Daniel R. *s.j.* '94 (BAL) [M] Baltimore, MD Jesuit Fathers and Brothers Maryland Provincial Curia.
Sweeney, Denis J. *c.ss.r.* '81 (TOL) [2] Lima, OH St. Gerard Church.
Sweeney, Denis R. '58 (GBG) Freeport, PA St. Mary Church.
Sweeney, Msgr. Donald F. '41 (DUB) Retired.
Sweeney, Edward '88 (AMA) Friona, TX St. Teresa of Jesus Church.
Sweeney, Edward J. *s.j.* '46 (NY) [DD] New York, NY Jesuit Community at Fordham University.
Sweeney, Ernest S. *s.j.* '63 (LA) [C] Los Angeles, CA Loyola Marymount University.
Sweeney, Eugene *s.m.* '78 (FWT) Denton, TX St. Mark Church.
Sweeney, Eugene J. '65 (PBL) Retired.
Sweeney, Francis M. *c.s.p.* '61 (BO) [P] Boston, MA Paulist Center; [W] Boston, MA Paulist Fathers Residence.
Sweeney, Francis W. *s.j.* '44 (BO) [W] Chestnut Hill, MA The Jesuit Community at Boston College.
Sweeney, Frederick E. '52 (BO) [3] Haverhill, MA St. John the Baptist Church.
Sweeney, James *m.h.m.* (CHI) [182] Chicago, IL St. Rene Goupil Church.
Sweeney, James '45 (MRY) Retired.
Sweeney, James '80 (BRK) [67] Brooklyn, NY St. John Cantius Church.
Sweeney, James E. '59 (ALN) Retired; [J] Bethlehem, PA Holy Family Villa.
Sweeney, James H. '81 (BRK) [101] Brooklyn, NY Our Lady of Mercy Church.
Sweeney, James P. '63 (BRK) [U] Jamaica, NY Parsons Manor.
Sweeney, Msgr. John A. '41 (STP) Retired.
Sweeney, John D. '56 (NEW) West Orange, NJ St. Joseph's Church.
Sweeney, John P. *s.m.a.* '34 (BO) [W] Dedham, MA African Mission House.
Sweeney, John P. '73 (PIT) Aliquippa, PA St. Titus Church.
Sweeney, John T. '70 (GBG) Lower Burrell, PA St. Margaret Mary Church.
Sweeney, Joseph F. *s.j.* '57 (WDC) [M] Washington, DC The Jesuit Community at Georgetown University.
Sweeney, Msgr. Kenny C. '53 (IND) Retired.
Sweeney, Kevin '94 (ORG) Military Chaplains.
Sweeney, Kevin J. '97 (BRK) [205] Queens, NY St. Nicholas of Tolentine Church.
Sweeney, Lawrence '88 (SD) Leave of Absence.
Sweeney, Lawrence P. '54 (SLC) [1] Ogden, UT Holy Family Church.
Sweeney, Leo C. *s.j.* '49 (CHI) [C] Chicago, IL Jesuit Community at Loyola University of Chicago.
Sweeney, Michael *o.p.* (OAK) [N] Oakland, CA Western Dominican Province.
Sweeney, Michael '79 (KNX) Harriman, TN Blessed Sacrament Church; Lancing, TN St. Ann Church.
Sweeney, Patrick E. '72 (PH) [121] Philadelphia, PA Our Lady of Lourdes Church.
Sweeney, Peter J. '61 (WDC) Damascus, MD St. Paul Church.
Sweeney, Reginald *o.f.m.conv.* '44 (TR) Seaside Park, NJ St. Catharine of Siena Church.
Sweeney, Robert J. '69 (RCK) Pecatonica, IL St. Mary Church.
Sweeney, Robert J. '82 (NY) Greenwood Lake, NY Holy Rosary Church.
Sweeney, Robert L. '48 (BWN) Retired.
Sweeney, Robert P. *s.s.c.* '59 (FgM) St. Columban's Foreign Mission.
Sweeney, Timothy *o.s.b.* '61 (IND) [J] St. Meinrad, IN St. Meinrad Archabbey.
Sweeney, Timothy *o.s.b.* '61 (OWN) [3] Owensboro, KY The Immaculate Church.
Sweeney, William *s.s.c.* '75 (OM) [K] St. Columbans, NE St. Columban's Foreign Mission Society.
Sweeney, William *s.a.c.* '77 (LUB) Seminole, TX St. James Church.
Sweeney, William '81 (BRK) [G] Fresh Meadows, NY St. Francis Preparatory School.
Sweeney, William F. '81 (BRK) [163] Queens, NY St. Clare Church.
Sweeny, Msgr. Edward (RVC) Graduate Studies.
Sweeny, Msgr. Edward A. '57 (RVC) Long Beach, NY St. Ignatius Martyr Church.
Sweeny, John J. '48 (SJ) [5] Santa Clara, CA Our Lady of Peace Church; [A] Santa Clara, CA Shrine of Our Lady of Peace.
Sweeny, Louis L. '48 (STO) Newman, CA St. Joachim Church.
Sweeny, Richard R. '86 (TR) Fair Haven, NJ Nativity Church.
Sweet, Douglas S. '95 (PRO) [2] Westerly, RI Immaculate Conception Church.
Sweetser, Thomas P. *s.j.* '70 (MIL) [P] Milwaukee, WI Jesuit Provincial Office, Wisconsin Province.
Sweitzer, Raymond M. *s.j.* (NY) [B] Bronx, NY Ciszek Hall.
Sweitzer, Raymond M. *s.j.* '75 (NY) [F] New York, NY Fordham Preparatory School.
Swencki, John T. '79 (BO) Emergency Response Group.
Swendrowski, Patrick R. '63 (MAD) Clinton, WI St. Stephen Church.
Swengros, William '91 (SP) Dunedin, FL Our Lady of Lourdes Church.
Swenson, Frederick O. '67 (LAF) Church Point, LA Our Lady of the Sacred Heart Church.
Swenson, James L. '74 (LAV) [7] Las Vegas, NV St. Bridget Church.
Swenson, Roger A. '70 (NO) [43] New Orleans, LA St. Leo the Great Church; [A] New Orleans, LA Notre Dame Seminary Graduate School of Theology.
Swenson, Walter '50 (NEW) Retired.
Swenson, Walter J.F. '50 (NEW) [22] Jersey City, NJ Our Lady of Victories Church.
Swertz, Thaddeus S. *c.s.c* '54 (BGP) [O] Bridgeport, CT Provincial Offices of the Priests and Brothers of Holy Cross, Eastern Province.
Swertz, Thaddeus (Ted) *c.s.c.* '40 (NOR) [D] Deep River, CT Mount St. John.
Swetland, Stuart W. (PEO) [O] Champaign, IL St. John's Catholic Student Chapel and Newman Foundation, University of Illinois.
Swetland, Stuart W. '91 (PEO) [2] Champaign, IL St. John's Catholic Chapel Church.
Swetnam, James H. *s.j.* '58 (FgM) Provinces.
Swetnam, R. William '73 (STL) Military Chaplains.
Swett, Charles J. '57 (TLS) Tahlequah, OK St. Brigid Church; [H] Tahlequah, OK Northeastern State University Catholic Student Organization.
Swett, Msgr. Ronald J. '67 (FRS) [6] Bakersfield, CA St. Philip the Apostle Church.
Swiader, Msgr. James P. '75 (RVC) Merrick, NY Cure of Ars Church.
Swiat, James R. '67 (LAN) Grand Blanc, MI Holy Family Church.
Swiatecki, Emilian '56 (VEN) Moore Haven, FL St. Joseph the Worker Church.
Swiatek, Emil P. '65 (BUF) Elma, NY Annunciation of the Blessed Virgin Mary Church.
Swiatek, Nicholas *o.f.m. conv.* '68 (BAL) [M] Ellicott City, MD Order of Friars Minor Conventual.
Swiatek, Nicholas *o.f.m.conv.* '68 (FgM) Conventual Franciscan Foreign Missions.
Swiatkowski, Msgr. Francis M. '44 (BUF) Retired; [O] Tonawanda, NY O'Hara Residence.
Swiatocha, Bruno '56 (RVC) Retired.
Swichtenberg, William '83 (GB) Howard, WI St. John the Baptist Church.
Swickard, John L. '74 (COL) [6] Columbus, OH Saint Anthony Church.
Swiderski, Gregory (PIT) [K] Pittsburgh, PA Vincentian Home Inc.
Swiderski, Gregory '72 (PIT) Wildwood, PA St. Catherine of Sweden Church; Allegheny County, PA Regency Hall Nursing Home; Allegheny County, PA Vincentian Home for the Chronically Ill.
Swiderski, Gregory C. '72 (PIT) [L] Allison Park, PA Regency Hall Nursing Home, Inc.
Swiderski, Stan *s.d.s* '63 (LR) Mountain Home, AR St. Peter the Fisherman Church.
Swiercz, Pawel A. (FR) [C] Taunton, MA Taunton Catholic Middle School.
Swiercz, Pawel A. '94 (FR) Raynham, MA St. Ann Church.
Swierczynski, Joseph E. '64 (PIT) [17] Pittsburgh, PA Immaculate Heart of Mary Church.
Swierz, Michael '85 (Y) Poland, OH Holy Family Church.
Swierzbinski, Edward '51 (NEW) Retired.
Swierzbiolek, Waclav *s.d.b.* '62 (NY) [DD] New Rochelle, NY Salesian Provincial House.
Swierzowski, Stanislaus J. '56 (ALB) [2] Amsterdam, NY St. John the Baptist Church.
Swierzy, Michael W. '75 (PH) Absent on Leave.
Swietek, Walter '62 (VEN) Lehigh Acres, FL St. Raphael Church.
Swietochowski, Andrew K. '78 (SFS) Jefferson, SD St. Peter Church.
Swift, Bruce *o.s.b.* '60 (SPC) Buffalo, MO St. William Church; Conway, MO Sacred Heart Church.
Swift, Bruce *o.s.b.* '90 (SPC) Fordland, MO Ozark Correctional Center.
Swift, Daniel (TR) Leave of Absence.
Swift, Gerald *s.t.* '46 (WDC) [M] Adelphi, MD Missionary Servants of the Most Holy Trinity.
Swift, James E. *c.m.* '78 (STL) [A] St. Louis, MO Kenrick-Glennon Seminary; [P] St. Louis, MO Vincentian Residence.
Swift, John *s.v.d.* '75 (CHI) [B] Techny, IL Divine Word Residence.
Swift, Walter A. '69 (SPR) Brimfield, MA St. Christopher's Church.
Swift, William J. '44 (TLS) [11] Tulsa, OK Church of St. Mary.
Swigan, James Mc. *c.ss.r.* '55 (MGZ) Aguadilla, PR St. Charles Borromeo Church.
Swiger, Msgr. Charles W. '63 (RVC) Farmingdale, NY St. Kilian Church.
Swing, R. John '70 (LC) Babcock, WI All Saints Church; Nekoosa, WI Sacred Heart of Jesus Church; Port Edwards, WI St. Alexander Church.
Swirski, Thaddeus M. '54 (CLV) [6] Akron, OH St. Hedwig Church.
Swisshelm, Germain *o.s.b.* '60 (IND) [J] St. Meinrad, IN St. Meinrad Archabbey.
Switalksi, Casimir S. '40 (SPR) Retired.
Switalski, Bruno (CHI) [198] Chicago, IL St. Tarcissus Church.
Switalski, Casimir S. '40 (SPR) [H] Holyoke, MA Sisters of Providence Care Centers, Inc.
Switanowski, Robert Joseph *o.f.m.conv.* '90 (MIL) [45] Milwaukee, WI Basilica of St. Josaphat Church.
Swizdor, Matthew *o.f.m.conv.* '43 (ROC) [6] Auburn, NY St. Hyacinth Church.
Swoger, John W. '63 (E) Youngsville, PA St. Luke Church.
Swoger, Mark S. '85 (E) Du Bois, PA St. Michael Church; [C] Du Bois, PA Du Bois Area Catholic Schools; [K] Du Bois, PA Christ the King Manor, Inc.
Swolek, Richard L. '63 (OM) [43] Omaha, NE St. Stanislaus Church.
Swope, John W. *s.j.* '86 (BAL) [M] Baltimore, MD Jesuit Fathers and Brothers Maryland Provincial Curia.
Swope, John W. *s.j.* '86 (FgM) Provinces.
Swope, Mark G. '90 (PH) Springfield, PA Holy Cross Church.
Swope, Msgr. Timothy J. '66 (ALT) Meyersdale, PA SS. Philip and James Church.
Sybertz, Donald F. *m.m.* '55 (FgM) Maryknoll Foreign Missions.
Sykes, Gregory '77 (KCK) Fort Leavenworth, KS St. Ignatius Chapel Church.
Sykes, Gregory '77 (OG) Military Chaplains.
Sykora, Paul M. *m.m.* '76 (FgM) Maryknoll Foreign Missions.
Sylva, Eugene R. '93 (PAT) Hawthorne, NJ St. Anthony's Church.

Sylvester, J. Wilfred '52 (LAF) Retired.
Sylvestre, Ernest *o.m.i.* '61 (SD) [1] Chula Vista, CA Most Precious Blood Church.
Sylvia, Albert A. '66 (BO) [11] Lawrence, MA SS. Peter and Paul Church.
Sylvia, Edmund J. '77 (STU) [A] Steubenville, OH Franciscan University of Steubenville.
Symes, David L. *c.m.* '47 (PH) [AA] Philadelphia, PA Congregation of the Mission.
Symes, Joseph J. *c.m.* '50 (PH) [AA] Philadelphia, PA Congregation of the Mission.
Symolon, Lawrence '75 (HRT) [5] West Haven, CT St. Paul's Church.
Synowiak, Msgr. Edward F. '51 (BUF) [23] Buffalo, NY St. Florian Church.
Sypek, Msgr. Stanislaus T. '43 (BO) [2] Boston, MA St. Adalbert Church.
Sypko, Tadeusz Marek '92 (NEW) On Duty Outside the Archdiocese.
Sypko, Tadeusz Marek '92 (TUC) Safford, AZ St. Rose of Lima Church.
Syracuse, Ross *o.f.m.conv.* '53 (BAL) [90] Baltimore, MD St. Stanislaus Kostka Church.
Syracuse, Ross *o.f.m.conv.* '78 (BAL) [20] Baltimore, MD St. Casimir Church.
Syrianey, Robert '45 (DEN) [2] Aurora, CO St. Michael the Archangel Church; Retired.
Sys, Joseph *m.afr.* '41 (SP) [O] St. Petersburg, FL Missionaries of Africa.
Syslo, Alan M. *c.s.v.* '66 (CHI) [N] Arlington Heights, IL Viatorian Province Center-Clerics of St. Viator.
Sysol, Steven M. *o.f.m.* '79 (NY) [DD] New York, NY Franciscan Province of the Immaculate Conception.
Syverstad, Daniel *o.p.* (OAK) [N] Oakland, CA Western Dominican Province.
Syverstad, Daniel *o.p.* '82 (FgM) Dominican - Order of Preachers Foreign Missions.
Syvinski, Henry B. *o.s.a.* '47 (PH) [AA] Villanova, PA St. Thomas Monastery.
Szabelski, Joseph R. '70 (CHI) [98] Chicago, IL St. James Church.
Szabo, Edward J. '57 (CLV) Stow, OH Holy Family Church.
Szabo, Msgr. Julius J. '36 (BUF) Retired; [O] Tonawanda, NY O'Hara Residence.
Szabo, Marcel '71 (PSC) Passaic, NJ St. Michael Cathedral; Mahwah, NJ Holy Spirit Church.
Szada, John A., Jr. '78 (HBG) Harrisburg, PA Harrisburg Hospital; Harrisburg, PA Polyclinic Medical Clinic.
Szadiak, Frank *c.ss.r.* '73 (PHU) Newark, NJ St. John the Baptist Church.
Szafranski, Richard T. '75 (SAG) Vassar, MI St. Frances Xavier Cabrini Church.
Szakaly, Anthony V. *c.s.c.* '92 (FTW) [12] South Bend, IN St. Joseph Church.
Szal, George *s.m.* (BO) [4] Methuen, MA St. Theresa Church.
Szal, Ignatius J. '44 (PH) Oreland, PA Holy Martyrs Church; Retired.
Szamocki, Piotr '91 (CAM) Westville Grove, NJ Most Holy Redeemer Church.
Szamreta, John *o.f.m.cap.* '81 (FgM) Capuchin Foreign Missions.
Szanto, Hubert S. *o.praem.* '48 (ORG) [A] Silverado, CA St. Michael's Norbertine Postulancy, Novitiate and Juniorate; [H] Silverado, CA Norbertine Fathers of Orange Inc.; [N] El Toro, CA Aid to the Church In Need, Inc.
Szantyr, Eugene R. '78 (BGP) [17] Bridgeport, CT St. Patrick Church; Bridgeport, CT Bridgeport Hospital.
Szantyr, John '57 (WOR) Absent on Leave.
Szanyi, Mark *o.f.m.conv.* '78 (PMB) Boynton Beach, FL St. Mark Church.
Szapka, Msgr. Edward J. '38 (TYL) Retired.
Szarek, Eugene *c.r.* '67 (CHI) [74] Chicago, IL St. Hedwig Church.
Szarek, Joseph '39 (ALB) Retired.
Szarek, Mitchell '57 (DET) [19] Detroit, MI St. Cunegunda Church.
Szarka, Balthasar *o.cist.* '49 (DAL) [M] Irving, TX Cistercian Abbey of Our Lady of Dallas.
Szarnicki, Henry '56 (PIT) Allegheny County, PA Marian Manor, Inc.; [L] Pittsburgh, PA Marian Manor Corp.
Szarnicki, Zygmunt V. '45 (PIT) Retired; [O] Pittsburgh, PA St. John Vianney Manor.
Szaroleta, Andrew L. '77 (MET) Clinton, NJ Immaculate Conception Church; Clinton, NJ Hunterdon State School.
Szarwark, Stan *c.i.c.m.* '64 (FgM) Missionhurst Foreign Missions.
Szatkowski, Casimir M. (CHI) Retired.
Szatkowski, Casimir M. '50 (CHI) [61] Chicago, IL St. Florian Church.
Szczapa, Stanley J. '71 (NOR) Vernon, CT Sacred Heart Church.
Szczepanik, John J. '88 (MET) Lambertville, NJ St. John the Evangelist Church.
Szczepankiewicz, Gary '75 (BUF) [1] North Tonawanda, NY Ascension Church.
Szczerbicki, Thaddeus P. '40 (LC) Retired.
Szczesniak, Harry F. '72 (BUF) [8] Cheektowaga, NY Our Lady of Czestochowa Church.
Szczesny, John S. '75 (GBG) Brownsville, PA St. Mary Church.
Szczesny, Michael S. '36 (GI) Retired.
Szczesny, Walter J. '90 (BUF) Hamburg, NY SS. Peter and Paul Church.
Szczkowski, Jan '88 (MAR) Engadine, MI Our Lady of Lourdes Church.
Szczygiel, Edwin A. '47 (DET) [38] Detroit, MI St. John Cantius Church.
Szczykutowicz, Francis S. '58 (PT) Sunny Hills, FL St. Theresa Church.
Szebenyi, Andrew L. *s.j.* '61 (SY) [S] Syracuse, NY Jesuits at LeMoyne, Inc.
Szekula, Augustin '44 (ARM) [A] La Crescenta, CA Mekhitarist School.
Szelest, Theodore A. '47 (NEW) Dumont, NJ St. Mary's Church; Retired.
Szeman, Stephen '53 (SEA) Retired.
Szemborski, Chester *s.d.b.* '50 (NY) [FF] West Haverstraw, NY Don Bosco Retreat Center and Marian Shrine; [FF] West Haverstraw, NY Marian Shrine.
Szemla, Patrick *o.f.m.* '43 (GRY) [J] Cedar Lake, IN Our Lady of Lourdes Friary.
Szepe, Ladislaus *s.f.o.* '35 (GB) [I] Pulaski, WI Assumption of B.V.M. Friary.
Szewczyk, Grzegorz *s.d.s.* '91 (NEW) [N] Verona, NJ The Salvatorian Fathers.
Szewczyk, Joseph '55 (DET) New Boston, MI St. Stephen Church; [H] Pontiac, MI St. Joseph Mercy - Oakland.
Szewczyk, Stanley M. '69 (SY) [25] Syracuse, NY Transfiguration Church.
Szews, George R. '78 (LC) [2] Eau Claire, WI Newman Community Church; [L] Eau Claire, WI Newman Parish.
Szippl, Richard *s.v.d.* '81 (FgM) Society of the Divine Word Foreign Missions.
Szklarski, Joseph '62 (NEW) Lyndhurst, NJ St. Michael's Church.
Szlanga, Edmund S. '48 (CHI) [33] Chicago, IL St. Bruno Church; [99] Chicago, IL St. Jane de Chantal Church; Retired.
Szleszinski, Peter F. '56 (SUP) Hudson, WI St. Patrick Church.
Szlezak, Emeric *o.f.m.* '44 (BGP) [3] Fairfield, CT St. Emery's Church.
Szmutko, Stephen *s.v.d.* '44 (TR) [14] Trenton, NJ St. Gregory the Great Church; [M] Bordentown, NJ Society of the Divine Word.
Szmyd, John '96 (CHI) Wilmette, IL St. Joseph Church.
Szodenyi, Damian *o.cist.* '38 (DAL) [M] Irving, TX Cistercian Abbey of Our Lady of Dallas.
Szolack, Joseph T. '88 (CAM) Merchantville, NJ St. Peter's Church.
Szolack, Joseph T. '88 (PH) [A] Wynnewood, PA Theological Seminary of St. Charles Borromeo, Overbrook.
Szopa, Daniel F. '76 (MAN) [10] Nashua, NH St. Stanislaus Church.
Szostak, Msgr. Daniel J. '54 (BUF) North Collins, NY Holy Spirit Church.
Szott, Timothy J. '70 (DET) Utica, MI St. Lawrence Church.
Szpiech, Edward P. '67 (NEW) [4] Garfield, NJ St. Stanislaus Kostka Church.
Szpieg, Edmund L. '94 (PMB) Royal Palm Beach, FL Our Lady Queen of the Apostles Church.
Szpilski, Joseph *c.m.* '56 (HRT) [4] Ansonia, CT St. Joseph's Church.
Sztorc, Richard E. '69 (CHI) Northbrook, IL Our Lady of the Brook Church.
Sztuczko, Thaddeus J. *f.d.p.* '53 (EVN) [F] Jasper, IN Providence Home, Nursing Home for the Needy.
Sztybel, Jaroslaw '97 (SP) Valrico, FL St. Stephen Church.
Szudarek, Ronald J. '81 (CLV) [19] Cleveland, OH Corpus Christi Church.
Szudera, Ted '77 (GF) Centerville, MT Holy Trinity Church.
Szudera, Ted F. '77 (GF) Belt, MT St. Mark the Evangelist Church.
Szufel, Adam *o.f.m.* '64 (GB) [I] Pulaski, WI Assumption of B.V.M. Friary.
Szufel, Adam E. *o.f.m.* '64 (GB) [I] Pulaski, WI Assumption of B.V.M. Friary.
Szukalski, John '97 (WDC) [M] Washington, DC Divine Word College.
Szulecki, Raymond L. '46 (MET) Retired.
Szulwach, Joseph B. '87 (MET) [2] New Brunswick, NJ St. John the Baptist Church.
Szumilo, Julian *c.m.* '50 (PRT) Lisbon Falls, ME Holy Trinity Church.
Szupa, Joseph '92 (PHU) Passaic, NJ St. Nicholas Church.
Szupper, Michael F. (WIL) [O] Newark, DE Univ. of Delaware Newman Center.
Szupper, Michael F. '57 (WIL) Newark, DE St. Thomas More Oratory Church; Dover, DE Wesley College; Newark, DE University of Delaware; [O] Newark, DE Univ. of Delaware Newman Center.
Szura, Carl A. *t.o.r.* '71 (ALT) [A] Loretto, PA St. Francis College; [A] Loretto, PA St. Francis College; [F] Loretto, PA St. Francis Friary, Third Order Regular of St. Francis of Penance; [H] Hollidaysburg, PA Campus Ministry.
Szura, John Paul *o.s.a.* '66 (JOL) New Lenox, IL St. Jude Church.
Szura, Thomas *c.m.m.* '78 (DET) [K] Dearborn Heights, MI Our Lady of Grace Monastery.
Szwach, Joseph F. '55 (WOR) Dudley, MA St. Andrew Bobola Church.
Szybka, Joseph P. '83 (TOL) Attica, OH SS. Peter and Paul Church; Republic, OH St. Aloysius Church; St. Stephen, OH St. Stephen Church.
Szybka, Stanley S. '80 (TOL) Lexington, OH Resurrection Church.
Szych, Mark *o.f.m.* '53 (MIL) [P] Burlington, WI Queen of Peace Friary.
Szydlowski, Gregory *s.o.cist.* '63 (CHI) [N] Willow Springs, IL Cistercian Fathers.
Szydlowski, Joel *o.f.m.* '67 (PH) [AA] Philadelphia, PA St. Pius X Friary.
Szydlowski, Joel F. *o.f.m.* '67 (TR) Trenton, NJ St. Francis Medical Center; [I] Trenton, NJ St. Francis Medical Center.
Szydlowski, Robert L. '62 (STL) [50] St. Louis, MO SS. Mary and Joseph Church.
Szymanski, Bronislaus '34 (PRO) Retired.
Szymanski, Edgar S. *c.s.c.* '43 (FTW) [J] South Bend, IN Congregation of Holy Cross Indiana Province Provincial House.
Szymanski, Msgr. John B. '57 (MET) Old Bridge, NJ St. Thomas the Apostle Church.
Szymaszek, Leszek '97 (BGP) Ridgefield, CT St. Mary's Church.
Szymborski, Alexander *c.r.l.* '54 (SPR) [1] Pittsfield, MA Holy Family Church.
Szymcik, Mark M. '75 (WOR) South Barre, MA St. Thomas-A-Becket Church.
Szymkowiak, Gerard J. *c.ss.r.* '68 (HBG) Lititz, PA St. James Church; [H] Ephrata, PA St. Clement's Mission House.
Szymusiak, Bruno '59 (SP) Retired.
Szyszko, Brian J. '83 (MIL) [6] Sheboygan, WI St. Peter Claver Church.

T

Ta, Binh Thanh *c.ss.r.* '93 (NO) [23] New Orleans, LA St. Alphonsus Church.
Taaffe, Charles '55 (P) Retired.
Tabak, Thaddeus *s.d.s.* '77 (AUS) Rosebud, TX St. Ann's Church.
Tabbert, Robert D. '79 (VEN) [1] Naples, FL St. Ann Church.
Taberski, Richard M. '64 (HRT) [16] Waterbury, CT St. Patrick Church.
Tabing, Omar '77 (OKL) Calumet, OK Immaculate Heart of Mary Church.
Tabit, Michael J. '39 (COL) Retired.
Tabit, Michael J. '39 (MIA) [12] Miami, FL Our Lady of the Holy Rosary Church.
Tabon, Raymond *o.s.j.* '60 (SCR) Exeter, PA St. Anthony of Padua Church.
Tabone, Marcel '85 (CAM) Washington Township, NJ Holy Family Church.
Tabor, Charlotte (ALB) [S] Loudonville, NY Siena College.
Tabor, Kenneth F. '75 (CHI) Northbrook, IL Our Lady of the Brook Church.
Tabor, Paul J. *s.j.* '88 (BO) [W] Boston, MA The Society of Jesus of New England-Provincial Offices.
Tabor, Paul J. *s.j.* '88 (NY) [DD] New York, NY St. Ignatius Loyola Residence.
Tabujara, Oscar D. '75 (SJ) Mountain View, CA St. Joseph the Worker Church.
Tacaw, Pius Mahn '67 (DOD) Great Bend, KS St. Rose of Lima Church.
Tacderas, Joseph '66 (LA) On Duty Outside the Archdiocese.
Tacelli, Ronald K. *s.j.* '82 (BO) [W] Chestnut Hill, MA The Jesuit Community at Boston College.
Tachias, Alfred A. '59 (GLP) [A] Gallup, NM Diocesan Diaconate Formation Program; [E] Gallup, NM Villa Guadalupe Home for the Aged.
Tacito, Nicholas M. *o.praem* '96 (ORG) [D] Siverado, CA St. Michael's College Preparatory High School; [H] Silverado, CA Norbertine Fathers of Orange Inc.
Tack, Theodore E. *o.s.a.* '53 (TLS) [B] Tulsa, OK Cascia Hall Preparatory School.
Tackaberry, John P. *c.m.* '41 (STL) [P] Perryville, MO Congregation of The Mission.
Tackney, John P. '74 (BO) [14] Cambridge, MA Sacred Heart of Jesus Church.
Taddy, Jerome '60 (GB) Green Bay, WI Green Bay Correctional Institution.
Tadeusz, Majcher *s.d.s.* '87 (NEW) [N] Verona, NJ The Salvatorian Fathers.
Tadla, Casimir *c.r.* '48 (CHI) [N] Chicago, IL Provincial Office of the Congregation of the Resurrection.

Tadyszak, Leonard *s.c.j.* '51 (SP) [O] Pinellas Park, FL Priests of the Sacred Heart.
Taft, Robert F. *s.j.* '63 (BO) [W] Boston, MA The Society of Jesus of New England-Provincial Offices.
Taft, William A. '94 (TUC) Kearny, AZ Infant Jesus of Prague Church.
Tagg, Joseph L., III '88 (MEM) [9] Memphis, TN Holy Names of Jesus and Mary Church.
Taggart, Bruce *o.carm.* '97 (WDC) [B] Washington, DC Whitefriars Hall.
Taggart, Frederick H. *o.s.a.* '65 (LAN) [11] Flint, MI St. Matthew Church.
Taggart, J. Vincent *s.j.* '67 (PH) [AA] Philadelphia, PA St. Joseph's Preparatory School Jesuit Community, Arrupe House.
Taggart, James E. *o.m.i.* '85 (MIA) Miramar, FL St. Stephen Church.
Taggart, John *c.r.i.c.* '42 (LA) [B] Los Angeles, CA Canons Regular of the Immaculate Conception-Novitiate.
Taggart, John L. '70 (WIL) [13] Wilmington, DE St. Thomas Church.
Taggart, Msgr. Paul J. '51 (WIL) Retired.
Tague, Charles *s.t.* '44 (WDC) [M] Adelphi, MD Missionary Servants of the Most Holy Trinity.
Tahaney, Msgr. James L. '63 (BRK) [U] Douglaston, NY Bishop Mugavero Residence.
Taheny, Mark V. '95 (SFR) [17] San Francisco, CA Church of the Epiphany.
Taheny, Robert R. *s.j.* '59 (SJ) [25] San Jose, CA St. Victor Church.
Taheny, Theodore T. *s.j.* '56 (FgM) Jesuit Foreign Missions.
Taheny, Theodore T. *s.j.* '56 (SFR) [N] San Francisco, CA Jesuit Community at University of San Francisco.
Taillez, Daniel *o.m.i.* '63 (STP) [28] St. Paul, MN St. Mary Church.
Taillon, Marcel L. '94 (PRO) [1] East Providence, RI St. Brendan Church; [C] Warwick, RI Bishop Hendricken High School.
Tajak, Ralph *o.s.b.* '94 (GBG) [H] Latrobe, PA Saint Vincent Archabbey.
Tajc, Edward C. '69 (GBG) Masontown, PA All Saints Church.
Takach, Brinstan G. *o.s.b.* '48 (GBG) Bovard, PA St. Bede Church; [H] Latrobe, PA Saint Vincent Archabbey.
Takeuchi, Osamu *s.j.* '96 (OAK) [N] Berkeley, CA Jesuit Community at Jesuit School of Theology at Berkeley.
Takuski, Walter J. '95 (CHI) [58] Chicago, IL St. Ferdinand Church.
Takyi, John K. '90 (PIT) Mt. Lebanon, PA St. Winifred Church.
Talafous, Don *o.s.b.* '52 (SCL) [I] Collegeville, MN St. John's Abbey, of the Order of St. Benedict.
Talar, Charles J.T. '79 (BAL) [A] Baltimore, MD St. Mary's Seminary and University.
Talar, Charles J.T. '79 (BGP) On Duty Outside the Diocese.
Talarico, Anthony M. '70 (CHI) [85] Chicago, IL Holy Rosary Church.
Talaska, Richard J. '68 (MIL) Greenfield, WI St. John the Evangelist Church.
Talavera, Carlos S. '97 (HT) [4] Thibodaux, LA St. Genevieve Church.
Talbot, Felix F. *s.j.* '44 (BO) [W] Chestnut Hill, MA The Jesuit Community at Boston College.
Talbot, Francis A. '63 (MAN) Manchester, NH V.A. Hospital.
Talbot, James F. *s.j.* '68 (PRT) [C] Portland, ME Cheverus High School; [I] Portland, ME St. Ignatius Residence.
Talbot, John *s.j.* (SJN) [C] Rio Piedras, PR Jesuit Novitiate.
Talbot, John F. *s.j.* '59 (FgM) Provinces.
Talbott, Ronald *o.f.m.cap.* (SFR) [N] Burlingame, CA Capuchin Provincial House.
Talcott, Peter '75 (SR) Unassigned.
Talentino, William *o.f.m.cap.* '67 (PIT) [S] Pittsburgh, PA The Capuchin Franciscan Volunteer Corps, Inc.
Talesfore, John '89 (SFR) [52] San Francisco, CA St. Thomas More Church; Special Assignment.
Talesfore, John J. '89 (SFR) [S] San Francisco, CA Newman Center, San Francisco State University.
Taliercio, Pasquale *m.s.a.* '92 (NOR) New London, CT St. Mary, Star of the Sea Church; [F] Cromwell, CT Missionaries of the Holy Apostles.
Talkin, Ralph H. *s.j.* (CHY) Glenrock, WY St. Louis Church.
Tallarida, Thomas *c.s.c.* '51 (FTW) [B] Notre Dame, IN University of Notre Dame Du Lac; [J] Notre Dame, IN Holy Cross Community, Corby Hall, University of Notre Dame.
Talley, David P. '89 (ATL) On Duty Outside the Archdiocese.
Tallman, Gilmary *o.f.m.cap.* '60 (STL) Arnold, MO Immaculate Conception Church; [P] Arnold, MO Immaculate Conception Friary.
Tallman, John (ALB) Albany, NY St. Peter's Hospital.
Tallman, John '88 (ALB) [5] Albany, NY St. Catherine of Siena Church.
Tallman, Stephen '59 (HEL) Stevensville, MT St. Mary Church.
Talloen, Jerome G. '45 (OKL) Retired.
Talocci, Peter J. '86 (PH) [94] Philadelphia, PA St. Martin of Tours Church.
Tam, Francis (TR) Keyport, NJ St. Joseph Church.
Tam, Thomas '50 (STP) [19] St. Paul, MN St. Columba Church.
Tamalis, John J. '71 (SCR) Unassigned or Leave of Absence.
Tamayo, Alfredo (SAC) Folsom, CA St. John the Baptist Church.
Tamayo, Elias '72 (PAT) Dover, NJ Our Lady Queen of the Most Holy Rosary Church.
Tamborino, James *s.o.l.t.* '91 (CC) [H] Robstown, TX Society of Our Lady of the Most Holy Trinity.
Tamburello, Dennis *o.f.m.* '80 (ALB) [B] Loudonville, NY Siena College.
Tamburello, Dominic J. *o.p.* '49 (NO) [30] New Orleans, LA St. Dominic Church.
Tamburrini, Joseph '64 (Y) Retired.
Tamburro, Francis (HBG) Danville, PA Geisinger Medical Center.
Tamburro, Francis '74 (HBG) [G] Danville, PA Maria Joseph Manor.
Tamm, Thaddeus *c.p.* '39 (BIR) [7] Birmingham, AL Holy Family Church.
Tamminga, Robert G. '71 (TUC) [13] Tucson, AZ St. Francis de Sales Church.
Tampe, Eric *s.a.* '49 (NY) [DD] Garrison, NY Generalate of the Franciscan Friars of the Atonement-St. James Friary.
Tamulis, Anthony J. '48 (SFD) Retired.
Tamulis, John J. '40 (GAY) Retired.
Tan, John '86 (BRK) [T] Brooklyn, NY Catholic Migration & Refugee Office, Catholic Migration Services, Inc.
Tancrede, Msgr. Roland '47 (MAN) [11] Manchester, NH St. John the Baptist Church; Retired.
Tancredi, Carl T. '67 (HBG) [4] York, PA St. Rose of Lima Church; [K] Harrisburg, PA Catholic Campus Ministry; [K] Harrisburg, PA Catholic Campus Ministry.
Tancrell, William Luke *o.p.* '59 (COL) [36] Columbus, OH St. Patrick Church.
Tandoh, Francis *c.s.sp.* '93 (CIN) [16] Dayton, OH St. James Church; [26] Dayton, OH Resurrection of Our Lord Church.
Taney, Francis J. *m.m.* '58 (HON) [H] Honolulu, HI Maryknoll Fathers House.
Tang, Emery *o.f.m.* '52 (ORG) [3] Huntington Beach, CA SS. Simon and Jude Church.
Tanghal, Albert '91 (CHI) [176] Chicago, IL St. Priscilla Church.
Tanguay, Andre *o.m.i.* '53 (FgM) Oblates Foreign Missions.
Tanguay, Andre *o.m.i.* '53 (MIA) Homestead, FL Sacred Heart Church.
Tanguay, William H. '69 (CHL) Hickory, NC St. Aloysius Church.
Tanguay, William H. '69 (PRO) [11] Pawtucket, RI Sacred Heart of Jesus Church; On Duty Outside the Diocese.
Tanilong, Gerardo J. '62 (ORG) Garden Grove, CA St. Callistus Church.
Tank, Thomas '67 (KCK) [1] Kansas City, KS Cathedral of St. Peter the Apostle.
Taormina, Andrew C. '62 (NO) [9] Metairie, LA St. Francis Xavier Church.
Tapella, Joseph J. '78 (JOL) [1] Joliet, IL The Cathedral of St. Raymond.
Taphorn, Joseph C. '97 (OM) Norfolk, NE Sacred Heart Church.
Tapp, John G. '84 (SP) [16] Tampa, FL St. Timothy Church; [F] Tampa, FL St. Timothy Catholic Early Childhood Learning Center.
Tappe, Walter J. '85 (WDC) Greenbelt, MD St. Hugh Church; Pastoral Center Special Ministries.
Tapper, John W. '61 (CHI) Hanover Park, IL St. Ansgar Church.
Taraborelli, Arthur I. '64 (PH) [151] Philadelphia, PA St. Thomas Aquinas Church.
Taraborelli, Carmen F. '70 (PH) [28] Philadelphia, PA St. Callistus Church.
Tarallo, Philip *s.s.j.* '36 (BR) New Roads, LA St. Augustine Church.
Taran, Peter *s.a.* '60 (NY) [DD] Garrison, NY Franciscan Friars of the Atonement.
Tarantino, James '81 (SFR) Tiburon, CA St. Hilary Church.
Tarantino, James A. '72 (NO) [19] New Orleans, LA Our Lady Of The Rosary Church.
Tarantino, John A. '78 (PAT) Montville, NJ St. Pius X Church.
Taranto, James '81 (KC) [25] Kansas City, MO St. Matthew The Apostle Church.
Tarasi, Carlo D. '72 (CHL) On Duty Outside the Diocese.
Tarasiw, Ihor '90 (STF) Riverhead, NY St. John the Baptist Church.
Tardiff, Charles *m.afr.* '47 (SP) [O] St. Petersburg, FL Missionaries of Africa.
Tardiff, Edward *c.s.s.r.* '42 (ALB) [L] Saratoga Springs, NY St. John Neumann Residence.
Tardivo, Mario *c.s.* '38 (BO) [67] Boston, MA Sacred Heart Church.
Targonski, Conrad *o.f.m.* '75 (GB) [I] Pulaski, WI Assumption of B.V.M. Friary.
Tarimo, Aquilene *s.j.* '95 (OAK) [N] Berkeley, CA Jesuit Community at Jesuit School of Theology at Berkeley.
Tarlizzo, David *o.m.i.* '68 (SAT) Eagle Pass, TX Sacred Heart Church.
Tarlton, Allen *o.s.b.* '55 (SCL) [I] Collegeville, MN St. John's Abbey, of the Order of St. Benedict.
Tarnawski, Wiktor '80 (ARE) Ciales, PR N.S. Madre del Redentor Church.
Tarrant, Msgr. Edward L. '50 (RVC) Hicksville, NY St. Ignatius Loyola Church.
Tarrant, Patrick '53 (BO) Lexington, MA Sacred Heart Church.
Tarrant, Patrick J. '53 (GF) Retired.
Tarrier, William Brandon *o.p.* '47 (L) [4] Springfield, KY St. Rose Church.
Tarrillion, Joseph A. *s.m.* '66 (SAT) [F] San Antonio, TX Central Catholic High School; [M] San Antonio, TX Chaminade Community House.
Tarro, Michael *c.s.* '58 (HRT) [15] New Haven, CT St. Michael's Church.
Tartaglia, Paul '58 (ALB) Retired.
Tartaglia, Richard V. '72 (PAT) Denville, NJ St. Mary's Church.
Tasch, Hugh *o.s.b.* '48 (KC) [J] Conception, MO Conception Abbey.
Tasch, Hugh *o.s.b.* '57 (KC) [A] Conception, MO Conception Seminary College.
Taschetta, Anthony '71 (JOL) [5] Kankakee, IL St. Teresa Church.
Tascon, Wilson *m.s.c.* '90 (FgM) Missionaries of the Sacred Heart Foreign Missions.
Tascon, Wilson *m.s.c.* '90 (RCK) [H] Aurora, IL Missionaries of the Sacred Heart Community.
Tash, Msgr. Joseph T. '62 (AMA) [11] Amarillo, TX St. Thomas the Apostle Church.
Tasker, Franklin R. *o.carm.* '56 (JOL) Glendale Heights, IL St. Matthew Church.
Tasler, Mak A. '90 (LIN) Nebraska City, NE St. Benedict's Church.
Tassone, Salvatore A. *s.j.* '63 (SJ) [B] Santa Clara, CA Santa Clara University.
Tasto, Harold J. '68 (STP) Blaine, MN St. Timothy's Church.
Tasto, John P. *o.s.a.* '67 (CHI) [N] Olympia Fields, IL The Augustinian Provincialate Tolentine Center.
Tasto, John P. *o.s.a.* '82 (FgM) Foreign Missions.
Tasy, Msgr. Francis G. *v.s.* '52 (FRS) Reedley, CA St. Anthony Church.
Tatarczuk, Msgr. Vincent A. '49 (PRT) [4] Portland, ME St. Louis Church; Retired.
Tate, Joseph H. *c.s.c.* '81 (BUR) Wilmington, VT Our Lady of Fatima Church.
Tatel, Orlando '65 (STP) [3] St. Paul, MN Blessed Sacrament Church.
Taton, Thomas P. '60 (BUF) [8] Lackawanna, NY Queen of All Saints Church.
Tatro, Kenneth J. '76 (SPR) Feeding Hills, MA Sacred Heart Church.
Tatum, Gregory *o.p.* '81 (OAK) [A] Berkeley, CA Dominican School of Philosophy and Theology.
Tatum, Gregory *o.p.* '89 (OAK) [4] Berkeley, CA St. Mary Magdalen Church.
Taube, Sylvester '64 (DET) Special Assignment.
Tauber, Gregory J. '77 (ALN) [1] Pottsville, PA St. John the Baptist Church.
Taubitz, Leo A. '56 (KAL) Dowagiac, MI Holy Maternity of Mary Church.
Taufen, Daniel '56 (SCL) Special Assignment.
Taugher, Timothy J. '78 (SY) Johnson City, NY Wilson Memorial Hospital; Special Assignment.
Tauke, Michael L. '74 (DUB) Bluffton, IA St. Bridget Church; Cresco, IA Assumption of the Blessed Virgin Mary Church; Cresco, IA St. Joseph's Church; [F] Cresco, IA Notre Dame System of Education.
Taurasi, David '88 (CC) Sinton, TX Our Lady of Guadalupe Church.
Tauro, Reginald J. *s.j.* '96 (MIL) [P] Milwaukee, WI Jesuit Community at Marquette University.
Tauscher, Donald *o.s.b.* '65 (SCL) [I] Collegeville, MN St. John's Abbey, of the Order of St. Benedict.
Tavai, Van Camp '89 (SPP) [4] Pago Pago, AS Church of St. Paul.
Tavard, George *a.a.* '47 (BO) [W] Brighton, MA Assumptionist Center.
Tavares, Antonino C. '43 (FR) [6] New Bedford, MA Our Lady of Mt. Carmel Church; Retired.
Tavares, Evaristo '60 (FR) [7] Fall River, MA Our Lady of the Angels Church.
Tavares, Msgr. John E. '55 (PRO) Retired.
Tavarro, Elly S. (ORG) [F] Orange, CA St. Joseph Health System.
Tavella, Thomas *c.s.p.* '62 (KNX) [K] Knoxville, TN Calvary.

Tavella, Thomas A. *c.s.p.* '81 (KNX) [3] Knoxville, TN Immaculate Conception Church.
Tavera, Joseph *s.x.* '71 (PAT) [M] Wayne, NJ Xaverian Missionary Fathers.
Tavis, Gordon *o.s.b.* '58 (SCL) [I] Collegeville, MN St. John's Abbey, of the Order of St. Benedict.
Tay, Msgr. Peter '54 (PBR) [2] Pittsburgh, PA Holy Ghost Church.
Taylor, Anthony B. '80 (OKL) Edmond, OK St. Monica Church; Special Assignment.
Taylor, Augustus R., Jr. '66 (PIT) On Duty Outside the Diocese.
Taylor, Benedict M. *o.f.m.* '60 (NY) [DD] New York, NY Franciscan Friars, Order of Friars Minor, Holy Name Province.
Taylor, Charles F. '53 (CHY) Kemmerer, WY St. Patrick's Church.
Taylor, Daniel '75 (TUC) Yuma, AZ St. Francis of Assisi Church.
Taylor, David H. '74 (PIT) [8] Pittsburgh, PA St. Charles Lwanga Parish.
Taylor, Donn J. '53 (KAL) Battle Creek, MI St. Joseph Church; Retired.
Taylor, Douglas '97 (TOL) Findlay, OH St. Michael Church.
Taylor, Eamon G. *s.j.* '51 (NY) [DD] New York, NY Jesuit Community at Fordham University.
Taylor, Gordon '85 (B) Bonners Ferry, ID St. Ann's Church.
Taylor, James B. '54 (BLX) Pascagoula, MS Sacred Heart Church; Retired.
Taylor, James E. *o.m.i.* '56 (BEL) [F] Belleville, IL Missionary Oblates of Mary Immaculate - St. Henry's Oblate Residence; [J] Belleville, IL Missionary Association of Mary Immaculate-Missionary Oblates of Mary Immaculate.
Taylor, Jon '64 (GF) Special Assignment; [A] Great Falls, MT University of Great Falls.
Taylor, Jon '64 (LAN) On Duty Outside the Diocese.
Taylor, Joseph C. '53 (CHI) [52] Chicago, IL St. Edward Church; Retired.
Taylor, Kenneth E. '78 (IND) [8] Indianapolis, IN Holy Trinity Church.
Taylor, Mel *o.s.b.* '67 (SCL) [I] Collegeville, MN St. John's Abbey, of the Order of St. Benedict.
Taylor, Michael *o.f.m.conv.* '86 (SY) [2] Syracuse, NY Assumption B.V.M. Church.
Taylor, Michael '93 (ARL) Springfield, VA St. Bernadette's Church.
Taylor, Michael J. *s.j.* '54 (SEA) [A] Seattle, WA Seattle University.
Taylor, Michael S. '97 (MAN) Keene, NH St. Bernard Church.
Taylor, Paul R. *o.s.b.* '92 (GBG) [H] Latrobe, PA Saint Vincent Archabbey.
Taylor, Peter (PHX) Bagdad, AZ St. Francis of Assisi Church.
Taylor, Peter '74 (GB) On Duty Outside the Diocese.
Taylor, Robert H. *s.j.* '52 (LA) [C] Los Angeles, CA Loyola Marymount University.
Taylor, Robert H. *s.j.* '52 (SAC) Placerville, CA St. Patrick's Church.
Taylor, Robert H. '56 (WIN) Absent on Leave.
Taylor, Roger H. '64 (MAD) Muscoda, WI St. John the Baptist Church.
Taylor, Samuel (NY) [107] New York, NY Resurrection Church.
Taylor, Senan *o.f.m.cap.* '70 (NY) [DD] Yonkers, NY St. Clare Friary.
Taylor, Thomas '83 (PEO) Absent on Leave.
Taylor, Vincent A. *s.j.* '45 (NY) [F] New York, NY Xavier High School.
Taylor, William '64 (B) Saint Maries, ID St. Mary's Church.
Taylor, William R. '67 (SAG) [2] Saginaw, MI Holy Family Church.
Teague, Bruce N. '80 (SPR) Amherst, MA St. Brigid's Church.
Teahan, Timothy J. '70 (BRK) Military Chaplains.
Teall, Richard *c.s.c.* '50 (AUS) Buda, TX Santa Cruz Church.
Tebangura, Francis '68 (SFD) Granite City, IL St. Elizabeth Church.
Tebbe, Francis *o.f.m.* '75 (DET) [C] Livonia, MI Madonna University.
Tebbe, Francis S. *o.f.m.* '75 (CHI) [U] Chicago, IL National Organization for Continuing Education of Roman Catholic Clergy, Inc.
Tebbe, Francis S. *o.f.m.* '75 (CIN) [M] Cincinnati, OH St. Francis Seraph Friary.
Tebes, Stephen J. '68 (CHI) Norridge, IL Divine Savior Church.
Teczar, Thomas '80 (WOR) Absent on Leave.
Tederous, Elias J. *m.m.* '55 (HON) Waianae, HI Sacred Heart Church; [H] Honolulu, HI Maryknoll Fathers House.
Tedesco, Joseph A. '79 (TR) Medford, NJ St. Mary of the Lakes Church.
Tedesco, Joseph P. *s.m.* (CIN) [M] Dayton, OH Marianist Provincialate.
Tedone, Michael G. '91 (BRK) [234] Queens, NY St. Rita Church; Special Assignment.
Teeling, John P. *s.j.* '55 (DEN) [M] Denver, CO Xavier Jesuit Center.
Tegeder, Michael V. '78 (STP) Mound, MN Our Lady of the Lake Church.
Tegeder, Vincent *o.s.b.* '37 (SCL) [I] Collegeville, MN St. John's Abbey, of the Order of St. Benedict.
Tegeler, Herbert L. '53 (DUB) Lansing, IA Immaculate Conception Church; [E] Lansing, IA Lansing School of Religion.
Tegels, Aelred '48 (SCL) [I] Collegeville, MN St. John's Abbey, of the Order of St. Benedict.
Tegmeyer, Mark *o.f.m.conv.* '95 (SAT) [M] San Antonio, TX San Damiano Friary.
Teichert, Isaiah *o.s.b.cam.* '90 (MRY) [G] Big Sur, CA New Camaldoli Hermitage.
Tejada, Denis '72 (LSC) [5] Las Cruces, NM St. Genevieve Church.
Tejeda, Jose Francisco '74 (MGZ) [C] Mayaguez, PR Opus Dei (Prelature of the Holy Cross and Opus Dei).
Tekippe, Terry T. '65 (NO) [A] New Orleans, LA Notre Dame Seminary Graduate School of Theology.
Teknipp, Robert J. '46 (CLV) Green, OH Queen of Heaven Church; Retired.
Teles, Dennis J. '65 (GRY) [4] Merrillville, IN Ss. Peter and Paul Church.
Telesz, Msgr. Leo '39 (CLV) [14] Cleveland, OH St. Casimir Church.
Teletchea, Msgr. Joseph L. '44 (WDC) Hyattsville, MD St. Jerome Church; Retired.
Telken, Paul E. '73 (STL) St. Clair, MO St. Clare Church.
Tellers, Marven *o.s.c.* '50 (STP) Shoreview, MN St. Odilia Church; [N] Shoreview, MN Crosier Community of Shoreview.
Telles, John '75 (ELP) [14] El Paso, TX Our Lady of Assumption Church.
Tellez, Eric '86 (PHX) [7] Scottsdale, AZ St. Patrick Church.
Tellez, Jairo '62 (SAT) Military Chaplains.
Telnack, Methodius *o.c.s.o.* '57 (ATL) [I] Conyers, GA The Monastery of the Holy Spirit.
Telthorst, Msgr. James T. '68 (STL) [1] St. Louis, MO Cathedral Basilica of St. Louis Church.
Teluma, Lukas Bao *s.v.d.* '75 (LA) [R] Los Angeles, CA Casa Guadalupe.
Temme, Roger *o.m.i.* '76 (SAT) [K] San Antonio, TX Oblate Madonna Residence.
Tempel, Theodore G. '64 (EVN) [5] Evansville, IN Good Shepherd Church.
Temple, Matthew *o.carm.* '82 (ROC) [I] Rochester, NY Whitefriars Priory.
Templeton, Edward J. *s.m.* '53 (WDC) [M] Washington, DC Marist Provincial House.
Templeton, Robert E. '88 (NEW) [5] Union City, NJ St. Rocco's Church.
Templin, Kenneth *s.m.* (CIN) [Q] Dayton, OH University of Dayton Campus Ministry.
Templin, Kenneth A. *s.m.* '79 (CIN) [M] Dayton, OH Marianist Provincialate.
Tenbarge, Timothy '73 (EVN) St. Anthony, IN St. Anthony Church.
Tengler, Msgr. Alvin '49 (CC) Retired.
Tenhundfeld, Carl '55 (GAL) [2] Houston, TX All Saints Church.
Tenhundfeld, Paul F. '54 (COV) Camp Springs, KY St. Joseph Church; Retired.
Tenorio, Roger P.T. '93 (CHK) San Vicente Village, District 10, MP San Vicente Ferrer Parish.
Tensi, Lawrence R. '77 (CIN) On Special and Diocesan Assignment.
Tentori, Franco *o.s.m.* '54 (ELP) [24] El Paso, TX St. Ignatius of Loyola Church.
Terdine, Richard '65 (PIT) Allegheny County, PA UPMC University of Pittsburgh Medical Center.
Terentieff, Robert '62 (BAL) [B] Emmitsburg, MD Mount Saint Mary's College.
Terentieff, Robert J. '62 (BGP) On Duty Outside the Diocese.
Terga, Richard '73 (NY) [85] New York, NY Our Lady of Good Counsel Church.
Terico, Nicholas R. *o.praem.* '89 (PH) Paoli, PA St. Norbert Church.
Terlecky, John '76 (STF) [1] Stamford, CT St. Vladimir Cathedral; [A] Stamford, CT St. Basil College.
Termine, Vincent J. '44 (BRK) Retired.
Termini, Mario '79 (BR) Retired.
Termyna, James J. '70 (PAT) Boonton, NJ SS. Cyril and Methodius Church.
Ternes, Cletus *o.m.i.* '61 (FgM) Oblates Foreign Missions.
Ternes, Gary '79 (SFS) [6] Sioux Falls, SD St. Mary Church.
Ternes, Gary '81 (SFS) [D] Sioux Falls, SD McKennan Hospital.
Ternullo, Joseph P. '73 (SAC) Winters, CA St. Anthony Church.
Tero, Richard D. '74 (ANC) Soldotna, AK Our Lady of Perpetual Help Church.
Terra, Joseph P. *f.s.s.p.* '89 (PAT) Pequannock, NJ Our Lady of Fatima Chapel (Tridentine) Church.
Terra, Joseph P. *f.s.s.p.* '89 (SCR) [M] Elmhurst, PA Priestly Fraternity of St. Peter (F.S.S.P.), North American District Headquarters.
Terra, Msgr. Russell G. '62 (SAC) Redding, CA St. Joseph Church.
Terranova, Robert P. *o.s.a.* '73 (FgM) Foreign Missions.
Terrassa, Antonio *t.o.r.* '47 (NEW) [20] Newark, NJ Immaculate Heart of Mary Church.
Terrebonne, Burnick J. '77 (NO) [3] Marrero, LA St. Joachim Church.
Terrero, Reynaldo '85 (MIA) [11] Miami, FL Our Lady of Divine Providence Church.
Terrien, Douglas J. '79 (DET) Lapeer, MI Immaculate Conception of the Blessed Virgin Mary Church.
Terrill, Richard F. '54 (IND) Retired.
Terrillion, Albert *o.s.b.* '96 (NO) [P] St. Benedict, LA St. Joseph Abbey.
Terriquez, Enrique '63 (B) Caldwell, ID St. Mary Church; [F] Caldwell, ID Albertson's College of Idaho.
Terry, Brian '97 (NY) [DD] Garrison, NY Generalate of the Franciscan Friars of the Atonement-St. James Friary.
Terry, Christopher *o.p.* '89 (P) [18] Portland, OR Holy Rosary Parish & Dominican Priory Church.
Terry, John S. '75 (SCR) Sugar Notch, PA Holy Family Church; [Q] Wilkes-Barre, PA Catholic Youth Center.
Tertzakian, Hovhannes *o.m.ven.* '48 (ARM) New York, NY St. Ann's Cathedral.
Terwilliger, Msgr. John G. '42 (SAC) Retired and in Senior Ministry.
Terza, William R. '69 (PIT) [3] McKees Rocks, PA St. John of God Church.
Terzano, John D. '74 (CLV) Peninsula, OH Mother of Sorrows Church.
Tesek, Albert J. '51 (CLV) North Royalton, OH St. Albert the Great Church.
Teske, Roland J. *s.j.* '65 (MIL) [P] Milwaukee, WI Jesuit Community at Marquette University.
Teslovic, Eugene J. '77 (RIC) [8] Virginia Beach, VA St. Luke Church.
Tessarolo, Giulivo *c.s.* '39 (NY) [94] New York, NY Our Lady of Pompeii Church.
Tessmer, Richard A. (CHI) Retired.
Testa, David '67 (ALB) On Duty Outside the Diocese.
Testa, David '67 (STU) [A] Steubenville, OH Franciscan University of Steubenville; [F] Steubenville, OH Holy Spirit Monastery.
Testa, Genaro J. '47 (HRT) Retired.
Testa, Jess '88 (JOL) Clarendon Hills, IL Notre Dame Church.
Testa, Richard '67 (ALB) Special Assignment.
Testa, Msgr. Steve J. *v.f.* '64 (ALX) Bunkie, LA St. Anthony of Padua Church.
Testagrossa, Joseph *o.f.m.cap.* '57 (SP) [O] Seminole, FL Capuchin Franciscan Residence.
Teta, Michael J. '74 (TUC) Absent on Leave.
Teter, Patrick A. '93 (SPC) [5] Springfield, MO St. Elizabeth Ann Seton Church.
Teti, James '97 (NEW) Ridgefield Park, NJ St. Francis of Assisi Church.
Tetlow, John H. '84 (STA) [3] Jacksonville, FL Christ the King Church.
Tetlow, Joseph A. *s.j.* '60 (NO) [P] New Orleans, LA Jesuit Provincial Office.
Tetrault, Ralph D. '65 (FR) Retired.
Tetrault, Raymond L. '60 (PRO) [32] Providence, RI St. Teresa of Avila Church.
Tetreault, Msgr. Jean C. '49 (BGP) Newtown, CT St. Rose of Lima Church; Retired.
Tetreault, Maynard *o.f.m.* '60 (DET) [B] Detroit, MI Duns Scotus.
Tetreault, Maynard *o.f.m.* '60 (LEX) Cumberland, KY St. Stephen Church.
Tetreault, Raymond A. '71 (PRO) North Smithfield, RI St. John the Evangelist Church.
Tetzlaff, Joseph W. '39 (LC) Retired.
Teufel, Charles B. '62 (WH) Wellsburg, WV St. John The Evangelist Church; [S] Wheeling, WV Mount Calvary.
Tevaga, Emani '86 (SPP) [2] Pago Pago, AS Co-Cathedral of St. Joseph the Worker.
Teverzczuk, William J. '73 (PH) Penndel, PA Our Lady of Grace Church.
Tevington, Thomas *o.s.a.* '34 (ORG) Buena Park, CA St. Pius V Church.
Tewes, John Edwin Thayer '96 (ARL) Fredericksburg, VA St. Mary Church.
Tewes, Msgr. Thomas J. '63 (BAL) [70] Baltimore, MD Our Lady of Hope Church.
Texada, David Ker '80 (NO) Retired.
Tey, Jose R. *s.j.* '59 (MIA) [D] Miami, FL Belen Jesuit Preparatory School; [H] Miami, FL Villa Javier.
Tezie, John M. '59 (CLV) Grafton, OH Assumption Church.
Tezie, William F. '56 (CLV) [38] Cleveland, OH St. John Nepomucene Church.
Thaar, Gerald *o.s.c.* '65 (DET) Royal Oak, MI St. Dennis Church; [K] Riverview, MI Crosier Community of Riverview.
Thachet, Joseph '60 (KAL) Retired.

Thaden, Roy W. *s.j.* '73 (FgM) Provinces.

Thaden, William A. '88 (CLV) El Salvador, C.A., OH Parroquial Inmaculada Concepcion.

Thadeu, Joseph S. '47 (PRO) Retired.

Thai, Thomas Vu Minh '54 (LEX) Carlisle, KY Shrine of Our Lady of Guadalupe Church; Paris, KY Annunciation of the Blessed Virgin Mary Church.

Thai Minh Tran, Joseph *s.s.s.* '94 (SFE) [23] Albuquerque, NM St. Charles Borromeo Church.

Thainese, Arulando '82 (FAR) Larimore, ND St. Stephen's Church.

Thainese, Joachim *s.j.* (MIL) [P] Milwaukee, WI Jesuit Community at Marquette University.

Thalanany, Joseph *v.c.* (SFS) [F] Emery, SD Vincentian Congregation.

Thalanany, Joseph *v.c.* '67 (SFS) Emery, SD St. Martin Church.

Thaler, Joseph L. *m.m.* '70 (NY) [DD] Maryknoll, NY Maryknoll Fathers and Brothers.

Thall, Apollinaris I. *s.j.* '83 (CI) Nemar, FM St. Mary Church.

Thalman, Eugene A. *m.m.* '60 (FgM) Maryknoll Foreign Missions.

Thalman, Eugene A. *m.m.* '60 (NY) [DD] Maryknoll, NY Maryknoll Fathers and Brothers.

Thamert, Mark *o.s.b.* '69 (SCL) [D] Collegeville, MN St. John's Preparatory School.

Thamert, Mark *o.s.b.* '79 (SCL) [I] Collegeville, MN St. John's Abbey, of the Order of St. Benedict.

Thames, Robert '64 (FWT) On Duty Outside the Diocese.

Thanh, Mark Tran-Xuan '59 (IND) [22] Indianapolis, IN St. Joseph Church.

Thanh, Nguyen Duc *c.ss.r.* '96 (LA) [R] Baldwin Park, CA Vietnamese Redemptorist Mission.

Thanh, Nguyen Van (ORG) [7] Santa Ana, CA St. Barbara's Church.

Thanh Hung, John B. '54 (MIL) [7] Milwaukee, WI St. Anthony Church.

Thannickal, Joseph *s.d.b.* '82 (SFR) [8] San Francisco, CA St. Brendan Church.

Thanugundla, Joseph '75 (CHI) [94] Chicago, IL Immaculate Heart of Mary Church.

Thapwa, Stephen M. '76 (WCH) Cherryvale, KS St. Francis Xavier's Church; Independence, KS St. Andrew Church.

Tharappel, Augustine '70 (TYL) [1] Tyler, TX Cathedral of the Immaculate Conception.

Tharayil, John *c.m.i.* '74 (PH) Croydon, PA St. Thomas Aquinas Church.

Tharp, Larry R. '77 (CIN) [84] Cincinnati, OH St. Teresa Church.

That Son, Nguyen Ngoc '90 (WH) Gary, WV Our Lady of Victory Church; Powhatan, WV Sacred Heart Church.

Thatcher, John R. *s.j.* '47 (SPK) [K] Spokane, WA Regis Community.

Thawale, P.J. (NY) [8] Yonkers, NY St. Eugene Church.

Thayer, David D. *s.s.* '75 (BAL) [A] Baltimore, MD St. Mary's Seminary and University.

Thayer, David D. *s.s.* '75 (HRT) On Duty Outside the Archdiocese.

Thayer, David D. *s.s.* '75 (WDC) [A] Washington, DC Theological College of the Catholic University of America.

Thein, Edward '79 (ATL) [1] Marietta, GA Holy Family Church.

Theis, Gerald *s.v.d.* '80 (FgM) Society of the Divine Word Foreign Missions.

Theis, Gerald J. *o.s.a.* '53 (JOL) [C] New Lenox, IL Providence Catholic High School; [J] New Lenox, IL Augustinian Friary.

Theis, Jeffrey '83 (ORG) Inactive Leave.

Theisen, Donald J. '42 (LC) Retired.

Theisen, Eugene A. *m.m.* '53 (FgM) Maryknoll Foreign Missions.

Theisen, John J. '59 (MIL) Retired.

Theisen, Kenneth *o.s.b.* '84 (RCK) [A] Aurora, IL Marmion Abbey; [H] Aurora, IL Marmion Abbey-St. Augustine's Abbey.

Theisen, Roman G. *m.m.* '54 (FgM) Maryknoll Foreign Missions.

Theisen, Wilfred *o.s.b.* '56 (SCL) [I] Collegeville, MN St. John's Abbey, of the Order of St. Benedict.

Theiss, Daniel *c.m.* '90 (CHI) [N] Chicago, IL Vincentian Community, Congregation of the Mission, Midwest Province.

Thekkedam, George '60 (LUB) Special Assignment; [B] Lubbock, TX St. Mary of the Plains Hospital.

Thekkeveetil, Bonaventure '63 (RVC) Dix Hills, NY St. Matthew Church.

Thekumthala, Ouseph '75 (TYL) Canton, TX St. Theresa Church.

Thelakkart, Xavier '80 (STP) [C] St. Paul, MN University of St. Thomas.

Thelen, Albert R. *s.j.* '68 (OM) [K] Omaha, NE Jesuit Community At Creighton University.

Thelen, Bert *s.j.* '68 (OM) [23] Omaha, NE St. John Church.

Thelen, Frederick L. '80 (LAN) [8] Lansing, MI Cristo Rey Church.

Thelen, Jerome *o.f.m.* '66 (SHP) Ruston, LA St. Thomas Aquinas Church; [G] Ruston, LA E. Donn Piatt Catholic Student Center at Louisiana Tech University.

Thelen, Msgr. Robert J. '70 (BRK) [204] Queens, NY Nativity of the Blessed Virgin Mary Church.

Thell, Richard *o.s.b.* '74 (OM) [C] Elkhorn, NE Mount Michael High School; [K] Elkhorn, NE Mount Michael Abbey.

Thelly, Matthew (TR) Deal, NJ St. Mary of the Assumption Church.

Thelly, Matthew '71 (SY) Utica, NY St. Elizabeth Hospital.

Thenen, James '58 (NY) Retired.

Thenen, John T. '58 (NY) [224] Staten Island, NY St. Peter Church.

Thennattil, George *t.o.r.* '76 (FWT) Carrollton, TX St. Catherine of Siena Church.

Thennes, Clarence J. '38 (RCK) Retired; [E] Freeport, IL St. Vincent's Community Living Facility and Supported Living Arrangement; [G] Freeport, IL St. Joseph Center; [G] Freeport, IL St. Joseph Adult Day Care Center.

Theobald, Charles F. '58 (NEW) Lodi, NJ St. Francis de Sales Church.

Theobald, Vincent *s.v.d.* '49 (NO) [N] New Orleans, LA St. John Berchmans Manor.

Thepe, Theodore C. *s.j.* '55 (CIN) [M] Cincinnati, OH Jesuit Community at Xavier University.

Theriault, A. Francis *s.v.d.* '55 (BLX) Bay St. Louis, MS St. Rose De Lima Church.

Theriault, Frank *c.s.c.* '53 (SD) [1] San Diego, CA St. Joseph Cathedral.

Theriault, H. *m.div.* '60 (NY) Tivoli, NY St. Sylvia Church.

Theriot, Donald C. '57 (LAF) Abbeville, LA St. Mary Magdalen Church.

Therly, Paul *o.praem.* '90 (CHI) [N] Chicago, IL Premonstratensian Fathers and Brothers (Norbertines).

Theroux, Bertrand L. '67 (PRO) [4] Warren, RI St. Mary of the Bay Church.

Theroux, David J. *s.s.e.* '74 (NO) [I] New Orleans, LA Bishop Perry Middle School.

Theroux, Denis B. (DET) Novi, MI Holy Family Church.

Theroux, J. Raymond '65 (PRO) [3] Cumberland, RI St. John Baptist Mary Vianney Church.

Theroux, Normand *m.s.* '54 (FR) [J] Attleboro, MA La Salette Shrine; [L] Attleboro, MA La Salette Center for Christian Living.

Theroux, Msgr. Paul D. '77 (PRO) Lincoln, RI St. Jude Church.

Therrien, Shawn M. '87 (MAN) Charlestown, NH St. Catherine Church.

Thesing, Gilbert *o.p.* '75 (FgM) Dominican - Order of Preachers Foreign Missions.

Thesing, Kenneth F. *m.m.* '69 (FgM) Maryknoll Foreign Missions.

Thesing, Kenneth F. *m.m.* '69 (NY) [DD] Maryknoll, NY Maryknoll Fathers and Brothers.

Thesing, Mark B. *c.s.c.* '86 (FTW) [A] Notre Dame, IN Moreau Seminary; [J] South Bend, IN Congregation of Holy Cross Indiana Province Provincial House.

Thesing, Mark B. *c.s.c.* '86 (R) [E] Chapel Hill, NC Jesuit Residence, Robert Southwell House.

Thessing, Charles J. '88 (LR) Carlisle, AR St. Rose of Lima Church; Jacksonville, AR St. Jude the Apostle Church.

Thevarkunnel, Anselm '57 (DUL) Deer River, MN St. Mary's Church.

Thevenin, C. '91 (BRK) [65] Brooklyn, NY St. Jerome's Church.

Thevis, Charles '92 (LAF) Loreauville, LA St. Joseph Church.

Thi, Andrew '85 (NY) [102] New York, NY St. Patrick Old Cathedral.

Thibault, Armand *s.m.* '85 (BO) [59] Boston, MA Our Lady of Victories Church; [W] Boston, MA Marist Fathers and Brothers Provincial House; [W] Boston, MA Marist Fathers of Our Lady of Victories (Boston Prov.).

Thibault, Camillus *a.a.* '56 (BO) [W] Brighton, MA Assumptionist Center.

Thibault, Donald P. *o.p.* '68 (WDC) [11] Washington, DC St. Dominic Church & Priory Church.

Thibeau, Richard *s.v.d.* '57 (FgM) Society of the Divine Word Foreign Missions.

Thibeault, Raoul *o.s.cam.* '55 (MIL) [P] Wauwatosa, WI St. Camillus Community House.

Thibeault, W. Timothy '72 (MAN) Londonderry, NH St. Jude Church.

Thibedeau, Vianney '88 (GB) [I] Appleton, WI St. Fidelis Friary.

Thibodeau, Andre M. '71 (MAN) Henniker, NH St. Theresa Church; [N] Durham, NH Campus Ministries; [N] Henniker, NH New England College Newman Center.

Thibodeau, Clement D. '58 (PRT) Gardiner, ME St. Joseph's Church.

Thibodeau, Kenneth *s.m.* (BO) [59] Boston, MA Our Lady of Victories Church.

Thibodeau, Kenneth *s.m.* '68 (BO) [W] Boston, MA Marist Fathers and Brothers Provincial House; [W] Boston, MA Marist Fathers of Our Lady of Victories (Boston Prov.).

Thibodeau, Raynold J. '85 (MAN) [N] Durham, NH Campus Ministries.

Thibodeau, Raynold P. *o.f.m.cap.* '85 (MAN) [N] Hanover, NH The Catholic Student Center at Dartmouth, Aquinas House, Aquinas at Dartmouth, Inc.

Thibodeau, Richard *c.ss.r.* '76 (DEN) [M] Denver, CO The Redemptorists/Denver Province.

Thibodeau, Richard *c.ss.r.* '76 (FgM) Redemptorist Foreign Missions.

Thibodeaux, Charles B. *s.j.* '59 (FgM) Provinces.

Thibodeaux, Charles B. *s.j.* '59 (NO) [P] New Orleans, LA Jesuit Provincial Office.

Thibodeaux, Paul A. '48 (LAF) Coteau, LA Our Lady of Prompt Succor Church.

Thibodeaux, Roger '79 (BEA) Corrigan, TX St. Martin de Porres Mission Church; Livingston, TX St. Joseph Church; Woodville, TX Our Lady of the Pines Church.

Thiel, Chris *o.f.m.cap.* '90 (LA) [F] La Canada Flintridge, CA St. Francis High School.

Thiel, Harold *c.ss.r.* '56 (CHI) [N] Chicago, IL Redemptorists:; [N] Bodija, Ibadan, Oyo State, Nigeria.

Thiel, Harold *c.ss.r.* '56 (DEN) [M] Denver, CO The Redemptorists/Denver Province.

Thiel, Harold J. *c.ss.r.* '56 (FgM) Redemptorist Foreign Missions.

Thiel, Lloyd *o.f.m. cap.* '56 (DET) Detroit, MI Beaumont Hospital; [K] Detroit, MI St. Bonaventure Friary.

Thiele, Richard *c.ss.r.* '54 (FgM) Redemptorist Foreign Missions.

Thiele, Robert A. (SC) Retired.

Thielemann, William A. *s.s.* '42 (BAL) [J] Baltimore, MD St. Charles Villa; [M] Baltimore, MD St. Charles Villa.

Thielen, Jeffrey M. '74 (MIL) [8] Racine, WI St. Lucy Church.

Thielen, Martin '35 (P) Retired.

Thielman, Kenneth '55 (SCL) Browerville, MN Christ the King Church; Sauk Centre, MN State Home School for Girls.

Thieman, Anthony J. '89 (SFD) Camp Point, IL St. Thomas Church; Liberty, IL St. Brigid Church.

Thieman, Donald J. *c.pp.s.* '53 (CIN) [M] Dayton, OH Provincial House of the Cincinnati Province of the Society of the Precious Blood.

Thiers, George G. '70 (PH) [47] Philadelphia, PA St. Francis Xavier Church; [AA] Philadelphia, PA Archdiocesan Oratory of St. Philip Neri (C.O.).

Thieryoung, John '96 (PEO) Bradford, IL St. John the Baptist Church.

Thiesing, Robert J. *s.j.* '76 (CIN) [28] Cincinnati, OH St. Francis Xavier Church.

Thiessen, Dennis D. *s.d.s.* '78 (FgM) Salvatorian Foreign Missions.

Thiessen, Dennis D. *s.d.s.* '78 (MIL) [P] Milwaukee, WI Salvatorian Provincial Residence.

Thill, Richard '81 (PBL) Absent on Leave.

Thillo, Marcel Van *c.i.c.m.* '56 (ARL) [J] Arlington, VA Missionhurst, C.I.C.M.-Central House and Provincialate.

Thimm, Donald H. '76 (MIL) Pleasant Prairie, WI St. Anne Church; Special Assignment.

Thimmesh, Hilary *o.s.b.* '54 (SCL) [I] Collegeville, MN St. John's Abbey, of the Order of St. Benedict.

Thinnes, John M. '64 (CHI) Deerfield, IL Holy Cross Church.

Thirukudumbam, Xavier *s.v.d.* '87 (WDC) [M] Washington, DC Divine Word College.

Thissen, Donald R. '70 (WCH) Arma, KS St. Joseph Church; Girard, KS St. Michael Church.

Thissen, Kevin C. *o.p.* '63 (GAL) Sugar Land, TX St. Thomas Aquinas Church.

Thoa, Ngo Dinh *c.ss.r.* '62 (LA) [R] Baldwin Park, CA Vietnamese Redemptorist Mission.

Thoennes, James '64 (SCL) Special Assignment.

Thoennes, Roger '90 (SCL) Harding, MN Holy Cross Church; Lastrup, MN St. John Nepomuk Church.

Thole, Simeon *o.s.b.* '62 (SCL) [I] Collegeville, MN St. John's Abbey, of the Order of St. Benedict.

Thole, Simeon J. *o.s.b.* '62 (SP) [O] St. Leo, FL St. Leo Abbey.

Thole, Thomas *o.s.b.* '58 (SCL) [I] Collegeville, MN St. John's Abbey, of the Order of St. Benedict.

Tholen, John (YAK) Retired.

Thom, Elmer D. '43 (SC) Retired.

Thom, William *s.j.* '58 (LA) [F] Los Angeles, CA Loyola High School.

Thoma, Anthony '37 (GB) [I] Appleton, WI St. Fidelis Friary.

Thoma, Steven R. *c.r.* '91 (STL) Spanish Lake, MO Our Lady of Loretto Church.

Thoman, Dwayne J. '76 (DUB) Andrew, IA St. John Church; La Motte, IA Holy Rosary Church.

Thoman, James *c.p.* '75 (CHI) [N] Chicago, IL Passionist Provincial Office; [N] Chicago, IL Immaculate

Conception Monastery.
Thoman, Robert A. '28 (PH) [AA] Philadelphia, PA Jesuit Community at St. Joseph's University.
Thomas, Alan E. '92 (ALT) [1] Johnstown, PA St. John Gualbert Cathedral; [B] Ebensburg, PA Bishop Carroll High School.
Thomas, Aquinas *s.a.* '48 (NY) [O] Barryville, NY New Hope Manor; [HH] Barryville, NY New Hope Manor.
Thomas, Msgr. Arthur S. '65 (NU) Military Chaplains.
Thomas, Charles Theodore '73 (COL) Mt. Vernon, OH St. Vincent de Paul Church; [J] Columbus, OH Campus Ministry.
Thomas, Curtis R. '87 (NO) [5] Metairie, LA St. Catherine of Siena Church.
Thomas, Msgr. Daniel E. '85 (PH) On Duty Outside the Archdiocese.
Thomas, David T. '52 (STL) [2] Creve Coeur, MO St. John Bosco Church.
Thomas, Delroy E. (PCE) [B] Ponce, PR The Pontifical Catholic University of Puerto Rico.
Thomas, Donald *m.s.* '57 (LKC) [3] Sulphur, LA Our Lady of Prompt Succor Church.
Thomas, Donald '85 (HON) Retired.
Thomas, Donald N. '68 (SAM) Olean, NY St. Joseph Church.
Thomas, Gary R. '83 (SJ) Los Altos, CA St. Nicholas Church.
Thomas, George '76 (SEA) Snoqualmie, WA Our Lady of Sorrows Church; Special Assignment.
Thomas, George L. '48 (SFR) [2] Menlo Park, CA St. Denis Church; Retired.
Thomas, Jacob '76 (ALX) Campti, LA Nativity of The Blessed Virgin Mary Church.
Thomas, James J. '76 (ALN) Military Chaplains.
Thomas, Jerald F. '56 (SR) [1] Santa Rosa, CA Cathedral of St. Eugene.
Thomas, John '93 (IND) [A] St. Meinrad, IN St. Meinrad Seminary.
Thomas, John '93 (OWN) On Duty Outside the Diocese.
Thomas, John A. '62 (TOL) Perrysburg, OH St. Rose Church.
Thomas, John D. '54 (WOR) Paxton, MA St. Columba's Church.
Thomas, John E. '50 (BO) [72] Boston, MA St. Thomas Aquinas Church.
Thomas, John M. '66 (SC) Bancroft, IA St. John the Baptist's Church; Ledyard, IA Sacred Heart Church.
Thomas, Joseph *b.s.o.* '91 (NTN) Akron, OH St. Joseph Church.
Thomas, Joseph S. '52 (CHI) Northlake, IL St. John Baptist Vianney, Cure of Ars Church.
Thomas, Juniper Jones '70 (RVC) [I] Port Jefferson, NY St. Charles Hospital, Port Jefferson, New York.
Thomas, Kevin *m.m.* '88 (DET) Macomb, MI St. Isidore Church.
Thomas, Kevin T. *m.m.* '88 (NY) [DD] Maryknoll, NY Maryknoll Fathers and Brothers.
Thomas, LaVerne, III '86 (SHP) [7] Shreveport, LA St. Elizabeth Ann Seton Church.
Thomas, Leo *o.p.* '54 (SEA) [22] Seattle, WA Blessed Sacrament Church.
Thomas, Mark '93 (PIT) [6] Ambridge, PA Good Samaritan Church.
Thomas, Mark A. '96 (PIT) [47] Pittsburgh, PA Guardian Angels Church.
Thomas, Merwyn J. *c.s.c.* '67 (FTW) [B] Notre Dame, IN University of Notre Dame Du Lac; [J] Notre Dame, IN Holy Cross Community, Corby Hall, University of Notre Dame.
Thomas, Michael G. '83 (SAM) Miami, FL Our Lady of Lebanon Church.
Thomas, Milton A. *o.s.c.* '64 (LIN) [A] Hastings, NE Crosier Monastery.
Thomas, Norman P. '55 (DET) [69] Detroit, MI Sacred Heart of Jesus Church.
Thomas, Park Seong Yeol (STA) [15] Jacksonville, FL St. Francis Choe Chapel Church.
Thomas, Paschal *o.s.b.* '57 (KC) [J] Conception, MO Conception Abbey.
Thomas, Paul '42 (ALT) Retired.
Thomas, Paul '63 (BAL) Special Assignment.
Thomas, Paul *o.s.b.* '82 (P) [L] St. Benedict, OR Mt. Angel Abbey.
Thomas, Philip *o.c.d.* '79 (MIL) [24] Milwaukee, WI St. Florian Church; [P] Milwaukee, WI Provincial Offices - Discalced Carmelites.
Thomas, Ralph W. '65 (CLV) Gates Mills, OH St. Francis of Assisi Church.
Thomas, Raymond E. '71 (COL) Leave of Absence.
Thomas, Raymond J. '72 (Y) Orwell, OH St. Mary Church.
Thomas, Richard M. *s.j.* '58 (ELP) [N] El Paso, TX Our Lady's Youth Center.
Thomas, Richardl L. '66 (GB) Oneida Township, WI Immaculate Conception Church.
Thomas, Robert '60 (TUC) Sabbatical Leave.
Thomas, Robert '61 (FgM) Society of St. James the Apostle.
Thomas, Robert R. '60 (TOL) On Duty Outside the Diocese.
Thomas, Robert W. '76 (BO) Society of St. James the Apostle.
Thomas, Msgr. Royce R. '69 (LR) Fort Smith, AR Christ the King Church; [B] Fort Smith, AR Trinity Junior High.
Thomas, Sylvester J. '55 (LA) Retired; [DD] San Pedro, CA Apostleship of the Sea, Catholic Maritime Ministry.
Thomas, Wilbur N. '73 (CHL) Hickory, NC St. Aloysius Church.
Thomas, William F. (LR) West Memphis, AR St. Michael's Church.
Thomas, William V. '62 (CIN) Jamestown, OH St. Augustine Church; South Charleston, OH St. Charles Borromeo Church.
Thome, Edwin A. '54 (GAY) Acme, MI Christ the King Church.
Thome, Edwin J. '51 (LC) Onalaska, WI St. Patrick Church; Retired.
Thome, Francis E. '89 (MRY) San Luis Obispo, CA San Luis Obispo Church.
Thome, John J. '46 (SAG) Retired.
Thommai, Raian A. *s.d.b.* '92 (NY) [99] New York, NY Our Lady of Victory Church.
Thompson, Andrew *c.ss.r.* '81 (FgM) Redemptorist Foreign Missions.
Thompson, August L. '57 (ALX) Retired.
Thompson, Augustine *o.p.* '85 (P) [6] Eugene, OR St. Thomas More Church.
Thompson, Charles C. '87 (L) Lebanon, KY St. Augustine Church.
Thompson, D. Timothy '82 (FWT) [14] Fort Worth, TX St. Peter The Apostle Church.
Thompson, Damien *o.c.s.o.* '61 (L) [L] Trappist, KY Abbey of Our Lady of Gethsemani, of the Order of Cistercians of the Strict Observance.
Thompson, David '92 (WDC) Forestville, MD Mt. Calvary Church.
Thompson, Dennis *o.f.m.conv.* '89 (STP) St. Louis Park, MN Most Holy Trinity Church.
Thompson, Edward C, '59 (NEW) Dumont, NJ St. Mary's Church.
Thompson, Edward J. '51 (ORL) Altamonte Springs, FL St. Mary Magdalen Church.
Thompson, George M. '52 (PEO) Retired.
Thompson, Msgr. George P. '65 (NY) [60] New York, NY St. John the Martyr Church.
Thompson, J. Garret '81 (BO) [2] Marlboro, MA Immaculate Conception Church.
Thompson, J. Noel '54 (SD) Retired.
Thompson, J. Timothy *s.j.* '70 (FgM) Provinces.
Thompson, J. Vincent *c.s.b.* '49 (GAL) [Q] Sugar Land, TX Basilian Mission Center.
Thompson, James *o.s.a.* '71 (CHI) [N] Chicago, IL St. John Stone Friary.
Thompson, James A. '44 (TR) Retired.
Thompson, James W. '44 (L) Retired; [L] Louisville, KY Bishop David Apartments.
Thompson, Jerald W. '94 (LA) Simi Valley, CA St. Rose of Lima Church.
Thompson, Jerome F. '66 (MIL) On Duty Outside the Archdiocese.
Thompson, Jerome H. '60 (LA) Retired.
Thompson, John *s.d.b.* '79 (FgM) Salesians of Don Bosco Foreign Missions.
Thompson, John A. '79 (BRK) [88] Brooklyn, NY St. Michael Archangel and St. Edward Church; [166] Queens, NY St. Elizabeth's Church.
Thompson, Kevin *o.f.m.conv.* '97 (BAL) [48] Baltimore, MD St. Jerome Church; [58] Baltimore, MD St. Martin Church; [80] Baltimore, MD St. Peter the Apostle Church.
Thompson, Kizito *o.c.s.o.* '70 (WOR) [N] Spencer, MA St. Joseph's Abbey.
Thompson, Matthew E. '79 (WDC) Hilltop, MD St. Ignatius Loyola Church; McConchie, MD St. Catherine of Alexandria Church.
Thompson, Melvin F. '67 (DEN) [3] Lakewood, CO Our Lady of Fatima Church.
Thompson, Michael '96 (STA) [1] Gainesville, FL St. Patrick's Church.
Thompson, Nils Francis *o.f.m.* '63 (SFE) [4] Albuquerque, NM Holy Family Church; Albuquerque, NM U.S.P.H. Indian Hospital.
Thompson, Msgr. Patrick '60 (LA) Lomita, CA St. Margaret Mary Alacoque Church; San Fernando, CA Santa Rosa Church.
Thompson, Philip '78 (DUB) [D] Gilbertville, IA Don Bosco High School.
Thompson, Philip E. '78 (DUB) Gilbertville, IA Immaculate Conception Church.
Thompson, Richard *o.s.c.* '78 (DET) [K] Riverview, MI Crosier Community of Riverview.
Thompson, Richard '95 (P) Beaverton, OR St. Cecilia Church.
Thompson, Richard B. '69 (MAN) Plaistow, NH Holy Angels Church.
Thompson, Richard J. '96 (PIT) Wexford, PA St. Alphonsus Church.
Thompson, Richard R. '59 (SY) Fulton, NY Holy Family Church.
Thompson, Robert '65 (GB) Absent on Leave.
Thompson, Thomas (SD) San Diego, CA Scripps Hospital.
Thompson, Thomas '82 (SD) La Jolla, CA All Hallows Church.
Thompson, Thomas A. *s.m.* '68 (CIN) [D] Dayton, OH The University of Dayton; [D] Dayton, OH The University of Dayton; [M] Dayton, OH Marianist Provincialate.
Thompson, Thomas E. '92 (SUP) Chelsea, WI Assumption of the Blessed Virgin Mary Church; Rib Lake, WI St. John the Baptist Church; Westboro, WI St. Theresa Church; Whittlesey, WI Our Lady of Perpetual Help Church.
Thompson, Thomas W. '64 (LAN) Brighton, MI St. Patrick Church.
Thompson, Msgr. William '54 (CC) [5] Corpus Christi, TX Most Precious Blood Church.
Thompson, William D. '69 (BGP) Military Chaplains.
Thompson, William L. *o.s.b.* '44 (PBL) [F] Canon City, CO Holy Cross Abbey.
Thomsen, Stephen '86 (LAN) On Duty Outside the Diocese.
Thomson, Edward A. '80 (PRT) Sabbatical.
Thomson, Paul van K. '83 (PRO) Retired.
Thomson, Richard *c.p.* '69 (FgM) Mission Procurators.
Thomson, Richard G. *o.s.c.* (DET) Special Assignment.
Thon, Andrew J. *s.j.* '74 (MIL) [P] Milwaukee, WI Jesuit Community at Marquette University.
Thong, John the Baptist '68 (BAL) [Q] Baltimore, MD Vietnamese Catholic Community at Baltimore (VC-CAB).
Thong, Nguyen Duc *c.ss.r.* '56 (LA) [R] Baldwin Park, CA Vietnamese Redemptorist Mission; [DD] Baldwin Park, CA The Redemptorist Vietnamese Mission Corporation.
Thongamphai, Peter B. '48 (JOL) Retired.
Thoni, Philip F. '49 (KNX) Fairfield Glade, TN St. Francis of Assisi Church.
Thonikuzhiyil, Mathai J. *c.m.i.* '77 (NSH) Madison, TN St. Joseph's Church.
Thoomkuzhy, George '72 (STP) Cologne, MN St. Bernard Church.
Thoonkuzhy, Joseph (KCK) [I] Leavenworth, KS Motherhouse of the Sisters of Charity of Leavenworth.
Thoonkuzhy, Joseph '58 (BEL) Special Assignment.
Thorburn, Msgr. Timothy J. '83 (LIN) [F] Waverly, NE Our Lady of Good Counsel Retreat House.
Thoren, Guy S. '71 (MAR) [4] Marquette, MI St. Louis Church.
Thorne, Carrol *c.p.* '60 (MET) [H] South River, NJ Passionist Provincial Office.
Thorne, Thomas P. '76 (BGP) [9] Stamford, CT St. Leo's Church.
Thorne, Vance *s.v.d.* '53 (TR) [M] Bordentown, NJ Society of the Divine Word.
Thornsberry, John J. '91 (BAL) [L] Sparks, MD Msgr. Clare J. O'Dwyer Retreat House.
Thornton, James W. *c.s.c.* (FTW) [B] Notre Dame, IN University of Notre Dame Du Lac; [J] Notre Dame, IN Holy Cross Community, Corby Hall, University of Notre Dame.
Thornton, Lawrence *s.v.d.* '54 (CHI) [B] Techny, IL Divine Word Residence.
Thornton, Msgr. Michael '69 (JKS) [H] Jackson, MS Nuestra Senora Del Perpetuo Socorro.
Thorsen, Henry '53 (BIR) Retired.
Thorsen, Robert J. '56 (CIN) Retired.
Thorton, James W. *c.s.c.* '64 (FTW) Notre Dame, IN Sacred Heart Church.
Thottakara, Daniel *c.m.i.* '62 (DET) Detroit, MI Clinton Valley Center.
Thottapally, James '71 (SR) Fortuna, CA St. Joseph Church; [G] Eureka, CA St. Joseph Hospital of Eureka.
Thottungal, Thomas '70 (NEW) [2] Jersey City, NJ St. Aloysius Church.
Thozhuthumparambil, Sebastian *c.m.* '62 (NY) [229] Staten Island, NY St. Sylvester Church.
Thrasher, Robert W. '62 (SPR) [3] Holyoke, MA Holy Family Church.
Thro, Edward A. *s.j.* '42 (DEN) [M] Denver, CO Xavier Jesuit Center.
Thro, Edward A. *s.j.* '42 (STL) [O] St. Louis, MO Fusz Pavilion.
Thro, Linus J. *s.j.* '44 (STL) [P] St. Louis, MO Jesuit Community Corporation at St. Louis University - Jesuit Hall.
Thro, Thomas *s.j.* '51 (SPC) Shell Knob, MO Holy Family Church.
Thuer, William J. '46 (HRT) Retired.
Thuerauf, Jeffrey P. '89 (TUC) Coolidge, AZ St. James Church.
Thul, Joseph T. '55 (MET) Retired.
Thul, Robert C. *s.j.* '61 (CHI) [D] Chicago, IL St. Ignatius College Prep; [D] Chicago, IL St. Ignatius Jesuit Community.
Thuma, Clifton M. '96 (BO) [3] Peabody, MA St. John the Baptist Church.
Thumma, Peter *j.c.d.* (NY) [170] Bronx, NY Our Lady of the Assumption Church.

Thurmer, William H. '48 (STL) Des Peres, MO St. Clement Church; Retired.
Thurmond, Benton A. '46 (VIC) Inez, TX St. Joseph's Church.
Thurner, Robert M. '51 (STP) Retired.
Thurston, Anthony '82 (WH) Follansbee, WV St. Anthony's Church.
Thury, Gerald '67 (SFS) Woonsocket, SD St. Wilfrid Church.
Thuy, Pham Quang '73 (RIC) On Duty Outside the Diocese.
Thychary, George (LAF) Morrow, LA St. Peter Church.
Thychery, George '60 (LAF) Franklin, LA St. Jules Church.
Thylstrup, Edward J. *s.j.* '67 (SJ) [M] Los Gatos, CA Sacred Heart Jesuit Center.
Tiano, Christopher M. '89 (HRT) [2] Hartford, CT Holy Trinity Church; Special and other (Arch)Diocesan Assignment.
Tibay, Ernesto '76 (NEW) Bergenfield, NJ St. John the Evangelist Church.
Tibbs, Thomas T. '74 (GRY) Kouts, IN St. Mary Church.
Tibesar, Leo J. '68 (STP) [24] Minneapolis, MN St. Frances Cabrini Church; Minneapolis, MN Riverside Medical Center.
Tiboni, Vito '69 (NEW) On Duty Outside the Archdiocese.
Tibudan, Tomasito '73 (AGN) Dededo, GU Santa Barbara Church.
Tice, Cecil W. '81 (CHL) [3] Charlotte, NC Our Lady of Consolation Church.
Tichacek, Charles P. '94 (STL) On Duty Outside the Archdiocese.
Tickerhoof, Bernard *t.o.r.* '77 (PIT) [O] Pittsburgh, PA Franciscan Friars, T.O.R.
Tickerhoof, David *t.o.r.* '67 (SFS) Lake Andes, SD St. Mark Church; Wagner, SD St. John the Baptist Church.
Tiedeman, Edmund '66 (SC) Mapleton, IA St. Mary's Church.
Tiedemann, Neil *c.p.* '75 (BRK) [U] Jamaica, NY Immaculate Conception Monastery.
Tiegs, James R. '74 (OM) [H] Omaha, NE New Cassel Retirement Center.
Tiell, Maurice J. '50 (OWN) Eddyville, KY St. Mark Church.
Tiemann, Stephen E. '89 (GAL) [1] Houston, TX Sacred Heart Co-Cathedral.
Tiemeyer, Bertram *o.f.m.* '47 (FgM) Franciscan Foreign Missions.
Tien, Msgr. Peter Nguyen Duc '60 (ORG) [G] Santa Ana, CA Vietnamese Catholic Center.
Tiercelin, Harry '47 (NY) [DD] New York, NY Pope John Paul II Residence.
Tiernan, John A. '96 (ALT) Hollidaysburg, PA St. Mary's Church.
Tierney, Berard *c.p.* '48 (SCR) [M] Scranton, PA Saint Ann's Passionist Monastery.
Tierney, Charles *o.m.i.* '73 (FgM) Oblates Foreign Missions.
Tierney, Francis J. *s.j.* '42 (NY) [DD] New York, NY Murray-Weigel Hall.
Tierney, Gary M. '67 (DET) Clawson, MI Guardian Angels Church.
Tierney, Msgr. James E. '50 (BO) [Z] Boston, MA Regina Cleri, Inc.
Tierney, Joachim *o.c.s.o.* '40 (ATL) [I] Conyers, GA The Monastery of the Holy Spirit.
Tierney, Joseph P. '86 (NY) [A] Yonkers, NY St. Joseph's Seminary.
Tierney, Michael '69 (KC) Grandview, MO Coronation of Our Lady Church.
Tierney, Michael J. '67 (RCK) Algonquin, IL St. Margaret Mary Church.
Tierney, Patrick '89 (DEN) Littleton, CO Light of the World Parish.
Tierney, Patrick J. '69 (BIR) Tuscumbia, AL Our Lady of the Shoals Church.
Tierney, Msgr. Patrick M. '57 (CAM) Avalon, NJ Maris Stella Church.
Tierney, Robert G. '67 (SY) [2] Endicott, NY St. Ambrose Church.
Tierney, Thomas J. *s.j.* '62 (RC) [B] Howes, SD Kino Jesuit Community.
Tierney, Thomas M. '70 (WOR) [2] Fitchburg, MA St. Bernard's Church; Gardner, MA Massachusetts Correctional Institution.
Tiesi, Samuel *t.o.r.* '63 (ARL) [J] Winchester, VA Sacred Heart Friary.
Tietjen, Kenneth F. *o.c.s.o.* '56 (DUB) [K] Peosta, IA New Melleray Abbey, Order of Cistercians of the Strict Observance.
Tiffany, Eugene W. '72 (STP) Lakeville, MN All Saints Church.
Tifft, Thomas W. '69 (CLV) [A] Wickliffe, OH St. Mary Seminary and Graduate School of Theology.
Tigges, James '71 (SC) Alton, IA St. Mary's Church; Hospers, IA St. Anthony's Church.
Tighe, Msgr. Benedict F. '59 (BGP) [9] Stamford, CT St. Leo's Church.
Tighe, Dermot F. '54 (DOD) Great Bend, KS St. Patrick Church.
Tighe, Msgr. Emmett F. '51 (WIN) Retired.
Tighe, James L. '70 (BRK) [96] Brooklyn, NY Our Lady of Grace Church.
Tighe, Leonard J. (BO) Jamaica Plain, MA Lemuel Shattuck Hospital; Jamaica Plain, MA Shattuck Hospital Correctional Unit.
Tighe, Timothy P. *c.s.p.* '69 (NY) [104] New York, NY St. Paul the Apostle Church.
Tigreros, Ernesto *s.s.p.* '66 (DET) [K] Dearborn, MI Society of St. Paul.
Tigyer, Paul '54 (PSC) Retired.
Tikalsky, Russell F. '56 (MIL) [K] Milwaukee, WI St. Mary's Hospital of Milwaukee.
Tilford, John E. '66 (CHI) [139] Chicago, IL St. Michael the Archangel Church.
Till, Joseph E. '46 (GRY) Retired.
Tilley, Charles J. *s.j.* '85 (MRY) San Luis Obispo, CA San Luis Obispo Church; [C] San Luis Obispo, CA Mission College Preparatory Catholic High School.
Tillia, Marc '59 (KCK) On Duty Outside the Archdiocese.
Tillman, Msgr. Clyde '34 (SFR) [K] San Rafael, CA Nazareth House.
Tillman, Msgr. Clyde F. '37 (SR) Retired.
Tillman, Richard H. '65 (BAL) Columbia, MD St. John the Evangelist Church.
Tillman, Richard J. '65 (STL) [1] St. Charles, MO St. Charles Borromeo Church.
Tillman, Robert J. *s.j.* '77 (OM) [C] Omaha, NE Creighton Preparatory School.
Tillman, Stanley *s.j.* '45 (LEX) Barbourville, KY St. Gregory Church; [L] Barbourville, KY St. Gregory Church-Union College.
Tillotson, Frederick *o.carm.* '69 (LA) [F] Encino, CA Crespi Carmelite High School.
Tillrock, Raymond J. '69 (CHI) [22] Chicago, IL St. Barnabas Church.
Tillyer, Msgr. Herbert K. '68 (PAT) Parsippany, NJ St. Peter the Apostle Church; [P] Paterson, NJ Martin de Porres Village Corporation.
Tilp, John R. '69 (DUB) Clutier, IA Immaculate Conception Church; Traer, IA St. Paul's Church; Vining, IA St. Mary's Church.
Timar, Frank *m.s.c.* '58 (RCK) [H] Aurora, IL Missionaries of the Sacred Heart Community.
Timar, Frank John *m.s.c.* '58 (RCK) Sycamore, IL St. Mary Church.
Timbre, Roland '61 (HT) Chackbay, LA Our Lady of Prompt Succor Church.
Timby, Bryan P. '83 (MEM) [10] Memphis, TN Holy Rosary Church.
Timchak, Robert M. '92 (SCR) [8] Wilkes-Barre, PA Holy Saviour Church; [D] Wilkes-Barre, PA Bishop Hoban High School.
Timko, Philip S. *o.s.b.* '69 (JOL) [A] Lisle, IL Benedictine University; [J] Lisle, IL St. Procopius Abbey; [K] Lisle, IL Benedictine Sisters of the Sacred Heart, Sacred Heart Monastery.
Timlin, Anthony J. '56 (SB) Palm Desert, CA Sacred Heart Church.
Timlin, John P. *c.m.* '79 (BRK) [66] Brooklyn, NY St. John the Baptist Church; [U] Brooklyn, NY St. John the Baptist Rectory.
Timlin, Thomas D. '55 (CHR) Anderson, SC St. Joseph's Church.
Timm, Richard W. *c.s.c.* '49 (FgM) Holy Cross Foreign Missions.
Timmel, Gerald L. (L) [23] Louisville, KY St. Elizabeth Ann Seton Church.
Timmerman, David W. '87 (MAD) Bloomington, WI St. Mary Church.
Timmerman, Gerard *s.m.* '75 (BO) [W] Boston, MA Marist Fathers and Brothers Provincial House.
Timmerman, Randy J. '93 (MAD) [7] Madison, WI St. Dennis Church.
Timmermans, Msgr. John '52 (ALX) Retired; [E] Moreauville, LA St. John's Village.
Timmings, Thomas '70 (FRS) Atwater, CA St. Anthony Church.
Timock, Ronald K. '83 (MAR) On Duty Outside the Diocese.
Timock, Ronald K. '83 (PRM) Cleveland, OH St. Mary Church.
Timone, Donald '60 (NY) [4] Newburgh, NY Sacred Heart Church.
Timone, Richard F. *s.j.* '64 (NY) [DD] New York, NY Murray-Weigel Hall.
Timoney, Brian '56 (OAK) Piedmont, CA Corpus Christi Church.
Timoney, Christopher *o.c.d.* '62 (SAT) [18] San Antonio, TX Our Lady of Mt. Carmel and St. Therese, Discalced Carmelite Fathers National Shrine of the Little Flower Church; [M] San Antonio, TX Discalced Carmelites (Prov. of St. Therese).
Timoney, Conan H. *c.p.* '68 (BAL) [11] Baltimore, MD Ascension Church; Baltimore, MD Veterans Hospital, Fort Howard; Baltimore, MD Veterans Hospital, Baltimore; [Q] Baltimore, MD Catholic War Veterans, Inc.
Timoney, Conan H. *c.p.* '68 (PSC) Baltimore, MD Patronage of the Mother of God Church.
Timoney, Francis '69 (LAV) [5] Las Vegas, NV Prince of Peace Church.
Timp, Frederick *s.v.d.* '71 (FgM) Society of the Divine Word Foreign Missions.
Timperman, Robert *c.i.c.m.* '49 (SAT) [K] San Antonio, TX Padua Place.
Tinajero, Frank *s.v.d.* (PBL) [1] Pueblo, CO Sacred Heart Cathedral.
Tindall, Harold '78 (SD) Retired.
Tindall, William H. '89 (DET) Newport, MI St. Charles Borromeo Church.
Tinder, F. Dennis '68 (BAL) Pasadena, MD St. Jane Frances de Chantal Church.
Tingerthal, James *o.s.b.* '61 (SCL) [I] Collegeville, MN St. John's Abbey, of the Order of St. Benedict.
Tinh, Joseph Nguyen '57 (SJ) On Duty Outside the Diocese.
Tinney, Edward J. *s.j.* '44 (ALN) [A] Wernersville, PA Novitiate of St. Isaac Jogues.
Tinney, Richard W. '65 (BUR) Rutland, VT Immaculate Heart of Mary Church.
Tino, Robert '71 (SEA) Steilacoom, WA Western State Hospital.
Tino, Robert F. '71 (MIL) On Duty Outside the Archdiocese.
Tinsley, Msgr. Edmond T. '51 (WOR) [I] Leicester, MA McAuley Nazareth Home for Boys; [R] Worcester, MA Monsignor Thomas Griffin Foundation.
Tintle, Raymond *o.f.m.* '69 (LA) [72] Los Angeles, CA St. Joseph Church.
Tiongson, Joselito '92 (SD) [33] San Diego, CA St. Michael Church.
Tippmann, Laurence '69 (FTW) [8] Fort Wayne, IN St. Joseph Church.
Tippmann, Lawrence '69 (FTW) [C] Fort Wayne, IN Bishop Luers High School.
Tipton, Grover B. '96 (STA) Special Assignment.
Tirabassi, Camillo '59 (FTW) [7] South Bend, IN Corpus Christi Church.
Tirado, James '56 (SJN) [26] San Juan, PR San Jose Church.
Tirado, Ramon O. *c.m.* '86 (ARE) [3] Manati, PR Sagrada Familia Church.
Tirone, Seraphin *o.f.m.cap.* '40 (NY) [B] Beacon, NY St. Lawrence of Brindisi Friary.
Tirpak, Adrian *t.o.r.* '60 (ALT) [3] Windber, PA St. Anthony of Padua Church.
Tiscornia, Thomas A. *m.m.* '73 (FgM) Maryknoll Foreign Missions.
Tissera, Edward '89 (NY) [202] Staten Island, NY St. Clare Church.
Titko, Stephen J. '79 (GRY) Saint John, IN St. John Evangelist Church.
Titland, Peter R. *s.j.* '70 (FgM) Provinces.
Titmas, William D. '63 (CAM) [I] Cherry Hill, NJ St. Mary's Nursing Home; [M] Cherry Hill, NJ Vianney Villa.
Tito, Joseph '88 (NOR) Baltic, CT St. Mary of the Immaculate Conception Church.
Tito, Joseph '96 (CHI) [196] Chicago, IL St. Sylvester Church.
Tito, Rocco A. '55 (E) Titusville, PA St. Walburga Church.
Titone, Robert '71 (BRK) [170] Queens, NY St. Gabriel Church.
Titta, Santino '60 (ALB) Cherry Valley, NY St. Thomas the Apostle Church.
Tittler, Leo R. '63 (BAL) Emmitsburg, MD St. Anthony Shrine Church; Thurmont, MD Our Lady of Mount Carmel Church.
Titus, Austin E. '92 (NY) [225] Staten Island, NY St. Rita Church.
Titus, John '89 (SFD) [6] Springfield, IL St. Aloysius Church.
Titus, John M. '89 (SFD) [7] Springfield, IL St. Frances Cabrini Church.
Titus, Rodney Q. '95 (PMB) Port St. Lucie, FL St. Lucie Church.
Tivenan, John J. '72 (B) [B] Nampa, ID Mercy Medical Center.
Tivenan, John J. '72 (BRK) Released from Diocesan Assignment.
Tivnan, Paul J. '63 (BO) Awaiting Assignment.
Tivy, Gerald '64 (JOL) Aurora, IL Our Lady of Mercy Church.
Tivy, Thomas A. '62 (CHI) [148] Chicago, IL Our Lady of Grace Church.
Tix, Michael '92 (STP) Richfield, MN Assumption of the B.V.M. Church.
Tizio, John G. *c.ss.r.* '85 (BAL) Annapolis, MD St. Mary Church; [M] Annapolis, MD Saint Mary Rectory.
Tizio, Joseph *c.ss.r.* '75 (NY) [78] New York, NY Most Holy Redeemer Church.
Tizio, Joseph C. *c.ss.r.* '75 (PH) [135] Philadelphia, PA St. Peter the Apostle Church.
Tkach, Norman A. '56 (SLC) On Duty Outside the Diocese.
Tkachuk, William '81 (CHI) Schaumburg, IL Church of the Holy Spirit.

Tlapa, Richard J. (CHI) Retired.
Tlucek, Edward *o.f.m.* '78 (GB) Pulaski, WI Assumption of the Blessed Virgin Mary Church; [I] Pulaski, WI Assumption of B.V.M. Friary.
To, Joseph Lien *i.c.m.* '62 (BR) [H] Baton Rouge, LA Incarnation Consecratio Mission.
Toal, Bernard *s.s.c.* '43 (DAL) Grand Prairie, TX Immaculate Conception Church.
Toal, James '58 (LA) [K] Burbank, CA Providence Saint Joseph Medical Center.
Toal, James '75 (ALB) [B] Loudonville, NY Siena College; [B] Loudonville, NY Siena College.
Toale, Thomas E. '81 (DUB) Temple Hill, IA St. Peter's Church.
Toan, Francis '34 (MRY) Retired.
Toan, John Hoang '68 (GAL) [54] Houston, TX Notre Dame Church.
Toan, John Hoang Minh (GAL) [15] Houston, TX Christ, The Incarnate Word Mission Church.
Tobar, Marcelo '88 (BWN) Escobares, TX Sacred Heart Church; Grulla, TX Holy Family Church; Rio Grande City, TX Immaculate Conception Church; San Isidro, TX St. Isidore Church.
Tobias, Humphrey '48 (MIL) [P] Burlington, WI Queen of Peace Friary.
Tobias, Joseph *m.s.c.* '66 (PH) Ottsville, PA St. John the Baptist Church.
Tobin, Chuck '68 (KC) Maryville, MO St. Gregory Barbarigo Church.
Tobin, Douglas R. '81 (CAM) Oaklyn, NJ St. Aloysius Church.
Tobin, Eamon '72 (ORL) Cocoa Beach, FL Church of Our Saviour.
Tobin, Flavian *o.f.m.* '45 (BO) [BB] Boston, MA St. Anthony Shrine.
Tobin, George W. '50 (OG) Cadyville, NY St. James Minor Church.
Tobin, James B. '52 (NY) Retired; [E] White Plains, NY Archbishop Stepinac High School.
Tobin, James E. *c.s.c.* '47 (FR) [A] North Easton, MA Holy Cross Fathers Religious.
Tobin, James M. *s.m.* '69 (STL) [4] Creve Coeur, MO Our Lady of the Pillar Church.
Tobin, Jeremy *o.praem.* '69 (CHI) [N] Chicago, IL Premonstratensian Fathers and Brothers (Norbertines).
Tobin, Joseph *c.ss.r.* '62 (LA) Whittier, CA St. Mary of the Assumption Church; [R] Whittier, CA Redemptorist Fathers Mission House.
Tobin, Joseph G. *c.s.sp.* (SB) [E] Hemet, CA Holy Ghost Fathers.
Tobin, Joseph W. *c.ss.r.* '78 (DEN) [M] Denver, CO The Redemptorists/Denver Province.
Tobin, Msgr. Neil W. '57 (DUB) Castle Grove, IA Immaculate Conception Church; Monticello, IA Sacred Heart Church.
Tobin, Paul R. '64 (Y) Geneva, OH Assumption B.V.M. Church.
Tobin, Robert E. *m.m.* '57 (FgM) Maryknoll Foreign Missions.
Tobin, T. Michael '93 (L) [49] Louisville, KY St. Margaret Mary Church.
Tobin, Terence *o.f.m.conv.* (FgM) Conventual Franciscan Foreign Missions.
Tobin, Thomas '59 (GF) Baker, MT St. John the Evangelist Church.
Tobin, Thomas F. *s.j.* '65 (FgM) Provinces.
Tobin, Thomas H. *s.j.* '73 (CHI) [C] Chicago, IL Jesuit Community at Loyola University of Chicago.
Tobin, Thomas J. '55 (FR) [J] North Dartmouth, MA Holy Cross Mission House.
Tobin, Vincent *o.s.b.* '59 (IND) [J] St. Meinrad, IN St. Meinrad Archabbey.
Tobolski, James F. '84 (SUP) [5] Superior, WI St. Francis Xavier Church.
Tobolski, Robert *m.s.c.* '55 (ALN) [K] Reading, PA Missionaries of the Sacred Heart.
Tocco, Msgr. Anthony M. '65 (DET) Bloomfield Hills, MI St. Hugo of the Hills Church.
Tochtrop, Randolph '96 (SPC) [1] Cape Girardeau, MO Cathedral of St. Mary.
Toczek, Melchior *o.f.m.* '49 (CHI) Oak Forest, IL Oak Forest Hospital; [N] Oak Forest, IL St. Roch Friary-Franciscan Fathers.
Todd, Richard J. *c.m.f.* '55 (CHI) [N] Oak Park, IL Claretian Fathers Headquarters of U.S.A. Eastern Province.
Todd, Terence N. *s.j.* (FgM) Provinces.
Todd, Wilmer '63 (HT) [5] Houma, LA St. Bernadette Church.
Toelle, William L. '56 (MIL) Ripon, WI St. Wenceslaus Church.
Toepfer, John *o.f.m.cap.* (DEN) [3] Denver, CO Annunciation Church.
Toepfer, John *o.f.m.cap.* '86 (DEN) [M] Denver, CO Annunciation Friary.
Tofani, Msgr. Richard L. '79 (TR) [2] Trenton, NJ Blessed Sacrament Church.
Togni, Peter J. *s.j.* '85 (SFR) [N] San Francisco, CA Jesuit Community at University of San Francisco.
Tojc, Edward C. '69 (GBG) Donegal, PA St. Raymond Church.
Tokarczyk, Joseph (NY) Florida, NY St. Joseph Church.
Tokarski, Stephen L. '69 (GF) [6] Billings, MT St. Pius X Church.
Tokarz, David J. '91 (MOB) [3] Montgomery, AL St. Bede Church.
Tokarz, John '39 (SPR) Retired; [H] Springfield, MA St. Michael's Residence.
Tokarz, Robert J. '96 (GRY) [2] Gary, IN Blessed Sacrament Church.
Tokarz, Thomas M. '77 (WOR) [2] Gardner, MA St. Joseph's Church.
Tokaz, John *o.f.m.cap.* '78 (PRT) [3] Portland, ME St. Joseph's Church; [M] Standish, ME Saint Joseph's College.
Tokus, William J. *m.m.* '60 (NY) [DD] Maryknoll, NY Maryknoll Fathers and Brothers.
Tolaas, Gregory '83 (STP) [32] Minneapolis, MN St. Philip Church; [C] St. Paul, MN University of St. Thomas.
Toland, Eugene W. *m.m.* '64 (FgM) Maryknoll Foreign Missions.
Toland, Paul L. (BO) Retired.
Toland, Terrence *s.j.* '52 (WDC) [M] Washington, DC The Jesuit Community at Georgetown University.
Tolang, Jaime '58 (SEA) [26] Seattle, WA Immaculate Conception Church; Retired.
Tolbert, George T. *s.j.* '45 (DET) [P] Clarkston, MI Colombiere Center.
Tolczyk, Marion M. *o.f.m.conv.* '54 (BUF) [O] Athol Springs, NY Father Justin Rosary Hour Radio Apostolate.
Tolentino, Eddie '84 (WDC) [16] Washington, DC Holy Comforter—St. Cyprian Church.
Tolentino, Thomas J. '56 (NY) Scarsdale, NY Immaculate Heart of Mary Church.
Tolentino de la Rosa, Lorenzo Maria, Jr. *o.cart.* '92 (BUR) [E] Arlington, VT Carthusian Foundation, Charterhouse of the Transfiguration.
Toliusis, Msgr. Casimir '36 (SFD) Retired.
Tolland, Cyril E. '44 (BO) Permanent Disability.
Tollini, Frederick P. *s.j.* '65 (SJ) [B] Santa Clara, CA Santa Clara University.
Tollner, Gary B. '61 (OAK) [S] Oakland, CA Catholic Ladies' Aid Society, Grand Chaplain.
Toloczko, Bernard A. '58 (SCR) [2] Nanticoke, PA Holy Trinity Church; [J] Nanticoke, PA Mercy Health Care Center.
Tolosa, Braulio '64 (DM) [D] Des Moines, IA Mercy Hospital Medical Center.
Tolve, Paul *o.f.m.cap.* '84 (NY) Valhalla, NY Westchester County Medical Center; [DD] White Plains, NY St. Conrad Friary.
Tomaino, Peter *s.a.* '47 (NY) [DD] Garrison, NY Generalate of the Franciscan Friars of the Atonement-St. James Friary.
Tomalonis, John '51 (PBL) Retired.
Toman, Edward A. *s.d.s.* '83 (NEW) [N] Verona, NJ The Salvatorian Fathers.
Tomasek, Richard A. *s.j.* '73 (MIL) [P] Milwaukee, WI Jesuit Provincial Office, Wisconsin Province.
Tomasek, Richard J. *s.j.* '73 (COL) [A] Columbus, OH Pontifical College Josephinum.
Tomaselli, Msgr. Samuel J. '59 (ALT) Somerset, PA St. Peter's Church.
Tomasi, Lydio *c.s.* '63 (NY) [DD] Staten Island, NY Scalabrinian Missionaries.
Tomasi, Noel *s.x.* '60 (FgM) Xaverian Foreign Missions.
Tomasi, Noel *s.x.* '60 (PAT) [M] Wayne, NJ Xaverian Missionary Fathers.
Tomasiewicz, Edward J. *c.m.* '74 (CHI) [C] Chicago, IL Vincentian Community at DePaul University.
Tomasiewicz, Frank S. '65 (SCL) Kimball, MN Church of Saint Anne.
Tomasiewicz, Mark '91 (OM) St. Helena, NE Immaculate Conception Church.
Tomasiewicz, Mark A. '91 (OM) Bow Valley, NE SS. Peter and Paul Church.
Tomasko, Andrew J. '91 (DET) [6] Warren, MI St. Leonard of Port Maurice Church; [T] Lake Orion, MI Guest House Alumni Association.
Tomaskovic, Emil F. *s.a.* '71 (NY) [DD] Garrison, NY Generalate of the Franciscan Friars of the Atonement-St. James Friary.
Tomasone, Richard C. '80 (E) [4] Farrell, PA St. Ann Church; [C] Hermitage, PA Kennedy Christian High School.
Tomasovich, Msgr. John A. '48 (NO) [24] New Orleans, LA St. Andrew the Apostle Church.
Tomassetti, Berard *o.f.m.cap.* '53 (SAL) [D] Victoria, KS St. Fidelis Friary.
Tomasso, Paul J. (ROC) [L] Rochester, NY Family Rosary For Peace, Inc.
Tomasso, Paul J. '81 (ROC) [6] Rochester, NY St. Anthony of Padua Church; [15] Rochester, NY St. Francis Assisi Church; [20] Rochester, NY Holy Apostles Church; [51] Rochester, NY SS. Peter and Paul Church.
Tomasulo, Anthony J. *o.s.a.* '61 (PH) [130] Philadelphia, PA Our Mother of Consolation Church.
Tomaszewski, Mariano '91 (LA) Pasadena, CA St. Philip the Apostle Church.
Tomaszewski, Msgr. Michael J. '58 (GRY) [4] Michigan City, IN St. Stanislaus Kostka Church.
Tomatis, Christopher F. *o.f.m.* '65 (OAK) [N] Oakland, CA Franciscan Friars Provincial Office, Province of St. Barbara.
Tombasco, Anthony R. '51 (SCR) [6] Dunmore, PA St. Rocco's Church.
Tomc, Victor N. '43 (CLV) [47] Cleveland, OH St. Mary Church; Retired.
Tomiak, Walter L. '40 (BUF) Retired.
Tomich, Daniel M. '76 (CHI) Riverdale, IL Queen of Apostles Church.
Tomichek, Msgr. George (PH) [135] Philadelphia, PA St. Peter the Apostle Church.
Tomicky, Ronald '75 (CLV) Retired.
Tomiczek, Damian *s.d.s.* '82 (SAT) Cestohowa, TX Nativity of the Blessed Virgin Mary Church; Hobson, TX St. Boniface Church.
Tomkins, Robert '88 (SB) Grand Terrace, CA Christ the Redeemer Church.
Tomlian, Robert J. '53 (NY) [59] New York, NY St. John Nepomucene Church.
Tomlinson, Brian *o.f.m.cap.* '65 (FgM) Capuchin Foreign Missions.
Tomlinson, Brian *o.f.m.cap.* '65 (PAT) [M] Lafayette, NJ St. Francis Center.
Tompkins, John-Mary *o.s.b.* '93 (GBG) [2] Latrobe, PA St. Vincent Basilica Church; [H] Latrobe, PA Saint Vincent Archabbey.
Tompkins, Regis C. *o.c.s.o.* '54 (ROC) [I] Piffard, NY Abbey of the Genesee.
Tompkins, Terry '82 (OAK) Danville, CA St. Isidore's Church.
Tompson, Harry W. *s.j.* '67 (NO) [11] New Orleans, LA Immaculate Conception Church.
Toms, Larry '88 (OM) [44] Omaha, NE St. Stephen the Martyr Church.
Tomsmeire, Sidney A. *s.j.* '43 (MOB) [B] Mobile, AL Spring Hill College.
Tomzik, Fred W. '84 (CHI) La Grange Park, IL St. Louise de Marillac Church.
Ton, Anthony '66 (SEA) [2] Vancouver, WA St. James Church.
Tonary, David *m.s.f.* '81 (CC) [15] Corpus Christi, TX St. Joseph Church.
Tonelli, Robert F. '72 (CHI) Streamwood, IL St. John the Evangelist Church.
Toner, Donald *c.s.s.* '62 (BO) [W] Waltham, MA Stigmatine Fathers & Brothers Provincial House.
Toner, Donald *c.s.s.* '62 (NY) [4] White Plains, NY Our Lady of Mt. Carmel Church.
Toner, Edward R. '52 (COV) Retired.
Toner, Msgr. Francis X. '55 (NY) [132] Bronx, NY St. Barnabas Church.
Toner, John G. *m.s.* '44 (HRT) [M] Hartford, CT Missionaries of LaSalette Provincial Secretary.
Toner, Jules J. '45 (DET) [P] Clarkston, MI Colombiere Center.
Toner, Oliver *o.carm.* '71 (VEN) [2] Fort Myers, FL Church of the Resurrection of Our Lord.
Toner, Patrick A. '75 (COL) Plain City, OH St. Joseph Church; London, OH London Correctional Institution.
Toner, Raphael F. *s.t.* '41 (JKS) Philadelphia, MS Holy Rosary Church.
Tong, Peter *o.c.s.o.* '68 (L) [L] Trappist, KY Abbey of Our Lady of Gethsemani, of the Order of Cistercians of the Strict Observance.
Tongotani, Celestin *c.i.c.m.* '96 (SAT) [15] San Antonio, TX Our Lady of Good Counsel Church.
Tonne, Msgr. Arthur '32 (WCH) Retired.
Tonos, Joseph '94 (JKS) [E] Jackson, MS Priory of St. Moses the Black.
Tonry, Patrick J. *s.m.* '65 (BAL) Sykesville, MD St. Joseph Church.
Toof, Daniel R. '94 (ATL) Toccoa, GA St. Mary's Church.
Toohey, Jerome '77 (BAL) Absent on Leave.
Toohey, Mark F. *s.j.* '90 (SFR) [E] San Francisco, CA St. Ignatius College Preparatory (Coed); [N] San Francisco, CA Jesuit Community at St. Ignatius College Preparatory.
Toohey, Timothy J. '65 (STL) Washington, MO St. John's Hospital; [K] Washington, MO St. John's Mercy Hospital.
Toohig, Timothy E. *s.j.* '65 (BGP) [A] Fairfield, CT Fairfield University; [O] Fairfield, CT The Fairfield Jesuit Community-Fairfield University.
Toohy, Msgr. William J. (NY) [I] New York, NY The Catholic Charities of the Archdiocese of New York.
Toohy, Msgr. William J. '61 (NY) [18] New York, NY Blessed Sacrament Church; [I] New York, NY The Catholic Charities of the Archdiocese of New York.
Tooker, Martin J. *c.p.* '46 (FgM) Passionist Foreign Missions.
Toolan, David S. *s.j.* '67 (NY) [DD] New York, NY West Side Jesuit Community.
Toolan, John A. *c.s.v.* '43 (CHI) [N] Arlington Heights, IL Viatorian Province Center-Clerics of St. Viator.
Toole, Arthur A. '58 (ALB) Voorheesville, NY St.

Matthew Church.
Toole, Lawrence E. '67 (PRO) [3] Westerly, RI St. Pius X Church.
Toolis, Martin '70 (GR) Retired.
Tooman, Robert '77 (NEW) [27] Newark, NJ Our Lady of Good Counsel Church.
Toomey, Charles B. *s.j.* '41 (BO) [W] Chestnut Hill, MA The Jesuit Community at Boston College.
Toomey, Gregory *o.f.m.* '48 (PAT) [M] Ringwood, NJ Holy Name Friary, Inc.
Toomey, John M. '61 (BO) [38] Boston, MA St. Joseph Church.
Toomey, Msgr. Leonard R. '48 (TR) Retired; [M] Trenton, NJ Villa Vianney.
Toomey, Thomas *o.s.b.* '50 (PAT) [M] Clifton, NJ Holy Face of Jesus Monastery.
Toonen, Harvey H. *o.praem.* '41 (GB) [17] Green Bay, WI St. Willebrord Church; [I] De Pere, WI St. Joseph Priory.
Topak, John *o.f.m.cap.* '78 (PRT) [A] Standish, ME Saint Joseph's College.
Topel, L. John *s.j.* '65 (SEA) [A] Seattle, WA Seattle University.
Topf, Thomas J. '63 (SC) Fort Dodge, IA Holy Rosary Church.
Topmoeller, William G. '52 (DET) [P] Clarkston, MI Colombiere Center.
Topper, Charles J. '68 (HBG) On Duty Outside the Diocese.
Topper, Charles J. '68 (HRT) [C] West Hartford, CT Saint Joseph College.
Topper, John M. *o.s.m.* '87 (CHI) [N] Chicago, IL Servite Friars - Eastern Province.
Topper, John M. *o.s.m.* '87 (ORG) [H] Buena Park, CA Servite Fathers And Brothers.
Topper, John M. *o.s.m.* '87 (P) [L] Portland, OR The Grotto, The National Sanctuary of Our Sorrowful Mother.
Topper, Msgr. Vincent J. '36 (HBG) Retired; [G] Lebanon, PA Villa Vianney.
Topping, Msgr. Joseph '47 (SD) Retired.
Torborg, Elmer J. '55 (SCL) Duelm, MN St. Lawrence's Church; Sauk Rapids, MN St. Patrick Church.
Torgerson, Msgr. Lloyd A. '65 (LA) Santa Monica, CA St. Monica Church.
Torina, Ronald F. *s.j.* (DET) [E] Detroit, MI University of Detroit Jesuit High School and Academy.
Torm, Agustin '93 (CHR) Military Chaplains.
Torma, Andrew *m.s.c.* '76 (Y) [A] Youngstown, OH Sacred Heart Retreat House & Renewal Center; [N] Youngstown, OH Sacred Heart Retreat and Renewal Center.
Tormey, Daniel '55 (ROC) Retired.
Tormey, James D. '78 (SY) [12] Binghamton, NY St. Thomas Aquinas Church.
Tornes, Dale F. '70 (STU) Belle Valley, OH Corpus Christi Church; Caldwell, OH St. Stephen Church.
Torney, Msgr. John R. *p.a.* '39 (MET) Bernardsville, NJ Our Lady of Perpetual Help Church; Retired; [H] Somerset, NJ Maria Regina Residence.
Toro, Emilio '60 (SJN) Luquillo, PR San Jose Church.
Torok, Bela E. '43 (SAG) Retired.
Torok, Delso '48 (Y) East Palestine, OH Our Lady of Lourdes Church.
Torok, Dezso '48 (Y) Retired.
Torok, George J. '58 (NY) [HH] Sparkill, NY Hallel Institute.
Torpey, Charles L. '69 (GI) Kearney, NE St. James Church.
Torpey, James M. '83 (ALN) Summit Hill, PA St. Joseph Church; Summit Hill, PA St. Stanislaus Church.
Torpey, Matt G. *o.c.s.o.* '56 (ATL) [I] Conyers, GA The Monastery of the Holy Spirit.
Torpey, Michael J. '68 (RVC) Sea Cliff, NY St. Boniface Martyr Church.
Torquato, James R. '89 (PIT) Glenshaw, PA St. Bonaventure Church.
Torralba, Antolin B. '48 (LA) Santa Fe Springs, CA St. Pius X Church.
Torralba, Julio *sch.p.* '58 (PCE) [C] Coto Laurel, PR Colegio Ponceno.
Torre, Emilio Diaz *l.c.* '93 (HRT) [V] Orange, CT Legion of Christ, Inc.
Torre, Jesse *o.f.m.cap.* '61 (DAL) [8] Dallas, TX Our Lady of Lourdes Church.
Torrelas, Eduardo '85 (CGS) [C] Humacao, PR San Antonio Abad Abbey of the Order of St. Benedict.
Torrens, James S. *s.j.* '61 (NY) [DD] New York, NY "America;" Residence and publication office of the America Press.
Torrente, Lorenzo '75 (RNO) Lovelock, NV St. John the Baptist Church.
Torres, Adrian '75 (PMB) [5] West Palm Beach, FL St. Juliana Church.
Torres, Daniel A. '96 (LKC) [8] Lake Charles, LA Our Lady Queen of Heaven Church.
Torres, E. Fernando (R) Lumberton, NC St. Francis De Sales Church.
Torres, Ernesto '72 (DAL) [13] Dallas, TX St. Augustine Church.
Torres, Fernado *sch.p.* '93 (PCE) [C] Coto Laurel, PR Colegio Ponceno.
Torres, Frank D. (GRY) [4] Gary, IN Holy Rosary Church.
Torres, Gabriel M. '95 (ARE) Ciales, PR Holy Rosary Church.
Torres, Hipolito '85 (CGS) Naranjito, PR San Miguel Arcangel Church.
Torres, Ivan '89 (SJN) On Duty Outside the Archdiocese.
Torres, Jose *o.m.i.* '74 (FgM) Oblates Foreign Missions.
Torres, Luis Angel '85 (SJN) [17] Carolina, PR Santisima Trinidad Church.
Torres, Mario A. '96 (LA) Huntington Park, CA St. Matthias Church.
Torres, Martin Betances '87 (NY) [96] New York, NY Our Lady of the Rosary Church.
Torres, Orlando *s.j.* '73 (SJN) [C] Rio Piedras, PR Jesuit Novitiate.
Torres, Pablo *c.m.* '88 (SJN) [55] San Juan, PR Sagrado Corazon de Jesus Church.
Torres, Robert A. '66 (LR) Retired.
Torres, Ruben M. *o.s.m.* '89 (ELP) [18] El Paso, TX Our Lady of Sorrows Church.
Torres Pagan, P. William (SJN) [8] San Juan, PR Nuestra Senora del Carmen Church.
Torretto, Joseph '75 (RIC) Charlottesville, VA Church of the Holy Comforter.
Torrez, Basil '56 (SAL) Collyer, KS St. Michael's Church; St. Peter, KS St. Anthony's Church.
Torsiello, Ralph C. '58 (WDC) Bryantown, MD St. Mary Church.
Torson, Daniel *c.pp.s.* '90 (KC) [B] Kansas City, MO Avila College; [N] Kansas City, MO Avila College Campus Ministry.
Tortora, James F. '72 (NEW) [8] Bayonne, NJ St. Michael's Church.
Tortora, Raymond '52 (RVC) Retired.
Tortorelli, Kevin *o.f.m.* '73 (NY) [35] New York, NY St. Francis of Assisi Church.
Tortorici, James D. '95 (PH) Yardley, PA St. Ignatius of Antioch Church.
Tortorici, Joseph *o.p.* '72 (WDC) [B] Washington, DC Dominican House of Studies.
Toruno, Jorge R. *s.j.* '44 (FgM) Provinces.
Tos, Aldo J. '53 (NY) [61] New York, NY St. Joseph Church.
Tosatto, Lawrence *f.d.p.* '65 (BO) [U] Boston, MA Don Orione Nursing Home.
Toscani, Peter J. *o.s.a.* '47 (PH) [111] Philadelphia, PA St. Nicholas of Tolentine Church.
Toscano, Eduardo '73 (SJN) [18] Carolina, PR Cristo Rey Church.
Toscano, Pasquale A. '44 (HRT) Retired.
Tosco, Lawrence *c.s.j.* '70 (CLV) [P] Avon, OH Congregation of St. Joseph.
Tosco, Lorenzo *c.s.j.* '70 (CLV) [A] Wickliffe, OH St. Mary Seminary and Graduate School of Theology.
Tosello, Matthew '62 (PIT) Prospect, PA St. Christopher Church.
Tosi, Msgr. John C. '73 (BRK) [1] Brooklyn, NY The Cathedral-Basilica of St. James Church; [Y] Brooklyn, NY St. James Cathedral Foundation, Inc.
Tosti, Anthony F. '65 (SY) Canastota, NY St. Agatha Church.
Tosti, Ronald A. '62 (FR) Mashpee, MA Christ The King Church.
Tosto, Louis F. '97 (RCK) [4] Elgin, IL St. Thomas More Church.
Totah, Sami '71 (NY) [9] Yonkers, NY Immaculate Conception Church.
Totaro, Dominic J. *s.j.* '67 (BAL) [M] Baltimore, MD Jesuit Fathers and Brothers Maryland Provincial Curia.
Totaro, Dominic J. *s.j.* '67 (FgM) Provinces.
Toth, Joseph A. '83 (PH) Downingtown, PA St. Joseph Church.
Toth, Julius *o.f.m.conv.* '53 (TR) Riverside, NJ St. Peter Church.
Toth, Michael A. '74 (OG) Mineville, NY The Church of All Saints; Port Henry, NY St. Patrick Church.
Toth, Simon J. *o.s.b.* '59 (GBG) [5] Latrobe, PA St. Boniface Church; [H] Latrobe, PA Saint Vincent Archabbey.
Toth, Victor '48 (HT) Retired.
Totten, Raymond F. '48 (COL) Retired.
Tottle, Gregg '91 (SP) Safety Harbor, FL Espiritu Santo Church.
Tou, John '57 (NY) On Duty Outside the Archdiocese.
Tou, Louis '56 (WDC) Retired.
Tou, Louis A. '56 (WDC) [K] Silver Spring, MD Holy Cross Hospital of Silver Spring, Inc.
Touchette, Marc L. '57 (ALB) [2] Cohoes, NY St. Bernard Church.
Tougas, Paul J. '64 (WOR) Boylston, MA St. Mary of the Hills Church.
Tougas, Roger *a.a.* '60 (BO) [W] Brighton, MA Assumptionist Center.
Toulas, James J. *c.ss.r.* '54 (BRK) [C] Whitestone, NY St. Alphonsus Formation Residence.
Toups, David '97 (SP) Graduate Studies.
Toups, Earl *c.ss.r.* '48 (BLX) [E] Biloxi, MS St. John Neumann Residence.
Tourangeau, John M. '86 (SFE) Ranchos De Taos, NM San Francisco de Asis Church.
Tourigney, Ernest E. '61 (BO) Permanent Disability.
Tourigny, William '80 (SPR) [11] Springfield, MA Our Lady of the Sacred Heart Church.
Tourneir, Msgr. Andre '48 (SFR) [K] San Rafael, CA Nazareth House.
Tournier, Msgr. Andre '48 (SR) Retired.
Tovar, Emilio *c.m.* '43 (ARE) [1] Manati, PR La Candelaria Church.
Towell, Stephen '33 (CLV) [N] Cleveland, OH Sts. Mary and Joseph Home for the Aged.
Towell, Stephen A. '33 (CLV) South Euclid, OH St. Gregory the Great Church; Retired.
Towey, Cyprian *c.p.* '42 (LA) [R] Pasadena, CA Passionist Community.
Towey, Damian *c.p.* '58 (PMB) [G] North Palm Beach, FL Our Lady of Florida Spiritual Center.
Towle, Joseph C. *s.j.* '66 (NY) [DD] New York, NY Jesuit Provincial's Office.
Towle, Joseph W. *m.m.* '65 (NY) [DD] Maryknoll, NY Maryknoll Fathers and Brothers.
Townsend, C. Frederick '83 (KC) Leave of Absence.
Townsend, Charles P. '91 (LIN) Mead, NE St. James Church.
Townsend, Joe C. '88 (TLS) Pawnee, OK St. John Church; Stillwater, OK St. John University Parish and Catholic Student Center Church; [H] Stillwater, OK St. John's University Parish and Catholic Student Center.
Townsend, Ralph V. *o.p.* '50 (PH) [61] Philadelphia, PA Holy Name of Jesus Church; [AA] Philadelphia, PA Holy Name Priory, Dominican Friars.
Towsley, Peter J. '91 (BGP) [5] Fairfield, CT Holy Family Church.
Toye, D. Richard *s.j.* '65 (GAL) [F] Houston, TX Strake, Jesuit College Preparatory Inc.
Tra, John *s.v.d.* '44 (DUB) [B] Epworth, IA Divine Word College.
Trabold, Alphonsus A. *o.f.m.* '51 (BUF) [O] St. Bonaventure, NY St. Bonaventure Friary.
Trabold, Alphonus A. *o.f.m.* (BUF) [C] St. Bonaventure, NY St. Bonaventure University.
Trabold, Msgr. George R. '73 (NEW) Bergenfield, NJ St. John the Evangelist Church.
Trac, Peter Vu Dinh '54 (ORG) [2] Orange, CA La Purisima Church.
Tracey, Bernard M. *c.m.* (BRK) [D] Staten Island, NY St. John's University, Staten Island Campus; [D] Jamaica, NY St. John's University.
Tracey, Bernard M. *c.m.* '74 (BRK) [U] Jamaica, NY St. Vincent's House.
Tracey, Michael J. '72 (BLX) Hattiesburg, MS St. Thomas Aquinas Church; Hattiesburg, MS University of Southern Mississippi; [G] Hattiesburg, MS University of Southern Mississippi.
Tracey, Philip A. '88 (PRT) [M] Brunswick, ME Bowdoin College; [M] Lewiston, ME Bates College.
Tracey, Terence '52 (SFD) Retired; [L] Springfield, IL St. Francis Convent.
Tracey, Thomas S. '63 (CAM) Wildwood Crest, NJ Assumption B.V.M. Church.
Tracy, Charles '63 (SR) Retired.
Tracy, David W. '63 (BGP) On Duty Outside the Diocese.
Tracy, Eugene '91 (SPK) [18] Spokane, WA St. Peter Church.
Tracy, George E. '84 (PRT) Retired.
Tracy, Msgr. James R. '60 (CAM) [3] Cherry Hill, NJ St. Peter Celestine Church.
Tracy, John *o.m.i.* '33 (BO) [Z] Tewksbury, MA Immaculate Heart of Mary Novitiate-Infirmary.
Tracy, John A. '52 (NEW) Retired.
Tracy, John P. '48 (HRT) [11] Hartford, CT St. Lawrence O'Toole Church; [3] West Hartford, CT St. John the Evangelist Church; Retired.
Tracy, Joseph A. '92 (PH) Cheltenham, PA Presentation of Blessed Virgin Mary Church; Graduate Studies.
Tracy, Laurence '63 (ROC) [36] Rochester, NY Our Lady of Mount Carmel Church.
Tracy, Laurence '66 (ROC) [25] Rochester, NY Holy Redeemer-St. Francis Xavier Church; [47] Rochester, NY St. Michael Church.
Tracy, Norbert J. *s.j.* '55 (FgM) Provinces.
Tracy, Philip Michael '60 (PRT) South Berwick, ME St. Michael Church.
Tracy, Robert P. *o.carm.* '63 (NY) Tarrytown, NY Transfiguration Church.
Tracy, T. Shawn *o.s.a.* '66 (PH) [C] Villanova, PA Villanova University; [AA] Villanova, PA St. John Stone Friary.
Tracy, Theodore J. *s.j.* '50 (CHI) [C] Chicago, IL Jesuit Community at Loyola University of Chicago.
Trad, John '41 (OLL) Retired.
Trader, William A. '74 (PH) Westtown, PA St. Maximilian Kolbe Church.
Traeger, Gregory *o.s.b.* '42 (SP) [O] St. Leo, FL St. Leo Abbey.
Traenkle, Mark *s.a.* '56 (OG) Harrisville, NY St.

Francis Solanus Church.
Trah, Luc *s.v.d.* '96 (LA) [25] Los Angeles, CA Our Lady of Loretto Church.
Trahan, Charles Nicholas '81 (LAF) [1] Opelousas, LA St. Landry Church.
Trahan, Harold '69 (LAF) [10] Lafayette, LA St. Elizabeth Seton Church.
Trahan, Romeo A. *s.s.e.* '45 (BUR) [E] Colchester, VT Society of St. Edmund.
Trahon, Basil *c.p.* '62 (HRT) [M] West Hartford, CT Holy Family Monastery/Retreat.
Trainer, Eugene '58 (STO) Modesto, CA Our Lady of Fatima Church.
Trainor, Daniel M. '61 (PRO) [6] Providence, RI Assumption of the Blessed Virgin Mary Church.
Trainor, Herny J. '73 (SFR) [41] San Francisco, CA St. Patrick Church.
Trainor, James F. '64 (WIL) [8] Wilmington, DE St. Mary of the Immaculate Conception Church; [9] Wilmington, DE St. Patrick Church; [G] Wilmington, DE St. Patrick's House, Inc.
Trainor, James T. '44 (PRO) Retired; [P] Providence, RI St. John Vianney Residence.
Trainor, John J. *c.m.* '43 (BUF) [C] Niagara University, NY Niagara University; [O] Niagara University, NY Vincentian Community at Niagara University.
Trainor, Michael P. *o.p.* '75 (PRO) [29] Providence, RI St. Pius V Church; [P] Providence, RI St. Pius Priory.
Trainor, Msgr. Patrick '44 (SP) Retired.
Trainor, Msgr. Patrick '45 (SP) St. Pete Beach, FL St. John Church.
Trainor, Richard F. '75 (WOR) Auburn, MA St. Joseph's Church.
Trainor, Msgr. Robert M. '57 (NY) [125] Bronx, NY St. Ann Church.
Trame, Richard H. *s.j.* '52 (LA) [C] Los Angeles, CA Loyola Marymount University.
Tran, Anh Q. '90 (FWT) Breckenridge, TX Sacred Heart Church; Dodson Prairie, TX St. Boniface Church; Graford, TX St. Francis of Assisi Church; Throckmorton, TX San Patricio Church.
Tran, Anthony Doan '88 (BLX) Bay St. Louis, MS Our Lady of the Gulf Church.
Tran, Anthony Hung Ngoc *o.p.* '92 (GAL) [57] Houston, TX Our Lady of Lavang Church.
Tran, Binh K. '92 (PEO) Ohio, IL Immaculate Conception Church; Walnut, IL St. John's Church.
Tran, Dac *o.f.m.* '89 (BO) [BB] Boston, MA St. Anthony Shrine.
Tran, Dac Tat *o.f.m.* (BO) Boston, MA New England Medical Center.
Tran, John '95 (NY) [127] Bronx, NY St. Anthony Church.
Tran, John Chinh Chan (GAL) Retired.
Tran, John Diem Dihn *c.m.c.* '96 (ALB) [15] Albany, NY Sacred Heart of Jesus Church.
Tran, John Kha '89 (GAL) [A] Houston, TX St. Mary's Seminary.
Tran, John Nghi '71 (LA) Rancho Palos Verdes, CA St. John Fisher Church.
Tran, John Tinh '96 (SY) [7] Syracuse, NY Our Lady of Pompei Church.
Tran, John-Hue *s.v.d.* '95 (DUB) [B] Epworth, IA Divine Word College.
Tran, Joseph '78 (LAN) [2] Lansing, MI St. Casimir Church.
Tran, Joseph '95 (NY) [168] Bronx, NY St. Nicholas of Tolentine Church.
Tran, Joseph Duykim '90 (NEW) Oradell, NJ St. Joseph's Church.
Tran, Joseph Huynh *s.v.d.* '93 (FgM) Society of the Divine Word Foreign Missions.
Tran, Joseph Thang Dinh '96 (NO) [31] New Orleans, LA St. Frances Xavier Cabrini Church.
Tran, Kiem Van '91 (ORG) [7] Santa Ana, CA St. Barbara's Church.
Tran, Liem *o.p.* '93 (WDC) [B] Washington, DC Dominican House of Studies.
Tran, Luan '94 (P) [1] Portland, OR Cathedral of the Immaculate Conception.
Tran, Luong Quane '89 (BEA) [1] Beaumont, TX St. Anthony Cathedral.
Tran, Luong Quang '89 (BEA) [G] Beaumont, TX St. Thomas More Society of Southeast Texas.
Tran, Martin Duc '90 (BAL) [M] Baltimore, MD Sulpician Provincial House.
Tran, Michael Mai *c.m.c.* '93 (BEA) [2] Port Arthur, TX Queen of Vietnam Church.
Tran, Michael X. '93 (SD) [4] Chula Vista, CA St. Rose of Lima Church.
Tran, Paul *o.p.* '86 (PHX) [5] Phoenix, AZ Most Holy Trinity Church; [5] Phoenix, AZ Most Holy Trinity Church.
Tran, Paul *s.d.b.* '95 (SFE) [18] Albuquerque, NM San Jose Church.
Tran, Peter '73 (RIC) [2] Newport News, VA Our Lady of Mount Carmel Church.
Tran, Peter Nam Van '84 (NO) [3] Kenner, LA St. Elizabeth Ann Seton Church.
Tran, Philip '92 (NY) [6] Poughkeepsie, NY St. Martin de Porres Church.
Tran, Phuong Duc '65 (SEA) [Q] Seattle, WA Seattle, Vietnamese Catholic Center.
Tran, Quan '96 (PH) Exton, PA SS. Philip and James Church.
Tran, Quynh Dinh '93 (SPR) [20] Springfield, MA St. Thomas Aquinas Church.
Tran, Quynh Dinh '93 (WOR) [21] Worcester, MA St. Charles Borromeo Church.
Tran, Sang V. '92 (LA) Sepulveda, CA Our Lady of Peace Church.
Tran, Tan Van '92 (DM) Bayard, IA St. Patrick Church.
Tran, Tan Van '96 (DM) [12] Des Moines, IA St. Theresa of the Child Jesus Church.
Tran, Tuan Quoc '97 (ATL) [3] Marietta, GA St. Joseph Church.
Tran Cao Tuong, Andrew '75 (NO) [2] Marrero, LA St. Agnes Le Thi Thanh Church.
Tran Dien, Peter (SPC) [E] Carthage, MO Congregation of the Mother Co-Redemptrix, United States Assumption Province.
Tran Dinh Diem, John Eudes M. *c.m.c.* (SPC) [E] Carthage, MO Congregation of the Mother Co-Redemptrix, United States Assumption Province.
Tran Ngoc Diep, Joseph M. *c.m.c.* '83 (SPC) [E] Carthage, MO Congregation of the Mother Co-Redemptrix, United States Assumption Province.
Tran Ngoc Thoai, Aloysius M. *c.m.c.* '92 (SB) [E] Corona, CA Congregation of the Mother Coredemptrix.
Tran Thanh Liem, Aloysius M. *c.m.c.* (SPC) [E] Carthage, MO Congregation of the Mother Co-Redemptrix, United States Assumption Province.
Tran Van Dong, Alphonsus '63 (BGP) [1] Bridgeport, CT St. Augustine Cathedral.
Tran Van Phat, Peter '67 (NY) Nanuet, NY St. Anthony Church.
Tran-cong-Ly, Hilary M. *c.m.c.* '77 (FWT) [5] Arlington, TX St. Matthew Church.
Tran-Khac-Hy, Hilarius '57 (WDC) Retired.
Trance, F. Raymond '94 (PIT) Bethel Park, PA St. Valentine Church.
Tranchida, Blaise *o.f.m.* '50 (NY) [DD] New York, NY Franciscan Province of the Immaculate Conception.
Tranchina, Joseph '68 (NO) Retired.
Trancone, Gerard A. '69 (WDC) Special Ministries; [S] Washington, DC Archdiocesan Campus Ministry; [V] Landover Hills, MD Catholic Deaf Center.
Tranel, Daniel D. '56 (RCK) Galena, IL St. Mary Church; Galena, IL St. Michael Church.
Tranel, Don *glmy.* '88 (WH) Spencer, WV Holy Redeemer Church.
Tranel, Dorrance E. '49 (RCK) Wonder Lake, IL Christ the King Church.
Trapani, Anthony (RVC) Priests Released from Diocesan Assignment.
Trapasso, Msgr. Thomas J. '49 (PAT) Netcong, NJ St. Michael's Church.
Trapini, Anthony '73 (RVC) Military Chaplains.
Trapold, John T. '60 (WDC) Retired.
Trapp, Arthur L. *c.m.* '56 (STL) [P] Perryville, MO Congregation of The Mission.
Trapp, Daniel J. '84 (DET) [11] Detroit, MI St. Augustine and St. Monica Church; [A] Detroit, MI Sacred Heart Major Seminary, Inc.
Trapp, Joseph John, II '96 (COL) [8] Columbus, OH St. Catharine Church.
Trapp, Joseph L. '59 (BEL) Elizabethtown, IL St. Joseph Church; Metropolis, IL St. Rose of Lima Church.
Traser, Anthony *c.pp.s.* '40 (CIN) [B] Carthagena, OH St. Charles.
Trask, David R. '86 (CLV) Strongsville, OH St. John Neumann Church.
Traub, George W. *s.j.* '67 (CIN) [P] Milford, OH Milford Spiritual Center.
Traub, Robert L. '39 (FTW) [9] Fort Wayne, IN St. Jude Church.
Traudt, Robert *o.carm.* '82 (NEW) Leonia, NJ St. John the Evangelist's Church.
Traufler, John F. '57 (WIN) Winnebago, MN St. Mary's Church.
Trauger, Francis X. '72 (PH) Levittown, PA St. Michael the Archangel Church.
Traupman, Robert '69 (ORL) On Duty Outside the Diocese.
Trausch, Dennis '78 (DM) Carter Lake, IA Our Lady of Carter Lake Church; [D] Council Bluffs, IA Bergan Mercy-Alegant Health System: Mercy Hospital.
Trautner, Kevin C. '74 (PH) [2] Norristown, PA St. Francis of Assisi Church.
Travaglione, Michael *o.f.m.* '66 (NY) [DD] New York, NY Franciscan Province of the Immaculate Conception.
Travasses, Horace J. '73 (FR) [22] Fall River, MA St. William's Church.
Travers, Alan F. '83 (NY) Yorktown Heights, NY St. Patrick Church.
Travers, David O. *s.j.* '68 (BO) [W] Boston, MA The Society of Jesus of New England-Provincial Offices.
Travers, David O. *s.j.* '68 (HON) [17] Honolulu, HI Saints Peter and Paul Church.
Travers, Gerard P. '65 (NY) Highland Mills, NY St. Patrick Church.
Travers, John J. *c.ss.r.* '59 (BRK) [107] Brooklyn, NY Our Lady of Perpetual Help Basilica Church.
Travers, Joseph A. *o.s.f.s.* (FgM) Oblates of St. Francis de Sales Foreign Missions.
Travers, Joseph A. *o.s.f.s.* '48 (CAM) [M] Pittsgrove, NJ Villa St. Joseph.
Travers, Luke *o.s.b.* '86 (PAT) [D] Morristown, NJ Delbarton School.
Travers, Luke L. *o.s.b.* '86 (PAT) [M] Morristown, NJ St. Mary's Abbey.
Travers, Patrick *ss.cc.* '62 (LA) [D] La Verne, CA Damien Boys High School; [R] La Verne, CA Congregation of the Sacred Hearts.
Travers, Patrick J. *o.m.i.* '93 (JUN) Petersburg, AK St. Catherine of Siena Church.
Travers, Tomas J. *c.ss.r.* '62 (SJN) [2] San Juan, PR San Agustin Church.
Traverso, Leonard '72 (SJ) San Jose, CA Notre Dame Villa; Saratoga, CA Our Lady of Fatima Villa; [I] Saratoga, CA Our Lady of Fatima Villa.
Travieso, Ernesto *s.j.* '73 (OM) [K] Omaha, NE Jesuit Community At Creighton University.
Travis, Francis J. '81 (CHR) Pickens, SC Holy Cross Church.
Travis, Herbert A. '42 (BRK) [10] Brooklyn, NY St. Anselm's Church; Retired.
Travis, Leo *c.ss.r.* '54 (FgM) Redemptorist Foreign Missions.
Travis, Msgr. Terrance A. (STU) Absent on Leave.
Travnikar, Rock *o.f.m.* (CIN) [M] Cincinnati, OH St. Francis Seraph Friary.
Trawick, Gregory G. (OWN) Studying Outside the Diocese.
Trawinski, Joseph *o.f.m.conv.* '40 (BUF) [21] Buffalo, NY Corpus Christi Church.
Traxl, William L. '60 (HRT) Glastonbury, CT St. Dunstan Church.
Trayers, Kevin (WCH) Retired.
Trayers, Kevin '52 (WCH) Cherryvale, KS St. Francis Xavier's Church.
Traylor, William A. '76 (EVN) Sabbatical.
Traynor, Anthony '58 (SAC) [6] Sacramento, CA Our Lady of Lourdes Church; Special Assignment.
Traynor, John '45 (RVC) Retired.
Traynor, Joseph P. '82 (GBG) Clymer, PA Church of the Resurrection.
Traynor, Patrick *c.s.p.* '68 (NY) [41] New York, NY Good Shepherd Church.
Traynor, Vincent dePaul *o.s.b.* '43 (OKL) Walters, OK St. Patrick Church; [I] Shawnee, OK St. Gregory Abbey.
Treacy, Canice '52 (WDC) Olney, MD St. Peter Church; Retired.
Treacy, Jerome F. '61 (DET) [P] Clarkston, MI Colombiere Center.
Treacy, William '44 (SEA) Retired.
Treanor, Boniface J. *o.s.b.* '56 (NEW) [N] Newark, NJ Newark Abbey.
Trebtoske, Everett (AUS) Wimberley, TX St. Mary Church.
Trejo, Ramiro M. '77 (CHI) [6] Cicero, IL Our Lady of the Mount Church.
Trela, Norman J. '66 (CHI) [197] Chicago, IL St. Symphorosa and Seven Sons Church.
Trela, Tadeusz '82 (NEW) [19] Jersey City, NJ Our Lady of Czestochowa Church.
Treleaven, Michael *s.j.* '83 (SPK) [C] Spokane, WA Gonzaga University.
Treloar, John L. *s.j.* '70 (MIL) [P] Milwaukee, WI Arrupe House Jesuit Community.
Trembaly, Albert J., Jr. '97 (MAN) Rochester, NH Holy Rosary Church.
Tremblay, Albert (MAN) [C] Dover, NH St. Thomas Aquinas High School.
Tremblay, Donat E. '82 (MAN) Retired.
Tremblay, Eugene *o.m.i.* '74 (BUF) [27] Buffalo, NY Holy Angels Church.
Tremblay, J. Normand '53 (WOR) Charlton City, MA St. Joseph's Church.
Tremblay, Jean A. '54 (MAN) Retired.
Tremblay, Leger '48 (SHP) Retired.
Tremblay, Marc P. '80 (FR) Somerset, MA St. Patrick's Church.
Tremblay, Nellis J. '54 (ALB) Warrensburg, NY St. Cecilia Church.
Trementozzi, Paul *o.c.d.* '55 (BO) [W] Brighton, MA Carmelite Monastery.
Tremie, Eugene R. '71 (LAF) Rayne, LA St. Joseph Church.
Tremmel, Benjamin *o.s.b.* '66 (KCK) [H] Atchison, KS St. Benedict's Abbey.
Tremonte, Pasquale *c.ss.r.* '81 (WIL) Seaford, DE Our Lady of Lourdes Church.
Tremonti, Joseph B. '41 (CHI) [N] Arlington Heights, IL Viatorian Province Center-Clerics of St. Viator.
Trempe, James F. '96 (LC) [6] Eau Claire, WI St. Patrick Church; [D] Eau Claire, WI Eau Claire Coordinated Catholic Schools.
Trench, Msgr. Edmond J. '57 (RVC) Southampton, NY

Sacred Hearts of Jesus and Mary Church.
Trenchard, Dawson D. '58 (HRT) Wallingford, CT Resurrection Church.
Trenchera, Manuel '80 (AGN) Malojlo, GU San Isidro Church.
Trenchs, Juan *sch.p.* '40 (LA) [R] Los Angeles, CA Piarist Fathers.
Trenier, Anthony S. '66 (MIL) Retired; [Y] Milwaukee, WI Archdiocesan Marian Shrine.
Trenkenschuh, Frank *o.s.c.* '66 (SCL) [I] Onamia, MN Crosier Monastery.
Trenor, Msgr. Edward F. '58 (COL) [10] Columbus, OH Christ the King Church.
Trent, James F. '62 (DET) On Duty Outside the Archdiocese.
Trepanier, James *c.s.c.* '55 (FTW) [A] Notre Dame, IN Moreau Seminary.
Trepanier, Thomas A. '75 (MIL) [4] South Milwaukee, WI St. Sylvester Church.
Trepanier, Thomas J. '64 (PRO) Lincoln, RI St. Ambrose Church.
Treppa, Terence F. '67 (DET) Washington, MI SS. John and Paul Church.
Trese, John A. '48 (DET) Birmingham, MI St. Columban Church.
Tressic, David L. '96 (ALB) Latham, NY Our Lady of the Assumption Church.
Tressler, Carl '91 (LA) [35] Los Angeles, CA Resurrection Church.
Tressler, David L. '85 (SCR) [4] Hazleton, PA Holy Trinity Church; [D] Hazleton, PA Bishop Hafey Junior/Senior High School.
Tressler, Robert '80 (ORG) Inactive Leave.
Treston, Msgr. James A. '60 (ALN) Sinking Spring, PA St. Ignatius Loyola Church.
Treston, Kevin *o.f.m.* '81 (WDC) [M] Washington, DC Commissariat of the Holy Land, Franciscan Monastery - Mount St. Sepulchre.
Treu, Stanislaus K. *o.s.a.* '37 (NY) [DD] New York, NY Our Lady of Consolation Residence.
Trevett, Msgr. Cyril I. '48 (BUF) Retired; [P] Orchard Park, NY Sisters of Mercy-Regional Community Offices.
Trevino, Alberto T., Jr. *m.s.f.* '84 (SAT) [B] San Antonio, TX MSF Formation Community.
Trevino, Richard *c.m.f.* '42 (SAT) [12] San Antonio, TX Immaculate Heart of Mary Church.
Trevizo, Raul P. '88 (TUC) [14] Tucson, AZ St. John the Evangelist Church.
Treyes, Reynaldo B. (CHI) Orland Park, IL St. Michael Church.
Trezza, Richard *o.f.m.* '87 (NEW) Wood-Ridge, NJ Our Lady of the Assumption Church.
Triano, Joseph A. *s.s.p.* '59 (DET) [K] Dearborn, MI Society of St. Paul.
Triatmoko, Benedict *s.j.* '94 (BO) [W] Chestnut Hill, MA The Jesuit Community at Boston College.
Tribou, George W. '49 (LR) [B] Little Rock, AR Catholic High School.
Tribuiani, Raymond F. '73 (PH) Oreland, PA Holy Martyrs Church.
Tribunal, Hien Nguyen '57 (SJ) Special Assignment.
Trieu Ngoc Le, '58 (PIT) Verona, PA St. Joseph Church.
Triggs, Thomas J. '75 (TR) Cinnaminson, NJ St. Charles Borromeo Church.
Trigilio, John, Jr. '88 (HBG) Hershey, PA St. Joan of Arc Church.
Trigueros, Raul '69 (ELP) [7] El Paso, TX Cristo Rey Church.
Trimaglio, John *c.s.j.* '68 (LA) San Pedro, CA St. Peter Church; [R] Los Angeles, CA Congregation of St. Joseph Casa Nazareth.
Trimbur, Edwin H. '51 (COV) Retired.
Trimbur, John S. '74 (Y) Campbell, OH St. John the Baptist Church.
Trimbur, Lee Francis '54 (LEX) Middlesboro, KY St. Julian Church.
Trinchard, Paul '66 (NO) Retired.
Trindad, Mel *s.d.b.* '86 (OAK) [E] Richmond, CA Salesian High School.
Trindade, Leonard J. '95 (FRS) [4] Bakersfield, CA St. Francis Church.
Tringhese, James D. '74 (GBG) Trafford, PA St. Regis Church.
Trinh, Joseph T. '91 (PH) [156] Philadelphia, PA Visitation B.V.M. Church.
Trinh, Loc '92 (GR) [17] Grand Rapids, MI St. Mary Magdalen Church.
Trinh, Paul Hao '90 (CAM) Swedesboro, NJ St. Joseph's Church.
Trinh, Thai (RIC) [4] Hampton, VA Our Lady of Viet Nam Chapel Church; [6] Norfolk, VA Our Lady of Lavang Church.
Trinidad, Nelson '86 (LA) [67] Los Angeles, CA St. Ignatius of Loyola Church.
Trinity, Msgr. Bernard J. '54 (PH) Southampton, PA Our Lady of Good Counsel Church.
Trinka, Joseph C. '59 (SUP) Clear Lake, WI St. John Church; Stanton, WI St. Bridget Church.
Trinkle, Clarence M. '92 (ARL) On Duty Outside the Diocese.
Trinkle, Donald F. '63 (CAM) [3] Cherry Hill, NJ St. Peter Celestine Church.
Tripi, Ronald R. *c.s.c.* '62 (FTW) [18] South Bend, IN St. Stanislaus Church.
Tripodi, Frank J. '88 (RCK) Absent on Leave.
Tripole, Martin R. *s.j.* '67 (PH) [C] Philadelphia, PA St. Joseph's University; [AA] Philadelphia, PA Jesuit Community at St. Joseph's University.
Tripp, Kevin F. '68 (FR) Absent on Leave.
Trippel, Edward '55 (CIN) [9] Cincinnati, OH Annunciation of the Blessed Virgin Mary Church.
Trippel, Edward G. (CIN) Retired.
Trippel, Jack '95 (LFT) Kokomo, IN St. Patrick Church.
Trisco, Msgr. Robert F. '54 (CHI) On Duty Outside the Archdiocese.
Trisco, Robert F. '54 (WDC) [C] Washington, DC Catholic University of America, The.
Trisolini, John *s.d.b.* '67 (FgM) Salesians of Don Bosco Foreign Missions.
Trivison, Louis J. '48 (CLV) Solon, OH Resurrection of Our Lord Church; Retired.
Troche, Sigfried *m.ss.cc.* (CAM) [M] Linwood, NJ Villa Pieta.
Trocinski, LaVern E. '60 (WIN) [2] Rochester, MN Pax Christi Church.
Troha, Michael J. '80 (CLV) [34] Cleveland, OH Immaculate Conception Church.
Troiand, Msgr. Leonard '79 (TR) [11] Trenton, NJ Sacred Heart Church.
Troiano, Louis *o.f.m.* '57 (NY) [79] New York, NY Most Precious Blood Church.
Trojan, Columban *o.s.b.* (JOL) [J] Lisle, IL St. Procopius Abbey.
Trojanowski, Miroslaw '87 (STF) Yonkers, NY St. Michael Church.
Trojcak, Ronald '62 (SFD) On Duty Outside the Diocese.
Trombetta, Paul N. '79 (BRK) Released from Diocesan Assignment.
Trombley, Edward '50 (SAG) [F] Saginaw, MI St. Francis Nursing Home.
Trombley, J. Edward '50 (SAG) Retired.
Trombley, Joseph P. '65 (OG) Bloomingdale, NY St. Paul Church; Gabriels, NY Gabriel's Correctional Facility; [G] Ellenburg Center, NY Our Lady of the Adirondack's Inc. House of Prayer, Franciscan Sisters of the Atonement.
Trompeter, Arthur J. '33 (KCK) [7] Topeka, KS St. Joseph's Church.
Troncale, F. Charles '65 (MOB) Prattville, AL St. Joseph Church.
Trong, John T.B. '71 (ARL) [5] Arlington, VA Holy Martyrs of Vietnam Church.
Trong, Joseph '46 (SB) Retired.
Trongo, Nicholas '67 (GBG) Mount Pleasant, PA Visitation of the Blessed Virgin Mary Church; Connellsville, PA Highlands Hospital & Health Center; Mount Pleasant, PA Frick Community Health Center.
Trosch, David '82 (MOB) On Leave from the Archdiocese.
Troska, Llewelyn J. '86 (CR) Leave of Absence.
Trosley, Anthony J. '78 (PEO) Oglesby, IL Holy Family Church.
Trotta, Louis P. *c.m.* '52 (BUF) [C] Niagara University, NY Niagara University; [O] Niagara University, NY Vincentian Community at Niagara University.
Trouille, Alan P. '97 (LKC) [5] Lake Charles, LA St. Margaret Church.
Troung, Dien *c.pp.s.* '97 (KC) Liberty, MO St. James Church.
Trout, Richard W. '85 (ORL) Sanford, FL All Souls Church.
Troutman, Richard E. '68 (TUC) [18] Tucson, AZ Saint Odilia Church.
Trovato, Joseph A. *c.s.b.* '56 (ROC) [13] Rochester, NY Christ the King Church.
Troy, Gabriel '66 (BO) [70] Boston, MA St. Stephen Church; Society of St. James the Apostle; [W] Boston, MA The Society of St. James the Apostle, Inc.
Troy, Gabriel '66 (FgM) Society of St. James the Apostle.
Troy, Henry A. '41 (CHI) Retired.
Troy, Joseph F. *c.s.p.* '34 (NY) [104] New York, NY St. Paul the Apostle Church; [DD] Jamaica Estates, NY Paulist Fathers Generalate.
Troy, Leander *o.carm.* '42 (CHI) [D] Chicago, IL Mt. Carmel High School; [N] Chicago, IL Carmelite Priory of St. Cyril.
Troy, Thomas B. '73 (PH) Ambler, PA St. Anthony of Padua Church.
Troyan, Daniel '82 (PHU) Centralia, PA Assumption of B.V.M. Church; Mount Carmel, PA SS. Peter and Paul Church.
Trucksis, Frederick '64 (Y) Absent on Leave.
Trudeau, Marc V. '91 (LA) Pasadena, CA St. Philip the Apostle Church.
Trudel, Lionel G. *m.m.* '56 (NY) Kingston, NY Benedictine Hospital; [W] Kingston, NY Benedictine Hospital; [DD] Maryknoll, NY Maryknoll Fathers and Brothers.
True, David H. '88 (OKL) Kingfisher, OK SS. Peter and Paul Church.
True, Isaac *o.s.b.* '66 (KC) [A] Conception, MO Conception Seminary College; [J] Conception, MO Conception Abbey.
Truhan, Luke *o.c.s.o.* '82 (WOR) [A] Spencer, MA St. Joseph's Abbey School of Theology and Institute of Monastic Studies; [N] Spencer, MA St. Joseph's Abbey.
Trujillo, Amando *t.o.r.* '88 (FWT) [2] Fort Worth, TX All Saints Church.
Trujillo, Antonio *o.f.m.* '89 (GLP) Acoma, NM San Esteban, Acoma Catholic Indian Mission Church; Laguna, NM St. Joseph Church.
Trujillo, Carlos B. '76 (PBL) Center, CO St. Francis Jerome Church; Del Norte, CO Holy Name of Mary Church; Monte Vista, CO St. Joseph Church.
Trujillo, Daniel '53 (SJN) [7] Bayamon, PR Santa Elena Church.
Trujillo, Francisco Javier '57 (LA) Lynwood, CA St. Philip Neri Church.
Trujillo, Ivan R. '85 (BUF) [3] Batavia, NY St. Mary Church.
Trujillo, Vincent *o.s.b.* '82 (P) [L] St. Benedict, OR Mt. Angel Abbey.
Trunk, Dale (SFR) [B] San Francisco, CA Capuchin House of Studies.
Trunk, Vincent E. *c.m.* '52 (PH) [AA] Philadelphia, PA Congregation of the Mission.
Truong, Dien *c.pp.s.* '96 (KC) [J] Liberty, MO Precious Blood Center.
Trupia, Msgr. Robert C. '73 (TUC) Absent on Leave.
Trupkovich, Joseph V. '97 (GBG) Murrysville, PA Mother of Sorrows Church.
Trupkovich, Thomas S. '97 (GBG) North Huntingdon, PA St. Agnes Church.
Trussel, Christopher '92 (SCL) [8] St. Cloud, MN St. Paul Church; Special Assignment; [C] St. Cloud, MN Cathedral High and John XXIII Middle School.
Trutter, Carl B. *o.p.* '60 (NO) [25] New Orleans, LA St. Anthony Of Padua Church; [P] New Orleans, LA Dominican Fathers & Brothers, Southern Dominican Province; [S] Metairie, LA Southern Dominican Foundation.
Trutter, Richard '57 (SFD) [H] Taylorville, IL St. Vincent Memorial Hospital.
Trzeciakowski, Edward J. '55 (PIT) McDonald, PA St. Alphonsus Church.
Trzecieski, Stephen P. *c.m.* '60 (PH) [AA] Philadelphia, PA Congregation of the Mission.
Trzil, Louis J. '50 (DUB) Harpers Ferry, IA St. Ann-St. Joseph Church; Wexford, IA Immaculate Conception Church.
Tsang, Augustine *s.j.* '94 (BO) [W] Cambridge, MA Faber House.
Tsang, Peter '59 (LA) Rowland Heights, CA St. Elizabeth Ann Seton Church.
Tsau, Paul '64 (WDC) [3] Rockville, MD St. Mary Church.
Tschakert, Gregory '82 (SFS) Hartford, SD St. George Church; [C] Sioux Falls, SD Sioux Falls Catholic School System.
Tscherne, David D. '77 (TOL) Junction, OH St. Mary Church; St. Michael's Ridge, OH St. Michael Church.
Tschudi, Michael '84 (PMB) North Palm Beach, FL St. Paul of the Cross Church.
Tseu, Msgr. Andrew '56 (LA) Pomona, CA St. Madeleine Church.
Tsoi, Peter '64 (NY) [64] New York, NY St. Joseph Church.
Tsung, Basil *o.f.m.* '53 (FgM) Franciscan Foreign Missions.
Tsung-Li-Chuen, Basil *o.f.m.* '53 (STL) [P] St. Louis, MO Franciscan Friary of St. Anthony of Padua.
Tu, Joachim Vu '63 (ORG) Absent on Sick Leave; [G] Santa Ana, CA Vietnamese Catholic Center.
Tu, Raymond '95 (KC) [15] Kansas City, MO Holy Cross Church; [17] Kansas City, MO Church of the Holy Martyrs.
Tuan, Bui quang *c.ss.r.* '96 (LA) [R] Baldwin Park, CA Vietnamese Redemptorist Mission.
Tubbs, Leo *o.p.* '66 (OAK) [N] Oakland, CA Dominican Order, Siena House.
Tubridy, James J. '53 (NY) Retired.
Tucceri, Robert A. '79 (TOL) Bellevue, OH Immaculate Conception Church.
Tucci, Bruno M. '71 (ALN) Nesquehoning, PA Immaculate Conception of B.V.M. Church; Nesquehoning, PA Our Lady of Mount Carmel Church.
Tucci, Italo '48 (DET) Retired.
Tuchalski, Stanley T. '90 (WH) Westover, WV St. Elizabeth Ann Seton Church.
Tuchols, Franklin J. '71 (BUF) Absent on Leave.
Tuchscherer, Vincent J. '55 (FAR) Balta, ND Our Lady of Mount Carmel Church.
Tucker, James *s.s.* '69 (SJ) Special Assignment.
Tucker, James S. '69 (LA) On Duty Outside the Archdiocese.
Tucker, John J. *s.j.* '55 (BO) [W] Weston, MA Campion Center.
Tucker, Mark *c.ss.r.* '89 (WDC) [M] Washington, DC Holy Redeemer College.

Tucker, Michael '77 (SEA) Unassigned.
Tucker, Patrick M. '74 (CHI) Forest Park, IL St. Bernardine Church.
Tucker, Richard '58 (ORL) [2] Lakeland, FL St. Anthony's Church; Retired.
Tucker, Richard '58 (SY) Retired.
Tucker, Rick '76 (LFT) Dunkirk, IN St. Mary Church.
Tucker, Robert *s.c.j.* '82 (GAL) [48] Houston, TX St. Matthew the Evangelist Church.
Tucker, Robert F. '70 (HRT) Litchfield, CT St. Anthony's Church.
Tucker, Robert G. '89 (LIN) McCook, NE St. Patrick Church.
Tucker, Thomas J. *o.s.f.s.* '66 (WIL) [B] Wilmington, DE Salesianum School.
Tueth, Michael V. *s.j.* '71 (NY) [DD] New York, NY Xavier Jesuit Community.
Tufaro, Douglas J. '83 (BGP) [5] Danbury, CT St. Peter's Church.
Tufts, Donn P. '80 (GR) Brunswick, MI St. Michael's Church.
Tugwell, Michael W. '75 (PT) [1] Tallahassee, FL Co-Cathedral of St. Thomas More.
Tugwood, James C. '60 (BRK) [220] Queens, NY Our Lady of the Snows Church.
Tuite, Howard A. '54 (CHI) [47] Chicago, IL Corpus Christi Church.
Tuite, Thomas P. '86 (RVC) Massapequa, NY St. Rose of Lima Church.
Tulko, Richard *o.f.m.* '64 (GB) [I] Pulaski, WI Assumption of B.V.M. Friary.
Tull, Terry *c.ss.r.* '85 (CGS) [B] Aguas Buenas, PR Casa Cristo Redentor.
Tuller, Eugene *o.f.m.cap.* '49 (MIL) [P] Mount Calvary, WI St. Lawrence Friary.
Tuller, Jerome '55 (GB) [I] Appleton, WI St. Fidelis Friary.
Tuller, Joel '51 (GB) [I] Appleton, WI St. Fidelis Friary.
Tuller, John J. '84 (CHL) Winston-Salem, NC St. Leo's Church.
Tulley, Edward M. '39 (CLV) Parma Heights, OH St. John Bosco Church; Retired.
Tullius, Richard '73 (DAL) Absent on Leave.
Tully, Eugene D. '68 (BO) Billerica, MA St. Theresa of Lisieux Church.
Tully, Eugene M. '73 (PH) [102] Philadelphia, PA St. Matthew Church.
Tully, Gerard *c.s.p.* '94 (NY) [41] New York, NY Good Shepherd Church.
Tully, Henry F. '77 (IND) [7] Indianapolis, IN Holy Spirit Church.
Tully, James *s.x.* '75 (FgM) Xaverian Foreign Missions.
Tully, James J. '44 (BRK) Retired.
Tully, John P. '69 (Y) [4] Massillon, OH St. Mary's Church.
Tully, Raymond M. *s.j.* '40 (STL) [P] St. Louis, MO Hallahan House.
Tully, Ronald J. '66 (PAT) Dover, NJ Sacred Heart Church.
Tully, Terence '42 (SPK) Retired.
Tully, Thomas S. '85 (R) Wake Forest, NC St. Catherine of Siena Church.
Tuma, Anthony F. '31 (OM) Retired.
Tumicki, Ted F. '97 (NOR) Willimantic, CT St. Joseph Church.
Tumminelli, Lawrence *b.s.o.* '96 (NTN) [B] Methuen, MA Basilian Salvatorian Order.
Tumosa, John Joseph '69 (CAM) Newfield, NJ St. Rose of Lima Church.
Tumulty, Matt '59 (P) [Q] Portland, OR Franciscan Ministry Network.
Tumulty, Michael J. *c.m.* (BUF) [O] Niagara University, NY Vincentian Community at Niagara University.
Tumulty, Michael J. *c.m.* '51 (BUF) [C] Niagara University, NY Niagara University.
Tung, Paul Nguyen Van '79 (NO) Waggaman, LA Our Lady of the Angels Church.
Tung, Vincent Pham The '85 (PH) Hatfield, PA St. Maria Goretti Church.
Tungol, Eugene D. '75 (SFR) [3] South San Francisco, CA St. Augustine Church.
Tunink, Wilfrid *o.s.b.* '45 (SFE) [L] Pecos, NM Our Lady of Guadalupe Benedictine Abbey.
Tunney, Michael F. *s.j.* '88 (BUF) [O] Buffalo, NY Canisius Jesuit Community.
Tunney, Thomas P. *c.s.sp.* (WDC) [B] Wheaton, MD Holy Ghost Fathers Development Office.
Tunney, Thomas P. '60 (ARL) [7] Arlington, VA Our Lady, Queen of Peace Church.
Tunny, Kenneth J. '63 (ALB) [16] Schenectady, NY St. Paul the Apostle Church; Schoharie, NY St. Joseph Church; Special Assignment.
Tuoc, Ignatius '71 (SP) [3] Tampa, FL Epiphany Church.
Tuohey, John '81 (OKL) [E] Oklahoma City, OK Mercy Memorial Health Center.
Tuohey, John F. '81 (SPR) On Duty Outside the Diocese.
Tuohey, John J. '81 (WDC) [C] Washington, DC Catholic University of America, The.
Tuohy, Edward *s.v.d.* '58 (BO) [W] Duxbury, MA Society of the Divine Word.
Tuohy, Msgr. Francis R. '61 (IND) [2] Indianapolis, IN Christ The King Church.
Tuozzolo, Leonard *c.s.sp.* '59 (NY) [69] New York, NY St. Mark the Evangelist Church.
Tupa, Jerome *o.s.b.* '82 (SCL) [I] Collegeville, MN St. John's Abbey, of the Order of St. Benedict.
Tupa, Michael J. '91 (SUP) Bloomville, WI St. John the Baptist Church; Harrison, WI St. Augustine Church; Pier-Willow, WI St. Francis of Assisi Church; Tomahawk, WI St. Mary Church.
Tupper, Dale E. '67 (WIN) [1] Rochester, MN Holy Spirit Church.
Tupper, John B. '60 (GAY) Empire, MI St. Philip Neri Church.
Tuptynski, Marek S. '97 (FR) [6] New Bedford, MA Our Lady of Mt. Carmel Church.
Turati, Fortunato *s.c.* '67 (LAN) [E] Chelsea, MI St. Louis Center for Exceptional Children & Adults.
Turbek, Aloysius *s.v.d.* '40 (TR) [M] Bordentown, NJ Society of the Divine Word.
Turci, Vitaliano *o.s.cam.* '44 (MIL) [P] Wauwatosa, WI St. Camillus Community House.
Turcich, Ronald R. *o.s.a.* '58 (CHI) Norridge, IL Divine Savior Church.
Turco, Alfredo *s.x.* '88 (MIL) [B] Franklin, WI Xaverian Missionary Fathers College Seminary.
Turczany, Christopher J. '83 (BRK) [235] Queens, NY St. Robert Bellarmine Church.
Turek, Michael E. '76 (STL) [8] Florissant, MO St. Norbert Church.
Turek, Ronald J. '74 (CLV) [9] Lorain, OH Nativity of the Blessed Virgin Mary Church.
Tureman, Thomas '88 (PHX) [4] Mesa, AZ Queen of Peace Church.
Tureman, Thomas M. *c.s.p.* '88 (NY) [DD] Jamaica Estates, NY Paulist Fathers Generalate.
Turgeon, Armand A. '43 (MAN) Retired.
Turi, John J. '55 (SCR) Matamoras, PA St. Joseph's Church.
Turillo, B. Samuel '46 (PRO) Retired.
Turk, Damian C. *o.c.s.o.* '69 (ATL) [I] Conyers, GA The Monastery of the Holy Spirit.
Turk, John P. '50 (Y) [5] Warren, OH St. Joseph Church.
Turley, Daniel T. *o.s.a.* '68 (CHI) [N] Olympia Fields, IL The Augustinian Provincialate Tolentine Center.
Turley, Sean F. '71 (WIL) On Duty Outside the Diocese.
Turlik, Andrew J. '46 (PIT) Retired; [O] Pittsburgh, PA St. John Vianney Manor.
Turlo, Walter J. '70 (CHI) Bridgeview, IL St. Fabian Church.
Turnbull, David *o.f.m.* '57 (FgM) Franciscan Foreign Missions.
Turnbull, John B. *o.f.m.* '55 (CIN) Centerville, OH St. Francis of Assisi Church.
Turnbull, Paul E. '73 (ALT) [10] Altoona, PA St. John the Evangelist Church.
Turnbull, Robert A. *o.s.a.* '65 (PH) [B] Villanova, PA St. Augustine Friary.
Turnbull, William D. '67 (ALB) [16] Albany, NY St. Teresa of Avila Church.
Turner, Bernard (ALB) Schaghticoke, NY St. John the Baptist Church.
Turner, Bernard R. '77 (ALB) Johnsonville, NY St. Monica's Church; [T] Albany, NY Diocesan HIV/AIDS Ministries.
Turner, David *o.s.b.* '63 (JOL) [J] Lisle, IL St. Procopius Abbey.
Turner, Edward '66 (HON) Retired.
Turner, George F. '60 (LR) Retired.
Turner, James '84 (PHX) [6] Glendale, AZ St. Thomas More Church.
Turner, James M. *o.s.f.s.* '81 (CHL) High Point, NC Immaculate Heart of Mary Church.
Turner, Jerome '64 (RIC) Norfolk, VA Depaul Medical Center.
Turner, Jerome R. '64 (MAD) Military Chaplains.
Turner, Joseph *s.d.s.* (WDC) [B] Silver Spring, MD Salvatorian Community.
Turner, Joseph *s.d.s.* '58 (MIL) [P] Milwaukee, WI Salvatorian Provincial Residence.
Turner, Patrick '72 (BEA) Orangefield, TX St. Helen Church.
Turner, Paul '79 (KC) [22] Kansas City, MO St. John Francis Regis Church.
Turner, Richard M. '80 (SPR) South Hadley, MA St. Patrick's Church.
Turner, Richard W. (R) Rocky Mount, NC Our Lady of Perpetual Help Church.
Turner, Robert '62 (GR) On Duty Outside the Diocese.
Turner, Robert '88 (GLP) On Duty Outside of Diocese.
Turner, Robert D. '82 (SPK) Okanogan-Omak, WA Our Lady of the Valley Church.
Turner, Robert D. '88 (MIL) [13] Milwaukee, WI Blessed Sacrament Church.
Turner, Robert G. '59 (PIT) [4] West Mifflin, PA Resurrection Church.
Turner, Thomas W. '82 (KC) Leave of Absence; [O] Kansas City, MO Bishop Sullivan Center.
Turner, Wayne A. '50 (MAD) Retired.
Turner, William J. '75 (IND) New Alsace, IN St. Paul Church; Yorkville, IN St. Martin Church.
Turner, William J. '79 (LAN) Fenton, MI St. John Church.
Turon, L. L. *o.p.* '55 (FgM) Dominican - Order of Preachers Foreign Missions.
Turowski, Joseph *m.m.* '84 (BUF) [O] Buffalo, NY Maryknoll House.
Turowski, William M. '85 (MET) South Amboy, NJ Sacred Heart Church.
Turro, Msgr. James C. *s.t.l., s.s.l., a.m.* '48 (BGP) [O] Stamford, CT St. John Fisher Seminary Residence.
Turro, Msgr. James C. *s.t.l., s.s.l., a.m.* '48 (NEW) Park Ridge, NJ Our Lady of Mercy Church; Retired; [A] South Orange, NJ Immaculate Conception Seminary; [B] South Orange, NJ Seton Hall University.
Turtora, Msgr. Dominic A. '48 (MET) [1] Metuchen, NJ Cathedral of St. Francis; Retired; [H] Somerset, NJ Maria Regina Residence.
Turula, Juan *s.j.* '70 (BAK) Hermiston, OR Our Lady of Angels Church.
Tushar, David (DUL) [1] Duluth, MN Cathedral of Our Lady of the Rosary.
Tushar, David '76 (DUL) [G] Duluth, MN The Human Life and Development Fund of the Diocese of Duluth.
Tusky, Richard J. '73 (PIT) Burgettstown, PA Our Lady of Lourdes Church.
Tustin, Joseph E. *o.s.f.s.* '67 (CHL) Kernersville, NC Holy Cross Church.
Tutas, Stephen *s.m.* '53 (SJ) [M] Cupertino, CA Villa Saint Joseph.
Tutokie, Msgr. Michael E. '45 (E) Winburne, PA SS. Cyril and Methodius Church; Retired.
Tutone, John J. '71 (RVC) Island Park, NY Sacred Heart Church.
Tuttle, Arthur *c.ss.r.* '65 (ALB) Saratoga Springs, NY St. Clement Church.
Tuttle, Charles W. '74 (BEL) Sandoval, IL St. Lawrence Church; [A] Breese, IL Mater Dei High School.
Tuttle, Patrick E. *o.f.m.* (R) [3] Durham, NC Immaculate Conception Church.
Tuttle, Richard '76 (STU) [2] Steubenville, OH Holy Family Church.
Tuugusamusu, Paulo '86 (HON) Pearl City, HI Our Lady of Good Counsel Church; [F] Honolulu, HI St. Francis Healthcare System of Hawaii.
Tuxbury, James C. *o.f.m.* '63 (FR) Buzzards Bay, MA St. Margaret Church.
Tuyn, William R. '62 (BUF) North Evans, NY St. Vincent Church.
Tuzeneu, Kenard J. '79 (TR) Barnegat, NJ St. Mary Church.
Tuzicka, Fred M. '51 (DOD) Retired.
Tuzik, Robert L. '73 (CHI) [2] Mt. Prospect, IL St. Emily Church.
Tvrdik, Roy *s.m.m.* '93 (BRK) [U] Ozone Park, NY Montfort Missionaries Provincialate - for Nation Community.
Tvrdy, Julius '73 (LIN) [5] Lincoln, NE Sacred Heart Church.
Twaddell, Gerald '67 (COV) [A] Covington, KY Thomas More College; [A] Covington, KY.
Twardzik, Francis M. *s.d.b.* '70 (PSC) Scranton, PA St. Mary's Byzantine Catholic Church.
Twardzik, Michael (SPR) [P] Amherst, MA University of Massachusetts and Amherst College, Newman Center.
Twardzik, Michael '70 (SPR) [2] North Adams, MA Notre Dame Church; [4] North Adams, MA Our Lady of Mercy Church; [5] North Adams, MA Our Lady of Mercy Shrine Church.
Twardzik, Michael W.T. '70 (SPR) [7] North Adams, MA St. Francis Church.
Twarog, Jerome *c.r.* '82 (CHI) [D] Chicago, IL Weber High School.
Twarog, Theodore S. '50 (SD) Absent on Sick Leave.
Twele, Robert *o.f.m.conv.* '81 (BAL) [M] Ellicott City, MD Order of Friars Minor Conventual.
Twele, Robert Augustine *ofm conv.* '81 (BUF) [D] Athol Springs, NY St. Francis High School.
Twiddy, Paul '52 (WDC) Retired.
Twigg-Porter, George M. *s.j.* '53 (SFR) [N] San Francisco, CA Jesuit Community at University of San Francisco; [U] San Francisco, CA Apostleship of Prayer.
Twiggs, Matthew J. '73 (PAT) Stockholm, NJ St. John Vianney Church.
Twiss, Francis *s.m.* '60 (HON) Kapaa, HI St. Catherine Church.
Twohig, Christopher T. '50 (WDC) On Duty Outside the Archdiocese.
Twohig, Michael J. '83 (SPR) West Springfield, MA Immaculate Conception Church.
Twohig, Richard H. *s.j.* '65 (FgM) Provinces.
Twohy, Patrick *s.j.* '70 (SEA) LaConner, WA St. Paul Church.
Twohy, Richard E. *s.j.* '42 (SPK) [C] Spokane, WA Gonzaga University.
Twomey, Daniel F. '75 (BO) Natick, MA St. Patrick Church.

Twomey, Dermot J. *s.c.j.* '76 (JKS) Walls, MS Sacred Heart Church; [E] Nesbit, MS St. Michael Community House.
Twomey, Gerald S. '81 (RVC) Brentwood, NY St. Anne's Church.
Twomey, John E. '52 (MIL) Retired.
Twomey, Msgr. John P. '63 (LA) [3] Long Beach, CA St. Barnabas Church.
Twomey, Simon D. '70 (SAC) [7] Sacramento, CA Presentation of the Blessed Virgin Mary Church.
Twomey, Thomas G. '65 (NOR) East Hampton, CT St. Patrick Church.
Twomey, Timothy *s.a.c.* '60 (RNO) Sparks, NV Immaculate Conception Church.
Tyburski, Zbigniew '73 (PAT) Newton, NJ St. Joseph's Church.
Tydlacka, Msgr. George '44 (AUS) Retired.
Tykhovytch, Ivan (STF) Spring Valley, NY SS. Peter and Paul Church.
Tyl, Albert '54 (FWT) [1] Fort Worth, TX St. Patrick Cathedral.
Tylawskyj, Ivan '50 (SJP) North Port, FL Entrance of B.V.M. into the Temple Church.
Tylenda, Joseph N. *s.j.* '60 (WDC) [M] Washington, DC The Jesuit Community at Georgetown University; [V] Washington, DC Woodstock Theological Center.
Tyler, Benedict E. *o.s.b.* '52 (NEW) [N] Newark, NJ Newark Abbey.
Tyler, Bernard L. '61 (LAN) Dexter, MI St. Joseph Church.
Tyler, Thomas L. '79 (E) New Bethlehem, PA St. Charles Church.
Tylka, Louis J. '96 (CHI) Orland Park, IL St. Michael Church.
Tyma, John A. *o.s.a.* '59 (CHI) [N] Olympia Fields, IL The Augustinian Provincialate Tolentine Center.
Tyma, John A. *o.s.a.* '59 (FgM) Foreign Missions.
Tyman, Gary L. '86 (ROC) [4] Rochester, NY St. Anne Church; [M] Rochester, NY Diocesan Office of Campus Ministry.
Tyminski, Joseph *s.d.b.* '49 (NEW) Mahwah, NJ Immaculate Heart of Mary Church.
Tymkiw, Msgr. Leo '48 (SJP) [2] Parma, OH St. Andrew Church.
Tynan, Desmond '67 (FgM) Society of St. James the Apostle.
Tynan, Desmond A. '67 (BO) Society of St. James the Apostle.
Tynan, John C. *m.m.* '62 (FgM) Maryknoll Foreign Missions.
Tynan, John C. *m.m.* '62 (NY) [DD] Maryknoll, NY Maryknoll Fathers and Brothers; [DD] Maryknoll, NY Maryknoll Fathers and Brothers.
Tynan, Joseph F. *o.c.s.o.* '47 (ATL) [I] Conyers, GA The Monastery of the Holy Spirit.
Tyne, John *s.s.j.* '63 (JKS) Fayette, MS St. Anne Church.
Tyne, John J. *s.s.j.* '63 (JKS) Natchez, MS Holy Family Church.
Tyrasinski, Lucius *o.s.p.p.e.* '56 (PH) [AA] Doylestown, PA Pauline Fathers Monastery, Shrine of Our Lady of Czestochowa.
Tyrell, Robert D. '67 (BO) Weston, MA St. Julia Church.
Tyrrell, Anthony *o.s.* '95 (PCE) [11] Ponce, PR San Jose Obrero Church.
Tyrrell, Bernard J. *s.j.* '65 (SPK) [C] Spokane, WA Gonzaga University.
Tyrrell, Joseph '89 (NY) [185] Bronx, NY St. Raymond Church.
Tyrrell, Michael *s.j.* '76 (SPK) [E] Spokane, WA Gonzaga Preparatory School.
Tyrrell, Michael A. *s.j.* '76 (P) [L] Portland, OR Jesuit Provincial Office (Society of Jesus, Oregon Prov.).
Tyrrell, Wilfred *s.a.* '94 (LA) [83] Los Angeles, CA St. Odilia Church.
Tysmans, Louis *c.i.c.m.* '47 (ARL) [J] Arlington, VA Missionhurst, C.I.C.M.-Central House and Provincialate; [J] Falls Church, VA Missionhurst-C.I.C.M.
Tyson, David T. *c.s.c.* '75 (FTW) [J] South Bend, IN Congregation of Holy Cross Indiana Province Provincial House.
Tyson, David T. *c.s.c.* '75 (P) [B] Portland, OR University of Portland; [L] Portland, OR Holy Cross Fathers & Brothers, C.S.C. - University of Portland.
Tyson, Joseph (SEA) [9] Seattle, WA St. George Church; [18] Seattle, WA St. Paul Church.
Tyson, Joseph '89 (SEA) [8] Seattle, WA St. Edward Church.
Tyson, Joseph V. *s.s.j.* '55 (LAF) Eunice, LA St. Mathilda Church.
Tyson, Michael *o.f.m.* '67 (WDC) [3] Silver Spring, MD St. Camillus Church.
Tywoniak, Robert F. '83 (MIA) [6] Fort Lauderdale, FL St. George Church.
Tzanakas, George M. '62 (AUS) Retired.
Tzecieski, Stephen *c.m.* '60 (PMB) [A] Boynton Beach, FL St. Vincent de Paul Regional Seminary.

U

Ubalde, Ulysses L. '93 (NEW) Paramus, NJ Our Lady of the Visitation Church.
Ubel, John '89 (STP) [A] St. Paul, MN St. John Vianney Seminary; [C] St. Paul, MN University of St. Thomas.
Ubinger, Herman F. *o.s.b.* '58 (GBG) [H] Latrobe, PA Saint Vincent Archabbey.
Uboldi, Victor '45 (SD) Retired.
Ubowski, Chester '49 (CHI) Retired; [J] Chicago, IL Resurrection Medical Center.
Ucbaghiorghis, Teclezghi *o.cist.* '78 (TR) Mount Laurel, NJ St. John Neumann Church; [M] Mount Laurel, NJ Cistercian Monastery of Our Lady of Fatima.
Uchendu, Okechukwu '92 (NY) [3] New Rochelle, NY St. Joseph Church.
Udick, William S. *s.j.* '55 (DEN) [M] Denver, CO Xavier Jesuit Center.
Udo, Emmanuel '18 (MIL) [4] Wauwatosa, WI St. Jude the Apostle Church.
Udovic, Edward *c.m.* '84 (CHI) [N] Chicago, IL Vincentian Community, Congregation of the Mission, Midwest Province.
Udovic, Edward R. *c.m.* '84 (CHI) [C] Chicago, IL De Paul University.
Udulutach, Irvin *o.f.m.cap.* (GB) Kaukauna, WI St. Mary of the Annunciation Church.
Udulutsch, Robert *o.f.m.cap.* '56 (GB) Kaukauna, WI St. Mary of the Annunciation Church.
Uebler, Michael G. '82 (BUF) Arcade, NY SS. Peter and Paul Church; East Arcade, NY St. Mary's Church; [D] Lancaster, NY St. Mary's High School.
Uecker, Joseph H. *c.pp.s.* '68 (SAN) [3] Abilene, TX St. Francis of Assisi Church; [4] Abilene, TX St. Vincent Pallotti Church.
Uehlein, Christopher *o.s.b.* '60 (SFS) [F] Marvin, SD Blue Cloud Abbey.
Uftring, Richard A. '76 (BO) Awaiting Assignment.
Ugah, Gregory (PIT) [8] Pittsburgh, PA St. Charles Lwanga Parish.
Ugliano, Bruno A. *o.s.b.* '67 (PAT) [M] Morristown, NJ St. Mary's Abbey.
Uglietto, Peter '77 (BO) [A] Weston, MA Pope John XXIII National Seminary.
Ugobueze, John '85 (PIT) Verona, PA St. Joseph Church.
Ugochukwu, John '84 (BRK) [217] Queens, NY Our Lady of Perpetual Help Church.
Ugochukwu, Sebastian (CHI) [8] Chicago, IL St. Aloysius Church.
Ugolik, Richard '54 (DET) Retired.
Ugomadi, Kevin '84 (CHI) [208] Chicago, IL Transfiguration of Our Lord Church.
Ugwuanya, Valentine C. '94 (NEW) Hillside, NJ Christ the King Church.
Ugwuegbu, Ambrose '87 (SAC) Carmichael, CA St. John the Evangelist Church.
Uhde, Peter M. '81 (NEW) [13] Newark, NJ Epiphany Church; [16] Newark, NJ Holy Trinity Church.
Uhen, Cletus V. '42 (MIL) Retired.
Uhen, Timothy J. '96 (BO) [V] Chestnut Hill, MA Opus Dei.
Uhl, Anthony C. '68 (COS) Salida, CO St. Joseph Church.
Uhlenkott, Gary D. *s.j.* '80 (SPK) [C] Spokane, WA Gonzaga University.
Uhler, Carl A. '56 (CLV) West Salem, OH St. Stephen Church.
Uhlik, Charles R. '92 (OM) West Point, NE Assumption B.V.M. Church; [G] West Point, NE Franciscan Care Services, Inc., dba St. Francis Memorial Hospital.
Uhlman, Laurence *t.o.r.* '90 (STU) [A] Steubenville, OH Franciscan University of Steubenville; [F] Steubenville, OH Holy Spirit Monastery.
Uhran, Vernon (ORL) Sabbatical.
Uhrig, A. Gregory '73 (MET) Three Bridges, NJ St. Elizabeth Ann Seton Church.
Uitendaal, Pius *o.f.m.conv.* (FgM) Conventual Franciscan Foreign Missions.
Ukwuoma, Augustine '83 (CLV) [1] Akron, OH Annunciation Church.
Ulahannan, Luka K. *m.s.f.s.* '88 (TYL) Atlanta, TX St. Catherine of Siena Church.
Ulak, Robert T. '70 (NEW) [3] Irvington, NJ Sacred Heart of Jesus Church.
Ulatowski, Donald F. (CHI) Retired.
Ulincy, Andrew A. '66 (ALN) [10] Reading, PA St. Paul Church.
Ullery, Kirk '65 (SFR) [40] San Francisco, CA Our Lady of Lourdes Church.
Ullman, Earl L. '38 (SD) Retired.
Ulloa, Daniel *o.p.* '70 (GAL) [Q] Houston, TX Dominican Fathers and Brothers, St. Mark Priory, Inc.
Ullrich, David *o.m.i.* '71 (FgM) Oblates Foreign Missions.
Ullrich, David *o.m.i.* '71 (OAK) [N] Oakland, CA Oblate Provincial House & Procure.
Ullrich, John R. *o.f.m.* (BO) [BB] Boston, MA St. Anthony Shrine.
Ullrich, Peter *o.s.b.* '59 (KC) [J] Conception, MO Conception Abbey.
Ullrich, Peter *o.s.b.* '87 (KC) [A] Conception, MO Conception Seminary College.
Ulm, John Francis '58 (GAL) [4] Spring, TX St. James the Apostle Church.
Ulman, Stanley A. '73 (DET) Hamtramck, MI St. Ladislaus Church.
Ulrich, Carl G. '43 (SCR) Retired; [N] Dunmore, PA Villa St. Joseph.
Ulrich, Eugene P. '74 (BUF) Almond, NY SS. Brendan and Jude Church; [R] Williamsville, NY Campus Ministry.
Ulrich, Hugh *c.pp.s.* '36 (CIN) [B] Carthagena, OH St. Charles.
Ulrich, James E. '60 (CIN) [41] Cincinnati, OH St. James Church.
Ulrich, Steve '90 (OWN) Calhoun, KY St. Sebastian Church; Livermore, KY St. Charles Church.
Ulrick, Stephen D. '82 (STP) Chanhassen, MN St. Hubert Church.
Ulrickson, Brian *s.j.* '78 (P) [L] Portland, OR Jesuit Provincial Office (Society of Jesus, Oregon Prov.).
Ulrickson, Brian L. *s.j.* '78 (P) [L] Portland, OR Colombiere Community.
Ulses, Eugene J. '69 (SC) Humboldt, IA St. Mary's Church; Livermore, IA Sacred Heart Church.
Ulshafer, Thomas *s.s.* '70 (WDC) On Duty Outside the Archdiocese.
Ulshafer, Thomas R. *s.s.* '70 (BAL) [A] Baltimore, MD St. Mary's Seminary and University; [M] Baltimore, MD Sulpician Provincial House.
Ulto, Victor A. (BRK) [120] Brooklyn, NY Queen of All Saints Church.
Umana, Miguel '96 (WDC) [4] Rockville, MD St. Raphael Church.
Umana, Pedro *o.f.m.* '89 (LA) [72] Los Angeles, CA St. Joseph Church.
Umberg, Andrew J. '91 (CIN) On Duty Outside the Archdiocese.
Umberg, Andrew J. '91 (COL) [A] Columbus, OH Pontifical College Josephinum.
Umberger, Patrick A. '80 (LC) Plover, WI St. Bronislava Church.
Umbras, Thomas *s.v.d.* '81 (FgM) Society of the Divine Word Foreign Missions.
Ume, Michael '93 (LA) [69] Los Angeles, CA St. Jerome Church.
Umhoefer, Stephen J. '66 (MAD) Monroe, WI St. Victor Church.
Umrahn, Kaleem '58 (BRK) [201] Queens, NY St. Michael Church.
Umwech, Adalbert *s.j.* (NY) [DD] New York, NY Murray-Weigel Hall.
Underdahl, Mark J. '96 (STP) Lake Elmo, MN Guardian Angels Church.
Underwood, Fred *s.o.l.t.* (FAR) Belcourt, ND St. Ann Church; Turtle Mountain Reservation, ND (Chippewa Indians) Church.
Underwood, Gary E. '80 (TUC) On Duty Outside the Diocese.
Underwood, Joseph '63 (BIR) Retired.
Underwood, Scott J. *o.s.b.* '76 (NO) [A] St. Benedict, LA St. Joseph's Seminary College; [P] St. Benedict, LA St. Joseph Abbey.
Ungashick, Thomas J. '76 (Y) Leetonia, OH St. Patrick's Church.
Unger, John M. '42 (PIT) Retired; [O] Pittsburgh, PA St. John Vianney Manor.
Unger, Msgr. John M. '65 (STL) [D] St. Louis, MO Paul VI Institute of Catechetical and Pastoral Studies; [R] St. Louis, MO School Sisters of Notre Dame.
Unger, Todd J. '82 (BAK) Madras, OR St. Patrick's Church.
Ungerleider, David L. *s.j.* '77 (BAL) [M] Baltimore, MD Jesuit Fathers and Brothers Maryland Provincial Curia.
Ungerleider, David L. *s.j.* '77 (FgM) Provinces.
Uniac, Tim *c.r.* '86 (SP) Ruskin, FL St. Anne Church.
Uniowski, Peter '75 (ORL) [3] Lakeland, FL St. John Neumann Church.
Universal, Patrick J. '75 (GLP) Crownpoint, NM St. Paul Church.
Unsworth, John E. '76 (PRO) [1] East Providence, RI St. Brendan Church.
Unterreiner, Glennon T. '46 (STL) Retired.
Unterreiner, James J. '70 (SPC) Ironton, MO Ste. Marie Du Lac Church.
Unverdorben, Ernest *o.c.d.* '66 (MIL) [P] Holy Hill, WI Discalced Carmelite Monastery.
Unverferth, Steven R. '89 (BEL) Leave of Absence.
Unwin, Rick '79 (CIN) Piqua, OH St. Boniface Church.
Unz, Thomas E. '83 (CHI) Stickney, IL St. Pius X Church.
Uong, Luong *c.ss.r.* '95 (NO) [23] New Orleans, LA St. Alphonsus Church.
Uppena, James '68 (MAD) [I] Madison, WI Bishop O'Connor Catholic Pastoral Center.
Upson, Michael G. '76 (BRK) Released from Diocesan Assignment.
Upson, Michael G. '76 (ROC) [27] Rochester, NY Immaculate Conception Church.
Upson, Wilfrid *o.m.i.* '56 (DUL) International Falls, MN St. Thomas Aquinas Church.
Upton, Edward F. '69 (CHI) Orland Park, IL St. Francis of Assisi Church.

Upton, John C. '83 (GAL) [41] Houston, TX St. John Vianney Church.
Uraban, Joseph '72 (NEW) [10] Newark, NJ St. Casimir's Church.
Uralikunnel, George '67 (BIS) Bowbells, ND St. Joseph Church.
Uram, Msgr. Kenneth '59 (STU) Richmond, OH St. John Fisher Church.
Urarte, Carmelo '59 (ARE) Quebradillas, PR Sacred Heart Church.
Urbain, Joseph V. '32 (CIN) Retired.
Urban, Anthony M. '73 (SCR) Bear Creek Township, PA St. Elizabeth Church.
Urban, Carl A. '66 (ALB) [1] Schenectady, NY Church of St. Adalbert.
Urban, Charles T. *o.praem.* '54 (PH) [AA] Paoli, PA Daylesford Abbey.
Urban, John L. '59 (MAD) Boscobel, WI Immaculate Conception Church.
Urban, Lawrence *s.d.b.* '77 (SP) [E] Tampa, FL Mary Help of Christians School.
Urban, Lonnie A. '67 (AUS) Taylor, TX St. Mary's Church.
Urban, Peter '58 (DEN) [15] Denver, CO Montbello Catholic Parish-Church of the Ascension.
Urban, Reginald A. '77 (GI) Loup City, NE St. Josaphat's Church.
Urban, Robert M. '60 (SUP) Retired.
Urbaniak, Msgr. Bernard J. '68 (E) [29] Erie, PA St. Stanislaus Church.
Urbaniak, Jan *c.m.* '71 (BRK) [134] Brooklyn, NY St. Stanislaus Kostka Church.
Urbaniak, Lawrence M. '61 (RCK) Hartland, IL St. Patrick Church.
Urbaniak, Lucian '85 (SY) [11] Utica, NY St. Mark Church.
Urbanik, Stanley J. '61 (NEW) Retired.
Urbano, Claudio '84 (CHI) [W] Chicago, IL Northview University Center.
Urbanowicz, Msgr. Francis J. '39 (PH) Clifton Heights, PA Sacred Heart Church; Retired.
Urbanowski, Konrad *s.ch.* '23 (DET) [8] Sterling Heights, MI Our Lady of Czestochowa Church.
Urbanski, Louis J. '64 (P) [36] Portland, OR St. Therese of the Child Jesus Church.
Urbine, Gordon *o.f.m.* '42 (OAK) [9] Oakland, CA St. Elizabeth's Church; [N] Oakland, CA Franciscan Friars.
Urbine, Richard '48 (FTW) Retired.
Urbonas, Msgr. Ignatius L. '35 (GRY) [9] Gary, IN St. Casimir Church.
Urdiain, Angelo *c.r.* '66 (DEN) [A] Denver, CO St. Andrew's Theatine House.
Ureel, Wayne G. '90 (DET) Dryden, MI St. Cornelius Church.
Urell, Msgr. John '78 (ORG) Laguna Beach, CA St. Catherine of Siena Church.
Urian, Thomas R. '90 (PH) Secane, PA Our Lady of Fatima Church; [D] Springfield, PA Cardinal O'Hara High School.
Uribe, Arturo *c.ss.r.* '95 (LA) Whittier, CA St. Mary of the Assumption Church; [R] Whittier, CA Redemptorist Fathers Mission House.
Uribe, Saul de Jesus '80 (ELP) [34] El Paso, TX Sts. Peter and Paul Church.
Urizalqui, Richard '77 (FRS) Tulare, CA St. Aloysius Church.
Urlage, Robert J. '58 (COV) Retired.
Urmston, Benjamin J. *s.j.* '59 (CIN) [M] Cincinnati, OH Jesuit Community at Xavier Unversity.
Urnick, Charles B. '74 (NEW) Norwood, NJ Immaculate Conception Church.
Uroda, Stanley *s.v.d.* '74 (CHI) [B] Techny, IL Divine Word Residence; [N] Techny, IL Society of the Divine Word, Provincial Headquarter-Chicago Prov.
Uroda, Stanley *s.v.d.* '74 (FgM) Society of the Divine Word Foreign Missions.
Urrea, Miguel '87 (SB) [2] San Bernardino, CA Christ the King Church.
Urriza, Luis *o.s.a.* '44 (BEA) [4] Beaumont, TX Cristo Rey Church.
Urrutigoity, Carlos (SCR) On Special or Other Diocesan Assignment.
Uschold, Raymond F. '64 (BUF) Delevan, NY Blessed Sacrament Church; Machias, NY Holy Family Church.
Useldinger, Karl J. '77 (COS) Woodland Park, CO Our Lady of the Woods Church.
Usenza, Robert J. '61 (BGP) Retired.
Ustaski, William '77 (LA) Canyon Country, CA St. Clare Church.
Ustaski, William B. *c.r.i.c.* '77 (LA) [B] Los Angeles, CA Canons Regular of the Immaculate Conception-Novitiate.
Utendorf, James M. *c.s.p.* '78 (NY) [DD] Jamaica Estates, NY Paulist Fathers Generalate.
Uter, Frank M. '69 (BR) Gramercy, LA Most Sacred Heart of Jesus Church; Paulina, LA St. Joseph Church.
Utrup, Eugene E. '59 (STL) Chesterfield, MO Incarnate Word Church.
Utz, Raymond Michael '63 (PIT) Penn Hills, PA St. Susanna Church.
Utzig, Albert *s.s.c.* '83 (FgM) St. Columban's Foreign Mission.
Uvietta, Joseph *s.m.* '61 (STL) [T] Eureka, MO Marianist Retreat & Conference Center.
Uzdrowski, Mel R. *o.s.b.* '56 (JOL) [J] Lisle, IL St. Procopius Abbey.
Uzoh, Louis '73 (BRK) [163] Queens, NY St. Clare Church; [T] Brooklyn, NY Catholic Migration & Refugee Office, Catholic Migration Services, Inc.
Uzzilio, Robert A. '65 (BGP) [5] Stamford, CT St. Gabriel Church.

V

Vaca, Modesto *o.de.m.* '56 (PCE) [9] Ponce, PR La Merced Church.
Vacca, Bernard '52 (Y) Retired.
Vaccarella, Samuel *t.o.r.* '77 (WDC) [M] Washington, DC St. Louis Friary.
Vaccari, Andrew J. '86 (BRK) [215] Queens, NY Our Lady of the Miraculous Medal Church.
Vaccari, Peter I. '77 (BRK) Released from Diocesan Assignment.
Vaccari, Peter I. '77 (RVC) [A] Huntington, NY Diocesan Seminary of the Immaculate Conception.
Vaccaro, Guy '78 (JOL) Winfield, IL St. John the Baptist Church.
Vaccaro, Joseph V. '58 (NEW) On Duty Outside the Archdiocese.
Vaccaro, Joseph V. '58 (STP) [T] Lake Elmo, MN Hermits of the Most Blessed Virgin Mary of Mount Carmel.
Vacco, James *o.f.m.* '82 (BUF) [R] Williamsville, NY Campus Ministry.
Vacco, James *o.f.m.* '82 (NY) [DD] New York, NY Franciscan Friars, Order of Friars Minor, Holy Name Province.
Vacek, Carl *t.o.r.* '79 (ORL) [D] Winter Park, FL San Pedro Spiritual Development Center; [F] Winter Park, FL San Pedro Center, Third Order Regular of St. Francis; [F] Winter Park, FL Franciscan Friars, T.O.R., Provincial Residence, San Pedro Friary.
Vacek, Edward V. *s.j.* '73 (BO) [W] Cambridge, MA Weston Jesuit Community.
Vacek, Edward V. *s.j.* '73 (MIL) [P] Milwaukee, WI Jesuit Provincial Office, Wisconsin Province.
Vachon, Robert *m.s.* '55 (FR) [J] Attleboro, MA La Salette Provincial House.
Vadakel, George T. '59 (NY) New City, NY St. Augustine Church.
Vadakethayil, George (RVC) Uniondale, NY St. Martha Church.
Vadakin, Msgr. Royale M. '64 (LA) [42] Los Angeles, CA St. Anastasia Church.
Vadakkedath, Vincent '72 (LKC) Grand Chenier, LA St. Eugene Church.
Vadakkekara, J. Philip '69 (MET) Bloomsbury, NJ Church of the Annunciation.
Vadakkekudy, Jacob '61 (HEL) Harlowton, MT St. Joseph Church.
Vadakkumpadan, Davis T. *c.m.i.* (PH) [63] Philadelphia, PA Holy Spirit Church.
Vader, Anthony J. '52 (CHI) [83] Chicago, IL Holy Name of Mary Church; [190] Chicago, IL Sacred Heart Mission of Holy Name of Mary Church; Retired.
Vadino, Joseph A. '63 (PH) Center Square, PA St. Helena Church.
Vaeth, Paul *c.p.* '68 (MET) [H] South River, NJ Passionist Provincial Office.
Vaeth, Paul *c.p.* '68 (R) [H] Greenville, NC Catholic Student Center for Students at East Carolina University.
Vaghetto, Benedetto P. '78 (PIT) [10] New Castle, PA St. Vincent de Paul Church.
Vaghi, Msgr. Peter J. '85 (WDC) [36] Washington, DC St. Patrick Church; [V] Washington, DC The John Carroll Society.
Vago, John C. '70 (ALT) Bedford, PA St. Thomas Church.
Vail, John D. '67 (WDC) Issue, MD Holy Ghost Church.
Vail, Nathan R. *f.s.s.p.* '94 (SCR) [M] Elmhurst, PA Priestly Fraternity of St. Peter (F.S.S.P.), North American District Headquarters.
Vail, Thomas '51 (ALB) Retired.
Vaillancourt, Joseph *o.m.i.* '46 (FgM) Oblates Foreign Missions.
Vaillancourt, Mark G. '94 (NY) [200] Staten Island, NY St. Charles Church.
Vaillancourt, Raymond *m.s.* '89 (FR) Brewster, MA Our Lady of the Cape Church.
Vaillancourt, Robert C. '82 (PRT) [1] Old Town, ME Holy Family Church.
Vainavicz, Anthony C. '61 (GR) Spring Lake, MI St. Mary's Church.
Vairo, Carmine *s.d.b.* '64 (LA) [D] Rosemead, CA Don Bosco Technical Institute.
Vairo, Carmine *s.d.b.* '78 (LA) [C] Rosemead, CA Don Bosco Technical Institute.
Vaisnoras, Boniface *m.i.c.* '47 (CHI) [N] Chicago, IL Congregation of Marian Fathers of the Immaculate Conception.
Vaisnoras, Boniface *m.i.c.* '47 (JOL) Plano, IL St. Mary Church.
Vaisnys, Juozas *s.j.* '43 (CHI) [N] Chicago, IL Lithuanian American Jesuits.
Vakoc, Henry T. '92 (STP) Military Chaplains.
Vakulskas, John A., Jr. '69 (SC) Milford, IA St. Joseph's Church.
Vala, John B. '39 (NY) [DD] New York, NY Pope John Paul II Residence.
Vala, John B. '40 (NY) Retired.
Valades, Reuben '70 (RC) New Underwood, SD St. John the Evangelist Church.
Valainis, Vitolds '66 (DAV) Iowa City, IA State University of Iowa Hospital.
Valasek, Donald '74 (PBR) Barnesboro, PA St. John the Baptist Church; Patton, PA SS. Peter and Paul Church.
Valasek, Edward A. '46 (LIN) Retired.
Valastro, Msgr. George J. '56 (NY) Middletown, NY St. Joseph Church.
Valbuena, Luis *o.m.i.* '55 (LA) Pacoima, CA Mary Immaculate Church.
Valdazo, Stephen '58 (BRK) [184] Queens, NY St. Joan of Arc Church.
Valderrama, Viliulfo '96 (TUC) [17] Tucson, AZ St. Monica Church.
Valdes, Msgr. Angel (SJN) Resident Chaplains; [E] Rio Piedras, PR Hospital del Maestro.
Valdes, Bert W. '62 (WH) Ona, WV St. Stephen Church.
Valdes, Luis '45 (SB) Retired.
Valdes, Nicanor '60 (SJN) [30] San Juan, PR San Juan Evangelista Church; [30] San Juan, PR San Juan Evangelista Church.
Valdez, Antonio *o.f.m.* '61 (SFE) [1] Santa Fe, NM The Cathedral of San Francisco de Asis.
Valdez, John '91 (AMA) Canadian, TX Sacred Heart Church; Pampa, TX St. Vincent de Paul Church.
Valdez, Jose R. '89 (MIL) Retired.
Valdez, Max E. '44 (GI) Retired.
Valdez, Patrick *c.r.* (DEN) [A] Denver, CO St. Andrew's Theatine House.
Valdez, Patrick M. *c.r.* '75 (PBL) San Luis, CO Sangre de Cristo Church.
Valdez, Paul R. '82 (MRY) [2] Salinas, CA Sacred Heart Church.
Valdez, Salvador *o.f.m.* (CHI) [D] Chicago, IL Hales Franciscan High School, Inc.
Valdez, Salvador *o.f.m.* '97 (STP) [10] St. Paul, MN Sacred Heart Church.
Valdivia, Adolfo A. '81 (SAT) [48] San Antonio, TX St. Lawrence Church.
Valdivia, Antonio A. '63 (OAK) Richmond, CA St. Cornelius Church; Richmond, CA St. Mark's Church.
Valdivia, Sergio '83 (MRY) [3] Salinas, CA St. Mary of the Nativity Church.
Valencia, Carlos '85 (BRK) [185] Queens, NY St. John Vianney Church.
Valencia, Thaddeus T. *c.s.b.* '79 (GAL) Missouri City, TX Holy Family Church.
Valenta, John G. '62 (STL) [P] St. Louis, MO Jesuit Community Corporation at St. Louis University - Jesuit Hall.
Valente, John B. *o.f.m.* '41 (PRO) [P] Providence, RI St. Francis Friary.
Valente, Michael (JOL) Winfield, IL St. John the Baptist Church.
Valente, Michael '58 (JOL) Winfield, IL Central DuPage Hospital.
Valente, Palmo *s.f.* '52 (WDC) [B] Silver Spring, MD Holy Family Seminary.
Valenti, Thomas (NY) [GG] New York, NY University Apostolate.
Valenti, Thomas '76 (NY) [82] New York, NY Notre Dame Church.
Valentine, Charles R. '54 (TR) Englishtown, NJ Our Lady of Mercy Church.
Valentine, Daniel '74 (PIT) [R] Slippery Rock, PA Office for Campus Ministry.
Valentine, Daniel A. '74 (PIT) [2] West Mifflin, PA Holy Spirit Church.
Valentine, John C. '85 (WH) Benwood, WV St. John's Church; McMechen, WV St. James Church.
Valentine, Joseph R. '93 (CHL) On Duty Outside the Diocese.
Valentine, Lambert F. *o.f.m.* '43 (NY) [35] New York, NY St. Francis of Assisi Church.
Valentine, Leroy A. '77 (STL) Absent on Sick Leave.
Valentine, Richard A. '74 (PRO) Smithfield, RI St. Michael Church.
Valentine, Robert J. '69 (BGP) New Canaan, CT St. Aloysius Church.
Valentine, Timothy *s.j.* '85 (NY) [82] New York, NY Notre Dame Church.
Valentini, Francis M. '44 (CLV) Retired.
Valentino, Dominic '47 (JOL) Retired.
Valentino, Francis P. *s.j.* '68 (NEW) [C] Jersey City, NJ St. Peter's Preparatory School.
Valentino, Frederick (TR) Leave of Absence.
Valentino, Msgr. Frederick A. '50 (TR) Lavallette, NJ

St. Bonaventure Church.
Valenzano, Msgr. Arthur '75 (BAL) Westminster, MD St. John Church.
Valenzuela, Adolfo L. '80 (SAN) Big Spring, TX St. Thomas Church.
Valenzuela, Luciano '87 (SAC) Fairfield, CA Holy Spirit Church.
Valenzuela, Pablo '53 (SJN) [11] San Juan, PR Corpus Christi Church.
Valera, Ramon (LA) Woodland Hills, CA St. Mel Church.
Valerio, Raymond A. (MAR) Retired.
Valerio, Thomas A. (PAT) On Duty Outside the Diocese.
Valero, Isidro Giber '73 (SJN) [3] Trujillo Alto, PR San Francisco de Asis Church.
Valero, Pedro Ruiz *o.m.* '88 (CGS) Cayey, PR Nuestra Senora de la Asuncion Church.
Valiquette, Hilaire *o.f.m.* '64 (SFE) Pena Blanca, NM Nuestra Senora De Guadalupe Church.
Valiquette, Thomas M. *s.j.* '64 (FgM) Provinces.
Valit, Robert L. '61 (STP) Edina, MN Our Lady of Grace Church.
Valker, Richard J. '57 (CHI) Northbrook, IL St. Norbert Church.
Valko, George '77 (ALT) Hollidaysburg, PA St. Michael's Church.
Valko, George J. '77 (ALT) [A] Cresson, PA Mount Aloysius College; [H] Hollidaysburg, PA Campus Ministry.
Valko, Robert A. '65 (PIT) Military Chaplains.
Valla, Dominic J. '63 (HRT) Oxford, CT St. Thomas the Apostle Church.
Vallamattam, Thomas *s.j.* '64 (FgM) Provinces.
Valle, Msgr. Fernando '56 (LA) Retired.
Vallecorsa, Daniel '93 (PIT) [10] New Castle, PA St. Vincent de Paul Church.
Vallee, Gerald A. '85 (STA) [4] St. Augustine, FL San Sebastian Church.
Vallee, Robert '87 (MIA) [A] Miami, FL St. John Vianney College Seminary.
Vallejo, Jesus (SJN) [E] Santurce, PR Hospital de Diego.
Vallejos, Francisco "Paco" '87 (SFE) Roy, NM Holy Family-St. Joseph Church.
Vallelonga, J. Stephen '90 (WH) Weirton, WV Sacred Heart of Mary Church.
Vallely, James P. '49 (PRT) Retired.
Valleroy, Paul '74 (KNX) Signal Mountain, TN St. Augustine Church.
Valleroy, Rickey J. '93 (STL) Manchester, MO St. Joseph Church.
Valles, Carlos *c.ss.r.* '67 (CGS) Aguas Buenas, PR Church of Tres Santos Reyes.
Valley, John '60 (CLV) Released from Diocesan Assignment.
Valley, Paul *s.p.* '64 (SFE) [J] Jemez Springs, NM The Jemez Program, Our Lady of Lourdes Novitiate.
Vallier, John F. '87 (GR) Rothbury, MI Our Lady of the Assumption Church; Shelby, MI Our Lady of Fatima Church.
Valliere, Romeo J. '63 (MAN) Absent on Sick Leave.
Valliere, Timothy C. '91 (NOR) Somersville, CT All Saints Church.
Vallina, Alfredo *o.p.* '57 (PCE) Yauco, PR Holy Rosary Church.
Vallina, Msgr. Emilio '52 (MIA) [22] Miami, FL St. John Bosco Church.
Vallocheril, George Sebastian '84 (MIL) [P] Milwaukee, WI Jesuit Community at Marquette University.
Vallone, Louis A. '48 (BUF) Retired.
Vallone, Louis F. '73 (PIT) [56] Pittsburgh, PA St. Mary of the Mount Church.
Vallooram, Pius *c.m.i.* (LAF) Mamou, LA St. Ann Church.
Vallooran, Joseph '59 (SR) Crescent City, CA Pelican Bay State Prison.
Vallor, Robert '55 (GBG) Retired.
Valls, Richard G. *sch.p.* '57 (KAL) Delton, MI St. Ambrose Church.
Valois, Normand W. '46 (PRO) [1] Providence, RI Cathedral of SS. Peter and Paul; Retired.
Valone, Fred P. '94 (GAL) [50] Houston, TX St. Michael Church.
Valoret, Joseph '83 (MIA) Retired.
Valtierra, David D. *c.o.* '76 (CHR) [D] Rock Hill, SC Oratory of St. Philip Neri, Congregation of the Oratory of Pontifical Rite; [G] Rock Hill, SC Winthrop University, York Co. Tech Center Newman Center.
Valtierra, J. Antonio '79 (GRY) [1] Hammond, IN All Saints Church.
Vamos, Joseph E. '66 (GRY) [1] Merrillville, IN Our Lady of Consolation Church.
Vamos, Joseph L. '61 (TOL) [16] Toledo, OH St. Agnes Church.
Van Acker, Michael R. '81 (PEO) [J] Galesburg, IL St. Mary Medical Center.
van Ackeren, Leonard J. *o.s.b.* '38 (MIL) [P] Benet Lake, WI St. Benedict's Abbey.
Van Ban, Martin Tran *c.m.c.* '94 (BEA) [2] Port Arthur, TX Queen of Vietnam Church.
Van Beck, Alfred F. '50 (MIL) Retired.
van Beeck, Frans J. *s.j.* '63 (CHI) [C] Chicago, IL Jesuit Community at Loyola University of Chicago.
Van Beek, Alois R. '73 (MIL) Nabob, WI St. Matthias Church; St. Lawrence, WI St. Lawrence Church.
Van Beek, Dennis E. '69 (MIL) Waterford, WI St. Thomas Aquinas Church.
Van Bergen, Francis G. '56 (CLV) South Euclid, OH St. Gregory the Great Church.
Van Boxel, Msgr. W. H. '40 (LAF) Retired.
Van Breda, William C. *o.s.a.* '50 (PH) [AA] Villanova, PA St. Thomas Monastery.
Van Bui, Joseph Dung '95 (ORL) [7] Orlando, FL St. Charles Borromeo Church.
Van Cauwenburgh, Roger *c.i.c.m.* '51 (ARL) [J] Arlington, VA Missionhurst, C.I.C.M.-Central House and Provincialate.
Van Coillie, Paul *c.i.c.m.* '47 (SAT) [15] San Antonio, TX Our Lady of Good Counsel Church.
van de Crommert, Paul H. '88 (NU) Canby, MN St. Peter Church; St. Leo, MN St. Leo Church.
Van De Kreeke, William (GB) [4] Oshkosh, WI St. Vincent de Paul Church.
Van De Kreeke, William L. '63 (GB) [5] Oshkosh, WI St. John Church.
Van De Loo, Willard '55 (GB) [17] Green Bay, WI St. Willebrord Church; Special Assignment.
Van de Paer, John *c.i.c.m.* '47 (ARL) [J] Arlington, VA Missionhurst, C.I.C.M.-Central House and Provincialate.
Van De Paer, John *c.i.c.m.* '47 (PH) Parkesburg, PA Our Lady of Consolation Church.
Van De Ven, Kenneth A. '71 (PHX) [3] Glendale, AZ St. James Church.
Van De Voord, Simeon *o.s.b.* '61 (B) [1] Boise, ID Cathedral of St. John the Evangelist.
Van den Bussche, Hugo *o.m.i.* '53 (BWN) Roma, TX Our Lady of Refuge Church.
Van den Eynde, Stephen *ss.cc.* '48 (HON) [H] Honolulu, HI St. Patrick's Monastery.
Van Der Horst, John G. '65 (GB) [13] Green Bay, WI SS. Peter and Paul Church.
Van Der Linden, Peter J. '55 (DET) Retired.
Van Der Paalen, Pieter *c.i.c.m.* '55 (SAT) [M] San Antonio, TX Missionhurst Community Residence.
Van Der Peet, Michael *s.c.j.* (GAL) Retired.
van der Peet, Michael *s.c.j.* '53 (SP) [O] Pinellas Park, FL Priests of the Sacred Heart.
Van Der Poel, Cornelius *c.s.sp.* '47 (VEN) [G] Sarasota, FL Congregation of the Holy Ghost.
Van Der Zanden, Edmund '38 (P) Retired.
Van Derdys, Carlos Jimenez '67 (SJN) Dorado, PR San Antonio de Padua Church.
Van Deuren, John (GB) [16] Green Bay, WI St. Elizabeth Ann Seton Church.
Van Deuren, John H. '59 (GB) [F] Green Bay, WI St. Mary's Hospital-Medical Center.
Van Doan, Vincent '86 (LAN) Ann Arbor, MI Veterans' Hospital.
Van Dyke, James R. *s.j.* '93 (BUF) [D] Buffalo, NY Canisius High School; [O] Buffalo, NY Canisius Jesuit Community.
Van Gastel, William *m.h.m.* '86 (LA) [9] Long Beach, CA St. Lucy Church.
Van Gorder, John '53 (KC) Retired.
Van Guilder, Alphonse *o.f.m.conv.* '64 (MRY) Pismo Beach, CA St. Paul the Apostle Church; San Luis Obispo, CA California Men's Colony East.
Van Haegenborgh, Ward *c.i.c.m.* '55 (FgM) Missionhurst Foreign Missions.
Van Handorf, Jay '75 (LEX) [5] Lexington, KY St. Elizabeth Ann Seton Church.
Van Hee, Francis *c.i.c.m.* '48 (SAT) [M] San Antonio, TX Missionhurst Community Residence.
Van Hoof, Achilles E. *o.praem.* '48 (GB) [I] De Pere, WI St. Norbert Abbey.
Van Hoof, Gordon *o.s.c.* '53 (CHI) [J] Chicago, IL Resurrection Medical Center.
Van Hoof, Gordon *o.s.c.* '53 (DET) [K] Riverview, MI Crosier Community of Riverview.
Van Hook, John E. *o.f.m.* '55 (ALB) [B] Loudonville, NY Siena College.
Van Houtteghem, Paul *c.i.c.m.* '48 (FgM) Missionhurst Foreign Missions.
van Kaam, Adrian *c.s.sp.* '46 (PIT) [B] Pittsburgh, PA Duquesne University of the Holy Ghost.
Van Kempen, Robert A. '93 (FTW) Hessen Cassel, IN St. Joseph Church.
Van Kuren, Corey S. '86 (SY) [10] Binghamton, NY St. Paul Church.
Van Lai, Joseph Khuyen '74 (SD) [6] San Diego, CA Holy Family Church.
van Lare, John *c.m.* '47 (SAT) Cotulla, TX Sacred Heart Church.
Van Lente, Richard J. '66 (GR) Fremont, MI All Saints Church.
Van Liefde, Msgr. Christian M. '73 (LA) Los Angeles, CA L.A. City Fire Dept.
Van Linden, Phil *c.m.* '70 (FRS) [3] Fresno, CA The Catholic Community of Mt. Carmel & St. Alphonsus Church.
Van Meter, Eric '97 (FTW) [9] Fort Wayne, IN St. Jude Church.
Van Mullekom, Richard '56 (SAG) Retired.
Van Nevel, Msgr. Albert H. '42 (GRY) Retired.
Van Nguyen, Joseph Huyen '95 (SAC) Chico, CA Our Divine Savior Church.
Van Nguyen, Peter '60 (PMB) Lake Worth, FL Sacred Heart Church.
Van Nguyen, Peter Phan *c.s.s.r.* (CC) Rockport, TX St. Peter Indo-Chinese Parish.
Van Nguyen, Phuong '93 (WOR) [4] Worcester, MA Christ the King Church.
Van Ommeren, Msgr. William '52 (SPK) [M] Spokane, WA Immaculate Heart Retreat Center.
Van Oosbree, Christian J. (SC) On Duty Outside the Diocese.
Van Oss, James R. '64 (BEL) Posen, IL Our Lady of Perpetual Help Church; Todd's Mill, IL St. Mary Magdalen Church; [J] Belleville, IL Catholic Committee on Scouting of the Diocese of Belleville.
van Oudheusden, Henry L. '79 (LA) [R] Los Angeles, CA Amat House.
Van Overbeel, Gerald *o.s.a.* (CHI) [J] Chicago, IL Holy Cross Hospital.
Van Phuong, Msgr. Francis Pham (ATL) [M] Riverdale, GA Our Lady of Vietnam Catholic Church - Pastoral Center.
Van Roo, William A. *s.j.* '47 (MIL) [P] Milwaukee, WI Jesuit Community at Marquette University.
Van Sickler, Robert '93 (BAK) John Day, OR St. Elizabeth's Church.
van Sloun, Eugene G. '48 (DOD) Retired.
Van Sloun, Michael *o.s.c.* '95 (STP) Anoka, MN St. Stephen Church; [N] Anoka, MN Crosier Community of Anoka.
Van Stone, John J. '48 (PH) Retired.
van Straaten, Werenfried P. *o.praem.* '40 (ORG) [H] Silverado, CA Norbertine Fathers of Orange Inc.
Van Thanh, Louis '94 (NY) [1] Newburgh, NY St. Patrick Church.
Van Thuyne, Dennis G. '77 (PH) Glenside, PA St. Luke the Evangelist Church.
Van Trieste, Martin *s.t.* '45 (SJN) [2] Canovanas, PR Resurreccion del Senior Church.
Van Ty, Nguyen '85 (HT) [2] Thibodaux, LA St. Charles Borromeo Church.
Van Vlaenderen, Leonard S. '88 (MIL) Special Assignment.
Van Vurst, James *o.f.m.* '61 (CIN) [L] Centerville, OH The Franciscan at St. Leonard.
Van Winkle, Charles E. *c.s.c.* '78 (AUS) Killeen, TX St. Joseph Church; [H] Austin, TX Congregation of Holy Cross - Southern Province.
van-Ackeren, Leonard *o.s.b.* '38 (MAD) [J] Baraboo, WI St. Marys Ringling Convent.
Van-Hoorn, Leo '55 (ALX) Retired.
Vanagas, Albeyro *c.s.v.* '90 (CHI) [N] Arlington Heights, IL Viatorian Province Center-Clerics of St. Viator.
VanAmburgh, Donald C. '61 (SY) Vestal, NY Our Lady of Sorrows Church.
Vanasse, Bernard '78 (FR) Dighton, MA St. Peter's Church.
Vanasse, Hervey '77 (SEA) Buckley, WA St. Aloysius Church.
Vanasse, Roman R. *o.praem.* '60 (GB) [I] De Pere, WI St. Norbert Abbey.
Vance, Charles P. '70 (PH) Lenni, PA St. Francis de Sales Church.
Vance, James *c.ss.r.* '35 (OM) [19] Omaha, NE Holy Name Church; [31] Omaha, NE Mother of Perpetual Help Church.
Vance, James L. '63 (SFE) Raton, NM St. Patrick/St. Joseph Church.
Vance, Leslie A. '76 (SAT) Kirby, TX St. Joan of Arc Church.
Vancik, Vladimir '34 (PRM) Retired.
Vandal, Roland *m.s.* '49 (FR) [J] Attleboro, MA La Salette Provincial House.
VanDamme, Larry P. '93 (MAR) Houghton, MI St. Albert the Great University Parish; [G] Houghton, MI St. Albert the Great, University Parish.
VanDane, Louis L. *m.s.* '45 (STL) [P] St. Louis, MO La Salette Missionaries.
Vande Castle, Louis J. *o.praem.* '50 (GB) [I] De Pere, WI St. Joseph Priory.
Vande Hey, Robert *o.praem.* '49 (GB) [I] De Pere, WI St. Joseph Priory.
Vandeberg, Joseph '89 (SCL) Villard, MN St. Bartholomew's Church; West Union, MN St. Alexius Church.
Vandebroek, Felix J. *ss.cc.* '54 (HON) Koloa, HI St. Raphael Church.
Vandegrift, Raymond *o.p.* (WDC) [11] Washington, DC St. Dominic Church & Priory Church.
Vandegrift, William S. (CAM) Penns Grove, NJ St. James Church.
Vandegrift, William S. '80 (CAM) Ocean City, NJ St. Augustine's Church.
Vandehey, Ervin S. '46 (P) Retired.
Vandehey, Kelly '96 (P) Medford, OR Sacred Heart of Jesus Church.

Vandehey, Scott '66 (P) [3] Eugene, OR St. Mary Church.
Vandeloo, Melvin B. '53 (BEL) Mount Vernon, IL St. Mary Church.
Vanden Heuvel, Jeffrey M. '86 (GB) [7] Oshkosh, WI St. Raphael Church; Special Assignment.
Vanden Hogen, Msgr. James '64 (GB) Little Chute, WI St. John Church; [O] Green Bay, WI The Diocesan Charismatic Renewal Center.
Vanden Hogen, Paul A. '54 (GB) King, WI St. George Church; King, WI Wisconsin Veterans Home.
Vandenberg, James '77 (PBL) Absent on Leave.
Vandenberg, Robert H. '58 (GB) Combined Locks, WI St. Paul Church.
Vandenberg, Thomas L. '62 (SEA) Federal Way, WA St. Vincent De Paul Church.
VanDenBogaard, Joseph E. *m.m.* '37 (NY) [DD] Maryknoll, NY Maryknoll Fathers and Brothers.
VandenBossche, John V. *c.s.c.* '51 (FTW) [J] South Bend, IN Congregation of Holy Cross Indiana Province Provincial House.
Vander Heyden, William F. '70 (GB) On Duty Outside the Diocese.
Vander Woude, Thomas '92 (ARL) Great Falls, VA St. Catherine of Siena Church.
Vandergeest, Peter J. '40 (ALN) Retired.
Vanderholt, James (BEA) Sabine Pass, TX St. Paul Mission Church.
Vanderholt, James '57 (BEA) [5] Port Arthur, TX St. James Church.
Vanderkolk, Peter J. '83 (LFT) Delphi, IN St. Joseph Church.
Vanderlay, Louis R. *o.s.b.* '66 (LA) Montebello, CA St. Benedict Church.
Vanderlin, Philip *o.s.b.* '70 (BIS) [A] Richardton, ND Assumption Abbey.
Vanderlin, Philip *o.s.b.* '80 (FgM) American - Cassinese Congregation Foreign Missions.
VanderVennet, Timothy *o.c.s.o.* '35 (SAC) [A] Vina, CA Abbey of New Clairvaux, Trappist Seminary.
VanderVennett, Timothy *o.c.s.o.* '35 (SAC) [G] Vina, CA Abbey of New Clairvaux, Trappist.
VanderWeel, Richard L. *s.s.e.* '62 (BUR) [E] Colchester, VT Society of St. Edmund.
VandeVelde, J. Richard *s.j.* '68 (CHI) [C] Chicago, IL Jesuit Community at Loyola University of Chicago.
VanDeVoord, Simeon *o.s.b.* '61 (B) [C] Jerome, ID Ascension Priory.
VandeWalle, Victor '40 (OKL) Retired.
VandeWeyer, Vincent *c.i.c.m.* '48 (FgM) Missionhurst Foreign Missions.
Vandreuil, Paul '64 (WOR) Fiskdale, MA St. Anne's and St. Patrick's Church.
Vandrovec, Jerry C. '78 (STP) Mahtomedi, MN St. Jude of the Lake Church.
Vanecko, William E. '65 (CHI) [114] Chicago, IL St. Kilian Church.
Vang, Chue Ying '92 (STP) [36] St. Paul, MN St. Vincent de Paul Church.
VanGorder, John '53 (KC) [28] Kansas City, MO Our Lady of Good Counsel Church.
VanHaverbeke, Kenneth S. '91 (WCH) [5] Wichita, KS Church of the Magdalen.
Vanhee, Francis *c.i.c.m.* '48 (SAT) Lytle, TX St. Andrew Church.
Vanhoomissen, Bernard *c.ss.r.* '42 (SEA) [32] Seattle, WA Sacred Heart of Jesus Church.
VanHove, Brian *s.j.* '82 (WDC) [M] Washington, DC Carroll House.
Vanin, Dino S. *p.i.m.e.* '72 (COL) [H] Newark, OH P.I.M.E. Mission & Prayer Center.
Vanissery, Matthew '64 (WIN) St. Clair, MN Immaculate Conception Church.
Vanitvelt, Milton H. '49 (MAR) Retired.
Vankeirsbilck, Paul *e.c.* '90 (STU) [F] Bloomingdale, OH Holy Family Hermitage.
Vanleeuwen, Joseph *c.p.* '64 (CHI) [N] Chicago, IL Passionist Provincial Office.
VanLente, Richard J. '66 (GR) White Cloud, MI St. Joseph's Church.
Vanleuwen, Joseph *c.p.* '64 (FgM) Mission Procurators.
VanLiefde, Msgr. Christian '73 (LA) Pico Rivera, CA St. Hilary Church.
VanLoon, Msgr. Neil J. *v.f.* '79 (SCR) Kingston, PA St. Ignatius Church.
VanMalderen, Paul *c.i.c.m.* '40 (FgM) Missionhurst Foreign Missions.
Vann, Alfred *ss.cc.* '43 (HON) [H] Honolulu, HI St. Patrick's Monastery.
Vann, John C. '42 (MIA) Retired.
Vann, Kevin W. '81 (SFD) [2] Decatur, IL Our Lady of Lourdes Church.
VanNuffelen, Albert *c.i.c.m.* '41 (ARL) [J] Arlington, VA Missionhurst, C.I.C.M.-Central House and Provincialate.
VanNufflen, Albert *c.i.c.m.* '41 (ORL) Retired.
Vano, Roque P. '79 (SD) Brawley, CA St. Margaret Mary Church.
Vanoncini, Robert R. '63 (FRS) Dos Palos, CA Sacred Heart Church.
VanOverbeek, Gerald *o.s.a.* '65 (CHI) [N] Chicago, IL St. Rita Monastery.
VanSmoorenburg, Matthew *l.c.* (MAD) [I] Edgerton, WI Legion of Christ, Inc.
Vanthu, Joseph N. (SJ) [21] San Jose, CA Our Lady Queen of Martyrs, Vietnamese Mission Church.
VanWiel, John E. *c.s.v.* '66 (CHI) [D] Arlington Heights, IL St. Viator High School.
Vanyo, Leo V. '52 (PIT) [1] Pittsburgh, PA St. Paul Cathedral.
Vanzillotta, Gino *o.m.* '54 (LA) [3] Los Angeles, CA All Saints Church; [R] Los Angeles, CA Minim Fathers.
Vap, Gerald F. '65 (LIN) Orleans, NE St. Mary's Church.
Vap, Msgr. Ivan F. '54 (LIN) Geneva, NE St. Joseph's Church.
Varady, Michael *c.ss.r.* '87 (CHR) Sumter, SC St. Jude Church; [G] Sumter, SC Morris College.
Varakukala, George *h.g.n.* '62 (TYL) Clarksville, TX St. Joseph Church.
Varano, Andrew R. '58 (BRK) [46] Brooklyn, NY St. Francis of Paola Church.
Varas, Felix '50 (SJN) [51] San Juan, PR Maria Reina del Mundo Church.
Varble, Edward F. '50 (Y) Middlebranch, OH St. Therese Little Flower Church; Retired.
Varela, Jose *o.r.c.* (SB) Mecca, CA Our Lady of Guadalupe Shrine Church; [E] Riverside, CA Operarios Del Reino De Cristo, O.R.C.
Varettoni, Msgr. Julian B. '55 (PAT) [1] Clifton, NJ Sacred Heart Church.
Varga, Andrew G. '78 (BGP) Westport, CT St. Luke Church.
Varga, George '42 (E) Retired.
Varga, Paul *o.f.m.conv.* (TR) [5] Trenton, NJ Immaculate Conception Church.
Varga, Wayne M. '74 (PAT) Parsippany, NJ St. Peter the Apostle Church.
Vargas, Eric P. *s.v.d.* '76 (SB) [7] San Bernardino, CA St. Anthony Church.
Vargas, Gabriel Francesco (NEW) [7] Bayonne, NJ Our Lady of the Assumption Church.
Vargas, German '63 (SJN) [60] San Juan, PR Santa Teresa Jornet Church.
Vargas, John '66 (DET) [4] Sterling Heights, MI St. Jane Frances de Chantal Church.
Vargas, John C. *c.ss.r.* (STL) [P] Liguori, MO Alphonsian Foundation Office.
Vargas, John C. *c.ss.r.* '78 (BR) [H] Baton Rouge, LA Redemptorist Vice Province.
Vargas, Jose Carlos '92 (PCE) Aguirre, PR Sacred Heart Church.
Vargas, Roberto *o.s.a.* '55 (CC) [17] Laredo, TX St. Vincent de Paul Church.
Vargas Agudelo, German '63 (CGS) [B] Aibonito, PR Casa Manresa.
Vargas Oliveras, Jose C. '92 (PCE) [B] Ponce, PR The Pontifical Catholic University of Puerto Rico.
Varghese, Benedict C. *c.m.i.* '90 (NY) [166] Bronx, NY St. Michael Church.
Vargo, Edward *s.v.d.* '63 (FgM) Society of the Divine Word Foreign Missions.
Vargo, Robert B. '89 (HRT) Poquonock, CT St. Joseph's Church; Special and other (Arch)Diocesan Assignment.
Varickamackal, Joseph '84 (HRT) [7] New Britain, CT St. Jerome's Church.
Varlea, Jose *o.r.c.* (SB) [1] Riverside, CA Our Lady of Guadalupe Shrine Church.
Varley, John J. '59 (SPR) [10] Pittsfield, MA St. Teresa Church.
Varna, Msgr. Leons '29 (BRK) [Y] Brooklyn, NY Latvian Roman Catholic Mission.
Varney, Lawrence F. '64 (TOL) Assumption, OH St. Mary of Assumption Church.
Varni, Msgr. Edward '39 (OAK) [3] Concord, CA St. Francis of Assisi Church; Retired.
Varno, John J. '66 (ALB) Wynantskill, NY St. Jude the Apostle Church.
Varo, Jose Luis *o.f.m.* '56 (FRS) McFarland, CA St. Elizabeth Church.
Varone, Normand G. '75 (SPC) Benton, MO St. Denis Church.
Varsany, Msgr. William I. '52 (NY) [HH] New York, NY Hungarian Catholic League of America, Inc.
Varsanyi, Msgr. William I. '46 (PRO) [24] Providence, RI Our Lady of Charity Church; [M] Pawtucket, RI Jeanne Jugan Residence.
Varvaro, Msgr. William A. '63 (BRK) [192] Queens, NY St. Margaret Church.
Varvaro, Msgr. William A. '63 (NY) [HH] Middle Village, NY National Italian Apostolate Conference.
Vas, Joseph S. '79 (OKL) Special Assignment; [E] Oklahoma City, OK St. Anthony Hospital.
Vasa, Msgr. Robert F. '76 (LIN) [13] Lincoln, NE Bishop Bonacum Chancery Church.
Vasaturo, Anthony J. '55 (BO) [5] Medford, MA Sacred Heart Church; Retired.
Vaschetto, Bernardo *o.f.m.cap.* '62 (BO) [60] Boston, MA St. Patrick Church.
Vasek, Stephen *o.m.i.* '71 (BUF) [27] Buffalo, NY Holy Angels Church.
Vasil, James D. '74 (GBG) Smithton, PA St. Timothy Church.
Vasile, Louis A. '72 (ROC) Fairport, NY Church of the Resurrection.
Vasilj, Kvirin *o.f.m.* '40 (CHI) [N] Chicago, IL Croatian Franciscan Custody of the Holy Family.
Vaske, Martin O. *s.j.* '47 (OM) [K] Omaha, NE Jesuit Community At Creighton University.
Vasko, Christopher P. *j.c.l.* (TOL) Continental, OH St. John the Baptist Church.
Vasko, Christopher P. *j.c.l.* '83 (TOL) Cloverdale, OH St. Barbara Church.
Vasko, Peter *o.f.m.* '87 (FgM) Custody of St. Mary of the Angels. Byzantine-Slavonic.
Vasquez, Joe S. '84 (SAN) [5] San Angelo, TX St. Joseph Church.
Vasquez, Pedro *o.f.m.* (SJ) [18] San Jose, CA Our Lady of Guadalupe Church.
Vass, Robert *s.d.v.* '87 (PAT) [M] Florham Park, NJ Father Justin Vocationary.
Vasti, Michael *m.s.c.* '56 (ALN) [A] Center Valley, PA Missionaries of the Sacred Heart.
Vasti, Michael J. *m.s.c.* '56 (ALN) [G] Allentown, PA Sacred Heart Hospital.
Vater, Robert L. '45 (COV) Fort Thomas, KY St. Catherine of Siena Church; Retired.
Vath, Aloysius H. '40 (PH) [47] Philadelphia, PA St. Francis Xavier Church.
Vath, William R. '72 (LFT) [3] Lafayette, IN St. Boniface Church; Special Assignment.
Vattakudiyil, Francis P. '63 (RVC) Kings Park, NY St. Joseph's Church.
Vattakunnel, Jose '90 (LKC) Elton, LA St. Joseph's Church.
Vatter, Joseph E. (BUF) [2] Depew, NY St. Barnabas Church.
Vaughan, Gregory D. '72 (TR) [21] Trenton, NJ St. Raphael Church.
Vaughan, James '50 (ALB) [13] Troy, NY Sacred Heart Church.
Vaughan, Msgr. John J. '67 (MIA) [4] Miami Beach, FL St. Patrick Church.
Vaughan, John R. '74 (OWN) [1] Owensboro, KY St. Stephen Cathedral.
Vaughan, Msgr. Richard F. '47 (AMA) On Special or Other Diocesan Assignment.
Vaughan, Richard P. *s.j.* '50 (LA) [C] Los Angeles, CA Loyola Marymount University.
Vaughan, Thomas *s.s.c.* '56 (OM) [K] St. Columbans, NE St. Columban's Foreign Mission Society.
Vaughan, William L. '95 (SFR) [3] San Rafael, CA St. Raphael Church.
Vaughey, Msgr. James K. (NY) On Special or Other (Arch)Diocesan Assignment.
Vaughey, Msgr. James K. '65 (NY) Briarcliff Manor, NY St. Theresa Church.
Vaughn, John *o.f.m.* '55 (MRY) [G] San Miguel, CA Franciscan Friars, O.F.M.; [G] San Miguel, CA Novitiate House for the Franciscan Friars, O.F.M.; [I] San Miguel, CA San Miguel Retreat House.
Vaughn, Mason L. '50 (SAG) Birch Run, MI Sacred Heart Church.
Vaughn, Robert William *o.p.* '71 (NY) [DD] New York, NY St. Vincent Ferrer Priory.
Vaughn, Roger *o.s.c.* '77 (NY) [DD] New York, NY Crosier (Canons Regular of the Order of the Holy Cross).
Vaughn, Roland '71 (LKC) Hackberry, LA St. Peter Apostle Church.
Vaught, Michael R. '73 (OKL) Clinton, OK St. Mary's Church.
Vavasseur, David A. '66 (BR) Baker, LA St. Isidore the Farmer Church; Baton Rouge, LA Nursing Homes not under Catholic auspices.
Vavasseur, Henry C. '58 (BR) Port Allen, LA Holy Family Church.
Vaverek, Gavin '90 (TYL) Longview, TX St. Mary Church.
Vaverek, Hayden J. '94 (CHR) Greenwood, SC Our Lady of Lourdes Church; [G] Greenwood, SC Lander College Newman Center.
Vaverek, Timothy V. '85 (AUS) [5] Waco, TX St. Joseph Church.
Vavonese, Charles S. '73 (SY) Special Assignment; [S] East Syracuse, NY Bishop Grimes Priests Residence.
Vavrick, Eugene '93 (TR) Lakewood, NJ St. Mary of the Lake Church.
Vavrina, Kenneth '62 (OM) Silver Creek, NE St. Lawrence Church.
Vavrina, Kenneth P. '62 (OM) Clarks, NE St. Peter Church.
Vayalil, Thomas '63 (JOL) Steger, IL St. Liborius Church.
Vaz, Francis F. '61 (MET) Oxford, NJ St. Rose of Lima Church.
Vaz, Rock I. '71 (AUS) Belton, TX Christ the King Church.
Vaze Parampil, Thomas '69 (LUB) Retired.
Vazhapilly, Paul '61 (BRK) [55] Brooklyn, NY Holy Family Church; [133] Brooklyn, NY SS. Simon and Jude Church; [T] Brooklyn, NY Catholic Migration &

Refugee Office, Catholic Migration Services, Inc.
Vazhappily, Mathew *c.m.i.* '74 (SFS) Conde, SD St. John the Baptist Church.
Vazquez, Albert M. *c.m.f.* '55 (LA) [28] Los Angeles, CA Our Lady Queen of the Angels Church.
Vazquez, Antonio J. (PCE) [B] Ponce, PR The Pontifical Catholic University of Puerto Rico.
Vazquez, Antonio J. '91 (ARE) [4] Camuy, PR Our Lady of Monserrate Church.
Vazquez, Carlos R. '89 (WIL) [1] Wilmington, DE Cathedral of St. Peter; New Castle, DE Delaware State Hospital.
Vazquez, Enrique '89 (SJN) [4] Bayamon, PR Cristo Salvador Church.
Vazquez, Harry Lopez '93 (MGZ) Sabana Grande, PR Church of San Isidro.
Vazquez, Jose '89 (Y) Absent on Leave.
Vazquez, Jose Natividad *m.sp.s.* '76 (LA) [3] Oxnard, CA Our Lady of Guadalupe Parish.
Vazquez, Luis A. '90 (ARE) Corozal-Padilla, PR Our Lady of the Seven Sorrows Church.
Vazquez, Msgr. Perfecto '56 (BRK) [52] Brooklyn, NY Guardian Angel Church.
Vazquez, Roman *o.f.m.* (CAM) On Duty Outside the Diocese.
Vazquez, Virginio '73 (TYL) Lovelady, TX Eastham Unit, Texas Department of Corrections.
Vazquez-Vega, Edwin '95 (PCE) Salinas, PR Our Lady of Monserrat Church.
Vead, Victor P. '92 (ALX) Isle Brevelle, LA St. Augustine's Church.
Vecchio, Egidio A. *m.s.* '55 (LKC) [1] Sulphur, LA Immaculate Conception of the B.V.M. Church.
Vecchio, Michael J. '50 (PIT) Retired.
Vecsey, Stephen N. '73 (LA) Retired.
Vedro, James A. *o.s.c.* '65 (DET) Trenton, MI St. Joseph Church; [K] Riverview, MI Crosier Community of Riverview.
Veeneman, Dismas J. *o.f.m.conv.* '69 (IND) Clarksville, IN St. Anthony of Padua Church.
Veerkamp, Teodoro *o.p.* (SJN) [A] Bayamon, PR Bayamon Central University.
Vega, Carlos '89 (MIA) [1] Miami, FL St. Mary's Cathedral.
Vega, Donald *s.j.* '65 (SJN) [22] San Juan, PR San Ignacio de Loyola Church.
Vega, Donald M. *s.j.* '65 (FgM) Provinces.
Vega, Fernando *c.m.f.* '40 (FRS) [8] Fresno, CA St. Anthony Claret Church.
Vega, Hector *isch.* (CC) [J] Corpus Christi, TX Secular Institute of the Schoenstatt Fathers aka Schoenstatt Fathers.
Vega, Hector *i.sch.* '74 (CC) On Special Assignment.
Vega, Hector R. *c.c.* '74 (MIL) [T] Waukesha, WI Secular Institute of Schoenstatt Fathers.
Vega, Jose L. *o.m.* '69 (LA) [3] Los Angeles, CA All Saints Church; [R] Los Angeles, CA Minim Fathers.
Vega, Jose Luis '54 (FRS) Cutler, CA St. Mary Church.
Vega, Juan Ramon '55 (BR) Paincourtville, LA St. Elizabeth Church.
Vega, Raymond *s.c.j.* '73 (SP) [O] Pinellas Park, FL Priests of the Sacred Heart.
Vega, Richard '83 (LA) Lompoc, CA La Purisima Concepcion Church.
Vega, Richard J. '83 (LA) Lompoc, CA Lompoc Federal Correctional Institution.
Vega, Roberto '87 (ARE) [1] Arecibo, PR Cathedral of San Felipe Apostol.
Vega (Vega-Montalbo), Jose (Giuseppe) '73 (SEA) Unassigned.
Vehovec, Valentine '43 (SB) Retired.
Veich, Vincent J. '71 (BGP) [1] Stamford, CT St. Benedict's Church.
Veigas, Albert '80 (CLV) [3] Garfield Heights, OH St. Therese Church.
Veik, Al *o.f.m.cap.* '67 (MIL) [Y] Milwaukee, WI House of Peace.
Veilleux, Dom Armand *o.c.s.o* (ATL) [I] Conyers, GA The Monastery of the Holy Spirit.
Veith, William E. '70 (CHI) [J] Elk Grove Village, IL Alexian Brothers Medical Center, Inc.
Vekemans, Roger *s.j.* (MIL) [Y] Milwaukee, WI International Institute of the Heart of Jesus.
Vela, Fabian '56 (MRY) Hollister, CA Sacred Heart Church.
Vela, Rudy *s.m.* '84 (SAT) [M] San Antonio, TX Marianist Woodlawn Community.
Vela, William *c.s.b.* '90 (GAL) [F] Houston, TX St. Thomas High School.
Velandria, Eric *s.j.* '96 (SFR) [N] San Francisco, CA Jesuit Community at University of San Francisco.
Velas, Vincent '64 (PIT) Ellwood City, PA St. Agatha Church.
Velasco, Arturo '86 (LA) [67] Los Angeles, CA St. Ignatius of Loyola Church.
Velasco, Jose' J. *s.j.* '57 (LA) Monterey Park, CA St. Stephen Church.
Velasquez, Charles J. '85 (CHY) Wheatland, WY St. Patrick's Church.
Velasquez, Jose '67 (ELP) Canutillo, TX St. Patrick Church.
Velasquez, Marcos C. '89 (TUC) Nogales, AZ Sacred Heart Church.
Velasquez, Rodrigo '58 (RVC) Glen Cove, NY St. Patrick's Church.
Velazquez, David Mateo *m.sp.s.* '80 (LA) Huntington Park, CA St. Martha Church.
Velazquez, Luis '78 (ARE) [7] Vega-Baja, PR Our Lady of Mt. Carmel Church.
Velez, Andrew '96 (PAT) Morristown, NJ St. Margaret's Church.
Velez, Msgr. Francisco '58 (PCE) Juana Diaz, PR St. Raymond Nonato Church.
Velie, Richard '79 (MIA) Absent on Leave.
Vella, Msgr. Desmond J. '59 (NY) [52] New York, NY Immaculate Conception Church.
Vella, Edward *c.ss.r.* '85 (FgM) Redemptorist Foreign Missions.
Vella, Francis (OAK) On Special Assignment.
Vella, Francis M. (HRT) Newington, CT Department of Veteran Affairs Medical Center.
Vella, Joseph C. '68 (BRK) Military Chaplains.
Vellankal, James '58 (LAF) [2] Opelousas, LA Our Lady of Mercy Church; On Special Assignment.
Vellaramparampil, Aaron '71 (RVC) East Meadow, NY St. Raphael Church.
Vellardita, Guy *o.f.m.* '58 (FgM) Franciscan Foreign Missions.
Vellenga, R. Stephen '81 (CLV) Painesville, OH St. Mary Church.
Vellooratil, George (CHI) [179] Chicago, IL Queen of All Saints Basilica Church.
Vellucci, Dennis C. '75 (LA) Walnut, CA St. Lorenzo Ruiz Church.
Velo, Msgr. Kenneth J. '73 (CHI) [U] Chicago, IL The Catholic Church Extension Society.
Velozo, Msgr. Donald D. '65 (CAM) Cape May Court House, NJ Our Lady of the Angels Church; Northfield, NJ St. Bernadette Church.
Velten, Robert *o.s.b.* '54 (SP) [O] St. Leo, FL St. Leo Abbey.
Veltri, Dennis J. '93 (E) Greenville, PA St. Michael Church.
Veltrie, James V. *s.j.* (STL) [C] St. Louis, MO Saint Louis University.
Veltrie, James V. *s.j.* '65 (STL) [P] St. Louis, MO Jesuit Community Corporation at St. Louis University - Jesuit Hall.
Velutis, John (CHI) Retired.
Vendetti, Michael A. '64 (BRK) Released from Diocesan Assignment.
Venditti, J. Michael '87 (MET) On Duty Outside the Diocese.
Venditti, J. Michael '87 (PSC) Edison, NJ St. Nicholas Church.
Vendramin, Aldo *c.s.* '75 (CHI) [N] Stone Park, IL Scalabrini Mission Center.
Venegoni, John L. '95 (BEL) Pinckneyville, IL St. Bruno Church.
Veneklase, Michael G. *o.c.d.* '93 (GRY) [J] Munster, IN Discalced Carmelite Fathers Monastery.
Veneroso, Joseph R. *m.m.* '78 (NY) [DD] Maryknoll, NY Maryknoll Fathers and Brothers.
Veneto, Joseph P. '46 (BO) Retired.
Venette, Howard J. '84 (OG) Colton, NY St. Patrick Church.
Venezia, Arthur '71 (PMB) North Palm Beach, FL St. Paul of the Cross Church.
Vengayil, Thomas '59 (PMB) Tequesta, FL St. Jude Church.
Venglarik, Daniel M. '73 (Y) Boardman, OH St. Charles Borromeo's Church.
Venker, Josef V. *s.j.* '87 (SEA) [A] Seattle, WA Seattle University.
Venne, Douglas F. *m.m.* '59 (FgM) Maryknoll Foreign Missions.
Venne, R. Thomas '62 (MIL) [2] Pewaukee, WI St. Anthony Church.
Venne, Samuel J. '78 (BUF) [46] Buffalo, NY St. Martin Church.
Venneri, Michael D. '82 (SPK) Special Ministry; [G] Spokane, WA Sacred Heart Medical Center.
Vennitti, Thomas A. '73 (STU) Cadiz, OH St. Teresa Church; Hopedale, OH Sacred Heart Church.
Vennix, James F. '56 (GB) Waupaca, WI St. Mary Magdalene Church.
Venters, Darrell '89 (OWN) [5] Owensboro, KY Precious Blood Church.
Ventiquattro, Jude *t.o.r.* '88 (ALT) [F] Loretto, PA St. Francis Friary, Third Order Regular of St. Francis of Penance; [H] Hollidaysburg, PA Campus Ministry.
Ventre, Armand V. '57 (PRO) [K] North Providence, RI St. Joseph Health Services of Rhode Island - Our Lady of Fatima Hospital.
Ventresca, A. Andrew '57 (HRT) Retired.
Ventura, Anthony C. '78 (HRT) Retired.
Ventura, Gennaro J. '43 (ROC) Retired.
Ventura, John '68 (BIR) Absent on Leave.
Ventura, Mauro '81 (STU) [F] Bloomingdale, OH Holy Family Hermitage.
Ventura, Thomas F. '61 (CHI) Winnetka, IL SS. Faith, Hope and Charity Church.
Venus, Charles C., Jr. '80 (BLX) Leakesville, MS South Mississippi Correctional Institution.
Venust Lobo, Mauro Raul '62 (NO) Violet, LA Our Lady of Lourdes Church.
Venuti, Angelo A. '61 (BRK) [81] Brooklyn, NY St. Mary Mother of Jesus Church.
Venvertloh, Ken J. '67 (SFD) Jacksonville, IL Our Saviour Church; Virginia, IL St. Luke Church.
Venza, Felix F. '72 (TR) Florence, NJ St. Clare Church.
Venzor, Jesse C. '80 (FRS) Woodlake, CA St. Frances Cabrini Church.
Ver Bust, Richard M. '58 (GB) Special Assignment; [B] De Pere, WI St. Norbert College.
Ver-Schneider, Neil *s.j.* '66 (PH) [I] Philadelphia, PA The Gesu School.
Vera, Luis A. *o.s.a.* '95 (NY) [216] Staten Island, NY Our Lady of Good Counsel Church.
Vera, Romulo E. *c.s.c.* '89 (FTW) [J] South Bend, IN Congregation of Holy Cross Indiana Province Provincial House.
Veras, Richard (NY) [211] Staten Island, NY St. Joseph, St. Thomas Church.
Verbeke, Albert *c.i.c.m.* '46 (FgM) Missionhurst Foreign Missions.
Verberg, Richard R. '71 (MIL) Greenfield, WI St. John the Evangelist Church.
Verboomen, Willy *c.i.c.m.* '63 (BWN) McAllen, TX McAllen Medical Center.
Verbrugghe, Albert E. '50 (TUC) [F] Tucson, AZ Regina Cleri Center.
Verbryke, William L. *s.j.* '83 (CIN) [F] Cincinnati, OH St. Xavier High School; [M] Cincinnati, OH Jesuit Community at St. Xavier High School.
Vercek, Alphonse *sch.p.* '38 (BUF) [O] Derby, NY Piarist Fathers.
Verdegan, Albert L. '60 (SUP) Radisson, WI Sacred Heart Church; Winter, WI St. Peter Church.
Verdelotti, Anthony W. '86 (PRO) East Greenwich, RI Our Lady of Mercy Church.
Verdelotti, James J. '78 (PRO) Bristol, RI Our Lady of Mount Carmel Church.
Verdi, Ralph C. *c.pp.s.* '71 (LFT) [A] Rensselaer, IN Saint Joseph's College.
Verdia, Carlos *c.m.f.* '85 (SJN) [5] Toa Alta, PR N. Sra. de la Providencia Church.
Verdick, James *o.f.m.* '40 (MIL) [P] Burlington, WI Queen of Peace Friary.
Verdick, Jerome '58 (WIN) Jackson, MN Good Shepherd Church.
Verdick, Jerome F. '58 (WIN) Absent on Leave.
Verdoon, Cornelius '51 (SPK) Retired.
Verdun, Gerald J. '72 (PEO) Pekin, IL St. Joseph's Church.
Vereb, Jerome *c.p.* '72 (PIT) [O] Pittsburgh, PA St. Paul of the Cross Monastery.
Vereb, John '47 (PMB) [4] West Palm Beach, FL St. John Fisher Church; Retired.
VerEecke, Robert F. *s.j.* '78 (BO) [3] Newton, MA St. Ignatius Church.
Vereker, Tobias '58 (SAC) Vallejo, CA St. Vincent Ferrer Church.
Verespy, Joseph D. '79 (SCR) Hughestown, PA Blessed Sacrament Church.
Vergara, Armando '73 (STO) Linden, CA Holy Cross Church.
Vergauwen, Peter '42 (SAN) Retired.
Vergauwen, Peter '42 (SAT) [K] San Antonio, TX Padua Place.
Verhaeghe, Ronald '92 (KC) Special Assignment.
Verhagen, Donald *s.d.s.* '45 (MIL) [P] Milwaukee, WI Salvatorians - Jordan Hall.
Verhagen, Norbert M. *m.m.* '39 (SJ) [M] Los Altos, CA Maryknoll.
Verhalen, Charles J. '47 (MIL) Retired.
Verhalen, Peter *o.cist.* '81 (DAL) [D] Irving, TX Cistercian Preparatory School; [G] Irving, TX Cistercian Preparatory School; [M] Irving, TX Cistercian Abbey of Our Lady of Dallas.
Verhasselt, David A. '89 (MIL) Mapleton, WI St. Catherine Church.
Verheggen, Peter *o.f.m.* '49 (TUC) [4] Tucson, AZ Mission San Xavier del Bac Church.
Verhelst, Steven J. '90 (NU) Benson, MN St. Francis Church; Clontarf, MN St. Malachy Church; Danvers, MN Church of the Visitation; De Graff, MN St. Bridget Church; Murdock, MN Church of the Sacred Heart.
Verhoff, Melvin '91 (TOL) [19] Toledo, OH St. Catherine of Siena Church.
Verhoff, Werner F. *c.pp.s.* '43 (FTW) [11] Fort Wayne, IN Most Precious Blood Church.
Verhoye, Gerard A. '49 (PEO) Retired.
Verkamp, Bernard J. '64 (EVN) On Leave of Absence.
Verley, Jude *o.s.c.* '79 (DET) Riverview, MI St. Cyprian Church; [K] Riverview, MI Crosier Community of Riverview.
Vermiglio, Tom *m.c.c.j.* '72 (CHI) [N] La Grange Park, IL Comboni Mission Center.
Vernon, Donald B. '55 (LFT) Dunnington, IN St. Mary Church; Fowler, IN Sacred Heart of Jesus Church.
Vernon, John E. '54 (OM) [46] Omaha, NE St. Thomas

More Church.
Vernon, William F. '97 (HEL) [6] Butte, MT St. Ann Church.
Verostko, Remigius B. *o.s.b.* '57 (GBG) [H] Latrobe, PA Saint Vincent Archabbey.
Verrecchia, James A. '83 (ARL) Manassas, VA All Saints Church.
Verrett, Joseph C. *s.s.j.* '55 (BAL) [M] Baltimore, MD St. Joseph Society of the Sacred Heart House of Central Administration.
Verrier, John M. '95 (PEO) [15] Peoria, IL St. Vincent De Paul Church.
Verrigni, Robert J. '77 (NY) Larchmont, NY SS. John and Paul Church.
Verrill, Wendell '63 (BO) [4] Waltham, MA St. Mary Church.
Verrilli, William F. '79 (BGP) Darien, CT St. Thomas More Church; [C] Stamford, CT Trinity Catholic High School.
Verruni, Samuel A. '86 (PH) Exton, PA SS. Philip and James Church; [EE] Philadelphia, PA Newman Apostolate.
Verschaeve, C. Michael '77 (DET) [1] Taylor, MI St. Alfred Church.
Verstreken, Alfred *c.j.* '73 (LA) [D] Santa Barbara, CA Bishop Garcia Diego High School.
Verstynen, Robert J. '47 (RCK) Retired.
Verswyvel, Joseph *c.i.c.m.* '52 (FgM) Missionhurst Foreign Missions.
Vertzelis, George D. '53 (BO) Wellesley, MA St. James the Great Church.
Vesbit, Thomas S. '64 (GR) [15] Grand Rapids, MI St. Jude Church.
Vescera, Giuseppe *c.p.* (BO) [53] Boston, MA Our Lady of the Assumption Church.
Veselenak, Stephen *o.s.b.* '67 (PBR) McKeesport, PA St. Nicholas Church.
Vesely, James J. '54 (CLV) Brooklyn, OH St. Thomas More Church.
Vesely, Stanley G. *o.s.b.* '40 (JOL) [A] Lisle, IL Benedictine University; [J] Lisle, IL St. Procopius Abbey.
Vesga, Mario '62 (SD) [2] Chula Vista, CA Our Lady of Guadalupe Church.
Vespa, Bauttista '34 (FRS) Faculties Only.
Vessels, John L. *s.j.* '57 (ATL) [K] Atlanta, GA Ignatius House.
Vessels, John L. *s.j.* '57 (NO) [C] New Orleans, LA Loyola University.
Vest, Joseph E. '81 (L) [15] Louisville, KY St. Bernard Church.
Veszelovszky, Albin V. *o.praem.* '44 (GB) [17] Green Bay, WI St. Willebrord Church; [I] De Pere, WI St. Norbert Abbey; [O] De Pere, WI Canons Regular of Magnovarad, Ltd.
Vetrano, Anthony *o.f.m.cap.* '92 (NY) [DD] Garrison, NY St. Francis Friary.
Vetrano, Michael A. '79 (RVC) Melville, NY St. Elizabeth Church.
Vetter, Austin A. '93 (BIS) Center, ND St. Martin Church.
Vetter, Matthew *c.p.* '38 (FgM) Mission Procurators.
Vetter, Msgr. Wendelyn '60 (FAR) Hillsboro, ND St. Rose of Lima Church.
Vettese, Donald *s.j.* '82 (TOL) [C] Toledo, OH St. John's Jesuit High School.
Vettiyankal, Abraham *c.m.i.* '70 (NY) Irvington-on-the-Hudson, NY Immaculate Conception Church.
Veverka, Floribert *o.f.m.* '48 (STL) [P] St. Louis, MO Franciscan Friary of St. Anthony of Padua.
Vevik, Paul '77 (SPK) [12] Spokane, WA St. Francis Xavier Church.
Vezhaparambil, Paul *c.m.i.* '64 (NY) Bronxville, NY St. Joseph Church; Bronxville, NY Lawrence Hospital.
Via, Anthony P. *s.j.* '62 (SPK) [C] Spokane, WA Gonzaga University.
Viale, Paul (NEW) Newark, NJ Essex County Youth Detention Center.
Viale, Paul A. '67 (NEW) [7] Newark, NJ St. Augustine's Church.
Viall, James A. '54 (CLV) [68] Cleveland, OH St. Rose Church.
Viall, John L. '59 (CLV) North Royalton, OH St. Albert the Great Church.
Viallis, Didier-Marie Dugas '94 (CC) [H] Laredo, TX St. John's Priory, (F.J.).
Vialpando, Kenneth L. '91 (SLC) [2] Salt Lake City, UT Our Lady of Guadalupe Church.
Vianney, Peter J. '65 (NY) Hyde Park, NY Regina Coeli Church.
Viau, Msgr. Roger '43 (SPR) Retired; [H] Springfield, MA St. Michael's Residence.
Viberti, Victor L. *s.s.p.* '38 (NY) [B] New York, NY Society of St. Paul.
Vicari, Marc A. '97 (NEW) South Orange, NJ Our Lady of Sorrows Church.
Vicchio, Stephen J. (BAL) [A] Baltimore, MD St. Mary's Seminary and University.
Vicente, Francisco '49 (OAK) Antioch, CA Holy Rosary Church.
Vicente, Isidore V. *o.p.* '64 (GAL) [Q] Houston, TX Dominican Fathers and Brothers, St. Mark Priory, Inc.; [T] Houston, TX University of Houston Central Campus Catholic Newman Association.
Vicente, Julian (SJN) On Duty Outside the Archdiocese.
Vichas, Walter A. '49 (HRT) [1] Waterbury, CT Blessed Sacrament Church.
Vichich, Michael T. '74 (MAR) Hermansville, MI St. John Neumann Church.
Vicini, Andrea *s.j.* '96 (BO) [W] Chestnut Hill, MA The Jesuit Community at Boston College.
Vickery, Richard F. '48 (MAN) Retired.
Victor, Al '76 (PMB) Retired.
Victor, Ronald J. '78 (DET) [3] St. Clair Shores, MI St. Isaac Jogues Church.
Victoria, Robert '91 (LA) Rowland Heights, CA St. Elizabeth Ann Seton Church.
Vida, Msgr. George N. '57 (VNN) Anaheim, CA Annunciation Church.
Vidal, Gustavo A. '97 (SLC) [3] Ogden, UT St. Joseph's Church; [C] Ogden, UT St. Joseph Regional School.
Vidal, Robert S. '66 (ORG) Seal Beach, CA St. Anne's Church.
Vidiella, Felix '52 (CC) Retired.
Vidmar, John C. *o.p.* '80 (WDC) [B] Washington, DC Dominican House of Studies.
Vidra, Msgr. Thomas J. '59 (SD) El Centro, CA St. Mary Church.
Vidrine, Msgr. Curtis S. '45 (LKC) Retired.
Vieages, Harold '64 (RNO) Leave of Absence.
Vieck, Hilary F. '55 (EVN) Bloomfield, IN Holy Name Church; Linton, IN St. Peter Church.
Vieira, John S. '97 (SB) [2] Corona, CA St. Edward Church.
Vieira, Victor M. '67 (PRO) [2] East Providence, RI St. Francis Xavier Church.
Vieites, Jesus *ss.cc.* '62 (SJN) [1] Guaynabo, PR Corazon de Jesus Church.
Vielgus, Thaddeus A. '54 (MET) Retired.
Vien, John R. '93 (STL) [14] St. Louis, MO Our Lady of Sorrows Church.
Vier, Msgr. Henry J. '40 (NY) [185] Bronx, NY St. Raymond Church; Retired; [E] White Plains, NY Archbishop Stepinac High School.
Viera, Manuel *o.f.m.* '82 (SFE) [1] Santa Fe, NM The Cathedral of San Francisco de Asis.
Vierling, Ronald M. *p.f.* (NY) Suffern, NY Sacred Heart Church.
Viero, James *c.s.* '45 (NY) [DD] Staten Island, NY Scalabrinian Missionaries.
Vierra, Theodore A. '60 (LA) [86] Los Angeles, CA St. Paul the Apostle Church; [CC] Los Angeles, CA Archdiocesan Office for Campus Ministry.
Vieson, Paul F. *s.m.* '84 (CIN) [D] Dayton, OH The University of Dayton; [M] Dayton, OH Marianist Provincialate.
Viet Tran, Bac-Hai '84 (NO) Pearl River, LA SS. Peter and Paul Church.
Viet-Chau, Joachim *s.s.s.* '72 (CLV) [P] Cleveland, OH Congregation of the Blessed Sacrament Provincial House.
Vieweg, Robert R. '64 (CLV) Grafton, OH Immaculate Conception Church.
Vigeant, Wilfred J. *s.j.* (BO) [W] Weston, MA Campion Center.
Vigil, Joe D. '80 (SFE) [5] Albuquerque, NM Holy Ghost Church.
Vigil, Michael A. '85 (GLP) Winslow, AZ St. Joseph's Church.
Vigil, Paul '91 (LA) Redondo Beach, CA St. Lawrence Martyr Church.
Vigilanti, John A. '72 (NY) Chappaqua, NY St. John and St. Mary Church; [GG] New York, NY University Apostolate.
Vigliotta, Thomas F. *o.f.m.* '85 (CHR) Anderson, SC St. Mary of the Angels Church.
Vigliotta, William J. *s.m.m.* '54 (RVC) [N] Eastport, NY Shrine of Our Lady of the Island.
Vignoe, Joseph M. '58 (BUR) Poultney, VT St. Raphael Church; [H] Burlington, VT University of Vermont-The Catholic Center at UVM.
Vignola, Robert R. *c.m.* '50 (BRK) [U] Jamaica, NY St. Vincent's House.
Vignone, John J. '75 (CAM) Runnemede, NJ St. Teresa of the Infant Jesus Church.
Vigues, Gabriel '93 (MIA) Coral Springs, FL St. Andrew Church.
Vila-Cha, Joao J. *s.j.* '91 (BO) [W] Chestnut Hill, MA The Jesuit Community at Boston College.
Viladesau, Richard R. *s.t.d.* '69 (RVC) Saltaire, NY Our Lady Star of the Sea, Mission Chapel Church; Priests Released from Diocesan Assignment.
Vilano, Anthony '96 (SAT) Kerrville, TX Notre Dame Church.
Vilaplana, Jose *s.j.* '63 (NY) [3] White Plains, NY St. Bernard Church.
Vileo, Stephen '87 (DET) [A] Detroit, MI Sacred Heart Major Seminary, Inc.
Vilie, Richard '79 (PMB) Hobe Sound, FL St. Christopher Church.
Vilkauskas, Edward J. *c.s.sp.* '73 (CHL) Monroe, NC Our Lady of Lourdes Church.
Villa, Angelo *p.i.m.e.* '51 (DET) [K] Detroit, MI P.I.M.E. Missionaries of SS. Peter and Paul.
Villa, Aurelio *o.f.m.* '64 (SR) Boyes Hot Springs, CA St. Leo Church; Sonoma, CA St. Francis Solano Church.
Villa, James *o.f.m.* '69 (NY) [4] Mt. Vernon, NY Our Lady of Mount Carmel Church.
Villa, Joseph L. '97 (IND) Graduate Studies.
Villa, Leonard F. '86 (NY) [8] Yonkers, NY St. Eugene Church.
Villa Gomez, Nemorio '56 (LA) Retired.
Villabon, German *o.s.a.* '54 (RVC) [1] Rockville Centre, NY St. Agnes Cathedral.
Villada, Luis Eduardo '95 (SJN) Dorado, PR San Antonio de Padua Church.
Villafranca, Eugenio *c.m.* '62 (PCE) [14] Ponce, PR San Vicente-Cantera Church.
Villagomez, Jose *o.f.m.cap.* '74 (AGN) Agat, GU Our Lady of Mount Carmel Church.
Villagomez, Jose *o.f.m.cap.* '74 (FgM) Capuchin Foreign Missions.
Villalba, Angel *o.m.i.* '39 (CC) Sarita, TX Our Lady of Guadalupe Church.
Villalobos, Alberto '85 (LA) [D] Mission Hills, CA Alemany High School.
Villalobos, David '96 (SR) [3] Santa Rosa, CA St. Rose of Lima Church.
Villalon, Jose M. (BWN) [5] Brownsville, TX Our Lady of Good Counsel Church; [6] Brownsville, TX Our Lady of Guadalupe Church.
Villalon, Jose M., Jr. '89 (BWN) Ranchito, TX St. Ignatius Church.
Villalta, Moises *o.f.m.cap.* '95 (WDC) [39] Washington, DC Shrine of the Sacred Heart Church.
Villamide, Msgr. Aniceto '67 (BGP) [18] Bridgeport, CT St. Peter's Church; [W] Bridgeport, CT Hispanic Social Ministries of Fairfield County, Inc.
Villani, Ralph A. '68 (NY) Mt. Kisco, NY St. Francis of Assisi Church.
Villani, Msgr. Rocco D. '61 (BRK) [81] Brooklyn, NY St. Mary Mother of Jesus Church.
Villano, Mark A. '88 (LA) [86] Los Angeles, CA St. Paul the Apostle Church; [CC] Los Angeles, CA Archdiocesan Office for Campus Ministry.
Villano, Richard R. '58 (STP) [26] Minneapolis, MN St. Helena Church.
Villanova, Richard A. '67 (NEW) Hillside, NJ St. Catherine of Siena Church.
Villanueva, Alfred '96 (ELP) [1] El Paso, TX St. Patrick's Cathedral.
Villanueva, Camilo P. (SJ) [5] Santa Clara, CA Our Lady of Peace Church.
Villanueva, Jose Antonio '63 (SAT) [13] San Antonio, TX Our Lady of the Angels Church.
Villar, Msgr. Demetrio '46 (RVC) Retired.
Villar, Vincent *s.d.b.* '55 (MIA) [25] Miami, FL St. Kieran Church.
Villareal, Louis *o.m.i.* '65 (BEA) Mont Belvieu, (1991) Holy Trinity Mission Church.
Villaronga, Angel *o.f.m.* '51 (MIA) [H] Miami, FL Franciscan Fathers' Residence.
Villarreal, Louis J. *o.m.i.* '65 (BEA) Anahuac, TX Our Lady of Light Church.
Villarroya, Ernesto '63 (DAL) [1] Garland, TX Good Shepherd Church.
Villarroya, Pedro *c.m.* '59 (LA) [R] Los Angeles, CA Vincentian Fathers and Brothers.
Villaruel, Alvin M. '94 (SR) [B] Santa Rosa, CA Cardinal Newman High School.
Villaruel, Salvador *m.s.c.* '79 (LA) Cudahy, CA Cudahy Mission Church.
Villaverde, Alberto *s.j.* '56 (SJN) [22] San Juan, PR San Ignacio de Loyola Church.
Villaverde, Antonio E. '55 (ALX) Retired.
Villaverde, Tirso S. '96 (CHI) [164] Chicago, IL St. Pascal Church.
Villegas, Efraim *o.s.b.* '88 (BIS) [A] Richardton, ND Assumption Abbey.
Villegas, Efraim *o.s.b.* '88 (FgM) American - Cassinese Congregation Foreign Missions.
Villegas, Gonzalo J. '92 (TUC) [1] Tucson, AZ St. Augustine's Cathedral.
Villegas, Hernando '57 (MIA) Coral Gables, FL Little Flower Church.
Villegas, Jorge C. '66 (E) [30] Erie, PA St. Stephen Church.
Villegas, Juan C. *s.j.* '75 (FgM) Provinces.
Villegas, Rafael '90 (ORL) [1] Orlando, FL St. James Cathedral.
Villegas, Robert *c.s.c.* '63 (LSC) Chamberino, NM San Luis Rey Church.
Villegas, Samuel '65 (LA) Huntington Park, CA St. Matthias Church.
Villegas, Samuel C. '56 (LA) Retired.
Villemaire, Arthur M. '51 (SP) St. Joseph, FL Sacred Heart Church; [F] Dade City, FL Sacred Heart Child Care Center.
Villerot, Henry E. '41 (DET) Retired.
Villerot, Msgr. Thomas H. '43 (DET) Royal Oak, MI St. Mary Church; Retired.

Vima, Amalor '71 (TLS) McAlester, OK St. John Church.
Vinasco, Diego H. '97 (CHR) Absent On Leave.
Vincent, Msgr. Amos J. '49 (LKC) Westlake, LA St. John Bosco Church.
Vincent, David P. '64 (CIN) [3] Springfield, OH St. Mary Church.
Vincent, John F. '54 (WIN) Retired.
Vincent, John J. *o.s.c.* '58 (LIN) [A] Hastings, NE Crosier Monastery.
Vincent, Michael *s.j.* '82 (CLV) [E] Cleveland, OH St. Ignatius High School.
Vincent, Robert G. *v.f.* '57 (NO) La Place, LA St. Joan of Arc Church.
Vincenzo, Dennis J. '91 (HRT) [1] Hartford, CT Cathedral of St. Joseph.
Vinci, Msgr. Guy S. '59 (NY) [102] New York, NY St. Patrick Old Cathedral; Harrison, NY St. Gregory the Great Church.
Vinci, Terzo *s.a.c.* '58 (NY) [13] Yonkers, NY Our Lady of Mt. Carmel Church.
Vincze, Michael A. '40 (MET) Retired.
Vincze, Michael M. '40 (MET) Woodbridge, NJ Our Lady of Mt. Carmel Church.
Vinsko, John J. *m.m.* '62 (SJ) [M] Los Altos, CA Maryknoll.
Vinslauski, Robert '71 (SFS) Aberdeen, SD St. Mary Church.
Vinyard, Barry '75 (SD) Lakeside, CA Our Lady of Perpetual Help Church.
Viola, William *o.f.m.conv.* (BAL) [90] Baltimore, MD St. Stanislaus Kostka Church.
Viola, William *s.s.* '84 (WDC) [C] Washington, DC Catholic University of America, The.
Viola, William L. '94 (BAL) Columbia, MD St. John the Evangelist Church.
Violette, Lawrence '93 (ARL) Annandale, VA St. Ambrose Church.
Violette, Tex '75 (HT) On Leave.
Virella, Jorge '97 (ARE) Hatillo, PR Our Lady of Mt. Carmel Church.
Virella, Miguel A. *s.v.d.* '96 (TR) Freehold, NJ St. Rose of Lima Church.
Virgen, Javier G. '93 (SLC) Provo, UT St. Francis of Assisi Church; Gunnison, UT State Penitentiary.
Virgets, Edward J. *c.m.* '46 (STL) [P] St. Louis, MO Vincentian Bellerive Residence.
Virginia, Stephen G. '79 (COL) Leave of Absence.
Virnig, Laurn '63 (SCL) Royalton, MN Holy Trinity Church.
Virtue, William D. '75 (PEO) Earlville, IL St. Theresa's Church.
Virus, Keith M. '92 (GRY) Munster, IN St. Thomas More Church.
Visbisky, Richard (BO) Brockton, MA Good Samaritan Medical Center.
Visbisky, Richard W. '62 (BO) [Q] Brockton, MA Good Samaritan Medical Center.
Viscardi, Christopher J. *s.j.* '76 (MOB) [B] Mobile, AL Spring Hill College.
Viscardi, Robert *i.m.c.* '63 (MET) [H] Somerset, NJ Consolata Society for Foreign Missions.
Visconti, Luciano M. *c.r.s.p.* '42 (BUF) [B] Youngstown, NY St. Anthony M. Zaccaria Seminary.
Visich, Eduard C. '53 (BRK) Absent on Leave.
Vita, Mariano L. '42 (CHI) Bellwood, IL St. Simeon Church; Retired.
Vitacolonna, Xavier *c.p.* '74 (PIT) [O] Pittsburgh, PA St. Paul of the Cross Monastery.
Vitaglione, Robert '76 (BRK) [70] Brooklyn, NY St. Joseph's Church.
Vitale, Louis *o.f.m.* '63 (SFR) [7] San Francisco, CA St. Boniface Church.
Vitali, James V. *o.s.a.* '81 (VEN) Golden Gate, FL St. Elizabeth Seton Church.
Vitali, John *c.r.s.* '71 (MAN) [H] Allenstown, NH Pine Haven Boys Center.
Vitali, Theodore *c.p.* '69 (MET) [H] South River, NJ Passionist Provincial Office.
Vitaliano, Dominic '91 (PEO) Philo, IL St. Thomas Church.
Vitaliano, Dominic J. '91 (PEO) Eureka, IL St. Luke's Church.
Vitela, Francisco '68 (LA) Compton, CA Sagrado Corazon, Sacred Heart Church.
Vitillo, Robert J. '72 (PAT) On Duty Outside the Diocese.
Vitka, Stephen G. '41 (HRT) Retired.
Vito, Alfred J. '84 (SCR) Canadensis, PA St. Bernadette Church.
Vitro, Thomas J. '66 (CHI) Other Assignments.
Vitsas, John P. '46 (RVC) Wading River, NY St. John Baptist Church; Retired; [N] Uniondale, NY St. Pius X Residence.
Vitte, Jules '49 (NO) Retired.
Vittengl, Donald J. *m.m.* '56 (FgM) Maryknoll Foreign Missions.
Vitturino, Saverio T. '67 (WDC) Benedict, MD St. Francis de Sales Church.
Vitucci, James '72 (MIA) Pembroke Pines, FL St. Maximilian Kolbe Church.
Vitus, Frank K. '75 (JOL) Minooka, IL St. Mary Church.
Viveiros, Joseph F. '74 (FR) [1] Swansea, MA St. Dominic's Church; [M] Fall River, MA Special Apostolates, Department of.
Vivero, David (ORL) Sanford, FL All Souls Church.
Viviano, Benedict T. *o.p.* '66 (CHI) [N] Chicago, IL Dominicans (Provincial Office).
Viviano, Charles '89 (ORL) Titusville, FL St. Teresa Church.
Viviano, Nino '60 (SP) [5] Clearwater, FL St. Michael The Archangel Church.
Viviano, Nino '64 (ALX) On Duty Outside the Diocese.
Vivona, Anthony '53 (BRK) Retired.
Vivona, Francis '69 (VNN) Las Vegas, NV Our Lady of Wisdom Italo-Greek Mission Church.
Vizcaino, Mario B. *sch.p.* '60 (MIA) [K] Miami, FL Southeast Pastoral Institute; [K] Miami, FL Southeast Regional Office for Hispanic Ministry, Inc.; [L] Miami, FL SEPI Evangelization and Education Foundation, Inc.
Vizcaino, Mario B. *sch.p.* '60 (PH) [AA] Devon, PA Piarist Fathers (Order of the Pious Schools).
Vizcaino, Mario B. *sch.p.* '60 (WDC) [B] Washington, DC Queen of Pious Schools House of Studies-Piarist Fathers.
Vizcarra, Angel *o.p.* '46 (NO) [25] New Orleans, LA St. Anthony Of Padua Church.
Vizzard, Msgr. James J. '48 (PH) Bala Cynwyd, PA St. Matthias Church; Retired.
Vjecha, Michael J. *s.j.* '87 (CLV) [C] Cleveland, OH John Carroll Jesuit Community.
Vjecha, Michael J. *s.j.* '87 (DET) [K] Detroit, MI Jesuit Provincial Office-Detroit Province of the Society of Jesus.
Vjecha, Michael J. *s.j.* '87 (FgM) Provinces.
Vlasz, Melvyn J. '63 (RCK) On Disability Leave; [G] Rockford, IL Cor Mariae Center.
Vlaun, James C. '88 (RVC) West Islip, NY Our Lady of Lourdes Church; [C] West Islip, NY St. John the Baptist.
Vliet, Charles Van *f.s.s.p.* (SCR) [M] Elmhurst, PA Priestly Fraternity of St. Peter (F.S.S.P.), North American District Headquarters.
Vo, Peter De Ta *s.v.d.* '87 (WDC) [M] Washington, DC Divine Word College.
Vo, Peter Phong '88 (MET) Port Reading, NJ St. Anthony of Padua Church.
Vodoklys, Edward J. *s.j.* '91 (WOR) [N] Worcester, MA Jesuits of Holy Cross College, Inc.
Voegele, Fridolin *o.f.m.* '58 (CIN) [24] Cincinnati, OH Corpus Christi Church.
Voelker, David A. '74 (BEL) Military Chaplains.
Voelker, Harold H. '54 (STL) Gardenville, MO St. George Church.
Voelker, James A. '69 (BEL) Beckemeyer, IL St. Anthony Church; [4] East St. Louis, IL St. Patrick Church; [5] East St. Louis, IL St. Philip Church.
Voelker, Karl *s.j.* '72 (WIN) [1] Mankato, MN SS. Peter and Paul's Church.
Voelker, Lawrence '66 (IND) [5] Indianapolis, IN Holy Cross Church; [6] Indianapolis, IN Holy Rosary Church; Indianapolis, IN Indiana Women's Prison.
Voelker, Peter H. *c.ss.r.* '61 (GAL) [34] Houston, TX Holy Ghost Church.
Voellmecke, Francis W. '59 (CIN) [60] Cincinnati, OH Old St. Mary Church.
Vogan, Howard L. '69 (DET) South Lyon, MI St. Joseph Church.
Vogan, Robert C. '70 (PH) Aston, PA St. Joseph Church.
Vogel, Arthur '57 (SCL) Retired.
Vogel, Charles P. '43 (BRK) [137] Brooklyn, NY St. Sylvester Church; Retired.
Vogel, Edward A. '50 (MIL) [3] Racine, WI Holy Name Church.
Vogel, F. Philip *s.d.s.* '69 (BAL) Baltimore, MD Spring Grove Center Hospital.
Vogel, Gerhard *s.v.d.* '65 (TR) Asbury Park, NJ St. Peter Claver Church.
Vogel, J. Carl '50 (DAL) McKinney, TX St. Michael Church.
Vogel, John '86 (LA) Burbank, CA St. Robert Bellarmine Church.
Vogel, Joseph '87 (SFS) Westport, SD Sacred Heart of Westport Church; [H] Aberdeen, SD Diocesan Newman Apostolate; [H] Aberdeen, SD Aquinas Student Center.
Vogel, Marcel (GF) Special Assignment.
Vogel, Marcel J. (GF) Chinook, MT St. Gabriel's Church.
Vogel, Murel R. *s.j.* '37 (CHI) [C] Chicago, IL Jesuit Community at Loyola University of Chicago.
Vogel, Philip *s.d.s.* '69 (WDC) [B] Silver Spring, MD Salvatorian Community.
Vogel, Walter J. '58 (MIL) Richfield, WI St. Mary Church; Thompson, WI St. Patrick Church.
Vogel, Walter P. *o.s.a.* '63 (SD) [B] San Diego, CA Austin House - House of Formation; [C] San Diego, CA St. Augustine High School; [H] San Diego, CA Augustinian Community.
Vogel, William '49 (DOD) Kinsley, KS St. Nicholas Church; Offerle, KS St. Joseph Church.
Vogel, William *s.j.* '75 (YAK) [4] Yakima, WA St. Joseph's Church.
Vogelgesang, John *s.v.d.* '42 (CHI) [B] Techny, IL Divine Word Residence.
Vogelpohl, Daniel J. '75 (COV) Fort Thomas, KY St. Catherine of Siena Church.
Vogelpohl, Msgr. Henry J. '39 (CIN) Retired.
Vogelpohl, Herbert '39 (LR) [A] Subiaco, AR Subiaco Monastery.
Vogelsang, Clifford R. '63 (IND) Jeffersonville, IN St. Augustine Church.
Vogl, Msgr. Robert R. '47 (DUB) Retired; [C] Dubuque, IA Loras College; [I] Dubuque, IA Marian Hall Infirmary.
Vogler, Harold *o.f.m.cap.* '28 (SAL) [D] Victoria, KS St. Fidelis Friary.
Vogler, Jean '70 (EVN) On Leave of Absence.
Vogler, John E. (STL) Retired.
Vogler, John E. '52 (STL) Bellefontaine Neighbors, MO Our Lady of Good Counsel Church.
Voglio, John *s.d.b.* '87 (NY) [136] Bronx, NY St. Clare of Assisi Church.
Vogrin, Joseph '44 (SCL) Retired.
Vogt, Daniel *c.m.f.* '89 (CHI) [N] Oak Park, IL Claretian Fathers Headquarters of U.S.A. Eastern Province.
Vogt, Emmerich *o.p.* '78 (OAK) [N] Oakland, CA Dominican Order, Siena House.
Vogt, Eric *o.s.b.* '79 (PIT) [81] Pittsburgh, PA St. Peter Church.
Vogt, Eric T. *o.s.b.* '79 (PIT) [R] Slippery Rock, PA Office for Campus Ministry.
Vogt, Francis (ROC) Canandaigua, NY Veteran's Hospital.
Vogt, Francis H. '38 (ROC) Palmyra, NY St. Anne Church; Retired.
Vogt, John '62 (PHX) Wickenburg, AZ St. Anthony of Padua Church.
Vogt, Otto J. '50 (ROC) [34] Rochester, NY Our Lady of Lourdes Church; Retired.
Vogt, Richard J. *s.j.* '63 (CHI) [145] Chicago, IL Our Lady of Fatima Church; [D] Chicago, IL St. Ignatius Jesuit Community.
Vogt, Robert W. '62 (BUF) [4] Tonawanda, NY St. Francis of Assisi Church.
Vogt, William '56 (FRS) Faculties Only.
Vogt, William E. '46 (GRY) Retired.
Vohsing, William J. '78 (ORG) [4] Anaheim, CA San Antonio Church.
Voight, Richard A. *s.d.b.* '78 (SFR) [N] San Francisco, CA Salesian Provincial Residence.
Voiland, Msgr. George T. '50 (BRK) [203] Queens, NY Most Precious Blood Church; Retired.
Voiss, James K. *s.j.* '88 (P) [L] Portland, OR Jesuit Provincial Office (Society of Jesus, Oregon Prov.).
Voity, Maurice '79 (SAN) [1] San Angelo, TX Cathedral of the Sacred Heart.
Vojtek, John '76 (PIT) Etna, PA All Saints Church.
Vojtik, James '62 (MIL) [1] Sheboygan, WI St. Clement Church.
Volino, Michael J. '92 (ROC) [41] Rochester, NY St. Lawrence Church.
Volk, Edwin '56 (BIS) Beulah, ND St. Joseph Church.
Volk, Marvin C. '74 (BEL) [2] Belleville, IL Blessed Sacrament Church.
Volk, Michael '92 (MRY) Gonzales, CA St. Theodore Church.
Volk, Norman *o.m.i.* '68 (SUP) [G] River Falls, WI St. Thomas More Newman Center.
Volk, William *c.pp.s.* '50 (CIN) [B] Carthagena, OH St. Charles.
Volkert, James T. '90 (MIL) Brighton, WI St. Francis Xavier Church.
Volkmer, Michael *c.pp.s.* '68 (KC) [3] St. Joseph, MO St. Francis Xavier Church.
Voll, Walter Urban *o.p.* '49 (PRO) [P] Providence, RI St. Thomas Aquinas Priory at Providence College.
Vollenweider, Roy W. *s.j.* '47 (NO) [P] New Orleans, LA Ignatius Residence.
Vollkommer, Andrew J. '86 (CHR) Chapin, SC Our Lady of the Lake Church.
Vollmer, Anthony L. *c.pp.s.* '53 (SLC) Kanab, UT St. Christopher's Church.
Vollmer, Caron *o.f.m.* (GLP) [F] Gallup, NM Southwest Indian Foundation.
Vollmer, Caron *o.f.m.* '47 (GLP) Lukachukai, AZ St. Isabel Mission for Navajo Indians Church.
Vollmer, Eugene C. '78 (RVC) Port Washington, NY St. Peter of Alcantara Church.
Vollmer, Gary '77 (LAV) [12] Las Vegas, NV St. Joseph, Husband of Mary Church.
Vollmer, Gary l. '77 (STL) On Duty Outside the Archdiocese.
Vollmer, Raymond A. '40 (PIT) Retired.
Vollmer, Msgr. Roman '45 (EVN) Retired.
Vollmer, William J. '97 (CHI) Arlington Heights, IL St. James Church.
Vollor, John '79 (JKS) West Point, MS Immaculate Conception Church.
Vollor, William '63 (BLX) Hattiesburg, MS Holy Rosary Church.

Volmi, Dennis G. '75 (WIL) Military Chaplains.
Volpe, Alphonse M. '83 (LKC) Cameron, LA Our Lady Star of the Sea Church.
Volpe, Philip *o.f.m.cap.* '43 (NEW) [5] Hoboken, NJ St. Ann's Church.
Volpe, Rocco C. *c.s.b.* '57 (GAL) Retired; [Q] Houston, TX Dominican Fathers and Brothers, St. Mark Priory, Inc.; [Q] Houston, TX Dillon House.
Volpert, R. Cass '61 (L) [25] Louisville, KY Epiphany Church.
Volskis, Aloyzas (DET) [3] Southfield, MI Divine Providence Church.
Voltaggio, Fred '71 (CAM) Pennsauken, NJ St. Cecilia's Church.
Volungis, Alphonse A. '45 (WOR) [15] Worcester, MA Our Lady of Vilna Church.
Volz, Anthony '85 (IND) [29] Indianapolis, IN St. Michael the Archangel Church.
Volz, Edward *o.s.p.p.e.* '88 (GBG) Cadogan, PA St. Lawrence Church; [H] Kittanning, PA Pauline Fathers Monastery.
Volz, Gerald '92 (KCK) Olathe, KS Prince of Peace Church; [B] Overland Park, KS Saint Thomas Aquinas High School, Inc.
Vomund, Jeffrey G. '97 (STL) Chesterfield, MO Ascension Church.
Von Ah, Richard J. '58 (DAV) [L] Davenport, IA Kahl Home for the Aged and Infirm.
von Arx, Jeffrey *s.j.* '81 (WDC) [M] Washington, DC The Jesuit Community at Georgetown University.
von Behren, Thomas R. *c.s.v.* '83 (LAV) [D] Las Vegas, NV Clerics of St. Viator.
von Drehle, James '81 (DET) [H] Pontiac, MI St. Joseph Mercy - Oakland.
von Duerbeck, Julian *o.s.b.* '76 (JOL) [J] Lisle, IL St. Procopius Abbey.
Von Essen, Pacificus *s.a.* '53 (NY) [DD] Garrison, NY Generalate of the Franciscan Friars of the Atonement-St. James Friary.
Von Essen, Peter *o.f.m.cap.* '56 (FgM) Capuchin Foreign Missions.
Von Euw, Vincent P. '66 (BO) [4] Boston, MA St. Ambrose Church.
von Fauer, Stephen C. '41 (STF) [E] West Burke, VT Mary Theotokos Centre.
Von Fauer, Stephen C. '53 (BUR) Retired.
Von Hagel, Davin W. *o.f.m.* '47 (GLP) Navajo, NM St. Berard Church.
von Hartleben, Msgr. Joseph A. '55 (CAM) [2] Vineland, NJ Sacred Heart Church.
Von Kaenel, George E. *s.j.* '58 (OM) [K] Omaha, NE Jesuit Community At Creighton University.
Von Kerssenbrock, Joachim *s.j.* '59 (NY) [HH] Bronx, NY American St. Boniface Society, Incorporated.
Von Kobs, Allan G. *o.f.m.* '82 (NY) [35] New York, NY St. Francis of Assisi Church.
Von Lehmen, Jeffrey D. '85 (COV) Edgewood, KY St. Pius X Church.
von Nell, Boniface *o.s.b.* '91 (WDC) [M] Washington, DC St. Anselm's Abbey.
von Phul Mouton, Msgr. Richard '55 (LAF) [16] Lafayette, LA St. Pius X Church.
Von Son, Msgr. Henry A. '49 (LA) Retired.
Von Tobel, James E. *s.j.* '67 (DET) [K] Detroit, MI Jesuit Provincial Office-Detroit Province of the Society of Jesus; [P] Clarkston, MI Colombiere Center.
Vona, Michael S. '68 (TR) Farmingdale, NJ St. Catherine of Siena Church.
vonBehren, Thomas R. *c.s.v.* '83 (LAV) [A] Las Vegas, NV Bishop Gorman High School.
Vonderhaar, Eugene F. '59 (CIN) Russia, OH St. Remy Church.
Vonderhaar, Ralph E. *s.j.* '57 (STL) [P] St. Louis, MO Hallahan House.
VonderHaar, Msgr. Roland '48 (LSC) Retired.
Vondras, John J. '85 (NY) [2] Newburgh, NY St. Francis of Assisi Church.
Vonnahmen, Robert J. '56 (BEL) Leave of Absence.
Voor, Joseph H. '50 (L) [17] Louisville, KY St. Brigid Church; [40] Louisville, KY St. James Church; Louisville, KY Vencor Hospital; Retired.
Voorhes, Msgr. Fred R. '71 (BUF) [P] Williamsville, NY Sisters of St. Francis of the Third Order Regular, St. Mary of the Angels.
Voorhies, Bennett J. '83 (LAF) On Duty Outside the Diocese.
Voorhies, Bennett J. '83 (SFE) Pecos, NM St. Anthony Church.
Voorhies, Louis '67 (ALX) Retired.
Voorhies, Thomas P. '90 (LAF) Delcambre, LA Our Lady of the Lake Church; Delcambre, LA Saint Martin de Porres Church.
Voors, David '81 (FTW) [12] Fort Wayne, IN Our Lady of Good Hope Church.
Voors, Msgr. William J. '39 (FTW) Retired.
Vorderlandwehr, Adrian *o.s.b.* '67 (OKL) Prague, OK St. Wenceslaus, National Shrine of the Infant Jesus of Prague Church.
Voris, Francis *o.f.m.cap.* '86 (SAG) Sanford, MI St. Agnes Church; [G] Saginaw, MI Queen of Angels Friary and Retreat House.
Vorisek, Rudolph T. *c.s.p.* '56 (NY) [104] New York, NY St. Paul the Apostle Church; [DD] Jamaica Estates, NY Paulist Fathers Generalate.
Vorwald, Aloysius J. '64 (DUB) Independence, IA St. John Evangelist Church; Rowley, IA All Saints Church.
Vorwerk, James *s.v.d.* '69 (TR) Neptune, NJ Our Lady of Providence Church.
Vorwoldt, James F. *s.j.* '71 (CHI) [D] Chicago, IL St. Ignatius Jesuit Community.
Vos, Thomas *o.f.m.* '61 (KNX) Mountain City, TN St. Anthony of Padua Catholic Church; [F] Mountain City, TN Franciscan Friars.
Vos, William (NY) [HH] Maryknoll, NY Maryknoll Mission Association of the Faithful.
Vos, William '64 (SCL) On Duty Outside the Diocese.
Vos, William A. *m.m.* '64 (FgM) Maryknoll Foreign Missions.
Vosen, Gerald P. '61 (MAD) Baraboo, WI St. Joseph Church.
Vosko, Richard '69 (ALB) Special Assignment.
Voss, Bernard L. '66 (BEL) [5] Belleville, IL St. Henry Church; [J] Belleville, IL Serra Club of St. Clair County.
Voss, Dennis F. '64 (BEL) [D] Belleville, IL St. Elizabeth Hospital.
Voss, Donald J. '93 (PBR) Clarence, PA St. Mary's Church; Hawk Run, PA St. John the Baptist Church.
Voss, Marcus J. *o.s.b.* '71 (BIR) [B] Cullman, AL St. Bernard Preparatory School, Inc.; [E] Cullman, AL St. Bernard Abbey.
Voss, Robert '70 (PHX) [4] Scottsdale, AZ St. Bernard of Clairvaux Church.
Voss, Robert D. *s.j.* '72 (FgM) Provinces.
Vossler, Brian E. '91 (E) Clarion, PA Immaculate Conception Church; [P] Erie, PA Newman Centers and Campus Ministry.
Vota, Paul *m.j.* '85 (PCE) On Duty Outside the Diocese.
Votraw, Thomas G. '60 (OG) [1] Ogdensburg, NY St. Mary's Cathedral; Absent on Sick Leave.
Votraw, Wilbur J. '55 (SY) [24] Syracuse, NY St. Vincent de Paul Church; Syracuse, NY Loretto Geriatric Center; [P] Syracuse, NY Loretto; [P] Syracuse, NY Loretto Rest, Inc.
Votraw, William J. '55 (SY) Special Assignment.
Votruba, George L. '54 (SUP) [2] Superior, WI Assumption of the B.V.M. Church; [9] Superior, WI St. William Church.
Votta, Robert '79 (LAV) [6] Las Vegas, NV St. Anne Church.
Vouk, William, III '86 (SCL) St. Anthony, MN St. Anthony's Church; St. Francis, MN St. Francis of Assisi Church.
Vovk, Joseph '32 (DUL) Retired.
Vowells, John *s.j.* (DEN) [P] Denver, CO Regis University (Denver).
Vowells, John J. *s.j.* '90 (DEN) [M] Denver, CO Regis Jesuit Community (The Jesuits at Regis University).
Vowels, G. Timothy '77 (STL) Hazelwood, MO St. Martin de Porres Church.
Vowra, Clarence (STP) Shieldsville, MN St. Patrick Church.
Voyt, Stephen A. '85 (PT) Military Chaplains.
Voytek, Leonard E. '74 (ALT) [1] Windber, PA St. John Cantius Church; [4] Windber, PA St. Mary's Church.
Voytko, Geo. '49 (STU) Retired.
Vrabel, George A. '87 (CLV) North Olmsted, OH St. Richard Church.
Vrabely, George M. '53 (GRY) La Porte, IN St. Peter Church.
Vrablic, Cyril *o.s.b.* '51 (IND) [J] St. Meinrad, IN St. Meinrad Archabbey.
Vrana, Francis R. '53 (STP) Retired.
Vrana, John G. '67 (CLV) Maple Heights, OH St. Martin of Tours Church.
Vrana, John P. '56 (OKL) Ardmore, OK St. Mary Church.
Vrana, Joseph L. '65 (VIC) Wharton, TX Holy Family Church.
Vrazel, Edward '58 (CC) [5] Laredo, TX Our Lady of Guadalupe Church.
Vrba, James J. '77 (DAV) [2] Iowa City, IA St. Patrick's Church.
Vreteau, Robert *o.m.i.* '49 (SAN) [2] Midland, TX Our Lady of Guadalupe Church.
Vu, An Ngoc '95 (WDC) Riverdale, MD St. Bernard Church.
Vu, Ignatius '94 (NY) [5] White Plains, NY Our Lady of Sorrows Church.
Vu, Joseph '90 (BRK) [10] Brooklyn, NY St. Anselm's Church.
Vu, Joseph Khai '96 (NEW) Newark, NJ St. Michael Medical Center.
Vu, Joseph Thanh '75 (GAL) [28] Houston, TX St. Frances Cabrini Church.
Vu, Khai (NEW) [2] Newark, NJ St. Patrick's Pro-Cathedral.
Vu, Lieu '91 (SJ) [4] San Jose, CA Christ the King Church.
Vu, Louis Lam '85 (LAF) Youngsville, LA St. Anne Church.
Vu, Minh Xuan '94 (STP) Roseville, MN St. Rose of Lima Church.
Vu, Peter (GR) [9] Grand Rapids, MI Immaculate Heart of Mary Church.
Vu, Peter Duc '96 (ATL) [2] Atlanta, GA Holy Cross Church.
Vu, Than N. '84 (BR) [17] Baton Rouge, LA St. Patrick Church.
Vu, Toan Viet (HT) Thibodaux, LA Thibodaux General Hospital.
Vu Dao, Joseph *s.v.d.* '88 (FgM) Society of the Divine Word Foreign Missions.
Vu Dinh Huyen, Leo M. *c.m.c.* (SPC) [E] Carthage, MO Congregation of the Mother Co-Redemptrix, United States Assumption Province.
Vu Dinh Huyen, Leo M. *c.m.c.* '94 (SB) [E] Corona, CA Congregation of the Mother Coredemptrix.
Vu Han, John Baptist '65 (NO) [2] Marrero, LA St. Agnes Le Thi Thanh Church; [2] Marrero, LA St. Agnes Le Thi Thanh Church.
Vu Quang Huy, John Eudes M. *c.m.c.* (SPC) [E] Carthage, MO Congregation of the Mother Co-Redemptrix, United States Assumption Province.
Vu Thanh Thien, Cyril M. *c.m.c.* (SPC) [E] Carthage, MO Congregation of the Mother Co-Redemptrix, United States Assumption Province.
Vucinovich, Albert '64 (SFR) Fairfax, CA St. Rita Church.
Vuelvas-Arias, David '75 (ORG) [2] Anaheim, CA St. Boniface Church.
Vujs, Joseph E. '57 (HRT) [5] Meriden, CT St. Rose of Lima Church.
Vujs, Robert W. *m.m.* '61 (FgM) Maryknoll Foreign Missions.
Vuketich, Donald F. *t.o.r.* '53 (PH) [AA] Fairless Hills, PA St. Anthony Friary.
Vukoja, Valentin *o.f.m.* '96 (NY) [29] New York, NY SS. Cyril and Methodius - St. Raphael Church.
Vuletic, Petar '62 (LA) [45] Los Angeles, CA St. Anthony Church.
Vuoso, Pasquale *c.r.i.c.* '87 (LA) [64] Los Angeles, CA St. Francis of Assisi Church; [B] Los Angeles, CA Canons Regular of the Immaculate Conception-Novitiate; [R] Los Angeles, CA Canons Regular of the Immaculate Conception.
Vuturo, Paul '73 (MIA) Miramar, FL St. Bartholomew Church.
Vye, Francis W. *s.j.* '65 (BO) [W] Chestnut Hill, MA The Jesuit Community at Boston College.
Vyoral, Louis *s.d.b.* '50 (NY) [DD] New Rochelle, NY Salesian Provincial House.
Vyverman, Mark J. '93 (KAL) Gull Lake, MI St. Ann Church.

W

Waago, Per *o.m.i.* (FgM) Oblates Foreign Missions.
Wababa, John *c.s.c.* '92 (PHX) [J] Phoenix, AZ Andre House of Arizona.
Wababa, John B. *c.s.c.* '92 (PHX) [F] Phoenix, AZ Holy Cross Congregation of Casa Santa Cruz.
Wach, Anthony J. *s.j.* '72 (FgM) Provinces.
Wach, Anthony J. *s.j.* '72 (MIL) [P] Milwaukee, WI Jesuit Provincial Office, Wisconsin Province.
Wachdorf, Paul H. '75 (CHI) [A] Mundelein, IL University of St. Mary of the Lake-Mundelein Seminary.
Wachira, Patrick Kanja '83 (SY) [3] Utica, NY Our Lady of Lourdes Church.
Wachtel, Dominic *o.f.m.* (CIN) [K] Cincinnati, OH Franciscan Hospital, Mt. Airy Campus.
Wachtel, Dominic *o.f.m.* '81 (CIN) [M] Cincinnati, OH St. Ann Friary.
Wachter, Robert B. (WCH) [4] Wichita, KS Christ the King Church.
Wack, William A. *c.s.c.* (FTW) [B] Notre Dame, IN University of Notre Dame Du Lac; [J] Notre Dame, IN Holy Cross Community, Corby Hall, University of Notre Dame.
Wack, William A. *c.s.c.* '94 (FTW) [A] Notre Dame, IN Moreau Seminary.
Wackenheim, Apollinaris *o.f.m.* '34 (SFD) [K] Sherman, IL Our Lady of Angels Friary.
Waclawski, Msgr. Joseph P. '42 (BUF) [39] Buffalo, NY St. John Kanty Church; Retired.
Waczula, Michael F. '66 (GBG) On Duty Outside the Diocese.
Wadas, Msgr. Ignatius C. '53 (ALT) Central City, PA Sacred Heart Church; Central City, PA St. John the Baptist Church.
Wadas, Joseph S. '91 (MOB) Eufaula, AL Holy Redeemer Church; Clayton, AL Ventress Correctional Institution; Union Springs, AL Bullock County Correctional Facility.
Wadas, Raymond J. '72 (WDC) [43] Washington, DC St. Thomas More Church.
Waddell, Chrysogonus *o.c.s.o.* '58 (L) [L] Trappist, KY Abbey of Our Lady of Gethsemani, of the Order of Cistercians of the Strict Observance.
Waddill, Dale T. '64 (P) [27] Portland, OR St. Peter Church.
Wade, Edward C. '72 (CAM) On Duty Outside the Diocese.

Wade, Gerald T. *s.j.* '68 (SJ) [D] San Jose, CA Bellarmine College Preparatory.
Wade, Hubert, Jr. '77 (SAN) Ballinger, TX St. Mary Star of the Sea Church.
Wade, Msgr. James J. '33 (OAK) Pleasant Hill, CA Christ the King Church; Retired.
Wade, Jarrell D. *s.j.* '65 (FgM) Provinces.
Wade, John '56 (TLS) [E] Tulsa, OK St. John Medical Center, Inc.
Wade, Michael J. '89 (BAL) Absent on Leave.
Wadell, John '40 (SB) Retired.
Wadell, Paul *c.p.* '78 (CHI) [B] Chicago, IL The Catholic Theological Union at Chicago.
Wadowicz, Msgr. Joseph M. '45 (STU) Retired.
Wadsworth, Msgr. James '41 (DM) Retired.
Waechter, Ernest *o.f.m.conv.* (IND) St. Peter, IN.
Waechter, Ernest *o.f.m.conv.* '59 (IND) Corydon, IN St. Joseph Church; New Middletown, IN Most Precious Blood Church; [I] Mount Saint Francis, IN Mount Saint Francis Friary and Retreat Center.
Wafzig, James E. '55 (L) [9] Louisville, KY St. Athanasius Church; Louisville, KY University Hospital; [O] Louisville, KY Catholic Charismatic Renewal.
Wagener, Clarence M. *s.j.* '53 (OM) [K] Omaha, NE Jesuit Community At Creighton University.
Wagener, John M. '61 (NU) Military Chaplains.
Wagenhoffer, Josef A. '65 (CAM) Somers Point, NJ St. Joseph's Church.
Wager, Terence J. *o.s.b.* '64 (SEA) Yelm, WA St. Columban Church.
Waggenor, William L. '52 (HEL) Retired.
Waggett, George *o.m.i.* '42 (BO) [Z] Tewksbury, MA Immaculate Heart of Mary Novitiate-Infirmary.
Wagman, Msgr. Cletus H. '42 (HBG) [5] Lancaster, PA St. Joseph Church.
Wagman, Stephen *o.s.b.* '48 (CR) [C] Detroit Lakes, MN St. Mary's Regional Health Center.
Wagner, Alan *s.d.s.* '76 (TUC) Vail, AZ Shrine of St. Rita in the Desert Church.
Wagner, Alfred S. '48 (STP) Retired.
Wagner, Bernard *o.f.m.cap.* '63 (FgM) Capuchin Foreign Missions.
Wagner, Cyril J. *o.f.m.* '67 (MEM) [16] Memphis, TN St. Louis Church; Somerville, TN St. Philip the Apostle Church; [J] Memphis, TN Franciscan Friars (Sacred Heart Prov.) of Memphis.
Wagner, Dennis A. '76 (GR) On Special Assignment.
Wagner, Donald '87 (SCL) St. Wendel, MN St. Columbkille's Church; Special Assignment.
Wagner, Edward *o.s.s.t.* '80 (BAL) [M] Baltimore, MD Holy Trinity Monastery.
Wagner, Eugene L. '40 (BUF) Olcott, NY St. Charles Borromeo Church; Retired.
Wagner, Frank *o.m.i.* '57 (SD) [1] Chula Vista, CA Most Precious Blood Church.
Wagner, Greta '91 (TOL) [H] Lima, OH St. Rita's Medical Center.
Wagner, Msgr. Harold '55 (BUF) [F] Buffalo, NY Cantalician Center for Learning, Inc.
Wagner, Jerome A. '72 (MIL) [2] Fond du Lac, WI St. Louis Church; St. Peter, WI St. Peter Church.
Wagner, John '49 (SAT) Charlotte, TX St. Rose of Lima Church.
Wagner, John '64 (SB) [4] Corona, CA St. Matthew Church.
Wagner, John C. '73 (MIL) On Leave.
Wagner, John J., III '87 (RIC) Portsmouth, VA Holy Angels Church.
Wagner, John P. '62 (SY) Baldwinsville, NY St. Elizabeth Ann Seton Church; On Duty Outside the Diocese.
Wagner, Joseph '65 (SFS) Military Chaplains.
Wagner, Joseph F. '44 (CLV) [46] Cleveland, OH St. Mark Church; Brunswick, OH St. Colette Church; Retired.
Wagner, Lawrence *s.v.d.* '44 (FgM) Society of the Divine Word Foreign Missions.
Wagner, Lawrence L. *o.s.b.* '54 (BIS) Lefor, ND St. Elizabeth Church; Lefor, ND St. Elizabeth Church.
Wagner, Leon R. '49 (CHI) Riverside, IL St. Mary Church; Retired.
Wagner, Mark (STO) Escalon, CA St. Patrick Church.
Wagner, Raymond J. '52 (LC) Retired.
Wagner, Richard '61 (DM) [8] Des Moines, IA Basilica of Saint John Church.
Wagner, Richard F. *s.s.j.* '59 (LAF) Breaux Bridge, LA St. Francis of Assisi Church.
Wagner, Robert F. '60 (SPR) Monson, MA State Hospital; [N] Holyoke, MA Bureau for Exceptional Children and Adults Inc.; [N] Pittsfield, MA Bureau for Exceptional Children and Adults.
Wagner, Robert J. '57 (LC) Trempealeau, WI St. Bartholomew Church.
Wagner, Ronald F. '79 (SAG) Palms, MI St. Patrick Church; Ruth, MI SS. Peter and Paul Church.
Wagner, Terence *o.s.b.* '64 (SEA) [M] Lacey, WA St. Martin's Abbey.
Wagner, Thomas A. '83 (PIT) Pleasant Hills, PA St. Elizabeth Church.
Wagner, Urban S. *o.f.m.conv.* '41 (STP) Bloomington, MN St. Bonaventure Church.
Wagner, Van A. '61 (TUC) [20] Tucson, AZ Saints Peter and Paul Church.
Wagner, Vernon *o.f.m.cap.* '53 (SAG) [G] Saginaw, MI Queen of Angels Friary and Retreat House.
Wagner, Walter C. *o.p.* '93 (BO) [W] Dover, MA St. Stephen Priory; [Y] Dover, MA St. Stephen Priory Spiritual Life Center.
Wagner, Wilbert *s.v.d.* '40 (FgM) Society of the Divine Word Foreign Missions.
Wagner, William C. '73 (CIN) Milford, OH St. Andrew Church.
Wagner, William F. '63 (L) [70] Louisville, KY SS. Simon and Jude Church.
Wagoner, Gordon P. (IND) Indianapolis, IN Veterans' Administration Hospital.
Waguespack, Clarence J. '62 (BR) Vacherie, LA Our Lady of Peace Church.
Wahl, Joseph A. *c.o.* '56 (CHR) [D] Rock Hill, SC Oratory of St. Philip Neri, Congregation of the Oratory of Pontifical Rite.
Wahl, Raymond J. '37 (ROC) Retired.
Wahl, Msgr. Raymond J. '52 (RCK) [4] Rockford, IL St. Edward Church.
Wahl, Richard A. *c.s.b.* (ROC) [B] Rochester, NY The Aquinas Institute; [I] Rochester, NY Residence of Basilian Fathers-The Aquinas Institute.
Wahl, Thomas *o.s.b.* '58 (FgM) American - Cassinese Congregation Foreign Missions.
Wahl, Thomas *o.s.b.* '58 (SCL) [I] Collegeville, MN St. John's Abbey, of the Order of St. Benedict.
Wahmhoff, Andrew *o.s.b.* '58 (RCK) [H] Aurora, IL Marmion Abbey-St. Augustine's Abbey.
Waibel, Kenneth '84 (LEX) Richmond, KY St. Mark Church; [L] Richmond, KY Catholic Newman Center-St. Mark Church.
Waibel, Philip *o.s.b.* '83 (P) [A] St. Benedict, OR Mount Angel Seminary; [L] St. Benedict, OR Mt. Angel Abbey.
Waickman, Thomas L. '84 (JC) Louisiana, MO St. Joseph Church.
Wainwright, Walter L. '65 (ROC) Canandaigua, NY St. Mary Church.
Waiss, John R. '87 (LA) [Y] Los Angeles, CA Opus Dei. Prelature of the Holy Cross and Opus Dei.
Wait, Dennis '72 (KCK) [8] Kansas City, KS St. Mary-St. Anthony Church.
Waite, Patrick J. '54 (SC) Retired.
Waitekus, Christopher '90 (SPR) [9] Chicopee, MA St. Rose de Lima Church.
Waiwood, Richard '73 (ELP) [9] El Paso, TX Holy Family Church.
Wajda, Edward J. '56 (PHX) Retired.
Wajda, Joseph L. '73 (STP) Special Assignment.
Wake, John F. '92 (TR) Browns Mills, NJ St. Ann Church.
Wakefield, Christopher L. (ALN) [11] Reading, PA St. Peter Church.
Wakefield, Michael '81 (LA) [41] Los Angeles, CA St. Ambrose Church; [2] North Hollywood, CA St. Charles Borromeo Church.
Wakeman, Msgr. John J. '56 (ALX) Retired.
Wakim, Rodolph '96 (SAM) Roanoke, VA St. Elias Church.
Wal, Eduardo '79 (SP) [4] Clearwater, FL St. Cecelia Church.
Walas, Joseph '59 (RVC) Riverhead, NY St. Isidore's Church.
Walaszek, Luke A. *o.p.* '58 (NOR) Willimantic, CT St. Joseph Church.
Walbe, John '44 (LR) [A] Subiaco, AR Subiaco Monastery.
Walch, John '45 (OKL) Retired.
Walck, Edward F. *m.m.* '56 (NY) [DD] Maryknoll, NY Maryknoll Fathers and Brothers.
Walczak, Donald J. '63 (LC) [2] Stevens Point, WI St. Casimir Church; Torun, WI St. Mary Church.
Walczak, Melvin (ROC) Absent on Leave.
Wald, Jeffrey '92 (FAR) Devils Lake, ND St. Joseph's Church; Devils Lake, ND School for the Deaf; [I] Devils Lake, ND UND-Lake Region.
Wald, John *s.v.d.* '43 (FgM) Society of the Divine Word Foreign Missions.
Wald, Kenneth '57 (BIS) Kenmare, ND St. Agnes Church.
Walden, Ellsworth R. '71 (RVC) Hauppauge, NY St. Thomas More Church.
Waldie, Paul *o.m.i.* '65 (OAK) [N] Oakland, CA Oblate Provincial House & Procure.
Waldie, Paul *o.m.i.* '65 (SEA) [4] Seattle, WA St. Benedict Church.
Waldie, Thomas *s.s.s.* '38 (CLV) [P] Cleveland, OH Congregation of the Blessed Sacrament Provincial House.
Waldie, Thomas E. *s.s.s.* '38 (CLV) [P] Cleveland, OH Blessed Sacrament Community.
Waldie, Thomas E. *s.s.s.* '38 (NY) [8] New York, NY St. Andrew Church.
Walding, Eugene F. '66 (SC) Fort Dodge, IA Trinity Regional Hospital; [E] Fort Dodge, IA The Marian Home.
Waldmann, Robert J. '46 (B) Retired.
Waldon, Clarence R. '64 (IND) [4] Indianapolis, IN Holy Angels Church.
Waldow, Msgr. Harold L. '70 (AMA) [F] Amarillo, TX Baptist St. Anthony Health System.
Waldrep, Jeffrey '90 (JKS) [3] Jackson, MS St. Richard Church.
Waldrep, John W. *m.m.* '90 (FgM) Maryknoll Foreign Missions.
Waldron, John '66 (P) Beaverton, OR Holy Trinity Church.
Waldron, Msgr. John E. '66 (BRK) [145] Brooklyn, NY Visitation of the Blessed Virgin Mary Church.
Waldron, John F. '62 (ALB) Colonie, NY Our Lady of Mercy Church.
Waldron, John R. '56 (NEW) Retired.
Waldron, Richard P. '61 (HBG) Mechanicsburg, PA St. Elizabeth Ann Seton Church.
Waldron, Robert J. '68 (BO) [3] Waltham, MA St. Jude Church.
Waldron, Walter J. '64 (BO) [36] Boston, MA St. Joseph Church; [60] Boston, MA St. Patrick Church.
Waldron, William '50 (PHX) Sun City, AZ St. Elizabeth Seton Church.
Waldschmidt, Donald L. '55 (DAV) Retired; [M] Davenport, IA St. Vincent Center.
Waldschmidt, Valens J. *o.f.m.* '47 (CIN) [M] Cincinnati, OH St. Clement Friary; [V] Cincinnati, OH St. Dymphna Ministry.
Walega, Stanley J. '64 (MET) Bound Brook, NJ St. Mary of Czestochowa Church.
Walick, Stephen '69 (CLV) Cleveland, OH University Hospitals Bedford Medical Center; Cleveland, OH Meridia South Pointe Hospital.
Walick, Stephen J. (CLV) Maple Heights, OH St. Wenceslas Church.
Walijewski, Joseph A. '50 (LC) Foreign Missions.
Walk, Donald J. '67 (VEN) Priests Released from Diocesan Assignment.
Walk, Edward J. '78 (E) Du Bois, PA St. Catherine Church; [C] Du Bois, PA Du Bois Area Catholic Schools.
Walker, Anselm '56 (GAL) Retired.
Walker, Benjamin *o.s.b.* '60 (PIT) [81] Pittsburgh, PA St. Peter Church.
Walker, Brian *o.m.i.* (FgM) Oblates Foreign Missions.
Walker, Brian G. *o.p.* '86 (CHI) [24] Chicago, IL St. Basil/Visitation Church.
Walker, Carlos '83 (BRK) [48] Brooklyn, NY St. Gabriel The Archangel Church.
Walker, Charles D. '81 (L) [66] Louisville, KY St. Pius X Church.
Walker, David M. '64 (HRT) [6] Hamden, CT St. Rita's Church.
Walker, Msgr. Dean P. '47 (SC) Retired.
Walker, Donald L. '58 (DET) Redford Township, MI St. Robert Bellarmine Church.
Walker, Earl G. '48 (LA) [2] Los Angeles, CA Cathedral Chapel Church.
Walker, Edmund *o.f.m. cap.* '63 (CHL) [8] Charlotte, NC St. Matthew Church.
Walker, Msgr. Edward J. '36 (BUF) Retired.
Walker, Francisco '87 (BRK) [154] Queens, NY St. Bartholomew's Church.
Walker, Gerald '55 (LA) Irwindale, CA Our Lady of Guadalupe Church.
Walker, Gerard T. '80 (BRK) [150] Queens, NY St. Andrew Avellino Church.
Walker, Henry *o.m.i.* (GAL) [64] Houston, TX St. Patrick Church.
Walker, J. Kenneth '81 (EVN) Newburgh, IN St. John the Baptist Church; Special Assignment.
Walker, J. Patrick '88 (STO) [9] Stockton, CA St. Michael Church.
Walker, James '77 (Y) [4] Warren, OH St. James Church.
Walker, James B. '90 (SAV) Macon, GA St. Peter Claver Church.
Walker, John H. '53 (CLV) Sheffield, OH St. Teresa Church; Retired.
Walker, Kent A. '89 (ORL) Merritt Island, FL Divine Mercy Church.
Walker, Leonard *s.d.s.* '74 (MIL) [P] Milwaukee, WI Salvatorian Provincial Residence.
Walker, Michael '62 (KC) Mission Duty.
Walker, Norbert J. '44 (PH) Retired.
Walker, Paul '72 (STU) McConnelsville, OH St. James Church.
Walker, Robert F. '65 (CAM) Margate, NJ Blessed Sacrament Church.
Walker, Robert L. *o.p.* '56 (WDC) [11] Washington, DC St. Dominic Church & Priory Church.
Walker, Ronald *o.m.i.* '61 (FgM) Oblates Foreign Missions.
Walker, Thomas J. '74 (MIL) Sick Leave.
Walker, Thomas J. '90 (STP) Red Wing, MN St. Joseph Church.
Walkiewicz, Jacek *s.chr.* '93 (CHI) [87] Chicago, IL Holy Trinity Mission Church.
Walkowiak, David '79 (CLV) [A] Wickliffe, OH St. Mary Seminary and Graduate School of Theology.
Wall, Antoninus *o.p.* '50 (OAK) [N] Oakland, CA

Dominican Order (Western Province), St. Albert's Priory.
Wall, Barry W. '62 (FR) Mattapoisett, MA St. Anthony's Church.
Wall, Damian '65 (CGS) [1] Caguas, PR Cathedral Dulce Nombre de Jesus Church.
Wall, G. Warren '76 (MOB) [7] Mobile, AL St. Ignatius Church.
Wall, Gus *s.v.d.* '91 (DUB) [B] Epworth, IA Divine Word College.
Wall, Msgr. James E. '63 (BUF) [Q] Derby, NY St. Columban's Center.
Wall, John A. '60 (R) Cary, NC St. Michael the Archangel Church.
Wall, John E. '57 (CIN) [56] Cincinnati, OH St. Margaret Mary Church.
Wall, John J. '68 (CHI) [165] Chicago, IL St. Patrick Church.
Wall, Malachy *o.c.s.o.* '55 (CHR) [D] Moncks Corner, SC Mepkin Abbey.
Wall, Sherman B. *o.m.i.* '57 (SPC) Willow Springs, MO Sacred Heart Church.
Wall, Warren '76 (NY) [HH] New York, NY North American College of Rome, Alumni Assoc. of.
Wallace, Basil J. *o.s.b.* '78 (PAT) [M] Newton, NJ St. Paul's Abbey.
Wallace, Cavana '92 (SD) [5] San Diego, CA Good Shepherd Church.
Wallace, Donald L. '62 (JC) Absent on Leave.
Wallace, Francis K. *s.j.* '46 (FgM) Provinces.
Wallace, Msgr. Francis T. '63 (LA) La Canada Flintridge, CA St. Bede the Venerable Church.
Wallace, Francis X. '47 (FR) Retired.
Wallace, George *s.m.* '57 (PH) [U] Langhorne, PA St. Mary Medical Center; [AA] Langhorne, PA Society of Mary, Marist Fathers.
Wallace, Harry C. '56 (ORL) Deltona, FL Our Lady of the Lakes Church.
Wallace, Harry C. '56 (SY) On Duty Outside the Diocese.
Wallace, James *c.ss.r.* '70 (WDC) [M] Washington, DC Holy Redeemer College.
Wallace, John *f.m.s.i.* '60 (BO) [B] Framingham, MA Sylva Maria.
Wallace, Joseph D. '85 (CAM) Woodbury Heights, NJ St. Margaret's Church.
Wallace, Leonard P. '55 (DET) Lakeport, MI St. Edward's on the Lake Church.
Wallace, Msgr. Murrough C. '60 (SAC) South Lake Tahoe, CA St. Theresa Church.
Wallace, Philip D. '65 (SEA) Seahurst, WA St. Francis of Assisi Church.
Wallace, Regis P. *o.s.b.* '60 (PAT) [M] Morristown, NJ St. Mary's Abbey.
Wallace, Richard '86 (P) Stayton, OR Immaculate Conception Church.
Wallace, Tom '80 (SB) Blythe, CA St. Joan of Arc Church.
Wallace, William J. *o.s.a.* '74 (NY) [168] Bronx, NY St. Nicholas of Tolentine Church.
Wallaik, William H. '49 (MIL) Mequon, WI St. James Church; Retired.
Walle, Msgr. Julius G. '56 (ALX) Cheneyville, LA St. Joseph Church; Retired.
Walleman, Kenneth T. *s.j.* '59 (MIL) [P] Milwaukee, WI Jesuit Community at Marquette University.
Wallen, Charles L. *c.s.c.* '54 (FR) [J] North Dartmouth, MA Holy Cross Mission House.
Wallen, Clarence J. *s.j.* '51 (LA) [C] Los Angeles, CA Loyola Marymount University.
Wallenfelsz, Scott *s.d.s.* '69 (MIL) [P] Milwaukee, WI Salvatorian Provincial Residence.
Wallenhorst, George A. *s.j.* '39 (CHI) Chicago, IL Cook County Hospital.
Waller, Charles J. '73 (PAT) [16] Paterson, NJ St. Therese Church.
Waller, Robert C. '75 (CIN) [48] Cincinnati, OH St. John Neumann Church.
Wallin, Msgr. Kevin W. '84 (BGP) [5] Danbury, CT St. Peter's Church; [R] Bridgeport, CT Inner-City Foundation for Charity & Education.
Walling, Gerald C. *s.j.* (CHI) [D] Chicago, IL St. Ignatius College Prep.
Walling, Gerald C. *s.j.* '61 (CHI) [C] Chicago, IL Jesuit Community at Loyola University of Chicago.
Walling, Larry E. *o.s.m.* (DEN) [22] Denver, CO Our Lady of Mt. Carmel Church.
Walling, Norman *s.j.* '61 (FgM) Provinces.
Walling, Richard W. '78 (CIN) [5] Springfield, OH St. Teresa of the Child Jesus Church.
Wallis, William H. '82 (SPR) Great Barrington, MA St. Peter's Church.
Walljasper, Mark A. '55 (LC) Sparta, WI St. Patrick Church; [G] Sparta, WI Franciscan Skemp Healthcare, Mayo Health System, Sparta Campus Nursing Home.
Wallner, Francis A. *s.j.* '51 (ALN) [A] Wernersville, PA Novitiate of St. Isaac Jogues.
Wallner, Gerhard '89 (FBK) Leave of Absence.
Wallroth, Joseph *o.carm.* '70 (JOL) [J] Darien, IL Carmelite Provincial Office.
Walls, Msgr. David E. '60 (PH) Bryn Mawr, PA St. John Neumann Church; Absent on Leave.
Walmesley, Jack '74 (SEA) Kent, WA St. John the Baptist Church.
Walmsley, Gerard *s.j.* '82 (BO) [W] Chestnut Hill, MA The Jesuit Community at Boston College.
Walpole, Donald *o.s.b.* '43 (IND) [B] St. Meinrad, IN St. Meinrad Seminary-College of Liberal Arts; [J] St. Meinrad, IN St. Meinrad Archabbey.
Walsh, Aidan J. (BO) Boston, MA Veterans Administration Hospital.
Walsh, Albert '92 (GAL) Wallis, TX Guardian Angel Church.
Walsh, Arthur '85 (CC) On Duty Outside the Diocese.
Walsh, Austin *s.t.* (WDC) [M] Riverdale, MD Holy Spirit Missionary Cenacle.
Walsh, Bernard '55 (SY) Retired.
Walsh, Bernard F. '55 (SY) [S] Syracuse, NY St. Pius X Home, Inc.
Walsh, Brendan J. '93 (LAN) [6] Lansing, MI St. Gerard Church.
Walsh, Broderick M. *c.s.p.* '92 (KNX) [3] Knoxville, TN Immaculate Conception Church.
Walsh, Msgr. Bryan O. '54 (MIA) Retired.
Walsh, Msgr. Charles F. '51 (WCH) El Dorado, KS St. John Church.
Walsh, Christopher J. '87 (BGP) [O] Stamford, CT St. John Fisher Seminary Residence.
Walsh, Clyde J. '51 (PRO) Retired; [P] Providence, RI St. John Vianney Residence.
Walsh, Daniel *c.s.sp.* '91 (SD) [19] San Diego, CA St. Agnes Church.
Walsh, Daniel M. '59 (SHP) Vivian, LA St. Clement Church.
Walsh, Daniel P. '68 (BUF) Fredonia, NY St. Anthony Church.
Walsh, David *c.ss.r.* '47 (CC) [8] Corpus Christi, TX Our Lady of Perpetual Help Church; On Special Assignment.
Walsh, David I. *m.m.* '42 (NY) [DD] Maryknoll, NY Maryknoll Fathers and Brothers.
Walsh, David I. '46 (SFR) Retired; [K] San Francisco, CA Home for the Aged of the Little Sisters of the Poor.
Walsh, Denis '66 (TYL) [B] Palestine, TX Hermitage.
Walsh, Dennis *c.ss.r.* '92 (NY) [150] Bronx, NY Immaculate Conception Church.
Walsh, Donal C. '55 (SD) Julian, CA St. Elizabeth Church.
Walsh, E. Corbett *s.j.* '71 (BO) [W] Weston, MA Campion Center.
Walsh, Edward J. '64 (CAM) Woodlynne, NJ Immaculate Heart of Mary Church.
Walsh, Edward J. '91 (PH) On Duty Outside the Archdiocese.
Walsh, Edward J. '91 (RVC) Franklin Square, NY St. Catherine of Sienna Church.
Walsh, Flannan J. '65 (STA) On Duty Outside the Diocese.
Walsh, Flavian *o.f.m.* '56 (PAT) Little Falls, NJ Our Lady of the Holy Angels Church.
Walsh, Francis (WDC) Cheverly, MD St. Ambrose Church.
Walsh, Francis *s.j.* '53 (SEA) [C] Tacoma, WA Bellarmine Preparatory School.
Walsh, Francis E. '66 (SPR) Military Chaplains.
Walsh, Francis M. *c.s.c.* '56 (FR) [A] North Easton, MA Stonehill College; [A] North Easton, MA Holy Cross Fathers Religious.
Walsh, Francis M. '67 (WDC) Hospital & Nursing Home Ministries.
Walsh, Francis P. '57 (CLV) [5] Lakewood, OH St. Luke Church.
Walsh, Frederick P. *o.s.b.* '38 (BR) [I] Tickfaw, LA Our Lady Queen Contemplative Monastery.
Walsh, Frederick P. *o.s.b.* '38 (IND) [J] St. Meinrad, IN St. Meinrad Archabbey.
Walsh, George J. '52 (PH) Retired.
Walsh, Gerald *c.s.sp.* '42 (PIT) [B] Pittsburgh, PA Duquesne University of the Holy Ghost.
Walsh, Gerald '95 (CHI) Tinley Park, IL St. George Church.
Walsh, Msgr. Gerald J. '55 (BIS) Special Assignment.
Walsh, Gerard P. '74 (WOR) Oxford, MA St. Roch's Church.
Walsh, Msgr. Gerard W. '46 (NEW) Retired.
Walsh, Harry A. '60 (STP) Special Assignment.
Walsh, J. Daniel *c.s.c.* '60 (BR) [2] Baton Rouge, LA St. Agnes Church; Jackson, LA East Feliciana Chronic Disease Hospital and Rehabilitation Center.
Walsh, J. Patrick *s.j.* '63 (DEN) [31] Denver, CO St. Ignatius Loyola Church.
Walsh, J. Patrick *s.j.* '66 (PBL) Springfield, CO Annunciation Church.
Walsh, J. Thomas '89 (HRT) [5] New Britain, CT St. Ann Church.
Walsh, James '66 (DUL) Pequot Lakes, MN St. Alice's Church.
Walsh, James '69 (SJ) [11] San Jose, CA St. Christopher Church.
Walsh, James A. '54 (TOL) Milan, OH St. Anthony Church.
Walsh, James F. *s.j.* '72 (BO) [W] Boston, MA The Society of Jesus of New England-Provincial Offices.
Walsh, James G. *c.s.p.* '41 (NY) [DD] Jamaica Estates, NY Paulist Fathers Generalate.
Walsh, Msgr. James J. '36 (NY) Retired; [E] White Plains, NY Archbishop Stepinac High School.
Walsh, James J. '68 (CIN) On Duty Outside the Archdiocese.
Walsh, James J. '73 (SCR) Jermyn, PA Sacred Heart of Mary Church.
Walsh, James J. '93 (ALB) Delmar, NY St. Thomas the Apostle Church.
Walsh, James P. *s.j.* '62 (BO) [W] Weston, MA Campion Center; [Y] Weston, MA Campion Renewal Center.
Walsh, James P. *s.j.* '66 (DEN) [M] Denver, CO Xavier Jesuit Center.
Walsh, James P. '73 (MAN) [6] Manchester, NH St. Catherine Church.
Walsh, James P.M. *s.j.* '70 (WDC) [M] Washington, DC The Jesuit Community at Georgetown University.
Walsh, Jeffrey J. '94 (SCR) [1] Scranton, PA St. Peter's Cathedral; [D] Scranton, PA Bishop Hannan High School.
Walsh, Jeffrey T. '89 (HRT) [1] East Hartford, CT Blessed Sacrament Church.
Walsh, Jerome '69 (DET) On Duty Outside the Archdiocese.
Walsh, Joachim E. *o.s.b.* '37 (BR) [I] Tickfaw, LA Our Lady Queen Contemplative Monastery.
Walsh, Joachim E. *o.s.b.* '37 (IND) [J] St. Meinrad, IN St. Meinrad Archabbey.
Walsh, John *s.j.* '45 (NY) [62] New York, NY St. Joseph Church.
Walsh, John '55 (PIT) [J] Pittsburgh, PA St. Francis Central Hospital.
Walsh, John '55 (SAL) Norton, KS St. Francis of Assisi Church.
Walsh, John '76 (PIT) Allegheny County, Pa UPMC Southside Hospital; Allegheny County, PA St. Francis Central Hospital.
Walsh, John A. '61 (SCR) On Duty Outside the Diocese.
Walsh, John A. '80 (E) Fryburg, PA St. Michael Church.
Walsh, John B. '57 (MAD) Lake Mills, WI St. Francis Xavier Church.
Walsh, John D. *m.m.* '56 (FgM) Maryknoll Foreign Missions.
Walsh, John F. '70 (BRK) Absent on Leave.
Walsh, John F. '76 (PIT) [11] Pittsburgh, PA Epiphany Church.
Walsh, John F. '84 (BO) [8] Lowell, MA St. Margaret Church.
Walsh, John J. *c.s.sp.* (GAL) [T] Houston, TX Texas Southern University Catholic Newman Hall.
Walsh, John J. *s.j.* '45 (STL) [P] St. Louis, MO Jesuit Community Corporation at St. Louis University - Jesuit Hall.
Walsh, John J. *s.j.* '46 (BO) [23] Boston, MA St. Francis de Sales Church; Rockland, MA Holy Family Church; [W] Weston, MA Campion Health Center, Inc.
Walsh, John J. *c.s.sp.* '48 (GAL) [B] Houston, TX Holy Ghost Fathers.
Walsh, John J. '57 (DUB) Webster City, IA St. Thomas Aquinas Church.
Walsh, John J. *m.m.* '61 (NY) [DD] Maryknoll, NY Maryknoll Fathers and Brothers.
Walsh, John Joseph *s.j.* '71 (BO) [E] Boston, MA Boston College High School & Jesuit Community; [W] Boston, MA The Society of Jesus of New England-Provincial Offices.
Walsh, John Kelly *m.m.* '33 (NY) [DD] Maryknoll, NY Maryknoll Fathers and Brothers.
Walsh, John M. '47 (PH) Retired.
Walsh, John P. (ATL) Peachtree City, GA Holy Trinity Catholic Church.
Walsh, John T. '44 (ROC) [43] Rochester, NY St. Margaret Mary Church; Retired.
Walsh, Joseph '64 (SFR) Special Assignment.
Walsh, Joseph E. '47 (PH) Lenni, PA St. Francis de Sales Church; Retired.
Walsh, Joseph M. '86 (LIN) [11] Lincoln, NE St. Teresa's Church; [K] Lincoln, NE Catholic Social Services; [L] Lincoln, NE Catholic Social Services.
Walsh, Joseph R. '64 (SFR) [49] San Francisco, CA St. Stephen Church.
Walsh, Kenneth *c.p.* '50 (BAL) [M] Baltimore, MD St. Joseph's Passionist Community.
Walsh, Kevin '78 (RVC) Priests Released from Diocesan Assignment.
Walsh, Kevin '92 (ARL) [8] Alexandria, VA St. Rita's Church.
Walsh, Kevin V. '78 (HRT) [17] Waterbury, CT SS. Peter and Paul Church.
Walsh, Laurence '45 (NO) Retired.
Walsh, Laurence E. *s.j.* '54 (STL) [P] St. Louis, MO Jesuit Community Corporation at St. Louis University - Jesuit Hall.
Walsh, Msgr. Lawrence '54 (SAT) [16] San Antonio, TX Our Lady of Grace Church.
Walsh, Msgr. Lawrence J. '63 (STL) [39] St. Louis, MO

St. Joan of Arc Church.
Walsh, Leo A., Jr. '94 (ANC) [2] Anchorage, AK St. Anthony Church.
Walsh, Marion *o.s.b.* '42 (IND) [J] St. Meinrad, IN St. Meinrad Archabbey.
Walsh, Marion C. *o.s.b.* '42 (BR) [I] Tickfaw, LA Our Lady Queen Contemplative Monastery.
Walsh, Martin *o.p.* '50 (OAK) [N] Oakland, CA Dominican Order (Western Province), St. Albert's Priory.
Walsh, Martin *o.m.i.* '54 (BO) Tewksbury, MA St. William Church.
Walsh, Msgr. Martin E. (OAK) Military Chaplains.
Walsh, Msgr. Martin E. '43 (OAK) Retired; [M] Oakland, CA Bishop Begin Villa.
Walsh, Martin J. '74 (BO) Absent on Leave.
Walsh, Maurice B. *s.j.* '46 (FgM) Provinces.
Walsh, Msgr. Michael '38 (LA) Retired.
Walsh, Michael '53 (DEN) [4] Englewood, CO St. Thomas More Church.
Walsh, Michael *o.f.m.cap.* '58 (BAK) Bend, OR St. Francis of Assisi Church.
Walsh, Michael '71 (SAC) Awaiting Assignment.
Walsh, Michael A. '72 (PAT) Military Chaplains.
Walsh, Michael E. *s.j.* '62 (SEA) [Q] Tacoma, WA Catholic Pastoral Care-Hospital Tacoma Ministry.
Walsh, Michael F. *c.m.* '72 (LA) [A] Camarillo, CA St. John's Seminary.
Walsh, Michael J. '38 (BRK) Retired.
Walsh, Michael J. '56 (CHI) Palos Hills, IL Sacred Heart Church.
Walsh, Michael J. '70 (BRK) [242] Queens, NY St. Stanislaus Kostka Church.
Walsh, Msgr. Michael J. '73 (TR) Lakewood, NJ St. Mary of the Lake Church.
Walsh, Michael L. '45 (PH) Retired; [V] Immaculata, PA Camilla Hall Nursing Home.
Walsh, Michael P. '88 (NY) [DD] Maryknoll, NY Maryknoll Fathers and Brothers.
Walsh, Miles D. '80 (BR) Special Assignment.
Walsh, Milton '78 (SFR) [A] Menlo Park, CA St. Patrick Seminary.
Walsh, Milton T. '78 (SFR) San Francisco, CA Knights of Malta.
Walsh, Patrick *s.a.* '63 (NY) [DD] Garrison, NY Franciscan Friars of the Atonement.
Walsh, Patrick '72 (P) Springfield, OR St. Alice Church.
Walsh, Patrick *c.s.c.* '81 (PRT) Saco, ME Most Holy Trinity Church.
Walsh, Patrick *l.c.* '91 (MAN) [A] Center Harbor, NH Immaculate Conception Apostolic School.
Walsh, Patrick A. *s.m.a.* '65 (NY) Tuckahoe, NY Immaculate Conception Church.
Walsh, Patrick E. *s.j.* '60 (MIL) [29] Milwaukee, WI Gesu Parish.
Walsh, Patrick J. '58 (LA) [60] Los Angeles, CA St. Eugene Church.
Walsh, Patrick P. *o.p.* '34 (NY) Valhalla, NY Holy Name of Jesus Church.
Walsh, Patrick R. '69 (SC) [B] Fort Dodge, IA St. Edmond High School.
Walsh, Paul '66 (RVC) Smithtown, NY St. Patrick Church.
Walsh, Paul *c.s.b.* '87 (ROC) Fairport, NY Assumption of the Blessed Virgin Mary Church.
Walsh, Paul F. *c.s.b.* '87 (ROC) [I] Rochester, NY Basilian Residence.
Walsh, Peter '59 (JC) Bonnots Mill, MO St. Louis Church; Frankenstein, MO Our Lady of Help Church.
Walsh, Peter *o.f.m.* '82 (NY) [DD] New York, NY Padua Friary.
Walsh, Peter *c.s.c.* '89 (BO) [18] Boston, MA St. Cecilia Church.
Walsh, Peter J. *c.s.c.* '89 (FR) [A] North Easton, MA Holy Cross Fathers Religious.
Walsh, Raymond D. '54 (BUR) West Rutland, VT St. Bridget Church.
Walsh, Richard '68 (ORL) Winter Park, FL St. Margaret Mary Church; Special Assignment.
Walsh, Richard '83 (JOL) Romeoville, IL St. Andrew the Apostle Church.
Walsh, Richard A. '62 (PRO) [6] Cranston, RI St. Matthew Church.
Walsh, Msgr. Richard J. '44 (ALT) Retired.
Walsh, Richard J. *c.s.p.* '44 (NY) [104] New York, NY St. Paul the Apostle Church; [DD] Jamaica Estates, NY Paulist Fathers Generalate.
Walsh, Msgr. Robert '46 (LA) Arcadia, CA Holy Angels Church; Retired.
Walsh, Robert A. '77 (CHI) [J] Chicago, IL St. Joseph Hospital.
Walsh, Robert J. '44 (RIC) Portsmouth, VA St. Paul Church; Retired.
Walsh, Robert P. *s.j.* '60 (FgM) Provinces.
Walsh, Robert T. *s.j.* '80 (LA) [F] Los Angeles, CA Loyola High School.
Walsh, Terrance G. *s.j.* '82 (BO) [W] Boston, MA The Society of Jesus of New England-Provincial Offices.
Walsh, Theodore *c.p.* '59 (BRK) [U] Jamaica, NY Immaculate Conception Monastery.
Walsh, Thomas '42 (PHX) [1] Scottsdale, AZ Blessed Sacrament Church.
Walsh, Thomas *s.s.c.* '57 (FgM) St. Columban's Foreign Mission.
Walsh, Thomas '72 (STA) [21] Jacksonville, FL San Jose Church.
Walsh, Thomas *o.f.m.conv.* '80 (BAL) [M] Baltimore, MD Immaculate Heart of Mary Friary.
Walsh, Thomas A. '42 (PHX) Retired.
Walsh, Thomas E. *o.f.m.conv.* '80 (BAL) [C] Baltimore, MD Archbishop Curley High School.
Walsh, Thomas F. *o.m.i.* '41 (BO) [Z] Tewksbury, MA Immaculate Heart of Mary Novitiate-Infirmary.
Walsh, Thomas F. '45 (PH) Retired.
Walsh, Thomas F. '46 (PH) Valley Forge, PA St. Teresa of Avila Church.
Walsh, Thomas F. *s.j.* '55 (PAT) [I] Morristown, NJ Loyola House of Retreats.
Walsh, Thomas J. *o.carm.* '50 (VEN) Englewood, FL St. Raphael Church.
Walsh, Thomas J. '67 (BO) Franklin, MA St. Mary Church.
Walsh, Thomas J. '94 (MET) East Brunswick, NJ St. Bartholomew Church.
Walsh, Thomas P. '86 (CHI) [175] Chicago, IL Presentation Church.
Walsh, Thomas R. '53 (CHL) Retired.
Walsh, Thomas R. '94 (LIN) Wallace, NE St. Mary's Church.
Walsh, Thomas V. '67 (WOR) Clinton, MA St. John the Evangelist Church.
Walsh, Ulich (WCH) Retired.
Walsh, Vincent '64 (SD) [B] San Diego, CA University of San Diego.
Walsh, Vincent '64 (SY) On Duty Outside the Diocese.
Walsh, Msgr. Vincent M. '62 (PH) Wynnewood, PA Presentation B.V.M. Church.
Walsh, William D. '66 (BO) [13] Cambridge, MA St. Peter Church.
Walsh, William J. *s.j.* '54 (WDC) [M] Washington, DC Woodstock Jesuit Community; [V] Washington, DC Woodstock Theological Center.
Walsh, William K. '49 (SAC) Rio Vista, CA St. Joseph Church; Retired and in Senior Ministry.
Walsh, William M. '71 (BO) Danvers, MA St. Mary of the Annunciation Church.
Walsh, William P. *s.j.* '67 (PAT) [I] Morristown, NJ Loyola House of Retreats.
Walsman, Paul *o.f.m.* '58 (CIN) [K] Cincinnati, OH Franciscan Hospital, Western Hills Campus.
Walter, Anthony *o.f.m.* '59 (BR) [F] Baton Rouge, LA Our Lady of the Lake Regional Medical Center; [H] Baton Rouge, LA Franciscan Residence.
Walter, Charles W. '74 (MIL) Sick Leave.
Walter, Chris B. '58 (BIS) [4] Minot, ND St. Leo Church.
Walter, David A. '63 (STL) Affton, MO St. Timothy Church.
Walter, Eugene *s.d.b.* (NY) [FF] West Haverstraw, NY Marian Shrine.
Walter, Eugene *s.d.b.* '83 (NY) [FF] West Haverstraw, NY Don Bosco Retreat Center and Marian Shrine.
Walter, Francis *o.f.m.* '77 (TR) Roebling, NJ Holy Assumption Church.
Walter, James A. '62 (COL) Sunbury, OH St. John Neumann Church.
Walter, James A. '69 (BUF) Springbrook, NY St. Vincent Church.
Walter, John F. '44 (MIL) Retired.
Walter, Joseph J. *s.j.* '45 (NY) [F] New York, NY Xavier High School; [DD] New York, NY Xavier Jesuit Community.
Walter, Joseph L. *c.s.c.* '61 (FTW) [B] Notre Dame, IN University of Notre Dame Du Lac; [J] Notre Dame, IN Holy Cross Community, Corby Hall, University of Notre Dame.
Walter, Mark J. '88 (CHI) [3] Oak Lawn, IL St. Germaine Church.
Walter, Raymond F. *c.ss.r.* '41 (STL) [P] Liguori, MO St. Clement Health Care Center.
Walter, Msgr. Robert J. '45 (DAV) Retired.
Walter, Steven P. '77 (CIN) [74] Cincinnati, OH Our Mother of Sorrows Church.
Walter, William P. *c.pp.s.* '61 (KC) Warrensburg, MO Sacred Heart Church; [A] Liberty, MO Society of the Precious Blood Provincial Offices.
Walters, Frederick (PAT) McAfee, NJ St. Francis de Sales Church.
Walters, Gary R. '79 (TOL) Bethlehem, OH Sacred Heart of Jesus Church; Crestline, OH St. Joseph Church.
Walters, Hilarion *c.p.* '47 (FgM) Passionist Foreign Missions.
Walters, James '59 (LR) Retired.
Walters, James *s.c.j.* '78 (SFS) Stephan, SD Immaculate Conception Church.
Walters, James L. *s.c.j.* '78 (RC) Lower Brule, SD St. Mary's Church; Lower Brule, SD Lower Brule Reservation Church; [B] Lower Brule, SD SCJ Community House.
Walters, John F. *s.j.* '71 (NY) [DD] New York, NY Jesuit Provincial's Office.
Walters, Michael M. '81 (NEW) Ridgefield, NJ St. Matthew's Church.
Walters, Neil G. '89 (CLV) [17] Akron, OH St. Sebastian Church.
Walters, Ronald F. *o.f.m.* '78 (GRY) [J] Cedar Lake, IN San Damiano Friary.
Walters, Theodore W. *s.j.* (DET) [K] Detroit, MI Jesuit Provincial Office-Detroit Province of the Society of Jesus.
Walters, Theodore W. *s.j.* '56 (FgM) Provinces.
Walters, Thomas J. *o.f.m.* '80 (NY) [35] New York, NY St. Francis of Assisi Church.
Walters, Vincent '54 (SB) Retired.
Waltersheid, William '92 (HBG) [5] Steelton, PA Prince of Peace Church.
Walther, James A. *o.m.v.* '95 (MET) Avenel, NJ St. Andrew Church.
Walton, James *o.f.m.* '91 (CHI) [N] Countryside, IL St. Gratian Friary, Franciscan Friars.
Walton, James *o.f.m.* '91 (JOL) Hinsdale, IL Hinsdale Hospital.
Walton, Robert '74 (SAC) Elk Grove, CA St. Joseph Church.
Walz, Julius J. '46 (FAR) Retired.
Walz, Richard *o.s.b.* '67 (FgM) American - Cassinese Congregation Foreign Missions.
Walz, Richard '88 (SCL) On Duty Outside the Diocese.
Walz, Msgr. W. Dean (DUB) [1] Waterloo, IA St. Joseph's Church.
Walz, Msgr. W. Dean '53 (DUB) On Special or Other (Arch)Diocesan Assignment.
Wambach, John W. *s.j.* '64 (LC) Prairie du Chien, WI St. Gabriel Church; Prairie du Chien, WI St. John Nepomucene Church.
Wampach, Frank J. '84 (STP) Watertown, MN Immaculate Conception Church.
Wanat, Edward *s.d.s.* '75 (SAT) Kosciuszko, TX St. Ann's Church.
Wanat, Mitchell J. *c.m.* '71 (MAN) [2] Concord, NH St. Peter Church.
Wanaurny, John *s.s.c.* (ELP) Fabens, TX Our Lady of Guadalupe Church.
Wanaurny, John '59 (OM) [K] St. Columbans, NE St. Columban's Foreign Mission Society.
Wancewicz, Walter '92 (OM) [25] Omaha, NE St. Joseph Church.
Wancewicz, Walter G. '92 (OM) [B] Omaha, NE Daniel J. Gross Catholic High School of Omaha.
Wanda, Michael J. '91 (CHI) La Grange Park, IL St. Louise de Marillac Church.
Wander, Paul H. '90 (B) St. Anthony, ID Mary Immaculate Church.
Wandless, John H. '75 (KC) Blue Springs, MO St. John La Lande Church.
Wang, Andrew (SD) [6] San Diego, CA Holy Family Church.
Wang, Barnabas '52 (BRK) Retired; [U] Douglaston, NY Bishop Mugavero Residence.
Wang, Francis X. *s.j.* '52 (SJ) [M] Los Gatos, CA Sacred Heart Jesuit Center.
Wang, Msgr. Ignatius '59 (SFR) [23] San Francisco, CA Holy Name of Jesus Church; Special Assignment; [U] San Francisco, CA Holy Childhood Pontifical Association.
Wang, John '54 (HEL) Retired.
Wangler, Msgr. Alex '41 (SAT) Retired.
Wangler, Brian *o.s.b.* '69 (BIS) Richardton, ND St. Mary Church; [A] Richardton, ND Assumption Abbey.
Wangler, Msgr. Donald L. '43 (BUF) [2] Lockport, NY St. John the Baptist Church.
Wangler, Leonard '70 (LR) [A] Subiaco, AR Subiaco Monastery.
Wangler, Msgr. William O. '63 (BUF) Olean, NY St. John Church.
Wankerl, Gary A. '80 (MAD) Montello, WI St. John the Baptist Church.
Wannemuehler, Robert '51 (EVN) [15] Evansville, IN St. Boniface Church; Retired.
Wanser, George V. *s.j.* '76 (SAC) [C] Sacramento, CA Jesuit High School; [G] Carmichael, CA Jesuit High School Community of Sacramento.
Wanstreet, Msgr. Joseph W. '40 (WH) Retired.
Wantland, Thomas '67 (MAR) On Duty Outside the Diocese.
Wantland, Thomas '67 (VEN) Port Charlotte, FL St. Charles Borromeo Church.
Wanzong, Gary F. '82 (GAL) [32] Houston, TX St. Gregory the Great Church.
Waozer, Finnian N. '91 (LIN) [2] Lincoln, NE Blessed Sacrament Church.
Wapen, Francis A. '70 (SY) Taberg, NY St. Patrick Church.
Waraska, Alex '90 (KNX) Cleveland, TN St. Therese of Lisieux Church.
Warburton, John C. *o.s.j.* '80 (SAC) [A] Loomis, CA Mount St. Joseph Novitiate and Seminary.
Warczynski, Leo '42 (BAL) [88] Baltimore, MD Sacred Heart of Mary Church.
Warczynski, Leon '42 (BAL) Retired.
Ward, Austin T. '70 (STP) Maplewood, MN Holy Redeemer Church.

Ward, Bernardine *o.f.m.* '42 (FgM) Franciscan Foreign Missions.
Ward, Bruce *s.t.* '60 (FgM) Trinity Missions.
Ward, Daniel *o.s.b.* '71 (FgM) American - Cassinese Congregation Foreign Missions.
Ward, Daniel *o.s.b.* '71 (SCL) [I] Collegeville, MN St. John's Abbey, of the Order of St. Benedict.
Ward, Donal '63 (BUR) Vergennes, VT St. Peter Church.
Ward, Donald *s.j.* '70 (CAM) [4] Camden, NJ Holy Name Church.
Ward, Edward *o.m.i.* '67 (CC) [5] Laredo, TX Our Lady of Guadalupe Church.
Ward, Edward *o.carm.* '73 (NEW) Bogota, NJ St. Joseph's Church.
Ward, Gerald T. '79 (PEO) [4] Bloomington, IL St. Patrick Church of Merna.
Ward, James Garcia *c.m.* '77 (NO) [61] New Orleans, LA St. Stephen Church.
Ward, James J. '48 (SFR) San Mateo, CA Serra Club of El Camino Real.
Ward, James J. '73 (ALN) [1] Saint Clair, PA St. Boniface Church; [4] Saint Clair, PA St. Mary Church; [5] Saint Clair, PA SS. Peter and Paul Church.
Ward, Jerome A. *o.m.i.* '67 (STP) [N] St. Paul, MN Oblate Residence.
Ward, John *o.m.i.* (GAL) [T] Houston, TX University of Houston, Clear Lake City Newman Center.
Ward, John *o.m.i.* '49 (GAL) [S] Dickinson, TX Christian Renewal Center.
Ward, John '86 (BAL) [42] Baltimore, MD Immaculate Heart of Mary Church.
Ward, John A. *s.s.* '39 (BAL) [J] Baltimore, MD St. Charles Villa; [M] Baltimore, MD St. Charles Villa.
Ward, John B. '86 (BAL) Special Assignment.
Ward, Msgr. John C. '45 (NU) Retired.
Ward, John F. '58 (HEL) Three Forks, MT Holy Family Church.
Ward, John J. '55 (SFR) Retired; [D] Kentfield, CA Marin Catholic College Preparatory (Coed).
Ward, John J. *c.s.b.* '70 (DET) [E] Redford, MI Catholic Central High School.
Ward, John P. '65 (CAM) Pine Hill, NJ St. Edward's Church.
Ward, Mark *c.p.* '76 (PIT) [O] Pittsburgh, PA St. Paul of the Cross Monastery; [Q] Pittsburgh, PA St. Paul of the Cross Retreat Center.
Ward, Martin de Porres *o.f.m.conv.* '55 (FgM) Conventual Franciscan Foreign Missions.
Ward, Michael '97 (NEW) Kearny, NJ St. Cecilia's Church.
Ward, Neal A. '57 (WDC) Morganza, MD St. Joseph Church.
Ward, Richard '93 (SEA) [1] Seattle, WA St. James Cathedral.
Ward, Richard E. '68 (PIT) Scott Township, PA SS. Simon and Jude Church.
Ward, Robert *o.m.i.* '61 (FgM) Oblates Foreign Missions.
Ward, Robert A. '74 (BO) [4] Somerville, MA St. Catherine of Genoa Church.
Ward, Sebastian *o.f.m.cap.* '47 (LA) [B] Santa Ynez, CA San Lorenzo Novitiate and Seminary.
Ward, Serge E. '95 (ATL) Greensboro, GA Christ Our King and Savior Church.
Ward, Thomas '62 (KC) Retired.
Ward, Thomas I. '97 (SY) Manlius, NY St. Ann Church.
Ward, Thomas R. '65 (OM) Bellevue, NE St. Mary Church.
Ward, William G. '50 (BUF) Retired.
Ward, William J. '63 (STP) [10] Minneapolis, MN Our Lady of Lourdes Church.
Ward, Msgr. William P. '57 (SCR) Milford, PA St. Vincent de Paul Church.
Wardanski, Msgr. Joseph '67 (E) [K] Erie, PA St. Mary's Home of Erie.
Wardanski, Msgr. Joseph V. '67 (E) [27] Erie, PA St. Patrick/St. Hedwig Church.
Warden, Daniel L. '66 (GAL) Rosenberg, TX Holy Rosary Church.
Warden, T. Patrick *c.s.b.* '65 (GAL) [Q] Houston, TX Residence of the Basilian Fathers of the University of St. Thomas.
Wardenski, Robert W. '72 (BUF) Le Roy, NY St. Peter Church.
Wardrope, Juan *c.m.* '89 (FgM) Vincentian Foreign Missions.
Ware, Donald *c.p.* '25 (NY) [FF] New York, NY Cardinal Spellman Retreat House.
Ware, Donald *c.p.* '72 (NY) [DD] New York, NY Passionist Spiritual Center.
Ware, Joseph F. '48 (ATL) Retired.
Ware, Joseph F. '48 (SAV) [7] Savannah, GA St. Frances Xavier Cabrini Church.
Wargel, William '65 (EVN) [6] Evansville, IN Holy Redeemer Church.
Wargo, Msgr. Robert J. '72 (ALN) Orefield, PA St. Joseph The Worker Church.
Waris, Gerald R. '67 (KC) [35] Kansas City, MO St. Peter's Church.
Warman, William '64 (MET) Lyons, NJ U.S. Veterans Medical Center.
Warman, William C. '64 (BAL) On Duty Outside the Archdiocese.
Warmuz, Wojciech *o.cist.* (CHI) [61] Chicago, IL St. Florian Church.
Warnakula, Antony B. '88 (SAC) Carmichael, CA Our Lady of the Assumption Church.
Warner, Carroll L. *o.f.m.cap.* '36 (WDC) [B] Washington, DC St. Francis Friary-Capuchin College.
Warner, James L. '69 (GI) Ord, NE Our Lady of Perpetual Help Church.
Warner, John '70 (Y) North Canton, OH St. Paul's Church.
Warner, John B. *s.j.* '74 (FgM) Provinces.
Warner, Richard V. *c.s.c.* '66 (FTW) [B] Notre Dame, IN University of Notre Dame Du Lac; [J] Notre Dame, IN Holy Cross Community, Corby Hall, University of Notre Dame.
Warnimont, Ronald R. '76 (TOL) [1] Toledo, OH Queen of the Most Holy Rosary Cathedral.
Warnisher, Maximilian M. *f.f.i.* (FR) [J] New Bedford, MA Marian Friary of Our Lady, Queen of the Seraphic Order.
Warnken, Edward L. '88 (ALN) [A] Northampton, PA Mary Immaculate Seminary.
Warnken, Edward L. *m.div.* '88 (NY) [A] Yonkers, NY St. Joseph's Seminary; [A] Bronx, NY St. John Neumann Residence.
Warnock, Damian J. *o.s.b.* '79 (GBG) [H] Latrobe, PA Saint Vincent Archabbey.
Warnstedt, Mark A. '96 (LA) Arcadia, CA Holy Angels Church.
Warosh, James *s.j.* '67 (MIL) [29] Milwaukee, WI Gesu Parish.
Warren, Arthur (LAF) Retired.
Warren, Clarence A. *s.s.p.* '85 (NY) [B] New York, NY Society of St. Paul.
Warren, Edward V. *s.j.* '52 (SJ) [B] Santa Clara, CA Santa Clara University.
Warren, Martin L. '78 (STP) [29] St. Paul, MN St. Matthew Church.
Warren, Robert '64 (RIC) Retired.
Warren, Robert *s.a.* '81 (NY) [DD] Garrison, NY Franciscan Friars of the Atonement; [DD] Garrison, NY St. Christopher's Friary.
Warren, Ronald J. '62 (BAK) Chiloquin, OR Our Lady of Mt. Carmel Church.
Warren, Thomas '66 (LA) Sick Leave.
Warren, William E. '69 (NY) [161] Bronx, NY St. Margaret of Cortona Church.
Warrington, Bede '87 (LA) [41] Los Angeles, CA St. Ambrose Church.
Warsey, Robert M. *o.s.m.* '85 (CHI) [N] Chicago, IL Servite Friars - Eastern Province.
Warzocha, Frank S. '53 (BUR) West Rutland, VT St. Stanislaus Kostka Church.
Wasek, Stanislaus *c.p.* '53 (BRK) [U] Jamaica, NY Immaculate Conception Monastery.
Waseline, Nicholas R. *o.s.f.s.* '80 (PH) [D] Philadelphia, PA Northeast Catholic High School for Boys; [AA] Philadelphia, PA Oblates of St. Francis De Sales.
Waser, Frank A. '79 (RCK) Absent on Leave.
Wash, Pat J. '68 (WH) Absent on Leave.
Washabaugh, Robert '78 (NOR) [1] Middletown, CT St. Francis Church.
Washington, Freddy *c.s.sp.* '92 (CIN) [16] Dayton, OH St. James Church; [26] Dayton, OH Resurrection of Our Lord Church.
Washko, Robert M. '77 (GBG) Mount Pleasant, PA Transfiguration Church.
Washko, Stephen G. '78 (VNN) Phoenix, AZ St. Stephen Church.
Wasiecko, Allan *o.f.m.cap.* '68 (FgM) Capuchin Foreign Missions.
Wasiel, Michael '33 (CHI) Harvey, IL St. John the Baptist Church.
Wasiel, Michael J. '33 (CHI) Retired.
Wasielewski, Henry R. '64 (PHX) Retired.
Wasikowski, Ronald S. '75 (OM) Elkhorn, NE St. Patrick Church.
Wasilewski, John D. '97 (CAM) Stratford, NJ St. Luke Church.
Wasinger, Msgr. Alfred J. (SAL) Retired.
Wasinger, Mark Shane '94 (STP) White Bear Lake, MN St. Pius X Church.
Waska, Raymond (FBK) Emmonak, AK Sacred Heart Church.
Wasko, Anthony J. *o.s.a.* '58 (LA) [31] Los Angeles, CA Mother of Good Counsel Church.
Waslo, Peter '86 (SJP) [2] Parma, OH St. Andrew Church.
Wasnewski, Richard P. (BO) Retired.
Wasnie, Blane *o.s.b.* '66 (SCL) [I] Collegeville, MN St. John's Abbey, of the Order of St. Benedict.
Wasowski, Ronald J. *c.s.c.* '73 (SCR) [C] Wilkes-Barre, PA Kings College.
Wassel, Msgr. Anthony F. '60 (ALN) [5] Mahanoy City, PA St. Joseph Church.
Wassel, Eugene A. '52 (PH) [30] Philadelphia, PA St. Casimir Church; Retired.
Wasser, James '74 (SAT) New Braunfels, TX Holy Family Church.
Wassie, Stephen M. '79 (Y) Jefferson, OH St. Joseph Calasanctius Church.
Wassmuth, Dennis '73 (B) [4] Boise, ID Our Lady of the Rosary Church.
Wastag, Michael *o.carm.* '97 (NEW) [P] Mahwah, NJ Carmel Retreat House.
Waszak, Norbert J. '53 (CHI) Argo, IL St. Blase Church.
Waszczenko, Andrzej *s.d.s.* '89 (BRK) [187] Queens, NY St. Joseph Church.
Waszczenko, Andrzej *s.d.s.* '89 (NEW) [N] Verona, NJ The Salvatorian Fathers.
Watanabe, Philip '77 (KC) [39] Kansas City, MO St. Therese Parish.
Watanabe, Msgr. Terrence A.M. '77 (HON) [12] Honolulu, HI St. Philomena Church.
Waterfall, Richard A. '49 (SB) Retired.
Waterman, Gerald *o.f.m.conv.* (BGP) [6] Danbury, CT Sacred Heart Church.
Waterman, Thomas '56 (KC) Hirlingen, MO Seven Dolors Church.
Waters, J. Kevin *s.j.* '64 (SPK) [C] Spokane, WA Gonzaga University.
Waters, John *s.j.* '64 (PBL) [8] Pueblo, CO Our Lady of Mt. Carmel Church.
Waters, Joseph '56 (CHL) Lenoir, NC St. Francis of Assisi Church.
Waters, Joseph '87 (MIA) [A] Miami, FL St. John Vianney College Seminary.
Waters, Joseph '87 (SP) On Duty Outside the Diocese.
Waters, Joseph L. *s.s.j.* '49 (BAL) [M] Baltimore, MD St. Joseph Society of the Sacred Heart House of Central Administration.
Waters, Mark S. '90 (STA) Fernandina Beach, FL St. Michael's Church.
Waters, Philip J. *o.s.b.* '72 (NEW) [23] Newark, NJ St. Mary's Church; [N] Newark, NJ Newark Abbey.
Waters, Robert E. '69 (BUF) Corfu, NY St. Francis of Assisi Church.
Waters, Robert J. '60 (SC) Absent on Leave.
Waters, William F. *o.s.a.* (BO) [9] Lawrence, MA St. Mary Immaculate Conception Church.
Wathen, Ambrose *o.s.b.* '65 (NO) [P] St. Benedict, LA St. Joseph Abbey.
Wathen, Ambrose G. *o.s.b.* '65 (NO) [A] St. Benedict, LA St. Joseph's Seminary College.
Wathier, Douglas O. '84 (DUB) [C] Dubuque, IA Loras College; [L] Dubuque, IA Mt. Loretto Convent.
Watkins, Clarence N. '67 (ARL) [8] Alexandria, VA St. Rita's Church.
Watkins, James D. '89 (WDC) [1] Washington, DC St. Matthew Cathedral.
Watkins, Jean '82 (ORG) [F] Fullerton, CA St. Jude Medical Center.
Watkins, Mark T. '91 (CIN) [75] Cincinnati, OH Sts. Peter and Paul Church.
Watkins, Paul D. *o.p.* '90 (NO) [P] New Orleans, LA Dominican Fathers & Brothers, Southern Dominican Province.
Watkins, Thomas '64 (R) Lumberton, NC St. Francis De Sales Church.
Watkins, Thomas '96 (R) Awaiting Assignment.
Watrin, Bernardo *o.s.b.* '41 (CGS) [C] Humacao, PR San Antonio Abad Abbey of the Order of St. Benedict.
Watrin, Clarence E. *c.s.b.* '59 (GAL) [Q] Sugar Land, TX Basilian Mission Center.
Watrin, Eugene L. *s.j.* '52 (FgM) Provinces.
Watroba, Boleslaus M. '35 (ALB) [2] Watervliet, NY Immaculate Conception Church; Retired.
Watson, Cletus M. *t.o.r.* '66 (STA) [4] Jacksonville, FL Crucifixion Church.
Watson, David *s.j.* '92 (TOL) [C] Toledo, OH St. John's Jesuit High School.
Watson, Douglas *s.c.j.* (SAT) On Educational Leave of Absence.
Watson, Douglas *s.c.j.* '83 (MIL) [P] Hales Corners, WI Priests of the Sacred Heart.
Watson, Edwin P. *o.s.b.* '45 (KCK) Basehor, KS Holy Angels Church.
Watson, Edwin P. *o.s.b.* '52 (KCK) [H] Atchison, KS St. Benedict's Abbey; [K] Atchison, KS The Maur Hill Prep School Endowment Association, Inc.
Watson, J. Timothy *c.ss.r.* '90 (LA) Whittier, CA St. Mary of the Assumption Church.
Watson, Msgr. James P. '54 (MAN) [1] Concord, NH St. John the Evangelist Church.
Watson, James Vincent *o.p.* '63 (L) [47] Louisville, KY St. Louis Bertrand Church.
Watson, Joseph G. '92 (PH) Malvern, PA St. Patrick Church.
Watson, Joseph T. *s.j.* '52 (NEW) [C] Jersey City, NJ St. Peter's Preparatory School.
Watson, Mark A. '96 (SHP) [7] Shreveport, LA St. Elizabeth Ann Seton Church.
Watson, Michael B. '86 (COL) [29] Columbus, OH St. Mary Church.
Watson, Stephen *o.c.d.* '84 (LA) Alhambra, CA St. Therese Church.
Watson, Timothy *c.ss.r.* '90 (LA) [R] Whittier, CA

Redemptorist Fathers Mission House.
Watson, Walter *s.j.* '70 (DEN) Arvada, CO St. Joan of Arc Church.
Watson, William *s.j.* '85 (WDC) [M] Washington, DC The Jesuit Community at Georgetown University.
Watson, William A. '62 (PEO) [14] Peoria, IL St. Thomas Church.
Watt, Gerald *c.r.* '67 (CHI) [N] Chicago, IL Provincial Office of the Congregation of the Resurrection.
Watt, Joseph '68 (MRY) Retired.
Watters, Joseph '88 (PT) Retired.
Watters, Timothy J. '71 (CHR) [B] Charleston, SC Bon Secours-St. Francis Xavier Hospital.
Watters, William J. *s.j.* '65 (BAL) [39] Baltimore, MD St. Ignatius Church; [E] Baltimore, MD St. Ignatius Loyola Academy; [Q] Baltimore, MD Radio Mass of Baltimore, Inc.
Watterson, John E. '62 (PRO) [9] Pawtucket, RI St. Mary of the Immaculate Conception Church; Cranston, RI Rhode Island State Institutions.
Wattigny, Patrick B. '94 (NO) [5] Marrero, LA The Visitation of Our Lady Church.
Watts, Albert W. '59 (BGP) [L] Norwalk, CT Notre Dame Convalescent Home; [P] Norwalk, CT Regional House of Sisters of St. Thomas of Villanova.
Watts, Msgr. Roger J. '59 (BGP) [3] Stamford, CT St. Cecilia's Church.
Watts, Thomas H. '57 (ROC) Van Etten, NY St. Pius the Tenth Church; Waverly, NY St. James Church.
Watts, Trent L. '93 (R) Dunn, NC Sacred Heart Church.
Watts, Wayne F. '90 (CHI) [179] Chicago, IL Queen of All Saints Basilica Church; [A] Chicago, IL Archbishop Quigley Preparatory Seminary.
Watzke, James N. *c.s.c.* '63 (FTW) [J] South Bend, IN Congregation of Holy Cross Indiana Province Provincial House.
Waudby, Lawrence '90 (BAL) [1] Baltimore, MD Cathedral of Mary Our Queen.
Waugh, John G. '55 (PEO) Wedron, IL St. Joseph's Church; Sheridan, IL Illinois Industrial School for Boys.
Wawerski, Msgr. Edward '61 (RVC) Hempstead, NY St. Ladislaus Church.
Wawiorka, Ray W. '56 (MIL) [1] Kenosha, WI St. Anthony Church.
Wawrzycki, Andrew '70 (ORL) Clermont, FL Blessed Sacrament Church.
Wawrzyniakowski, Edward J. '57 (MIL) Cedarburg, WI St. Francis Borgia Church.
Wawrzynski, Edward A. '60 (YAK) Retired.
Way, Edmund J. *o.p.* '43 (WDC) [11] Washington, DC St. Dominic Church & Priory Church.
Wayda, Henry A. '41 (SCR) Retired.
Wayne, David A. *s.j.* '68 (DEN) [M] Aurora, CO Regis Jesuit High School - Jesuit Community.
Waznak, Robert J. *s.s.* '64 (SCR) On Duty Outside the Diocese.
Waznak, Robert P. *s.s.* '64 (BAL) [M] Baltimore, MD Sulpician Provincial House.
Wdowiak, Boleslaw '65 (SAC) Retired and in Senior Ministry.
Wdzieczny, Gilbert *o.f.m.conv.* (HRT) [K] New Britain, CT St. Lucian's Home for the Aged.
Wdzieczyny, Gilbert *o.f.m.conv.* '42 (HRT) [M] New Britain, CT Conventual Franciscans.
Wea, Raymundus Bhia *s.v.d.* '82 (LA) [R] Los Angeles, CA Casa Guadalupe.
Weakley, Robert *o.f.m.* '68 (PEO) Metamora, IL St. Mary of Lourdes Church.
Wearden, Msgr. Francis G. (GAL) Retired.
Wearsch, Ronald '92 (CLV) Willowick, OH St. Mary Magdalene Church.
Weary, William M. '84 (HBG) Danville, PA St. Joseph Church.
Weaver, Cyprian *o.s.b.* '72 (FgM) American - Cassinese Congregation Foreign Missions.
Weaver, Cyprian *o.s.b.* '72 (SCL) [I] Collegeville, MN St. John's Abbey, of the Order of St. Benedict.
Weaver, Jeffrey M. '82 (CLV) Willoughby, OH Immaculate Conception Church.
Weaver, John G. '70 (HRT) [1] Torrington, CT St. Francis of Assisi Church; [3] Torrington, CT St. Mary's Church.
Weaver, Mark *o.f.m.conv.* (FgM) Conventual Franciscan Foreign Missions.
Weaver, Patrick '63 (CAM) On Leave of Absence.
Weaver, Richard (DAL) [2] Dallas, TX All Saints Church.
Webb, Raymond J. '67 (CHI) [A] Mundelein, IL University of St. Mary of the Lake-Mundelein Seminary.
Webber, Donald A. *c.p.* '73 (SAC) [G] Citrus Heights, CA Christ the King Retreat; [I] Citrus Heights, CA Christ the King Retreat Center.
Webber, Lawrence *o.f.m.cap.* '80 (FgM) Capuchin Foreign Missions.
Weber, Alan '84 (SP) [S] Tampa, FL Catholic Student Center, University of South Florida.
Weber, Allen *o.f.m.* (BUF) [C] St. Bonaventure, NY St. Bonaventure University.
Weber, Allen *o.f.m.* '65 (BUF) [O] St. Bonaventure, NY St. Bonaventure Friary.
Weber, Arnold *o.s.b.* '52 (STP) Wayzata, MN Holy Name Church.
Weber, Bernard *c.p.* (GAL) [S] Houston, TX Holy Name Retreat Center.
Weber, Charles A. *o.s.b.* '45 (GBG) [H] Latrobe, PA Saint Vincent Archabbey.
Weber, Charles E. '53 (COV) Covington, KY Children's Psychiatric Hospital of Northern Kentucky; Florence, KY St. Luke West; [I] Covington, KY St. Charles Care Center, Inc.
Weber, Charles P. '57 (BO) Permanent Disability.
Weber, Daniel C. *s.j.* '60 (P) [Q] Portland, OR Jesuit Development & Communications Office.
Weber, Daniel C. *s.j.* '60 (SEA) [C] Tacoma, WA Bellarmine Preparatory School.
Weber, David C. (CLV) [Z] Cleveland, OH St. John Cathedral Endowment Trust.
Weber, David C. '77 (CLV) [1] Cleveland, OH Cathedral of St. John the Evangelist.
Weber, Donald C. '53 (BUF) Sheldon, NY St. Cecilia Church.
Weber, Donald E. '58 (GR) [7] Grand Rapids, MI Holy Name of Jesus Church; On Special Assignment.
Weber, Donald N. '47 (MIL) Retired.
Weber, Edward J. '76 (NY) West Nyack, NY St. Francis of Assisi Church.
Weber, Eugene J. '72 (WH) [1] Fairmont, WV St. Peter's Church.
Weber, Fidelis F. *t.o.r.* '55 (PH) [D] Fairless Hills, PA Conwell-Egan Catholic High School; [AA] Fairless Hills, PA St. Anthony Friary.
Weber, Msgr. Francis J. '59 (LA) Mission Hills, CA San Fernando Rey Mission Church.
Weber, Frank (GB) New Holstein, WI Holy Rosary Church; St. Anna, WI St. Ann Church.
Weber, Frank W. '62 (PAT) [3] Clifton, NJ St. Brendan Church.
Weber, Gabriel M. *o.s.m.* (DEN) [22] Denver, CO Our Lady of Mt. Carmel Church.
Weber, George A. '60 (CAM) Retired.
Weber, George J. *c.m.* '54 (DAL) [6] Dallas, TX Holy Trinity Church; [M] Dallas, TX Congregation of the Mission, Southern Province.
Weber, George J. *c.m.* '54 (FgM) Vincentian Foreign Missions.
Weber, Gerald *o.m.i.* '62 (SAT) [T] San Antonio, TX Oblate Lourdes Grotto Shrine of the Southwest.
Weber, Gerard *o.m.i.* '62 (SAT) [M] San Antonio, TX Oblate Benson Residence (Southern Prov.).
Weber, Gerard P. '43 (CHI) Retired; [X] Chicago, IL Foundation for Adult Catechetical Teaching Aids.
Weber, Gordon A. '52 (MIL) [2] Waukesha, WI St. Mary Church.
Weber, Harold J. *s.j.* '44 (FgM) Provinces.
Weber, Herbert F. '74 (TOL) Mansfield, OH St. Peter Church.
Weber, James H. '43 (E) Retired.
Weber, Jerome F. '56 (SY) [3] Utica, NY Our Lady of Lourdes Church; Special Assignment.
Weber, John *o.f.m.conv.* '61 (LSC) Mesilla Park, NM Shrine and Parish of Our Lady of Guadalupe Church.
Weber, Msgr. John A. '45 (BR) Retired.
Weber, Msgr. John George '43 (SAL) Retired.
Weber, John R. *c.s.sp.* '61 (PIT) [3] Millvale, PA Holy Spirit Church.
Weber, John-Benedict *o.carm.* '77 (CHI) [N] Mundelein, IL Carmelite Monastery.
Weber, Joseph A. '76 (PRM) St. Louis, MO St. Louis Mission Church.
Weber, Joseph A. '76 (STL) New Melle, MO Immaculate Heart of Mary Church.
Weber, Joseph J. '66 (BRK) [57] Brooklyn, NY Holy Innocents Church.
Weber, Joseph O. '57 (SCR) Carverton, PA St. Frances Cabrini Church.
Weber, Keith '83 (SAL) Manhattan, KS St. Isidore Church; [G] Manhattan, KS St. Isidore's Catholic Student Center.
Weber, Kevin '92 (SAL) Ellis, KS St. Mary's Church.
Weber, Leo F. *s.j.* '56 (FgM) Provinces.
Weber, Mark *s.v.d.* '82 (CHI) [B] Techny, IL Divine Word Residence; [N] Techny, IL Society of the Divine Word, Provincial Headquarter-Chicago Prov.
Weber, Mark E. *s.v.d.* '82 (CHI) [N] Chicago, IL Divine Word Theologate.
Weber, Matthew *s.c.* '90 (LAN) [E] Chelsea, MI St. Louis Center for Exceptional Children & Adults.
Weber, Michael J. *o.praem.* '77 (GB) [I] De Pere, WI St. Norbert Abbey.
Weber, Norbert *m.s.c.* '57 (ALN) Nazareth, PA Holy Family Church.
Weber, Robert C. '81 (SY) [2] Rome, NY St. Mary of the Assumption Church; Marcy, NY Mid-State Correctional Facility; Special Assignment.
Weber, Robert P. '65 (CAM) Bridgeton, NJ Immaculate Conception Church; Delmont, NJ Southern State Correctional Facility; Leesburg, NJ New Jersey State Medium Security Prison.
Weber, Samuel *o.s.b.* '96 (IND) [J] St. Meinrad, IN St. Meinrad Archabbey.
Weber, Samuel *o.s.b.* '96 (MEM) [16] Memphis, TN St. Louis Church.
Weber, Terry '85 (SFS) Humboldt, SD St. Ann Church; Montrose, SD St. Patrick Church.
Weber, Theodore R. '55 (P) Redland, OR St. Philip Benizi Church.
Weber, Thomas H. '57 (CLV) [A] Wickliffe, OH St. Mary Seminary and Graduate School of Theology.
Weber, Thomas L. '74 (CLV) [6] Parma, OH Holy Family Church.
Weber., Jacques *s.j.* '49 (GAL) [24] Houston, TX St. Cyril of Alexandria Church.
Webre, Jerome '67 (HT) Grand Caillou, LA Holy Family Church.
Webster, Msgr. John C. '76 (SFR) Pacifica, CA St. Peter Church.
Webster, Robert '86 (ORL) Special Assignment.
Webster, Robert E. '86 (ORL) Daytona Beach, FL St. Paul's Church.
Wechter, David *o.c.s.o.* '58 (WIN) [G] Houston, MN Hermits of St. Mary of Carmel, H.S.M.C.
Weckbach, Hanford E. *s.j.* '43 (LA) [C] Los Angeles, CA Loyola Marymount University.
Weckerle, Leo F. '58 (BAK) Redmond, OR St. Thomas Church.
Weckesser, James R. *m.m.* '55 (FgM) Maryknoll Foreign Missions.
Wedeking, Patrick C. '88 (GLP) Aragon, NM Santo Nino Church.
Wedig, Mark *o.p.* '86 (MIA) [18] Miami, FL St. Dominic Church; [B] Miami, FL Barry University.
Weeg, Edmund J. '45 (DAV) Retired.
Weeke, James L. '86 (OM) [11] Omaha, NE St. Bridget Church.
Weeks, James '62 (WOR) [6] Fitchburg, MA St. Joseph's Church.
Weeks, Leonard (COS) [D] Colorado Springs, CO The Medalion (East); [D] Colorado Springs, CO The Medalion (West).
Weeks, William H. *s.j.* '44 (BO) [W] Weston, MA Campion Health Center, Inc.
Weerakkody, Don Oliver '65 (AUS) [F] Austin, TX Seton Medical Center.
Weerakkody, Oliver '65 (AUS) Austin, TX Brackenridge Hospital.
Weerasinghe, Felix (RVC) Islip Terrace, NY St. Peter the Apostle Church.
Weezorak, Dennis R. '86 (MET) South Amboy, NJ St. Mary Church.
Wegg, Mark '87 (NEW) On Duty Outside the Archdiocese.
Wegher, William F. (LAN) [12] Flint, MI St. Michael Church.
Wegierski, Blase *o.f.m.conv.* '71 (ALT) Boswell, PA All Saints Church.
Weglicki, Michael '79 (LEX) Lancaster, KY St. William Church; Ottenheim, KY St. Sylvester Church.
Wegman, Richard H. '90 (MAN) Alton, NH St. Joan of Arc Church.
Wegner, Gary *o.f.m.cap.* '89 (MIL) [B] Mount Calvary, WI St. Lawrence Seminary; [P] Mount Calvary, WI St. Lawrence Friary.
Wegner, Laurian *o.f.m.* '78 (FgM) Franciscan Foreign Missions.
Wehage, Robert C. '71 (COV) Erlanger, KY St. Henry Church.
Wehby, Albert *b.a.o.* '63 (NTN) Northlake, IL St. John the Baptist Church.
Wehinger, Thomas '61 (TOL) [11] Toledo, OH Our Lady of Lourdes Church.
Wehman, Jack W. '80 (CIN) [70] Cincinnati, OH Our Lady of the Sacred Heart Church.
Wehn, Timothy C. *s.a.c.* '79 (LAV) Ely, NV Sacred Heart Church.
Wehner, Edwin P. '69 (BIS) [4] Bismarck, ND St. Anne Church.
Wehner, Eugene C. *o.c.d.* '75 (BIS) On Duty Outside the Diocese.
Wehnert, Donald R. '63 (JOL) [2] Kankakee, IL St. Patrick Church.
Wehning, Jose *c.s.sp.* '37 (SJN) [F] Dorado, PR Santuario del Espiritu Santo.
Wehr, Arthur J. *s.j.* '90 (PHX) [11] Phoenix, AZ St. Francis Xavier Church.
Wehri, Francis *o.s.b.* '61 (BIS) [A] Richardton, ND Assumption Abbey.
Wehri, Francis *o.s.b.* '61 (FgM) American - Cassinese Congregation Foreign Missions.
Wehrle, Jonathan '78 (LAN) Okemos, MI St. Martha Church.
Wehrlen, Msgr. John B. '59 (PAT) Flanders, NJ St. Elizabeth Ann Seton Church.
Wehrlin, Leo J. '93 (Y) Ravenna, OH Immaculate Conception Church.
Wehrmeyer, Richard L. *c.m.* '91 (PBL) Rocky Ford, CO St. Peter Church.
Wei, Luke '60 (BRK) [38] Brooklyn, NY St. Finbar's Church.
Weibel, George L. '48 (DEN) [1] Boulder, CO Sacred Heart of Jesus Church; Retired.
Weibel, John F. '72 (E) Coudersport, PA St. Eulalia Church.

Weibl, Nicholas '64 (TOL) Sandusky, OH Holy Angels Church.
Weible, Thomas C. '59 (LA) Retired.
Weibler, William F. '55 (DAV) On Duty Outside the Diocese.
Weider, Gregory '63 (ALB) [9] Troy, NY Our Lady of Victory Church; Troy, NY Samaritan Hospital; Special Assignment.
Weider, William *t.o.r.* '41 (TR) Marlboro, NJ St. Gabriel Church.
Weidert, Richard J. '95 (BEL) Beckemeyer, IL St. Anthony Church.
Weidman, Michael J. '95 (CHI) Orland Park, IL St. Francis of Assisi Church.
Weidner, Halbert *c.o.* '74 (CHR) [D] Rock Hill, SC Oratory of St. Philip Neri, Congregation of the Oratory of Pontifical Rite.
Weidner, Halbert *c.o.* '74 (HON) [8] Honolulu, HI Holy Trinity Church; [J] Honolulu, HI Leadership Association of Religious Congregation (LARC).
Weidner, Larry W. '80 (PHX) [14] Phoenix, AZ St. Joan of Arc Church.
Weidner, Mark *o.c.s.o.* '54 (P) [L] Lafayette, OR The Cistercian (Trappist) Abbey of Our Lady of Guadalupe.
Weidner, William F. '64 (OM) Madison, NE St. Leonard Church.
Weier, Msgr. John A. '43 (DET) Retired.
Weigand, Dom Peter *o.s.b.* '70 (WDC) [E] Washington, DC St. Anselm's Abbey School.
Weigand, John J. '67 (CLV) [4] Lakewood, OH St. James Church.
Weigand, Joseph C. '62 (CLV) [4] Elyria, OH St. Mary Church.
Weigand, Peter *o.s.b.* '70 (WDC) [M] Washington, DC St. Anselm's Abbey.
Weigel, Edmund *c.pp.s.* '58 (KC) [J] Liberty, MO Precious Blood Center.
Weigel, Jovian C. *o.f.m.* '48 (CIN) [L] Cincinnati, OH Archbishop Leibold Home for the Aged; [M] Cincinnati, OH Pleasant Street Friary.
Weiglein, John *s.m.* '50 (WH) [I] Wheeling, WV Good Shepherd Nursing Home.
Weigman, Joseph '91 (TOL) Bowling Green, OH St. Thomas More University Parish; [N] Bowling Green, OH Bowling Green State University Campus Ministry.
Weiher, Charles F. *c.s.c.* '53 (FTW) [B] Notre Dame, IN University of Notre Dame Du Lac; [J] Notre Dame, IN Holy Cross Community, Corby Hall, University of Notre Dame.
Weihrer, John A. (GAL) Retired; [N] Houston, TX Pope John XXIII Priest Residence.
Weihrer, John A. '83 (TYL) Retired.
Weik, Terence P. *s.m.* '80 (BAL) Sykesville, MD St. Joseph Church.
Weiksnar, Jud *o.f.m.* '94 (WDC) [3] Silver Spring, MD St. Camillus Church.
Weiksner, Jerome M. '55 (GBG) Retired.
Weil, Frank *o.carm.* '67 (JOL) [J] Darien, IL Carmelite Provincial Office.
Weil, Msgr. H. Gil '56 (BUF) [1] Orchard Park, NY Nativity Church.
Weil, Robert L. '88 (MET) South River, NJ St. Mary of Ostrabrama Church.
Weiland, Duane J. '62 (DM) On Special Assignment.
Weiler, Anthony (BO) [9] Brockton, MA St. Theresa Church.
Weiler, Anthony '90 (SAM) Brockton, MA St. Theresa Church.
Weiler, Michael F. *s.j.* '88 (LA) [C] Los Angeles, CA Loyola Marymount University.
Weimer, Allen (CIN) [T] Dayton, OH Franciscan Health System of the Ohio Valley operations in Dayton, OH.
Weimer, Allen '71 (CIN) [K] Dayton, OH Franciscan Medical Center - Dayton Campus.
Weimer, Msgr. John C. '58 (BUF) [R] Williamsville, NY Campus Ministry.
Weinandy, Thomas *o.f.m.cap.* '72 (WDC) [39] Washington, DC Shrine of the Sacred Heart Church.
Weinberger, Paul L. '89 (DAL) [3] Dallas, TX Blessed Sacrament Church.
Weiner, James J. '88 (NEW) Glen Rock, NJ St. Catharine Church.
Weiner, Philip '91 (STF) Elmira Heights, NY St. Nicholas Church.
Weinert, Allan *c.ss.r.* '72 (STL) [P] Liguori, MO Liguori Mission House/Redemptorists.
Weingartz, Francis A. '54 (DET) [4] Warren, MI St. Dorothy Church.
Weinholtz, Bernard *o.f.m.* '40 (SP) [O] St. Petersburg, FL St. Anthony Friary.
Weinlader, Wayne T. *m.m.* '68 (NY) [DD] Maryknoll, NY Maryknoll Fathers and Brothers.
Weinlich, Alfred J. '35 (BRK) Retired; [R] Queens Village, NY Queen of Peace Residence.
Weir, Bernard E. '86 (DAV) Columbus Junction, IA St. Joseph Church; Wapello, IA St. Mary's Church.
Weirauch, William P. '35 (PIT) Retired.
Weis, Denis P. '63 (MIL) [38] Milwaukee, WI Holy Spirit Church.
Weis, Earl A. *s.j.* '54 (CHI) [C] Chicago, IL Jesuit Community at Loyola University of Chicago.
Weis, Earl A. *s.j.* '54 (DET) [K] Detroit, MI Jesuit Provincial Office-Detroit Province of the Society of Jesus.
Weis, Ivan '80 (BLX) White Cypress, MS St. Matthew the Apostle Church.
Weis, John '66 (SAG) Rapson, MI St. Joseph Church.
Weis, John H. '66 (PAT) On Duty Outside the Diocese.
Weis, Patrick *s.j.* '94 (DEN) [31] Denver, CO St. Ignatius Loyola Church.
Weis, Paul L. '57 (DUB) [9] Dubuque, IA Holy Trinity Church.
Weisbeck, Paul P. '70 (SJ) [9] San Jose, CA Holy Spirit Church.
Weisbecker, Thomas '96 (OM) Ralston, NE St. Gerald Church.
Weiscopf, Daniel '90 (BRK) [218] Queens, NY Our Lady, Queen of Martyrs Church.
Weise, David *c.s.b.* (OAK) [C] Oakland, CA Bishop O'Dowd High School.
Weise, Thomas D. '62 (MOB) Phenix City, AL St. Patrick Church.
Weisenbaugh, Robert *s.j.* '71 (CHL) [L] Charlotte, NC Diocesan Office of Campus Ministry.
Weisenbaugh, Robert D. *s.j.* '71 (CHL) [J] Charlotte, NC Jesuit Community.
Weisenbeck, Jude *s.d.s.* '60 (MIL) [P] Milwaukee, WI Salvatorian Provincial Residence.
Weisenberger, Gary '77 (SEA) Gig Harbor, WA St. Nicholas Church.
Weisenberger, Leon *m.s.c.* '59 (FgM) Missionaries of the Sacred Heart Foreign Missions.
Weisenberger, Leon *m.s.c.* '59 (RCK) [H] Aurora, IL Missionaries of the Sacred Heart Community.
Weisenberger, Raymond *s.v.d.* '39 (MIL) [P] East Troy, WI Divine Word Seminary.
Weisenberger, Richard J. '79 (LFT) [1] Lafayette, IN St. Mary Cathedral.
Weisenburger, Edward J. '87 (OKL) Okarche, OK Holy Trinity Church.
Weisensel, Cyril O. '67 (MAD) Hazel Green, WI St. Francis de Sales Church.
Weiser, Charles B. '66 (TR) [4] Long Branch, NJ St. Michael Church.
Weishaar, Leo '84 (MOB) [E] Mobile, AL Providence Hospital.
Weishaar, Ralph *o.f.m.* '44 (LA) [X] Malibu, CA Serra Retreat.
Weishar, John A. '43 (PEO) Retired.
Weishar, Paul M. '48 (MIL) Retired.
Weisman, Raymond F. '76 (WIL) Pocomoke City, MD Holy Name of Jesus Church.
Weisner, David E. '55 (DET) [53] Detroit, MI Our Lady of Good Counsel Church; [66] Detroit, MI St. Raymond Church.
Weiss, Charles W. *s.j.* (SPK) [C] Spokane, WA Gonzaga University.
Weiss, James F. '90 (E) On Leave of Absence.
Weiss, Jerome P. '77 (DUL) [9] Duluth, MN St. John's Church.
Weiss, John C. '67 (KC) [9] Kansas City, MO Christ the King Church.
Weiss, Joseph E. *s.j.* '85 (OM) Papillion, NE St. Columbkille Church; [K] Omaha, NE Jesuit Community At Creighton University.
Weiss, Nicholas *o.f.m.conv.* '58 (ALB) [12] Albany, NY Our Lady of Angels Church.
Weiss, Patrick J. *s.j.* '94 (DEN) [D] Aurora, CO Regis Jesuit High School.
Weiss, Peter C. *s.s.j.* '79 (NO) [39] New Orleans, LA St. Joan Of Arc Church.
Weiss, Richard (ELP) [38] El Paso, TX San Judas Tadeo Church.
Weiss, Richard '80 (ELP) [38] El Paso, TX San Judas Tadeo Church.
Weiss, Robert *c.p.* '65 (DET) [K] Detroit, MI St. Paul of the Cross Community, Congregation of the Passion.
Weiss, Robert E. '73 (BGP) Shelton, CT St. Joseph's Church.
Weiss, Robert F. *s.j.* '59 (STL) [P] St. Louis, MO Hallahan House; [P] St. Louis, MO The Jesuits of the Missouri Province.
Weissbeck, Reinhold B. '72 (DEN) Brighton, CO St. Augustine Church.
Weissler, John A. *o.m.i.* '43 (STP) [N] St. Paul, MN Oblate Residence.
Weist, Edward F. '69 (CLV) Litchfield, OH Our Lady Help of Christians Parish.
Weitensteiner, Joseph M. '66 (SPK) [H] Manito Station, WA Spokane Boys' Ranch, Inc.
Weithman, Martin V. '80 (COL) Lancaster, OH St. Mary Church.
Weithman, Raymond *c.ss.r.* '56 (NY) [DD] Esopus, NY Redemptorist Priests and Brothers C.Ss.R. (Province of Baltimore).
Weithman, Robert '55 (TOL) [3] Fremont, OH St. Casimir Church.
Weitzel, Eugene J. *c.s.v.* '59 (SFD) Arenzville, IL St. Fidelis Church; Beardstown, IL St. Alexius Church.
Weitzel, Stephen D. '90 (HBG) Hershey, PA St. Joan of Arc Church; Hershey, PA Milton J. Hershey Medical Center; [K] Harrisburg, PA Catholic Campus Ministry.
Weitzel, Theodore '68 (JOL) Hinsdale, IL St. Isaac Jogues Church.
Weixelman, Richard *o.m.i.* '65 (FgM) Oblates Foreign Missions.
Wekerle, Ronald '90 (B) Graduate Studies.
Welbers, Thomas '68 (LA) Claremont, CA Our Lady of the Assumption Church.
Welch, Msgr. Aloysius '40 (NEW) [N] Rutherford, NJ St. John Vianney Residence for Priests.
Welch, Bernard J. '81 (PRT) Military Chaplains.
Welch, Christopher (DET) Detroit, MI Beaumont Hospital.
Welch, Christopher '94 (ALB) Loudonville, NY St. Francis de Sales Church.
Welch, D. Michael '70 (IND) [18] Indianapolis, IN St. Christopher Church.
Welch, Eugene A. *s.j.* '60 (BAL) [M] Baltimore, MD Jesuit Fathers and Brothers Maryland Provincial Curia.
Welch, Eugene A. *s.j.* '60 (FgM) Provinces.
Welch, Gregory T. '67 (STP) [18] Minneapolis, MN St. Austin Church.
Welch, J. Paul *s.s.* '39 (BAL) [J] Baltimore, MD St. Charles Villa; [M] Baltimore, MD St. Charles Villa.
Welch, John *o.carm.* '65 (WDC) [B] Washington, DC Whitefriars Hall; [V] Washington, DC Carmelite Institute.
Welch, John A. *m.s.* '83 (ATL) Smyrna, GA St. Thomas the Apostle Church.
Welch, John E. *m.s.* (NOR) Danielson, CT St. James Church.
Welch, John J. *s.j.* '55 (FgM) Provinces.
Welch, Joseph *c.s.s.* '37 (BO) [Z] Waltham, MA Stigmatine Fathers and Brothers.
Welch, Joseph '91 (OAK) [4] Concord, CA Queen of All Saints Church.
Welch, Paul *s.s.* '39 (SEA) Retired.
Welch, Robert J. *s.j.* '60 (LA) [C] Los Angeles, CA Loyola Marymount University.
Welch, Thomas David '56 (RIC) Retired.
Welch, William '55 (GLP) Winslow, AZ Madre de Dios Church.
Welch, William F. '36 (DET) Retired.
Weldgen, Msgr. Francis G. '59 (BUF) [2] Tonawanda, NY St. Christopher Church.
Welding, Brian J. '91 (PIT) Graduate Studies.
Weldishofer, Bernard '92 (CIN) [72] Cincinnati, OH Our Lady of Visitation Church.
Weldon, Michael *o.f.m.* '81 (SFR) [5] San Francisco, CA St. Anthony Church.
Weligala, Joseph '59 (CHI) [98] Chicago, IL St. James Church.
Weling, John B. *s.j.* '81 (LA) [C] Los Angeles, CA Loyola Marymount University.
Welk, Thomas *c.pp.s.* '69 (WCH) [H] Wichita, KS Provincialate of the Sisters Adorers of the Blood of Christ.
Welkie, Paul P. '57 (ALN) Nesquehoning, PA Sacred Heart Church; Retired.
Wellar, Thomas '80 (CC) Ingleside, TX Our Lady of the Assumption Church.
Welle, Jacob *m.s.c.* '50 (ALN) [A] Center Valley, PA Missionaries of the Sacred Heart; [B] Center Valley, PA Allentown College of St. Francis de Sales.
Wellems, Bruce *c.m.f.* '86 (CHI) [80] Chicago, IL Holy Cross/Immaculate Heart of Mary Church.
Weller, Andre *o.f.m.cap.* '63 (FgM) Capuchin Foreign Missions.
Weller, Arnold *o.c.s.o.* '38 (P) [L] Lafayette, OR The Cistercian (Trappist) Abbey of Our Lady of Guadalupe.
Weller, Msgr. Arnold J. '32 (DOD) Retired.
Weller, Harold E. '45 (LFT) Retired.
Weller, Joseph W. (KAL) Retired.
Wellisch, Robert B. '69 (STP) [C] St. Paul, MN University of St. Thomas.
Wellman, Msgr. Dale L. '64 (PEO) Milan, IL St. Ambrose Church.
Wellmeier, Herbert J. '56 (SAV) Richmond Hill, GA St. Anne Church.
Wells, Jack M. '72 (P) Newport, OR Sacred Heart Parish.
Wells, James *o.f.m.* '82 (NY) [DD] New York, NY Franciscan Province of the Immaculate Conception.
Wells, Morris *o.carm.* '64 (VEN) Grove City, FL St. Francis of Assisi Church.
Wells, Patrick R. '93 (GAL) [30] Houston, TX St. Francis of Assisi Church.
Wells, Peter B. '91 (TLS) On Duty Outside the Diocese.
Wells, Peter V.B. '84 (PAT) Madison, NJ St. Vincent Martyr Church.
Wells, Philip '83 (SAC) Elk Grove, CA Good Shepherd Catholic Church.
Wells, Msgr. Thomas M. '71 (WDC) [4] Bethesda, MD Our Lady of Lourdes Church.
Wells, Walter '31 (BUR) [D] Burlington, VT St. Joseph's Home for Aged.
Welna, Floyd '50 (SAG) Retired.

Welp, Msgr. Harry J. '45 (COV) Retired.
Welsch, Gerard R. '66 (STL) Manchester, MO St. Joseph Church.
Welsch, John '46 (Y) Retired.
Welsh, Msgr. Aloysius J. '40 (NEW) Retired; [N] Caldwell, NJ The Rev. Msgr. James F. Kelley Residence for Retired Priests.
Welsh, Bart *o.f.m.* '43 (MRY) [I] San Juan Bautista, CA St. Francis Retreat Center.
Welsh, Canice T. *o.s.b.* '47 (GBG) [H] Latrobe, PA Saint Vincent Archabbey.
Welsh, Charles *s.j.* '72 (FgM) Provinces.
Welsh, Msgr. David B. '37 (NY) [7] Yonkers, NY St. Denis Church; Retired.
Welsh, John *s.j.* '56 (LAF) Grand Coteau, LA St. Charles Borromeo Church.
Welsh, Joseph L. '66 (BO) Abington, MA St. Nicholas Church.
Welsh, Peter J. *m.div., ph.d.* (ALN) [A] Northampton, PA Mary Immaculate Seminary.
Welsh, Peter J. '80 (PH) [A] Wynnewood, PA Theological Seminary of St. Charles Borromeo, Overbrook.
Welsh, Richard C. '60 (DET) [4] Roseville, MI Holy Innocents Church.
Welsh, Msgr. Robert E. '44 (BRK) [50] Brooklyn, NY Good Shepherd Church; Retired.
Welsh, Robert J. *s.j.* '67 (CLV) [E] Cleveland, OH St. Ignatius High School.
Welsh, Timothy L. *o.c.s.o.* '51 (DUB) [K] Peosta, IA New Melleray Abbey, Order of Cistercians of the Strict Observance.
Welsh, Vincent F. '89 (PH) [35] Philadelphia, PA St. Christopher Church.
Welsh, William P. '60 (CHI) Skokie, IL St. Lambert Church.
Welshons, Glendon R. *s.j.* '62 (RC) St. Francis, SD Rosebud Reservation Church.
Welsmiller, Francis F. '44 (SAG) Retired.
Welstead, Flavian *o.f.m.cap.* '67 (SFR) [N] Burlingame, CA Capuchin Provincial House.
Welter, Charles J. *c.m.* '45 (CHI) [C] Chicago, IL Vincentian Community at DePaul University.
Weltin, Richard W. '83 (SFD) Oblong, IL Our Lady of Lourdes Church; Robinson, IL St. Elizabeth Church.
Welton, Arthur T. '69 (NY) [193] Bronx, NY Visitation Church.
Welton, Paul D. '60 (STU) Shadyside, OH St. Mary Church.
Weltzer, Arthur '32 (SAV) [1] Columbus, GA Holy Family Church; Retired.
Welzbacher, George A. '51 (STP) New Market, MN St. Nicholas Church.
Wempe, Michael '66 (LA) [41] Los Angeles, CA St. Ambrose Church; Los Angeles, CA Cedar Sinai Medical Center.
Wempe, Richard C. '52 (KCK) Retired.
Wendel, Alfred W. '78 (ATL) [4] Atlanta, GA Immaculate Heart of Mary Church.
Wendel, Fred '78 (CHY) On Duty Outside the Diocese.
Wendel, Paul G. *c.s.c.* '55 (FTW) [L] Notre Dame, IN Holy Cross Mission House; [M] Notre Dame, IN Our Lady of Fatima Retreat Center.
Wendelken, Robert M. '61 (CLV) Solon, OH St. Rita Church.
Wenderoth, Joseph '84 (BAL) Special Assignment.
Wenderoth, Joseph R. '62 (BAL) Baltimore, MD Dismas House; [I] Baltimore, MD Dismas House East; [I] Baltimore, MD Dismas House West.
Wendland, Msgr. Thomas A. '52 (GAL) [73] Houston, TX St. Rose of Lima Church.
Wendrychowicz, John B. '73 (PH) [109] Philadelphia, PA Mother of Divine Grace Church; [D] Philadelphia, PA Cardinal Dougherty High School.
Wendt, Frank (Gregory) '70 (PSC) [C] Miami, FL Holy Cross Community.
Wendt, Patrick R. '79 (MIL) West Bend, WI Immaculate Conception Church.
Wendzikowski, Msgr. Mecislaus S. '59 (BUF) Holland, NY St. Joseph Church.
Wenig, Laurin J. '73 (MIL) Whitefish Bay, WI Holy Family Church.
Weninger, Ronald *c.ss.r.* '49 (FgM) Redemptorist Foreign Missions.
Wenke, Leonard C. '79 (CIN) [10] Cincinnati, OH St. Anthony Church; On Duty Outside the Archdiocese.
Wenning, Grigion '54 (GB) [I] Appleton, WI St. Fidelis Friary.
Wenning, Paul A. '45 (SPK) Retired.
Wenninger, Magnus *o.s.b.* '45 (SCL) [I] Collegeville, MN St. John's Abbey, of the Order of St. Benedict.
Wenninger, William '54 (SUP) Retired.
Wenrick, Patrick *s.v.d.* '82 (BO) [W] Duxbury, MA Society of the Divine Word.
Wenrick, Patrick *s.v.d.* '82 (TR) [M] Bordentown, NJ Society of the Divine Word.
Wensing, Michael G. '76 (SFS) [7] Sioux Falls, SD St. Michael Church.
Wenting, James J. '46 (JC) [A] Hannibal, MO St. Thomas Aquinas Seminary.
Wentink, William R. '70 (RCK) [D] Rockford, IL Saint Anthony Medical Center.
Wentz, Aelred W. '85 (ROC) [I] Piffard, NY Abbey of the Genesee.
Wenz, Robert '82 (CLV) [15] Cleveland, OH St. Catherine Church; Bedford, OH St. Pius X Church.
Wenzel, Edward J. '51 (MAR) Retired.
Wenzel, Timothy '66 (SCL) Sauk Centre, MN St. Paul's Church.
Wenzinger, George E. '71 (TOL) Defiance, OH St. John the Evangelist Church.
Wenzinger, Mark *o.s.b.* '95 (WDC) [B] Washington, DC Dominican House of Studies.
Wenzinger, Mark Edward *o.s.b.* '95 (GBG) [H] Latrobe, PA Saint Vincent Archabbey.
Wenzinger, Robert D. '82 (FRS) [5] Bakersfield, CA St. Joseph Church.
Werbylo, Walter M. *c.s.b.* '90 (GAL) [Q] Houston, TX Residence of the Basilian Fathers of the University of St. Thomas.
Werling, Norman G. *o.carm.* '41 (NEW) Paramus, NJ Carmelite Chapel of St. Therese Church.
Werner, Ben '64 (LAN) Ann Arbor, MI University of Michigan Hospitals/Pastoral Care Dept.
Werner, Benjamin '64 (LAN) Retired.
Werner, Msgr. Cyril J. '45 (OM) Retired.
Werner, George J. *s.m.m.* '57 (RVC) [N] Bay Shore, NY Montfort Missionaries.
Werner, John P. '51 (COV) Retired; [H] Edgewood, KY St. Elizabeth Medical Center, South.
Werner, Jon P. '82 (SY) [1] Liverpool, NY Christ the King Church.
Werner, Justin N. '58 (GB) Special Assignment.
Werner, Leo E. '51 (WH) Retired.
Werner, Msgr. Martin E. '35 (GF) Retired.
Werr, Donald *o.f.m.* '46 (FWT) [G] Crowley, TX St. Francis Village, Inc.; [H] Crowley, TX St. Maximilian Kolbe Friary.
Werra, Bogdan '81 (KAL) Mattawan, MI St. John Bosco Church.
Werring, Edward J. '71 (RVC) Patchogue, NY Our Lady of Mt. Carmel Church; [Q] Rockville Centre, NY The Campus Parish of Long Island.
Wersing, Richard F. *c.s.sp.* '37 (PIT) [B] Pittsburgh, PA Duquesne University of the Holy Ghost.
Wert, William *o.carm.* '77 (LA) [F] Encino, CA Crespi Carmelite High School.
Wertanen, Steven A. '97 (DET) [9] Sterling Heights, MI St. Rene Goupil Church.
Werth, Alvin '62 (SAL) Phillipsburg, KS SS. Philip and James Church.
Werth, Charles M. '53 (BUF) Retired.
Werth, Loren J. '56 (SAL) Clay Center, KS SS. Peter and Paul Church.
Werth, Robert '79 (ROC) [49] Rochester, NY Roman Catholic Community of the 19th Ward Church.
Werthman, Robert R. '60 (PIT) Brentwood, PA St. Sylvester Church.
Wertin, George P. '63 (STP) [27] Minneapolis, MN St. Joan of Arc Church.
Wertman, Raymond '72 (OG) Special Assignment.
Wesely, Eugene L. '57 (CR) Lake Eunice Township, MN St. Mary of the Lakes Church.
Wesely, Mark '93 (SAL) Bird City, KS St. Joseph's Church.
Weseman, Alan R. '86 (NO) Madisonville, LA St. Anselm Church.
Wesley, Andrew '80 (DET) [75] Detroit, MI Transfiguration Church.
Weslin, Norman U. *o.s.* '86 (PCE) On Duty Outside the Diocese.
Wesloh, Ferdinand J. '64 (STL) [3] Florissant, MO St. Angela Merici Church.
Wesnofske, Matthias *o.f.m.cap.* '67 (NY) [57] New York, NY St. John the Baptist Church.
Wesoloski, Richard J. (PIT) Imperial, PA St. Columbkille Church.
Wesolowski, Anthony P. *o.s.b.* '72 (SAV) [B] Savannah, GA Benedictine Military School; [F] Savannah, GA The Benedictine Priory.
Wesolowski, Edmund C. '48 (PH) [68] Philadelphia, PA Immaculate Conception Church; Absent on Sick Leave.
Wessel, John F. '57 (CLV) Avon, OH St. Mary of the Immaculate Conception Church.
Wesselsky, Msgr. Emil J. '56 (SAT) [40] San Antonio, TX St. Henry Church.
Wessling, Floyd A. '64 (OM) Clarkson, NE SS. Cyril and Methodius Church.
Wessling, John E. '58 (CIN) [72] Cincinnati, OH Our Lady of Visitation Church; [F] Cincinnati, OH Ursuline Academy of Cincinnati.
West, David F. '64 (DET) Farmington, MI Our Lady of Sorrows Church.
West, Gerald '59 (BAL) Retired; [N] Baltimore, MD Franciscan Sisters of Baltimore-General Motherhouse and Novitiate.
West, H. Gregory '93 (CHR) Bluffton, SC St. Andrew's Church.
West, James P. '86 (LR) Hot Springs National Park, AR St. John the Baptist Church.
West, John H. '80 (DET) Special Assignment.
West, Joseph *o.f.m.conv.* '92 (STP) Bloomington, MN St. Bonaventure Church.
West, Mauricio W. '79 (CHL) Special Assignment.
West, Norbert '56 (SUP) Retired.
West, Norbert R. '57 (Y) [I] Canton, OH House of Loreto.
West, Patrick (BRK) [F] Brooklyn, NY Bishop Loughlin Memorial High School.
West, Patrick J. '81 (BRK) [117] Brooklyn, NY St. Peter Claver Church.
West, Peter '91 (NEW) Bloomfield, NJ Sacred Heart Church.
West, Stephen C. '79 (GBG) [3] Latrobe, PA St. John the Evangelist Church; [I] Greensburg, PA Sisters of Charity.
West, Thomas *o.f.m.* '86 (OAK) [A] Berkeley, CA Franciscan School of Theology.
West, Tom *o.f.m.* '86 (OAK) [N] Oakland, CA Franciscan Friars.
West, Msgr. Willis W. '63 (NOR) Willimantic, CT St. Joseph Church.
Westbrook, James Severyn '62 (SPK) Cheney, WA St. Rose of Lima Church; [N] Cheney, WA Catholic Newman Center at Eastern Washington University.
Wester, Charles H. '59 (MIL) Mayville, WI St. Mary Church.
Wester, Donald R. '78 (STL) Bellefontaine Neighbors, MO Our Lady of Good Counsel Church.
Wester, Msgr. John '76 (SFR) Special Assignment.
Wester, Kevin J. '90 (MIL) Armstrong, WI Our Lady of Angels Church; Dotyville, WI St. Michael Church.
Westerberg, Eric *o.m.i.* '86 (FgM) Oblates Foreign Missions.
Westerhoff, Ralph A. '62 (CIN) [52] Cincinnati, OH St. Lawrence Church.
Westfall, Joseph B. '93 (LFT) On Duty Outside the Diocese.
Westfield, Carlton J. '71 (BUF) Falconer, NY Our Lady of Loreto Church; Frewsburg, NY Our Lady of Victory Church.
Westhoff, Donald F. '46 (STP) Retired.
Westhoff, Francis *m.s.c.* '35 (FgM) Missionaries of the Sacred Heart Foreign Missions.
Westhoff, Francis *m.s.c.* '35 (RCK) [H] Aurora, IL Missionaries of the Sacred Heart Community.
Westhoff, Frank D. '61 (SFD) On Duty Outside the Diocese.
Westhoven, Thomas *s.c.j.* '66 (RC) Eagle Butte, SD All Saints Church; Eagle Butte, SD Cheyenne River Reservation Church; [B] Eagle Butte, SD Sacred Heart Community House.
Westhues, Msgr. John H. '48 (SPC) Mount Vernon, MO St. Susanne Church.
Weston, Thomas C. *s.j.* '78 (OAK) [N] Oakland, CA Murray Residence Community.
Westray, Kenneth M. '81 (SFR) [47] San Francisco, CA Sacred Heart Church.
Wethington, Paul V. '47 (LEX) Retired.
Wetmore, John J. '73 (STL) Manchester, MO St. Joseph Church.
Wetter, Msgr. Richard L. '57 (BUF) Clarence, NY Our Lady of Peace Church.
Wetterer, Msgr. Edward V. '64 (BRK) [201] Queens, NY St. Michael Church.
Wetterholm, Lawrence J. '56 (BO) [1] Ipswich, MA Our Lady of Hope Church.
Wetzel, Leo *o.m.i.* '52 (BO) [16] Lowell, MA Sacred Heart Church.
Wetzel, William I. '55 (STL) Retired.
Wetzler, Daniel E. '63 (SPK) [16] Spokane, WA St. Paschal Church.
Wevita, Bede '91 (LAV) [4] Las Vegas, NV Our Lady of Las Vegas Church.
Wewer, Andrew '43 (LR) [A] Subiaco, AR Subiaco Monastery.
Wewers, Damian '37 (LR) [A] Subiaco, AR Subiaco Monastery.
Wewers, William '67 (LR) [A] Subiaco, AR Subiaco Monastery.
Wey, Richard '50 (SCL) Retired.
Weyand, John '62 (ALB) Greenfield Center, NY St. Joseph Church.
Weydert, Donald D. '43 (DUB) Retired.
Weyer, John T. '73 (GAL) Sugar Land, TX St. Laurence Church.
Weyhing, John '51 (L) Retired.
Weyker, James *s.d.s.* '69 (FgM) Salvatorian Foreign Missions.
Weyls, Richard C. '93 (COL) Newark, OH St. Francis de Sales Church.
Weymes, Gerald '74 (ARL) Stafford, VA St. William of York Church.
Weyrens, Ronald '82 (SCL) Waite Park, MN St. Joseph's Church.
Weyts, Albert *c.i.c.m.* '44 (FgM) Missionhurst Foreign Missions.
Whalen, Charles W. '44 (DUB) Retired.
Whalen, David M. *o.s.f.s.* (TOL) [K] Toledo, OH Oblates of St. Francis de Sales.
Whalen, Msgr. Earl L. '40 (CIN) Retired.
Whalen, Edmund J. (NY) [D] New York, NY Department of Education.

Whalen, Edmund J. '84 (NY) [A] Yonkers, NY St. Joseph's Seminary; [HH] New York, NY North American College of Rome, Alumni Assoc. of.
Whalen, Frank J. '68 (CIN) Military Chaplains.
Whalen, James R. '47 (GI) Retired.
Whalen, James W. '58 (STP) Coates, MN St. Agatha Church; Retired.
Whalen, John '94 (OM) Fremont, NE St. Patrick Church.
Whalen, John J. '69 (DAV) North English, IA St. Joseph's Church; Parnell, IA St. Joseph's Church.
Whalen, John P. '53 (ALB) Retired.
Whalen, John S. '39 (ROC) [60] Rochester, NY St. Thomas More Church; Retired.
Whalen, Joseph E. '89 (GI) On Duty Outside the Diocese.
Whalen, Joseph E. '89 (LEX) [D] Lexington, KY St. Joseph Hospital.
Whalen, Joseph F. *m.s.* '89 (NOR) Danielson, CT St. James Church.
Whalen, Joseph J. '71 (ALN) West Reading, PA Sacred Heart Church.
Whalen, Msgr. Joseph M. '66 (ALN) [J] Bethlehem, PA Holy Family Villa.
Whalen, Msgr. Leslie G. '38 (ROC) Retired; [E] Rochester, NY St. Ann's Home for the Aged.
Whalen, Michael D. *c.m.* '83 (BRK) [U] Jamaica, NY Vincentian Residence.
Whalen, Norman M. '54 (TUC) Retired.
Whalen, Paul A. '82 (GBG) Farmington, PA St. Joan of Arc Church.
Whalen, Robert J. *s.j.* '62 (ALN) [A] Wernersville, PA Novitiate of St. Isaac Jogues.
Whalen, Msgr. Thomas J. '67 (BGP) Shelton, CT St. Margaret Mary Church.
Whalen, Timothy F. '78 (PIT) California, PA St. Thomas Aquinas Church; [R] Slippery Rock, PA Office for Campus Ministry.
Whalen, William C. '92 (HRT) On Duty Outside the Archdiocese.
Whalen, William F. (ALB) Retired.
Whalen, William H. '59 (MIL) [12] Milwaukee, WI St. Bernadette Church.
Wharton, Joseph E. '92 (WIL) [6] Wilmington, DE St. Hedwig Church.
Wharton, Paul J. '82 (WH) Hurricane, WV Catholic Church of the Ascension.
Wharton, Robert H. '54 (WDC) Retired; [L] Washington, DC Cardinal O'Boyle Residence for Priests.
Whatley, Christopher J. '70 (BAL) Glyndon, MD Sacred Heart Church.
Whatley, Francis *o.ss.t.* '88 (NO) [16] New Orleans, LA Our Lady Of Good Counsel Church; [N] New Orleans, LA Mary-Joseph Residence for the Elderly.
Whealen, Martin *s.j.* '62 (DEN) [4] Englewood, CO St. Thomas More Church.
Whealen, Martin J. *s.j.* '62 (STL) [P] St. Louis, MO De Smet Jesuit High School Community.
Wheatley, Carroll '75 (OWN) Military Chaplains.
Wheatley, Charles J. '68 (MIL) Special Assignment.
Wheatley, Dennis *o.f.m.* '84 (BO) [W] Andover, MA St. Francis Friary.
Wheatley, Herbert *o.f.m.* '67 (P) [J] Portland, OR Providence Portland Medical Center.
Wheaton, William '92 (SLC) Price, UT Notre Dame de Lourdes Church; [C] Price, UT Notre Dame Regional School; [H] Price, UT College of Eastern Utah, Newman Club.
Whedbee, Dominic *o.c.s.o.* '77 (WOR) [A] Spencer, MA St. Joseph's Abbey School of Theology and Institute of Monastic Studies; [N] Spencer, MA St. Joseph's Abbey.
Whedbee, George *c.m.f.* '69 (LA) [K] Los Angeles, CA Queen of Angels-Hollywood Presbyterian Medical Center; [R] Los Angeles, CA Claretian Retreat Center Community.
Wheelahan, Michael '80 (OKL) Anadarko, OK St. Patrick's Church.
Wheeland, Thomas H. '66 (ROC) [21] Rochester, NY Holy Cross Church.
Wheeler, Ambrose J. *c.s.c.* '47 (PHX) [F] Phoenix, AZ Holy Cross Congregation of Casa Santa Cruz.
Wheeler, Arthur F. *c.s.c.* '84 (P) [B] Portland, OR University of Portland; [L] Portland, OR Holy Cross Fathers & Brothers, C.S.C. - University of Portland.
Wheeler, Charles '79 (JOL) [3] Kankakee, IL St. Rose of Lima Church.
Wheeler, Clarence '54 (JC) Retired.
Wheeler, Daniel '75 (LAN) Tecumseh, MI St. Elizabeth Church.
Wheeler, Msgr. David A. '52 (DUB) [L] Dubuque, IA St. Joseph's Convent, Mount Carmel.
Wheeler, James D. *s.j.* '54 (KC) [B] Kansas City, MO Rockhurst College; [J] Kansas City, MO Rockhurst College - Jesuit Community.
Wheeler, James J. *s.j.* '68 (NY) [DD] New York, NY Murray-Weigel Hall.
Wheeler, James J. *s.j.* '68 (RVC) [P] Melville, NY St. Joseph's Prayer Center.
Wheeler, John '47 (SD) Coronado, CA Sacred Heart Church; Retired.
Wheeler, Thomas F.X. *s.j.* '62 (PH) [BB] Merion Station, PA Religious Sisters of Mercy.
Wheeler, Wayne B., Jr. '79 (GR) Parnell, MI St. Patrick's Church.
Wheelock, Joseph P. '96 (OG) [1] Ogdensburg, NY St. Mary's Cathedral.
Wheelock, Robert *o.f.m.cap.* '64 (MIL) [25] Milwaukee, WI St. Francis of Assisi Church; [Y] Milwaukee, WI Franciscan Peacemakers, Inc., Milwaukee.
Whelan, Charles M. *s.j.* '58 (NY) [DD] New York, NY "America;" Residence and publication office of the America Press; [HH] New York, NY America Press, Inc., The.
Whelan, Dennis '65 (RVC) Franklin Square, NY St. Catherine of Sienna Church.
Whelan, Edward J. *m.m.* '61 (FgM) Maryknoll Foreign Missions.
Whelan, Fintan *o.f.m.cap.* '60 (BAK) Bend, OR St. Francis of Assisi Church.
Whelan, Gerald J. *c.s.c.* '55 (FgM) Holy Cross Foreign Missions.
Whelan, Gerald J. *c.s.c.* '55 (FTW) [J] South Bend, IN Congregation of Holy Cross Indiana Province Provincial House.
Whelan, James J. '73 (PH) Manoa, PA Sacred Heart Church.
Whelan, James P. '93 (NEW) Midland Park, NJ Nativity Church.
Whelan, John F. '58 (RVC) Malverne, NY Our Lady of Lourdes Church.
Whelan, Robert J. '83 (BRK) [14] Brooklyn, NY St. Augustine Church.
Whelan, Steve *s.d.b.* '34 (SFR) [45] San Francisco, CA SS. Peter and Paul Church.
Whelan, Thomas '45 (KC) Retired.
Whelan, Thomas J. *o.s.a.* '62 (P) [C] Medford, OR St. Mary's School; [L] Gold Hill, OR Augustinian Community; [N] Gold Hill, OR St. Rita's Retreat Center.
Whelan, Thomas J. '81 (BO) Awaiting Assignment.
Whelan, William S. '57 (OM) Schuyler, NE St. Augustine Church.
Whelton, Daniel P. '70 (SR) Occidental, CA St. Philip Church.
Whetstone, Richard J. *j.c.o.l.* '83 (PBR) Uniontown, PA St. John the Baptist Church.
Whipkey, Robert G., Jr. '83 (DEN) Iliff, CO St. Catherine of Siena Church; Peetz, CO Sacred Heart Church; Sterling, CO St. Anthony Church; [P] Sterling, CO Northeastern Junior College (Sterling).
Whipple, Donald W. *c.s.c.* '57 (ORL) Retired; [F] Cocoa Beach, FL Holy Cross Fathers, Eastern Priests Province.
Whistle, J. Brad '81 (OWN) Hardinsburg, KY St. Romuald Church; Irvington, KY Holy Guardian Angels Church.
White, A. Paul '59 (BO) [25] Boston, MA Gate of Heaven Church.
White, Anthony J. '55 (NO) [50] New Orleans, LA St. Patrick Church.
White, Bernard C. '52 (CHI) Elmwood Park, IL St. Celestine Church; Retired.
White, Bernard L. '77 (ALT) West Salisbury, PA St. Michael's Church.
White, Cajetan *o.s.b.* '65 (IND) [A] St. Meinrad, IN St. Meinrad Seminary; [B] St. Meinrad, IN St. Meinrad Seminary-College of Liberal Arts; [J] St. Meinrad, IN St. Meinrad Archabbey.
White, Charles G. '55 (OKL) Retired.
White, Charles H. '65 (BRK) [248] Queens, NY St. Virgilius Church.
White, Charles S. *c.s.p.* '48 (NY) [104] New York, NY St. Paul the Apostle Church; [DD] Jamaica Estates, NY Paulist Fathers Generalate.
White, Clark S. '74 (OG) Brasher Falls, NY St. Patrick Church; North Lawrence, NY St. Lawrence Church.
White, Cosmas *o.s.b.* '61 (P) [2] Portland, OR St. Agatha Church; [L] St. Benedict, OR Mt. Angel Abbey.
White, David '52 (SEA) [7] Seattle, WA St. Catherine Church.
White, David F. *s.j.* '67 (NY) [F] New York, NY Xavier High School.
White, David P. '94 (BO) [8] Quincy, MA Sacred Heart Church.
White, Denis E. '67 (JOL) Hopkins Park, IL Sacred Heart Church; Momence, IL St. Patrick Church.
White, Donald C. '93 (LA) Westlake Village, CA St. Jude Church.
White, Msgr. Francis A. '49 (OG) Elizabethtown, NY St. Elizabeth Church.
White, Francis P. *c.s.v.* '44 (LAV) [1] Las Vegas, NV Guardian Angel Cathedral.
White, Gale '56 (DAL) Retired.
White, George M. *o.m.i.* '45 (HRT) [2] Waterbury, CT Immaculate Conception Church.
White, George M. *o.m.i.* '45 (NY) [FF] Newburgh, NY Our Lady of Hope Center.
White, Gervase *o.f.m.* '54 (BUF) [O] St. Bonaventure, NY St. Bonaventure Friary.
White, Gervase F. *o.f.m.* (BUF) [C] St. Bonaventure, NY St. Bonaventure University.
White, Gregory A. '96 (PAT) Sparta, NJ Blessed Kateri Tekakwitha Church.
White, James *c.ss.r.* '81 (MIL) [S] Oconomowoc, WI Our Mother of Perpetual Help Retreat Center.
White, Msgr. James (NY) [D] New York, NY Department of Education.
White, James D. '69 (TLS) [10] Tulsa, OK Church of the Madalene; Special Assignment.
White, Msgr. James E. '83 (NY) [A] Bronx, NY St. John Neumann Residence.
White, James F. '55 (FTW) [B] Notre Dame, IN University of Notre Dame Du Lac.
White, James R. '80 (NEW) Mahwah, NJ Immaculate Conception Church; [C] Oradell, NJ Bergen Catholic.
White, Joanna (NY) [W] New York, NY Saint Vincent's Medical Center of Richmond.
White, John J. (BO) Retired.
White, John J. *s.m.* '45 (WDC) [M] Washington, DC Marist Provincial House.
White, John J. '55 (NOR) Rockville, CT St. Bernard Church.
White, John R. (CIN) [33] Cincinnati, OH Holy Angels Church.
White, John V. *s.j.* '65 (CLV) University Heights, OH Gesu Church.
White, John W. '83 (RVC) [H] Hicksville, NY Catholic Charities Central Administration.
White, Joseph L. *s.s.* '33 (BAL) [J] Baltimore, MD St. Charles Villa; [M] Baltimore, MD St. Charles Villa.
White, Joseph M. '92 (BO) Hull, MA St. Mary of the Assumption Church.
White, Kenneth R. '68 (PIT) Bethel Park, PA St. Thomas More Church.
White, Kris '41 (SB) Retired.
White, Lawrence E. '70 (CC) [14] Corpus Christi, TX SS. Cyril and Methodius Church.
White, Leland J. '65 (CHR) On Duty Outside the Diocese.
White, Msgr. Leo J. '56 (BRK) Released from Diocesan Assignment.
White, Leroy E. '56 (KAL) Retired.
White, Leroy E. '56 (LAN) Davison, MI St. John Church.
White, LLoyd W. '58 (SC) Retired.
White, Marcellus *c.p.* '34 (BO) [W] Brighton, MA St. Gabriel's Passionist Community.
White, Marcellus R. *c.p.* '34 (BO) [W] Brighton, MA St. Gabriel's Residence.
White, Michael *c.s.sp.* '83 (SD) [C] San Diego, CA University of San Diego High School.
White, Michael J. '48 (BIR) Retired.
White, Michael J. '84 (BAL) Timonium, MD Church of the Nativity.
White, Michael T. *c.s.sp.* '83 (SD) [31] San Diego, CA St. Mary Magdalene Church.
White, Paul *s.s.c.* '58 (LA) [66] Los Angeles, CA St. Gregory Nazianzen Church.
White, Paul C. '89 (RCK) Sterling, IL Sacred Heart Church.
White, Paul R. *c.pp.s.* '53 (LFT) Francesville, IN St. Francis Solano Church; Medaryville, IN St. Henry Church; [A] Rensselaer, IN Saint Joseph's College.
White, Peter H. '62 (WOR) Rochdale, MA St. Aloysius-St. Jude Church.
White, Ralph *o.f.m.conv.* '83 (SY) Bridgeport, NY St. Francis of Assisi Church.
White, Raymond F. *c.m.* '45 (CHI) [C] Chicago, IL Vincentian Community at DePaul University.
White, Richard *c.m.f.* '79 (CHI) [149] Chicago, IL Our Lady of Guadalupe Church.
White, Robert '70 (SD) San Diego, CA Mercy Hospital; [F] San Diego, CA Mercy Hospital and Medical Center dba Mercy Healthcare San Diego.
White, Robert A. *s.j.* '62 (FgM) Provinces.
White, Robert H. *o.f.m.* (BUF) [C] St. Bonaventure, NY St. Bonaventure University.
White, Robert H. *o.f.m.* '51 (BUF) [O] St. Bonaventure, NY St. Bonaventure Friary.
White, Robert H. '60 (DEN) Absent on Leave.
White, Robert K. '61 (SFR) Tomales, CA Church of the Assumption.
White, Robert L. '74 (STP) Victoria, MN St. Victoria Church.
White, Robert S. *c.s.s.* '73 (BO) [W] Waltham, MA Stigmatine Fathers & Brothers Provincial House.
White, Roger *o.f.m.cap.* '65 (FgM) Capuchin Foreign Missions.
White, Stephen *m.s.c.* '46 (SAT) [M] San Antonio, TX Missionaries of the Sacred Heart.
White, Stephen C. '86 (PH) [60] Philadelphia, PA Holy Innocents Church.
White, Thomas '64 (BLX) [3] Gulfport, MS St. John the Evangelist Church.
White, Thomas *l.c.* '78 (LA) [R] Pasadena, CA Legionaries of Christ; [CC] Los Angeles, CA Archdiocesan Office for Campus Ministry.
White, Thomas J. '59 (JOL) Wheaton, IL St. Daniel the Prophet Church.
White, William '58 (NY) On Duty Outside the Archdiocese.
White, Msgr. William '58 (PMB) [A] Boynton Beach, FL

St. Vincent de Paul Regional Seminary.
White, William A. '90 (NY) Pine Plains, NY St. Anthony Church.
White, William J. '52 (CHI) [2] Oak Lawn, IL St. Gerald Church; Retired.
White, William M. '58 (JOL) Braidwood, IL Immaculate Conception Church.
Whited, Msgr. Walter M. '66 (STL) Cottleville, MO St. Joseph Church.
Whiteing, Richard J. '80 (OM) Fullerton, NE St. Peter Church.
Whiteside, Daniel R. '92 (CHI) [109] Chicago, IL St. Josaphat Church.
Whiteside, David '97 (PEO) Oglesby, IL Holy Family Church.
Whitestone, David A. '89 (ARL) Falls Church, VA St. Philip Church.
Whitley, Edward D. *c.s.p.* '51 (NY) [DD] Jamaica Estates, NY Paulist Fathers Generalate.
Whitley, John R. *c.s.b.* '54 (GAL) [Q] Sugar Land, TX Basilian Mission Center.
Whitley, Rufus *o.m.i.* '76 (SAT) [M] San Antonio, TX Provincial Administration Office, Oblates of Mary Immaculate (Southern Prov.); [S] San Antonio, TX Missionary Oblates of Mary Immaculate of Texas Continuing Care Foundation.
Whitley, Rufus J. *o.m.i.* '76 (SAT) [B] San Antonio, TX Joseph Gerard House of Studies.
Whitlock, Joseph E. '55 (PRT) Bridgton, ME St. Joseph Church.
Whitlow, Ronald F. '61 (NO) [28] New Orleans, LA St. Cecilia Church.
Whitman, Andrew P. *s.j.* '63 (TUC) [F] Tucson, AZ Jesuit Community of the Vatican Observatory.
Whitman, Dan G. '83 (KNX) Clinton, TN St. Therese Church; Helenwood, TN St. Jude Parish; [K] Knoxville, TN Diocesan Council of Catholic Women.
Whitman, Glenn R. '75 (E) Girard, PA St. John the Evangelist Church.
Whitman, Mark G. '95 (STL) Des Peres, MO St. Clement Church.
Whitman, Thomas J. '87 (E) [21] Erie, PA St. Jude the Apostle Church.
Whitmore, James R. *m.m.* '59 (SJ) [M] Los Altos, CA Maryknoll.
Whitmore, Msgr. Paul E. '54 (OG) Port Leyden, NY St. Martin Church.
Whitney, A. Peter '84 (TYL) Fairfield, TX St. Bernard of Clairvaux Church; Fairfield, TX Boyd Unit, Texas Department of Criminal Justice.
Whitney, John D. *s.j.* '94 (SEA) [A] Seattle, WA Seattle University.
Whitney, Patrick J. '68 (RVC) Lake Ronkonkoma, NY St. Elizabeth Ann Seton Church.
Whitney, Msgr. Paul J. '58 (BUF) Medina, NY St. Mary Church.
Whitney, Philip '47 (HT) Retired.
Whitney, Richard P. '87 (RVC) Seaford, NY St. James Church.
Whitsell, John '96 (TYL) Kilgore, TX Christ the King Church.
Whitson, Robley E. '58 (NY) On Duty Outside the Archdiocese.
Whitt, D. Reginald *o.p.* '76 (FTW) [B] Notre Dame, IN University of Notre Dame Du Lac.
Whittaker, Kenneth '77 (MIA) Deerfield Beach, FL St. Ambrose Church.
Whitten, Carlton E. *s.j.* '61 (SAC) [C] Sacramento, CA Jesuit High School; [G] Carmichael, CA Jesuit High School Community of Sacramento.
Whittier, James E. (BO) Retired.
Whittington, Kenneth L. '88 (CHL) Morganton, NC St. Charles Borromeo Church.
Whittington, Paul *o.p.* '97 (CHI) [D] Oak Park, IL Fenwick High School.
Whittington, Paul DePorres *o.p.* '97 (CHI) [N] Chicago, IL Dominicans (Provincial Office).
Whyte, Edmond F. '64 (MIA) [10] Fort Lauderdale, FL St. Mark Church.
Wiant, George '61 (ROC) Victor, NY St. Patrick Church.
Wiatrowski, Ralph E. '74 (CLV) [5] Lakewood, OH St. Luke Church.
Wible, Charles M. '96 (BAL) Hydes, MD St. John the Evangelist Church.
Wichlan, David L. '57 (STL) Vinita Park, MO St. Rita Church.
Wichman, Edwin J. '80 (PIT) Verona, PA St. Joseph Church.
Wichmann, Edward W. '52 (BWN) [E] Brownsville, TX El Rancho Grande Apartments.
Wichmann, Edward W. '52 (PBL) Retired.
Wichmanowski, Walter F. '52 (PIT) Retired; [O] Pittsburgh, PA St. John Vianney Manor.
Wicht, Robert *s.d.s.* '67 (TUC) Vail, AZ Shrine of St. Rita in the Desert Church.
Wickenhauser, Gerald M. *m.m.* '62 (FgM) Maryknoll Foreign Missions.
Wicker, Paul F. '63 (COS) [4] Colorado Springs, CO Holy Apostles Church.
Wickers, Amideus M. *o.s.m.* '49 (CHI) [N] Chicago, IL Servite Friars - Eastern Province.
Wickey, Harold '55 (KCK) [14] Kansas City, KS St. Patrick's Church.
Wickham, William E. *c.s.c.* '81 (P) [13] Portland, OR St. Elizabeth of Hungary Church; Portland, OR Department of Veterans' Affairs Medical Center.
Wicki, Ted *c.r.* '88 (SB) [1] Fontana, CA Church of the Resurrection.
Wicklum, Paul R. '61 (LFT) De Motte, IN St. Cecilia Church.
Wickman, Robert '49 (RVC) Retired.
Wickowski, Leroy '66 (CHI) [4] Oak Park, IL St. Giles Church.
Wickrematunge, Vernon '87 (NY) Monroe, NY Sacred Heart Church.
Wicks, Jared W. *s.j.* '62 (CHI) [C] Chicago, IL Jesuit Community at Loyola University of Chicago.
Wicks, W. Jared *s.j.* '62 (DET) [K] Detroit, MI Jesuit Provincial Office-Detroit Province of the Society of Jesus.
Widacki, Msgr. Roman '57 (AUS) Retired.
Widera, Siegfried '67 (ORG) Inactive Leave.
Widhammer, Nicholas *o.f.m.cap.* '63 (FgM) Capuchin Foreign Missions.
Widmann, Phillip A. '77 (FTW) Nix Settlement, IN St. Catharine Church; Roanoke, IN St. Joseph Church.
Widmer, Edward *c.m.f.* '51 (LA) [R] Rancho Dominguez, CA Dominguez Seminary Inc.
Widner, Thomas '69 (CIN) [P] Milford, OH Milford Spiritual Center.
Widomski, Stanislaus '62 (FgM) Franciscan Foreign Missions.
Wieber, Donald A. '57 (KAL) Watervliet, MI St. Joseph Church.
Wieber, Elmer F. '54 (KAL) Retired.
Wieber, Robert *o.s.b.* '67 (SCL) [I] Collegeville, MN St. John's Abbey, of the Order of St. Benedict.
Wiecek, Ronald P. *c.pp.s.* '71 (OAK) Newark, CA St. Edward's Church; [N] Berkeley, CA Society of the Precious Blood.
Wiecki, Donald J. '58 (MAD) Reedsburg, WI Sacred Heart Church.
Wieckowski, Msgr. John F. '38 (CAM) Retired.
Wieczorek, Anthony J. *o.praem.* '85 (GB) [I] De Pere, WI St. Norbert Abbey.
Wieczorek, Edward R. '65 (Y) Randolph Township, OH St. Joseph Church.
Wieczorek, Matthew S. '59 (SY) [5] Rome, NY Transfiguration Church.
Wiedel, Thomas L. '90 (LIN) Alma, NE St. Joseph's Church.
Wieder, Henry '89 (OWN) LaCenter, KY St. Mary Church; [4] Paducah, KY St. Thomas More Church.
Wiederholt, Clarence E. '55 (JC) St. Anthony, MO St. Anthony Church.
Wiederholt, Thomas W. '63 (KC) Gladstone, MO St. Andrew the Apostle Church.
Wiedmann, Paul A. '63 (PH) Levittown, PA Queen of the Universe Church.
Wiegenstein, Francis J. '59 (HEL) Whitehall, MT St. Teresa Church.
Wieging, James F. '67 (DET) River Rouge, MI Our Lady of Lourdes Church.
Wiejata, Sylwester '96 (PH) [114] Philadelphia, PA Our Lady of Calvary Church.
Wiekierak, Joseph F. '46 (GAY) Retired.
Wieland, Bernard F. *m.m.* '38 (NY) [DD] Maryknoll, NY Maryknoll Fathers and Brothers.
Wieland, Dennis J. '91 (CR) Thief River Falls, MN St. Bernards Church.
Wieland, Edward R. '56 (MIL) New Berlin, WI Holy Apostles Church.
Wielebski, John T. '78 (BAL) Glyndon, MD Sacred Heart Church.
Wielgus, Msgr. Bronislaw '62 (NEW) [7] Elizabeth, NJ St. Hedwig's Church.
Wieliczko, Christopher *o.s.p.* '87 (NY) [113] New York, NY St. Stanislaus Church.
Wieling, Raymond P. '49 (SC) Retired.
Welinski, Alan '84 (SCL) Elizabeth, MN St. Elizabeth Church; Pelican Rapids, MN St. Leonard's Church.
Wielosinski, Robert J. '80 (CHI) [1] Chicago, IL Cathedral of the Holy Name.
Wielunski, Gregory '78 (BRK) [192] Queens, NY St. Margaret Church.
Wiemeyer, Raymond G. '52 (CIN) Retired.
Wienhoff, Paul R. '78 (BEL) Dupo, IL Sacred Heart of Jesus Church.
Wiera, Stefan '68 (SAT) San Antonio, TX Methodist Hospital.
Wierenga, Paul *o.p.* '63 (SFE) [M] Albuquerque, NM St. Thomas Aquinas.
Wierenga, Paul J. *o.p.* '63 (CHI) [N] Chicago, IL Dominicans (Provincial Office).
Wierichs, Paul *c.p.* '78 (NY) [HH] New York, NY Passionist Residence.
Wiersgalla, Joseph '51 (SCL) Retired.
Wierzbicki, Melvin *o.f.m.* '53 (GB) [I] Pulaski, WI Assumption of B.V.M. Friary.
Wierzbinski, Zeno (SPR) [H] Holyoke, MA Sisters of Providence Care Centers, Inc.
Wierzbinski, Zeno *o.f.m.conv.* '37 (SPR) [A] Granby, MA St. Hyacinth College and Seminary.
Wiese, Melvern '57 (OM) Olean, NE Sacred Heart Church.
Wiese, Melvern A. '57 (OM) Dodge, NE St. Wenceslaus Church.
Wiese, Miro *o.f.m.* '57 (GAY) Klacking Creek, MI Holy Family Church.
Wiese, Steve *s.c.j.* '63 (MIL) [P] Milwaukee, WI St. Joseph House of Formation.
Wiese, Thomas *s.s.s.* '75 (CLV) [P] Cleveland, OH Congregation of the Blessed Sacrament Provincial House.
Wieseler, Lawrence A. '69 (CR) On Duty Outside the Diocese.
Wiesenbaugh, Robert D. *s.j.* '71 (CHL) Mooresville, NC St. Therese Church.
Wieser, Francis '44 (SB) Retired.
Wieser, Stanley '68 (SCL) Kent, MN St. Thomas Church; [G] Breckenridge, MN St. Francis Medical Center; [H] Breckenridge, MN St. Francis Home.
Wieslaw, Strzadala *s.d.s.* '90 (NEW) [N] Verona, NJ The Salvatorian Fathers.
Wiesler, Willard F. '47 (TUC) Apache Junction, AZ St. George Church; Retired.
Wiesmann, Gary '83 (MIA) Plantation, FL St. Gregory Church.
Wiesner, James F. *c.s.p.* '83 (STP) [29] Minneapolis, MN St. Lawrence Church; [N] Minneapolis, MN Paulist Fathers.
Wiesner, Louis *s.m.* '40 (CIN) [M] Cincinnati, OH Marianist Community.
Wiesner, Mark '95 (OAK) [1] Hayward, CA All Saints Church.
Wiest, Donald *o.f.m.cap.* '34 (DET) [K] Detroit, MI St. Bonaventure Friary.
Wiest, Msgr. John J. '41 (RVC) Manhasset, NY St. Mary's Church; Retired.
Wieszczck, Rudolph *o.f.m.* '54 (TR) Trenton, NJ St. Francis Medical Center.
Wieszczek, Rudolph *o.f.m.* '54 (PH) [AA] Philadelphia, PA St. Pius X Friary.
Wieszczek, Rudolph *o.f.m.* '54 (TR) [I] Trenton, NJ St. Francis Medical Center.
Wietensteiner, Joseph M. '66 (SPK) Retired.
Wigand, William J. '83 (STL) [1] Jennings, MO Corpus Christi/St.Lucy Church.
Wigger, Brian K. '97 (COV) Southgate, KY St. Therese of the Infant Jesus Church.
Wiggins, Charles W. '85 (WIL) Garfield Park, DE Holy Spirit Church.
Wiggins, Frank '86 (RIC) [4] Richmond, VA Our Lady of Lourdes Church.
Wigginton, Ellsworth T. '76 (FWT) [13] Fort Worth, TX St. Paul Church.
Wiggs, Msgr. Joel M. '49 (MEM) Retired.
Wight, Jonathan C. '86 (TOL) [24] Toledo, OH St. Hyacinth Church.
Wightman, John H. '43 (NEW) Retired.
Wightman, Paul *o.m.i.* '42 (JUN) Sitka, AK St. Gregory of Nazianzen Church.
Wijoyo, Alex Soesilo *s.j.* '82 (BRK) [T] Brooklyn, NY Catholic Migration & Refugee Office, Catholic Migration Services, Inc.
Wiktor, Ronald A. *c.m.* '63 (HRT) Derby, CT St. Michael Church.
Wilber, Stewart A. '91 (ATL) Douglasville, GA St. Theresa Church.
Wilbers, Michael J. '72 (JC) [1] Jefferson City, MO St. Joseph Cathedral; Russellville, MO St. Michael Church.
Wilbright, Stephen *c.s.c.* '97 (PHX) Goodyear, AZ Saint John Vianney Church.
Wilbright, Stephen Sullivan *c.s.c.* '97 (FTW) On Duty Outside the Diocese.
Wilbur, David F. '36 (MIL) Retired.
Wilburn, Nathan *c.s.p.* '89 (NY) [DD] Jamaica Estates, NY Paulist Fathers Generalate.
Wilcox, C. Thomas *m.m.* '51 (FgM) Maryknoll Foreign Missions.
Wilcox, C. Thomas *m.m.* '51 (NY) [DD] Maryknoll, NY Maryknoll Fathers and Brothers.
Wilcoxson, Thomas J. '89 (COV) Leave of Absence.
Wilczek, Walter *c.r.* '53 (CHI) [74] Chicago, IL St. Hedwig Church.
Wilczynski, Casimir J. *c.r.* '40 (MOB) [8] Montgomery, AL Resurrection Catholic Church.
Wilczynski, Richard J. '55 (SY) [2] Utica, NY Holy Trinity Church.
Wild, Alexander '89 (DUB) [7] Dubuque, IA Sacred Heart Church.
Wild, David D. '53 (FAR) Retired.
Wild, J. Jerome '81 (PH) Maple Glen, PA St. Alphonsus Church.
Wild, Jon '82 (DUL) [6] Duluth, MN St. Benedict's Church.
Wild, Joseph C. *o.m.i.* '40 (BO) [Z] Tewksbury, MA Immaculate Heart of Mary Novitiate-Infirmary.
Wild, Michael L. '84 (MIL) Allenton, WI Resurrection Church.
Wild, Robert A. *s.j.* '57 (MIL) [C] Milwaukee, WI Marquette University.

Wild, Robert A. '67 (BUF) On Duty Outside the Diocese.
Wild, Robert A. *s.j.* '70 (MIL) [P] Milwaukee, WI Jesuit Community at Marquette University.
Wilde, Dennis G. *o.s.a.* '70 (PH) [C] Villanova, PA Villanova University; [AA] Villanova, PA St. Thomas Monastery.
Wildeman, Richard J. '77 (EVN) St. Joseph, IN St. Joseph's Church.
Wilder, Alfred W. *o.p.* '65 (NO) [P] New Orleans, LA Dominican Fathers & Brothers, Southern Dominican Province.
Wilder, Daniel '96 (PEO) Lincoln, IL Holy Family Church.
Wilder, Frank T. *o.a.r.* '91 (ORG) Fullerton, CA St. Mary's Church.
Wilderotter, Paul C. '74 (CHL) On Duty Outside the Diocese.
Wilders, Msgr. James G. '39 (NY) [96] New York, NY Our Lady of the Rosary Church; Retired.
Wildes, Kevin W. *s.j.* '86 (WDC) [M] Washington, DC The Jesuit Community at Georgetown University.
Wildgruber, Francis C. '60 (BRK) Absent on Sick Leave.
Wildonger, Lawrence H. *m.s.c.* '79 (ALN) [K] Reading, PA Missionaries of the Sacred Heart.
Wiles, Arthur W. '67 (COL) [11] Columbus, OH St. Christopher Church.
Wiley, James A. '58 (E) Grove City, PA Beloved Disciple Church.
Wiley, Joseph '44 (E) Retired.
Wiley, Leo A. '56 (OG) Croghan, NY St. Stephen Church.
Wiley, Robert E. '60 (STP) [16] St. Paul, MN St. Bernard Church.
Wilgenbusch, Lyle L. '66 (DUB) [11] Dubuque, IA St. Joseph the Worker Church.
Wilger, Donald F. '57 (LC) [E] Marshfield, WI St. Joseph's Hospital.
Wilger, John J. *t.o.r.* '48 (ALT) [F] Loretto, PA Mount Assisi Friary.
Wilger, Norbert J. '49 (LC) Altoona, WI St. Mary Church.
Wilhelm, Chad '94 (FAR) Sanborn, ND Sacred Heart Church.
Wilhelm, Dean E. '88 (AUS) College Station, TX St. Thomas Aquinas Church.
Wilhelm, Edward *c.ss.r.* '47 (CHI) [136] Chicago, IL St. Michael Church.
Wilhelm, H. Joseph *s.m.* '59 (WH) [11] Wheeling, WV St. Vincent de Paul's Church.
Wilhelm, Patrick R.C. '71 (NEW) Kearny, NJ St. Cecilia's Church; Kearny, NJ West Hudson Hospital.
Wilhelm, Paul W. *o.m.i.* '68 (LA) San Fernando, CA Santa Rosa Church.
Wilhelm, Paul W. *o.m.i.* '68 (STP) [N] St. Paul, MN Oblate Residence.
Wilhelm, Ray *o.m.i.* '58 (SAN) Colorado City, TX St. Ann's Church.
Wilhelm, Robert J. '59 (TOL) [12] Toledo, OH Our Lady of Perpetual Help Church.
Wilhelm, Thomas *o.s.a.* '73 (NY) [168] Bronx, NY St. Nicholas of Tolentine Church.
Wilhelmi, Richard *o.s.b.* '55 (BIS) [A] Richardton, ND Assumption Abbey; [B] Bismarck, ND University of Mary.
Wilhite, Philip A. *s.t.l.* '90 (GAL) [5] Houston, TX St. Ambrose Church.
Wilimek, Louis J. '50 (MIL) Kohler, WI St. John Evangelist Church.
Wilk, Edward J. '47 (DET) [1] Clinton Twp., MI St. Claude Church.
Wilk, Joseph M. '87 (CHI) Schaumburg, IL St. Matthew Church.
Wilk, Mitchell S. '70 (SPC) Military Chaplains.
Wilke, David M. '95 (BEL) Fairmont City, IL Holy Rosary Church.
Wilke, James B. '89 (STL) Concord Village, MO St. Simon the Apostle Church.
Wilke, Peter B. '77 (RC) [1] Rapid City, SD Cathedral of Our Lady of Perpetual Help.
Wilkening, David F. '79 (DAV) Farmington, IA St. Boniface Church; West Point, IA Assumption of the Blessed Virgin Mary Church.
Wilkening, Henry '47 (JOL) Carol Stream, IL Corpus Christi Church; Retired.
Wilker, Ronald H. '71 (CIN) Coldwater, OH Holy Trinity Church.
Wilkerson, Msgr. Gerald E. '65 (LA) Encino, CA Our Lady of Grace Church.
Wilkerson, Msgr. Jerome F. '50 (STL) Clayton, MO St. Joseph Church.
Wilkes, Robert *o.s.b.* '47 (CLV) [P] Cleveland, OH Benedictine Order of Cleveland.
Wilkie, John '92 (SEA) Port Angeles, WA Queen of Angels Church.
Wilkie, William E. '54 (DUB) [C] Dubuque, IA Loras College; [I] Dubuque, IA Holy Family Hall Infirmary.
Wilkiemeyer, Victor L. '43 (SJ) [4] Santa Clara, CA St. Lawrence the Martyr Church; Retired.
Wilkins, Bernard J. '61 (STL) Brentwood, MO St. Mary Magdalen Church.
Wilkinson, Bruce W. '81 (ATL) [5] Atlanta, GA Most Blessed Sacrament Church.
Wilkinson, James '42 (WCH) [3] Wichita, KS Blessed Sacrament Church.
Wilkinson, John (NY) City, NY Adolescent Remand & Detention Center.
Wilkinson, John H. '59 (BRK) [24] Brooklyn, NY St. Brigid Church; Queens, NY Queens House of Detention.
Wilkinson, Msgr. John V. '48 (NY) Hartsdale, NY Sacred Heart Church.
Wilkinson, Richard S. *c.s.c.* '79 (COS) [E] Cascade, CO Holy Cross Novitiate.
Wilkosz, William '95 (CHI) [67] Chicago, IL St. Gall Church.
Wilks, Bede *o.p.* '92 (P) [6] Eugene, OR St. Thomas More Church.
Wilkuski, Leonard F. '63 (SAG) Midland, MI St. Brigid Church.
Will, Anthony *o.f.m.cap.* '47 (MIL) [P] Mount Calvary, WI St. Lawrence Friary.
Will, Carl G. '49 (CIN) Retired.
Will, Gerald T. '80 (STL) [56] St. Louis, MO St. Simon of Cyrene Church.
Will, Msgr. Irvin R. '37 (SFD) Retired.
Will, Lowell '68 (EVN) Cannelburg, IN All Saints Church.
Will, Lowell C. '68 (EVN) Montgomery, IN St. Peter Church.
Will, Ron *c.pp.s.* '75 (KC) Liberty, MO St. James Church.
Will, Ronald *c.pp.s.* '75 (KC) [A] Liberty, MO Society of the Precious Blood Provincial Offices; [J] Liberty, MO Precious Blood Society Provincial Office; [J] Liberty, MO Precious Blood Center.
Will, Tony *o.f.m.cap.* '47 (MIL) [Q] Fond du Lac, WI Convent of the Sisters of St. Agnes.
Willard, Stephen '93 (PEO) [B] Bloomington, IL Central Catholic High School.
Willathgamuwa, Flavin *c.m.f.* '83 (LA) [R] Rancho Dominguez, CA Dominguez Seminary Inc.
Wille, Arthur H. *m.m.* '51 (SFR) [N] San Francisco, CA Maryknoll Fathers and Brothers, Catholic Foreign Mission Society of America, Inc.
Willemsen, Andrew J. '54 (AUS) On Duty Outside the Diocese.
Willenbring, Mark '57 (SCL) Princeton, MN St. Edward's Church.
Willenburg, Msgr. Francis J. '54 (SY) [5] Utica, NY St. Agnes Church.
Willett, Henry L. '45 (OWN) Retired.
Willett, John *c.ss.r.* '61 (CHI) [N] Chicago, IL Redemptorists:.
Willett, John *c.ss.r.* '61 (DEN) [M] Denver, CO The Redemptorists/Denver Province.
Willett, John *c.ss.r.* '61 (FgM) Redemptorist Foreign Missions.
Willett, Robert '68 (OWN) On Sabbatical.
Willett, William D. '79 (OWN) Military Chaplains.
Willette, Donald '84 (DEN) Louisville, CO St. Louis Church.
Willey, Dennis B. '94 (CHR) [1] Charleston, SC Cathedral of St. John the Baptist.
Willger, Gerard I. '86 (SUP) Barron, WI St. Joseph Church; Cameron, WI St. Peter Church; Chetek, WI St. Boniface Church.
Willhite, Robert J. '63 (RCK) [8] Aurora, IL St. Rita of Cascia Church.
Williams, Alfred '39 (P) Retired.
Williams, Anthony '83 (KCK) Military Chaplains.
Williams, Anthony C. (BIS) [1] Minot, ND Minot Air Force Base Chapel Church.
Williams, Bruce A. *o.p.* '67 (BO) [W] Dover, MA St. Stephen Priory.
Williams, Msgr. Charles M. '45 (NSH) Retired.
Williams, Clarence E. *c.pp.s.* '78 (CIN) [M] Dayton, OH Provincial House of the Cincinnati Province of the Society of the Precious Blood.
Williams, Clarence E. *c.pp.s.* '78 (DET) Special Assignment; [T] Detroit, MI The Black Catholic Televangelization Network.
Williams, Edward *o.m.i.* '57 (FgM) Oblates Foreign Missions.
Williams, Edward J. '93 (SCR) [1] Freeland, PA St. Ann's Church.
Williams, Edward T. '69 (CIN) Retired.
Williams, Francis '77 (LAN) Retired.
Williams, Gary (CC) Military Chaplains.
Williams, George J. '39 (BO) Retired.
Williams, George S. *s.j.* '72 (ALN) [A] Wernersville, PA Novitiate of St. Isaac Jogues; [N] Wernersville, PA Jesuit Center for Spiritual Growth.
Williams, George W. '96 (DET) Grosse Pointe Farms, MI St. Paul Catholic Church.
Williams, Gerald *o.carm.* (JOL) [J] Darien, IL Carmelite Community.
Williams, Germain *o.f.m.conv.* '48 (ALB) [12] Albany, NY Our Lady of Angels Church.
Williams, Glenn F. *s.j.* '56 (CLV) [E] Cleveland, OH St. Ignatius High School.
Williams, H. Brendan '65 (TR) Howell Township, NJ St. Veronica Church.
Williams, Ian J. '96 (GRY) Munster, IN St. Thomas More Church.
Williams, J. Craig '83 (PT) Niceville, FL Christ Our Redeemer Church.
Williams, James '65 (SEA) [5] Seattle, WA St. Bernadette Church.
Williams, James '74 (COS) Parker, CO Ave Maria Church.
Williams, James F. '69 (LA) La Mirada, CA Beatitudes of Our Lord Church.
Williams, James M. '70 (MAR) Mackinac Island, MI Ste. Anne de Michilimackinac Church.
Williams, Jerry *o.carm.* (JOL) [M] Darien, IL Carmelite Visitor Center (National Shrine & Museum of St. Therese).
Williams, Jerry *o.carm.* '80 (CHI) [N] Chicago, IL Carmelite Priory of St. Cyril.
Williams, John '78 (R) Clinton, NC Immaculate Conception Church.
Williams, John J. '91 (HRT) Wallingford, CT Holy Trinity Church.
Williams, John Mark '89 (PEO) [12] Peoria, IL St. Peter's Church.
Williams, Jonathan *o.f.m.cap.* '71 (FgM) Capuchin Foreign Missions.
Williams, Joseph *c.m.* (SPC) [2] Cape Girardeau, MO St. Vincent de Paul Church.
Williams, Kenneth '63 (SHP) Noble, LA St. Ann Church.
Williams, Manuel *c.r.* '87 (MOB) [8] Montgomery, AL Resurrection Catholic Church; [8] Montgomery, AL Resurrection Catholic Church; [F] Marbury, AL Resurrection Catholic Nursing Home; [F] Montgomery, AL Father Walter Memorial Center for Handicapped Children.
Williams, Matthew *o.c.d.* '90 (SEA) Stanwood, WA St. Cecilia's Church.
Williams, McKinley '83 (RIC) On Duty Outside the Diocese.
Williams, Michael A. *s.j.* '75 (MOB) [B] Mobile, AL Spring Hill College.
Williams, Michael E. '97 (OWN) [1] Owensboro, KY St. Stephen Cathedral.
Williams, Michael J. '95 (LAN) Flushing, MI St. Robert Church.
Williams, Michael S. '64 (STA) [2] Gainesville, FL Holy Faith Church.
Williams, Oliver F. *c.s.c.* '70 (FTW) [B] Notre Dame, IN University of Notre Dame Du Lac; [J] Notre Dame, IN Holy Cross Community, Corby Hall, University of Notre Dame.
Williams, Patrick J. '93 (NO) [A] New Orleans, LA Notre Dame Seminary Graduate School of Theology.
Williams, Paul D., Jr. '95 (ATL) [1] Marietta, GA Holy Family Church.
Williams, Paul M. *o.f.m.* '86 (CHR) Greenville, SC St. Anthony of Padua Church; [G] Greenville, SC Furman University Newman Center.
Williams, Peter '83 (SY) [13] Utica, NY St. Mary of Mt. Carmel Church.
Williams, Peter A. '83 (SY) Special Assignment.
Williams, Peter Y. '87 (BUR) [H] Burlington, VT University of Vermont-The Catholic Center at UVM.
Williams, Rayner F. *o.f.m.* '56 (NY) [35] New York, NY St. Francis of Assisi Church.
Williams, Rayner F. *o.f.m.* '56 (PAT) [P] Paterson, NJ St. Anthony's Guild.
Williams, Richard B. *o.p.* '71 (SAT) [26] San Antonio, TX St. Ann Church; [B] San Antonio, TX Dominican Priory of Juan Macias.
Williams, Richard C. '65 (PH) Chester Heights, PA St. Thomas the Apostle Church.
Williams, Robert '91 (DAL) Corsicana, TX Immaculate Conception Church.
Williams, Robert A. (BIS) Retired.
Williams, Robert Hayes '82 (DET) Hazel Park, MI St. Justin Church; Special Assignment.
Williams, Robert L. '68 (LFT) Anderson, IN St. Mary Church.
Williams, Ronald R. '79 (DET) [48] Detroit, MI St. Mary's of Redford Church.
Williams, Steven T. '91 (MOB) [12] Mobile, AL St. Mary Church; [C] Mobile, AL McGill-Toolen High School.
Williams, Thomas G. *s.j.* '60 (FgM) Provinces.
Williams, Walter Ray '97 (CHL) [1] Charlotte, NC St. Patrick Cathedral.
Williams, William '96 (ATL) [10] Atlanta, GA St. Jude Church.
Williams, Msgr. William E. '59 (NY) Centerville, NY St. John the Evangelist Church.
Williams, William G. '69 (BO) Hull, MA St. Mary of the Assumption Church.
Williams, William W. *s.j.* '68 (COS) [E] Sedalia, CO Sacred Heart Retreat House - Jesuit Community; [G] Sedalia, CO Sacred Heart Jesuit Retreat House.
Williamson, Bruce *o.m.v.* '82 (BO) [B] Boston, MA Oblate Provincialate.
Williamson, Christopher (ATL) Blue Ridge, GA St. Anthony's Church.
Williamson, Christopher '88 (ATL) Lawrenceville, GA St. Lawrence Church.

Williamson, G. Michael '86 (CLV) El Salvador, C.A., OH Senora del Pilar, Villa de Zaragoza.
Williamson, Harry A. *s.j.* '39 (BO) [W] Weston, MA Campion Center.
Williamson, Msgr. Robert J. '62 (BUF) Akron, NY St. Teresa of Avila Church.
Williamson, Thomas '96 (CHL) Absent On Leave.
Willig, James '77 (CIN) [64] Cincinnati, OH St. Michael Church.
Willig, James M. '77 (CIN) [1] Cincinnati, OH St. Peter in Chains Cathedral.
Willingham, Charles *o.praem.* '95 (ORG) Costa Mesa, CA Fairview Developmental Center.
Willingham, Charles W. *o.praem.* '95 (ORG) [D] Siverado, CA St. Michael's College Preparatory High School; [H] Silverado, CA Norbertine Fathers of Orange Inc.
Willingham, Jeffrey '97 (MET) [A] South Amboy, NJ St. Mary Regional High School.
Willingham, Jeffrey R. '97 (MET) Sayreville, NJ Our Lady of Victories Church.
Willis, Eugene F. '55 (ALB) Walton, NY St. John the Baptist Church.
Willis, Glen *s.d.s.* '69 (WDC) [B] Silver Spring, MD Salvatorian Community; [G] Rockville, MD The Frost Center; [V] Silver Spring, MD Camp St. Charles, Inc.
Willis, John R. *s.j.* '62 (BO) [W] Chestnut Hill, MA The Jesuit Community at Boston College.
Willis, Kevin '93 (FAR) La Moure, ND Holy Rosary Church; Oriska, ND St. Bernard's Church.
Willis, Lawrence R. *o.s.b.* '66 (CHL) [J] Belmont, NC Belmont Abbey.
Willis, Nathan S. '66 (Y) Conneaut, OH St. Mary's Church; Kingsville, OH St. Andrew Church.
Willis, Thomas S. '84 (STA) [10] Jacksonville, FL Most Holy Redeemer Church.
Willlard, Stephen A.. '93 (PEO) Downs, IL St. Mary's Church.
Willman, Herbert '57 (TOL) Norwalk, OH St. Paul Church.
Willmann, Robert E. '92 (COL) [2] Columbus, OH St. Agatha Church.
Willmering, John H. *s.j.* '68 (FgM) Provinces.
Willmes, Joseph F. *s.j.* '48 (FgM) Provinces.
Willmes, Robert J. *s.j.* '40 (CHI) [C] Chicago, IL Jesuit Community at Loyola University of Chicago.
Willoughby, Malcolm S. *o.p.* '49 (DET) [20] Detroit, MI St. Dominic Church.
Wilmer, Heiner T. *s.j.* '87 (NY) [DD] New York, NY Jesuit Community at Fordham University.
Wilmes, James J. '52 (CHL) Andrews, NC Holy Redeemer Church.
Wilmot, John P. *m.h.m.* '77 (WIN) Easton, MN Our Lady of Mount Carmel Church; Minnesota Lake, MN St. John the Baptist Church.
Wilmoth, James '65 (IND) Indianapolis, IN Indianapolis Fire Department.
Wilmoth, James R. '65 (IND) [35] Indianapolis, IN St. Roch Church; Indianapolis, IN Marion County Sheriff Department.
Wilmsen, Gerald *s.s.c.* (DAL) Grand Prairie, TX Immaculate Conception Church.
Wilson, Albert '51 (L) Retired.
Wilson, Albert L. '51 (L) Rhodelia, KY St. Theresa Church.
Wilson, Anthony *o.f.m.* '87 (FgM) Franciscan Foreign Missions.
Wilson, Brian *l.c.* '77 (LA) [R] Pasadena, CA Legionaries of Christ; [CC] Los Angeles, CA Archdiocesan Office for Campus Ministry.
Wilson, Cedric M. *o.s.a.* '78 (WDC) [B] Silver Spring, MD Austin Friars Hall, Order of St. Augustine.
Wilson, Clarence E. *c.s.p.* '43 (NY) [DD] Jamaica Estates, NY Paulist Fathers Generalate.
Wilson, David J. '88 (E) Johnsonburg, PA Holy Rosary Church.
Wilson, Dennis M. *o.f.m.* '92 (NY) [35] New York, NY St. Francis of Assisi Church.
Wilson, E. James '91 (DAV) [6] Davenport, IA St. Joseph's Church.
Wilson, Edward M. '56 (E) Retired.
Wilson, F. Philip *o.s.b.* '53 (PRO) [P] Portsmouth, RI Abbey of St. Gregory the Great.
Wilson, Gene *c.pp.s.* '60 (OAK) Newark, CA St. Edward's Church.
Wilson, George B. *s.j.* '59 (BAL) [M] Baltimore, MD Jesuit Fathers and Brothers Maryland Provincial Curia.
Wilson, George B. *s.j.* '59 (CIN) [M] Cincinnati, OH Jesuit Community at Xavier Unversity.
Wilson, George W. '92 (WDC) [7] Washington, DC St. Augustine Church; [34] Washington, DC Our Lady Queen of Peace Church.
Wilson, Guy *s.t.* '78 (FgM) Trinity Missions.
Wilson, James R. '54 (B) Lewiston, ID Our Lady of Lourdes Church.
Wilson, Jerome *c.s.c.* '49 (FTW) [A] Notre Dame, IN Moreau Seminary.
Wilson, John '46 (CLV) [4] Garfield Heights, OH St. Timothy Church.
Wilson, John F. '46 (CLV) Retired; [N] Fairlawn, OH St. Edward Home dba The Village at Saint Edward Nursing Care and Assisted Living.
Wilson, Msgr. John F. '48 (BRK) [58] Brooklyn, NY Holy Name Church; Retired.
Wilson, John H. *c.s.c.* '41 (FTW) [L] Notre Dame, IN Holy Cross Mission House.
Wilson, Joseph B. '94 (SCR) [2] Williamsport, PA Ascension Church.
Wilson, Joseph F. '86 (BRK) [191] Queens, NY St. Luke Church.
Wilson, Kent '90 (NY) Fishkill, NY Church of St. Mary, Mother of the Church.
Wilson, Leland '93 (LA) Pomona, CA Sacred Heart Church.
Wilson, Method *o.f.m.* '52 (LFT) [F] Kokomo, IN Maria Regina Mater Monastery.
Wilson, Michael '75 (WDC) [4] Rockville, MD St. Raphael Church.
Wilson, Richard D. '97 (FR) Special Assignment.
Wilson, Robert '57 (FWT) Colleyville, TX Good Shepherd Church.
Wilson, Ser Khu '79 (WCH) Piqua, KS St. Martin Church; Yates Center, KS St. Joseph Church.
Wilson, Stuart T. '67 (BAL) Military Chaplains.
Wilson, Thomas R. '75 (PIT) Mt. Lebanon, PA St. Bernard Church.
Wilson, Thomas W. '96 (STP) Coon Rapids, MN Church of the Epiphany.
Wilson, William '45 (SD) Retired; [G] San Diego, CA Nazareth House Retirement Home.
Wilson, William P. '69 (NEW) On Duty Outside the Archdiocese.
Wilson, Willian (SD) San Diego, CA Nazareth House.
Wilt, George A. '59 (PIT) Mt. Lebanon, PA St. Bernard Church.
Wilt, John E. '57 (GBG) Seward, PA Holy Family Church.
Wiltgen, Ralph *s.v.d.* '50 (MIL) [P] East Troy, WI Divine Word Seminary.
Wilton, David M. *c.p.m.* '46 (OWN) [F] South Union, KY Fathers of Mercy.
Wiltz, George *s.j.* '65 (FWT) [J] Lake Dallas, TX Montserrat Jesuit Retreat House.
Wiltz, George F. *s.j.* '65 (NO) [C] New Orleans, LA Loyola University.
Wilus, Msgr. John M. '37 (TR) Retired.
Wilutis, John P. '51 (RVC) [N] Uniondale, NY St. Pius X Residence.
Wilutis, John P. '55 (RVC) Retired.
Wilwerding, Anthony P. '46 (OM) Retired.
Wilwerding, James '92 (DM) [J] Panora, IA St. Thomas More Center.
Wilz, John C. '64 (PH) [3] Phoenixville, PA St. Mary of the Assumption Church.
Wimett, Leo J. '60 (SY) North Bay, NY St. John Church.
Wimmer, Joseph F. *o.s.a.* '64 (PH) [C] Villanova, PA Villanova University.
Wimmer, Joseph F. *o.s.a.* '64 (WDC) [B] Silver Spring, MD Austin Friars Hall, Order of St. Augustine.
Wimsett, Scott J. (L) On Special Assignment.
Winance, Eleutherius *o.s.b.* '35 (LA) [R] Valyermo, CA St. Andrew's Abbey.
Winaski, William '76 (FWT) Wichita Falls, TX Our Lady Queen of Peace Church.
Winca, George F. '38 (Y) Retired.
Winca, Harry S. '45 (CLV) Middlefield, OH St. Lucy Church; Parkman, OH St. Edward Church.
Winchester, George P. *s.j.* '65 (BO) Boston, MA Brigham and Women's Hospital; [W] Boston, MA Jesuit Urban Center & Immaculate Conception Community.
Winczewski, Andrew *o.s.b.* '43 (SCL) [I] Collegeville, MN St. John's Abbey, of the Order of St. Benedict.
Wind, John F. '67 (DEN) Littleton, CO St. Mary Church.
Windbacher, Ambrose *o.p.* '54 (FgM) Dominican - Order of Preachers Foreign Missions.
Windbacher, Ambrose P. *o.p.* '54 (CHI) [N] Chicago, IL Dominicans (Provincial Office).
Windhaus, Edward A. '72 (PH) Hatfield, PA St. Maria Goretti Church.
Windholtz, Barry M. '88 (CIN) [54] Cincinnati, OH St. Louis Church.
Windhotz, Barry M. '88 (CIN) [S] Cincinnati, OH Archdiocesan Central Council of Cincinnati.
Windisch, Adolf M. *s.m.* '60 (CIN) [M] Dayton, OH Marianist Provincialate.
Windisch, Adolf M. *s.m.* '60 (STL) [P] St. Louis, MO Provincialate of the Society of Mary, Province of St. Louis.
Windle, John J. '43 (CHI) Retired.
Windle, Raymond L. *s.j.* '59 (STL) [P] St. Louis, MO Jesuit Community Corporation at St. Louis University - Jesuit Hall.
Windolph, George *o.f.m.* '48 (SFD) [B] Quincy, IL Quincy University.
Windolph, Joseph '48 (CHI) [N] Chicago, IL St. Peter's Friary.
Windolph, Michael *o.f.m.* '51 (CHI) Oak Forest, IL Oak Forest Hospital; [N] Oak Forest, IL St. Roch Friary-Franciscan Fathers.
Windolph, Nestor *o.f.m.* '55 (FgM) Franciscan Foreign Missions.
Windy, Jeff '96 (PEO) [B] Peoria, IL Notre Dame High School.
Windy, Jeffrey I. '96 (PEO) [10] Peoria, IL St. Mark's Church.
Winel, Msgr. Roland T. '39 (COL) Retired.
Wines, Frank (PT) Tiger Point, FL St. Sylvester Church.
Wing, Kenneth A. '59 (GR) Retired.
Wingate, Arthur K. '56 (FR) [I] Fall River, MA Catholic Memorial Home Inc.
Wingert, D. William '60 (SC) Retired.
Wingert, Gerald R. '47 (SC) Retired.
Wingert, La Vern '57 (DM) [J] Griswold, IA Wakonda Prayer House.
Wingfield, Harvey J. *o.s.b.* '81 (SEA) [M] Lacey, WA St. Martin's Abbey.
Winiarski, James *m.s.* '66 (MIL) [65] Milwaukee, WI St. Paul Church; [P] Milwaukee, WI La Salette Fathers.
Winkel, Thomas J. '71 (CLV) Bedford, OH St. Mary Church.
Winkelbauer, Phillip '75 (KCK) Baldwin, KS Annunciation Church; [3] Topeka, KS Holy Name Church.
Winkelbauer, Phillip J. '75 (KCK) Edgerton, KS Assumption of the Blessed Virgin Mary Church.
Winkels, Michael *o.p.* (CHI) [N] Oak Park, IL Dominican Community of St. Martin de Porres.
Winkels, Michael A. *o.p.* '76 (CHI) [N] Chicago, IL Dominicans (Provincial Office).
Winkels, Robert H. *m.m.* '41 (NY) [DD] Maryknoll, NY Maryknoll Fathers and Brothers.
Winkler, Daryold *c.s.b.* (LSC) [4] Las Cruces, NM St. Albert the Great Newman Parish.
Winkler, Daryold *c.s.b.* '97 (LSC) [B] Las Cruces, NM Basilian Fathers.
Winkler, Edward J. '86 (VIC) Eagle Lake, TX Parish of the Nativity Church.
Winkler, Eugene D. '50 (MIL) Lima, WI St. Rose Church; St. George, WI St. George Church; [W] Milwaukee, WI Council of Catholic Women.
Winkler, Jude *o.f.m.conv.* (BAL) [M] Ellicott City, MD St. Joseph Cupertino Friary, Friars Minor Conventual of St. Francis of Assisi.
Winkler, Kenneth H. '81 (RVC) Mineola, NY Corpus Christi Church.
Winkowski, Eugene R. '71 (CHI) [213] Chicago, IL St. Wenceslaus Church.
Winkowski, Michael J. *c.pp.s* '70 (FTW) Walkerton, IN St. Patrick Church.
Winne, George R. '83 (ALN) [9] Allentown, PA Sacred Heart of Jesus Church; [C] Allentown, PA Allentown Central Catholic High School.
Winnenberg, John O. '55 (WDC) Retired.
Winnikates, Thomas '70 (CHI) Flossmoor, IL Infant Jesus of Prague Church.
Winrich, Walter W. *m.m.* '50 (NY) [DD] Maryknoll, NY Maryknoll Fathers and Brothers.
Winshman, Alfred O. *s.j.* '65 (BO) [W] Boston, MA Loyola House.
Winston, William L. '86 (PAT) Morristown, NJ Assumption of the Blessed Virgin Mary Church.
Winter, Donald *c.ss.r.* '55 (RIC) [2] Hampton, VA St. Joseph Church.
Winter, Harry *o.m.i.* '64 (WDC) [B] Washington, DC Oblate College/Oblate Center for Mission Studies.
Winterer, Michael J. '60 (SLC) Cedar City, UT Christ the King Church.
Wintergalen, Edward H. *s.j.* '37 (STL) [O] St. Louis, MO Fusz Pavilion.
Winterlin, John R. '68 (GRY) [2] Hammond, IN Our Lady of Perpetual Help Church.
Wintermeyer, John S. '62 (WDC) [S] Washington, DC Archdiocesan Campus Ministry.
Wintermeyer, William P. '49 (CIN) Retired.
Wintermyer, John S. '62 (WDC) [13] Washington, DC St. Francis de Sales Church; Washington, DC Washington Hospital Center; Hospital & Nursing Home Ministries.
Winter, Pius *o.f.m.* (CIN) [L] Cincinnati, OH St. Margaret Hall.
Winters, Alfred H. '62 (CLV) [1] Lakewood, OH St. Clement Church.
Winters, Arthur *s.v.d.* '45 (BLX) [A] Bay St. Louis, MS St. Augustine's.
Winters, Bartholomew S. *m. div.* '83 (CHI) [A] Mundelein, IL University of St. Mary of the Lake-Mundelein Seminary.
Winters, Daniel *s.m.* '63 (CIN) [M] Cincinnati, OH Marianist Community.
Winters, Francis X. *s.j.* '64 (BAL) [M] Baltimore, MD Jesuit Fathers and Brothers Maryland Provincial Curia.
Winters, Martin N. '52 (CHI) Retired; [O] Oak Forest, IL Our Lady of Sorrows Priory, Benedictine Sisters of Pontifical Jurisdiction.
Winters, Richard *s.v.d.* '41 (SB) [A] Riverside, CA Divine Word Seminary.
Winters, Sean G. '87 (MET) Bridgewater, NJ Holy Trinity Church; Somerville, NJ Somerset Medical Center.

Winters, Vaughn '93 (LA) [2] North Hollywood, CA St. Charles Borromeo Church.
Winters, William *o.f.m.cap.* '64 (RVC) East Patchogue, NY St. Joseph the Worker Church.
Wintz, Jack R. *o.f.m.* '63 (CIN) [M] Cincinnati, OH Pleasant Street Friary.
Winzenburg, George E. *s.j.* '74 (MIL) [29] Milwaukee, WI Gesu Parish.
Winzerling, James L. '61 (STL) St. Louis, MO Christian Hospital Northeast-Northwest.
Wiorkiewicz, Marek *s.d.s.* '89 (GRY) [J] Merrillville, IN Salvatorian Fathers (Society of the Divine Savior).
Wippel, Msgr. John '60 (STU) On Duty Outside the Diocese.
Wippel, Msgr. John '60 (WDC) [C] Washington, DC Catholic University of America, The.
Wirkes, Stephen E. '80 (SY) Mexico, NY St. Mary, Star of the Sea Church.
Wironen, John B. *c.s.c.* '79 (P) [13] Portland, OR St. Elizabeth of Hungary Church; Portland, OR Oregon Health Sciences University.
Wirth, Geoffrey '67 (RCK) Crystal Lake, IL St. Thomas the Apostle Church.
Wirth, Jerry E. '68 (BEL) Olney, IL St. Joseph Church.
Wirth, John J. '52 (STP) Retired.
Wirth, Richard P. '56 (STP) [35] St. Paul, MN St. Thomas The Apostle Church.
Wirth, Robert *c.ss.r.* '64 (CHI) [N] Chicago, IL Redemptorists:.
Wirth, Robert *c.ss.r.* '64 (DEN) [M] Denver, CO The Redemptorists/Denver Province.
Wirth, Robert *c.ss.r.* '64 (FgM) Redemptorist Foreign Missions.
Wischmeyer, Amos H. '51 (LAN) Swartz Creek, MI St. Mary Church.
Wise, Carl A. *c.pp.s.* '56 (CIN) Montezuma, OH Our Lady of Guadalupe Church.
Wise, Joseph *c.r.* '41 (CHI) [88] Chicago, IL St. Hyacinth Church.
Wise, Kenneth F. '47 (COL) Dennison, OH Immaculate Conception Church; Retired.
Wise, Marcos *c.ss.r.* '72 (CGS) [B] Aguas Buenas, PR Casa Cristo Redentor.
Wise, Neal *o.p.* '67 (AUS) [H] Austin, TX Dominican Fathers.
Wise, Paul C. '74 (CAM) [5] Atlantic City, NJ Our Lady Star of the Sea Church.
Wise, Richard P. '81 (ATL) Decatur, GA Sts. Peter and Paul Church.
Wise, Thomas F. *c.s.v.* '56 (SFD) Granite City, IL Holy Family Church.
Wiseman, James A. *o.s.b.* '70 (WDC) [C] Washington, DC Catholic University of America, The; [M] Washington, DC St. Anselm's Abbey.
Wiseman, Joseph '52 (BRK) Retired.
Wiseman, Joseph F. '52 (BRK) [197] Queens, NY Mary's Nativity Church.
Wiseman, Robert *c.s.c.* '77 (ORL) Winter Park, FL St. Margaret Mary Church.
Wiseman, Robert A., C.S.C. '77 (ORL) [E] Winter Park, FL Rollins College Campus Ministry.
Wiseman, Thomas '41 (P) Retired.
Wiseman, Vincent *o.p.* '71 (WDC) [B] Washington, DC Dominican House of Studies.
Wishard, John W. '62 (LA) Retired.
Wiskirchen, George C. *c.s.c.* '55 (FTW) [B] Notre Dame, IN University of Notre Dame Du Lac; [J] Notre Dame, IN Holy Cross Community, Corby Hall, University of Notre Dame.
Wisner, John H. '72 (KCK) Roeland Park, KS St. Agnes Church.
Wisneske, S. Patrick '50 (MAR) Menominee, MI Holy Spirit Church.
Wisneski, Edward '67 (NOR) Retired.
Wisneski, John A. '57 (LC) Blenker, WI St. Kilian Church; Junction City, WI St. Michael Church; Milladore, WI St. Wenceslaus Church.
Wisneski, John J. '64 (GR) [5] Grand Rapids, MI Blessed Sacrament Church.
Wisniefski, Robert W. '80 (PAT) [9] Paterson, NJ St. Joseph's Church.
Wisniewski, David '81 (OG) Glenfield, NY St. Mary Church; Houseville, NY St. Hedwig Church; Lowville, NY St. Peter Church.
Wisniewski, Joseph *c.m.* '65 (BRK) [134] Brooklyn, NY St. Stanislaus Kostka Church.
Wisniewski, Robert W. '89 (CLV) [1] Barberton, OH St. Augustine Church.
Wisniewski, Stanley T. *s.j.* '64 (RNO) Fallon, NV St. Patrick Church.
Wisniewski, Theodore '47 (BAL) Retired.
Wisniewski, Theodore M. '47 (BAL) [Q] Baltimore, MD Johns Hopkins Hospital Apostolate.
Wisniewski, Thomas '76 (MIA) Parkland, FL Mary Help of Christians Church.
Wisniewski, Thomas '80 (NEW) Maplewood, NJ St. Joseph's Church.
Wisniewski, Thomas J. '74 (PH) Penn Valley, PA St. Justin Martyr Church.
Wissel, Msgr. Francis C. '77 (BGP) [T] Bridgeport, CT St. Peter's Parish, St. Maximillian Kolbe House of Studies.
Wissel, Msgr. Frank C. *d.min.* (BGP) [1] Greenwich, CT St. Mary's Church.
Wissler, Thomas J. '83 (STL) Farmington, MO St. Joseph Church.
Wissman, J. Patrick '64 (SPC) Scott City, MO St. Joseph Church.
Wister, Msgr. Robert J. '68 (NEW) [A] South Orange, NJ Immaculate Conception Seminary; [B] South Orange, NJ Seton Hall University.
Wisz, Dominic *o.f.m.conv.* '47 (RCK) [2] Rockford, IL St. Anthony of Padua Church.
Witalec, Dennis J. '82 (PH) [78] Philadelphia, PA St. John Cantius Church.
Witcoskie, Stanley '93 (CAM) Wildwood, NJ St. Ann's Church.
Witczak, Msgr. Edward '60 (GB) Absent on Leave.
Witczak, Michael G. '77 (MIL) [A] Milwaukee, WI St. Francis Seminary.
Witek, John W. *s.j.* '65 (WDC) [M] Washington, DC The Jesuit Community at Georgetown University.
Witek, Stanley '87 (GRY) [13] East Chicago, IN St. Stanislaus Church.
With, William A. '72 (BRK) [214] Queens, NY Our Lady of Mercy Church.
Withers, Mark *c.s.j.* '79 (CLV) [D] Lorain, OH Lorain Catholic High School; [P] Avon, OH Congregation of St. Joseph.
Witherup, Ronald D. *s.s.* '76 (BAL) [M] Baltimore, MD Sulpician Provincial House.
Witherup, Ronald D. *s.s.* '76 (SFR) [A] Menlo Park, CA St. Patrick Seminary.
Withrow, Justin *o.s.b.* '90 (GBG) Greensburg, PA Westmoreland Hospital; Latrobe, PA Latrobe Area Hospital; Jeannette, PA Jeannette District Memorial Hospital; Jeannette, PA Monsour Medical Center; [H] Latrobe, PA Saint Vincent Archabbey.
Witkowski, Msgr. Bernard E. '62 (PH) [78] Philadelphia, PA St. John Cantius Church.
Witkowski, Phillip J. '75 (GR) [7] Muskegon, MI St. Thomas the Apostle Church.
Witkowski, Raymond A. '42 (MIL) Retired.
Witkowski, Robert J. '61 (DET) [5] Warren, MI St. Edmund Church.
Witmer, Joseph W. '67 (Y) Aurora, OH Our Lady of Perpetual Help Church.
Witon, Russell F. '63 (MIL) [N] Milwaukee, WI St. Anne's Home for the Elderly.
Witsken, Gary J. '69 (CIN) [87] Cincinnati, OH St. Vincent de Paul Church.
Witt, Christopher P. *c.s.p.* '79 (NY) [DD] Jamaica Estates, NY Paulist Fathers Generalate.
Witt, Edward G. *s.j.* '91 (MIL) [E] Milwaukee, WI Marquette University High School; [P] Milwaukee, WI Pere Marquette House Jesuit Community.
Witt, Michael J. '90 (STL) [8] St. Louis, MO Most Blessed Sacrament Church.
Witt, Paul K. '71 (LIN) [8] Lincoln, NE St. Mary Church.
Witt, Robert G. '50 (COV) Retired.
Witt, William '49 (Y) Retired.
Wittbrod, Joseph *o.c.s.o.* '49 (SAC) [A] Vina, CA Abbey of New Clairvaux, Trappist Seminary.
Wittbrod, Joseph J. *o.c.s.o.* '49 (SAC) [G] Vina, CA Abbey of New Clairvaux, Trappist.
Witte, Clarence J. *m.m.* '35 (FgM) Maryknoll Foreign Missions.
Witte, D. Steven '92 (BEL) Coulterville, IL St. Anthony Church; Lively Grove, IL St. Anthony Church.
Witte, Msgr. John C. '45 (GRY) Retired.
Witte, Mark '95 (COV) [C] Covington, KY Academy of Notre Dame.
Witte, Mark G. '95 (COV) Fort Mitchell, KY Blessed Sacrament Church.
Wittemann, Paul J. '56 (MIL) Retired.
Wittenbrink, Boniface *o.m.i.* '41 (BEL) [F] Belleville, IL Shrine of Our Lady of the Snows.
Witterholt, Herbert M. '40 (BRK) Retired.
Witthauer, Paul G. '60 (BAL) [70] Baltimore, MD Our Lady of Hope Church.
Witting, Martin *o.s.b.* '51 (RCK) [H] Aurora, IL Marmion Abbey-St. Augustine's Abbey.
Wittliff, Thomas F. '64 (MIL) [9] Milwaukee, WI St. Augustine Church.
Wittman, Christopher *s.m.* (CIN) [E] Dayton, OH Chaminade-Julienne High School.
Wittman, Karl M. '46 (STP) [20] St. Paul, MN St. Francis De Sales Church; Retired.
Wittman, Michael A. '88 (CLV) Litchfield, OH Our Lady Help of Christians Parish.
Wittman, Peter C. '75 (STP) Savage, MN St. John the Baptist Church.
Wittmann, Christopher T. *s.m.* '94 (CIN) [M] Dayton, OH Marianist Provincialate.
Wittosch, Paul '75 (JOL) Rockdale, IL St. Joseph Church.
Wittouck, Frank *s.c.j.* '65 (GAL) [27] Houston, TX St. Elizabeth Ann Seton Church.
Wittreich, John A. '47 (CLV) Norton, OH St. Andrew the Apostle Church; Retired.
Wittrock, Daniel L. '94 (OM) [38] Omaha, NE St. Pius X Church.
Wittstock, John J. '36 (DET) Retired.
Wittstock, Joseph *o.c.s.o.* '84 (ARL) [J] Berryville, VA Cistercian Abbey of Our Lady of the Holy Cross.
Witz, Dennis M. '76 (MIL) [42] Milwaukee, WI Immaculate Conception Church.
Witzemann, B. Gerald '61 (COV) Taylor Mill, KY St. Patrick Church.
Witzmann, Hugh *o.s.b.* '55 (SCL) [I] Collegeville, MN St. John's Abbey, of the Order of St. Benedict.
Wixted, Matthew O. '62 (SLC) Tooele, UT St. Marguerite's Church.
Wleczyk, Msgr. Leo '65 (GAL) Lake Jackson, TX St. Michael Church.
Wlodyka, Stanley *o.f.m.conv.* '41 (BO) [5] Haverhill, MA St. Michael Church.
Wodarski, Msgr. John P. *s.t.d.* '31 (HRT) [5] Bristol, CT St. Stanislaus Church; Retired.
Wodniak, John L. '43 (CHI) [98] Chicago, IL St. James Church; Retired.
Wodziak, Michael '48 (RVC) Retired.
Woefl, Paul A. *s.j.* '44 (TOL) [6] Toledo, OH Gesu Church.
Woempner, Michael A. '79 (MAR) White Pine, MI St. Jude Church.
Woerth, Thomas J. '66 (DEN) Denver, CO Veterans Hospital.
Wohinc, Karl R. '63 (WH) Shinnston, WV St. Ann's Church.
Wohler, Gil *o.f.m.* '62 (FgM) Franciscan Foreign Missions.
Wohlfeil, Steve (SFS) [I] Sioux Falls, SD St. Francis House.
Wohlrab, Paul G. '41 (ROC) Spencerport, NY St. John the Evangelist Church; Retired; [L] Spencerport, NY Legion of Mary.
Wohlwend, Paul W. *c.pp.s.* '54 (CIN) Fort Recovery, OH Mary Help of Christians Church.
Wohman, Andrew B. *c.s.c.* '44 (FTW) [J] South Bend, IN Congregation of Holy Cross Indiana Province Provincial House.
Wojcicki, Miroslaus A. '62 (PIT) East Pittsburgh, PA Holy Cross Church.
Wojcicki, Msgr. Ted L. '75 (STL) [62] St. Louis, MO St. Stanislaus Kostka Church.
Wojcicki, Wojciech '90 (DET) Hamtramck, MI Our Lady Queen of Apostles Church.
Wojciechowski, Christian *o.f.m.conv.* '53 (TR) [22] Trenton, NJ St. Stanislaus Church.
Wojciechowski, Edward C. '81 (PRM) Minneapolis, MN St. John the Baptist Church.
Wojciechowski, Richard P. '63 (BAL) [23] Baltimore, MD Christ the King Church.
Wojciechowski, Robert J. '83 (DET) [22] Detroit, MI St. Francis D'Assisi Church.
Wojciechowski, Thomas *o.f.m.* '75 (GB) [H] Manitowoc, WI St. Mary's Home for the Aged; [I] Pulaski, WI Assumption of B.V.M. Friary.
Wojciehowski, Msgr. Thaddeus J. '36 (TR) Retired.
Wojciehowski, Msgr. Thaddeus J. '42 (TR) [M] Trenton, NJ Villa Vianney.
Wojcik, Eugene J. '74 (BEL) Tipton, IL St. Patrick Church.
Wojcik, Joseph J. '69 (CHI) Westchester, IL Divine Providence Church.
Wojcik, Richard J. (CHI) Retired.
Wojcik, Richard J. '49 (CHI) [A] Mundelein, IL University of St. Mary of the Lake-Mundelein Seminary.
Wojcinski, Anthony A. '85 (PBL) [1] Pueblo, CO Sacred Heart Cathedral.
Wojnicki, Richard J. *o.s.f.s.* '85 (VEN) [3] Fort Myers, FL St. Cecilia Church.
Wojtewicz, Eugene E. '57 (DET) Southgate, MI St. Hugh Church.
Wojtowicz, Edward L. '44 (NU) Retired.
Wojtowicz, John E. *o.f.m.* '80 (CHI) [N] Chicago, IL Holy Name Friary.
Wojtunik, Henry *m.s.* '60 (MIL) [P] Twin Lakes, WI La Salette Missionaries Shrine.
Wojtus, Anthony '58 (WH) Retired.
Wojtycha, Msgr. Edward F. '38 (NEW) [2] Bayonne, NJ St. Andrew's Church; Retired.
Wolak, Edmund '92 (SY) [7] Oswego, NY St. Stephen the King Church.
Wolan, Stephen J. '58 (WH) Retired.
Wolanski, Edward *c.p.* '72 (WOR) [N] Shrewsbury, MA Passionist Fathers of Shrewsbury, Inc., Calvary Retreat Center; [P] Shrewsbury, MA Calvary Retreat Center, Passionist Community.
Wolbach, Richard A. '56 (OM) Retired.
Wolbang, Charles A. *c.m.* '41 (MET) [H] Plainsboro, NJ Vincentian Residence.
Wolber, Ferdinand A. '40 (DET) Retired.
Wolbert, John R. '74 (CIN) Owensville, OH St. Louis Church; Stonelick, OH St. Philomena Church.
Wolensky, Paul '94 (STF) Brooklyn, NY Holy Ghost Church.
Wolesky, John '67 (SAL) [3] Salina, KS St. Mary's Church.

Wolf, Adam *o.f.m.* (CHI) Oak Forest, IL Oak Forest Hospital.
Wolf, Anthony J. '96 (LC) [1] La Crosse, WI St. Joseph the Workman Cathedral.
Wolf, Charles E. *s.j.* (BAL) [M] Baltimore, MD Jesuit Fathers and Brothers Maryland Provincial Curia.
Wolf, Charles E. *s.j.* '46 (FgM) Provinces.
Wolf, Charles E. *s.j.* '49 (FgM) Provinces.
Wolf, David *o.s.b.* '52 (BIS) [A] Richardton, ND Assumption Abbey.
Wolf, Dennis G. '72 (BUF) Wellsville, NY Immaculate Conception Church.
Wolf, Don '81 (OKL) Special Assignment.
Wolf, Eugene *o.f.m.cap.* '54 (MIL) [P] Mount Calvary, WI St. Lawrence Friary.
Wolf, Eugene J. '63 (LC) Seneca, WI St. Patrick Church; Wauzeka, WI Sacred Heart Church.
Wolf, George *o.s.b.* '44 (FgM) American - Cassinese Congregation Foreign Missions.
Wolf, George '44 (SCL) [I] Collegeville, MN St. John's Abbey, of the Order of St. Benedict.
Wolf, George '80 (P) Salem, OR Queen of Peace Church.
Wolf, George C. '63 (RNO) Sparks, NV Holy Cross Catholic Community Church.
Wolf, James '48 (SFS) Retired.
Wolf, James *o.f.m.cap.* '57 (DET) [K] Detroit, MI St. Bonaventure Friary; [K] Detroit, MI St. Bonaventure Friary.
Wolf, Msgr. James J. (FTW) [H] Fort Wayne, IN St. Anne Home of the Diocese of Fort Wayne - South Bend.
Wolf, Msgr. James J. '69 (FTW) [1] Fort Wayne, IN Cathedral of the Immaculate Conception.
Wolf, John *c.pp.s.* '69 (KC) [8] Kansas City, MO St. Charles Borromeo Church.
Wolf, Msgr. John V. '45 (COL) Retired.
Wolf, John W. '38 (CLV) Chagrin Falls, OH St. Joan of Arc Church; Retired.
Wolf, Joseph *o.f.m.cap.* '64 (FgM) Capuchin Foreign Missions.
Wolf, Joseph '94 (DAV) Blue Grass, IA St. Andrew Church.
Wolf, Joseph A. '68 (MIL) [58] Milwaukee, WI Our Lady of Good Hope Church.
Wolf, Joseph B. '54 (STL) Retired.
Wolf, Joseph D. '87 (BUF) [3] Orchard Park, NY Our Lady of the Sacred Heart Church.
Wolf, Joseph M. '94 (DAV) [4] Davenport, IA St. Alphonsus Church.
Wolf, Lawrence *o.s.b.m.* '75 (PSC) Roebling, NJ St. Nicholas Church.
Wolf, Lawrence Robert *o.s.b.m.* '75 (PSC) [A] Matawan, NJ Basilian Fathers of Mariapoch.
Wolf, Michael H. '42 (SAG) Essexville, MI St. John the Evangelist Church; Retired.
Wolf, Msgr. Michael O.J. '38 (EVN) [1] Evansville, IN Pro-Cathedral of the Most Holy Trinity.
Wolf, Norbert K. '47 (E) Wilcox, PA St. Anne Church.
Wolf, Paul L. '83 (NU) Seaforth, MN St. Mary Church; Wabasso, MN St. Anne Church; Wabasso, MN St. Anne Church.
Wolf, Peter (BO) [6] Newton, MA Our Lady Help of Christians Church.
Wolf, Robert J. '44 (MIL) Retired.
Wolf, Ronald D. *s.j.* '74 (SJ) [M] Los Gatos, CA Sacred Heart Jesuit Center.
Wolf, Stephen J. '97 (NSH) [1] Nashville, TN Cathedral of the Incarnation.
Wolf, Werner *o.f.m.cap.* '58 (GB) [M] Appleton, WI Monte Alverno Retreat Center.
Wolfe, Allan F. (HBG) [3] Lancaster, PA Assumption of the Blessed Virgin Mary Church; [J] Lancaster, PA Iglesia de San Juan Bautista.
Wolfe, James T. '55 (ROC) Avon, NY St. Agnes Church.
Wolfe, Joseph M. *m.f.v.a.* '93 (BIR) [E] Birmingham, AL Franciscan Missionaries of the Eternal Word, A Public Association of the Christian Faithful.
Wolfe, Robert *o.carm.* '75 (NEW) Bogota, NJ St. Joseph's Church.
Wolfe, William P. '70 (LA) La Mirada, CA St. Paul of the Cross Church.
Wolfel, Daniel C. *o.s.b.* '54 (ALT) Summerhill, PA St. John Church.
Wolfer, Paul J. '45 (CIN) [68] Cincinnati, OH Our Lady of Lourdes Church; Retired.
Wolfer, Robert R. '48 (CIN) [68] Cincinnati, OH Our Lady of Lourdes Church; Retired.
Wolff, Alec J. '81 (CHI) Highland Park, IL Immaculate Conception Church; [X] Wilmette, IL Musica Pacis.
Wolff, Msgr. Robert C. '50 (CLV) Copley, OH Guardian Angels Church; Retired.
Wolfgram, Daniel '97 (SFS) Awaiting Assignment.
Wolford, Charles '80 (OWN) Retired.
Wolford, Donald L. '79 (SFD) [3] Decatur, IL St. Patrick Church.
Wolfram, Frank A. *s.d.b.* '62 (NY) [FF] West Haverstraw, NY Don Bosco Retreat Center and Marian Shrine.
Wolfram, Frank R. *s.d.b.* '62 (NY) [FF] West Haverstraw, NY Marian Shrine.
Wolken, Gary P. '93 (STL) [3] University City, MO Our Lady of Lourdes Church.
Wolken, Louis J. *m.m.* '46 (FgM) Maryknoll Foreign Missions.
Wolkovich, William L. '53 (BO) [2] Norwood, MA St. George Church.
Wolkovits, Paul D. '93 (LA) Panorama City, CA St. Genevieve Church.
Woll, Peter J. '44 (CLV) [31] Cleveland, OH Holy Trinity - St. Edward Church; [5] Euclid, OH St. Robert Bellarmine Church; Retired.
Wollering, Carl J. '66 (CIN) [32] Cincinnati, OH Guardian Angels Church; [42] Cincinnati, OH St. Jerome Church.
Wollersheim, David '77 (GLP) Absent on Leave.
Wollesen, Charles A. *s.j.* '52 (P) [L] Portland, OR Colombiere Community.
Wollet, George H. '32 (MIL) Retired.
Wollmering, Bruce *o.s.b.* '67 (SCL) [I] Collegeville, MN St. John's Abbey, of the Order of St. Benedict.
Wolnowski, Kenneth J. '65 (CLV) [10] Lorain, OH St. Peter Church.
Woloszczuk, Wolodymyr '81 (SJP) Retired.
Woloszyk, Ignatius J. '38 (SAG) Retired.
Wolsin, Msgr. Carl J. '45 (PAT) Retired; [P] Chester, NJ Nazareth Village.
Wolski, Adalbert *t.o.r.* '59 (ALT) [F] Hollidaysburg, PA St. Joseph Friary.
Wolski, Mark J. '67 (BUF) [38] Buffalo, NY St. John the Evangelist Church.
Wolter, Alan *o.f.m.* (BUF) [C] St. Bonaventure, NY St. Bonaventure University.
Wolter, Allan *o.f.m.* '40 (BUF) [O] St. Bonaventure, NY St. Bonaventure Friary.
Wolter, Allan *o.f.m.* '40 (LA) [R] Santa Barbara, CA Franciscan Friary, Order of Friars Minor (Old Mission).
Wolter, Allan *o.f.m.* '40 (STL) [P] St. Louis, MO Franciscan Friary of St. Anthony of Padua.
Wolter, Martin *o.f.m.* '46 (STL) [P] St. Louis, MO Franciscan Friary of St. Anthony of Padua.
Wolter, Richard J. '59 (STP) Centerville, MN St. Genevieve Church.
Wolter, Thomas '66 (JOL) Elmhurst, IL Mary, Queen of Heaven Church; Elmhurst, IL Elmhurst Memorial Hospital.
Wolters, Gilbert *o.s.b.* '34 (KCK) [H] Atchison, KS St. Benedict's Abbey.
Wolverton, R. Ambrose *o.s.b.* '65 (PRO) [P] Portsmouth, RI Abbey of St. Gregory the Great.
Womack, Emil *c.p.* '44 (DET) [K] Detroit, MI St. Paul of the Cross Community, Congregation of the Passion.
Womack, Warren *c.p.* '49 (CHI) [N] Chicago, IL Passionist Provincial Office.
Womack, Warren *c.p.* '49 (FgM) Mission Procurators.
Won, Msgr. John P. '58 (LA) West Covina, CA St. Christopher Church.
Wondolowski, Robert '76 (WOR) Absent on Leave.
Wong, George *s.j.* '51 (SJ) [M] Los Gatos, CA Sacred Heart Jesuit Center.
Wong, Maurice *s.j.* '67 (BGP) [A] Fairfield, CT Fairfield University; [O] Fairfield, CT The Fairfield Jesuit Community-Fairfield University.
Wong, Victor '50 (WDC) [5] Washington, DC St. Anthony Church.
Woo, Henry *s.d.b.* '93 (OAK) [N] Berkeley, CA Salesian Community.
Wood, Bruce Michael '84 (BUR) Brattleboro, VT St. Michael Church.
Wood, Dennis '68 (SEA) Medical Leave.
Wood, Drew '73 (GAL) [A] Houston, TX St. Mary's Seminary.
Wood, Edson J. *o.s.a.* '72 (NY) West Point, NY Catholic Chapel of the Most Holy Trinity Church.
Wood, Edson J. *o.s.a.* '72 (PH) [C] Villanova, PA Villanova University.
Wood, Gregg D. *s.j.* '75 (FBK) Chevak, AK Sacred Heart Church; Scammon Bay, AK Blessed Sacrament Church; [E] St. Marys, AK Brother Joe Prince Jesuit Community.
Wood, Gregg D. *s.j.* '95 (FBK) Hooper Bay, AK Little Flower of Jesus Church.
Wood, James L. '72 (RVC) Bohemia, NY St. John Nepomucene Church.
Wood, John M. '83 (SY) [1] Rome, NY St. John the Baptist Church.
Wood, Kenneth E. '89 (RIC) Harrisonburg, VA Blessed Sacrament Church.
Wood, Mark '87 (LR) Fayetteville, AR St. Joseph's Church; Fayetteville, AR St. Thomas Aquinas University Parish; [J] Little Rock, AR Catholic Campus Ministries.
Wood, Michael Bruce '84 (AMA) On Duty Outside the Diocese.
Wood, Norbert G. *o.praem.* '81 (ORG) [H] Silverado, CA Norbertine Fathers of Orange Inc.
Wood, Paul (BRK) [E] Brooklyn, NY Office of Religious Education: Evangelization and Catholic Formation.
Wood, Paul A. '80 (BRK) [189] Queens, NY St. Kevin Church.
Wood, Paul F. '58 (BRK) Absent on Leave.
Wood, Peter N. '82 (PT) On Leave of Absence.
Wood, Raymond B. '64 (SY) Jamesville, NY St. Mary Church.
Wood, Robert *c.m.* '56 (FgM) Vincentian Foreign Missions.
Wood, Robert J. '44 (NOR) Retired.
Wood, Robert T. '87 (OKL) [16] Oklahoma City, OK St. Philip Neri Church.
Wood, Robert W. '74 (BUF) Elma, NY Annunciation of the Blessed Virgin Mary Church.
Wood, Simon *c.p.* '43 (BAL) [M] Baltimore, MD St. Joseph's Passionist Community.
Wood, William J. *s.j.* '65 (SFR) [N] San Francisco, CA Jesuit Community at University of San Francisco.
Wood, William T. *s.j.* '48 (FgM) Jesuit Foreign Missions.
Wood, William T. *s.j.* '48 (NY) [DD] New York, NY Jesuit Provincial's Office; [DD] New York, NY St. Ignatius Loyola Residence; [HH] New York, NY Catholic Medical Mission Board, Inc.
Woodarek, Richard *c.s.s.* '57 (BO) [W] Waltham, MA Stigmatine Fathers & Brothers Provincial House.
Woodcock, Michael '73 (PMB) Royal Palm Beach, FL Our Lady Queen of the Apostles Church.
Woodeshick, Martin E. '69 (PH) Sharon Hill, PA Holy Spirit Church.
Woodka, Raymond A. *s.s.j.* '66 (BR) New Roads, LA St. Augustine Church.
Woodland, Stephen '88 (LA) Compton, CA St. Albert the Great Church.
Woodman, Gerald '78 (SEA) Renton, WA St. Anthony's Church.
Woodruff, Mark '72 (SAN) [3] Odessa, TX St. Elizabeth Ann Seton Church.
Woodruff, William F. '82 (NY) Mahopac, NY St. John the Evangelist Church.
Woods, Curtis '80 (SHP) [8] Shreveport, LA St. Joseph Church.
Woods, Msgr. Earl C. '57 (NO) Retired.
Woods, James A. *s.j.* '61 (BO) [C] Chestnut Hill, MA Boston College. [W] Chestnut Hill, MA The Jesuit Community at Boston College.
Woods, Joseph E. *o.s.f.s.* '44 (WIL) [I] Childs, MD Oblates of St. Francis De Sales.
Woods, Keith A. '95 (WDC) La Plata, MD Sacred Heart Church.
Woods, Lawrence H. '56 (KAL) Retired.
Woods, Michael A. '66 (ATL) On Duty Outside the Archdiocese.
Woods, Michael A. '66 (KNX) Oak Ridge, TN St. Mary Church.
Woods, Patrick F. *c.ss.r.* '75 (BRK) [U] Brooklyn, NY Our Lady of Good Counsel Residence.
Woods, Randall *s.t.* '67 (WDC) [M] University Park, MD Holy Trinity Missionary Cenacle.
Woods, Richard J. *o.p.* '69 (CHI) [N] Chicago, IL Dominicans (Provincial Office).
Woods, Walter J. '69 (BO) [A] Boston, MA St. John's Seminary School of Theology.
Woods, Warren L. '50 (SFR) [34] San Francisco, CA St. Monica Church.
Woodward, John B. *s.j.* '58 (WDC) [E] Washington, DC Gonzaga College High School.
Woolever, James '74 (SY) On Duty Outside the Diocese.
Woollett, D. Mathew '82 (ALX) Cottonport, LA St. Mary Assumption Church.
Woolsey, Msgr. John G. '65 (NY) [60] New York, NY St. John the Martyr Church; [190] Bronx, NY St. Theresa of the Infant Jesus Church.
Woolson, Herbert *c.pp.s.* '82 (LFT) Winamac, IN St. Peter Church.
Woolway, John S. '80 (LA) Los Nietos, CA Our Lady of Perpetual Help Church.
Woost, David G. (CLV) [D] Mentor, OH Lake Catholic High.
Woost, David G. '91 (CLV) Concord Twp., OH St. Gabriel Church.
Woost, Michael G. '84 (CLV) Graduate Studies.
Woost, Thomas G. '97 (CLV) Cuyahoga Falls, OH Immaculate Heart of Mary Church.
Wooton, Jerry A. '96 (ARL) Leesburg, VA St. John the Apostle Church.
Wopperer, Thomas J. '64 (BUF) [4] Dunkirk, NY St. Elizabeth Ann Seton Church.
Worcester, Thomas W. *s.j.* '91 (WOR) [N] Worcester, MA Jesuits of Holy Cross College, Inc.
Worch, Donald P. '67 (WDC) Derwood, MD St. Francis of Assisi Church.
Worczak, Paul F. '68 (OG) Norwood, NY St. Andrew Church.
Wordekemper, Thomas *o.s.b.* '94 (BIS) [A] Richardton, ND Assumption Abbey.
Wordeman, John J. '57 (LEX) Ashland, KY Holy Family Church.
Worm, Paul F. '88 (LR) [9] Little Rock, AR St. Mary Church; [12] Little Rock, AR St. Patrick's Church.
Worman, Jeremiah F. '67 (GB) Antigo, WI St. Mary Church; Neva, WI St. Wenceslaus Church.
Wormek, Joseph E. '76 (STL) Manchester, MO Christ, Prince of Peace Church.
Worn, G. Peter '77 (SY) Special Assignment; [V] Oswego, NY Newman Foundation, Inc., State University of New York.

Worner, William H. '45 (SFR) Special Assignment; Retired.
Woroniewicz, Michael A. '85 (DET) Royal Oak, MI St. Mary Church.
Worry, Benedict *o.s.b.* (NEW) [1] Linden, NJ St. Elizabeth's Church.
Worry, Benedict Michael *o.s.b.* '87 (PAT) [M] Morristown, NJ St. Mary's Abbey.
Worschak, George D. '78 (PHU) Absent on Leave.
Worsley, Stephen C. '84 (R) Ahoskie, NC St. Charles Borromeo Church.
Worster, John '87 (B) Soda Springs, ID St. Mary's Church.
Worthy, Donald '62 (DET) [H] Pontiac, MI St. Joseph Mercy - Oakland.
Wortmann, Edgar J. '48 (OM) [10] Omaha, NE Blessed Sacrament Church.
Wortmann, Joseph F. '58 (NEW) [B] South Orange, NJ Seton Hall University; [C] West Orange, NJ Seton Hall Preparatory School.
Worzalla, Dennis '50 (GB) Retired.
Worzalla, Dennis A. '50 (LC) [4] Stevens Point, WI St. Peter Church.
Wosman, Richard *s.m.* '92 (STL) [F] Kirkwood, MO Vianney High School.
Woster, Msgr. Michael '82 (RC) [D] Rapid City, SD Priest Retirement and Aid Association.
Wotelko, Matthew S. *o.s.b.* '67 (NEW) [N] Newark, NJ Newark Abbey.
Woulfe, Cornelius C. *c.s.sp.* '44 (NY) [4] Kingston, NY St. Mary Church; Kingston, NY Kingston City Hospital.
Woy, Richard '79 (BAL) Special Assignment.
Woytek, Robert '91 (PSC) Swoyersville, PA St. Nicholas Church.
Woytyna, Chistopher *o.s.b.m.* '61 (STF) Long Island City, NY Holy Cross Church; [E] New York, NY Provincialate of Basilian Fathers.
Wozniak, Aloysius (LC) Cashton, WI Sacred Heart of Jesus Church.
Wozniak, Aloysius A. '52 (LC) Retired.
Wozniak, Anthony A. '59 (GBG) Fairchance, PA SS. Cyril and Methodius Church.
Wozniak, Casimir J. '68 (E) [B] Erie, PA Gannon University.
Wozniak, James E. '97 (GRY) Schererville, IN St. Michael Church.
Wozniak, Msgr. Louis J. '51 (AUS) Georgetown, TX St. Helen's Church.
Wozniak, Richard *c.m.f.* '52 (ORG) [2] Orange, CA La Purisima Church.
Wozniak, Robert A. '88 (BUF) [4] Cheektowaga, NY St. Josaphat Church.
Wozniak, Ronald E. *s.j.* '77 (BO) [W] Boston, MA The Society of Jesus of New England-Provincial Offices.
Wozniak, Timothy J. '74 (STP) St. Paul Park, MN St. Thomas Aquinas Church.
Wozniczka, Stephen Z. *o.s.p.p.e.* '60 (PH) [AA] Doylestown, PA Pauline Fathers Monastery, Shrine of Our Lady of Czestochowa.
Wozny, William J. '48 (CHI) Retired.
Wraszczak, Chester '43 (P) Retired.
Wray, Joseph M. '96 (OM) [1] Omaha, NE St. Cecilia's Cathedral.
Wreisner, Hugh *o.p.* '88 (MAD) [3] Madison, WI Blessed Sacrament Church.
Wreisner, Hugo *o.p.* '88 (MAD) [G] Madison, WI St. Marys Hospital Medical Center.
Wren, Benjamin L. *s.j.* '61 (NO) [C] New Orleans, LA Loyola University.
Wrenn, Lawrence '77 (WH) Princeton, WV Sacred Heart Church; [Q] Athens, WV Concord College Newman Center.
Wrenn, Lawrence G. '53 (HRT) Special and other (Arch)Diocesan Assignment.
Wrenn, Msgr. Michael J. '61 (NY) [58] New York, NY St. John the Evangelist Church.
Wright, Addison G. *s.s.* '60 (BAL) [M] Baltimore, MD Sulpician Provincial House.
Wright, Arthur F. '67 (BO) [7] Cambridge, MA Immaculate Conception Church.
Wright, Charles *o.s.b.* '70 (SD) [H] Oceanside, CA Prince of Peace Abbey, Benet Hill.
Wright, D. Ralph *o.s.b.* '70 (STL) [1] Creve Coeur, MO St. Anselm Church; [F] Creve Coeur, MO St. Louis Priory School; [P] St. Louis, MO The Abbey of St. Mary and St. Louis.
Wright, David F. *o.p.* '68 (CHI) [N] Chicago, IL Dominicans (Provincial Office).
Wright, Msgr. Edward S. '54 (RCK) North Aurora, IL Blessed Sacrament Church.
Wright, Francis W. *c.s.sp.* (WDC) [V] Washington, DC Holy Childhood Association.
Wright, Gary R. *s.j.* (DET) *[S] Detroit, MI University of Detroit Mercy Campus Ministry.*
Wright, Gary R. *s.j.* '80 (DET) [K] Detroit, MI Jesuit Community at the University of Detroit.
Wright, Gerald *o.m.v.* '80 (BO) [W] Milton, MA Oblate Residence (St. Joseph House); [BB] Boston, MA St. Francis Chapel.
Wright, James B. '69 (DET) Farmington Hills, MI St. Alexander Church.
Wright, John '56 (CHY) [E] Powell, WY NorthWest College.
Wright, John A. '56 (CHY) Powell, WY St. Barbara Church.
Wright, John A. '82 (MAN) Hillsborough, NH St. Mary Church.
Wright, John C. *s.j.* '55 (SJ) [M] Los Gatos, CA Sacred Heart Jesuit Center.
Wright, John H. *s.j.* '52 (OAK) [A] Berkeley, CA The Jesuit School of Theology at Berkeley; [N] Berkeley, CA Jesuit Community at Jesuit School of Theology at Berkeley.
Wright, John H. '62 (HBG) [H] Ephrata, PA St. Clement's Mission House.
Wright, John J. '78 (CLV) [Q] Cleveland, OH Motherhouse and Novitiate of the Sisters of the Holy Spirit; [AA] Cleveland, OH The Greater Cleveland/Akron Corporation United for Education; [AA] Cleveland, OH Ninth Street CDC.
Wright, John M. (IND) Retired.
Wright, Joseph R. *c.m.* '54 (BAL) Emmitsburg, MD St. Joseph Church; [M] Emmitsburg, MD Vincentian House.
Wright, Michael '95 (SEA) [4] Vancouver, WA St. Joseph Church.
Wright, Patrick J. *v.f.* '54 (SFD) [5] Springfield, IL St. Agnes Church.
Wright, Richard J. '45 (PH) Ardmore, PA St. Colman Church; Retired.
Wright, Robert '54 (SY) Retired.
Wright, Robert E. *o.m.i.* '74 (SAT) [B] San Antonio, TX George Sexton House of Studies; [C] San Antonio, TX Oblate School of Theology.
Wright, Robert P. '54 (SY) [S] Syracuse, NY St. Pius X Home, Inc.
Wright, Msgr. Rupert A. '56 (BUF) Williamsville, NY St. Gregory the Great Church.
Wright, Tennant C. *s.j.* '62 (SJ) [B] Santa Clara, CA Santa Clara University.
Wright, Thomas E. '55 (RNO) Yerington, NV Holy Family Church.
Wright, Thomas M. *s.m.a.* '92 (NEW) [N] Tenafly, NJ Society of African Missions, Provincialate, S.M.A. Fathers.
Wright, Vincent L. '57 (BUF) Retired.
Wright, Warren J. *s.j.* '82 (SFR) [E] San Francisco, CA St. Ignatius College Preparatory (Coed); [N] San Francisco, CA Jesuit Community at St. Ignatius College Preparatory.
Wright, William *c.ss.r.* '60 (FgM) Redemptorist Foreign Missions.
Wright, William A. '65 (PH) [2] Drexel Hill, PA St. Bernadette Church.
Wrightson, Mark *o.s.f.s.* '86 (VEN) [6] Fort Myers, FL Our Lady of Light Church.
Wrigley, Franklin '52 (OKL) Retired.
Wrobleski, Edward D. *c.s.p.* '62 (LA) [86] Los Angeles, CA St. Paul the Apostle Church.
Wroblewski, Anthony *o.m.i.* '95 (DUL) [3] Duluth, MN Holy Family, Church.
Wroblewski, Brendan *o.f.m.* (GB) [10] Green Bay, WI St. Mary of the Angels Church; [I] Green Bay, WI St. Mary of the Angels Friary.
Wroblewski, Edward D. *c.s.p.* '62 (NY) [DD] Jamaica Estates, NY Paulist Fathers Generalate.
Wroblewski, Edward M. *m.m.* '52 (NY) [DD] Maryknoll, NY Maryknoll Fathers and Brothers.
Wroblewski, John J. '92 (NY) [194] Staten Island, NY St. Adalbert Church.
Wroblewski, Lawrence J. *s.j.* '74 (ROC) [B] Rochester, NY McQuaid Jesuit High School.
Wroblewski, Marion *c.r.* '65 (CHI) [192] Chicago, IL St. Stanislaus, Bishop and Martyr Church.
Wrozek, Timothy A. '88 (FTW) Wabash, IN St. Bernard Church.
Wrynn, John F. *s.j.* '70 (NEW) [N] Jersey City, NJ Jesuits of Saint Peter's College, Inc.
Wrynn, John P. '70 (NEW) [B] Jersey City, NJ Saint Peter's College.
Wtorek, Krzysztof '94 (CAM) Haddon Heights, NJ St. Rose's Church.
Wtulich, John S. '72 (BRK) [26] Brooklyn, NY St. Catharine of Alexandria Church.
Wu, Peter A. *m.m.* '61 (FgM) Maryknoll Foreign Missions.
Wu, Stanley '76 (SFR) [51] San Francisco, CA St. Thomas, The Apostle Church.
Wudarski, Dariusz P. '96 (SPR) Longmeadow, MA St. Mary's Church.
Wuellner, George E. '54 (PEO) Seymour, IL St. Boniface Church; Retired.
Wuerth, James E. *m.s.f.* '71 (SAT) Seguin, TX Our Lady of Guadalupe Church.
Wuertz, Richard '68 (YAK) Bridgeport, WA St. Anne's Church.
Wuertz, Richard A. '68 (YAK) Chelan, WA St. Francis de Sales Church.
Wuest, George *s.j.* '58 (PHX) El Mirage, AZ Santa Teresita Church.
Wueste, Andy *o.m.i.* '54 (SAN) [E] San Angelo, TX Christ the King Retreat Center.
Wulinski, Stanley F. '80 (BRK) Released from Diocesan Assignment.
Wulsch, Michael A. '72 (CHI) [140] Chicago, IL St. Monica Church.
Wummer, Robert P. '56 (WDC) Fort Washington, MD St. Ignatius Church.
Wunderlich, Dale P. '74 (STL) [2] St. Louis, MO Epiphany of Our Lord Church.
Wunderlich, Daniel F. (LAN) Ovid, MI Holy Family Church.
Wunderlich, Donulus *o.f.m.* '46 (SFD) [K] Sherman, IL Our Lady of Angels Friary.
Wunsch, Richard J. *c.s.c.* '66 (FgM) Holy Cross Foreign Missions.
Wurm, Robert L. '60 (DET) Ferndale, MI St. James Church.
Wurm, William *o.s.b.* '79 (GBG) [H] Latrobe, PA Saint Vincent Archabbey.
Wurst, Wayne H. '80 (CHI) Other Assignments.
Wurth, Elmer P. *m.m.* '56 (FgM) Maryknoll Foreign Missions.
Wurth, M. Philip *o.c.d.* '59 (DAL) [K] Dallas, TX Mount Carmel Center.
Wurtz, Camillus *o.s.b.* '52 (KCK) [E] Atchison, KS Maur Hill Prep School.
Wurtz, Msgr. Robert C. '58 (BUF) [1] Lackawanna, NY Basilica of Our Lady of Victory Church; [J] Lackawanna, NY Baker Victory Services; [K] Lackawanna, NY Our Lady of Victory Hospital; [T] Lackawanna, NY Our Lady of Victory Homes of Charity.
Wurz, George E. '60 (SY) [3] Oswego, NY St. Louis Church; [6] Oswego, NY St. Peter Church.
Wurzel, Richard T. '59 (TOL) Sylvania, OH St. Joseph Church.
Wutscheck, John J. '61 (MIL) [2] Milwaukee, WI St. Adalbert Church.
Wyckoff, Eric T. *s.d.b.* '92 (NO) [D] Marrero, LA Archbishop Shaw High School.
Wyczawski, Stanley '73 (DET) Port Huron, MI St. Mary Church.
Wydeven, John (OAK) Military Chaplains.
Wyen, Larry *c.pp.s.* '69 (CIN) St. Henry, OH St. Henry Church.
Wyffels, Robert J. '60 (NU) Winsted, MN Holy Trinity Church; Winsted, MN Holy Trinity Church.
Wylie, Stephen '41 (DOD) Retired.
Wymelenberg, M. John *s.j.* '60 (OM) [K] Omaha, NE Jesuit Community At Creighton University.
Wymes, John F. *m.m.* '54 (NY) [DD] Maryknoll, NY Maryknoll Fathers and Brothers.
Wymes, John F. *m.m.* '54 (RVC) Malverne, NY Our Lady of Lourdes Church.
Wynants, Paul G. *c.i.c.m.* (ARL) [N] Vienna, VA Mount Tabor Society, Inc.
Wyndaele, Bill *c.i.c.m.* '59 (ARL) [J] Arlington, VA Missionhurst, C.I.C.M.-Central House and Provincialate.
Wyndham, Thomas F. '69 (BO) [4] Weymouth, MA St. Jerome Church.
Wynne, James J. *o.m.i.* '55 (BEL) [F] Belleville, IL Missionary Oblates of Mary Immaculate - St. Henry's Oblate Residence.
Wynne, James J. *o.m.i.* '55 (STP) [N] St. Paul, MN Oblate Residence.
Wynne, Robert F. *m.m.* '68 (HON) Kamuela, HI Church of the Annunciation; [H] Honolulu, HI Maryknoll Fathers House.
Wynne, William J. *o.s.a.* '44 (BO) [C] North Andover, MA Merrimack College.
Wynnycky, John P. '92 (DET) Pontiac, MI St. Joseph Church; Pontiac, MI St. Michael Church; Pontiac, MI St. Vincent de Paul Church.
Wypych, Andrew P. '79 (CHI) [60] Chicago, IL Five Holy Martyrs Church; [163] Chicago, IL St. Pancratius Church.
Wyrsch, Thomas W. '78 (STL) [16] St. Louis, MO Resurrection of Our Lord Church.
Wyse, Alexander *o.f.m.* '43 (BO) [BB] Boston, MA St. Anthony Shrine.
Wyse, James B. '87 (GR) [3] Muskegon, MI St. Jean Baptiste Church.
Wysochansky, Constantine *o.s.b.m.* '62 (STN) Hamtramck, MI Immaculate Conception of B.V.M. Church.
Wysochansky, Demetrius *o.s.b.m.* '59 (STN) [7] Palos Park, IL Nativity of B. V. M. Church.
Wysochansky, John '57 (PHU) St. Clair, PA St. Nicholas Church; St. Clair, PA Holy Trinity Church.
Wysochansky, Walter J. '64 (SJP) [5] Austintown, OH St. Anne Church.
Wysocki, James R. '67 (DET) Marine City, MI Holy Cross Church.
Wysocki, Joseph A. '71 (SCR) On Duty Outside the Diocese.
Wysocki, Marek (NEW) [2] Elizabeth, NJ St. Adalbert's Church.
Wysocki, Paul J. '64 (CLV) Orrville, OH St. Agnes Church.
Wysocki, Paul P. '54 (HRT) [3] New Britain, CT Sacred

Heart of Jesus Church.
Wysong, William H. '72 (CIN) [J] Cincinnati, OH St. Rita School for the Deaf.
Wyszynski, Darius W. '58 (LAN) [5] Jackson, MI St. Stanislaus Kostka Church.
Wytish, Michael Jude '90 (PBR) [3] Pittsburgh, PA St. John the Baptist Church.
Wytrwal, Alexander J. '50 (DET) New Boston, MI St. Stephen Church.
Wyvill, Christopher *o.s.b.* '65 (WDC) [M] Washington, DC St. Anselm's Abbey.
Wyzgoski, Robert F. '59 (DET) Birmingham, MI Our Lady Queen of Martyrs Church.
Wyzykiewicz, Richard *sch.p.* (PH) [AA] Devon, PA Piarist Fathers (Order of the Pious Schools).
Wyzykiewicz, Richard S. *sch.p.* (PH) [AA] Devon, PA Piarist Fathers (Order of the Pious Schools).
Wyzykiewicz, Richard S. *sch.p.* '71 (PH) [G] Devon, PA Devon Preparatory School.

X

Xavier, Antony '60 (RVC) Manhasset, NY North Shore Univ. Hospital.
Xavier, Francis '41 (WOR) [N] Still River, MA Benedictine Monks, St. Benedict Abbey.
Xavier, Godwin '85 (SAC) Downieville, CA Immaculate Conception Church.
Xavier, Lawrence '79 (NY) Rhinebeck, NY The Good Shepherd Church.
Xuereb, Paul (DET) Retired.
Xuereb, Publius '68 (FWT) The Colony, TX Holy Cross Church.

Y

Yabes, Arthur *s.v.d.* '87 (SJ) [15] San Jose, CA St. Maria Goretti Church.
Yablonsky, Gabriel '59 (Y) Retired.
Yackanich, Eugene P. '65 (PBR) Munhall, PA St. Elias Church.
Yacobi, Francis *o.f.m.cap.* '90 (WDC) [B] Washington, DC St. Francis Friary-Capuchin College.
Yadegar, Benn Beth '93 (EST) On Assignment Outside the Diocese.
Yadrich, John B. '51 (KCK) Retired.
Yadron, Michael J. '83 (GRY) [3] Michigan City, IN Queen of All Saints Church.
Yadron, Raymond A. '63 (CHI) Palatine, IL St. Thomas of Villanova Church.
Yaeger, Gerald '66 (PHX) Prescott Valley, AZ St. Germaine Church.
Yaeger, Joseph J. '89 (R) Newton Grove, NC Our Lady of Guadalupe Church.
Yager, James P. '41 (GR) Retired.
Yagesh, Richard C. '78 (PIT) Military Chaplains.
Yaghi, Milad T. *m.l.m.* '88 (OLL) Houston, TX Our Lady of the Cedars Mission Church; [A] San Antonio, TX The Congregation of Maronite Lebanese Missionaries.
Yagley, Carl J. '53 (DET) Centerline, MI St. Clement Church.
Yahn, George '50 (SB) Retired.
Yahner, Gordon A. '63 (CLV) [7] Akron, OH St. Hilary Church.
Yakaitis, Michael T. '78 (CHI) [21] Chicago, IL St. Barbara Church; [141] Chicago, IL Nativity of the Blessed Virgin Mary Church.
Yaksick, Michael L. '94 (PIT) Castle Shannon, PA St. Anne Church.
Yallaly, Jules G. *c.m.* '36 (STL) [K] Bridgeton, MO De Paul Health Center; [P] St. Louis, MO Vincentian Bellerive Residence.
Yamada, John *ss.cc.* '71 (FR) [J] Fairhaven, MA Sacred Hearts Provincial House.
Yanas, John '84 (ALB) Frankfort, NY Our Lady Queen of Apostles Church; [H] Albany, NY Mercycare Corporation, St. Peter's Hospital.
Yance, Eugenio '92 (SLC) Wendover, UT Mission San Felipe Church.
Yandrisevits, Philip *m.s.c.* '42 (ALN) [K] Reading, PA Missionaries of the Sacred Heart.
Yanez, Horacio V. '75 (SEA) Bellevue, WA St. Louise Church.
Yanez, Jaime *o.f.m.* '47 (ELP) [B] El Paso, TX St. Anthony's School of Theology.
Yanez, Jose *c.m.* (SJN) [55] San Juan, PR Sagrado Corazon de Jesus Church.
Yang, David '94 (NEW) [6] Orange, NJ St. Andrew Kim Church.
Yang, Paul '48 (RVC) Retired.
Yangas, Peter M. '64 (CHI) Schaumburg, IL St. Marcelline Church.
Yaniak, Frank J. '49 (MIL) [51] Milwaukee, WI St. Mary Magdalen Church.
Yankauskas, Albin J. '51 (WOR) Retired.
Yankevitch, Robert *s.j.* '69 (PH) [82] Philadelphia, PA Old St. Joseph's Church.
Yannarell, James J. *s.j.* '71 (NY) [DD] New York, NY Xavier Jesuit Community.
Yanos, Richard M. '83 (CHI) Lake Villa, IL Prince of Peace Church.
Yanovski, Stepan '90 (STF) [3] Bridgeport, CT Protection of B.V.M. Church.
Yanus, Gary D. '81 (CLV) [33] Cleveland, OH St. Ignatius Church.
Yaoch, Felix K. *s.j.* '67 (CI) Koror, FM Sacred Heart Church; [C] Koror, Palau, PW Manresa Jesuit House.
Yarbrough, Michael H. '80 (SAT) Jourdanton, TX St. Matthew's Church.
Yardemian, Dadjad '71 (ARM) [C] Glendale, CA Mekhitarian Educational Foundation.
Yargeau, Ronald G. '73 (SPR) Haydenville, MA St. Mary's Church.
Yarno, Kenneth *c.s.v.* '59 (JOL) St. George, IL St. George Church.
Yarnold, Edward *s.j.* '60 (MIL) [P] Milwaukee, WI Jesuit Community at Marquette University.
Yarnovitz, Msgr. Robert '57 (PRM) Parma, OH Saint John the Baptist, Cathedral.
Yaroch, Kenneth E. '67 (SAG) Albee, MI St. Mary Church.
Yaroch, Paul *o.f.m.cap.* '64 (MIL) [P] Mount Calvary, WI St. Lawrence Friary.
Yarrish, Msgr. Bernard E. '76 (SCR) On Duty Outside the Diocese.
Yarrosh, Ronald J. '74 (ALN) [8] Reading, PA St. Margaret Church; [O] Kutztown, PA Christopher House.
Yasso, Jacob O. '60 (DET) [68] Detroit, MI Sacred Heart-Chaldean Parish.
Yasso, Jacob O. '60 (EST) Detroit, MI Sacred Heart Chaldean Parish.
Yast, Robert A. '56 (FTW) [2] Mishawaka, IN St. Joseph Church.
Yastishock, Charles '77 (PSC) Toms River, NJ Our Lady of Perpetual Help Church.
Yaszcz, Thomas A. '75 (SCR) On Special or Other Diocesan Assignment.
Yates, John *c.ss.p.* '54 (LR) Conway, AR St. Joseph's Church.
Yates, John *c.ss.p.* '54 (SB) Beaumont, CA San Gorgonio Church.
Yates, M. Clark *s.m.a.* '56 (WDC) [M] Takoma Park, MD Society of African Missions (S.M.A.).
Yates, Msgr. Robert J. '41 (MIA) Hollywood, FL St. Bernadette Church.
Yates, Msgr. Robert J. '41 (TOL) Retired.
Yates, Simeon *o.f.m.conv.* '63 (STP) [Q] Prior Lake, MN Franciscan Retreat House.
Yatkauskas, Matthew '89 (NY) Croton-on-Hudson, NY Holy Name of Mary Church.
Yavorsky, James A. '34 (CLV) [2] Barberton, OH SS. Cyril and Methodius Church; Retired.
Yavorsky, Stephen T. *s.j.* '77 (DEN) [M] Denver, CO Xavier Jesuit Center.
Yazawa, Francis R. *o.f.m.* (BO) [BB] Boston, MA St. Anthony Shrine.
Ybarra, Manuel *o.f.m.* '86 (WDC) [M] Washington, DC Commissariat of the Holy Land, Franciscan Monastery - Mount St. Sepulchre.
Ycoback, John D. '60 (PBR) [1] Youngstown, OH Assumption of the Blessed Virgin Church.
Ye Swe, Xeno (DOD) Ashland, KS St. Joseph Church.
Ye Swe, Zeno (DOD) Ashland, KS Holy Spirit Station Church.
Yeager, Robert J. '62 (TOL) Special Assignment; [O] Maumee, OH Diocesan Fiscal Management Conference - National Office.
Yeaglin, Armand *o.f.m.cap* '38 (PIT) [O] Pittsburgh, PA St. Augustine Friary.
Yeakel, James R. *o.s.f.s.* '79 (WDC) [B] Washington, DC Oblates of St. Francis de Sales.
Yeazel, J. Robert '67 (SY) Special Assignment; [S] East Syracuse, NY Bishop Grimes Priests Residence.
Yee Mon, Ronald '85 (FAR) Towner, ND St. Cecilia's Church.
Yehl, Msgr. Addison *m.s.* '51 (E) [B] Erie, PA Gannon University.
Yelinko, Flavian G. *o.s.b.* '33 (GBG) [H] Latrobe, PA Saint Vincent Archabbey.
Yelle, Ronald R. '79 (HRT) Granby, CT St. Therese's Church.
Yender, Basil *o.s.b.* '71 (RCK) [C] Aurora, IL Marmion Academy; [H] Aurora, IL Marmion Abbey-St. Augustine's Abbey.
Yenkevich, Daniel J. '90 (SCR) On Duty Outside the Diocese.
Yennock, Msgr. Eugene M. '50 (SY) [15] Syracuse, NY St. Daniel Church.
Yenushosky, Daniel J. '77 (ALN) [5] Allentown, PA Our Lady Help of Christians Church.
Yeo, William '58 (NEW) Hackensack, NJ Hackensack Medical Center.
Yerrnini, Chinnaiah *o.s.s.* '90 (PRO) North Smithfield, RI St. John the Evangelist Church.
Yesalonia, Dennis J. *s.j.* '85 (BO) [W] Chestnut Hill, MA The Jesuit Community at Boston College.
Yescas, Higinio M. *s.v.d.* '87 (CHI) [B] Techny, IL Divine Word Residence; [N] Chicago, IL Divine Word Theologate.
Yescas, Higinlo M. *s.v.d.* '87 (CHI) [N] Techny, IL Society of the Divine Word, Provincial Headquarter-Chicago Prov.
Yetmar, J. Charles '57 (SC) Sioux Rapids, IA St. Joseph's Church.
Yetsko, Robert K. *t.o.r.* '84 (PIT) [27] Pittsburgh, PA St. Matthew Church.
Yetter, Robert M. '73 (BUF) Swormville, NY St. Mary Church.
Yiengst, Msgr. George B. '62 (BUF) Getzville, NY St. Pius X Church.
Yiftheg, Cuthbert '89 (CI) Udot, FM St. Francis Assisi Church.
Yim, Louis H. '57 (HON) [16] Honolulu, HI St. Pius X Church.
Yncierto, Frank S. '75 (LAV) [9] Las Vegas, NV St. Francis de Sales Church.
Yocis, David A. '87 (BGP) Leave of Absence.
Yock, Peter *o.s.b.* '95 (IND) [J] St. Meinrad, IN St. Meinrad Archabbey.
Yockey, Gregory *o.s.b.* '93 (CC) [H] Sandia, TX Corpus Christi Abbey.
Yockey, John G. '70 (MIL) [B] Hales Corners, WI Sacred Heart School of Theology.
Yockey, John G. '97 (MIL) Oconomowoc, WI St. Jerome Church.
Yoelker, James A. '69 (BEL) Washington Park, IL St. Martin of Tours Church.
Yogus, Ronald B. '75 (ALT) [4] Portage, PA St. John the Baptist Church; Cresson, PA State Correctional Institution.
Yohe, Robert A. '89 (HBG) [1] Mount Carmel, PA Divine Redeemer Church.
Yom, Lawrence *s.j.* '97 (BAL) [B] Baltimore, MD Loyola College; [M] Baltimore, MD Jesuit Community of Loyola College, Inc.
Yonkovig, John R. '77 (OG) [5] Plattsburgh, NY St. Peter Church.
Yonson, Wenceslaus '46 (BRK) Retired.
Yontz, Msgr. George W. '59 (STU) [7] Steubenville, OH St. Peter's Church; [9] Steubenville, OH St. Stanislaus Church.
Yontz, Msgr. William C. '50 (STU) Byesville, OH Holy Trinity Church.
Yoo, Augustine '79 (SEA) Special Assignment.
Yoo, Matthew (LA) [47] Los Angeles, CA St. Basil's Church.
Yoon, Titus *o.f.m.conv.* (WDC) [B] Washington, DC St. Francis Friary-Capuchin College.
Yore, Lambert *o.carm.* '45 (WDC) [B] Washington, DC Whitefriars Hall.
Yori, Robert '61 (CAM) Woodbine, NJ St. Casimir's Church; Woodbine, NJ State Colony.
York, Edward '47 (WCH) Retired.
York, Kenneth J. '88 (BEL) [1] East St. Louis, IL Immaculate Conception Church; Smithton, IL St. John the Baptist Church.
York, Patrick G. '90 (WCH) Frontenac, KS Sacred Heart Church; [K] Pittsburg, KS St. Pius X Center (Pittsburg State University).
York, Paul H. '64 (LIN) Plattsmouth, NE Church of the Holy Spirit.
York, Richard R. '73 (PH) [27] Philadelphia, PA St. Bridget Church; [EE] Philadelphia, PA Newman Apostolate.
York, Vincent P. '68 (ALN) Fountain Hill, PA St. Ursula Church.
Yossa, Kenneth F. '88 (ROM) Special Assignment.
Yost, Charles *s.c.j.* '58 (JKS) Hernando, MS Holy Spirit Church; [E] Nesbit, MS St. Michael Community House.
Yost, Herbert C. *c.s.c.* '75 (FTW) [J] South Bend, IN Congregation of Holy Cross Indiana Province Provincial House.
Yost, Richard J. *o.s.f.s.* '76 (DET) [Q] Warren, MI St. John's Deaf Center.
Young, Anthony J. '44 (MAD) Retired.
Young, Arthur *o.f.m.conv.* '49 (RNO) [1] Reno, NV St. Thomas Aquinas Cathedral.
Young, Bernard L. '63 (NO) Military Chaplains.
Young, Bernard L. '63 (PHX) Phoenix, AZ United States Veterans Affairs Medical Center.
Young, Carl A. '53 (NEW) Retired.
Young, Charles H., Jr. '43 (BAL) [70] Baltimore, MD Our Lady of Hope Church.
Young, Msgr. Charles P. '50 (SD) [4] Chula Vista, CA St. Rose of Lima Church; Retired.
Young, Clyde *o.f.m.* '54 (CIN) [C] Cincinnati, OH St. Anthony Shrine, Franciscan Candidacy.
Young, Daniel A. (BUF) Pavilion, NY St. Mary Church.
Young, Daniel A. '95 (BUF) Harris Hill, NY Nativity of the Blessed Virgin Mary Church.
Young, David (MI) Special Assignment.
Young, David E. '95 (COL) Otway, OH Our Lady of Lourdes Church; West Portsmouth, OH Our Lady of Sorrows Church.
Young, Dennis M. (HBG) Lebanon, PA Veterans Administration Hospital.
Young, Dennis M. '80 (HBG) Annville, PA St. Paul the Apostle Church.

Young, Dennis M. '80 (STA) On Duty Outside the Diocese.
Young, DeSales *o.f.m.cap.* '48 (PIT) [O] Pittsburgh, PA St. Augustine Friary.
Young, Dismas *o.f.m.cap.* '66 (GBG) Export, PA St. Mary Church.
Young, Dominic '79 (LFT) Monterey, IN St. Anne Church.
Young, Edward '83 (STF) [A] Stamford, CT St. Basil College.
Young, Edward J. '53 (SC) Retired.
Young, Eugene '86 (PHX) [1] Scottsdale, AZ Blessed Sacrament Church.
Young, Frank '70 (SY) North Syracuse, NY St. Rose of Lima Church.
Young, Gary *c.r.* '76 (L) [M] Nazareth, KY Generalate, Motherhouse and Novitiate of the Sisters of Charity of Nazareth.
Young, Gerald A. '72 (DEN) Wray, CO St. Andrew Church; Yuma, CO St. John Church.
Young, Gerald A. '72 (LA) On Duty Outside the Archdiocese.
Young, Gerard F. '63 (BR) [1] Baton Rouge, LA St. Joseph Cathedral.
Young, James *s.m.* '45 (FWT) [A] Fort Worth, TX Nolan Catholic High School; [I] Fort Worth, TX Provincialate, Our Lady of Victory Center.
Young, Msgr. James E. '74 (TYL) Nacogdoches, TX Sacred Heart Church.
Young, James G. '69 (PIT) Washington, PA Immaculate Conception Church.
Young, Jerome *o.s.b.* '86 (P) [L] St. Benedict, OR Mt. Angel Abbey.
Young, John *s.c.j.* '74 (JKS) Olive Branch, MS Queen of Peace Church.
Young, John E. '57 (KAL) South Haven, MI St. Basil Church.
Young, Msgr. John M. '47 (LA) Retired.
Young, Larry '81 (OAK) [2] Fremont, CA Holy Spirit Church.
Young, Peter '70 (SP) [5] St. Petersburg, FL St. Joseph Church.
Young, Peter G. '47 (PRO) [2] North Providence, RI St. Lawrence Church; Retired.
Young, Peter G. '59 (ALB) Bolton Landing, NY Blessed Sacrament Church.
Young, Richard *o.f.m.* '95 (LSC) Roswell, NM St. Peter Church; Roswell, NM St. John the Baptist Church.
Young, Richard K. '95 (ATL) Cedartown, GA St. Bernadette's Church.
Young, Robert '53 (BRK) [U] Douglaston, NY Bishop Mugavero Residence.
Young, Robert *o.f.m.* '82 (LSC) Tularosa, NM St. Francis de Paula Church.
Young, Robert '94 (SP) [12] Tampa, FL St. Mary Church.
Young, Robert J. '53 (BRK) Retired.
Young, Ronald E. '75 (DAV) Clinton, IA Jesus Christ, Prince of Peace Church.
Young, Sam '90 (BAL) Glen Burnie, MD Holy Trinity Church.
Young, Samuel V., Jr. '90 (BAL) [70] Baltimore, MD Our Lady of Hope Church.
Young, Msgr. Terry W. '72 (ATL) Duluth, GA St. Benedict Church.
Young, Valentine *o.f.m.cap.* '49 (STL) [54] St. Louis, MO St. Patrick Church; [P] St. Louis, MO St. Patrick Friary; [W] St. Louis, MO Catholic Information Center.
Young, Valentine *o.f.m.* '56 (GLP) Houck, AZ St. John Church.
Young, Vincent J. *o.m.v.* '78 (SCR) [M] Little Meadows, PA St. Joseph's House.
Young, Walter J. *s.j.* '65 (BO) [W] Boston, MA The Society of Jesus of New England-Provincial Offices.
Young, William *s.s.s.* '64 (CLV) Highland Heights, OH St. Paschal Baylon Church.
Young, William '76 (SFR) Absent on Leave.
Young, William E. '90 (NY) On Duty Outside the Archdiocese.
Young, William E. '90 (SFE) Questa, NM St. Anthony Church.
Young, William J. *c.s.b.* '51 (GAL) [C] Houston, TX University of St. Thomas; [Q] Houston, TX Residence of the Basilian Fathers of the University of St. Thomas.
Young, William L., III '70 (GAL) [77] Houston, TX St. Thomas More Church.
Young, William T. *s.s.s.* '64 (CLV) [P] Cleveland, OH Blessed Sacrament Community.
Young, William W. '76 (SFR) [35] San Francisco, CA Most Holy Redeemer Church.
Youngberg, Vincent *c.p.* '67 (NY) [DD] Pelham Manor, NY St. Vincent's Residence.
Youngkamp, Vincent J. *s.s.c.* '59 (FgM) St. Columban's Foreign Mission.
Youngs, Fred '90 (BR) Baker, LA St. Isidore the Farmer Church.
Youssef, Youssef A. *b.s.o.* (BO) [8] Lawrence, MA St. Joseph Church.
Youssef, Youssef A. *b.s.o.* '86 (NTN) Lawrence, MA St. Joseph Church; [E] Lawrence, MA St. Joseph's Plains Community Center.
Youtz, Msgr. Richard A. '66 (HBG) [4] Lancaster, PA St. John Neumann Church.
Yrarrazaval, Diego J. *c.s.c.* '84 (FTW) [J] South Bend, IN Congregation of Holy Cross Indiana Province Provincial House.
Yrigan, Msgr. Pedro '47 (ORG) Retired.
Yrlas, Raynaldo, Jr. '97 (CC) Alice, TX St. Joseph Church.
Yslas, Martin *o.s.b.* '87 (LA) [R] Valyermo, CA St. Andrew's Abbey.
Ytsen, Robert A. *s.j.* '82 (CHI) [D] Wilmette, IL Loyola Academy.
Yu, Chang (PH) [56] Philadelphia, PA Holy Angels Church.
Yu, Reynaldo '55 (SEA) Everett, WA St. Mary Magdalen Church.
Yudin, Raynald *o.f.m.conv.* '62 (TR) [5] Trenton, NJ Immaculate Conception Church.
Yuen, Thomas '58 (SCR) [21] Scranton, PA St. Patrick's Church.
Yuhas, Edward L. '97 (PIT) Unity, PA St. John the Baptist Church.
Yuhaus, Cassian J. *c.p.* '51 (SCR) [M] Scranton, PA Saint Ann's Passionist Monastery; [R] Clarks Summit, PA Ministry for Religious Research and Consultancy.
Yulfo, Nestor '92 (SJN) [26] Bayamon, PR Santo Domingo De Guzman Church.
Yunk, Msgr. Michael J. '57 (BUF) [4] Lockport, NY St. Mary Church.
Yurchak, Thomas D. '76 (P) Canby, OR St. Patrick Church.
Yurco, Roy *ss.cc.* '62 (FR) [I] Fairhaven, MA Our Lady's Haven of Fairhaven Inc.; [J] Fairhaven, MA Sacred Hearts Provincial House.
Yurgel, Robert *o.f.m. cap.* '96 (CHL) [8] Charlotte, NC St. Matthew Church.
Yurgel, Robert *o.f.m.cap.* '96 (NY) [DD] New York, NY Immaculate Conception Friary.
Yurista, Michael '67 (PSC) Bayonne, NJ St. John the Baptist Church.
Yurko, William '48 (Y) [4] Youngstown, OH Immaculate Heart of Mary Church; Retired.
Yurkovic, Dale E. '91 (GF) Livingston, MT St. Mary's Church.
Yuse, Raymond B. '58 (HRT) Retired.

Z

Zabala, Efrain '67 (CGS) [12] Barrio Rio Canas, PR Santisima Trinidad Church.
Zabala, Luis *o.f.m.* (SJN) [52] San Juan, PR Resurreccion del Senor Church.
Zaballa, Pedro L. (SJN) [E] San Juan, PR Centro Medico de P.R.
Zabelskas, John A. '56 (GAL) Highlands, TX St. Jude Thaddeus Church.
Zabinski, Claude A. *o.f.m.* '40 (GB) Eland, WI St. William Church; Wittenberg, WI Holy Family Church.
Zabkiewicz, Stanislaus *o.f.m.conv.* (FgM) Conventual Franciscan Foreign Missions.
Zabler, Charles G. '77 (MIL) West Allis, WI West Allis Memorial Hospital.
Zaborowski, Paul *o.f.m.cap.* '97 (WDC) [39] Washington, DC Shrine of the Sacred Heart Church.
Zabowski, Theodore P. '70 (PIT) Washington, PA Immaculate Conception Church.
Zabrocki, Patrick '88 (GF) Havre, MT St. Jude Thaddeus Church.
Zabrocki, Stephen J. '89 (GF) Wolf Point, MT Immaculate Conception Church.
Zaccagnigno, Raffaele '68 (BRK) Released from Diocesan Assignment.
Zaccagnini, Kenneth G. '82 (GBG) Derry, PA St. Joseph Church.
Zaccardo, Peter J. '64 (NEW) Nutley, NJ Holy Family Church.
Zaccone, Paul C. '87 (OM) [38] Omaha, NE St. Pius X Church.
Zach, Charles *o.s.b.* '73 (OM) [C] Elkhorn, NE Mount Michael High School; [K] Elkhorn, NE Mount Michael Abbey.
Zach, Placidus *o.s.b.* '56 (P) [L] St. Benedict, OR Mt. Angel Abbey.
Zach, Roger *o.f.m.cap.* (GB) Champion, WI St. Joseph Church; New Franken, WI St. Kilian Church.
Zachar, Msgr. Albert L. '39 (DUB) Retired.
Zachariadis, Nicholas '86 (VNN) [A] Newberry Springs, CA Holy Resurrection Monastery.
Zacheis, Dennis B. '75 (STL) Krakow, MO St. Gertrude's Church.
Zachman, Clarence *o.m.i.* '48 (BEL) [F] Belleville, IL Shrine of Our Lady of the Snows.
Zacker, Mark A. *m.s.c.* '96 (OG) [2] Watertown, NY Our Lady of the Sacred Heart, Missionaries of the Sacred Heart Church.
Zadora, Bill *s.d.s.* '74 (SAT) St. Hedwig, TX Annunciation of the Blessed Virgin Mary Church.
Zadora, Charles J. '67 (BUF) Springville, NY St. Aloysius Church.
Zafe, Peter V. '64 (TOL) Clyde, OH St. Mary Church.
Zagar, Janko *o.p.* '48 (OAK) [N] Oakland, CA Dominican Order (Western Province), St. Albert's Priory.
Zagar, John T. '61 (OKL) Retired.
Zagarella, John *o.praem* '86 (PH) [D] Philadelphia, PA St. John Neumann High School.
Zagarella, John C. *o.praem.* '88 (PH) [AA] Philadelphia, PA St. Norbert Priory.
Zagari, Joseph '52 (CC) Retired.
Zagone, Frederick P. *s.j.* '93 (SCR) [C] Scranton, PA University of Scranton.
Zagorc, Francis D. *c.s.c.* '58 (PHX) Grand Canyon, AZ El Cristo Rey Church.
Zagorski, Thomas *o.f.m.conv.* '51 (LA) New Cuyama, CA Immaculate Conception Church.
Zagst, Bernard L. '61 (ALX) Boyce, LA St. Margaret Church.
Zahler, Paul *o.s.b.* '62 (OKL) [L] Shawnee, OK Oklahoma Benedictine Institute on Mental Retardation, Inc.
Zahler, Paul J. *o.s.b.* '62 (OKL) [I] Shawnee, OK St. Gregory Abbey.
Zahn, George E. '68 (RIC) [15] Richmond, VA St. Paul Church.
Zahn, John H. (LFT) Kewanna, IN St. Ann Church.
Zahn, John H. '72 (LFT) Rochester, IN St. Joseph Church.
Zahn, Robert R. *m.m.* '55 (FgM) Maryknoll Foreign Missions.
Zahner, William '45 (L) Retired; [L] Louisville, KY Bishop David Apartments.
Zahonski, Paul A. *s.j.* (BGP) [D] Fairfield, CT Fairfield College Preparatory School.
Zahorchak, Michael '56 (STU) Retired.
Zaiats, Volodymyr (STN) Milwaukee, WI St. Michaels Church.
Zaidan, Abdallah E. *m.l.m.* '86 (OLL) Los Angeles, CA Our Lady of Mt. Lebanon-St. Peter Cathedral; Denver, CO Maronite Catholic Community Church; [A] San Antonio, TX The Congregation of Maronite Lebanese Missionaries.
Zajac, Richard E. '76 (BUF) [K] Buffalo, NY Sisters of Charity Hospital of Buffalo, NY.
Zajdel, Bernard *o.f.m.conv.* '64 (STP) Bloomington, MN St. Bonaventure Church.
Zajdel, Robert J. '80 (PIT) Braddock, PA Good Shepherd Church.
Zak, Msgr. Casimir A. '45 (BUF) Retired; [O] Tonawanda, NY O'Hara Residence.
Zak, Daniel J. '67 (TOL) Swanton, OH St. Richard Church.
Zak, Stan '71 (OAK) [4] Concord, CA Queen of All Saints Church.
Zak, Steven B. '88 (LA) On Duty Outside the Archdiocese.
Zak, Timothy *s.d.b.* (NEW) [S] South Orange, NJ Salesians of Don Bosco, S.D.B.
Zakarauskas, Anthony J. '41 (CHI) [141] Chicago, IL Nativity of the Blessed Virgin Mary Church; Retired.
Zakarauskas, Vaclovas '31 (CHI) [141] Chicago, IL Nativity of the Blessed Virgin Mary Church; Retired.
Zake, Louis J. '60 (CHI) [14] Chicago, IL St. Ann Church; [A] Chicago, IL Archbishop Quigley Preparatory Seminary.
Zakens, Michael '45 (ALB) [12] Schenectady, NY St. Mary Church.
Zakens, Michael W. (ALB) Retired.
Zakowicz, Giles *o.f.m.conv.* '75 (BAL) [M] Ellicott City, MD Order of Friars Minor Conventual.
Zakowicz, Giles *o.f.m.conv.* '75 (FgM) Conventual Franciscan Foreign Missions.
Zakshesky, Francis '81 (TYL) Absent on Sick Leave.
Zalecki, Dennis M. '76 (CHI) [A] Mundelein, IL University of St. Mary of the Lake-Mundelein Seminary.
Zalecki, Marian *o.s.p.p.e.* '62 (PH) [AA] Doylestown, PA Pauline Fathers Monastery, Shrine of Our Lady of Czestochowa.
Zalenski, Gary A. '77 (STU) Ironton, OH St. Joseph Church; Ironton, OH St. Lawrence Church.
Zaleski, Daniel '80 (DET) [6] Westland, MI St. Theodore of Canterbury Church.
Zalewski, Francis '78 (TR) [20] Trenton, NJ SS. Peter and Paul Church; [23] Trenton, NJ St. Stephen Church.
Zalewski, Peter '97 (PT) Fort Walton Beach, FL St. Mary Church.
Zalewski, Thomas *o.carm.* '79 (PMB) [B] Boca Raton, FL Pope John Paul II High School; [G] Boca Raton, FL St. Elias Priory-Order of Carmelites, NY.
Zaloga, Daniel S. '67 (MAR) Iron Mountain, MI St. Mary and St. Joseph Church.
Zalonis, Jerome A. *m.i.c.* '59 (JOL) Plano, IL St. Mary Church.
Zalotay, Joseph '51 (WDC) Derwood, MD St. Francis of Assisi Church.
Zamborsky, Bill '74 (ORL) Mims, FL Holy Spirit Church.
Zamborsky, Leonard J. '76 (CLV) Cleveland Heights, OH St. Louis Church.
Zamborsky, Stephen A. *c.s.sp.* '36 (PH) [AA] Bensalem,

PA Congregation of the Holy Ghost.
Zammit, Francis X. '66 (ORL) Retired.
Zammit, Msgr. Joseph J. '56 (NY) [105] New York, NY St. Peter Church; New York, NY New York Police Department.
Zamora, Marcos *c.s.p.* '90 (NY) [41] New York, NY Good Shepherd Church.
Zamorano, Richard '93 (ELP) [33] El Paso, TX St. Thomas Aquinas Church; [39] El Paso, TX Santa Lucia Church.
Zamorski, Msgr. Robert J. '72 (MET) Fords, NJ Our Lady of Peace Church.
Zampelli, Michael *s.j.* '93 (BO) [W] Chestnut Hill, MA The Jesuit Community at Boston College.
Zampino, Ignatius *o.f.m.cap.* '61 (CHL) [10] Charlotte, NC St. Thomas Aquinas Church.
Zamudio, Ruben *o.s.a.* '73 (CC) [4] Laredo, TX Holy Redeemer Church.
Zanabria Vergara, Juan M. *o.s.a.* '85 (FgM) Foreign Missions.
Zanatta, Albert *c.r.s.* '74 (HRT) [6] Hartford, CT Sacred Heart Church.
Zanavich, Albert J. '41 (HRT) [1] Ansonia, CT Assumption Church; Retired.
Zancan, Robert D. '82 (BUF) Retired.
Zandri, William A. '84 (RC) Lead, SD St. Patrick's Church.
Zandy, Edward J. '70 (SY) [4] Binghamton, NY St. Christopher Church.
Zanetti, Humberto C. *o.f.m.* '55 (SD) Oceanside, CA St. Mary Star of the Sea Church.
Zang, Richard P. *c.s.c.* '69 (FTW) [12] South Bend, IN St. Joseph Church.
Zangari, Salvatore V. '44 (HBG) Retired.
Zaniolo, Michael G. '88 (CHI) [214] Chicago, IL St. William Church; Calumet City, IL St. Andrew the Apostle Church.
Zankl, Angelo *o.s.b.* '26 (SCL) [I] Collegeville, MN St. John's Abbey, of the Order of St. Benedict.
Zanni, Frank '90 (Y) Girard, OH St. Rose Church.
Zanni, James '96 (Y) [8] Canton, OH St. Joseph's Church.
Zanon, Romano '66 (BRK) [239] Queens, NY Sacred Heart Church; [Y] Flushing, NY Mount St. Mary.
Zanoni, Charles *c.s.* '62 (WDC) [19] Washington, DC Holy Rosary Church.
Zanoni, John '60 (JOL) Lombard, IL Sacred Heart Church.
Zanoni, Richard J. *s.j.* '75 (BUF) [50] Buffalo, NY St. Michael Church; [D] Buffalo, NY Canisius High School.
Zanotti, Charles F. '53 (NY) Glasco, NY St. Joseph Church.
Zanotti, Richard *c.s.* '80 (CHI) Melrose Park, IL Our Lady of Mount Carmel Church.
Zanotto, Luigi *m.c.c.j.* '68 (LA) [55] Los Angeles, CA St. Cecilia Church.
Zans, Florentino (SJN) [E] San Juan, PR Centro Medico de P.R.
Zaorski, Edward F. '90 (DET) [2] Detroit, MI All Saints Church; [5] Detroit, MI SS. Andrew and Benedict Church.
Zapalac, David J. *c.s.b.* '93 (GAL) [7] Houston, TX St. Anne Church.
Zapalac, William '70 (BWN) Weslaco, TX St. Pius X Church.
Zapata, Antonio '68 (ORG) [3] Anaheim, CA St. Justin Martyr Church.
Zapata, Emiliano *o.p.* '95 (MIA) [18] Miami, FL St. Dominic Church; [B] Miami, FL Barry University.
Zape, Juan de la Cruz '85 (STO) Riverbank, CA St. Frances of Rome Church.
Zapf, Albert L. '80 (PIT) Braddock, PA Good Shepherd Church; Braddock Hills, PA Sacred Heart Church.
Zapfel, Robert E. '81 (BUF) On Duty Outside the Diocese.
Zapotocki, Henry E. '48 (SCR) Tannersville, PA Our Lady of Victory Church.
Zapp, John '72 (Y) Uniontown, OH Holy Spirit Church.
Zappa, James C., Jr. '76 (STP) Burnsville, MN Mary, Mother of the Church.
Zappitelli, Francis R. '62 (PHX) [5] Scottsdale, AZ St. Daniel the Prophet Church.
Zaragoza, Rufino *o.f.m.* (OAK) [P] Danville, CA San Damiano Retreat.
Zarama, Luis '93 (ATL) Clarkesville, GA St. Mark's Church.
Zarate, Raymond J. *c.pp.s.* '79 (CIN) [57] Cincinnati, OH St. Mark Church.
Zarate-Suarez, Jose Edmundo '96 (SD) Escondido, CA Church of the Resurrection.
Zaratti, Elio '40 (SB) Retired.
Zaratti, Filiberto '40 (CHR) On Duty Outside the Diocese.
Zareski, Joseph S. '80 (SY) [3] Syracuse, NY Blessed Sacrament Church.
Zarichny, Steven '78 (SJP) [7] Cleveland, OH Ss. Peter and Paul Church.
Zarkoski, Donald *s.d.b.* '62 (MIA) [25] Miami, FL St. Kieran Church.
Zarlenga, Vincent I. *o.p.* '51 (CHI) River Forest, IL St. Vincent Ferrer Priory Church; [N] Chicago, IL Dominicans (Provincial Office).
Zasacki, Robert E. '67 (STP) Robbinsdale, MN Sacred Heart Church.
Zastawny, Kazimierz '57 (BO) [5] Lynn, MA St. Michael Church.
Zastoupil, Stephen R. '61 (BIS) [3] Bismarck, ND Corpus Christi Church.
Zastrow, John A. '56 (LIN) Holdrege, NE All Saints Church.
Zatalava, James D. '70 (ALT) State College, PA Our Lady of Victory Church.
Zatarga, George F. '68 (BRK) [162] Queens, NY Christ the King Church.
Zatina, Gregory E.J. '87 (SPC) Bolivar, MO Sacred Heart Church.
Zaucha, Finian *o.f.m.* '68 (GB) [10] Green Bay, WI St. Mary of the Angels Church; [I] Green Bay, WI St. Mary of the Angels Friary.
Zavacki, Richard A. '58 (SCR) Kingston, PA St. Hedwig's Church.
Zavala, Jesus Gusman *o.s.a.* '60 (FgM) Foreign Missions.
Zavaski, William J. '69 (CHI) Arlington Heights, IL St. James Church.
Zavattaro, Gabriel J. *s.d.b.* '34 (SFR) [45] San Francisco, CA SS. Peter and Paul Church.
Zavell, Edward '61 (PRM) Fairview Park, OH St. Mary Magdalene Church.
Zavelli, J. Keith '87 (MEM) [22] Memphis, TN Our Lady Of Perpetual Help Church.
Zavodny, Msgr. Francis J. '51 (ALN) [4] Allentown, PA St. John the Baptist Church.
Zawacki, Casimir J. '50 (GAY) Retired.
Zawacki, Robert *s.s.j.* (GAL) Huntsville, TX Ellis II Unit; Huntsville, TX Walls Unit; Huntsville, TX Wynne Unit.
Zawacki, Robert P. *s.s.j.* '77 (GAL) Huntsville, TX St. Thomas the Apostle Church.
Zawada, Jerome *o.f.m.* '64 (MIL) [P] Milwaukee, WI Francis and Clare House.
Zawada, Joseph F. *o.c.d.* '64 (STA) [J] Bunnell, FL Discalced Carmelite Fathers of Florida.
Zawadzki, Justin '68 (SJ) Los Gatos, CA St. Mary of the Immaculate Conception Church.
Zawadzki, Piotr '97 (VEN) [1] Venice, FL Epiphany Cathedral.
Zawadzki, Victor C. '50 (SCR) Retired.
Zawistanowicz, Norbert J. '49 (CHI) [94] Chicago, IL Immaculate Heart of Mary Church; [161] Chicago, IL Our Lady of Victory Church; Retired.
Zawodniak, Edward J. '47 (SCR) Retired.
Zayas, Antonio '59 (PCE) On Duty Outside the Diocese.
Zayas, Hector '93 (ARE) [3] Utuado, PR Our Lady of Angels Church.
Zazella, Msgr. Thomas J. '78 (PAT) [5] Clifton, NJ SS. Cyril and Methodius Church.
Zbieranski, Roman *o.f.m.* '61 (GB) [3] Manitowoc, WI St. Mary Church.
Zbin, Raphael *o.s.b.* '47 (CLV) [5] Cleveland, OH St. Andrew Church; [P] Cleveland, OH Benedictine Order of Cleveland.
Zboroswki, Richard M. '78 (CHI) Hoffman Estates, IL St. Hubert Church.
Zbrun, Reinaldo *s.v.d.* '72 (CHI) [N] Chicago, IL Divine Word Theologate.
Zdancewicz, Carl *o.f.m.conv.* '77 (ATL) Lithia Springs, GA St. John Vianney Church.
Zdilla, Valentine D. '96 (LA) [2] Oxnard, CA Santa Clara Church.
Zdrodowski, Francis '43 (DET) Retired.
Zebron, Sam *o.f.m.conv.* (SAV) [2] Augusta, GA St. Joseph's Church.
Zebron, Samuel *o.f.m.* '58 (CIN) [L] Centerville, OH The Franciscan at St. Leonard.
Zebrowski, Arnold '73 (VEN) Cape Coral, FL St. Andrew Church.
Zebrowski, Roy *o.f.m.* '58 (GAY) Lake City, MI St. Stephen Church.
Zebrowski, Roy *o.f.m.* '59 (GAY) Manton, MI St. Theresa Church.
Zec, John J. '70 (BAL) [B] Emmitsburg, MD Mount Saint Mary's College.
Zec, John J. '70 (TR) On Duty Outside the Diocese.
Zecharia, Boban '84 (BRK) [38] Brooklyn, NY St. Finbar's Church.
Zeck, George '70 (DUL) Two Harbors, MN Holy Spirit Church.
Zedar, Thomas J. '65 (VEN) Port Charlotte, FL San Antonio Church.
Zee, Louis C. '59 (DUB) Blairstown, IA St. John Church; Newhall, IA St. Paul's Church; Van Horne, IA Immaculate Conception Church.
Zeeb, Charles '56 (DET) Retired.
Zega, Eugene M. *o.s.a.* '36 (PH) [AA] Villanova, PA St. Thomas Monastery.
Zegar, David '79 (P) Woodburn, OR St. Luke Church.
Zegers, Msgr. James J. '40 (CAM) Retired.
Zegers, Paul A. *ss.cc.* '49 (HON) Hana, HI St. Mary Church.
Zehe, Ralph *o.f.m.cap.* '50 (PIT) [29] Pittsburgh, PA Our Lady of the Angels Church; Allegheny County, PA Department of Veterans Affairs Medical Center Aspinwall; Allegheny County, PA Department of Veterans Affairs Medical Center Oakland.
Zeihen, Joseph N. '50 (MIL) Retired.
Zeimet, Richard E. *m.m.* '64 (FgM) Maryknoll Foreign Missions.
Zeis, Gabriel *t.o.r.* (PH) [D] Fairless Hills, PA Conwell-Egan Catholic High School.
Zeis, Gabriel *t.o.r.* '80 (PH) [AA] Fairless Hills, PA St. Anthony Friary.
Zeisig, B. Thomas '57 (CLV) Cuyahoga Falls, OH St. Eugene Church.
Zeisler, Warren *o.f.m.* '50 (CIN) [M] Cincinnati, OH St. Clement Friary.
Zeitler, Msgr. Edward J. '58 (E) Grove City, PA Beloved Disciple Church.
Zeitler, Msgr. John W. '64 (BUF) Lake View, NY Our Lady of Perpetual Help Church.
Zekas, Msgr. Stanley '49 (STU) Retired.
Zeleznik, Clement *o.s.b.* (CLV) Broadview Heights, OH Assumption Church.
Zeleznik, Clement *o.s.b.* '59 (CLV) [P] Cleveland, OH Benedictine Order of Cleveland.
Zelik, Richard J. *o.f.m.cap.* '77 (WH) [2] Charleston, WV St. Anthony Church; [N] Charleston, WV Capuchins-St. Anthony Friary.
Zelinski, James *o.f.m.cap.* '61 (DET) [K] Detroit, MI St. Mary's Friary.
Zelinski, James *o.f.m.cap.* '61 (FgM) Capuchin Foreign Missions.
Zelinski, Thomas *o.f.m.cap.* '72 (FTW) Huntington, IN SS. Peter and Paul Church.
Zelker, Thomas '83 (ALB) Granville, NY Roman Catholic Community of Granville Church.
Zell, Charles Felix *o.c.s.o.* '80 (ATL) [I] Conyers, GA The Monastery of the Holy Spirit.
Zeller, Joseph E. '58 (RC) Timber Lake, SD Holy Cross Church.
Zeller, Leonard H. '73 (BAL) Military Chaplains.
Zelonis, Richard *s.c.j.* '79 (MIL) [N] Racine, WI St. Monica's Senior Citizens Home, Inc.; [P] Hales Corners, WI Sacred Heart Monastery.
Zemaitis, Kestutis '65 (CLV) [N] Cleveland, OH Jennings Hall Inc.
Zeman, Gerald L. '63 (SC) Sutherland, IA Sacred Heart Church.
Zemanick, Peter *o.c.s.o.* '44 (SP) [L] St. Petersburg, FL Bon Secours-Maria Manor Nursing Care Center, Inc.
Zemanick, Peter *o.c.s.o.* '44 (WOR) [N] Spencer, MA St. Joseph's Abbey.
Zemanik, Edward S. '81 (ALN) [3] McAdoo, PA St. Patrick Church.
Zembal, Theodore E. *s.j.* '68 (SEA) [A] Seattle, WA Seattle University.
Zembrzuski, Michael *o.s.p.p.e.* '34 (PH) [AA] Doylestown, PA Pauline Fathers Monastery, Shrine of Our Lady of Czestochowa.
Zemeikis, Alfred '36 (NEW) [13] Elizabeth, NJ SS. Peter and Paul's Church.
Zemelko, John J. '87 (GRY) Chesterton, IN St. Patrick Church.
Zemula, Anthony *s.a.c.* '78 (BUF) [O] North Tonawanda, NY Society of the Catholic Apostolate.
Zender, Gary M. '86 (SEA) Enumclaw, WA Sacred Heart of Jesus Church.
Zendzian, Peter '79 (SAT) [T] San Antonio, TX Polish American Priest Association (P.A.P.A.).
Zendzian, Peter W. '79 (BRK) [94] Brooklyn, NY Our Lady of Czestochowa-St. Casimir Church; [T] Brooklyn, NY Catholic Migration & Refugee Office, Catholic Migration Services, Inc.
Zengierski, Patrick '91 (BUF) [2] Cheektowaga, NY Infant of Prague Church.
Zeni, Msgr. Dino M. '59 (BRK) [126] Brooklyn, NY St. Rosalia-Regina Pacis Church.
Zenk, Donald W. '54 (WIN) Twin Lakes, MN St. James Church; Retired.
Zenk, Richard E. '54 (SC) Akron, IA St. Patrick's Church.
Zenkel, Edward B. '62 (ROC) Honeoye, NY St. Mary, Our Lady of the Hills Church.
Zenorini, Henry J. *s.j.* '61 (NY) [DD] New York, NY Xavier Jesuit Community.
Zens, Roger A. '57 (MIL) Retired.
Zensen, Gerald '24 (SC) Mapleton, IA St. Mary's Church.
Zensen, Gerald F. '49 (SC) Retired.
Zentner, Miguel '88 (NY) [131] Bronx, NY St. Augustine Church.
Zenz, Msgr. John P. '78 (DET) Special Assignment.
Zenz, Msgr. John P. '82 (DET) [Q] Detroit, MI Catholic Community Services of the Archdiocese of Detroit, Inc.; [T] Detroit, MI Christ Child Society.
Zenz, Louis '39 (FTW) [H] Fort Wayne, IN Saint Anne Home & Retirement Community.
Zepczyk, Gabriel C. '62 (SUP) Ino, WI St. Florian Church; Moquah, WI Ss. Peter and Paul Church.
Zepecki, Ronald P. '95 (HRT) [9] Hartford, CT SS. Cyril and Methodius Church.
Zepeda, Luis '94 (SAN) [2] Odessa, TX St. Anthony

Church; [4] Odessa, TX St. Joseph Church.
Zepp, Anthony W. '56 (CLV) [2] Garfield Heights, OH SS. Peter and Paul Church.
Zeps, Michael J. *s.j.* '71 (MIL) [P] Milwaukee, WI Jesuit Community at Marquette University.
Zercie, David '75 (NOR) [F] Cromwell, CT Missionaries of the Holy Apostles.
Zerfas, Msgr. Herman H. '47 (GR) Retired.
Zerhusen, Msgr. Henry F. '53 (BAL) [57] Baltimore, MD St. Mark Church.
Zeringue, Guy P. '75 (HT) Bourg, LA St. Ann Church.
Zerkel, Donald F. '57 (MIL) Byron, WI St. John Church; Oakfield, WI St. James Church.
Zerner, Harry B. *s.j.* '63 (R) Chapel Hill, NC St. Thomas More Church; [E] Chapel Hill, NC Jesuit Residence, Robert Southwell House; [E] Raleigh, NC Jesuit Community.
Zerr, Gary '97 (P) Hillsboro, OR St. Matthew Church.
Zerr, Maurice J. *m.m.* '51 (FgM) Maryknoll Foreign Missions.
Zerwas, Rick '91 (SFE) Los Lunas, NM St. Clement Church.
Zeth, Allen P. (ALT) [H] Hollidaysburg, PA Campus Ministry.
Zeth, Allen P. '86 (ALT) [13] Altoona, PA St. Therese of the Child Jesus Church; [H] Hollidaysburg, PA Campus Ministry.
Zettel, David H. '66 (L) [B] Louisville, KY Trinity High School.
Zetzl, Ralph '65 (SFD) [K] Sherman, IL Our Lady of Angels Friary.
Zeugner, Raymond J. '67 (MAR) Crystal Falls, MI Guardian Angels Church.
Zeuner, Karl A. '71 (PH) [3] Philadelphia, PA St. Agatha-St. James Church.
Zewe, M. Donald *s.j.* '56 (SY) [S] Syracuse, NY Jesuits at LeMoyne, Inc.
Zeyack, John *s.t.l.* '65 (PSC) Rahway, NJ St. Thomas the Apostle Church.
Zeyen, Thomas E. *s.j.* '54 (P) [L] Portland, OR Jesuit Provincial Office (Society of Jesus, Oregon Prov.).
Zglejszewski, Andrzej '90 (RVC) West Hempstead, NY St. Thomas, the Apostle Church.
Zgunda, Ronald S. '77 (EVN) Washington, IN Immaculate Conception Church.
Zhang, Dehua *c.s.j.b.* '76 (BRK) [U] Elmhurst, NY Congregation of St. John the Baptist of China.
Zibert, Jack *o.f.m.* (BUF) [C] St. Bonaventure, NY St. Bonaventure University.
Zibert, Jack *o.f.m.* '78 (BUF) [O] St. Bonaventure, NY St. Bonaventure Friary.
Zicarelli, Mario '47 (NY) Haverstraw, NY St. Mary Church.
Ziccardi, C. Anthony '90 (NEW) [A] South Orange, NJ Immaculate Conception Seminary; [B] South Orange, NJ Seton Hall University.
Zich, John '57 (WCH) St. Paul, KS St. Francis Church.
Zich, John S. '57 (WCH) Erie, KS St. Ambrose Church.
Zickert, John *o.f.m.cap.* (GB) Greenville, WI St. Mary Church.
Zidek, Vincent E. *o.s.b.* '91 (ALT) Carrolltown, PA St. Benedict's Church.
Zieba, Jerzy *c.r.* '92 (CHI) [88] Chicago, IL St. Hyacinth Church.
Ziebacz, Wieslaw '92 (SCR) Honesdale, PA St. John the Evangelist Church.
Ziebert, George M. *s.j.* '41 (FgM) Provinces.
Ziegelmaier, David A. '60 (LC) Alma Center, WI Immaculate Conception Church; Fairchild, WI St. John Cantius Church; Fairview, WI St. Joseph Church.
Ziegler, Ambrose M. '61 (LFT) Lake Village, IN St. Augusta Church.
Ziegler, Anthony '59 (OWN) Waverly, KY Sacred Heart Church; Waverly, KY St. Peter Church.
Ziegler, John '96 (ARL) [5] Alexandria, VA St. Lawrence Church.
Ziegler, Thomas G. '69 (Y) Columbiana, OH St. Jude Church.
Ziegmann, Msgr. Leonard M. '59 (SC) Laurens, IA Sacred Heart Church.
Zielezienski, Ray '81 (OAK) [4] Hayward, CA St. Joachim Church.
Zielinski, Brian A. *o.praem.* '71 (WIL) [B] Claymont, DE Archmere Academy; [I] Claymont, DE Immaculate Conception Priory of the Canons Regular of Premontre.
Zielinski, Chad W. '96 (GAY) Traverse City, MI Immaculate Conception Church.
Zielinski, Francis A. '62 (DET) Columbus, MI St. Philip Neri Church.
Zielinski, Martin '78 (CHI) [A] Mundelein, IL University of St. Mary of the Lake-Mundelein Seminary.
Zielke, Michael *o.f.m.conv.* (PAT) [6] Clifton, NJ St. John Kanty Church.
Zielonka, Darius J. '95 (BGP) [2] Stratford, CT St. James Church.
Zielonka, Dariusz J. '95 (BGP) New Canaan, CT St. Aloysius Church.
Ziemba, Anthony F. '43 (PH) [86] Philadelphia, PA St. Laurentius Church; Retired.
Ziemba, Herman J. *o.f.m.* '48 (GB) [I] Pulaski, WI Assumption of B.V.M. Friary.
Ziemba, Howard '79 (Y) Absent on Leave.
Ziemba, Walter J. '51 (DET) Retired; [A] Orchard Lake, MI SS. Cyril and Methodius Seminary.
Ziemkiewicz, Frank E. *o.s.b.* '84 (GBG) [H] Latrobe, PA Saint Vincent Archabbey.
Ziemnicki, Edward '96 (HRT) [2] New Britain, CT Holy Cross Church.
Zientek, Msgr. Benedict '58 (SAN) Brownwood, TX St. Mary's Church.
Zientek, Msgr. Boleslaus '59 (GAL) Danbury, TX St. Anthony de Padua Church.
Zientek, Timothy *o.f.m.conv.* '49 (BAL) [20] Baltimore, MD St. Casimir Church.
Ziezulewicz, George F. '64 (HRT) Union City, CT St. Hedwig Church; [18] Waterbury, CT St. Stanislaus Kostka Church.
Zigmond, Kenneth *o.s.b.* '57 (JOL) Lisle, IL St. Joan of Arc Church; [J] Lisle, IL St. Procopius Abbey.
Zilbert, Jack *o.f.m.* '78 (BUF) [C] St. Bonaventure, NY St. Bonaventure University.
Ziliak, Jerome *s.v.d.* '47 (FgM) Society of the Divine Word Foreign Missions.
Ziliak, Joseph L. '62 (EVN) Newburgh, IN St. John the Baptist Church.
Zilonka, Paul *c.p.* '71 (NEW) [N] Union City, NJ Congregation of the Passion (Passionists)-St. Michael's Residence.
Zilonka, Paul *c.p.* '71 (NY) [A] Yonkers, NY St. Joseph's Seminary.
Ziminski, James C. '91 (MAR) [5] Marquette, MI St. Michael Church; Special Assignment; [G] Marquette, MI Catholic Campus Ministry-Northern Michigan University.
Zimmer, Anthony S. '86 (MIL) [D] Milwaukee, WI Pius XI High School.
Zimmer, David L. '88 (BIS) New Salem, ND St. Pius V Church.
Zimmer, Edward A. '47 (ROC) [29] Rochester, NY St. John the Evangelist Church; Retired.
Zimmer, Ellis *o.f.m.cap.* '55 (GB) [M] Appleton, WI Monte Alverno Retreat Center.
Zimmer, Eric A. *s.j.* (DET) [K] Detroit, MI Jesuit Provincial Office-Detroit Province of the Society of Jesus.
Zimmer, Eric A. *s.j.* '94 (PH) [AA] Philadelphia, PA Jesuit Community at St. Joseph's University.
Zimmer, Joseph H. *s.a.c.* '56 (FAR) Dunseith, ND St. Louis Church.
Zimmer, Luke *ss.cc.* '54 (LA) [R] Fillmore, CA Apostolate of Christian Renewal Holy Family.
Zimmer, Nicholas M. '57 (SCL) Braham, MN St. Peter & Paul Church.
Zimmer, Thomas J. '52 (LFT) Retired.
Zimmer, William '91 (CHI) [143] Chicago, IL St. Nicholas of Tolentine Church.
Zimmer, William H. '60 (GB) [4] Manitowoc, WI Sacred Heart Church.
Zimmerman, Albert J. '45 (GRY) Retired.
Zimmerman, David (GB) [1] Marinette, WI Holy Family Church.
Zimmerman, David '97 (SFD) [3] Springfield, IL Christ The King Church.
Zimmerman, Donald D. '73 (SAL) Hays, KS Immaculate Heart of Mary Church.
Zimmerman, Msgr. Donald F. '73 (DAL) [4] Dallas, TX Christ the King Church.
Zimmerman, Eugene *s.j.* '51 (CHY) St. Stephens, WY St. Stephen's Church; [C] St. Stephens, WY St. Stephens Mission - Jesuit Community; [F] St. Stephens, WY St. Stephens Indian Mission Foundation.
Zimmerman, John F. *c.m.* '34 (STL) [P] Perryville, MO Congregation of The Mission.
Zimmerman, Joseph *o.f.m.* '62 (SFD) [B] Quincy, IL Quincy University.
Zimmerman, Lee B. *c.m.* '41 (NO) [P] New Orleans, LA Vincentian Fathers.
Zimmerman, Ralph '76 (SCL) [A] Collegeville, MN St. John's Seminary.
Zimmerman, Ralph G. '76 (SCL) Special Assignment.
Zimmerman, Rex A. '67 (LC) Bevent, WI St. Ladislaus Church; Galloway, WI St. Joseph Church.
Zimmerman, Msgr. Roland G. '51 (LA) Arcadia, CA Annunciation Church; Retired.
Zimmermann, P. Francis *c.m.* '39 (NO) [P] New Orleans, LA Vincentian Fathers.
Zimmers, Eugene R. *s.j.* '51 (OAK) [A] Oakland, CA Graduate School of Theology, School of Applied Theology; [S] Oakland, CA Institute of Lay Theology.
Zimmers, Eugene R. *s.j.* '51 (SFR) [N] San Francisco, CA Jesuit Community at University of San Francisco.
Zimmers, Michael J. *s.j.* '54 (OAK) [S] Oakland, CA Institute of Lay Theology.
Zimmers, Michael J. *s.j.* '54 (SFR) [N] San Francisco, CA Jesuit Community at University of San Francisco.
Zimmers, Michael J. *s.j.* '54 (SJ) [M] Los Gatos, CA Sacred Heart Jesuit Center.
Zimmerschied, Daniel W. '97 (DEN) [37] Denver, CO St. Vincent De Paul Church.
Zimney, Robert J. *c.m.* '42 (STL) [P] Perryville, MO Congregation of The Mission.
Zimpfer, Eugene A. *s.j.* '65 (BUF) [D] Buffalo, NY Canisius High School; [O] Buffalo, NY Canisius Jesuit Community.
Zina, George '86 (SAM) Orlando, FL St. Jude Mission Church; Jacksonville, FL St. Maron Maronite Church.
Zingales, Jonathan A. '76 (CLV) Released from Diocesan Assignment.
Zingaro, Joseph J. '78 (PH) Swedesburg, PA Sacred Heart Church.
Zink, David '90 (CIN) [Q] Urbana, OH Urbana University Campus Ministry.
Zink, David L. '90 (CIN) St. Paris, OH Sacred Heart Church; Sidney, OH Holy Angels Church; Urbana, OH St. Mary Church.
Zink, Harold G. *c.s.c.* '51 (AUS) [13] Austin, TX St. Ignatius Martyr Church.
Zink, William F. '68 (GR) Remus, MI St. Michael's Church.
Zinkan, Matthias *o.s.b.* '40 (FgM) American - Cassinese Congregation Foreign Missions.
Zinkan, Matthias *o.s.b.* '40 (RCK) [H] Aurora, IL Marmion Abbey-St. Augustine's Abbey.
Zinkle, Ronald T. *s.j.* '59 (LC) Lyndon Station, WI St. Mary Church.
Zinkula, Thomas R. '90 (DUB) Graduate Studies.
Zinn, Donald *c.r.* '72 (CHI) [D] Chicago, IL Gordon Technical High School.
Zinnamon, Brian F. *s.j.* '79 (GAL) [F] Houston, TX Strake, Jesuit College Preparatory Inc.
Zinno, Henry P., Jr. '82 (PRO) [2] Tiverton, RI Holy Ghost Church.
Zins, Charles '77 (BIS) Bowman, ND St. Charles Church.
Zinser, Robert E. '68 (STL) [64] St. Louis, MO St. Teresa of Avila Church.
Zinthefer, Neil G. '69 (MIL) Fredonia, WI St. Rose of Lima Church; Holy Cross, WI Holy Cross Church; Little Kohler, WI Mother of Sorrows Church.
Zinzer, Walter A. '64 (STL) Military Chaplains.
Ziobro, Joseph M. '73 (SCR) Unassigned or Leave of Absence.
Ziolkowski, Adam *o.f.m.conv.* '72 (SPR) [5] Holyoke, MA Mater Dolorosa Church.
Ziolkowski, Waldek *m.i.c.* '90 (CHL) [1] Greensboro, NC Our Lady of Grace Church.
Ziomek, David F. '94 (BO) Franklin, MA St. Mary Church.
Ziomek, Dennis A. '78 (CHI) [158] Chicago, IL Our Lady of the Snows Church; [A] Chicago, IL Archbishop Quigley Preparatory Seminary.
Zipay, Michael J. '68 (SCR) [3] Swoyersville, PA Holy Trinity Church.
Zipple, Frank '49 (LAN) Retired.
Ziqrang, Stephen P. *j.c.l.* '78 (GAL) Channelview, TX St. Andrew Church.
Zirnheld, Matthew J. '93 (BUF) [1] Lackawanna, NY Basilica of Our Lady of Victory Church.
Zitek, Bradley J. '89 (LIN) Steinauer, NE St. Anthony Church.
Ziter, Nelson B. *s.s.e.* '47 (MOB) [H] Selma, AL Edmundite Fathers.
Zitko, Msgr. Aloysius '28 (OAK) Retired.
Zitz, Nicholas *c.p.* '56 (BRK) [U] Jamaica, NY Immaculate Conception Monastery.
Ziuraitis, Gary *c.ss.r.* '78 (STL) [P] St. Louis, MO St. Alphonsus Rectory of the Redemptorist.
Zivic, Richard (ATL) Released from Archdiocesan Assignment.
Zivjak, John *c.pp.s.* '63 (CLV) [53] Cleveland, OH Our Lady of Good Counsel Church.
Zivkovic, Robert M. *o.s.m.* '66 (ORG) [H] Buena Park, CA Servite Fathers And Brothers.
Zizka, Peter J. '75 (HRT) [2] Manchester, CT St. Bartholomew's Church.
Zlock, Charles J. '94 (PH) [94] Philadelphia, PA St. Martin of Tours Church.
Zlotkowski, Francis T. *c.s.c.* (BO) Boston, MA Brigham and Women's Hospital.
Zlotkowski, Francis T. *c.s.c* '76 (BGP) [O] Bridgeport, CT Provincial Offices of the Priests and Brothers of Holy Cross, Eastern Province.
Zlotkowski, Francis T. *c.s.c.* '76 (FR) [A] North Easton, MA Holy Cross Fathers Religious.
Zmerlicki, Andrew '92 (NEW) Hasbrouck Heights, NJ Corpus Christi Church.
Zmija, Walter J. '42 (CHI) [115] Chicago, IL St. Ladislaus Church; Retired.
Zmozynski, Francis J. '57 (BUF) [60] Buffalo, NY St. Rose of Lima Church.
Znotinas, John '40 (WDC) Retired.
Zodrow, Nathan *o.s.b.* '88 (P) [L] St. Benedict, OR Mt. Angel Abbey.
Zoeller, Ben '65 (OKL) Yukon, OK St. John Nepomuk Church.
Zoeller, Eugene L. '58 (L) [A] Louisville, KY Bellarmine College.
Zoellner, Michael *o.s.b.* '80 (KCK) [H] Atchison, KS St.

Benedict's Abbey.
Zogby, Edward G. *s.j.* '67 (NY) [DD] New York, NY West Side Jesuit Community.
Zoghby, James F. '71 (MOB) [3] Mobile, AL Corpus Christi Church.
Zoghby, Paul G. '93 (MOB) [12] Mobile, AL St. Mary Church.
Zogheib, Hares '54 (SAM) Retired.
Zohlen, Raym J. '53 (SFR) [23] San Francisco, CA Holy Name of Jesus Church.
Zollinger, Msgr. Richard F. '55 (GRY) Knox, IN St. Thomas Aquinas Church.
Zolnerovicz, Nicolas (PAT) Pequannock, NJ Our Lady of Fatima Chapel (Tridentine) Church.
Zolnierzak, Stanislaus J. '36 (PIT) Retired; [O] Pittsburgh, PA St. John Vianney Manor.
Zolnowski, Wojciech J. '96 (DET) [2] Dearborn, MI St. Barbara Church.
Zombe, Omer-Luzolo Lwa-Lu *o.p.* '90 (SB) Chino, CA St. Margaret Mary Church.
Zona, James '73 (BRK) [210] Queens, NY Our Lady of Fatima Church.
Zonneveld, Leo J. *c.i.c.m.* '58 (ARL) Culpeper, VA Precious Blood Church; [J] Arlington, VA Missionhurst, C.I.C.M.-Central House and Provincialate.
Zonta, Angelo *c.s.j.* '68 (LA) Lancaster, CA Blessed Junipero Serra Church; [D] Lancaster, CA Paraclete High School.
Zoph, John L. '36 (SFR) Retired; [D] San Mateo, CA Junipero Serra High School (Boys).
Zorbach, Msgr. Francis X. '52 (BAL) Linthicum Heights, MD St. Philip Neri Church.
Zore, Richard I. '57 (IND) Plainfield, IN St. Susanna Church.
Zorichak, William '39 (DUL) Retired.
Zorman, Fortunat *o.f.m.* '40 (CHI) [N] Lemont, IL The Slovene Franciscan Fathers, Order of Friars Minor, Commissariat of the Holy Cross.
Zoromski, Herbert P. '51 (LC) Retired.
Zoshak, William H. '62 (NY) Military Chaplains.
Zotter, Thomas A. '76 (SFE) [22] Albuquerque, NM St. Bernadette Church.
Zoubek, Ronald '89 (BAL) [57] Baltimore, MD St. Mark Church.
Zoufal, Michael L. '87 (CHI) Calumet City, IL Our Lady of Knock Church; [G] Chicago, IL Catholic Charities of the Archdiocese of Chicago-Archdiocesan Offices.
Zsolczai, Raymond *o.f.m.* '83 (CHI) [J] Oak Park, IL Oak Park Hospital.
Zube, Joseph '53 (PEO) Special Residence.
Zuber, Marti G. '76 (BWN) Absent.
Zuber, Thaddeus F. '50 (NEW) Retired; [N] Rutherford, NJ St. John Vianney Residence for Priests.
Zuberbueler, Matthew H. '96 (ARL) Chantilly, VA St. Timothy Church.
Zubik, Rudolf '64 (NEW) Harrison, NJ Our Lady of Czestochowa Church.
Zuchowski, Robert J. '72 (GAY) Elk Rapids, MI Sacred Heart Church.
Zudaire, Claudio *o.f.m.cap.* '54 (FWT) [6] Fort Worth, TX Our Lady of Guadalupe Church.
Zuelke, Michael *o.f.m.cap.* '74 (MIL) [25] Milwaukee, WI St. Francis of Assisi Church.
Zuercher, John D. *s.j.* '59 (OM) [K] Omaha, NE Jesuit Community At Creighton University.
Zuerlein, Damian J. '81 (OM) [32] Omaha, NE Our Lady of Guadalupe Church.
Zuerlein, Damian Z. '81 (OM) [3] Omaha, NE St. Agnes Church.
Zuern, Theodore F. *s.j.* '57 (MIL) [P] Milwaukee, WI Jesuit Provincial Office, Wisconsin Province.
Zuern, Theodore F. *s.j.* '57 (WDC) [M] Washington, DC Leonard Neale House.
Zuffoletto, Michael P. '72 (BUF) Military Chaplains.
Zugelter, Alvin T. '46 (CIN) Retired.
Zugger, Christopher L. '81 (VNN) Albuquerque, NM Our Lady of Perpetual Help Church.
Zuhlsdorf, John '91 (STP) Crystal, MN St. Raphael Church.
Zukas, Stephen P. '92 (BO) Graduate Studies.
Zukowski, Nicholas '82 (DET) New Baltimore, MI St. Mary Queen of Creation Church.
Zuleger, Donald M. '76 (GB) [5] Appleton, WI St. Pius X Church.
Zuleta, Nondier '92 (B) Weiser, ID St. Agnes Church.
Zuliani, Vincent *s.d.b.* '56 (NEW) [3] Elizabeth, NJ St. Anthony's Church.
Zulkie, Lambert *o.carm.* (BO) [BB] Peabody, MA St. Theresa Carmelite Chapel.
Zulkie, Lambert *o.carm.* '88 (BO) [P] Peabody, MA Catholic Information Center.
Zuluaga, Jose Omar '84 (PRO) [5] Pawtucket, RI St. John the Baptist Church.
Zumaya, David G. '77 (SAT) Nixon, TX St. Joseph's Church; Smiley, TX St. Philip Benizi Church.
Zummach, Jerome A. *s.j.* '45 (STL) [O] St. Louis, MO Fusz Pavilion.
Zuniga, Domingo *c.m.f.* '52 (LA) [28] Los Angeles, CA Our Lady Queen of the Angels Church.
Zuniga, Juan M. *m.m.* '88 (SFR) [N] San Francisco, CA Maryknoll Fathers and Brothers, Catholic Foreign Mission Society of America, Inc.
Zunno, Michael O. *m.m.* '53 (FgM) Maryknoll Foreign Missions.
Zupa, Msgr. Emil P. '48 (BUF) Le Roy, NY St. Joseph Church.
Zupez, John H. *s.j.* '67 (FgM) Provinces.
Zupka, Anselm *o.s.b.* '67 (CLV) [E] Cleveland, OH Benedictine High School; [P] Cleveland, OH Benedictine Order of Cleveland.
Zurat, Hugh *o.f.m.* '62 (FgM) Franciscan Foreign Missions.
Zurat, Hugh *o.f.m.* '62 (MIL) [P] Milwaukee, WI Francis and Clare House.
Zuraw, Msgr. John Andrew '86 (Y) Girard, OH St. Rose Church.
Zurawski, Lawrence '85 (DET) Berkley, MI Our Lady of La Salette Church.
Zurcher, Thomas K. *c.s.c.* (PHX) [F] Phoenix, AZ Holy Cross Congregation of Casa Santa Cruz.
Zurek, Lawrence W. *o.f.m.* '85 (DET) [5] Southfield, MI St. Michael Church.
Zurek, Patrick J. '75 (AUS) [14] Austin, TX St. John Neumann Church.
Zuromskis, John D. '41 (BO) Retired.
Zurutuza, Juan M. *c.m.* '58 (PCE) [8] Ponce, PR La Milagrosa Church.
Zuscak, Richard T. '84 (WOR) Clinton, MA Our Lady of Jasna Gora Church.
Zuschmidt, Joseph C. *o.s.f.s.* '65 (CHL) High Point, NC Immaculate Heart of Mary Church.
Zusy, Dennis R. *o.p.* '55 (CHI) [N] Chicago, IL Dominicans (Provincial Office).
Zusy, James *o.p.* '59 (LEX) [6] Lexington, KY St. Paul Church.
Zuziak, Joseph R. *s.d.s.* '66 (GRY) [J] Merrillville, IN Salvatorian Fathers (Society of the Divine Savior).
Zuzik, John E. '91 (Y) [2] Canton, OH Our Lady of Peace Church.
Zvinklys, Antanas '39 (LC) Retired; [I] La Crosse, WI Holy Cross (Seminary) Diocesan Center.
Zwack, Jeffrey A. '84 (BIS) Hazelton, ND St. Paul Church; Linton, ND St. Anthony Church.
Zwahl, Eugene *o.f.m.conv.* '42 (TR) Seaside Park, NJ St. Catharine of Siena Church.
Zwaska, Victor L. '56 (MIL) Retired.
Zweber, Clement J. '49 (STP) Retired.
Zweber, Raymond J. '54 (STP) South St. Paul, MN St. Augustine Church.
Zwers, John B. '50 (DET) Redford Township, MI St. Robert Bellarmine Church.
Zwiefka, William L. '83 (GAY) Manistee, MI St. Joseph Church; Special Assignment.
Zwifka, David *m.a., j.c.d.* '81 (BUF) [A] East Aurora, NY Christ the King Seminary.
Zwinger, Msgr. Leonard '51 (SFS) Retired.
Zwirn, Ralph H. '85 (CHI) [131] Chicago, IL St. Mary, Star of the Sea Church.
Zwolenkiewicz, Raphael *o.f.m.conv.* '79 (SPR) [5] Holyoke, MA Mater Dolorosa Church.
Zygadlo, Mitchell '82 (ROC) [56] Rochester, NY St. Stanislaus Church.
Zyla, Jeffrey L. '92 (OM) [26] Omaha, NE St. Leo
Zylla, Paul '45 (SCL) Retired.
Zylla, Robert V. *o.s.c.* '51 (BAL) [A] Emmitsburg, MD Mount St. Mary's Seminary.
Zylla, Robert V. *o.s.c.* '51 (PHX) [F] Phoenix, AZ Crosier Community of Phoenix (Canons Regular of the Order of the Holy Cross).
Zywan, Paul J. '86 (PIT) [1] Pittsburgh, PA St. Paul Cathedral.

Necrology

ARCHBISHOPS

✠ Murphy, Thomas J. (SEA) Archbishop of Seattle. —Died June 26, 1997

BISHOPS

✠ Boudreaux, Most Rev. Warren Louis (HT) (Retired). —Died Oct. 6, 1997
✠ Brown, Most Rev. Charles A., *m.m.* (FgM) Retired Bishop of Bolivia. —Died May 14, 1997
✠ Brzana, Most Rev. Stanislaus J. (OG) (Retired). —Died March 1, 1997
✠ Curtis, Most Rev. Walter William (BGP) Retired Bishop Emeritus of the Diocese of Bridgeport. —Died Oct. 18, 1997
✠ Flanagan, Most Rev. Bernard J. (WOR) Retired Bishop of the Diocese of Worcester. —Died Jan. 28, 1997
✠ Francis, Most Rev. Joseph A., *s.v.d.* (NEW) Retired Auxilary Bishop of the Archdiocese of Newark. —Died Sept. 1, 1997
✠ Harrington, Most Rev. Timothy J. (WOR) Retired Bishop of the Diocese of Worcester. —Died March 23, 1997
✠ Lambert, Most Rev. Francis, *s.m.* (FgM) Retired Bishop Emeritus of Port Vila, Vanuatu, South Pacific. —Died Oct. 29, 1997
✠ McManus, Most Rev. William E. (FTW) (Retired). —Died March 3, 1997
✠ Nolan, Most Rev. John G. (MO) Auxiliary Bishop of the Archdiocese for the Military Services, U.S.A. —Died Nov. 19, 1997
✠ O'Keefe, Most Rev. Joseph T. (SY) Retired Bishop of the Diocese of Syracuse. —Died Sept. 2, 1997
✠ Power, Most Rev. Cornelius (P) (Retired). —Died May 22, 1997
✠ Scanlon, Most Rev. John J. (SFR) (Retired). —Died Jan. 31, 1997

PRIESTS

† (FgM) Mineiros, Goias, Brazil St. Joseph Priory. —Died Oct. 11, 1997
† Abi-Nader, Maroun (SAM) (Retired). —Died Dec. 29, 1996
† Ackerman, Raymond J. (CHI) (Retired). —Died Oct. 6, 1997
† Adams, Cletus A., *t.o.r.* (ALT) Retired. —Died Dec. 30, 1996
† Adams, Rev. Msgr. Oliver Edward (MOB) Mobile, AL St. Catherine of Siena. —Died July 21, 1997
† Alonso Ordonez, Juan Nicasio (CGS) Caguas, PR Sagrado Corazon de Jesus. —Died Sept. 20, 1997
† Andrews, William L. (CLV) Lakewood, OH St. James. —Died June 18, 1997
† Armijo, Walter F., *o.f.m.* (BO) Boston, MA St. Anthony Residence. —Died Aug. 9, 1996
† Ashline, Alfred (ALB) (Retired). —Died March 30, 1997
† Augustyn, Albert J. (SCR) Inkerman, PA St. Mark. —Died July 29, 1997
† Augustyn, Cyril, *o.f.m.conv.* (FR) Taunton, MA Our Lady of the Holy Rosary. —Died Sept. 11, 1997
† Autard, Joseph (OAK) (Retired). —Died March 7, 1997
† Avery, Joseph E., *m.m.* (NY) Maryknoll, NY Maryknoll Fathers and Brothers. —Died Aug. 15, 1997
† Ayers, Fabian, *c.r.* (L) Louisville, KY St. Cecilia's. —Died March 9, 1997
† Bachman, Paul (SFS) (Retired). —Died April 16, 1997
† Baggio, John A. (BEL) West Frankfort, IL St. John the Baptist. —Died June 1, 1997
† Baglio, Joseph L. (STP) (Retired). —Died Aug. 23, 1997
† Banasiak, Julian, *o.s.p.p.e.* (TR) Trenton, NJ St. Peter & Paul. —Died Nov. 27, 1997
† Barrette, Rev. Msgr. Dacian (Y) Brewster, OH St. Therese. —Died Oct. 4, 1997
† Barry, George F., *s.j.* (BO) Weston, MA Campion Center. —Died Nov. 1, 1996
† Baseheart, Edward J. (CHI) (Retired). —Died Jan. 31, 1997
† Batza, Rev. Msgr. Joseph (PHU) (Retired). —Died March 2, 1997
† Bauler, Robert John (BIR) (Retired). —Died June 26, 1997
† Bauman, Richard, *o.f.m.* (GLP) Retired. —Died Nov. 27, 1996
† Baumgartner, John (BAK) (Retired). —Died Feb. 9, 1997
† Beattie, Rev. Msgr. John (LA) Los Angeles, CA St. Ambrose. —Died July 9, 1997
† Beatty, John M. (SD) (Retired). —Died July 17, 1997
† Beaumont, Joseph (VEN) (Retired). —Died June 22, 1997
† Beauvais, Leon F. (BO) Boston, MA Sacred Heart. —Died March 23, 1997
† Bechtel, Francis (PHX) (Retired). —Died Nov. 10, 1997
† Bednar, Merrick J. (BUF) Tonawanda, NY St. Francis of Assisi. —Died May 12, 1997
† Begley, Patrick (BAL) (Retired). —Died May 30, 1997
† Bell, Arthur (DET) (Retired). —Died Aug. 12, 1997
† Benassu, Gregory R. (ATL) Kennasaw, GA St. Catherine of Siena. —Died March 30, 1997
† Benitez, Andres, *s.j.* (MIA) Miami, FL Belen Jesuit Preparatory School. —Died April 9, 1997
† Berberich, Peter Kurt (CHR) (Retired). —Died Jan. 20, 1997
† Berger, Lawrence Joseph (CC) (Retired). —Died July 24, 1997
† Bergeron, Arthur I. (BO) (Retired). —Died Oct. 25, 1996
† Bergthold, LeRoy (DAV) (Retired). —Died Jan. 29, 1997
† Bertolina, Thomas J. (GBG) North Huntingdon, PA St. Agnes. —Died Dec. 2, 1996
† Bessette, Ernest N. (FR) (Retired). —Died July 17, 1997
† Bianco, Hamilcar (P) (Retired). —Died April 6, 1997
† Bickford, Robert M., *s.j.* (SEA) Spokane, WA Gonzaga University. —Died Feb. 28, 1997
† Bienek, Dacien, *o.f.m.* (DET) Retired. —Died May 28, 1997
† Bier, Joseph V. (MIL) (Retired). —Died Oct. 31, 1997
† Biller, James C. (PIT) Cranberry Twp., PA St. Ferdinand. —Died Aug. 28, 1996
† Billig, Cloud, *o.f.m.* (SFD) Sherman, IL Our Lady of Angels Friary. —Died March 8, 1997
† Bilos, Rt. Rev. Mitred Arch Leo (STN) Palatine, IL Immaculate Conception. —Died July 31, 1997
† Bilotta, Anthony J. (BUF) (Retired). —Died Aug. 17, 1997
† Birdsall, Richard W. (SC) (Retired). —Died July 11, 1997
† Bisciglia, Francis X., *s.j.* (SEA) Tacoma, WA Bellarmine Prep School. —Died Nov. 5, 1996
† Blaney, Philip L. (HRT) (Retired). —Died May 21, 1997
† Blenner, Richard Stephen, *o.s.f.s.* (SLC) Salt Lake City, UT Villa St. Joseph. —Died June 30, 1997
† Bodart, William D. (TOL) Upper Sandusky, OH St. Peter. —Died Oct. 5, 1997
† Boehmicke, George (OWN) (Retired). —Died Nov. 6, 1996
† Bolds, Bernard L. (LR) (Retired). —Died Feb. 23, 1997
† Bonk, Matthew, *o.s.b.* (CLV) Retired. —Died Nov. 9, 1996
† Bonnet, Christian L., *s.j.* (STL) St. Louis, MO Fusz Pavilion. —Died Nov. 9, 1996
† Borsa, Rev. Msgr. Anthony (PHU) Marlboro, NJ St. Wolodymyr. —Died March 12, 1997
† Boskamp, Charles (MIL) Waukesha, WI Secular Institute of Schoenstatt Fathers. —Died Feb. 28, 1997
† Boudreaux, Rev. Msgr. Edward L. (NO) New Orleans, LA Our Lady of the Rosary Church. —Died Sept. 4, 1997
† Bovankovich, John (PSC) (Retired). —Died Nov. 11, 1997
† Boyea, Ivan G. (OG) Watertown, NY St. Patrick Church. —Died Oct. 31, 1996
† Boyle, James Leo (BO) (Retired). —Died Nov. 25, 1996
† Boysak, Basil (PSC) (Retired). —Died Aug. 20, 1997
† Brackin, Rev. Msgr. Francis A. (CHI) (Retired). —Died Oct. 10, 1997
† Bradley, John J. (PH) Philadelphia, PA St. Aloysius. —Died March 5, 1997
† Braud, Edmond P. (BR) (Retired). —Died March 10, 1997
† Braun, Warren (Y) (Retired). —Died Jan. 14, 1997
† Brendel, John A. (RVC) (Retired). —Died March 25, 1997
† Brennan, Jeremiah J., *m.m.* (NY) Maryknoll, NY Maryknoll Fathers and Brothers. —Died Sept. 20, 1997
† Bridge, Raphael G., *o.s.b.* (CHL) Belmont, NC Belmont Abbey. —Died Nov. 24, 1996
† Brochtrup, Eugene, *s.d.s.* (GB) Manitowoc, WI St. Mary's Home of the Aged. —Died Jan. 10, 1997
† Brochtrup, Eugene (MIL) Milwaukee, WI Salvatorians- Jordan Hall. —Died Jan. 10, 1997
† Broderick, John D. (PRO) Newport, RI Jesus Saviour. —Died Sept. 5, 1997
† Brogan, Edward P. (NY) (Retired). —Died July 24, 1997
† Broker, Ralph H. (STP) (Retired). —Died June 3, 1997
† Brou, Hubert J. (BR) Baton Rouge, LA St. Aloysius. —Died March 24, 1997
† Brown, Bonaventure, *o.f.m.* (PAT) Ringwood, NJ Holy Name Friary. —Died Dec. 28, 1996
† Brown, Francis (STU) (Retired). —Died Nov. 9, 1996
† Brug, Theodore R. (STL) University City, MO St. Patrick's. —Died Dec. 20, 1996
† Brumleu, Ernest J. (GAL) (Retired). —Died Nov. 10, 1997
† Bruns, J. Edgar (NO) New Orleans, LA Notre Dame Seminary. —Died May 29, 1997
† Bucher, Vitus, *o.s.b.* (SCL) Retired. —Died Dec. 5, 1996
† Buck, Francis C., *s.j.* (GLP) Gallup, NM St. Eleanor. —Died Aug. 16, 1997
† Bucki, Peter, *o.f.m.conv.* (BAL) Ellicott City, MD Order of Friars Minor Conventual. —Died Oct. 21, 1996
† Buckley, Robert G. (BO) Methuen, MA St. Monica. —Died June 20, 1997
† Buggy, Leon, *s.t.* (WDC) University Park, MD Holy Trinity Missionary Cenacle. —Died Oct. 9, 1996
† Bukowski, Vincent J. (NEW) (Retired). —Died May 9, 1997
† Bullwinkel, Andrew (SEA) Seattle, WA Christ the King. —Died Oct. 19, 1997
† Bungay, Eugene L. (BEL) (Retired). —Died Feb. 1, 1997
† Burke, Edward J., *c.m.* (BUF) Niagara University, NY Niagara University. —Died April 22, 1997
† Burke, Edward W., *s.j.* (DET) Clarkston, MI Colombiere Jesuit Community. —Died Oct. 10, 1997
† Burke, Rev. Msgr. Richard J. (ARL) Arlington, VA Cathedral of St. Thomas More. —Died Nov. 30, 1996
† Burns, Robert E. (CHI) (Retired). —Died Oct. 28, 1997
† Burns, Rev. Msgr. Vincent L. (PH) Drexil Hill, PA St. Andrew. —Died March 6, 1997
† Burton, John F.X., *s.j.* (DEN) Lakewood, CO Christ on the Mountain. —Died March 12, 1997
† Butler, Francis T. (HRT) (Retired). —Died Sept. 29, 1997
† Byrne, John H. (STL) (Retired). —Died Dec. 26, 1996
† Byrne, Robert B. (KC) (Retired). —Died Oct. 13, 1997
† Byron, Joseph F. (WDC) Potomac, MD Our Lady of Mercy. —Died Sept. 29, 1997
† Caballe, Peter, *c.m.f.* (SAT) San Antonio, TX Immaculate Heart of Mary. —Died May 6, 1997
† Cabaong, Henry (HEL) Helena, MT Warm Springs Hospital & Montana State Prison. —Died Aug. 17, 1997
† Caffarelli, Theodore C., *s.s.c.* (BUF) West Seneca, NY Fourteen Holy Helpers. —Died July 31, 1997
† Caine, John W., *c.m.* (PH) Philadelphia, PA St. Vincent's Seminary. —Died Nov. 18, 1996
† Calhoun, William E. (ATL) (Retired). —Died Jan. 4, 1997
† Calkins, Lawrence M., *o.s.m.* (P) Roseburg, OR Veterans' Administration Hospital. —Died Oct. 21, 1997

† Callaghan, Philip P., *s.j.* (SAC) Applegate, CA Our Lady of the Oaks Villa. —Died Dec. 7, 1996
† Callahan, Francis F., *s.j.* (BO) Weston, MA Campion Center. —Died Feb. 26, 1997
† Callahan, Raymond J., *s.j.* (BO) Boston, MA Nativity Prep. —Died July 25, 1997
† Campbell, William J. (TR) (Retired). —Died Oct. 7, 1997
† Cannon, William B. (CAM) (Retired). —Died Feb. 1, 1998
† Capuano, John J. (WOR) Worcester, MA Our Lady of Mount Carmel - St. Ann. —Died Feb. 7, 1997
† Carel, William L. (SC) (Retired). —Died June 10, 1997
† Carew, Cyprian E., *o.c.s.o.* (ATL) Retired. —Died June 14, 1997
† Carpanese, Mario, *s.d.b.* (BO) Boston, MA Don Bosco Tech. —Died Feb. 27, 1997
† Carr, James M. (ALN) (Retired). —Died May 15, 1997
† Carroll, Clement D. (CHI) (Retired). —Died Jan. 11, 1997
† Carroll, John D. (CHI) Chap., Veterans Admin. —Died July 28, 1997
† Carroll, W. Russell, *o.f.m.* (NY) New York, NY Franciscan Friars, Order of Friars Manor. —Died May 8, 1997
† Carter, William H. (ALN) Shenandoah, PA Annunciation/St. Mary Magdalen. —Died May 22, 1997
† Cassidy, Joseph L. (NEW) (Retired). —Died June 1, 1997
† Cassidy, Joseph A. (PAT) Budd Lake, NJ St. Jude. —Died Oct. 21, 1997
† Caster, Thomas Kevin (L) Louisville, KY St. Albert the Great. —Died July 31, 1997
† Cattaert, Michael, *c.i.c.m.* (SAT) San Antonio, TX St. John Berchman's. —Died March 17, 1997
† Cefai, John M. (TLS) (Retired). —Died June 28, 1997
† Cekovsky, Andrew (ALB) (Retired). —Died May 24, 1997
† Ceponis, Joseph A. (HBG) Lebanon, PA St. Benedict the Abbot. —Died June 11, 1997
† Chase, Chan H. (R) (Retired). —Died April 1, 1997
† Chavez, Very Rev. Msgr. Albert (LSC) (Retired). —Died Nov. 20, 1997
† Choquette, Paul A. (WOR) Fitchburg, MA Immaculate Conception. —Died Nov. 20, 1996
† Churchhill, Raymond (HON) (Retired). —Died June 9, 1997
† Cinque, Ralph G., *o.s.b.* (MAN) Manchester, NH St. Anselm Abbey. —Died March 24, 1997
† Clark, Emmanuel, *o.s.b.* (P) St. Benedict, OR Mount Angel Abbey. —Died Oct. 27, 1997
† Clark, Michael J., *o.m.i.* (BEL) Belleville, IL St. Henry's Oblate Residence. —Died April 19, 1997
† Clasen, Leonard A. (WIN) (Retired). —Died Nov. 22, 1996
† Clemens, Thomas Kirk, *s.m.* (B) Retired. —Died Feb. 9, 1997
† Colavecchio, John A. (SFD) (Retired). —Died March 26, 1997
† Colbert, C. Francis (WCH) (Retired). —Died April 7, 1997
† Colburn, Harold (ALB) (Retired). —Died November 13, 1996
† Cole, J. Gerard (WDC) (Retried). —Died Oct. 6, 1997
† Coll, Charles, *s.m.* (PH) Holland, PA St. Joseph Home for the Aged. —Died Aug. 10, 1997
† Collins, Rev. Msgr. Thomas J. (SAT) (Retired). —Died July 13, 1997
† Colloty, Ronald, *o.f.m.* (ORG) Huntington Beach, CA SS. Simon and Jude. —Died Feb. 25, 1997
† Coneglio, Andrew F. (CHI) (Retired). —Died May 1, 1997
† Conley, Joseph J. (MIL) (Retired). —Died March 5, 1997
† Conlin, Raymond E. (PAT) Clifton, NJ St. Philip the Apostle. —Died Sept. 19, 1997
† Conlin, Robert P. (BUF) Pavilion, NY St. Mary. —Died Dec. 9, 1997
† Conn, Thomas V., *s.j.* (LA) Santa Paula, CA Thomas Aquinas College. —Died Oct. 17, 1997
† Connolly, Rev. Msgr. James M. (NY) Bronxville, NY St. Joseph. —Died Dec. 15, 1997
† Connors, Francis P. (BO) (Retired). —Died Oct. 7, 1996
† Conroy, Rev. Msgr. Walter Richard (BGP) Newton, CT Saint Rose of Lima. —Died July 17, 1997
† Conway, John J., *c.m.* (PH) Philadelphia, PA St. Catherine's Infirmary. —Died Jan. 21, 1997
† Cooke, Rev. Msgr. Vincent W. (CHI) (Retired). —Died May 30, 1997
† Cooper, Harold L., *s.j.* (NO) New Orleans, LA Ignatius Residence. —Died Feb. 19, 1997
† Cordy, Robert J. (MAR) (Retired). —Died Jan. 14, 1997
† Cormier, Joseph (P) (Retired). —Died June 28, 1997
† Coronel, Juan S. (LA) (Retired). —Died Dec. 17, 1996
† Cortelyou, John R., *c.m.* (CHI) Chicago, IL DePaul Vincentian Residence. —Died Nov. 9, 1996
† Coseo, Rev. Msgr. Francis G. (OG) (Retired). —Died Feb. 5, 1997
† Costa, Salvatore, *o.m.i.* (BO) Tweksbury, MA Oblate Residence. —Died Jan. 10, 1997
† Costello, Daniel T., *s.j.* (STL) St. Louis, MO Jesuit Hall. —Died March 8, 1997
† Courtney, Paul J. (IND) (Retired). —Died Feb. 2, 1997
† Cox, James, *t.o.r.* (ALT) Retired. —Died March 31, 1997
† Coyle, Rev. Msgr. James A. (PH) (Retired). —Died Sept. 20, 1997
† Craycraft, Duane M. (LFT) Marion, IN St. Paul. —Died Sept. 29, 1997
† Crossan, Seamus S. (PHX) Williams, AZ St. Joseph. —Died April 15, 1997
† Crotti, Rev. Msgr. William A. (SCR) Dunmore, PA St. Anthony of Padua. —Died Dec. 13, 1996
† Cunningham, William (DET) Detroit, MI Church of the Madonna. —Died May 26, 1997
† Curran, Joseph B. (PH) Springfield, PA Holy Cross. —Died Jan. 4, 1997
† Cusick, William F. (DAL) Dallas, TX Gate of Heaven. —Died May 1, 1997
† Cusick, William F. (SCR) Dallas, PA Gate of Heaven. —Died May 1, 1997
† Cwalina, Rev. Msgr. John F. (RVC) (Retired). —Died April 11, 1997
† Cyr, Andre, *o.f.m.* (FgM) Retired. —Died June 16, 1996
† D'Alonges, John P. (HRT) (Retired). —Died Nov. 1, 1997
† Dacier, Gerard A. (BO) (Retired). —Died June 18, 1997
† Dagher, Joseph, *b.s.o.* (NTN) Retired. —Died May 18, 1997
† Dagwell, Robert A. (LR) (Retired). —Died Feb. 26, 1997
† Dal Maso, John, *s.d.b.* (LA) Los Angeles, CA St. John Bosco High School. —Died April 6, 1997
† Dalbec, John, *s.c.j.* (MIL) Retired. —Died Nov. 21, 1996
† Dale, James E. (NY) (Retired). —Died April 10, 1997
† Daly, Thomas J., *s.s.c.* (BUF) Retired. —Died Sept. 29, 1997
† Darcy, Rev. Msgr. Harold P. (NEW) Closter, NJ St. Mary. —Died Dec. 24, 1997
† Davey, John J. (PRO) Providence, RI St. Ann. —Died July 18, 1997
† David, Basilio (DET) (Retired). —Died Jan. 23, 1997
† David, Raymond J. (RVC) (Retired). —Died Sept. 25, 1997
† Degnan, Rev. Msgr. Paul (SAC) (Retired). —Died Aug. 16, 1997
† Delaney, John J. (LA) (Retired). —Died Feb. 17, 1997
† Delaney, Ralph B., *s.j.* (BO) Weston, MA Campion Center. —Died Dec. 26, 1996
† Della Penna, Marshall, *o.f.m.* (NY) New York, NY St. Francis if Assisi. —Died Oct. 8, 1996
† DeMarcelli, Evasio (TR) Princeton, NJ St. Paul. —Died March 10, 1997
† DeMarco, Nathan I. (CAM) West Collingswood, NJ Transfiguration. —Died Dec. 13, 1997
† Dempster, A. Patrick (Y) (Retired). —Died Dec. 7, 1997
† DeNapoli, Ettore J. (PIT) Butler, PA St. Michael. —Died May 15, 1997
† Dennis, Allan J., *m.m.* (NY) Maryknoll, NY Maryknoll Fathers and Brothers. —Died Oct. 2, 1997
† DeRuntz, Clarence Maximillian (KCK) Worthington, KS Pontifical College Josephinum. —Died May 5, 1997
† Dery, Jean-Pierre (PRO) Nasonville, RI St. Theresa of the Child Jesus. —Died Dec. 4, 1996
† Deters, Richard T., *s.j.* (DET) Clarkston, MI Colombiere Jesuit Community. —Died Jan. 15, 1997
† Detloff, Edward X. (CHI) Chicago, IL St. Tarcissus. —Died March 6, 1997
† Devenny, Joseph A., *s.j.* (BO) Weston, MA Campion Center. —Died Nov. 9, 1997
† Dierker, Louis P. (STL) Florissant, MO St. Christopher. —Died April 19, 1997
† Dietrich, Michael A. (SY) Chap. Syracuse, NY Psychiatric Center. —Died Aug. 8, 1997
† Dinan, Paul (JOL) (Retired). —Died Dec. 6, 1996
† Dion, Gerald C. (WOR) Oxford, MA St. Roach. —Died Jan. 10, 1997
† DiRaffaele, William F. (NY) Yonkers, NY Christ the King. —Died Jan. 28, 1997
† Dockers, Anthony R. (OKL) (Retired). —Died Dec. 14, 1996
† Doherty, Francis A., *ss.cc.* (OAK) Alameda, CA St. Joseph Basilica. —Died Aug. 4, 1997
† Domench, Jesus, *o.a.r.* (LA) Oxnard, CA St. Augustine Priory. —Died Aug. 8, 1997
† Dondero, Joseph L., *s.j.* (SJ) Los Gatos, CA Sacred Heart Jesuit Center. —Died June 28, 1997
† Donnelly, James (PAT) Paterson, NJ St. Stephen. —Died Sept. 24, 1997
† Donohue, Raymond J. (R) (Retired). —Died Oct. 10, 1997
† Doran, John (PHX) (Retired). —Died April 20, 1997
† Dorrity, Daniel K. (MIA) (Special Assignment). —Died March 16, 1997
† Dougherty, Francis D., *o.s.f.s.* (WIL) Retired. —Died Dec. 20, 1996
† Dowd, Patrick A. (MIL) (Retired). —Died March 5, 1997
† Downey, Patrick Michael (DOD) Dubuque, KS St. Catherine. —Died Jan. 1, 1997
† Downs, Leroy J. (WCH) (Retired). —Died Aug. 17, 1997
† Doyle, Robert A. (NEW) Jersey City, NJ Our Lady of Mercy. —Died July 18, 1997
† Duda, Stanislaus J. (FAR) (Retired). —Died March 3, 1997
† Duffy, Gabriel F. (WDC) Washington, DC Epiphany. —Died May 20, 1997
† Duignan, Rev. Msgr. Kevin Francis (MOB) Montgomery, AL St. Peter's. —Died Sept. 19, 1997
† Dumas, Alfred J. (MAN) (Retired). —Died Dec. 1, 1996
† Dunegan, Bertrand H., *o.s.b.* (GBG) Retired. —Died Dec. 18, 1996
† Dunleavy, Rev. Msgr. Joseph J. (MAR) (Retired). —Died Oct. 19, 1997
† Eagen, Rev. Msgr. Isaac Brent (SD) San Diego, CA University of San Diego. —Died Oct. 14, 1997
† Echle, Rev. Msgr. Edward V. (BAL) (Retired). —Died May 16, 1997
† Eckart, Stephen, *o.s.b.* (LR) Subiaco, AR Subiaco Abbey. —Died May 7, 1997
† Edwards, John G. (BO) (Retired). —Died Sept. 3, 1997
† Eichhoff, William M. (OKL) Oklahoma City, OK St. Francis of Assisi. —Died April 8, 1997
† Emmert, Roger A. (COL) Columbus, OH St. Joseph Cathedral. —Died Feb. 1, 1997
† Endal, George S., *s.j.* (ANC) Retired. —Died Nov. 15, 1996
† Enderle, Rev. Msgr. Marvin F. (BEA) Orange, TX St. Mary. —Died Jan. 16, 1997
† England, Robert Ellis (SD) (Absent on Sick Leave). —Died Jan. 31, 1997
† Eno, Robert B., *s.s.* (WDC) Washington, DC Theological College. —Died Feb. 13, 1997
† Erkens, William J. (PIT) Churchill, PA St. John Fisher. —Died Feb. 6, 1997
† Eschweiler, Francis L. (MIL) (Retired). —Died Dec. 27, 1997
† Esparza, Luis, *o.f.m.cap.* (ARE) Retired. —Died Jan. 1997
† Evett, Lester J., *s.j.* (DET) Clarkston, MI Colombiere Jesuit Community. —Died June 1, 1997
† Faase, Albert Anthony (CHR) (Retired). —Died April 11, 1997
† Fabing, Charles (HEL) (Retired). —Died May 15, 1997
† Fader, John J. (LA) (Retired). —Died Feb. 17, 1997
† Fagan, Bernard D., *s.j.* (RC) Rapid City, SD St. Isaac Jogues. —Died Nov. 10, 1997
† Fagan, Harry J. (CLV) Madison, OH Immaculate Conception. —Died Oct. 14, 1997
† Fagnani, Anthony G. (NY) (Retired). —Died Jan. 4, 1998
† Fahey, William M. (PH) Eddystone, PA St. Rose of Lima. —Died Oct. 4, 1997
† Fallon, Joseph M., *s.j.* (BO) Chestnut Hill, MA Boston College. —Died Jan. 29, 1997
† Farina, Edward R. (PIT) (Retired). —Died March 19, 1997
† Farmer, Matthew P. (LEX) (Special Assignment). —Died Feb. 10, 1997
† Fearon, John F. (CHI) (Retired). —Died Feb. 10, 1997
† Fecci, Albert A., *o.m.i.* (SAT) San Antonio, TX Oblate Madonna Residence. —Died April 23, 1997
† Fechhelm, Richard A. (MIL) (Retired). —Died March 26, 1997
† Felock, Michael (PRM) Barberton, OH St. Nicholas. —Died May 12, 1997
† Fennessey, Luke Thomas (SPR) (Retired). —Died June 14, 1997
† Fernandez, Pedro Barbero, *o.f.m.* (FgM) Retired. —Died April 1, 1997
† Ferrell, William F., *s.j.* (STL) St. Louis, MO Fusz Pavilion. —Died Oct. 21, 1996
† Fierro, Paul, *s.d.s.* (MIL) Milwaukee, WI Jordan Hall. —Died July 20, 1997
† Finn, Rev. Msgr. Cecil E. (TLS) (Retired). —Died Oct. 31, 1996
† Finnerty, Rev. Msgr. Edward M. (NY) (Retired). —Died Oct. 8, 1997
† Finnerty, Edward G. (NY) (Retired). —Died Oct. 8, 1997
† Fischer, Joseph A. (MIL) (Retired). —Died May 4, 1997
† Fisher, Joseph P., *s.j.* (STL) St. Louis, MO Fusz Pavilion. —Died Feb. 24, 1997
† FitzGerald, Bernard J., *c.m.* (STL) Perryville, MO St. Mary's of the Barrons. —Died April 23, 1997
† Fitzgerald, James C. (LAN) (Retired). —Died Oct. 18, 1997

† Fitzpatrick, Joseph (SFR) (Retired). —Died Dec. 1997
† Flanagan, Francis, *o.m.i.* (BO) Tewksbury, MA Oblate Residence. —Died Sept. 2, 1997
† Flattery, James M. (OG) (Retired). —Died Aug. 9, 1997
† Flavin, Daniel (BIS) (Retired). —Died April 8, 1997
† Fleck, Raymond S., *o.s.f.s.* (CAM) Retired. —Died Feb. 21, 1997
† Flynn, Fabian A., *o.f.m.* (NY) Obernburg, NY St. Mary. —Died Feb. 15, 1997
† Flynn, James (STL) (Retired). —Died April 2, 1997
† Flynn, Rev. Msgr. John A. (OM) Omaha, NE Archdiocesan Community Foundation. —Died Sept. 15, 1997
† Flynn, Thomas Valerian, *o.p.* (DEN) Retired. —Died Feb. 4, 1997
† Foley, James F. (NEW) (Retired). —Died Oct. 29, 1997
† Foley, John J. (BO) (Retired). —Died Jan. 22, 1996
† Foley, John (DET) (Retired). —Died March 29, 1997
† Forster, Andrew A., *s.s.* (BAL) Retired. —Died Sept. 17, 1997
† Foster, William A. (OM) (Retired). —Died May 14, 1997
† Foxxe, *o.s.b.* (SCL) Retired. —Died May 12, 1997
† Frain, Rev. Msgr. Thomas J. (TR) (Retired). —Died Jan. 17, 1997
† Fraser, Thomas (DET) (Retired). —Died May 31, 1997
† Froehlich, Raymond P. (PIT) Sewickley, PA St. James. —Died May 8, 1997
† Funk, Louis F. (CIN) (Retired). —Died Jan. 24, 1997
† Gaffigan, Aloysius J., *o.s.f.s.* (WIL) Retired. —Died Feb. 18, 1997
† Gagnon, John L. (BUR) (Retired). —Died Nov. 13, 1996
† Galvin, Paul G. (CIN) Cincinnati, OH St. John Fisher. —Died Nov. 13, 1997
† Garvey, John (OKL) (Retired). —Died Oct. 3, 1996
† Gates, Gabriel, *o.c.d.* (MIL) Millwaukee, WI Provincial Offices - Discalced Carmelites. —Died June 9, 1997
† Gaughan, Rev. Msgr. Francis J. (PH) Philadelphia, PA St. Matthew. —Died Nov. 19, 1996
† Gauthier, Joseph D., *s.j.* (BO) Chestnut Hill, MA Boston College. —Died Aug. 19, 1997
† Gauthier, Rene G. (FR) Fall River, MA St. Jean Baptiste. —Died Jan. 6, 1997
† Gawin, George H., *s.a.c.* (MIL) Milwaukee, WI St. Joan Antida. —Died July 11, 1997
† Gaynor, William (ROC) Auburn, NY St. Alphonsus. —Died Sept. 12, 1997
† Geary, Mark, *o.p.* (NSH) Nashville, TN St. Thomas Hospital. —Died Sept. 7, 1997
† Geisen, Bernard Sylvester (CC) (Retired). —Died Jan. 12, 1997
† Gentner, John F. (SAG) Essexville, MI St. John the Evangelist. —Died May 4, 1997
† Geraghty, Walter F. (HRT) Southington, CT St. Dominic. —Died Feb. 23, 1997
† Getlik, Stephen B. (TR) (Retired). —Died July 20, 1997
† Ghirlando, Gabriel, *s.j.* (BO) Weston, MA Campion Center. —Died Feb. 9, 1997
† Gill, Joseph Cecil (MOB) (Retired). —Died Dec. 7, 1996
† Gillgannon, Patrick (AUS) (Retired). —Died Sept. 11, 1997
† Gillgannon, Patrick (GAL) (Retired). —Died Sept. 11, 1997
† Gillick, Thomas A. (NEW) Rutherford, NJ St. John Vianney. —Died June 19, 1997
† Gilligan, Francis J. (STP) (Retired). —Died April 6, 1997
† Glavin, Rev. Msgr. Edward R. (ALB) Amsterdam, NY St. Mary. —Died June 21, 1997
† Gleeson, John P. (STO) (Retired). —Died May 1, 1997
† Gluchowski, Joseph, *c.r.* (CHI) Retired. —Died Feb. 19, 1997
† Gluszek, W. Adalbert (SFR) (Retired). —Died Feb. 22, 1997
† Glynn, Myles, *o.f.m.* (FgM) Retired. —Died Oct. 17, 1997
† Goedert, Edmund N., *c.s.c.* (FTW) Notre Dame, IN Holy Cross House. —Died Nov. 3, 1996
† Goode, Athanasius E., *s.t.* (SJN) San Juan, PR Padre Gerardo Fredericks Mission Center. —Died Oct. 14, 1996
† Goodwine, Rev. Msgr. John (NY) (Retired). —Died Dec. 2, 1997
† Gordon, Rev. Msgr. John T. (DET) Dir. Southfield, MI Archdiocesan Cemeteries. —Died Oct. 27, 1997
† Gordon, Rev. Msgr. John J. (NY) (Retired). —Died Jan. 20, 1998
† Gorney, Rev. Msgr. Francis L. (ALT) (Retired). —Died Feb. 19, 1997
† Gradeck, A. Edward (HRT) (Retired). —Died Nov. 12, 1997
† Graham, James M. (SPR) (Retired). —Died July 3, 1997
† Graham, Robert A., *s.j.* (SJ) Los Gatos, CA Sacred Heart Jesuit Center. —Died Feb. 11, 1997
† Greinader, Rev. Msgr. Linford F. (ALT) (Retired). —Died July 29, 1997
† Gremillion, Rev. Msgr. John Edward (LAF) (Retired). —Died Feb. 21, 1997
† Grey, Thomas J., *s.j.* (BO) Chestnut Hill, MA Boston College. —Died March 27, 1997
† Griese, Roger E. (CIN) (Retired). —Died March 4, 1997
† Grimillion, Rev. Msgr. John E. (ORL) (Retired). —Died Feb. 21, 1997
† Grogan, Patrick (ORL) Rockledge, FL St. Mary. —Died Aug. 12, 1997
† Grogan, Richard (IND) (Retired). —Died Oct. 4, 1997
† Gross, Justin, *s.c.j.* (MIL) Retired. —Died Oct. 5, 1997
† Gryga, Stanislaus (JOL) (Retired). —Died Nov. 15, 1996
† Guillemette, Joseph H. (STP) (Retired). —Died Dec. 2, 1997
† Guillette, Ronald P. (GB) Reedsville, WI St. Mary-St. Patrick. —Died Jan. 7, 1997
† Haen, Edmund H. (MIL) (Retired). —Died Oct. 23, 1997
† Hagerty, Francis O., *s.j.* (BO) Boston, MA Boston College High School. —Died April, 24, 1997
† Hagmann, James J. (LC) Whitehall, WI St. John the Apostle. —Died Oct. 3, 1997
† Hale, Francis A. (HRT) (Retired). —Died March 30, 1997
† Hall, Finbar (LA) (Retired). —Died March 16, 1997
† Hall, Francis J. (BUF) (Retired). —Died Feb. 13, 1997
† Halmo, John F. (MIL) (Retired). —Died May 10, 1997
† Hammond, Henry E. (ARL) Alexandria, VA St. Lawrence. —Died Nov. 9, 1996
† Hanafin, Reverend Father William (BEA) (Retired). —Died Dec. 27, 1996
† Hanly, John G. (NEW) (Retired). —Died Oct. 16, 1997
† Harcar, Anthony J. (OAK) (Retired). —Died Dec. 17, 1997
† Harding, Bernard (BAL) (Retired). —Died Sept. 13, 1997
† Harding, Bernard, *o.ss.t.* (BAL) Retired. —Died Sept. 13, 1997
† Harper, Rev. Msgr. James J. (KC) (Retired). —Died Oct. 19, 1997
† Harrington, Emmet (P) (Retired). —Died July 14, 1997
† Harrington, Eugene J., *s.j.* (WOR) Worchester, MA Holy Cross College. —Died Sept. 30, 1997
† Harvanek, Robert F., *s.j.* (CHI) Chicago, IL Loyola University. —Died Nov. 22, 1996
† Haungs, Edwin C., *s.j.* (BUF) Buffalo, NY c/o St. Michael's. —Died Nov. 16, 1997
† Hayden, Ambrose V. (STP) (Retired). —Died June 24, 1997
† Hayden, Guy B. (SJ) (Retired). —Died May 31, 1997
† Hayes, James E. (FTW) (Retired). —Died Jan. 30, 1997
† Hayes, John S. (ROC) (Retired). —Died May 20, 1997
† Healy, James K., *c.s.sp.* (ARL) Arlington, VA Our Lady, Queen of Peace. —Died Jan. 10, 1997
† Heffernan, John J. (CHI) (Retired). —Died June 6, 1997
† Heide, Rev. Msgr. Herman L. (NY) (Retired). —Died May 17, 1997
† Hein, George J. (RVC) Commack, NY Christ the King. —Died June 22, 1997
† Heinrichs, Very Rev. Joseph L., *s.a.c.* (MIL) Milwukee, WI Pallotti House. —Died June 26, 1996
† Heisel, Raymond (ROC) Rochester, NY Our Mother of Sorrows. —Died July 22, 1997
† Hemauer, William G. (GB) (Retired). —Died Sept. 21, 1997
† Henkel, Albert J. (KNX) Knoxville, TN Holy Ghost. —Died Dec. 26, 1996
† Heppler, Richard Leo, *o.f.m.* (PAT) Ringwood, NJ Holy Name Friary. —Died April 21, 1997
† Herber, Leo, *c.pp.s.* (CIN) Carthagena, OH St. Charles. —Died Jan. 12, 1997
† Herledan, John F. (AUS) (Retired). —Died Sept. 17, 1997
† Herrera, Henry, *c.m.f.* (PHX) Seligman, AZ St. Francis. —Died Nov. 30, 1996
† Hesse, Harold W. (NU) (Retired). —Died Sept. 20, 1997
† Hiltz, Peter M. (BAL) (Retired). —Died Dec. 5, 1996
† Hinton, James, *c.pp.s.* (CIN) Retired. —Died July 14, 1997
† Hoffman, Rev. Msgr. Robert F. (DEN) (Retired). —Died May 12, 1997
† Hoffmann, Edward D. (SC) (Retired). —Died Nov. 22, 1996
† Hogan, Michael Jerome (DUL) (Retired). —Died May 8, 1997
† Holden, Peter, *s.t.* (WDC) Adelphi, MD Father Judge Missionary Cenacle. —Died Jan. 22, 1997
† Holleran, Edward J., *o.f.m.* (PAT) Ringwood, NJ Holy Name Friary. —Died Sept. 12, 1997
† Hosty, Edward M. (CHI) (Retired). —Died Feb. 24, 1997
† Houle, John A., *s.j.* (LA) Los Angeles, CA Colombiere House. —Died Aug. 9, 1997
† Hourihan, Rev. Msgr. James (LA) (Retired). —Died July 8, 1997
† Houser, Joseph F., *c.s.c.* (FTW) Notre Dame, IN Holy Cross House. —Died June 25, 1997
† Howe, John H. (LIN) (Retired). —Died April 4, 1997
† Hudson, Charles J. (NEW) Westfield, NJ St. Helen's. —Died Jan. 21, 1997
† Huels, Vincent P. (STL) (Retired). —Died July 7, 1997
† Hughes, James (SFD) (Retired). —Died April 30, 1997
† Hulsman, Rev. Msgr. Francis J. (OM) (Retired). —Died Sept. 14, 1997
† Humphrey, Robert (SB) Riverside, CA St. Catherine of Alexandria. —Died Nov. 1, 1997
† Hurley, John D. (ROC) (Retired). —Died March 8, 1997
† Hyland, Rev. Msgr. Charles H. (BO) (Retired). —Died Dec. 22, 1996
† Imperiale, Roger A., *o.f.m.* (NY) Mount Vernon, NY Siena Friary. —Died Aug. 11, 1997
† Iocco, Vincent V. (WIL) New Castle, DE St. Peter the Apostle. —Died July 11, 1997
† Iscla-Rovira, Luis F., *s.j.* (DET) Clarkston, MI Colombiere Jesuit Community. —Died Jan. 24, 1997
† Isermann, William D. (PEO) (Retired). —Died Dec. 9, 1996
† Izquierdo, Jose Maria, *s.j.* (MIA) Miami, FL Belen Jesuit Preparatory School. —Died May 21, 1997
† Jacobowski, Raymond G. (PEO) On Duty Outside the Diocese. —Died Feb. 23, 1997
† Jacobs, Charles E. (LAN) (Retired) Flushing, MI St. Robert. —Died Dec. 12, 1996
† Jamula, Joseph M. (WH) (Retired). —Died June 14, 1997
† Janczukowicz, Rev. Msgr. Chester J. (WOR) Worcester, MA Our Lady of Czestochowa. —Died May 20, 1997
† Janson, John, *o.f.m.* (FgM) Retired. —Died Dec. 20, 1996
† Jasinaki, Kazimierz, *s.ch.* (DET) Livonia, MI St. Mary Hospital. —Died April 1, 1997
† Jenkins, Paul D. (RIC) Hopewell, VA St. James. —Died Jan. 8, 1997
† Johnson, Francis D., *s.j.* (CIN) Cincinnati, OH Xavier University. —Died Oct. 14, 1996
† Johnson, William G. (P) Portland, OR Mt. St. Joseph. —Died Jan. 18, 1997
† Joseph, Karunei (MIA) Coral Springs, FL St. Andrew. —Died Sept. 24, 1997
† Joyce, Richard C. (NY) Patterson, NY Sacred Heart. —Died Feb. 22, 1997
† Joyce, William J., *c.s.sp.* (PIT) Bethel Park, PA Holy Ghost Animation Center. —Died Feb. 24, 1997
† Joyce, William J., *s.j.* (SEA) Spokane, WA Seattle University. —Died Dec. 17, 1996
† Kaczorowski, Rev. Msgr. Theodore A. (CHI) (Retired). —Died Jan. 12, 1996
† Kalinowski, Anthony David, *o.p.* (DEN) Denver, CO Notre Dame. —Died March 22, 1997
† Kampsen, Frederick (SCL) (Retired). —Died Nov. 7, 1997
† Kane, Rev. Msgr. Bartholomew, P.A. (DM) (Retired). —Died April 23, 1997
† Kapica, Francis A. (MET) (Retired). —Died March 5, 1997
† Karier, Raymond, *s.s.c.* (OM) Retired. —Died Feb. 9, 1997
† Kasak, Andrew, *o.f.m.conv.* (BAL) Baltimore, MD St. Stanislaus Kostka. —Died July 3, 1997
† Kasch, John (SFS) Howard, SD St. Agatha. —Died March 15, 1997
† Kealy, Rev. Msgr. Joseph P. (HBG) (Retired). —Died July 19, 1997
† Keaney, Joseph F., *s.j.* (BO) Boston, MA Loyola House. —Died Aug. 18, 1997
† Keeley, James T. (OAK) Oakland, CA St. Mary, Immaculate Conception-St. Francis De Sales. —Died Jan. 3, 1997
† Keeshan, Paul J. (ALB) (Retired). —Died May 31, 1997
† Kehoe, Joseph A., *c.s.c.* (FTW) Notre Dame, IN Holy Cross House. —Died Oct. 18, 1997
† Kelly, Francis Joseph (COV) (Retired). —Died April 14, 1997
† Kelly, Jerome, *o.f.m.* (PAT) Ringwood, NJ Holy Name Friary. —Died Aug. 30, 1997
† Kelly, John A., *s.j.* (SAC) Sacramento, CA Jesuit High School. —Died Oct. 28, 1996
† Kelly, Joseph A. (CHI) (Retired). —Died April 4, 1997
† Kelsch, Emmanuel, *o.s.b.* (SCL) Retired. —Died Oct. 16, 1997
† Kennedy, Vincent A. (RVC) (Retired). —Died Feb. 22, 1997
† Keogh, Rev. Msgr. John P. (NY) (Retired). —Died Nov. 21, 1997

† Kerivan, William C. (BO) (Permanent Disability). —Died Dec. 3, 1996
† Kesterson, James (LA) Van Nuys, CA St. Bridget of Sweden. —Died July 7, 1997
† Kevane, Rev. Msgr. M. Eugene (SC) (Retired). —Died Nov. 20, 1996
† Kiernan, Patrick Joseph (P) North Bend, OR Holy Redeemer Parish. —Died Sept. 3, 1997
† Kilgarriff, John J. (PH) Morton, PA Our Lady of Perpetual Help. —Died March 11, 1997
† Kinsella, Gerald A., *s.j.* (BO) Weston, MA Campion Center. —Died Sept. 20, 1996
† Kippes, Albert J., *o.m.i.* (SAT) San Antonio, TX Oblate Madonna Residence. —Died May 17, 1997
† Kissling, Joseph L. (DUB) (Retired). —Died June 16, 1997
† Kleem, Ferris (OLL) Detroit, MI St. Maron Church. —Died Sept. 23, 1997
† Kleem, Ferris (SAM) (Retired). —Died Sept. 23, 1997
† Kleffman, William C. (OM) Omaha, NE St. Agnes. —Died Aug. 21, 1997
† Klister, Irving (SFE) Springer, NM St. Joseph. —Died April 19, 1997
† Kmiecik, Joseph M., *c.s.c.* (FTW) Retired. —Died July 8, 1997
† Knopke, Kenneth, *o.f.m.* (SP) St. Petersburg, FL St. Anthony's Friary. —Died April 10, 1996
† Knorr, Rev. Msgr. Joseph H. (PIT) Bloomfield, PA Immaculate Conception/St. Joseph. —Died Sept. 28, 1996
† Koch, J. Robert, *s.j.* (DET) Clarkston, MI Colombiere Jesuit Community. —Died Dec. 6, 1996
† Koenig, Rev. Msgr. William A. (PH) (Retired). —Died Nov. 5, 1996
† Koesler, Leo, *o.s.b.* (LR) Subiaco, AR Subiaco Abbey. —Died Aug. 1, 1997
† Koll, Jude Thaddaeus, *o.s.b.* (SCL) Retired. —Died Oct. 19, 1997
† Koopman, Bernard (IND) Bradford, IN St. Michael. —Died Feb. 26, 1997
† Koren, Louis F. (MIL) (Retired). —Died March 13, 1997
† Kosmal, John (JOL) (Retired). —Died Aug. 18, 1997
† Kowalchik, Demetrius, *o.s.b.* (JOL) Lisle, IL St. Procopius Abbey. —Died June 24, 1997
† Kowalski, John, *c.m.* (SY) Utica, NY St. Vincent's Mission House. —Died Dec. 16, 1996
† Krakovsky, Reginald, *t.o.r.* (ALT) Retired. —Died July 14, 1997
† Kramer, Bernard, *s.m.* (STL) Retired. —Died April 28, 1997
† Kress, Joseph (DET) (Retired). —Died May 27, 1997
† Krupa, Rev. Msgr. Francis A. (BUF) (Retired). —Died June 8, 1997
† Krusling, Rev. Msgr. James L. (CIN) (Retired). —Died April 27, 1997
† Kuechmann, Theodore M., *m.m.* (NY) Maryknoll, NY Maryknoll Fathers and Brothers. —Died Oct. 16, 1997
† Kunsch, William C. (DUB) (Retired). —Died April 29, 1997
† Kupinski, Raymond P. (CHI) (Retired). —Died Dec. 19, 1996
† Kurtz, Rev. Msgr. George (STL) (Retired). —Died June 20, 1997
† Kuzy, Paul S., *c.pp.s.* (SLC) St. George, UT St. George's. —Died March 27, 1997
† Kylius, Ferdinand W. (CIN) (Retired). —Died Jan. 19, 1997
† Lab, Robert J., *s.j.* (CHI) Barrington, IL Bellarmine Hall. —Died Jan. 31, 1997
† Lane, Andrew, *c.p.* (CHI) Chicago, IL Immaculate Conception Monastery. —Died Feb. 19, 1997
† Lane, Thomas (SEA) (Retired). —Died Aug. 11, 1997
† Laner, Leander, *o.f.m.* (LA) Santa Barbara, CA Franciscan Friary, Order of Friars Minor (Old Mission). —Died Oct. 9, 1996
† Langlois, Robert, *s.m.* (BO) Cambridge, MA Marist Novitiate. —Died Aug. 20, 1997
† Lapean, Gerald J. (SPR) Springfield, MA Our Lady of the Sacred Heart. —Died Jan. 21, 1997
† LaRue, Joseph, *o.f.m.* (LA) Santa Barbara, CA Franciscan Friary, Order of Friars Minor (Old Mission). —Died Dec. 22, 1996
† Latterell, Glenn F. (SFS) (Retired). —Died July 20, 1997
† Lautner, Rev. Msgr. William A. (EVN) (Retired). —Died May 15, 1997
† Lavallee, Henri, *o.m.i.* (BO) Retired. —Died Nov. 21, 1996
† Lazek, Aleck (AUS) (Retired). —Died Aug. 16, 1997
† Le, John Thang (CHI) Berwyn, IL St. Mary of Celle. —Died Nov. 11, 1997
† Leahy, Thomas W., *s.j.* (SJ) Los Gatos, CA Sacred Heart Jesuit Center. —Died Dec. 14, 1996
† Lebel, Guy, *s.m.* (BO) Framingham, MA The Marist House. —Died May 4, 1997
† Lee, Joseph (SFR) (Retired). —Died May 13, 1997
† Lees, Charles J., *s.m.* (CIN) Retired. —Died Oct. 16, 1996
† Leibinger, Arthur (STL) (Retired). —Died April 2, 1997
† Leiblinger, Frank J. (LIN) (Retired). —Died Feb. 4, 1997
† Leiker, Alexander, *c.pp.s.* (SAL) Retired. —Died May 4, 1997
† Lentocha, Rev. Msgr. George V. (HBG) Middletown, PA Seven Sorrows of the B.V.M.. —Died May 26, 1997
† Leonard, Rev. Msgr. Francis X. (NY) Pine Island, NY St. Stanislaus. —Died March 22, 1997
† LeSage, Joseph Vincent (PMB) Sebastian, FL St. Sebastian. —Died Nov. 29, 1997
† Lewers, William M., *c.s.c.* (FTW) Notre Dame, IN University of Notre Dame. —Died April 19, 1997
† Liepold, Donald F. (SFS) (Retired). —Died June 15, 1997
† Like, Wayne L., *o.m.i.* (BEL) Belleville, IL King's House. —Died March 24, 1997
† Linehan, William J. (BO) (Retired). —Died Oct. 3, 1997
† Linn, Rev. Msgr. Francis J. (BAL) (Retired). —Died Dec. 16, 1996
† Lister, Alfred Q., *o.p.* (NO) New Orleans, LA Dominican Fathers and Brothers, Southern Dominican Province. —Died Aug. 16, 1997
† Litzau, John B. (MIL) (Retired). —Died June 8, 1997
† Llanos, Theodore (LA) Longbeach, CA St. Lucy. —Died Dec. 30, 1996
† Lo Cascio, Thomas M., *o.s.m.* (CHI) Retired. —Died May 6, 1997
† Lockwood, Charles (ALB) Altamont, NY St. Lucy. —Died March 18, 1997
† Loehr, Alfred M. (GB) (Retired). —Died July 30, 1997
† Loftus, Joseph V., *s.j.* (DET) Clarkston, MI Colombiere Jesuit Community. —Died Oct. 13, 1997
† Long, Florent, *o.f.m.* (PRO) Retired. —Died April 27, 1996
† Loreti, Rev. Msgr. Joseph F. (NEW) Roselle Park, NJ Assumption. —Died Nov. 22, 1997
† Lorigan, Thomas (PT) Milton, FL St. Rose of Lima. —Died Sept. 8, 1997
† Louis, Anthony M. (STP) (Retired). —Died May 2, 1997
† Lowry, Rev. Msgr. James M. (SCR) Scranton, PA St. Vincent de Paul. —Died Aug. 13, 1997
† Lucey, John P., *c.s.c.* (FTW) Retired. —Died May 17, 1997
† Luszczak, Francis J. (ALN) (Retired). —Died Nov. 24, 1996
† Lyddy, Vincent E. (HRT) (Retired). —Died Nov. 22, 1997
† Lynch, Thomas J. (HRT) Newington, CT St. Mary. —Died Jan. 25, 1997
† Maguire, Crispin, *o.f.m.* (SP) St. Petersburg, FL St. Anthony Friary. —Died Dec. 28, 1996
† Magyar, Ladislaus, *sch.p.* (PH) Devon, PA Devon Preparatory School. —Died Oct. 31, 1997
† Mahler, Joachim, *o.f.m.* (PAT) Ringwood, NJ Holy Name Friary. —Died March 14, 1997
† Mahon, Rev. Msgr. David (PAT) Mountain Lakes, NJ St. Catherine of Siena. —Died July 15, 1997
† Mahrer, James Albert, *o.s.b.* (PBL) Westcliffe, CO Our Lady of the Assumption. —Died April 5, 1997
† Majdanik, Albin J. (SY) Binghamton, NY St. Stanislaus. —Died April 20, 1997
† Malek, Eugene, *o.f.m.* (PRO) Providence, RI St. Francis Chapel. —Died Jan. 16, 1997
† Malinak, Joseph G. (PIT) Tarentum, PA St. Clement. —Died May 14, 1997
† Maltese, Rev. Msgr. Anthony L. (NY) Tuckahoe, NY Immaculate Conception. —Died June 15, 1997
† Manders, Norbert R., *o.praem.* (SFE) Albuquerque, NM Santa Maria de la Vid Priory. —Died Aug. 14, 1997
† Mandl, Maximus J., *o.f.m.* (TR) Roebling, NJ Holy Assumption. —Died Dec. 11, 1997
† Mangan, Eugene (NY) Staten Island, NY St. Sylvester. —Died June 25, 1997
† Mangan, Joseph T., *s.j.* (DET) Clarkston, MI Colombiere Jesuit Community. —Died Oct. 8, 1996
† Manning, Thomas, *o.m.i.* (BO) Tewksbury, MA Oblate Residence. —Died Feb. 8, 1997
† Marquis, Paul, *o.m.i.* (BO) Retired. —Died Oct. 8, 1997
† Marrer, Robert (STU) (Retired). —Died Sept. 27, 1996
† Marshall, Albert, *s.d.b.* (SFR) San Francisco, CA Salesian Provincial Residence. —Died May 16, 1997
† Martin, Bernard E. (WDC) Silver Spring, MD St. Bernadette. —Died April 26, 1997
† Martin, Rev. Msgr. Myron (SFS) (Retired). —Died Jan. 28, 1997
† Martin, Rev. Msgr. William C. (SAT) San Antonio, TX St. Pius X. —Died Sept. 17, 1997
† Martinez, Armando (SFE) Santa Rosa, NM St. Rose of Lima. —Died May 3, 1997
† Martinez, Rev. Msgr. George W. (SHP) Monroe, LA St. Matthew. —Died June 23, 1997
† Martusevich, Rev. Msgr. Vito J. (PH) Philadelphia, PA St. George. —Died Aug. 23, 1997
† Marusa, Henry, *s.v.d.* (ORG) Santa Ana, CA Divine Word. —Died May 31, 1997
† Mastey, Walter S. (GRY) (Retired). —Died April 14, 1997
† Matheson, Paul (DET) (Retired). —Died April 25, 1997
† Mattie, Rev. Msgr. John G. (SEA) (Retired). —Died May 6, 1997
† Mayer, John, *o.f.m.* (FgM) Retired. —Died March 28, 1996
† Mayrand, Paul, *o.m.i.* (BO) Retired. —Died Dec. 9, 1996
† Maziarz, Edward, *c.pp.s.* (CHI) Retired. —Died July 11, 1997
† McAllister, Forest, *o.f.m.* (SFE) Rio Rancho, NM Felician Sisters. —Died July 26, 1997
† McAndrews, Walter J. (BO) (Retired). —Died June 14, 1997
† McCabe, Edwin J., *o.c.s.o.* (SAC) Vina, CA Abbey of New Clairvaux. —Died July 20, 1997
† McCall, Rev. Msgr. John H. (BAL) Fallston, MD St. Mark. —Died May 19, 1997
† McCarthy, John P. (BUF) (Retired). —Died Oct. 11, 1997
† McCarthy, Stanislaus, *o.carm.* (NY) Retired. —Died June 15, 1997
† McCarthy, William R., *m.m.* (NY) Maryknoll, NY Maryknoll Fathers and Brothers. —Died July 21, 1997
† McClintock, Robert J. (SC) Odebolt, IA St. Martin. —Died Aug. 29, 1997
† McCloskey, Henry Francis, *s.m.* (HON) Retired. —Died March 3, 1997
† McCloskey, James F. (NEW) (Retired). —Died Feb. 22, 1997
† McCluskey, Vincent S. (PAT) Denville, NJ Morris Catholic High School. —Died April 7, 1997
† McDonald, John James, *o.p.* (CHI) Retired. —Died Dec. 20, 1996
† McDonald, Michael J. (PRT) Portland, ME Cathedral of the Immaculate Conception. —Died June 20, 1997
† McElaney, Robert (PRM) Indianapolis, IN St. Athanasius. —Died Oct. 8, 1997
† McEnaney, Owen (NY) (Retired). —Died Sept. 3, 1997
† McEneany, Joseph K., *ss.cc.* (ORG) Costa Mesa, CA Fairview State Hospital. —Died Feb. 25, 1997
† McFarland, H. James, *s.j.* (SAC) Sacramento, CA Sutter General Hospital. —Died Feb. 22, 1997
† McFarlane, Dale Floyd (GF) (Retired). —Died April 25, 1997
† McGinty, Vincent T., *s.j.* (SJ) Los Gatos, CA Sacred Heart Jesuit Center. —Died March 18, 1997
† McGough, Rev. Msgr. Thomas J. (HBG) (Retired). —Died Aug. 29, 1997
† McGowan, Norbert, *o.s.b.* (SAV) Savannah, GA Benedictine Military School. —Died Jan. 2, 1962
† McGrenehan, Rev. Msgr. Bernard Joseph (PMB) Pastor Emeritus Palm Beach, FL St. Edward. —Died Aug. 31, 1997
† McGuinness, Fergus, *c.p.* (LA) Pomona, CA Passionist Community. —Died Nov. 12, 1996
† McHale, Rev. Msgr. James J. (ALN) Bath, PA Sacred Heart. —Died Oct. 25, 1997
† McHarness, Paul, *o.s.b.* (SFS) Marvin, SD Blue Cloud Abbey. —Died March 8, 1997
† McHatton, James S., *o.p.* (NO) New Orleans, NO St. Anthony of Padua. —Died June 16, 1997
† McKenna, Rev. Msgr. Edward I. (NOR) Middletown, CT St. John. —Died June 26, 1997
† McLaughlin, Francis J. (CAM) Barrington, NJ St. Francis de Sales. —Died Oct. 7, 1997
† McLaughlin, James E., *m.m.* (NY) Maryknoll, NY Maryknoll Fathers and Brothers. —Died June 3, 1997
† McLean, Edward J. (ARL) Arlington, VA St. Charles Borromeo. —Died Oct. 14, 1997
† McMahan, Frederick (DAV) Davenport, IA St. Ambrose University. —Died Aug. 15, 1997
† McManus, Edward A. (ALB) (Retired). —Died March 7, 1997
† McMullan, Rev. Msgr. Seamus (FRS) (Retired). —Died Nov. 27, 1997
† McNamara, Thomas E. (NY) Bronx, NY Sts. Philip & James. —Died Nov. 25, 1997
† McNeill, Rev. Msgr. Robert W. (BO) Kingston, MA St. Joseph. —Died Dec. 15, 1996
† McNerney, Malachy, *o.s.b.* (LR) Booneville, AR Church of the Assumption. —Died July 24, 1997
† McNicholas, Timothy J. (CIN) (Retired). —Died March 29, 1997
† McNulty, Michael A. (MET) Blairstown, NJ St. Jude. —Died April 19, 1997
† McNulty, William C. (STP) (Retired). —Died May 26, 1997
† McPeak, George H., *m.m.* (NY) Maryknoll, NY Maryknoll Fathers and Brothers. —Died Sept. 24, 1997

† McPeak, William J. (NY) (Retired). —Died Aug. 9, 1997
† McShane, Vincent J. (NY) Croton-on-Hudson, NY Holy Name of Mary. —Died March 11, 1997
† Mealey, John H. (ALB) Albany, NY St. Teresa of Avila. —Died Aug. 25, 1997
† Melycher, Stephen D. (BAL) (Retired). —Died Jan. 20, 1997
† Mendonca, Rev. Msgr. Luiz G. (FR) (Retired). —Died Feb. 21, 1997
† Merino, Zenon R. (BR) (Retired). —Died July 25, 1997
† Merkel, Francis J. (SCR) Scranton, PA St. John the Baptist. —Died July 30, 1997
† Merth, John P. (CR) (Retired). —Died March 30, 1997
† Messier, Bernard H. (BUR) Barre, VT St. Monica. —Died Dec. 28, 1996
† Mifkovic, Francis F. (KC) (Retired). —Died Aug. 7, 1997
† Mihai, Eugen (ROM) Astoria, NY St. Mary Mission. —Died Oct. 2, 1997
† Mihelko, John J., *m.m.* (NY) Maryknoll, NY Maryknoll Fathers and Brothers. —Died April 13, 1997
† Mihm, Xavier R., *o.s.b.* (GBG) Retired. —Died Oct. 29, 1996
† Miller, Rudolph H., *c.m.* (NO) New Orleans, LA St. Joseph. —Died Sept. 8, 1997
† Miller, Wayne E. (COL) Columbus, OH Our Lady of Victory. —Died May 28, 1997
† Minigan, Frederick J. (BO) (Retired). —Died July 27, 1997
† Mobley, William M. (SLC) (Retired). —Died Dec. 24, 1996
† Moffitt, Venard J., *t.o.r.* (SP) Tampa, FL St. Patrick. —Died Feb. 13, 1997
† Molloy, William T. (MET) (Retired). —Died April 24, 1997
† Monahan, John, *c.s.v.* (JOL) St. Anne, IL St. Anne. —Died Oct. 6, 1996
† Montalbano, Daniel F. (CHI) Chicago, IL Resurrection. —Died May 25, 1997
† Mooney, Charles A., *s.j.* (DET) Clarkston, MI Colombiere Jesuit Community. —Died Jan. 17, 1997
† Moore, Rev. Msgr. Robert E. (NY) Gardiner, NY St. Charles Borromeo. —Died March 22, 1997
† Moran, Donald V. (MAD) Ridgeway, WI St. Bridget. —Died Aug. 5, 1997
† Moras, Edward (OKL) Oklahoma City, OK St. James. —Died July 3, 1997
† Morello, Rev. Msgr. Amedeo L. (TR) (Retired). —Died Nov. 3, 1997
† Mores, Bernard, *c.pp.s.* (CIN) Carthagena, OH St. Charles. —Died Feb. 1, 1997
† Morkunas, Rev. Msgr. Simon (SC) (Retired). —Died July 5, 1997
† Morrell, Joseph J. (ALN) Allentown, PA St. Francis of Assisi. —Died Dec. 11, 1996
† Moskva, Emil (PSC) (Retired). —Died Jan. 26, 1997
† Mraz, Method J., *o.s.b.* (GBG) Retired. —Died June 9, 1997
† Mueller, Peter F., *c.s.c.* (FTW) Notre Dame, IN Holy Cross House. —Died July 16, 1997
† Murphy, Rev. Msgr. John E. (LR) (Retired). —Died May 14, 1997
† Murphy, Rev. Msgr. John J. (WDC) (Retired). —Died Sept. 15, 1997
† Murphy, Joseph B., c.s.sp. (SB) Retired. —Died Jan. 12, 1997
† Murphy, Kenneth G. (RVC) Great Neck, NY St. Aloysius. —Died Feb. 2, 1997
† Murphy, Thomas W. (NOR) Somersville, CT All Saints. —Died April 15, 1997
† Murray, Edmund J., *c.s.c.* (FTW) Notre Dame, IN Holy Cross House. —Died Nov. 12, 1996
† Murray, Edward L., *c.s.sp.* (PIT) Pittsburgh, PA Duquesne University. —Died Aug. 28, 1997
† Murray, John J. (CHL) Morganton, NC St. Charles Borromeo. —Died Sept. 29, 1997
† Murray, Rev. Msgr. Patrick J. (SAT) (Retired). —Died March 28, 1997
† Murray, Robert P. (TR) (Retired). —Died Nov. 24, 1997
† Murtaugh, Daniel J. (CHI) (Retired). —Died Dec. 30, 1996
† Myers, Edward F. (CHI) (Retired). —Died Aug. 20, 1997
† Nadrach, Adolph W. (KAL) (Retired). —Died June 15, 1997
† Napierkowski, Joseph J., *s.m.* (HON) Wailuku, Maui St. Anthony. —Died Jan. 19, 1997
† Nealen, Giles L., *o.s.b.* (GBG) Retired. —Died Dec. 29, 1996
† Nesevitch, Joseph (SJP) (Retired). —Died Oct. 4, 1997
† Neumann, Charles, *s.m.* (SAT) San Antonio, TX St. Mary's University. —Died May 9, 1997
† Nicholas, John J., *c.m.* (BIR) Alexander City, AL St. John the Apostle. —Died May 4, 1997
† Nicolas, Marcos (LA) (Retired). —Died June 16, 1997
† Niemeyer, Elmer (SFE) Albuquerque, NM St. Therese. —Died Feb. 19, 1997
† Niemeyer, John (JKS) (Retired). —Died March 8, 1997
† Nintemann, George Bernard, *o.p.* (WIN) Rochester, MN St. Bridget's. —Died Nov. 30, 1996
† Nolan, Rev. Msgr. Michael (SB) (Retired). —Died March 23, 1997
† Nytes, Raymond, *o.f.m.* (FWT) Crowley, TX St. Francis Village, Inc. —Died Jan. 5, 1997
† O'Brien, Rev. Msgr. Edward M. (NY) New York, NY Guardian Angel. —Died April 3, 1997
† O'Brien, Hugh V. (CHI) (Retired). —Died Jan. 21, 1997
† O'Brien, Rev. Msgr. John F. (NEW) (Retired). —Died Feb. 6, 1997
† O'Brien, John G. (R) (Retired). —Died Feb. 2, 1997
† O'Brien, Joseph A. (STL) (Retired). —Died June 23, 1997
† O'Brien, Robert E. (BO) Boston, MA St. Andrew. —Died Dec. 28, 1996
† O'Connell, Maurice J. (TLS) Broken Arrow, OK St. Anne. —Died Nov. 27, 1996
† O'Doherty, Dermot Augustine (DUL) (Retired). —Died June 25, 1997
† O'Donell, Daniel, *s.d.b.* (NY) Retired. —Died Feb. 4, 1997
† O'Donnell, Gregory, *o.f.m.* (PAT) Ringwood, NJ Holy Name Friary. —Died Aug. 5, 1997
† O'Dougherty, Rev. Msgr. Loyola (TUC) San Manuel, AZ St. Bartholomew. —Died April 9, 1997
† O'Flaherty, John P. (WOR) North Grafton, MA St. Mary's. —Died Nov. 21, 1996
† O'Hara, Maurice, *o.f.m.* (PAT) Ringwood, NJ Holy Name Friary. —Died May 1, 1997
† O'Hara, Michael J. (NOR) Killingworth, CT St. Lawrence. —Died Jan. 29, 1997
† O'Neil, Charles H. (SAG) Auburn, MI St. Joseph. —Died April 5, 1997
† O'Neil, William J. (Y) (Retired). —Died Jan. 16, 1997
† O'Neill, Michael (HEL) (Special Assignment). —Died Sept. 27, 1997
† O'Roake, Patrick J., *o.s.b.* (MIL) Benet Lake, WI St. Benedict's Abbey. —Died Jan. 28, 1997
† O'Sullivan, Carroll M., *s.j.* (SJ) Los Gatos, CA Sacred Heart Jesuit Center. —Died Oct. 9, 1996
† O'Sullivan, Laurence (MRY) (Retired). —Died Feb. 18, 1997
† O'Sullivan, Rev. Msgr. Thomas J. (LA) Los Angeles, CA Visitation. —Died Oct. 30, 1997
† Ohlenforst, J. William (LAF) Morse, LA Immaculate Conception. —Died Jan. 3, 1997
† Ondik, Michael J. (CLV) Avon, OH Holy Trinity. —Died Jan. 16, 1997
† Ormsby, Rev. Msgr. Basil A. (BUF) (Retired). —Died June 14, 1997
† Ornelas, Angel (CHY) Laramie, WY St. Lawrence O'Toole. —Died March 19, 1997
† Osendorf, Cassian, *o.s.b.* (SCL) Retired. —Died Oct. 19, 1996
† Ossowski, Rev. Msgr. Casimir B. (ALT) Johnstown, PA St. Casimir. —Died Jan. 28, 1997
† Otazua-Pena, Francisco, *s.j.* (SJ) Los Gatos, CA Sacred Heart Jesuit Center. —Died Feb. 11, 1997
† Otero, Neil (HRT) (Retired). —Died Jan. 15, 1998
† Overman, Conleth, *c.p.* (ORL) Orlando, FL Bethany House of Beutel. —Died June 5, 1997
† Owens, Edward M. (JC) (Retired). —Died Jan. 4, 1997
† Pachorek, Joseph (CHI) (Retired). —Died Dec. 23, 1996
† Padberg, John R., *s.j.* (STL) St. Louis, MO Fusz Pavilion. —Died Sept. 15, 1997
† Palmer, Edwin G. (KAL) Battle Creek, MI St. Jerome. —Died Feb. 13, 1997
† Palmer, Martin E., *s.j.* (STL) St. Louis, MO Saint Louis University. —Died Aug. 7, 1997
† Paloma, Jesus Pastor, *o.a.r.* (NY) Suffern, NY Tagaster Monastery. —Died Nov. 9, 1996
† Pandola, Oreste, *s.a.c.* (BAL) Baltimore, MD St. Leo's. —Died Jan. 17, 1997
† Pangelinan, Ferdinand S., *o.f.m.cap.* (AGN) Agana Heights, GU St. Fidelis Friary. —Died Jan. 8, 1997
† Pank, William H. (L) (Retired). —Died Sept. 28, 1997
† Pansza, Ralph C., *c.m.* (CHI) Chicago, IL DePaul Vincentian Residence. —Died Feb. 14, 1997
† Pasura, John G. (ALN) (Retired). —Died Sept. 23, 1996
† Patacconi, Noel, *o.s.b.* (DET) Oxford, MI Saint Benedictine Priory. —Died Sept. 26, 1996
† Patrick, Maurice C. (SFS) (Retired). —Died Oct. 20, 1997
† Pattok, Raymond J. (GR) (Retired). —Died Oct. 14, 1997
† Pavalkis, Victor (SJ) Milpitas, CA St. John the Baptist. —Died Dec. 4, 1996
† Pawelko, Mitchell, *c.r.* (CHI) Retired. —Died Dec. 26, 1996
† Pazera, Casimir A., *o.s.a.* (JOL) New Lennox, IL Providence Catholic High School. —Died July 16, 1997
† Peacock, Joseph L. (ATL) Decatur, GA St. Thomas More. —Died Sept. 31, 1997
† Pease, Anthony F. (OG) Combermere, Ontario Madonna House. —Died Jan. 8, 1997
† Pekar, Rev. Msgr. Gilbert F. (GAL) (Retired). —Died July 31, 1997
† Pellett, Marcian, *o.f.m.cap.* (AGN) Agana Heights, GU St. Fidelis Friary. —Died Nov. 18, 1996
† Pepel, Anthony (SY) Oswego, NY St. Stephen. —Died Aug. 7, 1997
† Perri, Joseph E., *s.j.* (P) Dexter, OR St. Henry. —Died March 7, 1997
† Peschel, Joseph E., *s.j.* (CIN) Milford, OH Milford Jesuit Community. —Died July 4, 1997
† Peters, John M. (DUB) (Retired). —Died May 31, 1997
† Petit, Clement P. (RCK) (Retired). —Died Sept. 4, 1997
† Petta, LeRoy A. (MIL) Milwaukee, WI St. Stanislaus. —Died Oct. 19, 1997
† Pfeifer, William A. (TOL) (Retired). —Died Sept. 4, 1997
† Phelan, Reginald L. (TUC) (Retired). —Died Jan. 1, 1997
† Phillips, Robert W. (SC) (Retired). —Died Dec. 7, 1996
† Picher, Leo J. (HRT) (Retired). —Died Aug. 13, 1997
† Piechocinski, Thomas A. (MET) Monmouth Junction, NJ St. Cecilia. —Died March 25, 1997
† Pierce, William Jean (SHP) (Retired). —Died Nov. 5, 1996
† Placek, Paul, *c.p.* (CHI) Chicago, IL Passionist Provincial Office. —Died Nov. 23, 1996
† Plafcan, Paul J. (CLV) Lorain, OH St. John. —Died May 26, 1997
† Pohorlak, John Gregory (PBR) Newton Falls, OH St. Michael. —Died Dec. 21, 1996
† Poirier, Raoul J., *m.afr.* (OG) Retired. —Died Jan. 5, 1997
† Pollack, Andrew, *c.pp.s.* (CIN) Carthagena, OH St. Charles. —Died June 19, 1997
† Pollard, Martin, *o.s.b.* (P) St. Benedict, OR Mount Angel Abbey. —Died Feb. 8, 1997
† Pondant, Anthony W. (DAL) Wylie, TX St. Anthony. —Died Aug. 24, 1997
† Ponisciak, Cyril S. (PH) Coatesville, PA St. Joseph. —Died May 17, 1997
† Ponsiglione, Attilio, *o.m.i.* (BO) Tewksbury, MA Oblate Residence. —Died June 15, 1997
† Poole, Rev. Msgr. James D. (SAC) (Retired). —Died Nov. 10, 1997
† Porter, Thomas, *o.c.s.o* (SLC) Huntsville, UT Abbey of Our Lady of the Holy Trinity. —Died Oct. 15, 1997
† Posluszny, Sylvester (GAL) (Retired). —Died Jan. 7, 1997
† Powers, James E., *s.j.* (BO) Weston, MA Campion Center. —Died Jan. 17, 1997
† Prather, Edward (OKL) (Retired). —Died Nov. 26, 1996
† Prendiville, Joseph A. (L) (Retired). —Died May 25, 1997
† Presinell, Joseph C. (SFS) (Retired). —Died Aug. 8, 1997
† Prill, John, M.A. (GAL) Houston, TX St. John Neumann.
† Pritchard, James F. (ALB) (Retired). —Died June 10, 1997
† Procopio, Charles A. (HBG) Mount Carmel, PA Our Lady of Mt. Carmel. —Died July 18, 1997
† Protomastro, Camillus, *o.f.m.cap.* (NY) Bronx, NY Immaculate Conception. —Died Jan. 15, 1997
† Provenzano, Francis A., *c.s.c.* (FTW) South Bend, IN Congregation of Holy Cross Indiana Province Provincial House. —Died June 12, 1997
† Provosty, William B. (ALX) Cottonport, LA St. Mary's Assumption. —Died April 3, 1997
† Przybyla, Raymond E. (TOL) (Retired). —Died Jan. 8, 1997
† Przydacz, John (TYL) Chap. Tyler, TX Mother Francis Hospital. —Died Sept. 28, 1997
† Przysucha, Joseph, *c.r.* (CHI) Chicago, IL Archbishop Weber High School. —Died Oct. 10, 1997
† Pucci, Rev. Msgr. Anthony (NY) Yonkers, NY Most Holy Trinity. —Died May 27, 1997
† Pyne, William F. (PRO) North Smithfield, RI St. Antoine Residence. —Died March 14, 1997
† Pysz, Bruno E., *o.f.m.conv.* (BUF) Buffalo, NY Corpus Christi. —Died Nov. 18, 1997
† Quinn, Patrick (JKS) (On Duty Outside the Diocese). —Died Jan. 9, 1997
† Quintana, Edward (GLP) (Retired). —Died Oct. 6, 1997
† Reagan, Oliver, *s.m.* (STL) Retired. —Died Dec. 21, 1996
† Rebain, Daniel (DET) Auburn Hills, MI Sacred Heart. —Died Jan. 18, 1997
† Reddington, Rev. John A. (ROC) Pittsford, NY St. Louis. —Died Dec. 30, 1997
† Reese, Harry A., *s.j.* (BUF) Williamsville, NY Canisius Jesuit Community. —Died April 29, 1997
† Regan, William (STL) (Retired). —Died Feb. 18, 1997

† Reid, Rev. Msgr. Marion M. (NO) (Retired). —Died Oct. 26, 1997
† Reilly, Peter J. (NEW) Rutherford, NJ St. Mary. —Died Feb. 21, 1997
† Reyna, Joseph A. (SAT) Pearsall, TX Immaculate Heart of Mary. —Died June 28, 1997
† Rezabek, Rev. Msgr. William J. (LIN) (Retired). —Died Oct. 29, 1997
† Richard, Rev. Msgr. Eugene (NY) New Rocelle, NY Blessed Sacrament. —Died Oct. 6, 1997
† Ricke, Peter, *o.f.m.* (SFE) Retired. —Died March 12, 1997
† Ridge, Thomas P. (TR) (Retired). —Died Oct. 6, 1997
† Riggie, Kloman F. (BAL) Hagerstown, MD St. Joseph. —Died Dec. 2, 1996
† Ring, Michael J. (SAV) Augusta, GA St. Joseph. —Died July 13, 1997
† Rivard, Robert J., *c.m.* (BRK) Jamaica, NY St. John's University. —Died Feb. 25, 1997
† Roberts, Edward Francis (KCK) (Retired). —Died Sept. 18, 1997
† Robertson, Kenneth, *o.f.m.* (GLP) Retired. —Died Oct. 20, 1996
† Robertson, Theophane, *o.f.m.* (LA) Santa Barbara, CA Franciscan Friary, Order of Friars Minor (Old Mission). —Died July 20, 1997
† Roche, Allan E. (BO) (Retired). —Died Aug. 10, 1997
† Romagno, Michael (ALN) (Retired). —Died Feb. 10, 1997
† Romero, Oswald E. (PIT) (Retired). —Died Feb. 7, 1997
† Rooney, Leo J. (SJ) Cupertino, CA St. Joseph of Cupertino. —Died Jan. 14, 1997
† Rowley, Charles, *o.f.m.* (PAT) Ringwood, NJ Holy Name Friary. —Died Nov. 20, 1996
† Ruffalo, Richard (JOL) Joliet, IL Holy Cross. —Died Feb. 21, 1997
† Ruhl, George J. (PH) Milmont Park, PA Our Lady of Peace. —Died Feb. 24, 1997
† Ruppe, Thomas G. (MAR) (Retired). —Died Nov. 20, 1997
† Rupprecht, Norbert A., *o.s.b.* (GBG) Retired. —Died Dec. 28, 1996
† Ryan, Brian G. (PT) Crestview, FL Our Lady of Victory. —Died Nov. 12, 1996
† Sablica, Michael J. (MIL) (Retired). —Died June 15, 1997
† Salinas, Marcel H., *c.m.f.* (PHX) Mesa, AZ St. Timothy. —Died March 26, 1997
† Salmon, Albert G. (OG) Brushton, NY St. Mary's Church. —Died Aug. 21, 1997
† Salt, Donald L. (STP) (Retired). —Died Feb. 7, 1997
† Sanchez, Rev. Msgr. Carlos (BR) (Retired). —Died Feb. 7, 1997
† Sancho-Boyles, Anthony (FRS) (Retired). —Died Aug. 2, 1997
† Sanders, Robert E. (HRT) (Retired). —Died April 14, 1997
† Sanguinetti, Joseph Peter, *o.p.* (SFR) San Francisco, CA St. Dominic Priory. —Died Jan. 23, 1997
† Saunders, Robert E. (HRT) (Retired). —Died April 20, 1997
† Scanlan, Most Rev. John J., D.D. (HON) (Retired). —Died Jan. 31, 1997
† Scanlan, John (SHP) Lake Providence, LA St. Patrick. —Died March 18, 1997
† Scarff, Rev. Msgr. Stanley J. (BAL) (Retired). —Died March 6, 1997
† Schaefers, Rev. Msgr. Francis (P) (Retired). —Died Nov. 25, 1996
† Schaeper, Jerome A. (CIN) Cincinnati, OH Elder High School. —Died July 11, 1997
† Scheid, Bernard W. (CHI) (Retired). —Died April 25, 1997
† Scheljens, Carl, *c.j.* (MRY) Los Osos, CA St. Elizabeth Seton. —Died Aug. 14, 1996
† Scherrer, George, *s.m.* (SAT) San Antonio, TX St. Joseph's Community. —Died May 22, 1997
† Schlatter, Glen F. (P) (Retired). —Died June 26, 1997
† Schlich, James Lee (L) (Retired). —Died May 4, 1997
† Schmidt, Stanley Andrew (L) (Retired). —Died May 2, 1997
† Schmidt, Vincent Francis (COV) (Retired). —Died Jan. 27, 1997
† Schmit, Rev. Msgr. Jerome E. (TOL) (Retired). —Died April 10, 1997
† Schmit, Ronald N. (PRT) Brewer, ME St. Joseph. —Died June 13, 1997
† Schmitt, Bernard, *c.pp.s.* (CIN) Carthagena, OH St. Charles. —Died May 4, 1997
† Schmitt, Leo J. (GB) (Retired). —Died Feb. 5, 1997
† Schneider, Robert W. (MIL) (Retired). —Died June 25, 1997
† Schoenberg, Martin, *o.s.c.* (LIN) Hastings, NE Crosier Community of Hastings. —Died Nov. 11, 1996
† Schumacher, Bernard, *o.s.b.* (LR) Subiaco, AR Subiaco Abbey. —Died Feb. 1, 1997
† Schutzman, John Stanley (COV) (Retired). —Died Nov. 26, 1996
† Schwartz, Clarence Joseph (L) (Retired). —Died Aug. 26, 1997
† Segadelli, Joseph D. (BO) (Retired). —Died Feb. 28, 1997
† Senderak, Rev. Msgr. Casimir E. (GRY) (Retired). —Died Dec. 14, 1996
† Setlock, Rev. Msgr. William A. (BUF) (Retired). —Died Feb. 25, 1997
† Shanahan, Edward J. (RVC) (Retired). —Died Nov. 15, 1996
† Shank, Bernard F. (GRY) (Retired). —Died Sept. 13, 1997
† Shenk, Joseph D. (TOL) (Retired). —Died Jan. 14, 1997
† Sherpenski, Donald A.J., *s.j.* (BO) Boston, MA Boston College High School. —Died April 28, 1997
† Shilala, Robert N. (SCR) Dorrance, PA Our Lady Help of Christians. —Died Aug. 26, 1997
† Shillito, Edward D. (RVC) (Retired). —Died Oct. 20, 1997
† Shimkus, Bernard A. (PH) (Retired). —Died Nov. 10, 1996
† Shine, Bernardine, *o.s.b.* (SD) Oceanside, SD Prince of Peace Abbey. —Died Nov. 24, 1993
† Shine, Cornelius (LA) Silver Springs Shores, FL Immaculate Heart of Mary. —Died Dec. 4, 1996
† Siedling, Rudolph, *o.s.b.* (SD) Oceanside, SD Prince of Peace Abbey. —Died Oct. 11, 1989
† Sienkiewicz, Rev. Msgr. Alfred Joseph (BGP) Stamford, CT Holy Spirit. —Died Dec. 1, 1996
† Siesle, John W. (STL) Lemay, MO Mary, Queen of the Universe. —Died April 21, 1997
† Sigur, Rev. Msgr. Alexander Octave (LAF) (Retired). —Died Aug. 13, 1997
† Sikora, Rev. Msgr. Joseph G. (PH) Philadelphia, PA St. Dominic. —Died Jan. 11, 1997
† Sikorski, Andrew (GR) (Retired). —Died June 8, 1997
† Silvestri, Anthony F., *o.s.f.s.* (ORL) Retired. —Died Nov. 26, 1996
† Simodejka, Rev. Msgr. Michael Andrew (PBR) Aliquippa, PA St. George. —Died Oct. 2, 1997
† Sisk, William, *o.f.m.* (SPK) Spokane, WA St. Francis. —Died July 23, 1997
† Skelly, Laurence R., *s.j.* (BO) Weston, MA Campion Center. —Died July 12, 1997
† Slattery, Dennis J., *m.m.* (NY) Maryknoll, NY Maryknoll Fathers and Brothers. —Died Oct. 19, 1997
† Slegers, Gabriel, *ss.cc.* (FgM) Retired. —Died March 27, 1997
† Smith, Arnold R. (SCR) Luzerne, PA Sacred Heart of Jesus. —Died Feb. 1, 1997
† Smith, Mark, *o.f.m.* (BO) Boston, MA St. Anthony Shrine. —Died Jan. 5, 1997
† Smith, Paul B. (ALX) Chicago, IL Holy Angels. —Died Nov. 23, 1996
† Smith, Richard F., *s.j.* (STL) St. Louis, MO Jesuit Hall. —Died March 15, 1997
† Smolar, Joseph A., *c.pp.s.* (CIN) Retired. —Died Jan. 12, 1997
† Smyth, Rev. Msgr. Claude (DAL) Plano, TX St. Mark the Evangelist. —Died Nov. 11, 1997
† Snellenberg, John Van (SAC) (Retired). —Died Oct. 24, 1997
† Snoj, Joseph (SB) (Retired). —Died June 30, 1997
† Sommer, Paul J., *m.m.* (NY) Maryknoll, NY Maryknoll Fathers and Brothers. —Died June 11, 1997
† Soucy, Maurice P. (HRT) Meriden, CT St. Laurent. —Died Nov. 14, 1997
† Squire, Aelred, *o.s.b.cam.* (MRY) Big Sur, CA New Camaldoli Hermitage. —Died May 1, 1997
† Staber, Francis H. (SC) (Retired). —Died July 22, 1997
† Stadler, Joseph (SB) (Retired). —Died Sept. 20, 1997
† Stankevicius, John P. (CHI) (Retired). —Died April 24, 1997
† Stanton, Leonard F. (SFS) (Retired). —Died April 3, 1997
† Stauter, Rev. Msgr. Patrick C. (PBL) (Retired). —Died Jan. 24, 1997
† Stebler, Lawrence F. (PIT) Perrysville, PA St. Teresa of Avila. —Died June 9, 1997
† Steiner, William H., *s.j.* (KC) Kansas City, MO Arrupe Jesuit Community. —Died Feb. 13, 1997
† Steinert, Thomas J. (LC) Camp Douglas, WI St. James. —Died Aug. 27, 1997
† Stewart, Rev. Msgr. Dell F. (KAL) Kalamazoo, MI Chancellor-Diocese of Kalamazoo. —Died Feb. 27, 1997
† Stier, Joseph S. (MIL) (Retired). —Died May 24, 1997
† Strandenses, Lawrence (FAR) (Retired). —Died April 20, 1997
† Straub, Very Rev. Carrol C. (MIL) Vicar for Priest Personnel. —Died May 7, 1997
† Streeter, Gerald R., *s.j.* (DET) Clarkston, MI Colombiere Jesuit Community. —Died Oct. 31, 1996
† Suarez, Juan, *o.p.* (CC) San Diego, TX St. Francis de Paula. —Died Oct. 25, 1996
† Suddes, Rev. Msgr. James A. (SFD) (Retired). —Died Sept. 5, 1997
† Sulicki, Casimir F. (SCR) Forest City, PA St. Joseph (Slovenian). —Died Dec. 10, 1996
† Sulka, Stanley E. (KAL) (Absent on Sick Leave). —Died June 6, 1997
† Sullivan, Rev. Msgr. Bernard O. (BEL) (Retired). —Died Feb. 24, 1997
† Sullivan, Dennis L., *t.o.r.* (PH) Newtown Square, PA St. Anastasia. —Died Oct. 15, 1997
† Sullivan, Eugene, *c.s.v.* (JOL) Kankakee, IL St. Patrick. —Died Oct. 10, 1997
† Sullivan, Francis, *c.pp.s.* (HBG) Columbia, PA St. Joseph's Convent. —Died Jan. 9, 1997
† Sullivan, Walter A. (FR) South Dartmouth, MA St. Mary. —Died May 1, 1997
† Suppe, Joseph V. (HRT) (Retired). —Died Sept. 28, 1997
† Sweeney, Eugene P. (ROC) Ithaca, NY Immaculate Conception. —Died April 4, 1997
† Sweeney, Rev. Msgr. William J. (NY) New York, NY Our Lady of the Rosary. —Died April 4, 1997
† Sweeny, Robert S. (BUF) (Retired). —Died May 5, 1997
† Symes, David L., *c.m.* (PH) Philadelphia, PA St. Vincent's Seminary. —Died Sept. 25, 1997
† Synan, Rev. Msgr. Edward A. (NEW) (Retired). —Died Aug. 2, 1997
† Szarama, Roman J. (NY) Yonkers, NY St. Eugene. —Died July 8, 1997
† Tait, Alexander A., *s.j.* (SJ) Los Gatos, CA Sacred Heart Jesuit Center. —Died Oct. 1, 1996
† Tappe, Rev. Msgr. Walter J. (SR) Santa Rosa, CA St. Rose. —Died July 28, 1997
† Taylor, Rev. Msgr. E. Melville (BAL) (Retired). —Died May 19, 1997
† Taylor, Rev. Msgr. Francis J. (HBG) New Cumberland, PA St. Theresa of the Infant Jesus. —Died June 7, 1997
† Tearney, Thomas A. (MIL) Oconomowoc, WI St. Jerome. —Died Feb. 16, 1997
† Tecca, Felix R. (Y) (Absent on Sick Leave). —Died Aug. 22, 1997
† Teller, Rev. Msgr. Raymond J. (PH) Doylestown, PA Our Lady of Mount Carmel. —Died March 2, 1997
† Tenoever, Donald A. (CIN) (Retired). —Died July 21, 1997
† Thomas, Fred J. (ORL) (Retired). —Died Feb. 23, 1997
† Thomas, Frederick Joseph (GAY) (Retired). —Died Feb. 23, 1997
† Thomas, Joseph W. (PH) (Retired). —Died Dec. 8, 1996
† Tierney, John J. (BAL) (Retired). —Died June 20, 1997
† Tirone, Seraphin, *o.f.m.cap.* (NY) Beacon, NY St. Lawrence Friary. —Died Oct. 7, 1997
† Tomala, John C., *c.s.sp.* (ARE) Orocovis, PR Our Lady of Fatima. —Died Dec. 9, 1996
† Toner, Eugene G., *c.s.sp.* (FgM) Retired. —Died Aug. 25, 1997
† Toohey, Thomas F. (HRT) (Retired). —Died Feb. 12, 1997
† Toven, Ronald D. (E) (Retired). —Died Oct. 8, 1997
† Tracy, John, *o.m.i.* (BO) Tewksbury, MA Oblate Residence. —Died Dec. 28, 1997
† Trainor, Joseph P., *m.m.* (BO) Brookline, MA St. Mary of the Assumption. —Died March 28, 1997
† Tran, Mark That (GAL) (Retired). —Died Jan. 19, 1997
† Trant, John P. (LC) (Retired). —Died Aug. 28, 1997
† Travers, William, *o.carm.* (JOL) Darien, IL Carmelite Fathers Provincial Office. —Died July 14, 1997
† Tremblay, Russel J., *o.m.i.* (GB) Manitowoc, WI St. Mary's Home. —Died Sept. 17, 1997
† Tresnak, Anthony J. (OM) (Retired). —Died May 11, 1997
† Trizzino, Peter, *o.s.b.* (SAV) Savannah, GA Benedictine Military School. —Died Sept. 26, 1964
† Truczynski, Richard (STU) (Retired). —Died Oct. 25, 1996
† Tunesi, Enrico, *o.s.j.* (SAC) Sacramento, CA St. Mary's. —Died Jan. 23, 1997
† Tunny, John V. (RVC) Hicksville, NY St. Ignatius Loyola. —Died June 23, 1997
† Turck, Blaise, *o.s.b.* (P) St. Benedict, OR Mount Angel Abbey. —Died Oct. 18, 1996
† Uglesic, Leopold (SFR) (Retired). —Died Nov. 14, 1997
† Urban, Matthew J. (MIL) (Retired). —Died Dec. 16, 1997
† Valcovich, Giles, *o.f.m.* (SAC) Sacramento, CA St. Francis. —Died June 22, 1997
† Valladares, Herman (SAN) (Retired). —Died Sept. 22, 1997
† Van Den Bogaard, Joseph E., *m.m.* (NY) Maryknoll, NY Maryknoll Fathers and Brothers. —Died Oct. 4, 1997
† Van Den Boogaard, Henry, *m.s.f.* (RIC) Retired. —Died Sept. 22, 1997
† Van Duren, Charles (JOL) (Retired). —Died Aug. 30, 1997

† van Gogh, James (SEA) (Retired). —Died Feb. 27, 1997
† Van Raes, Michael T. (PEO) (Retired). —Died June 25, 1997
† Vazquez, Elion (PCE) (Retired). —Died Aug. 19, 1997
† Vazquez, Jose L., *o.p.* (MIA) Miami, FL St. Dominic. —Died Oct. 14, 1997
† Velesz, Dunstan, *o.f.m.* (SFD) Quincy, IL Quincy University. —Died Feb. 20, 1997
† Viramontes, David Enriquez (LSC) Las Cruces, NM St. Joseph Mission. —Died Aug. 13, 1997
† Volker, Edward H. (CIN) (Retired). —Died Oct. 3, 1997
† Volpe, Philip, *o.f.m.cap.* (NEW) Hoboken, NJ St. Ann's. —Died Jan. 25, 1997
† Wageman, Rev. Msgr. Raymond L. (LIN) (Retired). —Died Dec. 27, 1996
† Wagner, Elmer A., *o.f.m.* (ALB) Loudonville, NY Siena College. —Died May 21, 1996
† Wagner, Ralph J. (MIL) (Retired). —Died July 31, 1997
† Waldo, Cornelius, *o.s.b.* (SD) Oceanside, SD Prince of Peace Abbey. —Died Dec. 7, 1983
† Waldruff, Stephen C., *t.o.r.* (ALT) Retired. —Died April 3, 1997
† Walker, William, *o.s.b.* (SD) Oceanside, SD Prince of Peace Abbey. —Died Sept. 11, 1984
† Walsh, John Kelly, *m.m.* (NY) Maryknoll, NY Maryknoll Fathers and Brothers. —Died Jan. 24, 1997
† Walsh, Thomas P., *o.s.f.s.* (CHI) Retired. —Died Feb. 15, 1997
† Ward, Rev. Msgr. Edward F. (PRT) (Retired). —Died Feb. 18, 1997
† Ward, Guy F., *s.j.* (SEA) Spokane, WA Seattle University. —Died Oct. 20, 1996
† Warner, J. Anthony (RIC) Richmond, VA Our Lady of Lourdes. —Died May 8, 1997
† Watry, Jerome R. (GB) (Retired). —Died Nov. 9, 1997
† Weishaar, Berard, *o.f.m.* (LA) Santa Barbara, CA Franciscan Friary, Order of Friars Minor (Old Mission). —Died April 15, 1997
† Wellein, Rev. Msgr. William G. (CHL) (Retired). —Died Oct. 2, 1997
† Werling, Norman G., *o.carm.* (NEW) Retired. —Died March 7, 1997
† Wessel, Stephen L., *o.m.i.* (BEL) Belleville, IL St. Henry's Oblate Residence. —Died Aug. 8, 1997
† Whelan, Harold A., *ss.cc.* (LA) Retired. —Died Jan. 15, 1997
† White, Alphonse P. (DUB) (Retired). —Died July 10, 1997
† Wieber, Joseph E. (LAN) (Retired). —Died Feb. 9, 1997
† Wiegele, Lloyd, *o.carm.* (BO) Peabody, MA St. Theresa Carmelite Chapel. —Died Sept. 15, 1997
† Wiercioch, Casimir (DET) Maybee, MI St. Joseph. —Died July 10, 1997
† Wiest, Robert E. (GI) (Retired). —Died Jan. 3, 1997
† Wild, Joseph, *o.m.i.* (BO) Tewksbury, MA Oblate Residence. —Died Dec. 18, 1997
† Wilkiemeyer, Philip (OKL) (Retired). —Died Dec. 31, 1996
† Wilson, Ernest, *o.f.m.* (P) Retired. —Died March 17, 1997
† Wilson, Joseph C. (BO) Billerica, MA St. Andrew. —Died Feb. 17, 1997
† Winkler, Clarence E. (STL) (Retired). —Died Dec. 3, 1996
† Winter, Pius R., *o.f.m.* (GLP) Retired. —Died Sept. 27, 1997
† Wolbang, Charles A., *c.m.* (MET) Plainsboro, NJ St. Joseph's Seminary. —Died Oct. 10, 1997
† Wolf, Benedict L. (ALT) (Retired). —Died April 20, 1997
† Wolf, Theodore J., *s.j.* (P) Sublimity, OR Jesuit Provincial Office. —Died April 13, 1997
† Wolf, Rev. Msgr. Vincent Joseph (FWT) Fort Worth, TX Holy Family. —Died July 8, 1997
† Wood, John K., *s.j.* (SEA) Spokane, WA Regis Community. —Died March 11, 1997
† Woods, Rev. Msgr. Patrick J. (BUF) Arcade, NY SS. Peter and Paul. —Died Feb. 14, 1997
† Worland, T. Vincent (SFD) Altamont, IL St. Clare. —Died Aug. 3, 1997
† Wozniak, Louis B. (GRY) (Retired). —Died May 11, 1997
† Wuellner, Bernard J., *s.j.* (DET) Clarkston, MI Colombiere Jesuit Community. —Died March 3, 1997
† Wyse, Gregory, *o.f.m.* (PAT) Ringwood, NJ Holy Name Friary. —Died May 6, 1996
† Yadrich, John Branko (KCK) (Retired). —Died Dec. 29, 1997
† York, James E. (PH) (Retired). —Died April 29, 1997
† Zabicki, Paul, *o.f.m.conv.* (BAL) Ellicott City, MD Order of Friars Minor Conventual. —Died Oct. 29, 1996
† Zach, Hilary, *o.f.m.cap.* (MIL) Fond du Lac, WI Genesys HealthCare of Fond du Lac. —Died March 22, 1997
† Zajac, Rev. Msgr. Stephen (PSC) Old Forge, PA St. Nicholas of Myra. —Died Oct. 10, 1997
† Zajdel, Adam, *o.f.m.conv.* (BGP) Danbury, CT Sacred Heart. —Died Jan. 21, 1997
† Zaorski, Thaddeus L. (NEW) (Retired). —Died June 22, 1997
† Zarrilli, Very Rev. Frederick B., V.F. (LR) Forrest City, AR St. Francis of Assisi. —Died June 6, 1997
† Zegers, Rev. Msgr. James J. (CAM) (Retired). —Died June 14, 1997
† Zemites, Joseph Francis (KCK) (Retired). —Died May 23, 1997
† Zenz, Louis J. (FTW) (Retired). —Died Nov. 12, 1996
† Zimmer, Luke B., *ss.cc.* (LA) Fillmore, CA Apostolate of Christian Renewal. —Died Jan. 7, 1997
† Zukowski, John A. (CHI) (Retired). —Died May 4, 1997
† Zvirblis, John (GR) (Retired). —Died March 4, 1997
† Zwicky, Richard C. (NU) (Retired). —Died Dec. 7, 1996
† Zywicki, Francis S. (ALT) (Retired). —Died Sept. 15, 1997

ALPHABETICAL LIST OF INSTITUTIONS

(Letters in brackets designate categories in the Institutions Section; followed by the (Arch)Diocesan abbreviation code.)

A

A.B.L.E. Families, Inc., [L], (WH), Naugatuck, WV.
A.C.T. Child Case Management, [I], (CIN). See St. Joseph Orphanage.
A.I.I.L.S., [U], (GAL), Houston, TX.
Abba House of Prayer, [O], (ALB), Albany, NY.
ABBA House, Missionaries of Charity, [F], (LR), Little Rock, AR.
Abbey Christian Life Center, [R], (NO), St. Benedict, LA.
Abbey of New Clairvaux, Trappist, [G], (SAC), Vina, CA.
Abbey of New Clairvaux, Trappist Seminary, [A], (SAC), Vina, CA.
Abbey of Our Lady of Gethsemani, of the Order of Cistercians of the Strict Observance, [L], (L), Trappist, KY.
Abbey of Our Lady of the Holy Trinity, [A], (SLC), Huntsville, UT.
Abbey of Our Lady of the Holy Trinity of the Order of Cistercians, [F], (SLC), Huntsville, UT.
Abbey of Regina Laudis, [N], (HRT), Bethlehem, CT.
Abbey of St. Gregory the Great, [P], (PRO), Portsmouth, RI.
The Abbey of St. Mary and St. Louis, [P], (STL), St. Louis, MO.
Abbey of St. Walburga, [N], (DEN), Virginia Dale, CO.
Abbey of the Genesee, [I], (ROC), Piffard, NY.
The ABC's, Associates for Breast Cancer Studies, [K], (LA). See Saint John's Health Center.
Aberdeen Catholic Schools Education Office, [C], (SFS), Aberdeen, SD.
Aberdeen Living Center, [E], (SFS), Aberdeen, SD.
Abraham House, Inc., [HH], (NY), Bronx, NY.
Academia Cristo de los Milagros, [A], (CGS), Caguas, PR.
Academia Sagrado Corazon, [B], (SJN), Santurce, PR.
Academia San Alfonso, [A], (CGS), Aguas Buenas, PR.
Academia Santa Teresita, [A], (CGS), Naranjito, PR.
Academy and Boarding-School of the Holy Family, [C], (NOR), Baltic, CT.
Academy of American Franciscan History, [S], (OAK), Berkeley, CA.
Academy of Holy Angels, [F], (STP), Richfield, MN.
Academy of Mount St. Ursula, [F], (NY), New York, NY.
Academy of Notre Dame, [E], (BO), Tyngsboro, MA.
Academy of Notre Dame, [C], (COV), Covington, KY.
Academy of Notre Dame at Tyngsboro, [H], (BO), Tyngsboro, MA.
Academy of Notre Dame de Namur, [G], (PH), Villanova, PA.
Academy of Our Lady, [D], (CHI), Chicago, IL.
Academy of Our Lady of Good Counsel, [F], (NY), White Plains, NY.
Academy of Our Lady of Good Counsel, [H], (NY), White Plains, NY.
Academy of Our Lady of Guam, [A], (AGN), Agana, GU.
Academy of Our Lady of Mercy, [E], (HRT), Milford, CT.
Academy of Our Lady of Mercy, [C], (L), Louisville, KY.
Academy of Our Lady of Peace, [C], (SD), San Diego, CA.
Academy of St. Aloysius, [C], (NEW), Jersey City, NJ.
Academy of St. Dorothy, [H], (NY), New York, NY.
Academy of St. Dorothy, [EE], (NY), New York, NY.
Academy of St. Elizabeth, [D], (PAT), Convent Station, NJ.
Academy of St. Joseph, [D], (RVC), Brentwood, NY.
Academy of the Holy Angels, [C], (NEW), Demarest, NJ.
Academy of the Holy Cross Convent, [O], (WDC). See Sisters of the Holy Cross.
The Academy of the Holy Cross, Inc., [E], (WDC), Kensington, MD.
Academy of the Holy Names Elementary, [E], (SP), Tampa, FL.
Academy of the Holy Names High School, [C], (SP), Tampa, FL.
Academy of the Holy Names of New York, [M], (ALB). See Sisters of the Holy Names of Jesus and Mary.
Academy of the Holy Names Upper, Middle and Lower Schools, [D], (ALB), Albany, NY.
Academy of the Incarnate Word, [F], (GAL), Houston, TX.
Academy of the Sacred Heart, [E], (DET), Bloomfield Hills, MI.
Academy of the Sacred Heart, [G], (DET), Bloomfield Hills, MI.
Academy of the Sacred Heart, [E], (LAF), Grand Coteau, LA.
Academy of the Sacred Heart, [C], (NEW), Hoboken, NJ.
Academy of the Sacred Heart, [H], (NO), New Orleans, LA.
Academy of the Sacred Heart, [G], (STL), St. Charles, MO.
Academy of the Sacred Heart "The Rosary", [F], (NO), New Orleans, LA.
Academy of the Visitation, [D], (BAL), Frederick, MD.
The Achievement Center-St. Vincent's Home, Inc., [F], (RIC), Roanoke, VA.
Acorn Apartments (Crandon), [E], (SUP). See Catholic Charities Bureau, Inc.
Acorn Apartments (Minong), [E], (SUP). See Catholic Charities Bureau, Inc.
Acorn Apartments (Wisconsin Rapids), [E], (SUP). See Catholic Charities Bureau, Inc.
Ada S. Niles Senior Center and Adult Day Care Services, [G], (CHI). See Catholic Charities of the Archdiocese of Chicago-Archdiocesan Offices.
Addiction Consultation and Educational Services, [G], (CHI). See Catholic Charities of the Archdiocese of Chicago-Archdiocesan Offices.
Addiction Recovery Center, [L], (MIA). See St. Luke's Center, Inc.
Addiction Services, [D], (WIL). See Catholic Charities, Inc.
Addolorata Villa, [M], (CHI), Wheeling, IL.
ADESTE Child Care, [Z], (LA). See Catholic Charities of Los Angeles, Inc.
ADESTE Child Care Services, [Z], (LA). See Catholic Charities of Los Angeles, Inc.
Adirondack Community College, [S], (ALB), Glens Falls, NY.
Administrative Center of the Sisters of Mercy of the Americas, [O], (CHI), Chicago, IL.
Administrative Services, [H], (RVC). See Catholic Charities Central Administration.
Administrative/AIDS Services, [H], (RVC). See Catholic Charities Central Administration.
Admission & Family Services, [R], (NY). See Pius XII Youth and Family Services, Inc.
Adoption, [G], (RNO). See Catholic Community Services of Northern Nevada.
Adoption Program, [G], (BGP). See Catholic Charities of Fairfield County.
Adoption Services, [E], (HBG). See Department for Catholic Charities Counseling/Field Services.
Adoption Services, [J], (SLC). See Catholic Community Services.
Adoptions, Child Care Division, and Young Parents Program, [H], (BUF). See The Catholic Charities of the Diocese of Buffalo.
Adoration Convent and Church of Christ the King, [G], (LIN), Lincoln, NE.
Adorers of the Blood of Christ, [I], (HBG), Columbia, PA.
Adorers of the Blood of Christ, [C], (LSC), Carlsbad, NM.
Adorers of the Blood of Christ (A.S.C.), [K], (ELP), El Paso, TX.
Adrian Dominican Office of Development, [L], (LAN), Adrian, MI.
Adrian Dominican Sisters, [I], (AUS), Austin, TX.
Adrian Dominican Sisters, [H], (MRY), Santa Cruz, CA.
Adrian Dominican Sisters - Great Lakes Mission Chapter, [L], (DET), Detroit, MI.
Adrian Dominican Sisters (O.P.), [K], (ELP), El Paso, TX.
Adrian Dominican Sisters of the Most Holy Rosary, [F], (R), Garner, NC.
Adrian Dominican Sisters, Florida Mission Chapter, [H], (PMB), West Palm Beach, FL.
Adrian Dominican Sisters, Mid-Atlantic Mission Chapter, [J], (ATL), Gainesville, GA.
Adrian Dominican Sisters, Midwest Dominican Mission Chapter, [O], (CHI). See Adrian Dominican Sisters, Upper Midwest Mission Chapter.
Adrian Dominican Sisters, Nokomis Mission Chapter, [L], (DET), Dearborn Heights, MI.
Adrian Dominican Sisters, Southeast Adrian Mission Chapter, [L], (DET), Farmington Hills, MI.
Adrian Dominican Sisters, Southwest Mission Chapter, [G], (PBL), Grand Junction, CO.
Adrian Dominican Sisters, Upper Midwest Mission Chapter, [O], (CHI), Hometown, IL.
Adrian Dominicans, [I], (ORG), Orange, CA.
Adrian Dominicans, [I], (ORG), Tustin, CA.
Adult Day Health Center, [U], (BO). See St. Joseph Manor Nursing & Extended Care Facility.
Adult Day Services, [L], (IND), Indianapolis, IN.
Adult Day Services, [J], (WCH). See Catholic Charities.
Adult Day Services, [L], (WCH). See Catholic Charities, Inc.
Adult Day Services and Resource Center, [N], (MIL), Milwaukee, WI.
Adult Reading Program, [K], (SAC). See Catholic Charities of Sacramento, Inc.
Adventus, [S], (OAK), Oakland, CA.
Affiliated Health Services, Inc., Detroit, [H], (DET). See St. John Hospital and Medical Center.
Affinity Health System, [O], (GB), Oshkosh, WI.
Affirmation Counseling Center, [J], (NOR), Portland, CT.
*Africa Faith & Justice Network, [V], (WDC), Washington, DC.
African Mission House, [W], (BO), Dedham, MA.
After School Programs, [R], (NY). See Pius XII Youth and Family Services, Inc.
Agape Community Center of Milwaukee, Inc., [Y], (MIL), Milwaukee, WI.
Agape Convent, [BB], (PH). See Religious Sisters of Mercy.
Agape Institute of St. Teresa of Jesus, [I], (BIR), Birmingham, AL.
Agnesian HealthCare, Inc., [K], (MIL), Fond du Lac, WI.
Agrupacion Catolica Universitaria, Inc., [J], (MIA). See John Paul II Retreat House.
AHA-Pierce County Association, [E], (SEA). See Catholic Community Services of Western Washington.
*Aid for Women, [X], (CHI), Chicago, IL.
Aid to the Church in Need, [R], (RVC), Deer Park, NY.
Aid to the Church In Need, Inc., [N], (ORG), El Toro, CA.
*Aid to the Church in Russia, [R], (SCR), Scranton, PA.
"Aimin' High" Family Service Center, [R], (NY). See Pius XII Youth and Family Services, Inc.
Aina Kupaa O Maili, [J], (HON), Honolulu, HI.
Air Force Base, Our Lady of the Snows Catholic Community, [I], (FAR), Grand Forks, ND.
AJT, Inc., [W], (STL), Arnold, MO.
Akron District Council, [V], (CLV). See Society of St. Vincent de Paul, Diocesan Central Council.
Alabama Southern Community College Newman Center, [K], (MOB), Monroeville, AL.
Alabama State University Newman Center, [K], (MOB), Montgomery, AL.
Alameda, [H], (OAK). See Catholic Charities of the Diocese of Oakland, Inc.
Alameda County Area Supervisor, [H], (OAK). See Catholic Charities of the Diocese of Oakland, Inc.
Alamo Catholic High School and Amarillo Catholic Middle School, [A], (AMA), Amarillo, TX.
Alaska Radio Mission, Station KNOM, [E], (FBK), Nome, AK.
Albany Area Hospital, [G], (SCL), Albany, MN.
Albergue La Providencia, Inc., [H], (PCE), Ponce, PR.
Alberta Health Center, [I], (MOB), Alberta, AL.
Albertine Home, [H], (GRY), Hammond, IN.
Albertine Sisters (Prov. of Krakow, Poland), [K], (GRY), Hammond, IN.
Albertson's College of Idaho, [F], (B), Caldwell, ID.
Albertus Magnus, [F], (NY), Bardonia, NY.
Albertus Magnus College, [C], (HRT), New Haven, CT.
Albertus Magnus College, [N], (HRT). See St. Joseph Convent.
Alcohol & Substance Abuse Services, [H], (RVC). See Catholic Charities Central Administration.
Alcohol Clinic, [R], (NY). See Pius XII Youth and Family Services, Inc.
Alderson-Broaddus College Newman Center, [Q], (WH), Philippi, WV.
Alee Shelter Program for Spouse Abuse, [D], (AGN). See Catholic Social Services of Guam.
Alegent Health - Bergen Mercy Health System, [G], (OM), Omaha, NE.
Alemany High School, [D], (LA), Mission Hills, CA.
Alexian Brothers, [F], (KNX), Signal Mountain, TN.
Alexian Brothers Community, [P], (MIL), Milwaukee, WI.
Alexian Brothers Health Management, Inc., (ABHM), [X], (CHI), Elk Grove Village, IL.
*Alexian Brothers Health System Inc., Investment Trust, [X], (CHI), Elk Grove Village, IL.
*Alexian Brothers Health System, Inc. Investment Trust, [X], (CHI), Elk Grove Village, IL.
Alexian Brothers Hospital, [H], (SJ), San Jose, CA.
Alexian Brothers Hospital, [K], (STL), St. Louis, MO.
Alexian Brothers Lansdowne Village, [O], (STL), St. Louis, MO.
Alexian Brothers Medical Center, Inc., [J], (CHI), Elk Grove Village, IL.
Alexian Brothers of America, Inc., [X], (CHI), Elk Grove Village, IL.
Alexian Brothers of Elizabeth, Inc., [S], (NEW), Elizabeth, NJ.
Alexian Brothers of Missouri, Inc., [W], (STL), St. Louis, MO.
Alexian Brothers of New Jersey, Inc., [S], (NEW), Elizabeth, NJ.

[L], (WCH). See Catholic Charities, Inc.
Anthony Square - Assisted Living, [L], (IND). See Catholic Charities of Terre Haute.
Antioch, [H], (OAK). See Catholic Charities of the Diocese of Oakland, Inc.
Antioch College Campus Ministry, [Q], (CIN), Yellow Springs, OH.
The Antonian, [G], (WIL), Wilmington, DE.
Antonian College Preparatory High School, [D], (SAT), San Antonio, TX.
Antonian Towers, [I], (ALN), Easton, PA.
Antonine Maronite Sisters of Youngstown, Inc., [B], (OLL), North Jackson, OH.
Apostles in the Marketplace (A.I.M.), [Q], (BAL), Baltimore, MD.
Apostles of Jesus, [P], (ALN), Shenandoah, PA.
Apostles of the Sacred Heart of Jesus, [I], (GBG), Greensburg, PA.
Apostles of the Sacred Heart of Jesus, [G], (NOR), Higganum, CT.
Apostles of the Sacred Heart of Jesus, [H], (SAC), Sacramento, CA.
Apostleship of Prayer, [V], (CIN), Cincinnati, OH.
Apostleship of Prayer, [P], (DAL), Commerce, TX.
Apostleship of Prayer, [L], (MOB), Daphne, AL.
Apostleship of Prayer, [FF], (PH), Philadelphia, PA.
Apostleship of Prayer, [L], (ROC), Rochester, NY.
Apostleship of Prayer, [U], (SFR), San Francisco, CA.
Apostleship of Prayer, [V], (WDC), Silver Spring, MD.
Apostleship of Prayer, National Office for the U.S., [R], (RVC), New Hyde Park, NY.
Apostleship of the Sea, [T], (BRK). See Catholic Migration & Refugee Office, Catholic Migration Services, Inc.
Apostleship of the Sea, [Y], (MIL), Milwaukee, WI.
Apostleship of the Sea (Baltimore), [Q], (BAL), Baltimore, MD.
Apostleship of the Sea, Catholic Maritime Ministry, [DD], (LA), San Pedro, CA.
Apostolate for Family Consecration, [N], (ARL), Woodbridge, VA.
Apostolate for Family Consecration, [H], (PCE), Ponce, PR.
Apostolate for Family Consecration, [J], (STU), Bloomingdale, OH.
Apostolate for Family Consecration, Inc., [HH], (NY), New York, NY.
Apostolate for Persons with Developmental Disabilities, [M], (FR). See Special Apostolates, Department of.
Apostolate for the Most Holy Rosary and the Brown Scapular Association, [I], (TLS), Claremore, OK.
Apostolate for the Suffering, [T], (ALB), Cohoes, NY.
Apostolate of Christian Action, [J], (FRS), Fresno, CA.
Apostolate of Christian Renewal Holy Family, [R], (LA), Fillmore, CA.
Apostolate of Christian Renewal/Holy Family Home of Peace, [DD], (LA), Fillmore, CA.
Apostolate of Suffering, [W], (MIL), Wauwatosa, WI.
Apostolate of the Handicapped, [X], (CHI), Chicago, IL.
Apostolate to Aid the Dying, [V], (CIN), Cincinnati, OH.
Apostolic Endowment Trust, [O], (SR), Santa Rosa, CA.
Apostolic Oblates, [M], (OM), Omaha, NE.
Apostolic Oblates, [N], (ORG), Fullerton, CA.
Apostolic Society of the Crusade of the Holy Spirit, [DD], (NY), New York, NY.
Apostolic Sodales - Secular Institute for Priests, [M], (OM). See Institute of the Apostolic Oblates.
*Appalachia Science in the Public Interest, [J], (LEX), Mount Vernon, KY.
Appalachian Apostolate, Inc., [O], (COV), Vanceburg, KY.
Apple River, Inc. (Amery), [E], (SUP). See Catholic Charities Bureau, Inc.
Appleton Catholic Educational System (ACES), [E], (GB), Appleton, WI.
Aquin Central Catholic Junior-Senior High School, [B], (RCK), Freeport, IL.
Aquin Elementary School, [F], (DUB), Cascade, IA.
The Aquin Guild, [X], (CHI), Chicago, IL.
Aquin Religious Education Center, [E], (DUB), Cascade, IA.
Aquinas Academy, [D], (GBG), Greensburg, PA.
Aquinas Center for Continuing Religious Education, [E], (IND), Clarksville, IN.
Aquinas Center of Theology at Emory University, [A], (ATL), Atlanta, GA.
Aquinas College, [B], (GR), Grand Rapids, MI.
Aquinas College, [A], (NSH), Nashville, TN.
Aquinas College at Milton, [I], (BO), Milton, MA.
Aquinas College at Milton Campus Ministry, [CC], (BO), Milton, MA.
Aquinas College at Newton, [I], (BO), Newton, MA.
Aquinas College at Newton Campus Ministry, [CC], (BO), Newton, MA.
Aquinas East and West, [G], (DAV), Fort Madison, IA.
Aquinas High School, [D], (DET), Southgate, MI.
Aquinas High School, [C], (LC), La Crosse, WI.
Aquinas High School, [F], (NY), New York, NY.
Aquinas High School, [A], (SAV), Augusta, GA.
Aquinas High School, [B], (SB), San Bernardino, CA.
Aquinas High School and Aquinas Schools Foundation, [M], (LC), La Crosse, WI.
Aquinas High School Endowment Fund, [L], (LIN), David City, NE.
The Aquinas Institute, [B], (ROC), Rochester, NY.
Aquinas Institute of Theology, [B], (STL), St. Louis, MO.
Aquinas Junior-Senior High School, [E], (DAV), Fort Madison, IA.
Aquinas Middle School, [D], (LC), La Crosse, WI.
Aquinas School, [G], (ARL), Woodbridge, VA.
Aquinas Student Center, [H], (SFS), Aberdeen, SD.
Aquinas West, [G], (DAV). See Aquinas East and West.
Aquinas/St. Mary's Schools, [C], (LIN), David City, NE.
Aquinata Hall, [I], (GR), Grand Rapids, MI.
Arapahoe Community College, [P], (DEN), Littleton, CO.
Arbor House, [P], (ALB), Albany, NY.
Arcadia Catholic School Endowment Trust Fund, [M], (LC), Arcadia, WI.
Arcadia Valley Hospital, [C], (SPC), Pilot Knob, MO.
Arch I, [I], (DAV). See Arch Office.
Arch II, [I], (DAV). See Arch Office.
Arch III, [I], (DAV). See Arch Office.
Arch Office, [I], (DAV), Clinton, IA.
Archabbey Guest House, [I], (IND), St. Meinrad, IN.
Archbishop Alter High School, [E], (CIN), Dayton, OH.
*Archbishop Bergan Mercy Medical Center, [G], (OM), Omaha, NE.
Archbishop Blenk High School, [D], (NO), Gretna, LA.
Archbishop Carroll High School, [D], (WDC), Washington, DC.
Archbishop Carroll High School, [V], (WDC), Washington, DC.
Archbishop Chapelle High School, [D], (NO), Metairie, LA.
The Archbishop Charity Fund, [S], (SAT), San Antonio, TX.
Archbishop Curley High School, [C], (BAL), Baltimore, MD.
Archbishop Curley-Notre Dame High School, [C], (MIA), Miami, FL.
Archbishop Damiano School/St. John of God Community Services, [F], (CAM), Westville Grove, NJ.
Archbishop Flores Charity Fund, [S], (SAT), San Antonio, TX.
Archbishop Hannan High School, [D], (NO), Meraux, LA.
Archbishop Hennessy Catholic School, [F], (DUB), New Vienna, IA.
Archbishop Hoban High School, [E], (CLV), Akron, OH.
Archbishop James P. Lyke Elementary School, [G], (CLV), Cleveland, OH.
Archbishop John Carroll High School, [D], (PH), Radnor, PA.
Archbishop Leibold Home for the Aged, [L], (CIN), Cincinnati, OH.
Archbishop Mitty High School, [C], (SJ), San Jose, CA.
Archbishop Molloy, [G], (BRK), Briarwood, NY.
Archbishop O'Hara High School, [C], (KC), Kansas City, MO.
Archbishop of Baltimore Annual Appeal Trust, [P], (BAL). See Chancery Office.
Archbishop Prendergast High School, [D], (PH), Drexel Hill, PA.
Archbishop Quigley Preparatory Seminary, [A], (CHI), Chicago, IL.
Archbishop Riordan High School (Boys), [D], (SFR), San Francisco, CA.
Archbishop Rummel High School, [D], (NO), Metairie, LA.
Archbishop Rummel Junior High School, [G], (NO), Metairie, LA.
Archbishop Ryan High School, [D], (PH), Philadelphia, PA.
Archbishop Ryan School for Children with Hearing Impairment, [J], (PH), Norwood, PA.
Archbishop Shaw High School, [D], (NO), Marrero, LA.
Archbishop Shaw Junior High School, [G], (NO), Marrero, LA.
Archbishop Sheehan Adult Education Fund, [N], (OM). See The Omaha Archdiocesan Educational Foundation, Inc.
Archbishop Spalding High School, [C], (BAL), Severn, MD.
Archbishop Stepinac High School, [E], (NY), White Plains, NY.
Archbishop Thomas A. Donnellan School, [D], (ATL), Atlanta, GA.
Archbishop Walsh High School, [D], (BUF), Olean, NY.
Archbishop Williams' High School, [D], (BO), Braintree, MA.
Archbishop Wood Catholic High School, [D], (PH), Warminster, PA.
Archbishop's School Fund, [N], (SFE), Albuquerque, NM.
Archdiocesan AIDS Ministry Office, [G], (CHI). See Catholic Charities of the Archdiocese of Chicago-Archdiocesan Offices.
Archdiocesan Association of Ladies of Charity, [I], (WDC), Washington, DC.
Archdiocesan Black Catholics Concerned, [O], (IND), Indianapolis, IN.
Archdiocesan Campus Ministry, [Q], (NEW), Newark, NJ.
Archdiocesan Campus Ministry, [S], (WDC), Washington, DC.
Archdiocesan Catechetical Office, [D], (NY). See Department of Education.
Archdiocesan Catholic Campus Ministry Association, Gabriel Richards Campus Ministry, [T], (DET), Dearborn, MI.
Archdiocesan Central Council of Cincinnati, [S], (CIN), Cincinnati, OH.
Archdiocesan Central High Schools, Inc., [D], (BO), Brighton, MA.
Archdiocesan Charitable Bequest Council, [W], (STL), St. Louis, MO.
Archdiocesan Consultation Service, [O], (OM), Omaha, NE.
Archdiocesan Council of Catholic Nurses, [HH], (NY), New York, NY.
Archdiocesan Council of Catholic Women, [U], (SFR), San Francisco, CA.
Archdiocesan Department of Special Education, [I], (NO), New Orleans, LA.
Archdiocesan Development Appeal, [W], (STL), St. Louis, MO.
Archdiocesan Drug Abuse Prevention Program, [D], (NY). See Department of Education.
Archdiocesan Endowment Fund, [S], (SAT), San Antonio, TX.
Archdiocesan Health Plan Trust Fund Agreement, [P], (BAL). See Chancery Office.
Archdiocesan Hispanic Ministry Office, [O], (OM), Omaha, NE.
Archdiocesan Housing Authority (AHA), [E], (SEA). See Catholic Community Services of Western Washington.
Archdiocesan Housing Committee, [K], (DEN), Denver, CO.
Archdiocesan Housing Committee, Inc.: Archdiocesan Family Housing, Inc., [L], (DEN). See Catholic Charities and Community Services of the Archdiocese of Denver, Inc.
Archdiocesan Housing Committee, Inc.: Cathedral Plaza, Inc., [L], (DEN). See Catholic Charities and Community Services of the Archdiocese of Denver, Inc.
Archdiocesan Housing Committee, Inc.: Holy Family Plaza, Inc., [L], (DEN). See Catholic Charities and Community Services of the Archdiocese of Denver, Inc.
Archdiocesan Housing Committee, Inc.: Marian Plaza, Inc., [L], (DEN). See Catholic Charities and Community Services of the Archdiocese of Denver, Inc.
Archdiocesan Information Center, [P], (BO), Boston, MA.
Archdiocesan Marian Committee, [Q], (L), New Haven, KY.
Archdiocesan Marian Shrine, [Y], (MIL), Milwaukee, WI.
Archdiocesan Office for Campus Ministry, [CC], (LA), Los Angeles, CA.
Archdiocesan Office-Newman Center, [O], (BAL), Baltimore, MD.
Archdiocesan Oratory of St. Philip Neri (C.O.), [AA], (PH), Philadelphia, PA.
Archdiocesan Pastoral Center, [G], (OKL), Oklahoma City, OK.
Archdiocesan Retreat Center at Archbishop Cousins Catholic Center, [S], (MIL), Milwaukee, WI.
Archdiocesan Spiritual Life Center, [V], (HRT), Bloomfield, CT.
Archdiocesan Spirituality Center, [DD], (LA), Los Angeles, CA.
Archdiocesan Spirituality Center, [R], (NO), New Orleans, LA.
Archdiocesan Stewardship Education Committee, [W], (STL), St. Louis, MO.
Archdiocesan Union of Holy Name Societies, [T], (SAT), San Antonio, TX.
The Archdiocese of Boston Self-Insurance Group, Inc., [DD], (BO), Boston, MA.
Archdiocese of Cotabato, [V], (WDC), Washington, DC.
Archdiocese of Dubuque Deposit and Loan Fund, [O], (DUB), Dubuque, IA.
Archdiocese of Dubuque Education Fund, [O], (DUB), Dubuque, IA.
Archdiocese of Dubuque Perpetual Care Fund, [O],

B

B.G.S. Charitable Trust, [M], (JOL), Momence, IL.
B.R.E.M. Catholic Social Ministry, [W], (STL), St. Louis, MO.
Babson College Campus Ministry, [CC], (BO), Wellesley, MA.
*Backbone Housing, Inc., [P], (BAL). See Chancery Office.
Bahamas Mission of Florida, Inc., [L], (MIA), Coral Gables, FL.
Baker Hall School (ages 5-21), [J], (BUF). See Baker Victory Services.
Baker Victory Services, [J], (BUF), Lackawanna, NY.
Bakersfield Big Brothers, [E], (FRS), Bakersfield, CA.
Bakersfield College Newman Center, [H], (FRS), Bakersfield, CA.
Bakersfield St. Vincent de Paul Thrift Store, [I], (FRS), Bakersfield, CA.
Ballentine Stepping Stones, [D], (LAN). See Catholic Social Services-St. Vincent Home, Inc.
Balltown-Sherrill Catholic School, [F], (DUB), Balltown, IA.
Bambino Gesu Child Development Center, [T], (PH), Philadelphia, PA.
The Banquet, [I], (SFS), Sioux Falls, SD.
*Baptist St. Anthony Health System, [F], (AMA), Amarillo, TX.
Baptist/St. Vincent's Primary Care System, [E], (STA). See St. Vincent's Medical Center, Inc.
Barat College, [C], (CHI), Lake Forest, IL.
Barat College, [V], (CHI). See Ministry in Higher Education.
The Barnabite Fathers Barnabite Spiritual Center, [K], (ALN), Bethlehem, PA.
Barnes Avenue Program, [O], (NY). See Beacon of Hope House.
Barry Manor, [G], (STA). See Jacksonville, Family Housing Management Co.
Barry University, [B], (MIA), Miami, FL.
Bartell Road Housing Development Fund Co., Inc., [Q], (SY), Brewerton, NY.
Bartlett Learning Center, [L], (CHI), Bartlett, IL.
The Basileiad Library, [G], (PHU), Jenkintown, PA.
Basilian Fathers, [B], (LSC), Las Cruces, NM.
Basilian Fathers Novitiate of the Order of St. Basil the Great, [B], (STF), Glen Cove, NY.
Basilian Fathers of Connecticut, Inc., [M], (NOR), Cromwell, CT.
Basilian Fathers of Mariapoch, [A], (PSC), Matawan, NJ.
Basilian Fathers Residence, [J], (GRY), Merrillville, IN.
The Basilian Fathers' Monastery of Citeaux, [Q], (GAL), Manvel, TX.
Basilian Mission Center, [Q], (GAL), Sugar Land, TX.
Basilian Residence, [I], (ROC), Rochester, NY.
Basilian Salvatorian Order, [B], (NTN), Methuen, MA.
Basilica of the Assumption Historic Trust, Inc., [P], (BAL). See Chancery Office.
Basilica of the National Shrine of the Immaculate Conception, [Q], (WDC), Washington, DC.
Batavia, [H], (BUF). See The Catholic Charities of the Diocese of Buffalo.
Bates College, [M], (PRT), Lewiston, ME.
Batesville Deanery Counseling & Family Mediations, [L], (IND), Greensburg, IN.
Bath County Medical Clinic, [E], (LEX), Owingsville, KY.
Baton Rouge Chancery Office, [M], (BR), Baton Rouge, LA.
Baton Rouge/Southwest Regional Office, [I], (BR), Baton Rouge, LA.
Battle Creek Health System, [D], (KAL), Battle Creek, MI.
Bay County Jail Ministry, [I], (SAG), Bay City, MI.
Bay Harbor Hospital, [K], (LA). See Little Company of Mary Health Services.
Bay View Community, [J], (PRT), Saco, ME.
Bay View Villa, Guest and Retreat House, [L], (PRT), Saco, ME.
Bay Webster Corporation, Inc., [Y], (BRK), Brooklyn, NY.
Bayamon Central University, [A], (SJN), Bayamon, PR.
Bayley Seton Hospital, [W], (NY), New York, NY.
Bayley-Ellard High School, [C], (PAT), Madison, NJ.
*Bayside Settlement House, [J], (SD), San Diego, CA.
Bayview Detention Center Ministry, [C], (BWN), Brownsville, TX.
BCACS Foundation, Inc., [I], (KAL), Battle Creek, MI.
Beacon House, House of Prayer, [O], (DAV), Burlington, IA.
Beacon of Hope House, [O], (NY), New York, NY.
Beatitude House, [M], (Y), Youngstown, OH.
Beaumont School, [E], (CLV), Cleveland, OH.
Beaven Kelly Home, [H], (SPR). See Sisters of Providence Care Centers, Inc.
Beaver College, Glenside, [EE], (PH). See Newman Apostolate.
Becker College, [Q], (WOR). See Campus Ministry.
Becker College at Leicester, [Q], (WOR). See Campus Ministry.
Becket Hall, [I], (ROC), Rochester, NY.
Becket House Apartments, [D], (PHX), Lake Havasu City, AZ.
Beckman High School, [D], (DUB), Dyersville, IA.
Bede House, Trenton State College, [S], (TR). See Campus Ministry for the Diocese of Trenton.
Bee Still Studio, [B], (WDC). See Oblates of St. Francis de Sales.
Beginning Experience, [K], (FWT). See The Catholic Renewal Center of North Texas, Inc.
Beginning Experience, [O], (OM), Omaha, NE.
Behavioral Health Services, [H], (RVC). See Catholic Charities Central Administration.
Belen Jesuit Alumni Association, [H], (MIA). See Villa Arrieta.
Belen Jesuit Preparatory School, [D], (MIA), Miami, FL.
Belhaven, [F], (CHL). See Holy Angels, Inc.
Belhaven College Newman Center, [G], (JKS), Jackson, MS.
Bell Tower Residence, Inc., [D], (SUP). See Holy Cross Provincial Office.
Bellarmine College, [A], (L), Louisville, KY.
Bellarmine College Preparatory, [D], (SJ), San Jose, CA.
Bellarmine Hall, [T], (CHI), Barrington, IL.
Bellarmine House, [W], (BO), Cohasset, MA.
Bellarmine House of Studies, [P], (STL), St. Louis, MO.
Bellarmine Jefferson High School, [D], (LA), Burbank, CA.
Bellarmine Preparatory School, [C], (SEA), Tacoma, WA.
Bellerose Senior Housing, HDFC, Inc., [L], (BRK). See Catholic Charities.
Bellevue Area Catholic Elementary School, [F], (DUB), Bellevue, IA.
Bellmore Campus, [E], (RVC). See St. Elizabeth Ann Seton Regional School.
Belmont Abbey, [J], (CHL), Belmont, NC.
*Belmont Abbey College, [A], (CHL), Belmont, NC.
Belmont House Aids Hospice, [Q], (SFR). See Catholic Charities of the Archdiocese of San Francisco.
Beloit District Office, [K], (MAD). See Catholic Charities, Inc.
Bend Social Services Conference, [C], (BAK). See Saint Vincent de Paul Society - District Council of Central Oregon.
Bender Memorial Academy, [E], (NEW), Elizabeth, NJ.
Benedict Court, [H], (SCL). See St. Benedict's Center.
Benedict Homes, [H], (SCL). See St. Benedict's Center.
Benedict Inn Retreat & Conference Center, [I], (IND), Beech Grove, IN.
Benedict Village, [H], (SCL). See St. Benedict's Center.
Benedicta Riepp Priory, [M], (E). See Om Shanti.
Benedictine Academy, [C], (NEW), Elizabeth, NJ.
Benedictine Center - St. Paul's Monastery, [Q], (STP), St. Paul, MN.
Benedictine Center, Inc., [P], (PIT). See St. Benedict Monastery.
Benedictine Center, Inc., [I], (SFS), Yankton, SD.
Benedictine Chinese Mission, [J], (JOL). See St. Procopius Abbey.
Benedictine College, [A], (KCK), Atchison, KS.
Benedictine Convent of Perpetual Adoration, [K], (KC), Clyde, MO.
Benedictine Convent of Perpetual Adoration, [R], (STL), St. Louis, MO.
*Benedictine Convent of St. Martin, [C], (RC), Rapid City, SD.
Benedictine Convent of St. Martin Retirement Trust, [C], (RC). See Benedictine Convent of St. Martin.
Benedictine Counseling and Consulting Institute, [O], (KC), Kansas City, MO.
Benedictine Early Learning Center, [C], (PBR), Warren, OH.
Benedictine Foundation of Oregon, [Q], (P), Mt. Angel, OR.
Benedictine Foundation, Inc., [G], (DUL). See Benedictine Sisters Benevolent Association.
The Benedictine Grange, [N], (BGP), West Redding, CT.
Benedictine Health Center, [D], (DUL), Duluth, MN.
Benedictine Health Center, [G], (DUL). See Benedictine Sisters Benevolent Association.
Benedictine Health Foundation, Inc., [I], (SFS), Yankton, SD.
Benedictine Health System, [G], (DUL). See Benedictine Sisters Benevolent Association.
Benedictine Health System, [I], (SFS), Yankton, SD.
Benedictine High School, [E], (CLV), Cleveland, OH.
Benedictine High School, [B], (RIC), Richmond, VA.
Benedictine Hospital, [W], (NY), Kingston, NY.
Benedictine Housing, Inc., [Q], (P), Mt. Angel, OR.
Benedictine Living Center of Garrison fka Garrison Nursing Center, [E], (BIS), Garrison, ND.
Benedictine Manor Retirement Home, Inc., [I], (BIR), Cullman, AL.
Benedictine Military School, [B], (SAV), Savannah, GA.
Benedictine Mission House, [K], (OM), Schuyler, NE.
Benedictine Monastery, [H], (NOR), Ashford, CT.
Benedictine Monastery, [G], (TUC), Tucson, AZ.
The Benedictine Monastery of Erlac in Sonoita, [F], (TUC), Sonoita, AZ.
Benedictine Monastery of Hawaii, [H], (HON), Waialua, Oahu, HI.
Benedictine Monks, St. Benedict Abbey, [N], (WOR), Still River, MA.
Benedictine Monks, St. Benedict Abbey, [P], (WOR), Still River, MA.
Benedictine Nursing Center, [K], (P), Mt. Angel, OR.
Benedictine Order of Cleveland, [P], (CLV), Cleveland, OH.
The Benedictine Priory, [F], (SAV), Savannah, GA.
Benedictine Resource Center, [T], (SAT), San Antonio, TX.
Benedictine Retreat Center, [G], (CC), Sandia, TX.
The Benedictine School for Exceptional Children, [C], (WIL), Ridgely, MD.
Benedictine School for Exceptional Children Foundation, Inc., [C], (WIL), Ridgely, MD.
The Benedictine School Habilitation Center, [B], (WIL), Ridgely, MD.
Benedictine Services Corporation, [Q], (P), Mt. Angel, OR.
Benedictine Sisters (Eichstatt, Bavaria), [I], (GBG), Greensburg, PA.
Benedictine Sisters Benevolent Association, [E], (DUL), Duluth, MN.
Benedictine Sisters Benevolent Association, [G], (DUL), Duluth, MN.
Benedictine Sisters of Chicago, St. Scholastica Monastery, [O], (CHI), Chicago, IL.
Benedictine Sisters of Denver, Inc., [N], (DEN), Lakewood, CO.
The Benedictine Sisters of Elizabeth, NJ, [N], (CAM), Ventnor, NJ.
Benedictine Sisters of Elk County O.S.B. St. Joseph Monastery, [M], (E), St. Marys, PA.
Benedictine Sisters of Glendora, [I], (SD), Chula Vista, CA.
Benedictine Sisters of Perpetual Adoration, [D], (CHY), Dayton, WY.
Benedictine Sisters of Perpetual Adoration, [G], (TLS), Sand Springs, OK.
Benedictine Sisters of the Good Shepherd, [F], (BWN), Rio Grande City, TX.
Benedictine Sisters of the Sacred Heart, Sacred Heart Monastery, [K], (JOL), Lisle, IL.
Benedictine Sisters of Virginia, St. Gertrude Convent, [M], (RIC), Richmond, VA.
Benedictine Sisters Shalom Prayer Center, [N], (P), Mt. Angel, OR.
Benedictine Spirituality and Conference Center, [I], (BIR), Cullman, AL.
Benedictine Spirituality Center, [L], (OKL), Piedmont, OK.
Benedictine University, [A], (JOL), Lisle, IL.
Benedictine University, [J], (JOL). See St. Procopius Abbey.
Benedictines, [I], (ORG), Laguna Beach, CA.
Benedictines of Jesus Crucified, [Q], (PRO), Newport, RI.
*Benedictus, [N], (SD), Escondido, CA.
Benefis Health Care, [G], (GF), Great Falls, MT.
Benefit Trust for Non-Incardinated Priests, [DD], (BO). See Chancery Office.
Benefit Trust of the Adrian Dominican Congregation (Adrian), [K], (LAN). See Chancery Office.
Benet Academy, [C], (JOL), Lisle, IL.
Benet Academy, [J], (JOL). See St. Procopius Abbey.
*Benet Hill Monastery, [F], (COS), Colorado Springs, CO.
*Benet Pines, [G], (COS), Colorado Springs, CO.
*Benet Place, [H], (SCL). See St. Benedict's Center.
Benet Place, [I], (SFS). See St. Ann's Corporation.
*Benetwood Apartments for Persons Elderly and Handicapped, [I], (E), Harborcreek, PA.
The Benilde Religious & Charitable Trust, [S], (OAK), Oakland, CA.
Benilde-St. Margaret's School, [E], (STP), St. Louis Park, MN.
Benincasa Family Services, Inc., [R], (RVC), Amityville, NY.
Benincasa-Dominican Renewal Center, [N], (SFD), Riverton, IL.
Benitia Family Center, [T], (SAT), San Antonio, TX.
Bentley College Campus Ministry, [CC], (BO), Waltham, MA.
Berakah, [L], (MAN), Pittsfield, NH.
Berakah Alternative Investment Fund, [U], (GAL), Houston, TX.
The Berakkah House, [I], (SFS), Sioux Falls, SD.
Berg Retreat Center, [M], (WIL), Ridgely, MD.
Bergamo, [P], (CIN), Dayton, OH.

C

C'est La Vie Center of the Sisters Marianites of Holy Cross, [G], (LAF), Opelousas, LA.
C.A.R.E. Child Case Management, [I], (CIN). See St. Joseph Orphanage.
C.C. Medical Associates, Inc., [FF], (BO). See Caritas Christi - A Catholic Health Care System.
C.C.M. of Schodack, Inc., [T], (ALB), Castleton-on-Hudson, NY.
C.N.C. Inc., [Q], (SY), Rome, NY.
C.N.D. Early Learning Center, [G], (SFR), Belmont, CA.
C.S.C. Housing Development Fund Co., Inc., dba Sanderson Court Senior Apts., [K], (ALB), Albany, NY.
C.S.S. of Washtenaw County, [D], (LAN), Ann Arbor, MI.
C.Y.O. Boys Camp, [R], (DET), Detroit, MI.
C.Y.O. Camp Christina, [M], (IND), Nashville, IN.
C.Y.O. Camp Rancho Framasa, [M], (IND), Nashville, IN.
C.Y.O. Girls Camp, [R], (DET), Detroit, MI.
c/o Immaculate Conception Church, [G], (BLX), Laurel, MS.
Cabrini Center/Boysville of Michigan, Inc., [O], (DET). See Boysville of Michigan, Inc.
Cabrini College, [C], (PH), Radnor, PA.
Cabrini Hall Maternity Home, [K], (PEO), Peoria, IL.
Cabrini Head Start, [J], (NO), New Orleans, LA.
Cabrini High School, [F], (NO), New Orleans, LA.
Cabrini High School, [H], (NO), New Orleans, LA.
Cabrini High School, Inc., [F], (NO). See Cabrini High School.
Cabrini Medical Center (Cabrini Development Council, Inc.), [W], (NY), New York, NY.
Cabrini Retreat Center, [T], (CHI), Des Plaines, IL.
Cabrini-on-Hudson, [R], (NY). See St. Cabrini Home.
Calais House, Inc., of Our Lady of the Lake Medical Center, [G], (BR). See Assisi Homes, Inc., of Our Lady of the Lake Medical Center.
Calasanzian Fathers (Piarists), [DD], (NY), New York, NY.
Caldwell College, [B], (NEW), Caldwell, NJ.
California Handicapables, Inc., [U], (SFR), San Francisco, CA.
California Institute of the Sisters of the Blessed Virgin Mary, I.H.M., [S], (LA), Los Angeles, CA.
California Province of the Society of Jesus, Jesuit Provincial Office, [M], (SJ), Los Gatos, CA.
California State University Fullerton, Newman Center, [L], (ORG), Fullerton, CA.
California State University/Campus Ministry Center, [Q], (OAK), Hayward, CA.
Calmar-Festina-Spillville (CFS) Catholic Elementary School, [F], (DUB), Calmar, IA.
Calumet College of St. Joseph, [A], (GRY), Whiting, IN.
Calvary Cemetery and Mausoleum Association, [L], (LIN), Lincoln, NE.
Calvary Fund, Inc., [HH], (NY), New York, NY.
Calvary Hospital, [X], (NY), New York, NY.
Calvary Retreat Center, Passionist Community, [P], (WOR), Shrewsbury, MA.
Calvert County Office, [H], (WDC). See Catholic Charities of the Archdiocese of Washington, Inc.
Calvert Hall College, [C], (BAL), Baltimore, MD.
Calvert High School, [B], (TOL), Tiffin, OH.
The Cambridge Center for the Study of Faith and Culture, Inc., [FF], (BO). See Our Lady of Kazan Russian Greek Catholic Mission.
Camden Catholic High School, [A], (CAM), Cherry Hill, NJ.
Camden Center for Law and Social Justice, Inc., [T], (CAM), Camden, NJ.
Camden Diocesan Center, [R], (CAM), Camden, NJ.
Camilla Hall Nursing Home, [V], (PH), Immaculata, PA.
Camillus Corporation, [I], (HRT). See Saint Francis Hospital and Medical Center.
Camillus Health Concern, Inc., [F], (MIA). See Camillus House, Inc.
Camillus House, Inc., [F], (MIA), Miami, FL.
Camp Alvernia, [Q], (BRK), Centerport, NY.
Camp Alvernia, [R], (RVC). See Mt. Alvernia, Inc.
Camp Auxilium Center, [G], (PAT), Newton, NJ.
Camp Bernadette, [Q], (MAN), Gilmanton Iron Works, NH.
Camp Christopher, [V], (CLV). See Catholic Charities Services Corporation.
Camp Corde, [V], (CLV). See Catholic Charities Services Corporation.
Camp Don Bosco, [G], (SB), Arrow Bear Lake, CA.
Camp Don Bosco, [O], (SEA), Seattle, WA.
Camp Fatima, [Q], (MAN), Gilmanton Iron Works, NH.
Camp Hamilton, [O], (SEA), Monroe-Duvall, WA.
Camp Holy Cross, Inc., [G], (BUR), Burlington, VT.
Camp Hope, [F], (CHL). See Holy Angels, Inc.
Camp Lawrence, [O], (GRY), Valparaiso, IN.
Camp Little Flower, [O], (KC), Kansas City, MO.
Camp Mariastella, [AA], (LA). See Scouting and Camp Fire Ministry/Catholic Youth Camps.
Camp Mariastella, Inc., [G], (SB), Los Angeles, CA.
Camp Marist, [Q], (MAN), Center Ossipee, NH.
Camp Marymount, [J], (NSH), Fairview, TN.
Camp Nazareth, [M], (SY), Utica, NY.
Camp Neringa, [D], (LIT), West Brattleboro, VT.
Camp Neumann Conference Center, [DD], (PH), Jamison, PA.
*Camp Oliver, [L], (SD), Descanso, CA.
Camp Ozanam, [R], (DET), Detroit, MI.
Camp St. Andrew, [Q], (SCR), Tunkhannock, PA.
Camp St. Charles, Inc., [V], (WDC), Silver Spring, MD.
Camp St. Francis, [I], (MRY), Aptos, CA.
Camp St. Michael, [J], (SR), Leggett, CA.
Camp Salesian, [J], (SR), Middletown, CA.
Camp Sancta Maria, [H], (GAY), Gaylord, MI.
Camp Santa Maria, [L], (DEN). See Catholic Charities and Community Services of the Archdiocese of Denver, Inc.
Camp Scully, [U], (ALB), Albany, NY.
Camp Stanislaus, [H], (BLX). See SSC Progression Corporation.
Camp Stapleton-St. Vincent de Paul Society, [R], (DET), Detroit, MI.
Camp Stella Maris, [G], (ROC), Livonia, NY.
Camp Tall Trees, [Q], (L), Louisville, KY.
Camp Tara, [G], (BUR), Burlington, VT.
Camp Tecaboca, [T], (SAT), Mountain Home, TX.
Camp Tekawitha, [K], (GB), Shawano, WI.
Camp Teresita Pines, [AA], (LA). See Scouting and Camp Fire Ministry/Catholic Youth Camps.
Camp Turner, [S], (BUF), Allegany State Park, NY.
Camp Tygart, [L], (WH), Huttonsville, WV.
Camp We-Ha-Kee, [I], (SUP), Winter, WI.
Campaign for Human Development, [Q], (SFR). See Catholic Charities of the Archdiocese of San Francisco.
Campaign for Human Development, [J], (STU), Steubenville, OH.
Campaign for Human Development (CHD), [H], (OAK). See Catholic Charities of the Diocese of Oakland, Inc.
Campaign For Human Development Apostolate, [M], (FR). See Special Apostolates, Department of.
Campbell Lodge Boys Home, [J], (COV), Cold Spring, KY.
Campion Center, [W], (BO), Weston, MA.
Campion Health Center, Inc., [W], (BO), Weston, MA.
Campion House, [K], (OM), Omaha, NE.
Campion Renewal Center, [Y], (BO), Weston, MA.
Campus Ministers and Ministry Centers, [E], (BRK). See Office of Religious Education: Evangelization and Catholic Formation.
Campus Ministries, [N], (MAN), Durham, NH.
Campus Ministry, [H], (ALT), Hollidaysburg, PA.
Campus Ministry, [L], (ATL), Atlanta, GA.
Campus Ministry, [R], (BUF), Williamsville, NY.
Campus Ministry, [J], (COL), Columbus, OH.
Campus Ministry, [K], (NOR), Willimantic, CT.
Campus Ministry, [Q], (WOR), Worcester, MA.
Campus Ministry - Diocese of Pueblo, [H], (PBL), Gunnison, CO.
Campus Ministry Center, [Q], (CIN), Fairborn, OH.
Campus Ministry Center, [G], (VIC), Victoria, TX.
Campus Ministry for the Archdiocese of Oklahoma City, [K], (OKL), Norman, OK.
Campus Ministry for the Diocese of Trenton, [S], (TR), Princeton, NJ.
Campus Ministry, Newman Center, University of Guam, [G], (AGN), Mangilao, GU.
Campus Ministry, University of Memphis, Rhodes College, [L], (MEM), Memphis, TN.
Campus Ministry-Diocese of Orange, [L], (ORG), Irvine, CA.
The Campus Parish of Long Island, [Q], (RVC), Rockville Centre, NY.
Cana, [N], (HRT), New Britain, CT.
Cana, [J], (SPR), West Springfield, MA.
Canaan House, Inc., [S], (NEW). See New Jersey Caritas Corporation, Inc.
Canevin Catholic High School, [C], (PIT), Pittsburgh, PA.
Canisius College, [C], (BUF), Buffalo, NY.
Canisius High School, [D], (BUF), Buffalo, NY.
Canisius House, [N], (CHI), Evanston, IL.
Canisius Jesuit Community, [O], (BUF), Buffalo, NY.
Canons Regular of Magnovarad, Ltd., [O], (GB), De Pere, WI.
Canons Regular of the Immaculate Conception, [R], (LA), Los Angeles, CA.
Canons Regular of the Immaculate Conception-Novitiate, [B], (LA), Los Angeles, CA.
Canossian Daughters of Charity, [H], (SAC), Sacramento, CA.
Cantalician Center for Learning, Inc., [F], (BUF), Buffalo, NY.
Canterbury School, [E], (HRT), New Milford, CT.
Canterbury School, [M], (HRT), New Milford, CT.
The Canticle, [N], (DAV), Clinton, IA.
Canticle Court, Inc., [N], (MIL), St. Francis, WI.
Canticle Hall, [N], (HRT). See Convent of Mary Immaculate, Provincial House of the Sisters of St. Joseph of Chambery.
Canticle Place, Inc., [M], (JOL), Wheaton, IL.
Cantwell Sacred Heart of Mary High School, [D], (LA), Montebello, CA.
Cape Cod Community College Newman Center, [O], (FR), West Barnstable, MA.
Capital Area Interfaith Respite, [D], (LAN). See Catholic Social Services-St. Vincent Home, Inc.
Capital Region Office, [E], (HBG). See Department for Catholic Charities Counseling/Field Services.
Capuchin Center for Spiritual Life, [F], (SAL), Victoria, KS.
The Capuchin Formation Trust of Puerto Rico, [H], (SJN), San Juan, Puerto Rico.
Capuchin Franciscan Friars, St. Francis Renewal Center, [I], (WIL), Wilmington, DE.
Capuchin Franciscan Friars, Vice Province of Texas, [M], (DAL), Dallas, TX.
Capuchin Franciscan Order, House of Studies, [N], (OAK), Berkeley, CA.
Capuchin Franciscan Residence, [O], (SP), Seminole, FL.
Capuchin Franciscan Tertiary Province of St. Joseph of Wisconsin, Inc., [Y], (MIL), Milwaukee, WI.
Capuchin Franciscan Volunteer Corps, Inc., [Y], (MIL), Milwaukee, WI.
The Capuchin Franciscan Volunteer Corps, Inc., [S], (PIT), Pittsburgh, PA.
Capuchin Friars - Province of the Sacred Stigmata of St. Francis, [N], (NEW), Union City, NJ.
Capuchin House of Studies, [B], (SFR), San Francisco, CA.
Capuchin Provincial House, [N], (SFR), Burlingame, CA.
Capuchin Retreat, [P], (DET), Washington, MI.
Capuchin Soup Kitchen, [Q], (DET), Detroit, MI.
Capuchins-St. Anthony Friary, [N], (WH), Charleston, WV.
Cara Program, [G], (CHI). See Catholic Charities of the Archdiocese of Chicago-Archdiocesan Offices.
CARA, Center for Applied Research in the Apostolate, [V], (WDC), Washington, DC.
*Cardijn Associates, Inc., [Q], (BAL), Baltimore, MD.
Cardinal Brennan Jr./Sr. High School, [C], (ALN), Ashland, PA.
Cardinal Club, [T], (DET), Detroit, MI.
Cardinal Cooke Guild, [HH], (NY), New York, NY.
Cardinal Cooke Memorial Foundation, [HH], (NY), New York, NY.
Cardinal Cushing General Hospital Foundation, Brockton, [DD], (BO). See Chancery Office.
Cardinal Cushing School and Training Center, Inc., [H], (BO), Hanover, MA.
Cardinal Dougherty High School, [D], (PH), Philadelphia, PA.
Cardinal Gibbons High School, [C], (MIA), Fort Lauderdale, FL.
Cardinal Gibbons Memorial High School, [A], (R), Raleigh, NC.
Cardinal Gibbons School for Boys, [C], (BAL), Baltimore, MD.
Cardinal Glennon Children's Hospital, [L], (STL), St. Louis, MO.
Cardinal Glennon Children's Hospital Foundation, [W], (STL), St. Louis, MO.
Cardinal Glennon College, [A], (STL). See Kenrick-Glennon Seminary.
Cardinal Hayes High School, [E], (NY), New York, NY.
Cardinal Hayes Home for Children, [S], (NY), Millbrook, NY.
Cardinal Hayes School for Special Children, [G], (NY), Millbrook, NY.
Cardinal Krol Center, [M], (PH), Springfield, PA.
Cardinal McCloskey Emergency Residential School, [R], (NY). See Cardinal McCloskey Services.
The Cardinal McCloskey Emergency Residential School, [U], (NY), Ossining, NY.
Cardinal McCloskey Services, [R], (NY), White Plains, NY.
Cardinal Medeiros Residence-Retirement Facility for Priests, [J], (FR), Fall River, MA.
The Cardinal Medeiros Trust, [DD], (BO). See Chancery Office.
Cardinal Mooney Catholic College Preparatory School, [D], (DET), Marine City, MI.
Cardinal Mooney High School, [A], (VEN), Sarasota, FL.
Cardinal Mooney High School, [C], (Y), Youngstown, OH.
Cardinal Mooney High School Foundation, [K], (VEN), Venice, FL.
Cardinal Muench Seminary, [A], (FAR), Fargo, ND.
Cardinal Newman High School, [A], (CHR), Columbia, SC.
Cardinal Newman High School, [B], (PMB), West Palm Beach, FL.
Cardinal Newman High School, [B], (SR), Santa Rosa, CA.

(STL). See Catholic Community Services Administration.
Catholic Community Services (C.C.S.) Mt. Carmel Guild Hospital, [G], (NEW), Newark, NJ.
Catholic Community Services Administration, [W], (STL), St. Louis, MO.
Catholic Community Services in Western Arizona, [D], (TUC). See Social Service Agencies: Pima County.
Catholic Community Services Northwest, [E], (SEA). See Catholic Community Services of Western Washington.
Catholic Community Services of Cochise County, [D], (TUC). See Social Service Agencies: Pima County.
Catholic Community Services of King County, [E], (SEA). See Catholic Community Services of Western Washington.
Catholic Community Services of Lane County, [G], (P). See Catholic Charities of the Archdiocese of Portland in Oregon.
Catholic Community Services of Mid-Willamette Valley and the Central Coast, [G], (P). See Catholic Charities of the Archdiocese of Portland in Oregon.
Catholic Community Services of Northern Nevada, [G], (RNO), Reno, NV.
Catholic Community Services of Southern Oregon, [G], (P). See Catholic Charities of the Archdiocese of Portland in Oregon.
Catholic Community Services of Stark County, Inc., [L], (Y), Canton, OH.
Catholic Community Services of the Archdiocese of Detroit, Inc., [Q], (DET), Detroit, MI.
Catholic Community Services of Western Washington, [E], (SEA), Seattle, WA.
Catholic Community Services of Western Washington Long Term Care System, [E], (SEA). See Catholic Community Services of Western Washington.
Catholic Community Services Southwest, [E], (SEA). See Catholic Community Services of Western Washington.
Catholic Community Services, Inc. of Trumbull County, [L], (Y), Warren, OH.
Catholic Conference Center, [P], (CHL), Hickory, NC.
Catholic Conference of Illinois, [X], (CHI), Chicago, IL.
Catholic Construction Services, Inc., [M], (ATL), atlanta, GA.
Catholic Counseling Services, [J], (DAL), Dallas, TX.
Catholic Counseling Services, Inc., [N], (ELP), El Paso, TX.
Catholic County Jail Ministry, [O], (OM), Omaha, NE.
Catholic Cursillo of Cincinnati, [V], (CIN), Cincinnati, OH.
Catholic Daughters of the America, [J], (STU), Martins Ferry, OH.
Catholic Daughters of the Americas, [Q], (BAL), Joppa, MD.
Catholic Daughters of the Americas, [J], (BEL), Belleville, IL.
Catholic Daughters of the Americas, [B], (STV). See Miscellaneous Organizations.
Catholic Daughters of the Americas and Its Courts, [HH], (NY), New York, NY.
Catholic Day Care Center, [C], (BEL), East St. Louis, IL.
Catholic Deaf Center, [V], (WDC), Landover Hills, MD.
Catholic Deaf Ministry, [W], (STL), St. Louis, MO.
Catholic Deaf of Baltimore, [Q], (BAL), Baltimore, MD.
Catholic Development Foundation, [I], (FAR), Fargo, ND.
The Catholic Diocese of El Paso Foundation, [N], (ELP), El Paso, TX.
The Catholic Diocese of Knoxville Foundation, Inc., [K], (KNX), Knoxville, TN.
Catholic Diocese of Las Cruces Foundation, Inc., [E], (LSC), Las Cruces, NM.
Catholic Diocese of Pittsburgh Foundation, [S], (PIT), Pittsburgh, PA.
*Catholic Diocese of Pueblo Foundation, [J], (PBL), Pueblo, CO.
The Catholic Distance University fka The Catholic Home Study Institute, [C], (ARL), Hamilton, VA.
Catholic East Elementary, [H], (MIL), Milwaukee, WI.
Catholic Eastside Apostolate, [T], (SAT), San Antonio, TX.
Catholic Education Foundation, Inc., [J], (EVN), Evansville, IN.
Catholic Education Foundation, Inc., [T], (SP). See Chancery Office.
The Catholic Education Fund, Inc., [D], (RC), Rapid City, SD.
Catholic Education Ministries of Western Maryland, [Q], (BAL), Cumberland, MD.
Catholic Education Office, [W], (STL). See Catholic High School Association.
Catholic Eldercare, Inc., [W], (STP), Minneapolis, MN.
Catholic Elementary Education Foundation of Hampton Roads, [O], (RIC), Portsmouth, VA.
Catholic Elementary School of Pointe Coupee, [D], (BR), New Roads, LA.
Catholic Elementary Schools-Region I, [E], (BGP), Greenwich, CT.
Catholic Elementary Schools-Region II, [E], (BGP), Stamford, CT.
Catholic Elementary Schools-Region III, [E], (BGP), Norwalk, CT.
Catholic Elementary Schools-Region IV, [E], (BGP), Wilton, CT.
Catholic Elementary Schools-Region IX and XI, [E], (BGP), Danbury, CT.
Catholic Elementary Schools-Region V, [E], (BGP), Fairfield, CT.
Catholic Elementary Schools-Region VI, [E], (BGP), Stratford, CT.
Catholic Elementary Schools-Region VII, [E], (BGP), Trumbull, CT.
Catholic Elementary Schools-Region VIII, [E], (BGP), Shelton, CT.
Catholic Elementary Schools-Region X, [E], (BGP), Bridgeport, CT.
Catholic Engaged Encounter of Oregon, Inc., [Q], (P), Corbett, OR.
Catholic Evangelization Fund, [J], (LIN). See Chancery.
*The Catholic Evidence Guild, [L], (LAN), Ann Arbor, MI.
Catholic Evidence League, [Q], (BAL), Baltimore, MD.
Catholic Family and Child Service, [C], (YAK), Yakima, WA.
Catholic Family and Child Service, [C], (YAK), Ephrata, WA.
Catholic Family and Child Service, [C], (YAK), Grandview, WA.
Catholic Family and Child Service, [C], (YAK), Richland, WA.
Catholic Family and Child Service, [C], (YAK), Wenatchee, WA.
Catholic Family and Child Service of Moses Lake-Ephrata, [C], (YAK), Moses Lake, WA.
Catholic Family Fraternal of Texas. KJZT, [N], (AUS), Austin, TX.
Catholic Family Service, [I], (FAR), Fargo, ND.
Catholic Family Service, [M], (GRY). See Catholic Charities.
Catholic Family Service, [H], (SPK), Spokane, WA.
*Catholic Family Service, Inc., [E], (AMA), Amarillo, TX.
Catholic Family Services, [G], (BIR), Birmingham, AL.
Catholic Family Services, [G], (BIR), Huntsville, AL.
Catholic Family Services, [G], (BIR), Tuscaloosa, AL.
Catholic Family Services, [C], (KAL), Kalamazoo, MI.
Catholic Family Services, [W], (STL), St. Louis, MO.
Catholic Family Services, Bridgeport, [G], (BGP). See Catholic Charities of Fairfield County.
Catholic Family Services, Danbury, [G], (BGP). See Catholic Charities of Fairfield County.
Catholic Family Services, Norwalk, [G], (BGP). See Catholic Charities of Fairfield County.
Catholic Family Services, Stamford, [G], (BGP). See Catholic Charities of Fairfield County.
The Catholic Foreign Mission Society of America, Inc., [M], (CIN), Cincinnati, OH.
The Catholic Foundation for Eastern South Dakota, [I], (SFS), Sioux Falls, SD.
Catholic Foundation for the Dominican Republic, [HH], (NY), New York, NY.
The Catholic Foundation for the People of the Diocese of Rockford, [L], (RCK), Rockford, IL.
Catholic Foundation of Alaska, [K], (ANC), Anchorage, AK.
The Catholic Foundation of Broome County, [H], (SY), Binghamton, NY.
Catholic Foundation of East Tennessee, [K], (KNX), Knoxville, TN.
Catholic Foundation of Eastern Oklahoma, Inc., [I], (TLS), Tulsa, OK.
Catholic Foundation of North Georgia, Inc., [M], (ATL), Atlanta, GA.
Catholic Foundation of Northcentral Indiana, Inc., [I], (LFT), Lafayette, IN.
Catholic Foundation of Northeast Kansas, [K], (KCK), Kansas City, KS.
Catholic Foundation of Tennessee, Inc., [L], (NSH), Nashville, TN.
Catholic Foundation of the Archdiocese of Boston, [DD], (BO). See Chancery Office.
The Catholic Foundation of the Diocese of Colorado Springs, Inc., [H], (COS), Colorado Springs, CO.
Catholic Foundation of the Diocese of Toledo, [O], (TOL), Toledo, OH.
The Catholic Foundation of the Spokane Diocese, [O], (SPK), Spokane, WA.
The Catholic Foundation of West Michigan, [L], (GR), Grand Rapids, MI.
The Catholic Foundation of Western Kentucky, [J], (OWN), Owensboro, KY.
Catholic Foundation, Diocese of Lubbock, [E], (LUB), Lubbock, TX.
Catholic Fraternity, [Q], (BAL), Baltimore, MD.
Catholic Gay & Lesbian Family Ministry, [L], (ROC), Rochester, NY.
Catholic Guardian Society, [T], (NY), New York, NY.
Catholic Guidance Center, [H], (STL), St. Louis, MO.
Catholic Guild for the Blind, [H], (BUF). See The Catholic Charities of the Diocese of Buffalo.
*Catholic Guild for the Blind, [U], (CHI), Chicago, IL.
Catholic Guild for the Blind, [O], (NY), New York, NY.
Catholic Guild for the Blind, Diocese of Brooklyn, Inc., [L], (BRK). See Catholic Charities.
Catholic Health Alliance for Metropolitan Chicago, [X], (CHI), Chicago, IL.
Catholic Health Association of Kansas, [K], (KCK), Topeka, KS.
The Catholic Health Association of the United States, [W], (STL), St. Louis, MO.
Catholic Health Association of Wisconsin, Inc., [M], (MAD), Madison, WI.
Catholic Health Care Federation, [G], (OM). See Catholic Health Corp.
Catholic Health Care Network, [HH], (NY), New York, NY.
Catholic Health Care West-Southern California, [K], (LA), Lynwood, CA.
Catholic Health Corp., [G], (OM), Omaha, NE.
Catholic Health Corporation Retirement Plan, [G], (OM). See Catholic Health Corp.
Catholic Health East, [FF], (PH), Radnor, PA.
Catholic Health Initiatives, [Q], (DEN), Denver, CO.
Catholic Health Partners Services, [X], (CHI), Chicago, IL.
Catholic Health Services of Long Island, Inc., [I], (RVC), Rockville Centre, NY.
Catholic Healthcare Network of Long Island, [I], (RVC), Rockville Centre, NY.
Catholic Healthcare Partners, [T], (CIN), Cincinnati, OH.
Catholic Healthcare West, [U], (SFR), San Francisco, CA.
Catholic Healthcare West Southern California, [DD], (LA), Los Angeles, CA.
Catholic Healthcare West System San Joaquin-Sierra Region, [C], (STO), Stockton, CA.
Catholic High School, [A], (BIR), Huntsville, AL.
Catholic High School, [C], (BR), Baton Rouge, LA.
Catholic High School, [B], (LAF), New Iberia, LA.
Catholic High School, [B], (LR), Little Rock, AR.
Catholic High School, [C], (MAD), Beloit, WI.
Catholic High School, [A], (RIC), Virginia Beach, VA.
Catholic High School Association, [W], (STL), St. Louis, MO.
Catholic High School Association of New York, [HH], (NY), New York, NY.
The Catholic High School of Baltimore, [C], (BAL), Baltimore, MD.
Catholic High School of Pointe Coupee, [B], (BR), New Roads, LA.
Catholic High Schools Alumni Association of Mobile, [L], (MOB), Mobile, AL.
Catholic High Schools' Athletic Association of the Archdiocese of New York, [HH], (NY), New York, NY.
Catholic Hispanic Community of Memphis (Comunidad Catolica Hispana de Memphis), [M], (MEM), Memphis, TN.
Catholic Hispanic Social Services, [J], (VEN), Fort Myers, FL.
Catholic Historical Society of the Roanoke Valley, [O], (RIC), Roanoke, VA.
Catholic Historical Society of Washington, [V], (WDC), Washington, DC.
The Catholic Historical Society of Western Pennsylvania, [S], (PIT), Pittsburgh, PA.
Catholic Home Bureau, [T], (NY), New York, NY.
Catholic Home Care, [R], (CHI), Chicago, IL.
Catholic Home Care Home Services, [R], (CHI), Chicago, IL.
Catholic Home Care, Inc., [G], (CHI). See Catholic Charities of the Archdiocese of Chicago-Archdiocesan Offices.
Catholic Home for Girls, [L], (PH), Philadelphia, PA.
Catholic Home Study Service, [W], (STL), Perryville, MO.
Catholic Horizons, Inc., [I], (BIR), Birmingham, AL.
Catholic Hospital Ministries, [Q], (SEA), Seattle, WA.
Catholic Housing Corporation, [I], (R), Raleigh, NC.
Catholic Housing of Birmingham, Inc., [I], (BIR), Birmingham, AL.
The Catholic Housing, Inc., [P], (BAL). See Chancery Office.
Catholic Human Services, [G], (GAY), Gaylord, MI.
Catholic Immigrant Ministries, Inc., [T], (BRK). See Catholic Migration & Refugee Office, Catholic Migration Services, Inc.
Catholic Information Center, [P], (BO), Peabody, MA.
Catholic Information Center, [Y], (MIL), Milwaukee, WI.
Catholic Information Center, [W], (STL), St. Louis, MO.

Chardon, OH.
Christ House, Inc., [HH], (NY), New York, NY.
Christ in the Wilderness, [N], (RCK), Stockton, IL.
Christ of the Desert Newman Center, [H], (SB), Palm Desert, CA.
Christ the Divine Teacher School, [D], (GBG), Latrobe, PA.
Christ the King, [G], (BRK), Middle Village, NY.
Christ The King, [C], (BUR), Burlington, VT.
Christ the King, [C], (BUR), Rutland, VT.
Christ the King (FOCUS), [I], (SAV), Hamilton, GA.
Christ the King Cathedral School Foundation, [E], (LUB), Lubbock, TX.
Christ the King Catholic Center, [L], (LAN), Ann Arbor, MI.
Christ the King Community, [I], (HON). See Sisters of St. Joseph of Carondelet CSJ, Hawaii Vice-Province.
Christ the King Educational Endowment Trust, [N], (OM). See The Omaha Archdiocesan Educational Foundation, Inc.
Christ the King Elementary School, [C], (SFS). See Sioux Falls Catholic School System.
Christ the King Extended Care, [G], (RIC), Norfolk, VA.
Christ the King Housing II, Inc. dba Kings Manor, [M], (SP), Tampa, FL.
Christ the King Housing, Inc. dba Kings Arms, [M], (SP), Tampa, FL.
Christ the King Learning Center, [C], (CC), Laredo, TX.
Christ the King Manor, Inc., [K], (E), Du Bois, PA.
Christ the King Monastery of St. Clare, [H], (PMB), Delray Beach, FL.
Christ the King Parish and Catholic Student Center, [K], (BR), Baton Rouge, LA.
Christ the King Parish Conference, [E], (YAK), Richland, WA.
Christ the King Regional School, [E], (CAM), Haddonfield, NJ.
Christ the King Retreat, [G], (SAC), Citrus Heights, CA.
Christ the King Retreat Center, [I], (SAC), Citrus Heights, CA.
Christ the King Retreat Center, [E], (SAN), San Angelo, TX.
Christ the King Retreat Center, [Q], (STP), Buffalo, MN.
Christ the King Retreat House, [U], (SY), Syracuse, NY.
Christ the King School, [D], (ALN), Whitehall, PA.
Christ the King School, [B], (CC), Corpus Christi, TX.
Christ the King Seminary, [A], (BUF), East Aurora, NY.
Christ the King University Parish - Ohio University, [I], (STU), Athens, OH.
Christa Center, [AA], (CLV), Cleveland, OH.
Christa House, Inc., [R], (RVC), West Babylon, NY.
*Christamore House Incorporated, [I], (DAV). See Young House Family Services, Inc.
Christendom College, [A], (ARL), Front Royal, VA.
Christian Brothers, [J], (ELP), El Paso, TX.
Christian Brothers (F.S.C.), [AA], (PH), Audubon, PA.
Christian Brothers (F.S.C.), [AA], (PH), Wyndmoor, PA.
Christian Brothers (F.S.C.)- St. Joseph Community, [M], (DEN), Denver, CO.
Christian Brothers Academy, [D], (SY), Syracuse, NY.
Christian Brothers Academy, [F], (SY), Syracuse, NY.
Christian Brothers Academy, [C], (TR), Lincroft, NJ.
Christian Brothers Center, [J], (JOL), Romeoville, IL.
Christian Brothers College High School (C.B.C.), [F], (STL), St. Louis, MO.
Christian Brothers Community Support Charitable Trust, [P], (BAL). See Chancery Office.
Christian Brothers Counseling Center, Inc., [X], (CHI), Westchester, IL.
Christian Brothers Employee Benefit Trust, [M], (JOL), Romeoville, IL.
Christian Brothers Employee Retirement Plan Trust, [M], (JOL), Romeoville, IL.
Christian Brothers Foundation, [S], (NO), New Orleans, LA.
The Christian Brothers Foundation, Inc., [HH], (NY), New Rochelle, NY.
Christian Brothers Fund, Inc., [M], (JOL), Romeoville, IL.
*Christian Brothers High School, [C], (MEM), Memphis, TN.
Christian Brothers High School of Sacramento, Inc., [C], (SAC), Sacramento, CA.
Christian Brothers Institute of California, Inc. dba Palma High School, [B], (MRY), Salinas, CA.
Christian Brothers Provincial Office (Midwest Province), [J], (JOL), Burr Ridge, IL.
Christian Brothers Provincialate, [M], (BAL), Adamstown, MD.
Christian Brothers Religious Comprehensive Trust, [M], (JOL), Romeoville, IL.
Christian Brothers Religious Deductible Trust, [M], (JOL), Romeoville, IL.
Christian Brothers Residence, [U], (BRK), Brooklyn, NY.
Christian Brothers Retreat and Conference Center, [L], (SR), Napa, CA.
Christian Brothers Retreat Center, [Q], (STP), Marine on St. Croix, MN.
Christian Brothers School, [H], (NO), New Orleans, LA.
*Christian Brothers Services, [M], (JOL), Romeoville, IL.
Christian Brothers Spiritual Center, [L], (BAL), Adamstown, MD.
*Christian Brothers University, [A], (MEM), Memphis, TN.
Christian Brothers Youth Home, [W], (STP), St. Paul, MN.
Christian Brothers' Academy, [D], (ALB), Albany, NY.
Christian Brothers' Center, [P], (PRO), Narragansett, RI.
Christian Brothers, St. La Salle Auxiliary, [M], (TR), Lincroft, NJ.
Christian Care and Share Center, [N], (LAF), Ville Platte, LA.
Christian Center of Concern, [G], (BIR), Hamilton, AL.
Christian Center of Concern, [G], (BIR), Winfield, AL.
Christian Center of Concern, [G], (BIR), Sulligent, AL.
Christian Center of Concern, [G], (BIR), Fayette, AL.
Christian Community Center, [L], (GR), Muskegon Heights, MI.
Christian Community of God's Delight, [P], (DAL), Dallas, TX.
Christian Family Movement (CFM), [O], (OM), Omaha, NE.
Christian Family School, [E], (DUB), Calmar, IA.
Christian Family Services of Lapeer County, Inc., [N], (DET), Lapeer, MI.
The Christian Institute for the Study of Human Sexuality, [V], (WDC), Washington, DC.
Christian Life Center, [P], (MAN), Berlin, NH.
Christian Life Center, [P], (MAN), Durham, NH.
Christian Life Center, [P], (MAN), Keene, NH.
Christian Life Center, [P], (MAN), Laconia, NH.
Christian Life Center, [P], (MAN), Salem, NH.
Christian Life Center, [L], (PRT), Upper Frenchville, ME.
Christian Life Center, [G], (SPR), Northampton, MA.
Christian Life Communities, [V], (WDC), Washington, DC.
Christian Life Community Regional Information Center, [Q], (BAL), Silver Spring, MD.
Christian Live Communities (Sodalities), [U], (SFR), Los Angeles, CA.
Christian Renewal Center, [S], (GAL), Dickinson, TX.
Christian Renewal Center, [A], (LUB), Lubbock, TX.
Christian Service Center, [N], (LAF), Abbeville, LA.
The Christian Sisters, [U], (MIL), Milwaukee, WI.
Christian Urban Education Service, [O], (OM), Omaha, NE.
Christian Urban Education Service Foundation, [F], (OM), Omaha, NE.
Christians Encounter Christ, [O], (OM), Omaha, NE.
Christina House, [M], (WCH), Wichita, KS.
Christlife, Inc., [Q], (BAL), Ellicott City, MD.
Christmas House, [L], (IND). See Catholic Charities of Terre Haute.
Christopher Assurance, Inc., [T], (SP). See Chancery Office.
Christopher Columbus High School, [D], (MIA), Miami, FL.
Christopher Community, Inc., [Q], (SY), Syracuse, NY.
The Christopher Home, [E], (PRT). See Catholic Charities Maine.
Christopher Homes of Arkansas, Inc., [L], (LR), Little Rock, AR.
Christopher Homes of Augusta, Inc., [L], (LR). See Christopher Homes of Arkansas, Inc.
Christopher Homes of Brinkley, Inc., [L], (LR). See Christopher Homes of Arkansas, Inc.
Christopher Homes of Camden, Inc., [L], (LR). See Christopher Homes of Arkansas, Inc.
Christopher Homes of Clarendon, Inc., [L], (LR). See Christopher Homes of Arkansas, Inc.
Christopher Homes of El Dorado, Inc., [L], (LR). See Christopher Homes of Arkansas, Inc.
Christopher Homes of Elaine, Inc., [L], (LR). See Christopher Homes of Arkansas, Inc.
Christopher Homes of Forrest City, Inc., [L], (LR). See Christopher Homes of Arkansas, Inc.
Christopher Homes of Hot Springs, Inc., [L], (LR). See Christopher Homes of Arkansas, Inc.
Christopher Homes of Jonesboro, Inc., [L], (LR). See Christopher Homes of Arkansas, Inc.
Christopher Homes of Marianna, Inc., [L], (LR). See Christopher Homes of Arkansas, Inc.
Christopher Homes of Monette, Inc., [L], (LR). See Christopher Homes of Arkansas, Inc.
Christopher Homes of North Little Rock, Inc., [L], (LR). See Christopher Homes of Arkansas, Inc.
Christopher Homes of Palestine, Inc., [L], (LR). See Christopher Homes of Arkansas, Inc.
Christopher Homes of Paragould, Inc., [L], (LR). See Christopher Homes of Arkansas, Inc.
Christopher Homes of Parkin, Inc., [L], (LR). See Christopher Homes of Arkansas, Inc.
Christopher Homes of Searcy, Inc., [L], (LR). See Christopher Homes of Arkansas, Inc.
Christopher Homes of Strong, Inc., [L], (LR). See Christopher Homes of Arkansas, Inc.
Christopher Homes of West Helena, Inc., [L], (LR). See Christopher Homes of Arkansas, Inc.
Christopher Homes of Wynne, Inc., [L], (LR). See Christopher Homes of Arkansas, Inc.
Christopher House, [O], (ALN), Kutztown, PA.
Christopher House-College Department of St. Joseph's Seminary, [A], (GR), Grand Rapids, MI.
Christopher Inn Apts., [N], (NO), New Orleans, LA.
The Christophers, [HH], (NY), New York, NY.
CHS Foundation, [M], (BR). See Baton Rouge Chancery Office.
Church of St. Boniface of Menominee, [N], (OM). See The Omaha Archdiocesan Educational Foundation, Inc.
Church of St. Francis of Assisi Parish Educational Endowment, [N], (OM). See The Omaha Archdiocesan Educational Foundation, Inc.
Church of St. Francis of Assisi Parish Endowment Fund, [N], (OM). See The Omaha Archdiocesan Educational Foundation, Inc.
Church of St. Theresa of Avila Educational Endowment, [N], (OM). See The Omaha Archdiocesan Educational Foundation, Inc.
Church of St. Theresa of Avila Parish Endowment, [N], (OM). See The Omaha Archdiocesan Educational Foundation, Inc.
Church of the Assumption of the B.V.M. Parish Endowment Trust, [N], (OM). See The Omaha Archdiocesan Educational Foundation, Inc.
Church of the Assumption Scholarship Educational Endowment, [N], (OM). See The Omaha Archdiocesan Educational Foundation, Inc.
The Church of the Immaculate Conception, North Providence, [U], (PRO). See Miscellaneous Listings for the Diocese of Providence.
Church of the Resurrection Educational Trust Fund (Church of the Resurrection, Lansing), [K], (LAN). See Chancery Office.
Churchill Manor, Inc., [Q], (SY), Syracuse, NY.
Ciara House, [L], (NO), New Orleans, LA.
Cicero Housing Development Fund Company Inc., [Q], (SY), Cicero, NY.
Cincinnati Catholic Women's Association, [V], (CIN), Cincinnati, OH.
Cincinnati Regional Community, Institute of the Sisters of Mercy of the Americas, [N], (CIN), Cincinnati, OH.
The Cistercian (Trappist) Abbey of Our Lady of Guadalupe, [L], (P), Lafayette, OR.
Cistercian Abbey of Our Lady of Dallas, [M], (DAL), Irving, TX.
Cistercian Abbey of Our Lady of the Holy Cross, [J], (ARL), Berryville, VA.
Cistercian Conventual Priory, St. Mary's Priory, [K], (ALN), New Ringgold, PA.
Cistercian Fathers, [N], (CHI), Willow Springs, IL.
Cistercian Monastery of Our Lady of Fatima, [M], (TR), Mount Laurel, NJ.
Cistercian Nuns of the Strict Observance (Virginia), [M], (RIC), Crozet, VA.
Cistercian Preparatory School, [D], (DAL), Irving, TX.
Cistercian Preparatory School, [G], (DAL), Irving, TX.
Cistercian Publications, Inc., [R], (WOR), Spencer, MA.
Cistercian Studies Quarterly, Inc., [J], (TUC), Sonoita, AZ.
Ciszek Hall, [B], (NY), Bronx, NY.
The Citadel, [G], (CHR), Charleston, SC.
Citizenship Services, [Q], (SFR). See Catholic Charities of the Archdiocese of San Francisco.
Citrus Valley Health Partners, Queen of the Valley Campus, [K], (LA), West Covina, CA.
City College of New York, [GG], (NY). See University Apostolate.
City Hospital Chaplaincy Service, [J], (DM), Des Moines, IA.
The City of St. Jude, Inc., [L], (MOB), Montgomery, AL.
City of St. Jude, Inc., The, [F], (MOB), Montgomery, AL.
City of the Lord, [J], (PHX), Tempe, AZ.
Civitas Dei Foundation, [X], (CHI), Mundelein, IL.
Clairvaux Commons, [K], (GBG), Indiana, PA.
Clairvaux House, [H], (MET), Raritan, NJ.
Clara Pfaender Fund, Inc., [M], (JOL), Wheaton, IL.
Clare Gardens, Inc., [K], (DEN), Denver, CO.
Clare House, [F], (ANC), Anchorage, AK.
Clare House, [CC], (PH), Aston, PA.
Clare of Assisi Homes - Westminster, Inc., [K], (DEN), Westminster, CO.
Clare Towers II, Inc. dba Clare Woods, [Y], (MIL), Milwaukee, WI.
Clare Towers, Inc., [Y], (MIL), Milwaukee, WI.

Claret Center, [X], (CHI), Chicago, IL.
Claretian Associates, Inc., [X], (CHI), Chicago, IL.
Claretian Educational and Renewal Center, Inc., [R], (LA). See Missionary Sons of the Immaculate Heart of Mary.
Claretian Fathers Headquarters of U.S.A. Eastern Province, [N], (CHI), Oak Park, IL.
Claretian Missionaries, [H], (ORG), Orange, CA.
Claretian Missionaries (Missionary Sons of the Immaculate Heart of Mary), [R], (LA), San Gabriel, CA.
Claretian Missionaries Community Support Trust, [N], (CHI). See Claretian Fathers Headquarters of U.S.A. Eastern Province.
Claretian Missionaries, St. Jude League, Inc., [N], (CHI), Chicago, IL.
Claretian Missionary, Sisters of Florida, Inc., [H], (PMB), Delray Beach, FL.
Claretian Missions, Inc., [L], (MIA), Miami, FL.
Claretian Retreat Center (All Groups), [X], (LA), Los Angeles, CA.
Claretian Retreat Center Community, [R], (LA), Los Angeles, CA.
Claretian Tape Ministry, Inc., [R], (LA). See Missionary Sons of the Immaculate Heart of Mary.
Claretian Volunteers and Lay Missionaries, [X], (CHI), Chicago, IL.
Claretians Missionaries' Residence-Villa Claret, [E], (SPC), Springfield, MO.
Clark Street House of Mercy, [D], (DM). See Mercy Hospital Medical Center.
Clark Street Jesuit Residence, [N], (CHI). See Chicago Province of the Society of Jesus-Provincial Office.
Clark University, [Q], (WOR). See Campus Ministry.
Clarke College, [C], (DUB), Dubuque, IA.
Clearview of Colorado, Tertiary Substance Abuse Facility, [E], (PBL). See Centura Health-St. Joseph Manor.
Clearwater Central Catholic High School, [B], (SP), Clearwater, FL.
Cleary Deaf Child Center, Inc., [G], (RVC), Nesconset, NY.
Clelian Adult Day Center, [H], (HRT), Hamden, CT.
Clelian Heights School for Exceptional Children, [E], (GBG), Greensburg, PA.
Clement Manor Health Center, [N], (MIL), Greenfield, WI.
Clement Manor Retirement Community, [N], (MIL), Greenfield, WI.
Clemons Productions, Inc., [W], (BGP), Greenwich, CT.
Clemson University, Southern Wesleyan University, [G], (CHR), Clemson, SC.
Clergy Assistance Trust, [DD], (BO), Brighton, MA.
Clergy Benefit Trust, [DD], (BO). See Chancery Office.
Clergy Fund Society, [DD], (BO). See Chancery Office.
Clergy Health Plan, [T], (DET), Detroit, MI.
Clergy Medical-Hospitalization Trust, [DD], (BO). See Chancery Office.
The Clergy Retirement Plan of Diocese of Raleigh, [I], (R), Raleigh, NC.
Clergy Retirement-Disability Trust, [DD], (BO). See Chancery Office.
Clerics of St. Viator, [D], (LAV), Las Vegas, NV.
Clerics of St. Viator Retirement Home, [D], (LAV), Las Vegas, NV.
Clerics of St. Viator-Provincial Residence, [N], (CHI), Arlington Heights, IL.
Clermont Mercy Hospital, [K], (CIN), Batavia, OH.
Clermont Residence, [Y], (BRK), Brooklyn, NY.
Cleveland Central Catholic High School, [D], (CLV), Cleveland, OH.
Cleveland District Council, [V], (CLV). See Society of St. Vincent de Paul, Diocesan Central Council.
Cliffview Retreat Center, [K], (LEX), Danville, KY.
Clinic For Kids, [F], (SFD). See Catholic Charities of Springfield.
Clinton Office, [H], (WOR). See Catholic Charities.
Clothesbasket, [I], (SAV), Claxton, GA.
Clothing Program, [K], (SAC). See Catholic Charities of Sacramento, Inc.
The Clubhouse, [O], (NY). See Beacon of Hope House.
Cluny Provincial House, [Q], (PRO), Newport, RI.
Coal City Family Health Center, [G], (JOL). See St. Joseph Medical Center.
COAR Children's Village, [AA], (CLV). See COAR Peace Mission, Inc.
COAR Peace Mission, Inc., [AA], (CLV), Cleveland, OH.
Coastal Carolina University, [G], (CHR), Conway, SC.
Coatesville Area Catholic Elementary School, [H], (PH), Coatesville, PA.
Cochise Community College, [I], (TUC), Douglas, AZ.
Cohoes Catholic School, [F], (ALB), Cohoes, NY.
Coker College Newman Center, [G], (CHR), Hartsville, SC.
Colby College, [M], (PRT), Waterville, ME.
Colby-Sawyer College Newman Center, [N], (MAN), New London, NH.
Colegio Catolico Notre Dame Elemental, [A], (CGS), Caguas, PR.
Colegio Catolico Notre Dame Superior, [A], (CGS), Caguas, PR.
Colegio Corazon de Maria, [A], (CGS), Juncos, PR.
Colegio El Ave Maria, [C], (PCE), Ponce, PR.
Colegio La Inmaculada, [B], (SJN), Santurce, PR.
Colegio La Milagrosa, [B], (SJN), Rio Piedras, PR.
Colegio Lourdes, [B], (SJN), Hato Rey, PR.
Colegio Maria Auxiliadora, [B], (SJN), Santurce, PR.
Colegio Marista, [B], (SJN), Guaynabo, PR.
Colegio Ntra. Sra. De La Caridad, [B], (SJN), Guaynabo, PR.
Colegio Ntra. Sra. De Pilar, [A], (CGS), Gurabo, PR.
Colegio Ntra. Sra. del Rosario, [B], (SJN), Bayamon, PR.
Colegio Nuestra Senora de la Merced, [A], (CGS), Cayey, PR.
Colegio Nuestra Senora De La Providencia, [B], (SJN), Rio Piedras, PR.
Colegio Nuestra Senora Del Carmen, [B], (SJN), Rio Piedras, PR.
Colegio Nuestra Senora del Perpetuo Socorro de Humacao, Inc., [A], (CGS), Humacao, PR.
Colegio Parroquial San Jose, [A], (CGS), Aibonito, PR.
Colegio Parvulos Inmaculada Corazon de Maria, [B], (SJN), San Juan, PR.
Colegio Ponceno, [C], (PCE), Coto Laurel, PR.
Colegio Sagrado Corazon, [C], (PCE), Ponce, PR.
Colegio San Antonio Abad, [A], (CGS), Humacao, PR.
Colegio San Benito, [A], (CGS), Humacao, PR.
Colegio San Francisco de Asis Elemental y Superior, [A], (CGS), Barranquitas, PR.
Colegio San Jose, [B], (SJN), Rio Piedras, PR.
Colegio San Jose Elemental, [A], (CGS), Caguas, PR.
Colegio San Jose Superior, [A], (CGS), Caguas, PR.
Colegio San Juan Apostol y Evangelista, [A], (CGS), Caguas, PR.
Colegio Santa Rosa, [B], (SJN), Bayamon, PR.
Colegio Santiago Apostol, [A], (CGS), Fajardo, PR.
Collaborative Project for Aging Religious, [DD], (LA), Los Angeles, CA.
College Formation Program, [A], (MIL). See St. Francis Seminary.
College Misericordia, [C], (SCR), Dallas, PA.
The College of Arts and Sciences, [C], (CHI). See Loyola University-Chicago.
College of Arts and Sciences, [D], (CIN). See The University of Dayton.
College of Arts and Sciences, [B], (NEW). See Seton Hall University.
College of Commerce, [C], (CHI). See De Paul University.
College of Eastern Utah, Newman Club, [H], (SLC), Price, UT.
College of Education and Human Services, [B], (NEW). See Seton Hall University.
College of Law, [C], (CHI). See De Paul University.
The College of Liberal Arts, [A], (DET). See Sacred Heart Major Seminary, Inc.
College of Liberal Arts and Sciences, [C], (CHI). See De Paul University.
College of Mount St. Joseph, [D], (CIN), Cincinnati, OH.
College of Mt. St. Joseph Campus Ministry, [Q], (CIN), Cincinnati, OH.
College of Mount Saint Vincent, [C], (NY), New York, NY.
College of Mt. St. Vincent, [GG], (NY). See University Apostolate.
*College of New Rochelle, [C], (NY), New Rochelle, NY.
College of New Rochelle, [GG], (NY). See University Apostolate.
College of Notre Dame, [C], (SFR), Belmont, CA.
College of Notre Dame of Maryland, [B], (BAL), Baltimore, MD.
College of Nursing, [B], (NEW). See Seton Hall University.
College of Our Lady of the Elms, [B], (SPR), Chicopee, MA.
College of St. Benedict, [B], (SCL), St. Joseph, MN.
College of St. Catherine, [C], (STP), St. Paul, MN.
The College of St. Catherine-Minneapolis, [C], (STP), Minneapolis, MN.
College of Saint Elizabeth, [B], (PAT), Morristown, NJ.
College of St. Elizabeth Newman Center, [O], (PAT), Convent Station, NJ.
College of St. Francis, [A], (JOL), Joliet, IL.
College of St. Joseph in Vermont, [A], (BUR), Rutland, VT.
College of St. Mary, [A], (OM), Omaha, NE.
The College of Saint Rose, [B], (ALB), Albany, NY.
College of St. Scholastica, [A], (DUL), Duluth, MN.
College of Santa Fe, [C], (SFE), Santa Fe, NM.
College of Southern Idaho, [F], (B), Twin Falls, ID.
College of the Holy Cross, Inc, [B], (WOR), Worcester, MA.
College Seminary, [B], (NEW). See Seton Hall University.
Collegiate Religious Center, [Q], (WOR). See Campus Ministry.
Collier Group Home, [K], (TR), Red Bank, NJ.
Collier Services, [K], (TR), Wickatunk, NJ.
Collin County Catholic High School Campaign, Inc., [P], (DAL), Dallas, TX.
Colombiere Center, [P], (DET), Clarkston, MI.
Colombiere Community, [L], (P), Portland, OR.
Colorado Affordable Catholic Housing Corporation, [K], (DEN). See Archdiocesan Housing Committee.
Colorado Mountain College, [P], (DEN), Steamboat Springs, CO.
Colorado Northwestern Community College (Rangely), [P], (DEN), Rangely, CO.
Colorado School of Mines (Golden), [P], (DEN), Golden, CO.
Colorado Springs Council of Black Catholics, [H], (COS), Colorado Springs, CO.
Colorado Springs Diocesan Council of Catholic Women, [H], (COS), Colorado Springs, CO.
Colorado State University (Fort Collins), [P], (DEN), Fort Collins, CO.
*Colorado Vincentian Volunteers, [Q], (DEN), Denver, CO.
Columba Hall, [J], (FTW). See Congregation of Holy Cross, Midwest Province.
Columban Fathers, [H], (ORG), Westminster, CA.
Columban Fathers Mission Center, [N], (CHI), Chicago, IL.
Columban Fathers Regional Administration, [N], (OM), St. Columbans, NE.
Columban Fathers Theologate, [N], (CHI), Chicago, IL.
Columban Fathers, Procure House, [R], (LA), Los Angeles, CA.
Columban Sisters, [X], (BO), Boston, MA.
Columbia Nursing Home Ministry, [D], (JC), Stoutsville, MO.
Columbia University, [GG], (NY). See University Apostolate.
Columbia-Greene Community College, [S], (ALB), Hudson, NY.
Columbian House, [J], (ORG). See Catholic Charities of Orange County, Inc.
Columbian House, [J], (ORG). See Catholic Charities of Orange County, Inc.
Columbiere House, [R], (LA), Los Angeles, CA.
Columbus High School, [D], (DUB), Waterloo, IA.
Columbus High School, [C], (LC), Marshfield, WI.
Columbus High School Foundation, [M], (LC), Marshfield, WI.
Columbus Home, Inc., [E], (KNX), Knoxville, TN.
Columbus Hospital, [J], (CHI), Chicago, IL.
Columbus Park Plaza, [I], (KC), Kansas City, MO.
The Comboni Lay Missionaries Association, [V], (CIN), Cincinnati, OH.
Comboni Mission Center, [N], (CHI), La Grange Park, IL.
Comboni Missionaries, [DD], (LA), Covina, CA.
Comboni Missionaries (Verona Fathers)-Comboni Mission Center, [M], (CIN), Cincinnati, OH.
The Comboni Missionaries Auxiliary, Inc., [V], (CIN), Cincinnati, OH.
Comboni Missionaries of the Heart of Jesus (Verona Fathers), [N], (NEW), Montclair, NJ.
Comboni Missionaries Theologate (M.C.C.J.), Verona Fathers, [N], (CHI), Chicago, IL.
Comboni Missionary Sisters, [O], (CHI), Chicago, IL.
Comboni Missionary Sisters, [BB], (PH), Coatesville, PA.
Comboni Missionary Sisters, Provincial House, [M], (RIC), Richmond, VA.
Comeau Catholic Campus Center at Fort Hays State University, [G], (SAL), Hays, KS.
Comfort House/Casa del Conseulo, [I], (BWN), McAllen, TX.
Commissariat of the Holy Land, Franciscan Monastery - Mount St. Sepulchre, [M], (WDC), Washington, DC.
Commission on Church Music, [D], (NY). See Department of Education.
Commission on Ecumenism, [P], (DAL), Dallas, TX.
Commission on Education for Jordan Catholic School, [E], (PEO). See Jordan Catholic School of Rock Island, Inc.
Commitment, [P], (DAV), Davenport, IA.
Committe for Mission Responsibility Society, Inc., [HH], (NY), New York, NY.
Common Fund for Schools, [P], (WH), Wheeling, WV.
Common Ground Center for Community Renewal, [AA], (CLV), Oberlin, OH.
Common Sense Parenting, [I], (SAT). See Father Flanagan's Boys' Town of San Antonio.
Commonwealth Catholic Charities, [K], (RIC), Richmond, VA.
Communio: International Catholic Review, [V], (WDC), Washington, DC.
Community, [N], (HRT). See Sisters of Notre Dame de Namur.
Community Action for Better Housing, Inc., [P], (FR), Fall River, MA.

Community and Family Support Services, [D], (WIL). See Catholic Charities, Inc.
Community Catholic School, [D], (L), Louisville, KY.
Community Clinical Services, Inc., [H], (PRT), Lewiston, ME.
Community College of Denver, [P], (DEN). See Auraria Campus.
Community College of Philadelphia, [EE], (PH). See Newman Apostolate.
Community College of R.I., [S], (PRO), Warwick, RI.
Community Counseling & Education Svcs., [F], (SJ). See Catholic Charities of Santa Clara County.
Community Family Service Center, [G], (CHI). See Catholic Charities of the Archdiocese of Chicago-Archdiocesan Offices.
Community Food Depots, [Q], (DET), Detroit, MI.
Community Foundation of St. Joseph's Hospital of Marshfield, Inc., [M], (LC), Marshfield, WI.
Community Foundation of Saint Michael's Hospital, [M], (LC), Stevens Point, WI.
Community Health Partners, [AA], (CLV). See CHP - Humility of Mary Health Partners.
Community Health Partners Foundation, [AA], (CLV), Lorain, OH.
Community Health Partners of Ohio, [J], (CLV), Lorain, OH.
Community Hospice of Texas, [N], (FWT), Fort Worth, TX.
Community House at St. Thomas, [N], (MET), East Brunswick, NJ.
Community House Inc., [L], (E), Erie, PA.
Community Institute of Behavorial Services (CIBS), [H], (BAL). See Bon Secours Baltimore Health Corporation, Inc.
Community Integration Program, [L], (OKL). See Oklahoma Benedictine Institute on Mental Retardation, Inc.
Community of the Resurrection, [J], (PRT), Casco, ME.
Community of Christ, [U], (WDC), Washington, DC.
Community of Christ the Redeemer, [T], (STP), West St. Paul, MN.
The Community of God's Love, [S], (NEW), Rutherford, NJ.
Community of Hope, [J], (MAD), Baraboo, WI.
Community of Jesus Crucified, [M], (LAF), Lafayette, LA.
Community of Little Brothers and Sisters of the Eucharist, Inc., [T], (CLV), Cleveland, OH.
Community of Our Lady, [I], (GB), Oshkosh, WI.
Community of St. Egidio, U.S.A., Inc., [HH], (NY), New York, NY.
The Community of St. John, [V], (WDC), Washington, DC.
Community of Teresian Carmelites, [P], (WOR), Worcester, MA.
Community of the Holy Spirit, [I], (ORG), Newport Beach, CA.
Community of the Holy Spirit, [I], (SD), San Diego, CA.
Community of the Holy Spirit, [N], (SJ), San Jose, CA.
Community of the Holy Spirit, C.H.S., [U], (LA), Los Angeles, CA.
Community of the Mother of God of Tenderness, [C], (NTN), Danbury, CT.
Community of the Sisters of Saint Anne, [X], (BO). See Sisters of St. Anne, Provincialate.
Community of the Way, [I], (NOR), Hampton, CT.
Community Organizing Center, [L], (DEN). See Catholic Charities and Community Services of the Archdiocese of Denver, Inc.
Community Outreach, [I], (SFS), Sioux Falls, SD.
Community Outreach Program for the Deaf, [D], (TUC). See Social Service Agencies: Pima County.
Community Residence Program, [H], (SY), Norwich, NY.
Community Service Center, [K], (KCK), Emporia, KS.
Community Service Center, [K], (KCK), Lawrence, KS.
Community Service Center, [K], (KCK), Leavenworth, KS.
Community Services, [F], (SFD). See Catholic Charities of Springfield.
Community Services of Catholic Charities, [F], (SCL), St. Cloud, MN.
Community Support Center, [H], (BAL). See Bon Secours Baltimore Health Corporation, Inc.
Community Support Charitable Trust, [U], (CIN), Cincinnati, OH.
Community Support Charitable Trust, [U], (CIN), Dayton, OH.
Companions of Christ, [J], (PRT), Auburn, ME.
The Companions of Christ, [T], (STP), St. Paul, MN.
Companions of Christ the Lamb, [T], (DET), Newport, MI.
Company of St. Paul, [HH], (NY), White Plains, NY.
Comtemplative Sisters of the Good Shepherd, [O], (WDC), Baltimore, MD.
Con El, Inc., [J], (PMB), Palm Beach Gardens, FL.
Conception Abbey, [J], (KC), Conception, MO.
Conception Benedictine Trust, [O], (KC), Conception, MO.
Conception Seminary College, [A], (KC), Conception, MO.
Concord, [H], (OAK). See Catholic Charities of the Diocese of Oakland, Inc.
Concord College Newman Center, [Q], (WH), Athens, WV.
Conference of Regional Treasurers, [U], (PRO), Burrillville, RI.
Congregacion de Santa Cruz, [J], (FTW). See Congregation of Holy Cross Indiana Province Provincial House.
Congregation of Alexian Brothers Immaculate Conception Province, Inc., [N], (CHI), Elk Grove Village, IL.
Congregation of Alexian Brothers-Alexian Brothers Novitiate, [N], (CHI), Chicago, IL.
Congregation of Armenian Catholic Sisters of Immaculate Conception, Inc., [X], (BO), Lexington, MA.
Congregation of Christian Brothers, [H], (HON), Honolulu, HI.
Congregation of Christian Brothers, [N], (NEW), East Orange, NJ.
Congregation of Christian Brothers, [N], (NEW), Oradell, NJ.
Congregation of Christian Brothers, [DD], (NY), West Park, NY.
Congregation of Christian Brothers, [M], (SEA), Seattle, WA.
Congregation of Christian Brothers, Brother Rice Community, [N], (CHI), Chicago, IL.
Congregation of Christian Brothers, Brother Rice Community, [K], (DET), Bloomfield Hills, MI.
Congregation of Christian Brothers, Brother Rice Provincialate, [J], (JOL), Joliet, IL.
Congregation of Divine Providence, [F], (BWN), Pharr, TX.
Congregation of Divine Providence (C.D.P.), [R], (GAL), Houston, TX.
Congregation of Divine Providence, C.D.P., [Q], (NO), New Orleans, LA.
Congregation of Holy Cross - Formation Community, [B], (SAT), San Antonio, TX.
Congregation of Holy Cross - Southern Province, [H], (AUS), Austin, TX.
Congregation of Holy Cross Indiana Province Provincial House, [J], (FTW), South Bend, IN.
Congregation of Holy Cross, Midwest Province, [J], (FTW), Notre Dame, IN.
Congregation of Humility of Mary, [F], (BLX), Biloxi, MS.
Congregation of Jesus and Mary, Provincialate, [O], (WDC), Mount Rainier, MD.
Congregation of Marian Fathers of the Immaculate Conception, [N], (CHI), Chicago, IL.
Congregation of Marians, [I], (SPR), Stockbridge, MA.
The Congregation of Maronite Lebanese Missionaries, [A], (OLL), San Antonio, TX.
Congregation of Mary Queen, [F], (SPC), Springfield, MO.
Congregation of Mary Queen (Vietnam), [G], (LIN), Lincoln, NE.
Congregation of Mary, Queen of the World Community, [R], (STL), St. Louis, MO.
Congregation of Mother Co-Redemptrix, Our Lady of the Rosary House, [E], (SPC), Springfield, MO.
Congregation of Notre Dame, [N], (HRT), Southington, CT.
Congregation of Notre Dame of Montreal, [F], (BWN), La Feria, TX.
The Congregation of Our Lady of Charity of the Good Shepherd, Community Support Trust, [U], (CIN), Cincinnati, OH.
Congregation of Our Lady of Mount Carmel, O.Carm., [Q], (NO), Lacombe, LA.
Congregation of Our Lady of the Retreat in the Cenacle, [T], (CHI), Chicago, IL.
Congregation of Our Lady of the Retreat in the Cenacle, [L], (JOL), Warrenville, IL.
Congregation of St. Agnes, [F], (R), Tarboro, NC.
Congregation of Saint Basil, [A], (VNN), Phoenix, AZ.
Congregation of St. Dominic General Motherhouse of the Sisters of St. Dominic of Blauvelt, [EE], (NY), Blauvelt, NY.
Congregation of St. John the Baptist, [DD], (LA), Monterey Park, CA.
Congregation of St. John the Baptist of China, [U], (BRK), Elmhurst, NY.
Congregation of St. Joseph, [P], (CLV), Avon, OH.
Congregation of St. Joseph Casa Nazareth, [R], (LA), Los Angeles, CA.
Congregation of the Benedictines of Jesus Crucified, O.S.B., [BB], (PH), Devon, PA.
Congregation of the Blessed Sacrament Provincial House, [P], (CLV), Cleveland, OH.
Congregation of the Brothers of St. Francis Xavier, [F], (NOR), Middletown, CT.
Congregation of the Divine Spirit, [M], (E), Erie, PA.
Congregation of the French-Cuban Dominican Sisters of Holy Rosary, Inc., [I], (MIA), Miami, FL.
Congregation of the Handmaids of the Holy Child Jesus, [O], (STP), Minneapolis, MN.
Congregation of the Holy Ghost, [AA], (PH), Bensalem, PA.
Congregation of the Holy Ghost, [G], (VEN), Sarasota, FL.
Congregation of the Holy Infancy of Jesus Regional House, [I], (MET), North Plainfield, NJ.
Congregation of the Holy Redeemer, [M], (HRT), Suffield, CT.
Congregation of the Holy Rosary, [F], (BLX), Long Beach, MS.
Congregation of the Humility of Mary Charitable Trust, [P], (DAV), Davenport, IA.
Congregation of the Humility of Mary, CHM, [B], (SAN), Midland, TX.
Congregation of the Incarnate Word & Blessed Sacrament (C.V.I.) (Houston), [R], (GAL), Houston, TX.
Congregation of the Infant Jesus, [V], (BRK), Brooklyn, NY.
Congregation of the Lovers of the Cross of Thaibinh Diocese, N. Vietnam, [R], (GAL), Houston, TX.
Congregation of the Marianites of Holy Cross, [G], (ALX), Alexandria, LA.
Congregation of the Marianites of Holy Cross, [G], (ALX), Cottonport, LA.
Congregation of the Mission, [AA], (PH), Philadelphia, PA.
Congregation of The Mission, [P], (STL), Perryville, MO.
Congregation of the Mission International Fund, [W], (STL), Earth City, MO.
Congregation of the Mission Midwest Province (Vincentians), [P], (STL), Earth City, MO.
Congregation of the Mission Midwest Province: De Paul House, [M], (DEN), Denver, CO.
Congregation of the Mission, Southern Province, [M], (DAL), Dallas, TX.
Congregation of the Most Holy Rosary, [H], (LAN). See Motherhouse of the Sisters of St. Dominic.
Congregation of the Mother Coredemptrix, [Q], (GAL), New Canen, TX.
Congregation of the Mother Coredemptrix, [E], (SB), Corona, CA.
Congregation of the Mother Co-Redemptrix, [A], (SPC), Carthage, MO.
Congregation of the Mother Coredemptrix Formation House, [B], (NO), Metairie, LA.
Congregation of the Mother Co-Redemptrix, United States Assumption Province, [E], (SPC), Carthage, MO.
Congregation of the Oratory of St. Philip Neri, [O], (PIT), Pittsburgh, PA.
Congregation of the Passion, [N], (CHI). See Passionist Provincial Office.
Congregation of the Passion (Passionists)-St. Michael's Residence, [N], (NEW), Union City, NJ.
Congregation of the Passion: Holy Family Community, Inc., [I], (BIR), Birmingham, AL.
Congregation of the Poor Sisters of Nazareth Motherhouse, U.S.A. and Novitiate, [S], (LA), Los Angeles, CA.
Congregation of the Priests of the Sacred Heart Support and Maintenance Trust, [Y], (MIL), Franklin, WI.
Congregation of the Sacred Heart of Jesus & Mary and of Perpetual Adoration, Inc., [EE], (LA). See Chancery Office.
Congregation of the Sacred Hearts, [R], (LA), La Verne, CA.
Congregation of the Sacred Hearts, [R], (LA), Mission Hills, CA.
Congregation of the Sacred Hearts and of Perpetual Adoration, [I], (HON), Honolulu, HI.
Congregation of the Sacred Hearts of Jesus and Mary (Hawaii Province SS.CC.), [H], (HON), Kaneohe, HI.
Congregation of the Sacred Hearts, SS.CC., [E], (SB), Hemet, CA.
Congregation of the Sisters of Charity of the Incarnate Word, [G], (ALX), Alexandria, LA.
Congregation of the Sisters of Charity of the Incarnate Word (C.C.V.I.), [R], (GAL), Houston, TX.
Congregation of the Sisters of Mercy, [F], (SB), San Bernardino, CA.
Congregation of the Sisters of St. Felix, St. Ignatius Convent, [BB], (PH), Philadelphia, PA.
Congregation of the Sisters of St. Joseph, [Y], (BRK), Brentwood, NY.
Congregation of the Sisters of St. Joseph Generalate, [P], (BUF), Buffalo, NY.
Congregation of the Sisters of the Holy Cross, [I], (CC), Corpus Christi, TX.
Congregation of the Sisters of the Holy Cross, [H], (LAN), Ann Arbor, MI.
Congregation of the Sisters of the Holy Cross, [H], (MRY), Salinas, CA.
Congregation of the Sisters of the Holy Cross (C.S.C.), [J], (SCL), St. Joseph, MN.
Congregation of the Sisters of the Holy Faith, C.H.F., [Q], (NO), New Orleans, LA.

D

Dominican Village, Inc., [J], (RVC), Amityville, NY.
Dominican Vocation Sponsors, [P], (NO). See Dominican Fathers & Brothers, Southern Dominican Province.
Dominicans (Dominican Community-Jordan House), [F], (PHX), Tempe, AZ.
Dominicans (Provincial Office), [N], (CHI), Chicago, IL.
Dominicans, Mission San Jose, [I], (ORG), Anaheim, CA.
Dominicans, Mission San Jose, [I], (ORG), Santa Ana, CA.
DominiCare, [H], (SPK), Chewelah, WA.
Dominicas De La Doctrina Cristiana, [C], (LSC), Chapparal, NM.
Dominicas de la Inmaculada Concepcion, [L], (MIA), Hialeah, FL.
Domus Corporation, Inc., [S], (NEW). See New Jersey Caritas Corporation, Inc.
Domus Transitional Housing of Catholic Charities, [M], (SCL), St. Cloud, MN.
Don Bosco Camp, [U], (STL), Hillsboro, MO.
Don Bosco Hall, Inc., [O], (DET), Detroit, MI.
*Don Bosco Harlem Association, Inc., [HH], (NY), New York, NY.
Don Bosco High School, [D], (DUB), Gilbertville, IA.
Don Bosco High School, [C], (LA). See Don Bosco Technical Institute.
Don Bosco Home Children's Center, [C], (BEL), Belleville, IL.
Don Bosco Preparatory High School for Boys, [C], (NEW), Ramsey, NJ.
Don Bosco Preparatory School, [E], (BO), Boston, MA.
Don Bosco Retreat Center and Marian Shrine, [FF], (NY), West Haverstraw, NY.
Don Bosco Technical High School, [D], (PAT), Paterson, NJ.
Don Bosco Technical Institute, [C], (LA), Rosemead, CA.
Don Bosco Technical Institute, [D], (LA), Rosemead, CA.
Don Bosco Volunteers, Inc., [D], (PAT). See Don Bosco Technical High School.
Don Guanella Center, Inc., Daughters of St. Mary of Providence, [X], (BO), Chelsea, MA.
Don Guanella House of Formation, [B], (PH), Springfield, PA.
Don Guanella School for Retarded Boys, [M], (PH), Springfield, PA.
Don Orione Center, [Y], (BO), Bradford, MA.
Don Orione Nursing Home, [U], (BO), Boston, MA.
Donnelly College, [A], (KCK), Kansas City, KS.
Donovan-Mayotte Catholic School, [C], (LAN), Flint, MI.
Dooley Center, Inc., [I], (KCK), Atchison, KS.
Doran Hall, [I], (GBG), Greensburg, PA.
Dorn Day Care Center (dba Gingerbread House Day Care Center), [L], (SY). See Sister Patricia Ann's Preschool dba Gingerbread House Preschool.
Dorothy Day Catholic Worker, [V], (WDC), Washington, DC.
Dorothy Miler House (mother & child group residence), [J], (BUF). See Baker Victory Services.
Dothan Office of Catholic Social Services, [J], (MOB), Dothan, AL.
Douglas County Correction Center, [O], (OM). See Omaha Catholic Jail Ministry.
The Dove Agency, Inc., [E], (SUP). See Catholic Charities Bureau, Inc.
The Dove, Inc., [E], (SUP). See Catholic Charities Bureau, Inc.
Dover General Campus-Dover, [J], (PAT). See Northwest Covenant Medial Center.
Dowagiac Nursing Home, [F], (KAL), Dowagiac, MI.
Dowling High School, [C], (DM), West Des Moines, IA.
Dowling-St. Joseph Alumni Foundation, [J], (DM), Des Moines, IA.
Downeast Big Brothers - Big Sisters, [E], (PRT). See Catholic Charities Maine.
*Downtown Women's Center and Abba House, Inc., [E], (AMA). See Catholic Family Service, Inc.
Drew University Catholic Campus Ministry, [O], (PAT), Madison, NJ.
Drew-Hamilton CYO Center, [CC], (NY), New York, NY.
Drexel University, [EE], (PH). See Newman Apostolate.
Driscoll Catholic High School, [C], (JOL), Addison, IL.
Drueding Center, [S], (PH), Philadelphia, PA.
Du Bois Area Catholic Schools, [C], (E), Du Bois, PA.
Dubuque Council, [O], (DUB). See St. Vincent de Paul Society of the Archdiocese of Dubuque.
Duchesne Academy of the Sacred Heart, [F], (GAL), Houston, TX.
Duchesne Academy of the Sacred Heart, [G], (GAL), Houston, TX.
Duchesne Academy of the Sacred Heart, [C], (OM), Omaha, NE.
Duchesne Clinic, [K], (KCK), Kansas City, KS.
Duchesne High School, [E], (STL), St. Charles, MO.
Duchesne High School Endowment Fund Inc., [W], (STL), St. Charles, MO.
Dujarie House, Infirmary, [J], (FTW). See Congregation of Holy Cross, Midwest Province.
Dukette Catholic School, [C], (LAN), Flint, MI.
Dukette Intercultural Center for Black Catholic Ministry, [L], (LAN), Flint, MI.
Dunkirk, [H], (BUF). See The Catholic Charities of the Diocese of Buffalo.
Dunn Tower Apartments, Inc., [L], (ROC), Rochester, NY.
Duns Scotus, [B], (DET), Detroit, MI.
Duquesne Catholic School, [F], (PIT), Duquesne, PA.
Duquesne University of the Holy Ghost, [B], (PIT), Pittsburgh, PA.
Dutchess & Ulster Counties, [D], (NY). See Department of Education.
The Dwelling Place, [F], (JKS), Brooksville, MS.
The Dwelling Place, [S], (MIL), Milwaukee, WI.
The Dwelling Place, [AA], (NY), New York, NY.
The Dwelling Place, [N], (RIC), Richmond, VA.
The Dwelling Place of New York, Inc., [EE], (NY), New York, NY.

E

E. Donn Piatt Catholic Student Center at Louisiana Tech University, [G], (SHP), Ruston, LA.
E.D. White Catholic High School Alumni Association, [A], (HT). See Edward Douglas White Catholic High.
E.D. White Catholic High School Foundation, Inc., [A], (HT). See Edward Douglas White Catholic High.
Earlham College Newman Center, [N], (IND), Richmond, IN.
Earthworks, Inc., [N], (FTW), Plymouth, IN.
East Bay Services to the Developmentally Disabled, [S], (OAK), Concord, CA.
East Bronx Supported Housing, [O], (NY). See Beacon of Hope House.
East Catholic Elementary, [D], (OM), Hartington, NE.
East Catholic Elementary School Endowment, [N], (OM). See The Omaha Archdiocesan Educational Foundation, Inc.
East Catholic High School, [D], (DET), Detroit, MI.
East Catholic High School, [D], (HRT), Manchester, CT.
East Central Community College Newman Center, [G], (JKS), Forest, MS.
East Greenbush Housing Development Fund Co., Inc. dba Branson Manor Senior Apartment, [K], (ALB), Rensselaer, NY.
East Main Family Practice, [J], (PEO). See United Samaritans Medical Center.
East Meadow Campus, [E], (RVC). See St. Elizabeth Ann Seton Regional School.
East Oakland, [H], (OAK). See Catholic Charities of the Diocese of Oakland, Inc.
East Side Service for Senior Citizens, [Y], (MIL), Milwaukee, WI.
East Valley Catholic Social Service, [J], (PHX). See Catholic Social Services of Central and Northern Arizona, Inc.
Eastern Arizona Junior College, [I], (TUC), Thatcher, AZ.
Eastern Catholic Associates, [C], (PSC), Passaic, NJ.
Eastern Illinois University Newman Center, [M], (SFD), Charleston, IL.
*Eastern Mercy Health System, [FF], (PH), Radnor, PA.
Eastern Point Retreat House, [Y], (BO), Gloucester, MA.
Eastern Province of the Oblates of St. Joseph, [M], (SCR), Pittston, PA.
Eastern Region, [N], (SY), Syracuse, NY.
Eastern Shore Co-op, [J], (WIL), Easton, MD.
Easton Catholic Elementary School, [D], (ALN), Easton, PA.
Eastside Catholic Community of Great Falls, [K], (GF), Great Falls, MT.
Eastside Catholic High School, [C], (SEA), Bellevue, WA.
Eastside Neighborhood Center, [F], (SJ). See Catholic Charities of Santa Clara County.
Eastside Nutrition Site, [F], (SJ). See Catholic Charities of Santa Clara County.
Eastwood-Oxford Network of Care, Detroit, [H], (DET). See St. John Hospital and Medical Center.
Eau Claire Coordinated Catholic Schools, [D], (LC), Eau Claire, WI.
Ecclesia Center/Renewal Center, [O], (E), Erie, PA.
Ecclesial Consultants, Inc., [L], (BRK). See Catholic Charities.
Echo House-Inner City Apostolate, [F], (CHR), Charleston, SC.
Eckerd College - Campus Ministry, [S], (SP), St. Petersburg, FL.
The Ecumenical Institute of Wake Forest University and Belmont Abbey College, [A], (CHL). See Belmont Abbey College.
Edgewood Campus School, [F], (MAD), Madison, WI.
Edgewood College, [B], (MAD), Madison, WI.
Edgewood High School, [D], (MAD), Madison, WI.
Edgewood Incorporated, [M], (MAD), Madison, WI.
Edinboro University of PA, [K], (BUF). See Our Lady of Victory Hospital.
Edith Stein House of Studies, [N], (CHI), Chicago, IL.
Edmonds Dominicans, Holy Angels Alumnae Assoc., [Q], (SEA), Edmonds, WA.
Edmundite Fathers, [H], (MOB), Selma, AL.
Edmundite House of Formation, [A], (MOB), Selma, AL.
Edmundite Seminary Guild, [A], (NOR), Mystic, CT.
Edu Care Pre-School and Daycare, [A], (NU). See New Ulm Area Catholic Schools.
Education & Training, [Z], (LA). See Catholic Charities of Los Angeles, Inc.
*Education for Parish Service Programs, [V], (WDC), Washington, DC.
Education Foundation of the Diocese of Galveston-Houston, [U], (GAL), Houston, TX.
Education Through the 90's Foundation, [L], (RCK), Freeport, IL.
The Education/Sustaining Endowment Trust, [M], (LC), Chippewa Falls, WI.
Educational Endowment Trust of Eau Claire Coordinated Catholic Schools, [M], (LC), Eau Claire, WI.
Educational Foundation of St. Francis Xavier School, Inc., [L], (GR), Grand Rapids, MI.
Educational Services for Blind and Visually Impaired Children, [E], (PRT). See Catholic Charities Maine.
Educational Services for Blind and Visually Impaired Children-Instructional Materials Center, [E], (PRT). See Catholic Charities Maine.
Educational Services for Blind and Visually Impaired Children-Satellite Office, [E], (PRT). See Catholic Charities Maine.
Educational Services for Blind and Visually Impaired Children-Satellite Office, [E], (PRT). See Catholic Charities Maine.
Edward Douglas White Catholic High, [A], (HT), Thibodaux, LA.
Edward McGuinn House of Studies, [N], (CHI). See Society of the Divine Word, Provincial Headquarter-Chicago Prov.
Efharisto Studio, Inc., [Q], (BAL), Baltimore, MD.
El Carmelo Residence, [AA], (NY), New York, NY.
El Carmelo Retreat House, [G], (SB), Redlands, CA.
El Carmen Sister's Residence, [N], (SAT), San Antonio, TX.
El Centro De La Causa, [G], (CHI). See Catholic Charities of the Archdiocese of Chicago-Archdiocesan Offices.
El Centro de Servicios Para Hispanos, [K], (KCK), Topeka, KS.
El Centro Del Cardenal/Catholic Charities, [N], (BO), Boston, MA.
El Centro, Inc., [K], (KCK), Kansas City, KS.
El Mirage Senior Village, [J], (PHX), Phoenix, AZ.
El Rancho Grande Apartments, [E], (BWN), Brownsville, TX.
El Rosario Charitable Trust, [I], (BWN), Mission, TX.
El Yo Yo Bilingual Day Care Center, [J], (NO), New Orleans, LA.
Elbert House, [K], (SEA), Bellevue, WA.
Elder Abuse Program, [B], (STO). See The Catholic Charities of the Diocese of Stockton.
Elder Abuse Program, [B], (STO). See The Catholic Charities of the Diocese of Stockton.
Elder Care of North La Crosse, Inc. (Village on St. James), [G], (LC), La Crosse, WI.
Elder Care of Sparta, Inc., [G], (LC), Sparta, WI.
Elder High School, [E], (CIN), Cincinnati, OH.
Elder Hospitality of Iowa II, Inc., [J], (DUB). See Elder Hospitality of Iowa, Inc.
Elder Hospitality of Iowa, Inc., [J], (DUB), Cresco, IA.
Eldercare Foundation, Inc. c/o CHI, [U], (CIN), Cincinnati, OH.
Eldercare Management, [B], (STO). See The Catholic Charities of the Diocese of Stockton.
Elementary School, [C], (PBL). See John Neumann Catholic Schools.
Elementary Schools: Shelby County Catholic Schools, [A], (DM). See Shelby County Board of Catholic Education.
Elizabeth Ann Seton Catholic School, [B], (BEL), Fairview Heights, IL.
Elizabeth Ann Seton Center, [K], (RIC), Richmond, VA.
Elizabeth Ann Seton Center, [K], (RIC), Charlottesville, VA.
Elizabeth House, [W], (STL), St. Louis, MO.
Elizabeth Seton Center Inc., [S], (PIT), Pittsburgh, PA.
The Elizabeth Seton Federation, Inc., [EE], (NY). See Sisters of Charity Center.
Elizabeth Seton High School, [E], (WDC), Bladensburg, MD.
*The Elizabeth Seton Housing Development Fund Corporation, [HH], (NY), New York, NY.
Elizabeth Seton Montessori School of Westmoreland County, Inc., [E], (GBG), Greensburg, PA.

Elizabeth Seton Residence, Inc., [X], (BO), Wellesley, MA.
Elizabethport Catholic School, [E], (NEW), Elizabeth, NJ.
Elk County Christian High School, [C], (E), Saint Marys, PA.
Elkhart Community Service Center, [N], (FTW). See Catholic Charities.
Ellendale Nursing Center, [E], (FAR), Ellendale, ND.
Elliot County Medical Clinic, [E], (LEX), Sandy Hook, KY.
Elmbrook Memorial Hospital, Inc., [K], (MIL), Brookfield, WI.
Elmwood Apartments, [E], (SUP). See Catholic Charities Bureau, Inc.
Elon College, [H], (R), Elon College, NC.
Elyria Catholic High School, [D], (CLV), Elyria, OH.
Embry-Riddle Aeronautical University, [E], (ORL), Daytona Beach, FL.
Emergency Assistance, [G], (RNO). See Catholic Community Services of Northern Nevada.
Emergency Assistance, [J], (VEN). See Catholic Charities of Collier County.
Emergency Assistance Program, [G], (CHI). See Catholic Charities of the Archdiocese of Chicago-Archdiocesan Offices.
Emergency Food Distribution, [B], (STO). See The Catholic Charities of the Diocese of Stockton.
Emergency Foster Care, [E], (PRT). See Catholic Charities Maine.
Emergency Services, [H], (OAK). See Catholic Charities of the Diocese of Oakland, Inc.
Emergency Services Division, [F], (TR). See Catholic Charities.
Emergency Shelter for Women, [D], (LAN). See Shelter of Flint, Inc.
Emma McRedmond Manor, [K], (SEA), Redmond, WA.
Emmanuel College, [C], (BO), Boston, MA.
Emmanuel College Campus Ministry, [CC], (BO), Boston, MA.
Emmanuel Community, [I], (MOB), Vredenburgh, AL.
Emmanuel House, [X], (BO), Wayland, MA.
Emmanuel House, [E], (JKS), Greenville, MS.
Emmanuel House, [Q], (PRO), Woonsocket, RI.
Emmanuel House Family Shelter, [N], (LAF). See Lafayette Catholic Service Centers, Inc.
Emmanuel House Kindergarten, [I], (BO), Boston, MA.
Emmanuel House of Prayer Country Retreat and Solitude Center, [O], (DAV), Iowa City, IA.
Emmanuel House/Catholic Charities - Community Social Service Center, [N], (BO), Boston, MA.
Emmanuel Monastery, [N], (BAL), Lutherville, MD.
Emmanuel, Inc., [V], (WDC), Gaithersburg, MD.
Emmaus Community, [F], (BLX), Pascagoula, MS.
Emmaus Community, [N], (CAM), Maple Shade, NJ.
Emmaus Community, [G], (NOR), Uncasville, CT.
Emmaus Conference Center, [AA], (CLV), Bedford, OH.
Emmaus Convent, [BB], (PH), Philadelphia, PA.
Emmaus East Harlem, [D], (NTN), New York, NY.
Emmaus House, [T], (ALB), Albany, NY.
Emmaus House, [H], (DM), Des Moines, IA.
Emmaus House, [F], (DOD), Garden City, KS.
Emmaus House, [E], (LFT), Lafayette, IN.
Emmaus House, [M], (MAN), Manchester, NH.
Emmaus House, [J], (MET), Perth Amboy, NJ.
Emmaus House, [I], (SAG), Saginaw, MI.
Emmaus House, [T], (TR), Elberon, NJ.
Emmaus House, [I], (Y), Louisville, OH.
Emmaus House, Rider College, [S], (TR). See Campus Ministry for the Diocese of Trenton.
Emmaus House/Harlem, [D], (NTN), New York, NY.
Emmaus Inns, AIDS Ministry, [D], (NTN), New York, NY.
Emmaus Ministries, [N], (E), Erie, PA.
*Emmaus Ministries, [I], (LAN), Howell, MI.
Emmaus of the Diocese of Brooklyn, Inc., [L], (BRK). See Catholic Charities.
Emmaus Place, [G], (BIS), Bismarck, ND.
Emmaus Residence, [J], (PMB), West Palm Beach, FL.
Emmaus Youth Center - Region 4, [N], (PRO), East Providence, RI.
Emmaus-Diocesan Spiritual Life Center, [J], (NOR), Uncasville, CT.
Employee Assistance Services Office, [R], (NY). See Pius XII Youth and Family Services, Inc.
Employment and Education Program & Career Center, [F], (SJ). See Catholic Charities of Santa Clara County.
Employment and Training Program, [G], (CHI). See Catholic Charities of the Archdiocese of Chicago-Archdiocesan Offices.
Employment Integration Program, [L], (OKL). See Oklahoma Benedictine Institute on Mental Retardation, Inc.
Employment Resource Center, [L], (DEN). See Catholic Charities and Community Services of the Archdiocese of Denver, Inc.
Employment Services, [J], (ORG). See Catholic Charities of Orange County, Inc.
Employment Training and Job Placement, [R], (NY). See Pius XII Youth and Family Services, Inc.
En El, Inc., [Y], (BRK), Brooklyn, NY.
Endowment Foundation of Thomas More Prep-Marian, Inc., [B], (SAL). See Thomas More Prep-Marian.
Endowment Fund for the Catholic Diocese of Victoria in Texas, [H], (VIC), Victoria, TX.
Endowment Trust of the Friends and Parishioners of St. Patrick Parish, [M], (LC), Sparta, WI.
Energy Assistance, [D], (WIL). See Catholic Charities, Inc.
Enfield Montessori School, [N], (HRT). See Felician Sisters - Our Lady of the Angels.
Enfield Montessori School, [N], (HRT), Enfield, CT.
Engaged Encounter, [L], (AMA), Amarillo, TX.
Engaged Encounter, [J], (BEL), Belleville, IL.
Engaged Encounter of North Texas, [K], (FWT). See The Catholic Renewal Center of North Texas, Inc.
English Action Center, [H], (OAK). See Catholic Charities of the Diocese of Oakland, Inc.
English Action Center, [H], (OAK). See Catholic Charities of the Diocese of Oakland, Inc.
English Action Center-Verde School, [H], (OAK). See Catholic Charities of the Diocese of Oakland, Inc.
Ennis Hall, [I], (GBG), Greensburg, PA.
Enserv Inc., [FF], (PH), Immaculata, PA.
Ephpheta Center and Hearing Conservation Service, [L], (CHI), Oak Park, IL.
The Epiphany Association, [S], (PIT), Pittsburgh, PA.
Epiphany Center for Families in Recovery, [L], (SFR). See Mount St. Joseph-St. Elizabeth.
Epiphany Housing of Tampa, Inc., [T], (SP), Tampa, FL.
Epiphany Manor, [C], (ORL), Port Orange, FL.
Epiphany Monastery, [F], (HEL), Columbia Falls, MT.
Epiphany Monastery, [M], (MAN), New Boston, NH.
Episcopal Catholic Apartments, [C], (ORL), Winter Haven, FL.
Equestrian Order of the Holy Sepulcher of Jerusalem, [DD], (LA), Los Angeles, CA.
Equestrian Order of the Holy Sepulchre, [S], (NO), New Orleans, LA.
Equestrian Order of the Holy Sepulchre of Jerusalem, [FF], (BO), Boston, MA.
Equestrian Order of the Holy Sepulchre of Jerusalem, [S], (CHI), Chicago, IL.
Equestrian Order of the Holy Sepulchre of Jerusalem, [U], (GAL), Houston, TX.
Equestrian Order of the Holy Sepulchre of Jerusalem - Middle Atlantic Lieutenancy of the U.S., [V], (WDC), Washington, DC.
Equestrian Order of the Holy Sepulchre of Jerusalem - Northwest Lieutenancy, [U], (SFR), San Francisco, CA.
Erie Community College, [K], (BUF). See Our Lady of Victory Hospital.
Erie Dawn, [M], (E), Erie, PA.
Erie East Coast Migrant Programs, [F], (E), Erie, PA.
Erskine College Newman Center, [G], (CHR), Due West, SC.
Escuela Nuestra Sra. de la Providencia, [A], (CGS), Caguas, PR.
Escuela Superior Catolica de Bayamon, Jazmin Esq. Millones, [B], (SJN), Bayamon, PR.
Espousal Retreat House and Conference Center, [Y], (BO), Waltham, MA.
Essex County College, Rutgers University/Newark, NJIT, [Q], (NEW), Newark, NJ.
Establishing Mission Churches with Lay Leaders, [L], (NSH). See Glenmary Department of Pastoral Services.
Estrella del Mar, Inc. dba Regis House, [V], (LA), Los Angeles, CA.
Ethiopian and Eritrean Catholic Mission, USA, [V], (WDC), Washington, DC.
ETSU-Catholic Center, [J], (KNX), Johnson City, TN.
Eucharistic Franciscan Missionary Sisters, [S], (LA), Los Angeles, CA.
Eucharistic Franciscan Missionary Sisters, [N], (SAT), San Antonio, TX.
Eucharistic Franciscan Missionary Sisters, [E], (STO), Stockton, CA.
Eucharistic Franciscan Missionary Sisters of Los Angeles, [S], (LA). See Eucharistic Franciscan Missionary Sisters.
Eucharistic Missionaries of St. Dominic, [F], (BLX), Gulfport, MS.
Eucharistic Missionaries of St. Dominic, [I], (LAF), Lafayette, LA.
Eucharistic Missionaries of St. Dominic, [I], (LAF), Duson, LA.
Eucharistic Missionaries of St. Dominic, O.P., [Q], (NO), New Orleans, LA.
Eucharistic Missionaries of St. Theresa, [W], (STL), St. Louis, MO.
Eucharistic Missionaries of St. Theresa-Mexico (M.E.S.T.), [R], (GAL), Houston, TX.
Eucharistic Missionaries of the Most Holy Trinity, [I], (ORG), Garden Grove, CA.
Eucharistic Missionaries of the Most Holy Trinity, [N], (SJ), San Jose, CA.
Eucharistic Shrine of the Adorable Face of Jesus, [R], (NEW), Kearny, NJ.
Eugene Kennedy Residence, [L], (PAT), Pompton Lakes, NJ.
Euphrasia Hall, [N], (HRT). See Convent of Mary Immaculate, Provincial House of the Sisters of St. Joseph of Chambery.
Euphrasia House, Inc., [FF], (PH), Philadelphia, PA.
Evelyn Malloy Education Fund for The Sisters of Charity of the Incarnate Word, [R], (GAL). See Congregation of the Sisters of Charity of the Incarnate Word (C.C.V.I.).
Evergreen Apartments (Chetek), [E], (SUP). See Catholic Charities Bureau, Inc.
Evergreen Apartments (Shell Lake), [E], (SUP). See Catholic Charities Bureau, Inc.
Evergreen Assisted Living, [I], (SFS). See St. Ann's Corporation.
Evergreen Court for Retirement Living, Inc., [K], (P), North Bend, OR.
Evergreen House and Day Care Program, [E], (HBG). See Department for Catholic Charities Counseling/Field Services.
Everitt Academy, [N], (MET), Peapack, NJ.
Evodia House, [E], (PRT). See Catholic Charities Maine.

F

F.A.I.T.H. Services Inc., [S], (NEW), Hoboken, NJ.
F.A.I.T.H. Services., [N], (NEW), Hoboken, NJ.
F.I.R.E., [J], (STU), Steubenville, OH.
Fa'asao High School, [C], (SPP), Lepuapua, AS.
Faber House, [W], (BO), Cambridge, MA.
Faber Jesuit Community, [M], (CIN), Cincinnati, OH.
Faces Intermediate Campus, [H], (MIL). See Fond du Lac Area Catholic Education System (FACES).
Faces Middle School Campus, [H], (MIL). See Fond du Lac Area Catholic Education System (FACES).
Faces Primary Campus, [H], (MIL). See Fond du Lac Area Catholic Education System (FACES).
Facilities Operations, [G], (CHI). See Catholic Charities of the Archdiocese of Chicago-Archdiocesan Offices.
Fahy Garden Apartments, [I], (SPK), Spokane, WA.
Fahy West Apartments, [I], (SPK), Spokane, WA.
Fairfield College Preparatory School, [D], (BGP), Fairfield, CT.
Fairfield Foundation of the Diocese of Bridgeport, Inc., [R], (BGP), Bridgeport, CT.
The Fairfield Jesuit Community-Fairfield University, [O], (BGP), Fairfield, CT.
*Fairfield University, [A], (BGP), Fairfield, CT.
Fairleigh Dickinson Univ.-Teaneck Campus, [Q], (NEW), Teaneck, NJ.
Fairleigh Dickinson University and Drew University, [O], (PAT), Madison, NJ.
Fairmont Catholic Grade School, [D], (WH), Fairmont, WV.
Fairmont State College Newman Center, [Q], (WH), Fairmont, WV.
Fairview Developmental Center, [H], (ORG), Costa Mesa, CA.
Faith and Light U.S.A., Inc., [AA], (CLV), Euclid, OH.
Faith House, Inc., [V], (WDC), Hyattsville, MD.
Faith in the Future Fund, Inc., [W], (BGP), Bridgeport, CT.
Faith Regional Health Services, [G], (OM), Norfolk, NE.
Faithful Shepherd Catholic School, [H], (STP), Eagan, MN.
Fall Lane Medical Center, [H], (BAL). See Bon Secours Baltimore Health Corporation, Inc.
Fall River Area Catholic Youth Organization, [N], (FR). See Diocesean Catholic Youth Organization.
Familia USA, Inc., [HH], (NY), Thornwood, NY.
Families Together, [L], (BRK). See Catholic Charities.
Family & Community Services, [H], (WOR). See Catholic Charities.
Family and Community Services of Catholic Charities, [L], (Y), Kent, OH.
Family and Counseling Services, [J], (SLC). See Catholic Community Services.
Family & Individual Services (including Family Life Bureau), [D], (WIL). See Catholic Charities, Inc.
Family Based Services, [G], (CHI). See Catholic Charities of the Archdiocese of Chicago-Archdiocesan Offices.
Family Care Center, [J], (PEO). See United Samaritans Medical Center.
The Family Center, [L], (DEN). See Catholic Charities and Community Services of the Archdiocese of Denver, Inc.
Family Counseling, [I], (GAL). See Associated Catholic Charities of the Diocese of Galveston-Houston.
Family Counseling and Guidance Centers, [K], (BO), Boston, MA.
Family Counseling Endowment Fund, Inc., [DD], (BO). See Chancery Office.

Family Counseling Service, [S], (HRT). See Catholic Charities-Catholic Family Services (Archdiocese of Hartford).
Family Crisis Center, [F], (DOD), Great Bend, KS.
Family Division, Catholic Charities, [K], (SY), Syracuse, NY.
Family Focus, [O], (RIC), Newport News, VA.
Family Focus Program, [H], (BUF). See The Catholic Charities of the Diocese of Buffalo.
Family Growth Division, [F], (TR). See Catholic Charities.
Family Health Service, Inc.; Little Sisters of the Assumption, [Y], (NY), New York, NY.
Family Life Education, [N], (SY), Syracuse, NY.
Family Life Ministry, [G], (BGP). See Catholic Charities of Fairfield County.
Family Life Ministry, [M], (GRY). See Catholic Charities.
Family Life Ministry, [K], (MIA), Miami, FL.
Family Life Office, [G], (ALT), Ebensburg, PA.
Family Life/Respect Life Catholic Center, [G], (BGP). See Catholic Charities of Fairfield County.
Family Life/Respect Life Office, [D], (NY). See Department of Education.
Family Mental Health Clinic, [D], (LAN). See Catholic Social Services-St. Vincent Home, Inc.
The Family of Nazareth, Inc., [S], (NEW), Kearny, NJ.
Family of the Americas Foundation, Inc., [Q], (BAL), Dunkirk, MD.
Family Practice Associates of Kenosha, [K], (MIL). See St. Mary's Medical Center, Inc.
Family Practice Center, [J], (PEO). See United Samaritans Medical Center.
Family Preservation Services, [I], (SAT). See Father Flanagan's Boys' Town of San Antonio.
Family Resource Center, [J], (ORG). See Catholic Charities of Orange County, Inc.
Family Rosary For Peace, Inc., [L], (ROC), Rochester, NY.
The Family Rosary Worldwide Office, [T], (ALB), Albany, NY.
Family Service Center, [J], (ORG). See Catholic Charities of Orange County, Inc.
Family Service Office, [E], (MET), Bridgewater, NJ.
Family Service Office, [E], (MET), Edison, NJ.
Family Service Office, [E], (MET), Milford, NJ.
Family Service Office, [E], (MET), Perth Amboy, NJ.
Family Service Office, [E], (MET), Phillipsburg, NJ.
Family Shelter for the Homeless, [Z], (LA). See Catholic Charities of Los Angeles, Inc.
Family Support Center, [J], (ORG). See Catholic Charities of Orange County, Inc.
Family Support Center, [E], (SR). See Diocese of Santa Rosa, Catholic Charities.
Family Ties Therapeutic Foster Care, [I], (CIN). See St. Joseph Orphanage.
Family Unity International, Inc., [V], (MIL), Elm Grove, WI.
Fanny Allen Hospital, [I], (BUR), Colchester, VT.
Fargo Catholic Schools Network, [B], (FAR), Fargo, ND.
Faribault B.A., Inc., [F], (STP), Faribault, MN.
Farley Health Care Corp., [O], (TOL), Toledo, OH.
Farmingdale Campus, [E], (RVC). See St. John Baptist de LaSalle Regional School.
Farren Care Center, Inc., [F], (SPR), Turners Falls, MA.
Fashion Institute of Technology (SUNY), [GG], (NY). See University Apostolate.
Father Al Miller Educational Trust Fund (St. Mary Parish, Westphalia), [K], (LAN). See Chancery Office.
Father Andre Coindre Charitable Trust, [U], (PRO), Burrillville, RI.
Father Barry CYO Center, [N], (PRO), Pawtucket, RI.
Father Dempsey's Hotel, Inc., [S], (STL), St. Louis, MO.
The Father Duenas Memorial School, [A], (AGN), Agana, GU.
Father Dunne's News Boys Home, [N], (STL), Florissant, MO.
Father Farrell Spiritual Life Center, [K], (LEX), Hazard, KY.
Father Flanagan's Boys' Home, [C], (OM), Boys Town, NE.
Father Flanagan's Boys' Home, [E], (OM), Boys Town, NE.
*Father Flanagan's Boys' Home, [I], (OM), Boys Town, NE.
Father Flanagan's Boys' Town of San Antonio, [I], (SAT), San Antonio, TX.
The Father Flohe Foundation, [L], (GR), Portland, MI.
Father Gabriel Richard High School, [B], (LAN), Ann Arbor, MI.
Father Gabriel Richard High School Trust Fund (Fr. Gabriel Richard H.S., Ann Harbor), [K], (LAN). See Chancery Office.
Fr. Hannibal House Social Service Center, [J], (FRS), Sanger, CA.
Father Holland Catholic Regional Elementary School, [H], (PRO), Burriliville, RI.
Fr. James E. Fitzgerald Educational Memorial, [N], (OM). See The Omaha Archdiocesan Educational Foundation, Inc.
Father James Fitton House of Priestly Formation, [N], (WOR), Leicester, MA.
Father Jim's Home, [S], (STL), St. Louis, MO.
Father John C. Silva Education Foundation, [G], (STO), Modesto, CA.
Father John Rossiter and Friends Endowment Trust of St. Patrick Parish, [M], (LC), Onalaska, WI.
Father Judge Apostolic Center, [P], (PAT), Stirling, NJ.
Father Judge Faculty House, [AA], (PH), Philadelphia, PA.
Father Judge High School for Boys, [D], (PH), Philadelphia, PA.
Father Justin Rosary Hour Radio Apostolate, [O], (BUF), Athol Springs, NY.
Father Justin Vocationary, [M], (PAT), Florham Park, NJ.
Father Kolbe Interparochial School, [E], (BAL), Baltimore, MD.
Fr. Kolbe Missionaries of the Immaculata, [T], (LA), West Covina, CA.
Father Lopez High School, [A], (ORL), Daytona Beach, FL.
Father Magsam Center for Spiritual Direction, [J], (CC), Corpus Christi, TX.
Fr. Marot CYO Center, [N], (PRO), Woonsocket, RI.
Fr. Marquette Catholic Central Schools System, [A], (MAR), Marquette, MI.
Fr. McKenna St. Vincent de Paul Shoppe, [W], (BGP), Shelton, CT.
Father Purcell Memorial Exceptional Children Center, [F], (MOB), Montgomery, AL.
Father Raphael Piperni Charitable Trust, [U], (SFR), San Francisco, CA.
Father Ryan Board of Trust, [B], (NSH). See Father Ryan High School.
Father Ryan High School, [B], (NSH), Nashville, TN.
Father Sweeney School, [D], (PEO), Peoria, IL.
Father Thomas O'Keeffe Missionary Cenacle, [M], (WDC), Adelphi, MD.
Father Thomas Scecina Memorial High School, [C], (IND), Indianapolis, IN.
Father Tolton Catholic Community Services, [W], (STL). See Catholic Community Services Administration.
Father Toubia Retirement Home, [E], (OLL), North Jackson, OH.
Father Walter J. Ciszek Elementary School, [D], (ALN), Shenandoah, PA.
Father Walter Memorial Center for Handicapped Children, [F], (MOB), Montgomery, AL.
Father Yermo Elementary School, [E], (ELP), El Paso, TX.
Father Yermo High School, [D], (ELP), El Paso, TX.
Fathers of Mercy, [F], (OWN), South Union, KY.
Fatima Community Center, [V], (CLV). See Catholic Charities Services Corporation.
Fatima Family Apostolate, [I], (SFS), Alexandria, SD.
Fatima Renewal Center, [H], (SCR), Dalton, PA.
Featherbed Lane Day Care Center, [V], (NY), New York, NY.
Federation of Catholic Parent Teacher Clubs of the Archdiocese of San Antonio, [T], (SAT), San Antonio, TX.
Federation of Catholic School Parents, Diocese of Buffalo, NY, [T], (BUF), Buffalo, NY.
Felician Adult Day Care, [N], (HRT). See Felician Sisters - Our Lady of the Angels.
Felician College, [B], (NEW), Lodi, NJ.
Felician Retreat House, [I], (PAT), Mount Arlington, NJ.
The Felician School for Exceptional Children, [E], (NEW), Lodi, NJ.
Felician Sisters, [N], (SAT), San Antonio, TX.
Felician Sisters, [K], (SFE), Rio Rancho, NM.
Felician Sisters - Our Lady of the Angels, [N], (HRT), Enfield, CT.
Felician Sisters Infirmary, [N], (HRT). See Felician Sisters - Our Lady of the Angels.
Felician Sisters of St. Francis of Assisi Convent, [N], (PAT), Mount Arlington, NJ.
Felician Village Inc., [H], (GB), Manitowoc, WI.
Felix Varela Foundation, Inc., The, [HH], (NY), New York, NY.
The Fellowship House, [E], (PRT). See Catholic Charities Maine.
Fellowship of Catholic Scholars, [V], (WDC), Washington, DC.
The Fellowship of the Beloved Disciple, [HH], (NY), Chelsea, NY.
Fenwick High School, [D], (CHI), Oak Park, IL.
Ferdinand Wheeler Jesuit Community, [M], (BAL), Baltimore, MD.
Ferncliff Nursing Home, [Z], (NY), Rhinebeck, NY.
Ferrini Welfare League, [L], (BRK). See Catholic Charities.
Field Neurosciences Institute, [E], (SAG). See St. Mary's Medical Center of Saginaw, Inc.
Fields-Wright Medical Facility, Inc., [N], (SFD), Sullivan, IL.
The 1540 House, [N], (NO), New Orleans, LA.
50-60 Kosciuzko Street Housing Development Fund Company, Inc., [T], (BUF), Buffalo, NY.
Filipino Apostolate, [T], (BRK). See Catholic Migration & Refugee Office, Catholic Migration Services, Inc.
Filipino Cursillo Secretariat, [U], (SFR), San Francisco, CA.
Filipino Pastoral Ministry, [DD], (LA), Los Angeles, CA.
Finance, [H], (RVC). See Catholic Charities Central Administration.
Finance Dept., [H], (BUF). See The Catholic Charities of the Diocese of Buffalo.
Financial Services, [G], (CHI). See Catholic Charities of the Archdiocese of Chicago-Archdiocesan Offices.
*First Care North, Inc., [O], (GB), Appleton, WI.
Fitchburg State College (Fitchburg), [Q], (WOR). See Campus Ministry.
Fitzgerald Charitable Trust, [N], (SFE), Jemez Springs, NM.
Fitzgerald Middle School, [C], (WIN). See Mankato Area Catholic Schools.
Flaget Center for Spirituality and Ministry Formation, [O], (L), Louisville, KY.
Flaget Memorial Hospital, [H], (L), Bardstown, KY.
Flagler College Newman Center, [L], (STA), St. Augustine, FL.
Flint-Goodridge Day Care Center, [J], (NO), New Orleans, LA.
Flintridge Sacred Heart Academy, [F], (LA), La Canada Flintridge, CA.
The Florida Catholic AIDS Network, [K], (STA), Jacksonville, FL.
The Florida Catholic of Palm Beach, Inc., [J], (PMB), Palm Beach Gardens, FL.
Florida Head Start, [J], (NO), New Orleans, LA.
Florida Institute of Technology Campus Ministry, [E], (ORL), Melbourne, FL.
Florida Southern College Newman Center, [E], (ORL), Lakeland, FL.
Flowers With Care Youth Services, Diocese of Brooklyn, Inc., [Y], (BRK), Astoria, NY.
Flowers With Care, Diocese of Brooklyn, Inc., [L], (BRK). See Catholic Charities.
FMOL Health Systems, Inc., [L], (BR), Baton Rouge, LA.
Focolare Movement, [FF], (BO), Newton, MA.
Focolare Movement, [Y], (BRK), Queens, NY.
Focolare Movement, [X], (CHI), Chicago, IL.
Focolare Movement, [T], (SAT), San Antonio, TX.
Focolare Movement National Center, [HH], (NY), Hyde Park, NY.
The Focolare Movement, Men's Branch (California) (Work of Mary), [DD], (LA), Los Angeles, CA.
Focolare Movement-Mariapolis Center, [T], (CHI), Chicago, IL.
Focus for Work, [F], (SJ). See Catholic Charities of Santa Clara County.
Focus Foundation (Federation of Catholic Urban Schools), [W], (STL). See Catholic High School Association.
*Focus Syndicate, Inc., [S], (NO), New Orleans, LA.
Fond du Lac Area Catholic Education System (FACES), [H], (MIL), Fond du Lac, WI.
Fontbonne Academy, [E], (BO), Milton, MA.
Fontbonne College, [C], (STL), St. Louis, MO.
Fontbonne Hall, [X], (BO), Framingham, MA.
Fontbonne Hall, [G], (BRK), Brooklyn, NY.
Food Distribution Center Program, [K], (SAC). See Catholic Charities of Sacramento, Inc.
Food for the Starving, [J], (LIN). See Chancery.
Food for Thought, Inc., [Q], (BAL), Baltimore, MD.
Food Pantry, [H], (SY). See Catholic Charities of Cortland County.
Fordham Preparatory School, [F], (NY), New York, NY.
*Fordham University, [C], (NY), Bronx, NY.
Fordham University at Lincoln Center, [GG], (NY). See University Apostolate.
Fordham University at Rosehill, [GG], (NY). See University Apostolate.
Forest Ridge School of the Sacred Heart, [C], (SEA), Bellevue, WA.
Forever Free Phase II-Transitional Housing For Women, [G], (CHI). See Catholic Charities of the Archdiocese of Chicago-Archdiocesan Offices.
Forever Free-Women's Wholistic Recovery Home, [G], (CHI). See Catholic Charities of the Archdiocese of Chicago-Archdiocesan Offices.
Formation Community, Religious of the Sacred Heart of Mary, [S], (LA), Los Angeles, CA.
Formation House, [A], (CHK), Saipan, MP.
Formation House, [Q], (NO). See Teresian Sisters (Society of St. Teresa of Jesus), S.T.J.
Formation Office, [B], (WDC). See Oblates of St. Francis de Sales.
Fort Wayne Community Service Center, [N], (FTW). See Catholic Charities.

G

Gwynedd-Mercy Academy, [I], (PH), Spring House, PA.
Gwynedd-Mercy College, [C], (PH), Gwynedd Valley, PA.

H

H.M. Center for Women and Children, [AA], (CLV), Cleveland, OH.
H.M. Housing Development Corporation, [AA], (CLV), Akron, OH.
H.M. Life Opportunity Services, [AA], (CLV), Akron, OH.
Haddon HealthCare, [H], (CAM). See Our Lady of Lourdes Medical Center, Inc.
Haitian Apostolate, [T], (BRK). See Catholic Migration & Refugee Office, Catholic Migration Services, Inc.
Haitian Center, [L], (BRK). See Catholic Charities.
Haitian Multi-Service Center/Catholic Charitable Bureau of Boston, [N], (BO), Boston, MA.
Haitian Office, [L], (NSH), Nashville, TN.
Halcyon, [K], (SEA), Bellevue, WA.
Hale Lokepa Community, [I], (HON). See Sisters of St. Joseph of Carondelet CSJ, Hawaii Vice-Province.
Hale Medaille Community, [I], (HON). See Sisters of St. Joseph of Carondelet CSJ, Hawaii Vice-Province.
Hale O Kamalii Montessori Preschool, [E], (HON), Hilo, HI.
*Hales Franciscan High School, Inc., [D], (CHI), Chicago, IL.
Halfmoon Housing Development Fund Co., Inc. dba Bishop Hubbard Senior Apartments/De Paul Management Corp., [K], (ALB), Clifton Park, NY.
Hallahan House, [P], (STL), St. Louis, MO.
Hallel Institute, [HH], (NY), Sparkill, NY.
Hallmar-Mercy Medical Center, [J], (DUB), Cedar Rapids, IA.
Hamilton College Newman Center, [V], (SY), Clinton, NY.
The Hamlet, [G], (BEA), Orange, TX.
Handicapables Program, [F], (SJ). See Catholic Charities of Santa Clara County.
Handmaids of Mary Immaculate, [I], (MET), Washington, NJ.
Handmaids of Mary Immaculate, [L], (MET), Washington, NJ.
Handmaids of Mary Novitiate, [EE], (NY). See Franciscan Handmaids of Mary Convent.
Handmaids of the Most Holy Trinity Monastery-Hermitage, [K], (FTW), South Bend, IN.
Handmaids of the Precious Blood-Priory of the Heart of Mary, [O], (CHI), Lake Villa, IL.
Handmaids of the Sacred Heart of Jesus, [BB], (PH), Philadelphia, PA.
Handmaids of the Sacred Heart of Jesus, [BB], (PH), Wyncote, PA.
Handmaids of the Sacred Heart of Jesus A.C.J., [I], (MIA), Miami, FL.
Handmaids of the Sacred Heart of Jesus, Mary and Joseph, [S], (LA), Ventura, CA.
Handmaids of the Sacred Heart of Pohang (H.S.H.), [R], (GAL), Houston, TX.
Hanna Boys Center, [H], (SR), Sonoma, CA.
Hannah House, [BB], (PH), Philadelphia, PA.
Hanover College Newman Center, [N], (IND), Madison, IN.
Harbor House, [J], (WCH). See Catholic Charities.
Harbor House, [L], (WCH). See Catholic Charities, Inc.
Harborcreek Youth Services, [H], (E), Harborcreek, PA.
Harborview Group Home-Handicapped, [E], (SUP). See Catholic Charities Bureau, Inc.
Harcar House, [M], (SAT), San Antonio, TX.
Harcum Junior College, [EE], (PH). See Newman Apostolate.
Harding University (Searcy) Campus Ministry, [J], (LR). See Catholic Campus Ministries.
Harmony Hill Center-Mt. Marty Branch Campus, [B], (SFS), Watertown, SD.
Harold C. and Connie Brand Early Child Development Center, [L], (OKL). See Oklahoma Benedictine Institute on Mental Retardation, Inc.
Harper Residence, [O], (WOR), Worcester, MA.
Harrington Homes Program, [O], (OM), Omaha, NE.
Harrison Co. Catholic School System. Notre Dame High School, [B], (WH), Clarksburg, WV.
Harrison County Catholic Education Foundation, Inc., [P], (WH), Clarksburg, WV.
Harrison County Catholic School System. St. Mary's Central Grade School, [D], (WH), Clarksburg, WV.
Hartford, [S], (HRT). See Catholic Charities-Catholic Family Services (Archdiocese of Hartford).
Hartford Place (Developmentally Disabled Housing), [K], (SAC). See Northern Valley Catholic Social Service.
Harvard-Radcliffe Catholic Student Center, [CC], (BO), Cambridge, MA.
Harvest House, [J], (WCH). See Catholic Charities.
Haskell Catholic Campus Center, [J], (KCK), Lawrence, KS.
Haven of Our Lady of Peace, [D], (PT), Pensacola, FL.
Haverford College, [EE], (PH). See Newman Apostolate.
*Havican Insurance Co., [Q], (DEN), Glendale, CO.
Hawley Winton Housing Development Fund, Inc., [Q], (SY), Syracuse, NY.
Hawley Youth Organization, [K], (SY), Syracuse, NY.
*Hawthorne Community Hospital, Inc., [K], (LA), Hawthorne, CA.
Haydel Heights Apartments, [N], (NO), New Orleans, LA.
Hayden High School, [B], (KCK), Topeka, KS.
Hayden High School Foundation, [B], (KCK). See Hayden High School.
Hayes Elementary School, [G], (DAV), Muscatine, IA.
Hayes Manor, [G], (CHI). See Catholic Charities of the Archdiocese of Chicago-Archdiocesan Offices.
Hayes Nursery School and Day Care Center, [V], (NY), Millbrook, NY.
Hayward, [H], (OAK). See Catholic Charities of the Diocese of Oakland, Inc.
Hazel Crest (Alcohol, Drug Dependency Program), [J], (CHI). See Mercy Hospital and Medical Center.
Hazleton-Saint Joseph Medical Center, [I], (SCR), Hazleton, PA.
Hazotte Ministries, Inc., [Y], (MIL), Fond du Lac, WI.
Head Start Catholic Center, [I], (CLV), Cleveland, OH.
Head Start Office, [N], (DET). See Catholic Social Services of Monroe County.
Head Start Program, [D], (NY). See Department of Education.
Head Start Services, [G], (CHI). See Catholic Charities of the Archdiocese of Chicago-Archdiocesan Offices.
Headquarters of Glenmary Home Missioners, [M], (CIN), Fairfield, OH.
Headwaters. Inc. (Rhinelander), [E], (SUP). See Catholic Charities Bureau, Inc.
Healing Through God Word Ministries, Inc., [HH], (NY), New York, NY.
Health and Retirement Planning: Inter-community Project, [T], (TR), Lakewood, NJ.
Health & Wellness Program, [H], (PRT). See Sisters of Charity Health System, Inc.
Health Care Endowment Fund, [F], (WIN). See Madonna Towers of Rochester, Inc.
Health Care Endowment Fund of the Reverend Oblate Fathers, [J], (BEL), Belleville, IL.
Health Facilities, Inc., [G], (OM). See Catholic Health Corp.
Health Services for Senior Citizens, [F], (HON). See St. Francis Healthcare System of Hawaii.
Health Services Self Protection Fund, [G], (OM). See Catholic Health Corp.
Health System of Mercy, [O], (OM), Omaha, NE.
Healthcare Center (general medicine, pediatrics, ob/gyn, and dental services), [J], (BUF). See Baker Victory Services.
Healy-Murphy Center, Inc., [F], (SAT), San Antonio, TX.
The Heart And Lung Institute, Inc., [E], (STA). See St. Vincent's Medical Center, Inc.
Heart of Jesus Retreat Center, [K], (ORG), Santa Ana, CA.
Heart of Mary Center, [R], (STL), St. Louis, MO.
Heart of Mary Convent (Residence for Bernardine Sisters), [P], (BGP), Stamford, CT.
Heart of Mary Publishing Company, Incorporated dba Heart of Mary Ministry, [O], (OM), Omaha, NE.
Heartbeats, [AA], (CLV), Cleveland, OH.
Heartland Center, [O], (GRY), Hammond, IN.
Heartland Center for Spirituality, [B], (DOD), Great Bend, KS.
Heartland Housing Initiative, [O], (DUB), Dubuque, IA.
HeartShare Human Services - 35th Avenue Residence, [O], (BRK). See HeartShare Human Services of New York, Roman Catholic Diocese of Brooklyn.
HeartShare Human Services - Adult Day Habilitation Program, [O], (BRK). See HeartShare Human Services of New York, Roman Catholic Diocese of Brooklyn.
HeartShare Human Services - Adult Day Habilitation Program, [O], (BRK). See HeartShare Human Services of New York, Roman Catholic Diocese of Brooklyn.
HeartShare Human Services - Antonetta Ferraro Residence, [O], (BRK). See HeartShare Human Services of New York, Roman Catholic Diocese of Brooklyn.
HeartShare Human Services - Bay Ridge Early Childhood Center, [O], (BRK). See HeartShare Human Services of New York, Roman Catholic Diocese of Brooklyn.
HeartShare Human Services - Beacon & Family Services Program at P.S. 288 Surfside Family Services, [O], (BRK). See HeartShare Human Services of New York, Roman Catholic Diocese of Brooklyn.
HeartShare Human Services - Bensonhurst Family Services, [O], (BRK). See HeartShare Human Services of New York, Roman Catholic Diocese of Brooklyn.
HeartShare Human Services - Clermont Residence, [O], (BRK). See HeartShare Human Services of New York, Roman Catholic Diocese of Brooklyn.
HeartShare Human Services - Clinton Residence, [O], (BRK). See HeartShare Human Services of New York, Roman Catholic Diocese of Brooklyn.
HeartShare Human Services - Community Follow-up Program, [O], (BRK). See HeartShare Human Services of New York, Roman Catholic Diocese of Brooklyn.
HeartShare Human Services - Dr. Catherine White Residence, [O], (BRK). See HeartShare Human Services of New York, Roman Catholic Diocese of Brooklyn.
HeartShare Human Services - Dolly and Frank Russo Sr. First Step Early Childhood Center, [O], (BRK). See HeartShare Human Services of New York, Roman Catholic Diocese of Brooklyn.
HeartShare Human Services - Doonan-Drake Residence, [O], (BRK). See HeartShare Human Services of New York, Roman Catholic Diocese of Brooklyn.
HeartShare Human Services - East Brooklyn Family Services, [O], (BRK). See HeartShare Human Services of New York, Roman Catholic Diocese of Brooklyn.
HeartShare Human Services - Eileen and William Lavin Day Treatment Center, [O], (BRK). See HeartShare Human Services of New York, Roman Catholic Diocese of Brooklyn.
HeartShare Human Services - Family Support Services Program, [O], (BRK). See HeartShare Human Services of New York, Roman Catholic Diocese of Brooklyn.
HeartShare Human Services - First Step Early Childhood Evaluation Center, [O], (BRK). See HeartShare Human Services of New York, Roman Catholic Diocese of Brooklyn.
HeartShare Human Services - Foster Care/Adoption Services (Brooklyn Office), [O], (BRK). See HeartShare Human Services of New York, Roman Catholic Diocese of Brooklyn.
HeartShare Human Services - Foster Care/Adoption Services (Queens Office), [O], (BRK). See HeartShare Human Services of New York, Roman Catholic Diocese of Brooklyn.
HeartShare Human Services - Frances Aiello Day Treatment Center, [O], (BRK). See HeartShare Human Services of New York, Roman Catholic Diocese of Brooklyn.
HeartShare Human Services - Harry Hoffman Day Treatment Center, [O], (BRK). See HeartShare Human Services of New York, Roman Catholic Diocese of Brooklyn.
HeartShare Human Services - Hart Street Residence, [O], (BRK). See HeartShare Human Services of New York, Roman Catholic Diocese of Brooklyn.
HeartShare Human Services - James and Kathleen Buckley Residence, [O], (BRK). See HeartShare Human Services of New York, Roman Catholic Diocese of Brooklyn.
HeartShare Human Services - John and Lillian Sharkey, Sr. Residence, [O], (BRK). See HeartShare Human Services of New York, Roman Catholic Diocese of Brooklyn.
HeartShare Human Services - Lefferts/Liberty Kiwanis First Step Early Childhood Center, [O], (BRK). See HeartShare Human Services of New York, Roman Catholic Diocese of Brooklyn.
HeartShare Human Services - Matilda Raffa Cuomo First Step Early Childhood Center, [O], (BRK). See HeartShare Human Services of New York, Roman Catholic Diocese of Brooklyn.
HeartShare Human Services - Msgr. Thomas G. Hagerty Residence, [O], (BRK). See HeartShare Human Services of New York, Roman Catholic Diocese of Brooklyn.
HeartShare Human Services - Red Hook Family Services, [O], (BRK). See HeartShare Human Services of New York, Roman Catholic Diocese of Brooklyn.
HeartShare Human Services - Residential Housing Program, [O], (BRK). See HeartShare Human Services of New York, Roman Catholic Diocese of Brooklyn.
HeartShare Human Services - Rita Short Hegarty Residence, [O], (BRK). See HeartShare Human Services of New York, Roman Catholic Diocese of Brooklyn.
HeartShare Human Services - Rocco Anthony Torre Residence, [O], (BRK). See HeartShare Human Services of New York, Roman Catholic Diocese of Brooklyn.
HeartShare Human Services - South Brooklyn Family

St. Petersburg, FL.
Holy Cross Kindergarten, [F], (MAN), Manchester, NH.
Holy Cross Long Term Care, Inc., [G], (MIA). See Holy Cross Hospital.
Holy Cross Middle School, [G], (LA), Los Angeles, CA.
Holy Cross Ministries, [D], (SLC), Murray, UT.
Holy Cross Mission House, [J], (FR), North Dartmouth, MA.
Holy Cross Mission House, [L], (FTW), Notre Dame, IN.
Holy Cross Novitiate, [E], (COS), Cascade, CO.
Holy Cross Provincial Office, [D], (SUP), Merrill, WI.
Holy Cross Regional School, [A], (RIC), Lynchburg, VA.
Holy Cross Retreat and Friary, [D], (LSC), Mesilla Park, NM.
Holy Cross School, [H], (MIL), South Milwaukee, WI.
Holy Cross School, [F], (NO), New Orleans, LA.
Holy Cross School, [H], (NO), New Orleans, LA.
Holy Cross School/Clete and Claire Haney Memorial, [N], (OM). See The Omaha Archdiocesan Educational Foundation, Inc.
Holy Cross Seminary Education Fund Endowment Trust, [M], (LC), La Crosse, WI.
Holy Cross Seminary House of Formation, [A], (LC), La Crosse, WI.
Holy Cross Services Corp., [N], (FTW), Notre Dame, IN.
Holy Cross Sisters, [E], (STO), Stockton, CA.
Holy Dormition Monastery, [E], (PHU), Sybertsville, PA.
Holy Dormition Monastery, [A], (PSC), Sybertsville, PA.
The Holy Evangelists Friary, [N], (CHI), Chicago, IL.
Holy Face of Jesus Monastery, [M], (PAT), Clifton, NJ.
Holy Family, [J], (PRT), Lewiston, ME.
Holy Family (Middle) School, [C], (OWN), Owensboro, KY.
Holy Family Academy, [C], (MET), Bound Brook, NJ.
Holy Family Academy, [C], (NEW), Bayonne, NJ.
Holy Family Adoption Foundation, Inc., [N], (LA). See Holy Family Services, Adoption & Foster Care.
Holy Family Adult Day Care, [I], (ALN), Bethlehem, PA.
Holy Family Adult Day Care, [M], (ALN). See St. Francis Center.
Holy Family Adult Day Care at St. Francis Center, [I], (ALN), Orwigsburg, PA.
Holy Family Apartments, [I], (ALN), Bethlehem, PA.
Holy Family Apartments, [I], (ALN), New Philadelphia, PA.
Holy Family Catholic Consolidated School, [F], (DUB), Cedar Rapids, IA.
Holy Family Catholic School, [D], (COV), Covington, KY.
Holy Family Catholic School of Coeur d'Alene, [A], (B), Coeur d'Alene, ID.
Holy Family Catholic School System-Diocese of Rochester, [D], (ROC), Rochester, NY.
Holy Family Center, [P], (OAK), Pleasant Hill, CA.
Holy Family Center, [K], (PH). See The Catholic Social Services of the Archdiocese of Philadelphia.
Holy Family Center, Inc., [E], (TUC). See Carondelet Health Network.
Holy Family Child Care Center, [I], (SFS), Sioux Falls, SD.
Holy Family Child Care Center, Inc., [S], (WH), Wheeling, WV.
Holy Family Church Inc., [X], (CHI), Chicago, IL.
Holy Family College, [C], (PH), Philadelphia, PA.
Holy Family Community, [Q], (PRO). See Franciscan Missionaries of Mary.
Holy Family Community, [M], (SR), Napa, CA.
Holy Family Convent, [E], (LAV), Las Vegas, NV.
Holy Family Convent, [Q], (PRO), North Kingstown, RI.
Holy Family Convent, [O], (SFR), South San Francisco, CA.
Holy Family Convent, [N], (SR), Crescent City, CA.
Holy Family Convent and Infirmary, [G], (HBG), Danville, PA.
Holy Family Convent of Franciscan Sisters of Christian Charity, [J], (GB), Manitowoc, WI.
Holy Family Day Care Center, [C], (LAV), Las Vegas, NV.
Holy Family Day Home, [I], (SFR), San Francisco, CA.
Holy Family Day Nursery and Convent, [J], (NEW), Nutley, NJ.
Holy Family Educational Foundation, [I], (BIR), Birmingham, AL.
Holy Family Elementary School, [B], (GAY), East Tawas, MI.
Holy Family Emergency Shelter, [L], (IND), Indianapolis, IN.
Holy Family Endowment Trust Fund, [M], (LC), St. Mary's Ridge, WI.
Holy Family Foundation, [S], (PIT), Pittsburgh, PA.
Holy Family Friary, [O], (PIT), Avalon, PA.
Holy Family Hall Infirmary, [I], (DUB), Dubuque, IA.
Holy Family Health Center, [M], (CHI), Des Plaines, IL.
Holy Family Hermitage, [F], (STU), Bloomingdale, OH.
Holy Family High School, [B], (BIR), Birmingham, AL.
Holy Family High School, [C], (DEN), Denver, CO.
Holy Family Home, [R], (BRK), Brooklyn, NY.
Holy Family Home, [M], (BUF), Williamsville, NY.
Holy Family Home, [L], (CLV), Cleveland, OH.
Holy Family Home, [M], (COV), Melbourne, KY.
Holy Family Home, [Y], (PH), Philadelphia, PA.
Holy Family Home, [G], (PT), Tallahassee, FL.
Holy Family Home and Shelter, Inc., [E], (NOR), Willimantic, CT.
Holy Family Home Health and Hospice Care, [H], (ALN), Orwigsburg, PA.
Holy Family Home Health Care, [M], (ALN). See St. Francis Center.
Holy Family Hospital, [D], (SC), Estherville, IA.
Holy Family Hospital, [G], (SPK), Spokane, WA.
Holy Family Hospital, [A], (SUP), New Richmond, WI.
Holy Family Hospital Adult Day Health, [G], (SPK), Spokane, WA.
Holy Family Hospital and Medical Center, [Q], (BO), Methuen, MA.
Holy Family Hospital Auxiliary, [FF], (BO). See Valley Regional Health System, Inc.
Holy Family Hospital Foundation, Inc., [DD], (BO). See Chancery Office.
Holy Family Hospital Foundation, Inc., [DD], (BO), Methuen, MA.
Holy Family Hospital Foundation, Inc., [I], (SUP), New Richmond, WI.
Holy Family Hospital Foundation., [D], (SC). See Holy Family Hospital.
Holy Family Hospital Men's Guild, [FF], (BO), Methuen, MA.
Holy Family Hospital, Inc., [FF], (BO). See Valley Regional Health System, Inc.
Holy Family House Convent, S.S.J., [K], (ARL), Falls Church, VA.
Holy Family Institute, [I], (PIT), Emsworth, PA.
Holy Family Manor, [H], (ALN), Bethlehem, PA.
Holy Family Manor, [P], (PIT), Pittsburgh, PA.
Holy Family Medical Center, [J], (CHI), Des Plaines, IL.
Holy Family Memorial, Inc., [F], (GB), Manitowoc, WI.
Holy Family Middle School, [D], (LC), Marshfield, WI.
Holy Family Middle School, [B], (SAG), Bay City, MI.
Holy Family Monastery, [M], (E), Erie, PA.
Holy Family Monastery/Retreat, [M], (HRT), West Hartford, CT.
Holy Family Monastery/Retreat, [N], (HRT), West Hartford, CT.
Holy Family Motherhouse, [G], (NOR), Baltic, CT.
Holy Family Parish Conference, [E], (YAK), Yakima, WA.
Holy Family Parish, Willard Endowment Trust, [M], (LC), Willard, WI.
Holy Family Plaza, Inc., [K], (DEN). See Archdiocesan Housing Committee.
Holy Family Regional School, [F], (DET), Rochester, MI.
Holy Family Regional School, [E], (RVC), Commack, NY.
Holy Family Regional School Foundation, [I], (BIR), Huntsville, AL.
Holy Family Residence, [I], (ALN), Orwigsburg, PA.
Holy Family Residence, [M], (ALN). See St. Francis Center.
Holy Family Residence, [L], (PAT), West Paterson, NJ.
Holy Family Residence, [M], (STP), St. Paul, MN.
Holy Family Retreat, [N], (RIC), Hampton, VA.
Holy Family Retreat Center, [F], (BEA), Beaumont, TX.
Holy Family Retreat House, [Q], (HRT), Farmington, CT.
Holy Family School, [D], (ALN), Frackville, PA.
Holy Family School, [B], (CC), Corpus Christi, TX.
Holy Family School, [C], (LAF), Lafayette, LA.
Holy Family School, [C], (PCE), Ponce, PR.
Holy Family School, [H], (PH), Phoenixville, PA.
Holy Family School, [E], (SCL), Sauk Centre, MN.
Holy Family School, [D], (SEA), Lacey, WA.
Holy Family School, [G], (SY), Norwich, NY.
Holy Family School Endowment Fund, Inc., [B], (MAR), Sault Sainte Marie, MI.
Holy Family Seminary, [B], (WDC), Silver Spring, MD.
Holy Family Services, Adoption & Foster Care, [N], (LA), Pasadena, CA.
Holy Family Services, Adoption and Foster Care, [G], (ORG), Santa Ana, CA.
Holy Family Sisters, [O], (OAK), Pleasant Hill, CA.
Holy Family Sisters, [E], (STO), Stockton, CA.
Holy Family Soup Kitchen, [I], (SAV), Columbus, GA.
Holy Family Spiritual Renewal Center, [H], (SCR), Nanticoke, PA.
Holy Family Villa, [J], (ALN), Bethlehem, PA.
Holy Family Villa, [G], (CHI). See Catholic Charities of the Archdiocese of Chicago-Archdiocesan Offices.
Holy Family Villa, [M], (CHI), Lemont, IL.
Holy Family Villa, [C], (LIT), Lemont, IL.
Holy Family, Seaside Convent, [N], (CAM), Ventnor, NJ.
Holy Ghost, [D], (LC). See Chippewa Area Catholic Schools.
Holy Ghost Animation Center, [Q], (PIT), Bethel Park, PA.
Holy Ghost Educational Endowment, [N], (OM). See The Omaha Archdiocesan Educational Foundation, Inc.
Holy Ghost Fathers, [B], (GAL), Houston, TX.
Holy Ghost Fathers, [AA], (PH), Philadelphia, PA.
Holy Ghost Fathers, [E], (SB), Hemet, CA.
Holy Ghost Fathers and Brothers Provincialate, [O], (PIT), Bethel Park, PA.
Holy Ghost Fathers Development Office, [B], (WDC), Wheaton, MD.
Holy Ghost Fathers Home, Maison Brothier, [F], (ALX), Natchitoches, LA.
Holy Ghost Fathers of Ireland, [U], (BRK), Long Island City, NY.
Holy Ghost Preparatory School, [G], (PH), Bensalem, PA.
Holy Heart of Mary Novitiate, [I], (RCK), Batavia, IL.
Holy Hill National Shrine of Mary Help of Christians, [P], (MIL). See Discalced Carmelite Monastery.
Holy Infant Apartments, Inc., [I], (STL). See Cardinal Ritter Institute.
Holy Innocents Day Care Center, [N], (BUF), Buffalo, NY.
Holy Innocents Foundation, [HH], (NY), Riverdale, NY.
Holy Innocents House, [N], (HRT). See Sisters of Notre Dame de Namur.
Holy Land Convent, [N], (HRT), Waterbury, CT.
Holy Martyrs of Vietnam Church Child Enrichment Day Care Center, [H], (ARL), Arlington, VA.
Holy Name, [D], (LC). See Wausau Area Catholic Schools.
Holy Name Academy Child Care Center dba Benedictine Sisters of Florida, [F], (SP), San Antonio, FL.
Holy Name Central Catholic Junior/Senior High School, [C], (WOR), Worcester, MA.
Holy Name Central Endowment Fund, Inc., [B], (MAR), Escanaba, MI.
Holy Name Central Grade School, [A], (MAR), Escanaba, MI.
Holy Name Centre for Homeless Men, Inc., [I], (NY). See The Catholic Charities of the Archdiocese of New York.
Holy Name College, [B], (WDC), Silver Spring, MD.
Holy Name Friary, [N], (CHI), Chicago, IL.
Holy Name Friary, Inc., [M], (PAT), Ringwood, NJ.
Holy Name Health Care Foundation, [S], (NEW), Teaneck, NJ.
Holy Name High School, [C], (ALN), Reading, PA.
Holy Name High School, [D], (CLV), Parma Heights, OH.
Holy Name High School, [E], (OAK), Oakland, CA.
Holy Name Hospital, [G], (NEW), Teaneck, NJ.
Holy Name Housing Corp., [O], (OM), Omaha, NE.
Holy Name Loaves and Fishes Community Meal, [L], (NSH), Nashville, TN.
Holy Name Monastery, [P], (SP), St. Leo, FL.
Holy Name of Jesus Hospital Trust, [I], (BIR), Birmingham, AL.
Holy Name Priory, Dominican Friars, [AA], (PH), Philadelphia, PA.
Holy Name Province, [W], (PH), Philadelphia, PA.
Holy Name Province - Provincial Motherhouse, [P], (BUF), Buffalo, NY.
Holy Name Retreat Center, [S], (GAL), Houston, TX.
Holy Name Retreat House, [M], (GB), Chambers Island, WI.
Holy Name Scholarship Foundation, [B], (MAR). See Holy Name Central Endowment Fund, Inc.
Holy Name Society, [J], (STU), Steubenville, OH.
Holy Name Society (Union), [Q], (BAL), Baltimore, MD.
Holy Names Academy, [C], (SEA), Seattle, WA.
Holy Names College, [B], (OAK), Oakland, CA.
Holy Names College, [G], (OAK), Oakland, CA.
Holy Names College Campus Ministry, [Q], (OAK), Oakland, CA.
Holy Names Foundation, [L], (SPK), Spokane, WA.
Holy Names Music Center, [O], (SPK), Spokane, WA.
Holy Names Preschool & After School Program, [G], (MEM), Memphis, TN.
Holy Names Sisters, [O], (OAK), Oakland, CA.
Holy Names Sisters, [O], (OAK), Hayward, CA.
Holy Names Sisters, [O], (OAK), Kensington, CA.
Holy Nativity Monastery, [B], (RC), Bethlehem, SD.
Holy Nativity Monastery, [C], (SAM), Bethlehem, SD.
Holy Peace Friary, [C], (BUF). See St. Bonaventure University.
Holy Redeemer College, [M], (WDC), Washington, DC.

Holy Redeemer Educational Trust Fund (Holy Redeemer Parish, Burton), [K], (LAN). See Chancery Office.
Holy Redeemer Foundation, [U], (PH), Huntingdon Valley, PA.
Holy Redeemer Foundation, [FF], (PH). See Holy Redeemer Health System, Inc.
*Holy Redeemer Health System, Inc., [FF], (PH), Huntingdon Valley, PA.
Holy Redeemer Home Health and Hospice Services, [FF], (PH). See Holy Redeemer Health System, Inc.
Holy Redeemer Hospice, [FF], (PH). See Holy Redeemer Health System, Inc.
Holy Redeemer Hospital and Medical Center, [U], (PH), Meadowbrook, PA.
Holy Redeemer Hospital and Medical Center, [FF], (PH). See Holy Redeemer Health System, Inc.
Holy Redeemer Multicare, [FF], (PH). See Holy Redeemer Health System, Inc.
Holy Redeemer Parish Conference, [E], (YAK), Yakima, WA.
*Holy Redeemer Physician Services, [FF], (PH), Huntingdon Valley, PA.
*Holy Redeemer Physician Services, [FF], (PH), Philadelphia, PA.
Holy Redeemer Rehabilitation Center, [J], (CAM), Cape May, NJ.
Holy Redeemer Rehabilitation Center, [T], (TR). See Holy Redeemer Visiting Nurse Agency, Inc.
Holy Redeemer Retreat and Conference Center, [N], (OAK). See Redemptorists.
Holy Redeemer Support Services, [FF], (PH). See Holy Redeemer Health System, Inc.
Holy Redeemer Transitional Care Unit, [FF], (PH). See Holy Redeemer Health System, Inc.
Holy Redeemer Visiting Nurse Agency, [FF], (PH). See Holy Redeemer Health System, Inc.
Holy Redeemer Visiting Nurse Agency, Inc., [J], (CAM), Swainton, NJ.
Holy Redeemer Visiting Nurse Agency, Inc., [T], (TR), Swainton, NJ.
*Holy Redeemer, Nazareth & St. Mary Home Health Services, [W], (PH), Philadelphia, PA.
Holy Resurrection Monastery, [A], (VNN), Newberry Springs, CA.
Holy Rosary Academy, [B], (ANC), Anchorage, AK.
Holy Rosary Academy, [C], (L), Louisville, KY.
Holy Rosary Academy, [E], (NEW), Union City, NJ.
Holy Rosary Academy, [I], (NO), New Orleans, LA.
Holy Rosary Catholic School "Vision 2000" Educational Trust Fund, [L], (LR), Stuttgart, AR.
Holy Rosary Child Care Center, [G], (RIC), Richmond, VA.
Holy Rosary Convent, [F], (JKS), Philadelphia, MS.
Holy Rosary Convent, [O], (NEW), Jersey City, NJ.
Holy Rosary Convent, [O], (NEW), Union City, NJ.
Holy Rosary Convent, [N], (SAT), San Antonio, TX.
Holy Rosary Elementary, [B], (GAY), Cedar, MI.
Holy Rosary Health Center, [G], (GF), Miles City, MT.
Holy Rosary Institute, [M], (LAF), Lafayette, LA.
Holy Rosary Marianist Community, [M], (SAT), San Antonio, TX.
Holy Rosary Parish Endowment Fund, [G], (DUL), Duluth, MN.
Holy Rosary Parish, R.E. Program, [B], (CR), Detroit Lakes, MN.
Holy Rosary Priory, [L], (P), Portland, OR.
Holy Rosary School, [C], (WIN). See Mankato Area Catholic Schools.
Holy Savior Menard Central, [A], (ALX), Alexandria, LA.
Holy Saviour-St. John Fisher School, [H], (PH), Linwood, PA.
Holy Shroud Guild, [HH], (NY), Esopus, NY.
Holy Spirit, [E], (BAL), Baltimore, MD.
Holy Spirit Academy, [F], (SCR), Hazleton, PA.
Holy Spirit Campus, [C], (MET), Perth Amboy, NJ.
Holy Spirit Central School Educational Fund, [A], (MAR), Norway, MI.
Holy Spirit Central School Educational Fund, [B], (MAR), Norway, MI.
Holy Spirit Community, [L], (SPK), Spokane, WA.
Holy Spirit Consolidated School, [B], (HBG), Mount Carmel, PA.
Holy Spirit Convent, [G], (OG), Tupper Lake, NY.
Holy Spirit Convent, [L], (PRO), Providence, RI.
Holy Spirit Convent, [F], (R), Jacksonville, NC.
Holy Spirit Convent, [H], (SAC). See Institute of the Sisters of Mercy of the Americas.
Holy Spirit Convent, Daughters of the Holy Spirit, [P], (BGP), Bridgeport, CT.
Holy Spirit Elementary School, [D], (COV), Newport, KY.
Holy Spirit Friary, [D], (CHI). See Hales Franciscan High School, Inc.
The Holy Spirit Health Care Center, Inc., [M], (NOR), Putnam, CT.
Holy Spirit Hermitage, [G], (WH), Old Fields, WV.
Holy Spirit High School, [A], (BIR), Tuscaloosa, AL.
Holy Spirit High School, [A], (CAM), Absecon, NJ.
Holy Spirit Hospital and Community Mental Health Center, [F], (HBG), Camp Hill, PA.
Holy Spirit Junior High School, [D], (COV), Newport, KY.
Holy Spirit Missionary Cenacle, [I], (MOB), Dothan, AL.
Holy Spirit Missionary Cenacle, [M], (PAT), Stirling, NJ.
Holy Spirit Missionary Cenacle, [M], (WDC), Riverdale, MD.
Holy Spirit Missonary Cenacle, [AA], (PH), Philadelphia, PA.
Holy Spirit Monastery, [F], (STU), Steubenville, OH.
Holy Spirit Motherhouse, [N], (SAT), San Antonio, TX.
Holy Spirit Newman Center, [F], (CR), Bemidji, MN.
Holy Spirit Provincial House, [G], (NOR), Putnam, CT.
Holy Spirit Regional School Foundation, [I], (BIR), Huntsville, AL.
Holy Spirit Retirement Home, [E], (SC), Sioux City, IA.
Holy Spirit Retirement Home Foundation, Inc., [H], (SC), Sioux City, IA.
Holy Spirit Retreat and Conference Center, [G], (CC), Laredo, TX.
Holy Spirit Retreat Center, [X], (LA), Encino, CA.
Holy Spirit Retreat House, [G], (ANC), Anchorage, AK.
Holy Spirit Retreat House, [I], (ANC), Anchorage, AK.
Holy Spirit School, [D], (ALN), Allentown, PA.
Holy Spirit School, [C], (WIN). See Rochester Catholic Schools.
Holy Spirit School of Tuscaloosa Endowment Foundation, [I], (BIR), Tuscaloosa, AL.
Holy Spirit Sisters Charitable Trust, [I], (SAG), Saginaw, MI.
Holy Spirit Sisters' Trust, [S], (SAT), San Antonio, TX.
Holy Spirit/Rego Park, [L], (BRK). See Catholic Charities.
Holy Transfiguration Monastery, [A], (STN), Redwood Valley, CA.
Holy Trinity, [E], (MAN), Laconia, NH.
Holy Trinity, [C], (RVC), Hicksville, NY.
Holy Trinity, [D], (TOL), Swanton, OH.
Holy Trinity Catholic, [D], (GBG), Mount Pleasant, PA.
Holy Trinity Catholic Church Endowment Trust, [M], (LC), La Crosse, WI.
Holy Trinity Catholic High School, [C], (AUS), Temple, TX.
Holy Trinity Catholic Mission School, [G], (DAV), Davenport, IA.
Holy Trinity Catholic School, [G], (CIN), Springfield, OH.
Holy Trinity Catholic School, [C], (FWT), Grapevine, TX.
Holy Trinity Community, [I], (HON). See Sisters of St. Joseph of Carondelet CSJ, Hawaii Vice-Province.
Holy Trinity Convent, [N], (HRT), Wallingford, CT.
Holy Trinity Convent, [O], (NEW), Fort Lee, NJ.
Holy Trinity Convent, [N], (PAT), Stirling, NJ.
Holy Trinity Friary, [M], (DEN), Denver, CO.
Holy Trinity High School, [D], (CHI), Chicago, IL.
Holy Trinity Manor, [B], (CHY), Cheyenne, WY.
Holy Trinity Middle School, [D], (CHL). See Mecklenburg Area Catholic Schools (M.A.C.S.).
Holy Trinity Middle School, [A], (NU). See New Ulm Area Catholic Schools.
Holy Trinity Missionary Cenacle, [M], (WDC), University Park, MD.
Holy Trinity Monastery, [M], (BAL), Baltimore, MD.
Holy Trinity Monastery, [D], (PBR), Butler, PA.
Holy Trinity Monastery, [F], (TUC), St. David, AZ.
Holy Trinity Parish Endowment, [N], (OM). See The Omaha Archdiocesan Educational Foundation, Inc.
Holy Trinity Place - Adult Day Care Center, [L], (IND). See Adult Day Services.
Holy Trinity School, [E], (SCL), Pierz, MN.
Holy Trinity Seminary, [A], (DAL), Irving, TX.
Holy Trinity Spiritual Center, [L], (BAL), Baltimore, MD.
Holy Trinity Student Chapel, [J], (LAN), Ypsilanti, MI.
Holy Trinity-Sacred Heart Consolidation, [F], (DUB), Dubuque, IA.
Holy Union Provincialate, [K], (FR), Fall River, MA.
Holyoke Catholic High School, [C], (SPR), Holyoke, MA.
Hombre Nueva (RI), Inc., [U], (PRO), South Kingston, RI.
Hombre Nuevo, [DD], (LA), El Monte, CA.
Home and Family, Inc., [M], (ATL), Dunwoody, GA.
Home Care Services, [H], (BUF). See The Catholic Charities of the Diocese of Buffalo.
Home Care Services, [H], (WOR). See Catholic Charities.
Home for Aged and Infirm, [D], (PCE), Ponce, PR.
Home for Aged of the Little Sisters of the Poor, Holy Family Residence, [L], (SCR), Scranton, PA.
The Home for the Aged of the Little Sisters of the Poor, [K], (HRT), Enfield, CT.
Home for the Aged of the Little Sisters of the Poor, [L], (PIT), Pittsburgh, PA.
Home for the Aged of the Little Sisters of the Poor, [K], (SFR), San Francisco, CA.
Home Integration Program, [L], (OKL). See Oklahoma Benedictine Institute on Mental Retardation, Inc.
Home of Divine Providence, [D], (PHU), Philadelphia, PA.
Home of Divine Providence, Inc.-Bayard House, [F], (WIL), Wilmington, DE.
Home of the Daughters of Charity, [G], (SLC), Price, UT.
Home of the Good Shepherd, [L], (STP), St. Paul, MN.
Home On The Range, [F], (BIS), Sentinel Butte, ND.
Home Start Program, [L], (OKL). See Oklahoma Benedictine Institute on Mental Retardation, Inc.
Homeless Haven (Transitional Housing Program), [K], (SAC). See Catholic Charities of Sacramento, Inc.
Homeless Prevention Services, [L], (DEN). See Catholic Charities and Community Services of the Archdiocese of Denver, Inc.
Homeless Service Center, [E], (SR). See Diocese of Santa Rosa, Catholic Charities.
Homeless Services, [H], (SFR). See San Mateo County District Council.
Homemaker Program, Cabrini League, [E], (FRS), Bakersfield, CA.
Homemaker-Companion Program, [B], (STO). See The Catholic Charities of the Diocese of Stockton.
Homes Again Program, [Q], (DEN). See Mercy Housing, Inc.
Homes for Hope Foundation, [U], (PRO). See Miscellaneous Listings for the Diocese of Providence.
Homes of Hope, Inc., [Q], (PEO), Bloomington, IL.
Honoratus Residence, [J], (PRT), Standish, ME.
Hood College, [O], (BAL). See Archdiocesan Office-Newman Center.
Hoosier Boys' Town, [G], (GRY), Schererville, IN.
Hope Community of Hicksville, Inc., [R], (RVC), Hicksville, NY.
The Hope Guild, [K], (LA). See Saint John's Health Center.
Hope Haven Center, [I], (NO), Marrero, LA.
Hope Haven Center, [K], (NO), Marrero, LA.
HOPE House, [E], (HBG). See Department for Catholic Charities Counseling/Field Services.
Hope Manor, [O], (TOL), Toledo, OH.
Hope Nursing Home, Inc., [N], (MIL), Lomira, WI.
Hope of Buffalo, Inc., [T], (BUF), Buffalo, NY.
Hope Rural School, [C], (PMB), Indiantown, FL.
Hope, Faith & Love, Inc., [J], (CC), Corpus Christi, TX.
Horizons Institute, Inc., [V], (HRT), Orange, CT.
Horizons Institute, Inc., [V], (HRT), Hamden, CT.
Hospice, [H], (ALB). See Mercycare Corporation, St. Peter's Hospital.
Hospice of Peace, [J], (DEN), Denver, CO.
Hospice of Rensselaer Co., [H], (ALB). See Mercycare Corporation, St. Peter's Hospital.
Hospital and Health Services Liaison, [U], (SFR), Mountain View, CA.
Hospital de Diego, [E], (SJN), Santurce, PR.
Hospital del Maestro, [E], (SJN), Rio Piedras, PR.
Hospital of St. Raphael, [I], (HRT), New Haven, CT.
Hospital of the Immaculate Conception, [A], (MGZ), San German, PR.
Hospital Sisters Health Care-West, Inc., [P], (LC), Eau Claire, WI.
Hospital Sisters Health System, [N], (SFD), Springfield, IL.
Hospital Sisters of St. Francis, [G], (BEL), Belleville, IL.
Hospital Sisters of St. Francis, [G], (BEL), Belleville, IL.
Hospital Sisters of St. Francis Foundation, Inc., [N], (SFD), Springfield, IL.
Hospital Sisters of the Third Order of St. Francis, [O], (CHI), Alsip, IL.
Hospital Sisters of the Third Order of St. Francis, [J], (GB), Green Bay, WI.
Hospital Sisters of the Third Order of St. Francis, [Q], (MIL), Sheboygan, WI.
Hospital Sisters Services, Inc., [N], (SFD), Springfield, IL.
Hospitaler Sisters of Mercy Novitiate, [N], (CAM), Pleasantville, NJ.
Hospitality Center, Inc., [G], (BEA), Port Arthur, TX.
Hospitality House Therapeutic Community Inc., [Q], (ALB), Albany, NY.
Hospitaller Brothers Healthcare, Inc., [R], (LA). See Brothers of John of God, Inc., The.
Hospitaller Brothers of St. John of God, [R], (LA), Los Angeles, CA.
Hospitaller Brothers St. John of God, [E], (SB), Apple Valley, CA.
Hospitaller Foundation of California, Inc., [R], (LA). See Brothers of John of God, Inc., The.
Hospitaller Foundation of California, Inc., The, [DD], (LA), Los Angeles, CA.
Hospitaller Order of St. John of God, [M], (CAM),

Westville Grove, NJ.
Hostos Community College, [GG], (NY). See University Apostolate.
House of Charity, [H], (SPK), Spokane, WA.
House of Discernment, [J], (PRT), Lewiston, ME.
House of Formation, [R], (LA). See Missionaries of Charity Brothers.
House of Formation, [J], (PRT), Portland, ME.
House of Joseph II, [F], (WIL). See Ministry of Caring, Inc.
House of Joseph Transitional Residence, [F], (WIL). See Ministry of Caring, Inc.
House of Loreto, [I], (Y), Canton, OH.
The House of Mary Shrine, Inc., [I], (SFS), Yankton, SD.
House of Mercy, [F], (DM), Des Moines, IA.
House of Mercy, Inc., [Q], (BAL), Baltimore, MD.
House of Mercy, Inc., [Q], (CHL), Belmont, NC.
House of Nazareth (Casa Nazaret), [L], (ALN), Reading, PA.
House of Nazareth Life Institute Ltd. (Nazareth Life Center), [HH], (NY), Garrison, NY.
House of Peace, [Y], (MIL), Milwaukee, WI.
House of Peace & Education, Inc., [R], (WOR), Gardner, MA.
House of Peace, Inc., [HH], (NY), New York, NY.
House of Prayer, [E], (FBK), Fairbanks, AK.
House of Prayer for Priests, [I], (OKL), Oklahoma City, OK.
House of Prayer for Priests, [K], (ORG), Orange, CA.
House of Providence, [L], (SY), Syracuse, NY.
House of Religious Men: Divine Word Theologate, [N], (CHI). See Society of the Divine Word, Provincial Headquarter-Chicago Prov.
House of the Good Shepherd, [L], (CHI), Chicago, IL.
House of the Holy Family School, [I], (NO), New Orleans, LA.
House of the Holy Innocents, Inc., [P], (RVC), Mount Sinai, NY.
House of the Holy Shroud, [H], (GAY), Prescott, MI.
House of the Lord Retreat Center, Inc., [M], (SPK), Tum Tum, WA.
Household Exchange, [L], (IND). See Catholic Charities of Terre Haute.
Housing and Supportive Services, [H], (BUF). See The Catholic Charities of the Diocese of Buffalo.
Housing Association of the Diocese of Saint Augustine, [G], (STA), Jacksonville, FL.
Housing Counseling Program, [E], (SUP). See Catholic Charities Bureau, Inc.
The Housing Fund of the Archdiocese of New York, [HH], (NY), New York, NY.
Housing Options, [E], (SR). See Diocese of Santa Rosa, Catholic Charities.
Housing Services, [H], (OAK). See Catholic Charities of the Diocese of Oakland, Inc.
Housing Services, [H], (RVC). See Catholic Charities Central Administration.
Howard Univ. Newman Center, [S], (WDC). See Archdiocesan Campus Ministry.
Howells Community Catholic School, [D], (OM), Howells, NE.
HRH Management Corporation, [U], (PH), Huntingdon Valley, PA.
Hudson Catholic High School, [D], (NEW), Jersey City, NJ.
Hudson Day Care Center (Hudson), [E], (SUP). See Catholic Charities Bureau, Inc.
Hudson Valley Community College, [S], (ALB), Troy, NY.
The Human Life and Development Fund of the Diocese of Duluth, [G], (DUL), Duluth, MN.
Human Life International, [V], (WDC), Front Royal, VA.
Human Resources, [G], (CHI). See Catholic Charities of the Archdiocese of Chicago-Archdiocesan Offices.
Human Services, [H], (RVC). See Catholic Charities Central Administration.
Human Services Division/Pierre Toussaint Haitian Catholic Center, Inc., [L], (MIA), Miami, FL.
Humility Convent, [N], (DAV), Davenport, IA.
Humility of Mary Center-Motherhouse of the Congregation of the Humility of Mary, [N], (DAV), Davenport, IA.
Humility of Mary Housing, Inc., [AA], (CLV), Akron, OH.
Humility of Mary Information Systems, Inc., [P], (Y), Youngstown, OH.
Humility of Mary Novitiate, [N], (DAV), Davenport, IA.
Hungarian Catholic League of America, Inc., [HH], (NY), New York, NY.
Hunger, Inc., [N], (SFD), Springfield, IL.
Hunter/Baruch College, [GG], (NY). See University Apostolate.
Hunterdon County Services, [E], (MET), Flemington, NJ.
Huntington College Newman Center, [K], (MOB), Montgomery, AL.
Hurley Manor I, [G], (STA). See Jacksonville, Family Housing Management Co.
Hurley Manor II, [G], (STA). See Jacksonville, Family Housing Management Co.
Huron House/Boysville of Michigan, Inc., [E], (GAY), Alpena, MI.

I

I'm Home Alone, [E], (SR). See Diocese of Santa Rosa, Catholic Charities.
I.H.M. Congregation Charitable Trust, [R], (SCR), Scranton, PA.
Idaho State University, St. John's Community, [F], (B), Pocatello, ID.
Idente Missionaries - Santa Maria Residence, [DD], (NY), Bronx, NY.
Iglesia de San Juan Bautista, [J], (HBG), Lancaster, PA.
Ignatian Lay Volunteer Corps, [Q], (BAL), Baltimore, MD.
Ignatius House, [K], (ATL), Atlanta, GA.
Ignatius House, The Novitiate of the California Province, Society of Jesus, [R], (LA), Culver City, CA.
Ignatius Residence, [P], (NO), New Orleans, LA.
IHM Center for Literacy and GED Programs, [FF], (PH), Philadelphia, PA.
IHM/St. Luke's Consolidated School, [H], (STP), St. Paul, MN.
III Order of St. Dominic, [N], (SEA), Tacoma, WA.
Il Ritiro-The Little Retreat, [T], (STL), Dittmer, MO.
Illinois College Newman Center, [M], (SFD), Jacksonville, IL.
Imani Center, [H], (BAL). See Bon Secours Baltimore Health Corporation, Inc.
Immacolata Manor Foundation, [H], (KC), Liberty, MO.
Immacolata Retreat Center, [O], (KC), Kansas City, MO.
Immaculata Academy, [D], (BUF), Hamburg, NY.
Immaculata College, [C], (PH), Immaculata, PA.
Immaculata Congretional Home, [O], (CHI), Bartlett, IL.
Immaculata Convent, [L], (OM), Norfolk, NE.
Immaculata Hall Convent, [K], (FTW). See Saint Mary's of the Immaculate Conception.
Immaculata High School, [B], (KCK), Leavenworth, KS.
Immaculata High School, [E], (NO), Marrero, LA.
Immaculata Retreat House, [I], (NOR), Willimantic, CT.
Immaculate Care Preschool, [G], (SCR), Scranton, PA.
Immaculate Conception Academy, [E], (PRO), Smithfield, RI.
Immaculate Conception Academy, (Girls), [E], (SFR), San Francisco, CA.
Immaculate Conception Apostolic School, [A], (MAN), Center Harbor, NH.
Immaculate Conception Cathedral Middle and High School, [C], (MEM), Memphis, TN.
Immaculate Conception Catholic School, [C], (FWT), Denton, TX.
Immaculate Conception Convent, [X], (BO), Boston, MA.
Immaculate Conception Convent, [P], (BUF), Belmont, NY.
Immaculate Conception Convent, [P], (BUF), Hamburg, NY.
Immaculate Conception Convent, [D], (DOD), Great Bend, KS.
Immaculate Conception Convent, [D], (FBK), Fairbanks, AK.
Immaculate Conception Convent, [O], (NEW), Irvington, NJ.
Immaculate Conception Convent, [O], (NEW), Lodi, NJ.
Immaculate Conception Convent, [N], (PEO), Peoria, IL.
Immaculate Conception Convent, [G], (TUC), Yuma, AZ.
Immaculate Conception Convent, Spiritual Renewal Center and Novitiate, [G], (NOR), Putnam, CT.
Immaculate Conception Friary, [DD], (NY), New York, NY.
Immaculate Conception Friary, [P], (STL), Arnold, MO.
Immaculate Conception Grade School, [B], (FBK), Fairbanks, AK.
Immaculate Conception High School, [C], (NEW), Lodi, NJ.
Immaculate Conception Home for Girls, [P], (LA), Los Angeles, CA.
Immaculate Conception Kindergarten and Nursery, [J], (SAT), San Antonio, TX.
Immaculate Conception Middle School, [A], (GAY), Traverse City, MI.
Immaculate Conception Monastery, [U], (BRK), Jamaica, NY.
Immaculate Conception Monastery, [N], (CHI), Chicago, IL.
Immaculate Conception Monastery Passionist Nuns, [R], (STL), Ellisville, MO.
Immaculate Conception Pastoral Center, [A], (BRK), Douglaston, NY.
Immaculate Conception Pre-Kindergarten, [E], (PEO), Peoria, IL.
Immaculate Conception Pre-School, [F], (SP), St. Petersburg, FL.
Immaculate Conception Priory, [I], (LC), St. Mary's Ridge, WI.
Immaculate Conception Priory of the Canons Regular of Premontre, [I], (WIL), Claymont, DE.
Immaculate Conception Prov. House and Novitiate of the Dominican Sisters, [O], (CHI), Justice, IL.
Immaculate Conception Provincialate, [X], (BO), Newton, MA.
Immaculate Conception Provincialate, [F], (STF), Sloatsburg, NY.
Immaculate Conception Rectory, [M], (HRT). See Missionaries of LaSalette Provincial Secretary.
Immaculate Conception Rectory, [M], (HRT), Waterbury, CT.
Immaculate Conception Regional School, [E], (CAM), Bridgeton, NJ.
Immaculate Conception Regional School, [F], (PAT), Franklin, NJ.
Immaculate Conception School, [D], (ALN), Pen Argyl, PA.
Immaculate Conception School, [C], (GLP), Cuba, NM.
Immaculate Conception School Endowment-Heine Memorial, [N], (OM). See The Omaha Archdiocesan Educational Foundation, Inc.
Immaculate Conception School Foundation, Inc., [I], (SFS), Watertown, SD.
Immaculate Conception Seminary, [A], (NEW), South Orange, NJ.
Immaculate Conception Trust Fund, [L], (LR), Blytheville, AR.
Immaculate Conception-St. Joseph School, [F], (DUB), Gilbertville, IA.
Immaculate Heart Academy, [D], (NEW), Washington Township, NJ.
Immaculate Heart Academy, [C], (TUC), Tucson, AZ.
Immaculate Heart Central High School, [C], (OG), Watertown, NY.
Immaculate Heart Claretian Seminary, [B], (SAT), San Antonio, TX.
Immaculate Heart Convent, [BB], (PH), Philadelphia, PA.
Immaculate Heart Convent, [BB], (PH), Norristown, PA.
Immaculate Heart Elementary School, [D], (ALN), Girardville, PA.
Immaculate Heart High School, [F], (LA), Los Angeles, CA.
Immaculate Heart High School, [B], (TUC), Tucson, AZ.
Immaculate Heart Lodge Convent, [G], (TUC), Tucson, AZ.
Immaculate Heart Monastery of the Poor Clares, [N], (SJ), Los Altos Hills, CA.
Immaculate Heart Novitiate, [EE], (NY). See Sisters of St. John the Baptist.
Immaculate Heart Novititate, [G], (TUC), Tucson, AZ.
Immaculate Heart of Mary Center, Marywood, [O], (SCR), Scranton, PA.
Immaculate Heart of Mary Convent, [I], (HBG), Harrisburg, PA.
Immaculate Heart of Mary Convent, [BB], (PH), Springfield, PA.
Immaculate Heart of Mary Convent, [BB], (PH), Warminster, PA.
Immaculate Heart of Mary Convent, [F], (SCR). See Monsignor McHugh Elementary School.
Immaculate Heart of Mary Convent, [G], (TUC), Somerton, AZ.
Immaculate Heart of Mary Friary, [M], (BAL), Baltimore, MD.
Immaculate Heart of Mary High School, [D], (CHI), Westchester, IL.
Immaculate Heart of Mary Home for Children, Inc., [T], (BUF), Buffalo, NY.
Immaculate Heart of Mary Novitiate, [A], (SFD), Godfrey, IL.
Immaculate Heart of Mary Novitiate-Infirmary, [Z], (BO), Tewksbury, MA.
Immaculate Heart of Mary Nursery, School & Kindergarten, [J], (NEW), Elizabeth, NJ.
Immaculate Heart of Mary Provincial House, [G], (TUC), Tucson, AZ.
Immaculate Heart of Mary Provincial House and Convent, [P], (BUF), Buffalo, NY.
Immaculate Heart of Mary St. Casimir School Mary Goeddeke Educational Trust Fund, [K], (LAN). See Chancery Office.
Immaculate Heart of Mary Seminary, [A], (SFE), Santa Fe, NM.
Immaculate Heart of Mary Seminary, [A], (WIN), Winona, MN.
The Immaculate Heart of Mary Spiritual Renewal Center, [H], (SCR), Cresco, PA.

of Saint Charles.
Italian-American Housing Development Fund Co., Inc. dba Cabrini Acres Senior Apts., [K], (ALB), Watervliet, NY.
Ittawamba Community College Newman Center, [G], (JKS), Amory, MS.
Ivrea Sisters of Charity of the Immaculate Conception, [I], (GBG), Mount Pleasant, PA.
IWHS Fort Worth Health Care Corporation, [H], (SAT). See Incarnate Word Health System.

J

J.K. Mullen High School, Corp., [D], (DEN), Denver, CO.
Jackson Catholic Middle School, [C], (LAN), Jackson, MI.
Jackson School Elementary, [H], (BO), Newton, MA.
Jackson State University Newman Center, [G], (JKS), Jackson, MS.
Jacksonville State University, [H], (BIR), Jacksonville, AL.
Jacksonville Univ. & Univ. of North Florida Catholic Campus Ministry, [L], (STA), Jacksonville, FL.
Jacksonville, Family Housing Management Co., [G], (STA), Jacksonville, FL.
Jail Ministries, [H], (COS), Colorado Springs, CO.
Jail Ministry, [I], (SAG). See Emmaus House.
Jail Ministry, [H], (SY), Syracuse, NY.
Jamestown, [H], (BUF). See The Catholic Charities of the Diocese of Buffalo.
Jamestown College, [I], (FAR), Jamestown, ND.
Jan Beyzym Society, Inc., [N], (CHI). See Sacred Heart Mission House.
Jan Beyzym Society, Inc., [U], (CHI), Chicago, IL.
Janesville District Office, [K], (MAD). See Catholic Charities, Inc.
Jasper Memorial Hospital, [C], (BEA), Jasper, TX.
Jean Francois Rivet High School, [A], (EVN), Vincennes, IN.
Jeanne Chezard De Matel Fund, [H], (VIC), Victoria, TX.
Jeanne d'Arc Convent, [H], (BO), Milton, MA.
Jeanne d'Arc Manor, [J], (SJ), San Jose, CA.
The Jeanne d'Arc Residence, [AA], (NY), New York, NY.
Jeanne Jugan Apartments, [M], (PRO), Pawtucket, RI.
Jeanne Jugan Center, [I], (KC), Kansas City, MO.
Jeanne Jugan Pavilion, [U], (BO), Somerville, MA.
Jeanne Jugan Residence, [U], (BO), Somerville, MA.
Jeanne Jugan Residence, [Z], (NY), Bronx, NY.
Jeanne Jugan Residence, [M], (PRO), Pawtucket, RI.
Jeanne Jugan Residence, [G], (WIL), Newark, DE.
Jeanne Jugan Residence-St. Joseph's Villa, [L], (WDC), Washington, DC.
Jeannette District Memorial Hospital, [F], (GBG), Jeannette, PA.
Jefferson Care Center, [L], (NO), Marrero, LA.
Jefferson County Catholic Community Services, [W], (STL). See Catholic Community Services Administration.
Jefferson County Technical Institute, [I], (STU), Steubenville, OH.
Jefferson House, [Q], (DET). See Capuchin Soup Kitchen.
The Jemez Program, Our Lady of Lourdes Novitiate, [J], (SFE), Jemez Springs, NM.
Jenkins Apartments, Inc., [P], (BAL). See Chancery Office.
Jenkins Housing, Inc., [P], (BAL). See Chancery Office.
Jennings Hall Inc., [N], (CLV), Cleveland, OH.
Jennings Hall, Inc., [V], (CLV). See Catholic Charities Services Corporation.
Jennings Manor Housing Corporation, [AA], (CLV), Garfield Heights, OH.
Jersey City State College, [Q], (NEW), Jersey City, NJ.
Jessie Albert Memorial Dental Center, [E], (PRT). See Catholic Charities Maine.
Jesu Children's Enrichment Centers, [I], (PEO), West Peoria, IL.
Jesuit Center for Spiritual Growth, [N], (ALN), Wernersville, PA.
Jesuit College Preparatory School, [D], (DAL), Dallas, TX.
Jesuit Community, [J], (CHL), Charlotte, NC.
Jesuit Community, [N], (FTW), Granger, IN.
Jesuit Community, [C], (LA). See Loyola Marymount University.
Jesuit Community, [DD], (NY). See Jesuit Provincial's Office.
Jesuit Community, [E], (R), Raleigh, NC.
Jesuit Community, [M], (SEA), Seattle, WA.
Jesuit Community, [B], (SJ). See Santa Clara University.
Jesuit Community - Casa Claver, [F], (SJN), Hato Rey, PR.
The Jesuit Community at Boston College, [W], (BO), Chestnut Hill, MA.
Jesuit Community At Creighton University, [K], (OM), Omaha, NE.
Jesuit Community at Fordham University, [DD], (NY), New York, NY.
The Jesuit Community at Georgetown University, [M], (WDC), Washington, DC.
Jesuit Community at Jesuit School of Theology at Berkeley, [N], (OAK), Berkeley, CA.
Jesuit Community at Loyola University of Chicago, [C], (CHI), Chicago, IL.
Jesuit Community at Marquette University, [P], (MIL), Milwaukee, WI.
Jesuit Community at St. Camillus, [P], (MIL), Wauwatosa, WI.
Jesuit Community at St. Ignatius College Preparatory, [N], (SFR), San Francisco, CA.
Jesuit Community at St. Joseph's University, [AA], (PH), Philadelphia, PA.
Jesuit Community at St. Xavier High School, [M], (CIN), Cincinnati, OH.
Jesuit Community at the University of Detroit, [K], (DET), Detroit, MI.
Jesuit Community at University of San Francisco, [N], (SFR), San Francisco, CA.
Jesuit Community at Xavier Unversity, [M], (CIN), Cincinnati, OH.
Jesuit Community Corporation at St. Louis University - Jesuit Hall, [P], (STL), St. Louis, MO.
Jesuit Community of Holy Rosary Mission, [B], (RC), Pine Ridge, SD.
Jesuit Community of Loyola College, Inc., [B], (BAL). See Loyola College.
Jesuit Community of Loyola College, Inc., [M], (BAL), Baltimore, MD.
Jesuit Community of Pittsburgh, [S], (PIT), Pittsburgh, PA.
Jesuit Community of the Vatican Observatory, [F], (TUC), Tucson, AZ.
Jesuit Conference, Inc., [V], (WDC), Washington, DC.
Jesuit Development & Communications Office, [Q], (P), Portland, OR.
Jesuit Development Office, [V], (CIN), Cincinnati, OH.
Jesuit Educational Association of Maryland, Inc., [Q], (BAL), Baltimore, MD.
The Jesuit Educational Center for Human Development, [V], (WDC), Washington, DC.
Jesuit Fathers and Brothers, [H], (AUS), Temple, TX.
Jesuit Fathers and Brothers Maryland Provincial Curia, [M], (BAL), Baltimore, MD.
Jesuit Fathers House, [H], (HON), Honolulu, HI.
Jesuit Fathers of the Province of the Antilles, Inc., [J], (MIA). See John Paul II Retreat House.
Jesuit Health Trust, [P], (NO). See Jesuit Provincial Office.
Jesuit High School, [F], (NO), New Orleans, LA.
Jesuit High School, [H], (NO), New Orleans, LA.
Jesuit High School, [D], (P), Portland, OR.
Jesuit High School, [C], (SAC), Sacramento, CA.
Jesuit High School, [C], (SP), Tampa, FL.
Jesuit High School Community of Sacramento, [G], (SAC), Carmichael, CA.
Jesuit House, [G], (ANC), Anchorage, AK.
Jesuit House, [C], (CI), Kolonia, Pohnpei, FM.
*Jesuit House of Prayer, [M], (CHL), Hot Springs, NC.
Jesuit House, Seattle, [M], (SEA), Seattle, WA.
Jesuit Institute for Family Life, [P], (SJ), Los Altos, CA.
Jesuit International Missions, [T], (DET). See Jesuit Seminary Association.
Jesuit International Missions, Inc., [X], (CHI), Chicago, IL.
Jesuit Jamshedpur Mission Society, Inc., [Q], (BAL), Baltimore, MD.
Jesuit Lithuanian Center, [D], (LIT), Chicago, IL.
The Jesuit Middle School of Omaha, [F], (OM), Omaha, NE.
Jesuit Mission Bureau, Maryland Province, Inc., [Q], (BAL), Baltimore, MD.
Jesuit Missions, Inc., [V], (WDC), Washington, DC.
Jesuit Novitiate, [C], (SJN), Rio Piedras, PR.
Jesuit Novitiate, [B], (STP), St. Paul, MN.
Jesuit Novitiate of St. Francis Xavier, [A], (P), Portland, OR.
The Jesuit Partnership, [Y], (MIL), Milwaukee, WI.
Jesuit Program for Living and Learning of New Orleans, Inc., [S], (NO), New Orleans, LA.
Jesuit Provincial Office, [P], (NO), New Orleans, LA.
Jesuit Provincial Office (Society of Jesus, Oregon Prov.), [L], (P), Portland, OR.
Jesuit Provincial Office, Wisconsin Province, [P], (MIL), Milwaukee, WI.
Jesuit Provincial Office-Detroit Province of the Society of Jesus, [K], (DET), Detroit, MI.
Jesuit Provincial's Office, [DD], (NY), New York, NY.
Jesuit Refugee Service, [V], (WDC), Washington, DC.
Jesuit Residence, [G], (ANC), Anchorage, AK.
Jesuit Residence, [C], (FBK), Fairbanks, AK.
Jesuit Residence, [DD], (NY). See Xavier Jesuit Community.
Jesuit Residence, Robert Southwell House, [E], (R), Chapel Hill, NC.
Jesuit Retreat House, [U], (CLV), Cleveland, OH.
Jesuit Retreat House, [M], (GB), Oshkosh, WI.
Jesuit Retreat House, [L], (SJ), Los Altos, CA.
Jesuit Retreat House, [Q], (STP), Lake Elmo, MN.
Jesuit Retreat House for Priests, Religious and Lay People, [O], (ALB), Auriesville, NY.
The Jesuit School of Theology at Berkeley, [A], (OAK), Berkeley, CA.
Jesuit Secondary Education Association, [V], (WDC), Washington, DC.
Jesuit Seminary and Mission Bureau, Inc., [HH], (NY), New York, NY.
Jesuit Seminary and Mission Fund, [S], (NO), New Orleans, LA.
Jesuit Seminary Association, [T], (DET), Detroit, MI.
Jesuit Seminary Guild, Maryland Province, Inc., [Q], (BAL), Baltimore, MD.
Jesuit Social Ministries-National Office, [V], (WDC), Washington, DC.
Jesuit Spirituality Center, [J], (LAF), Grand Coteau, LA.
The Jesuit Spirituality Center, [N], (P), Portland, OR.
Jesuit Urban Center & Immaculate Conception Community, [W], (BO), Boston, MA.
Jesuit Volunteer Corps Southwest, [P], (OAK), Berkeley, CA.
Jesuit Volunteer Corps. Midwest, Inc., [T], (DET), Detroit, MI.
*Jesuit Volunteer Corps: Northwest, [Q], (P), Portland, OR.
Jesuit Volunteer Corps: South, [U], (GAL), Houston, TX.
Jesuit Volunteers: International, [V], (WDC), Washington, DC.
Jesuits, [H], (ORG), Laguna Niguel, CA.
Jesuits, [H], (ORG), Orange, CA.
Jesuits at LeMoyne, Inc., [S], (SY), Syracuse, NY.
Jesuits of Holy Cross College, Inc., [N], (WOR), Worcester, MA.
Jesuits of Saint Peter's College, Inc., [N], (NEW), Jersey City, NJ.
The Jesuits of the Missouri Province, [P], (STL), St. Louis, MO.
The Jesuits of the Missouri Province, [W], (STL), St. Louis, MO.
Jesus and Mary Mission Center, [X], (BO), Plainville, MA.
Jesus Redeemer Convent, [P], (PIT), Pittsburgh, PA.
The Jesus School, [N], (MET), Lambertville, NJ.
Joan Ann Kennedy Memorial Preschool, [D], (NY). See Department of Education.
Joan Kroc Homeless Center, [J], (SD). See St. Vincent de Paul Management Inc.
Joan of Arc Residence, [J], (SD), San Diego, CA.
Jogues Retreat, [DD], (NY), Cornwall, NY.
John A. Coleman Catholic High School, [E], (NY), Hurley, NY.
John Cardinal Wright Vocation and Prayer Center, [Q], (PIT), Gibsonia, PA.
John Carroll Catholic Education Foundation, Inc., [I], (BIR), Birmingham, AL.
John Carroll Foundation of the Roman Catholic Archdiocese of Baltimore, [P], (BAL). See Chancery Office.
John Carroll High School, [A], (BIR), Birmingham, AL.
John Carroll High School, [B], (PMB), Fort Pierce, FL.
John Carroll Jesuit Community, [C], (CLV), Cleveland, OH.
The John Carroll School, [C], (BAL), Bel Air, MD.
The John Carroll Society, [V], (WDC), Washington, DC.
John Carroll University, [C], (CLV), Cleveland, OH.
John Courtney Murray Newman Center, [S], (DET), Port Huron, MI.
John F. Kennedy Catholic High School, [E], (STL), Manchester, MO.
John F. Kennedy High School, [E], (NY), Somers, NY.
John F. Kennedy High School, [C], (Y), Warren, OH.
John F. Kennedy Memorial High School, [B], (SEA), Seattle, WA.
John Flynn Family Endowment Trust, [N], (OM). See The Omaha Archdiocesan Educational Foundation, Inc.
John Gazzola Trust Estate, [L], (LR), Little Rock, AR.
John Ireland Schools, [H], (STP), Hopkins, MN.
John LaFarge Institute, The, [HH], (NY), New York, NY.
John Lewis Coffee Shop/Miriam House, [K], (DAV), Davenport, IA.
John Neumann Catholic School (Administration & Middle School), [J], (PBL), Pueblo, CO.
John Neumann Catholic Schools, [C], (PBL), Pueblo, CO.
John of the Cross Monastery Hermitage, [K], (PRT), Orland, ME.
John Paul Apartments, [H], (SCL), Cold Spring, MN.
John Paul II Catholic School, [G], (GAL), Houston, TX.
John Paul II Center for Special Learning, [E], (ALN), West Reading, PA.

K

L

Visitation Hospitality House of San Antonio, Texas and La Posada Transitional Housing.
La Providencia Spiritual Renewal Center, [K], (SD), Alpine, CA.
La Reina High School, [F], (LA), Thousand Oaks, CA.
La Roche College, [B], (PIT), Pittsburgh, PA.
La Salette Center for Christian Living, [L], (FR), Attleboro, MA.
La Salette Community, [M], (WDC), Washington, DC.
La Salette Fathers, [P], (MIL), Milwaukee, WI.
La Salette Ministries Development Center, [P], (STL). See La Salette Missionaries.
La Salette Missionaries, [P], (STL), St. Louis, MO.
La Salette Missionaries Shrine, [P], (MIL), Twin Lakes, WI.
La Salette Missionary Association, [J], (FR), Attleboro, MA.
La Salette Provincial House, [J], (FR), Attleboro, MA.
La Salette Shrine, [J], (FR), Attleboro, MA.
La Salette Shrine and Center of Enfield, [M], (MAN), Enfield, NH.
La Salette Shrine and Seminary, [A], (ALB), Altamont, NY.
La Salette Spirituality Center, [P], (STL). See La Salette Missionaries.
La Salle Academy, [F], (NY), New York, NY.
La Salle Academy, [E], (PRO), Providence, RI.
La Salle Academy, [F], (SCR), Jessup, PA.
La Salle Academy and Early Childhood Center, [D], (ALN), Shillington, PA.
La Salle Catholic School, [E], (PEO), La Salle, IL.
La Salle High School, [F], (LA), Pasadena, CA.
La Salle High School, [C], (MIA), Miami, FL.
La Salle High School, Yakima, Inc., [H], (YAK), Yakima, WA.
La Salle House, [J], (JOL), Romeoville, IL.
La Salle Institute, [T], (STL), Glencoe, MO.
La Salle Manor Christian Brothers Retreat House, [L], (JOL), Plano, IL.
La Salle Provincialate Inc., [M], (TR), Lincroft, NJ.
The La Salle School Foundation of Albany, [G], (ALB). See LaSalle School, Inc.
La Salle Warren, Inc., [E], (DET), Warren, MI.
La Storta Jesuit Community, [N], (STP), Minneapolis, MN.
La Verna Heights Provincial House, [K], (KC), Savannah, MO.
La Verna Heights Retirement Center, Inc., [I], (KC), Savannah, MO.
La Verna Village Apartments, [I], (KC), Savannah, MO.
La Verna Village Nursing Home, [I], (KC), Savannah, MO.
La'ialoha Community, [I], (HON). See Sisters of St. Joseph of Carondelet CSJ, Hawaii Vice-Province.
LAAR House, [F], (LC). See St. Francis Community Programs, Inc.
The Laboure Center/Catholic Charities, [M], (BO), Boston, MA.
The Laboure Center/Catholic Charities, [S], (BO), Boston, MA.
Laboure College, Inc., [I], (BO), Boston, MA.
Laboure Complex Foundation, [G], (MOB), Montgomery, AL.
Lackawanna Family Counseling Center, [H], (BUF). See The Catholic Charities of the Diocese of Buffalo.
Lacordaire Academy, Secondary Division, [C], (NEW), Upper Montclair, NJ.
Lacordaire Academy-Elementary Division, [E], (NEW), Upper Montclair, NJ.
Ladies of Bethany, [P], (PIT), Pittsburgh, PA.
Ladies of Charity, [N], (AUS), Austin, TX.
Ladies of Charity, [Q], (BAL), Baltimore, MD.
Ladies of Charity, [H], (BUF). See The Catholic Charities of the Diocese of Buffalo.
Ladies of Charity, [K], (GBG), Smock, PA.
Ladies of Charity, [K], (KNX), Knoxville, TN.
Ladies of Charity, [K], (KNX), Chattanooga, TN.
Ladies of Charity, [L], (MOB), Prichard, AL.
Ladies of Charity, [L], (MOB), Mobile, AL.
Ladies of Charity, [FF], (PH), Philadelphia, PA.
Ladies of Charity, [W], (SY), Binghamton, NY.
Ladies of Charity Center, Inc., [L], (NSH), Nashville, TN.
Ladies of Charity of Dallas, [P], (DAL), Dallas, TX.
Ladies of Charity of El Carmen, [T], (SAT), San Antonio, TX.
Ladies of Charity of Keokuk, [P], (DAV), Keokuk, IA.
Ladies of Charity of Memphis, [M], (MEM), Memphis, TN.
Ladies of Charity of Metropolitan Kansas City, [O], (KC), Kansas City, MO.
Ladies of Charity of Sacred Heart Church, [I], (CHR), Charleston, SC.
Ladies of Charity of St. Catherine Laboure, [W], (STL), St. Louis, MO.
Ladies of Charity of St. Vincent de Paul Oakland County Associaton, [T], (DET), Bloomfield Hills, MI.
Ladies of Charity of St. Vincent de Paul Parish, [W], (STL), Perryville, MO.
Ladies of Charity of St. Vincent-Guardian Angel, [W], (STL), St. Louis, MO.
The Ladies of Charity of the Catholic Charities of the Archdiocese of New York, [I], (NY). See The Catholic Charities of the Archdiocese of New York.
Ladies of Charity of the United States of America, [W], (STL), St. Louis, MO.
Ladies of Charity Welfare Agency, Inc., [L], (NSH), Nashville, TN.
Ladycliff College Alumnae Association, [HH], (NY), Tarrytown, NY.
Ladycliff College Alumnae Association, Inc., [HH], (NY), Highland Falls, NY.
Ladyfield School, [E], (TOL), Toledo, OH.
Ladywood High School, [E], (DET), Livonia, MI.
*LaFarge Lifelong Learning Institute, Inc., [Y], (MIL), Milwaukee, WI.
The Lafayette - Redeemer, [FF], (PH). See Holy Redeemer Health System, Inc.
Lafayette Catholic Service Centers, Inc., [N], (LAF), Lafayette, LA.
Lafayette Grand Hospital, [K], (STL), St. Louis, MO.
The Lafayette Redeemer, [Y], (PH). See Redeemer Long Term Care & Elder Services.
Lafon Child Development Center, [J], (NO), New Orleans, LA.
Lafon Nursing Home of the Holy Family, [N], (NO), New Orleans, LA.
Lake Catholic High, [D], (CLV), Mentor, OH.
Lake County Services, [G], (CHI). See Catholic Charities of the Archdiocese of Chicago-Archdiocesan Offices.
Lake Michigan Catholic Junior High and High School, [A], (KAL), St. Joseph, MI.
Lake Michigan Catholic Schools, [B], (KAL), St. Joseph, MI.
Lake St. Joseph Center, [O], (L), Crestwood, KY.
Lake Shore Catholic Academy, [X], (CHI), Waukegan, IL.
Lake Superior State University, Newman Center, [G], (MAR), Sault Sainte Marie, MI.
Lake Vineyard Camps, Inc., (Camp de Sales), [L], (LAN), Brooklyn, MI.
Lakemary Center, Inc., [K], (KCK), Paola, KS.
Lakeshore Health System Incorporated (the "Corporation"), [O], (GRY), East Chicago, IN.
Lakewood, [F], (CHL). See Holy Angels, Inc.
Lakewood Care Center, [C], (CR). See Lakewood Health Centers.
Lakewood Health Centers, [C], (CR), Baudette, MN.
Lakewoods Apartments, [E], (SUP). See Catholic Charities Bureau, Inc.
Lamar University-Catholic Student Center, [E], (BEA), Beaumont, TX.
LAMP Ministries, Inc., [HH], (NY), New York, NY.
Lancaster Catholic High School, [A], (HBG), Lancaster, PA.
Lancaster In-Home Intensive Services, [E], (HBG). See Department for Catholic Charities Counseling/Field Services.
Lancaster Office, [E], (HBG). See Department for Catholic Charities Counseling/Field Services.
Lander College Newman Center, [G], (CHR), Greenwood, SC.
Langlade Memorial Hospital, [F], (GB), Antigo, WI.
Lansdale Catholic High School, [F], (PH), Lansdale, PA.
Lansing Catholic Central High School, [B], (LAN), Lansing, MI.
Lansing School of Religion, [E], (DUB), Lansing, IA.
Lanteri House, [H], (MET), Asbury, NJ.
LaPaz Community Inc., [F], (SCL), St. Cloud, MN.
LaRisa Apartments Marianist Community, [M], (SAT), San Antonio, TX.
Las Casas Dominican Ministry Among the Cheyenne and Arapaho, [L], (OKL), Canton, OK.
Las Hermanas U.S.A., [T], (SAT), San Antonio, TX.
LaSalette Missionaries, [M], (PEO), Georgetown, IL.
LaSalette Retreat House at Newman Hall, [Y], (BO), Ipswich, MA.
Lasallain Educational Opportunities, Inc., [S], (OAK), Emeryville, CA.
LaSalle Academy, [U], (PRO). See Miscellaneous Listings for the Diocese of Providence.
LaSalle Albany, Inc., [T], (ALB), Albany, NY.
LaSalle Center, [M], (GB), Menasha, WI.
LaSalle College High School, [G], (PH), Wyndmoor, PA.
LaSalle High School, [E], (CIN), Cincinnati, OH.
LaSalle High School, [D], (P), Milwaukie, OR.
LaSalle High School Center, [D], (DUB). See Xavier High School dba Regis High School and LaSalle High School Center.
LaSalle Institute, [D], (ALB), Troy, NY.
LaSalle Lincroft, Inc., [M], (TR). See Christian Brothers, St. La Salle Auxiliary.
LaSalle New York City, Inc., [HH], (NY), New York, NY.
LaSalle School, Inc., [G], (ALB), Albany, NY.
Lasalle Syracuse, Inc., [W], (SY), Syracuse, NY.
LaSalle University, [C], (PH), Philadelphia, PA.
LaSalle, A Global Learning Community, [D], (RVC), Oakdale, NY.
Lasallian Education Corporation, [M], (SR). See De La Salle Institute/Provincial Office.
Lassen Community Hospital, [F], (SAC), Susanville, CA.
Latin America Fund, [J], (LIN). See Chancery.
Latino Catholic Pastoral Center, [T], (DET), Detroit, MI.
Latvian Roman Catholic Mission, [Y], (BRK), Brooklyn, NY.
The Laura, [Q], (L), Lebanon, KY.
Laura's House, [B], (STO). See The Catholic Charities of the Diocese of Stockton.
Laurel Lake Retirement Community, [AA], (CLV). See CHP - Humility of Mary Health Partners.
*Laurel Lake Retirement Community, Inc., [AA], (CLV), Hudson, OH.
Lavelle School for the Blind, [S], (NY), New York, NY.
LaVerna Terrace Apartments, [H], (FTW), Avilla, IN.
Lawrence University Newman Center, [N], (GB). See University of Wisconsin G.B. Ecumenical Center.
Lay Employees Pension Plan, [J], (STU), Steubenville, OH.
Lay Mission Program, [M], (WDC). See Society of African Missions (S.M.A.).
Lay Missionaries of the Passion (Passionist Secular Institute), [R], (SCR), Nanticoke, PA.
Lay Pastoral Ministry Program, [A], (CIN). See The Athenaeum of Ohio.
Lay Women's Association, [V], (WDC), Bethesda, MD.
Lazarist Trust Fund, [W], (STL), Earth City, MO.
Le Mans Academy, [D], (GRY), Rolling Prairie, IN.
Le Moyne College, [B], (SY), Syracuse, NY.
Leadership Association of Religious Congregation (LARC), [J], (HON), Honolulu, HI.
Leadership Conference of Women Religious in the U.S.A., [V], (WDC), Silver Spring, MD.
Leadership Conference of Women Religious Region 8, [N], (SFD), Springfield, IL.
League of Catholic Women of the Archdiocese of Boston, [FF], (BO), Boston, MA.
Leaven International Corporation, [M], (WCH), Wichita, KS.
Lebanon Family FOCUS, [E], (HBG). See Department for Catholic Charities Counseling/Field Services.
Lebanon Office, [E], (HBG). See Department for Catholic Charities Counseling/Field Services.
Lebh Shomea House of Prayer, [G], (CC), Sarita, TX.
Lebh Shomea, House of Prayer, [I], (CC), Sarita, TX.
The LeBlond Housing Corporation, [V], (CLV). See Catholic Charities Services Corporation.
Lee Memorial Hospital, [D], (KAL), Dowagiac, MI.
Legacies, The Foundation of St. Joseph's Mercy Hospital, [J], (DAV). See St. Joseph's Mercy Hospital.
Legacy of Catholic Learning Endowment Program, [K], (COL). See The Foundation of the Catholic Diocese of Columbus.
Legal Advocacy Program, [B], (STO). See The Catholic Charities of the Diocese of Stockton.
The Legion of Christ (RI) Incorporated, [U], (PRO), South Kingstown, RI.
Legion of Christ, Inc., [M], (ATL), Dunwoody, GA.
The Legion of Christ, Inc., [T], (DET), Bloomfield Hills, MI.
Legion of Christ, Inc., [V], (HRT), Orange, CT.
Legion of Christ, Inc., [I], (MAD), Edgerton, WI.
Legion of Christ, Incorporated, [HH], (NY), Rye, NY.
Legion of Mary, [Q], (BAL), Baltimore, MD.
Legion of Mary, [V], (CIN), Cincinnati, OH.
Legion of Mary, [W], (MIL), Horicon, WI.
Legion of Mary, [L], (NSH), Hendersonville, TN.
Legion of Mary, [L], (ROC), Spencerport, NY.
Legion of Mary, [N], (SFD), Springfield, IL.
Legion of Mary, [U], (SFR), San Francisco, CA.
Legion of Mary, [B], (STV). See Miscellaneous Organizations.
Legion of Mary, Office, [HH], (NY), New York, NY.
Legionaries of Christ, [M], (DAL), Irving, TX.
Legionaries of Christ, [M], (HRT), Cheshire, CT.
Legionaries of Christ, [R], (LA), Pasadena, CA.
Legionaries of Christ, [DD], (NY), Rye, NY.
Legionaries of Christ, [M], (WDC), Potomac, MD.
Legiondaries of Christ, [I], (ATL), Dunwoody, GA.
Lehman High School, [E], (CIN), Sidney, OH.
Leland Avenue Project, [Q], (SFR). See Catholic Charities of the Archdiocese of San Francisco.
LeMoyne College Newman Center, [V], (SY), Syracuse, NY.
Leo Brown Jesuit Community, [P], (STL), St. Louis, MO.
Leo High School, [D], (CHI), Chicago, IL.
Leo House, [AA], (NY), New York, NY.
Leo XIII Society, [T], (DET), Dearborn, MI.
Leonard Neale House, [M], (WDC), Washington, DC.
Leonora Hall, [S], (CLV), Akron, OH.
Leonora Hall, [V], (CLV), Akron, OH.
Leprosy Relief Society, [T], (DET), Detroit, MI.
Leslie Day Care Center, [J], (NO), New Orleans, LA.
Leviticus 25:23 Alternative Fund, Inc., [HH], (NY), Yonkers, NY.

Lewis and Clark District Council of St. Vincent de Paul, [G], (B), Clarkston, WA.
Lewis and Clark District Council of St. Vincent de Paul, [H], (SPK), Clarkston, WA.
Lewis and Clark Junior College Newman Center, [M], (SFD), Godfrey, IL.
Lewis and Clark State College, [F], (B), Lewiston, ID.
Lewis University, [A], (JOL), Romeoville, IL.
Lexington Catholic High School, [A], (LEX), Lexington, KY.
Lial Elementary School, [E], (TOL), Whitehouse, OH.
Lial Residence, Sisters of Notre Dame, [L], (TOL), Whitehouse, OH.
Libermann House, [H], (MET), Metuchen, NJ.
Libertas Treatment Center for Chemically Dependent, [F], (GB), Green Bay, WI.
Libertas-L.E. Phillips Treatment Center for the Chemically Dependent, [F], (LC), Chippewa Falls, WI.
*Liberty Medical Center, Inc., [H], (BAL). See Bon Secours Baltimore Health Corporation, Inc.
Lieut. Joseph P. Kennedy, Jr. Memorial Community Center, [CC], (NY), New York, NY.
Lt. Joseph P. Kennedy Jr. School, Palos Hills, [L], (CHI). See St. Coletta's of Illinois.
Lt. Joseph P. Kennedy, Jr., Institute, [G], (WDC), Washington, DC.
Lt. Joseph P. Kennedy, Jr., Memorial School, [H], (BO), Boston, MA.
LIFE, [F], (ROC). See St. Joseph's Villa of Rochester.
Life America, Inc., [L], (BR), Baton Rouge, LA.
Life Choices Vocational Program, [F], (CHL). See Holy Angels, Inc.
Life Experience and Faith Sharing Association, [CC], (NY), New York, NY.
Life in the Spirit Community, Inc., [J], (DM), Des Moines, IA.
Life Resources, Inc., [O], (BO), Boston, MA.
Life Resources/Alpha-Omega, [O], (BO), Littleton, MA.
Lifeline, [H], (PRT). See Sisters of Charity Health System, Inc.
Life-Line, [H], (WOR). See Catholic Charities.
Light of Christ Preschool, [F], (SP), Clearwater, FL.
Light of Hearts Villa, Inc., [N], (CLV), Bedford, OH.
Liguori Mission House/Redemptorists, [P], (STL), Liguori, MO.
Lima Central Catholic Educational Foundation, [O], (TOL), Lima, OH.
Limestone College Newman Center, [G], (CHR), Gaffney, SC.
Lincoln Hall, [T], (NY), Lincolndale, NY.
Lincoln Junior College Newman Center, [G], (JKS), Brookhaven, MS.
Lincoln University, [EE], (PH). See Newman Apostolate.
Lincoln University-Newman Center, [F], (JC), Jefferson City, MO.
Linda Vista Catholic School, [G], (STL), Chesterfield, MO.
The Linden House of Hobart, Inc., [F], (GRY). See St. Mary Medical Center.
Lindenwood Retreat, [M], (FTW), Donaldson, IN.
Lindenwood, Retreat & Conference Center, [K], (FTW). See Convent Ancilla Domini.
Link Community School, Inc., [E], (NEW), Newark, NJ.
Linton Hall, [F], (ARL), Bristow, VA.
Linus Oakes, Inc., [J], (P). See Mercy Medical Center, Inc.
Linwood Spiritual Center, [EE], (NY), Rhinebeck, NY.
Lisieux Pastoral Center, [M], (JOL), Kankakee, IL.
"The Listening Place", [W], (BO). See Franciscan Community (Province of Immaculate Conception).
Literacy Volunteers, [H], (WOR). See Catholic Charities.
Lithuanian American Jesuits, [N], (CHI), Chicago, IL.
Lithuanian Cultural Institution, [D], (LIT), Chicago, IL.
Lithuanian Youth Center, [N], (CHI). See Lithuanian American Jesuits.
Little Angel Day Care, [D], (LR), Little Rock, AR.
Little Angels Child Development Center, [F], (CHL). See Holy Angels, Inc.
Little Brothers of St. Francis, [W], (BO), Boston, MA.
Little Brothers of the Good Shepherd, [J], (SFE), Albuquerque, NM.
The Little Brothers of the Good Shepherd, B.G.S., [W], (LA), Los Angeles, CA.
Little Brothers of the Good Shepherd, Inc. of Illinois, [M], (JOL), Momence, IL.
Little Brothers of the Gospel, [U], (BRK), Brooklyn, NY.
Little Children's Aid, Junior Auxiliary, [Q], (SFR). See Catholic Charities of the Archdiocese of San Francisco.
Little Company of Mary Affiliated Services, Inc., [J], (CHI). See Little Company of Mary Hospital and Health Care Centers.
Little Company of Mary Auxiliary, [J], (CHI). See Little Company of Mary Hospital and Health Care Centers.
Little Company of Mary Convent, [S], (LA), Torrance, CA.
Little Company of Mary Health Services, [K], (LA), Torrance, CA.
Little Company of Mary Hospital, [K], (LA). See Little Company of Mary Health Services.
Little Company of Mary Hospital and Health Care Centers, [J], (CHI), Evergreen Park, IL.
Little Company of Mary Hospital and Health Care Centers, [X], (CHI), Evergreen Park, IL.
Little Company of Mary Hospital Foundation, [J], (CHI). See Little Company of Mary Hospital and Health Care Centers.
Little Flower Catholic High School for Girls, [D], (PH), Philadelphia, PA.
Little Flower Children's Services, [O], (BRK), Brooklyn, NY.
Little Flower Children's Services of New York, [G], (RVC), Wading River, NY.
Little Flower Clinic for the Poor, [K], (LR). See Brothers and Sisters of Charity at Little Portion Hermitage.
Little Flower Convent (S.M.), [E], (RNO), Reno, NV.
Little Flower Day Care, [F], (GF), Billings, MT.
Little Flower Development Center, [K], (P). See Maryville Nursing Home.
Little Flower Haven, [G], (SD), La Mesa, CA.
Little Flower Manor, [Y], (PH), Darby, PA.
Little Flower Manor of the Diocese of Scranton, [L], (SCR), Wilkes-Barre, PA.
Little Flower Missionary House, [P], (LA), Los Angeles, CA.
Little Flower of Jesus School Foundation, Inc., [I], (SFS), Sioux Falls, SD.
Little Flower School, [J], (BIS). See Minot Catholic Schools Corporation.
Little Franciscan Family, [L], (NOR), Cromwell, CT.
Little Franciscans of Mary, [O], (WOR), Worcester, MA.
Little Franciscans of Mary, [O], (WOR), Worcester, MA.
Little House, [A], (CHK), Saipan, MP.
Little Missionary Sisters of Charity, Immaculate Conception Convent, [X], (BO), East Boston, MA.
Little Nazareth Early Childhood Center, [F], (SP), Clearwater, FL.
Little Portion Franciscans, [F], (SPC), Republic, MO.
Little Portion Retreat and Training Center at More Mt., [K], (LR), Eureka Springs, AR.
Little Portion Retreat Center, [G], (SPC), Republic, MO.
Little Saints Preschool, [D], (ALN), Pottsville, PA.
Little Servant Sisters of the Immaculate Conception, [N], (CAM), Cherry Hill, NJ.
Little Servant Sisters of the Immaculate Conception (L.S.I.C.), [O], (NEW), Elizabeth, NJ.
Little Servants of the Holy Family of Seoul, [BB], (PH), Philadelphia, PA.
Little Sisters of Jesus, [G], (ALT), Gallitzin, PA.
Little Sisters of Jesus, [O], (CHI), Chicago, IL.
Little Sisters of Jesus, [D], (FBK), Nome, AK.
Little Sisters of Jesus, [O], (WDC), Washington, DC.
Little Sisters of Jesus-Regional Residence, [N], (BAL), Baltimore, MD.
Little Sisters of the Assumption, [EE], (NY), New York, NY.
Little Sisters of the Assumption, [EE], (NY), Walden, NY.
Little Sisters of the Assumption, [BB], (PH), Philadelphia, PA.
Little Sisters of the Assumption (L.S.A.), [BB], (PH), Overbrook, PA.
Little Sisters of the Assumption Convent, [X], (BO), Boston, MA.
Little Sisters of the Assumption of Woonsocket, [U], (PRO). See Miscellaneous Listings for the Diocese of Providence.
Little Sisters of the Assumption, Family Health Service, Inc., [S], (BO), Dorchester, MA.
Little Sisters of the Assumption, Pernet Family Health Service, Inc., [O], (WOR), Worcester, MA.
Little Sisters of the Poor, [V], (BRK), Queens Village, NY.
Little Sisters of the Poor, [J], (DET), Allen Park, MI.
Little Sisters of the Poor, [N], (HRT), Enfield, CT.
Little Sisters of the Poor, [Q], (LA), San Pedro, CA.
Little Sisters of the Poor, [S], (LA), San Pedro, CA.
Little Sisters of the Poor, [BB], (PH), Philadelphia, PA.
Little Sisters of the Poor, [O], (WDC), Washington, DC.
Little Sisters of the Poor Center for the Aging, [M], (CHI), Chicago, IL.
Little Sisters of the Poor, Home for the Aged, [O], (STL), St. Louis, MO.
Little Sisters of the Poor, Home For the Aged, Inc., [F], (MOB), Mobile, AL.
Little Sisters of the Poor, L.S.P., [Q], (NO), New Orleans, LA.
Little Sisters of the Poor, The, [O], (CHI), Chicago, IL.
Little Sisters of the Poor-Provincial Residence, [N], (BAL), Baltimore, MD.
Little Workers of the Sacred Hearts, [BB], (PH), Philadelphia, PA.
Liturgical Fabric Arts, [R], (STL). See School Sisters of Notre Dame.
Livermore, [H], (OAK). See Catholic Charities of the Diocese of Oakland, Inc.
Living His Life Abundantly, [Q], (SP). See Our Lady of Divine Providence, House of Prayer, Inc.
Living Monuments of Reparation, [V], (CIN), Cincinnati, OH.
Living Waters Catholic Reflection Center, [N], (CHL), Maggie Valley, NC.
Living Waters Convent, [K], (CHL), Maggie Valley, NC.
*Living Waters International, Inc., [O], (GB), Deerbrook, WI.
Livingston County Catholic Social Services, [D], (LAN), Brighton, MI.
Loaves and Fishes, [N], (FWT), Fort Worth, TX.
*Loaves & Fishes, [O], (SAC), Sacramento, CA.
Loaves & Fishes Dining Room, [O], (SAC). See Loaves & Fishes.
Lock Haven University (Lock Haven), [H], (ALT). See Campus Ministry.
Logos, Inc., [V], (HRT), Cheshire, CT.
Logos, Inc. (Michigan), [T], (DET), Bloomfield Hills, MI.
London, Marymount dba Marymount Medical Center, [D], (LEX), London, KY.
Long Beach Catholic Regional School, [E], (RVC), Long Beach, NY.
Long Island City Senior House, [L], (BRK). See Catholic Charities.
Long Term Care Ombudsman Program, [F], (SJ). See Catholic Charities of Santa Clara County.
Long Term Care Ombudsman Program, [B], (STO). See The Catholic Charities of the Diocese of Stockton.
Long Term Care Ombudsman Program, [B], (STO). See The Catholic Charities of the Diocese of Stockton.
*Longview Catholic School Endowment Fund, [E], (TYL), Longview, TX.
Lonsdale, New Market, Veseli Area Catholic School, [H], (STP), Lonsdale, MN.
Lorain Catholic High School, [D], (CLV), Lorain, OH.
Lorain Community/St. Joseph Regional Health Center, [J], (CLV), Lorain, OH.
Lorain District Council, [V], (CLV). See Society of St. Vincent de Paul, Diocesan Central Council.
Loras College, [C], (DUB), Dubuque, IA.
Loreto House, [G], (SPR). See Providence Ministries for the Needy, Inc.
Loretta Young Auxiliary, [P], (LA). See St. Anne's.
Loretto, [P], (SY), Syracuse, NY.
Loretto Academy, [D], (ELP), El Paso, TX.
Loretto Academy Middle School, [E], (ELP), El Paso, TX.
Loretto Apartments Housing Development Fund Co., Inc., [W], (SY), Syracuse, NY.
Loretto Center, [N], (DEN), Littleton, CO.
Loretto Center, [R], (STL), St. Louis, MO.
Loretto Conference Center, [K], (JOL). See Loretto Convent, Religious of the Institute of the Blessed Virgin Mary.
Loretto Convent, [K], (FTW). See Saint Mary's of the Immaculate Conception.
Loretto Convent, [Q], (MIL), Mount Calvary, WI.
Loretto Convent, [G], (TUC), Douglas, AZ.
Loretto Convent, Religious of the Institute of the Blessed Virgin Mary, [K], (JOL), Wheaton, IL.
Loretto Elementary School-Loretto Academy, [E], (ELP), El Paso, TX.
Loretto Geriatric Community Residences, Inc., [P], (SY), Syracuse, NY.
Loretto High School, [C], (SAC), Sacramento, CA.
Loretto Home for Aged, [D], (BUR), Rutland, VT.
Loretto House of Prayer, [J], (STA), Jacksonville, FL.
Loretto Rest, Inc., [P], (SY), Syracuse, NY.
Los Amigos del Peru, Inc., [O], (GB), De Pere, WI.
The Los Angeles Orphan Asylum, [I], (LA). See Maryvale.
Los Angeles Orphanage Guild, [I], (LA). See Maryvale.
LOSS (Loving Outreach to Survivors of Suicide), [G], (CHI). See Catholic Charities of the Archdiocese of Chicago-Archdiocesan Offices.
Louise Day Care Center, [J], (NO), New Orleans, LA.
Louisiana State University at Alexandria, [J], (ALX), Alexandria, LA.
Louisville High School, [F], (LA), Woodland Hills, CA.
Lourdes Alzheimers Special Care Center, [Q], (DET), Waterford, MI.
Lourdes Ancillary Services, Inc., [H], (CAM). See Our Lady of Lourdes Medical Center, Inc.
Lourdes Bureau, [FF], (BO), Boston, MA.
Lourdes Camp, [M], (SY), Syracuse, NY.
Lourdes Central High School Endowment Fund, [L], (LIN), Nebraska City, NE.
Lourdes College, [A], (TOL), Sylvania, OH.

Lourdes College Foundation, [O], (TOL), Sylvania, OH.
Lourdes Convent, [K], (FTW). See Saint Mary's of the Immaculate Conception.
Lourdes Elementary, [B], (LIN), Nebraska City, NE.
Lourdes Health Care Center, [P], (BGP), Wilton, CT.
Lourdes High School, [D], (CHI), Chicago, IL.
Lourdes High School, [C], (GB), Oshkosh, WI.
Lourdes High School of Rochester, Inc., [C], (WIN). See Rochester Catholic Schools.
Lourdes HomeHealth Services, [H], (CAM). See Our Lady of Lourdes Medical Center, Inc.
Lourdes Hospital, [D], (OWN), Paducah, KY.
Lourdes in Litchfield, [M], (HRT). See Montfort Missionaries.
Lourdes Junior-Senior High School, [C], (LIN), Nebraska City, NE.
Lourdes Nursing Home, [I], (DET), Waterford, MI.
Lourdes Primary, [B], (LIN), Nebraska City, NE.
Lourdes Shrine Guild, Inc., [V], (HRT), Litchfield, CT.
Lourdeshouse Maternity Services, [E], (HBG). See Department for Catholic Charities Counseling/Field Services.
Lourdesmont, [K], (SCR), Clarks Green, PA.
Lovers of the Holy Cross, [I], (ORG), Santa Ana, CA.
Lovers of the Holy Cross Sisters, [S], (LA), Los Angeles, CA.
Lovers of the Holy Cross, L.H.C., [Q], (NO), Marrero, LA.
Lowell Catholic High School, Inc., [E], (BO), Lowell, MA.
Lower Campus, [E], (NEW). See Elizabethport Catholic School.
Lower East Side Catholic Area Conference-Pastoral Center, [HH], (NY), New York, NY.
Lower Naugatuck Valley, [S], (HRT). See Catholic Charities-Catholic Family Services (Archdiocese of Hartford).
Lower School, [B], (HBG). See Cathedral School.
Lowndes County Catholic Center, [L], (MOB), Hayneville, AL.
Loyola, [Q], (STP), St. Paul, MN.
Loyola Academy, [D], (CHI), Wilmette, IL.
*Loyola College, [B], (BAL), Baltimore, MD.
Loyola College Business Center, [B], (BAL). See Loyola College.
Loyola College Prep, [A], (SHP), Shreveport, LA.
Loyola High School, [C], (BAL), Baltimore, MD.
Loyola High School, [E], (DET), Detroit, MI.
Loyola High School, [F], (LA), Los Angeles, CA.
Loyola High School, [C], (WIN). See Mankato Area Catholic Schools.
Loyola House, [W], (BO), Boston, MA.
Loyola House, [B], (DET), Berkley, MI.
Loyola House of Retreats, [I], (PAT), Morristown, NJ.
Loyola Institute, [O], (SR), Santa Rosa, CA.
Loyola Law School, [CC], (LA). See Archdiocesan Office for Campus Ministry.
Loyola Marymount University, [C], (LA), Los Angeles, CA.
Loyola Marymount University, [CC], (LA). See Archdiocesan Office for Campus Ministry.
Loyola of the Lakes Jesuit Retreat House, Inc., [U], (CLV), Akron, OH.
Loyola on the Potomac Retreat House, [P], (WDC), Faulkner, MD.
Loyola Parish - Jesuit Community, [M], (DEN), Denver, CO.
Loyola Press, [X], (CHI), Chicago, IL.
Loyola Sacred Heart High School, [C], (HEL), Missoula, MT.
Loyola School, [F], (NY), New York, NY.
Loyola School of Law, [C], (LA). See Loyola Marymount University.
Loyola University, [C], (NO), New Orleans, LA.
Loyola University Medical Center, [V], (CHI). See Ministry in Higher Education.
Loyola University of Chicago, [V], (CHI). See Ministry in Higher Education.
Loyola University of Chicago, University Ministry Dept., [V], (CHI). See Ministry in Higher Education.
Loyola University-Chicago, [C], (CHI), Chicago, IL.
Loyola-Sacred Heart High School Foundation, [I], (HEL), Missoula, MT.
Lucy Eaton Smith, The, [Z], (PH), Philadelphia, PA.
Ludden Housing Development Fund Company, Inc., [Q], (SY), Syracuse, NY.
*Lufkin School Foundation, [E], (TYL), Lufkin, TX.
Luke M. Powers Catholic High School, [B], (LAN), Flint, MI.
Luke M. Powers Educational Trust Fund (Flint), [K], (LAN). See Chancery Office.
Lumen 2000/Caribbean Region, [B], (STV). See Miscellaneous Organizations.
Lumen Catechetical Consultants, Inc., [V], (WDC), Silver Spring, MD.
Lumen Christi High School, [B], (LAN), Jackson, MI.
Lumen Christi High School Endowment Fund (Lumen Christi H.S., Jackson), [K], (LAN). See Chancery Office.
Lumen Christi Jr./Sr. High School, [B], (ANC), Anchorage, AK.
Lumen Christi Retreat Center, [C], (HT), Schriever, LA.
Lumen Christi Retreat House, [I], (BUR), Benson, VT.
Lumen Dei, [HH], (NY), New York, NY.
LUX ET VITA, INC., [V], (HRT), Orange, CT.
Luz De Cristo USA, [DD], (LA), Los Angeles, CA.
Lyle H. Boren Child Development Center, [L], (OKL). See Oklahoma Benedictine Institute on Mental Retardation, Inc.

M

M.F.S.I., Inc., [Y], (MIL), Milwaukee, WI.
*M.I. Adult Day Health Center, Inc., [U], (BO), Lawrence, MA.
M.I. Nursing-Restorative Center, Inc., [U], (BO), Lawrence, MA.
M.I. Residential Community II, Inc., [U], (BO), Lawrence, MA.
M.I. Residential Community III, Inc., [U], (BO), Lawrence, MA.
M.I. Residential Community, Inc., [U], (BO), Lawrence, MA.
*M.I. Transportation, Inc., [U], (BO), Lawrence, MA.
M.M.A.F. Charitable Trust, [DD], (NY), Maryknoll, NY.
Mabel Mosler Auxiliary, [P], (LA). See St. Anne's.
Macdonald Center, [O], (P), Portland, OR.
Machebeuf Catholic High School, [C], (DEN), Denver, CO.
MacMurray College Newman Center, [M], (SFD), Jacksonville, IL.
Macomb Community College Campus Ministry, [S], (DET), Warren, MI.
Macon Social Apostolate (SERVE), [I], (SAV), Macon, GA.
Madison Acquisition Company dba St. Francis Health Center, [J], (GAL), Madisonville, TX.
Madison County Catholic Charities, [H], (SY), Oneida, NY.
*Madonna Circle, Inc., [M], (MEM), Memphis, TN.
Madonna Day Care Center, [S], (WH), Clarksburg, WV.
Madonna Del Sasso Convent, [H], (MRY), Salinas, CA.
Madonna High School, [D], (CHI), Chicago, IL.
Madonna High School, [B], (WH), Weirton, WV.
Madonna Home, [H], (RIC), Norfolk, VA.
Madonna Homes, Inc., [O], (TOL), Toledo, OH.
Madonna House, [G], (R), Raleigh, NC.
Madonna House, [N], (RIC), Roanoke, VA.
Madonna House, [R], (WDC), Washington, DC.
Madonna House Apostolate, [H], (GAY), Alpena, MI.
Madonna House Apostolate, [L], (GR), Muskegon Heights, MI.
Madonna Learning Center for Retarded Children, [E], (MEM), Germantown, TN.
Madonna Manor Inc., [I], (FR), North Attleboro, MA.
Madonna Manor Retirement Home, [K], (MRY), Salinas, CA.
Madonna Manor, Inc., [I], (COV), Covington, KY.
Madonna Neighborhood Center, [T], (SAT), San Antonio, TX.
Madonna of Peace Renewal Center, [F], (STO), Copperopolis, CA.
Madonna Plaza, Inc., [K], (DEN). See Archdiocesan Housing Committee.
Madonna Queen Shrine, [BB], (BO), Boston, MA.
Madonna Rehabilitation Hospital, [E], (LIN), Lincoln, NE.
Madonna Residence, [K], (SFR), San Francisco, CA.
Madonna Retreat and Conference Center, [L], (SFE), Albuquerque, NM.
Madonna School for Exceptional Children, [F], (OM), Omaha, NE.
Madonna Shop, [F], (OM), Omaha, NE.
Madonna Towers of Rochester, Inc., [G], (DUL). See Benedictine Sisters Benevolent Association.
Madonna Towers of Rochester, Inc., [F], (WIN), Rochester, MN.
Madonna University, [C], (DET), Livonia, MI.
Madonna University Newman Center, [S], (DET), Livonia, MI.
Madonna Villa, [J], (DET). See Ryan Senior Residences of the Archdiocese of Detroit. Inc.
Madonna/Saint Joseph Center, [G], (CHI). See Catholic Charities of the Archdiocese of Chicago-Archdiocesan Offices.
Madres Clarisas Capuchinas, Capuchin Nuns of St. Clare, [J], (AMA), Amarillo, TX.
Magdalen College, [B], (MAN), Warner, NH.
Magic Kingdom Day Care Nursery School, [G], (PAT), Florham Park, NJ.
Magnificat - Joyful Visitation Chapter, Inc., [M], (ATL), Jackson, GA.
Magnificat - Mississippi Gulf Coast Chapter, [H], (BLX), Biloxi, MS.
Magnificat - Tucson Chapter, [J], (TUC), Tucson, AZ.
Magnificat Center of the Holy Spirit, [R], (NO), Ponchatoula, LA.
Magnificat High School, [E], (CLV), Cleveland, OH.
Magnificat Inc., Lower Pinellas Deanery Chapter of the Diocese of St. Petersburg, Florida, [T], (SP), St. Petersburg, FL.
Magnificat of the Houma-Thibodaux Diocese, [E], (HT), Thibodaux, LA.
Magnificat the Monterey Bay Chapter, [L], (MRY), Watsonville, CA.
Magnificat, Inc., [L], (MIA), Coral Gables, FL.
Magnificat: Mary, Woman of Faith Chapter, [I], (BIR), Birmingham, AL.
MAGNIFICAT-Baton Rouge Chapter, [L], (BR), Baton Rouge, LA.
Mahanoy City Catholic Elementary School, [D], (ALN), Mahanoy City, PA.
Maine Maritime Academy, [M], (PRT), Castine, ME.
Maintenance and Custodial Care Trust of the Franciscan Sisters of Savannah, MO, [K], (KC). See La Verna Heights Provincial House.
Maisha House of Prayer, Inc., [K], (ATL), Atlanta, GA.
Maison Marcotte, [G], (PRT), Lewiston, ME.
Majorie J. Gardner Wellness Center for Women, [F], (LAN), Okemos, MI.
Making the Right Connections, [B], (STO). See The Catholic Charities of the Diocese of Stockton.
Malachi House, Inc., [V], (CLV), Cleveland, OH.
Malden Catholic High School, [E], (BO), Malden, MA.
Mali O Ka Malu Community, [I], (HON). See Congregation of the Sacred Hearts and of Perpetual Adoration.
Mallinckrodt Campus, [C], (CHI). See Loyola University-Chicago.
Mallinckrodt Convent-Motherhouse and Novitiate of the Sisters of Christian Charity, [N], (PAT), Mendham, NJ.
The Malta Center, [J], (PHX), Phoenix, AZ.
Malvern Preparatory School for Boys, [G], (PH), Malvern, PA.
Mana'olana Community, [I], (HON). See Sisters of St. Joseph of Carondelet CSJ, Hawaii Vice-Province.
Managed Care Division, [I], (OM). See Father Flanagan's Boys' Home.
Manchester Convent of the Sisters of Mercy, [L], (MAN). See Sisters of Mercy of the Americas.
Manhattan College, [C], (NY), Bronx, NY.
Manhattan College, [GG], (NY). See University Apostolate.
Manhattan North Community Services, Inc., [HH], (NY), New York, NY.
Manhattanville College, [GG], (NY). See University Apostolate.
Manistee Catholic Central Schools, [A], (GAY), Manistee, MI.
Manitowoc Area Catholic System (MACS), [E], (GB), Manitowoc, WI.
Mankato Area Catholic Schools, [C], (WIN), Mankato, MN.
Manna Community Meal, [Q], (DET), Detroit, MI.
Manna House, [F], (DOD), Dodge City, KS.
Manna House of Prayer, [F], (SAL), Concordia, KS.
The Manor at St. Mary's, [K], (CAM), Cherry Hill, NJ.
Manor Junior College, [B], (PHU), Jenkintown, PA.
Manor St. Joseph, [E], (FAR), Edgeley, ND.
Manresa Jesuit House, [C], (CI), Koror, Palau, PW.
Manresa Jesuit Retreat House, [P], (DET), Bloomfield Hills, MI.
Manresa, House of Retreats, [J], (BR), Convent, LA.
Mantellate Sisters Servants of Mary of Plainfield, [K], (JOL), Plainfield, IL.
Maple Tree: Priory Childcare Center, [W], (STP), Maplewood, MN.
Maranatha, [N], (HRT). See Sisters of Mercy of the Americas of Connecticut.
Marbella Condominium 207 Association, Inc., [L], (MIA), Miami Shores, FL.
Marcellus Apartments Housing Development Fund Company, Inc., [Q], (SY), Syracuse, NY.
Marcum and Wallace Memorial Hospital, [D], (LEX), Irvine, KY.
Mareda, Inc., [O], (TOL), Toledo, OH.
Margaret's Pantry, [G], (SPR). See Providence Ministries for the Needy, Inc.
Marguerite's Place, [J], (MAN), Nashua, NH.
Maria Artero Nursery, [C], (AGN), Agana Heights, GU.
Maria Care, [E], (BEL), Red Bud, IL.
Maria Center, [K], (FTW). See Convent Ancilla Domini.
Maria Center, [R], (STL). See School Sisters of Notre Dame.
Maria College, [B], (ALB), Albany, NY.
Maria Community, [G], (TUC), Tucson, AZ.
Maria Droste Residence, [S], (STL), Normandy, MO.
Maria Droste Services, [HH], (NY), New York, NY.
Maria Hall, [G], (HBG), Danville, PA.
Maria Health Care Center, Inc., [N], (BAL), Baltimore, MD.
Maria High School, [D], (CHI), Chicago, IL.
Maria High School, [A], (LIT), Chicago, IL.
Maria Immaculata Convent, [O], (CHI), Wilmette, IL.

Marist Foreign Missions, [C], (NY). See Marist College.
Marist High School, [D], (CHI), Chicago, IL.
Marist High School, [D], (P), Eugene, OR.
Marist High School, [C], (SPP), Malaeloa, AS.
Marist High Schoool, [C], (NEW), Bayonne, NJ.
The Marist House, [Y], (BO), Framingham Centre, MA.
Marist Missionary Sisters, [X], (BO), Waltham, MA.
Marist Provincial House, [DD], (NY). See Marist Brothers Residence.
Marist Provincial House, [M], (WDC), Washington, DC.
Marist Residence, [DD], (NY). See Marist Brothers Residence.
Marist School, [C], (ATL), Atlanta, GA.
Marist Sisters, [B], (SAN), Abilene, TX.
Marist Volunteer Program, [X], (CHI), Chicago, IL.
Maristhill Nursing & Rehabilitation Center, [U], (BO), Waltham, MA.
Mark Seven - DePaul House of Studies, [A], (NY). See St. Joseph's Seminary.
Marksville Catholic School, [B], (ALX), Marksville, LA.
Marlborough Manor, [I], (KC), Kansas City, MO.
Marmion Abbey, [A], (RCK), Aurora, IL.
Marmion Abbey-St. Augustine's Abbey, [H], (RCK), Aurora, IL.
Marmion Academy, [C], (RCK), Aurora, IL.
The Marnee and John DeVine Foundation, [L], (LAN), Ann Arbor, MI.
Marquette Area Catholic Education Fund, [B], (MAR), Marquette, MI.
Marquette Catholic High School, [B], (GRY), Michigan City, IN.
Marquette Catholic High School, [D], (SFD), Alton, IL.
Marquette Catholic School, [B], (DUL), Virginia, MN.
Marquette Foundation, [P], (DAV), West Point, IA.
Marquette High School, [D], (DUB), Bellevue, IA.
Marquette High School, [B], (PEO), Ottawa, IL.
Marquette School System: Marquette Intermediate, [G], (DAV). See Marquette School, Inc.
Marquette School System: Marquette Jr./Sr. High, [G], (DAV). See Marquette School, Inc.
Marquette School System: Marquette Primary, [G], (DAV). See Marquette School, Inc.
Marquette School, Inc., [E], (DAV), West Point, IA.
Marquette School, Inc., [G], (DAV), West Point, IA.
*Marquette University, [C], (MIL), Milwaukee, WI.
Marquette University High School, [E], (MIL), Milwaukee, WI.
Marquette University Ministry, [X], (MIL), Milwaukee, WI.
Marriage Counseling Center, [H], (BUF). See The Catholic Charities of the Diocese of Buffalo.
Marriage Counseling Service, [G], (SPR), Springfield, MA.
Marriage Encounter, [L], (AMA), Amarillo, TX.
Marriage Encounter, [O], (OM), Omaha, NE.
Marriage Encounter, [J], (STU), Beverly, OH.
Marriage Encounter Apostolate, [L], (ROC), Rochester, NY.
Marriage Preparation Program, [M], (MEM), Memphis, TN.
Marshall Newman Center, [Q], (WH), Huntington, WV.
Marshalltown Area Consolidated Catholic School, [F], (DUB), Marshalltown, IA.
Martha W. Davis Cancer Center, [H], (RIC). See Bon Secours-Maryview Nursing Care.
Martha's Kitchen, [F], (SJ). See Catholic Charities of Santa Clara County.
Martha's Kitchen Food Services, [U], (GAL), Houston, TX.
The Martin Center, [H], (SEA), Bellingham, WA.
Martin De Porres Brothers Community, [U], (BRK), Springfield Gardens, NY.
Martin De Porres Group Homes, [P], (BRK), Springfield Gardens, NY.
Martin de Porres House, [X], (CHI), Chicago, IL.
Martin de Porres School, [I], (BRK), Springfield Gardens, NY.
Martin de Porres Village Corporation, [P], (PAT), Paterson, NJ.
Martin House, [F], (PT), Apalachicola, FL.
Martin House, [J], (RCK), Rockford, IL.
Martin House, [T], (TR), Trenton, NJ.
Martin House Learning Center, [T], (TR), Trenton, NJ.
Martin Luther King, Jr. Student Center, [K], (BR), Baton Rouge, LA.
Martin Luther King. Jr., Day Home Center, [F], (SEA), Seattle, WA.
Martina Place Assisted Living Residence, [E], (DM). See Bishop Drumm Retirement Center.
Martina Spiritual Renewal Center, Inc., [Q], (PIT), Pittsburgh, PA.
Mary and Joseph Retreat Center, [X], (LA), Rancho Palos Verdes, CA.
Mary and Joseph Trust, [W], (STL), St. Louis, MO.
*Mary Conrad Center, [E], (ANC), Anchorage, AK.
Mary Health of the Sick Convalescent and Nursing Hospital, [L], (LA), Newbury Park, CA.
Mary Help of Christians Academy, [D], (PAT), North Haledon, NJ.
Mary Help of Christians School, [B], (CC), Laredo, TX.
Mary Help of Christians School, [E], (SP), Tampa, FL.
Mary House, Inc., [P], (WOR), Spencer, MA.
Mary Immaculate Academy, [E], (HRT), New Britain, CT.
Mary Immaculate Convent, [BB], (PH), Philadelphia, PA.
Mary Immaculate Hospital, [E], (RIC), Newport News, VA.
Mary Immaculate Hospital Division, [N], (BRK). See Catholic Medical Center of Brooklyn & Queens.
Mary Immaculate Hospital Home Health Agency, [N], (BRK). See Catholic Medical Center of Brooklyn & Queens.
Mary Immaculate School, [F], (TOL), Toledo, OH.
Mary Immaculate Seminary, [A], (ALN), Northampton, PA.
Mary Immaculate Seminary, [M], (ALN), Northhampton, PA.
Mary Immaculate Star of the Sea, [E], (MIA), Key West, FL.
Mary Immaculate, Inc., [Y], (BRK), Jamaica, NY.
Mary Katherine Convent, Poor Handmaids of Jesus Christ, [G], (BEL), Cairo, IL.
*Mary Lay Center, [O], (TOL), Bellevue, OH.
The Mary Louis Academy (College Preparatory), [G], (BRK), Jamaica Estates, NY.
The Mary Magdalen Foundation, [M], (WCH), Wichita, KS.
Mary Manning Walsh Home, [Z], (NY), New York, NY.
Mary Mother of Hope House Transitional Residence, [F], (WIL). See Ministry of Caring, Inc.
Mary Mother of the Church Abbey, [L], (RIC), Richmond, VA.
Mary of Lourdes Elementary and Middle School, [E], (SCL), Little Falls, MN.
Mary of the Angels Convent, [L], (SPK), Spokane, WA.
Mary Our Queen Educational Endowment Trust, [N], (OM). See The Omaha Archdiocesan Educational Foundation, Inc.
Mary Queen and Mother Center, [O], (STL), St. Louis, MO.
Mary Queen of Peace Child Development Center, [J], (NO), New Orleans, LA.
Mary Rondorf Retirement Home of Sacred Heart Parish, [H], (SCL), Staples, MN.
Mary Star of the Sea Apartments, HFDC, Inc., [L], (BRK). See Catholic Charities.
Mary The Mother Montessori Pre-School, [A], (SPP), Pago Pago, AS.
Mary Theotokos Centre, [E], (STF), West Burke, VT.
Mary's Center, [K], (BAL), Pasadena, MD.
Mary's Hall, Inc., [L], (BRK). See Catholic Charities.
Mary's Home, Transitional Housing, La Habra, [G], (ORG). See St. Vincent de Paul Society.
Mary's House, [H], (ANC), Anchorage, AK.
Mary's Shelter, [P], (ALN), Reading, PA.
Mary's Solitude, [K], (FTW). See Saint Mary's of the Immaculate Conception.
Mary's Solitude-Prayer Center, [M], (FTW), Notre Dame, IN.
Mary, Help of Christians Convent, [I], (CC), Laredo, TX.
Mary, Mother of the Church Convent, [N], (HRT), Hamden, CT.
Mary, Mother of Youth Center, [U], (PRO). See Miscellaneous Listings for the Diocese of Providence.
Mary, Queen and Mother Nursing Center, [O], (STL), St. Louis, MO.
Marybrook Manor, [H], (DET). See Marian Village Corporation.
Marybrook Manor, [J], (DET), Livonia, MI.
Marycrest, [M], (CLV), Independence, OH.
Marycrest Convent Franciscan Sisters, [N], (DEN), Denver, CO.
Marycrest Health System, [Q], (DEN), Denver, CO.
Marycrest Manor, [I], (DET), Livonia, MI.
Marycrest Manor, Convalescent Home, [L], (LA), Culver City, CA.
Marydale Center, [J], (DET). See Ryan Senior Residences of the Archdiocese of Detroit. Inc.
Marydale Retirement Village, [G], (WIL), Newark, DE.
Marydale Retreat Center, [P], (COV), Erlanger, KY.
Marydell Faith & Life Center, [EE], (NY). See Sisters of Our Lady of Christian Doctrine aka Institute of Christian Doctrine.
Maryfield Nursing Home, [I], (CHL), High Point, NC.
Marygrove College, [C], (DET), Detroit, MI.
Marygrove College Campus Ministry, [S], (DET), Detroit, MI.
Marygrove Retreat Center, [F], (MAR), Garden, MI.
Marygrove Services, Inc., [N], (STL), Florissant, MO.
Marygrove, Inc., [W], (STL), Florissant, MO.
Maryhaven, [J], (DET). See Ryan Senior Residences of the Archdiocese of Detroit. Inc.
Maryhaven Center of Hope, [G], (RVC), Port Jefferson, NY.
Maryhaven Inc., [M], (CHI), Glenview, IL.
Maryhaven, Inc., [G], (CHI). See Catholic Charities of the Archdiocese of Chicago-Archdiocesan Offices.
Maryhill, [Q], (STP), St. Paul, MN.
Maryhill Hermitage, [G], (WH), Wheeling, WV.
Maryhill Manor (SNF), [H], (GB), Niagara, WI.
Maryhill Renewal Center, [H], (ALX), Pineville, LA.
Maryhouse, [N], (HRT), Newington, CT.
Maryhouse, [O], (SAC). See Loaves & Fishes.
Maryhouse Residence for Women, [S], (PIT). See St. Joseph's House of Hospitality, Inc.
Maryhouse Residential Nursing Facility, [D], (SFS), Pierre, SD.
Maryhurst, [J], (L), Louisville, KY.
Mary-Joseph Residence for the Elderly, [N], (NO), New Orleans, LA.
Maryknoll, [M], (HRT), Wolcott, CT.
Maryknoll, [M], (SJ), Los Altos, CA.
Maryknoll Communiti, Inc., [EE], (NY), Maryknoll, NY.
Maryknoll Department of Development, [W], (BO), East Walpole, MA.
Maryknoll Fathers, [P], (CLV), Cleveland, OH.
Maryknoll Fathers, [M], (SEA), Seattle, WA.
Maryknoll Fathers & Brothers, [N], (CHI), Chicago, IL.
Maryknoll Fathers and Brothers, [K], (DET), Detroit, MI.
Maryknoll Fathers and Brothers, [Q], (GAL), Houston, TX.
Maryknoll Fathers and Brothers, [R], (LA), Los Angeles, CA.
Maryknoll Fathers and Brothers, [DD], (NY), Maryknoll, NY.
Maryknoll Fathers and Brothers, [DD], (NY). See Maryknoll Fathers and Brothers.
Maryknoll Fathers & Brothers, [H], (STA), Jacksonville, FL.
Maryknoll Fathers and Brothers, [B], (WDC), Washington, DC.
The Maryknoll Fathers & Brothers Charitable Trust, [DD], (NY). See Maryknoll Fathers and Brothers.
Maryknoll Fathers and Brothers, Catholic Foreign Mission Society of America, [N], (STP), Minneapolis, MN.
Maryknoll Fathers and Brothers, Catholic Foreign Mission Society of America, Inc., [N], (SFR), San Francisco, CA.
Maryknoll Fathers House, [H], (HON), Honolulu, HI.
Maryknoll Fathers, Catholic Foreign Mission Society of America (Legal Title), [M], (DEN), Denver, CO.
Maryknoll House, [O], (BUF), Buffalo, NY.
Maryknoll House, [DD], (NY), New York, NY.
Maryknoll House, [AA], (PH), Philadelphia, PA.
Maryknoll House, [P], (STL), St. Louis, MO.
Maryknoll Mission Association of the Faithful, [HH], (NY), Maryknoll, NY.
Maryknoll Mission Association of the Faithful, Inc., [HH], (NY). See Maryknoll Mission Association of the Faithful.
Maryknoll Missioners, [N], (SJ), Gilroy, CA.
Maryknoll Residence, [N], (RVC), West Hempstead, NY.
Maryknoll Residential Care, [EE], (NY), Maryknoll, NY.
Maryknoll St. Teresa's Residence, [DD], (NY). See Maryknoll Fathers and Brothers.
Maryknoll Schools, [C], (HON), Honolulu, HI.
Maryknoll Sisters, [D], (CI), Colonia, Yap, FM.
Maryknoll Sisters, [I], (HON). See Maryknoll Sisters of St. Dominic M.M.
Maryknoll Sisters, [C], (LSC), Las Cruces, NM.
Maryknoll Sisters, [I], (SD), San Diego, CA.
Maryknoll Sisters, [E], (STO), Stockton, CA.
Maryknoll Sisters Charitable Trust, [EE], (NY), Maryknoll, NY.
Maryknoll Sisters Contemplative Community, [EE], (NY), Maryknoll, NY.
Maryknoll Sisters of St. Dominic, [N], (HRT), Wethersfield, CT.
Maryknoll Sisters of St. Dominic, [N], (HRT), New Britain, CT.
Maryknoll Sisters of St. Dominic, [N], (HRT), Terryville, CT.
Maryknoll Sisters of St. Dominic, [N], (HRT), Waterbury, CT.
Maryknoll Sisters of St. Dominic (M.M.), [R], (GAL), Houston, TX.
Maryknoll Sisters of St. Dominic Inc., [EE], (NY), Maryknoll, NY.
Maryknoll Sisters of St. Dominic M.M., [I], (HON), Honolulu, HI.
Maryknoll Sisters of St. Dominic, Inc., [F], (BWN), McAllen, TX.
Marylake - Carmelite Novitiate, [A], (LR), Little Rock, AR.
Maryland Catholic Health Care Consortium, Inc., [Q], (BAL), Baltimore, MD.
Maryland Health Center, [V], (WDC). See Spanish

Catholic Center.
Maryland Province Center, [N], (BAL), Stevenson, MD.
Marylawn of the Oranges Convent, [O], (NEW), South Orange, NJ.
Marylawn of the Oranges, High School for Girls, [C], (NEW), South Orange, NJ.
Marylhurst College, [B], (P), Marylhurst, OR.
Marymount Academy, [H], (LA), Santa Barbara, CA.
Marymount Child Care Center, [I], (CLV), Garfield Heights, OH.
Marymount College, [C], (NY), Tarrytown, NY.
Marymount College, [GG], (NY). See University Apostolate.
Marymount College, Palos Verdes, California, [C], (LA), Rancho Palos Verdes, CA.
Marymount Congregational Home, [Q], (CLV), Cleveland, OH.
Marymount Diocesan Activities Center, Inc., [H], (SAL), Salina, KS.
Marymount Health Care Systems, [AA], (CLV), Garfield Heights, OH.
Marymount Hermitage, Inc., Hermit Sisters of Mary, [D], (B), Mesa, ID.
Marymount High School, [F], (LA), Los Angeles, CA.
Marymount Hospital, Inc., [J], (CLV), Cleveland, OH.
Marymount Manhattan College, [C], (NY), New York, NY.
Marymount Manhattan College, [GG], (NY). See University Apostolate.
Marymount Memorial Educational Trust Fund, [H], (SAL), Salina, KS.
Marymount School, [H], (NY), New York, NY.
Marymount School of Practical Nursing, [K], (CLV), Cleveland, OH.
Marymount University, [A], (ARL), Arlington, VA.
Marytown, Our Lady of Fatima Friary, [N], (CHI), Libertyville, IL.
Marytown, U.S. National Center of the Militia of the Immaculata Movement, [Q], (CHI), Libertyville, IL.
Maryvale, [I], (LA), Rosemead, CA.
Maryvale Educational Fund, Inc., [P], (BAL). See Chancery Office.
Maryvale Motherhouse, [K], (CHL), Vale, NC.
Maryvale Preparatory School, [C], (BAL), Brooklandville, MD.
Maryview Employee Assistance Program, [H], (RIC). See Bon Secours-Maryview Nursing Care.
Maryview Hospice Program, [H], (RIC). See Bon Secours-Maryview Nursing Care.
Maryview MedCare Centers (Urgent Care), [H], (RIC). See Bon Secours-Maryview Nursing Care.
Maryview Medical Center, [E], (RIC), Portsmouth, VA.
Maryview Psychiatric Hospital, [O], (RIC), Portsmouth, VA.
Maryview Wellspring Home Health Agency, [H], (RIC). See Bon Secours-Maryview Nursing Care.
Maryville Academy, [H], (CHI), Des Plaines, IL.
Maryville Novitiate and Provincial House, [I], (BR), Baton Rouge, LA.
Maryville Nursing Home, [K], (P), Beaverton, OR.
Marywood Academy, [L], (GR), Grand Rapids, MI.
Marywood Apartments, [H], (RIC), Richmond, VA.
Marywood Center for Spirituality and Ministry, [J], (STA), Jacksonville, FL.
Marywood Children & Family Services, [E], (AUS), Austin, TX.
Marywood Convalescent Center, [G], (LC), Wausau, WI.
Marywood Early Childhood Center, [G], (SCR), Scranton, PA.
Marywood Eastern Region Center, [D], (SUP), Arbor Vitae, WI.
Marywood Franciscan Spirituality Center, [F], (SUP), Arbor Vitae, WI.
Marywood Nursing Care Center, [I], (DET), Livonia, MI.
Marywood Residential Community, [E], (CR), Crookston, MN.
Marywood Retreat Center, [K], (ORG), Orange, CA.
Marywood University, [C], (SCR), Scranton, PA.
Masmitja Hall Community, [G], (TUC). See Immaculate Heart Lodge Convent.
Mass of the Air, [Q], (L), Louisville, KY.
Mass Stipends, [J], (LIN). See Chancery.
Massachusetts Institute of Technology Catholic Community, [CC], (BO), Cambridge, MA.
Massachusetts Maritime Academy Newman Center, [O], (FR), Buzzards Bay, MA.
Mater Christi School, [C], (BUR), Burlington, VT.
Mater Dei College, [B], (OG), Ogdensburg, NY.
Mater Dei College, Sisters of St. Joseph, [G], (OG), Ogdensburg, NY.
Mater Dei High School, [A], (BEL), Breese, IL.
Mater Dei High School, [E], (DAV), Clinton, IA.
Mater Dei High School, [A], (EVN), Evansville, IN.
Mater Dei High School, [C], (ORG), Santa Ana, CA.
Mater Dei High School, [B], (TR), New Monmouth, NJ.
Mater Dei Institute, [C], (SPK), Spokane, WA.
Mater Dei Missionary Cenacle, [I], (MOB), Montgomery, AL.
Mater Dei Nursing Home, [I], (CAM), Newfield, NJ.
Mater Dei School, Inc., [E], (WDC), Bethesda, MD.
Mater Dolorosa Retreat Center, [X], (LA), Sierra Madre, CA.
"Mater Ecclesiae" International Formation Center, [U], (PRO), South Kingstown, RI.
Mater Ecclesiae, Inc., [U], (PRO), South Kingstown, RI.
Mater Spei Day Camp, [N], (PRO), Burrillville, RI.
Maternity Services, [H], (RVC). See Catholic Charities Central Administration.
Maternity/Adoption Services, [G], (CHI). See Catholic Charities of the Archdiocese of Chicago-Archdiocesan Offices.
Matignon High School, [D], (BO), Cambridge, MA.
Matt Talbot Inn, [V], (CLV). See Catholic Charities Services Corporation.
Matthew Manor, [G], (CHI). See Catholic Charities of the Archdiocese of Chicago-Archdiocesan Offices.
Matulaitis Institute, [D], (LIT), Chicago, IL.
Matulaitis Nursing Home Inc., [G], (NOR), Putnam, CT.
Maturana House of Prayer, [A], (CHK), Saipan, MP.
Maulaitis Nursing Home, [C], (LIT), Putnam, CT.
Maur Hill Prep School, [E], (KCK), Atchison, KS.
The Maur Hill Prep School Endowment Association, Inc., [K], (KCK), Atchison, KS.
*The Maura Clarke Ita Ford Center, [Y], (BRK), Brooklyn, NY.
Maxis Medical Services, [I], (SCR), Carbondale, PA.
May Forest, Generaltae and Motherhouse of the Sisters of Charity of Our Lady of Mercy, [E], (CHR), Charleston, SC.
Mayfair Auction, Billings Catholic Schools, [K], (GF), Billings, MT.
Mayfield Junior School, [H], (LA), Pasadena, CA.
Mayfield Senior School of the Holy Child Jesus, [F], (LA), Pasadena, CA.
Mayslake Marmion Ministries, Inc., [L], (JOL), Downers Grove, IL.
Mayslake Village, [I], (JOL), Oak Brook, IL.
Mayville State University Newman Center, [H], (FAR), Mayville, ND.
Maywood Apartments, [E], (SUP). See Catholic Charities Bureau, Inc.
Maywood Apartments (Plover), [E], (SUP). See Catholic Charities Bureau, Inc.
MCA Foundation, [S], (NO), New Orleans, LA.
McAdoo Catholic Elementary School, [D], (ALN), McAdoo, PA.
McAuley Bergan Center, [O], (OM), Omaha, NE.
The McAuley Center, [N], (CHL), Belmont, NC.
McAuley Center, Inc., [L], (HRT), West Hartford, CT.
McAuley Charitable Trust, [W], (STL), St. Louis, MO.
McAuley Clinic Corporation, [F], (LAN), Ann Arbor, MI.
McAuley Convent, [N], (CIN), Cincinnati, OH.
McAuley Convent, [V], (PH), Merion Station, PA.
McAuley Convent, [I], (RCK), Aurora, IL.
McAuley Convent, [H], (SAC). See Institute of the Sisters of Mercy of the Americas.
McAuley Fund, [N], (OM). See The Omaha Archdiocesan Educational Foundation, Inc.
McAuley Hall, [G], (ALT), Cresson, PA.
McAuley Hall Foundation, Inc., [N], (MET), Watchung, NJ.
McAuley Hall Inc., [I], (MET), Watchung, NJ.
McAuley High School, [E], (CIN), Cincinnati, OH.
McAuley Home, Sisters of Mercy Retirement Home, [F], (JKS), Vicksburg, MS.
McAuley House, [N], (CAM), Ventnor, NJ.
McAuley House, [N], (PRO), Providence, RI.
McAuley Manor, [F], (ANC), Anchorage, AK.
McAuley Manor, [G], (RCK), Aurora, IL.
McAuley Mercy Corporation, [K], (BUF), Buffalo, NY.
McAuley Nazareth Home for Boys, [I], (WOR), Leicester, MA.
McAuley Regional High School, [B], (SPC), Joplin, MO.
McAuley Residence, Inc., [F], (PRT), Portland, ME.
McAuley School for Exceptional Children, [D], (MET), Watchung, NJ.
McAuley Terrace Apts., [E], (DM). See Bishop Drumm Retirement Center.
McAuley Village, [N], (PRO), Providence, RI.
McAuley-Seton Home Care, [K], (BUF), Cheektowaga, NY.
McCabe Renewal Center, [G], (DUL), Duluth, MN.
McCarrick Care Center, [G], (MET), Somerset, NJ.
McCloskey Community Service Corporation, [T], (ALB), Albany, NY.
McClosky Program, Inc., [G], (GB), Green Bay, WI.
McCormick Catholic Academy, [F], (DET), Port Huron, MI.
The McCormick Memorial Home for the Aged, [H], (GB), Green Bay, WI.
McCorristin High School, [B], (TR), Trenton, NJ.
McDermott Place, [O], (OM), Omaha, NE.
McDonell Central Catholic High School, [C], (LC), Chippewa Falls, WI.
The McElligott Sacred Heart School Foundation, [G], (STO), Turlock, CA.
McFadden Home, [J], (DET). See St. Jude Home, Inc.
McGill-Toolen High School, [C], (MOB), Mobile, AL.
McGuire Memorial, [H], (PIT), New Brighton, PA.
McGurk House Apartments, [H], (RIC), Lynchburg, VA.
MCH, Inc. Court/Trezevant Apartments, [M], (MEM), Memphis, TN.
McHenry County Catholic Education Foundation, [L], (RCK), Woodstock, IL.
McKeesport Central Catholic, [F], (PIT), McKeesport, PA.
McKenna House, [V], (WDC), Washington, DC.
McKennan Hospital, [D], (SFS), Sioux Falls, SD.
McNicholas High School, [E], (CIN), Cincinnati, OH.
McNickols Campus, [S], (DET). See University of Detroit Mercy Campus Ministry.
McPherson Hospital, [F], (LAN), Howell, MI.
McQuaid Jesuit High School, [B], (ROC), Rochester, NY.
The Meadows at Maria Joseph Manor, [G], (HBG). See Maria Joseph Manor.
Meals on Wheels, [Q], (SFR). See Catholic Charities of the Archdiocese of San Francisco.
Mecklenburg Area Catholic Schools (M.A.C.S.), [D], (CHL), Charlotte, NC.
Medaille Center, [E], (SAL), Salina, KS.
Medaille Corporation, [FF], (BO), Boston, MA.
The Medalion (East), [D], (COS), Colorado Springs, CO.
The Medalion (West), [D], (COS), Colorado Springs, CO.
Media Production Center "In A Word", [E], (BLX), Bay St. Louis, MS.
Medical Mission Sisters, [N], (HRT), Hartford, CT.
Medical Mission Sisters, [C], (LSC), Las Cruces, NM.
Medical Mission Sisters, [BB], (PH), Brandamore, PA.
Medical Mission Sisters, [BB], (PH), Glenside, PA.
Medical Mission Sisters, [I], (SD), La Mesa, CA.
Medical Mission Sisters, [N], (SJ), Cupertino, CA.
Medical Mission Sisters, [R], (STL), St. Louis, MO.
Medical Mission Sisters (M.M.S.), [BB], (PH), Philadelphia, PA.
Medical Mission Sisters of Philadelphia (PA) M.M.S., [K], (MEM), Memphis, TN.
Medical Mission Sisters, North American Sector, [BB], (PH), Philadelphia, PA.
Medical Missionaries of Mary, [O], (CHI), Chicago, IL.
Medical Missionaries of Mary, [Z], (NY), Bronx, NY.
Medical Missionaries of Mary, [I], (SD), San Ysidro, CA.
Medical Missionaries of Mary, Inc., [X], (BO), Somerville, MA.
Medical Park Foundation, Inc., [P], (WH), Wheeling, WV.
Medical Sisters of St. Joseph-United States Foundation, [H], (WCH), Wichita, KS.
Medjugorje Group, [N], (SFE), Santa Fe, NM.
*Mekhitarian Educational Foundation, [C], (ARM), Glendale, CA.
Mekhitarist School, [A], (ARM), La Crescenta, CA.
Melita House for Pregnant Women, [L], (ROC), Rochester, NY.
Memorial Hospital, [B], (KNX), Chattanooga, TN.
Memorial Hospital and Health Care Center, Little Company of Mary of Indiana, Inc., [E], (EVN), Jasper, IN.
Memorial Hospital Convent, [N], (SR), Santa Rosa, CA.
Memorial Hospital Foundation, Inc., [E], (EVN), Jasper, IN.
Memphis Catholic High School and Middle School, [B], (MEM), Memphis, TN.
Men's House, [Y], (BRK). See The Roman Catholic Pontifical Lay Association Memores Domini.
Menifee Medical Center, [E], (LEX), Frenchburg, KY.
Menominee Catholic Central, [A], (MAR), Menominee, MI.
*Menominee Catholic Education Fund, Inc., [B], (MAR), Menominee, MI.
Mental Health Center, [E], (MET), East Brunswick, NJ.
Mental Health Outreach: Danbury, [G], (BGP). See Catholic Charities of Fairfield County.
Mental Health Services, [H], (RVC). See Catholic Charities Central Administration.
Mepkin Abbey, [D], (CHR), Moncks Corner, SC.
Merced Housing Texas, [T], (SAT), San Antonio, TX.
Mercedarian Missionaries Convent, [D], (LUB), Slaton, TX.
Mercedarian Missionaries of Berriz, [F], (AGN), Agana Heights, GU.
Mercedarian Missionaries of Berriz, [D], (CI), Weeno, Chuuk, FM.
Mercedarian Missionaries of Berriz, [D], (CI), Tol, Chuuk, FM.
Mercedarian Missionaries of Berriz, [D], (CI), Kolonia, Pohnpei, FM.

Mercedarian Missionaries of Berriz, [D], (CI), Koror, Palau, PW.
Mercedarians, [P], (CLV), Cleveland, OH.
Mercederian Missionaries of Berriz, [K], (KC), Kansas City, MO.
Mercedes Molina - Instituto Santa Mariana de Jesus, [Q], (MIL), Milwaukee, WI.
Merced-Mariposa District Council, [I], (FRS). See Society of St. Vincent de Paul.
Mercer Behavioral Healthcare Division, [F], (TR). See Catholic Charities.
Mercer County Community College, [S], (TR). See Campus Ministry for the Diocese of Trenton.
Mercer University, Wesleyan College Newman Center, [H], (SAV), Macon, GA.
Mercy Affordable Housing, Inc., [G], (B). See Mercy Housing Idaho, Inc.
Mercy Ambulatory Surgery Center, [K], (CIN), Fairfield, OH.
Mercy American River/Mercy San Juan Hospital/ Mercy American River Campus, [F], (SAC), Carmichael, CA.
Mercy By-the-Sea, [N], (CAM), Ventnor, NJ.
Mercy Catholic Medical Center, [U], (PH), Darby, PA.
Mercy Center, [N], (CIN), Cincinnati, OH.
Mercy Center, [L], (DET), Farmington Hills, MI.
The Mercy Center, [D], (DM). See Bergan Mercy-Alegant Health System: Mercy Hospital.
Mercy Center, [O], (SCR), Dallas, PA.
Mercy Center, [T], (STL), St. Louis, MO.
Mercy Center Convent, [O], (SCR), Dallas, PA.
Mercy Center for Women, [L], (E), Erie, PA.
Mercy Center for Women, [N], (E), Erie, PA.
Mercy Center Nursing Unit, Inc., [L], (SCR), Dallas, PA.
Mercy Center of the Arts, [F], (E), Erie, PA.
Mercy Center on Aging, [N], (E), Erie, PA.
Mercy Center, Inc., [T], (TR), Asbury Park, NJ.
Mercy Center, Incorporated, [Q], (HRT), Madison, CT.
Mercy Center, Spirituality and Conference Center, [M], (SFR), Burlingame, CA.
Mercy Central School of Nursing, [E], (GR). See St. Mary's Health Services.
Mercy Centre (Developmental Disabilities), [H], (WOR). See Catholic Charities.
Mercy Chicago Region Healthcare System, [M], (JOL), Naperville, IL.
Mercy Child Development Center, [J], (DM), Des Moines, IA.
Mercy Clinic (Mercy Hospital), [F], (SD). See Mercy Hospital and Medical Center dba Mercy Healthcare San Diego.
Mercy Clinics, Inc., [D], (DM). See Mercy Hospital Medical Center.
Mercy College in Dobbs Ferry, [C], (NY), Dobbs Ferry, NY.
Mercy College of Health Sciences, [B], (DM), Des Moines, IA.
Mercy College of Health Sciences, [D], (DM). See Mercy Hospital Medical Center.
Mercy College of Northwest Ohio, [H], (TOL). See Mercy Hospital.
Mercy Community Health, Inc., [V], (HRT), West Hartford, CT.
Mercy Community Home Care Services, Inc., [V], (HRT), West Hartford, CT.
Mercy Community Hospital, [W], (NY), Port Jervis, NY.
Mercy Connections, [R], (CIN), Cincinnati, OH.
*The Mercy Conservatory of Music, [S], (NEW), Scotch Plains, NJ.
Mercy Convent, [I], (FWT), Wichita Falls, TX.
Mercy Convent, [H], (GF), Billings, MT.
Mercy Convent, [E], (LAV), Ely, NV.
Mercy Convent, [I], (NSH), Nashville, TN.
Mercy Convent, [J], (PRT), Portland, ME.
Mercy Convent, [H], (SAC). See Institute of the Sisters of Mercy of the Americas.
Mercy Convent, [G], (SAV), Savannah, GA.
Mercy Convent and Formation House, [F], (AGN), Tai, GU.
Mercy Court, [D], (DM). See Mercy Hospital Medical Center.
Mercy Court, [FF], (PH), Yeadon, PA.
Mercy Crest of Arkansas, Inc., [G], (LR), Barling, AR.
Mercy Crestview Village, [O], (OM). See Mercy Housing dba Mercy House.
Mercy Cross Inter-Parochial High School, [B], (BLX), Biloxi, MS.
Mercy Development Office, [M], (NOR), Middletown, CT.
Mercy Diagnostic & Treatment Center, [J], (CHI). See Mercy Hospital and Medical Center.
*Mercy Education Project, [T], (DET), Detroit, MI.
Mercy Education Resource Center, [K], (SAC), Sacramento, CA.
Mercy Family Care Program Unit, [H], (DET), Detroit, MI.
Mercy Family Plaza, [U], (SFR). See Mercy/Charities Housing California.
Mercy Foundation - Bakersfield, [C], (FRS). See Mercy Healthcare Bakersfield.
Mercy Foundation of Des Moines - Affiliate of Catholic Health Initiatives, [J], (DM), Des Moines, IA.
Mercy Foundation, Inc., [J], (CHI). See Mercy Hospital and Medical Center.
Mercy Foundation, Inc., [J], (P). See Mercy Medical Center, Inc.
Mercy General Hospital, [F], (SAC), Sacramento, CA.
Mercy Green Mountain Manor, [Q], (DEN). See Mercy Properties, Inc.
Mercy Hall, [N], (CIN), Cincinnati, OH.
Mercy Haverford Hospital, [U], (PH), Haverford, PA.
Mercy Health & Rehabilitation Center Nursing Home Co., Inc., [H], (ROC), Auburn, NY.
Mercy Health Care & Rehabilitation Center, [J], (CHI). See Mercy Hospital and Medical Center.
Mercy Health Care and Rehabilitation Center, [M], (CHI), Homewood, IL.
Mercy Health Care Center, [J], (SCR), Nanticoke, PA.
Mercy Health Care Corp., [J], (CHI). See Mercy Hospital and Medical Center.
Mercy Health Center St. Mary's Unit-Oakcrest Manor, [J], (DUB), Dyersville, IA.
Mercy Health Center-St. Joseph's Unit, [H], (DUB), Dubuque, IA.
Mercy Health Center-St. Mary's Unit, [H], (DUB), Dyersville, IA.
Mercy Health Corp. of Southeastern PA, [FF], (PH), Bala Cynwyd, PA.
Mercy Health Corporation, [D], (RCK), Aurora, IL.
Mercy Health Foundation, [T], (DET), Farmington Hills, MI.
Mercy Health Foundation, [J], (PBL), Durango, CO.
Mercy Health Services (Formerly Sisters of Mercy Health Corporation), [T], (DET), Farmington Hills, MI.
Mercy Health System, [T], (CIN), Cincinnati, OH.
Mercy Health System - Western Ohio, Sisters of Mercy, [T], (CIN), Springfield, OH.
Mercy Health System of Kansas, Inc., [E], (WCH), Fort Scott, KS.
Mercy Health System of Western New York, [K], (BUF), Buffalo, NY.
Mercy Health System of Western New York, [T], (BUF), Buffalo, NY.
Mercy Health Systems of Kansas, Inc.-Independence, [E], (WCH), Independence, KS.
Mercy Healthcare Bakersfield, [C], (FRS), Bakersfield, CA.
Mercy Healthcare Center, Inc., [E], (OG), Tupper Lake, NY.
Mercy Healthcare Sacramento, [F], (SAC), Rancho Cordova, CA.
Mercy Healthcare, Inc., [J], (P). See Mercy Medical Center, Inc.
Mercy Heights Convent, [F], (AGN), Perezville-Tamuning, GU.
Mercy Heights Nursery and Kindergarten, Inc., [C], (AGN), Perezville-Tamuning, GU.
Mercy High School, [C], (BAL), Baltimore, MD.
Mercy High School, [B], (NOR), Middletown, CT.
Mercy High School, [C], (OM), Omaha, NE.
Mercy High School, [D], (RVC), Riverhead, NY.
Mercy High School, [B], (SAC), Red Bluff, CA.
Mercy High School (Girls), [E], (SFR), San Francisco, CA.
Mercy High School (Girls), [E], (SFR), Burlingame, CA.
Mercy High School for Girls, [E], (DET), Farmington Hills, MI.
Mercy High, Private School for Girls, [D], (ALB), Albany, NY.
Mercy Holly Park East, [Q], (DEN). See Mercy Properties, Inc.
Mercy Holly Park West, [Q], (DEN). See Mercy Properties, Inc.
The Mercy Home and School, [U], (PRO). See Miscellaneous Listings for the Diocese of Providence.
Mercy Home Care, [C], (FRS). See Mercy Hospital & Health Services.
Mercy Home for Children, [O], (BRK), Brooklyn, NY.
Mercy Home Health Services, Inc., [Q], (BAL), Baltimore, MD.
Mercy Hospice, [S], (PH), Philadelphia, PA.
Mercy Hospice, [K], (RVC), Uniondale, NY.
Mercy Hospice Foundation of Horry County, [I], (CHR), Myrtle Beach, SC.
Mercy Hospital, [D], (BIS), Williston, ND.
Mercy Hospital, [K], (BUF), Buffalo, NY.
Mercy Hospital, [J], (DAV), Iowa City, IA.
Mercy Hospital, [H], (DET), Detroit, MI.
Mercy Hospital, [D], (FAR), Devils Lake, ND.
Mercy Hospital, [D], (FAR), Valley City, ND.
Mercy Hospital, [C], (GAY), Cadillac, MI.
Mercy Hospital, [C], (GAY), Grayling, MI.
Mercy Hospital, [E], (GR), Muskegon, MI.
Mercy Hospital, [G], (MIA), Miami, FL.
*Mercy Hospital, [H], (PRT), Portland, ME.
Mercy Hospital, [I], (SCR), Scranton, PA.
Mercy Hospital, [I], (SCR), Wilkes-Barre, PA.
Mercy Hospital, [F], (SPR), Springfield, MA.
Mercy Hospital, [H], (TOL), Toledo, OH.
Mercy Hospital, [H], (TOL), Tiffin, OH.
Mercy Hospital & Health Services, [C], (FRS), Merced, CA.
Mercy Hospital and Medical Center, [J], (CHI), Chicago, IL.
Mercy Hospital and Medical Center dba Mercy Healthcare San Diego, [F], (SD), San Diego, CA.
Mercy Hospital Anderson, [K], (CIN), Cincinnati, OH.
Mercy Hospital Anderson Foundation, [U], (CIN), Cincinnati, OH.
Mercy Hospital Convent, [Q], (NO). See Sisters of Mercy of the Americas, R.S.M.
Mercy Hospital Convent, Sisters' Retirement Center, [I], (CC). See Sisters of Mercy of the St. Louis Regional Community, Inc.
Mercy Hospital Foundation, [P], (DAV), Iowa City, IA.
Mercy Hospital Foundation, [F], (SD). See Mercy Hospital and Medical Center dba Mercy Healthcare San Diego.
Mercy Hospital Foundation, Council Bluffs, [J], (DM), Council Bluffs, IA.
Mercy Hospital Guild of Iowa City, Iowa, [P], (DAV). See Mercy Hospital Foundation.
Mercy Hospital Medical Center, [D], (DM), Des Moines, IA.
Mercy Hospital of Folsom, [F], (SAC), Folsom, CA.
Mercy Hospital of Franciscan Sisters, [H], (DUB), Oelwein, IA.
Mercy Hospital of Hamilton-Fairfield, [K], (CIN), Hamilton, OH.
Mercy Hospital of Philadelphia, [U], (PH), Philadelphia, PA.
Mercy Hospital of Pittsburgh, [J], (PIT), Pittsburgh, PA.
The Mercy Hospital of Pittsburgh, [J], (PIT). See Pittsburgh Mercy Health System, Inc.
Mercy Hospital of Port Huron, [H], (DET), Port Huron, MI.
Mercy Hospital of Willard, [H], (TOL), Willard, OH.
Mercy Hospital School of Nursing Alumni Association, [S], (PIT), Pittsburgh, PA.
Mercy Hospital, Iowa City, Iowa, [P], (DAV). See Mercy Hospital Foundation.
Mercy Housing & Shelter Corporation, [V], (HRT), Hartford, CT.
Mercy Housing Arizona, [J], (PHX), Phoenix, AZ.
Mercy Housing Colorado, [Q], (DEN). See Mercy Housing, Inc.
Mercy Housing Corporation, [X], (CHI), Chicago, IL.
Mercy Housing dba Mercy House, [O], (OM), Omaha, NE.
Mercy Housing Development Fund Co., Inc., [Q], (SY), Auburn, NY.
Mercy Housing Idaho Properties, Inc., [G], (B). See Mercy Housing Idaho, Inc.
Mercy Housing Idaho, Inc., [G], (B), Nampa, ID.
Mercy Housing Michigan, [H], (GAY), Farmington Hills, MI.
*Mercy Housing Midwest, [O], (OM). See Mercy Housing dba Mercy House.
Mercy Housing, Inc., [Q], (DEN), Denver, CO.
Mercy Information Systems, [T], (DET), Farmington Hills, MI.
Mercy International Health Services, [T], (DET), Farmington Hills, MI.
Mercy Life Center Corporation, [J], (PIT). See Pittsburgh Mercy Health System, Inc.
Mercy Lodge, [R], (PRO), Cumberland, RI.
Mercy Long Term Care Initiatives dba Providence Retirement Home, [H], (IND), New Albany, IN.
Mercy McAuley Center-Mercy Health Systems, [L], (CIN), Urbana, OH.
Mercy Med-Care, Inc., [I], (SCR), Wilkes-Barre, PA.
Mercy Medical, [F], (MOB), Daphne, AL.
Mercy Medical at Presidential Towers, [J], (CHI). See Mercy Hospital and Medical Center.
Mercy Medical Center, [B], (B), Nampa, ID.
Mercy Medical Center, [K], (CIN), Springfield, OH.
Mercy Medical Center, [H], (DEN), Denver, CO.
Mercy Medical Center, [F], (GB), Oshkosh, WI.
Mercy Medical Center, [I], (RVC), Rockville Centre, NY.
Mercy Medical Center, [F], (SAC), Mt. Shasta, CA.
Mercy Medical Center, [F], (SAC), Redding, CA.
Mercy Medical Center - Affiliate of Catholic Health Initiatives, [D], (BIS), Williston, ND.
Mercy Medical Center Malpractice Self-Insurance Trust, [P], (BAL), Baltimore, MD.
Mercy Medical Center, Cedar Rapids, Iowa, [H], (DUB), Cedar Rapids, IA.
Mercy Medical Center, Cedar Rapids, Iowa, Endowment Foundation, Inc., [H], (DUB), Cedar Rapids, IA.
Mercy Medical Center, Inc., [H], (BAL), Baltimore, MD.
Mercy Medical Center, Inc., [J], (P), Roseburg, OR.
Mercy Medical Center, Wittenberg University Campus Ministry, [Q], (CIN), Springfield, OH.
Mercy Medical Foundation, [D], (BIS), Williston, ND.
Mercy Medical in Chatham, [J], (CHI). See Mercy

Misioneras Eucaristicas Franciscanas, [F], (BWN), Mission, TX.
Misioneras Guadalupanas del Espiritu Santo, [K], (FR), New Bedford, MA.
Misioneros Hijos del Inmaculado Corazon de Maria (Claretianos), [C], (CGS), Caguas, PR.
Mission College Preparatory Catholic High School, [C], (MRY), San Luis Obispo, CA.
*Mission Health Corporation, [T], (DET), Novi, MI.
Mission Helper Center, [N], (BAL), Baltimore, MD.
Mission Helper Productions, Inc., [Q], (BAL), Baltimore, MD.
Mission Helpers of the Sacred Heart, [O], (WDC), Lanham-Seabrook, MD.
Mission Helpers of the Sacred Heart Convent, [F], (PT), Marianna, FL.
Mission Helpers of the Sacred Heart-Our Lady of Pompei Convent, [N], (BAL), Baltimore, MD.
Mission Holding Corporation, [U], (SFR), San Rafael, CA.
Mission Hospital Regional Medical Center, [F], (ORG), Mission Viejo, CA.
Mission International, Inc., [N], (MET), Somerset, NJ.
Mission of Our Lady of Mercy-Mercy Home for Boys and Girls, [H], (CHI), Chicago, IL.
Mission of the Holy Cross, [G], (CHI). See Catholic Charities of the Archdiocese of Chicago-Archdiocesan Offices.
Mission of the Immaculate Virgin, [S], (NY), New York, NY.
Mission Office Fund, [J], (LIN). See Chancery.
Mission Project Service, [J], (OG), Watertown, NY.
Mission Promotion, [DD], (BO). See Chancery Office.
Mission Resource Center, [U], (PRO). See Franciscan Missionaries of Mary.
Mission San Luis Rey, [H], (SD), San Luis Rey, CA.
Mission San Luis Rey Retreat, [K], (SD), San Luis Rey, CA.
Mission Share, [S], (COV), Fort Thomas, KY.
Missionaries of Africa, [N], (CHI), Chicago, IL.
Missionaries of Africa, [H], (ORG), Orange, CA.
Missionaries of Africa, [O], (SP), St. Petersburg, FL.
Missionaries of Africa, [M], (WDC), Washington, DC.
Missionaries of Charity, [J], (ATL), Atlanta, GA.
Missionaries of Charity, [N], (BAL), Baltimore, MD.
Missionaries of Charity, [O], (CHI), Chicago, IL.
Missionaries of Charity, [K], (CHL), Charlotte, NC.
Missionaries of Charity, [N], (DAL), Dallas, TX.
Missionaries of Charity, [N], (DEN), Denver, CO.
Missionaries of Charity, [L], (DET), Detroit, MI.
Missionaries of Charity, [P], (FR), New Bedford, MA.
Missionaries of Charity, [I], (LAF), Lafayette, LA.
Missionaries of Charity, [K], (MEM), Memphis, TN.
Missionaries of Charity, [I], (MIA), Miami, FL.
Missionaries of Charity, [BB], (PH), Norristown, PA.
Missionaries of Charity, [E], (PHX), Phoenix, AZ.
Missionaries of Charity, [I], (SD), San Diego, CA.
Missionaries of Charity, [O], (SFR), San Francisco, CA.
Missionaries of Charity, [R], (STL), St. Louis, MO.
Missionaries of Charity, [O], (WDC), Washington, DC.
Missionaries of Charity (Contemplatives), [O], (WDC), Anacostia, Washington, DC.
Missionaries of Charity Brothers, [R], (LA), Los Angeles, CA.
Missionaries of Charity Brothers, House of Formation, [W], (LA), Los Angeles, CA.
Missionaries of Charity Brothers, Regional Center and Novitiate, [W], (LA), Los Angeles, CA.
Missionaries of Charity Convent, [N], (PEO), Peoria, IL.
Missionaries of Charity, Contemplative Our Lady of Lourdes Convent, [V], (BRK), Brooklyn, NY.
Missionaries of Charity, Gift of Mary, [BB], (PH), Chester, PA.
Missionaries of Charity, Gift of Peace Convent, [O], (WDC), Washington, DC.
Missionaries of Charity, Inc., [EE], (NY), New York, NY.
Missionaries of Jesus, [F], (BWN), Brownsville, TX.
Missionaries of LaSalette, [M], (HRT). See Missionaries of LaSalette Provincial Secretary.
Missionaries of LaSalette Provincial Secretary, [M], (HRT), Hartford, CT.
The Missionaries of Our Lady of La Salette, Provincialate, [W], (STL), St. Louis, MO.
Missionaries of Our Lady of LaSalette Corp., [W], (BO), Ipswich, MA.
Missionaries of Pastoral Charity Society, [T], (SAT), San Antonio, TX.
Missionaries of Saint Charles, [N], (CHI), Oak Park, IL.
Missionaries of the Company of Mary-Montfort Missionaries, [M], (WDC), Washington, DC.
Missionaries of the Holy Apostles, [F], (NOR), Cromwell, CT.
Missionaries of the Holy Family, General Mission Office—M.S.F., Inc., [L], (RIC), West Point, VA.
Missionaries of the Kingship of Christ, [S], (OAK), Oakland, CA.
Missionaries of the Kingship of Christ, [P], (SFR), San Francisco, CA.
Missionaries of the Kingship of Christ, [W], (STL), St. Louis, MO.
Missionaries of the Kingship of Christ, [P], (STP), St. Paul, MN.
Missionaries of the Kingship of Christ, [U], (WDC), West Bethesda, MD.
Missionaries of the Sacred Heart, [A], (ALN), Center Valley, PA.
Missionaries of the Sacred Heart, [K], (ALN), Reading, PA.
Missionaries of the Sacred Heart, [M], (SAT), San Antonio, TX.
Missionaries of the Sacred Heart Community, [H], (RCK), Aurora, IL.
Missionaries of the Sacred Heart of Jesus and Our Lady of Guadalupe M.S.C.Gpe., [O], (CHI), Arlington Heights, IL.
Missionaries of the Sacred Heart, M.S.C., [H], (AUS), Blanco, TX.
Missionary Association of Catholic Women, [V], (MIL), Milwaukee, WI.
Missionary Association of Mary Immaculate-Missionary Oblates of Mary Immaculate, [J], (BEL), Belleville, IL.
Missionary Brothers of Charity, [P], (LA), Los Angeles, CA.
Missionary Carmelites of St. Teresa (C.M.S.T.), [R], (GAL), Houston, TX.
Missionary Catechist of the Poor, [N], (DAL), Dallas, TX.
Missionary Catechists of Divine Providence, [F], (BWN), Pharr, TX.
Missionary Catechists of Divine Providence, [B], (SAN), Odessa, TX.
Missionary Catechists of Divine Providence, [N], (SAT), San Antonio, TX.
The Missionary Catechists of St. Therese of the Infant Jesus, Inc., [O], (WDC), Fort Washington, MD.
Missionary Catechists of the Sacred Hearts of Jesus and Mary, [I], (FWT), Fort Worth, TX.
Missionary Catechists of the Sacred Hearts of Jesus and Mary, [E], (VIC), Victoria, TX.
Missionary Catechists of the Sacred Hearts of Jesus and Mary (M.C.S.H.S.M.), [R], (GAL), Houston, TX.
Missionary Cathechists of Divine Providence, [I], (AUS), Austin, TX.
Missionary Community of St. Paul the Apostle and Mary, Mother of the Church, Inc., [Y], (MIL), Racine, WI.
Missionary Daughters of the Most Pure Virgin Mary, [I], (CC), Kingsville, TX.
Missionary Ecumenical, [I], (AUS), Somerville, TX.
Missionary Franciscan Sisters of the Immaculate Conception, [N], (HRT), New Haven, CT.
Missionary Franciscan Sisters of the Immaculate Conception, [N], (HRT), East Haven, CT.
Missionary Fraternity of Mary, USA, Ltd., [I], (WIL), Seaford, DE.
Missionary Oblates of Mary Immaculate, [W], (BO), Lowell, MA.
Missionary Oblates of Mary Immaculate, [W], (BO), Lowell, MA.
Missionary Oblates of Mary Immaculate, [W], (BO). See Missionary Oblates of Mary Immaculate.
Missionary Oblates of Mary Immaculate, [K], (MAN), Hudson, NH.
Missionary Oblates of Mary Immaculate, [W], (STP), St. Paul, MN.
Missionary Oblates of Mary Immaculate, [M], (WDC), Washington, DC.
Missionary Oblates of Mary Immaculate - St. Henry's Oblate Residence, [F], (BEL), Belleville, IL.
Missionary Oblates of Mary Immaculate of Texas Continuing Care Foundation, [S], (SAT), San Antonio, TX.
Missionary Oblates of Mary Immaculate, Western Province, Inc., [EE], (LA). See Chancery Office.
Missionary Servant of the Most Blessed Trinity, [BB], (PH), Philadelphia, PA.
The Missionary Servants of Pope John Paul I, [O], (MAN), Gilford, NH.
Missionary Servants of the Most Blessed Trinity, [N], (HRT), New Hartford, CT.
Missionary Servants of the Most Blessed Trinity, [F], (R), Southern Pines, NC.
Missionary Servants of the Most Blessed Trinity Ascension Missionary Cenacle, [S], (LA), Los Angeles, CA.
Missionary Servants of the Most Holy Trinity, [P], (CLV), Cleveland, OH.
Missionary Servants of the Most Holy Trinity, [M], (WDC), Adelphi, MD.
Missionary Servants of the Most Holy Trinity, S.T., [J], (ARL), Arlington, VA.
Missionary Sisters of Christ the King, [O], (CHI), Chicago, IL.
Missionary Sisters of Christ the King (Poland), [S], (LA), Los Angeles, CA.
Missionary Sisters of Divine Providence, [N], (PAT), Passaic, NJ.
Missionary Sisters of Jesus, Mary & Joseph, [K], (ELP), Marfa, TX.
Missionary Sisters of Jesus, Mary & Joseph (M.J.M.J.), [K], (ELP), El Paso, TX.
Missionary Sisters of Mother of God, [F], (STF), Stamford, CT.
Missionary Sisters of Our Lady of Africa, [O], (WDC), Chevy Chase, MD.
Missionary Sisters of Our Lady of Africa (M.S.O.L.A.), [F], (BUR), Winooski, VT.
Missionary Sisters of St. Benedict, [O], (RVC), Huntington, NY.
Missionary Sisters of St. Columbans, St. Columban's on the Lake, [P], (BUF), Silver Creek, NY.
Missionary Sisters of St. Peter Claver, [R], (STL), Chesterfield, MO.
Missionary Sisters of the Holy Family, [Q], (MIL), West Allis, WI.
Missionary Sisters of the Holy Rosary, [BB], (PH), Bryn Mawr, PA.
Missionary Sisters of the Holy Rosary (M.S.H.R.), [BB], (PH), Ardmore, PA.
Missionary Sisters of the Immaculate Conception, [J], (PRT), Orland, ME.
Missionary Sisters of the Immaculate Conception, [F], (SB), Calimesa, CA.
Missionary Sisters of the Immaculate Conception (S.M.I.C.), [R], (GAL), Houston, TX.
Missionary Sisters of the Immaculate Conception of the Mother of God, [I], (AUS), Austin, TX.
Missionary Sisters of the Immaculate Conception of the Mother of God, [N], (PAT), West Paterson, NJ.
Missionary Sisters of the Immaculate Conception of the Mother of God, [N], (PAT), Paterson, NJ.
Missionary Sisters of the Immaculate Conception, Convent of the Immaculate Conception, [N], (PAT), West Paterson, NJ.
Missionary Sisters of the Immaculate Heart of Mary, [F], (BWN), Alamo, TX.
Missionary Sisters of the Immaculate Heart of Mary, [F], (BWN), McAllen, TX.
Missionary Sisters of the Immaculate Heart of Mary, [F], (BWN), San Benito, TX.
Missionary Sisters of the Immaculate Heart of Mary, [EE], (NY), New York, NY.
Missionary Sisters of the Immaculate of the Mother of God, [N], (PAT), Paterson, NJ.
Missionary Sisters of the Lady of the Holy Rosary, [B], (SAN), Ft. Stockton, TX.
Missionary Sisters of the Most Blessed Sacrament and Mary Immaculate, [O], (NEW), Newark, NJ.
Missionary Sisters of the Most Sacred Heart of Jesus, [L], (ALN), Allentown, PA.
Missionary Sisters of the Most Sacred Heart, Trinity House, [BB], (PH), Philadelphia, PA.
Missionary Sisters of the Sacred Heart (Cabrini Sisters), [BB], (PH), Philadelphia, PA.
Missionary Sisters of the Sacred Heart (Cabrini) M.S.C., [Q], (NO), New Orleans, LA.
Missionary Sisters of the Sacred Heart "Ad Gentes", [J], (ATL), Chamblee, GA.
Missionary Sisters of the Sacred Heart of Jesus, [O], (CHI), Chicago, IL.
Missionary Sisters of the Sacred Heart of Jesus (Cabrini Sisters), [BB], (PH), Radnor, PA.
Missionary Sisters of the Sacred Heart of Jesus "Ad Gentes", [G], (KNX), Chattanooga, TN.
Missionary Sisters Of The Society Of Mary (Waltham, MA) S.M.S.M., [K], (MEM), Memphis, TN.
Missionary Society of St. Paul, Inc. - U.S. Region, [Q], (GAL), Barrett Station, TX.
Missionary Sons of the Immaculate Heart of Mary, [R], (LA), Los Angeles, CA.
*Missionary Vehicle Association, Inc., [V], (WDC), Washington, DC.
Missionhurst Community Residence, [M], (SAT), San Antonio, TX.
Missionhurst Formation Community, [B], (SAT), San Antonio, TX.
Missionhurst, C.I.C.M.-Central House and Provincialate, [J], (ARL), Arlington, VA.
Missionhurst-C.I.C.M., [J], (ARL), Falls Church, VA.
Mississippi College Newman Center, [G], (JKS), Clinton, MS.
Mississippi State University Catholic Student Association, [G], (JKS), Starkville, MS.
Mississippi State University for Women Student Center, [G], (JKS), Columbus, MS.
Missouri Catholic Conference, [G], (JC), Jefferson City, MO.
Mobile Podiatry, Dentures and Eyeglasses Clinic, [D], (TUC). See Social Service Agencies: Pima County.
Moeller High School, [E], (CIN), Cincinnati, OH.
Mohawk Valley Community College, [V], (SY), Utica, NY.
Mohun Health Care Center, [E], (COL), Columbus, OH.
Mohun Health Care Center, [I], (COL). See St. Mary of the Springs.
Mokena Family Health Center, [G], (JOL). See St. Joseph Medical Center.

N

*Natural Family Planning, [J], (PHX), Phoenix, AZ.
Natural Family Planning, [J], (STU), Steubenville, OH.
Natural Family Planning Center of Washington, DC, Inc., [V], (WDC), Bethesda, MD.
Nazareth, [E], (B), Boise, ID.
Nazareth Academy, [D], (CHI), LaGrange Park, IL.
Nazareth Academy, [B], (VIC), Victoria, TX.
Nazareth Academy Grade School, [I], (PH), Philadelphia, PA.
Nazareth Academy High School, [G], (PH), Philadelphia, PA.
Nazareth Arts For Life, Inc., [Q], (L), Nazareth, KY.
Nazareth Convent, [BB], (PH), Philadelphia, PA.
Nazareth Convent, [J], (ROC), Rochester, NY.
Nazareth Day Care, [M], (BO), Jamaica Plain, MA.
Nazareth Family Foundation, [S], (PIT), Pittsburgh, PA.
Nazareth Family Services, [S], (PIT). See Mount Nazareth Center, Inc.
Nazareth Farm, [L], (WH), Salem, WV.
Nazareth Hall, [I], (ELP), El Paso, TX.
Nazareth Hall Elementary School, [D], (ROC), Rochester, NY.
Nazareth Hall Middle School, [D], (ROC). See Nazareth Hall Elementary School.
Nazareth Heights, Inc., [Q], (MIL), Fond du Lac, WI.
Nazareth Hermitage, [F], (SPC), Ava, MO.
Nazareth Home, [F], (GRY). See St. Catherine Hospital.
Nazareth Home, [K], (L), Louisville, KY.
Nazareth Home, Residence for Single Pregnant Women, [D], (SAV), Macon, GA.
Nazareth Hospital, [U], (PH), Philadelphia, PA.
Nazareth House, [D], (FRS), Fresno, CA.
Nazareth House, [Q], (LA), Los Angeles, CA.
Nazareth House, [H], (MAD), Stoughton, WI.
Nazareth House, [N], (MET), Perth Amboy, NJ.
Nazareth House, [E], (SD), San Diego, CA.
Nazareth House, [K], (SFR), San Rafael, CA.
Nazareth House, [D], (SPP), Pago Pago, AS.
Nazareth House Retirement Home, [G], (SD), San Diego, CA.
Nazareth Housing Services, [S], (PIT). See Mount Nazareth Center, Inc.
*Nazareth Housing, Inc., [HH], (NY), New York, NY.
Nazareth II, [N], (NO), New Orleans, LA.
Nazareth In The Woods, Inc., [O], (E), Du Bois, PA.
Nazareth Inn, [N], (NO), New Orleans, LA.
Nazareth Living Center, [O], (STL), Mehlville, MO.
Nazareth Montessori Children's Center, [E], (L), Nazareth, KY.
Nazareth Motherhouse for the Sisters of St. Joseph, Concordia, [E], (SAL), Concordia, KS.
Nazareth Nursery, [V], (NY), New York, NY.
Nazareth Nursing Home, [M], (BUF), Buffalo, NY.
Nazareth Regional, [G], (BRK), Brooklyn, NY.
Nazareth Residence for Mothers and Children, [M], (BO), Roxbury, MA.
Nazareth Schools: The Hall; The Academy, [B], (ROC), Rochester, NY.
Nazareth Spiritual Enrichment Center, [R], (PRO), Newport, RI.
Nazareth Towers, [G], (COL), Columbus, OH.
Nazareth Village, [P], (PAT), Chester, NJ.
Nazarethville, [M], (CHI), Des Plaines, IL.
Near East Side Adventures Program, [K], (SY), Syracuse, NY.
Needle Fund, Inc., [W], (BGP), Bridgeport, CT.
Negaunee St. Paul Endowment Fund, [B], (MAR), Negaunee, MI.
Neighborhood Division, Catholic Charities, [K], (SY), Syracuse, NY.
Neighborhood House-Inner City Apostolate, [F], (CHR), Charleston, SC.
Neighbors Together, [Y], (BRK), Brooklyn, NY.
Neringa, Inc., [I], (BUR), West Brattleboro, VT.
Nerinx Hall High School, [F], (STL), Webster Groves, MO.
Nestucca Sanctuary, [N], (P), Pacific City, OR.
NET Ministries, Inc., [T], (STP), West St. Paul, MN.
Network of Sacred Heart Schools, Inc., [W], (STL), St. Louis, MO.
Neumann Apartments, [I], (ALN), Saint Clair, PA.
Neumann College, [C], (PH), Aston, PA.
Neumann Convent Sisters of St. Francis of Philadelphia (Glen Riddle), [L], (ALN), Reading, PA.
Neumann Early Childhood Center, Inc., [G], (BAL), Cumberland, MD.
Neumann Early Childhood Center, Inc., [P], (BAL). See Chancery Office.
Neumann High School, [C], (LIN), Wahoo, NE.
Neumann House, [G], (GBG), Greensburg, PA.
Neumann House, Village of St. Mary, [M], (CAM), Cherry Hill, NJ.
Neumann Residence, [D], (NY). See Department of Education.
Neumann Services, Inc., [L], (HBG), Lancaster, PA.
New Albany Deanery/Catholic Youth Ministry, [E], (IND). See Aquinas Center for Continuing Religious Education.
New Albany Deanery-Catholic Youth Ministry, [O], (IND), New Albany, IN.
New Bedford Area Catholic Youth Organization, [N], (FR). See Diocesean Catholic Youth Organization.
New Britain, [S], (HRT). See Catholic Charities-Catholic Family Services (Archdiocese of Hartford).
New Camaldoli, [A], (MRY), Big Sur, CA.
New Camaldoli Hermitage, [G], (MRY), Big Sur, CA.
New Camaldoli Hermitage, [I], (MRY), Big Sur, CA.
New Cassel Retirement Center, [H], (OM), Omaha, NE.
New Covenant Center: Education for Justice and Peace, [O], (OM), Omaha, NE.
New Covenant House of Hospitality (Yerwood Center), [G], (BGP). See Catholic Charities of Fairfield County.
New Directions Adult Day Health Care Center, [M], (NO), New Orleans, LA.
New England College Newman Center, [N], (MAN), Henniker, NH.
New England Conference of Diocesan Directors of Religious Education, [U], (PRO). See Miscellaneous Listings for the Diocese of Providence.
A New Genesis (ANG), [O], (GB), Green Bay, WI.
New Hampshire Catholic Charities, [G], (MAN), Manchester, NH.
New Hampshire Food Bank, [G], (MAN), Manchester, NH.
New Haven, [S], (HRT). See Catholic Charities-Catholic Family Services (Archdiocese of Hartford).
New Hope Manor, [O], (NY), Barryville, NY.
New Hope Manor, [HH], (NY), Barryville, NY.
New Hope Program, [C], (STA), Jacksonville, FL.
New Hope Treatment Center, [H], (BAL). See Bon Secours Baltimore Health Corporation, Inc.
New Horizons Adult Education Program, Inc., [Y], (BRK), Brooklyn, NY.
New Horizons of Faith, Inc., [D], (DAV), Davenport, IA.
New Jersey Boystown, [K], (NEW), Kearny, NJ.
New Jersey Caritas Corporation, Inc., [S], (NEW), Newark, NJ.
New Jerusalem, [O], (RVC), Bay Shore, NY.
New Jerusalem Community, [V], (CIN), Cincinnati, OH.
New Lenox Family Health Center, [G], (JOL). See St. Joseph Medical Center.
New Melleray Abbey, Order of Cistercians of the Strict Observance, [K], (DUB), Peosta, IA.
New Melleray Guest House, [M], (DUB), Dubuque, IA.
New Pathways, Counseling Services, School-Based Counseling Program, [K], (SAC). See Catholic Social Service, Sacramento.
New Phases, [H], (BAL). See Bon Secours Baltimore Health Corporation, Inc.
New Ulm Area Catholic Schools, [A], (NU), New Ulm, MN.
The New World, [X], (CHI), Chicago, IL.
New York Catholic Deaf Center, [O], (NY), New York, NY.
New York Catholic Forum, [HH], (NY), New York, NY.
New York Foundling Charitable Corp., [S], (NY), New York, NY.
New York Foundling Charitable Corp., [HH], (NY), New York, NY.
New York Foundling Hospital for Pediatric, Medical and Rehabilitative Care, Inc., [S], (NY), New York, NY.
New York Foundling Hospital, The, [S], (NY), New York, NY.
New York Institute for Human Development, Inc., [N], (NY). See Catholic Charities Department of Social and Community Development.
New York Maritime College, [GG], (NY). See University Apostolate.
New York Medical College, [GG], (NY). See University Apostolate.
New York State Catholic Conference, [T], (ALB), Albany, NY.
New York State Catholic Healthcare Council, [T], (ALB), Albany, NY.
New York State Council of Catholic Charities Directors, [T], (ALB), Albany, NY.
New York State Council of Catholic School Superintendents, [T], (ALB), Albany, NY.
New York State University at Albany, [S], (ALB), Albany, NY.
New York State University at Oneonta and Hartwick College, [S], (ALB), Oneonta, NY.
New York University, [GG], (NY). See University Apostolate.
Newark Abbey, [N], (NEW), Newark, NJ.
Newark Catholic High School, [C], (COL), Newark, OH.
*Newark Catholic High School Endowment Fund, [K], (COL), Newark, OH.
Newberry College Newman Center, [G], (CHR), Newberry, SC.
*Newburgh Ministry, [HH], (NY), Newburgh, NY.
Newman Apostolate, [EE], (PH), Philadelphia, PA.
Newman Apostolate Center, [T], (GAL), Galveston, TX.
Newman Apostolate-Valparaiso University, [N], (GRY), Valparaiso, IN.
Newman Association at SUNY Morrisville, [V], (SY), Morrisville, NY.
Newman Catholic, [G], (DUB), Mason City, IA.
Newman Catholic Fellowship, [H], (SB), San Bernardino, CA.
Newman Catholic Student Center, [H], (DAV), Iowa City, IA.
Newman Catholic Student Center, [H], (R), Chapel Hill, NC.
Newman Catholic Student Center, [L], (SCL), Morris, MN.
The Newman Center, [I], (BEL), Carbondale, IL.
Newman Center, [K], (GF), Billings, MT.
Newman Center, [I], (WIN), Mankato, MN.
Newman Center at Wabash College, [H], (LFT), Crawfordsville, IN.
Newman Center at Youngstown State University, [O], (Y), Youngstown, OH.
Newman Center for the University of Evansville, [I], (EVN), Evansville, IN.
The Newman Center Holy Spirit Parish University of Kentucky, [L], (LEX), Lexington, KY.
Newman Center of Northern Illinois University Educational Program, [L], (RCK), DeKalb, IL.
Newman Center, Inc., [L], (SCL), St. Cloud, MN.
Newman Center, San Francisco State University, [S], (SFR), San Francisco, CA.
Newman Center, University of California Medical Center, [S], (SFR), San Francisco, CA.
The Newman Center/Catholic Campus Ministry, [O], (SJ), San Jose, CA.
Newman Centers - Campus Ministry, [V], (BGP), Fairfield, CT.
Newman Centers and Campus Ministry, [P], (E), Erie, PA.
Newman Central Catholic High School, [B], (RCK), Sterling, IL.
Newman Club, Missouri Southern College, [I], (SPC), Webb City, MO.
Newman Community, Humboldt State University, [K], (SR), Arcata, CA.
Newman Foundation at Bradley University & Illinois Central College, [O], (PEO), Peoria, IL.
Newman Foundation for Catholic Students of Northern Illinois University, [M], (RCK), DeKalb, IL.
Newman Foundation of Chattanooga, Inc., [J], (KNX), Chattanooga, TN.
Newman Foundation of Cortland, Inc. at the State University College of New York, [V], (SY), Cortland, NY.
Newman Foundation, Inc., State University of New York, [V], (SY), Oswego, NY.
Newman Hall, Sonoma State University, Intercollegiate Catholic Ministries, [K], (SR), Penngrove, CA.
Newman High School, [C], (LC), Wausau, WI.
The Newman House at Northwest Missouri State University, [N], (KC), Maryville, MO.
Newman House Catholic Center at Boston University, [CC], (BO), Boston, MA.
Newman Institute for Historical and Religious Studies, [L], (MRY), Monterey, CA.
Newman Parish, [L], (LC), Eau Claire, WI.
The Newman Parish - Eau Claire Endowment Trust, [M], (LC), Eau Claire, WI.
Newman University Parish, [L], (LC), Stevens Point, WI.
Newport Central Catholic High School, [B], (COV), Newport, KY.
Next Passage, [H], (BAL). See Bon Secours Baltimore Health Corporation, Inc.
NH Catholic Charities, [G], (MAN), Berlin, NH.
NH Catholic Charities, [G], (MAN), Concord, NH.
NH Catholic Charities, [G], (MAN), Keene, NH.
NH Catholic Charities, [G], (MAN), Laconia, NH.
NH Catholic Charities, [G], (MAN), Lebanon, NH.
NH Catholic Charities, [G], (MAN), Littleton, NH.
NH Catholic Charities, [G], (MAN), Nashua, NH.
NH Catholic Charities, [G], (MAN), Rochester, NH.
NH Catholic Charities, [G], (MAN), Salem, NH.
Niagara Catholic Junior-Senior School, [D], (BUF), Niagara Falls, NY.
Niagara Community College, [K], (BUF). See Our Lady of Victory Hospital.
Niagara Falls, [H], (BUF). See The Catholic Charities of the Diocese of Buffalo.
Niagara Health Corporation, [E], (COL). See Mount Carmel Health System.
Niagara Homemaker Services, dba Mercy Home Care of Western New York, [K], (BUF), Lockport, NY.
Niagara University, [C], (BUF), Niagara University, NY.
Nichols College (Dudley), [Q], (WOR). See Campus Ministry.
Nigerian Apostolate, [T], (BRK). See Catholic Migration & Refugee Office, Catholic Migration Services, Inc.
Nim Pecquet Holy Family School Foundation, [M],

(BR). See Baton Rouge Chancery Office.
Ninth Street CDC, [AA], (CLV), Cleveland, OH.
Niobrara Valley House of Renewal, [O], (OM), Lynch, NE.
Noah Homes, [E], (SD), Spring Valley, CA.
Nocturnal Adoration Society of the United States, [HH], (NY), New York, NY.
Nolan Catholic High School, [A], (FWT), Fort Worth, TX.
Nolan School Trust, [A], (FWT). See Nolan Catholic High School.
Non-Secure Detention/Boysville of Michigan, Inc., [E], (GAY), Traverse City, MI.
NORBERT & CO., [O], (GB), De Pere, WI.
Norbertine Association of St. Joseph, Inc., [N], (ORG), Silverado, CA.
Norbertine Center for Spirituality, [M], (GB), De Pere, WI.
Norbertine Community of New Mexico, Inc., [N], (SFE), Albuquerque, NM.
Norbertine Fathers of Delaware, Inc., [I], (WIL), Claymont, DE.
Norbertine Fathers of Orange Inc., [H], (ORG), Silverado, CA.
Norbertine Generalate, Inc., [O], (GB), De Pere, WI.
Norbertine Retirement Fund Trust, [O], (GB), De Pere, WI.
Norco Adult Day Care, [M], (NO), Norco, LA.
Noreen McKeen Residence for Geriatric Care, [E], (PMB), West Palm Beach, FL.
Norfolk Catholic High School, [B], (OM), Norfolk, NE.
Noriega Adult Day Support Center, [Q], (SFR). See Catholic Charities of the Archdiocese of San Francisco.
Norm Fournier Court, [K], (SEA), Tacoma, WA.
Norris Square Senior Citizens Center, [R], (PH), Philadelphia, PA.
North America Union Sisters of Our Lady of Charity, Inc., [O], (WH), Wheeling, WV.
North American Center for Marianist Studies, [M], (CIN). See Marianist Provincialate.
North American College of Rome, Alumni Assoc. of, [HH], (NY), New York, NY.
North American La Salette Mission Center, [M], (HRT). See Missionaries of LaSalette Provincial Secretary.
North American La Salette Mission Center, Inc., [V], (HRT), Hartford, CT.
North American Union of the Sisters of Our Lady of Charity, [P], (BUF), Hamburg, NY.
North American Union of the Sisters of Our Lady of Charity, Inc., [J], (MAD), Wisconsin Dells, WI.
North American Union Sisters of Our Lady of Charity, [M], (E), Erie, PA.
North American Union Sisters of Our Lady of Charity, [K], (ELP), El Paso, TX.
North American Union, Sisters of Our Lady of Charity, [N], (SAT), San Antonio, TX.
North American Union-Sisters of Our Lady of Charity, OLC Holy Angels Convent, [J], (ROC), Rochester, NY.
North American Ursuline Education Services, [V], (CIN), Cincinnati, OH.
North Area Cares Emergency Assistance, [L], (DEN). See Catholic Charities and Community Services of the Archdiocese of Denver, Inc.
North Bronx Family Service Center, [R], (NY). See Pius XII Youth and Family Services, Inc.
North Cambridge Catholic High School, [D], (BO), Cambridge, MA.
North Carolina Central University, [H], (R), Durham, NC.
North Catholic Endowment Fund, [S], (PIT), Pittsburgh, PA.
North Catholic High School, [C], (PIT), Pittsburgh, PA.
North Central Catholic School Corp., [N], (AUS), Austin, TX.
North City, [W], (STL). See Catholic Family Services.
North Country Independent Living, Inc., [E], (SUP). See Catholic Charities Bureau, Inc.
North County, [H], (SFR). See San Mateo County District Council.
North East Hispanic Catholic Center, Inc., [HH], (NY), New York, NY.
North End Soup Kitchen, [D], (LAN), Flint, MI.
North Harris College Newman Center, [T], (GAL), Spring, TX.
North Idaho College, [F], (B), Coeur D'Alene, ID.
North Iowa Mercy Health Center, [H], (DUB), Mason City, IA.
North Shore-Danvers, [K], (BO). See Family Counseling and Guidance Centers.
North Texas San Benito, Inc., [N], (FWT), Fort Worth, TX.
North Tonawanda Catholic, [G], (BUF), North Tonawanda, NY.
Northeast Catholic Counseling Center, [Q], (P), Portland, OR.
Northeast Catholic High School for Boys, [D], (PH), Philadelphia, PA.
Northeast E.A. Center, [L], (DEN). See Catholic Charities and Community Services of the Archdiocese of Denver, Inc.
Northeast Hispanic Catholic Center, [HH], (NY), New York, NY.
Northeast Mississippi Community College Catholic Student Center, [G], (JKS), Booneville, MS.
Northeast Regional Catholic School, [H], (STP), Minneapolis, MN.
Northeastern Catholic Jr. High, [C], (ROC), Rochester, NY.
Northeastern Junior College (Sterling), [P], (DEN), Sterling, CO.
Northeastern Oklahoma A & M College Newman Center, [H], (TLS), Miami, OK.
Northeastern State University Catholic Student Organization, [H], (TLS), Tahlequah, OK.
Northern Cambria Catholic School, [C], (ALT), Nicktown, PA.
Northern Chautauqua Catholic, [G], (BUF), Dunkirk, NY.
Northern Koolau Health Education Center, [F], (HON). See St. Francis Healthcare System of Hawaii.
Northern Office, [E], (HBG). See Department for Catholic Charities Counseling/Field Services.
Northern Region, [N], (SY), Syracuse, NY.
Northern Region Religious Education Office & Special Education for Catechetics, [N], (SY), Syracuse, NY.
Northern Valley Catholic Social Service, [K], (SAC), Redding, CA.
Northern Wisconsin Center for the Developmentally Disabled, [P], (LC), Chippewa Falls, WI.
Northern Worcester Co., [H], (WOR). See Catholic Charities.
Northland House, [K], (LC), Wausau, WI.
Northside Community Health Center, [E], (LR), Fort Smith, AR.
Northside CYO, [K], (SY), Syracuse, NY.
Northside Office of Christian Response, [Q], (PEO), Peoria, IL.
Northview University Center, [W], (CHI), Chicago, IL.
Northwest, [W], (STL). See Catholic Family Services.
Northwest Catholic High School, [D], (HRT), West Hartford, CT.
NorthWest College, [E], (CHY), Powell, WY.
Northwest Covenant Medial Center, [J], (PAT), Denville, NJ.
Northwest Mississippi Community College Newman Center, [G], (JKS), Senatobia, MS.
Northwest Suburban Family Shelter, [G], (CHI). See Catholic Charities of the Archdiocese of Chicago-Archdiocesan Offices.
Northwest Suburban Senior Services, [G], (CHI). See Catholic Charities of the Archdiocese of Chicago-Archdiocesan Offices.
Northwestern State University, [J], (ALX), Natchitoches, LA.
Northwood Park Apartments, [H], (MEM), Memphis, TN.
Norwood-Fontbonne Academy for Boys and Girls, [I], (PH), Philadelphia, PA.
Notre Dame Academy, [E], (BO), Hingham, MA.
Notre Dame Academy, [F], (LA), Los Angeles, CA.
Notre Dame Academy, [C], (TOL), Toledo, OH.
Notre Dame Academy, [E], (WOR), Worcester, MA.
Notre Dame Academy (Elementary), [H], (LA), Los Angeles, CA.
Notre Dame Academy High School, [F], (NY), New York, NY.
Notre Dame Academy, Middleburg, VA, [E], (ARL), Middleburg, VA.
Notre Dame Academy-Elementary School, [H], (NY), New York, NY.
Notre Dame Catholic High School, [C], (BGP), Fairfield, CT.
Notre Dame Children's Class, [G], (BO), Wenham, MA.
Notre Dame Children's Endowment Trust, [M], (LC), Chippewa Falls, WI.
Notre Dame College, [B], (MAN), Manchester, NH.
Notre Dame College of Ohio, [C], (CLV), Cleveland, OH.
Notre Dame Community, [F], (AGN). See S.S.N.D. Regional House.
Notre Dame Community, [F], (AGN), Talofofo, GU.
Notre Dame Convalescent Home, [L], (BGP), Norwalk, CT.
Notre Dame Convent, [I], (FWT), Wichita Falls, TX.
Notre Dame Convent, [N], (HRT), Waterbury, CT.
Notre Dame Convent, [L], (TOL), Toledo, OH.
Notre Dame Convent, Sisters of the Congregation of Notre Dame, [F], (PT), Pensacola, FL.
Notre Dame de la Baie Academy, [D], (GB), Green Bay, WI.
Notre Dame de la Mer Retirement Apartments, [D], (BLX), Bay St. Louis, MS.
Notre Dame de Lourdes, [J], (PRT), Saco, ME.
Notre Dame de Sion Elementary School, [F], (KC), Kansas City, MO.
Notre Dame de Sion High School, [D], (KC), Kansas City, MO.
Notre Dame Development Fund, Inc., [X], (BO), Lowell, MA.
Notre Dame Diocesan Convent, [N], (TR), Trenton, NJ.
Notre Dame Education Center, [D], (BO), Lawrence, MA.
*Notre Dame Education Center, [V], (WDC), Washington, DC.
Notre Dame Education Center, Inc., [H], (JKS), Canton, MS.
Notre Dame Elementary School, [F], (CLV), Chardon, OH.
Notre Dame Elementary School, [C], (FWT), Wichita Falls, TX.
Notre Dame Elementary School, [F], (SCR), East Stroudsburg, PA.
Notre Dame Elementary School, [G], (SFR), Belmont, CA.
Notre Dame Graduate School of Christendom College, [B], (ARL), Arlington, VA.
Notre Dame High School, [A], (AGN), Talofofo, GU.
Notre Dame High School, [C], (ALN), Easton, PA.
Notre Dame High School, [D], (CHI), Chicago, IL.
Notre Dame High School, [D], (CHI), Niles, IL.
Notre Dame High School, [C], (COL), Portsmouth, OH.
Notre Dame High School, [E], (DAV), Burlington, IA.
Notre Dame High School, [E], (DET), Harper Woods, MI.
Notre Dame High School, [E], (HRT), West Haven, CT.
Notre Dame High School, [A], (KNX), Chattanooga, TN.
Notre Dame High School, [F], (LA), Sherman Oaks, CA.
Notre Dame High School, [C], (MRY), Salinas, CA.
Notre Dame High School, [B], (PEO), Peoria, IL.
Notre Dame High School, [B], (ROC), Elmira, NY.
Notre Dame High School, [B], (SB), Riverside, CA.
Notre Dame High School, [D], (SJ), San Jose, CA.
Notre Dame High School, [F], (STL), St. Louis, MO.
Notre Dame High School, [B], (TR), Trenton, NJ.
Notre Dame High School (Girls), [E], (SFR), Belmont, CA.
Notre Dame High School Financial Board of Trustees, [A], (KNX). See Notre Dame High School.
Notre Dame High School of Acadia Parish, [B], (LAF), Crowley, LA.
Notre Dame High School of Batavia, [D], (BUF), Batavia, NY.
Notre Dame Housing, Inc., [O], (OM), Omaha, NE.
Notre Dame Institute, [I], (PRT), Alfred, ME.
Notre Dame Interparochial School, [D], (SP), Spring Hill, FL.
Notre Dame Jr./Sr. High School, [C], (SY), Utica, NY.
Notre Dame Junior/Senior High School, [D], (SCR), East Stroudsburg, PA.
Notre Dame Living Center, Inc., [O], (OM), Omaha, NE.
Notre Dame Long Term Care Center, [K], (WOR), Worcester, MA.
Notre Dame Loyalty & Endowment Fund, Inc., [E], (HRT). See Notre Dame High School.
Notre Dame Middle School, [D], (LC). See Chippewa Area Catholic Schools.
Notre Dame Middle School, Inc., [G], (MIL), Milwaukee, WI.
Notre Dame Middle-High School, [A], (FWT), Wichita Falls, TX.
Notre Dame Ministry Corporation, [W], (STL), St. Louis, MO.
Notre Dame Mission Volunteer Corporation, [FF], (BO), Cambridge, MA.
Notre Dame Montessori School, [F], (CLV), Chardon, OH.
Notre Dame of Dallas Schools, Inc., [H], (DAL), Dallas, TX.
Notre Dame of Elm Grove, [Q], (MIL), Elm Grove, WI.
Notre Dame Parish Endowment Trust, [M], (LC), Chippewa Falls, WI.
Notre Dame Plaza Corporation, [P], (SJ), Saratoga, CA.
Notre Dame Preparatory High School and Marist Academy, [D], (DET), Pontiac, MI.
Notre Dame Preparatory School, [C], (BAL), Towson, MD.
Notre Dame Preparatory School, [E], (WOR), Fitchburg, MA.
Notre Dame Provincialate, [L], (TOL), Toledo, OH.
Notre Dame Regional High School, [B], (SPC), Cape Girardeau, MO.
Notre Dame Regional School, [E], (CAM), Newfield, NJ.
Notre Dame Regional School, [G], (PRO), West Warwick, RI.
Notre Dame Regional School, [C], (SLC), Price, UT.
Notre Dame Residence, [O], (SP), St. Petersburg, FL.
Notre Dame Retreat & Spiritual Center, [L], (PRT), Alfred, ME.
Notre Dame Retreat House, [K], (ROC), Canandaigua, NY.

O

Olean, [H], (BUF). See The Catholic Charities of the Diocese of Buffalo.
Ollie Steele Burden Manor, [G], (BR), Baton Rouge, LA.
Om Shanti, [M], (E), Erie, PA.
The Omaha Archdiocesan Community Foundation and Donor Directed Depository, [O], (OM), Omaha, NE.
The Omaha Archdiocesan Educational Foundation, Inc., [N], (OM), Omaha, NE.
Omaha Archdiocesan Educational Foundation, Inc., [O], (OM), Omaha, NE.
Omaha Catholic Jail Ministry, [O], (OM), Omaha, NE.
Ombudsman, [Q], (SFR). See Catholic Charities of the Archdiocese of San Francisco.
Omega Retreat Center, [O], (SAT), Boerne, TX.
OMI Senior Center, [Q], (SFR). See Catholic Charities of the Archdiocese of San Francisco.
ONE (Opportunity Network in Economics), [W], (SY), Syracuse, NY.
1-800-Mass-Times Trust, [L], (MIA), Key Largo, FL.
158 Chenango Street Housing Development Fund Company, Inc., [T], (BUF), Buffalo, NY.
161-01 89th Avenue Corp., [L], (BRK). See Catholic Charities.
The One Thousand Corporation, [I], (HRT). See Saint Francis Hospital and Medical Center.
One Thousand One Corporation, [I], (HRT). See Saint Francis Hospital and Medical Center.
Oneness in Peace Center, Inc., [T], (ALB), Germantown, NY.
Onondaga Community College Newman Center, [V], (SY), Syracuse, NY.
Onondaga County Catholic School Foundation (Western Region Catholic School Foundation), [W], (SY), Syracuse, NY.
Opdyke, Inc., [T], (DET), Bloomfield Hills, MI.
Opelousas Catholic School, [B], (LAF), Opelousas, LA.
Opelousas Housing Corporation, [N], (LAF), Opelousas, LA.
Open Hand Kitchen, [P], (L). See Society of St. Vincent de Paul, Council of Louisville.
Open Window Book and Gift Shop of the Diocese of Springfield, Inc., [L], (SPR), Chicopee, MA.
The Opening Word Program, Inc., [R], (RVC), Wyandanch, NY.
Operarios Del Reino De Cristo, O.R.C., [E], (SB), Riverside, CA.
Opportunity for Parochial Education Network (OPEN), [Q], (E), St. Marys, PA.
Opus Dei, [V], (BO), Chestnut Hill, MA.
Opus Dei, [I], (BUR), Randolph, VT.
Opus Dei, [W], (CHI), Chicago, IL.
Opus Dei, [L], (DAL), Irving, TX.
Opus Dei, [P], (GAL), Houston, TX.
Opus Dei, [I], (GRY), Valparaiso, IN.
Opus Dei, [M], (NEW), South Orange, NJ.
Opus Dei, [P], (PEO), Urbana, IL.
Opus Dei, [N], (PIT), Pittsburgh, PA.
Opus Dei, [F], (PMB), Delray Beach, FL.
Opus Dei, [T], (SFR), San Francisco, CA.
Opus Dei, [G], (SJN), Guaynabo, PR.
Opus Dei, [Q], (STL), Kirkwood, MO.
Opus Dei, [R], (TR), Princeton, NJ.
Opus Dei, [D], (VIC), Schulenburg, TX.
Opus Dei, [T], (WDC), Washington, DC.
Opus Dei (Prelature of the Holy Cross and Opus Dei), [C], (MGZ), Mayaguez, PR.
Opus Dei (Prelature of the Holy Cross and Opus Dei), [II], (NY), New Rochelle, NY.
Opus Dei (Prelature of the Holy Cross and Opus Dei), [R], (OAK), Berkeley, CA.
Opus Dei (Prelature of the Holy Cross and Opus Dei), [R], (SAT), San Antonio, TX.
Opus Dei, Mathewson House, [O], (PRO), Providence, RI.
Opus Dei, Prelature of the Holy Cross and Opus Dei, [V], (BO), Cambridge, MA.
Opus Dei. Prelature of the Holy Cross and Opus Dei, [Y], (LA), Los Angeles, CA.
Opus Dei-Prelature of the Holy Cross and Opus Dei., [O], (MIL), Brookfield, WI.
Opus Spiritus Sancti, [G], (SC), Pocahontas, IA.
Opus Spiritus Sancti-East Coast USA Region, [T], (PRO), Providence, RI.
Orange & Rockland Counties, [D], (NY). See Department of Education.
Orange County Catholic Alumni Club, [N], (ORG), Anaheim, CA.
Oratorian Community-Congregation of the Oratory of Pontifical Right, [G], (MRY), Monterey, CA.
The Oratory, [J], (HON), Honolulu, HI.
Oratory Academy, [B], (BWN), Pharr, TX.
The Oratory Catholic Preparatory School, [D], (NEW), Summit, NJ.
Oratory of St. Philip Neri, Congregation of the Oratory of Pontifical Rite, [D], (CHR), Rock Hill, SC.
Oratory of Saint Philip Neri, Congregation Pontifical Rite, [U], (BRK), Brooklyn, NY.
Oratory of St. Philip Neri, of Pontifical Right, [E], (BWN), Pharr, TX.
Orchard View, Inc., [D], (SC). See St. Anthony Regional Hospital.
Orchard View, Inc., [H], (SC), Carroll, IA.
Order of Friars Minor, [H], (AUS), Brenham, TX.
Order of Friars Minor Conventual, [M], (BAL), Ellicott City, MD.
Order of Friars Minor Conventual Immaculate Conception Province Charitable Trust, [T], (ALB), Rensselaer, NY.
Order of Friars Minor of the Province of the Most Holy Name aka Holy Name Province, [AA], (PH), Philadelphia, PA.
Order Of Preachers (Southern Dominican Prov.), [J], (MEM), Memphis, TN.
Order of Preachers (Southern Province), [N], (OAK), Oakland, CA.
Order of St. Augustine, [E], (KAL), Douglas, MI.
Order of St. Augustine, [AA], (PH), Villanova, PA.
Order of St. Augustine, [AA], (PH), Willowburn, PA.
Order of St. Sharbel Trust Fund, [E], (SAM), Staten Island, NY.
Order of the BVM of Mercy/Mercedarian Friars, [O], (BUF), LeRoy, NY.
Order of The Holy Trinity, [J], (MEM), Memphis, TN.
The Order of the Legion of Little Souls of the Merciful Heart of Jesus, [Q], (PEO), Moline, IL.
Order of the Visitation of Holy Mary, [J], (SPR), Tyringham, MA.
*The Ordinary Mutual, RRG, [U], (SFR), San Francisco, CA.
Oregon Catholic Conference, [Q], (P), Portland, OR.
Osborn Family Health Center, Inc., [H], (CAM). See Our Lady of Lourdes Medical Center, Inc.
OSF Healthcare Foundation, [J], (PEO). See OSF Healthcare System.
OSF Healthcare System, [J], (PEO), Peoria, IL.
OSF St. Joseph Medical Center, [J], (PEO), Bloomington, IL.
Osmund Program, [V], (WDC), Seat Pleasant, MD.
Ostrich Outreach Program, [L], (OKL). See Oklahoma Benedictine Institute on Mental Retardation, Inc.
OSU Charitable Trust, [HH], (NY), Bronx, NY.
Otsego Senior Apts., Inc., [F], (KAL), Otsego, MI.
Ottawa Cardiology Clinic, [G], (JOL). See St. Joseph Medical Center.
Our Blessed Lady of Victory Mission, Inc., [V], (MIL), Milwaukee, WI.
Our Help of Christians Elementary School, [F], (DET), Detroit, MI.
Our House of Minnesota, Inc. I, [R], (STP), St. Paul, MN.
Our House of Minnesota, Inc. II, [R], (STP), St. Paul, MN.
Our Lady of Angels Association, [T], (BUF), Niagara University, NY.
Our Lady of Angels Friary, [K], (SFD), Sherman, IL.
Our Lady of Angels Retirement Home, [I], (JOL), Joliet, IL.
Our Lady of Bellefonte Hospital, Inc., [D], (LEX), Ashland, KY.
Our Lady of Bethlehem Convent, [I], (COL), Columbus, OH.
Our Lady of Bethlehem Early Child Education Center, [I], (COL). See Our Lady of Bethlehem Convent.
Our Lady of Black Rock, [G], (BUF), Buffalo, NY.
Our Lady of Calvary Retreat House, [Q], (HRT), Farmington, CT.
Our Lady of Charity Center, Inc., [G], (GB), Green Bay, WI.
Our Lady of Charity, Inc., [DD], (LA), Lancaster, CA.
Our Lady of Comfort Women's Center, [HH], (NY), Newburgh, NY.
Our Lady of Compassion, [D], (KCK), Maple Hill, KS.
Our Lady of Confidence Day School, [J], (PH), Philadelphia, PA.
Our Lady of Consolation Geriatric Care Center, [J], (RVC), West Islip, NY.
Our Lady of Consolation Residence, [DD], (NY), New York, NY.
Our Lady of Creek Bend, [I], (RCK), St. Charles, IL.
Our Lady of Czestochowa, [N], (SAT), San Antonio, TX.
Our Lady of Czestochowa Shrine, [W], (CLV), Garfield Heights, OH.
Our Lady of Divine Providence House of Prayer, [Q], (SP). See Our Lady of Divine Providence, House of Prayer, Inc.
Our Lady of Divine Providence, House of Prayer, Inc., [Q], (SP), Clearwater, FL.
Our Lady of Elms Elementary School, [F], (CLV), Akron, OH.
Our Lady of Elms Pre-School, [I], (CLV), Akron, OH.
Our Lady of Fatima Apts., HDFC, Inc., [L], (BRK). See Catholic Charities.
Our Lady of Fatima Convent, [F], (BLX), Biloxi, MS.
Our Lady of Fatima Convent, [H], (SAC). See Institute of the Sisters of Mercy of the Americas.
Our Lady of Fatima Convent, [J], (WIL), New Castle, DE.
Our Lady of Fatima High School, [E], (PRO), Warren, RI.
Our Lady of Fatima Parish Conference, [E], (YAK), Moses Lake, WA.
Our Lady of Fatima Retreat Center, [M], (FTW), Notre Dame, IN.
Our Lady of Fatima Retreat House, Inc., [I], (IND), Indianapolis, IN.
Our Lady of Fatima Shrine, [BB], (BO), Holliston, MA.
Our Lady of Fatima Shrine, [H], (STU), Fatima, OH.
Our Lady of Fatima Villa, [I], (SJ), Saratoga, CA.
Our Lady of Fatima Villa Convent, [N], (SJ), Saratoga, CA.
Our Lady of Florida Spiritual Center, [G], (PMB), North Palm Beach, FL.
Our Lady of Florida Spiritual Center, [I], (PMB), North Palm Beach, FL.
Our Lady of Good Counsel Camp, [R], (SP), St. Petersburg, FL.
Our Lady of Good Counsel Franciscan Friary, [G], (WH), Morgantown, WV.
Our Lady of Good Counsel Historic Trust, Inc., [P], (BAL). See Chancery Office.
Our Lady of Good Counsel Home, [K], (STP), St. Paul, MN.
Our Lady of Good Counsel Residence, [U], (BRK), Brooklyn, NY.
Our Lady of Good Counsel Retreat House, [F], (LIN), Waverly, NE.
Our Lady of Good Voyage Chapel, [BB], (BO), Boston, MA.
Our Lady of Grace Convent, [P], (BGP), Stamford, CT.
Our Lady of Grace Convent, [D], (LUB), Lubbock, TX.
Our Lady of Grace Day Nursery, [H], (BGP), Stamford, CT.
Our Lady of Grace Home for Children, Inc., [F], (WIL), Newark, DE.
Our Lady of Grace Monastery, [K], (DET), Dearborn Heights, MI.
Our Lady of Grace Monastery, [M], (HRT), North Guilford, CT.
Our Lady of Grace Monastery for Sisters of St. Benedict of Beech Grove, IN, Inc., [K], (IND), Beech Grove, IN.
Our Lady of Grace Montessori School and Center, [F], (RVC), Manhasset, NY.
Our Lady of Grace School, [E], (CAM), Somerdale, NJ.
Our Lady of Grace Seminary, [B], (BO), Boston, MA.
Our Lady of Guadalupe Benedictine Abbey, [L], (SFE), Pecos, NM.
Our Lady of Guadalupe Campus, [C], (AMA). See Amarillo Catholic Children's Development Centers.
Our Lady of Guadalupe Convent, [K], (CHL), Cherokee, NC.
Our Lady of Guadalupe Convent, [EE], (NY), Bronx, NY.
Our Lady of Guadalupe Convent, [O], (OAK). See Dominican Sisters of Mission San Jose.
Our Lady of Guadalupe Mission, [D], (ALX), Forest Hill, LA.
Our Lady of Guadalupe Prayer Center, Inc., [E], (LSC), Las Cruces, NM.
Our Lady of Guadalupe Renewal Center, [L], (BAL), Catonsville, MD.
Our Lady of Guadalupe School, [B], (AMA), Amarillo, TX.
Our Lady of Guadalupe School, [B], (CC), Laredo, TX.
Our Lady of Guadalupe School, [E], (KC), Kansas City, MO.
Our Lady of Guadalupe Seminary, [M], (SCR). See Priestly Fraternity of St. Peter (F.S.S.P.), North American District Headquarters.
Our Lady of Holy Cross College, [C], (NO), New Orleans, LA.
Our Lady of Hope Center, [FF], (NY), Newburgh, NY.
Our Lady of Hope Health Center, Inc., [H], (RIC), Richmond, VA.
Our Lady of Hope Residence, [J], (ALB), Latham, NY.
Our Lady of Hope, House of Prayer, [L], (MAN), New Ipswich, NH.
Our Lady of Hungary Regional School, [D], (ALN), Northampton, PA.
Our Lady of Kazan Russian Greek Catholic Mission, [FF], (BO), Braintree, MA.
Our Lady of Lebanon Maronite Seminary, [A], (SAM), Washington, DC.
Our Lady of Levocha, [W], (CLV), Bedford, OH.
Our Lady of Life Apartments, Inc., [O], (STL), St. Louis, MO.
Our Lady of Light Chapel, [F], (TR), Trenton, NJ.
Our Lady of Light Chapel, [O], (TR), Trenton, NJ.
Our Lady of Loretto, [G], (ALT), Loretto, PA.
Our Lady of Lourdes, [W], (CLV), Cleveland, OH.
Our Lady of Lourdes, [I], (SAV), Columbus, GA.
Our Lady of Lourdes, [G], (SY), Utica, NY.
Our Lady of Lourdes Academy, [C], (MIA), Miami, FL.
Our Lady of Lourdes Associates Foundation, Inc., [H], (CAM). See Our Lady of Lourdes Medical Center, Inc.
Our Lady of Lourdes Convent, [K], (FR), Taunton, MA.

Our Lady of the Springs Community, [K], (KC), Blue Springs, MO.
Our Lady of the Valley, [F], (SPC), Pilot Knob, MO.
Our Lady of the Valley Educational Foundation, [I], (BIR), Birmingham, AL.
Our Lady of the Valley Retirement Community, [H], (RIC), Roanoke, VA.
Our Lady of the Valley School, [D], (ALN), Lansford-Summit Hill, PA.
Our Lady of the Valley School, [B], (HBG), Lebanon, PA.
Our Lady of the Wasatch Convent, [G], (SLC), Salt Lake City, UT.
Our Lady of the Waters House of Prayer, [G], (AGN), Agana, GU.
Our Lady of the Way Hospital, Inc., [D], (LEX), Martin, KY.
Our Lady of the Way Residence, [AA], (BO), Boston, MA.
Our Lady of the Woods, [O], (WDC). See Sisters of the Holy Cross.
Our Lady of Unity School, [C], (KCK), Kansas City, KS.
Our Lady of Valley Regional Elementary School, [F], (WOR), Uxbridge, MA.
Our Lady of Victories Regional Primary School, [H], (PRO), Woonsocket, RI.
Our Lady of Victory Academy High School, [F], (NY), Dobbs Ferry, NY.
Our Lady of Victory Convent, [O], (CHI), Lemont, IL.
Our Lady of Victory Convent, [N], (HRT), West Haven, CT.
Our Lady of Victory Convent, [I], (SD), El Centro, CA.
Our Lady of Victory Elementary, [D], (FWT), Fort Worth, TX.
Our Lady of Victory Homes of Charity, [T], (BUF), Lackawanna, NY.
Our Lady of Victory Hospital, [K], (BUF), Lackawanna, NY.
Our Lady of Victory Hospital Auxiliary, [K], (BUF), Lackawanna, NY.
Our Lady of Victory Missionary Sisters, [I], (AUS), Luling, TX.
Our Lady of Victory Missionary Sisters, [F], (SB), Coachella, CA.
Our Lady of Victory Missionary Sisters, [F], (SB), Yucaipa, CA.
Our Lady of Victory Missionary Sisters Convent, [N], (SAT), San Antonio, TX.
Our Lady of Victory Nursing Home, [I], (JOL), Bourbonnais, IL.
Our Lady of Vietnam Catholic Church - Pastoral Center, [M], (ATL), Riverdale, GA.
Our Lady of Wisdom Catholic Student Center, [L], (LAF), Lafayette, LA.
Our Lady of Wisdom Convent, [J], (PRT), St. Agatha, ME.
Our Lady of Wisdom Regional School, [E], (RVC), Port Jefferson, NY.
Our Lady Preschool Learning Center, [H], (BO), Marlboro, MA.
Our Lady Queen Contemplative Monastery, [I], (BR), Tickfaw, LA.
Our Lady Queen of Heaven Manor, [E], (LKC), Lake Charles, LA.
Our Lady Queen of Peace, [H], (GAL), Richwood, TX.
Our Lady Queen of the Clergy Home, [O], (BGP), Stamford, CT.
Our Lady's Academy, [B], (BLX), Bay St. Louis, MS.
Our Lady's Cathedral Academy, [D], (TR), Trenton, NJ.
Our Lady's Family Center, [N], (AUS), Austin, TX.
Our Lady's Guest and Retreat House, [EE], (NY), Graymoor, NY.
Our Lady's Guild House - Residence for Women, [AA], (BO), Boston, MA.
Our Lady's Haven of Fairhaven Inc., [I], (FR), Fairhaven, MA.
Our Lady's House of Peace, [Q], (SP). See Our Lady of Divine Providence, House of Prayer, Inc.
Our Lady's Inn, [W], (STL), St. Louis, MO.
Our Lady's Manor, Inc., [E], (ALX), Alexandria, LA.
Our Lady's Residence, [I], (CAM), Pleasantville, NJ.
Our Lady's Rosary Makers, [Q], (L), Louisville, KY.
Our Lady's Youth Center, [N], (ELP), El Paso, TX.
Our Lady, Queen of Apostles Regional School, [E], (RVC), Center Moriches, NY.
Our Lady, Queen of Peace, Assisted Living Community, [Q], (PRO). See Franciscan Missionaries of Mary.
Our Lady, Queen of the Clergy, [U], (PRO). See Miscellaneous Listings for the Diocese of Providence.
Our Lady, Queen of the Holy Rosary, [W], (CLV), Parma, OH.
Our Lady, Star of the Sea, [E], (CAM), Cape May, NJ.
Our Mother of Good Counsel Monastery, [C], (BO). See Merrimack College.
Our Mother of Perpetual Help Retreat Center, [S], (MIL), Oconomowoc, WI.
Our Mother's House, [J], (VEN), Venice, FL.
Our Place Day Care, [F], (SEA), Seattle, WA.
Our Sunday Visitor, Inc., [N], (FTW), Huntington, IN.
Outer Drive Campus, [S], (DET). See University of Detroit Mercy Campus Ministry.
Outpatient Clinic, [J], (BUF). See Baker Victory Services.
The Outpost, [J], (EVN), Santa Claus, IN.
Outreach East, [L], (LAN), Davison, MI.
Outreach in Love, [J], (RIC), Richmond, VA.
Outreach Office, [S], (HRT). See Catholic Charities-Catholic Family Services (Archdiocese of Hartford).
Overbrook Academy at Our Lady of Providence Center, [G], (PRO), Warwick, RI.
Overbrook School, [D], (NSH), Nashville, TN.
Overbrook, Incorporated, [U], (PRO), South Kingstown, RI.
Owensboro Catholic Consolidated School System, [J], (OWN), Owensboro, KY.
Owensboro Catholic High School, [B], (OWN), Owensboro, KY.
Ozanam Center, [H], (SFR). See Society of St. Vincent de Paul Archdiocesan Council.
Ozanam Hall of Queens Nursing Home, Inc., [R], (BRK), Bayside, NY.
Ozanam Inn, [P], (L). See Society of St. Vincent de Paul, Council of Louisville.
Ozanam Inn, [L], (NO), New Orleans, LA.
The Ozanam Shelter for Families and Single Women, [N], (MET), Edison, NJ.
Oznam Geriatric Foundation, [Y], (BRK), Bayside, NY.

P

P.I.M.E. College Community, [K], (DET), Detroit, MI.
P.I.M.E. Mission & Prayer Center, [H], (COL), Newark, OH.
P.I.M.E. Missionaries, [G], (PMB), Tequesta, FL.
P.I.M.E. Missionaries of SS. Peter and Paul, [K], (DET), Detroit, MI.
P.I.M.E. Missionaries Residence, [M], (PAT), Wayne, NJ.
P.O.M., Inc., [L], (MIA), Miami Shores, FL.
P.S. 91, [R], (NY). See Pius XII Youth and Family Services, Inc.
PACE - Parents Alliance for Catholic Education, [R], (WOR), Worcester, MA.
Pace University, [GG], (NY). See University Apostolate.
Pace University-Westchester, Suny, Purchase, [GG], (NY). See University Apostolate.
Pacelli Catholic High School, [A], (SAV), Columbus, GA.
Pacelli High School, [C], (LC), Stevens Point, WI.
Pacelli High School Foundation, [M], (LC), Stevens Point, WI.
Pacelli Senior High School, [C], (WIN). See Austin Area Catholic Schools.
Pacem in Terris Center for Spirituality, [K], (SCL), St. Francis, MN.
Pacific Institute for Community Organization, [S], (OAK), Oakland, CA.
Padre Pio Health Care Center, Inc. dba Stonehill Care Center, [J], (DUB), Dubuque, IA.
Padre Pio Shelter for Homeless Men, [AA], (NY), New York, NY.
Padua Community Services Pediatric Residential Program, [K], (NO), Belle Chasse, LA.
Padua Franciscan Friary, [P], (CLV), Cleveland, OH.
Padua Franciscan High School, [E], (CLV), Cleveland, OH.
Padua Friary, [DD], (NY), New York, NY.
Padua Hills Apartments, [D], (PHX), Wickenburg, AZ.
Padua Place, [K], (SAT), San Antonio, TX.
Paewalani Community, [I], (HON). See Congregation of the Sacred Hearts and of Perpetual Adoration.
Pakistan Apostolate, [T], (BRK). See Catholic Migration & Refugee Office, Catholic Migration Services, Inc.
Pala Rey Youth Camp & Retreat Center, [K], (SD), Pala, CA.
Palisades Retreat House, [O], (SEA), Federal Way, WA.
Pallotine Charitable, Educational and Apostolic Ministry Trust, [P], (BAL), Baltimore, MD.
Pallotti Convent, [O], (WDC), Laurel, MD.
Pallotti House, [P], (MIL), Milwaukee, WI.
Pallottine Center for Apostolic Causes, [M], (BAL), Baltimore, MD.
Pallottine Charitable, Educational and Apostolic Ministry Trust, [P], (BAL). See Chancery Office.
Pallottine Fathers, [K], (DET), Wyandotte, MI.
Pallottine Fathers, [DD], (NY), New York, NY.
Pallottine Fathers and Brothers, Inc., Disability Trust, [Y], (MIL), Milwaukee, WI.
Pallottine Fathers and Brothers, Inc., Educational and Apostolic Ministry Trust, [Y], (MIL), Milwaukee, WI.
Pallottine Health Services, Inc., [K], (WH), Huntington, WV.
Pallottine Missionary Sisters-Frascati Community, [R], (STL), Lonedell, MO.
Pallottine Missionary Sisters-Queen of Apostles Province, [R], (STL), Florissant, MO.
Pallottine Renewal Center, [T], (STL), Florissant, MO.
Pallottine Seminary at Green Hill, [B], (WDC), West Hyattsville, MD.
The Pallottines of South Orange, Inc., [S], (NEW), South Orange, NJ.
Palma Community, [G], (MRY), Salinas, CA.
Palmetto Catholic Charities, [J], (VEN), Palmetto, FL.
Palo Alto/Los Altos Auxiliary, [F], (SJ). See Catholic Charities of Santa Clara County.
Pamphile and Mabyn Donaldson Trust for St. Louis King of France Church, [M], (BR). See Baton Rouge Chancery Office.
Paraclete High School, [D], (LA), Lancaster, CA.
Paradise School, [E], (HBG). See Department for Catholic Charities Counseling/Field Services.
Paramus Catholic High School, [D], (NEW), Paramus, NJ.
Paris Foreign Mission Society Residence, [N], (SFR), San Francisco, CA.
Parish Conferences, [P], (L). See Society of St. Vincent de Paul, Council of Louisville.
Parish Endowment Trust Fund of St. Michael Catholic Church, [N], (OM). See The Omaha Archdiocesan Educational Foundation, Inc.
Parish Kitchen, [O], (COV), Covington, KY.
Parish Mission Team Res., [DD], (NY), Suffern, NY.
Parish Outreach Program, [H], (BUF). See The Catholic Charities of the Diocese of Buffalo.
Parish Social Ministry, [I], (GAL). See Associated Catholic Charities of the Diocese of Galveston-Houston.
Parish Social Ministry, [D], (LAN). See Catholic Social Services-St. Vincent Home, Inc.
Parish Social Ministry, [M], (NY). See Catholic Charities Department of Parish and Community Outreach.
Parish Social Ministry, [E], (PRT). See Catholic Charities Maine.
Parish Social Ministry, [H], (RVC). See Catholic Charities Central Administration.
Parish Social Ministry Outreach, [Q], (BAL), Baltimore, MD.
Parish Social Ministry/Community Connections, [F], (ATL). See Catholic Social Services, Inc.
Parish Social Work Program, [H], (BUF). See The Catholic Charities of the Diocese of Buffalo.
Parish Visitors of Mary Immaculate, [EE], (NY), New York, NY.
Parish Visitors of Mary Immaculate, [EE], (NY), Monroe, NY.
Parish Visitors of Mary Immaculate, [O], (SCR), Scranton, PA.
Parish/Family Services, [E], (SR). See Diocese of Santa Rosa, Catholic Charities.
Parishes with Ministry to Spanish Speaking: St. Bernard, [X], (CLV). See Diocesan Hispanic Office.
Park Circle Health Center, [H], (BAL). See Bon Secours Baltimore Health Corporation, Inc.
Park Performing Arts, Inc., [S], (NEW), Union City, NJ.
Park Village Child Development Center, [H], (HRT), West Hartford, CT.
Parkersburg Catholic Elementary School, [D], (WH), Parkersburg, WV.
Parkersburg Catholic Junior-Senior High School, [B], (WH), Parkersburg, WV.
Parkersburg Catholic Schools Foundation, Inc., [P], (WH), Parkersburg, WV.
Parkland Hospital, [I], (DAL), Dallas, TX.
Parkville, HDFC, [L], (BRK). See Catholic Charities.
Parkwood Retirement Apartments, [D], (SFS), Pierre, SD.
Parmadale, [M], (CLV), Parma, OH.
Parmadale, [V], (CLV). See Catholic Charities Services Corporation.
Parsons Manor, [U], (BRK), Jamaica, NY.
Particular Council of Flint, [L], (LAN), Flint, MI.
Particular Council of Gary, [M], (GRY). See Catholic Charities.
Particular Council of Staten Island, [Q], (NY), Staten Island, NY.
Particular Council of the St. Vincent de Paul Society, [U], (HRT), Hartford, CT.
Particular Council of Wichita Falls, St. Vincent de Paul Society, [L], (FWT), Wichita Falls, TX.
*Partners in Housing, Inc., [H], (COS), Colorado Springs, CO.
Partnership for Quality Education, Inc., [HH], (NY), New York, NY.
Passaic Catholic Regional School, [F], (PAT), Passaic, NJ.
Passionist Communications Center, [HH], (NY). See Passionist Communications, Inc.
Passionist Communications, Inc., [HH], (NY), Pelham, NY.
Passionist Community, [R], (LA), Pasadena, CA.
Passionist Community-CTU, [N], (CHI), Chicago, IL.

Pro Sanctity Spirituality Center, Retreat House, [M], (ORG), Fullerton, CA.
Professional Counseling Services of Humboldt/Del Norte, [E], (SR). See Diocese of Santa Rosa, Catholic Charities.
Professional Foster Care, [E], (SR). See Diocese of Santa Rosa, Catholic Charities.
Professional Office Corporation, [C], (FRS). See Saint Agnes' Medical Center.
Program for the Medically Underserved of Cincinnati, [R], (CIN), Cincinnati, OH.
Progress for the Diocese of El Paso, [N], (ELP), El Paso, TX.
Progress of Peoples Development Corporation, [L], (BRK). See Catholic Charities.
Progress of Peoples Managment Corporation, [L], (BRK). See Catholic Charities.
PROJECT AIMM, [Q], (L), Louisville, KY.
Project Ayuda, [D], (TUC). See Social Service Agencies: Pima County.
Project Hope, Inc., [V], (HRT), West Hartford, CT.
Project Irish Outreach, [L], (NY). See Catholic Charities Department of Migration Services.
Project Lazarus, [L], (NO), New Orleans, LA.
Project REMAIN, [R], (SCR), Wilkes-Barre, PA.
Project Renewal of Davenport, Inc., [K], (DAV), Davenport, IA.
Project Timothy: Christian Service Center, [O], (SPK), Dayton, WA.
*The Promise Outreach, Inc., [S], (NEW), Lodi, NJ.
Pronto of Long Island, Inc., [R], (RVC), Bay Shore, NY.
Propagation of the Faith, [B], (STV). See Miscellaneous Organizations.
Propagation of the Faith and Holy Childhood Association & Society of St. Peter the Apostle, [FF], (BO), Boston, MA.
Propagation of the Faith Holy Childhood Association, [J], (STU), Cambridge, OH.
The Prout School, [C], (PRO), South Kingstown, RI.
Provenant Acute Long Stay Hospital, [H], (DEN), Denver, CO.
Provenant Home Health and Eldercare Services, [H], (DEN), Denver, CO.
Providence Alaska Foundation, [C], (ANC), Anchorage, AK.
Providence Alaska Medical Center, [C], (ANC), Anchorage, AK.
Providence Alaska Medical Center, [H], (ANC), Anchorage, AK.
*Providence Building Corporation, [L], (MOB), Mobile, AL.
Providence Care Center, [K], (LA). See Providence Health System.
Providence Care Centers (Springfield), [H], (SPR). See Sisters of Providence Care Centers, Inc.
Providence Care Centers (Washington), [H], (SPR). See Sisters of Providence Care Centers, Inc.
Providence Catholic High School, [C], (JOL), New Lenox, IL.
Providence Catholic Schools Collaborative, [U], (PRO). See Miscellaneous Listings for the Diocese of Providence.
Providence Center, [CC], (PH), Yardley, PA.
Providence Center, [G], (STA). See Jacksonville, Family Housing Management Co.
Providence Centralia Hospital, [G], (SEA), Centralia, WA.
Providence Child Care Center, [I], (PIT), Pittsburgh, PA.
Providence Child Care Center, South, [I], (PIT). See Providence Connections, Inc.
*Providence Child Center, [H], (P), Portland, OR.
Providence College, [B], (PRO), Providence, RI.
*Providence Community Health Foundation, Medford, [J], (P). See Providence Medford Medical Center.
Providence Connections, Inc., [I], (PIT), Allison Park, PA.
Providence Day Care Center, North, [I], (PIT). See Providence Connections, Inc.
Providence Extended Care Center, [D], (ANC), Anchorage, AK.
Providence Extended Care Center, [K], (WOR), Worcester, MA.
Providence Family Support Center, [I], (PIT). See Providence Connections, Inc.
Providence Foundation, [E], (MOB), Mobile, AL.
Providence Foundation, [I], (SCR), Williamsport, PA.
The Providence Fund, [P], (BUF). See Holy Name Province - Provincial Motherhouse.
The Providence Fund, [O], (TOL), Sandusky, OH.
Providence General Medical Center, [G], (SEA), Everett, WA.
Providence Health Center, [F], (AUS), Waco, TX.
Providence Health Foundation, [K], (WDC). See De Paul Foundation, Inc.
Providence Health Services, [I], (NY). See The Catholic Charities of the Archdiocese of New York.
Providence Health Services, Inc., [K], (WDC), Washington, DC.
Providence Health System, [K], (LA), Burbank, CA.
Providence Health System, Inc., [I], (SCR), Williamsport, PA.
Providence Healthcare Services, [E], (MOB), Mobile, AL.
Providence Heights Alpha School, [G], (PIT), Allison Park, PA.
Providence High School, [F], (LA), Burbank, CA.
Providence High School, [F], (SAT), San Antonio, TX.
Providence Holy Cross Medical Center, [K], (LA). See Providence Health System.
Providence Home & Family Services, Inc., [I], (SAT), San Antonio, TX.
Providence Home Care and Hospice of Snohomish County, [J], (SEA), Everett, WA.
Providence Home Services, [J], (SEA), Seattle, WA.
Providence Home, Nursing Home for the Needy, [F], (EVN), Jasper, IN.
Providence Horizon House, [K], (ANC), Anchorage, AK.
Providence Hospital, [H], (DET), Southfield, MI.
Providence Hospital, [E], (MOB), Mobile, AL.
Providence Hospital, [B], (YAK), Toppenish, WA.
Providence Hospital Campus of Mercy Hospital, [F], (SPR). See Mercy Hospital.
Providence Hospital Inc., [H], (TOL), Sandusky, OH.
Providence Hospital School of Nursing, [H], (TOL). See Providence Hospital Inc.
Providence Hospital School of Radiology, [H], (TOL). See Providence Hospital Inc.
Providence Hospitality House, [L], (SEA), Seattle, WA.
Providence House, [Q], (SP). See Our Lady of Divine Providence, House of Prayer, Inc.
Providence House Apartments, [Q], (SY), Syracuse, NY.
Providence House Division, [F], (TR). See Catholic Charities.
Providence House Nursing Home of Millbury, [K], (WOR), Millbury, MA.
Providence House Nursing Home of Southbridge, [K], (WOR), Southbridge, MA.
Providence House, Inc., [L], (BRK). See Catholic Charities.
Providence Housing Development Corporation, [L], (ROC), Rochester, NY.
Providence Marianwood, [I], (SEA), Issaquah, WA.
Providence Medford Medical Center, [J], (P), Medford, OR.
Providence Medical Center, [F], (KCK), Kansas City, KS.
Providence Medical Center, [G], (OM), Wayne, NE.
Providence Medical Center Foundation, [K], (KCK), Kansas City, KS.
Providence Medical Foundation, [J], (P). See Providence Portland Medical Center.
*Providence Milwaukie Foundation, Milwaukie, [J], (P). See Providence Milwaukie Hospital.
*Providence Milwaukie Hospital, [J], (P), Milwaukie, OR.
Providence Ministries for the Needy, Inc., [G], (SPR), Holyoke, MA.
Providence Ministries for the Needy, Inc., [J], (SPR). See Sisters of Providence Infirmary.
Providence Montessori School, [H], (P). See Providence Child Center.
Providence Mother Joseph Care Center, [J], (SEA), Olympia, WA.
Providence Mount St. Vincent, [I], (SEA), Seattle, WA.
Providence Mount St. Vincent, [K], (SEA), Seattle, WA.
Providence Newberg Hospital, [J], (P), Newberg, OR.
Providence Newman Center, [O], (RVC), Selden, NY.
Providence Place, [G], (KCK), Kansas City, KS.
Providence Place, [K], (SEA), Chehalis, WA.
Providence Portland Medical Center, [J], (P), Portland, OR.
Providence Rest, [Z], (NY), Bronx, NY.
Providence Rest Child Day Care Center, Inc., [V], (NY), New York, NY.
Providence Saint Joseph Medical Center, [K], (LA), Burbank, CA.
Providence St. Joseph Medical Center, [K], (LA). See Providence Health System.
Providence St. Peter Hospital, [G], (SEA), Olympia, WA.
Providence St. Vincent Medical Center, [J], (P), Portland, OR.
Providence Seaside Hospital, [J], (P), Seaside, OR.
*Providence Seaside Hospital Foundation, Inc., [J], (P). See Providence Seaside Hospital.
Providence Seattle Medical Center, [G], (SEA), Seattle, WA.
Providence Self-Sufficiency Ministries, Inc., [K], (IND). See Sisters of Providence General Administration.
Providence Services, [O], (SPK), Spokane, WA.
Providence Sisters, [O], (OAK), Oakland, CA.
Providence Sound Home Care and Hospice, [J], (SEA), Olympia, WA.
Providence Trust, [S], (SAT), Helotes, TX.
Providence Trust, [W], (STL), Eureka, MO.
Providence Yakima Medical Center, [B], (YAK), Yakima, WA.
Province Center, Adorers of the Blood of Christ, Province of Ruma, [G], (BEL), Ruma, IL.
Province Development Office, [E], (BLX). See Southern Province of St. Augustine - Provincial Residence.
Province of Our Lady of Consolation, Inc., [I], (IND). See Mount Saint Francis Friary and Retreat Center.
Provincial Administration Office, Oblates of Mary Immaculate (Southern Prov.), [M], (SAT), San Antonio, TX.
Provincial Center, Religious Sacred Heart of Mary, [EE], (NY), Tarrytown, NY.
Provincial Definitors of the Province of Saint Barbara, [DD], (LA). See St. Francis Center.
Provincial Headquarters for the Conventual Franciscan Province, [J], (IND), Mount Saint Francis, IN.
Provincial House, [X], (BO), Methuen, MA.
Provincial House, [N], (HRT), East Haven, CT.
Provincial House, [O], (RVC). See Religious of Our Lady of the Retreat in the Cenacle.
Provincial House and Formation House, [J], (SPR), Holyoke, MA.
Provincial House and Novitiate, [N], (HRT). See Felician Sisters - Our Lady of the Angels.
Provincial House and Novitiate of the Sisters of St. Felix, [L], (DET), Livonia, MI.
Provincial House of Daughters of the Charity of the Sacred Heart of Jesus, [L], (MAN), Littleton, NH.
Provincial House of the Cincinnati Province of the Society of the Precious Blood, [M], (CIN), Dayton, OH.
Provincial House of the Dallas Province, [N], (DAL). See School Sisters of Notre Dame.
Provincial House of the Missionary Sisters Servants of the Holy Spirit, [O], (CHI), Techny, IL.
Provincial House of the School Sisters of Notre Dame, [G], (WIN), Mankato, MN.
Provincial House of the Sisters of Notre Dame, Juniorate, Novitiate, [Q], (CLV), Chardon, OH.
Provincial House of the Sisters of St. Francis of Penance and Christian Charity, [O], (SFR), Redwood City, CA.
Provincial House of the Sisters of St. Joseph of Carondelet, [S], (LA), Los Angeles, CA.
Provincial House of the Sisters of St. Joseph of Carondelet (Albany Province), [M], (ALB), Latham, NY.
Provincial House of the Sisters of the Holy Family of Nazareth, [O], (CHI), Des Plaines, IL.
Provincial House of the Sisters of the Holy Family of Nazareth, [BB], (PH), Philadelphia, PA.
Provincial House, Congregation de Notre Dame, [P], (BGP), Ridgefield, CT.
Provincial House, Health Center of Sisters of Notre Dame de Namur, [N], (CIN), Cincinnati, OH.
Provincial House, Immaculate Heart of Mary Province, Sisters of the Holy Family of Nazareth, C.S.F.N., [P], (BGP), Monroe, CT.
Provincial House, Juniorate and Novitiate of the Sisters of Resurrection, [M], (ALB), Castleton-on-Hudson, NY.
Provincial House, Society of the Sacred Heart-United States Province, [R], (STL), St. Louis, MO.
Provincial Motherhouse and Novitiate of the Daughters of Divine Charity, [Q], (CLV), Akron, OH.
Provincial Motherhouse and Novitiate of the Notre Dame Sisters, [L], (OM), Omaha, NE.
Provincial Motherhouse of Brothers of Mercy, [O], (BUF), Clarence, NY.
Provincial Motherhouse of the Carmelite Sisters of the Divine Heart of Jesus, [Q], (MIL), Wauwatosa, WI.
Provincial Motherhouse of the Sisters of St. Basil the Great, [F], (PHU), Fox Chase Manor, PA.
Provincial Office of Lay Carmelites and Scapular Confraternity, [M], (JOL), Darien, IL.
Provincial Office of the Congregation of the Resurrection, [N], (CHI), Chicago, IL.
Provincial Offices - Discalced Carmelites, [P], (MIL), Milwaukee, WI.
Provincial Offices of the Order of St. Augustine, Province of St. Thomas of Villanova, [AA], (PH), Villanova, PA.
Provincial Offices of the Priests and Brothers of Holy Cross, Eastern Province, [O], (BGP), Bridgeport, CT.
Provincial Realty Associates, Inc., [L], (MIA), Miami Shores, FL.
Provincial Residence, [J], (PRT), Saco, ME.
Provincial Residence, [N], (SFR), San Francisco, CA.
Provincial Residence and Novitiate, [N], (RVC), Mineola, NY.
Provincial Residence of the Handmaids of the Sacred Heart of Jesus, [BB], (PH), Haverford, PA.
Provincial Residence, Sisters of Divine Providence, [X], (BO), Kingston, MA.
Provincial Vocation Office, [P], (STL). See La Salette Missionaries.

Q

R

S

St. Agnes Foundation, Inc., [H], (BAL). See St. Agnes HealthCare, Inc.
St. Agnes HealthCare, Inc., [H], (BAL), Baltimore, MD.
St. Agnes Home for the Elderly, [O], (STL), Kirkwood, MO.
Saint Agnes Home, Inc., [J], (HRT), West Hartford, CT.
St. Agnes Hospital and Children's Rehabilitation Center, [W], (NY), White Plains, NY.
St. Agnes Hospital Convent, [F], (FRS), Fresno, CA.
St. Agnes Hospital Foundation, Inc., [P], (BAL). See Chancery Office.
St. Agnes Medical Center, [U], (PH), Philadelphia, PA.
St. Agnes Nursing and Rehabilitation Center, [I], (BAL), Ellicott City, MD.
St. Agnes School of Omaha, Inc., [D], (OM), Omaha, NE.
St. Agnes Seminary, [J], (BRK), Brooklyn, NY.
Saint Agnes' Medical Center, [C], (FRS), Fresno, CA.
St. Agnes' Residence, [AA], (NY), New York, NY.
St. Agnes-Sacred Heart School, [H], (PH), Sellersvile, PA.
Saint Albert Catholic Schools, [C], (DM), Council Bluffs, IA.
St. Albert Educational Foundation, [J], (DM), Council Bluffs, IA.
St. Albert Hall dba St. Albert Early Learning Center, [J], (SAT), Boerne, TX.
St. Albert Intermediate School, [A], (DM). See Council Bluffs Area Catholic Education Systems, Inc.
St. Albert Junior High School, [A], (DM). See Council Bluffs Area Catholic Education Systems, Inc.
St. Albert Primary School, [A], (DM). See Council Bluffs Area Catholic Education Systems, Inc.
St. Albert School, [E], (MAN), West Stewartstown, NH.
St. Albert the Great Catholic Center, [K], (BR), Hammond, LA.
St. Albert the Great House of Studies, [H], (LAN), De Witt, MI.
St. Albert the Great Priory, [N], (STP), Minneapolis, MN.
St. Albert the Great, University Parish, [G], (MAR), Houghton, MI.
St. Albert's Priory, [DD], (NY), Middletown, NY.
St. Alexis Hospital Medical Center, [J], (CLV), Cleveland, OH.
St. Alexius Medical Center, [D], (BIS), Bismarck, ND.
St. Alice Convent, [D], (LUB), Plainview, TX.
St. Aloisius Medical Center, [D], (FAR), Harvey, ND.
St. Aloysius Academy, [I], (PH), Bryn Mawr, PA.
St. Aloysius Educational Foundation, [I], (BIR), Bessemer, AL.
St. Aloysius Novitiate, [EE], (NY), Hopewell Junction, NY.
St. Aloysius Orphanage, [I], (CIN), Cincinnati, OH.
St. Aloysius Parish Conference, [E], (YAK), Toppenish, WA.
St. Aloysius School Endowment Fund, [M], (BR). See Baton Rouge Chancery Office.
St. Alphonsus Formation Residence, [C], (BRK), Whitestone, NY.
St. Alphonsus House, [AA], (PH). See Jesuit Community at St. Joseph's University.
St. Alphonsus House, [AA], (PH), Philadelphia, PA.
St. Alphonsus Rectory of the Redemptorist, [P], (STL), St. Louis, MO.
St. Alphonsus Regional Medical Center Convent-Sisters of Holy Cross, [D], (B), Boise, ID.
St. Alphonsus Regional Medical Center, Inc., [B], (B), Boise, ID.
St. Alphonsus Residence, [G], (VEN), Venice, FL.
St. Alphonsus Villa-Redemptorist Fathers and Brothers, [F], (ORL), New Smyrna Beach, FL.
St. Ambrose, [E], (BGP). See Catholic Elementary Schools-Region X.
St. Ambrose University, [B], (DAV), Davenport, IA.
St. Ambrose University Seminary, [A], (DAV), Davenport, IA.
St. Andre Health Care Facility, [G], (PRT), Biddeford, ME.
St. Andre Home, Inc., [F], (PRT), Biddeford, ME.
St. Andre Housing, Inc., [N], (PRT), Biddeford, ME.
St. Andre's Group Home for Pregnant and Parenting Young Women, [F], (PRT), Biddeford, ME.
St. Andre's Group Home for Single Mothers with Infants, [F], (PRT), Bangor, ME.
St. Andre's Group Home for Troubled Girls, [F], (PRT), Lewiston, ME.
Saint Andrew Early Childhood Center, [B], (R), Apex, NC.
Saint Andrew Hall, [A], (SY), Syracuse, NY.
St. Andrew Home, [G], (CHI). See Catholic Charities of the Archdiocese of Chicago-Archdiocesan Offices.
St. Andrew Home for the Aged, [M], (CHI), Niles, IL.
St. Andrew Kim Korean Catholic Society, [V], (CIN), Cincinnati, OH.
St. Andrew Kim Roman Catholic Church Society of Amherst, NY, Diocese of Buffalo, [T], (BUF), Amherst, NY.
St. Andrew Legal Clinic, [Q], (P), Portland, OR.
St. Andrew's Abbey, [R], (LA), Valyermo, CA.
St. Andrew's Abbey Retreat House (All Groups), [X], (LA), Valyermo, CA.
St. Andrew's Health Center, [D], (FAR), Bottineau, ND.
St. Andrew's Retreat House, [FF], (NY), Walden, NY.
St. Andrew's Theatine House, [A], (DEN), Denver, CO.
St. Andrews Newman Center, [H], (SB), Riverside, CA.
St. Angela Education Center, [F], (L), Louisville, KY.
St. Angela Hall Academy, [J], (BRK), Brooklyn, NY.
St. Angela Merici School, [C], (OWN), Owensboro, KY.
St. Ann Center for Intergenerational Care, Inc., [N], (MIL), St. Francis, WI.
St. Ann Convent, [N], (HRT), New Britain, CT.
St. Ann Convent, [G], (TUC), Tucson, AZ.
St. Ann Day Care, [O], (NEW). See St. Joseph Province Shalom Center.
St. Ann Elementary, [B], (GAY), Cadillac, MI.
Saint Ann Foundation, [Q], (CLV). See Mount Augustine, Motherhouse of the Sisters of Charity of St. Augustine.
St. Ann Friary, [M], (CIN), Cincinnati, OH.
St. Ann Home, [J], (MAN), Dover, NH.
St. Ann Interparochial School, [C], (OWN), Morganfield, KY.
St. Ann Mission Center, [K], (AUS), Somerville, TX.
St. Ann Rest Home, [N], (MIL), Milwaukee, WI.
St. Ann School, [D], (CHL). See Mecklenburg Area Catholic Schools (M.A.C.S.).
*St. Ann School Foundation, Inc., [K], (VEN), Naples, FL.
St. Ann's Auxiliary, [E], (COL). See Mount Carmel Health System.
St. Ann's Care Center, Inc., [A], (JUN), Juneau, AK.
St. Ann's Convent, [J], (PRT), Indian Island, ME.
St. Ann's Convent, [J], (PRT), Pleasant Point, ME.
St. Ann's Corporation, [I], (SFS), Watertown, SD.
St. Ann's Educational Foundation, [I], (BIR), Decatur, AL.
St. Ann's Home, [G], (GR), Grand Rapids, MI.
St. Ann's Home, [F], (SCL), Cold Spring, MN.
St. Ann's Home for the Aged, [H], (NEW), Jersey City, NJ.
St. Ann's Home for the Aged, [O], (NEW). See St. Joseph Province Shalom Center.
St. Ann's Home for the Aged, [E], (ROC), Rochester, NY.
St. Ann's Home Inc., [F], (OKL), Oklahoma City, OK.
St. Ann's Home Special Needs School, [I], (BO), Methuen, MA.
St. Ann's Home, Inc., [M], (BO), Methuen, MA.
St. Ann's Hospital, [E], (COL). See Mount Carmel Health System.
St. Ann's Hospital - General Hospital, [E], (COL). See Mount Carmel Health System.
St. Ann's Infant and Maternity Home, [J], (WDC), Hyattsville, MD.
Saint Ann's Media, Inc., [R], (SCR), Scranton, PA.
St. Ann's Novitiate, Little Sisters of the Poor, [V], (BRK), Queens Village, NY.
St. Ann's Nursery School, [C], (STF), Stamford, CT.
St. Ann's Nursing Home, [D], (AMA), Panhandle, TX.
St. Ann's Nursing Home Co., Inc., [E], (ROC), Rochester, NY.
Saint Ann's Passionist Monastery, [M], (SCR), Scranton, PA.
St. Ann's Place - East, [L], (IND). See Adult Day Services.
St. Ann's Place - North, [L], (IND). See Adult Day Services.
St. Ann's Senior Residence, [D], (DUL), Duluth, MN.
St. Ann's University Parish, [CC], (BO), Boston, MA.
St. Ann-Bartlett Extended Care, [I], (MEM), Memphis, TN.
St. Anne, [M], (HRT). See Missionaries of LaSalette Provincial Secretary.
St. Anne Center, [G], (RCK), Rockford, IL.
St. Anne Convent, [M], (COV), Melbourne, KY.
St. Anne Division, [K], (STL). See De Paul Health Center.
St. Anne Elementary, [B], (GAY), Alpena, MI.
St. Anne Home, [G], (GBG), Greensburg, PA.
Saint Anne Home & Retirement Community, [H], (FTW), Fort Wayne, IN.
St. Anne Home of the Diocese of Fort Wayne - South Bend, [H], (FTW), Fort Wayne, IN.
St. Anne Hospice, Inc., [F], (WIN), Winona, MN.
Saint Anne Institute, [G], (ALB), Albany, NY.
St. Anne Monastery, [F], (SPC), Springfield, MO.
The St. Anne Montessori School, [G], (BO), Marlboro, MA.
St. Anne Place, [G], (RCK), Rockford, IL.
St. Anne Residential Treatment Center, [H], (PEO), West Peoria, IL.
St. Anne Villa, [N], (PAT), Convent Station, NJ.
St. Anne's, [P], (LA), Los Angeles, CA.
St. Anne's, [V], (LA), Los Angeles, CA.
St. Anne's, [D], (LC). See Wausau Area Catholic Schools.
St. Anne's Catholic School Foundation, [G], (BEA), Beaumont, TX.
St. Anne's Center, [R], (PH), Philadelphia, PA.
St. Anne's Children's Home, [H], (SPK), Spokane, WA.
St. Anne's Endowment, [G], (STO), Lodi, CA.
St. Anne's Foundation, [P], (LA). See St. Anne's.
St. Anne's Guest Home, [E], (FAR), Grand Forks, ND.
St. Anne's Guild, [P], (LA). See St. Anne's.
St. Anne's Guild of Ventura, [P], (LA). See St. Anne's.
Saint Anne's Health Care Management Services, Inc., [G], (FR), Fall River, MA.
Saint Anne's Health Care System, Inc., [G], (FR), Fall River, MA.
St. Anne's Home, [G], (HBG), Columbia, PA.
St. Anne's Home for the Elderly, [N], (MIL), Milwaukee, WI.
Saint Anne's Hospital, [G], (FR), Fall River, MA.
St. Anne's Junior Guild, [P], (LA). See St. Anne's.
St. Anne's Shrine, [I], (BUR), Isle La Motte, VT.
St. Anselm Abbey, [K], (MAN), Manchester, NH.
St. Anselm Abbey Seminary, [A], (MAN), Manchester, NH.
Saint Anselm College, [B], (MAN), Manchester, NH.
St. Anselm's Abbey, [M], (WDC), Washington, DC.
St. Anselm's Abbey School, [E], (WDC), Washington, DC.
The St. Ansgar Catholic Church Endowment Trust, [M], (LC), Blair, WI.
St. Ansgar Scandinavian Catholic League, [HH], (NY), New York, NY.
St. Ansgar's Health Center, [D], (FAR), Park River, ND.
St. Anthony, [J], (LAN), Hillsdale, MI.
St. Anthony, [G], (SY), Endicott, NY.
St. Anthony Cathedral School Foundation, [G], (BEA), Beaumont, TX.
St. Anthony Catholic High School, [F], (SAT), San Antonio, TX.
St. Anthony Catholic High School House, [M], (SAT), San Antonio, TX.
St. Anthony Church Endowment Trust, [N], (OM). See The Omaha Archdiocesan Educational Foundation, Inc.
Saint Anthony College of Nursing, [D], (RCK), Rockford, IL.
St. Anthony Community, [J], (PBL), Pueblo, CO.
St. Anthony Community Hospital, Inc., [W], (NY), Warwick, NY.
St. Anthony Convent, [N], (HRT), Winsted, CT.
St. Anthony Convent, [BB], (PH), Springfield, PA.
St. Anthony Convent, [N], (SAT), San Antonio, TX.
St. Anthony Convent, [G], (SLC), Helper, UT.
St. Anthony Day Care Learning Center; Infant and Toddler Center, [J], (SAT), San Antonio, TX.
St. Anthony Foundation, [H], (SC), Carroll, IA.
St. Anthony Foundation, [U], (SFR), San Francisco, CA.
St. Anthony Friary, [A], (ALB), Catskill, NY.
St. Anthony Friary, [H], (GBG), Uniontown, PA.
St. Anthony Friary, [M], (PAT), Butler, NJ.
St. Anthony Friary, [AA], (PH), Fairless Hills, PA.
St. Anthony Friary, [O], (SP), St. Petersburg, FL.
St. Anthony Friary (Formerly Morris School for Boys), [A], (LR), Searcy, AR.
St. Anthony Friary and Mission House, [O], (PIT), Ben Avon, PA.
St. Anthony Head Start, [J], (NO), New Orleans, LA.
St. Anthony Health Care, [D], (LFT), Lafayette, IN.
St. Anthony Health Professions & Nursing Institute, [N], (BRK). See Catholic Medical Center of Brooklyn & Queens.
St. Anthony High School, [C], (NEW), Jersey City, NJ.
St. Anthony High School, [D], (SFD), Effingham, IL.
St. Anthony Home, [I], (HON), Honolulu, HI.
St. Anthony Home, Inc., [H], (GRY), Crown Point, IN.
St. Anthony Hospital, [A], (BAK), Pendleton, OR.
St. Anthony Hospital, [J], (CHI), Chicago, IL.
St. Anthony Hospital, [E], (OKL), Oklahoma City, OK.
St. Anthony Hospital and Health Centers, [F], (GRY), Michigan City, IN.
St. Anthony Hospital Central, [H], (DEN), Denver, CO.
St. Anthony Hospital Convent, [P], (SP), St. Petersburg, FL.
St. Anthony Hospital North, [H], (DEN), Denver, CO.
St. Anthony Interparochial School, [D], (SP), San Antonio, FL.
St. Anthony Junior-Senior High School, [C], (HON), Wailuku, HI.
St. Anthony M. Zaccaria Seminary, [B], (BUF), Youngstown, NY.
St. Anthony Manor, [B], (CHY), Casper, WY.
St. Anthony Mary Claret Seminary, [B], (SAT), San Antonio, TX.
Saint Anthony Medical Center, [D], (RCK), Rockford, IL.
St. Anthony Medical Center Foundation, [N], (FTW). See Alverno Administrative Services, Inc.
St. Anthony Medical Center, Inc., [F], (GRY), Crown Point, IN.
St. Anthony Messenger, St. Anthony Messenger Press

St. Boniface School, [G], (CIN), Cincinnati, OH.
St. Boniface School Endowment Trust, [N], (OM). See The Omaha Archdiocesan Educational Foundation, Inc.
St. Brendan Apts., [G], (CHI). See Catholic Charities of the Archdiocese of Chicago-Archdiocesan Offices.
St. Brendan Convent, [N], (HRT), New Haven, CT.
St. Brendan High School, [C], (MIA), Miami, FL.
St. Brendans Apartments, HDFC, Inc., [L], (BRK). See Catholic Charities.
St. Bridget Regional School, [E], (CAM), Glassboro, NJ.
St. Bridget's Convent, [K], (FTW). See Saint Mary's of the Immaculate Conception.
St. Brigid Elementary School, [F], (SFR), San Francisco, CA.
St. Brigid's Convent, [N], (SAT), San Antonio, TX.
St. Brigid's Kindergarten, [J], (SAT), San Antonio, TX.
St. Bronislava, [D], (LC). See Stevens Point Area Catholic Schools.
St. Bruno Convent, [J], (PRT), Van Buren, ME.
St. Cabrini Home, [R], (NY), West Park, NY.
St. Cabrini Nursing Home, [Z], (NY), Dobbs Ferry, NY.
St. Camillus Academy, [C], (LEX), Corbin, KY.
St. Camillus Adult Day Care, [J], (BGP). See St. Camillus Health Center.
St. Camillus Auxiliary Committee, [J], (BGP). See St. Camillus Health Center.
St. Camillus Communities, Inc., [Y], (MIL), Wauwatosa, WI.
St. Camillus Community, [N], (WOR), Whitinsville, MA.
St. Camillus Community House, [P], (MIL), Wauwatosa, WI.
St. Camillus Formation Community, [P], (MIL), St. Francis, WI.
St. Camillus Foundation, [P], (SY). See St. Camillus Health & Rehabilitation Center.
St. Camillus Health & Rehabilitation Center, [P], (SY), Syracuse, NY.
St. Camillus Health Center, [J], (BGP), Stamford, CT.
St. Camillus Health Center, Inc., [N], (MIL), Wauwatosa, WI.
St. Camillus Home Foundation, Inc., [J], (BGP), Bridgeport, CT.
St. Camillus Hospice, Inc., [K], (WOR), Whitinsville, MA.
St. Camillus Institute, [K], (WOR). See St. Camillus Nursing Home Inc.
St. Camillus Institute, Inc., [Y], (MIL), Wauwatosa, WI.
St. Camillus Institute, Inc., [R], (WOR), Whitinsville, MA.
St. Camillus Ministries, Inc., [Y], (MIL), Wauwatosa, WI.
St. Camillus Monastery and Retreat Center, [A], (MAD), Durward's Glen, WI.
St. Camillus Nursing Home Inc., [K], (WOR), Whitinsville, MA.
St. Camillus Place, [F], (SCL), Little Falls, MN.
St. Camillus Provincialate, [P], (MIL), Wauwatosa, WI.
St. Camillus Rectory, [K], (WOR). See St. Camillus Nursing Home Inc.
St. Casimir School, [E], (MAN), Manchester, NH.
St. Casimir's Monastery, Printing Plant and Cultural Center, [U], (BRK), Brooklyn, NY.
St. Catharine Academy, [F], (NY), New York, NY.
St. Catharine College, [A], (L), St. Catharine, KY.
St. Catharine of Siena Convent, [M], (L), St. Catharine, KY.
St. Catharine of Siena School, [D], (ALN), Reading, PA.
St. Catherine, [G], (SY), Binghamton, NY.
St. Catherine Campus, [G], (CLV). See Archbishop James P. Lyke Elementary School.
St. Catherine Community Center, [E], (SHP), Shreveport, LA.
St. Catherine Convent, [K], (GRY), East Chicago, IN.
St. Catherine Convent, [M], (L), Louisville, KY.
St. Catherine Convent, [L], (MAN), Manchester, NH.
St. Catherine Convent, [G], (TUC), Topawa, AZ.
St. Catherine Hall, [BB], (PH), Elkins Park, PA.
St. Catherine Hospital, [A], (DOD), Garden City, KS.
St. Catherine Hospital, [F], (GRY), East Chicago, IN.
St. Catherine Hospital Foundation, Inc., [F], (GRY). See St. Catherine Hospital.
St. Catherine Indian Boarding School, Inc., Junior-Senior High Boarding School, [E], (SFE), Santa Fe, NM.
St. Catherine Infirmary, [AA], (PH). See Congregation of the Mission.
St. Catherine Laboure Manor, [F], (STA), Jacksonville, FL.
St. Catherine Laboure Manor, Inc., [E], (STA). See St. Vincent's Medical Center, Inc.
St. Catherine Nursing Home, [N], (BAL). See Villa Julie at Seven Oaks (Maryland Province).
St. Catherine of Siena Catholic Student Center, [I], (DM), Des Moines, IA.
St. Catherine of Siena Convent, [O], (SFR). See Dominican Sisters of San Rafael Generalate & Convent.
St. Catherine of Siena Priory, [DD], (NY), New York, NY.
St. Catherine of Siena Supervised Apartment, [L], (NO), Harvey, LA.
St. Catherine Preschool, [G], (SCR), Moscow, PA.
St. Catherine Residence, Inc., [Y], (MIL), Milwaukee, WI.
St. Catherine School, [E], (MAN), Manchester, NH.
St. Catherine School Foundation, [G], (BEA), Port Arthur, TX.
Saint Catherine's Center for Children, [G], (ALB), Albany, NY.
St. Catherine's Convent of Mercy, [N], (HRT), Bethlehem, CT.
St. Catherine's High School, [E], (MIL), Racine, WI.
St. Catherine's High School Corporation, [Y], (MIL), Racine, WI.
St. Catherine's High School of Racine, Inc., [Y], (MIL), Racine, WI.
St. Catherine's Hospital, [K], (MIL), Kenosha, WI.
St. Catherine's House, [J], (DET), Detroit, MI.
St. Catherine's Infirmary, Inc., [Y], (MIL), Racine, WI.
St. Catherine's Military School, [E], (ORG), Anaheim, CA.
St. Catherine's Montessori, [G], (GAL), Houston, TX.
St. Catherine's Residence, [J], (PRT), Portland, ME.
St. Catherine's Residence and Nursing Center, [K], (P), North Bend, OR.
St. Cecelia Interparochial School, [D], (SP), Clearwater, FL.
St. Cecilia Academy, [C], (NSH), Nashville, TN.
St. Cecilia Cathedral Endowment Trust, [N], (OM). See The Omaha Archdiocesan Educational Foundation, Inc.
St. Cecilia Convent, [I], (NSH), Nashville, TN.
St. Cecilia Friary, [O], (PIT), Rochester, PA.
St. Cecilia High School Endowment Fund, [L], (LIN), Hastings, NE.
St. Cecilia House/Boysville of Michigan, Inc., [O], (DET). See Boysville of Michigan, Inc.
St. Cecilia's Convent, [O], (WOR), Leominster, MA.
St. Cecilia's Day Nursery, [V], (NY), New York, NY.
St. Cecilia's Middle School/High School, [C], (LIN), Hastings, NE.
St. Charles, [B], (CIN), Carthagena, OH.
St. Charles, [W], (STL). See Catholic Family Services.
St. Charles Borromeo, [D], (LC). See Chippewa Area Catholic Schools.
St. Charles Borromeo Educational Foundation, Inc., [DD], (BO). See Chancery Office.
St. Charles Care Center, Inc., [I], (COV), Covington, KY.
St. Charles Catholic High School, [D], (NO), La Place, LA.
St. Charles Cemetery, [Y], (MIL), Taycheedah, WI.
St. Charles Center, [C], (LKC), Moss Bluff, LA.
St. Charles Children's Home, [H], (MAN), Rochester, NH.
St. Charles College, [A], (LAF), Grand Coteau, LA.
St. Charles County Catholic Community Services, [W], (STL). See Catholic Community Services Administration.
St. Charles Future Fund Trust, [M], (LC), Chippewa Falls, WI.
St. Charles Hospital, Port Jefferson, New York, [I], (RVC), Port Jefferson, NY.
Saint Charles House of Studies, [U], (BRK), Jamaica, NY.
St. Charles House, Inc., [Q], (BAL), Pikesville, MD.
St. Charles Housing I, Inc., [F], (VEN), Port Charlotte, FL.
St. Charles Housing II, Inc., [F], (VEN), Port Charlotte, FL.
St. Charles Lwanga Center, [W], (STL), St. Louis, MO.
St. Charles Medical Center, [A], (BAK), Bend, OR.
St. Charles Mercy Health Foundation, [O], (TOL), Toledo, OH.
St. Charles Mercy Hospital, [H], (TOL), Oregon, OH.
St. Charles Mission School, [E], (GF), Pryor, MT.
St. Charles Preparatory School, [C], (COL), Columbus, OH.
St. Charles Seminary College Program, [A], (ELP), El Paso, TX.
St. Charles Villa, [J], (BAL), Baltimore, MD.
St. Charles Villa, [M], (BAL), Baltimore, MD.
St. Charles Youth and Family Services, [M], (MIL), Milwaukee, WI.
St. Chretienne Convent, [X], (BO), Salem, MA.
St. Chretienne Provincialate, [X], (BO), Wrentham, MA.
St. Christopher Friary, [W], (BO), Boston, MA.
St. Christopher School, [E], (MAN), Nashua, NH.
St. Christopher's Friary, [DD], (NY), Garrison, NY.
St. Christopher's Inn, [AA], (NY), Garrison, NY.
St. Christopher's Inn, [DD], (NY). See Franciscan Friars of the Atonement.
St. Christopher-Ottilie, [O], (BRK), Sea Cliff, NY.
Saint Claire Medical Center, [D], (LEX), Morehead, KY.
St. Clare Apartments Housing Development, [H], (BUF). See The Catholic Charities of the Diocese of Buffalo.
St. Clare Center for Spirituality, [H], (LC), Polonia, WI.
St. Clare Church-Berea College, [L], (LEX), Berea, KY.
St. Clare Convent, [L], (ALN), Reading, PA.
St. Clare Convent, [B], (BAK), Baker City, OR.
St. Clare Convent, [F], (BLX), Waveland, MS.
St. Clare Convent, [J], (GB), Manitowoc, WI.
St. Clare Convent, [J], (LC), Polonia, WI.
St. Clare Convent, [Q], (MIL), Milwaukee, WI.
St. Clare Convent, [BB], (PH), Philadelphia, PA.
St. Clare Convent, [P], (SP), Tampa, FL.
St. Clare Convent, [T], (SY), Syracuse, NY.
St. Clare Convent, [G], (TLS), Broken Arrow, OK.
St. Clare Convent, Cutting Memorial, [Q], (PRO), Newport, RI.
St. Clare Convent, Franciscan Sisters of the Poor, [N], (CIN), Cincinnati, OH.
St. Clare Friary, [N], (CHI), Chicago, IL.
St. Clare Friary, [M], (CIN), Cincinnati, OH.
St. Clare Friary, [DD], (NY), New York, NY.
St. Clare Friary, [DD], (NY), Yonkers, NY.
St. Clare High School, [D], (BO), Boston, MA.
St. Clare Home, [M], (PRO), Newport, RI.
St. Clare Hospital, [G], (SEA), Lakewood, WA.
St. Clare Hospital and Health Services, [G], (MAD), Baraboo, WI.
St. Clare Hospital of Monroe, Wisconsin, Inc., dba The Monroe Clinic, Inc., [G], (MAD), Monroe, WI.
St. Clare House, [G], (STA). See Jacksonville, Family Housing Management Co.
St. Clare House of Prayer, [K], (JOL), Kankakee, IL.
St. Clare Management, Inc., [Y], (MIL), Milwaukee, WI.
St. Clare Manor, [M], (BUF), Lockport, NY.
St. Clare Meadows Care Center, [H], (MAD), Baraboo, WI.
St. Clare Medical Outreach, [F], (WIL). See Ministry of Caring, Inc.
St. Clare Sisters Retreat Ministry, [P], (SP). See St. Clare's Convent.
St. Clare Terrace, [N], (MIL). See St. Francis Home for Aged.
St. Clare's Convent, [P], (SP), Holiday, FL.
St. Clare's Evangelization-Community Center, [I], (SAV), Albany, GA.
St. Clare's Holding Company, Inc., [H], (ALB), Schenectady, NY.
St. Clare's Hospital, [H], (ALB), Schenectady, NY.
Saint Clare's Hospital, [N], (SFD), Alton, IL.
St. Clare's Hospital and Health Center, [W], (NY), New York, NY.
St. Clare's Monastery, [J], (SCL), Sauk Rapids, MN.
St. Clare's Monastery of the Blessed Sacrament, O.S.C., [Q], (NO), New Orleans, LA.
St. Clare's Monastery of the Infant Jesus, [O], (STP), Minneapolis, MN.
St. Clare's Retreat, [H], (MRY), Soquel, CA.
St. Clare's Retreat House, [I], (MRY), Soquel, CA.
St. Clares-Riverside Campus-Boonton Township, [J], (PAT). See Northwest Covenant Medial Center.
St. Clares-Riverside Campus-Denville, [J], (PAT). See Northwest Covenant Medial Center.
St. Clares-Riverside Campus-Sussex, [J], (PAT). See Northwest Covenant Medial Center.
St. Clares-Riverside Foundation, Inc., [J], (PAT). See Sisters of the Sorrowful Mother Ambulatory Care Corp.
St. Clement Friary, [M], (CIN), Cincinnati, OH.
St. Clement Health Care Center, [P], (STL), Liguori, MO.
St. Clement Health Services, [D], (BEL), Red Bud, IL.
St. Clement's Archdiocesan Eucharistic Shrine, [BB], (BO), Boston, MA.
St. Clement's Mission House, [H], (HBG), Ephrata, PA.
St. Cloud Children's Home of the Diocese of St. Cloud, [F], (SCL), St. Cloud, MN.
St. Cloud Hospital, [G], (SCL), St. Cloud, MN.
St. Coletta Day School of Milwaukee, [G], (MIL), Milwaukee, WI.
St. Coletta Day School, Inc., [H], (BO), Braintree, MA.
St. Coletta of Wisconsin, Inc., [K], (MAD), Jefferson, WI.
St. Coletta School, [I], (ARL), Alexandria, VA.
St. Coletta's of Illinois, [L], (CHI), Palos Park, IL.
St. Coletta's of Illinois Foundation, [L], (CHI). See St. Coletta's of Illinois.
St. Coletta's of Massachusetts, Inc., [DD], (BO), Hanover, MA.
St. Colman's Convent, [M], (ALB), Watervliet, NY.
St. Colman's Home, [G], (ALB), Watervliet, NY.
St. Columba Preschool, [L], (MOB), Dothan, AL.
St. Columban's Burse Estate Trust, [N], (OM). See Columban Fathers Regional Administration.
St. Columban's Center, [Q], (BUF), Derby, NY.

St. Francis Nursing Center, [H], (RIC), Newport News, VA.
St. Francis Nursing Center-East, [J], (PIT). See St. Francis Health System.
St. Francis Nursing Center-East, [J], (PIT), Pittsburgh, PA.
St. Francis Nursing Center-North, [J], (PIT). See St. Francis Health System.
St. Francis Nursing Center-North, [J], (PIT), Cranberry Township, PA.
St. Francis Nursing Home, [F], (SAG), Saginaw, MI.
St. Francis Nursing Home, [K], (SAT), San Antonio, TX.
St. Francis of Assisi Chapel and Catholic Information Center, [L], (SPR), Springfield, MA.
St. Francis of Assisi Church of South Omaha Educational Endowment Fund, [N], (OM). See The Omaha Archdiocesan Educational Foundation, Inc.
St. Francis of Assisi Convent, [N], (HRT), Torrington, CT.
St. Francis of Assisi Convent, School Sisters of Notre Dame, [N], (HRT), New Britain, CT.
St. Francis of Assisi Educational Trust Fund (St. Francis of Assisi Parish, Ann Harbor), [K], (LAN). See Chancery Office.
St. Francis of Assisi Friary, [O], (BUF), Athol Springs, NY.
St. Francis of Assisi Friary, [M], (DEN), Denver, CO.
St. Francis of Assisi Friary, [R], (HRT). See Central Connecticut State University Newman House.
St. Francis of Assisi Kitchen, [R], (SCR), Scranton, PA.
St. Francis of Assisi Newman Center, [O], (PEO), Macomb, IL.
St. Francis of Assisi Novitiate, [DD], (NY). See Franciscan Friars of the Atonement.
St. Francis of Assisi Novitiate-Franciscan Sisters of St. Elizabeth, [N], (PAT), Parsippany, NJ.
St. Francis of Assisi School, [E], (MAN), Manchester, NH.
St. Francis of Assisi University Church, [H], (LFT), Muncie, IN.
The St. Francis Parish Endowment Trust, [M], (LC), Ellsworth, WI.
*St. Francis Plaza, Inc., [J], (PIT). See St. Francis Health System.
*St. Francis Plaza, Inc., [L], (PIT), Pittsburgh, PA.
St. Francis Preparatory School, [G], (BRK), Fresh Meadows, NY.
St. Francis Primary School, [D], (GF), Billings, MT.
St. Francis Provincialate, [K], (FTW), Mishawaka, IN.
St. Francis R.C.I.A. Residence, [I], (MET), Metuchen, NJ.
St. Francis Regional Medical Center, [G], (DUL). See Benedictine Sisters Benevolent Association.
St. Francis Regional Medical Center, [J], (STP), Shakopee, MN.
St. Francis Renewal Center, [L], (WIL), Wilmington, DE.
St. Francis Residence, [P], (MIL), Franklin, WI.
St. Francis Residence, Inc., [K], (SP). See St. Joseph's Hospital, Inc.
St. Francis Respite Program, Inc., [T], (BUF), Buffalo, NY.
St. Francis Retreat Center, [I], (LAN), De Witt, MI.
St. Francis Retreat Center, [I], (MRY), San Juan Bautista, CA.
St. Francis Retreat House, [M], (ALN), Easton, PA.
St. Francis School, [B], (AGN), GMF, GU.
St. Francis School, [C], (GLP), Lumberton, NM.
St. Francis School, [D], (HON), Honolulu, HI.
St. Francis School, [D], (HON). See St. Francis School.
St. Francis School, [F], (SPK), Spokane, WA.
St. Francis School, [C], (WIN). See Rochester Catholic Schools.
Saint Francis School for Exceptional Children, [F], (RCK), Freeport, IL.
St. Francis School of Nursing, [J], (CHI). See Saint Francis Hospital of Evanston.
St. Francis Seminary, [A], (MIL), Milwaukee, WI.
St. Francis Seminary, [A], (SD), San Diego, CA.
St. Francis Seraph Friary, [M], (CIN), Cincinnati, OH.
St. Francis Social Adult Day Service, [W], (SY), Syracuse, NY.
St. Francis Solanus Friary, [K], (SFD), Quincy, IL.
*St. Francis Specialty Hospital, [B], (SHP), Monroe, LA.
St. Francis Thrift Shop, [J], (BEL), Belleville, IL.
St. Francis Transitional Residence, [F], (WIL). See Ministry of Caring, Inc.
St. Francis Upper School, [D], (GF), Billings, MT.
St. Francis Villa Custody House, [P], (BGP). See Sisters Minor of Mary Immaculate.
St. Francis Village, Inc., [G], (FWT), Crowley, TX.
St. Francis Villas, Inc., [O], (TOL), Tiffin, OH.
St. Francis Xavier, [C], (BUR), Winooski, VT.
St. Francis Xavier - Jesuit Community, [J], (KC), Kansas City, MO.
St. Francis Xavier Catholic School Education Foundation, [I], (BIR), Birmingham, AL.
St. Francis Xavier Elementary, [B], (GAY), Petoskey, MI.
*St. Francis Xavier Home Health Care, Inc., [B], (CHR). See Bon Secours-St. Francis Xavier Hospital.
St. Francis Xavier Regional School, [C], (SLC), Kearns, UT.
St. Francis Xavier School, [E], (GB). See Manitowoc Area Catholic System (MACS).
St. Francis Xavier School Foundation, [K], (VEN), Fort Myers, FL.
St. Francis Youth Center, [D], (MRY), Watsonville, CA.
St. Francis' Medical Center, [J], (PEO), Peoria, IL.
*St. Francis' Medical Center, [C], (SPC), Cape Girardeau, MO.
St. Francis' Residence, [P], (FR), Fall River, MA.
St. Francis/Marist, [B], (SPP), Lepua, AS.
St. Frederick High School, [A], (SHP), Monroe, LA.
St. Gabriel, [G], (CIN), Cincinnati, OH.
St. Gabriel House, [N], (HRT), Farmington, CT.
St. Gabriel School, [D], (CHL). See Mecklenburg Area Catholic Schools (M.A.C.S.).
St. Gabriel's, [H], (ARL), Alexandria, VA.
St. Gabriel's Convent, [K], (ARL), Alexandria, VA.
The St. Gabriel's Endowment Trust, [M], (LC), Prairie du Chien, WI.
St. Gabriel's Hall, [O], (PH), Audubon, PA.
St. Gabriel's Hospital, [G], (SCL), Little Falls, MN.
St. Gabriel's Monastery, [O], (SCR), Clarks Summit, PA.
St. Gabriel's Passionist Community, [W], (BO), Brighton, MA.
St. Gabriel's Residence, [W], (BO), Brighton, MA.
St. Gabriel's Retreat Center, [P], (SCR), Clarks Summit, PA.
St. Gabriel's System, [O], (PH), Philadelphia, PA.
St. Gabriel's Youth House, [P], (RVC), Shelter Island Heights, NY.
*St. Gaspar Society, [O], (KC), Liberty, MO.
St. George Chapel of Marianist Community, [M], (CIN), Huntsville, OH.
St. George Manor, [L], (MAN), Manchester, NH.
St. George's Rectory, [I], (ROC), Rochester, NY.
St. Gerard Catholic High School, [E], (SAT), San Antonio, TX.
St. Gerard Community Nursing Home, [E], (FAR), Hankinson, ND.
St. Gerard Educational Trust Fund (St. Gerard Parish, Lansing), [K], (LAN). See Chancery Office.
St. Gerard Majella Alternative School, [I], (NO), New Orleans, LA.
Saint Gertrude High School, [B], (RIC), Richmond, VA.
St. Gertrude Priory, [M], (CIN), Cincinnati, OH.
St. Gertrude School, [B], (CC), Kingsville, TX.
St. Gertrude's Convent, Benedictine Sisters, [Q], (NO), Mandeville, LA.
St. Gertrude's Health Center, [W], (STP), Shakopee, MN.
St. Gertrude's Monastery, Motherhouse and Novitiate of the Sisters of St. Benedict, [J], (WIL), Ridgely, MD.
St. Gratian Friary, Franciscan Friars, [N], (CHI), Countryside, IL.
St. Gregory Abbey, [I], (OKL), Shawnee, OK.
St. Gregory Church-Union College, [L], (LEX), Barbourville, KY.
Saint Gregory Early Childhood Center, [F], (SCR), Clarks Green, PA.
The St. Gregory Seminary Trust, [A], (CIN). See The Athenaeum of Ohio.
St. Gregory the Great Housing Committee, Inc., [P], (BAL). See Chancery Office.
St. Gregory the Great Seminary, [A], (LIN), Seward, NE.
St. Gregory the Great Seminary Fund, [J], (LIN). See Chancery.
St. Gregory's Academy, [E], (SCR), Moscow, PA.
St. Gregory's Priory (Priestly Fraternity of St. Peter), [M], (SCR), Scranton, PA.
Saint Gregory's School, [E], (ALB), Loudonville, NY.
St. Gregory's University, [A], (OKL), Shawnee, OK.
St. Hedwig Cemetery and Mausoleum Corporation, [N], (CHI). See Conventual Franciscans of St. Bonaventure Province.
Saint Hedwig's Church Corporation, Providence, [U], (PRO). See Miscellaneous Listings for the Diocese of Providence.
St. Hedwig's Industrial School for Girls, [X], (CHI), Chicago, IL.
St. Helen's, Sisters of St. Joseph, [G], (OG), Chasm Falls, NY.
The St. Helena Cathedral Foundation, Inc., [I], (HEL), Helena, MT.
St. Helena Convent, [N], (SR), St. Helena, CA.
St. Helena House, [AA], (BO), Boston, MA.
St. Henry Campus, [G], (CLV). See Archbishop James P. Lyke Elementary School.
St. Henry Day Care Center, [C], (BEL), Belleville, IL.
St. Henry District High School, [B], (COV), Erlanger, KY.
*St. Henry Property Development, Inc. dba The Cloister, [L], (NSH), Nashville, TN.
*St. Hilary Parish Foundation, [Z], (CLV), Akron, OH.
St. Hubert's Catholic High School for Girls, [D], (PH), Philadelphia, PA.
St. Hyacinth College and Seminary, [A], (SPR), Granby, MA.
St. Ignatius, [J], (PRT), Sanford, ME.
St. Ignatius College Prep, [D], (CHI), Chicago, IL.
St. Ignatius College Preparatory (Coed), [E], (SFR), San Francisco, CA.
Saint Ignatius Convent, [L], (ALN), West Lawn, PA.
St. Ignatius Day Care - Mobile, [L], (MOB), Mobile, AL.
St. Ignatius Early Childhood Center, [F], (SP), Tarpon Springs, FL.
St. Ignatius Elementary, [B], (GAY), Rogers City, MI.
St. Ignatius High School, [E], (CLV), Cleveland, OH.
St. Ignatius Jesuit Community, [D], (CHI), Chicago, IL.
St. Ignatius Loyola Academy, [E], (BAL), Baltimore, MD.
St. Ignatius Loyola Residence, [DD], (NY), New York, NY.
St. Ignatius Loyola School, [D], (ALN), Sinking Spring, PA.
St. Ignatius Nursing Home, [X], (PH), Philadelphia, PA.
St. Ignatius Residence, [I], (PRT), Portland, ME.
St. Ignatius Retreat House, Inisfada, [P], (RVC), Manhasset, NY.
St. Isaac House, Society of the Daughters of the Heart of Mary, [BB], (PH), Philadelphia, PA.
St. Isidore Church Endowment Trust, [N], (OM). See The Omaha Archdiocesan Educational Foundation, Inc.
St. Isidore Elementary School Endowment Trust, [N], (OM). See The Omaha Archdiocesan Educational Foundation, Inc.
St. Isidore's Catholic Student Center, [G], (SAL), Manhattan, KS.
St. James, [E], (CAM), Penns Grove, NJ.
St. James, [D], (LC). See Eau Claire Coordinated Catholic Schools.
St. James Cathedral Foundation, Inc., [Y], (BRK), Brooklyn, NY.
St. James Community Hospital, Inc., [E], (HEL), Butte, MT.
St. James Convent, [N], (HRT). See Sisters of Mercy of the Americas.
St. James Convent, [O], (NEW), Springfield, NJ.
St. James Convent, [N], (SAT), San Antonio, TX.
St. James Convent, Sisters of St. Joseph, [G], (OG), Carthage, NY.
St. James Educational Foundation, [I], (BIR), Gadsden, AL.
St. James Friary, [O], (SP), Belleair Bluffs, FL.
St. James High School, [A], (CAM), Carneys Point, NJ.
St. James Hospital, [G], (NEW), Newark, NJ.
Saint James Hospital, [J], (PEO), Pontiac, IL.
St. James Hospital and Health Centers, [J], (CHI), Chicago Heights, IL.
St. James Hospital Division, Newark, [F], (NEW). See Cathedral Healthcare System, Inc.
St. James Manor, [I], (JOL), Crete, IL.
St. James Manor, Inc., [O], (OM), Omaha, NE.
St. James Mercy Hospital, [H], (ROC), Hornell, NY.
St. James Middle School, [G], (SY), Johnson City, NY.
St. James Parish Endowment Trust, [M], (LC), La Crosse, WI.
St. James Residence, [P], (PRO), Manville, RI.
The St. James the Greater Catholic Church Endowment Trust, [M], (LC), Eau Claire, WI.
St. James' Convent, Sisters of St. Joseph, [G], (OG), Gouverneur, NY.
St. James/Seton School Endowment Fund, [N], (OM). See The Omaha Archdiocesan Educational Foundation, Inc.
St. James-Seton School, [D], (OM), Omaha, NE.
St. Jane Catholic Community Services, [W], (STL). See Catholic Community Services Administration.
St. Jane Frances Educational Endowment Trust, [P], (BAL). See Chancery Office.
St. Jane Francis Educational Endowment Trust, [P], (BAL), Pasadena, MD.
St. Jeanne de Lestonnac Kindergarten and Day Nursery, [J], (LA), Los Angeles, CA.
St. Jeanne de Lestonnac Preschool/Kindergarten - Second Grade, [F], (SB). See Sisters of the Company of Mary (O.D.N.).
Saint Jeanne de Lestonnac School, [E], (ORG), Tustin, CA.
St. Jerome Early Childhood Center, [F], (SP), Largo, FL.
St. Jerome Hospital, [K], (BUF), Batavia, NY.
St. Jerome Housing Corporation, Inc., [P], (BAL). See Chancery Office.
St. Jerome Regional School, [D], (ALN), Tamaqua, PA.

St. Pius X High School Foundation, Inc., [N], (SFE), Albuquerque, NM.
St. Pius X High School, Inc., [F], (GAL), Houston, TX.
St. Pius X Home, Inc., [S], (SY), Syracuse, NY.
St. Pius X Parish Endowment Trust, [M], (LC), La Crosse, WI.
St. Pius X Residence, [N], (RVC), Uniondale, NY.
St. Pius X Residence, Inc., [J], (PIT). See Pittsburgh Mercy Health System, Inc.
St. Pius X Residence, Inc., [L], (PIT), Pittsburgh, PA.
St. Pius X School, [B], (CC), Corpus Christi, TX.
St. Pius X School, [C], (WIN). See Rochester Catholic Schools.
Saint Pius X Seminary, [A], (SCR), Dalton, PA.
St. Pius X Spiritual Life Center, [O], (CAM), Blackwood, NJ.
St. Pius X-St. Leo School, [D], (OM), Omaha, NE.
St. Placid Priory, [N], (SEA), Lacey, WA.
St. Procopius Abbey, [J], (JOL), Lisle, IL.
St. Procopius Abbey Endowment, [J], (JOL). See St. Procopius Abbey.
St. Raphael Academy, [C], (PRO), Pawtucket, RI.
St. Raphael Catholic School and Early Childhood Center, [B], (R), Raleigh, NC.
St. Raphael Convent, [J], (PRT), Kittery, ME.
St. Raphael Family Life Center, [J], (PMB), Palm City, FL.
St. Raphael Home for the Aged, Inc., [G], (COL), Columbus, OH.
Saint Raphael's Industrial Home and School, [U], (PRO). See Miscellaneous Listings for the Diocese of Providence.
Saint Raphaela Center, [CC], (PH), Haverford, PA.
St. Raymond, [E], (CAM), Villas, NJ.
St. Raymond Nonnatus Novitiate, [O], (BUF), LeRoy, NY.
Saint Regis Health Center, Inc., [I], (HRT), New Haven, CT.
St. Regis Mission, [J], (OG), Hogansburg, NY.
St. Regis Residence for Ladies, [S], (PIT), Pittsburgh, PA.
St. Richard's School Endowment Foundation, [O], (TOL), Swanton, OH.
St. Richard's Special Kids Program, [B], (JKS), Jackson, MS.
St. Rita Convent, [N], (HRT), Hamden, CT.
St. Rita Convent, [BB], (PH), Flourtown, PA.
St. Rita High School, [D], (CHI), Chicago, IL.
St. Rita Home, [G], (COL), Columbus, OH.
St. Rita Monastery, [N], (CHI), Chicago, IL.
St. Rita School for the Deaf, [J], (CIN), Cincinnati, OH.
St. Rita's Home for Children, Inc., [T], (BUF), Buffalo, NY.
St. Rita's Medical Center, [H], (TOL), Lima, OH.
St. Rita's Retreat Center, [N], (P), Gold Hill, OR.
St. Rita's Senior Citizen Center, [R], (PH), Philadelphia, PA.
St. Robert Bellarmine Chapel, [M], (ARL). See George Mason University, Catholic Campus Ministry House.
St. Robert Bellarmine Church Educational Endowment Trust, [N], (OM). See The Omaha Archdiocesan Educational Foundation, Inc.
St. Robert Bellarmine Newman Center, Illinois State University, [O], (PEO), Normal, IL.
St. Robert Bellarmine Parish Endowment Trust, [N], (OM). See The Omaha Archdiocesan Educational Foundation, Inc.
St. Robert Bellarmine/Fr. Charles Jacobs Educational Trust Fund (St, Robert Bellarmine Parish, Flushing), [K], (LAN). See Chancery Office.
St. Robert's Holy Name Society Boosters, [AA], (CLV), Euclid, OH.
St. Roch Friary-Franciscan Fathers, [N], (CHI), Oak Forest, IL.
St. Romuald School, [C], (OWN), Hardinsburg, KY.
St. Rosalie, [L], (NO), Gretna, LA.
St. Rose Academy Corporation, [U], (SFR), San Francisco, CA.
St. Rose Catholic Urban Academy, [F], (MIL), Milwaukee, WI.
St. Rose Center, [I], (CHI), Chicago, IL.
St. Rose Convent, [N], (CIN), Cincinnati, OH.
St. Rose Convent, [J], (LC), La Crosse, WI.
St. Rose Dominican Hospital, [B], (LAV), Henderson, NV.
Saint Rose High School, [B], (TR), Belmar, NJ.
St. Rose Hospital, [K], (OAK), Hayward, CA.
St. Rose Hospital Foundation, [K], (OAK). See St. Rose Hospital.
St. Rose Lima Trust Fund, [I], (KAL), Hastings, MI.
St. Rose Medical Office Bldg., [K], (OAK). See St. Rose Hospital.
St. Rose of Lima Academy, [C], (BIR), Birmingham, AL.
St. Rose of Lima Catholic Church Endowment Trust, [M], (LC), Cadott, WI.
The St. Rose of Lima Grade School Education Endowment Fund, [C], (DOD), Great Bend, KS.
St. Rose of Lima Parish Endowment, [N], (OM). See The Omaha Archdiocesan Educational Foundation, Inc.
St. Rose Parish Endowment, [N], (OM). See The Omaha Archdiocesan Educational Foundation, Inc.
St. Rose Parish, R.E. Program, [B], (CR), Argyle, MN.
St. Rose's Home, [X], (NY), New York, NY.
St. Rose's Settlement, [HH], (NY), New York, NY.
St. Saviour, [H], (BRK), Brooklyn, NY.
St. Saviour's Day Nursery, [F], (FR), New Bedford, MA.
St. Scholastica Academy, [D], (CHI), Chicago, IL.
St. Scholastica Academy, [D], (NO), Covington, LA.
St. Scholastica Academy, [B], (PBL), Canon City, CO.
St. Scholastica Center, [K], (LR), Fort Smith, AR.
St. Scholastica Mission House, [J], (JOL). See St. Procopius Abbey.
St. Scholastica Monastery, [N], (SAT), Boerne, TX.
St. Scholastica Monastery-Motherhouse, [I], (LR), Fort Smith, AR.
St. Scholastica Priory, [M], (E), Erie, PA.
St. Scholastica Priory, [O], (WOR), Petersham, MA.
St. Sebastian School Endowment Fund, [B], (MAR), Bessemer, MI.
St. Sebastian's Country Day School, Inc., [E], (BO), Needham, MA.
St. Stanislaus, [D], (LC). See Stevens Point Area Catholic Schools.
St. Stanislaus B. M. Friary, [M], (PAT), Oak Ridge-Milton, NJ.
St. Stanislaus Church Educational Endowment Trust, [N], (OM). See The Omaha Archdiocesan Educational Foundation, Inc.
St. Stanislaus College, [C], (BLX), Bay St. Louis, MS.
Saint Stanislaus Community, [E], (BLX), Bay St. Louis, MS.
St. Stanislaus Convent, [N], (HRT), Meriden, CT.
St. Stanislaus Convent, [G], (OG), Keeseville, NY.
St. Stanislaus Friary, [P], (CLV), Cleveland, OH.
St. Stanislaus Kostka Soup Kitchen, [G], (CHI). See Catholic Charities of the Archdiocese of Chicago-Archdiocesan Offices.
St. Stanislaus Middle School, [C], (WIN). See Winona Area Catholic Schools.
St. Stanislaus Parish Endowment Trust, [N], (OM). See The Omaha Archdiocesan Educational Foundation, Inc.
St. Stanislaus Rectory, [M], (HRT). See DePaul Provincial Residence.
St. Stanislaus Rectory, [M], (HRT). See DePaul Provincial Residence.
St. Stanislaus School and Educational Endowment Trust, [N], (OM). See The Omaha Archdiocesan Educational Foundation, Inc.
St. Stephen, [D], (LC). See Stevens Point Area Catholic Schools.
St. Stephen Campus, [C], (MET), Perth Amboy, NJ.
St. Stephen Convent, [N], (HRT). See Sisters of Mercy of the Americas of Connecticut.
St. Stephen Convent, [A], (VNN), Phoenix, AZ.
St. Stephen Parish Endowment Trust, [M], (LC), Stevens Point, WI.
St. Stephen Priory, [W], (BO), Dover, MA.
St. Stephen Priory Spiritual Life Center, [Y], (BO), Dover, MA.
St. Stephen Regional School, [D], (ALN), Port Carbon, PA.
St. Stephen the Witness Catholic Student Center, University of Northern Iowa, [N], (DUB), Cedar Falls, IA.
St. Stephen University Parish, [H], (BIR), Birmingham, AL.
St. Stephen's Community House, [L], (COL), Columbus, OH.
St. Stephen's Diocesan Center, [A], (HON), Kaneohe, HI.
St. Stephen's League, [Y], (MIL), Milwaukee, WI.
St. Stephen's School, [E], (KC), Kansas City, MO.
St. Stephens Indian Mission Foundation, [F], (CHY), St. Stephens, WY.
St. Stephens Mission - Jesuit Community, [C], (CHY), St. Stephens, WY.
St. Sylvester Monastery, [K], (DET), Detroit, MI.
St. Teresa, [E], (CAM), Runnemede, NJ.
St. Teresa High School, [D], (SFD), Decatur, IL.
St. Teresa Manor, [F], (ATL). See Catholic Social Services, Inc.
St. Teresa of Avila School, [C], (GLP), Grants, NM.
St. Teresa's Academy, [D], (KC), Kansas City, MO.
St. Teresa's Convent, [N], (SAT), San Antonio, TX.
St. Teresa's Motherhouse, [M], (ALB), Germantown, NY.
St. Teresa's Nursing Home, [Z], (NY), Middletown, NY.
St. Teresas Manor & Bishop Primeau Apartments, [J], (MAN), Manchester, NH.
St. Thecla's Retreat House, [Y], (BO), Billerica, MA.
St. Theodore Apts., [G], (CHI). See Catholic Charities of the Archdiocese of Chicago-Archdiocesan Offices.
St. Theodore Catholic School Endowment, [J], (WIN), Albert Lea, MN.
St. Theodore School, [C], (WIN), Albert Lea, MN.
St. Theodore's Apartment Housing Development Fund Co., Inc. (Dunn Tower II Apts.), [L], (ROC), Rochester, NY.
St. Theresa, [B], (SPP), Leone, AS.
St. Theresa Carmelite Chapel, [BB], (BO), Peabody, MA.
St. Theresa Community, [I], (HON). See Sisters of St. Joseph of Carondelet CSJ, Hawaii Vice-Province.
St. Theresa Community, [J], (PRT), Oakland, ME.
St. Theresa House, [X], (BO), Boston, MA.
St. Theresa of Avila Catholic School Educational Foundation, [M], (BR). See Baton Rouge Chancery Office.
St. Theresa's Camp, Inc., [J], (ANC), Anchorage, AK.
St. Therese Catholic Church Endowment Fund, [M], (LC), Rothschild, WI.
St. Therese Center for Special Ministry, [M], (SCL), St. Cloud, MN.
St. Therese Convent, [G], (KNX), Clinton, TN.
St. Therese Educational Trust Fund (St. Therese Parish, Lansing), [K], (LAN). See Chancery Office.
St. Therese Little Flower Day Care Center, [G], (MEM), Memphis, TN.
Saint Therese Medical Center, [J], (CHI), Waukegan, IL.
St. Therese, Schofield, [D], (LC). See Wausau Area Catholic Schools.
The Saint Thomas Academy, [E], (STP), St. Paul, MN.
St. Thomas Aquinas, [GG], (NY). See University Apostolate.
St. Thomas Aquinas, [M], (SFE), Albuquerque, NM.
St. Thomas Aquinas, [G], (SY), Binghamton, NY.
St. Thomas Aquinas Church and Catholic Student Center (Iowa State University), [N], (DUB), Ames, IA.
St. Thomas Aquinas College, [C], (NY), Sparkill, NY.
St. Thomas Aquinas Convent, [I], (MET), Edison, NJ.
St. Thomas Aquinas Early Childhood Center, [F], (SP), New Port Richey, FL.
St. Thomas Aquinas Educational Foundation Trust (St. Thomas Aquinas Parish, East Lansing), [K], (LAN). See Chancery Office.
St. Thomas Aquinas Foundation, [X], (CHI), Chicago, IL.
St. Thomas Aquinas Foundation, [HH], (NY), New York, NY.
St. Thomas Aquinas High School, [E], (HRT), New Britain, CT.
St. Thomas Aquinas High School, [C], (MAN), Dover, NH.
St. Thomas Aquinas High School, [C], (MIA), Fort Lauderdale, FL.
St. Thomas Aquinas High School, [C], (Y), Louisville, OH.
St. Thomas Aquinas High School Endowment Fund, [P], (Y), Louisville, OH.
St. Thomas Aquinas High School Foundation, [B], (KCK). See Saint Thomas Aquinas High School, Inc.
Saint Thomas Aquinas High School, Inc., [B], (KCK), Overland Park, KS.
St. Thomas Aquinas Newman Center, [F], (CR), Moorhead, MN.
St. Thomas Aquinas Newman Center, [I], (WIN), Winona, MN.
St. Thomas Aquinas Parish and Foundation for Catholic Students Attending Purdue University, [H], (LFT), West Lafayette, IN.
St. Thomas Aquinas Priory, [N], (CHI), River Forest, IL.
St. Thomas Aquinas Priory at Providence College, [P], (PRO), Providence, RI.
St. Thomas Aquinas Regional Catholic High School, [B], (BR), Tangipahoa, LA.
St. Thomas Aquinas School, [E], (MAN), Derry, NH.
St. Thomas Aquinas Seminary, [A], (JC), Hannibal, MO.
St. Thomas Aquinas, Newman Center, [H], (SLC), Logan, UT.
St. Thomas Aquinas-Mercy High School, [E], (STL), Florissant, MO.
St. Thomas Assessment Center/Boysville of Michigan, Inc., [O], (DET). See Boysville of Michigan, Inc.
St. Thomas Child and Family Center, [F], (GF), Great Falls, MT.
St. Thomas Child Development Center, [B], (R), Wilmington, NC.
Saint Thomas Foundation, [F], (NSH). See St. Thomas Hospital.
St. Thomas Grade School Trust Agreement (St. Thomas the Apostle Parish, Ann Arbor), [K], (LAN). See Chancery Office.
St. Thomas High School, [F], (GAL), Houston, TX.
St. Thomas High School, Inc., [Y], (MIL), Sheboygan, WI.
St. Thomas Hospital, [F], (NSH), Nashville, TN.
St. Thomas Korean Catholic Center, [G], (ORG), Anaheim, CA.
St. Thomas Manor, [F], (ATL). See Catholic Social Services, Inc.
St. Thomas Monastery, [AA], (PH), Villanova, PA.
St. Thomas More, [B], (LAF), Lafayette, LA.

St. Thomas More Academy, [C], (LAN), Burton, MI.
St. Thomas More Academy, [A], (WIL), Wyoming, DE.
St. Thomas More Catholic Newman Center, [H], (SFS), Vermillion, SD.
St. Thomas More Catholic Student Center at the University of New Hampshire, [N], (MAN), Durham, NH.
St. Thomas More Center, [J], (DM), Panora, IA.
St. Thomas More Center, [G], (WH), Wheeling, WV.
St. Thomas More Chapel, [BB], (BO), Boston, MA.
St. Thomas More Friary, Third Order Regular of St. Francis, [B], (WDC), Wheaton, MD.
St. Thomas More High School, [A], (RC), Rapid City, SD.
St. Thomas More High-Boysville, [B], (LAN), Clinton, MI.
St. Thomas More Lawyers Society, [Y], (MIL), Milwaukee, WI.
St. Thomas More Newman Center, [G], (SUP), River Falls, WI.
St. Thomas More Parish Endowment Trust, [M], (LC), La Crosse, WI.
St. Thomas More School, [F], (SFR), San Francisco, CA.
St. Thomas More School Endowment Trust, [M], (BR). See Baton Rouge Chancery Office.
St. Thomas More School Endowment Trust, [N], (OM). See The Omaha Archdiocesan Educational Foundation, Inc.
St. Thomas More Sisters' Residence, [F], (R), Chapel Hill, NC.
St. Thomas More Society, [Q], (E), Erie, PA.
St. Thomas More Society, [L], (MRY), Watsonville, CA.
Saint Thomas More Society, [S], (PIT), Pittsburgh, PA.
St. Thomas More Society of Maryland, [Q], (BAL), Timonium, MD.
St. Thomas More Society of Southeast Texas, [G], (BEA), Beaumont, TX.
St. Thomas Orphan Society, Inc., [G], (L), Louisville, KY.
Saint Thomas Preparatory Seminary Fund, [W], (SY), Syracuse, NY.
St. Thomas Regional School, [G], (PRO), Providence, RI.
St. Thomas Seminary, [A], (HRT), Bloomfield, CT.
St. Thomas the Apostle School Foundation, Inc., [L], (RCK), Crystal Lake, IL.
St. Thomas University, [B], (MIA), Opa Locka, FL.
St. Thomas Villa, [EE], (NY), Monticello, NY.
St. Thomas-Good Counsel School, [H], (PH), Villanova, PA.
St. Timothy Campus, [G], (CLV). See Archbishop James P. Lyke Elementary School.
St. Timothy Catholic Early Childhood Learning Center, [F], (SP), Tampa, FL.
St. Timothy's Park Villa Housing Development Fund Company, Inc., [T], (BUF), Buffalo, NY.
St. Ursula Academy, [C], (TOL), Toledo, OH.
St. Ursula Academy High School, [F], (CIN), Cincinnati, OH.
St. Ursula Learning Center, [D], (NY). See Department of Education.
St. Ursula Retreat Center, Inc., [P], (RVC), Blue Point, NY.
St. Ursula Villa, [H], (CIN), Cincinnati, OH.
St. Valerians Catholic Indian Center, [D], (GLP), Gallup, NM.
St. Veronica Giuliani Friary, Capuchin Franciscan Friars, [N], (NEW), Orange, NJ.
St. Veronica's Headstart Center, [G], (BAL), Baltimore, MD.
St. Viator High School, [D], (CHI), Arlington Heights, IL.
St. Vincent Academy, [C], (NEW), Newark, NJ.
St. Vincent and Sarah Fisher Center, [O], (DET), Farmington Hills, MI.
St. Vincent Apartments Housing Development Fund Co., Inc., [K], (ALB), Albany, NY.
Saint Vincent Archabbey, [H], (GBG), Latrobe, PA.
*St. Vincent Cardiac Services, Inc., [F], (IND). See Seton Health Corporation of Central Indiana.
St. Vincent Center, [K], (DAV), Davenport, IA.
St. Vincent Center, [M], (DAV), Davenport, IA.
St. Vincent Church, [W], (STL). See Catholic Family Services.
St. Vincent College, [B], (GBG), Latrobe, PA.
St. Vincent Community, [P], (MIL), Milwaukee, WI.
St. Vincent Day Care Center, [D], (EVN), Evansville, IN.
St. Vincent Day Care Center, [J], (PRO), Providence, RI.
St. Vincent de Paul Camp, [S], (BUF), Angola, NY.
St. Vincent de Paul Center, [I], (CHI), Chicago, IL.
St. Vincent de Paul Center, [E], (FRS), Farmersville, CA.
St. Vincent de Paul Center, [N], (LAF), Abbeville, LA.
St. Vincent de Paul Center, [J], (SLC). See Catholic Community Services.
St. Vincent de Paul Center, [E], (YAK), Toppenish, WA.
St. Vincent de Paul Center for Community Reconciliation, [G], (ORG). See St. Vincent de Paul Society.
St. Vincent de Paul Convent, [G], (SLC), Salt Lake City, UT.
St. Vincent de Paul Dining Room, [H], (SFR). See St. Vincent de Paul Society Marin County District Council.
St. Vincent de Paul Dining Room at St. Francis of Assisi Church, [H], (SFR). See San Mateo County District Council.
St. Vincent de Paul Diocesan Council of Fort Worth, [L], (FWT), Fort Worth, TX.
St. Vincent de Paul Educational Foundation, [W], (STL), St. Louis, MO.
St. Vincent de Paul Furniture and Clothing Inc., [J], (SY), Syracuse, NY.
St. Vincent de Paul High School, [A], (RIC), Petersburg, VA.
St. Vincent De Paul Historic Trust, Inc., [P], (BAL). See Chancery Office.
St. Vincent de Paul Home, Woonsocket, [U], (PRO). See Miscellaneous Listings for the Diocese of Providence.
St. Vincent De Paul Kitchen, [R], (SCR), Wilkes-Barre, PA.
St. Vincent de Paul Management Inc., [J], (SD), San Diego, CA.
St. Vincent de Paul Nursing Home, [J], (MAN), Berlin, NH.
St. Vincent de Paul Particular Council, [L], (LAN), Lansing, MI.
St. Vincent de Paul Preschool, [G], (SCR), Milford, PA.
St. Vincent de Paul Ranch Camp & Retreat Center, [BB], (LA). See St. Vincent de Paul Society.
St. Vincent de Paul Referral Services, [N], (FTW), South Bend, IN.
St. Vincent de Paul Regional Seminary, [A], (PMB), Boynton Beach, FL.
St. Vincent de Paul Regional Seminary Endowment Trust, [J], (PMB), Boynton Beach, FL.
St. Vincent de Paul Rehabilitation Service, Inc., [O], (P), Portland, OR.
St. Vincent de Paul Social Service Office, [H], (SPK), Spokane, WA.
Saint Vincent de Paul Society, [G], (AGN), Agana, GU.
St. Vincent de Paul Society, [K], (ANC), Anchorage, AK.
St. Vincent de Paul Society, [G], (B), Boise, ID.
St. Vincent de Paul Society, [G], (B), Mountain Home, ID.
St. Vincent de Paul Society, [Q], (DET), Detroit, MI.
St. Vincent de Paul Society, [G], (DUL), Duluth, MN.
St. Vincent de Paul Society, [BB], (LA), Los Angeles, CA.
St. Vincent de Paul Society, [L], (LR), Eureka Springs, AR.
St. Vincent De Paul Society, [H], (MAR), Marquette, MI.
St. Vincent de Paul Society, [W], (MIL), Milwaukee, WI.
St. Vincent de Paul Society, [G], (ORG), Orange, CA.
St. Vincent De Paul Society, [Q], (PEO), Peoria, IL.
St. Vincent de Paul Society, [FF], (PH), Conshohocken, PA.
St. Vincent De Paul Society, [J], (PHX), Phoenix, AZ.
St. Vincent de Paul Society, [S], (PIT), Pittsburgh, PA.
St. Vincent De Paul Society, [C], (SAN), Abilene, TX.
St. Vincent De Paul Society, [C], (SAN), Big Spring, TX.
St. Vincent De Paul Society, [C], (SAN), Midland, TX.
St. Vincent De Paul Society, [C], (SAN), Stanton, TX.
St. Vincent de Paul Society, [H], (SPK), Spokane, WA.
St. Vincent de Paul Society, [G], (STO), Manteca, CA.
St. Vincent de Paul Society, [B], (STV). See Miscellaneous Organizations.
St. Vincent de Paul Society, [J], (SY), Syracuse, NY.
Saint Vincent de Paul Society - District Council of Central Oregon, [C], (BAK), Bend, OR.
Saint Vincent de Paul Society - Prineville Conference, [C], (BAK), Prineville, OR.
Saint Vincent de Paul Society - Redmond Conference, [C], (BAK), Redmond, OR.
Saint Vincent de Paul Society - The Dalles Conference, [C], (BAK), The Dalles, OR.
St. Vincent De Paul Society Archdiocese Council of Indianapolis, Inc., [O], (IND), Indianapolis, IN.
St. Vincent de Paul Society Marin County District Council, [H], (SFR), San Rafael, CA.
St. Vincent de Paul Society of Idaho Falls, [G], (B), Idaho Falls, ID.
St. Vincent de Paul Society of St. Joseph County, Inc., [N], (FTW), South Bend, IN.
St. Vincent de Paul Society of the Archdiocese of Dubuque, [O], (DUB), Dubuque, IA.
St. Vincent de Paul Society of Yellowstone County, [K], (GF), Billings, MT.
St. Vincent de Paul Society Store, [N], (FTW), Fort Wayne, IN.
St. Vincent de Paul Society, District Council of Santa Clara County, [P], (SJ), San Jose, CA.
St. Vincent De Paul Society, St. John the Baptist Church Conference, [P], (DAV). See Burlington Notre Dame Foundation.
Saint Vincent de Paul Society-Baraboo, [M], (MAD), Baraboo, WI.
St. Vincent de Paul Store, [G], (B), Coeur D'Alene, ID.
St. Vincent de Paul Store, [I], (SFS), Sioux Falls, SD.
St. Vincent de Paul Store, [H], (SPK), Dayton, WA.
St. Vincent de Paul Store, [H], (SPK), Pasco, WA.
St. Vincent de Paul Store, [H], (SPK), Walla Walla, WA.
St. Vincent de Paul Store, [C], (YAK), Yakima, WA.
St. Vincent de Paul Store, [C], (YAK), Chelan, WA.
St. Vincent de Paul Store, [C], (YAK), Ellensburg, WA.
St. Vincent de Paul Store, [C], (YAK), Kennewick, WA.
St. Vincent de Paul Store, [C], (YAK), Sunnyside, WA.
St. Vincent de Paul Store, [C], (YAK), Wenatchee, WA.
St. Vincent de Paul Store of Springfield, OH, [S], (CIN). See Archdiocesan Central Council of Cincinnati.
St. Vincent de Paul Stores, [BB], (LA). See St. Vincent de Paul Society.
St. Vincent de Paul Stores of Dayton, Ohio, Inc., [S], (CIN). See Archdiocesan Central Council of Cincinnati.
St. Vincent de Paul Stores, Inc., [S], (CIN). See Archdiocesan Central Council of Cincinnati.
St. Vincent de Paul Stores, Inc., [Q], (DEN), Denver, CO.
St. Vincent de Paul Thrift Shop, [N], (FTW), South Bend, IN.
St. Vincent de Paul Thrift Shop, [L], (LR), Berryville, AR.
St. Vincent de Paul Thrift Shop, [J], (SY), Fulton, NY.
St. Vincent de Paul Thrift Store, [G], (B), Blackfoot, ID.
St. Vincent de Paul Thrift Store, [I], (HEL), Butte, MT.
St. Vincent de Paul Thrift Store, [K], (SAC). See Society of St. Vincent de Paul, Sacramento District Council.
St. Vincent de Paul Thrift Stores, [V], (CLV). See Society of St. Vincent de Paul, Diocesan Central Council.
St. Vincent de Paul Village, [J], (SD). See St. Vincent de Paul Management Inc.
St. Vincent de Paul, St. Anne Conference, [I], (SAV), Columbus, GA.
St. Vincent dePaul Assistance Office, [L], (SEA), Bremerton, WA.
*St. Vincent DePaul Community Pharmacy, Inc., [L], (BR), Baton Rouge, LA.
St. Vincent DePaul Dining Room, [L], (BR), Baton Rouge, LA.
St. Vincent dePaul Parish Endowment Trust, [N], (OM). See The Omaha Archdiocesan Educational Foundation, Inc.
St. Vincent dePaul Ranch Camp, [AA], (LA). See Scouting and Camp Fire Ministry/Catholic Youth Camps.
St. Vincent dePaul Residence, [Z], (NY), New York, NY.
St. Vincent dePaul Residence, [DD], (NY), New York, NY.
St. Vincent dePaul School Educational Endowment, [N], (OM). See The Omaha Archdiocesan Educational Foundation, Inc.
St. Vincent DePaul Society, [F], (GLP), Pinetop, AZ.
St. Vincent DePaul Society, [N], (RCK), Sterling, IL.
St. Vincent DePaul Society Denver-Metro Council, [Q], (DEN), Denver, CO.
St. Vincent DePaul Store, [L], (BR), Baton Rouge, LA.
St. Vincent Division, [K], (STL). See De Paul Health Center.
Saint Vincent Elementary School, [F], (SCR), Honesdale, PA.
St. Vincent Ferrer House, [E], (SB), Riverside, CA.
St. Vincent Ferrer Priory, [DD], (NY), New York, NY.
Saint Vincent Foundation, [K], (GF), Billings, MT.
*Saint Vincent Health Center, [G], (E), Erie, PA.
Saint Vincent Health System, [G], (E). See Saint Vincent Health Center.
Saint Vincent Healthcare System, Inc., [J], (WOR). See Saint Vincent Hospital, Inc.
St. Vincent Home Corporation, [P], (DAV), Davenport, IA.
St. Vincent Home for Children, [N], (STL), Normandy, MO.
St. Vincent Home-Boysville of Michigan, Inc., [D], (SAG), Saginaw, MI.
St. Vincent Hospital, [F], (GB), Green Bay, WI.
St. Vincent Hospital and Health Care Center, Inc., [F], (IND), Indianapolis, IN.
Saint Vincent Hospital and Health Center, [G], (GF), Billings, MT.
Saint Vincent Hospital, Inc., [J], (WOR), Worcester, MA.
St. Vincent Hotel, Inc., [S], (CIN). See Archdiocesan Central Council of Cincinnati.
St. Vincent Infirmary Medical Center, [E], (LR), Little Rock, AR.
St. Vincent Medical Center, [K], (LA), Los Angeles, CA.

Servite Community, Sarpi Priory, [N], (OAK), Berkeley, CA.
Servite Development Office, [N], (CHI). See Servite Friars - Eastern Province.
Servite Fathers and Brothers, [H], (ORG), Anaheim, CA.
Servite Fathers And Brothers, [H], (ORG), Buena Park, CA.
Servite Fathers and Brothers, [H], (ORG), Fullerton, CA.
Servite Fathers and Brothers, [H], (ORG), Orange, CA.
Servite Friars - Eastern Province, [N], (CHI), Chicago, IL.
Servite Friars-Eastern Province Retirement Trust, [X], (CHI), Chicago, IL.
Servite Friars-Eastern Province, Inc., [X], (CHI), Chicago, IL.
Servite High School; Servite High School Development Fund, [D], (ORG), Anaheim, CA.
Seton Academy, [D], (CHI), South Holland, IL.
Seton Catholic Central, [C], (OG), Plattsburgh, NY.
Seton Catholic Central High School of Broome County, [C], (SY), Binghamton, NY.
Seton Catholic Elementary School, [F], (DUB), Epworth, IA.
Seton Catholic High School, [A], (PHX), Phoenix, AZ.
Seton Catholic High School, [D], (SCR), Pittston, PA.
Seton Catholic Jr. High School, [E], (GAL), Houston, TX.
Seton Catholic Middle School, [G], (SY), Endicott, NY.
Seton Catholic School, [G], (DAV), Ottumwa, IA.
Seton Catholic School, [E], (PEO), Moline, IL.
Seton Catholic School of Hudson, [F], (CLV), Hudson, OH.
Seton Center, [D], (WIL). See Catholic Charities, Inc.
*Seton Center Family & Health Services, [M], (KC), Kansas City, MO.
Seton Center, Inc., [K], (BAL), Emmitsburg, MD.
Seton Center, Sisters of Charity, [J], (WIL), Princess Anne, MD.
Seton Centers, Inc., [I], (ARL), Falls Church, VA.
Seton Children's School, Inc., [J], (MIL), Milwaukee, WI.
Seton Coshocton, Inc., [G], (COL), Coshocton, OH.
The Seton Cove - A Spirituality Center, [N], (AUS), Austin, TX.
Seton East Community Health Center, [F], (AUS), Austin, TX.
Seton Foundation for Learning, [D], (NY). See Department of Education.
Seton Foundation for Learning, Inc., [G], (NY), New York, NY.
Seton Hall Preparatory School, [C], (NEW), West Orange, NJ.
Seton Hall University, [B], (NEW), South Orange, NJ.
Seton Hall University College Seminary, [A], (NEW), South Orange, NJ.
Seton Haven, [G], (MOB), Montgomery, AL.
Seton Health Care of Northern Illinois, [J], (CHI). See St. Joseph Hospital.
Seton Health Care Services, Inc., [Y], (MIL), Milwaukee, WI.
Seton Health Care, Inc., [P], (PAT), Convent Station, NJ.
Seton Health Corp. of South Alabama, [E], (MOB), Mobile, AL.
Seton Health Corporation of Central Indiana, [F], (IND), Indianapolis, IN.
Seton Health Corporation of East Central Michigan, [I], (SAG), Saginaw, MI.
Seton Health Corporation of North Alabama, [D], (BIR), Birmingham, AL.
Seton Health Corporation of Southeast Michigan, [T], (DET), Southfield, MI.
Seton Health Corporation of Southern Indiana, [J], (EVN), Evansville, IN.
Seton Health Corporation of Wisconsin, [Y], (MIL), Milwaukee, WI.
Seton Health Services Foundation, [J], (SFR). See Seton Medical Center.
Seton Health System, Inc., [H], (ALB), Troy, NY.
Seton High School, [E], (CIN), Cincinnati, OH.
Seton High School Foundation, [U], (CIN), Cincinnati, OH.
Seton Hill College, [B], (GBG), Greensburg, PA.
Seton Home Endowment Fund, [S], (SAT), San Antonio, TX.
Seton Home for Homeless, Pregnant Young Women, [I], (SAT), San Antonio, TX.
Seton Home Study School, [N], (ARL), Front Royal, VA.
Seton Housing, Inc., [G], (COL), Zanesville, OH.
Seton Institute for International Development, [J], (SFR). See Seton Medical Center.
Seton Kenton, Inc., [G], (COL), Kenton, OH.
The Seton Keough High School, [C], (BAL), Baltimore, MD.
The Seton Keough High School Endowment Trust, [P], (BAL). See Chancery Office.
The Seton Keough High School Endowment Trust, [P], (BAL), Baltimore, MD.
Seton Lancaster, Inc., [G], (COL), Lancaster, OH.
Seton London, Inc., [G], (COL), Columbus, OH.
Seton Manor, [H], (RIC), Hampton, VA.
Seton Medical Center, [F], (AUS), Austin, TX.
Seton Medical Center, [J], (SFR), Daly City, CA.
Seton Medical Center, [J], (SFR). See Seton Medical Center.
Seton Medical Center Coastside, [J], (SFR), Moss Beach, CA.
Seton Medical Management, Inc., [E], (MOB), Mobile, AL.
Seton Northwest Hospital, [F], (AUS), Austin, TX.
Seton Nursery School and Infant-Toddler Child Care Center, [O], (DET), Farmington Hills, MI.
Seton Regional Foundation, Inc., [P], (BAL). See Chancery Office.
Seton Regional Health System, Inc., [P], (BAL). See Chancery Office.
Seton Residence, [F], (EVN), Evansville, IN.
Seton Retreat Center, [L], (BAL), Emmitsburg, MD.
Seton South Columbus, Inc., [G], (COL), Columbus, OH.
Seton South Community Health Center, [F], (AUS), Austin, TX.
Seton Square Dover, I, Inc., [G], (COL), Dover, OH.
Seton Square Dover, II, Inc., [G], (COL), Dover, OH.
Seton Square East, Inc., [G], (COL), Reynoldsburg, OH.
Seton Square Marion, Inc., [G], (COL), Marion, OH.
Seton Square North, [G], (COL), Columbus, OH.
Seton Square Wellston, Inc., [G], (COL), Wellston, OH.
Seton Villa, Inc., [E], (WIL), Wilmington, DE.
Seton Village Inc., [G], (PRT), Waterville, ME.
Seton Washington Court House, Inc., [G], (COL), Columbus, OH.
Seton-LaSalle Catholic High School, [C], (PIT), Mt. Lebanon, PA.
Shade Tree Family Resource Center, Inc., [Y], (MIL), Milwaukee, WI.
Shakopee Area Catholic School, [H], (STP), Shakopee, MN.
Shalem House, [K], (FTW). See Saint Mary's of the Immaculate Conception.
Shalom Catholic Worker House, [K], (KCK), Kansas City, KS.
Shalom Center, Inc., [O], (GAL), Splendora, TX.
Shalom Community, [N], (HRT). See Sisters of St. Joseph.
Shalom Convent, [EE], (NY), New York, NY.
Shalom Convent, [BB], (PH), Philadelphia, PA.
Shalom Convent, [O], (SFR), San Francisco, CA.
Shalom House, [N], (RIC), Montpelier, VA.
Shalom House Family Shelter, [N], (LAF). See Lafayette Catholic Service Centers, Inc.
Shalom House of Prayer, [S], (GAL), Houston, TX.
Shalom Retreat Center, [M], (DUB), Dubuque, IA.
Shanley High School, [B], (FAR), Fargo, ND.
Shantivanam Archdiocesan House of Prayer, [K], (KCK), Easton, KS.
SHARE Colorado, [L], (DEN). See Catholic Charities and Community Services of the Archdiocese of Denver, Inc.
SHARE Food Program of Central Illinois, Inc., [Q], (PEO), Peoria, IL.
SHARE Southern California, [J], (SD). See SHARE Southern California.
SHARE Southern California, [J], (SD). See St. Vincent de Paul Management Inc.
Shared Housing Program, [F], (SJ). See Catholic Charities of Santa Clara County.
The Sharkey Family Charitable Trust, [G], (CAM), Ocean City, NJ.
Shawe Memorial Junior-Senior High School, [C], (IND), Madison, IN.
Sheehan Residence for Priests, [O], (BUF), Buffalo, NY.
Shelby County Board of Catholic Education, [A], (DM), Panama, IA.
Shelby County Catholic Education Foundation, [J], (DM), Harlan, IA.
Shelter for Homeless, [L], (DEN). See Catholic Charities and Community Services of the Archdiocese of Denver, Inc.
Shelter for the Homeless, [H], (PCE), Ponce, PR.
Shelter Nursery for Drug Exposed Babies, [L], (SFR). See Mount St. Joseph-St. Elizabeth.
Shelter of Flint, Inc., [D], (LAN), Flint, MI.
Shelter Plus Housing, [J], (SLC). See Catholic Community Services.
Sheltering Arms, [J], (DET), Southfield, MI.
Sheltering Arms Adult Day Care, [N], (DET). See Catholic Social Services of Oakland County.
Shelters for the Homeless, Inc., [X], (CHI), Chicago, IL.
Sheptytsky Arms, [B], (SJP), Pittsburgh, PA.
Sherri Lyn Shaffer Trust for St. Thomas More Church, [M], (BR). See Baton Rouge Chancery Office.
Shevchenko Manor, [B], (SJP), Parma, OH.
Shoreless Lake School, [B], (MET), New Brunswick, NJ.
Short Journey Center, [I], (R), Smithfield, NC.
Shrine Chapel of the Blessed Sacrament, [K], (MET), Raritan, NJ.
Shrine High School, [D], (DET), Royal Oak, MI.
Shrine of Immaculate Heart of Mary, [H], (SPC), Carthage, MO.
Shrine of Our Lady of Charity, [K], (MIA), Miami, FL.
Shrine of Our Lady of Grace, [K], (MAN), Colebrook, NH.
Shrine of Our Lady of La Salette, [K], (MAN), Enfield, NH.
Shrine of Our Lady of Martyrs, [O], (ALB), Auriesville, NY.
Shrine of Our Lady of Peace, [A], (SJ), Santa Clara, CA.
Shrine of Our Lady of the Island, [N], (RVC), Eastport, NY.
Shrine of Our Lady of the Snows, [F], (BEL), Belleville, IL.
Shrine of Our Lady of Victories at St. Peter Claver, [FF], (PH), Philadelphia, PA.
Shrine of St. Joseph, [M], (PAT), Stirling, NJ.
Shrine of St. Jude Thaddeus, [U], (SFR), San Francisco, CA.
Shrine of St. Jude, Inc., [HH], (NY), New York, NY.
Shrine of St. Maximilian Kolbe, [N], (CHI). See Marytown, Our Lady of Fatima Friary.
Shrine of the Immaculate Heart of Mary, [K], (MET), Washington, NJ.
Shrine of the Infant Jesus, [T], (BUF), North Tonawanda, NY.
Shrine of the Weeping Madonna of Mariapoch, [B], (PRM), Burton, OH.
Siena - Francis House, Inc., [O], (OM), Omaha, NE.
Siena Club, [O], (KC), Kansas City, MO.
Siena College, [B], (ALB), Loudonville, NY.
Siena College, [S], (ALB), Loudonville, NY.
Siena Convent, [N], (SR), Napa, CA.
Siena Hall, [F], (LC). See St. Francis Community Programs, Inc.
Siena Hall, Inc., [E], (WIL), Wilmington, DE.
Siena Heights College - President, [A], (LAN), Adrian, MI.
Siena Heights College Newman Center, [J], (LAN), Adrian, MI.
Siena House, [O], (OAK). See Dominican Sisters of Mission San Jose.
Siena House, [O], (OM), Omaha, NE.
Siena Literacy Center, [T], (DET), Redford, MI.
Siena Spirituality Center, [P], (RVC), Water Mill, NY.
Siena Springs, [L], (CIN), Dayton, OH.
Siena Village, [P], (PAT), Wayne, NJ.
Silva Pediatric Clinic, [K], (OAK). See St. Rose Hospital.
Silver Lake College of the Holy Family, [B], (GB), Manitowoc, WI.
Silver Penny Farm Retreat Center, [M], (SFR), Petaluma, CA.
Simeon House I (St. Patrick Parish), [L], (IND). See Catholic Charities of Terre Haute.
Simon Hall, [P], (L). See Society of St. Vincent de Paul, Council of Louisville.
Simpatico School, [L], (SFR). See Mount St. Joseph-St. Elizabeth.
Sinclair Community College Campus Ministry, [Q], (CIN), Dayton, OH.
Sinsinawa Dominican Community Support Trust, [M], (MAD), Sinsinawa, WI.
Sinsinawa Dominican Congregation of the Most Holy Rosary, [N], (SJ), San Jose, CA.
Sinsinawa Dominican Congregation of the Most Holy Rosary, O.P., [Q], (NO), Harvey, LA.
Sinsinawa Dominican Sisters, [I], (AUS), Austin, TX.
Sinsinawa Dominican Sisters, [K], (MEM), Somerville, TN.
Sinsinawa Dominican Sisters, [I], (MOB), Ozark, AL.
Sioux Falls Catholic Junior High, [C], (SFS). See Sioux Falls Catholic School System.
Sioux Falls Catholic School Corporation, [I], (SFS), Sioux Falls, SD.
Sioux Falls Catholic School System, [C], (SFS), Sioux Falls, SD.
Sister Disciples of the Divine Master, [X], (BO), Boston, MA.
Sister Disciples of the Divine Master, [F], (FRS), Fresno, CA.
Sr. Elizabeth Boyle Child Learning Center, Inc., [V], (NY), New York, NY.
Sister Georgine School, [H], (TR), Trenton, NJ.
Sister Joanna House of Formation, [N], (PAT), Florham Park, NJ.
Sr. Lucian Apartments, HDFC, Inc., [L], (BRK). See Catholic Charities.
The Sister M. Athanasia Gurry Trust Fund of the Sisters of St. Joseph, [T], (ALB), Latham, NY.
The Sister Maureen Keleher Center (Hospice), [F], (HON). See St. Francis Healthcare System of Hawaii.
Sister of Charity of St. Charles Borromeo, Inc., [O],

Sisters Of St. Joseph Of Pennsylvania (Erie, PA) S.S.J., [K], (MEM), Memphis, TN.
Sisters of St. Joseph of Philadelphia, [I], (MOB), Camden, AL.
Sisters of St. Joseph of Philadelphia, [BB], (PH), Philadelphia, PA.
Sisters of St. Joseph of Philadelphia, [BB], (PH), Warminster, PA.
Sisters of St. Joseph of Philadelphia, Cecilian Academy, [BB], (PH), Philadelphia, PA.
Sisters of St. Joseph of Philadelphia, Fournier Community, [BB], (PH), Philadelphia, PA.
Sisters of St. Joseph of Philadelphia, Mt. St. Joseph Academy, [BB], (PH), Flourtown, PA.
Sisters of St. Joseph of Philadelphia, Nazareth House, [BB], (PH), Philadelphia, PA.
Sisters of St. Joseph of Philadelphia, St. Joseph Villa Staff, [X], (PH), Flourtown, PA.
Sisters of St. Joseph of St. Mark, [Q], (CLV), Cleveland, OH.
Sisters of St. Joseph of the Third Order of St. Francis, [N], (HRT), Beacon Falls, CT.
Sisters of St. Joseph of the Third Order of St. Francis, [N], (HRT), Forestville, CT.
Sisters of St. Joseph of the Third Order of St. Francis, [O], (OAK), Concord, CA.
The Sisters of St. Joseph of the Third Order of St. Francis Central Offices, S.S.J.-T.O.S.F., [K], (FTW), South Bend, IN.
Sisters of St. Joseph of the Third Order of St. Francis Residences, [K], (FTW). See The Sisters of St. Joseph of the Third Order of St. Francis Central Offices, S.S.J.-T.O.S.F.
Sisters of St. Joseph of the Third Order of St. Francis Residences S.S.J.-T.O.S.F., [K], (FTW), Fort Wayne, IN.
Sisters of St. Joseph of the Third Order of St. Francis, S.S.J.-T.O.S.F., [O], (OAK), El Sobrante, CA.
Sisters of St. Joseph of Wheeling Foundation, Inc., [P], (WH), Wheeling, WV.
Sisters of St. Joseph of Wichita, [O], (OAK), San Leandro, CA.
Sisters of St. Joseph of Wichita, [J], (OKL), Ponca City, OK.
Sisters of St. Joseph of Wichita, KS., [O], (OAK), Hayward, CA.
Sisters of St. Joseph Society, Inc., [F], (BUR), Rutland, VT.
Sisters of St. Joseph's Architectural Stained Glass, [G], (ORL), Winter Garden, FL.
Sisters of St. Joseph, Concordia, KS, [C], (LSC), Las Cruces, NM.
Sisters of St. Joseph, S.S.J., [O], (WOR), Worcester, MA.
Sisters of St. Joseph, T.O.S.F., [G], (NOR), Middletown, CT.
Sisters of St. Joseph, Third Order of St. Francis, [G], (KNX), Butler, TN.
Sisters of St. Joseph, Third Order of St. Francis, [G], (KNX), Jonesborough, TN.
Sisters of St. Louis, [S], (LA), Encino, CA.
Sisters of St. Louis, [I], (ORG), Tustin, CA.
Sisters of St. Louis Monaghan, Inc., [EE], (LA). See Chancery Office.
Sisters of St. Louis, Louisville Convent, [S], (LA), Woodland Hills, CA.
Sisters of St. Louis—California Region, [F], (R), Ahoskie, NC.
Sisters of St. Mary, [P], (BUF), Buffalo, NY.
Sisters of St. Mary Convent, [E], (CHR), Charleston, SC.
Sisters of St. Mary Namur, [I], (FWT), Fort Worth, TX.
Sisters of St. Mary of Namur, [P], (BUF), Derby, NY.
Sisters of St. Mary of Namur (S.S.M.N.), [R], (GAL), Houston, TX.
Sisters of St. Mary of Washington, [O], (WDC), Washington, DC.
Sisters of St. Paul de Chartres, [H], (ANC), Anchorage, AK.
Sisters of St. Philip Neri, [E], (RNO), Sparks, NV.
Sisters of St. Ursula, [F], (R), Wilmington, NC.
Sisters of Social Service, [I], (ORG), Fountain Valley, CA.
Sisters of Social Service, [I], (ORG), Dana Point, CA.
Sisters of Social Service, [H], (SAC), Sacramento, CA.
Sisters of Social Service, [I], (SD), San Diego, CA.
Sisters of Social Service, [O], (SFR), San Francisco, CA.
Sisters of Social Service District Residence, [P], (BUF), Buffalo, NY.
Sisters of Social Service of Los Angeles, [S], (LA), Los Angeles, CA.
Sisters of St Joseph of Carondelet, [H], (MRY), San Luis Obispo, CA.
Sisters of Ste. Chretienne, [X], (BO), Marlboro, MA.
Sisters of Ste. Chretienne, [X], (BO). See Sisters of Ste. Chretienne.
Sisters of the Annunciation of the Archdiocese of Omaha, [L], (OM), Omaha, NE.
Sisters of the Assumption, [N], (HRT), West Haven, CT.
Sisters of the Assumption of the Blessed Virgin, [O], (WOR), Worcester, MA.
Sisters of the Blessed Sacrament, [I], (LAF), Church Point, LA.
Sisters of the Blessed Sacrament, [I], (LAF), Rayne, LA.
Sisters of the Blessed Sacrament, [I], (LAF), St. Martinville, LA.
Sisters of the Blessed Sacrament, [BB], (PH), Philadelphia, PA.
Sisters of the Blessed Sacrament Novitiate, [BB], (PH), Bensalem, PA.
Sisters of the Blessed Sacrament, S.B.S., [Q], (NO), New Orleans, LA.
Sisters of the Blessed Virgin Mary, [I], (ORG), Cypress, CA.
Sisters of the Cenacle, [K], (ARL), Great Falls, VA.
Sisters of the Cenacle, [K], (ATL), Hoschton, GA.
Sisters of the Community of St. John, [N], (PEO), Brimfield, IL.
Sisters of the Company of Mary, [S], (LA), Los Angeles, CA.
Sisters of the Company of Mary, [I], (ORG), Costa Mesa, CA.
Sisters of the Company of Mary, [I], (ORG), Orange, CA.
Sisters of the Company of Mary, [I], (ORG), Santa Ana, CA.
Sisters of the Company of Mary, [I], (ORG), Tustin, CA.
Sisters of the Company of Mary (O.D.N.), [F], (SB), Tustin, CA.
Sisters of the Company of the Savior, [P], (BGP), Bridgeport, CT.
Sisters of the Cross and Passion, [N], (HRT), Hartford, CT.
Sisters of the Cross and Passion, [N], (HRT), New Britain, CT.
Sisters of the Cross and Passion, [N], (HRT), Farmington, CT.
Sisters of the Cross and Passion, [Q], (PRO), South Kingstown, RI.
Sisters of the Cross & Passion Convent, [Q], (PRO), Narragansett, RI.
Sisters of the Cross & Passion, C.P., [S], (LA), San Gabriel, CA.
Sisters of the Cross of the Sacred Heart of Jesus, [E], (STO), Modesto, CA.
Sisters of the Divine Compassion, [G], (KNX), Knoxville, TN.
Sisters of the Divine Redeemer, [BB], (PH), Darby, PA.
Sisters of the Divine Savior, [Q], (MIL), Milwaukee, WI.
Sisters of the Eucharistic Covenant, [M], (LAF), Lafayette, LA.
Sisters of the Good Shepherd, [N], (BAL), Baltimore, MD.
Sisters of the Good Shepherd, [X], (BO), Boston, MA.
Sisters of the Good Shepherd, [X], (BO), Marlboro, MA.
Sisters of the Good Shepherd, [V], (BRK), Brooklyn, NY.
Sisters of the Good Shepherd, [O], (CHI), Chicago, IL.
Sisters of the Good Shepherd, [N], (CIN), Cincinnati, OH.
Sisters of the Good Shepherd, [N], (CIN), Cincinnati, OH.
Sisters of the Good Shepherd, [I], (COL), Columbus, OH.
Sisters of the Good Shepherd, [M], (COV), Fort Thomas, KY.
Sisters of the Good Shepherd, [M], (L), Louisville, KY.
Sisters of the Good Shepherd, [S], (LA), Los Angeles, CA.
Sisters of the Good Shepherd, [EE], (NY), New York, NY.
Sisters of the Good Shepherd, [EE], (NY), Peekskill, NY.
Sisters of the Good Shepherd, [BB], (PH), Philadelphia, PA.
Sisters of the Good Shepherd, [O], (RVC), Dix Hills, NY.
Sisters of the Good Shepherd, [O], (SFR), San Francisco, CA.
Sisters of the Good Shepherd - St. Paul Province, [O], (STP), St. Paul, MN.
Sisters of the Good Shepherd (Contemplative), [BB], (PH), Philadelphia, PA.
Sisters of the Good Shepherd (R.G.S.), [L], (OM), Omaha, NE.
Sisters of the Good Shepherd (R.G.S.), [BB], (PH), Philadelphia, PA.
Sisters of the Good Shepherd Convent, [F], (AGN), Ordot, GU.
Sisters of the Good Shepherd, Marycrest, [Q], (CLV), Independence, OH.
Sisters of the Good Shepherd-St. Joseph Residence, [N], (BAL), Baltimore, MD.
Sisters of the Guardian Angel, [S], (LA), Los Angeles, CA.
The Sisters of the Handmaids of the Holy Child Jesus (of Nigeria, Africa), [G], (ALX), Alexandria, LA.
Sisters of the Heart of Jesus in the Blessed Sacrament, [I], (SD), National City, CA.
Sisters of the Holy Child, [BB], (PH), Philadelphia, PA.
Sisters of the Holy Child, [BB], (PH), Bryn Mawr, PA.
Sisters of the Holy Child Jesus, [BB], (PH), Bryn Mawr, PA.
Sisters of the Holy Child Jesus, [O], (RVC), Old Westbury, NY.
Sisters of the Holy Child Jesus, [O], (WDC), Washington, DC.
Sisters of the Holy Child Jesus (S.H.C.J.), [BB], (PH), Rosemont, PA.
Sisters of the Holy Child Jesus (S.H.C.J.), [BB], (PH), Drexel Hill, PA.
Sisters of the Holy Child Jesus-African Province Office, [HH], (NY), New York, NY.
Sisters of the Holy Cross, [K], (ARL), Alexandria, VA.
Sisters of the Holy Cross, [I], (AUS), Austin, TX.
Sisters of the Holy Cross, [I], (AUS), Waco, TX.
Sisters of the Holy Cross, [N], (BAL), Baltimore, MD.
Sisters of the Holy Cross, [F], (BWN), Raymondville, TX.
Sisters of the Holy Cross, [O], (CHI), Chicago, IL.
Sisters of the Holy Cross, [K], (FTW), Elkhart, IN.
Sisters of the Holy Cross, [M], (L), Tompkinsville, KY.
Sisters of the Holy Cross, [M], (L), Columbia, KY.
Sisters of the Holy Cross, [S], (LA), Mission Hills, CA.
Sisters of the Holy Cross, [S], (LA), Ventura, CA.
Sisters of the Holy Cross, [F], (LFT), Anderson, IN.
Sisters of the Holy Cross, [G], (NOR), Baltic, CT.
Sisters of the Holy Cross, [I], (ORG), Orange, CA.
Sisters of the Holy Cross, [I], (ORG), Rancho Santa Margarita, CA.
Sisters of the Holy Cross, [F], (R), Raleigh, NC.
The Sisters of the Holy Cross, [N], (SAT), San Antonio, TX.
Sisters of the Holy Cross, [I], (SD), La Jolla, CA.
Sisters of the Holy Cross, [E], (STO), Modesto, CA.
Sisters of the Holy Cross, [G], (TUC), Tucson, AZ.
Sisters of the Holy Cross, [O], (WDC), Kensington, MD.
Sisters of the Holy Cross, [O], (WDC). See Sisters of the Holy Cross.
Sisters of the Holy Cross Convents, [K], (FTW). See St. Joseph High School Convent.
Sisters of the Holy Cross, Inc., [F], (LFT). See Sisters of the Holy Cross.
Sisters of the Holy Cross, Our Lady of Mount Carmel Convent, [I], (COL), Columbus, OH.
Sisters of the Holy Faith, [H], (SAC), Fairfield, CA.
Sisters of the Holy Faith in California, [S], (LA), Downey, CA.
Sisters of the Holy Family, [I], (LAF), Opelousas, LA.
Sisters of the Holy Family, [O], (OAK), Castro Valley, CA.
Sisters of the Holy Family, [O], (OAK), Fremont, CA.
Sisters of the Holy Family, [I], (SD), San Diego, CA.
Sisters of the Holy Family, [O], (SFR), San Francisco, CA.
Sisters of the Holy Family (S.S.F.), [R], (GAL), Houston, TX.
Sisters of the Holy Family Convent, S.H.F., [E], (RNO), Reno, NV.
Sisters of the Holy Family Development Office, [Q], (NO). See Sisters of the Holy Family Motherhouse and Novitiate, S.S.F.
Sisters of the Holy Family Motherhouse and Novitiate, S.S.F., [Q], (NO), New Orleans, LA.
Sisters of the Holy Family of Nazareth, [N], (DAL), Grand Prairie, TX.
Sisters of the Holy Family of Nazareth, [BB], (PH), Philadelphia, PA.
Sisters of the Holy Family of Nazareth, [O], (WOR), Worcester, MA.
Sisters of the Holy Family of Nazareth - Blessed Frances Siedliska Province Charitable Trust, [P], (DAL), Grand Prairie, TX.
Sisters of the Holy Family of Nazareth (C.S.F.N.), [BB], (PH), Ambler, PA.
Sisters of the Holy Family of Nazareth of Western Pennsylvania, [P], (PIT), Pittsburgh, PA.
Sisters of the Holy Family Residences, [I], (HON), Mountain View, HI.
Sisters of the Holy Family, Holy Family Convent, [N], (SJ), San Jose, CA.
Sisters of the Holy Names (S.N.J.M.), [O], (WDC), Silver Spring, MD.
Sisters of the Holy Names of Jesus and Mary, [M], (ALB), Albany, NY.
Sisters of the Holy Names of Jesus and Mary, [T], (ALB), Albany, NY.
Sisters of the Holy Names of Jesus & Mary, [N], (SJ), Los Gatos, CA.
Sisters of the Holy Names of Jesus & Mary of the New York Province, Inc., [T], (ALB), Albany, NY.

Society of Our Lady of the Way, [T], (LA), Los Angeles, CA.
Society of Our Lady of the Way, [S], (NO), New Orleans, LA.
The Society of Our Lady of the Way, [P], (SFR), San Francisco, CA.
Society of Our Mother of Peace, [P], (STL), High Ridge, MO.
The Society of Our Mother of Peace, Daughters of Our Mother of Peace, [G], (SPC), Marionville, MO.
Society of Our Mother of Peace, Daughters of Our Mother of Peace, [R], (STL), High Ridge, MO.
The Society of Our Mother of Peace, Daughters of Our Mothers of Peace, [F], (SPC), Marionville, MO.
The Society of Our Mother of Peace, Sons of Our Mother of Peace, [E], (SPC), Marionville, MO.
Society of Our Mother of Peace-Maria Fonte Solitude, [T], (STL), High Ridge, MO.
Society of St. Edmund, [E], (BUR), Colchester, VT.
Society of St. Edmund, [E], (BUR). See Society of St. Edmund.
Society of St. Edmund, [F], (NOR), Mystic, CT.
Society of St. Edmund Residence, [G], (VEN), Englewood, FL.
The Society of St. James the Apostle, Inc., [W], (BO), Boston, MA.
Society of St. John (Brothers of Saint Benedict), [J], (DM), Des Moines, IA.
Society of St. Joseph the Worker, [AA], (CLV), Parma, OH.
Society of St. Paul, [O], (BUF), Derby, NY.
Society of St. Paul, [K], (DET), Dearborn, MI.
Society of St. Paul, [R], (LA), Los Angeles, CA.
Society of St. Paul, [B], (NY), New York, NY.
Society of St. Paul, [A], (Y), Canfield, OH.
Society of St. Teresa of Jesus, [N], (SAT), Uvalde, TX.
Society of St. Vincent de Paul, [N], (AUS), Austin, TX.
Society of St. Vincent de Paul, [G], (B), Kellogg, ID.
Society of St. Vincent de Paul, [G], (B), Caldwell, ID.
Society of St. Vincent de Paul, [I], (BIR), Huntsville, AL.
Society of St. Vincent de Paul, [H], (BUF). See The Catholic Charities of the Diocese of Buffalo.
Society of St. Vincent De Paul, [Q], (CHL), Greensboro, NC.
Society of St. Vincent de Paul, [N], (COV), Covington, KY.
Society of St. Vincent de Paul, [P], (DAL), Dallas, TX.
Society of Saint Vincent de Paul, [J], (DM), Des Moines, IA.
Society of St. Vincent de Paul, [I], (FRS), Fresno, CA.
Society of St. Vincent de Paul, [M], (JOL), West Chicago, IL.
Society of St. Vincent de Paul, [L], (LAN), Lansing, MI.
Society of St. Vincent de Paul, [L], (LAN), Jackson, MI.
Society of St. Vincent de Paul, [I], (LEX), Lexington, KY.
Society of St. Vincent de Paul, [K], (MAD), Madison, WI.
Society of St. Vincent de Paul, [L], (MOB), Mobile, AL.
Society of St. Vincent de Paul, [O], (P), Portland, OR.
Society of St. Vincent de Paul, [O], (P), Medford, OR.
*Society of St. Vincent de Paul, [O], (P), Salem, OR.
Society of St. Vincent de Paul, [O], (P), Eugene, OR.
Society of Saint Vincent de Paul, [S], (PIT), Pittsburgh, PA.
Society of St. Vincent de Paul, [I], (SAG), Bay City, MI.
Society of St. Vincent de Paul, [P], (SAT), San Antonio, TX.
Society of St. Vincent de Paul, [I], (SAV), Brunswick, GA.
Society of St. Vincent de Paul, [L], (SEA), Everett, WA.
Society of St. Vincent de Paul, [J], (TUC), Tucson, AZ.
Society of St. Vincent de Paul, [I], (WDC), Riverdale, MD.
Society of St. Vincent de Paul, [L], (WH), Wheeling, WV.
Society of St. Vincent de Paul - Archdiocesan Council, [L], (SEA), Bellevue, WA.
Society of St. Vincent de Paul - Particular Council of Tacoma, [L], (SEA), Tacoma, WA.
Society of St. Vincent de Paul - Stores, [L], (SEA). See Society of St. Vincent de Paul - Archdiocesan Council.
Society of St. Vincent de Paul (Diocesan Central Council), [F], (SFD), Springfield, IL.
The Society of St. Vincent de Paul (not under membership structure), [V], (CLV). See Catholic Charities Services Corporation.
Society of St. Vincent de Paul and Related Stores, [L], (SEA), Manchester, WA.
Society of St. Vincent de Paul Archdiocesan Council, [H], (SFR), San Francisco, CA.
Society of St. Vincent de Paul District - Council of Seattle Area, [L], (SEA). See Society of St. Vincent de Paul - Archdiocesan Council.
Society of St. Vincent De Paul District Council, [I], (BWN), Brownsville, TX.
Society of St. Vincent de Paul in Diocese of Brooklyn, [L], (BRK). See Catholic Charities.
Society of St. Vincent de Paul of Alameda County, [I], (OAK), Oakland, CA.
Society of St. Vincent de Paul of Alameda County, [I], (OAK). See Society of St. Vincent de Paul of Alameda County.
Society of St. Vincent De Paul of Chicago, [G], (CHI). See Catholic Charities of the Archdiocese of Chicago-Archdiocesan Offices.
Society of St. Vincent de Paul of Contra Costa County, [I], (OAK), Pittsburg, CA.
Society of St. Vincent de Paul Solano District Council, [K], (SAC), Vallejo, CA.
Society of St. Vincent de Paul Stores and Workshop, [L], (SEA), Tacoma, WA.
Society of St. Vincent De Paul, Archdiocesan Central Council of New York, [Q], (NY), New York, NY.
Society of St. Vincent de Paul, Council of Louisville, [P], (L), Louisville, KY.
Society of St. Vincent de Paul, Diocesan Central Council, [V], (CLV), Cleveland, OH.
Society of St. Vincent de Paul, District Council, [J], (PMB), Riviera Beach, FL.
Society of St. Vincent de Paul, District Council of Napa County, [F], (SR), Napa, CA.
Society of St. Vincent de Paul, District Council of Sonoma County, [F], (SR), Rohnert Park, CA.
Society of St. Vincent de Paul, District Council of the Redwood Region, [F], (SR), Eureka, CA.
Society of St. Vincent de Paul, Particular Council of Yakima, [E], (YAK), Yakima, WA.
Society of St. Vincent de Paul, Sacramento District Council, [K], (SAC), Sacramento, CA.
Society of St. Vincent de Paul, St. Sebastian Conference, [J], (PMB), Vero Beach, FL.
Society of Saint Vincent de Paul, Sauk-Prairie/Roxbury Area, [M], (MAD), Prairie du Sac, WI.
Society of St. Vincent DePaul, [M], (GRY). See Catholic Charities.
Society of St. Vincent DePaul, [M], (MEM), Memphis, TN.
Society of St. Vincent DePaul, [K], (SAC), Roseville, CA.
Society of St. Vincent DePaul, Central Office, [L], (BO), Boston, MA.
Society of St. Vincent DePaul, Council of the United States, [W], (STL), St. Louis, MO.
The Society of Sisters for the Church, [N], (PAT), West Paterson, NJ.
Society of the Brothers of the Holy Spirit (B.H.S.), [AA], (PH), Philadelphia, PA.
Society of the Catholic Apostolate, [O], (BUF), North Tonawanda, NY.
Society of the Divine Savior Ongoing Community Support Trust, [Y], (MIL), Milwaukee, WI.
Society of the Divine Word, [W], (BO), Duxbury, MA.
Society of The Divine Word, [O], (PIT), Pittsburgh, PA.
Society of the Divine Word, [M], (TR), Bordentown, NJ.
Society of the Divine Word, [F], (TUC), Tucson, AZ.
Society of the Divine Word Augustine Tolton House, [P], (NO), New Orleans, LA.
Society of the Divine Word Western Province, [R], (LA), Los Angeles, CA.
Society of the Divine Word, Provincial Headquarter-Chicago Prov., [N], (CHI), Techny, IL.
Society of the Helpers of the Holy Souls, [R], (STL), St. Louis, MO.
Society of the Holy Child Jesus, [C], (LSC), Las Cruces, NM.
Society of the Holy Child Jesus, [BB], (PH), Bryn Mawr, PA.
Society of the Holy Child Jesus, [BB], (PH), Drexel Hill, PA.
Society of the Holy Child Jesus, [I], (SD), San Diego, CA.
The Society of the Homeless Orphan of the Diocese of St. Cloud, [M], (SCL), St. Cloud, MN.
Society of the Immaculate Conception of Brooklyn, [Y], (BRK), Douglaston, NY.
Society of the Little Flower, [M], (JOL), Darien, IL.
Society of the Precious Blood, [N], (OAK), Berkeley, CA.
Society of the Precious Blood, [N], (OAK), San Leandro, CA.
Society of the Precious Blood Provincial Offices, [A], (KC), Liberty, MO.
Society of the Priests of St. Sulpice (Sulpicians) S.S., [H], (HON), Honolulu, HI.
Society of the Sacred Heart, [EE], (NY), Purchase, NY.
Society of the Sacred Heart, [N], (SJ), San Jose, CA.
Society of the Sacred Heart, [N], (SJ), Alviso, CA.
Society of the Sacred Heart, R.S.C.J., [EE], (NY), New York, NY.
Society of the Sisters for the Church, [G], (NOR), Mystic, CT.
Society of the Sisters of the Church, [N], (PAT), Oak Ridge, NJ.
Sojourner Place, [L], (SEA), Seattle, WA.
Solitary Hermitesses, [B], (BAK), La Pine, OR.
Somerset County Services, [E], (MET), Bridgewater, NJ.
Sommerset Place, [F], (DOD), Great Bend, KS.
Songcatchers, Inc., [HH], (NY), New Rochelle, NY.
Sons of Divine Providence School for Exceptional Boys, [B], (BO), Haverhill, MA.
Sophia Counseling Center, Inc., [M], (TOL), Sylvania, OH.
Sophia House, [M], (E). See Om Shanti.
Sophia Institute Press, [O], (MAN), Manchester, NH.
Sophie Barat House, [R], (NO), New Orleans, LA.
Sorrowful Mother Shrine, [M], (TOL), Bellevue, OH.
Soup Kitchen, [N], (FWT). See Loaves and Fishes.
Soup Kitchen for Men, [F], (MIA). See Gift of Hope, Missionaries of Charity.
South, [W], (STL). See Catholic Family Services.
South Arlington Catholic School, [C], (FWT), Arlington, TX.
South Bend Community Service Center, [N], (FTW). See Catholic Charities.
South Carolina State University Newman Center & Claflin College, [G], (CHR), Orangeburg, SC.
*South Central Los Angeles Ministry Project (LAMP), [DD], (LA), Los Angeles, CA.
South Chautauqua Elderly Project, [H], (BUF). See The Catholic Charities of the Diocese of Buffalo.
South County, [H], (SFR). See San Mateo County District Council.
South Day Care Center of St. Joseph, [J], (MIL), Milwaukee, WI.
South of Market Multi-Service Center, [H], (SFR). See Society of St. Vincent de Paul Archdiocesan Council.
South Point, [F], (CHL). See Holy Angels, Inc.
South Shore Braintree, [K], (BO). See Family Counseling and Guidance Centers.
South Side Catholic Child Care Center, [I], (PEO), Peoria, IL.
The South Texas Catholic Retirement Center, Inc., [K], (SAT), San Antonio, TX.
Southbridge Office, [H], (WOR). See Catholic Charities.
Southbury Office, [S], (HRT). See Catholic Charities-Catholic Family Services (Archdiocese of Hartford).
Southeast Kansas Counseling, [J], (WCH). See Catholic Charities.
Southeast Kansas Counseling, [L], (WCH). See Catholic Charities, Inc.
Southeast Missouri State University, Newman Center, [I], (SPC), Cape Girardeau, MO.
Southeast Pastoral Institute, [K], (MIA), Miami, FL.
Southeast Regional Office for Hispanic Ministry, Inc., [K], (MIA), Miami, FL.
Southern Connecticut State University Newman Center, [R], (HRT), New Haven, CT.
Southern Dominican Foundation, [P], (NO). See Dominican Fathers & Brothers, Southern Dominican Province.
Southern Dominican Foundation, [S], (NO), Metairie, LA.
Southern Dominican Global Missions, [P], (NO). See Dominican Fathers & Brothers, Southern Dominican Province.
Southern Dominican Global Missions, [S], (NO). See Southern Dominican Foundation.
Southern Dominican Ministries, Inc., [M], (ATL), Gainesville, GA.
Southern Dominican Volunteer Program, [U], (GAL), Houston, TX.
Southern Illinois University Catholic Campus Ministry, [M], (SFD), Edwardsville, IL.
Southern Maine Technical College, [M], (PRT), South Portland, ME.
Southern Maryland Regional Office, [H], (WDC). See Catholic Charities of the Archdiocese of Washington, Inc.
Southern New England Rehabilitation Center, [K], (PRO). See St. Joseph Health Services of Rhode Island - St. Joseph Hospital for Specialty Care.
Southern Province of St. Augustine - Provincial Residence, [E], (BLX), Bay St. Louis, MS.
Southern Region Family Life Education, [N], (SY), Syracuse, NY.
Southern Tier Catholic, [G], (BUF), Olean, NY.
Southside Catholic Community Services, [W], (STL). See Catholic Community Services Administration.
Southtowns Catholic, [G], (BUF), Lake View, NY.
Southwest Austin Catholic School, Inc dba St. Gabriel's Catholic School, [N], (AUS), Austin, TX.
*Southwest Catholic Health Network Corp., [J], (PHX), Phoenix, AZ.
Southwest Emergency Assistance Center, [L], (DEN). See Catholic Charities and Community Services of the Archdiocese of Denver, Inc.
Southwest Indian Foundation, [F], (GLP), Gallup, NM.
Southwest Marian Divine Mercy Center, [J], (SFE), Bernalillo, NM.
The Southwest Metro Catholic High School, [F], (STP), Excelsior, MN.

T

Taylor Manor Nursing Home, [F], (LEX), Versailles, KY.
TEC, [O], (OM), Omaha, NE.
TEC (Teens Encounter Christ), [J], (BEL), Belleville, IL.
Teen Mom Program, [E], (SR). See Diocese of Santa Rosa, Catholic Charities.
Teen Parent Initative Program, [G], (CHI). See Catholic Charities of the Archdiocese of Chicago-Archdiocesan Offices.
Teens Encounter Christ (TEC), Green Bay Chapter, [O], (GB), Green Bay, WI.
Tekakwitha Adolescent Treatment Center, [I], (SFS), Sisseton, SD.
Tekakwitha Conference, [K], (GF), Great Falls, MT.
Tekakwitha Housing Corp, [I], (SFS), Sisseton, SD.
Tekakwitha Indian Mission, Inc., [I], (SFS), Sisseton, SD.
Tekakwitha Nursing Center, Inc., [E], (SFS), Sisseton, SD.
Tekawitha Nursing Center, Inc., [G], (DUL). See Benedictine Sisters Benevolent Association.
Tekekwitha Fine Arts Center, [I], (SFS), Sisseton, SD.
Teleton Navideno, [T], (SAT), San Antonio, TX.
TELIcare of the Diocese of Rockville Centre, [R], (RVC), Uniondale, NY.
Telos, Inc., [Y], (MIL), Milwaukee, WI.
Temple University, [EE], (PH). See Newman Apostolate.
Temple University, Ambler Division, [EE], (PH). See Newman Apostolate.
Teologado Padre Liberman, [C], (SJN), Bayamon, PR.
The Tepeyac Corporation dba/La Clinica Guadalupana, [L], (SP), Clearwater, FL.
Terence Cardinal Cooke Health Care Center, [X], (NY), New York, NY.
Terence Cardinal Cooke Health Care Center, [Z], (NY), New York, NY.
Terence Cardinal Cooke Residence, [O], (NY). See Beacon of Hope House.
Teresian House, [J], (ALB), Albany, NY.
Teresian House Foundation, [J], (ALB). See Teresian House.
Teresian Institute, [Q], (CHI), Chicago, IL.
Teresian Institute, Inc. (Rome, Italy), Teresian Institute of Florida, Inc., [L], (MIA), Miami, Fl.
Teresian Sisters (Society of St. Teresa of Jesus), S.T.J., [Q], (NO), Covington, LA.
The Terrace at St. Francis, Inc., [N], (MIL), Milwaukee, WI.
Terre Haute Catholic Charities Foodbank, [L], (IND). See Catholic Charities of Terre Haute.
Terre Haute Deanery Pastoral Center, [E], (IND), Terre Haute, IN.
Teurlings Catholic High, [B], (LAF), Lafayette, LA.
Texas Catholic Conference, [N], (AUS), Austin, TX.
Texas Catholic Historical Society, [N], (AUS), Austin, TX.
Texas Center for Immigrant Legal Assistance, [I], (GAL). See Associated Catholic Charities of the Diocese of Galveston-Houston.
Texas Christian University Catholic Community, [M], (FWT), Fort Worth, TX.
Texas Conference of Catholic Health Facilities, [N], (AUS), Austin, TX.
Texas Southern University Catholic Newman Hall, [T], (GAL), Houston, TX.
Theatine Fathers, [H], (ORG), Orange, CA.
The Theatre School, [C], (CHI). See De Paul University.
Theological College of the Catholic University of America, [A], (WDC), Washington, DC.
Theological Seminary of St. Charles Borromeo, Overbrook, [A], (PH), Wynnewood, PA.
Theological Studies, Inc., [V], (WDC), Washington, DC.
Theology Digest, [W], (STL), St. Louis, MO.
Theophilus, [O], (E), Erie, PA.
Therapeutic Foster Care, [E], (PRT). See Catholic Charities Maine.
Therapeutic Preschool (ages 3-5), [J], (BUF). See Baker Victory Services.
Theresian Sisters, [DD], (LA), Monterey Park, CA.
Theresians of the United States aka Theresians World Ministry, [H], (COS), Colorado Springs, CO.
Thevenet Montessori School, [HH], (NY), Highland Mills, NY.
Thieltges-St. Thomas Camp, [K], (GF), Monarch, MT.
Third Order of St. Dominic Support and Charitable Trust Fund, [U], (SFR), San Rafael, CA.
Third Order Regular Common Franciscan Novitiate, Inc., [J], (WIN), Winona, MN.
Third Order Regular of Saint Francis - Province of the *Most Sacred Heart of Jesus*, [O], (PIT), Pittsburgh, PA.
Thomas Aquinas College, [C], (LA), Santa Paula, CA.
Thomas College, [M], (PRT), Waterville, ME.
Thomas I. Conerty Outreach Center of Brentwood, Inc., [R], (RVC), Brentwood, NY.
Thomas Jefferson University, [EE], (PH). See Newman Apostolate.
Thomas Merton Academy, [E], (L), Louisville, KY.
Thomas Merton Center, [G], (BGP). See Catholic Charities of Fairfield County.
Thomas Merton House, Inc., [K], (DAV), Davenport, IA.
Thomas More Center for Preaching and Prayer, Inc., [I], (SUP), Webster, WI.
Thomas More College, [A], (COV), Covington, KY.
The Thomas More College of Liberal Arts, [B], (MAN), Merrimack, NH.
Thomas More High School, [D], (MIL), Milwaukee, WI.
Thomas More Prep-Marian, [B], (SAL), Hays, KS.
Thorpe Family Residence, Inc., [AA], (NY), New York, NY.
Thorpe Family Residence, Inc., [HH], (NY), New York, NY.
Thresholds, [G], (BGP). See Catholic Charities of Fairfield County.
Thrift Store Pickups, [H], (SFR). See Society of St. Vincent de Paul Archdiocesan Council.
Thrift Store Pickups:, [H], (SFR). See San Mateo County District Council.
Thrift Stores, [J], (SD). See SHARE Southern California.
Thrift Stores, [J], (SD). See St. Vincent de Paul Management Inc.
Thrift Stores:, [H], (SFR). See Society of St. Vincent de Paul Archdiocesan Council.
Tides Family Services, [U], (PRO), West Warwick, RI.
*Tierra del Sol Foundation, [M], (LA), Sunland, CA.
Tierra Del Sol West, [M], (LA), Van Nuys, CA.
Tiffin Calvert Foundation, [O], (TOL), Tiffin, OH.
Timber Ridge Apartments Pontchartrain Housing Corp. III, [N], (NO), New Orleans, LA.
Timberlane Apartments, [E], (SUP). See Catholic Charities Bureau, Inc.
Timon Towers Housing Development Fund Company, Inc., [T], (BUF), Buffalo, NY.
Tioga County Rural Ministry, Inc., [L], (ROC), Owego, NY.
To Encounter Christ of the Archdiocese of St. Paul-Minneapolis, Minnesota, Inc., [W], (STP), Minneapolis, MN.
Today and Tomorrow Educational Foundation, [W], (STL). See Catholic High School Association.
"Today's Catholic", [T], (SAT), San Antonio, TX.
Toddler Development Group (ages birth to 3), [J], (BUF). See Baker Victory Services.
Together in the Mission of Education (T.I.M.E.), [U], (SFR), San Francisco, CA.
Toledo Catholic Charities Corporation, [O], (TOL), Toledo, OH.
Tolentine Monastery at Tolentine Center, [N], (CHI), Olympia Fields, IL.
*Tolentine-Zeiser Community Life Center, Inc., [HH], (NY), Bronx, NY.
Tolton Manor, [G], (CHI). See Catholic Charities of the Archdiocese of Chicago-Archdiocesan Offices.
Toner Trust, [S], (PIT), Pittsburgh, PA.
Toomey Residential and Community Services Corp., [K], (SY), Syracuse, NY.
TORCH (To Reach Children), [R], (NY). See St. Dominic Home.
Torrington, [S], (HRT). See Catholic Charities-Catholic Family Services (Archdiocese of Hartford).
Totino-Grace High School, [E], (STP), Minneapolis, MN.
Totus Tuus, Inc., [M], (WCH), Wichita, KS.
Tougaloo College Newman Center, [G], (JKS), Jackson, MS.
Toussaint Teen Center, [J], (SD). See SHARE Southern California.
Toussaint Teen Center, [J], (SD). See St. Vincent de Paul Management Inc.
Tower Hill Camp, [N], (PRO), South Kingstown, RI.
Towson University, [O], (BAL). See Archdiocesan Office-Newman Center.
Traditional and Specialized Foster Care Services, [G], (CHI). See Catholic Charities of the Archdiocese of Chicago-Archdiocesan Offices.
Training School for the Lay Apostolate (Hermanos Cheos), [H], (PCE), Penuelas, PR.
Tranquil House, [P], (L). See Society of St. Vincent de Paul, Council of Louisville.
Transcultural Health Outreach, [B], (STO). See The Catholic Charities of the Diocese of Stockton.
Transfiguration Convent, [BB], (PH). See Sisters of Mercy of the Americas, Annunciation Convent.
Transfiguration Hermitage, [K], (PRT), Thorndike, ME.
Transfiguration Monastery, [T], (SY), Windsor, NY.
Transitional Care Unit (TCU), [F], (GRY). See St. Catherine Hospital.
Transitional Housing, [L], (DEN). See Catholic Charities and Community Services of the Archdiocese of Denver, Inc.
Transitional Housing, [O], (RIC), Richmond, VA.
Transitional Living Center, [H], (SPK), Spokane, WA.
Transitional Living Center, [O], (SPK). See Transitional Program for Women.
Transitional Program for Women, [O], (SPK), Spokane, WA.
Transitions, [O], (SPK). See Transitional Program for Women.
Transitus House, [F], (LC), Chippewa Falls, WI.
Travelers Aid, [S], (HRT). See Catholic Charities-Catholic Family Services (Archdiocese of Hartford).
Treasure Cove Resale Store, [Q], (CLV). See Motherhouse of the Sisters of St. Joseph.
Treasure Cove Resale Store, [Z], (CLV). See Sisters of St. Joseph Community Support Charitable Trust.
Tremont Place, [I], (KC), Kansas City, MO.
Trexler Pavilion, Personal Care Residence of Holy Family Manor, [I], (ALN), Bethlehem, PA.
Tri-Cities Preparatory School, [O], (SPK), Pasco, WA.
Tri-College Newman Cluster-Bryn Mawr, Haverford and Swarthmore Colleges, [EE], (PH). See Newman Apostolate.
Trinidad Area Catholic Community, [F], (PBL), Trinidad, CO.
Trinidad Catholic Schools, [A], (PBL), Trinidad, CO.
Trinita, [Q], (HRT), New Hartford, CT.
Trinitarian Counseling Services, Inc., [K], (BAL), Baltimore, MD.
Trinitarian Missionaries/Missionary Servants of the Most Holy Trinity, [H], (ORG), Santa Ana, CA.
Trinity Catholic Academy, [C], (WOR), Southbridge, MA.
Trinity Catholic High School, [C], (BGP), Stamford, CT.
Trinity Catholic School, [F], (DUB), Protovin, IA.
Trinity Catholic School, [C], (LAF), St. Martinville, LA.
Trinity Catholic School, [H], (NY), Port Jervis, NY.
Trinity Catholic School, [H], (STP), St. Paul, MN.
Trinity Catholic School, [W], (STP), St. Paul, MN.
Trinity College, [C], (WDC), Washington, DC.
Trinity College of Vermont, [A], (BUR), Burlington, VT.
Trinity Community Medical Center of Brenham, [F], (AUS), Brenham, TX.
Trinity Community, Assisted Living Community, [Q], (PRO). See Franciscan Missionaries of Mary.
Trinity Early Learning Center, [F], (DAV), Clinton, IA.
Trinity Educational Trust Fund, [B], (LR). See Trinity Junior High.
Trinity Elementary, [F], (DAV). See Trinity Early Learning Center.
Trinity Health System, [E], (STU), Steubenville, OH.
Trinity High School, [C], (BIS), Dickinson, ND.
Trinity High School, [D], (CHI), River Forest, IL.
Trinity High School, [E], (CLV), Cleveland, OH.
Trinity High School, [A], (HBG), Camp Hill, PA.
Trinity High School, [D], (HBG), Camp Hill, PA.
Trinity High School, [B], (L), Louisville, KY.
Trinity High School, [C], (MAN), Manchester, NH.
Trinity High School, [B], (OWN), Whitesville, KY.
Trinity High School, [B], (WCH), Hutchinson, KS.
The Trinity High School Education Endowment Fund, [B], (WCH), Hutchinson, KS.
*Trinity House, [U], (CHI), Chicago, IL.
Trinity House, [F], (VIC), Victoria, TX.
Trinity Junior High, [B], (LR), Fort Smith, AR.
Trinity Medical Center, East, [E], (STU). See Trinity Health System.
Trinity Medical Center, West, [E], (STU). See Trinity Health System.
Trinity Mission Center, [P], (PAT), Stirling, NJ.
Trinity Montessori School, [D], (ROC), East Rochester, NY.
Trinity Mother Frances Health System, [A], (TYL), Tyler, TX.
Trinity Place Apartments, [H], (OKL), Oklahoma City, OK.
Trinity Regional School, [E], (RVC), East Northport, NY.
Trinity Retreat, [FF], (NY), Larchmont, NY.
Trinity Retreat House, [D], (NY). See Department of Education.
Trinity School, [D], (BAL), Ellicott City, MD.
Trinity School, [F], (SPK), Spokane, WA.
Trinity Spiritual Center, [L], (HBG), Shiremanstown, PA.
Trinity Villas I, Inc., [C], (ORL), Ocala, FL.
Trinity Villas II, Inc., [C], (ORL), Ocala, FL.
Tri-State Coalition for Responsible Investment, [HH], (NY), New York, NY.
Trocaire, [N], (HRT). See Sisters of Mercy of the Americas of Connecticut.
Trocaire College, [C], (BUF), Buffalo, NY.
Trocaire College, [K], (BUF). See Our Lady of Victory Hospital.
Troy CYO Day Camp, [U], (ALB), Troy, NY.
Troy Quasi-Endowment Trust, [M], (LC), Lyndon Station, WI.
Troy State University Newman Center, [K], (MOB), Troy, AL.
Trust for Theological Studies, [S], (PIT), Pittsburgh, PA.

Tufts University Catholic Center, [CC], (BO), Medford, MA.
The Tuition Assistance Fund, Inc., [G], (CAM), Camden, NJ.
Tumwater Apartments, [K], (SEA), Tumwater, WA.
Turner Carroll High School, [D], (BUF), Buffalo, NY.
Tuscarawas Central Catholic High School Endowment Fund, [K], (COL), New Philadelphia, OH.
Tusculum College Newman Center, [J], (KNX), Greeneville, TN.
Tuskegee University Newman Center, [K], (MOB), Tuskegee Institute, AL.
Tutwiler Clinic, Inc., [C], (JKS), Tutwiler, MS.
Twin Cities Catholic Alumni Club, [W], (STP), Minneapolis, MN.
Twin Cities Catholic Educational System (TCCES), [E], (GB), Neenah/Menasha, WI.
Twin-City Area Catholic School Fund, Inc., [I], (KAL), St. Joseph, MI.
*Tyler Catholic School Foundation, [E], (TYL), Tyler, TX.
Tyler Junior College and The University of Texas at Tyler Newman Center, [D], (TYL), Tyler, TX.
*Tyme Out Youth Ministry Center, Inc., [Y], (MIL), Stone Bank, WI.
Tyson Place Housing Development Fund Company, Inc., [Q], (SY), Syracuse, NY.

U

U.P. Catholic Education Endowment Fund, [B], (MAR), Marquette, MI.
U.T. Newman Foundation for Student Education and Development, [O], (TOL), Toledo, OH.
Uihlein Mercy Center, [E], (OG), Lake Placid, NY.
*Ukrainian Catholic Relief, Inc., [G], (STF), Stamford, CT.
Ulster Office, [D], (NY). See Department of Education.
Unaccompanied Juvenile Foster Care Program, [I], (GAL). See Associated Catholic Charities of the Diocese of Galveston-Houston.
UND-Lake Region, [I], (FAR), Devils Lake, ND.
Unified Catholic Parish Schools of Beaver Dam, [H], (MIL), Beaver Dam, WI.
Unified Catholic Schools of Oshkosh, [E], (GB), Oshkosh, WI.
UniMed Medical Center Foundation, [D], (BIS), Minot, ND.
Union Catholic Convent, [O], (NEW), Scotch Plains, NJ.
Union Catholic Regional High School, [D], (NEW), Scotch Plains, NJ.
Union College, Catholic Campus Ministry, [S], (ALB), Schenectady, NY.
Union County College, [Q], (NEW), Cranford, NJ.
Union Meadows Housing Development Fund Corp., [L], (ROC), Rochester, NY.
Union of Sisters of the Presentation of the Blessed Virgin Mary, [E], (PHX), Phoenix, AZ.
United Catholic Schools Foundation of Austin, MN, Inc., [C], (WIN). See Austin Area Catholic Schools.
The United Colleges of San Antonio, [C], (SAT), San Antonio, TX.
United Day Care, Inc., [E], (SUP). See Catholic Charities Bureau, Inc.
United Medical Management, [D], (PMB). See St. Mary's Hospital, Inc.
United Samaritans Medical Center, [J], (PEO), Danville, IL.
United Samaritans Medical Center Apothecary, [J], (PEO). See United Samaritans Medical Center.
United Samaritans Medical Center Foundation, [J], (PEO). See United Samaritans Medical Center.
United Stand Family Center, [X], (CHI), Chicago, IL.
U.S. Catholic China Bureau, [S], (NEW), South Orange, NJ.
United States Catholic Historical Society, The, [HH], (NY), New York, NY.
The United States Catholic Widows and Widowers Association, Inc., [HH], (NY), Scarsdale, NY.
U.S. Federation of Sisters of St. Joseph, [L], (BR), Baton Rouge, LA.
United States Military Academy, [GG], (NY). See University Apostolate.
United States Province, [Q], (MIL), Milwaukee, WI.
Unity Health System, [H], (ROC), Rochester, NY.
Unity Properties, Inc., [P], (BAL). See Bon Secours Baltimore Health Corp., Inc.
Univ. of Arkansas at Little Rock Campus Ministry, [J], (LR). See Catholic Campus Ministries.
Univ. of Delaware Newman Center, [O], (WIL), Newark, DE.
Univ. of Michigan, Dearborn, Henry Ford Community College Newman Center, [S], (DET), Dearborn, MI.
Univ. of North Dakota Newman Center, [H], (FAR), Grand Forks, ND.
University Apostolate, [GG], (NY), New York, NY.
University Catholic Center, [M], (AUS), Austin, TX.
University Catholic Center - St. Thomas More Chapel, [M], (SFE), Portales, NM.
University College, [B], (NEW). See Seton Hall University.
University Health Services, [G], (FTW), Notre Dame, IN.
University Health Services, Notre Dame, [K], (FTW). See Saint Mary's of the Immaculate Conception.
University Heights Day Care, [R], (NY). See Pius XII Youth and Family Services, Inc.
University of Alabama in Tuscaloosa, [H], (BIR), Tuscaloosa, AL.
University of Arizona, [I], (TUC), Tucson, AZ.
University of Arkansas, St. Thomas Aquinas University Parish, [J], (LR). See Catholic Campus Ministries.
University of California at San Diego (Campus Ministry), [M], (SD), San Diego, CA.
University of California, Irvine, [L], (ORG). See Campus Ministry-Diocese of Orange.
University of Central Arkansas & Hendrix College Campus Ministry, [J], (LR). See Catholic Campus Ministries.
University of Central Florida Newman Center, [E], (ORL), Orlando, FL.
University of Charleston Newman Center, [Q], (WH), Charleston, WV.
University of Cincinnati Newman Center, [Q], (CIN), Cincinnati, OH.
University of Colorado (Boulder), [P], (DEN), Boulder, CO.
University of Colorado at Denver, [P], (DEN). See Auraria Campus.
University of Dallas, [B], (DAL), Irving, TX.
The University of Dayton, [D], (CIN), Dayton, OH.
University of Dayton Campus Ministry, [Q], (CIN), Dayton, OH.
University of Denver, [P], (DEN), Denver, CO.
University of Detroit Jesuit High School and Academy, [E], (DET), Detroit, MI.
University of Detroit Mercy, [C], (DET), Detroit, MI.
University of Detroit Mercy Campus Ministry, [S], (DET), Detroit, MI.
University of Findlay Campus Ministry, [N], (TOL), Findlay, OH.
University of Florida-St. Augustine Parish and Student Center, [L], (STA), Gainesville, FL.
University of Great Falls, [A], (GF), Great Falls, MT.
University of Hartford Newman Center, [R], (HRT), Hartford, CT.
University of Houston Central Campus Catholic Newman Association, [T], (GAL), Houston, TX.
University of Houston Downtown Catholic Campus Ministry, [T], (GAL), Houston, TX.
University of Houston, Clear Lake City Newman Center, [T], (GAL), Houston, TX.
University of Idaho, St. Augustine Catholic Center, [F], (B), Moscow, ID.
University of Indianapolis Newman Center, [N], (IND), Indianapolis, IN.
University of Maine, [M], (PRT), Orono, ME.
University of Maine at Farmington, [M], (PRT), Farmington, ME.
University of Maine at Fort Kent, [M], (PRT), Fort Kent, ME.
University of Maine at Machias, [M], (PRT), Machias, ME.
University of Maine at Presque Isle, [M], (PRT), Presque Isle, ME.
University of Mary, [B], (BIS), Bismarck, ND.
University of Maryland Catholic Student Center, [S], (WDC). See Archdiocesan Campus Ministry.
University of Maryland-Baltimore County, [O], (BAL). See Archdiocesan Office-Newman Center.
University of Massachusetts and Amherst College, Newman Center, [P], (SPR), Amherst, MA.
University of Massachusetts at Boston Campus Ministry, [CC], (BO), Dorchester, MA.
University of Massachusetts Dartmouth Catholic Campus Ministry, [O], (FR), North Dartmouth, MA.
University of Massachusetts Medical School, [Q], (WOR). See Campus Ministry.
University of Minnesota Cooperative Campus Ministry, [F], (CR), Crookston, MN.
University of Minnesota Newman Center and Chapel, [V], (STP), Minneapolis, MN.
University of Mississippi Medical Center - Newman Center, [G], (JKS), Jackson, MS.
University of Mississippi Newman Center, [G], (JKS), Oxford, MS.
University of Missouri, St. Louis, Newman House, [V], (STL), St. Louis, MO.
University of Missouri-Columbia, Campus Ministry, [F], (JC), Columbia, MO.
University of Missouri-Rolla, [F], (JC), Rolla, MO.
University of MN-Duluth, [F], (DUL), Duluth, MN.
University of Montana, [H], (HEL), Missoula, MT.
University of Montevallo, [H], (BIR), Montevallo, AL.
University of Nebraska at Kearney Newman Apostolate, [D], (GI), Kearney, NE.
University of Nebraska, Newman Club, [I], (LIN), Lincoln, NE.
University of Nevada, Newman Club, [F], (RNO), Reno, NV.
University of New England, [M], (PRT), Biddeford, ME.
University of North Alabama, [H], (BIR), Florence, AL.
University of North Texas and Texas Woman's University, [M], (FWT), Denton, TX.
University of Northern Colorado (Greeley), [P], (DEN), Greeley, CO.
University of Notre Dame, [K], (FTW). See Saint Mary's of the Immaculate Conception.
*University of Notre Dame Du Lac, [B], (FTW), Notre Dame, IN.
University of Ozarks Campus Ministry (Clarksville), [J], (LR). See Catholic Campus Ministries.
University of Pennsylvania, [EE], (PH). See Newman Apostolate.
University of Pittsburgh at Johnstown, [H], (ALT). See Campus Ministry.
*University of Portland, [B], (P), Portland, OR.
University of Portland, [P], (P), Portland, OR.
University of Redlands Newman Community, [H], (SB), Redlands, CA.
University of Rhode Island Catholic Center, [S], (PRO), South Kingstown, RI.
University of St. Francis, [B], (FTW), Fort Wayne, IN.
University of St. Mary of the Lake-Mundelein Seminary, [A], (CHI), Mundelein, IL.
University of St. Thomas, [C], (GAL), Houston, TX.
University of St. Thomas, [C], (STP), St. Paul, MN.
University of St. Thomas Campus Ministry, [T], (GAL), Houston, TX.
University of San Diego, [B], (SD), San Diego, CA.
University of San Diego High School, [C], (SD), San Diego, CA.
*University of San Francisco, [C], (SFR), San Francisco, CA.
University of Scranton, [C], (SCR), Scranton, PA.
University of South Alabama Newman Center, [K], (MOB), Mobile, AL.
University of South Carolina, Aiken Extension Newman Center, [G], (CHR), Aiken, SC.
University of South Carolina, Beaufort Extension Newman Center, [G], (CHR), Beaufort, SC.
University of South Carolina, St. Thomas More Center, [G], (CHR), Columbia, SC.
University of Southern Indiana Newman Center, [I], (EVN), Evansville, IN.
University of Southern Maine, [M], (PRT), Portland, ME.
University of Southern Mississippi, [G], (BLX), Hattiesburg, MS.
University of Tampa, [S], (SP), Tampa, FL.
University of Texas at Arlington, [M], (FWT), Arlington, TX.
University of Texas at El Paso Catholic Campus Ministry, [M], (ELP), El Paso, TX.
University of Texas Pan American Campus at Edinburg, [H], (BWN), Edinburg, TX.
University of the Arts, [EE], (PH). See Newman Apostolate.
University of the Incarnate Word, [C], (SAT), San Antonio, TX.
University of Toledo Campus Ministry, [N], (TOL), Toledo, OH.
University of Tulsa Newman Center, [H], (TLS), Tulsa, OK.
University of Utah, Newman Center, [H], (SLC), Salt Lake City, UT.
University of Vermont-The Catholic Center at UVM, [H], (BUR), Burlington, VT.
University of Wisconsin Fox Valley Campus Newman Center, [N], (GB). See University of Wisconsin G.B. Ecumenical Center.
University of Wisconsin G.B. Ecumenical Center, [N], (GB), Green Bay, WI.
University of Wisconsin Manitowoc Campus Newman Center, [N], (GB). See University of Wisconsin G.B. Ecumenical Center.
University of Wisconsin Marinette Campus Newman Center, [N], (GB). See University of Wisconsin G.B. Ecumenical Center.
University of Wisconsin Newman Center, [N], (GB). See University of Wisconsin G.B. Ecumenical Center.
University of Wisconsin, Superior, Newman Community, [G], (SUP), Superior, WI.
University of Wyoming, [E], (CHY), Laramie, WY.
University Parish of Christ Sun of Justice, [S], (ALB). See Rensselaer Polytechnic Institute.
University San Tommaso, [P], (NO). See Dominican Fathers & Brothers, Southern Dominican Province.
Unwed Mothers Home, [L], (BR), Baton Rouge, LA.
Upper Campus, [E], (NEW). See Elizabethport Catholic School.
Upper Campus, [E], (RVC). See All Saints Regional Catholic School.
Upper Iowa University, [N], (DUB), West Union, IA.
The Upper Room Spiritual Center, [P], (TR), Neptune, NJ.
Upper School, [B], (HBG). See Cathedral School.
The Urban Center of St. Charles Parish, [U], (BGP),

Bridgeport, CT.
Urban Community School, [G], (CLV), Cleveland, OH.
Urban House of Prayer, [CC], (PH), Philadelphia, PA.
Urban Medical Institute (UMI), [H], (BAL). See Bon Secours Baltimore Health Corporation, Inc.
*The Urban Medical Institute Foundation, Inc., [H], (BAL). See Bon Secours Baltimore Health Corporation, Inc.
The Urban Medical Institute Foundation, Inc., [P], (BAL). See Bon Secours Baltimore Health Corp., Inc.
*Urban Medical Institute, Inc., [H], (BAL). See Bon Secours Baltimore Health Corporation, Inc.
Urbana University Campus Ministry, [Q], (CIN), Urbana, OH.
Ursinus College, [EE], (PH). See Newman Apostolate.
Ursuline Academy, [E], (BO), Dedham, MA.
Ursuline Academy, [D], (DAL), Dallas, TX.
Ursuline Academy, [N], (DAL). See Ursuline Convent.
Ursuline Academy, [F], (NO), New Orleans, LA.
Ursuline Academy, [H], (NO), New Orleans, LA.
Ursuline Academy, [D], (SFD), Springfield, IL.
Ursuline Academy, [F], (STL), Kirkwood, MO.
Ursuline Academy Inc., The, [J], (WIL), Wilmington, DE.
Ursuline Academy of Cincinnati, [F], (CIN), Cincinnati, OH.
Ursuline Academy of Wilmington, DE, Inc., [B], (WIL), Wilmington, DE.
Ursuline Bedford Park Convent, [EE], (NY), New York, NY.
Ursuline Campus Schools, Inc., [Q], (L), Louisville, KY.
Ursuline Center, [K], (Y). See Motherhouse and Educational Center of the Ursuline Sisters.
The Ursuline Center, [P], (Y), Canfield, OH.
Ursuline Child Development Center, [F], (L), Louisville, KY.
Ursuline College, [C], (CLV), Cleveland, OH.
Ursuline Communities, Inc., [EE], (NY), Bronx, NY.
Ursuline Community, Ursuline Nuns, [G], (OG), Malone, NY.
Ursuline Companions in Mission, Inc., [HH], (NY), New Rochelle, NY.
Ursuline Convent, [X], (BO), Dedham, MA.
Ursuline Convent, [I], (CC), Laredo, TX.
Ursuline Convent, [E], (CHR), Columbia, SC.
Ursuline Convent, [N], (DAL), Dallas, TX.
Ursuline Convent, [H], (GF), Great Falls, MT.
Ursuline Convent, [L], (SFD), Springfield, IL.
Ursuline Convent of St. Teresa, [EE], (NY), New Rochelle, NY.
Ursuline Convent of the Holy Family of the Ursuline Nuns of the Roman Union, [L], (SFD), Alton, IL.
Ursuline Convent of the Immaculate Heart of Mary, [N], (CIN), Saint Martin, OH.
Ursuline Convent of the Sacred Heart, [L], (TOL), Toledo, OH.
*Ursuline High School, [C], (SR), Santa Rosa, CA.
Ursuline High School, [C], (Y), Youngstown, OH.
*Ursuline Memorial Scholarship Fund, [C], (SR). See Ursuline High School.
Ursuline Montessori School, [E], (L), Louisville, KY.
Ursuline Motherhouse of the Immaculate Conception, [M], (L), Louisville, KY.
*Ursuline Parent Association of Santa Rosa, [C], (SR). See Ursuline High School.
Ursuline Preschool & Kindergarten, [F], (Y), Canfield, OH.
Ursuline Provincial Administration Office, [V], (BRK), Jamaica, NY.
Ursuline Provincialate, [X], (BO), Dedham, MA.
Ursuline Provincialate, [EE], (NY), New York, NY.
Ursuline Provincialate, [R], (STL), Crystal City, MO.
Ursuline Residence, [N], (SR), Windsor, CA.
Ursuline Residence, [N], (SR), Healdsburg, CA.
Ursuline Residence, Inc., [EE], (NY), New Rochelle, NY.
Ursuline Residences, [N], (SAT), San Antonio, TX.
Ursuline Retreat Centre, [J], (GF), Great Falls, MT.
Ursuline School, [F], (NY), New Rochelle, NY.
Ursuline School of Music and Drama, [F], (L), Louisville, KY.
Ursuline Sisters, [M], (L), Louisville, KY.
Ursuline Sisters, [H], (SAC), Pollock Pines, CA.
Ursuline Sisters Charitable Trust, [K], (KCK), Paola, KS.
Ursuline Sisters Infirmary, [J], (PRT), Waterville, ME.
Ursuline Sisters of Andrews Avenue, Inc., [EE], (NY). See Ursuline Provincialate.
Ursuline Sisters of the Congregation of Tildonk, Belgium, [N], (HRT), Meriden, CT.
Ursuline Sisters of the Congregation of Tildonk, Belgium, [N], (HRT), Oxford, CT.
Ursuline Sisters of the Roman Union, O.S.U., [Q], (NO), New Orleans, LA.
Ursuline Sisters' Residence, [J], (PRT), Waterville, ME.
Ursuline Sisters, St. Ursula Center, [O], (RVC), Blue Point, NY.
Ursuline Social Outreach, Inc., [HH], (NY), Bronx, NY.
Ursuline Society and Academy of Education, [Q], (L), Louisville, KY.
*Ursuline Sophia Center, [AA], (CLV), Pepper Pike, OH.
Ursulines of Cincinnati, [N], (CIN), Cincinnati, OH.
Ursulines of Cincinnati, Ohio Charitable Trust, [U], (CIN), Cincinnati, OH.
Ursulines of the Western Province, Inc., [EE], (LA). See Chancery Office.
USCC Refugee Resettlement, [F], (SJ). See Catholic Charities of Santa Clara County.
Utica College of Syracuse University Newman Center, [V], (SY), Utica, NY.
UT-Knoxville, Newman Foundation, Inc., [J], (KNX), Knoxville, TN.

V

V.J. & Angela Skutt Catholic High School of Omaha, [B], (OM), Omaha, NE.
VA Medical Center, [E], (SJN), San Juan, PR.
Valdosta State College Newman Center, [H], (SAV), Valdosta, GA.
Valley Camp, [BB], (NY). See The Catholic Camp Association Inc.
Valley Catholic Middle & High Schools, [D], (P), Beaverton, OR.
Valley Catholic Middle School, [F], (P). See St. Mary of the Valley School.
Valley City State University, [I], (FAR), Valley City, ND.
Valley Family Center, [DD], (LA), San Fernando, CA.
Valley of Our Lady Monastery, [J], (MAD), Prairie du Sac, WI.
Valley Regional Health System, Inc., [FF], (BO), Methuen, MA.
Valley Regional Support Services, Inc., [FF], (BO). See Valley Regional Health System, Inc.
Valley Vista Apartments of Browns Valley Inc., [M], (SCL), St. Cloud, MN.
Vallombrosa Center, [M], (SFR), Menlo Park, CA.
Vancouver Oratorian Community, [Q], (SEA), Vancouver, WA.
Vandebilt Catholic High, [A], (HT), Houma, LA.
Vassar College, [GG], (NY). See University Apostolate.
Vatican II Institute for Clergy Formation, [U], (SFR), Menlo Park, CA.
*Vatican Observatory Foundation, [F], (TUC). See Jesuit Community of the Vatican Observatory.
The Vaugirard Religious & Charitable Trust, [M], (TR), Lincroft, NJ.
Vehicle Donations, [H], (SFR). See Society of St. Vincent de Paul Archdiocesan Council.
Vehicle Sales, [H], (SFR). See Society of St. Vincent de Paul Archdiocesan Council.
Vehicle Sales, [H], (SFR). See San Mateo County District Council.
Venango Christian High School, [C], (E), Oil City, PA.
Venerable Merlini Foundation, [S], (OAK), San Leandro, CA.
Venerini Academy, [G], (WOR), Worcester, MA.
VENTURA COUNTY REGION, [Z], (LA). See Catholic Charities of Los Angeles, Inc.
Verbum Dei Community, [N], (SFR), San Francisco, CA.
Verbum Dei Community, [O], (SFR), San Francisco, CA.
Verbum Dei High School, [D], (LA), Los Angeles, CA.
Veritas Communications, Inc., [DD], (LA), Westlake Village, CA.
Veritas Foundation, [M], (BR). See Baton Rouge Chancery Office.
Verna Montessori School, [E], (GBG), Mount Pleasant, PA.
Veronica House, [W], (STL), St. Louis, MO.
VESS, Volunteers for Educational and Social Services, [N], (AUS), Austin, TX.
Vestiarki Sisters of Jesus (Poland), [F], (PT), Sunny Hills, FL.
Veteran Mission Crusade, Archdiocesan, [Q], (BAL), Baltimore, MD.
Via Caritas Health System, Inc., [P], (PAT), Wayne, NJ.
Via Christi Foundation, Inc., [M], (WCH), Wichita, KS.
Via Christi Health Partners, Inc., [M], (WCH), Wichita, KS.
Via Christi Health System, Inc., [M], (WCH), Wichita, KS.
Via Christi Property Services, Inc., [M], (WCH), Wichita, KS.
Via Christi Regional Medical Center, Inc., [E], (WCH), Wichita, KS.
Via Christi Rehabilitation Center, Inc., [E], (WCH), Wichita, KS.
Via Christi Senior Services, Inc., [M], (WCH), Wichita, KS.
Via Escondida, [Q], (L), New Haven, KY.
Vianney High School, [F], (STL), Kirkwood, MO.
Vianney House, [G], (WIL), Wilmington, DE.
Vianney House, [M], (WOR), Worcester, MA.
Vianney Oaks, [G], (RCK), Rockford, IL.
Vianney Renewal Center, [T], (STL), Dittmer, MO.
Vianney Villa, [M], (CAM), Cherry Hill, NJ.
Vianney Villas Apartments, [D], (PHX), Avondale, AZ.
Viatorian Mission House, [N], (CHI), Arlington Heights, IL.
Viatorian Province Center-Clerics of St. Viator, [N], (CHI), Arlington Heights, IL.
Viatorian Residence, [N], (CHI), Chicago, IL.
Viatorian Residence, [N], (CHI), Olympia Fields, IL.
Vicariate of Holy Rosary, [H], (CC), San Diego, TX.
Vicariate Residence, [C], (CI), Tunnuk, Chuuk, FM.
The Viceprovince of Saint John the Baptist, Puerto Rico, of the Order Friars Minor Capuchins, [H], (SJN), Rio Piedras, PR.
Vicksburg Catholic School, [A], (JKS), Vicksburg, MS.
Victim Offender Reconciliation Program, [H], (OAK). See Catholic Charities of the Diocese of Oakland, Inc.
Victorian Towers Associates, [K], (CAM), Cape May, NJ.
Victorious Missionaries, [J], (BEL), Belleville, IL.
Victorious Missionaries, [T], (BUF), West Seneca, NY.
*Victory Medical Center, Inc., [E], (LC), Stanley, WI.
Victory Noll—Motherhouse of Our Lady of Victory Missionary Sisters, [K], (FTW), Huntington, IN.
Vietnamese Apostolate, [T], (BRK). See Catholic Migration & Refugee Office, Catholic Migration Services, Inc.
Vietnamese Catholic Center, [G], (ORG), Santa Ana, CA.
Vietnamese Catholic Community at Baltimore (VC-CAB), [Q], (BAL), Baltimore, MD.
Vietnamese Dominican Sisters, [N], (HRT), West Hartford, CT.
Vietnamese Health Center, [W], (STL). See Catholic Community Services Administration.
Vietnamese Redemptorist Mission, [R], (LA), Baldwin Park, CA.
Vietnamese Senior Care Center, [S], (OAK), Oakland, CA.
Vietnamese Youth and Culture Association, [P], (SJ), San Jose, CA.
Vietnamese-Catholic Community, [V], (CIN), Cincinnati, OH.
*Vigil Light Apartments (The Vigil Light, Inc.), [I], (SR), Santa Rosa, CA.
Vilaseca Day Care Center, [F], (JOL), Joliet, IL.
The Villa, [N], (BAL), Baltimore, MD.
Villa Academy, [D], (SEA), Seattle, WA.
Villa Angela - St. Joseph High School Education Endowment Foundation, [Z], (CLV), Cleveland, OH.
Villa Angela-St. Joseph High School, [D], (CLV), Cleveland, OH.
Villa Arrieta, [H], (MIA), Miami, FL.
Villa Assumpta, Inc., [J], (PMB), Jensen Beach, FL.
Villa Augustina Convent, [L], (MAN), Goffstown, NH.
Villa Augustina School, [F], (MAN), Goffstown, NH.
Villa Aviat Convent, [J], (WIL), Childs, MD.
Villa Celine, [Q], (MIL), Delavan, WI.
Villa Clement Health Center, [N], (MIL), West Allis, WI.
Villa D'Ames Apartments, [N], (NO), Marrero, LA.
Villa De Marillac Nursing Home, [K], (PIT), Pittsburgh, PA.
Villa de Sales Oblate Residence, [AA], (PH), Wyndmoor, PA.
Villa Desiderata Retreat House, [H], (RCK), McHenry, IL.
Villa Divino Amore Convent, Little Workers of the Sacred Hearts of Jesus & Mary, [P], (BGP), Stamford, CT.
Villa Duchesne, [G], (STL), Frontenac, MO.
Villa Duchesne/Oak Hill, [F], (STL), Frontenac, MO.
Villa Fatima, [K], (FR), Taunton, MA.
Villa Ferretti, Religious Teachers Filippini, [N], (HRT), Winchester Center, CT.
Villa Frances at the Knolls, [Z], (NY), Warwick, NY.
Villa Francesca, [J], (DET), Bloomfield Hills, MI.
Villa Franciscan, Franciscan Sisters Health Care Corp., [I], (JOL), Joliet, IL.
Villa Franciscan, Inc., [J], (PMB), Riviera Beach, FL.
Villa Francisco, [F], (VEN), Fort Myers, FL.
Villa Fusco Child Day Care Center, [T], (ALB), Niskayuna, NY.
Villa Gesu, [R], (STL), St. Louis, MO.
Villa Guadalupe Home for the Aged, [E], (GLP), Gallup, NM.
Villa Guadalupe Senior Services Corporation, [X], (CHI), Chicago, IL.
Villa Holy Names, [L], (SJ), Los Gatos, CA.
Villa Isenbart, Inc., [H], (OKL), Oklahoma City, OK.
Villa Javier, [H], (MIA), Miami, FL.
Villa Joseph Marie, [BB], (PH), Holland, PA.
Villa Joseph Marie High School for Girls, [G], (PH), Holland, PA.
Villa Julie at Seven Oaks (Maryland Province), [N], (BAL), Stevenson, MD.

W

X

Y

Z

	*Mobile AL	Birmingham AL	ALABAMA TOTAL	*Anchorage AK	Fairbanks AK	Juneau AK	1998 U.S. GRAND TOTAL
Cardinals	–	–	–	–	–	–	10
Archbishops	1	–	1	1	–	–	49
Bishops	–	1	1	–	2	1	358
Abbots	–	4	4	1	–	–	114
Diocesan Priests	105	73	178	20	5	16	31,657
Religious Priests	47	44	91	10	23	4	15,925
Total Priests in Diocese	152	117	269	30	28	20	47,563
Newly Ordained Priests	2	1	3	–	–	–	509
Total Permanent Deacons	41	25	66	12	41	9	12,247
Total Brothers	16	22	38	1	4	–	6,115
Total Sisters	221	172	393	44	15	10	85,412
Number of Parishes	76	60	136	20	48	10	19,628
Missions	15	16	31	8	7	15	3,006
Pastoral Centers	3	–	3	–	1	–	1,259
New Parishes	–	–	–	–	–	–	37
Catholic Hospitals	1	1	2	1	–	1	601
Patients Assisted Annually	182,750	122,764	305,514	287,000	–	46,403	65,853,111
Health Care Centers	4	1	5	1	–	–	440
Patients Assisted Annually	4,211	880,527	884,738	380	–	–	5,058,274
Specialized Homes	5	–	5	4	–	1	1,359
Total Assisted Annually	438	–	438	4,361	–	102	494,308
Residential Care of Children (Orphanages)	1	–	1	–	–	–	156
Total Assisted Annually	200	–	200	–	–	–	74,918
Day Care and Extended Day Care Centers	4	–	4	–	–	1	1,156
Total Assisted Annually	234	–	234	–	–	100	96,413
Special Centers for Social Services	9	14	23	5	1	1	2,113
Total Assisted Annually	94,632	66,964	161,596	13,600	5,900	6,047	18,323,523
Diocesan Seminaries	–	–	–	–	–	–	75
Students	–	–	–	–	–	–	3,248
Religious Seminaries	–	–	–	–	–	–	122
Students	4	2	6	–	–	–	1,340
Colleges and Universities	1	–	1	–	–	–	240
Total Students	960	–	960	–	–	–	692,951
High Schools, Diocesan and Parish	3	4	7	–	1	–	790
Total Students	1,602	1,416	3,018	–	225	–	374,590
High Schools, Private	–	1	1	1	–	–	557
Total Students	–	111	111	60	–	–	285,993
Elementary Schools, Diocesan and Parish	21	19	40	2	1	1	6,818
Total Students	5,942	5,045	10,987	347	270	105	1,961,899
Elementary Schools, Private	–	1	1	1	–	–	333
Total Students	–	195	195	140	–	–	91,049
Non–residential Schools for the Disabled	–	1	1	–	–	–	75
Total Students	–	143	143	–	–	–	17,942
Religious Education High School Students	810	1,766	2,576	899	657	184	804,514
Religious Education Elementary Students	3,516	5,548	9,064	2,630	1,956	610	3,518,872
Priests Teaching	1	4	5	–	–	–	2,120
Scholastics Teaching	–	–	–	–	–	–	77
Brothers Teaching	2	2	4	–	–	–	1,176
Sisters Teaching	21	11	32	6	2	–	10,025
Lay Teachers	510	325	835	43	37	9	150,783
Infant Baptisms	1,215	1,336	2,551	562	427	128	1,040,837
Adult Baptisms	221	213	434	67	31	36	73,426
Received into Full Communion	353	445	798	69	50	37	88,161
First Communions	1,230	1,265	2,495	610	343	110	858,665
Confirmations	1,232	1,003	2,235	326	141	33	607,645
Marriages	480	457	937	159	70	43	288,593
Deaths	660	480	1,140	121	126	26	465,773
Totals Catholics	68,838	71,958	140,796	28,723	17,095	6,030	61,563,769
Total Population	1,452,506	2,644,644	4,097,150	384,209	141,759	74,217	270,536,283
Catholic Population Percentage	5	3	3	7	12	8	23

Archdioceses = 36; Dioceses = 164; Apostolates = 3

1998 GENERAL SUMMARY

	ALASKA TOTAL	Samoa-Pago Pago AS	Phoenix AZ	Tucson AZ	ARIZONA TOTAL	Little Rock AR	1998 U.S. GRAND TOTAL
Cardinals	–	–	–	–	–	–	10
Archbishops	1	–	–	–	–	–	49
Bishops	3	1	2	1	3	1	358
Abbots	1	–	–	–	–	2	114
Diocesan Priests	41	9	145	113	258	83	31,657
Religious Priests	37	1	113	73	186	65	15,925
Total Priests in Diocese	78	10	258	186	444	148	47,563
Newly Ordained Priests	–	–	2	4	6	–	509
Total Permanent Deacons	62	19	175	127	302	58	12,247
Total Brothers	5	–	5	8	13	47	6,115
Total Sisters	69	13	230	331	561	365	85,412
Number of Parishes	78	9	88	64	152	90	19,628
Missions	30	1	28	31	59	44	3,006
Pastoral Centers	1	–	–	15	15	–	1,259
New Parishes	–	1	2	–	2	–	37
Catholic Hospitals	2	–	1	3	4	10	601
Patients Assisted Annually	333,403	–	311,481	299,790	611,271	782,801	65,853,111
Health Care Centers	1	–	2	1	3	1	440
Patients Assisted Annually	380	–	99,340	33,476	132,816	3,000	5,058,274
Specialized Homes	5	1	17	–	17	6	1,359
Total Assisted Annually	4,463	26	992	–	992	372	494,308
Residential Care of Children (Orphanages)	–	–	–	–	–	–	156
Total Assisted Annually	–	–	–	–	–	–	74,918
Day Care and Extended Day Care Centers	1	1	26	–	26	8	1,156
Total Assisted Annually	100	105	983	–	983	232	96,413
Special Centers for Social Services	7	1	11	1	12	23	2,113
Total Assisted Annually	25,547	560	2,096,541	400,000	2,496,541	14,982	18,323,523
Diocesan Seminaries	–	–	–	–	–	–	75
Students	–	–	–	–	–	–	3,248
Religious Seminaries	–	–	–	–	–	–	122
Students	–	–	–	–	–	–	1,340
Colleges and Universities	–	–	–	–	–	–	240
Total Students	–	–	–	–	–	15	692,951
High Schools, Diocesan and Parish	1	2	4	1	5	5	790
Total Students	225	305	2,526	1,412	3,938	1,416	374,590
High Schools, Private	1	–	1	2	3	2	557
Total Students	60	–	1,170	184	1,354	788	285,993
Elementary Schools, Diocesan and Parish	4	2	23	22	45	31	6,818
Total Students	722	433	7,816	5,128	12,944	6,601	1,961,899
Elementary Schools, Private	1	–	–	2	2	1	333
Total Students	140	–	–	312	312	66	91,049
Non–residential Schools for the Disabled	–	–	–	–	–	–	75
Total Students	–	–	–	–	–	–	17,942
Religious Education High School Students	1,740	250	5,444	3,153	8,597	2,220	804,514
Religious Education Elementary Students	5,196	1,826	30,437	14,550	44,987	4,589	3,518,872
Priests Teaching	–	–	17	5	22	10	2,120
Scholastics Teaching	–	–	4	–	4	–	77
Brothers Teaching	–	–	2	1	3	9	1,176
Sisters Teaching	8	5	43	43	86	46	10,025
Lay Teachers	89	42	577	273	850	544	150,783
Infant Baptisms	1,117	302	11,557	7,009	18,566	2,002	1,040,837
Adult Baptisms	134	62	463	367	830	248	73,426
Received into Full Communion	156	62	724	681	1,405	465	88,161
First Communions	1,063	34	6,032	5,529	11,561	1,643	858,665
Confirmations	500	6	3,049	3,281	6,330	1,206	607,645
Marriages	272	45	1,703	1,291	2,994	641	288,593
Deaths	273	55	3,392	2,314	5,706	891	465,773
Totals Catholics	51,848	11,405	388,839	323,698	712,537	86,990	61,563,769
Total Population	600,185	58,070	3,109,820	1,277,646	4,387,466	2,509,791	270,536,283
Catholic Population Percentage	9	20	13	25	16	3	23

***Indicates Archdioceses.**

†Certain Dioceses traverse state lines.

	*Los Angeles CA	*San Francisco CA	Fresno CA	Monterey in California CA	Oakland CA	Orange in California CA	1998 U.S. GRAND TOTAL
Cardinals	1	–	–	–	–	–	10
Archbishops	–	2	–	–	–	–	49
Bishops	7	2	1	3	1	2	358
Abbots	1	–	–	1	–	2	114
Diocesan Priests	571	222	108	91	203	178	31,657
Religious Priests	662	187	44	24	101	94	15,925
Total Priests in Diocese	1,233	409	152	115	304	272	47,563
Newly Ordained Priests	8	10	3	1	3	3	509
Total Permanent Deacons	153	53	7	4	80	49	12,247
Total Brothers	171	38	10	26	16	7	6,115
Total Sisters	1,944	884	109	151	320	360	85,412
Number of Parishes	286	89	84	46	89	54	19,628
Missions	21	7	40	9	3	5	3,006
Pastoral Centers	1	3	–	–	11	4	1,259
New Parishes	1	–	–	–	–	–	37
Catholic Hospitals	20	3	3	1	1	1	601
Patients Assisted Annually	1,139,746	515,000	576,663	116,693	29,000	34,488	65,853,111
Health Care Centers	5	–	2	1	–	2	440
Patients Assisted Annually	12,000	–	–	46	–	170,986	5,058,274
Specialized Homes	18	15	2	3	8	6	1,359
Total Assisted Annually	3,194	7,266	224	422	21,221	15,856	494,308
Residential Care of Children (Orphanages)	2	2	–	–	–	–	156
Total Assisted Annually	500	334	–	–	–	–	74,918
Day Care and Extended Day Care Centers	81	2	–	–	5	1	1,156
Total Assisted Annually	4,256	120	–	–	1,400	100	96,413
Special Centers for Social Services	79	35	5	–	3	3	2,113
Total Assisted Annually	259,248	73,000	277,103	–	25,000	375,479	18,323,523
Diocesan Seminaries	2	1	–	–	–	–	75
Students	146	53	–	–	–	–	3,248
Religious Seminaries	15	–	–	–	–	1	122
Students	24	6	–	1	71	11	1,340
Colleges and Universities	5	3	–	–	3	–	240
Total Students	10,009	11,062	–	–	4,500	–	692,951
High Schools, Diocesan and Parish	29	4	1	2	3	3	790
Total Students	17,352	3,574	775	607	1,922	4,633	374,590
High Schools, Private	22	9	1	2	6	3	557
Total Students	13,115	4,255	719	776	4,090	1,076	285,993
Elementary Schools, Diocesan and Parish	221	60	23	12	51	35	6,818
Total Students	69,903	19,417	5,720	3,426	6,012	13,257	1,961,899
Elementary Schools, Private	9	6	–	3	–	2	333
Total Students	2,718	1,701	–	627	–	718	91,049
Non–residential Schools for the Disabled	–	–	–	–	–	–	75
Total Students	–	–	–	–	–	–	17,942
Religious Education High School Students	24,000	4,452	7,070	1,524	1,750	7,645	804,514
Religious Education Elementary Students	200,000	12,691	23,268	10,763	9,882	30,660	3,518,872
Priests Teaching	76	35	1	1	–	11	2,120
Scholastics Teaching	24	4	–	–	–	–	77
Brothers Teaching	25	10	4	6	16	1	1,176
Sisters Teaching	381	128	28	21	19	51	10,025
Lay Teachers	4,379	1,759	245	268	848	933	150,783
Infant Baptisms	101,126	7,078	17,707	5,757	9,443	17,767	1,040,837
Adult Baptisms	1,956	464	466	195	543	811	73,426
Received into Full Communion	2,051	262	593	193	1,028	652	88,161
First Communions	46,861	4,648	8,481	3,577	6,992	11,211	858,665
Confirmations	15,494	2,588	3,195	1,072	2,584	4,406	607,645
Marriages	12,094	1,729	2,319	965	1,645	3,714	288,593
Deaths	13,395	2,861	2,881	1,073	2,799	2,748	465,773
Totals Catholics	3,188,816	422,000	323,743	176,650	500,000	606,484	61,563,769
Total Population	10,603,000	1,700,000	2,225,050	883,250	2,209,629	2,636,888	270,536,283
Catholic Population Percentage	30	25	15	20	23	23	23

Archdioceses = 36; Dioceses = 164; Apostolates = 3

1998 GENERAL SUMMARY

	Sacramento CA	San Bernardino CA	San Diego CA	San Jose in California CA	Santa Rosa in California CA	Stockton CA	1998 U.S. GRAND TOTAL
Cardinals	–	–	–	–	–	–	10
Archbishops	–	–	–	–	–	–	49
Bishops	3	1	2	1	2	1	358
Abbots	1	–	2	–	–	–	114
Diocesan Priests	161	144	210	112	85	58	31,657
Religious Priests	72	87	96	185	20	22	15,925
Total Priests in Diocese	233	231	306	297	105	80	47,563
Newly Ordained Priests	–	5	1	1	–	1	509
Total Permanent Deacons	102	83	86	8	19	26	12,247
Total Brothers	30	21	22	40	45	4	6,115
Total Sisters	201	158	361	407	98	–	85,412
Number of Parishes	98	97	98	48	43	32	19,628
Missions	42	13	19	4	20	8	3,006
Pastoral Centers	2	–	2	1	13	2	1,259
New Parishes	–	–	–	3	–	–	37
Catholic Hospitals	8	2	1	3	4	3	601
Patients Assisted Annually	367,137	–	341,695	273,515	325,009	322,514	65,853,111
Health Care Centers	3	–	–	1	–	–	440
Patients Assisted Annually	13,751	–	–	85	–	–	5,058,274
Specialized Homes	1	–	13	1	2	2	1,359
Total Assisted Annually	118	–	1,767	47	99	283	494,308
Residential Care of Children (Orphanages)	2	–	1	–	1	–	156
Total Assisted Annually	21	–	120	–	107	–	74,918
Day Care and Extended Day Care Centers	3	–	–	1	2	–	1,156
Total Assisted Annually	372	–	–	250	80	–	96,413
Special Centers for Social Services	7	–	21	47	13	1	2,113
Total Assisted Annually	950,000	–	283,227	140,953	12,500	25,000	18,323,523
Diocesan Seminaries	–	1	1	–	–	–	75
Students	–	8	18	–	–	–	3,248
Religious Seminaries	2	–	–	–	–	–	122
Students	8	–	–	–	–	–	1,340
Colleges and Universities	–	–	1	1	–	–	240
Total Students	–	–	6,694	7,863	–	–	692,951
High Schools, Diocesan and Parish	4	2	3	2	3	2	790
Total Students	1,658	902	1,850	1,742	1,055	1,354	374,590
High Schools, Private	3	–	2	4	3	–	557
Total Students	2,348	–	1,326	3,996	1,012	–	285,993
Elementary Schools, Diocesan and Parish	48	34	43	30	13	12	6,818
Total Students	13,544	8,370	13,134	10,710	3,001	3,395	1,961,899
Elementary Schools, Private	–	–	1	1	1	–	333
Total Students	–	–	351	152	30	–	91,049
Non–residential Schools for the Disabled	–	–	1	–	–	–	75
Total Students	–	–	184	–	–	–	17,942
Religious Education High School Students	2,182	10,776	6,565	2,391	1,198	927	804,514
Religious Education Elementary Students	14,390	32,326	27,202	14,636	5,842	11,816	3,518,872
Priests Teaching	13	–	12	53	4	4	2,120
Scholastics Teaching	3	–	–	9	–	–	77
Brothers Teaching	7	–	–	5	–	2	1,176
Sisters Teaching	16	–	56	50	11	5	10,025
Lay Teachers	501	372	1,066	1,173	309	139	150,783
Infant Baptisms	8,742	10,306	11,794	9,208	2,852	4,303	1,040,837
Adult Baptisms	667	1,348	487	586	196	530	73,426
Received into Full Communion	649	917	637	410	182	538	88,161
First Communions	6,479	9,817	9,691	5,654	2,135	3,130	858,665
Confirmations	4,732	3,468	3,654	2,582	1,014	1,913	607,645
Marriages	1,690	1,886	2,283	1,860	823	933	288,593
Deaths	2,649	2,703	2,935	1,918	1,108	1,357	465,773
Totals Catholics	432,300	779,504	716,602	398,901	139,513	180,678	61,563,769
Total Population	2,882,000	3,784,000	2,798,114	1,599,604	772,859	1,051,540	270,536,283
Catholic Population Percentage	15	21	26	25	18	17	23

*Indicates Archdioceses.

†Certain Dioceses traverse state lines.

	CALIFORNIA TOTAL	The Caroline Islands CI	*Denver CO	Colorado Springs CO	Pueblo CO	COLORADO TOTAL	1998 U.S. GRAND TOTAL
Cardinals	1	–	–	–	–	–	**10**
Archbishops	2	–	1	–	–	1	**49**
Bishops	26	2	–	1	2	3	**358**
Abbots	7	–	1	–	1	2	**114**
Diocesan Priests	2,143	13	161	34	77	272	**31,657**
Religious Priests	1,594	14	133	19	39	191	**15,925**
Total Priests in Diocese	3,737	27	294	53	116	463	**47,563**
Newly Ordained Priests	36	1	5	4	–	9	**509**
Total Permanent Deacons	670	39	126	20	10	156	**12,247**
Total Brothers	430	2	22	4	13	39	**6,115**
Total Sisters	4,993	38	450	145	102	697	**85,412**
Number of Parishes	1,064	21	112	30	55	197	**19,628**
Missions	191	2	38	9	61	108	**3,006**
Pastoral Centers	39	–	–	–	–	–	**1,259**
New Parishes	4	–	–	–	–	–	**37**
Catholic Hospitals	50	–	3	3	5	11	**601**
Patients Assisted Annually	4,041,460	–	374,673	292,014	1,462,029	2,128,716	**65,853,111**
Health Care Centers	14	–	3	2	–	5	**440**
Patients Assisted Annually	196,868	–	490	113	–	603	**5,058,274**
Specialized Homes	71	–	13	2	4	19	**1,359**
Total Assisted Annually	50,497	–	1,485	103	–	1,588	**494,308**
Residential Care of Children (Orphanages)	8	–	1	–	–	1	**156**
Total Assisted Annually	1,082	–	70	–	–	70	**74,918**
Day Care and Extended Day Care Centers	95	–	24	–	–	24	**1,156**
Total Assisted Annually	6,578	–	1,890	–	–	1,890	**96,413**
Special Centers for Social Services	214	–	4	–	1	5	**2,113**
Total Assisted Annually	2,421,510	–	7,550	–	2,894	10,444	**18,323,523**
Diocesan Seminaries	5	–	–	–	–	–	**75**
Students	225	–	–	–	–	–	**3,248**
Religious Seminaries	18	–	2	–	–	2	**122**
Students	121	5	16	3	–	19	**1,340**
Colleges and Universities	13	–	1	–	–	1	**240**
Total Students	40,128	–	10,155	–	–	10,155	**692,951**
High Schools, Diocesan and Parish	58	3	2	–	–	2	**790**
Total Students	37,424	456	579	–	–	579	**374,590**
High Schools, Private	55	2	3	–	1	4	**557**
Total Students	32,713	341	1,950	–	92	2,042	**285,993**
Elementary Schools, Diocesan and Parish	582	4	36	4	3	43	**6,818**
Total Students	169,889	1,632	10,886	1,324	886	13,096	**1,961,899**
Elementary Schools, Private	23	1	1	–	1	2	**333**
Total Students	6,297	229	469	–	234	703	**91,049**
Non–residential Schools for the Disabled	1	–	–	–	–	–	**75**
Total Students	184	–	–	–	–	–	**17,942**
Religious Education High School Students	70,480	250	3,222	2,409	2,269	7,900	**804,514**
Religious Education Elementary Students	393,476	3,350	24,069	6,524	4,429	35,022	**3,518,872**
Priests Teaching	210	6	6	–	–	6	**2,120**
Scholastics Teaching	40	5	–	–	–	–	**77**
Brothers Teaching	76	1	8	–	1	9	**1,176**
Sisters Teaching	766	24	35	1	8	44	**10,025**
Lay Teachers	11,992	111	660	78	102	840	**150,783**
Infant Baptisms	206,083	1,522	9,778	1,170	1,979	12,927	**1,040,837**
Adult Baptisms	8,249	205	882	218	137	1,237	**73,426**
Received into Full Communion	8,112	22	969	399	377	1,745	**88,161**
First Communions	118,676	854	6,905	1,311	1,611	9,827	**858,665**
Confirmations	46,702	860	4,425	645	925	5,995	**607,645**
Marriages	31,941	251	2,153	358	433	2,944	**288,593**
Deaths	38,427	276	2,775	254	1,269	4,298	**465,773**
Totals Catholics	7,865,191	64,881	330,662	84,810	106,482	521,954	**61,563,769**
Total Population	33,145,934	127,855	2,537,500	669,303	547,287	3,754,090	**270,536,283**
Catholic Population Percentage	24	51	13	13	19	14	**23**

Archdioceses = 36; Dioceses = 164; Apostolates = 3

1998 GENERAL SUMMARY

	*Hartford CT	Bridgeport CT	† Norwich CT	CONNECTICUT TOTAL	† Wilmington DE	*† Washington DC	1998 U.S. GRAND TOTAL
Cardinals	–	–	–	–	–	1	10
Archbishops	1	–	–	1	–	1	49
Bishops	2	1	1	4	1	3	358
Abbots	–	–	–	–	–	3	114
Diocesan Priests	416	262	143	821	128	336	31,657
Religious Priests	113	76	60	249	91	565	15,925
Total Priests in Diocese	529	338	203	1,070	219	901	47,563
Newly Ordained Priests	3	7	2	12	4	11	509
Total Permanent Deacons	333	77	49	459	46	242	12,247
Total Brothers	46	2	27	75	33	149	6,115
Total Sisters	995	522	320	1,837	287	829	85,412
Number of Parishes	220	88	78	386	55	139	19,628
Missions	4	2	10	16	21	8	3,006
Pastoral Centers	–	–	23	23	10	1	1,259
New Parishes	–	–	–	–	–	–	37
Catholic Hospitals	3	2	–	5	1	3	601
Patients Assisted Annually	715,286	200,000	–	915,286	311,000	461,970	65,853,111
Health Care Centers	–	–	–	–	2	5	440
Patients Assisted Annually	–	–	–	–	200	92,338	5,058,274
Specialized Homes	7	25	3	35	5	18	1,359
Total Assisted Annually	863	892	250	2,005	755	2,125	494,308
Residential Care of Children (Orphanages)	1	–	–	1	4	1	156
Total Assisted Annually	500	–	–	500	127	382	74,918
Day Care and Extended Day Care Centers	1	21	–	22	1	5	1,156
Total Assisted Annually	80	373	–	453	161	770	96,413
Special Centers for Social Services	20	20	1	41	18	68	2,113
Total Assisted Annually	24,000	14,271	126	38,397	323,768	104,216	18,323,523
Diocesan Seminaries	1	1	–	2	–	1	75
Students	6	16	–	22	–	65	3,248
Religious Seminaries	1	–	1	2	–	30	122
Students	145	–	–	145	–	171	1,340
Colleges and Universities	3	3	–	6	–	3	240
Total Students	3,920	10,905	–	14,825	–	20,363	692,951
High Schools, Diocesan and Parish	4	5	3	12	4	1	790
Total Students	1,851	2,476	1,750	6,077	2,858	700	374,590
High Schools, Private	7	3	2	12	3	16	557
Total Students	3,062	1,013	321	4,396	1,695	7,755	285,993
Elementary Schools, Diocesan and Parish	70	33	23	126	25	78	6,818
Total Students	18,831	10,854	4,658	34,343	9,783	22,126	1,961,899
Elementary Schools, Private	2	2	–	4	4	9	333
Total Students	330	422	–	752	1,018	1,538	91,049
Non–residential Schools for the Disabled	1	–	–	1	1	1	75
Total Students	47	–	–	47	77	71	17,942
Religious Education High School Students	8,619	2,907	2,728	14,254	1,171	3,064	804,514
Religious Education Elementary Students	43,752	27,068	15,155	85,975	8,853	25,579	3,518,872
Priests Teaching	17	18	1	36	21	30	2,120
Scholastics Teaching	–	–	–	–	–	3	77
Brothers Teaching	4	1	1	6	8	16	1,176
Sisters Teaching	111	44	15	170	63	122	10,025
Lay Teachers	1,207	717	23	1,947	943	2,370	150,783
Infant Baptisms	10,956	6,160	3,165	20,281	3,051	7,011	1,040,837
Adult Baptisms	256	173	132	561	201	585	73,426
Received into Full Communion	370	128	203	701	320	693	88,161
First Communions	10,354	5,186	2,983	18,523	2,685	6,153	858,665
Confirmations	7,402	3,886	1,655	12,943	2,055	4,826	607,645
Marriages	3,333	2,273	1,013	6,619	1,025	2,051	288,593
Deaths	8,840	3,616	2,082	14,538	1,428	2,878	465,773
Totals Catholics	756,663	360,918	223,511	1,341,092	166,059	495,321	61,563,769
Total Population	1,806,705	833,761	625,829	3,266,295	1,089,820	2,388,916	270,536,283
Catholic Population Percentage	42	43	36	41	15	21	23

*Indicates Archdioceses.

†Certain Dioceses traverse state lines.

	*Miami FL	Orlando FL	Palm Beach FL	Pensacola-Tallahassee FL	St. Augustine FL	St. Petersburg FL	1998 U.S. GRAND TOTAL
Cardinals	–	–	–	–	–	–	10
Archbishops	2	–	–	–	–	–	49
Bishops	3	2	1	1	1	3	358
Abbots	–	–	–	–	–	1	114
Diocesan Priests	265	134	96	74	90	130	31,657
Religious Priests	122	65	42	9	26	147	15,925
Total Priests in Diocese	387	199	138	83	116	277	47,563
Newly Ordained Priests	2	–	2	1	–	3	509
Total Permanent Deacons	128	123	37	45	23	86	12,247
Total Brothers	56	13	3	5	2	49	6,115
Total Sisters	345	142	183	61	111	359	85,412
Number of Parishes	108	70	46	49	50	72	19,628
Missions	5	10	5	9	9	5	3,006
Pastoral Centers	1	–	–	–	–	1	1,259
New Parishes	–	–	–	–	–	–	37
Catholic Hospitals	2	–	1	1	1	2	601
Patients Assisted Annually	573,198	–	15,862	20,269	192,700	2,343,257	65,853,111
Health Care Centers	3	–	–	–	–	7	440
Patients Assisted Annually	17,575	–	–	–	–	39,007	5,058,274
Specialized Homes	9	2	2	3	2	10	1,359
Total Assisted Annually	94,615	105	136	186	702	2,811	494,308
Residential Care of Children (Orphanages)	2	–	–	–	–	–	156
Total Assisted Annually	303	–	–	–	–	–	74,918
Day Care and Extended Day Care Centers	7	9	2	3	–	13	1,156
Total Assisted Annually	3,345	900	120	366	–	1,456	96,413
Special Centers for Social Services	38	6	21	7	6	8	2,113
Total Assisted Annually	999,979	25,000	19,251	50,362	50,000	14,981	18,323,523
Diocesan Seminaries	1	–	1	–	–	–	75
Students	43	–	73	–	–	–	3,248
Religious Seminaries	–	–	–	–	–	–	122
Students	–	–	–	–	–	–	1,340
Colleges and Universities	2	–	–	–	–	1	240
Total Students	9,480	–	–	–	–	7,124	692,951
High Schools, Diocesan and Parish	7	4	3	1	2	3	790
Total Students	6,915	2,370	2,067	600	1,867	1,927	374,590
High Schools, Private	5	–	–	–	–	2	557
Total Students	2,949	–	–	–	–	989	285,993
Elementary Schools, Diocesan and Parish	54	32	14	8	21	40	6,818
Total Students	22,833	12,809	5,357	1,737	7,118	11,006	1,961,899
Elementary Schools, Private	3	–	2	–	–	4	333
Total Students	1,222	–	562	–	–	1,298	91,049
Non–residential Schools for the Disabled	2	1	–	1	1	2	75
Total Students	11,641	61	–	16	110	141	17,942
Religious Education High School Students	2,935	3,877	2,377	1,582	1,106	2,380	804,514
Religious Education Elementary Students	43,753	21,757	13,530	5,332	7,919	19,479	3,518,872
Priests Teaching	10	1	19	–	2	13	2,120
Scholastics Teaching	–	–	–	–	–	1	77
Brothers Teaching	21	–	–	–	–	4	1,176
Sisters Teaching	51	36	22	8	17	61	10,025
Lay Teachers	1,733	826	420	139	434	831	150,783
Infant Baptisms	16,788	5,926	4,397	1,139	2,022	4,451	1,040,837
Adult Baptisms	826	670	280	155	333	713	73,426
Received into Full Communion	1,019	917	349	254	439	592	88,161
First Communions	12,946	5,683	3,675	1,217	2,317	5,016	858,665
Confirmations	7,649	3,690	1,960	906	1,834	3,417	607,645
Marriages	3,379	1,599	1,157	407	785	1,978	288,593
Deaths	4,586	3,296	2,347	541	931	4,325	465,773
Totals Catholics	774,125	312,609	219,470	63,985	124,669	354,699	61,563,769
Total Population	3,595,133	2,992,581	1,438,844	1,256,474	1,528,377	2,364,659	270,536,283
Catholic Population Percentage	22	10	15	5	8	15	23

Archdioceses = 36; Dioceses = 164; Apostolates = 3

1998 GENERAL SUMMARY

	Venice FL	FLORIDA TOTAL	*Atlanta GA	Savannah GA	GEORGIA TOTAL	*Agana GUAM	1998 U.S. GRAND TOTAL
Cardinals	–	–	–	–	–	–	10
Archbishops	–	2	2	–	2	1	49
Bishops	1	12	–	2	2	–	358
Abbots	–	1	2	–	2	–	114
Diocesan Priests	89	878	111	66	177	27	31,657
Religious Priests	76	487	99	33	132	19	15,925
Total Priests in Diocese	165	1,365	210	99	309	46	47,563
Newly Ordained Priests	4	12	5	3	8	1	509
Total Permanent Deacons	59	501	136	37	173	10	12,247
Total Brothers	20	148	1	18	19	1	6,115
Total Sisters	141	1,342	123	133	256	120	85,412
Number of Parishes	50	445	69	53	122	24	19,628
Missions	10	53	22	28	50	–	3,006
Pastoral Centers	–	2	3	–	3	–	1,259
New Parishes	–	–	–	–	–	–	37
Catholic Hospitals	2	9	2	3	5	–	601
Patients Assisted Annually	197,439	3,342,725	132,736	241,423	374,159	–	65,853,111
Health Care Centers	8	18	2	8	10	–	440
Patients Assisted Annually	72,960	129,542	20,202	166,200	186,402	–	5,058,274
Specialized Homes	10	38	6	1	7	5	1,359
Total Assisted Annually	521	99,076	220	22	242	1,253	494,308
Residential Care of Children (Orphanages)	–	2	–	1	1	–	156
Total Assisted Annually	–	303	–	42	42	–	74,918
Day Care and Extended Day Care Centers	–	34	2	–	2	4	1,156
Total Assisted Annually	–	6,187	77	–	77	459	96,413
Special Centers for Social Services	10	96	12	19	31	1	2,113
Total Assisted Annually	29,809	1,189,382	46,500	358,746	405,246	5,345	18,323,523
Diocesan Seminaries	–	2	–	–	–	–	75
Students	–	116	–	–	–	–	3,248
Religious Seminaries	–	–	–	–	–	–	122
Students	–	–	–	–	–	2	1,340
Colleges and Universities	–	3	–	–	–	–	240
Total Students	–	16,604	–	–	–	–	692,951
High Schools, Diocesan and Parish	3	23	1	2	3	2	790
Total Students	1,600	17,346	1,023	613	1,636	817	374,590
High Schools, Private	–	7	1	3	4	1	557
Total Students	–	3,938	1,025	1,800	2,825	245	285,993
Elementary Schools, Diocesan and Parish	9	178	12	15	27	7	6,818
Total Students	3,483	64,343	4,497	4,731	9,228	2,557	1,961,899
Elementary Schools, Private	–	9	2	–	2	–	333
Total Students	–	3,082	1,361	–	1,361	–	91,049
Non–residential Schools for the Disabled	–	7	–	–	–	–	75
Total Students	–	11,969	–	–	–	–	17,942
Religious Education High School Students	2,743	17,000	4,731	935	5,666	1,680	804,514
Religious Education Elementary Students	9,512	121,282	27,342	4,316	31,658	6,620	3,518,872
Priests Teaching	5	50	2	6	8	1	2,120
Scholastics Teaching	–	1	–	–	–	–	77
Brothers Teaching	1	26	–	1	1	–	1,176
Sisters Teaching	20	215	8	29	37	45	10,025
Lay Teachers	295	4,678	364	386	750	253	150,783
Infant Baptisms	2,943	37,666	6,069	1,363	7,432	2,730	1,040,837
Adult Baptisms	254	3,231	469	233	702	30	73,426
Received into Full Communion	505	4,075	980	446	1,426	26	88,161
First Communions	2,733	33,587	4,111	1,194	5,305	1,502	858,665
Confirmations	2,193	21,649	3,086	1,046	4,132	747	607,645
Marriages	880	10,185	1,633	365	1,998	220	288,593
Deaths	2,116	18,142	789	496	1,285	434	465,773
Totals Catholics	174,548	2,024,105	292,300	74,716	367,016	115,080	61,563,769
Total Population	1,385,308	14,561,376	4,896,392	2,440,868	7,337,260	136,421	270,536,283
Catholic Population Percentage	13	14	6	3	5	84	23

*Indicates Archdioceses.

†Certain Dioceses traverse state lines.

	Honolulu HI	Boise ID	*Chicago IL	Belleville IL	Joliet in Illinois IL	Peoria IL	1998 U.S. GRAND TOTAL
Cardinals	–	–	1	–	–	–	10
Archbishops	–	–	–	–	–	–	49
Bishops	2	1	9	1	2	2	358
Abbots	–	–	–	–	3	2	114
Diocesan Priests	70	96	941	148	199	256	31,657
Religious Priests	79	18	811	38	112	57	15,925
Total Priests in Diocese	149	114	1,752	186	311	313	47,563
Newly Ordained Priests	–	1	15	1	2	10	509
Total Permanent Deacons	33	29	599	40	138	96	12,247
Total Brothers	52	9	366	10	95	9	6,115
Total Sisters	152	106	3,263	265	766	336	85,412
Number of Parishes	68	63	378	131	119	165	19,628
Missions	–	32	11	1	10	39	3,006
Pastoral Centers	–	17	8	–	–	5	1,259
New Parishes	–	–	–	–	1	–	37
Catholic Hospitals	2	5	19	7	3	8	601
Patients Assisted Annually	394,015	586,031	2,799,947	407,412	588,624	923,194	65,853,111
Health Care Centers	3	–	1	–	–	–	440
Patients Assisted Annually	10,434	–	4,500	–	–	–	5,058,274
Specialized Homes	3	–	50	5	11	4	1,359
Total Assisted Annually	32,018	–	17,000	558	2,266	293	494,308
Residential Care of Children (Orphanages)	–	–	–	–	–	1	156
Total Assisted Annually	–	–	–	–	–	58	74,918
Day Care and Extended Day Care Centers	3	4	11	4	3	3	1,156
Total Assisted Annually	195	138	2,100	566	1,126	363	96,413
Special Centers for Social Services	2	13	45	3	5	1	2,113
Total Assisted Annually	31,814	62,771	98,000	41,975	33,912	17,426	18,323,523
Diocesan Seminaries	–	–	3	–	–	–	75
Students	–	–	471	–	–	–	3,248
Religious Seminaries	–	–	1	–	–	–	122
Students	2	–	85	–	–	–	1,340
Colleges and Universities	1	–	6	–	3	1	240
Total Students	2,592	–	40,814	–	12,530	152	692,951
High Schools, Diocesan and Parish	3	1	8	3	4	6	790
Total Students	1,171	738	2,501	1,651	2,515	2,590	374,590
High Schools, Private	4	–	39	–	4	–	557
Total Students	2,439	–	30,303	–	3,080	–	285,993
Elementary Schools, Diocesan and Parish	24	13	273	38	62	48	6,818
Total Students	6,923	2,477	100,566	7,552	19,311	12,478	1,961,899
Elementary Schools, Private	1	–	1	–	–	–	333
Total Students	363	–	357	–	–	–	91,049
Non–residential Schools for the Disabled	–	–	7	–	–	–	75
Total Students	–	–	600	–	–	–	17,942
Religious Education High School Students	1,757	3,124	8,793	1,875	5,371	3,409	804,514
Religious Education Elementary Students	5,295	7,064	97,405	8,423	48,682	13,589	3,518,872
Priests Teaching	6	–	49	–	34	5	2,120
Scholastics Teaching	–	–	5	–	–	–	77
Brothers Teaching	15	–	72	–	22	–	1,176
Sisters Teaching	57	3	334	15	44	45	10,025
Lay Teachers	390	166	5,816	391	1,485	726	150,783
Infant Baptisms	3,220	2,487	39,134	1,711	10,458	3,216	1,040,837
Adult Baptisms	391	237	1,982	274	332	513	73,426
Received into Full Communion	286	197	1,914	207	914	578	88,161
First Communions	2,162	1,898	29,417	1,698	9,335	3,211	858,665
Confirmations	1,278	1,065	19,917	1,817	6,789	3,114	607,645
Marriages	1,081	697	10,564	713	2,536	1,270	288,593
Deaths	1,572	786	18,580	1,355	3,534	2,298	465,773
Totals Catholics	232,780	120,000	2,349,000	113,051	535,000	230,481	61,563,769
Total Population	1,178,600	1,218,000	5,729,000	855,645	1,494,978	1,436,473	270,536,283
Catholic Population Percentage	20	10	41	13	36	16	23

Archdioceses = 36; Dioceses = 164; Apostolates = 3

1998 GENERAL SUMMARY

	Rockford IL	Springfield in Illinois IL	ILLINOIS TOTAL	*Indianapolis IN	Evansville IN	Fort Wayne - South Bend IN	1998 U.S. GRAND TOTAL
Cardinals	–	–	1	–	–	–	**10**
Archbishops	–	–	–	1	–	–	**49**
Bishops	2	1	17	–	1	4	**358**
Abbots	3	–	8	3	–	–	**114**
Diocesan Priests	156	146	1,846	164	104	101	**31,657**
Religious Priests	61	65	1,144	115	10	178	**15,925**
Total Priests in Diocese	217	211	2,990	279	114	279	**47,563**
Newly Ordained Priests	6	3	37	5	–	5	**509**
Total Permanent Deacons	108	2	983	–	22	32	**12,247**
Total Brothers	15	19	514	53	2	225	**6,115**
Total Sisters	450	707	5,787	780	321	658	**85,412**
Number of Parishes	110	166	1,069	138	70	89	**19,628**
Missions	6	–	67	13	–	–	**3,006**
Pastoral Centers	–	–	13	–	6	2	**1,259**
New Parishes	–	–	1	–	–	–	**37**
Catholic Hospitals	4	8	49	2	2	5	**601**
Patients Assisted Annually	471,652	901,359	6,092,188	1,147,664	320,428	396,192	**65,853,111**
Health Care Centers	1	–	2	–	1	1	**440**
Patients Assisted Annually	375	–	4,875	–	60	20,000	**5,058,274**
Specialized Homes	5	4	79	8	3	5	**1,359**
Total Assisted Annually	988	449	21,554	1,485	249	534	**494,308**
Residential Care of Children (Orphanages)	–	1	2	–	–	–	**156**
Total Assisted Annually	–	130	188	–	–	–	**74,918**
Day Care and Extended Day Care Centers	1	1	23	5	1	2	**1,156**
Total Assisted Annually	8,403	12	12,570	348	432	428	**96,413**
Special Centers for Social Services	10	–	64	9	15	3	**2,113**
Total Assisted Annually	312,797	–	504,110	70,799	24,000	12,919	**18,323,523**
Diocesan Seminaries	–	–	3	–	–	–	**75**
Students	–	–	471	–	–	–	**3,248**
Religious Seminaries	–	1	2	1	–	1	**122**
Students	–	10	95	122	–	25	**1,340**
Colleges and Universities	–	2	12	3	–	5	**240**
Total Students	–	1,672	55,168	2,675	–	13,805	**692,951**
High Schools, Diocesan and Parish	6	4	31	6	4	4	**790**
Total Students	3,458	1,033	13,748	3,173	1,702	3,405	**374,590**
High Schools, Private	2	3	48	3	1	–	**557**
Total Students	894	1,655	35,932	1,948	133	–	**285,993**
Elementary Schools, Diocesan and Parish	41	54	516	62	24	40	**6,818**
Total Students	12,309	12,791	165,007	19,854	5,947	10,875	**1,961,899**
Elementary Schools, Private	–	–	1	–	–	–	**333**
Total Students	–	–	357	–	–	–	**91,049**
Non-residential Schools for the Disabled	–	–	7	–	1	–	**75**
Total Students	–	–	600	–	22	–	**17,942**
Religious Education High School Students	4,900	3,221	27,569	3,138	2,017	2,483	**804,514**
Religious Education Elementary Students	22,006	10,864	200,969	14,479	7,881	10,114	**3,518,872**
Priests Teaching	48	4	140	–	2	2	**2,120**
Scholastics Teaching	–	–	5	–	–	–	**77**
Brothers Teaching	–	1	95	5	2	1	**1,176**
Sisters Teaching	34	46	518	53	24	25	**10,025**
Lay Teachers	905	846	10,169	1,425	410	718	**150,783**
Infant Baptisms	5,975	2,481	62,975	4,350	1,524	2,679	**1,040,837**
Adult Baptisms	254	322	3,677	684	147	390	**73,426**
Received into Full Communion	476	524	4,613	852	173	456	**88,161**
First Communions	5,506	2,847	52,014	3,557	1,523	3,115	**858,665**
Confirmations	3,780	3,052	38,469	2,276	1,506	2,952	**607,645**
Marriages	1,410	1,118	17,611	1,415	595	1,104	**288,593**
Deaths	1,926	1,757	29,450	1,979	907	1,565	**465,773**
Totals Catholics	280,652	168,967	3,677,151	219,247	88,903	162,756	**61,563,769**
Total Population	1,079,500	1,106,124	11,701,720	2,201,503	475,953	1,156,129	**270,536,283**
Catholic Population Percentage	26	15	31	10	19	14	**23**

*Indicates Archdioceses.

†Certain Dioceses traverse state lines.

	Gary IN	Lafayette in Indiana IN	INDIANA TOTAL	*Dubuque IA	Davenport IA	Des Moines IA	1998 U.S. GRAND TOTAL
Cardinals	–	–	–	–	–	–	**10**
Archbishops	–	–	1	2	–	–	**49**
Bishops	2	1	8	–	2	1	**358**
Abbots	–	–	3	5	–	–	**114**
Diocesan Priests	128	121	618	263	145	116	**31,657**
Religious Priests	52	22	377	36	3	10	**15,925**
Total Priests in Diocese	180	143	995	299	148	126	**47,563**
Newly Ordained Priests	2	–	12	4	3	3	**509**
Total Permanent Deacons	25	5	84	66	48	61	**12,247**
Total Brothers	20	2	302	30	1	8	**6,115**
Total Sisters	126	92	1,977	1,040	250	119	**85,412**
Number of Parishes	78	62	437	212	90	87	**19,628**
Missions	3	1	17	2	–	1	**3,006**
Pastoral Centers	7	–	15	1	1	–	**1,259**
New Parishes	–	–	–	–	–	–	**37**
Catholic Hospitals	6	4	19	6	3	3	**601**
Patients Assisted Annually	513,939	207,767	2,585,990	880,423	276,000	302,963	**65,853,111**
Health Care Centers	–	–	2	3	–	1	**440**
Patients Assisted Annually	–	–	20,060	374	–	522,056	**5,058,274**
Specialized Homes	4	2	22	5	3	2	**1,359**
Total Assisted Annually	1,178	385	3,831	382	597	401	**494,308**
Residential Care of Children (Orphanages)	3	–	3	–	–	–	**156**
Total Assisted Annually	128	–	128	–	–	–	**74,918**
Day Care and Extended Day Care Centers	1	–	9	1	–	–	**1,156**
Total Assisted Annually	200	–	1,408	61	–	–	**96,413**
Special Centers for Social Services	7	–	34	–	–	4	**2,113**
Total Assisted Annually	10,000	–	117,718	–	–	37,082	**18,323,523**
Diocesan Seminaries	–	–	–	1	1	–	**75**
Students	–	–	–	6	4	–	**3,248**
Religious Seminaries	1	–	3	1	–	–	**122**
Students	7	–	154	112	–	–	**1,340**
Colleges and Universities	1	3	12	3	2	1	**240**
Total Students	1,035	6,969	24,484	4,074	3,358	440	**692,951**
High Schools, Diocesan and Parish	3	1	18	8	7	2	**790**
Total Students	2,007	364	10,651	3,181	1,683	1,468	**374,590**
High Schools, Private	–	–	4	–	–	–	**557**
Total Students	–	–	2,081	–	–	–	**285,993**
Elementary Schools, Diocesan and Parish	30	20	176	54	45	15	**6,818**
Total Students	8,039	3,934	48,649	12,446	4,976	4,644	**1,961,899**
Elementary Schools, Private	1	–	1	–	–	–	**333**
Total Students	110	–	110	–	–	–	**91,049**
Non–residential Schools for the Disabled	–	–	1	–	–	–	**75**
Total Students	–	–	22	–	–	–	**17,942**
Religious Education High School Students	693	2,950	11,281	5,515	3,200	2,099	**804,514**
Religious Education Elementary Students	10,125	9,271	51,870	14,932	9,600	9,822	**3,518,872**
Priests Teaching	6	–	10	2	1	5	**2,120**
Scholastics Teaching	–	–	–	–	–	–	**77**
Brothers Teaching	4	–	12	1	–	1	**1,176**
Sisters Teaching	16	–	118	45	12	11	**10,025**
Lay Teachers	550	235	3,338	976	355	302	**150,783**
Infant Baptisms	2,345	1,861	12,759	3,378	1,645	1,977	**1,040,837**
Adult Baptisms	210	292	1,723	164	217	238	**73,426**
Received into Full Communion	262	441	2,184	434	219	485	**88,161**
First Communions	2,393	1,842	12,430	3,677	2,122	2,054	**858,665**
Confirmations	2,048	1,252	10,034	2,806	1,957	1,985	**607,645**
Marriages	888	622	4,624	1,589	783	669	**288,593**
Deaths	1,641	780	6,872	2,167	1,105	738	**465,773**
Totals Catholics	184,106	94,512	749,524	217,856	106,460	95,596	**61,563,769**
Total Population	759,673	1,115,156	5,708,414	923,000	726,646	671,091	**270,536,283**
Catholic Population Percentage	24	8	13	24	15	14	**23**

Archdioceses = 36; Dioceses = 164; Apostolates = 3

1998 GENERAL SUMMARY

	Sioux City IA	IOWA TOTAL	*Kansas City in Kansas KS	Dodge City KS	Salina KS	Wichita KS	1998 U.S. GRAND TOTAL
Cardinals	–	–	–	–	–	–	**10**
Archbishops	–	2	2	–	–	–	**49**
Bishops	2	5	1	2	2	1	**358**
Abbots	–	5	3	–	–	–	**114**
Diocesan Priests	173	697	96	49	69	126	**31,657**
Religious Priests	–	49	77	2	16	9	**15,925**
Total Priests in Diocese	173	746	173	51	85	135	**47,563**
Newly Ordained Priests	2	12	1	–	1	2	**509**
Total Permanent Deacons	35	210	–	4	–	2	**12,247**
Total Brothers	–	39	20	–	1	–	**6,115**
Total Sisters	114	1,523	830	116	207	385	**85,412**
Number of Parishes	123	512	119	51	92	93	**19,628**
Missions	10	13	–	–	–	–	**3,006**
Pastoral Centers	–	2	–	–	–	–	**1,259**
New Parishes	–	–	–	–	–	–	**37**
Catholic Hospitals	3	15	3	3	–	5	**601**
Patients Assisted Annually	315,780	1,775,166	327,154	120,480	–	466,826	**65,853,111**
Health Care Centers	–	4	2	–	–	2	**440**
Patients Assisted Annually	–	522,430	13,375	–	–	22,670	**5,058,274**
Specialized Homes	4	14	4	–	3	3	**1,359**
Total Assisted Annually	259	1,639	575	–	238	288	**494,308**
Residential Care of Children (Orphanages)	–	–	–	–	–	–	**156**
Total Assisted Annually	–	–	–	–	–	–	**74,918**
Day Care and Extended Day Care Centers	–	1	–	–	–	–	**1,156**
Total Assisted Annually	–	61	–	–	–	–	**96,413**
Special Centers for Social Services	4	8	10	4	–	1	**2,113**
Total Assisted Annually	6,142	43,224	15,245	77,895	–	14,240	**18,323,523**
Diocesan Seminaries	–	2	–	–	–	–	**75**
Students	–	10	–	–	–	–	**3,248**
Religious Seminaries	–	1	–	–	–	–	**122**
Students	–	112	2	–	–	–	**1,340**
Colleges and Universities	1	7	3	–	–	1	**240**
Total Students	1,011	8,883	2,430	–	–	1,857	**692,951**
High Schools, Diocesan and Parish	8	25	5	–	4	4	**790**
Total Students	2,802	9,134	3,085	–	402	1,950	**374,590**
High Schools, Private	–	–	2	–	1	–	**557**
Total Students	–	–	337	–	305	–	**285,993**
Elementary Schools, Diocesan and Parish	28	142	40	10	12	32	**6,818**
Total Students	6,353	28,419	11,672	1,251	1,953	7,481	**1,961,899**
Elementary Schools, Private	–	–	1	–	–	–	**333**
Total Students	–	–	40	–	–	–	**91,049**
Non–residential Schools for the Disabled	–	–	–	–	–	–	**75**
Total Students	–	–	–	–	–	–	**17,942**
Religious Education High School Students	3,516	14,330	2,724	1,609	2,383	3,087	**804,514**
Religious Education Elementary Students	7,586	41,940	14,396	4,122	6,124	8,194	**3,518,872**
Priests Teaching	8	16	1	–	8	–	**2,120**
Scholastics Teaching	–	–	–	–	–	–	**77**
Brothers Teaching	–	2	1	–	–	–	**1,176**
Sisters Teaching	26	94	59	2	8	32	**10,025**
Lay Teachers	521	2,154	977	87	203	499	**150,783**
Infant Baptisms	1,691	8,691	3,675	842	1,005	2,513	**1,040,837**
Adult Baptisms	124	743	429	236	141	334	**73,426**
Received into Full Communion	358	1,496	588	97	185	368	**88,161**
First Communions	1,892	9,745	3,568	887	959	2,344	**858,665**
Confirmations	1,412	8,160	2,877	604	1,264	1,694	**607,645**
Marriages	678	3,719	1,224	220	534	875	**288,593**
Deaths	1,146	5,156	1,337	324	589	809	**465,773**
Totals Catholics	92,309	512,221	188,704	44,504	53,060	107,337	**61,563,769**
Total Population	472,307	2,793,044	952,000	215,920	331,427	911,091	**270,536,283**
Catholic Population Percentage	20	18	20	21	16	12	**23**

*Indicates Archdioceses.

†Certain Dioceses traverse state lines.

1998 GENERAL SUMMARY

	KANSAS TOTAL	*Louisville KY	Covington KY	Lexington KY	Owensboro KY	KENTUCKY TOTAL	1998 U.S. GRAND TOTAL
Cardinals	–	–	–	–	–	–	**10**
Archbishops	2	2	–	–	–	2	**49**
Bishops	6	1	2	1	1	5	**358**
Abbots	3	1	–	–	–	1	**114**
Diocesan Priests	340	191	117	50	84	442	**31,657**
Religious Priests	104	69	1	22	13	105	**15,925**
Total Priests in Diocese	444	260	118	72	97	547	**47,563**
Newly Ordained Priests	4	5	1	1	6	13	**509**
Total Permanent Deacons	6	101	18	29	–	148	**12,247**
Total Brothers	21	87	6	3	4	100	**6,115**
Total Sisters	1,538	1,049	440	176	239	1,904	**85,412**
Number of Parishes	355	112	48	60	79	299	**19,628**
Missions	–	12	9	6	–	27	**3,006**
Pastoral Centers	–	3	8	–	2	13	**1,259**
New Parishes	–	1	1	–	1	3	**37**
Catholic Hospitals	11	2	3	6	1	12	**601**
Patients Assisted Annually	914,460	150,302	323,402	410,631	85,000	969,335	**65,853,111**
Health Care Centers	4	1	–	4	2	7	**440**
Patients Assisted Annually	36,045	2,300	–	74,502	8,000	84,802	**5,058,274**
Specialized Homes	10	6	3	1	2	12	**1,359**
Total Assisted Annually	1,101	1,019	576	82	176	1,853	**494,308**
Residential Care of Children (Orphanages)	–	1	2	–	–	3	**156**
Total Assisted Annually	–	62	78	–	–	140	**74,918**
Day Care and Extended Day Care Centers	–	1	1	3	3	8	**1,156**
Total Assisted Annually	–	185	81	150	136	552	**96,413**
Special Centers for Social Services	15	1	4	1	2	8	**2,113**
Total Assisted Annually	107,380	3,521	81,269	8,179	16,000	108,969	**18,323,523**
Diocesan Seminaries	–	–	–	–	–	–	**75**
Students	–	–	–	–	–	–	**3,248**
Religious Seminaries	–	–	–	–	–	–	**122**
Students	2	–	–	–	–	–	**1,340**
Colleges and Universities	4	3	1	–	1	5	**240**
Total Students	4,287	4,108	1,505	–	750	6,363	**692,951**
High Schools, Diocesan and Parish	13	4	7	1	3	15	**790**
Total Students	5,437	2,066	2,450	758	1,064	6,338	**374,590**
High Schools, Private	3	6	2	2	–	10	**557**
Total Students	642	4,023	791	89	–	4,903	**285,993**
Elementary Schools, Diocesan and Parish	94	57	29	14	19	119	**6,818**
Total Students	22,357	17,354	8,049	2,894	4,434	32,731	**1,961,899**
Elementary Schools, Private	1	3	2	1	–	6	**333**
Total Students	40	542	498	148	–	1,188	**91,049**
Non–residential Schools for the Disabled	–	1	1	–	–	2	**75**
Total Students	–	63	20	–	–	83	**17,942**
Religious Education High School Students	9,803	1,212	425	753	1,354	3,744	**804,514**
Religious Education Elementary Students	32,836	8,392	4,267	2,865	3,774	19,298	**3,518,872**
Priests Teaching	9	7	–	2	1	10	**2,120**
Scholastics Teaching	–	–	–	–	–	–	**77**
Brothers Teaching	1	15	1	–	1	17	**1,176**
Sisters Teaching	101	28	63	22	14	127	**10,025**
Lay Teachers	1,766	1,269	647	215	353	2,484	**150,783**
Infant Baptisms	8,035	3,101	1,435	718	1,074	6,328	**1,040,837**
Adult Baptisms	1,140	367	216	142	155	880	**73,426**
Received into Full Communion	1,238	627	145	298	265	1,335	**88,161**
First Communions	7,758	3,159	1,545	1,027	1,020	6,751	**858,665**
Confirmations	6,439	2,649	1,620	720	1,250	6,239	**607,645**
Marriages	2,853	1,139	593	294	492	2,518	**288,593**
Deaths	3,059	1,875	844	212	567	3,498	**465,773**
Totals Catholics	393,605	181,896	83,997	41,977	51,932	359,802	**61,563,769**
Total Population	2,410,438	1,139,022	401,127	1,444,148	778,235	3,762,532	**270,536,283**
Catholic Population Percentage	16	16	21	3	7	10	**23**

Archdioceses = 36; Dioceses = 164; Apostolates = 3

1998 GENERAL SUMMARY

	*New Orleans LA	Alexandria LA	Baton Rouge LA	Houma–Thibodaux LA	Lafayette LA	Lake Charles LA	1998 U.S. GRAND TOTAL
Cardinals	–	–	–	–	–	–	**10**
Archbishops	2	–	–	–	–	–	**49**
Bishops	3	1	1	1	3	1	**358**
Abbots	1	–	–	–	–	–	**114**
Diocesan Priests	229	66	88	73	145	56	**31,657**
Religious Priests	217	16	45	7	56	18	**15,925**
Total Priests in Diocese	446	82	133	80	201	74	**47,563**
Newly Ordained Priests	1	3	2	3	6	1	**509**
Total Permanent Deacons	194	7	28	25	57	25	**12,247**
Total Brothers	141	3	11	12	32	4	**6,115**
Total Sisters	870	62	120	34	178	28	**85,412**
Number of Parishes	146	48	70	42	121	36	**19,628**
Missions	8	23	–	6	35	25	**3,006**
Pastoral Centers	1	1	–	–	–	–	**1,259**
New Parishes	–	–	–	–	–	–	**37**
Catholic Hospitals	–	1	1	–	1	1	**601**
Patients Assisted Annually	–	131,845	230,000	–	81,000	104,497	**65,853,111**
Health Care Centers	3	1	–	–	1	–	**440**
Patients Assisted Annually	5,180	312	–	–	16,000	–	**5,058,274**
Specialized Homes	21	2	9	2	7	–	**1,359**
Total Assisted Annually	6,711	164	1,820	65	2,250	–	**494,308**
Residential Care of Children (Orphanages)	2	–	–	–	–	–	**156**
Total Assisted Annually	201	–	–	–	–	–	**74,918**
Day Care and Extended Day Care Centers	17	–	–	1	–	1	**1,156**
Total Assisted Annually	1,136	–	–	96	–	57	**96,413**
Special Centers for Social Services	55	16	6	4	6	1	**2,113**
Total Assisted Annually	158,562	125,650	101,784	9,506	180,000	2,166	**18,323,523**
Diocesan Seminaries	2	–	–	–	–	–	**75**
Students	155	–	–	–	–	–	**3,248**
Religious Seminaries	3	–	–	–	1	–	**122**
Students	17	–	–	–	15	–	**1,340**
Colleges and Universities	3	–	1	–	–	–	**240**
Total Students	10,311	–	961	–	–	–	**692,951**
High Schools, Diocesan and Parish	10	3	6	3	9	1	**790**
Total Students	6,627	570	2,589	1,871	3,755	511	**374,590**
High Schools, Private	13	–	2	–	1	–	**557**
Total Students	9,810	–	1,542	–	130	–	**285,993**
Elementary Schools, Diocesan and Parish	74	9	26	10	29	8	**6,818**
Total Students	32,742	2,546	12,391	4,186	11,000	2,386	**1,961,899**
Elementary Schools, Private	6	–	–	–	2	–	**333**
Total Students	1,441	–	–	–	670	–	**91,049**
Non–residential Schools for the Disabled	1	–	–	–	–	–	**75**
Total Students	192	–	–	–	–	–	**17,942**
Religious Education High School Students	4,148	1,746	5,882	3,247	26,186	4,267	**804,514**
Religious Education Elementary Students	18,072	3,116	10,628	6,382	10,571	5,817	**3,518,872**
Priests Teaching	95	–	1	–	–	1	**2,120**
Scholastics Teaching	–	–	–	–	–	–	**77**
Brothers Teaching	40	2	1	7	3	1	**1,176**
Sisters Teaching	155	20	25	–	23	–	**10,025**
Lay Teachers	3,515	182	877	312	820	198	**150,783**
Infant Baptisms	7,060	788	2,870	1,768	5,853	1,772	**1,040,837**
Adult Baptisms	408	84	192	60	173	131	**73,426**
Received into Full Communion	365	133	359	159	220	225	**88,161**
First Communions	6,754	760	2,901	1,547	5,396	1,464	**858,665**
Confirmations	5,984	568	2,384	1,449	4,325	1,086	**607,645**
Marriages	2,400	272	1,206	481	1,831	456	**288,593**
Deaths	4,580	674	1,649	1,091	3,587	922	**465,773**
Totals Catholics	471,107	48,050	209,182	97,993	363,090	82,414	**61,563,769**
Total Population	1,335,563	393,880	763,545	208,185	545,000	259,425	**270,536,283**
Catholic Population Percentage	35	12	27	47	67	32	**23**

*Indicates Archdioceses.

†Certain Dioceses traverse state lines.

	Shreveport LA	LOUISIANA TOTAL	Portland (In Maine) ME	Marshall Islands	*Baltimore MD	*Boston MA	1998 U.S. GRAND TOTAL
Cardinals	–	–	–	–	1	1	10
Archbishops	–	2	–	–	1	–	49
Bishops	1	11	3	–	2	7	358
Abbots	–	1	–	–	–	1	114
Diocesan Priests	41	698	189	1	292	971	31,657
Religious Priests	12	371	53	5	250	874	15,925
Total Priests in Diocese	53	1,069	242	6	542	1,845	47,563
Newly Ordained Priests	1	17	4	–	2	9	509
Total Permanent Deacons	7	343	11	2	175	187	12,247
Total Brothers	–	203	28	2	73	178	6,115
Total Sisters	62	1,354	483	16	1,362	2,873	85,412
Number of Parishes	31	494	138	4	155	388	19,628
Missions	14	111	54	7	7	–	3,006
Pastoral Centers	2	4	–	1	3	–	1,259
New Parishes	–	–	1	–	2	1	37
Catholic Hospitals	3	7	3	–	5	10	601
Patients Assisted Annually	191,594	738,936	220,987	–	1,079,584	846,384	65,853,111
Health Care Centers	1	6	1	–	–	2	440
Patients Assisted Annually	30,163	51,655	73	–	–	253	5,058,274
Specialized Homes	3	44	12	–	24	29	1,359
Total Assisted Annually	152	11,162	1,009	–	3,317	3,927	494,308
Residential Care of Children (Orphanages)	–	2	–	–	3	1	156
Total Assisted Annually	–	201	–	–	612	441	74,918
Day Care and Extended Day Care Centers	1	20	4	–	9	10	1,156
Total Assisted Annually	130	1,419	530	–	2,048	1,862	96,413
Special Centers for Social Services	21	109	7	–	29	46	2,113
Total Assisted Annually	19,100	596,768	2,685	–	895,862	155,824	18,323,523
Diocesan Seminaries	–	2	–	–	2	3	75
Students	–	155	–	–	227	169	3,248
Religious Seminaries	–	4	–	–	–	4	122
Students	–	32	–	–	–	–	1,340
Colleges and Universities	–	4	1	–	3	9	240
Total Students	–	11,272	4,685	–	11,150	20,351	692,951
High Schools, Diocesan and Parish	2	34	1	2	9	17	790
Total Students	735	16,658	241	299	3,588	5,739	374,590
High Schools, Private	–	16	2	–	13	19	557
Total Students	–	11,482	631	–	7,236	9,010	285,993
Elementary Schools, Diocesan and Parish	10	166	18	6	67	119	6,818
Total Students	2,407	67,658	4,079	1,223	22,915	36,316	1,961,899
Elementary Schools, Private	–	8	1	–	6	11	333
Total Students	–	2,111	174	–	2,051	3,560	91,049
Non–residential Schools for the Disabled	–	1	–	–	5	–	75
Total Students	–	192	–	–	336	–	17,942
Religious Education High School Students	751	46,227	4,448	57	4,499	28,563	804,514
Religious Education Elementary Students	2,323	56,909	16,669	335	32,905	125,551	3,518,872
Priests Teaching	–	97	4	1	67	14	2,120
Scholastics Teaching	–	–	–	–	3	–	77
Brothers Teaching	–	54	–	1	26	35	1,176
Sisters Teaching	7	230	30	8	156	301	10,025
Lay Teachers	210	6,114	289	81	2,615	2,734	150,783
Infant Baptisms	521	20,632	3,134	152	8,475	29,282	1,040,837
Adult Baptisms	102	1,150	240	4	659	478	73,426
Received into Full Communion	318	1,779	364	30	1,237	350	88,161
First Communions	564	19,386	3,238	165	8,280	23,721	858,665
Confirmations	641	16,437	6,309	32	5,716	15,734	607,645
Marriages	215	6,861	1,359	19	2,690	8,896	288,593
Deaths	341	12,844	2,751	16	5,188	18,847	465,773
Totals Catholics	40,436	1,312,272	233,927	4,000	487,499	2,002,322	61,563,769
Total Population	772,938	4,278,536	1,227,927	50,000	2,845,181	3,764,400	270,536,283
Catholic Population Percentage	5	31	19	8	17	53	23

Archdioceses = 36; Dioceses = 164; Apostolates = 3

1998 GENERAL SUMMARY

	Fall River MA	Springfield in Massachusetts MA	Worcester MA	MASS. TOTAL	*Detroit MI	Gaylord MI	1998 U.S. GRAND TOTAL
Cardinals	–	–	–	1	1	–	10
Archbishops	–	–	–	–	–	–	49
Bishops	1	3	2	13	8	1	358
Abbots	–	–	3	4	–	–	114
Diocesan Priests	181	203	254	1,609	487	73	31,657
Religious Priests	103	52	116	1,145	236	16	15,925
Total Priests in Diocese	284	255	370	2,754	723	89	47,563
Newly Ordained Priests	5	–	1	15	8	3	509
Total Permanent Deacons	56	51	67	361	143	12	12,247
Total Brothers	31	10	78	297	97	2	6,115
Total Sisters	385	650	550	4,458	2,091	66	85,412
Number of Parishes	111	133	125	757	307	81	19,628
Missions	13	15	3	31	5	–	3,006
Pastoral Centers	–	1	–	1	6	–	1,259
New Parishes	–	–	–	1	1	–	37
Catholic Hospitals	1	1	1	13	11	3	601
Patients Assisted Annually	169,825	129,000	174,000	1,319,209	1,523,477	222,179	65,853,111
Health Care Centers	1	1	–	4	8	–	440
Patients Assisted Annually	120	140	–	513	9,927	–	5,058,274
Specialized Homes	5	7	9	50	21	2	1,359
Total Assisted Annually	988	1,131	25,280	31,326	4,015	417	494,308
Residential Care of Children (Orphanages)	1	1	1	4	8	–	156
Total Assisted Annually	150	125	18	734	1,456	–	74,918
Day Care and Extended Day Care Centers	2	1	6	19	2	–	1,156
Total Assisted Annually	60	102	450	2,474	529	–	96,413
Special Centers for Social Services	4	2	10	62	11	19	2,113
Total Assisted Annually	2,400	3,720	31,000	192,944	17,223	9,008	18,323,523
Diocesan Seminaries	–	–	1	4	2	–	75
Students	–	–	5	174	121	–	3,248
Religious Seminaries	–	1	–	5	2	–	122
Students	–	–	–	–	12	–	1,340
Colleges and Universities	1	1	3	14	4	–	240
Total Students	2,715	1,187	5,537	29,790	19,526	–	692,951
High Schools, Diocesan and Parish	4	4	4	29	18	4	790
Total Students	2,550	1,798	2,695	12,782	6,268	657	374,590
High Schools, Private	–	–	4	23	14	–	557
Total Students	–	–	1,260	10,270	7,778	–	285,993
Elementary Schools, Diocesan and Parish	24	34	21	198	132	18	6,818
Total Students	5,791	7,254	5,707	55,068	40,030	2,921	1,961,899
Elementary Schools, Private	1	–	2	14	6	–	333
Total Students	158	–	593	4,311	1,124	–	91,049
Non–residential Schools for the Disabled	–	1	1	2	–	–	75
Total Students	–	1,200	67	1,267	–	–	17,942
Religious Education High School Students	5,642	6,348	7,400	47,953	7,347	1,342	804,514
Religious Education Elementary Students	33,809	25,164	21,398	205,922	72,206	5,227	3,518,872
Priests Teaching	11	–	5	30	35	–	2,120
Scholastics Teaching	–	–	–	–	–	–	77
Brothers Teaching	4	–	13	52	21	–	1,176
Sisters Teaching	23	47	37	408	154	8	10,025
Lay Teachers	566	503	493	4,296	2,484	207	150,783
Infant Baptisms	5,391	4,286	4,786	43,745	16,907	1,021	1,040,837
Adult Baptisms	114	153	174	919	1,327	174	73,426
Received into Full Communion	132	233	253	968	1,846	267	88,161
First Communions	5,264	4,176	4,764	37,925	16,084	1,357	858,665
Confirmations	4,300	3,038	2,870	25,942	12,508	1,421	607,645
Marriages	2,079	1,464	1,411	13,850	6,007	614	288,593
Deaths	3,950	4,078	3,836	30,711	10,324	964	465,773
Totals Catholics	356,972	291,350	301,660	2,952,304	1,452,100	85,533	61,563,769
Total Population	718,000	800,600	790,700	6,073,700	4,266,650	458,130	270,536,283
Catholic Population Percentage	50	36	38	49	34	19	23

*Indicates Archdioceses.

†Certain Dioceses traverse state lines.

	Grand Rapids MI	Kalamazoo MI	Lansing MI	Marquette MI	Saginaw MI	MICHIGAN TOTAL	1998 U.S. GRAND TOTAL
Cardinals	–	–	–	–	–	1	**10**
Archbishops	–	–	–	–	–	–	**49**
Bishops	3	2	2	2	1	19	**358**
Abbots	–	–	–	–	–	–	**114**
Diocesan Priests	129	57	152	108	119	1,125	**31,657**
Religious Priests	21	10	28	12	15	338	**15,925**
Total Priests in Diocese	150	67	180	120	134	1,463	**47,563**
Newly Ordained Priests	2	1	4	–	1	19	**509**
Total Permanent Deacons	21	17	62	18	17	290	**12,247**
Total Brothers	2	5	9	–	1	116	**6,115**
Total Sisters	300	234	441	67	143	3,342	**85,412**
Number of Parishes	90	46	93	74	110	801	**19,628**
Missions	12	13	1	24	–	55	**3,006**
Pastoral Centers	2	1	2	–	–	11	**1,259**
New Parishes	–	–	1	–	–	2	**37**
Catholic Hospitals	2	3	9	1	1	30	**601**
Patients Assisted Annually	773,842	565,960	644,597	66,670	123,620	3,920,345	**65,853,111**
Health Care Centers	–	–	5	–	1	14	**440**
Patients Assisted Annually	–	–	8,000	–	10,330	28,257	**5,058,274**
Specialized Homes	10	7	2	1	2	45	**1,359**
Total Assisted Annually	802	1,243	250	123	147	6,997	**494,308**
Residential Care of Children (Orphanages)	–	–	3	–	3	14	**156**
Total Assisted Annually	–	–	250	–	96	1,802	**74,918**
Day Care and Extended Day Care Centers	–	2	1	–	7	12	**1,156**
Total Assisted Annually	–	85	150	–	151	915	**96,413**
Special Centers for Social Services	22	4	10	6	5	77	**2,113**
Total Assisted Annually	25,500	27,730	–	1,393	1,246	82,100	**18,323,523**
Diocesan Seminaries	1	–	–	–	–	3	**75**
Students	3	–	–	–	–	124	**3,248**
Religious Seminaries	–	–	–	–	–	2	**122**
Students	–	–	–	–	–	12	**1,340**
Colleges and Universities	1	–	1	–	–	6	**240**
Total Students	2,458	–	2,000	–	–	23,984	**692,951**
High Schools, Diocesan and Parish	4	3	4	–	3	36	**790**
Total Students	1,912	857	2,397	–	935	13,026	**374,590**
High Schools, Private	–	–	–	–	–	14	**557**
Total Students	–	–	–	–	–	7,778	**285,993**
Elementary Schools, Diocesan and Parish	41	21	38	10	31	291	**6,818**
Total Students	8,974	4,474	10,060	1,695	5,744	73,898	**1,961,899**
Elementary Schools, Private	–	–	1	–	–	7	**333**
Total Students	–	–	345	–	–	1,469	**91,049**
Non–residential Schools for the Disabled	–	–	–	–	–	–	**75**
Total Students	–	–	–	–	–	–	**17,942**
Religious Education High School Students	2,346	1,227	3,027	3,279	3,191	21,759	**804,514**
Religious Education Elementary Students	12,649	6,773	20,469	6,346	11,263	134,933	**3,518,872**
Priests Teaching	–	–	8	–	1	44	**2,120**
Scholastics Teaching	–	–	–	–	–	–	**77**
Brothers Teaching	1	–	1	–	–	23	**1,176**
Sisters Teaching	27	10	16	8	22	245	**10,025**
Lay Teachers	654	319	641	108	329	4,742	**150,783**
Infant Baptisms	3,188	1,587	596	1,071	2,245	26,615	**1,040,837**
Adult Baptisms	350	307	110	52	276	2,596	**73,426**
Received into Full Communion	–	252	1,061	159	301	3,886	**88,161**
First Communions	3,138	1,543	4,449	1,079	2,194	29,844	**858,665**
Confirmations	2,406	1,330	3,559	1,060	4,650	26,934	**607,645**
Marriages	1,133	542	1,741	459	961	11,457	**288,593**
Deaths	1,443	869	224	1,232	1,514	16,570	**465,773**
Totals Catholics	145,021	109,328	210,460	71,706	139,876	2,214,024	**61,563,769**
Total Population	1,167,900	912,044	1,668,243	309,000	685,532	9,467,499	**270,536,283**
Catholic Population Percentage	12	12	13	23	20	23	**23**

Archdioceses = 36; Dioceses = 164; Apostolates = 3

1998 GENERAL SUMMARY

	*St. Paul and Minneapolis MN	Crookston MN	Duluth MN	New Ulm MN	St. Cloud MN	Winona MN	1998 U.S. GRAND TOTAL
Cardinals	–	–	–	–	–	–	10
Archbishops	2	–	–	–	–	–	49
Bishops	3	1	1	1	2	1	358
Abbots	–	–	–	–	2	–	114
Diocesan Priests	350	47	81	93	143	129	31,657
Religious Priests	148	6	16	1	113	13	15,925
Total Priests in Diocese	498	53	97	94	256	142	47,563
Newly Ordained Priests	7	–	1	–	1	1	509
Total Permanent Deacons	170	8	22	3	35	3	12,247
Total Brothers	55	2	1	–	71	22	6,115
Total Sisters	1,093	182	179	91	562	496	85,412
Number of Parishes	222	73	94	80	141	118	19,628
Missions	5	–	3	2	–	1	3,006
Pastoral Centers	4	1	–	–	–	2	1,259
New Parishes	–	–	–	–	–	–	37
Catholic Hospitals	3	3	2	1	4	2	601
Patients Assisted Annually	141,444	53,505	158,000	7,750	164,957	62,617	65,853,111
Health Care Centers	–	–	2	2	–	1	440
Patients Assisted Annually	–	–	1,500	7,435	–	4,622	5,058,274
Specialized Homes	8	4	2	6	15	10	1,359
Total Assisted Annually	693	317	305	460	1,438	916	494,308
Residential Care of Children (Orphanages)	1	–	–	–	1	–	156
Total Assisted Annually	4,000	–	–	–	104	–	74,918
Day Care and Extended Day Care Centers	–	1	–	–	2	3	1,156
Total Assisted Annually	–	53	–	–	28	7,845	96,413
Special Centers for Social Services	5	–	–	–	8	5	2,113
Total Assisted Annually	–	–	–	–	34,412	10,283	18,323,523
Diocesan Seminaries	2	–	–	–	–	1	75
Students	263	–	–	–	–	32	3,248
Religious Seminaries	–	–	–	–	1	–	122
Students	–	–	–	–	1	–	1,340
Colleges and Universities	3	–	1	–	2	1	240
Total Students	15,288	–	1,749	–	3,803	1,462	692,951
High Schools, Diocesan and Parish	7	1	–	3	1	4	790
Total Students	4,498	148	–	554	579	1,195	374,590
High Schools, Private	4	–	–	–	1	–	557
Total Students	2,380	–	–	–	216	–	285,993
Elementary Schools, Diocesan and Parish	88	8	13	19	33	28	6,818
Total Students	27,375	1,188	1,938	3,049	6,193	5,429	1,961,899
Elementary Schools, Private	1	1	–	–	–	–	333
Total Students	261	80	–	–	–	–	91,049
Non–residential Schools for the Disabled	–	–	–	–	1	–	75
Total Students	–	–	–	–	25	–	17,942
Religious Education High School Students	21,618	2,458	4,605	3,883	8,890	5,339	804,514
Religious Education Elementary Students	64,230	3,523	5,385	8,807	16,263	12,209	3,518,872
Priests Teaching	2	–	1	1	24	11	2,120
Scholastics Teaching	–	–	–	–	–	–	77
Brothers Teaching	11	–	–	–	5	–	1,176
Sisters Teaching	91	6	2	11	29	22	10,025
Lay Teachers	2,375	87	161	211	567	322	150,783
Infant Baptisms	11,606	755	1,190	1,124	2,521	1,890	1,040,837
Adult Baptisms	416	20	52	66	81	83	73,426
Received into Full Communion	1,267	96	228	103	222	254	88,161
First Communions	11,725	651	1,269	1,282	2,816	2,189	858,665
Confirmations	7,413	750	1,241	1,269	2,838	2,029	607,645
Marriages	3,771	262	563	471	1,130	816	288,593
Deaths	4,865	606	1,468	736	1,436	1,129	465,773
Totals Catholics	747,660	42,807	81,878	73,202	145,702	148,445	61,563,769
Total Population	2,720,413	236,100	416,781	283,229	470,105	528,303	270,536,283
Catholic Population Percentage	27	18	20	26	31	28	23

*Indicates Archdioceses.

†Certain Dioceses traverse state lines.

1998 GENERAL SUMMARY

	MINNESOTA TOTAL	Biloxi MS	Jackson MS	MISSISSIPPI TOTAL	*St. Louis MO	Jefferson City MO	1998 U.S. GRAND TOTAL
Cardinals	–	–	–	–	1	–	10
Archbishops	2	–	–	–	1	–	49
Bishops	9	1	1	2	5	2	358
Abbots	2	–	–	–	2	–	114
Diocesan Priests	843	58	70	128	476	115	31,657
Religious Priests	297	27	30	57	373	8	15,925
Total Priests in Diocese	1,140	85	100	185	849	123	47,563
Newly Ordained Priests	10	2	–	2	10	1	509
Total Permanent Deacons	241	21	11	32	209	60	12,247
Total Brothers	151	34	9	43	179	7	6,115
Total Sisters	2,603	38	287	325	2,230	101	85,412
Number of Parishes	728	44	74	118	227	95	19,628
Missions	11	14	28	42	8	15	3,006
Pastoral Centers	7	–	3	3	–	–	1,259
New Parishes	–	–	–	–	–	–	37
Catholic Hospitals	15	–	1	1	12	1	601
Patients Assisted Annually	588,273	–	68,195	68,195	1,278,393	117,463	65,853,111
Health Care Centers	5	–	1	1	–	15	440
Patients Assisted Annually	13,557	–	7,655	7,655	–	151,155	5,058,274
Specialized Homes	45	7	6	13	31	2	1,359
Total Assisted Annually	4,129	636	2,225	2,861	34,784	210	494,308
Residential Care of Children (Orphanages)	2	–	2	2	10	–	156
Total Assisted Annually	4,104	–	168	168	2,771	–	74,918
Day Care and Extended Day Care Centers	6	–	2	2	16	9	1,156
Total Assisted Annually	7,926	–	200	200	1,348	1,062	96,413
Special Centers for Social Services	18	6	2	8	24	–	2,113
Total Assisted Annually	44,695	101,377	8,050	109,427	275,292	–	18,323,523
Diocesan Seminaries	3	–	–	–	2	1	75
Students	295	–	–	–	75	24	3,248
Religious Seminaries	1	–	–	–	5	–	122
Students	1	–	–	–	36	–	1,340
Colleges and Universities	7	–	1	1	2	–	240
Total Students	22,302	–	21	21	13,902	–	692,951
High Schools, Diocesan and Parish	16	4	4	8	14	2	790
Total Students	6,974	1,232	792	2,024	6,638	985	374,590
High Schools, Private	5	1	–	1	15	–	557
Total Students	2,596	548	–	548	8,846	–	285,993
Elementary Schools, Diocesan and Parish	189	14	16	30	147	37	6,818
Total Students	45,172	3,226	3,200	6,426	41,260	6,199	1,961,899
Elementary Schools, Private	2	–	–	–	6	–	333
Total Students	341	–	–	–	2,334	–	91,049
Non–residential Schools for the Disabled	1	–	–	–	8	–	75
Total Students	25	–	–	–	220	–	17,942
Religious Education High School Students	46,793	2,174	1,328	3,502	511	2,733	804,514
Religious Education Elementary Students	110,417	4,294	4,543	8,837	22,374	4,984	3,518,872
Priests Teaching	39	–	2	2	40	6	2,120
Scholastics Teaching	–	–	–	–	3	–	77
Brothers Teaching	16	7	1	8	17	5	1,176
Sisters Teaching	161	19	22	41	197	25	10,025
Lay Teachers	3,723	325	313	638	3,484	438	150,783
Infant Baptisms	19,086	794	757	1,551	7,546	1,392	1,040,837
Adult Baptisms	718	406	167	573	939	219	73,426
Received into Full Communion	2,170	216	311	527	726	284	88,161
First Communions	19,932	1,214	740	1,954	7,938	1,488	858,665
Confirmations	15,540	631	474	1,105	7,239	1,407	607,645
Marriages	7,013	428	326	754	4,064	646	288,593
Deaths	10,240	655	459	1,114	4,236	747	465,773
Totals Catholics	1,239,694	65,524	44,340	109,864	573,000	81,122	61,563,769
Total Population	4,654,931	715,740	1,980,025	2,695,765	2,072,868	861,940	270,536,283
Catholic Population Percentage	27	9	2	4	28	9	23

Archdioceses = 36; Dioceses = 164; Apostolates = 3

1998 GENERAL SUMMARY

	Kansas City-St. Joseph MO	Springfield-Cape Girardeau MO	MISSOURI TOTAL	Great Falls-Billings MT	Helena MT	MONTANA TOTAL	1998 U.S. GRAND TOTAL
Cardinals	–	–	1	–	–	–	10
Archbishops	–	–	1	–	–	–	49
Bishops	2	1	10	2	–	2	358
Abbots	2	3	7	1	–	1	114
Diocesan Priests	131	76	798	77	89	166	31,657
Religious Priests	100	67	548	14	9	23	15,925
Total Priests in Diocese	231	143	1,346	91	98	189	47,563
Newly Ordained Priests	3	2	16	1	2	3	509
Total Permanent Deacons	60	5	334	3	27	30	12,247
Total Brothers	36	83	305	–	2	2	6,115
Total Sisters	327	133	2,791	79	63	142	85,412
Number of Parishes	83	68	473	54	58	112	19,628
Missions	14	21	58	72	39	111	3,006
Pastoral Centers	–	–	–	–	14	14	1,259
New Parishes	–	–	–	–	–	–	37
Catholic Hospitals	3	5	21	2	3	5	601
Patients Assisted Annually	244,243	278,162	1,918,261	24,906	181,351	206,257	65,853,111
Health Care Centers	–	–	15	1	–	1	440
Patients Assisted Annually	–	–	151,155	18,400	–	18,400	5,058,274
Specialized Homes	14	2	49	–	–	–	1,359
Total Assisted Annually	1,232	356	36,582	–	–	–	494,308
Residential Care of Children (Orphanages)	–	–	10	–	–	–	156
Total Assisted Annually	–	–	2,771	–	–	–	74,918
Day Care and Extended Day Care Centers	14	1	40	8	2	10	1,156
Total Assisted Annually	303	50	2,763	476	150	626	96,413
Special Centers for Social Services	–	1	25	3	–	3	2,113
Total Assisted Annually	–	1,833	277,125	81,200	–	81,200	18,323,523
Diocesan Seminaries	–	–	3	–	1	1	75
Students	–	–	99	–	8	8	3,248
Religious Seminaries	1	2	8	–	–	–	122
Students	21	26	83	–	–	–	1,340
Colleges and Universities	2	–	4	1	1	2	240
Total Students	4,112	–	18,014	1,253	1,180	2,433	692,951
High Schools, Diocesan and Parish	5	3	24	1	2	3	790
Total Students	1,506	815	9,944	391	403	794	374,590
High Schools, Private	3	–	18	1	–	1	557
Total Students	1,669	–	10,515	154	–	154	285,993
Elementary Schools, Diocesan and Parish	33	23	240	8	4	12	6,818
Total Students	9,077	3,862	60,398	1,646	852	2,498	1,961,899
Elementary Schools, Private	1	–	7	3	–	3	333
Total Students	298	–	2,632	476	–	476	91,049
Non-residential Schools for the Disabled	–	–	8	–	–	–	75
Total Students	–	–	220	–	–	–	17,942
Religious Education High School Students	930	1,571	5,745	2,575	1,533	4,108	804,514
Religious Education Elementary Students	8,977	3,836	40,171	4,906	5,948	10,854	3,518,872
Priests Teaching	4	1	51	2	10	12	2,120
Scholastics Teaching	–	–	3	–	–	–	77
Brothers Teaching	2	–	24	–	–	–	1,176
Sisters Teaching	20	13	255	6	10	16	10,025
Lay Teachers	807	239	4,968	254	196	450	150,783
Infant Baptisms	2,437	694	12,069	872	952	1,824	1,040,837
Adult Baptisms	549	443	2,150	116	248	364	73,426
Received into Full Communion	389	232	1,631	187	115	302	88,161
First Communions	2,518	1,231	13,175	946	1,118	2,064	858,665
Confirmations	1,692	956	11,294	879	814	1,693	607,645
Marriages	982	400	6,092	351	353	704	288,593
Deaths	1,348	551	6,882	973	882	1,855	465,773
Totals Catholics	161,043	56,968	872,133	57,165	66,500	123,665	61,563,769
Total Population	1,299,555	1,050,206	5,284,569	392,900	424,372	817,272	270,536,283
Catholic Population Percentage	12	5	17	15	16	15	23

*Indicates Archdioceses.
†Certain Dioceses traverse state lines.

1998 GENERAL SUMMARY

	Chalan Kanoa MP	*Omaha NE	Grand Island NE	Lincoln NE	NEBRASKA TOTAL	Las Vegas NV	1998 U.S. GRAND TOTAL
Cardinals	–	–	–	–	–	–	10
Archbishops	–	2	–	–	2	–	49
Bishops	1	2	2	1	5	1	358
Abbots	–	2	–	–	2	–	114
Diocesan Priests	6	231	80	144	455	45	31,657
Religious Priests	1	132	1	11	144	19	15,925
Total Priests in Diocese	7	363	81	155	599	64	47,563
Newly Ordained Priests	–	7	–	7	14	–	509
Total Permanent Deacons	3	131	–	–	131	8	12,247
Total Brothers	–	26	–	11	37	6	6,115
Total Sisters	35	343	98	113	554	51	85,412
Number of Parishes	9	141	43	134	318	22	19,628
Missions	2	18	40	1	59	7	3,006
Pastoral Centers	–	–	–	–	–	–	1,259
New Parishes	1	–	–	–	–	–	37
Catholic Hospitals	–	4	–	3	7	1	601
Patients Assisted Annually	–	268,064	–	211,112	479,176	89,420	65,853,111
Health Care Centers	–	1	2	–	3	–	440
Patients Assisted Annually	–	220	136,368	–	136,588	–	5,058,274
Specialized Homes	–	5	1	3	9	–	1,359
Total Assisted Annually	–	361	69	244	674	–	494,308
Residential Care of Children (Orphanages)	–	–	–	–	–	–	156
Total Assisted Annually	–	–	–	–	–	–	74,918
Day Care and Extended Day Care Centers	–	5	–	–	5	–	1,156
Total Assisted Annually	–	–	–	–	–	–	96,413
Special Centers for Social Services	1	13	–	4	17	10	2,113
Total Assisted Annually	664	121,703	–	50,002	171,705	758,785	18,323,523
Diocesan Seminaries	–	–	–	1	1	–	75
Students	–	–	–	–	–	–	3,248
Religious Seminaries	–	1	–	–	1	–	122
Students	–	11	–	–	11	–	1,340
Colleges and Universities	–	2	–	–	2	–	240
Total Students	–	7,361	–	–	7,361	–	692,951
High Schools, Diocesan and Parish	1	12	4	6	22	1	790
Total Students	721	3,534	1,086	1,727	6,347	1,098	374,590
High Schools, Private	–	6	–	–	6	–	557
Total Students	–	2,704	–	–	2,704	–	285,993
Elementary Schools, Diocesan and Parish	2	60	7	24	91	6	6,818
Total Students	292	15,900	716	5,364	21,980	2,287	1,961,899
Elementary Schools, Private	–	3	–	–	3	–	333
Total Students	–	301	–	–	301	–	91,049
Non–residential Schools for the Disabled	–	1	–	1	2	–	75
Total Students	–	55	–	16	71	–	17,942
Religious Education High School Students	583	3,905	2,421	2,253	8,579	1,787	804,514
Religious Education Elementary Students	1,583	15,503	5,481	6,296	27,280	7,755	3,518,872
Priests Teaching	2	23	–	46	69	2	2,120
Scholastics Teaching	–	–	–	–	–	–	77
Brothers Teaching	–	4	–	–	4	3	1,176
Sisters Teaching	5	41	2	56	99	3	10,025
Lay Teachers	42	1,300	73	426	1,799	141	150,783
Infant Baptisms	586	4,447	1,152	1,448	7,047	4,503	1,040,837
Adult Baptisms	–	223	111	168	502	271	73,426
Received into Full Communion	–	545	143	174	862	243	88,161
First Communions	83	4,373	1,235	1,497	7,105	2,752	858,665
Confirmations	37	3,444	833	2,243	6,520	984	607,645
Marriages	33	1,466	378	440	2,284	837	288,593
Deaths	139	1,889	520	633	3,042	641	465,773
Totals Catholics	47,322	214,523	56,523	87,198	358,244	377,000	61,563,769
Total Population	56,189	818,677	290,429	516,662	1,625,768	1,300,000	270,536,283
Catholic Population Percentage	84	26	19	17	22	29	23

Archdioceses = 36; Dioceses = 164; Apostolates = 3

1998 GENERAL SUMMARY

	Reno NV	NEVADA TOTAL	Manchester NH	*Newark NJ	Camden NJ	Metuchen NJ	1998 U.S. GRAND TOTAL
Cardinals	–	–	–	–	–	–	**10**
Archbishops	–	–	–	2	–	–	**49**
Bishops	1	2	3	6	2	2	**358**
Abbots	–	–	2	1	–	–	**114**
Diocesan Priests	22	67	251	764	322	210	**31,657**
Religious Priests	13	32	78	250	48	46	**15,925**
Total Priests in Diocese	35	99	329	1,014	370	256	**47,563**
Newly Ordained Priests	–	–	4	14	3	3	**509**
Total Permanent Deacons	8	16	23	228	125	103	**12,247**
Total Brothers	4	10	46	124	15	23	**6,115**
Total Sisters	33	84	765	1,757	375	492	**85,412**
Number of Parishes	28	50	131	233	125	108	**19,628**
Missions	8	15	38	–	7	–	**3,006**
Pastoral Centers	–	–	–	172	24	–	**1,259**
New Parishes	–	–	–	1	–	–	**37**
Catholic Hospitals	1	2	2	7	1	1	**601**
Patients Assisted Annually	142,566	231,986	15,182	866,365	228,155	172,380	**65,853,111**
Health Care Centers	3	3	–	90	4	2	**440**
Patients Assisted Annually	9,539	9,539	–	24,665	11,164	2,500	**5,058,274**
Specialized Homes	–	–	6	11	6	7	**1,359**
Total Assisted Annually	–	–	433	665	2,012	492	**494,308**
Residential Care of Children (Orphanages)	–	–	2	–	–	–	**156**
Total Assisted Annually	–	–	62	–	–	–	**74,918**
Day Care and Extended Day Care Centers	1	1	1	126	1	7	**1,156**
Total Assisted Annually	187	187	310	3,000	60	1,859	**96,413**
Special Centers for Social Services	7	17	–	240	12	9	**2,113**
Total Assisted Annually	182,000	940,785	–	125,377	8,731	21,147	**18,323,523**
Diocesan Seminaries	–	–	–	3	–	–	**75**
Students	–	–	–	131	–	–	**3,248**
Religious Seminaries	–	–	–	1	–	–	**122**
Students	–	–	1	20	–	–	**1,340**
Colleges and Universities	–	–	6	4	–	–	**240**
Total Students	–	–	6,439	16,283	–	–	**692,951**
High Schools, Diocesan and Parish	1	2	3	18	8	4	**790**
Total Students	531	1,629	1,569	8,530	4,625	2,622	**374,590**
High Schools, Private	–	–	1	19	3	2	**557**
Total Students	–	–	780	7,343	1,169	1,132	**285,993**
Elementary Schools, Diocesan and Parish	4	10	34	140	61	42	**6,818**
Total Students	1,143	3,430	6,850	43,571	18,157	14,199	**1,961,899**
Elementary Schools, Private	–	–	3	6	–	1	**333**
Total Students	–	–	837	1,632	–	213	**91,049**
Non–residential Schools for the Disabled	–	–	–	5	1	1	**75**
Total Students	–	–	–	265	616	38	**17,942**
Religious Education High School Students	1,141	2,928	5,539	4,571	400	1,208	**804,514**
Religious Education Elementary Students	4,135	11,890	28,591	57,094	33,830	39,058	**3,518,872**
Priests Teaching	–	2	–	133	17	2	**2,120**
Scholastics Teaching	–	–	–	–	–	–	**77**
Brothers Teaching	1	4	6	39	4	9	**1,176**
Sisters Teaching	4	7	58	382	128	83	**10,025**
Lay Teachers	66	207	622	3,773	1,109	899	**150,783**
Infant Baptisms	1,782	6,285	5,169	18,425	6,980	7,311	**1,040,837**
Adult Baptisms	162	433	178	577	571	138	**73,426**
Received into Full Communion	132	375	–	712	432	293	**88,161**
First Communions	1,166	3,918	5,195	14,344	6,840	7,113	**858,665**
Confirmations	573	1,557	3,044	10,643	5,388	5,319	**607,645**
Marriages	260	1,097	1,443	5,505	1,927	1,892	**288,593**
Deaths	322	963	3,180	11,918	–	3,888	**465,773**
Totals Catholics	55,536	432,536	326,870	1,346,185	415,717	483,500	**61,563,769**
Total Population	513,019	1,813,019	1,162,000	2,649,657	1,287,805	1,188,671	**270,536,283**
Catholic Population Percentage	11	24	28	51	32	41	**23**

***Indicates Archdioceses.**

†Certain Dioceses traverse state lines.

	Paterson NJ	Trenton NJ	NEW JERSEY TOTAL	*Santa Fe NM	† Gallup NM	Las Cruces NM	1998 U.S. GRAND TOTAL
Cardinals	–	–	–	–	–	–	**10**
Archbishops	–	–	2	2	–	–	**49**
Bishops	1	2	13	–	1	1	**358**
Abbots	7	–	8	2	–	–	**114**
Diocesan Priests	263	235	1,794	106	58	27	**31,657**
Religious Priests	194	72	610	104	31	50	**15,925**
Total Priests in Diocese	457	307	2,404	210	89	77	**47,563**
Newly Ordained Priests	–	1	21	3	–	–	**509**
Total Permanent Deacons	138	225	819	135	32	26	**12,247**
Total Brothers	42	61	265	89	12	4	**6,115**
Total Sisters	944	487	4,055	287	155	78	**85,412**
Number of Parishes	111	128	705	91	59	44	**19,628**
Missions	–	15	22	216	41	45	**3,006**
Pastoral Centers	5	–	201	4	38	–	**1,259**
New Parishes	–	–	1	–	–	–	**37**
Catholic Hospitals	3	1	13	4	–	–	**601**
Patients Assisted Annually	701,290	143,858	2,112,048	17,508	–	–	**65,853,111**
Health Care Centers	–	1	97	1	–	3	**440**
Patients Assisted Annually	–	3,759	42,088	5,000	–	142,000	**5,058,274**
Specialized Homes	11	14	49	6	3	–	**1,359**
Total Assisted Annually	16,470	13,180	32,819	957	242	–	**494,308**
Residential Care of Children (Orphanages)	2	9	11	–	–	–	**156**
Total Assisted Annually	56	20	76	–	–	–	**74,918**
Day Care and Extended Day Care Centers	20	2	156	2	–	1	**1,156**
Total Assisted Annually	900	246	6,065	1,218	–	40	**96,413**
Special Centers for Social Services	13	13	287	5	4	1	**2,113**
Total Assisted Annually	37,500	23,000	215,755	236,389	22,348	3,000	**18,323,523**
Diocesan Seminaries	–	–	3	1	–	–	**75**
Students	–	–	131	34	–	–	**3,248**
Religious Seminaries	4	–	5	–	–	–	**122**
Students	8	–	28	–	–	–	**1,340**
Colleges and Universities	2	4	10	1	–	–	**240**
Total Students	1,793	2,422	20,498	1,417	–	–	**692,951**
High Schools, Diocesan and Parish	5	8	43	1	–	–	**790**
Total Students	2,424	6,363	24,564	1,003	–	–	**374,590**
High Schools, Private	5	3	32	2	3	–	**557**
Total Students	1,547	1,104	12,295	895	303	–	**285,993**
Elementary Schools, Diocesan and Parish	58	59	360	17	2	4	**6,818**
Total Students	15,946	21,126	112,999	4,515	302	635	**1,961,899**
Elementary Schools, Private	3	2	12	–	8	–	**333**
Total Students	578	462	2,885	–	1,320	–	**91,049**
Non–residential Schools for the Disabled	–	1	8	–	–	–	**75**
Total Students	–	20	939	–	–	–	**17,942**
Religious Education High School Students	9,281	705	16,165	5,712	1,030	2,983	**804,514**
Religious Education Elementary Students	33,290	58,584	221,856	18,387	3,400	8,344	**3,518,872**
Priests Teaching	37	–	189	4	–	–	**2,120**
Scholastics Teaching	–	–	–	–	–	–	**77**
Brothers Teaching	19	–	71	5	–	–	**1,176**
Sisters Teaching	206	–	799	34	22	–	**10,025**
Lay Teachers	1,171	–	6,952	386	102	41	**150,783**
Infant Baptisms	8,815	10,719	52,250	6,599	936	2,612	**1,040,837**
Adult Baptisms	166	414	1,866	268	298	72	**73,426**
Received into Full Communion	319	931	2,687	293	107	66	**88,161**
First Communions	7,500	11,175	46,972	5,508	914	2,346	**858,665**
Confirmations	4,163	9,278	34,791	2,831	667	1,231	**607,645**
Marriages	2,173	5,887	17,384	1,387	211	502	**288,593**
Deaths	3,716	6,437	25,959	2,707	512	946	**465,773**
Totals Catholics	380,293	701,557	3,327,252	271,698	43,824	126,349	**61,563,769**
Total Population	1,055,369	1,763,249	7,944,751	1,036,297	355,640	463,500	**270,536,283**
Catholic Population Percentage	36	40	42	26	12	27	**23**

Archdioceses = 36; Dioceses = 164; Apostolates = 3

1998 GENERAL SUMMARY

	NEW MEXICO TOTAL	*New York NY	Albany NY	Brooklyn NY	Buffalo NY	Ogdensburg NY	1998 U.S. GRAND TOTAL
Cardinals	–	1	–	–	–	–	**10**
Archbishops	2	–	1	–	–	–	**49**
Bishops	2	8	1	5	4	1	**358**
Abbots	2	–	–	–	–	–	**114**
Diocesan Priests	191	895	319	685	448	168	**31,657**
Religious Priests	185	1,021	120	206	199	17	**15,925**
Total Priests in Diocese	376	1,916	439	891	647	185	**47,563**
Newly Ordained Priests	3	8	3	9	6	2	**509**
Total Permanent Deacons	193	310	95	146	88	58	**12,247**
Total Brothers	105	414	90	188	47	12	**6,115**
Total Sisters	520	3,849	957	1,321	1,472	194	**85,412**
Number of Parishes	194	413	187	222	266	123	**19,628**
Missions	302	–	34	–	10	28	**3,006**
Pastoral Centers	42	–	43	–	–	9	**1,259**
New Parishes	–	–	–	–	–	–	**37**
Catholic Hospitals	4	17	4	4	7	–	**601**
Patients Assisted Annually	17,508	1,969,157	600,000	1,033,371	989,424	–	**65,853,111**
Health Care Centers	4	3	15	17	–	2	**440**
Patients Assisted Annually	147,000	157,310	35,000	509,521	–	48,100	**5,058,274**
Specialized Homes	9	22	27	41	19	3	**1,359**
Total Assisted Annually	1,199	21,424	3,100	14,619	2,039	880	**494,308**
Residential Care of Children (Orphanages)	–	14	–	18	–	–	**156**
Total Assisted Annually	–	40,456	–	7,340	–	–	**74,918**
Day Care and Extended Day Care Centers	3	15	7	20	2	1	**1,156**
Total Assisted Annually	1,258	1,744	89	2,100	203	26	**96,413**
Special Centers for Social Services	10	148	22	90	4	8	**2,113**
Total Assisted Annually	261,737	685,800	179,500	71,074	2,756	15,700	**18,323,523**
Diocesan Seminaries	1	2	–	1	2	1	**75**
Students	34	83	–	21	24	23	**3,248**
Religious Seminaries	–	2	–	2	–	–	**122**
Students	–	6	–	16	–	–	**1,340**
Colleges and Universities	1	12	4	3	7	1	**240**
Total Students	1,417	60,700	4,650	18,970	14,765	335	**692,951**
High Schools, Diocesan and Parish	1	25	4	4	–	2	**790**
Total Students	1,003	13,824	1,823	2,013	–	689	**374,590**
High Schools, Private	5	30	3	18	17	–	**557**
Total Students	1,198	14,597	1,192	15,990	6,046	–	**285,993**
Elementary Schools, Diocesan and Parish	23	223	38	155	88	24	**6,818**
Total Students	5,452	76,021	8,939	55,048	22,864	4,427	**1,961,899**
Elementary Schools, Private	8	15	2	3	6	–	**333**
Total Students	1,320	3,913	424	478	1,743	–	**91,049**
Non–residential Schools for the Disabled	–	4	–	1	–	–	**75**
Total Students	–	200	–	103	–	–	**17,942**
Religious Education High School Students	9,725	13,050	10,194	9,850	12,741	3,008	**804,514**
Religious Education Elementary Students	30,131	99,700	33,052	49,250	40,459	9,885	**3,518,872**
Priests Teaching	4	50	8	6	22	2	**2,120**
Scholastics Teaching	–	–	–	–	–	–	**77**
Brothers Teaching	5	49	19	78	6	1	**1,176**
Sisters Teaching	56	260	98	268	140	30	**10,025**
Lay Teachers	529	4,200	861	3,290	1,818	371	**150,783**
Infant Baptisms	10,147	35,883	5,859	22,457	8,140	1,989	**1,040,837**
Adult Baptisms	638	1,038	384	928	219	163	**73,426**
Received into Full Communion	466	541	–	1,165	521	94	**88,161**
First Communions	8,768	26,947	5,774	15,759	8,314	2,090	**858,665**
Confirmations	4,729	19,990	4,059	11,383	6,051	1,701	**607,645**
Marriages	2,100	9,207	2,183	4,683	3,043	764	**288,593**
Deaths	4,165	16,413	5,204	12,018	7,299	1,667	**465,773**
Totals Catholics	441,871	2,347,100	403,403	1,615,117	749,655	139,447	**61,563,769**
Total Population	1,855,437	5,213,513	1,340,388	4,254,609	1,603,544	495,263	**270,536,283**
Catholic Population Percentage	24	45	30	38	47	28	**23**

*Indicates Archdioceses.
†Certain Dioceses traverse state lines.

	Rochester NY	Rockville Centre NY	Syracuse NY	NEW YORK TOTAL	Charlotte NC	Raleigh NC	1998 U.S. GRAND TOTAL
Cardinals	–	–	–	1	–	–	10
Archbishops	–	–	–	1	–	–	49
Bishops	3	4	3	29	2	2	358
Abbots	1	–	–	1	2	–	114
Diocesan Priests	270	449	297	3,531	82	77	31,657
Religious Priests	62	74	44	1,743	55	52	15,925
Total Priests in Diocese	332	523	341	5,274	137	129	47,563
Newly Ordained Priests	1	–	1	30	2	–	509
Total Permanent Deacons	108	197	62	1,064	63	22	12,247
Total Brothers	32	99	18	900	1	7	6,115
Total Sisters	650	1,487	497	10,427	182	83	85,412
Number of Parishes	161	134	175	1,681	66	70	19,628
Missions	19	–	18	109	24	14	3,006
Pastoral Centers	–	–	–	52	4	10	1,259
New Parishes	–	–	–	–	–	–	37
Catholic Hospitals	3	4	3	42	1	1	601
Patients Assisted Annually	720,000	755,760	650,000	6,717,712	69,157	6,000	65,853,111
Health Care Centers	4	–	–	41	8	–	440
Patients Assisted Annually	1,500	–	–	751,431	142,685	–	5,058,274
Specialized Homes	11	7	59	189	3	–	1,359
Total Assisted Annually	2,000	7,478	401	51,941	205	–	494,308
Residential Care of Children (Orphanages)	1	4	–	37	–	–	156
Total Assisted Annually	400	8,499	–	56,695	–	–	74,918
Day Care and Extended Day Care Centers	–	103	1	149	4	6	1,156
Total Assisted Annually	–	4,723	99	8,984	381	705	96,413
Special Centers for Social Services	35	26	8	341	–	10	2,113
Total Assisted Annually	80,000	222,586	56,616	1,314,032	–	47,452	18,323,523
Diocesan Seminaries	1	1	–	8	–	–	75
Students	8	50	–	209	–	–	3,248
Religious Seminaries	–	–	1	5	–	–	122
Students	–	4	13	39	–	–	1,340
Colleges and Universities	–	2	1	30	2	–	240
Total Students	–	4,913	2,915	107,248	902	–	692,951
High Schools, Diocesan and Parish	–	4	5	44	2	1	790
Total Students	–	3,817	2,113	24,279	1,159	575	374,590
High Schools, Private	8	9	1	86	–	–	557
Total Students	3,509	7,134	482	48,950	–	–	285,993
Elementary Schools, Diocesan and Parish	50	63	43	684	15	17	6,818
Total Students	13,360	28,848	10,554	220,061	5,708	4,969	1,961,899
Elementary Schools, Private	5	4	1	36	–	–	333
Total Students	821	1,132	244	8,755	–	–	91,049
Non–residential Schools for the Disabled	1	3	–	9	–	–	75
Total Students	104	295	–	702	–	–	17,942
Religious Education High School Students	3,651	4,140	8,500	65,134	3,936	3,143	804,514
Religious Education Elementary Students	31,464	109,114	39,500	412,424	12,080	13,015	3,518,872
Priests Teaching	18	11	4	121	2	–	2,120
Scholastics Teaching	–	–	–	–	–	–	77
Brothers Teaching	14	60	3	230	–	2	1,176
Sisters Teaching	17	225	86	1,124	7	16	10,025
Lay Teachers	1,256	1,762	900	14,458	372	243	150,783
Infant Baptisms	5,624	21,582	5,691	107,225	2,865	3,211	1,040,837
Adult Baptisms	289	638	309	3,968	298	246	73,426
Received into Full Communion	645	442	646	4,054	452	350	88,161
First Communions	5,321	19,034	5,514	88,753	2,579	2,890	858,665
Confirmations	4,494	16,497	4,081	68,256	1,936	1,347	607,645
Marriages	1,962	7,184	2,263	31,289	770	764	288,593
Deaths	4,258	12,926	4,282	64,067	622	674	465,773
Totals Catholics	370,162	1,372,111	372,665	7,369,660	116,539	133,442	61,563,769
Total Population	1,481,007	2,899,195	1,223,591	18,511,110	3,784,559	3,590,238	270,536,283
Catholic Population Percentage	25	47	30	40	3	4	23

Archdioceses = 36; Dioceses = 164; Apostolates = 3

1998 GENERAL SUMMARY

	NORTH CAROLINA TOTAL	Bismarck ND	Fargo ND	NORTH DAKOTA TOTAL	*Cincinnati OH	Cleveland OH	1998 U.S. GRAND TOTAL
Cardinals	–	–	–	–	–	–	10
Archbishops	–	–	–	–	1	–	49
Bishops	4	1	1	2	1	3	358
Abbots	2	3	–	3	–	1	114
Diocesan Priests	159	68	156	224	352	501	31,657
Religious Priests	107	28	7	35	246	141	15,925
Total Priests in Diocese	266	96	163	259	598	642	47,563
Newly Ordained Priests	2	2	12	14	4	4	509
Total Permanent Deacons	85	54	35	89	126	164	12,247
Total Brothers	8	27	8	35	182	79	6,115
Total Sisters	265	162	153	315	1,439	1,617	85,412
Number of Parishes	136	65	159	224	235	237	19,628
Missions	38	39	–	39	–	1	3,006
Pastoral Centers	14	–	–	–	1	2	1,259
New Parishes	–	–	–	–	–	1	37
Catholic Hospitals	2	6	8	14	11	6	601
Patients Assisted Annually	75,157	283,790	77,712	361,502	162,504	635,704	65,853,111
Health Care Centers	8	–	51	51	2	–	440
Patients Assisted Annually	142,685	–	904	904	284	–	5,058,274
Specialized Homes	3	5	5	10	14	30	1,359
Total Assisted Annually	205	646	485	1,131	1,413	4,532	494,308
Residential Care of Children (Orphanages)	–	–	–	–	4	1	156
Total Assisted Annually	–	–	–	–	660	236	74,918
Day Care and Extended Day Care Centers	10	–	35	35	1	7	1,156
Total Assisted Annually	1,086	–	280	280	98	1,259	96,413
Special Centers for Social Services	10	–	2	2	6	21	2,113
Total Assisted Annually	47,452	–	16,071	16,071	95,450	457,521	18,323,523
Diocesan Seminaries	–	–	1	1	1	2	75
Students	–	–	20	20	26	53	3,248
Religious Seminaries	–	–	–	–	–	–	122
Students	–	1	4	5	–	6	1,340
Colleges and Universities	2	1	–	1	4	3	240
Total Students	902	2,016	–	2,016	19,329	6,309	692,951
High Schools, Diocesan and Parish	3	3	1	4	18	7	790
Total Students	1,734	1,230	318	1,548	12,874	4,436	374,590
High Schools, Private	–	–	–	–	4	16	557
Total Students	–	–	–	–	2,842	10,184	285,993
Elementary Schools, Diocesan and Parish	32	14	13	27	110	133	6,818
Total Students	10,677	1,950	2,022	3,972	39,712	49,540	1,961,899
Elementary Schools, Private	–	–	–	–	2	7	333
Total Students	–	–	–	–	1,025	2,469	91,049
Non–residential Schools for the Disabled	–	–	–	–	–	1	75
Total Students	–	–	–	–	–	72	17,942
Religious Education High School Students	7,079	3,094	4,073	7,167	5,678	6,889	804,514
Religious Education Elementary Students	25,095	7,694	7,652	15,346	35,105	45,214	3,518,872
Priests Teaching	2	6	–	6	11	15	2,120
Scholastics Teaching	–	–	–	–	–	–	77
Brothers Teaching	2	1	4	5	26	21	1,176
Sisters Teaching	23	10	9	19	129	233	10,025
Lay Teachers	615	182	174	356	3,231	3,196	150,783
Infant Baptisms	6,076	1,208	1,052	2,260	8,377	11,013	1,040,837
Adult Baptisms	544	98	48	146	1,196	1,057	73,426
Received into Full Communion	802	151	224	375	910	903	88,161
First Communions	5,469	1,435	1,409	2,844	9,399	12,336	858,665
Confirmations	3,283	1,376	1,748	3,124	8,699	9,620	607,645
Marriages	1,534	440	556	996	3,348	4,516	288,593
Deaths	1,296	697	857	1,554	4,709	8,876	465,773
Totals Catholics	249,981	66,956	79,141	146,097	547,000	831,887	61,563,769
Total Population	7,374,797	253,552	391,000	644,552	2,927,300	2,821,580	270,536,283
Catholic Population Percentage	3	26	20	23	19	29	23

*Indicates Archdioceses.

†Certain Dioceses traverse state lines.

1998 GENERAL SUMMARY

	Columbus OH	Steubenville OH	Toledo OH	Youngstown OH	OHIO TOTAL	*Oklahoma City OK	1998 U.S. GRAND TOTAL
Cardinals	–	–	–	–	–	–	10
Archbishops	–	–	–	–	1	2	49
Bishops	2	2	3	3	14	–	358
Abbots	–	–	–	–	1	4	114
Diocesan Priests	199	123	218	200	1,593	93	31,657
Religious Priests	41	26	57	31	542	24	15,925
Total Priests in Diocese	240	149	275	231	2,135	117	47,563
Newly Ordained Priests	1	–	4	1	14	2	509
Total Permanent Deacons	62	5	194	56	607	48	12,247
Total Brothers	8	8	9	23	309	10	6,115
Total Sisters	398	84	772	273	4,583	151	85,412
Number of Parishes	108	75	163	106	924	75	19,628
Missions	6	3	–	2	12	46	3,006
Pastoral Centers	–	–	–	–	3	1	1,259
New Parishes	–	–	–	1	2	–	37
Catholic Hospitals	4	2	8	2	33	6	601
Patients Assisted Annually	907,461	232,712	820,465	384,873	3,143,719	617,440	65,853,111
Health Care Centers	–	–	2	4	8	–	440
Patients Assisted Annually	–	–	424	90,623	91,331	–	5,058,274
Specialized Homes	17	1	3	12	77	5	1,359
Total Assisted Annually	1,510	87	459	1,080	9,081	333	494,308
Residential Care of Children (Orphanages)	–	–	1	–	6	–	156
Total Assisted Annually	–	–	75	–	971	–	74,918
Day Care and Extended Day Care Centers	2	–	–	3	13	2	1,156
Total Assisted Annually	331	–	–	199	1,887	374	96,413
Special Centers for Social Services	13	1	13	7	61	1	2,113
Total Assisted Annually	323,348	5,800	8,200	81,229	971,548	668	18,323,523
Diocesan Seminaries	1	–	–	–	4	–	75
Students	103	–	–	–	182	–	3,248
Religious Seminaries	–	–	–	–	–	–	122
Students	8	–	–	–	14	–	1,340
Colleges and Universities	1	1	2	1	12	1	240
Total Students	1,949	1,997	1,838	1,241	32,663	600	692,951
High Schools, Diocesan and Parish	11	3	10	6	55	1	790
Total Students	4,771	709	3,993	2,849	29,632	706	374,590
High Schools, Private	–	–	4	–	24	1	557
Total Students	–	–	2,884	–	15,910	250	285,993
Elementary Schools, Diocesan and Parish	45	15	84	45	432	18	6,818
Total Students	13,804	2,823	22,197	12,374	140,450	3,540	1,961,899
Elementary Schools, Private	1	–	3	–	13	1	333
Total Students	207	–	525	–	4,226	285	91,049
Non–residential Schools for the Disabled	–	–	–	–	1	–	75
Total Students	–	–	–	–	72	–	17,942
Religious Education High School Students	1,619	887	3,032	3,925	22,030	2,765	804,514
Religious Education Elementary Students	13,835	2,906	16,583	14,339	127,982	8,762	3,518,872
Priests Teaching	4	–	26	5	61	2	2,120
Scholastics Teaching	–	–	–	–	–	–	77
Brothers Teaching	–	–	–	–	47	–	1,176
Sisters Teaching	39	6	107	49	563	12	10,025
Lay Teachers	994	195	1,582	862	10,060	241	150,783
Infant Baptisms	3,995	681	4,479	3,523	32,068	2,174	1,040,837
Adult Baptisms	556	345	–	369	3,523	386	73,426
Received into Full Communion	790	1,026	702	795	5,126	572	88,161
First Communions	4,164	847	4,711	3,723	35,180	1,826	858,665
Confirmations	3,516	1,198	4,127	2,881	30,041	1,188	607,645
Marriages	1,300	389	2,024	1,390	12,967	762	288,593
Deaths	1,732	818	3,037	2,996	22,168	828	465,773
Totals Catholics	218,796	47,122	327,921	257,200	2,229,926	93,262	61,563,769
Total Population	2,297,396	526,097	1,479,041	1,224,766	11,276,180	2,029,229	270,536,283
Catholic Population Percentage	10	9	22	21	20	5	23

Archdioceses = 36; Dioceses = 164; Apostolates = 3

1998 GENERAL SUMMARY

	Tulsa OK	OKLAHOMA TOTAL	*Portland in Oregon OR	Baker OR	OREGON TOTAL	*Philadelphia PA	1998 U.S. GRAND TOTAL
Cardinals	–	–	–	–	–	1	10
Archbishops	–	2	1	–	1	–	49
Bishops	1	1	1	1	2	6	358
Abbots	–	4	3	–	3	1	114
Diocesan Priests	77	170	150	39	189	810	31,657
Religious Priests	20	44	193	8	201	439	15,925
Total Priests in Diocese	97	214	343	47	390	1,249	47,563
Newly Ordained Priests	1	3	3	1	4	10	509
Total Permanent Deacons	47	95	16	5	21	150	12,247
Total Brothers	5	15	84	–	84	137	6,115
Total Sisters	123	274	577	34	611	3,977	85,412
Number of Parishes	58	133	125	35	160	287	19,628
Missions	23	69	26	29	55	9	3,006
Pastoral Centers	6	7	1	–	1	18	1,259
New Parishes	1	1	–	–	–	–	37
Catholic Hospitals	2	8	9	4	13	8	601
Patients Assisted Annually	533,145	1,150,585	1,525,424	231,609	1,757,033	682,720	65,853,111
Health Care Centers	–	–	5	–	5	9	440
Patients Assisted Annually	–	–	1,692	–	1,692	–	5,058,274
Specialized Homes	3	8	11	1	12	22	1,359
Total Assisted Annually	229	562	4,275	130	4,405	8,439	494,308
Residential Care of Children (Orphanages)	–	–	–	–	–	5	156
Total Assisted Annually	–	–	–	–	–	931	74,918
Day Care and Extended Day Care Centers	–	2	4	3	7	12	1,156
Total Assisted Annually	–	374	1,585	270	1,855	521	96,413
Special Centers for Social Services	3	4	14	–	14	13	2,113
Total Assisted Annually	57,604	58,272	937,267	–	937,267	79,396	18,323,523
Diocesan Seminaries	–	–	1	–	1	1	75
Students	–	–	125	–	125	196	3,248
Religious Seminaries	–	–	–	–	–	1	122
Students	–	–	29	–	29	12	1,340
Colleges and Universities	–	1	2	–	2	11	240
Total Students	–	600	5,584	–	5,584	32,400	692,951
High Schools, Diocesan and Parish	1	2	3	–	3	25	790
Total Students	889	1,595	1,591	–	1,591	23,020	374,590
High Schools, Private	1	2	6	–	6	15	557
Total Students	363	613	3,171	–	3,171	6,640	285,993
Elementary Schools, Diocesan and Parish	9	27	41	3	44	221	6,818
Total Students	2,210	5,750	8,990	589	9,579	86,186	1,961,899
Elementary Schools, Private	2	3	1	–	1	21	333
Total Students	1,356	1,641	383	–	383	5,363	91,049
Non–residential Schools for the Disabled	–	–	–	–	–	5	75
Total Students	–	–	–	–	–	405	17,942
Religious Education High School Students	1,776	4,541	2,404	926	3,330	6,240	804,514
Religious Education Elementary Students	5,584	14,346	12,125	2,492	14,617	46,325	3,518,872
Priests Teaching	6	8	51	–	51	181	2,120
Scholastics Teaching	–	–	2	–	2	–	77
Brothers Teaching	4	4	8	–	8	64	1,176
Sisters Teaching	7	19	73	4	77	894	10,025
Lay Teachers	300	541	1,268	42	1,310	8,669	150,783
Infant Baptisms	1,038	3,212	5,092	985	6,077	20,260	1,040,837
Adult Baptisms	201	587	732	146	878	1,151	73,426
Received into Full Communion	321	893	637	142	779	744	88,161
First Communions	1,021	2,847	3,802	766	4,568	14,011	858,665
Confirmations	758	1,946	1,960	348	2,308	12,502	607,645
Marriages	412	1,174	1,301	253	1,554	7,225	288,593
Deaths	469	1,297	1,974	275	2,249	13,200	465,773
Totals Catholics	54,206	147,468	286,741	34,811	321,552	1,421,570	61,563,769
Total Population	1,478,542	3,507,771	2,767,100	413,900	3,181,000	3,723,835	270,536,283
Catholic Population Percentage	4	4	10	8	10	38	23

*Indicates Archdioceses.

†Certain Dioceses traverse state lines.

1998 GENERAL SUMMARY

	Allentown PA	Altoona-Johnstown PA	Erie PA	Greensburg PA	Harrisburg PA	Pittsburgh PA	1998 U.S. GRAND TOTAL
Cardinals	–	–	–	–	–	–	**10**
Archbishops	–	–	–	–	–	–	**49**
Bishops	1	2	2	1	1	4	**358**
Abbots	–	–	–	2	–	–	**114**
Diocesan Priests	247	154	249	156	162	513	**31,657**
Religious Priests	75	61	14	89	34	124	**15,925**
Total Priests in Diocese	322	215	263	245	196	637	**47,563**
Newly Ordained Priests	3	1	3	5	2	3	**509**
Total Permanent Deacons	84	18	4	–	63	22	**12,247**
Total Brothers	11	8	2	43	1	46	**6,115**
Total Sisters	690	155	550	291	564	1,837	**85,412**
Number of Parishes	153	112	127	107	89	218	**19,628**
Missions	12	5	24	–	7	–	**3,006**
Pastoral Centers	–	–	1	–	–	–	**1,259**
New Parishes	–	–	–	–	–	–	**37**
Catholic Hospitals	3	2	1	1	2	5	**601**
Patients Assisted Annually	672,650	219,121	223,178	53,926	335,772	666,923	**65,853,111**
Health Care Centers	1	–	–	–	–	1	**440**
Patients Assisted Annually	1,641	–	–	–	–	35	**5,058,274**
Specialized Homes	14	3	6	2	10	17	**1,359**
Total Assisted Annually	1,521	241	810	58	1,010	3,604	**494,308**
Residential Care of Children (Orphanages)	–	–	–	–	1	4	**156**
Total Assisted Annually	–	–	–	–	86	484	**74,918**
Day Care and Extended Day Care Centers	50	–	1	–	1	98	**1,156**
Total Assisted Annually	1,988	–	173	–	9	610	**96,413**
Special Centers for Social Services	14	2	9	–	6	4	**2,113**
Total Assisted Annually	71,535	57,904	110,067	–	2,801	64,355	**18,323,523**
Diocesan Seminaries	–	–	1	–	–	1	**75**
Students	–	–	15	–	–	11	**3,248**
Religious Seminaries	–	–	–	1	–	–	**122**
Students	–	–	–	15	–	–	**1,340**
Colleges and Universities	2	2	2	2	–	3	**240**
Total Students	3,508	3,953	6,177	2,302	–	13,436	**692,951**
High Schools, Diocesan and Parish	9	3	6	2	7	8	**790**
Total Students	4,140	1,194	1,773	795	3,708	3,700	**374,590**
High Schools, Private	–	–	2	–	1	3	**557**
Total Students	–	–	1,400	–	30	639	**285,993**
Elementary Schools, Diocesan and Parish	55	31	42	27	40	105	**6,818**
Total Students	14,410	5,537	10,521	5,708	10,864	28,435	**1,961,899**
Elementary Schools, Private	–	–	1	4	2	4	**333**
Total Students	–	–	411	302	47	792	**91,049**
Non-residential Schools for the Disabled	3	–	–	–	–	2	**75**
Total Students	126	–	–	–	–	158	**17,942**
Religious Education High School Students	1,732	4,794	7,092	1,314	2,104	6,988	**804,514**
Religious Education Elementary Students	16,546	9,283	12,658	10,824	20,899	49,083	**3,518,872**
Priests Teaching	23	5	31	22	2	7	**2,120**
Scholastics Teaching	–	–	–	–	–	–	**77**
Brothers Teaching	–	2	–	6	–	16	**1,176**
Sisters Teaching	98	19	27	34	99	155	**10,025**
Lay Teachers	905	495	793	311	743	2,027	**150,783**
Infant Baptisms	3,980	1,613	2,497	2,348	3,565	8,951	**1,040,837**
Adult Baptisms	181	139	326	144	297	484	**73,426**
Received into Full Communion	415	173	264	373	551	1,089	**88,161**
First Communions	–	1,885	2,949	2,592	3,816	9,295	**858,665**
Confirmations	3,445	2,443	2,574	2,828	3,432	8,643	**607,645**
Marriages	1,529	845	1,278	1,050	1,268	3,700	**288,593**
Deaths	3,195	1,665	2,643	2,827	2,221	9,465	**465,773**
Totals Catholics	259,729	117,493	230,848	193,098	230,871	754,149	**61,563,769**
Total Population	1,084,189	645,521	878,400	679,144	1,940,954	2,009,092	**270,536,283**
Catholic Population Percentage	24	18	26	28	12	38	**23**

Archdioceses = 36; Dioceses = 164; Apostolates = 3

1998 GENERAL SUMMARY

	Scranton PA	PENN. TOTAL	*San Juan, Puerto Rico	Arecibo, Puerto Rico	Caguas, Puerto Rico	Mayaguez, Puerto Rico	1998 U.S. GRAND TOTAL
Cardinals	–	1	1	–	–	–	10
Archbishops	–	–	1	–	–	–	49
Bishops	2	19	2	2	1	2	358
Abbots	–	3	–	–	1	–	114
Diocesan Priests	355	2,646	154	84	67	41	31,657
Religious Priests	108	944	145	43	53	35	15,925
Total Priests in Diocese	463	3,590	299	127	120	76	47,563
Newly Ordained Priests	2	29	2	4	3	6	509
Total Permanent Deacons	37	378	260	6	63	3	12,247
Total Brothers	9	257	36	7	1	5	6,115
Total Sisters	843	8,907	433	147	130	151	85,412
Number of Parishes	200	1,293	152	59	43	29	19,628
Missions	85	142	–	228	–	–	3,006
Pastoral Centers	25	44	150	1	–	154	1,259
New Parishes	–	–	–	–	–	–	37
Catholic Hospitals	7	29	2	–	–	1	601
Patients Assisted Annually	780,171	3,634,461	19,325	–	–	113,023	65,853,111
Health Care Centers	3	14	2	–	1	–	440
Patients Assisted Annually	98,235	99,911	381	–	100	–	5,058,274
Specialized Homes	16	90	7	5	–	1	1,359
Total Assisted Annually	2,228	17,911	1,014	840	–	150	494,308
Residential Care of Children (Orphanages)	9	19	3	2	–	–	156
Total Assisted Annually	1,176	2,677	110	48	–	–	74,918
Day Care and Extended Day Care Centers	8	170	37	–	–	–	1,156
Total Assisted Annually	313	3,614	1,295	–	–	–	96,413
Special Centers for Social Services	13	61	–	1	–	1	2,113
Total Assisted Annually	168,213	554,271	–	1,411	–	1,450	18,323,523
Diocesan Seminaries	1	4	2	1	1	–	75
Students	25	247	25	2	20	–	3,248
Religious Seminaries	1	3	6	–	–	–	122
Students	54	81	22	–	–	–	1,340
Colleges and Universities	4	26	2	1	–	1	240
Total Students	11,442	73,218	9,620	707	–	1,800	692,951
High Schools, Diocesan and Parish	9	69	20	14	1	3	790
Total Students	3,395	41,725	5,411	2,699	110	760	374,590
High Schools, Private	2	23	30	–	6	4	557
Total Students	747	9,456	6,780	–	2,851	1,170	285,993
Elementary Schools, Diocesan and Parish	50	571	27	14	4	3	6,818
Total Students	17,418	179,079	10,806	4,209	650	982	1,961,899
Elementary Schools, Private	–	32	42	–	13	7	333
Total Students	–	6,915	14,136	–	4,248	2,380	91,049
Non–residential Schools for the Disabled	1	11	–	–	–	–	75
Total Students	15	704	–	–	–	–	17,942
Religious Education High School Students	12,835	43,099	4,902	2,375	4,794	1,288	804,514
Religious Education Elementary Students	31,101	196,719	19,711	14,010	7,288	10,347	3,518,872
Priests Teaching	7	278	34	13	19	5	2,120
Scholastics Teaching	–	–	2	–	4	–	77
Brothers Teaching	–	88	20	5	4	3	1,176
Sisters Teaching	152	1,478	130	43	17	6	10,025
Lay Teachers	971	14,914	2,210	386	365	310	150,783
Infant Baptisms	4,737	47,951	12,642	3,427	7,670	5,063	1,040,837
Adult Baptisms	463	3,185	1,172	202	490	259	73,426
Received into Full Communion	540	4,149	–	23	8,160	134	88,161
First Communions	5,711	40,259	7,716	2,805	5,630	3,051	858,665
Confirmations	7,958	43,825	5,557	2,587	3,350	3,217	607,645
Marriages	2,113	19,008	2,546	701	1,204	1,073	288,593
Deaths	5,489	40,705	–	959	1,680	2,511	465,773
Totals Catholics	351,188	3,558,946	886,994	383,018	515,000	360,000	61,563,769
Total Population	1,054,814	12,015,949	1,233,743	550,678	653,012	491,518	270,536,283
Catholic Population Percentage	33	30	72	70	79	73	23

*Indicates Archdioceses.

†Certain Dioceses traverse state lines.

	Ponce, Puerto Rico	PUERTO RICO TOTAL	Providence RI	Charleston SC	Rapid City SD	Sioux Falls SD	1998 U.S. GRAND TOTAL
Cardinals	–	1	–	–	–	–	**10**
Archbishops	–	1	1	–	–	–	**49**
Bishops	2	9	3	1	–	2	**358**
Abbots	–	1	2	2	–	3	**114**
Diocesan Priests	82	428	316	98	41	119	**31,657**
Religious Priests	56	332	132	33	27	39	**15,925**
Total Priests in Diocese	138	760	448	131	68	158	**47,563**
Newly Ordained Priests	3	18	4	4	2	1	**509**
Total Permanent Deacons	56	388	83	64	26	24	**12,247**
Total Brothers	1	50	124	28	9	22	**6,115**
Total Sisters	225	1,086	769	162	72	449	**85,412**
Number of Parishes	40	323	158	84	63	157	**19,628**
Missions	2	230	8	27	17	–	**3,006**
Pastoral Centers	229	534	18	11	4	–	**1,259**
New Parishes	–	–	–	–	–	–	**37**
Catholic Hospitals	–	3	1	3	–	9	**601**
Patients Assisted Annually	–	132,348	201,000	399,254	–	485,000	**65,853,111**
Health Care Centers	–	3	1	1	–	–	**440**
Patients Assisted Annually	–	481	45	327	–	–	**5,058,274**
Specialized Homes	3	16	15	1	1	11	**1,359**
Total Assisted Annually	329	2,333	1,048	17	1,309	1,645	**494,308**
Residential Care of Children (Orphanages)	–	5	–	–	1	–	**156**
Total Assisted Annually	–	158	–	–	6	–	**74,918**
Day Care and Extended Day Care Centers	–	37	9	–	1	1	**1,156**
Total Assisted Annually	–	1,295	672	–	20	50	**96,413**
Special Centers for Social Services	1	3	11	7	2	5	**2,113**
Total Assisted Annually	3,540	6,401	57,522	102,880	3,170	112,000	**18,323,523**
Diocesan Seminaries	1	5	1	–	–	–	**75**
Students	11	58	2	–	–	–	**3,248**
Religious Seminaries	2	8	–	–	–	–	**122**
Students	9	31	–	–	–	–	**1,340**
Colleges and Universities	1	5	2	–	–	2	**240**
Total Students	10,801	22,928	7,781	–	–	2,350	**692,951**
High Schools, Diocesan and Parish	20	58	4	2	1	3	**790**
Total Students	3,393	12,373	1,923	1,291	265	986	**374,590**
High Schools, Private	–	40	8	–	1	–	**557**
Total Students	–	10,801	3,383	–	160	–	**285,993**
Elementary Schools, Diocesan and Parish	22	70	46	25	1	23	**6,818**
Total Students	6,244	22,891	11,735	6,448	555	4,196	**1,961,899**
Elementary Schools, Private	–	62	4	–	1	–	**333**
Total Students	–	20,764	1,419	–	378	–	**91,049**
Non–residential Schools for the Disabled	–	–	–	–	–	–	**75**
Total Students	–	–	–	–	–	–	**17,942**
Religious Education High School Students	–	13,359	11,117	2,057	2,106	7,882	**804,514**
Religious Education Elementary Students	–	51,356	31,383	9,928	4,451	10,811	**3,518,872**
Priests Teaching	14	85	37	2	–	1	**2,120**
Scholastics Teaching	–	6	–	–	–	–	**77**
Brothers Teaching	–	32	43	–	–	–	**1,176**
Sisters Teaching	50	246	110	14	10	12	**10,025**
Lay Teachers	1,040	4,311	1,356	407	121	282	**150,783**
Infant Baptisms	5,282	34,084	7,066	1,991	1,202	1,961	**1,040,837**
Adult Baptisms	3,146	5,269	223	244	47	101	**73,426**
Received into Full Communion	616	8,933	360	392	141	319	**88,161**
First Communions	5,516	24,718	6,624	2,304	906	2,164	**858,665**
Confirmations	5,151	19,862	4,809	1,878	482	1,949	**607,645**
Marriages	1,540	7,064	2,308	669	205	724	**288,593**
Deaths	–	5,150	5,672	783	416	997	**465,773**
Totals Catholics	442,000	2,587,012	632,978	116,726	37,702	121,811	**61,563,769**
Total Population	551,525	3,480,476	996,325	3,699,000	211,591	503,000	**270,536,283**
Catholic Population Percentage	80	74	64	3	18	24	**23**

Archdioceses = 36; Dioceses = 164; Apostolates = 3

1998 GENERAL SUMMARY

	SOUTH DAKOTA TOTAL	Knoxville TN	Memphis TN	Nashville TN	TENNESSEE TOTAL	*San Antonio TX	1998 U.S. GRAND TOTAL
Cardinals	–	–	–	–	–	–	10
Archbishops	–	–	–	–	–	1	49
Bishops	2	1	1	2	4	1	358
Abbots	3	–	–	–	–	–	114
Diocesan Priests	160	44	66	53	163	153	31,657
Religious Priests	66	15	11	20	46	213	15,925
Total Priests in Diocese	226	59	77	73	209	366	47,563
Newly Ordained Priests	3	–	–	2	2	2	509
Total Permanent Deacons	50	23	21	28	72	252	12,247
Total Brothers	31	16	42	2	60	93	6,115
Total Sisters	521	52	107	137	296	980	85,412
Number of Parishes	220	44	49	50	143	144	19,628
Missions	17	2	5	3	10	39	3,006
Pastoral Centers	4	2	1	–	3	2	1,259
New Parishes	–	1	–	–	1	–	37
Catholic Hospitals	9	2	1	1	4	5	601
Patients Assisted Annually	485,000	317,928	25,168	153,760	496,856	170,068	65,853,111
Health Care Centers	–	1	1	–	2	2	440
Patients Assisted Annually	–	103	335	–	438	12,410	5,058,274
Specialized Homes	12	2	9	4	15	13	1,359
Total Assisted Annually	2,954	777	1,640	697	3,114	3,621	494,308
Residential Care of Children (Orphanages)	1	–	1	–	1	2	156
Total Assisted Annually	6	–	236	–	236	90	74,918
Day Care and Extended Day Care Centers	2	–	9	2	11	13	1,156
Total Assisted Annually	70	–	2,224	300	2,524	1,932	96,413
Special Centers for Social Services	7	6	1	6	13	8	2,113
Total Assisted Annually	115,170	27,674	7,046	34,069	68,789	323,161	18,323,523
Diocesan Seminaries	–	–	–	–	–	1	75
Students	–	–	–	–	–	39	3,248
Religious Seminaries	–	–	–	–	–	10	122
Students	–	–	–	–	–	51	1,340
Colleges and Universities	2	–	1	1	2	4	240
Total Students	2,350	–	1,784	385	2,169	11,346	692,951
High Schools, Diocesan and Parish	4	2	4	1	7	2	790
Total Students	1,251	945	1,256	1,000	3,201	738	374,590
High Schools, Private	1	–	2	1	3	7	557
Total Students	160	–	1,132	200	1,332	2,440	285,993
Elementary Schools, Diocesan and Parish	24	8	11	13	32	38	6,818
Total Students	4,751	2,585	3,786	3,436	9,807	11,578	1,961,899
Elementary Schools, Private	1	–	2	2	4	4	333
Total Students	378	–	468	724	1,192	1,631	91,049
Non–residential Schools for the Disabled	–	–	1	–	1	–	75
Total Students	–	–	44	–	44	–	17,942
Religious Education High School Students	9,988	1,142	709	1,675	3,526	12,006	804,514
Religious Education Elementary Students	15,262	3,746	4,577	6,401	14,724	37,440	3,518,872
Priests Teaching	1	3	1	1	5	40	2,120
Scholastics Teaching	–	–	–	–	–	1	77
Brothers Teaching	–	1	10	–	11	32	1,176
Sisters Teaching	22	9	16	44	69	161	10,025
Lay Teachers	403	156	463	391	1,010	1,712	150,783
Infant Baptisms	3,163	786	1,075	1,670	3,531	13,960	1,040,837
Adult Baptisms	148	175	231	204	610	660	73,426
Received into Full Communion	460	284	363	439	1,086	716	88,161
First Communions	3,070	889	1,342	1,331	3,562	9,927	858,665
Confirmations	2,431	665	1,131	1,204	3,000	5,280	607,645
Marriages	929	273	383	446	1,102	2,878	288,593
Deaths	1,413	309	440	456	1,205	4,636	465,773
Totals Catholics	159,513	45,482	59,138	60,405	165,025	663,257	61,563,769
Total Population	714,591	2,012,885	1,426,923	1,803,687	5,243,495	1,869,329	270,536,283
Catholic Population Percentage	22	2	4	3	3	35	23

*Indicates Archdioceses.

†Certain Dioceses traverse state lines.

	Amarillo TX	Austin TX	Beaumont TX	Brownsville TX	Corpus Christi TX	Dallas TX	1998 U.S. GRAND TOTAL
Cardinals	–	–	–	–	–	–	10
Archbishops	–	–	–	–	–	–	49
Bishops	2	1	1	2	2	2	358
Abbots	–	–	–	–	2	1	114
Diocesan Priests	65	125	49	57	112	105	31,657
Religious Priests	6	57	23	47	57	81	15,925
Total Priests in Diocese	71	182	72	104	169	186	47,563
Newly Ordained Priests	1	2	3	1	9	5	509
Total Permanent Deacons	45	101	31	83	67	146	12,247
Total Brothers	1	40	3	16	18	5	6,115
Total Sisters	148	115	61	127	274	160	85,412
Number of Parishes	35	105	44	63	86	65	19,628
Missions	13	30	9	46	59	7	3,006
Pastoral Centers	–	1	2	1	10	–	1,259
New Parishes	–	2	–	–	–	1	37
Catholic Hospitals	1	4	3	–	6	1	601
Patients Assisted Annually	22,300	341,863	373,063	–	405,685	43,303	65,853,111
Health Care Centers	1	3	–	2	–	–	440
Patients Assisted Annually	730	64,000	–	265	–	–	5,058,274
Specialized Homes	3	2	1	3	4	1	1,359
Total Assisted Annually	606	492	12	2,032	1,271	58	494,308
Residential Care of Children (Orphanages)	–	–	–	–	1	–	156
Total Assisted Annually	–	–	–	–	59	–	74,918
Day Care and Extended Day Care Centers	6	4	–	1	3	5	1,156
Total Assisted Annually	493	187	–	81	215	802	96,413
Special Centers for Social Services	4	1	2	4	8	16	2,113
Total Assisted Annually	35,000	210	51,955	28,135	27,141	61,225	18,323,523
Diocesan Seminaries	–	–	–	–	1	1	75
Students	–	–	–	–	1	10	3,248
Religious Seminaries	–	–	–	–	1	–	122
Students	–	–	–	–	4	–	1,340
Colleges and Universities	–	1	–	–	–	1	240
Total Students	–	3,101	–	–	–	2,897	692,951
High Schools, Diocesan and Parish	1	1	1	–	1	3	790
Total Students	134	206	678	–	550	1,269	374,590
High Schools, Private	–	3	–	1	1	4	557
Total Students	–	403	–	669	423	1,844	285,993
Elementary Schools, Diocesan and Parish	8	16	7	6	22	30	6,818
Total Students	1,097	3,507	1,913	2,035	3,456	10,082	1,961,899
Elementary Schools, Private	–	1	–	2	5	3	333
Total Students	–	39	–	552	1,120	700	91,049
Non–residential Schools for the Disabled	–	–	–	–	–	1	75
Total Students	–	–	–	–	–	101	17,942
Religious Education High School Students	1,792	5,559	1,565	7,066	3,983	4,273	804,514
Religious Education Elementary Students	3,708	22,635	6,107	24,725	15,256	29,143	3,518,872
Priests Teaching	–	5	1	–	3	15	2,120
Scholastics Teaching	–	–	–	–	–	1	77
Brothers Teaching	–	–	2	3	–	2	1,176
Sisters Teaching	15	13	23	20	69	25	10,025
Lay Teachers	104	302	198	215	383	860	150,783
Infant Baptisms	1,122	6,710	1,233	5,607	5,497	10,644	1,040,837
Adult Baptisms	114	560	143	2,615	228	711	73,426
Received into Full Communion	147	931	203	486	1,025	656	88,161
First Communions	1,047	5,594	1,415	6,346	5,104	7,489	858,665
Confirmations	1,066	3,368	983	2,468	5,646	4,565	607,645
Marriages	217	1,476	377	1,493	1,245	1,993	288,593
Deaths	305	1,514	792	2,407	2,310	1,210	465,773
Totals Catholics	47,387	234,487	86,598	748,326	362,500	544,441	61,563,769
Total Population	396,914	1,915,392	574,240	923,859	808,146	2,815,732	270,536,283
Catholic Population Percentage	12	12	15	81	45	19	23

Archdioceses = 36; Dioceses = 164; Apostolates = 3

1998 GENERAL SUMMARY

	El Paso TX	Fort Worth TX	Galveston—Houston TX	Lubbock TX	San Angelo TX	Tyler TX	1998 U.S. GRAND TOTAL
Cardinals	–	–	–	–	–	–	10
Archbishops	–	–	–	–	–	–	49
Bishops	1	1	3	1	1	1	358
Abbots	–	–	–	–	–	–	114
Diocesan Priests	92	58	191	34	50	27	31,657
Religious Priests	40	50	225	10	19	22	15,925
Total Priests in Diocese	132	108	416	44	69	49	47,563
Newly Ordained Priests	3	1	3	1	–	2	509
Total Permanent Deacons	15	64	256	47	41	34	12,247
Total Brothers	17	11	19	–	–	2	6,115
Total Sisters	243	113	517	35	43	65	85,412
Number of Parishes	58	87	151	36	49	33	19,628
Missions	22	2	9	24	24	25	3,006
Pastoral Centers	–	–	18	1	–	3	1,259
New Parishes	–	–	1	–	–	3	37
Catholic Hospitals	–	1	4	1	–	4	601
Patients Assisted Annually	–	65,000	307,364	97,399	–	195,697	65,853,111
Health Care Centers	1	1	6	35	–	7	440
Patients Assisted Annually	18,870	1,200	68,946	451,178	–	376,638	5,058,274
Specialized Homes	3	5	7	–	–	–	1,359
Total Assisted Annually	164	506	1,703	–	–	–	494,308
Residential Care of Children (Orphanages)	–	–	3	–	–	–	156
Total Assisted Annually	–	–	166	–	–	–	74,918
Day Care and Extended Day Care Centers	1	1	34	–	–	–	1,156
Total Assisted Annually	73	63	3,184	–	–	–	96,413
Special Centers for Social Services	5	16	10	1	–	1	2,113
Total Assisted Annually	75,600	30,621	446,647	33,000	–	120	18,323,523
Diocesan Seminaries	1	–	1	–	–	–	75
Students	1	–	47	–	–	–	3,248
Religious Seminaries	2	–	5	–	–	–	122
Students	18	–	20	–	–	–	1,340
Colleges and Universities	–	–	1	–	–	–	240
Total Students	–	–	2,506	–	–	–	692,951
High Schools, Diocesan and Parish	1	4	2	1	–	1	790
Total Students	657	1,572	410	92	–	121	374,590
High Schools, Private	2	–	6	–	–	–	557
Total Students	340	–	3,142	–	–	–	285,993
Elementary Schools, Diocesan and Parish	9	15	47	2	3	4	6,818
Total Students	3,410	4,758	12,372	330	843	729	1,961,899
Elementary Schools, Private	3	1	3	–	–	–	333
Total Students	850	232	748	–	–	–	91,049
Non–residential Schools for the Disabled	–	–	–	–	–	–	75
Total Students	–	–	–	–	–	–	17,942
Religious Education High School Students	5,062	5,491	14,603	3,136	4,462	1,320	804,514
Religious Education Elementary Students	12,686	17,983	62,835	6,082	8,808	4,496	3,518,872
Priests Teaching	9	2	15	–	–	–	2,120
Scholastics Teaching	–	–	–	–	–	–	77
Brothers Teaching	9	8	3	–	–	1	1,176
Sisters Teaching	33	20	58	–	4	5	10,025
Lay Teachers	283	636	1,263	34	53	67	150,783
Infant Baptisms	8,473	4,891	17,053	1,526	1,966	1,433	1,040,837
Adult Baptisms	127	461	1,285	195	142	239	73,426
Received into Full Communion	256	649	955	91	139	271	88,161
First Communions	5,433	4,080	14,793	1,168	1,964	1,411	858,665
Confirmations	3,642	2,290	7,078	947	1,667	712	607,645
Marriages	1,264	1,137	3,791	314	551	264	288,593
Deaths	1,816	982	3,405	395	587	361	465,773
Totals Catholics	591,361	200,461	862,369	53,035	82,500	49,326	61,563,769
Total Population	780,608	2,264,487	4,298,663	451,995	696,093	1,185,155	270,536,283
Catholic Population Percentage	76	9	20	12	12	4	23

*Indicates Archdioceses.

†Certain Dioceses traverse state lines.

	Victoria in Texas TX	TEXAS TOTAL	Salt Lake City UT	Burlington VT	St. Thomas Virgin Islands	Arlington VA	1998 U.S. GRAND TOTAL
Cardinals	–	–	–	–	–	–	10
Archbishops	–	1	–	–	–	–	49
Bishops	1	20	2	1	1	1	358
Abbots	–	3	1	–	–	–	114
Diocesan Priests	56	1,174	55	140	11	142	31,657
Religious Priests	10	860	29	48	6	76	15,925
Total Priests in Diocese	66	2,034	84	188	17	218	47,563
Newly Ordained Priests	–	33	1	–	–	3	509
Total Permanent Deacons	21	1,203	24	38	22	50	12,247
Total Brothers	1	226	14	21	2	16	6,115
Total Sisters	131	3,012	65	254	14	215	85,412
Number of Parishes	50	1,006	43	99	8	62	19,628
Missions	21	330	19	39	2	6	3,006
Pastoral Centers	–	38	–	1	–	–	1,259
New Parishes	–	7	–	–	–	1	37
Catholic Hospitals	–	30	–	–	–	–	601
Patients Assisted Annually	–	2,021,742	–	–	–	–	65,853,111
Health Care Centers	–	58	–	–	–	–	440
Patients Assisted Annually	–	994,237	–	–	–	–	5,058,274
Specialized Homes	1	43	1	4	–	–	1,359
Total Assisted Annually	59	10,524	723	152	–	–	494,308
Residential Care of Children (Orphanages)	–	6	–	1	–	–	156
Total Assisted Annually	–	315	–	30	–	–	74,918
Day Care and Extended Day Care Centers	–	68	7	–	4	–	1,156
Total Assisted Annually	–	7,030	324	–	91	–	96,413
Special Centers for Social Services	–	76	2	1	6	7	2,113
Total Assisted Annually	–	1,112,815	209,274	4,971	754	30,991	18,323,523
Diocesan Seminaries	–	5	–	–	–	–	75
Students	–	98	–	–	–	–	3,248
Religious Seminaries	–	18	–	–	–	–	122
Students	2	95	–	4	–	–	1,340
Colleges and Universities	–	7	–	3	–	2	240
Total Students	–	19,850	–	4,005	–	3,065	692,951
High Schools, Diocesan and Parish	2	20	2	2	2	3	790
Total Students	166	6,593	1,159	734	282	3,393	374,590
High Schools, Private	1	25	–	–	–	1	557
Total Students	425	9,686	–	–	–	150	285,993
Elementary Schools, Diocesan and Parish	12	219	10	9	3	32	6,818
Total Students	2,208	58,318	2,767	1,816	584	12,740	1,961,899
Elementary Schools, Private	1	23	–	2	–	2	333
Total Students	500	6,372	–	560	–	535	91,049
Non–residential Schools for the Disabled	–	1	–	–	–	1	75
Total Students	–	101	–	–	–	56	17,942
Religious Education High School Students	2,991	73,309	1,287	1,118	226	9,235	804,514
Religious Education Elementary Students	7,167	259,071	6,656	5,846	993	16,910	3,518,872
Priests Teaching	–	90	2	1	2	7	2,120
Scholastics Teaching	–	2	–	–	–	1	77
Brothers Teaching	–	60	1	1	1	1	1,176
Sisters Teaching	23	469	5	21	2	69	10,025
Lay Teachers	213	6,323	239	211	58	840	150,783
Infant Baptisms	1,538	81,653	2,213	1,878	412	5,250	1,040,837
Adult Baptisms	80	7,560	359	82	25	1,953	73,426
Received into Full Communion	137	6,662	248	136	22	–	88,161
First Communions	1,619	67,390	1,758	1,942	295	7,702	858,665
Confirmations	1,253	40,965	1,269	1,233	194	4,997	607,645
Marriages	496	17,496	476	749	116	1,811	288,593
Deaths	964	21,684	628	1,662	164	1,382	465,773
Totals Catholics	108,562	4,634,610	94,700	147,624	30,000	326,398	61,563,769
Total Population	255,276	19,235,889	2,200,362	588,654	110,000	2,115,700	270,536,283
Catholic Population Percentage	43	24	4	25	27	15	23

Archdioceses = 36; Dioceses = 164; Apostolates = 3

1998 GENERAL SUMMARY

	Richmond VA	VIRGINIA TOTAL	*Seattle WA	Spokane WA	Yakima WA	WASHINGTON TOTAL	1998 U.S. GRAND TOTAL
Cardinals	–	–	–	–	–	–	10
Archbishops	–	–	2	–	–	2	49
Bishops	1	2	–	2	1	3	358
Abbots	–	–	3	1	–	4	114
Diocesan Priests	168	310	186	85	59	330	31,657
Religious Priests	33	109	141	97	11	249	15,925
Total Priests in Diocese	201	419	327	182	70	579	47,563
Newly Ordained Priests	1	4	3	2	4	9	509
Total Permanent Deacons	24	74	86	45	25	156	12,247
Total Brothers	9	25	33	15	3	51	6,115
Total Sisters	269	484	652	338	53	1,043	85,412
Number of Parishes	139	201	138	78	41	257	19,628
Missions	11	17	30	3	4	37	3,006
Pastoral Centers	5	5	7	1	2	10	1,259
New Parishes	2	3	–	–	–	–	37
Catholic Hospitals	9	9	9	7	3	19	601
Patients Assisted Annually	449,572	449,572	985,981	324,781	315,869	1,626,631	65,853,111
Health Care Centers	1	1	–	2	–	2	440
Patients Assisted Annually	32,359	32,359	–	16,114	–	16,114	5,058,274
Specialized Homes	16	16	19	13	–	32	1,359
Total Assisted Annually	1,590	1,590	972	1,817	–	2,789	494,308
Residential Care of Children (Orphanages)	1	1	1	–	–	1	156
Total Assisted Annually	90	90	48	–	–	48	74,918
Day Care and Extended Day Care Centers	5	5	5	14	2	21	1,156
Total Assisted Annually	615	615	1,854	911	230	2,995	96,413
Special Centers for Social Services	4	11	35	4	6	45	2,113
Total Assisted Annually	10,180	41,171	92,200	16,113	32,376	140,689	18,323,523
Diocesan Seminaries	–	–	–	1	–	1	75
Students	–	–	–	24	–	24	3,248
Religious Seminaries	–	–	–	1	–	1	122
Students	–	–	11	18	–	29	1,340
Colleges and Universities	–	2	2	1	–	3	240
Total Students	–	3,065	7,510	4,370	–	11,880	692,951
High Schools, Diocesan and Parish	5	8	3	1	–	4	790
Total Students	1,819	5,212	2,231	191	–	2,422	374,590
High Schools, Private	4	5	6	1	–	7	557
Total Students	901	1,051	3,042	950	–	3,992	285,993
Elementary Schools, Diocesan and Parish	22	54	53	16	7	76	6,818
Total Students	5,020	17,760	15,689	3,325	1,950	20,964	1,961,899
Elementary Schools, Private	–	2	2	–	–	2	333
Total Students	–	535	670	–	–	670	91,049
Non–residential Schools for the Disabled	–	1	–	–	–	–	75
Total Students	–	56	–	–	–	–	17,942
Religious Education High School Students	5,631	14,866	5,875	1,921	1,802	9,598	804,514
Religious Education Elementary Students	18,862	35,772	28,050	4,692	4,607	37,349	3,518,872
Priests Teaching	4	11	27	18	–	45	2,120
Scholastics Teaching	–	1	–	1	–	1	77
Brothers Teaching	2	3	15	14	–	29	1,176
Sisters Teaching	13	82	25	5	10	40	10,025
Lay Teachers	470	1,310	1,458	86	100	1,644	150,783
Infant Baptisms	3,377	8,627	6,653	1,291	2,963	10,907	1,040,837
Adult Baptisms	600	2,553	1,262	383	119	1,764	73,426
Received into Full Communion	1,028	1,028	769	121	156	1,046	88,161
First Communions	3,439	11,141	5,807	796	1,683	8,286	858,665
Confirmations	1,645	6,642	2,255	392	694	3,341	607,645
Marriages	1,212	3,023	2,074	463	502	3,039	288,593
Deaths	1,476	2,858	2,939	1,793	474	5,206	465,773
Totals Catholics	187,263	513,661	374,800	79,323	67,336	521,459	61,563,769
Total Population	4,706,300	6,822,000	4,277,700	710,789	461,000	5,449,489	270,536,283
Catholic Population Percentage	4	8	9	11	15	10	23

*Indicates Archdioceses.

†Certain Dioceses traverse state lines.

1998 GENERAL SUMMARY

	Wheeling-Charleston WV	*Milwaukee WI	Green Bay WI	La Crosse WI	Madison WI	Superior WI	1998 U.S. GRAND TOTAL
Cardinals	–	–	–	–	–	–	10
Archbishops	–	1	–	–	–	–	49
Bishops	2	2	3	3	2	1	358
Abbots	–	2	4	1	–	–	114
Diocesan Priests	123	474	235	196	156	80	31,657
Religious Priests	58	290	147	24	19	14	15,925
Total Priests in Diocese	181	764	382	220	175	94	47,563
Newly Ordained Priests	1	5	5	–	–	3	509
Total Permanent Deacons	29	154	79	22	1	40	12,247
Total Brothers	9	31	46	8	10	2	6,115
Total Sisters	309	2,235	690	542	402	125	85,412
Number of Parishes	115	274	201	178	137	115	19,628
Missions	29	–	4	–	–	–	3,006
Pastoral Centers	18	21	18	2	–	2	1,259
New Parishes	–	3	–	–	–	–	37
Catholic Hospitals	3	11	7	9	4	5	601
Patients Assisted Annually	293,161	1,912,592	493,106	313,632	241,348	105,263	65,853,111
Health Care Centers	2	1	–	–	2	–	440
Patients Assisted Annually	–	14,000	–	–	306	–	5,058,274
Specialized Homes	5	33	14	15	6	2	1,359
Total Assisted Annually	–	8,783	1,831	7,538	762	350	494,308
Residential Care of Children (Orphanages)	1	–	–	–	–	–	156
Total Assisted Annually	–	–	–	–	–	–	74,918
Day Care and Extended Day Care Centers	–	7	2	1	15	4	1,156
Total Assisted Annually	–	1,132	100	150	688	200	96,413
Special Centers for Social Services	5	45	8	2	7	4	2,113
Total Assisted Annually	–	222,895	218,575	1,000	47,154	4,300	18,323,523
Diocesan Seminaries	–	1	–	1	–	–	75
Students	–	23	–	8	–	–	3,248
Religious Seminaries	–	1	1	–	–	–	122
Students	–	5	4	–	–	–	1,340
Colleges and Universities	1	5	2	1	1	–	240
Total Students	1,556	21,491	5,066	1,637	2,056	–	692,951
High Schools, Diocesan and Parish	7	7	5	7	1	–	790
Total Students	1,718	4,450	1,483	1,897	92	–	374,590
High Schools, Private	1	6	1	–	1	–	557
Total Students	47	3,213	826	–	584	–	285,993
Elementary Schools, Diocesan and Parish	26	143	79	78	44	18	6,818
Total Students	5,248	32,830	13,333	10,600	7,378	3,082	1,961,899
Elementary Schools, Private	2	2	–	–	1	–	333
Total Students	235	92	–	–	253	–	91,049
Non-residential Schools for the Disabled	–	2	–	–	–	–	75
Total Students	–	17	–	–	–	–	17,942
Religious Education High School Students	1,987	14,556	8,961	8,749	11,254	3,932	804,514
Religious Education Elementary Students	6,649	38,445	18,584	17,125	16,108	8,874	3,518,872
Priests Teaching	4	85	1	6	–	–	2,120
Scholastics Teaching	–	–	–	–	–	–	77
Brothers Teaching	–	10	3	–	2	1	1,176
Sisters Teaching	14	181	39	21	32	13	10,025
Lay Teachers	486	2,847	926	594	551	194	150,783
Infant Baptisms	1,283	9,466	4,792	3,129	3,278	1,090	1,040,837
Adult Baptisms	340	510	187	140	439	229	73,426
Received into Full Communion	294	611	474	308	–	146	88,161
First Communions	1,794	9,779	5,304	3,345	3,181	1,483	858,665
Confirmations	1,536	6,046	3,914	3,318	2,580	1,116	607,645
Marriages	664	3,500	2,068	1,425	1,314	535	288,593
Deaths	1,320	6,046	3,296	2,248	1,650	1,266	465,773
Totals Catholics	103,069	680,170	387,868	231,064	258,594	88,575	61,563,769
Total Population	1,793,477	2,080,000	898,050	882,036	876,469	387,290	270,536,283
Catholic Population Percentage	6	33	43	26	30	23	23

Archdioceses = 36; Dioceses = 164; Apostolates = 3

1998 GENERAL SUMMARY

	WISCONSIN TOTAL	†Cheyenne WY	EASTERN RITE *Philadelphia	*Pittsburgh	Armenian	Lady of Deliverance	1998 U.S. GRAND TOTAL
Cardinals	–	–	–	–	–	–	10
Archbishops	1	–	1	1	–	–	49
Bishops	11	1	1	–	2	1	358
Abbots	7	–	–	1	–	–	114
Diocesan Priests	1,141	51	57	65	4	10	31,657
Religious Priests	494	9	5	8	8	1	15,925
Total Priests in Diocese	1,635	60	62	73	12	11	47,563
Newly Ordained Priests	13	–	–	2	–	2	509
Total Permanent Deacons	296	8	5	–	–	4	12,247
Total Brothers	97	1	3	4	–	–	6,115
Total Sisters	3,994	31	85	108	14	–	85,412
Number of Parishes	905	36	77	85	6	6	19,628
Missions	4	42	–	3	–	3	3,006
Pastoral Centers	43	–	–	–	–	–	1,259
New Parishes	3	–	–	–	–	–	37
Catholic Hospitals	36	–	–	–	–	–	601
Patients Assisted Annually	3,065,941	–	–	–	–	–	65,853,111
Health Care Centers	3	–	–	–	–	–	440
Patients Assisted Annually	14,306	–	–	–	–	–	5,058,274
Specialized Homes	70	3	1	3	–	–	1,359
Total Assisted Annually	19,264	194	55	295	–	–	494,308
Residential Care of Children (Orphanages)	–	–	–	–	–	–	156
Total Assisted Annually	–	–	–	–	–	–	74,918
Day Care and Extended Day Care Centers	29	5	2	3	–	–	1,156
Total Assisted Annually	2,270	250	40	83	–	–	96,413
Special Centers for Social Services	66	10	–	–	–	–	2,113
Total Assisted Annually	493,924	10,933	–	–	–	–	18,323,523
Diocesan Seminaries	2	–	1	1	–	–	75
Students	31	–	18	15	–	–	3,248
Religious Seminaries	2	–	–	–	–	–	122
Students	9	–	–	–	–	–	1,340
Colleges and Universities	9	–	1	–	–	–	240
Total Students	30,250	–	693	–	–	–	692,951
High Schools, Diocesan and Parish	20	–	–	–	–	–	790
Total Students	7,922	–	–	–	–	–	374,590
High Schools, Private	8	–	1	–	–	–	557
Total Students	4,623	–	371	–	–	–	285,993
Elementary Schools, Diocesan and Parish	362	7	7	3	4	–	6,818
Total Students	67,223	1,263	1,704	551	1,006	–	1,961,899
Elementary Schools, Private	3	–	–	–	–	–	333
Total Students	345	–	–	–	–	–	91,049
Non–residential Schools for the Disabled	2	–	–	–	–	–	75
Total Students	17	–	–	–	–	–	17,942
Religious Education High School Students	47,452	1,639	426	586	–	150	804,514
Religious Education Elementary Students	99,136	5,853	2,610	2,484	116	250	3,518,872
Priests Teaching	92	2	2	–	2	–	2,120
Scholastics Teaching	–	1	–	–	–	–	77
Brothers Teaching	16	–	–	–	–	–	1,176
Sisters Teaching	286	2	25	9	12	–	10,025
Lay Teachers	5,112	94	300	34	90	–	150,783
Infant Baptisms	21,755	995	315	301	60	60	1,040,837
Adult Baptisms	1,505	168	38	38	–	4	73,426
Received into Full Communion	1,539	286	6	73	–	48	88,161
First Communions	23,092	1,083	367	356	36	64	858,665
Confirmations	16,974	915	353	339	60	64	607,645
Marriages	8,842	315	145	143	25	17	288,593
Deaths	14,506	567	528	903	36	19	465,773
Totals Catholics	1,646,271	48,911	68,024	81,129	26,000	12,070	61,563,769
Total Population	5,123,845	481,400	–	–	–	–	270,536,283
Catholic Population Percentage	32	10	–	–	–	–	23

*Indicates Archdioceses.

†Certain Dioceses traverse state lines.

	EASTERN RITE (Cont.)						
	Lady of Lebanon	Newton	Parma	Passaic	Romanian	St. Josaphat	1998 U.S. GRAND TOTAL
Cardinals	–	–	–	–	–	–	10
Archbishops	–	1	–	–	–	–	49
Bishops	1	2	1	2	2	1	358
Abbots	–	–	–	–	–	–	114
Diocesan Priests	28	43	39	94	17	42	31,657
Religious Priests	7	19	2	7	1	1	15,925
Total Priests in Diocese	35	62	41	101	18	43	47,563
Newly Ordained Priests	1	1	–	1	–	–	509
Total Permanent Deacons	–	27	3	17	2	9	12,247
Total Brothers	8	1	–	4	–	10	6,115
Total Sisters	–	3	14	21	–	10	85,412
Number of Parishes	29	35	38	98	15	37	19,628
Missions	–	6	2	7	3	3	3,006
Pastoral Centers	–	–	–	5	–	–	1,259
New Parishes	1	–	–	–	–	–	37
Catholic Hospitals	–	–	–	–	–	–	601
Patients Assisted Annually	–	–	–	–	–	–	65,853,111
Health Care Centers	–	–	–	–	–	–	440
Patients Assisted Annually	–	–	–	–	–	–	5,058,274
Specialized Homes	–	2	–	–	–	2	1,359
Total Assisted Annually	–	5,500	–	–	–	156	494,308
Residential Care of Children (Orphanages)	–	–	–	–	–	–	156
Total Assisted Annually	–	–	–	–	–	–	74,918
Day Care and Extended Day Care Centers	1	–	1	–	–	–	1,156
Total Assisted Annually	55	–	101	–	–	–	96,413
Special Centers for Social Services	–	1	1	–	–	–	2,113
Total Assisted Annually	–	5,300	7,000	–	–	–	18,323,523
Diocesan Seminaries	–	1	–	–	–	–	75
Students	–	1	–	–	–	–	3,248
Religious Seminaries	–	1	–	–	–	–	122
Students	–	2	–	–	–	–	1,340
Colleges and Universities	–	–	–	–	–	–	240
Total Students	–	–	–	–	–	–	692,951
High Schools, Diocesan and Parish	–	–	–	–	–	–	790
Total Students	–	–	–	–	–	–	374,590
High Schools, Private	–	–	–	–	–	–	557
Total Students	–	–	–	–	–	–	285,993
Elementary Schools, Diocesan and Parish	–	–	2	1	–	2	6,818
Total Students	–	–	349	490	–	274	1,961,899
Elementary Schools, Private	–	–	–	–	–	–	333
Total Students	–	–	–	–	–	–	91,049
Non–residential Schools for the Disabled	–	–	–	–	–	–	75
Total Students	–	–	–	–	–	–	17,942
Religious Education High School Students	–	262	176	365	10	68	804,514
Religious Education Elementary Students	–	1,194	825	1,965	50	194	3,518,872
Priests Teaching	1	–	–	–	–	–	2,120
Scholastics Teaching	–	–	–	–	–	–	77
Brothers Teaching	–	–	–	–	–	–	1,176
Sisters Teaching	–	–	5	8	–	3	10,025
Lay Teachers	–	–	18	20	–	27	150,783
Infant Baptisms	363	456	145	351	29	137	1,040,837
Adult Baptisms	22	22	13	16	2	2	73,426
Received into Full Communion	41	9	34	79	5	–	88,161
First Communions	195	499	155	398	19	71	858,665
Confirmations	241	566	133	333	31	–	607,645
Marriages	143	140	62	148	8	92	288,593
Deaths	170	172	190	580	37	246	465,773
Totals Catholics	23,711	27,800	12,716	59,733	5,300	11,566	61,563,769
Total Population	–	–	–	–	–	–	270,536,283
Catholic Population Percentage	–	–	–	–	–	–	23

Archdioceses = 36; Dioceses = 164; Apostolates = 3

1998 GENERAL SUMMARY

	EASTERN RITE (Cont.)					EASTERN RITE TOTAL	1998 U.S. GRAND TOTAL
	St. Maron	St. Nicholas	St. Thomas	Stamford	Van Nuys		
Cardinals	–	–	–	–	–	–	10
Archbishops	1	–	–	–	–	4	49
Bishops	1	2	1	1	1	19	358
Abbots	1	1	–	–	–	3	114
Diocesan Priests	56	31	19	35	19	559	31,657
Religious Priests	10	13	–	17	4	103	15,925
Total Priests in Diocese	66	44	–	52	23	643	47,563
Newly Ordained Priests	–	1	–	–	1	9	509
Total Permanent Deacons	12	13	–	4	5	101	12,247
Total Brothers	–	10	–	5	4	49	6,115
Total Sisters	8	4	–	42	5	314	85,412
Number of Parishes	33	35	12	49	16	571	19,628
Missions	3	–	–	4	2	36	3,006
Pastoral Centers	–	–	–	2	2	9	1,259
New Parishes	–	–	–	–	–	1	37
Catholic Hospitals	–	–	–	–	–	–	601
Patients Assisted Annually	–	–	–	–	–	–	65,853,111
Health Care Centers	–	–	–	–	–	–	440
Patients Assisted Annually	–	–	–	–	–	–	5,058,274
Specialized Homes	–	–	1	1	–	10	1,359
Total Assisted Annually	–	–	–	28	–	6,034	494,308
Residential Care of Children (Orphanages)	–	–	–	–	–	–	156
Total Assisted Annually	–	–	–	–	–	–	74,918
Day Care and Extended Day Care Centers	–	–	1	1	–	9	1,156
Total Assisted Annually	–	–	–	44	–	323	96,413
Special Centers for Social Services	–	–	–	1	–	3	2,113
Total Assisted Annually	–	–	–	45	–	12,345	18,323,523
Diocesan Seminaries	1	–	–	1	–	5	75
Students	–	–	3	59	–	96	3,248
Religious Seminaries	–	–	–	–	–	1	122
Students	–	–	–	–	–	2	1,340
Colleges and Universities	–	–	–	–	–	1	240
Total Students	–	–	–	–	–	693	692,951
High Schools, Diocesan and Parish	–	1	–	1	–	2	790
Total Students	–	90	–	140	–	230	374,590
High Schools, Private	–	–	–	–	–	1	557
Total Students	–	–	–	–	–	371	285,993
Elementary Schools, Diocesan and Parish	–	2	–	4	–	25	6,818
Total Students	–	433	–	364	–	5,171	1,961,899
Elementary Schools, Private	–	–	–	–	–	–	333
Total Students	–	–	–	–	–	–	91,049
Non–residential Schools for the Disabled	–	–	–	–	–	–	75
Total Students	–	–	–	–	–	–	17,942
Religious Education High School Students	356	20	–	19	101	2,539	804,514
Religious Education Elementary Students	1,197	150	–	720	378	12,133	3,518,872
Priests Teaching	–	–	–	–	–	5	2,120
Scholastics Teaching	–	–	–	–	–	–	77
Brothers Teaching	–	–	–	–	–	–	1,176
Sisters Teaching	–	4	–	7	–	73	10,025
Lay Teachers	–	50	–	28	–	567	150,783
Infant Baptisms	439	101	989	181	84	4,011	1,040,837
Adult Baptisms	11	5	17	9	11	210	73,426
Received into Full Communion	40	–	–	3	21	359	88,161
First Communions	318	101	851	158	112	3,700	858,665
Confirmations	330	117	1,006	171	134	3,878	607,645
Marriages	141	63	390	100	15	1,632	288,593
Deaths	229	160	156	385	25	3,836	465,773
Totals Catholics	29,206	10,186	65,000	16,399	2,905	451,745	61,563,769
Total Population	–	–	–	–	–	–	270,536,283
Catholic Population Percentage	–	–	–	–	–	–	23

*Indicates Archdioceses.

†Certain Dioceses traverse state lines.

1998 GENERAL SUMMARY

	*Military Archdiocese	1988 GRAND TOTALS	1997 GRAND TOTALS	1998 U.S. GRAND TOTAL
Cardinals	–	7	9	**10**
Archbishops	3	47	50	**49**
Bishops	3	342	358	**358**
Abbots	–	112	112	**114**
Diocesan Priests	–	34,791	31,977	**31,657**
Religious Priests	–	18,731	16,120	**15,925**
Total Priests in Diocese	–	53,522	48,097	**47,563**
Newly Ordained Priests	–	461	521	**509**
Total Permanent Deacons	–	8,512	11,788	**12,247**
Total Brothers	–	7,069	6,293	**6,115**
Total Sisters	–	106,912	87,644	**85,412**
Number of Parishes	–	19,596	19,677	**19,628**
Missions	–	3,137	3,051	**3,006**
Pastoral Centers	–	819	1,229	**1,259**
New Parishes	–	41	39	**37**
Catholic Hospitals	–	646	590	**601**
Patients Assisted Annually	–	40,039,956	61,489,163	**65,853,111**
Health Care Centers	–	162	366	**440**
Patients Assisted Annually	–	1,509,143	4,861,384	**5,058,274**
Specialized Homes	–	688	1,252	**1,359**
Total Assisted Annually	–	109,723	946,572	**494,308**
Residential Care of Children (Orphanages)	–	222	178	**156**
Total Assisted Annually	–	75,680	74,324	**74,918**
Day Care and Extended Day Care Centers	–	245	1,110	**1,156**
Total Assisted Annually	–	23,509	126,432	**96,413**
Special Centers for Social Services	–	1,542	2,014	**2,113**
Total Assisted Annually	–	4,979,995	18,262,444	**18,323,523**
Diocesan Seminaries	–	74	77	**75**
Students	–	4,981	3,149	**3,248**
Religious Seminaries	–	176	129	**122**
Students	–	2,531	1,496	**1,340**
Colleges and Universities	–	233	241	**240**
Total Students	–	563,799	690,826	**692,951**
High Schools, Diocesan and Parish	–	840	794	**790**
Total Students	–	424,729	369,281	**374,590**
High Schools, Private	–	551	563	**557**
Total Students	–	283,460	283,406	**285,993**
Elementary Schools, Diocesan and Parish	–	7,387	6,822	**6,818**
Total Students	–	1,933,915	1,960,274	**1,961,899**
Elementary Schools, Private	–	272	343	**333**
Total Students	–	55,551	93,545	**91,049**
Non-residential Schools for the Disabled	–	–	80	**75**
Total Students	–	–	19,198	**17,942**
Religious Education High School Students	21,000	804,775	804,759	**804,514**
Religious Education Elementary Students	44,200	3,044,832	3,445,153	**3,518,872**
Priests Teaching	–	3,483	2,174	**2,120**
Scholastics Teaching	–	140	51	**77**
Brothers Teaching	–	2,139	1,191	**1,176**
Sisters Teaching	12	23,153	11,217	**10,025**
Lay Teachers	220	134,317	152,165	**150,783**
Infant Baptisms	5,896	937,947	1,044,304	**1,040,837**
Adult Baptisms	1,045	81,739	75,645	**73,426**
Received into Full Communion	493	–	85,970	**88,161**
First Communions	3,316	–	846,104	**858,665**
Confirmations	2,385	–	592,399	**607,645**
Marriages	1,281	341,622	300,582	**288,593**
Deaths	–	453,290	472,126	**465,773**
Totals Catholics	1,194,000	53,496,862	61,207,914	**61,563,769**
Total Population	–	240,252,322	268,299,833	**270,536,283**
Catholic Population Percentage	–	22	23	**23**

Archdioceses = 36; Dioceses = 164; Apostolates = 3

1. U.S. Census Bureau estimate of Total Population as of Jan. 1, 1998: 268,921,733
2. U.S. Census Bureau estimate of Total Population as of Jan. 1, 1997: 266,490,000
3. U.S. Census Bureau estimate of Total Population as of Jan. 1, 1988: 244,427,098

CATHOLIC DIOCESAN AND PROVINCE BOUNDARIES
IN THE UNITED STATES

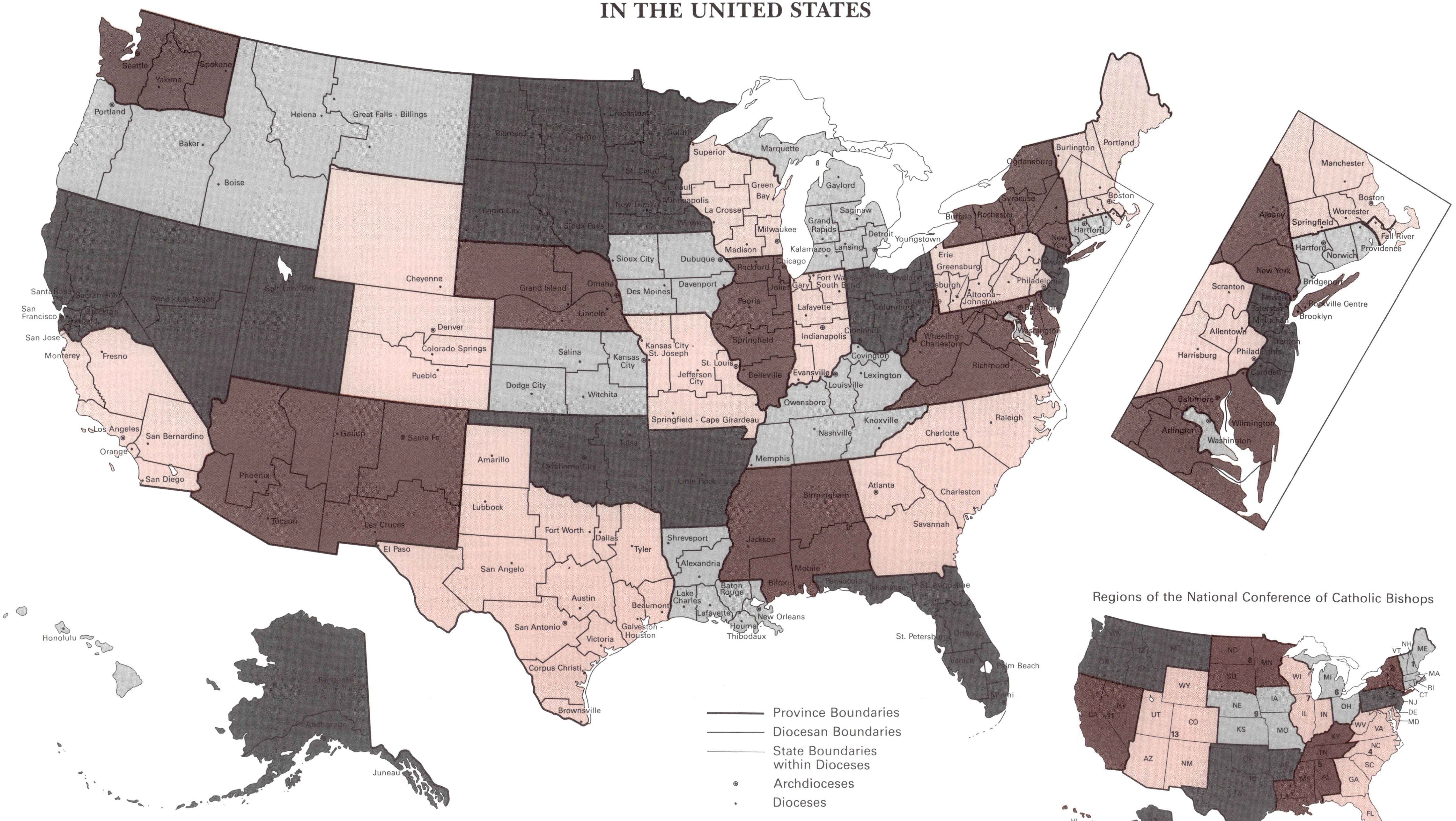

The Official Catholic Directory
P.J. Kenedy & Sons 1998

DUCTS AND SERVICES

THE COPYPRINTER CHURCHES HAVE FAITH IN.

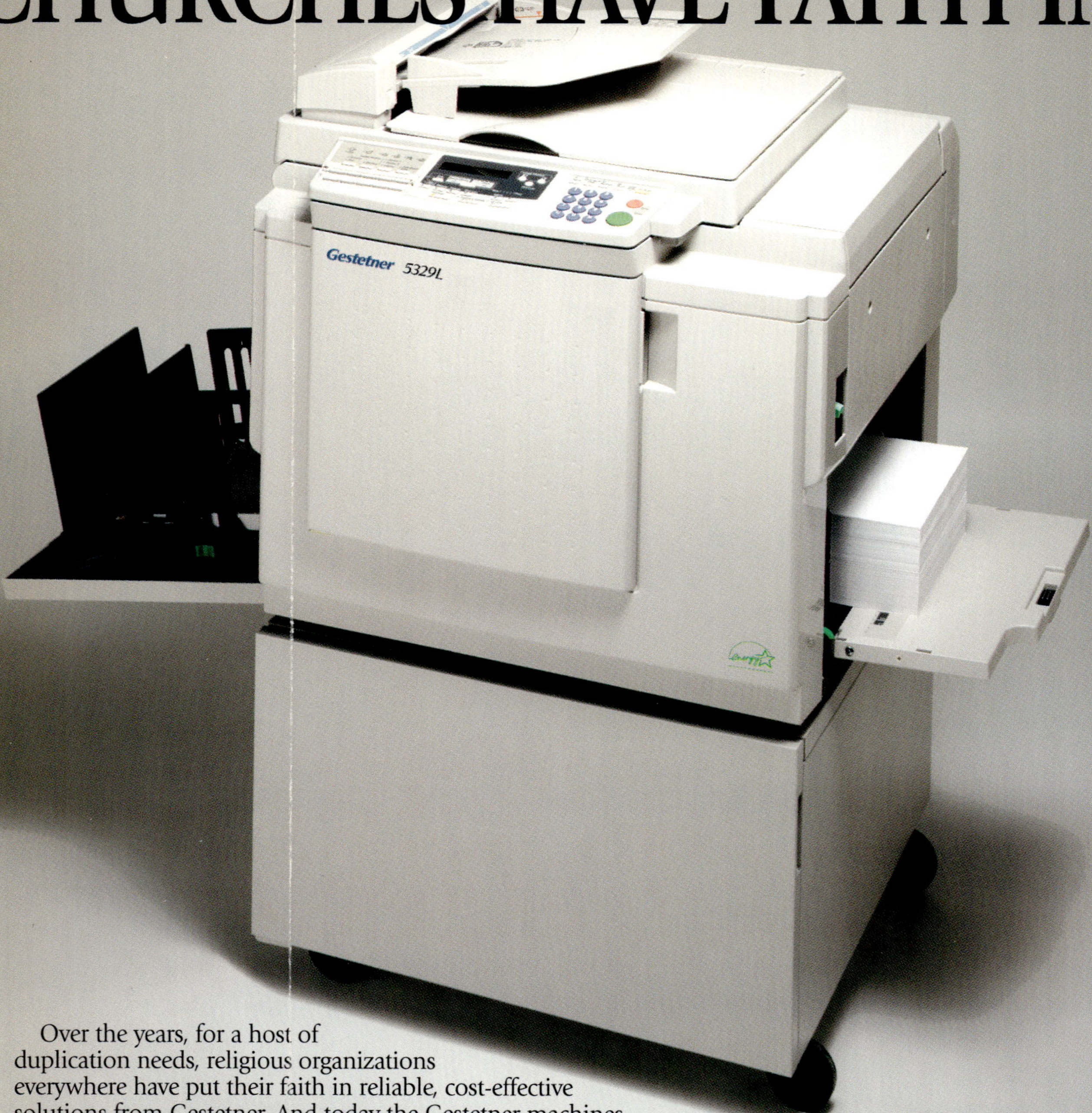

Over the years, for a host of duplication needs, religious organizations everywhere have put their faith in reliable, cost-effective solutions from Gestetner. And today the Gestetner machines more and more churches are placing their faith in are Gestetner CopyPrinters.

After all, every Gestetner CopyPrinter is a fast, efficient digital duplicator that creates crisp, clean multiple prints at speeds of up to 130 pages per minute, for less than a penny a page. And they come with some very heavenly productivity-enhancing options, like an automatic document feeder, the ability to connect to a computer, even the option of printing in up to 11 eye-catching colors.

Just as important, the Gestetner CopyPrinter is a tireless worker. With scheduled Gestetner maintenance required only every 300,000 copies.

For more information about Gestetner CopyPrinters, copiers, fax machines or other digital products you can have faith in, call **1-800-765-7746** or visit our website at www.gestetnerusa.com.

Gestetner

599 W. PUTNAM AVE., PO BOX 2656, GREENWICH, CT 06836-2656

The Official Catholic Directory

Products & Services Guide

1998

P.J. Kenedy & Sons
121 Chanlon Road, New Providence, NJ 07974
(908) 665-3563

THE OFFICIAL CATHOLIC DIRECTORY PRODUCTS & SERVICES GUIDE TABLE OF CONTENTS

AUDIO & VIDEO

AUDIO EQUIPMENT

ALL PRO SOUND

ALL PRO SOUND
806 Beverly Pkwy.
Pensacola, FL 32505
Tel.: 800-925-9822; FAX: 850-432-0844

Personnel:
Richard Couture . . . . Owner
Chuck Walthall . . . . Head Engineer

Type of Business:
All Pro Sound is a full service audio/video company. We specialize in custom design and installation of church, auditorium, stadium and school systems along with a national mail order service. All Pro Sound has over 17 years experience in all facets of the audio industry. We put this experience to use everyday by simply offering the best design, installation, training, and product services available anywhere.

CASSETTES, AUDIO & VIDEO

CATHEDRAL MUSIC PRESS
#4 Industrial Dr.
Pacific, MO 63069-0066
Tel.: 1-800-863-5229; 314-257-3970; FAX: 314-257-5062
Web: http://www.melbay.com; e-mail: email@melbay.com

Personnel:
William Bay . . . . President
L. Dean Bye . . . . General Manager
Michael Entsminger . . . . Marketing Coordinator
Ginny Patterson . . . . Sales

Type of Business:
A leading music publisher specializing in instrumental and instructional material for the church. A complete line of piano, organ, flute, clarinet, trumpet, saxophone, guitar, and other fretted instruments along with beautifully recorded CDs and cassettes are available. Write or phone for our most recent catalog at 1-800-863-5229.

J.S. PALUCH COMPANY

J.S. PALUCH CO., INC.
3825 N. Willow Rd.
Schiller Park, IL 60176
Tel.: 800-621-5197; FAX: 847-671-5715

Personnel:
Liturgy and Music Resources Customer Service 1-800-566-6150
Parish Bulletins; Calendars; Computer Software:1-800-621-5197
. . . . Fax: 847-671-5715

Type of Business:
Serving the Church for over 80 years. Liturgy and Music Resources; Parish Sundays - Laser ComExpress; National Vocations Awareness and Religious Art Calendars; Computer Software for parish management.

INTERCOM SYSTEMS

ALL PRO SOUND

ALL PRO SOUND
806 Beverly Pkwy.
Pensacola, FL 32505
Tel.: 800-925-9822; FAX: 850-432-0844

Personnel:
Richard Couture . . . . Owner
Chuck Walthall . . . . Head Engineer

Type of Business:
All Pro Sound is a full service audio/video company. We specialize in custom design and installation of church, auditorium, stadium and school systems along with a national mail order service. All Pro Sound has over 17 years experience in all facets of the audio industry. We put this experience to use everyday by simply offering the best design, installation, training, and product services available anywhere.

LOUDSPEAKER SYSTEMS

ALL PRO SOUND

ALL PRO SOUND
806 Beverly Pkwy.
Pensacola, FL 32505
Tel.: 800-925-9822; FAX: 850-432-0844

Personnel:
Richard Couture . . . . Owner
Chuck Walthall . . . . Head Engineer

Type of Business:
All Pro Sound is a full service audio/video company. We specialize in custom design and installation of church, auditorium, stadium and school systems along with a national mail order service. All Pro Sound has over 17 years experience in all facets of the audio industry. We put this experience to use everyday by simply offering the best design, installation, training, and product services available anywhere.

PRE-RECORDED CASSETTES & VIDEO

Cathedral MUSIC PRESS

CATHEDRAL MUSIC PRESS
#4 Industrial Dr.
Pacific, MO 63069-0066
Tel.: 1-800-863-5229; 314-257-3970; FAX: 314-257-5062
Web: http://www.melbay.com; e-mail: email@melbay.com

Personnel:
William Bay . . . . President
L. Dean Bye . . . . General Manager
Michael Entsminger . . . . Marketing Coordinator
Ginny Patterson . . . . Sales

Type of Business:
A leading music publisher specializing in instrumental and instructional material for the church. A complete line of piano, organ, flute, clarinet, trumpet, saxophone, guitar, and other fretted instruments along with beautifully recorded CDs and cassettes are available. Write or phone for our most recent catalog at 1-800-863-5229.

RENEWAL MUSIC

RENEWAL MUSIC
1000 Cody Rd.
Mobile, AL 36695
Tel.: 800-223-7333; FAX: 334-633-0882

Type of Business:
Blending texture of liturgy with the wind that is renewing the heart of the Church, Renewal Music's latest project, Behold The Lamb, opens wide timeless doors to reveal an intimate place of worship. Well-known singers and composers Jim Cowan, Don Moen and Steve Merkel take you on a rich journey of worship that exalts the Lamb of God who takes away the sins of the world. Look for more great projects coming from Renewal Music in 1998.

BUSINESS & FINANCE

The Catholic Software Co.

THE CATHOLIC SOFTWARE CO.
3768 Rocky River Dr., Suite 313
Cleveland, OH 44111-4050
Tel.: 800-428-3640; FAX: 216-671-1668

Personnel:
Rob Rhodes . . . . President
Peggy T.

Type of Business:
Offering software management solutions to Catholic parishes since 1991. Easy-to-use Window 95, Windows NT, Windows and Macintosh software products. Network ready at no additional cost! Software products available:

- Census, ministry, contribution & stewardship management
- Pledge campaign management
- Financial management: General Ledger with preloaded diocesan chart of accounts; Accounts Payable; Payroll
- School tuition and religious education management

CELEBRATING OUR 4TH ANNIVERSARY IN WINDOWS!

HARMONY
MEDIA

HARMONY MEDIA INC.
P.O. Box 138
Gervais, OR 97026
Tel.: 503-982-7675; FAX: 503-982-7833

Personnel:

William Van Smoorenburg . . . . President

Type of Business:

Bringing faith and technology together through computer CD-ROMs. This 100% Catholic company creates exciting catholic software for families, seminarians, priests, schools, parishes and all individuals that are interested in their faith. These programs contain hundreds of documents, illustrations and hyperlinks creating awesome collections. The New American Bible, RSV Catholic Edition Bible, Encyclicals, Catechism of the Catholic Church, John Paul II, Butler's, and Vatican II documents are just a few of the topics on CD-ROM!

CERTIFIED PUBLIC ACCOUNTANTS/ MANAGEMENT CONSULTING

CRAIG, FITZSIMMONS & MICHAELS
517 Route 111, Ste. 200
Hauppauge, NY 11788
Tel.: 516-360-1400; FAX: 516-360-7314

Personnel:

Robert R. Craig
Dennis Michaels
David P. Fitzsimmons

Type of Business:

Craig, Fitzsimmons & Michaels, Certified Public Accountants and Management Consultants exclusively serving Catholic Religious Not-for-Profit Organizations throughout the United States and internationally, with over 40 combined years of experience.

Our firm and clients have mutually benefited from our high quality of service which is a direct result of our philosophy of personal attention. Our services include accounting, auditing, computer systems, development office studies, investment monitoring, long-range strategic planning and feasibility studies, organization development, retirement planning and tax services.

CHURCH REGISTERS & PARISH OFFICE FORMS

Serving Catholic Parishes since 1873.

D.P. MURPHY CO., INC.
1221 Walt Whitman Rd.
Melville, NY 11747-3090
Tel: 516-673-9400; FAX: 516-673-1851

Personnel:

Peter Q. Murphy . . . . President

Type of Business:

Envelope mailing systems specifically designed to meet the needs of your parish — available at any frequency ... monthly, bi-monthly, quarterly, semi-annual, yearly sets. FREE List Maintenance. Contribution recording via fax, phone, mail, diskette, modem or E-Mail. Census, stewardship, tithing, and fundraising programs. Church stationery, registers, record books, mass cards and certificates. Specialists in old register rebinding.

F.J. REMEY CO., INC.
121 Willis Ave.
Mineola, NY 11501-0589
Tel.: 516-741-5112; FAX: 516-741-0523

Type of Business:
Serving Catholic parishes since 1921 by providing the following products: Envelope Mailing Systems, Annual Offering Envelope Boxsets, Bulk Collection Envelopes, Computer Recording, Collection Baskets, Parish Census, Church Record Books, Parish Office Forms, Church Stationery, Mass Cards, Raffle Tickets and Tuition Supplies.

COMMEMORATIVE KEEPSAKES

MESSERSMITH PROMOTIONS, INC.
P.O. Box 247
New Hampton, IA 50659-0247
Tel.: 800-726-1206; FAX: 515-394-4556

Personnel:
Bob Messersmith

Type of Business:
For over 30 years supplying churches with keepsakes to commemorate anniversaries. A large selection of mugs, plates, ornaments, etc

COMPUTERS & SOFTWARE

AGES Software
www.ageslibrary.com

AGES SOFTWARE
PO. Box 1926
Albany, OR 97321
Tel.: (800) 297-4307; FAX: (541) 917-0839
website: www.ageslibrary.com; e-mail: sales@ageslibrary.com

Personnel:
Steve Radda . . . . President
Tate Giersdorf . . . . Vice President

Type of Business:
Providers of electronic books to the Christian community on a CD-ROM, in a high value/low cost format. Over 330 important classic works such as *The Early Church Fathers* (38 vols.) and *The Works of Josephus* are available in a book-like, very easy to use format. A powerful search engine, copy/paste, and print features make this a must have tool for your research library. Compatible with Windows and Mac. Visit our website: www.ageslibrary.com.

Automated Church System

AUTOMATED CHURCH SYSTEM (ACS)
180 N. Dunbarton Dr.
PO Box 202010
Florence, SC 29502-2010
Tel.: (800) 736-7425; FAX: (800) 227-5990
website: www.acshome.com; e-mail: info@acshome.com

Personnel:
Hal Campbell . . . . President
Marvin Owen. . . . . . . Vice-President, Research & Development
Jim Brown. . . . . National Sales Manager
Pattie White . . . . Marketing Director

Type of Business:
Since 1978, ACS has been a leading provider of fully integrated, customizable software to help manage census, stewardship and financial information. Over 9000 religious organizations large and small count on ACS to help them be more effective in their ministry. Make the most of your investment with ACS Training, Forms & supplies, Support and other services. Regional representatives are located across the US to work with your parish or diocese. Available in DOS or Windows.

Catholic Church Windows

CATHOLIC CHURCH WINDOWS
Computer Helper Publishing
142 N High St., P.O. Box 30191
Columbus, OH 43230-0191
Tel.: (800) 533-5227; FAX: (614) 478-0621
website: www.churchwindows.com
e-mail: info@churchwindows.com

Personnel:
Maureen Wygant . . . . Dir. Marketing

Type of Business:
The best in census and financial Windows software designed specifically for Catholic parishes. Over 12 years in business with over 3,000 client churches. Available by the module or as an integrated package. Modules include: Membership, Contributions, Financial, and Payroll.
Ease of use and flexibility in:
- Mailing labels
- Financial Reporting
- Church Directories
- Sacramental Dates
- Giving Statements
- Visitation Tracking

Call today for a free preview or a free Web Site CD. Visit us on the Web at www.churchwindows.com.

The Catholic Software Co.

THE CATHOLIC SOFTWARE CO.
3768 Rocky River Dr., Suite 313
Cleveland, OH 44111-4050
Tel.: 800-428-3640; FAX: 216-671-1668

Personnel:
Rob Rhodes . . . . President
Peggy T.

Type of Business:
Offering software management solutions to Catholic parishes since 1991. Easy-to-use Window 95, Windows NT, Windows and Macintosh software products. Network ready at no additional cost! Software products available:
- Census, ministry, contribution & stewardship management
- Pledge campaign management
- Financial management: General Ledger with preloaded diocesan chart of accounts; Accounts Payable; Payroll
- School tuition and religious education management

CELEBRATING OUR 4TH ANNIVERSARY IN WINDOWS!

HARMONY MEDIA INC.

HARMONY MEDIA INC.
P.O. Box 138
Gervais, OR 97026
Tel.: 503-982-7675; FAX: 503-982-7833

Personnel:

William Van Smoorenburg . . . . President

Type of Business:

Bringing faith and technology together through computer CD-ROMs. This 100% Catholic company creates exciting catholic software for families, seminarians, priests, schools, parishes and all individuals that are interested in their faith. These programs contain hundreds of documents, illustrations and hyperlinks creating awesome collections. The New American Bible, RSV Catholic Edition Bible, Encyclicals, Catechism of the Catholic Church, John Paul II, Butler's, and Vatican II documents are just a few of the topics on CD-ROM!

NCS™

With Education in Mind™

NCS (National Computer Systems)
4401 West 76th St.
Edina, MN 55435
Tel.: 800-447-3269; FAX: 612-830-8564
e-mail: www@ncs.com

Personnel:

Mike Seeman. . . . . Marketing Manager, K-12
Fred Green . . . Marketing Mgr., Education Alternative Channels
For more information, contact NCS Telemarketing & Telesales

Type of Business:

For over 30 years, NCS has served the education market with optical mark reading (OMR) and imaging technology. NCS touches one of every two children in our nation's schools. NCS is the leading provider of scanning systems, software, and forms used to automate data collection and accurately report on assessment, instructional, and student records information. NCS scanners and forms are also compatible with most of the leading student administrative and testing software products on the market today.

RISO

IT IS NOT A COPIER!

RISO, INC.
300 Rosewood Dr.
Danvers, MA 01923
Tel.: 800-876-7476, ext. 705; 978-739-3553; FAX: 978-777-2517
website: http://www.riso.com

Personnel:

Kevin Thompson . . . . Church Market Manager
Richard Grassis . . . . Vice President, Marketing

Type of Business:

RISO, Inc. presents the Risograph, incorporating breakthrough technology in enhanced imaging for superior print quality, and new paper handling features that contribute to increased reliability and ease of use. The Risograph offers cost effective printing on a wide range of paper stocks from 14 to 110 lbs., in sizes from 4″ x 6″ to 11″ x 17″ in 17 different colors. The Risograph is compatible with PC or Macintosh computers or function as a stand-alone duplicator.

Ticketing Software for Windows®

TicketStop, Inc.

TICKETSTOP, INC.
14042 NE 8th St., Ste. 108
Bellevue, WA 98007
Tel.: 800-961-6111; FAX: 425-641-8151

Personnel:
Robin Nelson . . . . Account Executive
Jocelyn Ewert . . . . Marketing Coordinator

Type of Business:
TicketStop publishes TicketMaker™ Professional; ticketing and box office management software for Windows®. TMP supports advance sales and point-of-sale with capability for general admission and reserved seat events, series ticketing and patron management. Key features include: color seating charts, capability to track donations and down payments, & database integration with MS Access™. TMP works well with a wide range of thermal, laser, and dot matrix printers.
Call for a free demo of TicketMaker™ today!
1-800-961-6111
http://www.ticketstop.com

CONSULTANTS

CUNNEEN
PARISH
FUNDRAISING

CUNNEEN PARISH FUNDRAISING SERVICES, INC.
67 South Turnpike Rd.
Wallingford, CT 06492
Tel.: (800) 842-4488; FAX: (203) 284-3451
website: www.cunneenfundraising.com

Personnel:
Frank J. Cunneen . . . . President
John F. Cunneen, ... Vice President
James F. Cunneen . . . . Director of Operations
Daniel J. Wendt, ... Director of Mid-West Operations
Kevin R. Mancini. . . . . Director of Mid-Atlantic Operations

Type of Business:
Our company began serving Catholic parishes in 1981. Our approach is to provide the most effective, innovative and creative fundraising campaigns for client Catholic parishes. All our services, whether *Offertory Enhancement, Stewardship, In-Pew Capital Campaigns* or *On-Site Capital Campaigns* are infused with a commitment to providing fundraising that is firmly grounded in the principles of Biblical Stewardship. Over the past seventeen years, Cunneen has assisted over 5,000 Catholic parishes in all 50 states and Canada.

GG Guidance In Giving

GUIDANCE IN GIVING, INC.
225 Snedecor Ave.
Bayport, NY 11705
Tel.: 888-757-5444; FAX: 516-472-6109

8164 Sea Water Path
Columbia, MD 21045
Tel.: 888-869-5522; FAX: 410-799-9155

550 Camino De La Reina, Ste. 310
San Diego, CA 92108
Tel.: 800-993-3335; FAX: 619-491-0402

Personnel:
Michael R. Cusack . . . . President
Joseph W. Zamorano . . . . Executive Vice President
Michael V. Goodwin . . . . Executive Vice President

Type of Business:
Guidance In Giving is a Catholic Development and Stewardship firm specializing in Diocesan and Parish capital campaigns, annual appeals, and stewardship programs. Additionally, the firm assists Catholic schools with their development and fund raising programs. Executives of the firm have been conducting successful campaigns since 1980 and understand and respect the Mission of the Church. We welcome the opportunity to spend a day at your diocese, parish or school to discuss your development and stewardship efforts. We will prepare an honest objective appraisal of your program at no cost to you. If you are considering counsel, please call one of our office locations.

K E L L Y

PROFESSIONAL FUND RAISING CONSULTANTS

203 West Seventh St. • Traverse City, MI 49684 • 616/947-9636

KELLY-PROFESSIONAL FUND RAISING CONSULTANTS
203 W. Seventh St.
Traverse City, MI 49684
Tel.: 616-947-9636; FAX: 616-922-8120

Personnel:

Joe Kelly . . . . President
Al Kelly . . . . M.P.H., M.A., C.F.R.E.
Ed Kelly . . . . M.P.H., M.A.
Mike Kelly

WE RAISE FUNDS THE OLD FASHIONED WAY: WE ASK FOR THEM — PERSON TO PERSON. PEOPLE GIVE TO PEOPLE!

Type of Business:

Establishment of Development Office with on-site training of a local person as Development Director.

- Capital Campaigns
- Stewardship Programs/Annual Renewals
- Major Gifts
- Planned Giving
- Feasibility Studies

Services to Dioceses, Parishes, Elementary & Secondary Schools. 29 YEARS EXPERIENCE.

John V. McCarthy and Associates

JOHN V. McCARTHY & ASSOCIATES INC.
16250 Northland Dr., Ste. 200
Southfield, MI 48075-5266
Tel.: 800-444-1840; FAX: 248-552-0857 (eff. 5/97)

Personnel:

John V. McCarthy . . . . (President
Joseph H. Schram . . . . Vice President
Frank J. Krajca . . . . Vice President Marketing
Thomas A. Parker . . . . Vice President Operations

Type of Business:

Specialists in fund-raising: exclusively for Catholic parishes, dioceses, schools and other institutions. Individual program timetables are designed to allow for the composition of the parish or institution. Established in 1954, we have completed over 4,100 programs. We charge a flat fee with no additional costs for travel or living expenses. Our assigned Account Executive is on site full-time, except for small parish programs which can be designed on a consultation basis. We provide unmatched follow-up service for all clients.

FINANCIAL SERVICES

CFM

CRAIG, FITZSIMMONS & MICHAELS
517 Route 111, Ste. 200
Hauppauge, NY 11788
Tel.: 516-360-1400; FAX: 516-360-7314

Personnel:

Robert R. Craig
Dennis Michaels
David P. Fitzsimmons

Type of Business:

Craig, Fitzsimmons & Michaels, Certified Public Accountants and Management Consultants exclusively serving Catholic Religious Not-for-Profit Organizations throughout the United States and internationally, with over 40 combined years of experience.

Our firm and clients have mutually benefited from our high quality of service which is a direct result of our philosophy of personal attention. Our services include accounting, auditing, computer systems, development office studies, investment monitoring, long-range strategic planning and feasibility studies, organization development, retirement planning and tax services. .

FUND-RAISING COUNSEL

Kirby Smith Associates, Inc.
Ministry of Church Finance

KIRBY-SMITH ASSOCIATES, INC.
5 Fawn Dr.
Quarryville, PA 17566
Tel.: 1-800-762-3996; 717-284-3100; FAX: 717-284-3659
website: http://www.kirbysmith.com; e-mail: kirbysmith@aol.com

Personnel:

C. Eugene Musser . . . . President
Karl T. Frick . . . . Director Ministry Development

Type of Business:

Since our founding in 1938, Kirby-Smith Associates has served more than 5,000 parishes and schools, and has raised over two billion dollars. Our campaigns include detailed on-site counseling, organizational guidance, comprehensive materials, as well as long-term consultation and stewardship training. We offer a full range of services to better meet the needs of your parish or school; Capital and Budget Campaigns, Feasibility Studies, Pre-Campaign Planning and Strategic Planning. Meeting the needs of the Catholic community we serve is our ministry and the service we bring to you.

FUND-RAISING SERVICES

AMERICAN CITY BUREAU
1721 Moon Lake Blvd.
Hoffman Estates, IL 60194
Tel.: 800-786-GOAL; FAX: 847-490-5860

Personnel:
James J. Biggins . . . . Chairman and CEO
Leslie Biggins Mollsen . . . . Vice President

Type of Business:
Now celebrating its *85th year* of service to not-for-profit organizations, American City Bureau is the oldest, *most experienced* fund-raising consulting firm in the nation. Since 1913, we have helped raise more than $3 billion, providing more than 8,900 services, such as: Developmental Studies • Capital Campaign Direction • Major Gift/Planned Gift/Endowment Development • Communication Services • Video Productions • Development Office Audits & Strategic Planning.

FUND RAISING
& Public Relations Specialists

HANK BRANDT ASSOCIATES, INC.
P.O. Box 12383
Tucson, AZ 85732
Tel.: 520-745-9905; FAX: 520-747-7774

Personnel:
Bruce Brandt . . . . Vice President

Type of Business:
Established in 1958, Hank Brandt Associates provides highly personalized service, which is essential in reaching fund-raising potential. Each Hank Brandt Associates campaign is tailor-made to suit the client's needs. For 38 years, the firm has continuously attained top-notch results in conducting Annual Appeals, Capital Fund Campaigns and Increased Giving Programs along with public relations services and feasibility studies. Hank Brandt Associates offers in-depth experience and the edge to meet the most challenging financial objectives.

THE CATHOLIC SOFTWARE CO.
3768 Rocky River Dr., Suite 313
Cleveland, OH 44111-4050
Tel.: 800-428-3640; FAX: 216-671-1668

Personnel:
Rob Rhodes . . . . President
Peggy T.

Type of Business:
Offering software management solutions to Catholic parishes since 1991. Easy-to-use Window 95, Windows NT, Windows and Macintosh software products. Network ready at no additional cost! Software products available:
- Census, ministry, contribution & stewardship management
- Pledge campaign management
- Financial management: General Ledger with preloaded diocesan chart of accounts; Accounts Payable; Payroll
- School tuition and religious education management

CELEBRATING OUR 4TH ANNIVERSARY IN WINDOWS!

CCS CELEBRATES 50 YEARS

COMMUNITY COUNSELLING SERVICE CO., INC.
350 Fifth Ave., Ste. 7210
New York, NY 10118
Tel.: 800-223-6733; FAX: 212-967-6451

Personnel:
William B. Hanrahan . . . . President
Robert Kissane . . . . Executive Vice President
Patrick W. Moughan . . . . Managing Director Midwest Division
Joseph F. X. Lee . . . . Vice President

Type of Business:
CCS celebrates over 50 years of service to the Church. We have become one of the largest, most widely recommended fund raising firms in the world. CCS has successfully planned and managed fund raising campaigns for a variety of Catholic dioceses, parishes, universities, colleges, high schools, hospitals, homes for the aged, social service agencies, seminaries and religious communities. Regional offices in Chicago, San Francisco, London, Toronto and Dublin. Call 1-800-223-6733 for an estimate of your potential.

CRAIG, FITZSIMMONS & MICHAELS
517 Route 111, Ste. 200
Hauppauge, NY 11788
Tel.: 516-360-1400; FAX: 516-360-7314

Personnel:

Robert R. Craig
Dennis Michaels
David P. Fitzsimmons

Type of Business:

Craig, Fitzsimmons & Michaels, Certified Public Accountants and Management Consultants exclusively serving Catholic Religious Not-for-Profit Organizations throughout the United States and internationally, with over 40 combined years of experience.

Our firm and clients have mutually benefited from our high quality of service which is a direct result of our philosophy of personal attention. Our services include accounting, auditing, computer systems, development office studies, investment monitoring, long-range strategic planning and feasibility studies, organization development, retirement planning and tax services..

CUNNEEN
PARISH
FUNDRAISING

CUNNEEN PARISH FUNDRAISING SERVICES, INC.
67 South Turnpike Rd.
Wallingford, CT 06492
Tel.: (800) 842-4488; FAX: (203) 284-3451
website: www.cunneenfundraising.com

Personnel:

Frank J. Cunneen . . . . President
John F. Cunneen, ... Vice President
James F. Cunneen . . . . Director of Operations
Daniel J. Wendt, ... Director of Mid-West Operations
Kevin R. Mancini. . . . . Director of Mid-Atlantic Operations

Type of Business:

Our company began serving Catholic parishes in 1981. Our approach is to provide the most effective, innovative and creative fundraising campaigns for client Catholic parishes. All our services, whether *Offertory Enhancement, Stewardship, In-Pew Capital Campaigns* or *On-Site Capital Campaigns* are infused with a commitment to providing fundraising that is firmly grounded in the principles of Biblical Stewardship. Over the past seventeen years, Cunneen has assisted over 5,000 Catholic parishes in all 50 states and Canada.

FIRST COUNSEL, INC

FIRST COUNSEL, INC.
Stewardship Counsel Div.
428 E. Fourth St., Ste. 100
Charlotte, NC 28202
Tel.: 800-313-1645; FAX: 704-342-1700
www.firstcounsel.com

Personnel:

Dallas Mackey. . . . . Chairman, Executive Committee
Fred E. Beeson . . . . Chairman & CEO
Robert J. Simonds . . . . Chairman, FCI International and President, North Group
James L. Glass. . . . . President, West Group
Ronald C. Harding . . . . President, South Group
Alan W. Lee. . . . . President, South Atlantic

Type of Business:

First Counsel, Inc. provides comprehensive fundraising counsel to the non-profit sector. The STEWARDSHIP COUNSEL DIVISION was created by FCI to meet the unique fundraising needs of churches and church-related organizations. First Counsel has helped these Catholic institutions achieve their fundraising objectives:

- St. Barnabas Health System — Gibsonia, PA
- St. Anthony Hospital Foundation — Oklahoma City, OK
- St. Mary's Hospital Foundation — Knoxville, TN
- St. Joseph's Hospital Foundation — Asheville, NC
- Diocese of Greensburg — Greensburg, PA
- Christ Church Cathedral — Louisville, KY
- St. Mary's Catholic Church — Greenville, SC
- Charlotte Catholic High School — Charlotte, NC

FCI is a national network of experienced consultants. Our team of dynamic professionals is dedicated to integrity and results. FCI offers preliminary consultation without cost or obligation.
NEW YORK • CHARLOTTE • ATLANTA • LOS ANGELES

Ghiorse & Sorrenti INC.

FUND RAISING • MARKETING • PUBLIC RELATIONS

GHIORSE & SORRENTI, INC.
Cali Corporate Center
50 Tice Blvd.
Woodcliff Lake, NJ 07675
Tel.: 201-307-1970; FAX: 201-307-5632

Personnel:
Peter W. Ghiorse . . . . President & CEO
Dan Sorrenti. . . . . Executive Vice President & COO
Mary Ann Winters. . . . . Senior Vice President
Glenn Vallach . . . . VP for Public Relations & Communications

Type of Business:
Ghiorse & Sorrenti, Inc., is a full-service fund-raising and public relations firm specializing in capital campaigns for religious, healthcare, education and social service organizations. GSI offers highly tailored services, the personal involvement of the principals, and a team of seasoned fund raising and public relations executives. Resident campaign management and consulting services are available.

GG Guidance In Giving

GUIDANCE IN GIVING, INC.
225 Snedecor Ave.
Bayport, NY 11705
Tel.: 888-757-5444; FAX: 516-472-6109

8164 Sea Water Path
Columbia, MD 21045
Tel.: 888-869-5522; FAX: 410-799-9155

550 Camino De La Reina, Ste. 310
San Diego, CA 92108
Tel.: 800-993-3335; FAX: 619-491-0402

Personnel:
Michael R. Cusack. . . . . President
Joseph W. Zamorano . . . . Executive Vice President
Michael V. Goodwin . . . . Executive Vice President

Type of Business:
Guidance In Giving is a Catholic Development and Stewardship firm specializing in Diocesan and Parish capital campaigns, annual appeals, and stewardship programs. Additionally, the firm assists Catholic schools with their development and fund raising programs. Executives of the firm have been conducting successful campaigns since 1980 and understand and respect the Mission of the Church. We welcome the opportunity to spend a day at your diocese, parish or school to discuss your development and stewardship efforts. We will prepare an honest objective appraisal of your program at no cost to you. If you are considering counsel, please call one of our office locations.

HARVEST DEVELOPMENT, INC.

HARVEST DEVELOPMENT, INC.
200 Executive Way
Ponte Vedra Beach, FL 32082
Tel: (888) 322-9086; (904) 273-2108; FAX: (904) 285-1002

Personnel:
Paul D'Alessandro
John Patrick Alves
Martin Alves
Greg Switaj

Type of Business:
A full service fund raising and development consulting firm dedicated to helping our Catholic clients successfully achieve their development, strategic planning and campaign goals.

K E L L Y
PROFESSIONAL FUND RAISING CONSULTANTS
203 West Seventh St. • Traverse City, MI 49684 • 616/947-9636

KELLY-PROFESSIONAL FUND RAISING CONSULTANTS
203 W. Seventh St.
Traverse City, MI 49684
Tel.: 616-947-9636; FAX: 616-922-8120

Personnel:
Joe Kelly . . . . President
Al Kelly . . . . M.P.H., M.A., C.F.R.E.
Ed Kelly . . . . M.P.H., M.A.
Mike Kelly

WE RAISE FUNDS THE OLD FASHIONED WAY:
WE ASK FOR THEM — PERSON TO PERSON.
PEOPLE GIVE TO PEOPLE!

Type of Business:
Establishment of Development Office with on-site training of a local person as Development Director.
- Capital Campaigns
- Stewardship Programs/Annual Renewals
- Major Gifts
- Planned Giving
- Feasibility Studies

Services to Dioceses, Parishes, Elementary & Secondary Schools. 29 YEARS EXPERIENCE.

Kirby Smith
Associates, Inc.
Ministry of Church Finance

KIRBY-SMITH ASSOCIATES, INC.
5 Fawn Dr.
Quarryville, PA 17566
Tel.: 1-800-762-3996; 717-284-3100; FAX: 717-284-3659
website: http://www.kirbysmith.com; e-mail: kirbysmith@aol.com

Personnel:
C. Eugene Musser .... President
Karl T. Frick .... Director Ministry Development

Type of Business:
Since our founding in 1938, Kirby-Smith Associates has served more than 5,000 parishes and schools, and has raised over two billion dollars. Our campaigns include detailed on-site counseling, organizational guidance, comprehensive materials, as well as long-term consultation and stewardship training. We offer a full range of services to better meet the needs of your parish or school; Capital and Budget Campaigns, Feasibility Studies, Pre-Campaign Planning and Strategic Planning. Meeting the needs of the Catholic community we serve is our ministry and the service we bring to you.

John V. McCarthy
and Associates

JOHN V. McCARTHY & ASSOCIATES INC.
16250 Northland Dr., Ste. 200
Southfield, MI 48075-5266
Tel.: 800-444-1840; FAX: 810-552-0857 (eff. 5/97)

Personnel:
John V. McCarthy .... President
Joseph H. Schram .... Vice President
Frank J. Krajca .... Vice President Marketing
Thomas A. Parker .... Vice President Operations

Type of Business:
Specialists in fund-raising: exclusively for Catholic parishes, dioceses, schools and other institutions. Individual program timetables are designed to allow for the composition of the parish or institution. Established in 1954, we have completed over 4,100 programs. We charge a flat fee with no additional costs for travel or living expenses. Our assigned Account Executive is on site full-time, except for small parish programs which can be designed on a consultation basis. We provide unmatched follow-up service for all clients.

THE MARTIN J. MORAN CO.
Washington D.C. • San Diego • North Palm Beach • Boston
Catholic Fund-Raising Counsel

MARTIN J. MORAN CO.
One Pennsylvania Plaza
New York, NY 10119
Tel.: 212-736-9550

Type of Business:
The Moran Co. has been raising great amounts of money for its clients for a variety of needs. The key to success has been the design and conduct of a proven, time-tested Moran Co. Plan for generating both dollars and a high level of participation.

GRAHAM PELTON CONSULTING

GRAHAM-PELTON CONSULTING
89 Summit Ave., Ste. 161
Summit, NJ 07901
Tel.: 800-562-3695; FAX: 215-413-3268

Type of Business:
Graham-Pelton Consulting is a full-service fund-raising and non-profit management firm specializing in capital campaigns for religious, healthcare, educational and social service organizations. Graham-Pelton offers a team of seasoned fund-raising and public relations executives who have raised over 385 million dollars for the Catholic community including Catholic colleges, universities, secondary schools, dioceses and parishes. Graham-Pelton provides resident campaign management as well as a full range of consulting services.

RUOTOLO ASSOCIATES INC.
Horizon Square
29 Broadway, Ste. 210
Cresskill, NJ 07626
Tel.: 201-568-3898; FAX: 201-568-8783

Personnel:
George C. Ruotolo, Jr.. . . . . C.F.R.E., President

Type of Business:
Comprehensive development programs, capital campaigns, annual funds, planned giving, feasibility/planning studies, executive search, student recruitment, and marketing/public relations efforts. Specializing in service to Catholic institutions, including dioceses, schools, churches, religious orders, and social service and health organizations, serving the country through our four regional offices.

Walsh & Associates
"Helping Catholic Causes Reach New Heights"

WALSH & ASSOCIATES
12700 Nicollet Ave. So., Ste. 216
Burnsville, MN 55337
Tel.: 800-894-3863; FAX: 612-882-5270

Personnel:
Michael A. Walsh. . . . . President

Type of Business:
Walsh & Associates has been helping Catholic causes reach new heights since 1984 with our high quality, cost effective fund development and stewardship enhancement services. Our services include capital campaigns, feasibility/planning studies, stewardship education and enhancement efforts, planned giving programs and a variety of other services to help meet our clients' needs. So if you're ready to reach new heights in your fund development and stewardship efforts, give us a call. We'd be happy to help.

FUND RAISING SUPPLIES

AmericanChurch
a division of AmericanPaper Group, Inc.

AMERICAN CHURCH,
A DIVISION OF AMERICAN PAPER GROUP
8401 Southern Blvd.
Youngstown, OH 44512
Tel.: 800-228-6101; FAX: 330-758-9981

Personnel:
Ronald P. Blakeman. . . . . National Sales Manager
James P. Fitzgerald. . . . . Vice President — APG Direct
Rob Turnbull. . . . . Vice President — Direct Bank Giving

Type of Business:
Mailed Offering Envelope Systems
Boxed Set Systems
Direct Bank Giving
Mail Order Retail Catalog Systems

"Honor the Gift..................Honor the Giver"

B&D ... CONTRIBUTOR RECOGNITION PRODUCTS
119 South Mansfield Blvd.
Cherry Hill, NJ 08034-3611
1-800-873-3180; FAX: 609-429-3772

Honor those who Give, and they are your's forever ... Contributor Recognition is a key fund raising element that increases response and levels of giving. Our products create a permanent bond between the givers and their Church. Impressive, awe-inspiring and motivational, they enhance Church decor in an understated elegant manner. We can accommodate Churches of all sizes. Trees, Walls of Honor and Plaques are expandable, high quality and affordable.
We are as close as your telephone.

CARROLL ART, INC.
710 NE 26th St.
Fort Lauderdale, FL 33305
Tel.: 800-876-4569; FAX: 954-561-4098

Personnel:

David Nagle .... President Designer
Liza Palmer .... Sales Manager
Andrea Speier .... Sales Rep.
Robert Perkins .... Sales Rep.

Type of Business:

Carroll Art has been in business for 12 years. We design and custom build all types of plaques and memorials including the tree of life, plaques, recognition systems, church signs, donor plates, custom sculptures, and memorials are just a few of our products. We can provide you with the perfect fund raising tool.

HERSHEY

FUND RAISING

HERSHEY FUND RAISING
Hershey, Pennsylvania
Tel.: 800-217-8032

Type of Business:

Hershey's Fund Raising Products – Hershey's All American Candy Shoppe Assortment contains 40 assorted bars ($20 profit per box). Hershey's Candy Shoppe Max contains 50 assorted bars plus 2 free bars ($27 profit per box). Plus every box of $1.00 bars contains a free Hershey's All American Savings Card™ with discounts worth hundreds of dollars at national merchants and the chance to win $10,000 for your school. Contact your Fund Raising Distributor for information or call 800-217-8032.

TREES • OF • LIFE

A proven successful fund raiser whose strong lines and rich colors will enhance the space into which it is placed.

DAVID KLASS ART STUDIOS
136 West 24th St.
New York, NY 10011
Tel.: 212-243-7633; FAX: 212-243-7633

Personnel:

David Klass .... Owner, Designer

Type of Business:

Since 1968 David Klass has created numerous Trees of Life. Each one is custom designed to meet your needs. The finest select hardwoods, brasses and bronze are used.
Our beautiful designs and workmanship are ideal for donor recognition and fund raising drives. Special symbols and imagery meaningful to your parish can be incorporated into the design.

MESSERSMITH PROMOTIONS, INC.
P.O. Box 247
New Hampton, IA 50659-0247
Tel.: 800-726-1206; FAX: 515-394-4556

Personnel:
Bob Messersmith

Type of Business:
For over 30 years supplying churches with keepsakes to commemorate anniversaries. A large selection of mugs, plates, ornaments, etc.

F. J. REMEY CO., INC.
121 Willis Ave.
Mineola, NY 11501-0589
Tel.: 516-741-5112; FAX: 516-741-0523

Type of Business:
Serving Catholic parishes since 1921 by providing the following products: Envelope Mailing Systems, Annual Offering Envelope Boxsets, Bulk Collection Envelopes, Computer Recording, Collection Baskets, Parish Census, Church Record Books, Parish Office Forms, Church Stationery, Mass Cards, Raffle Tickets and Tuition Supplies.

THE PRINTERY HOUSE
Conception Abbey · CONCEPTION · MISSOURI 64433

THE PRINTERY HOUSE
Conception Abbey
Conception, MO 64433
Tel.: 800-322-2737 / 660-944-2632; FAX: 888-556-8262
e-mail: gnelson@msc-net.com

Personnel:
Gerald E. Nelson . . . . General Manager
Ron Riggs . . . . Director of Sales & Marketing

Type of Business:
The Printery House manufactures Christian greeting cards as a not-for-profit extension of the apostolic mission of Conception Abbey, a Benedictine community dedicated to a Christian life of work and prayer. We make our cards available to religious organizations to earn 50% with no risk, no prepayment. Call 800-889-0105 for your fund-raiser packet and more information.

THE ARTIST'S HAND MAKES THE DIFFERENCE
SANFORD WERFEL- ARTIST

SANFORD WERFEL - ARTIST
425 Old Georges Rd.,
North Brunswick, NJ 08902
Tel.: 800-443-3744; 732-297-1166; FAX: 732-297-7770

Type of Business:
Since 1968, Mr. Werfel's sculptures have been helping parishes to INSPIRE and MOTIVATE GIVING through the use of his original sculptures. Building drives, capital or endowment funds, sacrificial giving, and tithing programs all benefit from using Donor Recognition Sculptures. Call or write for FREE INFORMATION. Included will be costs and designs as well as a "HOW-TO-USE" guide that tells how your parish can use sculpture to raise funds. Good art is forever.

TESTAMINTS™

TESTAMINTS, INC.
1248 Sussex Tpke., Unit C-1
Randolph, NJ 07869
Tel.: 908-879-0400; FAX: 908-879-0321

Personnel:
Alfred Poe . . . . C.E.O.
Bill Tilley . . . . President
Juliet-Marie Adams . . . . Manager Fundraising Projects

Type of Business:
Testamints Inc., headquartered in Chester, NJ, was established by Christian investors in 1996. Our mission is to be the best at providing products that are daily encouragements and facilitate Christians sharing their faith with others.
Our fund raiser packs represent tremendous opportunities for Christian organizations to earn money with popular products that are also inspirational. We stand ready to develop a program that would meet the fund raising needs of your organization.
Call 1-888-879-0400 for further details.

INSURANCE

CATHOLIC ORDER OF FORESTERS
355 Shuman Blvd., P.O. Box 3012
Naperville, IL 60555-7012
Tel.: 630-983-4920; 800-552-0145; FAX: 630-983-5113

Type of Business:
Catholic Order of Foresters, a fraternal benefit society with 135,000 members nationwide, has been providing Catholics with financial protection since 1883. In addition to quality life insurance and annuity products, COF offers added value through fraternal benefits—parish and diocese loans, college scholarships, student loans, orphan benefits, local youth and adult court activities, and benevolence that includes a matching funds program.

Personnel:
Robert Ciesla . . . . High Chief Ranger
Armand R. Lemire . . . . Vice High Chief Ranger
Leo J. Beranek . . . . High Sec.-Treas.

INVESTMENT ADVISORS

CBIS Christian Brothers Investment Services, Inc.

CHRISTIAN BROTHERS INVESTMENT SERVICES
675 Third Ave., 31st Fl.
New York, NY 10017-5704
Tel.: 212-490-0800; FAX: 212-490-6092

Personnel:
Michael W. O'Hern, FSC . . . . President & CEO
Jessica W. Jennings. . . . . Vice President-Marketing

Type of Business:
Established in 1981, Christian Brothers Investment Services, Inc., (CBIS), acts as investment advisor exclusively to Catholic organizations throughout the world. As a registered investment advisor, we currently work with over 850 Catholic organizations representing total assets under advisement of $1.8 billion. CBIS offers individually managed portfolios as well as ten pooled investment funds which provide a wide range of risk and return characteristics and a broad choice of investment management styles.
Our comprehensive advisory services include: needs analysis, policy consulting, custody and reporting, investment management and performance evaluation. In addition, all investments made on behalf of participants are guided by CBIS's socially responsible investment principles. CBIS's "Faith and Finance" standards define our belief that investing and maintaining our Catholic ethics are not incompatible activities; they are indeed, our moral obligation.

INVESTMENT MANAGEMENT

CVIT Catholic Values Investment Trust

CATHOLIC VALUES INVESTMENT TRUST
1000 Lafayette Blvd.
Bridgeport, CT 06604
Tel.: 1-888-974-4486; 1-203-330-5197

Personnel:
Dr. Walter R. Miller, Ph.D. . . . . Secretary to the Board

Type of Business:
Catholic Values Investment Trust offers dioceses, parishes and other Catholic organizations and institutions a quality long-term growth mutual fund investment. What makes CVIT different from other investment options is that CVIT invests only in companies that conduct their business in a way consistent with the basic tenets and teachings of the Catholic Church.
The quality of the fund management and adherance to these Catholic views make this an investment you can put your faith in

LEGAL SERVICES

LEWIS, D'AMATO, BRISBOIS & BISGAARD LLP
221 North Figueroa St., Ste. 1200
Los Angeles, CA 90012
Tel.: 213-250-1800; FAX: 213-250-7900

Personnel:
Dennis R. Kasper, Esq.
Thomas H. Knudsen, Esq.

Type of Business:
Founded in 1979, we are a full-service law firm comprised of some 200 attorneys with offices in the heart of the business districts in Los Angeles, San Diego, San Francisco, Costa Mesa, Sacramento and San Bernardino. We work closely with clients through careful planning in order to achieve their goals, while remaining sensitive to the control of costs and fees. Among the areas in which we specialize are: churches and Christian schools representation, employment issues, and non-profit organizations; business, estate planning, health care law, intellectual property, real estate, taxation, trademarks, securities, worker's compensation.

MUTUAL FUNDS

CATHOLIC VALUES INVESTMENT TRUST
1000 Lafayette Blvd.
Bridgeport, CT 06604
Tel.: 1-888-974-4486; 1-203-330-5197

Personnel:
Dr. Walter R. Miller, Ph.D. . . . . Secretary to the Board

Type of Business:
Catholic Values Investment Trust offers dioceses, parishes and other Catholic organizations and institutions a quality long-term growth mutual fund investment. What makes CVIT different from other investment options is that CVIT invests only in companies that conduct their business in a way consistent with the basic tenets and teachings of the Catholic Church.
The quality of the fund management and adherance to these Catholic views make this an investment you can put your faith in.

OFFICE EQUIPMENT & SUPPLIES

AMERICAN CHURCH,
A DIVISION OF AMERICAN PAPER GROUP
8401 Southern Blvd.
Youngstown, OH 44512
Tel.: 800-228-6101; FAX: 330-758-9981

Personnel:
Ronald P. Blakeman. . . . . National Sales Manager
James P. Fitzgerald. . . . . Vice President — APG Direct
Rob Turnbull. . . . . Vice President — Direct Bank Giving

Type of Business:
Mailed Offering Envelope Systems
Boxed Set Systems
Direct Bank Giving
Mail Order Retail Catalog Systems

GESTETNER
333 Ludlow St.
Stamford, CT 06904-2270
Tel.: 1-800-765-7746

Type of Business:
Gestetner CopyPrinter digital duplicators have redefined the meaning of cost-effectiveness. Digital duplicators produce prints with high-quality text and image reproduction. They are ideal for jobs requiring large copy volumes — they can produce up to 130 prints per minute — while keeping costs at less than a penny a page. And since there are a variety of models available, you can be sure there's one to fit your organization's needs. The Gestetner name represents a long-standing tradition of excellence in the world of paper-based communication.

THE COPYPRINTER CHURCHES SWEAR BY.

For years Gestetner has been the name religious organizations swear by for reliable, cost-effective solutions to their duplication needs. And now Gestetner CopyPrinters are bringing more and more converts into the fold.

After all, every Gestetner CopyPrinter is a fast, efficient digital duplicator that creates crisp, clean multiple prints at speeds of up to 130 pages per minute, for less than a penny a page. And they come with some very heavenly productivity-enhancing options, like an automatic document feeder, the ability to connect to a computer, even the option of printing in up to 11 eye-catching colors.

Just as important, the Gestetner CopyPrinter is a tireless worker. With scheduled Gestetner maintenance required only every 300,000 copies.

For more information about Gestetner CopyPrinters, copiers, fax machines or other digital products, call **1-800-765-7746** or visit us at www.gestetnerusa.com. It just may be the answer to your prayers.

Gestetner

599 W. PUTNAM AVE., PO BOX 2656, GREENWICH, CT 06836-2656

RISO
IT IS NOT A COPIER!

RISO, INC.
300 Rosewood Dr.
Danvers, MA 01923
Tel.: 800-876-7476, ext. 705; 978-739-3553; FAX: 978-777-2517
website: http://www.riso.com

Personnel:
Kevin Thompson . . . . Church Market Manager
Richard Grassis . . . . Vice President, Marketing

Type of Business:
RISO, Inc. presents the Risograph, incorporating breakthrough technology in enhanced imaging for superior print quality, and new paper handling features that contribute to increased reliability and ease of use. The Risograph offers cost effective printing on a wide range of paper stocks from 14 to 110 lbs., in sizes from 4″ x 6″ to 11″ x 17″ in 17 different colors. The Risograph is compatible with PC or Macintosh computers or function as a stand-alone duplicator.

ORGANIZATIONAL DEVELOPMENT

HARVEST DEVELOPMENT, INC.

HARVEST DEVELOPMENT, INC.
200 Executive Way
Ponte Vedra Beach, FL 32082
Tel: (888) 322-9086; (904) 273-2108; FAX: (904) 285-1002

Personnel:
Paul D'Alessandro
John Patrick Alves
Jack Gibbons
Martin Alves
Greg Switaj

Type of Business:
A full service fund raising and development consulting firm dedicated to helping our Catholic clients successfully achieve their development, strategic planning and campaign goals.

STRATEGIC PLANNING

HARVEST DEVELOPMENT, INC.

HARVEST DEVELOPMENT, INC.
200 Executive Way
Ponte Vedra Beach, FL 32082
Tel: (888) 322-9086; (904) 273-2108; FAX: (904) 285-1002

Personnel:
Paul D'Alessandro
John Patrick Alves
Jack Gibbons
Martin Alves
Greg Switaj

Type of Business:
A full service fund raising and development consulting firm dedicated to helping our Catholic clients successfully achieve their development, strategic planning and campaign goals.

Kirby Smith
Associates, Inc.
Ministry of Church Finance

KIRBY-SMITH ASSOCIATES, INC.
5 Fawn Dr.
Quarryville, PA 17566
Tel.: 1-800-762-3996; 717-284-3100; FAX: 717-284-3659
website: http://www.kirbysmith.com; e-mail: kirbysmith@aol.com

Personnel:
C. Eugene Musser . . . . President
Karl T. Frick . . . . Director Ministry Development

Type of Business:
Since our founding in 1938, Kirby-Smith Associates has served more than 5,000 parishes and schools, and has raised over two billion dollars. Our campaigns include detailed on-site counseling, organizational guidance, comprehensive materials, as well as long-term consultation and stewardship training. We offer a full range of services to better meet the needs of your parish or school; Capital and Budget Campaigns, Feasibility Studies, Pre-Campaign Planning and Strategic Planning. Meeting the needs of the Catholic community we serve is our ministry and the service we bring to you.

CHURCH FURNISHINGS

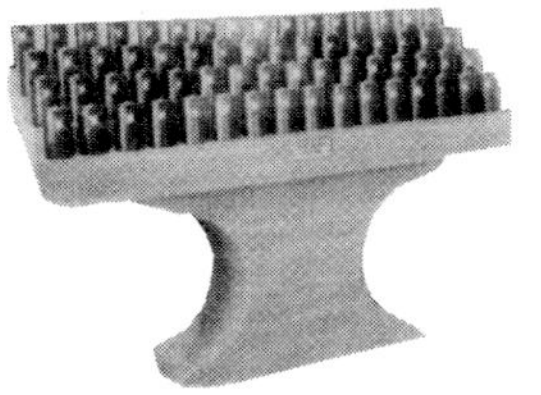

CARROLL ELECTRONICS INCORPORATED
710 Northeast 26th St.
Wilton Manors, FL 33305
Tel.: 800-331-0444; FAX: 954-561-4098

Personnel:
David Nagle . . . . President
Liza Palmer . . . . Sales Manager
Bob Perkins . . . . Sales Representative
John Lentz . . . . Service Engineer

Type of Business:
Carroll Electronics has been in business for 20 years designing and building Electronic Votive Candle Stands for thousands of churches throughout the United States.

CHURCH ORGAN SYSTEMS
630 Highway 12
P.O. Box 738
Baldwin, WI 54002
Tel.: 715-684-5397; FAX: 715-684-5297

Personnel:
Dwane Kuhn . . . . Vice President
Darlene Davis . . . . Administrative Assistant
Rodney Barbour . . . . Manager Sales & Service
David Wade . . . . Director Engrg.

Type of Business:
Church Organ Systems, a division of The Baldwin Piano and Organ Co., is dedicated to serving churches with products and programs designed to support music ministry.

MORODER-INTERNATIONAL STATUARY & ALTAR, INC.
7406 N. Santa Monica Blvd.
Milwaukee, WI 53217
Tel.: 414-351-0130

Type of Business:
Over 89 years of ecclesiastic service: Designers, Sculptors, Manufacturers—marble, wood, mosaic, bronze.

NATIONAL EQUIPMENT & CHURCH FURNISHINGS, INC.
449 North St. Francis
Wichita, KS 67202
Tel.: (316) 269-2121; FAX: (316) 269-9111

Personnel:
Milton Barkett . . . . President/Sales

Type of Business:
Pews are our specialty, nationwide. Be innovative with true curved pews. If you can imagine it, we can build it. For churches, courthouses, schools, universities, funeral homes, etc. Many styles of church furniture for total interiors. We offer classroom furniture, tables, chairs, portable partitions, stained glass windows, lighting, chalk and bulletin boards, baptisteries. Furniture of all designs and prices. Send your prints/specifications for delivery, installation and bid price. Call today.

NEW HOLLAND CUSTOM WOODWORK, LTD.
313 Prospect St., P.O. Box 217
New Holland, PA 17557-0217
Tel.: 800-648-9663; FAX: 717-354-2481
e-mail: nhcw@redrose.net
Website: http://www.newhollandwood.com

Personnel:
Jeff Lewis . . . . Director of Sales & Marketing

Type of Business:
New Holland Custom Woodwork has just written an all-new *"Guide to Designing and Buying Church Furniture"* This booklet is packed full of valuable information and it's yours free for the asking.
Since 1919, New Holland Custom Woodwork has supplied churches nationwide with both "custom" and standard church furniture. Today, we are America's only manufacturer of *"True Radius Pews."* We also offer: • interlocking stack chairs • standard & custom altar furnishings • full design assistance.
To order the new "Guide to Designing and Buying Church Furniture" as well as our Design and Specification Package, call, write or e-mail us.

Serenity® CHURCH FURNITURE

WALTER JACOBI AND SONS, INC.
1400 Elmer St. / P.O. Box 471
Belmont, CA 94002
Tel.: 800-522-6241; FAX: 650-592-2434
website: http://www.serenity-wjs.com

Personnel:
Arno M. Jacobi . . . . Sales
Albert O. Jacobi . . . . Sales

Type of Business:
Since 1921, MANUFACTURER: Devotional - Reverential - Furniture. MADE TO ORDER: Conducive to MEDITATION and PRAYER - ALL Wood, Cushion-loc, and Conventional Upholstered - Pews, Pewchairs, PewCHAR, Presider Chair, Clergy Chairs, Serenity Kneelers, Premium Kneelers, SKE Hydraulics, Kneeler Maintenance, Kneeler Parts and Repairs, Altar, Ambo, Lectern, Candlesticks, Crosses, Carvings. Seating Consultants to Church and/or Architect. Computer Layouts - send Plans or CAD Disk.

RAMBUSCH

RAMBUSCH
40 West 13th St.
New York, NY 10011
Tel.: 212-675-0400; FAX: 212-620-4687

Personnel:
Viggo Bech Rambusch . . . . Senior Project Director
Martin V. Rambusch . . . . Stained Glass Director

Type of Business:
Since 1898, creating church interiors, liturgical furnishings, and art work. Fine restoration of church interiors. In-house studios and shops for designing and executing stained glass, church lighting systems, art metal work, and decorative painting.

D.C. RIGGOTT INC.
3540 Neal Ave.
Afton, MN 55001
Tel.: 800-479-8777; FAX: 612-436-4769

Personnel:
Don Riggott . . . . Owner/President

Type of Business:
Specializing in vintage church accessories, architectural ornamentation and liturgical furnishings.
Stained Glass Windows • Altars • Lighting • Statuary • Stations of the Cross • Tabernacles • Monstranses • Fonts • Pews • Steeple Bells • Vestments • Books • Furniture • Candlesticks • Chalices, Please contact us with specific requests. We will be happy to send you photographs and specifics on any items in our inventory. You may have items in storage or not being used, please contact us as we are actively searching for vintage items to purchase for re-use in liturgical spaces.

Conrad Schmitt Studios Inc.

CONRAD SCHMITT STUDIOS, INC.
2405 S. 162nd St.
New Berlin, WI 53151
Tel.: 800-969-3033; 414-786-3030; FAX: 414-786-9036

Personnel:
Heidi Gruenke Emery . . . . Vice President & Marketing Director

Type of Business:
Since 1889, this family-owned Studio has restored and decorated hundreds of interiors across the country. Their scope of work includes the investigation and documentation of original decorative schemes; the restoration of those schemes through the application of various decorative techniques including gilding, glazing, marbleizing, stenciling, and graining, as well as the design, fabrication, conservation or replication of murals and stained glass. The Studio can assist projects in the early stages with architectural samples and rendering for fund-raising. Recently completed projects include St. Josaphat's Basilica, Milwaukee, WI; St. Ann's, Napoleanville, LA; and St. Bernard's, Akron, OH.

ALTARS, TABLERNACLES, ETC.

ECCLESIASTICAL ARTS, INC.
16 Herbert St.
Newark, NJ 07105
Tel: 973-491-0022; FAX: 973-491-0023

Personnel:
Joseph J. Zaky . . . . President

Type of Business:
Artists and Craftsmen specializing in custom designed and hand made furnishings in metal, wood, stone and glass. For interior design, fabrication, restoration and original sculpture, contact J.J. Zaky — the workshop/studio for design, fabrication, installation — nationwide.

Granda
Liturgical Arts, Inc.
TAG

GRANDA LITURGICAL ARTS, INC.
828 Davis St., Ste. 200
Evanston, IL 60201
Tel.: 800-425-0828; FAX: 847-492-1374
www.hispacom.es/granda; e-mail: ruf4granda@aol.com

Personnel:
Karen Johnson

Type of Business:
GRANDA LITURGICAL ARTS, Inc. is the USA branch of the largest supplier of church goods in the world: TALLERES DE ARTE GRANDA, S.A.
With 65 employees and sales all over the world, we can offer our experience in the manufacture of:
— metalware: chalices, tabernacles, etc.
— vestments
— wood carvings
— church decoration, interior design
Since 1891, we have been serving the church, combining modern techniques (computer aided design, projects in 3D ...) with artistic values.
Special custom orders are our specialty, styled and priced according to your needs.

ADRIAN HAMERS®
CHURCH INTERIORS

ADRIAN HAMERS INC.
2 Madison Ave.
Larchmont, NY 10538
Tel.: 914-834-7780; FAX: 914-834-0712

Type of Business:
Since 1887, the Hamers name has been synonymous with expert silversmithing throughout the world in the field of Liturgical Art. We are also experts in: Church Interiors from design to execution, Renovations, Altars, Sacred Vessels, Appraisals, Gold and Silver Plating & Repairing, Tabernacles, Marble, Woodwork & Woodcarving, Statuary, Stained Glass, Pews & Chairs, Gold Leafing, Frescoes, Restoration, Trompe-l'oeuil, Wall Murals (repair and conservation cleaning), Ornamental Plaster, Heraldic Designs & Bishop Regalia.

RAMBUSCH

RAMBUSCH
40 West 13th St.
New York, NY 10011
Tel.: 212-675-0400; FAX: 212-620-4687

Personnel:
Viggo Bech Rambusch. . . . . Senior Project Director
Martin V. Rambusch. . . . . Stained Glass Director

Type of Business:
Since 1898, creating church interiors, liturgical furnishings, and art work. Fine restoration of church interiors. In-house studios and shops for designing and executing stained glass, church lighting systems, art metal work, and decorative painting.

D.C. RIGGOTT INC.
3540 Neal Ave.
Afton, MN 55001
Tel.: 800-479-8777; FAX: 612-436-4769

Personnel:
Don Riggott . . . . Owner/President

Type of Business:
Specializing in vintage church accessories, architectural ornamentation and liturgical furnishings.
Stained Glass Windows • Altars • Lighting • Statuary • Stations of the Cross • Tabernacles • Monstranses • Fonts • Pews • Steeple Bells • Vestments • Books • Furniture • Candlesticks • Chalices, Please contact us with specific requests. We will be happy to send you photographs and specifics on any items in our inventory. You may have items in storage or not being used, please contact us as we are actively searching for vintage items to purchase for re-use in liturgical spaces.

Conrad Schmitt Studios Inc.

CONRAD SCHMITT STUDIOS, INC.
2405 S. 162nd St.
New Berlin, WI 53151
Tel.: 800-969-3033; 414-786-3030; FAX: 414-786-9036

Personnel:
Heidi Gruenke Emery . . . . Vice President & Marketing Director

Type of Business:
Since 1889, this family-owned Studio has restored and decorated hundreds of interiors across the country. Their scope of work includes the investigation and documentation of original decorative schemes; the restoration of those schemes through the application of various decorative techniques including gilding, glazing, marbleizing, stenciling, and graining, as well as the design, fabrication, conservation or replication of murals and stained glass. The Studio can assist projects in the early stages with architectural samples and rendering for fund-raising. Recently completed projects include St. Josaphat's Basilica, Milwaukee, WI; St. Ann's, Napoleanville, LA; and St. Bernard's, Akron, OH.

ANTIQUES, RELIGIOUS

Adrian Hamers®

One Hundred Years Serving the Clergy — Toujours 1887

Church Interiors

ADRIAN HAMERS INC.
2 Madison Ave.
Larchmont, NY 10538
Tel.: 914-834-7780; FAX: 914-834-0712

Type of Business:
Since 1887, the Hamers name has been synonymous with expert silversmithing throughout the world in the field of Liturgical Art. We are also experts in: Church Interiors from design to execution, Renovations, Altars, Sacred Vessels, Appraisals, Gold and Silver Plating & Repairing, Tabernacles, Marble, Woodwork & Woodcarving, Statuary, Stained Glass, Pews & Chairs, Gold Leafing, Frescoes, Restoration, Trompe-l'oeuil, Wall Murals (repair and conservation cleaning), Ornamental Plaster, Heraldic Designs & Bishop Regalia.

D.C. RIGGOTT INC.
3540 Neal Ave.
Afton, MN 55001
Tel.: 800-479-8777; FAX: 612-436-4769

Personnel:
Don Riggott . . . . Owner/President

Type of Business:
Specializing in vintage church accessories, architectural ornamentation and liturgical furnishings.
Stained Glass Windows • Altars • Lighting • Statuary • Stations of the Cross • Tabernacles • Monstranses • Fonts • Pews • Steeple Bells • Vestments • Books • Furniture • Candlesticks • Chalices, Please contact us with specific requests. We will be happy to send you photographs and specifics on any items in our inventory. You may have items in storage or not being used, please contact us as we are actively searching for vintage items to purchase for re-use in liturgical spaces.

GREG SPIESS & CO.

SPIESS ARCHITECTURAL ANTIQUES
230 East Washington St.
Joliet, IL 60433
Tel.: 815-722-5639; FAX: 815-722-0171

Type of Business:

Specializing in older and antique church furniture. Gothic, Romanesque and Classical styles in marble, wood, bronze etc. Altars, pews, communion rails, stained glass, lecterns, baptismals, vestment cases, confessionals, Stations of the Cross statuary. Lighting. Pew and wood restoration available.

SN STADELMAIER NIJMEGEN

STADELMAIER-NIJMEGEN-HOLLAND
P.O. Box 7063
6503 GN Nijmegen
Nijmegen, Holland 6501 BA
Tel.: 31-24-3791170; FAX: 31-24-3791171
e-mail: stadelmaier@telebyte.nl

Type of Business:

SN-Antiques offers, for the re-use in the Cath. Liturgy;
Completely restored, original, devotional interior-pieces. Altars, stations, candlesticks, perpetual lights, statues, reliquaries, ciboria, chalices, monstrances, censers, mission crosses, processional crosses, Saints, paintings, etc.
Different styles and age: Roman, baroque, neo-gothic, etc.
Please describe your interest directly to Mr. Ben Stadelmaier.

ART, STATUARY & DECORATIONS

ABBOTT INC.
Showroom 1515 Route 38
Cherry Hill, NJ 08002
Tel.: 800-522-2688; 609-662-6959; FAX: 609-665-5109
website: http://www.abbottsinc.com
e-mail: ACG.INC@internetMCI.com

Personnel:

Daniel J. Castonguay . . . . President
Joseph F. McKeaney . . . . General Manager
Michael W. Wasyluk . . . . Customer Service

Type of Business:

Purveyors of the Finest Vesture, Paraments, Statuary & Metalware since 1962. Unique and original creations, our specialty. Custom designs to complement your liturgical environment. Exclusive representatives of Slabbinck Master Collection & Original Collection.

THE BLACK FOREST BUILDING COMPANY

ANTHONY JOHN BELLOMO / THE BLACK FOREST CO.
310 Euclid
Mt. Clemens, MI 48043
Tel.: 810-954-4800; FAX: 810-954-4806

Personnel:

Anthony Bellomo . . . . President

Type of Business:

Anthony John Bellomo is a sculptor. He works in a wide variety of materials from wood and bronze to fibers, stone and living plant materials. Over the past twenty-five years he has developed the Black Forest Company. Black Forest is a group of artists and artisans, who along with Bellomo, design and build contemporary sculpture and furniture for liturgical spaces. He has developed a series of redwood sand carved exterior pieces for outdoor chapels and meditation gardens. Anthony, along with his team of dedicated crafts persons, pride themselves in listening to the individual community, designing and building pieces to help make their worship a deeper experience.

BOTTI STUDIO OF ARCHITECTURAL ARTS, INC.

BOTTI STUDIO OF ARCHITECTURAL ARTS, INC.
919 Grove St.
Evanston, IL 60201
Tel.: 800-524-7211; FAX: 847-869-5996
847-869-5933; e-mail: Boti@ix.netcom.com

East Coast Studio
1517 State St.
Sarasota, FL 33577
Tel.: 941-951-0978; FAX: 941-953-9078

West Coast Studio
1038 N Highway 101
Encinitas, CA 92024
Tel.: 619-753-0705; FAX: 619-753-0705

Personnel:
Staff includes internationlly recognized artists and designers working in conjunction with our highly skilled artisans and craftsmen.
Italo G. Botti . . . . President

Type of Business:
For generations Botti Studio has had a reputation for embodying all that is artistically creative in the traditional and contemporary ecclesiastical field. This field includes design and fabrication of stained and faceted glass windows, restoration of windows, church interiors, appointments, murals, sculpture, mosaic and marble. We are completely dedicated to both quality and satisfying our clients needs spiritually and liturgically. Botti Studio is nationwide, offering consultation and designs without obligation. Member Stained Glass Association of America.

DAPRATO RIGALI STUDIOS, INC.

DAPRATO RIGALI STUDIOS, INC.
7956 Oakton St.
Niles, IL 60714
Tel.: 847-692-6350; FAX: 847-692-3445

Personnel:
John Rigali
Robert Rigali
Lisa Rigali Galvin
Mike Rigali

Type of Business:
Daprato Rigali Studios Inc. has been beautifying Churches in America since 1860.
Today we find the Rigali Family restoring and renovating the churches originally decorated by their Great-Grandfather, John E. Rigali; aware of his reputation to create spiritually moving environments with quality material and craftsmanship.
Some of their most recent jobs include: decoration and stained glass restoration at St. Mary of the Lake Seminary, Mundelein, IL.; Marble renovation and decoration, St. Elizabeth's Mother House, Allegany, N.Y.; and General Contracting for complete renovation of St. Bernadette's Church, Rockford, IL.
The Daprato Rigali staff is equipped to take your project from start to finish. If you're interested in working with a fine interior design studio experienced in Ecclesiastical Artistries please call for consultation at no obligation. We deliver what we design.

D.M.S.

D.M.S. STUDIO
550 51st Ave.
Long Island City, NY 11101
Tel.: 718-937-5648; FAX: 718-937-2609

Personnel:
Daniel Sinclair . . . . President

Type of Business:
D.M.S. Studios specializes in the highest quality custom made products in limestone, marble and granite. Our specialties include classical statuary and architectural details. We are equipped to create any sculpture from models prepared in our studio to exacting specifications. D.M.S. Studios stands for superb craftsmanship in all of its undertakings and we guarantee absolute satisfaction for all our customers in jobs small or large.

Granda TAC
Liturgical Arts, Inc.

GRANDA LITURGICAL ARTS, INC.
828 Davis St., Ste. 200
Evanston, IL 60201
Tel.: 800-425-0828; FAX: 847-492-1374
www.hispacom.es/granda; e-mail: ruf4granda@aol.com

Personnel:
Karen Johnson

Type of Business:
GRANDA LITURGICAL ARTS, Inc. is the USA branch of the largest supplier of church goods in the world: TALLERES DE ARTE GRANDA, S.A.
With 65 employees and sales all over the world, we can offer our experience in the manufacture of:
— metalware: chalices, tabernacles, etc.
— vestments
— wood carvings
— church decoration, interior design
Since 1891, we have been serving the church, combining modern techniques (computer aided design, projects in 3D ...) with artistic values.
Special custom orders are our specialty, styled and priced according to your needs.

INSTITUTIONAL STATUARY
637 E. 132nd St.
Bronx, NY 10450
Tel.: 718-665-1125; FAX: 718-665-0956

Type of Business:
Distinctive religious works of art: Designers-Sculptors-Manufacturers. Full color catalog available upon request.

RAMBUSCH

RAMBUSCH
40 West 13th St.
New York, NY 10011
Tel.: 212-675-0400; FAX: 212-620-4687

Personnel:
Viggo Bech Rambusch . . . . Senior Project Director
Martin V. Rambusch . . . . Stained Glass Director

Type of Business:
Since 1898, creating church interiors, liturgical furnishings, and art work. Fine restoration of church interiors. In-house studios and shops for designing and executing stained glass, church lighting systems, art metal work, and decorative painting.

D.C. RIGGOTT INC.
3540 Neal Ave.
Afton, MN 55001
Tel.: 800-479-8777; FAX: 612-436-4769

Personnel:
Don Riggott . . . . Owner/President

Type of Business:
Specializing in vintage church accessories, architectural ornamentation and liturgical furnishings.
Stained Glass Windows • Altars • Lighting • Statuary • Stations of the Cross • Tabernacles • Monstranses • Fonts • Pews • Steeple Bells • Vestments • Books • Furniture • Candlesticks • Chalices,
Please contact us with specific requests. We will be happy to send you photographs and specifics on any items in our inventory. You may have items in storage or not being used, please contact us as we are actively searching for vintage items to purchase for re-use in liturgical spaces.

Conrad Schmitt Studios Inc.

CONRAD SCHMITT STUDIOS, INC.
2405 S. 162nd St.
New Berlin, WI 53151
Tel.: 800-969-3033; 414-786-3030; FAX: 414-786-9036

Personnel:
Heidi Gruenke Emery . . . . Vice President & Marketing Director

Type of Business:
Since 1889, this family-owned Studio has restored and decorated hundreds of interiors across the country. Their scope of work includes the investigation and documentation of original decorative schemes; the restoration of those schemes through the application of various decorative techniques including gilding, glazing, marbleizing, stenciling, and graining, as well as the design, fabrication, conservation or replication of murals and stained glass. The Studio can assist projects in the early stages with architectural samples and rendering for fund-raising. Recently completed projects include St. Josaphat's Basilica, Milwaukee, WI; St. Ann's, Napoleanville, LA; and St. Bernard's, Akron, OH.

Stadelmaier USA LLC

Unique Liturgical Solutions

A Division of Patrick Baker & Sons and Stadelmaier Nijmegen

STADELMAIER USA LLC
1650 West St., P.O. Box 1028
Southington, CT 06489-5028
Tel.: 1-800-243-6385; FAX: 860-276-9438

Type of Business:

A new and exquisite collection of original, limited edition, art pieces that is designed to enrich your pastoral environment and to compliment any architectural context. Our fresh approach in vision, iconography and execution goes well beyond the customary symbolic references. Don't make your next statuary selection without first seeing these fine works of art.

BAPTISMAL FONTS

DAPRATO RIGALI STUDIOS, INC.

DAPRATO RIGALI STUDIOS, INC.
7956 Oakton St.
Niles, IL 60714
Tel.: 847-692-6350; FAX: 847-692-3445

Personnel:

John Rigali
Robert Rigali
Lisa Rigali Galvin
Mike Rigali

Type of Business:

Daprato Rigali Studios Inc. has been beautifying Churches in America since 1860.

Today we find the Rigali Family restoring and renovating the churches originally decorated by their Great-Grandfather, John E. Rigali; aware of his reputation to create spiritually moving environments with quality material and craftsmanship.

Some of their most recent jobs include: decoration and stained glass restoration at St. Mary of the Lake Seminary, Mundelein, IL.; Marble renovation and decoration, St. Elizabeth's Mother House, Allegany, N.Y.; and General Contracting for complete renovation of St. Bernadette's Church, Rockford, IL.

The Daprato Rigali staff is equipped to take your project from start to finish. If you're interested in working with a fine interior design studio experienced in Ecclesiastical Artistries please call for consultation at no obligation. We deliver what we design.

D.C. RIGGOTT INC.
3540 Neal Ave.
Afton, MN 55001
Tel.: 800-479-8777; FAX: 612-436-4769

Personnel:

Don Riggott . . . . Owner/President

Type of Business:

Specializing in vintage church accessories, architectural ornamentation and liturgical furnishings.

Stained Glass Windows • Altars • Lighting • Statuary • Stations of the Cross • Tabernacles • Monstranses • Fonts • Pews • Steeple Bells • Vestments • Books • Furniture • Candlesticks • Chalices, Please contact us with specific requests. We will be happy to send you photographs and specifics on any items in our inventory. You may have items in storage or not being used, please contact us as we are actively searching for vintage items to purchase for re-use in liturgical spaces.

Conrad Schmitt Studios Inc.

CONRAD SCHMITT STUDIOS, INC.
2405 S. 162nd St.
New Berlin, WI 53151
Tel.: 800-969-3033; 414-786-3030; FAX: 414-786-9036

Personnel:

Heidi Gruenke Emery . . . . Vice President & Marketing Director

Type of Business:

Since 1889, this family-owned Studio has restored and decorated hundreds of interiors across the country. Their scope of work includes the investigation and documentation of original decorative schemes; the restoration of those schemes through the application of various decorative techniques including gilding, glazing, marbleizing, stenciling, and graining, as well as the design, fabrication, conservation or replication of murals and stained glass. The Studio can assist projects in the early stages with architectural samples and rendering for fund-raising. Recently completed projects include St. Josaphat's Basilica, Milwaukee, WI; St. Ann's, Napoleanville, LA; and St. Bernard's, Akron, OH.

BELLS, CARILLONS, ETC.

BROSAMER'S BELLS
207 Irwin St.
Brooklyn, MI 49230
Tel.: 517-592-9030; FAX: 517-592-4511

Personnel:
R.C. Brosamer and family

Type of Business:
BUYS & SELLS USED BELLS
We will purchase pre-owned bells and remove bells that are no longer needed by churches or other organizations. The bells will then be restored and kept until they are called on to serve someone else's needs. Our pre-owned cast bells are affordable. Check on new, then call us.

CHIME MASTER™ SYSTEMS
Automation ◆ Chimes ◆ Bells ◆ Carillons
America's Best Value
USA Toll Free 800-344-7464
CAN Toll Free 800-432-3977
www.ChimeMaster.com

CHIME MASTER SYSTEMS
P.O. Box 936
Lancaster, OH 43130
Tel.: 800-344-7464; FAX: 614-746-9566
e-mail: cmsinfo@ChimeMaster.com

Type of Business:
Manufacturers of carillons and bell automation controls. Forty years of church bell experience.
Electronic Carillons: 100% digital reproduction, choose CD or recordable solid state memory storage. Keyboards for live performance. Update existing systems or design new.
Cast Bell Automation: Automate 1 bell to 50 or more. Renovations for bells, chimes and carillons. Bells play from keyboard or automatically from memory. Angelus, hour strike, and sacred music.
"Beautiful sound, easy to use, unmatched warranty"

(See full-page display ad on preceding page)

MAAS ROWE

MAAS-ROWE CARILLONS, INC.
2255 Meyers Ave.
Escondido, CA 92029
Tel.: 800-854-2023; FAX: 760-747-2677

Personnel:
Paul Rowe . . . . President
Craig Johnson . . . . National Sales Manager

Type of Business:
Established 1922. Manufacturers of automatic (computerized) Carillon and Church Bell Systems using compact discs for ultra high quality sound. Factory direct sales, service and installation. Sales—National and International. Upgrading of older carillon systems (any brand) to compact disc with computer control. Producers of compact discs featuring carillon and organ church music designed to play automatically or manually in computer controlled carillon equipment. Manufacturers of Musical Handbells. Importers of European Cast Bronze Church Bells and accessories.

McSHANE BELL FOUNDRY CO., INC.
400 C Arundel Corporation Rd.
Glen Burnie, MD 21060
Tel.: 410-636-4390; FAX: 410-636-7533

Type of Business:
Manufacturer of bells, chimes and electric ringing equipment for both swinging and stationary systems. Complete bell restoration and bell repairs to all makes.

D.C. RIGGOTT INC.
3540 Neal Ave.
Afton, MN 55001
Tel.: 800-479-8777; FAX: 612-436-4769

Personnel:
Don Riggott . . . . Owner/President

Type of Business:
Specializing in vintage church accessories, architectural ornamentation and liturgical furnishings.
Stained Glass Windows • Altars • Lighting • Statuary • Stations of the Cross • Tabernacles • Monstranses • Fonts • Pews • Steeple Bells • Vestments • Books • Furniture • Candlesticks • Chalices, Please contact us with specific requests. We will be happy to send you photographs and specifics on any items in our inventory. You may have items in storage or not being used, please contact us as we are actively searching for vintage items to purchase for re-use in liturgical spaces.

Schulmerich Bells
Electronic Carillons • Handbells • Cast Bell Carillons
Carillon Hill • PO Box 903 • Sellersville, PA • 18960-0903
215/257-2771 • 800/772-3557 • Fax: 215/257-1910

SCHULMERICH CARILLONS INC.
Carillon Hill
Sellersville, PA 18960
Tel.: 800-772-3557 / 215-257-2771; FAX: 215-257-1910

Personnel:
Bern E. Deichmann . . . . President & CEO

Type of Business:
Enhance your worship celebration easily and affordably with the sound of Schulmerich Bells, a leader in bell music technologies since 1935. Schulmerich designs and manufactures cast bronze handbells, electronic carillons, MelodyChime™ Instruments (hand-held chimes), towers/cupolas, and liturgical bells. Also furnishes cast bells.

VERDIN
V
SINCE 1842

THE VERDIN CO.
444 Reading Rd.
Cincinnati, OH 45202
Tel.: 800-543-0488; 531-241-4010; FAX: 531-241-1855

Personnel:
Robert Verdin . . . . CEO
James Verdin . . . . President
David Verdin . . . . Vice President
Suzanne Sizer . . . . Sales/Mkt. Mgr.

Type of Business:
Combining 155 years of experience and tradition with 20th Century technical expertise makes The Verdin Company the leading supplier and manufacturer of bells, bell ringing equipment, carillons and clocks in the nation.

vanBergen
est 1795

THE VAN BERGEN COMPANY
P.O. Box 12928
Charleston, SC 29422-2928
Tel.: 800-544-8820; FAX: 803-559-0797

Personnel:
Harry van Bergen . . . . President
Peter Martin. . . . . General Manager

Type of Business:
Established in 1795, van Bergen celebrates over 200 years of service. We represent the famous Paccard Fonderie de Cloches. Van Bergen prides itself on providing the highest quality in cast bronze bells, electronic carillon instruments, clock and bell towers and electrification/renovation of existing cast bells. Van Bergen is committed to provide support, expert installation and superior service. OUR BELLS RING ROUND THE WORLD.

BENCHES, LECTERNS, PEWS

Hamlin
ATWOOD-HAMLIN MANUFACTURING

ATWOOD-HAMLIN MFG., INC.
P.O. Box 150
Richmond, IL 60071
Tel.: 1-800-545-8964

Type of Business:
Since 1948, Atwood-Hamlin Manufacturing has been your source for church furnishing. Our products include the famous **Hamlin Folding Pew Kneeler** as well as their replacement upholstered pads and parts. For your pews we also offer our comfortable, non-slip **Pew-Form Cushions** that do not have to be fastened to your pews. All reversible styles available. Our solid oak, stacking pew-chairs top our line of seating products. All upholstered products are available in hundreds of colors and fabric choices. We also offer pew refinishing services. Call for free product information.

CHURCH CHAIR INDUSTRIES INC.
7007 New Calhoun Hwy. NE
Rome, GA 30161
Tel.: 800-331-5411; FAX: 706-291-9277
e-mail: msammons@aol.com

Type of Business:
Church Chair is one of the largest chair manufacturers in the world. We build only chairs for churches and deal on direct basis with the church. We build 5 different metal chairs and 4 wood chairs. We build two types of pew chairs and three classroom type chairs.
We are a full scale manufacturer, not an assembler. We buy steel in the raw form and then form it into tubing with our tube mill. Then weld it with our 4 robotic welders, paint it with our power coating system and then on to final assembly, and finally to shipping on our trucks. We build and ship about 50,000 chairs each month all over the world.

Serenity® CHURCH FURNITURE

WALTER JACOBI AND SONS, INC.
1400 Elmer St. / P.O. Box 471
Belmont, CA 94002
Tel.: 800-522-6241; FAX: 650-592-2434
website: http://www.serenity-wjs.com

Personnel:
Arno M. Jacobi. . . . . Sales
Albert O. Jacobi . . . . Sales

Type of Business:
Since 1921, MANUFACTURER: Devotional - Reverential - Furniture. MADE TO ORDER: Conducive to MEDITATION and PRAYER - ALL Wood, Cushion-loc, and Conventional Upholstered - Pews, Pewchairs, PewCHAR, Presider Chair, Clergy Chairs, Serenity Kneelers, Premium Kneelers, SKE Hydraulics, Kneeler Maintenance, Kneeler Parts and Repairs, Altar, Ambo, Lectern, Candlesticks, Crosses, Carvings. Seating Consultants to Church and/or Architect. Computer Layouts - send Plans or CAD Disk.

D.C. RIGGOTT INC.
3540 Neal Ave.
Afton, MN 55001
Tel.: 800-479-8777; FAX: 612-436-4769

Personnel:
Don Riggott . . . . Owner/President

Type of Business:
Specializing in vintage church accessories, architectural ornamentation and liturgical furnishings.
Stained Glass Windows • Altars • Lighting • Statuary • Stations of the Cross • Tabernacles • Monstranses • Fonts • Pews • Steeple Bells • Vestments • Books • Furniture • Candlesticks • Chalices, Please contact us with specific requests. We will be happy to send you photographs and specifics on any items in our inventory. You may have items in storage or not being used, please contact us as we are actively searching for vintage items to purchase for re-use in liturgical spaces.

BISHOP'S REGALIA

ADRIAN HAMERS®
CHURCH INTERIORS

ADRIAN HAMERS INC.
2 Madison Ave.
Larchmont, NY 10538
Tel.: 914-834-7780; FAX: 914-834-0712

Type of Business:
Since 1887, the Hamers name has been synonymous with expert silversmithing throughout the world in the field of Liturgical Art. We are also experts in: Church Interiors from design to execution, Renovations, Altars, Sacred Vessels, Appraisals, Gold and Silver Plating & Repairing, Tabernacles, Marble, Woodwork & Woodcarving, Statuary, Stained Glass, Pews & Chairs, Gold Leafing, Frescoes, Restoration, Trompe-l'oeuil, Wall Murals (repair and conservation cleaning), Ornamental Plaster, Heraldic Designs & Bishop Regalia.

P. J. McDERMOTT & CO.
P.O. Box 950101
Fort Tilden, NY 11695
Tel.: 718-634-5583

Personnel:
Patrick J. McDermott . . . . President

Type of Business:
We are a major supplier of Ready-made suits, coats, slacks, blazers, R.J. Toomey Co. shirt fronts, French-cuff shirts, clerical vests ... "Beau-Veste" and Gammarelli (Rome) albs, surplices and rochets ... Fully custom tailored cassocks ... We are considered the leader in the U.S. and specialize in Bishops and Monsignors robes, all of which are custom tailored here. We also supply all Episcopal accessories; mitres, zuchettos, birettas, rochets, albs, pectoral cross, chains and cross cords, bishops rings, croziers.
HAVE TAPE MEASURE — WILL TRAVEL

D.C. RIGGOTT INC.
3540 Neal Ave.
Afton, MN 55001
Tel.: 800-479-8777; FAX: 612-436-4769

Personnel:
Don Riggott . . . . Owner/President

Type of Business:
Specializing in vintage church accessories, architectural ornamentation and liturgical furnishings.
Stained Glass Windows • Altars • Lighting • Statuary • Stations of the Cross • Tabernacles • Monstranses • Fonts • Pews • Steeple Bells • Vestments • Books • Furniture • Candlesticks • Chalices, Please contact us with specific requests. We will be happy to send you photographs and specifics on any items in our inventory. You may have items in storage or not being used, please contact us as we are actively searching for vintage items to purchase for re-use in liturgical spaces.

SN
STADELMAIER
NIJMEGEN

STADELMAIER-NIJMEGEN-HOLLAND
P.O. Box 7063
6503 GN Nijmegen
Nijmegen, Holland 6501 BA
Tel.: 31-24-3791170; FAX: 31-24-3791171
e-mail: stadelmaier@telebyte.nl

Type of Business:

SN mighty mitres are visibly the best.
SN crosiers have the SN-signature, to match the total design.
Ben Stadelmaier Sr. is the specialist.

INTERIOR DESIGN & RESTORATION

Your Supplier of Fine Ecclesiastical Interiors
CAVE CO.

CAVE COMPANY
P.O. Box 211
Old Westbury, NY 11568
Tel.: 800-989-CAVE / 516-333-3659; FAX: 516-338-4796
e-mail: www.csrr.com/caveco.html

Personnel:

Gregory P. Cave . . . . President

Type of Business:

Our company is a fourth-generation business whose specialty is in the ecclesiastical interior design and restoration field. Our staff prides itself in the complete restoration and decoration of the smallest chapel to the largest cathedral, offering such unique services and products as our "Tree of Life" for fund raising, and electrical devotional candle stands. Our true specialty is the personalized service we are committed to bring our customers in the professional fashion they deserve.

We specialize in:

- Tree of Life
- Electric Devotional Candles
- Painting & Decorating
- Poor Boxes
- Kneelers & Pews; Restoration & New
- Gold Leaf
- Statuary & Sculpture; Repair & Restoration
- Challices & Ciboria; 24 Karat Gold Plating

LAMPS & LIGHTING

CAPITOL LIGHTING & RESTORATION
500 W. Exchange St.
Spring Lake, MI 49456-2083
Tel.: 616-844-5000; FAX: 616-844-2228

Personnel:

Brenda Hoyt . . . . . . Managing Director — Sales and Marketing
John Fuchs. . . . . Managing Director — Design

Type of Business:

CAPITOL LIGHTING & RESTORATION is a company whose two founders and senior business associates have a history in the lighting industry dating back to the 1950's. It is a company totally dedicated to supplying quality products and delivering them on schedule. Due to the background of its founders, CAPITOL LIGHTING is sensitive to the needs of its clients. Designers need accurate drawings and information on time. Owners and contractors need adherence to schedules with equipment delivered in good condition and in conformance with approved coordination drawings.

CAPITOL LIGHTING & RESTORATION is owned and operated by Brenda Hoyt and John Fuchs. Both bring their own unique talents to the organization making it unrivaled in the lighting industry. CAPITOL LIGHTING's associates include a metal sculptor with a Master of Fine Arts degree; another metal sculptor whose special interest is 19th century gas and oil lighting fixtures and their early conversion to electric usage; two foundry specialists, one for short custom production runs, the other for production runs using the traditional lost wax process. In this process, CAPITOL LIGHTING & RESTORATION is able to offer bronze chandeliers of extraordinary quality. CAPITOL LIGHTING & RESTORATION has also successfully modified existing and antique lighting equipment to make use of newly developed light sources. It has always been a corporate philosophy to restore old fixtures rather than discard them and supply new replacements — it is a philosophy much appreciated by sensitive clients.

In addition to restoring and supplying ornamental lighting equipment, CAPITOL LIGHTING & RESTORATION has carved a niche for itself in the design of special lighting equipment largely unavailable from other suppliers. Whether it is the design of ornamental exit signs or small accent lights to be installed in very limited spaces — CAPITOL LIGHTING & RESTORATION has always prevailed in the face of difficult design challenges.

It is safe to say that no other ornamental lighting fixture supplier can claim to have this type of expertise at its disposal or within its own corporate structure — it is a fertile environment conducive to the promotion and fulfillment of the design process.

RAMBUSCH

RAMBUSCH
40 West 13th St.
New York, NY 10011
Tel.: 212-675-0400; FAX: 212-620-4687

PersonneL:
Viggo Bech Rambusch . . . . Senior Project Director
Martin V. Rambusch . . . . Stained Glass Director

Type of Business:
Since 1898, creating church interiors, liturgical furnishings, and art work. Fine restoration of church interiors. In-house studios and shops for designing and executing stained glass, church lighting systems, art metal work, and decorative painting.

D.C. RIGGOTT INC.
3540 Neal Ave.
Afton, MN 55001
Tel.: 800-479-8777; FAX: 612-436-4769

Personnel:
Don Riggott . . . . Owner/President

Type of Business:
Specializing in vintage church accessories, architectural ornamentation and liturgical furnishings.
Stained Glass Windows • Altars • Lighting • Statuary • Stations of the Cross • Tabernacles • Monstranses • Fonts • Pews • Steeple Bells • Vestments • Books • Furniture • Candlesticks • Chalices, Please contact us with specific requests. We will be happy to send you photographs and specifics on any items in our inventory. You may have items in storage or not being used, please contact us as we are actively searching for vintage items to purchase for re-use in liturgical spaces.

MOSAICS

ABBOTT CHURCH GOODS, INC.
Showroom: 1515 Route 38
Cherry Hill, NJ 08002
Tel.: 800-522-2688; 609-662-6959; FAX: 609-665-5109
website: http://www.abbottsinc.com
e-mail: ACG.INC@internetMCI.com

Personnel:
Daniel J. Castonguay . . . . President
Joseph F. McKeaney . . . . General Manager
Michael W. Wasyluk . . . . Customer Service

Type of Business:
Purveyors of the Finest Vesture, Paraments, Statuary & Metalware since 1962. Unique and original creations, our specialty. Custom designs to complement your liturgical environment. Exclusive representatives of Slabbinck Master Collection & Original Collection.

RAMBUSCH

RAMBUSCH
40 West 13th St.
New York, NY 10011
Tel.: 212-675-0400; FAX: 212-620-4687

Personnel:
Viggo Bech Rambusch . . . . Senior Project Director
Martin V. Rambusch . . . . Stained Glass Director

Type of Business:
Since 1898, creating church interiors, liturgical furnishings, and art work. Fine restoration of church interiors. In-house studios and shops for designing and executing stained glass, church lighting systems, art metal work, and decorative painting.

D.C. RIGGOTT INC.
3540 Neal Ave.
Afton, MN 55001
Tel.: 800-479-8777; FAX: 612-436-4769

Personnel:
Don Riggott . . . . Owner/President

Type of Business:
Specializing in vintage church accessories, architectural ornamentation and liturgical furnishings.
Stained Glass Windows • Altars • Lighting • Statuary • Stations of the Cross • Tabernacles • Monstranses • Fonts • Pews • Steeple Bells • Vestments • Books • Furniture • Candlesticks • Chalices, Please contact us with specific requests. We will be happy to send you photographs and specifics on any items in our inventory. You may have items in storage or not being used, please contact us as we are actively searching for vintage items to purchase for re-use in liturgical spaces.

CONRAD SCHMITT STUDIOS, INC.
2405 S. 162nd St.
New Berlin, WI 53151
Tel.: 800-969-3033; 414-786-3030; FAX: 414-786-9036

Personnel:
Heidi Gruenke Emery . . . . Vice President & Marketing Director

Type of Business:
Since 1889, this family-owned Studio has restored and decorated hundreds of interiors across the country. Their scope of work includes the investigation and documentation of original decorative schemes; the restoration of those schemes through the application of various decorative techniques including gilding, glazing, marbleizing, stenciling, and graining, as well as the design, fabrication, conservation or replication of murals and stained glass. The Studio can assist projects in the early stages with architectural samples and rendering for fund-raising. Recently completed projects include St. Josaphat's Basilica, Milwaukee, WI; St. Ann's, Napoleanville, LA; and St. Bernard's, Akron, OH.

ORGANS & PIANOS

ALLEN ORGAN CO.
P.O. Box 36
Macungie, PA 18062-0036
Tel.: 610-966-2202; FAX: 610-965-3098
e-mail: aosales@allenorgan.com
website: http://www.allenorgan.com

Personnel:
Barry Holben

Type of Business:
World's largest builder of church organs, with a variety of standard models and custom designs to meet every need.

CHURCH ORGAN SYSTEMS
422 Wards Corner Rd.
Loveland, OH 45140-8390
Tel.: 513-576-4660; FAX: 513-576-6871

Personnel:
Duane Kuhn . . . . Vice President
Darlene Davis . . . . Administrative Assistant
Rodney Barbour . . . . Manager Sales & Svc.
David Wade . . . . Director Engrg.

Type of Business:
Church Organ Systems, a division of The Baldwin Piano and Organ Co., is dedicated to serving churches with products and programs designed to support music ministry.

HAMMOND®

HAMMOND SUZUKI
733 Annoreno Dr.
Addison, IL 60101
Tel.: (630) 543-0277; FAX: (630) 543-0279

Personnel:
Mike Armstrong . . . . VP Sales

Type of Business:
Manufacturer and distributor of Hammond Institutional Organs, Hammond Digital Pianos, ProLine Keyboards, Sound Modules and Leslie Speaker Systems.

ORGAN CLEARING HOUSE
P.O. Box 104-RC
Harrisville, NH 03450-0104
Tel.: 603-827-3055; FAX: 603-827-3750

Personnel:
Alan Miller Laufman . . . . Exec. Director

Type of Business:
Urban renewal and church closings/mergers frequently make pipe organs available for recycling. Since 1959, we have relocated nationwide hundreds of carefully renovated instruments to churches which could not afford new ones. We are now listing more than 300 pipe organs, large and small, old and new. Please send $6 in stamps for our current brochure. Or let us know if you have a pipe organ for sale; we may be able to help.

RODGERS®
INSTRUMENT CORPORATION
The sound choice!

RODGERS INSTRUMENT CORPORATION
1300 N.E. 25th Ave.
Hillsboro, OR 97124
Tel.: 503-648-4181; FAX: 503-681-0444

Personnel:
Dennis Houlihan . . . . President
Jonas Nordwall. . . . . Product Marketing Manager
Donna Parker. Marketing Administrator
David Tomb . . . . Sales & Marketing Development Manager

Type of Business:
Rodgers Instrument Corporation is respected worldwide for technical leadership in the manufacturing of digital electronic, pipe and electronic/pipe combination organs using PDI (Parallel Digital Imaging) technology for church, home, schools, and concert halls. Rodgers also builds digital keyboards, MIDI sound modules and sequencers.

(See full-page display ad on next page)

WICKS PIPE ORGAN COMPANY

WICKS ORGAN CO.
1100 Fifth St.
Highland, IL 62249
Tel.: 618-654-2191; FAX: 618-654-3770

Personnel:
Martin Wick. . . . . President
Scott Wick . . . . Vice President
Jack Jenkins. . . . . Sales Manager

Type of Business:
Custom designed pipe organs and combination instruments to fit your space and budget. 100+ years experience in over 6,000 churches worldwide. Free on-site evaluations and proposal drawings. Highest levels of professionalism from beginning to end. 10-year warranty. Specialists in DIRECT-ELECTRIC™ and Mechanical Action organs. Financially sound company, AAA-#1 Dunn & Bradstreet rating. Also, pre-designed compact models for limited space, time or budget. Some available for immediate delivery. Literature and video available for committees and individuals. Call Wicks Organ Co. at 800-444-WICK or 618-654-2191.

PEW CUSHIONS

Hamlin
ATWOOD-HAMLIN MANUFACTURING

ATWOOD-HAMLIN MFG., INC.
P.O. Box 150
Richmond, IL 60071
Tel.: 1-800-545-8964

Type of Business:
Since 1948, Atwood-Hamlin Manufacturing has been your source for church furnishing. Our products include the famous **Hamlin Folding Pew Kneeler** as well as their replacement upholstered pads and parts. For your pews we also offer our comfortable, non-slip **Pew-Form Cushions** that do not have to be fastened to your pews. All reversible styles available. All upholstered products are available in hundreds of colors and fabric choices. We also offer pew refinishing services. Call for free product information.

CHURCH CHAIR INDUSTRIES INC.
7007 New Calhoun Hwy. NE
Rome, GA 30161
Tel.: 800-331-5411; FAX: 706-291-9277
e-mail: msammons@aol.com

Type of Business:

Church Chair is one of the largest chair manufacturers in the world. We build only chairs for churches and deal on direct basis with the church. We build 5 different metal chairs and 4 wood chairs. We build two types of pew chairs and three classroom type chairs.

We are a full scale manufacturer, not an assembler. We buy steel in the raw form and then form it into tubing with our tube mill. Then weld it with our 4 robotic welders, paint it with our power coating system and then on to final assembly, and finally to shipping on our trucks. We build and ship about 50,000 chairs each month all over the world.

PLAQUES & MEMORIALS

"Honor the Gift..................Honor the Giver"

B&D ... CONTRIBUTOR RECOGNITION PRODUCTS
119 South Mansfield Blvd.
Cherry Hill, NJ 08034-3611
1-800-873-3180; FAX: 609-429-3772

Honor those who Give, and they are your's forever ... Contributor Recognition is a key fund raising element that increases response and levels of giving. Our products create a permanent bond between the givers and their Church. Impressive, awe-inspiring and motivational, they enhance Church decor in an understated elegant manner. We can accommodate Churches of all sizes. Trees, Walls of Honor and Plaques are expandable, high quality and affordable.

We are as close as your telephone.

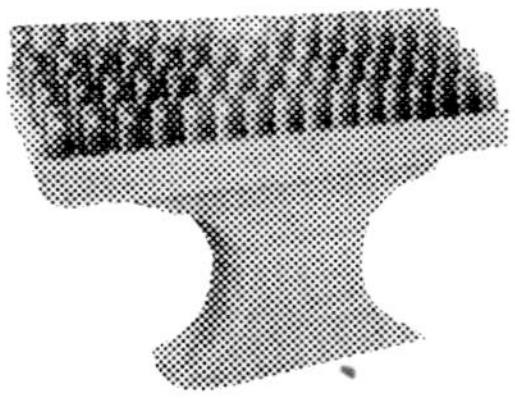

CARROLL ART INC.
710 NE 26th St.
Fort Lauderdale, FL 33305
Tel.: 800-876-4569; FAX: 954-561-4098

Personnel:

David Nagle . . . . President/Designer
Liza Palmer . . . . Sales Manager
Andrea Speier . . . . Sales Rep.
Robert Perkins . . . . Sales Rep.

Type of Business:

Carroll Art has been in business for 12 years. We design and custom build all types of plaques and memorials including the tree of life, plaques, recognition systems, church signs, donor plates, custom sculptures, and memorials are just a few of our products. We can provide you with the perfect fund raising tool.

TREES • OF • LIFE

A proven successful fund raiser whose strong lines and rich colors will enhance the space into which it is placed.

DAVID KLASS ART STUDIOS
136 West 24th St.
New York, NY 10011
Tel.: 212-243-7633; FAX: 212-243-7633

Personnel:

David Klass . . . . Owner, Designer

Type of Business:

Since 1968 David Klass has created numerous Trees of Life. Each one is custom designed to meet your needs. The finest select hardwoods, brasses and bronze are used.

Our beautiful designs and workmanship are ideal for donor recognition and fund raising drives. Special symbols and imagery meaningful to your parish can be incorporated into the design.

THE ARTIST'S HAND MAKES THE DIFFERENCE

SANFORD WERFEL- ARTIST

SANFORD WERFEL - ARTIST
425 Old Georges Rd.,
North Brunswick, NJ 08902
Tel.: 800-443-3744; 732-297-1166; FAX: 732-297-7770

Type of Business:

Since 1968, Mr. Werfel's sculptures have been helping parishes to INSPIRE and MOTIVATE GIVING through the use of his original sculptures. Building drives, capital or endowment funds, sacrificial giving, and tithing programs all benefit from using Donor Recognition Sculptures. Call or write for FREE INFORMATION. Included will be costs and designs as well as a "HOW-TO-USE" guide that tells how your parish can use sculpture to raise funds. Good art is forever.

CHECK OUT OUR NEW PILGRIMAGE DESTINATION GUIDE FOR 1998

NOW INCLUDED IN THIS SHIPMENT

ZAX Recognition Products

Donor Wall

Tree of Life

Book of Memory

The fine art of gratitude.

Commemorate Your Donors with handsomely presented Plaques by Zax.

DONOR WALLS OF DISTINCTION
BOOK OF MEMORIES
TREES OF LIFE • MULTI-NAME PLAQUES
ADD-ON DONOR PLAQUES • MARBLEGRAPH PLAQUES
BRONZE TABLETS • AWARDS

zax
Recognition Products

Call TOLL FREE for an Estimate: 800/258-1566
or Write for Our Comprehensive New Catalog.

ZAX Corporation, 20 Otterson Street, Nashua, NH 03061
Telephone: (603) 889-4126 Fax: (603) 883-6395

STRATEGIC PLANNING

Kirby Smith Associates, Inc.
Ministry of Church Finance

KIRBY-SMITH ASSOCIATES, INC.
5 Fawn Dr.
Quarryville, PA 17566
Tel.: 1-800-762-3996; 717-284-3100; FAX: 717-284-3659
website: http://www.kirbysmith.com; e-mail: kirbysmith@aol.com

Personnel:
C. Eugene Musser . . . . President
Karl T. Frick . . . . Director Ministry Development

Type of Business:
Since our founding in 1938, Kirby-Smith Associates has served more than 5,000 parishes and schools, and has raised over two billion dollars. Our campaigns include detailed on-site counseling, organizational guidance, comprehensive materials, as well as long-term consultation and stewardship training. We offer a full range of services to better meet the needs of your parish or school; Capital and Budget Campaigns, Feasibility Studies, Pre-Campaign Planning and Strategic Planning. Meeting the needs of the Catholic community we serve is our ministry and the service we bring to you.

TABLES & CHAIRS

CHURCH CHAIR INDUSTRIES INC.
7007 New Calhoun Hwy. NE
Rome, GA 30161
Tel.: 800-331-5411; FAX: 706-291-9277
e-mail: msammons@aol.com

Type of Business:
Church Chair is one of the largest chair manufacturers in the world. We build only chairs for churches and deal on direct basis with the church. We build 5 different metal chairs and 4 wood chairs. We build two types of pew chairs and three classroom type chairs.
We are a full scale manufacturer, not an assembler. We buy steel in the raw form and then form it into tubing with our tube mill. Then weld it with our 4 robotic welders, paint it with our power coating system and then on to final assembly, and finally to shipping on our trucks. We build and ship about 50,000 chairs each month all over the world.

clarin
a division of greenwich industries, l.p.

CLARIN, A DIVISION OF GREENWICH INDUSTRIES, L.P.
927 North Shore Dr.
Lake Bluff, IL 60044
Tel.: 847-295-2200; FAX: 847-234-9001

Personnel:
William P. Peterson . . . . President
Wilson J. Troup III . . . . Vice President Sales and Marketing
Greg Star. . . . . CFO
Evelyn Herron . . . . Vice President Human Resources

Type of Business:
Manufacturer of portable and fixed lecture room seating. Supplier of logo chairs and stools for schools and athletic teams, correct pitch music chairs, tablet arm chairs and other seating products for all uses. Our fabrics, colors and options provide the most contemporary seating environments available.
Since 1925 our commitment to excellence in service, product durability and style, enables Clarin to offer the ultimate in seating concepts to customers worldwide.

CLERICAL APPAREL

DQ
DUFFY & QUINN
Apparel for the Clergy

DUFFY & QUINN
307 5th Ave.
New York, NY 10016
Tel.: 800-425-3466 / 212-725-0213; FAX: 212-997-7318

Personnel:
John M. McGuinness . . . . Manager
Marvin Goldman . . . . Owner

Type of Business:
Duffy & Quinn is a leading supplier of religious apparel and accessories to the Reverend clergy — featuring suits, coats, clerical shirts, ready-made and custom-tailored cassocks. Monsignors and Bishops robes are made to order, with careful attention to detail, quality and on-time delivery. Full stocks of R.J. Toomey, Beau Veste, Gammarelli, and Barbiconi merchandise available for shipment at once. Mitres, zuchettos, birettas, vestments, pectoral crosses, chains, cross cords and Bishop's rings are our specialty.

THE HOLY+ROOD GUILD

THE HOLY ROOD GUILD
St. Joseph's Abbey
167 North Spencer Rd.
Spencer, MA 01562-1233
Tel.: 508-885-8750; FAX: 508-885-8758

Type of Business:
Designers and crafters of ecclesiastical vesture for over 40 years. Inspired by our monastic tradition, we seek to unite in our work simplicity in design, quality in materials and excellence in craftsmanship. The result is vesture that enhances the liturgical celebration with visual grace and order. Our artists—both monks and laypersons—are available for custom design work and consultation. We also provide an extensive selection of ready made items.

ADAM KOCHLIN
DESIGNS

ADAM KOCHLIN DESIGNS
33 Magee Ave., 2nd Fl.
Stamford, CT 06902
Tel.: 800-886-4668; FAX: 203-325-3755

Personnel:
Adam Kochlin . . . . Design Director
Michael Kirshbaum . . . . Executive Director
Regina Maguire . . . . Product Manager

Type of Business:
Adam Kochlin Designs creates a complete line of made to order vestments and hangings produced in our studio in Connecticut. Working with a number of artists we also create made to order sacred vessels and appointments including processional crosses, pacschal candlesticks, altar candlesticks, sanctuary lamps, incensors, chalices and patens, aumbrys, curets, and falgons in wood, ceramic, glass and metal. Call 800-886-4668 for free catalog and information.

P. J. McDERMOTT & CO.
P.O. Box 950101
Fort Tilden, NY 11695
Tel.: 718-634-5583

Personnel:
Patrick J. McDermott . . . . President

Type of Business:
We are a major supplier of Ready-made suits, coats, slacks, blazers, R.J. Toomey Co. shirt fronts, French-cuff shirts, clerical vests ... "Beau-Veste" and Gammarelli (Rome) albs, surplices and rochets ... Fully custom tailored cassocks ... We are considered the leader in the U.S. and specialize in Bishops and Monsignors robes, all of which are custom tailored here. We also supply all Episcopal accessories; mitres, zuchettos, birettas, rochets, albs, pectoral cross, chains and cross cords, bishops rings, croziers. HAVE TAPE MEASURE — WILL TRAVEL

MURPHY VESTMENTS®

MURPHY VESTMENTS
Murphy Cap & Gown Co.
4200 31st St. North
St. Petersburg, FL 33714
Tel.: 800-876-8774; 813-527-0696; FAX: 813-526-3528
website: www.murphyrobes.com; e-mail: murphyrb@gte.net

Personnel:
Don Camp . . . . President
Gary Bergamo . . . . Sales Manager
George Shahine . . . . Administrative Manager
Josephine DeFeo . . . . Vestment Designer

Type of Business:
Manufacturer of vestments, albs, cassocks, choir and acolyte robes and accessories, all value priced with guaranteed fit and quality. We supply a complete line of liturgical attire, custom tailored as well as many styles in stock and ready to ship within 24 hours of receipt of order. Available through your church goods dealer, or call or write for more information.

CLERGY SHIRTS

Stadelmaier USA LLC
Unique Liturgical Solutions
A Division of Patrick Baker & Sons and Stadelmaier Nijmegen

STADELMAIER USA LLC
1650 West St., P.O. Box 1028
Southington, CT 06489-5028
Tel.: 1-800-243-6385; FAX: 860-276-9438

Type of Business:
Finally, the generous shape and quality that allow for the greatest comfort and the highest performance. Silky smooth fabrics in black, french/blue and white, short and long sleeves, including Neckband dress shirts and the already famous Milano long sleeve tab collar shirt, made in 100% combed cotton fabric, "easy iron" in dark grey. All rich colors maintain their rich color after repeated washing, including black!

The Savior Processional Cross
Designed and made by Almy for the 1995 Papal Mass at St. Joseph's Seminary in New York. The Savior Cross is just one selection of Almy's exclusive offering of processional appointments, sacred vessels, eucharistic vestments and clerical clothing. Classic designs for today's church.
For a complimentary copy of the Almy Catalog, please call or write today.
C.M. ALMY & SON
OUTFITTERS TO THE CHURCH AND CLERGY SINCE 1892
10 GLENVILLE STREET DEPT YY GREENWICH CT 06836
1.800.225.ALMY E-MAIL almyaccess@almy.com

ROBES, VESTMENTS, ETC.

ABBOTT CHURCH GOODS, INC.
Showroom: 1515 Route 38
Cherry Hill, NJ 08002
Tel.: 800-522-2688; 609-662-6959; FAX: 609-665-5109
website: http://www.abbottsinc.com
e-mail: ACG.INC@internetMCI.com

Personnel:
Daniel J. Castonguay . . . . President
Joseph F. McKeaney . . . . General Manager
Michael W. Wasyluk . . . . Customer Service

Type of Business:
Purveyors of the Finest Vesture, Paraments, Statuary & Metalware since 1962. Unique and original creations, our specialty. Custom designs to complement your liturgical environment. Exclusive representatives of Slabbinck Master Collection & Original Collection.

C.M. ALMY & SON, INC.
10 Glenville St., P.O. Box 2644
Greenwich, CT 06836-2644
Tel.: 203-531-7600

Type of Business:
We make a complete line of eucharistic vestments, clerical haberdashery and choir robes; as well as sacred vessels worthy of the Lord's table. Chalices, ciboria and other metal appointments from ALMY are classic designs.

(See full-page display ad on preceding page)

T.M.

Bringing the Art Back into the Craft

BRAMANTE STUDIO
321 Wellington St. N.
Kitchener, ON, Canada N2H 5K8
Tel.: 800-295-6902; FAX: 519-570-2706

Personnel:
Abraham Mathew. . . . . President

Type of Business:
Every parish is unique, not only in terms of the parishioners who make up the body of the church, but also in terms of the art and architectural elements that define the worship space. At Bramante Studio we endeavour to capture this individuality in each fabric art piece we make. Using exceptional fabrics and old world craftsmanship, we create custom made hangings, tapestries, vestments, and altar cloths that seek to recognize the uniqueness of each parish.

Chagall Design Limited

CHAGALL DESIGN LIMITED
910 S. Los Angeles St., 9th Fl.
Los Angeles, CA 90015
Tel.: 800-947-7923; 213-624-7656; FAX: 213-624-8036

Type of Business:
Chagall Design is unique in its own right. Its reputation stems from the custom designs created here in America by European designer Jacques de Groot. These creations are designed for the individual and special needs of the Fathers and Parishes throughout the United States, Canada and Europe.
Working directly with the church, Chagall creates and custom makes the Chasubles, Banners, Altar Cloths and Stoles, which can be viewed on our web site, including the full Millennium collection and Millennium Banners both Old and New Testament. Chagall stands by our wide selection of fine fabrics and excellent craftsmanship with a full guarantee, and offer our beautiful designs to you at low prices.
To request a free catalogue or for more information on how our custom design house can best serve you, please call 1-800-947-7923 or E-mail to Chagall@IX.NETCOM.COM. Also, visit our web site WWW.CHAGALLDESIGN.COM.

Robert Gaspard Co.

ROBERT GASPARD CO., INC.
200 N. Janacek Rd.
Brookfield, WI 53045-6101
Tel.: 800-784-6868; 414-784-6800; FAX: 414-784-7567

Personnel:
Rose Gaspard . . . . President
John Andorfer . . . . Vice President
Jason R. Gaspard . . . . Sales & Marketing Mgr.

Type of Business:
The Robert Gaspard Co. was established in 1954. Over the past 43 years, we have grown to be a nationally-known company. We pride ourselves on the ability to create original custom designs to enrich your worship needs. Our complete line consists of all ecclesiastical vesture, as well as paraments, mass and altar linens, stoles, banners, chasubles, funeral palls, albs, cossacks, surplices, choir robes, acolyte robes and many accessories. Complimentary catalogs and fabric swatches sent on request.

Granda
Liturgical Arts, Inc.

GRANDA LITURGICAL ARTS, INC.
828 Davis St., Ste. 200
Evanston, IL 60201
Tel.: 800-425-0828; FAX: 847-492-1374
www.hispacom.es/granda; e-mail: ruf4granda@aol.com

Personnel:
Karen Johnson

Type of Business:
GRANDA LITURGICAL ARTS, Inc. is the USA branch of the largest supplier of church goods in the world: TALLERES DE ARTE GRANDA, S.A.
With 65 employees and sales all over the world, we can offer our experience in the manufacture of:
— metalware: chalices, tabernacles, etc.
— vestments
— wood carvings
— church decoration, interior design
Since 1891, we have been serving the church, combining modern techniques (computer aided design, projects in 3D ...) with artistic values.
Special custom orders are our specialty, styled and priced according to your needs.

HOUSE OF HANSEN
4223 W. Irving Park Rd.
Chicago, IL 60641
Tel.: 773-736-5858; FAX: 773-736-6715

Type of Business:
Clerical tailoring specialists for over 85 years. We specialize in Prelatial Appointments and Custom Tailored cassocks made by our professional staff. Custom tailored vestments and albs. A full line of ready-made clerical apparel. See our ad in the front section of this book.
(See display ad on preceding page)

ADAM KOCHLIN
DESIGNS

ADAM KOCHLIN DESIGNS
33 Magee Ave., 2nd Fl.
Stamford, CT 06902
Tel.: 800-886-4668; FAX: 203-325-3755

Personnel:
Adam Kochlin .... Design Director
Michael Kirshbaum .... Executive Director
Regina Maguire .... Product Manager

Type of Business:
Adam Kochlin Designs creates a complete line of made to order vestments and hangings produced in our studio in Connecticut. Working with a number of artists we also create made to order sacred vessels and appointments including processional crosses, pacschal candlesticks, altar candlesticks, sanctuary lamps, incensors, chalices and patens, aumbrys, curets, and falgons in wood, ceramic, glass and metal. Call 800-886-4668 for free catalog and information.

P. J. McDERMOTT & CO.
P.O. Box 950101
Fort Tilden, NY 11695
Tel.: 718-634-5583

Personnel:
Patrick J. McDermott .... President

Type of Business:
We are a major supplier of Ready-made suits, coats, slacks, blazers, R.J. Toomey Co. shirt fronts, French-cuff shirts, clerical vests ... "Beau-Veste" and Gammarelli (Rome) albs, surplices and rochets ... Fully custom tailored cassocks ... We are considered the leader in the U.S. and specialize in Bishops and Monsignors robes, all of which are custom tailored here. We also supply all Episcopal accessories; mitres, zuchettos, birettas, rochets, albs, pectoral cross, chains and cross cords, bishops rings, croziers.
HAVE TAPE MEASURE — WILL TRAVEL

SLABBINCK®

ART STUDIO SLABBINCK
Headquarters:
L. Bauwensstraat 18
8200 Brugge, Belgium
Tel.: 32-50-312557; FAX: 32-50-318358

Type of Business:
Belgian made vestments (chasubles, stoles, albs, copes, deacon-stoles, dalmatics, altar and lectern covers, altar linens and cloths, tapestries and banners). Chalices, ciboria, patens and pyxes also available. Slabbinck Speed Service offered for many items as advertised in our catalog. Also Dirk Slabbinck Master Collection, an exclusive collection of vestments and paraments created from the inspired imagination of master designer Dirk Slabbinck, or according to your own specifications. For information on the dealer nearest you, call 800-423-3224 or FAX 800-284-9000.

STADELMAIER
NIJMEGEN

STADELMAIER-NIJMEGEN-HOLLAND
P.O. Box 7063
6503 GN Nijmegen
Nijmegen, Holland 6501 BA
Tel.: 31-24-3791170; FAX: 31-24-3791171
e-mail: stadelmaier@telebyte.nl

Type of Business:
"LITURGICAL VESTMENTS OF INSPIRING BEAUTY"
A wide variety, sometimes handwoven, mostly hand-embroidered, sometimes bold, mostly elegant ... to serve all priests in different architectures. Always "QUALITY IN LITURGY," from Holland of course. Big enough, with a world wide reputation, to execute large orders with precision. Small enough to give orders the family touch and attention.
Parent Company of KREATON KEVELAER, GRAND GERMAN VESTMENTS.

CONSTRUCTION, MAINTENANCE & RENOVATION

RAMBUSCH

RAMBUSCH
40 West 13th St.
New York, NY 10011
Tel.: 212-675-0400; FAX: 212-620-4687

Personnel:
Viggo Bech Rambusch . . . . Senior Project Director
Martin V. Rambusch . . . . Stained Glass Director

Type of Business:
Since 1898, creating church interiors, liturgical furnishings, and art work. Fine restoration of church interiors. In-house studios and shops for designing and executing stained glass, church lighting systems, art metal work, and decorative painting.

ARCHITECTS

Conrad Schmitt Studios Inc.

CONRAD SCHMITT STUDIOS, INC.
2405 S. 162nd St.
New Berlin, WI 53151
Tel.: 800-969-3033; 414-786-3030; FAX: 414-786-9036

Personnel:
Heidi Gruenke Emery . . . . Vice President & Marketing Director

Type of Business:
Since 1889, this family-owned Studio has restored and decorated hundreds of interiors across the country. Their scope of work includes the investigation and documentation of original decorative schemes; the restoration of those schemes through the application of various decorative techniques including gilding, glazing, marbleizing, stenciling, and graining, as well as the design, fabrication, conservation or replication of murals and stained glass. The Studio can assist projects in the early stages with architectural samples and rendering for fund-raising. Recently completed projects include St. Josaphat's Basilica, Milwaukee, WI; St. Ann's, Napoleanville, LA; and St. Bernard's, Akron, OH.

ARTISTS & DECORATORS

BOTTI STUDIO OF ARCHITECTURAL ARTS, INC.

BOTTI STUDIO OF ARCHITECTURAL ARTS, INC.
919 Grove St.
Evanston, IL 60201
Tel.: 800-524-7211; FAX: 847-869-5996
847-869-5933; e-mail: Boti@ix.netcom.com

East Coast Studio
1517 State St.
Sarasota, FL 33577
Tel.: 941-951-0978; FAX: 941-953-9078

West Coast Studio
1038 N. Highway 101
Encinitas, CA 92024
Tel.: 619-753-0705; FAX: 619-753-0705

Personnel:
Staff includes internationlly recognized artists and designers working in conjunction with our highly skilled artisans and craftsmen.
Italo G. Botti . . . . President

Type of Business:
For generations Botti Studio has had a reputation for embodying all that is artistically creative in the traditional and contemporary ecclesiastical field. This field includes design and fabrication of stained and faceted glass windows, restoration of windows, church interiors, appointments, murals, sculpture, mosaic and marble. We are completely dedicated to both quality and satisfying our clients needs spiritually and liturgically. Botti Studio is nationwide, offering consultation and designs without obligation. Member Stained Glass Association of America.

Holy Land Art Company

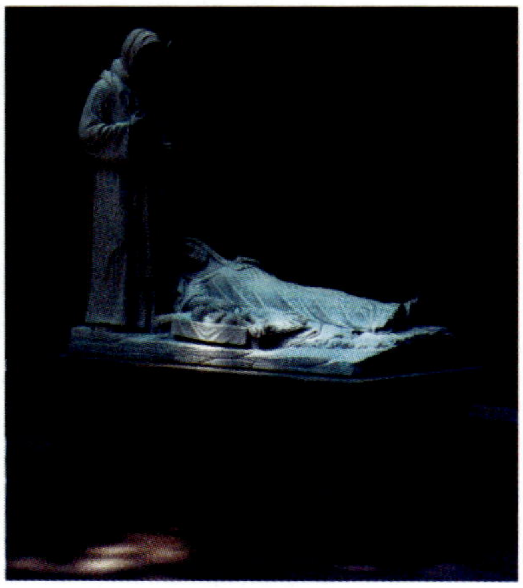

For over seventy years, Holy Land Art Company has been a leader in design and fabrication of liturgical furnishings and artwork.

Holy Land Art Company offers a full array of services:

- *Liturgical Designs*
- *Consultations*
- *Custom Wood*
- *Custom Metal*
- *Stone*
- *Fine Arts*
- *Stained Glass*
- *Seating*
- *Ecclesiastical Painting*

12 Sullivan Street
Westwood, NJ 07675
800-334-3621

300 Prosperity Farm Road
North Palm Beach, FL 33408
800-526-1294

Conrad Schmitt Studios Inc.

CONRAD SCHMITT STUDIOS, INC.
2405 S. 162nd St.
New Berlin, WI 53151
Tel.: 414-786-3030; 800-969-3033; FAX: 414-786-9036

Personnel:
Heidi Gruenke Emery . . . . Vice President & Marketing Director

Type of Business:
Since 1889, the Conrad Schmitt Studios has restored and decorated hundreds of interiors across the country. Their scope of work includes the investigation/documentation of original design schemes, the restoration of those schemes through the application of various decorative techniques including gilding, glazing, marbleizing, stencilling, and graining, as well as the conservation, restoration, and replication of murals and stained glass. Some of their recently completed projects include the Cathedral of the Assumption, Louisville, Kentucky; St. John's Cathedral, Shreveport, Louisiana; and Sacred Heart Church, New Philadelphia, Ohio.

DAPRATO RIGALI STUDIOS, INC.

DAPRATO RIGALI STUDIOS, INC.
7956 Oakton St.
Niles, IL 60714
Tel.: 847-692-6350; FAX: 847-692-3445

Personnel:
John Rigali
Robert Rigali
Lisa Rigali Galvin
Mike Rigali

Type of Business:
Daprato Rigali Studios Inc. has been beautifying Churches in America since 1860.
Today we find the Rigali Family restoring and renovating the churches originally decorated by their Great-Grandfather, John E. Rigali; aware of his reputation to create spiritually moving environments with quality material and craftsmanship.
Some of their most recent jobs include: decoration and stained glass restoration at St. Mary of the Lake Seminary, Mundelein, IL.; Marble renovation and decoration, St. Elizabeth's Mother House, Allegany, N.Y.; and General Contracting for complete renovation of St. Bernadette's Church, Rockford, IL.
The Daprato Rigali staff is equipped to take your project from start to finish. If you're interested in working with a fine interior design studio experienced in Ecclesiastical Artistries please call for consultation at no obligation. We deliver what we design.

Holy Land Art Company

HOLY LAND ART CO.
12 Sullivan St.
Westwood, NJ 07675
Tel.: 800-334-3621

Type of Business:
For over 70 years, a leader in design and fabrication of liturgical furnishings and artwork.

ALBERT MICHAELS CONSERVATION, INC.
1116 North Third St.
Harrisburg, PA 17102
Tel.: 717-232-9592; FAX: 717-234-0311

Personnel:
John M. DiTonno . . . . Projects Manager
John A. Rita. . . . . Conservator
William W. Tull. . . . . General Manager

Type of Business:
Founded in 1971, we offer a range of art and architectural conservation and restoration services, including PROJECT PLANNING and collection assessment, ANALYTICAL INVESTIGATION to determine original and subsequent finishes including techniques and materials employed. CONSERVATION & RESTORATION OF original artwork, ornamental plaster, painted surfaces, interior wood finishes, marble surfaces historic furniture, metal light fixtures, leaded glass windows, and REPRODUCTION OF ornamental plaster, architectural woodwork, decorative paint finishes, faux finishes, historic furnishings and fixtures, historic window treatments and carpets.
(See display ad on preceding page)

RAMBUSCH

RAMBUSCH
40 West 13th St.
New York, NY 10011
Tel.: 212-675-0400; FAX: 212-620-4687

Personnel:
Viggo Bech Rambusch . . . . Senior Project Director
Martin V. Rambusch . . . . Stained Glass Director

Type of Business:
Since 1898, creating church interiors, liturgical furnishings, and art work. Fine restoration of church interiors. In-house studios and shops for designing and executing stained glass, church lighting systems, art metal work, and decorative painting.

Winterich's
DESIGNERS AND CRAFTSMEN

JOHN W. WINTERICH & ASSOCIATES
9545 Midwest Ave., Ste. M
Cleveland, OH 44125
Tel.: 800-255-4544; FAX: 216-662-2509

Personnel:
John W. Winterich III
Greg M. Winterich
Bill O'Loughlin

Type of Business:
Founded in 1913, the Winterich Studio of Liturgical Art provides complete interior design and fabrication services for all aspects of new church projects and restoration and renovations. The award winning work of Winterich's is known nationwide. Our on-staff architect, liturgical consultants, designers and craftsmen are dedicated to excellence in Liturgical Art.

BELLTOWERS & STEEPLES

FIBERGLASS SPECIALTIES INCORPORATED

FIBERGLASS SPECIALTIES, INC.
P.O. Box 1340
Henderson, TX 75653
Tel.: 800-527-1459; FAX: 903-657-2318

Type of Business:
Fiberglass Specialties has been producing quality church steeples and cupolas for more than thirty years. They have the largest selection of standard designs in the industry, or they can custom build to your unique design. Their in-house sales staff combined with a nationwide network of local representatives are ready to assist you.

D.C. RIGGOTT INC.
3540 Neal Ave.
Afton, MN 55001
Tel.: 800-479-8777; FAX: 612-436-4769

Personnel:

Don Riggott . . . . Owner/President

Type of Business:

Specializing in vintage church accessories, architectural ornamentation and liturgical furnishings.
Stained Glass Windows • Altars • Lighting • Statuary • Stations of the Cross • Tabernacles • Monstranses • Fonts • Pews • Steeple Bells • Vestments • Books • Furniture • Candlesticks • Chalices, Please contact us with specific requests. We will be happy to send you photographs and specifics on any items in our inventory. You may have items in storage or not being used, please contact us as we are actively searching for vintage items to purchase for re-use in liturgical spaces.

vanBergen est 1795

THE VAN BERGEN COMPANY
P.O. Box 12928
Charleston, SC 29422-2928
Tel.: 800-544-8820; FAX: 803-559-0797

Personnel:

Harry van Bergen. . . . . President
Peter Martin. . . . . General Manager

Type of Business:

Established in 1795, van Bergen celebrates over 200 years of service. We represent the famous Paccard Fonderie de Cloches. Van Bergen prides itself on providing the highest quality in cast bronze bells, electronic carillon instruments, clock and bell towers and electrification/renovation of existing cast bells. Van Bergen is committed to provide support, expert installation and superior service. OUR BELLS RING ROUND THE WORLD.

VERDIN V SINCE 1842

THE VERDIN CO.
444 Reading Rd.
Cincinnati, OH 45202
Tel.: 800-543-0488; 531-241-4010; FAX: 531-241-1855

Personnel:

Robert Verdin . . . . CEO
James Verdin . . . . President
David Verdin . . . . Vice President
Suzanne Sizer . . . . Sales/Mkt. Mgr.

Type of Business:

Combining 155 years of experience and tradition with 20th Century technical expertise makes The Verdin Company the leading supplier and manufacturer of bells, bell ringing equipment, carillons and clocks in the nation.

CAPITAL CAMPAIGNS

GG Guidance In Giving

GUIDANCE IN GIVING, INC.
225 Snedecor Ave.
Bayport, NY 11705
Tel.: 888-757-5444; FAX: 516-472-6109

8164 Sea Water Path
Columbia, MD 21045
Tel.: 888-869-5522; FAX: 410-799-9155

550 Camino De La Reina, Ste. 310
San Diego, CA 92108
Tel.: 800-993-3335; FAX: 619-491-0402

Personnel:

Michael R. Cusack. . . . . President
Joseph W. Zamorano . . . . Executive Vice President
Michael V. Goodwin . . . . Executive Vice President

Type of Business:

Guidance In Giving is a Catholic Development and Stewardship firm specializing in Diocesan and Parish capital campaigns, annual appeals, and stewardship programs. Additionally, the firm assists Catholic schools with their development and fund raising programs. Executives of the firm have been conducting successful campaigns since 1980 and understand and respect the Mission of the Church. We welcome the opportunity to spend a day at your diocese, parish or school to discuss your development and stewardship efforts. We will prepare an honest objective appraisal of your program at no cost to you. If you are considering counsel, please call one of our office locations.

CHURCH SIGNS & BANNERS

the symbol of Regal Splendor

Robert Gaspard Co.

ROBERT GASPARD CO., INC.
200 N. Janacek Rd.
Brookfield, WI 53045-6101
Tel.: 800-784-6868; 414-784-6800; FAX: 414-784-7567

Personnel:

Rose Gaspard . . . . President
John Andorfer . . . . Vice President
Jason R. Gaspard . . . . Sales & Marketing Mgr.

Type of Business:

The Robert Gaspard Co. was established in 1954. Over the past 43 years, we have grown to be a nationally-known company. We pride ourselves on the ability to create original custom designs to enrich your worship needs. Our complete line consists of all ecclesiastical vesture, as well as paraments, mass and altar linens, stoles, banners, chasubles, funeral palls, albs, cossacks, surplices, choir robes, acolyte robes and many accessories. Complimentary catalogs and fabric swatches sent on request.

Wayne Industries Inc.
"Setting the Pace for the Future"

WAYNE INDUSTRIES, INC.
P.O. Drawer 2100
Clanton, AL 35046
Tel.: 205-755-5580; FAX: 205-755-1516

Personnel:

Diane Cleckler
Linda Coste
Monte Easterling

Type of Business:

For over thirty years, Wayne Industries, Inc. has been manufacturing attractive outdoor signage, an investment second to none. Your church will receive a sign constructed of the highest quality materials available. Your church will also be buying direct from the manufacturing plant. The salesperson you deal with will oversee the entire manufacturing process, assuring you receive exactly what you order. Factory-direct buying can amount to thousands of dollars in savings. Call TODAY for more information.

CONSERVATION

ALBERT MICHAELS CONSERVATION, INC.
1116 North Third St.
Harrisburg, PA 17102
Tel.: 717-232-9592; FAX: 717-234-0311

Personnel:

John M. DiTonno . . . . Projects Manager
John A. Rita. . . . . Conservator
William W. Tull. . . . . General Manager

Type of Business:

Founded in 1971, we offer a range of art and architectural conservation and restoration services, including PROJECT PLANNING and collection assessment, ANALYTICAL INVESTIGATION to determine original and subsequent finishes including techniques and materials employed. CONSERVATION & RESTORATION OF original artwork, ornamental plaster, painted surfaces, interior wood finishes, marble surfaces historic furniture, metal light fixtures, leaded glass windows, and REPRODUCTION OF ornamental plaster, architectural woodwork, decorative paint finishes, faux finishes, historic furnishings and fixtures, historic window treatments and carpets.

Conrad Schmitt Studios Inc.

CONRAD SCHMITT STUDIOS, INC.
2405 S. 162nd St.
New Berlin, WI 53151
Tel.: 800-969-3033; 414-786-3030; FAX: 414-786-9036

Personnel:

Heidi Gruenke Emery . . . . Vice President & Marketing Director

Type of Business:

Since 1889, this family-owned Studio has restored and decorated hundreds of interiors across the country. Their scope of work includes the investigation and documentation of original decorative schemes; the restoration of those schemes through the application of various decorative techniques including gilding, glazing, marbleizing, stenciling, and graining, as well as the design, fabrication, conservation or replication of murals and stained glass. The Studio can assist projects in the early stages with architectural samples and rendering for fund-raising. Recently completed projects include St. Josaphat's Basilica, Milwaukee, WI; St. Ann's, Napoleanville, LA; and St. Bernard's, Akron, OH.

DOORS & PARTITIONS

HUFCOR

HUFCOR INC.
P.O. Box 591
Janesville, WI 53547
Tel.: 800-542-2371, ext. 214; FAX: 608-758-8253

Personnel:

Elaine Masters . . . . Marketing Coordinator

Type of Business:

Hufcor operable and accordion partitions allow you the flexibility to create large or small spaces, fast. Our wide selection of models, sound control ratings, configurations, options, and finishes, lets you choose the right product for your budget and needs. Hufcor partitions are available through local, factory-trained Distributors who offer free design assistance as well as installation and service. Hufcor is a ISO 9001 registered company. Call our toll free number for the name of your nearest representative.

FACETED GLASS

Conrad Schmitt Studios Inc.

CONRAD SCHMITT STUDIOS, INC.
2405 S. 162nd St.
New Berlin, WI 53151
Tel.: 800-969-3033; 414-786-3030; FAX: 414-786-9036

Personnel:
Heidi Gruenke Emery . . . . Vice President & Marketing Director

Type of Business:
Since 1889, this family-owned Studio has restored and decorated hundreds of interiors across the country. Their scope of work includes the investigation and documentation of original decorative schemes; the restoration of those schemes through the application of various decorative techniques including gilding, glazing, marbleizing, stenciling, and graining, as well as the design, fabrication, conservation or replication of murals and stained glass. The Studio can assist projects in the early stages with architectural samples and rendering for fund-raising. Recently completed projects include St. Josaphat's Basilica, Milwaukee, WI; St. Ann's, Napoleanville, LA; and St. Bernard's, Akron, OH.

GENERAL CONTRACTORS

DAPRATO RIGALI STUDIOS, INC.

DAPRATO RIGALI STUDIOS, INC.
7956 Oakton St.
Niles, IL 60714
Tel.: 847-692-6350; FAX: 847-692-3445

Personnel:
John Rigali
Robert Rigali
Lisa Rigali Galvin
Mike Rigali

Type of Business:
Daprato Rigali Studios Inc. has been beautifying Churches in America since 1860.

Today we find the Rigali Family restoring and renovating the churches originally decorated by their Great-Grandfather, John E. Rigali; aware of his reputation to create spiritually moving environments with quality material and craftsmanship.

Some of their most recent jobs include: decoration and stained glass restoration at St. Mary of the Lake Seminary, Mundelein, IL.; Marble renovation and decoration, St. Elizabeth's Mother House, Allegany, N.Y.; and General Contracting for complete renovation of St. Bernadette's Church, Rockford, IL.

The Daprato Rigali staff is equipped to take your project from start to finish. If you're interested in working with a fine interior design studio experienced in Ecclesiastical Artistries please call for consultation at no obligation. We deliver what we design.

MONUMENTAL CHURCH ENTRANCES

THE BAUT STUDIOS, INC.
ECCLESIASTICAL CRAFTSMEN

THE BAUT STUDIOS, INC.
1095 Main St.
Swoyersville, PA 18704
Tel.: 800-326-9421; FAX: 717-288-0380

Personnel:
Heide Marie Cebrick . . . . Artisan/Designer
Conrad Dismas Baut . . . . President
Gerhard Francis Baut. . . . . Master Sculptor

Type of Business:
The Baut Studios, Inc., established in 1927, is a full service ecclesiastical studio that has been manufacturing and installing their own door systems for over 19 years. Baut recently introduced "BRONZFORM" entranceways featuring the attractive look of bronze doors but crafted in structural aluminum components. Richly sculpted design appliqués look like bronze castings and contain bronze alloys in a composite that is low maintenance, highly functional, extremely durable and very attractive. Baut decorative door inserts include "Structural" Stained Glass (a patented product of Baut), and Abrasively Etched Glass. Other product offerings include Single Glazed, Double Glazed, extremely large monumental Triple Glazed Church Windows and Ventilators, Restoration/New Traditional Stained Glass, Altars and Appointments, Crosses, Steeples, Glass Mosaics and Church Lighting. As with all Baut products, custom sizes, shapes and designs to match any decor, are available.

PARISHIONER SERVICE EQUIPMENT

Show you care
Koala

KOALA CORPORATION
11600 E. 53rd Ave., Bldg. D
Denver, CO 80239-2312
Tel.: 800-666-0363; FAX: 303-574-9000

Personnel:
Pamela Schmidt . . . . Director of Marketing
James Zazenski . . . . Executive Vice President
Mark Betker . . . . CEO
Jeff Vigil. . . . . Vice President/Finance

Type of Business:
The premier manufacturer of baby changing stations provides vertical, horizontal, and counter top designs in optional designer colors or stainless steel cladding. The Child Protection Seat is designed to minimize child risk and provide sanitary convenience in public bathroom stalls or vanity sink areas. The Koala family of products also includes the Koala Highchair, Infant Seat Kradle, Booster Buddy and Activity Systems. To order, call 800.666.0363.

RESTORATION

DAPRATO RIGALI STUDIOS, INC.

DAPRATO RIGALI STUDIOS, INC.
7956 Oakton St.
Niles, IL 60714
Tel.: 847-692-6350; FAX: 847-692-3445

Personnel:
John Rigali
Robert Rigali
Lisa Rigali Galvin
Mike Rigali

Type of Business:
Daprato Rigali Studios Inc. has been beautifying Churches in America since 1860.
Today we find the Rigali Family restoring and renovating the churches originally decorated by their Great-Grandfather, John E. Rigali; aware of his reputation to create spiritually moving environments with quality material and craftsmanship.
Some of their most recent jobs include: decoration and stained glass restoration at St. Mary of the Lake Seminary, Mundelein, IL.; Marble renovation and decoration, St. Elizabeth's Mother House, Allegany, N.Y.; and General Contracting for complete renovation of St. Bernadette's Church, Rockford, IL.
The Daprato Rigali staff is equipped to take your project from start to finish. If you're interested in working with a fine interior design studio experienced in Ecclesiastical Artistries please call for consultation at no obligation. We deliver what we design.

ADRIAN HAMERS®
CHURCH INTERIORS

ADRIAN HAMERS INC.
2 Madison Ave.
Larchmont, NY 10538
Tel.: 914-834-7780; FAX: 914-834-0712

Type of Business:
Since 1887, the Hamers name has been synonymous with expert silversmithing throughout the world in the field of Liturgical Art. We are also experts in: Church Interiors from design to execution, Renovations, Altars, Sacred Vessels, Appraisals, Gold and Silver Plating & Repairing, Tabernacles, Marble, Woodwork & Woodcarving, Statuary, Stained Glass, Pews & Chairs, Gold Leafing, Frescoes, Restoration, Trompe-l'oeuil, Wall Murals (repair and conservation cleaning), Ornamental Plaster, Heraldic Designs & Bishop Regalia.

KOLEY'S, INC.
2951 Harney St.
Omaha, NE 68131
Tel.: 402-341-9795; FAX: 402-341-5857

Personnel:
Tom Koley
Terry Goehring

Type of Business:
Quality, Care and Craftsmanship. For four generations these words have described Koley's, Inc. Since our very beginning in 1919, we have endeavored to serve the churches and clergy in repairing, polishing and replating of sacred vessels or other items of metal found in the Church. Our craftsmen strive to restore your cherished ecclesiastical items to its original condition whenever possible. We take pride in knowing that you have entrusted us with your items. Free estimates.

RAMBUSCH

RAMBUSCH
40 West 13th St.
New York, NY 10011
Tel.: 212-675-0400; FAX: 212-620-4687

Personnel:
Viggo Bech Rambusch . . . . Senior Project Director
Martin V. Rambusch . . . . Stained Glass Director

Type of Business:
Since 1898, creating church interiors, liturgical furnishings, and art work. Fine restoration of church interiors. In-house studios and shops for designing and executing stained glass, church lighting systems, art metal work, and decorative painting.

D.C. RIGGOTT INC.
3540 Neal Ave.
Afton, MN 55001
Tel.: 800-479-8777; FAX: 612-436-4769

Personnel:
Don Riggott . . . . Owner/President

Type of Business:
Specializing in vintage church accessories, architectural ornamentation and liturgical furnishings.
Stained Glass Windows • Altars • Lighting • Statuary • Stations of the Cross • Tabernacles • Monstranses • Fonts • Pews • Steeple Bells • Vestments • Books • Furniture • Candlesticks • Chalices, Please contact us with specific requests. We will be happy to send you photographs and specifics on any items in our inventory. You may have items in storage or not being used, please contact us as we are actively searching for vintage items to purchase for re-use in liturgical spaces.

Conrad Schmitt Studios Inc.

CONRAD SCHMITT STUDIOS, INC.
2405 S. 162nd St.
New Berlin, WI 53151
Tel.: 800-969-3033; 414-786-3030; FAX: 414-786-9036

Personnel:
Heidi Gruenke Emery.... Vice President & Marketing Director

Type of Business:
Since 1889, this family-owned Studio has restored and decorated hundreds of interiors across the country. Their scope of work includes the investigation and documentation of original decorative schemes; the restoration of those schemes through the application of various decorative techniques including gilding, glazing, marbleizing, stenciling, and graining, as well as the design, fabrication, conservation or replication of murals and stained glass. The Studio can assist projects in the early stages with architectural samples and rendering for fund-raising. Recently completed projects include St. Josaphat's Basilica, Milwaukee, WI; St. Ann's, Napoleanville, LA; and St. Bernard's, Akron, OH.

Stained Glass Associates

STAINED GLASS ASSOCIATES
P.O. Box 1531
Raleigh, NC 27602-1531
Tel.: 919-266-2493

Personnel:
Robert J. Wysocki .... Owner

Type of Business:
- Design, Fabrication and Installation of:
  - Leaded, Faceted and Painted Glass
- Restoration and Repair
  - Replacement Frames
  - Fire Damage
- Appraisals

About SGA:
- Established in 1958
- Studio Member of Stained Glass Association of America
- 957 Installations Nationally and Internationally

Stained Glass Associates is committed to maintaining the highest of ecclesiastical standards and the complete satisfaction of every client.

ROOFING

GERARD ROOFING TECHNOLOGIES, INC.
955 Columbia St.
Brea, CA 92821-2923
Tel.: 800-237-6637; FAX: 714-529-6643
e-mail: info@gerardusa.com; website: http://www.gerardusa.com

Personnel:
Matt Pritchard......................... Product Manageri

Type of Business:
The Gerard stone-coated steel roofing system is a durable, class "A" roof covering that has proven itself through nature's worst conditions. Manufactued to the strictest standards, Gerard has assembled a lightweight (1.4 lb/sq.ft.), interlocking roof system that won't dry up, burn, break, blow off, crack or curl ... offering a combination of properties that you can't get with other products. The Gerard panels are available in tile or shake profiles and in a variety of colors.

STAINED GLASS

BOTTI STUDIO OF ARCHITECTURAL ARTS, INC.

BOTTI STUDIO OF ARCHITECTURAL ARTS, INC.
919 Grove St.
Evanston, IL 60201
Tel.: 800-524-7211; FAX: 847-869-5996
847-869-5933; e-mail: Boti@ix.netcom.com

East Coast Studio
1517 State St.
Sarasota, FL 33577
Tel.: 941-951-0978; FAX: 941-953-9078

West Coast Studio
1038 N Highway 101
Encinitas, CA 92024
Tel.: 619-753-0705; FAX: 619-753-0705

Continued from previous column

Personnel:
Staff includes internationlly recognized artists and designers working in conjunction with our highly skilled artisans and craftsmen.
Italo G. Botti .... President

Type of Business:
For generations Botti Studio has had a reputation for embodying all that is artistically creative in the traditional and contemporary ecclesiastical field. This field includes design and fabrication of stained and faceted glass windows, restoration of windows, church interiors, appointments, murals, sculpture, mosaic and marble. We are completely dedicated to both quality and satisfying our clients needs spiritually and liturgically. Botti Studio is nationwide, offering consultation and designs without obligation. Member Stained Glass Association of America.
(See display ad on next page)

DAPRATO RIGALI STUDIOS, INC.

DAPRATO RIGALI STUDIOS, INC.
7956 Oakton St.
Niles, IL 60714
Tel.: 847-692-6350; FAX: 847-692-3445

Personnel:

John Rigali | Robert Rigali
Lisa Rigali Galvin | Mike Rigali

Type of Business:

Daprato Rigali Studios Inc. has been beautifying Churches in America since 1860.

Today we find the Rigali Family restoring and renovating the churches originally decorated by their Great-Grandfather, John E. Rigali; aware of his reputation to create spiritually moving environments with quality material and craftsmanship.

Some of their most recent jobs include: decoration and stained glass restoration at St. Mary of the Lake Seminary, Mundelein, IL.; Marble renovation and decoration, St. Elizabeth's Mother House, Allegany, N.Y.; and General Contracting for complete renovation of St. Bernadette's Church, Rockford, IL.

The Daprato Rigali staff is equipped to take your project from start to finish. If you're interested in working with a fine interior design studio experienced in Ecclesiastical Artistries please call for consultation at no obligation. We deliver what we design.

DIETERICH SPAHN & ASSOCIATES, INC.
605 Bushaway Rd.
Wayzata, MN 55391
Tel.: 612-475-2601; FAX: 612-930-3930
e-mail: dspahn@citilink.com

Personnel:

Dieterich Spahn . . . . Artist/Designer/Principal

Type of Business:

Group of skilled artisans & craftsmen — some are European trained.

Since 1961, creating new stained glass windows, mosaic icons and murals. Liturgical design for complete church interior with furnishings. Statues in wood or bronze. Liturgical art for the worship space. Fine restoration of early European stained glass and mosaics.

Dieterich Spahn & Associates, Inc. works nationwide.

References: completed church commissions throughout the country, upon request.

Emmanuel Studios, Inc.
STAINED GLASS WINDOWS

EMMANUEL STUDIOS
410 Maple Ave.
Nashville, TN 37210
Tel.: 800-326-2228; 615-255-5446; FAX: 615-255-5447

Personnel:

Dennis R. Harmon . . . . President
William B. Brimm Jr. . . . . Vice President

Type of Business:

Emmanuel Studios has been designing, fabricating, and installing stained glass for over twenty-two years. We create designs that are sensitive to and compatible with any architectural style. Our leaded and faceted windows are constructed with quality craftsmanship and careful attention to detail. An installation by Emmanuel Studios can help your building convey an uplifting atmosphere.

Hiemer & Company
Stained Glass Studio

HIEMER & CO. STAINED GLASS STUDIO
403 Crooks Ave. at Wabash
Clifton, New Jersey 07011
Tel.: 973-772-5081; FAX: 973-772-0325

Personnel:

Gerhard E. Hiemer . . . . President
Judith Hiemer Van Wie . . . . Designer

Type of Business:

Designers, fabricators and installers of ecclesiastical stained glass since the 1880's. The permanent staff of certified journeymen specialize in traditional and contemporary liturgical design. Highly skilled and experienced with large scale restorations, artistic replications and window renovations. Works may be seen in over 1,060 North American churches.
*Portland, OR rep: Steven Closs 503-253-6343
*Anchorage, AK rep: Rita Hiemer Lammot 907-746-4948
Information and quotations submitted without obligation. Member, National Glass Association

LYNCHBURG STAINED GLASS CO.
P.O. Box 4453
Lynchburg, VA 24502
Tel.: 800-237-6161; FAX: 804-525-6168

Type of Business:

Products Offered: Custom designed leaded and faceted stained glass windows. Aluminum frames and protective coverings.
Services Offered: On site design and consultation service. Complete delivery and installation. Repair and restoration service.
Recent Clients: Holy Spirit, Atlanta, GA; St. Joseph's, Cockeysville, MD; St. Andrew the Apostle, Silver Springs, MD; Immaculate Conception, Towson, MD; St. Anthonys, Atlanta, GA.
Free Information: Call for a free packet of information.

RAMBUSCH

RAMBUSCH
40 West 13th St.
New York, NY 10011
Tel.: 212-675-0400; FAX: 212-620-4687

Personnel:

Viggo Bech Rambusch . . . . Senior Project Director
Martin V. Rambusch . . . . Stained Glass Director

Type of Business:

Since 1898, creating church interiors, liturgical furnishings, and art work. Fine restoration of church interiors. In-house studios and shops for designing and executing stained glass, church lighting systems, art metal work, and decorative painting.

D.C. RIGGOTT INC.
3540 Neal Ave.
Afton, MN 55001
Tel.: 800-479-8777; FAX: 612-436-4769

Personnel:
Don Riggott . . . . Owner/President

Type of Business:
Specializing in vintage church accessories, architectural ornamentation and liturgical furnishings.
Stained Glass Windows • Altars • Lighting • Statuary • Stations of the Cross • Tabernacles • Monstranses • Fonts • Pews • Steeple Bells • Vestments • Books • Furniture • Candlesticks • Chalices, Please contact us with specific requests. We will be happy to send you photographs and specifics on any items in our inventory. You may have items in storage or not being used, please contact us as we are actively searching for vintage items to purchase for re-use in liturgical spaces.

ROHLF'S STAINED & LEADED GLASS STUDIO, INC.
783 South Third Ave.
Mt. Vernon, NY 10550
Tel.: 914-699-4848; FAX: 914-699-7091

Personnel:
Peter A. Rohlf . . . . President
Peter Hans Rohlf . . . . Vice President
Gregory Rohlf . . . . Secretary/Treasurer

Type of Business:
For Three Generations our family owned and operated Studio together with our affiliate, George L. Payne Studio have been dedicated to excellence in Stained Glass Art. Our team of International designers and Master Craftspersons have created stained glass windows for over a thousand Churches and Institutions Worldwide. Our reputation and experience in the field of Restoration, Replication and Preservation is well known. We would be pleased to assist you in the early stages of planning and design, working with your Architect and/or committee to achieve your desired goals.
From concept to completion, we are dedicated to serve you.

Conrad Schmitt Studios Inc.

CONRAD SCHMITT STUDIOS, INC.
2405 S. 162nd St.
New Berlin, WI 53151
Tel.: 800-969-3033; 414-786-3030; FAX: 414-786-9036

Personnel:
Heidi Gruenke Emery . . . . Vice President & Marketing Director

Type of Business:
Since 1889, this family-owned Studio has restored and decorated hundreds of interiors across the country. Their scope of work includes the investigation and documentation of original decorative schemes; the restoration of those schemes through the application of various decorative techniques including gilding, glazing, marbleizing, stenciling, and graining, as well as the design, fabrication, conservation or replication of murals and stained glass. The Studio can assist projects in the early stages with architectural samples and rendering for fund-raising. Recently completed projects include St. Josaphat's Basilica, Milwaukee, WI; St. Ann's, Napoleanville, LA; and St. Bernard's, Akron, OH.

GREG SPIESS & CO.

SPIESS ARCHITECTURAL ANTIQUES
230 East Washington St.
Joliet, IL 60433
Tel.: 815-722-5639; FAX: 815-722-0171

Type of Business:
Specializing in older and antique church furniture. Gothic, Romanesque and Classical styles in marble, wood, bronze etc. Altars, pews, communion rails, stained glass, lecterns, baptismals, vestment cases, confessionals, Stations of the Cross statuary. Lighting. Pew and wood restoration available.

Stained Glass Associates

STAINED GLASS ASSOCIATES
P.O. Box 1531
Raleigh, NC 27602-1531
Tel.: 919-266-2493

Personnel:
Robert J. Wysocki . . . . Owner

Type of Business:
- Design, Fabrication and Installation of:
  - Leaded, Faceted and Painted Glass
- Restoration and Repair
  - Replacement Frames
  - Fire Damage
- Appraisals

About SGA:
- Established in 1958
- Studio Member of Stained Glass Association of America
- 957 Installations Nationally and Internationally

Stained Glass Associates is committed to maintaining the highest of ecclesistical standards and the complete satisfaction of every client.

EDUCATION

HARMONY
MEDIA
INC.

HARMONY MEDIA INC.
P.O. Box 138
Gervais, OR 97026
Tel.: 503-982-7675; FAX: 503-982-7833

Personnel:
William Van Smoorenburg . . . . President

Type of Business:
Bringing faith and technology together through computer CD-ROMs. This 100% Catholic company creates exciting catholic software for families, seminarians, priests, schools, parishes and all individuals that are interested in their faith. These programs contain hundreds of documents, illustrations and hyperlinks creating awesome collections. The New American Bible, RSV Catholic Edition Bible, Encyclicals, Catechism of the Catholic Church, John Paul II, Butler's, and Vatican II documents are just a few of the topics on CD-ROM!

EDUCATIONAL OPPORTUNITIES

GUEST HOUSE, INC.
1601 Joslyn Rd., P.O. Box 420
Lake Orion, MI 48361
Tel.: 800-626-6910; 248-391-4445; FAX:248-391-0210
e-mail: ghouse@ic.net

LAKE ORION CENTER
(For Women Religious)
P.O. Box 68
Lake Orion, MI 48361
Tel.: 800-626-6910; 248-391-3100; FAX: 248-391-1553
e-mail: guestmae@ic.net

ROCHESTER TREATMENT CENTER
(For priests, deacons, brothers & seminarians)
P.O. Box 954
Rochester, MN 55903
Tel.: 800-634-4155; 507-288-4693; FAX: 507-288-1240
e-mail: ghousemn@infonet.isl.net

Personnel:

Daniel A. Kidd . . . . President and Chief Executive Officer
Sr. Mae Kierans, CSJ. Clinical Program Coord., Lake Orion, MI
Bill Morgan, C.C.D.C.R. . . . . VP Clinical Oper., Rochester, MN
Daniel Webster. . . . . Director of Communications

Type of Business:

Guest House, Inc. is a lay-owned, lay-operated nonprofit corporation established in 1956. With the approbation of the Catholic hierarchy, it operates special residential treatment centers for alcoholic Catholic priests, deacons, brothers, sisters and seminarians from all over the world.

Catholic women religious are treated in Guest House in Lake Orion, Michigan. The facility in Rochester, Minnesota has treatment programs for priests, deacons, brothers and seminarians.

An important part of the treatment is the beautiful environment of our facilities. Residents respond to the quiet serenity of the surroundings to help in their recovery not only physically and emotionally, but spiritually as well.

Surveys are conducted regularly to determine how our graduates are doing. The 1997 survey shows that after a year and a half, over 90% report they are doing well and abstaining from all drugs and alcohol.

No priest or religious will be denied treatment because of inability to pay. Our generous donors have established an endowment fund to provide financial assistance.

Accredited by JCAHO (Joint Commission on Accreditation of Healthcare Organizations) and licensed by the Department of Public Health in the states of Michigan and Minnesota respectively.

EDUCATIONAL SYSTEMS & SOFTWARE

With Education in Mind™

NCS (National Computer Systems)
4401 West 76th St.
Edina, MN 55435
Tel.: 800-447-3269; FAX: 612-830-8564
e-mail: www@ncs.com

Personnel:

Mike Seeman. . . . . Marketing Manager, K-12
Fred Green . . . Marketing Mgr., Education Alternative Channels
For more information, contact NCS Telemarketing & Telesales

Type of Business:

For over 30 years, NCS has served the education market with optical mark reading (OMR) and imaging technology. NCS touches one of every two children in our nation's schools. NCS is the leading provider of scanning systems, software, and forms used to automate data collection and accurately report on assessment, instructional, and student records information. NCS scanners and forms are also compatible with most of the leading student administrative and testing software products on the market today.

EDUCATIONAL TEST SCORING

With Education in Mind™

NCS (National Computer Systems)
4401 West 76th St.
Edina, MN 55435
Tel.: 800-447-3269; FAX: 612-830-8564
e-mail: www@ncs.com

Personnel:

Mike Seeman. . . . . Marketing Manager, K-12
Fred Green . . . Marketing Mgr., Education Alternative Channels
For more information, contact NCS Telemarketing & Telesales

Type of Business:

For over 30 years, NCS has served the education market with optical mark reading (OMR) and imaging technology. NCS touches one of every two children in our nation's schools. NCS is the leading provider of scanning systems, software, and forms used to automate data collection and accurately report on assessment, instructional, and student records information. NCS scanners and forms are also compatible with most of the leading student administrative and testing software products on the market today.

INSTRUCTIONAL MANAGEMENT & STUDENT RECORD SYSTEMS

NCS™

With Education in Mind™

NCS (National Computer Systems)
4401 West 76th St.
Edina, MN 55435
Tel.: 800-447-3269; FAX: 612-830-8564
e-mail: www@ncs.com

Personnel:

Mike Seeman . . . . Marketing Manager, K-12
Fred Green . . . Marketing Mgr., Education Alternative Channels
For more information, contact NCS Telemarketing & Telesales

Type of Business:

For over 30 years, NCS has served the education market with optical mark reading (OMR) and imaging technology. NCS touches one of every two children in our nation's schools. NCS is the leading provider of scanning systems, software, and forms used to automate data collection and accurately report on assessment, instructional, and student records information. NCS scanners and forms are also compatible with most of the leading student administrative and testing software products on the market today.

MINISTRY OPPORTUNITIES

AIR FORCE Chaplain SERVICE

AIR FORCE CHAPLAIN RECRUITING SERVICE
HQ AFRS/RSOCC
550 D Street West Ste 1
Randolph AFB TX 78150-4527
Tel.: 800-803-2452
kinneyj@afrs.rs.af.mil / lemonsr@afrs.rs.af.mil

Personnel:

Ch, Lt. Col. Rita A. Lemons
. . . . Chief, Chaplain Accessions Section
Ch, Capt. John M. Kinney
. . . . Deputy Chief, Chaplain Accessions Section

Type of Business:

Air Force chaplains ensure the free exercise of religion for the globally engaged Air Force community. Catholics make up approximately 30% of the military. Priest chaplains are particularly responsible for the spiritual and the sacramental needs of Catholics in the military setting. Because the Catholic Chaplain lives the same challenging demands of military life, he can truly respond. The Air Force offers the qualified priest many opportunities to serve both the Church and the country in a pluralistic global environment.

Chaplains remain steadfast witnesses of the holy in a changing world environment. Consider the possibility of serving as a priest and an officer in the United States Air Force. For more information, please contact the above office.

CRS

CATHOLIC RELIEF SERVICES' OPERATION RICE BOWL
209 W. Fayette St.
Baltimore, MD 21201
Tel.: 410-625-2220; FAX: 410-234-3183

Personnel:

Bill O'Keefe . . . . Director Church Outreach
Corryne Deliberto . . . . Director Operation Rice Bowl
Lisa D'Ambrogi . . . . Materials Order Coordinator

Type of Business:

Catholic Relief Services' Operation Rice Bowl program draws Catholics into the unique spirit of the Lenten season. It is an opportunity for families, communities, parishes, and other groups to reflect on, pray for, and assist the poor in this country and in the developing world. The program provides a forum to understand the values of self-sacrifice and concern for the poor everywhere. Call 1-800-222-0025 to order free materials for your parish or school.

HABITAT FOR HUMANITY INTERNATIONAL
121 Habitat St.
Americus, GA 31709
Tel.: 800-HABITAT / 912-924-6935; FAX: 912-924-6541

Personnel:
Millard Fuller . . . . Founder and President
Sr. Betsy Van Deusen, CSJ . . . . . . Director of Church Relations

Type of Business:
Habitat for Humanity International is an ecumenical Christian housing ministry founded in 1976 by Millard Fuller along with his wife, Linda. It works in partnership with people in need, building simple, decent shelter that is sold at no profit, through no-interest mortgages. With affiliates around the globe, Habitat for Humanity has built more than 60,000 houses, sheltering more than 300,000 people.

PAPERBACK SELECTIONS

HOLYOKE NEWS CO., INC.
720 Main St.
Holyoke Selections, MA 01040
Tel.: 800-628-8372; FAX: 413-538-7161

Personnel:
Mike Putira . . . . Vice President & Gen. Mgr.
Jim Morton . . . . Book Department Manager
John Hopkins . . . . Sales & Marketing
Barbara Kaak . . . . Customer Service

Type of Business:
Holyoke News Co. has been in business for almost 90 years. We have been distributing paperbacks to both private and public elementary, middle and secondary schools, as well as college and universities throughout the United States and overseas. We take pride in our extensive inventory, school catalog, maximum **40% discount** and ability to privide you with the finest in educational titles, all with the most complete and friendly service possible.
Your One Stop Educational Source

SPIRITUAL ENRICHMENT

SACRED HEART JESUIT RETREAT HOUSE
P.O. Box 185
Sedalia, CO 80135
Tel.: 303-688-4198; FAX: 303-688-9633

Type of Business:
The Retreat House is located on 280 acres in the foothills of the Rockies with easy transportation from Denver International Airport. Directed retreats of various lengths are offered for clergy, religious and laity throughout the year. Call or write for registration information: Reservations Coordinator, P.O. Box 185, Sedalia, CO 80135 (303) 688-4198. Visit our web site: http://gabrielmedia.org/shjrh/shjrh.html.

TUITION FINANCING

TUITION PROGRAM, INC.
521 S. Livingston Ave.
Livingston, NJ 07039
Tel.: 800-828-9944 / 973-535-2776
FAX: 800-432-9994 / 973-533-0086

Personnel:
Brendon & Cecilia Devlin

Type of Business:
Founded in 1985 by Catholic parents to serve Catholic Schools. There is absolutely no charge to the school. There is no charge to parents if payments are on time. Each student receives a Tuition Credit Line for present and future use. The school receives 100% tuition. Call today 1-800-828-9944 or fax 1-800-432-9994 or e-mail: tuition@ldt.net.

EMPLOYMENT

AIR FORCE CHAPLAIN SERVICE

AIR FORCE CHAPLAIN RECRUITING SERVICE
HQ AFRS/RSOCC
550 D Street West Ste 1
Randolph AFB TX 78150-4527
Tel.: 800-803-2452
kinneyj@afrs.rs.af.mil / lemonsr@afrs.rs.af.mil

Personnel:
Ch, Lt. Col. Rita A. Lemons
. . . . Chief, Chaplain Accessions Section
Ch, Capt. John M. Kinney
. . . . Deputy Chief, Chaplain Accessions Section

Type of Business:
Air Force chaplains ensure the free exercise of religion for the globally engaged Air Force community. Catholics make up approximately 30% of the military. Priest chaplains are particularly responsible for the spiritual and the sacramental needs of Catholics in the military setting. Because the Catholic Chaplain lives the same challenging demands of military life, he can truly respond. The Air Force offers the qualified priest many opportunities to serve both the Church and the country in a pluralistic global environment.
Chaplains remain steadfast witnesses of the holy in a changing world environment. Consider the possibility of serving as a priest and an officer in the United States Air Force. For more information, please contact the above office.

LITURGICAL & CHURCH GOODS

ABBOTT CHURCH GOODS, INC.
Showroom: 1515 Route 38
Cherry Hill, NJ 08002
Tel.: 800-522-2688; 609-662-6959; FAX: 609-665-5109
website: http://www.abbottsinc.com
e-mail: ACG.INC@internetMCI.com

Personnel:
Daniel J. Castonguay . . . . President
Joseph F. McKeaney . . . . General Manager
Michael W. Wasyluk . . . . Customer Service

Type of Business:
Purveyors of the Finest Vesture, Paraments, Statuary & Metalware since 1962. Unique and original creations, our specialty. Custom designs to complement your liturgical environment. Exclusive representatives of Slabbinck Master Collection & Original Collection.

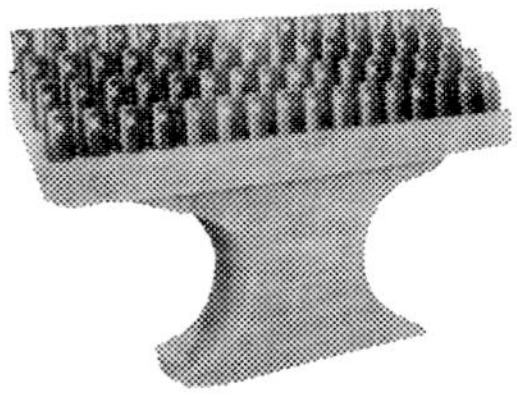

CARROLL ELECTRONICS INCORPORATED
710 Northeast 26th St.
Wilton Manors, FL 33305
Tel.: 800-331-0444; FAX: 954-561-4098

Personnel:
David Nagle . . . . President
Liza Palmer . . . . Sales Manager
Bob Perkins . . . . Sales Representative
John Lentz . . . . Service Engineer

Type of Business:
Carroll Electronics has been in business for 20 years designing and building Electronic Votive Candle Stands for thousands of churches throughout the United States.

THE HOLY ROOD GUILD
St. Joseph's Abbey
167 North Spencer Rd.
Spencer, MA 01562-1233
Tel.: 508-885-8750; FAX: 508-885-8758

Type of Business:
Designers and crafters of ecclesiastical vesture for over 40 years. Inspired by our monastic tradition, we seek to unite in our work simplicity in design, quality in materials and excellence in craftsmanship. The result is vesture that enhances the liturgical celebration with visual grace and order. Our artists—both monks and laypersons—are available for custom design work and consultation. We also provide an extensive selection of ready made items.

ADAM KOCHLIN DESIGNS
33 Magee Ave., 2nd Fl.
Stamford, CT 06902
Tel.: 800-886-4668; FAX: 203-325-3755

Personnel:
Adam Kochlin . . . . Design Director
Michael Kirshbaum . . . . Executive Director
Regina Maguire . . . . Product Manager

Type of Business:
Adam Kochlin Designs creates a complete line of made to order vestments and hangings produced in our studio in Connecticut. Working with a number of artists we also create made to order sacred vessels and appointments including processional crosses, pacschal candlesticks, altar candlesticks, sanctuary lamps, incensors, chalices and patens, aumbrys, curets, and falgons in wood, ceramic, glass and metal. Call 800-886-4668 for free catalog and information.

TERRA SANCTA GUILD
P.O. Box 300, 858 Sussex Blvd.
Broomall, PA 19008
Tel.: 800-523-5155; 610-544-9900; FAX: 610-544-6994

Personnel:
Ade Bethune . . . . Liturgical Art Director
I.A. Serot . . . . President
Sharon Shore . . . . General Manager

Type of Business:
Custom design and manufacture of awards and recognition items for benefactors and volunteers; fundraising incentives; insignia for religious communities; commemoratives for church expansion and anniversaries. Your logo adapted or a new design created by world renowned liturgical artist, Ade Bethune. All lettering in original calligraphy.

ALTAR BREADS

A Division of Patrick Baker & Sons and Stadelmaier Nijmegen

STADELMAIER USA LLC
1650 West St., P.O. Box 1028
Southington, CT 06489-5028
Tel.: 1-800-243-6385; FAX: 860-276-9438

Type of Business:
We import St. Michael Altar Bread from the St. Michael Bakery in St. Michielgestel, The Netherlands. Founded in 1844 by the Roman Catholic Institute for the deaf, the bakery generates funds to provide food, lodging and occupational therapy for deaf children and adults. The Institute also works closely with the International Assistance Program in achieving remarkable results in the Third World. St. Michael Altar Bread is made of only the finest pure wheat flour and natural spring water and is guaranteed to arrive fresh and unbroken in over 50 couintries worldwide.

ALTAR LINENS, LACES

STADELMAIER-NIJMEGEN-HOLLAND
P.O. Box 7063
6503 GN Nijmegen
Tel.: 31-24-3791170; FAX: 31-24-3791171
e-mail: stadelmaier@telebyte.nl

Type of Business:
SACRISTA, by Stadelmaier Nijmegen, a superb and complete line of communion linens and altar cloth. Made from 100% linen damask. We offer chalice palls, purificators, corporals and lavabo towels, with jacquard woven designs or with exquisite embroideries. Also altarcloth, handwoven or semi-handwoven, 63" wide, in wool/trevira and subtle designs woven in.
Please ask your SN-dealer.

BIBLE STUDY SOFTWARE

HERMENEUTIKA COMPUTER BIBLE RESEARCH SOFTWARE
P.O. BOX 2200
BIG FORK, MT 59911-2200
TEL.: 406-837-2244; FAX: 406-837-4433
website: http://www.bibleworks.com; e-mail: sales@bibleworks.com

Type of Business:
BibleWorks CD-ROM for Windows. Over 64 Bibles and Reference Works in 14 languages, including Greek NT, LXX, Hebrew OT, Latin Vulgate, English, Germany, French, Italian, Spanish, Indonesian. Rated best tool and most complete solution for exegesis, exposition, and comparative bible study. Lexical and grammatical concording. Interlinear, multiple lexigons. (By late 1998: NAB, NJB, Douay-Rheins; Portuguese, Polish, Russian, Ukrainian, etc.). Call, e-mail, or fax for free brochure.

BIBLES, HYMNALS, MISSALETTES

GIA PUBLICATIONS, INC.
7404 S. Mason Ave.
Chicago, IL 60638
Tel.: 1-800-GIA-1358; 708-496-3800; FAX: 708-496-3828
website: www.giamusic.com; e-mail: custserv@giamusic.com

Personnel:
Robert J. Batastini . . . . Senior Editor, V.P.
Michael Cymbala . . . . Marketing Director
David Anderson . . . . Workshop Coordinator
Mike O'Connell . . . . Hymnal Sales

Type of Business:
GIA offers church music in all styles and forms for today's "eclectic" church. In addition to a broad range of hymnals, including *Worship, Gather, Gather Comprehensive, RitualSong,* and *Lead Me, Guide Me,* GIA also offers liturgical planning software, worship calendars and other music supplies, innovative music education products, excellent recordings, and the *GIA Quarterly,* a liturgical music journal.
Composers & distribution rights include:
John Bell and the Iona Community, Jacques Berthier and the Taizé Community, Rory Cooney, Jeanne Cotter, Joseph Gelineau, David Haas, Marty Haugen, Howard Hughes, Michael Joncas, Alexander Peloquin, Donna Peña, and Richard Proulx.

OXFORD UNIVERSITY PRESS
198 Madison Ave.
New York, NY 10016-4314
Tel.: 800-451-7556; FAX: 919-677-1303

Type of Business:

Oxford University Press publishes a variety of books and Bibles which are of interest to Roman Catholic readers. The latter include *The Catholic Study Bible, New American Bible* (the first true study Bible for Catholics); *The Catholic Bible: Personal Study Edition, New American Bible* (an introductory Bible for teenagers, RCIA candidates and other adults); and, *The Complete Parallel Bible with the Apocryphal/Deuterocanonical Books* (featuring the texts of the New Revised Standard Version, Revised English Bible, New American Bible & New Jerusalem Bible).

BOOKS & RELIGIOUS ARTICLES

AGES Software
www.ageslibrary.com

AGES SOFTWARE
PO. Box 1926
Albany, OR 97321
Tel.: (800) 297-4307; FAX: (541) 917-0839
website: www.ageslibrary.com; e-mail: sales@ageslibrary.com

Personnel:

Steve Radda . . . . President
Tate Giersdorf . . . . Vice President

Type of Business:

Providers of electronic books to the Christian community on a CD-ROM, in a high value/low cost format. Over 330 important classic works such as *The Early Church Fathers* (38 vols.) and *The Works of Josephus* are available in a book-like, very easy to use format. A powerful search engine, copy/paste, and print features make this a must have tool for your research library. Compatible with Windows and Mac. Visit our website: www.ageslibrary.com.

D.C. RIGGOTT INC.
3540 Neal Ave.
Afton, MN 55001
Tel.: 800-479-8777; FAX: 612-436-4769

Personnel:

Don Riggott . . . . Owner/President

Type of Business:

Specializing in vintage church accessories, architectural ornamentation and liturgical furnishings.
Stained Glass Windows • Altars • Lighting • Statuary • Stations of the Cross • Tabernacles • Monstranses • Fonts • Pews • Steeple Bells • Vestments • Books • Furniture • Candlesticks • Chalices, Please contact us with specific requests. We will be happy to send you photographs and specifics on any items in our inventory. You may have items in storage or not being used, please contact us as we are actively searching for vintage items to purchase for re-use in liturgical spaces.

BULLETINS & CALENDARS

BARTON-COTTON

BARTON COTTON
1405 Parker Rd.
Baltimore, MD 21227
Tel.: 800-638-4652; FAX; 800-807-2954

Personnel:

Denise J. Payne. . . . . Vice President Marketing and Sales

Type of Business:

For more than 70 years, Barton-Cotton, Inc. has been proud to supply the finest selection of quality religious stationery products for the Catholic Clergy and Religious. More than 300 products are available including Mass cards, Certificates, Christmas and Easter cards, Mother's and Father's Day sets, Ordination/Jubilee products, Way of the Cross booklets, Rosary folders, Holy cards, Bookmarks, bulletins and offering envelopes, and many other items. To request a FREE catalog, call toll-free today at 1-800-638-4652.

J.S. PALUCH COMPANY

J.S. PALUCH CO., INC.
3825 N. Willow Rd.
Schiller Park, IL 60176
Tel.: 800-621-5197; FAX: 847-671-5715

Personnel:
Liturgy and Music Resources Customer Service 1-800-566-6150
Parish Bulletins 1-800 621-5197
Calendars Computer Software 1-800-621-5197

Type of Business:
Serving the church for over 80 years. Liturgy and Music Resources; Parish Sundays – Laser ComExpress; National Vocations Awareness and Religious Art Calendars; Computer Software for parish management.

CANDLES, INCENSE

ACADIAN
Candle Company

ACADIAN CANDLE COMPANY
6328 Penn Ave. So.
Richfield, MN 55423
Tel.: 888-424-9425; FAX: 612-861-1433

Personnel:
Scott Evenson . . . . President
Judy Hechtl. . . . . Customer Service

Type of Business:
Handcrafted, custom candles poured in layers of colors lathed to give them their unique and distinctive look. Slow-burning and dripless our candles are made of the finest raw materials available. Candles for every occasion — Paschal, Advent, Lent, RCJA, Baptism, Confirmation, Weddings, or custom silkscreened candles to fit any commemorative celebration or event. Call for a complete free color brochure.
Acadian Candles — Quality Candles Crafted By Hand.

ROOT™
CANDLES

THE A.I. ROOT CANDLE CO.
623 W. Liberty St.
Medina, OH 44258
Tel.: 800-289-7668; FAX: 330-725-5624

Personnel:
John Holodnak . . . . Sales Manager

Type of Business:
• **Merchandise Handled:** Full line of altar candles, Advent, wedding and sacrament candles. Devotional lights, sanctuary lights, altar wine/bread, palms/ashes, and church supplies.
• **Services Offered**: Replating/refinishing services. Personalized sales representation in most states. Two factory locations: Medina, OH; San Antonio, TX.
• **Recent Clients:** Serving over 12,000 churches nationwide.
• **Statement:** Craftsmen in wax since 1869. Root Quality - Root Service.
• **Free Literature:** Free color catalog, 800-BUY-ROOT.

CATHEDRAL CANDLE CO.
Now in stock at your nearest Church Goods dealer.

Type of Business:
Classical symbolism and expressive liturgical design in the luxurious hand decorated artistry of SCULPTWAX ... created and mastercrafted here in the United States, exclusively at Cathedral Candle Co.

See full-page display ad on page 11F.

Hand-tailoring, exquisite fabrics and attention to detail result in vesture that will last for years.
QUALITY
Designers & Crafters of Ecclesiastical Vesture
St. Joseph's Abbey Spencer, MA 01562-1233
T508-885-8750
F 508-885-8758
Our catalog of hand-tailored vesture and sanctuary accessories is available upon request.
THE HOLY+ROOD GUILD

THE HOLY ROOD GUILD
St. Joseph's Abbey
167 North Spencer Rd.
Spencer, MA 01562-1233
Tel.: 508-885-8750; FAX: 508-885-8758

Type of Business:

Designers and crafters of ecclesiastical vesture for over 40 years. Inspired by our monastic tradition, we seek to unite in our work simplicity in design, quality in materials and excellence in craftsmanship. The result is vesture that enhances the liturgical celebration with visual grace and order. Our artists—both monks and laypersons—are available for custom design work and consultation. We also provide an extensive selection of ready made items.

KERRY CANDLES
6070 Corte del Cedro
Carlsbad, CA 92009
Tel.: 619-931-0191

Type of Business:

So many churches have come to appreciate the cleanliness, safety, and beauty of Kerry Candles. The pure liquid inside lights their way without melted wax, smoke or odor. These handcrafted liquid candles are available in a variety of styles and sizes.

emkay

MUENCH KREUZER CANDLE CO.
P.O. Box 4969
Syracuse, NY 13221
Tel.: 315-471-4515; FAX: 315-471-4581

Type of Business:

Manufacturers of Church candles, altar, sanctuary, sacramental, votive & devotional candles of the highest quality. Emkay Candles ... available through your nearest Church Goods Dealer.

(See display ad on preceding page)

CHALICES, CROSSES & METAL WARE

ECCLESIASTICAL ARTS, INC.
16 Herbert St.
Newark, NJ 07105
Tel: 973-491-0022; FAX: 973-491-0023

Personnel:

Joseph J. Zaky .... President

Type of Business:

Artists and Craftsmen specializing in custom designed and hand made furnishings in metal, wood, stone and glass. For interior design, fabrication, restoration and original sculpture, contact J.J. Zaky — the workshop/studio for design, fabrication, installation — nationwide.

Granda
Liturgical Arts, Inc.

TAG

GRANDA LITURGICAL ARTS, INC.
828 Davis St., Ste. 200
Evanston, IL 60201
Tel.: 800-425-0828; FAX: 847-492-1374
www.hispacom.es/granda; e-mail: ruf4granda@aol.com

Personnel:

Karen Johnson

Type of Business:

GRANDA LITURGICAL ARTS, Inc. is the USA branch of the largest supplier of church goods in the world: TALLERES DE ARTE GRANDA, S.A.

With 65 employees and sales all over the world, we can offer our experience in the manufacture of:

— metalware: chalices, tabernacles, etc.
— vestments
— wood carvings
— church decoration, interior design

Since 1891, we have been serving the church, combining modern techniques (computer aided design, projects in 3D ...) with artistic values.

Special custom orders are our specialty, styled and priced according to your needs.

ADRIAN HAMERS®

CHURCH — ONE HUNDRED YEARS SERVING THE CLERGY — TOUJOURS 1887 — INTERIORS

ADRIAN HAMERS, INC.
2 Madison Ave.
Larchmont, NY 10538
Tel.: 914-834-7780; FAX: 914-834-0712

Type of Business:

Since 1887, the Hamers name has been synonymous with expert silversmithing throughout the world in the field of Liturgical Art. We are also experts in: Church Interiors from design to execution, Renovations, Altars, Sacred Vessels, Appraisals, Gold and Silver Plating & Repairing, Tabernacles, Marble, Woodwork & Woodcarving, Statuary, Stained Glass, Pews & Chairs, Gold Leafing, Frescoes, Restoration, Trompe-l'oeuil, Wall Murals (repair and conservation cleaning), Ornamental Plaster, Heraldic Designs & Bishop Regalia.

THE HOLY ROOD GUILD

THE HOLY ROOD GUILD
St. Joseph's Abbey
167 North Spencer Rd.
Spencer, MA 01562-1233
Tel.: 508-885-8750; FAX: 508-885-8758

Type of Business:
Designers and crafters of ecclesiastical vesture for over 40 years. Inspired by our monastic tradition, we seek to unite in our work simplicity in design, quality in materials and excellence in craftsmanship. The result is vesture that enhances the liturgical celebration with visual grace and order. Our artists—both monks and laypersons—are available for custom design work and consultation. We also provide an extensive selection of ready made items.

ADAM KOCHLIN
DESIGNS

ADAM KOCHLIN DESIGNS
33 Magee Ave., 2nd Fl.
Stamford, CT 06902
Tel.: 800-886-4668; FAX: 203-325-3755

Personnel:
Adam Kochlin . . . . Design Director
Michael Kirshbaum. Executive Director
Regina Maguire . . . . Product Manager

Type of Business:
Adam Kochlin Designs creates a complete line of made to order vestments and hangings produced in our studio in Connecticut. Working with a number of artists we also create made to order sacred vessels and appointments including processional crosses, pacschal candlesticks, altar candlesticks, sanctuary lamps, incensors, chalices and patens, aumbrys, curets, and falgons in wood, ceramic, glass and metal. Call 800-886-4668 for free catalog and information.

D.C. RIGGOTT INC.
3540 Neal Ave.
Afton, MN 55001
Tel.: 800-479-8777; FAX: 612-436-4769

Personnel:
Don Riggott . . . . Owner/President

Type of Business:
Specializing in vintage church accessories, architectural ornamentation and liturgical furnishings.
Stained Glass Windows • Altars • Lighting • Statuary • Stations of the Cross • Tabernacles • Monstranses • Fonts • Pews • Steeple Bells • Vestments • Books • Furniture • Candlesticks • Chalices,
Please contact us with specific requests. We will be happy to send you photographs and specifics on any items in our inventory. You may have items in storage or not being used, please contact us as we are actively searching for vintage items to purchase for re-use in liturgical spaces.

SN
STADELMAIER
NIJMEGEN

STADELMAIER-NIJMEGEN-HOLLAND
P.O. Box 7063
6503 GN Nijmegen
Tel.: 31-24-3791170; FAX: 31-24-3791171
e-mail: stadelmaier@telebyte.nl

Type of Business:
Our special department "SN-Sancta," carries chalices, ciboria, monstrances, etc., made in various technics and styles. Stainless steel, enamel-cloisonné or sterling silver. We have a small but beautiful collection to offer.

CHOIR ROBES

Robert Gaspard Co.

ROBERT GASPARD CO., INC.
200 N. Janacek Rd.
Brookfield, WI 53045-6153
Tel.: 800-784-6868; 414-784-6800; FAX: 414-784-7567

Personnel:

Rose Gaspard . . . . President
John Andorfer . . . . Vice President
Jason R. Gaspard . . . . Sales & Marketing Mgr.

Type of Business:

The Robert Gaspard Co. was established in 1954. Over the past 43 years, we have grown to be a nationally-known company. We pride ourselves on the ability to create original custom designs to enrich your worship needs. Our complete line consists of all ecclesiastical vesture, as well as paraments, mass and altar linens, stoles, banners, chasubles, funeral palls, albs, cossacks, surplices, choir robes, acolyte robes and many accessories. Complimentary catalogs and fabric swatches sent on request.

MURPHY VESTMENTS

MURPHY VESTMENTS
Murphy Cap & Gown Co.
4200 31st St. North
St. Petersburg, FL 33714
Tel.: 800-876-8774; 813-527-0696; FAX: 813-526-3528
website: www.murphyrobes.com; e-mail: murphyrb@gte.net

Personnel:

Don Camp . . . . President
Gary Bergamo . . . . Sales Manager
George Shahine . . . . Administrative Manager
Josephine DeFeo . . . . Vestment Designer

Type of Business:

Manufacturer of vestments, albs, cassocks, choir and acolyte robes and accessories, all value priced with guaranteed fit and quality. We supply a complete line of liturgical attire, custom tailored as well as many styles in stock and ready to ship within 24 hours of receipt of order. Available through your church goods dealer, or call or write for more information.

CHURCH REGISTERS

Serving Catholic Parishes since 1873.

D.P. MURPHY CO., INC.
1221 Walt Whitman Rd.
Melville, NY 11747-3090
Tel: 516-673-9400; FAX: 516-673-1851

Personnel:

Peter Q. Murphy . . . . President

Type of Business:

Envelope mailing systems specifically designed to meet the needs of your parish — available at any frequency ... monthly, bi-monthly, quarterly, semi-annual, yearly sets. FREE List Maintenance. Contribution recording via fax, phone, mail, diskette, modem or E-Mail. Census, stewardship, tithing, and fundraising programs. Church stationery, registers, record books, mass cards and certificates. Specialists in old register rebinding.

F.J. REMEY CO., INC.
121 Willis Ave.
Mineola, NY 11501-0589
Tel.: 516-741-5112; FAX: 516-741-0523

Type of Business:

Serving Catholic parishes since 1921 by providing the following products: Envelope Mailing Systems, Annual Offering Envelope Boxsets, Bulk Collection Envelopes, Computer Recording, Collection Baskets, Parish Census, Church Record Books, Parish Office Forms, Church Stationery, Mass Cards, Raffle Tickets and Tuition Supplies.

CLIP-ART

KINGDOM GRAPHICS TM

KINGDOM GRAPHICS
2713 Mt. Vernon Ave.
Willow Grove, PA 19090
Tel.: 800-618-3133; FAX: 215-657-4847
website: www.kingdomgraphics.com
e-mail: kingraph@cyberenet.net
VISA & MasterCard accepted.

Personnel:
Bert VandenBos . . . . Owner / Creative Director

Type of Business:
Kingdom Graphics has been serving the Christian community for over 10 years with professional products and services that are highly creative and practical. A free catalog, upon request, is available showing the following:
— Clip-Art (for IBM or Macintosh)
— Computer Papers (pre-designed, full-color, tri-fold brochures, etc.)
— Ministry & Friendship NoteCards (creative, inspirational)
— Ministry & Friendship NotePads (creative, inspirational)
— Custom Design & Graphic Arts Services (logos, brochures, etc.)

FABRIC ART HANGINGS & TAPESTRIES

ABBOTT CHURCH GOODS, INC.
Showroom: 1515 Route 38
Cherry Hill, NJ 08002
Tel.: 800-522-2688; 609-662-6959; FAX: 609-665-5109
website: http://www.abbottsinc.com
e-mail: ACG.INC@internetMCI.com

Personnel:
Daniel J. Castonguay . . . . President
Joseph F. McKeaney . . . . General Manager
Michael W. Wasyluk . . . . Customer Service

Type of Business:
Purveyors of the Finest Vesture, Paraments, Statuary & Metalware since 1962. Unique and original creations, our specialty. Custom designs to complement your liturgical environment. Exclusive representatives of Slabbinck Master Collection & Original Collection.

T.M.

Bringing the Art Back into the Craft

BRAMANTE STUDIO
321 Wellington St. N.
Kitchener, ON, Canada N2H 5K8
Tel.: 800-295-6902; FAX: 519-570-2706

Personnel:
Abraham Mathew. . . . . President

Type of Business:
Every parish is unique, not only in terms of the parishioners who make up the body of the church, but also in terms of the art and architectural elements that define the worship space. At Bramante Studio we endeavour to capture this individuality in each fabric art piece we make. Using exceptional fabrics and old world craftsmanship, we create custom made hangings, tapestries, vestments, and altar cloths that seek to recognize the uniqueness of each parish.

Chagall Design Limited

CHAGALL DESIGN LIMITED
910 S. Los Angeles St., 9th Fl.
Los Angeles, CA 90015
Tel.: 800-947-7923; 213-624-7656; FAX: 213-624-8036

Type of Business:
Chagall Design is unique in its own right. Its reputation stems from the custom designs created here in America by European designer Jacques de Groot. These creations are designed for the individual and special needs of the Fathers and Parishes throughout the United States, Canada and Europe.
Working directly with the church, Chagall creates and custom makes the Chasubles, Banners, Altar Cloths and Stoles, which can be viewed on our web site, including the full Millennium collection and Millennium Banners both Old and New Testament. Chagall stands by our wide selection of fine fabrics and excellent craftsmanship with a full guarantee, and offer our beautiful designs to you at low prices.
To request a free catalogue or for more information on how our custom design house can best serve you, please call 1-800-947-7923 or E-mail to Chagall@IX.NETCOM.COM. Also, visit our web site WWW.CHAGALLDESIGN.COM.

D.C. RIGGOTT INC.
3540 Neal Ave.
Afton, MN 55001
Tel.: 800-479-8777; FAX: 612-436-4769

Personnel:
Don Riggott . . . . Owner/President

Type of Business:
Specializing in vintage church accessories, architectural ornamentation and liturgical furnishings.
Stained Glass Windows • Altars • Lighting • Statuary • Stations of the Cross • Tabernacles • Monstranses • Fonts • Pews • Steeple Bells • Vestments • Books • Furniture • Candlesticks • Chalices,
Please contact us with specific requests. We will be happy to send you photographs and specifics on any items in our inventory. You may have items in storage or not being used, please contact us as we are actively searching for vintage items to purchase for re-use in liturgical spaces.

SN STADELMAIER NIJMEGEN

STADELMAIER-NIJMEGEN-HOLLAND
P.O. Box 7063, 6503 GN-Nijmegen
Nijmegen, Holland 6501 BA
Tel.: 31-24-3791170; FAX: 31-24-3791171

Type of Business:
Embroideries.
Executed in centuries-old techniques, SN tapestries are world-famous. Brilliant colour combinations function differently in churches.
Magnificent designs available of Stations of the Cross, pastoral themes, Blessed Mother, Holy Family, Risen Christ, and Saints.

GLASSWARE

Stadelmaier USA LLC
Unique Liturgical Solutions

A Division of Patrick Baker & Sons and Stadelmaier Nijmegen

STADELMAIER USA LLC
1650 West St., P.O. Box 1028
Southington, CT 06489-5028
Tel.: 1-800-243-6385; FAX: 860-276-9438

Type of Business:
From the earliest days, glassware has been a fascinating material for holding the precious gifts. It has so many spiritual qualities and unique shapes, finishes and sizes. Our handblown glass is noble in form, beautiful to look at, and precious enough to enhance the Liturgy of the Lord. The collection includes complete communion sets, bowls, cruets, decanters and crismatories, and is available in October 1998.

GOLD & SILVER PLATING RESTORATION & REPAIRS

ADRIAN HAMERS®

CHURCH INTERIORS
ONE HUNDRED YEARS SERVING THE CLERGY
TOUJOURS 1887

ADRIAN HAMERS, INC.
2 Madison Ave.
Larchmont, NY 10538
Tel.: 914-834-7780; FAX: 914-834-0712

Type of Business:
Since 1887, the Hamers name has been synonymous with expert silversmithing throughout the world in the field of Liturgical Art. We are also experts in: Church Interiors from design to execution, Renovations, Altars, Sacred Vessels, Appraisals, Gold & Silver Plating and Repairing, Tabernacles, Marble, Woodwork & Woodcarving, Statuary, Stained Glass, Pews & Chairs, Gold Leafing, Frescoes, Restoration, Trompe-l'oeuil, Wall Murals (repair and conservation cleaning), Ornamental Plaster, Heraldic Designs & Bishop Regalia.

OFFERING ENVELOPES

AMERICAN CHURCH,
A DIVISION OF AMERICAN PAPER GROUP
8401 Southern Blvd.
Youngstown, OH 44512
Tel.: 800-228-6101; FAX: 330-758-9981

Personnel:
- Ronald P. Blakeman . . . . National Sales Manager
- James P. Fitzgerald. . . . . Vice President — APG Direct
- Rob Turnbull . . . . Vice President — Direct Bank Giving

Type of Business:
- Mailed Offering Envelope Systems
- Boxed Set Systems
- Direct Bank Giving
- Mail Order Retail Catalog Systems

Cathedral
CORPORATION
Church Services Division

CATHEDRAL CORPORATION
P.O. Box 1293
Buffalo, NY 14240
Tel.: 800-828-7455; FAX: 716-667-7309

Personnel:
Marianne Gaige . . . . President
Stephen L. Miller . . . . Director of Marketing
Maurie L. Jachimiak . . . . Sales/Service Manager

Type of Business:
Cathedral Corporation has been a full-service supplier of products and services designed to enhance the financial health of parishes for over 60 years, including:
- Mailed envelopes; monthly, bi-monthly, quarterly, Custom and money-saving Compuset envelopes
- Boxed sets; adult, youth and children's
- Cost-effective offering envelope recording and reporting
- Stewardship, Weekly renewal, and Capital campaigns
- Laser personalized mailings for improved parishioner communications
- Offset printing, addressing and mailing to fill a variety of parish and school needs.

Serving Catholic Parishes since 1873.

D.P. MURPHY CO., INC.
1221 Walt Whitman Rd.
Melville, NY 11747-3090
Tel: 516-673-9400; FAX: 516-673-1851

Personnel:
Peter Q. Murphy . . . . President

Type of Business:
Envelope mailing systems specifically designed to meet the needs of your parish — available at any frequency ... monthly, bi-monthly, quarterly, semi-annual, yearly sets. FREE List Maintenance. Contribution recording via fax, phone, mail, diskette, modem or E-Mail. Census, stewardship, tithing, and fundraising programs. Church stationery, registers, record books, mass cards and certificates. Specialists in old register rebinding.

NATIONAL CHURCH SUPPLY CO.
P.O. Box 269
Chester, WV 26034
Tel.: 304-387-5200; FAX: 304-387-5266

Personnel:
Ms. Kathy Myers. . . . . Sales & Advertising Coordinator

Type of Business:
Nurturing Stewardship Growth in churches is a tradition at Catholic Envelope Service. A division of National Church Supply Co., we have been serving the Christian community for over 80 years. Every person in our family owned organization has the same goal: to help every church customer find the best possible solution to today's and tomorrow's stewardship challenges. Our innovative church offering envelopes and stewardship systems are geared to increase communications while improving parishioner commitment and response.

ONE-WRITE COMPANY
P.O. Box 310
Lancaster, OH 43130
Tel.: 1-800-268-6070; FAX: 800-504-2260

Type of Business:
Book Offering Envelopes, Tuition Payment Books, Mailing Plan for Offering Envelopes, and Contribution Report Forms. We invite you to compare the features and prices of the Book Offering Envelopes with your current system. The savings will be considerable. Write or call for a free catalog and quote today.

Our Sunday Visitor
Offering Envelopes

OUR SUNDAY VISITOR, INC.
200 Noll Plaza
Huntington, IN 46750
Tel.: 800-348-2886; FAX: 219-356-4584

Personnel:
Kyle Hamilton. . . . . Vice-President-General Manager
Sharon Kaiser . . . . Sales Manager
Julie Kenny . . . . Marketing Manager

Type of Business:
Only **Catholic, not-for-profit company** in the offering envelope business. Our Sunday Visitor provides a wide variety of offering envelope products and services for adults and children including Stewardship envelopes (English and Spanish/English) and inserts. We have an envelope solution to fit your needs whether your parish uses a mailing or boxed set program, or purchases in bulk.
(Also, see our display ad under "Liturgical and Church Goods" — Offering Envelopes)

F.J. REMEY CO., INC.
121 Willis Ave.
Mineola, NY 11501-0589
Tel.: 516-741-5112; FAX: 516-741-0523

Type of Business:
Serving Catholic parishes since 1921 by providing the following products: Envelope Mailing Systems, Annual Offering Envelope Boxsets, Bulk Collection Envelopes, Computer Recording, Collection Baskets, Parish Census, Church Record Books, Parish Office Forms, Church Stationery, Mass Cards, Raffle Tickets and Tuition Supplies.

SACRED VESSELS

ADRIAN HAMERS®
CHURCH INTERIORS

ADRIAN HAMERS INC.
2 Madison Ave.
Larchmont, NY 10538
Tel.: 914-834-7780; FAX: 914-834-0712

Type of Business:
Since 1887, the Hamers name has been synonymous with expert silversmithing throughout the world in the field of Liturgical Art. We are also experts in: Church Interiors from design to execution, Renovations, Altars, Sacred Vessels, Appraisals, Gold and Silver Plating & Repairing, Tabernacles, Marble, Woodwork & Woodcarving, Statuary, Stained Glass, Pews & Chairs, Gold Leafing, Frescoes, Restoration, Trompe-l'oeuil, Wall Murals (repair and conservation cleaning), Ornamental Plaster, Heraldic Designs & Bishop Regalia.

ADAM KOCHLIN
DESIGNS

ADAM KOCHLIN DESIGNS
33 Magee Ave., 2nd Fl.
Stamford, CT 06902
Tel.: 800-886-4668; FAX: 203-325-3755

Personnel:
Adam Kochlin . . . . Design Director
Michael Kirshbaum. . . . . Executive Director
Regina Maguire . . . . Product Manager

Type of Business:
Adam Kochlin Designs creates a complete line of made to order vestments and hangings produced in our studio in Connecticut. Working with a number of artists we also create made to order sacred vessels and appointments including processional crosses, pacschal candlesticks, alter candlesticks, sanctuary lamps, incensors, chalices and patens, aumbrys, curets, and falgons in wood ceramic, glass and metal. Call 800-886-4668 for free catalog and information.

D.C. RIGGOTT INC.
3540 Neal Ave.
Afton, MN 55001
Tel.: 800-479-8777; FAX: 612-436-4769

Personnel:
Don Riggott . . . . Owner/President

Type of Business:
Specializing in vintage church accessories, architectural ornamentation and liturgical furnishings.
Stained Glass Windows • Altars • Lighting • Statuary • Stations of the Cross • Tabernacles • Monstranses • Fonts • Pews • Steeple Bells • Vestments • Books • Furniture • Candlesticks • Chalices, Please contact us with specific requests. We will be happy to send you photographs and specifics on any items in our inventory. You may have items in storage or not being used, please contact us as we are actively searching for vintage items to purchase for re-use in liturgical spaces.

SN
STADELMAIER
NIJMEGEN

STADELMAIER-NIJMEGEN-HOLLAND
P.O. Box 7063
6503 GN Nijmegen
Tel.: 31-24-3791170; FAX: 31-24-3791171
e-mail: stadelmaier@telebyte.nl

Type of Business:
Our special department "SN-Sancta," carries chalices, ciboria, monstrances, etc., made in various technics and styles. Stainless steel, enamel-cloisonné or sterling silver. We have a small but beautiful collection to offer.

Stadelmaier USA LLC
Unique Liturgical Solutions

A Division of Patrick Baker & Sons and Stadelmaier Nijmegen

STADELMAIER USA LLC
1650 West St., P.O. Box 1028
Southington, CT 06489-5028
Tel.: 1-800-243-6385; FAX: 860-276-9438

Type of Business:
Our special department "SN-Sancta," carries items such as chalices, ciboria, monstrances, and much, much more, all made in varying styles and techniques. They are crafted in stainless steel, enamel-cloisonne or sterling silver. This is an exclusive and beautiful collection that we offer.

STATIONERY & GREETING CARDS

BC

BARTON-COTTON

BARTON COTTON
1405 Parker Rd.
Baltimore, MD 21227
Tel.: 800-638-4652; FAX; 800-807-2954

Personnel:
Denise J. Payne. . . . . Vice President Marketing and Sales

Type of Business:
For more than 65 years, Barton-Cotton, Inc. has been proud to supply the finest selection of quality religious stationery products for the Catholic Clergy and Religious. More than 300 products are available including Mass cards, Certificates, Christmas and Easter cards, Mother's and Father's Day sets, Ordination/Jubilee products, Way of the Cross booklets, Rosary folders, Holy cards, Bookmarks, bulletins and offering envelopes, and many other items. To request a FREE catalog, call toll-free today at 1-800-638-4652.

KINGDOM GRAPHICS™

KINGDOM GRAPHICS
2713 Mt. Vernon Ave.
Willow Grove, PA 19090
Tel.: 800-618-3133; FAX: 215-657-4847
website: www.kingdomgraphics.com
e-mail: kingraph@cyberenet.net
VISA & MasterCard accepted.

Personnel:
Bert VandenBos . . . . Owner / Creative Director

Type of Business:
Kingdom Graphics hs been serving the Christian community for over 10 years with professional products and services that are highly creative and practical. A free catalog, upon request, is available showing the following:
— Clip-Art (for IBM or Macintosh)
— Computer Papers (pre-designed, full-color, tri-fold brochures, etc.)
— Ministry & Friendship NoteCards (creative, inspirational)
— Ministry & Friendship NotePads (creative, inspirational)
— Custom Design & Graphic Arts Services (logos, brochures, etc.)

THE PRINTERY HOUSE
Conception Abbey · CONCEPTION · MISSOURI 64433

THE PRINTERY HOUSE
Conception Abbey
Conception, MO 64433
Tel.: 800-322-2737 / 660-944-2632; FAX: 888-556-8262
e-mail: gnelson@msc-net.com

Personnel:
Gerald E. Nelson . . . . General Manager
Ron Riggs . . . . Director of Sales & Marketing

Type of Business:
The Printery House manufactures Christian greeting cards as a not-for-profit extension of the apostolic mission of Conception Abbey, a Benedictine community dedicated to a Christian life of work and prayer. We make our cards available to religious organizations to earn 50% with no risk, no prepayment. Call 800-889-0105 for your fund-raiser packet and more information.

STEWARDSHIP

OurSundayVisitor
Offering Envelopes

OUR SUNDAY VISITOR, INC.
200 Noll Plaza
Huntington, IN 46750
Tel.: 800-348-2886; FAX: 219-356-4584

Personnel:
Kyle Hamilton. . . . . Vice-President-General Manager
Sharon Kaiser . . . . Sales Manager
Julie Kenny . . . . Marketing Manager

Type of Business:
Only **Catholic, not-for-profit company** in the offering envelope business. Our Sunday Visitor provides a wide variety of offering envelope products and services for adults and children including Stewardship envelopes (English and Spanish/English) and inserts. We have an envelope solution to fit your needs whether your parish uses a mailing or boxed set program, or purchases in bulk.
(Also, see our display ad under "Liturgical and Church Goods" — Offering Envelopes)

PUBLISHERS

BC

BARTON-COTTON

BARTON COTTON
1405 Parker Rd.
Baltimore, MD 21227
Tel.: 800-638-4652; FAX; 800-807-2954

Personnel:

Denise J. Payne. . . . . Vice President Marketing and Sales

Type of Business:

For more than 65 years, Barton-Cotton, Inc. has been proud to supply the finest selection of quality religious stationery products for the Catholic Clergy and Religious. More than 300 products are available including Mass cards, Certificates, Christmas and Easter cards, Mother's and Father's Day sets, Ordination/Jubilee products, Way of the Cross booklets, Rosary folders, Holy cards, Bookmarks, bulletins and offering envelopes, and many other items. To request a FREE catalog, call toll-free today at 1-800-638-4652.

BETHLEHEM BOOKS

Literature to feed the imagination

Specializing in reprinting quality children's books

BETHLEHEM BOOKS
15605 County Road 15
Minto, ND 58261
Tel.: (701) 248-3929; FAX: (701) 248-3940

Personnel:

Jack Sharpe . . . . General Manager

Type of Business:

Bethlehem Books is an apostolate dedicated to building Catholic Culture by publishing children's literature written to feed the imagination. Our business, a branch of Bethlehem Community, co-publishes with Ignatius Press a wide variety of wholesome well-written books, by such Catholic authors as Hilda vanStockum, Meriol Trevor and Ethel Pochocki. We offer a "Living History Library" series, picture books, adventure stories and more by both new and established authors. Call for a free catalog: 1-800-757-6831. 20% discount to libraries and schools.

THE LITURGICAL PRESS
P.O. Box 7500, St. John's Abbey
Collegeville, MN 56321
Tel.: 800-858-5450 / 320-363-2213; FAX: 800-445-5899
website: www.litpress.org; e-mail: sales@litpress.org

Personnel:
Ed Vessel .... Bookstore Sales
Carmen Donabauer .... Customer Service
Rita Groetsch .... Customer Service
Mary Ann Karasch .... Customer Service

Type of Business:
For over 70 years suppliers of liturgical, biblical, ritual, and instructional material to English-speaking countries. Products offered: *Celebrating the Eucharist* Mass Guide, *Bible and Liturgy Sunday Bulletins*, books, leaflets, video and audio cassettes, *Days of the Lord, Sacra Pagina, Collegeville Pastoral Dictionary of Biblical Theology, The Encyclopedia of American Catholic History, The International Catholic Bible Commentary,* and *The Bible Today, Sister's Today, Worship, New Theology Review, Liturgical Ministry,* and *Journal of Hispanic/Latino Theology* magazines. Call for a free catalog.

LITURGY TRAINING PUBLICATIONS

LITURGY TRAINING PUBLICATIONS
1800 N. Hermitage Ave.
Chicago, IL 60622-1101
Tel.: 800-933-1800; FAX: 800-933-7094
e-mail: orders@ltp.org

Personnel:
Gabe Huck.................................. Director
John D. Wright....................... Marketing Director

Type of Business:
LTP provides materials that assist parishes, institutions and households in the preparation and celebration of liturgy in Christian life. In its products and its operation, LTP strives to express the justice and beauty that are fundamental to the church and to its liturgy. Publications include *Workbook for Lectors and Gospel Readers, Sourcebook for Sundays and Seasons, At Home with the Word, Children's Daily Prayer, The Sunday Mass Video Series, Catechumenate* magazine, *Liturgy 90, E&A Newsletter.*

PAULIST PRESS
997 Macarthur Blvd.
Mahwah, NJ 07430
Tel.: 201-825-7300; FAX: 201-825-8345
website: www.paulistpress.com; e-mail: paulistp@pipeline.com

Personnel:
Kevin A. Lynch, CSP......................... Publisher
Don Brophy .... Managing Editor
John A. Thomas .... Marketing Director

Type of Business:
- Publishes Ordo; religious books; the Classics of Western Spirituality series; catechetical programs; pastoral resources; liturgical desk and pocket calendars; Paulist Bible Study Program; and children's books.
- Produces religious videos, audios and CD-ROMs.
- Provides Catholic books and magazines to parishes from a variety of Catholic publishers through its National Catholic Reading Distribution division.

TREEHAUS COMMUNICATIONS, INC.
906 W. Loveland Ave.
P.O. Box 249
Loveland, OH 45140-0249
Tel.: 800-638-4287; FAX: 513-683-2882

Personnel:
Gerard A. Pottebaum .... President
Kim Mathes............................. Office Manager

Type of Business:
Treehaus Communications, Inc. publisher of the internationally acclaimed Sunday Liturgy of the Word materials (English/ Spanish) that respect the child's natural relationship with God; Sunday readings adapted for children; Sunday liturgy planning guide with catochetical supplement; illustrated leaflets and posters for each Sunday; acclamations and responses as well as music children can sing drawn from parish hymnals; personal and family spiritual life journals. Selected resources, including the Catechesis of the Good Shepherd, that recognize the child's innate sense of the sacred.

BOOKS & RELIGIOUS ARTICLES

TREEHAUS COMMUNICATIONS, INC.
906 W. Loveland Ave.
P.O. Box 249
Loveland, OH 45140-0249
Tel.: 800-638-4287; FAX: 513-683-2882

Personnel:
Gerard A. Pottebaum .... President
Kim Mathes .... Office Manager

Type of Business:
Treehaus Communications, Inc. publisher of the internationally acclaimed Sunday Liturgy of the Word materials (English/ Spanish) that respect the child's natural relationship with God; Sunday readings adapted for children; Sunday liturgy planning guide with catochetical supplement; illustrated leaflets and posters for each Sunday; acclamations and responses as well as music children can sing drawn from parish hymnals; personal and family spiritual life journals. Selected resources, including the Catechesis of the Good Shepherd, that recognize the child's innate sense of the sacred.

MAGAZINES, JOURNALS

THE TABLET
the international Catholic weekly

THE TABLET PUBLISHNG COMPANY LTD.
1, King Street Cloisters, Clifton Walk
London, U.K. W6 0QZ
Tel.: (011 44) 181 748 8484; FAX: (011 44) 181-563-7644
website: http://www.thetablet.co.uk
e-mail: market@tablet.netkonect.co.uk

Personnel:
Hugh Kealy .... Publisher
Rebecca Cullen-Moreno .... Marketing Manager
Simon Lister .... Marketing Assistant
Conor Taaffe .... Advertising Manager

Type of Business:
The Tablet is the international Catholic weekly, reporting on world Church news as well as informing and entertaining on issues of the day. The discussion of politics, current affairs, religion, science, literature and biography provides a forum for international debate and is combined with a comprehensive books and arts review section.

(See display ad on next page)

MUSIC PUBLISHERS

CATHEDRAL MUSIC PRESS
#4 Industrial Dr.
Pacific, MO 63069-0066
Tel.: 1-800-863-5229; 314-257-3970; FAX: 314-257-5062
Web: http://www.melbay.com; e-mail: email@melbay.com

Personnel:
William Bay................................ President
L. Dean Bye .... General Manager
Michael Entsminger .... Marketing Coordinator
Ginny Patterson .... Sales

Type of Business:
A leading music publisher specializing in instrumental and instructional material for the church. A complete line of piano, organ, flute, clarinet, trumpet, saxophone, guitar, and other fretted instruments along with beautifully recorded CDs and cassettes are available. Write or phone for our most recent catalog at 1-800-863-5229.

RENEWAL MUSIC

RENEWAL MUSIC
1000 Cody Rd.
Mobile, AL 36695
Tel.: 800-223-7333; FAX: 334-633-0882

Type of Business:

Blending texturs of liturgy with the wind that is renewing the heart of the Church, Renewal Music's latest project, Behold The Lamb, opens wide timeless doors to reveal an intimate place of worship. Well-known singers and composers Jim Cowan, Don Moen and Steve Merkel take you on a rich journey of worship that exalts the Lamb of God who takes away the sins of the world. Look for more great projects coming from Renewal Music in 1998.

Voice of the Rockies

VOICE OF THE ROCKIES
P.O. Box 1043
Boulder, Colorado 80306
Tel.: 1-800-783-1233; 303-444-2475; FAX: 303-444-8334
website: http://www.voiceoftherockies.com
e-mail: Voiceofroc@AOL.com

Personnel:

Patricia T. Holmberg .... President
Russell K. Holmberg .... V. President
April Seawell .... Office Manager

Type of Business:

A publisher of printed music, Voice of the Rockies has a steadily growing catalog of choral music, as well as piano, organ, instrumental, chamber, orchestral and vocal music. Please look for our products in music stores, call for our catalog or look for our presence on the Internet at the above address.

PARISH DIRECTORIES

olan mills
CHURCH DIRECTORIES
We Make It Special

OLAN MILLS CHURCH DIVISION
4325 Amnicola Hwy.
Chattanooga, TN 37422
Tel.: 800-845-1157; FAX: 423-629-8106

Personnel:
. . . . V.P. Sales

Type of Business:
You can trust Americas' largest Church Directory publisher. A full color pictorial directory by Olan Mills, IS the Number One Parish communication tool. It's delivered in 45 days and we help you all the way. Each family receives an Olan Mills custom 8x10 portrait AND, a copy of the directory FREE.
Special for 1998-1999 directories:
Mention this offer: code KEN 598, and receive 2 Extra Color pages plus 50 additional directories FREE.

PHOTOGRAPHY

olan mills
PORTRAIT STUDIOS
We Make It Special

OLAN MILLS, INC.
4325 Amnicola Hwy.
Chattanooga, TN 37422
Tel.: 800-845-1157; FAX: 423-629-8106

Personnel:
Richard Restiano . . . . Dir. of Marketing

Type of Business:
Olan Mills is the premier portrait company in America, with studios across the nation. Families, for over 65 years, have enjoyed our professionalism and exceptional quality.
The Church Division provides this same quality product when photographing your families for a parish directory. All work is 100% satisfaction guaranteed. Special discount prices are made available to parish families.
The School Division brings the studio to the school, with money saving portrait packages, and fundraising potential.

TRANSLATIONS & EDITING

COME ALIVE

COMMUNICATIONS, INC.

"Multilingual Catholic Communication Experts"

COME ALIVE COMMUNICATIONS
289 Avondale Rd., P.O. Box 436
West Grove, PA 19390-0436
Tel.: 610-869-3660; FAX: 610-869-7557

Personnel:

Bridget G. Hylak . . . . Chief of Translation & Editing

Type of Business:

- Expert Catholic Translators
- Guaranteed Low Rates
- State-of-the-Art Equipment

All types of translation, editing, professional desktop publishing, advertising and graphic design: books, movies, brochures, newsletters, ads, etc. Top quality staff of native linguists and designers. Ample references available.

Call/FAX for a free estimate.

Come Alive is dedicated to serving the Catholic Community with theologically and linguistically impeccable documents in 14 languages. All translation assignments are conducted in complete obedience to the Vatican's official translation guidelines.

YEARBOOKS

olan mills

PORTRAIT STUDIOS

We Make It Special

OLAN MILLS SCHOOL DIVISION
5962 Brainerd Rd.
Chattanooga, TN 37421
Tel.: 800-472-4348; FAX: 423-499-8428

Personnel:

Randy Campbell . . . . V.P. Sales

Type of Business:

Olan Mills provides complete photographic programs for schools from pre-k through college. Products include not only yearbooks, but digital photo ID cards with bar codes, class composites and portraits on CD-ROM. Classbook programs offer "how-to" kits, exciting standard cover options and all the necessary tools for a successful sales campaign. Customer service dedicated to each account will provide complete support throughout the school year. Classbooks are available in B&W, full color or a combination.

PROFESSIONAL ASSOCIATIONS & ORGANIZATIONS

FRATERNAL ORGANIZATIONS

AIR FORCE Chaplain SERVICE

AIR FORCE CHAPLAIN RECRUITING SERVICE
HQ AFRS/RSOCC
550 D Street West Ste 1
Randolph AFB TX 78150-4527
Tel.: 800-803-2452
kinneyj@afrs.rs.af.mil / lemonsr@afrs.rs.af.mil

Personnel:

Ch, Lt. Col. Rita A. Lemons
. . . . Chief, Chaplain Accessions Section
Ch, Capt. John M. Kinney
. . . . Deputy Chief, Chaplain Accessions Section

Type of Business:

Air Force chaplains ensure the free exercise of religion for the globally engaged Air Force community. Catholics make up approximately 30% of the military. Priest chaplains are particularly responsible for the spiritual and the sacramental needs of Catholics in the military setting. Because the Catholic Chaplain lives the same challenging demands of military life, he can truly respond. The Air Force offers the qualified priest many opportunities to serve both the Church and the country in a pluralistic global environment.

Chaplains remain steadfast witnesses of the holy in a changing world environment. Consider the possibility of serving as a priest and an officer in the United States Air Force. For more information, please contact the above office.

CATHOLIC ORDER OF FORESTERS
355 Shuman Blvd., P.O. Box 3012
Naperville, IL 60555-7012
Tel.: 630-983-4920; 800-552-0145; FAX: 630-983-5113

Personnel:

Robert Ciesla . . . . High Chief Ranger
Armand R. Lemire . . . . Vice High Chief Ranger
Leo J. Beranek . . . . High Sec.-Treas.

Type of Business:

Catholic Order of Foresters, a fraternal benefit society with 135,000 members nationwide, has been providing Catholics with financial protection since 1883. In addition to quality life insurance and annuity products, COF offers added value through fraternal benefits—parish and diocese loans, college scholarships, student loans, orphan benefits, local youth and adult court activities, and benevolence that includes a matching funds program.

SCHOOL SUPPLIES & EQUIPMENT

GESTETNER
333 Ludlow St.
Stamford, CT 06904-2270
Tel.: 1-800-765-7746

Type of Business:

Gestetner CopyPrinter digital duplicators have redefined the meaning of cost-effectiveness. Digital duplicators produce prints with high-quality text and image reproduction. They are ideal for jobs requiring large copy volumes — they can produce up to 130 prints per minute — while keeping costs at less than a penny a page. And since there are a variety of models available, you can be sure there's one to fit your organization's needs. The Gestetner name represents a long-standing tradition of excellence in the world of paper-based communication.

CLASSROOM SEATING

CLARIN, A DIVISION OF GREENWICH INDUSTRIES, L.P.
927 North Shore Dr.
Lake Bluff, IL 60044
Tel.: 847-295-2200; FAX: 847-234-9001

Personnel:

William P. Peterson . . . . President
Wilson J. Troup III . . . . Vice President Sales and Marketing
Greg Star. . . . . CFO
Evelyn Herron . . . . Vice President Human Resources

Type of Business:

Manufacturer of portable and fixed lecture room seating. Supplier of logo chairs and stools for schools and athletic teams, correct pitch music chairs, tablet arm chairs and other seating products for all uses. Our fabrics, colors and options provide the most contemporary seating environments available.

Since 1925 our commitment to excellence in service, product durability and style, enables Clarin to offer the ultimate in seating concepts to customers worldwide.

DON'T BLAME THE BARTENDER

Tonight Was a Long Time Coming

Could this priest be heading for his car? Let's hope not. Clearly, he's drunk and he'd be putting in harm's way not only himself, but every occupant of every car on the road he drives.

Maybe he intends to walk. In which case, he might very well meet members of his congregation along the way. They can't fail to notice his unsteady gait and unfocused eyes. Will they feel shock or disappointment? More likely, what they'll feel is a sudden sense of abandonment.

Who's to blame? Alcoholism is a disease. The victim seldom is able to shake its tenacious grasp without a helping hand. Think about it. Didn't you notice, or at least suspect, ***before*** tonight, that Father had a chemical dependency problem? What steps have you taken?

One Out of Ten

Chemical dependency is a problem so widespread that at least ten percent of the Catholic clergy is afflicted. The popular impression is that men who are not treated are left to suffer the horrid consequences alone.

That's simply not true. They don't suffer alone. Members of their dioceses fall victims, too.

If this priest decides tonight to drive in his impaired condition and has a serious accident, it could cost his diocese tens of thousands of dollars in legal fees and lawsuits – programs will have to be eliminated, parish improvements canceled, needy people deprived.

Shame shared.

You Need to Act Now

Time and time again, the court says, "They're your employees. You're responsible." ***If they get in an accident, the diocese is going to pay.***

As for those parishioners the priest may encounter if he instead decides to walk – no monetary system can repay the damage done them.

No Priest Is an Island

In the end, of course, it's not a moral issue for the alcoholic, but for you. We're only following our Faith in giving troubled clergy the "hand up" they require to continue their work with success and sobriety. They need us. More importantly, we need them. Denial by the priest or deacon is generally part of the problem, so contact us at Guest House for help on how to proceed. Call now. We are able to provide a complete spiritual, psychological and medical evaluation at no charge.

GuestHouse®

Ph: 1-800-634-4155

4800 48th Street N.E.
Rochester, Minnesota 55903

SPECIAL CARE FACILITIES

GUEST HOUSE, INC.
1601 Joslyn Rd., P.O. Box 420
Lake Orion, MI 48361
Tel.: 800-626-6910; 810-391-4445; FAX: 810-391-0210

LAKE ORION CENTER
(For Women Religious)
P.O. Box 68
Lake Orion, MI 48361
Tel.: 800-626-6910; 810-391-3100; FAX: 810-391-1553

ROCHESTER TREATMENT CENTER
(For priests, deacons, brothers & seminarians)
P.O. Box 954
Rochester, MN 55903
Tel.: 800-634-4155; 507-288-4693; FAX: 507-288-1240

Personnel:

Richard K. Frisch, A.C.S.W. . . . . President & CEO
Danial A. Kidd. . . . . Chief Administrative Officer
Sr. Mae Kierans, C.S.J. . . . . Lake Orion Center
Bill Morgan, C.C.D.C.R.. . . . . Rochester Treatment Center
Daniel Webster. . . . . Director of Communications

Type of Business:

Guest House, Inc. is a lay-owned, lay-operated nonprofit corporation established in 1956. With the approbation of the Catholic hierarchy, it operates special residential treatment centers for alcoholic Catholic priests, deacons, brothers, sisters and seminarians from all over the world.

Catholic women religious are treated at Guest House in Lake Orion, Michigan. Our facility in Rochester, Minnesota has treatment programs for priests, deacons, brothers and seminarians.

Lovely buildings, spacious country landscape, comfortable rooms set in a serene, non-clinical setting all play an important role in reaffirming a sense of self-worth to a sick, chemically dependent priest or religious.

Accredited by JCAHO (Joint Commission on Accreditation of Healthcare Organizations) and licensed by the Department of Public Health in the states of Michigan and Minnesota respectively.

(See full-page display ad on preceding page)

CEMETERY MERCHANDISE/ CREMATION URNS & CREMATION URN VAULTS

F.H. NOBLE & COMPANY, INC.
P.O. Box 588, 888 Tower Rd., Unit "N"
Mundelein, IL 60060
Tel.: (800) 431-7690; FAX: (847) 566-0909

Personnel:

Frank N. Allen. . . . . President (Partner)
Kim J. Allen . . . . Vice President (Partner)

Type of Business:

F.H. Noble & Company manufactures two (2) urn vault lines. The versatile Convertible Urn Vault line for multiple use in stone front mausoleum niches, in-ground burial and in urn gardens. The new Global Urn Vault line will contain all sizes of urns intended for ground burial. Noble introduces the beautiful Natural Stone/Bronze urn line featuring urns of bronze and granite construciton for placement in glass front mausoleum and columbarium niches.

SAFE HOUSE & PERMANENT RESIDENCY

RECON, INC.
P.O. Box 220
Dittmer, MO 63023
Tel.: 314-285-1733; FAX: 314-285-1736

Personnel:

Fr. Bertin Miller. . . . . OFM
Mark T. Matousek . . . . MS, CCDC
Judy Dautenhahn. . . . . Clerical Assistant
Jim Funke . . . . Resident Manager

Type of Business:

RECON — a short term, long term and permanent residential recovery management program for priests and religious seeking a place to refine healthy skills in self management, vocational rehabilitation and occupational opportunities. The staff and community are skilled in support and encouragement in the resident's growth challenges. The program is Eucharist centered, assisted by professional and clinical resources and located on 280 acres of woods, lakes and rolling hills 39 miles southeast of St. Louis, Missouri. (314-285-1733)

TRAVEL & TOURISM

ABRATOURS

ABRATOURS

175 Main St.
White Plains, NY 10601
Tel.: (914) 949-3300; FAX: (914) 949-4154

Personnel:

Yaacov Amit . . . . President
Dalia Arcan . . . . Executive Vice President
Eitan Silberberg . . . . Sales and Marketing Director

Type of Business:

ARBRATOURS — Your Direct Link With the Holy Land. 800-ARBRATUR
Founded in 1933, Abratours is today's Number One specialist for the Pilgrim traveler!
Discover the Holy sites of Israel and Jordan with us.
Deluxe or Value tours, packages, guaranteed departures!
Taylor made tours and programs — enjoy the best hotels, private or shared cars, guides, and flights selected by our experienced staff to accommodate your needs and budget.
Specially customized tours and benefits for groups.

ALTURATOURS®
THE TOUR GENERATORS™

ALTURA TOURS

7270 NW 12th St., Ste. 545
Miami, FL 33126
Tel.: 800-242-4122; FAX: 305-470-9772
e-mail: altura@alturatours.com; www.alturatours.com

Personnel:

Diego Linares. . . . . President
Ivonne Gero. . . . . V.P. of Operations-Groups
Angie Novillo . . . . FIT Department

Type of Business:

Altura Tours is a full-service tour operator with over 45 years experience in international travel and tour operations. Our religious department's team of travel professionals has special ways to help you plan your next Christian pilgrimage to The Holyland and other Mediterranean and European destinations. Assistance in planning, personalized attention, competitive pricing,, rapid quotations and the best "Free Trip Incentive Program" guarantees that every group member enjoys a spiritually enriching travel experience. Call today for free brochures!

FTI
Fellowship
Travel International

FELLOWSHIP TRAVEL INTERNATIONAL, INC.

P.O. Box 15360
Richmond, VA 23227
Tel.: 800-2-FLY-FTI; FAX: 800-FAX-4-FTI
e-mail: mail@fellowship.com

Personnel:

Mr. Mike Bowles . . . . Individual Reservations Mgr.
Mr. Jeff Compton . . . . Group Reservations Mgr.
Ms. Teresa Faber. . . . . Operations Mgr.
Mr. G. Wayne Lawhorn . . . . President

Type of Business:

"Your Mission is Our Mission"

Fellowship Travel is the USA affiliate for the World InService Card Travel Savings Program. This provides both individuals and groups International Airfare discounts up to 75% on over 50 world carriers. We are your "low cost source for any type of international air or ground travel.

"Quality Tours & Pilgrimages Worldwide"

Our "total tour management" makes it easy for you to host a tour and pilgrimage. Our "volume buying power" gives you quality tours and pilgrimages at bargain prices.

ISRAEL
NO ONE BELONGS HERE MORE THAN YOU

ISRAEL TOURISM INFORMATION CENTER, N.A.

800 2nd Ave.
New York, NY 10017
Tel.: 888-77-ISRAEL; FAX: 212-499-5665

Type of Business:

Only Israel can offer you the chance to actually experience the wonders of The Bible. From walking the Vin Dolorosa to enjoying a sunset on the Mount of the Beatitudes, Israel has it all. Come visit the land that feels your body and soul. Israel. No one belongs here more than you. For more information on travel to Israel call toll-free 888-77-ISRAEL or visit us at www.goisrael.com.

206 TOURS
325 Middle Country Rd.
Smithtown, NY 11787
Tel.: 800-206-TOURS; FAX: 516-361-3682

Personnel:

Milanka Pauciullo .... CTC President, 206 Tours
Maria Ufret .... Manager
Elena Gorham-Rossi .... Sales
Jennifer Hangley .... Sales

Type of Business:

206 Tours have serviced hundreds of thousands of Catholic pilgrims to Medjugorje, Lourdes, the Holy Land, Italy and Fatima since 1985. We are dedicated to the needs of the Catholic pilgrim and are unparalleled in our service to these individuals who participate in these journeys of faith. Please feel free to call us for upcoming special Pilgrimages for 1998 through to the year 2000.

TWA GETAWAY VACATIONS
10 East Stow Rd.
Marlton, NJ 08053
Tel.: 1-800-GETAWAY; FAX: 609-984-4105

Personnel:

Peggie Montemurro .... Mgr. Int'l. Mktg.

Type of Business:

With TWA Getaway you can take advantage of great commissions up to 20%! For reservations and brochures call 1-800-GETAWAY.

Getaway Group Packages offer your clients:

- Design your own vacation
- Customize our brochure departures
- Exclusive occupancy on escorted tours of 36 passengers.
- Book by 8-31-98; get 1 free air for every 15 passengers and 1 free land package for every 20 passengers
- 5000 frequent flyer miles in addition to actual miles flown on TWA
- special group # 1-800-228-7600

CONFERENCE CENTERS

GLORIETA CONFERENCE CENTER
P.O. Box 8, I-25 North Exit 299
Glorieta, NM 87535
Tel.: (505) 757-6161; FAX: (505) 757-6149

Personnel:

Ray Ezelle .... Director of Sales and Marketing
Jennifer Venable .... National Sales Manager

Type of Business:

Glorieta Conference Center is the perfect setting for conferences, conventions, and church retreats. With three auditoriums ranging from 400 to 2,800 capacities and 60+ conference rooms. Glorieta offers ten distinctive styles of accommodations. Our professional staff will take care of your needs from audiovisual equipment to extra blankets. Glorieta's commitment to you: Our ministry is to serve your ministry, in a safe, secure Christian environment.

SAN DAMIANO CONFERENCE AND RETREAT CENTER
Rt. 1, Box 106
Golconda, IL 62938
Tel.: 618-385-3507; FAX: 618-285-3507

Personnel:

Mark Migas .... Manager
Margie Douglas .... Reservationist
Reverend Robert Vonnahmen .... Director
Craig Simoneaux .... Assistant Director

Type of Business:

San Damiano Retreat Center and Shrine of the Good Shepherd is located in Southern Illinois' Shawnee National Forest high on the bluffs overlooking the Ohio River and Western Kentucky. The shrine hosts seminars, retreats, concerts, conferences, and workshops for groups of all faiths. Featured on the grounds are 26 cottages, 35 foot bronze Good Shepherd statue, XXIII Psalm, Meditation Garden, Stations of the Cross, book and video library as well as conference and visitor center.

MASS TIMES

1-800-MASS-TIMES TRUST
67 N. Bounty Ln.
Key Largo, FL 33037
Tel.: 305-852-4530; FAX: 305-852-1582

Type of Business:

FREE Church/Mass lookup service for USA Parishes and travelers. Call 800-Mas-stim or 800-627-7846, or use the web sites listed below, find a Church Mass near your destination. Parishes can reduce their calls with NO cost to the Parish. Yearly updates of the diocesan directories of Parishes and the Internet access is provided to keep the church information current. Established in 1994, we have received 30,000 calls in 1997. The Trust is a not-for-profit trust and is listed in The Official Catholic Directory under the Miami Archdiocese. Please contact us if your Parish information is missing or needs updating.

67 N. Bounty Ln. or PO Box 2228
Key Largo, FL 33037
Office 305-852-4530 Fax 305-852-1582
Web sites: www.masstimes.org/parish, www.catholic-catalog.org
or www.catholic.net
e-mail blummel@aol.com

PILGRIMAGES

206 TOURS
325 Middle Country Rd.
Smithtown, NY 11787
Tel.: 800-206-TOURS; FAX: 516-361-3682

Personnel:

Milanka Pauciullo . . . . CTC President, 206 Tours
Maria Ufret . . . . Manager
Elena Gorham-Rossi . . . . Sales
Jennifer Hangley . . . . Sales

Type of Business:

206 Tours have serviced hundreds of thousands of Catholic pilgrims to Medjugorje, Lourdes, the Holy Land, Italy and Fatima since 1985. We are dedicated to the needs of the Catholic pilgrim and are unparalleled in our service to these individuals who participate in these journeys of faith. Please feel free to call us for upcoming special Pilgrimages for 1998 through to the year 2000.

ABRATOURS

ABRATOURS
175 Main St.
White Plains, NY 10601
Tel.: (914) 949-3300; FAX: (914) 949-4154

Personnel:

Yaacov Amit . . . . President
Dalia Arcan . . . . Executive Vice President
Eitan Silberberg . . . . Sales and Marketing Director

Type of Business:

ARBRATOURS — Your Direct Link With the Holy Land. 800-ARBRATUR
Founded in 1933, Abratours is today's Number One specialist for the Pilgrim traveler!
Discover the Holy sites of Israel and Jordan with us.
Deluxe or Value tours, packages, guaranteed departures!
Taylor made tours and programs — enjoy the best hotels, private or shared cars, guides, and flights selected by our experienced staff to accommodate your needs and budget.
Specially customized tours and benefits for groups.

ALTURA TOURS
7270 NW 12th St., Ste. 545
Miami, FL 33126
Tel.: 800-242-4122; FAX: 305-470-9772
e-mail: altura@alturatours.com; www.alturatours.com

Personnel:

Diego Linares. . . . . President
Ivonne Gero. V.P. of Operations-Groups
Angie Novillo . . . . FIT Department

Type of Business:

Altura Tours is a full-service tour operator with over 45 years experience in international travel and tour operations. Our religious department's team of travel professionals has special ways to help you plan your next Christian pilgrimage to The Holyland and other Mediterranean and European destinations. Assistance in planning, personalized attention, competitive pricing, rapid quotations and the best "Free Trip Incentive Program" guarantees that every group member enjoys a spiritually enriching travel experience. Call today for free brochures!

BALTIC TOURS

BALTIC TOURS
368 West Broadway
Boston, MA 02127
Tel.: 800-216-5987; 617-268-7999; FAX: 617-268-7325
website: http://www.quikpage.com/B/baltictours

Personnel:

Kristin Mitkus . . . . President
Birute Mitkus . . . . Vice President
Albina Rudziunas . . . . Director of Operations

Type of Business:

Since our beginning in 1975, Baltic Tours has been a specialist in group and individual travel arrangements to Lithuania, Latvia and Estonia. Baltic Tours has also custom designed tours for organizations such as Church, Pilgrimages, social clubs, fraternal, university and special interest groups. We also have an office in Vilnius, Lithuania as well as representation in both Riga, Latvia and Tallinn, Estonia to take care of all our client's needs.

Catholic Legacy Tours

CATHOLIC LEGACY TOURS
310 First Ave.
Needham, MA 02194
Tel.: 800-874-4445; FAX: 781-449-8988
website: www.catholic-legacytours.com
A division of the Interface Group

Type of Business:

"Our Precious Legacy Tours — Catholic Legacy Tours is committed to providing a special opportunity for all Catholics to share the beauty and legacy of the land of Israel. It is our goal and dream to allow each individual and family to experience the uniqueness of Israel's heritage in an atmosphere of sharing. As a company we stand behind the belief in the ability of a trip to Israel to foster the common bond that unites us all."

We specialize in providing the only deluxe, all-inclusive and personally guided tours of the Catholic sites in Israel, for individuals and small groups, with guaranteed weekly departures, available in the USA.

For Parish leaders we will create an educational, spiritual and fiscally rewarding pilgrimage to Israel, and other Catholic destinations upon request.

Catholic Travel Centre
Worldwide Tours and Pilgrimages

CATHOLIC TRAVEL CENTRE
7100 Hayvenhurst Ave., Ste. 107
Van Nuys, CA 91406
Tel.: 818-909-9910; FAX: 818-909-0486

Personnel:

J. Scott Scherer . . . . President
Inga Duranovic . . . . Director of Operations
Yvonne Hanratty . . . . Operations Assistant
Henry Nassim . . . . Business Manager

Type of Business:

Catholic Travel Centre's strong reputation derives from operating high quality, customized group tours and pilgrimages. Our President, Mr. J. Scott Scherer, has 13 years experience in leading and organizing religious group tours, part of that time in a development capacity for a Catholic diocese.

An intimate knowledge of Catholic sites permits us to design a one-of-a-kind itinerary that suits your group's unique interests. Our long list of repeat clientele includes parishes, religious orders, colleges, alumni associations, and schools of theology nationwide.

COLLETTE TOURS
Experience It!

COLLETTE TOURS
162 Middle St.
Pawtucket, RI 02860
Tel.: 800-972-7373; FAX: 401-727-1000

Type of Business:

First Class escorted travel around the world at reasonable prices. We provide safe quality vacations using unique itineraries that capture the flavor of the destination. Collette tours include first class centrally located accommodations, most meals, multiple night stays creating a leisurely pace, exciting entertainment, included features that are optional with most competitors, and knowledgeable friendly tour escorts. Tours available to the Oberammergau Passion Play, Italy, France, Portugal, Quebec and many other destinations. 1-800-972-7373.

DEPARTURE POINT
927 S. Walter Reed Dr., Suite 28
Arlington, VA 22204-2311
Tel.: (703) 271-6378 / (800) 764-6836; FAX: (703) 271-6379
website: meetpt@erols.com

Personnel:
Harry S. Benjamin . . . . M.A., S.T.L., S.S.L., President
Patrick B. Dunnigan. . . . . Vice President

Type of Business:
DEPARTURE POINT custom creates and operates worldwide international pilgrimages and programs of professional continuing education in the Roman Catholic tradition for dioceses, religious communities, parishes, and Catholic educational and health institutions. Each program is created to the client/leader's specific requests. Particular attention is given to liturgical aspects of DEPARTURE POINT pilgrimages, thus assuring the appropriate spiritual character of the journey.
DEPARTURE POINT is a division of The Shirben Group, Inc.

DURGAN TRAVEL SERVICE
125 Main St.
Stoneham, MA 02180
Tel.: 800-234-9959-Toll Free; 781-438-2224; FAX: 781-438-6772

Personnel:
Richard Durgan . . . . President
Matthew Lordan . . . . Group Sales
Cathy Briggs . . . . Retail Sales Manager

Type of Business:
Full service travel agency planning custom group travel (jet, cruise & domestic & international motorcoach trips). Many group priced trips are available for the individual traveler. We specialize in Italy, Greece/Turkey, The Holy Land, Medjugorje, and the British Isles. Please call for a competitive bid on your next tour.

EDUCATIONAL OPPORTUNITIES
PO Box 6067
Lakeland, FL 33807
Tel.: 941-644-8485; FAX: 941-647-5789
e-mail: eo@travelwithus.com
web site: www.eo.travelwithus.com

Personnel:
Dr. James Ridgway . . . . President

Type of Business:
EO is a not-for-profit Christian travel Organization established in 1974 and has grown into North America's **largest organizer of Christian groups to the Holy Land.** Our size gives you the best travel value at the lowest cost, the best guides and motor coaches, the best hotels. Despite our size, EO remains a traveler-friendly company. **Clergy and religious orders are eligible for a scholarship** on their first EO journey to the Holy Land. Group leaders can earn their trip. Contact us today for details.

FELLOWSHIP TRAVEL INTERNATIONAL, INC.
P.O. Box 15360
Richmond, VA 23227
Tel.: 800-2-FLY-FTI; FAX: 800-FAX-4-FTI
e-mail: mail@fellowship.com

Personnel:
Mr. Mike Bowles . . . . Individual Reservations Mgr.
Mr. Jeff Compton . . . . Group Reservations Mgr.
Ms. Teresa Faber. . . . . Operations Mgr.
Mr. G. Wayne Lawhorn . . . . President

Type of Business:
"Your Mission is Our Mission"
Fellowship Travel is the USA affiliate for the World InService Card Travel Savings Program. This provides both individuals and groups International Airfare discounts up to 75% on over 50 world carriers. We are your "low cost source for any type of international air or ground travel.
"Quality Tours & Pilgrimages Worldwide"
Our "total tour management" makes it easy for you to host a tour and pilgrimage. Our "volume buying power" gives you quality tours and pilgrimages at bargain prices.

(See full-page display ad on next page)

Donna Franca Tours

DONNA FRANCA TOURS
470 Commonwealth Ave.
Boston, MA 02215-2795
Tel.: (617) 375-9400 / (800) 225-6290; FAX: (617) 266-1062

Personnel:
Franca Franzaroli . . . . President
Leo Locke . . . . Vice President
Phil Fakir . . . . Operations Escorted/Independent Tours
Francesco Testa . . . . Group Operations Manager

Type of Business:
Leading tour specialist for Italy, Sicily, Malta, French Riviera. Escorted, independent and customized itineraries. Pilgrimages, Retreats, Fundraisers to suit all tastes and budgets.

GEORGE'S
INTERNATIONAL
TOURS & TRAVEL, Inc.

GEORGE'S INTERNATIONAL TOURS & TRAVEL, INC.
9265 Dowdy Dr., Ste. 232
San Diego, CA 92126
Tel.: 800-566-7499 / 619-566-9911; FAX: 619-271-6692

Personnel:
Garo Garabedian . . . . President
Steve Gureghian . . . . Director of Sales & Marketing
Ron Harris . . . . Operations Manager

Type of Business:
George's International Tours & Travel is a family owned and operated tour co.. For more than 65 years, we have been providing arrangements for Holy Land Pilgramages. Recently George's International has begun providing quality programs to other religious sites around the world, including the Marian Shrines of Europe, Betania, Medjugorje and more. Our reputation speaks for itself, references are available from the many thousands of Christian Pilgrims who have availed themselves of our service.

GOLDEN FRONTIER
4100 North Illinois St.
Swansea, IL 62226-1834
Tel.: 618-234-1445; FAX: 618-234-9861

Personnel:
Linda Davinroy. Domestic Reservations
Patti Grindstaff . . . . International Reservations
Reverend Robert Vonnahmen . . . . Director
Craig Simoneaux . . . . Assistant Director

Type of Business:
Golden Frontier has provided 19 years of spiritual renewal through travel to religious destinations throughout the world. A professional and knowledgeable staff are on hand here and at overseas destinations to assure your travel experience will be rewarding and uplifting. A priest chaplain accompanies each group to offer Holy Mass and spiritual guidance along the way. Customized group programs are available for parish groups and other religious organizations. See our accompanying ad.

Inspirational Tours, Inc.
Religious Group Tour Wholesaler Since 1972!

INSPIRATIONAL TOURS INC.
5433 Westheimer, Ste. 600
Houston, TX 77056
Tel.: 1-800-231-6287; FAX: 713-961-7496

Type of Business:
Specializes in Pilgrimage Tours to the Holy Land, Shrines of Italy, Shrines of France and Shrines of Europe, Fatima. For any special request and customized itinerary, please contact Mr. Moses Khano, President at 1-800-231-6287.

ISRAEL
NO ONE BELONGS HERE MORE THAN YOU

ISRAEL TOURISM INFORMATION CENTER, N.A.
800 2nd Ave.
New York, NY 10017
Tel.: 888-77-ISRAEL; FAX: 212-499-5665

Type of Business:

Only Israel can offer you the chance to actually experience the wonders of The Bible. From walking the Vin Dolorosa to enjoying a sunset on the Mount of the Beatitudes, Israel has it all. Come visit the land that feels your body and soul. Israel. No one belong here more than you. For more information on travel to Israel call toll-free 888-77-ISRAEL or visit us at www.goisrael.com.

Journeys Unlimited

JOURNEYS UNLIMITED
500 Eighth Ave.
New York, NY 10018
Tel.: 800-486-8359; 212-736-2028; FAX: 212-736-8959
e-mail: holytours@worldnet.att.net

Personnel:

Nicholas Mancino .... President
Raymond Masillo.................... Vice President
Lucille Sciabarassi .... Travel Consultant
Everett Mansfield .... Group Sales
Total Staff 16

Type of Business:

Journeys Unlimited was founded by Raymond Masillo & Nicholas Mancino in 1990 in cooperation with four other travel professionals. The Management has been arranging Pilgrimages since 1969 and has over 100 years of professional experience. The company's philosophy is that each Pilgrimage be escorted by a spiritual leader in order to transform our tours into Pilgrimages. Our Pilgrimages have been designed to give each participant comfort for recreation and spiritual guidance for RENEWAL. Our staff is dedicated to personal, efficient and economical group travel. We also offer tours to Italy, Greece, Turkey, Egypt, Syria, Fatima, Lourdes, Oberammer Gau, and other Marian Shrines.

nawas
INTERNATIONAL

NAWAS INTERNATIONAL TRAVEL
777 Post Rd., Third Floor
Darien, CT 06820-4721
Tel.: 800-221-4984; FAX: 203-655-1577

On the West Coast:
1100 Alma St., Ste. 100
Menlo Park, CA 94025-3344
Tel.: 800-288-2688; FAX: 650-322-6485

Personnel:

Soli Nawas.................... President
George Khoury........ Executive Vice President (Darien, CT)
Sami Nawas.................... Vice President
Neil Dellis .... Vice President

Type of Business:

Nawas International has designed and operated pilgrimages to the Holy Land, Italy, Fatima, Lourdes, Shrines of Europe and more since 1949. For the *Jubilee Year 2000*, Nawas has developed special pilgrimages to **Rome** and the **Passion Play of Oberammergau**. With our dedication to delivering **high quality** programs at **very competitive** prices and on-site quality control via our local, Nawas-owned offices, we provide the finest pilgrimages available. We also offer **excellent tour host benefits** — you can travel **FREE** with **as few as five** paying passengers! Thousands of church leaders have organized their travel plans through Nawas. Call us toll-free and we'll show you how to do it, too!

PILGRIMAGE
TOURS & TRAVEL

PILGRIMAGE INTERNATIONAL —
Catholic Pilgrimage Tours™
35 South 13th Street, Allentown, PA 18102
Tel.: (800) 455-5514; FAX: (610) 435-3874
website: www.CatholicPilgrimageTour.com

Personnel:
David Roth . . . . STD, President
Pilgrimage Planners and Associates through the USA

Type of Business:
PILGRIMAGE INTERNATIONAL is the new home of Catholic Pilgrimage Tours and the only tour company to offer bona fide Catholic Pilgrimage Tours™. These include the Cornerstones of Faith Pilgrimage™ to the Hole Land, Rome and Assisi, and the Ultimate European Pilgrimage™ to Fatima, Lourdes, Avila, Santo Domingo de Silos, Rome, Assisi and more.
We're the leader in no-nonsense pricing, and in all-inclusive, parish and Catholic group travel. Ask about our Pastors Go Free ... Guaranteed™ pilgrimages, as well as our generous tour host programs.
Settle for nothing less than a bona fide Catholic Pilgrimage Tour™.

SELECT International

SELECT INTERNATIONAL TOURS & CRUISES
116 US Highway 22 E.
North Plainfield, NJ 07060
Tel.: 800-571-0884; 908-412-0044; FAX: 908-412-0099

Personnel:
Edita Krunic. . . . . President
Maryanna Kosorich . . . . Manager

Type of Business:
For the past 10 years, our company has created programs for Catholic churches, choirs, schools and organizations to Europe, Holy Land, and Latin America. In addition to the 40 page catalogue featuring over 45 different itineraries we also offer cruises for groups and custom designed itineraries, based on the group's interests and preferences.
Pilgrimages to special events such as the World Youth Day, Eucharistic Congress, Exposition of the Holy Shroud in Turin in 1998, Oberammergau Passion Play and the Great Jubilee, Celebration 2000 in Rome and Holy Land, are also planned. With affiliate offices throughout Europe, Holy Land and Latin America and with a staff that has visited each destination we feature, you will benefit by receiving assistance for your groups from an experienced and friendly staff, staying at excellent hotels, traveling with knowledgeable guides and all at a superior value.

TWA
Getaway Vacations

TWA GETAWAY VACATIONS
10 East Stow Rd.
Marlton, NJ 08053
Tel.: 1-800-GETAWAY; FAX: 609-984-4105

Personnel:
Peggie Montemurro . . . . Mgr. Int'l. Mktg.

Type of Business:
With TWA Getaway you can take advantage of great commissions up to 20%! For reservations and brochures call 1-800-GETAWAY.
Getaway Group Packages offer your clients:
- Design your own vacation
- Customize our brochure departures
- Exclusive occupancy on escorted tours of 36 passengers.
- Book by 8-31-98; get 1 free air for every 15 passengers and 1 free land package for every 20 passengers
- 5000 frequent flyer miles in addition to actual miles flown on TWA
- special group # 1-800-228-7600

ESTABLISHED 1957
UNITOURS, inc.

UNITOURS, INC.
411 W. Putnam Ave.
Greenwich, CT 06830
Tel.: 800-777-7432; FAX: 203-629-1905
website: www.unitours.com; e-mail: unitoursus@aol.com

Personnel:
Larry Oliveri . . . . Sales Manager

Type of Business:
Unitours, Inc., a leader in Roman Catholic group travel since 1957, specializes in Israel travel and is a pioneer in Holy Land Pilgrimages. Unitours' experienced professionals lead travelers over the same paths and rocks that Jesus walked on, stirring feelings and inspiring memories that stay with you forever. Each touir is custom designed to satisfy your group's specific interests and priced to suit your budget. Holy Land, Rome, Fatima, Lourdes, Ireland, anywhere ... personal service, professionalism and quality give you the best value and the memorable experience of a lifetime. *SPECIAL HOLY YEAR 2000 TOURS AVAILABLE TO JERUSALEM, ITALY AND THE PASSION PLAY IN OBERAMMERGAU, GERMANY.* **Clergy that travel with their groups earn free travel and extra cash as well.**
NEW: ***Scripture cruises to Caribbean, Mediterranean and Alaska. Call for details.***

SHRINES

206 Tours

206 TOURS
325 Middle Country Rd.
Smithtown, NY 11787
Tel.: 800-206-TOURS; FAX: 516-361-3682

Personnel:
Milanka Pauciullo . . . . CTC President, 206 Tours
Maria Ufret. . . . . Manager
Elena Gorham-Rossi. . . . . Sales
Jennifer Hangley . . . . Sales

Type of Business:
206 Tours have serviced hundreds of thousands of Catholic pilgrims to Medjugorje, Lourdes, the Holy Land, Italy and Fatima since 1985. We are dedicated to the needs of the Catholic pilgrim and are unparalleled in our service to these individuals who participate in these journeys of faith. Please feel free to call us for upcoming special Pilgrimages for 1998 through to the year 2000.

ALTURA TOURS®
THE TOUR GENERATORS™

ALTURA TOURS
7270 NW 12th St., Ste. 545
Miami, FL 33126
Tel.: 800-242-4122; FAX: 305-470-9772
e-mail: altura@alturatours.com; www.alturatours.com

Personnel:
Diego Linares. . . . . President
Ivonne Gero. V.P. of Operations-Groups
Angie Novillo . . . . FIT Department

Type of Business:
Altura Tours is a full-service tour operator with over 45 years experience in international travel and tour operations. Our religious department's team of travel professionals has special ways to help you plan your next Christian pilgrimage to The Holyland and other Mediterranean and European destinations. Assistance in planning, personalized attention, competitive pricing, rapid quotations and the best "Free Trip Incentive Program" guarantees that every group member enjoys a spiritually enriching travel experience. Call today for free brochures!

Blue Army Shrine

THE BLUE ARMY OF OUR LADY OF FATIMA, U.S.A.
Shrine of the Immaculate Heart of Mary
P.O. Box 976 - Mountainview Rd.
Washington, N.J. 07882 (Warren County)
Tel.: 908-689-1700; FAX: 908-689-6279
Internet: Website: http://www.bluearmy.com
e-mail: bluearmy@ix.netcom.com

Personnel:
Most Rev. James S. Sullivan . . . . Blue Army President

Type of Business:
The Blue Army is a Church-approved non-profit Catholic organization with divisions in 70 United States dioceses. Our famous shrine honors Our Lady of Fatima. Perched upon a majestic country hillside, our shrine offers 72 acres of well-maintained countryside where you, or your group, can walk and pray. Mass is offered daily in our charming chapel. A unique Rosary garden allows an environment for outdoor prayer. Frequent exposition of the Blessed Sacrament. (Gift Shop.)

ISRAEL
NO ONE BELONGS HERE MORE THAN YOU.

ISRAEL TOURISM INFORMATION CENTER, N.A.
800 2nd Ave.
New York, NY 10017
Tel.: 888-77-ISRAEL; FAX: 212-499-5665

Type of Business:
Only Israel can offer you the chance to actually experience the wonders of The Bible. From walking the Vin Dolorosa to enjoying a sunset on the Mount of the Beatitudes, Israel has it all. Come visit the land that feels your body and soul. Israel. No one belong here more than you. For more information on travel to Israel call toll-free 888-77-ISRAEL or visit us at www.goisrael.com.

RAMBUSCH

RAMBUSCH
40 West 13th St.
New York, NY 10011
Tel.: 212-675-0400; FAX: 212-620-4687

PersonneL:
Viggo Bech Rambusch . . . . Senior Project Director
Martin V. Rambusch . . . . Stained Glass Director

Type of Business:
Since 1898, creating church interiors, liturgical furnishings, and art work. Fine restoration of church interiors. In-house studios and shops for designing and executing stained glass, church lighting systems, art metal work, and decorative painting.

TOURS

206 Tours

206 TOURS
325 Middle Country Rd.
Smithtown, NY 11787
Tel.: 800-206-TOURS; FAX: 516-361-3682

Personnel:
Milanka Pauciullo . . . . CTC President, 206 Tours
Maria Ufret. . . . . Manager
Elena Gorham-Rossi. . . . . Sales
Jennifer Hangley . . . . Sales

Type of Business:
206 Tours have serviced hundreds of thousands of Catholic pilgrims to Medjugorje, Lourdes, the Holy Land, Italy and Fatima since 1985. We are dedicated to the needs of the Catholic pilgrim and are unparalleled in our service to these individuals who participate in these journeys of faith. Please feel free to call us for upcoming special Pilgrimages for 1998 through to the year 2000.

INDEX OF DISPLAY ADVERTISERS

For Pages 1f to 46f see *front* advertising section.
For Pages 1r to 105r see *rear* advertising section.

Products & Services Section with company listings arranged by category begins on Page 1r.

NOTES

CONTENTS

SECTION 9 Problems of Ingestion, Digestion, Absorption, and Elimination

SECTION 10 Problems of Urinary Function

SECTION 11 Problems Related to Regulatory and Reproductive Mechanisms

SECTION 12 Problems Related to Movement and Coordination

APPENDIXES

Lewis'edical-Surgical Nursing

ASSESSMENMANAGEMENT OF CLINICAL PROBLEMS

A tailored education experience — *Sherpath book-organized collections*

Sherpath is the digital teaching and learning technology designed specifically for healthcare education.

ELSEVIER

Sherpath-organized collection:r:

Objective-based, di ons, mapped chapter-by-chapter t book, that make it easy to find applicabl assignment content.

Adaptive quizzing with alized questions that correlate directly to text ntent.

Teaching materials that a the text and are organized by chapter for c nd easy access to invaluable class activities a ources.

Elsevier ebooks that provide enient access to textbook content, even offlin

VISIT
myevolve.us/sherpath
today to learn more!

21-CS-0280 TM/AF 6/21

12TH EDITION

Lewis's Medical-Surgical Nursing

ASSESSMENT AND MANAGEMENT OF CLINICAL PROBLEMS

Mariann M. Harding, PhD, RN, CNE, FAADN
Professor of Nursing, Kent State University Tuscarawas, New Philadelphia, Ohio

SECTION EDITORS

Jeffrey Kwong, RN, DNP, MPH, ANP-BC, FAANP, FAAN
Professor, Division of Advanced Nursing Practice, School of Nursing, Rutgers University, Newark, New Jersey

Debra Hagler, PhD, RN, ACNS-BC, CNE, CHSE, ANEF, FAAN
Clinical Professor, Edson College of Nursing and Health Innovation, Arizona State University, Phoenix, Arizona

Courtney Reinisch, RN, DNP, FNP-BC
Associate Professor, School of Nursing, Montclair State University, Montclair, New Jersey

ELSEVIER

3251 Riverport Lane
St. Louis, Missouri 63043

LEWIS'S MEDICAL-SURGICAL NURSING,
TWELFTH EDITION

Single-volume ISBN: 978-0-323-78961-5
Two-volume ISBNs: 978-0-323-79236-3 (volume 1)
978-0-323-79237-0 (volume 2)

Notice

Practitioners and researchers must always rely on their own experience and knowledge in evaluating and using any information, methods, compounds or experiments described herein. Because of rapid advances in the medical sciences, in particular, independent verification of diagnoses and drug dosages should be made. To the fullest extent of the law, no responsibility is assumed by Elsevier, authors, editors or contributors for any injury and/or damage to persons or property as a matter of products liability, negligence or otherwise, or from any use or operation of any methods, products, instructions, or ideas contained in the material herein.

Previous editions copyrighted 2020, 2017, 2014, 2011, 2007, 2004, 2000, 1996, 1992, 1987, and 1983.

Executive Content Strategist: Lee Henderson
Senior Content Development Specialist: Rebecca Leenhouts
Publishing Services Manager: Julie Eddy
Book Production Specialist: Clay S. Broeker
Design Direction: Brian Salisbury

Printed in Canada

Last digit is the print number: 9 8 7 6 5 4 3 2

MARIANN M. HARDING, PhD, RN, CNE, FAADN

Mariann Harding is a Professor of Nursing and Nursing Program Director at Kent State University Tuscarawas, New Philadelphia, Ohio, where she has been faculty since 2005. She received her diploma in nursing from Mt. Carmel School of Nursing, her Bachelor of Science in nursing from Ohio University, her Master of Science in Nursing as an adult nurse practitioner from the Catholic University of America, and her doctorate in nursing from West Virginia University. Her nursing experience has primarily been in critical care nursing and teaching in licensed practical, associate, and baccalaureate nursing programs. Her research has focused on promoting student success and health promotion among persons with gout and facing cancer. Dr. Harding is co-author of *Clinical Reasoning Cases in Nursing and Conceptual Nursing Care Planning.* She is a Fellow in the Academy of Associate Degree Nursing.

JEFFREY KWONG, RN, DNP, MPH, ANP-BC, FAAN, FAANP

Jeffrey Kwong is a Professor in the Division of Advanced Nursing Practice in the School of Nursing at Rutgers, the State University of New Jersey. He has worked in adult primary care with a special focus on HIV for over 25 years. He received his undergraduate degree from the University of California–Berkeley, received his nurse practitioner degree from the University of California–San Francisco, and completed his doctoral training at the University of Colorado–Denver. He also has a Master of Public Health Degree from the University of California–Los Angeles. In addition to teaching, Dr. Kwong maintains a clinical practice in New York City where he provides care for the LGBTQ+ community. He is a Fellow in the American Association of Nurse Practitioners and the American Academy of Nursing.

DEBRA HAGLER, PhD, RN, ACNS-BC, CNE, CHSE, ANEF, FAAN

Debbie Hagler is a Clinical Professor in the Edson College of Nursing and Health Innovation at Arizona State University in Phoenix. Dr. Hagler earned a Practical Certificate in Nursing, Associate Degree in Nursing and Bachelor of Science in Nursing from New Mexico State University. She earned the Master of Science with concentrations in Adult Health and Nursing Education from the University of Arizona and a doctorate in Learning and Instructional Technology from Arizona State University. Dr. Hagler is a Clinical Nurse Specialist with experience in adult health and critical care nursing. Currently, she serves as Lead Faculty Honors Advisor for Edson College and teaches students in the undergraduate, master's, and doctoral programs. For many years, she has led writing groups to support nursing and health professions faculty members in becoming published authors. Dr. Hagler is the Associate Editor for Credentialing at *The Journal of Continuing Education in Nursing* and co-author of *Conceptual Nursing Care Planning.* Her research focuses on clinical decision making and supporting professional competency in nursing. She is a Fellow in the American Academy of Nursing.

COURTNEY REINISCH, RN, DNP, FNP-BC

Courtney Reinisch is an Associate Professor for the School of Nursing at Montclair State University. She earned her Bachelor of Arts in biology and psychology from Immaculata University. She received her Bachelor of Science in nursing and Master of Science in family practice nurse practitioner degree from the University of Delaware. She completed her Doctor of Nursing Practice degree at Columbia University School of Nursing. Dr. Reinisch's nursing career has focused on providing care for underserved populations in primary care and emergency settings. She has taught in undergraduate and graduate nursing programs in New York and New Jersey. She is an active advocate for the needs of students with learning differences and the LGBTQ+ community.

CONTRIBUTORS

Cynthia Amerson, MS, MSN, RN, CNE
Professor
Division of Nursing
Collin College
McKinney, Texas

Vera Barton-Maxwell, PhD, APRN, FNP-BC
Assistant Professor
Advanced Nursing Practice
Family Nurse Practitioner Program
Georgetown University
Washington, DC;
Nurse Practitioner
Wheeling Health Right
Wheeling, West Virginia

Cecilia Bidigare, DNP
Professor
Nursing
Sinclair Community College
Dayton, Ohio

Samantha J. Bonaduce, DNP
Associate Lecturer
Nursing Technology
Kent State University Tuscarawas
New Philadelphia, Ohio

Diana Taibi Buchanan, PhD, RN
Associate Professor and Mary S. Tschudin Endowed Professor of Nursing Education
Biobehavioral Nursing and Health Informatics
University of Washington
Seattle, Washington

Michelle Bussard, PhD, MSN, ACNS-BC, CNE
Director
School of Nursing
Associate Professor
College of Health and Human Services
Bowling Green State University
Bowling Green, Ohio

Mary M. Cameron, MSN, RN
Lecturer
Nursing Technology
Kent State University Tuscarawas
New Philadelphia, Ohio

Christine M. Cervini, DNP, APRN, ANP-BC
Associate Professor
Barbara H. Hagan School of Nursing and Health Sciences
Molloy University
Rockville Centre, New York;
Nurse Practitioner
Gastroenterology
Mount Sinai Beth Israel
New York, New York

Kristen J. Costello, DNP, ACNP-BC, PMHNP-BC, RNFA
Nurse Practitioner
Trauma and Acute Care Surgery
Banner Thunderbird Medical Center
Glendale, Arizona

Ann H. Crawford, PhD, RN, CNS, CEN, CPEN
Professor
Scott & White School of Nursing
University of Mary Hardin-Baylor
Belton, Texas;
Relief Charge/Staff Nurse
Emergency Department
Baylor Scott & White McLane Children's Medical Center
Temple, Texas

Kimberly Day, DNP, CHSE
Clinical Associate Professor
Edson College of Nursing and Health Innovation
Arizona State University
Phoenix, Arizona

Deena D. Dell, MSN, APRN, AOCN, LNC
Nurse in Professional Development Specialist
Oncology
Sarasota Memorial Hospital Brian D. Jellison Cancer Institute
Sarasota, Florida

Hazel A. Dennison, DNP, APNc, CHCP, CPHQ, CNE
Senior Manager
Accreditation
HealthStream
Nashville, Tennessee;
Faculty
College of Nursing
Walden University
Minneapolis, Minnesota

Jane K. Dickinson, PhD, RN, CDCES
Program Director and Senior Lecturer
Health and Behavior Studies
Teachers College
Columbia University
New York, New York

Susan Doyle-Lindrud, DNP, ANP
Assistant Dean of Academic Affairs
School of Nursing
Columbia University
New York, New York

Nathan J. Dreesmann, PhD, RN
Clinical Operations Specialist
Operations
Virtual Therapeutics
Kirkland, Washington

Marybeth Duffy, DNP, FNP, ACNP, ANCC
Associate Professor
School of Nursing
Montclair State University
Montclair, New Jersey

Rebekah Filson, DNP, ACNS-BC, ANP-BC
Clinical Outcomes Manager
Orthopedics and Neurosciences
Northside Hospital
Cumming, Georgia

Jessica I. Goldberg, PhD, NP, ACHPN
Nurse Practitioner
Supportive Care Service
Memorial Sloan Kettering Cancer Center
New York, New York

Sherry A. Greenberg, PhD, GNP-BC, FGSA, FNAP, FAANP, FAAN
Associate Professor
College of Nursing
Seton Hall University
South Orange, New Jersey

Diana Rabbani Hagler, MSN-Ed, RN, CCRN
Staff RN
Intensive Care Unit
Banner Health
Gilbert, Arizona;
Adjunct Faculty
Nursing
Grand Canyon University
Phoenix, Arizona;
Adjunct Faculty
Nursing
Gateway Community College and Maricopa Community College
Phoenix, Arizona

Julia A. Hitch, MS, FNP, CDCES
Nurse Practitioner
Diabetes
Level2
Minnetonka, Minnesota

Haley Hoy, PhD, NP
Associate Professor
Nursing
University of Alabama in Huntsville
Huntsville, Alabama;
Nurse Practitioner
Vanderbilt Lung Transplantation
Vanderbilt Medical Center
Nashville, Tennessee

Patricia Keegan, DNP, NP-C, FACC
Director of Strategic and Programmatic Initiatives
Heart and Vascular Center
Emory University
Atlanta, Georgia;
Operations and Clinical Lead
Emory Structural Heart and Valve Center
Emory Healthcare
Atlanta, Georgia

Anthony Lutz, MSN, NP-C, CUNP
Nurse Practitioner and Clinical Director of Outpatient Urology
Department of Urology
Columbia University Irving Medical Center
New York, New York

Thuy Lynch, PhD, RN
Assistant Professor
College of Nursing
University of Alabama in Huntsville
Huntsville, Alabama

Helen Miley, PhD, AG-ACNP
Critical Care
Robert Wood Johnson University Hospital
New Brunswick, New Jersey;
Adjunct Faculty
School of Nursing
Montclair State University
Montclair, New Jersey

Eugene Mondor, RN, MN, BScN, CNS, CNCC(C)
Clinical Nurse Specialist
Adult Critical Care
Royal Alexandra Hospital
Edmonton, Alberta, Canada

Brenda C. Morris, EdD, RN, CNE
Clinical Professor
Edson College of Nursing and Health Innovation
Arizona State University
Phoenix, Arizona

Janice A. Neil, PhD, RN, CNE
Associate Professor Emeritus
College of Nursing
East Carolina University
Greenville, North Carolina

Yeow Chye Ng, PhD, CRNP, CPC, AAHIVE, FAANP
Associate Professor
College of Nursing
University of Alabama in Huntsville
Huntsville, Alabama

Mary Olson, DNP, APRN, ANP-BC
Nurse Practitioner
Gastroenterology
School of Medicine
New York University
New York, New York

Shila Pandey, DNP, AGPCNP-BC, ACHPN
Nurse Practitioner
Supportive Care Service
Memorial Sloan Kettering Cancer Center
New York, New York

Amisha Parekh de Campos, PhD, MPH, RN, CHPN
Quality and Education Coordinator
Hospice Care at Home
Middlesex Health
Middletown, Connecticut;
Assistant Clinical Professor
School of Nursing
University of Connecticut
Storrs, Connecticut

Margaret R. Rateau, PhD, RN, CNE
Associate Professor
Nursing
Robert Morris University
Moon Township, Pennsylvania

Catherine R. Ratliff, PhD, GNP-BC, CWOCN, CFCN, FAAN
Clinical Associate Professor and Nurse Practitioner
Department of Surgery/Vascular Surgery
School of Nursing
University of Virginia Health
Charlottesville, Virginia

Dottie Roberts, EdD, MSN, MACI, RN, CMSRN, OCNS-C, CNE
Contributing Faculty
College of Nursing
Walden University
Minneapolis, Minnesota;
Editor
MEDSURG Nursing
Jannetti Publications, Inc.
Pitman, New Jersey;
Nursing Online Faculty
College of Online and Continuing Education
Southern New Hampshire University
Manchester, New Hampshire

Sandra Irene Rome, MN, AOCN
Clinical Nurse Specialist
Blood and Marrow Transplant Program
Cedars-Sinai Medical Center
Los Angeles, California;
Volunteer Assistant Clinical Professor
UCLA School of Nursing
Los Angeles, California

William E. Rosa, PhD, MBE, ACHPN, FAANP, FAAN
Chief Research Fellow
Department of Psychiatry & Behavioral Sciences
Memorial Sloan Kettering Cancer Center
New York, New York

Diane M. Rudolphi, MSN, RN
Senior Instructor
Nursing
University of Delaware
Newark, Delaware

Diane Ryzner, MSN, APRN, CNS-BC, OCNS-C
Clinical Practice Specialist
Professional Practice
Northwest Community Healthcare
Arlington Heights, Illinois

Janice A. Sarasnick, PhD, MSN, RN
Associate Professor
Nursing
Robert Morris University
Coraopolis, Pennsylvania

Andrew Scanlon, DNP, MNS, BN
Senior Lecturer
Nursing
University of Melbourne
Melbourne, Victoria, Australia;
Nurse Practitioner
Neurosurgery
Austin Health
Heidelberg, Victoria, Australia

Robyn Schafer, PhD, CNM, FACNM
RBHS Lecturer
Division of Advanced Nursing Practice
Rutgers School of Nursing
Newark, New Jersey;
Certified Nurse Midwife
Department of Obstetrics, Gynecology and Reproductive Sciences
Robert Wood Johnson Medical School
New Brunswick, New Jersey

Rose B. Shaffer, MSN, ACNP-BC, CCRN, FAHA
Nurse Practitioner
Cardiology
Thomas Jefferson University Hospital
Philadelphia, Pennsylvania

Cynthia Ann Smith, DNP, APRN, FNP-BC, CNN-NP, FNKF
Clinical Coordinator
Ambulatory Care
Hershel "Woody" Williams VA Medical Center
Huntington, West Virginia

Janice Smolowitz, PhD, DNP, EdD
Dean and Professor
School of Nursing
Montclair State University
Montclair, New Jersey

Ashton T. Strachan, DNP, FNP-c, WHNP-BC
Nurse Practitioner
Women's Health
Georgia Institute of Technology
Atlanta, Georgia;
Adjunct Professor
School of Nursing
University of Alabama at Birmingham
Birmingham, Alabama

Teresa Turnbull, DNP, MN
Clinical Assistant Professor
School of Nursing
Oregon Health & Science University
Portland, Oregon

Kara Ann Ventura, DNP, PNP, FNP
Director
Liver Transplant Program
Yale New Haven Hospital
New Haven, Connecticut

Colleen Walsh, DNP, ONC, ONP-C, CNS, ACNP-BC
Contract Assistant Professor of Nursing Emeritus
Graduate Nursing
University of Southern Indiana
Evansville, Indiana

Rita Wermers, DNP, ANP-BC
Nurse Practitioner and Clinic Manager
Health Services
Arizona State University
Phoenix, Arizona

Daniel P. Worrall, MSN, ANP-BC
Nurse Practitioner
Sexual Health Clinic
Massachusetts General Hospital
Boston, Massachusetts;
Nurse Practitioner
General and Gastrointestinal Surgery
Massachusetts General Hospital
Boston, Massachusetts;
Clinical Operations Manager
Ragon Institute of MGH, MIT and Harvard
Cambridge, Massachusetts

Janice A. Sarasnick, PhD, MSN, RN
Associate Professor
Nursing
Robert Morris University
Coraopolis, Pennsylvania

Andrew Scanlon, DNP, MNS, RN
Senior Lecturer
Nursing
University of Melbourne
Melbourne, Victoria, Australia
Nurse Practitioner
Neurosurgery
Austin Health
Heidelberg, Victoria, Australia

Robyn Schaiser, PhD, CNM, FACNM
RBHS Lecturer
Division of Advanced Nursing Practice
Rutgers School of Nursing
Newark, New Jersey
Certified Nurse-Midwife
Department of Obstetrics, Gynecology and Reproductive Sciences
Robert Wood Johnson Medical School
New Brunswick, New Jersey

Rose B. Shaffer, MSN, ACNP-BC, CCRN, FAHA
Nurse Practitioner
Cardiology
Thomas Jefferson University Hospital
Philadelphia, Pennsylvania

Cynthia Ann Smith, DNP, APRN, FNP-BC, CNN-NP, FNKF
Clinical Coordinator
Ambulatory Care
Hershel "Woody" Williams VA Medical Center
Huntington, West Virginia

Janice Smolowitz, PhD, DNP, EdD
Dean and Professor
School of Nursing
Montclair State University
Montclair, New Jersey

Ashton T. Strachan, DNP, FNP-C, WHNP-BC
Nurse Practitioner
Womens Health
Georgia Institute of Technology
Atlanta, Georgia
Adjunct Professor
School of Nursing
University of Alabama at Birmingham
Birmingham, Alabama

Teresa Turnbull, DNP, MN
Clinical Assistant Professor
School of Nursing
Oregon Health & Science University
Portland, Oregon

Kara Ann Ventura, DNP, PNP, FNP
Director
Liver Transplant Program
Yale New Haven Hospital
New Haven, Connecticut

Colleen Walsh, DNP, ONC, ONP-C, CNS, ACNP-BC
Contract Assistant Professor of Nursing
Emeritus
Graduate Nursing
University of Southern Indiana
Evansville, Indiana

Rita Wermers, DNP, ANP-BC
Nurse Practitioner and Clinic Manager
Health Services
Arizona State University
Phoenix, Arizona

Daniel P. Worrall, MSN, ANP-BC
Nurse Practitioner
Sexual Health Clinic
Massachusetts General Hospital
Boston, Massachusetts
Nurse Practitioner
General and Gastrointestinal Surgery
Massachusetts General Hospital
Boston, Massachusetts
Clinical Operations Manager
Ragon Institute of MGH, MIT and Harvard
Cambridge, Massachusetts

AUTHORS OF TEACHING AND LEARNING RESOURCES

Test Bank

Debra Hagler, PhD, RN, ACNS-BC, CNE, CHSE, ANEF, FAAN
Clinical Professor
Edson College of Nursing and Health Innovation
Arizona State University
Phoenix, Arizona

Case Studies (Interactive and Applying Clinical Judgment With Multiple Patients)

Mariann M. Harding, PhD, RN, CNE, FAADN
Professor of Nursing
Kent State University Tuscarawas
New Philadelphia, Ohio

Brenda C. Morris, EdD, RN, CNE
Clinical Professor
Edson College of Nursing and Health Innovation
Arizona State University
Phoenix, Arizona

PowerPoint Presentations

Jane Grages, MS, RN
Associate Professor of Nursing
Pennsylvania College of Technology
Williamsport, Pennsylvania

Michelle A. Walczak, MSN, RN
Associate Professor of Nursing
Pennsylvania College of Technology
Williamsport, Pennsylvania

TEACH for Nurses

Katrina Pyo, PhD, RN, CCRN
Associate Professor
School of Nursing, Education, and Human Studies
Robert Morris University
Moon Township, Pennsylvania

Margaret R. Rateau, PhD, RN, CNE
Associate Professor
Nursing
Robert Morris University
Moon Township, Pennsylvania

Janice A. Sarasnick, PhD, RN, CHSE
Associate Professor
Nursing
Robert Morris University
Moon Township, Pennsylvania

NCLEX® Examination Review Questions

Shelly Stefka, MSN, RN
Senior Lecturer
Nursing
Kent State University Tuscarawas
New Philadelphia, Ohio

Study Guide

Collin Bowman-Woodall, MS, RN
Assistant Professor
San Francisco Peninsula Campus
Samuel Merritt University
San Mateo, California

Clinical Companion

Debra Hagler, PhD, RN, ACNS-BC, CNE, CHSE, ANEF, FAAN
Clinical Professor
Edson College of Nursing and Health Innovation
Arizona State University
Phoenix, Arizona

Evidence-Based Practice Boxes

Dottie Roberts, EdD, MSN, MACI, RN, CMSRN, OCNS-C, CNE
Contributing Faculty
College of Nursing
Walden University
Minneapolis, Minnesota;
Editor
MEDSURG Nursing
Jannetti Publications, Inc.
Pitman, New Jersey;
Nursing Online Faculty
College of Online and Continuing Education
Southern New Hampshire University
Manchester, New Hampshire

Nursing Care Plans

Collin Bowman-Woodall, MS, RN
Assistant Professor
San Francisco Peninsula Campus
Samuel Merritt University
San Mateo, California

REVIEWERS

Katherine H. Lawson, BSN, DNP
Associate Director and Clinical Coordinator
School of Nursing
Southside Regional Medical Center
Southside College of Health Sciences
Colonial Heights, Virginia

Michele Terney Miller, DNP
Associate Professor of Nursing
Muskingum University
New Concord, Ohio

Diana Moxness, MSN, RN, CNE
Associate Professor
School of Nursing
Midland University
Fremont, Nebraska

Susan Patton, PhD, MHSA, CNS-BC, CNE
Assistant Professor
Nursing
University of Arkansas
Fayetteville, Arkansas

Julie S. Snyder, MSN, RN-BC
Visiting Professor
College of Nursing
Chamberlain University
Downers Grove, Illinois

Rebecca S. Zukowski, PhD, RN
Director
ABSN Program
Misericordia University
Coraopolis, Pennsylvania

PREFACE

The twelfth edition of *Lewis's Medical-Surgical Nursing: Assessment and Management of Clinical Problems* incorporates the most current medical-surgical nursing information in an easy-to-use format. This textbook is a comprehensive resource describing standards of nursing clinical practice for providing safe and comprehensive patient care. The text and accompanying resources include many features to help students learn key medical-surgical nursing content, including patient and caregiver teaching, gerontology, interprofessional care, diversity, patient safety, nutrition and drug therapy, evidence-based practice, and much more.

This edition features several important changes. Chapter 2, Social Determinants of Health, focuses on nursing awareness of patient circumstances on health outcomes. The discussion includes health status differences among groups of people related to access to care, economic aspects of health care, gender and cultural issues, and the nurse's role in promoting health equity.

New to this edition, Chapter 6, Caring for Lesbian, Gay, Bisexual, Transgender, Queer or Questioning, and Gender Diverse Patients, addresses the unique health care needs of the LGBTQ+ population with the goal of promoting high-quality care.

Another new chapter to this edition is Chapter 28, Supporting Ventilation. Promoting a concept-based approach to optimizing ventilation, this chapter focuses on various strategies used use to promote optimal ventilation and oxygenation. Covered content includes O_2 therapy, chest tubes, respiratory therapy, chest surgeries, and mechanical ventilation. Textbook reorganization to support a concept-based approach includes adding Acute Respiratory Failure and ARDS to the Ventilation Section and Shock, Sepsis, and MODS to the Perfusion Section.

Chapter 12, Inflammation and Healing, and Chapter 15, Infection, have been revised to include more concept-based care for the patient with an infection or experiencing inflammation. New tables addressing the nursing management of the patient with a fever and infection and antibiotic, antiviral, and antifungal Drug Therapy tables enhance the content. Care of the patient with COVID-19 infection is included.

Critical care nursing is now addressed throughout the textbook, an approach that reflects the needs of patients in various care environments. Varying levels of hemodynamic monitoring now occur outside the critical care unit and are included in the enhanced Cardiovascular System Assessment chapter. Similarly, advanced techniques to assess oxygenation are included in the new Supporting Ventilation chapter. Care of the patient experiencing problems such as pain, difficulty sleeping, and delirium are addressed in the respective textbook chapters.

Special content has been added to assist with NCLEX® preparation and the development of clinical judgment based on NCSBN's Clinical Judgment Measurement Model (CJMM). At the end of each unit, the reader will find Applying Clinical Judgment With Multiple Patients, featuring traditional and Next-Generation NCLEX® (NGN)–style questions. Discussion questions in the management chapters' Case Studies focus on the 6 cognitive skills identified in the CJMM: Recognize Cues, Analyze Cues, Prioritize Hypotheses, Generate Solutions, Take Actions, and Evaluate Outcomes.

Great effort has been put into continuing to improve readability and lower the reading level. Readers will find clearer and easier-to-read language, with an engaging conversational style. The narrative addresses the reader, helping make the text more personal and an active learning tool.

ORGANIZATION

Content is organized into 2 major divisions. The first division, Sections 1 through 3 (Chapters 1 through 17), discusses general concepts related to the care of adult patients. The second division, Sections 4 through 13 (Chapters 18 through 68), presents nursing assessment and nursing management of medical-surgical problems. At the beginning of each chapter, the Conceptual Focus helps students focus on the key concepts and integrate concepts with exemplars affecting different body systems. Learning Outcomes and Key Terms assist students in identifying the key content for that chapter.

The various body systems are grouped to reflect their interrelated functions. Each section is organized around 2 central themes: assessment and management. Chapters dealing with assessment of a body system include a discussion of the following:

1. A brief review of anatomy and physiology, focusing on information that will promote understanding of nursing care
2. Health history and noninvasive physical assessment skills to expand the knowledge base on which treatment decisions are made
3. Common diagnostic studies, expected results, and related nursing responsibilities to provide easily accessible information

Management chapters focus on the pathophysiology, clinical manifestations, diagnostic studies, interprofessional care, and nursing management of various problems. The conceptual focus at the beginning of each chapter helps students focus on the key concepts and integrate concepts with exemplars affecting different body systems. The nursing management sections are organized into assessment, clinical problem, planning, implementation, and evaluation. To emphasize the importance of patient care in and across various clinical settings, nursing implementation is organized by the following levels of care:

1. Health Promotion
2. Acute Care
3. Ambulatory Care

SPECIAL FEATURES

- Features that are focused on developing clinical judgment include:
  - **Applying Clinical Judgment With Multiple Patients**, featuring traditional and **Next-Generation NCLEX® (NGN)–style** questions at the end of each unit
  - Prioritization questions in case studies and Bridge to NCLEX® Examination Questions.
  - ***Enhanced!* Case Studies** help students learn how to prioritize care and manage patients in the clinical setting. Discussion questions focus on the 6 cognitive skills identified in the CJMM, with a special focus on patient safety. For clarity, they are identified as Recognize, Analyze, Prioritize, Plan, Act, and Evaluate. Answer guidelines are provided on the Evolve website.
- ***Expanded!* Nursing Management** tables focus on the actions nurses need to take to deliver safe, quality, effective patient care. Multiple new tables throughout the text focus on problems such as infection, fever, pressure injury, and inflammation.
- ***Expanded!* Drug Therapy** tables provide more detailed information on associated nursing considerations. Concise **Drug Alerts** highlight important safety considerations for key drugs.
- ***Enhanced!* Evidence-Based Practice** boxes use a case study approach to help students learn to use evidence in making decisions at the patient and systems levels.
- Interprofessional care delivered by physicians, nurses, and other health care team members is highlighted in **Interprofessional Care** tables throughout the text.
- **Safety Alert** boxes highlight important patient safety issues and focus on the US National Patient Safety Goals.
- **Bridge to NCLEX® Examination** questions at the end of each chapter match the Learning Outcomes and help students learn the important points in the chapter. Answers are provided just below the questions for immediate feedback, and rationales are provided on the Evolve website.
- Teaching is an ongoing theme and highlighted in **Patient & Caregiver Teaching** tables.
- Gerontology is addressed throughout the text under Gerontologic Considerations headings and in **Gerontologic Assessment Differences** tables.
- Nutrition is highlighted throughout the textbook. **Nutrition Therapy** tables summarize nutrition interventions and promote healthy lifestyles.
- **Promoting Population Health** boxes address strategies to improve health outcomes as they relate to specific disorders, such as diabetes and cancer, and to health promotion, such as preserving hearing and maintaining a healthy weight.
- **Check Your Practice** boxes challenge students to think critically, analyze patient assessment data, and implement the appropriate intervention. Scenarios and discussion questions are provided to promote active learning.
- **Ethical/Legal Dilemmas** boxes promote critical thinking for timely and sensitive issues that nursing students may deal with in clinical practice—topics such as informed consent, advance directives, and confidentiality.
- **Emergency Management** tables outline the emergency treatment of health problems most likely to require emergency intervention.
- **Nursing Care Plans** on the Evolve website focus on common problems. These care plans incorporate clinical problems, Nursing Interventions Classification (NIC), and Nursing Outcomes Classification (NOC) in a way that clearly shows the linkages among NIC, NOC, and clinical problems and applies them to nursing practice.
- **Nursing Assessment** and **Health History** tables summarize key subjective and objective data related to common problems. Subjective data are organized by functional health patterns.
- **Assessment Abnormalities** tables in assessment chapters alert the nurse to commonly encountered abnormalities and their possible etiologies.
- **Focused Assessment** boxes in all assessment chapters provide brief checklists that help students conduct a more practical "assessment on the run" or bedside approach to assessment. They can be used to evaluate the status of previously identified health problems and monitor for signs of new problems.
- Genetics content includes:
  - **Genetics in Clinical Practice** boxes that summarize the genetic basis, genetic testing, and clinical implications for genetic disorders that affect adults.
  - A genetics chapter that focuses on practical application of nursing care, as it relates to this important topic.
  - **Genetic Risk Alerts** in the assessment chapters, which highlight key genetic risks
  - **Genetic Link** headings in the management chapters, which highlight the specific genetic bases of many disorders.
- **Biologic Sex Considerations** boxes discuss how biologic women and men are affected differently by conditions such as pain and hypertension.

LEARNING SUPPLEMENTS FOR STUDENTS

- The **Clinical Companion** presents more than 200 common medical-surgical problems and procedures in a concise, alphabetical format for quick clinical reference. Designed for portability, this popular reference includes the essential, need-to-know information for treatments and procedures in which nurses play a major role. An attractive and functional full-color design highlights key information for quick, easy reference.
- The revised **Study Guide** contains more than 500 pages of review material that reflects the content found in the textbook. It features a wide variety of clinically relevant exercises and activities, including NCLEX®-format multiple choice and alternate format questions, anatomy review, critical thinking activities, and much more. The revised case studies mirror the NCLEX® examination, with NGN-style case studies and questions reflecting the cognitive skills of the CJMM. It features an attractive full-color design and many alternate-item format questions to better prepare students for the NCLEX® examination. An answer key is included to provide students with immediate feedback as they study.

- The **Evolve Student Resources** are available online at http://evolve.elsevier.com/Lewis/medsurg. They include the following valuable learning aids organized by chapter:
  - Printable **Key Points** summaries for each chapter.
  - 1000 NCLEX® examination **Review Questions.**
  - **Answer Guidelines** to the case studies in the textbook.
  - **Rationales for the Bridge to NCLEX® Examination Questions** in the textbook.
  - 55 **Interactive Case Studies** with state-of-the-art animations and a variety of learning activities, which provide students with immediate feedback. Ten of the case studies are enhanced with photos and narration of the clinical scenarios.
  - Customizable **Nursing Care Plans** for more than 60 common patient problems.
  - **Conceptual Care Map Creator.**
  - **Audio Glossary** of key terms, available as a comprehensive alphabetical glossary and organized by chapter.
  - **Content Updates.**

TEACHING SUPPLEMENTS FOR INSTRUCTORS

- The **Evolve Instructor Resources** (available online at http://evolve.elsevier.com/Lewis/medsurg) remain the most comprehensive set of instructor's materials available, containing the following:
  - **TEACH for Nurses Lesson Plans** with electronic resources organized by chapter help instructors develop and manage the course curriculum. This exciting resource includes:
    - Objectives
    - Pre-class activities
    - Nursing curriculum standards
    - Student and instructor chapter resource listings
    - Teaching strategies, with learning activities and assessment methods tied to learning outcomes
    - Case studies with answer guidelines.
- The **Test Bank** features more than 2000 NCLEX® test questions with text page references and answers coded for NCLEX® Client Needs category, nursing process, and cognitive level. The test bank includes hundreds of prioritization, delegation, and multiple patient questions. Alternate-item format questions are included. The ExamView software allows instructors to create new tests; edit, add, and delete test questions; sort questions by NCLEX® category, cognitive level, nursing process step, and question type; and administer and grade online tests.
- Unfolding and Standalone **Next-Generation NCLEX® (NGN) Examination–Style Case Studies** can be used to help strengthen students' clinical judgment and prepare them for NGN success.
- The **Image Collection** contains more than 800 full-color images for use in lectures.
- The **PowerPoint Presentations** include more than 125 different presentations focused on the most common patient problems. They feature unfolding case studies and NCLEX® examination questions for use with classroom response media.

ACKNOWLEDGMENTS

The editors are especially grateful to many people at Elsevier who assisted with this revision effort. In particular, we wish to thank the team of Lee Henderson, Rebecca Leenhouts, and Clay Broeker. We also thank our contributors and reviewers for their assistance with the revision process.

We hope that this book will assist both students and clinicians in practicing truly professional nursing.

Mariann M. Harding
Jeffrey Kwong
Debra Hagler
Courtney Reinisch

- The **Evolve Student Resources** are available online at http://evolve.elsevier.com/Lewis/medsurg. They include the following valuable learning aids organized by chapter:
- **Printable Key Points** summaries for each chapter
- 1000 NCLEX® examination **Review Questions**
- **Answer Guidelines** to the case studies in the textbook
- **Rationales** for the **Bridge to NCLEX® Examination Questions** in the textbook
- 55 **Interactive Case Studies** with state-of-the-art animations and a variety of learning activities, which provide students with immediate feedback. Ten of the case studies are enhanced with photos and narration of the clinical scenarios.
- **Customizable Nursing Care Plans** for more than 60 common patient problems
- **Conceptual Care Map Creator**
- **Audio Glossary** of key terms, available as a comprehensive alphabetical glossary and organized by chapter
- **Content Updates**

TEACHING SUPPLEMENTS FOR INSTRUCTORS

- The **Evolve Instructor Resources** (available online at http://evolve.elsevier.com/Lewis/medsurg/) remain the most comprehensive set of instructor's materials available, containing the following:
- **TEACH for Nurses Lesson Plans** with electronic resources organized by chapter help instructors develop and manage the course curriculum. This exciting resource includes:
  - Nursing curriculum standards
  - Student and instructor chapter resource listings
  - Teaching strategies with learning activities and assessment methods tied to learning outcomes
  - Case studies with answer guidelines
- The **Test Bank** features more than 2000 NCLEX test questions with text page references and answers coded for NCLEX® Client Needs category, nursing process, and cognitive level. The test bank includes hundreds of prioritization, delegation, and multiple patient questions. Alternate-item format questions are included. The ExamView software allows instructors to create new tests; edit, add, and delete test questions; sort questions by NCLEX® category, cognitive level, nursing process step, and question type; and administer and grade online tests.
- Unfolding and Standalone Next-Generation NCLEX® (NGN) Examination–Style Case Studies can be used to help strengthen students' clinical judgment and prepare them for NGN success.
- The **Image Collection** contains more than 800 full-color images for use in lectures.
- The **PowerPoint Presentations** include more than 120 different presentations focused on the most common patient problems. They feature unfolding case studies and NCLEX® examination questions for use with classroom response media.

ACKNOWLEDGMENTS

The editors are especially grateful to many people at Elsevier who assisted with this revision effort. In particular, we wish to thank the team of Lee Henderson, Rebecca Leenhouts, and Clay Broeker. We also thank our contributors and reviewers for their assistance with the revision process.

We hope that this book will assist both students and clinicians in practicing truly professional nursing.

Mariann M. Harding
Jeffrey Kwong
Debra Hagler
Courtney Reinisch

CONTENTS

SECTION 11 Problems Related to Regulatory and Reproductive Mechanisms

SECTION 12 Problems Related to Movement and Coordination

APPENDIXES

CONCEPT EXEMPLARS

Acid–Base Balance
Chronic Kidney Disease
Diarrhea
Metabolic Acidosis
Metabolic Alkalosis
Respiratory Acidosis
Respiratory Alkalosis

Cellular Regulation
Anemia
Breast Cancer
Cervical Cancer
Colon Cancer
Endometrial Cancer
Head and Neck Cancer
Leukemia
Lung Cancer
Lymphoma
Melanoma
Prostate Cancer

Clotting
Disseminated Intravascular Coagulopathy
Pulmonary Embolism
Thrombocytopenia
Venous Thromboembolism

Cognition
Alzheimer Disease
Delirium

Elimination
Benign Prostatic Hypertrophy
Chronic Kidney Disease
Constipation
Diarrhea
Intestinal Obstruction
Pyelonephritis
Prostatitis
Renal Calculi

Fluids and Electrolytes
Burns
Hyperkalemia
Hypernatremia
Hypokalemia
Hyponatremia

Gas Exchange
Acute Respiratory Failure
Acute Respiratory Distress Syndrome
Asthma
Chronic Obstructive Pulmonary Disease
Cystic Fibrosis
Lung Cancer
Pulmonary Embolism

Glucose Regulation
Cushing Syndrome
Diabetes

Hormonal Regulation
Addison Disease
Hyperthyroidism
Hypothyroidism

Immunity
Allergic Rhinitis
Anaphylaxis
HIV Infection
Organ Transplantation
Peptic Ulcer Disease

Infection
Antimicrobial Resistant Infections
COVID-19
Health Care–Associated Infections
Hepatitis
Pneumonia
Tuberculosis
Urinary Tract Infection

Inflammation
Appendicitis
Cholecystitis
Glomerulonephritis
Pancreatitis
Pelvic Inflammatory Disease
Peritonitis
Rheumatoid Arthritis

Intracranial Regulation
Brain Tumor
Head Injury
Meningitis
Seizure Disorder
Stroke

Mobility
Fractures
Low Back Pain
Multiple Sclerosis
Osteoarthritis
Parkinson Disease
Spinal Cord Injury

Nutrition
Gastroesophageal Reflux Disease
Inflammatory Bowel Disease
Metabolic Syndrome
Malnutrition
Obesity

Perfusion
Acute Coronary Syndrome
Atrial Fibrillation
Cardiogenic Shock
Endocarditis
Heart Failure
Hyperlipidemia
Hypertension
Hypovolemic Shock
Mitral Valve Prolapse
Peripheral Artery Disease
Septic Shock
Sickle Cell Disease

Reproduction
Early Pregnancy Loss
Ectopic Pregnancy
Infertility

Sleep
Insomnia
Sleep Apnea

Sensory Perception
Cataracts
Glaucoma
Hearing Loss
Macular Degeneration
Otitis Media

Sexuality
Erectile Dysfunction
Leiomyomas
Menopause
Sexually Transmitted Infection

Thermoregulation
Frostbite
Heat Stroke
Hyperthyroidism

Tissue Integrity
Burns
Pressure Injuries
Wound Healing

SPECIAL FEATURES

ASSESSMENT ABNORMALITIES TABLES

BIOLOGIC SEX CONSIDERATIONS BOXES

CASE STUDIES

End-of-Chapter Case Studies

Applying Clinical Judgment With Multiple Patients Case Studies

Assessment Case Studies

DIAGNOSTIC STUDIES TABLES

DRUG THERAPY TABLES

EMERGENCY MANAGEMENT TABLES

ETHICAL/LEGAL DILEMMAS BOXES

EVIDENCE-BASED PRACTICE BOXES

FOCUSED ASSESSMENT BOXES

GENETICS IN CLINICAL PRACTICE BOXES

GERONTOLOGIC ASSESSMENT DIFFERENCES TABLES

HEALTH HISTORY TABLES

INTERPROFESSIONAL CARE TABLES

NURSING ASSESSMENT TABLES

NURSING MANAGEMENT TABLES

NUTRITION THERAPY TABLES

PATIENT & CAREGIVER TEACHING TABLES

PROMOTING HEALTH EQUITY BOXES

PROMOTING POPULATION HEALTH BOXES

Lewis's Medical-Surgical Nursing

ASSESSMENT AND MANAGEMENT OF CLINICAL PROBLEMS

1

Professional Nursing

Mariann M. Harding

http://evolve.elsevier.com/Lewis/medsurg/

CONCEPTUAL FOCUS

Care Competencies
Leadership
Clinical Judgment
Professional Identity

LEARNING OUTCOMES

1. Describe the domain and definition of professional nursing practice.
2. Compare the different scopes of practice available to professional nurses.
3. Describe the role of clinical judgment skills and using a clinical practice framework to provide patient-centered care.
4. Apply the SBAR procedure and effective communication techniques in the clinical setting.
5. Explore the role of the professional nurse in delegating care to licensed practical/vocational nurses and assistive personnel.
6. Discuss the role of integrating safety and quality improvement processes into nursing practice.
7. Evaluate the role of informatics and health care technology in nursing practice.
8. Apply concepts of evidence-based practice to nursing practice.

KEY TERMS

advanced practice registered nurse (APRN)
clinical pathways
clinical judgment
delegation
electronic health records (EHRs)
evidence-based practice (EBP)
failure to rescue
interprofessional team
nursing
nursing process
patient handoff
SBAR (Situation-Background-Assessment-Recommendation)
serious reportable event (SRE)
telehealth

This chapter presents an overview of professional nursing practice, discussing the wide variety of roles and responsibilities nurses fulfill to meet society's health care needs. This overview includes the core abilities that are part of competent nursing practice. These include providing safe, patient-centered care and collaborating with others.

PROFESSIONAL NURSING PRACTICE

Domain of Nursing Practice

Today, nursing practice consists of a wide variety of roles and responsibilities necessary to meet society's health care needs. You have never been more important to health care than you are today. As a nurse, you are at the forefront of patient care (Fig. 1.1). Beyond nursing's reputation for compassion and dedication lies a highly specialized profession.[1] Nursing continues to evolve to meet society's health care needs.

As a nurse, you (1) offer skilled care to those recovering from illness or injury, (2) advocate for patients' rights, (3) teach patients to manage their health, (4) support patients and their caregivers at critical times, and (5) help them navigate the complex health care system. You can practice in virtually all health care settings and communities. Although many nurses

Fig. 1.1 Nurses are frontline professionals of health care. (© LightField-Studios/iStock/Thinkstock.)

work in acute care facilities, nurses may practice in long-term care, home care, community health, public health centers, schools, and ambulatory or outpatient clinics. Wherever you practice, recipients of your care include individuals, families, groups, or communities. Nurses work collaboratively with other health care providers to manage the needs of persons and groups.

Definitions of Nursing

Nursing is described as both an art and a science; a heart and a mind.[1] Well-known definitions of nursing show that the basic themes of caring, health, and illness have existed since Florence Nightingale first described nursing. Here are 2 such examples:

- Nursing is putting the patient in the best condition for nature to act (Nightingale).[2]
- The nurse's unique function is to aid patients, sick or well, in performing those activities contributing to health or its recovery (or to peaceful death) that they would perform unaided if they had the necessary strength, will, or knowledge—and to do this in such a way as to help them gain independence as rapidly as possible (Henderson).[3]

In 2010, the American Nursing Association (ANA) provided a new definition of nursing that reflects the ongoing evolution of nursing practice:

> **Nursing is the protection, promotion, and optimization of health and abilities, prevention of illness and injury, alleviation of suffering through the diagnosis and treatment of human response, and advocacy in the care of individuals, families, communities, and populations.**[4]

Nursing's View of Humanity

In this book, we believe 7 dimensions of wellness contribute to health and quality of life: Physical, psychologic, social, spiritual, intellectual, career, and environmental. These dimensions are interrelated and not separate entities. Thus, a problem in one dimension may affect one or more of the other dimensions. A person is in constant interaction with a changing environment. A person's behavior is meaningful and oriented toward fulfilling needs, coping with stress, and developing oneself. However, at times a person needs help to meet these needs, cope successfully, or develop their unique potential.

Scope of Nursing Practice

The essential core of nursing practice is to deliver holistic, patient-centered care. This includes assessment and evaluation, giving a variety of interventions, patient and caregiver teaching, and being a member of the interprofessional health care team.

The extent that nurses engage in their scope of practice depends on their educational preparation, experience, role, and state law. To enter practice, a nurse must complete an accredited program and pass the NCLEX-RN, a test that verifies the nurse has the basic knowledge needed to provide safe care. Entry-level nurses with associate or baccalaureate degrees are prepared to function as generalists. At this level, nurses provide direct health care and focus on ensuring coordinated, comprehensive care to patients in a variety of settings.

With experience and continued study, nurses may specialize in a specific practice area. Certification is a formal way for nurses to obtain professional recognition for having expertise in a specialty area. Many nursing organizations offer certification in specialty practice. Certification requires a certain amount of clinical experience and successfully passing a test. Recertification usually requires ongoing clinical experience and continuing education. Common nursing specialties include critical care, women's health, geriatric, medical-surgical, perinatal, emergency, psychiatric/mental health, and community health nursing.

More education and experience can prepare nurses for advanced practice. An **advanced practice registered nurse (APRN)** is a nurse educated at the master's or doctoral level. They have advanced education in pathophysiology, pharmacology, and health assessment and expertise in a specialized area of practice. APRNs include clinical nurse specialists, nurse practitioners, nurse midwives, and nurse anesthetists. APRNs play a vital role in the health care delivery system. Besides managing and delivering expert direct patient care, APRNs have roles in patient and staff education, leadership, quality improvement, research, and consulting.

The doctor of nursing practice (DNP) degree is a practice-focused terminal nursing degree. With raising the educational preparation for APRNs to the doctoral level, nursing is at the same level as other health professions that have practice doctorates (pharmacy [PharmD], physical therapy [DPT]). Nurses with a research-focused doctorate (PhD) typically work in health care settings as nurse faculty, clinical experts, researchers, and health care system executives.

Standards of Professional Nursing Practice

To guide nurses in how to perform professionally, the ANA defined Standards of Professional Nursing Practice. There are 2 parts, Standards of Practice and Standards of Professional Performance.[5] The Standards of Practice describe a competent level of nursing care based on the nursing process. The Standards of Professional Performance describe behavioral competencies expected of a nurse. You are following the performance standards when you practice ethically and use evidence-based practice. Communicating effectively and staying competent in practice are essential. You must be able to work in collaboration with other health care team members, patients, and caregivers.

INFLUENCES ON PROFESSIONAL NURSING PRACTICE

Expanding Knowledge and Technology

Ever-changing technology and rapidly expanding clinical knowledge add to the complexity of health care. The increased treatment, diagnostic, and care options available change care delivery and extend patients' lives. Discoveries in genetics are changing how we think about diseases such as cancer and heart disease. For example, genetic information guides breast cancer treatment. If a woman has cancer, this information allows for treatment and drug therapy based on genetic makeup. Ethical dilemmas arise about the use of new scientific knowledge and the disparities that exist in patients' access to advanced health care. Throughout this book, genetics and ethical/legal boxes highlight expanding knowledge and technology's impact on nursing practice.

Diverse Populations

Patient populations are more diverse than ever. People are living longer, with the number of people with chronic illnesses and multiple comorbidities increasing. Unlike those who receive acute, episodic care, patients with chronic illnesses have complex needs. They see different health care providers over an extended period and often move among health care settings. You need to be able to manage and coordinate care when patients transition among different settings.

At the same time, you will be caring for a more culturally and ethnically diverse population. When delivering care, you must consider the patient's and caregiver's cultural beliefs and values. Immigrants, particularly undocumented immigrants, often lack the resources necessary to access health care. Inability to pay for health care is related to a tendency to delay seeking care, resulting in more serious illnesses at the time of diagnosis. Boxes throughout this book emphasize the influence of such factors as gender, culture, and ethnicity on nursing practice.

Consumerism

Many patients today want to be more engaged in their health care. They want more control over their health care and expect high-quality, coordinated, and financially reasonable care. Health information is readily available. Many patients are very knowledgeable about their health and seek information about health problems and health care from media and Internet sources. They gather information so that they can have a voice in making decisions about their health care. As a nurse, you must be able to help patients access, interpret, and use safe health care information (Fig. 1.2).

Health Care Financing

High health care costs are a growing problem. There are many reasons for the continued increase in costs. These include the aging population, increased prescription medication use, administrative costs, and more expensive products and treatments. Many changes in health care systems that influence nursing care delivery are usually in an effort to contain spending and provide more cost-effective health care delivery.

The U.S. health system is a mix of public and private, for-profit and nonprofit insurers, and health care providers. Public and private insurers set their own cost-sharing structures within federal and state regulations. Historically, the most noted event related to reimbursement was the establishment of the Medicare prospective payment system (PPS). With PPS, payment for care for Medicare patients is based on flat fees determined by the diseases and problems treated during the admission. For example, if a patient had a total hip replacement, the hospital receives a set sum of money, such as $45,000, for the patient's care.

Other managed care systems also use PPS. In health maintenance organizations (HMOs) and preferred provider organizations (PPOs), charges are negotiated before delivering care using fixed reimbursement rates or capitation fees for medical care, hospitalization, and other health care services.

Now, quality initiatives have further changed health care financing. Value-based purchasing programs base payment to health care providers on their performance on certain quality measures. These measures include clinical outcomes, patient safety, patient satisfaction, and the provider's adherence to evidence-based practice. Those who provide quality care at a lower cost may receive more payment.

As part of value-based purchasing, payment for care can be withheld if a patient experiences events such as developing a pressure injury during a hospital stay or having something happen that is considered preventable (fall-related injury, having wrong-site surgery). This type of event is considered a serious reportable event (SRE). SREs are discussed later in this chapter.

Health Policy

Legislation has serious implications for health care delivery and nursing practice. The Affordable Care Act (ACA) was the most important health care legislation since the creation of Medicare in 1965. The ACA triggered changes throughout the health care system. The ACA's main goal was to increase access to health care. The ACA created new health care delivery and payment models that emphasized teamwork, care coordination, and quality care.

The ACA encourages the creation of accountable care organizations (ACOs). ACOs are groups of physicians, hospitals, and health care providers who unite to coordinate care for Medicare patients. The goal of an ACO is to see that patients, especially the chronically ill, get the right care at the right time while avoiding duplicate services and preventing errors. As a nurse, you must take a leadership role in creating health care systems that provide safe, quality, patient-centered care.

Professional Nursing Organizations

The ANA is the primary professional nursing organization. There are many professional specialty organizations, such as the American Association of Critical-Care Nurses (AACN), National Association of Orthopedic Nurses (NAON), and Oncology Nursing Society (ONS). Professional organizations

Fig. 1.2 The patient, caregiver, and nurse collaborate as part of coordinating care. (© monkeybusinessimages/iStock/Thinkstock.)

play a role in promoting quality patient care and professional nursing practice. These roles include developing standards of practice and codes of ethics, supporting research, and lobbying for legislation and regulations. Major nursing organizations research the causes of errors, develop strategies to prevent errors, and address nursing issues that affect the nurse's ability to deliver patient care safely. Nurses join a professional organization to keep current in their practice and network with others interested in a specific practice area.

A program that supports nurses is the American Nurses Credentialing Center's Magnet Recognition Program. Health care agencies that achieve Magnet designation have created environments in which high-quality nursing care is provided.[6] Magnet agencies provide a positive practice environment for nurses. Nurses who work in Magnet agencies have low turnover and burnout rates and more professional and personal growth opportunities. This leads to better patient outcomes and greater career satisfaction.

Nursing Core Competencies

Several high-profile reports over the past 25 years have highlighted problems with health care quality. One report, *The Future of Nursing: Leading Change, Advancing Health,* discussed how health care providers, including nurses, were not being prepared to provide the highest quality care possible in today's health care systems. The report recommended making changes so that nurses would have the skills to advance health care and play leadership roles in health care.[7]

The Robert Wood Johnson Foundation funded the *Quality and Safety Education for Nurses (QSEN) Institute* to address nursing's role in solving these problems. QSEN made a major contribution to nursing by defining specific competencies that nurses need to practice safely and effectively in today's complex health care system. These competencies have been integrated into prelicensure and graduate nursing education. The rest of this chapter describes 6 common nursing competencies and the knowledge, skills, and attitudes (KSAs) associated with each: (1) patient-centered care, (2) interprofessional partnerships, (3) safety, (4) quality improvement, (5) informatics, and (6) evidence-based practice (Table 1.1).[8] When you are licensed as a registered nurse, you accept responsibility to base your practice on these competencies.

PATIENT-CENTERED CARE

Nurses have long shown that they deliver compassionate and coordinated care based on each patient's unique needs and respect for their preferences and values. We build relationships that make the patient a full partner in their care. Patients and caregivers are involved in making decisions and coordinating care. Patient-centered care is interrelated with quality and safety. With patient-centered care, patients and caregivers seek and receive care from competent and knowledgeable health care professionals.

Clinical Judgment

Complex health care environments require that you use clinical judgment to make decisions that lead to the best patient outcomes. **Clinical judgment** is your ability to make decisions and solve problems by making sense of information in a situation. It is not memorizing a list of facts or the steps of a procedure. Instead, you use nursing knowledge to assess situations, identify priority problems, and generate the best possible solutions to deliver safe patient care.[9] It involves understanding the medical and nursing implications of a patient's situation when making decisions about patient care. You use clinical judgment when you identify a change in a patient's status, consider the context and patient and caregiver concerns, and decide what to do.

Because of the diversity and complexity of patient care, there may not be a right solution in each situation. Therefore, you need to learn and implement clinical judgment skills through experience. Various experiences in nursing school help you to learn to make decisions about patient care. Learning activities, including unfolding case studies and simulation, help you practice using clinical judgment. Throughout this book, case studies and practice questions promote your use of clinical judgment.

Clinical Practice Frameworks

Depending on the situation, nurses use different scientific models when providing patient care. Many use the nursing process. The **nursing process** is a problem-solving approach to the identification and treatment of patient problems. It is the foundation of nursing practice. The nursing process framework provides a structure for delivering nursing care and the knowledge, judgments, and actions that nurses use to achieve the best patient outcomes.

The nursing process consists of 5 phases: assessment, diagnosis, planning, implementation, and evaluation (ADPIE) (Fig. 1.3). The nursing process begins with assessment. *Assessment* is the collection of subjective and objective patient information on which you will base your care plan. *Diagnosing* is the act of analyzing the assessment data and making conclusions. During *planning,* you develop patient outcomes or goals and identify nursing interventions to accomplish the outcomes. Identifying the right expected outcomes provides criteria you can use to

TABLE 1.1 Core Nursing Competencies

Competency	Examples of Knowledge, Skills, and Attitudes
Patient-Centered Care Provide holistic, compassionate, and coordinated care based on respect for patient's preferences, values, and needs and guided by a scientific body of knowledge	• Provide care with sensitivity and respect • Consider the patient's perspectives, beliefs, and culture • Communicate effectively • Engage the patient in an active partnership that promotes health, well-being, and self-care management • Use assessment skills, diagnose health problems, and develop and deliver a plan of care
Interprofessional Partnerships Function effectively within nursing and interprofessional teams	• Value the expertise of each team member • Delegate work to team members based on their roles and competency • Initiate appropriate referrals • Follow communication practices that minimize risks associated with hand-offs and care transitions • Take part in interprofessional rounds • Manage conflict among team members
Safety Minimize risk of harm to patients and providers	• Follow national safety recommendations • Appropriately communicate concerns about hazards and errors • Contribute to designing systems to improve safety • Be accountable for reporting unsafe conditions and near misses • Promote policies to reduce workplace violence
Quality Improvement Use data to monitor the outcomes of care and to improve the quality and safety of health care systems	• Use outcome data to understand performance • Participate in implementing practice changes • Take part in investigating the circumstances surrounding a sentinel event or SRE
Informatics and Health Care Technology Use information and technology to communicate, manage knowledge, reduce errors, and support decision making	• Protect confidentiality of protected health information • Document appropriately in electronic health records • Use technology to coordinate patient care • Respond correctly to clinical decision-making alerts
Evidence-Based Practice Integrate best current evidence with clinical expertise and the patient/caregiver preferences and values for delivery of optimal health care	• Read research, clinical practice guidelines, and evidence reports related to area of practice • Base patient care plan on patient's values, clinical expertise, and evidence • Continuously improve clinical practice based on new knowledge

Source: QSEN competencies. Retrieved from www.qsen.org/competencies.

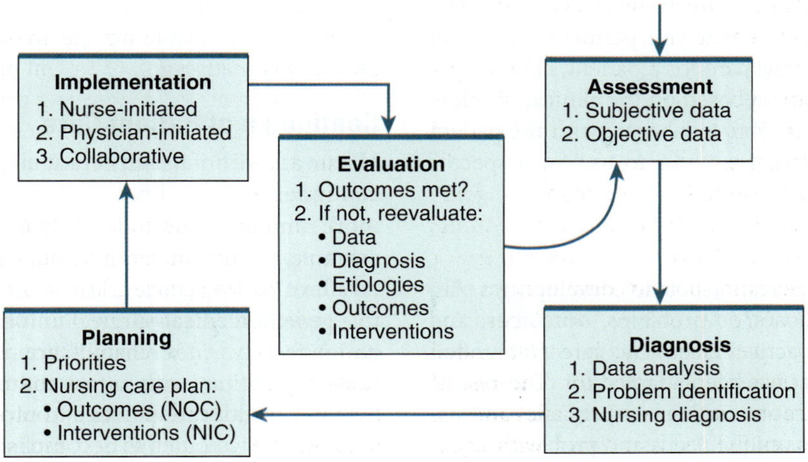

Fig. 1.3 Nursing process.

Model/theory	Components					
NCSBN clinical judgment model	Recognize cues	Analyze cues	Prioritize hypotheses	Generate solutions	Take action	Evaluate outcomes
Nursing process (ADPIE or AAPIE)	Assessment	Diagnosis or analysis		Planning	Implementation	Evaluation
Tanner model	Noticing	Interpreting		Responding		Reflecting

Fig. 1.4 Comparison of the phases of clinical practice frameworks. (From https://evolve.elsevier.com/education/next-generation-nclex/resources/continuing-nursing-education/.)

measure and evaluate the impact of the interventions you provide. *Implementation* is the action phase of the plan with the use of nursing interventions. *Evaluation* is a continual activity of deciding whether the patient outcomes were met. If the outcomes were not met, a review of the process helps to figure out why. You may need to obtain more assessments and revise diagnoses, outcomes, and interventions. Once started, the nursing process is continuous and cyclic.

There are other clinical practice frameworks. These include Tanner's Model of Clinical Judgment Model (with the phases of Noticing, Interpreting, Responding, and Reflecting) and the National Council of State Boards of Nursing's Clinical Judgment Model (CJM) (Fig. 1.4). The CJM was designed to test your clinical judgment on the NCLEX-RN. All 3 models emphasize assessment, making decisions, taking action, and evaluating outcomes. Many clinical facilities use a "shortened version" of the nursing process—Assess, Act, Reassess.[10]

In this book, we use an ADPIE format to help you learn how to care for patients with certain health problems. We use the term "clinical problem" to represent the diagnostic phase of nursing clinical practice (see Appendix B). It is intended to be a synonym for nursing diagnoses, nursing problems, patient problems, or any other label that describes patient problems, conditions, or diagnoses requiring health care.[11] Clinical problems can be diagnosed based on a single clinical finding, such as pain or anxiety, or result from a complex decision about a particular focus, such as impaired nutrition or musculoskeletal problem. Clinical problems are the basis for selecting nursing interventions to achieve patient outcomes for which nursing is accountable.

A nursing intervention is "a single nursing action, treatment, procedure, activity, or service designed to achieve an outcome of a nursing or medical diagnosis for which the nurse is accountable."[12] This includes treatments that you perform and direct or indirect care. When planning care for a patient, choose specific interventions for the patient based on the clinical problem and desired patient outcomes. You collaborate with the patient to decide when and which interventions to use for a specific patient and situation.

Nursing Care Plans

In any clinical setting, you are responsible for developing a plan of care that includes diagnoses or problems, outcomes, and interventions. In clinical practice, electronic care plans often follow a standard format that has been adapted for that specific setting. These plans are guides for routine nursing care. You customize each to your patient's unique needs and problems.

In nursing education, you will likely document the nursing process differently from clinical practice. The nursing process is often recorded in nursing care plans similar to those found on the website for this book (http://evolve.elsevier.com/Lewis/medsurg). These nursing care plans are teaching and learning tools. You practice and learn the nursing process by collecting assessment data, identifying clinical problems, and selecting patient outcomes and nursing interventions. You usually must give rationales for the interventions you choose.

The nursing care plans associated with this book list clinical problems, in order of priority, along with outcomes and interventions. When you use these care plans, you will need to customize the plan for your patient. You must use clinical judgment to continually evaluate the situation and revise the clinical problems, outcomes, and interventions to fit each patient's unique care needs.

A *concept map* is another way to record a nursing care plan. A concept map records the nursing process in a visual diagram. The map shows patient problems and interventions and relationships among clinical data. Nurse educators use concept mapping to teach nursing processes and care planning. Concept maps have various formats.

Conceptual care maps blend a concept map and a nursing care plan. On a conceptual care map, assessment data used to identify the patient's primary health concern are in the center. Diagnostic test data, treatments, and medications surround the assessment data. Positioned below are clinical problems or nursing diagnoses that represent the patient's responses to the health state. Listed with those are the supporting assessment data, outcomes, nursing interventions with rationales, and evaluation. After completing the map, you draw connections between identified relationships and concepts. A conceptual care map creator is available online on the website for this book. Concept maps for select case studies at the end of management chapters are available on the website at http://evolve.elsevier.com/Lewis/medsurg.

Continuum of Patient Care

Nursing is part of health care at all points along the patient care continuum. Depending on their health status, patients often move among a multitude of different health care settings. For example, a young man is in a trauma unit of an acute care hospital after a motor vehicle crash. After he is stable, he is transferred to a general medical-surgical unit and then to an acute rehabilitation facility. After rehabilitation is complete, he is discharged home to continue with outpatient rehabilitation, with follow-up by home health care nurses and care in an ambulatory clinic.

Decisions about the best setting for obtaining health care often depend on the cost of care and the patient's health insurance plan and personal finances. Although the hospital is the

NURSING CARE PLAN

Patient With Heart Failure

Clinical Problem
Impaired Respiratory Function
Etiology: Increased preload, alveolar-capillary membrane changes
Supporting data: Abnormal O_2 saturation, hypoxemia, dyspnea, tachypnea, tachycardia, restlessness, patient's statement, "I am so short of breath."

Patient Goal
Maintains adequate O_2/CO_2 exchange at the alveolar-capillary membrane to meet O_2 needs of the body

Outcomes (NOC)	Interventions (NIC) and *Rationales*
Respiratory Status: Gas Exchange • O_2 saturation ___ • Arterial pH ___ • PaO_2 ___ • $PaCO_2$ ___ • Chest x-ray findings ___ **Measurement Scale** 1 = Severe deviation from normal range 2 = Substantial deviation from normal range 3 = Moderate deviation from normal range 4 = Mild deviation from normal range 5 = No deviation from normal range • Dyspnea with exertion ___ • Dyspnea at rest ___ • Restlessness ___ • Impaired cognition ___ **Measurement Scale** 1 = Severe 2 = Substantial 3 = Moderate 4 = Mild 5 = None	**Respiratory Monitoring** • Monitor pulse oximetry, respiratory rate, rhythm, depth, and effort of respirations *to detect changes in respiratory status.* • Auscultate breath sounds, noting areas of decreased or absent ventilation and presence of adventitious sounds *to detect presence of pulmonary edema.* • Monitor for increased restlessness, anxiety, and work of breathing *to detect increasing hypoxemia.* **Oxygen Therapy** • Administer supplemental O_2 or other noninvasive ventilator support (e.g., bilevel positive airway pressure [BiPAP]) as needed *to maintain adequate O_2 levels.* • Monitor the O_2 liter flow rate and placement of O_2 delivery device *to ensure O_2 is adequately delivered.* • Change O_2 delivery device from mask to nasal prongs during meals as tolerated *to sustain O_2 levels while eating.* • Monitor the effectiveness of O_2 therapy *to identify hypoxemia and establish range of O_2 saturation.* **Positioning** • Position patient to alleviate dyspnea (e.g., semi-Fowler's position), as appropriate, to improve ventilation by decreasing venous return to the heart and increasing thoracic capacity.

mainstay for acute care interventions, community-based settings offer patients the opportunity to live or recover in settings that maximize their independence and preserve human dignity.

Community-based health care settings include ambulatory care, transitional care, and long-term care. *Transitional care* settings provide care in between the acute care and the home or long-term care setting. Patients may receive transitional care at an acute rehabilitation facility after head trauma or a spinal cord injury. *Long-term care* refers to the care of patients for a period longer than 30 days. It may be needed for those who are severely developmentally disabled, who are mentally impaired, or who have physical deficits requiring continuous medical and nursing care. These include patients who are ventilator dependent or have Alzheimer disease. Long-term care facilities include skilled nursing facilities, assisted living facilities, and residential care facilities.

There is a new emphasis on care coordination when patients transition between care settings. *Transitions of care* refer to patients moving among health care practitioners, settings, and home as their condition and care needs change.[13] As a nurse, you are an essential part of care coordination by stressing actions that meet patients' needs and facilitate safe, quality care. Collaborating with other members of the health care team is critical. A lack of communication can result in an ineffective care transition, leading to drug errors and higher hospital readmission rates. For example, you are a nurse in acute care admitting a long-term care patient who has been receiving propranolol 20 mg/5 mL twice a day. The admitting orders read, "propranolol 20 mg/mL, give 5 mL twice a day." Using communication to reconcile the difference averts a drug error. The patient would have received 100 mg instead of the 20 mg dose ordered.

Delivery of Nursing Care

Nurses deliver patient-centered care in collaboration with the interprofessional health care team and within the framework of a care delivery model. A care delivery model outlines how responsibilities and authority are structured to carry outpatient care. Better outcomes occur when the number and type of care providers match patient needs, and there is a designated care coordinator.

In acute care settings, 2 basic models are used: team care and total patient care. *Team care* models involve a group of providers who work together to deliver care. A professional nurse is usually the team leader. As the team leader, you manage and coordinate care with others, such as licensed practical/vocational nurses (LPN/VNs) and assistive personnel (AP). You have accountability for the quality of care delivered by team

Fig. 1.5 Patient in home quarantine videoconferencing with the nurse. (© valentinrussanov/iStock/Thinkstock.)

members during a work period. In total patient care models, you are responsible for planning and providing all care.

Case management involves managing the patient's care with other health care team members and available resources across multiple care settings and levels of care to meet their health needs. It is thought to promote quality, cost-effective outcomes. In nursing case management delivery systems, a registered nurse assumes the role of case manager. In this role, the nurse assesses the needs of patients and/or caregivers, coordinates services for them, makes appropriate referrals, and evaluates the progress toward meeting care goals. For example, a nurse case manager in an outpatient clinic has been working for 3 months with an older male patient with multiple comorbidities, including severe coronary artery disease, diabetes, and osteoarthritis. After he is scheduled for a coronary artery bypass, the nurse manager coordinates his care with other health care team members. She arranges his preoperative appointments and informs the other team members so that everyone understands the patient's unique needs. After the patient has surgery, he develops a deep venous thrombosis in his leg. The case manager then works with the health care team to evaluate the patient's discharge needs and decide whether rehabilitation or home health care is necessary for the patient. With the patient and caregiver, the team decides to discharge the patient to a rehabilitation facility. The case manager helps with the transition, again coordinating care so that the providers at the rehabilitation facility are aware of the patient's needs.

Telehealth nursing provides health care and information using telehealth technologies in virtual environments. These include smartphones and watches, kiosks, and Web-based or digital platforms. The type of telehealth visit depends on the setting and patient need.[14] Among the many uses are triaging patients, monitoring patients with chronic or critical conditions, helping patients manage symptoms, providing patient and caregiver education and emotional support, and providing follow-up care. Telehealth can increase access to care. The nurse engaged in telehealth can assess the patient's health status, deliver interventions, and evaluate the outcomes of nursing care while separated geographically from the patient (Fig. 1.5).

Supporting Caregivers

Caregivers play a valuable role in the patient's health and are members of the health care team. They contribute to the patient's well-being by (1) linking the patient to news from the outside world; (2) facilitating decision making and advising the patient; (3) helping with activities of daily living; (4) acting as liaisons to advise the health care team of the patient's wishes for care; and (5) providing safe, caring, familiar relationships for the patient.

When someone is ill, care extends beyond the patient to the patient's caregivers. Caregivers need your guidance and support. Anxiety and concerns about the patient's condition, prognosis, and pain are common. Caregivers may have a concern about financial issues related to a hospital stay. They often disrupt their daily routines to support the patient. Conduct a family assessment and intervene as needed. Recognize the caregivers' feelings, listen to them openly and without being judgmental, and acknowledge their decisions. Consult other team members, such as a chaplain or social worker, as needed to help caregivers cope.

The key needs of caregivers include information, communication, and access. Lack of information is a major source of anxiety. Assess their understanding of the patient's status, treatment plan, and prognosis and provide them with information. Identify a spokesperson to help coordinate information exchange between the health care team and caregivers. Have them meet team members. Include caregivers in rounds and patient care conferences. It helps caregivers cope when they see that the team is caring and competent, decisions are deliberate, and their input is valued. Invite the caregivers to take part in the patient's care if they want.

Caregivers need access to the patient. Assess the patient's and caregiver's needs and preferences and include these into the plan of care. Caregivers should have the option to be present at the bedside when patients are undergoing invasive procedures (central line insertion) or cardiopulmonary resuscitation (CPR). Even when the outcomes are not favorable, being present helps caregivers to (1) overcome doubts about the patient's condition, (2) reduce their anxiety and fear, (3) meet their need to be together with and to support their loved one, and (4) begin the grief process if death occurs.

INTERPROFESSIONAL PARTNERSHIPS

Interprofessional Team

To deliver high-quality care, you need to have effective working relationships with the health care team members. The **interprofessional team** is made up of providers from various disciplines, working together and sharing their expertise to provide customized care. It may consist of physicians, nurses, pharmacists, occupational and physical therapists, and others (Table 1.2). To be competent in interprofessional practice, you must collaborate in many ways by exchanging knowledge, sharing responsibility for problem solving, and making patient care decisions. You may be responsible for coordinating care among the team members, taking part in interprofessional team meetings or rounds, and making referrals when you need expertise in specialized areas to help the patient. To do so, you must be aware of the knowledge and skills of other team members and be able to communicate effectively with them.

To help you develop the competencies necessary to practice within an interprofessional clinical environment, you may take

TABLE 1.2 Interprofessional Health Care Team Members

Team Member	Services Provided
Dentist	Provides preventive and restorative treatments for problems affecting the teeth and mouth
Dietitian	Provides general nutrition services, including dietary consultation about health promotion or specialized diets
Occupational therapist (OT)	May help patient with fine motor coordination, performing activities of daily living, cognitive-perceptual skills, sensory testing, and the construction or use of assistive or adaptive equipment
Pastoral care	Offers spiritual support and guidance to patients and caregivers
Pharmacist	Prepares medications and infusion products
Physical therapist (PT)	Works with patients to improve strength and endurance, gait training, transfer training, and developing a patient education program
Physician (medical doctor [MD])	Practices medicine and treats illness and injury by prescribing medication, performing diagnostic tests and evaluations, performing surgery, and providing other medical services and advice
Physician assistant	Conducts physical exams, diagnoses and treats illnesses, and counsels on preventive health care in collaboration with a physician
Respiratory therapist	May provide oxygen therapy in the home, give specialized respiratory treatments, and teach the patient or caregiver about the proper use of respiratory equipment
Social worker	Assists patients with developing coping skills, meeting caregiver concerns, securing adequate financial resources or housing, or making referrals to social service or volunteer agencies
Speech pathologist	Focuses on treating speech defects and disorders, especially by using physical exercises to strengthen muscles used in speech, speech drills, and audiovisual aids that develop new speech habits

TABLE 1.3 Guidelines for Communicating Using SBAR

Purpose: SBAR is a model for effective transfer of information by providing a standard structure for concise factual communication from nurse-to-nurse, nurse-to-physician, or nurse-to–other health professionals.

Steps to Use: Before speaking with a physician or other health care professional about a patient problem, assess the patient yourself, read the most recent progress notes, and have the patient's health record available.

S Situation	• What is the situation you want to discuss? What is happening right now? • Identify self, unit. State: I am calling about: *patient, room number.* • Briefly state the problem: what it is, when it happened or started, and how severe it is. State: I have just assessed the patient and am concerned about: *describe why you are concerned.*

B
Background
	• What is the background or circumstances leading up to the situation? State pertinent background information related to the situation that may include:
	  • Admitting diagnosis and date of admission
	  • List of current medications, allergies, IV fluids
	  • Most recent vital signs
	  • Date and time of any laboratory testing and results of previous tests for comparison
	  • Synopsis of treatment to date
	  • Code status

A
Assessment
	• What do you think the problem is? What is your assessment of the situation? State what you think the problem is:
	  • Changes from prior assessments
	  • Patient condition unstable or worsening

R
Recommendation/Request
	• What should we do to correct the problem? What is your recommendation or request? State your request.
	  • Specific treatments
	  • Tests needed
	  • Patient needs to be seen now

Source: Institute for Health Care Improvement: SBAR technique for communication: a situational briefing model. Retrieved from www.ihi.org/resources/Pages/Tools/SBARTechniqueforCommunicationASituationalBriefingModel.aspx.

part in education activities with students from other disciplines. Throughout this book, case studies and review questions discuss the roles others have in managing patient care.

Coordinating Care

Communication

Effective communication is key to fostering teamwork and coordinating care. To provide safe, effective care, team members must exchange information clearly and accurately among team members. Everyone involved in a patient's care should understand the patient's condition and needs. Unfortunately, many issues result from a breakdown in communication.

One model used to improve communication is the **SBAR (Situation-Background-Assessment-Recommendation)** technique (Table 1.3). SBAR offers a structured way to discuss a patient's condition between team members. It allows you to communicate vital patient information that needs immediate attention and action. There will be times when you will be

TABLE 1.4 Communicating Using CUS

CUS: Concerned, Uncomfortable, Safety	
"I am **C**oncerned that..."	State your concern about the patient or situation.
"I am **U**ncomfortable because...!"	State why you feel uncomfortable with what is occurring.
"This is a **S**afety issue because..."	Describe why there is a safety issue and state what actions you think should be taken.

Example: "I'm concerned that the patient is more confused and having difficulty breathing. I am uncomfortable because of the sudden onset of these symptoms. I believe the patient is not safe; there may be something serious going on, and we need to call the rapid response team."

alarmed about a patient situation and need to alert team members. At those times, you can use another model: Concerned, Uncomfortable, Safety (CUS) (Table 1.4). With CUS you state that you are concerned, feel uncomfortable, or perceive a safety issue to stress important or critical information.

Poor communication can occur during transitions of care. Examples of transitions in care include shift changes and patient transfers. A **patient handoff** is the process of passing patient information to another team member during a transition.[15] The handoff should include information about the patient's condition and any recent or anticipated changes. There should be an opportunity to ask questions and a way to confirm information, such as read-back.

Huddles and rounds promote effective communication among team members. A huddle is a short, daily meeting that often happens at the start of each day.[16] Huddles let team members discuss patient concerns, safety concerns, and updates. They improve care quality by helping to solve problems that are affecting patient care (Box 1.1). Interprofessional rounds allow team members to discuss patient care and discharge plans. Rounding at the bedside involves the patient in planning care.

Clinical Pathways

Clinical pathways are interprofessional care plans that outline the care and desired outcomes for a specific time for patients with a specific diagnosis. Think of a clinical pathway as a road map the patient and health care team should follow. As the patient progresses along the road, the patient should receive specific care and meet specific goals. If a patient's progress differs from the planned path, a variance has occurred. A negative variance occurs when specific goals are not met. The nurse usually identifies when a negative variance is present and works with the team members to create a plan to address the issue.

The exact content and format of clinical pathways vary among agencies and settings. Each agency usually has its own pathways based on evidence-based practice guidelines. Common components include assessment guidelines, laboratory and diagnostic testing, medications, activity, diet, and teaching. In acute care, clinical pathways often describe which patient care components are needed at specific times (Fig. 1.6). The case types that have pathways are usually high volume or high risk and predictable, such as myocardial infarction and surgical procedures, like endoscopy, cholecystectomy, cataract surgery.

BOX 1.1 EVIDENCE-BASED PRACTICE

Participating in Post-Fall Huddles

You are caring for J.R., a 76-year-old female admitted for acute kidney injury. She has a history of falls at home, none of which have resulted in serious injury to date. Despite correct identification of her fall risk and implementation of the fall prevention bundle, J.R. fell trying to get up to the bedside commode without calling for assistance. Based on recent policy changes on your unit, a post-fall huddle is called after any patient fall to evaluate contributing circumstances and any unidentified patient risk factors. You are taking part in the fall huddle as J.R.'s assigned nurse. J.R. and her 52-year-old daughter are joining the huddle.

Making Clinical Decisions

Synthesis of Best Available Evidence

After-action reviews, also called huddles or debriefs, have been implemented in health care after a key event (e.g., a patient fall) to discuss contributing factors, identify lessons learned, and determine how those lessons can be implemented to avoid future incidents. Debriefing increases knowledge and improves patient outcomes. Debriefing is widely used as part of an evidence-based fall prevention program. The team members convened after a patient fall typically includes the assigned nurse, any AP, the charge nurse, as well as physical therapists, respiratory therapists, and pharmacists. A designated family member may be included. In particular, nursing staff and the family provide information about what the patient was doing at the time of the fall, the location of the fall, how it was discovered, the severity of any patient injury, interventions intended to be placed, and changes in the plan of care needed to decrease the risk of another fall.

Clinician Expertise

Although the research is limited and has not shown that post-fall huddles decrease fall occurrence, you know that the huddle is part of a unit culture of reflection and open communication. You review J.R.'s current medications and discuss with the pharmacist the potential impact on fall risk. The physical therapist and you discuss the potential value of a balance and core strengthening exercise plan for J.R.

Patient Preferences and Values

J.R. and her daughter express concern about the risk of injury with future falls, but they also want to preserve J.R.'s independence.

Implications for Nursing Practice

1. How does taking part in post-fall huddles encourage teamwork and a culture of patient safety?
2. How can the results of post-fall huddles be shared for wider learning by all staff?

Reference for Evidence

Jones KJ, Crowe J, Allen JA, et al.: The impact of post-fall huddles on repeat fall rates and perceptions of safety culture: A quasi-experimental evaluation of a patient safety demonstration project, *BMC Health Serv Res* 19:650, 2019.

Delegation and Assignment

As a registered nurse (RN), you will delegate nursing care and supervise those who are qualified to deliver care. **Delegation** allows a care provider to perform a specific nursing activity, skill, or procedure beyond their usual role.[17] Delegating and assigning nursing activities is a process that, when used appropriately, results in safe, effective, and efficient patient care. Delegating can allow you more time to focus on complex patient care needs. Delegating care and supervising others will be one of your essential roles as a professional nurse.

Patient Name ____________ Date ____________

DRG# ____________ Expected LOS <23 hours

	Preprocedure	Preoperative	Intraoperative	Postoperative PHASE I PACU	Postoperative PHASE II PACU	Discharge	Postoperative PHASE II PACU
Medication	Review medical history	Start IV	Administer meperidine, propofol, midazolam	Administer naloxone, flumazenil pm	Pain med prn	Start on Rx omeprazole	Continue medications
Diagnostic tests	H-&-P chest x-ray, ECG, blood work	Review tests	Endoscopy procedure	None, unless complications	None	None	None
Diet	Regular	NPO	NPO	NPO	Clear liquids & progress	Regular	Regular
Activity	Not restricted	Ambulate	None	Turn, cough, and deep breathe	Increase activity to ambulation	Normal ambulation	Not restricted
Nursing action	Assessment	Vital signs	Vital signs, O_2 saturation	Vital signs, level of consciousness, O_2 saturation	Monitor as before	Prepare for discharge	Follow-up evaluation via phone
Teaching/ discharge planning	Phone call	Patient education about procedure	Transport to PACU	Discharge when Aldrete criteria I met	Discharge when Aldrete criteria II met	Instructions reviewed	Phone call for follow-up

Fig. 1.6 Clinical pathway for endoscopy. (From Arnold EC, Boggs KU: *Interpersonal relationships,* ed 6, St Louis, 2011, Mosby.)

Delegation usually involves tasks and procedures that licensed LPN/VNs and AP perform. Nursing interventions that require independent nursing knowledge, skill, or judgment (initial assessment, patient teaching, evaluating care) are your responsibility and cannot be delegated. State nurse practice acts and agency policies identify what you can delegate to LPN/VNs and AP. You will use professional judgment to select which activities to delegate. Your decision will be based on the patient's needs, the LPN/VN's and AP's education and training, and the amount of supervision needed. The most common delegated nursing actions involve aspects of direct patient care. For example, you can delegate measuring oral intake and urine output to AP, but you use your nursing judgment to decide if the intake and output are adequate.

The general guideline for LPN/VN practice is that they can function independently in a stable, routine situation. However, they must work under the direct supervision of a professional nurse in acute, unstable situations in which a patient's condition can rapidly change. In most states, LPN/VNs may give medications, perform sterile procedures, and perform a wide variety of interventions planned by the RN. The procedure itself is not the issue when an RN is determining what to delegate. Instead, the patient's stability determines whether it is appropriate for an RN to delegate a procedure to an LPN/VN. For example, the LPN/VN can change an abdominal surgical wound dressing, but the RN should do the first dressing change and wound assessment.

AP holds many titles, including nurse aides, certified medication aides, nursing assistants, patient care assistants, or technicians. The activities AP perform typically include obtaining routine vital signs on stable patients, feeding and helping patients at mealtimes, ambulating stable patients, and helping patients with bathing and hygiene.

Delegation can occur among professional nurses. For example, if 1 RN has accountability for an outcome and asks another RN to perform a specific intervention related to that outcome, that is delegation. This type of delegation typically occurs when 1 RN leaves the unit/work area for a meal break.

Assignment is different from delegation. The term *assign* is used when you direct an LPN/VN or AP to do an activity or procedure that is part of their everyday job.[17] An assignment must be within the authorized scope of practice of the LPN/VN or part of the routine function of the AP. For example, you can assign an LPN/VN to give medications to a patient because this is within the LPN/VN's scope of practice. You cannot assign an LPN/VN to a patient who needs an admission assessment because an RN must perform the initial patient assessment.

Whether you delegate or assign staff tasks, you are responsible for the patient's total care during your work period. You need to decide what patient care tasks must be carried out during the

TABLE 1.5 The 5 Rights of Delegation

The registered nurse uses clinical judgment to be sure that the delegation or assignment is:

1. The right task
2. Under the right circumstances
3. To the right person
4. With the right directions and communication
5. Under the right supervision and evaluation

Right of Delegation	Description	Questions to Ask
Right Task	One that can be delegated for a specific patient	Is it appropriate to delegate based on legal and agency factors? Has the person been trained and evaluated in performing the task? Is the person able and willing to do this specific task?
Right Circumstances	Appropriate patient setting, available resources, and considering relevant factors, including patient stability	What are the patient's needs right now? Is staffing such that the circumstances support delegation strategies?
Right Person	Right person is delegating the right task to the right person to be performed on the right person	Is the prospective delegatee a willing and able employee? Are the patient needs a "fit" with the delegatee?
Right Directions and Communication	Clear, concise description of task, including its objective, limits, and expectations	Have you given clear communication about the task? With directions, limits, and expected outcomes? Does the delegatee know what and when to report? Does the delegatee understand what needs to be done?
Right Supervision and Evaluation	Appropriate monitoring, evaluation, intervention, and feedback	Do you know how and when you will interact about patient care with the delegatee? How often do you need to directly observe? Will you be able to give feedback to the staff member if needed?

Source: National Guidelines for Nursing Delegation. Retrieved from https://www.ncsbn.org/NGND-PosPaper_06.pdf.

given period, identify who will do them, and prioritize the order in which the tasks must be completed. You are responsible for supervising AP and LPN/VNs. Clearly communicate the tasks that need completed and give necessary guidance. Because you are accountable for ensuring that delegated tasks are completed competently, evaluate the care provided, follow up as needed, and make sure no care was missed.

You need to use clinical judgment to ensure that you follow the 5 Rights of Delegation (Table 1.5). Delegation is a skill that is learned, and you must practice it to be proficient in managing patient care. To help you learn to delegate, there is information on delegation in nursing management tables and case study questions at the end of the management chapters.

SAFETY

Preventable medical errors are a serious problem and a leading cause of death in the United States. Several groups address this issue by outlining safety goals for health care organizations and identifying safety competencies for health professionals. Implementing procedures and systems that improve patient safety minimizes the risk of harm to patients through effective health care systems and individual accountability.

Serious Reportable Events

The National Quality Forum (NQF) uses the term **serious reportable event (SRE),** also called a *never event,* to describe serious, largely preventable, and harmful clinical events.[18] The current list of SREs consists of 29 events. These events include a patient acquiring a stage 3 or greater pressure injury after admission and death or injury from a fall or hypoglycemia.

To reduce the occurrence of SREs, the NQF has a list of effective *Safe Practices* that health care settings should use to provide safe patient care (www.qualityforum.org). You are implementing NQF practices when you perform a time-out before a surgical procedure, reconcile medication records, and implement interventions to prevent hospital-acquired infections, pressure injuries, and falls.

National Patient Safety Goals

The Joint Commission (TJC), an accrediting agency for health care organizations, gathers and reports data on serious errors they call sentinel events. A *sentinel event* is a patient safety event unrelated to the patient's illness or underlying condition that results in death, permanent harm, or severe, temporary harm.[19] Events are "sentinel" because they signal the need for immediate investigation and response. Many sentinel events are also serious reportable events. If the patient has a wrong-site or wrong-procedure surgery, is assaulted in the health care setting, or receives an incompatible blood product, the occurrence is both a sentinel event, reportable to TJC, and a serious reportable event, reportable to NQF.

To address specific patient safety concerns, TJC issues National Patient Safety Goals (NPSGs).[20] NPSGs promote patient safety by giving evidence-based solutions to common safety problems. Table 1.6 lists the current NPSGs.

The latest safety goal, focusing on improving the safety of clinical alarm systems, greatly affects nursing. Patient monitoring systems provide vital information. Alarms that work well

TABLE 1.6 National Patient Safety Goals

Safety Goal	Examples
Identify patients correctly	• Use at least 2 ways to identify patients (have them state full name and date of birth). • Give the correct patient the correct blood with every blood transfusion.
Improve communication among the health care team	• Get critical test results to the right person on time.
Use medicines safely	• Before a procedure, label all medicines. Discard any found unlabeled. • Use proper precautions with patients who take anticoagulants. • Find out what medicines each patient is taking. Make certain that it is safe for the patient to take any new medicines with their current ones. • Give a medication list to the patient and the caregiver before discharge. Explain the list.
Use alarm systems safely	• Respond to alarms promptly. • Do not turn alarms off.
Prevent health care–associated infections	• Follow hand hygiene guidelines. • Use evidence-based practices to prevent infections related to central lines, indwelling urinary catheters, and multidrug-resistant organisms
Identify patient safety risks	• Assess patients at risk for suicide. • Assess any risks, such as fires, for patients who are getting home oxygen therapy. • Use measures to reduce fall risk.
Prevent mistakes in surgery	• Conduct a time-out before the start of any surgery. • Confirm correct patient, procedure, and site.

Adapted from The Joint Commission (TJC): National patient safety goals. Retrieved from https://www.jointcommission.org/standards/national-patient-safety-goals/.

improve patient safety and care by telling you when a patient needs your attention. However, so many alarms can go off that *alarm fatigue* occurs, and you can become less sensitive to the sounds. By better managing alarms, we reduce alarm fatigue and improve patient safety.

Failure to rescue (FTR) occurs when there is failure or delay in recognizing a patient has developed complications. As a result, the patient worsens and has an adverse outcome. FTR often involves subtle signs and symptoms that are thought to be of no concern or are missed entirely. You can prevent FTR by recognizing changes in a patient's condition, taking the right actions based on the problem, and activating a response team when needed.

Because you have the most interaction with patients, you play a key role in promoting safety. Many describe nurses as the patient's last line of defense. Every nurse has the responsibility to ensure the patient receives care in a manner that prevents errors and promotes patient safety. Throughout this book, safety alerts highlighting patient care issues and NPSGs will help you learn to apply safety principles.

QUALITY IMPROVEMENT

Quality care and safety are related: the higher the culture of safety, the better the quality of care. Quality improvement (QI) programs involve systematic actions that monitor, assess, and improve health care quality. Health care systems focused on quality outcomes use practice standards and protocols based on best evidence while considering the patient's unique preferences and needs. QI is an interprofessional team effort that accrediting agencies require.

As part of your nursing practice, you will coordinate the complex aspects of patient care, including monitoring the care delivered by others and looking for and correcting issues associated with poor quality or unsafe care. You need to be able to collect data using QI tools, implement interventions to improve patient care, and monitor patient outcomes. Think to yourself, "How can I do my job better?" Identify where changes can be made and be part of making them.

Patient outcomes are an important indicator of quality in health care. Several public and private groups focusing on improving health care quality have developed standard QI measures. These performance measures assess how well the health care team cares for a patient with a certain condition or receives a specific treatment. They describe what data the team must collect and monitor. Fig. 1.7 shows an example of a QI system for adult patients with asthma. In this example, you would review patient medical records to decide if flu vaccination rates exceed 90%. You would share the results with the team and work as a team to implement measures to correct the problem if the identified standard was not met.

National Database of Nursing Quality Indicators

The National Database of Nursing Quality Indicators (NDNQI) provides data on nursing-sensitive measures to evaluate the impact of nursing care on patient outcomes. Patient outcomes are nursing sensitive if they improve with a greater quantity or quality of nursing care. NDNQI outcomes are unique because they identify how nursing workforce factors, including nurse staffing and skill mix, directly influence patient outcomes. NDNQI data show the incidence of falls and health care–associated pressure injuries and infections decreases with adequate staffing and increased nurse education and satisfaction with the work environment. Table 1.7 lists the current NDNQI.

INFORMATICS

Nursing is an information-intense profession. Technology has changed the way nurses plan, deliver, document, and evaluate

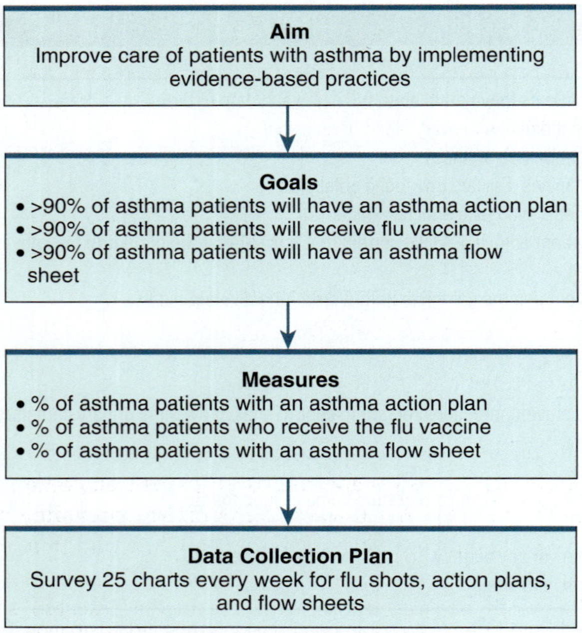

Fig. 1.7 Quality improvement system. (Adapted from Courtlandt CD, Noonan L, Leonard GF: Model for improvement—part 1: a framework for health care quality, *Pediatr Clin North Am* 56:757, 2009.)

TABLE 1.7 National Database of Nursing Quality Indicators

- Structure indicators
  - RN turnover rate
  - Nursing hours per patient day
  - RN education and certification
  - Staff mix: RNs, LPN/VNs, AP, agency staff
- Process and outcome indicators
  - Patient falls and falls with injury
  - Pressure injury rate
  - RN job satisfaction and practice environment survey results
- Outcome indicators
  - Physical/sexual assault rate
  - Restraint use
- Health care–associated infection rate

Source: National Database of Nursing Quality Indicators. Retrieved from https://nursingandndnqi.weebly.com/ndnqi-indicators.html.

care. All nurses, regardless of their setting or role, use informatics and technology every day in practice. You will use informatics to obtain and review diagnostic information, make clinical decisions, communicate with patients and health care team members, document, and provide care.

Technology advances have increased the efficiency of nursing care, improving the work environment and the care nurses provide. Computers and mobile devices allow you to document when you deliver care and give you quick and easy access to information, such as clinical decision-making tools, patient education materials, and references. Texting, video chat, and e-mail enhance communication among health care team members and help you deliver the right message to the right person at the right time.

Technology plays a key role in providing safe, quality patient care. Medication administration applications improve patient safety by flagging potential errors, such as look-alike and sound-alike medications and adverse drug interactions before they can occur. Computerized provider order entry (CPOE) systems can reduce errors caused by misreading or misinterpreting handwritten orders. Sensor technology can decrease the number of falls in high-risk patients. Care reminder systems give cues that decrease the amount of missed nursing care.

Using technology skills to communicate and access information is an essential part of your nursing practice. You must be able to use word processing software, communicate by e-mail and messaging, access information, and follow security and confidentiality rules. You need to have the ability to use patient care technologies and electronic documentation systems safely.

Protected health information (PHI) is highly sensitive. *The Health Insurance Portability and Accountability Act (HIPAA)* is part of federal legislation that addresses actions for how we use and disclose PHI. With the increased use of informatics and technology are concerns on how to comply with HIPAA regulations and maintain a patient's privacy. Wireless technologies, increased use of e-mail and computer networking, and the ongoing threat of computer viruses increase the need for properly protecting a patient's privacy. We must assure patients of their privacy and that only those with a right to know are accessing protected information.

As a nurse, you have an obligation to ensure the privacy of your patient's health information. To do so, you need to understand your agency's policies about the use of technology. You need to know the rules about accessing patient records and releasing PHI, what to do if information is released accidentally or intentionally, and how to protect all your passwords. If you are using social networking, you must not place PHI online (Box 1.2).

Electronic Health Records

The largest use of informatics is **electronic health records (EHRs)**, also called *electronic medical records.* An EHR is a computerized record of patient information. It is shared among all health care team members involved in a patient's care and moves with the patient—to other providers and across care settings. The ideal EHR is a single place for team members to review and update a patient's health record, document care given, and enter patient care orders, including medications, procedures, diets, and diagnostic and laboratory tests (Fig. 1.8).

Several obstacles are still in the way of fully implementing EHRs. EHRs are expensive and technologically complex. They require many resources and training to implement and maintain. Communication is still lacking among computer systems and software applications. Finally, challenges in the use of EHRs, including increased workload and the need for workarounds, affect implementation.

EVIDENCE-BASED PRACTICE

Evidence-based practice (EBP) is a problem-solving approach to clinical decision making. Using the best available evidence (e.g., research findings, QI data), combined with your expertise

BOX 1.2 ETHICAL/LEGAL DILEMMAS

Social Networking: HIPAA Violation

Situation

You log into a closed group on a social networking site and read a post from a fellow nursing student. The post describes in detail the complex care the student gave to a patient in a local hospital the previous day. The student comments on how stressful the day was and asks for advice on dealing with similar patients in the future.

Ethical/Legal Points for Consideration

- Protecting and maintaining patient privacy and confidentiality are basic obligations defined in the Code of Ethics for Nurses, which nurses and nursing students should uphold.[1]
- As outlined in the Health Insurance Portability and Accountability Act (HIPAA), a patient's private health information is any information that relates to the person's past, present, or future physical or mental health. This includes not only specific details such as a patient's name or picture but also information that gives enough details that someone may be able to identify that person.
- You may unintentionally breach privacy or confidentiality by posting patient information (diagnosis, condition, situation) on a social networking site. Using privacy settings or being in a closed group does not guarantee the secrecy of posted information. Others can copy and share any post without your knowledge.
- Potential consequences for not using social networking properly vary based on the situation. These may include (1) disciplinary action by the state board of nursing; (2) being disciplined, suspended, or fired by your employer; (3) dismissal from a nursing program; and (4) civil and/or criminal charges.
- A student nurse who had a stressful day and is looking for advice and support from peers (e.g., "Today my patient died. It made me cry.") could share by clearly limiting the post to the student's perspective and not sharing any identifying information.

Discussion Questions

1. How would you deal with the situation involving the fellow nursing student?
2. How would you handle a situation if you saw a staff member who violated HIPAA?

Reference

1. Code of Ethics for Nurses. Retrieved from www.nursingworld.org/DocumentVault/Ethics-1/Code-of-Ethics-for-Nurses.html.

Fig. 1.8 Members of the interprofessional team review a patient's electronic health record. (© Portra/iStock/Thinkstock.)

TABLE 1.8 Steps of the Evidence-Based Practice (EBP) Process

1. Ask the clinical question using the **PICOT** format:
   Patients/population
   Intervention
   Comparison or comparison group
   Outcome(s)
   Time (as applicable)
2. Search for the best evidence based on the clinical question.
3. Critically appraise and synthesize the evidence.
4. Implement the evidence in practice.
5. Evaluate the practice decision or change.
6. Share the outcomes of the decision or change.

and the patient's unique circumstances and preferences leads to better clinical decisions and improved patient outcomes. EBP closes the gap between research and practice, providing more reliable and predictable care than that based on tradition, opinion, and trial and error.

EBP does not mean that you conduct a research study. Instead, EBP means you take an active role in using the best available evidence when delivering care. You need to have an ongoing curiosity about what are the best nursing practices and routinely ask questions about your patient's care. Know when you need more information. When you base your practice on valid evidence, you are solving problems and supporting best patient outcomes.

Steps of EBP Process

The EBP process has 6 steps (Table 1.8).

Step 1

Step 1 is asking a clinical question in the PICOT format. Developing the clinical question is the key step in the EBP process. A good clinical question sets the context for integrating evidence, clinical judgment, and patient preferences. In addition, the question guides the literature search for the best evidence to influence practice.

An example of a clinical question in PICOT format is, "In adult abdominal surgery patients (**P** = patients/population) is splinting with an elasticized abdominal binder (**I** = intervention) or a pillow (**C** = comparison) more effective in reducing pain associated with ambulation (**O** = outcome) on the first postoperative day (**T** = time period)?" A clinical question may not have all components of PICOT. Some only include 4 components. The (T) timing and (C) comparison components are not appropriate for every question. The (C) component of PICOT may include a comparison with a specific intervention, the usual standard of care, or no intervention at all.

Step 2

Step 2 is searching for the best evidence that applies to the clinical question. Technology provides you with ready access to data. You can easily search online resources and collect large amounts of information and evidence. It is important to evaluate all data sources for their credibility and reliability. Not all evidence is equal. Fig. 1.9 presents the hierarchy of evidence. As

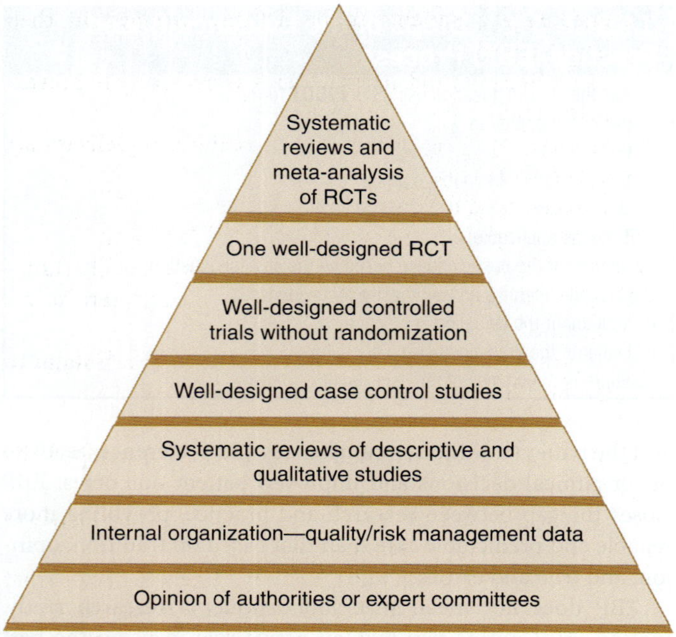

Fig. 1.9 **Hierarchy of evidence.** (Modified from Melnyk BM, Fineout-Overholt E: *Evidence-based practice in nursing and healthcare: a guide to best practice,* ed 3, Philadelphia, 2014, Lippincott Williams & Wilkins.)

you go down the pyramid, the strength of the evidence becomes weaker. Systematic reviews and evidence-based clinical practice guidelines save time and effort in the EBP process. However, they are available for only a limited number of clinical topics and may not suit all types of clinical questions. When insufficient research exists to guide practice, recommendations from expert panels and authority figures may be the best evidence available.

Step 3

Step 3 is to critically appraise the evidence you found. A successful critical appraisal process focuses on 3 essential questions: (1) What are the results? (2) Are the results reliable and valid? and (3) Will the results help me in caring for my patients? You decide the strength of the evidence and synthesize the findings related to the clinical question to conclude what the best practice is. For example, you find strong evidence supporting the effectiveness of elasticized binders and pillows in reducing pain associated with ambulation. However, binders appear to be most effective if the patient is obese or had prior abdominal surgery.

Step 4

Step 4 involves implementing the evidence in practice. The decision to implement change is made by combining the evidence, clinical judgment, and preferences and values of patients and caregivers. You may be part of an interprofessional team charged with implementing a practice change or applying evidence in a specific patient care situation. This may include developing clinical practice guidelines, policies, and procedures, or new assessment, teaching, or documentation tools. For example, you may be part of a team implementing a new postoperative protocol focused on using elasticized abdominal binders with patients who are obese or had prior abdominal surgery.

Step 5

Step 5 is evaluating the outcome of the practice change. After implementing the change for a specific period, you should monitor outcomes to determine whether the change has improved patient outcomes. Accrediting bodies require documentation of outcome measures to show that the organization is using evidence to improve patient care.

Step 6

Step 6 is sharing the results of the EBP change. If you do not share the outcomes of EBP, then other health care providers and patients cannot benefit from what you learned from your experience. You can share information locally using unit- or hospital-based newsletters and posters and regionally and nationally through journal publications and presentations at conferences.

Implementing EBP

To implement EBP, you must develop the skills to be able to seek and incorporate into practice scientific evidence that supports best patient outcomes. Throughout this book, Evidence-Based Practice boxes allow you to practice applying EBP to patient scenarios. To help you identify the use of evidence in this book, an asterisk (*) in the reference list at the end of each chapter indicates evidence-based information for clinical practice.

BRIDGE TO NCLEX EXAMINATION

The number of the question corresponds to the same-numbered outcome at the beginning of the chapter.

1. An example of a nursing activity that best reflects the American Nurses Association's definition of nursing is
   - **a.** treating dysrhythmias that occur in a patient in the coronary care unit.
   - **b.** diagnosing a patient with a feeding tube as being at risk for aspiration.
   - **c.** setting up protocols for treating patients in the emergency department.
   - **d.** offering antianxiety drugs to a patient with a disturbed sleep pattern.
2. A nurse working on the medical-surgical unit at an urban hospital would like to become certified in medical-surgical nursing. The nurse knows that this process would most likely require
   - **a.** a bachelor's degree in nursing.
   - **b.** formal education in advanced nursing practice.
   - **c.** experience for a specific period in medical-surgical nursing.
   - **d.** membership in a medical-surgical nursing specialty organization.

3. The nurse is assigned to care for a newly admitted patient. Number in order the steps for using the nursing process to prioritize care. (Number 1 is the first step, and number 5 is the last step.)
   ___ Determine whether the plan was effective.
   ___ Identify any clinical problems.
   ___ Collect patient information.
   ___ Carry out the plan.
   ___ Decide a plan of action.
4. Using the SBAR format, number in order the steps for how the nurse would communicate information with the provider. (Number 1 is the first step, and number 4 is the last step.)
   ____ "I would like you to order an IV medication and come evaluate the patient as soon as possible."
   ____ "This is Nurse M.H. I am calling from the unit because your patient, D.R., has a new onset of atrial fibrillation."
   ____ "The atrial fibrillation started about 10 minutes ago. The heart rate is 124; BP 90/60. The patient is reporting dizziness."
   ____ "D.R., who is 2 days postoperative for a bowel resection for an obstruction, has a history of mitral valve disease."
5. The nurse is caring for a patient with diabetes in the ambulatory surgical unit who had a wound debridement. Which task is appropriate for the nurse to delegate to assistive personnel (AP)?
   a. Check the patient's vital signs.
   b. Assess the patient's pain level.
   c. Palpate the patient's pedal pulses.
   d. Monitor the patient's IV catheter site.
6. The nurse's role in addressing the National Patient Safety Goals established by The Joint Commission includes *(select all that apply)*
   a. answering all patient monitoring alarms promptly.
   b. memorizing all the rules published by The Joint Commission.
   c. obtaining a correct list of the patient's medications on admission.
   d. encouraging patients to be actively involved in their health care.
   e. using side rails and alarm systems as necessary to prevent patient falls.
7. Advantages of using informatics in health care delivery are *(select all that apply)*
   a. reduced need for nurses in acute care.
   b. increased patient anonymity and confidentiality.
   c. the ability to deliver high standards of safe, quality care.
   d. access to decision-making tools for health care teams members.
   e. improved communication of the patient's health status to the health care team.
8. When using evidence-based practice, the nurse
   a. must use clinical practice guidelines developed by national health agencies.
   b. should use findings from randomized controlled trials to plan care for all patient problems.
   c. uses clinical decision making and judgment to decide what evidence is appropriate for a specific clinical situation.
   d. analyzes the relationship of nursing interventions to patient outcomes to discover evidence for patient interventions.

1. b, 2. c; 3. 5, 2, 1, 4, 3; 4. 4, 1, 3, 2. 5. a; 6. a, c, e; 7. c, d, e; 8. c.

For rationales to these answers and even more NCLEX review questions, visit http://evolve.elsevier.com/Lewis/medsurg.

EVOLVE WEBSITE/RESOURCES LIST

http://evolve.elsevier.com/Lewis/medsurg
Review Questions (Online Only)
Key Points
Answer Key for Questions
- Rationales for Bridge to NCLEX Examination Questions

Conceptual Care Map Creator
Audio Glossary
Content Updates

REFERENCES

1. American Nurses Association: What is nursing? Retrieved from https://www.nursingworld.org/practice-policy/workforce/what-is-nursing/.
2. Nightingale F: *Notes on nursing: what it is and what it is not (facsimile edition)*, Philadelphia, 1946, Lippincott. (Classic).
3. Henderson V: *The nature of nursing*, New York, 1966, Macmillan (Classic).
4. American Nurses Association: *Nursing: a social policy statement*, ed 3, Washington, DC, 2010, The Association. (Classic).
5. American Nurses Association: *Nursing: scope and standards of practice*, Washington, DC, 2010, The Association. (Classic).
6. ANCC Magnet Recognition Program. Retrieved from www.nursingworld.org/organizational-programs/magnet/.
7. Committee on the Robert Wood Johnson Foundation Initiative on the Future of Nursing at the Institute of Medicine: *The future of nursing: leading change, advancing health*, Washington, DC, 2011, National Academies Press. (Classic).
8. QSEN Institute. Retrieved from http://qsen.org.
9. National Council of State Boards of Nursing: Clinical judgment measuring model. Retrieved from https://www.ncsbn.org/NGN_Winter19.pdf.
10. Alfaro-LeFevre R: *Critical thinking, clinical reasoning, and clinical judgment: a practical approach*, ed 7, St. Louis, 2020, Elsevier.
11. Harding M, Hagler D: *Conceptual care planning*, St. Louis, 2021, Elsevier.
12. Clinical Care Classification: Nursing interventions. Retrieved from https://careclassification.org/framework/nursing-interventions/.
13. The Care Transitions Program. Retrieved from https://caretransitions.org/.
14. American Academy of Ambulatory Care Nursing: Telehealth. Retrieved from https://www.aaacn.org/practice-resources/telehealth.
15. The Joint Commission: Inadequate handoff communication. Retrieved from https://www.jointcommission.org/-/media/tjc/documents/resources/patient-safety-topics/sentinel-event/sea_58_hand_off_comms_9_6_17_final_(1).pdf.

16. Institute for Healthcare Improvement: Huddles. Retrieved from http://www.ihi.org/resources/Pages/Tools/Huddles.aspx.
17. National Guidelines for Nursing Delegation. Retrieved from https://www.ncsbn.org/NGND-PosPaper_06.pdf.
18. National Quality Forum: Serious reportable events. Retrieved from http://www.qualityforum.org/topics/sres/serious_reportable_events.aspx.
19. The Joint Commission: Sentinel events policy and procedures. Retrieved from www.jointcommission.org/sentinel_event_policy_and_procedures/.
20. The Joint Commission: National patient safety goals. Retrieved from www.jointcommission.org/standards_information/npsgs.aspx.

2

Social Determinants of Health

Andrew Scanlon and Courtney Reinisch

http://evolve.elsevier.com/Lewis/medsurg/

CONCEPTUAL FOCUS

Culture
Health Disparities
Population Health

LEARNING OUTCOMES

1. Identify the social determinants of health.
2. Describe the factors that contribute to health disparities and health equity.
3. Define cultural competence and its related terminology.
4. Explain how culture and ethnicity may affect a person's health.
5. Apply strategies for integrating social determinants of health in the nursing process.
6. Describe the role of nursing in promoting health equity.
7. Examine ways that your cultural background may influence nursing care.
8. Describe strategies for successfully communicating with a person who speaks a language that you do not understand.

KEY TERMS

acculturation
cultural competence
culture
ethnicity
ethnocentrism
folk healers
health disparities
health equity
health status
place
race
racism
social determinants of health
stereotyping
values

This chapter discusses social determinants of health (SDH), health disparities, and culture. The SDH serve as the foundation for how we express our culture. Understanding the SDH is needed to provide patient-centered care. Health is a cultural concept because culture frames and shapes our experiences. Cultural beliefs influence health promotion practices and attitudes about seeking health care. Social and cultural factors influence equity in health care. **Health disparities** are differences in the incidence, prevalence, mortality rate, and burden of diseases that exist among specific population groups. An inability to address the SDH results in health disparities and negatively impacts well-being.

SOCIAL DETERMINANTS OF HEALTH

Why are there differences in people's health status? How do these differences occur? The **social determinants of health** are nonmedical factors that (1) influence the health of persons and groups and (2) explain why some people have poorer health than others.[1] The SDH can be broken down into 5 groups. These are neighborhood, economic stability, education, health care access, and community context (Fig. 2.1). Where people are born, grow up, live, work, and age helps to determine their health status, behaviors, and care.

Health status is a holistic concept that is more than the presence or absence of disease. It encompasses life expectancy and self-assessment of health. Many measures make up the concept of health status. For a person, this means the sum of their current health problems plus their coping resources (e.g., family, financial resources). For a community, health status is the combination of health measures for all people living in the community. Community health measures include birth and death rates, life expectancy, access

Social determinants of health

Economic stability	Neighborhood	Education	Community context	Health care
Employment	Housing	Literacy	Social integration	Health coverage
Income	Transportation	Language	Support systems	HCP availability
Expenses	Safety	Early childhood education	Community engagement	Linguistic and cultural competency
Debt	Recreation	Vocational training	Discrimination	Quality of care
Medical bills	Walkability	Higher education	Stress	
Support	Zip code/ geography			
	Food			

Health outcomes
Mortality, morbidity, life expectancy, health status, functional limitations

Fig. 2.1 Social determinants of health.

to care, and morbidity and mortality rates related to disease and injury.

Factors in a person's social and physical environment, including personal relationships, workplace, housing, transportation, and neighborhood violence, contribute to health status.[1] For example, the risk of youth homicide is much higher in neighborhoods with gang activity and high crime rates. The physical environment in which one lives, works, and plays may expose a person to such risks as environmental hazards (workplace injuries), toxic agents (chemical spills, industrial pollution), unsafe traffic patterns (lack of sidewalks), or absence of fresh, healthy food choices.

A person's behavior is influenced by their environment, education, and economic status. Behaviors such as tobacco and drug use are strongly linked to many health conditions (e.g., lung cancer, liver disease). A person's biologic makeup, such as genetics and family history of disease (e.g., heart disease), can increase the risk for specific diseases.

Access to health care contributes to a person's health. Although government initiatives strive to reduce the number of uninsured Americans, millions still are uninsured and have limited access to care. This affects both individual and community health.

Neighborhood

Place refers to the geographic and environmental location where a person is born, grows, lives, works, and ages. Your neighborhood affects the use of health services, health status, and health behaviors.

Housing is a basic need. It protects us from environmental harm. Housing can contribute to poor health outcomes. Unsafe or poor-quality housing is associated with exposure to lead, indoor air pollution, and asthma triggers (dust, mold, rodents). Overcrowded living conditions can contribute to the spread of infectious disease. Living close to environmental hazards can affect pregnancy outcomes. It increases the risk of cancer and neurologic problems.

About 20% of Americans live in nonurban or rural areas.[2] Differences in access to health care services between rural and urban settings can create geographic health disparities. People in rural areas may need to travel long distances to receive health care.[2] This can result in inadequate or less-frequent access to health care services. Some parts of the rural United States are "medically underserved" because of low numbers of HCPs.

People in rural areas have higher rates of obesity and chronic disease. They are more likely to have cancer, heart disease, diabetes, depression, and injury-related deaths than people in urban areas. In rural Appalachia, the rates of lung, colon, cervical, and colorectal cancer are higher than average. Rural populations tend to be older than urban populations. The impact of social and physical environment on health choices can be illustrated by the problem of intimate partner violence in rural communities.[3] The decision to seek help is affected by geographic isolation, traditional gender roles, patriarchal attitudes, fear of lack of confidentiality, and economic factors that exist in some small rural communities.

Living in urban centers may predispose a person to other health disparities. People in high crime areas may not visit HCPs. High rates of chronic health problems and premature deaths occur in neighborhoods with social inequalities. These include high poverty rates, high crime rates, and residential segregation.

Among the most obvious health behaviors affected by place are physical activity and nutrition. Safe, walkable neighborhoods with playgrounds promote physical activity. Source and price of healthy foods affect diet intake and weight. Social support positively affects coping with illness. Social networks are more likely in communities where neighbors interact and rely on one another.

Economic Stability

The main nonmedical factor affecting health is socioeconomic status. Socioeconomic status is related to wealth, education, and occupation. Those living in poverty cannot afford healthy food,

Fig. 2.2 Interprofessional team working together in a multicultural health care environment. (© Thinkstock/Stockbyte/Thinkstock.)

health care, and safe housing. People of lower income report worse health and die at a younger age. Hazardous work environments and high-risk occupations increase health risk and contribute to higher rates of illness, injury, and death.

Health Care

Many people do not have access to quality health care. Health care coverage is a key factor that contributes to health disparities. People who are underinsured, have no insurance, or lack financial resources to pay for treatment of diseases may forgo health care visits, screenings, and treatments. Patients who lack the knowledge and/or access to apply for government aid programs (e.g., Medicaid) are also at risk.

The health care system may contribute to health disparities. For example, a clinic located in an area with a large population of non–English-speaking immigrants that does not provide interpreters or educational materials and financial forms in languages other than English may limit these families' ability to understand how to access health care.

Discrimination and *bias* based on a patient's race, ethnicity, gender, age, body size, sexual orientation, or ability to pay are likely to result in less aggressive or negative treatment practices. Discrimination can result in the delay of a diagnosis due to assumptions made about the patient. Sometimes discrimination is hard to recognize, especially when it occurs at the institutional level.

An HCP's discriminatory behavior may not be clear to the patient or yourself. It may be difficult to confront. Even well-intentioned HCPs who try to eliminate bias in their care can show their prior beliefs or prejudices through nonverbal communication. Many policies are in place to eliminate discrimination, but it still exists.

Poorer health outcomes for minorities are linked to the shortage of culturally and ethnically diverse HCPs, who are underrepresented in the health professions. A diversity gap exists between the ethnic composition of the health care team and the overall population in the United States (Fig. 2.2). For example, the diversity of nurses in the United States is increasing but still lags that of the overall population. Blacks, Hispanic/Latino Americans, and Native Americans make up more than 35% of the population but only 24% of the nation's nurses.[4] Biased behaviors against nurses of diverse cultural and ethnic backgrounds by patients and health care professionals may contribute to their underrepresentation.

Cultural differences affect how well patients think they can communicate with their HCP. In the United States, minority patients are more likely to have difficulty understanding and communicating with their HCP. Communication issues include not understanding the HCP, feeling that they are not listened to, and having questions but not asking them.

Education

Where you live influences your access to quality education. Some communities have better schools than others. People with higher levels of education tend to be healthier. Adults without a high school diploma or equivalent are 3 times more likely to die before age 65 than those with a college degree.

Health literacy is defined as the degree to which a person has the capacity to obtain, process, and understand basic health information and services needed to make appropriate health decisions. This includes the ability to (1) read, understand, and analyze information; (2) understand instructions; (3) weigh risks and benefits; and (4) make decisions and act. Low health literacy is related to more hospitalizations, greater use of emergency department care, decreased use of cancer screening and influenza vaccine, decreased ability to use medications correctly, and higher mortality rates among older adults.

Patients need to be able to self-manage conditions such as diabetes and asthma. Patients with diabetes may not be able to maintain adequate blood glucose levels if they cannot read or understand the numbers on the home glucose monitoring system. The inability to read and understand medication labels can result in taking medications at the wrong time or in the wrong dose. See Chapter 4 for more about health literacy.

Community

Our sense of connection with family, friends, coworkers, and community members affects our health and well-being. Positive relationships can improve health. Persons who are bullied may not get the support they need. Nurses can help people get social support in the community to reduce health disparities.

HEALTH DISPARITIES AND HEALTH EQUITY

In the United States, health disparities occur because of social, economic, or environmental disadvantages. They can affect population groups based on gender, age, ethnicity, socioeconomic status, education, location, sexual orientation, or disability status (Box 2.1).[5] **Health equity** is achieved when every person has the opportunity to attain their health potential, and no one is disadvantaged (Box 2.2).

Factors and Conditions Leading to Health Disparities

Many factors and conditions can lead to the development of health disparities (Table 2.1). Awareness of these factors will help you to provide optimal care for your patients.

BOX 2.1 ETHICAL/LEGAL DILEMMAS

Health Disparities

Situation

E.M., a 47-year-old Latino woman living with type 2 diabetes, comes to the clinic to have her blood glucose measured. It has been 12 months since her last visit. At that time, the nurse asked that she bring along her glucometer and strips to show how she checks her blood glucose because her glucose values were high at her previous visits.

When you check E.M.'s equipment and glucose strips, you find the strips are for a different machine and expired 2 years ago. When you inquire about the situation, E.M. says that she cannot afford to come to the clinic or to buy new equipment and supplies to check her blood glucose level. During the day, E.M. cares for her 3 grandchildren so her daughter can work. E.M. spends most of her income on food for her family, so she has little money left for her health care.

Ethical/Legal Points for Consideration

- Ethnic minorities and other vulnerable or disadvantaged groups have higher rates of certain chronic illnesses. Limited access to high-quality, accessible, and affordable health care services is related to an increased incidence of complications and a reduced life span.
- People with certain health problems such as diabetes may have difficulty obtaining health care insurance. Consider these issues in the broader context of social justice.
- The legal definition of the role of the professional nurse includes patient advocacy. Advocacy includes the obligation to provide adequate follow-up care for all patients, regardless of race, gender, or ability to pay.
- A nurse who sees disparities must consider the possibility of discrimination. Professional nurses are legally and ethically responsible for patient advocacy. The nurse may incur legal liability if failure to fulfill this obligation results in patient harm.

Discussion Questions

1. How would you work with E.M. to help her obtain the necessary resources and knowledge to care for her diabetes?
2. What can you do to begin working on the problems of health disparities in your community?

BOX 2.2 PROMOTING HEALTH EQUITY

Promoting Health Equity Boxes Throughout the Book

TABLE 2.1 Factors and Conditions Leading to Health Disparities

- Age
- Disability status
- Education
- Ethnicity and race
- Food insecurity
- HCP attitudes/biases
- Health literacy
- Income status
- Lack of health care services access
- Language barrier
- Occupation or unemployment
- Place
- Sexual orientation
- Unemployment
- Unstable housing

Ethnicity and Race

The terms **ethnicity** and **race** are subjective and based on self-report. We often use these terms interchangeably. They are not defined by genetic markers. Social context and lived experiences influence people's decision about the ethnic and race category to which they identify or are assigned. Ethnic and race categories may differ on a person's birth certificate and death certificate.

People often identify their own ethnicity and race for health data collection (e.g., health plans, birth certificates). Collection of health data based on self-reported ethnic and race categories is important for research, to inform policy, and to understand and eliminate disparities. People identify their race using 1 or more categories. Law requires federal agencies to list a minimum of 5 race categories: White, Black, American Indian or Alaska Native, Asian, and Native Hawaiian or other Pacific Islander. Federal agencies must also list a minimum of 2 ethnicities for people who self-identify as either *Hispanic or Latino* and *Not Hispanic or Latino.* A Hispanic or Latino is typically a person of Cuban, Mexican, Puerto Rican, South or Central American, or other Spanish descent, regardless of race. In this book, we use the terms *ethnicity* and *race* interchangeably or together.

Although dramatic improvements in treatments have prolonged and improved quality of life for many, racial and ethnic minorities have received less benefit from these advances. We generally determine disparities by comparing groups. In the United States, minority groups include Hispanic/Latino (19%), Black (13%), and Asian (6%).[6] Native Hawaiian and other Pacific Islander, Native American and Native Alaskan, and 2 or more

TABLE 2.2 Basic Characteristics of Culture

- Dynamic and ever-changing
- Not always shared by all members of a cultural group
- Adapted to specific conditions such as environmental factors
- Learned through oral and written histories, as well as socialization

races make up 4% of the population.[6] The number for most of these groups is expected to increase in the coming decades.

Obesity and chronic illness rates for diabetes, hypertension, chronic obstructive pulmonary diseases, cancer, and stroke are higher among minorities. Racial, ethnic, and cultural differences exist in health services, treatments provided, and access to HCPs. Race and ethnicity also influence disease risk and outcomes. For example, after myocardial infarction, minority patients are at greater risk of rehospitalization and death. They are less likely than nonminority patients to receive potentially beneficial treatments.[7] Native Americans have a higher incidence of several types of cancers.

Gender

Health disparities exist between men and women. Adult women use health care services more than men. Women may not receive the same quality of care. When we combine gender with racial and ethnic differences, the disparities are even greater. Biologic Sex Considerations boxes throughout this book highlight differences in disease risk, manifestations, and treatment.

Age

Older adults are at risk for experiencing health disparities in the number of diagnostic tests done and aggressiveness of treatments used. Biases toward older adults that affect their care, or ageism, are discussed in Chapter 5. Older people of low socioeconomic status have greater disability, more limitations in activities of daily living, and more frequent and rapid cognitive decline. Black and Latino older adults are disproportionately affected by chronic illnesses, disability, depression, and substandard quality of life.[8]

CULTURE

Culture is a way of life for a group of people. It includes the behaviors, beliefs, values, traditions, and symbols that the group accepts, generally without thinking about them. This way of life is passed along by communication and imitation from 1 generation to the next. You can also think of culture as behavior that one acquires through social learning. It is the totality of a person's learned, accumulated experience that is socially transmitted. The 4 basic characteristics of culture are described in Table 2.2.

Values are the sets of rules by which persons, families, groups, and communities live. They are the principles and standards that serve as the basis for beliefs, attitudes, and behaviors. Although all cultures have values, the types and expressions of those values differ from 1 culture to another. These cultural values develop over time, guide decision making and actions, and may affect a person's self-esteem. Cultural values often

Fig. 2.3 Members of this family share a common heritage. (© Jack Hollingsworth/Photodisc/Thinkstock.)

unconsciously develop early in life as a child learns about acceptable and unacceptable behaviors. The extent a person's cultural values are internalized influences that person's tendency toward judging other cultures. We usually use our own culture as the accepted standard.

Although persons within a cultural group may have many similarities through their shared values, beliefs, and practices, there is also diversity within groups (Fig. 2.3). Each person is culturally unique. Such diversity may result from different perspectives and interpretations of situations. These differences may be based on age, gender, marital status, family structure, income, education level, religious views, and life experiences. Within any cultural group, there are smaller groups that may not hold all the values of the dominant culture. These smaller cultural groups have experiences that differ from those of the dominant group. These differences may be related to ethnic background, residence, religion, occupation, health, age, gender, education, or other factors that unite the group. Members of a subculture share certain aspects of culture that are different from those of the overall cultural group. For example, people from a cultural group seek professional health care right away when symptoms appear. While others from the same culture rely first on folk healers. A third group may seek the opinion of family and friends before seeking formal health care.

Cultural beliefs about symptom tolerance and health care–seeking behavior can contribute to health disparities. Some cultures consider pain something to endure or ignore. As a result, the patient does not seek help. Some cultures may view diseases or problems fatalistically. This means there is no reason to seek treatment because they believe there is no hope. Some cultures view the signs and symptoms of an illness as "God's will" or as a punishment for some prior behavior. In some cultures, it may not be acceptable to see an HCP who is not of the same gender or ethnic group. Such beliefs can result in delays in seeking health care or inadequate treatment.

Acculturation is the lifelong process of incorporating cultural aspects of the contexts in which a person grows, lives, works, and ages. It is often bidirectional. In other words, the context changes as a person's culture influences it. Change may be in attitudes, behaviors, and values. For example, a sedentary person who loves to cook may change their attitude toward exercise when living with athletic roommates. They in turn also change as they begin to appreciate cooking. Behaviors change when an immigrant child learns the local language while influencing the conduct of classmates. A deeply held value such as self-sufficiency may change for a person exposed to a culture in which reliance on others dominates.

Newcomers may adopt both the strengths and limitations of the dominant culture. This is relevant when considering health behaviors and the quality of health care delivered by professionals. For example, an immigrant may be negatively influenced by a dominant cultural context in which unhealthy eating habits prevail.[9]

The result of acculturation may be new cultural variations in attitudes, behaviors, and values. All people take part in this process over their lives. People who move to a new cultural context are more aware of the acculturation experience than people who are not exposed to new experiences. Exposure to new cultural contexts increases a nurse's cultural competency.

Stereotyping refers to an overgeneralized viewpoint that members of a specific culture, race, or ethnic group are alike and share the same values and beliefs. This oversimplified approach does not consider the individual differences that exist within a culture. Being a member of a particular cultural, ethnic, or racial group does not make the person an expert on other members of that same group. Such stereotyping can lead to false assumptions and affect a patient's care. For example, it would be inappropriate for you to assume that just because a nurse is of a particular culture, they would know how a person of the same culture's beliefs may affect that patient's health care practices. As another example, a young Latino nurse born and raised in a large city experienced a different culture than the older patient who was born and raised in a rural area of the same country of origin.

Ethnocentrism refers to the belief that one's own culture and worldview are superior to those of others from different cultural, ethnic, or racial backgrounds.[9] Comparing others' ways to your own can lead to seeing others as different or inferior. HCP's ethnocentrism can result in poor communication, patient alienation, and potentially inadequate treatment. To avoid ethnocentrism, you need to remain open to a variety of perspectives and maintain a nonjudgmental view of the values, beliefs, and practices of others. Failure to do this can result in ethnic stereotyping or cultural imposition.

Cultural imposition occurs when we impose our own cultural beliefs and practices on another person or group of people. In health care, it can result in disregarding or trivializing a patient's health care beliefs or practices. Cultural imposition may happen when an HCP is unaware of the patient's cultural beliefs and plans and implements care without taking them into account.

Cultural safety describes care and advocacy for a person of another culture determined by that person or family. Care that is culturally safe prevents cultural imposition. Culturally safe care requires cultural competency and action to ensure that cultural histories, experiences, and traditions of patients, their families, and communities are valued and shape health care approaches and policies.[10]

Madeleine Leininger coined the term transcultural nursing in the 1950s. Transcultural nursing is a specialty that focuses on the study and analysis of cultures and subcultures. The goal of transcultural nursing is the discovery of culturally relevant facts that guide the nurse in providing culturally appropriate care.[9]

CULTURAL COMPETENCE

Cultural competence is the ability to understand, appreciate, and work with people from cultures other than your own. It involves an awareness and acceptance of cultural differences, self-awareness, knowledge of the patient's culture, and adaptation of skills to meet the patient's needs. The 4 components of cultural competence are (1) cultural awareness, (2) cultural knowledge, (3) cultural skill, and (4) cultural encounter (Table 2.3).

Providing culturally competent care may increase patient satisfaction, promote health equity, increase patient safety, and prevent misunderstandings between you and your patients. It also involves integrating cultural practices into Western medicine. For example, before some diagnostic procedures and interventions, it is typical to have patients remove personal objects they are wearing on the body. Ask patients whether they wear personal objects and the significance of their removal, since they may have cultural or spiritual significance. Know whether wearing these objects will affect patient safety, test results, or outcomes of the intervention.

When HCPs from different cultures work together as members of the health care team, opportunities for miscommunication and conflict can occur. We call this *cultural conflict*. The cultural origins of miscommunication and conflict in the workplace are often connected with cultural beliefs, values, and etiquette. Seeking clarification about misperceptions and misunderstandings is a communication strategy to foster effective teamwork among a multicultural health care team.

CULTURAL FACTORS AFFECTING HEALTH AND HEALTH CARE

Culture greatly affects health and health care. It affects perceptions of health, illness, and death; ideas about causes of disease; ways of promoting health; how one experiences and expresses illness and pain; where and when you seek help; and treatments we prefer. Potential factors are outlined in Table 2.4. It may be helpful to review general cultural characteristics associated with a cultural group when preparing to care a patient. However, remember that the patient may not identify with the assumed cultural group and the provider's own biases and stereotypes may affect the patient and result in more patient-provider barriers.

Folk Healers and Traditions

Many cultures have **folk healers**, who are also known as *traditional healers*. Most folk healers speak the person's native language and cost less than conventional HCPs. Among the many folk healers found worldwide, patients from regions in Mexico and Central and South America may choose to use a *curandero* (or *curandera*). Some cultures employ lay midwives (e.g., *parteras* for Latino women) in the care of pregnant women.

Folk medicine and traditions are culturally based forms of prevention and treatment. They traditionally rely on oral transmission of healing techniques from 1 generation to the next. The

TABLE 2.3 How to Develop Cultural Competence

Description	Role of Nurse
Cultural Awareness	
• Ability to understand patients' unique cultural needs	• Understand your own cultural background, values, and beliefs, especially as related to health and health care. • Examine your own cultural biases toward people whose cultures differ from your own culture.
Cultural Knowledge	
• Process of learning key aspects of a group's culture, especially as it relates to health and health care practices • Patients are best source of information about their culture	• Learn basic general information about predominant cultural groups in your geographic area. Cultural guides are a good resource. • Assess patients for presence or absence of cultural traits based on an understanding of generalizations about a cultural group. • Do not make assumptions based on cultural background because the degree of acculturation varies among persons. • Read research studies that describe cultural differences. • Read ethnic newspaper articles and books. • View documentaries about cultural groups.
Cultural Skill	
• Ability to collect relevant cultural data • Performance of a cultural assessment	• Be alert for unexpected responses with patients, especially as related to cultural issues. • Become aware of cultural differences in predominant ethnic groups. • Develop assessment skills to do a competent cultural assessment for any patient (see Table 2.7). • Learn assessment skills for different cultural groups, including cultural beliefs and practices.
Cultural Encounter	
• Direct cross-cultural interactions between people from culturally diverse backgrounds • Extended contact with a cultural group to enhance understanding of its values and beliefs	• Create opportunities to interact with predominant cultural groups. • Attend cultural events, such as religious ceremonies, significant life passage rituals, social events, and demonstrations of cultural practices. • Visit markets and restaurants in ethnic neighborhoods. • Explore ethnic neighborhoods, listen to different types of ethnic music, and learn games of various ethnic groups. • Visit or volunteer at health fairs in local ethnic neighborhoods. • Learn about prominent cultural beliefs and practices and include this knowledge when planning nursing care.

patient may not use the term *folk medicine* but thinks of these as cultural home remedies or treatment practices. A patient can be practicing folk medicine at home without using a folk healer. It is important to assess whether the patient is practicing traditional or folk healing. Some herbal remedies could pose potential interactions with medications.

Some traditions that are practiced as a rite of passage in some cultures are considered harmful in the dominant culture in the United States. For example, female genital cutting is a tradition that is illegal in most countries yet still practiced in many countries in Africa and the Middle East. It results in physical and emotional trauma and may affect childbirth. Nurses can advocate for immigrant women who went through this trauma and to prevent return of young girls to their country of origin for the procedure.

Spirituality and Religion

Spirituality refers to a person's effort to find purpose and meaning in life. It is influenced by a person's unique life experiences and reflects one's personal understanding of life's mysteries. Spirituality relates to the soul or spirit more than to the body. It may provide hope and strength for a person during an illness. *Religion* is a more formal and organized system of beliefs, including belief in or worship of God or gods. Religious beliefs include the cause, nature, and purpose of the universe and involve prayer and rituals. Religion is based on beliefs about life, death, good, and evil.

Spirituality and religion are aspects of culture that may affect a person's beliefs about health, illness, and end-of-life care (Table 2.5). They may also play a role in nutrition and decisions related to health, wellness, and how to respond to or treat an illness. You can use several interventions to meet a patient's religious and spiritual needs. These include prayer, scripture reading, listening, and referral to a chaplain, rabbi, or religious leader.

Many patients find that rituals help them during times of illness. Rituals help a person make sense of life experiences. They may take the form of prayer, meditation, or other rituals that the patient may create. Include spiritual questions in your patient assessment and plan care accordingly. Table 10.2 has a spiritual assessment guide you can use with patients.

Cross-Cultural Communication

Communication refers to an organized, patterned system of behavior that may be verbal or nonverbal (Fig. 2.4). *Verbal communication* includes not only one's language or dialect but also voice tone, volume, timing, and ability to share thoughts and feelings. More than 60 million people in the United States speak a language other than English in their home. Spanish is the most common. Hispanic people who do not speak English at home are less likely to receive a variety of health care services even if they are comfortable speaking English.

Nonverbal communication may take the form of writing, gestures, body movements, posture, facial expressions, and

TABLE 2.4 Cultural Factors Affecting Health and Health Care

Beliefs and Practices
- Care provided in established health care programs may not be perceived as culturally relevant.
- Religious reasons, beliefs, or practices may affect a person's decision to seek or not seek health care.
- Patients may delay seeking health care because of fear or dependence on folk medicine and herbal remedies.
- Patients may stop treatment or visits for health care because the symptoms are no longer present, and they think that further care is not needed.
- Some patients associate hospitals and extended care facilities with death.
- The patient may have had a previous negative experience with culturally incompetent HCPs or discriminatory practices.
- Some people mistrust the majority population and institutions dominated by them.
- Some patients may feel apprehensive about unfamiliar diagnostic procedures and treatment options.

Communication and Language
- Patients may not speak English and may not be able to communicate with the HCP.
- It may be hard to communicate, even with interpreters.

Economic Factors
- Patients may not get health care because they cannot pay for it or because of the costs of travel for health care.
- Refugee or undocumented immigrant status may deter some patients from using the health care system.
- Immigrant women who are heads of households or single mothers may not seek health care for themselves because of childcare costs.
- Patients may lack health insurance.

Health Care System
- Patients may not make or keep appointments because of the time lag between the onset of an illness and an available appointment.
- Hours of operation of health care facilities may not accommodate patients' need to work or use public transportation.
- Requirements to access some types of care may discourage some patients from taking the steps to qualify for health care or health care payment assistance.
- Some patients have a general distrust of HCPs and health care systems.
- Lack of ethnic-specific health care programs may deter some people from seeking health care.
- Transportation may be a problem for patients who must travel long distances for health care.
- Adequate interpreter services may be unavailable.
- Patients may not have a primary HCP. They may use emergency departments or urgent care centers for health care.
- Shortages of HCPs from specific ethnic groups may deter some people from seeking health care.
- Patients may lack knowledge about the availability of existing health care resources.
- Agency policies may not be culturally competent (e.g., hospital policy may limit the number of visitors, which is problematic for cultures that value having many family members present).

Time Orientation
- For some cultures, it is more important to attend to a social role than to arrive on time for an appointment with an HCP.
- Some cultures are future oriented; others are past or present oriented.

personal dress in some cultures. It includes eye contact, use of touch, body language, style of greeting, and spatial distancing. Eye contact varies greatly among cultural groups. Other variables to consider include the role of gender, age, acculturation, and status. For example, Muslim-Arab women exhibit modesty when avoiding eye contact with men other than their husbands and when in public situations.

Silence has many meanings. It is important to understand the meaning of silence for different cultural groups. Some people are comfortable with silence. Others become uncomfortable and may speak to decrease the amount of silent time. It is important to clarify what silence means in an interaction with a patient. Patients sometimes nod their head or say "yes" as if agreeing with you or to show they understand. Actually, they may be doing this because it is a culturally acceptable manner of showing respect, not because they understand or agree.

Many Native Americans are comfortable with silence and interpret silence as essential for thinking and carefully considering a response. In these interactions, silence shows respect for the other person and shows the importance of the remarks. In traditional Asian cultures, the speaker may stop talking and leave a period of silence for the listener to think about what was said before continuing. Silence may show respect for the speaker's privacy. In some cultures (e.g., French, Spanish, Russian) the person may interpret silence as meaning agreement. Asians may use silence to show respect for elders.

Racism and microaggression affect communication. **Racism** is a system that categorizes and ranks people based on race, culture, color, and ethnicity. The dominant group uses power to allocate resources in a way that unfairly disadvantages those who are inferior.[11] Structural or institutional racism are the processes of racism within institutions that are evident through laws, policies, and practices that provide advantages to certain racial groups over another.[11] These practices maybe overtly evident but due to antidiscriminatory laws are more likely covert in nature.

Microaggression is social exchanges in which a person says or does something that can either intentionally or unintentionally belittle or alienate a person, especially someone of a different racial/ethnic group. It is important that we seek to understand racism and microaggression through education, self-awareness, and open dialogue with peers.[12]

Family Roles and Relationships

Family roles differ from one culture to another (Fig. 2.5). It is important for you to determine who should be involved in communication and decision making related to health care. Some cultural groups emphasize interdependence rather than independence. In the United States, many in the mainstream culture have strong beliefs related to autonomy. We expect a patient to sign consent forms when receiving health care. In some cultural groups, the patient may expect a family member to make health care decisions. When you encounter a patient who values interdependence over independence, the health care system may have difficulty with how the patient makes decisions. We may have to delay treatment while the patient waits for family members to arrive before giving consent for a procedure

TABLE 2.5 Health-Related Beliefs and Practices of Selected Religious Groups

Amish
- Prohibit drinking alcohol
- Prohibit abortion, artificial insemination, and stem cell use
- Seldom buy commercial health insurance
- Prohibit drugs unless prescribed by HCPs

Buddhism
- Prohibit drinking alcohol and using illicit drugs
- Practice moderation in diet and avoidance of extremes
- Central tenets are maintaining right views, intentions, speech, actions, livelihood, effort, mindfulness, and concentration

Catholicism
- Fast and abstain from meat and meat products on Ash Wednesday and the Fridays of Lent
- Prohibit artificial contraception and direct abortion
- Indirect abortion (e.g., treatment of uterine cancer in a pregnant woman) may be morally justified
- Sacrament of the Sick includes anointing of sick with oil, blessing by a priest, and communion (unleavened wafer made of flour and water)

Church of Jesus Christ of Latter-Day Saints (Mormons)
- Strict diet code called Word of Wisdom prohibits all alcohol, hot drinks (non-herbal teas and coffee), tobacco, and recreational drugs
- Fast for a 24-h period each month on "Fast Sunday"
- During hospitalization or serious illness, an elder anoints the ill person with oil while a second elder seals the anointing with a prayer and blessing (laying on of hands)
- Prohibit abortion except when the mother's life is in danger

Hinduism
- Prohibit eating meat because it involves harming a living creature
- Cremation is the usual form of body disposal, but fetuses or newborns are sometimes buried

Islam
- Fasting during daytime hours occurs during a month-long period called Ramadan
- Perform a ritual cleansing with water before eating and before prayer
- Prohibit eating pork or taking medicines with pork derivatives
- Prohibit drinking alcohol
- Artificial insemination is permissible only if from the husband to his own wife

Jehovah's Witness
- Prohibit transfusions of blood in any form or agents in which blood is an ingredient
- Blood volume expanders are acceptable if they are not derivatives of blood
- Prohibit transplants that involve bodily mutilation
- Prohibit artificial insemination and therapeutic and on-demand abortions

Judaism
- Prohibit eating pork, shellfish, or predatory fowl or mixing milk dishes and meat dishes when preparing foods
- Certain foods and drinks are designated as kosher, which means "proper." All animals must be ritually slaughtered
- On the 8th day after birth, boys are circumcised in a ritual called Brit Milah. Girls are given a dedication ceremony involving prayers and blessings
- Prohibit abortion except when the mother's life is in danger
- Organized support system for the sick includes a visit from the rabbi.
  The rabbi may pray with the sick person alone or in a minyan, a group of 10 adults older than age 13
- If an autopsy is done, all body parts must be returned for burial

Seventh Day Adventism
- Encourage a vegetarian diet
- Nonvegetarian members do not eat foods derived from any animal having a cloven hoof that chews its cud (e.g., pigs, goats)
- Prohibit eating shellfish; eating fish with fins and scales is acceptable
- Prohibit drinking alcohol
- Healthy church members practice voluntary fasting

Source: Andrews MM, Boyle JS: *Transcultural concepts in nursing care,* ed 7, Philadelphia, 2016, Lippincott Williams & Wilkins.

or treatment. In other instances, the patient may make a decision that is best for the family despite adverse outcomes for the patient. Being aware of such values will better prepare you to advocate for the patient.

Some cultural differences relate to expectations of family members in providing care. In some cultures, family members expect to provide care for the patient even in the hospital. The patient may expect that the family, along with the HCPs, will provide all

Fig. 2.4 Coworkers from different cultures communicate with verbal and nonverbal cues. (© BananaStock/Thinkstock.)

Fig. 2.5 Family roles and relationships differ from among cultures. (© Jupiterimages/Photos.com/Thinkstock.)

care. This view is the opposite of the predominant Western expectation that the patient will assume self-care as quickly as possible.

Ask about culturally relevant gender relationships. For example, in some cultures, it is not appropriate for a man to be alone with a woman other than his wife. Nor is it appropriate for a woman other than a man's wife to provide physical care for him. The clinical implication of this cultural belief is that nurses cannot provide direct physical care for patients of the opposite gender. In some instances, patients may receive procedures or treatments only from providers of the opposite gender if a third party is present.

Personal Space

Personal space zones are the variable and subjective distance at which 1 person feels comfortable talking to another. A representative example of personal space zones for European Americans is shown in Fig. 2.6. Personal space distances vary from culture to culture, as well as within a culture. As a nurse, you often interact with patients in the intimate or personal distance, which may be uncomfortable for the patient.

Cultural groups have wide variations in their perception of appropriate distances. An American nurse of European descent may be comfortable with a certain distance. A person from a Hispanic or Middle Eastern background may believe that the distance is too far and will move closer. This may make you feel uncomfortable. If you then move away to a more comfortable distance, this may cause the other person to think that you are unfriendly, or the person may be offended.

Touch

Physical contact with patients conveys various meanings depending on the culture. Performing a physical assessment requires touching a patient. Many people of Asian and Hispanic heritage believe that touching a person's head is a sign of disrespect because the head is the source of one's strength and/or soul. Many people in the world believe in the evil eye, or *mal ojo.* In this culture-bound syndrome, the illness—usually in a child or a woman—resulted from excessive admiration by another person. In some cultures, the way to ward off the evil eye is to touch the area of admiration. For example, if the person admires the hair, the top of the head may be touched. It is important for you to ask permission before touching anyone, particularly if it is necessary to touch the person's head.

Nutrition

An important part of cultural practices is food, including both the foods that one eats and rituals and practices associated with food. Muslims fast during the daytime during the Islamic month of Ramadan. Such practices may affect when and how patients take medications. Patients may need to make major changes in their diets because of health problems. A person may use food to cope with life changes such as homesickness. Specific foods may be considered essential to good health during pregnancy or other life stages. The HCP should consider food-related cultural beliefs, practices, and habits when discussing nutrition with patients and planning their diets.

When people immigrate to an area that is very different from their country of origin, they may encounter unfamiliar foods, food-storage systems, and food-buying habits. They may come from countries that have limited food supplies because of poverty, wars, and poor sanitation. They may arrive with conditions such as malnutrition, diarrhea, and dental caries. Other problems may develop after the person arrives in the new country. For example, with obesity, second-generation immigrants have a greater chance of becoming overweight than their first-generation counterparts.[9] The increase in weight is related to the degree of acculturation the immigrant experiences.

Immigrants and Immigration

Several conditions drive migration, such as overcrowding, natural disasters, geopolitical conflict, persecution, and economic forces. Because of these migrations, a rich diversity of cultures exists in many communities and countries (Fig. 2.7).

Recent immigrants may be at risk for physical and mental health problems for many reasons. Conditions in their

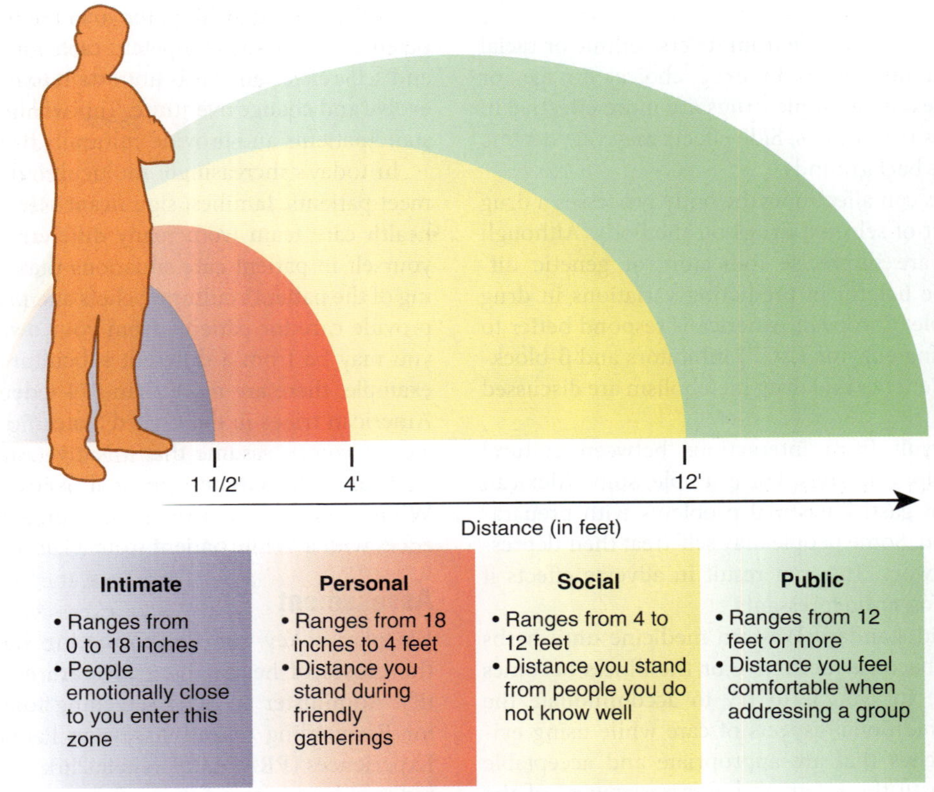

Fig. 2.6 Personal space zones.

Fig. 2.7 Recently arrived immigrants join a neighbor for a barbecue, a common American tradition. (© Jack Hollingsworth/Photodisc/Thinkstock.)

countries of origin (e.g., malnutrition, poor sanitation, civil war) may have resulted in chronic health problems. In addition, recent immigrants are at increased risk for health problems after arriving in a new area. Relocation is associated with many losses and can cause economic hardship, physical stress, and mental distress.

As new immigrants go through the acculturation process, many have cultural stress as they adjust to their new environment, especially if they have left relatives behind or are unable to return to their home country. Older immigrants are especially affected by changes in role and social position. This may result in depression. Immigrants who have survived wars and violence may have posttraumatic stress disorder. Immigrants may face barriers to social acceptance, such as prejudice or discrimination. There may be a lack of ethnic and cultural resources. For some, it may mean loss of the social status that they had in their country of origin.

Another potential problem is tuberculosis (TB). Persons born outside the United States have a TB rate 15.5 times higher than those born inside the country.[13] Those who have recently immigrated from areas that have a high endemic rate of TB are more likely to have TB. Foreign-born Hispanics and Asians combined account for 48% of the nation's TB cases. The top 5 countries of the origin of foreign-born people with TB are Mexico, Philippines, Vietnam, India, and China. Early identification and treatment is important for reducing the burden of TB.[14]

During the past 45 years, the migration pattern of North America has shifted. Once, most immigrants came from Europe. Now, most come from Asia, Latin America, and Africa. An increased number of first- and second-generation immigrants enter the United States after visiting friends and relatives. They have a higher risk for malaria, typhoid fever, cholera, and hepatitis A than people born in the United States. Many immigrants lack health insurance and may primarily obtain their health care in emergency departments and urgent care clinics. Therefore nurses in all settings need to be aware of refugee health screening, treatment recommendations, and resources for access to health care and social services.

Drugs

Genetic differences among people from diverse ethnic or racial groups may explain differences in drug choice, dosage, or administration. For example, some drugs are more effective in certain ethnic groups than others. Side effects may vary among persons from diverse backgrounds.

Genetic variations can affect how the body processes a drug and the overall effect of selected drugs on the body. Although race and ethnicity are imprecise indicators of genetic differences, they can be helpful in predicting variations in drug response. For example, European Americans respond better to angiotensin-converting enzyme (ACE) inhibitors and β-blockers than do Blacks. Genetics and drug metabolism are discussed in Chapter 13.

Problems can result from interactions between cultural remedies and prescription drugs. For example, some Mexican Americans may treat gastrointestinal problems with preparations that contain lead. Some people may self-treat their depression with St. John's wort. This can result in adverse effects if taken with prescription antidepressants.

Patients may avoid standard Western medicine until herbs and other remedies become ineffective or the illness becomes acute. The challenge for you is to try to accommodate the patient's desire for traditional aspects of care while using evidence-based approaches that are appropriate and acceptable to the patient. Evaluate the safety and appropriateness of the patient's traditional cultural healing therapies.

Develop a collaborative, trusting relationship with patients and encourage them to discuss their traditional approaches to healing. Seek out information on potential drug and herbal product interaction from the pharmacist. Honor the patient's choices if safe and effective. This will enhance collaboration and may have a positive impact on health outcomes.

Psychologic Factors

Symptoms are interpreted through a person's cultural norms and may vary from the recognized interpretations of Western medicine. All symptoms have meaning. The meanings may vary from one culture to another. For example, cultural views can affect the degree of depression after a cardiac diagnosis. It is important to ask patients what their illness means to them, what they believe is the cause, and what they think is the best treatment.

NURSING MANAGEMENT: SOCIAL DETERMINANTS OF HEALTH AND CULTURALLY COMPETENT CARE

Self-Assessment

The first step in promoting health equity and providing culturally competent care is for you to assess your own cultural background, values, and beliefs, especially those that are related to health and health care. Many tools are available to help you with this process. One is available through the Georgetown University National Center for Cultural Competence (http://nccc.georgetown.edu).

Table 2.3 suggests ways for you to improve your cultural competence. Culturally competent care requires continual learning and self-reflection.[15] It is important to understand that cultures evolve and change over time. This will help you to better understand patients and provide culturally competent care.

In today's increasingly multicultural environment, you will meet patients, families, significant others, and members of the health care team from many different cultures. You will find yourself in patient care situations that require an understanding of the patient's cultural beliefs and practices. Even when you provide care for patients from your own cultural background, you may be from a different subculture than the patient. For example, there are more than 574 federally recognized Native American tribes in the United States.[16] It would be inappropriate for you to assume that a Native American nurse can give culturally appropriate care to all Native American patients. A White nurse from an urban upbringing may find cultural differences with a White patient from a rural community.

Assessment

We play a key role in promoting health equity. However, the causes of health disparities are not always easy to identify. Administer an SDH screening tool, such as the Protocol for Responding to and Assessing Patient's Assets, Risks, and Experiences (PRAPARE) (Table 2.6). Assess patients for risk of reduced health care services because of limited access, inadequate resources, age, or low health literacy. Review the patient's eligibility for various resources, such as insurance, food assistance, and unemployment,

Include a cultural assessment.[15] Table 2.7 lists important components of the assessment. Determine the patient's (1) health beliefs and health care practices and (2) perspective of the meaning, cause, and preferred treatment of illness. Ask questions that you are comfortable with based on your own culture.

How can you be aware of the differences among ethnic groups? Using guides for cultural assessment will facilitate the nursing process when working with patients, families, or other groups who are from different cultures. Although guides can help in this process, you need to be careful not to stereotype or assume that common cultural characteristics pertain to each patient. Use guides to explore the degree to which patients share commonalities with the traits attributed to their cultural group. You need to know about traditional characteristics of cultural groups while recognizing that culture is constantly evolving and unique for each person.

Implementation

Although the issues associated with health disparities can seem overwhelming, several strategies are available to reduce and eliminate health disparities. Table 2.8 presents nursing interventions to promote health equity.

Advocacy

Strategies to increase health care access and insurance are critical for making sure more people get important health care services. The solutions to reduce health disparities often rest with

TABLE 2.6 Protocol for Responding to and Assessing Patient's Assets, Risks, and Experiences (PRAPARE)

Category	Question
Personal characteristics	Are you Hispanic or Latino? Which race(s) are you? At any point in the past 2 years, has seasonal or migrant farm work been your or your family's main source of income? Have you been discharged from the armed forces of the United States? What language are you most comfortable speaking?
Family and home	How many family members, including yourself, do you currently live with? What is your housing situation today? Are you worried about losing your housing? What address do you live at?
Money and resources	What is the highest level of school that you have finished? What is your current work situation? What is your main insurance? During the past year, what was the total combined income for you and your family members you live with? In the past year, have you or any family members you live with been unable to get food, clothing, utilities, child care, phone, medicine, or health care when it was really needed? Has lack of transportation kept you from medical appointments, meetings, work, or from getting things needed for daily living?
Social and emotional health	How often do you see or talk to people that you care about and feel close to? How stressed are you?

Adapted from the National PRAPARE® Social Determinants of Health Protocol developed by the National Association of Community Health Centers, Association of Asian Pacific Community Health Organizations, and Oregon Primary Care Organization and their development partners. www.nachc.org/prapare. Retrieved from http://www.nachc.org/wp-content/uploads/2019/04/NACHC_PRAPARE_Full-Toolkit.pdf.

TABLE 2.7 Cultural Assessment

A cultural assessment should include these areas:

- Communication
  - Languages spoken; skill in speaking, reading, and writing in English
  - Eye contact, interpersonal space
  - Preferred way to communicate with patient and family
- Cultural group person identifies with
- Cultural restrictions and taboos
- Decision making within the family
- Diet practices
- Organizations providing cultural support
- Personal beliefs about health and illness
  - Meaning and beliefs about cause of illness
  - Practices or rituals used to improve health
  - Use of alternative medicine
  - Acceptability of direct care by gender
- Presence of social network
- Religious affiliation, practices, and rituals
- Socioeconomic considerations
- Spiritual beliefs
- Where born; if in other country, length of time in United States and circumstances

TABLE 2.8 NURSING MANAGEMENT

Interventions to Promote Health Equity

- Treat all patients equally.
- Be aware of your own biases or prejudices and work toward eliminating them.
- Learn about services and programs that focus on specific cultural/ethnic groups.
- Inform patients about health care services available for their specific cultural/ethnic group.
- Make sure you follow the same standards of care for all patients regardless of culture or ethnicity.
- Recognize health care practices and cultural practices that are important to cultural and ethnic identity.
- Take part in research focused on understanding and improving care to culturally and ethnically diverse populations.
- Identify stereotypic attitudes toward a culture/ethnic group that may interfere with getting appropriate health care.
- Support patients who are fearful about traveling outside the accepted neighborhood for health care services.
- Advocate for patients of specific cultural/ethnic groups to receive health care services that pay special attention to English-language limitations and cultural health practices.
- Learn advocacy and interpersonal strategies from leaders of specific cultural/ethnic groups. For example, some cultures emphasize themes such as "do it for your loved ones."
- Ensure availability of culturally appropriate patient educational resources.

the policymakers. Economic issues often determine health care delivery. Access and public policy decisions determine who is eligible for federal and state health insurance coverage. You play an important role in improving health care access.

You, along with the social worker, can help by identifying key resources in the community, including transportation services, reduced-fee screening programs, and appropriate federal and state offices for Medicaid and Medicare. You can be an advocate in your health care setting by helping to create a community advisory group. Such a group can be helpful when setting up health programs within a community. This can increase the distribution of culturally sensitive information. Another powerful strategy is to increase the number of underrepresented populations in the health care professions (Fig. 2.8).

Standardized Guidelines

The use of standardized, evidence-based care guidelines can reduce disparities in diagnosis and treatments. For example, the management of hypertension should be based on guidelines and the patient's blood pressure, symptoms, history, and laboratory values rather than other characteristics such as gender, age, or culture. Following the guidelines reduces racial or cultural differences in outcomes. In addition, recommendations related to cultural competency will guide you in your learning and practice.

The National Standards for Culturally and Linguistically Appropriate Services in Health Care (CLAS standards) are guidelines that improve the quality of health care.[17] The CLAS standards provide practical guidance for care of people with limited English proficiency and of diverse cultural backgrounds.

Fig. 2.8 A Navajo nurse teaching a Navajo patient. (From Giger JN: *Transcultural nursing,* ed 7, St Louis, 2016, Mosby.)

Communication

Improving interpersonal skills is an important first step in providing culturally competent care. To show respect for the patient, consider the patient's usual communication style. For instance, conduct a health history in an unhurried manner and in a way that is appropriate for the culture. In some cultures, it is best to start with general rather than direct questions. For some cultures, it is most effective to engage in "small talk," with the discussion including answers that may seem to be unrelated to the questions. If you appear to be "too busy," communication may be impaired.

When meeting patients or family members, introduce yourself and indicate how you would like them to address you—whether they should use first names; Mr., Ms., or Mrs.; or a title, such as Doctor or Pastor. Ask the patient how they prefer to be addressed. This shows respect and will help you begin the relationship in a culturally appropriate manner.

If you need to gather personal information, it is important to understand the most effective approach to use. For instance, when talking with people from some cultural groups, it is imperative that you take time to establish trust and listen to the patient's responses to questions. There may be long silences as the person thinks about the question, showing respect by giving the question consideration before answering. Take time to listen and help establish trust.

Consider how the patient's age may affect their views and communication. For example, older adults with mental health concerns may struggle with shame, uncertainty, and lack of trust in the system.

Do not try to serve as an interpreter if your patient does not understand English, because this could lead to misunderstandings. Get the help of a person who is qualified to do medical interpretation when you cannot speak the patient's primary language (Table 2.9). Interpreters are available by phone anywhere in the United States through a fee-based service. Use them rather than a family member. Table 2.10 offers guidelines for communicating when no interpreter is available.

A dictionary that translates from both your language and the patient's language (e.g., Spanish-English/English-Spanish dictionary) is useful. Patients may find it helpful if you already have a prepared list of questions and potential answers in several languages. Many websites and applications can translate spoken words and documents from one language into another. However, be careful because some applications may not accurately reflect your intended question or statement. It is helpful to have resources for persons from cultural groups who often use your agency. This is especially beneficial when a qualified medical interpreter is not readily available, and you need to learn important phrases in another language.

TABLE 2.9 Using a Medical Interpreter

Choosing an Interpreter

- Use an agency interpreter if possible.
- Use a trained medical interpreter who knows how to interpret, has a health care background, understands patients' rights, and can help with advice about the cultural relevance or appropriateness of the health care plan and instructions.
- Use a family member only if necessary. Be aware of limitations if the family member does not understand medical terms, is younger or a different gender from the patient, or is not aware of the health care procedures or medical ethics.
- Interpreter should be able to do the following:
  - Interpret the patient's nonverbal as well as verbal communication.
  - Translate the message into understandable terms.
  - Act as a patient advocate to represent the patient's needs to the health care team.
  - Be culturally competent and understand how to give teaching instructions.

Strategies for Working With an Interpreter

- If possible, have the interpreter meet with the patient ahead of time to establish rapport before the interpreting begins.
- Speak slowly.
- Maintain eye contact with the patient.
- Talk to the patient, not the interpreter.
- Use simple language with as few medical terms as possible.
- Speak 1 or 2 sentences at a time to allow for easier interpretation.
- Avoid raising your voice during the interaction.
- Obtain feedback to be certain the patient understands.
- Plan to take twice as long to complete the interaction.

TABLE 2.10 Overcoming Language Barriers

1. Be polite and formal.
2. Pronounce name correctly. If unsure, ask about the correct pronunciation of the name. Use titles of respect, such as "Mr.," "Mrs.," "Ms.," or "Dr." Greet the person using the last or complete name.
3. Gesture to yourself and say your name.
4. Offer a handshake or nod. Smile.
5. Proceed in an unhurried manner. Pay attention to any effort by the patient or family to communicate.
6. Speak in a low, moderate voice and avoid excess hand gestures. Remember that there is a tendency to raise the volume and pitch of your voice when the listener appears not to understand. The listener may perceive that you are shouting or angry.
7. Use any words that you might know in the person's language. This shows that you are aware of and respect their culture.
8. Use simple words such as "pain" instead of "discomfort." Avoid medical jargon, idioms, and slang. Do not use contractions (e.g., don't, can't, won't). Use nouns repeatedly instead of pronouns. *Example:*
   Do not say: "He has been taking his medicine, hasn't he?"
   Do say: "Does Juan take medicine?"
9. Act out words and simple actions while you say them.
10. Give instructions in the right sequence. *Example:*
    Do not say: "Before you rinse the bottle, sterilize it."
    Do say: "First, wash the bottle. Second, rinse the bottle."
11. Discuss 1 topic at a time. Avoid using conjunctions. *Example:*
    Do not say: "Are you cold and in pain?"
    Do say: "Are you cold [while pantomiming]? Are you in pain?"
12. Validate whether the person understands by having them repeat instructions, demonstrate the procedure, or act out the meaning.
13. Write out several short sentences in English and determine the person's ability to read them.
14. Try a third language. Many Indochinese people speak French. Europeans often know 2 or more languages. Try Latin words or phrases. Use English words that have Latin roots (e.g., use precipitation instead of rain).
15. Ask the person's family and friends who could serve as an interpreter.
16. Use websites that translate words from 1 language to another. Some have audio to help you know how to say the word correctly.
17. Obtain phrase books from a library or bookstore or use flash cards. Many websites and applications can translate spoken words and documents.

Source: Jarvis C: *Physical examination and health assessment,* ed 8, Philadelphia, 2019, Saunders.

Case Study

Health Disparities

(© Luevanos/iStock/Thinkstock.)

Patient Profile

M.S. is an 81-year-old woman who came to the United States from India 4 years ago with her son and daughter-in-law and their 4 children. She has several health problems, including coronary artery disease, hypertension, osteoarthritis in her right hip, and diabetes. Her daughter-in-law is the primary caregiver and often brings her to the urban community health clinic for a variety of health-related problems. Recently, M.S. has been having memory problems.

The entire family comes to the health clinic with M.S. Because English is a second language (Hindustani is their first language) for all the adult family members, the staff relies on the oldest granddaughter to interpret.

At this clinic visit, M.S. is presenting with shortness of breath. Through her granddaughter's interpretation, she tells the nurse that she is having trouble walking up the stairs in the apartment building. The nurse does the history and assessment, checks her blood glucose (which is within normal limits), and tells her that she should get more exercise. Given M.S.'s memory problems and limited English, the nurse does not complete a 24-hour diet recall or teach her or the family about diabetes management. M.S. is scheduled for an appointment with the cardiologist for an evaluation of her hypertension and heart disease. Two weeks later, when she sees the cardiologist, her shortness of breath is much worse, and she is having chest pain. She is hospitalized immediately.

Meanwhile, the clinic supervisor is completing a chart audit for the clinic's quality review program. She is reviewing M.S.'s chart and notices that, although she has been a patient in the clinic for 3 years, she has never received instructions on blood glucose monitoring or general diabetes management. The clinic has a nurse diabetes educator who teaches individual patients and groups of patients with diabetes. The clinic manager reviews these findings with the nurse and asks why she has not recommended that M.S. see the diabetes educator. The nurse states that with M.S.'s memory problems and the language barrier, she assumed that M.S. and her family would not benefit from the consultation.

Discussion Questions

1. ***Recognize***: What type of health disparity has M.S. experienced?
2. ***Analyze***: What factors led to her not receiving the standard of care?
3. ***Analyze***: What other assessment should have been done at the initial visit?
4. ***Act***: What strategies may have worked to enhance patient education?
5. ***Act***: How would you consider M.S.'s religious and spiritual needs?
6. ***Evaluate***: If you were the clinic manager, how would you recommend that the nurse improve her practice?

Answers available at http://evolve.elsevier.com/Lewis/medsurg.

BRIDGE TO NCLEX EXAMINATION

The number of the question corresponds to the same-numbered outcome at the beginning of the chapter.

1. Which factors are part of the social determinants of a patient's health? *(select all that apply.)*
   a. Genetics
   b. Economic status
   c. Family history of disease
   d. Social and physical environment
   e. Type and quality of health care received
2. In identifying patients at the *greatest* risk for health disparities, the nurse would note that
   a. patients who live in urban areas have readily available access to health care services.
   b. cultural differences may exist in patients' ability to communicate with the health care provider.
   c. a patient receiving care from a health care provider of a different culture will have decreased quality of care.
   d. persons who immigrate to the United States are less likely to have health problems once they establish residency.

3. Forcing one's own cultural beliefs and practices on another person is an example of
   a. stereotyping.
   b. ethnocentrism.
   c. cultural relativity.
   d. cultural imposition.
4. Which statement *most* accurately describes cultural factors that may affect health?
   a. Diabetes and cancer rates differ by cultural/ethnic groups.
   b. There are limited ethnic variations in physiologic responses to drugs.
   c. Most patients find that religious rituals help them during times of illness.
   d. Silence after providing patient education means the patient understands the instructions.
5. As part of the nursing process, cultural assessment is *best* accomplished by
   a. judging the patient's cultural values based on observations.
   b. using a cultural assessment guide as part of the nursing process.
   c. seeking guidance from a nurse from the patient's cultural background.
   d. relying on the nurse's previous experience with patients from that cultural group.
6. An important mechanism in promoting health equity is to
   a. discourage use of evidence-based practice guidelines.
   b. insist that patients adhere to established clinical guidelines.
   c. teach patients to use the Internet to find resources related to their health.
   d. engage in active listening and establish relationships with patients and families.
7. What is the first step in developing cultural competence?
   a. Create opportunities to interact with a variety of cultural groups.
   b. Examine your own cultural background, values, and beliefs about health and health care.
   c. Learn about a multitude of folk medicines and herbal substances that different cultures use for self-care.
   d. Learn assessment skills for different cultural groups, including cultural beliefs and practices and physical assessments.
8. When communicating with a patient who speaks a language that the nurse does not understand, it is important to *first* attempt to
   a. have a family member interpret.
   b. use a trained medical interpreter.
   c. use specific medical terminology so there will be no mistakes.
   d. focus on the translation rather than nonverbal communication.

1. b, d, e; 2. b; 3. d; 4. a; 5. b; 6. d; 7. b; 8. b.

For rationales to these answers and even more NCLEX review questions, visit http://evolve.elsevier.com/Lewis/medsurg.

EVOLVE WEBSITE/RESOURCES LIST

http://evolve.elsevier.com/Lewis/medsurg
Review Questions (Online Only)
Key Points
Answer Keys for Questions
- Rationales for Bridge to NCLEX Examination Questions
- Answer Guidelines for Case Study

Conceptual Care Map Creator
Audio Glossary
Content Updates

REFERENCES

1. Office of Disease Prevention and Health Promotion: Social determinants of health. *Healthy People 2030.* Retrieved from https://health.gov/healthypeople/objectives-and-data/social-determinants-health.
*2. Centers for Disease Control and Prevention: Prevalence of disability and disability types by urban-rural county classification. Retrieved from https://www.cdc.gov/ncbddd/disabilityandhealth/features/disability-prevalence-rural-urban.html.
*3. RHI Hub: Violence and abuse in rural America. Retrieved from https://www.ruralhealthinfo.org/topics/violence-and-abuse.
*4. Nurse M: Nursing statistics, 2020. Retrieved from http://minoritynurse.com/nursing-statistics/.
5. Kaiser Family Foundation: Disparities in health and health care, *Disparities Policy,* 2020. Retrieved from https://www.kff.org/disparities-policy/issue-brief/disparities-in-health-and-health-care-five-key-questions-and-answers/.
6. U.S. Census Bureau: Quick facts. Retrieved from https://www.census.gov/quickfacts/fact/table/US/PST045219.
*7. Bromfield SG, Sullivan S, Saelee R, et al.: Race and gender differences in the association between experiences of everyday discrimination and arterial stiffness among patients with coronary heart disease, *Ann of Beh Med* 54:761, 2020.
*8. McGrath RP, Al Snih S, Markides KS, et al.: The burden of health conditions across race and ethnicity for aging Americans: disability-adjusted life years, *Medicine* 98:e17964, 2019.
9. Giger JN, Haddad L: *Transcultural nursing: assessment and intervention*, ed 8, Elsevier Health Sciences, 2020.
*10. Curtis E, Jones R, Tipene-Leach D, et al.: Why cultural safety rather than cultural competency is required to achieve health equity: a literature review and recommended definition, *International Jrnl Equity Hlth* 174, 2019.
11. Williams DR, Lawrence JA, Davis BA: Racism and health: evidence and needed research, *Ann Rev Pub Hlth* 40:105, 2019.
*12. Ackerman-Barger K, Boatright D, Gonzalez-Colaso R, et al.: Seeking inclusion excellence: understanding racial microaggressions as experienced by underrepresented medical and nursing students, *Jrnl of Assoc of Am Med Col* 95:758, 2020.
*13. Schwartz NG, Price S, Pratt RH, et al.: Tuberculosis—United States, 2019, *MMWR (Morb Mortal Wkly Rep)* 68:286, 2020.
14. CDC: Refugee health guidelines, 2020. Retrieved from https://www.cdc.gov/immigrantrefugeehealth/guidelines/refugee-guidelines.html.

15. AACN: Cultural competency in baccalaureate nursing education. Retrieved from https://www.aacnnursing.org/Portals/42/AcademicNursing/CurriculumGuidelines/Cultural-Competency-Bacc-Edu.pdf.
16. Saenz M: Federal and state recognized tribes, 2020. Retrieved from https://www.ncsl.org/research/state-tribal-institute/list-of-federal-and-state-recognized-tribes.aspx.
17. Office of Minority Health: Think cultural health, 2020. Retrieved from https://thinkculturalhealth.hhs.gov/.

*Evidence-based information for clinical practice.

3

Health History and Physical Examination

Courtney Reinisch

http://evolve.elsevier.com/Lewis/medsurg/

CONCEPTUAL FOCUS

Clinical Judgment
Collaboration
Communication

LEARNING OUTCOMES

1. Explain the purpose, components, and techniques of a patient's health history and physical examination.
2. Obtain a nursing history using a functional health pattern format.
3. Select appropriate techniques of inspection, palpation, percussion, and auscultation for the physical examination.
4. Distinguish among emergency, comprehensive, and focused assessments in terms of indications, purposes, and components.

KEY TERMS

auscultation
database
functional health patterns
inspection
nursing history
objective data
palpation
percussion
subjective data

During an assessment, you will obtain a patient's health history and perform a physical examination. This is part of the interprofessional team's patient evaluation. The interprofessional team, also known as an interdisciplinary or multidisciplinary team, is made up of health care professionals who provide care to a patient. The findings of your nursing assessment (1) contribute to a database that identifies the patient's current and past health status and (2) provide a baseline against which we evaluate future changes. The purpose of the nursing assessment is to enable you to make clinical judgments about your patient's health status.[1] Assessment is the first step of the nursing process. It is performed continually throughout the nursing process to evaluate nursing interventions and progress toward patient outcomes.

Assessment as a term is complex, with many meanings. In this text, *assessment* describes a hands-on data collection process. *Database* identifies a specific list of information (data) to collect.

DATA COLLECTION

The **database** is all the health information about a patient. It includes (1) nursing history and physical examination, (2) the medical history and physical examination, and (3) laboratory and diagnostic test results. A nurse and health care provider (HCP) perform a history and physical assessment using formats and data based on each discipline's focus.

Medical Focus

A *medical history* is used primarily by the HCP to determine risk for disease and diagnose medical conditions. The medical history is usually collected by a member of the health care team, such as a physician, advanced practice nurse (APN), resident, physician's assistant, or medical student. The HCP's physical examination and diagnostic tests aid in establishing medical diagnoses and implementing and monitoring the medical treatment plan. The information collected and reported by the HCP is used by nurses and other health care team members (e.g., pharmacist, physical therapist, dietitian, social worker) based on the focus of their care. For example, the abnormal results of a neurologic examination by an APN may help diagnose a stroke. You use the same results to identify fall risk in a patient. A physical therapist uses this information to plan therapy involving range-of-motion exercises.

TABLE 3.1 NURSING MANAGEMENT

Assessment and Data Collection

- On admission, complete a comprehensive admission assessment (see Table 3.5).
- Obtain patient's health history by interviewing patient and/or caregiver..
- Perform physical examination using inspection, palpation, percussion, and auscultation as appropriate.
- Record findings from the health history and physical examination in the patient's record.
- Organize patient data into functional health patterns (see Table 3.3).
- Develop and prioritize nursing problems for the patient.
- Throughout hospitalization, perform focused assessments based on patient's history or clinical manifestations (see Table 3.8).
- Refer patients to the appropriate community-based services.
- Supervise aspects of data collection by AP:
  - Vital signs, including oxygen saturation
  - Height and weight, oral intake, and output
  - Per agency policy, point-of-care testing, such as blood glucose

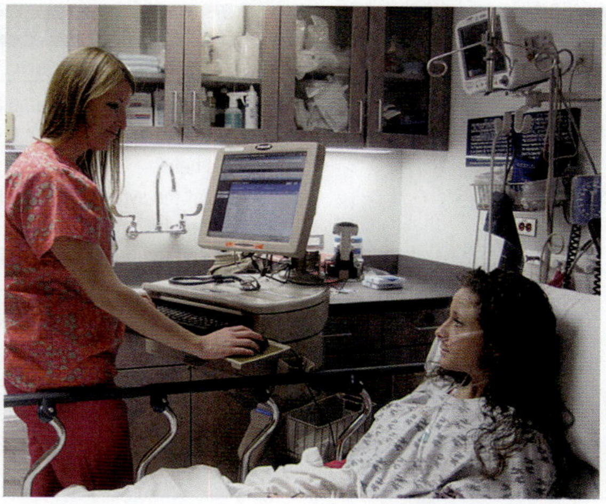

Fig. 3.1 Conducting a nursing focused interview. (Courtesy Linda Bucher, RN, PhD, CEN, CNE, Staff Nurse, Virtua Memorial Hospital, Mt. Holly, NJ.)

Nursing Focus

Nursing care is the diagnosis and treatment of human responses to actual or potential health problems or life processes. The information obtained from the **nursing history** and physical examination is used to determine the patient's strengths and responses to a health problem. For example, a patient with a diagnosis of diabetes may respond with anxiety or lack of knowledge about managing the condition. This patient may have the physical response of the abnormal fluid loss caused by hyperglycemia. These human responses to the condition of diabetes are diagnosed and treated by nurses. During the nursing history interview and physical examination, you will obtain and record the data to support decisions about nursing care (Table 3.1).

Types of Data

The database includes subjective and objective data. **Subjective data**, or *symptoms*, are collected by interviewing the patient and/or caregiver during the nursing history. This type of data includes information that can be described or verified only by the patient or caregiver. It is what the person tells you, either spontaneously or in response to a direct question.

Objective data, or *signs*, are data that we can observe or measure. You obtain objective data using inspection, palpation, percussion, and auscultation. Objective data are also obtained by diagnostic testing. Patients often provide subjective data while you are performing their assessment. You will observe objective signs while interviewing the patient. All the findings related to a specific problem, whether subjective or objective, are known as *clinical manifestations* of that problem.

Interview Considerations

The purpose of the patient interview is to obtain a health history (i.e., subjective data) about the patient's past and present health state (Fig. 3.1). Effective communication is used in the interview process. Creating a climate of trust and respect is critical to establishing a therapeutic relationship.[2] You need to communicate acceptance of the patient as a person by using an open, responsive, nonjudgmental approach. You communicate through spoken language and actions, including your manner of dress, gestures, and body language. Culture influences the words, gestures, and postures one uses and the information we share with others (see Chapter 2).

In addition to understanding the principles of effective communication, you will develop a personal style of relating to patients. One style of communication does not fit all. The wording of questions can increase the likelihood of obtaining the needed information. The ease of asking questions, particularly those related to sensitive areas such as sexual function, comes with training and experience.

The amount of time you need to complete a nursing history varies with the format used and your experience. The nursing history may be completed in 1 or several sessions, depending on the setting and patient. For example, an older adult patient with a low energy level may need a few brief interviews to allow time to give the needed information. You must judge the amount of information to collect on initial contact with the patient. In interviews with patients with chronic disease, patients in pain, and patients in emergency situations, ask only those questions that are pertinent to a specific problem. You can complete the health history interview at a more appropriate time.

Judge the reliability of the patient as a historian. An older adult may give a false impression about their mental status because of a prolonged response time or vision and hearing problems. The complexity and duration of health problems may make it hard for an older adult or a chronically ill younger patient to be an accurate historian.

It is important for you to determine the patient's priority concerns and expectations, since your priorities may be different from the patient's. For example, your priority may be to complete the health history, while the patient is interested only in relief from symptoms. Until the patient's priority need is met, you will probably be unsuccessful in obtaining complete and accurate data.

Symptom Investigation

At any time during the assessment, the patient may report a symptom such as pain, fatigue, or weakness. Because we do not

TABLE 3.2 Investigation of Patient-Reported Symptom

	Factor	Questions for Patient and Caregiver	Record
P	Precipitating and Palliative	Were there any events that came before the symptom? What makes it better? Worse? What have you done for the symptom? Did this help?	Influence of physical and emotional activities. Patient's attempts to alleviate or treat the symptom
Q	Quality	Tell me what the symptom feels like (e.g., aching, dull, pressure, burning, stabbing).	Patient's own words, such as "Like a pinch or stabbing feeling"
R	Radiation	Where do you feel the symptom? Does it move to other areas?	Region of body. Local or radiating, superficial or deep
S	Severity	On a scale of 0–10, with 0 meaning no pain and 10 being the worst pain you could imagine, what number would you give your symptom?	Pain rating number (e.g., 5/10)
T	Timing	When did the symptom start? Was it sudden or gradual? Any particular time of day, week, month, or year? Has the symptom changed over time? Has the symptom happened before? What are you doing when the symptom occurs?	Time of onset, duration, periodicity, and frequency. Course of symptoms. Where patient is and what patient is doing when the symptom occurs

observe symptoms patients experience, we need to ask further questions. Table 3.2 shows a mnemonic (PQRST) to help you remember the areas to explore when a symptom is reported. The information you receive may help determine the cause of the symptom. A common symptom that you will assess is pain (see Chapter 9). If a patient states he has "pain in his leg," you would assess and record the data using PQRST:

Patient has right midcalf pain that usually occurs at work when climbing stairs after lunch (P). Pain is alleviated by stopping and resting for 2 to 3 minutes. States he has been "eating a banana every day for extra potassium" but "it hasn't helped" (P). Describes pain as "stabbing" and non-radiating (Q, R). Pain is so severe (rating 9 on a 0 to 10 scale) that patient cannot continue activity (S). Onset is abrupt, occurring once or twice daily. It last occurred yesterday while cutting the lawn (T).

Data Organization

You must systematically obtain and organize assessment data so you can readily analyze and make judgments about the patient's health status and any health problems. Some assessment forms are organized by body system. Although helpful, these types of forms may be incomplete because they may omit areas, such as health promotion behaviors, sleep, coping, and values.

Functional health patterns, developed by Gordon, provide the framework used throughout this book for obtaining a nursing history.[3] This format includes an initial collection of important health information followed by assessment of 11 areas of health status or function (Table 3.3). Data organized in this format allow for the identification of areas of wellness (or positive function) and health problems.[2]

Culturally Competent Care: Assessment

The process of obtaining a health history and performing a physical examination is an intimate experience for you and the patient. Culture influences patterns of communication and the information one shares with others. During the interview and physical examination, be sensitive to issues of eye contact, space, modesty, and touching, as discussed in Chapter 2. Knowing the cultural norms related to male-female relationships is especially important during the physical assessment. To avoid violating any culturally based practices, ask the patient about cultural values. Determine if the patient would like to have someone present or someone of the same gender to perform the history and physical examination.[1]

NURSING HISTORY: SUBJECTIVE DATA

Important Health Information

Important health information offers an overview of past and present medical conditions and treatments. Health history, medications, allergies, and surgery or other treatments are included in this part of the history.

Health History

The health history provides information about the patient's prior state of health. Ask the patient about major childhood and adult illnesses, injuries, hospitalizations, and surgeries. Specific questions are more effective than simply asking whether the patient has had any illness or health problems in the past. For example, asking "Do you have a history of diabetes?" elicits better information than asking "Do you have any chronic health problems?"

Medications

Take a thorough medication history. Ask for specific details related to past and current medications, including prescription and illicit drugs, over-the-counter (OTC) drugs, and vitamins. Record the dose (if known), frequency, length of time taken, any side effects, and the reason for taking the medication. Encourage the patient to bring all medication bottles and any inhalers to each visit with an HCP. Ask about herbs and dietary supplement use. Patients often do not consider herbs and dietary supplements as drugs. It is important to specifically ask about them because they can interact adversely with existing or newly prescribed medications.

Ask older adults and patients with chronic illnesses about medication routines. Look for issues related to medication cost and polypharmacy. Changes in absorption, metabolism, and elimination of drugs can potentially pose serious problems for these patients.[4]

TABLE 3.3 HEALTH HISTORY

Functional Health Pattern Format

Demographic Data

Name, address, age, occupation, gender

Race, ethnicity, culture, spirituality

Health Perception–Health Management Pattern

1. Reason for visit?
2. General state of health?
3. Most important things done to keep healthy? Testicular self-examination? Colorectal cancer, hypertension, and heart disease risk screening? Papanicolaou (Pap) test? Immunizations such as tetanus, pneumonia, hepatitis, and flu vaccines?
4. Who is your primary health care provider?
5. Health adherence problems?
6. Cause of illness? Action taken? Results?
7. Things important to you while here?
8. Family health history (e.g., cardiovascular disease, hypertension, cancer, diabetes, psychiatric illness, genetic disorders)?
9. Illness and injury risk factors (e.g., sexual abuse, intimate partner abuse, violence, use of tobacco or alcohol, substance use)?

Nutritional-Metabolic Pattern

1. Typical daily food intake (describe)? Supplements?
2. Typical daily fluid intake (describe)?
3. Weight loss or gain (amount, time span, intentional)?
4. Desired weight?
5. Appetite?
6. Food or eating: Discomfort? Diet restrictions?
7. Change in appetite with anxiety?
8. Heal well or poorly?
9. Skin problems: Lesions? Dryness?
10. Dentition: Dental problems? Well-fitting dentures?
11. Food preferences?
12. Food allergies?

Elimination Pattern

1. Bowel elimination pattern (describe): Frequency? Character? Discomfort? Laxatives? Enemas?
2. Urinary elimination pattern (describe): Frequency? Problem in control? Diuretics?
3. Any external devices?
4. Excess perspiration? Odor problems? Itching?

Activity-Exercise Pattern

1. Sufficient energy for desired or required activities?
2. Exercise pattern? Type? Regularity?
3. Spare time (leisure) activities?
4. Dyspnea? Chest pain? Palpitations? Stiffness? Aching? At rest? With activity?
5. Perceived ability for (rate Functional Level 0–III for each):

   Eating __ Cooking __ Grooming __

   Transfer (e.g., bed to chair) __ Toileting __

   Bathing __Dressing __ Shopping __ General mobility __

   Functional Levels

   Level 0: Full self-care

   Level I: Requires use of equipment or device

   Level II: Needs help or supervision from another person

   Level III: Is dependent and does not participate

Important Health Information

Health history

Medications, supplements

Allergies

Surgery or other treatments

Sleep-Rest Pattern

1. Generally rested and ready for daily activities after sleep?
2. Sleep onset problems? Aids (drugs, CPAP)? Dreams (nightmares)? Early awakening?
3. Usual sleep rituals?
4. Usual sleep pattern?

Cognitive-Perceptual Pattern

1. Hearing impairment? Hearing aids?
2. Vision? Wear glasses? Wear contact lens? Last checked?
3. Any change in taste? Any change in smell?
4. Any recent change in memory?
5. Easiest way to learn things?
6. Any discomfort? Pain (rating on scale of 0–10)? How managed?
7. Ability to communicate (e.g., primary language)?
8. Understanding of illness?
9. Understanding of treatments?

Self-Perception–Self-Concept Pattern

1. Self-description? Self-perception?
2. Effect of illness on self-image?

Role-Relationship Pattern

1. Live alone? Family/caregiver? Family structure?
2. Family problems?
3. Family problem solving?
4. Family dependence on you for things? How managing?
5. Family's and others' feelings about illness or hospitalization?[a]
6. Problems with children? Hard to handle?[a]
7. Belong to social groups? Have close friends? Feel lonely (frequency)?
8. Work (school) satisfaction? Income sufficient for needs?[a]
9. Feel part of or isolated from neighborhood where living?

Sexuality-Reproductive Pattern

1. Any changes or problems in sexual relations?[a]
2. Effect of illness?
3. Use of contraceptives? Problems?
4. When menstruation started? Last menstrual period? Menstrual problems? Gravida? Para?[b]
5. Effect of present condition or treatment on sexuality?
6. Sexually transmitted infections?

Coping–Stress Tolerance Pattern

1. Tense a lot of the time? What helps? Use any drugs, alcohol?
2. Have someone to confide in? Available to you now?
3. Recent life changes?
4. Problem-solving techniques? Effective?

Value-Belief Pattern

1. Satisfied with life?
2. Religion important in your life?
3. Conflict between treatment and beliefs?

[a]If appropriate.

[b]For women.

CPAP, Continuous positive airway pressure.

Modified from Gordon M: *Manual of nursing diagnosis,* ed 13, Boston, 2016, Jones & Bartlett.

Allergies

Explore the patient's history of allergies to drugs, latex, contrast media, food, and the environment (e.g., pollen). Include a detailed description of any allergic reaction(s) reported by the patient.

Surgery and Other Treatments

Record all surgeries, along with the date, reason for the surgery, and outcome. The outcome includes whether the problem was resolved or has residual effects. Ask about and record any blood products the patient has received.

Functional Health Patterns

Assess the patient's functional health patterns to identify effective, dysfunctional, and potential dysfunctional health patterns. *Dysfunctional health patterns* occur with disease. *Potential dysfunctional patterns* identify risk conditions for problems. You may identify patients with effective health function who want a higher level of wellness. Table 3.3 gives examples of possible questions to ask the patient related to functional health patterns.

Health Perception–Health Management Pattern

This pattern focuses on the patient's perceived level of health and well-being and on personal practices for maintaining health. Ask the patient to describe their personal health and any concerns about it. Explore the patient's feelings of effectiveness at staying healthy by asking what helps and what hinders their well-being. Ask the patient to rate their health as excellent, good, fair, or poor. When possible, record this information in the patient's own words.

Next, ask about the type of HCP the patient uses. Patients may seek care from providers that are often used in their country of origin. They may see healers the family views as traditional. These providers may be viewed as alternative in Western culture but are accepted as the norm within certain populations. Respect the patient's wishes when they seek care from non-Western providers (see Chapter 2).

Other questions seek to identify risk factors by obtaining a thorough family history (e.g., heart disease, cancer, genetic disorders), history of personal health habits (e.g., tobacco, alcohol, drug use), and history of exposure to environmental hazards (e.g., asbestos). Ask the hospitalized patient about their expectations for this experience. Have the patient describe their understanding of the current health problem, including its onset, course, and treatment. These questions obtain information about a patient's knowledge of the health problem and ability to use appropriate resources to manage the problem.

Nutritional-Metabolic Pattern

This pattern assesses the processes of ingestion, digestion, absorption, and metabolism. Obtain a 24-hour diet recall from the patient to evaluate the quantity and quality of foods and fluids consumed. If there is a concern, ask the patient to keep a 3-day food diary for a more careful analysis of dietary intake. Assess the impact of psychologic factors such as depression, anxiety, stress, and self-concept on nutrition. Evaluate socioeconomic and cultural factors, such as food budget, who prepares the meals, and food preferences. Determine whether the patient's present condition has interfered with eating and appetite by exploring any symptoms of nausea, intestinal gas, or pain. Note any food allergies and food intolerances, such as lactose or gluten intolerance.

Elimination Pattern

The elimination pattern involves bowel, bladder, and skin function. Ask the patient about the frequency of bowel and bladder activity. Ask about urgency, incontinence, and diuretic use. Inquire about stool consistency, color, and laxative use. Assess the skin here in terms of its excretory function.

Activity-Exercise Pattern

Assessing this pattern looks at the patient's usual pattern of exercise, work activity, leisure, and recreation. Ask about the patient's ability to perform activities of daily living (ADLs) and note any specific problems. Table 3.3 includes a scale for rating the functional levels of common activities.

Sleep-Rest Pattern

The sleep-rest pattern describes the patient's perception of their pattern of sleep, rest, and relaxation in a 24-hour period. Elicit this information by asking, "Do you feel rested when you wake up?"

Cognitive-Perceptual Pattern

Assessing this pattern involves a description of the senses and cognitive functions. Assess pain as a sensory perception (see pain assessment in Chapter 9). Ask the patient about any sensory deficits that affect the ability to perform ADLs. Record ways in which the patient compensates for any sensory-perceptual problems. Ask the patient how they learn best and in what language. Assess what they understand about the illness and treatment plan. Plan patient teaching according to identified needs and preferences (see Chapter 4 for details on patient teaching).

Self-Perception–Self-Concept Pattern

The patient's self-concept is critical in determining the way the person interacts with others. Included in assessing this pattern are attitudes about self, perception of personal abilities, body image, and general sense of worth. Ask the patient for a self-description and about how their health condition affects self-concept. Patients' expressions of hopelessness or loss of control often reflect an inability to care for oneself.

Role-Relationship Pattern

This pattern reveals the patient's roles and relationships, including major responsibilities. Ask the patient to describe family, social, and work roles and relationships. Have the patient rate their performance of the expected behaviors. Determine whether patterns in these roles and relationships are satisfactory or whether strain is evident. Note the patient's feelings about how the present condition affects their roles and relationships.

Sexuality-Reproductive Pattern

This pattern describes satisfaction or dissatisfaction with personal sexuality and describes reproductive issues. Assessing this pattern is important because many illnesses, surgical procedures, and drugs affect sexual function. The patient may express sexual and reproductive concerns. You may identify teaching needs through the information you obtain.

You may feel uncomfortable obtaining information related to sexuality. However, it is important to take a health history and screen for sexual function and problems in a nonjudgmental way. Provide appropriate information or refer the patient to a more experienced HCP.

Coping–Stress Tolerance Pattern

This pattern describes the patient's general coping and the effectiveness of the coping mechanisms. Assessing this pattern involves analyzing the specific stressors or problems that confront the patient, the patient's perception of the stressors, and the patient's response to the stressors. Review any major losses or stressors experienced by the patient in the previous year. Note strategies used by the patient to deal with stressors and relieve tension. Ask about persons and groups that make up the patient's social support networks.

Value-Belief Pattern

This pattern describes the values, goals, and beliefs (including spiritual) that guide health-related choices. Document the patient's ethnic background and effects of culture and beliefs on health practices. Note and respect the patient's wishes about continuation of religious or spiritual practices and the use of religious articles.

PHYSICAL EXAMINATION: OBJECTIVE DATA

General Survey

After the nursing history, make a *general survey statement.* This is your general impression of a patient, including behavioral observations. The initial survey begins with your first encounter with the patient and continues during the health history interview.

The major areas included in the general survey statement are (1) body features, (2) mental state, (3) speech, (4) body movements, (5) obvious physical signs, (6) nutrition status, and (7) behavior. Vital signs and body mass index (BMI) (calculated from height and weight [kg/m^2]) may be included. The following is a sample of a general survey statement:

A.H. is a 34-year-old Hispanic woman, BP 130/84, P 88, R 18. No distinguishing body features. Alert but anxious. Speech rapid with trailing thoughts. Wringing hands and shuffling feet during interview. Skin flushed, hands clammy. Overweight relative to height (BMI = 28.3 kg/m^2). Sits with eyes downcast, shoulders slumped, and avoids eye contact.

Physical Examination

The *physical examination* is the systematic assessment of a patient's physical status. Explore any positive findings using the same criteria used when investigating a symptom in the nursing history (Table 3.2). A *positive finding* shows that the patient has or has had a particular problem or condition. For example, if the patient with jaundice has an enlarged liver, it is a positive finding. You then need to gather relevant information about this problem.

Negative findings may be significant. A pertinent *negative finding* is the absence of a sign or symptom usually associated with a problem. For example, peripheral edema is common with advanced liver disease. If edema is not present in a patient with advanced liver disease, specifically note this as "no peripheral edema."

Techniques

Four major techniques are used in assessment: inspection, palpation, percussion, and auscultation. The techniques are usually performed in the same sequence—inspection, palpation, percussion, and auscultation. The abdominal examination is an exception. Inspection is first, followed by auscultation, percussion, and palpation. Performing percussion and palpation before auscultation can alter bowel sounds and produce false findings. Not every assessment area requires the use of all 4 assessment techniques. The musculoskeletal system requires only inspection and palpation.

Inspection. **Inspection** is the visual assessment of a part or region of the body to assess normal conditions or deviations. Inspection is more than just looking. This technique is deliberate, systematic, and focused. Compare what is seen with the known, generally visible characteristics of the body part that you are inspecting. For example, most 30-year-old men have hair on their legs. Absence of hair may indicate a vascular problem and the need for further investigation, or it may be normal for a patient of a particular ethnicity. Always compare 1 side of the patient's body to the other to assess bilaterally for any abnormal findings.

Palpation. **Palpation** is the assessment of the body using touch. Using light and deep palpation can yield information about masses, pulsations, organ enlargement, tenderness or pain, swelling, muscular spasm or rigidity, elasticity, vibration of voice sounds, crepitus, moisture, and texture. Different parts of the hand are more sensitive for specific assessments. For example, use the dorsa (backs) of your hands and fingers to assess skin temperature and tips of your fingers to palpate pulses (Fig. 3.2).[1]

Percussion. **Percussion** is a technique that produces a sound and vibration to obtain information about the underlying area (Fig. 3.3). The sounds and vibrations are relative to the underlying structures. A change from an expected sound may indicate a problem. For example, you would need further assessment if you heard dullness in the right lower quadrant instead of the normal tympany. Specific percussion sounds of various body parts and regions are discussed in the appropriate assessment chapters.

Auscultation. **Auscultation** involves listening to sounds produced by the body with a stethoscope to assess normal and abnormal conditions. This technique is useful in evaluating sounds from the heart, lungs, abdomen, and vascular system (Fig. 3.4). The bell of the stethoscope is more sensitive to low-pitched sounds (e.g., heart murmurs). The diaphragm of the stethoscope is more sensitive to high-pitched sounds (e.g., bowel sounds). Some stethoscopes have only a diaphragm,

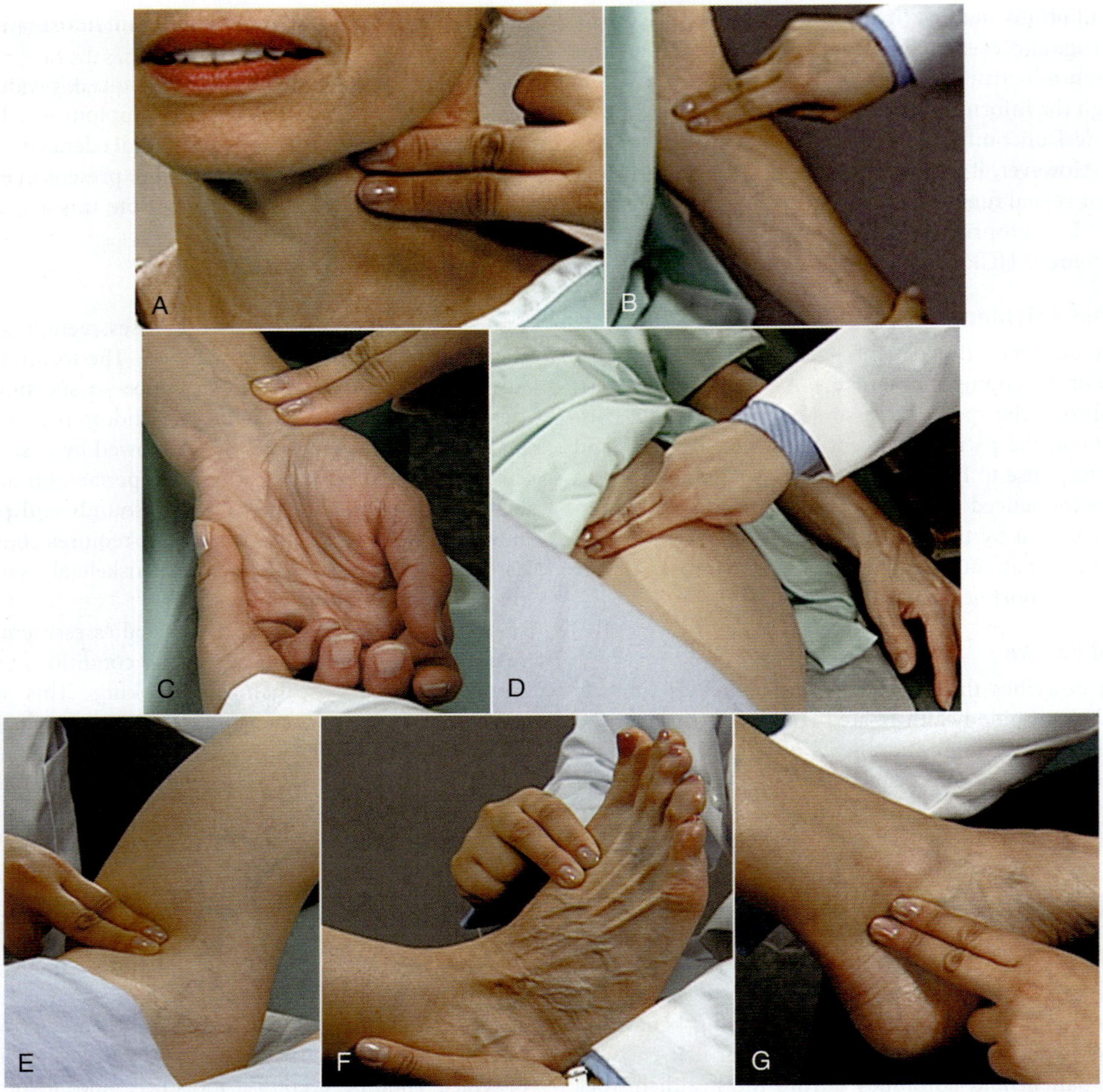

Fig. 3.2 Palpating peripheral pulses. (A) carotid, (B) brachial, (C) radial, (D) femoral, (E) popliteal, (F) dorsalis pedis, (G) posterior tibial. (From Ball JW, et al: *Seidel's guide to physical examination*, ed 9, St. Louis, 2018, Elsevier.)

designed to transmit low- and high-pitched sounds. To listen for low-pitched sounds, hold the diaphragm lightly on the skin. For high-pitched sounds, press the diaphragm firmly on the skin.[1] Specific sounds and auscultation techniques are discussed in the appropriate assessment chapters.

Equipment

Collect the equipment you need before you begin (Table 3.4). This saves time and energy for you and the patient. It promotes trust by showing a level of professionalism. The use of specific equipment is discussed in the appropriate assessment chapters.

Organization of Examination

Perform the physical examination systematically and efficiently. Give explanations to the patient as you proceed and consider the patient's comfort, safety, and privacy. Follow the same sequence every time to avoid omitting a procedure, a step in the sequence, or a part of the body. Table 3.5 presents a comprehensive, organized physical examination outline.

Adapting the physical examination is often useful for the older adult patient, who may have age-related problems, such as decreased mobility, limited energy, and perceptual changes.[5] An outline listing some useful adaptations is found in Table 3.6.

A nurse with appropriate education can perform advanced techniques. A retinal examination would be done with an eye examination. Speculum and bimanual examination of women and the prostate gland examination of men would be performed after inspecting the genitalia.

Documentation

At the end of the examination, record the normal and abnormal findings in the patient's health record. Table 3.7 shows an example of how to record findings of a normal physical examination of a healthy adult. See Table 5.5 to find age-related assessment findings in the book.

TYPES OF ASSESSMENT

We use different types of assessment to obtain patient information. There are 3 approaches: emergency, comprehensive, and focused (Table 3.8). Decide what type of assessment to perform based on the clinical situation. Sometimes the health care agency provides guidelines. Other times it is a nursing judgment.

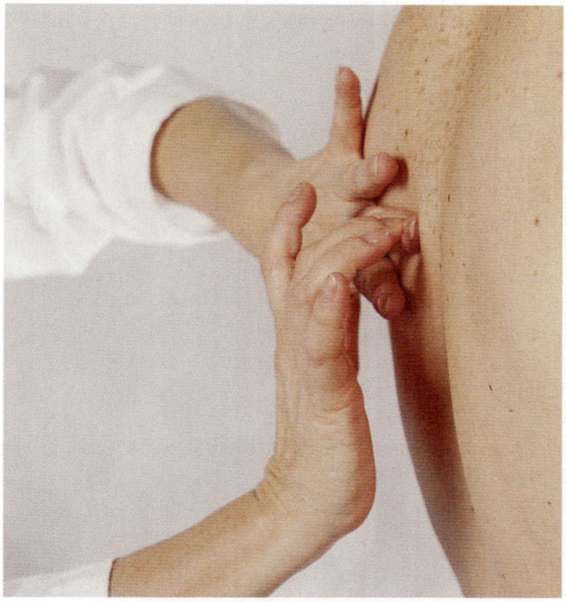

Fig. 3.3 Percussion is tapping of the patient's skin with the middle finger or striking finger of the dominant hand. Hyperextend the middle finger of the nondominant hand and place its distal joint and tip firmly on the patient's skin. Normal percussion sounds: *resonant*—lung tissue; *tympany*—air-filled viscus (e.g., intestines); *dull*—dense organs (e.g., liver); *flat*—no air present (e.g., bone, muscle). (Adapted from Jarvis C: *Physical examination and health assessment,* ed 7, St Louis, 2015, Saunders.)

Emergency Assessment

An *emergency assessment* may be done in an emergency or life-threatening situation. This involves a rapid history and examination of a patient while supporting vital functions.

Comprehensive Assessment

A *comprehensive assessment* includes a detailed health history and physical examination of all body systems. This is typically done on admission to the hospital or onset of care in a primary care setting.

Focused Assessment

A *focused assessment* is an abbreviated health history and examination. It is used to evaluate the status of previously identified

TABLE 3.4 Common Physical Examination Equipment

- Alcohol swabs
- Blood pressure cuff
- Cotton balls
- Examining table or bed
- Eye chart (e.g., Snellen eye chart)
- Paper cup with water
- Patient gown
- Pocket flashlight
- Reflex hammer
- Stethoscope (with bell and diaphragm or a dual-purpose diaphragm; tubing 15–18 inches [38–46 cm])
- Tongue blade
- Watch (with second hand or digital)

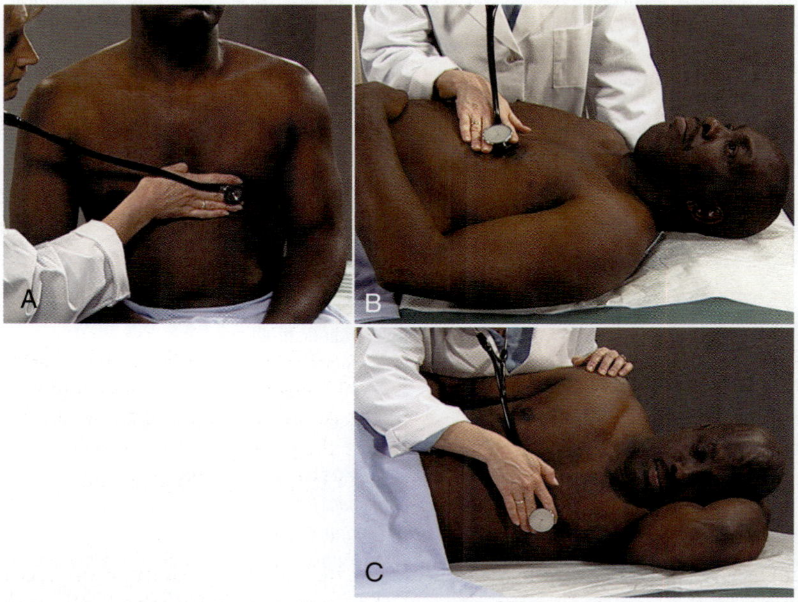

Fig. 3.4 Patient positions for auscultating heart sounds. (A) Sitting, (B) supine, and (C) left lateral. (From Ball JW, et al: *Seidel's guide to physical examination,* ed 9, St. Louis, 2018, Elsevier.)

TABLE 3.5 Physical Examination Outline

1. General Survey

Observe general state of health (with patient seated).
- Body features
- Mental state and level of orientation
- Speech
- Body movements
- Physical appearance
- Nutrition status
- Behavior

2. Vital Signs

Record vital signs.
- Blood pressure—both arms for comparison
- Apical/radial pulse
- Respiration
- Temperature
- Oxygen saturation

Record height and weight; calculate body mass index (BMI).

3. Skin

Inspect and palpate skin for the following:
- Color
- Integrity (e.g., lacerations, lesions, breakdown)
- Scars, tattoos, piercings
- Bruises, rash
- Edema
- Moisture
- Texture
- Temperature
- Turgor
- Vascularity

Inspect and palpate nails for the following:
- Color
- Lesions
- Size
- Shape
- Angle
- Capillary refill time

4. Head and Neck

Inspect and palpate head for the following:
- Shape and symmetry of skull
- Masses
- Tenderness
- Condition of hair and scalp
- Temporal arteries
- Temporomandibular joint
- Sensory (CN V, light touch, pain)
- Motor (CN VII, shows teeth, purses lips, raises eyebrows)
- Looks up, wrinkles forehead (CN VII)
- Raises shoulders against resistance (CN XI)

Inspect and palpate (occasionally auscultate) neck for the following:
- Skin (vascularity and visible pulsations)
- Symmetry
- Range of motion
- Pulses and bruits (carotid)
- Midline structure (trachea, thyroid gland, cartilage)
- Lymph nodes (preauricular, postauricular, occipital, mandibular, tonsillar, submental, anterior and posterior cervical, infraclavicular, supraclavicular)

Test visual acuity.

Inspect and lightly palpate eyes/eyebrows for the following:
- Position and movement of eyelids (CN VII)
- Visual fields (CN II)
- Extraocular movements (CN III, IV, VI)
- Cornea, sclera, conjunctiva
- Pupillary response (CN III)
- Red reflex

Inspect and palpate nose and sinuses for the following:
- External nose: Shape, blockage
- Internal nose: Patency of nasal passages, shape, turbinates or polyps, discharge
- Frontal and maxillary sinuses

Inspect and palpate ears for the following:
- Placement
- Pinna
- Auditory acuity (whispered voice, ticking watch) (CN VIII)
- Mastoid process
- Auditory canal
- Tympanic membrane

Inspect and palpate mouth for the following:
- Lips (symmetry, lesions, color)
- Buccal mucosa (Stensen's and Wharton's ducts)
- Teeth (absence, state of repair, color)
- Gums (color, receding from teeth)
- Tongue for strength (asymmetry, ability to stick out tongue, side to side, fasciculations) (CN XII)
- Palates
- Tonsils and pillars
- Uvular elevation (CN IX)
- Posterior pharynx
- Gag reflex (CN IX and X)
- Jaw strength (CN V)
- Moisture
- Color
- Floor of mouth

5. Extremities

Observe size and shape, symmetry and deformity, involuntary movements.

Inspect and palpate arms, fingers, wrists, elbows, shoulders for the following:
- Strength
- Range of motion
- Joint pain
- Swelling
- Pulses (radial, brachial)
- Sensation (light touch, pain, temperature)
- Test reflexes: Triceps, biceps, brachioradialis

Inspect and palpate legs for the following:
- Strength
- Range of motion
- Joint pain
- Swelling, edema
- Hair distribution
- Sensation (light touch, pain, temperature)
- Pulses (dorsalis pedis, posterior tibialis)
- Test reflexes: Patellar, Achilles, plantar

6. Posterior Thorax

Inspect for muscular development, scoliosis, respiratory movement, anteroposterior (AP) diameter.
- Palpate for symmetry of respiratory movement, CVA tenderness, spinous processes, tumors or swelling, tactile fremitus
- Percuss for pulmonary resonance
- Auscultate for breath sounds
- Auscultate for egophony, bronchophony, whispered pectoriloquy

TABLE 3.5 Physical Examination Outline—cont'd

7. Anterior Thorax • Assess breasts for configuration, symmetry, dimpling of skin • Assess nipples for rash, direction, inversion, retraction • Inspect for apical impulse, other precordial pulsations • Palpate the apical impulse and the precordium for thrills, lifts, heaves, tenderness • Inspect neck for venous distention, pulsations, waves • Palpate lymph nodes in the subclavian, axillary, brachial areas • Palpate breasts • Auscultate for rate and rhythm; character of S_1 and S_2 in the aortic, pulmonic, Erb's point, tricuspid, mitral areas; bruits at carotid, epigastrium **8. Abdomen** • Inspect for scars, shape, symmetry, bulging, muscular position and condition of umbilicus, movements (respiratory, pulsations, presence of peristaltic waves) • Auscultate for peristalsis (i.e., bowel sounds), bruits • Percuss then palpate to confirm positive findings; check liver (size, tenderness), spleen, kidney (size, tenderness), urinary bladder (distention) • Palpate femoral pulses, inguinofemoral nodes, abdominal aorta **9. Neurologic** *Observe motor status:* • Gait • Toe walk • Heel walk	• Drift *Observe coordination:* • Finger to nose • Romberg sign • Heel to opposite shin *Observe the following:* • Proprioception (position sense of great toe) **10. Genitalia** ***Male External Genitalia*** • Inspect penis, noting hair distribution, prepuce, glans, urethral meatus, scars, ulcers, eruptions, structural changes, discharge • Inspect epidermis of perineum, rectum • Inspect skin of scrotum; palpate for descended testes, masses, pain ***Female External Genitalia*** • Inspect hair distribution; mons pubis, labia (minora and majora); urethral meatus; Bartholin's, urethral, Skene's glands (palpate, if indicated); introitus; any discharge • Assess for presence of cystocele, prolapse • Inspect perineum, rectum

CN, Cranial nerve; *CVA,* costovertebral angle.

TABLE 3.6 GERONTOLOGIC ASSESSMENT DIFFERENCES

Adaptations in Physical Assessment Techniques

General Approach
Keep patient warm and comfortable because loss of subcutaneous fat decreases ability to stay warm. Adapt positioning to physical limitations. Avoid unnecessary changes in position. Perform as many activities as possible in the position of comfort for the patient.

Skin
Handle with care because of fragility and loss of subcutaneous fat.

Head and Neck
Provide a quiet environment free from distraction because of possible sensory impairments (e.g., decreased vision, hearing).

Extremities
Use gentle movements and reinforcement techniques. Avoid having patient hop on one foot or perform deep knee bends if patient has limited range of motion of the extremities, decreased reflexes, or diminished sense of balance.

Thorax
Adapt examination for changes related to decreased force of expiration, weakened cough reflex, and shortness of breath.

Abdomen
Use caution in palpating patient's liver because it is readily accessible because of a thinner, softer abdominal wall. The older adult patient may have diminished pain perception in the abdominal wall.

problems and monitor for signs and symptoms of new problems. It can be done when a specific problem (e.g., pneumonia) is identified. The patient's clinical manifestations guide a focused assessment. For example, abdominal pain signals the need for a focused assessment of the abdomen. Some problems need a focused assessment of more than one body system. A patient with a headache may need musculoskeletal, neurologic, and head and neck examinations. Examples of focused assessments for the various body systems are found in each assessment chapter of this book.

Using Assessment Approaches

Assessment in an inpatient, acute care hospital setting is different from assessment in other settings. Focused assessment of the hospitalized patient is frequent and performed by many different HCPs. A team approach demands a high degree of consistency among HCPs from a variety of disciplines.

As you gain experience, you will be able to form a mental image of a patient's status from a few basic details, such as "85-year-old Hispanic woman admitted for COPD exacerbation." Details from a complete verbal report, including length of stay, laboratory results, physical findings, and vital signs, will help you have a clearer picture. Next, perform your own assessment using a focused approach. During your assessment, you will confirm or revise the findings that you read in the medical record and what you heard from other HCPs.

Remember, the process does not end once you have done your first assessment on a patient during rounds. Continue to

TABLE 3.7 Findings From a Physical Examination of a Healthy Adult

Example

General Status
- Well-nourished, well-hydrated, well-developed white (woman) or (man) in no acute distress, appears stated age, speech clear and evenly paced; is alert and oriented ×3; cooperative, calm; BMI 23.8

Integument
- Skin clear s̄ lesions, warm and dry, trunk warmer than extremities, normal skin turgor, no ↑ vascularity, no varicose veins
- Nails well-groomed round 160-degree angle s̄ lesions, nail beds pink, capillary refill <2 s
- Hair thick, brown, shiny, normal (male, female) distribution

Head
- Normocephalic, nontender

Eyes
- Visual fields intact on gross confrontation

Visual acuity:	Right eye	20/20
	Left eye	20/20
	Both eyes	20/20
	s̄ glasses	

- EOM: Intact on all gazes s̄ ptosis, nystagmus
- Pupils: PERRLA, negative cover and uncover tests

Ears
- Pinna intact, in proper alignment; external canal patent; small amount of cerumen present bilaterally; TMs intact; pearly gray LM, light reflex visible, not bulging; whisper heard at 3 ft bilaterally

Nose
- Patent bilaterally; turbinates pink, no swelling
- Sinuses nontender

Mouth
- Moist and pink, soft and hard palates intact, uvula rises midline on "ahh," 24 teeth present and in good repair
- Tonsils surgically removed, no redness
- Tongue moist, pink, size appropriate for mouth, no lesions

Neck
- Supple, no masses or bruits, lymph nodes nonpalpable and nontender
- Thyroid: Palpable, smooth, not enlarged
- ROM: Full, intact strong
- Trachea: Midline, nontender

Breasts
- Soft, nonpendulous, no dimpling or puckering
- Nipples: Inversion, point in same direction, areola dark and symmetric, no discharge, no masses, nontender

Axilla
- Hair present, no lesions, no palpable lymph nodes

Thorax and Lungs
- Respiratory rate 18, regular rhythm, oxygen saturation 98% on room air; AP < transverse diameter, no ↑ in tactile fremitus, no tenderness, lungs resonant throughout, diaphragmatic excursion 4 cm bilaterally, chest expansion symmetric, lung fields clear throughout

Heart
- Rate 82, regular rate and rhythm; blood pressure: RA: 122/76, LA: 120/78; no lifts, heaves
- Apical impulse: 5th ICS at MCL; no palpable thrills; S_1, S_2 louder, softer in appropriate locations; no S_3, S_4; no murmurs, rubs, clicks
- Carotid, femoral, pedal, and radial pulses present; equal, 2+ bilaterally

Abdomen
- No pulsations visible, rounded, positive bowel sounds in 4 quadrants, no bruits or CVA tenderness, no palpable masses
- Liver lower border percussed at costal margin, smooth, nontender; approx. 9-cm span
- Spleen nonpalpable nontender

Neurologic System
- Cranial nerves I–XII intact
- Motor (drift, toe stand) intact
- Coordination (finger to nose, Romberg) intact
- Reflexes: See diagram

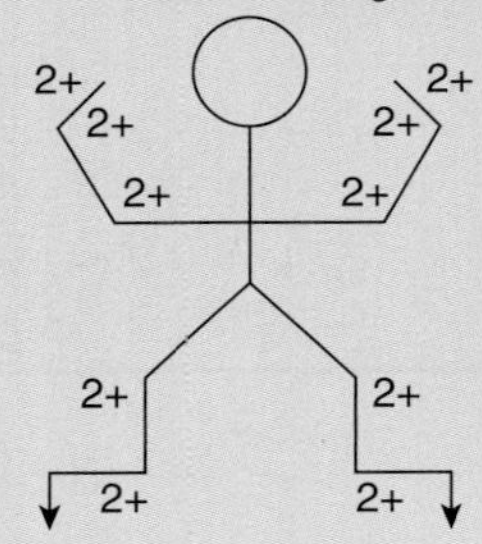

Grading Scale
- 0 No response
- 1+ Diminished
- 2+ Normal
- 3+ Increased
- 4+ Hyperactive
- Sensation (touch, vibration, proprioception) normal bilaterally, upper and lower extremities

Musculoskeletal System
- Well developed, no muscle wasting, crepitus, nodules, or swelling; no scoliosis
- ROM: Full and equal bilaterally, upper and lower extremities
- Strength: Equal, strong 5/5 bilaterally, upper and lower extremities
- Gait: Walks erect 2-foot steps, arms swinging at side s̄ staggering

Female Genitalia[a]
- External genitalia: No swelling, redness, tenderness in BUS; normal hair distribution, no cysts
- Vagina: No lesions, discharge; bulging, pink
- Cervix: Os closed; pink, no lesions, erosions, nontender
- Uterus: Small, firm, nontender
- Adnexa: No enlargement; nontender
- Rectovaginal: Sphincter intact; confirms above findings

Male Genitaliaa
- Normal male hair distribution, negative inguinal hernia
- Penis: Urethral opening patent; no redness, swelling, discharge; no lesions, structural changes
- Scrotum: Testes descended; no redness, masses, tenderness
- Rectal: No lesions, redness; sphincter intact; prostate small, nontender

[a]Some data would be obtained only if the nurse has the appropriate education.

AP, Anterior-posterior; *BMI,* body mass index; *BUS,* Bartholin's gland, urethral meatus, Skene's duct; *CVA,* costovertebral angle; *EOM,* extraocular movements; *ICS,* intercostal space; *LA,* left arm; *LM,* landmarks; *MCL,* midclavicular line; *PERRLA,* pupils equal, round, reactive to light and accommodation; *RA,* right arm; *ROM,* range of motion; S_1, S_2, S_3, and S_4, heart sounds; *TM,* tympanic membrane.

TABLE 3.8 Types of Assessment

The following describes types of assessment that you may use in various situations.

Description	When and Where Performed	Where to Find in Book
Emergency		
• Limited to assessing life-threatening conditions (e.g., inhalation injuries, anaphylaxis, myocardial infarction, shock, stroke) • Conducted to ensure survival. Focuses on elements in primary survey (e.g., airway, breathing, circulation, disability) • After life-saving interventions are started, perform brief systematic assessment to identify other injuries or problems	• Performed in any setting when signs or symptoms of a life-threatening condition appear (e.g., emergency department, critical care unit, surgical setting)	• Chapter 21, Table 21.3 and Table 21.5 • Emergency Management tables throughout the book and listed in Table 21.1
Comprehensive		
• Detailed assessment of all body systems (head-to-toe assessment)	• Onset of care in primary or ambulatory care setting • On admission to hospital, rehabilitation, or long-term care setting • On initial home care visit	• Assessment chapters for each body system • Physical examination outline (Table 3.4) • Findings from physical examination of a healthy adult (Table 3.6)
Focused		
• Abbreviated assessment that focuses on 1 or more body systems that are the focus of care • Includes an assessment related to a specific problem (e.g., pneumonia, specific abnormal laboratory findings) • Monitors for signs and symptoms of new problems	• Throughout hospital admission—at beginning of a shift and as needed throughout shift • Revisit in ambulatory care setting or home care setting	• Focused assessment tables in each assessment chapter • Tables on nursing assessment of specific diseases throughout book

TABLE 3.9 Clinical Applications for Types of Assessment

The following is an example of how different types of assessment would be used as a patient progresses from the emergency department to a clinical unit of a hospital.

Timeline	Type of Assessment
Emergency Department	
• Patient arrives in acute respiratory distress	• Perform emergency assessment (see Table 21.3)
• Problem is found, and critical interventions are performed	• Conduct a focused assessment of the respiratory and related body systems (e.g., cardiovascular)
• Patient stabilizes	• May begin comprehensive assessment of all body systems.
Clinical Unit	
Patient is admitted to a monitored clinical unit	• Complete comprehensive assessment of all body systems within proper timeframe
Beginning of each shift: Reassess per orders and more frequently as determined by the nurse	• Perform focused assessment of respiratory system and other related body systems per agency protocol • Perform focused assessment of appropriate body system(s) if new symptoms are reported

gather information about all your patients throughout your shift. You consider everything you learned previously about each patient in light of new information. For example, when you are doing a respiratory assessment on your patient with COPD, you hear crackles in her lungs. This finding should lead you to do a cardiovascular assessment because heart problems (e.g., heart failure) can also cause crackles. As you gain experience, the importance of new findings will be more obvious to you. Case studies integrated into all the assessment chapters will help you develop your assessment skills and knowledge.

Table 3.9 shows how you perform different types of assessments based on a patient's progress through a given hospitalization. When a patient arrives at the emergency department with a life-threatening condition, you will perform an emergency assessment based on the elements of a primary survey (e.g., airway, breathing, circulation, disability) (see Table 21.3). Once the patient is stable, you can begin a focused assessment of related body systems. After the patient is admitted, you perform a comprehensive assessment of all body systems.

BRIDGE TO NCLEX EXAMINATION

The number of the question corresponds to the same-numbered outcome at the beginning of the chapter.

1. The patient health history and physical examination provide the nurse with information primarily to
   - a. diagnose a medical problem.
   - b. investigate a patient's signs and symptoms.
   - c. classify subjective and objective patient data.
   - d. make clinical judgments about the patient's health.
2. The nurse would place information about the patient's concern that his illness is threatening his job security in which functional health pattern?
   - a. Role-relationship
   - b. Cognitive-perceptual
   - c. Coping–stress tolerance
   - d. Health perception–health management
3. The nurse is preparing to examine a patient's abdomen. Place in order the proper steps for an abdominal assessment, using the numbers 1–4, with 1 = the first technique and 4 = the last technique:
   - a. ___ Inspection
   - b. ___ Palpation
   - c. ___ Percussion
   - d. ___ Auscultation
4. Which situation would require the nurse to obtain a focused assessment? *(select all that apply)*
   - a. A patient denies a current health problem.
   - b. A patient reports a new symptom during rounds.
   - c. A previously identified problem needs reassessment.
   - d. A baseline health maintenance examination is needed.
   - e. A patient with an emergent problem needs immediate care.

1. d; 2. a; 3. 1, 4, 3, 2; 4. b, c.

For rationales to these answers and even more NCLEX review questions, visit http://evolve.elsevier.com/Lewis/medsurg.

EVOLVE WEBSITE/RESOURCES LIST

http://evolve.elsevier.com/Lewis/medsurg
Review Questions (Online Only)
Key Points
Answer Key for Questions
- Rationales for Bridge to NCLEX Examination Questions

Conceptual Care Map Creator
Audio Glossary
Content Updates

REFERENCES

1. Jarvis C: *Physical examination and health assessment*, ed 8, St Louis, 2019, Saunders.
2. Wilson S, Giddens J: *Health assessment for nursing practice*, ed 6, St Louis, 2016, Mosby.
3. Gordon M: *Manual of nursing diagnosis*, ed 13, Boston, 2016, Jones & Bartlett.
4. Lehne R: *Pharmacology for nursing care*, ed 10, St Louis, 2019, Saunders.
5. Touhy T, Jett J: *Ebersole and Hess' toward healthy aging*, ed 10, St Louis, 2020, Mosby.

4

Patient and Caregiver Teaching

Brenda C. Morris

http://evolve.elsevier.com/Lewis/medsurg/

CONCEPTUAL FOCUS

Adherence
Communication
Health Promotion
Patient Education
Self-Management

LEARNING OUTCOMES

1. Apply the teaching-learning process to diverse patient populations.
2. Select strategies to support patient learning.
3. Evaluate the role of the caregiver in patient teaching.
4. Relate the physical, psychologic, and sociocultural characteristics of the patient and caregiver to the teaching-learning process.
5. Prioritize patient teaching goals for patients and caregivers.
6. Choose appropriate teaching strategies for patients and their caregivers.
7. Choose appropriate methods to evaluate patient and caregiver learning.

KEY TERMS

caregivers
health literacy
learning
learning needs
motivational interviewing
positive reinforcement
self-efficacy
teaching
teaching plan
teaching process

This chapter describes the process of patient and caregiver teaching and strategies that contribute to successful teaching and learning experiences. The concept of patient and caregiver (family member or significant other) teaching is central to delivering quality patient care. It is a dynamic, interactive process that involves a change in a patient's knowledge, behavior, and/or attitude to maintain or improve health. You will find that teaching is a challenging and rewarding role. Teaching patients and caregivers is a key nursing intervention that makes a difference in their lives.

ROLE OF PATIENT AND CAREGIVER TEACHING

The general goals of patient teaching include health promotion, disease prevention, illness management, and appropriate choice and use of treatment options. In patients with acute and chronic health problems, your teaching can prevent complications and promote recovery, self-care, and independence. In the United States, 6 in 10 adults have a chronic disease and 4 in 10 adults have 2 chronic diseases.[1] Whether patients adequately manage their health problems and maintain quality of life depends on what they learn about their conditions and what they do with this knowledge. Patients who have the knowledge, skills, and desire to manage their health are less likely to be readmitted to the hospital.[2]

Teaching may occur wherever you work as a nurse. Although agencies may employ advanced practice nurses and patient educators to provide patient teaching programs, you are always responsible for patient and caregiver teaching.[3] Teaching is a responsibility that you cannot delegate to assistive personnel (AP).

Every interaction with a patient and a caregiver is a potential *teachable moment.* On any given day, more informal opportunities to teach occur than formal opportunities. Take advantage of and document all these moments. For example, when you teach a patient with asthma how to use a peak flow meter, you do not need a formal teaching plan. However, when your patient has a specific learning need about health promotion or managing a health problem, you should develop a teaching plan. A **teaching plan** includes (1) assessment of the patient's ability and readiness to learn, (2) identification of teaching needs, (3) development of learning goals with the patient, (4) implementation plans for the teaching, and (5) evaluation of the patient's learning.

TEACHING-LEARNING PROCESS

Teaching is the act of conveying information to facilitate learning. When a nurse is teaching a patient about health, the nurse becomes the teacher and the patient becomes the learner. Nurses often teach patients using methods such as direct instruction, coaching, counseling, and behavior modification. Teaching may be formal, such as giving a planned presentation to a group of patients and their caregivers, or informal, such as teaching a patient about medications before giving them.

Learning is the act of acquiring knowledge or skills that may produce a change in behavior. Observation of this change is an indication that learning has occurred. However, learning may not result in any observable change. A patient who understands the instruction and is fully informed may choose not to change behavior.

Although learning may occur without teaching, a teacher helps to organize information and skills to make learning more efficient. In patient teaching, the teaching-learning process involves the patient, the patient's caregiver(s), and you.

Adult Learner

Adult Learning Principles

Understanding how and why adults learn is important for you to effectively teach patients and their caregivers. Knowles identified 6 principles of *andragogy* (adult learning) that are important for you to consider when teaching adults (Table 4.1).[4]

Models to Promote Health

Patients and their caregivers may progress through a series of steps before they are willing or able to change their health behaviors. Prochaska and Velicer proposed 6 stages of change in their *Transtheoretical Model of Health Behavior Change* (Table 4.2).[5] This model is often used for planning to help patients stop smoking, manage diabetes, and lose weight.

Motivational interviewing is a nonconfrontational communication method to motivate patients to change behavior.[6] This strategy includes interventions that enhance the patient's motivation for change (Table 4.3). The techniques used in motivational interviewing are linked to the stages of change identified by Prochaska and Velicer.[5]

During the process of change, relapse and recycling through the stages are expected. Sometimes patients do not change behaviors. Some return to previous behaviors after a period of change. This may mean that the interventions used did not consider the patient's stage of change. Identify the patient's current stage of readiness for change and the stage to which the patient is moving. Patients who are in the early stages of change need and use different kinds of motivational support than patients at later stages of change.

For example, a hospitalized patient who smokes cigarettes may be in the *precontemplation* or *contemplation* stage of change. In the precontemplation stage, the patient is not concerned about their smoking and not considering quitting. During this stage, it is important to help the patient increase awareness of risks and problems related to smoking and create doubt about using cigarettes. Ask the patient what they think could happen if they continued smoking. Give evidence of the problem (e.g., x-ray changes). Share facts about the risks of smoking. Although they may not be ready to change behavior while experiencing an acute health problem, the seeds of doubt are sown. In other

TABLE 4.1 Adult Learning Principles Applied to Patient and Caregiver Teaching

Principles	Teaching Implications for Nurse	Examples
Need to know	• Patients need to know why they should learn something, what they need to learn, and how it will help them. • Ask the patient questions such as, "What do you think you need to learn about this topic?"	Your patient and his caregiver ask what they need to know about exercise guidelines after a heart attack.
Readiness to learn	• Readiness and motivation to learn are high when facing new tasks. • Health crises provide opportunities for patients to learn and change behavior. • Stress and anxiety may interfere with learning, thus requiring frequent reinforcement of content.	While recovering from a transient ischemic attack, your patient tells you that she is ready to learn about the changes she needs to take to reduce her risk for stroke.
Prior experiences	• Motivation is increased when one already knows something about the subject from past experiences. • Identification of past knowledge and experiences can help find familiar ground to increase patients' confidence.	Your patient needs to begin injections of enoxaparin. She tells you that she gives her father insulin injections and is ready to learn how to give this medication.
Motivation to learn	• Patients prefer to apply learning at once. • Long-term goals may have less appeal than short-term goals. • Focus teaching on information that the patient views as needed right now.	Your patient is scheduled for discharge in the morning. Both she and her caregiver have received instruction on wound care and have watched the procedure. The caregiver tells you that he wants to perform the wound care today.
Orientation to learning	• Patients seek out various resources for specific learning and prefer choices. • When the patient does not recognize the relevancy of the teaching, offer explanations of the value of the learning. • Teaching should target the specific problem or circumstance.	Your patient, who is newly diagnosed with diabetes, tells you that he is worried about the diet changes he will need to make. Share several options with him to learn about diet changes (e.g., cooking classes, Web-based tutorials, mobile applications, individual sessions with the dietitian, brochures).
Self-concept	• Patients need control and self-direction (sense of autonomy) to maintain their sense of self-worth. • Patients do not learn when we treat them like children and tell them what they must do.	Your patient has a temporary colostomy. She says she is not ready to look at the stoma. Work out a schedule with her for learning colostomy care that meets her need for control and prepares her for self-care.

TABLE 4.2 Stages of Change in Transtheoretical Model

Stage	Patient Behavior	Nursing Implications
1. **Precontemplation**	Is not considering a change. Is not ready to learn.	Provide support, increase awareness of condition. Describe benefits of change and risks of not changing.
2. **Contemplation**	Thinks about a change. May state recognition of need to change. Says "I know I should," but identifies barriers.	Introduce what is involved in changing the behavior. Reinforce the stated need to change.
3. **Preparation**	Starts planning the change, gathers information, sets a date to start change, shares decision to change with others.	Reinforce the positive outcomes of change, give information and encouragement, develop a plan, help set priorities, and identify sources of support.
4. **Action**	Begins to change behavior through practice. Tentative and may experience relapses.	Reinforce behavior with reward, encourage self-reward, discuss choices to help minimize relapses and regain focus. Help patient plan to deal with potential relapses.
5. **Maintenance**	Practices the behavior regularly. Able to sustain the change.	Continue to reinforce behavior. Provide more teaching on the need to maintain change.
6. **Termination**	Change has become part of lifestyle. Behavior no longer considered a change.	Evaluate effectiveness of the new behavior. No further intervention needed.

Adapted from Prochaska J, Velicer W: The transtheoretical model of health behavior change, *Am J Health Promot* 12:38, 1997. (Classic).

TABLE 4.3 Key Aspects of Motivational Interviewing

- Listen rather than tell.
- Adjust to, rather than oppose, patient resistance.
- Express empathy through reflective listening.
- Focus on the positive. Do not criticize the patient.
- Gently persuade with the understanding that change is up to the patient.
- Focus on the patient's strengths to support the hope needed to make changes.
- Avoid argument and direct confrontation. They can cause defensiveness and a power struggle.
- Help the patient recognize the "gap" between where they are and where they hope to be.

cases, such as when a patient has a life-threatening condition (e.g., heart attack), there may be an immediate awareness of the problem and motivation to change.

A patient in the *contemplation* stage of change often is ambivalent. The patient understands that the behavior is a problem and that change is necessary. However, they believe that change is too hard or that the pleasures of the behavior are worth the risks. This is seen in the patient who says, "I know that I have to stop smoking. This heart attack really scared me. I know I need to lose weight and start exercising, but I can't change everything all at once. Smoking helps me control my eating. I can't stop until I lose some weight." During this stage of change, help the patient consider the positive and negative aspects of their behavior (e.g., tobacco use). Gently try to tip the balance in favor of positive behavior. Helping the patient discover internal motivators in addition to those external motivators (e.g., second heart attack, lung disease) that push the patient toward change can move the patient from contemplating change to preparation and action. Throughout this process, emphasize the patient's personal choices and responsibilities for change.

As the patient moves from contemplation to *preparation,* we can help strengthen the commitment to change by helping the patient develop self-efficacy.[6] This is the belief that one can succeed in a given situation. In this case, it is the patient's belief that they can change tobacco-use behaviors. Support even the smallest effort to change. Movement through action and maintenance stages of change requires continued support for the patient's involvement and participation in treatment. You can find a comprehensive discussion of motivational interviewing in the Treatment Improvement Protocols at www.ncbi.nlm.nih.gov/books/NBK14856.

The resolution of acute health problems or discharge from the hospital often occurs before the patient moves to the preparation and action stages of change. As the patient develops readiness in the contemplative stage of change, provide referrals to appropriate community and outpatient resources.

Nurse as Teacher

Required Competencies

Knowledge of subject matter. Develop confidence as a teacher by becoming knowledgeable about the topic. For example, if you are teaching patients about managing hypertension, you must be able to explain what hypertension is and why treating it is important. Teach patients what they need to know about exercise, diet, medication side effects, monitoring BP, and situations that they must report to the health care provider (HCP). Provide the patient with resources such as credible websites, brochures, and information about support organizations (e.g., American Heart Association [AHA]).

Do not expect to be an expert in all subject areas. Sometimes you will not be able to answer patients' or caregivers' questions. Clarify the questions to be sure of what they are asking. When you do not know the answer, tell them this and that you will find out an answer. Seek help from co-workers, patient educators, and other reliable sources to answer the question.

Communication skills. Patient teaching depends on effective communication between you and the patient or caregiver. Medical jargon can be intimidating and frightening. Introduce medical words and define their meanings. Limit the use of acronyms (e.g., CABG for coronary artery bypass graft) and abbreviations (e.g., IV). Have the patient and caregiver clarify their understandings of the disease process. Ask them to explain what they know in their own words. For example, if a patient has leukopenia, define this term. Explain that *leuko-* refers to a leukocyte, a white blood cell that fights infections, and that *penia* refers to a shortage. To enhance learning, use a brief explanation such as, "You do not have enough white blood cells. They are cells that fight infection."

Nonverbal communication is critical when teaching. Cultural practices often guide nonverbal communication. For example, in Western culture, sitting in an open, relaxed position facing the patient with eyes at the same level delivers a positive nonverbal message (Fig. 4.1). Sit in a chair at the bedside and use open body gestures to communicate interest and a willingness to share. Patients from Eastern cultures may prefer that you avoid direct eye contact and give health information to a family spokesperson rather than directly to the patient.

Develop the art of active listening. Pay attention to what the patient says, observe the patient's nonverbal cues, and do not interrupt. Nod in response to the patient's statements and restate what the patient is saying to help clarify communication.

Empathy is the courage to enter the world of another in a manner that does not judge or correct but tries to understand. Empathy means putting aside your own self and stepping into the patient's shoes. Active listening, combined with empathy, is a powerful way to communicate caring and prepare the patient to learn.

Challenges to nurse-teacher effectiveness. Teaching patients and caregivers has many challenges, including (1) lack of time, (2) your own feelings as a teacher, (3) nurse-patient differences in learning goals, and (4) rapid or early discharge from the health care system.

Lack of time can be a barrier to effective teaching. For example, the patient's physical needs may compete for time that you could use for teaching. To make the most of limited time, set learning priorities with the patient. Tell the patient at the beginning of the interaction how much time you can devote to the session. Deliver or reinforce teaching during every contact with the patient or caregiver. For example, when giving a medication, explain the purpose and side effects. Reinforcing small pieces of information over time is an effective teaching strategy, especially if information is new or complex.

Other potential barriers are your own feelings as a teacher and insecurity about your knowledge and skill. Teaching is a skill that takes time to master. Consult with nurse educators or experienced co-workers for further help with developing your teaching skills. Become familiar with the resources for patient teaching available at your agency.

Fig. 4.1 Open, relaxed positioning of patient, spouse, and nurse at eye level promotes communication in teaching and learning. (© Jupiterimages/Photos.com/Thinkstock.)

Sometimes disagreements arise among the patient, the caregiver, and you about the expectations or outcomes of teaching. Having realistic discussions about discharge plans, timelines, and home care options can emphasize the need for learning. For example, after a diagnosis of heart failure due to aortic valve insufficiency and subsequent emergent valve surgery, the patient and caregiver may reject teaching efforts until they accept the seriousness of the patient's health problem.

Another important challenge to patient teaching relates to early and quick patient discharges from the health care system. Shorter lengths of hospital stays have resulted in patients having only basic teaching plans implemented. This makes it important to begin teaching patients soon after admission to the health care system.

Caregiver Support in the Teaching-Learning Process

The teaching and learning process applies to the caregiver as well as the patient. **Caregivers** are people who care for those who cannot care for themselves. Most caregivers are family members or significant others who (1) give or help with direct patient care; (2) provide emotional, social, spiritual, and possibly financial support for the patient; and (3) manage and coordinate health care services.

About 1 in 4 American adults serves as a caregiver to a person with a long-term disability or illness.[7] We often categorize caregivers by their relationship to the patient. The most common caregivers are spouses, adult children, parents, grandparents, and life partners. Identify the key caregiver(s) and assess their roles and relationships to the patient. Because the patient's health problem affects family roles and functions, it is important to identify the needs of caregivers. Caregivers with unmet needs may be unable to assist the patient (Table 4.4).

Consider cultural differences when assessing the caregiver. In some cultures, a male family member may be the designated spokesperson to receive and communicate information among family members and the patient. Assure that the family spokesperson and the caregivers who will actually provide care for the patient are included in discharge planning. See Chapter 2 for more information on culturally competent care.

TABLE 4.4 Assessment of Caregiver Needs

Ask caregivers the following questions:

1. How are you coping with your caregiver role?
2. Do you have any problems performing your caregiver responsibilities?
3. How much support do you get from outside sources (e.g., other family members, friends)?
4. Are you aware of and do you use community resources (e.g., disease-specific professional organizations [such as Alzheimer's Association, AHA, ACS], adult day care centers, religious/spiritual organizations)?
5. Do you know about resources that are available for respite (someone caring for your loved one while you have time to yourself)?
6. What kind of help or services do you need now and in the near future?
7. How can I or other health care providers help you in your caregiving role?

When possible, teach the caregiver along with the patient. Explain the goals of the teaching plan. Caregivers may need help to learn the physical and technical requirements of care, find resources for home care, find equipment and supplies, and rearrange the home to accommodate the patient. Sources of support for the transition from hospital to home include community-based agencies, Medicare and Medicaid offices, and case managers at the hospital and insurance companies.

Patients and caregivers may have different teaching needs. For example, the priority of an older patient with a diabetic leg ulcer may be to learn how to transfer from a bed to a chair in the least painful manner. On the other hand, the caregiver may be most concerned about learning the technique for dressing changes. Both the patient's and caregiver's learning needs are important. The patient and caregiver may also have different or conflicting views of the illness and treatment options. Developing a successful teaching plan requires you to view the patient's needs within the context of the caregiver's needs. For instance, you may teach a patient with right-sided *paresis* (weakness) self-feeding techniques with special tools. Then, at a home visit you find the caregiver feeding the patient. On questioning, the caregiver reveals that it is too hard to watch the patient struggle with feeding, it takes too long, and it is messy. As a result, the caregiver decided that it is easier to feed the patient. This is an example of a situation in which the patient and caregiver need more teaching about goals for self-care.

Discuss potential resources provided by support groups, family and friends, and community organizations. Support groups help by sharing experiences and information, offering understanding and acceptance, and suggesting solutions to common problems and concerns.

Regulatory Mandates for Patient Teaching

Several important agencies have specific mandates related to teaching hospitalized patients. The Joint Commission's (TJC's) accreditation standards, National Patient Safety Goals,[8] and the American Hospital Association's Patient Care Partnership[9] state that patients have a fundamental right to receive information about their care. This information includes their diagnosis, treatment, and prognosis in terms that they can understand. For example, written materials must be at the patient's reading level. One program started by TJC, Speak Up, was developed to encourage patients to become more involved and informed about their plan of care (Table 4.5).[10] Another program implemented by the Institute for Healthcare Improvement's National Patient Safety Foundation is Ask Me 3.[11] Both programs encourage patients to ask specific questions about their care.

PROCESS OF PATIENT TEACHING

We use many different approaches in patient teaching. However, the approach used most often by nurses parallels the nursing process. The **teaching process** includes assessment, goal setting, implementation, and evaluation. The teaching process, like the nursing process, may not always flow in linear order, but the steps serve as checkpoints.

TABLE 4.5 The Joint Commission's Speak Up Initiative

Speak up if you have questions or concerns. If you still do not understand, ask again. It is your body, and you have a right to know.
Pay attention to the care you get. Always make sure you are getting the right treatments and medicines by the right health care professionals. Do not assume anything.
Educate yourself about your illness. Learn about the medical tests you get and your treatment plan.
Ask a trusted family member or friend to be your advocate (advisor or supporter).
Know what medicines you take and why you take them. Medicine errors are the most common health care mistakes.
Use a hospital, clinic, surgery center, or other type of health care organization that has been carefully checked out.
Participate in all decisions about your treatment. You are the center of the health care team.

Source: The Joint Commission: To prevent health care errors, patients are urged to Speak Up (poster). Retrieved from www.jointcommission.org/assets/1/18/SpeakUp_Poster.pdf.

Assessment

During the general nursing assessment, determine if the patient has learning needs. For example, what does the patient know about the health problem? How do they perceive the problem? If you identify a learning need, conduct a more detailed assessment, and address that problem with a teaching plan. Include caregivers in the assessment as you determine their role and ability to care for the patient at home. Key questions to use in the assessment are outlined in Table 4.6.

Physical Factors

The patient's age is a factor to consider in the teaching plan. Age affects the patient's experiences and rate of learning. Some effects of increased age on learning may be obvious, but the inexperience of younger people can also affect learning. For example, a man in his twenties who has never thought about his own mortality may be unable to accept the long-term health implications of diabetes.

Sensory problems (e.g., hearing, or vision loss) that decrease sensory input can alter learning. Cognition may be affected by disorders of the nervous system (e.g., stroke, head trauma) and by other diseases (e.g., liver problems, heart failure). Patients with altered cognition may have a hard time learning and need more caregiver involvement in the teaching process. Manual dexterity is needed to perform skills such as giving injections or BP monitoring.

Pain, fatigue, and certain drugs influence the patient's ability to learn. No one can learn effectively when in pain. Provide teaching after the patient's pain is controlled. A tired, weak patient may be unable to concentrate. Sleep disruption is common during hospitalization, and patients are often sleep deprived at the time of discharge. Drugs that cause central nervous system depression, such as opioids and sedatives, decrease mental alertness and can affect the patient's ability to learn new information. Adjust the teaching plan by setting high-priority goals based on need-to-know information and realistic expectations. Patients often need a referral for follow-up care so that teaching continues and learning is confirmed after discharge.

TABLE 4.6 Assessment of Factors Affecting Patient Teaching

Key Factors and Questions

Physical
- What is the patient's age?
- Is the patient acutely ill?
- Is the patient fatigued or in pain?
- What is the primary diagnosis?
- Are there other medical problems?
- What is the patient's current mental status?
- What is the patient's hearing ability? Visual ability? Motor ability?
- What drugs does the patient take that may affect learning?

Psychologic
- Does the patient appear anxious, afraid, depressed, defensive?
- Is the patient in a state of denial?
- What is the patient's level of motivation? Self-efficacy?

Sociocultural
- What are the patient's beliefs about their illness or treatment?
- Is the proposed teaching consistent with the patient's cultural values?
- What is the patient's educational experience, reading ability, primary language?
- What is the patient's present or past occupation?
- How does the patient describe their financial status?
- What is the patient's living arrangement?
- Does the patient have family or close friends?

Learner
- What does the patient already know about the health problem?
- What does the patient think is most important to learn?
- What prior learning experiences could be a frame of reference for current learning needs?
- Is the patient ready to learn? Change behavior?
- How does the patient learn best (e.g., reading, listening, looking at pictures, doing, playing games)?
- In what kind of environment does the patient learn best? Formal classroom? Computer/Web-based setting? Informal setting, such as home? Alone or in a group?
- In what way should the caregiver(s) be involved in patient teaching?

Psychologic Factors

Psychologic factors have a major influence on the patient's ability to learn. Anxiety and depression are common reactions to illness. Although mild anxiety increases the learner's perceptual and learning abilities, moderate or severe anxiety limits learning. Anxiety and depression can negatively affect the patient's motivation and readiness to learn. For instance, the patient newly diagnosed with diabetes who is depressed about the diagnosis may not listen or respond to instructions about glucose testing. Discussions with the patient about these concerns or referrals to an appropriate support group may help the patient to learn that management of diabetes is possible.

Patients respond to the stress of illness with a variety of defense mechanisms, such as denial, rationalization, or even humor. A patient who denies having cancer will not be receptive to information related to treatment options. Similarly, a caregiver may have a hard time accepting a terminal diagnosis. A patient using rationalization will imagine any number of reasons for avoiding change or for rejecting teaching. For example, a patient with heart disease who does not want to change dietary habits will relate stories of people who have eaten bacon and eggs every day and lived to be 100 years old. Some patients use humor to filter reality or decrease anxiety. They may use laughter to escape from the experience of facing threatening situations. Humor in the teaching process is important and useful but notice when humor is used to avoid reality.

One key factor in successful adoption of new behaviors is the patient's sense of self-efficacy. There is a strong relationship between self-efficacy and outcomes of illness management. Self-efficacy increases when a person gains new skills in managing a threatening situation. It decreases if the person has repeated failure, especially early in the course of events. Plan easily achievable goals early in the teaching sessions. Proceed from simple to more complex content to support a feeling of success.

Sociocultural Factors

Health literacy. *Literacy* is the ability to use printed and written information to function in society. **Health literacy** is the degree to which a person can obtain and understand basic health information needed to make appropriate health decisions.[12] Almost 90% of US adults have limited health literacy skills.[13] Currently, only 69% of adults report receiving easy-to-understand instructions from their HCPs.[14] Only 31% report that a HCP asked them to describe how they will follow the instructions provided.[14] Patients with low levels of health literacy have trouble understanding and acting on health information, placing them at greater risk for hospital readmissions.[15] Even patients with high levels of health literacy may have a hard time understanding complex health information if they are sick or stressed. Health illiteracy results in poor patient outcomes, not following treatment plans, limited self-management skills, and increased health disparities.[15]

It is challenging to assess health literacy, because patients may be embarrassed to admit that they are having trouble understanding health information. Health professionals often over-estimate the health literacy of patients, so it is important to routinely assess health literacy level. Easy-to-use assessment tools are available. The Single-Item Literacy Screener (SILS) uses 1 question to identify adults who need help with reading.[16] The question is, "How often do you need to have someone help you when you read instructions, pamphlets, or other written material from your doctor or pharmacy?"

Another approach is to implement health literacy universal precautions. These are the steps to take when we assume that all patients may have difficulty understanding important health information and accessing health services. These include using simple communications about health information and verifying patient understanding.[13]

TJC states that we must tailor patient teaching to the patient's literacy needs. For example, teach patients and give them written materials in their primary language. Teaching materials are available in multiple languages. It is better to use medical interpreters instead of family members or friends, to protect patient privacy (Fig. 4.2). Medical interpreters are discussed in Table

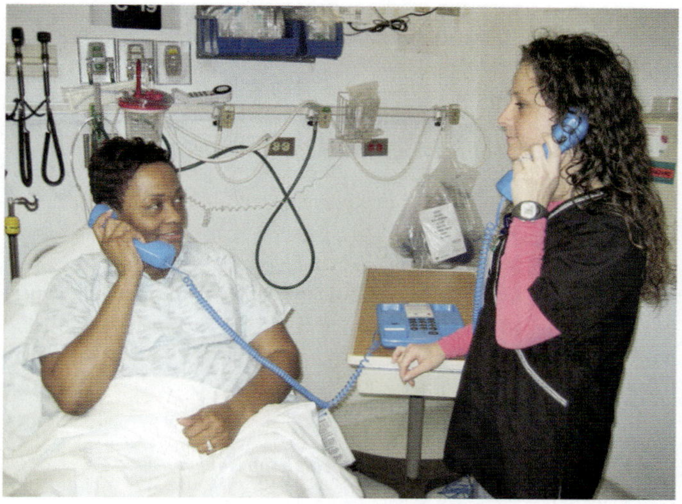

Fig. 4.2 Nurse communicating with a non–English-speaking patient using a translation phone service. (Courtesy Linda Bucher, RN, PhD, CEN, CNE, Staff Nurse, Virtua Memorial Hospital, Mt. Holly, NJ.)

2.9. Choose patient teaching materials written at the 5th grade or lower reading level. Other interventions to help patients with low levels of health literacy include using the teach-back method, highlighting key text, and teaching content in small increments.

Cultural considerations. Cultural traditions influence our health practices, beliefs, and behavior. These traditions, which can affect patient teaching, can be identified in a cultural assessment (see Table 2.5). TJC requires that we tailor patient teaching to the patient's cultural needs.[17] Ask patients to describe their beliefs about health and illness.

One cultural element that specifically affects the teaching-learning process is a conflict between the patient's cultural beliefs and values and the behaviors promoted by the health care team. For example, you can teach a patient who values having an average body weight to use diet and exercise to maintain the recommended weight to improve BP control. However, being heavier may be valued in another patient's culture. This patient may have more difficulty accepting the need for diet and exercise in BP control.

Assess the patient's use of cultural remedies and healing practices. Consider the cultural remedies that may conflict with the treatment plan.

Last, it is important to know who has authority in the patient's culture. The patient may defer to the authority, such as an elder or a spiritual leader, for decisions. In this case, identify and work with the patient and the decision makers in the patient's cultural group. See Chapter 2 for more information on cultural competence.

Socioeconomic considerations. Consider a variety of socioeconomic factors when preparing to teach patients. Knowing the patient's present or past occupation may help you determine the vocabulary to use during teaching. For example, an auto mechanic may understand the volume overload from heart failure as flooding an engine. An engineer may understand the principles of physics associated with gravity and pressures when discussing vascular problems.

Ask the patient about living arrangements. Whether the patient lives alone, with friends, or with family influences who you include in the teaching process. You may need to change the teaching plan if the patient does not have access to electricity or phones. If the patient has unmet learning needs at the time of discharge, arrange for ongoing teaching.

Learner Factors

Last, assess learner factors, including the patient's learning needs, readiness to learn, and learning style.

Learning needs. **Learning needs** are the new knowledge and skills that a person must have to meet a goal. Assess what the patient already knows and any past experiences with health problems. Patients with long-standing health problems may have different learning needs from those patients with newly diagnosed health problems.

What patients should learn about managing health and illness may seem obvious to you. However, what you think is important may be different from what patients want to know. Remember, adults learn best when given information that they view as being needed at once (see Table 4.1). Ask patients to prioritize what they see as the most critical information. Start by giving the patient a list of the recommended topics and then ask the patient to identify other topics not on the list. Having patients prioritize their own learning needs lets you begin with the patient's most important needs. Explain why critical information is "need to know."

Readiness to learn. Motivation and readiness to learn depend on multiple factors, such as perceived need, attitudes, and beliefs. When teaching adults, identify what information the person values. Readiness to learn increases when the patient perceives a need for information, has a belief that a behavior change has value, or perceives the learning activities as new and stimulating.[4]

Before implementing the teaching plan, determine where the patient is in the stages of change (see Table 4.2). If the patient is in the precontemplation stage, provide support and increase the patient's awareness of the problem until the patient is ready to consider a behavior change. Nurses in outpatient settings and home health care can continue to assess the patient's readiness to learn and implement the teaching plan as the patient moves through the stages of change. Reinforcement throughout the change process is a strong motivational factor for achieving a desired behavior. **Positive reinforcement** involves rewarding the target behavior with positive feedback or other rewards to maintain the behavior.[5]

Learning style. Each person has preferred styles of learning. The three general learning styles are (1) *visual* (reading, pictures), (2) *auditory* (listening), and (3) *physical* (doing things). People often use more than 1 learning style to gain new knowledge or skills. Ask how the patient likes to learn and has learned effectively in the past. Identify the patient who does not read or who has low health literacy. For example, the patient may tell you that they do not read much but likes to learn from television. In addition, assess the patient's *ehealth literacy*. This refers to the degree that patients use digital information (e.g.,

Fig. 4.3 Older couple accessing the Web for health information. (© monkeybusinessimages/iStock/Thinkstock.)

webinars, online health management tools) and communication technologies (e.g., online communication with HCP, online support groups) to improve their health (Fig. 4.3).[18] When possible, use the patient's or caregiver's preferred learning style in developing teaching plans.

Clinical Problems

Clinical problems for the patient and caregiver related to teaching include:

- Deficient knowledge
- Literacy problem

Planning

Prioritize the patient's learning needs and agree on learning goals. If the patient's condition prevents participation, involve the patient's caregiver(s) in the planning.

Setting Goals

It is important to have clear and measurable learning goals (Table 4.7). Learning goals relate to the intended outcome of the learning process, guide the choice of teaching strategies, and help evaluate the patient's progress. Learning goals are parallel to patient outcomes in the nursing care plan (NCP). Most settings have standardized NCPs with preset goals and interventions for specific learning needs. You will modify these NCPs based on the patient's unique sociocultural and learner characteristics.

Choosing Teaching Strategies

Three factors that influence the choice of teaching strategies are (1) patient characteristics (e.g., learning style, educational background, culture, language skills), (2) subject matter, and (3) available resources. Table 4.8 summarizes learner characteristics and recommended teaching approaches based on the generation of the patient or caregiver.

Consider various strategies (Table 4.9) in the teaching plan. We often use multiple teaching strategies to improve learning (Fig. 4.4). Discussion is the most common type of interaction used in teaching patients and caregivers. A type of group teaching involves *peer teaching,* as occurs in support groups. Patients

TABLE 4.7 Writing Learning Goals

Elements of Learning Goals

Learning goals are written statements that define exactly how patients demonstrate their knowledge of the content. Goals address the following 4 questions:

1. ***Who Will Perform the Activity or Acquire the Desired Behavior?***
   Examples:
   - I (the patient) will
   - I (the caregiver) will
   - We (patient's family/caregivers) will
2. ***What Is the Actual Behavior That the Learner Will Exhibit to Show Mastery of the Goal?***
   Examples:
   - List the symptoms.
   - Self-administer an insulin injection.
   - Choose from a hospital menu.
3. ***What Are the Conditions Under Which the Behavior Is to Be Demonstrated?***
   Examples:
   - In front of the nurse
   - From a random list
   - Using sterile technique
4. ***What Are the Specific Criteria That Will Be Used to Measure the Patient's Success, Such as Time and Degree of Accuracy?***
   Examples:
   - With 100% accuracy
   - Over the next week
   - Before discharge

Verbs in Learning Goals

Avoid vague, ambiguous verbs that are hard to measure:	*Use verbs that have precise descriptions with few interpretations:*
• Appreciate	• Identify
• Learn	• List
• Understand	• Describe
• Enjoy	• Demonstrate
• Feel	• Perform
• Value	• Choose

Poorly and Well-Written Learning Goals

Example of Poorly Written Learning Goal	Examples of Well-Written Learning Goals
• The patient will understand the importance of managing his own colostomy. *Analysis*: It is not clear how the patient will show that he "understands" the importance of managing his colostomy, when and to whom he will demonstrate this behavior, or what criteria will be used to determine whether the goal has been met.	• The patient will describe to the nurse the basic steps for changing the colostomy pouch and skin barrier by 2/14/21. • Using correct technique, the patient will empty his colostomy pouch when one-third full. • The patient's caregiver will perform colostomy care, including changing the pouch and skin barrier. • Given a list of signs and symptoms related to complications of a colostomy, the patient and caregiver will identify signs and symptoms to report to a health care provider before discharge. *Analysis*: When learning goals are clear and specific and documented in the patient's record, all members of the health care team can work together to achieve the same outcomes.

TABLE 4.8 Learner Characteristics and Teaching Strategies by Generation

Birth Year	Learner Characteristics	Recommended Teaching Strategies
Generation Z		
Late 1990s to mid-2010s	• Prefer intrapersonal or independent learning • Personal meaning-making • Hands-on or applied learning • Technology focused • Connected to the virtual world • View educators as supportive resources to enhance learning	• Alternate individual learning with educator-led teaching activities • Integrate technology and media in teaching • Use self-paced learning activities • Provide hands-on learning experiences
Millennials (Generation Y, Yers, Nexters, Digital Natives)		
1981–2000	• Multitaskers • Prefer interactive and virtual environments • Technologically focused • Need flexibility • Short attention span • Team players • Prefer more structured learning compared to Xers • Accustomed to learning whatever, wherever, whenever	• Integrate technology and media in teaching • Discuss reliable health-related mobile apps and websites • Download health information to smart phones, tablets, or similar devices • Consider group teaching • Consider active learning approaches
Generation X (Xers, Digital Natives)		
1965–1980	• Self-directed or self-paced learning • Self-reliant • Consumers of education • Short attention span	• Integrate technology and media in teaching • Discuss reliable websites • Consider health-related mobile applications • Give Web-based education materials • Provide education materials that are brief and easy to read • Encourage questions
Baby Boomers (Digital Immigrants)		
1946–1964	• Emphasis on self-knowledge • Solve problems by action • Acquisition of knowledge from authoritative sources • Receptive to feedback • Prefer text over graphics • Process (step-by-step) oriented	• Assess ehealth literacy and consider strategies as appropriate • Consider lecture or lecture-discussion (e.g., PowerPoint presentation) • Use patient education TV channels • Provide printed materials
Veterans (Traditionalists, Digital Immigrants)		
Born before 1946	• Emphasis on rote learning • Memorization of knowledge • Follow rules	• Assess ehealth literacy and consider strategies as appropriate • Consider lecture or lecture-discussion • Use pictures and printed materials such as books

Compiled from Ford C, Mosely L: Challenges to health professions education and strategies for moving forward, *New Direct Teach Learn* 162:199, 2020; Bradshaw M, Lowenstein A: *Innovative teaching strategies in nursing*, ed 7, Burlington, MA, 2017, Jones & Bartlett Learning; and Hart S: Today's learners and educators: bridging the generational gaps, *Teach Learn Nurs* 12:253, 2017.

dealing with common problems such as cancer, alcoholism, and eating disorders can receive help from peer teaching.

Adapt your teaching methods when teaching patients with a disability how to care for themselves or how to take part in their own care. It is essential to know how to modify teaching methods to meet the needs of patients with cognitive impairment, hearing loss, limited manual dexterity, or vision loss. Magnifying glasses, bright lighting, and materials printed in a large font may help the patient with impaired vision read teaching materials. More visual stimuli can help people with hearing loss. Using adaptive equipment may help those with problems performing manual skills. Table 4.10 presents strategies for teaching patients who have disabilities.

Learning materials. Use learning materials in multiple formats. Learn what resources are available in your agency and from support services and professional groups. The use of CDs/DVDs and online videos is helpful, particularly when teaching visual content such as the steps of a procedure (e.g., suctioning a tracheostomy). The health care agency's television system may show high-quality, professionally produced patient teaching programs on demand or on a rotating schedule (see Fig. 4.4).

Printed materials are useful for teaching patients and caregivers, especially for those whose preferred learning style is reading. Some health-related organizations, such as the American Cancer Society (ACS) and the AHA provide free, quality patient education materials. Some governmental organizations, such as the National Institutes of Health and the Centers for Disease Control and Prevention, have learning materials for patients and caregivers. These materials can be used with other teaching strategies. For instance, after a discussion on the effects of smoking on health, you may use material from the ACS to reinforce the information.

TABLE 4.9 Comparison of Teaching Strategies

Description	Advantages	Limitations
Discussion ("Teach Back")		
• Purpose is to exchange points of view about a topic or to arrive at a decision or conclusion • Can be done with patient, with patient and caregiver, or with group • *Example:* Weight loss	• Allows for an active exchange of information and experiences among participants • Good when patients have experience with subject and have information to share • Nonthreatening format • Can use peers (patients with common problems) to teach	• May need more time depending on topic and number of participants
Lecture-Discussion		
• Useful when group of patients and caregivers can benefit from basic information • Lecture portion is short (i.e., 15–20 min) • Discussion ("teach back") follows lecture • *Example:* Basic principles of cardiac rehabilitation (e.g., exercise, nutrition)	• Combines short lecture to present basic information with time for discussion • Provision of printed material related to lecture content is useful and recommended	• Need to limit number of lecture topics to 3–5 • May need more time depending on topic and number of participants
Demonstration/Return Demonstration ("Show Back")		
• Purpose is to teach patient and caregiver to perform a skill • Return demonstration ("show back") can show patient's ability to perform skill (see Fig. 4.5) • *Examples:* Dressing change, injection	• Provides for learning and practice of physical skills • Dividing skill into series of smaller steps helps mastery and provides reinforcement	• May need more time for practice needed to master skill • Patients with limited manual dexterity may have difficulty
Use of Teaching Resources		
• Audiovisual aids to supplement teaching • Printed materials (e.g., brochures) • CDs/DVDs • Hospital-based TV (see Fig. 4.4) • Digital and communication technologies (e.g., mobile applications, Web-based patient education programs, game-based education, online support groups) • Telehealth	• Enhances the presentation through visual and/or auditory stimulation • Best used in combination with other teaching strategies • Use of digital and communication technologies for health information is the preferred choice for many • Web access in patient rooms is standard in most health care agencies • Health information can be given and reinforced to patients remotely	• Review materials for accuracy, reading level, completeness, before using • Evaluate websites, games, applications, programs, for validity of information • May not be appropriate for all learners (e.g., lack of interest, decreased mental capacity) • Finances (e.g., equipment purchase, Internet service) may be a limiting factor to using digital technology

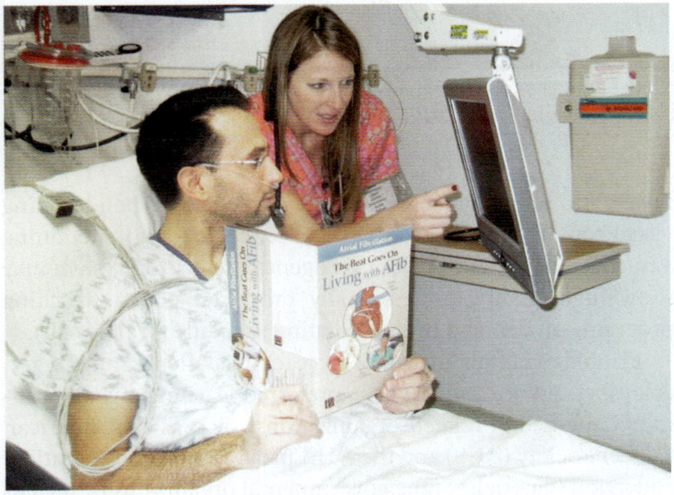

Fig. 4.4 Effective teaching using a variety of strategies (written materials, computer-based patient education programs). (Courtesy Linda Bucher, RN, PhD, CEN, CNE, Staff Nurse, Virtua Memorial Hospital, Mt. Holly, NJ.)

When writing teaching materials, use several techniques to keep the reading level at a fifth-grade level. These include (1) organize the content logically; (2) highlight or place key information in bold or italics; (3) use short, common words of 1 or 2 syllables; (4) define medical words in simple language; (5) keep sentences short, between 10 and 15 words; (6) use pictures or drawings; and (7) use active voice in the same manner in which you would normally speak.[12] Whenever possible, appraise written materials for readability level using word processing (e.g., Microsoft Word) or Web-based (e.g., www.wordscount.info) programs.

Using technology. Patients may use the Internet and other digital technology (e.g., smart phones) to obtain information and manage their health. Patients can quickly do a Web search or open a software application for access to information about diseases, drugs, treatments, and surgeries. Your job is to help patients sift through the information and determine if it is valid, reliable, and usable. Encourage patients to use websites maintained by the government, universities, or reputable health-related organizations (e.g., American Diabetes Association, AHA, ACS, National Institutes of Health, U.S. Food and Drug Administration). Teach patients to search for valid health information. The presence of Internet connections in patient rooms provides an opportunity to teach patients about their illness and how to find related information online.

Overall, the digital health divide for older adults has narrowed. However, there are racial and ethnic disparities amongst older adults' use of health technologies. Blacks and Hispanics are less likely than whites to use health-management sites or access the Internet for health-related uses.[19] Organizations dedicated to improving the quality of life for older adults publish guides to help evaluate Web-based health information (e.g., www.mlanet.org/resources/userguide.html).

The quantity and complexity of digital health care technology available to you and your patients will continue to increase. *Telehealth,* a broad term that refers to the delivery of health-related services and information via telecommunications technologies, allows for (1) remote HCP-patient consultations *(telemedicine);* (2) monitoring of physical parameters, such as vital signs, weight, heart rhythm, blood glucose, and (3) ongoing patient teaching.

TABLE 4.10 Teaching Patients With Disabilities

Hearing Loss[20]
- Sit in front of the patient at eye level with the light shining on your face
- Use assistive listening devices to amplify sound
- Speak slowly and clearly, using short, simple sentences
- Create a quiet environment that eliminates or minimizes background noises
- Assess patient's preferred communication method (sign language or lip reading)
- If patient prefers to use sign language:
  - Leave as much freedom as possible for their dominant hand to allow for signing
  - Use a sign language interpreter to preserve patient privacy and confidentiality
  - If using a sign language interpreter, speak to the patient, not the interpreter
- If the patient prefers lip-reading:
  - Make sure the patient can see your lips
  - Face the patient and maintain eye contact
  - Ensure there is good lighting on your lips
  - Speak in a normal rhythm and tone
  - Use facial expressions to help convey meaning

Limited Manual Dexterity
- Provide assistive (ease of use) devices to help the patient perform necessary tasks to perform a skill

Mild Cognitive Impairment[21]
- Explain what you will be doing
- Use simple wording
- Present one instruction at a time
- Ask yes/no questions
- Avoid open-ended questions
- Be patient
- Answer repeated questions as if it were the first time the question was asked
- Reinforce instructions often
- Create a quiet environment and minimize distractions

Vision Loss[22,23]
- Use low-vision aids, such as magnifiers, high-power reading glasses, or handheld or mounted telescopes
- Use technology, such as screen readers that read text on the computer screen using a speech synthesizer or convert text to braille
- Use electronic tablets or smart phones with adjustable text size
- Use large print publications
- Ensure that there is good lighting in the environment
- Minimize distractions and eliminate background noise
- Give educational materials available in braille
- Provide verbal or tactile instruction instead of written instruction

Implementation

During the implementation phase, use the planned strategies to present information and teach new skills. Include verbal and nonverbal communication skills, active listening, and empathy in the process. Based on the assessment of the patient's physical, psychologic, sociocultural, and learner characteristics, determine how much the patient can participate. Whenever possible and appropriate, involve the patient's caregiver(s) in the teaching-learning process.

Remember to respect the principles and characteristics of the adult learner. Although reinforcement and reward are important, phrases such as, "Aren't you doing well!" in a tone one would use with a child can seem condescending to adult learners.

Evaluation

Evaluation, the last step in the learning process, is a measure of the degree to which the patient has achieved the learning goals. You can use various evaluation techniques (Table 4.11).

TABLE 4.11 Evaluating Patient and Caregiver Learning

Technique	Strategy and Examples

Observe patient or caregiver directly	• Ask person to show you how to change the dressing
	• Return demonstration ("show back") determines whether:
	  • Skill has been mastered
	  • Further instruction is needed
	  • Patient and caregiver are ready for new or more content

Observe verbal and nonverbal cues	• Teaching may have to be delayed, more teaching needed, or different strategy used if patient or caregiver:
	  • Asks you to repeat instructions
	  • Loses eye contact
	  • Begins to doze in chair or bed
	  • Becomes restless or fidgety
	  • Does not speak English

Ask open-ended questions ("teach back")	• Open-ended questions provide more information about understanding than closed-ended questions, which need only a "yes" or "no"
	• Ask questions such as:
	  • "How often do you need to change the dressing?"
	  • "What will you do if you develop chest pain at home?"

Talk with caregiver ("teach back")	• Involve caregiver in the evaluation process
	• Ask questions such as:
	  • "What medications is she taking?"
	  • "When does he use his oxygen?"

Seek the patient's self-evaluation of progress	• Ask patient's opinion about their progress • Assess what evidence the patient has that the goals are being met • Assess if the patient is ready to learn new material

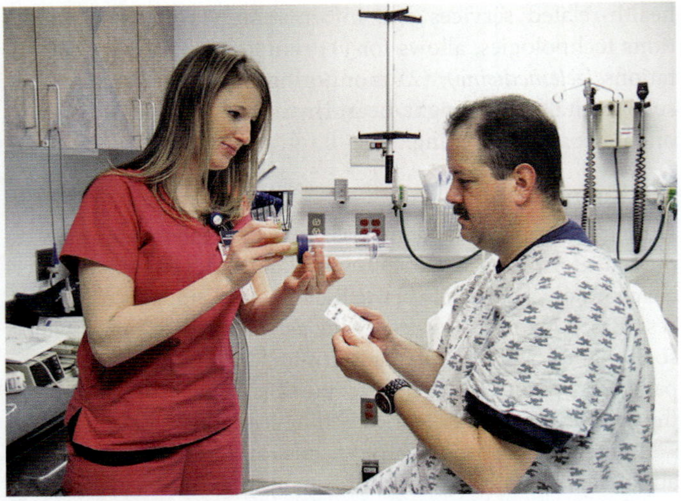

Fig. 4.5 Teaching using discussion ("teach back") and demonstration/return demonstration ("show back") increases successful learning by the patient. (Courtesy Linda Bucher, RN, PhD, CEN, CNE, Staff Nurse, Virtua Memorial Hospital, Mt. Holly, NJ.)

Use techniques such as "teach back" to determine the knowledge and skill levels of the patient and/or caregiver throughout the teaching and learning process (Fig. 4.5). If goals are not reached, reassess the patient and revise the teaching plan as needed.

Assumptions about a patient's knowledge and skills are dangerous. Confirm prior knowledge even as you are teaching and evaluating new skills.

Long-term evaluation of learning goals often requires follow-up after discharge. Provide a written schedule of visits and other appropriate referrals before the patient leaves the hospital or clinic. It is important to share this information with the patient's caregiver(s) so that everyone involved in the patient's long-term progress has the same information.

Documentation is an essential part in the teaching-learning process. Record the teaching goals, strategies, and evaluation results so that the information is clear, complete, and available to the team members.

CHECK YOUR PRACTICE

Your patient is a 53-year-old man with type 1 diabetes who entered the hospital with a blood glucose level of 550 mg/dL (30.53 mmol/L). He is now stable and soon will be discharged.

You prepare his insulin and plan to give him the syringe to let him do his own injection. Before you go to his room, your preceptor suggests that you observe his technique of preparing the insulin as well as the injection. This comment puzzles you because he has had diabetes for 32 years and should know how to do it.

When you go to his room, you ask him to prepare the insulin injection ("show back"). You notice that he filled the syringe with 30 units of insulin and 10 units of air, instead of 40 units of insulin. After correcting the dose and questioning the patient more fully ("teach back"), you wonder what happened.

What are possible reasons that he did not draw up the correct amount of insulin?

Case Study

Patient and Caregiver Teaching

(© azndc/iStock/Thinkstock.)

Patient Profile

M.L., a 60-year-old Asian woman, is admitted to the hospital with a diagnosis of exacerbation of chronic obstructive pulmonary disease (COPD).

Subjective Data

- History of COPD for 10 years. Admitted twice in the past 8 months for COPD exacerbations. Reports a chronic cough. Denies any recent change in sputum color. States: "I stopped smoking last year, but my son-in-law smokes in the house."
- Medical history: Gastroesophageal reflux disease; macular degeneration in right eye.
- Social history: Widowed 5 years ago. Lives with daughter and son-in-law, who work full time. Cares for 2 young grandchildren after school. English is M.L.'s second language.

Objective Data

Physical Assessment

- Alert, oriented, anxious, thin woman with dyspnea on minimal exertion. Speaks in short phrases. States: "I have no energy."
- Oxygen via nasal cannula at 2 L/min
- Weight 100 lb, height 5 ft 2 in

Diagnostic Studies

- Chest x-ray negative for acute infection
- Arterial blood gases on room air: pH 7.35, $PaCO_2$ 47 mm Hg, PaO_2 75 mm Hg, HCO_3^- 30 mEq/L
- O_2 saturation via pulse oximetry during 6-min walk test on room air = 83%
- Forced expiratory volume in 1 second of expiration (FEV_1) = 60% of predicted

Interprofessional Care

- Medications: bronchodilator therapy (inpatient nebulizer therapy, inhalers at home), oral corticosteroids
- Continuous home O_2 therapy 2 L/min via nasal cannula
- Pulmonary rehabilitation: inpatient and outpatient

Discussion Questions

1. ***Recognize:*** What potential challenges might you expect when planning to teach M.L.? How would you manage them?
2. ***Analyze:*** What factors (e.g., sociocultural, physical, psychologic) noted in the assessment may influence M.L.'s response to teaching?
3. ***Plan/Prioritize:*** Choose 2 of M.L.'s priority learning needs. Develop a teaching plan for M.L. for each of these needs.
4. ***Evaluate:*** What assessment data would you need to collect to decide if teaching was effective?

Answers available at http://evolve.elsevier.com/Lewis/medsurg.

BRIDGE TO NCLEX EXAMINATION

The number of the question corresponds to the same-numbered outcome at the beginning of the chapter.

1. A patient tells the nurse that he is ready to start a weight-loss program. Which nursing action would match this patient's readiness for change?
   - a. Confirm that the patient is serious about losing weight.
   - b. Assess the patient's awareness of his dietary behaviors.
   - c. Insist that the patient consider an organized group weight-loss program.
   - d. Focus on the patient's strengths to support his optimism that he can lose weight.
2. Which action would the nurse *prioritize* when limited time is available for patient teaching?
   - a. Setting realistic goals that have high priority for the patient
   - b. Referring the patient to a nurse educator for private practice
   - c. Asking more experienced nurses how to teach faster and more efficiently
   - d. Providing reading materials for the patient instead of discussing the information
3. Which rationale supports including caregivers in patient teaching? *(select all that apply.)*
   - a. Caregivers provide all the care for patients after discharge.
   - b. They might feel rejected if they are not included in the teaching.
   - c. Patients have better outcomes when their caregivers are involved.
   - d. The patient may be too ill or too stressed to fully understand the teaching.
   - e. Caregivers are responsible for the overall management of the patient's care.
4. Which patient characteristic enhances learning outcomes?
   - a. Feeling moderate anxiety
   - b. Developing high self-efficacy
   - c. Laughing about the current health problem
   - d. Being in the precontemplation stage of change
5. Which goal applies when planning to teach a middle-aged woman about ways to relieve symptoms of menopause?
   - a. Prevent the development of future disease.
   - b. Maintain the patient's current state of health.
   - c. Provide information on possible treatment options.
   - d. Change the patient's beliefs about herbal supplements.
6. A patient tells the nurse that she enjoys talking with others and sharing experiences but often falls asleep when reading. Which teaching strategy would the nurse plan for this patient?
   - a. Formal lecture
   - b. Journal writing
   - c. Digital technology
   - d. Small-group discussion
7. The nurse taught a caregiver how to administer insulin. Which action would the nurse take to evaluate the caregiver's learning?
   - a. Monitor the patient's glucose readings.
   - b. Arrange for follow-up with a home care nurse.
   - c. Ask the caregiver to "show back" the ability to administer insulin.
   - d. Assess what the caregiver thought was effective about the teaching.

1. d; 2. a; 3. c, d; 4. b; 5. c; 6. d; 7. c.

For rationales to these answers and even more NCLEX review questions, visit http://evolve.elsevier.com/Lewis/medsurg.

EVOLVE WEBSITE/RESOURCES LIST

http://evolve.elsevier.com/Lewis/medsurg
Review Questions (Online Only)
Key Points
Answer Key for Questions
- Rationales for Bridge to NCLEX Examination Questions

Conceptual Care Map Creator
Audio Glossary
Content Updates

REFERENCES

1. Centers for Disease Control and Prevention: Chronic disease prevention and health promotion. Retrieved from www.cdc.gov/chronicdisease/index.htm.

*2. Ryan CJ, Bierle RS, Vuckovic KM: The three Rs for preventing heart failure readmission: review, reassess, and reeducate, *Crit Care Nurse* 39:85, 2019.

3. American Nurses Association: *Nursing scope and standards of practice*, ed 3, Washington, DC, 2015, The Association. (Classic).

4. Knowles MS, Holton EF, Swanson RA: *The adult learner: the definitive classic in adult education and human resource development*, ed 7, St Louis, 2011, Mosby. (Classic).

5. Prochaska J, Velicer W: The transtheoretical model of health behavior change, *Am J Health Promotion* 12:38, 1997. (Classic).

6. Rollnick S, Miller WR, Yahne CE: *Motivational interviewing in health care: helping patients change behavior*, New York, 2008, Guilford Press. (Classic).

7. Centers for Disease Control and Prevention: Healthy aging, Caregiving. Retrieved from www.cdc.gov/aging/caregiving/index.htm.

8. The Joint Commission: National patient safety goals, 2020. Retrieved from. https://www.jointcommission.org/standards/national-patient-safety-goals/.

9. American Hospital Association: The patient care partnership. Retrieved from www.aha.org/advocacy-issues/communicatingpts/pt-care-partnership.shtml.

10. The Joint Commission: Speak Up initiatives, 2018. Retrieved from. https://www.jointcommission.org/resources/for-consumers/speak-up-campaigns/.

11. Institute for Healthcare Improvement, National Patient Safety Foundation: Ask Me 3. Retrieved from http://www.ihi.org/resources/Pages/Tools/Ask-Me-3-Good-Questions-for-Your-Good-Health.aspx.

12. National Institutes of Health: Health literacy. Retrieved from www.nih.gov/institutes-nih/nih-office-director/office-communications-public-liaison/clear-communication/health-literacy.

13. Agency for Healthcare Research and Quality: Health literacy universal precautions toolkit, ed 2. Retrieved from https://www.ahrq.gov/health-literacy/quality-resources/tools/literacy-toolkit/index.html.
14. Office of Disease Prevention and Health Promotion: Health communication and health information technology. Retrieved from www.healthypeople.gov/2020/topics-objectives/topic/health-communication-and-health-information-technology.
*15. Son YJ, Won MH: Gender differences in the impact of health literacy on hospital readmission among older heart failure patients: a prospective cohort study, *J Adv Nurs* 76:1345, 2020.
16. Morris NS, MacLean CD, Chew LD, et al.: The single item literacy screener: evaluation of a brief instrument to identify limited reading ability, *BMC Fam Pract* 7:21, 2006 (Classic).
17. The Joint Commission: Health equity. Retrieved from https://www.jointcommission.org/resources/patient-safety-topics/health-equity/#t=_StandardsFAQsTab.
18. Oh H, Rizo C, Enkin M, et al.: What is e-health: a systematic review of published definitions, *J Med Internet Res* 7:1, 2005. (Classic).
19. Uchechi AM, Perla GC, Ruggiero L, Muramatsu N: The digital divide in health-related technology use: the significance of race/ethnicity, *Gerontol* 59(6), 2019.
20. National Institutes of Health, National Institute on Deafness and Other Communication Disorders: Hearing loss and older adults. Retrieved from www.nidcd.nih.gov/health/hearing-loss-older-adults.
21. National Institute on Aging: Communicating with a confused patient. Retrieved from www.nia.nih.gov/health/communicating-confused-patient.
22. U.S. National Library of Medicine, Medline Plus: Living with vision loss. Retrieved from www.medlineplus.gov/ency/patientinstructions/000526.htm.
23. American Foundation for the Blind: Technology resources for people with vision loss. Retrieved from www.afb.org/info/living-with-vision-loss/using-technology/12.

*Evidence-based information for clinical practice.

5

Chronic Illness and Older Adults

Sherry A. Greenberg

http://evolve.elsevier.com/Lewis/medsurg/

CONCEPTUAL FOCUS

Cognition
Family Dynamics
Functional Ability
Mobility
Nutrition
Sensory Perception

LEARNING OUTCOMES

1. Explain the characteristics of a chronic illness.
2. Describe the prevention and major causes of chronic illness.
3. Describe the demographics of aging.
4. Explain the needs of special populations of older adults.
5. Describe types of elder mistreatment and appropriate nursing interventions.
6. Distinguish among care alternatives and ways to create systems of care to meet needs of older adults.
7. Describe common problems of older adults related to hospitalization and acute illness and the nurse's role in assisting them.
8. Describe the nurse's role in health promotion and managing the special needs of older adults.

KEY TERMS

ageism
elder mistreatment (EM)
ethnogeriatric
frail older adult
gerontologic nursing
Medicaid
Medicare
old-old adult
young-old adult

This chapter discusses issues related to chronic illness and aging. The older adult population is growing rapidly. You need to consider their multiple, complex health care conditions and needs when planning and providing comprehensive nursing care. Functional ability in those with chronic illness and older adults is interrelated with several concepts. These include mobility, perfusion, nutrition, cognition, and sensory perception. Family dynamics and caregiving shape the care provided to those who need help to meet their needs.

CHRONIC ILLNESS

Illness can be categorized as either acute or chronic (Table 5.1). The U.S. health care system faces a growing burden of chronic illness as the population ages. Chronic illnesses account for 70% of all deaths in the United States. Chronic illness results in limitations in physical functioning, work productivity, and quality of life for nearly 1 out of 10 Americans. Many older adults live with more than 1 chronic illness. Some live with 6 or more. In 2016, 38% of older adults age 65 and older had at least 1 chronic condition. 47% had 2 to 3 chronic conditions, and 15% had 4 or more chronic conditions.[1] A large portion of U.S. health care dollars goes toward treating chronic illnesses. Managing a chronic illness greatly affects the lives of older adults, families, and caregivers. Table 5.2 presents the impact of some chronic illnesses.

In addition to people living longer, other societal changes have contributed to the increase in chronic illnesses. These include insufficient physical activity, lack of access to fresh fruits and vegetables, and tobacco and alcohol use.[2]

Trajectory of Chronic Illness

The person with a chronic illness can move from a level of optimum functioning, with the illness well controlled, to a period of physical instability. Corbin and Strauss proposed a view of chronic illness as a trajectory (Fig. 5.1) with overlapping phases (Table 5.3).[3] This trajectory depicts the common course of most chronic conditions. In addition, Corbin and Strauss identified the 7 tasks of those who are chronically ill (Table 5.4). We discuss these tasks in the next sections.

Preventing and Managing a Crisis

Most chronic illnesses have the potential for an acute exacerbation of symptoms. This may result in further disability or death. Examples include the patient with heart disease who has another myocardial infarction or the patient with asthma who has a severe attack. A major task for the patient and caregiver is to learn to prevent or manage the crisis. First, they need to understand the potential for the crisis to occur. Second, they need to know ways to prevent or modify the threat. This often involves adhering to a prescribed medical and overall health plan. Patients need to know the signs and symptoms of the onset of a crisis or exacerbation. Depending on the chronic illness, signs and symptoms may occur suddenly (e.g., bleeding in a patient with inflammatory bowel disease) or slowly (e.g., heart failure in a person with untreated hypertension). It is important for the patient and caregiver to have a plan to manage a crisis that is likely to occur.

Carrying Out Prescribed Treatment Plan

Treatment plans vary in degree of difficulty and the impact they have on the person's lifestyle. Some plans may be perceived as challenging or time-consuming, such as changing a dressing multiple times a day or following a toileting program. However, they generally save time, prevent complications, and improve outcomes.

Controlling Symptoms

An important task for those with chronic illnesses is to learn to control symptoms so that they can continue to do what matters to them. Some alter their lifestyle by learning to plan ahead. People with heart failure adjust the time they take diuretics when going out for the day to avoid needing to rush to a bathroom. Encourage independence in decision making and collaborating with the health care provider (HCP) about treatment plans to avoid an exacerbation of the illness. Others may change their living space. Patients and their families need to learn about the pattern of symptoms, such as typical onset, duration, and severity, so that lifestyle may be changed accordingly while maintaining safety.

TABLE 5.1 Characteristics of Acute and Chronic Illness

Description	Characteristics
Acute Illness	
Diseases that have a rapid onset and short duration *Examples:* colds, influenza, acute gastroenteritis	• Usually self-limiting • Responds readily to treatment • Complications infrequent • After illness, return to previous level of functioning
Chronic Illness	
Diseases that are prolonged, do not resolve spontaneously, rarely cured completely *Examples:* Table 5.2	• Permanent impairments or deviations from normal • Irreversible pathologic changes • Residual disability • Special rehabilitation needed • Need for long-term medical and/or nursing management

TABLE 5.2 Impact of Chronic Illnesses

Chronic Illness	Impact	Chapter
Cancer	• 2nd leading cause of death • Risk increases with age	16
Cardiovascular disease, including heart disease and stroke	• Affects about 17 million adults • Account for 33% of U.S. deaths annually • Heart disease is leading cause of death in United States • Heart failure is a common cause of hospitalization and rehospitalization • Stroke is 5th leading cause of death • Stroke is a common cause of serious disability	37, 38, and 62
COPD	• Affects many older adults • 4th leading cause of death	31
Diabetes	• Affects >30 million Americans • 25% of adults in United States do not know they have diabetes • 7th leading cause of death	53
Human immunodeficiency virus (HIV)	• Nearly 50% of those living with HIV in the United States are over 50 years old • Older adults more likely to receive diagnosis of HIV infection later in course of disease	15
Obesity	• Affects 43% of adults age 60 and over • Major contributor to other health problems and chronic diseases	45

Data from Centers for Disease Control and Prevention: CDC's chronic disease press releases. Retrieved from www.cdc.gov/chronicdisease/resources/publications/aag.htm; www.cdc.gov/hiv/group/age/olderamericans/index.html; and https://www.cdc.gov/nchs/fastats/leading-causes-of-death.htm.

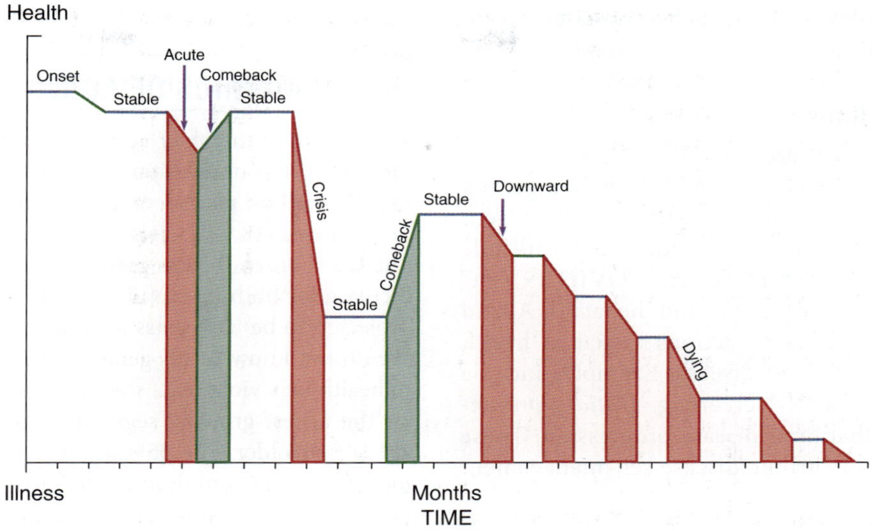

Fig. 5.1 The Chronic Illness Trajectory is a theoretical model of chronic illness. The trajectory model of chronic illness recognizes that chronic illness will have many phases (Table 5.3). (From Woog P: *The chronic illness trajectory framework: the Corbin and Strauss nursing model*, New York, 1992, Springer.)

TABLE 5.3 Chronic Illness Trajectory

Phases	Description
Onset	• Signs and symptoms are present • Disease diagnosed
Stable	• Illness course and symptoms controlled by treatment plan • Person maintains daily activities
Acute	• Active illness with severe and unrelieved symptoms or complications • Hospitalization may be needed for management
Comeback	• Gradual return to an acceptable way of life
Crisis	• Life-threatening situation occurs • Emergency services are necessary
Unstable	• Unable to keep symptoms or disease course under control • Life disrupted while patient works to regain stability • Hospitalization not required
Downward	• Gradual and progressive deterioration in physical or mental status • Accompanied by increasing disability and symptoms • Continuous changes in daily life activities
Dying	• Patient has to relinquish life interests and activities, let go, and die peacefully • Immediate weeks, days, hours preceding death

Source: Woog P: *The chronic illness trajectory framework: the Corbin and Strauss nursing model*, New York, 1992, Springer.

Reordering Time

People with chronic illness often report having too much or too little time. Treatment plans that require large amounts of time for the person, as well as caregivers, may require changing schedules or eliminating other activities. For example, the patient with a new ileostomy needs to plan for increased time in the bathroom to change the drainage bag.

TABLE 5.4 7 Tasks of People With Chronic Illness

- Prevent and manage a crisis
- Carry out prescribed treatment plan
- Control symptoms
- Reorder time
- Adjust to changes in course of disease
- Prevent social isolation
- Attempt to normalize interactions with others

Source: Corbin JM, Strauss A: A nursing model for chronic illness management based upon the trajectory framework, *Sch Inq Nurs Pract* 5:155, 1991.

Adjusting to Changes in the Course of Disease

Some diseases, such as multiple sclerosis, have unpredictable courses that make planning activities difficult. Part of the person's task is to develop a personal identity that includes the chronic illness and to adjust to the necessary lifestyle changes. For example, a person with a mechanical heart valve taking warfarin may need to avoid sports that have a high risk for injury.

Preventing Social Isolation

Social isolation may occur with chronic illness. The person may choose to withdraw from social activities. For example, a woman with aphasia after a stroke may not want to go out in public because she is embarrassed about communication issues. Sometimes others withdraw from the ill person.

Attempting to Normalize Interactions With Others

Most persons with chronic illness try to manage symptoms so that they can hide their disabilities or disfigurement. This may involve wearing a prosthesis. They may want to show they can function the same as a person without a disability or chronic illness. An example is a woman with heart failure who stops walking to catch her breath but appears to be inspecting a plant or looking in a store window.

Preventing Chronic Illness

Chronic illnesses are often preventable. *Primary prevention* refers to measures such as eating a healthy diet, getting proper exercise, and receiving immunizations that prevent a specific disease. Immunizations for older adults include influenza, pneumococcal, herpes zoster, COVID-19, tetanus/diphtheria/pertussis (Td/Tdap), and hepatitis A and B. *Secondary prevention* refers to actions aimed at health screening and early detection of disease. Examples include colon cancer and breast cancer screening. *Tertiary prevention* refers to activities that limit disease progression. These include rehabilitation and chronic disease self-management programs.

NURSING MANAGEMENT: CHRONIC ILLNESS

Diagnosis and treatment of the acute phase or acute exacerbations of a chronic illness sometimes take place in a hospital. Other phases of a chronic illness are regularly assessed and managed in an ambulatory care setting, at home, in an assisted living facility, or in a skilled nursing facility.

An assessment of health status, at least annually, includes a person's level of daily functioning and their perception of relative health, function, and/or illness. Health assessment includes activities of daily living (ADLs), such as bathing, dressing, eating, toileting, and transferring. It also includes instrumental ADLs (IADLs). These include activities such as shopping, preparing food, housekeeping, doing laundry, taking medications, and handling finances.

Because most chronic illnesses are treated in an ambulatory care setting, it is important for patients and caregivers to understand and manage their own health. The term *self-management* refers to the person's ability to manage their health, especially in response to living with a chronic illness. It includes the ability to manage symptoms, medications and treatment plans, physical and psychosocial consequences, and lifestyle changes. Self-management is done in conjunction with the family and HCP.

You play a key role in managing patients with chronic illness. This includes conducting a complete history and physical assessment, teaching the patient and caregiver about the treatment plan, implementing symptom management plans, and evaluating patient outcomes.

Family caregivers (e.g., spouses, partners, adult children) often have important roles in the life of the chronically ill person. The ideal situation is when family caregivers work together with the patient to manage the chronic condition(s). This collaboration begins under the direction of the health care team at the time of diagnosis. When the caregiver is a spouse or partner who is also older, they may have a chronic illness or multiple chronic conditions as well. This may add a level of complexity to the coordination of care.

OLDER ADULTS

DEMOGRAPHICS OF AGING

The growth of the older adult population continues to outpace the rest of the population. Nearly 1 in 7 U.S. residents, more than 52 million people, or 16% of the population, were age 65 or older in 2018.[4] This is projected to reach 95 million in 2060. The U.S. Census Bureau predicts life expectancy to continue to increase for both men and women. By 2060, life expectancy is projected to be 83.9 years for men and 87.3 years for women.[4] We do not know if this gender difference is due to differences in health behaviors (e.g., smoking, alcohol use) or occupation.

The fastest-growing segment of older Americans is people ages 85 or older. The 85 and older population is projected to increase from 6.5 million in 2017 to 14.4 million in 2040.[4] The increase in life span is due to declining infant mortality, new drug therapies, mechanical devices, and improved surgical interventions. A greater emphasis on health promotion, disease prevention, and earlier detection as well as better care management has led to more Americans living past 85 years.

The percent of older adults age 65 and older from racial and ethnically diverse populations is expected to grow too. By 2050, we estimate that persons of Hispanic ethnicity will increase to 19.5% of the population. Asians are expected to increase to 8.4%, and Blacks to increase to 11.8%.[5]

The terms **young-old adult** (65 to 74 years of age) and **old-old adult** (85 years of age and older) describe 2 groups of older adults with distinct characteristics, needs, and living arrangements. Young-old adults typically are healthier, independent, and typically maintain good cognitive function. The old-old adult is often a widowed, divorced, or single woman dependent on family for support or care. Many old-old adults have outlived children, spouses or partners, and siblings.

The **frail older adult** is usually over age 75 with multiple physical, cognitive, and/or mental conditions. These often interfere with

BOX 5.1 BIOLOGIC SEX CONSIDERATIONS

Older Adults

Men
- More likely to be married and living with spouse or partner
- More likely to have health insurance
- Higher income after retirement
- Less likely to be involved in caregiving
- Overall have fewer chronic health conditions

Women
- More likely to live alone
- More likely to be widowed
- Less likely to have health insurance
- More likely to live in poverty
- Poverty rates highest among minority women
- More likely to lack formal work experience, leading to lower income
- More likely to rely on Social Security as a major source of income
- More likely to be the caregiver of an ill spouse or partner
- Have a higher incidence of chronic health conditions such as arthritis, hypertension, stroke, and diabetes

self-management and the ability to perform daily activities independently. Frail older adults are discussed later in this chapter.

ATTITUDES TOWARD AGING

Who is old? The answer often depends on the respondent's age and attitude. Your "real" age is set by a date in time. Many factors influence how "old" you feel. These include emotional and physical health, developmental stage, socioeconomic status, culture, and ethnicity. We all age. As we do, we are exposed to new and different life experiences. The accumulation of these differences makes older adults more diverse than any other age group.

As you assess older adults, consider and value their diversity and life history. Assess their feelings of what it means to be an older adult. Most older adults report having good-to-excellent health despite having a chronic condition. However, those with poor health often report a higher perceived age and lower sense of well-being when compared with healthy older adults. Age is important, but it may not be the most relevant factor in determining the appropriate care of an individual older adult.

Myths and stereotypes about aging are often supported by media reports of older adults who are "problematic." These misconceptions may lead to omissions or errors in assessment and unnecessary limitations or interventions. For example, if you think that all older people are rigid in their thinking, you may not present new ideas to a patient.

Ageism is a negative attitude based on age. Ageism leads to discrimination and disparities in the care given to older adults. If you have negative attitudes, it may be because you fear your own aging process. Or you may not be knowledgeable about aging and the health care needs of the older adult.

BIOLOGIC AGING

From a biologic view, *aging* reflects the changes that occur over time. Biologic aging is a multifactorial process involving genetics, diet, and environment. In part, we view biologic aging as a balance of positive and negative factors (Fig. 5.2). Research is directed at increasing older adults' average life span, functional status, and quality of life. The hope is that we can develop new antiaging therapies to slow down or reverse age-related changes that result in chronic illness and disability.

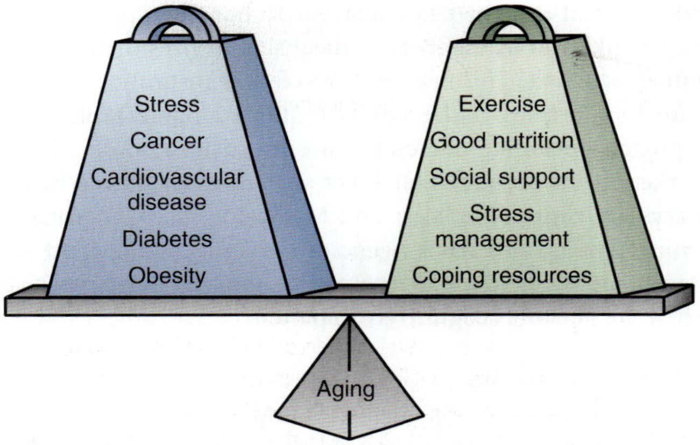

Fig. 5.2 The aging process can be viewed as a balance between negative and positive factors.

AGE-RELATED PHYSIOLOGIC CHANGES

Age-related changes affect every body system. These changes are normal and occur as people age. However, the age at which specific changes occur differs from person to person and within the same person. For instance, a person who has gray hair at age 45 may have fairly unwrinkled skin at age 80. As a nurse, you will assess for age-related changes. Table 5.5 shows where to find tables outlining age-related assessment findings.

SPECIAL OLDER ADULT POPULATIONS

Chronically Ill Older Adults

Daily living with chronic illness is a reality for many older adults; the incidence of chronic illness triples after age 45. Most people 65 years of age and older have at least 1 chronic condition. Many have multiple conditions.[1] The most common chronic conditions in older adults are hypertension, arthritis, heart disease (e.g., heart failure, coronary artery disease), diabetes, cancer, stroke, and chronic obstructive pulmonary disease (COPD). Other common chronic conditions include Alzheimer disease, vision and hearing deficits, osteoporosis, Parkinson disease, and depression.

Cognitively Impaired Older Adults

Most healthy older adults have no noticeable decline in cognitive abilities (Table 5.6). Older adults may have a mild decline in memory and may need more time to recall events or new information. This differs from cognitive impairment. New learning may be slower. Refer older adults with memory loss to their HCP for an evaluation. Teach them to use memory aids, attempt recall in a calm and quiet environment, and actively engage in enhancing memory. Memory aids include clocks, calendars, notes, marked pillboxes, safety alarms on stoves,

TABLE 5.5 GERONTOLOGIC ASSESSMENT DIFFERENCES

Tables Throughout the Book

Title	Chapter
Adaptations in Physical Assessment Techniques	3
Auditory System	23
Cardiovascular System	35
Cognitive Function	5
Effects of Aging on Hematologic Studies	33
Effects of Aging on the Immune System	14
Endocrine System	52
GI System	43
Integumentary System	24
Musculoskeletal System	66
Nervous System	60
Reproductive Systems	55
Respiratory System	27
Urinary System	49
Visual System	22

TABLE 5.6 GERONTOLOGIC ASSESSMENT DIFFERENCES

Cognitive Function

Effect of Aging	Cognitive Function
Improves with aging	• Vocabulary and verbal reasoning • Crystallized intelligence (ability to use skills, knowledge, experience)
Declines during middle age	• Mental performance speed • Synthesis of new information • Fluid intelligence (ability to think logically and solve problems in new situations)
Declines during old age	• Short-term recall memory
Constant (no changes with aging)	• Long-term recall memory

Fig. 5.3 Older adults living in rural areas often enjoy outside activities, such as gardening. (© arianarama/iStock.com.)

and identification necklaces or bracelets. Memory techniques include word association, mental imaging, and mnemonics.

Dementia, delirium, and depression can occur and may coexist in older adults. Declining physical health and acute illness are important factors that may influence cognition. For example, an older adult who has surgery may have an acute change in mental status called *delirium*.[6] Delirium superimposed on dementia may signify an acute or emergent condition such as heart failure. Hence, it is important to distinguish the signs and symptoms of each. Cognitive impairment, delirium, and dementia are discussed in Chapter 64.

Rural Older Adults

Key barriers to health care access for rural older adults are transportation, limited supply of health care workers and agencies, lack of quality health care, social isolation, and financial limitations. Particularly vulnerable are older adults of racial or ethnic minorities living in rural areas, who have even less access to HCPs. Older adults who live in rural areas may be less likely to engage in health-promoting activities.

When you work with older adults in rural areas, recognize lifestyle values and practices of rural life (Fig. 5.3). In planning care, be aware that transportation is the top barrier to health care for rural older adults. Alternative service approaches such as DVDs, radio, community centers, and church events may be used to promote healthy practices or to conduct health screening (Fig. 5.4).

Fig. 5.4 Older adults are using computers more often and accessing health care information on the Internet. (© iStockphoto/Thinkstock.)

The use of telehealth devices for monitoring patients in their home environments has enhanced the ability to provide care, including to those more isolated.[7] We must continue to develop innovative nursing practice models to help rural older adults. Older adults are increasingly using technology in their daily lives. Most older adults use the internet and a cell phone.

Homeless Older Adults

The number of older adults who are homeless is increasing. Key factors associated with homelessness include (1) having a low income, (2) having reduced cognitive capacity, (3) living alone, and (4) living in a community that lacks affordable housing. Homeless older adults may be chronically homeless or recently homeless because of a crisis in either health, economic, or social status.

Mortality rates for homeless older adults are higher than those who have housing. Older homeless adults are at higher risk for more health problems because many aging network services are not designed to reach out to homeless people. They are less likely to use shelters or meal site services than younger homeless people. This may be due to fear of institutionalization. Care for homeless older adults requires an interprofessional approach (including nurses, physicians, social workers, clerical workers, transporters) that links shelters with outreach, primary care clinics, Medicare and Medicaid offices, pharmacies, senior centers, and Area Agencies on Aging. Long-term care placement is often an alternative to homelessness, especially when the person is cognitively impaired.

Frail Older Adults

Frailty is a common clinical syndrome seen in older adults. We consider a person with 3 or more of these criteria as frail: (1) unintentional weight loss (10 pounds or more in a year);

TABLE 5.7 SCALES: Nutrition Assessment of Older Adults

The acronym SCALES can remind you to assess important nutrition indicators:
Sadness, or mood change
Cholesterol, high
Albumin, low
Loss or gain of weight
Eating problems (e.g., mechanical problems, such as impaired swallowing, poor dentition)
Shopping and food preparation problems

(2) self-reported exhaustion; (3) weakness (measured by grip strength); (4) slow walking speed; and (5) low level of physical activity.[8] Risk factors include disability, multiple chronic conditions, and dementia. People are more likely to become frail if they smoke, have a history of depression or long-term medical health problems, or are underweight. The old-old adult is most at risk for frailty, although many in this age group are healthy and robust.

Older frail adults often have declining function and decreasing daily energy. When stressful life events (e.g., death of a close friend) and daily strain (e.g., caring for an ill spouse) occur, frail older adults may have ineffective coping mechanisms. As a result, they may become ill themselves. Common health problems of frail older adults include mobility limitations, sensory impairment, cognitive decline, and falls.

Frail older adults may tire easily, have little physical reserve, and are at risk for physical dependence and institutionalization. They are especially at risk for malnutrition and dehydration. These are related to factors such as living alone, depression, and low socioeconomic status. Other factors, such as dementia, inadequate dental care, sensory deficits, fatigue, and limited mobility, increase the risk for malnutrition and dehydration. Monitor frail older adults for adequate calorie, protein, iron, calcium, vitamin D, and fluid intake. Use the *SCALES* tool to assess the risk factors for poor nutrition status in older adults (Table 5.7). Consider how to meet an older adult's nutrition needs. Common interventions include home-delivered meals, dietary supplements, Supplemental Nutrition Assistance Program (SNAP), dental referrals, and vitamin supplements. Because medications may affect appetite or interact with nutrients, obtain a thorough medication history. Nutrition is discussed in Chapter 44.

Culturally Competent Care: Older Adults

The term **ethnogeriatrics** describes the specialty area of providing culturally competent care to older adults.[9] As American society changes, ethnic institutions and neighborhoods may also change. For the older adult with strong ethnic and cultural roots, there may be a loss of friends who speak the native language, a loss of the religious institution that supports social, ethnic activities, and a loss of stores that carry desired ethnic foods. This sense of loss is increased when children and others deny or ignore ethnic and cultural practices. Support for older adults of racial or ethnic minority is most often found in the family, religious practices, and isolated geographic or community ethnic clusters.

Ethnic populations of older adults face unique situations. Older adults may live in neighborhoods where physical security and personal safety related to crime may be a concern. Those who identify with specific ethnic groups often have disproportionately lower incomes. They may not be able to afford Medicare deductibles or drugs needed to treat chronic illnesses. Older adults from minority populations may use health care services less often when compared to nonminority groups.[10]

Assess each older adult's ethnic and cultural background. Assume that ethnicity and culture are important and of value to them unless they tell you otherwise. For you to be effective with the ethnic older adult, a sense of respect and clear communication are critical. Culturally competent care is discussed in Chapter 2.

SOCIAL SUPPORT AND OLDER ADULTS

Social support for older adults occurs at 3 levels. First, family members are the primary and preferred providers of social support. Second, semiformal support is found in clubs, religious (faith-based) organizations, neighborhoods, adult day care, and senior centers. Third, older adults may be linked to formal systems of social welfare agencies, health agencies, and government support. Generally, you, as a nurse, are part of the formal support system.

Family Caregivers

Many older adults need caregiving by family members. This includes those with multiple chronic conditions, those who need help with ADLs and IADLs, and persons with dementia. The most common caregivers are spouses, adult children, parents, grandparents, and life partners. Older adult women, age 65 or older, are the most common family caregivers. Other examples include husbands who care for wives with Alzheimer disease, adult children who care for a parent with a stroke, grandparents who care for a grandchild with a developmental disorder, and parents who care for an adult child with a spinal cord injury. Many family caregivers are caring for themselves, their aging parents, and their children and grandchildren.

The caregiver usually takes on responsibilities gradually. For example, a caregiver may initially need only to adjust work schedules to accommodate a patient's health care appointments. Later, as the patient's needs become greater, the caregiver has to reduce work hours and provide more help with ADLs.

Caregiving is an experience for which most people are not prepared. It is common for caregivers to become physically, emotionally, and economically overwhelmed by the responsibilities and demands of caring for a loved one. The stress of caregiving may lead to emotional problems such as depression, anger, and resentment. Signs of caregiver stress include irritability, inability to concentrate, fatigue, and sleeplessness. The caregiver often experiences decreased social interactions and is at risk for social isolation. Multiple commitments, fatigue, and, at times, the patient's socially inappropriate behaviors contribute to the caregiver's social isolation. Stress can progress to burnout and result in negligence and abuse of the patient by the caregiver. Consider collaborating with a social worker if caregiver stress or strain is present and caregivers need respite.

Encourage caregivers to take care of themselves. Suggest journaling or joining a support group to help them share feelings. Remind caregivers that getting regular exercise and sleep and

TABLE 5.8 Types of Elder Mistreatment

Characteristic	Manifestations
Abandonment	
Desertion of an older person by a person who has assumed responsibility for providing care or by a person with physical custody	Older adult's reports of being abandoned; deserting an older adult at a hospital or skilled nursing facility, shopping center, or other public places
Financial Abuse	
Denying access to personal resources, stealing money or possessions. Coercing to sign contracts or durable power of attorney. Making changes in will or trust	Living situation below level of personal resources. Sudden change in personal finances, sudden transfer of assets
Neglect	
Failure or refusal to provide basic life needs, including food, water, medications, clothing, hygiene. Failure to provide physical aids such as dentures, eyeglasses, hearing aid. Failure to ensure safety	Older adult's report of being neglected. Untreated or infected pressure injuries on sacral area, heels. Weight loss, malnutrition. Laboratory values showing dehydration. Poor personal hygiene. Lack of adherence with medical treatment
Failure to provide social stimulation. Leaving alone for long periods. Failure to provide companionship	Depression, withdrawn behavior, agitation. Ambivalent attitude toward caregiver or family member
Physical Abuse	
Slapping, striking, restraining, incorrect positioning. Oversedation with medications	Bruises, bilateral injuries (upper arms, ankles, wrists), repeated injuries in various stages of healing, burn marks, oversedation. Use of several emergency departments
Psychologic Abuse	
Berating verbally, harassment, intimidation, threats of punishment, or deprivation. Childlike treatment, isolation	Depression, withdrawn behavior, agitation. Ambivalent attitude toward caregiver or family member
Sexual Abuse	
Nonconsensual sexual contact, including inappropriate touching. Forced sexual contact	Older adult's report of sexual abuse. Unexplained vaginal or anal bleeding, bruised breasts. Unexplained sexually transmitted or genital infections.
Violation of Personal Rights	
Denying right to privacy or right to make decisions about health care or living environment. Forcible eviction	Sudden inexplicable changes in living situation, confusion

eating balanced meals will enhance their well-being. Encourage contact with others to give emotional support. Finally, humor is important. Sometimes its use by caregivers can provide distraction and relieve stress-filled situations.

Elder Mistreatment

Elder mistreatment (EM) describes intentional acts of omission or commission by a caregiver or "trusted other" that cause harm or serious risk for harm to a vulnerable older adult. EM may occur in community (home, assisted living facility) or long-term care (institutional) settings.

Between 2% and 10% of community-dwelling older adults in the United States are abused, neglected, or exploited by trusted others.[11] The prevalence of EM in institutional settings is unknown, but it is thought to be widespread. Although EM rates are similar in women and men, most victims are women because of the larger number of older women. Victims of EM have a mortality risk that is 3 times higher than those who are not mistreated. This higher risk is not due to the abuse or neglect itself but may be due to stress-related illnesses associated with prolonged mistreatment.

EM is a hidden problem. For every reported case in the community setting, more than 5 cases go unreported. Underreporting may be higher based on immigration status, ethnic background, or sexual orientation. Victims are unlikely to report mistreatment by "trusted others" because of isolation; impaired cognitive or physical function; feelings of shame, guilt, or self-blame; fear of reprisal; pressure from family members; fear of long-term care; or cultural norms. HCPs also underreport EM, possibly from a failure to suspect or recognize EM, perceived inability to successfully intervene, desire to avoid responsibility for further action, or ageism.

Family members are responsible for up to 90% of domestic EM. Adult children who abuse, neglect, or exploit their parents are usually dependent on their parent(s) for housing and financial support, have a history of violence, are unemployed, and/or are disabled from substance use or mental illness. Abusive spouses or partners may either begin intimate partner violence at an older age or continue a lifelong pattern of abuse.

Many factors put community-dwelling older adults at risk for domestic EM. These include (1) physical or cognitive problems that lead to an inability to perform ADLs (and thus produces dependence on others for care), (2) any psychiatric diagnoses, including dementia and depression, (3) alcohol use, (4) decreased social support, (5) living with a several household members other than a spouse, and (6) low income. In long-term care settings, the same factors that lead to institutionalization are risk factors for mistreatment by staff, visitors, and others. These include dependence on others for care because of physical or cognitive limitations.

Types of EM, characteristics, and manifestations are shown in Table 5.8. In institutional settings, EM includes the types

TABLE 5.9 NURSING MANAGEMENT

Elder Mistreatment

When elder mistreatment is suspected, it is important to do the following:

Screen for possible elder mistreatment, including domestic violence.

Conduct a thorough history and physical assessment. Document your findings, including any statements made by the patient and accompanying persons.

If the patient appears to be in immediate danger, develop and implement a safety plan in collaboration with the health care team members involved in the patient's care.

Identify, collect, and preserve physical evidence (e.g., dirty or bloody clothing).

After obtaining consent, take photographs to document physical findings of suspected abuse or neglect. If possible, do this before treating or bathing the patient.

If you suspect that mistreatment is occurring, report your findings to the state agency and/or law enforcement as mandated by state law.

Initiate needed consultations with social work, forensic nursing, and adult protective services.

described in Table 5.8 as well as failure to follow the plan of care, unauthorized use of physical or chemical restraints, overuse or underuse of medication, or isolation as punishment.

Follow your agency's protocols for EM screening and interventions. Perform a thorough history and physical assessment that includes screening for mistreatment. It is important that you interview people alone. If mistreatment is occurring, they may not disclose it in the presence of the person who is with them, especially if that person is the abuser. Be especially attentive to explanations about injuries that are not consistent with what you observe, contradictory explanations between the patient and caregiver, or behavior clues that suggest the patient is being threatened or intimidated. Other assessments and interventions are listed in Table 5.9. In most states, health care workers are among those mandated to report suspected or actual EM to Adult Protective Services (APS) and/or law enforcement. Know your legal responsibilities by checking the laws in your state.

Self-Neglect

Most referrals made to APS are for self-neglect. Older adults who self-neglect are often unable to meet their basic needs and refuse help; have multiple, untreated medical or psychiatric conditions; and live alone and often in squalor.[12] Older community-dwelling adults who self-neglect face a higher risk for mortality than peers who do not self-neglect. Nursing interventions include assessing for possible self-neglect and referring to long-term case management and APS as needed.

SOCIAL SERVICES FOR OLDER ADULTS

A network of services supports older adults in the community and health care agencies. In the United States, most older adults are the beneficiaries of at least 1 social or governmental service. To understand the older adult's situation, learn about government structures that fund and regulate programs for older adults.

MEDICARE AND MEDICAID

Medicare is a federally funded health insurance program for people ages 65 years or older.[13] It also covers people under age 65 with certain disabilities and those of any age with end-stage renal disease requiring dialysis or a kidney transplant.

Medicare has 4 options for coverage: A, B, C, and D. Part A covers inpatient hospital care and partially covers skilled nursing facility care, hospice, and home health care. Part A coverage is "free" because workers support Medicare through payroll taxes. Part B partially covers outpatient care, physicians' or primary care providers' services, and home health care. It also covers some preventive services, such as mammograms. Part B is voluntary and has a monthly premium. There is an annual deductible before payment begins. Medicare Advantage Plans, sometimes called "Part C" or "MA Plans," are offered by private companies approved by Medicare to provide Part A and Part B benefits. Part D is available to Medicare enrollees and provides a prescription drug benefit. Members pay a yearly deductible, monthly premium, and copayment. People with lower incomes and limited assets may qualify for extra help to pay for prescriptions.

Medicare does not cover long-term care, custodial ADLs or IADLs care, dental care or dentures, hearing aids, or eyeglasses. More information is available at www.medicare.gov. Out-of-pocket expenditures for people on Medicare continue to rise. The costs increase with age, functional disabilities, number of chronic conditions, and number of hospitalizations.[13]

Medicaid is a state-administered, needs-based program to help eligible low-income people, including Medicare beneficiaries, with certain medical expenses. Those who qualify for both Medicare and Medicaid are referred to as *dual-eligible.* Eligibility and coverage vary by state. For qualified Medicare beneficiaries, Medicaid pays Medicare premiums, deductibles, and co-insurance, as well as long-term care and home health expenses. In the United States, most long-term care is paid for by Medicaid or private pay. More information is available at www.medicaid.gov.

CARE ALTERNATIVES FOR OLDER ADULTS

Older adults with special care needs include people who are homeless, in need of help with ADLs, cognitively impaired, homebound, or no longer able to live at home. Older adults may be served by adult day care, adult day health care, home health care, and long-term care. Continuing care retirement communities, congregate housing, and assisted living facilities are housing options for older adults.

Adult Day Care and Adult Day Health Care

Adult day care centers provide social, recreation, and health-related services to people in a safe, community-based environment (Fig. 5.5). This includes daily supervision, social activities, opportunities for social interaction, and ADLs help. They serve 2 groups of adults: (1) those who are cognitively impaired and (2) those who have problems independently performing ADLs. Adult day care programs provide services based on need. Programs designed for adults who are cognitively impaired

Fig. 5.5 Senior centers offer places for older adults who live independently to meet and gather with friends. (© Jupiterimages/Comstock/Thinkstock.)

Fig. 5.6 Social interaction and acceptance are important for older adults. (© Morsa Images/iStock.com.)

offer therapeutic recreation, support for families, family counseling, and social involvement.

Adult day health care centers are like adult day care but provide care to meet the needs of older adults and people with disabilities who need a higher level of care. This might include health monitoring, therapeutic activities, 1-on-1 ADLs training, and personal services.

Adult day care centers and adult day health care centers may offer respite to allow continued employment for the caregiver and delay institutionalization. States set standards and regulate centers. Medicare does not cover costs. Adult day health care is tax-deductible as dependent care. Placement in an adult care program that matches the person's needs is important. You can help by knowing the available centers in your area and assessing the needs of older adults and their families. You will then be able to help them make good decisions about their care.

Home Health Care

Home health care (HHC) can be a cost-effective care alternative for older adults who are homebound, have health needs that are intermittent or acute, and have supportive caregiver involvement. HHC is not an alternative for adults in need of 24-hour help with ADLs or continuous safety supervision. Private duty care may be an alternative in these situations. HHC services require HCP orders and skilled nursing care for Medicare reimbursement. Unless one meets these requirements, Medicare will not pay for home health aides for ADLs management or a homemaker for IADLs management.

In addition to HHC, caregivers often seek homemaker services and respite and personal care through organizations that provide nonmedical assistance. These services help older adults stay at home.

Long-Term Care Facilities

Three factors appear to lead to placement in a long-term care facility: (1) rapid patient deterioration, (2) caregiver inability to continue care because of stress and burnout, and (3) a change in or loss of the family support system. Progressive dementia, urinary incontinence, or a major health event (e.g., stroke) can hasten long-term care placement.

The conflicts and fears faced by older adults and their families make placement a difficult transition. Common caregiver concerns include: (1) Will the older adult resist admission? (2) Will the level of care given by staff be sufficient? (3) Will the resident be lonely? and (4) Will care be affordable?

The physical relocation of the older adult may lead to adverse health effects. *Relocation stress syndrome* is associated with the disruption, confusion, and challenges that older adults face when moving to a new environment. Older adults may have anxiety, depression, and disorientation. Appropriate interventions can reduce the effects of relocation. Whenever possible, involve older adults in the decision to move and fully inform them about the location. Caregivers can share information, pictures, or a video recording of the new location. Staff members can send a welcome message. On arrival, they can greet new residents and provide orientation. To bridge the relocation, new residents can be "buddied" with seasoned residents (Fig. 5.6).

Programs for All-Inclusive Care for the Elderly

Programs for All-Inclusive Care for the Elderly (PACE) provide care for adults age 55 and older. PACE services include primary care, including prescription medications and wound care; physical, occupational, recreational, and speech therapy; adult day care; dental; podiatry; social services; and home health care. Respite care, hospitalization, short-term rehabilitation, and long-term care are provided as needed.[14]

A person who has Medicaid will not have to pay a monthly premium for the long-term portion of the PACE benefit. A person who does not qualify for Medicaid but has Medicare must pay a monthly premium to cover the long-term care portion.

Age-Friendly Health Systems

To address the challenges that older adults face as they age, especially the complexity of care, we have developed a new care model called the Age-Friendly Health System's Model of Care.[16] The aim of this initiative is to build a social movement so that all older adult care is age-friendly. This means care is guided by a set of evidence-based practices, causes no harm, and is consistent with what matters to the older adult and their family caregivers. The key components are the 4Ms: (1) *What Matters* to the older adult—considering what is most important

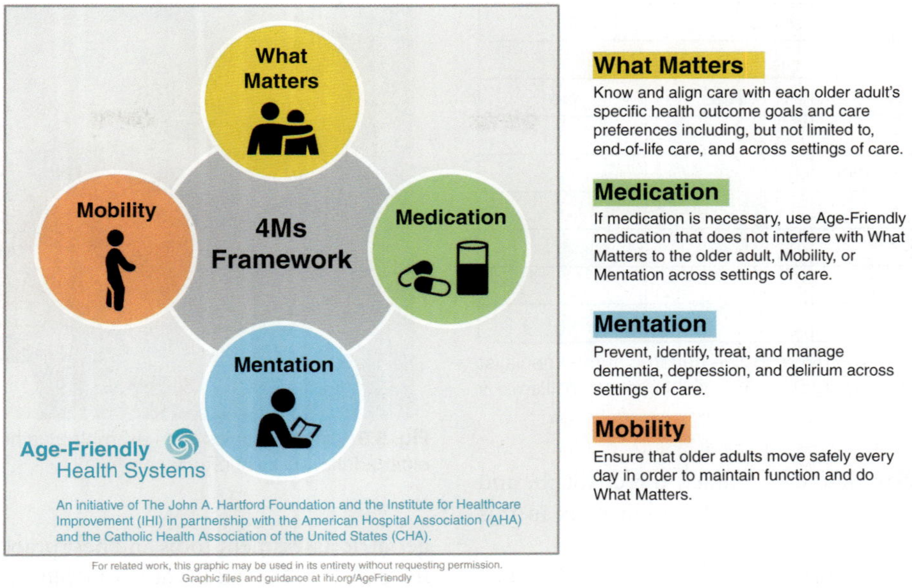

Fig 5.7 The 4M Framework of Age-Friendly Health Systems. (© Institute for Healthcare Improvement, http://www.ihi.org/Engage/Initiatives/Age-Friendly-Health-Systems/Pages/default.aspx.)

to the patient, family, and caregivers, including care goals and preferences; (2) *Medication*—making sure all medications have a clear indication, are prescribed at the lowest effective dose and frequency; (3) *Mentation*—assessing and managing dementia, delirium, and/or depression; and (4) *Mobility*—maintaining or improving mobility and function (Fig. 5.7). Use the 4M model to guide the care you provide older adults. Oftentimes, when using the 4Ms to plan care for a patient, it is necessary to work with other health care team members. This allows for a comprehensive, age-friendly assessment and plan for each older adult in your care.

LEGAL AND ETHICAL ISSUES

Legal guidance and assistance are needed by many older adults. Legal issues include advance directives, estate planning, taxation issues, appeals for denied services (e.g., disability), financial decisions, or exploitation by strangers or "trusted others."

Advance directives are written statements of a person's wishes about medical care. A health care proxy may be appointed to make medical decisions if a person is unable to make their own medical decisions. These documents allow people to direct their own care at end-of-life. Advance directives are discussed in detail in Chapter 10 and Table 10.3.

When working with older adults, you may find several ethical issues that influence practice, such as the assessment of older adults' ability to make decisions. Other ethical issues relate to end-of-life care. These include decisions about resuscitation, nutrition and hydration, and transfer to more intensive treatment units and the hospital. These situations are often complex, especially during emotionally difficult times.[15] You can assist the older adult, family, and other health care workers by (1) keeping current on the ethical issues, (2) acknowledging when an ethical dilemma is present, and (3) advocating for an institutional ethics committee to help provide guidance in making decisions and assist when differences of opinion occur.

NURSING MANAGEMENT: OLDER ADULTS

Gerontologic nursing is the care of older adults based on the specialty body of knowledge of gerontology and nursing. These specialty nurses provide care for older adults using a whole-person (e.g., physical, psychologic, functional, developmental, socioeconomic, cultural) perspective. Care of older adults is complex and presents challenges that require skilled assessment and interventions tailored to this population.

Diseases and conditions in older adults may be hard to accurately assess and diagnose. Older adults may underreport symptoms and try to manage these symptoms by changing their functional status. For example, a woman with a loss of feeling in her feet from neuropathy may start using a walker but not report the symptom to her HCP. The older adult may attribute a new symptom to "aging" and ignore it. Or someone may eat less, sleep more, or "wait it out."

In older adults, disease symptoms are often atypical. The most common atypical presentations are "delirium" or "acute change in mental status" and change in functional status. For example, confusion may be a sign of a urinary tract infection. A caregiver may say that a relative "is acting differently," "doesn't appear as themself," or is no longer taking part in usual activities or self-care. Pathologic conditions with similar symptoms can be confused. For example, depression may be misdiagnosed and treated as dementia.

In older adults, a *cascade disease pattern* may occur. For example, a person who has insomnia treats the condition with sleeping medication. They become lethargic and delirious and fall, sustaining a hip fracture. This decreases activity and mobility, leading to pneumonia and/or pressure injuries. Nurses play a vital role in preventing this downward trajectory.

For older adults, the stress of an illness may lead to fear and anxiety. They may view health care personnel as helpful but perceive institutions as negative and potentially harmful places. Communicate a sense of concern and care by use of direct and

Patient name:	Date:	
	EVIDENCE	
SPICES	Yes	No
Sleep disorders		
Problems with eating or feeding		
Incontinence		
Confusion		
Evidence of falls		
Skin breakdown		

Fig. 5.8 SPICES. (Adapted from Fulmer T: The geriatric nurse specialist role: a new model, *Nurs Manag* 22:91, 1991. © Lippincott Williams & Wilkins, www.lww.com.)

simple statements, appropriate eye contact, direct touch, and gentle humor. These actions help the older adult relax in this stressful situation.

Assessment

Prior to an assessment, attend to the person's primary needs. For example, ensure that older adults are comfortable and ask if they need to use the bathroom. If they normally use eyeglasses and hearing aids, ask them to use these during the assessment. Place all assistive devices, such as walkers, within reach. Assess your patient's level of fatigue and pause the assessment if necessary. Allow adequate time to offer information and time for the person to respond to questions—interview both the older adult and their family or caregivers. You can do this separately unless the patient is cognitively impaired or specifically requests the caregiver's presence.

The focus of a geriatric assessment is to determine interventions needed to support and enhance the health, quality of life, function, and independence of older adults. At a minimum, it includes the medical history, functional assessment, medication review, cognitive and mood evaluation, social resources, and physical assessment followed by recommended diagnostic tests. The assessment is often conducted by an interprofessional geriatric assessment team. This team minimally includes a staff nurse, an HCP such as a physician or advanced practice nurse, and a social worker. It may also include a physical and/or occupational therapist, dietitian, podiatrist, ophthalmologist, dentist, and pastoral care representative. After the assessment is complete, the team meets with the patient and family to present the team's findings and recommendations.

Specific elements in a complete nursing assessment include a thorough history, mood assessment, functional assessment including ADLs and IADLs, mental status evaluation, social-environmental assessment, and physical assessment. Although the health history may be lengthy, it is important to obtain. Review medical records and determine what information is most relevant or needs more detail.

Evaluation of mental status is particularly important for older adults because these results often determine the potential for independent living. *SPICES,* an effective tool for obtaining assessment data in older adults, may be used as an initial nursing assessment in any setting (Fig. 5.8). Multiple evidence-based

Fig. 5.9 Water aerobics is an example of a health promotion activity for older adults. (© kali9/iStock.com.)

geriatric assessment tools and best practice approaches to nursing care for older adults are available from the *Try This* Series at the Hartford Institute for Geriatric Nursing (available at https://hign.org/consultgeri/try-this).

Assess for fall risk, fear of falling, and cause(s) of past falls. Those at increased risk for falls have a history of falls or a fear of falling. Other factors that increase fall risk include use of certain drugs; infection; orthostatic hypotension; dehydration; electrolyte imbalance; arthritis; changes in gait, balance, and mobility; neurologic problems (e.g., stroke, Parkinson disease); decreased muscle strength; and decreased visual acuity. Assess for symptoms of dizziness or lightheadedness upon standing. Other risk factors include environmental hazards, feet abnormalities, poor footwear, clutter, throw rugs, incorrect use of an assistive device such as a walker or cane, shiny or waxy floors, slippery floors, poor lighting, bed in an incorrect position such as too high, and uneven pavement.

Evaluation of the results of the assessment helps determine needed services and potential long-term placement needs. Collect data about community resources that will help older adults and their caregivers in supporting maximal function. The goal is to plan and implement actions that help older adults stay as functionally independent as possible and to promote their quality of life.

Planning

When setting goals with older adults, identify their strengths and abilities. Include caregivers in planning. Priority goals may include gaining a sense of control, feeling safe, and reducing stress.

Implementation

When carrying out a plan of action for older adults, adjust your approach and actions based on their physical, functional, and mental status. The small body size of a frail older adult may require the use of pediatric equipment (e.g., BP cuff). Safety is a primary concern when caring for an older adult. Those with bone and joint changes often need transfer assistance, altered positioning, and the use of gait belts and lift devices. Older adults with declining energy reserves may need extra

TABLE 5.10 NURSING MANAGEMENT

Care of the Hospitalized Older Adult

Give special consideration to the following interventions when caring for hospitalized older adults:

- Identify older adults at risk for consequences of medical and/or surgical treatments.
- Consider discharge and post-acute needs early in the hospital stay, especially assistance with activities of daily living and medications.
- Encourage the development and use of interprofessional teams, special care units, and providers who focus on the special needs of older patients.
- Implement standard protocols to screen for at-risk conditions common in the hospitalized older adult, such as urinary tract infections and delirium.
- Implement mobility and exercise programs to prevent functional decline.
- Monitor for and prevent skin integrity changes.
- Implement measures focused on safety (e.g., fall prevention).
- Refer patients to the appropriate community-based services.

time to complete tasks. A slower approach and the use of other adaptive equipment may be needed. Cognitive impairment, if present, requires that you offer careful explanations and a calm approach to avoid producing anxiety and resistance. Depression can result in apathy and poor cooperation with the treatment plan.

Health Promotion

Health promotion and prevention of health problems for older adults focus on 3 areas: (1) increased participation in health promotion and disease prevention activities (Fig. 5.9), (2) reduction in diseases and health-related issues, and (3) increased use of services that reduce health hazards. Programs exist for screening for chronic health conditions, tobacco cessation, geriatric foot care, vision and hearing screening, stress reduction, exercise programs, fall prevention programs, drug use, crime prevention, elder mistreatment, and home safety assessment. Teach older adults about the need for preventive services and available programs (Box 5.2).

BOX 5.2 PROMOTING POPULATION HEALTH

Promoting Health in Older Adults

- Get recommended vaccines.
- Create an environment free of hazards to reduce the risk of falling.
- Drink plenty of liquids. Limit drinks with lots of added sugar or salt.
- Obtain at least 150 min of moderate-intensity exercise each week.
- Maintain an appropriate weight based on a nutrient-rich diet.
- Use medications, herbs, and supplements according to your HCP's direction.

Include health promotion and disease prevention in nursing interventions and plans at any setting or level of care in which nurses and older adults interact. You can use health promotion activities to increase personal responsibility for health and independent functioning. Teaching and reinforcement are important tools for you to use to enhance self-care practices by older adults. Patient teaching is discussed in Chapter 4.

Fig. 5.10 The nurse assists a patient in a geriatric rehabilitation facility. (© FG Trade/iStock.com.)

Acute and Ambulatory Care

The hospital may be the first point of contact for older adults with the health care system. Conditions that often result in hospitalization include falls, dysrhythmias, heart failure, stroke, fluid and electrolyte imbalances (e.g., hyponatremia, dehydration), pneumonia, urosepsis, and hip fractures. Hospitalized older adults often have multiple problems, acute and chronic.

When older adults are being cared for in the acute care setting, both patients and caregivers need help with a variety of functions (Table 5.10). The outcome of hospitalization for older adults varies. Of special concern are patients having high-risk surgeries (e.g., hip replacement) and those who have delirium while hospitalized.

Care transitions. The time of a care transition to another setting (e.g., acute care hospital to rehabilitation) is challenging for many older adults. While in the hospital, patients and caregivers are counseled on how to prepare for posthospital care. Those with multiple health conditions have a particularly high risk for rehospitalization.

Medicare regulations require a registered nurse, social worker, or qualified person to develop a care transition plan for patient discharge. Safe and effective care transitions are most likely to occur when health care team members work together with the patient and family to coordinate care.

The Transitional Care Model (TCM) is an evidence-based, innovative approach to care coordination and management of patients with complex needs. In the TCM, a transitional care nurse delivers and coordinates care by nurses and other team members throughout potential and acute episodes of illness. Those most likely to benefit from transitional care nursing include older adults and those with functional deficits, behavior or psychiatric issues, multiple chronic conditions, polypharmacy, a recent hospitalization, lack of a support system, low health literacy, and history of non-adherence to treatment.[17]

Rehabilitation. The goal of rehabilitation is to help older adults adapt to or recover from disability or an acute functional decline. Rehabilitation may occur in acute inpatient rehabilitation, subacute rehabilitation, or long-term care settings. With proper training, assistive equipment, and attendant personal care, people with functional deficits may live independently. Older adults, primarily through Medicare reimbursement, can receive rehabilitative assistance through acute inpatient rehabilitation (limited days) and home health care programs (Fig. 5.10).

Older adults with chronic conditions, such as arthritis, have an increased risk for functional decline. Decreased function or disabilities lead to increased self-care deficits, increased rates of institutionalization, decreased quality of life, and higher mortality rates.

Several factors influence the rehabilitation of older adults. First, preexisting conditions associated with decreased reaction time, visual acuity, fine motor ability, physical strength, and cognitive function affect the short- and long-term rehabilitation potential. Older adults may have anxiety, fear, or concern about falling. Poor nutrition and financial issues may limit the rehabilitation process. Encouragement, support, and acceptance from the health care team members and caregivers can help older adults remain motivated for potentially physically challenging rehabilitation.

Second, older adults often lose function because of inactivity and immobility. This deconditioning can occur because of unstable acute medical conditions, lack of assistive devices, and a lack of motivation to stay fit. The effect of inactivity leads to "use it or lose it" consequences. Older adults can improve flexibility, strength, and aerobic capacity even into very old age. Passive and active range-of-motion exercises are used with all older adults to preserve muscle tone and strength and prevent deconditioning and subsequent functional decline.

Last, the goal of rehabilitation is to strive for maximal function and physical capabilities considering the person's current health and functional status. For example, on admission to an acute or long-term care facility and home health services, assess for fall risk as well as the person's fear of falling. Initiate needed fall prevention interventions and assess for ongoing risk. Conduct foot and peripheral vascular assessments for all older adults, especially those with diabetes, and arrange needed follow-up care.

Assistive devices. Consider the use of assistive devices as interventions for older adults. Using assistive devices such as dentures, glasses, hearing aids, walkers, wheelchairs, adaptive utensils, elevated toilet seats, and skin protective devices can increase function. Include these tools and devices in the older adult's care plan when needed and teach the use of the devices. For example, using a cane correctly may decrease fall risk.

Technology can help with rehabilitation and living with functional impairments. For example, we can use electronic monitoring equipment to monitor heart rhythm and BP. Monitoring can locate a person with dementia who has wandered away from home or a long-term care facility. Computerized assistive devices may help patients with speech problems after a stroke. Small electronic devices can serve as memory aids.

Safety. Safety is crucial in maintaining an older adult's health. When compared to younger adults, older adults are at higher risk for accidents due to normal sensory changes, slowed reaction time, decreased thermal and pain sensitivity, changes in gait and balance, and drug effects. Most accidents occur in or around the home. Falls, motor vehicle accidents, and fires are common causes of accidental death in older adults. Declining thermoregulation impairs the older person's ability to adapt to extremes in environmental temperatures. An older adult's body can neither conserve nor dissipate heat as efficiently as a younger adult. Therefore, both hypothermia and hyperthermia occur more readily. The older adult age group accounts for most deaths during severe cold spells and heat waves.

Review the environment for needed changes that can improve safety for older adults. Measures such as colored step strips, tub and toilet grab bars, and stairway handrails can be effective in "safety-proofing" living spaces. Uncluttered floor space (e.g., removing throw rugs), railings, and increased lighting and nightlights are some of the easiest and most practical adaptations. Social workers may help older adults make these environmental changes. You can advocate for home fire and security alarms.

Other interventions to decrease the risk for falling include exercise, physical therapy, and management of foot and footwear issues. Encourage the patient's use of glasses and hearing aids as needed. Fear of falling can affect the older adults' decisions about the activities that they engage in and how active they remain.

Older adults who are new to inpatient or long-term care settings need a thorough orientation to the environment. Reassure the older adult that they are safe. Answer all questions and refer to team members and specialists as needed. Foster orientation by displaying large-print clocks, keeping wall designs simple, clearly designating doors and exits, and using simple bed and nurse or family-call controls. Provide diffuse lighting while avoiding glare.

Medication use. Medication use in older adults requires thorough and regular assessment, care planning, and evaluation. Nonadherence to medication plans by older adults may occur due to the inability to read prescription drug labels and/or understand the health information that we provide them.

Age-related changes alter the pharmacodynamics and pharmacokinetics of drugs. Drug-drug, drug-nutrient, and drug-disease interactions influence the absorption, distribution, metabolism, and excretion of drugs. The most dramatic changes with aging are related to drug metabolism (Fig. 5.11). Hepatic blood flow and the enzymes responsible for drug metabolism decrease markedly with aging. These increase drug half-life in older adults and lead to greater risk for drug toxicity and adverse drug events. Overall, by age 75 to 80, there is a 50% decline in the renal clearance of drugs. Older adults with altered renal function may need a lower dose and/or decreased frequency of administration of a drug excreted by the kidney. When drug level monitoring is available (e.g., digoxin), identify toxic levels by serum monitoring at regular intervals, especially when there is a change of dose and/or frequency of administration.

Older adults may have difficulty managing drug therapy due to cognitive impairment, altered sensory perception, and limited hand mobility or dexterity. Table 5.11 lists common reasons for drug errors made by older adults.

Polypharmacy (the use of multiple medications by a person who has more than 1 health problem), overdose, dependence, or addiction to prescription drugs are major causes of illness in older adults. Potential medication errors include (1) taking both

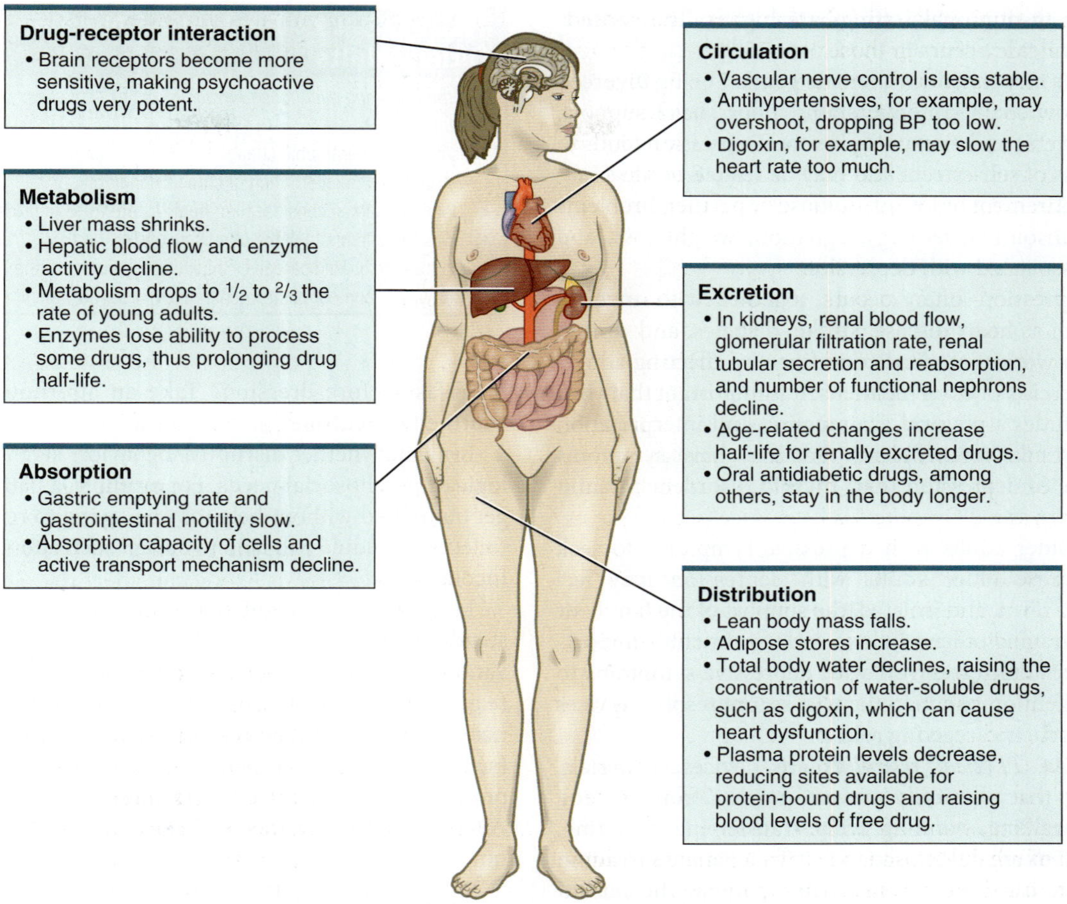

Fig. 5.11 The effects of aging on drug metabolism.

TABLE 5.11 Drug Therapy
Causes of Medication Errors by Older Adults

- Decreased vision
- Forgetting to take drugs
- Taking drugs incorrectly
- Use of drugs prescribed for someone else
- Lack of financial resources to obtain prescription drugs
- Refusal to take a drug because of undesirable side effects
- Failure to understand instructions or importance of drug treatment

brand and generic medications, (2) refilling medications too soon or too late (resulting in taking the medication incorrectly), and (3) drug-drug interactions. These errors can be prevented by having a pharmacist review medications regularly. Suggest the use of 1 pharmacy for filling all prescription medications.

The effects of medications in older adults with multiple health problems are particularly challenging to assess and manage. As 1 disease is treated, another may be affected. For example, the use of oxybutynin to treat overactive bladder may cause confusion. To accurately assess medication knowledge and use, ask older adults to bring all medications that they take regularly or occasionally to their health care appointment. You will then be able to accurately assess all medications that the patient is taking, including drugs that the person may have omitted or thought unimportant. The American Geriatrics Society (AGS) Beers Criteria are designed to reduce problems with medications in older adults.[18] Table 5.12 describes other nursing interventions to help older adults follow a safe medication routine.

TABLE 5.12 Drug Therapy
Safe Medication Use by Older Adults

When older adults are using medications, it is important to take the following measures to prevent medication errors:

- Assess cognitive function and monitor for changes.
- Assess their ability to self-administer medication
- Obtain and maintain a complete medication record.
- Assess for alcohol and illicit drug use.
- Encourage the use of written or electronic medication-reminder systems.
- Encourage the use of 1 pharmacy.
- Work with HCPs and pharmacists to set up routine drug profiles on all older adult patients.
- Try to reduce drug use that is not essential by consulting the HCP and pharmacist.
- Advocate for low-income prescription support services.

Depression. Depression is not a normal part of aging. However, it is often an underrecognized problem in older adults. Around 15% of older adults living in their homes have manifestations of depression. Rates of depressive symptoms in older adults in institutional settings are higher. The second-highest rate of suicide occurs in those over 75.[19]

Depression is associated with female gender, being divorced or separated, low socioeconomic status, poor social support, and a recent adverse and unexpected event. Depression tends to arise from a loss of self-esteem and may be related to life situations, such as retirement or loss of a spouse or partner. Problems such as pain, insomnia, lethargy, agitation, weight loss, and dementia are associated with depression.

Late-life depression often occurs together with medical conditions, such as heart disease, stroke, diabetes, and cancer. Depression can worsen medical conditions by affecting adherence to diet, exercise, or drug regimens. It is important that your assessment includes a physical examination and interpretation of laboratory results for problems that may have symptoms similar to those of depression (e.g., thyroid disorders, vitamin deficiencies).

Encourage older adults with depressive symptoms to seek treatment. Because older adults with depression may feel unworthy, withdrawn, and isolated, the support of the family or others in encouraging older adults to seek treatment is important. Assist older adult caregivers with depressive symptoms to seek medical attention and help them in secure respite services and support for their caregiving role.

Restraint use. *Physical restraints* are devices, materials, and equipment that physically prevent persons from moving freely, such as walking, standing, lying, transferring, or sitting. *Chemical restraints* are drugs used to restrict a patient's freedom of movement or, in some cases, to sedate a patient. The current standard is to provide safe care without using restraints of any form, whether physical or chemical. Restraints are a last resort. Only use restraints to ensure the person's safety or the safety of others.[20]

Before considering the use of any restraint, completely assess the perceived need for the restraint and document the assessment. Behavior symptoms, such as crying and shouting, may arise from co-morbidities, pain, medication effects, unmet needs, and/or environmental factors. When behavior manifestations are present, ask questions to better understand the patient's behavior: Is the person able to say what they need or want? People with dementia may respond by speaking, gesturing, nodding, or making eye contact. Questions that use "yes" or "no" answers are better than open-ended questions for gathering assessment information. Ask family, friends, or staff members from previous care settings about the patient's (1) history; (2) usual communication style and cues to indicate pain, fatigue, hunger, or a need to urinate or defecate; (3) abilities in ADLs; and (4) daily routines (e.g., "Is he often awake at night or an early riser?" "Does she eat breakfast before dressing? Take an afternoon nap? Have a routine for bedtime?").

TABLE 5.13 Evaluating Nursing Care for Older Adults

Use the following questions to evaluate the effectiveness of care for older adults:

- Is there an identifiable change in function, mental status, or signs and symptoms of exacerbation of chronic condition(s)?
- Does the person consider their health state to be improved?
- Does the person think the plan is helpful?
- Do the person and caregiver think the care is worth the time and cost?
- Can you document positive changes that support the interventions?

Evaluate whether disruptive behaviors signal unmet physiologic or psychosocial needs. For example, a patient who tries to get out of bed without help may be trying to reach the toilet. A toileting schedule will help to curtail such attempts and prevent incontinence.

Long-term care regulations and The Joint Commission set standards for restraint use. These include a time limit, observation, care, mandating the use of least restrictive measures (e.g., mittens), and alternatives to restraint use. Restraint alternatives include low beds, body props, and electronic devices (such as bed and chair alarm signaling). Such approaches support the development of a "restraint-free," safe environment. Alternatives to restraints require vigilant, creative, and sensitive nursing care.

All restraints require an order from an HCP. Carefully document restraint use and the reason for use. It is not appropriate to use restraints to prevent falls, avoid interference with medical devices, or reduce irritating behaviors, such as calling out. Frequent scheduled reviews of the ongoing need for the restraint are done with consideration of when to discontinue the restraint.

Sleep. Adequacy of sleep is often a concern for older adults because of altered sleep patterns. Older people have a marked decrease in deep sleep and are easily aroused. Many older adults report difficulty going to sleep and staying asleep. They may feel "unrefreshed" after sleep. See Chapter 8 for more about older adults' sleep problems.

Evaluation

The evaluation phase of the nursing process is similar for all patients. The results of the evaluation direct you to continue the plan of care or revise as needed. When evaluating nursing care with older adults, focus on functional improvement and quality of life. Useful questions to consider when evaluating the plan of care for older adults are outlined in Table 5.13.

Case Study

Older Adults

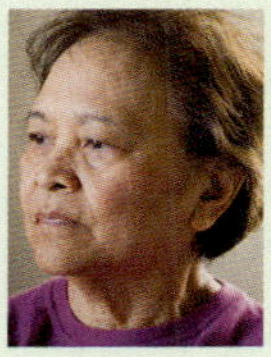

(©azndc/iStock/Thinkstock.)

Patient Profile

C.L., a 76-year-old Filipino woman, was admitted with confusion and found to have a urinary tract infection. Her medical history includes hypertension, diabetes, lung cancer, mild renal insufficiency, depression, macular degeneration, and significant hearing loss.

Subjective Data

- A stroke 5 years ago and has right-sided weakness
- A 100 pack-year history of tobacco use but quit smoking after her stroke
- Unplanned weight loss of 15 pounds in the past year
- Spends her days either in bed or in a recliner watching television
- Confusion and urinary incontinence for the past 3 days

Psychosocial Data

- Came to the United States 35 years ago from Manila
- Speaks Tagalog with limited English proficiency
- Lives with her unemployed adult son, who provides help with ADLs and IADLs
- Has 3 daughters who live within a 2-h drive
- Limited financial resources but has Medicare and Medicaid benefits
- Daughters raise concerns about their mother's care and safety at home, given their brother's history of anger issues and a gambling addiction
- When daughters ask their brother about how he is caring for his mother, he says, "I'm doing the best I can. She refuses help. She refuses to go to the doctor. What do you want me to do? She's old. She's crazy. She's going to die anyway!"
- Daughters state their mother does not want to go to a nursing home

Objective Data

Physical Assessment

- Unwashed, matted hair, poor oral hygiene, overgrown toenails
- 2 stage 3 sacral pressure injuries
- Unstageable right heel pressure injury
- Multiple small bruises on her forearms and shins
- 5 × 10 cm bruise in the middle of her back

Diagnostic Tests

- Serum albumin 2.4 g/dL
- Creatinine 1.3 mg/dL
- BUN 26 mg/dL
- Urinalysis reveals + leucocytes, + nitrites, 3+ blood, + bacteria

Discussion Questions

1. ***Recognize***: Describe what additional history you need to fully assess C.L.'s condition? What issues would you be most concerned about?
2. ***Recognize:*** What risk factors does C.L. have for developing frailty? Which factors are modifiable?
3. ***Analyze:*** Define ageism and explain how it may be manifested in this case.
4. ***Analyze:*** What are important findings regarding C.L.'s ability to manage her chronic illnesses?
5. ***Plan:*** Identify the stage of Corbin and Strauss chronic illness trajectory that describes C.L.'s status. Which stage is the goal of your nursing care?
6. ***Plan:*** Based on your assessment of C.L., what will you include in your care planning to optimize her self-care ability?
7. ***Plan:*** Because she has an expressed desire to return home, what referrals would be indicated if this were the plan?
8. ***Prioritize:*** What are the interprofessional team's priorities for C.L.?
9. ***Act:*** What role do assistive personnel (AP) have in this situation?
10. ***Safety:*** To ensure C.L.'s safety, what interventions are necessary during her hospitalization?
11. ***Safety:*** What risk factors does C.L. have for becoming a victim of elder mistreatment? List and provide the rationale for nursing interventions and legal and ethical responsibilities in this case.
12. ***Evaluate:*** What care setting would be best for C.L. upon hospital discharge?

Answers available at http://evolve.elsevier.com/Lewis/medsurg.

BRIDGE TO NCLEX EXAMINATION

The number of the question corresponds to the same-numbered outcome at the beginning of the chapter.

1. The trajectory of chronic illness includes *(select all that apply)*
   - **a.** periods of crisis.
   - **b.** episodes of exacerbations and stability.
   - **c.** a gradual return to an acceptable way of life.
   - **d.** a straight trajectory without overlapping phases.
   - **e.** symptoms that can be controlled by proper treatment.
2. A patient is ordered cardiac rehabilitation following cardiac bypass surgery. The nurse recognizes this as
   - **a.** primary prevention for atelectasis.
   - **b.** secondary prevention for atherosclerosis.
   - **c.** tertiary prevention to reduce the progression of heart disease.
   - **d.** a recommended treatment to prevent deep vein thrombosis.
3. Demographic trends among older Americans in the United States suggests
   - **a.** there are fewer people living past age 85.
   - **b.** more frailty in persons between 65 and 75 years.
   - **c.** a growth in racial and ethnically diverse populations.
   - **d.** women having a decreased life expectancy when compared to men.
4. A nurse is discharging an older adult patient who is homeless. Which actions demonstrate the nurse's understanding of the needs of this population? *(select all that apply)*
   - **a.** instructs the patient to check his blood pressure daily
   - **b.** asks the patient if they have a social worker or case manager
   - **c.** inquires if the patient has concerns about staying in the local shelter
   - **d.** asks the physician if enoxaparin can be changed to an oral anticoagulant
   - **e.** informs the patient that the hospital will call with his culture test results next week

BRIDGE TO NCLEX EXAMINATION—cont'd

5. In which situation would the nurse suspect elder mistreatment?
   a. Patient admitted with recurrent syncope
   b. Creatinine of 1.1 mg/dL and BUN of 10 mg/dL
   c. Sacral pressure injury on a patient who lives at home
   d. Patient with dementia who becomes more confused at night

6. Which action is aligned with the 4M model of an age-friendly health system?
   a. Silencing a bed alarm so the patient can sleep at night
   b. Assessing if the patient needs a mobility device, such as a walker
   c. Asking for haloperidol for a patient with dementia who is pulling on their IV
   d. Telling the patient that they need to eat their dinner in order to avoid a feeding tube

7. Which action is a *priority* for a newly admitted patient?
   a. checking for pressure ulcers
   b. planning for post-discharge needs
   c. administering an influenza vaccine
   d. assessing the patient's mental status

8. Nursing interventions directed at health promotion in the older adult are mainly focused on
   a. performing IADLs.
   b. symptom management.
   c. reducing risk for illness or injury.
   d. assessing if the patient has an advanced directive.

1. a, b, c, e; 2. c; 3. c; 4. b, c, d; 5. c; 6. b; 7. d; 8. c.

For rationales to these answers and even more NCLEX review questions, visit http://evolve.elsevier.com/Lewis/medsurg.

EVOLVE WEBSITE/RESOURCES LIST

http://evolve.elsevier.com/Lewis/medsurg
Review Questions (Online Only)
Key Points
Answer Keys for Questions
- Rationales for Bridge to NCLEX Examination Questions
- Answer Guidelines for Case Study

Conceptual Care Map Creator
Audio Glossary
Content Updates

REFERENCES

1. Administration on Aging: A profile of older Americans: 2019. Retrieved from https://acl.gov/sites/default/files/Aging%20and%20Disability%20in%20America/2019OlderAmericansProfile.pdf.
2. Centers for Disease Control and Prevention: Chronic diseases in America. Retrieved from *https://www.cdc.gov/chronicdisease/resources/infographic/chronic-diseases.htm*.
3. Corbin JM, Strauss A: A nursing model for chronic illness management based upon the Trajectory Framework, *Sch Inq Nurs Pract* 5:155, 1991. (Classic).
4. U.S. Census Bureau. Living longer: historical and projected life expectancy in the United States, 1960 to 2060. Retrieved from https://www.census.gov/content/dam/Census/library/publications/2020/demo/p25-1145.pdf.
5. American Society on Aging. Diversity and our common future: race, ethnicity, and the older American. Retrieved from https://www.asaging.org/blog/diversity-and-our-common-future-race-ethnicity-and-older-american.
6. Iamaroon A, Wongviriyawong T, Sura-arunsumrit P, et al.: Incidence of and risk factors for postoperative delirium in older adult patients undergoing noncardiac surgery: a prospective study, *BMC Geriatr* 20:40, 2020.
7. Evangelista L, Steinhubl SR, Topol EJ: Digital health care for older adults, *Lancet* 393:1493, 2019.
8. Quinn TJ, Mooijaart SP, Gallacher K, et al.: Acute care assessment of older adults living with frailty, *BMJ* 364:I13, 2019.
9. Stanford School of Medicine: Ethnogeriatrics. Retrieved from https://geriatrics.stanford.edu/culturemed/overview/introduction/field.html.
10. Chase JD, Russell D, Huang L, et al.: Relationships between race/ethnicity and health care utilization among older post-acute home health care patients, *J Appl Gerontol* 39:201, 2020.
11. National Council on Aging: Elder abuse facts. Retrieved from https://www.ncoa.org/public-policy-action/elder-justice/elder-abuse-facts/.
12. American Society on Aging. Elder self-neglect is a growing and largely hidden problem. Retrieved from https://www.asaging.org/blog/elder-self-neglect-growing-and-largely-hidden-problem.
13. U.S. Centers for Medicare and Medicaid Services. What Medicare covers. Retrieved from https://www.medicare.gov/what-medicare-covers.
14. National PACE Association: Eligibility requirements. Retrieved from www.npaonline.org.
15. Institute for Healthcare Improvement. Age-friendly health systems. Retrieved from http://www.ihi.org/Engage/Initiatives/Age-Friendly-Health-Systems/Pages/default.aspx.
16. Kim M, Oh Y, Kong B: Ethical conflicts experienced by nurses in geriatric hospitals in South Korea: if you can't stand the heat, get out of the kitchen, *Int J Environ Res Public Health* 12:442, 2020.
17. Dresden SM, Hwang U, Garrido MM, et al.: Geriatric emergency department innovations: the impact of transitional care nurses on 30-day readmissions for older adults, *Acad Emerg Med* 27:43, 2020.
18. The 2019 American Geriatrics Society (AGS) Beers Criteria® Update Expert Panel (2019): American Geriatrics Society 2019 updated AGS Beers Criteria® for potentially inappropriate medication use in older adults, *J Am Geriatr Soc* 67:674, 2019.
19. Dong L, Kalesnikava VA, Gonzalez R, et al.: Beyond depression: estimating 12-months prevalence of passive suicidal ideation in mid-and late-life in the health and retirement study, *Am J Geriatr Psychiatry* 27:1399, 2019.
*20. Lachance C, Wright MD: Avoidance of physical restraint use among hospitalized older adults: a review of clinical effectiveness and guidelines. Retrieved from https://www.ncbi.nlm.nihg.gov/books/NBK545889/.

*Evidence-based information for clinical practice.

6

Caring for Lesbian, Gay, Bisexual, Transgender, Queer or Questioning, and Gender Diverse Patients

Jeffrey Kwong

http://evolve.elsevier.com/Lewis/medsurg/

CONCEPTUAL FOCUS

Health Disparities

Sexuality

LEARNING OUTCOMES

1. Describe the difference between biologic sex, sexual orientation, and gender identity.
2. Explain how health disparities affect lesbian, gay, bisexual, transgender, queer or questioning, and gender diverse (LGBTQ+) populations.
3. Explain strategies to create an LGBTQ+ inclusive environment.
4. Discuss the options for gender affirming hormone therapy.
5. Discuss interprofessional management for persons undergoing gender confirming surgery.

KEY TERMS

biologic sex
cisgender
gender affirming hormone therapy
gender affirming surgery
gender dysphoria
gender identity
minority stress mode
sexual orientation
transgender

This chapter provides an overview of care considerations for persons who identify as lesbian, gay, bisexual, transgender, queer, questioning, or gender diverse (LGBTQ+). There is a growing recognition of the health disparities and needs of the LGBTQ+ community. Nurses need to be aware of best practices in order to provide care that is unconditional, inclusive, and respectful.

BIOLOGIC SEX, GENDER IDENTITY, AND SEXUAL ORIENTATION

Biologic sex, also called *sex assigned at birth,* is determined by a person's external genitalia, internal reproductive organs, and chromosomes. Persons born with a penis, testicles, and who have XY chromosomes are considered biologically male. Their sex assigned at birth is male. Persons born with a vagina, uterus, ovaries, and who have XX chromosomes are biologically female. Their sex assigned at birth is female. Some persons may have genitalia that we cannot categorize as either male or female or have a chromosomal make up that we cannot clearly categorize as one or the other sex. In these situations, we sometimes use the term *intersex.*[1]

Gender identity refers to a person's self-perceived gender. It may be the same or different than their sex assigned at birth. The term **cisgender** refers to persons whose gender identity aligns with their sex assigned at birth. **Transgender** refers to someone whose gender identity or gender expression is different than their sex assigned at birth. Someone whose sex assigned at birth is male but feels or identifies as female would be considered a transgender female. Someone whose sex assigned at birth is female but feels and identifies as male would be considered a transgender male. Some believe the term transgender to be an umbrella term that includes many different forms of gender identity and expression.[2] The term *transexual* is an old term that refers to persons who use medical interventions to change their bodies. Many transgender persons do not identify as transexual. We should not use this term when identifying a person. It is best to ask a person how they identify.

Gender is a socially constructed idea based on cultural standards. In traditional Western culture, there are 2 primary options for gender selection: male and female. However, this is beginning to change. In many cultures there is a recognition of genders beyond a binary (male/female) construct. People may take on more blended characteristics. For example, in the indigenous American culture, the term *two-spirit* is used to describe those who are born of one gender but who take on roles or identities of the opposite gender.[3] In India, *hijras* is a feminine gender identity that is taken on by persons whose sex assigned at birth was male or intersex. Within the Albanian culture, *burrnesha* are women who take a vow of celibacy and live their lives as men.

Gender expression refers to how someone expresses their gender in an outward appearance. It is a combination of a person's behavior, mannerisms, interests, and appearance associated with gender. An example is the use of clothing or accessories. We traditionally considered gender a binary category (meaning either male or female). Now, there is growing acceptance that gender can be considered along a continuum that may change over time. *Non-binary,* also termed *gender fluid* or *gender queer*, are terms that we use to describe someone who does not define themselves as completely one gender or the other. This term differs from *cross-dressing.* Cross-dressing typically refers to men (usually heterosexual) who wear women's clothing for pleasure or performance in specific settings and manner which may not lead to permanent changes to their appearance. They do not choose to live full-time in the opposite gender.

Gender dysphoria is a diagnostic classification that describes the distress that occurs when there is conflict between a person's gender identity and their sex assigned at birth.[4] There are defined diagnostic criteria for gender dysphoria, with specific criteria for children, adolescents, and adults (Table 6.1). Gender dysphoria differs from *gender non-conformity*. Gender non-conformity is the extent that a person's gender identity, role, or expression differs from expected cultural norms.[5] Gender non-conformity is not a mental health disorder.

Sexual orientation refers to how one identifies based on their sexual or romantic attraction to others. When thinking about sexual orientation, it is helpful to consider 3 different aspects – behavior, attraction, and identity. These 3 aspects are not always tied together. For instance, some men may have sex with other men but may not identify as gay. Sexual orientation and sexual behavior can be considered across a continuum. They can be influenced by social and cultural norms. Remember that having a gender identity as transgender is separate from sexual orientation. Transgender persons may identify as gay, lesbian, bisexual, or heterosexual.

The term heterosexual, or "straight," implies a person who has sex with or is attracted to persons of the opposite gender. The term homosexual is considered offensive by some due to the stigma and derogatory use of this word. The preferred terms used to describe persons who have sex with or are attracted to persons of the same gender include *gay man* or *lesbian*. Bisexual (or "bi") describes those who are sexually attracted to or have sex with persons of more than one gender. Besides the commonly accepted terms lesbian, gay, and bi, there are several other terms that are used to describe sexual orientation (Table 6.2).

TABLE 6.1 Diagnostic Criteria

Gender Dysphoria

The American Psychiatric Association uses the following as diagnostic criteria for gender dysphoria in adolescents and adults.

A. A marked incongruence between one's experienced/expressed gender and assigned gender, of at least 6 months' duration, as manifested by at least 2 of the following:
1. A marked incongruence between one's experienced/expressed gender and primary and/or secondary sex characteristics (or in young adolescents, the anticipated secondary sex characteristics)
2. A strong desire to be rid of one's primary and/or secondary sex characteristics because of a marked incongruence with one's experienced/expressed gender (or in young adolescents, a desire to prevent the development of the anticipated secondary sex characteristics)
3. A strong desire for the primary and/or secondary sex characteristics of the other gender
4. A strong desire to be of the other gender (or some alternative gender different from one's assigned gender)
5. A strong desire to be treated as the other gender (or some alternative gender different from one's assigned gender)
6. A strong conviction that one has the typical feelings and reactions of the other gender (or some alternative gender different from one's assigned gender)

B. The condition being associated with clinically significant distress or impairment in social, occupational, or other important areas of functioning

Adapted from American Psychiatric Association: *Diagnostic and statistical manual of mental disorders,* ed 5, Arlington, VA, 2013, American Psychiatric Publishing. Retrieved from https://www.psychiatry.org/psychiatrists/cultural-competency/education/transgender-and-gender-nonconforming-patients/gender-dysphoria-diagnosis.

LGBTQ+ HEALTH INEQUITIES

The LGBTQ+ population experiences various health inequities compared to non-LGBTQ+ populations. Many of the inequities stem from stigma and discrimination.[6] These issues are based on cultural, political, legal, and historic contexts. Researchers describe this phenomenon as the **minority stress model**. This model assumes that a large part of the health disparities experienced by the LGBTQ+ community stems from stressors associated with a culture that is hostile. It results in a lifetime of harassment and victimization.[7] For example, up until 1973 the American Psychiatric Association considered homosexuality a mental illness. This had far reaching impact by making people who identified as gay or lesbian believe they had a mental illness or that there was something "wrong with them."

Certain societal and cultural beliefs further perpetuate discrimination and stigma. Some religions do not acknowledge or accept same sex behaviors or feelings. People who do not identify as heterosexual may be excluded, shamed, or become targets of fear and hatred. Some laws and regulations have institutionalized these inequalities and stigma.

In some parts of the country, a person can be subject to criminal actions or denied certain privileges because of their sexual orientation. It was not until 2015 that the U.S. Supreme Court legalized same sex marriage. Federal recognition of same sex marriage represented a major milestone, not only in terms of recognition of same sex unions, but the legal right of marriage has implications that can affect the provision of health care. This

TABLE 6.2 Terms Used to Describe Gender and Sexual Identity[a]

Term	Meaning or Significance
Asexual	Not feeling sexual attraction or desire for partnered sexuality
Bi, Bisexual	A person who is emotionally, sexually, or affectionally attracted to more than one gender
Cis, Cisgender	Term to describe persons whose gender identity matches their physical sex assigned at birth
Gay male	A male who is sexually, romantically, or relationally attracted to other men
Gender Queer/Gender Non-Conforming	A person whose gender identity or expression falls outside the traditional male/female binary
Intersex	A person who has biologic or secondary sex traits that are inconsistent with what is typically considered male or female
Lesbian	A woman who is sexually, romantically, or relationally attracted to other women
LGBTQ+, LGBTQI+, LGBTQIA+	Abbreviation for Lesbian, Gay, Bisexual, Queer/Questioning (LGBTQ), Intersex (LGBTQI), Ally/Asexual (LGBTIA) The plus (+) acknowledges that there are more identities that exist
MSM	Men who have sex with men
Non-Binary	Refers to a spectrum of gender and not being in 1 of 2 categories. Typically, the 2 gender categories are male and female
Omnigender	Term that describes possessing all genders
Poly (Polyamorous)	Having more than 1 romantic relationship at the same time
Queer	A term that can mean people who identify as lesbian, gay, bisexual, transgender, or who identify outside of the traditional societal definitions of gender or sexual orientation Some consider term offensive as it was previously used as a slur Members of the LGBTQ+ community have taken back this term as a form of empowerment
Questioning	Persons who are in the process of examining or understanding their gender identity or sexual orientation
Same Gender Loving	Term to describe persons who are attracted physically, romantically, or relationally to persons of the same gender
Trans, Transgender	An umbrella term for people whose gender identity differs from their sex assigned at birth
Two Spirit	A term used by Native American and Canadian First Nation people to describe persons who identify with a 3rd gender that has both masculine and feminine qualities

[a]This table is not meant to be an exhaustive list of terms or definitions
Adapted from University of California San Francisco Lesbian Gay Bisexual and Transgender Resource Center. Retrieved from https://lgbt.ucsf.edu/glossary-terms.

includes who has legal visitation rights during a patient's hospitalization, who can make health care decision, and the ability to provide spousal coverage on a health insurance plan.[8] Surveys conducted among LGB persons found that 56% reported feeling discriminated by health care providers. Approximately 70% of transgender persons reported similar experiences.[9]

Poverty stems from stigma and discrimination. Research shows that there are inequities in the socioeconomic status of LGBTQ+ persons compared to non-LGBTQ+ persons. An analysis found that 22% of lesbian, gay, bisexual and 29% of transgender people live in poverty in the U.S. compared to 16% of cisgender straight people.[10] Poverty is associated with lack of access to health insurance and a lower likelihood of engaging in wellness behaviors. Both can affect health outcomes.

Other health inequities and disparities that occur within the LGBTQ+ population include higher rates of substance use, tobacco use, depression, anxiety, violence, and victimization. We estimate that rates of substance use, including alcohol and tobacco use, are nearly twice as high among LGBTQ+ persons compared to non-LGBTQ+ persons.[11] Similarly, mental health issues, such as depression and anxiety, are more prevalent among persons who identify as LGBTQ+. A recent national survey conducted by the U.S. Department of Health and Human Services Substance Abuse and Mental Health Administration found nearly 1 out of every 3 lesbian, gay, or bisexual adults experienced a mental health disorder compared to 1 out of every 5 heterosexuals. The rate of mental health disorders was higher among transgender persons. Nearly 40% reported having had psychologic distress.[12]

Among LGBTQ+ youth, the rates of mental health disorders are higher than non-LGBTQ+ youth (Fig. 6.1). A 2019 national survey of LGBTQ+ youth found that over 70% reported feeling down or hopeless for at least 2 weeks in the preceding year.[13] Nearly 40% of LGBTQ+ youth considered attempting suicide. More than 50% of transgender and non-binary youth have seriously considered suicide.[13]

Rates of violence and victimization are higher among LGBTQ+ populations compared to heterosexual populations. Hate-crimes and intimate partner violence rates greatly affect LGBTQ+ persons. The rates of violence among transgender persons are also much higher compared to their cisgender counterparts. A disproportionate number of violent crimes are committed against transgender and gender nonconforming persons of color.[14] Recent data found that nearly 40% of LGBTQ+ related homicides occurred in transgender women of color.

Certain cancers occur at a high rate within the LGBTQ+ community. We believe that lesbians may have a higher incidence of breast cancer. Risk factors associated with these higher rates include tobacco use, obesity, and nulliparity. Men who have sex with men (MSM), especially those living with HIV, have nearly twice the rate of anal cancer from human papilloma virus infection. Lung cancer rates are also higher. This is in part due to higher rates of tobacco use.[15]

Lesbian and bisexual women have higher rates of being overweight or obese compared to heterosexual women.[16] Obesity itself is a risk factor for other chronic conditions. These include diabetes, heart disease, hypertension, and osteoarthritis.

HIV and sexually transmitted infections (STIs), such as syphilis, are disproportionately higher, especially among MSM

Fig. 6.1 Rates of mental health disorders are higher among LGBTQ+ youth. (© franckreporter/iStock.com.)

Fig. 6.2 Older LGBTQ+ adults tend to rely on partners or friends for caregiving. (© SilviaJansen/iStock.com.)

and transgender women. In the United States, the majority of new HIV infections occur among MSM. Among Black communities, the rates are even more staggering. We estimate the lifetime risk of acquiring HIV among Black MSM to be as high as 1:2 compared to 1:4 for Hispanic/Latino men and 1:11 for White MSM.[17]

One of the structural barriers that contributes to health disparities is the limited amount of training that health professionals receive in how to provide LGBTQ+ culturally appropriate care. Studies estimate that medical providers receive less than 5 hours of clinical training in LGBTQ+ health. Lack of knowledge about care considerations and a lack of preparation in how to communicate with LGBTQ+ patients contribute to the challenges and barriers LGBTQ+ people experience.

GERONTOLOGIC CONSIDERATIONS

Older LGBTQ+ adults (those age 65 years or older) experience different challenges with their health and caregiving. Many older LGBTQ+ adults do not have children to help support them as they age. Thus, more than half of older LGBTQ+ adults rely on a partner or friend to help or care for them (Fig. 6.2). The aging population also lived through the early years of the HIV epidemic. Many people lost their friends, partners, and social networks. This has implications for higher rates of isolation as that generation reaches older adulthood. Some who need to receive care at a long-term care facility go "back in the closet" and again hide their sexual orientation or gender identity due to negative and sometimes violent reactions from other residents or care staff. These issues add to the physical and mental health disparities between LGBTQ+ and non-LGBTQ+ persons.

ESTABLISHING INCLUSIVE ENVIRONMENTS

The Joint Commission developed guidelines to improve the health care experience of LGBTQ+ patients. These guidelines are part of the accreditation process. Examples include having hospitals post non-discrimination visitation policies, having unisex or single stall bathrooms, and using patient intake forms that collect information on sexual and gender identity.[18]

Establishing a Welcoming Environment

Creating a welcoming environment starts the moment a patient enters a health care agency or makes contact with a facility (Table 6.3). For instance, when patients enter a building or a hospital unit, displaying an inclusive patient bill of rights is important. Have signs or symbols that indicate a safe space for LGBTQ+ persons. This can be in the form of signage or visual cues that have the rainbow flag (a universal symbol of LGBTQ+ pride), advertisements or posters that include same sex couples or transgender persons, all-inclusive or non-gender specific restrooms, or having LGBTQ+ literature or magazines in the waiting areas. Staff can incorporate visual cues on ID badges. These strategies help establish a welcoming environment before having any direct interaction with patients or their caregivers.

CHECK YOUR PRACTICE

You are getting report from the emergency department for a new admission. The patient is a 22-year-old who attempted an overdose with acetaminophen. The nurse giving report says, "the patient says he is 'non-binary'—whatever that means. He looks like a guy to me."
How would you respond?

Health History and the Intake Process

As part of a comprehensive health history, establish the patient's identity. Introduce yourself. Ask the patient their preferred name, gender identity, and pronouns. Using a patient's chosen name is important as it shows recognition for the person's identity. This is true for all persons, not just LGBTQ+ persons. For example, some people may have the legal name Jennifer, but they prefer you call them Jen or Jenny. Some people may go by their middle name or a nick name.

For transgender persons, they may still have their legal name on their insurance cards, but no longer wish to use this name. They sometimes refer to that name as their "dead name." Having legal documents with a given name (which may be a different gendered name) poses a challenge for transgender persons as they begin the transition process or even years after. Some agencies now include a preferred name on the electronic health

TABLE 6.3 Promoting an Inclusive Environment

- Post the agency's nondiscrimination policy and patient bill of rights.
- See that waiting rooms and common areas reflect and are inclusive of LGBTQ+ patients and caregivers.
- Create or designate unisex or single-stall restrooms.
- Allow the patient to identify a support person of their choice.
- Implement visitation polices in a fair and nondiscriminatory manner.
- Honor and respect the patient's decision and pacing in providing information.
- Make sure all forms use inclusive, gender-neutral language that allows for self-identification.
- Provide information and guidance for the specific health concerns facing LGBTQ+ people.
- Ensure that the disclosure of sexual orientation and gender identity information is voluntary.
- Make sure that strong privacy protections for all patient data are in place.

Source: The Joint Commission: Advancing effective communication, cultural competence, and patient-and-family centered care for the lesbian, gay, bisexual, and transgender (LGBT) community: a field guide. Retrieved from https://www.jointcommission.org/-/media/deprecated-unorganized/imported-assets/tjc/system-folders/topics-library/lgbtfieldguidepdf.pdf?db=web&hash=224B46C31193399359B8113698971F26.

record. Verify this before starting the health history. The easiest way to obtain the name a person wishes to use is to ask, "Is there a name you would like for us to use for you while you are here with us?" This will include those whose legal name is William and use Bill as well as those whose legal name is William but use the name Jennifer. The crucial element is that the question needs to be asked of everyone.

Asking about gender identity is important. Some agencies include this information on an intake form and patients can complete the information directly. If the information is pre-entered into the electronic health record, verify that the information is correct before proceeding. If this information is not pre-entered into the medical record system, use a 2-step process for asking about gender identity. Ask the patient their sex assigned at birth and their current gender identity. Ask if the patient has any gender specific pronouns (e.g., he/him, she/her, they/them). Make note to use these pronouns when talking about the patient. If you make a mistake and misgender a person or address them by the wrong name, acknowledge your error right away. Apologize to the patient. Table 6.4 describes other ways to be more inclusive in your communication.

Social History

As part of the social history, use gender neutral terms when asking about a patient's relationship status or living situation. For example, when asking about a patient's partner or spouse, do not assume that a male patient will have a wife or a girlfriend. Rather, you can either wait for the patient to disclose the gender of their partner, or if you are unclear or they do not specify, then you can ask the patient to clarify for you. It is better to ask for clarification versus making an automatic

TABLE 6.4 Inclusive Communication Strategies

Use these strategies to be more inclusive and welcoming when communicating with patients.

Do

Use a 2-step gender question:
- "What was your sex assigned at birth?"
- "What is your current gender?"

Ask and use a patient's preferred name and pronoun:
- "Do you have a preferred name that you would like me to use?"
- "Do you have any preferred pronouns?"

Avoid using gender terms with new patients until all information is known:
- Instead of "how may I help you, sir?" ask "how may I help you?"
- Use the patient's preferred first and last name instead of "Mr. or Ms."
- Instead of saying "He is here for his appointment" say "the patient is here."
- Use the term "transition" to accurately reflect the process and continuum of change that transgender person's experience.

Avoid
- Asking unnecessary questions. Stay focused on why the patient is being seen or evaluated. Remember not every problem or issue is related to one's sexual orientation or gender identity.
- Referring to a patient as "it."
- Asking a transgender person for their "real" name. This may offend some people who no longer identify with their given name.

Terms to Avoid
- "*Sexual preference*"—Alludes to the concept that sexual orientation is a choice.
- "*Transgendered*"—Transgender is an adjective, not a noun. Avoid referring to someone as "a transgender," just like you would not call someone "a straight."
- Do not add "-ed" at the end of transgender. This makes it sound like a condition.
- Do not use these terms "*preop*" or "*postop sex change*" when referring to a transgender person. These terms are outdated and considered offensive.

Adapted from Centers for Disease Control and Prevention: Patient-centered care for transgender people: recommended practices for health care settings. Retrieved from https://www.cdc.gov/hiv/clinicians/transforming-health/health-care-providers/affirmative-care.html; GLAAD: An ally's guide to terminology: talking about LGBT people and equality. Retrieved from https://www.glaad.org/sites/default/files/allys-guide-to-terminology_1.pdf.

assumption. If you make a mistake, acknowledge the error and apologize.

In the absence of people to rely on from their families of origin, LGBTQ+ persons often have a family of choice, often made up of friends, partners, and perhaps a few relatives. Ask the patient who is part of their family of choice and if they have any advance directives. LGBTQ+ patients are especially vulnerable if they do not have advance directives in place. Without an advance directive naming a surrogate decision maker, LGBTQ+ patients who are single or not legally married are at risk of having someone from their family of origin rather than their family of choice make health care decisions if they cannot make decisions for themselves (Box 6.1).

BOX 6.1 ETHICAL/LEGAL DILEMMAS

Durable Power of Attorney for Health Care

Situation

G.V., a 64-year-old woman, is admitted to the ICU with HF. She has many complications from a long-term history of type 1 DM and hypertension, including a right leg above-the-knee amputation and blindness related to retinopathy. She severed ties with her family 30 years ago. She has a life partner of 35 years whom she chose as her proxy in her signed Durable Power of Attorney. She has said many times that she would rather die than have renal dialysis. She has been sedated and intubated for 3 days. The HCP plans to extubate her and resuscitate her so that she can start dialysis. Her brother shows up at the hospital and supports the HCP's decision. Her partner disagrees with the decision. The HCP refuses to recognize her partner as proxy because she is not a blood relative.

Ethical/Legal Points for Consideration

The Patient Self-Determination Act (1990) requires all health care agencies receiving Medicare and Medicaid funding to make available advance directives allowing persons to state their preferences or refusals of health care in the event that they are incapable of consenting for themselves. Durable Power of Attorney for health care is one type of advance directive in which people, when they are competent, identify someone else to make decisions for them, should they lose their decision-making ability in the future (see Table 10.3). A Living Will, another type of advance directive, permits people to state their own preferences and refusals.

Within your scope of nursing practice, you need to know the decision-making laws and regulations in your own state and make advance directive documents available to patients. In addition, you need to (1) teach patients and their families about advance directives, (2) make sure that HCPs are aware of and follow advance directives, (3) assist the patient and family in communicating with the HCPs when a "No Code" order is requested, and (4) assist a conflicted family in obtaining appropriate counseling whenever needed.

Many HCPs mistakenly think that proxies must be family members or blood relatives. Lesbian, gay, bisexual, transgender, queer or questioning, and gender diverse (LGBTQ+) persons often have difficulty having their partnership recognized as valid, especially if the patient's family disputes their rights. Counsel LGBTQ+ patients on the importance of having a health care proxy and a will to legally protect their end-of-life choices.

Discussion Questions

1. How can you assess the patient and family's understanding of durable power of attorney and assist them in understanding their role in decision making?
2. What should you do when an HCP orders dialysis to be started when you know that this goes against the patient's advance directive?

Sexual and Reproductive Health History

Taking a sexual history is an important aspect of providing holistic care. The most important element to taking an inclusive sexual history is to understand, before asking questions, what it is you need to know to provide care to that person. Although sexual history taking may not be done in all clinical settings, when obtaining a sexual history use nonjudgmental language. Be sensitive to the range of sexual practices for *all* patients, not just the LGBTQ+ community.[19] You need to feel comfortable asking these questions. If you appear uncomfortable, patients will sense your uneasiness. They may choose not to disclose information.

Fig. 6.3 A growing number of LGBTQ+ persons are having and raising families. (© Jelena Stanojkovic/iStock.com.)

BOX 6.2 PROMOTING POPULATION HEALTH

Improving the Health and Well-Being of LGBTQ+ Persons

- Provide supportive social services to reduce suicide among LGBTQ+ persons.
- Implement antibullying policies in schools and the workplace.
- Provide health care professionals with knowledge of the health needs of the LGBTQ+ community and training on related mental health issues.
- Continue efforts to expand domestic partner health insurance coverage.
- Establish community advisory boards and LGBTQ+ health centers.
- Disseminate effective HIV and sexually transmitted infection interventions.

Consider asking questions that speak specifically to pregnancy (prevention, family planning) or STI risk and prevention. This will help guide your conversation to the sexual practices and away from questions that seem probing or unnecessary.

Questions about fertility and family planning are important to ask regardless of sexual orientation or practices. LGBTQ+ persons may have children or have an interest in parenting children (Fig. 6.3). You can find more information on sexual history taking in Chapter 55.

PREVENTIVE HEALTH

Preventive health is an important part of providing care (Box 6.2). In addition to standard guidelines for preventive health screenings, offer MSM vaccinations for hepatitis A and B. Rates of these preventable forms of viral hepatitis are higher among MSM due to sexual practices. Although not a vaccine-preventable form of hepatitis, the rate of hepatitis C infection among MSM and transgender women, especially those living with HIV, is higher than for heterosexual men.[20] Screening for HCV antibodies is recommended for those at risk.

Given the higher rates of HIV infection and STIs among MSM and transgender women, assess the patient's awareness of their HIV and STI status. Teach those without HIV about strategies to prevent HIV. Include pre-exposure prophylaxis (PrEP) and post-exposure prophylaxis (PEP) (see Chapter 15).

TABLE 6.5 Gender Affirming Hormone Therapy

Masculinizing Hormone Therapy Options		
Hormone	**Anticipated Effects**	**Nursing Considerations**
Testosterone *Available Formulations:* • Injectable testosterone Topical testosterone	• ↑ Abdominal fat • Acne • Amenorrhea • Clitoromegaly • Deepening voice • ↑ Facial hair • ↑ Hemoglobin and hematocrit • ↑ Muscle mass • Vaginal dryness • Oily skin	When given IM or SC, teach injection techniques. Review importance of rotating injection sites. For topical therapy, apply daily. Avoid skin contact with others until testosterone has dried to avoid unintentional transfer of testosterone. Contraindications include pregnancy, unstable coronary artery disease, and untreated polycythemia with a hematocrit of 55% or higher. Patients with history of breast or estrogen dependent cancers should consult with an oncologist before hormone use. Obtain a cardiology consult for those with cardiovascular or cerebrovascular disease. Although menses may cease, persons at risk for pregnancy should consider an additional method of birth control.
Feminizing Hormone Therapy Options		
Hormone	**Anticipated Effects**	**Considerations for Care**
Estradiol *Available Formulations:* • Oral or sublingual estradiol • Injectable estradiol valerate • Transdermal estradiol patch	• Breast growth • Erectile dysfunction • Fat redistribution from the abdomen to the hips • ↓ Libido • ↓ Prostate and testicular size • Skin softens • Slowing of androgenetic hair loss	Bioidentical forms are preferred. Take oral/sublingual formulations daily. ↑ Risk of venous thromboembolic events. Contraindicated in persons with previous venous thromboembolic events related to an underlying hypercoagulable condition, history of estrogen-sensitive cancers, or end-stage chronic liver disease. For persons using injectable therapy, teach injection techniques. Some patients on estrogen therapy are at potential risk of prolactinomas. Refer for evaluation patients with new onset galactorrhea, vision changes, or headaches. Estrogen therapy may worsen migraines. Patients with pre-existing migraines should be started on lower doses of estrogen and titrated upwards as needed.
Anti-Androgen *Available Formulations:* • Spironolactone		Monitor potassium levels for persons on spironolactone, especially those with renal disease, or who are on ACE or ARBs
• Finasteride/dutasteride		Preferred for patients unable to tolerate or with contraindications to spironolactone.

References: Hembree WC, Cohen-Kettenis PT, Gooren L, et al: Endocrine Treatment of gender-dysphoric/gender-incongruent persons: an Endocrine Society clinical practice guideline, *J Clin Endocrinol Met* 102:3869, 2017; Radix A: Hormone therapy for transgender adults, *Urologic Clinics* 46:467, 2019.

Breast and cervical cancer screenings are important for lesbian and bisexual women. Ensuring that women receive appropriate preventive screening and early detection can help reduce the complications associated with these cancers.

Remember that not all transgender people undergo surgical transition. In fact, many choose not to undergo surgical transition for a variety of reasons. Thus, a transgender woman may still have a prostate and be at risk for prostate cancer. Similarly, a transgender man with a cervix should have a screening for cervical cancer. Do not assume that a transgender patient has had gender affirming surgery.

Tobacco use is thought to be 2 to 3 times higher among LGBTQ+ persons. Tobacco use increases the risk for conditions such as pulmonary and cardiovascular problems. Screening for tobacco use should be part of routine care. For those who report using tobacco, provide education and assistance by referring them to a tobacco cessation program or specialist. See more about cessation in Chapter 11.

GENDER AFFIRMATION THERAPY

Gender Affirming Hormone Therapy

Testosterone and estrogen are both naturally occurring hormones in those assigned male and female at birth. Testosterone is higher in cisgender males. It is responsible for physical attributes such as increased muscle mass, facial hair, and a lower voice. Estrogen produces female characteristics. These include softer skin, breast development, and changes in the distribution of body fat.

Gender affirming hormone therapy (GAHT) provides transgender persons the opportunity to transition from their sex assigned at birth to the gender that aligns with their sense of being. Table 6.5 provides a summary of GAHT options for transgender persons. For a person whose sex assigned at birth was female but who identifies as male, testosterone therapy is used. A person who was assigned male sex at birth but whose gender is female is prescribed feminizing hormone therapy with estrogen and an anti-androgen.[21] The goal of GAHT is to align

Fig. 6.4 The goal of gender affirming hormone therapy is to align a person's hormones and physical appearance with their identified gender. (© TwilightShow/iStock.com.)

a person's hormones and physical attributes with their affirmed gender (Fig. 6.4).

The physical changes of GAHT occur over an extended period of time, much like puberty. Transgender men who start testosterone therapy will typically experience cessation of menses and increased body hair within the first few months of starting therapy. Transgender women who are starting feminizing hormones with estrogen and an anti-androgen agent may develop breast buds after several months of therapy. For many people, the maximum of effects of hormone therapy can take several years.

Several guidelines for the care and management of transgender persons exist. The World Professional Association for Transgender Health (WPATH) is an international organization of health professionals who have developed standards of care for transgender persons.[5] The Endocrine Society and Transline (a collaborative of transgender medicine specialists) have published guidelines on the use of GAHT and gender affirming surgery. [22,23]

As part of an initial assessment before GAHT, ask patients about their desires for future fertility and reproductive health. Hormone or medical therapy may impact future fertility.

We should have a conversation and provide resources about sperm or egg preservation for those who are interested.

Counsel and teach patients starting GAHT about anticipated side effects and the importance of adherence to hormone therapy. Teach patients who receive injectable therapy how to properly inject hormones if they are going to be doing self-injections. If someone on GAHT is hospitalized, maintain their hormone therapy during their hospitalization if there are no contraindications.

Nonsurgical Gender Affirming Interventions

Some transgender persons may choose to begin their transition process by including nonsurgical or nonhormonal interventions to help align their physical appearances with their gender identity.[24] Examples include chest binding of the breasts for transgender men who desire to have a more masculine appearing chest. Transgender women with a penis may "tuck" their penis to flatten the front part of their genital area. Those who do chest binding or tucking may develop skin irritation in these areas. Assess if they have any issues with skin infections, rashes, or irritations and intervene as needed.

Other nonsurgical interventions include cosmetic fillers. Transgender women can use these to feminize facial features. Silicone is one of the fillers used. When implanted correctly, fillers are a safe and effective way to create wanted changes to the appearance of the body in a similar manner to non-transgender people. Refer patients to a qualified professional as serious complications can occur.

Vocal therapy is an intervention used by transgender women to help feminize their voices. Typically, a speech pathologist who is trained in working with transgender patients can help patients achieve a higher pitch to their voice. In some cases, the person may have vocal surgery.[25]

Gender Affirming Surgery

Gender affirming surgery (sometimes called gender reconstructive surgery) are surgical procedures performed to create either more masculinizing features in a transgender man or feminizing features in a transgender woman.[2] There are a number of gender affirming surgical options for transgender persons. The range and type of surgery depends on several factors. The main one is patient desires and goals. Not all transgender persons wish to have gender affirming surgery. Table 6.6 outlines the types of gender affirming surgeries and procedures. Depending on the type of procedure done, a person may need to have several procedures over time to achieve the desired outcome.

More hospitals are performing gender affirming surgery. Nurses caring for patients having gender affirming surgery need to be familiar with providing appropriate and supportive care before surgery and through the recovery period. For patients who require more extensive wound care after surgery, home care nurses and office-based primary care nurses may need to provide wound care teaching as part of the continuum of care.

Chest Masculinization Surgery

Chest masculinization surgery is a surgical intervention for transgender men. As part of this procedure, breast tissue is removed. The nipples are repositioned to provide a more masculine appearing chest. There are several surgical approaches and techniques based on the patient's anatomy and surgical preference. These include variation in incision site, incision size, and preservation of nerve sensation in the nipples. Previous hormone therapy with testosterone is not a requirement.

Feminizing Breast Augmentation

Feminizing breast surgery provides transgender women an opportunity to augment their breasts with implants to create a more feminine appearance. Although GAHT can cause breast development in transgender women, in some people hormone therapy alone does not produce the desired results for breast development. Some surgical centers require a person to

TABLE 6.6 Gender Affirming Surgical Procedures

Feminizing Surgical Procedures	
Breast augmentation/feminizing augmentation mammoplasty	• Implants (saline or silicone) are placed under the breast muscle to enhance breast size • May be done using fat transferred from another part of the body
Facial feminization surgery	• Surgical procedures done to make the face softer and more feminine in appearance • Includes brow lifts, hairline adjustment, nose reshaping, cheek implants, blepharoplasty, mandibular angle reduction, chin width reduction, lip reshaping, tracheal shave (thyroid chondroplasty)
Orchiectomy	• Removal of the testicles
Vaginoplasty	• Creates a vagina • During the procedure, the penis, testicles, and scrotum are removed. The tissue is then reshaped to create a neo-vagina. May have skin grafting from the abdomen or thigh • Dilators are used afterwards to help keep the graft from contracting and improves the elasticity of the vagina
Masculinizing Surgical Procedures	
Hysterectomy and oophorectomy	• Removal of the uterus and ovaries
Masculinizing chest reconstruction (mastectomy)	• Breast tissue is removed and reshaped to have a more masculine appearance
Metoidioplasty (also called meta)	• Creation of a penis from existing genital tissue including the clitoris
Pectoral implants	• Implants used to create a more masculine chest
Phalloplasty	• A multi-stage procedure that creates a penis. • Typically involves lengthening the urethra, creating a scrotum, removing the vagina, and placing erectile and testicular implants • Several techniques exist. Involves grafting additional skin and muscle from another part of the body, such as the forearm, thigh, or latissimus dorsi
Scrotoplasty	• Creation of a scrotum • Typically includes testicular implants

Source: Chen ML, Reyblat P, Poh MM, et al: Overview of surgical techniques in gender-affirming genital surgery, *Transl Androl Urol* 8:191, 2019.

be on hormone therapy at least 12 months to allow for maximal breast growth before surgery. Options for breast implants include gel or saline implants and fat transfer. With fat transfer, body fat is removed from one part of the body and injected or placed around the breast to enhance or augment the shape.

NURSING MANAGEMENT: GENDER AFFIRMING SURGERY

Assessment

Current guidelines for transgender care recommend that patients undergoing either chest masculinization or breast augmentation surgery have persistent and well-documented gender dysphoria, the capacity and ability to provide informed consent, be the age of majority, and have any medical or mental health concerns well controlled.[5] The surgical team should work closely with the patient's hormone therapy and mental health providers to make sure that the patient is a good candidate for surgery and prepared for the procedure and post-surgical recovery period.

Implementation

Acute Care

After surgery, provide general postoperative care as described in Chapter 20. Some patients having chest masculinization or breast augmentation surgery may have surgical drains. If drains are present, assess for the amount and type of drainage. A chest binder or other supportive dressings are in place until the surgical wounds are healed. Assess the dressing for signs of excess bleeding.

Pain management during the recovery period is important for patients having either chest masculinization or breast augmentation surgery. Assess the patient's pain level. Give analgesics as ordered to keep the patient comfortable.

Ambulatory Care

Possible post-procedure complications include seromas, hematomas, and infection. Teach and monitor patients for signs or symptoms of infection. Patients will often have limited range of motion for several weeks afterwards. Teach the patient how to minimize movement. Have the patient avoid activities such as heavy lifting or reaching. They may need help with certain activities or must make modifications in the home or work environment. For example, relocating items from a high shelf to a lower shelf or countertop will help avoid stretching.

Although breast tissue is removed with chest masculinization surgery, there is still a potential for breast cancer development. Counsel those with a history of breast cancer or a high risk for breast cancer on the importance of regular screening. There is limited data on persons who had feminizing breast augmentation surgery about breast cancer prevalence. Current guidelines recommend that breast cancer screening in transgender women begin at age 50 if the person has been on estrogen therapy for at least 5 years.[27] The length of exposure to feminizing hormones influences the risk of breast cancer.

Case Study

Anal Cancer

(© azndc/iStock.com.)

Patient Profile

J.B. is a 61-year-old cisgender, gay-identified man with a history of well-controlled HIV. He was recently diagnosed with Stage III squamous cell carcinoma of the anus. He had an abdominal peritoneal resection with diverting colostomy to remove the cancer.

Subjective Data

- Diagnosed with HIV 25 years ago
- Doing well on antiretroviral therapy
- Noted a mass in his rectum for several years but did not seek care until recently when he started having rectal pain
- Completed 5 weeks of external beam radiation before surgery
- Has a male partner of 15 years

Objective Data

- Temperature: 98.9°F, BP: 116/80 mmHg, heart rate 80 beats/min, respiratory rate is 18 breaths/min and unlabored
- Reports 6/10 pain in his abdomen
- Stoma is moist appearing, with minimal drainage
- Has a flattened affect and is tearful

Discussion Questions

1. ***Recognize***: What do you know about the rates of cancer in the LGBTQ+ community?
2. ***Recognize***: What factors may have caused J.B. to delay seeking care?
3. ***Plan***: What other interprofessional team members might be useful to involve?
4. ***Prioritize***: Based on the information provided, what are the priority nursing interventions for this patient?
5. ***Act:*** J.B. tells you that he is concerned about how his surgery will impact his sexual relationship with his partner. How would you respond?

BRIDGE TO NCLEX EXAMINATION

The number of the question corresponds to the same-numbered outcome at the beginning of the chapter.

1. The nurse caring for a patient who identifies as bisexual understands that bisexuality refers to
   - **a.** a person who was born female but uses testosterone to grow facial hair.
   - **b.** a person born male who uses estrogen to achieve feminine characteristics.
   - **c.** a person who is sexually or affectionately attracted to more than one gender.
   - **d.** a person who expresses their gender by wearing both male and female clothing.
2. A nurse is caring for a young man admitted with pneumonia. The patient discloses that he identifies as a gay male. Which statement by the nurse demonstrates an understanding of health disparities and the LGBTQ+ community?
   - **a.** "Have you been vaccinated for measles?"
   - **b.** "When was the last time you were tested for HIV?"
   - **c.** "Do you need a referral to a hormone therapy specialist?"
   - **d.** "When was the last time you received colon cancer screening?"
3. A nurse is leading a committee to improve LGBTQ+ inclusiveness on an inpatient medical unit. Which strategies are recommended for creating an inclusive LGBTQ+ environment? (*select all that apply*)
   - **a.** Use a patient's preferred name and pronoun.
   - **b.** Allow staff to wear a rainbow pin on their name badges.
   - **c.** Assign a transgender patient to a private room, when possible.
   - **d.** Make single stall public bathrooms to be all-gender bathrooms.
   - **e.** Only allow a patient's immediate biologic family visiting rights.
4. Expected effects of masculinizing hormone therapy include
   - **a.** iron-deficiency anemia
   - **b.** increased body and facial hair
   - **c.** elevated thyroid stimulating hormone
   - **d.** increased risk of pulmonary embolism and stroke
5. You are caring for a transgender woman who recently underwent vaginoplasty. What information should the nurse include as part of the patient's discharge instructions?
   - **a.** You will need regular cervical cancer screening.
   - **b.** Let me show you how to do testosterone injections.
   - **c.** If you find the dilators difficult to use, contact your surgeon.
   - **d.** You should anticipate your first menstrual cycle to begin soon.

1. c; 2. b; 3 a, b, c, d; 4. b; 5. c.

For rationales to these answers and even more NCLEX review questions, visit http://evolve.elsevier.com/Lewis/medsurg.

EVOLVE WEBSITE/RESOURCES LIST

http://evolve.elsevier.com/Lewis/medsurg
Review Questions (online only)
Key Points
Answer Key for Questions
- Rationales for Bridge to NCLEX Examination Questions
- Answer Guidelines for Case Study

Conceptual Care Map Creator
Audio Glossary
Content Updates

REFERENCES

1. Lee PA, Fuqua JS, Houk CP, et al.: Individualized care for patients with intersex, *J Pediatr Urol* 16:230, 2020.
2. Fausto-Sterling A: Gender/sex, sexual orientation, and identity are in the body: how did they get there? *J Sex Res* 56:529, 2019.
3. Robinson M: Two-spirit identity in a time of gender fluidity, *J Homosex* 1675, 2020.
4. American Psychiatric Association: What is gender dysphoria? Retrieved from https://www.psychiatry.org/patients-families/gender-dysphoria/what-is-gender-dysphoria.
*5. World Professional Association for Transgender Health: *Standards of care for the health of transsexual, transgender, and gender nonconforming people*, ed 7, 2012. (Classic).
6. Valdiserri RO, Holtgrave DR, Poteat TC, et al.: Unraveling health disparities among sexual and gender minorities: a commentary on the persistent impact of stigma, *J Homosex* 66:571, 2019.
7. Bailey JM: The minority stress model deserves reconsideration, not just extension, *Arch Sex Behav* 49:2265, 2019.
8. Ball CA: *After marriage equality: the future of LGBT rights*, New York, 2019, NYU Press.
9. Human Rights Campaign: Health Care Equality Index 2020. Retrieved from https://hrc-prod-requests.s3-us-west-2.amazonaws.com/resources/HEI-2020-FinalReport.pdf?mtime=20200830220806&focal=none.
10. SAGE: The facts on LGBT aging. Retrieved from https://www.sageusa.org/wp-content/uploads/2018/05/sageusa-the-facts-on-lgbt-aging.pdf.
11. National Institute on Drug Abuse: Substance use and SUDs in LGBTQ populations. Retrieved from https://www.drugabuse.gov/drug-topics/substance-use-suds-in-lgbtq-populations.
12. Substance Abuse and Mental Health Association: Lesbian, gay, bisexual, and transgender (LGBT). Retrieved from https://www.samhsa.gov/behavioral-health-equity/lgbt.
*13. Ream JL: What's unique about lesbian, gay, bisexual, and transgender (LGBT) youth and young adult suicides? Findings from the National Violent Death Reporting System, *J Adolesc Health* 64:602, 2019.
*14. National Coalition of Anti-Violence Programs: Lesbian, gay, bisexual, transgender, queer and HIV-affected hate and intimate partner violence in 2017. Retrieved from https://avp.org/2017-hv-ipv-report/.
15. National LGBT Cancer Network. LGBT cancer information. Retrieved from https://cancer-network.org/cancer-information/cancer-resources-for-the-lgbt-community/.
*16. Azagba S, Shan L, Latham K: Overweight and obesity among sexual minority adults in the United States, *Int J Environ Res Public Health* 16:1828, 2019.
17. Centers for Disease Control and Prevention: Gay and bisexual men's health - Sexually transmitted diseases. Retrieved from https://www.cdc.gov/msmhealth/STD.htm.
18. The Joint Commission: Advancing effective communication, cultural competence, and patient-and-family centered care for the lesbian, gay, bisexual, and transgender (LGBT) community: a field guide. Retrieved from https://www.jointcommission.org/-/media/deprecated-unorganized/imported-assets/tjc/system-folders/topics-library/lgbtfieldguidepdf.pdf?db=web&hash=224B46C31193399359B8113698971F26.
19. Thompson J: Taking a sexual history with sexual and gender minority individuals. Retrieved from https://www.lgbtqiahealtheducation.org/wp-content/uploads/2020/03/6.-Taking-an-Affirming-Sexual-History.min_.pdf.
20. Njimeijer BM, Koopsen J, Schinkel J, et al.: Sexually transmitted hepatitis C virus infections: current trends, and recent advances in understanding the spread in men who have sex with men, *J Int AIDS Soc* 22, 2019.
21. Radix A: Hormone therapy for transgender adults, *Urol Clin North Am* 46:467, 2019.
*22. Hembree WC, Cohen-Kettenis PT, Gooren L, et al.: Endocrine treatment of gender-dysphoric/gender-incongruent persons: an Endocrine Society clinical practice guideline, *J Clin Endocrinol* 102:3869, 2017. (Classic).
23. TransLine: Hormone therapy. Retrieved from https://transline.zendesk.com/hc/en-us/categories/204099748-Hormone-Therapy.
24. Deutsch MB: Binding, packing, tucking. Retrieved from https://transcare.ucsf.edu/guidelines/binding-packing-and-tucking.
25. Nolan IT, Morrison SD, Arowojolu O, et al.: The role of voice therapy and phonosurgery in transgender vocal feminization, *J Carniofac Surg* 30:1368, 2019.
26. Chen ML, Reyblat P, Poh MM, et al.: Overview of surgical techniques in gender-affirming genital surgery, *Transl Androl Urol* 8:191, 2019.
*27. Deutch MB: Screening for breast cancer in transgender women. Retrieved from https://transcare.ucsf.edu/guidelines/breast-cancer-women.

*Evidence-based information for clinical practice.

7

Stress Management

Margaret R. Rateau

http://evolve.elsevier.com/Lewis/medsurg/

CONCEPTUAL FOCUS

Risk for Disease

Stress and Coping

LEARNING OUTCOMES

1. Distinguish between the terms *stressor* and *stress.*
2. Describe the role of the nervous and endocrine systems in the stress process.
3. Describe the effects of stress on the immune system.
4. Discuss the effects of stress on health.
5. Explain the role of coping in managing stress.
6. Select coping and relaxation strategies that you, a patient, or a caregiver experiencing stress can use.
7. Describe the assessment and management of a patient experiencing stress.

KEY TERMS

biofeedback
coping
emotion-focused coping
imagery
massage
meditation
mind-body-spirit connection
problem-focused coping
psychoneuroimmunology (PNI)
relaxation breathing
stress
stressors

All people have stress. Stress has a powerful effect on the mind and a significant effect on one's health and well-being. The concept of stress directly relates to multiple other concepts. Chronic stress is a major factor in causing and worsening chronic health conditions. This in turn is a major driver of soaring health care costs.

High levels of stress are common among patients and caregivers. How they deal with their stress is critical to their well-being. As a nurse, you play a key role in helping them recognize stress and manage stressful events. This chapter focuses on how stress can affect the mind, body, and spirit and how a person can effectively cope with stress.

WHAT IS STRESS?

Stress is the inability to cope with perceived (real or imagined) demands or threats to one's mental, emotional, or spiritual well-being.[1] Stress is more prevalent in women and reported through physical symptoms such as anxiety and depression. More women seek help for stress-related symptoms. Men are more likely to die from stress-related illnesses.[2]

Many different events or factors can be **stressors.** They can be physiologic (e.g., acute pain) or emotional/psychologic (e.g., death of a child, loss of a home through fire, fear) (Fig. 7.1). Emotional/psychologic stressors can be positive or negative. For example, the birth of a baby is usually a positive stressor. Marital discord is a negative stressor.

Perception of the potential stressor influences the way a person responds to that stressor. Responses to the same stressor vary greatly. What one person perceives as stressful may not be perceived as stressful to someone else. This is shown in the following examples:

- B.J., a 43-year-old woman, becomes depressed after a laparoscopic hysterectomy for fibroids. She is unwilling to take part in normal self-care activities. You are surprised by her response. You think she had a simple surgery and should get on with life. After further assessment, you discover that removing her uterus is a great psychologic stressor because she perceives it as a loss of her womanhood and femininity.

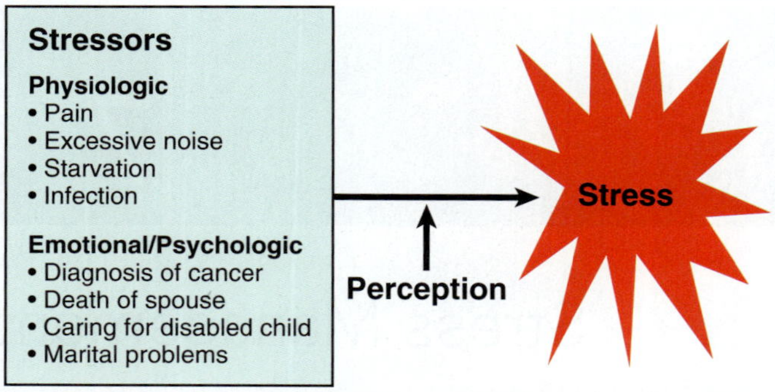

Fig. 7.1 Stressors can be physiologic or emotional/psychologic. Events or circumstances become stressful when you perceive them to be.

- K.R., a 52-year-old woman, has just been told by her health care provider (HCP) of her new diagnosis of type 2 diabetes. After the HCP's visit with her, you are prepared to provide emotional support. However, you are puzzled when she is smiling and feeling relieved. You think that this diagnosis should be stressful. However, K.R. tells you that she is so relieved because for weeks she was worried that her symptoms were caused by cancer.

Is Stress Bad or Good?

We tend to think of stress as bad or a threat. Actually, any event or situation that is out of the ordinary can be a stressor. This includes events that we normally consider happy or enjoy, such as getting married or going on a vacation. Stress can be helpful. A little stress can motivate you. Stress can actually inspire you to achieve a goal, become more confident, or stronger physically.

The body cannot tell between bad and good stress or real or imaginary stress. It responds to the stressor with the same stress response. This stress response is the way our bodies react both physically and emotionally to any change, be it good, bad, real, or imagined.

For you as a nursing student, a test can be a stressful situation. A little bit of stress related to an upcoming test makes you study and become better prepared. If you feel mildly stressed during the test, it may help your test performance. A little stress heightens your awareness and increases your mental acuity. However, if you are overly stressed, it causes mental blocks, lack of concentration, and inability to remember things.

Stress is a key for survival, but too much stress can be detrimental. That is why it is important for you and your patients to learn to cope more effectively with the stressors in life.

Factors Affecting Response to Stress

Why do people respond so differently to stress? Why do some people cope better with stress than others? Interestingly, some people experience significant adverse life events but do not succumb to the effects of stress. It is important to use a holistic approach when assessing the impact of stress on a person because of the number of factors that influence a person's response to stress. Important variables include the type of stressor, duration (acute or chronic), and intensity (mild, moderate, or severe).

TABLE 7.1 Factors Affecting Response to Stress

Internal
- Age
- Attitude
- Genetic background
- Hardiness
- Health status
- Nutrition status
- Optimistic outlook
- Personality characteristics
- Previous experience with stressors
- Resilience
- Sleep status

External
- Cultural and ethnic influences
- Number of stressors present
- Religious or spiritual influences
- Socioeconomic status
- Social support
- Timing of stressors

Fig. 7.2 During stressful situations, demands may exceed resources. (© SDI Productions/iStock.com.)

Internal and external factors play a vital role in one's ability to cope with stress (Table 7.1). Being surrounded by a strong social support system and receiving positive support from friends and family have a large impact on a person's ability to cope with stressors (Fig. 7.2).

Key personal characteristics that buffer the effects of stress are attitude, hardiness, being optimistic, and resilience. *Resilience* is being resourceful and flexible and having good problem-solving skills. People who have a high degree of resilience are not as likely to perceive an event as stressful.

Hardiness is a combination of 3 characteristics: commitment, control, and openness to change. Together they give the courage and motivation needed to turn stressful circumstances from potential calamities into opportunities for personal growth.

Attitude can influence the effect of stress on a person. People with positive attitudes view situations differently from those with negative attitudes. A person's attitude also influences how

PATHOPHYSIOLOGY MAP

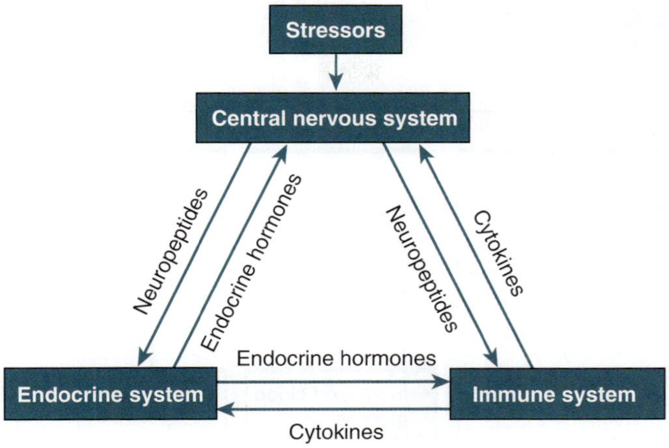

Fig. 7.3 Neurochemical links among the nervous, endocrine, and immune systems. The communication among the systems is bidirectional.

they manage stress. To some extent, positive attitudes can prevent disease and prolong life.[3]

Being optimistic can help you cope more effectively with stress. Optimism also reduces a person's chances of developing stress-related illnesses. When optimistic people do become ill, they tend to recover more quickly. Pessimists are likely to deny the problem, distance themselves from the stressful event, focus on stressful feelings, or allow the stressor to interfere with achieving a goal. Those with a more pessimistic attitude tend to report poorer health than those with optimistic attitudes.[3]

PHYSIOLOGIC RESPONSE TO STRESS

The nervous, endocrine, and immune systems are primarily involved in the stress response. These systems are interrelated. This interrelationship is reflected in a person's physiologic response to stress (Fig. 7.3). Further, stress activation of these systems affects other body systems, such as the cardiovascular, respiratory, gastrointestinal (GI), renal, and reproductive systems. A person's response to a stressor determines the impact that stress will have on the body.

Nervous System

Cerebral Cortex

The areas of the cerebral cortex, or cerebrum, involved in the control of cognition, affect, and movement influence how we perceive stressors. We evaluate the stressor in light of past experiences and future consequences. This gives us some control over our response to stress. The motor areas also send signals to the adrenal medulla that directly relate to how stressors are managed.

Limbic System

The *limbic system* lies in the inner midportion of the brain near the base of the brain. The limbic system is an important mediator of emotions and behavior. When the limbic system is stimulated, emotions, feelings, and behaviors can occur that ensure survival and self-preservation.

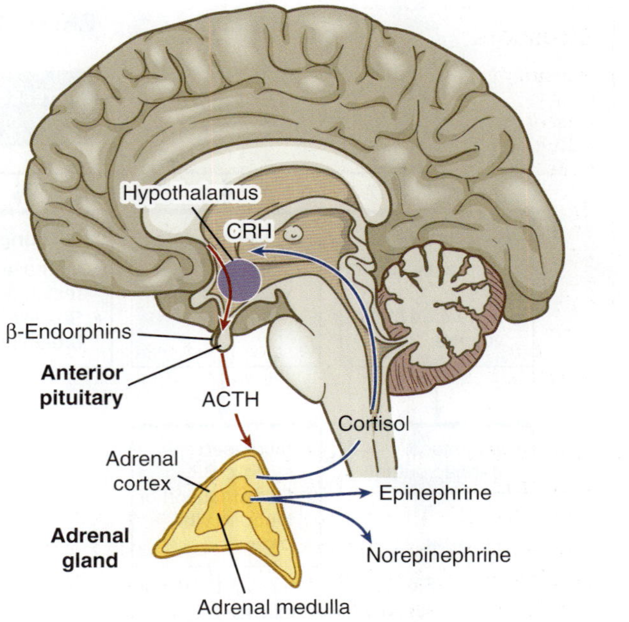

Fig. 7.4 Hypothalamic-pituitary-adrenal axis. *ACTH,* Adrenocorticotropic hormone; *CRH,* corticotropin-releasing hormone.

Reticular Formation

The *reticular formation* is located between the lower end of the brainstem and thalamus. It contains the *reticular activating system* (RAS), which sends impulses contributing to alertness to the limbic system and cerebral cortex. When the RAS is stimulated, it increases its output of impulses, leading to wakefulness. Stress usually increases the degree of wakefulness and can lead to sleep problems.

Hypothalamus

The hypothalamus, which lies at the base of the brain just above the pituitary gland, has many functions that aid in adaptation to stress. Stress activates the limbic system, which in turn stimulates the hypothalamus. Because the hypothalamus secretes neuropeptides that regulate the release of hormones by the anterior pituitary, it is central to the connection between the nervous and endocrine systems in responding to stress (Fig. 7.4).

The hypothalamus plays a primary role in the stress response by regulating the function of both the sympathetic and parasympathetic branches of the autonomic nervous system. When a person perceives a stressor, the hypothalamus sends signals that initiate both the nervous and endocrine responses to the stressor. It does this mainly by sending signals via nerve fibers to stimulate the sympathetic nervous system (SNS) and by releasing corticotropin-releasing hormone (CRH). CRH stimulates the pituitary to release adrenocorticotropic hormone (ACTH) (see Chapter 52).

Endocrine System

Once the hypothalamus is activated in response to stress, the endocrine system becomes involved. The SNS stimulates the adrenal medulla to release epinephrine and norepinephrine (catecholamines). The effect of catecholamines and the activation of the SNS, including the response of the adrenal medulla,

PATHOPHYSIOLOGY MAP

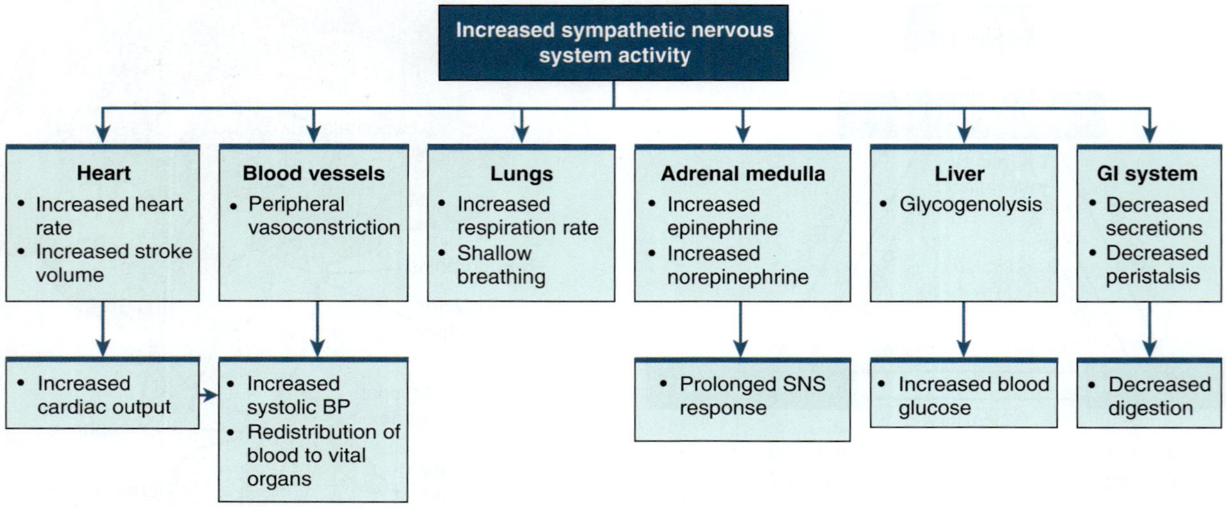

Fig. 7.5 "Fight-or-flight" reaction. Alarm reaction responses resulting from increased sympathetic nervous system *(SNS)* activity.

is referred to as the *sympathoadrenal response.* Epinephrine and norepinephrine prepare the body for the *fight-or-flight response* (Fig. 7.5).

Stress activates the hypothalamic-pituitary-adrenal (HPA) axis. In response to stress, the hypothalamus releases CRH, which stimulates the anterior pituitary to release proopiomelanocortin (POMC). Both ACTH (a hormone) and β-endorphin (a neuropeptide) are derived from POMC. Endorphins have analgesic-like effects and blunt pain perception during stress situations involving pain stimuli. ACTH in turn stimulates the adrenal cortex to synthesize and secrete corticosteroids (e.g., cortisol) and, to a lesser degree, aldosterone.

Corticosteroids are essential for the stress response. Cortisol produces several physiologic effects, such as increasing blood glucose levels, intensifying the action of catecholamines on blood vessels, and inhibiting the inflammatory response. Corticosteroids play an important role in "turning off" or blunting the stress response, which, if uncontrolled, can become self-destructive. This is shown by their ability to suppress the release of proinflammatory mediators, such as the cytokines tumor necrosis factor (TNF) and interleukin-1 (IL-1). The persistent release of these mediators is thought to initiate organ dysfunction in conditions such as sepsis or autoimmune disease. Thus, corticosteroids act not only to support the body's adaptive response to a stressor but also to suppress an overzealous and potentially self-destructive response.

The stress response involves increases in (1) cardiac output (from the increased heart rate and increased stroke volume), (2) blood glucose levels, (3) oxygen consumption, and (4) metabolic rate (Fig. 7.5). In addition, dilation of skeletal muscle blood vessels increases blood supply to the large muscles and supports quick movement. Increased cerebral blood flow increases mental alertness. For example, in the case of stressful situations (e.g., blood loss from trauma), the increased blood volume (from increased extracellular fluid and the shunting of blood away from the GI system) helps to maintain adequate circulation to vital organs.

Summary of Stress Response

In summary, the fight-or-flight response is an important and necessary adaptive mechanism of the body to acute stress. We activate this response to stressors whether they are physiologic or emotional/psychologic. Acute stress leads to physiologic changes that are important to a person's survival. This is your "alarm system." It puts you on high alert. The acute stress response is a state of physiologic and psychologic arousal characterized by increased SNS activity that leads to increased heart and respiratory rate, increased BP, increased muscle tension, increased brain activity, and decreased skin temperature.

Immune System

Stress has an impact on the immune system. **Psychoneuroimmunology (PNI)** is an interdisciplinary science that studies the interactions among psychologic, neurologic, and immune responses. Because neuroanatomic and neuroendocrine pathways connect the brain to the immune system, stressors have the potential to lead to changes in immune function (Fig. 7.6).

Nerve fibers extend from the nervous system and synapse on cells and tissues of the immune system (i.e., spleen, lymph nodes). In turn, the cells of the immune system have receptors for many neuropeptides and hormones. This allows them to respond to nervous and neuroendocrine signals. As a result, the mediation of stress by the central nervous system leads to corresponding changes in immune cell activity.

Both acute and chronic stress can cause immunosuppression. Stress affects immune function by (1) decreasing the number and function of natural killer cells; (2) decreasing lymphocyte proliferation; (3) altering production of *cytokines* (soluble factors secreted by white blood cells and other cells, e.g., interferon, interleukins); and (4) decreasing phagocytosis by neutrophils

PATHOPHYSIOLOGY MAP

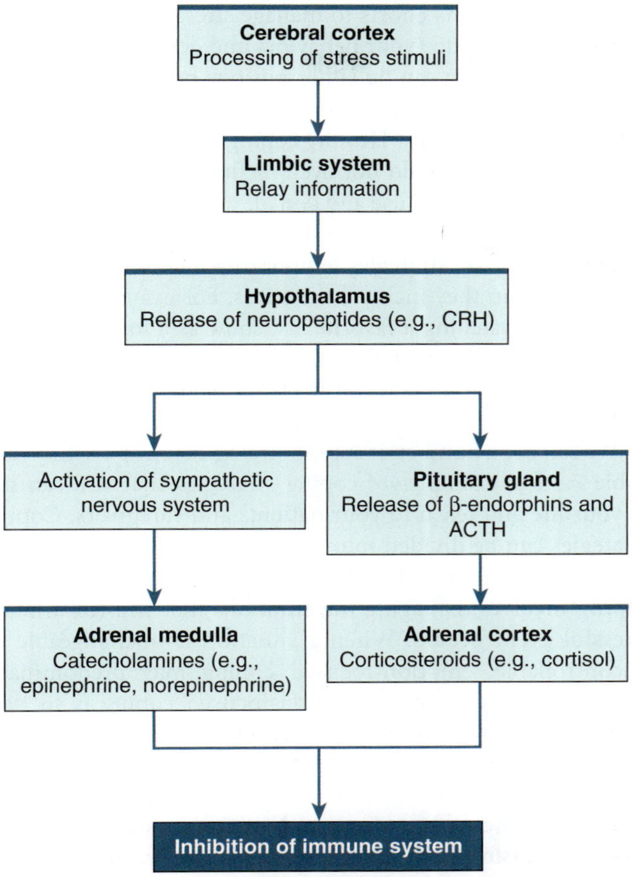

Fig. 7.6 The cerebral cortex processes stressful stimuli and relays the information via the limbic system to the hypothalamus. Corticotropin-releasing hormone *(CRH)* stimulates the release of adrenocorticotropic hormone *(ACTH)* from the pituitary gland. ACTH stimulates the adrenal cortex to release corticosteroids. Sympathetic nervous system stimulation results in the release of epinephrine and norepinephrine from the adrenal medulla. The result is the inhibition of the immune system.

and monocytes. Stress-induced immunosuppression may worsen or increase the risk for progression of immune-related diseases such as multiple sclerosis, asthma, rheumatoid arthritis, and cancer.[4] Natural killer cells, lymphocytes, and cytokines are discussed in Chapter 14.

Importantly, the network that links the brain and immune system is bidirectional (Fig. 7.3). Signals from these systems travel back and forth, allowing for communication between these systems. Consequently, not only do emotions influence the immune response, but products of immune cells send signals back to the brain and alter its activity. Many of the communication signals sent from the immune system to the brain are mediated by cytokines, which are central to the coordination of the immune response. For example, IL-1 (a cytokine made by monocytes) acts on the temperature regulatory center of the hypothalamus and initiates the febrile response to infectious pathogens (see Fig. 12.4).

Many questions about stress and the immune response are unanswered. For example, it is not known how much stress (intensity, chronicity) is needed to cause changes or how much of a change in the immune system is necessary before disease susceptibility occurs.

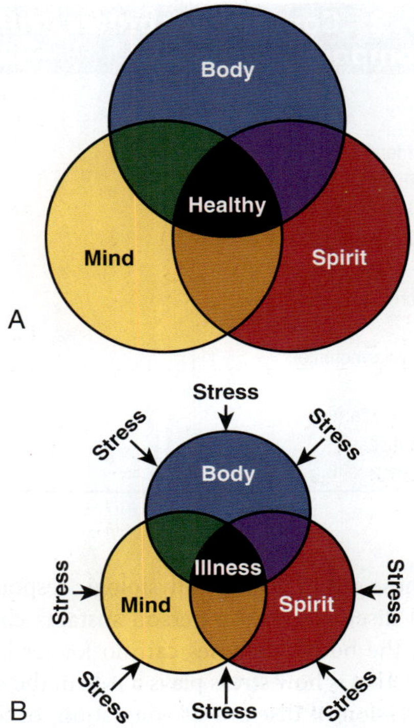

Fig. 7.7 The connections among the mind, body, and spirit can lead to a person being healthy (A) or the effects of stress on the mind, body, and spirit connections can lead to illness (B).

MIND-BODY-SPIRIT CONNECTION

The **mind-body-spirit connection** involves the relationship and interconnectedness among the parts that make up a person: mind, body, and spirit (Fig. 7.7). All 3 parts are important in your life and in determining who you are. What goes on in your mind influences every part of the body. Your mind is the most powerful weapon that you have to deal with and conquer stress. You have a choice in how you respond to a crisis or a difficult time. Even if the outcome of the situation is not what you wanted, you can emerge with a winning attitude.

How you deal with difficult situations or stressful times greatly influences your overall well-being: your mind, body, and spirit. When your mind is healthy, your body can resist illness better. When your body is healthy, your feelings are more positive. Your spirit is renewed and energized.

As a nurse, stress can have a significant effect on you. A primary source of stress for a nurse can be the work environment. This includes extreme physical demands when caring for patients and tensions among co-workers and supervisors.[5] The mind-body-spirit connection also influences your ability to provide nursing care. Your ability to maintain the mind-body-spirit balance is important in providing proper care to your patients and in maintaining a healthy and meaningful life for yourself.

EFFECTS OF STRESS ON HEALTH

As previously mentioned, the acute stress response is your alarm system and puts you on alert. However, your body was not meant to be on high alert all the time. If stress is excessive or

TABLE 7.2 Common Disorders With a Stress Component

- Depression
- Dyspepsia
- Eating disorders
- Erectile dysfunction
- Fatigue
- Fibromyalgia
- Headaches
- Hypertension
- Insomnia
- Irritable bowel syndrome
- Low back pain
- Menstrual irregularities
- Peptic ulcer disease
- Sexual problems

prolonged, these same "helpful" physiologic responses can lead to harm and disease. When a person sustains chronic, unrelieved stress, the body's defenses can no longer keep up with the demands. This is how stress plays a role in the development and/or progression of diseases of adaptation, or stress-related illnesses (Table 7.2).

Stress is linked to leading causes of death, including cancer, accidents, and suicides. Stress can have effects on cognitive function, including poor concentration, memory problems, distressing dreams, sleep problems, and impaired decision making. It can also cause a wide variety of changes in behavior. These include people withdrawing from others, decreased interest in physical appearance, changing eating habits, drinking alcohol excessively, or becoming irritable.[6] Long-term exposure to catecholamines from excessive SNS activation may increase the risk for cardiovascular diseases such as atherosclerosis and hypertension.[7] Other conditions that are precipitated or worsened by stress include diabetes, asthma, and anxiety disorder. Behavior interventions aimed at stress reduction and relaxation have helped manage these diseases in conjunction with standard medical therapy.[8]

Stressful life events can make a person more susceptible to infection. For example, psychologic stress may increase the risk for developing the common cold. In a landmark study, researchers intranasally inoculated healthy people with low doses of upper respiratory tract viruses. The people underwent psychologic testing to measure the occurrence of stressful events in their lives and their reactions to such stresses. The results showed that the rates of both viral infection and clinical colds increased with the degree of psychologic stress. In this study, social support buffered the harmful effects of stress.[9]

At the cellular level, stress may promote earlier onset of age-related diseases. There is a link between stress and telomere length. Telomeres are the protective end caps on chromosomes. Their diminishing size is a sign of age. Telomeres are highly susceptible to stress. Telomeres are shorter in people who are stressed than in healthy people. Thus, chronic stress can have a long-term effect on our overall health by changing our DNA and accelerating the rate at which our cells age.[10]

COPING STRATEGIES

Coping is a person's efforts to manage stressors. *Coping strategies* are what you do (your behaviors and actions) to help deal with stress. Coping can be either positive or negative. Positive coping includes activities such as exercise and spending time with friends and family. Healthy coping helps you handle your stressors so that they do not overwhelm you. Negative coping may include substance use and denial.

Unfortunately, some coping strategies make the stress worse. Sometimes coping strategies temporarily relieve the stress, but in the long run they increase the stress. For example, you may really enjoy watching a favorite TV show as a form of coping. However, if you become fixated on several reality shows, then TV becomes an addiction and an escape from dealing with your real stressors.

We can use a number of coping strategies to cope with stress. Table 7.3 has examples of coping strategies that you can use in your life and teach to your patients and caregivers. Coping strategies can be divided into 2 broad categories: emotion-focused coping and problem-focused coping. **Emotion-focused coping** involves managing the emotions that you feel when a stressful event occurs. When a situation is unchangeable or uncontrollable, emotion-focused coping may predominate. The primary purpose of emotion-focused coping is to help decrease negative emotions and create a feeling of well-being. Examples include discussing feelings with a friend or taking a hot bath.

Problem-focused coping involves attempts to resolve the problems causing the stress. If you can change or control a problem, this strategy is the most helpful. Problem-focused coping strategies allow a person to look at a challenge objectively, act to address the problem, and thereby reduce the stress. Setting priorities, collecting information, and seeking advice are examples of problem-focused coping.

We often use a combination of strategies to cope with the same stressor. Table 7.4 gives examples of emotion- and problem-focused coping when applied to the same stressful situation.

RELAXATION STRATEGIES

The *relaxation response* is a state of physiologic and psychologic rest. It is opposite of the stress response. The relaxation response is characterized by decreased SNS activity. This leads to decreased heart and respiratory rate, decreased BP, decreased muscle tension, decreased brain activity, and increased skin temperature.

We can use various relaxation strategies to elicit the relaxation response (Table 7.5). Regularly eliciting the relaxation response is an effective treatment for a wide range of stress-related disorders, including chronic pain, insomnia, and hypertension. People who regularly engage in relaxation strategies cope better with everyday life and can decrease their stress levels in their bodies and minds.[11]

Relaxation Breathing

The way you breathe affects every aspect of life. When a person is stressed, muscles tense and breathing becomes shallow and

TABLE 7.3 Coping Strategies

Strategy	Description	How to Implement
Aromatherapy	• Use of essential oils (fragrant molecules from plants) for inhalation or topical application • Variety of essential oils, including lavender, peppermint, rosemary, eucalyptus, tea tree	• Place 5–8 drops in a full bath and agitate water before bathing • Place a few drops on a tissue or in diffuser or vaporizer
Art therapy	• Allows a person to nonverbally express and communicate feelings, emotions, and thoughts • Can reduce stress, promote relaxation, and help process experiences • Based on the belief that the creative process is healing and life enhancing	• Close your eyes and draw a line on a piece of paper Open your eyes. Continue to build on that line and draw whatever comes to mind • Get a piece of paper and doodle. Do not edit • Get a coloring book and crayons and just start coloring
Exercise	• Any form of movement, especially aerobic movement • Can be viewed as meditation in motion	• Walk, swim, garden, bicycle, dance, climb stairs, take part in group exercises
Humor	• Can take the form of laughter, cartoons, funny movies, videos, riddles, comic books, and joke books	• Keep a "tickler" scrapbook with funny photos, cartoons • Humor carts can be set up in the clinical setting for patient and family use
Journaling	• Allows a person to express self in writing • Enhances personal development and awareness through self-reflection	• Use a journaling notebook or computer to write down thoughts, feelings, memories, and perceptions
Pet therapy (animal-assisted therapy) (Fig. 7.8)	• Use of animals as a form of treatment • Improves a patient's social, emotional, or cognitive functioning	• Pet therapist or family member or friend brings a pet with which patient can socialize
Social support	• Relationships with family and friends • Self-help groups and professional help	• Get together with family and friends on a regular basis • Join a support group that specifically helps to meet needs (e.g., grief support group)

TABLE 7.4 Problem- and Emotion-Focused Coping

Stressor	Problem-Focused Coping	Emotion-Focused Coping
Failing an examination	Obtaining a tutor	Going for a run
Being diagnosed with diabetes	Attending education classes about diabetes	Getting a massage
Receiving questionable mammogram results	Scheduling follow-up testing for ultrasound	Expressing feelings of anxiety to friends and nurse

TABLE 7.5 Common Relaxation Strategies

- Biofeedback
- Imagery
- Massage
- Meditation
- Muscle relaxation
- Music
- Qigong
- Relaxing breathing
- Tai Chi
- Yoga

rapid. So, a simple and effective way to stop the stress response is to breathe deeply and slowly. It is hard to stay tense when breathing in a slow, deep, and relaxed pattern. **Relaxation breathing** forms the basis for most relaxation strategies. It is especially useful during a stressful or anxious situation to reduce stress. You can do relaxation breathing while sitting, standing, or lying down. It is natural for newborns and sleeping adults.

Fig. 7.8 Pet therapy can be used in a variety of settings including stress management counseling. (© NoSystem images/iStock.com.)

Before practicing relaxation breathing, it is important to assess one's normal breathing pattern (Table 7.6). Chest breathing, which involves the upper chest and shoulders, is inefficient. We often use it during times of anxiety and distress.

Relaxation breathing is a more efficient type of breathing. It involves the primary use of the diaphragm and less use of the upper chest and shoulders to help in each breath. In this type of breathing, the abdomen gently moves in and out during exhalation and inhalation. The breaths should be slow, steady, and deep.

A basic technique for relaxation breathing is as follows: (1) Inhale slowly and deeply, pushing the abdomen out. Think about breathing in peace. (2) Exhale slowly, letting the abdomen come in and all the muscles relax. Think about breathing out tension. (3) Repeat these deep breaths 10 times without interruption. As with any breathing exercise, if a light-headed feeling arises, stop for 30 seconds, and then start again. Other methods used to teach relaxation breathing are the 4 × 4 technique and relaxation sigh.

At first, relaxation breathing may feel unusual. With practice it becomes easier, and its relaxing benefits are soon obvious. You should personally learn to use relaxation breathing before teaching it to patients and their caregivers. Once learned, you can easily teach relaxation breathing to patients in a variety of settings, particularly when they are undergoing stressful and painful procedures.

Biofeedback

Biofeedback helps a person become more aware of involuntary body responses such as breathing, heart rate, and muscle activity. Electrodes attached to the skin or, in some cases, hand-held sensors measure these processes and display them on a monitor. This feedback allows the person to learn to control their responses. This gives a person the power to use thoughts to control the body, often to improve a health condition or physical performance.[12]

Meditation

Meditation is a practice of concentrated focus on a sound, object, visualization, the breath, or movement. The purpose of meditation is to increase awareness, reduce stress, promote relaxation, and enhance personal and spiritual growth.

It is best to practice meditation in a quiet place, free of distractions. Table 7.7 gives some basic guidelines on how to meditate. Meditation is often practiced while seated. It is important to maintain a comfortable posture. Meditation can be done while walking and focusing on a single action such as the movement of the feet. In the beginning, you typically start with just 5 to 10 minutes of meditation at a time. Increase the time as the practice becomes more comfortable.

Imagery

Imagery is the use of your mind to generate images that have a calming effect on the body. It involves focusing the mind and incorporates all the senses to create physiologic and emotional changes. It is a simple relaxation technique that needs no equipment other than an active imagination. *Guided imagery* is a variation of imagery in which another person (either live or through technology) suggests the images to you.

You can use imagery in your own life or use guided imagery with your patients. One use of imagery is to create a special place for a mental retreat. Table 7.8 describes the steps involved in creating a special place. It is best to perform imagery in a comfortable position. Take slow, deep breaths. Focus should involve all senses (sight, hearing, touch, smell). For example, you can use an image, such as Fig. 7.9, engaging all the senses as you focus on the image.

Imagery can be used in many clinical settings for stress reduction and pain relief. Benefits of imagery include reduced anxiety, decreased muscle tension, improved comfort during procedures, enhanced immune function, decreased recovery time after surgery, and fewer sleeping problems. It can specifically target a disease, problem, or stressor. Table 7.9 describes some suggestions for using imagery in specific diseases or disorders.

A person can use imagery to enhance performance or process stressful or difficult tasks. For example, an athlete or musician can use imagery to achieve greater success. Imagery allows you to mentally rehearse a difficult or challenging situation. Imagery can help you start an IV line or perform a difficult procedure. It can be used with a patient who is afraid to have a stressful or painful procedure, such as a bone marrow biopsy.

TABLE 7.6 Relaxation Breathing Techniques

Breathing Assessment

1. Begin by placing 1 hand gently on your abdomen below your waistline.
2. Place the other hand on the center of your chest on the sternum.
3. Without changing the normal breathing pattern, take several breaths. During inhalation notice which hand rises the most.
4. When relaxation breathing is done properly, the hand on the abdomen should rise more than the hand on the chest.

4 × 4 Technique

1. Sit up straight with your back flush to the support of the chair and your feet flat on the floor.
2. Rest your arms on your lap, thighs, or arms of the chair.
3. Take in a deep breath through your nose to a count of 4 (1 ... 2 ... 3 ... 4).
4. Hold your breath to a count of 4 (1 ... 2 ... 3 ... 4).
5. Release your breath through your mouth to a count of 4 (1 ... 2 ... 3 ... 4).
6. Rest for a count of 4 (1 ... 2 ... 3 ... 4).
7. Repeat the cycle 4 times.

Relaxing Sigh

1. Sit up straight with your back against the support of the chair and your feet flat on floor.
2. Inhale a natural breath and then sigh deeply. Let out a sound of relief as the air rushes out of your lungs.
3. Do not think about inhaling at the end of the sigh; just let the air come in naturally as you breathe deeply.
4. Repeat this sigh about 4 to 6 times very slowly.
5. You can repeat this exercise whenever you need it.

TABLE 7.7 Guide to Meditation

You can teach yourself the basics of meditation by following a few simple steps:

1. Find a quiet place.
2. Make sure there are no distractions.
3. Sit in a comfortable position.
4. Close your eyes.
5. Shut out the world so that your brain can stop processing information coming from your senses.
6. Pick a focus word, short phrase, song verse (melody), or prayer that is firmly rooted in your belief system, such as *one, peace, The Lord is my shepherd, Hail Mary full of grace,* or *shalom.*
7. Breathe slowly and practice relaxation breathing. Say your focus word, short phrase, song verse, or prayer silently to yourself as you exhale.
8. Say the word or phrase again and again.
9. Try saying the word or phrase silently to yourself with every exhalation. The monotony will help you focus.
10. Relax your muscles, progressing from your feet to your calves, thighs, abdomen, shoulders, head, and neck.
11. Do not be concerned when other thoughts come to mind. Just acknowledge them and return calmly to your word or phrase.
12. Continue for 10–20 min, but even 5 min can leave you feeling calm and refreshed. Rise slowly.
13. Practice once or twice daily.

Massage

Massage includes a range of techniques that manipulate the soft tissues and joints of the body through touch and movement. It is typically delivered with the hands. Massage reduces muscle tension and positively affects mental and emotional states.

Massage is an important form of touch. It is a form of caring, communication, and comfort. Your role related to massage differs from that of the registered massage therapist. A massage therapist can provide more comprehensive massage therapies. As a nurse, you can use specific massage techniques as part of nursing care. For example, you can give a back massage to help promote sleep. For a bedridden patient, gentle massage can stimulate circulation and help prevent skin breakdown. A simple hand massage can have a calming and relaxing effect, especially for patients who are anxious or agitated. During end-of-life care, hospice nurses may include massage into their nursing care as massaging touch can lessen pain and restlessness.

When you identify that massage may be useful, first assess the patient's preference about touch and massage. Consider cultural and social beliefs and discuss potential benefits with the patient. You can teach family members to massage their loved one, giving a way for family members to take part in patient care. This can be therapeutic for the patient and family, even when the loved one is cognitively impaired or unresponsive.

TABLE 7.8 Imagery

Creating Your Special Place

1. Begin by closing your eyes and taking several slow, deep breaths.
2. Imagine a place where you feel completely comfortable and peaceful. It may be a real place or one you imagine. Use a place from your past or a place you have always wanted to go.
3. Allow this special place to take form, slowly. As it takes form, look around to your left, to your right. Enjoy the scenery: the colors, the texture, the shapes.
4. Listen carefully to the sounds of your place. What do you hear?
5. Is there a gentle breeze or sunshine warming your face? Pick up or touch some favorite objects from your special place.
6. Take in a deep breath through your nose and notice the rich smells around you. Perhaps your favorite flower is in bloom, or you smell the scents of the ocean.
7. Take another deep breath and relax. Enjoy the peace, comfort, and safety of your special place.
8. This is your special place. You relax and feel thankful that you are here, in your special place.
9. You can return to this place any time that you wish.

Fig 7.9 In imagery, special places are created involving all the senses, such as a place where you can hear flowing water, smell flowers, feel the wind, and see a colorful landscape. (© LanaCanada/iStock.com.)

Music

Music can help achieve relaxation and bring about healthy changes in emotional or physical states. Listening to relaxing music can divert one's focus from a stressful situation. Music can be used in many clinical settings. It is noninvasive, safe, inexpensive, and easy to use. Music decreases anxiety and elicits the relaxation response. It helps people with insomnia go to sleep. Music can improve your state of mind and trigger the relaxation response.[13]

Each person considers different types of music to be relaxing. Music that has 60 to 80 beats/min is considered soothing. Many find low-pitched tones and music without words best for relaxation. Mozart's music is popular for relaxation. On the other hand, fast-tempo music can stimulate and uplift a person. Assess each patient's interest and preference in music. Find music that best matches the person's needs and circumstance. Create a listening environment by helping the patient find a comfortable position and minimizing interruptions. Evaluate patients' responses to the music, asking them how it sounds and how it makes them feel.

Prayer

Prayer can be a form of meditation. It is a spiritual communion with God or an object of worship. Many people find deep comfort in their faith. Religious services, conversations with clergy, and personal worship and prayer may help to ease a person's stress and give greater perspective, strength, and inspiration.

TABLE 7.9 Examples of Imagery

Imagery can be used to relieve stress and promote health and healing in conjunction with regular medical care. Special images can be created to ease symptoms or treat diseases or disorders. The image should be strong and vivid for the person, using many senses to create the image. Below are some examples that may be useful.

Problem	Images
Arthritis	• Cells working as carpenters to rebuild their bones, tendons, and ligaments
Asthma	• Tiny elastic rubber bands that constrict the airways pop open
Cancer	• Shark gobbles up cancer cells • Radiation or chemotherapy treatments enter the body like healing rays of light; they destroy cancer cells
Depression	• Attach troubles and feelings of sadness to big colorful helium balloons that float off into a clear blue sky
Infection	• White blood cells are warriors who are attacking invaders
Pain	• Place painful sensations on a raft and watch them float away on a river
Peptic ulcer disease	• A cold mountain stream extinguishing a fire
Weakened immune system	• White blood cells rapidly multiply like millions of seeds bursting from a ripe seed pod

❖ NURSING MANAGEMENT: STRESS

◆ Assessment

Patients and caregivers face many potential stressors that can have health consequences. As a nurse, you are in a key position to (1) assess stress in patients and caregivers, (2) help them identify high-risk periods for stress, and (3) implement stress management strategies that can prevent the negative consequences of stress on their health (Fig. 7.10).

The first step in managing stress is to become aware of its presence. This includes identifying what the stressors are and the person's response to them. Be aware of situations that are likely to result in stress. Assess the number of stressors, duration of these stressors, and prior experience with similar demands. Assess the personal and cultural meaning attached to the stressful situation to provide useful insight for planning stress management strategies with the patient.

Be specific with your questions: Have you experienced this stressor before? How did you handle it? What worked well and what did not? Although the manifestations of stress vary from person to person, assess the patient for the signs and symptoms of the stress response. These include an increased heart rate and BP, hyperventilation, sweating, headache, musculoskeletal pain, GI upset, loss of appetite, insomnia, and fatigue. In addition, the patient may show stress-related illness (Table 7.2).

Behavior manifestations of stress may include an inability to concentrate, accident proneness, impaired speech, anxiety, crying, frustration, and irritability. Work-related responses to stress may include absenteeism or tardiness at work, decreased productivity, and job dissatisfaction. Cognitive responses include self-reports about the inability to make decisions and forgetfulness. Some of these responses may be apparent to others.

Consider the caregivers' responses to the stressors. A patient's illness often causes stress for the caregiver and other family members. Assess what aspects of the illness are the most stressful for the patient and caregiver. These may include the patient's physical health, job responsibilities, finances, and children. This information is valuable because it helps you to understand the patient's perspective of the stressors. Knowledge of stressors, the feelings these stressors evoke, and the psychologic effects they can produce will help you recognize potential and actual sources of stress and their effect on the patient.

Fig. 7.10 As a nurse, you have a key role in helping patients deal with stress. (© fizkes/iStock.com.)

◆ Clinical Problems

Clinical problems for the patient with stress include:

- Difficulty coping
- Spiritual problem

◆ Planning

Nursing care focuses on helping persons recognize stress and implanting measures to help manage stress. The overall goals are that the patient with stress will (1) report decreased levels of stress, (2) use positive coping strategies, and (3) be free from complications resulting from stress.

◆ Implementation

Your role is to facilitate and enhance the patient's coping and adaptation. Nursing interventions depend on the severity of the stress experience. For example, a patient with multiple trauma expends energy to physically survive. As a nurse, you direct efforts toward life-supporting interventions and approaches aimed at reducing added stressors for the patient. The patient is much less likely to adapt or recover if faced with more stressors, such as sleep deprivation or an infection. You can assume a primary role in implementing stress management strategies.

Ideas for how to include stress management strategies into nursing practice are described in Table 7.10. Although some require additional training, many stress management strategies are within the scope of nursing practice. These include relaxation breathing, imagery, music, exercise, massage, meditation, art therapy, and journaling.

Coping strategies used should be helpful and not a source of added stress for the patient. You can teach most coping and relaxation strategies to patients in 10 to 15 minutes. Choose a coping or relaxation strategy to best suit the patient and situation. Effective stress management provides a sense of control of the stressful situation. As stress management practices become part of daily activities, the person can increase their confidence and self-reliance and limit the emotional response to the stressful circumstances. Having a sense of control can prevent the harmful effects of a stress response.

As a nurse, you are in an ideal situation to integrate stress management in clinical practice. You are well equipped to

TABLE 7.10 How to Implement Stress Management in Practice

1. Learn relaxation breathing. It is the easiest method of relaxation to use.
2. Practice teaching relaxation breathing with peers, then patients.
3. Pick coping strategies (Table 7.3) and relaxation strategies that are appropriate for your clinical area.
4. Practice using the strategy yourself. It becomes easier with time.
5. Take advantage of opportunities to teach coping and relaxation strategies to patients.
6. If you have setbacks, think about what went wrong. Do NOT quit!
7. Attend seminars and workshops on stress management to learn more.

TABLE 7.11 Personal Tips for Handling Stress

- Do not try to be superhuman.
- Learn to "let go" of things that are outside of your control.
- Learn acceptance of yourself.
- Exercise regularly.
- Share your feelings.
- Keep a sense of humor; laugh often.
- Learn relaxation breathing.
- Use imagery.
- Meditate or pray.
- Get adequate sleep.
- Live a healthy lifestyle.
- Try to look at change as a positive challenge, not as a threat.
- Solve the little problems, since this can help you gain a feeling of control.
- Work to resolve conflicts with other people.
- If needed, get counseling.

develop and test the effectiveness of new ways to manage stress and promote positive health outcomes. However, it is very important to recognize when you need to refer the patient or caregiver to a professional with advanced training in counseling.

Some personal tips for handling stress are shown in Table 7.11. These tips will help you personally and enhance your own level of health and wellness. It is essential that you first care for yourself before you can help the patients who need your care. Many professional organizations, such as the American Nurses Association, offer resources to help you manage stress (www.nursingworld.org). Once you include these strategies into your life, you can share them with patients and caregivers.

Case Study

Stress-Induced Illness

(© JackF/ iStock/ Thinkstock.)

Patient Profile

K.F., a 48-year-old woman, recently moved to the United States from Romania with her 2 teenage children. She has no family in the country and was recently divorced. She works as a server in a hectic restaurant and as a seamstress out of her home in the evenings. K.F. must maintain these 2 jobs so that she can provide for her rent and other financial responsibilities. K.F.'s family remain in Romania, and she tries to visit them every 6 months.

She has developed some unusual symptoms and comes to see the nurse practitioner at a community clinic. Although she says that she was in good health when she left Romania, she now presents with fatigue, inability to sleep, and aches all over her body. Even when she gets some extra sleep, she still feels exhausted. Her coworker told her she has fibromyalgia.

Discussion Questions

1. ***Recognize:*** Considering K.F.'s situation, what risk factors can you identify that led to her current condition? Describe the possible effects of these stressors on her health.
2. ***Plan:*** What limitations should you consider when discussing specific coping strategies?
3. ***Prioritize:*** What are the priority coping strategies that you should include in K.F.'s plan of care?
4. ***Act:*** What cultural considerations should you include when delivering care?

Answers available at http://evolve.elsevier.com/Lewis/medsurg.

BRIDGE TO NCLEX EXAMINATION

The number of the question corresponds to the same-numbered outcome at the beginning of the chapter.

1. Determination of whether an event is a stressor is based on a person's
   a. tolerance
   b. perception
   c. adaptation
   d. stubbornness
2. The nurse would expect which finding in a patient due to the physiologic effect of stress on the reticular formation?
   a. An episode of diarrhea while awaiting painful dressing changes
   b. Refusal to communicate with nurses while awaiting a cardiac catheterization
   c. Inability to sleep the night before beginning to self-administer insulin injections
   d. Increased blood pressure, decreased urine output, and hyperglycemia after a car accident
3. The nurse uses the knowledge of stress on the immune system through the understanding of which process?
   a. Infection risk increases with prolonged exposure to stress.
   b. The body's stress response does not affect cytokine production.
   c. Phagocytosis by neutrophils and monocytes are strengthened when illness occurs.
   d. Natural killer cells remain constant during both relaxation and stress periods.
4. The nurse understands that a person who has chronic stress could be at higher risk for *(select all that apply)*
   a. asthma.
   b. osteoporosis.
   c. fibromyalgia.
   d. colds and influenza.
   e. high blood pressure.
5. The nurse recognizes that a patient with newly diagnosed breast cancer is using an emotion-focused coping process when she
   a. joins a support group for women with breast cancer.
   b. considers the pros and cons of the various treatment options.
   c. delays treatment until her family can take a weekend trip together.
   d. tells the nurse that she has a good prognosis because the tumor is small.

6. During a stressful circumstance that is unchangeable, which type of coping strategy is the *most* effective?
   a. Avoidance
   b. Coping flexibility
   c. Emotion-focused coping
   d. Problem-focused coping
7. An appropriate nursing intervention for a hospitalized patient who says she cannot cope with her illness is
   a. controlling the environment to prevent sensory overload and promote sleep.
   b. encouraging the patient's family to offer emotional support by frequent visiting.
   c. arranging for the patient to phone family and friends to maintain emotional bonds.
   d. asking the patient to describe previous stressful situations and how she managed to resolve them.

1. b; 2. c; 3. a; 4. a, d, e; 5. a; 6. c; 7. d.

For rationales to these answers and even more NCLEX review questions, visit http://evolve.elsevier.com/Lewis/medsurg.

EVOLVE WEBSITE/RESOURCES LIST

http://evolve.elsevier.com/Lewis/medsurg
Review Questions (Online Only)
Key Points
Answer Keys for Questions
- Rationales for Bridge to NCLEX Examination Questions

Answer Guidelines for Case Study
Conceptual Care Map Creator
Audio Glossary
Content Updates

REFERENCES

1. Seward BL: *Managing stress: principles and strategies for health and well-being*, ed 9, Burlington, MA, 2017, Jones & Bartlett.
2. Health Day New for Healthier Living: Gender and stress. Retrieved from https://consumer.healthday.com/encyclopedia/men-s-health-28/men-s-problems-health-news-469/gender-and-stress-645980.html.
3. Mayo Clinic: Positive thinking. Retrieved from www.mayoclinic.org/healthy-living/stress-management/in-depth/positive-thinking/art-20043950.
4. American Institute of Stress: Effects of stress. Retrieved from www.stress.org.
5. Registered Nursing.org: How to manage your stress as a nurse. Retrieved from https://www.registerednursing.org/how-manage-stress-nurse/.
6. The American Institute of Stress: 50 common signs and symptoms of stress. Retrieved from https://www.stress.org/stress-effects.
7. American Heart Association: Stress and heart health. Retrieved from www.heart.org/HEARTORG/Conditions/More/MyHeartandStrokeNews/Stress-and-Heart-Health_UCM_437370_Article.jsp.
8. Medical News Today. Stress symptoms: what to watch for. Retrieved from: https://www.medicalnewstoday.com/articles/stress-symptoms.

*9. Cohen S, Tyrrell DA, Smith AP: Psychological stress and susceptibility to the common cold, *N Engl J Med* 325:606, 1991. (Classic).

10. American Institute of Stress: Stress, aging and telomeres. Retrieved from https://www.stress.org/stress-aging-and-telomeres.
11. Mayo Clinic: Relaxation techniques: try these steps to reduce stress. Retrieved from https://www.mayoclinic.org/healthy-lifestyle/stress-management/in-depth/relaxation-technique/art-20045368.
12. Dr. Axe: Biofeedback therapy: a proven therapy for 16+ medical conditions. Retrieved from https://draxe.com/health/biofeedback-therapy/.
13. Verywell Mind: How music can be therapeutic. Retrieved from https://www.verywellmind.com/how-and-why-music-therapy-is-effective-3145190.

*Evidence-based information for clinical practice.

8

Sleep and Sleep Disorders

Diana Taibi Buchanan and Nathan J. Dreesmann

http://evolve.elsevier.com/Lewis/medsurg/

CONCEPTUAL FOCUS

Functional Ability
Mood and Affect
Sleep

LEARNING OUTCOMES

1. Define sleep.
2. Describe the stages of sleep.
3. Explain the relationship of various health problems and sleep disorders.
4. Describe the etiology, clinical manifestations, and interprofessional and nursing management of insomnia.
5. Describe the etiology, clinical manifestations, and interprofessional and nursing management of obstructive sleep apnea.
6. Describe clinical manifestations and interprofessional management of narcolepsy, parasomnias, and circadian rhythm disorders.
7. Select strategies for managing sleep problems associated with shift work sleep disorder.

KEY TERMS

circadian rhythms
continuous positive airway pressure (CPAP)
insomnia
jet lag disorder
narcolepsy
obstructive sleep apnea (OSA)
parasomnias
periodic limb movement disorder (PLMD)
shift work sleep disorder
sleep
sleep-disordered breathing (SDB)
sleep disorders
sleep disturbance
sleep hygiene
wake behavior

SLEEP

Sleep is a state in which a person lacks conscious awareness of environmental surroundings but can be easily aroused. Sleep is distinct from unconscious states such as coma, in which the person cannot be aroused. Sleep is a basic, dynamic, highly organized, and complex behavior that is essential for healthy functioning and survival. Over a life span of 80 years, a person who sleeps 7 hours each night will spend around 24 years sleeping. Sleep influences mood, behavior, and physical functioning. Some functions sleep affects are memory, mood, hormone secretion, glucose metabolism, immune function, and body temperature.

Most adults need 7 to 8 hours of sleep within a 24-hour period.[1] *Sleep insufficiency* is sleep that does not support optimal alertness, functioning, and health. It may be caused by sleep deprivation or sleep fragmentation. *Sleep deprivation* is too little sleep to meet the person's needs. *Sleep fragmentation* means a person frequently wakes up or almost wakes (called an arousal), interrupting continuous sleep. Sleep fragmentation may create negative outcomes even when a person gets the right amount of sleep.

Sleep disturbance is a broad term that refers to poor sleep quality from various causes. Sleep disturbance may be related to environmental factors such as noise or light. It can be caused by health-related factors such as pain or by **sleep disorders**. Sleep

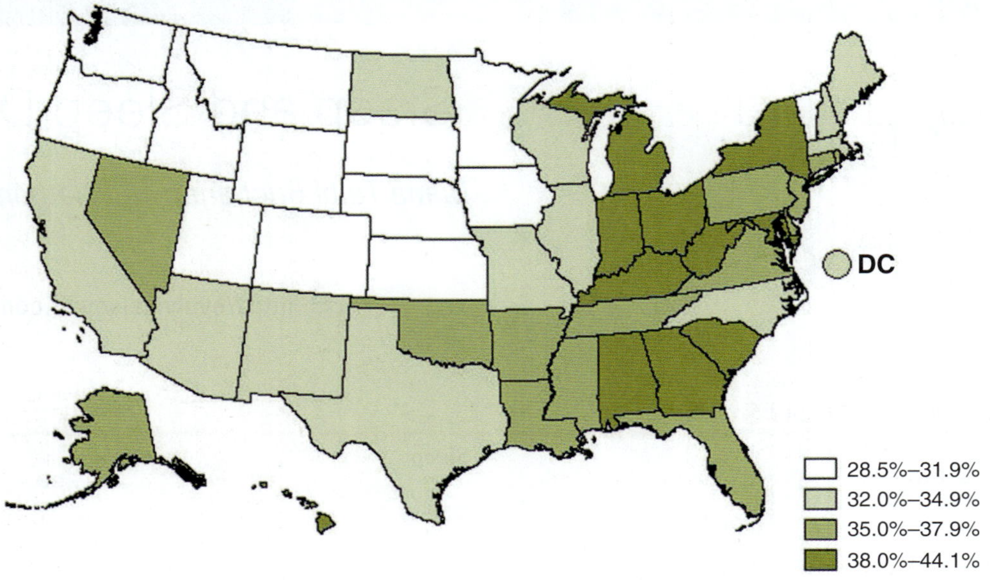

Fig. 8.1 US adults that obtain less than 7 hours of sleep each night. (Modified from www.cdc.gov/sleep/data_statistics.html.)

disorders include insomnia, obstructive sleep apnea syndrome, periodic limb movement disorder, circadian sleep disorders, narcolepsy, and parasomnias.

Sleep disturbances and sleep disorders can result in insufficient sleep. Many people get insufficient sleep because they simply are not in bed long enough to allow for an adequate amount of sleep. About 35% of Americans get less than the recommended 7 hours of sleep per night. An estimated 50 to 70 million people in the United States have a sleep disorder.[2] Many are unaware that they have a problem (Fig. 8.1). People with chronic illnesses have the greatest risk for sleep disturbances.

Untreated sleep disorders cause considerable health, safety, and economic consequences. Severe daytime sleepiness can interfere with work and social functioning. Driving while drowsy is related to around 90,000 accidents and nearly 800 deaths per year.[3] Sleep disorders, sleep loss, and excessive daytime sleepiness cost the United States billions of dollars each year in health care, work-related accidents, and lost productivity.[4] Opportunities to address sleep problems are often missed because health care providers (HCPs) do not ask, and patients do not readily talk about them.

PHYSIOLOGIC SLEEP MECHANISMS

Sleep-Wake Cycle

The brain controls the cyclic changes between sleep and waking. Complex networks in the areas of the forebrain (cerebral cortex, hypothalamus, thalamus) and brainstem interact to regulate the sleep-wake cycle.

Wake Behavior

Wake behavior is maintained by an integrated network of arousal systems from the brainstem and forebrain. A cluster of neuron structures in the brainstem, called the *ascending reticular activating system (ARAS),* promote general activation of the cerebral cortex, which is responsible for higher brain functions. This activation gives rise to typical wake behaviors such as alertness and attention. Various neurotransmitters (glutamate, acetylcholine, norepinephrine, dopamine, histamine, serotonin) promote wake behavior.[5]

People with Alzheimer disease lose cholinergic neurons in the forebrain, which results in sleep disturbances. In Parkinson disease, wake-promoting dopamine neurons in the ARAS degenerate. This causes daytime sleepiness. Histamine neurons in the hypothalamus also stimulate cortical activation and wake behavior. The sedating properties of certain sleep medications result from inhibiting histamine-related arousal.[6]

Orexin (also called hypocretin) is a neuropeptide found in the hypothalamus. Orexin is involved in regulating the sleep-wake cycle. It plays an important role in keeping people awake. Orexin inhibitors, a newer class of prescription sleep medication, block the wake-promoting effects of orexin. Decreased levels of orexin or its receptors lead to problems staying awake, which is a syndrome called *narcolepsy*.[6]

Sleep Behavior

An area in the hypothalamus just above the optic chiasm contains many sleep-promoting neurons. These neurons inhibit the ARAS and promote sleep. A variety of neurotransmitters and peptides promote sleep. These include γ-aminobutyric acid (GABA), galanin, melatonin, adenosine, somatostatin, growth hormone–releasing hormone (GHRH), delta-sleep–inducing peptide, prostaglandins, and proinflammatory cytokines. When a person has an infection, proinflammatory cytokines (interleukin-1, tumor necrosis factor, interleukin-6) contribute to sleepiness and lethargy.[5]

Melatonin is a hormone made by the pineal gland in the brain. Melatonin secretion is linked to the environmental light-dark

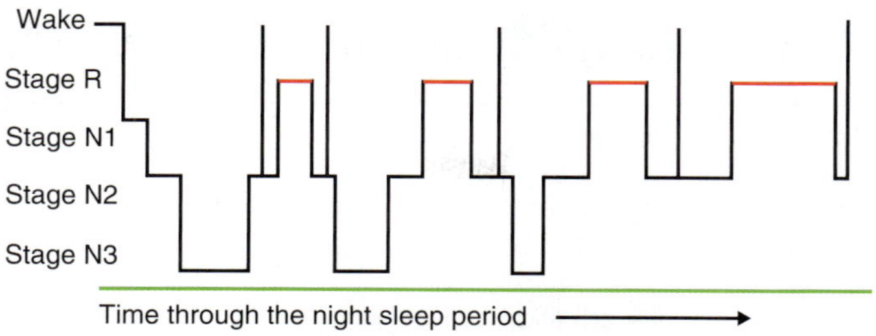

Fig. 8.2 Sleep stages graphed across a complete sleep cycle. (From Goldman L, Schafer AI: *Goldman's Cecil medicine*, ed 26, Philadelphia, 2019, Saunders.)

cycle. Its release signals the time for sleep by "turning off" the mechanisms that promote wakefulness. Under normal day-night conditions, we release melatonin in the evening as it gets dark. Light exposure at night can suppress melatonin secretion.[7]

Circadian Rhythms

Many biologic rhythms of behavior and physiology fluctuate within a 24-hour period. These 24-hour patterns are called **circadian** (meaning, *about a day*) **rhythms**.[8] The suprachiasmatic nucleus (SCN) in the hypothalamus is the master clock of the body. The SCN synchronizes the genetic clocks within individual cells and regulates the 24-hour sleep-wake cycle. Circadian rhythm timing is synchronized to the environmental light and dark periods through specific light detectors in the retina. Pathways from the retina reach the SCN, and pathways from the SCN innervate brain regions controlling wake and sleep behavior.[7]

Light is the strongest cue for the sleep-wake rhythm. Thus, we can use light as a therapy to shift the timing of the sleep-wake rhythm. For example, bright light used early in the morning will cause the sleep-wake rhythm to move to an earlier time. Bright light used in the evening will cause the sleep-wake rhythm to move to a later time. For some people, being outside in daylight without sunglasses may be helpful. Others need light therapy given with a device that provides very bright light.

Sleep Architecture

Sleep architecture refers to the pattern of nighttime sleep recorded from physiologic measures using *polysomnography* (PSG). PSG measures we record include (1) muscle tone with an electromyogram (EMG), (2) eye movements with an electrooculogram (EOG), and (3) brain activity recorded through electroencephalograph (EEG).

Sleep consists of 2 basic states: *rapid eye movement (REM) sleep* and *non–rapid eye movement (NREM) sleep*. During sleep, the body cycles between NREM and REM sleep. Once asleep, a person goes through 4 to 6 NREM and REM sleep cycles, each cycle lasting 60 to 110 minutes (Fig. 8.2).

NREM Sleep

Healthy adults spend about 75% to 80% of sleep time in NREM sleep. NREM sleep is divided into 3 stages.[8] However, you may see the older version of sleep staging that used 4 stages. The newer, 3-stage approach combines the old stages 3 and 4 into N3.

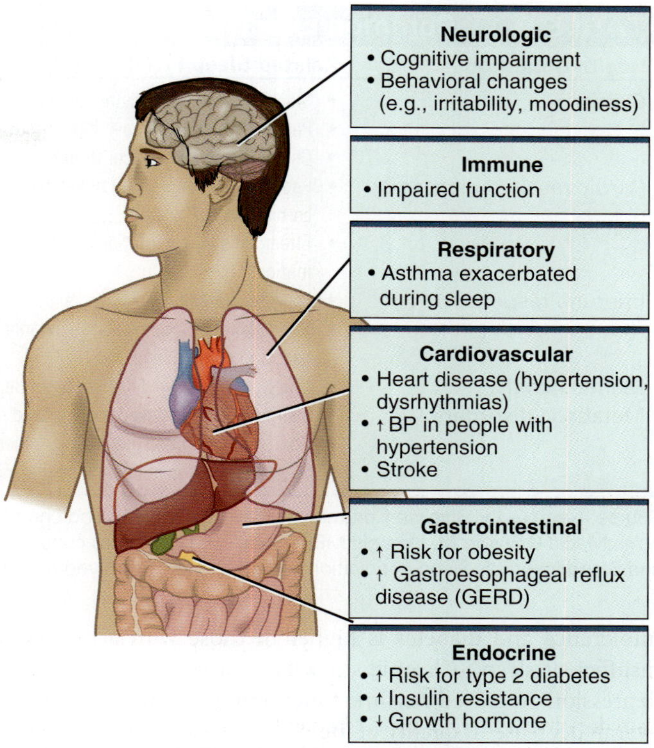

Fig. 8.3 Effects of sleep deprivation and sleep disorders on the body.

- *N1* is the stage that occurs at the beginning of sleep. It is characterized by slow eye movements. N1 is a transition phase from wakefulness to sleep. During N1 the person can be easily awakened.
- *N2* is the stage that takes up most of the night's sleep. The heart rate slows down and body temperature drops. N2 is associated with specific brain wave forms measured by EEG that represent sleep-maintaining neural activity.
- *N3* is the deepest stage of sleep. We call N3 slow-wave sleep (SWS) because of the characteristic large, low-frequency EEG waves. These delta waves are a measure of sleep intensity. SWS declines as people age. Most adults over 60 years of age have little N3 sleep.

REM Sleep

REM sleep accounts for 20% to 25% of sleep. REM sleep follows NREM sleep in a sleep cycle. In this stage, brain waves resemble wakefulness. Postural muscles are inhibited, leading to greatly reduced skeletal muscle tone. During REM sleep a person cannot initiate muscle movement (e.g., cannot stand up). REM sleep is the period when most vivid dreaming occurs.

INSUFFICIENT SLEEP AND SLEEP DISTURBANCES

Insufficient sleep is associated with changes in body function (Fig. 8.3) and health problems (Table 8.1). Impaired cognitive function and impaired performance on simple behavioral tasks occur within 24 hours of sleep loss. The effects of sleep loss are cumulative. Those who report less than 6 hours of sleep a night are more likely to be obese. The risk for developing glucose

TABLE 8.1 **Common Effects of Sleep on Health**

Health Condition	Related Sleep Problems/Effects
Cancer	• Sleep and circadian rhythm disruption increase cancer risk and progression • Persons with cancer have higher rates of insomnia • Chemotherapy for cancer treatment can cause fragmented sleep and fatigue
Cardiovascular disease	• People with sleep apnea or sleep disorders are at increased risk for CV disorders, including hypertension, dysrhythmias, and coronary artery disease • Effects of sleep disruption on CV health likely are due to sympathetic activation, impaired glucose metabolism, and inflammation
Immune response	• Long-term sleep deficiency can suppress the immune response to infection • Sleep deficiency can increase inflammation, which contributes to CV disease, metabolic syndrome, and other conditions associated with sleep loss
Mental health	• Sleep disturbance is a symptom of depression but can also worsen depression
Metabolic disorders	• Insufficient sleep linked to increased risk for type 2 diabetes • Short sleep duration may result in metabolic changes that are linked to obesity • Sleep deprivation in healthy people increases insulin resistance and leads to increased food intake

Source: Centers for Disease Control and Prevention: Sleep and chronic disease. Retrieved from www.cdc.gov/sleep/about_sleep/chronic_disease.html; Medic G, Willie M, Hemels MEH: Short- and long-term consequences of sleep disruption, *Nat Sci Sleep* 9:151, 2017; National, Health, Lung, and Blood Institute: Sleep deprivation and deficiency. Retrieved from https://www.nhlbi.nih.gov/health-topics/sleep-deprivation-and-deficiency.

intolerance and diabetes is higher in those with a history of insufficient sleep.[9] Chronic sleep loss places people at risk for depression, impaired daytime functioning, social isolation, and overall decrease in quality of life.[10]

SLEEP DISTURBANCES IN THE HOSPITAL

Hospitalized patients, especially in the intensive care unit (ICU), may have decreased total sleep time, disrupted normal sleep stages, and disordered circadian rhythms.[11] In the hospital, disruptive environmental factors, psychoactive medications, and acute and critical illness contribute to poor sleep. Disruptive environmental factors include around-the-clock noise, light, and patient care activities. Hospital and ICU noise often persists both day and night from sources such as ventilator alarms, bedside monitors, infusion alarms, and staff conversations in hallways. Bright lights during the night disrupt sleep and reduce melatonin levels. Patient care activities including dressing changes, blood draws, vital sign monitoring, and medication administration often disrupt patients' and their roommates' ability to get sound, continuous sleep. Inactivity, boredom, and napping during the day and evening can affect nighttime sleep. Patient symptoms, including pain, dyspnea, and nausea, can contribute to sleep loss in the acutely ill patient. Commonly used medications can further contribute to sleep loss. Preexisting sleep disorders may worsen or be triggered in hospitalized patients.

Sleep problems can cause delirium and delayed recovery. Decreased sleep duration and sleep loss cause patients to be more sensitive to pain and less able to tolerate pain.[12] Adequate pain management may improve total sleep time. But many pain medications, especially opioids, alter sleep quality, and place a person at risk for sleep-disordered breathing.

You play a key role in creating an environment conducive to sleep. This includes how you schedule medications and procedures, including those performed by assistive personnel (AP). Reducing light and noise levels at night can promote opportunities for sleep. Other measures include scheduling rest periods, getting physiologic measurements without disturbing the patient, opening curtains during the daytime, providing eye masks/ear plugs to encourage sleep, and providing comfort measures (e.g., massage). Hypnotic sleep-aid medications may be available on an as-needed basis or can be discussed with the HCP.

SLEEP DISORDERS

INSOMNIA

The most common sleep disorder, insomnia, affects 1 in 3 adults.[13] **Insomnia** is characterized by difficulty falling asleep, difficulty staying asleep, waking up too early, or waking up feeling unrefreshed.[13] People with insomnia report overall dissatisfaction with sleep quality and quantity.

Short-term insomnia disorder refers to problems falling or remaining asleep at least 3 nights per week for less than 3 months. *Chronic insomnia disorder* is defined by the same symptoms and a daytime problem related to poor sleep (e.g., fatigue, poor concentration, interference with social or family activities) that persist for 3 months or longer. Chronic insomnia occurs in 10% of Americans. It is more common in women than men.[13] Insomnia is more common in those who are divorced, widowed, and separated than in those who are married. It is more prevalent in people with low socioeconomic status and less education.[13]

Etiology and Pathophysiology

Behaviors, lifestyle, diet, physical and mental conditions, and medications may contribute to insomnia. Insomnia is worsened by behaviors such as varying bedtime and rise time, taking long naps in the afternoon, spending time awake in bed trying to sleep, sleeping late in the morning, and exercising near bedtime.

Lifestyle factors can contribute to insomnia. Although the sedative effects of alcohol help people fall asleep, it suppresses REM sleep and causes restlessness and awakenings later in the night. Use of stimulants including nicotine in tobacco products, caffeine, or methamphetamine can cause restlessness and sleep disruption, which worsen insomnia.[14] Insomnia is a common side effect of many medications (e.g., antidepressants, antihypertensives, corticosteroids, psychostimulants, analgesics).

Chronic insomnia may be related to varied factors. Often people report that the insomnia symptoms started after a stressful life event, such as losing a job or the death of a loved one. In other cases, psychiatric illnesses, medical conditions, medications, or substance use may initially cause insomnia. Patients with psychiatric or medical conditions are more likely to have insomnia than those without these conditions. Once insomnia becomes chronic, symptoms are likely to persist.

Clinical Manifestations

Manifestations of insomnia include 1 or more of the following symptoms: (1) difficulty falling asleep (long sleep latency), (2) prolonged nighttime awakenings or awakening too early and not being able to fall back to sleep (difficulty maintaining sleep), (3) awakening earlier than desired, (4) avoidance or resistance to a scheduled bedtime, and (5) inability to sleep without intervention.[13] Daytime or functional consequences include fatigue, having trouble concentrating at work or school, impaired functional performance, and having an altered mood. Behavioral manifestations include irritability, sleepiness during the day, heightened states of arousal (e.g., aggression or hyperactivity), reduced energy, and problems with attention and concentration.

Diagnostic Studies

Self-Report

The diagnosis of insomnia is made based on subjective reports and an evaluation of a 1- or 2-week sleep diary completed by the patient. A diary or log usually includes the number and times of naps; times of going to bed, awakening, and getting up; number of awakenings; and overall sleep quality ratings.

In ambulatory care settings, the evaluation of insomnia requires a comprehensive sleep history. This establishes the type of insomnia and screens for possible psychiatric, medical, or other sleep disorders requiring specific treatment. We often use questionnaires to assess sleep quality and negative daytime symptoms related to insomnia. Examples include the Pittsburgh Quality Sleep Index, Insomnia Severity Index, and Epworth Daytime Sleepiness.

Actigraphy

Actigraphy is a method of monitoring rest and activity cycles. An actigraph is a device worn on the wrist that measures overall motor activity. Actigraphs used for sleep medicine and research are more accurate and sensitive than consumer-based devices. The unit continuously records the patient's movements. This data is downloaded to a computer and analyzed. Activity corresponds to time spent awake. Continuous inactivity corresponds to time spent asleep. Actigraphy is not necessary for diagnosing insomnia. It is useful for confirming patient's sleep self-reports and monitoring the effects of treatments.

Interprofessional Care

Insomnia treatments are directed toward changing behaviors that perpetuate insomnia and managing symptoms (Table 8.2). The goal is to (1) prevent short-term insomnia from becoming chronic and (2) treat chronic insomnia. An important first step is teaching about sleep and behavioral strategies. **Sleep hygiene** is a variety of practices that are important to normal, quality nighttime sleep and daytime alertness (Table 8.3). Patients are often familiar with some sleep hygiene principles. They may benefit from coaching on using the principles effectively.

TABLE 8.2 Interprofessional Care
Insomnia

Diagnostic Assessment

History
- Self-report sleep log or diary
- Sleep assessment (Table 8.5)
- Pittsburgh Sleep Quality Index
- Insomnia Severity Index
- Epworth Sleepiness Scale

Management

Nondrug Therapy
- Sleep hygiene (Table 8.3)
- Cognitive-behavioral therapies for insomnia (CBT-I)

Drug Therapy (Table 8.4)
- Benzodiazepines
- Benzodiazepine-receptor–like agents
- Orexin-receptor antagonist
- Melatonin-receptor agonist
- Antidepressants

Cognitive-Behavioral Therapy for Insomnia

Those with chronic insomnia need more in-depth *cognitive-behavioral therapy for insomnia (CBT-I)*.[14] CBT-I is based on structured treatment plans that include cognitive and behavioral components. The cognitive part may include stress management techniques (e.g., relaxation breathing, imagery) or strategies to address misconceptions about sleep. The specific approach used varies based on the patient's need. The behavioral part includes instructions to (1) limit the amount of time in bed, (2) set a scheduled time to get up in the morning, (3) go to bed only when feeling sleepy, and (4) get out of bed when unable to sleep. CBT-I includes focused teaching and coaching on how to effectively use sleep hygiene practices (Table 8.3). CBT-I requires behavior change, which can be hard.

A trained HCP should deliver CBT-I treatment. CBT-I has become more accessible to patients through health technologies. It can be offered via telehealth sessions. There are also several online interactive programs developed by sleep experts. These include Sleepio (https://www.sleepio.com/) and Sleep Healthy Using the Internet (SHUTi, https://support.myshuti.com/hc/en-us).

You can apply many CBT-I principles to help patients. Teach the person with insomnia to avoid naps. Older adults may have difficulty fully avoiding naps. You can teach them that naps are less likely to affect nighttime sleep if they are less than 15 to 20 minutes, once per day, and occur within 7 to 9 hours after waking in the morning. Regular exercise may enhance sleep quality but should not be done within several hours of bedtime.

TABLE 8.3 PATIENT & CAREGIVER TEACHING

Sleep Hygiene

Include the following instructions when teaching a patient who has a sleep disturbance or disorder:

- Do not go to bed unless you are sleepy.
- If you are not asleep after 20 min, get out of bed and do a nonstimulating activity. Return to bed only when you are sleepy.
- Adopt a regular pattern in terms of bedtime and awakening.
- Begin rituals (e.g., warm bath, light snack, reading) that help you relax each night before bed.
- Get a full night's sleep on a regular basis.
- Make your bedroom quiet, dark, and a little bit cool.
- Do not read, write, eat, watch TV, talk on the phone, or use technologies such as smart phones and tablet computers in bed.
- Avoid caffeine, nicotine, and alcohol starting 4–6 hours before bedtime.
- Do not go to bed hungry, but do not eat a big meal near bedtime.
- Avoid strenuous exercise within 6 hours of your bedtime.
- Avoid sleeping pills or use them cautiously.
- Practice relaxation techniques (e.g., relaxation breathing) to help you cope with stress.

Adapted from American Academy of Sleep Medicine: Healthy sleep habits. Retrieved from www.sleepeducation.org/treatment-therapy/healthy-sleep-habits/.

Drug Therapy

Drug therapy is useful in treating insomnia in certain situations.[13] Most medications for insomnia work by producing sleepiness to promote the onset or maintenance of sleep. Based on the characteristics (onset, half-life, mechanism of action), certain medications may be used for specific patterns of insomnia but not for others. They can treat problems falling asleep (sleep onset), waking during the night and having trouble falling back asleep (sleep maintenance), or both. Medications that treat insomnia can cause next-day drowsiness and impair driving and other activities that require alertness. People can be impaired even when they feel fully awake. Many people who take over-the-counter (OTC) or prescription medications to treat insomnia risk becoming psychologically and physically dependent on them. *Rebound insomnia* is worsening of sleep problems that may occur when one abruptly stops certain sleep medications.

Medications are generally recommended for short-term treatment of insomnia. There is little evidence to support the use of medications for chronic insomnia. Initial drug classes used to treat insomnia are benzodiazepine-receptor agonists, followed by an orexin-receptor antagonist, melatonin receptor agonists, or antidepressants.[5] Benzodiazepines, antihistamines, and antipsychotics require special considerations and may be less effective (Table 8.4).[13]

Benzodiazepine-receptor agonists. Benzodiazepine-receptor agonists are considered first-line for pharmacologic treatment of insomnia. They act at GABA receptors more selectively than benzodiazepines, resulting in better safety. Zaleplon (Sonata) is used for sleep onset insomnia. Zolpidem (Ambien) and eszopiclone (Lunesta) are used for sleep onset and sleep maintenance insomnia.[13] There is some evidence that these drugs may be safe for prolonged use, but intermittent (rather than daily) use is still recommended.[5] They should not be taken with food as it can delay the onset of action. These agents have a short duration of action that reduces the risk for daytime sedation. Newer formulations have improved specific therapeutic uses. A controlled-release formulation of zolpidem (Ambien CR) lengthens the action of the medication, improving its use for sleep maintenance insomnia. A dissolvable tablet form of zolpidem (Edluar) and an oral spray formulation (ZolpiMist) may be used with those who have trouble swallowing pills or are on restricted oral fluid intake.

TABLE 8.4 Drug Therapy

Insomnia

Benzodiazepine-Receptor–Like Agents
- Zolpidem (Ambien, Ambien CR, Edluar, ZolpiMist)
- Zaleplon (Sonata)
- Eszopiclone (Lunesta)

Orexin-Receptor Antagonist
- Lemborexant (Dayvigo)
- Suvorexant (Belsomra)

Melatonin-Receptor Agonist
- Melatonin (controlled release)
- Ramelteon (Rozerem)
- Tasimelteon

Antidepressants
- Amitriptyline
- Doxepin (Silenor)
- Mirtazapine
- Trazodone

Benzodiazepines
- Temazepam (Restoril)
- Triazolam (Halcion)

Antihistamines
- Diphenhydramine
- Doxylamine (Unisom)
- Hydroxyzine (Vistaril)

Antipsychotics
- Quetiapine
- Olanzapine

Source: Bragg S, Benich JJ, Christian N, et al: Updates in insomnia diagnosis and treatment, *Int J Psychiatry Med* 54:275, 2019.

DRUG ALERT

- Sleepwalking, sleep driving, and engaging in other activities while not fully awake may occur after taking a benzodiazepine-receptor agonist.
- Tell patients to stop taking the drug immediately if they have such an episode.

Orexin-receptor antagonist. Suvorexant (Belsomra) and lemborexant (Dayvigo) promote sleep by blocking the wake-promoting effects of orexin. They should be taken once per night, within 30 minutes of going to bed, with at least 7 hours remaining before the planned time of waking. Use is best for sleep onset or sleep maintenance insomnia.[5] The most common side effect is drowsiness.

Melatonin-receptor agonist. Ramelteon (Rozerem) is a prescription melatonin-receptor agonist. It has a rapid onset. Ramelteon is recommended for insomnia with difficulty falling asleep, not for insomnia due to waking up during the night. Ramelteon does not cause tolerance, but it is not always effective in improving sleep quality.[5]

Antidepressants. Certain tricyclic antidepressants (e.g., doxepin, amitriptyline) are used as sleep aids due to their side effect of sedation. The insomnia dose is much lower than the antidepressant dose. Doxepin is used for sleep maintenance insomnia.[13] It improves sleep without next-day drowsiness in older and middle-aged adults with chronic primary insomnia.

Trazodone, an atypical antidepressant, is a common agent prescribed to treat insomnia, especially in older adults. However, giving this drug to older adults is controversial. Daytime sleepiness is a common side effect. Tolerance can develop within a few weeks. Trazodone is not recommended because there is not enough research to determine if the benefit outweighs risks for side effects.[13]

Benzodiazepine hypnotics. Benzodiazepines activate GABA receptors to promote sleep. These drugs are not part of first-line therapy for insomnia. Only 2 benzodiazepines are approved for insomnia: triazolam (Halcion) is recommended for sleep onset insomnia. Temazepam (Restoril) is used for both sleep onset and sleep maintenance insomnia.[13] Some benzodiazepines are recommended for treating anxiety but not insomnia (e.g., diazepam, alprazolam). However, you may still see patients who are prescribed these medications for insomnia. Other benzodiazepines (estazolam, flurazepam, oxazepam) lack enough research to support clinical recommendations. The prolonged half-life of some of these drugs can result in daytime sleepiness, amnesia, dizziness, and rebound insomnia. Tolerance develops. There is a risk for dependence and the potential for misuse. These drugs should be used for only 2 to 3 weeks. In addition, they can cause dangerous levels of sedation if used with alcohol and other central nervous system (CNS) depressants.

Antihistamines. Many people self-medicate with OTC sleep aids such as doxylamine (Unisom) and diphenhydramine. Diphenhydramine is in many "nighttime" pain medicines. Research does not show that diphenhydramine improves sleep. It should not be used by older adults. Antihistamines have anticholinergic side effects, including daytime sleepiness, impaired cognitive function, blurred vision, urinary retention, constipation, and risk for increased intraocular pressure.[13]

Complementary and Alternative Therapy

People use many types of complementary and alternative therapies as sleep aids. Melatonin may be effective for circadian rhythm disorders (e.g., jet lag).[15] It can help night shift workers sleep during the daytime. Melatonin can allow for slight decreases in time-to-sleep and increase amount of sleep. It is not a recommended treatment for insomnia. Issues with OTC melatonin products include a lack of US Food and Drug Administration (FDA) regulation and purity concerns in many products.

Herbal remedies are another means of treating insomnia. While we now better understand the mechanisms behind many herbal remedies, further testing in clinical trials is needed to guide clinical use.[16]

TABLE 8.5 NURSING ASSESSMENT

Sleep

Use the following questions to do an initial sleep assessment.

1. What time do you normally go to bed at night? What time do you normally wake up in the morning?
2. Do you often have trouble falling asleep at night?
3. About how many times do you wake up at night?
4. If you do wake up during the night, do you usually have trouble falling back asleep?
5. Does your bed partner say or are you aware that you frequently snore, gasp for air, or stop breathing?
6. Does your bed partner say or are you aware that you kick or thrash about while asleep?
7. Are you aware that you ever walk, eat, punch, kick, or scream during sleep?
8. Are you sleepy or tired during much of the day?
9. Do you usually take 1 or more naps during the day?
10. Do you usually doze off without planning to during the day?
11. How much sleep do you need to feel alert and function well?
12. Are you currently taking any type of medication or other preparation to help you sleep?

NURSING MANAGEMENT: INSOMNIA

Assessment

As a nurse, you are in a key position to assess sleep problems in patients and their caregivers. Sleep assessment is important in helping patients identify personal habits and environmental factors that contribute to poor sleep. Family caregivers may have sleep disruptions from the need to provide care to patients in the home. These sleep disruptions can increase the burden of caregiving.

We use self-report and objective data to assess sleep duration and quality. Many patients do not tell their HCP about their sleep problems. Make sure to ask patients about their sleep and problems with sleep. A sleep history includes characteristics of sleep such as sleep duration, the pattern of sleep, and daytime alertness (Table 8.5). Healthy adults should have 7 to 8 hours of sleep a night.[1] Occasional difficulty getting to sleep or awakening during the night is not unusual. However, sleep disturbances longer than 1 month are problematic. Be sure to assess diet and caffeine intake.

Ask the patient about sleep aids including OTC and prescription medications. Note the drug dose, frequency of use, and any side effects (e.g., daytime drowsiness, dry mouth). Ask about alcohol use and whether it is used as a sleep aid. Many people use herbal or dietary supplements that they believe will improve sleep. Common supplements include valerian, melatonin, hops, passion flower, kava, and skullcap. Tell the patient that many of these products are sold as dietary supplements and do not have FDA approval or regulatory oversight. The exact components and concentrations of herbs and supplements often are unknown. Patients may have adverse effects or herb-drug interactions. Certain agents such as kava can cause liver toxicity.

Encourage the patient to keep a sleep diary for 1 to 2 weeks. Free sleep diaries are available from the National Sleep Foundation (https://www.sleepfoundation.org/articles/nsf-official-sleep-diary) or the National Institutes of Health (https://www.nhlbi.nih.gov/health-topics/all-publications-and-resources/sleep-diary). You can help the patient choose a sleep diary smartphone application that tracks sleep information. Activity monitors can track sleep, but these vary in accuracy. Encourage people with sleep problems to share this information with their HCP to help identify sleep patterns.

The patient's medical history can provide important information about factors related to poor sleep. For example, a man with benign prostatic hyperplasia may report frequent awakenings during the night for voiding. Mental health problems (e.g., depression, anxiety, posttraumatic stress disorder [PTSD], drug use) are associated with sleep disturbances. Sleep disturbances often develop as a result or complication of a chronic or terminal condition (e.g., heart disease, dementia, cancer). Painful conditions such as arthritis may contribute to nighttime awakenings.

Shift work contributes to reduced or poor-quality sleep. Ask about work schedules and cross-country and international travel. Work-related behaviors resulting from poor sleep may include poor performance, decreased productivity, and job absenteeism.

◆ Clinical Problems

Clinical problems related to sleep include:

- Impaired sleep
- Fatigue

◆ Implementation

Care depends on the severity and duration of the sleep problem. Although teaching about sleep hygiene practices (Table 8.3) is beneficial, patients with chronic insomnia need more in-depth intervention using CBT-I strategies. An important part of sleep hygiene is reducing intake of caffeine-containing substances (Table 8.6). Caffeine has a half-life of about 6 hours and possibly as long as 9 hours in older adults. Patients should avoid caffeinated beverages starting 6 to 9 hours before bedtime.

Suggest and implement changes in home and institutional environments to enhance sleep. Reducing light and noise levels enhances sleep. Some people sleep better when they do not look at the clock during the night. Awareness of time passing and watching the clock adds to anxiety about not falling asleep or returning to sleep. Keeping the bedroom dark and cool is conducive to good sleep.

Teach patients about sleep medications. With benzodiazepines, non-benzodiazepine hypnotics, and melatonin-receptor agonists, teach patients to take medications right before bedtime and prepare to get a full night's sleep of at least 6 to 8 hours. Tell patients not to plan activities the next morning that require highly skilled psychomotor coordination. Teach patients not to take these medications with high-fat food (delays absorption), alcohol, or other CNS depressants. Follow-up about medications is important. Ask patients about daytime sleepiness, nightmares, and any problems with activities of daily living.

TABLE 8.6 Caffeine Content of Select Beverages

Beverage	Caffeine (mg)
Coffee, brewed (8 oz)	96
Coffee, instant (8 oz)	62
Coffee, espresso (1 oz)	64
Coffee, decaffeinated	2
Cola (8 oz)	22
Energy drink (8 oz)	29
Energy shot (1 oz)	215
Tea, black (8 oz)	47
Tea, green (8 oz)	28

Source: Mayo Clinic: Caffeine content for coffee, tea, soda and more, 2020. Retrieved from www.mayoclinic.org/healthy-lifestyle/nutrition-and-healthy-eating/in-depth/caffeine/art-20049372.

OBSTRUCTIVE SLEEP APNEA

The term **sleep-disordered breathing (SDB)** describes abnormal respiratory patterns associated with sleep. These include snoring, apnea, and hypopnea. Apnea and hypopnea involve respiratory airflow that is reduced (hypopnea) or absent (apnea). SDB results in frequent sleep disruptions and changes in sleep stages. Obstructive sleep apnea, the most diagnosed SDB problem, occurs in about 25% of adults in the United States.[17]

Obstructive sleep apnea (OSA), also called *obstructive sleep apnea–hypopnea syndrome* (OSAHS), is characterized by partial or complete upper airway obstruction during sleep. *Apnea* is the cessation of respiratory airflow (90% or greater decrease) lasting longer than 10 seconds. *Hypopnea* is a condition characterized by shallow respirations (30% to 90% decrease in airflow). Airflow obstruction in OSA occurs because of (1) narrowing of the air passages with relaxation of muscle tone during sleep and/or (2) the tongue and soft palate falling backward and partially or completely obstruct the pharynx (Fig. 8.4).[17] Each obstruction may last from 10 to 90 seconds. During the apneic period the patient can have *hypoxemia* (decreased PaO_2 or SpO_2) and *hypercapnia* (increased $PaCO_2$). These changes stimulate ventilation and cause brief arousals which end the apnea or hypopnea episode. Arousals are often under the threshold of awakening. Therefore, persons with OSA might not remember these events the next day.

When an arousal occurs, the person with OSA resumes regular ventilation with a generalized startle response. This event includes snorts and gasps, which cause the tongue and soft palate to move forward and the airway to open. Apnea and arousal cycles occur repeatedly throughout the night. Apneic episodes occur most often during REM sleep, when airway muscle tone is lowest.

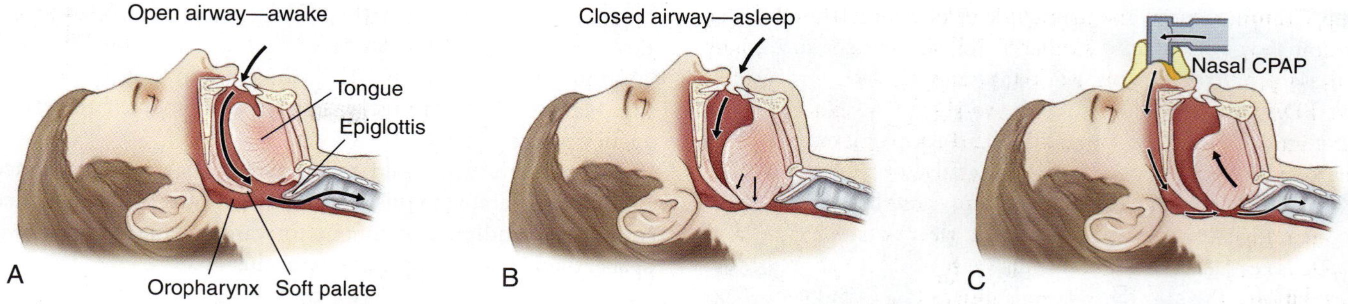

Fig. 8.4 How sleep apnea occurs. (A) The patient predisposed to obstructive sleep apnea (OSA) has a small pharyngeal airway. (B) During sleep, the pharyngeal muscles relax, allowing the airway to close. Lack of airflow results in repeated apneic episodes.(C) CPAP splints the airway open, preventing airflow obstruction. (Modified from LaFleur Brooks M: *Exploring medical language: a student-directed approach,* ed 8, St Louis, 2012, Mosby.)

There is no single cause for OSA. The condition is related to multiple factors that influence airway patency and airway muscle tone. Risk factors include obesity (body mass index [BMI] greater than 30 kg/m^2), age older than 65 years, neck circumference 16 inches or larger, male sex, and postmenopausal status in women.

Clinical Manifestations

Clinical manifestations include frequent arousals during sleep, insomnia, excessive daytime sleepiness, and witnessed apneic episodes. The patient's bed partner may complain about the patient's loud snoring. Morning headaches are common. They are caused by hypercapnia or increased blood pressure that causes vasodilation of cerebral blood vessels. Persons with OSA may display personality changes or irritability.

Untreated OSA can lead to serious health consequences. Apnea during sleep causes hypoxia, nocturnal arousals, and increased pressure in the thoracic cavity. These events can lead to negative physiologic patterns, including over-activation of the sympathetic nervous system, increased vascular resistance, and reduced oxygenation of the heart muscle. Long-term effects include hypertension, type 2 diabetes, dysrhythmias, coronary heart disease, arteriosclerosis, heart failure, and cardiovascular-related mortality.[17]

Chronic sleep loss predisposes the person to diminished ability to concentrate, impaired memory, failure to complete daily tasks, and interpersonal problems. Men may have impotence. Hypercapnia and arousals contribute to daytime sleepiness. Driving accidents may occur due to excessive daytime sleepiness. Family life and the patient's ability to maintain employment may be compromised. As a result, the patient may become depressed. The bed partner's awareness of apnea episodes is usually a source of anxiety because of fear that breathing may not resume.

Diagnostic Studies

Assessment of the patient with OSA includes a thorough sleep and medical history. Tools used to screen for OSA are the Berlin and STOP-BANG questionnaires. Each assesses manifestations highly suspicious of OSA, including snoring, known apneic episodes, sleepiness/fatigue, hypertension, obesity, older age, neck size, and sex. The Epworth Sleepiness Scale may be used to check for sleepiness associated with OSA.[17]

Typically, OSA is diagnosed by PSG done in a clinical sleep laboratory. Home testing may be done for patients with high likelihood of OSA based on our assessment. In a PSG study, electrodes simultaneously record physiologic measures (muscle tone, eye movement, and brain activity) that define the main stages of sleep and wakefulness. In laboratory and home testing, key measurements include chest and abdominal movement, oral and nasal airflow, and SpO_2. In the laboratory, additional measures include limb movements, EEG, and heart rate.

A diagnosis of sleep apnea is based on calculation of the apnea-hypopnea index (AHI). This is an hourly average of apneic events or hypopneas of at least 10 seconds' duration. OSA is defined as an AHI greater than 5 events per hour with a 3% to 4% decrease in oxygen saturation. Severe apnea can be associated with more than 30 to 50 apneic events per hour of sleep.[8]

NURSING AND INTERPROFESSIONAL MANAGEMENT: SLEEP APNEA

Behavioral Treatment

Mild sleep apnea (AHI of 5 to 10) may respond to simple behavioral measures. In some persons, OSA occurs primarily when sleeping in the prone position. Sleeping on one's side rather than on the back (called *positional therapy*) can be effective in such cases by reducing the effects of gravity on the airway. Elevating the head of the bed may eliminate OSA in some patients.

Behavioral treatment may involve weight loss and avoiding medications or substances that make apnea worse. Excess body weight worsens sleep apnea. The pressure of adipose tissue in the neck and on the chest restricts ventilation. Referral to a weight loss program may be needed. Substances that relax airway muscle tone often make OSA worse. Teach the patient to avoid taking sedatives or drinking alcoholic beverages for 3 to 4 hours before sleep. Sleep medications often make OSA worse.

Teach the patient the dangers of driving or using heavy equipment due to the profound sleepiness that is common in people with OSA. Some find a support group helpful to express

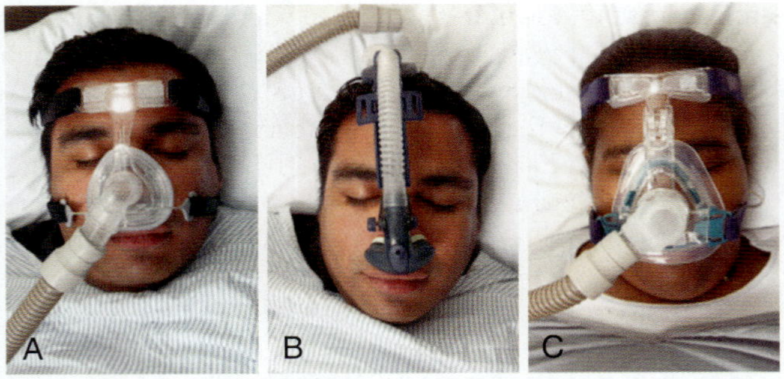

Fig. 8.5 Examples of positive airway pressure devices for sleep apnea. (A) Patient wearing a nasal mask and headgear (positive pressure only through nose). (B) Patient wearing nasal pillows (positive pressure only through nose). (C) Patient wearing a full face mask (positive pressure to nose and mouth). (From Goldman L, Schafer AI: *Goldman's Cecil medicine*, ed 24, Philadelphia, 2012, Saunders.)

concerns and feelings and discuss strategies for resolving problems. Insomnia is common in people with OSA. They may need specific treatment for the insomnia (such as CBT-I).

Medical Devices

Medical devices are key to managing OSA. For persons with more severe symptoms (>15 apnea/hypopnea events/hour), treatment guidelines recommend the use of devices that deliver positive airway pressure.[17] The most common device is a **continuous positive airway pressure (CPAP)** machine. With CPAP, the patient applies a nasal or oral-nasal mask that is attached to a high-flow blower (Fig. 8.5). The blower is adjusted to maintain enough positive pressure (5 to 25 cm H_2O) in the airway during inspiration and expiration to prevent airway collapse.

Some patients cannot adjust to wearing a mask over the nose or mouth or to exhaling against the high pressure. A technologically more sophisticated therapy, bilevel positive airway pressure (BiPAP), can deliver a higher inspiration pressure and a lower expiration pressure. The lower mean pressure of BiPAP can relieve apnea symptoms. It may be better tolerated.

CPAP reduces apnea episodes, daytime sleepiness, and fatigue. It improves quality of life and returns cognitive functioning to normal. Benefits of CPAP are dose-dependent based on how long the patient uses CPAP during the night. Although CPAP is a highly effective treatment, patients have problems with using it every day. Many of those using CPAP report side effects such as nasal stuffiness. We define proper CPAP adherence as 5 days or more each week with at least 4 hours per night of use.[17]

Assess the patient's knowledge about OSA and CPAP. Involve the bed partner in teaching. Assess the patient for nasal resistance. To ensure successful adherence to CPAP treatment, involve the patient in choosing the mask and device before the start of therapy. Patient-centered care may improve patient outcomes given that OSA treatment requires behavioral and lifestyle changes. You can facilitate goal-setting discussions between patients and HCPs to arrive at feasible and mutually agreed upon treatment plans.

When patients with a history of OSA are hospitalized, be aware that giving opioid analgesics and sedating medications that depress respiration may worsen OSA symptoms. Collaborate to determine if a patient who uses home CPAP or BiPAP should continue this therapy in the hospital when resting or sleeping. Many patients can use their own equipment if allowed by agency policy.

For patients with mild to moderate OSA, oral appliances might be preferable to positive airway pressure. Oral appliances bring the mandible and tongue forward to enlarge the airway space, thereby preventing airway occlusion.

Surgical Treatment

If other measures fail, OSA can be managed surgically. The goal of OSA surgery is to reduce collapsibility and increase patency of the upper airway, including oral, nasal, and pharyngeal passages. The most common procedures are uvulopalatopharyngoplasty (UPPP or UP3) and genioglossal advancement and hyoid myotomy (GAHM). UPPP involves removal of obstructing tissue from the tonsillar pillars, uvula, and posterior soft palate. GAHM involves advancing the attachment of the muscular part of the tongue on the mandible. When GAHM is performed, UPPP is generally done as well. Depending on the site of the obstruction, symptoms are relieved in up to 80% of patients.

Radiofrequency ablation (RFA) is the least invasive surgical intervention. RFA of obstructive tissues is used alone or in combination with other surgical techniques. New treatments involve surgically implanted neurostimulators. One type stimulates the hypoglossal nerve to increase the tone of airway muscles. We are still testing this treatment for effectiveness and safety. It tends to be more expensive than other treatment options.

Complications of airway obstruction or hemorrhage occur most often in the immediate postoperative period. Patients are usually discharged home within 1 day after surgery. Teach the patient what to expect during the postoperative recovery period. Tell patients to expect a sore throat. A foul breath odor may be reduced by rinsing with diluted mouthwash and then salt water for several days. Snoring may persist until the inflammation has subsided. Follow-up care after surgery is important, including a repeat PSG in 3 to 4 months.

PERIODIC LIMB MOVEMENT DISORDER

Periodic limb movement disorder (PLMD) is characterized by *periodic limb movements in sleep* (PLMS): involuntary, repetitive movement of the limbs that affects people only during sleep.[13] PLMD usually involves the legs and rarely involves the arms. Sometimes abdominal, oral, and nasal movement accompanies PLMD. Movements typically occur for 0.5 to 10 seconds, in intervals separated by 5 to 90 seconds. PLMD causes poor-quality sleep and excessive daytime sleepiness.

We do not know the cause of PLMD. Iron deficiency and dopamine dysfunction in the CNS might contribute.[13] PLMS can occur with sleep disorders (e.g., sleep apnea, narcolepsy) and certain medications (e.g., antidepressants). For a diagnosis of PLMD, the occurrence of PLMS must not be due to another disorder. PLMS affects many people with restless legs syndrome (RLS). RLS is discussed in Chapter 58.

PLMD is diagnosed using a detailed history from the patient and/or bed partner and doing PSG. PLMD is treated by medications aimed at reducing or eliminating the limb movements or the arousals. The benzodiazepine clonazepam is used to treat PLMD. It likely helps patients by improving sleep quality rather than reducing limb movements. Other medications shown to be effective are valproic acid, an antiseizure drug that reduces muscle activity, and selegiline, a dopaminergic agent. Dopamine agonists (pramipexole, ropinirole) are used to treat RLS, but there is little research on their efficacy for PLMD. However, it is common practice for HCPs to prescribe these drugs to treat PLMD.

CIRCADIAN RHYTHM DISORDERS

Circadian rhythm disorders can occur when the circadian time-keeping system loses alignment with the time cues from the environment such as light/dark phases indicating day and night. We call this loss of synchrony. Lack of synchrony between the circadian time-keeping system and environment disrupts the sleep-wake cycle and affects the patient's ability to have quality sleep. The common symptoms are insomnia and excessive sleepiness. Jet lag disorder and shift work sleep disorder (see the Special Sleep Needs of Nurses section) are the most common types of circadian rhythm disorders.

Jet lag disorder occurs when a person travels across multiple time zones. The result is the body's time and the environmental time are not synchronized. Most persons crossing at least 3 time zones have jet lag. The number of time zones crossed affects the symptom severity and the recovery time. Resynchronization of the body's clock occurs at a rate of about 1 hr/day when traveling eastward and 1.5 hr/day when traveling westward. Melatonin and exposure to daylight help to synchronize the body's rhythm.

Several strategies may help to reduce the risk for developing jet lag. Before travel, the person can begin harmonizing with the time schedule of the destination. When time at the destination is brief (i.e., 2 days or less), keeping home-based sleep hours rather than adopting destination sleep hours may reduce sleepiness and jet lag symptoms.

NARCOLEPSY

Narcolepsy is a chronic neurologic disorder caused by the brain's inability to regulate sleep-wake cycles normally. At various times throughout the day, people with narcolepsy have uncontrollable urges to sleep. Patients with narcolepsy often go directly into REM sleep from wakefulness.[13] This unique feature of narcolepsy does not occur in normal sleep. Patients with narcolepsy also have fragmented and disturbed nighttime sleep. There are 2 types of narcolepsy: with cataplexy *(type 1)* and without cataplexy *(type 2)*.[13] Cataplexy is a brief and sudden loss of skeletal muscle tone. It can manifest as a brief episode of muscle weakness or complete postural collapse and falling. Laughter, anger, or surprise often triggers episodes.

The onset of narcolepsy typically occurs in adolescence or early in the patient's 20s. Head trauma, a sudden change in sleep-wake habits, and infection may trigger the onset. The cause of narcolepsy is unknown. It is associated with destruction of neurons that make orexin, thought to be due to an autoimmune process.[18] The resulting deficiency of orexin causes transitions from wake to sleep that occur unpredictably.

Narcolepsy is diagnosed based on a history of sleepiness, PSG, and daytime *multiple sleep latency tests* (MSLTs).[13] For the MSLT, patients undergo an overnight PSG evaluation followed by 4 or 5 naps scheduled every 2 hours during the next day. Short sleep latencies and onset of REM sleep in more than 2 MSLTs are diagnostic signs of narcolepsy.

Narcolepsy cannot be cured. Management focuses on common symptoms: excessive daytime sleepiness, nighttime sleep disturbance, and cataplexy (Table 8.3). Provide teaching about sleep and sleep hygiene. Teach the patient to take 2 to 3 short (15 to 20 minute) naps throughout the day. You can play a key role in ensuring patient safety by teaching safety behaviors and encouraging adherence to the prescribed medication plan. Safety precautions, especially when driving, are critically important for patients with narcolepsy. The behavioral therapies for insomnia are also used to address the sleep disturbances. Stimulants are used to counter daytime sleepiness.

Modafinil (Provigil) and armodafinil (Nuvigil) are nonamphetamine wake-promotion drugs that are part of first-line drug therapy. Newer wake-promoting drugs are available. These include pitolisant (Wakix), which exerts effects at the histamine receptor, and solriamfetol (Sunosi). It is thought to inhibit norepinephrine and dopamine reuptake.[18] Sodium oxybate (Xyrem), a metabolite of GABA, is another wake-promoting medication that is effective for treating both daytime sleepiness and cataplexy. Antidepressants, including tricyclics and selective serotonin reuptake inhibitors (SSRIs), are used to treat cataplexy.[18]

PARASOMNIAS

Parasomnias are unusual and often undesirable behaviors that occur while falling asleep, transitioning between sleep stages, or arousing from sleep.[13] They are due to CNS activation and often involve complex behaviors. The parasomnia is generally goal directed, although the person is not aware or conscious of the act. Parasomnias may result in fragmented sleep and fatigue.

Sleepwalking and sleep terrors are arousal parasomnias that occur during NREM sleep. *Sleepwalking* behaviors can range from sitting up in bed, moving objects, and walking around the room to driving a car. During a sleepwalking event the person may not speak and may have limited or no awareness of the event. On awakening, the person does not remember the event. In the ICU, a parasomnia may be misinterpreted as ICU psychosis. Sedated ICU patients can have manifestations of a parasomnia.

Sleep terrors (night terrors) are characterized by a sudden awakening from sleep along with a loud cry and signs of panic. The person has marked increases in heart rate and respiration and diaphoresis. Factors in the ICU such as sleep disruption and deprivation, fever, stress, and exposure to noise and light can contribute to sleep terrors.

Fig. 8.6 Many older people have sleep problems. (© Studio-Annika/iStock/Thinkstock.)

Nightmares are a parasomnia characterized by recurrent awakening with recall of a frightful or disturbing dream. These normally occur during REM sleep during the final third of sleep. In critically ill patients, nightmares are common and likely due to medications. Drug classes most likely to cause nightmares are sedative-hypnotics, β-adrenergic antagonists, dopamine agonists, and amphetamines.

Gerontologic Considerations: Sleep

Older age is associated with overall shorter total sleep time, decreased sleep efficiency, and more awakenings (Fig. 8.6). A common misconception is that older people need less sleep than younger people. In fact, the amount of sleep needed as a person ages stays relatively constant. Other sleep disorders (e.g., sleep-disordered breathing) increase with age and may manifest with symptoms of insomnia. Some older adults have a shift in their circadian sleep timing so that they get sleepy earlier in the evening and awaken early in the morning.

Multiple factors impair older adults' ability to obtain quality sleep. Insomnia symptoms often occur with depression, cardiovascular disease, pain, and cognitive problems. Chronic conditions that are common in older adults (chronic obstructive pulmonary disease [COPD], diabetes, dementia, chronic pain, cancer) can affect sleep quality.[19] Medications used to treat these conditions and OTC medications can contribute to sleep problems as well. Stimulating OTC medications include (1) cough and cold medications, especially those containing pseudoephedrine; (2) caffeine-containing drugs; and (3) drugs containing nicotine (e.g., nicotine gum, transdermal patches).

Awakening and getting out of bed during the night (e.g., to use the bathroom) increases the risk for falls. Older adults' use of OTC medications or alcohol as sleep aids further increase the risk for falls at night. Chronic, disturbed sleep in older adults can result in disorientation, delirium, impaired intellect, disturbed cognition, and an increased risk for accidents and injury.[19]

Because older adults may attribute their disturbed sleep to normal aging, they may not report symptoms of sleep disorders to their HCPs. Alternatively, providers may overlook sleep disorders by attributing symptoms to other health issues.[20] Use a sleeping assessment (Table 8.5) to detect sleep problems in older adults.

Sleep medications should be used with great caution in older adults. Metabolism of most hypnotic drugs decreases with aging. Thus, drug therapy for sleep disturbances are started at lower doses and monitored carefully.[20] Whenever possible, long-acting benzodiazepines should be avoided. Older adults receiving benzodiazepines are at increased risk of daytime sedation, falls, and cognitive and psychomotor impairment. Diphenhydramine, alone or in combination with other drugs, is sedating with anticholinergic effects. Any OTC medication labeled "PM" may have diphenhydramine and should be used cautiously by older adults.

Fig. 8.7 Sleep problems are common among nurses. (© iStock.com/kupicoo.)

SPECIAL SLEEP NEEDS OF NURSES

In many settings, nurses work alternating and rotating day and night shifts. Unfortunately, nurses who work these shifts often report less job satisfaction, less social engagement, and more job-related stress.[21]

Nurses on permanent night or rapidly rotating shifts are at increased risk for **shift work sleep disorder**. It is characterized by insomnia, sleepiness, and fatigue. Nurses on rotating shifts get the least amount of sleep. With repeated periods of inadequate sleep, the sleep debt grows. Chronic fatigue in nurses doing shift work poses challenges for the individual nurse's health and for patient safety (Fig. 8.7).[21]

Shift work alters the synchrony between circadian rhythms and the environment, leading to sleep disruption. Nurses working the night shift are often too sleepy to be fully alert at work and too alert to sleep soundly the next day. Sustained changes in circadian rhythms such as those with rotating shift work are linked to increased morbidity and mortality risks from cardiovascular problems. Mood disorders such as anxiety are higher in nurses who work rotating shifts.[21]

From a safety perspective, disturbed sleep and subsequent fatigue can result in errors and accidents that affect nurses and their patients. Fatigue diminishes or distorts perceptual skills, judgment, and decision-making capabilities. Lack of sleep reduces the ability to cope and handle stress, which may result in physical, mental, and emotional exhaustion.

The problem of sleep disruption is important to nursing. Several strategies may help reduce the problems with rotating shift work. These include brief periods of on-site napping. Maintaining a consistent sleep-wake schedule even on days off is best but hard to do. For night shift work, scheduling the sleep period just before going to work increases alertness and vigilance, improves reaction times, and decreases accidents during night shift work. Nurses who have control over their work schedules appear to have less sleep disruption. As a nurse, you need to manage the impact of sleep disruption by using sleep hygiene practices.

Case Study

Insomnia

(© JackF/ iStock/ Thinkstock.)

Patient Profile

G.P. is a 49-year-old woman who is being seen in the primary care clinic for chronic fatigue and disturbed sleep. Currently she is taking OTC diphenhydramine for sleep. Her partner, who has accompanied her to the clinic, states that her snoring has gotten worse, and it is interfering with his sleep.

Subjective Data

A focused subjective assessment of G.P. revealed the following:

Medical History: Postmenopausal based on self-report. Does not report any other health problems. Takes a multivitamin and uses diphenhydramine, 25 mg, each night at bedtime to help her sleep

Health Perception-Health Management: Reports that she feels generally healthy and able to manage her own health except for problems related to her sleep

Sleep-Rest: States she was a sound sleeper prior to the menopausal transition. Now awakens 5 or more times during the night. Attributes her awakenings to hot flashes. Has difficulty falling asleep, usually taking 30–60 min. Has trouble falling back asleep after waking during the night. Says she is very sleepy during the day. Falling asleep in the evening when watching television and has occasionally fallen asleep at work. Her partner reports that her snoring has gotten much worse in the last year. States she stops breathing for around 30 sec.

Cognitive-Perceptual: Reports feeling sleepy and fatigued during the day. Has difficulty concentrating on her work at times due to fatigue

Nutritional-Metabolic: On a usual workday drinks 2 cups of hot tea in the morning and a can of diet cola in the late afternoon

Objective Data

Physical Assessment:

- Alert and oriented but appears tired
- Height is 5′6″; weight 190 lb (BMI = 30.7)

Vital signs: BP 140/88 mm Hg, HR 80/min, respiratory rate 18/min, temp 36.8°C, SpO2 97% on room air

Diagnostic Studies

A nighttime PSG study revealed an apnea-hypopnea index of 24 with reduced pulse oxygen readings. This indicates moderate obstructive sleep apnea.

Interprofessional Care

A patient-centered plan of care was developed by G.P. and her health care team. Treatment will include CPAP nightly, referral for weight reduction counseling, and teaching about sleep hygiene.

Discussion Questions

1. ***Recognize:*** What are G.P.'s risk factors for sleep apnea?
2. ***Analyze:*** What are the major health risks for G.P. from sleep apnea?
3. ***Plan:*** What referrals may be indicated for G.P.?
4. ***Prioritize:*** Based on the assessment data provided, what are the priority clinical problems?
5. ***Act:*** What teaching will you provide so G.P. can successfully self-manage care and improve her sleep quality?
6. ***Evaluate:*** What assessment data would you need to collect to decide if care was effective?
7. ***Safety:*** What safety concerns should you address with the patient?

Answers available at http://evolve.elsevier.com/Lewis/medsurg.

BRIDGE TO NCLEX EXAMINATION

The number of the question corresponds to the same-numbered outcome at the beginning of the chapter.

1. Which statement *best* describes sleep?
   a. A loosely organized state similar to coma
   b. A quiet state in which there is little brain activity
   c. A state in which a person has reduced sensitivity to pain
   d. A state lacking conscious awareness of the environment
2. Which statements are true about rapid eye movement (REM) sleep? *(select all that apply)*
   a. The EEG pattern is quiescent.
   b. Muscle tone is greatly reduced.
   c. It occurs only once in the night.
   d. It is physiologically similar to NREM sleep.
   e. The most vivid dreaming occurs during this phase.
3. Which factors does the nurse associate with insufficient sleep? *(select all that apply)*
   a. Increased body mass index
   b. Increased insulin resistance
   c. Impaired cognitive functioning
   d. Enhanced immune responsiveness
   e. Increased daytime body temperature
4. When teaching the patient with insomnia about sleep hygiene, which information would the nurse emphasize?
   a. The importance of daytime naps
   b. The need for long-term use of hypnotics
   c. Planning for exercise about 1 hour before bedtime
   d. The importance of avoiding caffeine 6 to 9 hours before bedtime

5. An overweight patient with sleep apnea would like to avoid using a nasal CPAP device. Which recommendation would the nurse make to help the patient manage sleep apnea without using CPAP?
   a. Lose excess weight
   b. Take a nap each afternoon
   c. Eat a high-protein snack at bedtime
   d. Use mild sedatives or alcohol at bedtime
6. While caring for a patient with a history of narcolepsy with cataplexy, which activity can the nurse delegate to the assistive personnel (AP)?
   a. Teaching about the timing of medications
   b. Walking the patient to and from the bathroom
   c. Developing a plan of care with a family member
   d. Planning a diet that avoids caffeine-containing foods
7. Which strategy reduces drowsiness on the job for night shift workers?
   a. Exercising before going to work
   b. Taking melatonin before working the night shift
   c. Sleeping for at least 2 hours immediately before work time
   d. Walking for 10 minutes every 4 hours during the night shift

1. d; 2. b, e; 3. a, b, c; 4. d; 5. a; 6. b; 7. c.

For rationales to these answers and even more NCLEX review questions, visit http://evolve.elsevier.com/Lewis/medsurg.

EVOLVE WEBSITE/RESOURCES LIST

http://evolve.elsevier.com/Lewis/medsurg
Review Questions (Online Only)
Key Points
Answer Keys for Questions
- Rationales for Bridge to NCLEX Examination Questions
- Answer Guidelines for Case Study Conceptual Care Map Creator

Audio Glossary
Content Updates

REFERENCES

1. National Heart, Lung, and Blood Institute: How much sleep is enough? Retrieved from http://www.nhlbi.nih.gov/health-topics/sleep-deprivation-and-deficiency.
2. Centers for Disease Control and Prevention: Short sleep duration among U.S. adults. Retrieved from http://www.cdc.gov/sleep/data_statistics.html.
3. National Highway Traffic Safety Administration: Drowsy driving. Retrieved from https://www.nhtsa.gov/risky-driving/drowsy-driving.

*4. Barnes CM, Watson NF: Why healthy sleep is good for business, *Sleep Med Rev* 47:112, 2019.
*5. Venner A, Todd WD, Fraigne J, et al.: Newly identified sleep-wake and circadian circuits as potential therapeutic targets, *Sleep* 42:023, 2019.
*6. Dujardin S, Pijpers A, Pevernagie D: Prescription drugs used in insomnia, *Sleep Med Clin* 5:133, 2020.
*7. Schwartz WJ, Klerman EB: Circadian neurobiology and the physiologic regulation of sleep and wakefulness, *Neurol Clin* 37:475, 2019.
*8. Berry RB, Brooks R, Gamaldo C, et al.: *The AASM manual for the scoring of sleep and associated events*, Westchester, IL, 2017, American Academy of Sleep Medicine.
*9. Wilms B, Chamorro R, Hallschmid M, et al.: Timing modulates the effect of sleep loss on glucose homeostasis, *J Clin Endocrinol Metab* 104:2801, 2019.
10. Chaput JP, Shiau J: Routinely assessing patients' sleep health is time well spent, *Prev Med Rep* 14:100851, 2019.
*11. Ye L, Owens RL, Dykes P: Individualized sleep promotion in acute care hospitals: identifying factors that affect patient sleep, *Appl Nurs Res* 48:63, 2019.
*12. Krause AJ, Prather AA, Wager TD, et al.: The pain of sleep loss: a brain characterization in humans, *J Neurosci* 39:2291, 2019.
13. American Academy of Sleep Medicine: *International classification of sleep disorders*, ed 3, Westchester, IL, 2014, American Academy of Sleep Medicine. (Classic).
*14. Baglioni C, Altena E, Bjorvatn B, et al.: The European Academy for cognitive Behavioural therapy for insomnia: an initiative of the European insomnia network to promote implementation and dissemination of treatment, *J Sleep Res* 29:e12967, 2020.
15. Bragg S, Benich JJ, Christian N, et al.: Updates in insomnia diagnosis and treatment, *Int J Psychiatry Med* 54:275, 2019.
*16. Cheng B, Liu Y, Tian J, et al.: Complementary and alternative medicine for the treatment of insomnia: an overview of scientific evidence from 2008 to 2018, *Curr Vasc Pharmacol* 18:307, 2020.
*17. Gottlieb DJ, Punjabi NM: Diagnosis and management of obstructive sleep apnea: a review, *J Am Med Assoc* 323:1389, 2020.
18. Reading PJ: Update on narcolepsy, *J Neurol* 266:1809, 2019.
19. Hamilton C, Christmas C: Evaluation and management of difficult symptoms in older adults in primary care, *Med Clin North Am* 104:885, 2019.
20. Dzierzewski JM, Dautovich ND: Who cares about sleep in older adults? *Clin Gerontol* 41:109, 2018.
21. Cheng P, Drake C: Shift work disorder, *Neurol Clin* 37:563, 2019.

*Evidence-based information for clinical practice.

9

Pain

Jessica I. Goldberg and William E. Rosa

http://evolve.elsevier.com/Lewis/medsurg/

CONCEPTUAL FOCUS

Coping
Functional Ability
Pain

LEARNING OUTCOMES

1. Define pain.
2. Describe the neural mechanisms of pain and pain modulation.
3. Distinguish between nociceptive and neuropathic types of pain.
4. Explain the physical and psychologic effects of unrelieved pain.
5. Interpret data from a comprehensive pain assessment.
6. Describe effective interprofessional pain management techniques.
7. Describe drug and nondrug methods of pain relief.
8. Explain your role and responsibility in pain management.
9. Discuss ethical and legal issues related to pain and pain management.
10. Evaluate the influence of one's own knowledge, beliefs, and attitudes about pain assessment and management.

KEY TERMS

analgesic ceiling
breakthrough pain (BTP)
central sensitization
complex regional pain syndrome (CRPS)
equianalgesic dose
modulation
multimodal analgesia
neuropathic pain
nociception
nociceptive pain
pain
patient-controlled analgesia (PCA)
patient-controlled epidural analgesia (PCEA)
peripheral sensitization
transduction
transmission
trigger point

Pain is a complex, multidimensional experience that is closely related to suffering and decreased quality of life. Pain is a major reason that people seek health care. To effectively assess and manage patients with pain, you need to understand the physiologic and psychosocial dimensions of pain. Pain is interrelated with many concepts. Culture and spirituality influence the expression of pain. Acute pain adversely affects mobility and sleep, leading to fatigue. Having pain is a stressor that can lead to depression. Those with severe or chronic pain are more likely to describe their health as poor and may have increased mortality. This chapter presents information to help you assess and safely manage pain in collaboration with other interprofessional team members.

EXTENT OF PAIN PROBLEM

Millions of people suffer from pain. Each year in the US, at least 25 million people have acute pain from an injury or surgery. Common chronic pain conditions, such as arthritis, migraine headache, and back pain, affect more than 1 million American adults. Pain is a common symptom experienced by patients with cancer.[1] Despite the high prevalence of acute and chronic pain, many people experience inadequate pain management. Consequences of unrelieved acute pain are shown in Table 9.1.

DEFINITIONS AND DIMENSIONS OF PAIN

The International Association for the Study of Pain (IASP) defines **pain** as "an unpleasant sensory and emotional experience associated with actual or potential tissue damage." This definition emphasizes the subjective nature of pain, in which the patient's self-report is the most valid means of assessment. Although understanding the patient's experience and relying on self-report is essential, this view is problematic for many patients. For example, patients who are comatose or who have

TABLE 9.1 Negative Consequences of Unrelieved Acute Pain

Response	Possible Consequences
Cardiovascular	
↑ Cardiac output	Deep vein thrombosis
↑ Coagulation	Hypertension
↑ Heart rate	Myocardial infarction
↑ Myocardial O_2 consumption	Unstable angina
↑ Peripheral vascular resistance	
Endocrine and Metabolic	
↑ Adrenocorticotropic hormone (ACTH)	↑ BP
	Fluid overload
↑ Aldosterone	↑ Heart rate
↑ Antidiuretic hormone (ADH)	Hyperglycemia
↑ Cortisol	↑ Respiratory rate
↑ Epinephrine and norepinephrine	Shock
Gluconeogenesis	Urinary retention, ↓ urine output
Glycogenolysis	Weight loss (from ↑ catabolism)
↓ Insulin	
Muscle protein catabolism	
Gastrointestinal	
↓ Gastric and intestinal motility	Anorexia
	Constipation
	Obstruction
	Paralytic ileus
Immunologic	
↓ Immune response	Infection
Musculoskeletal	
Impaired muscle function	Immobility
Muscle spasm	Weakness and fatigue
Neurologic	
Impaired cognitive function	Confusion
	Impaired ability to think, reason, make decisions
Renal and Urologic	
↓ Urine output	Electrolyte imbalance
Urinary retention	Fluid imbalance
Respiratory	
↓ Cough with sputum retention	Atelectasis
Hypoxemia	Pneumonia
↓ Tidal volume	

dementia, who are mentally disabled or challenged, or have expressive aphasia have varying abilities to report pain. In these instances, you must include nonverbal information, such as observed behaviors, in your pain assessment.

The emotional distress of pain can cause suffering, especially when the pain is unrecognized or undertreated.[2] Suffering can result in a sense of insecurity, lack of control, and spiritual distress. It is important to assess the ways in which a person's spirituality influences and is influenced by pain.

The biopsychosocial model of pain includes the physiologic, affective, cognitive, behavior, and sociocultural dimensions of pain (Table 9.2). Each person understands and conceptualizes their pain in their own way. For example, a woman in labor will have pain. She may choose to manage it without analgesics because she associates it with a joyful event. She may feel control over her pain because of the training she received in prenatal classes and the knowledge that the pain is time limited. In contrast, a woman with chronic, undefined musculoskeletal pain may be stressed by thoughts that others think that her pain is "not real," is uncontrollable, or is caused by her own actions. Perceptions influence the ways in which a person responds to pain. We must consider perceptions in a comprehensive treatment plan.

TABLE 9.2 Dimensions of Pain

Dimension	Description
Affective	• Emotional responses to pain include anger, fear, depression, anxiety • Negative emotions impair patient's quality of life
Behavior	• Observable actions (e.g., grimacing, irritability, coping skills) are used to express or control pain • People unable to communicate may have behavior changes (e.g., agitation, combativeness)
Cognitive	• Beliefs, attitudes, memories, and meaning attributed to pain influence the ways in which a person responds to pain
Physiologic	• Genetic, anatomic, and physical determinants of pain influence how we process, recognize, and describe painful stimuli
Sociocultural	• Age and gender influence nociceptive processes and responses to opioids • Families and caregivers influence patient's response to pain through their beliefs, behaviors, and support • Culture affects pain expression, medication use, pain-related beliefs, and coping methods

Some people cope with pain by distracting themselves. Others convince themselves that the pain is permanent and untreatable. People who believe their pain is uncontrollable and overwhelming are more likely to have poor outcomes.

Families and caregivers influence the patient's response to pain through their beliefs and behaviors. For example, families may discourage the patient from taking opioids because they fear that the patient may become addicted. Understanding these beliefs helps you address them through patient and family teaching.

Pain Mechanisms

Nociception is the physiologic process by which we communicate information about tissue damage to the central nervous system (CNS). It involves 4 processes: (1) transduction, (2) transmission, (3) perception, and (4) modulation (Fig. 9.1).

Transduction

Transduction involves the conversion of a noxious (tissue-damaging) stimulus into an electrical signal called an action potential. Noxious stimuli can be thermal (e.g., sunburn), mechanical (e.g., surgical incision), or chemical (e.g., toxic substances).

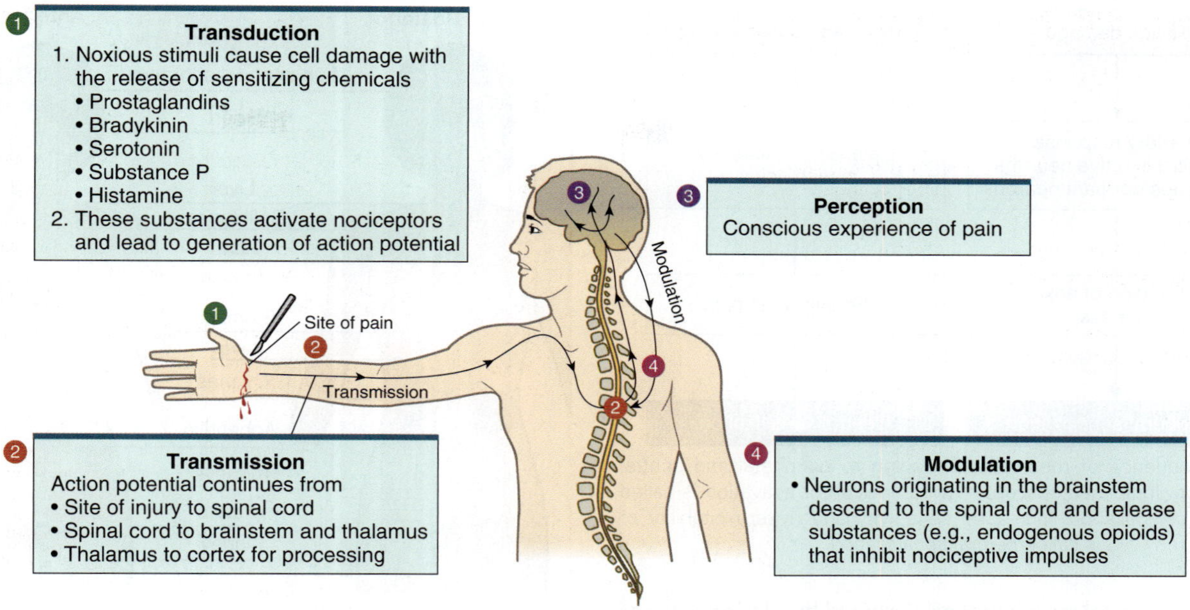

Fig. 9.1 Nociceptive pain originates when tissue is injured. (1) Transduction occurs when there is release of chemical mediators. (2) Transmission involves the conduct of the action potential from the periphery (injury site) to the spinal cord and then to the brainstem, thalamus, and cerebral cortex. (3) Perception is the conscious awareness of pain. (4) Modulation involves signals from the brain going back down the spinal cord to modify incoming impulses. (Developed by McCaffery M, Pasero C, Paice JA. Modified from McCaffery M, Pasero C: *Pain: clinical manual,* ed 2, St Louis, 1999, Mosby.)

They cause the release of chemicals, such as substance P and adenosine triphosphate (ATP), into the damaged tissues. Other chemicals are released by mast cells (e.g., serotonin, histamine, prostaglandins) and macrophages (e.g., cytokines). These chemicals activate nociceptors (specialized receptors), or free nerve endings, which respond to painful stimuli. Activating the nociceptors results in an action potential. It is carried from the nociceptors to the spinal cord by small, rapidly conducting, myelinated A-delta fibers and slowly conducting unmyelinated C fibers.

Besides stimulating nociceptors, inflammation and the subsequent release of chemical mediators lower nociceptor thresholds. As a result, nociceptors may fire in response to stimuli that previously were insufficient to elicit a response. They may also fire in response to nonnoxious stimuli, such as light touch. We call this increased susceptibility to nociceptor activation **peripheral sensitization**. Leukotrienes, prostaglandins, cytokines, and substance P are involved in peripheral sensitization. Cyclooxygenase (COX), produced in the inflammatory response, also plays a key role in peripheral sensitization. A clinical example of this process is sunburn. Thermal injury causes inflammation that results in pain when the affected skin is lightly touched. Peripheral sensitization amplifies signal transmission. This contributes to central sensitization (discussed under Dorsal Horn Processing). The pain from activation of peripheral nociceptors is called nociceptive pain.

Therapies that change either the local environment or sensitivity of the peripheral nociceptors can prevent transduction and initiation of an action potential. Decreasing the effects of chemicals released at the periphery is the basis of several drug approaches to pain relief. For example, nonsteroidal antiinflammatory drugs (NSAIDs), such as ibuprofen, exert their analgesic effects by blocking the action of COX-2 enzymes.

Transmission

Transmission is the process by which we relay pain signals from the periphery to the spinal cord and then to the brain. Nerves that carry pain impulses from the periphery to the spinal cord are called *primary afferent fibers*. These include A-delta and C fibers. Each is responsible for a different pain sensation. A-delta fibers conduct pain rapidly. They are responsible for the initial, sharp pain that accompanies tissue injury. C fibers transmit painful stimuli more slowly. They produce pain that is typically aching or throbbing. Primary afferent fibers end in the dorsal horn of the spinal cord. Activity in the dorsal horn integrates and modulates pain inputs from the periphery.

Fig. 9.1 shows the movement of pain impulses from the site of transduction to the brain. Three segments are involved in nociceptive signal transmission: (1) transmission along the peripheral nerve fibers to the spinal cord, (2) dorsal horn processing, and (3) transmission to the thalamus and cerebral cortex.

Drugs that stabilize the neuronal membrane act on peripheral sodium channels to inhibit movement of nerve impulses. These medications include local anesthetics (e.g., injectable or topical lidocaine, bupivacaine) and antiseizure drugs (e.g., gabapentin).

Transmission to spinal cord. The *first-order neuron* extends the entire distance from the periphery to the dorsal horn with no synapses. For example, an afferent fiber travels from the great toe through the 5th lumbar nerve root into the spinal cord. It is a single cell. Once generated, an action potential travels all the way to the spinal cord unless it is blocked by a sodium channel

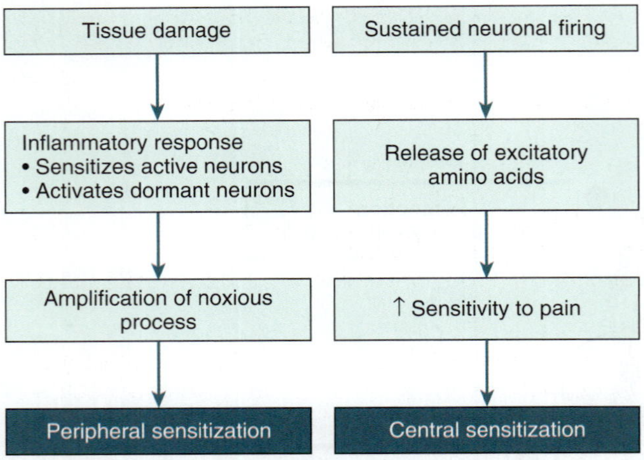

Fig. 9.2 Sequence of mechanisms leading to peripheral and central sensitization. Increased susceptibility to nociceptor activation is called *peripheral sensitization.* Increased sensitivity and hyperexcitability of neurons in the CNS is called *central sensitization.*

inhibitor (e.g., local anesthetic) or disrupted by a lesion, such as a dorsal root entry zone lesion.

The way nerve fibers enter the spinal cord is central to the notion of spinal dermatomes. *Dermatomes* are areas on the skin that are innervated primarily by a single spinal cord segment. They determine the distinct pattern of the rash caused by herpes zoster (shingles) across the back and trunk. Different dermatomes and their innervations are shown in Fig. 60.7.

Dorsal horn processing. Once a nociceptive signal arrives in the spinal cord, it is processed within the dorsal horn. Neurotransmitters released from the afferent fiber bind to receptors on nearby cells. Some of these neurotransmitters (e.g., glutamate, substance P) cause activation. Others (e.g., γ-aminobutyric acid [GABA], serotonin) inhibit activation. In this area, exogenous and endogenous opioids (e.g., encephalin, β-endorphin) play a vital role by binding to opioid receptors and blocking the release of neurotransmitters, especially substance P. They produce analgesic effects like those of exogenous opioids, such as morphine. We call the neurons that project to the thalamus *second-order neurons.*

Increased sensitivity and hyperexcitability of neurons in the CNS are called **central sensitization**. With central sensitization, the central processing circuits are altered. Peripheral tissue damage or nerve injury can cause central sensitization. Continued nociceptive input from the periphery maintains it (Fig. 9.2). In some cases, central sensitization can be long lasting due to multiple changes that occur in the periphery and CNS.

Because of the increased excitability of CNS neurons, normal sensory inputs cause abnormal sensing and responses to painful and other stimuli. This explains why some people have significant pain from touch or tactile stimulation that is not typically painful. We call this *allodynia*. It also explains why some people have *hyperalgesia,* an exaggerated or increased pain response to noxious stimuli.

With ongoing stimulation of slowly conducting unmyelinated C-fiber nociceptors, firing of specialized dorsal horn neurons gradually increases. These inputs can lead to the sprouting of wide dynamic range (WDR) neuron dendrites and

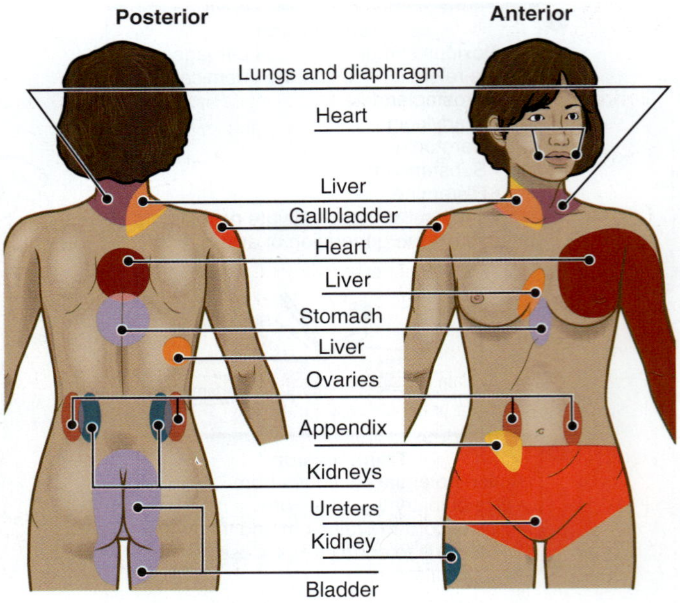

Fig. 9.3 Typical areas of referred pain.

the induction of glutamate-dependent *N*-methyl-D-aspartate (NMDA) receptors. This results in an increased capacity to transmit a broader range of stimuli-producing signals, which we then pass up the spinal cord and to the brain. This process is known as *wind-up.* Activation of NMDA receptors also plays a role in wind-up. NMDA receptor antagonists, such as ketamine, potentially interrupt or block mechanisms that lead to or sustain central sensitization. Wind-up is like central sensitization and hyperalgesia in that it occurs in response to C-fiber inputs. Wind-up is different in that it can be short-lasting, while central sensitization and hyperalgesia persist over time.

It is important to understand that acute, unrelieved pain leads to chronic pain through central sensitization. Even brief intervals of acute pain can induce long-term neuronal remodeling and sensitization *(plasticity),* chronic pain, and lasting psychologic distress.

Neuroplasticity refers to processes that allow neurons in the brain to compensate for injury and adjust their responses to new situations or changes in their environment. Neuroplasticity contributes to adaptive mechanisms for reducing pain. It can also result in maladaptive mechanisms that enhance pain sensitivity.

Genetic variability may play a key role in changes that occur in the CNS and the response to different analgesic therapies to treat pain. Understanding this phenomenon helps explain patients' differences in response to pain and why some patients develop chronic pain conditions and others do not.

We must consider the possibility of referred pain when interpreting the location of pain reported by the person with an injury or a disease involving visceral organs. The location of a stimulus may be distant from the pain location reported by the patient (Fig. 9.3). For example, the patient often reports pain from liver disease in the right upper abdominal quadrant. It can be referred to the anterior and posterior neck region, shoulder area, and posterior flank area. If we do not consider referred

TABLE 9.3 **Comparison of Nociceptive and Neuropathic Pain**

	Nociceptive Pain	Neuropathic Pain[a]
Definition	Normal processing of stimulus that damages normal tissue or has the potential to do so if prolonged	Abnormal processing of sensory input by the peripheral or CNS
Treatment	Usually responsive to nonopioid and/or opioid drugs	Usually treated with adjuvant analgesics May be responsive to opioid drugs
Types	**Superficial Somatic Pain** Pain arising from skin, mucous membranes, subcutaneous tissue. Tends to be well localized *Examples:* Sunburn, skin contusions	**Central Pain** Caused by primary lesion or CNS problems *Examples:* Poststroke pain, pain associated with multiple sclerosis
		Peripheral Neuropathies Pain felt along the distribution of 1 or many peripheral nerves caused by damage to the nerve *Examples:* Diabetic neuropathy, alcohol-nutritional neuropathy, trigeminal neuralgia, postherpetic neuralgia
	Deep Somatic Pain Pain arising from muscles, fasciae, bones, tendons. Localized or diffuse and radiating *Examples:* Arthritis, tendonitis, myofascial pain	
	Visceral Pain Pain arising from visceral organs, such as the GI tract and bladder. Well or poorly localized. Often referred to cutaneous sites *Examples:* Appendicitis, pancreatitis, cancer affecting internal organs, irritable bowel and bladder syndromes	**Deafferentation Pain** Pain resulting from a loss of or altered afferent input *Examples:* Phantom limb pain, postmastectomy pain, spinal cord injury pain
		Sympathetically Maintained Pain Pain that persists due to autonomic nervous system dysfunction *Examples:* Phantom limb pain, complex regional pain syndrome

[a]Some types of neuropathic pain (e.g., postherpetic neuralgia) are caused by more than 1 neuropathologic mechanism.

pain when evaluating a pain location report, diagnostic tests and therapy could be misdirected.

Transmission to thalamus and cortex. From the dorsal horn, nociceptive stimuli are communicated to the *third-order neuron,* primarily in the thalamus. Fibers of dorsal horn projection cells enter the brain through several pathways, including the spinothalamic tract and spinoreticular tract. Distinct thalamic nuclei receive nociceptive input from the spinal cord and have projections to several regions in the cerebral cortex. This is where we presume that pain perception occurs.

Therapeutic approaches that target pain transmission include opioid analgesics. They bind to opioid receptors on primary afferent and dorsal horn neurons. These agents mimic the inhibitory effects of endogenous opioids. Baclofen inhibits pain transmission by binding to GABA receptors, thus mimicking the inhibitory effects of GABA.

Perception

Perception occurs when pain is recognized, defined, and assigned meaning by the person experiencing the pain. In the brain, nociceptive input is perceived as pain. Pain perception involves several brain structures. We think that the reticular activating system warns the person to address the pain stimulus. The somatosensory system is responsible for localization and characterization of pain. Our emotional and behavior responses may originate in the limbic system.

Cortical structures are crucial to constructing the meaning of the pain.[3] This makes behavior strategies, such as distraction and relaxation, effective pain-reducing therapies for many people. Meditation and imagery can affect pain perception. By directing attention away from the pain sensation, patients can reduce the sensory and affective components of pain.

Modulation

Modulation involves the activation of descending pathways that exert inhibitory or facilitatory effects on pain transmission (Fig. 9.1). Depending on the type and degree of modulation, we may or may not perceive nociceptive stimuli as pain. Modulation of pain signals can occur at the level of the periphery, spinal cord, brainstem, and cerebral cortex. Descending modulatory fibers release chemicals, such as serotonin, norepinephrine, GABA, and endogenous opioids, which can inhibit pain transmission.

Several antidepressants exert their effects through the modulatory systems. For example, tricyclic antidepressants (TCAs) (e.g., amitriptyline) and serotonin norepinephrine reuptake inhibitors (SNRIs) (e.g., venlafaxine) are used to manage chronic noncancer and cancer pain. These agents interfere with the reuptake of serotonin and norepinephrine. This increases their availability to inhibit noxious stimuli.

CLASSIFICATION OF PAIN

We classify pain in several ways. Most often, we classify pain as nociceptive or neuropathic based on underlying pathology (Table 9.3). Another useful scheme is to classify pain as acute or chronic (Table 9.4).

Nociceptive Pain

Nociceptive pain is caused by damage to somatic or visceral tissue. *Somatic pain* often is further described as superficial or deep. *Superficial pain* arises from skin, mucous membranes, and subcutaneous tissues. It is often described as sharp, burning, or prickly. *Deep pain* is often described as aching or throbbing. It originates in bone, joint, muscle, skin, or connective tissue.

TABLE 9.4 Differences Between Acute and Chronic Pain

	Acute Pain	Chronic Pain
Onset	Sudden	Gradual or sudden
Duration	<3 mo or as long as it takes for normal healing to occur	>3 mo. May start as acute injury or event but continues past the normal time for recovery
Severity	Mild to severe	Mild to severe
Cause of pain	Usually can identify a precipitating event (e.g., illness, surgery)	May not be known. Original cause of pain may differ from mechanisms that maintain the pain.
Course of pain	Decreases over time and goes away as recovery occurs	Typically pain does not go away Characterized by periods of increasing and decreasing pain
Typical physical and behavior manifestations	Manifestations vary but can reflect sympathetic nervous system activation: • ↑ Heart rate, respiratory rate, BP • Confusion, anxiety, agitation • Diaphoresis, pallor • Urine retention	Common behavior manifestations: • Fatigue • Flat affect • ↓ Physical activity • Withdrawal from social interaction
Usual goals of treatment	Pain control with ability to take part in recovery activities Minimize side effects of treatment	Pain control to the extent possible Focus on enhancing function and quality of life Minimize side effects of treatment

Visceral pain results from the activation of nociceptors in the internal organs and lining of the body cavities, such as the thoracic and abdominal cavities. Visceral nociceptors respond to inflammation, stretching, and ischemia. Stretching of hollow viscera in the intestines and bladder that occurs from tumor involvement or obstruction can cause intense cramping pain. Examples of visceral nociceptive pain include pain from a surgical incision, pancreatitis, and inflammatory bowel disease.

Neuropathic Pain

Neuropathic pain is caused by damage to peripheral nerves or structures in the CNS. It is often associated with diabetic neuropathy and other neuropathic pain syndromes. Around 8% of the general population has pain with neuropathic characteristics. It is typically described as numbing, hot, burning, shooting, stabbing, sharp, or electric shock–like. Neuropathic pain can be sudden, intense, short lived, or lingering. Paroxysmal firing of injured nerves is responsible for shooting and electric shock-like sensations. Common causes include trauma, inflammation, metabolic diseases (e.g., diabetes), alcohol use disorder, nervous system infections (e.g., herpes zoster), tumors, toxins some chemotherapy agents, and neurologic diseases (e.g., multiple sclerosis). Examples of neuropathic pain conditions include phantom limb sensation, diabetic neuropathy, and trigeminal neuralgia.

CNS lesions or dysfunction cause *central pain. Deafferentation pain* results from loss of or altered afferent input from either peripheral nerve injury (e.g., amputation) or CNS damage, including a spinal cord injury. Painful peripheral polyneuropathies (pain felt along the distribution of multiple peripheral nerves) and painful mononeuropathies (pain felt along the distribution of a damaged nerve) arise from damage to peripheral nerves. They generate pain that people may describe as burning, paroxysmal, or shock-like. The patient may have positive or negative motor and sensory signs, including numbness, allodynia, or change in reflexes and motor strength.

Sympathetically maintained pain is associated with a group of conditions that have a degree of change in autonomic nervous system. One especially debilitating type is **complex regional pain syndrome (CRPS).**[4] Typical features include dramatic changes in the color and temperature of the skin over the affected limb or body part, accompanied by intense burning pain, skin sensitivity, sweating, and swelling. Triggers for CRPS type I include tissue injury, surgery, or a vascular event, such as stroke. CRPS type II includes all these features and a peripheral nerve lesion.

Opioid analgesics alone are often not effective in treating neuropathic pain. Treatment often requires a multimodal approach combining various adjuvant analgesics from different drug classes. These include TCAs (e.g., amitriptyline), SNRIs (e.g., bupropion [Wellbutrin]), antiseizure drugs (e.g., pregabalin [Lyrica]), transdermal lidocaine, and α_2-adrenergic agonists (e.g., clonidine). NMDA receptor antagonists, such as ketamine, have shown promise in alleviating neuropathic pain refractory to other drugs.[5]

Acute and Chronic Pain

Acute pain and chronic pain differ in their cause, course, manifestations, and treatment (Table 9.4). Acute pain functions as a signal, warning the person of potential or actual tissue damage. Examples include postoperative pain, labor pain, pain from trauma (e.g., lacerations, fractures, sprains), pain from infection (e.g., dysuria from cystitis), and pain from acute ischemia. For acute pain, treatment includes analgesics and treatment of the underlying cause (e.g., splinting for a fracture, antibiotic therapy for an infection). Normally, acute pain decreases over time as healing occurs. Sometimes acute pain can persist and lead to a disabling chronic pain state. For example, pain from herpes zoster subsides as the acute infection resolves, usually within a month. Sometimes the pain persists and develops into a chronic pain state called *postherpetic neuralgia.* Because of the connection between inadequately treated acute pain and chronic pain, it is important to treat acute pain aggressively.

TABLE 9.5 Principles of Pain Assessment

Principle	Nursing Implications
1. Patients have the right to appropriate assessment and management of pain.	• Assess pain in *all* patients.
2. Pain is always subjective.	• Patient's self-report of pain is the single most reliable indicator of pain. • Accept and respect this self-report unless there are clear reasons for doubt.
3. Physiologic and behavior signs of pain (e.g., tachycardia, grimacing) are not reliable or specific for pain.	• Do not rely primarily on observations and objective signs of pain unless the patient is unable to self-report pain.
4. Pain is an unpleasant sensory and emotional experience.	• Address physical and psychologic aspects of pain when assessing pain.
5. Assessment approaches, including tools, must be appropriate for the patient population.	• Special considerations are needed for assessing pain in patients with difficulty communicating. • Include family members in the assessment process (when appropriate).
6. Pain can exist even when no physical cause can be found.	• Do not attribute pain that does not have an identifiable cause to psychologic causes.
7. Different patients have different levels of pain in response to comparable stimuli.	• A uniform pain threshold does not exist.
8. Patients with chronic pain may be more sensitive to pain and other stimuli.	• Pain tolerance varies among and within persons depending on several factors (e.g., genetics, energy level, coping skills, prior experience with pain).
9. Unrelieved pain has adverse consequences. Acute pain that is not adequately controlled can result in physiologic changes that increase the chance of developing persistent pain.	• Encourage patients to report pain, especially patients who are reluctant to discuss pain, deny pain when it is probably present, or fail to follow through on prescribed treatments.

Chronic pain, or *persistent pain,* lasts for longer periods. We often define this as longer than 3 months or past the time when an expected acute pain or acute injury should subside. The severity and functional impact of chronic pain are often disproportionate to objective findings because of changes in the nervous system that are not detectable with standard tests. Chronic pain does not appear to have an adaptive role. It can be disabling. The patient may experience anxiety and depression.

PAIN ASSESSMENT

Assessment is an essential step in pain management. It is important to regularly screen all patients for pain. When present, perform a more thorough pain assessment. The key to accurate and effective pain assessment is to consider the principles of pain assessment (Table 9.5).

The goals of a nursing pain assessment are to (1) describe the patient's pain experience in order to implement appropriate pain management techniques and (2) identify the patient's goal for therapy and resources for self-management.

Elements of a Pain Assessment

Most components of a pain assessment involve direct interview or patient observation. Diagnostic studies and physical assessment findings complete the initial assessment. The assessment differs with the clinical setting, patient population, and point of care (e.g., whether the assessment is part of an initial workup or a reassessment of pain following therapy). Your evaluation of pain should always be multidimensional (Table 9.6).

Before beginning any assessment, recognize that patients may use words other than "pain."[6] For example, some older adults may deny that they have pain but respond positively when asked if they have soreness or aching. Record the specific words that the patient uses to describe pain. Then consistently ask the patient about pain using their words.

Document the pain assessment. This is critical to ensure safe, effective communication among interprofessional team members. Many health care facilities have adopted specific tools to record an initial pain assessment, treatment, and reassessment. There also are many multidimensional pain assessment tools, such as the Brief Pain Inventory, the McGill Pain Questionnaire, and the Neuropathic Pain Scale.

Pain Pattern

Assessing pain *onset* involves determining when the pain started. Patients with acute pain resulting from injury, acute illness, or treatment (e.g., surgery) often know exactly when their pain began. Those with chronic pain may be less able to relate when the pain started. Establish the *duration* of the pain (how long it has lasted). This information helps to determine whether the pain is acute or chronic and helps identify the cause of the pain. For example, a patient with advanced cancer who has chronic low back pain from spinal stenosis reports a sudden, severe pain in the back that began a week ago. Knowing the onset and duration leads to a diagnostic workup that reveals new metastatic disease in the spine.

The pain pattern gives clues about the cause of the pain and directs its treatment. Many types of chronic pain (e.g., arthritis pain) can increase and decrease over time. A patient may have pain all the time (around-the-clock pain), as well as periods of intermittent pain.

Breakthrough pain (BTP) is transient, moderate to severe pain that occurs in patients with stable chronic pain. The average peak of BTP can be 3 to 5 minutes. It can last up to 30 minutes or even longer. BTP can be either predictable or unpredictable. Patients can have 1 to many episodes per day. Short-acting analgesics (e.g., hydromorphone) can be effective to treat BTP.

End-of-dose failure is pain that occurs before the expected duration of a specific analgesic. It should not be confused with

TABLE 9.6 NURSING ASSESSMENT

Pain

Subjective Data

Important Health Information

Health history: Pain history includes onset, location, intensity, quality, patterns, aggravating and alleviating factors, and expression of pain. Coping strategies. Past treatments and their effectiveness. Review health care use related to the pain problem (e.g., emergency department visits, treatment at pain clinics, visits to primary health care providers and specialists)

Medications: Use of any prescription or over-the-counter, illicit, or herbal products for pain relief. Alcohol and marijuana use

Nondrug measures: Use of therapies, such as massage, heat or ice, Reiki, aromatherapy, acupuncture, hypnosis, yoga, or meditation

Functional Health Patterns

Health perception–health management: Social and work history, mental health history, smoking history. Effects of pain on emotions, relationships, sleep, and activities. Interviews with family members. Records from psychological treatment related to the pain. Knowledge and beliefs about pain and expectations about pain management.

Elimination: Constipation related to opioid drug use, other medication use, or pain related to elimination

Activity-exercise: Fatigue, limitations in ability to perform activities of daily living (ADLs), instrumental activities of daily living (IADLs), and pain related to use of muscles

Sexuality-reproductive: Decreased libido

Coping–stress tolerance: Psychologic evaluation using standardized measures to examine depression, anxiety. Current and past use of stress management and coping strategies.

Objective Data

Physical assessment, including evaluation of functional limitations

Psychosocial evaluation, including mood

BTP. Pain that occurs at the end of the duration of an analgesic often leads to a prolonged increase in the baseline persistent pain. For example, in a patient on transdermal fentanyl (Duragesic patches), the typical duration of action is 72 hours. An increase in pain after 48 hours on the drug would be an end-of-dose failure. End-of-dose failure signals the need for changes in the dose or scheduling of the analgesic.

Episodic, procedural, or *incident pain* is a transient increase in pain caused by a specific activity or event. Examples include dressing changes, movement, position changes, and procedures, such as catheterization.

Location

Determining the *location* of pain helps us identify possible causes and treatment. Some patients may be able to specify the precise location(s) of their pain. Others may describe general areas or comment that they "hurt all over." The location of the pain may be referred from its origin to another site (Fig. 9.3). For example, myocardial infarction can result in pain in the left shoulder. Pain can radiate from its origin to another site. For example, angina pectoris can radiate from the chest to the jaw or down the left arm. *Sciatica* is pain that follows the course of the sciatic nerve. It may originate from joints or muscles around the back or from compression or damage to the sciatic nerve. The pain is projected along the course of the peripheral nerve. This causes painful shooting sensations down the back of the thigh and inside of the leg to the foot.

Obtain information about the location of pain by asking the patient to (1) describe the site(s) of pain, (2) point to painful areas on the body, or (3) mark painful areas on a pain map. Because many patients have more than 1 site of pain, make sure that the patient describes every location.

Intensity

Assessing the severity, or *intensity,* of pain provides a reliable measure to determine the type of treatment and its effectiveness. Pain scales help the patient communicate pain intensity. Base your choice of a scale on the patient's developmental needs and cognitive status (Fig. 9.4). Many adults can rate their pain intensity using a numeric rating scale (e.g., 0 = no pain, 10 = the worst pain). Patients who wish to have word choices to quantify pain may prefer a verbal descriptor scale (e.g., none, mild, moderate, severe). For those oriented to vertical representations, the Pain Thermometer Scale is an option. Other visual pain measures, such as the Wong-Baker FACES pain tool, are useful for patients with cognitive or language barriers to describe their pain. Pain assessment measures for cognitively impaired adults and nonverbal adults are addressed later in this chapter.

Although intensity is a key factor in determining analgesic approaches, do not dose patients with opioids solely based on reported pain scores. Opioid "dosing by numbers" can lead to unsafe practices and serious adverse events. We can achieve safe analgesic administration by balancing an amount of pain relief with analgesic side effects and using a multimodal approach. We can adjust therapy to promote better pain control and minimize adverse outcomes.

Quality

The pain *quality* refers to the nature or characteristics of the pain. For example, patients often describe neuropathic pain as burning, numbing, shooting, stabbing, electric shock–like, or itchy. Nociceptive pain may be described as sharp, aching, throbbing, dull, and cramping. Since the quality of pain relates to a degree to the classification of pain (e.g., neuropathic, nociceptive),

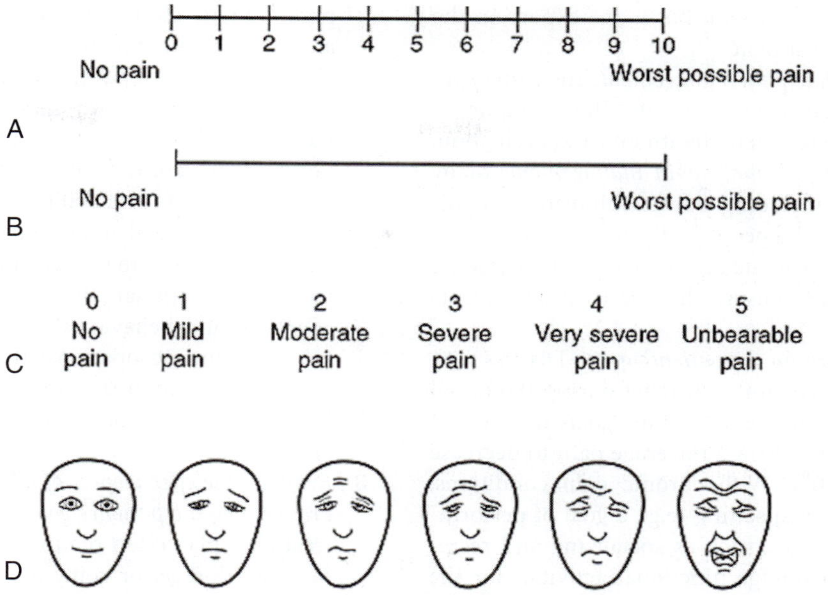

Fig. 9.4 Pain intensity scales. (A) 0 to 10 numeric scale. (B) Visual analog scale. (C) Descriptive scale. (D) Faces Pain Scale. (Modified from Baird M: *Manual of critical care nursing: nursing interventions and collaborative management*, ed 7, St Louis, 2016, Elsevier.)

these descriptors can help to guide treatment options that best address the specific mechanism of pain.

Associated Symptoms

Pain may worsen associated symptoms, such as anxiety, fatigue, and depression. Patients with pain often report poor sleep and subsequent daytime sleepiness. Poor sleep can further increase pain perception. Ask about aggravating factors that increase pain as well as activities and situations that alleviate pain. For example, musculoskeletal pain may increase or decrease with movement and ambulation. Resting or immobilizing a painful body part can decrease pain. Knowing what makes pain better or worse can help characterize the type of pain and be helpful in selecting treatments.

Management Strategies

As people experience and live with pain, they may cope differently and have varying levels of willingness to try pain management strategies. To maximize the effectiveness of the pain treatment plan, ask patients what they are using now to control pain, what they have used in the past, and the outcomes of these methods. Strategies include prescription and nonprescription drugs and nondrug therapies, such as hot and cold applications, complementary and alternative therapies (e.g., acupuncture), and relaxation strategies (e.g., imagery). It is important to document both those that work and those that are ineffective.

Impact of Pain

Pain can have a profound influence on a patient's quality of life and functioning. Assess the effect of the pain on the patient's ability to sleep, enjoy life, interact with others, perform work and household duties, and engage in physical and social activities. Assess the impact of pain on the patient's mood.

In an acute care setting, time limitations may dictate a shortened assessment. At a minimum, assess the effects of the pain on the patient's sleep and daily activities, relationships with others, physical activity, and emotional well-being. Include the ways in which the patient describes the pain and strategies used to cope with and control the pain.

Patient's Beliefs, Expectations, and Goals

Patient and family beliefs, attitudes, and expectations influence responses to pain and pain treatment. Assess for attitudes and beliefs that may hinder effective treatment (e.g., belief that opioid use will result in addiction). Ask about expectations and goals for pain management.

Reassessment

It is critical for you to reassess pain at appropriate intervals. Reassessment provides real-time evaluation data on the efficacy of pain management interventions. The frequency and scope of reassessment are guided by factors such as pain severity, physical and psychosocial condition, type of intervention, risks for adverse effects, and agency policy. For example, we frequently reassess a postoperative patient for the effectiveness of each analgesic dose. In a long-term care facility, residents with chronic pain are reassessed at least quarterly or with a change in condition or functional status.

PAIN TREATMENT

Basic Principles

All pain treatment plans are based on the following 10 principles and practice standards:

1. *Follow the principles of pain assessment* (Table 9.5). Remember that pain is a subjective experience. The patient is not

only the best judge of their pain but is the expert on the effectiveness of pain treatment.

2. *Use a holistic approach to pain management.* The pain experience affects all aspects of a person's life. Thus it requires a holistic approach to assessment, treatment, and evaluation.
3. *Every patient deserves adequate pain management.* Many patient populations, including ethnic minorities, cognitively impaired adults, and people with substance use problems, are at risk for inadequate pain management. Be aware of your own biases and ensure that we treat all patients respectfully.
4. *Base the treatment plan on the patient's goals.* Discuss with the patient realistic goals for pain relief during the initial pain assessment. We can describe some goals in terms of pain intensity (e.g., the desire for average pain to decrease from "8/10" to "3/10"). With chronic pain conditions, encourage functional goal setting (e.g., a goal of performing certain daily activities, such as socializing and recreational activities). Encourage functional activities for the patient with acute pain as well. For example, the pain must be at a level that allows the patient to use the incentive spirometer, get out of bed, and ambulate. Over time, reassess these goals and progress made toward meeting them. The patient, in collaboration with the health care team, determines new goals. If the patient has unrealistic goals for therapy, such as wanting to be completely rid of all chronic arthritis pain or be completely pain free after a major surgery, work with the patient to establish a more realistic goal.
5. *Use both drug and nondrug therapies.* Although we consider analgesics the mainstay of therapy, include self-care activities and nondrug therapies to increase the overall effectiveness of therapy and minimize adverse drug effects.
6. *When appropriate, use a multimodal approach to analgesic therapy.* **Multimodal analgesia** uses 2 or more classes of analgesic agents to take advantage of the various mechanisms of action. The goal is to combine analgesics from different classes to achieve maximum pain relief with minimal adverse effects. For acute, postoperative pain, a multimodal approach may include the use of an opioid (morphine), NSAID, and/or antiseizure drug (e.g., gabapentin). Regional anesthesia and continuous peripheral neural blockade used with local anesthetics are part of multimodal regimens. Factors such as age, organ function, type of surgery, risk for developing chronic pain, and coexisting conditions are all considered when designing a multimodal analgesic regimen.
7. *Address pain using an interprofessional approach.* The expertise and perspectives of an interprofessional team are often necessary to provide effective assessment and therapies for patients with both acute and chronic pain. For hospitalized patients or those with complex acute or chronic pain issues, anesthesiology-based pain services may be available to manage patients with technology-supported pain care (e.g., patient-controlled analgesia [PCA] or regional analgesia). Palliative care teams may be useful to help manage complex pain symptoms in the those with serious illness. Team members may include pain management nurses, nurse practitioners, clinical nurse specialists, anesthesiologists, and clinical pharmacists. These teams help to establish realistic goals with patients and families to facilitate recovery and discharge. Many patients have access to outpatient pain management centers or clinics. Some provide comprehensive pain care and employ multiple providers, including anesthesiologists, rehabilitation physicians, nurses, psychologists, physical and occupational therapists, and social workers. Services may focus on medication management, pain interventional therapies, psychologic counseling, cognitive and behavior therapies, rehabilitative therapies (physical and occupational therapy), and social services. Specialized pain treatment centers may also offer more holistic therapies, such as massage, music and art therapy, and acupuncture.
8. *Evaluate the effectiveness of all therapies to ensure that they are meeting the patient's goals.* Achievement of an effective treatment plan often requires trial and error. Adjustments in drug, dosage, or route are common to achieve maximal benefits while minimizing adverse effects. This trial-and-error process can become frustrating for the patient and caregivers. Reassure them that pain relief, if not pain cessation, is usually possible and that the health care team will continue to work with them to achieve adequate pain relief.
9. *Prevent and/or manage medication side effects.* Side effects or adverse events are a major reason for treatment failure and nonadherence. Side effects are managed in several ways (Table 9.7). You play a key role in monitoring for and treating side effects and in teaching patients and caregivers how to minimize these effects.
10. *Include patient and caregiver teaching throughout assessment and treatment.* Teach the patient and caregiver about the causes of the pain, pain assessment methods, treatment goals and options, expectations of pain management, safe use of drugs, side effect management, and nondrug and self-help pain relief measures. Document the teaching and include evaluation of patient and caregiver comprehension.

Drug Therapy for Pain

We generally divide pain medications into 3 categories: nonopioids, opioids, and adjuvant drugs. Patient-centered treatment plans may include medications from 1 or more of these groups. Mild pain often can be relieved using nonopioids alone. Moderate to severe pain usually requires an opioid. Some types

TABLE 9.7 Drug Therapy
Managing Side Effects of Pain Medications

Side effects can be managed by 1 or more of the following methods:

- Decreasing the dose of analgesic by 10%–15%
- Changing to a different agent in the same class
- Adding a drug to counteract the adverse effect of the analgesic (e.g., using a stimulant laxative for patients with opioid-induced constipation)
- Using an administration route that minimizes drug concentrations (e.g., intraspinal opioid administration used to minimize high drug levels that produce sedation, nausea, and vomiting)

of pain, such as neuropathic pain, typically require adjuvant drug therapy alone or in combination with an opioid or another class of analgesics. We may treat pain caused by cancer with analgesics as well as chemotherapy or radiation therapy.

Nonopioids

Nonopioid analgesics include acetaminophen, aspirin and other salicylates, and NSAIDs (Table 9.8).[7] As a group, these drugs do not produce tolerance or physical dependence. Many are available without a prescription. To provide safe care, monitor over-the-counter (OTC) analgesic use to avoid serious problems related to drug interactions, side effects, and overdose.

Nonopioids are effective for mild to moderate pain. They are often used in conjunction with opioids because they allow for effective pain relief using lower opioid doses (thereby causing fewer opioid side effects). This phenomenon is called the *opioid-sparing effect*. They have an **analgesic ceiling**. This means that increasing the dose beyond an upper limit provides no greater analgesia.

Aspirin is effective for mild pain. Its use is limited by its common side effects, including increased risk for bleeding, especially gastrointestinal (GI) bleeding. Acetaminophen (Tylenol) has analgesic and antipyretic effects.[8] Unlike aspirin, it has no antiplatelet or antiinflammatory effects. Acetaminophen is often well tolerated. It is metabolized by the liver. Liver toxicity may result from chronic dosing of more than 3 g/day, acute overdose, or use by patients with severe liver disease. Adding acetaminophen to opioid therapy produces an opioid-sparing effect, lower pain scores, and fewer side effects. This is the reason for opioid-acetaminophen combinations.

IV acetaminophen (Ofirmev) is used alone for treating acute mild to moderate pain, as an adjunct to opioid analgesics, or part of a multimodal analgesic regimen for moderate to severe pain. It has a short duration of action.

NSAIDs represent a broad class of drugs with varying efficacy and side effects. All NSAIDs inhibit COX. It is the enzyme that converts arachidonic acid into prostaglandins and related compounds. The enzyme has 2 forms: COX-1 and COX-2. COX-1 is found in almost all tissues. It is responsible for several protective physiologic functions. In contrast, COX-2 is made mainly at the sites of tissue injury, where it mediates inflammation (Fig. 9.5). Inhibiting COX-1 causes many of the untoward effects of NSAIDs, such as renal problems, bleeding tendencies, GI irritation, and ulceration. COX-2 inhibition is associated with the therapeutic, antiinflammatory effects of NSAIDs. Celecoxib (Celebrex) is a COX-2 inhibitor. Older NSAIDs, such as ibuprofen, inhibit both forms of COX. We call these nonselective NSAIDs.

Patient response to a specific NSAID varies greatly. So, we should suggest another NSAID if the first one does not provide relief. NSAIDs have many side effects. They can cause cognitive problems and hypersensitivity reactions with asthma-like symptoms.

NSAID-associated GI toxicity ranges from dyspepsia to life-threatening ulceration and hemorrhage. Patients at risk include those who have a recent history of peptic ulcer disease, patients who are older than 65, and those also using corticosteroids or anticoagulants. When patients at risk for GI bleeding use NSAIDs, they should also receive misoprostol (Cytotec) or a proton pump inhibitor, such as omeprazole. NSAIDs should not be given with aspirin since this increases the risk for GI bleeding.

TABLE 9.8 Drug Therapy

Select Nonopioid Analgesics

Drug	Nursing Considerations
Nonsalicylates	
acetaminophen (Tylenol)	• Sustained release, rectal suppository, and IV forms available • Maximum daily dose of 3 g/day for adults ≥50 kg • Oral doses of >3 g may cause liver toxicity • Acute overdose: Acute liver failure • Give IV form over 15 min
Nonsteroidal Antiinflammatory Drugs (NSAIDs)	
celecoxib (Celebrex)	• Causes fewer GI side effects (e.g., bleeding) than other NSAIDs, but risk still present • More costly than other NSAIDs • May increase risk for serious cardiovascular thrombotic events, myocardial infarction, and stroke • Risks may increase with duration of use, preexisting cardiovascular disease, or risk factors for cardiovascular disease
diclofenac K	• Use lowest effective dose for shortest possible duration • Available in oral, ophthalmic, topical preparations
ibuprofen (Advil)	• Use lowest effective dose for shortest possible duration • Increased risk for serious GI adverse events (bleeding, ulceration, perforation), especially in older adults • May increase risk for serious cardiovascular thrombotic events, myocardial infarction, and stroke • May increase risk for hypertension and renal insufficiency
ketorolac	• Limit treatment to 5 days • May cause renal failure in dehydrated patients
naproxen (Naprosyn, Aleve)	• Use lowest effective dose for shortest possible duration • Increased risk for serious GI adverse events (bleeding, ulceration, perforation), especially in older adults • Contraindicated for treating pain after coronary artery bypass graft (CABG) surgery
Salicylates	
aspirin	• Rectal suppository and sustained-release preparations available • Chance of upper GI bleeding • Used more often in low doses as a cardioprotective measure than for its analgesic properties

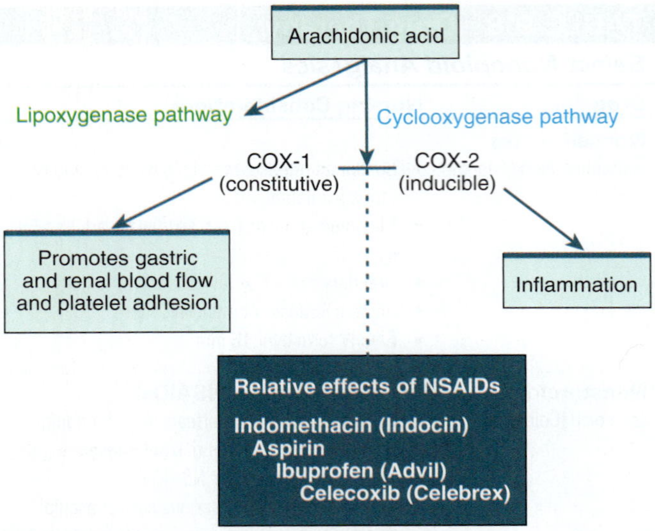

Fig. 9.5 Arachidonic acid is oxidized by 2 different pathways: lipoxygenase and cyclooxygenase. The cyclooxygenase *(COX)* pathway leads to 2 forms of the enzyme COX: COX-1 and COX-2. COX-1 is *constitutive* (always present). COX-2 is *inducible* (its expression varies markedly depending on the stimulus). NSAIDs differ in their actions, with some having more effects on COX-1 and others more on COX-2. Indomethacin acts primarily on COX-1. Ibuprofen is equipotent on COX-1 and COX-2. Celecoxib primarily inhibits COX-2.

DRUG ALERT

NSAIDs

- NSAIDs, except aspirin, are linked to a higher risk for cardiovascular events, such as myocardial infarction, stroke, and heart failure.
- Patients who have just had heart surgery should not take NSAIDs.

Opioids

Opioids (Table 9.9) produce their effects by binding to receptors in the CNS. This results in (1) inhibition of the transmission of nociceptive input from the periphery to the spinal cord, (2) altered limbic system activity, and (3) activation of the descending inhibitory pathways that modulate transmission in the spinal cord. Thus opioids act on several nociceptive processes.

Types of opioids. Opioids are categorized by their physiologic action (e.g., agonist, antagonist) and binding at specific opioid receptors (e.g., mu, kappa, delta). The most common subclass of opioids is the pure opioid agonists, or morphine-like opioids. They bind to mu receptors.

Opioids are used for acute and chronic pain. Although nociceptive pain seems to be more responsive to opioids than neuropathic pain, opioids may be used to treat both types of pain. Pure opioid agonists include morphine, oxycodone (OxyContin), hydrocodone, codeine, methadone, hydromorphone (Dilaudid), and levorphanol (Table 9.9). These drugs are effective for moderate to severe pain because they are potent, theoretically have no analgesic ceiling, and can be given by several routes. When opioids are prescribed for moderate pain, they are usually combined with a nonopioid analgesic, such as acetaminophen or ibuprofen.

Methadone has a unique mechanism of action as an NMDA receptor antagonist and mu opioid receptor agonist.[9] It is most often a treatment for chronic pain but can be used for acute pain. It produces analgesic effects independent of its action as an opioid.

Mixed agonist-antagonists (e.g., butorphanol) bind as agonists on kappa receptors and as weak antagonists or partial agonists on mu receptors. Because of this difference in binding, they cause less respiratory depression than drugs that act only at mu receptors. However, these drugs cause more dysphoria and agitation. Opioid agonist-antagonists have an analgesic ceiling and can precipitate withdrawal if used by a patient who is physically dependent on mu agonist drugs. Partial opioid agonists (e.g., buprenorphine [Buprenex]) can produce some pain relief but bind tightly to mu receptors and block the effect of other drugs. Agonist-antagonists and partial agonists currently have limited clinical application in pain management.

Dual-mechanism agents. Some opioid analgesics have 2 distinct actions, or dual mechanisms. Tramadol (Ultram) is a weak mu agonist and inhibits the reuptake of norepinephrine and serotonin.[10] It can be effective in treating low back pain, osteoarthritis, fibromyalgia, diabetic peripheral neuropathic pain, polyneuropathy, and postherpetic neuralgia. The most common side effects are like those of other opioids, including nausea, constipation, dizziness, and sedation. As with other drugs that increase serotonin and norepinephrine, patients with a history of seizures should avoid this drug because it lowers the seizure threshold.

Tapentadol (Nucynta) is a centrally acting opioid analgesic that works at mu receptors and inhibits norepinephrine reuptake.[11] It is approved for managing moderate to severe acute pain. For chronic moderate to severe pain, an extended-release formula is available. The side effects are similar to those of conventional opioids except that this drug causes less nausea and constipation.

Opioids to avoid. Some opioids should be avoided for pain relief because of limited efficacy and/or toxicities. The American Pain Society does not recommend the use of meperidine (Demerol) as an analgesic. It can cause neurotoxicity (e.g., seizures) from the accumulation of its metabolite, normeperidine. When given, use is limited to the very short-term (less than 48 hours) treatment of acute pain when other opioid agonists are contraindicated.

Opioid side effects. Common side effects include constipation, nausea and vomiting, sedation, respiratory depression, and pruritus.[12] With continued use, many side effects diminish. The exception is constipation. Less common side effects include urinary retention, myoclonus, dizziness, confusion, and hallucinations.

Constipation is the most common side effect of opioids. Left untreated, it may increase the person's pain and can lead to fecal impaction and paralytic ileus. A bowel regimen should be started at the beginning of opioid therapy and continued for as long as the person takes opioids.[13] Although diet fiber, fluids, and exercise should be encouraged, these measures alone may not be enough. Most patients should use a gentle stimulant laxative (e.g., senna). A stool softener (e.g., docusate sodium) may be added if the patient has hard stools. Be aware that a stool softener will not increase the number of bowel movements. Other agents (e.g., Milk of Magnesia, bisacodyl, polyethylene glycol, lactulose) can be added if needed. Methylnaltrexone (Relistor), naldemedine (Symproic), and naloxegol (Movantik)

TABLE 9.9 Drug Therapy

Opioid Analgesics

Drug	Routes of Administration	Nursing Considerations
Mu Agonists		
codeine oral (with acetaminophen [Tylenol #3]), codeine injectable	PO, subcutaneous	• Associated with higher incidence of nausea and constipation than other mu agonists • Many codeine preparations are combined with acetaminophen • 5%–10% of European Americans lack the enzyme to metabolize codeine to morphine
fentanyl (Sublimaze [IV]), Duragesic [transdermal], Actiq [transmucosal], Fentora [buccal tablet], Lazanda [nasal spray]	IV, epidural, intrathecal, transmucosal, transdermal	• Immediate onset after IV route, 7–8 min after IM route, 5–15 min after transmucosal route, up to 6 hr after transdermal route • For procedures, IV fentanyl often combined with benzodiazepines for analgesia and sedation • Very potent; dosage is in micrograms (mcg) • Transdermal fentanyl used only for chronic pain and should not be given to opioid-naive patients
hydrocodone with acetaminophen (Norco), hydrocodone with bitartrate (Hysingla ER, Zohydro ER), hydrocodone with ibuprofen (Reprexain)	PO (short acting and long acting)	• Used for moderate or moderately severe pain • For short-term management of acute pain (e.g., trauma, musculoskeletal)
hydromorphone (Dilaudid)	PO (short-acting and long-acting forms), rectal, IV, subcutaneous, epidural, intrathecal	• Slightly shorter duration than morphine • For moderate to severe pain • Tablets for sustained-release preparations are to be swallowed whole and must not be broken, chewed, dissolved, or crushed • Preparations for neuraxial administration must be preservative free
levorphanol	PO, IV, IM, subcutaneous	• Accumulates with repeated dosing
methadone (Dolophine)	PO, IV, IM	• High oral and rectal bioavailability • Accumulates with repeated dosing • Use with caution in older adults • Risk for QT interval prolongation
morphine (MS Contin, Kadian, Duramorph)	PO (short-acting and sustained-release forms), rectal, IV, subcutaneous, epidural, intrathecal, sublingual, intranasal	• Standard of comparison for opioid analgesics (Table 9.12) • For moderate to severe pain • Can stimulate histamine release, leading to pruritus, with systemic administration • Tablets for sustained-release preparations are to be swallowed whole and must not be broken, chewed, dissolved, or crushed • Preparations for neuraxial administration must be preservative free
oxycodone (Roxicodone) oxycodone extended release (OxyContin) oxycodone plus acetaminophen (Percocet) oxycodone plus aspirin (Percodan)	PO (short-acting and extended-release forms)	• Available as single entity and in combination with a nonopioid • Used similarly for moderate to severe pain • Often combined with a nonopioid for acute, moderate pain • Extended release indicated for chronic pain
tapentadol (Nucynta)	PO (short-acting and extended release)	• Dual mechanism of action: Mu opioid agonist and blocks reuptake of norepinephrine and serotonin
tramadol (Ultram)	PO (short-acting and extended release)	• Dual mechanism of action: Mu opioid agonist and blocks reuptake of norepinephrine and serotonin • Used for moderate pain
Mu Mixed Agonist-Antagonists		
butorphanol	Nasal spray, injectable form Not available orally	• Psychotomimetic effects lower than with pentazocine • May precipitate withdrawal in opioid-dependent patients • Injectable used for acute pain • Nasal spray given for migraine headaches
Partial Agonists		
buprenorphine buprenorphine plus naloxone sublingual (Suboxone)	Sublingual, injectable, implant	• Sublingual form should not be chewed or swallowed • Lower abuse potential than morphine • Does not produce psychotomimetic effects • May precipitate withdrawal in opioid-dependent patients. Not readily reversed by naloxone • Buprenorphine plus naloxone used as a sublingual preparation to treat opioid dependence for easier withdrawal when necessary to taper from opioids

are peripheral opioid receptor antagonists used for opioid-induced constipation when the response to laxative and stool softener therapy is insufficient. The absence of a bowel regimen may lead to serious complications, including bowel obstruction.

Nausea is often a problem in opioid-naive patients. The use of an antiemetic, such as ondansetron (Zofran), metoclopramide (Reglan), transdermal scopolamine, or hydroxyzine (Vistaril), can prevent or minimize nausea and vomiting until tolerance develops. This usually occurs within 1 week. Opioids delay gastric emptying. The patient may report gastric fullness. Metoclopramide can reduce this effect. If nausea and vomiting are severe and persistent, changing to a different opioid may be needed.

Sedation usually occurs in opioid-naive patients being treated for acute pain. Regularly monitor patients receiving opioid analgesics, especially in the first few days after starting therapy (e.g., after surgery). Be aware that the risk for unintended sedation in postoperative patients is greatest within 4 hours after leaving the postanesthesia care unit. Opioid-induced sedation resolves as tolerance develops. Persistent sedation with chronic opioid use can often be treated with psychostimulants, such as caffeine, dextroamphetamine (Dexedrine), methylphenidate (Ritalin), or the anticataleptic drug modafinil (Provigil).

The risk for *respiratory depression* is higher in opioid-naive, hospitalized patients being treated for acute pain. Clinically significant respiratory depression is rare in opioid-tolerant patients and when opioids are titrated to analgesic effect. Patients most at risk for respiratory depression include those who are age 65 or older, have a history of snoring or witnessed apneic episodes, report excessive daytime sleepiness, have underlying heart or lung disease, are obese (body mass index greater than 30 kg/m^2), have a history of smoking (more than 20 pack-years), or are receiving other CNS depressants (e.g., sedatives, benzodiazepines, antihistamines). For postoperative patients, the greatest risk for opioid-related respiratory adverse events is within the first 24 hours after surgery.

Frequently monitor both the sedation level and respiratory rate in patients receiving opioid analgesics. Use a sedation scale for monitoring and providing appropriate interventions based on the level of sedation (Table 9.10).

CHECK YOUR PRACTICE

A 61-year-old patient returns to the unit after spinal surgery with a PCA pump. Her wife tells you that the patient seems groggy and is difficult to arouse. She also tells you that the O_2 saturation monitor became disconnected. When you reconnect it, you see that the patient's O_2 saturation is 89% and her respiratory rate ranges from 8 to 10 breaths/min.

- What should you do?

SAFETY ALERT

Sedation and Respiratory Depression

- If the patient's respiratory rate falls below 8 or 10 breaths/min and the sedation level is 3 or greater, vigorously stimulate the patient and try to keep the patient awake.
- If the patient becomes oversedated (respiratory rate less than 8–10 breaths/min or obtunded), follow agency protocol and prepare to administer naloxone.

TABLE 9.10 Pasero Opioid-Induced Sedation Scale (POSS) With Interventions

Level of Sedation	Nursing Intervention
S = Sleep, easy to arouse	• Acceptable • No action necessary • May increase opioid dose if needed
1. Awake and alert	• Acceptable • No action necessary • May increase opioid dose if needed
2. Slightly drowsy, easily aroused	• Acceptable • No action necessary • May increase opioid dose if needed
3. Frequently drowsy, arousable, drifts off to sleep during conversation	• Unacceptable • Monitor respiratory status and sedation level closely until sedation level is stable at <3 and respiratory status is satisfactory • Decrease opioid dose 25%–50% or notify HCP or anesthesiologist for orders • Consider giving a non-sedating, opioid-sparing nonopioid, such as acetaminophen or an NSAID, if not contraindicated
4. Somnolent, minimal or no response to verbal or physical stimulation	• Unacceptable • Stop opioid • Consider giving naloxone • Notify HCP or anesthesiologist • Monitor respiratory status and sedation level closely until sedation level is stable at <3 and respiratory status is satisfactory

Adapted from Pasero C: Assessment of sedation during opioid administration for pain management, *J PeriAnesthesia Nurs* 24:186, 2009.

For patients who are excessively sedated or unresponsive, we can give naloxone, an opioid antagonist that rapidly reverses the effects of opioids. It can be given by IV, subcutaneous, or intranasal routes. A hand-held autoinjector containing naloxone (Evzio) can be used by a caregiver or family member to treat a person known or suspected to have had an opioid overdose. Since naloxone is an opioid antagonist, its use can precipitate severe, agonizing pain, profound withdrawal symptoms, hypertension, and pulmonary edema. Because naloxone's half-life is shorter than that of most opioids, it is important to frequently monitor the patient. You may need to give repeated doses.

Pruritus (itching) is another common side effect of opioids. It occurs most often when patients receive opioids by neuraxial (i.e., epidural, intrathecal) routes. Managing opioid-induced pruritus in noncancer patients may include low-dose infusions of naloxone.

A rare but concerning problem with long-term and sometimes short-term use of high-dose opioids is *opioid-induced hyperalgesia* (OIH).[14] OIH is a state of nociceptive sensitization caused by opioid exposure. It is a paradoxical response in which patients become more sensitive to certain painful stimuli and report increased pain with opioid use. We do not understand the exact cause of OIH. It may be due to neuroplasticity changes.

Adjuvant Analgesic Therapy

Analgesic adjuvants drugs are used alone or in conjunction with opioid and nonopioid analgesics (Table 9.11). Most of

TABLE 9.11 Drug Therapy

Adjuvant Drugs Used for Pain

Drug	Specific Indication	Nursing Considerations
α_2-Adrenergic Agonists		
clonidine (Duraclon) tizanidine (Zanaflex)	Especially useful for neuropathic pain when given intrathecally	• Side effects include sedation, orthostatic hypotension, dry mouth • Often combined with anesthetics (e.g., bupivacaine)
Anesthetics: Local		
capsaicin (active compound of chili peppers)	Pain associated with arthritis, postherpetic neuralgia, diabetic neuropathy	• Apply very sparingly onto affected area. • Use gloves or wash hands with soap and water after application • Monitor for side effects: Skin irritation (burning, stinging) at application site and cough when inhaled
lidocaine (L-M-X)	Topical local anesthetic cream applied to intact skin before venipuncture or lumbar puncture. May be effective for postherpetic neuralgia	• Apply bubble layer to intact skin and wait at least 20–30 min before wiping and performing painful procedure • Duration is around 60 min after wiped from skin • Available without prescription
lidocaine 2.5% + prilocaine 2.5% (topical eutectic mixture of local anesthetics [EMLA])	Longer time to take effect than L-M-X	• Apply under an occlusive dressing (e.g., Tegaderm, DuoDerm) or on an anesthetic disk • Side effects include mild erythema, edema, skin blanching
Anesthetics: Oral or Systemic		
5% lidocaine-impregnated transdermal patch (Lidoderm patch)	Postherpetic neuralgia	• Local skin reactions (e.g., change in color, colored spots, irritation, itching, rash, burning) occur at the site of application; typically mild
mexiletine	Diabetic neuropathy Neuropathic pain	• Monitor for side effects: High incidence of nausea, dizziness, perioral numbness, paresthesia, tremor, seizures (at high doses), dysrhythmias, and myocardial depression • Avoid in patients with preexisting heart disease
Antidepressants		
Tricyclic Antidepressants (TCAs)		
amitriptyline desipramine (Norpramin) doxepin imipramine (Tofranil) nortriptyline (Pamelor)	Neuropathic pain	• Side-effect profile differs for each agent and is often dose-dependent • Common side effects include anticholinergic effects (e.g., dry mouth) and sedation • Monitor for anticholinergic side effects • Titrate slowly over days to weeks to reach optimal therapeutic doses
Serotonin Norepinephrine Reuptake Inhibitor (SNRI) Antidepressants		
duloxetine (Cymbalta) milnacipran (Savella) venlafaxine (Effexor)	Neuropathic pain Multimodal therapy for acute pain (venlafaxine) Fibromyalgia (duloxetine, milnacipran)	• Side effects vary with each agent • Decreased arousal and desire for sex
Other Antidepressants		
bupropion (Wellbutrin)	Neuropathic pain Headaches	• Low risk for sexual problems and sedation • Distinguished from TCAs and SNRIs as an inhibitor of norepinephrine and dopamine uptake
Antiseizure Drugs		
First generation: carbamazepine (Tegretol), phenytoin (Dilantin) Second generation: gabapentin (Neurontin), lamotrigine (Lamictal), pregabalin (Lyrica)	Neuropathic pain Multimodal therapy for acute pain (gabapentin, pregabalin) Fibromyalgia (pregabalin)	• Start with low doses, increase slowly • Side effects vary with each agent
Cannabinoids		
dronabinol (Marinol)	Neuropathic pain Certain pain syndromes	• May relieve nausea and increase appetite • May have opioid-sparing effects, possibly reducing opioid tolerance and symptoms of opioid withdrawal
Corticosteroids		
dexamethasone (Decadron)	Inflammation	• Avoid high doses for long-term use
γ-Aminobutyric Acid (GABA)-Receptor Agonist		
baclofen (Lioresal)	Neuropathic pain Muscle spasms	• Monitor for weakness, urinary problems • Avoid abrupt discontinuation because of central nervous system irritability

Adapted from Portenoy RK, Ahmed E, Keilson YY: Cancer pain management: adjuvant analgesics. Retrieved from https://www.uptodate.com/contents/cancer-pain-management-adjuvant-analgesics-coanalgesics.

these drugs were developed for other purposes (e.g., antiseizure drugs, antidepressants) and found to be effective for treating pain. Antidepressants and antiseizure drugs are the recommended first-line agents for treating neuropathic pain.[15]

α_2-Adrenergic agonists. Clonidine and tizanidine (Zanaflex) are the most widely used α_2-adrenergic agonists. They likely work on the central inhibitory α-adrenergic receptors. These agents may also decrease norepinephrine release peripherally. They are helpful in treating chronic headache and neuropathic pain.

Antidepressants. TCAs enhance the descending inhibitory system by preventing the cellular reuptake of serotonin and norepinephrine. Higher levels of serotonin and norepinephrine in the synapse inhibit the transmission of nociceptive signals in the CNS. Other potential beneficial actions include sodium channel modulation, α_1-adrenergic antagonist effects, and a weak NMDA receptor modulation. They are effective for a variety of pain syndromes, especially neuropathic pain syndromes. However, side effects, such as sedation, dry mouth, blurred vision, and weight gain, limit their use. Antidepressants that selectively inhibit reuptake of serotonin and norepinephrine (SNRIs) are effective for many neuropathic pain syndromes and have fewer side effects than the TCAs. These agents include venlafaxine, desvenlafaxine (Pristiq), milnacipran (Savella), and bupropion.

Antiseizure drugs. Antiseizure drugs affect peripheral nerves and the CNS in several ways. These include sodium channel modulation, central calcium channel modulation, and changes in excitatory amino acids and other receptors. Agents such as gabapentin (Neurontin), lamotrigine (Lamictal), and pregabalin (Lyrica) are valuable adjuvant agents in chronic pain therapy. We are using them more for treating acute pain.

GABA-receptor agonist. Baclofen, an agonist at GABA receptors, can interfere with the transmission of nociceptive impulses. It helps manage muscle spasms and neuropathic pain. It crosses the blood-brain barrier poorly and is much more effective for spasticity when delivered intrathecally.

Corticosteroids. Corticosteroids include dexamethasone, prednisone, and methylprednisolone (Medrol). They are used for managing acute and chronic cancer pain, pain from spinal cord compression, and inflammatory joint pain syndromes. Mechanisms of action may be related to the ability of corticosteroids to decrease edema and inflammation.

Corticosteroids have many side effects, especially when given chronically in high doses. These include hyperglycemia, fluid retention, dyspepsia and GI bleeding, impaired healing, muscle wasting, osteoporosis, adrenal suppression, and susceptibility to infection. Because they act through the same final pathway as NSAIDs, do not give corticosteroids at the same time as NSAIDs.

Local anesthetics. Local anesthetics, such as bupivacaine and ropivacaine, can be given epidurally by continuous infusion or by intermittent or continuous infusion with regional nerve blocks to manage acute pain from surgery or trauma. A systemic lidocaine IV infusion is sometimes used for neuropathic and postoperative visceral pain. Topical applications interrupt transmission of pain signals to the brain. For example, 5% lidocaine patch (Lidoderm) is a first-line agent for treating several types of neuropathic pain. Oral therapy with mexiletine (Mexitil) may be an option for treating chronic severe neuropathic pain that is refractory to other analgesics.

Cannabinoids. Cannabinoid-derived medications show promise in treating neuropathic pain, certain pain syndromes, and some symptoms.[16] Synthetic cannabinoids (e.g., dronabinol [Marinol]) have been approved for medical use. Smoking marijuana or cannabis rapidly increases plasma levels of tetrahydrocannabinol (THC). The increase depends on composition of the marijuana cigarette and inhalation technique. As a result, this form has variable pain relief. With commercially available oral preparations, the absorption and bioavailability are more reliable and predictable.

Cannabinoids exert their analgesic effects primarily through the cannabinoid-l (CB1) and CB2 receptors. Activation of cannabinoid receptors modulates neurotransmission in the serotoninergic, dopaminergic, and glutamatergic systems, as well as other systems. Cannabinoids also enhance the endogenous opioid system. Other beneficial effects include alleviating nausea and increased appetite. They may have opioid-sparing effects, possibly reducing opioid tolerance and symptoms of opioid withdrawal.

Administration

Scheduling. Appropriate analgesic scheduling focuses on preventing or controlling pain, rather than providing analgesics only after the patient's pain has become severe. An example is premedicating a patient before a procedure or activity that will likely cause pain. Similarly, a patient with constant pain should receive analgesics around the clock rather than on an "as needed" (PRN) basis. These strategies control pain before it starts and usually result in lower analgesic requirements.

Titration. *Analgesic titration* is dose adjustment based on assessment of the adequacy of analgesic effect versus the side effects produced. The amount of analgesic needed to manage pain varies widely. Titration is an important strategy in addressing this variability. An analgesic can be titrated upward or downward, depending on the situation. For example, in a postoperative patient the dose of analgesic decreases over time as the acute pain resolves. On the other hand, opioids for chronic, severe cancer pain may be titrated upward many times over the course of the disease to maintain adequate pain control. The goal of titration is to use the smallest dose of analgesic that provides effective pain control with the fewest side effects.

Equianalgesic dosing. The term **equianalgesic dose** refers to a dose of one analgesic that is equivalent in pain-relieving effects to a given dose of another analgesic (Table 9.12). This equivalence helps guide opioid dosing when changing routes or opioids when a specific drug is ineffective or causes intolerable side effects. Equianalgesic charts and conversion programs are widely available in clinical guidelines, in agency pain protocols, and on the Internet. They are useful tools, but you need to understand their limitations since these doses are estimates. To ensure safety, carefully monitor the patient with all changes in opioid therapy and adjust as needed.

Administration routes. We can deliver opioids and other analgesic agents by many routes. This flexibility allows the

TABLE 9.12 Opioid Equianalgesic Doses

	DOSE EQUAL TO PARENTERAL MORPHINE 10 mg	
Drug	**Oral (mg)**	**Parenteral (IM, IV, Subcutaneous) (mg)**
Codeine	200	120–130
Fentanyl	NA	0.1 (100 mcg)
Hydrocodone	30	NA
Hydromorphone	7.5	1.5
Levorphanol	4	2
Morphine	30	10
Oxycodone	20	NA

[a]All equivalencies are approximations. These amounts can be affected by many factors, including interpatient variability, type of pain, and tolerance. Monitor patients for effectiveness and adverse reactions and adjust the dose accordingly.

HCP to (1) target a particular anatomic source of the pain, (2) achieve therapeutic blood levels rapidly when necessary, (3) avoid certain side effects through localized administration, and (4) provide analgesia when patients are unable to swallow. The next section highlights the uses and nursing considerations for analgesic agents delivered through a variety of routes.

Oral. Oral administration is the route of choice for the person with a functioning GI system. Most pain medications are available in oral preparations, such as liquid and tablet. For opioids, larger oral doses are needed to achieve the equivalent analgesia of doses given IM or IV (Table 9.12). For example, 5 mg of IV morphine is equivalent to around 15 mg of oral morphine. The reason larger doses are needed is related to the *first-pass effect* of hepatic metabolism. This means that oral opioids are absorbed from the GI tract into the portal circulation and shunted to the liver. Partial metabolism in the liver occurs before the drug enters the systemic circulation and becomes available to peripheral receptors or can cross the blood-brain barrier and access CNS opioid receptors, which is needed to produce analgesia. Oral opioids are as effective as parenteral opioids if the dose is large enough to compensate for the first-pass metabolism.

Many opioids are available in short-acting (immediate-release) and long-acting (sustained-release or extended-release) oral preparations. Immediate-release products are effective in providing rapid, short-term pain relief. Sustained-release or extended-release preparations are often given every 8 to 12 hours. Some preparations (e.g., Kadian) may be dosed every 24 hours.

! SAFETY ALERT

Sustained-Release or Extended-Release Preparations

- These drugs are not to be crushed, broken, dissolved, or chewed. They should be swallowed whole.
- If all the drug is released into a person at once, serious side effects can occur, including death from overdose.

Transmucosal and buccal routes. Although we have historically given morphine sublingually to people with cancer pain who have problems swallowing, little of the drug is absorbed from the sublingual tissue. Instead, most of the drug dissolves in saliva and is swallowed, making its absorption like that of oral morphine.

Several transmucosal fentanyl products are options in treating BTP. Oral transmucosal fentanyl citrate (Actiq) contains fentanyl in a flavored lozenge on a stick. The lozenge is rubbed against the buccal surface (not sucked as a lollipop), allowing the buccal mucosa to absorb the fentanyl. Fentanyl buccal tablet (Fentora) is a quickly dissolving a buccal tablet. Transmucosal absorption allows the drug to enter the bloodstream and travel directly to the CNS. Pain relief typically occurs 5 to 7 minutes after administration. These agents should be used only for patients who are already receiving and are tolerant to opioid therapy.

Intranasal route. Intranasal administration allows delivery of medication to highly vascular mucosa and avoids the first-pass effect. Butorphanol is given for acute headache and other intense, recurrent types of pain. A transmucosal fentanyl nasal spray (Lazanda) is available for treating BTP.

Rectal. We often overlook the rectal route. It is especially useful when the patient cannot take an analgesic by mouth, such as with severe nausea and vomiting or at end of life. Analgesics that are available as rectal suppositories include hydromorphone, oxymorphone, morphine, and acetaminophen. If rectal preparations are not available, many oral agents can be given rectally if the patient is unable to take medications by mouth.

Transdermal route. Transdermal patches offer systemic or local delivery. Fentanyl (Duragesic) is useful for the patient who cannot tolerate oral analgesic drugs. Absorption from the patch is slow. It takes 12 to 17 hours to reach full effect with the first application. Therefore transdermal fentanyl is not suitable for rapid dose titration but better if the patient's pain is stable and the dose needed to control it is known. Patches may have to be changed every 48 hours rather than the recommended 72 hours based on the patient's response. Patches should be applied to intact, nonhair skin on the upper extremities or back. Rashes caused by the patch's adhesive may be reduced by preparing the skin 1 hour before placement with a weak corticosteroid cream. Biocclusive dressings are available if the patch falls off because of sweating. Remove a fentanyl patch if the patient has a fever. The elevated body heat can cause increased absorption of the medication and lead to increased side effects. In addition, teach patients to avoid heat application over the patch for extended periods of time (e.g., heating pad, long hot showers). A transdermal PCA system (iontophoretic transdermal system [ITS]) is available.

A 5% lidocaine-impregnated transdermal patch (Lidoderm patch) can be used for local delivery of pain medication. The patch is placed directly on the intact, nonhair skin in the area of pain and left in place for up to 12 hours. There are few systemic side effects, even with chronic use.

Creams and lotions containing 10% trolamine salicylate (e.g., Aspercreme) are available for joint and muscle pain. This aspirin-like substance is absorbed locally. This route avoids GI irritation but not the other side effects of high-dose salicylates. Topical diclofenac solution or a diclofenac patch (Flector) can be effective in treating local pain, for example, in patients with osteoarthritic knee pain.

Other topical analgesic agents, such as capsaicin (e.g., Zostrix) and lidocaine (L-M-X cream), also provide analgesia. Derived from red chili pepper, capsaicin acts on C-fiber heat receptors. If used 3 or 4 times a day for 4 to 6 weeks, it will cause the C nociceptor fibers to become inactive. The result is neuronal resistance to painful stimuli. Capsaicin may control pain from diabetic neuropathy, arthritis, and postherpetic neuralgia. We can apply L-M-X cream to control pain from venipunctures. Cover the targeted area of intact skin with a layer of L-M-X for at least 20 to 30 minutes, then wipe it off prior to beginning.

Parenteral routes. Parenteral routes include IV and subcutaneous administration. Single, repeated, or continuous dosing is possible with parenteral routes. IV administration is the best route when immediate analgesia and rapid titration are needed. Continuous IV infusions provide excellent steady-state analgesia through stable blood levels.

Onset of analgesia after subcutaneous administration is slow. Thus we rarely use the subcutaneous route for acute pain management. Continuous subcutaneous infusions are effective for pain management at the end of life. This route is especially helpful for people with abnormal GI function and limited venous access.

The IM route is not recommended. Injections cause significant pain and result in unreliable absorption. With chronic use, IM injections can result in abscesses and fibrosis.

Intraspinal delivery. Intraspinal or neuraxial opioid therapy involves inserting a catheter into the subarachnoid space *(intrathecal delivery)* or the epidural space *(epidural delivery)* (Fig. 9.6). Analgesics are injected either by intermittent bolus doses or continuous infusion.

Percutaneously placed temporary catheters are used for short-term therapy (2 to 4 days). While the lumbar region is the most common site of placement, epidural catheters may be placed at any point along the spinal column (cervical, thoracic, lumbar, or caudal). The tip of the epidural catheter is placed as close to the nerve supplying the painful dermatome as possible. For example, a thoracic catheter is placed for upper abdominal surgery, and a high lumbar catheter is used for lower abdominal surgery. Fluoroscopy ensures correct placement of the catheter.

Intraspinal analgesics are highly potent because they are delivered close to the receptors in the spinal cord dorsal horn. Smaller doses of analgesics are needed than with other routes, including IV. For example, 1 mg of intrathecal morphine equals 10 mg of epidural morphine, and 100 mg of IV morphine. Intraspinal analgesics include morphine, fentanyl, sufentanil (Sufenta), alfentanil (Alfenta), hydromorphone, clonidine, and ziconotide. Ziconotide is a calcium channel receptor modulator for treating neuropathic pain syndromes. Nausea, itching, and urinary retention are common side effects of intraspinal opioids.

Complications of intraspinal analgesia include catheter displacement and migration, accidental infusions of neurotoxic agents, epidural hematomas, and infection. Clinical manifestations of catheter displacement or migration depend on

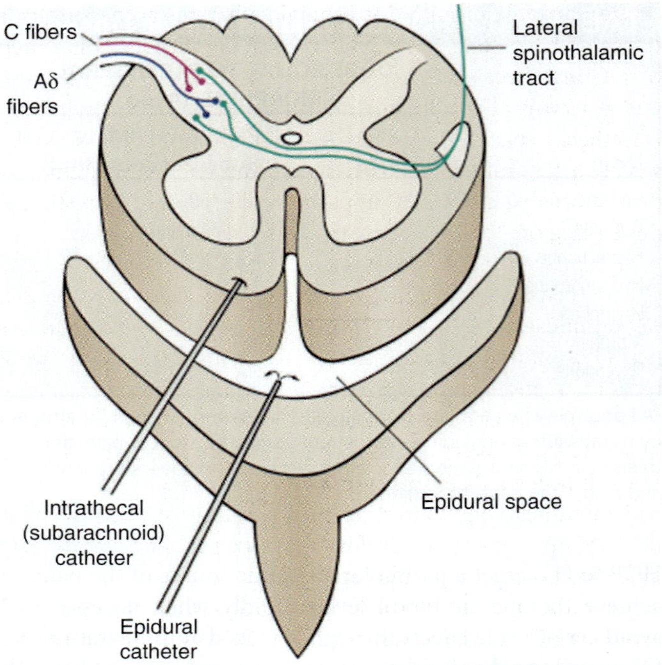

Fig. 9.6 Cross section of spinal cord with placement of catheters into the subarachnoid space (intrathecal delivery) and the epidural space (epidural delivery). (From Urden LD, Stacy KM, Lough ME: *Critical care nursing: diagnosis and management*, ed 8, St Louis, 2018, Elsevier.)

catheter location and the drug. A catheter that migrates out of the intrathecal or epidural space causes a decrease in pain relief with no improvement with more boluses or increases in the infusion rate. If an epidural catheter migrates into the subarachnoid space, increased side effects become quickly apparent. Somnolence, confusion, and increased anesthesia (if the infusion contains an anesthetic) may occur. Follow agency policy for aspirating cerebrospinal fluid to determine intrathecal catheter placement. Migration of a catheter into a blood vessel may cause an increase in side effects because of systemic drug distribution.

Many drugs and chemicals are highly neurotoxic when given intraspinally. These include antibiotics, chemotherapy agents, potassium, parenteral nutrition, and many preservatives, such as alcohol and phenol. To avoid accidental injection of IV drugs into an intraspinal catheter, clearly mark the catheter as an intraspinal access device.

Infection is a rare but serious complication of intraspinal analgesia. Assess the skin around the exit site for inflammation, drainage, or pain. Manifestations of an intraspinal infection include diffuse back pain, pain or paresthesia during bolus injection, and unexplained sensory or motor deficits in the lower limbs. Fever may or may not be present. Acute bacterial infection (meningitis) is manifested by photophobia, neck stiffness, fever, headache, and altered mental status. Regular, meticulous wound care and using sterile technique when caring for the catheter and injecting drugs reduces infection risk.

Long-term epidural catheters may be placed for terminal cancer patients or patients with certain pain syndromes that are unresponsive to other treatments. If a long-term indwelling epidural catheter is used, bacterial filters are recommended.

Implantable pumps. Intraspinal catheters can be surgically implanted for long-term pain relief. The surgical placement of an intrathecal catheter to a subcutaneously placed pump and reservoir allows for the delivery of drugs directly into the intrathecal space. The pump is normally placed in a pocket made in the subcutaneous tissue of the abdomen. It may be programmable or fixed. Pumps are refilled every 30 to 90 days, depending on flow rate, mixture, and reservoir size.

Patient-controlled analgesia. Patient-controlled analgesia (PCA) (demand analgesia) is a method that allows the patient to self-administer preset doses of an analgesic within a prescribed time period by activating an infusion pump. Routes of administration include IV and epidural (patient-controlled epidural analgesia [PCEA]). PCA also can be adapted for oral administration. With PCA/PCEA, a dose of opioid is delivered when the patient decides a dose is needed. PCA/PCEA uses an infusion system in which the patient pushes a button to receive a bolus infusion of an analgesic. PCA/PCEA is used widely for the management of acute pain, including postoperative and cancer pain.

Opioids, such as morphine and hydromorphone, are often given via PCA therapy. Sometimes IV PCA is given with a continuous or background infusion called a *basal rate,* depending on the patient's opioid requirement. Adding a basal rate in opioid-naive patients and those at risk for adverse respiratory outcomes (e.g., older age, obstructive sleep apnea, lung disease) may lead to serious respiratory events.

PCEA often combines an opioid and local anesthetic. Basal rates are often used with PCEA. Because the medication is delivered directly into the epidural space, the amount of opioid is 10 times less than is needed by IV route. This lessens the risk for respiratory depression but does not eliminate it.

Patient teaching is very important with the use of PCA/PCEA. Help the patient understand the mechanics of the machine. Teach the patient to self-administer the analgesic before pain is severe. Assure the patient that they cannot "overdose" because the pump is programmed to deliver a maximum number of doses per hour. The patient will not receive more analgesic once they reach the maximum dose. If the maximum dose is inadequate to relieve pain, we can reprogram the pump to increase the amount or frequency of dosing. In addition, you can give bolus doses if they are part of the HCP's orders. To make a smooth transition from infusion PCA to oral drugs, the patient should receive increasing doses of oral drug while we taper the PCA analgesic.

Patient-controlled delivery systems are intended for use by the patient. An *authorized agent-controlled analgesia (AACA)* is a method of delivery performed by a consistently available and competent person for patients who are unable to independently activate PCA devices. This authorized agent must be carefully selected, taught the principles of PCA, and capable of recognizing pain and the appropriate times to give medication via the PCA device. Understand your agency's policies about PCA and AACA.

Interventional Therapy

Therapeutic Nerve Blocks

Nerve blocks involve 1-time or continuous infusion of local anesthetics into an area to produce pain relief. We also call these techniques *regional anesthesia.* Nerve blocks interrupt all afferent and efferent transmission to the area and are not specific to nociceptive pathways. They include local infiltration of anesthetics into a surgical area (e.g., chest incisions, inguinal hernia) and injection of anesthetic into a specific nerve (e.g., occipital, pudendal nerve) or nerve plexus (e.g., brachial, celiac plexus). Nerve blocks can be used during and after surgery to manage pain. For longer-term relief of chronic pain syndromes, we can give local anesthetics by a continuous infusion.

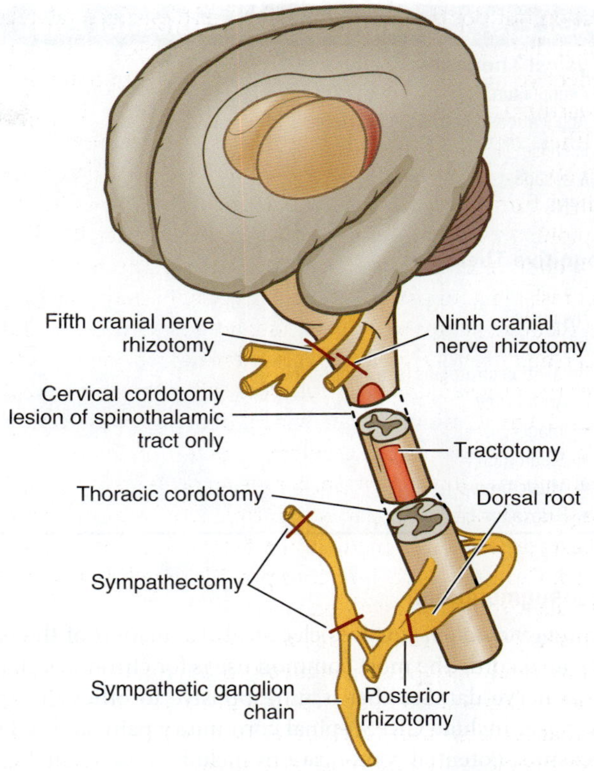

Fig. 9.7 Sites of neurosurgical procedures for pain relief.

Adverse effects of nerve blocks are like those for local anesthetics delivered by other systemic routes. Effects include systemic toxicity resulting in dysrhythmias, confusion, nausea and vomiting, blurred vision, tinnitus, and metallic taste. Temporary nerve blocks affect motor function and sensation and typically last 2 to 24 hours, depending on the agent and the site of injection. Motor ability generally returns before sensation.

Neuroablative techniques. *Neuroablative interventions* are done for severe pain that is unresponsive to all other therapies. They involve destroying nerves, thereby interrupting pain transmission. Destruction is by surgical resection or thermocoagulation, including radiofrequency coagulation. Neuroablative interventions that destroy the sensory division of a peripheral or spinal nerve are classified as *neurectomies, rhizotomies,* and *sympathectomies.* Neurosurgical procedures that ablate the lateral spinothalamic tract are classified as *cordotomies* if the tract is interrupted in the spinal cord or *tractotomies* if the interruption is in the medulla or midbrain of the brainstem (Fig. 9.7). Cordotomy and tractotomy can be done with the aid of local anesthesia by a percutaneous technique under fluoroscopy.

TABLE 9.13 Nondrug Therapies for Pain

Physical Therapies
- Acupuncture
- Application of heat and cold (Table 9.14)
- Exercise
- Massage
- TENS

Cognitive Therapies
- Distraction
- Hypnosis
- Imagery
- Relaxation strategies (see Chapter 7)
  - Art therapy
  - Imagery
  - Meditation
  - Music therapy
  - Relaxation breathing

Neuroaugmentation

Neuroaugmentation involves electrical stimulation of the brain and spinal cord. The most common use is for chronic back pain due to nerve damage that is unresponsive to other therapies. Other uses include CRPS, spinal cord injury pain, and interstitial cystitis. Potential complications include those related to the surgery (bleeding, infection), migration of the generator (which usually is implanted in the subcutaneous tissues of the upper gluteal or pectoralis area), and nerve damage.

Nondrug Therapies for Pain

Nondrug strategies play an important role in pain management (Table 9.13). They can reduce the dose of an analgesic needed to relieve pain and thereby minimize side effects of drug therapy. Moreover, they increase the patient's sense of personal control about managing pain and increase coping skills. We think some strategies alter ascending nociceptive input or stimulate descending pain modulation mechanisms. These nondrug therapies are useful for both acute and chronic pain.

Physical Pain Relief Strategies

Massage. Massage may be useful to alleviate certain types of acute and chronic pain.[17] Many different massage techniques exist. These include moving the hands or fingers over the skin slowly or briskly with long strokes or in circles (superficial massage) or applying firm pressure to the skin to maintain contact while massaging the underlying tissues (deep massage). Another type is trigger point massage. A **trigger point** is a circumscribed hypersensitive area within a tight band of muscle. It is caused by acute or chronic muscle strain. It feels like a tight knot under the skin. Trigger point massage is done by applying strong, sustained digital pressure; deep massage; or gentler massage with ice followed by muscle heating. See more about massage in Chapter 7.

Exercise. Exercise is an essential part of the treatment plan for patients with chronic pain, especially those with musculoskeletal pain.[18] Many patients become physically deconditioned from their pain, which in turn leads to more

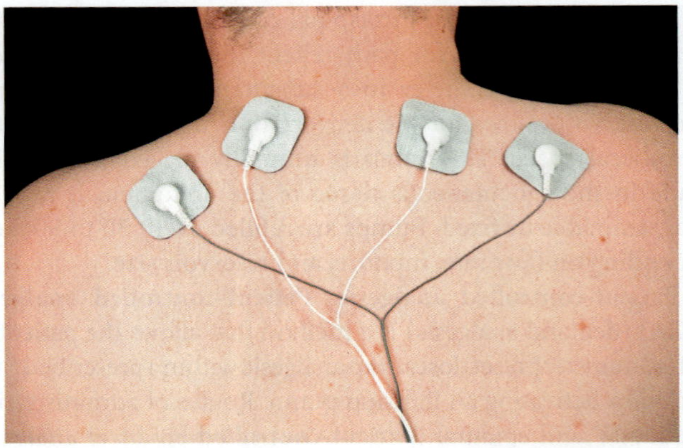

Fig. 9.8 Treatment of pain with TENS treatment after shoulder surgery. (© Noel Moore/Hemera/Thinkstock.)

pain. Exercise acts via many mechanisms to relieve pain. It enhances circulation and cardiovascular fitness, reduces edema, increases muscle strength and flexibility, and enhances physical and psychosocial functioning. It is important to tailor an exercise program to the patient's physical needs and lifestyle. It may include aerobic exercise, stretching, and strengthening exercises. Trained personnel (e.g., physical therapist) should supervise the program.

Transcutaneous electrical nerve stimulation. *Transcutaneous electrical nerve stimulation* (TENS) involves the delivery of an electric current through electrodes applied to the skin surface over the painful region, at trigger points, or over a peripheral nerve.[19] A TENS system consists of 2 or more electrodes connected by lead wires to a small, battery-operated stimulator (Fig. 9.8). A physical therapist is often responsible for delivering TENS therapy, although nurses can be trained in the technique. TENS may be used for acute pain, including postoperative pain and pain from physical trauma. The effects of TENS on chronic pain are less clear, but it may be effective in these cases.

Acupuncture. Acupuncture is a technique of traditional Chinese medicine in which very thin needles are inserted into the body at designated points.[20] It is used for many kinds of pain. Acupuncture is described in Chapter 7.

Heat therapy. Heat therapy is the application of either moist or dry heat to the skin. Heat therapy can be either superficial or deep. We can apply heat using an electric heating pad (dry or moist), a hot pack, hot moist compresses, warm wax (paraffin), or a hot water bottle. To expose large areas of the body, patients can immerse themselves in a hot bath, shower, or whirlpool. Physical therapy departments provide deep-heat therapy through techniques such as short-wave diathermy, microwave diathermy, and ultrasound therapy. Patient and caregiver teaching about heat therapy is described in Table 9.14.

Cold therapy. Cold therapy involves the application of either moist or dry cold to the skin. Dry cold can be applied by using an ice bag. Moist cold can be applied by using towels soaked in ice water, cold hydrocollator packs, or immersion in a bath or under running cold water. Icing with ice cubes or blocks of ice made to resemble popsicles is another technique used for pain relief. Patient and caregiver teaching about cold therapy is described in Table 9.14.

TABLE 9.14 PATIENT & CAREGIVER TEACHING

Heat and Cold Therapy

Include the following instructions when teaching the patient and caregiver about superficial heat or cold techniques:

Heat Therapy

- Do not use heat on an area that is being treated with radiation therapy, is bleeding, has decreased sensation, or has been injured in the past 24 hours.
- Do not use any menthol-containing products (e.g., Ben-Gay, Vicks, Icy Hot) with heat applications because this may cause burns.
- Cover the heat source with a towel or cloth before applying to the skin to prevent burns.

Cold Therapy

- Cover the cold source with a cloth or towel before applying to the skin to prevent tissue damage.
- Do not apply cold to areas that are being treated with radiation therapy, have open wounds, or have poor circulation.
- If it is not possible to apply the cold directly to the painful site, try applying it right above or below the painful site or on the opposite side of the body on the corresponding site (e.g., left elbow if the right elbow hurts).

Cognitive Therapies

Techniques to alter the affective, cognitive, and behavior components of pain include a variety of cognitive strategies and behavior approaches.[21] For example, patients can identify and challenge negative pain-related thoughts and replace them with more positive coping thoughts. Some techniques need little training. They may be adopted independently by the patient. For others, a trained therapist is needed.

Distraction. Distraction involves redirection of attention away from the pain and onto something.[22] It is a simple but powerful strategy to relieve pain. Distraction involves engaging the patient in any activity that can hold their attention (e.g., watching TV or a movie, conversing, listening to music). It is important to match the activity with the patient's energy level and ability to concentrate.

Hypnosis. Hypnotherapy is a structured technique that enables a patient to achieve a state of heightened awareness and focused concentration that can be used to alter the patient's pain perception.[23] Hypnosis should be delivered and monitored only by specially trained clinicians.

Relaxation strategies. Relaxation strategies reduce stress, decrease acute anxiety, distract from pain, ease muscle tension, combat fatigue, promote sleep, and enhance the effectiveness of other pain relief measures. Relaxation strategies include relaxation breathing, music, imagery, meditation, muscle relaxation, and art (see Chapter 7).

❖ NURSING AND INTERPROFESSIONAL MANAGEMENT: PAIN

You are an important member of the interprofessional pain management team. You provide input into the assessment and reassessment of pain (Table 9.15). You help in planning and implementing treatments, including teaching, advocacy, and support of the patient, caregiver, and family. Because patients in any care setting can have pain, you must be knowledgeable about current therapies and flexible in trying new approaches to pain management.

TABLE 9.15 NURSING MANAGEMENT

Pain Management

- Assess pain characteristics (pattern and onset, area or location, intensity, quality, associated symptoms, and management strategies) (Table 9.6).
- Collaborate with patient, caregivers, and interprofessional team members to develop treatment plan for patient's pain (including drug and nondrug therapies).
- Give ordered analgesia. Base the decision on administering range orders on a thorough pain assessment and knowledge of the medication being given.
- Adhere to system safeguards that minimize the potential for misuse of controlled substances.
- Implement measures to reduce or eliminate common side effects of drug therapy.
- Give pretreatment analgesia and/or nonpharmacologic strategies before painful procedures.
- Collaborate with the patient, caregiver, and other health professionals to select and implement nondrug pain relief measures (Table 9.13, 9.14, and 9.15).
- Evaluate whether current treatment plan is effective through ongoing assessment.
- Implement measures to address problems that precipitate or increase the pain experience, such as depression.
- Help the patient develop strategies to help with participation in activities of daily living in the home, work, and socially.
- Promote adequate periods of rest and sleep and institute measures to address impaired sleep if present.
- Help the patient and caregivers cope with the pain experience by using positive coping and stress management behaviors.
- Teach patient and caregiver about treatment plan (Tables 9.16 and 9.17).
- Implement discharge teaching about pain management.
- Provide effective supervision of AP:
  - Help with screening for pain, and notify RN if patient expresses pain.
  - Take and report vital signs before and after pain medications are given.
  - Note and report if patient is refusing to take part in ordered activities, such as ambulation (since this may indicate inadequate pain management).

Together with the patient, develop a written agreement or treatment plan that describes the pain management. The plan should ensure that pain will be treated based on the patient's perception and report of pain. When appropriate, the plan should outline the gradual tapering of the analgesic dose, with eventual substitution of parenteral analgesics with long-acting oral preparations and possibly cessation of opioids.

Many nursing roles are described earlier in this chapter, including assessing pain, giving treatment, monitoring for side effects, and teaching patients and caregivers. However, the success of these actions depends on your ability to establish a trusting relationship with the patient and caregiver and address their concerns about pain and its treatment.

◆ Effective Communication

Because pain is a subjective, patients need to feel confident that their reporting of pain will be believed and will not be perceived

TABLE 9.16 PATIENT & CAREGIVER TEACHING

Pain Management

Include the following information in the teaching plan for the patient with pain and caregiver:

- Cause of the pain, if known, and how long it may last
- Factors that may be contributing to pain
- Pain assessment methods and reason for frequent monitoring of pain
- Expectations about pain management
- Self-management techniques
- Realistic goals for pain control
- Negative consequences of unrelieved pain
- Need to maintain a record of pain level and effectiveness of treatment
- Safe use of analgesia
- Treat pain with drugs and/or nondrug therapies before it becomes severe
- Medication may stop working after it is taken for a time period. Dosages may need adjusted
- Potential side effects and complications associated with pain therapies can include nausea and vomiting, constipation, sedation and drowsiness, itching, urinary retention, and sweating
- Need to report when pain is not relieved to tolerable levels

as "complaining." The patient and caregiver need to know that you consider the pain significant and understand that pain may profoundly disrupt a person's life. Communicate concern and commit to helping the patient obtain pain relief and cope with any unrelieved pain. Support the patient and caregiver through the period of trial and error that may be necessary to implement an effective therapeutic plan. It is important to clarify responsibilities in pain relief. Help the patient understand the role of the interprofessional team members, as well as the patient's roles and expectations.

Evaluate the impact that the pain has on the lives of the patient and caregiver. Table 9.16 addresses teaching needs of patients and caregivers related to pain management.

◆ Challenges to Effective Pain Management

Common challenges to effective pain management include misunderstandings about tolerance, physical dependence, and addiction. It is important for you to understand and be able to explain these concepts. Table 9.17 lists barriers to pain management and strategies to address them.

◆ Tolerance

Tolerance occurs with chronic exposure to a variety of drugs. In the case of opioids, tolerance to analgesia is characterized by the need for an increased opioid dose to maintain the same degree of analgesia. The incidence of clinically significant analgesic opioid tolerance in chronic pain patients is unknown, since dosage needs may increase as the disease (e.g., cancer) progresses. It is essential to assess for increased analgesic needs in patients on long-term therapy. The interprofessional team must evaluate and rule out other causes of increased analgesic needs, such as disease progression or infection.

If significant tolerance to opioids develops and the opioid is losing its effectiveness or if intolerable side effects occur with dose escalation, the practice of *opioid rotation* may be considered. This involves switching from one opioid to another, assuming that the new opioid will be more effective at lower equianalgesic doses. However, very high opioid doses can result in OIH rather than pain relief. This means that increases in the dose can lead to higher pain levels.

◆ Physical Dependence

Like tolerance, physical dependence is a normal physiologic response to ongoing exposure to drugs. It is manifested by a withdrawal syndrome when the drug is abruptly decreased. Manifestations of opioid withdrawal are listed in Table 9.18. When opioids are no longer needed to provide pain relief, a tapering schedule should be used with careful monitoring. A typical tapering schedule may involve reducing the dose by 20% to 50% per day. The goal is to reduce the amount of medication and at the same time minimize adverse and withdrawal effects.

◆ Pseudoaddiction

Inadequate treatment of pain can lead to a phenomenon called *pseudoaddiction*. This occurs when patients show behaviors associated with addiction (e.g., frequent requests for analgesic refills or higher dosages), but the behaviors resolve with adequate treatment of the patient's pain. These patients are often labeled as drug seeking. This can result in mistrust between the patient and HCP. Effective communication strategies and optimal pain management can help avoid this problem.

◆ Addiction

Addiction is a complex neurobiologic condition characterized by aberrant behaviors arising from a drive to obtain and take substances for reasons other than the prescribed therapeutic value (see Chapter 11). Tolerance and physical dependence are not indicators of addiction. Rather, they are normal physiologic responses to chronic exposure to certain drugs, including opioids. If we suspect addiction, it must be investigated and appropriately diagnosed. The hallmarks of addiction include (1) compulsive use, (2) loss of control of use, and (3) continued use despite risk of harm.

INSTITUTIONALIZING PAIN EDUCATION AND MANAGEMENT

Besides patient and caregiver barriers, other barriers to effective and safe pain management include inadequate HCP education and lack of agency support. Traditionally, medical and nursing school curricula have spent little time teaching future physicians and nurses about pain and symptom management. The lack of emphasis on pain has contributed to inadequate training.

We have made progress overcoming these barriers. Medical and nursing schools devote more time to addressing pain. Numerous professional organizations have published evidence-based guidelines for assessing and managing pain in many patient populations and clinical settings.

Agency commitment and practices are changing clinical practice. One major step is the development and adoption of The Joint Commission (TJC) guideline on pain. Under these standards, health care agencies are required to (1) recognize

TABLE 9.17 PATIENT & CAREGIVER TEACHING

Reducing Barriers to Pain Management

When teaching the patient and caregiver about pain management discuss the following barriers:

Barrier	Nursing Considerations
Fear of addiction	• Acknowledge and normalize fears. • Reinforce that health care team members will be monitoring for signs of addiction.
Fear of tolerance	• Teach that tolerance is a normal physiologic response to chronic opioid therapy. If tolerance does develop, the drug may have to be changed (e.g., morphine in place of oxycodone). • Teach that there is no absolute upper limit to pure opioid agonists (e.g., morphine). Dosages can be increased, and patient should not save drugs for when the pain is worse. • Teach that tolerance develops more slowly to analgesic effects of opioids than to side effects (e.g., sedation, respiratory depression). Tolerance does not develop to constipation, so a regular bowel program should be started early.
Concern about side effects	• Teach methods to prevent and to treat common side effects. • Stress that side effects, such as sedation and nausea, decrease with time. • Explain that different drugs have unique side effects, and other pain drugs can be tried to reduce the specific side effect.
Fear of injections	• Explain that oral medicines are preferred. • Stress that even if oral route becomes unusable, transdermal or indwelling parenteral routes can be used rather than injections.
Desire to be "good" patient	• Discuss that patients are partners in their care and that partnership requires open communication by both patient and nurse. • Stress to patients that they have a responsibility to keep you informed about their pain.
Desire to be stoic	• Explain that although stoicism is a valued behavior in many cultures, failure to report pain can result in undertreatment and severe, unrelieved pain.
Forgetting to take analgesic	• Provide and teach use of pill containers. • Provide methods of record keeping for drug use. • Recruit caregivers to help with the analgesic regimen.
Concern that pain indicates disease progression	• Explain that increased pain or the need for analgesics may reflect tolerance. • Stress that new pain may come from a non–life-threatening source (e.g., muscle spasm, urinary tract infection). • Use drug and nondrug strategies to reduce anxiety. • Ensure that patient and caregivers have current, accurate, comprehensive information about the disease and prognosis. • Provide psychologic support.
Sense of fatalism	• Explain that pain can be managed in most patients. • Explain that most therapies require a period of trial and error. • Stress that side effects can be managed.
Ineffective medication	• Teach that there are multiple options within each category of medication (e.g., opioids, NSAIDs), and another medication from the same category may provide better relief. • Discuss that finding the best treatment regimen may require trial and error. • Include nondrug approaches in treatment plan.

the patient's right to appropriate assessment and management of pain; (2) identify pain in patients during their initial assessment and as needed, during ongoing, periodic reassessments; (3) teach HCPs about pain assessment and management and ensure competency; and (4) teach patients and their families about pain management.

A common concern of health care professionals and caregivers is that giving enough drug to relieve pain will hasten or precipitate death of a terminally ill person. However, there is no scientific evidence that opioids can hasten death, even among patients at the very end of life. Moreover, you have a moral obligation to provide comfort and pain relief at the end of life. Even if there is a concern about the possibility of hastening death, the rule of double effect provides ethical justification. This rule states that if an unwanted consequence (i.e., hastened death) occurs because of an action taken to achieve a moral good (i.e., pain relief), the action is justified if the nurse's intent is to relieve pain and not to hasten death.

MANAGING PAIN IN SPECIAL POPULATIONS

Older Adults

Persistent pain is a common problem in older adults. It is often associated with physical disability and psychosocial problems. The prevalence of chronic pain among community-dwelling older adults exceeds 50%. Among older nursing home patients, it is around 80%. The most common painful conditions among older adults are musculoskeletal conditions, such as osteoarthritis and low back pain. Chronic pain often results in depression, sleep problems, decreased mobility, increased health care

TABLE 9.18 Manifestations of Opioid Withdrawal Syndrome

	Early Response (6–12 hr)	Late Response (48–72 hr)
Psychosocial	• Anxiety	• Excitation
Secretions	• Diaphoresis • Lacrimation • Rhinorrhea	• Diarrhea
Other	• Anorexia • Chills, shaking • Dilated pupils • Piloerection • Tremor • Yawning	• Abdominal pain, cramping • ↑BP • Fever • ↑HR • Insomnia • Nausea and vomiting • Restlessness

use, and physical and social role problems. Despite its high prevalence, pain in older adults is often inadequately assessed and treated.

Several barriers to pain assessment in the older patient exist. Older adults and their HCPs often believe that pain is a normal, inevitable part of aging and that nothing can be done to relieve the pain. Older adults may not report pain for fear of being a "burden" or a "complainer." They may fear taking opioids. In addition, older patients are more likely to use words such as "aching," "soreness," or "discomfort" rather than "pain." Be persistent in asking older adults about pain. Perform your assessment in an unhurried, supportive manner.

Another barrier is the increased prevalence of cognitive, sensory-perceptual, and motor problems that interfere with a person's ability to process information and communicate. Examples include dementia and delirium and poststroke aphasia. Hearing and vision deficits may complicate assessment. Therefore pain assessment tools may have to be adapted for older adults. For example, you many need to use a large-print pain intensity scale. Most older adults, even those with mild to moderate cognitive impairment, can use quantitative scales accurately and reliably.

In older patients with chronic pain, perform a thorough physical assessment and history to identify causes of pain, possible therapies, and potential problems. Assess for depression and functional impairments. They are common among older adults with pain.

Treatment of pain in older adults is complicated by several factors. First, older adults metabolize drugs more slowly than younger people. Thus they are at greater risk for higher blood levels and adverse effects. Apply the adage "start low and go slow" to analgesic therapy in this age group. Second, the use of NSAIDs in older adults is associated with a high frequency of GI bleeding. Third, older adults often are taking many drugs for 1 or more chronic conditions. The addition of analgesics can result in dangerous drug interactions and increased side effects. Last, analgesics, such as opioids, antidepressants, and antiseizure drugs can worsen cognitive problems and ataxia. This requires that HCPs titrate drugs slowly and monitor carefully for side effects.

Treatment plans for older adults must include nondrug modalities. Exercise and patient teaching are important nondrug interventions for older adults with chronic pain. Include family and caregivers in the treatment plan (Tables 9.16 and 9.17).

Patients Unable to Self-Report Pain

Although the patient's self-report is the gold standard of pain assessment, many illnesses and conditions affect a patient's ability to report pain. These diagnoses and conditions include dementia and delirium. For these people, behavior and physiologic changes may be the only indicators of pain. You must be astute at recognizing behavior symptoms of pain

A guide for assessing pain in nonverbal patients is outlined in Table 9.19. Several scales are available to assess pain-related behaviors in nonverbal patients, especially those with advanced dementia and the critically ill. Links to several pain assessment tools are available at the City of Hope Pain and Palliative Care Resource Center website (http://prc.coh.org).

BOX 9.1 EVIDENCE-BASED PRACTICE

Managing Pain in the Patient With Communication Problems

You are caring for G.V., a 70-year-old patient who had an ischemic stroke. G.V. is intermittently awake, able to respond to simple questions, but does not initiate conversation. Based on behavior cues, you believe G.V. is experiencing pain. She is moaning softly when you enter the room for initial assessment at the start of the shift. She appears tense and shifts restlessly in the bed. After reviewing vital signs with the nursing assistant, you determine both her BP and heart rate are elevated since the previous assessment 4 hours ago.

Making Clinical Decisions

Synthesis of Best Available Evidence

Poststroke pain commonly manifests as headache or musculoskeletal pain. Communication problems are assumed to be the cause of our underrecognizing pain. Reliable, validated assessment tools may be lacking for use in patients who are not able to consistently report their pain.

Clinician Expertise

Six months ago, your unit educator and manager worked with the EBP Committee to start standardized pain assessment for patients who cannot consistently report their pain experience. You use the new Numeric Rating Scale to assess G.V.'s pain based on her behavior. You determine analgesia is needed to manage G.V.'s assessed level of pain and document your assessment and intervention. When you reassess G.V.'s pain in 1 hour, you find her awake and resting quietly with her daughter at her side.

Patient Preferences and Values

G.V.'s daughter comments to you, "My mother seems much calmer and more comfortable. I was really concerned to see her so restless and unsettled." You ask G.V. how she feels; she haltingly responds, "Better."

Implications for Nursing Practice

1. How often should pain be assessed in patients with communication problems?
2. Describe your assessment and treatment of pain in a patient with communication problems.

Reference for Evidence

Schuster J, Hoyer C, Ebert A, et al.: Use of analgesics in acute stroke patients with inability to self-report pain: a retrospective cohort study, *BMC Neurol* 20(18), 2020.

TABLE 9.19 Assessing Pain in Nonverbal Patients

The following assessment techniques are recommended:

- Obtain a self-report when possible.
- Never assume a nonverbal person is unable to communicate pain; blinking, writing, hand gestures, or nodding can be ways to express pain or the absence of pain.
- Investigate potential causes of pain.
- Observe patient behaviors that indicate pain (e.g., grimacing, frowning, rubbing a painful area, groaning, restlessness).
- Obtain surrogate reports of pain from professional and family caregivers.
- Try to use analgesics and reassess the patient to observe for a decrease in pain-related behaviors.

Modified from Herr K, Coyne PJ, Ely E, et al.: Pain assessment in the patient unable to self-report: clinical practice recommendations in support of the ASPMN 2019 position statement, *Pain Manag Nurs* 20:404, 2019.

Patients in the Critical Care Unit

Unrelieved pain is common among critical care patients and can lead to poor outcomes. Inadequate pain control is linked with agitation, fear, and anxiety and adds to the stress response. Patients at high risk for pain include those who (1) have medical conditions that include ischemic, infectious, or inflammatory processes; (2) are immobilized; (3) have invasive monitoring devices, including endotracheal tubes (ETs); and (4) undergo procedures.

For many critically ill patients (e.g., those intubated), continuous IV sedation (e.g., propofol [Diprivan]) and an analgesic agent (e.g., fentanyl) provide sedation and pain control. However, patients getting deep sedation are often unresponsive. This prevents us from fully assessing the patient's neurologic status. To address this issue, all patients who can safely tolerate an interruption in sedation usually receive a daily, scheduled interruption of sedation, or "sedation holiday." These allow you to awaken the patient to conduct a neurologic examination.

Patients With Substance Abuse Problems

HCPs are often reluctant to give opioids to patients at risk for addiction or those with substance use problems for fear of promoting or worsening addictions. However, there is no evidence that providing opioid analgesia to these patients in any way worsens their addictive disease. In fact, the stress of unrelieved pain may contribute to relapse in the recovering patient or increased drug use in the patient who actively misuses drugs.

The American Society for Pain Management Nursing has established guidelines for pain management in patients with addiction. These guidelines reflect your role in a team approach in which patients with addictive disease and pain have the right to be treated with dignity, respect, and the same quality of pain assessment and management as all other patients.

CHECK YOUR PRACTICE

A 36-year-old male patient is recovering from abdominal surgery to remove his spleen after an automobile accident. He is a known drug user. You are taking care of him, and he is very irritable because he is not getting enough pain medication. You are reluctant to give him his PRN morphine for fear that you will contribute to his addiction problem.

- What should you do?

Several opioid risk assessments are available to help us assess patients for misuse and addiction. Other tools assess for the risk of addiction with opioid analgesia. These include the Opioid Risk Tool (www.drugabuse.gov/sites/default/files/files/OpioidRiskTool.pdf) and the Screener and Opioid Assessment for Patient Pain (www.nhms.org/sites/default/files/Pdfs/SOAPP-14.pdf). We may use a controlled substance agreement for those at risk. Patient monitoring with urine drug screens and access to state prescription monitoring programs to track prescriptions are effective in detecting misuse of drugs.

If the patient acknowledges substance use, determine the types and amounts of drugs used. Avoid exposing the patient to the misused drug. Effective equianalgesic doses of other opioids may be determined if daily drug doses are known. If a history of drug use is unknown or if the patient does not acknowledge substance use, be suspect when normal doses of analgesics do not relieve the patient's pain.

Aggressive behavior patterns and signs of withdrawal may occur. Withdrawal symptoms can worsen pain and lead to drug-seeking behavior or illicit drug use. Toxicology screens may be helpful in determining recently used drugs. Discussing these findings with the patient may help gain the patient's cooperation in pain control.

Severe pain should be treated with opioids. They will likely need to be at much higher doses than those used with drug-naive patients. The use of a single opioid is best. Avoid using a mixed opioid agonist-antagonist (e.g., butorphanol) or a partial agonist (e.g., buprenorphine), because these drugs may precipitate withdrawal symptoms. Nonopioid and adjuvant analgesics and nondrug pain relief measures may be used as needed. To maintain opioid blood levels and prevent withdrawal symptoms, provide analgesics around the clock. Use supplemental doses to treat BTP. IV or PCA infusions may be an option for acute pain management.

Pain management for people with addiction is challenging and needs an interprofessional team approach. When possible, the team includes pain management and addiction specialists. Team members need to be aware of their own attitudes about people with substance use problems, which may result in undertreatment of pain.

Case Study

Pain

© ajr_images/iStock.com)

Patient Profile

R.W. is a 135-lb (61-kg) 71-year-old woman with diabetes, peripheral neuropathy, hypertension, and depression. She was admitted for repair of an abdominal wound dehiscence. She is being discharged on her 3rd postoperative day. Her daughter will perform dressing changes at home.

Subjective Data

- Lives alone
- Desires 0 pain but will accept 1 or 2 on a scale of 0–10
- Reports incision area pain as a 2 or 3 between dressing changes and as a 6 during dressing changes
- States sharp pain persists 1 to 2 hours after dressing change
- Reports pain between dressing changes controlled by 2 oxycodone tablets
- Has history of peripheral neuropathy and describes chronic pain in her feet
- Her daughter tells you that her mother does not like taking pain medications

Objective Data

- Needs dressing changes 4 times per day after discharge
- For discharge, prescribed oxycodone 1 tablet oral every 4 hr as needed for pain

Discussion Questions

1. ***Recognize***: Describe the assessment data that are important for determining whether R.W. has adequate pain management.
2. ***Analyze***: What can you do to respect R.W.'s beliefs about using pain medication?
3. ***Plan:*** What other pain therapies might you plan to help R.W. through the dressing change?
4. ***Prioritize:*** Based on the data presented, what are the priority clinical problems?
5. ***Prioritize:*** What are the priority nursing interventions for R.W.?
6. ***Safety***: How long should the daughter wait after giving the oxycodone to begin the dressing change?
7. ***Safety:*** What side effects might she have because of her pain medication? How can these be safely managed?
8. ***Act:*** To whom can you delegate teaching R.W. and her daughter the plan of care at home?

Answers available at www.evolve.elsevier.com/Lewis/medsurg.

BRIDGE TO NCLEX EXAMINATION

The number of the question corresponds to the same-numbered outcome at the beginning of the chapter.

1. The nurse provides comprehensive pain management based on which principles? *(select all that apply)*
   - **a.** Pain does not have an emotional component.
   - **b.** Pain consists of an unpleasant sensory experience.
   - **c.** Families and caregivers do not play a role in pain response.
   - **d.** Self-report is one of the most valid means of pain assessment.
   - **e.** Observed behaviors are used to assess pain in nonverbal patients.
2. A patient is receiving a patient-controlled analgesia (PCA) infusion after spinal surgery. She is sleeping soundly, awakens when the nurse speaks to her in a normal tone of voice, and reports her pain as "mild and tolerable." Her respirations are 8 breaths/min. The *most* appropriate nursing action in this situation is to
   - **a.** stop the PCA infusion.
   - **b.** obtain an oxygen saturation level.
   - **c.** continue to closely monitor the patient.
   - **d.** administer naloxone and contact the provider.
3. A patient with pancreatitis reports abdominal pain. The nurse knows that this type of pain
   - **a.** is described as an electrical shock.
   - **b.** arises from damage to peripheral nerves.
   - **c.** is associated with visceral nociceptive pain.
   - **d.** is best treated with adjuvant therapies, such as gabapentin.
4. Unrelieved pain is
   - **a.** inevitable in persons in hospice.
   - **b.** expected in a person with peripheral neuropathy.
   - **c.** something to expect because of the opioid addiction epidemic.
   - **d.** dangerous and can lead to many physical and psychologic complications.
5. The nurse is assessing a postoperative patient for the presence of pain. The best approach to assess this patient's pain is to
   - **a.** take the patient's vital signs.
   - **b.** observe for nonverbal pain behaviors.
   - **c.** ask the patient to rate their pain on a 0 to 10 scale.
   - **d.** question the caregiver as to their belief if the patient is in pain.
6. A patient with an epidural catheter reports increased pain in their lower extremities. The best action by the nurse caring for this patient is to
   - **a.** administer naloxone.
   - **b.** assess the catheter for correct placement.
   - **c.** ask the physician for an IV bolus of morphine.
   - **d.** encourage the patient to take try a visualization technique.
7. A patient with cancer who reports constant, moderate pain with short periods of severe pain during dressing changes. The best approach in managing this patient's pain is
   - **a.** intermittent heat and cold therapy.
   - **b.** acetaminophen only when the patient asks for it.
   - **c.** as needed long-acting opioids and topical lidocaine.
   - **d.** best treated by receiving a long-acting and a short-acting opioid.

BRIDGE TO NCLEX EXAMINATION—cont'd

8. An *important* nursing responsibility related to pain is to *(select all that apply)*
   a. reassess the effect of analgesia.
   b. investigate potential causes of pain.
   c. trust the subjective pain report of the patient.
   d. perform pain assessments on nonverbal patients.
   e. withhold pain medication for patients with addiction.
9. Giving opioids to an actively dying patient who is reporting moderate to severe pain
   a. is ineffective.
   b. can lead to addiction.
   c. will hasten the person's death.
   d. is an appropriate and ethically justified nursing action.
10. A nurse believes that all patients recovering from hip replacement surgery should have the same amount of pain. This statement reflects
    a. a belief that results in effective pain management.
    b. a lack of knowledge about factors affecting pain, leading to poor pain management.
    c. a belief that will not have any effect on the type of care provided to patients in pain.
    d. an accurate statement about pain mechanisms and the expected goals of pain therapy.

1. b, d, e; 2. c; 3. c; 4. d; 5. c; 6. b; 7. d; 8. a, b, c, d; 9. d; 10. b.

For rationales to these answers and even more NCLEX review questions, visit http://evolve.elsevier.com/Lewis/medsurg.

EVOLVE WEBSITE/RESOURCES LIST

http://evolve.elsevier.com/Lewis/medsurg
Review Questions (Online Only)
Key Points
Answer Keys for Questions
- Rationales for Bridge to NCLEX Examination Questions
- Answer Guidelines for Case Study

Student Case Study
- Patient with Pain

Conceptual Care Map Creator
Audio Glossary
Content Updates

REFERENCES

1. Russo MM, Sundaramurthi T: An overview of cancer pain: epidemiology and pathophysiology, *Semin Oncol Nurs* 35:223, 2019.
2. Siler S, Borneman T, Ferrell B: Pain and Suffering, *Semin Oncol Nurs* 35:310, 2019.
3. Ong WY, Stohler CS, Herr DR: Role of the prefrontal cortex in pain processing, *Mol Neurobiol* 56:1137, 2019.
4. Shim H, Rose J, Halle S, et al.: Complex regional pain syndrome: a narrative review for the practicing clinician, *Br J Anaesth* 123:424, 2019.
5. Kamp J, Van Velzen M, Olofsen E, et al.: Pharmacokinetic and pharmacodynamic considerations for NMDA-receptor antagonist ketamine in the treatment of chronic neuropathic pain: an update of the most recent literature, *Expert Opin Drug Metab Toxicol* 15:1033, 2019.
6. Munday I, Kneebone I, Newton-John T: The language of chronic pain, *Disabil Rehabil* 43:354, 2021.
7. Finnerup NP: Nonnarcotic methods of pain management, *N Engl J Med* 380:2440, 2019.
8. Saragiotto BT, Abdel Shaheed C, Maher CG: Paracetamol for pain in adults, *BMJ* 367:16693, 2019.
9. Kreutzwiser D, Tawfic QA: Methadone for pain management: a pharmacotherapeutic review, *CNS Drugs* 34:827, 2020.
10. Barakat A: Revisiting tramadol: a multi-modal agent for pain management, *CNS Drugs* 33:481, 2019.
*11. Romualdi P, Grilli M, Canonico PL, et al.: Pharmacological rationale for tapentadol therapy: a review of new evidence, *J Pain Res* 121513, 2019.
12. Mercadante S: Opioid analgesics adverse effects: the other side of the coin, *Curr Pharm Des* 25:3197, 2019.
*13. Crockett S, Greer KB, Sultan S: Opioid-induced constipation (OIC) guideline, *Gastroenterol* 156:228, 2019.
14. Mercadante S, Arcuri E, Santoni A: Opioid-induced tolerance and hyperalgesia, *CNS Drugs* 33:943, 2019.
15. Attal N: Pharmacological treatments of neuropathic pain: the latest recommendations, *Rev Neuro* 175:46, 2019.
16. Urtis I, Borchart M, Hasegawa M, et al.: An update of current cannabis-based pharmaceuticals in pain medicine, *Pain Ther* 8:41, 2019.
*17. Miake-Lye IM, Mak S, Lee J, et al.: Massage for pain: an evidence map, *J Altern Complement Med* 25:475, 2019.
*18. Polaski AM, Phelps AL, Kostek MC, et al.: Exercise-induced hypoalgesia: A meta-analysis of exercise dosing for the treatment of chronic pain, *PLoS One* 14, 2019:e0210418.
*19. Gibson W, Wand BM, Meads C, et al.: Transcutaneous electrical nerve stimulation (TENS) for chronic pain: an overview of Cochrane Reviews, *Cochrane Database Syst Rev* 4:Cd011890, 2019.
20. Kelly RB, Willis J: Acupuncture for pain, *Am Fam Physician* 100:89, 2019.
*21. Urtis I, Hubble A, Peterson E, et al.: An update on cognitive therapy for the management for chronic pain: a comprehensive review, *Curr Pain Headache Rep* 23:57, 2019.
*22. Thompson T, Terhune DB, Oram C, et al.: The effectiveness of hypnosis for pain relief: a systematic review and meta-analysis of 85 controlled experimental trials, *Neurosci Biobehav Rev* 99:298, 2019.
23. Andres TM, McGrane T, McEvoy MD, et al.: Geriatric pharmacology: an update, *Anesthesiol Clin* 37:475, 2019.

*Evidence-based information for clinical practice.

10

Palliative and End-of-Life Care

Amisha Parekh de Campos, Shila Pandey, and William E. Rosa

http://evolve.elsevier.com/Lewis/medsurg/

CONCEPTUAL FOCUS

Coping
Ethics
Family Dynamics
Health Care Organizations
Palliative Care
Spirituality

LEARNING OUTCOMES

1. Distinguish the purpose of palliative care and hospice care.
2. Describe the physical and psychologic manifestations at the end of life.
3. Discuss ethical and legal issues related to palliative care.
4. Describe the nursing management of the dying patient.
5. Explore the special needs of family caregivers in palliative care.
6. Explain the process of grief and bereavement at the end of life.
7. Discuss the special needs of the nurse who cares for dying patients and their families.
8. Examine cultural and spiritual issues related to palliative care.

KEY TERMS

advance care planning
advance directives
anticipatory grief
bereavement
brain death
death
do-not-resuscitate (DNR) order
end of life
grief
hospice
palliative care
primary palliative care
spirituality

PALLIATIVE CARE

Palliative care is the active holistic care of persons with serious health-related suffering from severe illness.[1] The severe illness may be acute or chronic, with a high mortality rate. Patients with serious illnesses experience a significant burden of suffering. The illness may impact quality of life and role function, and create increased burden related to symptoms, treatment, or caregiver stress.

It is estimated that by 2060, 48 million people will die annually with serious health-related suffering.[2] While palliative care can be started at any time, optimal benefits occur when it begins following the diagnosis of a serious illness. These include neurodegenerative diseases, cancer, heart failure, chronic obstructive pulmonary disease (COPD), dementia, or end-stage kidney disease.[3] The growing number of people with conditions such as diabetes and heart disease contribute to the increased need for and use of palliative care.[4]

Palliative care involves assessment and management of pain and other symptoms, support of caregiver needs, and care coordination. The approach to care is patient- and family-centered. The goal is to reduce the burden of health-related suffering while improving quality of life (Fig. 10.1). Palliative care has been shown to (1) improve quality of life for those with chronic illness, (2) decrease costs for their health care, and (3) ease caregiver burden.[5]

Palliative care can be provided as the primary focus of care or concurrently with medical/curative treatment (Table 10.1). Ideally, all patients receiving curative or restorative health care should receive palliative care at the same time. Care is provided based on individual needs. Palliative care extends into the period of end-of-life (EOL) care and offers patient and family support while planning for EOL needs.[6] Grief and bereavement care follows the patient's death (Fig. 10.2).

The American Nurses Association (ANA) and the Hospice and Palliative Nurses Association suggest that every nurse should deliver primary palliative care, regardless of setting. In

Fig. 10.1 One goal of palliative care is to improve the quality of the patient's remaining life. (© FatCamera/iStock.com)

TABLE 10.1 Goals of Palliative Care

- Provide relief from pain and other physical symptoms
- Maximize quality of life
- Provide psychosocial and spiritual care
- Help patients and their families determine goals of care
- Neither hasten nor postpone death; recognize dying as a natural process
- Provide support to the family and the caregivers during the patient's illness and in bereavement
- Recognize and respect the cultural values and beliefs of the patient and the family

Adapted from International Association for Hospice and Palliative Care (IAHPC): *Global consensus based palliative care definition*, Houston, TX, 2018, The International Association for Hospice and Palliative Care. Retrieved from https://hospicecare.com/what-we-do/projects/consensus-based-definition-of-palliative-care/definition/.

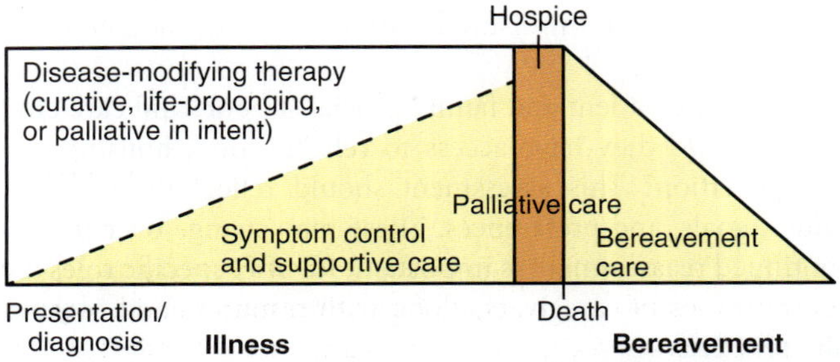

Fig. 10.2 Continuum-of-care model showing integration of curative care, palliative and end-of-life/hospice care, and bereavement care. (Redrawn from Robert Wood Johnson Foundation: The EPEC Project: Elements and models of end-of-life care, 1999.)

other words, all who care for seriously ill patients should provide basic palliative care interventions.[7] **Primary palliative care** (or *generalist palliative care*) includes basic symptom management, routine discussions about care goals, and the assessment of psychologic, social, cultural, and spiritual care.[8] Specialist palliative care clinicians offer complex symptom management, have difficult discussions and clarify care goals, and help with accessing the appropriate level of care.

The palliative care team is an interprofessional collaboration. The team often includes nurses, advanced practice nurses, social workers, pharmacists, physicians, chaplains, and other

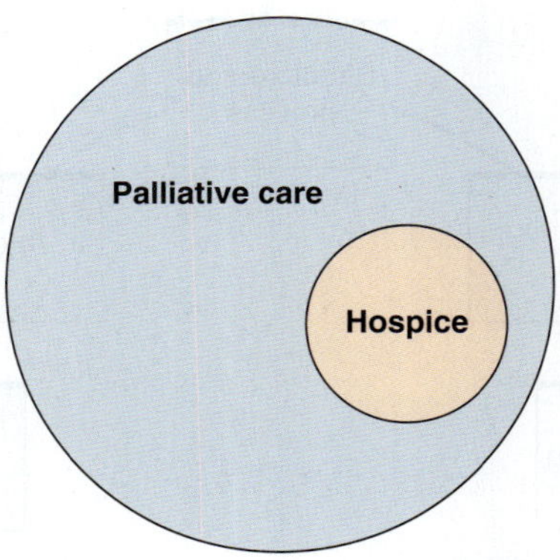

All hospice is palliative care, but not all palliative care is hospice.

Fig. 10.3 Relationship of palliative care and end-of-life care/hospice. (From Limerick M, Sutton M: Palliative care, *J Oncol Navig Surviv* 11:123, 2020. Reprinted with permission.)

health care professionals.[8] Empathetic, respectful, and reflective communication among the patient, family, and the team is vital to ensuring patient- and family-centered care. Patients receive palliative care services in multiple settings. These include the home, long-term and acute care, mental health agencies, rehabilitation centers, and prisons. Many agencies have established palliative care teams.

HOSPICE CARE

Hospice care is a subcategory of palliative care (Fig. 10.3). **Hospice** is a concept of EOL care with an emphasis on symptom management, advance care planning, spiritual care, and family support.[9] Hospice clinicians provide compassion, concern, and support for patients in the last phases of a serious illness. The main goal of hospice care is to help the patient to live as fully and comfortably as possible while dying with dignity.

Hospice care is an option when a patient has a limited life expectancy—specifically 6 months or less. The overall care focuses on improving quality of life and maintaining comfort while forgoing curative treatment. Hospice is often underused. Many wrongly assume the patient must be actively dying. On the contrary, it is important that the patient be referred to hospice as early as possible to ease the physical, emotional, and spiritual distress so common at the EOL.

Almost half of the patients who die in the United States are in hospice care. More than 75% of patients in hospice are over the age of 65 years. Most patients have cancer, dementia, stroke, or heart or respiratory conditions.[9] Often hospice and palliative care are used interchangeably. Palliative care is considered supportive care when a serious illness is diagnosed and there is a need to manage symptoms and delineate care goals. All hospice patients are under the philosophical umbrella of palliative care but not all palliative patients receive hospice care.

DOMAINS OF PALLIATIVE CARE

The National Consensus Project for Quality Palliative Care Guidelines outline 8 key domains for quality palliative care: (1) care structure and processes, (2) physical aspects of care, (3) psychologic and psychiatric aspects, (4) social aspects of care,

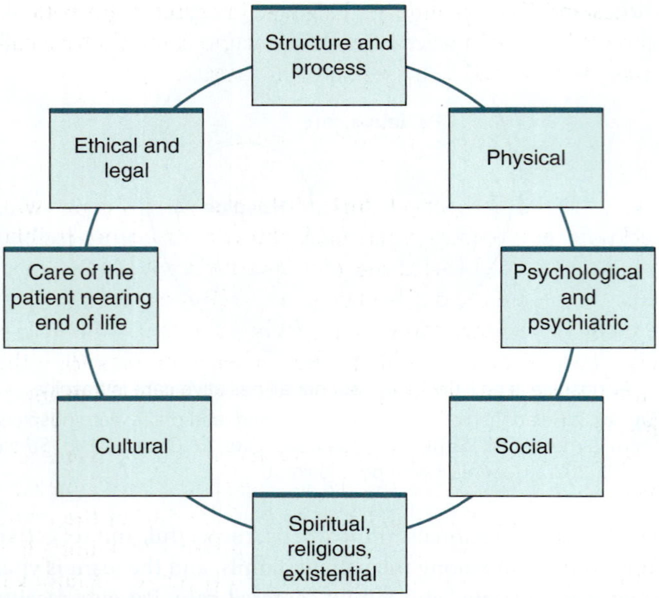

Fig. 10.4 8 Domains of palliative care. (Created from National Consensus Project for Quality Palliative Care: Clinical practice guidelines for quality palliative care, ed 4, Richmond, VA, 2018, National Coalition for Hospice and Palliative Care. Retrieved from https://www.nationalcoalitionhpc.org/ncp.)

(5) spiritual, religious, and existential aspects of care, (6) culture care, (7) care of the patient nearing end of life, and (8) ethical and legal aspects (Fig. 10.4).[5]

Domain 1: Care Structure and Processes

Palliative care is coordinated and provided holistically. The interprofessional team (IPT) works together to support the patient and family across all settings throughout the illness trajectory. Nurses serve as advocates, provide direct care, coordinate additional care, teach, and continually re-evaluate patient and family needs. The IPT establishes a plan of care and continually refines the plan based on the goals of the patient and communication with IPT members.

The initial patient assessment includes a history, examination, and discussions with the patient and family. Assess their understanding of the serious illness. Discuss advance care planning, including care goals and treatment preferences, and review advanced directives. Obtain the patient's medical history, medication record, and laboratory and diagnostic results. Note the specific event or change that brought the patient into the health care setting. Do a brief review of systems. Note any current symptoms. Assess for discomfort, pain, nausea, and dyspnea. Evaluate for comorbidities or acute episodes of problems, such as diabetes or headache. Ask about the patient's food and fluid intake and sleep patterns. How are they responding to the stress of a serious illness diagnosis? Consider factors related to the social determinants of health, caregiver support, and emotional and spiritual concerns.

Domain 2: Physical Aspects of Care

Symptom management can improve the patient's physical well-being and function. You can anticipate and prevent some symptoms with continued assessment and monitoring. Symptom management considers physical, emotional, spiritual, and cultural factors that can contribute to the burden of pain and suffering related to serious illness.

Pay close attention to the onset, quality, and severity of symptoms. Note factors that worsen or relieve the symptom and prior treatment such as medications or interventions. Consider the impact of symptoms on function and quality of life. Timely reassessment is needed to determine if treatments are effective, if new symptoms arise, and if the patient and family can manage the plan of care.

Domain 3: Psychologic and Psychiatric Aspects

A diagnosis of serious illness can impact the mental health of a patient and family. Anxiety, depression, delirium, posttraumatic stress disorder, and substance use may be a factor in the progression of the patient's illness. The IPT can support, provide treatment, and coordinate care to manage emotional, psychosocial, and/or existential distress.

The nurses' role is to ensure support for the patient and family during their journey with serious illness. A social worker can help manage psychologic symptoms and refer to counseling if needed. Discuss any sign of suicidal ideation or a serious and/or persistent mental illness immediately with the IPT. Treatment of psychologic or mental health issues can include behavior, therapeutic, and pharmacologic interventions. Cultural or complementary therapies may be used.

Domain 4: Social Aspects of Care

Social aspects include environmental and social factors that affect the quality of life. Issues to address include access to medication and treatment, transportation to appointments, financial constraints, and other social factors that surround persons who are uninsured, under-insured, homeless, or undocumented.

Assess the patient and family's social support and care environment. Do they have access to reliable food, housing, and transportation? This assessment should reflect their culture, values, goals, and preferences. These may change over time so continued reassessment is important. Identify specific roles and contributions of caregivers, along with resources and community services.

Domain 5: Spiritual, Religious, and Existential Aspects of Care

Spiritual care is fundamental to addressing the suffering associated with serious illness.[10] **Spirituality** is a broad concept that encompasses beliefs, values, and purpose related to the search for existential meaning and purpose. Some define spirituality as a relationship with a supreme being that directs beliefs and practices. Spiritual needs do not necessarily equate to religious beliefs in a higher power. A patient may not practice a particular religion but have a deep spirituality. The IPT should care for patients and families in a manner that respects their spiritual beliefs and practices. The team should also respect when patients and families decline to discuss their beliefs or accept spiritual support.

TABLE 10.2 Spiritual Assessment

Obtain basic spiritual-related information, including:
- Religious preference
- If the patient is part of a spiritual or religious community
- If religion is significant to them
- Whether the patient would like a chaplain or other person involved
- Whom the patient turns to when they need help
- Use of spiritual-related coping strategies
- Any religious or spiritual practices the patient wants to participate in
- Presence of any concerns or conflicts between spiritual or religious beliefs and health care
- Sources of hope, strength, comfort, and peace

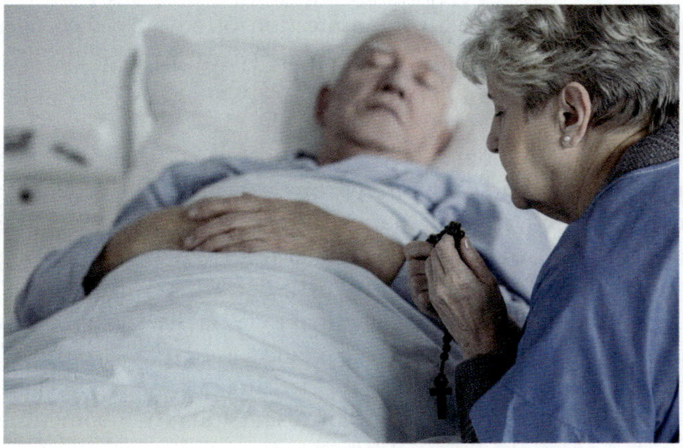

Fig. 10.5 Spiritual needs are an important consideration in end-of-life care. (© KatarzynaBialasiewicz/iStock.com)

Assess spiritual needs (Table 10.2). Assess the patient's and family's preferences related to spiritual guidance or pastoral care services and make needed referrals. Spiritual distress is a state of suffering related to meaning of connectedness to self, others, or a higher power. Patients may question their beliefs about their journey through life, religion, and an afterlife (Fig. 10.5). *Existential distress* may occur as the person re-examines their lives and questions their prior understandings of meaning.[10] Professional chaplains are trained to address spiritual issues.

Domain 6: Cultural Care

Cultural beliefs affect a patient's values and traditions related to health, illness, family caregiving roles, and decision making. Acknowledge and respect a patient and family's culture and provide care that is sensitive to these needs.

Cultural variations exist in symptom expression (e.g., pain expression), communication, and use of health care services. Providing culturally competent care requires assessment of nonverbal cues, such as grimaces, body position, and decreased or guarded movements. See Chapter 9 for issues related to pain assessment and management. Careful consideration should take place about a patient's language, cognitive capacity, disabilities, and developmental stage. Communicate with attention to verbal, non-verbal, and symbolic details. Use medical interpreter services when communicating with those that do not understand English and sign language interpreters for patients who are hearing impaired. Teaching materials should have culturally representative images and language.

Domain 7: Care of the Patient Nearing the End of Life

End of life is the period during which a patient copes with declining health from a terminal illness or from the frailties associated with advanced age, even if death is not clearly imminent.[11] In some cases it is obvious to HCPs that the patient is at the EOL. In other cases, they may be uncertain if the EOL is near. This uncertainty adds to the challenge of answering the common question asked by the patient and family, "How much time is left?"

End-of-life care (EOL care) is the term used for issues and services related to death and dying. The goals for EOL care are to (1) provide comfort and supportive care during the dying process, (2) improve the quality of the patient's remaining life, (3) help ensure a dignified death, and (4) provide emotional support to the family.

Discussions about hospice should be started early so that patients can understand the philosophy, services, benefits, and limitations. The decision to begin hospice care is hard for several reasons. Many patients, families, and HCPs lack information about hospice care. Some cultural/ethnic groups may not use hospice because of a lack of awareness of hospice services, a desire to continue with potentially curative treatment, and concerns about lack of minority hospice workers. HCPs may be reluctant to give referrals if they view a patient's functional decline as their personal failure. Some patients or family members see hospice care as "giving up" or receiving second-rate care. Openly discuss this concern and provide reassurance in the quality of hospice care.

Hospice services are available 24 hours a day, 7 days a week to help patients and families in their homes. Inpatient hospice settings often have a relaxed and homelike atmosphere (Fig. 10.6).

It is important to consider potential barriers to hospice care for vulnerable populations. These may include veterans, immigrants, and persons who are impoverished, uninsured, disabled, institutionalized, or incarcerated. The hospice team may need to collaborate with community partners to facilitate support services.

In the United States, Medicare, Medicaid, and many private insurance agencies cover hospice services. Admission to a hospice program has 2 criteria. The first criterion is that the patient must want the services and agree in writing to use only hospice care, not curative care, to treat the terminal illness. The second criterion is that the patient must be medically eligible for hospice. This means that 2 physicians certify that the patient's prognosis is terminal, with less than 6 months to live. After this initial certification, only 1 physician (e.g., the hospice medical director) is needed to recertify the patient. It is important to realize that the physician who certifies that a hospice patient is terminal does not "guarantee" death within 6 months. If a patient in hospice survives beyond 6 months, Medicare and other organizations will continue to reimburse if the patient still meets enrollment criteria.

Fig. 10.6 Inpatient hospice settings are designed to make the atmosphere as relaxed and homelike as possible. (© KatarzynaBialasiewicz/iStock.com)

Hospice patients can receive care for other health problems that are not related to the terminal illness. However, the hospice, Medicare, Medicaid, or patient's insurance company may not cover those services.[12] Occasionally, a patient's condition stabilizes, and the patient may be discharged from hospice care after review of the treatment plan and input from the hospice team. Patients can voluntarily withdraw from the program at any time.

The hospice nurse plays a key role in coordinating the hospice team. Hospice nurses focus on pain control and symptom management, spiritual assessment, and assessment and management of family needs. To meet patient and family needs, the hospice nurse needs excellent teaching skills, compassion, flexibility, cultural competence, and adaptability.

Domain 8: Ethical and Legal Aspects of Care

Patients and families struggle with many decisions associated with a serious illness or EOL experience. Palliative care focuses on honoring patient preferences. Decisions may involve the choice for (1) advance directives (e.g., living wills), (2) specific treatments (e.g., chemotherapy, surgery) (3) cardiopulmonary resuscitation (CPR), (4) organ and tissue donations, and (5) feeding tube placement. Provide information to help patients with these decisions.

Decisional capacity refers to the ability to consent to or refuse care. It means that the patient has an understanding and appreciation of the information received and has the capacity to engage in the reasoning process.

Advance Care Planning and Advance Directives

Advance care planning is a process of having patients (1) think through their values and goals for treatment, (2) talk about their values and goals with others, and (3) document their preferences. **Advance directives** are the written documents that provide information about the patient's wishes and designated spokesperson (Table 10.3). Under the 1990 Patient Self Determination Act (PSDA), patients must receive information on advance directives from health care agencies.

Each state has specific advance directive forms. A *living will* is used to detail a person's wishes to avoid, limit, or withhold interventions. These forms are often combined with a *durable power of attorney for health care* (DPAHC), *medical power of attorney* (MPOA), and *power of attorney for health care* (POAH) or *health care proxy*. If the patient is unable to communicate or is incapacitated, the DPAHC allows the agent to make all health care decisions. Patients may change their minds about desired treatments as their disease state progresses, so it is important to reassess the advance directives. For cognitively impaired older adults who lack decision making capacity, consider the patient's values, collaborate with the IPT, and engage the surrogates in medical decisions.

In addition to state-specific advance directive forms, documents such as the Five Wishes help people discuss their care preferences with their loved ones and HCP.[13] Verbal directives can be given to the attending physician in the presence of 2 witnesses. To improve communication of advance directives, the Physician Order for Life-Sustaining Treatment (POLST) or Medical Order for Life-Sustaining Treatment (MOLST) outline the patient's desire for treatment (Table 10.3).

The patient should keep a copy of all advance directives and let family know where the copy is kept. In the absence of advance directives and if the patient is not capable of communicating, the surrogate decision maker (most often family or significant other) will be asked to make decisions. Surrogates rely on information from the IPT to make crucial decisions. Record discussions and decisions in the medical record to keep the IPT informed and assure appropriate care.

CPR is an important topic of discussion. HCP sometimes avoid discussing CPR, which can lead to inappropriate or unwanted use of resuscitation methods. Patients and families may have unrealistic expectations about survival potential after CPR. The patient with no preferred limits on life support has a *full code* status. This choice allows for resuscitation attempts with chest compressions, defibrillation, intubation, vasopressors, and other life-sustaining interventions.

After considering health problems, prognosis, and personal values, some patients may request a **do-not-resuscitate (DNR) order**. A DNR order is a written medical order that documents a patient's wishes about resuscitation and the patient's desire to avoid CPR.[14] Use language cautiously. Terms such as *do not attempt resuscitation (DNAR)* or *allow natural death (AND)* may more accurately reflect the meaning of this intervention.

Some hospitals may define a DNR order as only cardiac resuscitation attempts and use a *do not intubate (DNI)* order for patents who decline intubation or mechanical ventilation efforts. A *chemical code* may involve the use of drugs for resuscitation, such as vasopressors without the use of CPR. Some health care settings may have a *comfort measures only* (CMO) order, or an EOL order set that assists with selecting only interventions that will provide comfort and limit invasive measures. Some states have implemented a form called *out-of-hospital DNR* for use by terminally ill patients who wish to have no heroic measures used to prolong life after they leave an acute care agency.

Do not hospitalize (DNH) is a status used by skilled nursing agencies if a patient does not want to go to the hospital for treatment. These terms never mean to indicate care is withheld,

TABLE 10.3 **Common Legal Documents Used in Palliative Care**

Term	Description	Special Considerations
Advance directive	Written documents that state information about the patient's future health care decisions or choices. Guide for families, HCP, and caregivers on the patients' goals and wishes for care.	• Document takes various forms • Should adhere to guidelines in the state of residence
Allow natural death (AND)	Preferred term for a do-not-resuscitate order. Acknowledges the patient's wish to avoid aggressive measures. May be associated with care focusing on dignity and comfort.	• May be called do not attempt resuscitation (DNAR) in some states or agencies
Combined directives	Includes more than 1 form. Contain directives about health care, values/goals, and/or appointed health care proxy. Example includes the "Five Wishes" advance directive.	• Not considered a legal document in all states • May be used to start discussion about advance directives between patient, family, and HCP
Do not resuscitate (DNR)	Written order reflecting a patient's wish to avoid or not attempt CPR.	• Signed by a physician or nurse practitioner (varies by state) • Record that discussion was held
Durable power of attorney for health care (DPAHC)	Defines who will serve as the surrogate decision-maker when the patient loses decision-making capacity.	• Also called medical power of attorney, health care proxy, appointment of a health care agent or surrogate • Does not include financial decisions
Living will	Lay term for a written legal document that describes the patient's preferences about future health care decisions or choices.	• Must identify specific treatments that a person wants or does not want at EOL
Physician/Practitioner Order for Life-Sustaining Treatment (POLST)	Legal form completed by the patient and HCP listing treatments wanted, not wanted, or limited. Guides current treatment and acts as medical orders across health care settings.	• State specific form • May be signed by a physician and/or nurse practitioner (varies by state), and patient or patient surrogate • Also called Medical Order for Life-Sustaining Treatment (MOLST)

rather care is focused to relieve suffering and promote dignity at the EOL.

An advance directive may include withholding or withdrawing treatments such as a ventilator, artificial hydration, and nutrition. The ANA states that the decision to withhold artificial nutrition and hydration should be made by the patient or surrogate together with the IPT. The nurse continues to provide expert care for patients who are withdrawing treatments.

Organ and Tissue Donation

Patients may choose organ donation of a body part or the entire body. Advance directives and organ donor information should be in the medical record and identified on the patient's care plan. The decision to donate organs may also be made by immediate family after the patient's death. Next of kin permission must be obtained at the time of donation.[15] Organ and tissue donations follow specific legal guidelines and agency policies. Prompt notification to the right personnel when organ donation is intended is important since some tissues must be used within hours after death.

Euthanasia and Physician-Assisted Suicide

Euthanasia is the deliberate act of hastening death. It is not legal in the United States. The ANA statement on requests for medical aid in dying clearly state euthanasia is inconsistent with the core commitments of the nursing profession. Nurses are ethically prohibited from giving aid-in-dying medication.[16] *Physician-assisted suicide,* or *aid-in-dying laws,* are offered in some states. In this case, the physician provides the means and/or information for a terminally ill patient to self-administer medication to hasten death.

Nurses have the obligation to support patients at the EOL by understanding these laws and providing prompt, humane, and comprehensive EOL care. *Palliative sedation* refers to giving medications to intentionally produce sedation to relieve distressing symptoms in a patient who is imminently dying. The intent of palliative sedation is to relieve unmanageable pain and suffering. It is not to shorten life or to hasten death.

The use of opioids for symptom management at the EOL is often misunderstood and feared by patients, families, and HCPs. Many patients refuse opioids for pain, which leads to physical and emotional suffering. However, opioids for pain management and shortness of breath are the gold standard in EOL care. Relieving patient suffering includes giving medications such as opioids that have the potential to produce harm (Box 10.1). Teach the patient and family about addiction, tolerance, and dependence on medications. Opioids should not be withheld at the end of life, even for those with a history of addiction. Pain management is discussed in Chapter 9.

DEATH

Death occurs when all vital organs and body systems cease to function. It is the irreversible cessation of cardiovascular, respiratory, and brain function. In some states and under specific circumstances, a registered nurse is legally allowed to pronounce death. Policies and procedures vary by state and among health care agencies.

BOX 10.1 ETHICAL/LEGAL DILEMMAS

Pain Management at End of Life

Situation

A.P. is a terminally ill 50-year-old woman with metastatic breast cancer who is hospitalized with severe bone pain. She has had multiple complications including respiratory failure, infections, and difficult to manage pain. Goals of care discussions led to decisions to focus exclusively on comfort measures. She continues to moan at rest and shows signs of severe pain with any movement. The team recently increased the doses of pain medications. She is intermittently awake, and her family are at the bedside. Some of the nurses do not feel comfortable giving the high doses of opioid for fear they will hasten death.

Ethical/Legal Points for Consideration

- Adequate pain relief at EOL is fundamental to the quality life of the patient and experience of family caregivers.
- The *Code of Ethics for Nurses* and position statement from the ANA address the ethical responsibility of the nurse to relieve pain and suffering it causes, along with counseling patients and families about pain and symptom management.[1,2]
- The goal of adequate pain control in seriously ill or terminally ill is based on the *principle of nonmaleficence, to ease suffering* (preventing or reducing harm to the patient). Access to adequate pain and symptom management at EOL follows the *principle of beneficence,* which includes promoting good. Since the intent of this action is to ease suffering, not hasten death, it is ethically justified by the principle of *double effect.* Though administering opioids and sedatives at the end of life may cause sedation, it is justified to relieve suffering.
- Nurses are responsible for providing comprehensive and compassionate end of life care. Legally, the *standard of care* is used to define the nursing acts required for safe and competent nursing practice. Nursing care that is below the standard is considered negligent and unsafe.
- In A.P.'s situation the standard of care includes access to opioids for relief of pain at the EOL. Failure of the nurse to act assertively to achieve pain relief for the patient and failure to effectively use resources to obtain that pain relief will be considered below the standard of care and unsafe and incompetent practice. Nurse should seek counsel of mentors and the IPT to gain comfort with providing this care.

Discussion Questions

1. What types of discussions should occur among the health care team, patient, and family as this patient approaches EOL?
2. How can nurses reduce moral distress when managing patients' pain at the EOL?
3. What training is needed for nurses to safely give opioids at the EOL?

References

ANA: *The code of ethics for nurses with interpretive statements,* 2015. Retrieved from https://www.nursingworld.org/practice-policy/nursing-excellence/ethics/code-of-ethics-for-nurses/.

ANA: *Position statement: The ethical responsibility to manage pain and the suffering it causes,* 2018. Retrieved from https://www.nursingworld.org/practice-policy/nursing-excellence/official-position-statements/id/the-ethical-responsibility-to-manage-pain-and-the-suffering-it-causes/.

Brain death is an irreversible loss of all brain functions, including those of the brainstem. Brain death is a clinical diagnosis. It occurs when the cerebral cortex stops functioning or is irreversibly destroyed. The diagnostic criteria for clinical diagnosis of brain death include coma or unresponsiveness, absence of brainstem reflexes, and apnea.[17] Physicians perform specific assessments to confirm each criterion. Current legal and medical standards require that all brain function cease to be able to pronounce brain death. Diagnosing brain death is of special importance when organ donation is an option.

Physical Manifestations at End of Life

As death approaches, the body gradually slows down until all functions end. Respiratory changes are common. Respirations may be rapid or slow, shallow, and irregular. Breath sounds may become wet and noisy, both audibly and on auscultation. Mouth breathing and mucus accumulation in the airways cause noisy, wet-sounding respirations. We call these terminal secretions or *the death rattle.* Cheyne-Stokes respiration is a pattern of breathing characterized by alternating periods of apnea and deep, rapid breathing. When respirations cease, the heart stops beating within a few minutes. The physical manifestations of approaching death are listed in Table 10.4.

Psychosocial Manifestations at End of Life

A variety of feelings and emotions can affect the patient and family at the EOL (Table 10.5). The patient and family may feel overwhelmed, fearful, powerless, and fatigued. They may also feel at peace with death and feel gratitude for a "life well lived." The family's response depends in part on the type and length of the illness and their relationship with the patient.

We must respect the patient's needs and wishes. Patients need time to think and express their feelings. Response time to questions may be sluggish from fatigue, weakness, and confusion.

Bereavement and Grief

Although we often use the terms interchangeably, *bereavement* refers to the state of loss and *grief* refers to the reaction to loss. **Bereavement** is the period after the death of a loved one during which we experience grief and mourning occurs. The time spent in bereavement depends on several factors. These include how attached one was to the person who died and how much time one spent expecting the loss.

Grief is a normal reaction in response to the real loss of a loved one and the loss of what might have been. Psychologic responses include anger, guilt, anxiety, sadness, depression, and despair. Physiologic reactions include sleeping problems, changes in appetite, physical problems, and illness.

Grief is a complex and intense emotional experience. Many describe grief as a pattern with phases (Table 10.6).[18] Not every person goes through all the phases of grieving, and they are not always progressive. It is common to be in a phase and then go backward. For example, a person may be in the bargaining phase and then revert to the anger phase.

Another model of grief is seen in the grief wheel (Fig. 10.7). After a loss, the person feels *shock* (numbness, denial, inability to think straight). Next is the *protest* stage, in which a person may have anger, guilt, sadness, fear, and searching. Then comes the *disorganization* stage, with despair, apathy, anxiety, and confusion. In the *reorganization* stage, a person gradually returns to normal functioning, but feels different. The last stage is the *new normal.* Eventually the destabilization experienced in grief resolves and the challenge is to accept the new normal. Trying to

TABLE 10.4 Physical Manifestations at End of Life

System	Manifestations
Cardiovascular	• ↑ Heart rate; later slowing and weakening of pulse • Irregular rhythm • ↓ BP • Delayed absorption of drugs given IM or subcutaneous
Gastrointestinal	• Hypoactive bowel sounds, constipation, abdominal distention • Anorexia, no oral intake • Loss of sphincter control with incontinence • Bowel movement before imminent death or at time of death
Musculoskeletal	• Gradual immobility • Sagging of jaw resulting from loss of facial muscle tone • Difficulty speaking • Swallowing becoming more difficult • Difficulty maintaining body posture and alignment • Loss of gag reflex • Jerking seen in patients on high doses of opioids
Nervous	• ↑ confusion or delirium, hallucinations, impaired cognition • Temperature swings: hypothermia and fever • Possible seizures, non-reactive pupils
Respiratory	• ↑ respiratory rate, tachypnea • Irregular breathing, Cheyne-Stokes respiration, periods of apnea, episodic deep, rapid breaths • Inability to cough or clear secretions resulting in grunting, gurgling, or noisy congested breathing (death rattle or terminal secretions)
Sensory	• Hearing is usually last to disappear • ↓ Taste and smell • ↓ Sensation • ↓ Response to tactile stimuli • Blurred vision • Sinking and glazing of eyes • Blink reflex absent • Inability to close eyelids
Skin	• Mottling on hands, feet, coccyx, arms, and legs • Skin breakdown, especially in pressure areas • Peripheral cyanosis of nose, nail beds, knees • Cold, clammy skin or "waxlike" skin when death is imminent
Urinary system	• Gradual decrease in urine output • Incontinence • Inability to urinate

TABLE 10.5 Psychosocial Manifestations at End of Life

Dimension	Manifestations
Dealing with change and redefining self	• Acceptance of mortality, engage in planning for one's death, experience peacefulness • Denial, defensiveness, maladaptive coping • Frustration with changes, anger about situation • Worry about burdening others
Impact of illness on finding meaning and hope	• Enhanced meaning of life, ability to talk about the future or death • Deep expressions of loss, signs of depression
Relationships with loved ones	• Lack of or poor communication, unresolved conflicts, estrangement • Engagement of loved ones, able to say goodbye or give/receive forgiveness • Expressions of love to significant persons
Preparing for death	• Legacy work and life review • Reconciling unfinished business or incomplete life tasks • Developmental issues expressed as anger, sorrow, grief, and/or sadness

Adapted from Block SD: Psychological issues in end-of-life care, *J Palliat Med* 9(3), 751–772, 2006.

go back to the "old" normal (which is not there anymore) causes a great deal of anxiety and stress.

The way a person grieves depends on factors such as the relationship with the person who has died (e.g., spouse, parent), physical and emotional coping resources, concurrent life stresses, cultural beliefs, and personality. Other factors that affect the grief response include mental and physical health, economic resources, religious or spiritual beliefs, family relationships, social support, and time spent preparing for the death. Conflict may affect the grief response.[19]

The grief experience for the caregiver or family of the patient with a severe illness often begins long before the actual death. We call this **anticipatory grief**. Patients at the EOL also can have anticipatory grief.

Working in a positive way through the grief process helps to adapt to the loss. Grief that helps the person accept the reality of death is a healthy response called *adaptive grief*. It may be grieving before death occurs or when the death is expected. Signs of adaptive grief include the ability to see some good resulting from the death and positive memories of the deceased person.

Dysfunctional reactions to loss can occur. The physical and psychologic impact of the loved one's death may persist for years. *Prolonged grief disorder*, formerly called *complicated grief*, is a term for lengthy and intense mourning. Prolonged grief disorder can include recurrent and severe distressing emotions and intrusive thoughts related to the loss of a loved one, self-neglect, and denial of the loss for longer than 6 months. About 1 in 5 bereaved persons has prolonged grief disorder. They have a higher risk for illness and may have impaired work and social role function.

Bereavement and grief counseling are core parts of palliative care. The goal of a bereavement program is to provide support and to help survivors in the transition to a life without the deceased person. Include grief support into the plan of care for the family and significant others during the patient's illness and after the death.

Priority interventions for grief focus on providing an environment that allows the patient and family to express their feelings, such as anger, fear, and guilt. Discussing feelings helps

TABLE 10.6 **Phases of Grief**

Phase	What Person May Say	Characteristics
Shock	I can't believe this. This isn't happening.	React to the learning of a loss with numbness. Shock may provide an emotional buffer and protect the person from being overwhelmed.
Denial	I'm doing fine. The results are wrong.	Denies the loss has taken place. Feelings of defensiveness may be present or act withdrawn. Temporary response may last minutes to months.
Anger	Why me? This is not fair. Why could this happen? Who is to blame?	Emotional response as the realization of severity of illness increases. Feelings of anger may be directed at inanimate objects, friends, family, strangers, or HCPs. May be angry at the person who inflicted the hurt (even after death) or at the world for letting it happen. May be angry with self for letting an event (e.g., car accident) take place, even if nothing could have stopped it. Loved ones may be angry at the dying or deceased patient.
Bargaining	If I could trade their life for mine... I promise to quit smoking. If only I had seen the oncologist sooner...	Normal reaction to feeling helpless and vulnerable. Statements made out of sense to regain control. Attempts to rationalize current state. Associated with feelings of guilt. May make bargains with God.
Depression	I'm dying, so what's the point? I'm so sad, so why bother with anything?	Feelings of sadness, despair, and regret as one recognizes mortality. Patients and families may be quiet, seek isolation, or appear mournful.
Acceptance	I'm okay with it all. It's going to be okay.	Embracing of mortality and inevitable death. Able to engage in life review and feel at peace with one's death or death of a loved one.

Adapted from Oates JR, Maan-Fogelman PA: Nursing grief and loss. Retrieved from https://www.ncbi.nlm.nih.gov/books/NBK518989/.

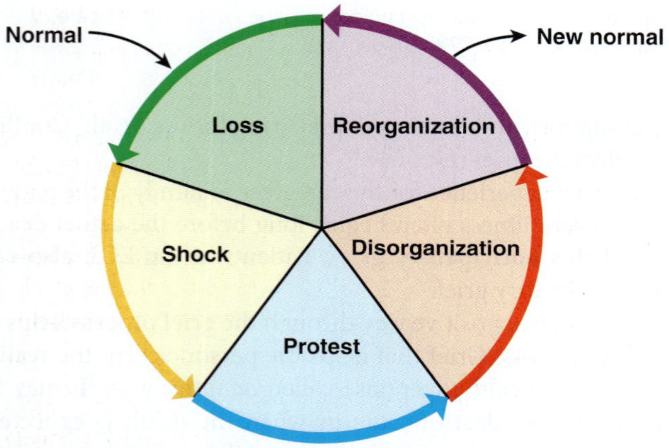

Fig. 10.7 The grief wheel model begins with the normal state at the bottom. After a person goes through the grief process, eventually the grief will resolve. Because of the loss, the normal state is different from before. The challenge is to accept the "new normal."

them work toward resolution of the grief process. Respect the patient's privacy and need to talk or remain silent. Be honest in answering questions and giving information.

Spirituality and religion may offer meaning and are associated with decreased despair in patients at EOL.[20] Some dying patients are secure in their faith about the future. It is common to see patients give away material possessions and focus on values that they believe will lead them on to another place. Religion may offer a meaning and a sense of peace and recognition in the broader cosmic context.[20]

Culturally Competent Care: End of Life

Culture and ethnicity are important considerations for patients receiving palliative and EOL care and their families. Cultural beliefs affect a person's understanding of and reaction to death or loss. Culture and ethnicity affect decision making about life support, withholding and withdrawing treatments, and using palliative or hospice care.[21] Perform a cultural assessment and tailor care to the patient and family.

Rituals associated with dying are part of all cultures. Many differences exist among cultural beliefs and values in relation to death and dying. Being aware of specific cultural traditions may help to anticipate patient and family needs. For example, some in the Jewish faith may not engage in organ donation. They may keep constant vigil during end of life and 7 days after burial. Some Hindus and Buddhists may believe in karma or reincarnation and prefer cremation. In many Islamic cultures, the traditional rites of washing, shrouding, funeral prayers, and burial are done as soon as possible.

Make accommodations related to the patient's language, diet, and cultural beliefs and practices. Families with non–English-speaking members are at risk for receiving less information about their family member's critical illness and prognosis.[21] Access medical interpreter services, if needed, so that the patient's wishes are known. Culturally competent care is discussed in Chapter 2.

NURSING MANAGEMENT: END OF LIFE

Nurses spend more time with patients near the EOL than any other health care professionals. Respect, dignity, and comfort are important for the patient and family. Although there is no cure for the patient's disease, the treatment plan still consists of assessment, planning, implementation, and evaluation. The main difference is that the focus of care is on the management of the symptoms.

Assessment

Be sensitive and do not perform repeated, unnecessary assessments. When possible, use health history data available in the medical record rather than tiring the patient with an interview. Assess the patient's functional status, intake, patterns of sleep and rest, and response to the stress of terminal illness. Review their ability to cope with the diagnosis and prognosis. Assess the family's ability to manage the needed care and to cope with the illness and its consequences.

The physical assessment focuses on changes that accompany terminal illness and the specific disease process (Table 10.4). The frequency depends on the patient's stability. Assessment is done at least every 8 hours in the agency setting. For patients cared for in their homes by hospice programs, assessment may occur weekly. Pay attention to patients who are nonverbal for subtle changes in their condition. As changes occur, you may assess and document more often.

Key elements of a social assessment include the relationships and patterns of communication among the family. Listen to concerns. Evaluate the goals of the patient and family. Differences in expectations and interpersonal conflict can produce disruptions during the dying process and after the death of the loved one.

Monitor the patient for multiple systems failing with attention to subtle physical changes. Neurologic assessment is especially important and includes level of consciousness, presence of reflexes, and pupil responses. Vital signs, skin color, and temperature show changes in circulation. Monitor and describe respiratory status, character and pattern of respirations, and characteristics of breath sounds. Assess nutrition and fluid intake, urine output, and bowel function since this gives data about renal and gastrointestinal functioning. Assess skin condition on an ongoing basis since fragile skin may easily break down.

In the last hours of life, limit assessments to those that determine patient comfort. Assessment of pain and respiratory status may be the most important during this time. It may be more peaceful and comforting to the patient and family if you refrain from measuring BP or checking for pupillary response. As death approaches, provide emotional and psychosocial support to the patient and family. Limit tasks that will not impact the comfort or outcome for the patient.

◆ Clinical Problems

Clinical problems for the patient who is dying and their family includes:

- Grief
- Dying process

◆ Planning

The overall goals are that the patient who is dying will (1) make decisions about EOL care and (2) experience a peaceful death. Involve the patient and family in planning and coordinating EOL care. Develop a comprehensive plan to support, teach, and evaluate patients and families. Care goals during the last stages of life involve comfort and safety measures and care of the patient's emotional and physical needs. These may include determining where the patient would like to die and whether this is possible. For example, the patient may want to die at home, but the family may object or be unable to manage the physical care.

◆ Implementation

Advocate for the patient's wishes to be met where possible. Patients and families need ongoing information on the disease, the dying process, the care you will be providing, and how to cope. Denial and grieving may be barriers to learning for both the patient and family.

◆ Psychosocial Care

As death approaches, respond appropriately to the patient's psychosocial manifestations at the EOL (Table 10.7).

TABLE 10.7 NURSING MANAGEMENT

Psychosocial Care at End of Life

Dimensions	Nursing Management
Preparing for Death	
Serious illness can create strain on relationships. It is important to facilitate meaningful discussions for the patient and family to prepare for death. They may reconcile the past to find meaning in the present.	Encourage the patient and family to share their feelings of love, sadness, loss, forgiveness. Saying goodbye can be therapeutic. Encourage the use of physical touch (e.g., hand holding, hugging) and expressions such as crying. Allow the patient and family privacy to express their feelings and comfort one another.
Spiritual Needs	
Religion, faith, and spirituality may be sources of strength for patients and families. Patients and family members may experience spiritual longing.	Assess spiritual needs, cultural norms, hopes, values, and fears. Address the needs of the family and caregivers. Allow patient to express concerns about quality of life, fear of death or dying, spiritual practices, and significant relationships. Recognize the presence of spiritual or existential distress. Promote visits by spiritual care service provider, chaplain, family member.
Unusual Communication	
This may indicate altered coping that may prevent the patient from resolving issues and letting go. Comorbid psychiatric conditions may worsen. Patients may become restless and agitated, which may be a manifestation of terminal delirium.	Assess for depression, anxiety, and/or delirium. Encourage the family to talk with and reassure the patient. Coordinate with the IPT to assist with counseling and communication.
End-of-Life Dreams and Visions	
Patients may be seen talking to persons who are not there or seeing places and objects not visible. They may report dreams of living or deceased loved ones. These experiences may comfort the patient in coming to terms with meaning in life and transition from it.	Assess for the presence, distress, or comfort from these visions. Affirm the patient's experience as a part of transition from this life. Teach families and caregivers about the patient's experiences.
Withdrawal	
This may be an emotional response or part of grieving. Patient near death may seem withdrawn from the physical environment, maintaining the ability to hear but unable to respond.	Allow the patient to sleep and rest. Converse as though the patient were alert, using a soft voice and gentle touch. Provide education to families and caregivers. Encourage meaningful tasks and discussions during periods of wakefulness.

Anxiety and depression. Patients often show signs of anxiety and depression during the EOL period. Causes of anxiety and depression may include uncontrolled pain and dyspnea, psychosocial factors related to the disease process or impending death, altered physiologic states, and drugs used in high dosages. Anxiety is often related to fear. Encouragement, support, and teaching may help. Management may include both medications and nonpharmacologic interventions. Relaxation strategies, such as relaxation breathing, muscle relaxation, music, and imagery, may be useful (see Chapter 7).

Anger. Anger is a common and normal response to grief. A grieving person cannot be forced to accept the loss. The surviving family members may be angry with the dying loved one who is leaving them. Encourage the expression of feelings, but it is hard to come to terms with loss. As a nurse, you may be the target of the anger. Understand the anger response and avoid reacting on a personal level.

Hopelessness and powerlessness. Feelings of hopelessness and powerlessness are common during the EOL period. Encourage realistic hope within the limits of the situation. Support the patient's involvement in decision making about care to foster a sense of control and autonomy. Allow the patient and family to deal with what is within their control. Help them recognize what is beyond their control.

Fear. Fear is a typical feeling associated with dying. Specific fears include fear of pain, fear of shortness of breath, fear of loneliness and abandonment, and fear of meaninglessness.

Many people assume that pain accompanies death. However, there is no evidence that death is always painful. Most patients want their pain relieved without the side effects of grogginess or sleepiness. Pain relief measures do not have to deprive the patient of the ability to interact with others. Assure the patient and family that drugs will be given promptly when needed and that any side effects will be managed. As many EOL patients are unable to swallow, other routes, such as patches, sublingual, and rectal routes, may be used. Consider alternative methods like massage, music, aromatherapy, and mindfulness.

Respiratory distress and dyspnea are common near the EOL. The sensation of air hunger results in anxiety for the patient and family. Current treatments include opioids, bronchodilators, and oxygen, depending on the cause of the dyspnea. Anxiety-reducing agents (e.g., anxiolytics) may help produce relaxation.

Most terminally ill and dying people do not want to be alone. Many dying patients are afraid that loved ones who are unable to cope with the patient's imminent death will abandon them. Simply being present offers support and comfort (Fig. 10.8). Holding hands, touching, and listening are important nursing interventions. Providing companionship allows the patient a sense of security.

Fear of meaninglessness leads people to review their lives. Assist patients with *life review* to help them recognize the value of their lives. Practical ways of helping may include looking at photo albums or collections of important mementos while sharing thoughts and feelings.

Empathy and active listening are essential. Often silence is related to the overwhelming feelings experienced at the EOL.

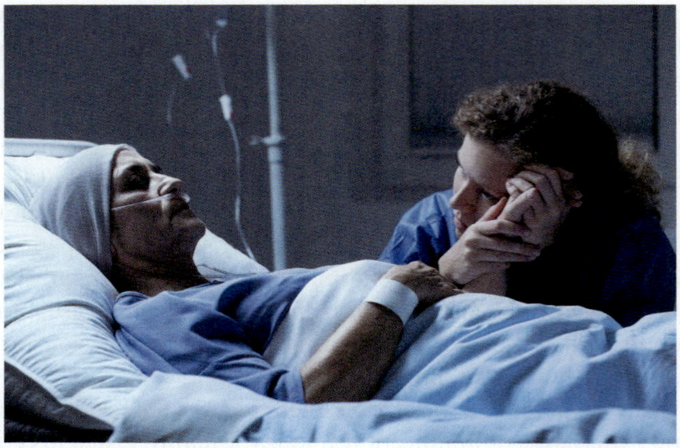

Fig. 10.8 Dying patients often want someone whom they know and trust to stay with them. (© KatarzynaBialasiewicz/iStock.com)

Silence can also allow time to gather thoughts. Listening to the silence sends a message of acceptance and comfort.

Patients and family members may have difficulties expressing themselves. Allow time for them to express their feelings and thoughts. Listen and interact in a sensitive way to enhance the relationship among you, the patient, and the family. A family conference can create a good environment for communication.

Prepare family members for changes in the patient's emotional and cognitive function as death nears. The patient's speech may become confused, disoriented, or garbled. Patients may speak to or about family members or others who have predeceased them or give instructions to those who will survive them.

◆ Physical Care

Physical care at the EOL focuses on symptom management and comfort (Table 10.8). The priority is meeting the patient's physiologic and safety needs. Physical care focuses on the needs for oxygen, nutrition, pain relief, mobility, elimination, and skin care. People who are dying deserve and require the same physical care as people who are expected to recover. Discuss the goals of care with the patient and family before treatment begins.

Postmortem care. After a patient is pronounced dead, you will need to prepare or delegate preparing the patient's body for immediate viewing by the family. Consider cultural customs and follow your agency policy for postmortem care (Table 10.9). In some cultures, such as Hinduism and Judaism, it may be important to allow the family to prepare or help in caring for the patient's body.[22] When the death is unexpected, preparing the patient's body for viewing or release to a funeral home depends on state law and agency policy.

Care of and discussion related to the patient should continue to be respectful even after death. Allow the family privacy and as much time as they need with the deceased patient. Never refer to the deceased patient as "the body."

SPECIAL NEEDS OF CAREGIVERS AND NURSES IN END-OF-LIFE CARE

Special Needs of Family Caregivers

Family caregivers are important in meeting the patient's physical and psychosocial needs. Their role includes working and

TABLE 10.8 NURSING MANAGEMENT

Physical Care at End of Life

Manifestation	Nursing Management
Anorexia, Dehydration, Nausea, and Vomiting	
• May be caused by complications of disease process • Hunger and thirst significantly decrease in the last days of life • Dehydration is common • Medications contribute to nausea • Constipation, impaction, and bowel obstruction can cause anorexia, nausea, vomiting	• Assess the patient for nausea or vomiting, and possible contributing causes • Provide antiemetics as needed and before meals if ordered • Offer and provide frequent meals with small portions of favorite foods. Offer culturally appropriate foods • Do not force the patient to eat or drink • Provide frequent mouth care • Encourage consumption of ice chips and sips of fluids or use moist cloths to moisten the mouth • Use moist cloths and swabs for unconscious patients to avoid aspiration • Apply lubricant to the lips and oral mucous membranes as needed • Ensure uninterrupted mealtimes • Teach family that hunger and thirst naturally decreases at end of life
Bowel Patterns	
• Immobility, opioid use, depression, lack of dietary fiber in the diet, dehydration, obstructive cancer can cause constipation • Diarrhea may occur from laxative use, obstruction, fecal impaction, infection, medications, chemotherapy	• Assess bowel function and associated symptoms • Assess for and remove fecal impactions • Encourage movement and physical activities as tolerated • Encourage fiber in the diet if appropriate. Discuss the role of IV fluids in context of goals of care • Use suppositories, stool softeners, laxatives, and/or enemas as ordered, especially if on opioids • Assess for confusion, agitation, restlessness, and pain, which may be signs of constipation • Encourage the intake of simple carbohydrates, if appropriate, and use of antidiarrheals as needed
Oral Conditions	
• Candidiasis may be present due to chemotherapy, immunosuppression • Xerostomia or dry mouth is common. This may be due to comorbidities, medication, radiation, dehydration	• Assess oral cavity and cause of problem • If ordered, give oral antifungal • Clean dentures and other dental appliances to prevent reinfection • Provide oral hygiene and use soft toothbrush or sponge
Delirium and Restlessness	
• Develops over a short period of time with severity fluctuating through the day • Characterized by confusion, disorientation, restlessness, clouding of consciousness, incoherence, fear, anxiety, excitement, hallucinations • May be misidentified as depression, psychosis, anger, anxiety • Contributing factors include medications, underlying disease, environment, sensory impairment, metabolic problems • Associated with adverse outcomes • Considered reversible • Common in final days of life	• Perform a thorough assessment for delirium using a validated tool • Assess for risk factors for delirium, including pain, constipation, and urinary retention and treat as needed • Include nonpharmacologic interventions as appropriate • Provide a room that is quiet, well lit, and familiar to reduce the effects of delirium • Reorient the patient to person, place, and time with each encounter • Give ordered antipsychotics, benzodiazepines, and sedatives as needed • Stay physically close to frightened patient. Reassure in a calm, soft voice with touch and slow strokes of the skin • Avoid physical restraints whenever possible • Provide family with emotional support and encouragement in their efforts to cope with the behaviors associated with delirium
Difficulty Swallowing	
• May occur due to cancer, neurologic problems, weakness • Common at EOL • May lead to aspiration of liquids and/or solids, pneumonia, malnutrition, dehydration, death • Drooling/inability to swallow secretions may be present	• Assess level of alertness and safety of oral intake • Collaborate with IPT for evaluation based on goals of care. Referral for speech-language pathologist • If needed, use alternative routes for (rectal, buccal, transdermal, IV) drug administration for symptom management • Modify diet to focus on comfort or pleasure, as tolerable by patient • Teach family on safety and risk for aspiration • Review medications and stop nonessential • Hand feed small meals • Elevate the head for meals and at least 30 minutes after

TABLE 10.8 NURSING MANAGEMENT—cont'd

Physical Care at End of Life

Manifestation	Nursing Management
Dyspnea, Terminal Secretions, and Cough • Can significantly impair quality of life. • Dyspnea is often accompanied by chest tightness, fear of suffocation, anxiety • Terminal secretions, or death rattle, is noisy breathing from secretion accumulation. Very common in the hours before death • Presence of terminal secretions can be distressing to family members • Cough is a reaction to an irritation of the respiratory tract, and can be debilitating	• Assess respiratory status regularly • Assess for anxiety and other associated symptoms including pain and fatigue • Elevate the head and/or position patient on side to improve chest expansion • Use a fan or air conditioner to help movement of cool air • Teach and encourage the use of pursed-lip breathing • Teach relaxation and guided imagery techniques for relaxation • Administer opioids as ordered for dyspnea • Administer benzodiazepines for associated anxiety • Administer anticholinergic medications such as glycopyrrolate or atropine for secretion management • Administer antitussives, expectorants, mucolytics, opioids, or inhaled anesthetics for cough • O_2 use should be based on the goals of care at the EOL • Avoid deep suctioning. Gentle oral suctioning may be used • Teach the patient and family on these symptoms and treatments. Provide emotional support for caregivers
Myoclonus • Mild to severe abnormal movement that may be a brief jerking, twitching, or movement of the extremities • Can be caused by medications, metabolic imbalances, central nervous system damage	• Assess for onset, duration, any discomfort or distress • Review potential causes, including medications • Treat symptoms with benzodiazepines • Provide education and emotional support to patient and family
Pain • Is a major symptom at EOL, can contribute to suffering, and the most feared • Often associated with other symptoms and sources of distress • Can be acute or chronic, neuropathic, nociceptive, inflammatory, and/or mechanical • Often requires opioids for management • Bone pain can be caused by metastases, fractures, arthritis, immobility • Physical and emotional stressors can worsen pain	• Assess pain thoroughly and regularly to determine the onset, duration, quality, intensity, location, and aggravating and alleviating factors • Assess for associated symptoms including anxiety, social or spiritual distress • Give medications around the clock, in a timely manner, and on a regular basis to provide constant relief rather than waiting until the pain is unbearable and then trying to relieve it • Provide nonpharmacologic interventions, such as guided imagery, massage, and relaxation techniques as needed (see Chapter 7) • Frequently evaluate effectiveness of pain relief measures • Ensure that the patient is on a correct, adequate drug regimen • Monitor for side effects of opioids, such as nausea or constipation, and treat as appropriate • Teach the patient and family on all interventions and medications • Do not delay or deny pain relief measures to a terminally ill patient
Skin Breakdown • Skin integrity is hard to maintain at the end of life • Immobility, urinary and bowel incontinence, dry skin, malnutrition, anemia, friction, and shearing forces lead to a high risk for skin breakdown • Disease and other processes may impair skin integrity • In the last days of life, circulation to the extremities decreases and they become cool, mottled, cyanotic	• Assess skin for signs of breakdown or injury • Assess risk factors for skin breakdown and implement protocols to prevent • Perform wound assessments as needed • Follow protocols for dressing wounds • Premedicate if turning, repositioning, or wound care cause discomfort • Follow protocols to prevent skin irritation and breakdown from urinary and bowel incontinence • Use blankets to cover for warmth. Use lotions to prevent dryness
Urinary and Bowel Incontinence • May result from disease progression or changes in the level of consciousness, medications, decreased mobility • As death becomes imminent, the perineal muscles relax, causing incontinence of bowel and bladder • Urine production is decreased at EOL	• Assess urinary and bowel function • Use absorbent pads for incontinence and barrier creams to prevent irritation • Follow protocols for the use and management of indwelling or external catheters • Follow protocols to prevent skin irritation and breakdown from urinary and bowel incontinence
Weakness and Fatigue • Decline in mental status and energy is expected • Causes include metabolic demands related to disease, underlying chronic condition, cancer, malnutrition, insomnia, infection	• Assess the patient's tolerance for physical and mental activities • Help the patient identify and complete valued or desired activities • Modify and time nursing interventions to conserve energy • Refer to physical and occupational therapy for safe movement • Review nutrition and hydration based on goals of care • Give frequent rest periods and adjust environment to allow for quiet surroundings

TABLE 10.9 NURSING MANAGEMENT
Postmortem Care

- Provide privacy throughout the process. Teach family and caregivers on process if present.
- Assess cultural and/or religious preferences or rituals about this process from family or caregivers before starting.
- Obtain supplies needed before starting. This may include a kit or individual items. Ask for help if needed.
- Wash hands, and use protective equipment as needed.
- Close the patient's eyes and jaw.
- Replace dentures; if unable, place in labeled cup.
- Remove jewelry, eyeglasses, and other personal belongings.
- Remove tubes and dressings (per policy).
- Wash the body as needed then apply clothes selected by the patient or family (home), or a clean gown (agency). Comb and arrange the hair neatly.
- Place a waterproof pad or incontinence brief to absorb urine and feces.
- Straighten the body, placing the arms at their sides or across the abdomen with palms down.
- Follow instructions per policy in home or agency setting.

communicating with the patient and other family members, supporting the patient's concerns, and helping the patient resolve any unfinished business. Families often face emotional, physical, and economic consequences from caring for a family member who is dying. The caregiver's responsibilities do not end when the patient is admitted to an acute care, inpatient hospice, or long-term care agency.[23]

Being present during a family member's dying process can be highly stressful. Recognize signs and behaviors of abnormal grief reactions among family members. Warning signs may include dependency and negative feelings about the dying patient, inability to express feelings, sleep problems, a history of depression, difficult reactions to previous losses, perceived lack of social or family support, low self-esteem, multiple previous bereavements, or alcohol or substance use. Caregivers with concurrent life crises (e.g., divorce) are especially at risk.

Encourage family caregivers and other family members to continue their usual activities where possible to maintain some control over their lives. Inform caregivers about resources for support, including respite care, community counseling, and local support in working through grief. Encourage caregivers to build a support system of extended family, friends, faith community, and clergy to call on to express any feelings they are experiencing.

Special Needs of Nurses

Nurses who care for the dying need to recognize their own needs when dealing with grief and dying. Caring for patients and their families at the EOL is challenging and rewarding but also intense and emotionally charged. A bond or connection may develop between you and the patient or family. When you provide care for terminally ill or dying patients, you are not immune to feelings of loss. Be aware of how grief personally affects you. It is common to feel helpless and powerless when dealing with death. Be aware of what you can and cannot control. Express feelings of sorrow, guilt, and frustration. Recognize your own values, attitudes, and feelings about death. Realizing that it is okay to cry with the patient or family during the EOL may be important for your well-being.

To meet your personal needs, focus on interventions to decrease your stress. Get involved in hobbies or other interests, schedule time for yourself, ensure time for sleep, maintain a peer support system, and develop a support system beyond the workplace. Many hospice agencies offer support groups and discussion sessions that can help you cope.

Case Study
Spiritual Distress at End of Life

(© XiXinXing/ iStock.com)

Patient Profile

G.M. is a 42-year-old man with end-stage liver disease and recently diagnosed liver cancer. He could not receive any therapy and is now enrolled in hospice. He has a history of excessive alcohol use. He reports increased abdominal pain, nausea, vomiting, and anorexia. Current medications include fentanyl transdermal patch and hydromorphone for pain, ondansetron for nausea and vomiting, sertraline for depression, and mirtazapine for appetite. He is divorced with 2 children, age 10 and 8. He was raised Christian but says faith is not important to his care.

Subjective Data

- Reports pain at 7 (0- to 10-point scale) not relieved by medication
- Reports feeling that he is being punished for his previous lifestyle and getting divorced
- Asks why God would leave his children without a father and questions if there "is a God"
- States he is worried about the loss of his health benefits and what will happen to his children

Objective Data

Assessment

- Dry skin with scratch marks
- Weight 145 lb., height 5 ft 10 in
- Yellow sclera

Interprofessional Care

- Review pain medications usage and assess for dosage adjustment
- Consult chaplaincy and review ways to address distress
- Social work consult to review medical benefits and disability application
- Psychology consult for counseling and promoting discussions with ex-wife and children
- Ensure that advance directives are in place

Discussion Questions

1. ***Recognize:*** What are G.M.'s risk factors for spiritual and existential distress?
2. ***Analyze:*** Based on the data given, what are the major health problems for G.M.?
3. ***Plan:*** What cultural considerations should be included when planning care?
4. ***Prioritize:*** Based on your assessment of G.M., what are the top 3 priority nursing interventions?
5. ***Act:*** What teaching will be important so the patient can self-manage symptoms and care?
6. ***Evaluate:*** What outcomes would indicate interprofessional care was effective?
7. ***Safety:*** Describe specific nursing actions you would take to promote patient safety.

Answers available at http://evolve.elsevier.com/Lewis/medsurg.

BRIDGE TO NCLEX EXAMINATION

The number of the question corresponds to the same-numbered outcome at the beginning of the chapter.

1. A 77-year-old man with emphysema is receiving palliative care along with pulmonary management. Which statements provide accurate information for planning this patient's care? *(select all that apply)*
   a. This patient does not need palliative care.
   b. The pulmonologist can provide primary palliative care.
   c. Palliative care can help improve coping and quality of life.
   d. Palliative care can help with symptom burden, such as dyspnea.
   e. The patient is at end of life since palliative care is only for those who are dying.
2. The nurse explains to a patient with advanced prostate cancer about the differences between hospice and palliative care. Which patient statement indicates teaching was effective?
   a. "Hospice care is not available if I am in the hospital."
   b. "Palliative care provides better methods of pain control."
   c. "Hospice care can help me stay home and die naturally."
   d. "Palliative care does not include any advance directives."
3. A woman has been widowed for 2 years after her husband died from glioblastoma. The woman stopped working, does not leave the house often, has not removed her husband's items from the home, and cries daily about her loss. How would the nurse characterize this woman's grieving?
   a. Adaptive grief
   b. Disruptive grief
   c. Anticipatory grief
   d. Prolonged grief disorder
4. A patient on home hospice tells the nurse, "I can't believe God would do this to me. I've always been healthy until this cancer. I don't understand!" Which state is the patient exhibiting? *(select all that apply)*
   a. Denial
   b. Loneliness
   c. Fear of death
   d. Spiritual distress
   e. Existential distress
5. A nurse is completing the admission assessment for an 88-year-old woman admitted with heart failure. The nurse asks about advance directives, and the patient does not know what this means. Which response would accurately describe advance directives?
   a. "These are forms that tell your doctor when you want to withdraw care."
   b. "These forms will tell your loved ones where your money goes after you die."
   c. "There are forms such as a living will where you detail your treatment preferences."
   d. "You cannot fill out any advance directives right now since you are in the hospital."
6. A 35-year-old woman with sarcoma arrives to the clinic for chemotherapy. She reports severe pain at a level of 7 (0- to 10-point scale) in her right lower extremity. Which action would the nurse take before starting the chemotherapy?
   a. Auscultate for bowel sounds.
   b. Ask her about advance directives.
   c. Administer chemotherapy premedications.
   d. Review orders and give prescribed pain medications.
7. Which clinical manifestations are common in a patient who is actively dying? *(select all that apply)*
   a. Noisy secretions
   b. Increased sensation
   c. Mottling of hands and feet
   d. Cheyne-Stokes respirations
   e. Increased response to tactile stimuli
8. The nurse is assigned a 49-year-old patient with breast cancer who speaks only Cantonese. There are several family members at bedside. Which action would the nurse take first?
   a. Call a pastor or priest for the family to help them cope.
   b. Avoid using a translator for fear of offending the family.
   c. Ask for a different nurse to have this patient assignment.
   d. Assess the language preferences and beliefs of the patient and family.

1. b, c, d; 2. c; 3. d; 4. d, e; 5. c; 6. d; 7. a, c, d; 8. d.

For rationales to these answers and even more NCLEX review questions, visit http://evolve.elsevier.com/Lewis/medsurg.

EVOLVE WEBSITE/RESOURCES LIST

http://evolve.elsevier.com/Lewis/medsurg
Review Questions (Online Only)
Key Points
Answer Keys for Questions
- Rationales for Bridge to NCLEX Examination Questions
- Answer Guidelines for Case Study

Student Case Study
- Patient With Chronic Myelogenous Leukemia Including End-of-Life Care

Conceptual Care Map Creator
Audio Glossary
Content Updates

REFERENCES

*1. Radbruch L, De Lima L, Knaul F, et al.: Redefining palliative care: a new consensus-based definition, *J Pain Symptom Manage* 20:S0885–3924, 2020.
*2. Knaul FM, Bhadelia A, Rodriguez NM, Arreola-Ornelas H, Zimmerman C: The Lancet Commission on palliative care and pain relief-findings, recommendations, and future directions, *Lancet* 6:s5, 2018.
*3. Institute for Clinical Systems Improvement: *Palliative care for adults*, ed 6, Bloomington, MN, 2020.

4. Center to Advance Palliative Care: Palliative care facts and stats. Retrieved from https://media.capc.org/filer_public/68/bc/68b-c93c7-14ad-4741-9830-8691729618d0/capc_press-kit.pdf.

*5. National Coalition for Hospice and Palliative Care: Clinical practice guidelines for quality palliative care. Retrieved from www.nationalcoalitionhpc.org/ncp/.

6. American Nurses Association & Hospice and Palliative Nurses Association: Call for action: Nurses lead and transform palliative care. Retrieved from https://www.nursingworld.org/~497158/globalassets/practiceandpolicy/health-policy/palliativecareprofessionalissuespanelcallforaction.pdf

7. Quill TE, Abernathy AP: Generalists plus specialists palliative care – creating a more sustainable model, *N Engl J Med* 368:1173, 2013. (Historical).

8. Mazanec P, Reimer R, Bullington J, et al.: Interdisciplinary palliative care teams. In Ferrell BR, Paice J, editors: *Oxford textbook of palliative nursing*, ed 5, New York, 2019, Oxford University Press.

9. National Hospice and Palliative Care Organization: Facts on hospice and palliative care. Retrieved from www.nhpco.org/hospice-statistics-research-press-room/facts-hospice-and-palliative-care.

*10. Rosa W: Spiritual care intervention. In Ferrell BR, Paice JA, editors: *Oxford textbook of palliative nursing*, ed 5, New York, 2019, Oxford University Press.

11. Field M, Cassel C: *Approaching death: Improving care at the end of life*, Washington, DC, 1997, National Academy Press. (Classic).

12. National Hospice and Palliative Care Organization: Palliative care costs and benefits. Retrieved from www.caringinfo.org/i4a/pages/index.cfm?pageid=3297.

13. Aging with Dignity: Five Wishes. Retrieved from https://fivewishes.org.

14. George LS, Breitbart W, Prigerson HG: "My family wants something different": Discordance in perceived personal and family treatment preference and its association with do-not-resuscitate order placement, *J Oncol Pract* 15:11, 2019.

15. U.S. Department of Health and Human Services: U.S. government information on organ donation and transplantation. Retrieved from www.organdonor.gov/index.html.

16. American Nurses Association: The nurse's role when a patient requests medical aid in dying, 2019. Retrieved from https://www.nursingworld.org/~49e869/globalassets/practiceandpolicy/nursing-excellence/ana-position-statements/social-causes-and-health-care/the-nurses-role-when-a-patient-requests-medical-aid-in-dying-web-format.pdf.

17. American Academy of Neurology: Brain injury and brain death. Retrieved from https://www.aan.com/Guidelines/home/ByTopic?topicId=13.

18. Oates JR, Maan-Fogelman PA: Nursing grief and loss. Retrieved from https://www.ncbi.nlm.nih.gov/books/NBK518989/.

19. National Cancer Institute: PDQ: Grief, bereavement, and coping with loss. Retrieved from www.cancer.gov/cancertopics/pdq/supportivecare/bereavement/HealthProfessional.

20. Vail KE, Routledge C: *The science of religion, spirituality, and existentialism*, New York, 2020, Elsevier.

21. American Psychological Association: Culturally diverse communities and palliative and end-of-life care. Retrieved from https://www.apa.org/pi/aging/programs/eol/end-of-life-diversity.

22. Center to Advance Palliative Care: Increasing awareness of palliative care for minorities. Retrieved from https://www.capc.org/blog/increasing-awareness-palliative-care-minorities/.

*23. Becque YN, Rietjens J, van Driel A, et al.: Nursing interventions to support family caregivers in end-of-life at home: a systematic review, *Int J Nurs Stud* 97:28, 2019.

*Evidence-based information for clinical practice.

11

Substance Use Disorders in Acute Care

Mariann M. Harding

ⓔ http://evolve.elsevier.com/Lewis/medsurg/

CONCEPTUAL FOCUS

Addiction
Cognition
Stress and Coping

LEARNING OUTCOMES

1. Relate the effects of substance use to its resulting major health complications.
2. Discern among the effects of the use of stimulants, depressants, and cannabis.
3. Explain your role in promoting the cessation of smoking and tobacco use.
4. Summarize the nursing and interprofessional management of patients with toxicity or withdrawal from stimulants and depressants.
5. Apply the Screening, Brief Intervention, and Referral to Treatment approach in clinical situations.
6. Describe the incidence and effects of substance use in the older adult.

KEY TERMS

acute alcohol toxicity
alcohol use disorder (AUD)
alcohol withdrawal syndrome (AWS)
binge drinking
Screening, Brief Intervention, and Referral to Treatment (SBIRT)
substance use disorder (SUD)
tobacco use disorder (TUD)
vaping

Substance use is a serious problem affecting society and the health care system. Substance-related disorders involve several types of substances. These range from widely used and accepted tobacco and alcohol to illegal, brain-altering drugs such as heroin and cocaine. **Substance use disorder (SUD)** occurs when the use of alcohol and/or drugs causes significant impairment, including health problems and failure to meet responsibilities (Table 11.1).[1]

Some describe SUD as mild, moderate, or severe, depending on the pattern of use and its impact on the person's daily life. Knowing the severity of substance use allows the health care team to tailor treatment to the patient's needs. For example, a person who binge drinks may not have alcohol SUD but is at increased risk for SUD. On the other hand, a person who uses heroin or cocaine is likely to have severe SUD because these substances are highly addictive.

Many patients with substance use problems receive acute care for problems associated with substance use. SUD does not exist in isolation. There are many interrelated problems depending on the patient's situation. Every drug associated with SUD harms some tissue or organ. Substance use causes specific health problems, such as liver damage related to alcohol use or lung cancer related to smoking. Other problems result from injuries associated with substance use, such as falls or motor vehicle accidents. Common health problems related to substance use are outlined in Table 11.2.

This chapter focuses on the nurse's role in identifying and managing the patient with SUD in the acute care setting. A hospitalized patient who uses substances can develop withdrawal when substance use abruptly stops. You need to be able to recognize substance use and its effects on health problems and manage withdrawal. The health care setting offers an opportunity for screening and teaching about substance use. It is your responsibility to motivate the patient to change behavior and refer the patient to treatment programs.

TABLE 11.1 Diagnostic Criteria

Substance Use Disorder

The following general criteria can be used to identify the presence of SUD:

Impaired Control

- Taking more or for longer than intended
- Not quitting use despite multiple times of trying
- Spending a great deal of time obtaining, using, or recovering from use
- Urge or craving to use the substance

Social Impairment

- Missing school, work, or other responsibilities due to use
- Continuing use despite problems caused or worsened by use
- Giving up or reducing important activities because of use
- Use takes precedence over other interests or enjoyments, daily activities, or health or personal care
- Use takes a central role in the person's life

Dependence

- Physical tolerance to effects of the substance
- Presence of withdrawal symptoms when not using or using less
- Repeated use to prevent or alleviate withdrawal symptoms.

Source: Saunders JB, Latt NC: Diagnosis and classification of substance use disorders. In *Addiction medicine: Science and practice*, 2020, Elsevier.

DRUGS ASSOCIATED WITH SUBSTANCE USE DISORDER

NICOTINE

You are most likely to encounter people with **tobacco use disorder (TUD)**. People with TUD are dependent on the drug nicotine from using tobacco products. Products that contain nicotine include smoked tobacco (cigarettes, cigars, pipes), smokeless tobacco (chew, snuff, dip), and some electronic cigarettes. Cigarette smoking is the main form of tobacco use in the United States.

Effects of Use and Complications

Nicotine is a central nervous system stimulant. Within seconds of entering the body, nicotine reaches the brain, causing the release of adrenaline and creating feelings of a "high" or a "buzz." The effects last about 1 to 2 hours before withdrawal symptoms occur, leaving the person feeling tired, irritable, and anxious. The need to have the "high" or "buzz" feelings again makes the person crave more nicotine, leading to addiction.

Smoked tobacco is the most harmful method of nicotine use. Smoking harms nearly every organ in the body and reduces the person's general health. More than 16 million persons in the United States have a smoking-related disease.[2] Smoking causes lung disease, lung and other cancers, and heart disease and is a major factor in many other conditions (Fig. 11.1).

Although those who use smokeless tobacco have less risk for lung disease, use can cause serious health problems. Holding tobacco in the mouth is associated with periodontal disease and cancer of the mouth, cheek, tongue, throat, and esophagus. The nicotine in smokeless tobacco affects the cardiovascular system, increasing the risk for high blood pressure, heart attack, and stroke.

Vaping, or the use of electronic cigarettes or e-cigs, continues to increase. E-cigs have a similar look and feel of regular cigarettes. These battery-operated devices turn nicotine and other chemicals into an inhaled vapor. Vaping is associated with health risks. It can cause e-cig vaping-associated lung injury (EVALI) and other lung and cardiovascular problems. It can harm adolescent brain development and negatively influence pregnancy outcomes.[3] Although some believe e-cigs may aid in smoking cessation, they are not FDA-approved as a smoking cessation aid. Instead, you should encourage those who vape to stop using the same cessation strategies recommended for TUD.

TABLE 11.2 Health Problems Related to Substance Use

	Health Problems[a]
Substance	
Amphetamines	• Dysrhythmias, myocardial ischemia, and infarction • Liver, lung, kidney damage • Mood changes, violent behavior, psychoses
Cannabis	• Bronchitis, chronic cough • Depression, anxiety, schizophrenia • Impaired memory
Cocaine	• Dysrhythmias, myocardial ischemia and infarction • Psychosis • Seizures, stroke
Inhalants	• Acute and chronic kidney injury • Cognitive and motor impairment
Opioids	• Gastric ulcers • Glomerulonephritis • Sexual problems
Sedative-hypnotics	• Impaired memory • Personality changes, depression
Behaviors	
Injecting drugs	• Blood clots, phlebitis, skin infections • Hepatitis B and C • HIV/AIDS • Other infections: endocarditis, tuberculosis, pneumonia, meningitis, tetanus, bone and joint infections, lung abscesses
Personal neglect	• Accidental injuries • Malnutrition
Risky sexual behavior	• Hepatitis B and C • HIV/AIDS • Sexually transmitted infections
Snorting drugs	• Chronic sinusitis • Nasal sores, septal necrosis, perforation

[a]Health problems related to SUD are discussed in the appropriate chapters throughout the text, where they are identified as risk factors for these problems.

Adapted from National Institute on Drug Abuse: Medical consequence of drug abuse. Retrieved from www.drugabuse.gov/related-topics/medical-consequences-drug-abuse.

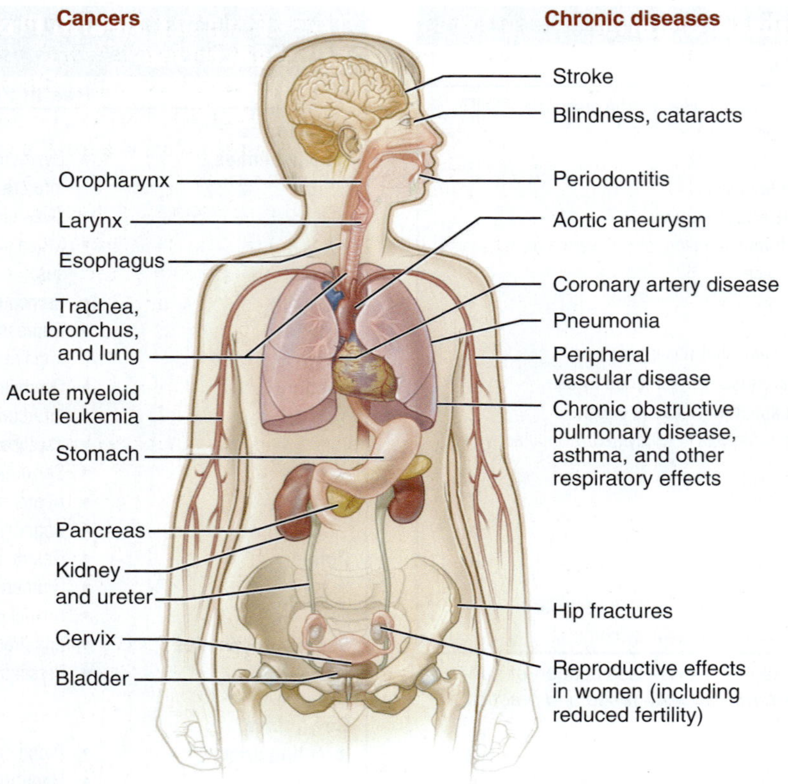

Fig. 11.1 Health effects of smoking. (From Samet JM: Tobacco smoking, *Thorac Surg Clin* 23[2]:103, 2013.)

NURSING AND INTERPROFESSIONAL MANAGEMENT: TOBACCO USE DISORDER

◆ Tobacco Cessation

As a nurse, you have a professional responsibility to help people stop smoking or using tobacco. The Joint Commission mandates that every health professional identify tobacco users and provide them with information on ways to stop using tobacco. Patients who receive even brief advice and intervention from you are more likely to quit than those who receive no intervention.

With each patient encounter, encourage the patient to quit and offer specific smoking cessation interventions. There are several tools we can use to encourage users to quit (Tables 11.3 and 11.4).[4] Use the brief clinical intervention the "5 *A*s and 5 *R*s" with each patient encounter. It will help you identify tobacco users, encourage them to quit, determine their willingness to quit, assist them in quitting, and arrange for follow-up. A patient teaching guide (Table 11.5) expands on the fourth strategy, *Assist,* to help you when the user is willing to quit. If a tobacco user is not willing to quit, using the "5 *Rs*" may encourage them to quit in the future.

A variety of smoking cessation products are available to help support users in quitting. These include prescription medicines and over-the-counter (OTC) products such as skin patches, lozenges, and gum. Nicotine replacement products are a common smoking cessation product. They reduce the craving and withdrawal symptoms of cessation by supplying the body with smaller amounts of nicotine (Table 11.6).

TABLE 11.3 5 *A*s and 5 *R*s

Brief TUD Intervention

The 5 *A*s for Users Who Want to Quit	The 5 *R*s for Users Unwilling to Quit
1. **Ask:** Identify all tobacco users at every contact.	1. **Relevance:** Ask the patient to say why quitting is personally relevant (e.g., health).
2. **Advise:** Strongly urge all tobacco users to quit.	2. **Risks:** Ask the patient to identify their potential risks/consequences of tobacco use.
3. **Assess:** Determine willingness to make a quit attempt.	3. **Rewards:** Ask the patient to relate potential benefits of stopping tobacco use.
4. **Assist:** Develop a plan with the patient to help the patient quit (e.g., counseling, medication).	4. **Roadblocks:** Ask patient to identify barriers or impediments to quitting.
5. **Arrange:** Schedule follow-up contact.	5. **Repetition:** Repeat process every clinic visit.

Source: Agency for Healthcare Research and Quality: *AHCPR supported clinical practice guideline: Treating tobacco use and dependence—2008 update,* Washington, DC, 2008, U.S. Public Health Service.

Because most health care agencies are tobacco-free, admitted patients addicted to nicotine may have withdrawal symptoms since they are unable to smoke. These symptoms are the same as for the person who stops using tobacco "cold turkey." Offering nicotine replacement therapy to every patient who wants to quit will help control withdrawal symptoms while hospitalized and promote continued cessation after discharge.

TABLE 11.4 Inpatient Tobacco Cessation Interventions

Take the following steps for every hospitalized patient:

- Ask each patient on admission if they use tobacco, and document tobacco use status.
- For current tobacco users, list tobacco use status on the admission problem list and as a discharge diagnosis.
- Use counseling and medication to help all tobacco users stay abstinent and to treat withdrawal symptoms.
- Give advice and assistance on how to quit while hospitalized and stay abstinent after discharge.
- Arrange for follow-up about smoking status. Provide supportive contact for at least a month after discharge.

Source: Agency for Healthcare Research and Quality: *AHCPR supported clinical practice guideline: Treating tobacco use and dependence: 2008 update,* Washington, DC, 2008, US Public Health Service.

Non-nicotine products also play a role in helping users quit. Varenicline (Chantix) is a drug used to aid smoking cessation. Varenicline is unique in that it has both agonist and antagonist actions. Its agonist activity at 1 subtype of nicotinic receptors provides some nicotine effects to ease withdrawal symptoms. If the person does resume smoking, its antagonist action blocks the effects of nicotine at another subtype of nicotinic receptor, making smoking less enjoyable. Bupropion (Zyban), an antidepressant drug, reduces the urge to smoke, reduces some withdrawal symptoms, and helps prevent weight gain from smoking cessation.

DRUG ALERT

Varenicline (Chantix) and Bupropion (Zyban)

- Behavior changes, hostility, aggression, depression, anxiety, suicidal thoughts, attempted suicide, and delusions have been reported.
- Tell patients to stop taking these drugs and contact the HCP at once if they have any of these manifestations.

TABLE 11.5 PATIENT & CAREGIVER TEACHING

Smoking and Tobacco Use Cessation

The following interventions are methods that work for quitting tobacco use. Tobacco users have the best chance of quitting if they use more than 1 method.

Develop a Quit Plan

- Set a quit date, ideally within 2 weeks.
- Talk to your HCP about getting help to quit.
- Tell family, friends, and coworkers about quitting and request understanding and support.
- Expect withdrawal symptoms and challenges when quitting.
- Before quitting, avoid smoking in places where you spend a lot of time (work, car, home).
- Throw away all tobacco products from your home, car, and work.
- Have support options in place by your quit date.

Use Approved Nicotine Replacement Systems

- Use a nicotine replacement agent unless you are a pregnant or nursing woman (Table 11.6).
- Do not use other forms of tobacco when using nicotine replacement systems.

Support and Encouragement

- Joining a quit-tobacco support group will increase your chances of stopping permanently.
- If you get the urge for tobacco, call someone to help talk you out of it—preferably an ex-user.
- Be proud every time you reach a quit milestone and reward yourself.
- Do not be afraid to talk about how you feel while quitting, especially fears of not being able to quit for good. Ask your spouse or partner, friends, and coworkers to support you. Self-help materials, mobile phone applications, and hotlines are available:
  - American Lung Association: 800-LUNGUSA; www.lung.org
  - American Cancer Society: 800-227-2345; www.cancer.org
  - National Cancer Institute: LiveHelp; www.smokefree.gov

Dealing With Urges to Use Tobacco

- Identify situations that may cause you to want to smoke or use other tobacco, such as being around other smokers, being under time pressure, feeling sad or frustrated, and drinking alcohol.
- Avoid difficult situations while you are trying to quit. Try to lower your stress level.
- Exercise can help, such as walking, jogging, or bicycling.
- Distract yourself from thoughts of smoking and the urge to use tobacco by talking to someone, going to a movie, getting busy with a task, or having a game night with friends.
- Drink a lot of water.
- Keep your hands busy with a pen or toothpick.

Avoiding Relapse

Most relapses occur within the first 3 months after quitting. Do not be discouraged if you start using tobacco again. Remember, most people try several times before they finally quit. Explore different ways to break habits. You may have to deal with triggers that cause relapse.

- *Change your environment.* Get rid of cigarettes, tobacco (in any form), and ashtrays in your home, car, and place of work. Get rid of the smell of cigarettes in your car and home.
- *Alcohol.* Consider limiting or stopping alcohol use while you are quitting tobacco.
- *Other smokers at home.* Encourage housemates to quit with you. Work out a plan to cope with others who smoke and avoid being around them.
- *Weight gain.* Tackle 1 problem at a time. Work on quitting tobacco first. You will not necessarily gain weight, and increased appetite is often temporary. Eat healthy and exercise.
- *Negative mood or depression.* If these symptoms persist, talk to your HCP. You may need treatment for depression.
- *Withdrawal symptoms.* Your body will go through many changes when you quit tobacco. You may have a dry mouth, cough, or scratchy throat, and you may feel irritable. The nicotine patch or gum may help with cravings (Table 11.6).
- *Focus on the benefits of quitting:*
  - Your BP and heart rate will lower almost at once.
  - Your risk for a heart attack declines within 24 hours. The blood will become less likely to clot, making dangerous blood clots less likely.
  - Within a few weeks, you will be less short of breath, cough less, and have more energy. Your ability to smell and taste should improve.
  - Your immune system will be stronger, so you will be less likely to be sick.
  - Quitting will improve your night vision and help preserve your overall vision.

Adapted from National Cancer Institute: Quit Smoking. Retrieved from https://smokefree.gov/quit-smoking.

Along with using a smoking cessation product, users who wish to quit are most likely to succeed if they take part in a tobacco cessation program.[5] You should be aware of available community resources. Cessation programs may involve behavior counseling, aversion therapy, group support, individual therapy, and self-help options. Many of these programs teach users to avoid high-risk situations for smoking relapse, such as those that promote cue-induced craving. They help them develop coping skills, such as cigarette refusal skills, assertiveness, alternative activities, and peer support systems.

ALCOHOL

Of Americans ages 18 and older, 70% consume alcohol. Most people use alcohol in moderation.[6] *Moderate drinking* is up to 1 drink per day for women and up to 2 drinks per day for men (Fig. 11.2). **Alcohol use disorder (AUD)**, or alcoholism, affects about 5.8% of U.S. adults.[6] A higher percent engages in periodic excess alcohol use. **Binge drinking** is consuming 5 or more alcoholic drinks for males or 4 or more alcoholic drinks for females on the same occasion at least once per month. AUD and binge drinking can have harmful physical, emotional, and social consequences.

Effects of Use and Complications

Alcohol affects almost all cells of the body. It changes neurotransmitter levels in the central nervous system (CNS), affecting all areas and functions of the CNS. These include centers that control our impulses, mood, and behavior; coordinate motor activity; and promote respiratory and cardiac function. The immediate effects of alcohol depend on a person's susceptibility to alcohol and the blood alcohol concentration (BAC).

For the person who is not dependent on alcohol, the BAC generally predicts alcohol's effects. The relationship between BAC and behavior is different in a person who has developed tolerance to alcohol and its effects. The *tolerant person* can usually drink large amounts without obvious impairment and perform complex tasks without problems at BAC levels much

TABLE 11.6 Drug Therapy

Smoking Cessation[a]

Agents	Side Effects	Considerations
Nicotine Replacement Agents		
Nicotine Gum (OTC)		
Nicorette, Thrive 2 mg, 4 mg • Use for 12 wk • Use 1 piece q1–2hr for 6 wk then q2–4hr for 3 wk • Maximum dose: 24 pieces/day	Hiccups, mouth/jaw pain, mouth ulcers, heartburn, throat irritation, nausea	Use "chew and park," alternating chewing with periods of holding the gum between cheek and teeth. Do not eat or drink 15 min before and during use. Chew at least 9 pieces/day the first 6 wk.
Nicotine Lozenge (OTC)		
Commit 2 mg, 4 mg; Thrive 1 mg, 2 mg • Use 8–12 wk • Use 1 lozenge q1–2hr for 6 wk tapering to 1 lozenge q4–8hr by 12 wk	Insomnia, nausea, sore throat, hiccups, cough, heartburn, headache	Dissolves in mouth in 20–30 min. Do not chew or swallow. Do not eat or drink 15 min before and during use. Occasionally rotate around the mouth.
Nicotine Patch (OTC)		
NicoDerm CQ, Habitrol, Nicotine transdermal system • 18- or 24-hr doses • Use 6-20 wk	Local skin irritation, insomnia, nausea, headache	Provides steady level of nicotine. Easy to use. Do not use if allergic to adhesive. Rotate sites to decrease skin irritation.
Nicotine Nasal Spray		
Nicotrol NS • 1–2 doses (2 sprays)/hr • Use ≥6 mo	Nose and throat irritation, sneezing, rhinitis, headache, cough	Requires a prescription. Provides fastest nicotine delivery. Do not sniff, swallow, or inhale while spraying. Tilt head back slightly for best results.
Nicotine Inhaler		
Nicotrol nicotine inhalation system • Use 1 cartridge q1–2hr • Use 3–6 mo	Cough, mouth and throat irritation, headache, nausea, hiccups	Requires a prescription. Simulates smoking with mouthpiece and nicotine cartridge. Use with caution in those with heart disease, asthma, or lung disease.
Non-Nicotine Agents		
bupropion (Zyban) 150 mg/day for 3 days, then 150 mg bid Use 12 wk; can use up to 6 mo	Insomnia, dry mouth, irritability, rash, tremors, anorexia	Contraindicated with history of seizures or eating disorders. Promotes weight loss. First choice for those with depression.
varenicline (Chantix) 0.5 mg/day for 3 days, 0.5 mg bid for 4 days, then 1 mg bid Use 12 wk; additional 12 wk may be used in select patients	Nausea, insomnia, constipation, flatulence, vomiting, headache	Increased incidence of side effects when taken concurrently with other nicotine replacement products.

[a]OTC nicotine replacement agents are also available in generic forms. More information and patient instructions are available from the American Lung Association at www.lung.org.

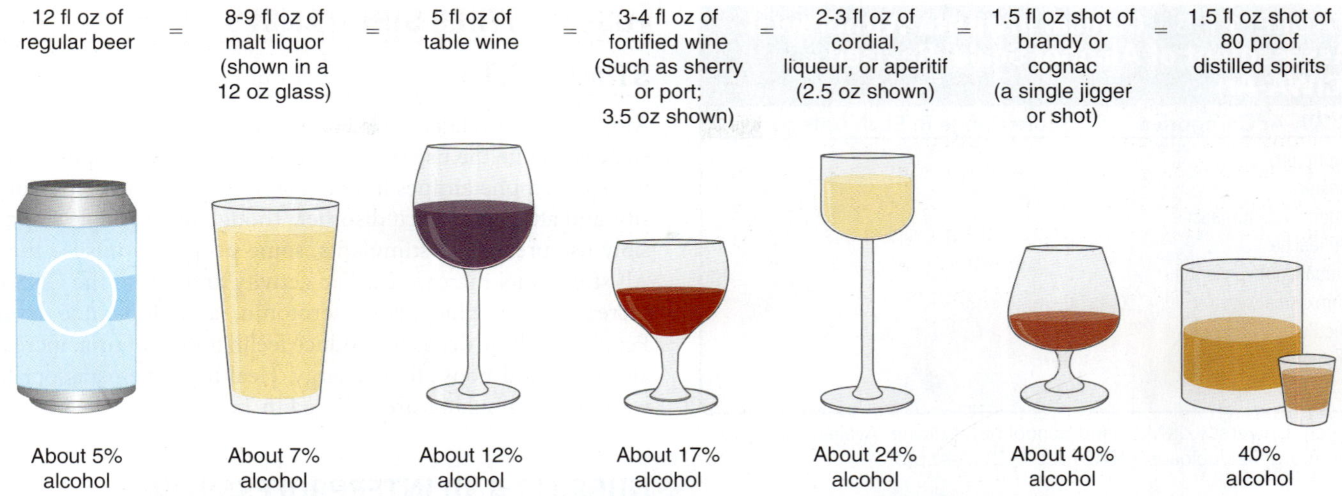

Fig. 11.2 US standard drink equivalents. Each beverage represents 1 alcoholic drink equivalent, defined in the United States as any beverage containing 0.6 fl oz or 14 g of pure alcohol. (Adapted from NIAAA: *What's a standard drink?* Retrieved from https://www.niaaa.nih.gov/what-standard-drink.)

TABLE 11.7 Effects of Chronic Alcohol Use

Body System	Effects
Cardiac	Hypertension, atrial fibrillation, cardiomyopathy, stroke, coronary artery disease, sudden cardiac death
Gastrointestinal (GI)	Gastritis, gastroesophageal reflux disease (GERD), peptic ulcer, esophagitis, esophageal varices, GI bleeding, pancreatitis, oropharyngeal cancer, colorectal cancer
Hematologic	Bone marrow depression, anemia, leukopenia, thrombocytopenia, blood clotting problems
Hepatic	Alcoholic hepatitis, cirrhosis, liver cancer
Musculoskeletal	Myopathy, osteoporosis, gout
Neurologic	Alcoholic dementia, Wernicke-Korsakoff syndrome, impaired cognitive function, psychomotor skills, abstract thinking, and memory. Depression, anxiety, attention deficit, labile moods, seizures, insomnia, peripheral neuropathy, chronic headache
Nutrition	Diabetes, anorexia, malnutrition, vitamin deficiencies (especially thiamine)
Reproductive	Breast cancer, testicular atrophy, decreased beard growth, decreased libido, decreased sperm count, gynecomastia
Skin	Palmar erythema, spider angiomas, rosacea, rhinophyma
Urinary	Diuretic effect from inhibition of antidiuretic hormone

higher than levels that would produce obvious impairment in the *nontolerant drinker*. Women have higher blood alcohol levels than men do after the same amount of alcohol intake.

Alcohol use is linked to many health problems (Table 11.7). These problems are often the reason that people seek health care. Long-term alcohol use can lead to hypertension, heart disease, stroke, liver disease, and digestive problems. Short-term, excess alcohol use increases the risk for injury from motor vehicle crashes, falls, firearms, assault, drowning, and burns. Patients with AUD undergoing surgery have increased in-hospital death rates and longer lengths of stay.

Complications may arise from the interaction of alcohol with commonly prescribed or OTC medications. Those that interact with alcohol in an additive manner include antihypertensives, antihistamines, and antianginals. Alcohol taken with aspirin may cause or worsen GI bleeding. Alcohol taken with acetaminophen may increase the risk of liver damage. Taking a CNS depressant with alcohol can increase, or potentiate, the effect of both. An alcohol-dependent person may have cross-tolerance, needing higher doses of CNS depressants to achieve the desired effect.

❖ NURSING AND INTERPROFESSIONAL MANAGEMENT: ALCOHOL USE DISORDER

◆ Alcohol Toxicity

Acute alcohol toxicity occurs when a person has a high blood alcohol level, generally after ingesting a large amount of alcohol. This leads to behavior changes and alcohol-induced CNS depression, resulting in respiratory and circulatory failure. Unconsciousness, coma, and death can occur. Other common effects include hypokalemia, hypomagnesemia, and hypoglycemia.

Obtain a health history as able and assess for injuries, diseases, and hypoglycemia. No antidote for alcohol is available. Implement supportive care measures to maintain airway, breathing, and circulation (the ABCs) until the alcohol metabolizes. Frequently monitor vital signs and level of consciousness. Treat alcohol-induced hypotension with IV fluids.

Patients with hypoglycemia may receive glucose-containing IV solutions. IV thiamine may be given before or with IV glucose solutions to prevent *Wernicke-Korsakoff syndrome,* which can cause seizures and brain damage. Many patients have low

TABLE 11.8 Clinical Institute Withdrawal Assessment of Alcohol Scale, Revised (CIWA-Ar)

CIWA-Ar Categories	Score Range in Each Category
Agitation	0–7
Anxiety	0–7
Auditory disturbances	0–7
Headache	0–7
Clouding of sensorium	0–4
Paroxysmal sweats	0–7
Tactile disturbances	0–7
Tremor	0–7
Visual disturbances	0–7

Source: University of Maryland School of Medicine. Available at www.umem.org/files/uploads/1104212257_CIWA-Ar.pdf.

serum magnesium levels and other signs of malnutrition, so HCPs often add multivitamins and magnesium to the IV fluids.

Agitation and anxiety are common. Stay with the patient as much as possible, orienting as necessary. Assess the patient for increasing anger and the potential for violence. Use protective measures since the patient is at risk for injury because of lack of coordination and impaired judgment.

◆ Alcohol Withdrawal Syndrome

Alcohol withdrawal syndrome (AWS) can develop in a hospitalized patient when the use of alcohol abruptly stops. The onset of AWS depends on the quantity, frequency, pattern, and duration of alcohol use. The early signs often develop within a few hours after the last drink. They peak after 24 to 48 hours and then disappear unless the withdrawal progresses to alcohol withdrawal delirium.

Alcohol withdrawal delirium is a serious complication that can occur from 2 to 3 days after the last drink and last 2 to 3 days—the greater the patient's dependence on alcohol, the greater the risk for alcohol withdrawal delirium. Death may result from multiorgan failure, dysrhythmias, or peripheral vascular collapse.

Management begins with identifying at-risk persons. Use a symptom assessment tool, such as the Clinical Institute Withdrawal Assessment of Alcohol Scale, Revised (CIWA-Ar), to determine treatment (Table 11.8).[7] Table 11.9 outlines the clinical manifestations and treatment for AWS. A nursing care plan (see eNursing Care Plan 11.1) for a patient with AWS is available on the website at http://evolve.elsevier.com/Lewis/medsurg.

CHECK YOUR PRACTICE

A 34-year-old male patient was admitted for multiple trauma after a car accident. His girlfriend tells you that he drinks too much, and she knew he would get in trouble someday.

- What signs and symptoms would alert you to the presence of AWS?
- What measures would you use to protect his safety?
- How would you involve members of the health care team in planning patient care?

USE OF OTHER SUBSTANCES

STIMULANTS

Amphetamine-related stimulants are highly addictive substances. While the use of crack cocaine and methamphetamine is illegal, amphetamines have a role in treating narcolepsy, obesity, and attention deficit disorder. Though most people responsibly use prescribed stimulants, some people do misuse them. All stimulants increase cardiac activity and excite the CNS by increasing norepinephrine, serotonin, and dopamine levels. People use these drugs to produce feelings of euphoria, increase alertness, and boost their energy. Health problems associated with using stimulants are outlined in Table 11.2.

❖ NURSING AND INTERPROFESSIONAL MANAGEMENT: STIMULANT USE

◆ Toxicity

Patients with stimulant toxicity present with *sympathetic overdrive* (increased stimulation of the sympathetic nervous system). The patient has restlessness, agitation, impaired judgment, and paranoia with psychotic symptoms. Physical effects include hypertension, tachycardia, fever, seizures, and confusion. Death may occur from stroke, dysrhythmias, or myocardial infarction.[1]

The emergency management depends on the clinical manifestations at the time of treatment (Table 11.10). A specific antidote for stimulant toxicity is not available. Treatment focuses on supportive care measures.

◆ Withdrawal

Stimulant withdrawal is usually not an emergency. Abrupt cessation can lead to a "crash." The patient may be depressed and have fatigue, disturbed sleep, vivid dreams, general aching, irritability, increased appetite, and mood swings.[8] Craving for the drug is intense during the first hours to days of drug cessation and may continue for weeks. Supportive care includes providing a safe, quiet environment and allowing the patient to sleep and eat as desired. If a patient has severe depression, implement suicide precautions and refer for further treatment.

DEPRESSANTS

Commonly used depressants include sedative-hypnotics and opioids. Depressants have rapid development of tolerance and dependence. Their use is associated with many medical emergencies involving toxicity and withdrawal. Most overdose deaths involve an opioid, either alone or in combination with another depressant, such as an opioid and benzodiazepine.[9] Common health problems resulting from depressant use are outlined in Table 11.2.

Sedative-Hypnotics

Common sedative-hypnotic agents include barbiturates, benzodiazepines, and barbiturate-like drugs. Sedative-hypnotic

TABLE 11.9 Manifestations and Treatment of Alcohol Withdrawal

Manifestations	Interprofessional Care	Nursing Management
Alcohol Withdrawal Syndrome		
• Agitation • Anxiety • ↑ BP • ↑ Heart rate • Hyperactivity • Insomnia • Nausea • Sweating • Tremors	• Benzodiazepines (lorazepam, diazepam) to prevent seizures and delirium • Thiamine to prevent Wernicke-Korsakoff syndrome • Multivitamins (folate, B vitamins) • Magnesium sulfate to treat low serum magnesium • IV glucose solution to treat hypoglycemia • β-Blockers (atenolol) or α_2-agonists (clonidine) to stabilize vital signs • Respiratory support	• Monitor vital signs and neurologic status. • Infuse thiamine before dextrose-containing IV solutions. • Maintain NPO status. • Implement seizure precautions. • Determine CIWA-Ar score q 4 hr until it is less than 8 for 24 hr. • Use measures to manage any fever and pain. • Provide a quiet, nonstimulating, well-lit environment. • Maintain adequate nutrition and fluid intake.
Alcohol Withdrawal Delirium		
• Disorientation • Seizures • Visual, tactile, or auditory hallucinations	• Continued use of benzodiazepines • Valproic acid or gabapentin to treat seizures • Antipsychotic agents (haloperidol [Haldol]) • Chlordiazepoxide if psychosis persists after receiving benzodiazepines	• Orient the patient as needed. • Provide a safe environment. • Implement measures to address any hallucinations.

TABLE 11.10 EMERGENCY MANAGEMENT

Stimulant Toxicity

Assessment Findings	Interventions
Cardiovascular • ↑ BP • Chest pain • Diaphoresis • Dysrhythmias • ↑ HR • Myocardial ischemia • Palpitations **Central Nervous System** Agitation Combativeness Confusion Fever Hallucinations Impaired judgment Insomnia Paranoia Pupil dilation Seizures	• Ensure patent airway. • Establish IV access and start fluid replacement. • Obtain a 12-lead ECG and start ECG monitoring. • Treat dysrhythmias as needed. • Treat hypertension and chest pain with nitrates or calcium channel blockers. • Aspirin may be given to lower the risk for myocardial infarction. • Give IV diazepam or lorazepam for seizures. • Give IV antipsychotic drugs for psychosis and hallucinations. • Monitor vital signs and level of consciousness. • Use cooling measures for fever. • Implement measures to treat insomnia. • Start gastric lavage in cases of recent ingestion.

drugs depress the CNS, causing sedation at low doses and sleep at high doses. Their use produces euphoria and intoxication that resembles that of alcohol. Tolerance develops rapidly to the effects of these drugs, requiring higher doses to achieve euphoria. However, tolerance may not develop to the brainstem-depressant effects. As a result, an increased dose may trigger hypotension and respiratory depression, resulting in death.

Opioids

Opioids include substances directly derived from the opium poppy (morphine), semisynthetics (heroin, hydromorphone), and synthetic compounds (fentanyl). Persons dependent on opioids include those who use illegal drugs sold on the street and those who misuse prescription opioids. Opioids act on opiate receptors and neurotransmitter systems in the CNS, causing sedation and analgesia. The person taking an opioid has euphoria, mood changes, mental clouding, drowsiness, and pain reduction. While this makes prescription opioids useful in treating some medical problems, their pleasurable effects promote misuse. Misusing oxycodone or fentanyl can result in the same harmful consequences as using heroin.

NURSING AND INTERPROFESSIONAL MANAGEMENT: DEPRESSANT USE

Toxicity

Overdoses can occur when a person purposefully misuses a depressant or takes 1 prescribed for someone else. Unintentional overdose often occurs, especially when depressants are used with alcohol or other drugs. Depressant toxicity can cause death from respiratory and CNS depression. The priority of care is the patient's ABCs. Supporting respiratory and cardiovascular function and continuous monitoring of neurologic status is critical until the patient is stable. The emergency management depends on the substance used and the clinical manifestations (Table 11.11).

Sedative-Hypnotics

On occasion, a patient with a benzodiazepine overdose may receive flumazenil, a specific benzodiazepine antagonist. Because flumazenil may have a shorter duration of action than some benzodiazepines, repeated doses may be needed until the benzodiazepine is metabolized. Place the patient on safety precautions as flumazenil can cause seizures.

There are no antagonists for barbiturates or other sedative-hypnotic drugs. The patient receives supportive care, including respiratory care, hydration, vasopressors, and treatments to

TABLE 11.11 EMERGENCY MANAGEMENT

Depressant Toxicity

Assessment Findings	Interventions
• Aggressive behavior • Agitation • ↓ BP • Cold, clammy skin • Confusion • Depression • Dysrhythmias • ECG changes • Hallucinations • ↑ HR • Lethargy • Nystagmus • ↓ O_2 saturation • Pinpoint pupils • Respiratory or cardiac arrest • Seizures • Slow or rapid shallow respirations • Slurred speech • Stupor • Seizures	• Ensure patent airway. • Expect intubation if respiratory distress is present. • Establish IV access. • Monitor vital signs, level of consciousness, and O_2 saturation. • Obtain 12-lead ECG and start continuous ECG monitoring. • Obtain information about substance (name, route, when taken, amount). • Obtain drug levels or comprehensive toxicology screen. • Obtain a health history, including drug use and allergies. • Give the right antidotes. • Perform gastric lavage if necessary. • Give activated charcoal and cathartics if ordered.

promote drug elimination. If the airway is maintained, some may receive activated charcoal. Dialysis is used in some situations.

Opioids

Overdose in the inpatient setting may occur when a patient inadvertently receives an incorrect dose or when opioids are aggressively dosed, given to patients with new kidney or liver impairment, or given with drugs that enhance respiratory depression.[10] Treatment includes supporting respiratory function and giving the opioid antagonist naloxone. Naloxone reverses respiratory depression and other manifestations of toxicity. Monitor the patient closely because naloxone has a shorter duration of action than most opioids. Repeated doses or IV infusion of naloxone may be needed until the opioid is metabolized.

Overdose in the community setting can occur when a person deliberately misuses an illegal or prescription opioid, takes an opioid in combination with other depressants, or takes an opioid prescribed for someone else. In many areas, naloxone is publicly available. This allows police, first responders, family members, and friends to give someone naloxone in emergencies, thus reversing the effects of an overdose sooner. As a result, you may see more patients who need post reversal care.

Withdrawal

Sedative-Hypnotics

Withdrawal from sedative-hypnotics can be life threatening. The manifestations and treatment are similar to those of AWS. Early, the patient may have tremors, anxiety, insomnia, fever, and disorientation. Delirium, seizures, and respiratory and cardiac arrest may occur within 24 hours after the last dose. Treatment consists of tapering doses of a long-acting benzodiazepine. IV diazepam is an option for severe manifestations. Closely monitor the patient. Supportive care includes implementing patient safety and comfort measures, frequently assessing neurologic status and vital signs, and providing reassurance and orientation.

Opioids

Opioid withdrawal symptoms depend on the opioid used, route of use, and duration of use. It is usually not life threatening but can be very uncomfortable. With short-acting drugs, withdrawal begins 6 to 12 hours after the last dose. Early symptoms include craving, anorexia, anxiety, sweating, increased respirations and blood pressure, tremor, and irritability. After 2 to 3 days, the symptoms progress and include vomiting, diarrhea, insomnia, tachycardia, abdominal cramps, and muscle spasms. While these subside over 5 to 7 days, craving, depression, and irritability can last for months. With longer-acting drugs, manifestations may begin 24 to 48 hours after the last dose and may last 3 weeks or more.[11]

Treatment focuses on relieving symptoms and often requires drug therapy. Substituting a long-acting opioid (methadone, buprenorphine) at low doses or α_2-adrenergic agonists (e.g., clonidine) decreases withdrawal symptoms. Other therapies include medications for GI distress (loperamide, ondansetron), acetaminophen or nonsteroidal antiinflammatory agents for muscle aches and fever, and antihistamines for acute anxiety and sleep disturbances.

INHALANTS

Persons with inhalant use disorder inhale hydrocarbon-based fumes, such as those found in glues or paints, to change their mental state.[1] Inhalants are rapidly absorbed and reach the CNS quickly. Most are depressants with effects like those of alcohol. They cause a brief period of euphoria, followed by drowsiness and lightheadedness. Long-term use can result in neurologic problems, including damage to parts of the brain that control cognition, movement, vision, and hearing (Table 11.2).

The patient with inhalant toxicity may have lethargy, dizziness, slurred speech, blurry vision, tremors, and impaired coordination.[1] The effects usually resolve within minutes to a few hours. Inhalant toxicity is managed with supportive care. However, in rare cases, users need emergency treatment for dysrhythmias, heart failure, or CNS hyperactivity (e.g., seizures). Using some inhalants, like toluene, can result in kidney damage; so, monitor renal function. Withdrawal is rare as most inhaled substances have a very short duration. Any manifestations that may occur require supportive care.

CANNABIS

The use of cannabis, or marijuana or weed, continues to increase in the United States. Cannabis is available in forms that can be smoked, vaporized, or ingested. The main ingredient is tetrahydrocannabinol (THC). At low to moderate doses, THC produces euphoria, reduced anxiety, and improved appetite.

Adverse effects include impaired memory, impaired motor coordination, altered judgment, and, in high doses, paranoia and psychosis. Long-term use is associated with a wide range of effects, particularly on cardiopulmonary and mental health (Table 11.2). Illegal synthetic cannabinoid drugs (e.g., K2, Spice) have some of the same properties as THC. They contain varying amounts of different ingredients. The result is that these products have unpredictable effects and are more toxic. Sometimes, death has occurred with 1 use.

More than half of the states have legalized use for specific medical reasons. If an HCP in 1 of those states determines a patient has a disorder that qualifies for medical cannabis use, the HCP can give the patient an *authorization for use*. This form allows the patient to buy cannabis at special dispensaries or have a limited number of cannabis plants. There are 2 THC-based medications, dronabinol (Marinol) and nabilone (Cesamet). They are used for chemotherapy-induced nausea and vomiting and to promote appetite in those with acquired immunodeficiency syndrome (AIDS) or cancer.[12]

Patients with *acute marijuana toxicity* may have acute psychotic episodes, especially if the patient used a synthetic derivative. Tachycardia and hypertension can trigger dysrhythmias and myocardial infarction. Support the patient's ABCs. Panic and flashbacks are managed by maintaining a quiet environment and reassuring the patient. Benzodiazepines give symptom relief.

Withdrawal can occur in a hospitalized patient who uses cannabis. The patient may have irritability, insomnia, anorexia, anger, anxiety, and restlessness. Symptoms begin within a week and last a few weeks.[13] There is no specific drug therapy for treating withdrawal. Supportive care includes measures to promote sleep, safety, and patient comfort, including analgesics and hydration.

CAFFEINE

Caffeine is the most widely used psychoactive substance in the world. It is very weak when compared with the other stimulants. Most people use it to promote wakefulness. Other uses include promoting motor activity and treating headaches. Its use is safe for most people. Problems from high doses of caffeine have occurred from "energy" drinks. A large caffeine intake can cause dysrhythmias, hypertension, disturbed sleep, seizures, and anxiety. Treatment consists of seizure control with benzodiazepines and supportive care until the effects wear off. In a hospitalized patient, caffeine withdrawal can result in muscle pain or stiffness, drowsiness, irritability, and headaches after general anesthesia or during restrictions on usual caffeine intake.[1]

NURSING MANAGEMENT: SUBSTANCE USE

Assessment

You need to be able to determine if patients use substances in a way that places them at risk or if SUD is present. Screening is a simple, effective way to identify patients who need further assessment. Use the **Screening, Brief Intervention, and Referral to Treatment (SBIRT)** approach (Fig. 11.3). SBIRT consists of 3 parts: (1) screening to quickly identify and assess the severity of any substance use problems, (2) providing a brief intervention or teaching patients about the consequences of substance use, and (3) referring those who screen positive for further treatment.[14]

Screening is the first part of SBIRT. Use screening tools to identify those who may have problems with substance use. As a baseline, ask every patient about the use of all substances, including prescribed medications, OTC medications, caffeine, tobacco, and recreational drugs. Use simple 1 or 2 question screening tests to detect alcohol, tobacco, and other substance use problems (Table 11.12). If a patient has a positive screen, follow up with a detailed assessment to identify specific problems. A screening tool for AUD, the Alcohol Use Disorders Identification Test, is shown in Table 11.13. A score of 8 points or more in men or 7 or more in women is concerning. Another useful tool is the Drug Abuse Screening Test (DAST-10), shown in Table 11.14.

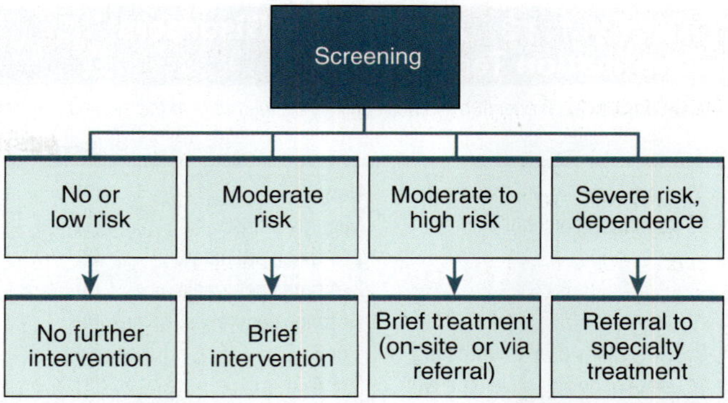

Fig. 11.3 Screening, brief intervention, and referral to treatment approach. (From Substance Abuse and Mental Health Services Administration [SAMHSA]: Systems-level implementation of screening, brief intervention, and referral to treatment, Technical Assistance Publication [TAP] Series 33. HHS Publication No. 13-4741, Rockville, MD, 2013, SAMHSA.)

TABLE 11.12 Brief Screening Tools for Substance Use

Single Question Tests

Use 1 of these questions to screen for the presence of alcohol, drug, or tobacco use.

- How often in the past year have you had 5 (men) or 4 (women) or more drinks in a day?
- How many times in the past year have you used illegal drugs or prescription medications for nonmedical reasons?
- In the past year, how often have you used tobacco products?

2-Question Tests

Use the following 2 questions to screen for alcohol or drug use.

- In the past year, have you ever drunk or used drugs more than you meant to?
- Have you felt you wanted or needed to cut down on your drinking or drug use in the past year?

Adapted from Strobbe S: Prevention and screening, brief intervention, and referral to treatment for substance use in primary care, *Prim Care Clin Office Pract* 41:185, 2014.

TABLE 11.13 Alcohol Use Disorders Identification Test (AUDIT)

Please answer each question by checking 1 of the numbers in the second column.

		Score
1. How often do you have a drink containing alcohol?	Never	(0)
	Monthly or less	(1)
	2–4 times per month	(2)
	2–4 times per week	(3)
	4+ times per week	(4)
2. How many drinks containing alcohol do you have on a typical day when you are drinking?	1 or 2	(0)
	3 or 4	(1)
	5 or 6	(2)
	7 to 9	(3)
	10 or more	(4)
3. How often do you have 6 or more drinks on 1 occasion?	Never	(0)
	Less than monthly	(1)
	Monthly	(2)
	Weekly	(3)
	Daily or almost daily	(4)
4. How often during the last year have you found that you were not able to stop drinking once you had started?	Never	(0)
	Less than monthly	(1)
	Monthly	(2)
	Weekly	(3)
	Daily or almost daily	(4)
5. How often in the last year have you failed to do what was normally expected of you because you were drinking?	Never	(0)
	Less than monthly	(1)
	Monthly	(2)
	Weekly	(3)
	Daily or almost daily	(4)
6. How often during the last year have you needed a first drink in the morning to get yourself going after a heavy drinking session?	Never	(0)
	Less than monthly	(1)
	Monthly	(2)
	Weekly	(3)
	Daily or almost daily	(4)
7. How often during the last year have you had a feeling of guilt or remorse about drinking?	Never	(0)
	Less than monthly	(1)
	Monthly	(2)
	Weekly	(3)
	Daily or almost daily	(4)
8. How often during the last year have you been unable to remember what happened the night before because you had been drinking?	Never	(0)
	Less than monthly	(1)
	Monthly	(2)
	Weekly	(3)
	Daily or almost daily	(4)
9. Have you or someone else been injured as a result of your drinking?	No	(0)
	Yes, but not in the last year	(2)
	Yes, during the last year	(4)
10. Has a relative, friend, or other health worker been concerned about your drinking or suggested that you cut down?	No	(0)
	Yes, but not in the last year	(2)
	Yes, during the last year	(4)

Scoring for AUDIT: Questions 1 through 8 are scored 0, 1, 2, 3, or 4. Questions 9 and 10 are scored 0, 2, or 4 only. The minimum score (nondrinkers) is 0, and the maximum possible score is 40. A score of 9 or more indicates hazardous or harmful alcohol consumption.

Source: Babor TF, Higgins-Biddle JC, Saunders JB, Monteiro M: *The alcohol use disorders identification test,* ed 2, Geneva, Switzerland, 2001, WHO Press.

TABLE 11.14 Drug Abuse Screening Test (DAST-10)

In the last 12 months:

1. Have you used drugs other than those required for medical reasons?	No	Yes
2. Do you use more than 1 drug at a time?	No	Yes
3. Are you always able to stop using drugs when you want to?	No	Yes
4. Have you had "blackouts" or "flashbacks" as a result of drug use?	No	Yes
5. Do you ever feel bad or guilty about your drug use?	No	Yes
6. Does your spouse (or parents) ever complain about your involvement with drugs?	No	Yes
7. Have you neglected your family because of your use of drugs?	No	Yes
8. Have you engaged in illegal activities in order to obtain drugs?	No	Yes
9. Have you ever had withdrawal symptoms or felt sick when you stopped taking drugs?	No	Yes
10. Have you had medical problems because of your drug use?	No	Yes

Score 1 point for each question answered: "Yes," except for question 3, for which a "No" receives 1 point.

Score	Degree of Problem	Suggested Action
0	None	None at this time
1–2	Low	Monitor, reassess later
3–5	Moderate	Investigate further
6–8	Substantial	Intensive assessment
9–10	Severe	Intensive assessment

Retrieved from https://cde.drugabuse.gov/sites/nida_cde/files/DrugAbuseScreeningTest_2014Mar24.pdf.

If there is any sign of substance use, determine when the patient last used the substance. Knowing this information will let you know when to expect the onset of withdrawal and help you anticipate drug interactions. Assess for other factors that influence withdrawal. These include the dose taken, method of intake, and length of time the patient has used the substance. You may find that the patient is dealing with *polysubstance use,* or the use of more than 1 substance. Alert the HCP as these patients need care tailored to the combination of substances used.

You may find problems associated with substance use during your physical assessment. Assess the patient's general appearance and nutrition status. Examine the abdomen, skin, and cardiovascular, respiratory, and neurologic systems. The presence of a mental health disorder, such as anxiety, bipolar disorder, or depression, increases the risk for SUD. Serum and urine drug screens can identify the type and amounts of drugs present in the body. A complete blood count, serum electrolytes, blood urea nitrogen, creatinine, and liver function tests evaluate for electrolyte imbalances and cardiac, kidney, or liver problems.

During your assessment, look for patient behaviors such as denial, avoidance, underreporting or minimizing substance use, or giving inaccurate information. Behaviors and physical manifestations suggesting substance use are outlined in Table 11.15. Remember, these behaviors are not all inclusive.

TABLE 11.15 Findings Suggesting Substance Use

Physiologic

- Fatigue
- Insomnia
- Headaches
- Changes in mood
- Anorexia, weight loss
- Vague physical problems
- Appearing older than stated age, unkempt appearance
- Sexual problems, decreased libido, erectile dysfunction
- Standard doses of sedatives do not have a therapeutic effect

Behavior

- Mouthwash or toiletries overuse
- Trauma from falls, auto accidents, fights, or burns
- Citations for driving while intoxicated or impaired
- Leisure activities that involve alcohol or other drugs
- Financial problems, including those related to spending on substances
- Defensive or evasive answers to questions about substance use and its importance in the person's life
- Problems in areas of life function, such as frequent job changes; marital problems; work-related accidents, tardiness, absenteeism; legal problems; social isolation, estranged from friends or family

◆ Clinical Problems

Clinical problems for the patient with substance use disorder include

- Substance use
- Risk for injury
- Impaired cognition
- Neurologic problem

◆ Planning

Nursing care focuses on the priority problems of reducing the risk for injury and managing acute confusion. The overall goals are that the patient with a substance use problem will (1) have normal physiologic functioning, (2) be free from complications resulting from withdrawal, (3) admit to a substance use problem, (4) abstain from substance use, and (5) cooperate with the proposed treatment plan.

◆ Implementation

◆ Health Promotion

Your role in health promotion includes prevention and early detection of substance use. Prevention measures include abstaining from harmful substances and limiting alcohol use. These measures decrease the risk for substance-related injury or illness. You can help prevent substance use problems by (1) teaching about the effects and negative outcomes of substance use and (2) providing support. Through screening, you have an opportunity to prevent patients from becoming dependent on alcohol and drugs. You can do this by using brief intervention techniques and helping patients access appropriate care through referral to treatment if they show risky behaviors or are already dependent (Table 11.16).

BOX 11.1 ETHICAL/LEGAL DILEMMAS

Board of Nursing Disciplinary Action

Situation

The State Board of Nursing has received multiple complaints about J.R., an RN who works in a long-term care agency. J.R. has signed off on 3 controlled substances counts that have been inaccurate. The investigation revealed that several members of the nursing staff knew about J.R.'s reported behavior, but they did not report their observations to the unit administrator because the administrator is J.R.'s aunt. After the investigation, the board of nursing subpoenas J.R. to a meeting to discuss charges in preparation for a disciplinary hearing.

Ethical/Legal Points for Consideration

- Regulation of professional nursing practice is the right of each of the 50 states. Most have regulatory agencies charged with writing regulations and rules to implement the State Nurse Practice Act. The regulations approved by these agencies carry the weight of the law. Failure to behave accordingly places a nurse at risk for disciplinary action.
- The RN charged with unprofessional behavior has been charged with an offense and is entitled to the same legal rights as any other person. This includes a fair and timely hearing, opportunity to confront the accusers, right to be represented by an attorney, and right to prepare a defense.
- Possible disciplinary actions include temporary suspension of the nursing license, revocation of the nursing license, mandatory rehabilitation for substance use, and mandated supervision and evaluation of practice. Sometimes the disciplinary action includes fines and requires reeducation. The State Board of Nursing may report the action to the state attorney general if evidence suggests the person committed a crime. The RN who is found guilty of unprofessional practice must report this action on all future applications for nursing positions.
- All RNs should be familiar with their state's nurse practice act and regulations and the composition and actions of the State Board of Nursing. Nurses should pay attention to the regulation that lists examples of actionable behavior and disciplinary actions sanctioned by the state.
- RNs have a legal and ethical obligation to report suspected illegal behavior to their administrators and to continue reporting until the situation is resolved. By failing to report, the RN may be charged as an accessory to the act or aiding and abetting the behavior. The RN here may be charged with unprofessional behavior and risks losing their nursing license. Shifting the obligation to someone else to report or failure to continue reporting each incident does not satisfy this duty.

Discussion Questions

1. What would you do if you suspect a coworker of substance use?
2. How would you handle a situation where retaliation for reporting unprofessional behavior may occur?

◆ Acute Intervention

The immediate result of overconsumption is acute toxicity or overdose. The patient may also present with trauma or injuries. The priority of care is supporting the patient's ABCs, especially respiratory status. In addition to treating injuries, provide supportive care until detoxification can occur. Nursing care includes frequently assessing neurologic status and vital signs, giving IV fluids to prevent dehydration, orienting to time and place, and implementing patient safety measures.

Sometimes, uncertainty exists as to what substances are involved. If the patient used multiple substances, a complex clinical picture could result. For example, a patient presents with toxicity, and we do not know what substances are involved. Although blood and urine tests will help identify the substances, treatment is started while waiting for the test results. The patient in this situation would usually receive naloxone. If the substance used is a barbiturate or another CNS depressant, naloxone will not help the patient, but it will not hurt the patient either. If the patient does not respond to a total dose of 10 mg of naloxone, opioids are likely not involved.

Once acute health issues are resolved, provide a brief intervention to teach patients about the consequences of substance use and support behavior change. When patients have a substance use problem, help the patient become motivated to engage in treatment. You are in a unique position to empower behavior change. When a patient seeks care for health problems related to substance use or when hospitalization interferes with the usual pattern of use, the patient's awareness of any substance use problem increases. Intervention at this time can promote behavior change. Take an active role in performing motivational interviewing and providing counseling aimed at cessation.[15] Motivational interviewing is discussed in Chapter 4. Discuss the risks associated with substance use and provide feedback and advice. If the patient agrees, assist with referral to counseling or behavior therapy.

Gerontologic Considerations: Substance Use

Substance use in older adults is a fast-growing and often hard to recognize problem. Older adults do not fit the image of users. For example, older users are less likely to binge drink and use different substances than younger users. The effects of alcohol and drugs can be mistaken for medical conditions common among older adults, such as dementia. So, we may attribute substance use problems to another cause and not offer treatment. Some use alcohol or drugs to cope with grief and loss, such as the death of a spouse.

Because of the higher rate of coexisting medical problems, older adults are at greater risk for medical problems from substance use. Common problems include liver damage and cardiovascular, GI, and endocrine problems. Substance use may cause confusion, delirium, memory loss, and neuromuscular impairment. Physiologic changes may lead to toxicity at levels that may not have been a problem at a younger age. Withdrawal symptoms may be more severe than in younger persons.

It is important to screen older adults for substance use. Family members are important sources of information. Other potential sources include friends, home health aides, meal delivery personnel, and staff members at senior citizen centers and long-term care agencies. It is important for you to discuss drug and alcohol use with older adult patients, including OTC drug use. Assess the patient's knowledge of currently used drugs. Common screening questionnaires may not identify an older adult with a substance use problem. The Short Michigan Alcoholism Screening Test–Geriatric version (SMAST-G) is a short-form alcoholism screening instrument for older adults that can identify potential AUD.

Smoking and other tobacco use is another issue. Those who have smoked for decades may feel unable to stop or believe there is no benefit to stopping at an advanced age. However, smoking contributes to and worsens many chronic illnesses found in older adults. Smoking cessation at any age is beneficial. The information about smoking cessation discussed earlier is appropriate for helping older adults with smoking cessation (Tables 11.3 to 11.6).

Patient teaching for the older adult includes teaching about the desired effects, possible side effects, and proper use of prescribed and OTC drugs. When you suspect alcohol or substance use, refer the patient for treatment. It is a mistaken belief that older people have little to gain from alcohol and drug dependence treatment. The rewards of treatment can lead to greater quality and quantity of life for older adults.

Case Study

Substance Use Disorder

(© JPC-PROD/iStock/Thinkstock.)

Patient Profile

C.M., a 78-year-old woman, was admitted to the emergency department after falling and injuring her right hip. She has been widowed for 4 years and lives alone. Recently her best friend died. Her only family is a daughter who lives out of town. When contacted by phone, the daughter tells the nurse that her mother has appeared more disoriented and confused over the past few months when she has talked to her on the phone.

Subjective Data

- Describing severe pain in her right hip
- Admits she had some wine in the late afternoon to stimulate her appetite
- Has had several falls in the past 2 months
- Reports that she fell after taking a prescribed sleeping pill because she does not sleep well
- Speech is hesitant and slurred
- Says she smokes about a 1/2 pack of cigarettes a day

Objective Data

Physical Assessment

- Oriented to person and place, but not time
- BP 162/94, pulse 92, respirations 24
- Severe pain and tenderness in the right hip region
- Bilateral hand tremors

Diagnostic Tests

- X-ray reveals a subtrochanteric fracture of the right femur requiring surgical repair
- Blood alcohol concentration (BAC) 120 mg/dL (0.12%)
- Complete blood count: Hemoglobin 10.6 g/dL, hematocrit 33%

Discussion Questions

1. ***Recognize:*** What other information is needed to assess C.M.'s condition?
2. ***Recognize:*** What risk factors for substance use do you identify?
3. ***Analyze***: What possible complications and injury risks may occur during C.M.'s postoperative recovery?
4. ***Plan:*** What treatment will C.M. need for substance use?
5. ***Plan:*** What referrals are indicated?
6. ***Prioritize:*** Based on the assessment data given, what are the priority clinical problems?
7. ***Prioritize:*** What are the priority nursing interventions during C.M.'s preoperative period?
8. ***Act:*** How would you use the assistive personnel (AP) on the postoperative unit to carry out the interventions you identified in question 6?
9. ***Safety:*** To ensure C.M.'s safety, what nursing interventions are necessary after surgery?

Answers available at http://evolve.elsevier.com/Lewis/medsurg.

BRIDGE TO NCLEX EXAMINATION

The number of the question corresponds to the same-numbered outcome at the beginning of the chapter.

1. When admitting a patient, the nurse must assess the patient for substance use based on the knowledge that long-term use of addictive substances leads to
   a. the development of coexisting psychiatric illnesses.
   b. a higher risk for complications from underlying health problems.
   c. potentiation of effects of similar drugs taken when the person is drug-free.
   d. increased availability of dopamine, resulting in decreased sleep requirements.
2. The nurse would suspect cocaine toxicity in the patient who is experiencing
   a. agitation, confusion, and seizures.
   b. diarrhea, nausea and vomiting, and confusion.
   c. blurred vision, constricted pupils, and paranoia.
   d. slow, shallow respirations; bradycardia; and hypotension.
3. The *most* appropriate nursing intervention for a patient who is being treated for an exacerbation of emphysema and is not interested in quitting smoking is to
   a. accept the patient's decision and not intervene until the patient expresses a desire to quit.
   b. realize that some smokers never quit, and trying to assist them increases the patient's frustration.
   c. ask the patient to identify the risks and benefits of quitting and what barriers to quitting are present.
   d. motivate the patient to quit by describing how continued smoking will worsen the breathing problems.
4. While caring for a patient with alcohol withdrawal, the nurse should *(select all that apply)*
   a. monitor neurologic status on a routine basis.
   b. provide a quiet, nonstimulating, dimly lit environment.
   c. pad the side rails and place suction equipment at the bedside.
   d. orient the patient to the environment and person with each contact.
   e. give antiseizure drugs and sedatives to relieve withdrawal symptoms.
5. A patient admitted for scheduled surgery has a positive brief screening test for alcohol use disorder. Which initial action is *most* appropriate?
   a. Notify the health care provider.
   b. Complete a detailed alcohol use assessment.
   c. Initiate a referral to a specialty treatment center.
   d. Provide patient teaching on postoperative health risks.
6. Substance use problems in older adults are usually related to
   a. use of drugs and alcohol as a social activity.
   b. continuing the use of illegal drugs started during middle age.
   c. misuse of prescribed and over-the-counter medications and alcohol.
   d. a pattern of binge drinking for weeks or months with periods of sobriety.

1. b; 2. a; 3. c; 4. a, c, d, e; 5. b; 6. c.

For rationales to these answers and even more NCLEX review questions, visit http://evolve.elsevier.com/Lewis/medsurg.

EVOLVE WEBSITE/RESOURCES LIST

http://evolve.elsevier.com/Lewis/medsurg
Review Questions (Online Only)
Key Points
Answer Keys for Questions
- Rationales for Bridge to NCLEX Examination Questions
- Answer Guidelines for Case Study
- Answer Guidelines for Managing Care of Multiple Patients Case Study (Section 2) Nursing Care Plan
- eNursing Care Plan 11.1: Patient in Alcohol Withdrawal

Conceptual Care Map Creator
Audio Glossary
Content Update

REFERENCES

1. Substance Abuse and Mental Health Services Administration: Mental health and substance use disorders. Retrieved from https://www.samhsa.gov/find-help/disorders.
2. Centers for Disease Control and Prevention: Adult cigarette smoking in the U.S. Retrieved from www.cdc.gov/tobacco/data_statistics/fact_sheets/adult_data/cig_smoking.

*3. Agarwal S, Trolice MP, Lindheim SR: E-cigarette use in reproductive-aged women and pregnancy: a rising health concern, *Fertil Steril* 113:1133, 2020.

4. Centers for Disease Control and Prevention: Smoking and tobacco use: Clinical tools. Retrieved from https://www.cdc.gov/tobacco/basic_information/for-health-care-providers/clinical-tools/index.html.
5. U.S. Department of Health and Human Services: Smoking cessation: A report of the Surgeon General. Retrieved from: https://www.hhs.gov/sites/default/files/2020-cessation-sgr-executive-summary.pdf.
6. National Institute on Alcohol Abuse and Alcoholism: Alcohol facts and statistics. Retrieved from www.niaaa.nih.gov/alcohol-health/overview-alcohol-consumption/alcohol-facts-and-statistics.
7. University of Maryland School of Medicine: CIWA-Ar. Retrieved from www.umem.org/files/uploads/1104212257_CIWA-Ar.pdf.
8. Srinivasan J, Chaves C, Scott B, Small JE, editors: *Netter's Neurology*, ed 3, St. Louis, MO, 2020, Elsevier.
9. Centers for Disease Control and Prevention: Understanding the epidemic. Retrieved from www.cdc.gov/drugoverdose/epidemic/index.html.

*10. Danovitch I, Vanle B, Van Groningen N, Ishak W, Nuckols T: Opioid overdose in the hospital setting: a systematic review, *J Addict Med* 14:39, 2020.

11. Renner JA, Suzuki J: *Opiates and prescription drugs in addiction medicine: Science and practice*, ed 2, St Louis, MO, 2020, Elsevier.

*12. Levinsohn EA, Hill KP: Clinical uses of cannabis and cannabinoids in the United States, *J Neurol Sci* 411:116717, 2020.

13. Danovitch I, Mooney LJ: *The assessment and treatment of addiction*, St. Louis, MO, 2019, Elsevier.

14. SAMSA-HRSA Center for Integrated Health Solutions: SBIRT. Retrieved from www.samhsa.gov/sbirt.

*15. Brown KG, Capili B: CE: Opioid use disorder: Pathophysiology, assessment, and effective interventions, *Am J Nurs* 120:38, 2020.

* Evidence-based information for clinical practice.

Case Study

Applying Clinical Judgment With Multiple Patients

It is 0715. The following 3 patients are among the 6 you are assigned to care for today on the medical unit. You have an experienced AP assigned to assist you. A float RN can be paged if needed.

 (© Luevanos/iStock/Thinkstock.)	M.S., an 81-year-old woman, was admitted yesterday with heart failure. She came to the United States from India 4 years ago. She speaks minimal English, relying on her oldest granddaughter to translate. M.S. has a history of diabetes and, recently, some memory problems. Vital signs: 152/78, 96, RR 24, and O_2 saturation 96% on 2 L/min via nasal cannula.
 (© azndc/iStock/Thinkstock.)	C.L. is a 73-year-old Filipino woman admitted with confusion. She was found to have a urinary tract infection and is receiving IV antibiotics. The next dose is due at 1000. Her history includes hypertension, diabetes, stroke, and significant hearing loss. Lives with her son; daughters raise concerns about her care and safety at home.
 (© JPC-PROD/iStock/Thinkstock.)	C.M. is a 78-year-old woman admitted the previous evening with a right hip fracture. She is in Buck's traction. Surgery is scheduled later this morning. She has a history of substance use. Her blood alcohol content (BAC) was 120 mg/dL (0.12 %) on admission. The nurse reports she has been confused and restless overnight. She is receiving IV morphine as needed for pain. The last dose was at 0530.

1. Highlight all the findings above that require your follow-up.
2. Which patient would you see first? Why?
3. The AP tells you that you need to see M.S. immediately. You enter M.S.'s room and find her sitting up in bed with labored respirations. Although you cannot understand what she is saying, you note that she is unable to say more than a few words without stopping for a breath. Use an X for the nursing actions listed below that are Indicated (appropriate or necessary), Contraindicated (could be harmful), or Nonessential (makes no difference or not necessary) for M.S. at this time.

Nursing Action	Indicated	Contraindicated	Nonessential
Perform a respiratory assessment.			
Direct the AP to stay with M.S. while you contact the HCP.			
Obtain a glucose measurement.			
Access the hospital's translation services.			
Place the head of the bed flat.			
Obtain vital signs with O_2 saturation.			
Encourage M.S. to use the incentive spirometer every hour.			

Case Study Progression

M.S.'s assessment reveals bibasilar crackles, 2+ dependent pitting edema, BP 175/84, pulse 116, RR 32, temp 98.2°F (36.8°C), and pulse oximetry 90% on 2 L/min via nasal cannula. You increase the O_2 to 4 L/min per protocol and obtain an order from M.S.'s HCP for furosemide 40 mg IV stat. After giving the diuretic, M.S.'s granddaughter arrives, and you discuss her grandmother's condition. She tells you that her grandmother asked her to bring in potato chips and soda yesterday. She did not think her grandmother should be eating salt, but M.S. insisted that the dietitian said that she could eat them.

4. On further investigation, the dietitian tells you that a translator was not available when she saw M.S. yesterday. Because the dietitian did not understand what M.S. was saying, she could not respond to her questions. She planned to visit M.S. today when the granddaughter is present. Being a culturally competent nurse, you realize that M.S. most likely interpreted the dietitian's silence as
   a. agreement with what M.S. was asking.
   b. demonstrating a lack of respect for M.S.'s wishes.
   c. a lack of understanding by the dietitian as to what M.S. was asking.
   d. a need for the dietitian to get more information before answering questions.

Case Study Progression

Knowing that C.M.'s confusion and restlessness may indicate acute alcohol withdrawal, you go to perform her assessment. You find C.M. trying to pull out the IV line and remove the Buck's traction.

5. What action would you take *first*?
   a. Have the AP stay with C.M.
   b. Ask C.M.'s daughter to stay with her.
   c. Obtain a restraint order from the HCP.
   d. Move C.M. to a room closer to the nurse's station.
6. Your assessment reveals a score of 11 on the CIWA-Ar Scale. Choose the most *likely* option for the information missing from statement below by selecting from the lists of options provided.

Case Study—cont'd

Based on C.M.'s condition, the priority need will be prevention of ________1_______. To reduce this risk, you would plan to give _____2_____ per the HCP's prescription.

Options for 1	Options for 2
alcohol withdrawal delirium	enoxaparin
deep vein thrombosis	lorazepam
respiratory depression	naloxone

Case Study Progression

You find yourself falling behind in the care you need to provide for your assigned patients. The charge nurse tells you that the float RN is free to assist you for an hour.

7. Insert an X in each row to indicate which interventions you would include delegate to the AP and which interventions to the float RN.

Intervention	AP	RN
Reapply C.L.'s external urinary incontinence device.		
Titrate M.S.'s O_2 to maintain a pulse oximetry reading of 95%.		
Reassess M.S. after having administered furosemide.		
Move C.M. to a room closer to the nurse's station.		
Reinforce diet teaching for M.S. and her granddaughter.		
Assess C.L.'s IV site for signs of phlebitis or infiltration.		
Assist C.M. with morning care.		

8. As you assess C.L., you are concerned about the possibility of elder abuse. Which assessment findings would suggest mistreatment by C.L.'s son with whom she lives *(select 5 correct options)*?
   a. Two sacral ulcers
   b. Asking when her son is coming to visit
   c. Appears to have symptoms of depression
   d. Multiple small bruises on her forearms and shins
   e. Matted hair, poor oral hygiene, overgrown toenails
   f. C.L. becomes totally silent when her son comes to visit
9. The float RN informs you that the AP is not following C.L.'s fall risk protocol. What is the *most* appropriate action?
   a. Notify the unit manager as soon as possible.
   b. Ask the float RN to explain hospital protocol to the AP.
   c. Write up the AP's actions so they will be included in her evaluation.
   d. Talk to the AP about the importance of following protocol to prevent C.L. from sustaining a fall-related injury.

Answers available at http://evolve.elsevier.com/Lewis/medsurg.

12 Inflammation and Healing

Catherine R. Ratliff

http://evolve.elsevier.com/Lewis/medsurg/

CONCEPTUAL FOCUS

Health Promotion
Inflammation
Nutrition
Pain
Perfusion
Sensory Perception
Tissue Integrity

LEARNING OUTCOMES

1. Describe the inflammatory response, including vascular and cellular responses and exudate formation.
2. Explain local and systemic manifestations of inflammation and their physiologic bases.
3. Describe the drug therapy, nutrition therapy, and nursing management of inflammation.
4. Distinguish among healing by primary, secondary, and tertiary intention.
5. Describe the factors that delay wound healing and common complications of wound healing.
6. Describe the nursing and interprofessional management of wound healing.
7. Explain the etiology and clinical manifestations of pressure injuries.
8. Apply a patient risk assessment to measures used to prevent the development of pressure injuries.
9. Discuss nursing and interprofessional management of a patient with pressure injuries.

KEY TERMS

dehiscence, Table 12.9
evisceration, Table 12.9
fibroblasts
inflammatory response
pressure injury
regeneration
repair
shear

This chapter focuses on inflammation, wound healing, and pressure injury prevention and management. Maintaining skin and tissue integrity is a key nursing role. Multiple concepts are closely related to tissue integrity. Adequate nutrition and perfusion are essential so that the body has the needed factors to promote healing when an injury occurs. Impaired mobility and sensory perception increase the risk for injury. When an injury does occur, pain and problems regulating temperature and fluid and electrolyte balance are common.

INFLAMMATORY RESPONSE

The **inflammatory response** is a sequential reaction to cell injury. It neutralizes and dilutes the inflammatory agent, removes necrotic materials, and sets up an environment suitable for healing and repair. Some use the term *inflammation* incorrectly as a synonym for *infection.* Inflammation is always present with infection, but infection is not always present with inflammation. An infection involves the invasion of tissues or cells by microorganisms, such as bacteria, fungi, and viruses. In contrast, heat, radiation, trauma, chemicals, allergens, and an autoimmune reaction also can cause inflammation. A person who is neutropenic may have an infection but not be able to mount an inflammatory response.

The intensity of the inflammatory response depends on the extent and severity of the injury and the person's reactive capacity. The inflammatory response is divided into a vascular

PATHOPHYSIOLOGY MAP

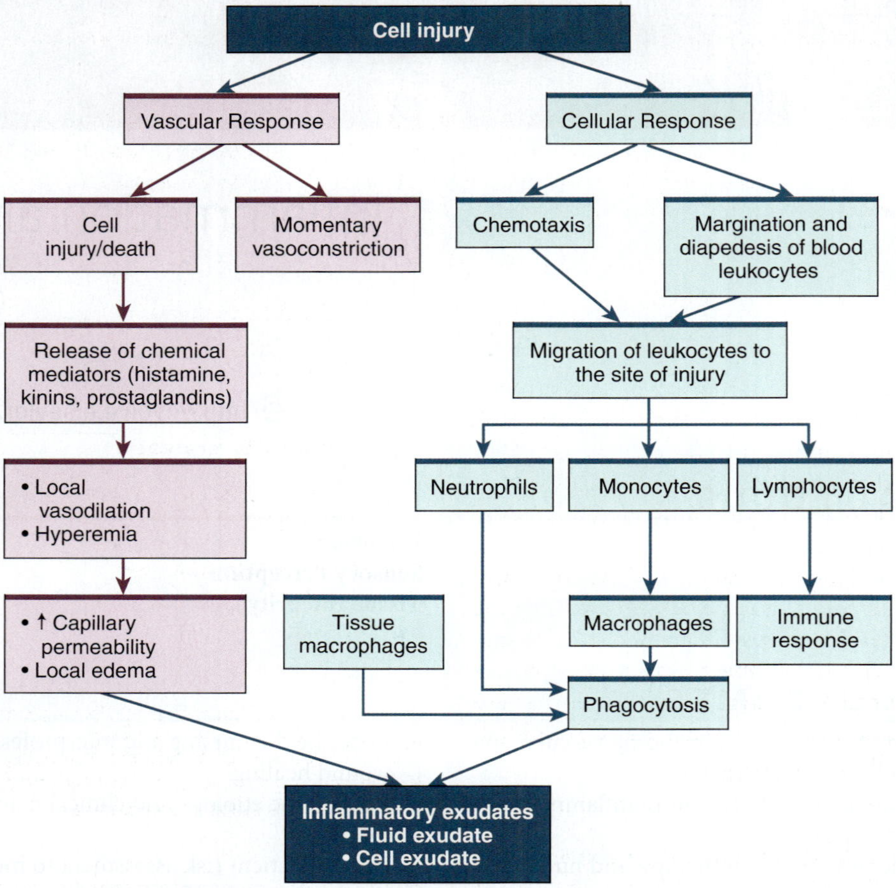

Fig. 12.1 Vascular and cellular responses to tissue injury.

response, cellular response, exudate formation, and healing. Fig. 12.1 shows the vascular and cellular response to injury.

Vascular Response

After cell injury, local arterioles briefly undergo transient vasoconstriction. After release of histamine and other chemicals by the injured cells, the vessels dilate. Chemical mediators cause increased capillary permeability and promote fluid movement from capillaries into tissue spaces. At first, this inflammatory exudate is made up of serous fluid. Later, it contains plasma proteins, primarily albumin. These proteins exert oncotic pressure that further draws fluid from blood vessels. Both vasodilation and increased capillary permeability are responsible for redness, heat, and swelling at the site of injury and the surrounding area.

As the plasma protein fibrinogen leaves the blood, it is activated to fibrin by the products of the injured cells. Fibrin strengthens a blood clot formed by platelets. In tissues, the clot functions to trap bacteria, prevent their spread, and serves as a framework for the healing process. Platelets release growth factors that start the healing process.

Cellular Response

Neutrophils and monocytes move from circulation to the site of injury (Fig. 12.1). *Chemotaxis* is the directional migration of white blood cells (WBCs) to the site of injury. This results in an accumulation of neutrophils and monocytes at the site.

Neutrophils

Neutrophils are the first WBCs to arrive at the injury site (usually within 6 to 12 hours). They phagocytize (engulf) bacteria, other foreign material, and damaged cells. With their short life span (24 to 48 hours), dead neutrophils soon accumulate. In time, a mix of dead neutrophils, digested bacteria, and other cell debris accumulate as a creamy substance called *pus*.

To keep up with the demand for neutrophils, the bone marrow releases more neutrophils into circulation. This results in a high WBC count, especially the neutrophil count. Mature neutrophils are called *segmented neutrophils*. Sometimes the demand for neutrophils increases to the extent that the bone marrow releases immature neutrophils *(bands)* into circulation. We call an increased number of band neutrophils in circulation a *shift to the left*. This is common in patients with acute bacterial infections.

Monocytes

Monocytes are the second type of phagocytic cells that migrate from circulating blood. They usually arrive at the site within 3 to 7 days after the onset of inflammation. On entering the tissue

TABLE 12.1 Mediators of Inflammation

Mediator	Source	Mechanisms of Action
Complement components (C3a, C4a, C5a)	Anaphylatoxic agents generated from complement pathway activation	Stimulate histamine release and chemotaxis
Cytokines	See Table 14.3	
Histamine	Stored in granules of basophils, mast cells, platelets	Cause vasodilation and increased capillary permeability
Kinins (e.g., bradykinin)	Produced from precursor factor kininogen because of activation of Hageman factor (XII) of clotting system	Cause contraction of smooth muscle and vasodilation. Result in stimulation of pain
Prostaglandins (PGs) **and leukotrienes** (LTs)	Produced from arachidonic acid (Fig. 12.2)	PGs cause vasodilation. LTs stimulate chemotaxis
Serotonin	Stored in platelets, mast cells, enterochromaffin cells of GI tract	Same as histamine. Stimulate smooth muscle contraction

spaces, monocytes transform into macrophages. Together with the tissue macrophages, these new macrophages help with phagocytosis of the inflammatory debris. Because the area must be clean so it can heal, they play a key role in the healing process. Macrophages have a long life span. They can multiply and may stay in the damaged tissues for weeks.

When particles are too large for a single macrophage, macrophages accumulate and fuse to form a *multinucleated giant cell.* Collagen encapsulates this giant cell, leading to the formation of a granuloma. A classic example of this process occurs in tuberculosis of the lung. While the *Mycobacterium* bacillus is walled off, a chronic state of inflammation exists. The granuloma formed is a cavity of necrotic tissue.

Lymphocytes

Lymphocytes arrive later at the site of injury. Their primary role is related to humoral and cell-mediated immunity (see Chapter 14).

Chemical Mediators

Table 12.1 describes inflammatory response mediators.

Complement System

The complement system is an enzyme cascade (C1 to C9) consisting of pathways to mediate inflammation and destroy invading pathogens. Major functions of the complement system are enhanced phagocytosis, increased vascular permeability, chemotaxis, and cellular lysis. These activities are important mediators of the inflammatory response and healing.

Cell lysis occurs when the final components create holes in the cell membranes and cause targeted cell death by membrane rupture. In autoimmune disorders, complement activation and the resulting inflammatory response can damage healthy tissue. Examples of this include rheumatoid arthritis and systemic lupus erythematosus.

Prostaglandins and Leukotrienes

With cell injury, the arachidonic acid in the cell membrane is rapidly converted to produce prostaglandins (PGs), thromboxane, and leukotrienes (Fig. 12.2). PGs are considered proinflammatory. They are potent vasodilators contributing to increased blood flow and edema formation.

Some subtypes of PGs form when platelets are activated. They can inhibit platelet and neutrophil aggregation. PGs have a significant

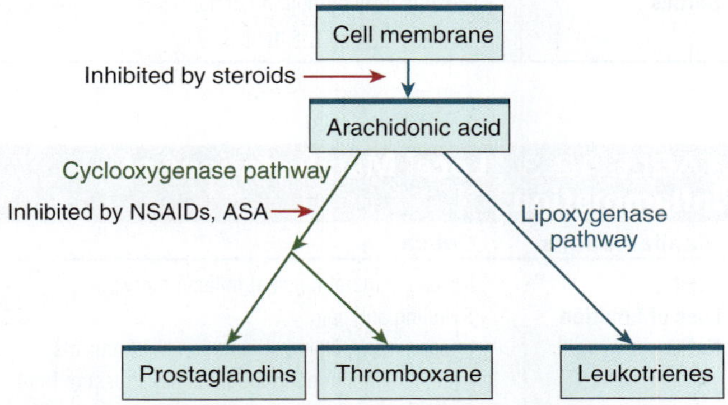

Fig. 12.2 Pathway of generation of prostaglandins, thromboxane, and leukotrienes. Corticosteroids, *NSAIDs,* and acetylsalicylic acid *(ASA)* act to inhibit various steps in this pathway.

role in sensitizing pain receptors to arousal by stimuli that would normally be painless. PGs stimulate the temperature-regulating area of the hypothalamus, producing a febrile response.

Thromboxane is a powerful vasoconstrictor and platelet-aggregating agent. It causes brief vasoconstriction and skin pallor at the injury site and promotes clot formation. It has a short half-life. The pallor soon gives way to vasodilation and redness, which is caused by PGs and histamine.

Leukotrienes form the slow-reacting substance of anaphylaxis (SRS-A). SRS-A constricts smooth muscles of the bronchi, causing narrowing of the airway, and increases capillary permeability. This leads to airway edema.

Exudate Formation

Exudate consists of fluid and WBCs that move from the circulation to the site of injury. The nature and quantity of exudate depend on the type and severity of the injury and tissues involved (Table 12.2).

Types of Inflammation

The basic types of inflammation are acute, subacute, and chronic. In *acute inflammation,* the healing occurs in 2 to 3 weeks and usually leaves no residual damage. Neutrophils are the main cell type at the site of inflammation. *Subacute inflammation* has the features of the acute process but lasts longer. For example, subacute infective endocarditis has acute inflammation, but it can last for weeks or months (see Chapter 40).

TABLE 12.2 Types of Inflammatory Exudate

Type	Description	Examples
Catarrhal	Found in tissues where cells produce mucus Inflammatory response accelerates mucus production	Runny nose from an upper respiratory tract infection
Fibrinous	Occurs with increasing vascular permeability and fibrinogen leakage into interstitial spaces Excessive amounts of fibrin that coats tissue surfaces may cause them to adhere	Adhesions, gelatinous ribbons seen in surgical drain tubing Frequently covers fluid-exuding wounds, such as venous injuries
Hemorrhagic	Results from rupture or necrosis of blood vessel walls	Hematoma, bleeding after surgery or tissue trauma
Purulent (pus)	Consists of WBCs, microorganisms (dead and alive), liquefied dead cells, and other debris	Furuncle (boil), abscess, cellulitis (diffuse inflammation in connective tissue)
Serosanguinous	Found during the midpoint in healing after surgery or tissue injury Composed of RBCs and serous fluid, which is semiclear pink and may have red streaks	Surgical drain fluid
Serous	Results from outpouring of fluid. Seen in early stages of inflammation or when injury is mild	Skin blisters, pleural effusion

TABLE 12.3 Local Manifestations of Inflammation

Manifestations	Cause
Heat	Increased metabolism at inflammatory site
Loss of function	Swelling and pain
Pain	Change in pH. Nerve stimulation by chemicals (e.g., histamine, prostaglandins). Pressure from fluid exudate
Redness	Hyperemia from vasodilation
Swelling	Fluid shift to interstitial spaces. Fluid exudate accumulation

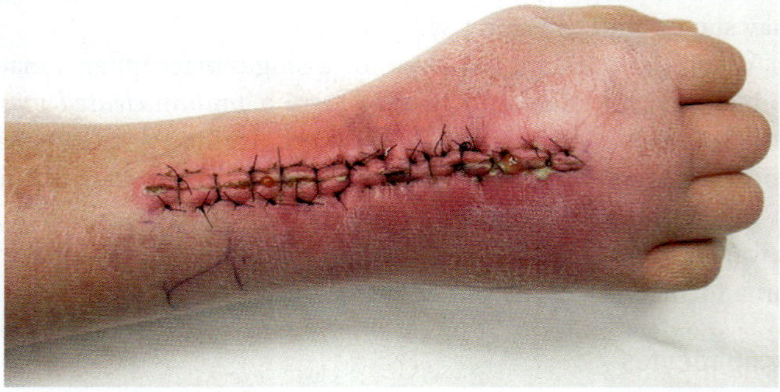

Fig. 12.3 Inflammation with a deep wound infection after wrist surgery. (From Hayden RJ, Jebson PJL: Wrist arthrodesis, *Hand Clin* 21[4]:631, 2005.)

Chronic inflammation lasts for weeks, months, or even years. The injurious agent persists or repeatedly injures tissue. The main cell types present at the site of inflammation are lymphocytes and macrophages. Examples include rheumatoid arthritis and osteomyelitis. Chronic inflammation may result from an alteration in the immune response (e.g., autoimmune disease) and can lead to physical deterioration.

Clinical Manifestations

The *local* manifestations of inflammation include redness, heat, pain, swelling, and loss of function (Table 12.3 and Fig. 12.3). *Systemic* manifestations include an increased WBC count with a shift to the left, fatigue, nausea and anorexia, increased pulse and respiratory rate, and fever.

Leukocytosis results from the increased release of WBCs from the bone marrow. The causes of other systemic manifestations may be related to complement activation and the release of *cytokines*. Cytokines are soluble factors secreted by WBCs and other types of cells that act as intercellular and intracellular messengers. Some cytokines (e.g., interleukins [ILs], tumor necrosis factor [TNF]) are important in causing fever and other systemic manifestations of inflammation. An increase in pulse and respiration follows the rise in metabolism because of an increase in temperature.

Fever

The release of cytokines triggers the onset of fever. Cytokines cause fever by initiating metabolic changes in the temperature-regulating center in the hypothalamus (Fig. 12.4). PG synthesis is the most critical metabolic change. PGs act directly to increase the thermostatic set point. The hypothalamus then activates the autonomic nervous system to stimulate increased muscle tone and shivering and decrease perspiration and peripheral blood flow. Epinephrine released from the adrenal medulla increases the metabolic rate. The net result is fever.

With the physiologic thermostat raised to a higher-than-normal temperature, the body increases heat production and conservation until the temperature reaches that new set point. At this point, the person feels chilled and shivers. The shivering response is the body's way of raising the body's temperature to the new set point. This seeming paradox is dramatic. The body is hot, yet the person piles on blankets and may go to bed to get warm. When the temperature reaches the setpoint, the chills and warmth-seeking behavior cease.

The released cytokines and the fever that they trigger activate the body's defense mechanisms. Beneficial aspects of fever include increased killing of microorganisms, increased phagocytosis by neutrophils, and increased proliferation of T cells.[1]

PATHOPHYSIOLOGY MAP

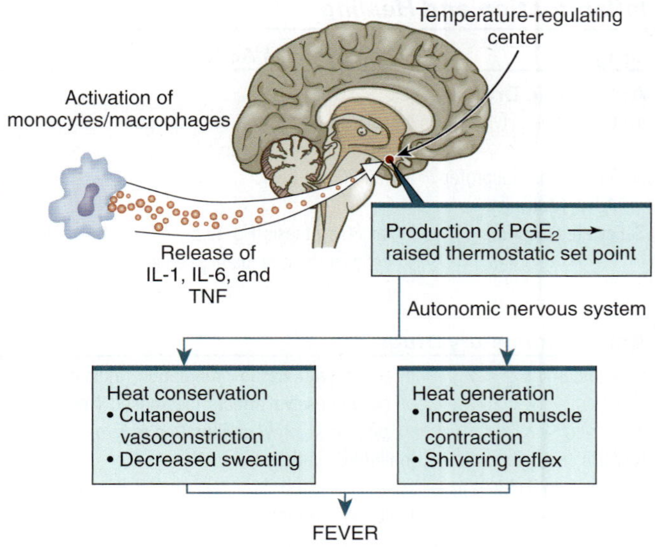

Fig. 12.4 Production of fever. When monocytes/macrophages are activated, they secrete cytokines such as interleukin-1 *(IL-1)*, interleukin-6 *(IL-6)*, and tumor necrosis factor *(TNF)*, which reach the hypothalamic temperature-regulating center. These cytokines promote the synthesis and secretion of prostaglandin E_2 *(PGE_2)* in the anterior hypothalamus. PGE_2 increases the thermostatic set point. This stimulates the autonomic nervous system, resulting in shivering, muscle contraction, and peripheral vasoconstriction.

Fever may enhance the activity of interferon, the body's natural virus-fighting substance (see Chapter 14).

NURSING MANAGEMENT: INFLAMMATION

Assessment

Early recognition of inflammation is important so that proper treatment can begin. Assess for the potential cause of the inflammation (Table 12.4). Are there any risk factors that may limit the patient's ability to respond to any inflammation? In the immunosuppressed person (e.g., taking corticosteroids, receiving chemotherapy), the classic manifestations of inflammation may be masked. The only early symptoms may be malaise or "just not feeling well."

Vital signs are important to note with any inflammation, especially when infection is present. With infection, the temperature, pulse, and respiratory rate may increase.

Clinical Problems

Clinical problems for the patient with inflammation include:

- Inflammation
- Altered temperature
- Impaired tissue integrity

A nursing care plan for a patient with a fever (eNursing Care Plan 12.1) is available on the website for this chapter at http://evolve.elsevier.com/Lewis/medsurg.

Implementation

Most treatment of inflammation depends on the cause. The care of the patient with acute inflammation is directed at mediating the inflammatory process to promote tissue healing. This may include rest, drug therapy, or specific treatment of the injured site. Immediate treatment may prevent the extension and complications of inflammation. Interventions for those with chronic inflammation aim to prevent or slow tissue damage.

Adequate nutrition is essential so that the body has the necessary factors to promote healing when injury occurs. A high fluid intake will replace fluid loss from perspiration. There is a 7% increase in metabolism for every 1°F increase in temperature above 100°F (37.8°C), or a 13% increase for every 1°C increase. The increased metabolic rate increases a patient's need for calories.

TABLE 12.4 Common Causes of Inflammation

Acute Inflammation	Chronic Inflammation
• Allergic reaction	• Asthma
• Anaphylaxis	• Chronic obstructive pulmonary disease (COPD)
• Appendicitis	• Cirrhosis
• Burn injury	• Diverticulitis
• Cholecystitis	• Fibromyalgia
• Foreign-body injury	• Inflammatory bowel disease
• Infection	• Multiple sclerosis
• Insect bite or sting	• Myasthenia gravis
• Joint strain or sprain	• Osteoarthritis
• Nephritis	• Psoriasis
• Septic shock	• Rheumatoid arthritis
• Trauma	• Systemic lupus erythematosus
• Upper respiratory infection	• Tuberculosis

Fever

The nursing management of the patient with a fever is outlined in Table 12.5. Although many regard fevers as harmful, an increase in temperature is an important host defense mechanism. We often take steps to lower a fever to relieve anxiety of the patient and health care professionals.

Because mild to moderate fever usually does little harm, imposes no great discomfort, and may help host defense mechanisms, antipyretic drugs are rarely essential to patient welfare. Moderate fevers (up to 103°F [39.4°C]) usually cause few problems in most patients.[1] However, if the patient is very young or very old, is very uncomfortable, or has a significant medical problem (e.g., severe heart or lung disease, brain injury), antipyretic use should be considered. Fever in the immunosuppressed patient should be treated immediately with antibiotic therapy because infections can rapidly progress to septicemia. Neutropenia is discussed in Chapter 34.

Fever, especially if greater than 104°F (40°C), can damage body cells. Delirium and seizures can occur. At temperatures greater than 105.8°F (41°C), the hypothalamic temperature control center becomes impaired. Damage can occur to many cells, including those in the brain.

Older adults have a blunted febrile response to infection. The temperature may not rise to the level expected for a younger adult, or there may be a delay in the onset of the rise. The blunted response can delay diagnosis and treatment. By the

TABLE 12.5 NURSING MANAGEMENT

Patient With a Fever

- Notify the HCP of a temperature per agency policy.
- Monitor the patient with a temperature up to 103°F (39.4°C) without trying to lower it. Focus interventions on patient comfort.
- Give medications as prescribed, including antipyretics, anti-inflammatories, and antibiotics.
- Assure adequate fluid intake through oral or IV fluid therapy as prescribed.
- Implement measures to decrease temperature if temperature is 103°F (39.4°C) or higher, such as:
- Applying cooling blankets
- Providing a tepid bath
- Applying cold packs
- Using a fan to cool the environment
- Keep linens and clothing clean and dry with diaphoresis.
- Initiate fall and seizure precautions for the patient with neurologic or neuromuscular manifestations.
- Provide optimal skin and oral care.
- Maintain a quiet, nonstimulating, well-lit environment.

time fever (as defined for younger adults) is present, the illness may be more severe. Patients who are taking nonsteroidal anti-inflammatory drugs (NSAIDs) on a regular basis may have a blunted febrile response.

Although sponge baths increase evaporative heat loss, they may not decrease the temperature unless the person receives antipyretic drugs to lower the set point. Otherwise, the body will use compensatory mechanisms (e.g., shivering) to restore body heat. The same principle applies to the use of cooling blankets. They are most effective in lowering temperature after the setpoint has been lowered.

◆ Drug Therapy

Drugs can decrease the inflammatory response and lower the temperature (Table 12.6). Aspirin blocks PG synthesis in the hypothalamus and elsewhere in the body. Acetaminophen acts on the heat-regulating center in the hypothalamus. Some NSAIDs (e.g., ibuprofen) have antipyretic effects. Corticosteroids are antipyretic through the dual actions of preventing cytokine production and PG synthesis. This results in dilation of superficial blood vessels, increased skin temperature, and sweating.

CHECK YOUR PRACTICE

A 76-year-old female patient has acute osteomyelitis after a fractured femur. You are checking her temperature every 2 hours and giving acetaminophen when it is higher than 102°F. However, you notice that her temperature fluctuates from 96°F to 103°F.

- What should you do?

Antipyretics cause a sharp decrease in temperature. They should be given regularly at 2- to 4-hour intervals to prevent acute swings in temperature. Given intermittently, they can induce or perpetuate chills. When the antipyretic wears off, the body may initiate a compensatory involuntary muscular contraction (i.e., chill) to raise the body temperature back up to its previous level.

TABLE 12.6 Drug Therapy

Inflammation and Healing

Drug	Mechanism of Action
Antipyretic Drugs	
acetaminophen (Tylenol)	Inhibits PG synthesis. Lower temperature by action on heat-regulating center in hypothalamus
NSAIDs (e.g., ibuprofen [Advil, Motrin])	Inhibit PG synthesis
Salicylates (aspirin)	Inhibit PG synthesis (Fig. 12.2). Lower temperature by action on heat-regulating center in hypothalamus, resulting in peripheral vasodilation and heat loss
Anti-Inflammatory Drugs	
Corticosteroids	Interfere with tissue granulation, induce immunosuppressive effects (decreased lymphocyte synthesis), prevent liberation of lysosomes
NSAIDs (e.g., ibuprofen, piroxicam [Feldene])	Inhibit PG synthesis
Salicylates (aspirin)	Inhibit PG synthesis, reduce capillary permeability
Vitamins	
Vitamin A	Accelerate epithelialization
Vitamin B complex	Act as coenzymes
Vitamin C	Aid in synthesis of collagen and new capillaries
Vitamin D	Facilitate calcium absorption

◆ RICE

Rest, **I**ce, **C**ompression, **E**levation (RICE) is a key concept in treating soft tissue injuries and related inflammation.

Rest. Rest, or immobilization, prevents further injury and gives the body time to heal. It decreases the tissues' metabolic needs and helps the body use its nutrients and O_2 for healing. The repair process is facilitated by allowing fibrin and collagen to form across the wound edges with little disruption. Applying a cast or splint supports fractured bones and prevents further tissue injury from sharp bone fragments that could sever nerves or blood vessels, causing bleeding (see Chapter 67).

Ice (thermal therapy). Cold application is usually best at the time of the initial trauma. Cold promotes vasoconstriction and decreases swelling, pain, and congestion from increased metabolism in the area of inflammation. Heat may be used later (e.g., after 24 to 48 hours) to promote healing by increasing circulation to the inflamed site. This promotes the removal of debris. Heat can localize inflammatory agents. Warm, moist heat may help debride the wound if necrotic material is present.

Compression. Compression counters the vasodilation effects and development of edema. Compression by direct pressure over a laceration occludes blood vessels and stops bleeding. Compression bandages support injured joints when tendons and muscles are unable to provide support on their own. Assess distal pulses and capillary refill before and after applying compression to make sure the compression does not compromise circulation (e.g., pale color of skin, loss of feeling).

Elevation. Elevating the injured extremity above the level of the heart reduces edema at the inflammatory site by increasing venous and lymphatic return. It helps reduce pain from blood

TABLE 12.7 Regenerative Ability of Different Types of Tissues

Tissues	Cell Type	Description
Skin, lymphoid organs, bone marrow, and mucous membranes	Labile cells	Cells divide constantly. Injury to these organs is followed by rapid regeneration.
Liver, pancreas, kidney, and bone cells	Stable cells	Retain their ability to regenerate but do so only if the organ is injured. Regeneration is slow.
Neurons of the central nervous system (CNS) and skeletal and cardiac muscle cells	Permanent cells	Do not divide. Damage to CNS neurons or skeletal or heart muscle can lead to permanent loss. Healing of skeletal and cardiac muscle will occur by repair with scar tissue. If neurons in the CNS are destroyed, the tissue is generally replaced by glial cells. Neurogenesis may occur from stem cells (see Chapter 60).

engorgement at the injury site. Elevation may be contraindicated in patients with significantly reduced arterial circulation.

HEALING PROCESS

The last phase of the inflammatory response is healing. Healing includes 2 major components: regeneration and repair.

Regeneration

Regeneration is the replacement of lost cells and tissues with cells of the same type. The ability of cells to regenerate depends on the cell type (Table 12.7).

Repair

Repair is healing, with connective tissue replacing lost cells. Repair is the more common type of healing and usually results in scar formation. Repair is a more complex process than regeneration. Most injuries heal by connective tissue repair. Repair healing occurs by primary, secondary, or tertiary intention (Fig. 12.5).

Primary Intention

Primary intention healing takes place when wound margins are neatly approximated, as in a surgical incision or a paper cut. A continuum of processes is associated with primary healing (Table 12.8). These include 3 phases.

Initial phase. In the *initial* (inflammatory) phase, the edges of the incision are aligned and sutured (or stapled) in place. The incision area fills with blood from the cut blood vessels. Blood clots form, and platelets release growth factors to begin the healing process. This forms a matrix for WBC migration. An acute inflammatory reaction occurs.

The area of injury is composed of fibrin clots, red blood cells (RBCs), neutrophils (dead and dying), and other debris. Macrophages ingest and digest cellular debris, fibrin fragments, and RBCs. Extracellular enzymes derived from macrophages and neutrophils help digest fibrin. As the wound debris is removed, the fibrin clot serves as a meshwork for future capillary growth and migration of epithelial cells.

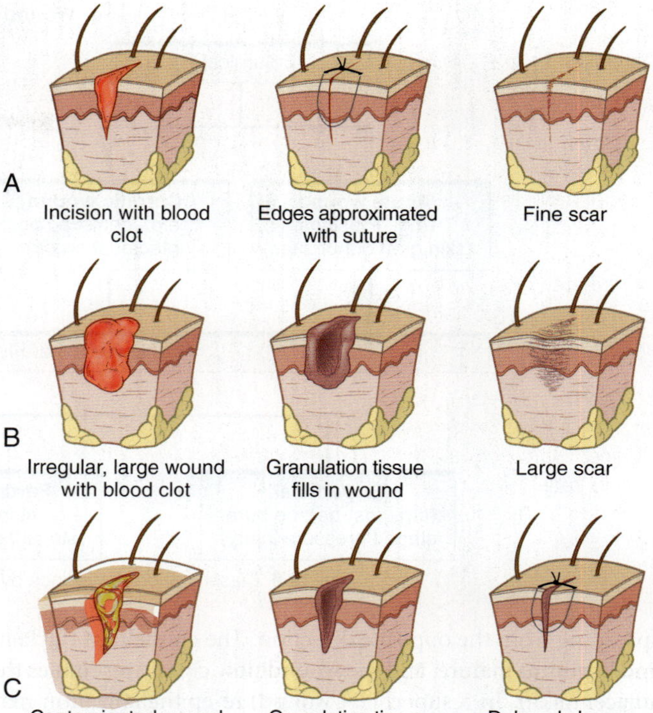

Fig. 12.5 Types of wound healing. (A) Primary intention. (B) Secondary intention. (C) Tertiary intention.

TABLE 12.8 Phases in Primary Intention Healing

Phase	Duration	Description
Initial	3–5 days	Approximation of incision edges. Migration of epithelial cells. Clot serving as meshwork for starting capillary growth
Granulation	5 days to 4 weeks	Migration of fibroblasts. Secretion of collagen. Abundance of capillary buds. Wound fragile
Maturation and scar contraction	7 days to several months	Remodeling of collagen. Strengthening of scar

Granulation phase. The *granulation* phase is the second step. The components of granulation tissue include proliferating fibroblasts; proliferating capillary sprouts *(angioblasts);* various WBCs; exudate; and loose, semifluid, ground substance.

Fibroblasts are immature connective tissue cells that migrate into the healing site and secrete collagen. In time, the collagen is organized and restructured to strengthen the healing site. At this stage, we call it *fibrous* or *scar tissue.*

During the granulation phase, the wound is pink and vascular. Numerous red granules (young budding capillaries) are present. At this point, the wound is friable, at risk for dehiscence, and resistant to infection.

Surface epithelium at the wound edges begins to regenerate. In a few days, a thin layer of epithelium migrates across the wound surface in a 1-cell-thick layer until it contacts cells

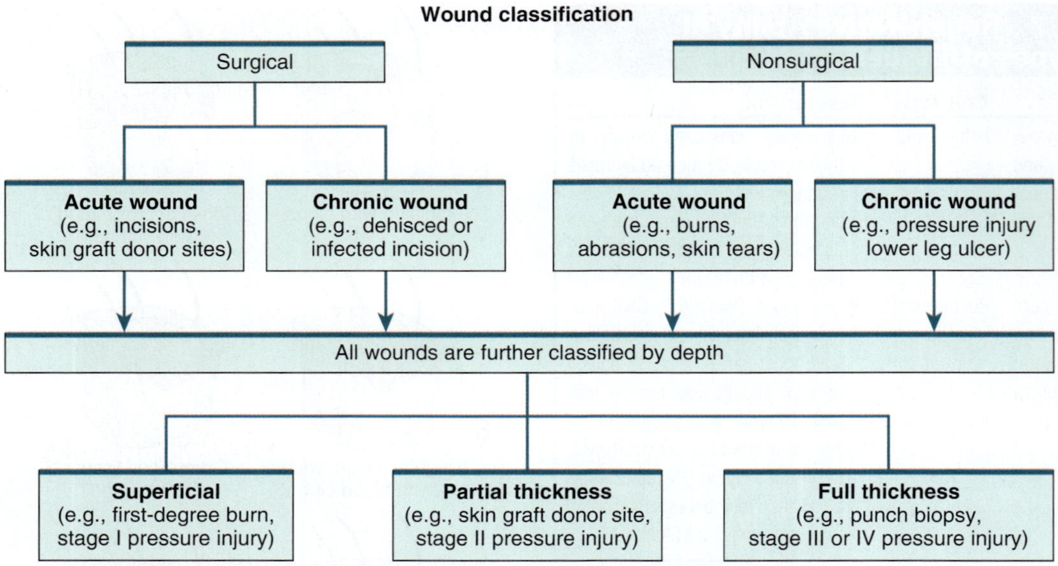

Fig. 12.6 Classification of wounds by their cause and the depth of tissue affected.

spreading from the opposite direction. The epithelium thickens and begins to mature, and the wound now closely resembles the adjacent skin. In a superficial wound, re-epithelialization may take 3 to 5 days.

Maturation phase and scar contraction. The *maturation* phase, during which scar contraction occurs, overlaps with the granulation phase. It may begin 7 days after the injury and continue for several months or years.

Collagen fibers are further organized, and remodeling occurs. Fibroblasts disappear as the wound becomes stronger. The active movement of the myofibroblasts causes contraction of the healing area, helping to close the defect and bring the skin edges closer together. A mature scar is then formed. In contrast to granulation tissue, a mature scar is virtually avascular and pale. The scar may be more painful at this phase than in the granulation phase.

Secondary Intention

Wounds that occur from trauma, injury, and infection have large amounts of exudate and wide, irregular wound margins with extensive tissue loss. These wounds may have edges that cannot be approximated or brought together. The inflammatory reaction may be greater than in primary healing. This results in more debris, cells, and exudate. We may have to clear the debris away *(debride)* before healing can take place.

Healing by secondary intention is basically the same as healing by primary intention. The major differences are the greater defect and the gaping wound edges. Healing and granulation take place from the edges inward and from the bottom of the wound upward until the wound is filled. There is more granulation tissue. The result is a much larger scar.

Tertiary Intention

Tertiary intention (delayed primary intention) healing occurs with delayed suturing of a wound in which 2 layers of granulation tissue are sutured together. This occurs when a contaminated wound is left open and sutured closed after the infection is controlled. It also occurs when a primary wound becomes infected, is opened, allowed to granulate, and then sutured. Tertiary intention usually results in a larger and deeper scar than primary or secondary intention.

Wound Classification

A *wound* is a break or opening into the skin. Wounds often occur because of surgery, accidents, or injuries. Types of wounds can range from minor scrapes to deep wounds involving bones, blood vessels, and nerves.

Knowing the cause of a wound is essential to classifying the wound properly. We can classify wounds by their cause (surgical or nonsurgical; acute or chronic) and the depth of tissue affected (superficial, partial thickness, or full thickness) (Fig. 12.6). A *superficial wound* involves only the epidermis. *Partial-thickness* wounds extend into the dermis. *Full-thickness* wounds have the deepest layer of tissue destruction. They involve the subcutaneous tissue and sometimes extend into the fascia and underlying structures, including muscle, tendon, or bone.

A *skin tear* is a wound caused by shear, friction, and/or blunt force resulting in the separation of skin layers. A skin tear can be partial thickness or full thickness. This type of wound is common, especially in older adults and critically or chronically ill adults.[2]

Complications of Healing

Factors that can impede wound healing and lead to complications are described in Table 12.9.

❖ NURSING AND INTERPROFESSIONAL MANAGEMENT: WOUND HEALING

◆ Assessment

In general, you are responsible for assessing wounds and managing wound care (Table 12.10). You may work with a Wound, Ostomy, and Continence Nurse (WOCN) or HCP specializing

TABLE 12.9 Complications of Wound Healing

Adhesions
- Bands of scar tissue that form between or around organs
- May occur in the abdominal cavity or between the lungs and the pleura
- In the abdomen may cause an intestinal obstruction

Contractions
- Wound contraction is a normal part of healing
- Complications occur when excessive contraction results in deformity
- Shortening of muscle or scar tissue, especially over joints, results from excessive fibrous tissue formation

Dehiscence
- Separation and disruption of previously joined wound edges
- Usually occurs when a primary healing site bursts open
- May be caused by:
  - Infection causing inflammation
  - Granulation tissue not strong enough to withstand forces imposed on wound
  - Obesity, because adipose tissue has less blood supply and may slow healing
  - Pocket of fluid (seroma, hematoma) developing between tissue layers and preventing the edges of the wound from coming together

Evisceration
- Occurs when wound edges separate to the extent that intestines protrude through wound
- Usually needs immediate surgical treatment

Excess Granulation Tissue
- Excess granulation tissue protrudes above surface of healing wound
- If the tissue is cauterized or cut off, healing continues in normal manner

Fistula Formation
- An abnormal passage between organs or a hollow organ and skin (abdominal or perianal fistula)

Infection (Fig. 12.3)
- Increased risk for infection when wound contains necrotic tissue, or with impaired blood supply, impaired immune function (e.g., from immunosuppressive drugs), undernutrition, multiple stressors, hyperglycemia

Hemorrhage
- Causes of bleeding include suture failure, clotting problems, dislodged clot, infection, erosion of a blood vessel by a foreign object (tubing, drains), infection

Hypertrophic Scars
- Inappropriately large, raised red and hard scars
- Occur when an overabundance of collagen is made during healing

Keloid Formation
- Great protrusion of scar tissue that extends beyond wound edges and may form tumor-like masses of scar tissue
- Permanent without any tendency to subside
- May be tenderness, pain, and paresthesia, especially in early stages
- Thought to be a hereditary condition occurring most often in persons with dark skin

TABLE 12.10 NURSING MANAGEMENT

Wound Care

- Assess all patients at risk for pressure injury at time of first hospital and/or home visit or whenever the patient's condition changes. Thereafter, assess at regular intervals based on care setting (every 24 hrs for acute care or every visit in home care).
- Assess patients for factors that may delay wound healing and develop a plan of care to address these factors.
- Assess and document initial wound appearance, including wound size, depth, color, and drainage.
- Develop a plan of care to prevent the development of pressure injuries.
- Provide appropriate wound care, choosing dressings and therapies for wound treatment in conjunction with the HCP or WOCN.
- Implement measures to promote wound healing and prevent further injury, including positioning devices to reduce shear and pressure, and nutrition care.
- Implement needed infection control measures.
- Assist the patient with managing any body image concerns and fears.
- Provide effective pain management.
- Evaluate whether wound care is effective in promoting wound healing.
- Teach patient and caregivers about wound care and pressure injury prevention.
- Supervise LPN/VN:
  - Perform dressing changes.
  - Apply ordered topical agents to wounds.
  - Apply prescribed medications for wound debridement.
  - Collect and record wound assessment data.
- Collaborate with dietitian to:
  - Assess and monitor patient's nutrition status.
  - Outline diet to support proper wound healing.

in wound management to treat and manage chronic wounds, traumatic or draining wounds, pressure injuries, and fistulas.

Assess the wound on admission or first clinic visit and then on a regular basis. Begin by obtaining a history of the wound. What is the cause of the wound? If it is a chronic wound, how long has it been present? In healthy people, wounds heal at a normal, predictable rate. Assess for factors that may delay wound healing or contribute to a wound not healing as expected (Table 12.11). Continually assess for complications (e.g., infection) associated with healing (Table 12.9). If wound deterioration occurs, assess and document changes more often.

Perform a thorough wound assessment (Table 12.12). Determine the type of wound and its involvement (Table 12.13).[3] Note the location and size. There are several ways to measure a wound. One way is shown in Fig. 12.7. Assess the wound margin and wound bed. Record the consistency, color, approximate amount, and odor of any drainage. Report if abnormal for the situation. *Staphylococcus* and *Pseudomonas* are common organisms that cause purulent, draining wounds.

◆ Implementation

The type of wound management and dressings needed depend on the type, extent, and characteristics of the wound and the phase of healing.[4] The purposes of wound management include (1) protecting a clean wound from trauma so that it can heal normally, (2) cleaning a wound to remove any dirt and debris from the wound bed, and (3) preventing and treating infection.[5] There are many wound products available (Table 12.14).

TABLE 12.11 Factors Delaying Wound Healing

Factor	Effect on Wound Healing
Advanced age	Slows collagen synthesis by fibroblasts, impairs circulation, needs longer time for epithelialization of skin, alters phagocytic and immune responses
Anemia	Supplies less O_2 at tissue level
Corticosteroid drugs	Impair phagocytosis by WBCs, inhibit fibroblast proliferation and function, depress formation of granulation tissue, inhibit wound contraction
Diabetes	Decreases collagen synthesis, delays capillary growth, impairs phagocytosis (result of hyperglycemia), reduces supply of O_2 and nutrients due to vascular disease
Inadequate blood supply	Decreases supply of nutrients to injured area, decreases removal of exudative debris, inhibits inflammatory response
Infection	Increases inflammatory response and tissue destruction
Mechanical friction on wound	Destroys granulation tissue, prevents apposition of wound edges
Nutrition deficiencies	
Vitamin C	Delays formation of collagen fibers and capillary development
Protein	Decreases supply of amino acids for tissue repair
Zinc	Impairs epithelialization
Obesity	Decreases blood supply in fatty tissue
Poor general health	Causes generalized absence of factors necessary to promote wound healing
Smoking	Nicotine, a potent vasoconstrictor, impedes blood flow to healing areas

TABLE 12.12 NURSING ASSESSMENT

Wound Assessment

Include the following when performing a wound assessment and monitoring for wound healing:

- Location of the wound
- Type of wound
- Measure the depth, length (head to toe), and width of the wound (see Fig. 12.7)
- Wound bed (e.g., granulation tissue, eschar, slough)
- Wound margins for tunneling, undermining, rolling (epibole), fibrotic changes, not attached
- Presence, type, and amount of drainage:
  - Serous, serosanguineous, sanguineous, purulent
  - None, scant, minimal, moderate, large
- Presence of odor after cleansing the wound
- Perfusion to the wound and surrounding tissue
- Condition of surrounding tissue
- Signs and symptoms of infection
- Associated symptoms, including pain, loss of function

Adapted from Nagle SM, Waheed A, Wilbraham SC: Wound Assessment. Retrieved from https://www.ncbi.nlm.nih.gov/books/NBK482198/.

TABLE 12.13 Wound Classifications by Degree of Tissue Involvement

Involved Tissues	Types of Wounds
Epidermis	Grade 0 diabetic foot ulcer Partial thickness, superficial burn Stage 1 pressure injury Superficial injury, abrasions Type 1a skin tear
Epidermis, dermis	Grade 1 diabetic foot ulcer Partial thickness, deep burn Skin graft donor site Stage 2 pressure injury Type 1b, 2, and 3 skin tears
Epidermis, dermis, subcutaneous tissue, and fascia	Grade 2 diabetic foot ulcer Full-thickness burn Punch biopsy Stage 3 pressure injury
Epidermis, dermis, subcutaneous tissue and fascia, deep fascia, underlying structures (muscle, bone, tendon)	Dehisced surgical wound Full-thickness burn Grade 3 diabetic foot ulcer Stage 4 pressure injury

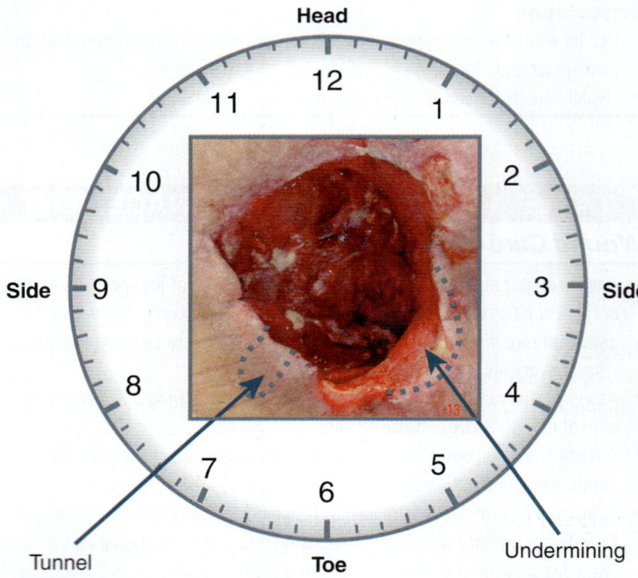

Fig. 12.7 Wound measurements are made in centimeters. The first measurement is oriented from head to toe, the second is from side to side, and the third is the depth (if any). Chart any tunneling or undermining in respect to a clock, with 12 o'clock being toward the patient's head. You would chart this wound as a full-thickness, red wound, 7 × 5 × 3 cm, with a 3-cm tunnel at 7 o'clock and 2 cm undermining from 3 o'clock to 5 o'clock. (Courtesy Robert B. Babiak, RN, BSN, CWOCN, San Antonio, TX.)

◆ Clean Wounds

Superficial skin injuries may only need cleansing. Materials used to close wounds include adhesive strips (e.g., Steri-Strips), sutures (stitches), staples, and tissue adhesives (fibrin sealants). We use adhesive strips for some injuries because they decrease scarring and are easy to care for. Sutures are used to close wounds that need mechanical support to sustain closure. A wide variety of

TABLE 12.14 Types of Wound Dressings

Type of Dressing	Description	Uses	Considerations
Alginates *Examples:* Algisite, CalciCare, Kalginate, Melgisorb	Derived from processed seaweed or kelp. Form a nonstick gel on contact with draining wound. Highly absorbent. Hemostatic.	Wounds with moderate to heavy exudates (e.g., pressure injuries, infected wounds).	Easy to use over irregular-shaped wounds. Require a secondary dressing. Nonadherent. Usually changed every 24-48 hr. Do not use in dry wounds or wounds with minimal drainage.
Antimicrobials *Examples*: Aquacel, Acticoat, Curity AMD, Iodoflex, Medi-honey, SilverSorb, Silvercel	Alter the wound bed bioburden. Often contain silver, iodine, chlorhexidine, honey, or polyhexamethylene biguanide (PHMB). Available as sponges, impregnated woven gauzes, film dressings, absorptive products, nylon fabric, nonadherent barriers, or a combination of materials	Locally infected or colonized wounds. May be used prophylactically in non-healing or non-healable wounds to prevent wound infection.	Absorbent ability varies. Must come into direct contact with the wound bed to be effective.
Foams *Examples:* Allevyn, Cutimed, Hydrocell, Lyofoam, Mepilex, Permafoam,	Film-coated gel or polyurethane.	Primary dressing for absorption, secondary dressing for wounds with packing. Used to prevent sacral pressure injuries.	Nonadherent. May need a secondary dressing. Can absorb large amount exudate. Some cause a foul-smelling discharge.
Gauze *Examples:* Curity, Kerlix	Made of woven or nonwoven material.	Can be a primary dressing on almost any wound. Cleanse and pack a wound, usually moistened. Often combined with another kind of dressing.	Absorbs exudate. If unmoistened, gauze can adhere and damage wound base. Dressings must be changed often because gauze tends to dry out quickly.
Hydrocolloids *Examples:* Bursamed, Comfeel, DuoDerm, Hydrocoll, PrimaCol	Gelatin, pectin, or carboxymethylcellulose bonded to a film or sheet. Produce a flat occlusive dressing that forms a gel on wound surface. Occlusion does not interfere with wound healing. Autolytic debridement. Prevents secondary infections.	Wounds with light to moderate drainage, such as small abrasions, superficial burns, pressure injuries	Avoid with wound infection. Some leave a foul-smelling residue on the wound surface. Change dressing every 3–5 days. Comfortable.
Hydrogels *Examples:* Aquasite, Curasol, IntraSite, Purilon, Solosite	Available in gels, gel-covered gauze, or sheets. Give moisture to a dry wound and maintain a moist environment. Can rehydrate wound tissue. Autolytic debridement from moisturizing effects.	Dry wounds. Wounds with minimal drainage. Necrotic wounds.	May have a soothing effect in a painful wound. Dressings often changed daily. Do not apply the gel to the surrounding skin as maceration can occur. Requires a secondary dressing.
Nonadherent *Examples:* Adaptic, Vaseline gauze, Xeroform	Woven or nonwoven dressings. May be impregnated with saline, petrolatum, or antimicrobials.	Applied over skin tears, open wounds, minor wounds or as a second dressing.	Dressing changes needed every 24-48 hr to prevent product from drying and adhering to wound bed. Minimally absorbent. Does not harm intact skin.
Transparent films *Examples:* Bioclusive, Biofilm, OpSite, Tegaderm, Transeal	Generally composed of polyurethane. Transparency allows wound visualization. Enhance autolytic debridement. Varying degrees of permeability.	Dry, uninfected wounds or wounds with minimal drainage. Often used as a secondary dressing to secure other dressing materials, such as foams.	Can result in further tissue loss in fragile wounds (e.g., skin tears) when removed. Can draw in moisture, increasing risk for infection. Minimally absorbent. Easy to apply, flexible.

suturing materials are available. Tissue adhesives are a biologic adhesive that is applied alone or with sutures or tape.

A dressing material that keeps the wound surface clean and slightly moist is best to promote epithelialization. For wounds that heal by primary intention, we often cover the wound or incision with a dry, sterile dressing. It is removed as soon as the drainage stops or in 2 to 3 days. Transparent film or adhesive semipermeable dressings are common choices. Sometimes an HCP will leave a surgical wound uncovered or remove the dressing within 48 hours after surgery. Medicated sprays that form a transparent film on the skin may be used as a dressing on a clean incision or injury.

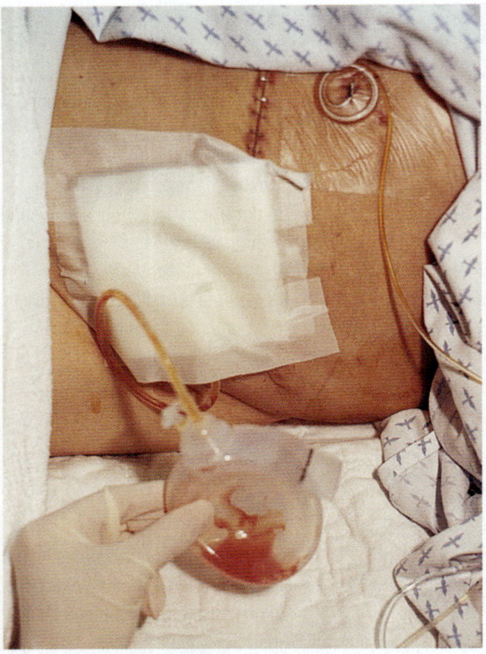

Fig. 12.8 Jackson-Pratt drainage device. (From Perry AG, Potter PA, Elkin MK: *Nursing interventions and clinical skills*, ed 5, St Louis, 2012, Mosby.)

Keep clean wounds that are granulating and re-epithelializing, slightly moist and protected from further trauma until they heal naturally. Do not let a wound that has the potential to heal dry out. Dryness is an enemy of wound healing. "Airing out" a wound is a great mistake. Wounds need a moist environment to heal.[6] Unnecessary manipulation during dressing changes may destroy new granulation tissue and break down fibrin formation.

Sometimes drains are inserted into the wound to help remove fluid. The Jackson-Pratt drain is a suction drainage device consisting of a flexible plastic bulb connected to an internal plastic drainage tube (Fig. 12.8).

TABLE 12.15 Types of Debridement

Type	Description
Autolytic debridement	• Slow debridement that occurs naturally • Can be aided by using topical agents and moisture-retentive semiocclusive or occlusive dressings (e.g., hydrocolloids, transparent films, hydrogels) (Table 12.14) that soften dry eschar by autolysis • Need a moist wound environment so assess area around wound for maceration
Biologic debridement (larval therapy)	• Use of living organisms, such as maggots, to remove necrotic or dead tissue from a wound • Applied either free range (direct contact method) or via a biobag (indirect contact method) dressing
Conservative sharp	• May be done at the bedside • Use of scalpels, curettes, scissors to remove nonviable tissue • Ensure adequate vascular blood supply
Enzymatic/chemical debridement	• Drug applied topically to dissolve necrotic tissue and then covered with moist dressing (e.g., saline-moistened gauze) • Process can be slow, and thick eschar may have to be scored with scalpel

Mechanical debridement	• Methods:
	  • *Wet-to-dry dressings,* in which open-mesh gauze is moistened with normal saline, lightly packed into wound surface, and outer layer allowed to dry. Wound debris adheres to dressing, and then dressing is removed
	  • *Wound irrigation.* Make certain bacteria are not driven into wound with high irrigation pressure
	• Noncontact low-frequency ultrasound and ultrasonic mist

Surgical debridement	• Done in the operating room • Quick method of debridement to prevent, control, or remove infection • Used when large amounts of nonviable tissue are present • Prepares wound bed for healing, skin grafting, or flaps

◆ Contaminated Wounds

A contaminated wound must be converted into a clean wound before healing can occur normally. Debridement of a wound that has debris or dead tissue may be needed. The debridement method used depends on the type of wound, amount of debris, and the condition of the wound tissue (Table 12.15).

One option is absorptive dressings. They can absorb exudate and clean the wound surface. These dressings work by drawing excess drainage from the wound surface. The amount of wound drainage and type of dressing dictates the frequency of dressing changes.

In hydrocolloid dressings, the inner part of the dressing interacts with the exudate, forming a hydrated gel over the wound. When we remove the dressing, the gel separates and stays over the wound. The wound must be cleaned gently to prevent damage to newly formed tissue. We can leave these dressings in place for up to 7 days or until leakage occurs around the dressing.

◆ Negative-Pressure Wound Therapy

Negative-pressure wound therapy (NPWT) is used to treat acute and chronic wounds (Box 12.1). A vacuum source creates continuous or intermittent negative pressure inside the wound to remove fluid, exudates, and infectious materials to promote wound healing. We do not know exactly how NPWT promotes healing. We think that NPWT pulls excess fluid from the wound, reduces bacterial load, and increases blood flow into the wound base.[7]

NPWT systems consist of a vacuum pump, drainage tubing, a foam dressing, and an adhesive film dressing that covers and seals the wound.[7] In NPWT, we cleanse the wound, then cut a foam dressing to fit the dimensions of the wound. A larger occlusive dressing is applied, with a small hole made over the foam dressing where the tubing is attached (Fig. 12.9). The tubing connects to the vacuum pump, which creates a negative pressure in the wound bed.

BOX 12.1 EVIDENCE-BASED PRACTICE

Use of Negative Pressure Wound Therapy (NPWT)

A.C. is a 64-year-old male admitted to the hospital for unhealed diabetic foot ulcers (DFUs). He has had type 2 diabetes since age 38. He has retinopathy and moderate vision loss from microvascular complications of the disease. You find that A.C. that he has difficulty preparing food due to vision loss. He often eats frozen convenience foods at home. He has mobility problems because of pain from the DFUs. The HCP has ordered NPWT to treat the DFUs. Because of your membership on the unit's EBP Committee, you are interested in reviewing the evidence related to this use of NPWT.

Making Clinical Decisions

Synthesis of Best Available Evidence

Traditionally, we use wet gauze dressings to treat DFUs. You take the question of NPWT effectiveness in treating DFUs to the EBP Committee and work with a peer to complete a literature search. Although you find several studies addressing NPWT with and without irrigation, most are small cohort studies or low-quality randomized trials. Many studies had methodologic problems, including premature end or treatment changes. Few studies addressed NPWT as a treatment for DFUs.

Clinician Expertise

You learn that some research findings were clinically important. Compared to standard wet-to-dry dressings, some studies have found NPWT decreases costs and treatment time. Patients have reported greater satisfaction with their wound treatment. The EBP Committee discusses the concept of clinical importance, including implications for current practice.

Patient Preferences and Values

A.C. expresses concern about past failed treatments and shares his hopes that the NPWT will speed healing of the ulcers.

Implications for Nursing Practice

1. How should you consider clinical important research findings for patients such as A.C.?
2. How can you use the evidence to maximize A.C.'s treatment?
3. What could committee members do with the results of the evidence review?

Reference for Evidence

Seidel D, Storck M, Lawall H, et al.: Negative pressure wound therapy compared with standard moist wound care on diabetic foot ulcers in real-life practice: Results of the German Dia-FU RCT, *BMJ Open* 10:e026345, 2020.

◆ Hyperbaric Oxygen Therapy

Hyperbaric O_2 therapy (HBOT) is the delivery of O_2 at increased atmospheric pressures. It can be given topically by creating a chamber around the injured limb. It also can be given systemically with the patient in an enclosed chamber, receiving 100% O_2 at 1.5 to 3 times the normal atmospheric pressure. Most systemic treatments last from 90 to 120 minutes. The number of treatments is highly variable (from 10 to 60), depending on the condition being treated.

HBOT allows O_2 to diffuse into the serum, rather than RBCs, and be transported to the tissues. By increasing O_2 content in the serum, HBOT moves the O_2 past narrowed arteries and capillaries where RBCs cannot go.

The high O_2 levels stimulate angiogenesis, kill anaerobic bacteria, and increase the killing power of WBCs and certain antibiotics (e.g., fluoroquinolones, aminoglycosides). HBOT accelerates granulation tissue formation and wound healing.[8]

◆ Drug Therapy

Platelet-derived growth factor is released from the platelets. It stimulates cell proliferation and migration. Becaplermin (Regranex), a recombinant human platelet-derived growth factor gel, actively stimulates wound healing. It is used to treat patients with diabetic foot ulcers. Becaplermin should be used only when the wound is free of dead tissue and infection.

◆ Nutrition Therapy

Special nutrition care promote wound healing. A high fluid intake is needed to replace fluid loss from perspiration and exudate formation. An increased metabolic rate intensifies water loss. Persons at risk for wound healing problems are those with malabsorption problems (e.g., Crohn disease, GI surgery, liver disease), deficient intake or high energy demands (e.g., cancer, major trauma or surgery, sepsis, fever), and diabetes.

Undernutrition puts a person at risk for poor healing. A diet high in protein, carbohydrates, and vitamins with moderate fat intake is necessary to promote healing. Protein is needed to correct the negative nitrogen balance resulting from the increased metabolic rate. It is also needed for the synthesis of immune factors, WBCs, fibroblasts, and collagen, which are the building blocks for healing. Carbohydrates are needed to meet the increased metabolic energy needed for healing. If there is a carbohydrate deficit, the body will break down protein for the needed energy. Fats help in the synthesis of fatty acids and triglycerides, which are part of the cell membrane.

Vitamin C is needed for capillary synthesis and collagen production by fibroblasts. The B-complex vitamins are necessary as coenzymes for many metabolic reactions. If a vitamin B deficiency develops, disruption of protein, fat, and carbohydrate metabolism will occur. Vitamin A aids in epithelialization. It increases collagen synthesis and tensile strength of the healing wound.

If the patient is unable to eat, enteral nutrition (EN) and oral supplements should be the first choice if the GI tract is functional. Parenteral nutrition (PN) is indicated when EN is contraindicated or not tolerated. EN and PN are discussed in Chapter 44.

◆ Infection Prevention and Control

You and the patient must follow aseptic procedures, including handwashing, to keep the wound free from infection. Do not allow the patient to touch a recently injured area. The patient's environment should be as free as possible from contamination from items introduced by roommates and visitors. Some patients may receive prophylactic antibiotics.

If an infection develops, a culture and sensitivity test can determine the organism and the most effective antibiotic for that specific organism. Obtain the culture before giving the first dose of antibiotic. We can obtain cultures by needle aspiration, tissue culture, or swab technique. HCPs perform needle and tissue punch biopsies.

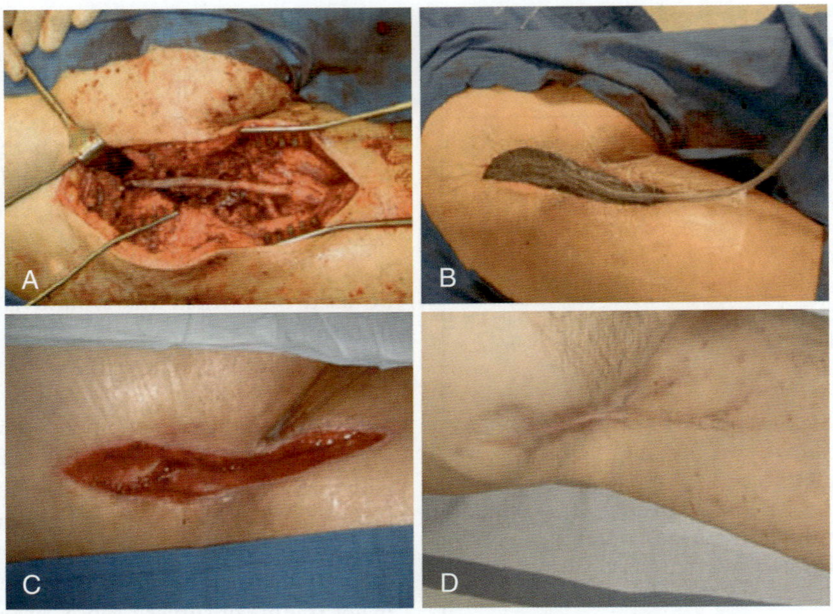

Fig. 12.9 Negative-pressure wound therapy in woman with history of IV drug use. (A) The destroyed femoral artery was reconstructed with a homograft. (B) A black open-pore polyurethane foam was directly applied to the vascular reconstruction and negative pressure applied to wound. (C) Wound site 16 days after surgery. (D) Healed wound at 28 months without reinfection. (Reprinted from Mayer D, Hasse B, Koelliker J, et al: Long-term results of vascular graft and artery preserving treatment with negative pressure wound therapy in Szilagyi grade III infections justify a paradigm shift, *Ann Surg* 254:754, 2011. © Southeastern Surgical Congress.)

You can obtain cultures using the swab technique. Rotate a culture swab over a cleansed 1-cm^2 area near the center of the wound. Use enough pressure to extract wound fluid from deep tissue layers. Take a culture of the clean tissue because exudate and necrotic tissue will not provide an accurate sample. Send the sample to the laboratory within 30 minutes.

◆ Psychologic Implications

The patient may be distressed at the sight of an incision or wound or fear scarring or disfigurement. Drainage and odor from a wound often cause alarm. The patient needs to understand the healing process and normal changes that occur as the wound heals.

When changing a dressing, avoid inappropriate facial expressions that may alert the patient to problems with the wound or raise doubts about your ability to care for it. Wrinkling your nose may convey disgust to the patient. Be careful not to focus on the wound to the extent that you are not treating the patient as a total person.

◆ Patient Teaching

The patient and caregiver must know how to care for the wound and perform dressing changes. Wound healing may not be complete for 4 to 6 weeks or longer. Emphasize the importance of adequate rest and good nutrition throughout this time. Physical and emotional stress should be minimized. Observing the wound for complications, such as contractures, adhesions, and secondary infection, is important. Teach the patient and caregiver the signs and symptoms of infection. Have them note changes in the wound color and amount of drainage. Teach them to notify the HCP of any signs of abnormal wound healing.

Drugs may be given for a time after recovery from the acute infection. Review drug-specific side effects and adverse effects with the patient and caregiver, as well as methods to prevent side effects (e.g., taking with food). Teach the patient to contact the HCP if any of these effects occur. Discuss the need to complete the entire course of therapy. This will help prevent a more severe, drug-resistant infection.

PRESSURE INJURIES

Etiology and Pathophysiology

A **pressure injury** is localized damage to the skin and/or underlying soft tissue. It usually occurs over a bony prominence or is related to a medical or other device. The injury occurs because of intense and/or prolonged pressure or pressure in combination with shear. The most common site for pressure injuries is the sacrum, with heels being second.

Factors that influence the development of pressure injuries include the amount of pressure (intensity), length of time the pressure is exerted on the skin (duration), and ability of the patient's tissue to tolerate the externally applied pressure. Other contributing factors include *excessive moisture* (increases risk for skin breakdown) and **shear**. Shear is the pressure exerted on the skin when it adheres to the bed, and the skin layers slide in the direction of body movement. This may occur when pulling the patient up in bed. The tolerance of soft tissue for pressure and shear is affected by microclimate, nutrition, perfusion, co-morbidities, and condition of the soft tissue.[9]

Factors that put a patient at risk for developing a pressure injury are outlined in Table 12.16. Patients at risk include those who are older, incontinent, unable to reposition or unaware of

TABLE 12.16 Risk Factors for Pressure Injuries

- Advanced age
- Anemia
- Cognitive impairment
- Critically ill, cared for in critical care setting
- Diabetes
- Fever
- Friction (rubbing of surfaces together)
- Hip fracture
- Immobility
- Incontinence
- Long and/or extensive surgical procedure
- Low diastolic blood pressure (<60 mm Hg)
- Major trauma
- Malnourished
- Musculoskeletal problems
- Neurologic problems
- Peripheral vascular disease
- Spinal cord injury

the need to reposition (e.g., spinal cord injury), and bed- or wheelchair-bound.

Clinical Manifestations

The manifestations of pressure injuries depend on the extent of the tissue involved. The injury can present as intact skin or an open injury and may be painful. We stage pressure injuries based on the visible or palpable tissue in the wound bed. Table 12.17 shows the stages of pressure injury.

A medical device-related pressure injury results from the use of devices designed and applied for diagnostic or therapeutic purposes.[10] The resulting injury generally conforms to the pattern or shape of the device. The most implicated devices include splints, braces, indwelling lines, and respiratory devices. The most common site is the ears, from O_2 tubings and masks. Another common site is the feet, from casts and splints. A mucosal membrane pressure injury (MMPI) can occur on mucous membranes with a history of a medical device in use at that site.

If the pressure injury becomes infected, the patient may have signs of infection (e.g., leukocytosis, fever). The pressure injury may increase in size, odor, and drainage; have necrotic tissue; and be indurated, warm, and painful. Untreated pressure injuries may lead to *cellulitis*, chronic infection, sepsis, and possibly death. The most common complication of a pressure injury is recurrence. It is important to note the location of previously healed pressure injuries on a patient's admission assessment.

NURSING MANAGEMENT: PRESSURE INJURIES

You play a key role in preventing and treating pressure injuries. Other members of the health team, such as the wound care specialist, plastic surgeon, WOCN, dietitian, and physical therapist, can provide valuable input into the complex treatment necessary to prevent and treat pressure injuries.

SAFETY ALERT

Pressure Injuries

- A Stage 3 or 4 (full skin–thickness injury) pressure injury acquired after admission to a health care setting is a serious reportable event (SRE) (see Chapter 1).

Assessment

Assess patients for pressure injury risk initially on admission and at periodic intervals based on the patient's condition. Use a validated assessment tool, such as the Braden Scale (available at www.bradenscale.com). Knowing the level of risk can help determine how aggressive preventive measures should be. Conduct a thorough head-to-toe assessment on admission to identify and document any pressure injuries. After admission, conduct periodic reassessments of the skin and wounds.

SAFETY ALERT

Assessing for Pressure Injuries

- In acute care, reassess patients for pressure injuries every 24 hours.
- In long-term care, reassess residents weekly for the first 4 weeks after admission and then at least monthly or quarterly.
- In home care, reassess patients at every nurse visit.

Identifying skin changes may be hard in patients with dark skin. Chapter 24 presents information on assessing patients with dark skin tones.

Subjective and objective data you should obtain from a person with or at risk for a pressure injury are outlined in Table 12.18.

Clinical Problems

Clinical problems for the patient with a pressure injury may include:

- Impaired tissue integrity
- Risk for infection

The eNursing Care Plan 12.2 (available on the website for this chapter at http://evolve.elsevier.com/Lewis/medsurg) outlines the care for the patient with a pressure injury.

Planning

The overall goals are that the patient with a pressure injury will (1) have no deterioration of the wound, (2) not develop an infection in the pressure injury, (3) have healing of pressure injuries, and (4) have no recurrence.

Implementation

Health Promotion

The main nursing responsibilities are (1) identifying patients at risk for developing pressure injuries (Tables 12.16 and 12.18) and (2) implementing pressure injury prevention strategies for those at risk (Table 12.19). Prevention is the best treatment for pressure injuries. Implementing evidence-based pressure injury prevention programs can reduce the occurrence of health-care-acquired pressure injuries.[11]

TABLE 12.17 Diagnostic Criteria

Staging of Pressure Injuries

Stage 1: Non-Blanchable Erythema of Intact Skin

Intact skin with non-blanchable redness of a localized area, usually over a bony prominence. Blanchable redness or changes in sensation, temperature, or firmness may precede visual changes. May be hard to detect in persons with dark skin tones.

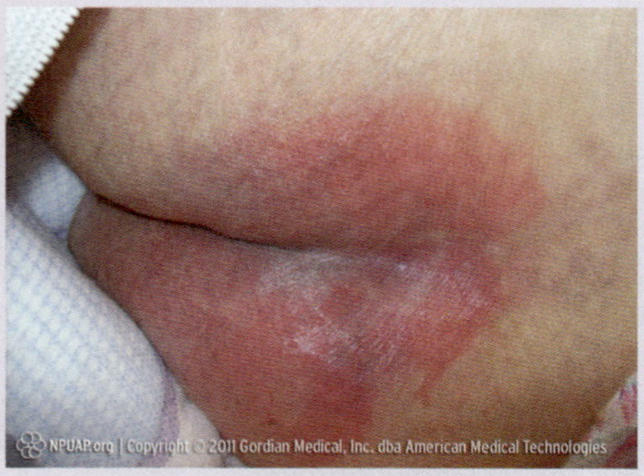

Stage 2: Partial-Thickness Skin Loss With Exposed Dermis

Blister or partial thickness loss of skin with exposed dermis. The wound bed is viable, pink or red, and moist. There is no slough, eschar, or granulation tissue.

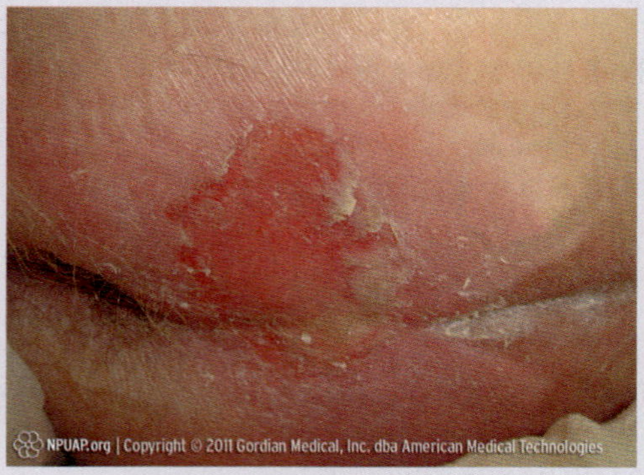

Stage 3: Full-Thickness Tissue Loss

Full-thickness tissue loss, in which subcutaneous fat may be visible. Granulation tissue and rolled wound edges are often present. Slough and/or eschar may be visible. Depth of tissue damage varies by anatomic location. Areas of significant adiposity can develop deep wounds. Undermining and tunneling may occur.

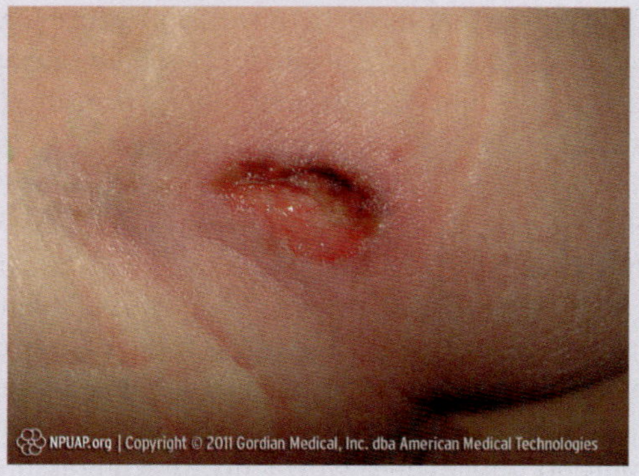

Stage 4: Full-Thickness Skin and Tissue Loss

Full-thickness skin and tissue loss with involvement of muscle, tendon, ligament, cartilage, or bone. Slough and/or eschar may be visible. Often includes undermining and/or tunneling. Depth varies by anatomical location.

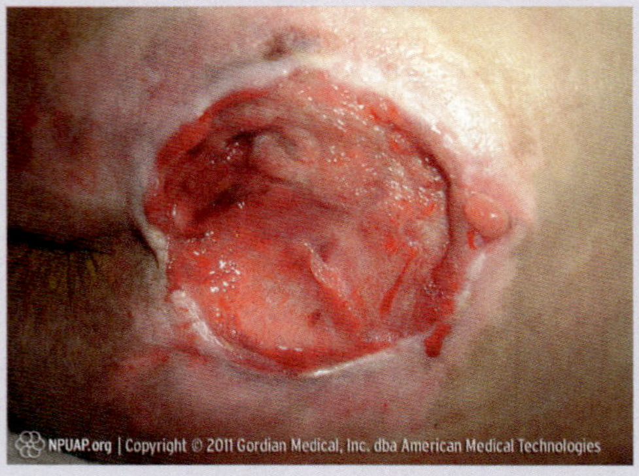

Unstageable: Obscured Full-Thickness Skin and Tissue Loss

Full-thickness skin and tissue loss in which the extent of the injury cannot be determined because the base of the injury is covered by slough or eschar. A Stage 3 or Stage 4 pressure injury is present after removing slough or eschar. Stable eschar (i.e., dry, adherent, intact without redness or fluctuance) on the heel or ischemic limb should not be softened or removed.

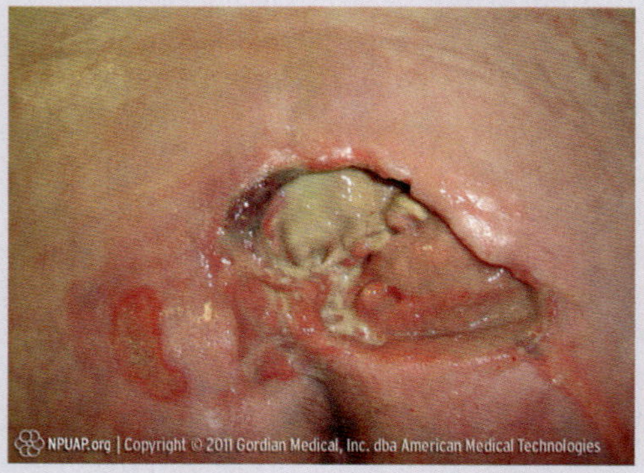

Deep Tissue Pressure Injury (DTPI): Persistent Non-Blanchable Deep Red, Maroon, or Purple Discoloration

Intact or non-intact skin with localized area of persistent non-blanchable deep red, maroon, purple discoloration, or epidermal separation revealing a dark wound bed or blood-filled blister. Pain and temperature changes often precede skin color changes. May be hard to detect in persons with dark skin. May evolve rapidly to reveal the actual extent of tissue injury or may resolve without tissue loss. Visible necrotic tissue, subcutaneous tissue, granulation tissue, fascia, muscle, or other underlying structures indicates a full thickness pressure injury (Unstageable, Stage 3, or Stage 4).

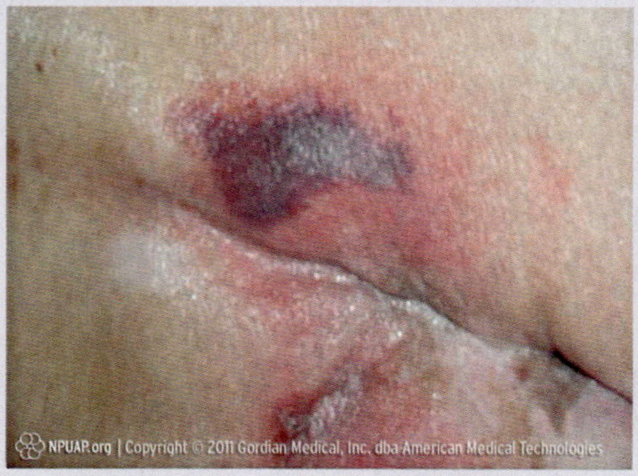

Source: European Pressure Ulcer Advisory Panel, National Pressure Injury Advisory Panel, and Pan Pacific Pressure Injury Alliance: *Prevention and treatment of pressure ulcers/injuries: quick reference guide.* Used with permission from the National Pressure Injury Advisory Panel (NPIAP). Copyright 2021 NPIAP.

TABLE 12.18 NURSING ASSESSMENT

Pressure Injuries

Subjective Data

Important Health Information

Health history: Stroke, spinal cord injury; prolonged bed rest or immobility; impaired circulation; poor nutrition; altered level of consciousness; prior history of pressure injury; immunologic problems; advanced age; diabetes; anemia; trauma

Medications: Use of opioids, hypnotics, systemic corticosteroids

Surgery or other treatments: Recent surgery

Functional Health Patterns

Nutritional-metabolic: Obesity, emaciation; decreased fluid, calorie, or protein intake; vitamin or mineral deficiencies; significant malnutrition; decreased body weight (15% less than ideal body weight)

Elimination: Incontinence of urine, feces, or both

Activity-exercise: Weakness, debilitation, inability to turn and position body; contractures

Cognitive-perceptual: Pain or altered cutaneous sensation in pressure injury area; decreased awareness of pressure on body areas; ability to follow treatment plan

Objective Data

General

Fever

Skin

Diaphoresis, edema, and discoloration, especially over bony areas, such as sacrum, hips, elbows, heels, knees, ankles, shoulders, and ear rims, progressing to increased tissue damage characteristic of injury stages

Possible Diagnostic Findings

Leukocytosis, positive cultures for microorganisms from pressure injury

TABLE 12.19 Preventing Pressure Injuries

The plan of care for a patient who is at risk for pressure injury should include:

- Skin inspection, skin cleansing, care for dry skin, use of moisture barriers
- Nutrition support based on an individualized nutrition assessment
- A plan to maintain and, when appropriate, increase mobility
- Positioning, repositioning, transferring, and turning techniques that reduce friction and shear
- Devices to reduce pressure and shear (e.g., low-air-loss mattresses, foam mattresses, wheelchair cushions, padded commode seats, boots [foam, air], lift sheets) as needed.
- Measures to reduce exposure to excessive moisture

In the past, standard care was to turn and reposition patients every 2 hours. However, this practice is not evidence-based. Individualize time schedules and frequency based on risk factors, patient's overall condition, and type of mattress and support surface. For example, we may need to turn and reposition some high-risk patients every hour, while we may turn and reposition others at lower risk only every 3 to 4 hours.[12]

◆ Acute Care

Care of a patient with a pressure injury requires wound care and support measures of the whole person, including adequate nutrition, pain management, control of other medical conditions, and redistributing pressure. Both conservative and surgical strategies are used in treating a pressure injury, depending on the stage and condition of the injury.

We base our interventions on the injury characteristics (e.g., stage, size, location, amount of exudate, type of wound, presence of infection or pain) and the patient's general status (e.g., nutrition state, age, cardiovascular status, level of mobility). Document the size of the pressure injury. Documentation of the healing wound can be done using several available pressure injury healing tools, such as the NPUAP Pressure Injury Scale for Healing (PUSH) tool (available at https://npiap.com/page/PUSHTool). Some agencies require taking pictures of the pressure injury initially and at regular intervals during treatment.

Pressure injuries generally heal by secondary intention. Care may involve debridement, wound cleaning, application of a dressing, and offloading pressure. It is important to choose the right pressure-redistributing techniques (e.g., mattress replacement, mattress overlay, integrated bed system, seat cushion, seat cushion overlay) to move pressure off areas of pressure injury. Whenever possible, do not turn the patient onto a body surface that has blanchable redness. Massage is contraindicated in acute inflammation and where there is the possibility of damaged blood vessels or fragile skin.

A pressure injury that has necrotic tissue or eschar (except for dry, stable necrotic feet or heels) should have the tissue removed by surgical, mechanical, enzymatic, or autolytic debridement methods (Table 12.15). Once the pressure injury has been successfully debrided and has a clean granulating base, the goal is to provide a wound environment that supports moist wound healing and prevents disruption of the newly formed granulation tissue. Reconstruction of the pressure injury site by surgical repair, including skin grafting, skin flaps, musculocutaneous flaps, or free flaps, may be necessary.

Clean pressure injuries with noncytotoxic solutions (e.g., normal saline) that do not kill or damage cells, especially fibroblasts. Cytotoxicity is a concern when applying a topical agent to a pressure injury. Use enough irrigation pressure (4 to 15 psi) to clean the pressure injury without causing trauma or damage to the wound. You can achieve this pressure using a 30-mL syringe and a 19-gauge needle.

After cleansing the pressure injury, cover it with a proper dressing. Keep a pressure injury slightly moist rather than dry to enhance re-epithelialization. Some factors to consider when choosing a dressing are maintaining a moist environment, preventing the wound from drying out, ability to absorb the wound drainage, location of the wound, amount of caregiver time needed to change the dressing, cost of the dressing, presence of infection, clean versus sterile dressings, and care delivery setting. Dressings are described in Table 12.14.

Stages 2 through 4 pressure injuries are considered contaminated or colonized with bacteria. Remember that in people who have chronic wounds or are immunocompromised, the signs and symptoms of infection (purulent exudate, odor, redness, warmth, tenderness, edema, pain, fever, high WBC count) may not be present even when the pressure injury is infected.

Maintaining adequate nutrition is an important nursing responsibility for the patient with a pressure injury. Often the patient is debilitated and has a poor appetite from inactivity. Oral feedings must be adequate to meet the patient's nutrition requirements. The caloric intake needed to correct and maintain

TABLE 12.20 PATIENT & CAREGIVER TEACHING

Pressure Injury

When teaching the patient and caregiver to prevent and care for pressure injuries, do the following:

1. Identify and explain risk factors and cause of pressure injuries.
2. Teach the caregiver techniques for incontinence. If incontinence occurs, cleanse skin at time of soiling and use absorbent pads or briefs.
3. Demonstrate correct positioning to decrease risk for skin breakdown. NEVER position the patient directly on the pressure injury if possible.
4. Teach caregiver to reposition a bed-bound patient at least every 2 hours and a chair-bound patient every hour.
5. Review the available resources (i.e., caregiver's availability and skill, finances, equipment) of patients who need pressure injury care at home.
6. Teach patient and/or caregiver to place clean dressings over sterile dressings using "no touch" technique when changing dressings. Review the disposal of contaminated dressings.
7. Teach patient and caregiver to inspect skin daily. Tell them to report any significant changes to the HCP.
8. Review the importance of good nutrition to enhance injury healing.

nutrient balance may be 30 to 35 calories/kg/day and 1.25 to 1.50 g of protein/kg/day.[13]

EN can supplement oral feedings. When oral feedings and EN are inadequate, PN with amino acid and glucose solutions is given. PN and EN are discussed in Chapter 44.

◆ Ambulatory Care

Pressure injuries affect the quality of life of patients and their caregivers. Because pressure injuries often recur, teaching prevention techniques to the patient and caregiver is important (Table 12.20). The caregiver needs to know the cause of pressure injuries, prevention techniques, early signs, nutrition support, and care techniques for actual pressure injuries. Because the patient with a pressure injury often needs extensive care for other health problems, it is important that the nurse support the caregiver with the added responsibility for pressure injury treatment.

◆ Evaluation

The expected outcomes are that the patient with a pressure injury will have

- Healing of pressure injury(s)
- Intact skin with no further breakdown

Case Study

Pressure Injury

(© iStockphoto/ Thinkstock.)

Patient Profile

G.N., a 62-year-old man, is being admitted to the medical unit with a urinary tract infection. He has multiple sclerosis, which has led to a loss of feeling and mobility in his lower extremities. During the admission assessment, you discover a Stage 2 sacral pressure injury. His wife, who has been caring for him at home, is with him.

Subjective Data

- Wheelchair-bound for 8 years
- Requires 1 person to assist with transferring
- Reports a decreased appetite and problems swallowing
- Drinks 2 oral nutrition supplements daily
- Had been using a trapeze to help with repositioning in bed, but states that its use has become harder lately due to feeling weaker

Objective Data

Physical Assessment

- Vital signs: 118/62, 88 and regular, 18, 100.4°F (38°C)
- Wound dimensions are 2.8 × 2.0 × 1.0 cm
- Continent of urine and stool

Laboratory Studies

- WBC count 16,400/μL (26.4×10^9/L) with 80% neutrophils (10% bands)

Discussion Questions

1. ***Recognize***: What risk factors contributed to his developing a pressure injury?
2. ***Recognize***: Describe the assessment you need to obtain in relation to his pressure injury.
3. ***Analyze***: What would you expect a Stage 2 pressure injury to look like?
4. ***Analyze***: Why does he have a fever?
5. ***Analyze***: What is the significance of his WBC count and differential?
6. ***Plan***: What are your options for dressing G.N.'s wound?
7. ***Prioritize***: What are the priority clinical problems?
8. ***Act***: What referrals could you initiate?
9. ***Act:*** What interventions would you implement to promote wound healing?
10. ***Evaluation:*** What outcomes would indicate that interprofessional care was effective?

Answers available at http://evolve.elsevier.com/Lewis/medsurg.

BRIDGE TO NCLEX EXAMINATION

The number of the question corresponds to the same-numbered outcome at the beginning of the chapter.

1. A patient 1 day postoperative after abdominal surgery has incisional pain, 99.5°F temperature, slight redness at the incision margins, and 30 mL serosanguinous drainage in the Jackson-Pratt drain. Based on this assessment, what conclusion would the nurse make?
   - **a.** The patient has a normal inflammatory response.
   - **b.** The abdominal incision shows signs of an infection.
   - **c.** The abdominal incision shows signs of impending dehiscence.
   - **d.** The patient's health care provider must be notified about their condition.

2. The nurse assessing a patient with a chronic leg wound finds redness and edema. The patient reports pain at the wound site. What would the nurse expect to be ordered to assess the patient's systemic response?
   a. Serum protein analysis
   b. WBC count and differential
   c. Punch biopsy of the center of the wound
   d. Culture and sensitivity of the wound
3. A patient in the unit has a 103.7°F temperature. Which intervention would be *most* effective in restoring normal body temperature?
   a. Using a cooling blanket while the patient is febrile
   b. Giving antipyretics on an around-the-clock schedule
   c. Providing increased fluids and have the AP give sponge baths
   d. Giving prescribed antibiotics and placing warm blankets for comfort
4. A nurse is caring for a patient who has a pressure injury that is treated with debridement, irrigations, and moist gauze dressings. How would the nurse expect healing to occur?
   a. Cell regeneration
   b. Tertiary intention
   c. Secondary intention
   d. Remodeling of tissues
5. Which patient has the *greatest* risk for delayed wound healing?
   a. A 65-year-old woman with stress incontinence
   b. A 52-year-old obese woman with type 2 diabetes
   c. A 78-year-old man who has a history of hypertension
   d. A 30-year-old man who drinks 2 alcoholic beverages per day
6. Which order should a nurse question in the plan of care for an older adult, immobile stroke patient with a pink, clean stage 3 pressure injury?
   a. Pack the wound with foam dressing.
   b. Turn and position the patient every hour.
   c. Clean the wound daily with a cytotoxic solution.
   d. Assess for pain and medicate before dressing change.
7. An 85-year-old patient has a score of 16 on the Braden Scale. What should the nurse include in the plan of care?
   a. Implementing a 1-hour turning schedule with skin assessment.
   b. Elevating the head of the bed 90 degrees when the patient is supine.
   c. Continuing with weekly skin assessments with no special precautions.
   d. Placing a silicone foam dressing on the patient's sacrum to prevent breakdown.
8. Which patients are at *most* risk for pressure injuries? *(select all that apply)*
   a. A patient with right sided-paralysis and fecal incontinence
   b. An older adult who is alert and needs assistance to ambulate
   c. A young adult patient with paraplegia after a gunshot wound
   d. A morbidly obese patient who has an open abdominal wound
   e. An ambulatory patient who has occasional stress incontinence
   f. A young adult with a tibial fracture from a motor vehicle accident
9. An 82-year-old man is being cared for at home by his family. A pressure injury on his right buttock measures 1 × 2 × 0.8 cm, and pink subcutaneous tissue is completely visible on the wound bed. Which stage would the nurse document on the wound assessment form?
   a. Stage 1
   b. Stage 2
   c. Stage 3
   d. Stage 4

1. a; 2. b; 3. b; 4. c; 5. b; 6. c; 7. a; 8. a, c, d; 9. c.

For rationales to these answers and even more NCLEX review questions, visit http://evolve.elsevier.com/Lewis/medsurg.

EVOLVE WEBSITE/RESOURCES LIST

http://evolve.elsevier.com/Lewis/medsurg
Review Questions (Online Only)
Key Points
Answer Keys for Questions
- Rationales for Bridge to NCLEX Examination Questions
- Answer Guidelines for Case Study

Student Case Study
- Patient With Pressure Injury

Nursing Care Plans
- eNursing Care Plan 12.1: Patient With a Fever
- eNursing Care Plan 12.2: Patient With a Pressure Injury

Conceptual Care Map Creator
Audio Glossary
Content Updates

REFERENCES

*1. Vijapura P, Cowart JB, Kashiwagi DT, et al.: Things We Do For No Reason™: treatment of infection-related fever in hospitalized patients, *J Hosp Med* 15:269, 2020.
2. Idensohn P, Beeckman D, Conceição VL, et al.: Ten top tips: skin tears, *Wounds Int* 10:10, 2019.
3. Nagle SM, Waheed A, Wilbraham SC: Wound assessment. Retrieved from https://www.ncbi.nlm.nih.gov/books/NBK482198/.
*4. Axibal E, Brown M: Surgical dressings and novel skin substitutes, *Dermatol Clin* 37:349, 2019.
5. Cox J: Wound care 101, *Nursing2020* 49:32, 2020.
6. Nuutila K, Eriksson E: Moist wound healing with commonly available dressings, *Adv Wound Care* 10:685–698, 2021.
7. Dehn R, Asprey D: *Essential clinical procedures*, ed 4, St. Louis, 2021, Elsevier.
*8. Memar MY, Yekani M, Alizadeh N, Baghi HB: Hyperbaric oxygen therapy: antimicrobial mechanisms and clinical application for infections, *Biomed Pharmacother* 109:440, 2019.

*9. National Pressure Injury Advisory Panel: Prevention and treatment of pressure ulcers. Retrieved from www.npuap.org/resources/educational-and-clinical-resources/.

*10. Gefen A, Alves P, Ciprandi G, et al.: Device-related pressure ulcers: SECURE prevention, *J Wound Care* 29:S1, 2020.

*11. Miller MW, Emeny RT, Freed GL: Reduction of hospital-acquired pressure injuries using a multidisciplinary team approach: a descriptive study, *Wounds* 31:108, 2019.

*12. Blackburn J, Ousey K, Taylor L, et al.: The relationship between common risk factors and the pathology of pressure ulcer development: a systematic review, *J Wound Care* 29:S4, 2020.

*13. European Pressure Ulcer Advisory Panel, National Pressure Injury Advisory Panel and Pan Pacific Pressure Injury Alliance. *Prevention and treatment of pressure ulcers/injuries: clinical practice guideline*. The International Guideline. Emily Haesler (Ed.). EPUAP/NPIAP/PPPIA; 2019.

*Evidence-based information for clinical practice.

13

Genetics

Janice Smolowitz and Marybeth Duffy

http://evolve.elsevier.com/Lewis/medsurg/

CONCEPTUAL FOCUS

Cellular Regulation

Ethics

LEARNING OUTCOMES

1. Describe common terms related to genetics and genetic disorders.
2. Distinguish between the 2 common causes of genetic mutations.
3. Compare and contrast the 3 most common inheritance patterns of genetic disorders.
4. Describe common classifications of genetic disorders.
5. Explore the complex ethical and social implications of genetic testing.
6. Analyze the role of pharmacogenomics and pharmacogenetics in personalized drug therapy.
7. Discuss your role in assisting the patient and family in dealing with genetic and genomic issues.

KEY TERMS

epigenetics
genes
genetics
genome
genomics
hereditary, Table 13.1
heterozygous, Table 13.1
homozygous, Table 13.1
mutation
pharmacogenetics
pharmacogenomics

GENETICS AND GENOMICS

Genes are the basic units of heredity. They are composed of sequences of deoxyribonucleic acid (DNA) that are arranged along a person's chromosomes. Genes are passed from 1 generation to the next. The **genome** is the complete set of DNA. It includes all the organism's genes. An organism's genome has all the information it needs to build and maintain itself.[1]

Genetics is the study of genes and their role in inheritance. Genetics determines the way that certain traits or conditions are passed down through genes. A person's genes can have a profound impact on health and disease. We think more than 4000 diseases are related to altered genes.

Genomics is the study of all a person's genes (the *genome*), including interactions of these genes with each other and with the person's environment. Genomics includes the study of complex diseases, such as heart disease, diabetes, and cancer. These diseases are typically caused by a combination of genetic and environmental factors rather than by a single gene. Genomics may help us understand why some people who eat healthy diets and exercise die at a young age of heart disease, while others eat unhealthy diets and never exercise and live to old age.[2] Table 13.1 presents common terms used in genetics and genomics.

Advances in genetic and genomic research and technology have affected health care delivery.[3] In response to these scientific advances, nursing organizations have established practice standards that provide a framework for caring for persons with genetic and genomic concerns. Other standards outline competencies and education in relation to professional practice and genetics.[3]

Identifying a genetic basis for many diseases has the potential to influence the care of patients at risk for or diagnosed with a disease that has a genetic link. You need to know the basic genetic principles, be familiar with the impact that genetics has on health and disease, and be prepared to aid the patient and family with genetic issues.

TABLE 13.1 Glossary of Genetic and Genomic Terms

Term	Definition
Allele	One of a series of alternative forms (genotypes) at a specific region (locus) of a chromosome
Autosome	A chromosome other than X or Y. The human genome has 44 autosomes (22 pairs of autosomes)
Carrier	A person who is heterozygous for a gene variant that causes autosomal recessive or X-linked recessive disease. Used to describe heterozygotes for risk alleles of complex traits with variable penetrance, regardless of inheritance type
Carrier rate	Frequency of carriers in a population
Carrier testing	Clinical method used to identify at-risk family members of populations who are usually asymptomatic but may have a pathogenic variant for an autosomal recessive or X-linked disorder
Chromosome	Microscopic structures in the cell nucleus composed of chromatin, which contain genetic information. Each cell normally has 46 chromosomes in 23 pairs (22 autosome pairs and 2 sex chromosomes)
Codominance	Expression of each pair of alleles when present in the heterozygous state (e.g., AB blood type)
Congenital	Present at birth
Consanguineous	Reproduction between 2 persons from the same bloodline, such as 1st or 2nd cousins. Consanguineous parentage increases the probability of a rare recessive disease
Dominant allele	Gene that is expressed in the phenotype of a heterozygous person
Familial disorder	A trait that appears with higher frequency among close relatives than in the general population
Gene	Functional unit of heredity. A gene is a unit of DNA sequence that encodes for a specific functional product, such as RNA
Genetic risk	Probability that a trait will occur or recur in a family, based on knowledge of its genetic pattern of transmission
Genetics	Study of genes and their role in inheritance
Genome	All the DNA contained in a person. A person's genetic constitution
Genome-wide association study (GWAS)	A type of genetic mapping study design that involves scanning complete sets of DNA (genomes) of many people to find genetic variations associated with a particular disease
Genomics	Study of how genes interact and influence people's biologic and physical characteristics
Genotype	Genetic identity of a person, comprised of the entire complex of genes inherited from both parents
Haploid	Cells or organisms that have 1 copy of each autosomal chromosome and 1 copy of each sex chromosome. Ova and sperm are haploid. Fertilization results in an embryo with 1 set of chromosomes from each parent (diploid embryo)
Hereditary	Transmission of a disease, condition, or trait from parent to children
Heterozygous	Having 2 different alleles for 1 given gene, 1 inherited from each parent
Homozygous	Having 2 identical alleles for 1 given gene, 1 inherited from each parent
Locus	Position of a gene on a chromosome
Mutation	A change in a gene that affects function. Types include nonsense, missense silent, and frameshift. A *pathogenic variant* is a mutation associated with a disease. Sometimes parents pass mutations to children.
Oncogene	Gene that contributes to the conversion of normal cells to cancer cells. Usually dominant
Pedigree	A graphic representation that shows family relationships, gender, age, and presence of diseases for each family member
Pharmacogenetics	Study of variability of drug metabolism related to variations in single genes
Pharmacogenomics	Study of variability of drug metabolism in relation to variations in and interactions of multiple genes or the person's genome
Phenotype	Observable characteristics of a person. Measured categorically or quantitatively
Protooncogene	Genes that can be turned into oncogenes by a dominant activating mutation. Oncogenes produce structurally altered proteins that result in cancer
Recessive allele	Allele that has no noticeable effect on the phenotype in a heterozygous person
Trait	Physical characteristics a person inherits, such as hair or eye color
X-linked gene	Gene found on the X chromosome rather than an autosome. In general, sex-linked disorders occur in males

Basic Principles of Genetics

Chromosomes

Chromosomes are found in the cell nucleus. They occur in pairs. Humans have 23 pairs of chromosomes. Twenty-two of the 23 pairs of chromosomes are *homologous autosomes.* This means the pair of chromosomes has corresponding DNA sequences. Autosomes are the same in both males and females. The sex chromosomes make up the 23rd pair. A female has 2 X chromosomes, and a male has 1 X and 1 Y chromosome. One chromosome of each pair is inherited from the mother and one from the father. Half of each child's chromosomes (and therefore the genetic makeup) come from their father and half from their mother.

Genes

We think there are around 30,000 genes in each person's genome. Genes carry the instructions (encode) for making proteins that direct the activities of cells. Genes control how a cell functions, including how quickly it grows, how often it divides, and how long it lives. To control these functions, genes make proteins that perform specific tasks and act as messengers for the cell. Each gene must have the correct instructions, or "code," for making its protein so that the protein can perform the proper function for the cell.

Genes are arranged in a specific linear formation along a chromosome (Fig. 13.1). Each gene has a specific location on a chromosome, called the *locus.* An *allele* is 1 of 2 or more

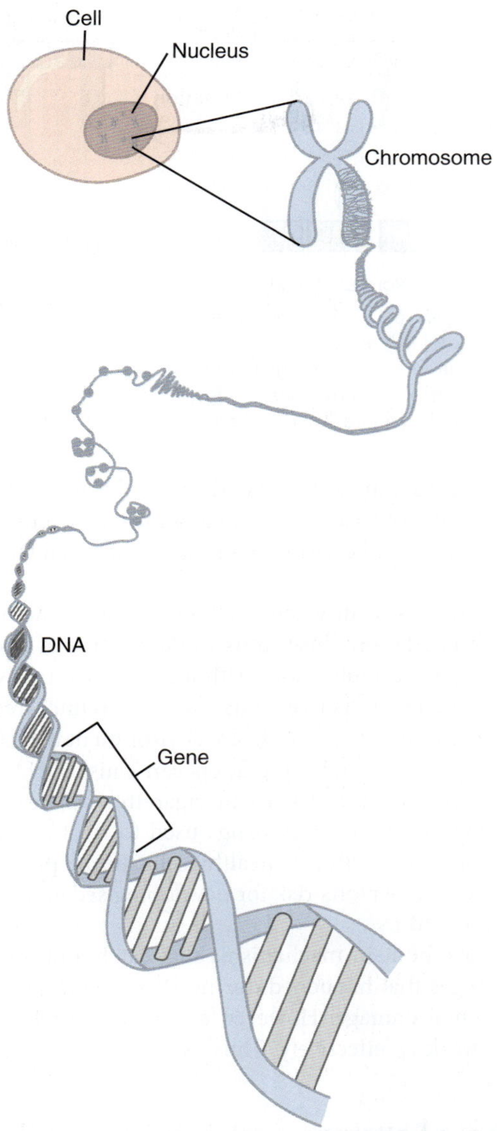

Fig. 13.1 The long, stringy DNA that makes up genes is spooled within chromosomes inside the nucleus of a cell. Note: A gene would be a much longer stretch of DNA than what we show here.

alternative forms of a gene that occupy corresponding loci on homologous chromosomes. Each allele codes for a specific inherited characteristic.

When the alleles are different, the allele that is fully expressed is the *dominant allele.* The allele that cannot express itself in the presence of a dominant allele is the *recessive allele.* The actual genetic makeup of the person is the *genotype.* Physical traits expressed by a person are the *phenotype.*

DNA

Genes are made up of a nucleic acid called DNA. DNA stores genetic information and encodes the instructions for producing specific proteins needed to maintain life. It also dictates the rate at which one makes proteins. Every somatic cell in a person's body has the same DNA.

The information in DNA is stored as a code made up of 4 nitrogenous bases: adenine (A), guanine (G), cytosine (C), and thymine (T). Human DNA consists of about 3 billion bases. More than 99% of those bases are the same in all people. The order, or sequence, of these bases, determines the information for building and maintaining an organism. This is similar to the way we use letters of the alphabet to create words and sentences.

DNA bases pair up with each other, A with T and C with G, to form units called *base pairs.* Each base is attached to a sugar molecule and a phosphate molecule (Fig. 13.2). Together, a base, sugar, and phosphate form a *nucleotide.* Nucleotides are arranged in 2 long strands that form a spiral called a *double helix.* The structure of the double helix is like a ladder. The base pairs form the ladder's rungs. The sugar and phosphate molecules form the ladder's vertical sidepieces.

DNA can *replicate* or make copies of itself. Each DNA strand in the double helix can serve as a pattern for duplicating the sequence of bases. When cells divide, each new cell must have an exact copy of the DNA that was in the parent (original) cell.

If you uncoil the chromosomes in a cell and place them end to end, the DNA would be about 6 feet long. If you connected all the DNA in your body, it would stretch about 67 billion miles.[4]

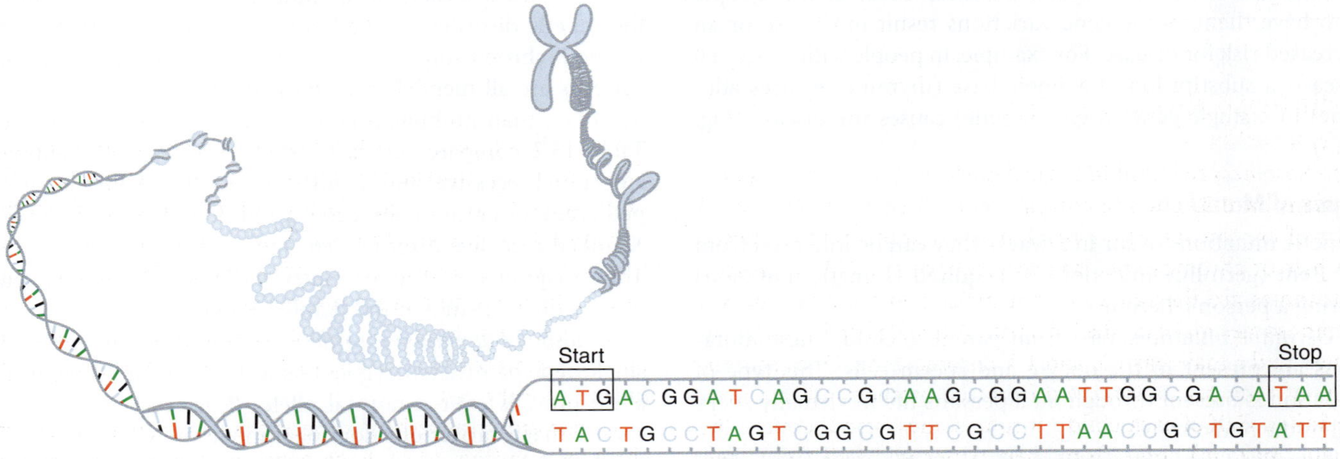

Fig. 13.2 DNA consists of 2 long, twisted chains made up of nucleotides. Each nucleotide contains a base, a phosphate molecule (P), and the sugar molecule deoxyribose (S). The bases in DNA nucleotides are adenine (A), thymine (T), cytosine (C), and guanine (G).

RNA

Ribonucleic acid (RNA) is similar to DNA but with some major differences. RNA contains the nitrogenous bases adenine, guanine, and cytosine, but it contains uracil instead of thymine. RNA is single, not double, stranded. It contains ribose instead of deoxyribose sugar. RNA transfers the genetic information obtained from DNA to the proper location for protein synthesis.

Protein Synthesis

Protein synthesis, or the making of proteins, occurs in 2 steps: *transcription* and *translation*. Transcription is the process by which messenger RNA (mRNA) is made from single-stranded DNA. The mRNA becomes attached to a ribosome, where translation occurs. At this point, another specialized type of RNA, transfer RNA (tRNA), arranges the amino acids in the correct sequence to assemble the protein. Once the protein is complete, the ribosome releases the protein. It can perform its specific function in the cell.

Mitosis

Mitosis is a type of cell division that results in the formation of genetically identical daughter cells. Before cell division, the chromosomes duplicate, and each new cell (called *daughter cells*) receives an exact replica of the chromosomes from the original cell (called the *parent cell*).

Meiosis

Meiosis occurs only in germline or sexual reproductive cells. Two consecutive nuclear divisions, meiosis I and meiosis II, occur without chromosomes replicating in between. This process results in the production of 4 haploid sex cells. Each has 1 copy of each chromosome.

Genetic Mutations

A **mutation** is any change in the usual DNA sequence. Mutations range in size from a single DNA base (building block) to a large segment of a chromosome. The change in gene structure may change the type and/or amount of protein made. The protein may not work at all, or it may work incorrectly. In some cases, genetic mutations do not have a visible effect on the people who have them. Some gene variations result in disease or an increased risk for disease. For example, in people with sickle cell disease, a substitution of a single base (thymine replaces adenine) in a single gene (β-globin gene) causes the disease (Fig. 13.3).

Types of Mutations

Genetic mutations occur in 2 ways. They can be inherited from a parent (germline mutation) or acquired (somatic mutation) during a person's lifetime.

Germline mutations pass from parent to child. These mutations are present in the oocyte and sperm cells. This type of mutation is present throughout a person's life in virtually every cell in the body.

Acquired (somatic) mutations occur in the DNA of a cell at some time during a person's life. An acquired mutation passes on to all cells that develop from that single cell. These mutations in somatic cells cannot be passed on to the next generation. Acquired mutations can occur if (1) a mistake occurs as DNA replicates during cell division or (2) environmental factors alter the DNA.

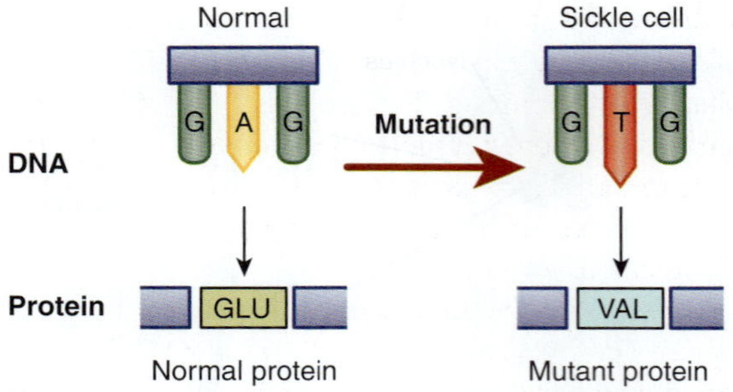

Fig. 13.3 In sickle cell disease, a single gene mutation leads to mutant (incorrect) protein. The substitution of valine *(VAL)* for glutamic acid on the β-globin chain of hemoglobin produces abnormal hemoglobin, hemoglobin S (Hb S). In response to low O_2 levels, erythrocytes with Hb S stiffen and elongate, taking on a sickle shape.

Mutations can occur when a cell is dividing. Sometimes mistakes, such as deletions, insertions, or duplication of DNA material, occur during replication. Although DNA repair enzymes can correct replication errors, mistakes can go uncorrected.

DNA damage can occur from environmental factors. For example, ultraviolet (UV) radiation can cause DNA damage, leading to skin cancer. Toxins in cigarettes can lead to lung cancer. Many chemotherapy drugs used to treat cancer target the DNA of cancer cells and healthy cells. In the process, these drugs increase a person's risk for developing secondary cancers (see Chapter 16).

Cells have built-in mechanisms that catch and repair most of the changes that happened during DNA replication or from environmental damage. However, as we age, our DNA repair does not work as effectively. Thus, we accumulate changes in our DNA.

Inheritance Patterns

We can inherit genetic conditions in several ways. These include autosomal dominant, autosomal recessive, X-linked, and Y-linked disorders. If the mutant gene is on an autosome, the genetic disorder is called *autosomal*. If the mutant gene is on the X chromosome, it is an *X-linked* genetic disorder. These patterns are all mendelian patterns of inheritance. They occur less often than multifactorial or complex traits and disorders. Table 13.2 compares characteristics of autosomal dominant, autosomal recessive, and X-linked recessive conditions. Family pedigrees for autosomal recessive and dominant disorders and X-linked recessive disorders are shown in Figs. 13.4 and 13.5. These diagrams are discussed later in this chapter in the context of recording a pedigree and family history.

Autosomal dominant disorders are caused by a mutation of a single gene pair (heterozygous) on a chromosome. A dominant allele prevails over a normal allele. *Penetrance* describes the chance that a carrier of a dominant mutation will show signs of the disorder. *Incomplete penetrance* occurs when a person with a genetic mutation does not have signs of the disorder. It explains why a parent who has a genetic disorder may not have signs of the disorder, but the child does. Autosomal dominant disorders show variable expressivity. *Expressivity* describes the way the phenotype manifests. This accounts for how symptoms of a disorder vary from person to person, even though they have the same mutated gene. Symptoms are also influenced by other, usually unknown, genetic factors, gene-environment interactions, and chance events.

Autosomal recessive disorders are caused by mutations of 2 gene pairs (homozygous) on a chromosome. A person who inherits 1 copy of the recessive allele does not develop the disease because the normal allele predominates. However, this person is a *carrier.* A couple who are carriers may have affected children. These disorders occur in 1 generation and more often among children of parents who are blood relatives, such as 1st cousins. Disorders affect males and females with equal frequency and severity.

X-linked recessive disorders are caused by a mutation on the X chromosome. They can severely affect men because they have only 1 X chromosome. Women who carry the mutated gene on 1 X chromosome have another X chromosome to compensate for the mutation. Women who carry the mutated gene can transmit it to their offspring.

Y chromosomal inheritance occurs for genes that are only on the Y chromosome. They only affect men. An affected father transmits the disorder to all his sons.

TABLE 13.2 Comparison of Genetic Disorders

Characteristics	Examples
Autosomal Dominant	
• Males and females are affected or have the disease equally • More common than recessive disorders and usually less severe • Affected persons show variable expression • Affected persons may have an affected parent • Children of a heterozygous (affected) parent have a 50% chance of being affected • Affects persons in successive generations	• Breast and ovarian cancer related to *BRCA* genes • Familial hypercholesterolemia • Hereditary nonpolyposis colorectal cancer • Huntington disease • Neurofibromatosis • Marfan syndrome
Autosomal Recessive	
• Affects males and females equally • Heterozygotes are carriers and usually asymptomatic • Affected persons may have unaffected parents who are heterozygous for trait • Children of 2 heterozygous parents have a 25% chance of being affected and a 50% chance of being carriers (Fig. 13.9) • Often no family history of disease	• Cystic fibrosis • Phenylketonuria • Sickle cell disease • Tay-Sachs disease • Thalassemia
X-Linked Recessive	
• Most affected persons have unaffected parents • Affected persons are usually male • Daughters of affected males are carriers • Sons of affected males are unaffected (unless mother is a carrier)	• Duchenne muscular dystrophy • Hemophilia • Wiskott-Aldrich syndrome

Human Genome Project

The Human Genome Project (HGP), completed in 2003, mapped the entire human genome.[5] The knowledge gained through the HGP (1) helps improve the diagnosis of diseases, (2) allows for earlier detection of genetic predisposition to diseases, and (3) plays a key role in determining risk assessment for genetic-related diseases. In addition, the results of the HGP help match organ donors with transplant recipients.

GENETIC DISORDERS

A *genetic disorder* is caused in whole or in part by a change in the DNA sequence. They can be inherited (person born with altered genetic code) or acquired (e.g., replication errors, toxic damage to DNA).[1] Genetic disorders can be caused by (1) a mutation in 1 gene (single gene disorder); (2) mutations in multiple genes (multifactorial inheritance disorder), which are often related to environmental factors; or (3) damage to chromosomes (changes in the number or structure of chromosomes).

Classification of Genetic Disorders

Single Gene Disorders

Some genetic disorders result from a single gene mutation (Fig. 13.6A). Examples include cystic fibrosis, sickle cell disease, and polycystic kidney disease. The pattern of inheritance for single-gene disorders can be autosomal dominant, autosomal recessive, or X-linked. Single gene disorders are relatively rare compared with more common multifactorial genetic disorders.

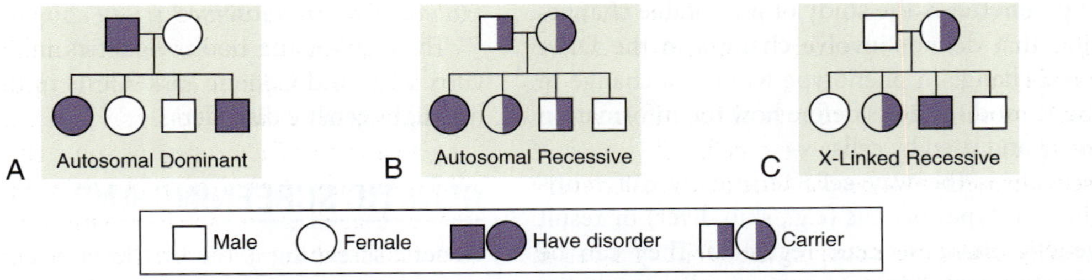

Fig. 13.4 Examples of family pedigrees showing inheritance of (A) autosomal dominant, (B) autosomal recessive, and (C) X-linked recessive disorders.

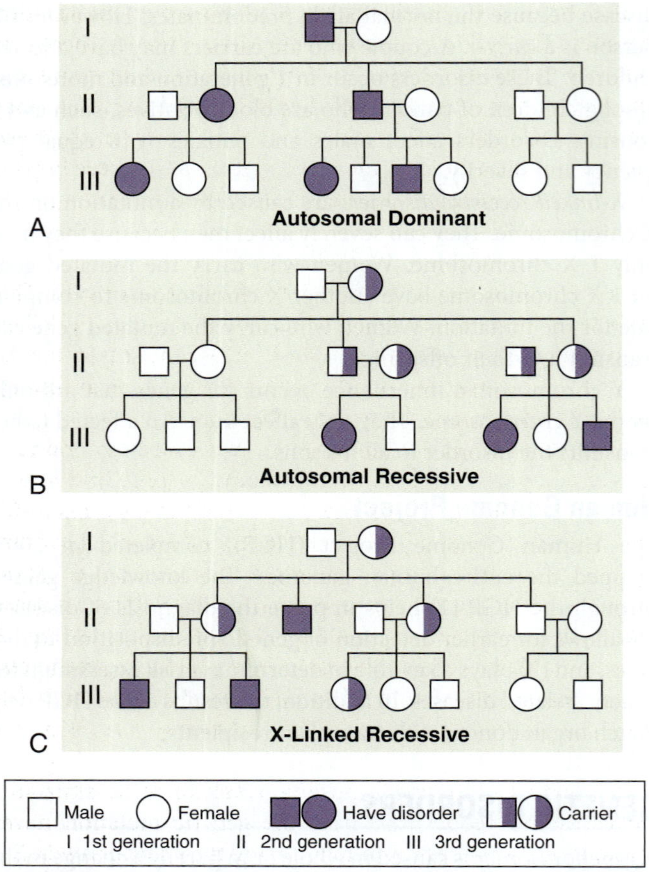

Fig. 13.5 Family pedigrees showing 3 generations. (A) Family pedigree suggestive of an autosomal dominant disorder. (B) Family pedigree suggestive of an autosomal recessive disorder. (C) Family pedigree suggestive of an X-linked recessive disorder.

Multifactorial Inherited Conditions

Multifactorial inherited conditions are complex diseases that result from inherited variations in genes acting together with environmental factors (Fig. 13.6B). These disorders run in families but do not show the same inherited characteristics as the single gene mutation conditions. Examples include heart disease, diabetes, and most cancers.[1]

Rare hereditary mutations in a single gene can cause disease. In these cases, genetic mutations that cause or strongly predispose a person to these diseases run in a family. These mutations can significantly increase each family member's risk of developing the disease. One example is breast cancer. Inheriting a mutated *BRCA1* or *BRCA2* gene confers a significant risk for developing breast cancer.[6]

Epigenetics. Epigenetics is the study of inheritable changes in gene expression that do not involve changes in the DNA sequence. There is a change in phenotype without a change in genotype. Epigenetic modifications define how the information in genes is expressed and used by cells.

Epigenetics influences the way cells terminally differentiate to become different types of cells (e.g., skin, liver) or result in disease. Epigenetic changes occur regularly. They can be influenced by age, the environment, exercise, diet, and disease. Identical twins, who have the same genetic makeup, do not always develop the same diseases or at the same rate. Twins share the same genes, but their environments become different as they age. This unique aspect of twins makes them an excellent model for understanding how genes and the environment contribute to certain traits, especially complex behaviors, and diseases.[7]

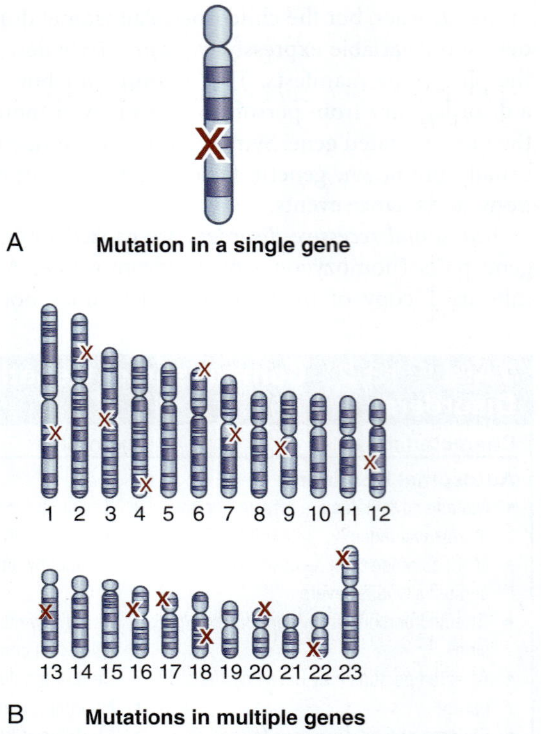

Fig. 13.6 (A) Genetic disorders can be caused by a mutation in a single gene (e.g., sickle cell disease, cystic fibrosis, hemophilia). (B) Most genetic disorders are multifactorial genetic disorders caused by a combination of mutations in multiple genes, often interacting with environmental factors. Examples include cancer, diabetes, obesity, and hypertension.

Chromosome Disorders

Chromosome disorders are caused by structural changes within chromosomes or an excess or deficiency of the genes on chromosomes. For example, an extra copy of chromosome 21 causes Down syndrome (called *trisomy 21*). There are 3 copies of this chromosome instead of 2. In Down syndrome, there is no individual abnormal gene on the chromosome.

Chromosomal translocation, in which portions of 2 chromosomes (chromosomes 9 and 22) are switched, can cause chronic myelocytic leukemia. This translocation is called the *Philadelphia chromosome*.[8]

Throughout the book, Genetics in Clinical Practice boxes (Box 13.1) and Genetic Risk Alerts in the assessment chapters highlight genetic disorders.

GENETIC SCREENING AND TESTING

Genetic screening is the first level of detection. It is offered to general or targeted populations who are at risk for a disorder but do not have symptoms or have a family history of the disorder.

BOX 13.1 GENETICS IN CLINICAL PRACTICE

Genetics in Clinical Practice Boxes Throughout the Book

Title	Chapter
α_1-Antitrypsin Deficiency	31
AD	64
Ankylosing Spondylitis (AS)	69
Breast Cancer	56
Cystic Fibrosis	31
Diabetes	53
Duchenne and Becker Muscular Dystrophy (MD)	68
Familial Adenomatous Polyposis (FAP)	47
Familial Hypercholesterolemia	37
Genetic Information Nondiscrimination Act (GINA)	13
Hemochromatosis	34
Hemophilia A and B	34
Hereditary Nonpolyposis Colorectal Cancer (HNPCC) or Lynch Syndrome	47
Huntington Disease (HD)	63
Ovarian Cancer and BRCA Genetic Mutations	58
Polycystic Kidney Disease (PKD)	50
Sickle Cell Disease	34

An example is α-fetoprotein screening, which we offer to pregnant women to detect fetal anomalies. Community groups, hospitals, or governmental agencies may offer screenings.

Genetic testing focuses on persons and families for a specific reason. Symptoms or family history may show an increased risk for a specific condition. Testing procedures analyze chromosomes, genes, or any gene product that can determine whether a mutation or predisposition to a condition exists. We can obtain samples for genetic testing from a person's blood, skin, hair, or saliva. We can also obtain tissues and cells prenatally. In many cases, insurance companies do not cover the cost of genetic testing.

Genetic testing has become important in health care (Table 13.3). Genetic tests are available for more than 2000 diseases. Most tests assess single genes. They can help diagnose genetic disorders, such as cystic fibrosis or Duchenne muscular dystrophy.[1] Some genetic tests look at rare inherited mutations of otherwise protective genes, such as *BRCA1* and *BRCA2*. They are responsible for some types of hereditary breast and ovarian cancers.[1]

Test results are used to assess risk or diagnose a disorder, a key step in providing ongoing care for the person and family. They help us to identify people at high risk for conditions that may be preventable. For example, persons who have inherited a gene for familial adenomatous polyposis (FAP) need ongoing monitoring.[1]

Genetic testing may raise ethical questions. People considering genetic testing should receive counseling about the various issues. They should be aware that test results in their medical records might not be private, and there is the potential for discrimination by employers and insurance companies. To protect people from this discrimination, the federal government passed the Genetic Information Nondiscrimination Act (GINA) in 2008 (Box 13.2).[9]

If a person has genetic testing, it may uncover information that may affect a family member who was not tested. These persons may not have taken part in the decision-making process to have testing. Similarly, if a whole family is tested, the results may show that a biologic relationship is not what the family believed it to be. For more information about genetic testing, see https://www.cdc.gov/genomics/gtesting/genetic_testing.htm.

Interpreting Genetic Test Results

The results of genetic tests are not always straightforward. This often makes them challenging to interpret and explain. When interpreting test results, we need to consider the reason for the test, pretest counseling provided, the person's medical history, the family history, and the type of genetic test.[1]

A *positive test* result means that the laboratory found a change in a particular gene, chromosome, or protein that was being tested. Depending on the purpose of the test, this result may confirm a diagnosis (e.g., Huntington disease), show that a person is a carrier of a particular genetic mutation (e.g., cystic fibrosis), identify an increased risk for developing a disease (e.g., breast cancer), or suggest a need for further testing. A positive result of a predictive or presymptomatic genetic test usually cannot establish the absolute risk for developing a disorder. A positive test cannot predict the course or severity of a condition.

It is hard to interpret a positive result in some situations because some people who have the genetic mutation never develop the disease. For example, having the *apolipoprotein E-4 (Apo E-4)* allele increases the risk of developing Alzheimer disease. However, many people who test positive for *Apo E-4* never develop Alzheimer disease (see Chapter 64).

A *negative test* result means that the laboratory did not find an altered form of the gene, chromosome, or protein under consideration. This result generally means a person is not affected by a particular disorder, is not a carrier of a specific genetic mutation, or does not have an increased risk for developing a certain disease. It is possible that the test missed a disease-causing genetic alteration. Many tests cannot detect all the genetic changes that cause a specific disorder. The person may need more testing to confirm a negative result.[10]

Direct-to-Consumer Genetic Tests

Direct-to-consumer genetic tests are marketed directly to people (consumers) via television, print advertisements, or the Internet. The person receives the test kit directly rather than from an HCP's office. The test typically involves collecting a DNA sample at home, often by swabbing the inside of the cheek, and mailing the sample back to the laboratory. In some cases, the person must visit a health clinic to have blood drawn. People receive their results by mail, over the telephone, or online. In some cases, a genetics counselor or other HCP is available to explain the results and answer questions.[11]

Direct-to-consumer genetic tests have risks and limitations. People may want their genetic information, but they may not understand what it means. They may be misled by unproven or invalid test results. Without guidance from an HCP, they may make important decisions about disease treatment or prevention based on inaccurate, incomplete, or misunderstood

TABLE 13.3 Use of Genetic Tests

Type of Test	Description	Examples
Carrier screening	• Used to identify unaffected persons who carry 1 copy of a gene • Offered to persons who have a family history of a genetic disorder and to those in ethnic groups with an increased risk for specific genetic conditions • If both parents are tested, the test can provide information about a couple's risk for having a child with a genetic condition	• Cystic fibrosis • Sickle cell disease • Hemophilia
Diagnostic testing	• Used to diagnose, rule out, or confirm a specific genetic or chromosomal condition • Used to confirm findings when patient's signs and symptoms suggest a genetic disorder • Can be done at any time during a person's life but is not available for all genes or all genetic conditions	• Cystic fibrosis • Sickle cell disease • Polycystic kidney disease • Hemophilia • Familial hypercholesterolemia
Forensic testing	• Done to identify a person for legal purposes	• Identify crime or victims in catastrophic situations • Rule out or implicate a crime suspect
Newborn screening	• Most widespread use of genetic testing • Early intervention to treat these disorders can eliminate or reduce symptoms that may otherwise cause a lifetime of disability	• Phenylketonuria • Congenital hypothyroidism • Cystic fibrosis
Parental testing	• Establish biologic relationships between people	• Paternity testing
Pharmacogenomic testing	• Identifies genetic variations that influence a person's response to drugs • Results provide information to help choose drug therapy that is best for the person	• Warfarin (Coumadin) dose
Predictive testing	• Can identify mutations that increase a person's risk for developing disorders • If results are positive, person can have prophylactic measures (e.g., mastectomy, oophorectomy) to prevent development of cancer	• Breast cancer • Ovarian cancer
Preimplantation genetic diagnosis (PGD)	• Fertilized embryos tested before implantation and pregnancy • Allows embryos free of a particular disorder to be placed into the uterus • Embryos that test positive for genetic disorders can be destroyed	• For persons known to have or be a carrier for a genetic mutation (e.g., Huntington disease)
Prenatal diagnostic testing	• Fluid obtained from amniocentesis or tissue from chorionic villus used to obtain fetal cells. Can obtain fetal samples from mother's blood • Used to detect changes in genes or chromosomes of fetus before birth • Testing offered to a couple with an increased risk for having a baby with a genetic or chromosomal disorder • Can decrease a couple's uncertainty or help them decide whether to end a pregnancy	• Down syndrome • Other genetic alterations in fetuses
Presymptomatic testing	• Used to detect genetic mutations associated with disorders that appear later in life • Can be helpful to people who have a family member with a genetic disorder but who have no features of the disorder themselves at the time of testing • Results can provide information about a person's risk for developing a specific disorder and help with making decisions about treatment	• Huntington disease • Adult polycystic kidney disease • Hemochromatosis • Familial adenomatous polyposis • Hereditary nonpolyposis colorectal cancer syndrome

information about their health. People may experience an invasion of genetic privacy if testing companies use their genetic information in an unauthorized way. When people are considering using these kinds of genetic tests, nurses should provide education and suggest they discuss the issue with their HCP or a genetics counselor. Teaching related to genetic testing is outlined in Table 13.4.

Genetic Technology

DNA Fingerprinting

DNA (genetic) fingerprinting begins by extracting DNA from the cells in a sample of blood, saliva, semen, or other appropriate fluid or tissue. *Polymerase chain reaction (PCR)* is a quick, easy method to provide unlimited copies of a DNA or RNA sequence using only a small sample. PCR involves the artificial replication of a DNA or RNA sequence. The DNA or RNA strands can be separated to form new templates that are used for replication.

PCR is a key element in *genetic fingerprinting.* It is an essential technique for finding mutations in genes. We use it in forensic medicine to identify the DNA of criminal suspects by using samples from blood, hair, saliva, and semen. Results have freed persons who are wrongly incarcerated. PCR is used in paternity testing and as a confirmatory test in human immunodeficiency virus (HIV) testing. This is especially important when an infant of a mother who is HIV-antibody positive tests HIV positive. In this situation, PCR will determine if the baby is infected with HIV or if the antibodies are from the mother.

DNA Microarray (DNA Chip)

Although all a person's somatic cells have identical genetic material, the same genes are not active in every cell. Studying which genes are active and inactive in different cell types helps to understand (1) how these cells function normally and (2) how they are affected when various genes do not perform properly.

Gene expression profiling uses a technology called *DNA microarrays* (DNA chips). DNA chips can identify changes in gene sequences or if certain genes are turned off in cells and tissues. It can serve as a diagnostic test or determine if certain medications might have a better therapeutic effect for certain people. The chip is a small glass plate enclosed in plastic. The surface of each chip has thousands of short, synthetic, single-stranded DNA sequences. Together they represent the normal gene, as well as known variations of the gene.

To determine if a mutation is present for a specific disease, we obtain a sample of DNA from the blood of the person with suspected disease and a control sample, which does not have a gene mutation. The DNA in the samples is separated into single-stranded molecules and then cut into small fragments. The fragments are labeled using fluorescent dye. Different colors identify the control and test samples. Both sets are inserted into the chip, where they bind to the synthetic DNA on the chip. If the person does not have a mutation for the gene, both samples will bind to the normal sequences on the chip. If a mutation is present, the person's DNA will bind to the sequence on the chip that represents the mutated DNA.[12]

Genome-Wide Association Study (GWAS)

Genome-wide association study (GWAS) is an approach that involves rapidly scanning complete sets of DNA, or genomes, of many people to find genetic variations associated with the development or progression of a specific disease.

With GWAS, researchers can study large numbers of genes and proteins, including how they act and interact. This gives us a more complete picture of what goes on in a person. We may learn how to stop or jump-start genes on demand, change the course of a disease, or prevent it from ever happening. GWAS is particularly useful in finding genetic variations that contribute to multifactorial inherited disorders, such as cancer and heart disease.

Researchers use 2 groups of people to carry out a GWAS: those with the disease and similar people without the disease. Each person's complete set of DNA, or genome, is purified from the blood or cells, placed on tiny chips, and scanned on automated laboratory machines. The machines quickly survey each person's genome for strategically selected markers of genetic variation.

If certain genetic variations are significantly more common in people with the disease than those without the disease, the variations are "associated" with the disease. The associated genetic variations can serve as powerful pointers to the human genome region where the disease-causing problem exists.

BOX 13.2 GENETICS IN CLINICAL PRACTICE

Genetic Information Nondiscrimination Act (GINA)

The GINA is a federal law prohibiting discrimination in health care coverage and employment based on genetic information. Genetic information is any data about a person's genetic tests, family members' genetic tests, and family history of a genetic disease or disorder.[9]

- Addresses concerns about discrimination that might prevent people from seeking genetic tests
- Enables people to take part in research studies without fear that their DNA information may be used against them in the workplace or prevent them from getting health insurance
- Prevents health insurers from denying health insurance coverage and discriminating against a person based on genetic or family history information
- Prevents health insurers from asking that a person have a genetic test
- Prohibits most employers from using genetic information for hiring, firing, or promotion decisions and any decisions about terms of employment
- Protection does not extend to life insurance, disability insurance, or long-term care insurance

For more information, see Genetic Discrimination. Retrieved from www.genome.gov.

TABLE 13.4 PATIENT & CAREGIVER TEACHING

Genetic Testing

Genetic Counselors	General Information
• People considering genetic testing should meet with a genetics counselor who is specially trained in medical genetics and counseling. • Counseling can help you understand the purpose of genetic testing, considerations before testing, and the emotional and medical impact of the test results. • Genetics counseling can help you understand the pros and cons of genetic testing before deciding to undergo a genetic test.	*The following includes some important general information about genetic testing:* • Genetic testing can be expensive. Your health insurance may not cover the cost. • Genetic testing may determine whether you are predisposed to developing an inherited disease. • A particular genetic test will only tell you whether there is a specific genetic variant or mutation. Positive tests do not mean you will develop that disease or disorder. Neither can the results tell you when you will develop the disease. • If a genetic test shows a genetic predisposition to an inherited disorder, the news can be depressing. • Knowledge of a genetic predisposition to a disease may motivate you to take preventive measures (e.g., taking drugs for familial hypercholesterolemia) or make lifestyle changes to lower the risk for a disease (e.g., exercising to decrease the risk for type 2 diabetes). • If a genetic test reveals you are at risk for a specific genetic disorder, there is the chance that other family members may be at risk. • If a genetic test reveals you are at risk for developing an inherited disease, whether you decide to share that information with family members is a personal and ethical decision that you will have to make. • Genetic testing may provide important information that you can use when making decisions about having children.

The potential impact of GWAS is substantial since it lays the groundwork for personalized medicine. This changes the "1-size-fits-all" approach to health care. It provides a mechanism for providing more individualized care. The information will help the HCP tailor prevention programs.[13]

PHARMACOGENOMICS AND PHARMACOGENETICS

Patients vary widely in their response to drugs. Although the reasons for this are complex, genetic factors may account for a large percentage of individual variability. **Pharmacogenomics** looks at how drugs affect and interact with the genome and output expression. Pharmacogenomics allows for the identification of variations in multiple genes that affect drug response. **Pharmacogenetics** is the study of variable drug responses, including adverse events from differences in inheritable genes. Many use these terms interchangeably when describing the relationship between pharmacology and genetic variability in determining a person's response to drugs. Pharmacogenetics has a narrower focus than pharmacogenomics.[1]

Pharmacogenetic and pharmacogenomic studies could lead to the development of drugs that can be tailor-made or adapted to each person's particular genetic makeup. This will make it possible to have personalized medicine by choosing the right drug and the right dose for the right person.[11] HCPs are starting to use pharmacogenomic information to prescribe drugs. Examples are shown in Table 13.5.

One important area of study has focused on the hepatic cytochrome P450 (CYP450) enzyme system. It is responsible for oxidizing many drugs and chemicals.[11] The enzymes in this system share certain amino acid sequences. Each is coded by a separate gene. People with a less active form of the enzyme (who metabolize the drug slowly) may get too much of the drug. People with a more active form of the enzyme (who metabolize the drug quickly) may get too little of the drug. It may appear that the medication is not effective. These persons may need more frequent dosing. So, pharmacogenomic testing can help HCPs in prescribing the right dose of medicine based on a patient's particular genetic makeup (Fig. 13.7).

TABLE 13.5 Examples of Pharmacogenomics

Drug	Role of Pharmacogenetics
abacavir (Ziagen)	• Some people are at greater risk for serious allergic reactions when first starting treatment with this drug. • Genetic testing for *HLA-B*5701* before taking the drug can identify those who carry a genetic marker associated with life-threatening hypersensitivity reactions.
clopidogrel (Plavix)	• For clopidogrel to work, cytochrome P450 enzymes in the liver (particularly CYP2C19) must convert the drug to its active form. • About 2%–14% of the population are poor metabolizers of the drug. These patients may not receive the full benefits of the drug. • Genetic tests are available to identify genetic differences in CYP2C19 function.
crizotinib (Xalkori)	• Used to treat patients with late-stage, non–small cell lung cancers (NSCLCs) who express the abnormal anaplastic lymphoma kinase *(ALK)* gene. • *ALK* gene abnormality causes cancer development and growth. • Blocks certain proteins called *kinases,* including the protein made by the abnormal *ALK* gene. • Approved for use with a companion genetic diagnostic test that determines whether a patient with NSCLC has the abnormal *ALK* gene.
trastuzumab (Herceptin)	• In breast cancer, drug works only for women whose tumors have genes that lead to the overproduction of a protein called HER-2. • Drug is a monoclonal antibody to HER-2. After the antibody attaches to the antigen, it kills the cells. • Genetic testing provides information on which women are good candidates for treatment with drug. • Drug does not work for women whose tumor genes do not express HER-2.
vemurafenib (Zelboraf)	• Approved for patients with late-stage (metastatic) or unresectable melanoma. • Indicated for the treatment of patients with melanoma whose tumors express a gene mutation called *BRAF V600E.* • To be considered for treatment, patients must first have genetic testing to determine whether melanoma cells have the *BRAF V600E* mutation.
warfarin (see Fig. 13.7)	• Genetic variants in the genes *VKORC1* and cytochrome P450 2C9 *(CYP2C9)* significantly impact people's sensitivity to warfarin (Fig. 13.7). • Persons with specific variations in these genes need a lower warfarin dose to maintain therapeutic levels of anticoagulation. • Persons with other variations need higher doses. • Together, these genetic variations explain about 50% of the required dose difference between persons. • Testing for *CYP2C9* and *VKORC1* genotype information can assist in choosing the starting dose.

GENE THERAPY

Gene therapy is an experimental technique used to treat the underlying cause of a disease. Gene therapy may be able to supply a missing gene, provide the missing gene's role, or enhance the treatment of a disease. The goal is to provide a normally functioning gene to a person with a pathogenic gene variant.

A carrier molecule called a *vector* must be used to deliver the therapeutic gene to the person's target cells.[1] Currently, the most common vector is a genetically altered virus to carry normal human DNA.[1] The vector is given IV or directly injected into tissue.[1] The vector unloads its genetic material containing the therapeutic human gene into the target cell. If the treatment is successful, the new gene will make a functional protein and restore the target cell to normal. A diagram of gene therapy is shown in Fig. 13.8.

Gene therapy is a promising treatment for several diseases, including inherited disorders, some types of cancer, and certain viral infections. Right now, the use of gene therapy is limited. Tisagenlecleucel (Kymriah) is an FDA-approved gene therapy used to treat some pediatric and young adult patients with a form of acute lymphoblastic leukemia.[14] Another gene therapy treats vision loss from a congenital retinal degenerative disorder.[15]

Metabolism of Drug	Genetic Variants of Cytochrome P450	Drug Dose Based on Genetic Testing of Cytochrome P450
Normal metabolism		Normal dose
Some people metabolize the drug quickly (fast metabolizers) and need higher doses		Higher dose
Some people metabolize the drug slowly (slow metabolizers) and need lower doses		Lower dose

Fig. 13.7 People respond differently to the drug warfarin. The diversity of responses is partially due to genetic variants in 1 of the cytochrome P450 genes.

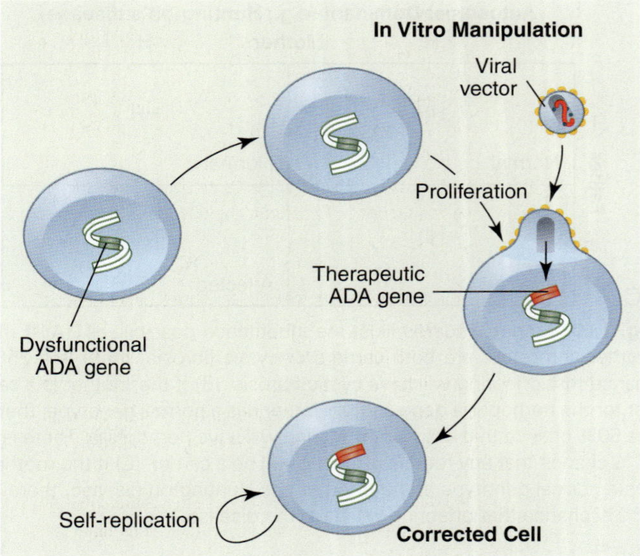

Fig. 13.8 Gene therapy for adenosine deaminase *(ADA)* deficiency tries to correct this immunodeficiency state. The viral vector containing the therapeutic ADA gene is inserted into the patient's lymphocytes. These cells can then make the ADA enzyme.

STEM CELL THERAPY

Stem cells are unspecialized cells in the body that have the ability to (1) remain in their unspecialized state and divide or (2) differentiate and develop into specialized cells. The use of stem cells may allow for the regeneration of lost tissue and restoration of function in various diseases. Stem cells can be derived from human embryos or adult somatic tissues. Stem cells can be totipotent, pluripotent, multipotent, or unipotent. Totipotent cells can produce all the cell types of the developing organism. Pluripotent cells can make any body cell because they make all cells of the embryo. Multipotent cells only make cells within a specific germ layer. Unipotent cells make a single cell type.[16]

Adult stem cells are undifferentiated cells that exist in small numbers in many organs and tissues. These include the brain, bone marrow, peripheral blood, blood vessels, skeletal muscle, skin, teeth, heart, GI tract, liver, ovarian epithelium, and testes. The primary roles of adult stem cells are to maintain and repair the tissues in which they are found. They are generally multipotent cells, giving rise to a closely related family of cells within the tissue. For example, skin stem cells produce new skin cells. Hematopoietic stem cells found within the bone marrow can form all the various blood cells. These cells are prolific by design.[16]

We use stem cells to treat persons with many different disorders, including severe burns and orthopedic conditions requiring bone grafting. Hematopoietic stem cell transplantation is a standard treatment for hematologic cancers and bone marrow failure (see Chapter 16). We are researching the use of stem cells to repair or replace damaged body tissues, similar to whole organ transplants.[16]

❖ NURSING MANAGEMENT: GENETICS AND GENOMICS

You need to understand genetics and genomics to assist persons and families seeking information and making decisions related to genetic issues.[1,3] By understanding the influence that genetics has on health and illness, you can aid the patient and family in making critical decisions related to genetic issues, such as genetic testing. You can facilitate access to resources and provide education in response to questions.

You will collaborate with other health care team members, including genetics nurses and genetics counselors. A genetics nurse is a nurse with specialized education and training in genetics. Nurses with *GCN* after their names are baccalaureate-prepared RNs who have specialty credentialing as a Genetic Clinical Nurse (GCN). Nurses with *APNG* after their names are RNs with a master's degree who have specialty credentialing as an Advanced Practice Nurse in Genetics (APNG).

The special knowledge and counseling skills of a genetics nurse or genetics counselor are often important in genetic testing. Genetic testing may raise many emotional issues. Knowledge of the carrier status of a genetic disorder may influence a person's career, marriage, and childbearing decisions. It may affect family members as they contemplate potentially serious life and health care issues.

For example, how should a wife deal with a husband who has tested positive for Huntington disease and shows early signs of cognitive impairment? Should their children be tested for the disease? Consider the situation of a woman with a family history of breast cancer who now has breast cancer. She asks whether she and her daughters should have *BRCA* testing. What do you tell her?

Genetic testing raises ethical questions. Who should know the results of a genetic test? Who should protect the privacy of test results and prevent persons from discrimination? People may not want to share or disclose information about family history or genetic test results. They may fear they are vulnerable to discrimination based on their DNA. As a nurse, you need to understand how different health care policies relate to genetic testing. Discuss how the GINA protects persons from discrimination by employers and health care insurance companies (Box 13.3).[9]

BOX 13.3 ETHICAL/LEGAL DILEMMAS

Genetic Testing

Situation

A 30-year-old woman tells you that she is 3 months pregnant. She and her husband have 2 children. This pregnancy was unplanned, and her youngest child has cystic fibrosis (CF). She expresses concern about the chance of having another child with CF. She mentions that she would like to have genetic testing on her fetus. Her husband asks you what the chance is of having another child with CF.

Ethical/Legal Points for Consideration

- With genetic testing, the couple can find out whether their child will have CF. They can then make an informed decision.
- Genetic counseling is recommended before and after genetic testing because of the complexity of the information and the emotional issues involved with implications and options.
- Knowing that CF is an autosomal recessive condition, you can use Punnett squares (Fig. 13.9) or a family pedigree (Figs. 13.4 and 13.5) to show them the probability of having another child with CF.
- Be mindful of the privacy and confidentiality of genetic information and the potential conflict between 1 person's right to privacy and another person's right to information.

Discussion Questions

1. What information would you give the patient and her husband about genetic testing for them to make an informed decision?
2. What options are available for this couple?
3. How would you help this couple as they are considering ending the pregnancy if the genetic test results reveal that the fetus has CF?

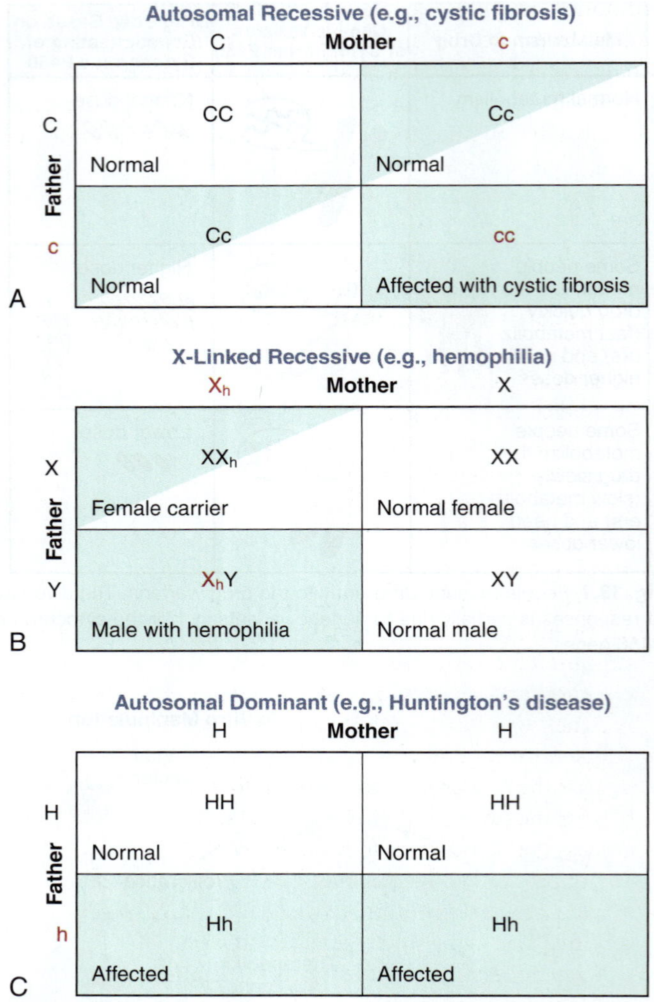

Fig. 13.9 Punnett squares illustrate inheritance possibilities. (A) If the mother and father are both carriers of cystic fibrosis, there is a 25% chance that offspring will have cystic fibrosis. (B) If the mother is a carrier for the hemophilia gene and the father has a normal genotype, there is a 50% chance that any male offspring will have hemophilia. There is a 50% chance that any female offspring will be a carrier. (C) If the mother has a normal genotype and the father has Huntington disease, there is a 50% chance that offspring will have the disease.

◆ Family History

It is important that you ask patients about their family history and identify and assess inheritance patterns. The family health history is a written or graphic record of the health problems present in one's family (see Chapter 3). You may construct a family pedigree (Figs. 13.4 and 13.5). A pedigree is a graphic representation of the family health history. The family health history and pedigree should include a minimum of 3 generations.[1,3]

To help people record information about their family history, the Centers for Disease Control and Prevention (CDC) collaborated with the US Surgeon General and other federal agencies to develop a Web-based tool called My Family Health Portrait (https://phgkb.cdc.gov/FHH/html/index.html). Other Web-based programs are available to help create pedigree diagrams based on the information entered.

When constructing the pedigree, start with the proband or person being interviewed. For each family member, record date of birth, health problems and the age when diagnosed, and age and cause of death if the person is deceased. Note racial and ethnic information and information that is unknown, and whether there are any shared ancestors. Review the information to identify key features that may increase a person's risk for genetic-related diseases. These include:

- Disease in more than 1 close relative
- Disease that does not usually affect a certain gender (e.g., breast cancer in a male)
- Disease that occurs at an earlier age than expected (e.g., myocardial infarction before age 35)
- Certain combinations of diseases within a family (e.g., breast and ovarian cancer, heart disease and diabetes)

If we identify 1 or more of these features, the family history may hold important clues about a person's risk for a genetic disease. These persons may benefit from further clinical investigation, screening, and diagnostic testing. As a nurse, you may refer these persons to a specialist for information about the benefits and risks of genetic screening and testing.

Genetic Risk Alert boxes in the assessment chapters of this book highlight persons' risks related to genetic diseases and disorders. You can use the information in these boxes to assess family history.

As a nurse, you can support the person and family by providing education and reinforcing the information they receive throughout the process. Use the family history, pedigree, and Punnett squares (Fig. 13.9) to explain the risk for inheritable disease. When a diagnosis is confirmed, you can discuss health promotion activities. People with multifactorial disorders may benefit from lifestyle modification that addresses unhealthy behaviors (e.g., smoking, poor eating habits). You can help the person and family understand how we use evidence-based guidelines for monitoring, screening, and ongoing follow-up. For example, it is important to monitor cholesterol levels in a person with a family history of familial hypercholesterolemia. Throughout this process, maintain the person's confidentiality and respect their values and beliefs.

BRIDGE TO NCLEX EXAMINATION

The number of the question corresponds to the same-numbered outcome at the beginning of the chapter.

1. If a person is heterozygous for a given gene, it means that the person
   - **a.** is a carrier for a genetic disorder.
   - **b.** is affected by the genetic disorder.
   - **c.** has 2 identical alleles for the gene.
   - **d.** has 2 different alleles for the gene.
2. Common causes of genetic mutations include *(select all that apply)*
   - **a.** DNA damage from toxins.
   - **b.** DNA damage from UV radiation.
   - **c.** inheritance of altered genes from father.
   - **d.** inheritance of altered genes from mother.
   - **e.** inheritance of somatic mutations from either parent.
3. A father who has an X-linked recessive disorder and a wife with a normal genotype will
   - **a.** pass the carrier state to all his children.
   - **b.** pass the carrier state to his male children.
   - **c.** pass the carrier state to his female children.
   - **d.** not pass on the genetic mutation to any of his children.
4. What characterizes multifactorial genetic disorders?
   - **a.** Often caused by single-gene alterations
   - **b.** Genetic testing available for most disorders
   - **c.** Many family members report having the disorder
   - **d.** Caused by complex interactions of genetic and environmental factors
5. If a person tests positive for a genetic mutation, it means *(select all that apply)*
   - **a.** the laboratory found an alteration in a gene.
   - **b.** the person is predisposed to develop a genetic disease.
   - **c.** there is the chance other family members may be at risk.
   - **d.** the person will definitely develop the disease at some point.
   - **e.** the person should not have any children or any more children.
6. What role does pharmacogenomics have in health care?
   - **a.** It can assess individual variability to many drugs.
   - **b.** Information can assess the effectiveness of a drug.
   - **c.** It provides important assessment data for gene therapy.
   - **d.** It can assess the variability of drug responses due to single genes.
7. A couple who recently had a son with hemophilia A is consulting with a nurse. They want to know if their next child will have hemophilia A. The nurse can tell the parents that if their child is a
   - **a.** boy, he will have hemophilia A.
   - **b.** boy, he will be a carrier of hemophilia A.
   - **c.** girl, she will be a carrier of hemophilia A.
   - **d.** girl, there is a 50% chance she will be a carrier of hemophilia A.

1. d; 2. a, b, c, d; 3. c; 4. d; 5. a, c; 6. d; 7. d.

For rationales to these answers and even more NCLEX review questions, visit http://evolve.elsevier.com/Lewis/medsurg.

EVOLVE WEBSITE/RESOURCES LIST

http://evolve.elsevier.com/Lewis/medsurg
Review Questions (Online Only)
Key Points
Answer Key for Questions
- Rationales for Bridge to NCLEX Examination Questions

Conceptual Care Map Creator
Audio Glossary
Content Updates

REFERENCES

1. Gunder McClary LM: *Essentials of medical genetics for nursing and health professionals: an interprofessional approach*, Burlington, MA, 2020, Jones & Bartlett Learning.
2. National Human Genome Research Institute: Genetics vs. genomics fact sheet. Retrieved from https://www.genome.gov/about-genomics/fact-sheets/Genetics-vs-Genomics.
3. International Society of Nurses in Genetics: Position statements: Privacy and confidentiality of genetic information. Retrieved from www.isong.org/resources/Documents/PS_Privacy_Confidentiality.pdf.
4. National Institute of General Medical Sciences: Genetics by the number. Retrieved from https://www.nigms.nih.gov/education/Inside-Life-Science/Pages/genetics-by-the-numbers.aspx.
5. National Human Genome Research Institute: The Human Genome Project. Retrieved from https://www.genome.gov/human-genome-project.
6. Centre for Genetics Education: Fact sheet 11: Environmental and genetic interactions. Retrieved from https://www.genetics.edu.au/publications-and-resources/facts-sheets/fact-sheet-11-environmental-and-genetic-interactions.
7. National Human Genome Research Institute: Epigenomics fact sheet. Retrieved from https://www.genome.gov/about-genomics/fact-sheets/Epigenomics-Fact-Sheet.

8. National Center for Advancing Translational Sciences: Genetic and rare diseases information center. Retrieved from https://rarediseases.info.nih.gov/diseases/diseases-by-category/36/chromosome-disorders.
9. National Human Genome Research Institute: Genetic Information Nondiscrimination Act. Retrieved from https://www.genome.gov/genetics-glossary/Genetic-Information-Nondiscrimination-Act.
10. US National Library of Medicine: What do the results of genetic tests mean? Retrieved from https://medlineplus.gov/genetics/understanding/testing/interpretingresults/.
11. US Food and Drug Administration: Direct to consumer testing. Retrieved from www.fda.gov/medical-devices/vitro-diagnostics/direct-consumer-tests
12. National Human Genome Research Institute: DNA microarray technology fact sheet. Retrieved from https://www.genome.gov/about-genomics/fact-sheets/DNA-Microarray-Technology.
13. National Human Genome Research Institute: Genome wide association studies fact sheet. Retrieved from https://www.genome.gov/about-genomics/fact-sheets/Genome-Wide-Association-Studies-Fact-Sheet.
14. US Food & Drug Administration: FDA continues strong support of innovation in development of gene therapy products. Retrieved from https://www.fda.gov/news-events/press-announcements/fda-continues-strong-support-innovation-development-gene-therapy-products.
15. US Food & Drug Administration: Approved cellular and gene therapy products. Retrieved from https://www.fda.gov/vaccines-blood-biologics/cellular-gene-therapy-products/approved-cellular-and-gene-therapy-products.
16. US National Library of Medicine: Stem cells. Retrieved from https://medlineplus.gov/stemcells.html.

14

Immune Responses and Transplantation

Thuy Lynch, Yeow Chye Ng, and Haley Hoy

http://evolve.elsevier.com/Lewis/medsurg/

CONCEPTUAL FOCUS

Functional Ability
Immunity
Infection
Inflammation
Tissue Integrity

LEARNING OUTCOMES

1. Describe the components and functions of the immune system.
2. Characterize the 5 types of immunoglobulins.
3. Distinguish among the 4 types of hypersensitivity reactions in terms of immunologic mechanisms and resulting alterations.
4. Outline the clinical manifestations and emergency management of a systemic anaphylactic reaction.
5. Describe the assessment and interprofessional care of a patient with chronic allergies.
6. Describe the etiologic factors, clinical manifestations, and treatment of autoimmune diseases.
7. Discern the etiologic factors and categories of immunodeficiency disorders.
8. Explain the relationship between the human leukocyte antigen system and certain diseases.
9. Distinguish among the types of rejections after transplantation.
10. Identify the types and side effects of immunosuppressive therapy.

KEY TERMS

anergy
antigen
autoimmunity
cell-mediated immunity
cytokines
human leukocyte antigen (HLA)
humoral immunity
hypersensitivity reactions
immunocompetence
immunodeficiency
immunosuppressive therapy

Our bodies have several defense mechanisms for protecting ourselves. One of the most complex is the immune response. Immune processes must be functioning properly for the body to defend itself against the presence of foreign substances. This response is critical to maintaining health. Thus, many problems occur when the immune response is altered. These problems are closely related to the concepts of inflammation, infection, and tissue integrity. You will find that the care of patients with immune disorders discussed in this chapter is similar to the care of patients with inflammation (see Chapter 12), neutropenia (see Chapter 34), and general infection (see Chapter 15).

NORMAL IMMUNE RESPONSE

Immunity is the body's ability to resist disease. Immune responses serve the following 3 functions:

1. *Defense:* The body protects against invasions by microorganisms and prevents the development of infection by attacking foreign antigens and pathogens.
2. *Homeostasis:* Damaged cellular substances are digested and removed. Through this mechanism, the body's different cell types stay uniform and unchanged.
3. *Surveillance:* Mutations continually arise. They are recognized as foreign cells and destroyed.

Antigens

An **antigen** is a substance that elicits an immune response. Most antigens are composed of protein. However, other substances such as large polysaccharides, lipoproteins, and nucleic acids can act as antigens. All the body's cells have antigens on their surface. They are unique to that person and enable the body to recognize itself. The immune system normally becomes "tolerant" to the body's own molecules. This makes us nonresponsive to "self" antigens.

Types of Immunity

We classify immunity as innate or acquired.

Innate Immunity

Innate immunity is present at birth. Its primary role is first-line defense against pathogens. This type of immunity involves a nonspecific response. Neutrophils and monocytes are the primary white blood cells (WBCs) involved. Innate immunity is not antigen specific. So, it can respond within minutes to an invading pathogen without prior exposure to that organism.

Acquired Immunity

Acquired immunity is the development of either active or passive immunity (Table 14.1).

Active acquired immunity. *Active acquired immunity* results from the invasion of the body by foreign substances such as microorganisms and the subsequent development of antibodies and sensitized lymphocytes. With each reinvasion of the microorganisms, the body responds more rapidly and vigorously to fight off the invader. Active acquired immunity may result naturally from a disease or artificially through immunization. Because the body makes antibodies, immunity takes time to develop but is long lasting.

Passive acquired immunity. In *passive acquired immunity,* the host receives antibodies to an antigen rather than making them. This may take place naturally through the transfer of immunoglobulins across the placental membrane from mother to fetus. Artificial passive acquired immunity occurs through injection with gamma globulin (serum antibodies). The benefit of this immunity is its immediate effect. Unfortunately, passive immunity is short lived because the person does not make the antibodies and memory cells for the antigen.

TABLE 14.1 Types of Acquired Specific Immunity

Type	Natural	Artificial
Active	Natural contact with antigen through actual infection (e.g., chickenpox, measles, mumps)	Immunization with antigen (e.g., vaccines for chickenpox, measles, mumps)
Passive	Transplacental and colostrum transfer from mother to child (e.g., maternal immunoglobulins passed to baby)	Injection of serum with antibodies from 1 person (e.g., injection of hepatitis B immune globulin) to another person who does not have antibodies

Lymphoid Organs

The lymphoid system is composed of central (or primary) and peripheral lymphoid organs. The *central lymphoid organs* are the thymus gland and bone marrow. The *peripheral lymphoid organs* are the lymph nodes; tonsils; spleen; and gut-, genital-, bronchial-, and skin-associated lymphoid tissues (Fig. 14.1).

We make lymphocytes in the bone marrow. They eventually migrate to the peripheral organs. The thymus is involved in the differentiation and maturation of T lymphocytes. This makes it essential for a cell-mediated immune response. The thymus is its largest during childhood. After puberty, the thymus starts to slowly shrink and become replaced by fat. By age 75, the thymus is little more than fatty tissue and makes few T lymphocytes.

When antigens enter the body, they may be carried by the bloodstream or lymph channels to regional lymph nodes. The antigens interact with B and T lymphocytes and macrophages in the lymph nodes. The 2 major functions of lymph nodes are (1) filtration of foreign material brought to the site and (2) circulation of lymphocytes.

The tonsils are an example of lymphoid tissue. The spleen, a peripheral lymph organ, is important as the primary site for filtering foreign antigens from the blood. We have lymphoid tissue in the submucosa of the GI (gut-associated), genitourinary (genital-associated), and respiratory (bronchial-associated) tracts. This tissue protects the body from external microorganisms.

The skin-associated lymph tissue consists primarily of lymphocytes and Langerhans cells (type of dendritic cell) found in the epidermis of skin. When Langerhans cells are depleted, the skin cannot initiate an immune response. Therefore, a delayed hypersensitivity reaction (as determined by skin testing with injected antigens) does not occur.

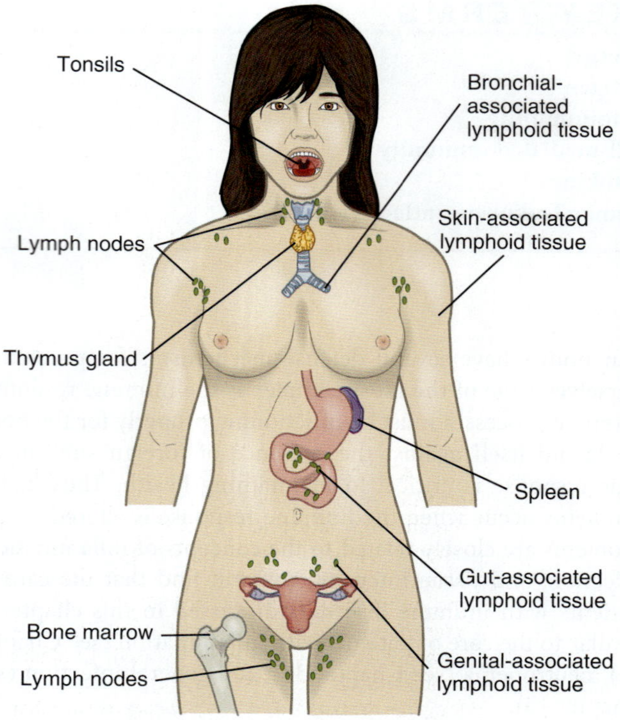

Fig. 14.1 Organs of the immune system.

Cells Involved in Immune Response

Mononuclear Phagocytes

The *mononuclear phagocyte system* includes monocytes in the blood and macrophages found throughout the body. Mononuclear phagocytes have a critical role in the immune system. They are responsible for capturing, processing, and presenting the antigen to the lymphocytes. This stimulates a humoral or cell-mediated immune response. Capturing is accomplished through phagocytosis. The macrophage-bound antigen, which is highly immunogenic, is presented to circulating T or B lymphocytes and thus triggers an immune response (Fig. 14.2).

Lymphocytes

We make lymphocytes in the bone marrow (Fig. 14.3). They then differentiate into B and T lymphocytes.

B lymphocytes. B cells differentiate into *plasma cells* when activated. Plasma cells make antibodies (immunoglobulins) (Table 14.2).

T lymphocytes. Cells that migrate from the bone marrow to the thymus differentiate into *T lymphocytes* (thymus-dependent cells). The thymus secretes hormones, including thymosin, that stimulate the maturation and differentiation of T lymphocytes. T cells make up 70% to 80% of the circulating lymphocytes. They are mainly responsible for immunity to intracellular viruses, tumor cells, and fungi. T cells can live from a few months to the life span of a person. They account for long-term immunity.

We categorize T lymphocytes as T cytotoxic and T helper cells. Antigenic characteristics of WBCs can be classified using monoclonal antibodies. These antigens are classified as *clusters of differentiation*, or *CD antigens*. We refer to many types of

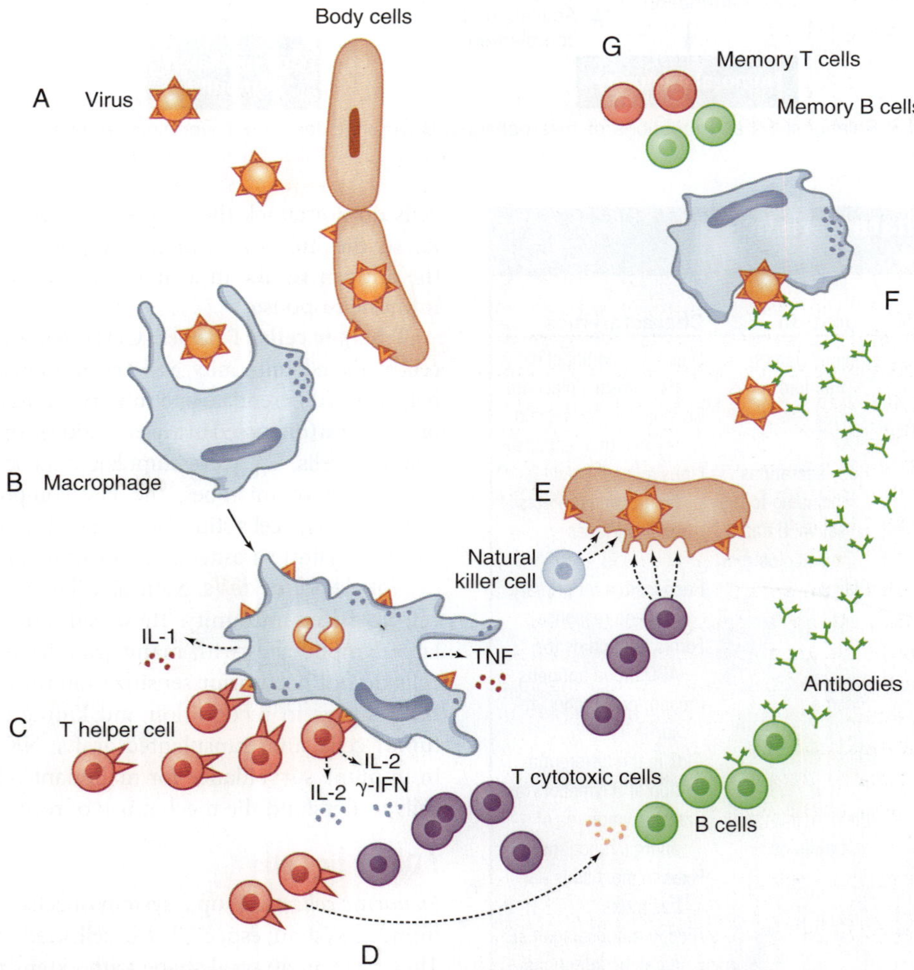

Fig. 14.2 The immune response to a virus. (A) A virus invades the body through a break in the skin or another portal of entry. The virus must make its way inside a cell to replicate itself. (B) A macrophage recognizes the antigens on the surface of the virus. The macrophage digests the virus and displays pieces of the virus (antigens) on its surface. (C) T helper cell recognizes the antigen displayed and binds to the macrophage. This binding stimulates the production of cytokines (interleukin-1 *[IL-1]* and tumor necrosis factor *[TNF]*) by the macrophage and interleukin-2 *(IL-2)* and γ-interferon *(γ-IFN)* by the T cell. These cytokines are intracellular messengers that provide communication among the cells. (D) IL-2 instructs other T helper cells and T cytotoxic cells to proliferate (multiply). T helper cells release cytokines, causing B cells to multiply and make antibodies. (E) T cytotoxic cells and natural killer cells destroy infected body cells. (F) The antibodies bind to the virus and mark it for macrophage destruction. (G) Memory B and T cells stay behind to respond quickly if the same virus attacks again.

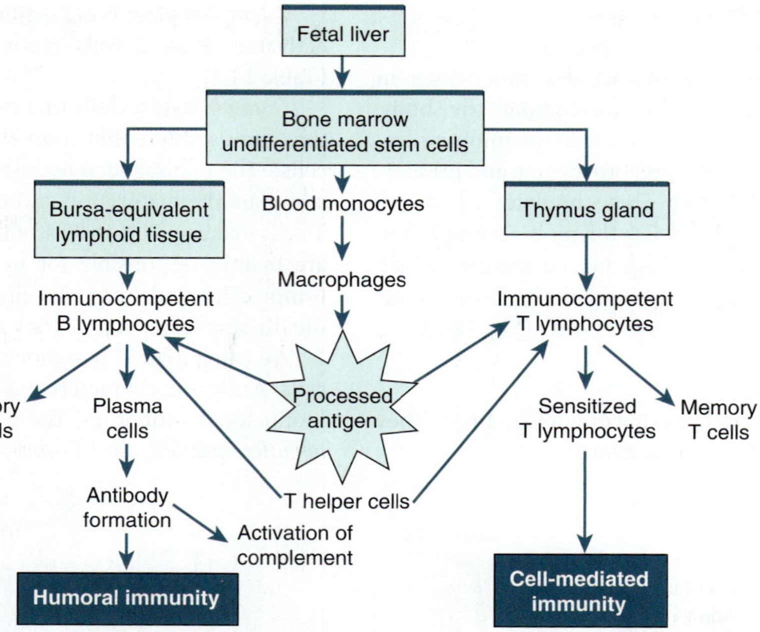

Fig. 14.3 Relationships and functions of macrophages, B lymphocytes, and T lymphocytes in an immune response.

TABLE 14.2 Characteristics of Immunoglobulins

Class	Serum Concentration (%)	Location	Characteristics
IgG	76	Plasma, interstitial fluid	Only immunoglobulin that crosses placenta Responsible for secondary immune response
IgA	15	Body secretions, including tears, saliva, breast milk, colostrum	Lines mucous membranes and protects body surfaces
IgM	8	Plasma	Responsible for primary immune response Forms antibodies to ABO blood antigens
IgD	1	Plasma	Present on lymphocyte surface Aids in the differentiation of B lymphocytes
IgE	0.002	Plasma, interstitial fluids	Causes symptoms of allergic reactions Fixes to mast cells and basophils Aids in defense against parasitic infections

WBCs, especially lymphocytes, by their CD designations. All mature T cells have the CD3 antigen.

T cytotoxic cells. T cytotoxic (CD8) cells are involved in attacking antigens on the cell membrane of foreign pathogens and releasing cytolytic substances that destroy the pathogen. These cells have antigen specificity and are sensitized by exposure to the antigen. Much like B cells, some sensitized T cells do not attack the antigen but remain as memory T cells. As in the humoral immune response, a second exposure to the antigen results in a more intense and rapid cell-mediated immune response.

T helper cells. T helper (CD4) cells are involved in regulating cell-mediated immunity and the humoral antibody response. T helper cells differentiate into subsets of cells that make distinct types of cytokines (discussed in a later section). These subsets are T_H1 cells and T_H2 cells. T_H1 cells stimulate phagocyte-mediated ingestion and killing of microbes, the key component of cell-mediated immunity. T_H2 cells stimulate eosinophil-mediated immunity. It is effective against parasites and is involved in allergic responses.

Natural killer cells. Natural killer (NK) cells are involved in cell-mediated immunity. These cells are not T or B cells but are large lymphocytes with many granules in their cytoplasm. NK cells do not need prior sensitization for their generation. These cells engage in recognition and killing of virus-infected cells, tumor cells, and transplanted grafts. NK cells have a vital role in immune surveillance for malignant cell changes. We do not fully understand the mechanism of recognition.

T Dendritic Cells

Dendritic cells make up a system of cells that is important to the immune system, especially the cell-mediated immune response. They have an atypical shape with extensive dendritic processes that form and retract. They are found in many places in the body, including the skin (where they are called *Langerhans cells*) and the lining of the nose, lungs, stomach, and intestine. There are many immature dendritic cells in the blood.[1]

Dendritic cells function primarily to capture antigens at sites of contact with the external environment (e.g., skin, mucous membranes) and then transport the antigen until it meets a T cell with specificity for that antigen. In this role, they have an important function in activating the immune response.

TABLE 14.3 Types and Functions of Cytokines

Type	Primary Functions
Colony-Stimulating Factors (CSFs)	
Erythropoietin	Stimulates erythroid progenitor cells in bone marrow to make red blood cells
Granulocyte colony-stimulating factor (G-CSF)	Stimulates proliferation and differentiation of neutrophils, enhances functional activity of mature PMNs
Granulocyte-macrophage colony-stimulating factor (GM-CSF)	Stimulates proliferation and differentiation of PMNs and monocytes
Macrophage colony-stimulating factor (M-CSF)	Promotes proliferation, differentiation, and activation of monocytes and macrophages
Interferons (IFNs)	
α-IFN β-IFN	Inhibits viral replication, activates NK cells and macrophages, antiproliferative effects on tumor cells
γ-IFN	Proinflammatory mediator. Activates macrophages, neutrophils, and NK cells. Promotes B-cell differentiation. Inhibits viral replication
Interleukins (ILs)	
IL-1	Proinflammatory mediator. Promotes proliferation of B cells. Activates T cells, NK cells, and macrophages
IL-2	Activates T cells, NK cells, and macrophages. Stimulates release of other cytokines (α-IFN, TNF, IL-1, IL-6)
IL-3	Hematopoietic growth factor for hematopoietic precursor cells
IL-4	Antiinflammatory mediator. B-cell growth and differentiation. Induces differentiation into T_H2 cells. Stimulates growth of mast cells
IL-5	B-cell growth and differentiation. Promotes growth and differentiation of eosinophils
IL-6	Proinflammatory mediator. T- and B-cell growth factor, promotes differentiation of B cells into plasma cells and stimulates antibody secretion. Induces fever. Synergistic effects with IL-1 and TNF
Tumor Necrosis Factor (TNF)	Proinflammatory mediator. Activates macrophages and granulocytes. Promotes immune and inflammatory responses. Kills tumor cells. Responsible for weight loss with chronic inflammation and cancer

NK, Natural killer; *PMNs,* polymorphonuclear neutrophils.

Cytokines

The immune response involves complex interactions of T cells, B cells, monocytes, and neutrophils. These interactions depend on **cytokines** (soluble factors secreted by WBCs and a variety of other cells in the body) that act as messengers among the cell types. Cytokines instruct cells to alter their proliferation, differentiation, secretion, or activity.

Currently, we know of more than 100 different cytokines. They are classified into distinct categories. Table 14.3 lists some of these cytokines. In general, the interleukins (ILs) act as immunomodulatory factors. Colony-stimulating factors act as growth-regulating factors for hematopoietic cells. Interferons are antiviral and immunomodulatory.

TABLE 14.4 Clinical Uses of Cytokines

Cytokine	Clinical Uses
Colony-Stimulating Factors	
Erythropoietin epoetin alfa (Epogen, Procrit) Darbepoetin alfa (Aranesp)	Anemia related to chronic kidney disease, cancer, and chemotherapy
G-CSF filgrastim (Neupogen) pegfilgrastim (Neulasta)	Chemotherapy-induced neutropenia
GM-CSF sargramostim (Leukine)	Neutropenia, myeloid recovery after bone marrow transplantation
IL-1 Receptor Antagonist anakinra (Kineret)	Rheumatoid arthritis
Interferons	
α-Interferon (Roferon-A, Intron A)	Hairy cell leukemia, chronic myelogenous leukemia, malignant melanoma, renal cell cancer, ovarian cancer, multiple myeloma, Kaposi sarcoma, hepatitis B and C
β-Interferon (Betaseron, Avonex, Rebif)	Multiple sclerosis
Interleukins	
IL-2 aldesleukin (Proleukin)	Metastatic renal cell cancer, metastatic melanoma
IL-11 (platelet growth factor) oprelvekin (Neumega)	Thrombocytopenia related to chemotherapy
Soluble TNF Receptor etanercept (Enbrel)	Rheumatoid arthritis

G-CSF, Granulocyte colony-stimulating factor; *GM-CSF,* granulocyte-macrophage colony-stimulating factor; *TNF,* tumor necrosis factor.

The net effect of an inflammatory response is determined by a balance between proinflammatory and antiinflammatory mediators. We sometimes classify cytokines as proinflammatory or antiinflammatory. However, it is not that clear-cut, since many other factors (e.g., target cells, environment) influence the inflammatory response to a given injury or insult.

Cytokines have a beneficial role in hematopoiesis and immune function. They can have detrimental effects such as those seen in chronic inflammation, autoimmune diseases, and sepsis. Cytokines such as colony-stimulating factors, interferons, and IL-2 have clinical uses (Table 14.4).

Interferon helps the body's natural defenses attack tumors and viruses. We know of 3 types of interferon (Table 14.3). Interferon is not directly antiviral. It produces an antiviral effect in cells by reacting with them and inducing the formation of a second protein termed *antiviral protein* (Fig. 14.4). This protein mediates the antiviral action of interferon by changing the cell's protein synthesis and preventing new viruses from becoming assembled.

Comparison of Humoral and Cell-Mediated Immunity

We need both humoral and cell-mediated immunity to remain healthy. Each type of immunity has unique properties, different methods of action, and reactions against particular antigens. Table 14.5 compares humoral and cell-mediated immunity.

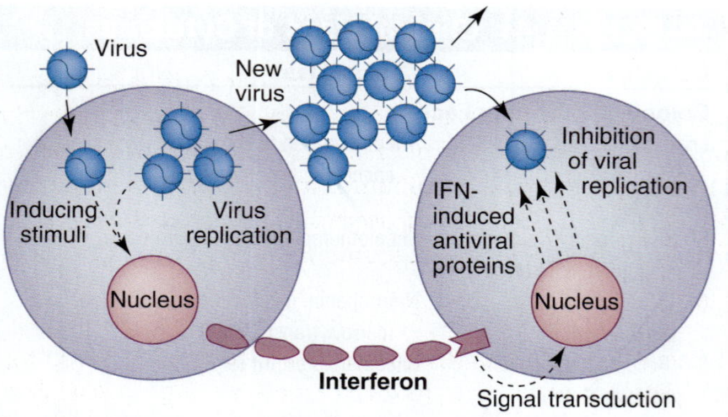

Fig. 14.4 Mechanism of action of interferon *(IFN)*. When a virus attacks a cell, the cell begins to make viral DNA and IFN. IFN serves as an intercellular messenger and induces the production of antiviral proteins. Then the virus is not able to replicate in the cell.

TABLE 14.5 Comparison of Humoral and Cell-Mediated Immunity

Characteristics	Humoral Immunity	Cell-Mediated Immunity
Cells involved	B lymphocytes	T lymphocytes, macrophages
Products	Antibodies	Sensitized T cells, cytokines
Memory cells	Present	Present
Protection	Bacteria	Chronic infectious agents
	Respiratory and GI pathogens	Fungi
		Tumor cells
	Viruses (extracellular)	Viruses (intracellular)
Examples	Anaphylactic shock	Contact dermatitis
	Atopic diseases	Destruction of cancer cells
	Bacterial infection	Fungal infection
	Transfusion reaction	Graft rejection
		Tuberculosis

Humoral Immunity

Humoral immunity consists of antibody-mediated immunity. The term *humoral* comes from the Greek word *humor,* which means body fluid. Since antibodies are made by plasma cells (differentiated B cells) and found in plasma, we use the term *humoral immunity*. Antibody production is an essential part of the humoral immune response. Each of the 5 classes of immunoglobulins (IgG, IgA, IgM, IgD, IgE) has specific characteristics (see Table 14.2).

When a pathogen (especially bacteria) enters the body, it may encounter a B cell that is specific for antigens found on that bacterial cell wall. In addition, a monocyte or macrophage may phagocytize the bacteria and present its antigens to a B cell. The B cell recognizes the antigen because it has receptors on its cell surface specific for that antigen. When the antigen comes in contact with the cell surface receptor, the B cell becomes activated, and most B cells differentiate into plasma cells (Fig. 14.3). The mature plasma cell secretes immunoglobulins. Some stimulated B cells remain memory cells.

The primary immune response becomes evident 4 to 8 days after the first exposure to the antigen (Fig. 14.5). IgM is the first type of antibody formed. Because of its large size, IgM molecule

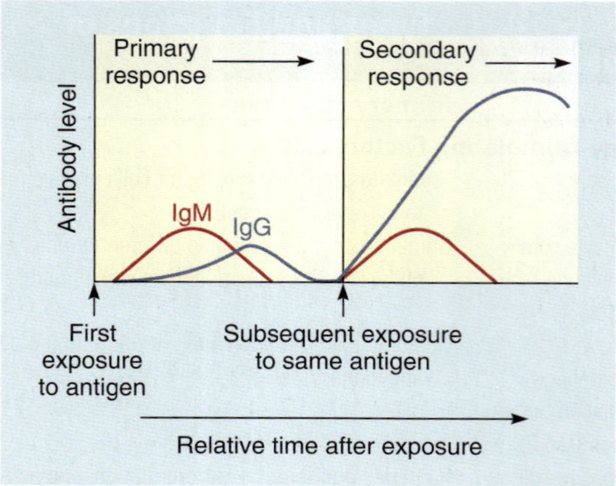

Fig. 14.5 Primary and secondary immune responses. The introduction of antigen induces a response dominated by 2 classes of immunoglobulins, IgM and IgG. IgM dominates in the primary response, with some IgG appearing later. After the host's immune system is primed, another challenge with the same antigen induces the secondary response, in which some IgM and large amounts of IgG are made.

is confined to the intravascular space. As the immune response progresses, we make IgG. IgG can move from intravascular to extravascular spaces.

When a person is exposed to the antigen the second time, a secondary antibody response occurs. This response occurs faster (1 to 3 days), is stronger, and lasts for a longer time than a primary response. Memory cells account for the memory of the first exposure to the antigen and the more rapid production of antibodies. IgG is the primary antibody found in a secondary immune response.

IgG crosses the placental membrane. It provides the newborn with passive acquired immunity for at least 3 months. Infants may get some passive immunity from IgA in breast milk and colostrum.

Cell-Mediated Immunity

Immune responses that we initiate through specific antigen recognition by T cells are termed **cell-mediated immunity**. Several cell types and factors are involved in cell-mediated immunity. These include T cells, macrophages, and NK cells. Cell-mediated immunity is of primary importance in (1) immunity against pathogens that survive inside of cells, including viruses and some bacteria (e.g., mycobacteria); (2) fungal infections; (3) rejection of transplanted tissues; (4) contact hypersensitivity reactions; and (5) tumor immunity.

Gerontologic Considerations: Effects of Aging on the Immune System

With advancing age, there is a decline in the function of the immune response (Table 14.6). The main evidence of *immunosenescence* is the high incidence of cancer in older adults. Older people are also more susceptible to infections (e.g., influenza, pneumonia) from pathogens that they were more immunocompetent against earlier in life. Bacterial pneumonia is the leading cause of death from infections in older adults. The antibody response to immunizations (e.g., flu vaccine) in older adults is much lower than in younger adults.[1]

The bone marrow is unaffected by increasing age. Immunoglobulin levels decrease with age, leading to a suppressed humoral immune response in older adults. The thymus shrinks with age, along with decreased numbers of T cells. These changes in the thymus gland are a primary cause of immunosenescence. Both T and B cells show deficiencies in activation, transit time through the cell cycle, and differentiation. However, the most significant changes involve T cells. As thymic output of T cells diminishes, the differentiation of T cells increases. Consequently, there is an accumulation of memory cells rather than new precursor cells responsive to previously unencountered antigens.

The delayed hypersensitivity reaction, as determined by skin testing with injected antigens, is often decreased or absent in older adults. This altered response reflects **anergy** (an immunodeficient condition characterized by lack of or diminished reaction to an antigen or a group of antigens).

TABLE 14.6 GERONTOLOGIC ASSESSMENT DIFFERENCES

Effects of Aging on the Immune System

- ↑ Autoantibodies
- ↓ Cell-mediated immunity
- ↓ Delayed hypersensitivity reaction
- ↓ IL-1 and IL-2 synthesis
- ↓ Expression of IL-2 receptors
- ↓ Primary and secondary antibody responses
- ↓ Proliferative response of T and B cells
- Thymic shrinkage

IL, Interleukin.

ALTERED IMMUNE RESPONSE

Immunocompetence exists when the body's immune system can identify and inactivate or destroy foreign substances. When the immune system is incompetent or under responsive, severe infections, cancers, and immunodeficiency diseases may occur. When the immune system overreacts, hypersensitivity disorders such as allergies and autoimmune diseases may develop.

Hypersensitivity Reactions

Sometimes the immune response is overreactive against foreign antigens or reacts against its own tissue, resulting in tissue damage. These responses are termed **hypersensitivity reactions**. *Autoimmune disease,* a type of hypersensitivity response, occurs when the body does not recognize self-proteins and reacts against self-antigens.

We can classify hypersensitivity reactions by the source of the antigen, time sequence (immediate or delayed), or immunologic mechanisms causing the injury. Four types of hypersensitivity reactions exist (Table 14.7). Types I, II, and III are immediate and are examples of humoral immunity. Type IV is a delayed hypersensitivity reaction and is related to cell-mediated immunity.

Type I: IgE-Mediated Reactions

Anaphylactic reactions are type I reactions that occur only in susceptible people who are highly sensitized to specific allergens. IgE antibodies, made in response to the allergen, have a characteristic property of attaching to mast cells and basophils (Fig. 14.6). Within these cells are granules that contain potent

TABLE 14.7 Types of Hypersensitivity Reactions

Type I: IgE-Mediated	Type II: Cytotoxic	Type III: Immune-Complex	Type IV: Delayed Hypersensitivity
Antigen			
Pollen, food, drugs, dust	Cell surface of RBCs Cell basement membrane	Extracellular fungal, viral, bacterial	Intracellular or extracellular
Rate of Development			
Immediate	Minutes to hours	Hours to days	Several days
Complement Involved			
No	Yes	Yes	No
Mediators of Injury			
Histamine Leukotrienes Mast cells Prostaglandins	Complement lysis Macrophages in tissues	Complement lysis Lysosomal enzymes Monocytes, macrophages Neutrophils	Cytokines T cytotoxic cells
Examples			
Allergic rhinitis Angioedema Asthma Atopic dermatitis Hives	Goodpasture syndrome Graves disease Immune thrombocytopenic purpura Transfusion reaction	Acute glomerulonephritis Rheumatoid arthritis SLE	Contact dermatitis (e.g., to poison ivy)
Skin Test			
Wheal and flare	None	Erythema and edema in 3–8 h	Erythema and edema in 24–48 h (e.g., TB test)

chemical mediators (histamine, serotonin, leukotrienes, eosinophil chemotactic factor of anaphylaxis [ECF-A], kinins, bradykinin). Chemical mediators of inflammation are discussed in Chapter 12 and Table 12.1.

On the first exposure to the allergen, IgE antibodies are made and bind to mast cells and basophils. On any subsequent exposures, the allergen links with the IgE bound to mast cells or basophils and triggers degranulation of the cells and the release of chemical mediators from the granules. In this process, the mediators that are released attack target tissues, causing clinical symptoms of an allergic response. These effects include smooth muscle contraction, increased vascular permeability, vasodilation, hypotension, increased secretion of mucus, and itching. Fortunately, mediators are short acting and their effects are reversible. Table 14.8 lists these mediators.

A genetic predisposition to the development of allergic diseases exists. The capacity to become sensitized to an allergen, rather than the specific allergic disorder, appears to be an inherited trait. For example, a father with asthma may have a son who has allergic rhinitis.

The manifestations of an anaphylactic reaction depend on whether the mediators stay localized or become systemic and whether they affect specific organs. When the mediators are localized, a skin response called a *wheal-and-flare reaction* occurs. This reaction is characterized by a pale wheal containing edematous fluid surrounded by a red flare from the hyperemia. The reaction occurs in minutes or hours and is usually not dangerous. A classic example of a wheal-and-flare reaction is a mosquito bite. The wheal-and-flare reaction serves a diagnostic purpose by showing allergic reactions to specific allergens during skin tests.

Common allergic reactions include anaphylaxis and atopic reactions.

Anaphylaxis. *Anaphylaxis* can occur when mediators are released systemically (e.g., after injection of a drug, after an insect sting). The reaction occurs within minutes. It can be life threatening because of bronchial constriction and subsequent airway obstruction and vascular collapse. The target organs affected are shown in Fig. 14.7. Initial symptoms include edema and itching at the site of exposure to the allergen. Shock can occur rapidly. It is manifested by rapid, weak pulse; hypotension;

TABLE 14.8 Allergic Response Mediators

- Anaphylatoxins (C3a, C4a, C5a from complement activation)
- Histamine
- Kinins
- Leukotrienes
- Platelet-activating factor
- Prostaglandins
- Serotonin

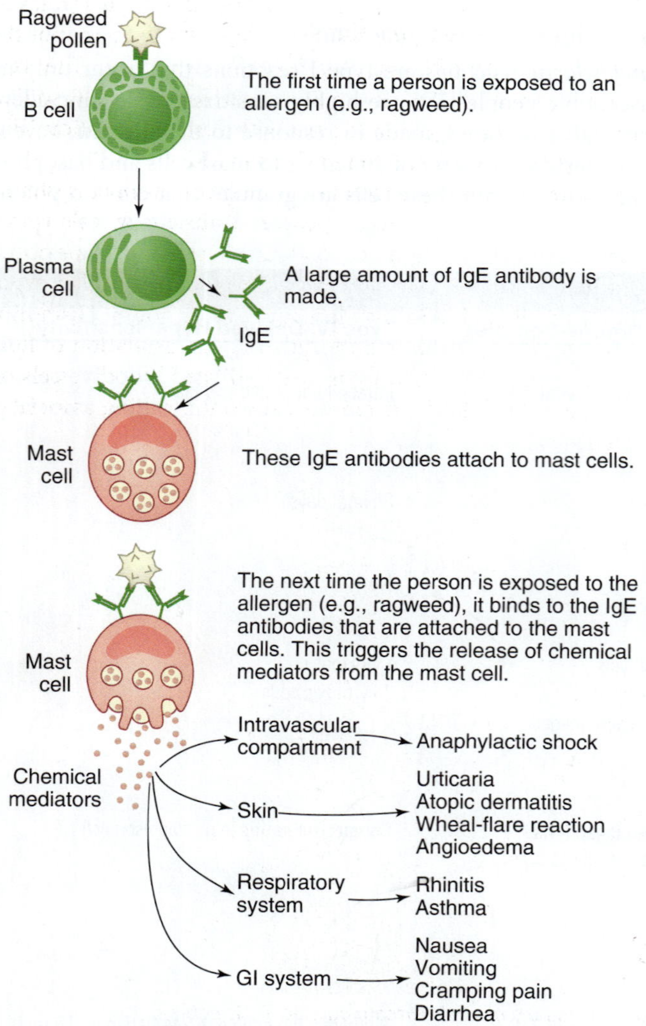

Fig. 14.6 Steps in a Type I allergic reaction.

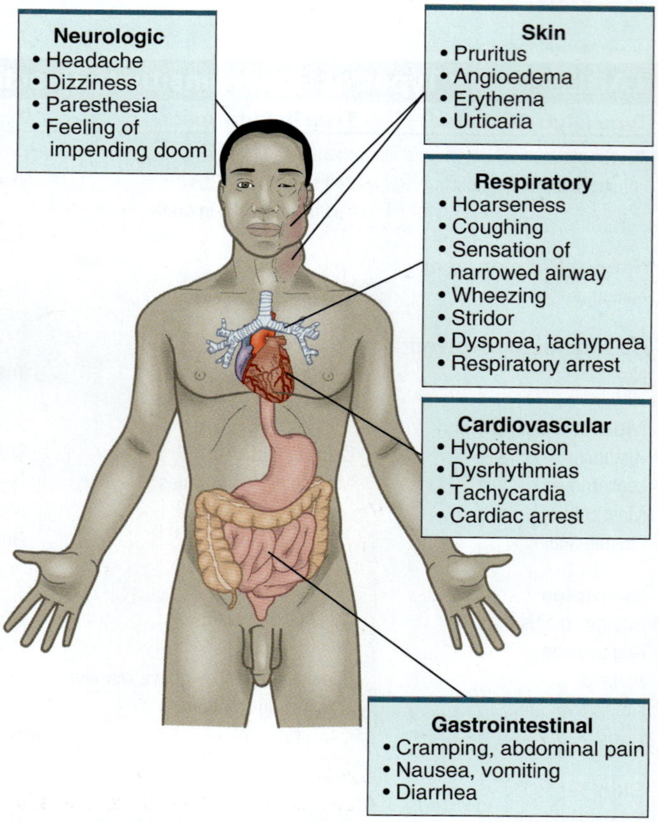

Fig. 14.7 Manifestations of a systemic anaphylactic reaction.

dilated pupils; dyspnea; and possibly cyanosis. Bronchial edema and angioedema can compound shock. Death will occur without emergency treatment. Table 14.9 lists some common allergens that can cause anaphylactic shock in hypersensitive people. Drugs are the leading cause of anaphylaxis-related deaths.[2]

Atopic reactions. Around 20% of the population is *atopic*. This means they have an inherited tendency to become sensitive to environmental allergens. The atopic diseases that can result are allergic rhinitis, asthma, atopic dermatitis, hives, and angioedema.

TABLE 14.9 Allergens Causing Anaphylactic Shock

Animal Sera
- Diphtheria antitoxin
- Rabies antitoxin
- Snake venom antitoxin
- Tetanus antitoxin

Drugs
- Aspirin
- Cephalosporins
- Chemotherapy drugs
- Insulins
- Local anesthetics
- Nonsteroidal antiinflammatory drugs
- Penicillins
- Sulfonamides
- Tetracycline

Foods
- Eggs, milk, nuts, peanuts, shellfish, fish, chocolate, strawberries

Insect Venoms
- Wasps, hornets, yellow jackets, bumblebees, ants

Treatments
- Allergy extracts used in immunotherapy
- Blood products (whole blood and components)
- Iodine-contrast media for CT scan or other radiologic procedures

Allergic rhinitis, or hay fever, is the most common type I hypersensitivity reaction. It may occur year-round (perennial allergic rhinitis) or be seasonal (seasonal allergic rhinitis). Airborne substances such as pollens, dust, and molds are the primary causes of allergic rhinitis. Dust, molds, and animal dander often cause perennial allergic rhinitis. Pollens from trees, weeds, or grasses often cause seasonal allergic rhinitis. The target areas affected are the conjunctiva and the mucosa of the upper respiratory tract. Symptoms include nasal discharge; sneezing; tearing; mucosal swelling with airway obstruction; and itching of the eyes, nose, throat, and mouth. Treatment of allergic rhinitis is discussed in Chapter 29.

Many patients with *asthma* have an allergic component to their disease. These patients often have a history of atopic disorders (e.g., infantile eczema, allergic rhinitis, food intolerances). Inflammatory mediators cause bronchial smooth muscle constriction, excess secretion of thick mucus, edema of the mucous membranes of the bronchi, and decreased lung compliance. These changes cause dyspnea, wheezing, coughing, tightness in the chest, and thick sputum. Asthma is discussed in depth in Chapter 31.

Atopic dermatitis is a chronic, inherited skin disorder characterized by exacerbations and remissions. It is caused by environmental allergens. These allergens are often hard to identify. Although patients with atopic dermatitis have high IgE levels and positive skin tests, the histopathologic features are not the typical, localized wheal-and-flare type I reactions. The skin lesions are more generalized and involve blood vessel vasodilation. This causes interstitial edema with vesicle formation (Fig. 14.8). Dermatitis is discussed in Chapter 25.

Urticaria (hives) is a cutaneous reaction against systemic allergens occurring in atopic people. Transient wheals (pink, raised, edematous, itchy areas) that vary in size and shape occur. They may be all over the body. Hives develop rapidly after exposure to an allergen and may last minutes or hours. Histamine causes localized vasodilation (erythema), transudation of fluid (wheal), and flaring. Flaring is due to dilated blood vessels on the edge of the wheal. Histamine causes the itching associated with the lesions.

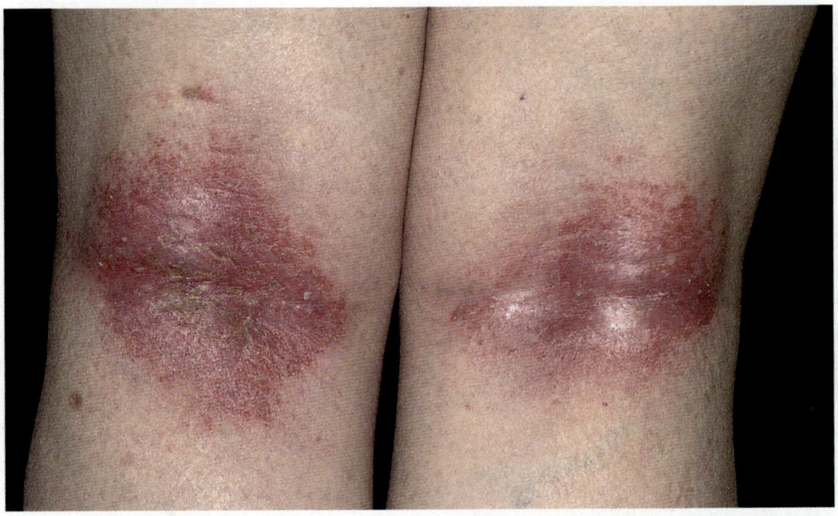

Fig. 14.8 Atopic dermatitis behind the knees. (From Dinulos J: *Habif's clinical dermatology,* ed 7, St Louis, 2021, Elsevier.)

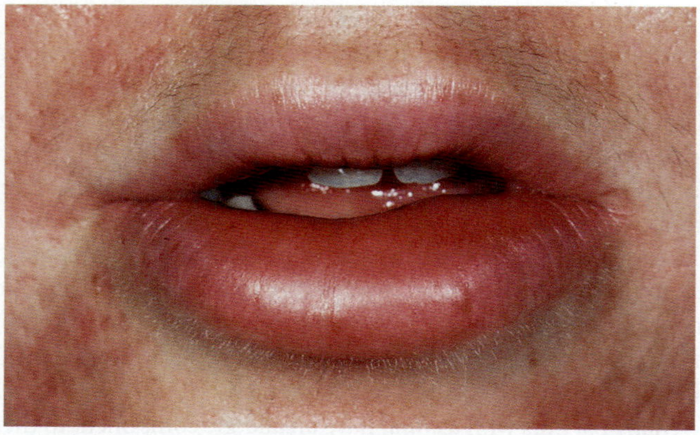

Fig. 14.9 Allergic reaction with angioedema of the lip. (From Habif TP: *Clinical dermatology,* ed 6, Philadelphia, 2016, Saunders.)

Angioedema is a localized cutaneous lesion similar to hives but involving deeper layers of the skin and submucosa. The principal areas involved include the eyelids, lips, tongue, larynx, hands, feet, GI tract, and genitalia (Fig. 14.9). Swelling usually begins in the face and then progresses to the airways and other parts of the body. Dilation and engorgement of the capillaries from the release of histamine causes the diffuse swelling. Welts are not present as in hives. The outer skin appears normal or has a reddish hue. The lesions may burn, sting, or itch. It can cause acute abdominal pain if in the GI tract. The swelling may occur suddenly or over several hours. It usually lasts for 24 hours.

Type II: Cytotoxic and Cytolytic Reactions

Cytotoxic and cytolytic reactions are type II hypersensitivity reactions involving the direct binding of IgG or IgM antibodies to an antigen on the cell surface. Antigen-antibody complexes activate the complement system, which mediates the reaction. Cellular tissue is destroyed by either (1) activation of the complement system resulting in cytolysis or (2) enhanced phagocytosis.

Target cells often destroyed in type II reactions are erythrocytes, platelets, and leukocytes. The tissue damage usually occurs rapidly. Some of the antigens involved are the ABO blood group, Rh factor, and drugs. Pathophysiologic disorders characteristic of type II reactions include ABO incompatibility transfusion reaction, Rh incompatibility transfusion reaction, autoimmune and drug-related hemolytic anemias, leukopenia, thrombocytopenia, erythroblastosis fetalis (hemolytic disease of the newborn), and Goodpasture syndrome.

Hemolytic transfusion reactions. A classic type II reaction occurs when a recipient receives ABO-incompatible blood from a donor. Naturally acquired antibodies to antigens of the ABO blood group are in the recipient's serum but are not present on the erythrocyte membranes. For example, a person with type A blood has anti-B antibodies, a person with type B blood has anti-A antibodies, a person with type AB blood has no antibodies, and a person with type O blood has anti-A and anti-B antibodies.

If the recipient is transfused with incompatible blood, antibodies immediately coat the foreign erythrocytes, causing *agglutination* (clumping). The clumping of cells blocks small blood vessels in the body, uses existing clotting factors, and depletes them. This leads to bleeding. Within hours, neutrophils and macrophages phagocytize the agglutinated cells. The complement system is activated. Cell lysis occurs, which causes the release of hemoglobin into the urine and plasma. Acute kidney injury can result from the hemoglobinuria. See Chapter 34 for more about blood transfusions.

Goodpasture syndrome. *Goodpasture syndrome* is a disorder involving the lungs and kidneys. An antibody-mediated autoimmune reaction occurs involving the glomerular and alveolar basement membranes. The circulating antibodies combine with tissue antigen to activate the complement system. This causes deposits of IgG to form along the cell basement membranes of the lungs or kidneys. This may result in pulmonary hemorrhage and glomerulonephritis. Goodpasture syndrome is discussed in Chapter 50.

Type III: Immune-Complex Reactions

Tissue damage in immune-complex reactions, which are type III reactions, results from antigen-antibody complexes. Soluble antigens combine with IgG and IgM to form complexes that are too small for the mononuclear phagocyte system to effectively remove them. Therefore, the complexes deposit in tissue or small blood vessels. They cause activation of the complement system and release of chemotactic factors that lead to inflammation and destruction of the involved tissue.

Type III reactions may be local or systemic and immediate or delayed. The manifestations depend on the number of complexes and the location in the body. Common sites for deposit are the kidneys, skin, joints, blood vessels, and lungs. Severe type III reactions are associated with autoimmune disorders such as systemic lupus erythematosus (SLE), acute glomerulonephritis, and rheumatoid arthritis. See more about SLE and rheumatoid arthritis in Chapter 69. Acute glomerulonephritis is discussed in Chapter 50.

Type IV: Delayed Hypersensitivity Reactions

A *delayed hypersensitivity reaction*—a type IV reaction—is a *cell-mediated immune response.* Although cell-mediated responses are usually protective mechanisms, tissue damage occurs in delayed hypersensitivity reactions.

The tissue damage in a type IV reaction does not occur in the presence of antibodies or complement. Rather, sensitized T cells attack antigens or release cytokines. Some of these cytokines attract macrophages into the area. The macrophages and the enzymes they release cause most of the tissue destruction. In the delayed hypersensitivity reaction, it takes 24 to 48 hours for a response to occur.

Examples of delayed hypersensitivity reactions include contact dermatitis (Fig. 14.10); hypersensitivity reactions to bacterial, fungal, and viral infections; and transplant rejections. Some drug sensitivity reactions also fit this category.

Contact dermatitis. *Allergic contact dermatitis* is an example of a delayed hypersensitivity reaction involving the skin. The reaction occurs when the skin is exposed to substances that easily penetrate the skin to combine with epidermal proteins. The substance then becomes antigenic. Over a period of 7 to 14

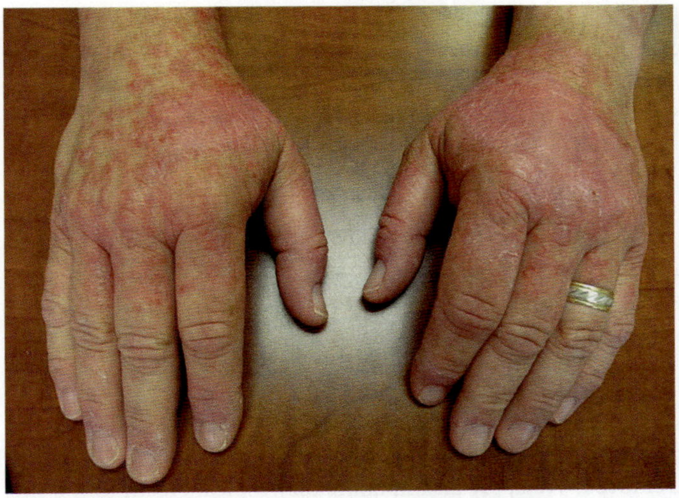

Fig. 14.10 Contact dermatitis to rubber. (From Rich R, Fleisher AT, Shearer WT, et al.: *Clinical immunology: principles and practice*, ed 5, St. Louis, 2019, Elsevier.)

days, memory cells form to the antigen. On subsequent exposure to the substance, a sensitized person develops eczematous skin lesions within 48 hours. The most common antigenic substances are metal compounds (e.g., those containing nickel or mercury); rubber compounds; poison ivy, poison oak, and poison sumac; cosmetics; and some dyes.

In acute contact dermatitis, the skin lesions appear red and swollen and are covered with papules, vesicles, and bullae. The involved area itches. It may burn or sting. When contact dermatitis becomes chronic, the lesions resemble atopic dermatitis because they are thickened, scaly, and lichenified. The main difference between contact dermatitis and atopic dermatitis is that contact dermatitis is localized and restricted to the area exposed to the allergens. Atopic dermatitis is usually widespread.

Microbial hypersensitivity reactions. The classic example of a microbial cell-mediated immune reaction is the body's defense against the tubercle bacillus. Tuberculosis results from invasion of lung tissue by the highly resistant tubercle bacillus. The organism itself does not directly damage the lung tissue. However, antigenic material released from the tubercle bacilli reacts with T cells, initiating a cell-mediated immune response. The resulting response causes extensive caseous necrosis of the lung.

After the first cell-mediated reaction, memory cells persist. Subsequent contact with the tubercle bacillus or an extract of purified protein from the organism causes a delayed hypersensitivity reaction. This is the basis for the purified protein derivative (PPD) tuberculosis skin test, which we read 48 to 72 hours after injecting the PPD intradermally. See Chapter 30 for more about tuberculosis.

ALLERGIC DISORDERS

Assessment

For a thorough assessment of a patient with allergies, obtain a complete history and perform a comprehensive physical assessment, diagnostic workup, and skin testing for allergens. Obtain information from the patient about family allergies, social and environmental factors, and a complete history of known allergies (Table 14.10).

TABLE 14.10 NURSING ASSESSMENT

Allergies

Subjective Data

Important Health Information

Health history: Details about past and present allergies, including associated symptoms and their severity, age symptoms started, speed of symptom onset after contact with allergen, duration of symptoms, frequency of occurrence, reproducibility of symptoms with further exposure, seasonal exacerbations. Details of any previous treatment, including the use of over-the-counter and prescription medications to treat allergies.

Recurrent respiratory problems: Unusual reactions to insect bites or stings

Medications: Unusual reactions to any medications

Functional Health Patterns

Health perception–health management: Family history of allergies or atopic disease; malaise

Nutritional-metabolic: Food intolerances, vomiting

Elimination: Abdominal cramps, diarrhea

Activity-exercise: Fatigue; hoarseness, cough, dyspnea

Cognitive-perceptual: Itching, burning, stinging of eyes, nose, throat, or skin; chest tightness

Role-relationship: Altered home and work environment, presence of pets

Objective Data

Eyes, Ears, Nose, and Throat

Eyes: Conjunctivitis, lacrimation, rubbing or excessive blinking, dark circles under the eyes ("allergic shiner")

Ears: Diminished hearing, immobile or scarred tympanic membranes, recurrent ear infections

Nose: Nasal polyps, nasal voice, nose twitching, itchy nose, rhinitis; pale, boggy mucous membranes; sniffling, repeated sneezing; swollen nasal passages; recurrent, unexplained nosebleeds; crease across the bridge of nose ("allergic salute")

Throat: Continual throat clearing, swollen lips or tongue, red throat, palpable neck lymph nodes

Respiratory

Wheezing, stridor; thick sputum

Skin

Rashes, including hives, wheal and flare, papules, vesicles, bullae; dryness, scaliness, scratches, irritation

Possible Diagnostic Findings

Eosinophilia of serum, sputum, or nasal and bronchial secretions; increased serum IgE levels; positive skin tests; abnormal chest and sinus x-rays

Family history, including information about atopic reactions in relatives, is especially important in identifying at-risk patients. Note past and present allergies. Obtain information about the manifestations and course of allergic reaction. The time of year when an allergic reaction occurs can be a clue to a seasonal allergen. Ask about all medications used to treat the allergies.

Social and environmental factors, especially the physical environment, are important. Ask about pets, trees and plants on the property, pollutants in the air, floor coverings, houseplants, and cooling and heating systems in the home and workplace.

Note any reactions to medication. A daily or weekly food diary with a description of any untoward reactions may be useful.[3] Ask about the patient's lifestyle and stress level in connection with the allergic symptoms.

It is important to list all the patient's allergies on the chart, nursing care plan, and medication record. During the physical assessment, focus attention on the site of the allergic manifestations (Table 14.10).

Diagnostic Studies

We use various immunologic techniques to detect abnormalities of lymphocytes, eosinophils, and immunoglobulins. A complete blood count (CBC) with WBC differential is done, with an absolute lymphocyte count and eosinophil count. Immunodeficiency is diagnosed if the lymphocyte count is below 1200/μL (1.2×10^9/L). T-cell and B-cell quantification can diagnose specific immunodeficiency syndromes. The eosinophil count and serum IgE level are high in type I hypersensitivity reactions. The serum IgE level also serves as a diagnostic indicator of atopic diseases.

We can test sputum and nasal and bronchial secretions for the presence of eosinophils. Pulmonary function tests, especially for forced expiratory volume, are helpful for patients with asthma.

Of primary importance is the need to identify the offending allergen. Sometimes we can do this with skin testing. In the case of food allergies an elimination diet is an option. If an allergic reaction occurs, the patient should stop all foods eaten shortly before the reaction and gradually reintroduce them 1 at a time until the offending food is detected.

Skin Tests

Skin testing can identify the specific allergens that are causing the allergy symptoms. With the use of empiric allergy medications as the treatment of choice for most allergic rhinitis, it has become more common to omit skin testing for specific allergens in these patients. However, diagnosing an allergy to a specific antigen allows the patient to avoid an allergen and makes them a candidate for immunotherapy.

Unfortunately, we cannot do skin testing on patients who cannot stop taking drugs that suppress the histamine response or patients with food allergies. In these instances, blood allergy testing is used. Blood testing may be done if a person cannot tolerate the many needle scratches needed for skin testing or has a skin disorder (e.g., severe eczema, dermatitis, psoriasis).

Procedure. We can do skin testing by 3 different methods: (1) a scratch or prick test, (2) an intradermal test, or (3) a patch test. The areas of the body usually used in skin testing are the arms and back. Allergen extracts are applied to the skin in rows with a corresponding control site opposite the test site. Saline or another diluent is applied to the control site. In the *scratch test* a drop of allergen is placed on the skin, and then a pricking device is used so that the allergen can enter the skin. In the *intradermal test* the allergen extract is injected under the skin, similar to a PPD test for TB. In the *patch test* an allergen is applied to a patch that is placed on the skin.

Results. In the scratch and intradermal tests, the reaction occurs in 5 to 10 minutes. In the patch test the patches must be worn for 48 to 72 hours. If the person is hypersensitive to the allergen, a positive reaction will occur within minutes after insertion in the skin. It may last for 8 to 12 hours. We will see a local wheal-and-flare response with a positive reaction.

The size of the positive reaction does not always correlate with the severity of allergy symptoms. False-positive and false-negative results may occur. Negative results from skin testing do not always mean the person does not have an allergic disorder. Positive results do not always mean that the allergen was causing the manifestations. Positive results imply that the person is sensitized to that allergen. Therefore, correlating skin test results with the patient's history is important.

Precautions. A highly sensitive person is always at risk for developing an anaphylactic reaction to skin tests. Therefore, never leave a patient during the testing period. If a severe reaction does occur with a skin test, the extract is immediately removed. We apply antiinflammatory topical cream to the site. For intradermal testing, the arm is best so that a tourniquet can be applied during a severe reaction. The patient may need a subcutaneous injection of epinephrine.

Interprofessional and Nursing Management

After an allergic disorder is diagnosed, treatment is aimed at reducing exposure to the offending allergen, treating the symptoms, and, if needed, desensitizing the person through immunotherapy.

Anaphylaxis

Anaphylactic reactions occur suddenly in hypersensitive patients after exposure to the offending allergen. They may occur after parenteral injection of drugs (especially antibiotics) or blood products and after insect stings. All health care workers must be prepared for the rare but life-threatening anaphylactic reaction. The key principle in management is speed in (1) recognizing signs and symptoms of an anaphylactic reaction, (2) maintaining a patent airway, (3) giving drugs, and (4) treating for shock. Table 14.11 outlines the emergency treatment of anaphylactic shock.

Epinephrine is the drug of choice to treat an anaphylactic reaction. It must be given parenterally (IM, IV). Patients receiving β-blockers may be resistant to treatment with epinephrine. They can develop refractory hypotension and bradycardia. Those patients should receive glucagon. Its inotropic and chronotropic effects are not mediated through β-receptors. Severe cases of anaphylaxis may result in hypovolemic shock because of the loss of intravascular fluid into interstitial spaces that occurs due to increased capillary permeability.[4] Peripheral vasoconstriction and stimulation of the sympathetic nervous system occur to compensate for the fluid shift. However, unless shock is treated early, the body will no longer be able to compensate and irreversible tissue damage will occur, leading to death. You can read about hypovolemic shock in Chapter 42.

CHECK YOUR PRACTICE

You are caring for a patient who has been receiving IV antibiotic therapy for 2 days. Several minutes after starting the latest infusion, the patient states that his chest feels tight and begins coughing. You take his BP, and it is 100/64 and his pulse is 124.

- What should you do?

TABLE 14.11 EMERGENCY MANAGEMENT

Anaphylactic Shock

Cause
- Injection of, inhalation of, ingestion of, or topical exposure to substance that produces profound allergic response (Table 14.9)

Assessment Findings
- Fig. 14.7

Interventions

Initial
- Ensure patent airway. Intubation if evidence of impending obstruction
- Remove insect stinger if present
- Establish IV access
- Give epinephrine, options include:
- 0.3-0.5 mg (0.3-0.5 mL) subcut or IM, preferably in the mid-outer thigh. Repeat every 5–10 min.
- 0.1mg/mL IV at rate of 1-4 mcg/min over 5 min or continuous infusion at 5-15 mcg/min
- Give high-flow O_2 (8–10 L/min) via face mask. Can give up to 100% as needed
- Nebulized albuterol for bronchospasm resistant to epinephrine
- IV diphenhydramine for hives and itching
- IV corticosteroids

Hypotension
- Place recumbent and elevate legs
- IV normal saline rapid bolus of 1–2 L
- Maintain BP with fluids, volume expanders, vasopressors (e.g., dopamine)

Ongoing Monitoring
- Monitor vital signs, respiratory effort, O_2 saturation, level of consciousness, heart rhythm, and urine output
- Anticipate intubation with severe respiratory distress
- Anticipate cricothyrotomy or tracheostomy with severe laryngeal edema

Chronic Allergies

Most allergic reactions are chronic. Periods of remissions and exacerbations of symptoms occur. Treatment focuses on identification and control of allergens, relief of symptoms through drug therapy, and hyposensitization of a patient to an offending allergen.

Allergen recognition and control. You play a key role in helping the patient make lifestyle adjustments so that there is minimal exposure to offending allergens. Reinforce that, even with drug therapy and immunotherapy, the patient will never be totally desensitized or completely symptom free. Help the patient use various preventive measures to control the allergic symptoms.

Many allergic reactions, especially asthma and hives, may worsen with fatigue and emotional stress. Help the patient plan a stress management program. Have the patient practice relaxation techniques when coming in for immunotherapy.

Sometimes control of allergic symptoms requires environmental control. This might include changing an occupation, moving to a different climate, or giving up a favorite pet. In the case of airborne allergens, sleeping in an air-conditioned room, damp dusting daily, covering mattresses and pillows with hypoallergenic covers, and wearing a mask outdoors may be helpful.

If the allergen is a drug, have the patient avoid the drug. The patient has the responsibility to make any drug allergies known to all health care team members. The patient should wear a Medic Alert bracelet listing the drug allergy and have the drug allergy listed on all medical and dental records.

For a patient allergic to insect stings, commercial kits containing automatic injectable epinephrine are available. Teach the patient and family how to use the injector and have them practice assembling and using the training device (Table 14.12). This patient should wear a Medic Alert bracelet and carry an insect-sting kit whenever going outdoors.

TABLE 14.12 PATIENT & CAREGIVER TEACHING

Automatic Epinephrine Injectors

Include the following information when teaching the patient and caregiver how to use an automatic epinephrine injector:

1. Fill the prescription at once and keep at least 2 doses available.
2. Always keep at least 1 autoinjector with you.
3. Keep an autoinjector in a place where others can easily find it in case of an emergency. Tell family and friends where it is stored.
4. Keep the autoinjector in the original case, at room temperature, away from extremes of cold and heat.
5. Mark on your calendar when the autoinjector expires, although you can use an expired autoinjector if there is no alternative. Replace solutions that are discolored or contain particles.
6. Use the device if you have any sign of anaphylaxis, such as trouble breathing or feeling tightness in the throat or lightheaded.
7. When needed:
   - Inject the drug into the top of the thigh, slightly to the outside, at a 90-degree angle. Hold in place for at least 2–3 sec.
   - You can inject the drug through clothes. Avoid pockets and seams where the fabric is thick.
   - After use, call 911 and get to the nearest hospital for monitoring. Take the autoinjector with you.

Drug Therapy

The major categories of drugs used for symptomatic relief of chronic allergic disorders include antihistamines, sympathomimetic/decongestant drugs, corticosteroids, antipruritic drugs, and mast cell–stabilizing drugs. Many of these drugs are available OTC.

Antihistamines. Antihistamines are the best drugs for treating allergic rhinitis, itching, and hives (see Table 29.2). They are less effective for severe allergic reactions and do not prevent bronchoconstriction. They act by competing with histamine for H_1-receptor sites, thus blocking the effect of histamine. Results are best if they are taken as soon as allergy symptoms appear. With seasonal rhinitis, antihistamines should be taken during peak pollen seasons.

Sympathomimetic/decongestant drugs. The major sympathomimetic drug is epinephrine. Epinephrine is made by the adrenal medulla and stimulates α- and β-adrenergic receptors. Stimulation of the α-adrenergic receptors causes vasoconstriction of peripheral blood vessels. β-Receptor stimulation relaxes bronchial smooth muscles. Epinephrine also acts directly on mast cells to stabilize them against further degranulation. The action of epinephrine lasts only a few minutes.

Minor sympathomimetic agents include drugs containing phenylephrine and pseudoephedrine. They differ from epinephrine because they are taken orally or nasally. Their effects last several hours. These drugs are mainly used to treat allergic rhinitis (see Table 29.2).

Corticosteroids. Nasal corticosteroid sprays are effective in relieving the symptoms of allergic rhinitis. Sometimes patients have such severe allergy manifestations that they are truly incapacitated. In these situations, a brief course of oral corticosteroids can be used.

Antipruritic drugs. Antipruritic drugs provide relief from itching and protect the skin. They are most effective when applied topically to intact skin. Common OTC drugs include calamine lotion, coal tar solutions, and camphor. Menthol and phenol may be added to other lotions to relieve itching.

Mast cell–stabilizing drugs. Cromolyn is a mast cell–stabilizing agent that inhibits the release of histamines, leukotrienes, and other agents from the mast cell after antigen-IgE interaction. It is available as an inhalant nebulizer solution or a nasal spray. Cromolyn is used in the management of allergic rhinitis (see Table 29.2).

Leukotriene receptor antagonists. Leukotriene receptor antagonists (LTRAs) block leukotriene, a major mediator of the allergic inflammatory process. These medications can be taken orally. They are used to treat allergic rhinitis and asthma.

Immunotherapy

Immunotherapy is the recommended treatment for control of allergic symptoms when the allergen cannot be avoided, and drug therapy is not effective. Few patients with allergies have symptoms so intolerable that they need allergy immunotherapy. Immunotherapy is definitively indicated for those with anaphylactic reactions to insect venom.

Immunotherapy involves giving small titers of an allergen extract in increasing strengths until hyposensitivity to the specific allergen is achieved. For best results, teach the patient to avoid the offending allergen whenever possible because complete desensitization is impossible. Unfortunately, not all allergy-related conditions respond to immunotherapy. Food allergies cannot be safely treated with this therapy. Eczema may worsen with immunotherapy.

Mechanism of action. The IgE level is high in atopic people. When IgE combines with an allergen in a hypersensitive person, a reaction occurs, releasing histamine in various body tissues. Allergens more readily combine with IgG than with other immunoglobulins. Therefore, immunotherapy involves injecting allergen extracts that will stimulate increased IgG levels. The goal of long-term immunotherapy is to keep "blocking" IgG levels high. By increasing IgG levels, IgE is blocked from binding to the allergen. This prevents mast cell degranulation. In addition, allergen-specific T suppressor cells develop in those receiving immunotherapy. The allergens included in immunotherapy are based on the results of skin testing.

Method of administration

Subcutaneous immunotherapy. *Subcutaneous immunotherapy (SCIT)* involves the subcutaneous injection of titrated amounts of allergen extracts biweekly or weekly. The dose is small at first, then increased slowly until a maintenance dosage is reached. It often takes 1 to 2 years of immunotherapy to reach the maximal therapeutic effect. Therapy may continue for about 5 years. After that, some patients may stop therapy. Many have a sustained decrease in symptoms after the treatment is stopped. Those with severe allergies or sensitivity to insect stings may continue maintenance therapy indefinitely.

Sublingual immunotherapy. *Sublingual immunotherapy (SLIT)* involves allergen extracts taken under the tongue. Sublingual products include a 5-grass pollen tablet (Oralair), a single-grass pollen tablet (Grastek), and a ragweed pollen tablet (Ragwitek).[5]

Patients usually take SLIT once daily at home. The first dose is usually given under medical supervision. Some patients have local application site reactions (e.g., oral pruritus, throat irritation, tongue swelling). Local reactions subside in many patients within a few days to a week. Systemic allergic reactions are markedly fewer than with SCIT. SLIT has the advantage of being a convenient, self-administered oral therapy. Its primary disadvantage is that the patient must consistently adhere to the therapy.[6]

❖ NURSING MANAGEMENT: IMMUNOTHERAPY

You will often be the person responsible for giving SCIT. Immunotherapy always carries the risk for a severe anaphylactic reaction. Therefore, an HCP, emergency equipment, and essential drugs should be available whenever injections are given. Always anticipate adverse reactions, especially when using a new dose strength, after a previous reaction, or after a missed dose. Early manifestations of a systemic reaction include itching, hives, sneezing, laryngeal edema, and hypotension. If these occur, begin emergency measures for anaphylactic shock at once.

Describe any local reaction according to the degree of redness and swelling at the injection site. If the area is greater than the size of a quarter in an adult, report the reaction to the HCP. The allergen dosage may need decreased.

Accurate record keeping can help prevent an adverse reaction to the allergen extract. Before giving an injection, check the patient's name against the name on the vial. Next, determine the vial strength, amount of last dose, date of last dose, and any reaction information.

Always give the allergen extract in an extremity away from a joint so you can apply a tourniquet for a severe reaction. Rotate the site for each injection. After giving the injection, observe the patient for 20 to 30 minutes, since systemic reactions are most likely to occur immediately. However, teach the patient that a delayed reaction can occur up to 24 hours later.

◆ Latex Allergies

Allergies to latex products have become an increasing problem for patients and health care workers. The increase coincides with the sharp increase in glove use. The more frequent and prolonged the exposure to latex, the greater the risk for developing a latex allergy.[7]

Besides gloves, we use many other latex-containing products in health care. These include BP cuffs, stethoscopes, tourniquets, IV tubing, syringes, electrode pads, O_2 masks, tracheal tubes, colostomy and ileostomy pouches, urinary catheters, anesthetic masks, and adhesive tape. Latex proteins can become aerosolized through powder on gloves and can result in serious reactions when inhaled by sensitized persons. All health care agencies should use powder-free gloves to avoid respiratory exposure to latex proteins.[8]

◆ Types of Latex Allergies

Two types of latex allergies can occur: type IV allergic contact dermatitis and type I allergic reactions. *Type IV contact dermatitis* is caused by the chemicals used in manufacturing latex gloves. It is a delayed reaction that occurs within 6 to 48 hours. Typically, the person first has dryness, itching, fissuring, and cracking of the skin, followed by redness, swelling, and crusting at 24 to 48 hours. Chronic exposure can lead to lichenification, scaling, and hyperpigmentation. The dermatitis may extend beyond the area of physical contact with the allergen.

A *type I allergic reaction* is a response to the natural rubber latex proteins. It occurs within minutes of contact with the proteins. The manifestations can vary from skin redness, hives, rhinitis, conjunctivitis, or asthma to full-blown anaphylactic shock. Systemic reactions to latex may result from exposure to latex protein via various routes, including the skin, mucous membranes, inhalation, and blood.

◆ Latex-Food Syndrome

Because some proteins in rubber are similar to food proteins, some foods may cause an allergic reaction in people who are allergic to latex. We call this *latex-food syndrome*. The most common of these foods are banana, avocado, chestnut, kiwi, tomato, water chestnut, guava, hazelnut, potato, peach, grape, and apricot. Most people with latex allergy have a positive allergy test to at least 1 related food.

❖ NURSING MANAGEMENT: LATEX ALLERGIES

Identifying patients and health care workers sensitive to latex is crucial to prevent adverse reactions. Obtain a thorough health history and history of any allergies, especially for patients with any history of latex contact symptoms. The greatest risk factor is long-term multiple exposures to latex products (e.g., health care personnel, those who have had multiple surgeries, rubber industry workers). Other risk factors include a patient history of allergic rhinitis, asthma, and allergies to those latex-related foods.

Use latex precaution protocols for those patients with a positive latex allergy test or a history of signs and symptoms related to latex exposure. Many health care agencies have created latex-free product carts to use with patients with latex allergies. Since we cannot identify all latex-sensitive people, even with a careful and thorough history, follow general recommendations for preventing allergic reactions to latex (Table 14.13).

Because of the potential for severe symptoms of food allergy, teach patients to avoid those foods. Other recommendations for people with latex and food allergies include wearing a Medic Alert bracelet or necklace and carrying an injectable epinephrine pen.

◆ Multiple Chemical Sensitivity

Multiple chemical sensitivity (MCS) is a subjective illness marked by recurrent, vague, nonspecific symptoms attributed to low levels of chemical, biologic, or physical agents.

Commonly accused substances include smoke, pesticides, plastics, synthetic fabrics, scented products, petroleum products, and paint fumes. Women between the ages of 30 and 50 are more likely to develop the symptoms. MCS is a controversial diagnosis. The American Medical Association and many other authorities do not recognize it as an illness.[9]

People report a wide range of nonspecific symptoms. These include headache, fatigue, dizziness, nausea, congestion, itching, sneezing, sore throat, chest pain, breathing problems, muscle pain or stiffness, skin rash, diarrhea, bloating, gas, confusion, difficulty concentrating, memory problems, and mood changes. These symptoms are usually subjective. There is no evidence of a pathologic or physiologic problem.

Diagnosis is usually made based on a patient's health history. There are no tests to diagnose MCS. The most effective treatment is to avoid the chemicals that may trigger symptoms and create a chemical-free and odor-free home and workplace.

Psychotherapy is recommended. In patients who are unwilling to undergo psychotherapy but willing to accept medications, antidepressants, including selective serotonin reuptake inhibitors (SSRIs) (e.g., citalopram [Celexa]), are options. Drugs for anxiety and sleep also have been used.

AUTOIMMUNITY

Autoimmunity is an immune response against self in which the immune system no longer differentiates self from nonself. For some unknown reason, immune cells that are normally unresponsive (tolerant to self-antigens) are activated. In autoimmunity, autoantibodies and autosensitized T cells cause tissue damage.

TABLE 14.13 Guidelines for Preventing Allergic Latex Reactions

- Use nonlatex gloves for activities that are not likely to involve contact with infectious materials (e.g., food preparation, housekeeping).
- If you choose latex gloves, use powder-free gloves.
- Do not use oil-based hand creams or lotions when wearing latex gloves.
- Wash hands with soap and water after wearing gloves.
- Frequently clean work areas that are contaminated with latex-containing dust (e.g., carpets, ventilation ducts).
- Frequently change the ventilation filters and vacuum bags used in latex-contaminated areas.
- Learn to recognize the symptoms of latex allergy: Skin rash; hives; flushing; itching; nasal, eye, or sinus symptoms; asthma.
- If symptoms of latex allergy develop, avoid direct contact with latex gloves and products.
- Wear a Medic Alert bracelet and carry an epinephrine pen.

The cause of autoimmune diseases is still unknown. Age may play some role because the number of circulating autoantibodies increases in people over age 50. We think the main factors in the development of autoimmunity are (1) the inheritance of susceptibility genes, which contribute to the failure of self-tolerance, and (2) initiation of autoreactivity by triggers, such as infections, which activate self-reactive lymphocytes.

Autoimmune diseases tend to cluster. A given person may have more than 1 autoimmune disease (e.g., rheumatoid arthritis, Addison disease). Other family members may have the same or related autoimmune diseases. This observation has led to the concept of genetic predisposition to autoimmune disease. Most of the genetic research correlates certain human leukocyte antigen (HLA) types with an autoimmune condition. HLAs and disease association are discussed later in this chapter.

Even in a genetically predisposed person, some trigger is needed to initiate autoreactivity. This may include infectious agents such as a virus. Viral infections can change cells or tissues that are not normally antigenic. The virally induced changes make the cells or tissues antigenic. Viruses may be involved in the development of diseases such as type 1 diabetes. Rheumatic fever and rheumatic heart disease are autoimmune responses triggered by streptococcal infection. Antibodies against group A β-hemolytic streptococci cross-react with heart muscles, heart valves, and synovial membranes.

Drugs can be precipitating factors in autoimmune disease. Hemolytic anemia can result from methyldopa administration. Procainamide can induce the formation of antinuclear antibodies and cause a lupus-like syndrome.

Gender and hormones have a role in autoimmune disease. More women have autoimmune disease. During pregnancy, many autoimmune diseases get better. After delivery, the woman with an autoimmune disease often has an exacerbation.

TABLE 14.14 Examples of Autoimmune Diseases

Systemic Diseases
- Rheumatoid arthritis
- Scleroderma (systemic sclerosis)
- Systemic lupus erythematosus

Specific Diseases

Blood
- Autoimmune hemolytic anemia
- Hemochromatosis
- Immune thrombocytopenic purpura (ITP)
- Pernicious anemia

CNS
- Guillain-Barré syndrome
- Multiple sclerosis
- Myasthenia gravis

Endocrine System
- Addison disease
- Graves disease
- Hypothyroidism
- Thyroiditis
- Type 1 diabetes

Eye
- Uveitis

GI System
- Celiac disease
- Inflammatory bowel disease

Heart
- Rheumatic fever

Kidney
- Glomerulonephritis
- Goodpasture syndrome

Liver
- Autoimmune hepatitis
- Primary biliary cirrhosis

Autoimmune Diseases

We often group autoimmune diseases according to organ-specific and systemic diseases (Table 14.14). SLE is a classic example of a systemic autoimmune disease characterized by damage to multiple organs. The cause is unknown, but there appears to be a loss of self-tolerance for the body's own DNA antigens.

In SLE, tissue injury appears to result from the formation of antinuclear antibodies. For some reason (possibly a viral infection), the cell membrane is damaged, and DNA is released into the systemic circulation. There it is viewed as nonself. This DNA is normally sequestered in the cell nucleus. On release into the circulation, the DNA antigen reacts with an antibody. Some antibodies are involved in immune complex formation, and others cause damage directly. Once the complexes are deposited, the complement system is activated and further damages the tissue, especially the renal glomerulus. See more about SLE in Chapter 69.

Apheresis

Apheresis is a procedure to separate components of the blood followed by the removal of 1 or more of these components. It is an effective treatment for several autoimmune diseases and other diseases and disorders. Compound words are often used to describe a specific apheresis procedure, depending on the blood components being collected. *Plateletpheresis* is the removal of platelets. It often involves collecting platelets from normal persons to infuse into patients with low platelet counts (e.g., patients taking chemotherapy who develop thrombocytopenia). *Leukocytapheresis* is a general term describing the removal of WBCs. It is used in chronic myelogenous leukemia to remove high numbers of leukemic cells.

Apheresis is used in hematopoietic stem cell transplantation to collect stem cells from peripheral blood. These stem cells can then be used to repopulate a person's bone marrow after high-dose chemotherapy. See Chapter 16 for more on hematopoietic stem cell transplants.

Plasmapheresis

Plasmapheresis is the removal of plasma containing components causing or thought to cause disease. It can be used to get plasma from healthy donors to give to patients as replacement therapy.

Plasmapheresis involves removing whole blood through an IV device, then circulating the blood through an apheresis machine. Inside the machine the blood is divided into plasma and its cellular components by centrifugation or membrane filtration. The plasma is replaced with normal saline, lactated Ringer's solution, fresh-frozen plasma, plasma protein fractions, or albumin. When we manually remove blood, we can only take 500 mL at 1 time. However, with the use of apheresis procedures, more than 4 L of plasma can be pheresed in 2 to 3 hours.

Plasmapheresis has been used to treat autoimmune diseases such as SLE, glomerulonephritis, Goodpasture syndrome, myasthenia gravis, rheumatoid arthritis, and Guillain-Barré syndrome. Many of these disorders have circulating autoantibodies (usually of the IgG class) and antigen-antibody complexes. The reason for performing therapeutic plasmapheresis in autoimmune disorders is to remove pathologic substances present in plasma. Immunosuppressive therapy has been used to prevent recovery of IgG production, and plasmapheresis to prevent antibody rebound.

Plasmapheresis may remove inflammatory mediators (e.g., complement) that cause tissue damage. In the treatment of SLE, plasmapheresis is usually reserved for the patient having an acute attack who is unresponsive to conventional therapy.

You need to be aware of side effects associated with plasmapheresis. The most common complications are hypotension and citrate toxicity. Hypotension is usually the result of a vasovagal reaction or transient volume changes. Citrate, used as an anticoagulant, may cause hypocalcemia. The patient may have a headache, paresthesias, and dizziness.

IMMUNODEFICIENCY DISORDERS

When the immune system does not adequately protect the body, **immunodeficiency** exists. Immunodeficiency disorders involve an impairment of 1 or more immune mechanisms, which include (1) phagocytosis, (2) humoral response, (3) cell-mediated response, (4) complement, and (5) a combined humoral and cell-mediated deficiency. Immunodeficiency disorders are *primary* if the immune cells are improperly developed or absent and *secondary* if an illness or treatment causes the deficiency. Primary immunodeficiency disorders are rare and often serious. Secondary disorders are more common and less severe.

Primary Immunodeficiency Disorders

The basic categories of primary immunodeficiency disorders are (1) phagocytic defects, (2) B-cell deficiency, (3) T-cell deficiency, and (4) a combined B-cell and T-cell deficiency (Table 14.15).

Secondary Immunodeficiency Disorders

Key factors that may cause secondary immunodeficiency disorders are shown in Table 14.16. Drug-induced immunosuppression is the most common. Immunosuppressive therapy is prescribed for patients to treat autoimmune disorders and prevent transplant rejection. Immunosuppression is a serious side effect of drugs used in cancer chemotherapy. Generalized leukopenia often results, leading to a decreased humoral and cell-mediated response. Therefore, secondary infections are common in immunosuppressed patients.

TABLE 14.15 Primary Immunodeficiency Disorders

Disorder	Affected Cells	Genetic Basis
Ataxia-telangiectasia	B, T	Autosomal recessive
Bruton's X-linked agammaglobulinemia	B	X-linked
Chronic granulomatous disease	PMNs, monocytes	X-linked
Common variable hypogammaglobulinemia	B	—
DiGeorge syndrome (thymic hypoplasia)	T	—
Graft-versus-host disease	B, T	—
Job syndrome	PMNs, monocytes	—
Severe combined immunodeficiency disease	Stem, B, T	X-linked or autosomal recessive
Selective IgA, IgM, or IgG deficiency	B	Some X-linked
Wiskott-Aldrich syndrome	B, T	X-linked

Ig, Immunoglobulin; *PMNs,* polymorphonuclear neutrophils.

TABLE 14.16 Causes of Secondary Immunodeficiency

Age
- Infants
- Older adults

Conditions
- Acquired immunodeficiency syndrome (AIDS)
- Burns
- Cancers
- Chronic kidney disease
- Cirrhosis
- Diabetes
- Hodgkin lymphoma
- Severe infection
- Systemic lupus erythematosus
- Trauma

Drug-Induced Immunodeficiency
- Chemotherapy drugs
- Corticosteroids

Malnutrition
- Cachexia
- Dietary deficiency

Stress
- Chronic stress
- Trauma (physical or emotional)

Therapies
- Anesthesia
- Radiation
- Surgery

Malnutrition alters cell-mediated immune responses. When protein is deficient over a prolonged period, the thymus gland atrophies, and lymphoid tissue decreases. In addition, an increased susceptibility to infections always exists.

Hodgkin lymphoma impairs the cell-mediated immune response, and patients may die from severe viral or fungal infections (see Chapter 34). Viruses, especially rubella, may cause immunodeficiency by direct cytotoxic damage to lymphoid cells. Systemic infections can place such a demand on the immune system that resistance to a secondary or another infection is impaired.

Radiation can destroy lymphocytes either directly or through depletion of stem cells. As the radiation dose is increased, more bone marrow atrophies. This leads to severe pancytopenia and suppression of immune function. Splenectomy in children is especially dangerous. They may develop sepsis from a simple respiratory tract infection.

Stress may alter the immune response. This response involves interrelationships among the nervous, endocrine, and immune systems (see Chapter 7).

HUMAN LEUKOCYTE ANTIGEN SYSTEM

The antigens responsible for rejection of genetically unlike tissues are called the *major histocompatibility antigens.* These antigens are products of histocompatibility genes. In humans, they are called the **human leukocyte antigen (HLA)** system. The genes for the HLA antigens are linked and occur together on the sixth chromosome. HLAs are present on all nucleated cells and platelets. We primarily use the HLA system in matching organs and tissues for transplantation.

An important characteristic of HLA genes is that they are highly *polymorphic* (variable). Each HLA locus can have many possible alleles, so many combinations exist. Each person has 2 alleles for each locus, 1 inherited from each parent. Both alleles of a locus are expressed independently, meaning they are codominant. The proteins encoded by certain genes are known as *antigens*.

The entire set of A, B, C, D, and DR genes (the HLA genes) on 1 chromosome is a *haplotype*. A complete set is inherited as a unit (haplotype). One haplotype is inherited from each parent (Fig. 14.11). This means that a person has HLA genes that are half identical to those of each parent. The HLA genes of 1 person have a 25% chance of being identical to the HLA genes of a sibling. In organ transplantation we primarily use A, B, and DR for compatibility matching. The specific allele at each locus is identified by a number. For example, a person could have an HLA of A2, A6, B7, B27, DR4, and DR7. Currently more than 8000 HLA alleles have been identified for the various HLA genes.

Human Leukocyte Antigen and Disease Associations

Several diseases show significant associations with specific HLA alleles. People who have these alleles are much more likely to develop the associated disease than those who do not have the alleles. However, having a particular HLA allele does not mean

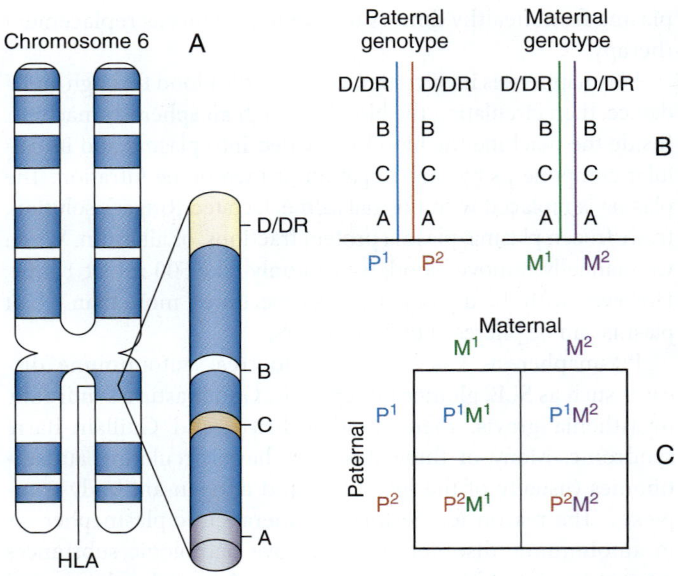

Fig. 14.11 Patterns of human leukocyte antigen (HLA) inheritance. (A) HLA genes are found on chromosome 6. (B) The 2 haplotypes of the father are labeled P^1 and P^2, and the haplotypes of the mother are labeled M^1 and M^2. Each child inherits 2 haplotypes, 1 from each parent. (C) Only 4 combinations—P^1M^1, P^1M^2, P^2M^1, and P^2M^2—are possible, and 25% of the offspring will have identical HLA haplotypes.

that the person will necessarily develop the associated disease—only that the risk is greater than in the general population. Most people who inherit a specific HLA type that is associated with a disease will never develop that disease.

Many of the HLA-associated diseases are autoimmune disorders. Examples of HLA types and disease associations include (1) HLA-B27 and ankylosing spondylitis; (2) HLA-DR2, HLA-DR3, and SLE; (3) HLA-DR3, HLA-DR4, and diabetes; and (4) HLA-DR2 and narcolepsy.

Currently the association between HLAs and certain diseases is of minimal practical clinical importance. But there is promise for the development of future clinical applications. For example, with some autoimmune diseases, it may be possible to identify members of a family at greatest risk for developing the same or a related autoimmune disease. These people would need close medical supervision, implementation of preventive measures (if possible), and early diagnosis and treatment to prevent chronic complications.

ORGAN TRANSPLANTATION

Transplantation success has improved with advances in surgical technique, advances in histocompatibility testing, and more effective immunosuppressant drugs. Common tissue transplants include corneas, skin, bone marrow, heart valves, bone, and connective tissues (Fig. 14.12). Corneal transplants can prevent or correct blindness. Skin grafts are used in managing burn patients. Donated bone marrow can help patients with leukemias and other cancers.

Transplanted organs currently come from many different body systems. These organs include the heart, lung, liver, kidney, pancreas, and intestine. Multiple organs can be transplanted

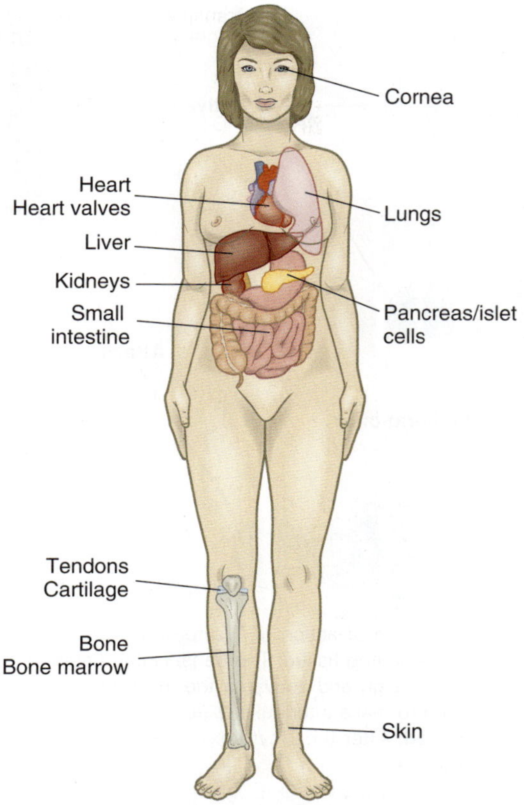

Fig. 14.12 Tissues and organs that can be transplanted.

together, such as kidney and pancreas, kidney and liver, kidney and heart, or the complete intestinal tract. For example, some patients with diabetes who receive a pancreas transplant also receive a kidney transplant because the diabetes also led to kidney failure.

Some organs can be transplanted in parts or segments instead of transplanting an entire organ. Examples include transplanting liver and lung lobes or segments of an intestine. This allows for 1 person's organ donation to help many recipients. This technique also allows living donors to donate part of an organ or 1 of their organs, in the case of kidneys.

Organ donations come from either deceased (cadaver) or living donors. Most organs and tissues currently come from deceased donors. However, because of the shortage of organs from deceased donors, the use of related and living unrelated donor organs is increasing.

People can show their wish to become a donor when they sign a donor card or driver's license or join a donor registry (depending on the state). However, on their death or imminent death, the person's legal next of kin may need to consent to the donation regardless of the donor's wishes. Legal requirements and the agency's policy for the legal next of kin to consent varies from state to state and from agency to agency.

Currently more than 116,000 people are on the organ procurement and transplantation network's national waiting list. The United Network for Organ Sharing (UNOS) maintains this list. However, fewer than 35,000 people receive transplants annually. The organs in highest demand are kidneys, hearts, and livers. These are also the most often transplanted organs.[10] The Uniform Anatomical Gift Act regulates organ and tissue donations to allow for fair and consistent transplantation laws among all states.[11] Patients are matched to available donors based on several factors: ABO blood and HLA typing, medical urgency, time on the waiting list, and geographic location.

Tissue Typing

The recipient usually receives a transplant from an ABO blood group–compatible donor. The donor and recipient do not need to share the same Rh factor.

HLA Typing

HLA typing is done on potential donors and recipients. Currently we think only the A, B, and DR antigens are clinically significant for transplantation. Because each locus has 2 alleles that encode for antigens, there are a total of 6 antigens. In transplantation we try to match as many antigens as possible between the HLA-A, HLA-B, and HLA-DR loci. Antigen matches of 5 and 6 antigens and some 4-antigen matches have better clinical outcomes. This means the patient is less likely to reject the transplanted organ.

The degree of HLA matching needed or suitable for successful transplantation depends on the type of organ and degree of acceptable risk. Certain organ and tissue transplants need a closer histocompatibility match than other organs. For example, nearly anyone can accept a cornea transplant. Corneas are avascular so no antibodies can reach the cornea and cause rejection. In kidney and bone marrow transplantation, HLA matching is very important, since these transplants are at high risk for graft rejection. HLA mismatches have little impact on graft survival for liver transplants. Heart and lung transplants fall somewhere in between but minimizing HLA mismatches significantly improves survival. For liver, lung, and heart transplants, few donors are available, and it is hard to get good HLA matches.

Transporting and storing donated organs can take time. The "best" match may live many miles from the "ideal" recipient. The need to have the "best" matches must be balanced against the time it takes to obtain and transport a donated organ and then transplant it.

Panel of Reactive Antibodies

A *panel of reactive antibodies (PRA)* shows the recipient's sensitivity to various HLAs before receiving a transplant. PRA allows us to determine whether a recipient is of high or low reactivity to potential donors. To detect preformed antibodies to HLA, the recipient's serum is mixed with a randomly selected panel of donor lymphocytes to determine reactivity. Patients awaiting transplantation usually have a PRA panel done on a regular basis.

We calculate the results for the PRA in percentages. A high PRA means that the person has many cytotoxic antibodies and is highly sensitized. There will be a poor chance of finding a crossmatch-negative donor. They may have been exposed to HLA antigens by previous blood transfusions, pregnancy, or a previous organ transplant. In highly sensitized patients (high

PRA), plasmapheresis and IV immunoglobulin (IVIG) are options to lower the number of antibodies.

Crossmatch

A crossmatch is done to determine the existence of antibodies against the potential donor. A crossmatch uses serum from the recipient mixed with donor lymphocytes to test for any preformed anti-HLA antibodies to the potential donor organ. The crossmatch can be used as a screening test when possible living donors are being considered or once a cadaver donor is chosen.

A negative crossmatch means that no preformed antibodies are present, and it is safe to go ahead with transplantation. A positive crossmatch means that the recipient has cytotoxic antibodies to the donor. This is an absolute contraindication in living donor transplants. Live donor transplants may be done for patients with a positive crossmatch if no other live donors (with a negative crossmatch) exist. In this situation, plasmapheresis or IVIG can remove antibodies.

It is not always possible to complete a crossmatch prior to transplantation. If a crossmatch is done after, the results will have implications for immunosuppression protocols after the transplant. A prospective crossmatch is especially important for kidney transplants. It is not an option for lung, liver, and heart transplants.

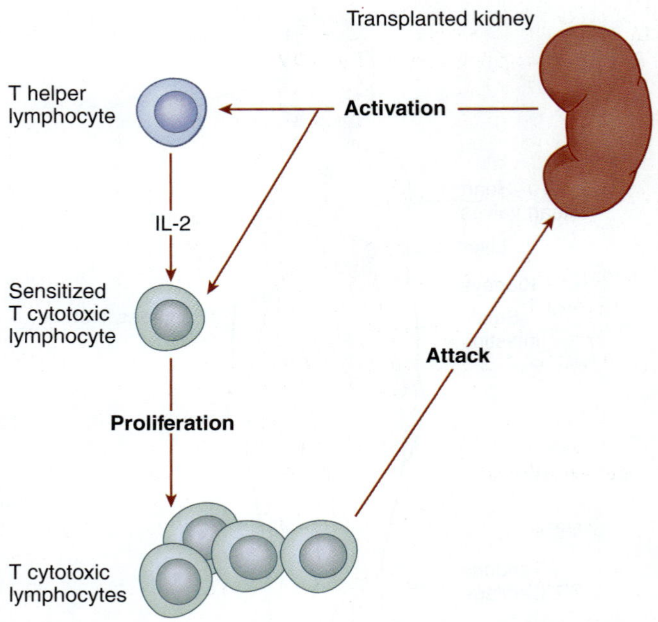

Fig. 14.13 Mechanism of action of T cytotoxic lymphocyte activation and attack of transplanted tissue. The transplanted organ (e.g., kidney) is recognized as foreign and activates the immune system. T helper cells are activated to make interleukin-2 *(IL-2),* and T cytotoxic lymphocytes are sensitized. After the T cytotoxic cells proliferate, they attack the transplanted organ.

Transplant Rejection

Rejection is a major problem after organ transplantation. Organ rejection occurs as a normal immune response to foreign tissue. Immunosuppression therapy, performing ABO and HLA matching, and ensuring that the crossmatch is negative reduces the risk for rejection. Unfortunately, many different HLAs exist. A perfect match is nearly impossible unless the tissue is from one's self, an identical twin, or in some cases a sibling. Rejection can be hyperacute, acute, or chronic. Prevention, early diagnosis, and treatment of rejection are essential for long-term graft function.

Hyperacute Rejection

Hyperacute rejection occurs within 24 hours after transplantation. It occurs because the person had preexisting antibodies against the transplanted tissue or organ. There is no treatment for hyperacute rejection. We must remove the transplanted organ. Fortunately, hyperacute rejection is a rare event because of improved immunosuppression medications and because the final testing before transplantation usually determines whether the recipient is sensitized to any of the donor HLAs.

Acute Rejection

Acute rejection most often occurs in the first 6 months after transplantation. This type of rejection is usually a cell-mediated immune response by the recipient's lymphocytes, which are activated against the donated (foreign) tissue or organ (Fig. 14.13). In addition to cell-mediated rejection, another type of acute rejection occurs when the recipient develops antibodies to the transplanted organ (humoral rejection).

It is common to have at least one rejection episode, especially with organs from deceased donors. These episodes are usually reversible with additional immunosuppressive therapy. This may include increased corticosteroid doses or polyclonal or monoclonal antibodies. Unfortunately, immunosuppressants increase the risk for infection. To combat acute rejection, all patients with transplants need long-term use of immunosuppressants, putting them at a high risk for infection, especially in the first few months after transplant when the immunosuppressive doses are highest.

Chronic Rejection

Chronic rejection is a process that occurs over months or years. It is irreversible. Chronic rejection can occur for unknown reasons or from repeated episodes of acute rejection. Large numbers of T and B cells infiltrate the transplanted organ, with ongoing, low-grade, immune-mediated injury. Chronic rejection results in fibrosis and scarring. In heart transplants it manifests as accelerated coronary artery disease. In lung transplants it manifests as bronchiolitis obliterans. In liver transplants, we see a loss of bile ducts. In kidney transplants it manifests as fibrosis and glomerulopathy.

There is no definitive treatment for chronic rejection. Treatment is primarily supportive. Chronic rejection is hard to manage and does not have the optimistic prognosis of acute rejection.

Immunosuppressive Therapy

Immunosuppressive therapy requires a lifelong balance between rejection and infection. The immune response must be suppressed to prevent rejection of the transplanted organ. On the other hand, an adequate immune response must be maintained to prevent overwhelming infection and the development of cancers.[12]

TABLE 14.17 **Drug Therapy**

Immunosuppressive Therapy

Agent	Route	Mechanism of Action	Side Effects
Calcineurin Inhibitors			
cyclosporine (Gengraf, Neoral, Sandimmune)	PO, IV	Acts on T helper cells to prevent production and release of IL-2 T- and B-cell proliferation	Kidney toxicity, ↑ infection risk, neurotoxicity (tremors, seizures), liver toxicity, lymphoma, ↑ BP, tremors, hirsutism, leukopenia, gingival hyperplasia
tacrolimus (Astagraf XL, Envarsus XR, Prograf)	PO, IV	Same as cyclosporine but more effective	Same as cyclosporine
Corticosteroids			
prednisone, methylprednisolone	PO, IV	Suppress inflammatory response Inhibit cytokine production (IL-1, IL-6, TNF) and T-cell activation and proliferation	Peptic ulcers, ↑ BP, osteoporosis, Na^+ and H_2O retention, muscle weakness, easy bruising, delayed healing, hyperglycemia, ↑ infection risk
Cytotoxic (Antiproliferative) Drugs			
azathioprine (Imuran)	PO, IV	Inhibits purine synthesis Suppresses proliferation of T and B cells	Bone marrow suppression (neutropenia, anemia, thrombocytopenia)
cyclophosphamide	PO, IV	Cross-links DNA, leading to cell injury and death. Results in decrease in number and activity of T and B cells	Neutropenia, hemorrhagic cystitis
everolimus (Afinitor, Zortress)	PO	Binds to mechanistic target of rapamycin (mTOR), thereby suppressing T-cell activation and proliferation	Peripheral edema, constipation, ↑ BP, nausea, anemia, urinary tract infection, hyperlipidemia
mycophenolate mofetil (CellCept, Myfortic)	PO, IV	Inhibits purine synthesis Suppresses T- and B-cell proliferation	Diarrhea, nausea and vomiting, neutropenia, thrombocytopenia, ↑ infection risk, ↑ cancer risk
sirolimus (Rapamune, Torisel)	PO	Same as everolimus	↑ Infection risk, leukopenia, anemia, thrombocytopenia, hyperlipidemia, hypercholesterolemia, arthralgias, diarrhea. ↑ cancer risk
Monoclonal Antibodies			
alemtuzumab (Campath, Lemtrada)	IV	Monoclonal antibody that targets the CD52 antigen on T and B cells, monocytes, and macrophages Causes prolonged T-cell depletion	Fever, chills, dyspnea, chest pain, nausea, vomiting. Neutropenia, anemia, thrombocytopenia ↑ risk for opportunistic infections
basiliximab (Simulect)	IV	Monoclonal antibody that targets IL-2 receptor and inhibits T-cell activation and proliferation	Can cause acute hypersensitivity reaction, including anaphylaxis
Other			
belatacept (Nulojix)	IV	Prevents T-cell activation	Anemia, diarrhea, constipation, urinary tract infection, peripheral edema
Polyclonal Antibodies			
Horse antithymocyte globulin (Atgam) Rabbit antithymocyte globulin (Thymoglobulin, ATG)	IV	Prepared by immunizing horse or rabbit with human thymocytes or T cells. Polyclonal antibodies directed against T cells, thus depleting them	Fever, chills, dyspnea, myalgia, chest pain, nausea and vomiting, anaphylaxis, leukopenia, thrombocytopenia, rash, ↑ infection risk

Many of the drugs used to achieve immunosuppression have significant side effects. Because transplant recipients must take immunosuppressants for life, the risk for toxicity continues for the rest of their lives.

Immunosuppressant drugs are listed in Table 14.17.[13] With the use of a combination of agents that work during different phases of the immune response (see Fig. 14.13), we can give lower doses of each drug to produce effective immunosuppression while minimizing side effects.

The major immunosuppressive agents are (1) calcineurin inhibitors; (2) corticosteroids (prednisone, methylprednisolone); (3) purine synthesis antagonists, including mycophenolate mofetil (CellCept, Myfortic) and azathioprine (Imuran); and (4) sirolimus. IV Muromonab-CD3 and either horse antithymocyte globulin (Atgam) or rabbit antithymocyte globulin (ATG) are used for short periods to prevent early rejection or reverse acute rejection.

Immunosuppression protocols are highly variable among transplant centers, with different drug combinations being used. Most patients are initially on triple therapy. The standard triple therapy usually includes a calcineurin inhibitor, a corticosteroid, and mycophenolate mofetil.

The doses of immunosuppressant drugs are reduced over time after the transplant. The trend in many transplant centers is to follow an immunosuppression protocol that uses minimal corticosteroids because of their many side effects. Patients taking corticosteroids may be weaned off after a few years.

Calcineurin Inhibitors

This group of drugs includes tacrolimus (Prograf, Envarsus XR) and cyclosporine (Sandimmune). They are the most effective agents and serve as the foundation of most immunosuppression regimens. Calcineurin inhibitors work by preventing a cell-mediated attack against the transplanted organ (Fig. 14.14). They

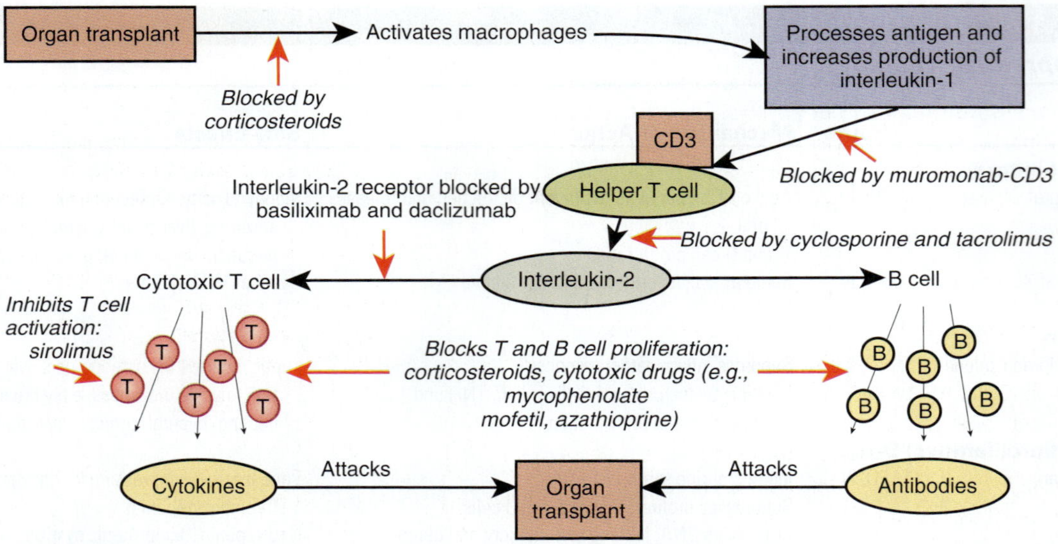

Fig. 14.14 Sites of action for immunosuppressive agents. (Adapted from McKenry L, Tessier E, Hogan M: *Mosby's pharmacology in nursing,* St Louis, 2006, Mosby.)

are usually used in combination with corticosteroids, mycophenolate mofetil, and sirolimus. Tacrolimus is the most widely used. Envarsus XR is an extended-release long-acting formulation of tacrolimus that is dosed once daily. Cyclosporine is being used less often as a first-line drug choice.

DRUG ALERT

Tacrolimus and Cyclosporine

- A substance in grapefruit and grapefruit juice prevents metabolism of these drugs.
- Consuming grapefruit or grapefruit juice while using these drugs can increase their toxicity.

Mycophenolate Mofetil

Mycophenolate mofetil inhibits purine synthesis with suppressive effects on T and B cells. The major limitation of this drug is GI toxicity, including nausea, vomiting, and diarrhea. In many cases the side effects can be lessened by lowering the dose or giving smaller doses more often.

DRUG ALERT

Mycophenolate Mofetil

- When given IV, it can only be reconstituted in D_5W.
- Do not give as IV bolus. Give over 2 or more hours.

Sirolimus

Sirolimus suppresses T-cell activation and proliferation. It is used in combination with corticosteroids, cyclosporine, and/or tacrolimus.

Monoclonal Antibodies

Monoclonal antibodies are used to prevent and treat acute rejection episodes. Muromonab-CD3 was the first monoclonal antibody to be used in transplantation. It is a mouse monoclonal antibody that binds with the CD3 antigen found on the surface of human thymocytes and mature T cells. It interferes with the function of T cells, the pivotal cells involved in rejection. They affect all T cells, not just the subset active in graft rejection. It is given by IV bolus. Within minutes after the first infusion, the number of circulating T cells decreases significantly.

A flu-like syndrome occurs during the first few days of treatment because of cytokine release. Side effects include fever, chills, headache, myalgias, and various GI problems. To reduce the expected side effects, give patients acetaminophen, diphenhydramine, and IV methylprednisolone beforehand.

Newer generation monoclonal antibodies are a hybrid of mouse and human antibodies. They have fewer side effects than muromonab-CD3 because they have been "humanized." Agents include basiliximab (Simulect), which targets the IL-2 receptor and impairs lymphocyte proliferation. Another monoclonal antibody is alemtuzumab (Campath). It targets the CD52 antigen found on T and B cells, monocytes, and macrophages. Prolonged T-cell depletion can result.

Polyclonal Antibodies

Polyclonal antibodies to T cells include horse antithymocyte globulin (Atgam) and rabbit antithymocyte globulin (thymoglobulin, ATG). These agents are derived by injecting animals (rabbit or horse) with human lymphoid cells, then procuring and purifying the resultant antibody. They are often used for induction immunosuppression and treating acute rejection.

Allergic reactions to the foreign proteins from the host animal are common but usually not severe enough to prevent use. Manifestations include fever, arthralgias, and tachycardia. These effects can be decreased by giving the preparation slowly, over 4 to 6 hours, and premedicating patients with acetaminophen, diphenhydramine, and methylprednisolone. The main toxicities of polyclonal antibodies are leukopenia and thrombocytopenia. They are caused by antibody contaminants that are not completely removed during preparation of the antibodies.

GRAFT-VERSUS-HOST DISEASE

Graft-versus-host disease (GVHD) occurs when an immunodeficient patient receives immunocompetent cells. In most transplantation situations, the biggest concern is the patient's (host's) rejection of the organ or transplant. However, in GVHD disease, the graft (donated tissue) rejects the host (recipient) tissue.[13] A GVHD response is most common in hematopoietic stem cell transplants.

The GVHD response may begin 7 to 30 days after transplantation. Once the reaction is started, little can be done to change its course. We do not completely understand the exact mechanisms involved. It does involve donor T cells attacking and destroying vulnerable host (recipient) cells.

The target organs for the GVHD phenomenon are the skin, liver, and GI tract. The skin disease may be a maculopapular rash, which may be itchy or painful. It initially involves the palms and soles of the feet. It can progress to a generalized erythema with bullous formation and desquamation (shedding of the outer layer of skin). The liver disease may range from mild jaundice with high liver enzymes to hepatic coma. GI manifestations may include mild to severe diarrhea, severe abdominal pain, GI bleeding, and malabsorption.

The biggest problem with GVHD is infection, with different types of infections seen in different periods. Bacterial and fungal infections can occur right after transplantation when granulocytopenia exists. Interstitial pneumonitis is the primary concern later.

There is no adequate treatment of GVHD once it is established. Although corticosteroids are often used, they enhance the susceptibility to infection. The use of immunosuppressive agents (e.g., methotrexate, cyclosporine) has been most effective as a preventive rather than a treatment measure. Radiating blood products before they are given is another way to prevent T-cell replication. Ibrutinib (Imbruvica), a kinase inhibitor that is used to treat several forms of leukemia and lymphoma, is an option for some patients with chronic GVHD

Case Study

Anaphylaxis

(© shironosov/ iStock.com.)

Patient Profile

J.S., a 43-year-old female, presents to the emergency department with an anaphylaxis reaction. Her symptoms started while she was wearing latex gloves at work.

Subject Data

- Works as a construction site manager
- Reports tightness in the vocal cord, dizziness
- States she is having difficulty breathing
- Both hands are "itchy" with burning sensations

Objective Data

Physical Assessment

- BP 80/40 mm Hg, temp 100.1°F (37.8°C), O_2 saturation 94% on room air
- Wheezing noted throughout all lung fields
- Heart rate is 110 and regular
- Both upper hands have erythema, with irregular shaped wheals that are warm to touch

Interprofessional Care

- Epinephrine (1 mg/mL preparation). 0.5 mg IM in vastus lateralis. Repeat q 15 minutes
- Diphenhydramine 50 mg IV now
- 1 liter IV normal saline by rapid bolus
- Place patient in a recumbent position and elevate legs
- Monitor vital signs and O_2 saturation

Discussion Questions

1. ***Recognize:*** What clinical manifestations of anaphylaxis does J.S. have?
2. ***Analyze***: How would IgE Antibody Immunoassays be beneficial in the diagnose of latex sensitivity?
3. ***Plan***: Provide the rationale for each of the HCP's orders.
4. ***Prioritize***: What are your priority nursing interventions for J.S.?
5. ***Act***: Which interventions can you delegate to AP or other members of the health care team?
6. ***Evaluate***: What outcomes would indicate nursing interventions were successful?

BRIDGE TO NCLEX EXAMINATION

The number of the question corresponds to the same-numbered outcome at the beginning of the chapter.

1. A patient with a low number of monocytes would have a decreased ability to
   a. stimulate the production of T and B lymphocytes.
   b. make antibodies after exposure to foreign substances.
   c. bind antigens and stimulate natural killer cell activation.
   d. capture antigens by phagocytosis and present them to lymphocytes.
2. Newborns are protected for the first 3 months of life from bacterial infections because of the maternal transmission of
   a. IgA.
   b. IgE.
   c. IgG.
   d. IgM.
3. In a type I hypersensitivity reaction the primary immunologic disorder appears to be
   a. binding of IgG to an antigen on a cell surface.
   b. deposit of antigen-antibody complexes in small vessels.
   c. release of cytokines used to interact with specific antigens.
   d. release of chemical mediators from IgE-bound mast cells and basophils.
4. The nurse would be alerted to possible anaphylactic shock after a patient has received IM penicillin by the development of
   a. edema and itching at the injection site.
   b. sneezing and itching of the nose and eyes.
   c. a wheal-and-flare reaction at the injection site.
   d. chest tightness and production of thick sputum.

5. The nurse tells a friend who asks him to administer his allergy shots that
   a. it is illegal for nurses to administer injections outside of a medical setting.
   b. he is qualified to do it if the friend has epinephrine in an injectable syringe provided with his extract.
   c. avoiding the allergens is a more effective way of controlling allergies, and allergy shots are not usually effective.
   d. immunotherapy should only be administered in a setting where emergency equipment and drugs are available.
6. A patient is undergoing plasmapheresis for treatment of systemic lupus erythematosus. The nurse explains that plasmapheresis is used in treatment to
   a. remove T lymphocytes in her blood that are producing antinuclear antibodies.
   b. remove normal particles in her blood that are being damaged by autoantibodies.
   c. exchange her plasma that contains antinuclear antibodies with a substitute fluid.
   d. replace viral-damaged cellular components of her blood with replacement whole blood.
7. The *most* common cause of secondary immunodeficiencies is
   a. drugs.
   b. stress.
   c. malnutrition.
   d. human immunodeficiency virus.
8. Association between HLA antigens and diseases is *most* often found in what disease conditions?
   a. Cancers
   b. Infectious diseases
   c. Neurologic diseases
   d. Autoimmune disorders
9. What accurately describes rejection after transplantation?
   a. Hyperacute rejection can be treated with antimetabolites.
   b. Acute rejection can be treated with sirolimus or tacrolimus.
   c. Chronic rejection can be treated with tacrolimus or cyclosporine.
   d. Hyperacute reaction can be avoided if crossmatching is done before transplantation.
10. In a person having an acute rejection of a transplanted kidney, what would help the nurse understand the course of events? *(select all that apply)*
   a. A new transplant should be considered.
   b. Acute rejection can be treated with mycophenolate.
   c. Repeated episodes of acute rejection can lead to chronic rejection.
   d. Corticosteroids are the most successful drugs used to treat acute rejection.
   e. Acute rejection is common after a transplant and can be treated with drug therapy.

1. d; 2. c; 3. d; 4. a; 5. d; 6. c; 7. a; 8. d; 9. d; 10. b, c, e.

For rationales to these answers and even more NCLEX review questions, visit http://evolve.elsevier.com/Lewis/medsurg.

EVOLVE WEBSITE/RESOURCES LIST

http://evolve.elsevier.com/Lewis/medsurg
Review Questions (Online Only)
Key Points
Answer Key for Questions
- Rationales for Bridge to NCLEX Examination Questions

Conceptual Care Map Creator
Audio Glossary
Content Updates

REFERENCES

1. McCance K: *Pathophysiology*, ed 8, St. Louis, 2019, Elsevier.
*2. Shaker MS, Wallace DV, Golden D, et al.: Anaphylaxis—a 2020 practice parameter update, systematic review, and Grading of Recommendations, Assessment, Development and Evaluation (GRADE) analysis, *J Allergy Clin Immunol* 145:1082, 2020.
3. American Academy of Allergy, Asthma, & Immunology (AAAAI): Food allergy. Retrieved from https://www.aaaai.org/conditions-and-treatments/allergies/food-allergies.
4. AAAAI: Anaphylaxis. Retrieved from https://www.aaaai.org/conditions-and-treatments/library/allergy-library/anaphylaxis.
5. AAAAI: SLIT treatment for allergic rhinitis. Retrieved from https://www.aaaai.org/conditions-and-treatments/library/allergy-library/sublingual-immunotherapy-for-allergic-rhinitis.
*6. AAAAI: Practice parameters and other guidelines. Retrieved from https://www.aaaai.org/practice-resources/statements-and-practice-parameters/practice-parameter-guidelines.
7. Asthma and Allergy Foundation of America: Latex allergy. Retrieved from https://www.aafa.org/latex-allergy/.
8. Centers for Disease Control and Prevention: Preventing allergic reactions to natural rubber latex in the workplace. Retrieved from www.cdc.gov/niosh/docs/97-135/pdfs/97-135.pdf.
9. U.S. Department of Labor: Multiple chemical sensitivities. Retrieved from https://www.osha.gov/multiple-chemical-sensitivities.
10. United Network for Organ Sharing (UNOS). Retrieved from www.unos.org.
11. U.S. Department of Health and Human Services: Organ procurement and transplantation network. Retrieved from https://optn.transplant.hrsa.gov/.
12. Cupples SA, Lerret S, McCalmont V, et al.: *Core curriculum for transplant nurses*, ed 2, Philadelphia, 2017, Wolters Kluwer.
*13. Chen Y, Rogers C: New treatment options for the management of acute graft-versus-host disease, *Clin Adv Hematol Oncol* 17:482, 2019.
14. Skidmore-Roth L: *Mosby's 2021 Nursing drug reference*, ed 34, St. Louis, 2021, Elsevier.

*Evidence-based information for clinical practice.

15

Infection

Jeffrey Kwong

http://evolve.elsevier.com/Lewis/medsurg/

CONCEPTUAL FOCUS

Adherence
Coping
Functional Ability
Immunity
Infection
Inflammation
Nutrition

LEARNING OUTCOMES

1. Discuss principles of epidemiology related to infectious disease.
2. Describe the impact of emerging and reemerging infections on health care.
3. Identify interventions to reduce health care–associated infections.
4. Evaluate methods health care workers can take to protect themselves from infection.
5. Describe the manifestations, diagnosis, treatment, and prevention options for COVID-19.
6. Describe methods used to diagnose and monitor HIV infection.
7. Discuss the role of HIV antiretroviral therapy.
8. Summarize the characteristics of opportunistic diseases associated with AIDS.
9. Describe the potential complications of long-term treatment of HIV infection.
10. Describe the nursing management of patients with HIV and those at-risk for HIV infection.

KEY TERMS

acquired immunodeficiency syndrome (AIDS)
emerging infection
epidemiology
health care–associated infections (HAIs)
human immunodeficiency virus (HIV)
incidence
nonoccupational postexposure prophylaxis (nPEP)
opportunistic diseases
personal protective equipment (PPE)
postexposure prophylaxis (PEP)
preexposure prophylaxis (PrEP)
prevalence
SARS-CoV-2
standard precautions
transmission-based precautions
viral load
viral vector vaccines
window period

This chapter presents a brief overview of the concept of emerging and health care–associated infections (HAIs). This includes identifying persons most at risk, recognizing signs and symptoms of infection, and understanding ways to treat or manage infection. Infection, immunity, and inflammation are closely related. The chapter closes with a discussion of human immunodeficiency virus (HIV) infection.

INFECTIONS

Infections, such as pneumonia, COVID-19, malaria, HIV, and tuberculosis (TB), are responsible for a significant number of deaths worldwide. Infection occurs when a *pathogen* (a microorganism that causes disease) invades the body, multiplies, and causes disease, usually causing harm to the host. The signs and symptoms of infection are a result of specific pathogen activity, which triggers inflammation and other immune responses.

We categorize infections as localized, disseminated, or systemic. A *localized* infection is limited to a small area. A *disseminated* infection has spread to areas of the body beyond the initial site of infection. *Systemic* infections have spread extensively throughout the body, often via the blood.

EPIDEMIOLOGY CONCEPTS

Epidemiology is the study of the distribution and determinants of health conditions, such as infections or diseases.[1] Important concepts include incidence and prevalence. **Incidence** is the number of new cases of a health-related issue or problem that occur during a specific time period. For example, the annual incidence of new HIV cases in the United States is around 36,400 cases per year. This means that each year, about 36,400 people are diagnosed with HIV. **Prevalence** is the total number of people who have a specific health-related issue, problem, disease, or illness at any given time. For example, in the United States, we think the prevalence, or the total number of people living with HIV, is 1.2 million.

Endemic is a term that describes the baseline level of disease in a particular area. *Epidemic* refers to a rise or increase of a disease or condition within a certain community or area. For example, the 2014 whooping cough outbreak is an example of an epidemic. *Pandemic* is a type of epidemic that has significant geographic spread and affects entire countries or the world. COVID-19 in 2020 is an example of a pandemic.

TYPES OF PATHOGENS

A pathogen is an agent that causes disease. Bacteria, viruses, fungi, protozoa, and prions are all types of pathogens. *Bacteria* are one-celled organisms that are common throughout nature. Many bacteria are normal flora. They live harmoniously in or on the human body without causing disease under normal circumstances. Normal flora protect the human body by preventing the overgrowth of other microorganisms. For example, *Escherichia coli* is part of the normal flora in the large intestine.

Bacteria cause disease in 2 ways: by entering the body and growing inside human cells (e.g., TB) or by secreting toxins that damage cells (e.g., *Staphylococcus aureus*). Bacteria are classified based on the shape of their cells. *Cocci,* such as streptococci and staphylococci, are round. *Bacilli* are rod shaped and include tetanus and TB. *Curved rods* include *Vibrio* bacteria, one of which causes cholera. *Spirochetes* are spiral shaped. They include the organisms that cause leprosy and syphilis. Table 15.1 lists common bacteria that cause disease.

Viruses, unlike bacteria, do not have a cellular structure. They are simple infectious particles that consist of a small amount of genetic material (either ribonucleic acid [RNA] or deoxyribonucleic acid [DNA]) and a protein envelope. Viruses can reproduce only after releasing their genetic material into the cell of another living organism. Table 15.2 shows some diseases that are caused by viruses.

Fungi are organisms similar to plants, but they lack chlorophyll. *Mycosis* is any disease caused by a fungus. Pathogenic fungi cause infections that are usually local. Tinea pedis (athlete's foot) and tinea corporis (ringworm) are two common examples. Systemic infections occur much less often but are much more dangerous. This can happen in an immunocompromised person. Some fungi are normal flora in the body, but when overgrowth occurs, disease can result. For example, overgrowth of *Candida albicans* can cause candidiasis in the mouth (thrush), esophagus, intestines, and vagina. Table 15.3 lists other fungi and the infections they cause.

Protozoa are single-cell, animal-like microorganisms. Protozoa normally live in soil and bodies of water. If they enter the body, they can cause infection. Protozoal parasites cause amoebic dysentery and giardiasis. A sporozoan called *Plasmodium malariae* causes malaria.

Prions are infectious particles that have abnormally shaped proteins. Not all prions cause disease. Those that do often affect the nervous system. They can cause a group of illnesses called *transmissible spongiform encephalopathies (TSEs).* Examples of TSEs are Creutzfeldt-Jakob disease and bovine spongiform encephalopathy in cattle (mad cow disease).

TABLE 15.1 Disease-Causing Bacteria

Bacteria	Diseases Caused
Chlamydia trachomatis	Chlamydia, lymphogranuloma venereum
Clostridia	
• *Clostridium botulinum*	Food poisoning with progressive muscle paralysis
• *Clostridium tetani*	Tetanus (lockjaw)
Corynebacterium diphtheriae	Diphtheria
Escherichia coli	UTIs, peritonitis, hemolytic-uremic syndrome
Haemophilus	
• *Haemophilus influenzae*	Nasopharyngitis, meningitis, pneumonia
• *Haemophilus pertussis*	Pertussis (whooping cough)
Helicobacter pylori	Peptic ulcers, gastritis
Klebsiella-Enterobacter organisms	UTIs, peritonitis, pneumonia
Legionella pneumophila	Pneumonia (Legionnaires disease)
Mycobacteria	
• *Mycobacterium leprae*	Hansen disease (leprosy)
• *Mycobacterium tuberculosis*	TB
Neisseriae	
• *Neisseria gonorrhoeae*	Gonorrhea, pelvic inflammatory disease, proctitis
• *Neisseria meningitidis*	Meningococcemia, meningitis
Proteus species	UTIs, peritonitis
Pseudomonas aeruginosa	UTIs, meningitis
Salmonella	
• *Salmonella typhi*	Typhoid fever
• Other *Salmonella* organisms	Food poisoning, gastroenteritis
Shigella	Shigellosis; diarrhea, abdominal pain, and fever (dysentery)
Staphylococcus aureus	Skin infections, pneumonia, UTIs, acute osteomyelitis, toxic shock syndrome
Streptococci	
• *Streptococcus faecalis*	Genitourinary infection, surgical wound infections
• *Streptococcus pneumoniae*	Pneumococcal pneumonia
• *Streptococcus pyogenes* (group A β-hemolytic streptococci)	Pharyngitis, scarlet fever, rheumatic fever, acute glomerulonephritis, erysipelas, pneumonia
• *S. pyogenes* (group B β-hemolytic streptococci)	UTIs
• *Streptococcus viridans*	Bacterial endocarditis
Treponema pallidum	Syphilis

SPECIFIC TYPES OF INFECTIONS

Emerging Infections

An **emerging infection** is an infectious disease that has recently increased in incidence or that threatens to increase in the immediate future.[2] They can originate from unknown sources, from contact with animals, changes in known diseases, or

TABLE 15.2 Disease-Causing Viruses

Virus	Diseases Caused
Adenoviruses	Upper respiratory tract infection (URI), pneumonia
Arbovirus	Syndrome of fever, malaise, headache, myalgia; aseptic meningitis; encephalitis
Coronavirus	Respiratory tract infection
• SARS-CoV-2	COVID-19
• SARS	Severe Acute Respiratory Syndrome (SARS) Middle Eastern Respiratory Syndrome (MERS)
Coxsackieviruses A and B	URI, gastroenteritis, acute myocarditis, aseptic meningitis
Ebola	Hemorrhagic fever
Echoviruses	URI, gastroenteritis, aseptic meningitis
Hepatitis A, B, C	Viral hepatitis
Herpesviruses	
• Cytomegalovirus (CMV)	Gastroenteritis; pneumonia and retinal damage in immunosuppressed persons, infectious mononucleosis-like syndrome
• Epstein-Barr	Mononucleosis, Burkitt lymphoma (possibly)
• Herpes simplex type 1	Herpes labialis ("fever blisters"), genital herpes infection
• Herpes simplex type 2	Genital herpes infection
• Varicella-zoster	Chickenpox, shingles
Human immunodeficiency virus (HIV)	HIV infection, AIDS
Influenza A and B	URI, H1N1 (swine) flu, H5N1 avian (bird) flu
Mumps	Parotitis, orchitis in postpubertal males
Papillomavirus	Genital warts, cervical and anal cancer
Parainfluenza 1-4	URI
Parvovirus	Gastroenteritis
Poliovirus	Poliomyelitis
Pox viruses	Smallpox, Molluscum contagiosum
Reoviruses 1, 2, 3	URI
Respiratory syncytial virus	Gastroenteritis, respiratory tract infection
Rhabdovirus	Rabies
Rhinovirus	URI, pneumonia
Rotaviruses	Gastroenteritis
Rubella	German measles
Rubeola	Measles
West Nile virus	Flu-like symptoms, meningitis, encephalitis
Zika virus	Flu-like symptoms, fetal microcephaly

TABLE 15.3 Disease-Causing Fungi

Fungi	Diseases Caused	Organs Affected
Aspergillus fumigatus	Aspergillosis	Lungs[a]
	Otomycosis	Ears
Blastomyces dermatitidis	Blastomycosis	Lungs,[a] various organs
Candida albicans	Candidiasis	Intestines
	Vaginitis	Vagina
	Thrush	Skin,[b] mouth
Coccidioides immitis	Coccidioidomycosis	Lungs[a]
Epidermophyton	Tinea corporis	Skin[b]
Microsporum	Tinea capitis	Skin[b]
Pneumocystis jiroveci	Pneumocystis pneumonia (PCP)	Lungs[a]
Sporothrix schenckii	Sporotrichosis	Skin, lymph vessels
Trichophyton	Tinea pedis	Skin[b]

[a]See Table 30.15: Fungal Infections of the Lungs.
[b]See Table 25.8, Common Fungal Infections of the Skin and Nails.

biologic warfare. Table 15.4 lists examples of emerging infections. COVID-19 (caused by SARS-CoV-2) and Ebola virus are examples. Other emerging infections occur when a previously treatable organism develops resistance to antibiotics, such as carbapenum-resistant enterobacteriaceae (CRE).

Studies in *zoonosis* (science of transmission of diseases from animals to humans) have shown that many infectious diseases come from animal and insect vectors. Rabies, Lyme disease, West Nile, Ebola, and severe acute respiratory syndrome (SARS) are examples of zoonotic infections.

Ebola virus has been an ongoing public health challenge since we first saw it in 1976. In 2014, rates of Ebola increased significantly in East Africa and the first cases of Ebola occurred in the United States. These first cases were from travelers or medical aid workers who were working in Africa. Ebola virus can cause severe hemorrhagic fever. It is usually lethal. Treatments are limited. The natural reservoir and path of transmission are unknown, which makes it impossible to effectively combat Ebola virus and the disease it causes.

West Nile virus is carried and transmitted by mosquitoes. Mosquitoes acquire the virus as they draw blood from infected animals and humans. The virus does not cause illness in the mosquito. The mosquito transfers the virus to uninfected animals and humans when it feeds. Bird deaths are an early warning sign of a West Nile virus outbreak, which can spread quickly without prompt action.

TABLE 15.4 Emerging Infections

Microorganism	Related Disease
Bacteria	
Borrelia burgdorferi	Lyme disease
Campylobacter jejuni	Diarrhea
Escherichia coli 0157:H7	Hemorrhagic colitis, hemolytic-uremic syndrome
Helicobacter pylori	Peptic ulcer disease
Legionella pneumophila	Pneumonia (Legionnaires disease)
Vibrio cholerae 0139	New strain of epidemic cholera
Virus	
Chikungunya	Fever, muscle aches, rash
Ebola virus	Ebola hemorrhagic fever
H1N1	H1N1 (swine) flu
Hantavirus	Hemorrhagic fever with severe pulmonary syndrome
Hepatitis C virus	Parenterally transmitted hepatitis
Hepatitis E virus	Enterically transmitted hepatitis
Human immunodeficiency virus (HIV)	HIV infection and AIDS
Human herpesvirus 6 (HHV-6)	Roseola subitum
Human herpesvirus 8 (HHV-8)	Causes Kaposi sarcoma in immunosuppressed patients, including people with HIV infection
SARS-Cov-2	COVID-19
West Nile virus	West Nile fever
Zika virus	Fever, rash, muscle aches; microcephaly in children born to infected mothers
Parasite	
Cryptosporidium parvum	Acute and chronic diarrhea

Influenza viruses are examples of how disease can spread between animals and humans. Variants of influenza A viruses are responsible for many influenza epidemics. We traced the 2009 influenza A (H1N1) outbreak to pigs, hence the name *swine flu.* In 1997 and 2003, outbreaks of the influenza A (H5N1) strain of avian flu resulted from transmission of influenza virus from chickens to humans.

Coronaviruses are a group of viruses that can circulate between animals and humans. These viruses get their name because of their crown-like structure. Most coronaviruses cause respiratory illnesses in humans, including pneumonia. The most notable coronavirus is SARS-CoV-2. It is the virus that causes COVID-19.

Unlike other recent infectious disease outbreaks, the COVID-19 pandemic was unique. The rapid spread of the infection, high mortality rate, unexpected strain on the health care system, massive quarantine initiatives, and global response had not been seen with other infectious disease outbreaks. Major issues at the beginning of the pandemic included the limited amount of information about how the virus was transmitted and how to treat and prevent infection. Researchers and clinicians worked rapidly to develop and deploy diagnostic tests, effective treatments, and preventive vaccines.

Reemerging Infections

While vaccines and treatments have led to the near eradication of some infections (e.g., smallpox, polio), infective agents can reemerge under the right conditions. Factors such as population density, inadequate sanitation, antibiotic misuse, and bioterrorism have increased the risk for widespread distribution of these infections. Domestic outbreaks have typically occurred in areas with low vaccination rates. For example, infections such as measles, diphtheria, and pertussis have had sporadic resurgences. This is in part due to people not receiving recommended vaccines.

International travel is an obstacle for the eradication of some diseases. For example, measles is no longer endemic in the United States but is still a leading cause of death in developing countries. Some cases occurred in people who have recently traveled to measles-endemic areas outside the United States.

Antimicrobial-Resistant Infections

Resistance occurs when pathogenic organisms change in ways that decrease the ability of a drug (or a family of drugs) to treat disease.[3] Microorganisms can become resistant to classic treatments (e.g., penicillin) as well as to newer antimicrobial agents. Microorganisms are highly adaptable. They have evolved genetic and biochemical mechanisms to defend against antimicrobials. Genetic mechanisms include mutation and acquisition of new DNA or RNA. Biochemically, bacteria can resist antibiotics by making enzymes that destroy or inactivate the drugs. Drug target sites are then altered so that the antibiotic cannot bind to or enter the bacteria. If the drug cannot enter the cell, it cannot kill the bacteria. Table 15.5 describes common antibiotic-resistant bacteria.

TABLE 15.5 Common Antibiotic-Resistant Organisms and Treatment

Bacteria	Resistant to	Preferred Treatment
Enterococcus faecalis	vancomycin streptomycin gentamicin	daptomycin (Cubicin) linezolid (Zyvox) oritavancin (Orbactiv) tigecycline (Tygacil)
Enterococcus faecium	vancomycin streptomycin gentamicin	daptomycin (Cubicin) linezolid (Zyvox) tigecycline (Tygacil)
Klebsiella pneumoniae	carbapenems (e.g., imipenem, meropenem)	ceftazidime and avibactam (Avycaz)
Streptococcus pneumoniae	penicillin G	ceftriaxone cefotaxime

Drug-resistant bacteria were first seen in health care settings but are becoming more prevalent in the community. For example, we initially considered methicillin-resistant *S. aureus* (MRSA), a form of *S. aureus* that does not respond to methicillin- or penicillin-based therapies, a health care–associated infection (HA-MRSA). However, a variant strain of MRSA that is primarily acquired in the community (community-acquired MRSA [CA-MRSA]) has emerged.[4] This strain of MRSA is more *virulent* (able to cause disease or infection) compared with HA-MRSA. CA-MRSA can cause rapidly forming skin infections and systemic diseases, including pneumonia and sepsis. Vancomycin-resistant enterococci (VRE) infection is another concern for patients and health care workers. VRE are more virulent than MRSA and can survive on environmental surfaces for weeks. Although antibiotic-resistant bacteria can infect anyone, hospitalized patients and those with a suppressed immune system are more likely to be exposed to these bacteria and develop infection.

HCPs have contributed to the development of drug-resistant microorganisms by (1) giving antibiotics for viral infections, (2) succumbing to patient pressure to prescribe unnecessary antibiotic therapy, (3) using inadequate drug regimens to treat infections, or (4) using broad-spectrum or combination agents for infections that should be treated with first line agents.

Patients can contribute to resistance development by (1) skipping doses, (2) not taking antibiotics for the full duration of prescribed therapy, or (3) saving unused antibiotics "in case I need them later." In addition, limited resources and access to care make it hard for some patients to get adequate treatment for infections. The Centers for Disease Control and Prevention (CDC), the Infectious Diseases Society of America (IDSA), and many health care organizations campaign for the proper use of antibiotics in reaction to this problem.

Although antibiotics are a class of drugs that we typically think of when discussing drug-resistant organisms, any organism (virus, fungi, parasite) can develop drug resistance to agents typically used to treat them. This is why we now use the term *antimicrobial resistance* to describe resistance across different classes of organisms.

Health Care–Associated Infections

Health care–associated infections (HAIs) are infections that are acquired because of exposure to microorganisms in a health care setting.[5] About 722,000 HAIs occur annually. Nearly 1 in every 25 hospitalized patients has at least 1 HAI. Around one-third of HAIs are preventable. HCPs often transmit HAIs from patient to patient through direct contact. Improvements in infection control have resulted in fewer infections in recent years. We have seen decreases in several major types of HAIs. These include central line–associated bloodstream infections (CLABSIs), catheter-associated urinary tract infections (CAUTIs), surgical site infections (SSIs), *Clostridioides difficile* infections, and MRSA bacteremia.

Any organism can cause HAIs, but certain bacteria, including *E. coli, S. aureus, Enterobacter aerogenes,* and various types of streptococci, are most common. Some bacteria that do not normally cause disease can cause infections in high-risk patients because of illness or treatment of illness. Surgical and immunocompromised patients are at highest risk.

NURSING MANAGEMENT: INFECTION

You play a key role in reducing the risk of infection by prioritizing infection control in practice. Assess the patient's risk for infection, noting factors that increase risk (Table 15.6). Monitor for signs and symptoms of infection on an ongoing basis. Create a safe environment that addresses the patient's risks (Table 15.7). Provide education to patients and caregivers aimed at reducing infection risk.

Infections vary by severity, location, the patient's response to treatment, and the potential for harm. Managing infections requires both treating the infection and providing supportive care. The main treatment goal is to eradicate the infection.

Many nursing interventions are supportive. Provide measures to manage pain, fatigue, and fever (see Table 12.5). Monitor for problems with fluid and electrolyte balance. Administer antimicrobials and IV fluids as prescribed. Helping the patient maintain adequate nutrition and rest is important.

Antimicrobial Therapy

Antimicrobial therapy is the main treatment for many infections. Laboratory testing helps to determine the right antimicrobial. Common classes of antibiotics are shown in Table 15.8. Antibiotics within a class tend to have similar effectiveness, side effects, and allergic potential.

Spectrum refers to the number of organisms affected by an antibiotic (broad or narrow spectrum). Activity refers to how an antibiotic kills bacteria. Bactericidal agents attack and kill the bacteria directly. Bacteriostatic agents interfere with bacterial replication.

Before giving any antibiotic, obtain a history of any allergic reactions. Have you collected any needed cultures? Perform baseline and infection-specific assessments. Ensure baseline laboratory results, such as liver function tests, are done. Set up an around the clock dosing schedule to maintain effective blood levels. Review all drugs the patient is taking to make sure oral agents are not given at the same time as antacids and products containing calcium, iron, or magnesium.

During therapy, monitor the patient for adverse effects, including allergic reactions and superinfections. Superinfections can occur when antibiotics reduce or eliminate the normal bacterial flora. This allows other bacteria or fungi to take over and cause infection. Teaching patients and caregivers the proper use

TABLE 15.6 Risk Factors for Infection

- Age
- Autoimmune disease
- Being unimmunized
- Burns
- Cancer and its treatment
- Chronic kidney disease
- Chronic obstructive pulmonary disease (COPD)
- Crowded or unsanitary living conditions
- Debilitation
- Diabetes
- High-risk sexual behavior
- Impaired immune function
- Impaired nutrition
- Indwelling urinary catheter
- Invasive lines and mechanical ventilation
- IV drug use
- Lack of preventative health care
- Liver disease
- Low socioeconomic status
- Medications: Antimicrobials, biologic response modifiers, corticosteroids
- Poor hand hygiene
- Recent surgery
- Recent travel, especially outside the United States or to an underdeveloped area
- Recurrent infections
- Trauma (physical, emotional)

TABLE 15.7 NURSING MANAGEMENT

Infection Prevention

- Perform screening and assess for signs and symptoms of infection, implementing appropriate actions as needed.
- Perform hand washing or use an alcohol-based hand sanitizer before and after patient contact or procedures.
- Appropriately use PPE.
- Change gloves and wash hands when moving between tasks, even when working with the same patient.
- Implement appropriate transmission-based precautions.
- Ensure all reusable equipment is properly cleaned before use with a new patient.
- Avoid or limit use of invasive interventions when possible.
- Give antimicrobial therapy as prescribed (Table 15.8).
- Use proper technique when performing procedures that require aseptic technique.
- Ensure all environmental surfaces are properly cleaned, disinfected, and maintained.
- Implement specific care bundles to prevent CAUTI, SSI, CLABSI, and VAP.
- Properly dispose of patient-care equipment contaminated with blood, body fluid, secretions, and excretions.
- Maintain closed catheter systems, such as those used for hemodynamic monitoring, chest tubes, urinary catheters, and IV infusions, when possible.

TABLE 15.8 Drug Therapy

Antibiotics

Drug	Action	Side Effects	Considerations
Aminoglycosides amikacin gentamycin neomycin tobramycin	Bacteriocidal Inhibits protein synthesis of many gram-negative bacteria	GI distress Kidney toxicity Ototoxicity	Encourage fluids Monitor kidney function and hearing Give IM dose by deep injection
Cephalosporins 1st-generation: cefazolin, cephalexin 2nd-generation: cefaclor, cefoxitin, cefuroxime 3rd-generation: cefdinir, ceftriaxone 4th-generation: cefepime 5th-generation: ceftaroline	Bacteriocidal Inhibits bacterial cell wall synthesis	Allergic reactions Bleeding GI distress Rash	Take with food Avoid alcohol while taking Monitor kidney function Cross allergy with penicillins Have Vitamin K available if bleeding occurs
Fluoroquinolones ciprofloxacin levofloxacin	Bacteriocidal Interferes with DNA replication in gram-negative bacteria	GI distress Headache Kidney toxicity Photosensitivity Rash Tendonitis	Monitor kidney function tests Take 1 hr before or 2 hr after meals Encourage fluids
Lincosamides clindamycin	Bacteriostatic and bacteriocidal Inhibits bacterial protein synthesis	Allergic reactions Colitis GI distress Liver toxicity Rash	Monitor liver function tests Take with a full glass of water Give IM dose by deep injection
Macrolides azithromycin erythromycin	Bacteriostatic and bacteriocidal Inhibits bacterial protein and cell wall synthesis	GI distress Liver toxicity Mental status changes	Take 1 hr before or 2 hr after meals Take with a full glass of water, avoiding juice Monitor liver function tests
Penicillins amoxicillin ampicillin nafcillin penicillin G penicillin V	Bacteriocidal Inhibits bacterial cell wall synthesis	Allergic reactions GI distress Rash	Give IM dose by deep injection, rotating sites Take with a full glass of water, avoid juice Monitor IV site frequently
Sulfonamides trimethoprim/ sulfamethoxazole	Bacteriostatic Prevent bacterial synthesis of folic acid	Allergic reactions GI distress Liver toxicity Kidney toxicity Peripheral neuropathy Photosensitivity Stomatitis	Take with food and a full glass of water Protect from sunlight exposure Monitor liver and kidney function tests
Tetracyclines doxycycline minocycline tetracycline	Bacteriostatic Inhibits bacterial protein synthesis	GI distress Photosensitivity Rash	Avoid use in pregnancy Protect from sunlight exposure Take 1 hr before or 2 hr after meals Avoid dairy products, antacids, iron
Vancomycin	Bacteriocidal Inhibits bacterial cell wall synthesis	Kidney toxicity Ototoxicity Rash Thrombophlebitis	Monitor kidney function and hearing Monitor IV site frequently

of antibiotics (Table 15.9) is crucial to treatment success and preventing drug-resistant pathogens.

Currently, antiviral therapy is available for a small number of viral infections. These drugs target viruses that cause herpes, hepatitis, varicella, and some influenza infections. Most antiviral drugs work by suppressing viral replication. Table 15.10 shows some common drugs used to treat herpes and cytomegalovirus infections. See Table 48.7 for the drug therapy for hepatitis infection and Chapter 29 for information about influenza treatment.

Antifungals are a fairly small group of drugs (Table 15.11). They fall into 2 major groups: drugs for systemic infections and drugs for local infections. A few drugs treat both. Systemic fungal infections and some localized ones are

TABLE 15.9 PATIENT & CAREGIVER TEACHING

Decreasing the Risk for Antibiotic-Resistant Infection

Include the following instructions when teaching patients or their caregivers how to decrease the risk for antibiotic-resistant infection:

1. Only Take Antibiotics Prescribed for You
   - This decreases your risk for developing resistant infection.
   - You may need antibiotics before surgery or dental work or in the presence of immune dysfunction.
2. Wash Your Hands Frequently
   - Hand washing is the single most important thing you can do to prevent infection.
3. Follow Directions When Taking Antibiotics
   - Not taking your antibiotic as prescribed or skipping doses can allow antibiotic-resistant bacteria to develop.
4. Do Not Request an Antibiotic for Flu or Colds
   - If your HCP says that you do not need an antibiotic, chances are you do not.
   - Antibiotics are effective against bacterial infections but not viruses, which cause colds and flu.
5. Finish Your Antibiotic
   - Do not stop taking your antibiotic when you feel better.
   - If you stop taking your antibiotic early, the hardiest bacteria survive and multiply.
   - Eventually you could develop an infection resistant to any antibiotics. You should never have leftover antibiotics.
6. Do Not Take Leftover Antibiotics
   - Do not save unfinished antibiotics for later use or borrow leftover drugs from family or friends.
   - This is dangerous because (1) the leftover antibiotic may not be appropriate for you, (2) your illness may not be a bacterial infection, (3) old antibiotics can lose their effectiveness and, in some cases, can be fatal, and (4) there will not be enough doses in a leftover bottle to provide full treatment.

TABLE 15.10 Drug Therapy

Antivirals for Herpes and Cytomegalovirus Infections

Drug	Indications	Side Effects	Considerations
acyclovir (Zovirax)	CMV HSV VZV	Diarrhea Headache Irritation (topical)	Given PO, IV, topical. Encourage fluids. Monitor kidney function. Monitor IV site frequently. Give IV dose over at least 1 hr.
cidofovir	CMV	GI distress Kidney toxicity	Given IV. Monitor kidney function.
famciclovir	HSV VZV	Fatigue Fever GI distress Headache	Given PO. Encourage fluids. Monitor CBC and kidney function.
foscarnet (Foscavir)	CMV HSV VZV	Electrolyte imbalances GI distress Headache Liver toxicity Kidney toxicity Seizures	Given IV. Monitor kidney and liver function. Monitor serum electrolytes.
ganciclovir	CMV	Bleeding Neutropenia Sore throat	Given IV, PO, ocular. Monitor CBC. Avoid use in pregnancy. Monitor IV site frequently.
valacyclovir (Valtrex)	HSV VZV	GI distress Headache	Given PO. Encourage fluids. Monitor CBC and kidney function.
valganciclovir (Valcyte)	CMV	Anemia GI Distress	Given PO. Monitor CBC. Do not crush; avoid contact with powder. Avoid use in pregnancy. Encourage fluids.

CMV, Cytomegalovirus; *HSV*, herpes simplex virus; *VZV*, varicella-zoster virus.

treated with oral or IV drugs. Fungi are often very difficult to kill, and resistance is common. Many drugs have potential toxicity problems.

Occupational Safety and Health Administration (OSHA) Guidelines

OSHA is a federal agency that protects workers from injury and illness in places of employment and supports activities that minimize or eliminate exposure to infectious materials in the workplace. OSHA mandates that any employer whose employees could be exposed to potentially infectious materials implement standard policies and procedures to protect those employees. Employees must be provided with appropriate **personal protective equipment (PPE)**, which are items that prevent infection or injury to the wearer.[6] PPE includes gloves, gowns, facial protection, and disposal systems for sharps (Table 15.12). PPE also must be provided in the right sizes. Hypoallergenic gloves or similar alternatives must be made available to those who have an allergic sensitivity to gloves.

Appropriate PPE varies depending on the situation. You need to use sound judgment when deciding when and how to use PPE. Knowing how to properly put on and take off PPE is important for the health and safety of you and your patients. Isolated infections can be caused when bacteria that normally stay in one area of the body are introduced into another area. Therefore you must take care to change gloves and wash hands when moving from one task to another, even when working with the same patient.

Infection Precautions

The CDC has established guidelines with 2 levels of precautions: (1) **standard precautions**, designed for the care of all patients in hospitals and health care facilities, and (2) **transmission-based precautions**, designed for specific diseases.[7] The purpose of precautions is to prevent the transmission of organisms from patients to HCPs, from HCPs to patients, from patients to other patients, and from health care personnel and patients to people outside of the hospital (Table 15.13).

TABLE 15.11 Antifungals

Drug	Route	Side Effects	Considerations
Echinocandins			
anidulafungin (Eraxis)	IV	GI distress Hypokalemia Liver toxicity Peripheral edema	Encourage fluid intake. Monitor CBC, electrolytes, and liver function tests. Avoid use in pregnancy.
caspofungin (Cancidas)	IV	GI distress Infusion-related reaction Liver toxicity	Monitor CBC and liver function tests. Monitor for problems during IV infusion. Avoid use in pregnancy.
micafungin (Mycamine)	IV	Cognitive changes GI distress Liver toxicity Kidney toxicity	Monitor kidney and liver function tests. Infuse over at least 1 hr. Avoid use in pregnancy.
Imidazoles			
ketoconazole (Extina, Xolegel)	PO, topical	GI distress Rash, burning (topical)	Do not take PO within 2 hr of drugs that affect stomach acid.
Polyenes			
amphotericin B (Abelcet, Ambisome)	IV	Bone marrow suppression Dysrhythmias Electrolyte imbalances Infusion-related reaction Kidney toxicity	Monitor CBC, electrolytes, and kidney function. Pretreat before IV dose with antipyretics, antihistamines, antiemetics, and/or corticosteroids as ordered. Monitor vital signs and IV site frequently during infusion.
nystatin	PO, Topical	GI distress Rash, burning	Do not eat or drink 30 min after oral treatment. Remove dentures before oral treatment. Do not use while breast feeding.
Triazoles			
fluconazole (Diflucan)	IV, PO	Bone marrow suppression Dysrhythmias GI distress Liver toxicity	Monitor CBC and liver function tests.
isavuconazonium (Cresemba)	IV, PO	Cognitive changes GI distress Liver toxicity Infusion-related reaction Kidney toxicity Peripheral edema	Monitor kidney and liver function tests. Monitor I and O, daily weights. Avoid use in pregnancy.
itraconazole (Sporanox, Tolsura)	PO	GI distress Hepatitis	Take tablets with food. Take solution on an empty stomach. Monitor liver function tests. Avoid use in pregnancy.
posaconazole (Noxafil)	IV, PO	BP changes Cough Dysrhythmias Edema Fatigue GI distress Musculoskeletal pain	Monitor vital signs and ECG frequently. May need antiemetic agent. Give PO with food. Avoid use in pregnancy.
voriconazole (Vfend)	IV, PO	Dysrhythmias GI distress Hallucinations Liver toxicity Kidney toxicity Photophobia, vision changes	Monitor kidney and liver function tests. Monitor vision function with long-term therapy. Take on empty stomach. Avoid use in pregnancy.

TABLE 15.12 OSHA Requirements for PPE

The following equipment minimizes exposure to blood-borne pathogens.

Equipment	Indications for Use
Gloves	• Must be used when the employee can reasonably expect having contact with blood or other potentially infectious materials, when performing vascular access procedures, and when handling or touching contaminated items or surfaces. • Gloves must be replaced if torn, punctured, or contaminated or their ability to function as a barrier is compromised.
Clothing (gowns, aprons, caps, boots)	• Must be used when occupational exposure is expected. • The type and characteristics depend on the task and degree of exposure expected.
Face protection (mask and glasses with solid side shields or a chin-length face shield)	• Must be used when splashes, sprays, spatters, or droplets of blood or other potentially infectious materials pose a hazard to the eyes, nose, or mouth.

Source: Occupational Safety and Health Administration (OSHA): Blood-borne pathogens and needlestick prevention. Retrieved from www.osha.gov/SLTC/bloodbornepathogens.

TABLE 15.13 Isolation Precautions Used in Health Care Settings

Type	Examples
Standard Precautions	
• Used for care of all patients, regardless of diagnosis or presumed infection status	Includes the use of hand washing and appropriate PPE
Transmission-Based Precautions	
• Provides additional precautions beyond standard precautions to prevent transmission of pathogens • Used for patients known or suspected to be infected or colonized with pathogens that can be transmitted by airborne or droplet transmission, or by contact with dry skin or contaminated surfaces • Used in addition to standard precautions	**Airborne precautions:** Used for infections spread in small particles in the air, such as chickenpox (varicella), measles, TB **Droplet precautions:** Used for infections spread in large droplets by coughing, talking, or sneezing, such as influenza and bacterial meningitis **Contact precautions:** Used for infections spread by skin-to-skin contact or contact with other surfaces, such as *C. difficile*, MRSA, and VRE

Standard precautions apply to (1) blood; (2) all body fluids, secretions, and excretions; (3) nonintact skin; and (4) mucous membranes. Standard precautions are designed to reduce the risk for transmission of microorganisms in hospitals. They should be applied to *all* patients regardless of diagnosis or presumed infection status. Standard precautions include all the OSHA blood-borne pathogens standard requirements.

Transmission-based precautions are used for patients known to be or suspected of being infected with highly transmissible or epidemiologically important pathogens that require additional precautions to interrupt transmission and prevent infection. Transmission-based precautions include airborne precautions, droplet precautions, and contact precautions. *Airborne precautions* are used if the organism can cause infection over long distances when suspended in the air (e.g., TB, rubeola). *Droplet precautions* minimize contact with pathogens that spread through the air at close contact and that affect the respiratory system or mucous membranes (e.g., influenza, pertussis). *Contact precautions* minimize the spread of pathogens that are acquired from direct or indirect contact, especially multidrug-resistant organisms (e.g., MRSA, VRE, CRE). Transmission-based precautions may be combined for diseases with multiple routes of transmission. Whether used alone or in combination, transmission-based precautions should always be used in conjunction with standard precautions.

CHECK YOUR PRACTICE

You are caring for a patient on contact precautions and need assistance with lifting the patient up in bed. You ask the AP for help. After helping you, the AP leaves the room and only removes their gloves without removing their protective gown. The AP then enters another patient's room with the gown still on.

What should you do in this situation?

Gerontologic Considerations: Infections in Older Adults

The rate of HAIs is 2 to 3 times higher in older adults. This risk is higher for persons in long-term care facilities. Age-related changes (e.g., impaired immune function) and co-morbidities, such as diabetes and physical disabilities, contribute to the higher infection rates.

Infections common in older adults include pneumonia, urinary tract infections (UTIs), skin infections, and TB. UTIs are more common in those who live in long-term care facilities. Patients with indwelling catheters are at particular risk.

Infections in older adults often have atypical manifestations, such as cognitive and behavior changes, before they develop fever, pain, or changes in laboratory values. Do not rely on the presence of fever to indicate infection in older adults. Many have lower core body temperatures and decreased immune responses. We should suspect a problem if a patient shows changes in the ability to perform daily activities or cognitive function. Underlying diseases and increased frequency of drug reactions can complicate the treatment of an older adult with infection.

COVID-19

The COVID-19 pandemic forever impacted communities worldwide. Since the infection was first recognized in 2019, it has caused significant morbidity and mortality globally. During the first year of the pandemic, we estimate 2.33 million people died from COVID-19 infection. That number has exponentially

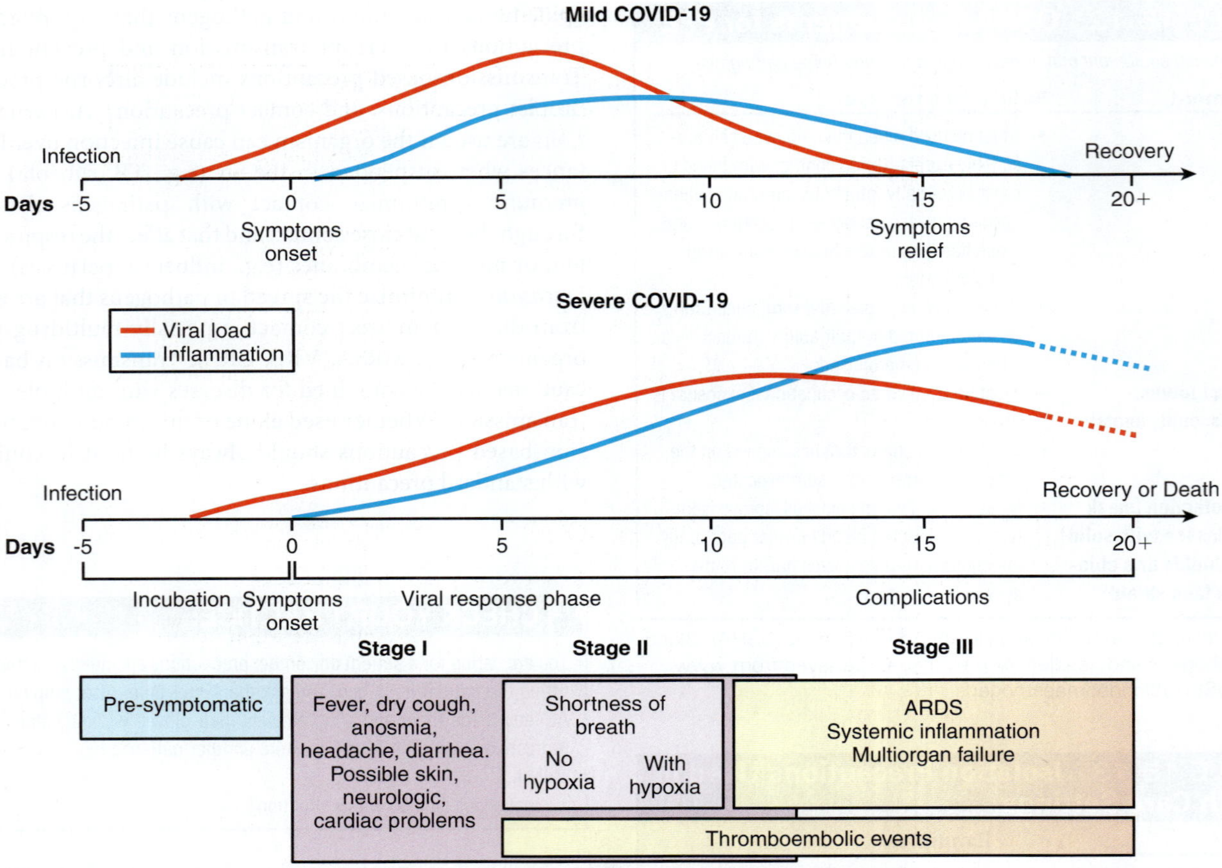

Fig. 15.1 The time course of the immune response in COVID-19 infection.

increased. COVID-19 mainly spreads through respiratory droplets. Once infected, the incubation period can be up to 14 days. During this period, persons with COVID-19 may not show any symptoms but can transmit the infection to others.

Pathophysiology

Like other coronaviruses, SARS-CoV-2 is an RNA virus that is surrounded by a protein envelope that has "spikes" on the outer surface.[8] These spikes give the virus a crown-like appearance (hence the name "corona," which means crown). The spikes from the virus's outer envelope bind with angiotensin-converting enzyme 2 (ACE2) receptors in the host, which allow entry of virus into cells. The virus tends to infect cells within the upper respiratory tract. Research suggests that cells within the conjunctiva and gastrointestinal tract may also be sites of entry. Once infected, cell-mediated and humoral immune responses occur. These immune responses lead to a release of cytokines and disruption of cellular integrity.

The time from infection to initial symptoms is thought to be about 5 days. For mild cases of COVID-19, symptoms and immune response peak within the first week. In more severe cases, a significant inflammatory cascade is triggered, leading to acute respiratory distress syndrome (ARDS) and multiorgan dysfunction (MODS) (Fig. 15.1). See Chapter 32 for more about ARDS and Chapter 42 about MODS.

One of the challenges in battling COVID-19 is the appearance of viral variants. Variants occur when the virus mutates slightly. This can result in a variety of different outcomes, including a virus that is more infectious or one that may not respond to established treatments or vaccines. There is ongoing monitoring of viral variants across the globe.[9]

TABLE 15.14 Manifestations of COVID-19

- Cough
- Diarrhea
- Dyspnea
- Fatigue
- Fever
- Headache
- Muscle or body aches
- Nausea and vomiting
- New loss of taste or smell
- Sore throat
- Runny nose, congestion

Other symptoms may include:

- Malaise
- Mental status changes
- Respiratory distress
- Sputum production

Adapted from CDC. Retrieved from https://www.cdc.gov/coronavirus/2019-ncov/hcp/clinical-guidance-management-patients.html.

Clinical Manifestations and Complications

Manifestations vary widely (Table 15.14). Some patients may be asymptomatic or have a mild flu-like illness with fever, fatigue,

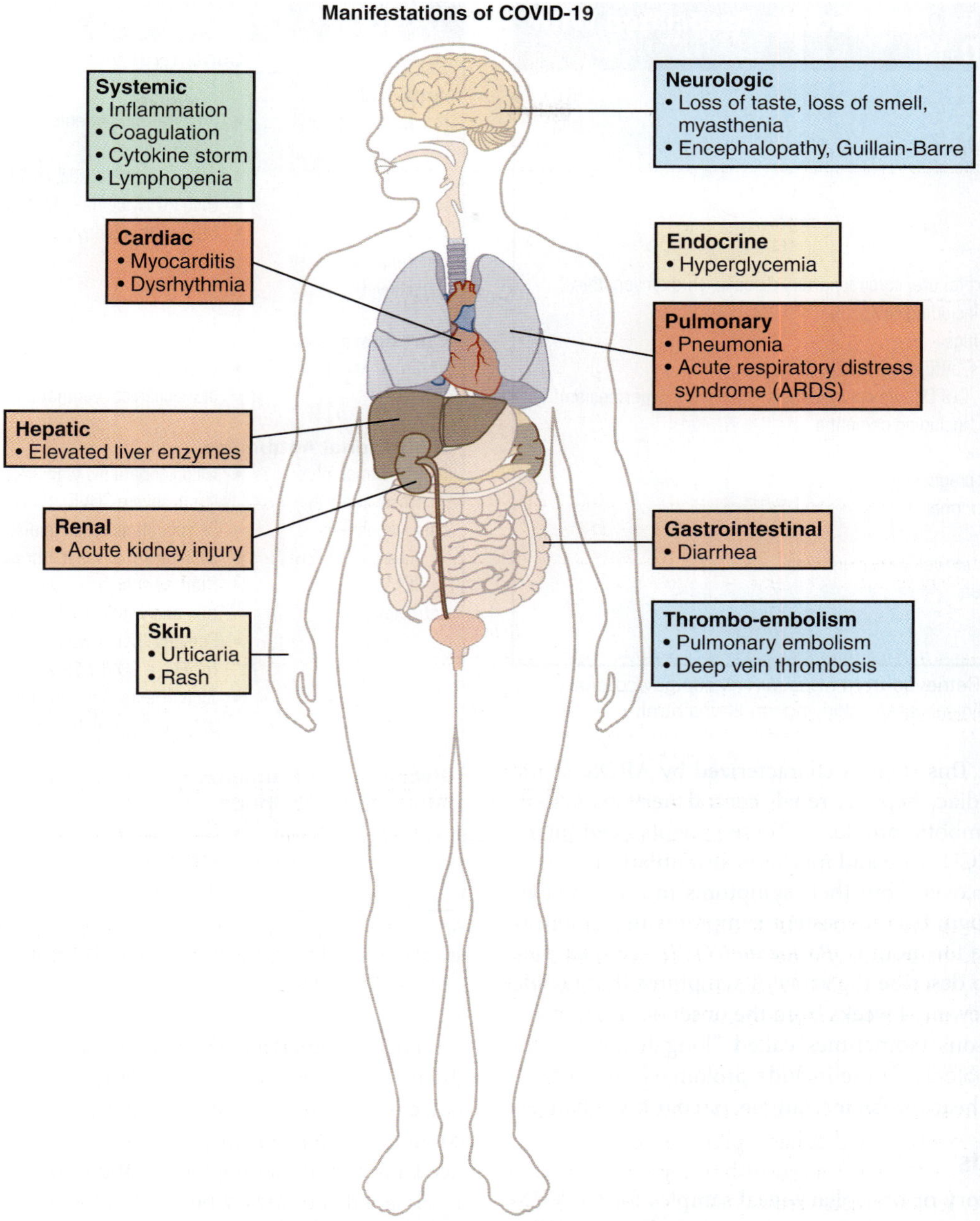

Fig. 15.2 Manifestations of COVID-19 infection.

and changes in taste or smell. Others develop serious pneumonia and respiratory failure. COVID-19 can also present with broad cardiac, neurologic, and skin manifestations (Fig. 15.2). COVID-19 is most severe in older persons and those with preexisting conditions (Table 15.15). Children infected with COVID-19 are more likely than adults to be asymptomatic or to have only mild symptoms.

The clinical spectrum of COVID-19 varies significantly. The range of illness has been classified into 5 categories:[10]

- Asymptomatic or presymptomatic infection. This occurs when someone has evidence of infection on a viral test for COVID-19 but has no symptoms.
- Mild illness. People with mild illness may have cough, fever, loss of taste or smell, general malaise, sore throat, or diarrhea. They usually do not have shortness of breath or abnormalities seen on radiographic testing. Most people with mild illness can be managed at home.
- Moderate illness. People have similar symptoms as those with mild illness, but they usually have more significant signs of respiratory illness, including signs of pneumonia.
- Severe illness. Patients with severe illness typically have decreased oxygenation (SpO_2 <94% on room air, respiratory rate >30 breaths/min, lung infiltrates >50%). They may have signs of sepsis.

TABLE 15.15 Risk Factors Associated With Severe COVID-19

Age (≥65 years)
Cancer
Cerebrovascular disease
Chronic kidney disease
Cystic fibrosis
Diabetes
Down syndrome
Heart conditions (heart failure, coronary artery disease, cardiomyopathies)
Immune deficiencies, including HIV
Immunosuppressive drugs
Liver disease (cirrhosis, autoimmune hepatitis)
Lung disease (asthma, COPD, pulmonary fibrosis, pulmonary hypertension)
Neurologic conditions, including dementia
Obesity, overweight
Pregnancy and recent pregnancy
Smoking (current and former)
Sickle cell disease
Solid organ or blood stem cell transplantation
Substance use disorders
Thalassemia
Tuberculosis

Adapted from CDC. Retrieved from https://www.cdc.gov/coronavirus/2019-ncov/hcp/clinical-care/underlyingconditions.html.

- Critical illness. This stage is characterized by ARDS, septic shock, and cardiac, hepatic, renal, central nervous system (CNS), or thrombotic problems. These patients need intensive care unit (ICU) care and mechanical ventilation.

Most people recover from their symptoms in a few weeks. Some people, though, have persistent symptoms or complications that continue for months. *Postacute COVID-19 syndrome* is the term used to describe the array of symptoms that people have that persist beyond 4 weeks from the onset of initial infection.[11] These persons (sometimes called "long haulers") can have lingering problems. These include prolonged loss of taste or smell, dyspnea, heart problems, fatigue, or cognitive changes.

Diagnostic Tests

Testing of respiratory or oral-pharyngeal samples for COVID-19 through reverse transcription polymerase chain reaction (RT-PCR), also known as nucleic acid amplification testing (NAAT), is the gold standard for diagnosis. Antigen testing is available but is less reliable. Antibody testing detects antibodies to COVID-19. It is used to determine past infection or can be seen in vaccinated persons.

Laboratory findings with COVID-19 include lymphopenia, increased liver enzymes, low albumin, low platelets, high inflammatory markers (C-reactive protein, ferritin, sedimentation rate), increased D dimer, and increased lactate dehydrogenase. Chest CT imaging may show diffuse may show opacities. In a small percent of people, imaging studies may be normal.[10]

Interprofessional and Nursing Management

Most patients with asymptomatic, mild, or moderate COVID-19 can be treated on an outpatient basis. Advise them to follow quarantine restrictions. Keep up to date with your agency and

TABLE 15.16 COVID-19 Therapy

Agent	Considerations
Antiviral	
remdesivir (Veklury)	• Hospitalized patients who need supplemental O_2 • IV infusion • Side effects: Nausea, increased liver function tests
molnupiravir	• Give PO twice daily for 5 days
ritonavir-boosted nirmatrelvir (Paxlovid)	• Start within 5 days of symptom onset
Corticosteroids	
dexamethasone	• Hospitalized patients who need supplemental O_2 or mechanical ventilation
Monoclonal Antibodies	
bamlanivimab plus etesevimab casirivimab plus imdevimab (REGEN-COV) sotrovimab	• Mild For patients who are at high-risk of progressing to severe COVID-19 and/or hospitalization • IV, subcutaneous administration • Monitor for at least 1 hr post IV infusion • Start as soon as possible after confirmed infection and within 10 days of symptom onset • Persons should wait 90 days after treatment to receive a COVID-19 vaccine • Side effects: Nausea, diarrhea, dizziness, headache, itching, vomiting, fever
Recombinant Humanized Anti-Interleukin-6 Receptor Monoclonal Antibody	
tocilizumab (Actemra)	• Can be added to patients receiving dexamethasone therapy who have rapid respiratory decompensation

Adapted from National Institutes of Health: COVID-19 treatment guidelines. Retrieved from https://www.covid19treatmentguidelines.nih.gov/therapeutic-management.

local health department's recommendations on quarantining as these policies may change regularly. Teach patients the importance of good hand washing and oral hygiene. Discuss when to contact the HCP for in-person evaluation. Some patients may need additional therapy for specific symptoms.

Hospitalization may be needed for the severely ill or debilitated patient. In the acute care setting it is important to follow agency policies for isolation and transmission-based precautions. Nursing care focuses on monitoring of respiratory status and hemodynamics. Patients may decline rapidly and need transition to the ICU. Provide measures to decrease symptoms, such as acetaminophen for fever.

Disease-specific treatments include monoclonal antibodies and antiviral agents (Table 15.16). Monoclonal antibodies are laboratory-made proteins that mimic the immune system and attack infectious agents, like COVID-19. Nausea and increased liver enzymes are possible with remdesivir. Given the rapidly evolving nature of the pandemic, many treatments are initially made available under an *emergency use authorization* (EUA) by the US Food and Drug Administration (FDA). An EUA provides early access to treatments during a public health emergency that have potential benefit but are not officially approved by the FDA. Access and availability of these treatment options may be limited depending on your work setting.

Vaccines

A little over a year after the first cases of COVID-19 were identified, the first vaccines for COVID-19 became available for general use. These vaccine mechanisms include messenger RNA (mRNA) vaccines and viral vector vaccines.[12] *mRNA vaccines* use a technology that provides instructions to the hosts' immune cells to create one of the "spike proteins" found on the outer coating of COVID-19. This helps the body create antibodies to the protein. The vaccines do not change your genes (it never gets inside the nucleus). The mRNA is destroyed soon after it completes giving instructions to the immune system. These vaccines do not contain any live virus. They do not cause someone to get COVID-19 infection.

Viral vector vaccines use a harmless version of another virus (in the case of COVID-19, adenovirus is used) to act as a transport mechanism to deliver genetic material to the cells. The viral vector vaccine contains a small piece of DNA that triggers the body's immune system to create antibodies to the spike protein found on COVID-19. The DNA does not change or interact with the host's DNA in any other way.

Common vaccine side effects are similar. They include injection site reactions, fatigue, tiredness, fever, and muscle pain. Teaching patients about vaccination and potential side effects is an important nursing action.

HUMAN IMMUNODEFICIENCY VIRUS INFECTION

Human immunodeficiency virus (HIV) is a retrovirus that causes immunosuppression. More than 1.2 million people are living with HIV in the United States. About 36,400 new infections occur annually.[13] In North America, men who have sex with men (MSM) account for the largest group of persons living with HIV. With effective treatment, HIV is considered a chronic condition.

HIV Transmission

HIV can be transmitted through contact with infected blood, semen, vaginal secretions, or breast milk. It is not spread by tears, saliva, urine, emesis, sputum, feces, sweat, respiratory droplets, or enteric routes. HIV is not spread casually. The virus cannot be transmitted through hugging, dry kissing, shaking hands, sharing eating utensils, or using toilet seats. Health care personnel have a low risk for acquiring HIV at work, even after a needle-stick injury.

Sexual Transmission

The most common mode of transmission is unprotected sexual contact with a person who has a high HIV viral load. It is not possible to transmit HIV sexually if the person with HIV has an undetectable viral load.[14] This concept of not being able to sexually transmit HIV with an undetectable viral load is also known as "U=U" or undetectable equals untransmittable. Sexual activity involves contact with semen, vaginal secretions, and/or blood, all of which have lymphocytes that may contain HIV. Sexual activities that cause trauma to local tissues increase the risk for transmission. Genital lesions from other sexually transmitted infections (STIs), such as herpes or syphilis, increase the chance of transmission.

Contact With Blood and Blood Products

HIV can be transmitted from exposure to blood when sharing drug-using paraphernalia. Needles, syringes, straws, and other equipment may be contaminated with HIV or other bloodborne organisms.

Routine screening of blood donors to identify at-risk persons and testing donated blood for the presence of HIV have improved the safety of the blood supply. In countries that routinely test donated blood, HIV infection because of blood transfusions or hemophilia clotting factors is unlikely.

Puncture wounds are the most common means of work-related HIV transmission. The risk for infection after a needlestick exposure to HIV-infected blood is around 0.3%.[15] The risk is higher if the exposure involves blood from a patient with a high level of circulating HIV, a deep puncture wound, a needle with a hollow bore and visible blood, or a device used for venous or arterial access. Splash exposures of blood on skin with an open lesion present some risk, but it is much lower than from a puncture wound.

Perinatal Transmission

Perinatal transmission from mother to child can occur during pregnancy, delivery, or breastfeeding. On average, 25% of infants born to women with untreated HIV infection are born with HIV. Fortunately, the risk for transmission is less than 1% when pregnant women are tested for HIV infection and, if found to be infected, treated with antiretroviral therapy (ART).

Pathophysiology

HIV is an RNA virus. RNA viruses are called *retroviruses* because they replicate in a "backward" manner (going from RNA to DNA). Like all viruses, HIV cannot replicate unless it is inside a living cell. The *CD4⁺ T cell (CD4 cell),* a type of lymphocyte, is the target cell for HIV. HIV enters the CD4 cell by binding to protein receptors on the outside of the cell (Fig. 15.3). This process is known as *fusion* (Fig. 15.4).

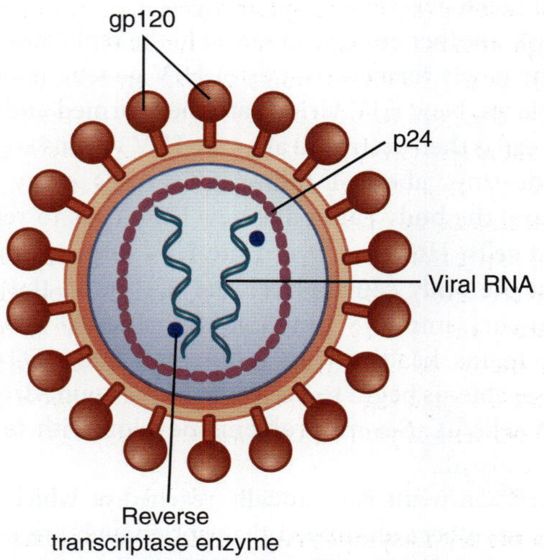

Fig. 15.3 HIV is surrounded by an envelope made up of proteins (including gp120) and a core of viral RNA and proteins.

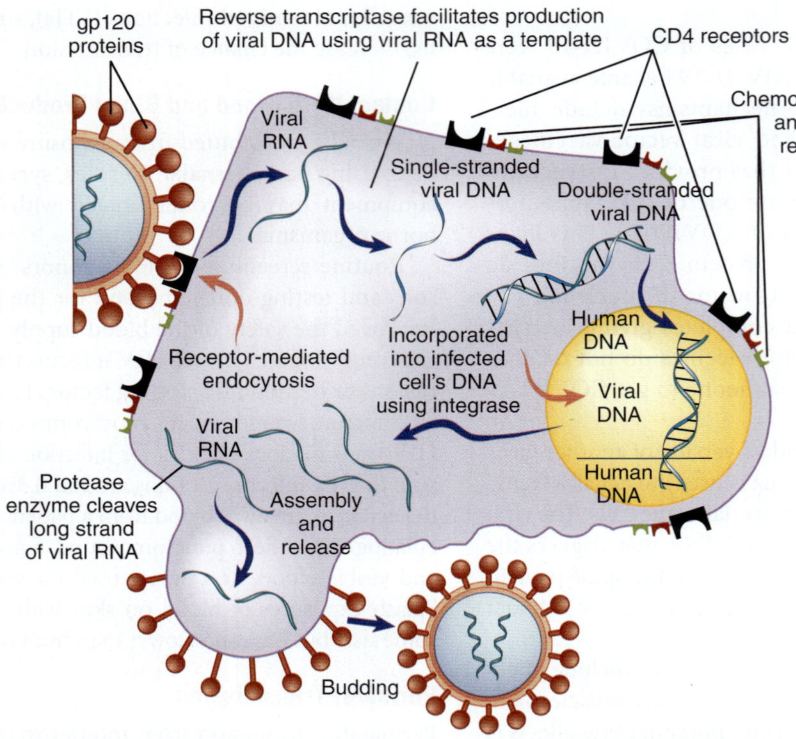

Fig. 15.4 HIV has gp120 glycoproteins that attach to CD4 and chemokine CXCR4 and CCR5 receptors on the surface of CD4 cells. Viral RNA then enters the cell and makes viral DNA in the presence of reverse transcriptase. It incorporates itself into the cellular genome in the presence of integrase, causing permanent cellular infection and the production of new virions. New viral RNA develops initially in long strands that are cut in the presence of protease and leave the cell through a budding process that contributes to cellular destruction.

Once HIV is attached and fused with the CD4 cell, HIV RNA enters the CD4 cell. This triggers the release of *reverse transcriptase,* an enzyme that transforms HIV RNA into a single strand of DNA. This strand copies itself, becoming double-stranded viral DNA. Another enzyme, called *integrase,* allows the newly formed double-stranded DNA to integrate itself into the host' genetic structure. This action has 2 consequences: (1) because all genetic material is replicated during cell division, all daughter cells are infected and (2) viral DNA in the genome directs the cell to make new HIV.

Protease, another enzyme involved in the replication process, cleaves the newly formed strands of HIV genetic material into smaller pieces. New HIV virions are then formed and released. The CD4 cell is then destroyed after the HIV virions are released.

HIV destroys about 1 billion CD4 cells every day. For many years, the body can make new CD4 cells to replace the destroyed cells. However, over time HIV destroys more CD4 cells than the body can replace. The decline in the CD4 cell count impairs immune function. In general, the immune system remains healthy with more than 500 CD4 cells/μL. Immune problems begin to occur when the count drops below 500 CD4 cells/μL. Severe problems develop with fewer than 200 CD4 cells/μL.

With HIV, a point is eventually reached at which so many CD4 cells have been destroyed that not enough are left to regulate immune responses (Fig. 15.5). This allows **opportunistic diseases** (infections and cancers that occur in immunosuppressed patients) to develop. Opportunistic diseases are the main cause of disease, disability, and death in patients with HIV infection.

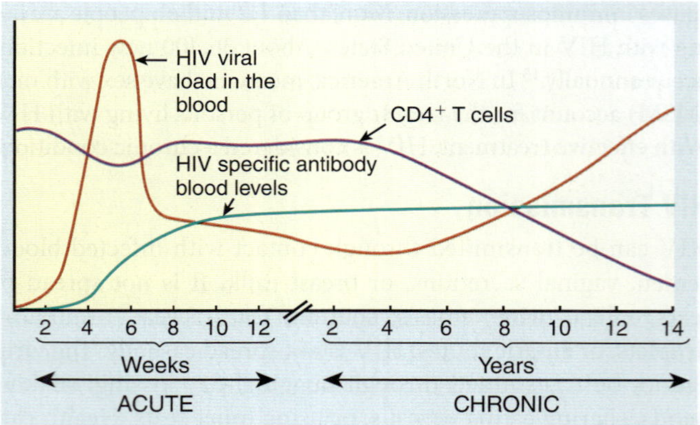

Fig. 15.5 Viral load in the blood in relationship to number of CD4 cells over the spectrum of untreated HIV infection.

Clinical Manifestations and Complications

The typical course of untreated HIV infection follows the pattern shown in Fig. 15.6.[16] Remember that (1) disease progression is highly individualized, (2) treatment can significantly alter this pattern, and (3) a person's prognosis is unpredictable.

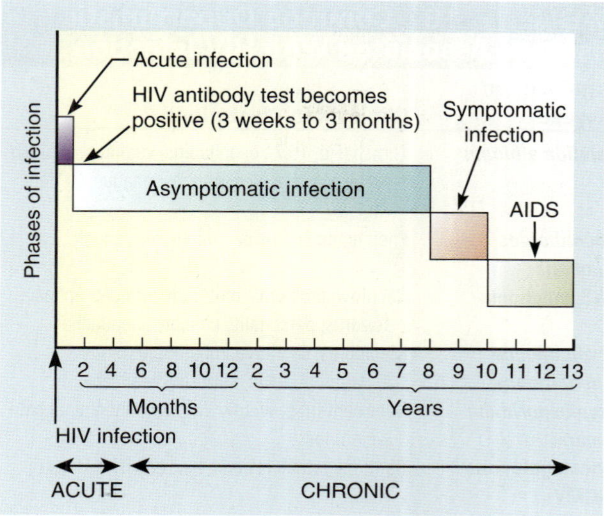

Fig. 15.6 Timeline for the spectrum of untreated HIV infection. The timeline represents the course of untreated illness from the time of infection to clinical manifestations of disease.

Acute Infection

About 2 to 4 weeks after someone becomes newly infected with HIV, they typically develop *acute HIV infection.* During this period, a person can have a mononucleosis-like syndrome of fever, swollen lymph nodes, sore throat, headache, malaise, nausea, muscle and joint pain, diarrhea, and/or a diffuse rash. Many people, including HCPs, mistake these symptoms for the flu. Some people have neurologic problems, such as aseptic meningitis, peripheral neuropathy, facial palsy, or Guillain-Barré syndrome. During acute infection, there is a high **viral load**, the amount of HIV circulating in the blood. This is why people are most infectious during this stage. CD4 cell counts fall temporarily but quickly return to baseline or near-baseline levels (see Fig. 15.5).

Chronic HIV Infection

Asymptomatic infection. The time between initial HIV infection and a diagnosis of AIDS is about 10 years in untreated infection. During the first several years after initial infection, people are typically asymptomatic and have no symptoms or limited signs of infection.

Since symptoms during early infection are vague and nonspecific for HIV, people may not be aware that they are infected. They continue their usual activities, which may include high-risk sexual and drug-using behaviors, and can transmit HIV to others even though they have no symptoms. Their personal health is affected because they are not receiving treatment that could improve the quality and length of their lives.

Symptomatic infection. As the CD4 cell count declines closer to 200 cells/μL and the viral load increases, HIV advances to a more active stage. Symptoms such as persistent fever, frequent night sweats, chronic diarrhea, recurrent headaches, and severe fatigue may develop.

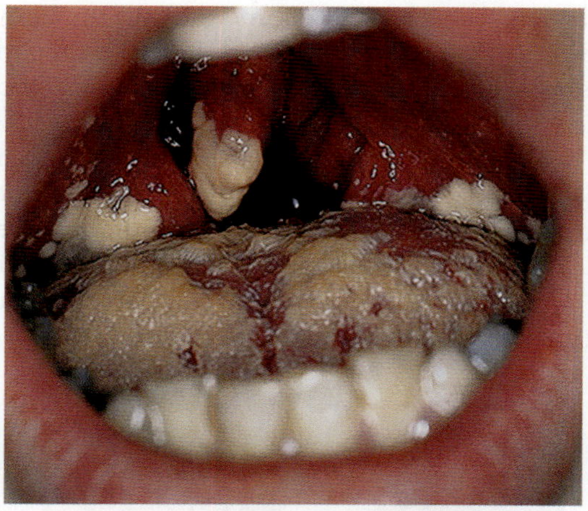

Fig. 15.7 Oral thrush involving hard and soft palate. (From Emond R, Welsby P, Rowland H: *Colour atlas of infectious diseases,* ed 4, Edinburgh, 2003, Mosby.)

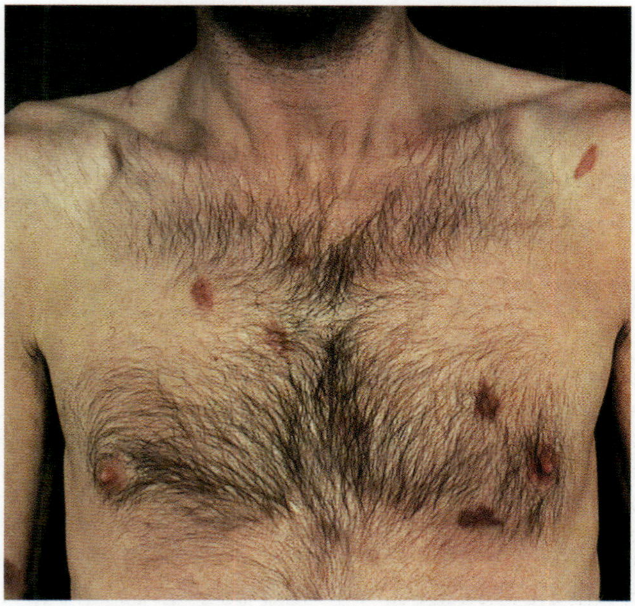

Fig. 15.8 Kaposi sarcoma (KS). KS lesions can appear anywhere on the skin surface or on internal organs. Lesions vary in size from pinpoint to large. They may appear in a variety of shades. (From Male DM, Peebles S, Male V: Secondary immunodeficiency and immunosuppression, *Immunology* 19:276, 2021.)

A common infection during this phase is oropharyngeal candidiasis (thrush) (Fig. 15.7). Other infections that can occur at this time include shingles (caused by the varicella-zoster virus); persistent vaginal candidal infections; outbreaks of oral or genital herpes; bacterial infections; and Kaposi sarcoma (KS), caused by human herpesvirus 8 (Fig. 15.8). *Oral hairy leukoplakia,* an Epstein-Barr virus infection that causes painless, white, raised lesions on the lateral aspect of the tongue (Fig. 15.9), is another sign of disease progression.

AIDS. A diagnosis of **acquired immunodeficiency syndrome (AIDS)** is made when a person with HIV meets criteria established by the CDC. This occurs when the immune system becomes severely compromised (Table 15.17). Opportunistic diseases generally do not occur in the presence of a functioning immune system. Many infections, a variety of cancers, wasting, and HIV-related cognitive changes can occur in patients with immune impairment (Table 15.18). Organisms that do not cause severe disease in people with functioning immune systems can cause debilitating, life-threatening infections during this stage. Several opportunistic diseases may occur at the same time, making diagnosis and treatment more difficult. Advances in

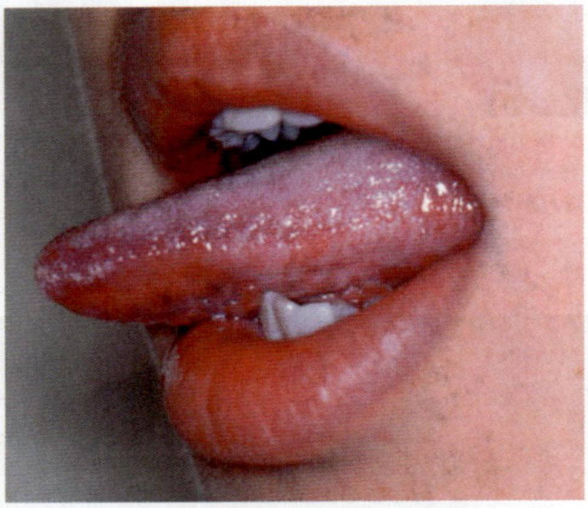

Fig. 15.9 Oral hairy leukoplakia on the lateral aspect of the tongue. (From: Chan R, Chio M, Koh HY: Cutaneous manifestations of HIV infection, *Dermatology* 78:1364, 2018.)

TABLE 15.17 Diagnostic Criteria AIDS

AIDS is diagnosed when a person with HIV develops at least one of the following conditions:

1. CD4+ T cell count drops below 200 cells/μL.
2. One of the following opportunistic infections (OIs):
   - *Bacterial:* TB (any site); any disseminated or extrapulmonary mycobacteria, including *Mycobacterium avium* complex (MAC) or *Mycobacterium kansasii;* recurrent pneumonia; recurrent *Salmonella* septicemia
   - *Fungal:* Candidiasis of bronchi, trachea, lungs, or esophagus; PCP; disseminated or extrapulmonary coccidioidomycosis; disseminated or extrapulmonary histoplasmosis
   - *Protozoal:* Toxoplasmosis of the brain, chronic intestinal isosporiasis, chronic intestinal cryptosporidiosis
   - *Viral:* Cytomegalovirus (CMV) disease other than liver, spleen, or nodes; CMV retinitis (with loss of vision); herpes simplex with chronic ulcer(s) or bronchitis, pneumonitis, or esophagitis; progressive multifocal leukoencephalopathy (PML); extrapulmonary cryptococcosis
3. One of the following opportunistic cancers:
   - Burkitt's lymphoma
   - Immunoblastic lymphoma
   - Invasive cervical cancer
   - Kaposi sarcoma
   - Primary lymphoma of the brain
4. Wasting syndrome. *Wasting* is defined as a loss of 10% or more of ideal body mass.

Modified from CDC: Revised surveillance case definition for HIV infection—United States, 2014. Retrieved from https://www.cdc.gov/mmwr/preview/mmwrhtml/rr6303a1.htm#Tab.

TABLE 15.18 Common Opportunistic Diseases Associated With HIV Infection

Organism or Disease	Clinical Manifestations
Candida albicans	Thrush (Fig. 15.7), esophagitis, vaginitis. Whitish yellow patches in mouth, esophagus, GI tract, vagina
Coccidioides immitis	Pneumonia and fever, weight loss, cough
CNS lymphoma	Cognitive problems, motor impairment, aphasia, seizures, personality changes, headache
Cryptococcus neoformans	Meningitis, cognitive impairment, motor impairment, fever, seizures, headache
Cryptosporidium muris	Gastroenteritis, watery diarrhea, abdominal pain, weight loss
Cytomegalovirus (CMV)	*Retinitis:* retinal lesions, blurred vision, loss of vision *Esophagitis, stomatitis:* difficulty swallowing, colitis or gastritis: bloody diarrhea, pain, weight loss *Pneumonitis:* respiratory symptoms *Neurologic disease:* CNS manifestations
Hepatitis B virus	Jaundice, fatigue, abdominal pain, loss of appetite, nausea, vomiting, joint pain. Some have no signs or symptoms
Hepatitis C virus	Jaundice, fatigue, abdominal pain, loss of appetite, nausea, vomiting, dark urine. Many have no signs or symptoms
Herpes simplex virus (HSV)	*HSV-1 (type 1):* orolabial and mucocutaneous vesicular and ulcerative lesions. Keratitis, vision changes, encephalitis, CNS manifestations *HSV-2 (type 2):* genital and perianal vesicular and ulcerative lesions
Histoplasma capsulatum	*Pneumonia:* fever, cough, weight loss *Meningitis:* CNS manifestations, disseminated disease
JC papovavirus	Progressive multifocal leukoencephalopathy (PML), CNS manifestations, mental and motor declines
Kaposi sarcoma (KS) caused by human herpesvirus 8 (HHV-8)	Vascular lesions on the skin (Fig. 15.6), mucous membranes, and viscera with wide range of presentation: firm, flat, raised, or nodular; pinpoint to several cm in size; hyperpigmented, multicentric. Can cause lymphedema and disfigurement. Usually not serious unless occurring in the respiratory or GI system
***Mycobacterium avium* complex (MAC)**	Gastroenteritis, watery diarrhea, weight loss
Mycobacterium tuberculosis (MTB, TB)	Respiratory and disseminated disease. Productive cough, fever, night sweats, weight loss
***Pneumocystis jiroveci* pneumonia (PCP)**	Pneumonia, nonproductive cough, hypoxemia, progressive shortness of breath, fever, night sweats, fatigue
Toxoplasma gondii	Encephalitis, cognitive problems, motor impairment, fever, headache, seizures, sensory problems
Varicella-zoster virus (VZV)	*Shingles:* red, maculopapular rash along dermatomal planes, pain, pruritus *Ocular:* progressive outer retinal necrosis (PORN)

HIV treatment have decreased the occurrence of opportunistic diseases.

Diagnostic Studies

Diagnosis of HIV infection is made by testing for HIV antibodies and/or antigens. HIV screening tests can be done using blood or saliva. It can take several weeks after infection before a screening test can detect evidence of HIV (Fig. 15.5). This delay is the **window period**. The typical window period is about 3 weeks (Table 15.19). If a newly infected person is tested during the window period, the test may not be able to detect infection and there will be a false negative result.

We monitor HIV progression by assessing CD4 cell count and viral load.[17] The CD4 cell count reflects immune function. The normal range for CD4 cells is 800 to 1200 cells/μL. As the disease progresses, the number of CD4 cells usually decreases (Fig. 15.5). Viral levels provide an assessment of disease progression. The lower the viral load, the less active the disease. In HIV, viral loads are reported as real numbers (e.g., 1260 copies/μL). The goal of treatment is to suppress the viral load to the lowest level possible, which is below the level of detection on a commercial assay. This is referred to as "undetectable." "Undetectable" does *not* mean that the virus has been eliminated from the body or that the person is cured of HIV. Rather, it means that the amount of circulating HIV in the blood is below the level of detection of the test.

Abnormal blood test results are common in HIV infection. They may be caused by HIV, opportunistic diseases, or complications of therapy. Decreased white blood cell (WBC) counts, with lymphopenia and neutropenia, often occur. HIV, antiplatelet antibodies, or drug therapy can cause low platelet counts. Anemia occurs from the chronic disease process and adverse effects of ART. Altered liver function, caused by HIV infection, drug therapy, or coinfection with a hepatitis virus, may be seen. Early identification of coinfection with hepatitis B or hepatitis C virus is important. These infections have a more serious course in patients with HIV, may limit options for ART, and can cause liver-related morbidity and mortality.[18]

Resistance tests can determine if a patient's HIV is resistant to drugs used for ART. *Genotype* and *phenotype* assays help HCPs to know which drugs can best control a patient's infection. These tests are similar to culture and sensitivity testing used for antibiotic selection.

TABLE 15.19 HIV Testing

HIV-Antibody/Antigen Testing

A highly sensitive test detects antibodies and antigens associated with HIV. Blood samples that are negative for HIV infection are reported as negative. The antigen/antibody testing algorithm includes confirmation with HIV viral load testing for any indeterminate results.

- If the patient has a negative HIV antibody/antigen test, but reports recent risky behaviors, encourage retesting in 4–6 weeks. Assess persons at ongoing risk and provide teaching for risk reduction interventions, including PrEP.
- If the results are positive and consistent with HIV infection, assist the patient in getting appropriate counseling, support, and follow-up HIV primary care.

1 Rapid HIV-Antibody Testing

1. The CDC strongly recommends rapid testing. Results are highly accurate. It can be done in a variety of settings (mobile health units, HCP offices, privacy of a person's home). Results are typically available within 20 minutes.
2. In-home HIV test kits are available. Testing is done on saliva.
3. Follow a negative rapid test with a risk assessment to determine the need for repeat tests.
4. Positive rapid tests can be disclosed to the patient but must be confirmed with a standard HIV assay. This step requires a blood draw and a return appointment to get results.

Interprofessional Care

HIV cannot be cured. Interprofessional care focuses on (1) monitoring HIV disease progression and immune function, (2) starting and monitoring ART, (3) preventing opportunistic diseases, (4) detecting and treating opportunistic diseases, (5) managing symptoms, (6) preventing or decreasing treatment complications, and (7) preventing further HIV transmission. To achieve these goals, ongoing assessment, clinician-patient interactions, and patient teaching and support are needed.

Drug Therapy for HIV Infection

ART is a combination of medications used to control and suppress HIV replication. The goals of ART are to (1) decrease the viral load, (2) maintain or increase CD4 cell counts, (3) prevent HIV-related symptoms and opportunistic diseases, (4) delay disease progression, and (5) prevent HIV transmission.[19] When taken consistently and correctly, ART can reduce viral loads by 90% to 99%. This makes adherence to treatment regimens very important.

A major principle of treating HIV is to use combination therapy with drugs from different classes. Drugs used to treat HIV work at various points in the HIV replication cycle (Tables 15.20 and 15.21). The major advantage of combination therapy is it inhibits viral replication in different ways. This makes it more difficult for the virus to recover and decreases the chance of drug resistance. Resistance can develop rapidly when drugs are used alone or taken in inadequate doses. Improvements in ART have simplified therapy so many persons can take combination therapy in a single tablet. Disadvantages of ART include drug side effects and expense.

! SAFETY ALERT

Interaction of ART With Other Drugs

- Many ARTs have interactions with other drugs and herbal therapies.
- Significant interactions occur with over-the-counter (OTC) drugs, including antacids and proton pump inhibitors.
- Be sure to ask patients about prescribed and OTC drugs as well as herbal products and supplements.

TABLE 15.20 **Drug Therapy**

HIV Infection

Drug Classification	Mechanism of Action	Considerations
Attachment Inhibitors fostemsavir (Rukobia) ibalizumab-uiyk (Trogarzo)	Interrupts the ability of HIV to attach to the CD4 cell	Fostemsavir taken twice daily PO. May cause heart and liver problems. Ibalizumab-uiyk given IV. An initial loading dose followed by 15–30 min infusion every 14 days. May ↑ glucose.
Entry Inhibitors enfuvirtide (Fuzeon) maraviroc (Selzentry)	Prevent binding of HIV to cells, thus preventing entry of HIV into cells where replication would occur	Enfuvirtide given subcut twice daily. May cause peripheral neuropathy. Maraviroc may cause heart and liver problems. Taken PO.
Integrase Inhibitors bictegravir cabotegravir (Vocabria) dolutegravir (Tivicay) elvitegravir raltegravir (Isentress)	Bind with integrase enzyme and prevent HIV from incorporating its genetic material into the host cell	Elvitegravir and bictegravir are available only in fixed-dose combinations with tenofovir AF and emtricitabine (Table 15.15). Cabotegravir available PO or a long-acting injectable. Can cause severe skin reactions, widespread inflammation.
Protease Inhibitors (PIs) atazanavir (Reyataz) darunavir (Prezista) fosamprenavir (Lexiva) indinavir (Crixivan) lopinavir/ritonavir (Kaletra) nelfinavir (Viracept) ritonavir (Norvir)[a] saquinavir (Fortovase, Invirase) tipranavir (Aptivus)	Prevent the protease enzyme from cutting HIV proteins into the proper lengths needed to allow viable virions to assemble and bud out from the cell membrane	Taken PO as tablets. All part of therapy with other HIV agents, either separately or in a fixed-dose agent. May cause liver problems, ↑ glucose, ↑ cholesterol. Should not take with most statins (e.g., lovastatin).
Reverse Transcriptase Inhibitors		
Nonnucleoside Reverse Transcriptase Inhibitors (NNRTIs) delavirdine (Rescriptor) efavirenz (Sustiva) etravirine (Intelence) nevirapine (Viramune XR) rilpivirine (Edurant)	Inhibit the action of reverse transcriptase	Taken PO. May cause liver problems and neuropsychiatric symptoms, such as nightmares, hallucinations, suicidal thoughts.
Nucleoside Reverse Transcriptase Inhibitors (NRTIs) abacavir (Ziagen) didanosine (Videx, Videx-EC) doravirine (Pifeltro) emtricitabine (Emtriva) lamivudine (Epivir) stavudine (Zerit) zidovudine (Retrovir)	Insert a piece of DNA into the developing HIV DNA chain, blocking further development of the chain and leaving the production of the new strand of HIV DNA incomplete	Can cause rashes and skin problems, liver problems, peripheral neuropathy, lactic acidosis. Abacavir, emtricitabine, lamivudine, stavudine, zidovudine taken PO as tablet or solution. Didanosine taken PO as tablet or oral powder. Doravirine taken PO as a tablet.
Nucleotide Reverse Transcriptase Inhibitor (NtRTI) tenofovir (Viread)	Combines with reverse transcriptase enzyme to block the process needed to convert HIV RNA into HIV DNA	Oral powder must be added to 2–4 ounces of soft food such as applesauce, baby food, or yogurt. Do not mix oral powder with liquid. May cause liver or kidney problems, lactic acidosis.

[a]Most often used in low doses with other PIs to boost effect.

Drug Therapy for Opportunistic Diseases

Management of HIV is complicated by the many opportunistic diseases that can develop as the immune system deteriorates (Table 15.18). Prevention is the preferred approach to opportunistic diseases. Several opportunistic diseases associated with HIV can be delayed or prevented with ART, vaccines (including hepatitis A, hepatitis B, influenza, pneumococcal), and disease-specific prevention measures.[20] Although it is usually not possible to eradicate opportunistic diseases once they occur, prophylactic therapy can decrease morbidity and mortality. Advances in managing opportunistic diseases have contributed significantly to increased life expectancy.

NURSING MANAGEMENT: HIV INFECTION

Assessment

Assessment of people without HIV infection should focus on behaviors that put the person at risk for HIV and other STIs and blood-borne infections. Assess risk by asking basic questions: (1) Have you ever had a blood transfusion or used clotting factors?

TABLE 15.21 Fixed-Dose Drug Combination Products

HIV Infection

Mechanism of Action

More than 1 drug combined into a single tablet or administered concurrently as a complete regimen. Drugs may be from the same or different classes.

Examples

Atripla (tenofovir DF + emtricitabine + efavirenz)
Biktarvy (tenofovir AF + emtricitabine + bictegravir)
Cabenuva (cabotegravir + rilpivirine)[a]
Combivir (lamivudine + zidovudine)
Complera (tenofovir DF + emtricitabine + rilpivirine)
Delstrigo (tenofovir DF + lamivudine + doravarine)
Descovy (tenofovir AF + emtricitabine)
Dovato (lamivudine + dolutegravir)
Epzicom (abacavir + lamivudine)
Evotaz (atazanavir + cobicistat[b])
Genvoya (tenofovir AF + emtricitabine + elvitegravir + cobicistat[b])
Juluca (dolutegravir + rilpivirine)
Odefsey (tenofovir AF + emtricitabine + rilpivirine)
Prezcobix (darunavir + cobicistat[b])
Temixys (tenofovir DF + lamivudine)
Triumeq (abacavir + lamivudine + dolutegravir)
Trizivir (abacavir + lamivudine + zidovudine)
Truvada (tenofovir DF + emtricitabine)
Stribild (tenofovir DF + emtricitabine + elvitegravir + cobicistat[b])
Symtuza (tenofovir AF + emtricitabine + darunavir + cobicistat[b])

[a]Injectable formulations must be given concurrently.
[b]Cobicistat is a pharmacologic booster that enhances the potency of some HIV antiretrovirals. It has no direct effects against HIV.
AF, Alafenamide; *DF,* disoproxil fumarate.

If so, was it before 1985? (2) Have you ever shared drug-using equipment with another person? (3) Have you ever had a sexual experience in which your penis, vagina, rectum, or mouth came into contact with another person's penis, vagina, rectum, or mouth? (4) Have you ever had an STI? (5) Have you ever had sexual contact with someone known to have HIV? Follow up a positive response to any question with an in-depth exploration of issues related to the identified risk (Box 15.1).

The first patient visit for a patient with HIV provides an opportunity to gather baseline data and start establishing rapport. A complete history and physical assessment, including an immunization history and psychosocial and diet evaluations, should be done (Table 15.22). Repeated assessments are essential because people's circumstances change. We can identify and address problems in a timely manner.

BOX 15.1 Ethical/Legal Dilemmas

Individual vs. Public Health Protection

Situation

A nurse in a community clinic is having a follow-up visit with V.T., a 38-year-old woman who was diagnosed with HIV infection during her annual physical 2 weeks ago. During the visit, V.T. discloses that her partner verbally and physically abuses her. V.T. says she had not yet told her partner about the HIV diagnosis because she is afraid that he will hurt her. She has not used any protection during sex with him since she learned of her test results because she suspects he infected her.

Ethical/Legal Points for Consideration

- You face a conflict between preventing further harm to V.T. (risk of intimate partner violence), providing care to her partner (his need for an HIV test, diagnosis, and treatment), and protecting the public health (potential spread of HIV infection to her partner or from her partner to others in the community). Patient teaching and support are essential because your primary obligation is to the patient.
- Because relevant laws vary, be familiar with your state law concerning mandated reporting for domestic partner abuse and infectious diseases.
- Federal laws about protection of privacy in HIV testing apply everywhere.
- In many states, reporting domestic abuse is mandatory only when the reporter witnesses the abuse or the immediate effects of the abuse (e.g., wounds, contusions, broken bones).[1]
- Be familiar with local crisis counseling services. Offer V.T. the following advice: Collect and stash a set of car keys or taxi money in a safe place, keep a bag packed and hidden or even stored in a locker somewhere accessible, develop a code phrase to use with a friend or family member to call for help, keep a cell phone charged, and have money hidden in a safe place.

Discussion Questions

1. How can you protect the patient's confidentiality to prevent further intimate partner violence?
2. What services does your state offer to notify a partner without disclosing the source patient's name? How would V.T. access those services in your state?
3. How can you protect the partner from possible infection while also protecting V.T. from further violence?
4. How can you best address the issue of intimate partner violence? What resources would V.T. have in your community?

Reference

1. National Coalition Against Domestic Violence. Retrieved from www.ncadv.com.

◆ Clinical Problems

Clinical problems for the patient with HIV may include:

- Risk for infection
- Deficient knowledge
- Difficulty coping
- Nutritionally compromised

◆ Planning

Nursing care can help the patient to (1) adhere to ART; (2) adopt a healthy lifestyle that includes avoiding exposure to other STIs and blood-borne diseases; (3) protect others from HIV; (4) have supportive relationships; (5) maintain activities and productivity; (6) explore spiritual issues; (7) come to terms with issues related to disease, disability, and death; and (8) cope with symptoms caused by HIV and its treatments.

◆ Implementation

The complexity of HIV disease is related to its chronic nature. Primary prevention and health promotion are the most effective health care strategies. Table 15.23 shows a summary of nursing goals, assessments, and interventions throughout the course of HIV infection.

◆ Health Promotion

Preventing HIV infection. HIV infection is preventable. The goal is to develop safer, healthier, and less risky behaviors (Box 15.2). The more consistently and correctly one uses prevention

TABLE 15.22 NURSING ASSESSMENT

Patient With HIV

Subjective Data

Important Health Information

Health history: Route of infection. Hepatitis, other STIs, tuberculosis. Frequent viral, fungal, and/or bacterial infections

Medications: Use of immunosuppressive drugs

Functional Health Patterns

Health perception–health management: Perception of illness. Alcohol and drug use. Malaise

Nutritional-metabolic: Weight loss, anorexia, nausea, vomiting. Lesions, bleeding, or ulcerations of lips, mouth, gums, tongue, or throat. Sensitivity to acidic, salty, or spicy foods. Difficulty swallowing, abdominal cramping. Skin rashes, lesions, or color changes

Elimination: Persistent diarrhea, change in character of stools. Painful urination, low back pain

Activity-exercise: Chronic fatigue, muscle weakness, difficulty walking. Cough, shortness of breath

Sleep-rest: Insomnia, night sweats, fatigue

Cognitive-perceptual: Headaches, stiff neck, chest pain, rectal pain, retrosternal pain. Blurred vision, photophobia, diplopia, loss of vision. Hearing impairment. Confusion, forgetfulness, attention deficit, changes in mental status, memory loss, personality changes. Paresthesias, hypersensitivity in feet, pruritus

Role-relationship: Support system(s), career or job, financial resources

Sexuality-reproductive: Lesions on genitalia or anus (internal or external), pruritus or burning in vagina, penis, or anus. Painful sexual intercourse, rectal pain or bleeding, changes in menstruation, vaginal or penile discharge. Use of birth control measures, pregnancies, desire for future children

Coping–stress tolerance: Stress levels, previous losses, coping patterns, self-concept; social withdrawal

Objective Data

Cardiovascular

Pericardial friction rub, murmur, bradycardia, tachycardia

Eyes

Presence of exudates, retinal lesions or hemorrhage, papilledema

GI

Mouth lesions, including blisters (HSV), white-gray patches (*Candida* infection), painless white lesions on the side of the tongue (hairy leukoplakia), discolorations (Kaposi sarcoma). Gingivitis, tooth decay or loosening. Redness or white patchy lesions of throat. Vomiting, diarrhea, incontinence, rectal lesions, hyperactive bowel sounds, abdominal masses, hepatosplenomegaly

General

Lethargy, persistent fever, lymphadenopathy, peripheral wasting, fat deposits in truncal areas and upper back

Musculoskeletal

Muscle wasting, weakness

Neurologic

Ataxia, tremors, lack of coordination. Sensory loss, slurred speech, aphasia. Memory loss, peripheral neuropathy, apathy, agitation, depression, inappropriate behavior. Decreasing levels of consciousness, seizures, paralysis, coma

Respiratory

Tachypnea, dyspnea, intercostal retractions. Crackles, wheezing, productive or nonproductive cough

Reproductive

Genital lesions or discharge, abdominal tenderness secondary to pelvic inflammatory disease

Skin

Dry skin, diaphoresis. Pallor, cyanosis. Lesions, eruptions, discolorations, bruising of skin or mucous membranes. Vaginal or perianal excoriation. Alopecia. Delayed wound healing

Possible Diagnostic Findings

Positive HIV antibody/antigen assay. Detectable viral load. ↓ CD4 cell count, ↓ WBC count, lymphopenia, anemia, thrombocytopenia. Electrolyte imbalances. ↑ liver function tests. ↑ cholesterol, ↑ triglycerides, ↑ glucose

methods, the more effective they are in preventing HIV infection. Nursing interventions to prevent HIV transmission are based on an assessment of the person's risk behaviors. Provide culturally sensitive, language-appropriate, and age-specific teaching and behavior change counseling. Nurses who are comfortable with and know how to talk about sensitive topics such as sexuality and drug use are best prepared to provide prevention education.

Biomedical Prevention

Preexposure prophylaxis (PrEP) is a prevention method in which people who do not have HIV take HIV medicine to reduce their risk for acquiring HIV sexually or through IV drug use.[21] PrEP should be used with other prevention interventions such as condoms, risk reduction counseling, and regular HIV testing. Two agents are approved for PrEP. Each consists of 2 drugs in 1 tablet, taken orally each day. Both contain emtricitabine. It is combined with either tenofovir disoproxil fumarate (Truvada) or tenofovir alafenamide (Descovy).

Nonoccupational postexposure prophylaxis (nPEP) is another prevention option. With nPEP, combination HIV ART is given to someone within 72 hours after a potential exposure to reduce the risk of HIV infection.[22] nPEP can be given to people who may have an unanticipated exposure through either sex, needlestick, or other blood-borne exposure. Treatment is typically given for 28 days after the exposure. Patients are monitored after the incident with repeat HIV testing.

Behavior Modification

A wide variety of activities can reduce the risk for HIV infection. Help people choose the methods that best fit their needs and circumstances. Prevention techniques are divided into *safer activities* (those that have minimal risk) and *risk-reducing activities* (those that decrease, but do not eliminate, risk). A combination of prevention methods (e.g., PrEP, using protective barriers, limiting the number of sex partners) increases the prevention effect.

TABLE 15.23 NURSING MANAGEMENT

HIV Infection

Nursing Care and Goals	Assessment	Interventions
Health Promotion		
Prevent HIV infection	*Risk factors:* What behaviors or social, physical, emotional, pathogenic, or immune factors place the patient at risk?	• Teaching, including knowledge, attitudes, and behaviors, with emphasis on risk reduction to the following: • *General population:* Cover general information • *Pregnant women:* General information and information specific to HIV infection and pregnancy • *Individual patient:* Specific to assessed need • Empower patients to take control of prevention measures.
Detect HIV infection early	Does the patient need to be tested for HIV?	• Provide HIV antibody/antigen testing with appropriate counseling.
Acute Care		
Promote health and limit disability	*Physical health:* Is the patient having problems? *Mental health:* How is the patient coping? *Resources:* Does the patient have family or social support? Is the patient accessing community services? Is money or insurance a problem? Does the patient have access to spiritual support as desired?	• Provide case management or appropriate referrals such as social work. • Teach about HIV, the spectrum of infection, options for care, signs and symptoms to report, treatment options, immune enhancement, risk reduction, and ways to adhere to treatment regimens. • Establish long-term, trusting relationship with patient, family, and significant others. • Provide emotional and spiritual support. • Develop resources for legal needs: discrimination prevention, wills, advance directives, childcare wishes. • Empower the patient to identify needs, direct care, and seek services.
Manage problems caused by HIV infection	*Physical health:* Has the patient had an acute exacerbation of problems related to immunodeficiency, opportunistic disease, or risk factors (e.g., substance use)? *Mental health status:* Has the patient's ability to cope with psychosocial issues deteriorated?	• Provide care during acute exacerbations: recognition of life-threatening developments, life support, rapid intervention with treatments and drugs, comfort, and hygiene needs. • Support patient and family during crisis. • Assist the patient with mental health issues and provide referral to mental health specialist as needed.
Ambulatory Care		
Maximize quality of life	*Physical health:* Are new symptoms developing? Are their drug side effects or interactions?	• Continue case management. • Teach about changing treatment options and continued adherence. • Empower patient to continue to direct care and to make desires known to family and significant others.
Resolve life and death issues	*Mental health:* How is the patient coping? What adjustments have been made? *Finances:* Can the patient maintain health care and basic standards of living? *Family, social, and community support:* Are these available? Is the patient using support in an effective manner? Do family or significant others need teaching, encouragement, or stress relief? *Spirituality issues:* Does the patient desire support from a religious organization or spiritual counselor? What assistance does the patient desire?	• Continue physical care for chronic disease process: treatments, drugs, comfort, and hygiene needs. • Refer the patient to resources to support finances. • Support patient and family or significant others in a trusting relationship. • Assist with end-of-life issues, including resuscitation orders, comfort measures, funeral plans, estate planning, childcare. • Assess desires and refer to resources that will help in meeting spiritual needs.

Decreasing risks related to sexual intercourse. *Safe sexual activities* eliminate the risk for exposure to HIV in semen and vaginal secretions. Abstaining from all sexual activity is an effective way to achieve this goal. There are safe options for those who cannot or do not wish to abstain. Limiting sexual behavior to activities in which the mouth, penis, vagina, or rectum does not come into contact with a partner's mouth, penis, vagina, or rectum eliminates contact with blood, semen, or vaginal secretions. Safe activities include masturbation, mutual masturbation ("hand job"), and other activities that meet the "no contact" requirements.

Risk-reducing sexual activities decrease the risk of contact with HIV. Protective barriers can be used when engaging in insertive sexual activity (oral, vaginal, anal) with a partner who has HIV or whose HIV status is not known. The most-used barrier is the male condom (Box 15.3). They offer protection during anal, vaginal, and oral intercourse. Female condoms are an alternative to male condoms. Squares of

BOX 15.2 PROMOTING POPULATION HEALTH

Prevention and Early Detection of HIV

- Increase safer sexual practices, including condom use
- Decrease equipment sharing among IV drug users
- Increase clinician skills to assess for risk factors for HIV infection, recommend HIV testing, and provide counseling for behavior change
- Make HIV testing a routine part of health care
- Increase access to new HIV testing technologies, especially rapid testing
- Increase access to HIV testing in traditional health care settings and alternative sites, such as drug and alcohol treatment facilities and community-based organizations
- Increase behavior change messages to people with HIV to prevent new infections
- Discuss and offer PrEP to persons at-risk for HIV infection
- Discuss the option of nPEP for persons at-risk for HIV who had an unanticipated exposure
- Decrease perinatal HIV infection by offering HIV testing as a part of routine prenatal care
- Counsel and support those with HIV to take ART as prescribed

BOX 15.3 EVIDENCE-BASED PRACTICE

Condom Use and HIV

As a nurse in an HIV clinic, you are counseling M.J., a 27-year-old man and his male partner. M.J. is on ART. His viral load is very low, and his CD4 cell count is normal. He tells you that since the drugs are working, he and his partner (who is HIV negative) are considering not using condoms in the future.

Making Clinical Decisions

Best Available Evidence

One of the best ways to prevent HIV transmission continues to be the consistent and correct use of latex condoms. Those with HIV who take ART and have an undetectable viral load (<200 copies/mL) have no risk for transmitting HIV to their sexual partners. Behavior change programs provided by HCPs, peers, and others can significantly reduce risk behaviors among those with HIV and the transmission of the virus to others.

Clinician Expertise

You know that risk-reducing sexual activities in this situation include the continued use of condoms. You also know that while an undetectable viral load decreases the risk for HIV transmission, the risk of transmission of other STIs is not completely eliminated.

Patient Preferences and Values

M.J. and his partner tell you that they are in a committed relationship and have no other partners. They do not like using condoms.

Implications for Practice

1. What information would you discuss related to HIV transmission, ART and viral load, and the risks of unprotected sexual activity?
2. What measures besides condom use would you discuss with them to reduce the risk for HIV transmission?

References for Evidence

CDC. Evidence of HIV treatment and viral suppression in preventing the sexual transmission of HIV. Retrieved from www.cdc.gov/hiv/pdf/risk/art/cdc-hiv-art-viral-suppression.pdf.

CDC. Proven HIV prevention methods. Retrieved from www.cdc.gov/nchhstp/newsroom/docs/factsheets/hiv-proven-prevention-methods-508.pdf.

latex (dental dams) can be used as a barrier during oral sexual activity.

Decreasing risks related to drug use. The major risk for HIV related to using drugs involves sharing equipment or having unsafe sexual experiences while under the influence of drugs. Basic risk reduction rules are (1) do not use drugs; (2) if you use drugs, do not share equipment; and (3) do not have sexual intercourse when under the influence of any drug, including alcohol, which impairs decision making.

The safest method is to abstain from drugs. This may not be a practical option for users who are not prepared to quit or have no access to drug treatment services. The risk for HIV infection for these persons is eliminated if they do not share equipment. Injecting equipment ("works") includes needles, syringes, cookers (spoons or bottle caps used to mix the drug), cotton, and rinse water. Blood can contaminate equipment used to snort (straws) or smoke (pipes) drugs and should not be shared.

Access to sterile equipment is an important risk elimination tactic. Some communities have needle and syringe exchange programs (NSEPs) that provide sterile equipment in exchange for used equipment. In communities with NSEPs, drug use does not increase, and rates of HIV and other blood-borne infections are controlled.[23] Proper cleaning of equipment can reduce risk by decreasing the chance of blood contact.

Decreasing perinatal transmission. The best way to prevent HIV infection in infants is to prevent HIV infection in women. We should ask women with HIV about their reproductive desires. Those who choose not to have children need to have family planning methods discussed in detail. Women who are pregnant or contemplating pregnancy should receive HIV counseling, be offered access to voluntary HIV-antibody testing, and, if infected, be offered optimal ART.[24] When women with HIV are treated with ART during pregnancy, the rate of perinatal transmission decreases from 25% to less than 1%.[24]

Decreasing risks at work. The risk for infection from occupational exposure to HIV is small but real. OSHA requires employers to protect workers from exposure to blood and other potentially infectious materials (Table 15.12). Precautions and safety devices decrease the risk for direct contact with blood and body fluids. Should exposure to HIV-infected fluids occur, **postexposure prophylaxis (PEP)** with combination ART can significantly decrease the risk for infection.[15] The need for timely treatment and counseling makes it critical for nurses to report all blood exposures.

HIV testing. Around 14% of people with HIV in the United States do not know they are infected. They are more likely to transmit the infection to others. Current guidelines recommend universal, voluntary testing as part of routine medical care.[25] The goal is to normalize the test, decrease the stigma related to HIV testing, find hidden cases, get infected persons into care, and prevent new cases of infection.

◆ Acute Care

Early intervention. Early intervention after detection of HIV infection can promote health and limit disability. Findings from the history, assessment, and laboratory tests help to determine patient needs. Ongoing assessment should focus on early detection of symptoms, opportunistic diseases, and psychosocial problems (Table 15.22). Begin teaching about HIV disease, prevention of transmission to others, health promotion, and family planning. Use patient input to develop a plan of care and determine the need for referrals. Remember that a newly diagnosed patient may not be able to retain or understand information. Be prepared to repeat and clarify information over the course of several months.

Provide teaching about ART. Include (1) advantages and disadvantages of treatments, (2) dangers of poor adherence to treatment plan, (3) how and when to take each drug, (4) drug interactions to avoid, and (5) side effects to report to the HCP. Table 15.24 outlines patient and caregiver teaching on HIV treatment and initial follow-up.

One of the most important components of successful treatment is adherence to ART. Nurses can promote adherence to ART (Table 15.25). Taking drugs as prescribed is important. Missing even a few doses can lead to drug resistance. Group support and individual counseling can help. The best approach is to learn about the patient's life and assist with problem solving related to taking medications within the confines of that life.

CHECK YOUR PRACTICE

You are caring for a 26-yr-old patient with HIV infection. When you ask them about their HIV treatment, they tell you, "I don't really feel sick, so I don't always take my meds."

How would you respond to this patient?

Teach patients to recognize symptoms that may indicate disease progression and drug side effects so that prompt medical care can be started. Table 15.26 gives an overview of symptoms that patients should report. Teach about hand hygiene and ways to avoid exposure to new infectious agents.

Promoting a healthy immune system may delay the progression of HIV disease. Nutrition support can help maintain lean body mass and ensure appropriate levels of vitamins and micronutrients. Encourage moderating or eliminating alcohol, tobacco, and drug use. Administer vaccines to keep the patient up to date with those that are recommended. Adequate rest provides the body with the energy needed for optimal immune function. Taking part in safe exercise and activities helps maintain physical and pulmonary function.

Reactions to HIV diagnosis. Reactions to an HIV diagnosis are similar to the reactions of people who are diagnosed with any life-threatening, debilitating, or chronic illness. These reactions include anxiety, panic, fear, depression, denial, hopelessness, anger, and guilt. Unfortunately, all these emotions

TABLE 15.24 PATIENT & CAREGIVER TEACHING

Antiretroviral Drugs

Resistance to antiretroviral drugs is a major problem in treating HIV infection. Include the following instructions when teaching the patient and/or caregiver to decrease the risk for developing resistance:

1. Discuss options with your HCP to find the best regimen for you.
2. Know the drugs you are taking and how to take them (some must be taken with food, some must be taken on an empty stomach, some cannot be taken together). If you do not understand, ask. Have your nurse write the instructions for you.
3. Take the full dose prescribed and take it on schedule. If you cannot take the drug because of side effects or other problems, report it to your HCP immediately.
4. Take all your medications as prescribed. Do not quit taking one drug while continuing the others. If you cannot tolerate any of your drugs, talk to your HCP, who will recommend a way to deal with the side effects or a new set of drugs.
5. Many antiretroviral drugs interact with other drugs, including many common drugs you can buy without a prescription. Be sure your HCP and pharmacist know all the drugs that you are taking. Do not take any new drugs without checking for possible interactions.
6. The goals of ART are to decrease the amount of virus in your blood (your viral load) and to keep your CD4 cell count high. The best results reduce your viral load below detectable levels and keep your CD4 cell count high. Most HCPs do routine laboratory work every 3 to 6 months whether you are taking antiretroviral drugs or not.
7. At 2 to 4 weeks after you start on drug therapy or change your therapy, your HCP will test your viral load to find out how the drugs are working.
   - Your viral load is reported in absolute numbers. All you need to know is that you want to see the viral load drop.
   - Your CD4 cell count is reported in absolute numbers or percentages. It is best for your CD4 cell count to be above 500 cells/μL. If reported in percentages, you would like your CD4 cell value to be above 14%.
8. An undetectable viral load means that the amount of virus is extremely low. HIV cannot be found in the blood using current testing technology. It does not mean that the virus is gone because the virus can be in lymph nodes and organs that blood tests cannot detect. HIV cannot be transmitted through sexual contact if you have an undetectable viral load. It is important to monitor your viral load and take your medications regularly.

TABLE 15.25 PATIENT & CAREGIVER TEACHING

Improving Adherence to ART

The following are strategies that you can use to improve a patient's adherence to ART:

1. Determine whether the patient understands the importance of adherence and is ready to start therapy.
2. Provide teaching on ART dosing.
3. Review potential ART side effects. Assure the patient that side effects can be treated. If not, ART regimens can be changed.
4. Use teaching and memory aids, including pictures, pillboxes, and calendars.
5. Engage family and friends in the teaching process. Solicit their support to help the patient take treatment.
6. Simplify regimens, dosing, and food requirements as much as possible.
7. Use a team of nurses, HCPs, pharmacists, case managers, and mental health and peer counselors to support the patient.
8. Help the patient integrate the medication regimen into their typical life activities and work schedules.

Modified from Panel on Antiretroviral Guidelines for Adults and Adolescents: Guidelines for the use of antiretroviral agents in adults and adolescents living with HIV. Retrieved from https://clinicalinfo.hiv.gov/en/guidelines/adult-and-adolescent-arv/whats-new-guidelines.

TABLE 15.26 PATIENT & CAREGIVER TEACHING

Signs and Symptoms Patients With HIV Need to Report

Teach the patient with HIV infection and the caregiver to report the following signs and symptoms:

Report Immediately

- Any change in level of consciousness: lethargic, hard to arouse, unable to arouse, unresponsive, unconscious
- Headache with nausea and vomiting, changes in vision, changes in ability to perform coordinated activities, or after any head trauma
- Vision changes: blurry or black areas in vision field, new floaters, double vision
- Persistent shortness of breath related to activity and not relieved by a short rest period
- Nausea and vomiting with abdominal pain
- Vomiting blood
- Dehydration: unable to eat or drink because of nausea or mouth lesions; severe diarrhea or vomiting; dizziness when standing
- Yellow skin discoloration
- Any rectal bleeding that is not related to hemorrhoids or trauma (e.g., from anal sexual intercourse)
- Pain in the flank with fever and inability to urinate for more than 6 hours
- Blood in the urine
- New onset of weakness in any part of the body, new onset of numbness that is not related to pressure, new onset of difficulty speaking
- Chest pain not related to a cough
- Seizures
- New rash with a fever
- New oral lesions with a fever
- Severe depression, anxiety, hallucinations, delusions, or thoughts of causing danger to self or others

Report the Following Signs and Symptoms Within 24 Hours

- New or different headache; constant headache not relieved by OTC medication
- Headache with fever, nasal congestion, or cough
- Burning, itching, or discharge from the eyes
- New or productive cough
- Vomiting 2 or 3 times a day
- Vomiting and fever
- New, significant, or watery diarrhea (more than 6 times a day)
- Painful urination, bloody urine, urethral discharge
- Significant new rash (widespread; painful; or following a path down the leg or arm, around the chest, or on the face)
- Problems eating or drinking because of mouth lesions
- Vaginal discharge, pain, or itching

are overlaid with the stigma and discrimination that continue to infuse societal reactions to HIV. The patient's family, friends, and caregivers have many of the same reactions.

Acute exacerbations. Nursing care becomes more complex as the patient's immune system declines and new problems arise to compound existing problems. Nursing care can help to prevent

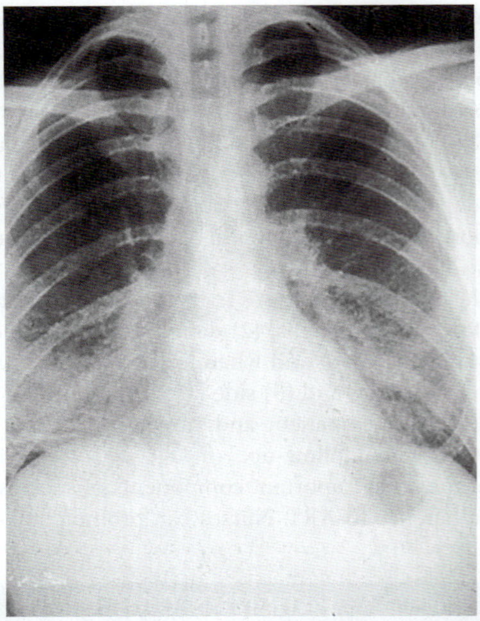

Fig. 15.10 Chest x-ray showing interstitial infiltrates from PCP. (From the CDC. Courtesy Jonathan W. M. Gold, MD, New York, NY.)

many opportunistic diseases associated with HIV infection. The best way to prevent opportunistic disease is to ensure that the patient is adhering ART regimen and, if appropriate, taking prophylactic therapy for opportunistic infections.

When opportunistic diseases or treatment side effects develop, the patient needs symptom management, teaching, and support. Help the patient adhere to therapy and provide supportive care specific to the opportunistic disease. For example, if the patient has *Pneumocystis jiroveci* pneumonia (PCP) (Fig. 15.10), nursing interventions can ensure adequate oxygenation. If the patient has cryptococcal meningitis, an important nursing concern is maintaining a safe environment for a confused patient.

◆ Ambulatory Care

HIV infection affects the entire range of a person's life from physical health to social, emotional, economic, and spiritual well-being. As a nurse, you are often the person who works most closely with patients who are coping with living with HIV.

Psychosocial care. As time passes, patients and their loved ones will be confronted with complex treatment decisions; feelings of loss, anger, powerlessness, depression, and grief; social isolation; the possibility of death; and/or thoughts of suicide. Infections, cancers, debility, and psychosocial or economic issues may interact to overwhelm the patient's ability to cope. Review coping and stress management strategies. Refer the patient to counseling as needed. Encourage them to get involved in support groups and community activities.

Patients with HIV share problems experienced by those with chronic diseases, but these problems are worsened by negative social attitudes and beliefs surrounding HIV. People with HIV may be thought to lack control over urges to have sex or use IV drugs. Some people conclude that people with HIV brought the disease on themselves and deserve to be sick. Some view behaviors related to HIV infection as immoral (e.g., same-sex activity, promiscuity). Other behaviors are sometimes illegal (e.g., using drugs, sex work). The fact that people with HIV can transmit the virus to others creates fear, which leads to stigma and discrimination in all areas of life.[26]

In the United States, people with HIV have lost jobs, homes, and insurance, although the Americans with Disabilities Act (ADA) prohibits these forms of discrimination. HIV-related stigma is a global problem that is often more severe for women. Discrimination can lead to social isolation, dependence, frustration, low self-image, loss of control, and economic pressures.

Disease and drug side effects. Physical problems related to HIV or its treatment can interfere with the patient's ability to maintain a desired lifestyle. Persons with HIV can suffer from anxiety, fear, depression, diarrhea, peripheral neuropathy, pain, nausea, vomiting, and fatigue. Nursing interventions for these symptoms are similar to what they would be for the patient who does not have HIV infection. For example, management of diarrhea includes recommending diet changes, encouraging fluid and electrolyte replacement, teaching about skin care, and managing any perianal skin breakdown. Approaches for fatigue include teaching patients to assess fatigue patterns; determine contributing factors; set activity priorities; conserve energy; schedule rest periods; and exercise regularly. The patient should avoid caffeine, nicotine, and alcohol.

Gerontologic Considerations: HIV Infection

The number of older adults who have HIV disease is increasing because (1) HIV treatment has been effective in reducing the number of deaths from HIV-related opportunistic infections and (2) people 60 and older are being infected at increasing rates. The number of older adults with HIV is expected to grow.

Older adults with HIV are susceptible to the same diseases as older adults without HIV. These include heart disease, cancer, diabetes, bone disease, arthritis, hypertension, kidney disease, and cognitive problems. However, people with HIV infection may develop these diseases at an earlier age (compared with people without HIV) and be at higher risk for comorbidities related to ART.[27] We do not know why this happens. It is likely a combination of factors including genetic predisposition, chronic stress, long-term infection with HIV, and side effects of ART.

Management of these other chronic conditions focuses on detecting problems early, dealing with modifiable risk factors, and helping the patient cope with emerging problems and changes to treatment plans. In addition to addressing modifiable risk factors, such as tobacco cessation, other interventions to help minimize the effects of co-occurring chronic conditions include changing ART because some drugs may contribute to these associated disorders.

> **CHECK YOUR PRACTICE**
>
> You are receiving report on a patient newly admitted to the rehabilitation unit. He is a 68-year-old male patient who had a hip replacement 3 days ago. The nurse giving the report casually mentions, "Oh, by the way, he has AIDS. Can you believe that an old man like that has HIV?"
>
> • How would you respond?

The impact of polypharmacy is another consideration with the aging HIV population. In general, older adults take multiple medications to manage various chronic diseases. Some agents may interact with or be potentiated by ART. Therefore careful monitoring and assessment of possible drug interactions are important when providing care.

Older adults may be ashamed and hesitate to tell anyone that they have an HIV infection. This may make it hard for them to get the appropriate health care and support. As a nurse, you need to recognize that HIV will affect an increasing number of older adults and be prepared to help the older person with HIV.

End-of-life care. Despite new developments in the treatment of HIV infection, many patients eventually have disease progression, disability, and death. Sometimes these occur because treatments do not work for the patient. Sometimes the patient's HIV becomes resistant to all available drug therapies. In addition, ART is now allowing people with HIV to live longer and to develop diseases of aging, such as cardiovascular and endocrine problems that lead to death.

Nursing care during the terminal phase of any disease should focus on keeping the patient comfortable, facilitating emotional and spiritual acceptance of the finite nature of life, helping the patient's significant others deal with grief and loss, and maintaining a safe environment. As a nurse, you are the pivotal care provider during this phase of illness, whether at home, through hospice, or in a health care facility. End-of-life care is discussed in Chapter 10.

◆ Evaluation

The expected outcomes are that the patient at risk for HIV infection will:

- Develop and implement a personal plan to decrease personal risk factors
- Have testing for HIV

The expected outcomes are that the patient with HIV infection will:

- Adhere to treatment for HIV disease
- Work with the health care team to achieve optimal health
- Prevent transmission of HIV to others

Case Study

HIV Infection

(© iStock.com/ Cecilie_Arcurs.)

Patient Profile

J.N. is a 56-year-old male with HIV, chronic hepatitis B, and hypertension. He was admitted 2 days ago with cellulitis of his right arm from an abscess he developed from injecting drugs.

Subjective Data

- Diagnosed with HIV infection at age 36 after his male partner was diagnosed with Kaposi sarcoma
- Has had issues taking ART consistently, "Too many side effects"
- Has fatigue and frequent oral candidiasis outbreaks
- Has a history of IV drug use
- Expresses concern about his future, "I don't know who will take care of me. I don't have any family around"

Objective Data

Physical Assessment

- 5 ft 10 in tall, 150 lb, temperature 100.4°F (38°C), O_2 saturation 98% on room air

Laboratory Studies

- CD4 cell count 285 cells/μL
- Viral load 2250 copies/μL
- Wound culture: + Methicillin-resistant *Staphylococccus aureus* (MRSA)

Interprofessional Care

- Vancomycin
- Combination ART: tenofovir alafenamide, emtricitabine, bictegravir (Biktarvy)

Discussion Questions

1. ***Recognize***: Why was vancomycin ordered, and what are its common side effects?
2. ***Analyze:*** What teaching needs should be covered before J.N. is discharged from the hospital to return home?
3. ***Plan:*** Older lesbian, gay, bisexual, transgender (LGBT) adults often lack familial social support as they age. What barriers could this cause for J.N.'s treatment? How could the interprofessional team assist in addressing these issues? What referrals may be made?
4. ***Prioritize:*** What are the priority nursing interventions? What nursing care will he need after discharge?
5. ***Act***: How can we help J.N. adhere to his ART schedule?
6. ***Evaluate:*** What assessment data would you need to collect to decide if care was effective?
7. ***Safety:*** The nurse needs to start an IV to administer the patient's antibiotic. Before inserting the IV what type of PPE is recommended for this situation?

Answers available at http://evolve.elsevier.com/Lewis/medsurg.

BRIDGE TO NCLEX EXAMINATION

The number of the question corresponds to the same-numbered outcome at the beginning of the chapter.

1. A surgical unit's quality improvement committee notes the number of new catheter-associated urinary tract infections (CAUTIs) increased over the past 6 months. The nurse understands that this means:
   a. There is CAUTI pandemic on the unit.
   b. There is a need to review unit practices.
   c. Droplet precautions are needed to prevent CAUTIs.
   d. The prevalence of antibiotic resistant CAUTI infections is decreasing.
2. Factors associated with an increase in reemerging infections include *(select all that apply)*
   a. international travel.
   b. poor immunization rates.
   c. poor sanitation standards.
   d. not completing a full course of antibiotics.
   e. correct use of personal protective equipment.
3. Interventions to prevent health care–associated infections include *(select all that apply)*
   a. following hand-washing protocols.
   b. limiting visitors to persons over age 18.
   c. giving all patients prophylactic antibiotics.
   d. placing all patients on contact precautions.
   e. decontaminating equipment used for patient care.
4. When working with a patient who has suspected tuberculosis, the nurse would
   a. wear a cloth mask.
   b. only use standard precautions.
   c. place the patient on airborne precautions.
   d. wear a new gown each time they enter the room.
5. Which factors place the patient at increased risk for severe COVID-19? *(select all that apply)*
   a. Obesity
   b. Thyroid disease
   c. Cigarette smoking
   d. Pernicious anemia
   e. Chronic kidney disease
6. The patient asks the nurse why they need viral load testing. The nurse responds that an undetectable HIV viral load *(select all that apply)*
   a. is the goal of HIV therapy.
   b. occurs with drug resistance.
   c. is a sign of disease progression.
   d. means that person is cured of HIV.
   e. means that someone is unable to sexually transmit HIV.
7. A basic principle to consider when planning treatment for HIV is
   a. stimulating the immune system to increase viral load.
   b. using a combination of drugs from more than one class.
   c. suppressing the replication of virus by decreasing the $CD4^+$ count.
   d. encouraging patients to use natural supplements, such as St. John's Wort.
8. Opportunistic diseases in HIV infection
   a. are usually benign.
   b. are slow to develop and progress.
   c. occur in the presence of immunosuppression.
   d. are curable with appropriate drug interventions.

9. The nurse caring for a patient with HIV who has been on ART for many years plans care with the knowledge that the patient
   - **a.** will inevitably develop drug resistance.
   - **b.** is less likely to develop problems such as hyperlipidemia.
   - **c.** is more likely to require treatment of opportunistic infections.
   - **d.** can develop other chronic conditions at an earlier age than someone without HIV.

10. What is the *most* appropriate nursing intervention to help patients with HIV adhere to their treatment plan?
   - **a.** Set up a drug pillbox for the patient every week.
   - **b.** Give the patient a video and a brochure to view and read at home.
   - **c.** Tell the patient that side effects of ART are bad but that they go away.
   - **d.** Assess the patient's routines and find adherence cues that fit into their life circumstances.

1. b; 2. a, b, c, d; 3. a, e; 4. c; 5. a, c, e; 6. a, e; 7. b; 8. c; 9. d; 10. d.

For rationales to these answers and even more NCLEX review questions, visit http://evolve.elsevier.com/Lewis/medsurg.

EVOLVE WEBSITE/RESOURCES LIST

http://evolve.elsevier.com/Lewis/medsurg
Review Questions (Online Only)
Key Points
Answer Keys for Questions
- Rationales for Bridge to NCLEX Examination Questions
- Answer Guidelines for Case Study

Student Case Study
- Patient With Human Immunodeficiency Virus (HIV) Infection and Acquired Immunodeficiency Syndrome (AIDS)

Conceptual Care Map Creator
Audio Glossary
Content Updates

REFERENCES

1. Centers for Disease Control and Prevention (CDC): Principles of epidemiology in public health practice. Retrieved from https://www.cdc.gov/careerpaths/k12teacherroadmap/classroom/principlesofepi.html.
2. CDC: National Center for Emerging and Zoonotic Infectious Diseases (NCEZID). Retrieved from https://www.cdc.gov/ncezid/index.html.
3. World Health Organization: Antimicrobial resistance. Retrieved from https://www.who.int/news-room/fact-sheets/detail/antimicrobial-resistance#:~:text=What%20is%20antimicrobial%20resistance%3F,spread%2C%20severe%20illness%20and%20death.

*4. Barcudi D, Sosa EJ, Lamberghini R, et al.: MRSA dynamic circulation between the community and the hospital setting: new insights from a cohort study, *J Infect* 80:24, 2020.

5. CDC: Healthcare-associated infections. Retrieved from www.cdc.gov/HAI.
6. U.S. Department of Labor Occupational Health and Safety Administration: PPE. Retrieved from https://www.osha.gov/personal-protective-equipment.
7. CDC: Using PPE. Retrieved from https://www.cdc.gov/coronavirus/2019-ncov/hcp/using-ppe.html.
8. Joost WW, Rhodes A, Cheng AC: Pathophysiology, transmission, diagnosis and treatment of coronavirus disease 2019 (COVID-19): a review, *JAMA* 324:782, 2020.
9. CDC: About variants of the virus that causes COVID-19. Retrieved from https://www.cdc.gov/coronavirus/2019-ncov/variants/variant.html.
10. NIH: Coronavirus Disease 2019 (COVID-19) treatment guidelines. Retrieved from https://www.covid19treatmentguidelines.nih.gov/.
11. CDC: Post-COVID conditions. Retrieved from https://www.cdc.gov/coronavirus/2019-ncov/long-term-effects.html.
12. CDC: Vaccines for COVID-19. Retrieved from https://www.cdc.gov/coronavirus/2019-ncov/vaccines/index.html.
13. CDC: HIV in the United States: At a glance. Retrieved from https://www.hiv.gov/hiv-basics/overview/data-and-trends/statistics.
14. National Institute of Allergy and Infectious Diseases: HIV undetectable=untransmittable (U=U), or treatment as prevention. Retrieved from https://www.niaid.nih.gov/diseases-conditions/treatment-prevention.
15. CDC: HIV and occupational exposure. Retrieved from www.cdc.gov/hiv/workplace/healthcareworkers.html.
16. National Institutes of Health Office of AIDS Research: The stages of HIV infection. Retrieved from https://hivinfo.nih.gov/understanding-hiv/fact-sheets/stages-hiv-infection
17. National HIV Curriculum: HIV diagnostic testing. Retrieved from https://www.hiv.uw.edu/go/screening-diagnosis/diagnostic-testing/core-concept/all
18. CDC: People coinfected with HIV and viral hepatitis. Retrieved from https://www.cdc.gov/hepatitis/populations/hiv.htm.

*19. Panel on Antiretroviral Guidelines for Adults and Adolescents: Guidelines for the use of antiretroviral agents in adults and adolescents living with HIV. Retrieved from https://clinicalinfo.hiv.gov/en/guidelines/adult-and-adolescent-arv/whats-new-guidelines

*20. Panel on Opportunistic Infections in HIV-Infected Adults and Adolescents: Guidelines for the prevention and treatment of opportunistic infections in adults and adolescents with HIV. Retrieved from https://clinicalinfo.hiv.gov/en/guidelines/adult-and-adolescent-opportunistic-infection/whats-new-guidelines.

*21. U.S. Public Health Service: PrEP for the prevention of HIV infection: a clinical practice guideline. Retrieved from https://clinicalinfo.hiv.gov/themes/custom/aidsinfo/documents/cdc-hiv-prep-guidelines-2017.pdf.

*22. CDC: Updated guidelines for antiretroviral PEP after sexual, drug use, or other nonoccupational exposure to HIV—United States, 2016. Retrieved from https://stacks.cdc.gov/view/cdc/38856.

23. U.S. Department of Health and Human Services HIV.gov: Syringe Services Programs. Retrieved from https://www.hiv.gov/federal-response/policies-issues/syringe-services-programs.

*24. Panel on Treatment of Pregnant Women with HIV Infection and Prevention of Perinatal Transmission: Recommendations for the use of antiretroviral drugs in in pregnant women with HIV infection and interventions to reduce perinatal HIV transmission in the United States. Retrieved from https://clinicalinfo.hiv.gov/sites/default/files/guidelines/documents/PerinatalGL.pdf.

*25. U.S. Public Health Service: Human immunodeficiency virus (HIV) infection: Screening. Retrieved from https://www.uspreventiveservicestaskforce.org/uspstf/recommendation/human-immunodeficiency-virus-hiv-infection-screening.

26. CDC: HIV stigma and discrimination. Retrieved from https://www.cdc.gov/hiv/basics/hiv-stigma/index.html.

*27. De Francesco D, Sabin C, Reiss P: Multimorbidity patterns in people with HIV, *Curr Opinion HIV AIDS* 15:110, 2020.

*Evidence-based information for clinical practice.

16

Cancer

Susan Doyle-Lindrud

http://evolve.elsevier.com/Lewis/medsurg/

CONCEPTUAL FOCUS

Cellular Regulation
Coping
Health Promotion

LEARNING OUTCOMES

1. Describe the incidence, survival, and mortality rates of cancer in the United States.
2. Discuss the processes involved in the biology of cancer.
3. Outline the stages of cancer development.
4. Describe the role of the immune system related to cancer.
5. Discuss the role of the nurse in the prevention, detection, and diagnosis of cancer.
6. Explain the use of surgery, chemotherapy, radiation therapy, immunotherapy, targeted therapy, and hormone therapy in treating cancer.
7. Identify the classifications of chemotherapy drugs and methods of administration.
8. Distinguish between external beam radiation and brachytherapy.
9. Describe the effects of radiation therapy and chemotherapy on normal tissues.
10. Identify the types and effects of immunotherapy and targeted therapy.
11. Describe the nursing management of patients receiving chemotherapy, radiation therapy, immunotherapy, and targeted therapy.
12. Describe nutrition therapy for patients with cancer.
13. Identify complications associated with cancer.
14. Describe support interventions for cancer patients, survivors, and their caregivers.

KEY TERMS

angiogenesis
brachytherapy
cancer
carcinogens
carcinoma in situ (CIS)
chemotherapy
external beam radiation
hematopoietic stem cell transplantation (HSCT)
histologic grading
immunologic surveillance
immunotherapy
malignant neoplasms
metastasis
oncogenes
peripheral stem cell transplantation (PSCT)
protooncogenes
staging
targeted therapy
vesicants

Cancer is a group of diseases characterized by uncontrolled and unregulated cell growth. The resulting problems may be directly related to the cancer, a consequence of cancer treatment, or a combination of both. The shared physiologic, psychologic, and social impact of cancer on patients and their caregivers is considerable. A lot of anxiety and fear are associated with a cancer diagnosis.

Educating health care professionals and the public is essential to promote realistic attitudes about cancer and cancer treatment. You are in a key position to lead efforts for changing attitudes about cancer. You can help people decrease their risk for cancer and take part in cancer screening. You need to know about types of cancer, treatment options, managing side effects of therapy, and supportive therapies. By supporting patients and caregivers as they cope with the effects of cancer and treatment, you are helping them adhere to cancer management plans and improve quality of life.

We often consider cancer a disease of aging. Most cases are diagnosed in those over age 55 years. However, it occurs in people of all ages. An estimated 1.8 million people in the

BOX 16.1 BIOLOGIC SEX CONSIDERATIONS

Cancer

Men

- More die from cancer-related deaths each year
- Have a higher mortality rate from lung cancer
- Prostate cancer has the highest incidence among men
- More likely to develop liver cancer
- More likely to be diagnosed with invasive cancer over their lifetime

Women

- Lung cancer has the highest death rate among women
- Breast cancer has the highest incidence among women
- Thyroid cancer is more prevalent in women
- Cancer incidence is higher in females during early adulthood (ages 20–49)

TABLE 16.1 Cancer Incidence by Site and Gender[a]

MALE		FEMALE	
Type	**%**	**Type**	**%**
Prostate	27	Breast	13
Lung	12	Lung	13
Colon/rectum	8	Colon/rectum	8
Urinary bladder	6	Uterus	7
Melanoma	6	Melanoma	5
Kidney and renal pelvis	5	Non-Hodgkin lymphoma	4
Non-Hodgkin lymphoma	4	Thyroid	3
Oral cavity and pharynx	4	Kidney and renal pelvis	3
Leukemia	4	Pancreas	3
Pancreas	3	Leukemia	3

[a]Numbers are estimates and exclude basal and squamous cell skin cancers and carcinoma in situ.
Source: National Cancer Institute: Cancer stat facts. Retrieved from https://seer.cancer.gov/statfacts.

United States are diagnosed each year with cancer. This number excludes basal and squamous cell skin cancers and carcinoma in situ of any site except the bladder.[1]

Overall, both the incidence and mortality rates of cancer have been declining.[2] The incidence of many cancers, such as colorectal, lung, and laryngeal cancers, have declined largely because of preventive efforts. The incidence of other cancers, such as kidney, pancreas, liver, uterus, melanoma, multiple myeloma, and oropharyngeal, is increasing.[3]

Overall cancer incidence is higher in men than women. Differences in incidence and death rates for specific cancers are shown in Box 16.1 and Tables 16.1 and 16.2.

Although mortality rates from all cancers combined are on the decline, it is still the second most common cause of death in the United States. Cancer is the leading cause of death of people 40 to 79 years of age. Each year about 606,520 Americans die from cancer. This is more than 1600 people per day.[1,2]

We have made great progress in controlling cancer for long periods. More than 16.9 million Americans with a history of cancer are alive today. This includes those who have cancer and are undergoing treatment, are disease free, or are in remission.[2]

TABLE 16.2 Cancer Deaths by Site and Gender

MALE		FEMALE	
Type	**%**	**Type**	**%**
Lung and bronchus	21	Lung and bronchus	21
Prostate	11	Breast	15
Colon/rectum	9	Colon/rectum	8
Pancreas	8	Pancreas	8
Liver and intrahepatic bile ducts	6	Ovary	4
Leukemia	4	Uterus	4
Esophagus	4	Liver and intrahepatic bile ducts	4
Urinary bladder	4	Leukemia	3
Non-Hodgkin lymphoma	4	Non-Hodgkin lymphoma	3
Brain & other nervous system	3	Brain and other nervous system	3

Source: National Cancer Institute: Cancer stat facts. Retrieved from https://seer.cancer.gov/statfacts.

BIOLOGY OF CANCER

Two major dysfunctions present in the process of cancer development are defective cell proliferation (growth) and defective cell differentiation.

Defect in Cell Proliferation

Normally, most tissues have a population of undifferentiated cells known as stem cells. These stem cells ultimately differentiate and become mature, functioning cells of a specific tissue.

Cell proliferation starts in the stem cell and begins when the stem cell enters the cell cycle (Fig. 16.1). The time from when a cell enters the cell cycle to when the cell divides into 2 identical cells is the *generation time* of the cell. A mature cell continues to function until it degenerates and dies.

All the body's cells are controlled by an intracellular mechanism that determines when cell proliferation is necessary. A state of dynamic equilibrium is present under normal conditions. This means cell proliferation equals cell degeneration or death. Normally, the process of cell division and proliferation is activated only in the presence of cell degeneration or death *(apoptosis).* Cell proliferation also occurs if the body has a physiologic need for more cells. For example, a normal increase in white blood cell (WBC) count occurs with infection.

Another means of proliferation control in normal cells is *contact inhibition*. Normal cells respect the boundaries and territory of the cells around them. They will not invade a territory that is not their own. We think the neighboring cells inhibit cell growth through the physical contact of their cell membranes. Cancer cells grown in tissue culture have a loss of contact inhibition. They have no regard for cell boundaries. They grow on top of one another and on top of or between normal cells.

The rate of cell proliferation from the time of cell birth to the time of cell death differs in each body tissue. In some tissues, such as bone marrow, hair follicles, and epithelial lining of the

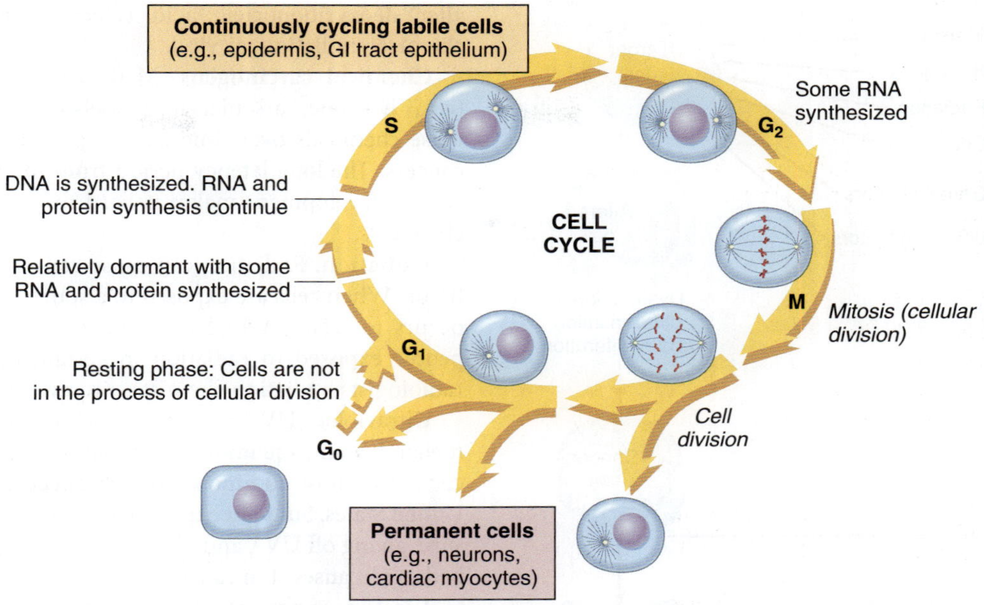

Fig. 16.1 Cell life cycle and metabolic activity. Generation time is the period from *M* phase to *M* phase. Cells not in the cycle but capable of division are in the resting phase *(G_0)*. (Adapted from Kumar V, Abbas AK, Fausto N, et al.: *Robbins and Cotran pathologic basis of disease,* ed 8, Philadelphia, 2010, Saunders.)

gastrointestinal (GI) tract, the rate of cell proliferation is rapid. In other tissues, such as myocardium and cartilage, cell proliferation does not occur or is slow.

Cancer cells proliferate at the same rate as the normal cells of the tissue from which they arise. However, cancer cells respond differently to the intracellular signals that regulate cell proliferation and death. The result is that cancer cell proliferation is indiscriminate and continuous. Sometimes they produce more than 2 cells at the time of mitosis. In this way, there is continuous growth of a tumor mass: $1 \times 2 \times 4 \times 8 \times 16$ and so on. We call this the *pyramid effect.* The time needed for a tumor mass to double in size is known as its *doubling time.*

Defect in Cell Differentiation

Cell differentiation is normally an orderly process that progresses from a state of immaturity to a state of maturity. Because all body cells are derived from the fertilized ova, all cells have the potential to perform all body functions. As cells differentiate, this potential is repressed. The mature cell can perform only specific functions. With cell differentiation, there is a stable and orderly phasing out of cell potential. Normally, the differentiated cell is stable and will not *dedifferentiate* or return to its previous undifferentiated state.

Genetic Link

Cancer involves the malfunction of genes that control differentiation and proliferation. Two types of normal genes that can be affected by mutation are *protooncogenes* and *tumor suppressor genes.* **Protooncogenes** are normal cell genes that are important regulators of normal cell processes. Protooncogenes promote growth. Mutations that change the expression of protooncogenes can cause them to function as **oncogenes** (tumor-inducing genes).

Think of the protooncogene as the genetic lock that keeps the cell in its mature functioning state. When this lock is "unlocked," which can occur through exposure to *carcinogens* (agents that cause cancer) or oncogenic viruses, genetic alterations and mutations occur. Thus oncogenes can change a normal cell to a malignant one. This cell regains a fetal appearance and function. For example, some cancer cells make new proteins characteristic of the embryonic and fetal periods of life. These proteins, found on the cell membrane, include carcinoembryonic antigen (CEA) and α-fetoprotein (AFP). They can be found in the blood by laboratory studies. Other cancer cells, such as small cell lung cancer, make hormones that are usually made by cells arising from the same embryonic cells as the tumor cells.

Tumor suppressor genes suppress growth. They prevent cells from going through the cell cycle. Mutations can change tumor suppressor genes and make them inactive. This results in a loss of their tumor-suppressing action. Examples of tumor suppressor genes are *BRCA1* and *BRCA2.* Alterations in these genes increase a person's risk for breast and ovarian cancer. Another tumor suppressor gene is the *APC* gene. *APC* mutations increase a person's risk for familial adenomatous polyposis, a precursor for colorectal cancer (see Chapter 47). Mutations in the *p53* tumor suppressor gene have been found in many cancers. These include bladder, breast, colorectal, esophageal, liver, lung, and ovarian cancers.

Development of Cancer

The following is a theoretical model of cancer development. The cause and development of each type of cancer are likely to be multifactorial. A common misbelief is that cancer development is a rapid, haphazard event. However, cancer is usually an orderly process that occurs over time. There are 3 stages: initiation, promotion, and progression (Fig. 16.2).

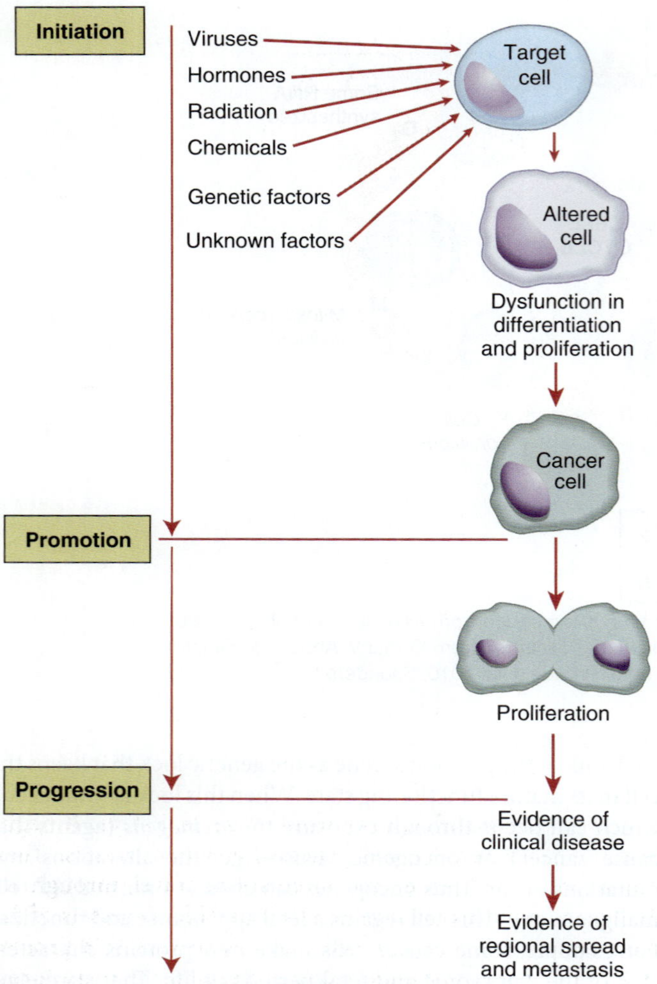

Fig. 16.2 Process of cancer development.

Initiation

Cancer cells arise from normal cells because of changes in genes. The first stage, *initiation*, involves a mutation in the cell's genetic structure. A *mutation* is any change in the usual DNA sequence.

Genetic Link

Gene mutations can occur in 2 ways: *inherited* from a parent (passed from one generation to the next) or *acquired* during a person's lifetime. See more about mutations in Chapter 13.

We think the genetic predisposition to cancer plays a role in about 5% to 10% of cancers. These genetic alterations lead to a high risk for developing a specific type of cancer. However, most cancers do not result from inherited genes. They are acquired from damage to genes occurring during one's lifetime. An acquired mutation is passed on to all cells that develop from that single cell. The damaged cell may die or repair itself. However, if cell death or repair does not occur before cell division, the cell will replicate into daughter cells, each with the same genetic alteration.

Carcinogens. **Carcinogens** are cancer-causing agents capable of producing cell alterations. Many are detoxified by protective enzymes and harmlessly excreted. If this protective mechanism fails, carcinogens can enter the cell's nucleus and alter deoxyribonucleic acid (DNA). Carcinogens may be chemical, radiation, or viral.

Chemical carcinogens. Many chemicals are carcinogens (e.g., benzene, arsenic, formaldehyde). People exposed to these chemicals over time have a greater incidence of certain cancers. The long latency period from the time of exposure to cancer development makes it hard to identify cancer-causing chemicals.

Radiation. Radiation can cause cancer in almost any body tissue. When cells are exposed to a source of radiation, damage occurs to DNA. A higher incidence of cancer may occur in people exposed to radiation in certain occupations, such as radiologists, radiation chemists, aircrews, and uranium miners.

Ultraviolet (UV) radiation has long been associated with melanoma and squamous and basal cell skin cancers. Skin cancer is the most common type of cancer among whites in the United States. Sunlight exposure is the main source of UV exposure, giving off UVA and UVB rays. UV radiation from tanning beds also causes skin cancer.[4]

Viral carcinogens. Certain DNA and ribonucleic acid (RNA) viruses, termed *oncogenic,* can alter the cells they infect and induce malignant transformation. These viruses have been identified as causative agents of cancer in animals and humans. Burkitt lymphoma is associated with Epstein-Barr virus (EBV).[5] People with acquired immunodeficiency syndrome (AIDS), caused by human immunodeficiency virus (HIV), have a high incidence of Kaposi sarcoma (see Chapter 15). Other viruses linked to cancer include hepatitis B virus, which is associated with primary liver cancer (hepatocellular cancer), and human papillomavirus (HPV). HPV can cause lesions that progress to squamous cell cancers, such as cervical, anal, and head and neck cancers.

Promotion

A single alteration of the cell's genetic structure is not enough to cause cancer. However, the odds of cancer development increase with the presence of promoting agents. *Promotion,* the second stage in cancer development, is characterized by the reversible proliferation of the altered cells. An increase in the altered cell population increases the likelihood of more mutations.

An important distinction between initiation and promotion is that the activity of promoters is reversible. This is a key concept in cancer prevention. Promoting factors include agents such as obesity, cigarette smoking, and alcohol use. Changing a person's lifestyle to modify these risk factors can reduce the chance of cancer development. Around 40% of newly diagnosed cancers in the United States are potentially avoidable. These include cancers caused by obesity, alcohol use, unhealthy diet, smoking, and physical inactivity.[1]

Several promoting agents have activity against specific body tissues. These agents tend to promote specific kinds of cancer. For example, cigarette smoke is a promoting agent in lung cancer. In conjunction with alcohol use, it promotes esophageal and bladder cancers.

Some carcinogens, termed *complete carcinogens,* are capable of both initiating and promoting cancer development. Cigarette smoke is an example of a complete carcinogen.

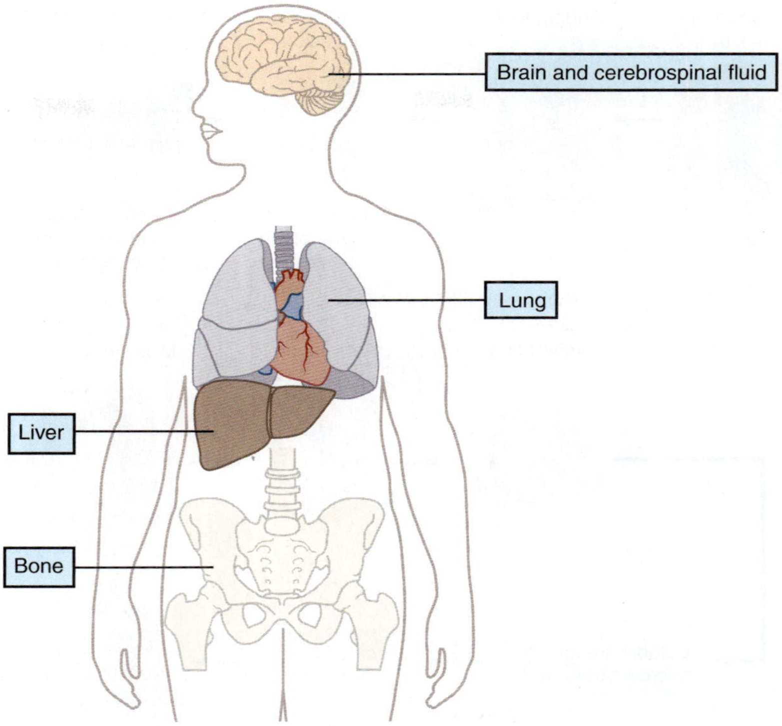

Fig. 16.3 Main sites of metastasis.

The time between the first genetic alteration and the actual clinical evidence of cancer is the *latent* period. It includes both the initiation and promotion stages. The variation in the length of time that elapses before the cancer becomes clinically evident is related to the mitotic rate of the tissue of origin and environmental factors. In most cancers, this process is years or even decades in length.

For the disease process to become clinically evident, the cells must reach a critical mass. A tumor that is 1.0 cm (0.4 inch) (the size usually detectable by palpation) has 1 billion cancer cells. A 0.5-cm tumor is the smallest that we can detect with current diagnostic measures, such as MRI.

Progression

Progression is the last stage. Here, we see increased growth rate of the tumor, increased invasiveness, and **metastasis** (spread of the cancer to a distant site). Some cancers have an affinity for a particular tissue or organ as a site of metastasis. For example, colon cancer often spreads to the liver. Other cancers are unpredictable in their pattern of metastasis. The most common sites of metastasis are lungs, liver, bone, and brain (Fig. 16.3).

Metastasis is a multistep process. It begins with the rapid growth of the primary tumor (Fig. 16.4). As the tumor increases in size, developing its own blood supply is critical to its survival and growth. The process of forming blood vessels within the tumor itself is termed tumor **angiogenesis**. It is facilitated by tumor angiogenesis factors made by the cancer cells.

Tumor cells can detach from the primary tumor, invade the tissue surrounding the tumor, and penetrate the walls of lymph or vascular vessels for metastasis to a distant site. Once free from the primary tumor, metastatic tumor cells often travel to distant sites by hematogenous or lymphatic routes.

Hematogenous metastasis involves several steps. It begins with primary tumor cells penetrating blood vessels. These tumor cells then enter the circulation, travel through the body, and adhere to and penetrate small blood vessels of distant organs. Most tumor cells do not survive this process. They are destroyed by mechanical mechanisms (e.g., turbulence of blood flow) and cells of the immune system. The formation of a combination of tumor cells, platelets, and fibrin deposits may protect some tumor cells from destruction in blood vessels.

In the lymphatic system, tumor cells can be "trapped" in the first lymph node to which cancer cells are most likely to spread from a tumor. This lymph node is the *sentinel lymph node*. A sentinel lymph node biopsy (SLNB) can help determine the extent of the cancer. A positive SLNB means cancer is present in the sentinel node and may have spread to other lymph nodes and organs. Sometimes, the tumor cells may bypass local lymph nodes and travel to distant lymph nodes. We call this phenomenon *skip metastasis*.

Tumor cells that survive the process of metastasis must create an environment in the distant organ site that promotes their growth and development. This is facilitated by the tumor cells' ability to evade cells of the immune system and produce a vascular supply within the metastatic site. Vascularization is critical to the supply of nutrients to the metastatic tumor and the removal of waste products.

Role of the Immune System

The immune system has the potential to tell normal (self) cells from abnormal (nonself) cells. For example, the immune system can recognize cells of transplanted organs as *nonself* and

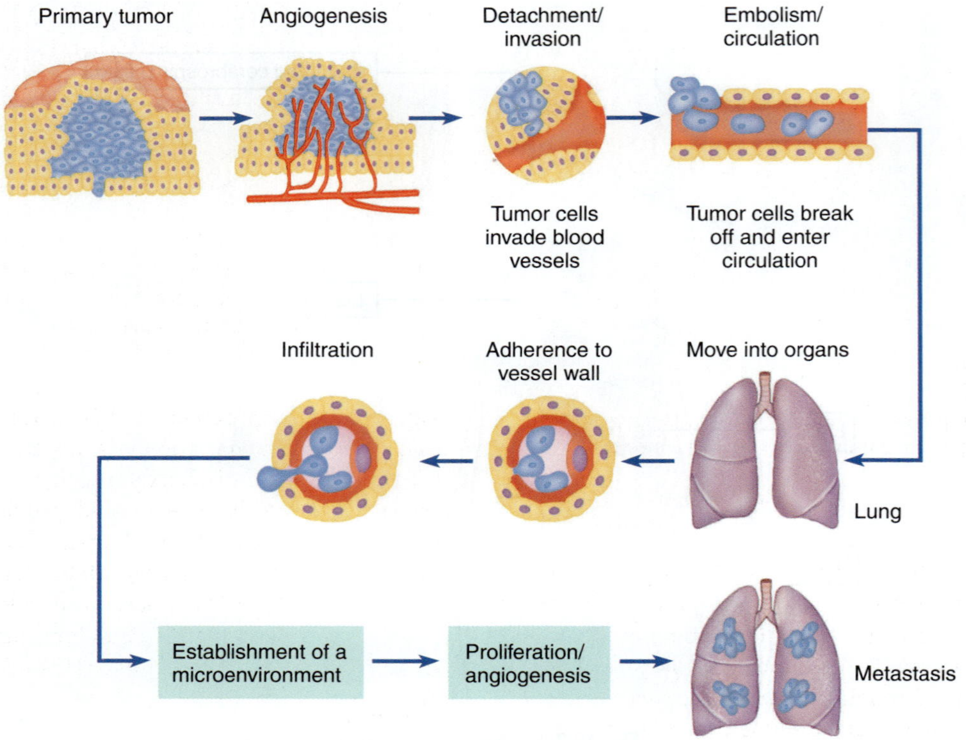

Fig. 16.4 The pathogenesis of cancer metastasis. To produce metastases, tumor cells must detach from the primary tumor and enter the circulation, survive in the circulation to rest in the capillary bed, adhere to capillary basement membrane, gain entrance into the organ parenchyma, respond to growth factors, proliferate, induce angiogenesis, and evade host defenses. (Adapted from Fidler IT: The pathogenesis of cancer metastasis: The "seed and soil" hypothesis revisited, *Nat Rev Cancer* 3:453, 2003.)

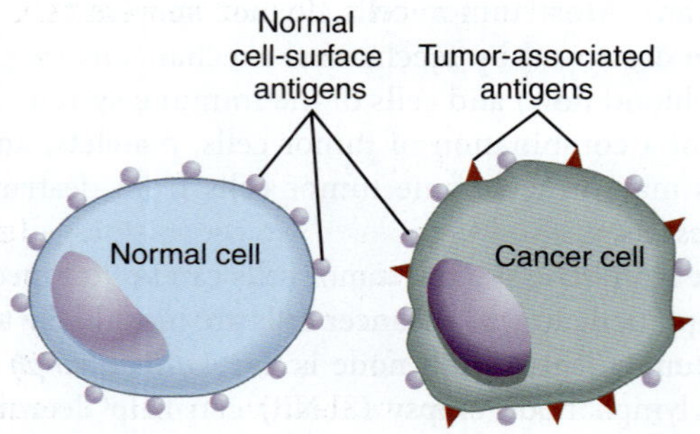

Fig. 16.5 Tumor-associated antigens appear on the cell surface of cancer cells.

thus elicit an immune response. This response can result in organ rejection. Similarly, cancer cells can be perceived as nonself. This can elicit an immune response, resulting in their rejection and destruction. However, cancer cells arise from normal human cells and, although they are mutated and thus different, the immune response that is mounted against cancer cells may be inadequate to effectively kill them.

Cancer cells may have altered cell-surface antigens because of malignant transformation. These antigens are termed *tumor-associated antigens (TAAs)* (Fig. 16.5). We think that the immune system responds to TAAs through a process termed **immunologic surveillance**. In this process, lymphocytes continuously check cell-surface antigens. They detect and destroy cells with abnormal or altered cell-surface antigens. Under most circumstances, immune surveillance prevents transformed cells from developing into detectable tumors.

Immune response to cancer cells involves cytotoxic T cells, natural killer (NK) cells, macrophages, and B cells. *Cytotoxic T cells* play a key role in resisting tumor growth. These cells can kill tumor cells. T cells are important in the production of cytokines (e.g., interleukin-2 [IL-2], γ-interferon), which stimulate T cells, NK cells, B cells, and macrophages. *NK cells* can directly kill tumor cells without any prior sensitization. γ-Interferon (made by T cells) and IL-2 (released from T cells) stimulate NK cells, resulting in increased cytotoxic activity.

Monocytes and *macrophages* have several important roles in tumor immunity. γ-Interferon can activate macrophages to become nonspecifically lytic for tumor cells. Macrophages secrete cytokines, including IL-1, tumor necrosis factor (TNF), and colony-stimulating factors (CSFs). The release of IL-1, coupled with the presentation of the processed antigen, stimulates T-cell activation and production. α-Interferon augments the killing ability of NK cells. TNF causes hemorrhagic necrosis of tumors and exerts cytocidal or cytostatic actions against tumor cells. CSFs regulate the production of various blood cells in the bone marrow and stimulate the function of various WBCs.

B cells can make specific antibodies that bind to tumor cells. These antibodies are often detectable in the patient's serum and saliva.

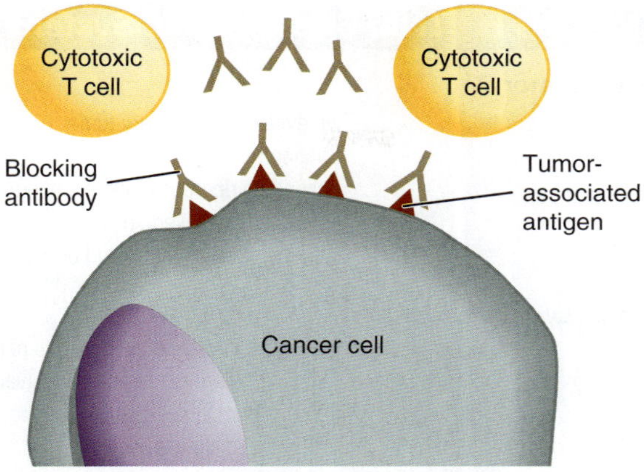

Fig. 16.6 Blocking antibodies prevent T cells from interacting with tumor-associated antigens and from destroying the cancer cell.

Escape Mechanisms From Immunologic Surveillance

Immunologic escape is the process by which cancer cells evade the immune system. Possible mechanisms for immunologic escape include (1) suppression of factors that stimulate T cells to react to cancer cells; (2) weak surface antigens allowing cancer cells to "sneak through" immunologic surveillance; (3) development of tolerance of the immune system to some tumor antigens; (4) suppression of the immune response by products secreted by cancer cells; (5) induction of suppressor T cells by the tumor; and (6) blocking antibodies that bind TAAs, thus preventing their recognition by T cells (Fig. 16.6).

Oncofetal Antigens and Tumor Markers

Oncofetal antigens are a type of tumor antigen. They are on the surfaces and the inside of cancer cells and fetal cells. These antigens are an expression of the shift of cancerous cells to a more immature metabolic pathway. This expression is usually associated with embryonic or fetal periods of life. We think the reappearance of fetal antigens is the result of the cell regaining its embryonic capability to differentiate into many different cell types.

Examples of oncofetal antigens are CEA and AFP. CEA is found on the surfaces of cancer cells from the GI tract and normal cells from the fetal gut, liver, and pancreas. Normally, CEA disappears during the last 3 months of fetal life. High CEA levels often occur with colorectal cancer. However, high CEA levels can occur in nonmalignant conditions (e.g., cirrhosis, ulcerative colitis, heavy smoking).

Oncofetal antigens can be used as *tumor markers* that may be clinically useful to monitor the effect of therapy and indicate tumor recurrence. However, they are not 100% specific for tumor recurrence. Various factors affect tumor markers. We must consider these factors when reviewing results. For example, high CEA titers that persist after surgery means that some cancer is still present. A rise in CEA levels after chemotherapy may mean recurrence or spread of the cancer, or it may be due to chronic lung disease and smoking.

AFP is made by malignant liver cells, metastatic liver growth, and fetal liver cells. AFP has diagnostic value in primary liver cancer. This makes AFP valuable in tumor detection and evaluating tumor progression. AFP levels are also high in some cases of testicular cancer and viral hepatitis.

Other examples of oncofetal antigens are CA-125 (ovarian cancer), CA-19-9 (pancreatic and gallbladder cancer), prostate-specific antigen (PSA) (prostate cancer), and CA-15.3 and CA-27-29 (breast cancer). Molecular markers for specific tumors include KRAS (an oncogene in colon cancer), epidermal growth factor receptor (EGFR) in lung cancer, and human epidermal growth factor receptor-2 (HER-2) expression in breast cancer.

TABLE 16.3 Comparison of Benign and Malignant Neoplasms

Characteristic	Benign	Malignant
Encapsulated	Usually	Rarely
Differentiated	Normally	Poorly
Metastasis	Absent	Capable
Recurrence	Rare	Possible
Vascularity	Slight	Moderate to marked
Mode of growth	Expansive	Infiltrative and expansive
Cell characteristics	Fairly normal, like parent cells	Cells abnormal, become more unlike parent cells

BENIGN VERSUS MALIGNANT NEOPLASMS

We classify tumors as benign or malignant. In general, *benign neoplasms* are well differentiated. **Malignant neoplasms** range from well-differentiated to undifferentiated. The ability of malignant tumor cells to invade and metastasize is the major difference between benign and malignant neoplasms. Other differences are outlined in Table 16.3.

CLASSIFICATION OF CANCER

Tumors can be classified by anatomic site, histology (grading), and extent of disease (staging). Tumor classification systems provide a standardized way to (1) communicate the status of the cancer to all members of the health care team, (2) assist in determining the most effective treatment plan, (3) evaluate the treatment plan, (4) predict prognosis, and (5) compare groups for statistical purposes.

Anatomic Site Classification

In the *anatomic classification* of tumors, the tumor is identified by the tissue of origin, anatomic site, and behavior of the tumor (benign or malignant) (Table 16.4). *Carcinomas* originate from embryonal *ectoderm* (skin and glands) and *endoderm* (mucous membrane linings of the respiratory tract, GI tract, and genitourinary [GU] tract). *Sarcomas* originate from embryonal *mesoderm* (connective tissue, muscle, bone, fat). Lymphomas and leukemias originate from the hematopoietic system.

Histologic Classification

In **histologic grading** of tumors, the appearance of cells and degree of differentiation are evaluated pathologically. Grading is based on the degree to which the cells resemble the tissue of

TABLE 16.4 Anatomic Classification of Tumors

Site	Benign	Malignant
Epithelial Tissue Tumors[a]	**-oma**	**-carcinoma**
Surface epithelium	Papilloma	Carcinoma
Glandular epithelium	Adenoma	Adenocarcinoma
Connective Tissue Tumors[b]	**-oma**	**-sarcoma**
Fibrous tissue	Fibroma	Fibrosarcoma
Cartilage	Chondroma	Chondrosarcoma
Striated muscle	Rhabdomyoma	Rhabdomyosarcoma
Bone	Osteoma	Osteosarcoma
Nervous Tissue Tumors	**-oma**	**-oma**
Meninges	Meningioma	Meningeal sarcoma
Nerve cells	Ganglioneuroma	Neuroblastoma
Hematopoietic Tissue Tumors		
Lymphoid tissue	—	Hodgkin lymphoma, non-Hodgkin lymphoma
Plasma cells	—	Multiple myeloma
Bone marrow	—	Lymphocytic and myelogenous leukemia

[a]Body surfaces, lining of body cavities, and glandular structures.
[b]Supporting tissue, fibrotic tissue, and blood vessels.

origin. Poorly differentiated (undifferentiated) tumors have a poorer prognosis than those that are closer in appearance to the normal tissue of origin (well-differentiated). We use 4 grades for many tumor types:

Grade I: Cells differ slightly from normal cells (mild dysplasia) and are well-differentiated (low grade).

Grade II: Cells are more abnormal (moderate dysplasia) and moderately differentiated (intermediate grade).

Grade III: Cells are very abnormal (severe dysplasia) and poorly differentiated (high grade).

Grade IV: Cells are immature, primitive *(anaplasia),* and undifferentiated. Cell origin is hard to determine (high grade).

Grade X: Grade cannot be assessed.

Extent of Disease Classification

Classifying the extent and spread of disease is termed **staging**. Staging is based on the anatomic extent of disease. Although there are similarities in the staging of various cancers, there are many differences for specific types of cancer. Staging can be done initially and at several points. Clinical staging is done at the completion of the diagnostic workup to guide treatment selection.

Clinical Staging

The clinical staging classification system determines the anatomic extent of the cancer by stages:

Stage 0: Cancer in situ

Stage I: Tumor limited to the tissue of origin; localized tumor growth

Stage II: Limited local spread

Stage III: Extensive local and regional spread

Stage IV: Metastasis

Clinical staging is used as a basis for staging a variety of tumor types. Look at the examples for colorectal cancer (see Table 47.26) and Hodgkin lymphoma (see Fig. 34.15). Other cancers (e.g., leukemia) do not use this staging approach. **Carcinoma in situ (CIS)** refers to a cancer whose cells are localized and show no tendency to invade or metastasize to other tissues.

TABLE 16.5 TNM Classification System

Primary Tumor (T)	
T_0	No evidence of primary tumor
T_{is}	Carcinoma in situ
T_{1-4}	Ascending degrees of increase in tumor size and involvement
T_x	Tumor cannot be measured or found
Regional Lymph Nodes (N)	
N_0	No evidence of disease in lymph nodes
N_{1-4}	Ascending degrees of nodal involvement
N_x	Regional lymph nodes unable to be assessed clinically
Distant Metastases (M)	
M_0	No metastases
M_{1-4}	Metastases present
M_x	Cannot be determined

TNM Classification System

We use the *TNM classification system* (Table 16.5) to determine the anatomic extent of cancer involvement. There are 3 parameters: tumor size and invasiveness (T), presence or absence of regional spread to the lymph nodes (N), and metastasis to distant organ sites (M). Examples of the TNM classification system are shown in Tables 30.26 and 56.7. We do not use TNM staging with all cancers. For example, we do not stage leukemias with TNM since they are not solid tumors. CIS has its own designation in the system (T_{is}). CIS has all the histologic characteristics of cancer except invasion, a key feature of the TNM staging system.

The latest cancer staging guidelines for some cancers add non-anatomic factors when making the final determination of stage. Staging is still based on the TNM classification, but it adds grade and hormone receptor expression. When appropriate, it also includes genomic profile results (e.g., Oncotype DX, Mammaprint). This information allows for a more accurate determination of prognosis and better guide therapy.

Surgical staging refers to the extent of the disease as determined by surgical excision, exploration, and/or lymph node sampling. For example, a laparotomy and splenectomy may be done to stage Hodgkin lymphoma. Lymph node biopsies may be done during a staging laparotomy. Margins of any masses may be marked with metal clips for use during radiation therapy. We use exploratory surgical staging less often as noninvasive diagnostic technology becomes more advanced.

After the extent of the disease is determined, the stage classification is set. The original description of the extent of the tumor stays part of the record. If the patient needs more treatment, or if treatment fails, retreatment staging is done to determine

BOX 16.2 PROMOTING POPULATION HEALTH

Prevention and Early Detection of Cancer

Teach patients and the public about cancer prevention and early detection. Points include:

- Limit alcohol use.
- Get regular physical activity (e.g., 30 min or more of moderate physical activity 5 times weekly).
- Maintain a normal weight.
- Have regular physical examinations.
- Obtain regular colorectal screenings.
- Avoid cigarette smoking and other tobacco use.
- Get regular mammography screening and Pap tests.
- Be familiar with your own family history and risk factors for cancer.
- Obtain adequate rest of at least 6–8 hours per night.
- Use sunscreen with a sun protection factor of 15 or higher. Avoid tanning beds.
- Eliminate, reduce, or change the perception of stressors and enhance the ability to effectively cope with stress (see Chapter 7).
- Eat a balanced diet that includes vegetables and fresh fruits, whole grains, and fiber. Reduce dietary fat and preservatives. Limit smoked and salt-cured meats with high nitrite concentrations.

the extent of the disease before retreatment. "Restaging" classification (rTNM) is distinguished from the stage at diagnosis since the clinical significance may be different. Staging cannot decrease, but the stage can increase. For example, a patient may initially be a stage 3. After treatment failure, the tumor metastasizes, and now the patient is a stage 4.

In addition to tumor classification systems, we can use other rating scales to describe and document the patient's status at the time of diagnosis, treatment, retreatment, and at each follow-up appointment. For example, the Karnofsky Performance Scale and Katz Index of Independence in Activities of Daily Living describe a patient's functional performance.

PREVENTION AND DETECTION OF CANCER

We can reduce the incidence of cancer through a stronger emphasis on prevention by promoting healthy lifestyles (Box 16.2). As a nurse, you have an essential role in the prevention and early detection of cancer. Reducing risk factors reduces the incidence of cancer. For example, smoking-related cancers (e.g., lung and bladder cancer) have declined with a reduction in smoking rates.[1]

Early detection and prompt treatment are responsible for increased survival rates. Colonoscopy is important in reducing colon cancer mortality both by early detection of colon cancer and prevention (e.g., excision of adenomatous polyps).

The goals of public education are to (1) motivate people to recognize behaviors that may negatively affect health and (2) encourage awareness of and participation in health-promoting behaviors. When you teach about cancer, try to lessen the fear that surrounds the diagnosis.

Teach people to be familiar with their bodies and how to perform self-examinations. Review the 7 warning signs of cancer (Table 16.6). Encourage them to seek immediate medical care if they notice a change in what is normal for them or if cancer is suspected. Following recommended cancer screening guidelines for breast, colon, cervical, and prostate cancer from the American Cancer Society (ACS) is important.[6]

TABLE 16.6 Warning Signs of Cancer

Change in bowel or bladder habits
A sore that does not heal
Unusual bleeding or discharge from any body orifice
Thickening or a lump in the breast or elsewhere
Indigestion or difficulty in swallowing
Obvious change in a wart or mole
Nagging cough or hoarseness

Diagnosis of Cancer

Facing a possible diagnosis of cancer is a stressful time for the patient and caregivers. Patients may undergo several days to weeks of diagnostic studies. During this time, fear of the unknown may be more stressful than the actual diagnosis of cancer. Patients may feel overwhelmed or confused by the need for multiple diagnostic studies and consultations. Help coordinate care among multiple specialists. Explain the purpose of required tests and any special preparation needed.

Some agencies have comprehensive oncology teams and services housed in the same building. This helps us coordinate care among cancer specialists. These centers combine appointments to make the experience convenient and comfortable for patients and their caregivers.

While patients are waiting for the results of diagnostic studies, actively listen to their concerns. Anxiety may arise from myths and misconceptions about cancer (e.g., cancer is a "death sentence," cancer treatment is "horrible"). Correcting those misconceptions can help lessen their anxiety.

Learn to manage your own discomfort during difficult conversations. Avoid communication that hinders exploration of feelings and meaning. These include providing false reassurances (e.g., "It's probably nothing"), redirecting the discussion (e.g., "Let's discuss that later"), and generalizing (e.g., "Everyone feels this way"). These strategies deny patients the opportunity to share the meaning of their experience. They can jeopardize your ability to build a trusting relationship with your patients.

During this time of high anxiety, the patient may need repeated explanations of the diagnostic plan. Include as much information as needed by the patient and caregivers. Give clear, understandable explanations and reinforce them as needed. Avoid using overly technical language. Written information is helpful to reinforce verbal information.

A diagnostic plan for the person suspected of having cancer includes the health history (including a history of present illness), identifying risk factors, the physical assessment, and specific diagnostic studies. Many people receive a cancer diagnosis after an abnormal screening test (e.g., mass on mammogram). Others are alerted to the presence of cancer by a presenting symptom or cluster of symptoms (e.g., cough and hemoptysis, anorexia, and weight loss).

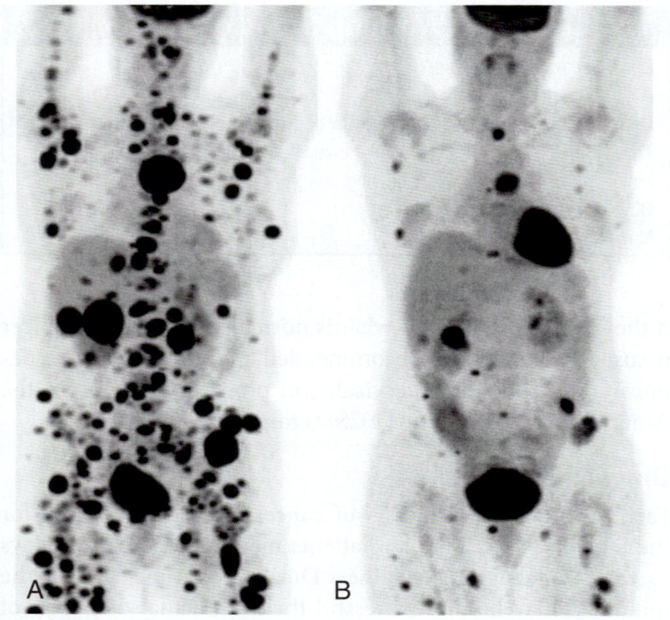

Fig. 16.7 PET scan before treatment (A) showing multiples metastases in the skeleton, soft tissues, muscles, mediastinum, lymph nodes, liver, kidneys, and thyroid gland. PET scan after treatment (B) shows the effects of therapy. (From Faria S, Devine C, Viswanathan C, et al.: FDG-PET assessment of other gynecologic cancers, *PET Clinics* 13:203, 2017.)

Concentrate on risk factors for cancer. Obtain information about any family and personal history of cancer. Is there any exposure to or use of known carcinogens (e.g., cigarette smoking, occupational pollutants or chemicals, radiation exposure)? Review the health history for diseases characterized by chronic inflammation or immunosuppression (e.g., ulcerative colitis) and treatments (e.g., hormone therapy, previous anticancer therapies). Assess factors that may call for additional supportive care during therapy, including alcohol or drug use, living situation, social support, and coping strategies for perceived stressors.

Diagnostic studies depend on the suspected primary or metastatic site(s) of the cancer. Examples include:

- Cytology studies (e.g., Pap test, bronchial washings)
- Chest x-ray
- Complete blood count (CBC), chemistry profile
- Liver function studies (e.g., aspartate aminotransferase [AST])
- Endoscopic examination: upper GI, sigmoidoscopy, or colonoscopy (including guaiac test for occult blood)
- Radiographic studies (e.g., mammography, ultrasound, CT scan, MRI)
- Radioisotope scans (e.g., bone, lung, liver, brain)
- PET scan (Fig. 16.7)
- Tumor markers (e.g., CEA, AFP, PSA, CA-125)
- Genetic markers (e.g., *BRCA1, BRCA2*)
- Molecular receptor status (e.g., estrogen and progesterone receptors)
- Bone marrow examination

Biopsy

A *biopsy* is the removal of a tissue sample for pathologic analysis. The method used to obtain a biopsy depends on the location and size of the suspected tumor. *Percutaneous biopsy* is often done for tissue that can be safely reached through the skin. *Endoscopic biopsy* may be used for lung or other intraluminal lesions (esophageal, colon, bladder). When a tumor is not easily accessible, surgery (laparotomy, thoracotomy, craniotomy) may be done to obtain a piece of the tumor tissue. Many radiographic techniques may be used to improve tissue localization with the biopsy. These include CT, MRI, ultrasound-guided biopsy, and stereotactic biopsy.

Various types and sizes of biopsy needles are available. The choice depends on the type of tissue to be sampled. *Fine-needle aspiration* (FNA) may be done with a small-gauge aspiration needle that provides cells from the mass for cytologic examination. *Large-core biopsy* cutting needles deliver an actual piece of tissue (core) for analysis. An advantage is that it preserves the histologic architecture of the tissue specimen. *Excisional biopsy* involves the surgical removal of the entire lesion, lymph node, nodule, or mass. So, it is therapeutic as well as diagnostic. If an excisional biopsy is not feasible, an *incisional biopsy* (partial excision) may be done with a scalpel or dermal punch.

Pathologic evaluation of a tissue sample is the only definitive way to diagnose cancer. The pathologist examines the tissue to determine (1) whether it is benign or malignant, (2) the anatomic tissue from which the tumor arises *(histology),* and (3) the degree of cell differentiation *(histologic grade).* Other information that we can obtain include the extent of malignant involvement (size of tumor and depth), evidence of invasiveness (extracapsular, lymphatic), adequacy of surgical excision (positive or negative surgical margin status), and nuclear grade (mitotic rate). Special staining techniques may give insight into responsiveness of the tumor to treatment or disease behavior (receptor status, tumor markers).

INTERPROFESSIONAL CARE

TREATMENT GOALS

The goals of cancer treatment are cure, control, and palliation (Fig. 16.8). When caring for the patient with cancer, knowing the treatment goals will help you appropriately communicate with, teach, and support the patient. The main factors that determine the therapy plan are tumor histology and staging outcomes. Other crucial factors are the patient's physiologic status (e.g., presence of co-morbid illnesses), psychologic status, and personal desires (e.g., active treatment versus palliation).

These factors influence (1) the treatment modalities (e.g., surgery, radiation therapy, chemotherapy), (2) how therapies are sequenced, and (3) the length of time of treatment. A therapy can be used alone or in any combination during initial treatment, as maintenance therapy, and in retreatment if the disease does not respond or recurs after remission.

Many patients receive 2 or more treatment modalities (known as *multimodality therapy* or *combined modality therapy*) to achieve the goal of cure or long-term control. Multimodality therapy has the benefit of being more effective because it takes advantage of more than one mechanism of action. Often, though, this is at the expense of greater toxicity.

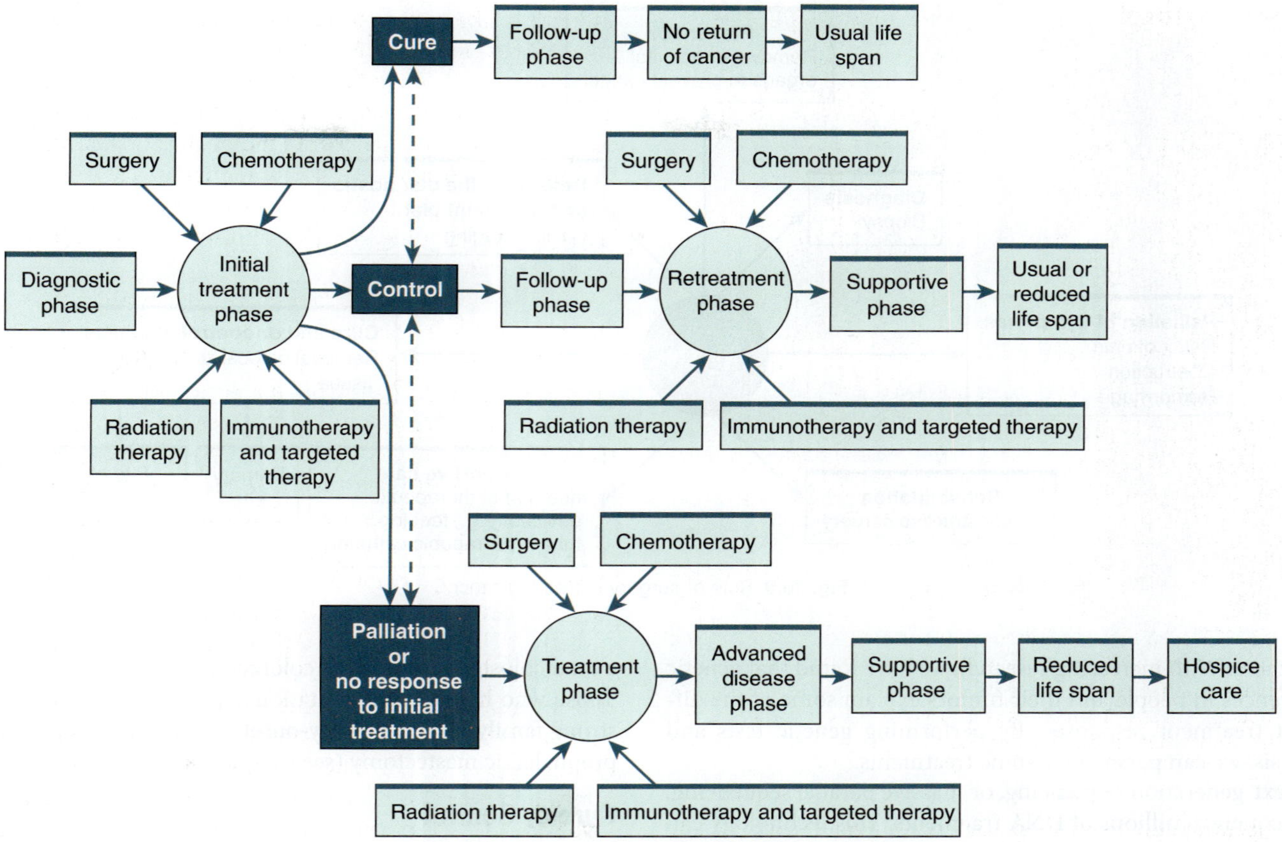

Fig. 16.8 Goals of cancer treatment.

Cure

When *cure* is the goal, we expect treatment to have the greatest chance of eradicating the cancer. Curative cancer therapy differs by the type of cancer. It may involve local therapies (e.g., surgery or radiation) alone or in combination, with or without adjunctive systemic therapy (e.g., chemotherapy).

For example, surgical excision usually cures basal cell skin cancer. If there is a high risk of recurrence, the patient may receive several weeks of radiation therapy. The treatment plan for acute promyelocytic leukemia (which has curative potential) includes several chemotherapy drugs given over many months to several years. Testicular cancer can be cured with a combination of surgery, chemotherapy, and radiation.

There is no benchmark that ensures "cure" for most cancers. In general, the risk for recurrent disease is highest after treatment completion. It gradually decreases the longer the patient is cancer free after treatment. Cancers with a higher mitotic rate (e.g., testicular cancer) are more likely to recur than cancers with slower mitotic rates (e.g., postmenopausal breast cancer). Thus, the timeframe to consider a person "cured" differs depending on the tumor and its characteristics.

Control

Control is the goal of treatment for cancers that we cannot completely eradicate but are responsive to anticancer therapies. As with other chronic illnesses (e.g., diabetes, heart failure), cancer can be controlled for long periods with therapy. Examples include multiple myeloma and chronic lymphocytic leukemia (see Chapter 34). Patients may receive an initial course of treatment followed by maintenance therapy for as long as the disease is responding. Patients are monitored closely for early signs and symptoms of cancer recurrence or progression and the cumulative effects of therapy. Evidence of tumor resistance (e.g., disease progression) may call for changing to a different therapy.

Palliation

Palliation is the goal of treatment when the goals are symptom control or relief and maintaining a satisfactory quality of life. Palliative care and treatment are not mutually exclusive and can take place concurrently. An example of treatment in which palliation is the goal includes using radiation therapy to reduce tumor size and relieve subsequent symptoms, like the pain of bone metastasis.

PERSONALIZED CANCER MEDICINE

Personalized medicine is an emerging trend in cancer treatment. It involves using the patient's genetic information to guide decisions about cancer prevention, diagnosis, and treatment. Many diagnostic studies (tumor markers, genetic markers, molecular receptor status) are useful in determining treatment options.

Before personalized medicine, most patients with a specific type and stage of cancer received the same treatment. However, some treatments worked well for some patients and not as well

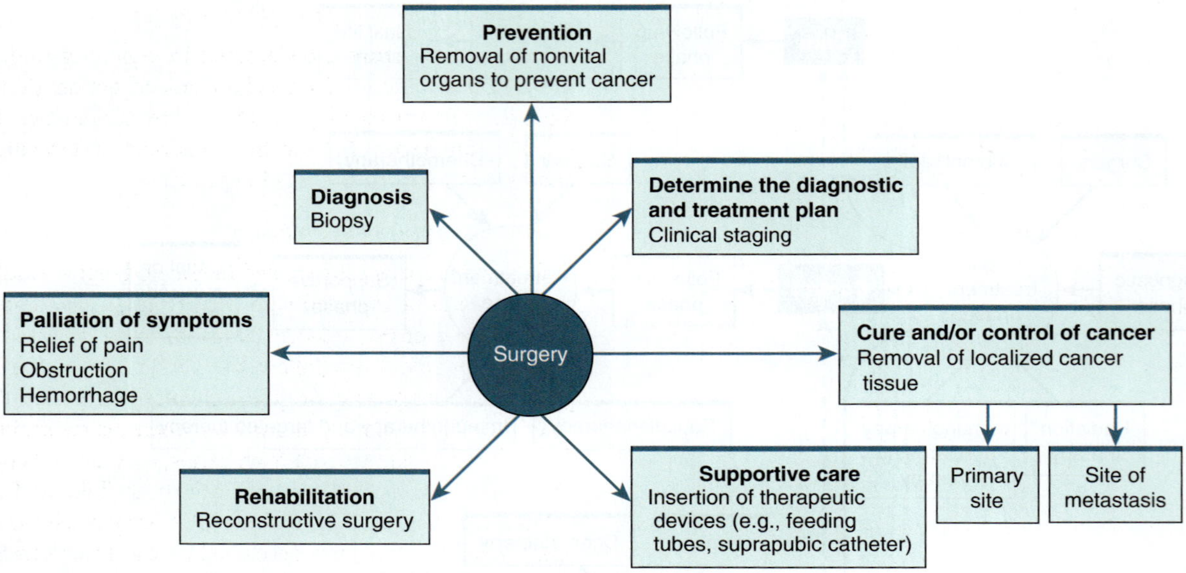

Fig. 16.9 Role of surgery in treating cancer.

for others. With increasing research, we have found that genetic differences in people and their tumors explain some of the different treatment responses. By performing genetic tests and analysis, we can personalize some treatments.[7]

Next-generation sequencing, or massive parallel sequencing, can sequence millions of DNA fragments. This technology can determine if a patient's cancer is caused by a hereditary cancer syndrome or if it is sporadic. Results guide which specific drugs target a patient's mutation and help identify clinical trials specific to the genetic mutation.[8]

Targeted therapy targets a cancer's specific genes or proteins that contribute to cancer growth and survival. Treatment with a targeted therapy depends on assessing whether the tumor has the specific target. This is usually done by testing a sample of the tumor obtained through a biopsy.

Pharmacogenomics and *pharmacogenetics* are the study of genomic variation in drug responses.[9] Examples of how the results of genetic testing can be applied to cancer drug therapy are shown in Table 13.5. For example, vemurafenib is a treatment for patients with metastatic melanoma. It is indicated only for those with tumors that express a gene mutation called *BRAF V600E.*

Not all types of cancer have personalized treatment options. Genetic testing may be costly and time consuming. Many insurance plans do not cover the costs of these tests. Some personalized treatments, such as targeted treatments, can be expensive.[7]

SURGICAL THERAPY

Surgery is the oldest form of cancer treatment. Today surgery can meet a variety of goals (Fig. 16.9).

Prevention

Surgery can eliminate or reduce the risk for cancer development. Prophylactic removal of nonvital organs has been successful in reducing the risk for some cancers. For example, patients with adenomatous familial polyposis may benefit from a total colostomy to prevent colorectal cancer (see Chapter 47). Those who have genetic mutations of *BRCA1* or *BRCA2* and a strong family history of early-onset breast cancer may consider prophylactic mastectomy (see Chapter 56).

Cure or Control

When the goal is cure or control, the objective is to remove all or as much resectable tumor as possible while sparing normal tissue. Examples of surgeries used for cure or control of cancer include radical neck dissection, mastectomy, thyroidectomy, nephrectomy, hysterectomy, and oophorectomy. The trend is toward less radical surgeries.

The patient may undergo a *debulking* or *cytoreductive procedure* if the tumor cannot be completely removed (e.g., a tumor attached to a vital organ). With debulking, as much tumor as possible is removed. The patient then receives chemotherapy and/or radiation therapy. This type of surgery can make chemotherapy or radiation therapy more effective, since the tumor mass is reduced before treatment is started. At other times, a patient may need to receive *neoadjuvant* (treatment before surgery) chemotherapy or radiation therapy to reduce tumor size and improve the surgical outcome.

Supportive and Palliative Care

When cure or control of cancer is no longer possible, the focus shifts to supportive care and palliation of symptoms. Surgical procedures can be part of supportive care that maximizes bodily function or facilitates cancer treatment. Examples of supportive surgeries include:

- Inserting a feeding tube to maintain nutrition during head and neck cancer treatment
- Placing a central venous access device to deliver chemotherapy
- Prophylactic surgical fixation of bones at risk for pathologic fracture

Effects of treatment or symptoms from metastatic cancer may require surgical intervention for palliation. Examples include (1)

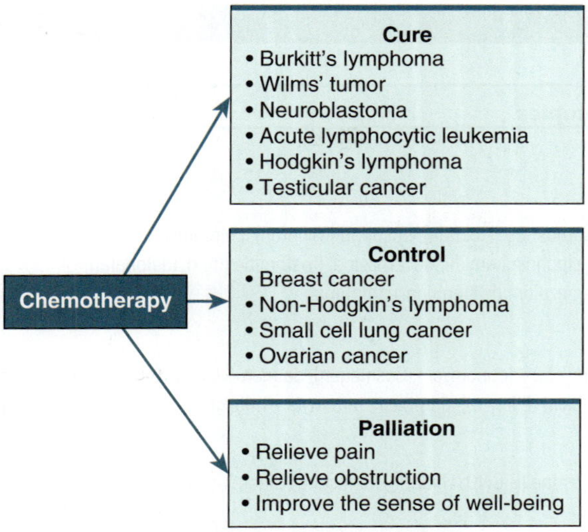

Fig. 16.10 Goals of chemotherapy.

tumor debulking to relieve pain or pressure, (2) colostomy for the relief of a bowel obstruction (see Chapter 47), and (3) laminectomy for the relief of a spinal cord compression (see Chapter 65).

CHEMOTHERAPY

Chemotherapy (antineoplastic therapy) is the use of chemicals as a systemic therapy for cancer. It is a mainstay of cancer treatment for most solid tumors and hematologic cancers (e.g., leukemias, lymphomas). Chemotherapy can offer cure for some cancers, control other cancers for long periods, and in some cases, offer palliative relief of symptoms when cure or control is no longer possible (Fig. 16.10).

Effect on Cells

The goal of chemotherapy is to eliminate or reduce the number of cancer cells in the primary and metastatic tumor site(s). All cells (cancer cells and normal cells) enter the cell cycle for replication and proliferation (Fig. 16.1). We describe the effects of the chemotherapy drugs in relation to the cell cycle.

The 2 major categories of chemotherapy drugs are cell cycle phase–nonspecific and cell cycle phase–specific drugs. *Cell cycle phase–nonspecific chemotherapy drugs* have their effect on the cells during all phases of the cell cycle. This includes the process of cell replication and proliferation and the resting phase (G_0). *Cell cycle phase–specific chemotherapy drugs* have their greatest effects during specific phases of the cell cycle (e.g., when cells are in the process of replication or proliferation during G_1, S, G_2, or M). Giving cell cycle phase–specific and cell cycle phase–nonspecific drugs together maximizes their effectiveness by using drugs that act in different ways and throughout the cell cycle.

When cancer first begins to develop, most of the cells are actively dividing. As the tumor increases in size, more cells become inactive and convert to a resting state (G_0). Because most chemotherapy drugs are only effective against dividing cells, cells can escape death by staying in the G_0 phase. A challenge is to overcome the effect of resistant resting and noncycling cells.

Classification of Chemotherapy Drugs

Chemotherapy drugs are classified in general groups by their molecular structure and mechanisms of action (Table 16.7). Each drug in a particular class has many similarities. However, there are differences in how the drugs work and the unique side effects associated with drugs in each class.

Chemotherapy Preparation

Only persons specifically trained in chemotherapy handling techniques should be involved with the preparation and administration of cancer drugs.[10] Cancer drugs may pose a hazard to health care persons who do not follow safe handling guidelines. A person preparing, transporting, or giving chemotherapy may absorb the drug through inhalation of particles when reconstituting a powder or through skin contact from exposure to droplets or powder. There may be some risk in handling the body fluids and excretions of people during the first 48 hours after they receive chemotherapy. We follow guidelines developed by the American Society of Clinical Oncology for the safe handling of chemotherapy.[11]

Methods of Administration

We give chemotherapy by multiple routes (Table 16.8). The IV route is the most common. Major concerns associated with IV chemotherapy administration include venous access problems, device- or catheter-related infection, and *extravasation*.[10] It is the infiltration of drugs into tissues surrounding the infusion site, causing local tissue damage (Fig. 16.11).

Many chemotherapy drugs are either irritants or vesicants. *Irritants* damage the intima of the vein, causing phlebitis and sclerosis and limiting future peripheral venous access. They will not cause tissue damage if infiltrated. **Vesicants**, if inadvertently infiltrated into the skin, may cause severe local tissue breakdown and necrosis. It is very important to monitor for and take prompt action if extravasation of a vesicant occurs. To lessen discomfort and risks of infection and infiltration, IV chemotherapy can be given through a *central venous access device* (CVAD). CVADs are placed in large blood vessels. They allow frequent, continuous, or intermittent administration of chemotherapy, immunotherapy, targeted therapy, and other products. This avoids multiple venipunctures for vascular access. See more about CVADs in Chapter 17.

With advances in drug formulation techniques, more oral chemotherapy drugs are available. An advantage to oral drugs is the patient takes them at home. This makes it easier for the patient.

Regional Chemotherapy Administration

Regional treatment with chemotherapy involves delivery of the drug directly to the tumor site. The advantage of this method is that we can deliver higher concentrations of the drug to the tumor with less systemic toxicity. Examples include intraarterial, intraperitoneal, intrathecal, intraventricular, and intravesical bladder chemotherapy.

Intraarterial Chemotherapy

Intraarterial chemotherapy delivers the drug to the tumor through the arteries supplying the tumor. This method is used

TABLE 16.7 Drug Therapy

Chemotherapy

Mechanisms of Action	Examples
Cell Cycle Phase–Nonspecific	
Alkylating	
Damage DNA by causing breaks in the double-stranded helix. If repair does not occur, cells will die immediately (cytocidal) or when they try to divide (cytostatic).	bendamustine (Treanda), busulfan (Myleran), chlorambucil (Leukeran), cyclophosphamide, dacarbazine, ifosfamide (Ifex), melphalan, temozolomide (Temodar), thiotepa
Antitumor Antibiotics	
Bind directly to DNA, thus inhibiting the synthesis of DNA and interfering with transcription of RNA.	bleomycin, dactinomycin (Cosmegen), daunorubicin, doxorubicin (Doxil), epirubicin (Ellence), idarubicin, mitomycin, mitoxantrone, valrubicin (Valstar)
Nitrosoureas	
Break DNA helix, interfering with DNA replication. Cross blood-brain barrier.	carmustine (BiCNU, Gliadel), lomustine (Gleostine), streptozocin (Zanosar)
Platinum Drugs	
Bind to DNA and RNA, miscoding information and/or inhibiting DNA replication, and cells die.	carboplatin, cisplatin, oxaliplatin
Cell Cycle Phase–Specific	
Antimetabolites	
Mimic naturally occurring substances, thus interfering with enzyme function or DNA synthesis. Primarily act during S phase. Purine and pyrimidine are building blocks of nucleic acids needed for DNA and RNA synthesis.	
• Interfere with purine metabolism	cladribine, clofarabine (Clolar), fludarabine, mercaptopurine (Purixan), nelarabine (Arranon), pentostatin (Nipent), thioguanine
• Interfere with pyrimidine metabolism	capecitabine (Xeloda); cytarabine, floxuridine, fluorouracil, gemcitabine (Gemzar)
• Interfere with folic acid metabolism	methotrexate (Trexall), pemetrexed (Alimta)
• Interfere with DNA synthesis	hydroxyurea (Hydrea, Droxia)
Mitotic Inhibitors	
Taxanes	albumin-bound paclitaxel (Abraxane), docetaxel (Taxotere)
Antimicrotubule agents that interfere with mitosis. Act during the late G_2 phase and mitosis to stabilize microtubules, thus inhibiting cell division.	
Vinca Alkaloids	vinblastine, vincristine, vinorelbine
Act in M phase to inhibit mitosis.	
Others	estramustine (Emcyt), ixabepilone (Ixempra), eribulin (Halaven)
Microtubular inhibitors.	
Topoisomerase Inhibitors	
Inhibit topoisomerases (normal enzymes) that function to make reversible breaks and repairs in DNA that allow for flexibility of DNA in replication.	etoposide, irinotecan (Camptosar), topotecan (Hycamtin)

TABLE 16.8 Drug Therapy

Methods of Chemotherapy Administration

Method	Examples
Oral	cyclophosphamide, capecitabine (Xeloda), temozolomide (Temodar)
Intraarterial	dacarbazine, fluorouracil, methotrexate
Intracavitary (pleural, peritoneal)	Radio isotopes, alkylating drugs, methotrexate
Intramuscular	bleomycin
Intrathecal	methotrexate (preservative free), cytarabine
Intravenous	doxorubicin, vincristine, cisplatin, fluorouracil
Perfusion	Alkylating drugs
Subcutaneous	cytarabine, bortezomib
Topical	fluorouracil

to treat osteogenic sarcoma; cancers of the head and neck, bladder, and cervix; melanoma; primary liver cancer; and retinoblastoma. One method of intraarterial drug delivery involves the surgical placement of a catheter that is connected to an external or implanted infusion pump for infusion of the chemotherapy agent.

Intraperitoneal Chemotherapy

Intraperitoneal chemotherapy involves the delivery of chemotherapy to the peritoneal cavity. It is a treatment for peritoneal metastases from primary colorectal and ovarian cancers and malignant ascites. For short-term chemotherapy administration, we can place temporary Silastic catheters (Tenckhoff, Hickman, Groshong) percutaneously or surgically into the peritoneal cavity. An implanted

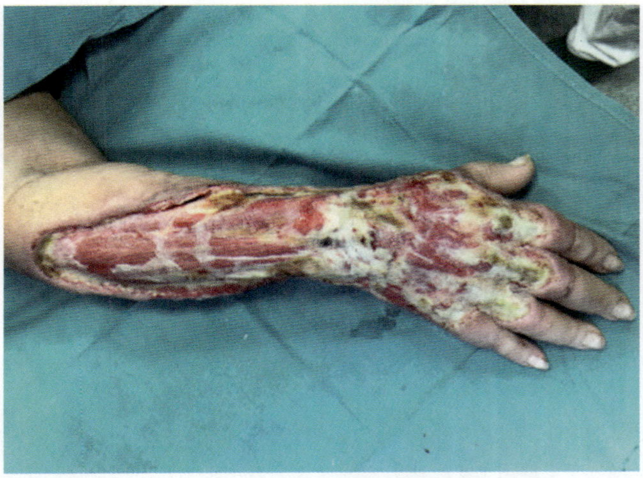

Fig. 16.11 Extravasation injury from infiltration of chemotherapy drug. (From Faenza M, Ferraro GA, Fonzone Caccese FP, et al.: Combined approach with negative pressure wound therapy and dermal substitute for extravasation injury. *JPRAS Open*, 25:62, 2020.)

port also can be used to give chemotherapy intraperitoneally. Chemotherapy is generally infused into the peritoneum in 1 to 2 L of fluid and allowed to *dwell* in the peritoneum for 1 to 4 hours. After the *dwell time,* the fluid is drained from the peritoneum.

Intrathecal or Intraventricular Chemotherapy

Cancers that metastasize to the central nervous system (CNS) are hard to treat because the blood-brain barrier often prevents distribution of chemotherapy to this area. One method used to treat metastasis to the CNS is intrathecal chemotherapy. This involves a lumbar puncture and injection of chemotherapy into the subarachnoid space. To reduce the need for repeated lumbar punctures, patients may have an Ommaya reservoir inserted. An Ommaya reservoir is a soft, plastic, dome-shaped disk with an extension catheter. It is surgically implanted through the cranium into a lateral ventricle.

Intravesical Bladder Chemotherapy

Intravesical bladder chemotherapy involves instilling chemotherapy into the bladder. This is done through a urinary catheter. The solution is retained for 1 to 3 hours.

Effects of Chemotherapy on Normal Tissues

Chemotherapy drugs cannot selectively distinguish between normal cells and cancer cells. Chemotherapy-induced side effects result from the destruction of normal cells, especially those that are rapidly proliferating. These include cells in the bone marrow, lining of the GI tract, and integument (skin, hair, nails) (Table 16.9). We classify the general and drug-specific adverse effects as acute, delayed, or chronic.

Acute toxicity occurs during and right after drug administration. It includes anaphylactic and hypersensitivity reactions, extravasation or flare reactions, anticipatory nausea and vomiting, and dysrhythmias.

Delayed effects are numerous. They include delayed nausea and vomiting, mucositis, alopecia, skin rashes, bone marrow suppression, altered bowel function (diarrhea, constipation), and various cumulative neurotoxicities.

TABLE 16.9 Cells With a Rapid Rate of Proliferation

Cells	Generation Time	Effect of Cell Destruction
Bone marrow stem cell	6–24 hr	Myelosuppression (infection, bleeding, anemia)
Epithelial cells lining the GI tract	12–24 hr	Anorexia, mucositis (including stomatitis, esophagitis), nausea, vomiting, diarrhea
Hair follicle cells	24 hr	Alopecia
Neutrophils	12 hr	Leukopenia, infection
Ova and testes	24–36 hr	Reproductive problems

Chronic toxicities involve damage to organs, such as the heart, liver, kidneys, and lungs. Chronic toxicities can be either long-term effects that develop during or right after treatment and persist or late effects that are absent during treatment and manifest later.

Some side effects fall into more than 1 category. For example, nausea, vomiting, and diarrhea can be both acute and delayed.

Treatment Plan

Although some patients receive single-drug chemotherapy, the most common treatment plans combine drugs in multidrug regimens. Multidrug plans target more than one signaling pathway. They are more effective in managing most cancers. The plans involve drugs with different mechanisms of action and varying toxicity profiles. However, when chemotherapy drugs are used in combination, patients can have an increase in toxicities.

Drug regimens are based on evidence supporting their use in specific cancers. Sometimes they are customized to meet specific patient needs. Chemotherapy is most effective when the tumor burden is low, therapy is not interrupted, and the patient receives the intended dose. Drug doses are based on the person's weight and height using the body surface area calculation.

Mutation of cancer cells within the tumor can result in cells that are resistant to chemotherapy. With multiple drugs working at different places in the cell cycle, cancer cells can be more effectively killed. This decreases mutation and resistance.

RADIATION THERAPY

Along with surgery, radiation therapy is one of the oldest methods of cancer treatment. Many cancer patients receive radiation therapy at some point in their treatment. Technologic advances have expanded and refined the sources and methods of delivering radiation therapy. This allows for more accurate and less invasive treatment options.

Radiation therapy uses high energy beams or waves, that when absorbed into tissue, produce ions in the cells. The energy in ionizing radiation acts to break the chemical bonds in DNA. The DNA is damaged, causing cell death.

Principles of Radiobiology

As the radiation beam passes through the treatment field, energy is deposited. *Low-energy beams* (e.g., electrons) expend energy

TABLE 16.10 Tumor Radiosensitivity

High Radiosensitivity
- Hodgkin lymphoma
- Neuroblastoma
- Non-Hodgkin lymphoma
- Ovarian dysgerminoma
- Testicular seminoma
- Wilms tumor

Moderate Radiosensitivity
- Bladder carcinoma
- Breast adenocarcinoma
- Esophageal carcinoma
- Oropharyngeal carcinoma
- Prostate carcinoma
- Uterine and cervical carcinoma

Mild Radiosensitivity
- Colon adenocarcinoma
- Gastric adenocarcinoma
- Renal adenocarcinoma
- Soft tissue sarcomas (e.g., chondrosarcoma)

Poor Radiosensitivity
- Osteosarcoma
- Malignant glioma
- Melanoma
- Testicular nonseminoma

quickly on impact with matter, so they penetrate only a short distance. They are clinically useful in treating superficial skin lesions. *High-energy beams* (e.g., photons) have greater depth of penetration, not reaching full intensity until they reach a certain depth. This makes them suitable for delivering optimal doses to internal targets while sparing the skin.

Technically, all cancer cells could be killed with radiation given in high enough doses. However, to avoid serious toxicity and long-term complications of treatment, radiation to surrounding healthy tissue must be limited to the *maximal tolerated dose* for that specific tissue. Advances in planning and in delivery technology (e.g., *intensity-modulated radiation therapy [IMRT]* and *image-guided radiation therapy [IGRT]*) have improved our ability to deliver maximal doses while sparing critical structures (e.g., spinal cord, carotid arteries, optic chiasm) as much as possible.

Radiation doses are expressed in units called a *gray* (Gy) or centigray (cGy). A *centigray* is equal to 1 rad; 100 centigray equals 1 gray. Once the total dose to be delivered is determined, that dose is divided into daily *fractions*. Doses between 180 and 200 cGy/day are considered *standard fractionation*. They are typically delivered once a day Monday through Friday for a period of 2 to 8 weeks, depending on the desired total dose.

Some cancers are more responsive to the effects of radiation than others (Table 16.10). Radiosensitivity is the relative responsiveness of cells and tissues to the effects of radiation. In highly responsive tumors (such as lymphomas), radiation therapy can affect even a large tumor. In less responsive tumors, there may be a slower or incomplete response. Localized prostate cancer responds very slowly to radiation (several months after treatment is completed).

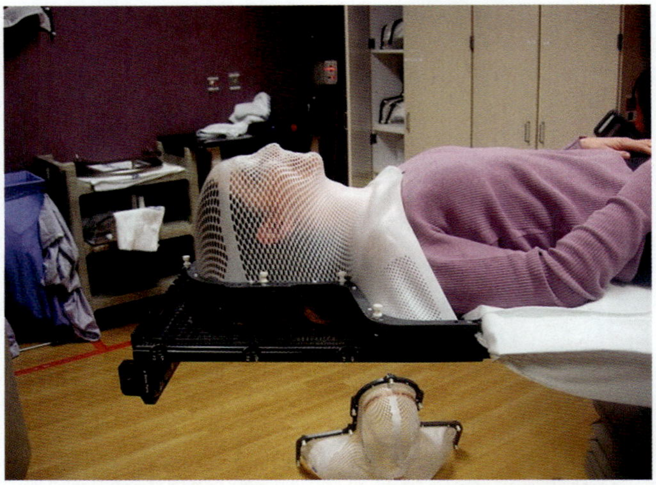

Fig. 16.12 Immobilization device. A head holder and an immobilization mask ensure accurate positioning for daily treatment of head and neck cancer. (Courtesy Jormain Cady, Virginia Mason Medical Center, Seattle, WA.)

Radiation is used to treat a carefully defined area of the body. Since radiation affects only tissues within the treatment field, it is not appropriate as the main treatment for systemic disease. However, radiation may be used by itself, in combination with chemotherapy or surgery to treat primary tumors, or for palliation of metastatic lesions.

Simulation and Treatment Planning

Simulation is a process by which the radiation treatment fields are defined, filmed, and marked out on the skin. The target is defined using a variety of imaging techniques (e.g., x-rays; CT, MRI, PET scans), physical assessment, and surgical reports. The radiation oncologist specifies the dose and volume of area to be treated. Treatment volumes include the (1) *gross target volume* (GTV), which is the gross extent of the tumor; (2) the *clinical target volume* (CTV), which is the GTV plus additional margin to encompass any potential microscopic or subclinical disease; and (3) the *planning target volume* (PTV). PTV is the GTV/CTV plus additional margin to allow for organ motion or variance in daily set-up position.

During the simulation, the patient is positioned on a simulator. It is a diagnostic x-ray machine that re-creates the actions of the linear accelerator. The radiation fields are marked on the patient's skin. Immobilization devices (e.g., casts, bite blocks, thermoplastic face masks) are often used to help the patient stay in a stable position (Fig. 16.12). Temporary tattoos may be placed to ensure the patient position is precisely reproduced with each treatment.

Treatment

Radiation is used to treat a carefully defined area of the body. Since radiation affects only tissues within the treatment field, it is not appropriate as the main treatment for systemic disease. However, radiation may be used by itself, in combination with chemotherapy or surgery to treat primary tumors, or for palliation of metastatic lesions.

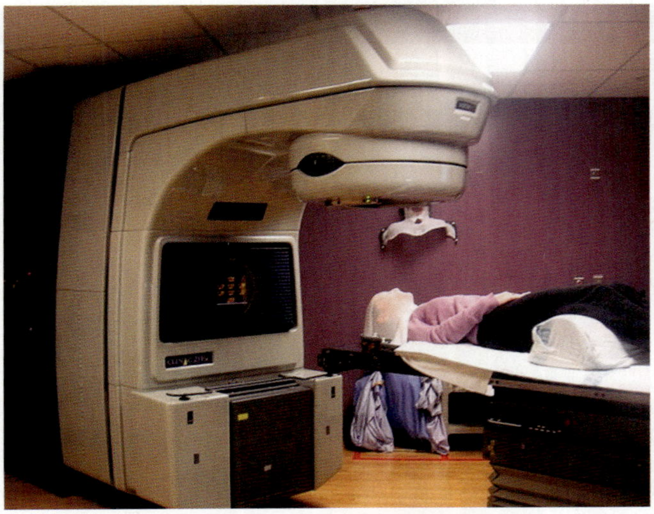

Fig. 16.13 Linear accelerator used to deliver radiation therapy. Patient is positioned on radiation treatment table for treatment of head and neck cancer. (Courtesy Jormain Cady, Virginia Mason Medical Center, Seattle, WA.)

External Radiation

Radiation can be delivered externally *(external beam radiation therapy)* or internally *(brachytherapy)*. **External beam radiation** is the most common form of radiation treatment delivery. With this technique, the patient is exposed to radiation from a megavoltage treatment machine. The beam passes through the external tissues to reach the internal target. A linear accelerator is the most commonly used machine for delivering external beam radiation (Fig. 16.13). *Gamma knife technology* (used to deliver highly accurate stereotactic treatment to a localized treatment volume) uses a cobalt source.

Internal Radiation

Radiation can be delivered as **brachytherapy**, which means "close" or internal radiation treatment. It consists of the implantation or insertion of radioactive materials directly into the tumor (interstitial) or near the tumor (intracavitary or intraluminal). This allows for direct delivery of radiation to the target with minimal exposure to surrounding healthy tissues. It is often used in combination with external radiation as a supplemental "boost" treatment. It may be a primary or adjuvant therapy.

Sources of radiation for brachytherapy include temporary sealed sources (e.g., iridium-192, cesium-137) and permanent sealed sources (e.g., iodine-125, gold-198, palladium-103). These are supplied in the form of seeds or ribbons. With a temporary implant, the source may be placed into a special catheter or metal tube that has been inserted into the tumor area. It is left in place until the prescribed dose of radiation has been reached in the calculated number of hours.

Brachytherapy may be delivered as high-dose-rate (HDR) treatment (e.g., several doses given at varying intervals over a few minutes each time) or low-dose-rate (LDR) treatment (e.g., continuous treatment over several hours or days). A remote "afterloading" technique (e.g., the source is inserted after the applicator is in place) is designed to enhance HCP and patient safety. It is used for HDR brachytherapy with iridium-192. These methods are often used for head and neck, lung, breast, and gynecologic cancers.

Permanent implants, such as for prostate brachytherapy, involve the insertion of radioactive seeds directly into the tumor tissue, where they stay permanently. As interstitial seeds used for treatment emit low energies with limited tissue penetration, patients are not considered radioactive. However, some initial radiation precautions may be recommended because of a small risk of seed dislodgement. Over time, the isotopes that are used decay and are no longer radioactive. The timeframe for side effects induced by treatment can be predicted based on the rate of decay for the specific isotope used.

Radioactive drugs, or radiopharmaceuticals, are used to treat some cancers systemically. They may be given orally as a capsule or drink (e.g., iodine-131 for thyroid cancer). IV examples include yttrium-90 for resistant lymphomas and radium-223 for bone metastases in prostate cancer. The drug is sometimes bound to monoclonal antibodies. The antibodies attach to the cancer cell, directly delivering the radiation. This may minimize the effects of the radiation on healthy cells.

Caring for the person undergoing brachytherapy or receiving radioactive drugs requires you to be aware when the patient is emitting radioactivity. Patients with temporary implants are radioactive only while the source is in place. In those with permanent implants, because the sources have short half-lives and are weak emitters, the radioactive exposure to the outside and to others is low. These patients may be discharged with minimal precautions.

The principles of *ALARA (as low as reasonably achievable)* and *time, distance,* and *shielding* are vital to our safety when caring for the person with a source of internal radiation. Organize care to limit the time spent in direct contact with the patient. To lessen anxiety and confusion, tell the patient the reason for time and distance limitations before the treatment.

The radiation safety officer will say how much time at a specific distance one can spend with the patient. This is determined by the dose delivered by the implant. Because the source is nonpenetrating, small differences in distance are critical. Only care that must be delivered near the source, such as checking placement of the implant, is done in proximity. Use shielding, if available. Do not deliver care without wearing a film badge (dosimeter) showing cumulative radiation exposure. Do not share the film badge. Do not wear it anywhere but at work and return it according to the agency's protocol.

NURSING MANAGEMENT: CHEMOTHERAPY AND RADIATION THERAPY

You play a key role in helping patients deal with the side effects of chemotherapy and radiation therapy. Before starting teaching, assess the patient's ability to process information. Tailor teaching to meet the patient's and caregiver's learning needs.

Table 16.11 outlines the common side effects of chemotherapy and radiation. Bone marrow suppression, fatigue, GI problems, skin and mucosal problems, and pulmonary and reproductive effects are discussed here.

TABLE 16.11 NURSING MANAGEMENT

Problems Caused by Chemotherapy and Radiation Therapy

Etiology	Nursing Management
Biochemical	
Hyperuricemia	
↑ Uric acid levels due to chemotherapy-induced cell destruction. Can cause secondary gout and obstructive uropathy.	• Monitor uric acid levels. • Allopurinol may be given as a prophylactic measure. • Maintain increased fluid intake.
Cardiovascular	
Cardiotoxicity	
Some chemotherapy drugs (e.g., anthracyclines, taxanes) can cause ECG changes and rapidly progressive heart failure.	• Monitor heart with ECG and cardiac ejection fractions. • Drug therapy may need to be changed for symptoms or deteriorating cardiac function studies. • Administer antidysrhythmic drugs as ordered.
Pericarditis and Myocarditis	
Inflammation from radiation injury. Complication from chest wall radiation. May occur up to 1 year after treatment. Side effect of some chemotherapy drugs.	• Monitor for manifestations of these problems (e.g., dyspnea).
Comfort	
Fatigue	
Anabolic processes result in accumulation of metabolites from cell breakdown.	• Assess for reversible causes of fatigue and address them as indicated. • Reassure patient that fatigue is a common side effect of therapy. • Encourage patient to rest when fatigued, to maintain usual lifestyle patterns, as much as possible, and to pace activities in accordance with energy level. • Encourage moderate exercise as tolerated.
Gastrointestinal System	
Anorexia	
Release of TNF and IL-1 from macrophages has appetite-suppressant effect. Therapy-induced GI effects (mucositis, nausea, vomiting, bowel problems) and anxiety reduce appetite.	• Monitor weight. • Encourage patient to eat small, frequent meals of high-protein, high-calorie foods. • Gently encourage patient to eat, but do not nag. • Recommend keeping a food diary to track daily calories and fluids. • Serve food in pleasant environment.
Constipation	
Autonomic nervous system dysfunction decreases intestinal motility. Caused by neurotoxic effects of plant alkaloids (vincristine, vinblastine).	• Teach patients to take stool softeners as needed, eat high-fiber foods, and increase fluid intake. • Increase activity (e.g., walking) if tolerated.
Diarrhea	
From denuding of epithelial lining of intestines. Side effect of chemotherapy. Follows radiation to abdomen, pelvis, lumbosacral areas.	• Give antidiarrheal drugs as needed. • Encourage low-fiber, low-residue diet. • Encourage fluid intake of at least 3 L/day.
Hepatotoxicity	
Toxic effects from chemotherapy drugs (usually transient and resolve when drug is stopped).	• Monitor liver function tests.
Nausea and Vomiting	
Release of intracellular breakdown products stimulates vomiting center in brain. Drugs stimulate vomiting center in brain. Radiation and chemotherapy destroy lining of GI tract.	• Encourage patient to eat and drink when not nauseated. • Give prophylactic antiemetics before chemotherapy and on as-needed basis. • Teach patients to take antiemetics on a scheduled basis for 2–3 days after highly emetogenic chemotherapy. • Use diversional activities (if appropriate).

TABLE 16.11 NURSING MANAGEMENT—cont'd

Problems Caused by Chemotherapy and Radiation Therapy

Etiology	Nursing Management
Stomatitis, Mucositis, and Esophagitis	
Chemotherapy or radiation treatment destroy epithelial cells located in field (e.g., head and neck, stomach, esophagus). Rapid cell destruction causes inflammation and ulceration.	• Assess oral mucosa daily and teach patient to do this. • Use nutrition supplements (e.g., Ensure, Boost) if intake is decreasing. • Be aware that eating, swallowing, and talking may be difficult and patient may need analgesics. • Teach avoidance of irritating spicy or acidic foods or too hot or too cold food (extremes in temperature). • Teach how to choose moist, bland, and softer foods. • Keep oral cavity clean and moist by frequent oral rinses with saline or salt and soda solution. • Use artificial saliva to manage dryness (radiation). • Discourage use of irritants, such as tobacco and alcohol. • Apply topical anesthetics (e.g., viscous lidocaine, oxethazaine).
Genitourinary Tract	
Hemorrhagic Cystitis	
Chemotherapy (e.g., cyclophosphamide, ifosfamide) destroys cells lining the bladder Side effect of radiation when in the treatment field.	• Increase fluid intake 24–72 hr after treatment as tolerated. • Monitor for urgency, frequency, and hematuria. • Give cytoprotectants (mesna [Mesnex]) and hydration. • Provide supportive care to manage symptoms (e.g., flavoxate).
Nephrotoxicity	
Exposure to nephrotoxic drugs (cisplatin and high-dose methotrexate) directly damages renal cells. Precipitation of metabolites of cell breakdown (tumor lysis syndrome [TLS]).	• Monitor BUN and serum creatinine levels. • Avoid potentiating drugs. • Alkalinize the urine by adding sodium bicarbonate to IV infusion • Give allopurinol or rasburicase for TLS prevention.
Reproductive Problems	
Therapy damages cells of testes or ova.	• Discuss risk with patients before starting treatment. • Offer opportunity for sperm and ova banking before treatment for patients of childbearing age.
Hematologic System	
Anemia	
Therapy causes bone marrow depression. Cancer cells infiltrate bone marrow.	• Monitor hemoglobin and hematocrit levels. • Give iron supplements and erythropoietin. • Encourage intake of foods that promote RBC production (see Table 34.5).
Leukopenia	
Chemotherapy or radiation therapy causes bone marrow depression. Infection most frequent cause of morbidity and death in cancer patients. Respiratory and genitourinary system are usual sites of infection.	• Monitor WBC count, especially neutrophils. • Tell patient to report temperature elevation and any other manifestations of infection. • Teach patient to avoid large crowds and people with infections. • Give WBC growth factors (Table 16.15). • For patient teaching, see Table 34.24.
Thrombocytopenia	
Chemotherapy causes bone marrow depression. Cancer cells infiltrate bone marrow. Spontaneous bleeding can occur with platelet counts ≤20,000/μL.	• Observe for signs of bleeding (e.g., petechiae, bruising). • Monitor platelet counts. • For patient teaching, see Table 34.15.
Integumentary System	
Alopecia	
Chemotherapy or radiation to scalp destroys hair follicles. Hair loss usually is temporary with chemotherapy, may be permanent with radiation.	• Suggest ways to cope with hair loss (e.g., hair pieces, scarves, wigs). • Cut long hair before therapy. • Avoid excessive shampooing, brushing, and combing of hair. • Avoid use of electric hair dryers, curlers, and curling rods. • Discuss impact of hair loss on self-image.

Continued

TABLE 16.11 NURSING MANAGEMENT—cont'd

Problems Caused by Chemotherapy and Radiation Therapy

Etiology	Nursing Management
Chemotherapy-Induced Skin Changes	
Acneiform eruptions. Acral erythema. Hyperpigmentation. Photosensitivity. Telangiectasia.	• Alert patient to potential skin changes. • Encourage patient to avoid sun exposure. • Implement symptomatic management as needed depending on specific skin effect (e.g., application of lotions, corticosteroid creams).
Radiation Skin Changes (dry to moist desquamation)	
Radiation damages skin.	• Table 16.12 describes patient management.
Nervous System	
Cognitive Changes ("chemo brain")	
Occur during and after treatment (especially with chemotherapy). Problems with concentration, memory lapses, trouble remembering details, taking longer to finish tasks. May happen quickly and last a short time. Some people have mild long-term effects.	• Teach patients to • Use detailed daily planner. • Get enough sleep and rest. • Exercise brain (learn something new, do word puzzles). • Focus on one thing (no multitasking).
Intracranial Pressure	
May result from radiation edema in central nervous system.	• Monitor neurologic status. • May be controlled with corticosteroids.
Peripheral Neuropathy	
Paresthesias, areflexia, skeletal muscle weakness, and smooth muscle dysfunction can occur as a side effect of plant alkaloids, taxanes, and cisplatin.	• Monitor for manifestations in patients on these drugs. • Consider temporary chemotherapy dose interruption or reduction until symptoms improve. • Antiseizure drugs (e.g., gabapentin) may be given.
Respiratory System	
Pneumonitis	
Radiation pneumonitis develops 2–3 mo after start of treatment. After 6–12 mo, fibrosis occurs and is evident on x-ray. Side effect of some chemotherapy and immunotherapy drugs.	• Monitor for dry, hacking cough; fever; and dyspnea with exertion. • Encourage activity and respiratory exercises.

◆ Implementation

◆ Bone Marrow Suppression

Myelosuppression is one of the most common effects of chemotherapy. To a lesser extent, it can occur with radiation. Treatment-induced myelosuppression can result in life-threatening and distressing effects. These include infection, hemorrhage, and overwhelming fatigue. The major difference in manifestations between radiation therapy and chemotherapy is that radiation (a local therapy) only affects bone marrow within the treatment field. Chemotherapy (a systemic therapy) affects bone marrow function throughout the body. When the therapies are combined, the risk for myelosuppression greatly increases.

In general, the onset of bone marrow suppression is related to the life span of the type of blood cell. WBCs (especially neutrophils) are affected first (within 1 to 2 weeks), platelets in 2 to 3 weeks, and red blood cells (RBCs), with a longer life span of 120 days, later. The severity of myelosuppression depends on the chemotherapy drugs used, drug dosages, and the radiation treatment field. Radiation to large marrow-containing regions of the body causes more clinically significant myelosuppression. In the adult, most of the active marrow is in the pelvis and thoracic and lumbar vertebrae.

Monitor the CBC, especially the neutrophil, platelet, and RBC counts. Patients often have the lowest blood cell counts (called the *nadir*) between 7 and 10 days after starting therapy. However, the exact onset depends on the drug regimen.

Neutropenia is more common in patients receiving chemotherapy. It is a serious risk factor for life-threatening infection and sepsis. Significant neutropenia will prompt treatment delay or adjustments (e.g., lower dosages). Take every measure to prevent infections in these patients. Hand hygiene is the mainstay of patient safety. Patients and their contacts, including health care team members, should follow hand-washing guidelines.

Monitor temperature routinely. Any sign of infection should be treated promptly. Fever in the presence of neutropenia is a medical emergency. WBC growth factors (e.g., filgrastim [Neupogen]) are often used to reduce the duration of chemotherapy-induced neutropenia. They are used as a prophylactic measure to prevent neutropenia when highly myelosuppressive chemotherapy drugs are used.[12] Neutropenia is discussed in Chapter 34. (See the patient teaching guide in Table 34.24 and eNursing Care Plan 34.3 on the website for Chapter 34.)

Thrombocytopenia can result in spontaneous bleeding or major hemorrhage. Avoid invasive procedures. Teach patients to avoid activities that place them at risk for injury or bleeding. Risk for serious bleeding is generally not present until the platelet count falls below 20,000/μL. When the count drops that low, we often give platelet transfusions. Thrombocytopenia is discussed in Chapter 34. See the patient teaching guide in Table 34.15 and eNursing Care Plan 34.2 on the website for Chapter 34.

Anemia is common in patients undergoing either radiation therapy or chemotherapy. It generally has a later onset (about 3 to 4 months after starting treatment). Patients with low hemoglobin levels may receive RBC growth factors (e.g., darbepoetin, epoetin [Procrit]). In extreme circumstances (e.g., symptomatic anemia), the patient may need RBC transfusions. However, in general, we avoid RBC transfusions.

Fatigue

Fatigue is the persistent sense of tiredness that interferes with usual day-to-day function. It is a nearly universal symptom affecting most patients with cancer. Many describe fatigue as the most disturbing of treatment-related side effects. Fatigue may persist long after treatment has ended.

Anemia is one cause of fatigue. Other causes may be related to the (1) toxic substances left in the body from cells killed by cancer treatment, (2) need for extra energy to repair and heal body tissue damaged by treatment, and (3) lack of sleep caused by some chemotherapy drugs or steroids. Assess for reversible causes of fatigue. These include anemia, hypothyroidism, depression, insomnia, dehydration, or infection.

Help patients recognize that fatigue is common. Teach them energy conservation strategies. Help patients identify days or times during the day when they typically feel better. Encourage them to be more active during those periods.

Patients may need to rest before activity and have others help with work or home tasks. Ignoring fatigue or overstressing the body when fatigue is tolerable may lead to an increase in symptoms. Maintaining exercise and activity within tolerable limits is often helpful in managing fatigue. Walking programs are a way for most patients to keep active without overtaxing themselves. Staying active helps improve mood and avoid the debilitating cycle of fatigue-depression-fatigue that can occur in patients with cancer. Use guidelines to evaluate and manage cancer-related fatigue.[13]

CHECK YOUR PRACTICE

Your 62-year-old male patient with diabetes and Stage III colorectal cancer has just completed adjuvant chemotherapy. At his clinic visit today, he reports being so tired that he "can barely get out of bed." He reports mucositis and ongoing nausea. The patient says to you, "Is this treatment worth it?"

- How would you respond?

GI Effects

The cells of the mucosal lining of the GI tract are highly proliferative. We replace the epithelial cells every 2 to 6 days. The intestinal mucosa is one of the most sensitive tissues to radiation and chemotherapy. GI problems include nausea and vomiting, diarrhea, mucositis, and anorexia. These problems can significantly affect the patient's hydration and nutrition status and sense of well-being.

There are several reasons GI problems occur. These include (1) the release of serotonin from the GI tract, which stimulates the chemoreceptor trigger zone (CTZ) and the vomiting center in the brain, and (2) cell death and resulting damage to GI mucosa. Radiation to treatment fields that contain GI structures (e.g., abdominopelvic, lumbosacral, lower thoracic areas) and selected chemotherapy drugs cause direct injury to GI epithelial cells.

Nausea and vomiting. Nausea and vomiting are common effects of chemotherapy and sometimes radiation therapy. Chemotherapy-induced nausea and vomiting (CINV) may occur within 1 hour of chemotherapy administration. Vomiting may start a few hours after radiation therapy to the chest or abdomen. It may persist for 24 hours or more. Several antiemetic drugs are available (see Table 46.1).

Serotonin (5-HT_3) receptor antagonists (ondansetron, palonosetron [Aloxi]) and neurokinin-1 receptor antagonists (NK_1RA) (e.g., aprepitant [Emend], rolapitant [Varubi]) can reduce CINV. Dexamethasone given with other antiemetics helps manage acute and delayed CINV. Akynzeo is a fixed combination of palonosetron (a 5-HT_3 receptor antagonist) and netupitant (a NK_1RA antagonist).

Anticipatory nausea and vomiting can develop if a patient had poorly controlled nausea and vomiting with prior chemotherapy administration. In this phenomenon, encountering the cues even without receiving treatment may precipitate nausea and vomiting. Preventing nausea and vomiting with the first cycle lowers the risk. If it does occur, we initiate aggressive emesis control. This includes giving prophylactic antiemetic and antianxiety medication 1 hour before treatment. The patient may find that eating a light meal of nonirritating food before treatment is helpful.

Delayed nausea and vomiting can develop 24 hours to a week after treatment. Assess patients who have nausea and vomiting for signs and symptoms of dehydration and metabolic alkalosis. Treatment includes antiemetic drugs, diet adjustments, and nondrug interventions (e.g., relaxation breathing).

Diarrhea. Diarrhea is a reaction of the bowel mucosa to radiation and some chemotherapy drugs. The patient can have an increase in frequency and liquidity of stool. The small bowel is very sensitive and does not tolerate significant radiation doses. With pelvic radiation, patients may receive treatment with a full bladder. This moves the small bowel out of the treatment field. Both radiation- and chemotherapy-induced diarrhea are best managed with diet adjustments, antidiarrheals, antimotility drugs, and antispasmodics (see Table 47.2).

Recommend a diet low in fiber and residue before chemotherapy known to cause diarrhea. This includes limiting foods high in roughage (e.g., fresh fruits, vegetables, seeds, nuts). To prevent diarrhea, other foods to avoid include fried, fatty, or highly seasoned foods, and foods that are gas-producing. Bowel mucosal injury from radiation may cause temporary lactose intolerance. Avoiding milk products is helpful for some patients during and right after treatment.

Depending on the severity of the diarrhea, the patient may need hydration and electrolyte supplements. Lukewarm sitz baths may ease discomfort and cleanse the rectal area if rectal irritation develops. The rectal area must be clean and dry to maintain skin integrity. Inspect the perianal area for evidence of skin breakdown. Systemic analgesia may be used for painful skin irritations. Note the number, volume, consistency, and character of stools per day. Have patients keep a diary or log to record episodes and aggravating and alleviating factors.

Mucositis. Mucositis is irritation, inflammation, and/or ulceration of the mucosa. Like the bowel mucosa, the mucosal linings of the oral cavity, oropharynx, and esophagus are very sensitive to the effects of radiation and chemotherapy. Patients diagnosed with head and neck cancer who receive radiation are at high risk.

Certain factors can compound the problem. For example, patients undergoing head and neck radiation may face the added challenge of radiation-induced parotid gland dysfunction. This may result in decreased salivary flow, causing acute or chronic *xerostomia* (dry mouth). Dryness or thick saliva compromises the protective salivary functions of assisting with cleansing teeth, moistening food, and swallowing. Meticulous oral care during and for a long time after treatment reduces the risk for cavities, which may occur due to decreased saliva. Teach patients to continue regular dental follow-up every 6 months. They should use fluoride supplements as recommended by their dentist. Saliva substitutes may help patients with xerostomia. Many patients find that drinking small amounts of water frequently has a similar effect.

Dysgeusia (taste loss) may develop during therapy. By the end of treatment, patients often report that all food has lost its flavor. Nutrition may be compromised. *Dysphagia* (difficulty swallowing), which marks pharyngeal and esophageal involvement, further impedes eating. Patients may report feeling that they have a "lump" as they swallow and that "foods get stuck." Patients with *odynophagia* (painful swallowing) caused by oropharyngeal or esophageal irritation and ulceration may need analgesics before meals.

Oral assessment and careful intervention to keep the oral cavity moist, clean, and free of debris are essential to prevent infection and promote nutrition intake. Implement standard oral care protocols that address prevention and management of mucositis.

Routinely assess the oral cavity, mucous membranes, characteristics of saliva, and ability to swallow. Referral to a dentist for all necessary dental work is common before starting treatment. Teach the patient to self-examine the oral cavity and how to perform oral care. They should perform oral care before and after each meal, at bedtime, and as needed throughout the day. A saline solution of 1 tsp of salt in 1 L of water is an effective cleansing agent. Adding 1 tsp of sodium bicarbonate to the oral care solution can decrease odor, ease pain, and dissolve mucin. Have the patient use a soft-bristled toothbrush.

Treat mucositis or pain in the throat with systemic and topical analgesics and antibiotics if infection is present. Monitor and get prompt treatment for oral candidiasis (which often occurs with mucositis). Frequent cleansing with saline and water and topical application of anesthetic gels directly to the lesions are standard care.

Anorexia. Anorexia (loss of appetite) is a common. It is a side effect of cancer and cancer treatment. Anorexia may be related to an inflamed mouth or esophagus, which creates difficulty chewing or swallowing, or to emotions, such as anxiety or depression. It is important to have a dietitian involved in patient care before cancer treatment starts.

Patients with nausea and vomiting, bowel problems, mucositis, and taste changes typically have little desire to eat. Anorexia seems to peak at about 4 weeks of treatment. It resolves more quickly than fatigue when treatment ends.

Monitor patients during and after treatment to ensure that weight loss does not become excessive. Observe for dehydration. Most tolerate small, frequent meals of high-protein, high-calorie foods best. Nutrition supplements can be helpful. The patient may need enteral (EN) or parenteral nutrition (PN) if they are severely malnourished, if symptoms will interfere with nutrition for a time, or if the bowel needs rest. Monitor for and manage other symptoms that interfere with appetite (e.g., nausea, vomiting, pain, depression).

◆ Skin Reactions

Radiation skin changes. With radiation therapy, skin effects are local, occurring only in the treatment field. Radiation-induced skin changes can be acute or chronic depending on the area irradiated, the dosage, and technique. The skin-sparing ability of modern radiation equipment limits the severity of these reactions.

Erythema may develop 1 to 24 hours after a single treatment. It generally occurs progressively as the treatment dose accumulates. It is an acute response followed by dry desquamation (Fig. 16.14). If the rate of cell sloughing is faster than the ability of the new epidermal cells to replace dead cells, a wet desquamation occurs with exposure of the dermis and weeping of serous fluid (Fig. 16.15). Skin reactions are especially evident in areas of skinfolds or where skin is subjected to pressure. This includes behind the ear; in gluteal folds; on the perineum, breast, or collar line; and bony prominences.

Although skin care protocols vary, basic skin care principles apply. The goal is to prevent infection and promote wound healing. Protect radiated skin from temperature extremes. Do not use heating pads, ice packs, and hot water bottles in the treatment field. Avoid constricting garments, rubbing, harsh chemicals, and deodorants since they may traumatize the skin. Dry reactions are uncomfortable and cause pruritus. Lubricate dry skin with a nonirritating lotion emollient that contains no metal, alcohol, perfume, or additives. These can be irritating. Calendula ointment and topical hyaluronic acid cream are effective for managing radiation dermatitis. Aloe vera gel is useful for preventing skin problems.

Wet desquamation generally causes pain, drainage, and increased risk for infection. Skin care for moist desquamation includes keeping tissues clean with normal saline compresses or modified Burow's solution soaks. Protect the skin from further damage with moisture vapor–permeable dressings or Vaseline petrolatum gauze. Because protocols vary widely, you should verify the guidelines in Table 16.12 with your agency's radiation oncology department.

Chemotherapy skin changes. Chemotherapy causes a wide range of skin problems. These can range from mild redness and hyperpigmentation to more serious acral erythema and

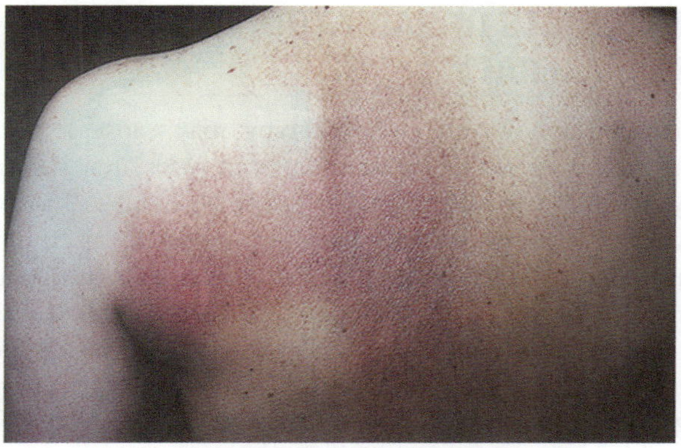

Fig. 16.14 Dry desquamation.

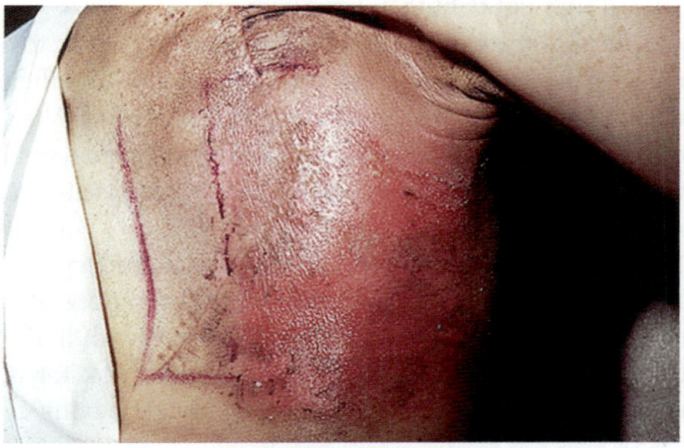

Fig. 16.15 Wet desquamation.

erythrodysesthesia syndrome (hand-foot syndrome). Hand-foot syndrome causes mild redness and tingling of the palms of the hands and soles of the feet. It may also cause painful moist desquamation, ulceration, blistering, and pain.

Alopecia is an easily recognizable effect of cancer treatment. Hair loss from radiation is local. Chemotherapy affects hair throughout the body. The degree and duration of hair loss depend on the type and dose of the chemotherapy agent. Scalp cooling may reduce alopecia. Cold caps are placed on the head before, during, and after chemotherapy treatment. Common side effects are headache and cold sensation.[14]

Alopecia from chemotherapy is usually reversible. Usually, the hair does not grow back until 3 to 4 weeks after the end of therapy. Sometimes the new hair is a different color and texture.

Patients have a range of emotions at the prospect of losing their hair and when hair loss occurs. These may include anger, grief, embarrassment, or fear. Hair loss is a visible reminder of their cancer and the challenges of treatment. For some people, hair loss is one of the most stressful events experienced during treatment. The ACS's "Look Good, Feel Better" program is excellent resource for people with hair loss and body image changes.

Pulmonary Effects

Both chemotherapy and radiation have the potential to cause irreversible and progressive lung damage. Distinguishing between the complications of treatment and those related to the disease is challenging. The effects of radiation on the lung include both acute and late reactions. Acute effects can be alarming to patients because they may mimic symptoms (e.g., cough, dyspnea) that led to the cancer diagnosis.

Pneumonitis is a delayed acute inflammatory reaction that may occur within 1 to 3 months after completing thoracic radiation. This reaction is often asymptomatic. An increase in cough, fever and night sweats may occur. Some patients may develop pulmonary fibrosis (with or without pneumonitis), a late effect of therapy.

The most common toxicities from chemotherapy include pulmonary edema (noncardiogenic) related to capillary leak syndrome or fluid retention, hypersensitivity pneumonitis, interstitial fibrosis, and pneumonitis due to an inflammatory reaction or destruction of alveolar-capillary endothelium.

Cardiovascular Effects

Radiation to the thorax can damage the pericardium, myocardium, valves, and coronary blood vessels. The pericardium is

TABLE 16.12 PATIENT & CAREGIVER TEACHING

Radiation Skin Reactions

Include the following instructions when teaching the patient and caregiver to clean and protect the skin in a radiation treatment area:

1. Gently cleanse the skin in the treatment field using a mild soap (Dove, Basis), tepid water, a soft cloth, and a gentle patting motion. Rinse thoroughly and pat dry.
2. Apply nonmedicated, nonperfumed, moisturizing lotion or cream, such as calendula ointment, aloe gel, Aquaphor, or Eucerin cream, to alleviate dry skin. Some substances must be gently cleansed from the treatment field before each treatment and reapplied. Over-the-counter hydrocortisone cream 1% may reduce itching.
3. Rinse the area with saline solution. Expose the area to air as often as possible. If copious drainage is present, use astringent compresses (such as Domeboro solution) and nonadhesive absorbent dressings. Change dressings as soon as they become wet.
4. Observe the area daily for signs of infection.
5. Avoid wearing tight-fitting clothing, including brassieres and belts, over the treatment field.
6. Avoid wearing harsh fabrics, such as wool and corduroy. A lightweight cotton garment is best. If possible, expose the treatment field to air.
7. Use gentle detergents (e.g., Tide Free and Gentle) to wash clothing that will come in contact with the treatment field.
8. Avoid direct exposure to the sun. If the treatment field is in an area that is exposed to the sun, wear protective clothing, such as a wide-brimmed hat, when out in the sun and apply sunscreen lotion.
9. Avoid all sources of excessive heat (hot water bottles, heating pads, sunlamps) on the treatment field.
10. Avoid exposing the treatment field to cold temperatures (ice bags or cold weather).
11. Avoid swimming in salt water or in chlorinated pools while in treatment.
12. Avoid using potential irritants (e.g., perfumes, powders, or cosmetics) on the skin in the treatment field. Use other topical medications or lotions as directed by the HCP. Avoid tape, dressings, and adhesive bandages unless allowed by the radiation therapist.
13. Continue to protect sensitive skin after the treatment is completed. Do the following:
    - Avoid direct exposure to the sun. A sunscreen agent and protective clothing must be worn if the potential of exposure to the sun is present.
    - Use an electric razor if shaving is needed in the treatment field.

most often involved. Pericardial effusion and pericarditis are key problems. Patients with preexisting coronary artery disease are especially at risk.

Anthracyclines (e.g., doxorubicin, daunorubicin) cause cardiotoxicity. Acute cardiotoxicities may cause electrocardiographic (ECG) changes. Late effects cause left ventricular dysfunction and heart failure. Baseline and periodic echocardiograms to monitor left ventricular function during treatment are usually done.

◆ Cognitive Effects

Cognitive effects can happen at any time during cancer, especially after treatment. Patients describe this change in mental function, often called *chemo brain*, as mental cloudiness, or fog.[15] Patients can have thinking and memory problems. These effects can last a short time or for years. They can be so severe that patients may be unable to be involved in any activities that need mental effort, including school, work, or social activities.

◆ Reproductive Effects

Reproductive problems from radiation and chemotherapy depend on the radiation treatment field and dosage, the chemotherapy drugs and dosage, and host factors (e.g., age). Treatment can cause temporary or permanent gonadal failure. Reproductive problems occur most often when reproductive organs are part of the radiation field or with alkylating drug treatment.

The testes are highly sensitive to radiation. We protect them with a testicular shield whenever possible. Pretreatment status may be a significant factor. A low sperm count and loss of motility occur with testicular cancer and Hodgkin lymphoma before starting any therapy. Combined modality treatment or prior chemotherapy with alkylating drugs enhances and prolongs the effects of radiation on the testes. When radiation is used alone with conventional doses and appropriate shielding, testicular recovery often occurs. Men may have erectile dysfunction after pelvic radiation.

The radiation dose that induces ovarian failure changes with age. With radiation therapy, we shield the ovaries whenever possible. Other factors that influence reproductive or sexual functioning in women include reactions in the cervix and endometrium. These tissues withstand a high radiation dose with minimal sequelae. This accounts for the ability to treat endometrial and cervical cancer with high external and brachytherapy doses. Acute reactions, such as tenderness, irritation, and loss of lubrication, compromise sexual activity. Late effects of combined internal and external radiation therapy include vaginal shortening related to fibrosis and loss of elasticity and lubrication. After pelvic radiation, specific suggestions include using a water-soluble vaginal lubricant and a vaginal dilator.

The patient and partner need information about the expected effects of treatment-related to reproductive and sexual issues. Encourage discussion of issues related to reproduction and sexuality. Potential infertility can be a significant consequence. Counseling may be needed. We should address fertility preservation before starting cancer treatment. Pretreatment harvesting of sperm, ova, or ovarian tissue may be considered.[16]

LATE EFFECTS OF RADIATION AND CHEMOTHERAPY

Radiation therapy and chemotherapy may cause long-term effects *(late effects)* that occur months to years after therapy.[17] They can affect every body system to some extent.

Acute radiation effects generally manifest as transient inflammatory changes in highly proliferative cells (e.g., epithelial tissues). In contrast, late radiation effects occur most often in post-mitotic cells (e.g., liver, kidney, lung, heart, muscle, bone, connective tissues). Once they occur, the late effects may be progressive and generally are permanent. Examples range from skin telangiectasias to strictures, fistulas, or radiation necrosis. Alteration of the lymphatic channels (e.g., axillary lymph node dissection) may contribute to lymphedema.

Long-term effects of chemotherapy include cardiac toxicity, cataracts, arthralgia, endocrine problems, renal insufficiency, hepatitis, osteoporosis, and neurocognitive problems. The additive effects of multiagent chemotherapy before, during, or after a course of radiation therapy can significantly increase the resulting late effects.

The cancer survivor may be at risk for secondary cancers, including leukemia, angiosarcoma, and skin cancer. Patients treated with alkylating drugs and those treated with high-dose radiation have an increased risk. The potential risk for developing secondary cancer does not contraindicate having cancer treatment.

IMMUNOTHERAPY AND TARGETED THERAPY

Immunotherapy uses the immune system, the body's main defense against infection and disease, to fight cancer. Some types of immunotherapy are called *biologic therapy*. Immunotherapy can (1) boost or manipulate the immune system and create an environment that is not conducive for cancer cells to grow or (2) attack cancer cells directly. Types of immunotherapy include cytokines, vaccines, and monoclonal antibodies (Table 16.13).

Monoclonal antibodies (drugs ending in -mab) are a very successful immunotherapy. Antibodies are proteins made by the immune system that bind to a target antigen on the cell surface. Because each antibody is specific to an antigen, that mechanism is used to develop specific drugs to treat cancer. Many of the monoclonal antibodies are targeted therapies.

Targeted therapy interferes with cancer growth by targeting specific cell receptors and pathways that are important in tumor growth.[18,19] Targeted therapies work at sites that are on the cell surface, at the intracellular level, or in the extracellular domain (Fig. 16.16 and Table 16.13). Targeted therapies are more selective for specific molecular targets than chemotherapy drugs. Thus, they act on specific targets that are associated with cancer. A major advantage of targeted therapy is that it does less damage to normal cells.

As we identify more oncogene targets, we are developing drugs that target those specific oncogenes. Targeted therapies personalize treatment based on the biology of the tumor.

A key class of targeted therapy is tyrosine kinase inhibitors (Table 16.13). Tyrosine kinases are enzymes responsible for

TABLE 16.13 Drug Therapy

Select Immunotherapies and Targeted Therapies

Mechanism of Action	Examples
Angiogenesis Inhibitors	
Bind vascular endothelial growth factor (VEGF), thereby inhibiting angiogenesis.	bevacizumab (Avastin) pazopanib (Votrient) ramucirumab (Cyramza)
CD20 Monoclonal Antibodies	
Bind CD20 antigen, causing cytotoxicity and radiation injury.	ibritumomab tiuxetan/yttrium-90 (Zevalin)
Bind CD20 antigen, causing cytotoxicity.	ofatumumab (Arzerra) rituximab (Rituxan)
CD52 Monoclonal Antibody	
Bind CD52 antigen (found on T and B cells, monocytes, natural killer [NK] cells, neutrophils).	alemtuzumab (Campath)
Cytokines (see Table 14.3)	
Inhibit DNA and protein synthesis. Suppress cell proliferation. ↑ Cytotoxic effects of NK cells.	α-interferon (Intron A)
Stimulate proliferation of T and B cells. Activate NK cells.	interleukin-2 (aldesleukin [Proleukin])
Human Epidermal Growth Factor Receptor-2 (HER-2)	
Monoclonal antibody to HER-2 that attaches to the antigen. It is taken into the cells and eventually kills them.	pertuzumab (Perjeta) trastuzumab (Herceptin)
Trastuzumab connected to a chemotherapy drug called DM1.	ado-trastuzumab emtansine (Kadcyla)
Immunomodulatory Drugs (IMiDs)	
Inhibit production of TNF, IL-6, and VEGF, leading to antiangiogenic effects. Stimulate T and NK cells. ↑ γ-interferon and IL-2 production.	apremilast (Otezla) lenalidomide (Revlimid) pomalidomide (Pomalyst) thalidomide (Thalomid)
Kinase Inhibitors	
Anaplastic Lymphoma Kinase (ALK) Inhibitors	
Inhibit anaplastic lymphoma kinase (ALK).	ceritinib (Zykadia) crizotinib (Xalkori) entrectinib (Rozlytrek)
BCR-ABL Tyrosine Kinase Inhibitors	
Inhibit BCR-ABL TK. Primarily used in chronic myeloid leukemia.	bosutinib (Bosulif) dasatinib (Sprycel) imatinib (Gleevec) nilotinib (Tasigna)
BRAF and MEK Kinase Inhibitors	
Inhibit BRAF and MEK enzymes.	dabrafenib (Tafinlar) trametinib (Mekinist) vemurafenib (Zelboraf) cobimetinib (Cotellic)
EGFR Tyrosine Kinase (TK) Inhibitors	
Inhibit epidermal growth factor receptor (EGFR) TK.	cetuximab (Erbitux) erlotinib (Tarceva) gefitinib (Iressa) panitumumab (Vectibix)
Inhibit EGFR-TK and binds HER-2.	lapatinib (Tykerb)
Multi-Tyrosine Kinase Inhibitors	
Inhibit multiple TKs.	axitinib (Inlyta) cabozantinib (Cometriq) pazopanib (Votrient) regorafenib (Stivarga) sorafenib (Nexavar) sunitinib (Sutent) vandetanib (Caprelsa)

Continued

TABLE 16.13 **Drug Therapy—cont'd**

Select Immunotherapies and Targeted Therapies

Mechanism of Action	Examples
mTOR Kinase Inhibitors	
Inhibit a specific protein known as the mechanistic target of rapamycin (mTOR).	everolimus (Afinitor) temsirolimus (Torisel)
Programmed Death Receptor (PD)-1 Blockers	
Block PD-1, a protein on T cells that normally helps keep these cells from attacking other cells. This boosts immune response against cancer cells.	nivolumab (Opdivo) pembrolizumab (Keytruda)
Proteasome Inhibitors	
Inhibit proteasome activity, which functions to regulate cell growth.	bortezomib (Velcade) carfilzomib (Kyprolis)
Vaccines	
Live attenuated strain of *Mycobacterium bovis* induces immune response. Used intravesically to treat bladder cancer (see Chapter 50).	BCG vaccine
Vaccine against prostate cancer that stimulates the immune system against the cancer (see Chapter 59).	sipuleucel-T (Provenge)

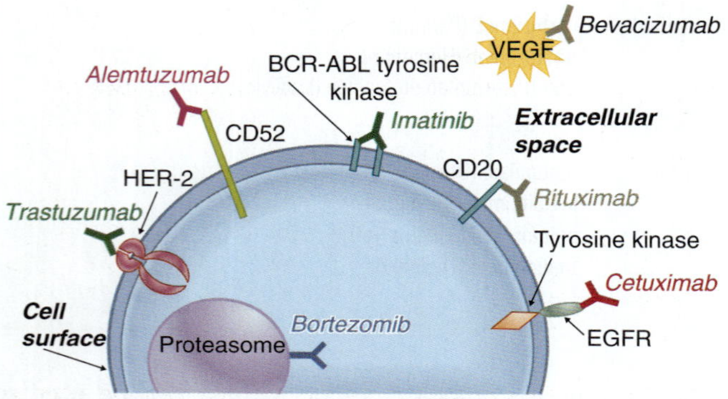

Fig. 16.16 Sites of action of targeted therapy. Examples of targeted therapy drugs that work at the specific site of action are shown in colored, italicized font. *EGFR,* Epidermal growth factor receptor; *HER-2,* human epidermal growth factor receptor-2; *VEGF,* vascular endothelial growth factor.

activating many proteins by signal transduction cascades. EGFR is a transmembrane molecule that works by activating intracellular tyrosine kinase (TK). Overexpression of EGFR is associated with unregulated cell growth and a poor prognosis. Drugs that inhibit EGFR suppress cell proliferation and promote *apoptosis* (programmed cell death).

EGFRs belong to the same receptor family as HER-2. It is the target for trastuzumab (Herceptin), a drug mainly used to treat breast cancer. HER-2 is overexpressed in certain cancers (especially breast cancers). It is associated with more aggressive disease and decreased survival. Trastuzumab is a monoclonal antibody (MoAb) that binds to HER-2. It is given IV to inhibit the growth of breast cancer cells that overexpress the HER-2 protein. Lapatinib (Tykerb) is an oral agent used for breast cancer that overexpresses HER-2.

Chronic myeloid leukemia (CML) cells make an abnormal active enzyme called BCR-ABL tyrosine kinase. Drugs, such as imatinib (Gleevec), that inhibit this enzyme suppress proliferation of CML cells and promote cell death.

Angiogenesis inhibitors work by preventing the mechanisms and pathways necessary for the vascularization of tumors. Bevacizumab (Avastin), a recombinant human MoAb, binds with vascular endothelial growth factor (VEGF), a compound that stimulates blood vessel growth. When bevacizumab binds with VEGF, it prevents VEGF from binding with its receptors on vascular endothelial cells and promoting new vessel formation. This inhibits further tumor growth.

Proteasomes are intracellular multienzyme complexes that degrade proteins. In cancer cells, proteasome inhibitors (e.g., bortezomib [Velcade]) promote the accumulation of proteins, leading to cell death.

Cancer cells can become resistant to targeted therapies. This can occur because the (1) target changes through mutation and the therapy no longer interact with it, and (2) the tumor finds a new growth pathway and no longer depends on the target. Because of the risk of resistance, targeted therapies work best in combination treatments such as with a chemotherapy drug.

Side Effects of Immunotherapy and Targeted Therapy

The administration of immunotherapy usually induces the endogenous release of other agents. The release and action of these agents result in systemic immune and inflammatory responses. The toxicities and side effects are related to dose and schedule.

Common side effects are flu-like symptoms, including headache, fever, chills, myalgias, fatigue, malaise, weakness, photosensitivity, anorexia, and nausea. Those receiving interferon therapy almost always have flu-like symptoms. The severity generally decreases over time. Acetaminophen given every 4 hours and large amounts of fluids often reduce the severity of the flu-like syndrome. The patient is often premedicated with acetaminophen to try to prevent or decrease the intensity of symptoms.

Tachycardia and orthostatic hypotension are common. IL-2 and MoAbs can cause *capillary leak syndrome,* which can result in pulmonary edema. A wide range of neurologic problems can occur with interferon and IL-2 therapy. They are frightening to the patient and caregivers. Teach them to observe for neurologic problems (e.g., confusion, memory loss, difficulty making decisions, insomnia), report their occurrence, and institute safety and support measures. Other side effects with interferons and IL-2 involve the renal, hepatic, and cardiovascular systems.

MoAbs are given IV. Patients may have infusion-related symptoms, including fever, chills, urticaria, mucosal congestion, nausea, diarrhea, and myalgias. Other toxicities of MoAbs include liver toxicity, bone marrow depression, and CNS effects.

Skin rashes are common in patients receiving EGFR inhibitors. They generally manifest as redness and acneiform-like rash that can cover a large part of the upper body. Angiogenesis inhibitors can cause arterial thrombi, hemorrhage, hypertension, impaired wound healing, and proteinuria.

NURSING MANAGEMENT: IMMUNOTHERAPY AND TARGETED THERAPY

Some problems experienced by the patient receiving immunotherapy and targeted therapy occur more acutely and are dose limited (e.g., effects resolve when therapy is over). Patients may be hesitant to inform the HCP of intolerable side effects. Some may be afraid to discuss side effects because they think that the drug will be stopped. Or they decide to stop the drug because of side effects. Assess and evaluate the patient's side effects and tolerance. Appropriate proactive nursing care can prevent these problems because you can intervene.

Capillary leak syndrome and pulmonary edema are problems that require critical care nursing. Bone marrow depression is generally more transient and less severe than that seen with chemotherapy. Fatigue from immunotherapy and targeted therapy can be so severe that it is a dose-limiting toxicity. Combining these agents with chemotherapy expands the spectrum of therapy-related effects.

Nursing interventions for flu-like syndrome include giving acetaminophen before treatment and every 6 hours after treatment. IV meperidine (Demerol) can help control the severe chills or rigors from some agents such as IL-2. Other care includes monitoring vital signs and temperature, planning for rest periods, assisting with activities of daily living (ADLs), and monitoring for adequate oral intake.

HORMONE THERAPY

The hormones estrogen and progesterone can enhance the growth of some breast cancers. Androgen (testosterone) can enhance the growth of some prostate cancers. When given as a cancer treatment, hormone therapy drugs can block the effects of the hormone and stop the growth of cancer cells (Table 16.14). Surgical interventions (oophorectomy, orchiectomy) can be used to remove the effects of the hormone on cancer growth.

HEMATOPOIETIC GROWTH FACTORS

Hematopoietic growth factors are used to support patients through their cancer treatment (Table 16.15). CSFs are a family of glycoproteins made by various cells. CSFs stimulate production, maturation, regulation, and activation of cells of the hematologic system. The name of the CSF is based on the specific cell line it affects.

TABLE 16.14 Drug Therapy

Hormone Therapy

Androgen Receptor Blockers	
Selectively attach to androgen receptors, blocking androgen from binding. Inhibits tumor growth.	bicalutamide (Casodex), enzalutamide (Xtandi), apalutamide (Erleada)
Aromatase Inhibitors	
Inhibit aromatase, thus preventing the production of estrogen.	anastrozole (Arimidex), exemestane (Aromasin), letrozole (Femara)
Corticosteroids	
Disrupt the cell membrane and inhibit synthesis of protein. ↓Circulating lymphocytes, inhibit mitosis, depress immune system, increase sense of well-being.	cortisone, dexamethasone, hydrocortisone, methylprednisolone, prednisone
Estrogens	
Interfere with the effect of testosterone.	estradiol, estramustine (Emcyt), estrogen (Menest)
Estrogen Receptor Blockers	
Selectively attach to estrogen receptors, blocking estrogen from binding. Inhibits tumor growth.	fulvestrant (Faslodex), tamoxifen, toremifene (Fareston)
Estrogen Receptor Modulator	
Has both estrogen-agonistic effects on bone and estrogen-antagonistic effects on breast tissue.	raloxifene (Evista)

Erythropoiesis-stimulating agents (ESAs) can be used to treat anemia from chemotherapy that is not intended to cure. ESA use has safety concerns when the target hemoglobin is greater than 12 g/dL. They can cause potential harm (thromboembolic and cardiovascular events) and increase the risk of death. Thus we give the lowest dose that will gradually increase hemoglobin to the lowest level sufficient to avoid the need for blood transfusion. Monitor the hemoglobin level regularly.

HEMATOPOIETIC STEM CELL TRANSPLANTATION

Hematopoietic stem cell transplantation (HSCT) and **peripheral stem cell transplantation (PSCT)** are effective, lifesaving treatments for several malignant and nonmalignant diseases (Table 16.16). Both allow for the safe use of very high doses of chemotherapy drugs and/or radiation therapy in patients whose tumors have developed resistance (refractory) or did not respond to standard doses of chemotherapy and radiation. Overall, cure rates are steadily increasing. Even when a cure is not achieved, transplantation can result in a period of remission. The drawback is that patients may have long-term or delayed complications that can affect their quality of life.

Many call either procedure a "bone marrow transplant." This is because when it was first developed, the bone marrow was the source of stem cells. However, advances in harvesting and cryopreservation have opened new pathways to collecting stem

TABLE 16.15 Drug Therapy

Hematopoietic Growth Factors Used in Cancer Treatment

Growth Factor	Drug Name	Indications	Side Effects
Erythropoietin	epoetin alfa (Epogen, Procrit)	Anemia of chronic cancer	↑ BP, thrombosis, headache
	darbepoetin alfa (Aranesp)	Anemia related to chemotherapy	↑ BP, thrombosis, headache
Granulocyte colony-stimulating factor (G-CSF)	filgrastim (Neupogen)	Chemotherapy-induced neutropenia	Bone pain, nausea, vomiting
	filgrastim-sndz (Zarxio)		
	pegfilgrastim (Neulasta)		
	tbo-filgrastim (Granix)		
Granulocyte-macrophage colony-stimulating factor (GM-CSF)	sargramostim (Leukine)	Myeloid cell recovery after bone marrow transplantation	Nausea, vomiting, diarrhea, fever, chills, myalgia, headache, fatigue
Interleukin-11 (platelet growth factor)	oprelvekin (Neumega)	Thrombocytopenia related to chemotherapy	Fluid retention, peripheral edema, dyspnea, ↑ heart rate, nausea, mouth sores

TABLE 16.16 Indications for Hematopoietic Stem Cell Transplantation

Malignant Diseases

- Acute and chronic lymphocytic leukemia
- Acute and chronic myelogenous leukemia
- Hodgkin lymphoma
- Multiple myeloma
- Myelodysplastic syndrome
- Non-Hodgkin lymphoma

Nonmalignant Diseases

- Aplastic anemia
- Chronic granulomatous disease
- Fanconi anemia
- Hematologic diseases
- Immunodeficiency diseases
- Severe combined immunodeficiency disease (SCID)
- Sickle cell disease (severe)
- Thalassemia
- Wiskott-Aldrich syndrome

cells from the peripheral blood.[20] Consequently, the terminology has changed.

The approach in HSCT is to eradicate diseased tumor cells and/or clear the bone marrow of its components to make way for engraftment of the transplanted, healthy stem cells. This is done by giving higher than usual dosages of chemotherapy with or without radiation therapy. Life-threatening consequences from pancytopenia and other adverse effects can result. After chemotherapy and radiation therapy are over, healthy stem cells are infused. These healthy stem cells "rescue" the damaged bone marrow through subsequent proliferation and differentiation of the donated stem cells in the recipient.

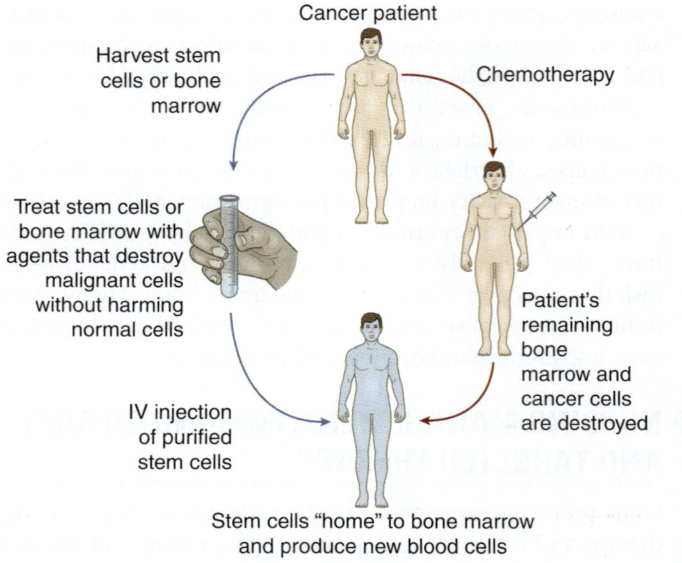

Fig. 16.17 Autologous stem cell transplant.

HSCT is an intensive procedure with many risks. Some patients die from treatment-related complications or from recurrence of the original disease. Because it is a highly toxic therapy, the patient must weigh the significant risks for treatment-related death or treatment failure (relapse) against the hope of a cure.

Types of Hematopoietic Stem Cell Transplants

We categorize HSCTs as allogeneic, syngeneic, or autologous. The sources of stem cells include the bone marrow, peripheral blood, and umbilical cord blood. In *allogeneic transplantation,* stem cells are acquired from a donor (graft) who, through human leukocyte antigen (HLA) tissue typing, has been determined to be HLA matched to the recipient (host). HLA typing involves testing WBCs to identify genetically inherited antigens common to both donor and recipient that are important in the compatibility of transplanted tissue. HLA tissue typing is discussed in Chapter 14. The donor is often a family member. It may be an unrelated donor found through a national or international bone marrow registry (e.g., National Marrow Donor Program). These are known as matched unrelated donor (MUD) transplants. Increased risks and toxicities may be associated with a MUD. Common indications for allogeneic transplant are certain leukemias, multiple myeloma, and lymphoma.

Syngeneic transplantation is a type of allogeneic transplant that involves obtaining stem cells from one identical twin and infusing them into the other. Identical twins have identical HLA types and are a perfect match

In *autologous transplantation,* patients receive their own stem cells back after *myeloablative* (destroying bone marrow) chemotherapy (Fig. 16.17). The aim of this approach is "rescue."

It allows patients to receive intensive chemotherapy and radiation by supporting them with their previously harvested stem cells until their marrow generates blood cells again on its own. Restoration usually takes about 4 to 6 weeks.

The newer, nonmyeloablative, or reduced-intensity transplant uses lower doses of radiation or chemotherapy that result in less toxicity and myelosuppression. HSCT continues to be researched in managing some solid tumors resistant to treatment.

Procedures

Harvest Procedures

Hematopoietic stem cells are *harvested* from a donor (for allogeneic transplantation) or the recipient (for autologous transplantation) via 2 methods. Harvesting stem cells from bone marrow is done in the operating room using general or spinal anesthesia. Multiple bone marrow aspirations (usually from the iliac crest, sometimes the sternum) are carried out to obtain stem cells. The harvested marrow is processed to strain out bone fragments. The entire bone marrow harvest procedure takes about 1 to 2 hours. The patient can be discharged after recovery. Postharvest, the donor may have pain at the collection site that lasts up to 7 days. It can be treated with mild analgesics. The donor's body will replenish the removed bone marrow in a few weeks.

Peripheral stem cell transplants are obtained from the peripheral blood in an outpatient procedure. Cell separator equipment automatically separates the stem cells from the blood circulating through the machine and returns the remaining blood components to the donor. The process takes about 2 to 4 hours. Sometimes it takes longer depending on donor factors and the quality of the venous access. Often it takes more than 1 procedure to obtain enough stem cells. Because the blood has fewer stem cells than the bone marrow, "mobilizing" stem cells from the bone marrow into the peripheral blood can be achieved with chemotherapy and/or hematopoietic growth factors.

Growth factors, such as granulocyte-macrophage colony-stimulating factor (GM-CSF) and granulocyte colony-stimulating factor (G-CSF), may be given to increase stem cell production for collection (Table 16.15). When patients receive growth factors for mobilization, stem cells are harvested 4 or 5 days after growth factor injections.

After collection, the marrow or peripheral stem cells are used immediately or bagged with preservatives for cryopreservation and stored until they are needed. Since they come from the patient, autologous stem cells are sometimes treated (purged) to remove undetected cancer cells. Many different pharmacologic, immunologic, physical, and chemical agents are used for this purpose.

Umbilical cord blood is rich in hematopoietic stem cells. Successful allogeneic transplants have been done using this source. Cord blood can be HLA-typed and cryopreserved. A disadvantage of cord blood is the risk of insufficient numbers of stem cells to allow a transplant to adults. Considerable research is currently ongoing to define the optimal use of this technology.

Preparative Regimens and Stem Cell Infusions

Patients receive myeloablative dosages of chemotherapy with or without adjunctive radiation to treat the underlying disease. Total-body irradiation (TBI) can be used for immunosuppression or to treat the disease. These preparative therapies are known as the *conditioning regimen*.

Stem cell infusions are given IV. They can be injected via the slow bolus method or infused, much like a blood transfusion (using tubing without a filter). The infused stem cells reconstitute the bone marrow elements, "rescuing" the recipient's hematopoietic system. It usually takes 2 to 4 weeks for the transplanted marrow to start making hematopoietic blood cells. During this period, the patient has pancytopenia. The patient must be protected from exposure to infection and supported with electrolyte supplements, nutrition, and blood component transfusions (as needed) to maintain adequate levels of circulating RBCs and platelets.

Complications

Bacterial, viral, and fungal infections are common after HSCT. Prophylactic therapies are used to reduce their incidence. A potentially serious complication of allogeneic transplant is graft-versus-host disease. This occurs when the T cells from the donated marrow (graft) recognize the recipient (host) as foreign and begin to attack certain organs, such as the skin, liver, and GI tract. Graft-versus-host disease is discussed in Chapter 14.

The occurrence and severity of posttransplant complications depend on the drugs used (some are more toxic than others) and the stem cell source. Because stem cells in the peripheral blood are more mature than those harvested from the marrow, the hematologic recovery period in PSCT is shorter, and fewer, less severe complications occur.

GENE THERAPY

Gene therapy is an experimental therapy that involves introducing genetic material (DNA or RNA) into a person's cells to fight disease. Gene therapy is discussed in Chapter 13.

COMPLICATIONS OF CANCER

The patient may develop complications related to the cancer growing into normal tissue or to the side effects of treatment.

NUTRITION PROBLEMS

Malnutrition

The patient with cancer may have protein and calorie malnutrition with fat and muscle depletion. The assessment of malnutrition is discussed in Chapter 44.

Soft, nonirritating high-protein, and high-calorie foods should be eaten throughout the day. Foods suggested for increasing protein intake are shown in Table 16.17. High-calorie foods that provide energy and lessen weight loss are shown in Table 16.18. Foods in a high-calorie, high-protein diet are outlined in Table 44.10.

Teach the patient to avoid extremes of temperature, tobacco, alcohol, spicy or rough foods, and other irritants. Encourage nutrition supplements (e.g., Ensure) as an adjunct to meals and fluid intake. Weigh the patient at least twice each week to monitor for weight loss.

TABLE 16.17 NUTRITION THERAPY

Protein Foods With High Biologic Value

Cheese

- Cottage: ½ cup = 15 g protein.
- American: 1 slice = 3 g protein.
- Cheddar: 1 slice = 6 g protein.
- Cream: 1 Tbsp = 1 g protein.
- Use cheese in a sandwich or as a snack.
- Add cheese to salads, casseroles, sauces, and baked potatoes.

Eggs

- Egg: 6 g protein.
- Eggnog: 1 cup = 15.5 g protein.
- Add eggs to salads, casseroles, and sauces. Deviled eggs are especially well tolerated.
- Desserts that contain eggs include angel food cake, sponge cake, custard, and cheesecake.

Meat, Poultry, and Fish

- Pork: 3 oz = approx. 19 g protein.
- Chicken: ½ breast = approx. 26 g protein.
- Fish: 3 oz = approx. 30 g protein.
- Tuna fish: 6½ oz = approx. 44.5 g protein.
- Add meat, poultry, and fish to salads, casseroles, and sandwiches.
- Add strained and junior baby meats to soups and casseroles.

Milk

- Whole milk: 1 cup = 9 g protein.
- Double-strength milk (1 quart of whole milk plus 1 cup of dried skim milk blended and chilled): 1 cup = 14 g protein.
- Milk shake (1 cup of ice cream plus 1 cup of milk): 15 g protein, 415 cal.
- Use evaporated milk, double-strength milk, or half-and-half to make casseroles, hot cereals, sauces, gravies, puddings, milk shakes, and soups.
- Yogurt (regular and frozen): Select brands with high protein content: 1 cup = 10 g protein

TABLE 16.18 NUTRITION THERAPY

High-Calorie Foods

Mayonnaise	1 Tbsp	=	101 cal
Butter or margarine	1 tsp	=	35 cal
Sour cream	1 Tbsp	=	72 cal
Peanut butter	1 Tbsp	=	94 cal
Whipped cream	1 Tbsp	=	53 cal
Corn oil	1 Tbsp	=	119 cal
Jelly	1 Tbsp	=	49 cal
Ice cream	1 cup	=	256 cal
Honey	1 Tbsp	=	64 cal

Suggest a referral for diet counseling to the patient or HCP as soon as a 5% weight loss is noted or if the patient has the potential for protein and calorie malnutrition. Monitor albumin and prealbumin levels. Once a 10-lb. (4.5-kg) weight loss occurs, it may be hard to maintain the patient's nutrition status.

Teach the patient to use nutrition supplements in place of milk when cooking or baking. Foods to which supplements can be easily added include scrambled eggs, pudding, custard, mashed potatoes, cereal, and cream sauces. Packages of instant breakfast can be used as indicated or sprinkled on cereals and other foods.

Caregivers may need to help the patient with eating. If the malnutrition cannot be treated with dietary intake, it may be necessary to use EN or PN. See more about EN and PN in Chapter 44.

Altered Taste (Dysgeusia)

Cancer cells may release substances that stimulate the bitter taste buds. The patient may have changes in the sweet, sour, and salty taste sensations. Meat may taste bitter or bland. We do not know the cause of these taste changes.

Teach patients with taste problems to avoid foods that they dislike. Often, the patient may feel compelled to eat certain foods they believe are beneficial. Tell the patient to try different ways to mask the taste changes. Some find stronger seasonings and spices effective. Others find it better to avoid strong flavors and eat more bland foods. Avoiding strong smells, drinking more water with food, oral care before eating, eating smaller amounts more often, and using plastic utensils may help.[21]

Cancer Cachexia

Cancer cachexia (wasting syndrome) is a complex, multifactorial syndrome characterized by anorexia and/or unintended loss of weight and appetite. It is accompanied by generalized tissue wasting, skeletal muscle atrophy, immune dysfunction, and metabolic problems. Nutrition therapy cannot reverse weight loss. Patients with upper GI and pancreatic cancers are prone to cachexia. As cancer progresses, cachexia can affect many cancer patients. It is associated with increased morbidity.[22]

The best way to manage cancer cachexia is to treat the cancer. Unfortunately, this is not a realistic goal for patients with advanced cancer. A second option is to increase intake, but this does not completely reverse the wasting from cachexia. A third option is to use megestrol acetate. It is a synthetic form of the hormone progesterone, which stimulates appetite in patients with cachexia.

INFECTION

Infection is a leading cause of death in the patient with cancer. Common sites of infection include the lungs, GU system, mouth, rectum, peritoneal cavity, and blood (septicemia). Infection occurs because of the ulceration and necrosis caused by the tumor, the tumor compressing vital organs, and neutropenia from the cancer or cancer treatment.

Teach patients at risk for neutropenia to call their HCP if they have a temperature of 100.4°F (38°C) or greater. Assessment often includes signs and symptoms of fever, determining the possible cause (e.g., sinuses, mucous membranes, respiratory, GI, urinary, sites of any tubes or lines), and CBC.

Many patients are neutropenic when an infection develops. In these persons, infection may cause significant morbidity. It may be rapidly fatal if not treated promptly. The classic manifestations of infection are often subtle or absent in a patient with neutropenia and a depressed immune system. Neutropenia is discussed in Chapter 34.

ONCOLOGIC EMERGENCIES

Oncologic emergencies are life-threatening emergencies that occur because of cancer or cancer treatment. Emergencies can be obstructive, metabolic, or infiltrative (Table 16.19).

Obstructive Emergencies

Obstructive emergencies are mainly caused by tumor obstruction of an organ or blood vessel. They include superior vena cava syndrome (Fig. 16.18), spinal cord compression syndrome, third space syndrome, and intestinal obstruction.

Metabolic Emergencies

Metabolic emergencies are caused by the production of ectopic hormones directly from the tumor or from metabolic problems caused by the cancer or cancer treatment. Ectopic hormones arise from tissues that do not normally make these hormones. Cancer cells return to a more embryonic form, thus allowing the cells' stored potential to become evident.

Metabolic emergencies include syndrome of inappropriate antidiuretic hormone secretion (see Chapter 54), hypercalcemia (see Chapter 17), tumor lysis syndrome, septic shock (see Chapter 44), and disseminated intravascular coagulation (see Chapter 34).

Infiltrative Emergencies

Infiltrative emergencies occur when cancer infiltrates major organs or from cancer treatment. The most common infiltrative emergencies are cardiac tamponade and carotid artery rupture.

CANCER PAIN

Moderate to severe pain occurs in around 50% of patients who are receiving active treatment for their cancer and 90% of patients with advanced cancer.[23] What is concerning is that these statistics have not changed in the past 30 years. Undertreatment of cancer pain is common. It causes needless suffering, decreases quality of life, and increases caregiver burden.

Pain Assessment

Inadequate pain assessment is the single greatest barrier to effective pain management. Data, such as vital signs and patient behaviors, are not reliable indicators of pain, especially long-standing, chronic pain. Determine if pain is persistent or episodic, positional, or breakthrough pain. Obtain a comprehensive pain assessment. Include the quality, location, intensity, duration, and precipitating and alleviating factors. Distinguishing between types of pain (e.g., visceral, somatic, neuropathic) is important in developing an effective pain management plan.

Assess pain on an ongoing basis to determine the effectiveness of the treatment plan. Obtain data and document at regular intervals the location and intensity of the pain, what it feels like, and how it is relieved. Assess change in pain (e.g., a change in the intensity, character, worsening, or location) to determine the cause (e.g., disease progression).

Always believe the patient's report. Table 16.20 presents assessment questions that may facilitate data collection. Have patients keep a pain management diary.[23]

Pain Management

Pain management for the cancer patient must address both persistent and breakthrough components of pain if they are present. Adjuvant therapies need to be delivered specific to the type or nature of the pain.

Drug therapy, including NSAIDs (e.g., ibuprofen), opioids (e.g., morphine), and adjuvant pain medications, should be used and selected based on the character and cause of the pain. Opioids normally are prescribed for the treatment of moderate to severe cancer pain. Corticosteroids are part of many drug regimens. They are anti-inflammatory, reducing swelling and inflammation, which may contribute to cancer pain.

Drug dosages are adjusted to control pain with the fewest side effects. Analgesic medications (e.g., morphine, fentanyl) should be given on a regular schedule (around the clock) with more doses available as needed for breakthrough pain. In general, oral administration is preferred. Other routes (e.g., transdermal, transmucosal) are options.

Treatment plans should be developed that balance analgesia and side effects to maintain optimal functional status. It is important for you to pay attention to common side effects of pain medications (e.g., constipation) to ensure the patient's well-being and adherence to the pain management program. NSAIDs often serve as helpful adjuncts to opioid therapy, especially for bone pain. Antidepressant and antiseizure drugs may be helpful in managing neuropathic pain, which is often resistant to opioids.

Radioactive drugs (e.g., samarium-153) may help patients with diffuse bone pain, especially if no further chemotherapy is planned. Patients may have an initial pain flare after administration. Nerve blocks or epidural or intrathecal analgesia may help patients with unrelieved pain or to minimize opioid use.

Discuss pain management goals with patients, especially those needing large or chronic doses of opioids. Assess for risk factors for opioid misuse. Clarify myths and misconceptions. Reassure patients and caregivers that cancer pain can be effectively relieved. Address any fear of addiction. It is a significant barrier for patients and nurses in appropriate pain management. Stress that addiction and tolerance are not problems associated with effective cancer pain management. Nondrug interventions, including relaxation therapy and imagery, are part of pain management (see Chapter 7). Other strategies to relieve pain are discussed in Chapter 9.

COPING WITH CANCER AND TREATMENT

You play a key role in helping patients cope with the psychosocial issues associated with cancer and cancer treatment. The patient may have a variety of concerns, including fears of dependency, loss of control, family and relationship stress, financial burden, and fear of death. Anxiety and fear may occur throughout the cancer continuum, including at diagnosis, during or after treatment, and in association with long-term follow-up.

Repetitive office visits or hospitalizations, continuing medications, and frequent laboratory testing force the patient to confront the cancer every day. Treatment-related uncertainties and fears are often most evident at the beginning of therapy. However, anxiety and fear may be present throughout treatment

TABLE 16.19 Oncologic Emergencies

Description	Manifestations	Management
Obstructive Emergencies		
Spinal Cord Compression		
• Neurologic emergency caused by cancer in epidural space of spinal cord. • Common causes are breast, lung, prostate, GI, renal cancers, melanoma. • Lymphomas can invade epidural space.	• Intense, localized, and persistent back pain with vertebral tenderness. • Motor weakness, sensory paresthesia, and loss. • Autonomic dysfunction (e.g., change in bowel or bladder function).	• Radiation therapy, corticosteroids. • Surgical decompressive laminectomy. • Activity limitations and pain management.
Superior Vena Cava Syndrome (SVCS)		
• Results from obstruction of superior vena cava by tumor or thrombosis. • Common causes are lung cancer, non-Hodgkin lymphoma, metastatic breast cancer. • Presence of central venous catheter and previous mediastinal radiation increase risk.	• Facial edema, periorbital edema. • Distention of veins of head, neck, and chest (see Fig. 15.18). • Headache, seizures. • Mediastinal mass on chest x-ray.	• Considered a serious medical problem. • Radiation therapy to site of obstruction. • Chemotherapy for tumors more sensitive to this therapy.
Third Space Syndrome		
• Shifting of fluid from vascular space to interstitial space. • Occurs due to extensive surgical procedures, immunotherapy, septic shock.	• Signs of hypovolemia: ↓ BP, ↑ heart rate, ↓ central venous pressure, ↓ urine output.	• Fluid, electrolyte, plasma protein replacement. • During recovery hypervolemia can occur, causing ↑ BP, ↑ central venous pressure, weight gain, shortness of breath.
Metabolic Emergencies		
Hypercalcemia		
• Occurs in metastatic bone disease, multiple myeloma, or when cancer cells secrete a parathyroid hormone–like substance. • Immobility and dehydration can contribute to or worsen hypercalcemia.	• Serum calcium higher than 12 mg/dL (3 mmol/L) often produces symptoms. • Apathy, depression, fatigue, muscle weakness, ECG changes, polyuria and nocturia, anorexia, nausea, vomiting. • High calcium elevations can be life threatening. • Chronic hypercalcemia can result in renal failure.	• Treat primary disease. • Hydration (3 L/day) • Diuretics (especially loop diuretics) used to prevent heart failure or edema. • Infusion of bisphosphonate zoledronate or pamidronate (Aredia). • RANKL inhibitor injection • Denosumab (Xgeva)
Syndrome of Inappropriate Antidiuretic Hormone (SIADH)		
• Tumor cells can produce abnormal or sustained production of antidiuretic hormone (ADH). • Many chemotherapy drugs may contribute to ectopic ADH production or potentiate ADH effects.	• Water retention and hyponatremia (hypotonic hyponatremia) (see Chapter 49). • Weight gain without edema, weakness, anorexia, nausea, vomiting, personality changes, seizures, oliguria, ↓ in reflexes, coma.	• Treat underlying cancer. • Take measures to correct sodium-water imbalance, including fluid restriction, oral salt tablets or isotonic (0.9%) saline administration, and IV 3% sodium chloride solution (severe cases). • Furosemide used in early phases. • Monitor sodium level. Correcting SIADH quickly may cause seizures or death.
Tumor Lysis Syndrome (TLS)		
• Metabolic complication characterized by rapid release of intracellular components in response to chemotherapy and radiation therapy (less often). • Massive cell destruction releases intracellular components (potassium, phosphate, DNA, RNA) that are metabolized to uric acid by liver.	• *Hallmark signs*: hyperuricemia, hyperphosphatemia, hyperkalemia, hypocalcemia. • Weakness, muscle cramps, diarrhea, nausea, vomiting, cardiac dysrhythmia, seizure, syncope. • Occurs within 24–48 hr after starting chemotherapy. • May last 5–7 days. • Metabolic abnormalities and concentrated uric acid (which crystallizes in distal tubules of kidneys) can lead to acute kidney injury.	• Identify patients at risk. • Monitor for and address abnormal electrolyte values. • Maintain high urine output with hydration therapy. • Decrease uric acid concentration with allopurinol. • Implement safety precautions.
Infiltrative Emergencies		
Cardiac Tamponade		
• Fluid accumulation in pericardium. • Caused by constriction of pericardium by tumor or pericarditis from radiation therapy to the chest.	• Heavy feeling over chest, shortness of breath, ↑ heart rate, cough, dysphagia, hiccups, hoarseness. • Nausea, vomiting, excessive perspiration. • ↓ Level of consciousness, distant or muted heart sounds. • Extreme anxiety.	• Decrease fluid around heart using (1) surgery to create a pericardial window or an (2) indwelling pericardial catheter. • Administer O_2 therapy, IV hydration, and vasopressor therapy.

TABLE 16.19 Oncologic Emergencies—cont'd

Description	Manifestations	Management
Carotid Artery Rupture		
• Invasion of arterial wall by tumor or erosion following surgery or radiation therapy. • Occurs most often in patients with head and neck cancer.	• Bleeding: ranges from minor oozing to spurting of blood in the case of a "blowout" of artery.	• Give IV fluids and blood products. • Surgery: ligation of carotid artery above and below rupture site and reduction of local tumor.

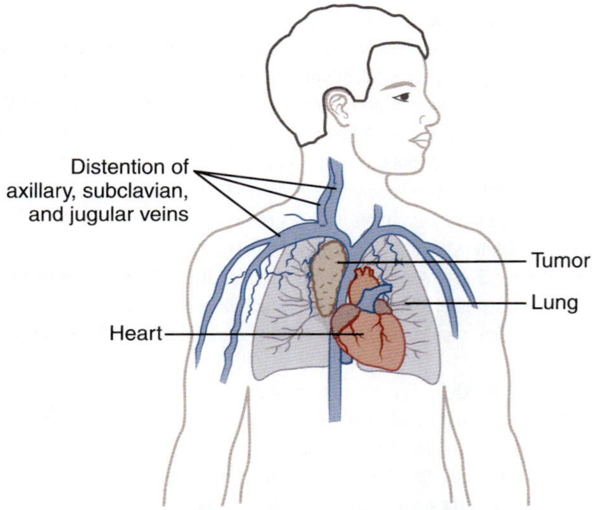

Fig. 16.18 Superior vena cava obstruction in bronchial cancer.

TABLE 16.20 Pain Assessment in Cancer Patients

Characteristic	Questions to Ask
Location	• Where is the pain? • Is the pain in more than one place? Is the pain in a new location? • Does location of pain correlate with known diagnosis?
Intensity	• How bad is the pain? • Rate the pain on a scale of 0–10.
Quality	• What does the pain feel like—sharp, dull, burning, shooting, aching, or other?
Pattern	• Has the pain changed? • Is the pain getting better, worse, or unchanged? • What makes the pain better or worse?
Relief measures	• What do you do to control your pain? • Do you use medications? • Do the relief measures help much? How much?

and when therapy is completed (e.g., fear of recurrence, less available support).

Several factors influence adaptation and coping with a cancer diagnosis. These include demographics, prior coping skills and strategies, social support, and religious and spiritual beliefs (Table 16.21). You are in a key position to assess the patient's and caregiver's responses and support positive coping strategies. To promote effective coping and to support them during the various stages of cancer, you should

- Be available and continue to be available, especially during difficult times.
- Exhibit a caring attitude.
- Listen actively to fears and concerns.
- Help provide relief from distressing symptoms.
- Provide accurate, essential information about cancer and cancer care.
- Help establish realistic expectations about what the patient will experience.
- Maintain a relationship based on trust and confidence. Be open, honest, and caring in the approach.
- Use touch to show caring. A squeeze of the hand or a hug may at times be more effective than words.
- Help the patient in setting realistic, reachable short-term and long-term goals.
- Help the patient maintain usual lifestyle patterns.
- Maintain hope, which is the key to effective cancer care.

Hope varies, depending on the patient's status—hope that the symptoms are not serious, hope that the treatment is curative, hope for independence, hope for relief of pain, hope for longer life, hope to achieve meaningful goals, or hope for a peaceful death. Hope provides control over what is occurring. It is the basis of a positive attitude toward cancer and cancer care.

Reassure patients that support is ongoing. Give information and support to help minimize the negative impact of cancer treatment on quality of life. Patient teaching and symptom management help patients to self-manage their illness (e.g., adjusting treatment schedules to allow patients to work when possible, making referrals to support groups). Work with the oncology nurse navigators, who serve as the liaison between the patient and the health care team.

Arrange for patients to meet with people who have successfully completed therapy. This can increase their hopefulness and confidence. Make regular supportive telephone contacts between office visits. Assist with planning for transportation, nutrition, and emotional support.

Do not forget the caregivers. They need education and support throughout the trajectory of diagnosis, treatment, and follow-up. Patients and caregivers may benefit from a variety of psychosocial interventions. These include supportive listening, stress management techniques, individual or group counseling, and cognitive-behavioral therapy. Assess the psychosocial concerns and emotional responses of patients, caregivers, and families so that you can connect them with appropriate supportive care resources. Use the available resources in the community, such as the ACS, Cancer Lifeline, churches, and other community resources.

TABLE 16.21 Factors Affecting How Patients Cope With Cancer

Factor	Description
Ability to cope with past stressful events	How patients coped with previous stressful events (e.g., loss of job, major disappointment, significant traumatic event) affects how they cope with diagnosis of cancer.
Ability to express feelings and concerns	Patients who express feelings and needs and ask for help cope better than those who internalize feelings and needs.
Age at the time of diagnosis	Age determines coping strategies to a great degree. For example, a young mother and a 70-year-old woman with cancer may have different concerns.
Attitude associated with the cancer	Patients who feel in control and have a positive outlook about cancer and cancer treatment cope better with the diagnosis and treatment of cancer than those who feel hopeless, helpless, and out of control.
Availability of significant others	Patients who have effective support systems cope better than those who do not.
Negative body image	Negative body image (e.g., deformity, ostomy, mastectomy) may intensify the psychologic impact of cancer.
Extent of disease	Cure or control of the disease process is usually easier to cope with than the reality of terminal illness.
Experience with cancer	Negative experiences with cancer (personal or with others) influence perceptions about the current situation.
Symptoms	Symptoms such as fatigue, nausea, diarrhea, and pain may intensify the psychologic impact of cancer.

Gerontologic Considerations: Cancer

Cancer is usually a disease of aging. Approximately 80% of cancers occur in people 55 years or older.[1] Of all deaths due to cancer, 70% occur in those over 65. This is especially important since the proportion of the population that is older than 65 years is increasing.

Manifestations of cancer in older adults may be mistakenly attributed to age-related changes and ignored by the person.[24] Older adults are especially at risk for complications of both cancer and cancer treatment. This is due to their decline in physiologic functioning, social and emotional resources, and cognitive function.

The older adult's functional status should be taken into consideration when developing a treatment plan. Age alone is not a good predictor of tolerance or response to treatment. Advances in cancer treatment are making cancer therapies beneficial to more older adults, including those with suboptimal health.

Assess the patient at the time of diagnosis to identify important issues that may affect decisions about treatment options. Include projected life expectancy, estimate of morbidity from cancer, co-morbidities that would affect treatment, and patient decision-making capacity and wishes.

Some important questions to consider when an older adult is diagnosed with cancer include: Will the treatment provide more benefits than harm? Will they be able to tolerate the treatment safely? Is there a need to treat co-morbidities or nutrition or functional status before starting treatment? What are the patient's preferences and wishes (Box 16.3)?

BOX 16.3 ETHICAL/LEGAL DILEMMAS

Medical Futility

Situation

D.M., a 65-year-old Asian woman, has breast cancer with metastasis to the liver and bone. The family asks you why their mother is not receiving chemotherapy. They want to make sure that she will be resuscitated should her heart stop. They are aware of her diagnosis and that she only has a few weeks to live. In morning rounds, you hear that D.M. does not want any more treatment that would prolong her life.

Ethical/Legal Points for Consideration

- Although court decisions have varied, legally there is substantial consensus about the right to privacy (a constitutional right), right to informed consent and refusal of treatment, and rights about end-of-life decision making. The *Code of Ethics for Nurses* addresses the key components in the informed consent process that nurses must address.[1]
- An adult patient who is competent (defined as capable of understanding and interpreting information, making choices, and communicating those choices) solely retains the right to make personal health care decisions.
- The Patient Self-Determination Act requires that we ask the patient on admission whether they have an advance directive. If available, place it in the medical record. Document if the patient does not have an advance directive.
- The National POLST Paradigm is an approach to end-of-life planning that emphasizes patients' wishes about the care they receive. The POLST Paradigm is an approach to end-of-life planning emphasizing the medical orders and includes coverage regardless of location (e.g., hospital, home, assisted living).[2]
- Families may difficulty accepting a terminal diagnosis.
- Sometimes family members have conflicting interests (e.g., finances, property, inheritance rights) that influence their decision-making abilities.

Discussion Questions

1. How can you help D.M. communicate her wishes to her family?
2. How can you help the family in planning end-of-life care that considers their mother's wishes?
3. What are the cultural issues in D.M.'s case?

References

1. Code of Ethics for Nurses. Retrieved from www.nursingworld.org/practice-policy/nursing-excellence/ethics/code-of-ethics-for-nurses/.
2. Physician Orders for Life Sustaining Treatment (POLST) Paradigm. Retrieved from www.polst.org.

CANCER SURVIVORSHIP

As the overall death rate from cancer decreases, the number of cancer survivors continues to increase. There are currently more than 16.9 million cancer survivors in the United States. Some of these persons are cancer free. Others still have evidence of cancer and may be receiving treatment. The increase in survivorship is attributed to the aging and growth of the population and improvements in early detection and treatment. Survival statistics vary by the type and stage of cancer.[1,2]

We are developing a greater awareness of the long-term health and quality-of-life issues that a cancer diagnosis imposes.

TABLE 16.22 PATIENT & CAREGIVER TEACHING

Cancer Survivors

You can help cancer survivors by doing the following:

1. Provide all cancer patients with a treatment summary and care plan outlining treatment exposures, risk for late effects, preventive care recommendations, and follow-up surveillance plan after completion of treatment.
   - Care plans should clearly identify all members of the interprofessional team and their responsibilities for follow-up care.
   - Include referrals to appropriate supportive care and community resources that would help the patient in recovery or ongoing care.
2. Coordinate care among the oncology team, primary HCP, and other specialists.
3. Teach HCPs about the needs of cancer survivors, including long-term effects of cancer and cancer treatments.
4. Teach cancer survivors to look for and report any ongoing symptoms resulting from treatment, including late effects of radiation therapy and chemotherapy.
5. Teach cancer survivors healthy behaviors:
   - *Prevention:* good nutrition, exercise, smoking avoidance, maintaining proper weight, cardiac risk reduction, bone health.
   - *Early detection:* routine health screenings (e.g., breast, colon), cholesterol, diabetes, osteoporosis screening as recommended.
6. Encourage cancer survivors to have regular follow-up examinations with their HCP.
7. Assess for psychologic, financial, health insurance, or vocational problems related to cancer. Assist patients in getting appropriate help if necessary.

Cancer survivors have a variety of long-term and late effects after treatment. You need to be aware of the effects of the various treatments so that you can teach patients and their caregivers.

The impact of cancer and its treatment confers greater risk for non–cancer-related death and co-morbidities (e.g., heart disease, diabetes, metabolic syndrome, endocrine dysfunction, osteoporosis) among survivors. They may continue to have symptoms or impaired function related to treatment for years after treatment. Emotional issues can play a profound role in a patient's life after cancer. Many find living in uncertainty challenging. Cancer survivors often report financial, vocational, marital, and spiritual concerns long after treatment is over.

Some patients may wish to return to their normal lives as soon as possible. They may not go to scheduled follow-up appointments. Others become cancer advocates or active members of a support group. Still, others allow their lives to revolve around the cancer and may even resist giving up the illness role.

Tips to help cancer survivors are described in Table 16.22. Connecting cancer survivors to online support and resources is a strategy to enhance positive health outcomes (Table 16.23).

TABLE 16.23 Resources for Cancer Survivors

Organization	Purpose
ACS Cancer Survivors Network	Provides survivorship information and resources and online forum for connecting with others affected by cancer. (https://csn.cancer.org/)
CancerCare	Provides a variety of free support services delivered by professional oncology social workers for patients and anyone else affected by cancer. (www.cancercare.org)
Cancer.Net	American Society of Clinical Oncology (ASCO) patient support site that includes extensive information and resources for cancer survivors. (www.cancer.net)
National Cancer Institute Office of Cancer Survivorship	Supports research into the short- and long-term physical, social, emotional, and economic effects of cancer survivorship. Offers educational and support resources for cancer survivors, caregivers, and advocates. (www.cancercontrol.cancer.gov/ocs/)
National Coalition for Cancer Survivorship	Advocates for quality cancer care. Seeks to teach patients and advocates about issues that affect the quality of life of cancer survivors. (www.canceradvocacy.org)
National Comprehensive Cancer Network	An alliance of leading cancer centers has developed patient and caregiver resources, including information to assist cancer survivors and their families with issues post treatment. (https://www.nccn.org/patients/resources/life_after_cancer/default.aspx)

BOX 16.4 PROMOTING HEALTH EQUITY

Cancer

- Cancer incidence and death rates for men are highest among Blacks, followed by Whites, Hispanics, and Asians/Pacific Islanders.
- Cancer incidence rates for women are highest among Whites, followed by Blacks, Hispanics, and Asians/Pacific Islanders.
- Cancer death rates for women are highest among Blacks, followed by Whites, Hispanics, and Asians/Pacific Islanders.

Social Determinants of Health: Cancer

Cancer incidence and death rates are disproportionately higher in Black and other minority persons (Box 16.4). Although overall racial disparities in cancer death rates have been declining, death rates continue to be higher among Blacks than Whites. Blacks are more likely to have later-stage disease at the time of diagnosis than whites.[1]

We attribute differences in survival rates from cancer to a combination of factors. These include poverty, difficult access to and poorer quality of health care, and more co-morbid conditions. Disparities in cancer care exist throughout the continuum, from prevention and screening to end-of-life care and survivorship. The disparity in prevention and screening results in cancer being in advanced stages at the time of diagnosis.[1,2]

BRIDGE TO NCLEX EXAMINATION

The number of the question corresponds to the same-numbered outcome at the beginning of the chapter.

1. Trends in the death rates from cancer that affect health promotion programs include
   a. more women die of colon cancer compared to men.
   b. prostate cancer is the leading cause of death in men.
   c. breast cancer is the leading cause of cancer deaths in women.
   d. lung cancer is a leading cause of death among men and women.
2. What features of cancer cells distinguish them from normal cells? *(select all that apply)*
   a. Cancer cells proliferate faster.
   b. Cancer cells lack contact inhibition.
   c. Cancer cells regain a fetal appearance and function.
   d. Cancer cells return to a previous undifferentiated state.
   e. Proliferation occurs when there is a need for more cells.
3. A characteristic of the *promotion* stage of cancer development is
   a. tumor cells detach from the primary tumor.
   b. tumor cells are trapped in a sentinel lymph node.
   c. genetic mutations of cells initially occur in this stage.
   d. cellular alterations that occur in this stage are reversible.
4. The immune system monitors and regulates proliferation of cancer cells through *(select all that apply)*
   a. suppressing cytotoxic T cells.
   b. deactivating natural killer cells.
   c. producing antibodies that bind to tumor cells.
   d. surveillance of cells with tumor-associated antigens.
   e. sensitizing natural killer cells before they lyse tumor cells.
5. The nurse is caring for a female who had surgery 1 day ago to remove a breast mass. The patient is awaiting the pathology report. She is tearful and says that she is scared to die. The *most* effective nursing intervention at this point is to use this opportunity to
   a. review the importance of advanced directives.
   b. provide reassurance that everything will be fine.
   c. discuss healthy stress relief and coping practices.
   d. let her communicate about the meaning of this experience.
6. Surgery is used in cancer care to (*select all that apply*)
   a. diagnose cancer.
   b. cure or control cancer.
   c. provide supportive care.
   d. prevent spread of cancer.
   e. assist with rehabilitation after treatment.
7. The *most* effective method of administering a chemotherapy agent that is a vesicant is to
   a. give it orally.
   b. give it intraarterially.
   c. use a central venous access device.
   d. use the smallest gauge needle through a peripheral line.
8. Principles of radiation treatment include (*select all that apply*)
   a. brachytherapy is delivered by an external beam.
   b. doses of radiation are expressed in units called gray or centigray.
   c. low energy beam radiation is ineffective on superficial skin lesions.
   d. the total dose for a radiation treatment is divided into daily fractions.
   e. radiosensitivity is the unresponsiveness of cells to the radiation treatment.
9. A patient on chemotherapy and radiation for head and neck cancer has a WBC count of $1.9 \times 10^3/\mu L$, hemoglobin of 10.8 g/dL, and a platelet count of $99 \times 10^3/\mu L$. Based on the CBC results, which are the *most* serious clinical findings?
   a. Anorexia and nausea
   b. Headache, mucositis, and constipation
   c. Fatigue and skin redness at site of radiation
   d. Temperature of 101.9°F, fatigue, and shortness of breath
10. To prevent fever and shivering during an infusion of rituximab (Rituxan), the nurse should premedicate the patient with
   a. aspirin.
   b. diazepam.
   c. acetaminophen.
   d. sodium bicarbonate.
11. The nurse, who is teaching a patient how to manage chemotherapy-induced diarrhea, determines that teaching is successful when the patient states
   a. "I will only drink two glasses of liquid a day."
   b. "I should eat more fresh fruits and vegetables."
   c. "I will decrease fried and fatty foods in my diet."
   d. "Increasing the fiber in my diet will bulk up my stools."
12. A patient receiving treatment for cancer is having problems maintaining their weight. What is the best option that the nurse can do for the patient?
   a. Counsel them to eat foods low in fiber.
   b. Recommend high-fat foods that are spicy.
   c. Contact the provider about a feeding tube.
   d. Suggest adding nutrition supplements with meals.
13. A patient who recently started chemotherapy has uncontrollable nausea, diarrhea, muscle cramps, and dizziness. Which complication of cancer is this *most* likely caused by?
   a. Tumor lysis syndrome
   b. Third space syndrome
   c. Spinal cord compression
   d. Superior vena cava syndrome
14. A woman has recently been diagnosed with early-stage uterine cancer. What can you do to promote effective coping strategies? *(select all that apply)*
   a. maintain the patient's hope.
   b. connect the patient to a support group.
   c. help the patient in setting realistic goals
   d. discuss replacement childcare for the patient's children.
   e. when patient begins to discuss her fears, change the topic to something uplifting.

1. d; 2. b, c, d; 3. d; 4. c, d; 5. d;
6. a, b, c, d, e; 7. c; 8. b, d; 9. d; 10. c; 11. c; 12. d; 13. a; 14. a, b, c

For rationales to these answers and even more NCLEX review questions, visit http://evolve.elsevier.com/Lewis/medsurg.

EVOLVE WEBSITE/RESOURCES LIST

http://evolve.elsevier.com/Lewis/medsurg
Review Questions (Online Only)
Key Points
Answer Keys for Questions
- Rationales for Bridge to NCLEX Examination Questions

Conceptual Care Map Creator
Audio Glossary
Content Updates

REFERENCES

1. American Cancer Society: Cancer facts & figures 2020. Retrieved from www.cancer.org/research/cancer-facts-statistics/all-cancer-facts-figures/cancer-facts-figures-2020.html.
2. Siegel RL, Miller KD, Jemal A: Cancer statistics 2020, *CA Cancer J Clin* 70:7–30, 2020.
3. National Cancer Institute: Cancer trends progress report. Retrieved from www.progressreport.cancer.gov.
4. Centers for Disease Control and Prevention: Skin cancer. Retrieved from www.cdc.gov/cancer/skin/.
5. Kanabar AH, Sacher RA, Besa EC: Burkitt lymphoma and Burkitt-like lymphoma. Retrieved from https://emedicine.medscape.com/article/1447602-overview.

*6. American Cancer Society: Cancer screening guidelines. Retrieved from www.cancer.org/healthy/find-cancer-early/cancer-screening-guidelines.html.

7. American Society of Clinical Oncology: What is personalized cancer medicine? Retrieved from www.cancer.net/navigating-cancer-care/how-cancer-treated/personalized-and-targeted-therapies/what-personalized-cancer-medicine.

*8. Zeng J, Johnson A, Shufean M, et al.: Operationalization of next-generation sequencing and decision support for precision oncology, *JCO Clin Cancer Inform* 3:1, 2019.

9. Crisci S, Amitrano F, Saggese M, et al.: Overview of current targeted anti-cancer drugs for therapy in onco-hematology, *Medicina* 55:414, 2019.

*10. Olsen M, LeFebvre K, Brassil K: *Chemotherapy and immunotherapy guidelines and recommendations for practice*, Pittsburgh, 2019, Oncology Nursing Society.

*11. Celano P, Fausel C, Kennedy E, et al.: Safe handling of hazardous drugs: ASCO standards, *J Clin Oncol* 37:598, 2019.

*12. Becker P, Griffiths EA, Alwan LM, et al.: NCCN guidelines insights: hematopoietic growth factors, *J Natl Compr Canc Netw* 18:12, 2020.

13. National Cancer Institute: Fatigue (PDQ[R])—Health professional version. Retrieved from www.cancer.gov/about-cancer/treatment/side-effects/fatigue/fatigue-hp-pdq.

*14. Silva GB, Hernandez KC, Donati A, et al.: Scalp cooling to prevent chemotherapy induced alopecia, *An Bras Dermatol*, 2020.

*15. Lange M, Joly F, Vardy J, et al.: Cancer–related cognitive impairment: an update on state of the art detection and management strategies in cancer survivors, *Ann Onco* 30:1925, 2019.

16. Dolmans MM, Manavella DD: Recent advances in fertility preservation, *J Obstet Gynaecol Res* 45:266, 2019.

*17. Miller K, Nogueira L, Mariotto A, et al.: Cancer treatment and survivorship statistics, 2019, *Ca Cancer J Clin* 69:5, 2019.

18. American Cancer Society (ACS): Targeted therapy. Retrieved from https://www.cancer.org/treatment/treatments-and-side-effects/treatment-types/targeted-therapy.html.
19. National Cancer Institute: Targeted cancer therapies. Retrieved from www.cancer.gov/about-cancer/treatment/types/targeted-therapies/targeted-therapies-fact-sheet.
20. Khaddour K, Hana CK, Mewawalla P: Hematopoietic stem cell transplantation, *StatPearls*, 2020. Retrieved from https://www.ncbi.nlm.nih.gov/books/NBK536951/.

*21. Pugnaloni S, Vignini A, Borroni F, et al.: Modifications of taste sensitivity in cancer patients: a method for the evaluations of dysgeusia, *Support Care Cancer* 28:1173, 2020.

22. Peixoto da Silva S, Santos JMO, Costa S, et al.: Cancer cachexia and its pathophysiology: links with sarcopenia, anorexia and asthenia, *J Cachexia, Sarcopenia and Muscle* 11:619, 2020.

*23. National Comprehensive Cancer Network: National clinical practice guidelines in oncology: Adult cancer pain, version 1; 2020. Retrieved from https://www.nccn.org/professionals/physician_gls/pdf/pain.pdf.

24. White M, Holman D, Goodman R, et al.: Cancer risk among older adults: time for cancer prevention to go sliver, *Gerontologist* 59:S1, 2019.

*Evidence-based information for clinical practice.

17

Fluid, Electrolyte, and Acid-Base Imbalances

Margaret R. Rateau

http://evolve.elsevier.com/Lewis/medsurg/

CONCEPTUAL FOCUS

Acid-Base Balance
Fluid and Electrolytes
Perfusion
Safety
Self-Management

LEARNING OUTCOMES

1. Describe the composition of the major body fluid compartments.
2. Define processes involved in regulating water and electrolyte movement between the body fluid compartments.
3. Describe the etiology, manifestations, and interprofessional management of:
   a. Extracellular fluid volume imbalances: fluid volume deficit and fluid volume excess
   b. Sodium imbalances: hypernatremia and hyponatremia
   c. Potassium imbalances: hyperkalemia and hypokalemia
   d. Magnesium imbalances: hypermagnesemia and hypomagnesemia
   e. Calcium imbalances: hypercalcemia and hypocalcemia
   f. Phosphate imbalances: hyperphosphatemia and hypophosphatemia
4. Identify the processes involved in maintaining acid-base balance.
5. Discuss the etiology, manifestations, and nursing and interprofessional management of acid-base imbalances: metabolic acidosis, metabolic alkalosis, respiratory acidosis, and respiratory alkalosis.
6. Describe the composition of and indications for common IV fluid solutions.
7. Discuss the types and nursing management of commonly used central venous access devices.

KEY TERMS

acidosis
alkalosis
buffers
central venous access devices (CVADs)
electrolytes
fluid spacing
hydrostatic pressure
hypercalcemia
hyperkalemia
hypernatremia
hypertonic
hypocalcemia
hypokalemia
hyponatremia
hypotonic
isotonic
osmolality

Body fluids and electrolytes play an important role in maintaining *homeostasis,* the body's stable internal environment. Body fluids are in constant motion transporting nutrients, electrolytes, and oxygen to cells and carrying waste products away from cells. The body uses many adaptive responses to keep the composition and volume of fluids and electrolytes within narrow limits to maintain homeostasis and promote health.

Fluid and electrolyte imbalances occur in most patients with a major illness or injury because illness disrupts normal homeostatic mechanisms. Illness or disease directly causes some fluid and electrolyte imbalances (e.g., burns, heart failure). Other times, therapeutic measures (e.g., colonoscopy preparation, diuretics) cause or contribute to imbalances. Perioperative patients are at risk for developing fluid and electrolyte imbalances because of fluid restrictions, blood or fluid loss, and the stress of surgery.

Conceptually, these imbalances are often reflected by changes in perfusion, gas exchange, mobility, and cognition. For example, a patient with metastatic colon cancer may develop hypercalcemia because of bone destruction from tumor invasion. They have severe muscle weakness and confusion. Chemotherapy used to treat the cancer may result in nausea and vomiting, causing dehydration and hypotension. When correcting dehydration with IV fluids, the patient needs close monitoring to prevent fluid overload.

We classify fluid and electrolyte imbalances as *deficits* or *excesses.* Fluid volume deficit *(hypovolemia)* and volume excess *(hypervolemia)* are common clinical conditions. Volume imbalances are usually accompanied by one or more electrolyte imbalances, especially changes in the serum sodium level.

Although each imbalance is discussed separately in this chapter, it is common for more than one imbalance to occur in the same patient. For example, a patient with prolonged nasogastric (NG) suction will lose sodium, potassium, hydrogen, and chloride. This may result in low sodium and potassium levels, fluid volume deficit, and metabolic alkalosis caused by the loss of HCl acid.

It is important to anticipate the potential for fluid and electrolyte imbalances associated with certain disorders and medical therapies, recognize the signs and symptoms of imbalances, and intervene with the appropriate action. This chapter describes the (1) normal control of fluids, electrolytes, and acid-base balance; (2) conditions that disrupt homeostasis and resulting manifestations; and (3) actions that the HCP and you can take to manage fluid, electrolyte, and acid-base imbalances and restore homeostasis.

WATER CONTENT OF THE BODY

The body is mainly composed of water. It accounts for about 50% to 60% of body weight in the adult. Water content varies with body mass, gender, and age (Fig. 17.1). Lean body mass has a higher percentage of water. Fat tissue has a lesser percentage of water. So, the more fat present in the body, the less the total water content. Women generally have a lower percentage of body water because they tend to have less lean body mass than men. Older adults also tend to have less lean body mass. This results in a lower percentage of body water when compared to younger adults. In older adults, body water content averages 45% to 50% of body weight. This places them at a higher risk for fluid-related problems than young adults.

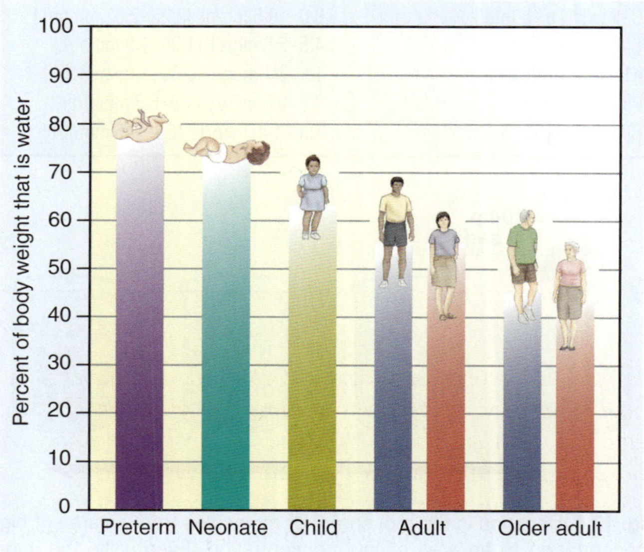

Fig. 17.1 Body water over the life span.

Body Fluid Compartments

The 2 fluid compartments in the body are the *intracellular space* (inside the cells) and the *extracellular space* (outside the cells) (Fig. 17.2). About two-thirds of body water is found within cells. It is the *intracellular fluid* (ICF). ICF makes up about 40% of body weight of an adult. This means a 70-kg person would have about 42 L of water, with about 28 L of that water within their cells.

The fluid in the extracellular space is *extracellular fluid* (ECF). The 2 main compartments containing ECF are the *interstitial fluid,* the fluid in the spaces between cells, and the intravascular fluid or *plasma,* the liquid part of blood. Other ECF compartments include lymph and *transcellular fluids.* Transcellular fluids include cerebrospinal fluid; fluid in the gastrointestinal (GI) tract and joint spaces; and pleural, peritoneal, intraocular, and pericardial fluid. ECF makes up about one-third of the body water. This amounts to about 14 L in a 70-kg person. About one-third of ECF is in the intravascular space as plasma (3 L in a 70-kg person). Two-thirds are in the interstitial space or about 10 L in a 70-kg person. The fluid in the transcellular spaces totals about 1 L at any given time.

Calculation of Fluid Gain or Loss

One liter of water weighs 2.2 lb (1 kg). Bodyweight change, especially a sudden change, is an excellent indicator of overall fluid volume loss or gain. For example, if a patient drinks 240 mL (8 oz) of fluid, weight gain will be 0.5 lb (0.23 kg). A patient receiving diuretic therapy who loses 4.4 lb (2 kg) in 24 hours has a fluid loss of about 2 L. An adult patient who is fasting may lose 1 to 2 lb/day. A weight loss exceeding this is likely due to loss of body fluid.

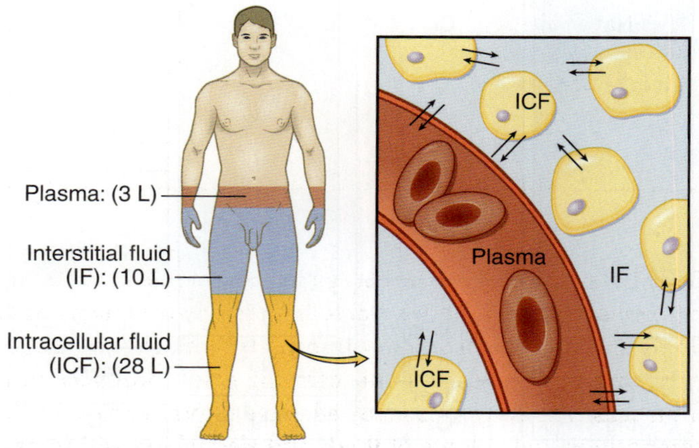

Fig. 17.2 Relative volumes of 3 body fluids. Values represent fluid distribution in a young male adult.

ELECTROLYTES

Electrolytes are substances whose molecules dissociate, or split, into ions when placed in water. *Ions* are electrically charged particles. *Cations* are positively charged ions. Examples include sodium (Na^+), potassium (K^+), calcium (Ca^{2+}), and magnesium (Mg^{2+}) ions. *Anions* are negatively charged ions. Examples include bicarbonate (HCO_3^-), chloride (Cl^-), and phosphate (PO_4^{3-}) ions. Most proteins bear a negative charge and thus are anions.

Measurement of Electrolytes

We express electrolyte concentration in body fluids as milliequivalents (mEq) per liter. Since electrolytes are active chemicals, we express their concentration according to their chemical activity, or the number of electrolytes able to combine chemically. Ions combine milliequivalent for milliequivalent. For example, 1 mEq (1 mmol) of sodium combines with 1 mEq (1 mmol) of chloride.

Electrolyte Composition of Fluid Compartments

Electrolyte composition varies between ECF and ICF. The overall concentration of electrolytes is nearly the same in the ECF and ICF. However, concentrations of specific ions differ greatly (Fig. 17.3). In ECF, the main cation is sodium, with small amounts of potassium, calcium, and magnesium. The primary ECF anion is chloride, with small amounts of bicarbonate, sulfate, and phosphate anions.

In ICF, the main cation is potassium, with small amounts of magnesium and sodium. The main ICF anion is phosphate, with some protein and a small amount of bicarbonate. Table 17.1 lists normal serum electrolyte values.

MECHANISMS CONTROLLING FLUID AND ELECTROLYTE MOVEMENT

The movement of electrolytes and water between ICF and ECF to maintain homeostasis involves many different processes. These include simple diffusion, facilitated diffusion, and active transport. Water moves as driven by two forces: hydrostatic pressure and osmotic pressure.

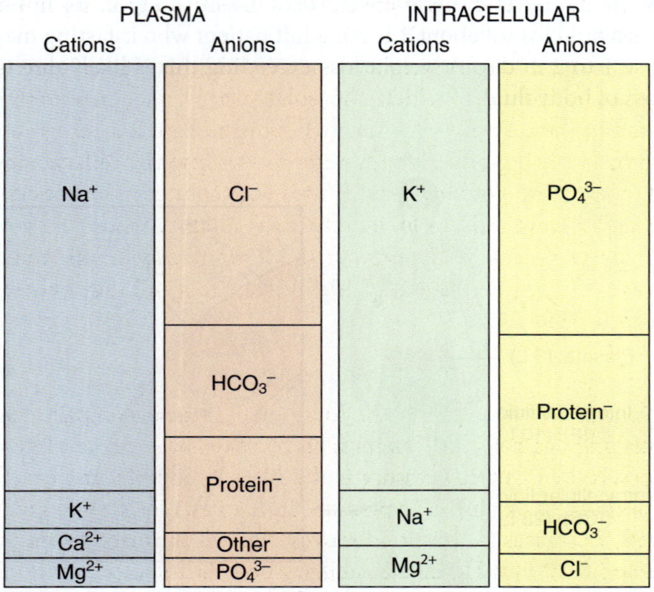

Fig. 17.3 The relative concentrations of the major cations and anions in the intracellular space and the plasma.

Diffusion

Diffusion is the movement of molecules from an area of high concentration to low concentration (Fig. 17.4). Net movement of molecules stops when the concentrations are equal in both areas. It occurs in liquids, gases, and solids. Simple diffusion requires no external energy.

Facilitated Diffusion

Facilitated diffusion involves the use of a protein carrier in the cell membrane. The protein carrier combines with a molecule, especially one too large to pass easily through the cell membrane and helps move the molecule across the membrane from an area of high to low concentration. Like simple diffusion, facilitated diffusion is passive and requires no energy. An example of facilitated diffusion is glucose transport into the cell. The large glucose molecule must combine with a carrier molecule to be able to cross the cell membrane and enter most cells.

Active Transport

Active transport is a process in which molecules move against the concentration gradient. External energy is needed for this process. An example is the sodium-potassium pump. The concentrations of sodium and potassium differ between the ICF and ECF (see Fig. 17.3). To maintain this concentration difference,

TABLE 17.1 Normal Serum Electrolyte Values

Electrolyte	Reference Interval
Anions	
Bicarbonate (HCO_3^-)	22–26 mEq/L (22–26 mmol/L)
Chloride (Cl^-)	98–106 mEq/L (98–106 mmol/L)
Phosphate (PO_4^{3-})	3.0–4.5 mg/dL (0.97–1.45 mmol/L)
Cations	
Calcium (Ca^{2+}) (total)	9.0–10.5 mg/dL (2.25–2.62 mmol/L)
Calcium (ionized)	4.5–5.6 mg/dL (1.05–1.3 mmol/L)
Magnesium (Mg^{2+})	1.3–2.1 mEq/L (0.65–1.05 mmol/L)
Potassium (K^+)	3.5–5.0 mEq/L (3.5–5.0 mmol/L)
Sodium (Na^+)	136–145 mEq/L (136–145 mmol/L)

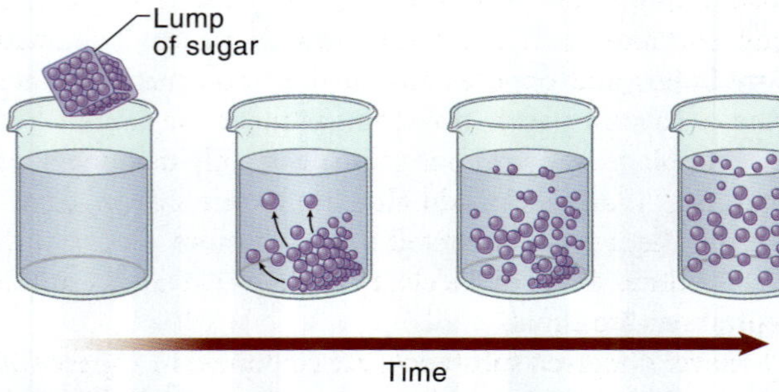

Fig. 17.4 Diffusion is the movement of molecules from an area of high concentration to an area of low concentration. Eventually, the sugar molecules are evenly distributed.

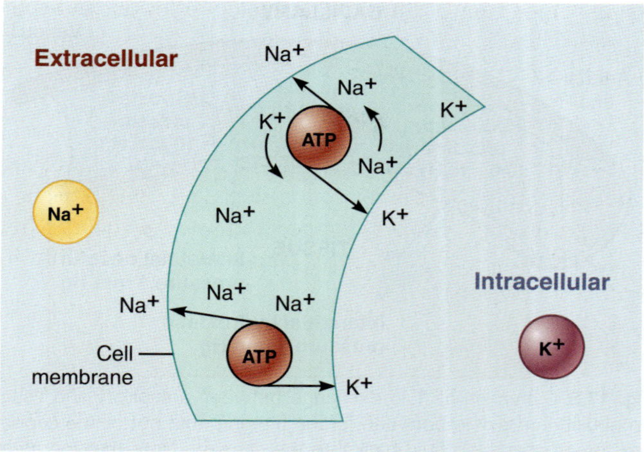

Fig. 17.5 Sodium-potassium pump. As sodium *(Na^+)* diffuses into the cell and potassium *(K^+)* diffuses out of the cell, an active transport system supplied with energy delivers Na^+ back to the extracellular compartment and K^+ to the intracellular compartment. *ATP,* Adenosine triphosphate.

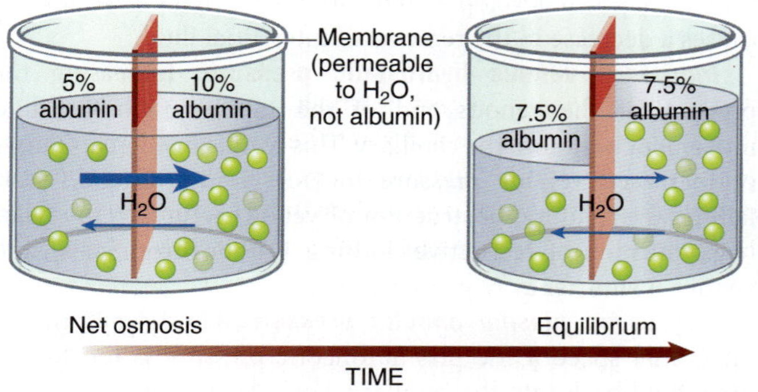

Fig. 17.6 Osmosis is the process of water movement through a semipermeable membrane from an area of low solute concentration to an area of high solute concentration.

the cell uses active transport to move sodium out of the cell and potassium into the cell (Fig. 17.5). The energy source for this movement is adenosine triphosphate (ATP). ATP is made in the cell mitochondria.

Osmosis

Osmosis is the movement of water "down" a concentration gradient, that is, from a region of low solute concentration to one of high solute concentration, across a semipermeable membrane. Osmosis requires no outside energy sources. It stops when the concentration differences disappear or when hydrostatic pressure builds and opposes any further movement of water. Imagine a chamber with two compartments separated by a semipermeable membrane, one that allows only the movement of water (Fig. 17.6). If you add albumin to one side, water will move from the less concentrated side (has more water) to the more concentrated side of the chamber (has less water) until the concentrations are equal.

Whenever dissolved substances are contained in a space with a semipermeable membrane, they can pull water into the space by osmosis. The concentration of the solution determines the strength of the osmotic pull. The higher the concentration, the greater a solution's pull or osmotic pressure. *Osmotic pressure* is measured in milliosmoles (mOsm). We express it as either fluid osmolarity or fluid osmolality. Although you will often see the terms *osmolarity* and *osmolality* used interchangeably, they are different measurements. *Osmolarity* measures the total milliosmoles per liter of solution or the concentration of molecules per volume of solution (mOsm/L). **Osmolality** measures the number of milliosmoles per kilogram of water or the concentration of molecules per weight of water. Osmolality is the preferred measure to evaluate the concentration of plasma, urine, and other body fluids. Changes in the ECF osmolality can cause significant changes in the ICF osmolality. These changes can affect normal cell function.[1]

Measurement of Osmolality

Osmolality is nearly the same in the various body fluid spaces. Therefore, measuring or estimating plasma osmolality is a good way to assess the state of the body's water balance. Calculate the plasma osmolality using the following formula.[2]

$$\text{Plasma osmolality} = (2 \times \text{Na}) + (\text{BUN}/2.8) + (\text{Glucose}/18)$$

Normal plasma osmolality is between 280 and 295 mOsm/kg. A value greater than 295 mOsm/kg means that the concentration of solute is too great, or the water content is too little. This condition is termed *water deficit.* A value less than 275 mOsm/kg means there is too little solute for the amount of water or too much water for the amount of solute. This is termed *water excess.* Both conditions are clinically significant.

Urine osmolality can range from 100 to 1300 mOsm/kg. It depends on fluid intake, the amount of antidiuretic hormone (ADH) in circulation, and the renal response to ADH.

Osmotic Movement of Fluids

The osmolality of the fluid surrounding cells affects them. Fluids with the same osmolality as the cell interior are **isotonic**. Normally, ECF and ICF are isotonic to one another, so no net movement of water occurs.

Changes in the osmolality of ECF change the volume of cells. Solutions in which the solutes are less concentrated than in the cells are **hypotonic** (hypoosmolar). If a cell is surrounded by hypotonic fluid, water moves into the cell, causing it to swell and possibly burst. Fluids with solutes more concentrated than in cells, or an increased osmolality, are **hypertonic** (hyperosmolar). If hypertonic fluid surrounds a cell, water leaves the cell to dilute ECF. The cell shrinks and may eventually die (Fig. 17.7).

Hydrostatic Pressure

Hydrostatic pressure is the force of fluid in a compartment pushing against a cell membrane or vessel wall. In the blood vessels, hydrostatic pressure is the BP generated by the heart's contraction. Hydrostatic pressure in the vascular system gradually decreases as the blood moves through the arteries until it is about 30 mm Hg in the capillary bed. At the capillary level, hydrostatic pressure is the major force that pushes water out of the vascular system and into the interstitial space.

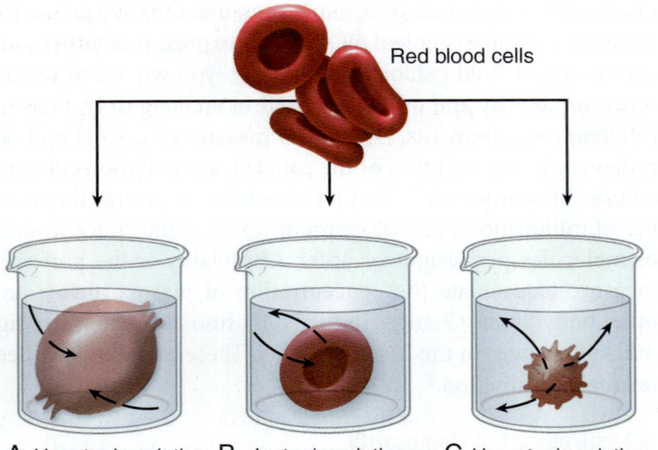

Fig. 17.7 Effects of water status on red blood cells. (A) Hypotonic solution (H_2O excess) results in cellular swelling. (B) Isotonic solution (normal H_2O balance) results in no change. (C) Hypertonic solution (H_2O deficit) results in cellular shrinking.

Oncotic Pressure

Oncotic pressure (colloidal osmotic pressure) is the osmotic pressure caused by plasma colloids (large molecules) in solution. The major colloids in the vascular system contributing to osmotic pressure are proteins, such as albumin. Plasma has large amounts of protein, while the interstitial space has little. Plasma protein molecules attract water, pulling fluid from the tissue space to the vascular space. Under normal conditions, plasma oncotic pressure is about 25 mm Hg. The small amount of protein found in the interstitial space has an oncotic pressure of about 1 mm Hg.

FLUID MOVEMENT IN CAPILLARIES

As plasma flows through the capillary bed, 4 factors determine if fluid moves out of the capillary and into the interstitial space or if fluid moves back into the capillary from the interstitial space. The amount and direction of movement are determined by the interaction of (1) capillary hydrostatic pressure, (2) plasma oncotic pressure, (3) interstitial hydrostatic pressure, and (4) interstitial oncotic pressure.

Capillary hydrostatic pressure and interstitial oncotic pressure move water out of the capillaries. Plasma oncotic pressure and interstitial hydrostatic pressure move fluid into the capillaries. At the arterial end of the capillary, capillary hydrostatic pressure exceeds plasma oncotic pressure, and fluid moves into the interstitial space. At the venous end of the capillary, the capillary hydrostatic pressure is lower than plasma oncotic pressure. The oncotic pressure created by plasma proteins draws fluid back into the capillary (Fig. 17.8).

Fluid Shifts

If capillary or interstitial pressures change, fluid may abnormally shift from one compartment to another. This shift results in edema or dehydration.

Shifts of Plasma to Interstitial Fluid

Edema is an accumulation of fluid in the interstitial space. It occurs if venous hydrostatic pressure increases, plasma oncotic pressure decreases, or interstitial oncotic pressure increases. Edema may also develop if an obstruction of lymphatic outflow causes a decrease in the removal of interstitial fluid.

Increased venous hydrostatic pressure. Increasing the pressure at the venous end of the capillary inhibits fluid movement back into the capillary. This results in edema. Causes of increased venous pressure include fluid overload, heart failure, liver failure, obstruction of venous return to the heart (e.g., tourniquets, restrictive clothing, venous thrombosis), and venous insufficiency (e.g., varicose veins).

Decreased plasma oncotic pressure. Fluid stays in the interstitial space if the plasma oncotic pressure is too low to draw fluid back into the capillary. Low plasma protein content decreases oncotic pressure. This can result from excess protein loss (renal problems), decreased protein synthesis (liver disease), and decreased protein intake (malnutrition).

Increased interstitial oncotic pressure. Trauma, burns, and inflammation can damage capillary walls and allow plasma proteins to accumulate in the interstitial space. This increases interstitial oncotic pressure, draws fluid into the interstitial space, and holds it there.

Shifts of interstitial fluid to plasma. An increase in the plasma osmotic or oncotic pressure draws fluid into the plasma from the interstitial space. This could happen when we give colloids, dextran, mannitol, or hypertonic solutions. Increasing the tissue hydrostatic pressure is another way of causing a shift of fluid into plasma. Wearing elastic compression gradient stockings or hose to decrease peripheral edema is a therapeutic application of this effect.

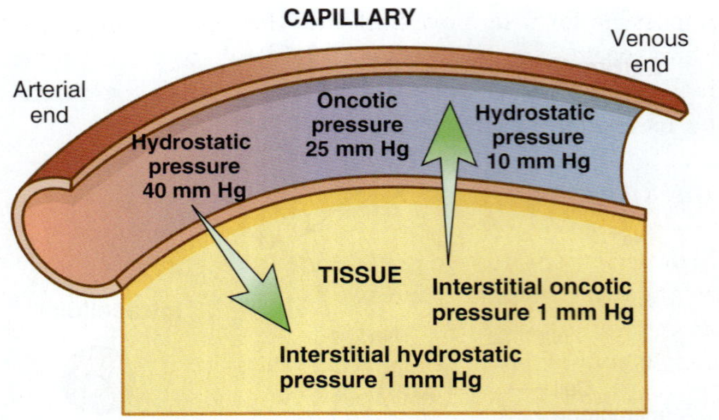

Fig. 17.8 Dynamics of fluid exchange between a capillary and tissue. An equilibrium exists between forces filtering fluid out of the capillary and forces absorbing fluid back into the capillary. Note that the hydrostatic pressure is greater at the arterial end of the capillary than at the venous end. The net effect of pressures at the arterial end of the capillary causes a movement of fluid into the tissue. At the venous end of the capillary, there is net movement of fluid back into the capillary.

FLUID SPACING

Fluid spacing is a term used to describe the distribution of body water. *First spacing* describes the normal distribution of fluid in ICF and ECF compartments. *Second spacing* refers to an abnormal accumulation of interstitial fluid (i.e., edema). *Third spacing* occurs when excess fluid collects in the nonfunctional area between cells. This fluid is trapped where it is difficult or impossible for it to move back into the cells or blood vessels. Third spacing occurs with ascites; fluid leaking into the abdominal cavity with peritonitis or pancreatitis; and edema from burns, trauma, or sepsis.

REGULATION OF WATER BALANCE

Many factors are involved in maintaining the finely tuned balance among water intake, use, and excretion. For proper fluid balance, an average healthy adult needs a daily water intake of between 2000 and 3000 mL (Table 17.2). This amount replaces what the body loses in urinary output and insensible losses. Oral fluid intake accounts for most of the water intake. Water intake also includes water from food metabolism and water present in solid foods.

Insensible water loss occurs with the invisible vaporization from the lungs and skin. It helps regulate body temperature. Accelerated body metabolism, which occurs with increased body temperature and exercise, increases the amount of water lost and may result in the need for additional water replacement.

Do not confuse water loss through the skin with the vaporization of water excreted by sweat glands. Insensible perspiration causes only water loss. Excess sweating *(sensible perspiration)* caused by exercise, fever, or high environmental temperatures may lead to large losses of water and electrolytes.

Hypothalamic-Pituitary Regulation

Water ingestion equals water loss in the person who has free access to water, intact thirst and ADH mechanism, and normally functioning kidneys. A body fluid deficit or increase in plasma osmolality activates osmoreceptors in the hypothalamus. This stimulates thirst and the release of ADH from the posterior pituitary gland. ADH acts on the distal tubules and collecting ducts in the kidney by making them more permeable to water. The result is increased water reabsorption from the tubular filtrate into the blood and decreased excretion in the urine. Because ADH is only able to regulate how much water the body holds onto, an intact thirst mechanism is our main protection against developing dehydration or hyperosmolality. Thirst causes us to increase the amount of water we drink. Together these result in increased free water in the body, decreasing plasma osmolality and restoring fluid volume.

Many factors influence ADH secretion and thirst. Decreased BP, nausea, pain, hypoglycemia, and hypoxemia stimulate ADH release. In the postoperative patient, the stress response to surgery and receiving analgesics and anesthesia cause ADH release and decreased osmolality. The unconscious or cognitively impaired patient is at increased risk for fluid deficit and hyperosmolality because of an inability to express thirst and act on it. A dry mouth will cause a person to drink, even when there is no body water deficit.

TABLE 17.2 Normal Fluid Balance in the Adult

Intake	
Fluids	1200 mL
Solid food	1000 mL
Water from oxidation	300 mL
Total	2500 mL
Output	
Insensible loss (skin and lungs)	900 mL
In feces	100 mL
Urine	1500 mL
Total	2500 mL

Renal Regulation

The primary function of the kidneys is to regulate fluid and electrolyte balance by adjusting urine volume and the excretion of most electrolytes (see Chapter 49). The kidneys filter the total plasma volume many times each day. In the average adult, the kidneys reabsorb 99% of this filtrate, producing around 1.5 L of urine per day. Under the influence of ADH, aldosterone, and other hormones, selective reabsorption and secretion of water and electrolytes in the renal tubules result in urine that is different in composition and concentration from plasma. This process helps maintain normal plasma osmolality, electrolyte balance, blood volume, and acid-base balance.

With severely impaired renal function, the kidneys cannot maintain fluid and electrolyte balance. This results in edema, potassium and phosphate retention, acidosis, and other electrolyte imbalances (see Chapter 51).

Adrenal Cortical Regulation

Glucocorticoids and mineralocorticoids secreted by the adrenal cortex help regulate water and electrolyte balance. The glucocorticoids (e.g., cortisol) mainly have an antiinflammatory effect and increase serum glucose levels. The mineralocorticoids (e.g., aldosterone) enhance sodium retention and potassium excretion (Fig. 17.9). When sodium is reabsorbed, water follows because of osmotic changes.

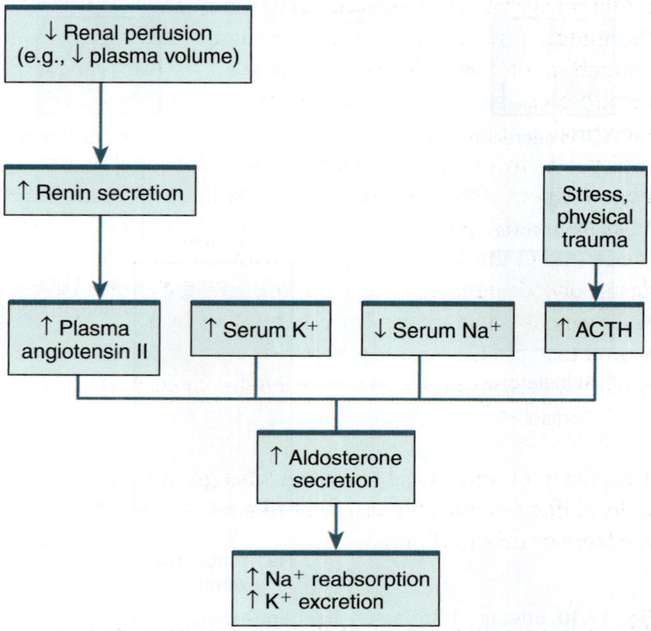

Fig. 17.9 Factors affecting aldosterone secretion. *ACTH,* Adrenocorticotropic hormone.

Aldosterone is a mineralocorticoid with strong sodium-retaining and potassium-excreting capabilities. Decreased renal perfusion or decreased sodium in the distal part of the renal tubule activates the renin-angiotensin-aldosterone system (RAAS), resulting in aldosterone secretion. In addition to the RAAS, increased serum potassium, decreased serum sodium, and adrenocorticotropic hormone (ACTH) stimulate aldosterone secretion. Aldosterone increases sodium and water reabsorption in the renal distal tubules, decreasing plasma osmolality and restoring fluid volume.

Cortisol is the most abundant glucocorticoid. In large doses, cortisol has both glucocorticoid (glucose-elevating, antiinflammatory) and mineralocorticoid (sodium-retention) effects. Normal cortisol secretion occurs in a diurnal or circadian pattern. Increased cortisol secretion occurs in response to physical and psychologic stress. This affects many body functions, including fluid and electrolyte balance (Fig. 17.10).

Cardiac Regulation

Natriuretic peptides, including atrial natriuretic peptide (ANP) and b-type natriuretic peptide (BNP), are hormones made by cardiomyocytes. They are made in response to increased atrial pressure (increased volume, such as occurs in heart failure) and high serum sodium levels. They are natural antagonists to the RAAS and suppress secretion of aldosterone, renin, and ADH, and the action of angiotensin II. In the renal tubules, peptides promote excretion of sodium and water, decreasing blood volume and BP.

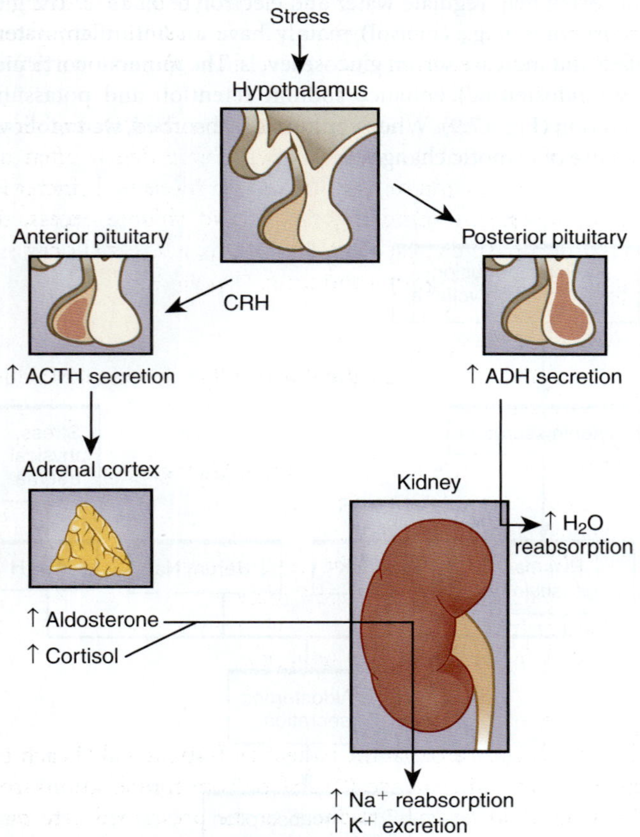

Fig. 17.10 Effects of stress on fluid and electrolyte balance. *ACTH,* Adrenocorticotropic hormone; *ADH,* antidiuretic hormone; *CRH,* corticotropin-releasing hormone.

Gastrointestinal Regulation

In addition to oral intake, the GI tract normally secretes around 8000 mL of digestive fluids each day. The GI tract normally reabsorbs most of this fluid, with only a small amount eliminated in feces. This is why diarrhea and vomiting, which prevent GI reabsorption of the secreted fluid, can lead to significant fluid and electrolyte loss.

Gerontologic Considerations: Fluid and Electrolytesicon

The older adult has normal physiologic changes that increase susceptibility to fluid and electrolyte imbalances. Structural changes to the kidneys and a decrease in the renal blood flow lead to decreased glomerular filtration rate and loss of the ability to concentrate urine and conserve water. Hormonal changes include a decrease in renin and aldosterone and an increase in ADH and ANP. Subcutaneous tissue loss and thinning of the dermis lead to increased moisture lost through the skin and an inability to respond quickly to heat or cold.

Do not automatically attribute older patients' fluid and electrolyte problems to aging. Throughout this chapter are suggestions for adapting your assessment and interventions when caring for the older adult.

FLUID VOLUME IMBALANCES

FLUID VOLUME DEFICIT

Fluid volume deficit can occur with abnormal body fluid loss (e.g., diarrhea, vomiting, hemorrhage, polyuria), inadequate fluid intake, or a shift from plasma to interstitial fluid. Though often used interchangeably, *fluid volume deficit* and *dehydration* are not the same. *Dehydration* refers to loss of pure water alone without the loss of sodium. Table 17.3 lists causes and manifestations of fluid volume deficit.

Interprofessional Care

We manage fluid volume deficit by correcting the underlying cause and replacing both water and any needed electrolytes. Replacement therapy depends on the severity and type of volume loss. In mild losses, we can use oral rehydration. If the deficit is more severe, we may replace volume with blood products or isotonic IV solutions (0.9% sodium chloride, lactated Ringer's solution). The choice of fluid depends on the cause and patient's electrolyte status. For rapid volume replacement, 0.9% sodium chloride is preferred. Blood is given when volume loss is due to blood loss.

FLUID VOLUME EXCESS

Fluid volume excess may result from excess fluid intake, abnormal fluid retention (e.g., heart failure, renal failure), or a shift of fluid from interstitial fluid into plasma fluid. Weight gain is the most consistent manifestation of fluid volume excess. Table 17.3 lists causes and manifestations of fluid volume excess.

TABLE 17.3 Extracellular Fluid Imbalances

Causes and Manifestations

ECF Volume Deficit	ECF Volume Excess
Causes	
• Diabetes insipidus	• Corticosteroids use long-term
• GI losses: vomiting, NG suction, diarrhea, fistula drainage	• Cushing syndrome
• Hemorrhage	• Heart failure
• Inadequate fluid intake	• Primary polydipsia
• ↑ Insensible water loss or perspiration (high fever, heatstroke)	• Renal failure
• Osmotic diuresis	• SIADH
• Overuse of diuretics	
• Third-space fluid shifts: burns, pancreatitis	
Manifestations	
• ↓ Capillary refill	• Bounding pulse, ↑ BP, ↑ CVP
• Confusion, restlessness, drowsiness, lethargy	• Confusion, headache, lethargy
• Cold clammy skin	• Dyspnea, crackles, pulmonary edema
• Postural hypotension, ↑ pulse, ↓ CVP	• Edema
• ↑ Respiratory rate	• JVD
• Seizures, coma	• Muscle spasms
• Thirst, dry mucous membranes	• Polyuria (with normal renal function)
• ↓ Urine output, concentrated urine	• S_3 heart sound
• Weakness, dizziness	• Seizures, coma
• Weight loss	• Weight gain

Interprofessional Care

We manage fluid volume excess by treating the underlying cause and removing fluid without causing abnormal changes in the electrolyte composition or osmolality of ECF. Diuretics and fluid restriction are the main therapies. Some patients also need sodium restrictions. If the fluid excess leads to ascites or pleural effusion, an abdominal paracentesis or thoracentesis may be needed. Careful assessment and management of fluid volume changes are needed (Table 17.4).

TABLE 17.4 NURSING MANAGEMENT

Fluid Volume Changes

- Assess patient for manifestations of fluid imbalances.
- Assess for the presence of risk factors for a fluid imbalance, including the patient's ability to self-manage hydration
- Give IV fluids and medications as ordered.
- Give O_2 therapy as ordered.
- Implement fall precautions.
- Provide prescribed diet appropriate for the specific fluid imbalance.
- Initiate referrals, such as dietitian and occupational therapy, as needed.
- Supervise AP:
  - Obtain daily weights and vital signs.
  - Offer frequent oral care.
  - Record accurate intake and output.
  - Protect skin and perform skin care.
  - Assist with frequent position changes and toileting, as needed.
  - Elevate edematous extremities.
  - Encourage oral fluids as appropriate.
- Monitor patient for effectiveness of therapy.

❖ NURSING MANAGEMENT: FLUID IMBALANCES

◆ Assessment

Question the patient about any history of problems involving the kidneys, heart, GI system, or lungs that could affect the present fluid balance. Ask about specific diseases such as diabetes, diabetes insipidus, renal failure, heart failure, and liver disease. Assess for any prior fluid balance problems. Ask the patient about any recent changes in body weight.

Ask about the patient's exercise pattern and any excess perspiration. Is the patient exposed to extremely high temperatures during leisure or work activity? Ask the patient what they do to replace fluid and electrolytes lost through excess perspiration. Assess the patient's activity level to determine any functional problems that could lead to the lack of ability to obtain food or fluids.[3]

Assess the patient's current and past use of medications. Many prescription drugs, including diuretics and corticosteroids, can cause fluid imbalance. Ask the patient about past or present renal dialysis, kidney surgery, or bowel surgery resulting in a temporary or permanent external collecting system, such as an ileostomy.

Perform a complete physical assessment because fluid imbalances can affect all body systems. As you assess each system, check for manifestations that you would expect with an imbalance (see Table 17.3).

Monitor available laboratory results and calculate the serum osmolality. The patient with a fluid volume deficit often has increased BUN, sodium, and hematocrit levels with increased plasma and urine osmolality. With fluid volume excess, the patient will have decreased BUN, sodium, and hematocrit levels, with decreased plasma and urine osmolality.

◆ Clinical Problems

Clinical problems for the patient with a fluid imbalance include

- Hypervolemia
- Hypovolemia
- Deficient Knowledge-Fluid Volume Management
- Impaired Tissue Perfusion
- Altered Blood Pressure
  - Impaired Respiratory System Function
  - Impaired Urinary System Function
- Risk for Injury
  - Risk for Impaired Skin Integrity

◆ Planning

The overall goals are that the patient with stress will (1) achieve and maintain fluid balance, (2) be free from complications from abnormal fluid levels, (3) adhere to the prescribed care plan, and (4) recognize factors that can lead to a fluid imbalance and take preventative action.

Implementation

Daily Weights

Daily weights are the most accurate measure of volume status. An increase of 1 kg (2.2 lb) is equal to 1000 mL (1 L) of fluid retention, provided the person has maintained usual dietary intake or has not been on NPO status. Obtain the weight under standard conditions. Weigh the patient at the same time every day, wearing the same clothes and on the same calibrated scale. Remove excess bedding and empty all drainage bags before the weighing. If items are present that are not there every day, such as bulky dressings or tubes, note this along with the weight.

Intake and Output

Intake and output records give valuable information about fluid and electrolyte balance. An accurately recorded intake and output will identify sources of excess intake or fluid losses. Intake should include oral and IV fluids, enteral nutrition (EN) or tube feedings, and retained irrigation solutions. Output includes urine, excess perspiration, wound or tube drainage, vomitus, and diarrhea. Estimate fluid loss from wounds and perspiration. Note the amount and color of the urine and measure the urine specific gravity. Readings greater than 1.025 mean urine is concentrated, while readings less than 1.010 mean urine is dilute.

Cardiovascular Care

Monitor vital signs and perform a thorough cardiovascular assessment as needed. Changes in BP, central venous pressure (CVP), pulse force, and jugular venous distention (JVD) reflect ECF volume imbalances. In fluid volume excess, the pulse is full, bounding, and not easily obliterated. Increased volume causes distended neck veins (JVD), increased CVP, and high BP. Auscultate heart sounds, being alert for the presence of an S_3.

In mild to moderate fluid volume deficit, sympathetic nervous system compensation increases the heart rate and results in peripheral vasoconstriction to try to keep BP within normal limits. Pulses may be weak and thready. Assess for orthostatic changes. A change in position from lying to sitting or standing may decrease BP or further increase the heart rate (orthostatic hypotension). In more severe deficits, hypotension may be present.

Respiratory Care

Monitor pulse oximetry and auscultate lung sounds as needed. ECF excess can cause pulmonary congestion and pulmonary edema, as increased hydrostatic pressure in the pulmonary vessels forces fluid into the alveoli. The patient will have shortness of breath and moist crackles on auscultation. The patient with ECF deficit will have an increased respiratory rate because of decreased tissue perfusion and resultant hypoxia. Give O_2 as ordered.

Patient Safety

The patient with fluid volume deficit is at risk for falls because of orthostatic hypotension, muscle weakness, and changes in level of consciousness. Assess level of consciousness, gait, and muscle strength. Implement fall precautions. If orthostatic hypotension is present, teach the patient to change positions slowly when rising from a bed or chair. Place alarm monitors on patients who are confused and try to get out of bed without help.

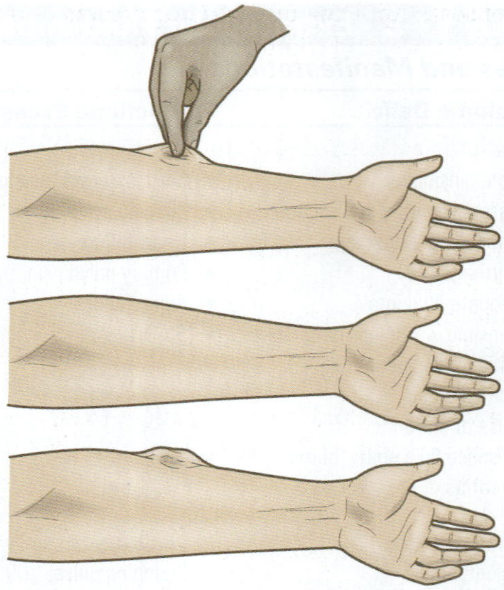

Fig. 17.11 Assessment of skin turgor. (A and B) When normal skin is pinched, it resumes shape in seconds. (C) If the skin stays wrinkled for 20 to 30 seconds, the patient has poor skin turgor.

Skin Care

Assess the skin for turgor and mobility. Normally, a fold of skin, when pinched, will readily move and, on release, rapidly return to its former position. In ECF volume deficit, there is diminished skin turgor with tenting or a lag in the pinched skinfold's return to its original state. Skin areas over the sternum, abdomen, and anterior forearm are the usual sites we use to assess turgor (Fig. 17.11). In older people, decreased skin turgor is less predictive of fluid deficit because of the loss of tissue elasticity.

In mild fluid deficits, the skin may appear warm, dry, and wrinkled. These signs may be hard to assess in the older adult because the person's skin may be normally dry, wrinkled, and non-elastic. In more severe deficits, the skin may be cool and moist if there is vasoconstriction to compensate for the decreased fluid volume. Oral mucous membranes will be dry, and the tongue may be furrowed. The person often is thirsty. Routine oral care is important for the comfort of a patient who is dehydrated or on a fluid restriction.

Edematous skin may feel cool because of fluid accumulation and a decrease in blood flow from the pressure of the fluid. The fluid can stretch the skin, causing it to feel taut and hard. Assess edema by pressing with a thumb or forefinger over the edematous area. Use a grading scale to standardize the description if an indentation (ranging from 1+ [slight edema; 2-mm indentation] to 4+ [pitting edema; 8-mm indentation]) remains when pressure is released. Assess for edema in areas where soft tissues overlie a bone, particularly the tibia, fibula, and sacrum.

Good skin care is important. Protect tissues from extremes of heat and cold, prolonged pressure, and trauma. Frequent skin care and changes in position will prevent skin breakdown. Elevate edematous extremities to promote venous return and fluid reabsorption. Dehydrated skin needs frequent care without the use of soap. Applying moisturizing creams or oils increases moisture retention and stimulates circulation.

Fluid Therapy

Give IV fluids as ordered. Carefully monitor the rates of infusion of IV fluid solutions, especially when you are giving large volumes of fluid. This is especially true in patients with heart, renal, or neurologic problems.

In the presence of fluid volume deficit, you can use several interventions to maintain adequate oral intake. Assess the patient's ability to obtain adequate fluids independently, express thirst, and swallow effectively. Fluids should be easily accessible. Provide a variety of fluids that the patient likes.[3] Serve fluids at a temperature preferred by the patient. Offer fluids every 1 to 2 hours and at select times, such as when giving medications. Remind the patient to finish all drinks.

If the patient is choosing to limit intake to decrease nocturia or incontinence, make it easier for the patient to reach the toilet when needed. Help those with physical limitations, such as arthritis, to open and hold containers. Involve the dietitian, speech therapist, or occupational therapist for help with patients with dysphagia or physical limitations.

SODIUM IMBALANCES

Sodium is the main cation of ECF. It plays a major role in maintaining the concentration and volume of ECF and influencing water distribution between ECF and ICF. Sodium is important in generating and transmitting nerve impulses, muscle contractility, and regulating acid-base balance.

The serum sodium level reflects the ratio of sodium to water, not necessarily the amount of sodium in the body. Changes in the serum sodium level can reflect a primary water imbalance, primary sodium imbalance, or combination of the two. Sodium imbalances are typically associated with imbalances in ECF volume (Figs. 17.12 and 17.13). Because sodium is the main

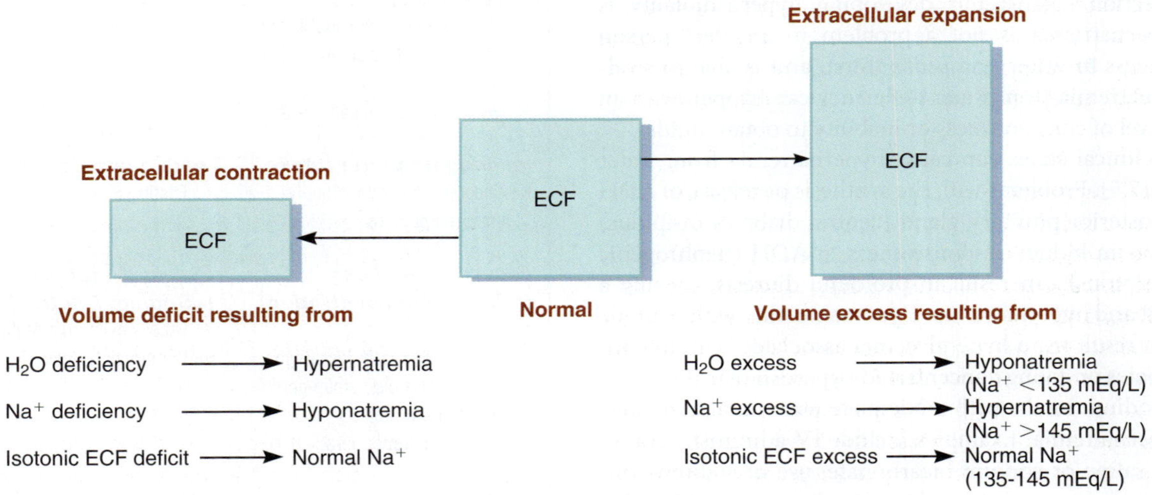

Fig. 17.12 Assessment of extracellular fluid *(ECF)* volume.

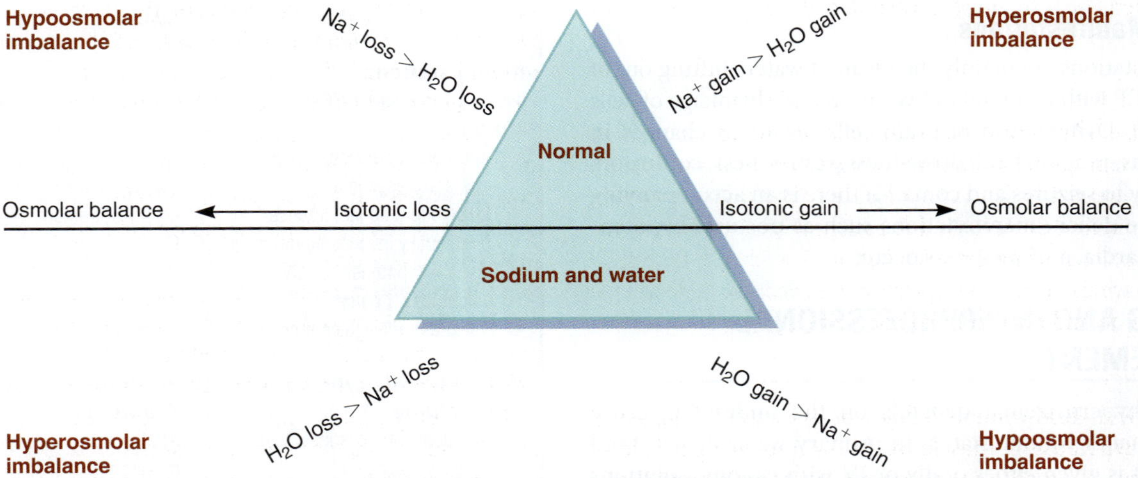

Fig. 17.13 Isotonic gains and losses affect mainly the extracellular fluid (ECF) compartment, with little or no water movement into the cells. Hypertonic imbalances cause water to move from inside the cell into the ECF to dilute the concentrated sodium, causing cell shrinkage. Hypotonic imbalances cause water to move into the cell, causing cell swelling.

determinant of ECF osmolality, sodium imbalances are typically associated with parallel changes in osmolality.

The GI tract absorbs sodium from foods. Typically, daily intake of sodium far exceeds the body's daily requirements. Sodium leaves the body through urine, sweat, and feces. The kidneys mainly regulate sodium balance. The kidneys control ECF sodium concentration by excreting or retaining water under the influence of ADH. Aldosterone plays a smaller role in sodium regulation by promoting sodium reabsorption from the renal tubules.

HYPERNATREMIA

Hypernatremia (high serum sodium) may occur with inadequate water intake, excess water loss, or, rarely, sodium gain. Because sodium is the main determinant of ECF osmolality, hypernatremia causes hyperosmolality. ECF hyperosmolality causes water to move out of the cells to restore equilibrium, leading to cellular dehydration. As discussed earlier, the primary protection against our developing hyperosmolality is thirst. Hypernatremia is not a problem in an alert person who has access to water, can sense thirst, and is able to swallow. Hypernatremia from water deficiency can happen with an impaired level of consciousness or inability to obtain fluids.

Several clinical states can cause hypernatremia from water loss (Table 17.5). Problems with the synthesis or release of ADH from the posterior pituitary gland (central diabetes insipidus) or a decrease in kidney responsiveness to ADH (nephrogenic diabetes insipidus) can result in profound diuresis, causing a water deficit and hypernatremia. Hyperosmolality with osmotic diuresis can result from hyperglycemia associated with uncontrolled diabetes or giving concentrated hyperosmolar EN.

Excess sodium intake with inadequate water intake can also lead to hypernatremia. Examples include IV administration of hypertonic saline or sodium bicarbonate, use of sodium-containing drugs, excess oral intake of sodium (e.g., ingesting seawater), and *primary aldosteronism* (excess aldosterone secretion) caused by a tumor of the adrenal glands.

Clinical Manifestations

The manifestations are mainly the result of water shifting out of cells into ECF with resultant dehydration and shrinkage of cells (Table 17.5). Dehydration of brain cells results in changes in mental status, ranging from drowsiness, restlessness, confusion, and lethargy to seizures and coma.[4] If there is an accompanying ECF volume deficit, manifestations such as postural hypotension, tachycardia, and weakness occur.

❖ NURSING AND INTERPROFESSIONAL MANAGEMENT

Managing hypernatremia depends on the underlying cause and the patient's volume status. In primary water deficit, fluid replacement is given either orally or IV with isotonic solutions such as 0.9% sodium chloride.[2] If the problem is sodium excess, expect diluting the high sodium concentration with sodium-free IV fluids, such as 5% dextrose in water, and promoting sodium excretion with diuretics. Dietary sodium intake is often restricted. If the patient has altered consciousness or is having seizures, initiate seizure precautions.

Monitor serum sodium levels, serum osmolality, and the patient's response to therapy. The serum sodium level should not decrease by more than 8 to 15 mEq/L in an 8-hour period.[2] Quickly reducing levels can cause a rapid shift of water back into the cells, causing cerebral edema and neurologic complications. This risk is greatest in the patient who developed hypernatremia over several days or longer.

TABLE 17.5 Sodium Imbalances

Causes and Manifestations

Hypernatremia (Na^+ >145 mEq/L [mmol/L])	Hyponatremia (Na^+ <136 mEq/L [mmol/L])
Causes	
Excess Sodium Intake	***Excess Sodium Loss***
• Hypertonic EN without water supplements	• *GI losses:* diarrhea, vomiting, fistulas, NG suction
• IV fluids: hypertonic NaCl, excess isotonic NaCl, IV sodium bicarbonate	• *Renal losses:* diuretics, adrenal insufficiency, Na^+ wasting renal disease
• Near-drowning in salt water	• *Skin losses:* burns, wound drainage
Inadequate Water Intake	***Inadequate Sodium Intake***
• Unconscious or cognitively impaired persons	• Fasting diets
Excess Water Loss (↑ Sodium Concentration)	***Excess Water Gain (↓ Sodium Dilution)***
• Diarrhea	• Excess hypotonic IV fluids
• ↑ Insensible water loss (high fever, heatstroke, prolonged hyperventilation)	• Primary polydipsia
• Osmotic diuretic therapy	
Diseases	***Diseases***
• Cushing syndrome	• Cirrhosis
• Diabetes insipidus	• Heart failure
• Primary hyperaldosteronism	• Primary hypoaldosteronism
• Uncontrolled diabetes	• SIADH
Manifestations	
With Decreased ECF Volume	***With Decreased ECF Volume***
• Agitations, restlessness, lethargy, seizures, coma	• Apprehension, irritability, confusion, dizziness, personality changes, tremors, seizures, coma
• Dry swollen tongue, intense thirst, sticky mucous membranes	• Cold and clammy skin
• Postural hypotension, ↓ CVP, weight loss, ↑ pulse	• Dry mucous membranes
• Weakness, muscle cramps	• Postural hypotension, ↓ CVP, ↓ jugular venous filling, ↑ pulse, thready pulse
With Normal or Increased ECF Volume	***With Normal or Increased ECF Volume***
• Agitations, restlessness, twitching, seizures, coma	• Apathy, headache, confusion, muscle spasms, seizures, coma
• Edema, peripheral and pulmonary	• Nausea, vomiting, diarrhea, abdominal cramps
• Intense thirst, flushed skin	
• Weight gain, ↑ BP, ↑ CVP	• Weight gain, ↑ BP, ↑ CVP

HYPONATREMIA

Hyponatremia (low serum sodium) may result from a loss of sodium-containing fluids, water excess in relation to the amount of sodium (dilutional hyponatremia), or a combination of both (Table 17.5). Hyponatremia is usually associated with ECF hypoosmolality from the excess water. To restore balance, fluid shifts out of the ECF and into the cells, leading to cellular edema.

Common causes of hyponatremia from loss of sodium-rich body fluids include draining wounds, diarrhea, vomiting, and primary adrenal insufficiency. Inappropriate use of sodium-free or hypotonic IV fluids causes hyponatremia from water excess. This may occur in patients after surgery or major trauma, or if we give fluids to patients with renal failure. Patients with psychiatric disorders may have an excess water intake. Syndrome of inappropriate antidiuretic hormone secretion (SIADH) results in dilutional hyponatremia caused by abnormal retention of water (see Chapter 54).

Clinical Manifestations

The manifestations are due to cellular swelling and first appear in the central nervous system (CNS). Mild hyponatremia has minor, nonspecific neurologic symptoms. These include headache, irritability, and difficulty concentrating. More severe hyponatremia can cause confusion, vomiting, seizures, and even coma. If hyponatremia is severe and develops rapidly, irreversible neurologic damage or death from brain herniation can occur.

❖ NURSING AND INTERPROFESSIONAL MANAGEMENT

We manage hyponatremia from fluid loss by replacing fluid using isotonic sodium-containing solutions, encouraging oral intake, and withholding all diuretics.[2] In mild hyponatremia caused by water excess, fluid restriction may be the only treatment. Loop diuretics and demeclocycline may be given. If hyponatremia is acute or more serious, small amounts of IV hypertonic saline solution (3% sodium chloride) can restore the serum sodium level while the body is returning to a normal water balance.

Vasopressor receptor antagonists block the activity of ADH. They are used to treat patients who cannot tolerate fluid restrictions or have more severe symptoms.[4] These drugs include conivaptan (Vaprisol) and tolvaptan (Samsca). Conivaptan is given IV to hospitalized patients with severe hyponatremia from water excess. Tolvaptan is given orally to treat hyponatremia from heart failure or SIADH.

Monitor serum sodium levels and the patient's response to therapy. Avoid rapid correction or overcorrection. The level should not increase by more than 10 to 12 mEq/L per hour in the first 24 hours and 18 mEq/L or less per hour within 48 hours.[5] Quickly increasing sodium levels can cause osmotic demyelination syndrome with permanent damage to nerve cells in the brain. An accurate urine output record is essential. The patient may need a urinary catheter placed if unable to help with monitoring output. If the patient has an altered consciousness or is having seizures, initiate seizure precautions.

POTASSIUM IMBALANCES

Potassium is the major ICF cation, with 98% of the body potassium being in cells. For example, potassium concentration within muscle cells is around 140 mEq/L; potassium concentration in ECF is 3.5 to 5.0 mEq/L. The sodium-potassium pump in cell membranes maintains this concentration difference by pumping potassium into the cell and sodium out. Insulin helps by stimulating the sodium-potassium pump.

Because the ratio of ECF to ICF potassium is the major factor in the resting membrane potential of nerve and muscle cells, potassium imbalances often affect neuromuscular and cardiac function. Potassium is involved with regulating intracellular osmolality and promoting cellular growth. It is required for glycogen to be deposited in muscle and liver cells. It also plays a role in acid-base balance (discussed in the section on Acid-Base Regulation later in this chapter).

Diet is the main source for potassium. The typical Western diet contains around 50 to 100 mEq of potassium daily. This mainly comes from protein-rich foods and various fruits and vegetables. Many salt substitutes used in low-sodium diets have substantial potassium. Patients may receive potassium from IV sources, including IV fluids; transfusions of stored, hemolyzed blood; and some medications (e.g., potassium penicillin).

The kidneys are the primary route for potassium loss, eliminating about 90% of the daily potassium intake. Potassium excretion depends on the serum potassium level, urine output, and renal function. When serum potassium is high, urine potassium excretion increases. When serum levels are low, excretion decreases. Large urine output can cause excess potassium loss. Impaired kidney function can cause potassium retention. An inverse relationship exists between sodium and potassium reabsorption in the kidneys. Factors that cause sodium retention (e.g., low blood volume, hyponatremia, aldosterone secretion) cause potassium excretion.

HYPERKALEMIA

Hyperkalemia (high serum potassium) may result from impaired renal excretion, a shift of potassium from ICF to ECF, a massive intake of potassium, or a combination of these factors (Table 17.6). The most common cause is renal failure. Adrenal insufficiency with subsequent aldosterone deficiency leads to potassium retention. Factors that cause potassium to move from ICF to ECF include acidosis, massive cell destruction (as in burn or crush injury, tumor lysis, severe infections), and intense exercise. In metabolic acidosis, potassium ions shift from ICF to ECF in exchange for hydrogen ions moving into the cell.

Digoxin-like drugs and β-adrenergic blockers (e.g., propranolol) can impair entry of potassium into cells, resulting in higher ECF potassium concentrations. Several drugs, such as NSAIDs, potassium-sparing diuretics, angiotensin II receptor blockers (e.g., losartan), and angiotensin-converting enzyme (ACE) inhibitors (e.g., lisinopril), can contribute to hyperkalemia by reducing the kidney's ability to excrete potassium.[6]

TABLE 17.6 Potassium Imbalances

Causes and Manifestations

Hyperkalemia (K⁺ >5.0 mEq/L [mmol/L])	Hypokalemia (K⁺ <3.5 mEq/L [mmol/L])
Causes	
Excess Potassium Intake	***Potassium Loss***
• Excess or rapid IV administration • Potassium-containing drugs (e.g., potassium penicillin) • Potassium-containing salt substitute	• Dialysis • Diaphoresis • *GI losses*: diarrhea, vomiting, fistulas, NG suction, ileostomy drainage • *Renal losses:* diuretics, hyperaldosteronism, magnesium depletion
Shift of Potassium Out of Cells	***Shift of Potassium into Cells***
• Acidosis • Intense exercise • Tissue catabolism (e.g., fever, crush injury, sepsis, burns) • Tumor lysis syndrome	• Alkalosis • ↑ Epinephrine (e.g., stress) • ↑ Insulin release (e.g., IV dextrose load) • Insulin therapy (e.g., with diabetic ketoacidosis)
Failure to Eliminate Potassium	***Lack of Potassium Intake***
• Adrenal insufficiency • *Medications:* Angiotensin II receptor blockers, ACE inhibitors, heparin, potassium-sparing diuretics, NSAIDs • Renal disease	• Diet low in potassium • Failure to include potassium in IV fluids if NPO • Starvation
Clinical Manifestations	
• Abdominal cramping, diarrhea, vomiting • Confusion • Fatigue, irritability • Irregular pulse • Loss of muscle tone • Muscle weakness, cramps • Paresthesias, decreased reflexes • Tetany	• Constipation, nausea, paralytic ileus • Fatigue • Hyperglycemia • Irregular, weak pulse • Muscles soft, flabby • Muscle weakness, leg cramps • Paresthesias, decreased reflexes • Shallow respirations
ECG Changes	***ECG Changes***
• Loss of P wave • Prolonged PR interval • ST segment depression • Widening QRS • Tall, peaked T wave • Ventricular fibrillation • Ventricular standstill	• Peaked P wave • Prolonged QRS • ST segment depression • Flattened T wave • Presence of U wave • Ventricular dysrhythmias • First- and second-degree heart block

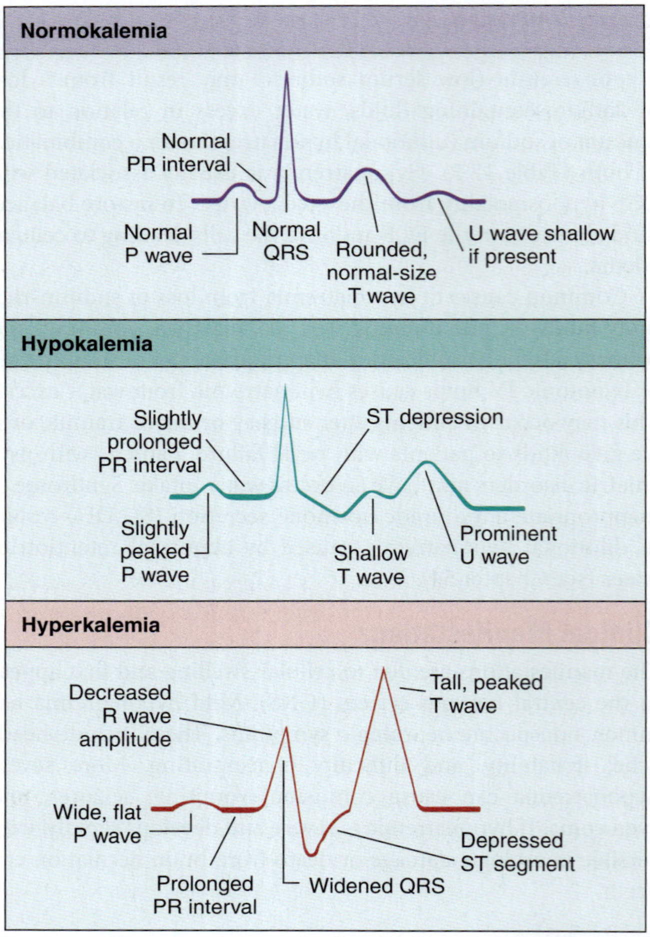

Fig. 17.14 ECG changes associated with changes in potassium levels.

Clinical Manifestations

The increased potassium concentration outside the cell changes the normal ECF and ICF ratio. This results in increased cell excitability and changes in impulse transmission to the nerves and muscles. The most clinically significant problems are the changes in cardiac conduction. The initial finding is tall, peaked T waves. As potassium increases, cardiac depolarization decreases. This leads to loss of P waves, a prolonged PR interval, ST segment depression, and widening QRS complex (Fig. 17.14). Life-threatening dysrhythmias may occur.[6]

The patient may have fatigue, confusion, tetany, muscle cramps, paresthesias, and weakness. As potassium increases, loss of muscle tone and weakness or paralysis of other skeletal muscles, including the respiratory muscles, can occur, leading to respiratory arrest. Abdominal cramping, vomiting, and diarrhea occur from hyperactivity of GI smooth muscles.

❖ NURSING AND INTERPROFESSIONAL MANAGEMENT

Therapies to manage hyperkalemia include:

1. Stop oral and IV potassium intake.
2. Increase potassium excretion. This may be done with loop or thiazide diuretics, dialysis, patiromer (Veltassa), sodium zirconium cyclosilicate (ZS-9, Lokelma), and/or sodium polystyrene sulfonate (Kayexalate). Kayexalate, given orally or rectally, is used acutely to bind potassium in the bowel. Each gram removes roughly 1 mEq of potassium and frees 1 to 2 mEq of sodium.[6] Patients with renal failure need hemodialysis.[6] Patiromer, given orally, exchanges calcium for potassium in the lower GI tract. It may take up to 7 hours to take initial effect and 2 days to see maximal results. It is best used for patients with chronic hyperkalemia due to chronic renal failure. Sodium zirconium cyclosilicate (ZS-9, Lokelma) traps potassium in the GI lumen, thereby increasing fecal

excretion.[6] Given orally, maximum drug effect occurs in 2 to 3 hours. The risk of toxicity is low since the drug is not absorbed systemically.

3. Force potassium from ECF to ICF. A combination of IV regular insulin with dextrose and a β-adrenergic agonist stimulates the sodium-potassium pump, shifting potassium into cells. Using these drugs together is more effective than using either alone. Metered-dose inhalers and nebulized β-adrenergic agonists (e.g., nebulized albuterol) are equally effective. IV sodium bicarbonate is an option if the patient is acidotic.[7]
4. Stabilize cardiac membranes. IV calcium chloride or calcium gluconate does not lower the potassium but serves as an antagonist to reverse the toxic effects on the cardiac cell membrane. This protects the patient from life-threatening dysrhythmias.[7]

When the potassium elevation is mild, and the kidneys are functioning, it may be enough to (1) withhold potassium from the diet and IV sources and (2) increase renal potassium excretion by giving fluids and loop or thiazide diuretics. Patients with severe hyperkalemia or symptomatic patients should receive treatment to force potassium into cells.

Use continuous ECG monitoring for all patients with clinically significant hyperkalemia to detect dysrhythmias and monitor the effects of therapy. The patient with dangerous dysrhythmias should receive IV calcium immediately. Monitor BP because giving calcium rapidly can cause hypotension. When giving insulin, monitor for hypoglycemia and give glucose as needed. Monitor serum potassium levels as appropriate.

HYPOKALEMIA

Hypokalemia (low serum potassium) can result from an increased loss of potassium, an increased shift of potassium from ECF to ICF, or, rarely, from decreased dietary potassium intake. The most common causes are abnormal losses from either the kidneys or GI tract. GI tract losses occur with diarrhea, laxative misuse, vomiting, and ileostomy drainage. Renal losses occur when a patient has increased urinary output, is using loop or other potassium depleting diuretics, or has a low magnesium level. Low magnesium levels stimulate renin and aldosterone release, resulting in potassium excretion.

Among the factors causing potassium to move from ECF to ICF are insulin therapy, especially in conjunction with diabetic ketoacidosis, and β-adrenergic stimulation (catecholamine release in stress, coronary ischemia). Alkalosis can cause a shift of potassium into cells in exchange for hydrogen, which lowers potassium in ECF.

Clinical Manifestations

Hypokalemia alters the resting membrane potential, resulting in hyperpolarization (an increased negative charge within the cell) and impaired muscle contraction. Therefore, the manifestations of hypokalemia involve changes in cardiac and muscle function (Table 17.6).

The most serious clinical problem is cardiac changes. These include impaired repolarization, resulting in a flattened T wave, depressed ST segment, and the presence of a U wave. The P waves peak and the QRS complex is prolonged (Fig. 17.14). There is an increased incidence of heart block and potentially lethal ventricular dysrhythmias.

As with hyperkalemia, skeletal muscle weakness and paresthesia may occur. Severe hypokalemia can cause paralysis. This usually involves the extremities but can involve the respiratory muscles, leading to shallow respirations and respiratory arrest. Changes in smooth muscle function may lead to decreased GI motility (e.g., constipation, paralytic ileus). Finally, hypokalemia impairs insulin secretion, leading to glucose intolerance and hyperglycemia.

❖ NURSING AND INTERPROFESSIONAL MANAGEMENT

We manage hypokalemia by giving oral or IV potassium chloride (KCl) supplements and increased dietary intake of potassium. Consuming potassium-rich foods can usually correct mild hypokalemia. See Table 17.7 for foods that are high in potassium. Clinically significant hypokalemia requires giving oral or IV KCl.

! SAFETY ALERT

IV KCl

- Always dilute IV KCl and do not give in concentrated amounts.
- Never give KCl via IV push or as a bolus.
- Invert IV bags containing KCl several times to ensure even distribution in the bag.
- Do not add KCl to a hanging IV bag to prevent giving a bolus dose.

IV KCl infusion rates should not exceed 10 mEq/hr unless the patient is in a critical care setting with continuous ECG monitoring and central line access for administration.[8] IV KCl must be given by infusion pump to ensure correct administration rate. Because KCl is irritating to the vein, assess IV sites at least hourly for phlebitis and infiltration. Infiltration can cause necrosis and sloughing of the surrounding tissue.

TABLE 17.7 NUTRITION THERAPY

High-Potassium Foods

Fruits	Vegetables	Other Foods
• Apricot, raw (medium) • Avocado (¼ whole) • Banana (¼ whole) • Cantaloupe • Dried fruits • Grapefruit juice • Honeydew • Orange (medium) • Orange juice • Prunes • Raisins	• Baked beans • Butternut squash • Refried beans • Black beans • Broccoli, cooked • Carrots, raw • Greens, except kale • Mushrooms, canned • Potatoes, white and sweet • Spinach, cooked • Tomatoes or tomato products • Vegetable juices	• Bran or bran products • Chocolate (1.5–2 oz) • Granola • Milk, all types (1 cup) • Nutrition supplements (use only under the direction of physician or dietitian) • Nuts and seeds (1 oz) • Peanut butter (2 Tbsp) • Salt substitutes, Lite Salt • Salt-free broth • Yogurt

Patients who are critically ill and those at risk for hypokalemia should have continuous ECG monitoring to detect cardiac changes. Monitor serum potassium levels and urine output as appropriate. KCl is usually given only if the urine output is at least 0.5 mL/kg of body weight per hour. Because patients on digoxin therapy have an increased risk for toxicity if their serum potassium level is low, monitor the patient for digitalis toxicity. Manifestations include confusion, lethargy, anorexia, nausea, and vomiting. Vision problems, including decreased acuity, blind spots, and yellow or halo vision, may be seen in digitalis toxicity.[9]

Teach patients ways to prevent hypokalemia (Table 17.8). Patients at risk should have regular monitoring of serum potassium levels. Teach the patient taking digitalis to report signs and symptoms of digoxin toxicity at once to the HCP.

CHECK YOUR PRACTICE

You are taking care of a 78-year-old female patient with heart failure. She is taking furosemide (Lasix) and digitalis.

- What should you be alert for in a patient who takes both drugs?

CALCIUM IMBALANCES

Calcium has a role in many metabolic processes. It is the main cation in bones and teeth. Calcium plays a role in blood clotting, transmission of nerve impulses, myocardial contractions, and muscle contractions. The major source for calcium is dietary intake. Calcium absorption requires the active form of vitamin D. Vitamin D is obtained from foods or made in the skin by the action of sunlight on cholesterol.

The total body content of calcium is about 1200 g. The bones contain 99% of the body's calcium; the rest is in plasma and body cells. Of the calcium in plasma, 50% is bound to plasma proteins, mainly albumin. Approximately 40% is in a free or ionized form, and the rest is found bound with phosphate, citrate, or carbonate. The ionized or free calcium is biologically active. The serum pH influences how much calcium is ionized or bound to albumin. A decreased plasma pH (acidosis) decreases calcium binding to albumin, leading to more ionized calcium. An increased plasma pH (alkalosis) increases calcium-binding, leading to decreased ionized calcium.

Serum calcium levels reflect the total level of all forms of plasma calcium. Serum albumin levels affect the interpretation of total calcium levels. Total calcium values increase or decrease directly with serum albumin levels. Ionized calcium levels are measured using special laboratory techniques or calculated using a formula. Albumin levels do not affect ionized calcium levels.

Parathyroid hormone (PTH) and calcitonin regulate calcium levels. Since the bones serve as a readily available store of calcium, the body can usually keep calcium levels normal by regulating the movement of calcium into or out of the bone. Low serum calcium levels stimulate the parathyroid glands to make and release PTH. PTH increases bone resorption (movement of calcium out of bones), increases GI absorption of calcium, and increases renal tubule reabsorption of calcium. High serum calcium levels stimulate the release of calcitonin from the thyroid gland. Calcitonin has the opposite effect of PTH. It lowers the serum calcium level by increasing calcium deposition into bone, increasing renal calcium excretion, and decreasing GI absorption.

TABLE 17.8 PATIENT & CAREGIVER TEACHING

Prevention of Hypokalemia

Include the following instructions when teaching at-risk patients how to prevent hypokalemia:

1. For all patients at risk:
    - Report the signs and symptoms of hypokalemia (Table 17.5) to the HCP.
    - Have serum potassium levels checked regularly.
    - Regularly include foods high in potassium in your diet (Table 17.6).
    - Drink alcohol in moderation.
    - Avoid eating large amounts of licorice.
2. For patients taking oral potassium supplements
    - Take the supplement as prescribed to prevent overdosing.
    - Take with a full glass of water. Do not crush or chew tablets.

HYPERCALCEMIA

Hypercalcemia (high serum calcium) is caused by hyperparathyroidism in about two-thirds of persons. Cancers, especially kidney, breast, prostate, ovarian, hematologic, and lung cancers, cause the remaining third. Cancers lead to hypercalcemia through tumor-producing factors that prompt osteoclastic activity and bone resorption.[10] Rare causes include thiazide diuretic use, prolonged immobilization, and increased calcium intake (e.g., calcium-containing antacids).

Excess calcium acts like a sedative, leading to reduced excitability of muscles and nerves. Neurologic manifestations begin with fatigue, lethargy, weakness, and confusion and progress to hallucinations, seizures, and coma. Changes in cardiac conduction can lead to dysrhythmias, including heart block and ventricular tachycardia. Table 17.9 lists the causes and manifestations of hypercalcemia.

NURSING AND INTERPROFESSIONAL MANAGEMENT: HYPERCALCEMIA

Management depends on the degree of hypercalcemia, patient's condition, and underlying cause. Patients with mild hypercalcemia should stop any medications related to hypercalcemia, start a diet low in calcium, increase weight-bearing activity, and maintain adequate hydration. The patient must drink 3000 to 4000 mL of fluid daily to promote the renal excretion of calcium and decrease the chance of kidney stones. Fluids that promote urine acidity (cranberry or prune juice) will help to prevent stone formation.

We manage severe hypercalcemia by giving IV isotonic saline, a bisphosphonate, and calcitonin. IV saline therapy requires careful monitoring. Fluid overload can occur in patients who cannot excrete the excess sodium because of impaired renal

TABLE 17.9 Calcium Imbalances

Causes and Manifestations

Hypercalcemia (Ca^{2+} >10.5 mg/dL [2.62 mmol/L])	Hypocalcemia (Ca^{2+} <9.0 mg/dL [2.25 mmol/L])
Causes	
Increased Total Calcium	***Decreased Total Calcium***
• Hyperparathyroidism	• Acute pancreatitis
• Adrenal insufficiency	• Chronic alcohol use
• Cancers with bone metastasis	• Diarrhea
• Excess dairy intake	• Malnutrition, vitamin D deficiency
• Hematologic cancer	• ↓ Magnesium level
• *Medications*: Thiazide diuretics, calcium-containing antacids, vitamin A, or D	• *Medications*: Bisphosphonates, loop diuretics
	• ↑ Phosphate level
• Mycobacterium infection	• Primary hypoparathyroidism
• Paget disease	• Renal insufficiency
• Prolonged immobilization	• ↓ Serum albumin
• Thyrotoxicosis	• Tumor lysis syndrome
Increased Ionized Calcium	***Decreased Ionized Calcium***
• Acidosis	• Alkalosis
	• Receiving excess citrated blood
Manifestations	
• ↑ BP	• ↓ BP
• Bone pain, fractures	• Chvostek sign
• Confusion, psychosis	• Confusion, depression, irritability
• Fatigue, lethargy, weakness	• Fatigue, weakness
• Depressed reflexes	• Hyperreflexia, muscle cramps
• Decreased memory	• Laryngeal and bronchial spasms
• Kidney stones	• Numbness and tingling in extremities and around mouth
• Nausea, vomiting, anorexia	
• Polyuria, dehydration	• Tetany, seizures
• Seizures, coma	• Trousseau sign
ECG Changes	***ECG Changes***
• Short ST segment	• Elongated ST segment
• Short QT interval	• Prolonged QT interval
• Ventricular dysrhythmias	• Ventricular tachycardia
• Increased digitalis effect	

function. Bisphosphonates (e.g., pamidronate, zoledronic acid) are the gold standard in treating hypercalcemia, particularly when caused by cancer. They interfere with the activity of osteoclasts, cells that break down bone. Because it takes 2 to 4 days for them to achieve maximum effect, patients receive calcitonin injections for an immediate effect. Calcitonin rapidly increases renal calcium excretion. However, therapy is effective for only a few days and may cause tachycardia. For patients who do not respond to bisphosphonates, have cancer-induced hypercalcemia, or have renal impairment, denosumab (Prolia) may be used as an alternative treatment.[11] Dialysis is an option in life-threatening situations.

HYPOCALCEMIA

Hypocalcemia (low serum calcium) can result from any condition associated with PTH deficiency. This may occur with surgical removal of part of or injury to the parathyroid glands during thyroid or neck surgery or with neck radiation. The patient who

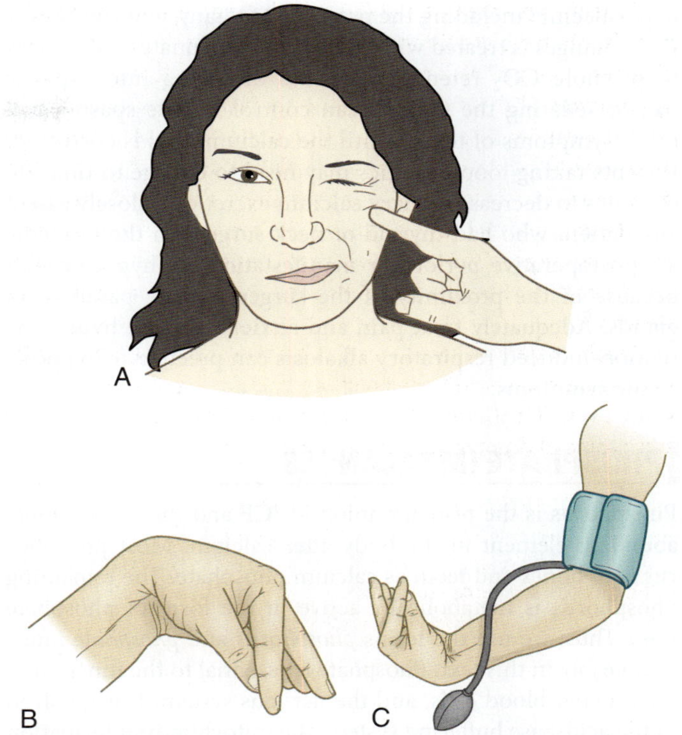

Fig. 17.15 Tests for hypocalcemia. (A) Chvostek sign is contraction of facial muscles in response to a light tap over the facial nerve in front of the ear. (B) Trousseau sign is a carpal spasm induced by (C) inflating a BP cuff above the systolic pressure for a few minutes.

receives multiple blood transfusions can develop hypocalcemia. This is because citrate, used as an anticoagulant in blood bags, binds with calcium, decreasing ionized calcium levels. Sudden alkalosis may result in symptomatic hypocalcemia despite a normal total serum calcium level. The high pH increases calcium binding to protein, decreasing the amount of ionized calcium. Table 17.9 lists causes and manifestations of hypocalcemia.

Low ionized calcium levels decrease the threshold for activating the sodium channels that cause cell membrane depolarization. This results in increased nerve excitability and sustained muscle contraction, or *tetany*. Clinical signs of tetany include Chvostek sign and Trousseau sign. *Chvostek sign* is contraction of facial muscles in response to a tap over the facial nerve in front of the ear (Fig. 17.15A). *Trousseau sign* refers to carpal spasms induced by inflating a BP cuff on the arm (Fig. 17.15B and C). When you inflate the cuff above the systolic pressure, carpal spasms occur within 3 minutes if hypocalcemia is present. Other manifestations of tetany are laryngeal stridor, dysphagia, paresthesia, and numbness and tingling around the mouth (circumoral) or in the extremities. Cardiac effects include decreased cardiac contractility and ECG changes. A prolonged QT interval may develop into ventricular tachycardia.

❖ NURSING AND INTERPROFESSIONAL MANAGEMENT: HYPOCALCEMIA

Managing hypocalcemia depends on the underlying cause and the presence of symptoms. We treat mild or asymptomatic hypocalcemia with a diet high in calcium-rich foods and calcium and vitamin D supplementation. Symptomatic hypocalcemia including the presence of tetany, and significant ECG changes is treated with IV calcium gluconate.[12] Measures to promote CO_2 retention, such as breathing into a paper bag or sedating the patient, can control muscle spasms and other symptoms of tetany until the calcium level is corrected. Patients taking loop diuretics may need to change to thiazide diuretics to decrease urinary calcium excretion. Closely assess any patient who had thyroid or neck surgery in the immediate postoperative period for manifestations of hypocalcemia because of the proximity of the surgery to the parathyroid glands. Adequately treat pain and anxiety because hyperventilation-induced respiratory alkalosis can precipitate hypocalcemic symptoms.

PHOSPHATE IMBALANCES

Phosphorus is the primary anion in ICF and the second most abundant element in the body after calcium. Most phosphorus is in bones and teeth as calcium phosphate. The remaining phosphorus is metabolically active in the form of phosphate salts. Thus, we use the terms *phosphorus* and *phosphate* interchangeably in this text. Phosphate is essential to the function of muscle, red blood cells, and the nervous system. It is involved in the acid-base buffering system; the mitochondrial formation of ATP; cellular uptake and use of glucose; and carbohydrate, protein, and fat metabolism.

PTH maintains serum phosphate levels and balance. Phosphate balance requires adequate renal functioning because the kidneys are the main route of phosphate excretion. When the phosphate level in the glomerular filtrate falls below normal, or PTH levels are low, the kidneys reabsorb more phosphate. A reciprocal relationship exists between phosphate and calcium. This means a low serum calcium level will result in a high phosphate level and vice-versa.[13]

TABLE 17.10 Phosphate Imbalances

Causes and Manifestations

Hyperphosphatemia PO_4^{3-} (>4.5 mg/dL [1.45 mmol/L])	Hypophosphatemia PO_4^{3-} (<3.0 mg/dL [0.97 mmol/L])
Causes	
• Excess ingestion (e.g., phosphate-containing laxatives)	• Chronic alcohol use
• Hyperthermia	• Chronic diarrhea
• Hypoparathyroidism	• Diabetic ketoacidosis
• Phosphate enemas (e.g., Fleet Enema)	• Malabsorption syndromes
• Renal failure	• Malnutrition, vitamin D deficiency
• Rhabdomyolysis	• Hyperparathyroidism
• Sickle cell anemia, hemolytic anemia	• Parenteral nutrition
• Tumor lysis syndrome	• Phosphate-binding antacids
• Thyrotoxicosis	• Refeeding syndrome
	• Respiratory alkalosis
Manifestations	
• Hyperreflexia, muscle cramps	• CNS depression (confusion, coma)
• Hypocalcemia	• Heart problems (dysrhythmias, heart failure)
• Numbness and tingling in extremities and around mouth	• Muscle weakness, including respiratory muscle weakness
• Tetany, seizures	• Polyneuropathy, seizures
• Calcium-phosphate precipitates in skin, soft tissue, cornea, viscera, blood vessels	• Rhabdomyolysis
	• Rickets, osteomalacia

HYPERPHOSPHATEMIA

Hyperphosphatemia (high serum phosphate) is common in patients with acute kidney injury or chronic kidney disease because both alter the kidney's ability to excrete phosphate. Other causes include excess phosphate intake from the use of phosphate-containing laxatives or enemas or a shift of phosphate from ICF to ECF. This may occur in patients with tumor lysis syndrome or rhabdomyolysis. Hypoparathyroidism and vitamin D intoxication cause increased kidney phosphate reabsorption. Table 17.10 describes causes and manifestations of hyperphosphatemia.

Hyperphosphatemia can be asymptomatic unless calcium binds with phosphate, leading to manifestations of hypocalcemia. These include tetany, muscle cramps, paresthesias, hypotension, dysrhythmias, and seizures.[14] Long-term, increased phosphate levels result in the development of calcified deposits outside of the bones. These calcium deposits can be found in soft tissues, such as joints, arteries, skin, corneas, and kidneys, and cause organ dysfunction, notably renal failure.

Management involves identifying and treating the underlying cause. Restrict the intake of foods and fluids high in phosphorus (e.g., dairy products). Oral phosphate-binding agents (e.g., calcium carbonate) limit intestinal phosphate absorption and increase phosphate secretion in the intestine. With severe hyperphosphatemia, hemodialysis may be used to rapidly decrease levels. Volume expansion and forced diuresis with a loop diuretic may increase phosphate excretion. If hypocalcemia is present, institute measures to correct calcium levels. See Chapter 51 for more information about treating hyperphosphatemia from kidney disease.

HYPOPHOSPHATEMIA

Hypophosphatemia (low serum phosphate) can result from decreased intestinal absorption, increased urinary excretion, or ECF to ICF shifts. Malabsorption, diarrhea, and phosphate-binding antacids lead to decreased absorption. Phosphate shifts occur in respiratory alkalosis, treatment of diabetic ketoacidosis, and refeeding syndrome (reinstitution of nutrition to patients who are severely malnourished). Hypophosphatemia may occur in those who are malnourished or receive parenteral nutrition (PN) with inadequate phosphorus replacement. Table 17.10 lists causes and manifestations of hypophosphatemia.

Most of the manifestations result from impaired cellular energy and O_2 delivery due to low levels of cellular ATP and 2,3-diphosphoglycerate (2,3-DPG). It is an enzyme in RBCs that facilitates O_2 delivery to the tissues. Mild to moderate hypophosphatemia is often asymptomatic. Severe hypophosphatemia may be fatal because of decreased cellular function. Acute manifestations include CNS depression, muscle weakness and pain, respiratory failure, and heart failure. Chronically low phosphate levels alter bone metabolism, causing rickets and osteomalacia.

We treat mild phosphate deficiency by increasing oral intake with dairy products or phosphate supplements. Dairy products are better tolerated because phosphate supplements often cause adverse GI effects, including diarrhea and bloating.[15] Symptomatic hypophosphatemia can be fatal and usually requires IV administration of sodium phosphate or potassium phosphate. During IV replacement, monitor serum calcium and phosphate levels every 6 to 12 hours and perform frequent assessments.[15] Complications include hypocalcemia, hyperkalemia, hypotension, and dysrhythmias.

MAGNESIUM IMBALANCES

Magnesium, the second most abundant intracellular cation, plays a key role in essential cellular processes. It is a cofactor in many enzyme systems, including those responsible for carbohydrate metabolism, DNA and protein synthesis, blood glucose control, and BP regulation. Magnesium is needed for the production and use of ATP, the energy source for the sodium-potassium pump. Muscle contraction and relaxation, normal neurologic function, and neurotransmitter release depend on magnesium.

About 50% to 60% of the body's magnesium is stored in muscle and bone. About 30% is in cells, with only 1% in ECF. The kidneys and GI system regulate serum magnesium by controlling the amount of magnesium reabsorbed in the ascending loop of Henle and distal tubules and absorption in the small intestine. GI absorption and renal reabsorption increase when magnesium levels are low.

HYPERMAGNESEMIA

Hypermagnesemia (high serum magnesium level) usually occurs only with increased magnesium intake accompanied by renal insufficiency or failure. A patient with chronic kidney disease who ingests products containing magnesium (e.g., Maalox, Milk of Magnesia) will have a problem with excess magnesium. Magnesium excess could develop in a pregnant woman receiving magnesium sulfate for the treatment of eclampsia or in patients taking laxatives and antacids that contain magnesium. Table 17.11 lists the causes and manifestations of hypermagnesemia.

Excess magnesium inhibits acetylcholine release at the myoneural junction and calcium movement into cells. This impairs nerve and muscle function. Initial manifestations include hypotension, facial flushing, lethargy, urinary retention, nausea, and vomiting. As the serum magnesium level increases, deep tendon reflexes are lost, followed by muscle paralysis and coma. Respiratory and cardiac arrest can occur.

Management begins with stopping magnesium-containing drugs and limiting dietary intake of magnesium-containing foods (e.g., green vegetables, nuts, bananas, oranges, peanut butter, chocolate). If renal function is adequate, increased fluids and diuretics promote urinary excretion of magnesium. The patient with impaired renal function may need dialysis. If the patient is symptomatic, giving IV calcium gluconate will oppose the effects of the excess magnesium on cardiac muscle.[16]

TABLE 17.11 Magnesium Imbalances

Causes and Manifestations

Hypermagnesemia (Mg^{+} >2.1 mEq/L [1.05 mmol/L])	Hypomagnesemia (Mg^{+} <1.3 mEq/L [0.65 mmol/L])
Causes	
• Adrenal insufficiency	• Acute pancreatitis
• Antacids, laxatives	• Chronic alcohol use
• Hypothyroidism	• GI tract fluid losses (e.g., diarrhea, NG suction)
• IV administration of magnesium, especially for treatment of eclampsia	• Hyperglycemia
	• Malabsorption syndromes
• Metastatic bone disease	• Prolonged malnutrition
• Renal failure	• Proton pump inhibitor therapy
• Tumor lysis syndrome	• ↑ Urine output
Manifestations	
• ↓ Deep tendon reflexes	• Chvostek and Trousseau signs
• Flushed, warm skin, especially facial	• Confusion
• Lethargy, drowsiness	• Hyperactive deep tendon reflexes
• Nausea, vomiting	• Muscle cramps
• Muscle weakness	• ↑ Pulse, ↑ BP, dysrhythmias
• ↓ Pulse, ↓ BP	• Tremors, seizures
• Urinary retention	• Vertigo

HYPOMAGNESEMIA

Hypomagnesemia (low serum magnesium level) occurs in patients with limited magnesium intake or increased GI or renal losses. Causes from insufficient food intake include prolonged fasting or starvation and chronic alcohol use. Another potential cause is prolonged PN without magnesium supplementation. Fluid loss from the GI tract, acute pancreatitis, and poorly controlled diabetes may contribute to low magnesium. Diuretics, proton pump inhibitors, and some antibiotics may lead to magnesium loss.[17] Table 17.11 lists the causes and manifestations of hypomagnesemia.

Clinically, hypomagnesemia resembles hypocalcemia. Neuromuscular manifestations are common. These include muscle cramps, tremors, hyperactive deep tendon reflexes, Chvostek sign, and Trousseau sign. Neurologic manifestations include confusion, vertigo, and seizures. Dysrhythmias, such as torsades de pointes and ventricular fibrillation, can occur.

Management depends on the underlying cause and the patient's symptoms. We treat mild magnesium deficiency with oral supplements and increased dietary intake of foods high in magnesium. We give IV magnesium (e.g., magnesium sulfate) if the deficiency is severe or if hypocalcemia is present.

! SAFETY ALERT

IV Magnesium

- Always give using an infusion pump.
- Monitor vital signs, level of consciousness, and reflexes frequently.
- Rapid administration can lead to hypotension and cardiac or respiratory arrest.
- Keep IV calcium gluconate on hand.

ACID-BASE IMBALANCES

The body normally maintains a steady balance between the acids continually produced during normal metabolism and the bases that neutralize and promote the excretion of the acids. Because these acids alter the body's internal environment, their regulation is necessary to maintain homeostasis and acid-base balance (Table 17.12). Many health problems may lead to acid-base imbalances. Patients with diabetes, chronic obstructive pulmonary disease (COPD), and kidney disease often develop acid-base imbalances.

Remember that an acid-base imbalance is not a disease but a symptom of an underlying health problem. Always consider the possibility of acid-base imbalance in patients with serious illnesses.

pH AND HYDROGEN ION CONCENTRATION

The acidity or alkalinity of a solution depends on its hydrogen ion (H^+) concentration. An increase in H^+ concentration leads to acidity. A decrease leads to alkalinity. We usually express H^+ concentration as a negative logarithm (symbolized as *pH*). The use of the negative logarithm means that the lower the pH, the higher is the H^+ concentration.

The pH of a chemical solution may range from 1 to 14. A solution with a pH of 7 is considered neutral. An acid solution has a pH less than 7, and an alkaline solution has a pH greater than 7. Blood is slightly alkaline and has a normal arterial pH of 7.35 to 7.45. Medically, if the pH drops below 7.35, a person

TABLE 17.12 Acid-Base Imbalances

Causes	Pathophysiology	Laboratory Findings
Respiratory Acidosis		
• Atelectasis • Chest wall abnormality • Chronic respiratory disease (e.g., COPD) • Mechanical hypoventilation • Pneumonia (severe) • Pulmonary edema • Respiratory muscle weakness • Sedative overdose	• ↑ CO_2 retention from hypoventilation • Compensatory response is ↑ HCO_3^- retention by kidney	↓ Plasma pH ↑ $PaCO_2$ HCO_3^- normal (uncompensated) ↑ HCO_3^- (compensated) *Sample ABG* Uncompensated: pH 7.31 $PaCO_2$ 54 mm Hg HCO_3^- 25 mEq/L
Respiratory Alkalosis		
• Hyperventilation (e.g., hypoxia, anxiety, fear, pain, exercise, fever) • Liver failure • Mechanical hyperventilation • Stimulated respiratory center (e.g., septicemia, stroke, meningitis, encephalitis, brain injury, salicylate poisoning)	↑ CO_2 excretion from hyperventilation Compensatory response is ↑ HCO_3^- excretion by kidney	↑ Plasma pH ↓ $PaCO_2$ HCO_3^- normal (uncompensated) ↓ HCO_3^- (compensated) *Sample ABG* Uncompensated: pH 7.52 $PaCO_2$ 27 mm Hg HCO_3^- 24 mEq/L
Metabolic Acidosis		
• Diabetic ketoacidosis • Diarrhea • GI fistulas • Lactic acidosis • Renal failure • Renal tubular acidosis • Shock • Starvation	• Gain of fixed acid, inability to excrete acid or loss of base • Compensatory response is ↑ CO_2 excretion by lungs	↓ Plasma pH $PaCO_2$ normal (uncompensated) ↓ $PaCO_2$ (compensated) ↓ HCO_3^- *Sample ABG* Uncompensated: pH 7.29 $PaCO_2$ 38 mm Hg HCO_3^- 18 mEq/L 18 mEq/L
Metabolic Alkalosis		
• Diuretic therapy • Excess $NaHCO_3$ intake • Hypokalemia • Mineralocorticoid use • NG suctioning • Vomiting	• Loss of strong acid or gain of base • Compensatory response is ↑ CO_2 retention by lungs	↑ Plasma pH $PaCO_2$ normal (uncompensated) ↑ $PaCO_2$ (compensated) ↑ HCO_3^- *Sample ABG* Uncompensated: pH 7.50 $PaCO_2$ 40 mm Hg HCO_3^- 34 mEq/L 34 mEq/L

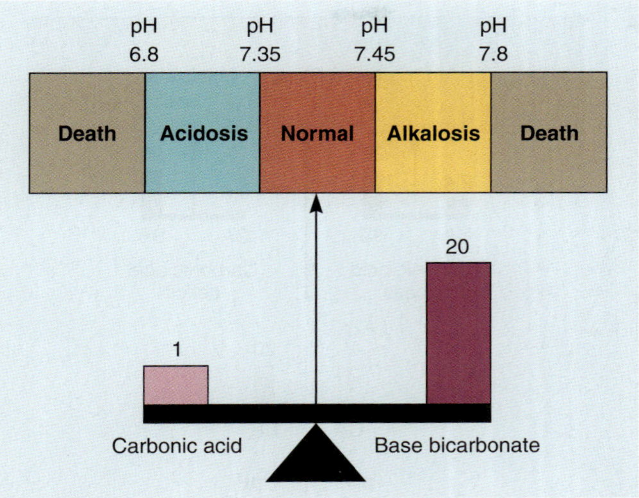

Fig. 17.16 The normal range of plasma pH is 7.35 to 7.45. A normal pH is maintained by a ratio of 1-part carbonic acid to 20 parts bicarbonate.

has **acidosis**. If the blood pH is greater than 7.45, the person has **alkalosis** (Fig. 17.16).

ACID-BASE REGULATION

The body uses 3 mechanisms to regulate acid-base balance and keep the pH between 7.35 and 7.45. These are the buffer systems, respiratory system, and renal system. Each mechanism reacts at different speeds. Buffers are the fastest, reacting immediately. The respiratory system responds in minutes and reaches maximum effectiveness in hours. The renal response occurs hours to days after a change in pH. The kidneys can maintain balance indefinitely in patients with chronic imbalances. But, if the person has impaired kidney function, the kidneys will not be effective in maintaining acid-base balance.

Buffer System

Buffering is the primary regulator of acid-base balance. **Buffers** act chemically to change strong acids into weaker ones or bind acids to neutralize them. This minimizes the effect of acids on blood pH until they can be excreted from the body. Buffers can maintain pH only if the respiratory and renal systems function adequately.

All body fluids contain buffers. The major buffer in ECF is the carbonic acid–bicarbonate system (H_2CO_3 / HCO_3^-). Other buffer systems include phosphate, protein, and hemoglobin. The cell can act as a buffer by shifting H^+ in and out of the cell. When ECF levels of H^+ are increased, H^+ enters the cell in exchange for potassium. This may result in hyperkalemia as potassium moves into the ECF. Conversely, with decreased H^+ levels, H^+ enters plasma in exchange for potassium. This is why a patient with alkalosis can develop hypokalemia.

A buffer consists of a weak acid, which releases H^+ when fluid is too alkaline, or a base and its salt, which takes up H^+ when fluid is too acidic. The carbonic acid–bicarbonate buffer system neutralizes hydrochloric acid (HCl), a strong acid, by combining it with a strong base. This prevents the acid from making a large decrease in pH.

$$\underset{\text{Strong Acid}}{HCL} + \underset{\text{Strong Base}}{Na_2CO_3} \rightarrow \underset{\text{Salt}}{NaCl} + \underset{\text{Weak Acid}}{H_2CO_3}$$

The carbonic acid is broken down into H_2O and CO_2. The lungs excrete CO_2, either combined with insensible H_2O as carbonic acid or alone as CO_2.

The phosphate, protein, and hemoglobin buffer systems act in the same way as the bicarbonate system. The main components of the phosphate system are monohydrogen phosphate (HPO_4^{2-}) and dihydrogen phosphate ($H_2PO_4^-$). A phosphate, combined with sodium, can neutralize a strong acid, such as HCl, by forming sodium chloride (NaCl) and sodium biphosphate (NaH_2PO_4), a weak acid. If a strong base, such as sodium hydroxide (NaOH), is present, sodium biphosphate (NaH_2PO_4) neutralizes it to a weaker base (Na_2HPO_4) and H_2O.

Intracellular and extracellular proteins can act as an acid or base. Because the chemical structure of amino acids has an acid and a base, they can accept H^+ if pH decreases or release H^+ if fluid is too alkaline. Some amino acids have basic radicals (NH_3OH [ammonium hydroxide]) that can dissociate into NH_3^+ (ammonia) and OH^- (hydroxide). The OH^- can combine with H^+ to form H_2O.

Hemoglobin can bind with both H^+, forming a weak acid, and CO_2, forming carbaminohemoglobin ($HbCO_2$). $HbCO_2$ dissociates in the lungs, releasing CO_2 for exhalation. Because H^+ can combine only with hemoglobin that has released its O_2, venous blood is a better buffer than arterial blood, which contains saturated hemoglobin. Hemoglobin also aids in controlling pH by shifting chloride in and out of RBCs in exchange for bicarbonate.

The buffer system maintains a 20:1 ratio between HCO_3^- and carbonic acid in ECF. The body's ability to keep this ratio is important in controlling pH. For example, excess carbonic acid increases the ratio and decreases pH, resulting in acidosis. In response, the body can increase HCO_3^- levels to keep the ratio 20:1 and keep the pH near normal, a state called *compensation*. For example, a ratio of 40:2 is present in compensated acid-base balance.

Respiratory System

The lungs help maintain a normal pH by excreting CO_2 and water, which are by-products of cellular metabolism. When released into the circulation, CO_2 enters RBCs and combines with H_2O to form H_2CO_3. Carbonic acid dissociates into H^+ and HCO_3^-. Hemoglobin buffers the free H^+, and the HCO_3^- diffuses into the plasma. This process is reversed in the pulmonary capillaries, forming CO_2 that is excreted by the lungs.

The amount of CO_2 in the blood directly relates to carbonic acid and H^+ concentration. With increased respirations, the lungs expel more CO_2, so less stays in the blood. This leads to less carbonic acid and less H^+. With decreased respirations, more CO_2 stays in the blood. This leads to increased carbonic acid and more H^+.

The respiratory center in the medulla controls the rate of excretion of CO_2. If increased amounts of CO_2 or H^+ are present, the respiratory center stimulates an increased rate and depth of breathing to "blow off" CO_2 through hyperventilation. If the center senses low H^+ or CO_2 levels, respirations are reduced, and CO_2 is retained. The older adult has an impaired compensatory ability due to decreased respiratory function.

Renal System

Under normal conditions, the body depends on the kidneys to reabsorb and conserve all the HCO_3^- they filter and excrete some of the acid produced by cellular metabolism. The 3 mechanisms of acid excretion include (1) secreting small amounts of free hydrogen into the renal tubule, (2) combining H^+ with ammonia (NH_3) to form ammonium (NH_4^+), and (3) excreting weak acids.

The kidneys normally excrete acidic urine (average pH is 6). As a compensatory mechanism, the pH of the urine can decrease to 4 or increase to 8. To compensate for acidosis, the kidneys can reabsorb more HCO_3^- and excrete excess H^+. This increases the blood pH and decreases the urine pH. In the older adult, the kidneys are less able to compensate for acid load.

ALTERATIONS IN ACID-BASE BALANCE

An acid-base imbalance results when there is a change in the ratio of 20:1 between base and acid content. This occurs when a disease or process alters one side of the ratio (e.g., CO_2 retention in pulmonary disease), and the compensatory processes that maintain the other side of the ratio (e.g., increased renal HCO_3^- reabsorption) either fail or are inadequate. The compensatory process may be inadequate because either the pathophysiologic activity is overwhelming or there is not enough time for the compensatory process to work.

Acid-base imbalances are classified as respiratory or metabolic. *Respiratory imbalances* result from changes in carbonic acid concentration. *Metabolic imbalances* affect the base HCO_3^-. Acidosis occurs with an increase in carbonic acid (respiratory acidosis) or decrease in HCO_3^- (metabolic acidosis). Alkalosis occurs with a decrease in carbonic acid (respiratory alkalosis) or an increase in HCO_3^- (metabolic alkalosis). We further classify Imbalances as acute or chronic. Chronic imbalances allow greater time for compensatory changes.

Respiratory Acidosis

Respiratory acidosis (carbonic acid excess) occurs when a person has hypoventilation (Table 17.12). Hypoventilation leads to a buildup of CO_2, resulting in an accumulation of carbonic acid in the blood. Carbonic acid dissociates, releasing H^+ and decreasing pH. If CO_2 is not eliminated from the blood, acidosis results from the accumulation of carbonic acid (Fig. 17.17A).

During acute respiratory acidosis, the renal compensatory mechanisms begin to work within 24 hours. The kidneys conserve HCO_3^- and secrete increased H^+ into the urine. Until the renal mechanisms have an effect, the serum HCO_3^- level will usually be normal and then increase.

Respiratory Alkalosis

Respiratory alkalosis (carbonic acid deficit) occurs with hyperventilation, or an increase in respiratory rate or volume (Table 17.12). The primary cause of respiratory alkalosis is hypoxemia from acute pulmonary disorders (e.g., pneumonia, pulmonary

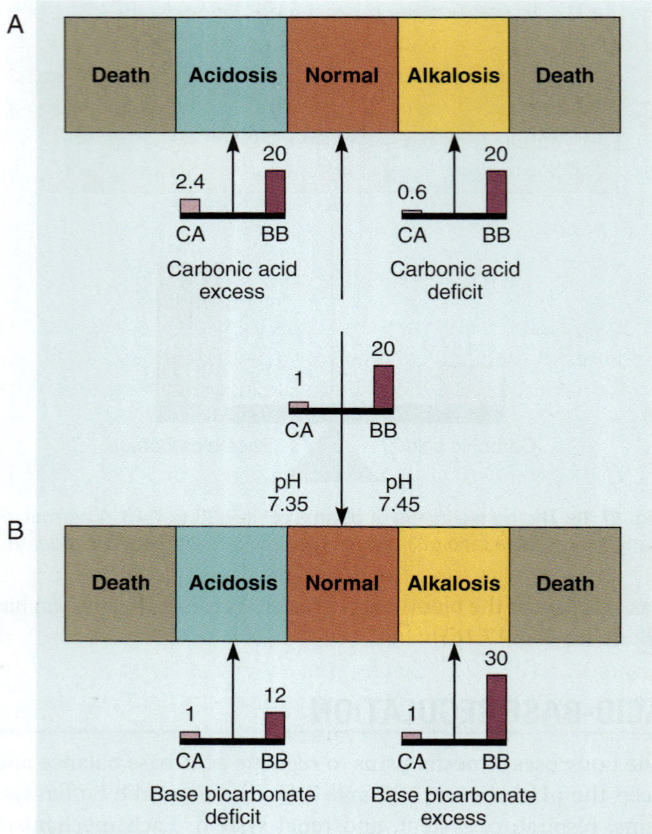

Fig. 17.17 Kinds of acid-base imbalances. (A) Respiratory imbalances caused by carbonic acid *(CA)* excess and carbonic acid deficit. (B) Metabolic imbalances caused by base bicarbonate *(BB)* deficit and base bicarbonate excess.

embolus). Hyperventilation can occur as a physiologic response to metabolic acidosis and increased metabolic demands (e.g., fever). Pain, anxiety, and some CNS disorders can increase respirations without a physiologic need. The decrease in the arterial CO_2 level leads to decreased carbonic acid concentration in the blood and an increased pH (see Fig. 17.17A).

Compensated respiratory alkalosis is rare. In acute respiratory alkalosis, aggressive treatment of the cause of hypoxemia is essential. This usually does not allow time for compensation to occur. If the respiratory alkalosis is caused by significant pain, anxiety, or panic, breathing into a closed system to rebreathe eliminated CO_2 can aid in the compensatory process. Some buffering may occur with the shifting of HCO_3^- into cells in exchange for chloride ions (Cl^-). In chronic respiratory alkalosis that occurs with pulmonary fibrosis or CNS disorders, compensation may include renal excretion of HCO_3^-.

Metabolic Acidosis

Metabolic acidosis (base bicarbonate deficit) occurs when an acid other than carbonic acid accumulates in the body or when bicarbonate is lost in body fluids (Table 17.12 and Fig. 17.17B). Ketoacid accumulation in diabetic ketoacidosis and lactic acid accumulation with shock are examples of acid accumulation. Severe diarrhea resulting in loss of HCO_3^- is an example of a base deficit. In renal disease, the kidneys lose their ability to reabsorb HCO_3^- and secrete H^+. To compensate for metabolic acidosis, the kidneys try to excrete extra acid, and the lungs increase CO_2 excretion. The patient often develops *Kussmaul respirations* (deep, rapid breathing) when trying to compensate for metabolic acidosis.

If metabolic acidosis is present, calculating the anion gap helps you figure out the source of the acidosis. The *anion gap* is the difference between the measured serum cations and anions in ECF

$$\text{Anion gap} = Na^+ - (HCO_3^- + Cl^-)$$

A normal anion gap is 8 to 12 mmol/L. The anion gap increases in metabolic acidosis from acid gain (e.g., lactic acidosis, diabetic ketoacidosis) but is normal in metabolic acidosis caused by bicarbonate loss (e.g., diarrhea).

Metabolic Alkalosis

Metabolic alkalosis (base bicarbonate excess) occurs when a loss of acid (e.g., from prolonged vomiting or gastric suction) or a gain in HCO_3^- (e.g., from ingestion of baking soda) occurs (Table 17.12 and Fig. 17.17B). Renal excretion of HCO_3^- occurs in response to metabolic alkalosis. The lung's compensatory response is limited. The respiratory rate decreases to retain plasma CO_2. However, once hypoxemia occurs or plasma CO_2 reaches a certain level, stimulation of chemoreceptors will increase respirations.

Mixed Acid-Base Disorders

A mixed acid-base disorder occurs when 2 or more disorders are present at the same time. The pH depends on the type, severity, and acuity of each disorder involved and any compensatory mechanisms at work. Respiratory acidosis combined with metabolic alkalosis (e.g., a patient with atelectasis and NG suction) may result in a near-normal pH. Respiratory acidosis combined with metabolic acidosis causes a greater decrease in pH than either disorder alone. An example of a mixed acidosis is a patient in severe shock with poor perfusion and hypoventilation. Mixed alkalosis can occur in a patient hyperventilating because of postoperative pain who is losing acid from NG suctioning.

CLINICAL MANIFESTATIONS

The manifestations of acidosis and alkalosis are outlined in Tables 17.13 and 17.14. In both respiratory and metabolic acidosis, the CNS is depressed. Headache, lethargy, weakness, and confusion develop, leading eventually to coma and death. Compensatory mechanisms also produce specific manifestations. For example, the deep, rapid (Kussmaul) respirations of a patient with metabolic acidosis occur with respiratory compensation.

In both types of alkalosis, symptoms usually result from an accompanying electrolyte abnormality rather than the alkalosis. Hypocalcemia occurs due to increased calcium binding with albumin, lowering the amount of ionized, active calcium. Therefore, muscle cramping and symptoms of CNS excitability, including tingling and numbness of the fingers and tetany, occur. While respiratory alkalosis itself is not usually life-threatening, the underlying cause may be.[18]

TABLE 17.13 Manifestations of Acidosis

Respiratory (↑ $PaCO_2$)	Metabolic (↓HCO_3^-)
Neurologic	
Lethargy	Lethargy
Confusion	Confusion
Dizziness	Dizziness
Headache	Headache
Coma	Coma
Cardiovascular	
↓ BP	↓ BP
Ventricular fibrillation (related to hyperkalemia from compensation)	Dysrhythmias (related to hyperkalemia from compensation)
Warm, flushed skin	Cold, clammy skin
Gastrointestinal	
No significant findings	Nausea, vomiting, diarrhea, abdominal pain
Neuromuscular	
Seizures	Muscle weakness
Respiratory	
Hypoventilation with hypoxia	Deep, rapid respirations

TABLE 17.14 Manifestations of Alkalosis

Respiratory (↓ $PaCO_2$)	Metabolic (↑ HCO_3^-)
Neurologic	
Dizziness	Irritability
Light-headedness	Lethargy
Confusion	Confusion
Headache	Headache
Cardiovascular	
Tachycardia	Tachycardia
Dysrhythmias (related to hypokalemia from compensation)	Dysrhythmias (related to hypokalemia from compensation)
Gastrointestinal	
Nausea, vomiting, diarrhea	Nausea, vomiting
Epigastric pain	Anorexia
Neuromuscular	
Tetany	Tetany
Numbness	Tremors
Tingling of extremities	Tingling of fingers and toes
Hyperreflexia	Muscle cramps, hypertonic muscles
Seizures	Seizures
Respiratory	
Hyperventilation (lungs are unable to compensate if there is a respiratory problem)	Hypoventilation (compensatory action by lungs)

Blood Gas Values

Arterial blood gas (ABG) values give objective information about a patient's acid-base status, the underlying cause of an imbalance, and the body's ability to regulate pH. Knowing the patient's clinical situation and the extent of renal and respiratory

TABLE 17.15 Normal Arterial Blood Gas Values

Parameter	Reference Interval
pH	7.35–7.45
$PaCO_2$	35–45 mm Hg
Bicarbonate (HCO_3^-)	22–26 mEq/L (mmol/L)
PaO_2[a]	80–100 mm Hg
SaO_2	>95%
Base excess	±2.0 mEq/L

[a]Decreases above sea level and with increasing age.

TABLE 17.16 ROME

Memory Device for Acid-Base Imbalances

For acid-base imbalances, use this quick memory device (mnemonic).

In ***Respiratory*** conditions, the pH and the $PaCO_2$ go in ***Opposite*** directions.

- In respiratory alkalosis, the pH is ↑ and the $PaCO_2$ is ↓.
- In respiratory acidosis, the pH is ↓ and the $PaCO_2$ is ↑.
- In ***Metabolic*** conditions, the pH and the HCO_3^- go in the same direction ***(Equal).*** The $PaCO_2$ may also go in the same direction.
- In metabolic alkalosis, pH and HCO_3^- are ↑ and the $PaCO_2$ is ↑ or normal.
- In metabolic acidosis, pH and HCO_3^- are ↓ and the $PaCO_2$ is ↓ or normal.

compensation allows you to identify acid-base disorders and the patient's ability to compensate. ABG analysis also shows the partial pressure of arterial O_2 (PaO_2) and O_2 saturation. Table 17.15 lists normal ABG values. These values help you evaluate the patient's overall oxygenation status and identify hypoxemia. Table 17.16 shows *ROME,* a quick memory device for understanding acid-base imbalances.

To interpret the results of an ABG, perform the following 5 steps:

1. Look at each of the values. If the pH is between 7.35 and 7.45, and the CO_2, HCO_3^-, and PaO_2 are within normal limits, the ABGs are normal. If any value is out of normal, then continue.
2. Look at the pH first. Values less than 7.35 indicate acidosis. Values greater than 7.45 indicate alkalosis. A normal pH means there is normal acid-base status, compensation is occurring, or a mixed disorder is present.
3. Use ROME (see Table 17.16) to figure out if the origin is respiratory or metabolic. Remember respiratory opposite and metabolic equal.
4. Once the metabolic or respiratory origin is determined, look at the remaining value, either the CO_2 or HCO_3^-, to figure the level of compensation. If the value is moving in the opposite direction, the body is trying to compensate. If the remaining value moving to compensate is abnormal and the pH is higher or lower than normal, *partial compensation* has occurred. If the pH is within normal limits, *full compensation* has occurred.
5. Assess the PaO_2 and O_2 saturation. If these values are abnormal, hypoxemia is present.

Table 17.17 explains how to analyze ABG results. The laboratory findings section of see Table 17.12 shows ABG findings of the 4 major acid-base imbalances. See Chapter 27 for further discussion of ABGs.

TABLE 17.17 Applying Arterial Blood Gas (ABG) Analysis

Sample ABG Values	Analysis
pH 7.32 $PaCO_2$ 30 HCO_3^- 16 PaO_2 95	1. Look at each of the values. If the pH is between 7.35 and 7.45, and the CO_2, HCO_3^-, and PaO_2 are within normal limits, the ABGs are normal. If any value is out of normal, then continue. *The pH, CO_2, HCO_3^- are all abnormally low. Continue with analysis.* 2. Look at the pH first. Values less than 7.35 indicate acidosis and values greater than 7.45. *The pH is below 7.35, indicating acidosis.* 3. Use ROME to figure out if the origin is respiratory or metabolic. Remember respiratory opposite and metabolic equal. *Using ROME, the pH and CO_2 are not going in the opposite direction (the disorder is not respiratory in origin). The pH and HCO_3^- are moving in the same or equal direction, so the disorder is metabolic in origin.* 4. Once the metabolic or respiratory origin is determined, look at the remaining laboratory value (either CO_2 or HCO_3^-) to determine the level of compensation. *Since the disorder is metabolic in origin, review the remaining laboratory value (in this case the CO_2). The CO_2 is low, meaning the lungs are trying to compensate by lowering acid levels.* 5. Assess the PaO_2 and O_2 saturation. If these values are abnormal, hypoxemia is present. *The PaO_2 is normal and does not indicate hypoxemia.*

Interpretation

This ABG shows metabolic acidosis with partial compensation. Partial compensation is occurring because the pH remains abnormal. Full compensation would occur after the pH returns within normal limits.

ASSESSMENT OF ELECTROLYTE AND ACID-BASE IMBALANCES

Assessing patients for electrolyte and acid-base imbalances is an important part of your nursing practice. In addition to assessing for the manifestations discussed earlier in this chapter, obtain subjective and objective data from any patient with suspected electrolyte or acid-base imbalances.

Subjective Data

Important Health Information

Health history. Question the patient about any history of problems involving the kidneys, heart, GI system, or lungs that could affect the present electrolyte and acid-base balance. Ask about specific diseases such as diabetes, endocrine problems, COPD, renal failure, liver disease, GI problems, and cancer. Assess for any prior electrolyte or acid-base problems.

Medications. Assess the patient's current and past use of medications. Many drugs, especially over-the-counter drugs, are hidden sources of sodium, potassium, calcium, magnesium, and other electrolytes. Other drugs, including diuretics, corticosteroids, and electrolyte supplements, can cause electrolyte imbalances.

Surgery or other treatments. Ask the patient about past or present renal dialysis, kidney surgery, or bowel surgery resulting in a temporary or permanent external collecting system, such as an ileostomy.

Functional Health Patterns

Health perception–health management pattern. If the patient currently has a problem related to electrolyte and acid-base balance, obtain a detailed description of the illness, including onset, course, and treatment.

Nutritional-metabolic pattern. Ask the patient about their usual diet and any special diet practices. Weight reduction diets, fad diets, or any eating disorders, such as anorexia or bulimia, can lead to electrolyte problems. If the patient is on a special diet, such as low sodium or high potassium, assess the ability to adhere to the dietary prescription. Ask if they add salt to their food.

Elimination pattern. Make note of the patient's usual bowel and bladder habits. Carefully document any problems, such as diarrhea, oliguria, polyuria, or incontinence.

Activity-exercise pattern. Ask about the patient's exercise pattern and any excess perspiration. Determine if the patient is exposed to extremely high temperatures during leisure or work activity. Ask the patient what they do to replace fluid and electrolytes lost through excess perspiration.

Cognitive-perceptual pattern. Ask about any changes in sensations, such as numbness, tingling, or muscle weakness, which could signal an electrolyte problem. Ask the patient and caregiver if there have been any changes in cognition, such as confusion or memory impairment, or lethargy.

Objective Data

Physical Assessment

Perform a complete physical assessment because electrolyte and acid-base balance affects all body systems. Identify patients in need of emergency management so that they can be immediately stabilized. As you assess each system, check for manifestations that you would expect with an imbalance. Common abnormal assessment findings of major body systems offer clues to possible imbalances (Table 17.18).

Laboratory Values

Assessing serum electrolyte values is a good starting point for evaluating fluid and electrolyte balance (Table 17.1). Serum electrolytes can also provide important information about a patient's acid-base balance. Changes in the serum HCO_3^- occur with metabolic acidosis (low HCO_3^- level) or alkalosis (high HCO_3^- level).

! SAFETY ALERT

Managing Critical Test Results

- Promptly report critical laboratory values to the HCP.
- Assess the patient and take appropriate actions (e.g., ECG monitoring).

Remember that serum electrolyte values often provide limited information. They reflect the concentration of that electrolyte in ECF but not necessarily in ICF. For example, most

TABLE 17.18 ASSESSMENT ABNORMALITIES

Fluid and Electrolyte Imbalances

Finding	Possible Cause
Blood Pressure	
Hypotension	Fluid volume deficit, low Ca^{2+}, high Mg^{2+}
Hypertension	Fluid volume excess, high Ca^{2+}, low Mg^{2+}
Muscular	
Chvostek sign	Low Ca^{2+}, high PO_4^{3-}, low Mg^{2+}
Muscle cramping	High K^+, low Ca^{2+}, high PO_4^{3-}, low Mg^{2+}
Muscle weakness	High or low K^+, high Ca^{2+}, low PO_4^{3-}, high Mg^{2+}
Trousseau sign	Low Ca^{2+}, high PO_4^{3-}, low Mg^{2+}
Neurologic	
Confusion	Fluid volume excess, high or low Na^+, high or low K^+, low Ca^{2+}, high or low Mg^{2+}, low PO_4^{3-}
Decreased level of consciousness	Fluid volume deficit or excess, high or low Na^+, low PO_4^{3-}
Fatigue	Fluid volume deficit, low K^+, high Ca^{2+}
Irritability	Low Na^+, high K^+, low Ca^{2+}, high PO_4^{3-}
Tremors, seizures	High Na^+, low K^+, low Ca^{2+}, high PO_4^{3-}, low Mg^{2+}
Respirations	
Crackles	Fluid volume excess
Dyspnea	Fluid volume excess
Rapid respirations	Fluid volume deficit
Restricted airway	Low Ca^{2+}, high PO_4^{3-}
Pulse	
Bounding pulse	Fluid volume excess
Rapid, weak, thready pulse	Fluid volume deficit
Weak, irregular, rapid pulse	Severe low K^+, low Mg^{2+}
Weak, irregular, slow pulse	Severe high K^+, high Mg^{2+}
Skin	
Cold, clammy skin	Fluid volume deficit, low Na^+
Flushed, dry skin	High Na^+, High Mg^{2+}
Pitting edema	Fluid volume excess
Poor skin turgor	Fluid volume deficit

potassium is found in the cells. Changes in serum potassium values may be the result of a true deficit or excess of potassium or reflect the movement of potassium into or out of the cell during acid-base imbalances. An abnormal serum sodium level may reflect a sodium problem or, more likely, a water problem.

Other useful laboratory tests include serum and urine osmolality, serum glucose, blood urea nitrogen, serum creatinine, ABG sampling, urine specific gravity, and urine electrolytes.

Clinical Problems

Clinical problems for the patient with an electrolyte or acid-base imbalance include:

- Electrolyte imbalance
- Acid-base imbalance
- Impaired cardiac function
- Impaired cognition
- Impaired respiratory system function
- Risk for injury
- Healthcare-associated complication

Planning

The overall goals are that the patient will (1) achieve and maintain electrolyte and acid-base balance, (2) be free from any complications, and (3) adhere to the prescribed therapies.

Implementation

The general considerations for the nursing care of the patient with electrolyte or acid-base imbalances are outlined in Table 17.19.

! SAFETY ALERT

Using Smart Infusion Pumps

- Smart infusion pumps can calculate IV drug dose and delivery rates.
- If you make an error and enter incorrect data, you will get incorrect results.
- Have a second RN confirm the settings for high-risk drugs.
- Use your best judgment when using smart infusion pumps and follow agency policy.

TABLE 17.19 NURSING MANAGEMENT

Electrolyte and Acid-Base Imbalances

- Assess patient for manifestations of electrolyte and acid-base imbalances.
- Determine risk factors and assess for the potential cause of an imbalance.
- Be prepared to institute resuscitation protocols and respiratory support.
- Give IV fluids and medications as prescribed.
- Treat dysrhythmias according to agency policy.
- Provide prescribed diet appropriate for specific electrolyte imbalance.
- Properly obtain laboratory specimens for electrolyte levels and ABG analysis.
- Provide a safe environment for the patient with neurologic or neuromuscular manifestations by instituting fall and seizure precautions.
- Monitor for complications from or measures to correct the balance.
- Implement measures to orient the patient as needed.
- Help the patient prioritize activities and alternate rest and activity periods.
- Implement measures to reduce or eliminate common side effects from prescribed supplemental electrolytes and other therapies.
- Evaluate response to therapies addressing the electrolyte or acid-base imbalance.

ORAL FLUID AND ELECTROLYTE REPLACEMENT

Oral rehydration solutions may be used to correct mild fluid and electrolyte deficits. They generally contain water, potassium, sodium, and glucose. Glucose not only provides calories but also promotes sodium and water absorption in the small intestine. Commercial oral rehydration solutions are now available for home use. Avoid cola drinks because they do not contain adequate electrolyte replacement, and the sugar content may lead to osmotic diuresis.

IV FLUID AND ELECTROLYTE REPLACEMENT

IV fluid and electrolyte therapy are necessary to treat many different fluid and electrolyte imbalances. Many patients need maintenance IV fluid therapy when they cannot take oral fluids (e.g., during and after surgery). Other patients need corrective or replacement therapy for losses that are ongoing or have already occurred. The amount and type of solution are determined by the normal daily maintenance requirements and by imbalances identified by laboratory results. We classify IV replacement solutions by their concentration or tonicity (Table 17.20). Tonicity is a key factor in determining the appropriate solution to correct imbalances.

Solutions

Hypotonic

A hypotonic solution has a lower osmolality when compared to plasma. Infusing a hypotonic solution dilutes ECF, lowering serum osmolality. Osmosis then produces a movement of water from ECF to interstitial spaces and cells, causing cells to swell. After achieving equilibrium, ICF and ECF have the same osmolality. Hypotonic solutions (e.g., 0.45% NaCl) are useful in treating patients with hypernatremia. They are a good maintenance fluid because normal daily losses are hypotonic. They are not good for replacement because they can deplete ECF and lower BP. Because hypotonic solutions have the potential to cause cellular swelling, monitor patients for changes in mentation that may signal cerebral edema.

Although 5% dextrose in water is technically an isotonic solution, the dextrose quickly metabolizes. The net result is the administration of hypotonic free water with equal expansion of ECF and ICF. One liter of a 5% dextrose solution provides 50 g of dextrose or 170 calories. While this amount of dextrose is not enough to meet caloric requirements, it helps prevent ketosis associated with starvation.

Isotonic

An isotonic solution has an osmolality similar to plasma. Because of this similarity, giving an isotonic solution expands only ECF, and the fluid does not move into cells. This makes isotonic solutions the ideal fluid replacement for patients with ECF volume deficits. Examples of isotonic solutions include 0.9% NaCl and lactated Ringer's solution.

Isotonic saline (0.9% NaCl), or *normal saline,* has a sodium concentration (154 mEq/L) slightly higher than that of plasma (135 to 145 mEq/L) and a chloride concentration (154 mEq/L) significantly higher than the plasma chloride level (96 to 106 mEq/L). Therefore, giving too much isotonic saline has the potential to increase sodium and chloride levels. Isotonic saline is used when a patient has had both fluid and sodium losses (e.g., diarrhea, vomiting).

Lactated Ringer's solution contains sodium, potassium, chloride, calcium, and lactate (the precursor of bicarbonate) in about the same concentrations as ECF. This makes it the ideal fluid in certain situations, such as surgery, burns, or GI fluid losses. Patients with liver problems, hyperkalemia, and severe hypovolemia should not receive lactated Ringer's because they have a decreased ability to convert the lactate to bicarbonate.

Hypertonic

A hypertonic solution has a higher osmolality than plasma. The higher osmotic pressure draws water out of the cells into ECF. It is useful in the treatment of hyponatremia and trauma patients with a head injury. Those receiving hypertonic solutions need frequent monitoring of BP, lung sounds, and serum sodium levels because of the risk for intravascular fluid volume excess.

TABLE 17.20 Common Crystalloid Solutions

Solution	Tonicity	mOsm/kg	Contents	Indications and Considerations
Dextrose in Water				
5%	Isotonic, but physiologically hypotonic	278	50 g/L dextrose	• Contains free water only, no electrolytes • Provides 170 cal/L • Used to replace water losses and treat hypernatremia
10%	Hypertonic	556	100 g/L dextrose	• Contains free water only, no electrolytes • Provides 340 cal/L • Used with PN
Saline				
0.45%	Hypotonic	154	77 mEq/L Na^+ 77mEq/L Cl^-	• Contains free water, Na^+, and Cl^-, no calories • Used to treat hypernatremia and uncontrolled hyperglycemia • Used as a maintenance solution
0.9%	Isotonic	308	154 mEq/L Na^+ 154mEq/L Cl^-	• Contains Na^+ and Cl^- in excess of plasma levels • Does not contain free water or calories • Used to expand intravascular volume and replace extracellular fluid losses • Only solution given with blood products • May cause volume overload in patients with heart or kidney disease
3.0%	Hypertonic	1026	513 mEq/L Na^+ 513 mEq/L Cl^-	• Contains Na^+ and Cl^- in excess of plasma levels • Used to treat symptomatic hyponatremia and trauma patients with head injury • Give slowly because it may cause volume overload and pulmonary edema
Dextrose in Saline				
5% in 0.225%	Isotonic	355	50 g/L dextrose 34 mEq/L Na^+ 34 mEq/L Cl^-	• Provides Na^+, Cl^-, and free water • Used to replace hypotonic losses and treat hypernatremia • Provides 170 cal/L
5% in 0.45%	Hypertonic	432	50 g/L dextrose 77 mEq/L Na^+ 77 mEq/L Cl^-	• Provides Na^+, Cl^-, and free water due rapid metabolism of the dextrose • Used as a maintenance solution
5% in 0.9%	Hypertonic	586	50 g/L dextrose 154 mEq/L Na^+ 154 mEq/L Cl^-	• Contains Na^+ and Cl^- in excess of plasma levels • Used to treat metabolic alkalosis and volume deficits in patients with hyponatremia
Multiple Electrolyte Solutions				
Ringer's solution	Isotonic	309	147 mEq/L Na^+ 156 mEq/L Cl^- 4 mEq/L K^+ 4 mEq/L Ca^{2+}	• Similar in composition to plasma except that it has excess Cl^-, no Mg^{2+}, no HCO_3^- • Does not provide free water or calories • Used to expand the intravascular volume and replace extracellular fluid losses
Lactated Ringer's (Hartmann's) solution	Isotonic	273	130 mEq/L Na^+ 109 mEq/L Cl^- 4 mEq/L K^+ 3 mEq/L Ca^{2+} 28 mmol/L lactate	• Similar in composition to normal plasma except does not contain Mg^{2+} • Does not provide free water or calories • Used to treat hypovolemia, burns, and GI fluid losses • Cannot be used in patients with alkalosis or lactic acidosis

Although concentrated dextrose and water solutions (10% dextrose or greater) are hypertonic solutions, once the dextrose is metabolized, the net result is the administration of water. This free water ultimately expands ECF and ICF. The primary use of these solutions is providing calories as part of PN (see Chapter 44). You may give solutions containing 10% dextrose or less through a peripheral line. You must use a central line to give solutions with dextrose concentrations greater than 10%.

IV Additives

Additives in basic IV solutions replace specific losses. KCl, calcium, magnesium, and HCO_3^- are common additives. The use of each was described earlier in the discussion of the specific electrolyte deficiencies. Many premixed IV solutions containing specific additives are available. Using these solutions reduces error as the solution contains the correct amount of the electrolyte in the right volume and type of IV solution.

Colloids

Colloid solutions contain large molecules that increase oncotic pressure and pull fluid into the blood vessels. Because this action restores blood volume, we also call colloids *volume expanders* or *plasma expanders.* Colloids include human plasma products (albumin, fresh frozen plasma, blood) and semisynthetic solutions (dextran, starches).

Albumin is available in 5% and 25% solutions. The 5% solution has an albumin concentration similar to that of plasma. Use results in plasma volume expansion equal to the volume infused. This makes it ideal for treating hypovolemic patients. In contrast, 25% albumin solution is hypertonic and draws fluid from the interstitial space. This makes it useful in treating patients with burns, hepatic failure, and ascites.

Dextran solutions are synthetic complex sugar solutions. There are 2 types: low-molecular-weight dextran (dextran 40) and high-molecular-weight dextran (dextran 70). Because dextran metabolizes slowly, it stays in the vascular system for a prolonged period. It pulls fluid into the intravascular space, expanding it by more volume than what is infused. Hydroxyethyl starches (e.g., Hespan) are synthetic colloids that work similarly to dextran to expand plasma volume.

Colloids can lead to circulatory overload because they pull fluid into ECF. Monitor vital signs and urine output frequently and assess for signs and symptoms of fluid volume excess. All colloids affect blood coagulation by interfering with coagulation factor VII.[19] Monitor coagulation times and implement any necessary precautions. Fatal anaphylactic reactions have occurred with Hespan and dextran. Monitor the patient closely for a hypersensitivity reaction and stop an infusion at once if a reaction occurs.

If the patient has lost blood, whole blood or packed RBCs are given. Packed RBCs have the advantage of giving the patient mostly RBCs rather than RBCs and fluid volume. Although packed RBCs have a decreased plasma volume, they increase the oncotic pressure and pull fluid into the intravascular space. The use of whole blood, with its added fluid volume, may cause circulatory overload, particularly in patients who are susceptible to complications from excess circulating volume (e.g., heart failure). To prevent fluid volume excess, loop diuretics may be given with blood and colloids. See Chapter 34 for more about giving blood and blood products. See Table 17.21 for nursing management of IV therapy.

CENTRAL VENOUS ACCESS DEVICES

Central venous access devices (CVADs) are catheters placed in large blood vessels (e.g., subclavian vein, jugular vein) of people who need frequent or special access to the vascular system. There are 3 main types of CVADs: centrally inserted catheters, peripherally inserted central catheters (PICCs), and implanted ports.

Advantages of CVADs include immediate access to the central venous system, a reduced need for multiple venipunctures, and decreased risk for extravasation injury. CVADs permit frequent, continuous, rapid, or intermittent administration of fluids and medications. They allow us to administer more safely drugs that are potential *vesicants* (agents that can cause tissue damage), blood and blood products, and PN. CVADs can provide a means to perform hemodynamic monitoring and obtain venous blood samples. They are useful with patients who have limited peripheral vascular access or who have a projected need for long-term vascular access. We can also use a CVAD to inject radiopaque contrast media. Table 17.22 gives examples of when we use CVADs.

The major disadvantages are an increased risk for systemic infection and the invasiveness of the procedure. Extravasation (leakage of fluid) can still occur if there is displacement of or damage to the device.

TABLE 17.21 NURSING MANAGEMENT

IV Therapy

- Assess patient for manifestations of fluid and electrolyte imbalances.
- Determine if ordered IV therapies are appropriate.
- Choose and insert appropriate IV catheters and infusion devices.
- Give IV fluids and medications.
- Monitor for adverse reactions to IV fluids or medications.
- Assess for fluid overload or hypovolemia and initiate appropriate changes in IV fluids.
- Evaluate if IV therapies are addressing patient's fluid and electrolyte needs.
- Collaborate with the pharmacist to:
  - Determine appropriateness of IV therapies and need for dose adjustments.
  - Prepare IV infusions and medications.
  - Screen for potential problems, such as compatibility issues.
  - Monitor response to therapy.

TABLE 17.22 Common Indications for Central Venous Access Devices (CVADs)

Condition	Indications for Use
Autoimmune disorders	Perform plasmapheresis
Blood sampling	Multiple blood draws for diagnostic tests over time
Blood transfusions	Infusion of blood or blood products
Heart failure	Perform ultrafiltration
Hemodynamic monitoring	Used to measure CVP and assess fluid balance
Medication administration	
• Cancer	Chemotherapy, infusion of irritating or vesicant medications
• Contrast media	Inject radiopaque contrast media for diagnostic testing
• Infection	Long-term administration of antibiotics
• Pain	Long-term administration of pain medication
• Drugs at risk for causing phlebitis	Epoprostenol (Flolan) Calcium chloride Potassium chloride Amiodarone
Nutrition replacement	PN IV high percentage dextrose solutions
Renal failure	Perform hemodialysis (especially on an acute basis) or continuous renal replacement therapy
Shock, burns	Infusion of high volumes of fluid and electrolyte replacement

Centrally Inserted Catheters

The tip of centrally inserted catheters (also called central venous catheters [CVCs]) rests in the distal end of the superior vena cava near its junction with the right atrium (Fig. 17.18). The other end of the catheter exits through a separate incision on the chest or abdominal wall. *Nontunneled catheters* are usually placed in the subclavian or internal jugular vein, more rarely in the femoral vein. They are best for patients with short-term needs in an acute care setting. *Surgically placed tunneled catheters* (e.g., Hickman, Broviac, Groshong) are suitable for long-term needs. Tunneling of the catheter through the subcutaneous tissue and the synthetic cuff used to anchor the catheter provide stability and decrease infection risk. After the site heals,

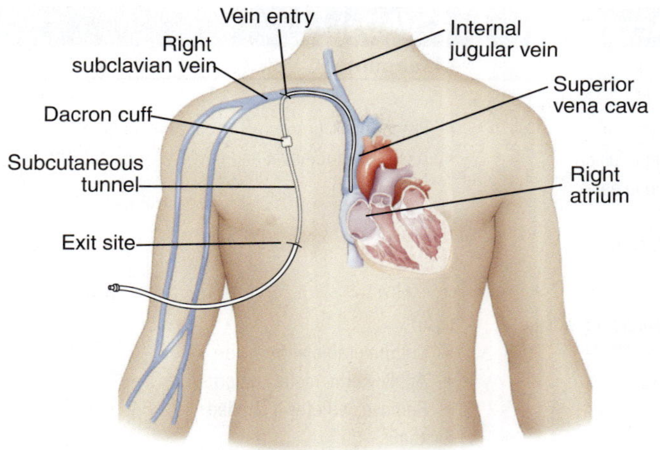

Fig. 17.18 Tunneled central venous catheter. Note tip of the catheter in the superior vena cava.

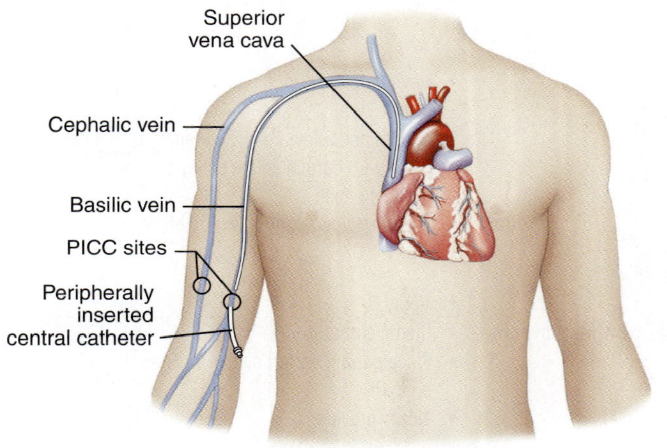

Fig. 17.19 Peripherally inserted central catheter *(PICC)* can be inserted using the basilic or cephalic vein.

the catheter does not need a dressing, making it easier for the patient to maintain the site at home.

CVCs are available with single-, double-, or triple-lumens. Multilumen catheters are used in the critically ill patient because each lumen can be used simultaneously to provide a different therapy. For example, incompatible drugs infuse in separate lumens without mixing, while a third lumen gives access for blood sampling.

Peripherally Inserted Central Catheters

PICCs are CVCs inserted into a vein in the arm. The basilic vein is best because of its large diameter (Fig. 17.19). The cephalic, median cubital, or brachial veins are other options. Single-, double-, or triple-lumens are available. Double lumens are preferred because they allow for simultaneous use. PICCs are used with patients who need vascular access for 1 week to 6 months, but they can be in place for longer periods.

Advantages of a PICC over a CVC are lower infection rate, fewer insertion-related complications, decreased cost, and ability to insert at the bedside or in an outpatient area. PICCs, however, have an increased risk for deep vein thrombosis and phlebitis (Table 17.23). If phlebitis occurs, it usually happens within 7 to 10 days after insertion. Do not use the arm with the PICC to take a BP reading or draw blood. When the BP cuff is inflated, the PICC can touch the vein wall, increasing the risk for vein damage and thrombosis.

Implanted Infusion Ports

An implanted infusion port consists of a surgically implanted CVC connected to a reservoir or port (Fig. 17.20A). The catheter tip lies in the desired vein. The port lies in a surgically created subcutaneous pocket on the upper chest or arm. It consists of a titanium or plastic reservoir covered with a self-sealing silicone septum. You access the port by using a special noncoring needle with a deflected tip. This prevents damage to the septum that could make the port useless (Fig. 17.20B).

We place drugs in the reservoir by a direct injection or through injection into an established IV line. The reservoir then slowly releases the medicine into the bloodstream. Implanted ports are good for long-term therapy and have a low risk for infection. The hidden port offers the patient cosmetic advantages and overall has less maintenance than other types of CVADs. Monitor accessed ports for infiltration that can occur if the needle is not in place or dislodges.

Midline Catheters

Midline catheters technically are peripheral catheters because they do not enter a central vein. However, their use and care are similar to a PICC. A specially trained nurse can insert a midline catheter. A catheter can be from 3 to 8 inches long and have single or double lumens. They are inserted in the antecubital area through either the basilic or cephalic vein, often under ultrasound guidance. The basilic vein is best since it has a larger diameter. The tip rests right below the axilla, staying below the shoulder joint to reduce the risk for vein irritation from moving the shoulder. These lines can stay in place for up to 4 weeks.

Complications

CVADs always have a potential for complications. Careful monitoring and assessment will help you to identify potential complications early. Table 17.23 lists common complications, potential causes, manifestations, and interventions.

❖ NURSING MANAGEMENT: CENTRAL VENOUS ACCESS DEVICES

Nursing management of CVADs includes assessment, dressing changes and cleansing, injection cap changes, and maintenance of catheter patency. The exact frequency and procedures for these requirements vary by type of CVAD and agency, so it is important to follow your agency's policies and procedures. The following section discusses some general guidelines.

Catheter and insertion site assessment includes inspecting the site for redness, edema, warmth, drainage, tenderness, or pain. Observing the catheter for misplacement or slippage is important. Perform a pain assessment, particularly noting any reports of chest or neck discomfort, arm pain, or pain at the insertion site. Do not use a newly placed CVAD until the tip position is verified with a chest x-ray.

TABLE 17.23 Complications of Central Venous Access Devices (CVADs)

Possible Cause	Manifestations	Management
Catheter Migration		
• Improper suturing • Insertion site trauma • Changes in intrathoracic pressure • Forceful catheter flushing • Spontaneous	• Sluggish infusion or aspiration • Edema of chest or neck during infusion • Patient reports gurgling sound in ear • Dysrhythmias • Increased external catheter length	• Prepare for fluoroscopy to confirm position • Assist with removal and new CVAD placement
Catheter-Related Infection (Local or Systemic)		
• Contamination during insertion or use • Migration of organisms along catheter • Immunosuppressed patient	• *Local:* redness, tenderness, purulent drainage, warmth, edema • *Systemic:* fever, chills, malaise	Local • Culture drainage from site • Apply warm, moist compresses • Remove catheter if needed Systemic • Take blood cultures • Give antibiotic therapy • Give antipyretic therapy • Remove catheter if needed
Catheter Occlusion		
• Clamped or kinked catheter • Tip against wall of vessel • Thrombosis • Precipitate buildup in lumen	• Sluggish infusion or aspiration • Inability to infuse and/or aspirate	• Have patient change position, raise arm, and cough • Assess and alleviate any clamping or kinking • Flush with normal saline using a 10-mL syringe. Do not force flush • Instill anticoagulant or thrombolytic agent
Embolism		
• Catheter breaking • Dislodgment of thrombus • Entry of air into circulation	• Chest pain • Respiratory distress (dyspnea, tachypnea, hypoxia, cyanosis) • ↓ BP • ↑ Pulse	• Apply O_2 • Clamp catheter • Place patient on left side with head down (air emboli) • Notify provider
Pneumothorax		
• Perforation of visceral pleura during insertion	• Decreased or absent breath sounds • Respiratory distress (cyanosis, dyspnea, tachypnea) • Chest pain • Distended unilateral chest	• Apply O_2 • Place in semi-Fowler's position • Prepare for chest tube insertion

CHECK YOUR PRACTICE

You are taking care of a 74-year-old patient with a left triple-lumen subclavian catheter. When you are changing the dressing, you note some redness at the site with a small amount of yellow, foul-smelling drainage.

- What should you do?

Before manipulating a catheter for any reason, perform hand hygiene. Perform dressing changes and cleanse the catheter insertion site using strict sterile technique. Typical dressings include transparent semipermeable dressings or gauze and tape. If the site is bleeding, a gauze dressing may be preferable. Otherwise, transparent dressings are best. They allow observation of the site without having to remove the dressing. Transparent dressings may be in place for up to 1 week. Change any dressing at once if it becomes damp, loose, or soiled.

Cleanse the skin around the catheter insertion site according to agency policy. A chlorhexidine-based preparation is the cleansing agent of choice. Its effects last longer than either povidone-iodine or alcohol, offering improved killing of bacteria.[20] When using chlorhexidine, cleansing the skin with friction is critical to preventing infection. When applying a new dressing, allow the area to air dry completely. Secure the lumen ports to the skin above the dressing site. Document the date and time of the dressing change and initial the dressing.

Disinfect catheter hubs, needleless connectors, and injection ports before accessing the catheter. Use an alcoholic chlorhexidine preparation, 70% alcohol, or povidone-iodine per agency policy. Change injection caps at regular intervals according to policy, or if they have damage from excess punctures. Use strict sterile technique. Teach the patient to turn the head to the opposite side of the insertion site during cap change. If you cannot clamp the catheter, have the patient lie flat in bed and

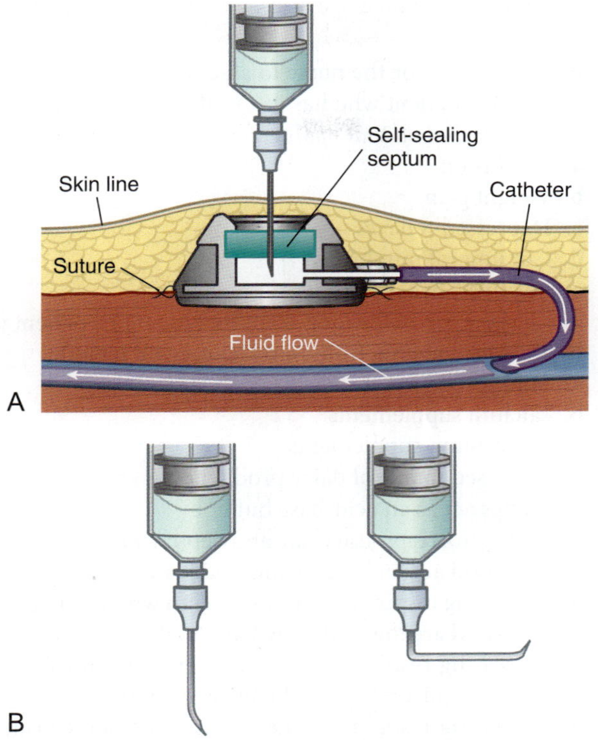

Fig. 17.20 (A) Cross section of implantable port displaying access of the port with the Huber-point needle. Note the deflected point of the Huber-point needle, which prevents coring of the port's septum. (B) 2 Huber-point needles used to enter the implanted port. The 90-degree needle is used for top-entry ports for continuous infusion.

perform the Valsalva maneuver whenever the catheter is open to air to prevent an air embolism.

Flushing is one of the most effective ways to maintain catheter patency. It also keeps incompatible drugs or fluids from mixing. Use a normal saline solution in a syringe that has a barrel capacity of 10 mL or more to avoid excess pressure on the catheter. If you feel resistance, do not apply force. This could result in a ruptured catheter or create an embolism if a thrombus is present. Because of the risk for contamination and infection, use solution from prefilled syringes or single-dose vials rather than multiple-dose vials when flushing catheters. If you are not using a positive-pressure valve cap, clamp any unused lines after flushing.

Use the push-pause technique when flushing all catheters. Push-pause creates turbulence within the catheter lumen, promoting the removal of debris that adheres to the catheter lumen and decreasing the chance of occlusion. This technique involves injecting saline with a rapid alternating push-pause motion, instilling 1 to 2 mL with each push on the syringe plunger. If you are using a negative-pressure cap or neutral pressure cap, clamp the catheter while maintaining positive pressure while instilling the last 1 mL of saline. This prevents reflux of blood back into the catheter. If a positive-pressure valve cap is present, it works to prevent the reflux of blood and resultant catheter lumen occlusion. Remove the syringe before clamping the catheter to allow the positive pressure valve to work correctly.

CVAD Removal

Removing a CVAD is done according to agency policy and the nurse's scope of practice. In many agencies, nurses with proven competency can remove PICCs and nontunneled CVCs. The procedure involves removing any sutures and then gently withdrawing the catheter. Have the patient perform the Valsalva maneuver as you withdraw the last 5 to 10 cm of the catheter. Immediately apply pressure to the site with sterile gauze to prevent air from entering and to control bleeding. Inspect the catheter tip to determine that it is intact. After bleeding has stopped, apply an antiseptic ointment and sterile dressing to the site.

Case Study

Fluid and Electrolyte Imbalance

(© Kevin Peterson/ Photodisc/ Thinkstock.)

Patient Profile

S.S., a 63-year-old woman with acute lymphocytic leukemia, has been receiving chemotherapy on an outpatient basis. She completed her 3rd treatment 5 days ago and has had nausea and vomiting for 2 days despite using ondansetron (Zofran). S.S.'s daughter brings her to the hospital, where she is admitted to the medical unit. As the admitting nurse, you perform an admission assessment.

Subjective Data

- Reports lethargy, weakness, dizziness, and dry mouth
- States she has been too nauseated to eat or drink anything for 2 days
- Reports "little urination" over the previous 24 hr

Objective Data

- Heart rate 110 beats/min, pulse thready
- BP 100/65
- Weight loss of 5 lb since she received her chemotherapy treatment 5 days ago
- Dry oral mucous membranes
- Delayed skin turgor

Discussion Questions

1. ***Recognize***: What are her risk factors for fluid and electrolyte imbalances?
2. ***Recognize***: What additional assessment data should you obtain?
3. ***Analyze***: Based on her manifestations, what fluid imbalance does S.S. have?
4. ***Analyze***: You draw blood for a serum chemistry evaluation. What electrolyte imbalances are likely and why?
5. ***Recognize***, *Analyze:* S.S. is at risk for which acid-base imbalance? Describe the changes that would occur in S.S.'s ABGs with this acid-base imbalance. How would the body compensate?
6. ***Prioritize***: What are the priority nursing interventions for S.S.?
7. ***Prioritize***, *Plan:* Who should be the primary members of the interprofessional team in caring for S.S.? What is the interprofessional team's priority at this time for S.S.?
8. ***Act***: The provider orders dextrose 5% in 0.45% saline to infuse at 100 mL/hr. What type of solution is this, and how will it help S.S.'s fluid imbalance?
9. ***Act***: S.S. has a double-lumen PICC in her left arm. One lumen is connected to the IV infusion; the other is unused. What is the recommended practice for maintaining the patency of the unused lumen?
10. ***Evaluate***: What outcomes will indicate that interprofessional care was effective?

Answers available at http://evolve.elsevier.com/Lewis/medsurg.

BRIDGE TO NCLEX EXAMINATION

The number of the question corresponds to the same-numbered outcome at the beginning of the chapter.

1. During the postoperative care of a 76-year-old patient, the nurse monitors the patient's intake and output carefully, knowing that the patient is at risk for fluid and electrolyte imbalances primarily because
- **a.** older adults have an impaired thirst mechanism and need reminding to drink fluids.
- **b.** older adults are more likely than younger adults to lose extracellular fluid during surgeries.
- **c.** water accounts for a greater percentage of body weight in the older adult than in younger adults.
- **d.** small losses of fluid are significant because body fluids account for 45% to 50% of body weight in older adults.

2. During administration of a hypertonic IV solution, the mechanism involved in equalizing the fluid concentration between ECF and the cells is (recognize)
- **a.** osmosis.
- **b.** diffusion.
- **c.** active transport.
- **d.** facilitated diffusion.

3a. An older adult is admitted to the medical unit with GI bleeding. Assessment findings that occur with fluid volume deficit include *(select all that apply)*
- **a.** weight loss.
- **b.** dry oral mucosa.
- **c.** full bounding pulse.
- **d.** engorged neck veins.
- **e.** orthostatic
- **f.** hypotension.
- **g.** increased central venous pressure.

3b. The nursing care for a patient with hyponatremia and fluid volume excess includes
- **a.** fluid restriction.
- **b.** administration of hypotonic IV fluids.
- **c.** administration of a cation-exchange resin.
- **d.** placement of an indwelling urinary catheter.

3c. The nurse should be alert for which manifestations in a patient receiving a loop diuretic?
- **a.** Restlessness and agitation
- **b.** Paresthesias and irritability
- **c.** Weak, irregular pulse and poor muscle tone
- **d.** Increased blood pressure and muscle spasms

3d. Which patient is at *greatest* risk for developing hypermagnesemia?
- **a.** 83-year-old man with lung cancer and hypertension
- **b.** 65-year-old woman with hypertension taking β-adrenergic blockers
- **c.** 42-year-old woman with systemic lupus erythematosus and renal failure
- **d.** 50-year-old man with benign prostatic hyperplasia and a urinary tract infection

3e. It is important for the nurse to assess for which manifestation(s) in a patient who has just undergone a total thyroidectomy? *(select all that apply)*
- **a.** Confusion
- **b.** Weight gain
- **c.** Depressed reflexes
- **d.** Circumoral numbness
- **e.** Positive Chvostek sign

3f. The nurse expects the long-term treatment of a patient with hyperphosphatemia from renal failure will include
- **a.** fluid restriction.
- **b.** calcium supplements.
- **c.** magnesium supplements.
- **d.** increased intake of dairy products.

4. The lungs act as an acid-base buffer by
- **a.** increasing respiratory rate and depth when CO_2 levels in the blood are high, reducing acid load.
- **b.** increasing respiratory rate and depth when CO_2 levels in the blood are low, reducing base load.
- **c.** decreasing respiratory rate and depth when CO_2 levels in the blood are high, reducing acid load.
- **d.** decreasing respiratory rate and depth when CO_2 levels in the blood are low, increasing acid load.

5. A patient has the following arterial blood gas results: pH 7.52, $PaCO_2$ 30 mm Hg, HCO_3^- 24 mEq/L. The nurse determines that these results indicate
- **a.** metabolic acidosis.
- **b.** metabolic alkalosis.
- **c.** respiratory acidosis.
- **d.** respiratory alkalosis.

6. The typical fluid replacement for the patient with a fluid volume deficit is
- **a.** dextran.
- **b.** 0.45% saline.
- **c.** lactated Ringer's solution.
- **d.** 5% dextrose in 0.45% saline.

7. The nurse is unable to flush a central venous access device and suspects occlusion. The *best* nursing intervention would be to
- **a.** apply warm moist compresses to the insertion site.
- **b.** try to force 10 mL of normal saline into the device.
- **c.** place the patient on the left side with the head down.
- **d.** have the patient change positions, raise arm, and cough.

1. d; 2. a; 3a. a, b, e; 3b. a; 3c. c; 3d. c; 3e. a, d, e; 3f. b; 4. a; 5. d; 6. c; 7. d.

For rationales to these answers and even more NCLEX review questions, visit http://evolve.elsevier.com/Lewis/medsurg.

EVOLVE WEBSITE/RESOURCES LIST

http://evolve.elsevier.com/Lewis/medsurg
Review Questions (Online Only)
Key Points

Answer Keys for Questions

- Answer Guidelines for Case Study
- Rationales for Bridge to NCLEX Examination Questions
- Answer Guidelines for Managing Care of Multiple Patients Case Study (Section 3)

Student Case Study

- Patient With Hyponatremia/Fluid Volume Imbalance

Conceptual Care Map Creator
Audio Glossary
Fluids and Electrolytes Tutorial
Content Updates

REFERENCES

1. Henderson R: Osmolality, osmolarity, and fluid homeostasis. Retrieved from www.patient.info/doctor/osmolality-osmolarity-and-fluid-homeostasis.
2. Reddi AS: *Fluid, electrolyte and acid-base disorders*, ed 2, New York, 2018, Springer.
*3. Mentes JC, Gaspar PM: Hydration management, *J Gerontol Nurs* 46:19, 2020.
4. Simon E, Hamrahian S, Teran F: Hyponatremia and treatment. Retrieved from https://emedicine.medscape.com/article/242166-treatment.
5. American Nurse: Beer potomania and hyponatremia. Retrieved from https://www.myamericannurse.com/beer-potomania-and-hyponatremia/.
6. Wooten JM, Kupferman FE, Kupferman JC: A brief review of the pharmacology of hyperkalemia: causes and treatment, *South Med J* 112:4, 2019.
7. Wooten J, Kupferman F, Kupferman J: A brief review of the pharmacology of hyperkalemia: causes and treatment, *South Med J* 112:228, 2019.
8. Drugs.com: Potassium chloride dosage. Retrieved from https://www.drugs.com/dosage/potassium-chloride.html.
9. Wik EM: Digoxin toxicity. Retrieved from https://www.wikem.org/wiki/Digoxin_toxicity.
10. Lewis, JL: Merck manual—professional version: hypercalcemia.. Retrieved from https://www.merckmanuals.com/professional/endocrine-and-metabolic-disorders/electrolyte-disorders/hypercalcemia.
11. Skugor, M: Cleveland Clinic Center for Continuing Education: Hypercalcemia. Retrieved from http://www.clevelandclinicmed.com/medicalpubs/diseasemanagement/endocrinology/hypercalcemia/.
12. Suneja, M: Medscape Nurses: What is the treatment for severe hypocalcemia? Retrieved from https://www.medscape.com/answers/241893-20177/what-is-the-treatment-for-severe-hypocalcemia.
13. Perdue C: Hypercalcemia of malignancy: causes and management, *Cancer Nurs Pract* 19:32, 2020.
14. Lewis J: Merck manual—professional version: hypophosphatemia. Retrieved from https://www.merckmanuals.com/professional/endocrine-and-metabolic-disorders/electrolyte-disorders/hyperphosphatemia.
15. Boyle SM, Goldfarb S: *Phosphate deficiency and the phosphate-depletion syndrome: pathophysiology, diagnosis, and treatment*, New York, 2017, Springer.
16. Cascella M, Sarosh V: StatPearls: Hypermagnesemia. Retrieved from https://www.ncbi.nlm.nih.gov/books/NBK549811/.
17. Gragosian M, Bashir K, Friede R: Hypomagnesemia. *StatPearls.* Retrieved from https://www.ncbi.nlm.nih.gov/books/NBK500003/.
18. Medical News Today. What to know about respiratory alkalosis. Retrieved from https://www.medicalnewstoday.com/articles/324539.
19. Lecturio. Types of intravenous fluids. Retrieved from https://www.lecturio.com/magazine/types-of-intravenous-fluids/.
*20. Shi Y, Yang N, Zhang L, et al.: Chlorhexidine disinfectant can reduce the risk of central venous catheter infection compared with povidone: a meta-analysis, *J Infect Control* 47:1255, 2019.

*Evidence-based information for clinical practice.

Case Study

Applying Clinical Judgment With Multiple Patients

It is 0715 and you are assigned to care for the following 3 patients in the step-down unit. You have an AP to assist you. You have just finished receiving change of shift report.

(© Stockphoto/Thinkstock.)

G.N., a 62-year-old man, was admitted with a urinary tract infection. He has multiple sclerosis and a Stage 2 sacral pressure injury. He is receiving O_2 at 4 L/min via nasal cannula. Vital signs: 118/62, 88 and regular, RR 18, 100.4°F (38°C), and O_2 saturation 93%. His WBC count is 26,400/μL (26.4×10^9/L) with 80% neutrophils (10% bands). The wound dressing needs changed.

(© iStock.com/Cecilie_Arcurs.)

J.N., a 56-year-old male with HIV, chronic hepatitis B, and hypertension, was admitted last night with MRSA cellulitis of his right arm from an abscess he developed from injecting drugs. He is to receive his first dose of IV Vancomycin at 0800. Vital signs: 124/72, 90 and regular, RR 20, 100.4°F (38°C), O_2 saturation 98%.

(© Kevin Peterson/Photodisc/Thinkstock.)

S.S., a 63-year-old woman with acute lymphocytic leukemia, has been receiving chemotherapy on an outpatient basis. She completed her 3rd treatment 5 days ago. She has had nausea and vomiting for 2 days despite using ondansetron. Vital signs: BP 90/50, 112 and regular, RR 22, O_2 saturation 95% on 2L/via nasal cannula. Her last emesis was 3 hours ago.

1. Highlight all the findings above that require your follow-up.
2. Which patient would you see first? Why?
3. Which nursing actions would you include in S.S.'s plan of care at this time? Use an X to indicate which actions listed in the left column would be included in the plan of care for S.S.

Continued

Case Study—cont'd

Nursing Actions	Relevant Nursing Actions
Place S.S. on strict NPO status.	
Suggest a referral to the dietitian for enteral nutrition.	
Provide oral care after episodes of emesis.	
Administer as ordered antiemetics.	
Administer IV fluid replacement therapy as ordered.	
Initiate daily weights and intake and output.	

4. Which morning tasks would you delegate to the AP? *(select all that apply)*
   a. Provide oral care for G.N.
   b. Change J.N.'s saturated arm dressing.
   c. Obtain strict intake and output on S.S.
   d. Take J.N. to radiology for a chest x-ray.
   e. Perform a respiratory assessment on G.N.

Case Study Progression

When preparing J.N.'s AM medications, you note that he is scheduled to receive the following antibiotics at 8 AM: vancomycin 1 gram in 150 mL normal saline over 60 minutes (twice daily) and cefazolin 1 gram in 100 mL normal saline over 30 minutes (every 8 hr). He has 1 IV site in the left arm.

5. Which action is *most* appropriate?
   a. Call the HCP to change the administration times.
   b. Obtain a second peripheral IV site in the right arm.
   c. Check with pharmacy to see if they can be mixed in the same IV bag.
   d. Administer the cefazolin first because it takes the least amount of time to infuse.

After you start J.N.'s IV antibiotic therapy, you ask the AP to obtain vital signs on your other patients while you begin a more thorough assessment of J.N. During your assessment of J.N., you note gray-white patches on the inside of his mouth.

6. You recognize these as *most* likely caused by
   a. *Candida albicans.*
   b. poor oral hygiene.
   c. *Coccidioides immitis.*
   d. irritation from recent mouth care.
7. Choose the most *likely* option for the information missing from statement below by selecting from the lists of options provided.

You receive notification that morning laboratory results are available. S.S.'s chemistry panel results show a serum potassium level of 2.8 mEq/L. Based on this result, the priority need will be prevention of _____1_____. To detect this complication, you will prioritize the assessment of S.S.'s _____2_____.

Options for 1	Options for 2
Diarrhea	Bowel function
Dysrhythmias	Cardiac rhythm
Respiratory depression	Muscle strength

8. Which medication would you administer first?
   a. *Daily* subcutaneous enoxaparin to J.N.
   b. IV Bactrim, ordered twice daily, to G.N.
   c. IV proton pump inhibitor, ordered twice daily, to S.S.
   d. As-needed IV morphine to J.N., who reports pain at a level 9 (1–10 scale)
9. As the day continues, you find that you are getting busy. Which nursing task should be your priority?
   a. Changing the dressing on G.N.'s sacral wound
   b. Reviewing new orders received from the HCP for J.N.
   c. Starting a 500-mL fluid bolus to S.S., whose most recent BP is 76/42
   d. Calling the hospital chaplain to speak with S.S., who is upset over her condition
10. By late morning, you are able to change G.N.'s dressing and perform his assessment. For each assessment finding, use an X to indicate whether the interventions were Effective (helped to meet expected outcomes), Ineffective (did not help to meet expected outcomes), or Unrelated (not related to the expected outcomes).

Assessment Finding	Effective	Ineffective	Unrelated
Urine output clear yellow			
Tunneling present in pressure injury			
Periodic diarrheal stools			
Normal temperature			
WBC count 14,600/μL (14.6×10^9/L)			
Bowel sounds hyperactive x 4 quadrants			

11. While sitting at the computer charting your patients' shift assessments, you overhear the AP telling a nursing student that J.N. deserves what he got because "HIV is God's way of punishing those who sin." Your *most* appropriate response would be to
    a. report the AP's actions to the supervisor.
    b. ask the AP to keep her opinions to herself.
    c. ignore the conversation because it does not affect patient care.
    d. talk to the AP and student about keeping personal feelings separate from patient care.

Answers available at http://evolve.elsevier.com/Lewis/medsurg.

18

Preoperative Care

Janice A. Neil

http://evolve.elsevier.com/Lewis/medsurg/

CONCEPTUAL FOCUS

Anxiety
Patient Education
Safety

LEARNING OUTCOMES

1. Distinguish the common purposes and settings of surgery.
2. Describe the purpose and components of a preoperative nursing assessment.
3. Interpret the significance of data related to the preoperative patient's health status and operative risk.
4. Analyze the components and purpose of the patient's informed consent for surgery.
5. Examine the nursing role in the preparation of the surgical patient.
6. Prioritize the nursing responsibilities related to day-of-surgery preparation for the surgical patient.
7. Discern the purposes and types of common preoperative drugs.
8. Plan care to include special considerations of preoperative preparation for the older adult surgical patient.

KEY TERMS

ambulatory surgery
elective surgery
emergency surgery
informed consent
perioperative
same-day admission
surgery

Surgery is the art and science of treating diseases, injuries, and deformities by operation and instrumentation. The **perioperative** period includes the time before surgery (preoperative period), the time spent during the actual surgical procedure (intraoperative period), and the period after the surgery is over (postoperative period).

The surgical experience involves an interprofessional team, including the patient, surgeon, anesthesia care provider (ACP), nurse, and other health care team members. Preparing patients for surgery is an important nursing role. This chapter discusses preoperative care that applies to all surgical patients. Preparation measures for specific surgeries (abdominal, thoracic, orthopedic surgery) are discussed in the appropriate chapters of this book.

Patients have surgery for many reasons. These include:

- *Diagnosis:* Determine the presence and extent of a pathologic condition (e.g., lymph node biopsy, bronchoscopy).
- *Cure:* Eliminate or repair a pathologic condition (e.g., remove a ruptured appendix or benign ovarian cyst).
- *Palliation:* Alleviate symptoms without cure (e.g., cutting a nerve root to reduce pain, creating a colostomy to bypass an inoperable bowel obstruction).
- *Prevention:* Reduce the risk of developing a condition (e.g., removal of a mole before it becomes malignant, removal of the colon in a patient with familial polyposis to prevent cancer).
- *Cosmetic improvement:* Alter physical appearance (e.g., repairing a burn scar, breast reconstruction after a mastectomy).
- *Exploration:* Determine the nature or extent of a disease (e.g., laparotomy). With the use of advanced diagnostic tests, exploration is less common because we can identify many problems noninvasively.

TABLE 18.1 Suffixes Describing Surgical Procedures

Suffix	Meaning	Example
-ectomy	Excision or removal of	Appendectomy
-lysis	Destruction of	Electrolysis
-orrhaphy	Repair or suture of	Herniorrhaphy
-oscopy	Looking into	Endoscopy
-ostomy	Creation of opening into	Colostomy
-otomy	Cutting into or incision of	Tracheotomy
-plasty	Repair or reconstruction of	Mammoplasty

Surgical procedures are usually described by combining specific suffixes with a body part or organ (Table 18.1).

SURGICAL SETTINGS

Surgery may be a carefully planned event (**elective surgery**) or may arise with unexpected urgency (**emergency surgery**). Both elective and emergency surgeries are done in a variety of settings. The type of surgery, potential complications, and the patient's health status influence the setting where a patient can safely have surgery.

For inpatient surgery, patients are usually admitted to the hospital on the day of surgery (**same-day admission**). Patients who are in the hospital before surgery are usually there because of acute or chronic medical conditions.

Most surgeries are performed as **ambulatory surgery** (also called *same-day* or *outpatient surgery*). Many of these use minimally invasive techniques such as laparoscopy. Ambulatory surgery often occurs in endoscopy clinics, health care providers' (HCP) offices, surgical clinics, and hospital outpatient surgery units. These procedures can involve the use of general, regional, or local anesthetic. Patients require less than a 24-hour stay after surgery. Many go home with a caregiver within hours of surgery.

Patients and HCPs often prefer ambulatory surgery. Generally, it requires fewer laboratory tests and medications. There is a lower risk for health care–associated infections. Patients like the convenience of recovering at home. HCPs prefer the flexibility in scheduling. The costs are usually less for the patient and the insurer.

You play an essential role in preparing the patient for surgery. To perform this function effectively, first identify the reason the patient is undergoing surgery and any comorbidities. Second, assess the patient's response to the stress of surgery. Third, review the results of preoperative diagnostic tests. Last, identify potential risks and complications of the surgical procedure and any special considerations for planning care. The patient is likely to receive care from several different nurses in the preoperative area, operating room (OR), postanesthesia care unit (PACU), surgical intensive care unit (SICU), and/or surgical unit. Document and directly communicate important assessment findings to health team members.

PATIENT INTERVIEW

The preoperative interview is an important nursing responsibility. The nurse who works in the HCP's office, ambulatory surgery center, or hospital may do the interview. It can occur in advance or on the day of surgery.

The primary purposes of the patient interview are to (1) obtain the patient's health information, including drug and food allergies; (2) provide and clarify information about the planned surgery, including anesthesia; and (3) assess the patient's emotional state and readiness for surgery, including their expectations about the surgical outcomes. The interview gives the patient and caregiver an opportunity to ask questions about the surgery, anesthesia, and postoperative care. Often patients ask about taking their routine drugs, such as insulin, anticoagulants, or heart medications, and if they will have pain. By being aware of the patient's and caregiver's needs, you can provide the information and support needed during the perioperative period.

ASSESSMENT OF PREOPERATIVE PATIENT

The overall goal of the preoperative assessment is to identify risk factors and plan care to ensure patient safety. To achieve this, you will need to do the following:

- Establish baseline data for comparison in the intraoperative and postoperative period.
- Determine the patient's psychologic status to reinforce the use of coping strategies.
- Determine physiologic factors related to the planned procedure that may contribute to operative risk factors.
- Participate in the identification and documentation of the surgical site according to agency protocol.
- Identify prescription drugs, over-the-counter (OTC) drugs, and herbs taken by the patient that may result in drug interactions affecting the surgical outcome.
- Review the results of all preoperative diagnostic studies in the patient's record and share this information with the appropriate HCPs.
- Identify cultural and ethnic factors that may affect the surgical experience.
- Determine if the patient received adequate information from the surgeon to make an informed decision to have surgery. Verify that the consent form is signed and witnessed.

Subjective Data

Psychosocial Assessment

Surgery is a stressful event, even for a minor procedure. The psychologic and physiologic reactions to surgery may elicit the stress response (e.g., increased BP and heart rate). The stress response enables the body to meet the perioperative demands, but excessive stressors or responses may affect recovery. Many factors influence the patient's reaction to stress, including age, their experiences with illness and pain, current health, and socioeconomic status. Avoid medical jargon. Use common words and language familiar to the patient. This promotes understanding and reduces anxiety.

Your role in psychologically preparing the patient for surgery is to assess the patient for potential or actual stressors that could negatively affect outcomes (Table 18.2). Communicate all concerns to the appropriate surgical team member, especially if the

TABLE 18.2 **Psychosocial Assessment of Preoperative Patient**

Situational Changes	Concerns With the Unknown	Concerns With Body Image	Experiences	Need for Information
• Define current degree of personal control, decision making, and independence • Determine the presence of hope and anticipation of positive results • Consider the impact of surgery and hospitalization and effects on lifestyle • Identify support systems, including family, other caregivers, and religious and spiritual groups	• Identify degree of anxiety and fears related to the surgery (e.g., pain) • Identify expectations of surgery, changes in current health status, effects on daily living, and sexual activity (if appropriate)	• Identify current roles or relationships and view of self • Determine perceived or potential changes in roles or relationships and their impact on body image	• Review previous surgical experiences, hospitalizations, and treatments • Determine responses to those experiences (positive and/or negative) • Identify perceptions of the planned procedure in relation to the above and information from others (e.g., a friend's view of a personal surgical experience)	• Determine the amount and type of information the patient wants • Assess understanding of surgical procedure, including preparation, care, interventions, preoperative activities, restrictions, and expected outcomes • Review the accuracy of information the patient has received from others, including health care team, family, friends, and media

concern requires intervention later in the surgical experience. Many patients are admitted directly into the preoperative area from their homes, so you must be skilled in quickly assessing important psychologic factors. The most common psychologic factors are anxiety, fear, and hope.

Anxiety. Most people are anxious when facing surgery because of the unknown. This is a normal survival mechanism. However, a high anxiety level can impair cognition, decision-making, and coping abilities.

Anxiety can arise from a lack of knowledge. This can range from not knowing what to expect to uncertainty about the outcome. Past experiences and stories from friends or the media can contribute. You can decrease some anxiety for the patient by giving information about what to expect. This is often done through classes or Web-based or print teaching materials before surgery. Inform the surgeon if the patient needs more information or has excessive anxiety (Box 18.1).

The patient may receive drugs that provide an amnesic effect, so they will not remember what occurs during surgery. Telling the patient this helps decrease anxiety.

Patients may have anxiety when surgery conflicts with their religious or cultural beliefs. For example, patients who are Jehovah's Witnesses may decline to receive blood or blood products.[1] Identify, record, and communicate patient decisions about the possibility of blood transfusions.

Common fears. Patients fear surgery for many reasons. The most common fear is the risk of death or permanent disability. Sometimes the fear comes after hearing or reading about the risks during the informed consent process. Other fears are related to pain, change in body image, or results of diagnostic procedures.

Fear of death can be extremely harmful. Notify the HCP if the patient has a strong feeling of impending death. The HCP may delay the surgery because the patient's emotional state and stress response influence the surgical outcome.

Fear of pain and discomfort during and after surgery is common. If the fear is extreme, notify the ACP or surgeon. Reassure the patient that drugs are available for anesthesia and analgesia during surgery. Tell the patient to ask for pain medication before pain becomes severe. Teach the patient how to use a pain intensity scale (e.g., 0 to 10, FACES). See Chapter 9 for more on pain scales.

BOX 18.1 **EVIDENCE-BASED PRACTICE**

Technology-Based Devices and Preoperative Anxiety

You are taking care of D.G., an 18-year-old woman scheduled for a renal mass biopsy. She was admitted early this morning to the preoperative unit. Unfortunately, an emergency surgery has resulted in at least a 4-hour delay of her procedure. You note that she has a high level of anxiety.

Making Clinical Decisions

Best Available Evidence

Complementary therapies include a variety of interventions such as mental imagery and music. Electronic devices with interactive components may be useful for delivering interventions such as music, games, or videos to help reduce anxiety. Music intervention in the preoperative period, including listening to pre-recorded or personally tailored music given by a trained therapist, can help reduce anxiety. While sedatives and antianxiety drugs are often given before surgery, these drugs can have negative side effects, especially in older adults.

Clinician Expertise

Anxiety can increase BP and pulse rate and may lengthen postoperative recovery. Excessive anxiety can even result in surgery being canceled.

Patient Preference and Values

D.G. tells you that she cannot relax and would like "a strong pill" to help her calm down. D.G.'s family mentioned to you earlier that she enjoys listening to classical music at home.

Implications for Practice

1. What information would you share with D.G. about the use of drugs to reduce her anxiety?
2. How would you respond to D.G. when she asks how an electronic device could help in reducing her anxiety?

Reference for Evidence

Kim J, Chiesa N, Raazi M, Wright KD: A systematic review of technology-based preoperative preparation interventions for child and parent anxiety, *Can J Anaesth* 66:966, 2019.

Fear of mutilation or *altered body image* can occur whether the surgery is radical, such as amputation, or minor, such as breast biopsy. Even a small scar on the body can upset some. Others fear keloid development (overgrowth of a scar). Listen to and assess the patient's concern about this fear with an accepting attitude.

Fear of anesthesia may arise from the unknown, personal experience, or tales of others' bad experiences. These concerns can also result from information about anesthesia risks (e.g., brain damage, paralysis). Many patients fear losing control while under anesthesia. If you identify any of these fears, ask the ACP to talk with the patient.

Fear of disruption of life functioning may range from fear of permanent disability to concern about limiting usual activities for a few weeks. You may find concerns about loss of role function, separation from family, and how the family will manage. Financial concerns include dealing with an expected loss of income and the costs of surgery.

Consulting with the patient's caregiver, a social worker, a spiritual advisor, or a psychologist may be appropriate. Financial advisors at the hospital may provide information about financial options and support.

CHECK YOUR PRACTICE

Your 19-year-old male patient is in the holding area. He is scheduled for an orchiectomy for testicular cancer. He is visibly sweating and agitated. When you ask him how he is doing, he responds, "I am scared. Wouldn't you be?"

- What can you do to reduce his fear?

Hope. Hope may be the patient's strongest method of coping. To deny or minimize hope may negate the positive mental attitude necessary for a quick and full recovery. Some patients hopefully anticipate surgery to repair (e.g., plastic surgery for burn scars), rebuild (e.g., total joint replacement to reduce pain and improve function), or save and extend life (e.g., repair an aneurysm, organ transplant). Assess and support the presence of hope and the patient's anticipation of positive results.

Health History

Ask the patient about health problems and surgeries. Determine if the patient understands the reasons for surgery. For example, the patient scheduled for a total knee replacement may say that relieving pain and restoring mobility are the reasons for the surgery.

Record the reason for any hospitalizations, including surgeries and the dates. Identify any problems with previous surgeries. For example, the patient may have had a wound infection or a reaction to a drug.

Ask women about their menstrual and obstetric history. This includes the date of their last menstrual period, the number of pregnancies, and any history of cesarean section.

When obtaining a family health history, ask the patient and caregiver about any inherited traits since they may contribute to the surgical outcome. Record family history of heart and endocrine diseases. For example, if a patient reports a parent with hypertension, sudden cardiac death, or myocardial infarction (MI), this should alert you that the patient may have a similar predisposition or condition. Obtain information about the patient's family history of adverse reactions to or problems with anesthesia. For example, malignant hyperthermia has a genetic predisposition. If present, measures will be taken to decrease complications associated with this condition (see Chapter 19).

TABLE 18.3 Common Drugs Requiring Preoperative Adjustment

- Angiotensin-converting enzyme (ACE) inhibitors
- Angiotensin II receptor blockers (ARBs)
- Anticoagulants
- Antidepressants
- Antidysrhythmics
- Antiplatelets
- Aspirin
- Corticosteroids
- Diuretics
- Erectile dysfunction drugs
- Estrogen replacement therapy
- Hypoglycemic drugs
- Insulin
- MAO Inhibitors
- NSAIDs
- Oral contraceptive therapy

Medications

Document all current medications, including OTC drugs and herbs. Many surgery centers ask patients to bring in their medications for accurate documentation of the names and dosages.

The interaction of the patient's current drugs and anesthetics can alter the effects of the anesthetics (Table 18.3). For example, some antidepressants potentiate the effect of opioid agents used for anesthesia or pain control. Antihypertensive drugs may predispose the patient to hypotension or shock from the combined effect of the drug and the vasodilator effect of some anesthetic agents. Insulin or oral hypoglycemic drugs may need adjustments during the perioperative period because of increased body metabolism, decreased oral intake, stress, and anesthesia. Antiplatelet drugs (e.g., aspirin, clopidogrel, nonsteroidal antiinflammatory drugs (NSAIDs) inhibit platelet aggregation and may contribute to postoperative bleeding.

HCPs may ask patients to withhold medications before surgery. Specific timeframes for withholding medications depend on the drug and the patient. Patients on long-term anticoagulation therapy (e.g., warfarin, rivaroxaban [Xarelto], apixaban [Eliquis]) present a unique challenge. Options for these patients include (1) continuing therapy, (2) withholding therapy for a time before and after surgery, or (3) withholding the therapy and starting subcutaneous or IV heparin therapy during the perioperative period. The strategy selected is based on the patient and the nature of the surgery.[2]

Ask about the use of herbs and diet supplements because their use is so common. Many patients do not think to include these on their medication list. They believe that herbal and diet supplements are "natural" and do not pose a surgical risk.[3] Herbal supplements taken with anticoagulants or antiplatelet drugs can cause excess postoperative bleeding that may require a return to the OR.[3]

Ask the patient about substance use. This includes tobacco, alcohol, opioids, marijuana, cocaine, and amphetamines. Ask in a frank manner. Stress that substance use may affect the type and amount of anesthesia the patient will need. When patients become aware of the potential interactions of these substances with anesthetics, most patients respond honestly about using them.

Chronic alcohol use can place the patient at risk because of lung, GI, or liver damage. Decreased liver function prolongs the metabolism of anesthetic agents, alters nutrition status, and increases the potential for postoperative complications. Alcohol withdrawal can occur during lengthy surgery or recovery. Proper planning and management help to prevent this life-threatening condition (see Chapter 11).

Record and share the patient's drug history with the perioperative health care team. The ACP will decide the best schedule and dose of the patient's routine drugs before and after surgery. Ensure that you identify all the patient's drugs, implement any changes in the medication plan, and monitor the patient for potential interactions and complications.

Allergies

Ask the patient about drug intolerances and drug allergies. Drug intolerance usually results in side effects that are unpleasant but not life threatening. These include nausea, constipation, diarrhea, or *idiosyncratic* (opposite than expected) reactions. A true drug allergy causes hives and/or an anaphylactic reaction, causing cardiopulmonary compromise (e.g., hypotension, tachycardia, bronchospasm). Being aware of drug intolerances and drug allergies helps the health care team maintain patient comfort and safety.

Record all drug intolerances and allergies and, if needed, place an allergy identification band on the patient on the day of surgery.

! SAFETY ALERT

Allergies

- Some local anesthetic agents contain bisulfite preservatives.
- Notify the ACP if the patient reports an allergy to sulfur-containing drugs.

Ask about nondrug allergies, specifically food and environmental (e.g., latex, pollen, animals) allergies. The patient with a history of any allergic reactions has a greater potential for hypersensitivity reactions to drugs given during anesthesia. Screen all patients for latex allergies by gathering data about:

- Risk factors
- Contact dermatitis
- Contact urticaria (e.g., hives)
- Aerosol reactions
- History of reactions that suggest an allergy to latex

Risk factors for latex allergy include long-term, multiple exposures to latex products, such as those experienced by health care and rubber industry workers. Other risk factors include a history of hay fever, asthma, and allergies to certain foods (e.g., eggs, avocados, bananas, chestnuts, potatoes, peaches).[4] Latex allergies are discussed in Chapter 14.

Review of Systems

The last part of the patient history is the body systems review. Ask specific questions to confirm the presence or absence of any diseases. Current health problems can alert you to areas that you will need to examine in the preoperative physical examination. The combined review of systems and patient history provide essential data to determine the specific preoperative tests that the patient needs.

Cardiovascular system. Evaluate cardiovascular (CV) function to determine preexisting disease or problems (e.g., coronary artery disease, prosthetic heart valve). In reviewing the CV system, you may find a history of hypertension, angina, dysrhythmias, heart failure, or MI. Ask about the patient's current treatment for any CV condition and the level of functioning. A cardiology consultation is often needed before surgery if the patient has a significant CV history (e.g., recent MI, valvular heart disease, implantable cardioverter-defibrillator).

If indicated, the patient should have a 12-lead electrocardiogram (ECG) and coagulation studies, and the results should be on the chart before surgery. The CV assessment provides data on what other measures the patient needs. For example, the patient who is on diuretic therapy needs to have a serum potassium level drawn before surgery. If the patient has hypertension, the ACP may give vasoactive drugs to control the BP during surgery. The patient with a prosthetic heart valve may receive antibiotic prophylaxis before surgery to decrease the risk for infective endocarditis (see Chapter 40).

Venous thromboembolism (VTE), a condition that includes deep vein thrombosis and pulmonary embolism, is a concern for any surgical patient. Immobility and positioning during the operative procedure increase the risk of VTE. Patients at high risk for VTE include those with a history of previous thrombosis, blood-clotting disorders, cancer, varicosities, obesity, tobacco use, heart failure, or chronic obstructive pulmonary disease (COPD).[5] Intermittent pneumatic compression devices (IPCs) may be applied in the preoperative holding area to decrease the risk of VTE.

Respiratory system. Ask the patient about any recent or chronic respiratory problems or infections. Elective surgery may be postponed if the person has an upper respiratory tract infection. Upper airway infections increase the risk for bronchospasm, laryngospasm, decreased O_2 saturation, and problems with respiratory secretions. Report a patient's history of dyspnea at rest or with exertion, coughing (dry or productive), or hemoptysis (coughing blood) to the ACP and surgeon.

If a patient has a history of asthma, ask about the use of inhaled or oral corticosteroids and bronchodilators, as well as the frequency and triggers of asthma attacks. The patient with a history of COPD is at high risk for pulmonary complications, including hypoxemia and atelectasis.

Gather information about the patient's tobacco use. The HCP and you should encourage the patient to stop smoking at least 6 weeks before surgery. Smoking increases the risk for pulmonary complications during and after surgery. Report conditions likely to affect respiratory function such as sleep apnea, obesity, and spinal, chest, and airway deformities. Patients are often asked to bring their sleep apnea devices with them to the hospital or surgical center. Depending on the patient's history and physical assessment, baseline pulmonary function tests and arterial blood gases may be done before surgery.

Neurologic system. Evaluation of neurologic functioning includes assessing the patient's ability to respond to questions, follow commands, and maintain orderly thought patterns. Changes in the patient's hearing and vision may affect responses and the ability to follow directions. Record the patient's ability to pay attention, concentrate, and respond appropriately to establish a baseline for postoperative comparison.

If you note deficits in cognitive function, determine the extent of the problems and whether they can be corrected before surgery. If the problems cannot be corrected, it is important to involve a legal guardian or person with durable power of attorney for health care to aid the patient and provide informed consent for surgery.

Preoperative assessment of the older person's baseline cognitive function is especially crucial for comparison during and after surgery. The older adult may have intact mental abilities before surgery but is more prone to adverse outcomes during and after surgery than the younger adult. This is due to the added stressors of surgery, dehydration, hypothermia, and anesthesia and adjunctive drugs. These factors contribute to *emergence delirium*, a condition that may be falsely labeled as senility or dementia.

Obtain information about any history of strokes, transient ischemic attacks, or spinal cord injury. Ask about neurologic problems, such as myasthenia gravis, Parkinson disease, and multiple sclerosis, and any treatments used.

Genitourinary system. Assess for a history of renal or urinary tract diseases, such as chronic kidney disease or repeated urinary tract infections. Renal problems are associated with fluid and electrolyte imbalances, coagulopathies, increased risk for infection, and impaired wound healing. The kidneys metabolize and excrete many drugs, so a decrease in renal function can lead to an altered response to drugs and unpredictable drug elimination. Many patients have renal function tests (e.g., serum creatinine, blood urea nitrogen [BUN]) before surgery.

Record and share with the perioperative team if the patient has problems voiding (e.g., incontinence, hesitancy). Older male patients may have an enlarged prostate that can interfere with the insertion of a bladder catheter or impair voiding after surgery.

For a woman of childbearing age, assess for pregnancy. Most agencies perform a pregnancy test for all women of childbearing age before surgery.[6] Immediately tell the surgeon if the patient states that she may be pregnant. Maternal and fetal exposure to anesthetics should be avoided during the first trimester.

Hepatic system. The liver is involved in glucose homeostasis, fat metabolism, protein synthesis, drug and hormone metabolism, and bilirubin formation and excretion. The liver detoxifies many anesthetics and adjunctive drugs. The patient with hepatic problems has an increased perioperative risk for clotting abnormalities and adverse responses to drugs. Consider the presence of liver disease if there is a history of jaundice, hepatitis, alcohol abuse, or obesity.

Skin. Ask about a history of skin problems. Assess the current condition of the skin, especially at the incision site, for rashes, breakdown, or other skin conditions. A patient with a history of pressure injuries may need extra padding during surgery. Skin problems can affect wound healing.

Body art such as tattoos and piercings are increasingly common. When possible, select pigment-free areas for injections, IV sites, and laboratory draws.

Musculoskeletal system. Note any musculoskeletal and mobility problems, especially in the older adult. Identify any joints affected by arthritis. Mobility restrictions may influence intraoperative and postoperative positioning and ambulation. Spinal anesthesia may be difficult if the patient cannot flex the lumbar spine enough to allow easy needle insertion. If the neck is affected, intubation and airway management may be difficult. Any mobility aids (e.g., cane, walker) should be with the patient on the day of surgery.

Endocrine system. The patient with diabetes is especially at risk for adverse effects of anesthesia and surgery. Hypoglycemia, hyperglycemia, delayed wound healing, and infection are common perioperative complications of diabetes. Clarify with the surgeon or ACP whether the patient should take the usual dose of insulin or oral hypoglycemic agents on the day of surgery. ACPs may vary the usual insulin dose based on the patient's status and history of glucose control. Measure serum or capillary glucose levels the morning of surgery to establish baseline levels. Assess the patient's glucose levels regularly and, if necessary, manage according to agency protocol.

Determine if the patient has a history of thyroid problems. Hyperthyroidism or hypothyroidism can place the patient at surgical risk because of changes in metabolic rate. If the patient takes a thyroid replacement drug, check with the ACP about giving the drug on the day of surgery. Laboratory tests may be done to determine current levels of thyroid function.

The patient with Addison disease needs special consideration during surgery. Addisonian crisis or shock can occur if a patient abruptly stops taking replacement corticosteroids. The patient may need additional IV corticosteroid therapy to manage the stress of surgery (see Chapter 54).[7]

Immune system. Note if the patient has a history of a compromised immune system or takes immunosuppressive drugs. Corticosteroids used in immunosuppressive doses may be tapered before surgery. An impaired immune system can lead to delayed wound healing and an increased risk for infections.[8] Elective surgery may be canceled if the patient has an acute infection (e.g., sinusitis, influenza). Patients with active chronic infections such as hepatitis B or C, acquired immunodeficiency syndrome, or tuberculosis may have surgery if needed. However, when preparing the patient for surgery, take infection control precautions to protect the patient and staff. Infection control guidelines are discussed in Chapter 15.

Fluid and electrolyte status. Ask the patient about any recent conditions that increase the risk for fluid and electrolyte imbalances, such as vomiting, diarrhea, or completing a bowel prep. Identify drugs that change fluid and electrolyte status, such as diuretics. Serum electrolyte levels are often assessed before surgery. Patients who have fluids restricted before surgery may develop dehydration if surgery is delayed. A patient with dehydration may need more fluids and electrolytes before or during surgery.

Complete a preoperative fluid balance history for all patients. The reduced adaptive capacity of older adults leaves a narrow margin of safety between overhydration and underhydration.

Nutrition status. Knowing that a patient has a nutrition problem can help the health care team provide more customized care. For example, if the patient is thin, place more padding than usual on the OR table. Notify the team if a patient is severely obese (body mass index [BMI] greater than 40 kg/m^2) to allow time to obtain special equipment needed for the patient's care (e.g., longer instruments for abdominal surgery).

Obesity stresses the heart and lungs and makes access to the surgical site and anesthesia administration more difficult.[9] The decreased perfusion of fat tissue predisposes the patient to wound dehiscence, wound infection, and incisional herniation after surgery. The patient may be slower to recover from anesthesia because fat tissue absorbs and stores inhalation agents. See Chapter 45 for the special needs of obese patients undergoing surgery.

Nutrition problems impair surgical recovery. Remember that the obese patient or the very thin patient can be protein and vitamin deficient. If the problem is severe, surgery may be postponed. Protein and vitamins A, C, and B complex deficiencies are particularly important because these substances are essential for wound healing.[10] The older adult is often at risk for malnutrition and fluid volume deficits. Patients who are malnourished may receive supplemental nutrition during the perioperative period.

Identify patients who consume large quantities of coffee or caffeinated drinks. Withholding caffeinated beverages before surgery or for some time after surgery can lead to severe withdrawal headaches.[11] These headaches can be confused with spinal headaches if the preoperative data are not recorded. Giving caffeinated beverages after surgery, when possible, may prevent these headaches.

Objective Data

Physical Examination

The Joint Commission requires that all patients admitted to the OR have a documented history and physical examination (H&P) in their chart.[12] This may be done before or on the day of surgery. Any qualified HCP, including advanced practice nurses, physicians, physician assistants, or ACPs, may perform the H&P. Findings from the H&P enable the ACP to assign the patient a physical status rating for anesthesia administration (Table 18.4). This rating is an indicator of the patient's perioperative risk and may influence perioperative decisions. The scale is P1 to P6. Patients undergoing surgery in ambulatory or outpatient settings generally have ratings of P1, P2, or P3. We can add other designations to the ASA status, such as an "E" to designate an "emergent" procedure.

Complete a physical assessment of the patient before surgery (Table 18.5). Review the documentation in the patient's chart, including the H&P. Record all findings and share any relevant findings at once with the surgeon or ACP.

Diagnostic Studies

Obtain and assess the results of diagnostic studies ordered before surgery (Table 18.6). For example, a patient taking an antiplatelet drug (e.g., aspirin) may have a coagulation profile done, or a patient on diuretic therapy may have a potassium level checked.

TABLE 18.4 American Society of Anesthesiologists' (ASA) Physical Classification System

Rating	Definition
P1 (ASA I)	Normal healthy person
P2 (ASA II)	Patient with mild systemic disease
P3 (ASA III)	Patient with severe systemic disease
P4 (ASA IV)	Patient with severe systemic disease that is a constant threat to life
P5 (ASA V)	Moribund patient who is not expected to survive without surgery
P6 (ASA VI)	Declared brain-dead patient whose organs are being removed for donor purposes

Source: American Society of Anesthesiologists: ASA physical status classification system, 2019. Retrieved from https://www.asahq.org/standards-and-guidelines/asa-physical-status-classification-system.

A woman of childbearing age may have a pregnancy test. An ECG is done for patients who take drugs for dysrhythmias or have high blood pressure. Patients with diabetes undergo blood glucose monitoring. Some settings test patients for methicillin-resistant *Staphylococcus aureus*. Those with positive results are prescribed antibiotics for several days before surgery.[13]

During periods of widespread communicable infections such as pandemics, patients may be tested for a specific organism before surgery. Those who test positive for infection may have non-emergent procedures rescheduled.

Ideally, preoperative tests are ordered based on the patient's H&P. Common tests are listed in Table 18.6. However, many agencies and insurers have protocols for preoperative tests, and some may be done days before surgery. Ensure that all laboratory and diagnostic reports are in the patient's chart. Missing reports may result in a delay or cancellation of the surgery.

NURSING MANAGEMENT: PREOPERATIVE PATIENT

Base the preoperative nursing interventions and patient teaching on the assessment of the patient's specific needs. The pending surgery and routines of the surgery setting guide the patient's physical preparation. The Association of periOperative Registered Nurses (AORN) provides standards and recommended practices to guide nursing interventions in all perioperative settings.[5]

Preoperative Teaching

The patient has a right to know what to expect and how to take part effectively during the surgical experience. Preoperative teaching increases patient satisfaction and can reduce postoperative fear, anxiety, and stress.[14] Teaching may decrease the development of complications, length of hospitalization, and recovery time after discharge.

In most surgical settings, patients arrive a short time before surgery. Preoperative teaching for these patients generally occurs in the surgeon's office or a preadmission surgical clinic. It is reinforced on the day of surgery. Discharge teaching is required for all patients (see Chapter 20). After ambulatory

TABLE 18.5 Preoperative Patient Assessment[a]

Cardiovascular System	• Identify acute or chronic problems. Note presence of angina, hypertension, heart failure, recent myocardial infarction. • Identify any drugs (e.g., aspirin) or herbs (e.g., ginkgo) that may affect coagulation. • Identify patients with prosthetic heart valves, pacemakers, or implantable cardioverter-defibrillators. • Assess for edema (including dependent areas), noting location and severity. • Inspect neck veins for distention. • Obtain bilateral baseline BPs. • Assess capillary refill and pulses for rate, rhythm, and quality: apical, radial, and pedal.
Gastrointestinal System	• Determine patterns of food and fluid intake and any recent changes in weight. • Review usual pattern of bowel movements, including date of last bowel movement. • Assess for presence of dentures and bridges (loose dentures or teeth may be dislodged during intubation). • Auscultate abdomen for presence of bowel sounds. • Weigh patient.
Genitourinary System	• Identify any infection or preexisting disease. • Determine ability to void. • Note color, amount, and characteristics of urine. • Determine pregnancy status (if appropriate).
Hepatic System	• Review any substance use, especially alcohol and IV drug use. • Inspect skin color and sclera of eyes for any signs of jaundice.
Immune System	• Note any immunodeficiency or autoimmune disorders. • Assess for use of corticosteroids or other immunosuppressant drugs.
Musculoskeletal System	• Examine skin around bone pressure points. • Assess for limitations in joint range of motion and muscle strength. • Assess for joint or muscle pain. • Assess mobility, gait, and balance.
Neurologic System	• Determine orientation to person, place, and time. • Assess baseline mental status. Note any confusion, disorderly thinking, or inability to follow commands. • Identify any history of strokes, transient ischemic attacks, or neurologic problems (e.g., Parkinson disease, multiple sclerosis).
Respiratory System	• Identify acute or chronic problems. Note presence of infection, COPD, or asthma. • Note use of continuous positive airway pressure (CPAP) machine. • Assess tobacco history, including date/time of last cigarette and number of pack-years. • Determine baseline O_2 saturation and respiratory rate and rhythm. • Observe for cough, dyspnea, and use of accessory muscles of respiration. • Auscultate lungs for normal and adventitious breath sounds.
Skin	• Determine skin status. Note any current or previous skin problems (e.g., pressure injuries, eczema, bruising). • Inspect skin for rashes, boils, or infection, especially around the planned surgical site. • Inspect mucous membranes and skin turgor for signs of dehydration. • Assess skin moisture and temperature.

[a]See specific body system chapters for more detailed assessments and related laboratory studies.

TABLE 18.6 Common Preoperative Diagnostic Studies

Test	Assessment
ABGs, pulse oximetry	Respiratory and metabolic function, oxygenation status
Blood glucose	Metabolic status, diabetes
Blood urea nitrogen, creatinine	Renal function
Chest x-ray	Lung disorders, cardiac enlargement, heart failure
CBC: RBCs, Hgb, Hct, WBCs	Anemia, immune status, infection
Electrocardiogram	Heart disease, dysrhythmias
Electrolytes	Metabolic status, renal function, diuretic side effects
hCG	Pregnancy status
Liver function tests	Liver status
PT, PTT, INR, platelet count	Coagulation status
Pulmonary function studies	Pulmonary status
Serum albumin	Nutrition status
Type and crossmatch	Blood available for replacement (elective surgery patients may have own blood available)
Urinalysis	Renal status, hydration, urinary tract infection
Test or culture for communicable disease	Presence or absence of communicable disease

TABLE 18.7 **PATIENT & CAREGIVER TEACHING**

Preoperative Preparation

Include the following information in the preoperative teaching plan for the patient and caregiver.

Sensory Information	• Preoperative holding area may be noisy • Drugs and cleaning solutions may be odorous • Operating room (OR) can be cold. Forced air warming devices may be used. Warm blankets are available • Talking may be heard but may be distorted because of masks. Ask questions if something is not understood • OR bed will be narrow. A safety strap will be applied over the thighs • Lights in the OR may be bright • Monitoring machines may be heard (e.g., beeping noises) when awake
Procedural Information	• What to bring and what type of clothing to wear to the surgery center • Any changes in time of surgery • Fluid and food restrictions • Physical preparation needed (e.g., shower, bowel, or skin preparation) • Purpose of frequent vital signs assessment • Pain control and other comfort measures • Why turning, deep breathing, and coughing after surgery are important. Do practice sessions • Insertion of IV lines • Procedure for anesthesia administration • Surgical site may be marked with indelible ink or marker
Process Information	
Information About General Flow of Surgery	• Admission area • Preoperative holding area, OR, and postanesthesia care unit (PACU) • Caregivers can usually stay in preoperative holding area until surgery • Caregivers will be able to see patient after discharge from the PACU or possibly in PACU once the patient is awake • Any technology that may be present on awakening, such as monitors, central lines, intermittent pneumatic compression devices
Where Caregivers Can Wait During Surgery	• Encourage caregivers to ask questions and express any concerns • OR staff will update caregivers during surgery and when surgery is over • Surgeon will usually talk with caregivers after surgery

surgery, the patient usually goes home several hours after recovery, depending on the patient's progress and procedure-specific needs. Teaching must include information that focuses on the patient's safety. Give written materials for patients and caregivers to use for review and reinforcement at home.

When delivering teaching, find a balance between explaining so much that the patient is overwhelmed and telling so little that the patient is unprepared. Observe and listen carefully to the patient to determine how much information is enough. Remember that anxiety and fear may limit learning ability. Assess what the patient wants to know and give priority to those concerns.

Generally, preoperative teaching includes 3 types of information: sensory, process, and procedural. Patients with varying cultures, backgrounds, and experiences may want different types of information. See Table 4.7 for factors affecting patient teaching.

With *sensory information,* patients find out what they will see, hear, smell, and feel during the surgery. For example, you may tell them that the OR will be cold, but they can ask for a warm blanket, and the lights in the OR are bright. Unfamiliar sounds and specific smells will be present.

Patients wanting *process information* may not want specific details but just the general flow of what is going to happen. This information would include the patient's transfer to the holding area, visits by the nurse and the ACP before transfer to the OR, and waking up in the PACU.

With *procedural information,* patients desire specific details. For example, this information would include saying an IV line will be started while the patient is in the holding area, and the surgeon will mark the operative area with an indelible marker to verify the surgical site.[15]

Share the preoperative teaching given to the patient with the nurses providing postoperative care to evaluate patient learning and avoid duplication of teaching. Because there is limited time for teaching, we often use a team approach. For example, teaching may start in the outpatient setting. Your responsibility is to assess the patient's understanding and fill in the gaps.

Record all teaching in the patient's chart. A guide for preoperative patient and caregiver teaching is outlined in Table 18.7. See Chapter 4 for more on patient and caregiver teaching.

◆ General Surgery Information

Unless it is contraindicated (e.g., after craniotomy, tonsillectomy), all patients should receive instruction about deep breathing, coughing, and early ambulation. This is essential because patients may not want to do these activities after surgery unless they know the reasons and practice before surgery. Tell patients and caregivers if tubes, drains, monitoring devices, or special equipment will be used after surgery and explain why. Specific

TABLE 18.8 **Preoperative Fasting Recommendations**

Liquid and Food Intake	Minimum Fasting Period (hr)
Clear liquids (e.g., water, clear tea, black coffee, carbonated beverages, fruit juice without pulp)	2
Breast milk	4
Nonhuman milk, including infant formula	6
Light meal (e.g., toast and clear liquids)	6
Regular meal (may include fried or fatty food, meat)	8 or more

Source: Practice guidelines for preoperative fasting and the use of pharmacologic agents to reduce the risk of pulmonary aspiration: application to healthy patients undergoing elective procedures, *Anesthesiology* 126:376, 2017.

teaching may include how to use incentive spirometers or patient-controlled analgesia pumps. Patients should have a clear understanding of how to rate their pain and how their pain will be managed (see Chapter 9).

The patient should also receive surgery-specific information. For example, a patient having a total joint replacement may wear an immobilizer after surgery. Tell a patient having open heart surgery about waking up in the intensive care unit.

◆ Ambulatory Surgery Information

The patient admitted to the hospital for ambulatory or day surgery needs to receive information before admission. Some ambulatory surgical centers telephone patients several days before the procedure to obtain health information, give instructions, and answer questions. In addition to specifics on the procedure, patients need information on day-of-surgery events such as arrival time, registration, parking, what to wear, what to bring, and the need to have a responsible adult provide transportation home after surgery.

Traditionally, we tell patients having elective surgery to have nothing by mouth (NPO) starting at midnight on the night before surgery. Evidence-based guidelines for healthy patients of all ages undergoing elective surgery (except women in labor) from the American Society of Anesthesiologists are less strict (Table 18.8).[16] Restricting fluids and food is designed to reduce the risk for pulmonary aspiration and nausea and vomiting. Protocols vary for patients having local anesthesia or surgery scheduled late in the day. Follow the protocol of your surgical setting. It is critical that the patient understands and follows all restrictions. The patient who has not followed the NPO instructions may have surgery delayed or canceled.

◆ Legal Preparation for Surgery

Legal preparation for surgery consists of checking that all required forms have been correctly signed and are present in the patient's chart and that the patient and caregiver clearly understand what is planned. Standard consent forms include the surgical procedure and blood transfusions. Other forms may include advance directives and durable power of attorney for health care (see Chapter 10).

◆ Consent for Surgery

Before nonemergency surgery can be legally performed, the patient must voluntarily sign an informed consent form in the presence of a witness. **Informed consent** is an active, shared decision-making process between the HCP and the recipient of care. Three conditions must be met for consent to be valid. First, there must be *adequate disclosure* of the (1) diagnosis; (2) nature and purpose of the proposed treatment; (3) risks and consequences of the proposed treatment; (4) probability of a successful outcome; (5) availability, benefits, and risks of alternative treatments; and (6) prognosis if treatment is not instituted. Second, the patient must show a clear *understanding* of the information before receiving sedating preoperative drugs. If a patient is sedated prior to signing the consent, surgery may be canceled or delayed. Third, the patient must *give consent voluntarily.* The patient must not be persuaded or coerced in any way by anyone to undergo the procedure.

The surgeon is ultimately responsible for obtaining the patient's consent for surgical treatment. You may be asked to witness the patient's signature on the consent form. Serve as a patient advocate, verifying that the patient understands the information in the consent and the implications of consent, and gives truly voluntary consent for surgery. If the patient is unclear about the surgical plans, contact the surgeon about the patient's need for more information. The patient should be aware that consent, even when signed, can be withdrawn at any time (Box 18.2).

If the patient is a minor, unconscious, or mentally incompetent to sign the permit, a legally appointed representative or responsible

BOX 18.2 **ETHICAL/LEGAL DILEMMAS**

Informed Consent

Situation

J.S., a 72-year-old woman, is waiting in the preoperative holding area. You are discussing her impending surgery when you realize that this competent adult does not fully understand her surgery and was not informed of the alternatives to this surgery. Although she has previously signed a consent form, your assessment is that she was not fully informed about her treatment options or does not recall them.

Ethical/Legal Points for Consideration

- Informed consent requires that patients have complete information about the proposed treatment, as well as alternative treatments, risks and benefits of each treatment option, and possible consequences of the surgery. The person (usually the surgeon) performing the procedure usually has this responsibility.
- An opportunity to have questions answered about the various treatment options and their possible outcomes is a crucial element of informed consent.
- A patient can revoke the consent at any time, even at the very last minute. It is essential that you report any circumstance that suggests that the patient does not understand the information or is revoking the informed consent to the person who obtained the consent.
- In most states, the registered nurse's legal role is to witness the signing of the document. This means that as a nurse, you attest to the fact that the patient's signature was valid.

Discussion Questions

1. What do you think you should do next?
2. What is your role as a patient advocate in the informed consent process?
3. What should you do if the patient states that she does not want to know about the surgical procedure or alternatives to surgery?

family member may give written permission. An *emancipated minor* is one who is younger than the legal age of consent but is recognized as having the legal capacity to provide consent. Follow your state's nurse practice act and agency's policies.

A true medical emergency may override the need to obtain consent. The next of kin may give consent when immediate medical treatment is necessary to preserve life or prevent serious impairment to life or limb, and the patient is incapable of giving consent. If reaching the next of kin is not possible, the HCP may begin treatment without written consent. A note in the chart must document the medical necessity of the procedure. In an emergency in which consent cannot be obtained, you will usually need to complete an event report because it is inconsistent with routine agency practices.

Day-of-Surgery Preparation

Nursing Role

Your responsibilities immediately before surgery include final preoperative teaching, assessment, and communication of pertinent findings. Ensure that all preoperative orders are done and that the chart is complete and goes with the patient to the OR. Verify the presence of a signed informed consent form, results of laboratory and diagnostic studies, an H&P, a record of any consultations, baseline vital signs, proper skin preparation, and completed nursing notes. The surgical site is identified and marked with an indelible marker by the surgeon and documented to show that the patient agrees.[15]

Hospitals often require that a patient wear a hospital gown with no underclothes. Surgical centers may allow the patient to wear underwear, depending on the procedure. The patient should remove any cosmetics to allow for observation of skin color. Remove nail polish and artificial nails so you can assess capillary refill and pulse oximetry. Place an identification band on the patient and, if needed, an allergy band (Fig. 18.1). Return all patient valuables to a caregiver or secure them according to agency policy. All prostheses, including dentures, contact lenses, and glasses, are generally removed to prevent loss or damage. If electrocautery devices will be used during surgery, jewelry in piercings must be removed as a safety measure. Leave hearing aids in place to allow the patient to hear instructions. Return eyeglasses to the patient as soon as possible after surgery.

Encourage the patient to void before you give preoperative drugs and before transfer to the OR. An empty bladder prevents involuntary elimination under anesthesia and reduces the risk for urinary retention during the early postoperative recovery.

Many preoperative drugs interfere with balance and increase the risk for a fall during ambulation. Carefully assess each patient for responses to drugs given and adjust the plan of care as needed.

CHECK YOUR PRACTICE

You are caring for an older female patient who received a dose of alprazolam (Xanax) for preoperative anxiety. One hour later, she requests to use the bathroom. You ask her if she can walk, and she replies, "yes." When helping her to stand, she becomes dizzy and almost falls. You return her to bed.

- Instead of trying to help this patient ambulate to the bathroom, what could have you done?

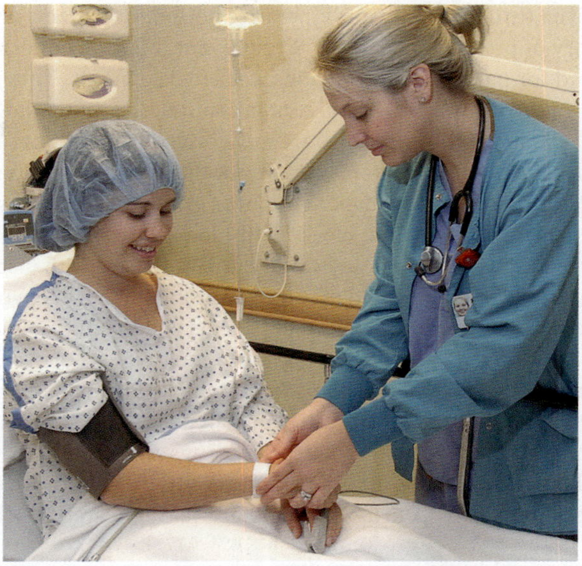

Fig. 18.1 The nurse performs a safety check by verifying that the patient has an identification band (wristband) as part of the preoperative preparations before she goes to surgery. (Courtesy Susan R. Volk, RN, MSN, CCRN, CPAN, Staff Development Specialist, Christiana Care Health System, Newark, DE.)

TABLE 18.9 Drug Therapy

Common Preoperative Agents

Class	Drug	Purpose
Antibiotics	cefazolin	Prevent postoperative infection
Anticholinergics	atropine glycopyrrolate	↓ Oral and respiratory secretions
	scopolamine (Transderm Scop)	Prevent nausea and vomiting Provide sedation
Antidiabetics	Insulin	Stabilize blood glucose
Antiemetics	metoclopramide (Reglan)	↑ Gastric emptying
	ondansetron (Zofran)	Prevent nausea and vomiting
Benzodiazepines	diazepam lorazepam (Ativan) midazolam	↓ Anxiety, induce sedation, amnesic effects
β-Blockers	labetalol	Manage hypertension
Histamine (H_2)-receptor antagonists	famotidine	↓ HCl acid secretion, ↑ pH, ↓ gastric volume
Opioids	fentanyl morphine	Relieve pain during preoperative procedures

Preoperative Medications

Preoperative medications are used for a variety of reasons (Table 18.9). A patient may receive a single drug or a combination. Benzodiazepines are used for their sedative and amnesic properties. Anticholinergics are sometimes given to reduce secretions. Opioids may be given to decrease pain and anesthetic requirements during surgery. Antiemetics can decrease nausea and vomiting.

Other drugs that may be given before surgery include antibiotics, eyedrops, and routine prescription drugs. Antibiotics may be given throughout the perioperative period for patients with a history of prosthetic heart valve to prevent infective endocarditis and for patients with previous joint replacements. They also may be given when wound contamination is a potential risk (e.g., GI surgery). Antibiotics are most often given IV as a single or first dose within 30 to 60 minutes of the surgical incision.

People with known hypertension or coronary artery disease may receive β-adrenergic blockers (β-blockers) to control BP or reduce the chances of MI and cardiac arrest.[17] Those with diabetes are carefully monitored and may receive insulin in the preoperative period. Eyedrops are often given to patients undergoing cataract or other eye surgery. The patient may need multiple sets of eyedrops given at 5-minute intervals. It is important to give these drugs as ordered and on time to adequately prepare the eye for surgery.

Patients may or may not receive drugs they routinely take on the day of surgery. To aid patient teaching and remove confusion about which drugs patients are taking, carefully check written preoperative orders and clarify the orders with the surgeon and/or ACP if needed.

Preoperative drugs may be given by mouth (PO), IV, or subcutaneously. Provide PO drugs with a small sip of water 60 to 90 minutes before the patient goes to the OR unless otherwise ordered. Subcutaneous injections (e.g., insulin) and IV drugs are usually given to the patient after arrival in the preoperative holding area. Teach the patient about the expected effects of the drugs (e.g., drowsiness).

! SAFETY ALERT

Preoperative Checklist

- Use a preoperative checklist (Table 18.10) to make sure you complete all required preparations.
- This is especially important to do before the patient receives any sedating drugs.

TABLE 18.10 Preoperative Checklist

Preoperative Data	Initials
Height _____ Weight _____	
Isolation Y or N Type _____	
Allergies noted on chart Y or N	
Vital signs (baseline)T _____ P _____ R _____ BP _____ Pulse Ox _____	
Chart Review	
H&P on chart	
H&P within 30 days? Y or N	
Signed and witnessed informed consent form on chart Y or N	
Signed consent for blood administration Y or NA	
Blood type and crossmatch Y or NA	
Diagnostic Results	
Hgb/Hct _____/_____ NA	
PT/INR/PTT _____/_____/_____ NA	
CXR _____ NA	
ECG _____ NA hCG _____ Negative _____ Positive _____NA	
Other labs: (example- test for communicable disease)	
Final Chart Review	
Additional forms attached:	

Day of Surgery	Initials
Surgical site marked Y or NA	
ID band on patient Y or N	
Allergy band on patient Y or NA	
Vital signs Time _____ T _____ P _____ R _____ BP _____ Pulse Ox _____	
Procedures	
NPO since _____	
Capillary blood glucose Time _______ Result: _____ NA	
Voided/catheter Time _____	
Preoperative drugs given Time _____ NA	
Preoperative antibiotics given Time _____ NA	
Preoperative skin prep Y or NA Shower_____ Scrub_____ Clip_____	
Makeup, nail polish, false fingernails, and false eyelashes removed Y or NA	
Hospital gown applied Y or NA	
Valuables	
Dentures Y or N	
Wig or hairpiece Y or N	
Eyeglasses Y or N	
Contact lenses Y or N	
Hearing aid Y or N	
Prosthesis Y or N	
Jewelry Y or N Piercings with jewelry Y or N	
Clothing Y or N	
Disposition of valuables: Hearing aid in place Y or NA	

Time to OR ____________________ Date ____________________

Transported to OR by ____________________

Final check by ____________________ RN ____________________

◆ Transportation to the Operating Room

For inpatients, transport staff move the patient by stretcher to the OR. Help the patient in moving from the bed to the stretcher and raise the side rails. Ensure that the completed chart and any needed equipment goes with the patient. In many agencies, the caregiver goes with the patient to the holding area.

In an ambulatory surgical center, the patient may go to the OR by stretcher or wheelchair. If no sedatives have been given, the patient may even walk with someone to the OR. In all cases, it is important to ensure patient safety during transport. Record the method of transportation and the person who transports the patient to the OR. Provide the hand-off communication to the nurse receiving the patient. This allows each of you to ensure you have shared all pertinent patient information. To avoid adverse events related to miscommunication, AORN recommends the use of the Situation-Background-Assessment-Recommendation (SBAR) model for the hand-off process in this setting (see Table 1.3).[18]

Show the caregiver where to wait for the patient during surgery. Many hospitals have a surgical waiting room where OR staff communicate the patient's status to the caregiver(s) and let them know when the surgery is complete. The surgeon can find the caregiver in this room after surgery to discuss the outcome. Some hospitals give pagers to caregivers so that they may eat or do errands during the surgery.

Culturally Competent Care: Preoperative Patient

Include cultural considerations when assessing and implementing preoperative patient care. For example, culture often determines one's expression of pain, family expectations, and ability to verbally express needs. One's culture may require that the family be included in any decision making. For example, many older Hispanic women may defer to their family for the decision of whether to have surgery. Respect these decisions. If the patient or caregiver does not speak English, use a qualified interpreter (translates orally) or translator (interprets written text) communication system. See more on culturally competent care in Chapter 2.

Gerontologic Considerations: Preoperative Patient

Frequently performed procedures in older adults include cataract extraction, coronary and vascular procedures, prostate surgery, cholecystectomy, and joint repair or replacement. Communication is important as the surgeon is usually not the patient's primary HCP. Often several HCPs are involved in the patient's care.

An event that has little effect on a younger adult may be overwhelming to the older patient. Hospitalization may represent a physical decline and loss of health, mobility, and independence. The older adult may view the hospital as a place to die or as a stepping-stone to a nursing home. Help to decrease anxieties and fears while maintaining the self-esteem of the older adult undergoing surgery.

The risks associated with anesthesia and surgery increase in older patients. In general, the older the patient, the greater are the risks for complications after surgery. In planning care, consider the patient's physiologic status, not only the chronologic age. The surgical risk in the older adult relates to normal physiologic aging and changes that compromise organ function, reduce reserve capacity, and limit the body's ability to adapt to stress. This decreased ability to cope with stress, often compounded by the burden of one or more chronic illnesses, and the surgery itself increase the risk for complications.

Confirm and document the patient's goals and treatment preferences. In those with advance directives, discuss any new risks associated with the planned surgery. Make sure the approach for treating any potential problems is consistent with the patient's preferences.

Older adults may have sensory deficits such as reduced vision and hearing. Bright lights may bother those with eye problems. Thought processes and cognitive abilities may be slowed or impaired. Assess and record baseline sensory and cognitive function. Physical reactions are often slowed because of mobility and balance problems. Because of these changes, the older adult may need more time to complete preoperative testing and understand preoperative instructions. These changes require you to pay more attention to promoting patient safety and preventing injury.

You may need to coordinate transportation from a long-term care or assisted living facility so that the patient's timely arrival allows for surgery preparation. A legal representative of the patient must be present to provide consent for surgery if the patient cannot provide informed consent.

Finally, determine the presence of or need for caregiver support for the older adult undergoing surgery. Caregiver support is critical for continuity of care after outpatient surgery and shorter inpatient length of stays.

Case Study

Preoperative Patient

(© Ryan McVay/ Photodisc/Thinkstock.)

Patient Profile

N.T., a 66-year-old retired registered nurse, is admitted to the ambulatory surgery center for a hysteroscopy and dilatation and curettage (D&C) to obtain uterine biopsies after episodes of post-menopausal bleeding. She is obese, has type 2 diabetes, hypertension, and a history of atrial fibrillation. She has been NPO since midnight and did not take her morning medications. It is now 1200.

Subjective Data

- History of hypertension for 20 years; states, "I can't get my blood pressure under control" despite 2 blood pressure medications (diltiazem and HCTZ).
- History of atrial fibrillation with successful cardioversion and control by medications 5 years ago
- History of obesity with adjustable gastric banding procedure 10 years ago.
- Surgical history: cesarean sections at age 30 and 32, gastric banding at age 53. Currently, the band is deflated due to severe acid reflux controlled with omeprazole.

Continued

Case Study—cont'd

Preoperative Patient

- Reports frequent burning in the chest due to reflux. Sleeps with her head elevated
- Lives alone
- Uses herbs to help her sleep.
- Former 1 pack/day cigarette smoker. Quit 5 years ago.
- Drinks 1 glass of wine every night

Objective Data

Physical Assessment

- Alert, cognitively intact, anxious, older woman
- Weight 205 lb, height 5 ft 2 in
- BP 180/94, pulse 84 and regular
- Oxygen saturation 95% on room air
- Medications:
  - Diltiazem 240 mg daily
  - Hydrochlorothiazide 25 mg daily
  - ASA 80 mg daily
  - Omeprazole 20 mg daily
  - Wears glasses. Has trouble seeing without them.

Diagnostic Studies

- Complete blood count values within normal limits
- Serum potassium 3.4, sodium 145, chem 12, PT, PTT, U/A, COVID test, MRSA swab
- Admission serum blood glucose level 120 mg/dL (15.2 mmol/L), glycosylated hemoglobin (Hb A1C) 5%
- Blood glucose level 120 mg/dL (11 mmol/L)
- Serum creatinine 1.2 mg/dL (176 mmol/L)
- Chest X-ray and ECG normal
- Pulmonary function tests negative

Interprofessional Care

- D&C scheduled at 1300 today

Discussion Questions

1. ***Recognize:*** What factors may influence N.T.'s response to hospitalization and surgery?
2. ***Analyze:*** What potential perioperative complications may you expect for N.T.?
3. ***Plan:*** What priority topics would you include in N.T.'s preoperative teaching plan?
4. ***Prioritize:*** Based on the assessment data presented, identify the priority clinical problems and related interventions.
5. ***Act:*** Given N.T.'s history, what priority preoperative assessments would you want to complete and why?
6. ***Evaluate:*** What do you need to continually monitor for N.T. prior to surgery?
7. ***Safety:*** To ensure N.T.'s safety, what preoperative nursing interventions are essential?

Answers available at http://evolve.elsevier.com/Lewis/medsurg.

BRIDGE TO NCLEX EXAMINATION

The number of the question corresponds to the same-numbered outcome at the beginning of the chapter.

1. A patient with obesity (BMI 42.1 kg/m^2) is scheduled for a laparoscopic cholecystectomy in an outpatient surgery setting. Which information would the nurse include in the plan of care?
- **a.** The patient will be in the hospital for several days.
- **b.** Surgery will involve removing a part of the liver.
- **c.** The setting is not appropriate for the planned procedure.
- **d.** Special equipment may be needed for the patient's care.

2. The patient reports that she has noticed a skin reaction when wearing disposable gloves. Which action would the nurse take?
- **a.** Notify the surgeon so that the surgery can be canceled.
- **b.** Ask further questions to assess for a possible latex allergy.
- **c.** Notify the OR staff at once so they can use latex-free supplies.
- **d.** No action is needed because the patient's reaction has no bearing on surgery.

3. A 59-year-old man scheduled for a herniorrhaphy in 2 days reports that he takes an anticoagulant agent daily. Which action would the nurse take?
- **a.** Inform the surgeon since the procedure may have to be rescheduled.
- **b.** Tell the patient to continue to take the drug up to the day before surgery.
- **c.** Ask the patient if he has any side effects from taking this drug supplement.
- **d.** Notify the anesthesia care provider since this drug may interfere with anesthetics.

4. A 17-year-old patient with a leg fracture who is scheduled for surgery is an emancipated minor. She has a statement from the court for verification. Which action would the nurse take?
- **a.** Witness the patient signing the permit after the surgeon obtains consent.
- **b.** Call a parent or legal guardian to sign the permit since the patient is under 18.
- **c.** Notify the hospital attorney that an emancipated minor is consenting for surgery.
- **d.** Obtain verbal consent since written consent is not necessary for emancipated minors.

5. Which intervention would the nurse *prioritize* to aid a preoperative patient in coping with the fear of postoperative pain?
- **a.** Inform the patient that pain medication will be available.
- **b.** Teach the patient to use guided imagery to help manage pain.
- **c.** Describe the type of pain expected after the patient's surgery.
- **d.** Explain the pain management plan and the use of a pain rating scale.

6. A patient is scheduled for surgery requiring general anesthesia at an ambulatory surgical center. The nurse asks him when he ate last. He replies that he had a light breakfast a couple of hours before coming to the surgery center. Which action would the nurse take?
- **a.** Tell the patient to come back tomorrow since he ate a meal.

   b. Have the patient void before giving any preoperative medication.
   c. Proceed with the preoperative checklist, including site identification.
   d. Notify the anesthesia care provider of when and what the patient last ate.
7. A patient who takes metformin 500 mg every morning for control of type 2 diabetes asks if she should take her medication the day of surgery. Which recommendation would the nurse make?
   a. Skip her medication the day of surgery.
   b. Get instructions from the surgeon about medication adjustments.
   c. Take her usual morning dose at bedtime the night before surgery.
   d. Take her medication as usual with a sip of water in the morning.
8. Which preoperative considerations would the nurse plan for the care of an older adult? *(Select all that apply.)*
   a. Using only large-print educational materials.
   b. Speaking louder for patients with hearing aids.
   c. Recognizing that sensory deficits may be present.
   d. Providing warm blankets to prevent hypothermia.
   e. Teaching important information early in the morning.

1. d; 2. b; 3. a; 4. a; 5. d; 6. d; 7. b; 8. c, d.

For rationales to these answers and even more NCLEX review questions, visit http://evolve.elsevier.com/Lewis/medsurg.

EVOLVE WEBSITE/RESOURCES LIST

http://evolve.elsevier.com/Lewis/medsurg
Review Questions (Online Only)
Key Points
Answer Keys for Review Questions
- Rationales for Bridge to NCLEX Examination Questions
- Answer Guidelines for Case Study Conceptual Care Map Creator

Audio Glossary
Content Updates

REFERENCES

1. Jehovah's Witnesses: Why don't Jehovah's Witnesses accept blood transfusions? Retrieved from www.jw.org/en/jehovahs-witnesses/faq/jehovahs-witnesses-why-no-blood-transfusions/.
*2. Patel RB, Tassiopoulos AK: Anticoagulants and surgery: so many agents, so many taking them, *Adv Surg* 53:235, 2019.
3. Society of Gastroenterology Nurses and Associates: Patient safety issues with use of herbal supplements. Retrieved from www.sgna.org/Practice/GI-Nurse-Sedation/Patient-Care-Safety.
4. American College of Allergy, Asthma, and Immunology: Latex allergy. Retrieved from https://acaai.org/allergies/types/latex-allergy.
*5. Hanh BM, Cuong LQ, Son NT, et al.: Determination of risk factors for venous thromboembolism by an adapted Caprini scoring system in surgical patients, *J Pers Med* 9:36, 2019.
*6. Kerai S, Saxena KN, Wadhwa B: Preoperative pregnancy testing in surgical patients: how useful is policy of routine testing, *Indian J Anaesth* 63:786, 2019.
*7. Bonnecaze AK, Reynolds P, Burns CA: Stress-dosed glucocorticoids and mineralocorticoids before intensive endurance exercise in primary adrenal insufficiency, *Clin J Sport Med* 29(6):e73, 2019.
8. Wound care centers: how diabetes affects wound healing. Retrieved from https://www.woundcarecenters.org/article/living-with-wounds/how-diabetes-affects-wound-healing.
*9. Pouwels S, Buise MP, Twardowski P, Stepaniak PS, Proczko M: Obesity surgery and anesthesiology risks: a review of key concepts and related physiology, *Obes Surg* 29:2670, 2019.
*10. Mohapatra S, Gangadharan K, Pitchumoni CS: Malnutrition in obesity before and after bariatric surgery, *Dis Mon* 66:100866, 2019.
11. Sajadi-Ernazarova KR, Anderson J, Dhakal A, Hamilton RJ: Caffeine withdrawal. In *StatPearls*, Treasure Island, FL, 2020, StatPearls Publishing.
12. The joint Commission: History and physical content. Retrieved from https://www.jointcommission.org/en/standards/standard-faqs/critical-access-hospital/medical-staff-ms/000002272/.
*13. Bauer A, Grünewald M, Eberhardt H, et al.: Ambulatory screening and decontamination to prevent *Staphylococcus aureus* complications in patients undergoing elective surgery, *BMC Infect Dis* 20:95, 2020.
14. Aronson S, Grocott M, Mythen MG: Preoperative patient preparation, programs, and education in the United States: state of the art, state of the science, and state of affairs, *Adv Anesth* 37:127, 2019.
15. Rothrock JC: *Alexander's care of the patient in surgery*, ed 16, Philadelphia, 2016, Elsevier.
16. Di Muzio M, Giannetta N, Figura M, et al.: Perioperative nutritional support or perioperative fasting? A narrative review, *G Chir* 40:377, 2019.
*17. Oprea AD, Lombard FW, Kertai MD: Perioperative β-adrenergic blockade in noncardiac and cardiac surgery: a clinical update, *J Cardiothorac Vasc Anesth* 33:817, 2019.
18. Association of periOperative Registered Nurses: *Guidelines for perioperative practice*, Denver, 2020, AORN.

*Evidence-based information for clinical practice.

19

Intraoperative Care

Kimberly Day and Debra Hagler

http://evolve.elsevier.com/Lewis/medsurg/

CONCEPTUAL FOCUS

Gas Exchange
Pain
Perfusion
Safety
Tissue Integrity

LEARNING OUTCOMES

1. Describe appropriate attire for various areas of the perioperative department.
2. Outline the roles and responsibilities of surgical team members.
3. Prioritize needs of patients undergoing surgery.
4. Analyze role of a perioperative nurse in managing patients undergoing surgery.
5. Apply basic principles of infection prevention and aseptic technique in the operating room.
6. Recognize operating room safety measures related to patients, equipment, and anesthesia.
7. Describe various anesthesia techniques and common anesthesia drugs.

KEY TERMS

anesthesia care provider (ACP)
anesthesiology
epidural block
general anesthesia
local anesthesia
malignant hyperthermia (MH)
nurse anesthetist
regional anesthesia
spinal anesthesia

Historically, surgery took place in the hospital operating room (OR). Now, many patients have surgery in outpatient settings. More surgeons are using *minimally invasive surgery* (MIS) techniques and advanced technologies such as endoscopes and robotics that decrease blood loss, incision size, pain, recovery time, and hospital length of stay. Hybrid ORs, which allow for MIS and traditional open incision approaches within the same room, are becoming more common. This chapter describes the basics of intraoperative care that apply to all surgical patients, regardless of where or how the surgery is done.

PHYSICAL ENVIRONMENT OF THE OPERATING ROOM

Department Layout

The surgery department is a controlled environment designed to minimize the spread of pathogens and allow a smooth flow of patients, staff, and equipment for safe surgical patient care. The department is divided into 3 distinct zones: (1) unrestricted, (2) semirestricted, and (3) restricted (Fig. 19.1). The *unrestricted zone* is where people in street clothes interact with those in scrub attire. These areas typically include the points of entry for patients (e.g., preoperative holding area), staff (e.g., locker rooms), and information (e.g., nursing station or control desk). The *semirestricted zone* includes the surrounding support areas and corridors. Only authorized staff are allowed access to semirestricted areas. All staff in the semirestricted area should wear clean surgical attire. This includes scrub attire that was laundered in an accredited laundry facility, long-sleeved jacket, shoes dedicated for surgery use or shoe covers, surgical head cover that covers all head and facial hair, and any appropriate personal protective equipment (e.g., face shield). The *restricted zone* is found within the semirestricted area. It includes the OR or surgical suite where the procedure takes place and the sterile core (Fig. 19.2). Masks should be worn and traffic minimized when sterile supplies are open in the restricted area.[1–3]

The physical layout is designed to reduce cross-contamination. The flow of clean and sterile supplies and equipment is separate from contaminated supplies, equipment, and waste. Staff move supplies from clean areas, such as the sterile core, through the OR for surgery, and on to the instrument decontamination and sterilization area (e.g., central processing department [CPD]).

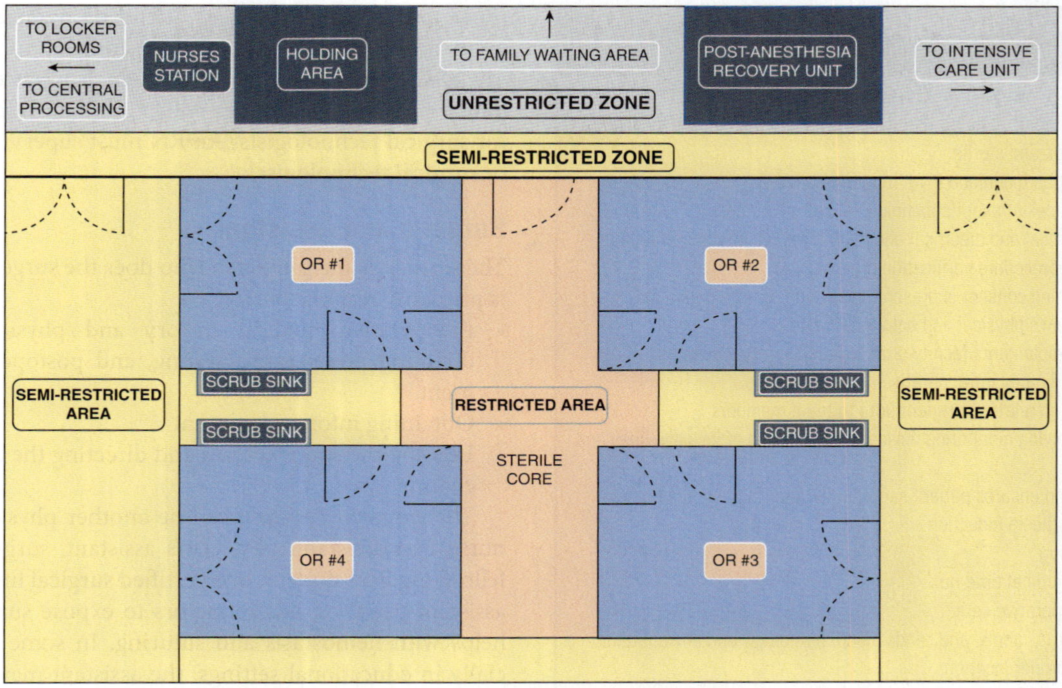

Fig. 19.1 Perioperative department layout.

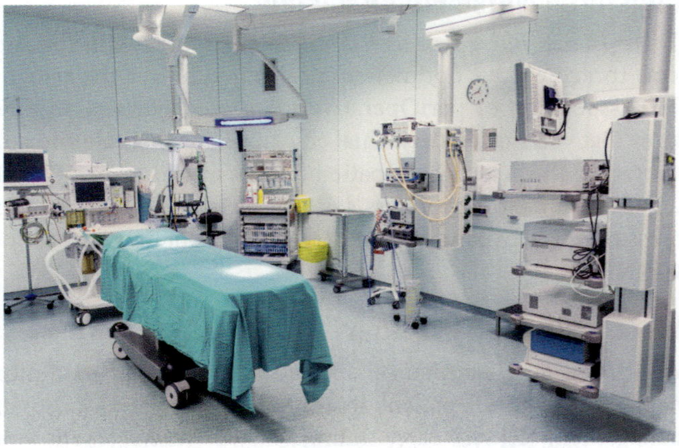
Fig. 19.2 Typical OR. (© iStock.com/windslegend.)

Preoperative Holding Area

The preoperative *holding area* is an unrestricted zone where patient identification and assessment take place. In some settings, the holding area is called the *admission, observation, and discharge* (AOD) unit. An AOD unit is designed to allow early morning admission for outpatient surgery, same-day admission, and inpatient holding before surgery. The patient is identified and assessed before and after surgery, before being discharged home or transferred to an inpatient room. The AOD unit is important in outpatient surgery and prevents unnecessary overnight stays in the inpatient setting.

Operating Room

The traditional OR is a unique setting separate from other clinical units. This restricted zone is controlled geographically, environmentally, and aseptically (Fig. 19.1). Having the OR next to the postanesthesia care unit (PACU) and the surgical intensive care unit allows for quick transport of the patient after surgery and close proximity to anesthesia staff if complications occur.

We use several methods to prevent the transmission of infection in the OR. Filters and controlled airflow in the ventilating systems provide dust control. Positive air pressure in the rooms prevent air from entering the OR from the halls and corridors. Temperature and humidity are controlled to prevent bacterial growth. Ultraviolet lighting reduces the number of microorganisms in the air. ORs have strict protocols for cleaning between cases and terminal cleaning at the end of the day.[1–3]

Furniture that is adjustable, easy to clean, and easy to move promotes safety and comfort. We check equipment frequently to ensure proper functioning and electrical safety. The lighting is designed for a precise view of the surgical site. A communication system offers a way to deliver routine and emergency messages.

SURGICAL TEAM

Registered Nurse

The *perioperative nurse* is a registered nurse (RN) who works with the rest of the surgical team and implements the patient's plan of care during the perioperative period. Depending on the size of the OR department, this role may include 3 domains: (1) preoperative RN, (2) OR RN, and (3) PACU RN. As an OR RN, you are the patient's advocate during surgery. This includes (1) maintaining the patient's safety, dignity, and confidentiality; (2) communicating with the patient, the surgical team, and other departments (e.g., CPD, PACU, laboratory); and (3) providing nursing care as described in this chapter.

During surgery, the OR RN assumes functions that involve either sterile or unsterile activities (Table 19.1). The *scrub nurse* (sterile) follows the designated surgical hand antisepsis with sterile glove and gown attire. They prepare and manage the

TABLE 19.1 Intraoperative Nursing Activities

Circulating, Nonsterile Activities

- Helps prepare room, ensuring that supplies and equipment are available, in working order, and sterile
- Maintains aseptic technique in all required activities
- Monitors practices of aseptic technique in self and others
- Checks mechanical and electrical equipment and environmental factors
- Conducts a preprocedure verification process
- Confirms informed consent is present and patient has no questions
- Assesses patient's physical and emotional status
- Confirms and implements facility protocols and safety measures
- Plans and coordinates intraoperative nursing care
- Checks chart and relates pertinent data to team members
- Helps with applying monitoring devices and insertion of invasive lines and other devices
- Assists with and ensures patient safety in transferring and positioning
- Aids with anesthesia induction
- Monitors draping
- Takes part in surgical time-out
- Records intraoperative care
- Prepares, records, labels, and sends blood, pathology, and any anatomic specimens to proper locations
- Confirms, dispenses, and records drugs used, including local anesthetics
- Coordinates all intraoperative activities with team members and other departments
- Works with scrubbed personnel to keep correct count of sponges, needles, instruments, and medical devices
- Facilitates patient transfer to PACU
- Gives hand-off report to PACU nurse with information relevant to care of patient

Scrubbed, Sterile Activities

- Helps prepare the OR
- Completes surgical hand antisepsis and gowns and gloves self and other members of surgical team
- Prepares instrument table and arranges sterile equipment for use
- Assists with draping
- Takes part in surgical time-out procedure
- Passes instruments to surgeon and assistants by anticipating their needs
- Keeps correct count of sponges, needles, instruments, and medical devices that could be retained in the patient
- Monitors practices of aseptic technique in self and others
- Keeps track of irrigation solutions used for calculation of blood loss
- Accepts, verifies, and reports drugs used by surgeon, including local anesthetics

sterile field and instrumentation. The *circulating nurse* stays in the unsterile field, facilitates the progress of the procedure, and keeps documentation. Examples of nursing activities that occur during each phase of surgery are outlined in Table 19.2.

After meeting specific criteria (e.g., 2 years of experience), perioperative RNs can earn OR certification (CNOR). CNOR certification validates a nurse has essential knowledge and skills in perioperative nursing.[4]

Licensed Practical/Vocational Nurse and Surgical Technologist

Depending on a state's nurse practice act, an LPN/VN or a surgical technologist may fill the role of the circulating or scrub nurse. Surgical technologists attend an associate degree program or a vocational, hospital, or military training program. The Association of Surgical Technologists sets education standards, provides continuing education, and offers certification for surgical technologists. An RN must supervise the LPN/VN or surgical technologist.

Surgeon and Assistant

The *surgeon* is the physician who does the surgery. The surgeon is primarily responsible for:

- Preoperative medical history and physical assessment, directing preoperative testing, and postoperative management
- Obtaining informed consent
- Leading the surgical team and directing the course of a procedure

The *surgeon's assistant* can be another physician, registered nurse first assistant, physician's assistant, surgical resident or fellow, medical student, or a certified surgical first assistant. The assistant usually holds retractors to expose surgical areas and helps with hemostasis and suturing. In some agencies, especially in educational settings, the assistant may perform some parts of the surgery under the surgeon's direct supervision.

Registered Nurse First Assistant

The *registered nurse first assistant* (RNFA) works with the surgeon to achieve an optimal surgical outcome for the patient. The Association of periOperative Registered Nurses (AORN) states that you must have formal education for this role and collaborate with the surgeon, patient, and surgical team.[5] CNOR nurses or nurse practitioners can complete an RNFA program to assume this expanded role. RNFAs can obtain certification (C-RNFA).

Anesthesia Care Provider

Anesthesiology is a medical specialty that focuses on clinical management of the patient in the perioperative period, pain management, critical care, trauma, airway management, and cardiopulmonary resuscitation. The **anesthesia care provider (ACP)** is responsible for administering anesthetic agents and managing vital life functions (e.g., breathing, BP) during the perioperative period. This can be an anesthesiologist, nurse anesthetist, or anesthesiologist assistant (AA).

A **nurse anesthetist** is a master's or a doctorate prepared RN who has graduated from an accredited nurse anesthesia program and completed a national certification examination to become a certified registered nurse anesthetist (CRNA).

The CRNA's scope of practice includes[6]:

- Performing and documenting a preanesthetic assessment and evaluation
- Developing and implementing a plan for delivering anesthesia
- Choosing, obtaining, and administering anesthesia, adjuvant drugs, and fluids
- Choosing, applying, and inserting appropriate monitoring devices
- Managing a patient's airway and pulmonary status

TABLE 19.2 Common Perioperative Nursing Activities

Before Surgery	During Surgery	After Surgery
Home, Clinic, Holding Area • Starts preoperative assessment • Plans teaching appropriate to patient's needs • Involves caregiver **Surgical Unit** • Completes preoperative assessment • Coordinates patient teaching with staff • Develops a plan of care that reflects patient's level of function and ability • Confirms informed consent is present and patient has no questions • Safely gives ordered drugs **Surgical Suite** • Conducts preprocedure verification • Assesses patient's level of consciousness, skin integrity, mobility, emotional status, functional limitations • Reviews chart • Ensures all supplies and equipment needed are available, functioning, and sterile, if appropriate	**Maintain Safety** • Ensures integrity of sterile field • Ensures that sponge, needle, instrument, and medical device counts are correct • Positions patient to ensure correct alignment, exposure of surgical site, prevention of injury • Prevents chemical injury from prepping solutions, drugs • Ensures safe use of electrical equipment • Safely gives ordered drugs **Monitor Physical Status** • Monitors and reports changes in vital signs • Monitors blood loss and urine output **Monitor Psychologic Status** • Gives emotional support to patient • Ensures patient's right to privacy • Communicates patient' emotional status to health care team	**Postanesthesia, Discharge Area** • Determines patient's response to surgical intervention • Monitors ABCs, vital signs, level of consciousness • Safely gives ordered drugs **Clinical Unit** • Evaluates effectiveness of nursing care in OR using patient outcome criteria • Determines patient's level of satisfaction with care given • Assesses patient's psychologic status • Helps with discharge planning **Home, Clinic** • Seeks patient's perception of surgery in terms of effects of anesthetic agents, impact on body image, immobilization • Determines caregiver's perceptions of surgery

- Managing emergence and recovery from anesthesia
- Releasing or discharging patients from a PACU
- Ordering, starting, or modifying pain relief therapy
- Responding to emergency situations by providing airway management

An AA is a master's-prepared health professional who serves under the direction of an anesthesiologist. AAs have completed an accredited program and passed a national certification examination. They take part in all types of anesthesia. This includes giving drugs, obtaining vascular access, applying and interpreting monitors, maintaining airways, and helping with preoperative assessment.

NURSING MANAGEMENT: PATIENT BEFORE SURGERY

The preoperative assessment of the surgical patient provides baseline data for planning intraoperative and postoperative care. Preoperative care of the patient is discussed in Chapter 18.

Assessment

Provide physical and emotional comfort for the patient and caregivers along with teaching about the upcoming surgery. This is particularly important for patients who are anxious and in the same-day surgery settings. There, caregivers must assume greater responsibility for postoperative care. You can usually answer general questions about surgery and anesthesia, such as "Who will be in the room?" "When will my surgeon arrive?" "How much of my body will be exposed?" Refer specific questions about the details of the surgery and anesthesia to the surgeon or ACP. For patients who do not speak English, use a qualified interpreter (see Table 2.9).

Separation from caregivers just before surgery can produce patient anxiety. Allowing the caregiver to wait with the patient in the preoperative holding area until the patient is transferred to the OR can reduce anxiety.

Perform a thorough physical assessment during the preoperative preparation of the patient (see Chapter 18).

Chart Review

Required chart data vary with agencies, patient conditions, and surgery. Table 18.5 provides an example of data obtained during the preoperative assessment. This information gives an understanding of past and present medical history and an opportunity to prepare for potential needs during surgery. Discuss abnormal findings or concerns for infection and other complications with the surgeon or ACP.

> **CHECK YOUR PRACTICE**
>
> Your patient has arrived in the holding area. As you review the chart, you realize the patient has not signed the consent for blood administration. You read that the patient has Alzheimer disease and is not mentally competent to give consent.
> - How would you proceed?

Admitting the Patient

Follow your agency's protocol when admitting the patient to the preoperative holding area and OR. A general routine includes initial greeting, proper identification, and a supportive welcome to the setting.

The admitting process continues with reassessment of the patient and time for last-minute questions. Determine if any other tasks need to be done. Complete the chart review and note any problems or changes. Ask the patient about valuables and prostheses. When was their last intake of food and fluid? Confirm that any ordered preoperative drugs were given. Provide a pillow or adjust the patient's position if requested. Most agencies require the patient's hair to be covered just before transfer to the OR suite to reduce any shedding.

You may offer complementary and alternative therapies, such as aromatherapy, music therapy, guided imagery, and distraction. These therapies may decrease anxiety, promote relaxation, and reduce pain. Some agencies start these therapies before the patient is admitted to the OR. In others, such as ambulatory settings, they may start after the patient arrives in the holding area.

NURSING MANAGEMENT: PATIENT DURING SURGERY

Patient care in the surgical setting is dynamic. Care depends on the nurse's knowledge, skills, and judgment. The circulating nurse is responsible for implementing the intraoperative plan of care and serving as the patient's advocate. The circulating nurse focuses on the whole patient. This involves ongoing assessment, reassessment, and adjusting the care plan to promote the best surgical outcomes.

Room Preparation

Before transferring the patient into the OR, prepare the room to ensure privacy, prevention of infection, and safety. When a patient is severely obese, extra staff and special equipment may be needed to safely position and transfer the patient to and from the OR bed. During surgery, special equipment (e.g., extra-long instrumentation, bariatric OR bed) may be used.

CHECK YOUR PRACTICE

A severely obese patient is admitted to the preoperative holding area before surgery.

- What special considerations are needed to promote a safe surgical experience for this patient?

All people entering the OR wear surgical attire (Fig. 19.3). All electrical and mechanical equipment is checked for proper functioning. Each surgical item is opened and placed on the instrument table using aseptic technique. Sponges, needles, instruments, and small medical devices (e.g., surgical clip cartridges, universal adapters) are counted according to strict processes to ensure accurate retrieval at the end of the procedure. Any retained surgical supplies, devices, or instruments are sentinel events (never events) or serious reportable events (SREs) that can result in negative patient outcomes.[7] Sentinel events and SREs are discussed in Chapter 1.

During room preparation and the surgery, the scrub person does surgical hand antisepsis, dons sterile gown and gloves, and touches only items in the sterile field. The circulating nurse stays in the unsterile field and does those activities that involve contact with all unsterile items and the patient. This coordinated effort allows for smooth work throughout the procedure.

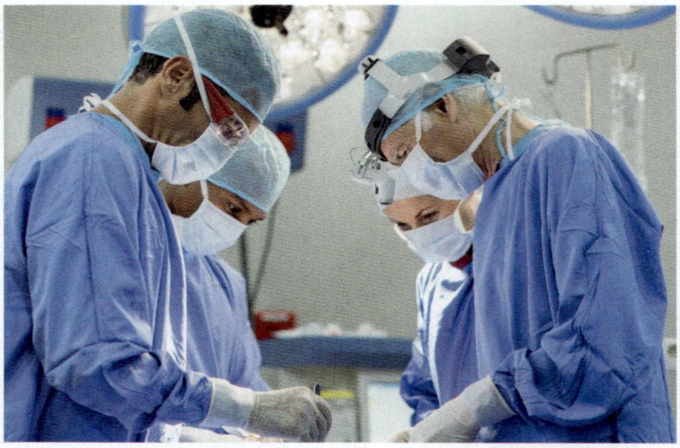

Fig. 19.3 All surgical personnel wear surgical attire. (© iStock.com/Ridofranz.)

Transferring the Patient

The patient is moved into the OR after the preoperative assessment is complete and the surgical suite is ready. Always maintain privacy during transfers through public areas. Cover the patient with a gown and/or blanket. Each time a patient is transferred between beds, the wheels of each bed must be locked. Enough staff using ergonomic tools for safe patient handling and movement should be available to lift, guide, and prevent accidental fall or injury to the patient and staff. Once the patient is on the OR bed, ensure that there is always someone on each side of the patient until a safety strap is secured to prevent falls. The monitor leads (e.g., ECG leads), BP cuff, and pulse oximeter are usually applied after the patient is safely on the OR bed.

Scrubbing, Gowning, and Gloving

Surgical hand antisepsis is required of all sterile members of the surgical team (scrub nurse, surgeon, assistant). When wet scrubbing is used, clean your fingernails first. Follow with scrubbing each plane of individual fingers, palms, and forearms in the distal to proximal fashion. Always hold your hands away from surgical attire and higher than the elbows. This prevents contamination from clothing or detergent suds and water draining from the unclean area above the elbows to the clean and previously scrubbed areas of the hands and fingers.

Waterless, alcohol-based agents are replacing soap and water in many agencies. When using an alcohol-based surgical hand-scrub product, prewash hands and forearms with soap and dry completely before applying the alcohol-based product. After applying the alcohol-based product, rub hands and forearms thoroughly until dry before donning sterile attire.[1]

Once surgical hand antisepsis is completed, the team members enter the OR to put on sterile gowns and 2 pairs of gloves. This protects patients and staff from the transmission of microorganisms.[1,4] Because the gowns and gloves are sterile, those who have scrubbed can touch and organize all sterile items for use during the procedure.

TABLE 19.3 Principles of Aseptic Technique in the Operating Room

- All materials that enter the sterile field must be sterile.
- If a sterile item comes in contact with an unsterile item, it is contaminated.
- Contaminated items are removed at once from the sterile field. If the unsterile item is small (e.g., unopened suture), once it is removed, the area is marked off (i.e., covered with a sterile drape). If the entire field is contaminated, it should be set up again with all new materials.
- The surgical team working in the operative field must wear sterile gowns and gloves. Once dressed for procedure, they must recognize that the only parts of the gown considered sterile are the front from chest to table level and sleeves to 2 inches above elbow.
- A wide margin of safety is maintained between sterile and unsterile fields.
- Tables are sterile only at tabletop level. Items extending beneath this level are contaminated.
- The edges of a sterile package are contaminated once the package has been opened. If a sterile package (e.g., package of sutures) is placed on the sterile field, that entire package stays sterile even when opened.
- Microorganisms travel on airborne particles and will enter the sterile field with excessive air movements and currents.
- Microorganisms travel by capillary action through moist fabrics, resulting in contamination.
- Microorganisms on the patient's and team members' hair, skin, and respiratory tracts must be confined by proper attire.

◆ Basic Aseptic Technique

Aseptic technique is practiced in the OR to prevent infection. This is done by creating and maintaining a sterile field. The center of the sterile field is the site of the surgical incision. Items used in the sterile field, including surgical instruments and equipment, have been sterilized.

Team members must understand specific principles to practice aseptic technique (Table 19.3). If team members do not follow these principles, the patient's safety is compromised and the risk for infection is increased.[1,4]

The surgical team must follow guidelines established by the U.S. Occupational Safety and Health Administration (OSHA) and the AORN to protect the patient and the team from exposure to blood-borne pathogens.[8] These guidelines emphasize (1) standard and transmission-based precautions; (2) engineering and work practice controls; and (3) using personal protective equipment, such as gloves, gowns, caps, face shields, masks, and protective eyewear. This is especially important in the OR because of the high risk for exposure to blood-borne pathogens.

◆ Assisting the ACP

While you check the OR to complete the final preparations, the ACP prepares the patient for receiving anesthesia. You need to understand the effects of the anesthetic agents and know the location of all emergency drugs and equipment.

If you are the circulating nurse, you may be involved in placing monitoring devices used during the procedure (e.g., ECG leads). If the patient is having general anesthesia, stay at the patient's side to ensure safety and aid the ACP. These responsibilities may include measuring BP and helping maintain the patient's airway. During the procedure, you are a vital communication link for the ACP to other departments, such as the laboratory or blood bank.

◆ Positioning the Patient

The surgical team carefully plans the patient's position and monitors the patient throughout the procedure. Positioning is a critical part of every procedure. It usually follows induction of anesthesia. The ACP says when to begin positioning. The position should allow for accessibility to the operative site, administering and monitoring of anesthetic agents, and maintaining the airway. There are a variety of surgical positions.[5] Supine is the most common position. It allows operating on most body systems, including the abdomen, heart, chest, or head. The prone position is often used in spine surgery (e.g., laminectomy). The lithotomy position is used for various gynecologic, genitourinary, and colon procedures. Other common positions include lateral and sitting.

With any position, take great care to prevent injury to the patient. Improper positioning can result in muscle strain, joint damage, pressure injuries, nerve damage, and other untoward effects.

Take care to provide correct musculoskeletal alignment. Prevent occlusion of arteries and veins and undue pressure on nerves, skin over bony prominences, earlobes, and eyes. Make sure there is room for adequate thoracic excursion. Provide modesty in exposure. Recognize and respect patient needs, such as previously assessed pain or deformities. It is your responsibility to secure the extremities, provide adequate padding and support, and have physical or mechanical help to avoid unnecessary straining of the staff and patient.

Because anesthesia blocks the sensory nerve impulses, the patient will not feel pain, discomfort, or stress placed on nerves, muscles, bones, and skin. General anesthesia causes peripheral vessels to dilate. Position changes affect where the pooling of blood occurs. If the head of the OR bed is raised, the lower torso will have increased blood volume and the upper torso may become compromised. Hypovolemia and cardiovascular disease can further compromise the patient's status.

◆ Electrosurgery and Smoke

Care must be taken to correctly place the grounding pad and all electrosurgical equipment to prevent injury from burns or fire. When an electrosurgical unit is in use, the patient must be properly grounded to prevent unintended injury (Fig. 19.4). Excess hair, adipose tissue, bony prominences, fluid (edema), adhesive failure, and scar tissue can compromise safety. Fire in the OR can have devastating consequences for the patient. We can prevent surgical fires with the use of safe practices.[2,3,9]

◆ Preparing the Surgical Site

The purpose of skin preparation, or "prepping," is to reduce the number of microorganisms available to migrate to the surgical wound. The circulating nurse, surgeon, or surgical assistant completes the task of prepping before surgery.

We prepare the skin by mechanically scrubbing or cleansing the surgical site with an antimicrobial agent specific to the

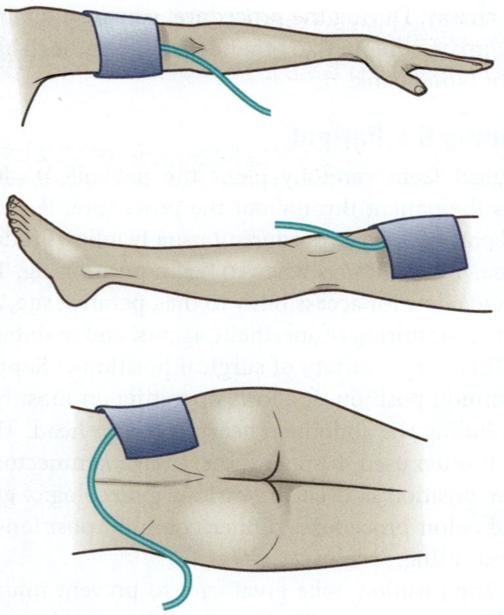

Fig. 19.4 A well-vascularized muscle mass is the best site for grounding. (Courtesy Covidien, Mansfield, MA.)

procedure. Follow manufacturer's instructions for proper application of the prepping agent. Follow the principle of scrubbing from the clean area (site of the incision) to the dirty area (distal to the incision).

Antiseptic agents used for skin preparation may contain alcohol and therefore are flammable. Skin injury can occur if these agents pool under the patient. Take care to ensure that these agents are properly confined and allowed to fully dry. After the skin is prepped, the fumes are allowed to dispel to reduce the risk for fire. The sterile members of the surgical team then drape the area. Only the site to be incised is left exposed.

◆ Safety Considerations

All procedures put the patient at risk for injury. Potential injuries include infection, physical trauma from positioning or equipment, or physiologic effects of surgery itself. Although technical skills, such as operating equipment or proper instrument handling, are a critical part of OR RN competency, nontechnical skills (NTS) also have a high impact on outcomes. These include proper and clear communication, teamwork, situational awareness, and stress and fatigue management.[8] Some agencies use special training programs to develop these NTS. Standard approaches and communication tools can promote safe patient care and minimize the risk for injury.

◆ Communication

Many team members care for the patient in the perioperative process. Chances for error arise whenever team members share information. The Joint Commission requires that all health care providers use a standardized approach to hand-off communication. As an RN, use SBAR (see Table 1.3) to ensure a complete and accurate hand-off every time patient care is transferred to another provider (e.g., change of shift, surgeon to nurse, OR RN to PACU RN).[10]

◆ Surgical Care Improvement Project

The *Surgical Care Improvement Project* (SCIP) is a national quality partnership of organizations focused on improving surgical care by reducing the number of complications from surgery. Specific SCIP measures include (1) a prophylactic antibiotic started within 30 to 60 minutes before the surgical incision to decrease risk for infection, (2) applying a warming blanket to prevent unintended hypothermia, and (3) applying intermittent pneumatic compression devices (IPCs) to minimize the risk for VTE.

◆ Time Out and Surgical Checklist

The National Patient Safety Goals (NPSGs) require a preprocedure verification process.[11] This includes verifying relevant documentation (e.g., history and physical assessment, signed consent forms, nursing and preanesthetic assessment) and the results of any diagnostic studies (e.g., x-rays, biopsy reports). Blood products, implants, devices, and special equipment we expect to be used must be available.

The *Universal Protocol,* one of the NPSGs, is followed to prevent wrong patient, wrong site, and wrong surgery.[6] Wrong surgical procedure and surgery on the wrong body part or wrong patient are *sentinel events (never events)* or *SREs* (described in Chapter 1). The surgeon marks the procedure site. If possible, the patient is involved in the marking.[1]

A patient safety checklist for ORs is the cornerstone of a major focus to make surgery safer. Using the World Health Organization (WHO) Surgical Safety Checklist has improved compliance with standards and decreased complications from surgery (Fig. 19.5). In addition, OR staff complete a fire risk assessment to identify and reduce the risk for a fire.

! SAFETY ALERT

Surgical Time-Out

- Before anesthesia induction, ask the patient to confirm name, birthdate, procedure, site, and consent.
- All surgical team members stop what they are doing just before the procedure starts to verify patient identification, procedure, and surgical site.

❖ MANAGEMENT: PATIENT AFTER SURGERY

Through constant observation of the surgical process, the ACP anticipates the end of the procedure. The ACP gives proper types and doses of anesthetic agents so that their effects will be minimal at the end of the surgery. This allows greater physiologic control of the patient during the transfer to the PACU.

The ACP and the OR RN or another member of the surgical team go with the patient to the PACU. The hand-off, including the patient's status and the procedure done, is communicated to the nurse receiving the patient in the PACU to promote safe, ongoing care.

ANESTHESIA

The American Society of Anesthesiologists (ASA) defines anesthesia according to the effect that it has on the patient's sensorium and

World Health Organization

SURGICAL SAFETY CHECKLIST (FIRST EDITION)

Before induction of anaesthesia ▶▶▶▶▶▶▶▶▶ Before skin incision ▶▶▶▶▶▶▶▶▶▶▶▶▶ Before patient leaves operating room

SIGN IN

- ☐ PATIENT HAS CONFIRMED
  - IDENTITY
  - SITE
  - PROCEDURE
  - CONSENT
- ☐ SITE MARKED/NOT APPLICABLE
- ☐ ANAESTHESIA SAFETY CHECK COMPLETED
- ☐ PULSE OXIMETER ON PATIENT AND FUNCTIONING

DOES PATIENT HAVE A:

KNOWN ALLERGY?
- ☐ NO
- ☐ YES

DIFFICULT AIRWAY/ASPIRATION RISK?
- ☐ NO
- ☐ YES,AND EQUIPMENT/ASSISTANCE AVAILABLE

RISK OF > 5000 ML BLOOD LOSS (7 ML/KG IN CHILDREN)?
- ☐ NO
- ☐ YES, AND ADEQUATE INTRAVENOUS ACCESS AND FLUIDS PLANNED

TIME OUT

- ☐ CONFIRM ALL TEAM MEMBERS HAVE INTRODUCED THEMSELVES BY NAME AND ROLE
- ☐ SURGEON, ANAESTHESIA PROFESSIONAL AND NURSE VERBALLY CONFIRM
  - PATIENT
  - SITE
  - PROCEDURE

ANTICIPATED CRITICAL EVENTS
- ☐ SURGEON REVIEWS: WHAT ARE THE CRITICAL OR UNEXPECTED STEPS, OPERATIVE DURATION, ANTICIPATED BLOOD LOSS?
- ☐ ANAESTHESIA TEAM REVIEWS: ARE THERE ANY PATIENT-SPECIFIC CONCERNS?
- ☐ NURSING TEAM REVIEWS: HAS STERILITY (INCLUDING INDICATOR RESULTS) BEEN CONFIRMED? ARE THERE EQUIPMENT ISSUES OR ANY CONCERNS?

HAS ANTIBIOTIC PROPHYLAXIS BEEN GIVEN WITH IN THE LAST 60 MINUTES?
- ☐ YES
- ☐ NOT APPLICABLE

IS ESSENTIAL IMAGING DISPLAYED?
- ☐ YES
- ☐ NOT APPLICABLE

SIGN OUT

NURSE VERBALLY CONFIRMS WITH THE TEAM:
- ☐ THE NAME OF THE PROCEDURE RECORDED
- ☐ THAT INSTRUMENT, SPONGE AND NEEDLE COUNTS ARE CORRECT (OR NOT APPLICABLE)
- ☐ HOW THE SPECIMEN IS LABELLED (INCLUDING PATIENT NAME)
- ☐ WHETHER THERE ARE ANY EQUIPMENT PROBLEMS TO BE ADDRESSED
- ☐ SURGEON, ANAESTHESIA PROFESSIONAL AND NURSE REVIEW THE KEY CONCERNS FOR RECOVERY AND MANAGEMENT OF THIS PATIENT

Fig. 19.5 WHO Surgical Safety Checklist.

pain perception. These definitions include minimal sedation (e.g., anxiolysis), moderate sedation/analgesia, deep sedation/analgesia, and general anesthesia. The science of providing anesthesia continues to evolve. For example, newer noninvasive technology allows ACPs to track the level of patient awareness (i.e., *awareness monitoring*) during surgery and adjust anesthesia as needed.

The anesthetic technique and agents are chosen by the ACP in collaboration with the surgeon and patient. The ACP has ultimate responsibility for the choice of anesthesia. Contributing factors include the patient's current physical and mental status, age, allergies, pain history, expertise of the ACP, and procedural factors (e.g., length, site, discharge plans). An absolute contraindication to any anesthetic technique or agent is patient refusal.

The ACP obtains anesthesia consent, writes orders for preoperative and postoperative drugs, and assigns the patient an anesthesia classification. The ASA physical status classification system is based on the patient's physiologic status. It uses a scale ASA1 to ASA6 (see Table 18.3).[2] An intraoperative complication is more likely to develop when a patient has a higher classification number.

ANESTHESIA TECHNIQUES

Types of anesthesia techniques include moderate to deep sedation, monitored anesthesia care (MAC), general anesthesia, and local and regional anesthesia (Table 19.4).[12]

Moderate to Deep Sedation

Moderate to deep sedation is used for procedures done outside of the OR (e.g., reducing a dislocated joint in the emergency department). The presence of an ACP is not needed. Trained RNs who are allowed by agency protocols and state nurse practice acts can provide this type of anesthesia under the direct supervision of a physician.

Monitored Anesthesia Care

Monitored anesthesia care (MAC) is used for diagnostic or therapeutic procedures done in or outside of the OR (e.g., endoscopy clinic). MAC includes varying levels of sedation, analgesia, and anxiolysis. A critical part of MAC is the assessment and management of any physiologic problems that may develop. The provider of MAC must be an ACP since it may be necessary to change to general anesthesia during the procedure.

General Anesthesia

General anesthesia is the technique of choice for patients who are having surgeries that are of significant duration, need skeletal muscle relaxation, require uncomfortable operative positions because of the location of the incision site, or need control of ventilation. Other reasons include patient refusal of local or regional techniques, contraindications to other techniques, and uncooperative patients. Patients may be uncooperative due to substance use, emotional lability, head injury, impaired cognition, or inability to remain immobile. Phases of general anesthesia are outlined in Table 19.5.

The goals of anesthesia include controlling biologic responses induced by a variety of stressors and protecting patients from stress-induced complications. To this end, *total intravenous anesthesia (TIVA)* and newer inhalation agents have a fast onset, fast elimination, and fewer undesirable side effects than earlier agents. These factors promote early discharge from the PACU and ambulatory surgery centers.

TABLE 19.4 Anesthesia Techniques and Effects

Technique	Effect on Patient
General anesthesia	• Loss of sensation with loss of consciousness • Combination of hypnosis, analgesia, and amnesia • Usually involves use of inhalation agents • Skeletal muscle relaxation • Eliminates coughing, gagging, vomiting, and sympathetic nervous system responsiveness • Requires advanced airway management
Local anesthesia	• Loss of sensation without loss of consciousness • Induced topically or via infiltration, intracutaneously, or subcutaneously • Topical applications may be aerosolized or nebulized
Moderate sedation/analgesia (formerly called *conscious sedation*)	• Sedative, anxiolytic, and/or analgesic drugs used • Does not include use of inhalation agents • Patient responsive and breathes without assistance • Not expected to induce level of sedation that would impair patients' ability to protect their airway • Most often used for minor therapeutic procedures (e.g., fracture realignment in the emergency department)
Monitored anesthesia care (MAC)	• Sedative, anxiolytic, and/or analgesic drugs used • Does not usually involve inhalation agents • Patient less responsive and may need airway management • Gives greatest flexibility to match sedation level to patient needs and procedural requirements • Often used in conjunction with regional or local anesthesia • Often used for minor therapeutic and diagnostic procedures (e.g., eye surgery, colonoscopy)
Regional anesthesia	• Loss of sensation to a region of body without loss of consciousness • Involves blocking a specific nerve or group of nerves by administering a local anesthetic • Includes spinal, caudal, and epidural anesthesia and IV and peripheral nerve blocks (e.g., interscalene, axillary, infra-/supra-clavicular, popliteal, femoral, sciatic)

Source: American Society of Anesthesiologists: Types of anesthesia, 2021. Retrieved from https://www.asahq.org/madeforthismoment/anesthesia-101/types-of-anesthesia/.

TABLE 19.5 Phases of General Anesthesia

Preinduction	Induction	Maintenance	Emergence
Description			
• Period starting with initiation of IV or arterial access, application of monitors (e.g., ECG), administration of preoperative drugs	• Initiation of drugs that make patient unconscious • Airway secured with airway assist devices (ETT, LMA)	• Period during which procedure is done • Patient stays in an unconscious state with measures to ensure airway safety	• Period when procedure is completed • Patient is prepared for return to consciousness and removal of airway assist devices
Role of Anesthesia Care Provider			
• Determine anesthetic care plan • Insert and monitor IV or arterial access • Confirm antibiotic prophylaxis • Give drugs for anxiety, pain, nausea, aspiration prophylaxis	• Give appropriate drugs • Secure airway • Position patient appropriately for procedure	• Monitor patient's physiologic status • Give drugs and titrate fluids as appropriate	• Reverse residual neuromuscular blocking agents • Assess for return of all protective reflexes • Remove airway assist devices • Assess pain
Role of Perioperative Nurse			
• Complete preoperative assessment • Check and confirm signed informed consent • Complete surgical time-out	• Help with application of monitors (noninvasive and invasive) • Assist with airway management	• Adjust patient position as needed • Monitor patient safety	• Help place dressing • Protect patient during return of reflexes • Prepare patient to move to PACU
Classes of Drugs Used			

• Benzodiazepines
• Opioids
• Antibiotics
• Aspiration prophylaxis:
  • H_2 receptor blockers (e.g., famotidine)
  • Anticholinergics (e.g., scopolamine)
  • 5HT3 antagonist (ondansetron)
	• Benzodiazepines
	• Opioids
	• Barbiturates
	• Hypnotics
	• Volatile gases
		• Benzodiazepines
		• Opioids
		• Barbiturates
		• Hypnotics
		• Volatile gases
		• Neuromuscular blocking agents
			• Reversal agents (PRN):
			  • Anticholinesterases (e.g., neostigmine)
			  • Opioid antagonists (e.g., naloxone)
			  • Benzodiazepine antagonists (e.g., flumazenil)
			  • Neuromuscular block reversal of rocuronium (Zemuron) and vecuronium (Norcuron) (e.g., sugammadex [Bridion])
			• Supplemental opioids (PRN)
			• Antiemetics (PRN)

General anesthesia may be induced by IV or inhalation and maintained by either or a combination of the two (Table 19.6). A *balanced technique,* using adjunctive drugs to complement the induction, is the most common approach for general anesthesia.

IV Agents

All routine general anesthetics begin with an IV induction agent. This agent may be a hypnotic, anxiolytic, or dissociative agent. When used during the initial period of anesthesia, these agents induce sleep rapidly. A single dose lasts only a few minutes. This is long enough for placement of a laryngeal mask airway (LMA) or an endotracheal (ET) tube. Once this is done, the ACP gives inhalation and IV agent(s).[12]

Inhalation Agents

Inhalation agents are the cornerstone of general anesthesia. They may be volatile liquids or gases. Volatile liquids are given through a specially designed vaporizer after being mixed with oxygen as a carrier gas. This gas mixture is delivered to the patient through the anesthesia circuit. Waste gases are removed using negative evacuation pressure venting to the outside of the agency.

Inhalation agents enter the body through the alveoli in the lungs. These agents are easily administered and rapidly excreted by ventilation. Some inhalation agents (e.g., desflurane [Suprane]) have an irritating effect on the respiratory tract. Complications include coughing, laryngospasm, and increased secretions.[12]

Once the patient has been induced with an IV agent, the inhalation agent is usually delivered through an ET tube or LMA. The ET tube allows control of ventilation and protects the airway from aspiration. LMAs are an important option for patients with difficult airways, but they do not provide access to the trachea or airway protection with the same certainty as ETs. Complications of ET tube or LMA use are mainly related to insertion and removal. These include failure to intubate, damage to teeth and lips, laryngospasm, laryngeal edema, sore throat, and hoarseness caused by injury or irritation of the vocal cords or surrounding tissues.

Adjuncts to General Anesthesia

General anesthesia is rarely limited to a single agent. Drugs added to an inhalation anesthetic (other than an IV induction drug) are termed *adjuncts*. Adjuncts are added to the anesthetic regimen to achieve unconsciousness, analgesia, amnesia, muscle relaxation, or autonomic nervous system control. They include opioids, benzodiazepines, neuromuscular blocking agents (muscle relaxants), and antiemetics (Table 19.7). These drugs may have synergistic or antagonistic effects. You may see deeper levels of sedation or more drug-related side effects beyond those seen with inhalation anesthetics alone. If needed, drugs are available to reverse the effects of some of these adjuncts.

Dissociative Anesthesia

Dissociative anesthesia interrupts associative brain pathways while blocking sensory pathways. The patient may appear catatonic, is amnesic, and has profound analgesia that lasts into the postoperative period. Ketamine (Ketalar) (given IV or IM) is a common dissociative anesthetic. It is a potent analgesic and amnesic. Ketamine is being used more often for general anesthesia as research shows it does not increase intracranial pressure. Because ketamine is a phenyl cyclohexyl piperidine (PCP) derivative, the drug may cause hallucinations and nightmares, limiting its usefulness. Concurrent use of midazolam (Versed) can reduce or eliminate the hallucinations. Providing a quiet, calm environment in the PACU is important for patients receiving dissociative anesthesia.

Local and Regional Anesthesia

Local anesthesia interrupts the generation of nerve impulses by changing the flow of sodium into nerve cells. The result is autonomic nervous system blockade, anesthesia, and skeletal muscle flaccidity or paralysis. Local anesthetics are topical, ophthalmic, nebulized, or injected. A local anesthetic is applied to a specific area of the body by the surgeon or ACP. It does not involve sedation or loss of consciousness.

Regional anesthesia (or block) using a local anesthetic is always injected. It involves a central nerve (e.g., spinal) or group of nerves (e.g., plexus) that innervate a site remote to the point of injection. We may administer a local or regional anesthetic concurrently with MAC or moderate to deep sedation (Table 19.4), either preinjection or intraoperatively. Regional blocks are used as preoperative analgesia, during surgery to manage surgical pain, and after surgery to control pain. Indwelling catheters that deliver local anesthetic to the surgical site through a pump implanted during surgery can give continuous pain relief up to 72 hours after surgery.

Advantages of local and regional anesthesia include rapid recovery and discharge with continued postoperative analgesia without any cognitive dysfunction. Local and regional routes can safely be used in those with comorbidities that prevent general anesthesia use.

Disadvantages include the risk for technical problems, discomfort at the injection site, and the inability to precisely match the duration of the procedure. The success of injected local anesthetics may be limited by prolonged duration of procedure or infection at the injection site that interferes with drug absorption. Another disadvantage is the risk for inadvertent vascular injection leading to local anesthetic systemic toxicity (LAST). LAST first presents as confusion, metallic taste, oral numbness, and dizziness.[13] Without treatment, seizures, coma, and dysrhythmias may occur. Treatment for LAST involves lipid emulsion infusion along with respiratory and cardiovascular support.[11]

Topical creams, ointments, aerosols, and liquids are standard ways to administer local anesthesia. These agents are applied directly to the skin, mucous membranes, or open surface. An example is EMLA cream, a combination of prilocaine and lidocaine. It is applied to the site 30 to 60 minutes before a procedure.

In ambulatory or outpatient procedures, you may aid the ACP in administering a peripheral or regional block. You must be familiar with the drugs, including the methods of administration and adverse and toxic effects. Initial patient assessment should include their history with the use of local anesthetics. Have there been any adverse events associated with their use by the patient or blood relatives?

Many patients report "allergies" to local anesthetics. True allergies to local anesthetics are rare. Allergies are likely to be a result of additives or preservatives in the preparation. Some local anesthetics are combined with epinephrine to provide localized vasoconstriction. This decreases absorption and extends the action of the agent. However, if the local anesthetic is absorbed in the tissues or inadvertently injected IV and enters the general

TABLE 19.6 Drug Therapy

General Anesthesia

Drugs	Advantages	Adverse Effects	Nursing Interventions
IV Agents			
Barbiturates			
methohexital (Brevital)	Rapid induction, duration of action <5 min	Cardiac effects (e.g., myocardial depression), ↑ heart rate, ↓ BP, respiratory depression, hiccups, excitation, involuntary movement	Usually have minimal effects after surgery because of short duration of action. ↑ of nausea in patients with barbiturate sensitivity, histamine-triggered nausea and vomiting.
Nonbarbiturate Hypnotics			
etomidate (Amidate)	Has little effect on cardiovascular function Useful for hemodynamically unstable patients. Minor respiratory depression. No histamine release.	Myoclonia, nausea and vomiting, hiccups, adrenocortical inhibition	Monitor vital signs. Observe for myoclonia, nausea and vomiting, hiccups, hypoglycemia.
propofol (Diprivan)	Ideal for short outpatient procedures because of rapid onset of action, metabolic clearance. May be used for induction and maintenance of anesthesia. Has antiemetic and antipruritic properties. No adjustment needed for liver or renal problems.	Bradycardia and other dysrhythmias, ↓ BP, apnea, transient phlebitis, pain during injection, hiccups. May cause hypertriglyceridemia.	Monitor vital signs. Monitor serum triglycerides q24hr when sedated >24 hr.
Inhalation Agents			
Gaseous Agents			
nitrous oxide	Potentiates volatile agents, thus speeding induction and reducing total dosage and side effects. Weak anesthetic, rarely used alone. Good analgesic potency. Anxiolytic properties. Minimal hemodynamic effects.	Little or no toxicity at therapeutic concentrations.	Avoid in patients with bone marrow depression. Must give with O_2 to prevent hypoxemia. Avoid in patients with strong history of nausea and vomiting.
Volatile Liquids			
desflurane (Suprane) isoflurane (Forane) sevoflurane (Ultane)	Cause skeletal muscle relaxation. *desflurane:* Fastest onset and emergence, widely used in ambulatory settings. Least postoperative cognitive dysfunction. *isoflurane:* No increase in ventricular irritability. Does not cause liver or renal toxicity. Resistant to metabolic breakdown. Used for surgical cases longer than 2 hours. *sevoflurane:* Predictable effects on cardiovascular and respiratory systems, rapid acting. Preferred for inhalation induction as nonirritating to respiratory tract. Used for procedures less than 2 hours	Triggers for malignant hyperthermia. All cause respiratory depression, ↓ BP, myocardial depression. *desflurane and isoflurane:* May be unsuitable for patients with coronary artery disease. *desflurane:* May see longer emergence times. Potential airway irritant. *sevoflurane:* May be associated with emergence delirium (see Chapter 20), atypical seizure-like activity.	Assess and treat pain during early anesthesia recovery. Assess vital signs. Observe for prolonged respiratory depression. Monitor for nausea and vomiting.
Dissociative Anesthetic			
ketamine (Ketalar)	Given IV or IM. Potent analgesic and amnesic. Used for patients with hypotension from hemorrhage, hypovolemia, sepsis, or severe cardiovascular compromise. Useful in people with asthma to prevent bronchospasm.	May cause hallucinations and nightmares (midazolam decreases these effects), ↑ heart rate, ↑ BP.	Anticipate use of a benzodiazepine if agitation and hallucinations occur. Calm, quiet environment is essential in postoperative care.

circulation, the patient may have tachycardia, hypertension, and a general feeling of panic.

Examples of common regional nerve blocks include brachial plexus block; IV regional anesthesia (IVRA) or Bier block anesthesia; and femoral, axillary, cervical, sciatic, ankle, and retrobulbar blocks. For IVRA or Bier block, the patient has a double-cuff tourniquet applied to prevent absorption of the drug into the systemic circulation.

You can promote the success of regional anesthesia by properly positioning the patient and using supporting devices (at

TABLE 19.7 Drug Therapy

Adjuncts to General Anesthesia

Agents	Intended Effect	Adverse Effects	Nursing Interventions
Antiemetics (see Table 46.1)			
aprepitant (Emend) granisetron ondansetron (Zofran) palonosetron prochlorperazine rolapitant (Varubi)	Counteract emetic effects of inhalation agents and opioids. Prevent nausea and vomiting related to histamine release, vagal stimulation, vestibular disturbance, procedure (e.g., abdominal laparoscopy).	Headache, dizziness, IV irritation, dysrhythmias, dysphoria, dystonia, dry mouth, central nervous system sedation	Monitor heart rhythm, cardiopulmonary status, level of central nervous system excitation or sedation, ability to move limbs, presence of nausea or vomiting.
Benzodiazepines			
diazepam (Valium) lorazepam (Ativan) midazolam (Versed)	Reduce anxiety. Induce and maintain anesthesia. Induce amnesia. Treat emergence delirium. Supplement sedation in local and regional anesthesia and MAC.	Synergistic effect with opioids, increasing risk for respiratory depression. ↓ BP, ↑ HR. Prolonged sedation or confusion.	Monitor level of consciousness. Assess vital signs and note any for respiratory depression. Reverse severe benzodiazepine-induced respiratory depression with flumazenil.
Neuromuscular Blocking Agents			
Depolarizing agent: succinylcholine (Anectine)	Promote endotracheal intubation. Promote skeletal muscle relaxation (paralysis) to enhance access to surgical sites.	Trigger for malignant hyperthermia. Apnea related to respiratory muscle paralysis. Duration of action of nondepolarizing agents may be longer than surgery. Reversal agents may not completely eliminate effects. Confusion and nausea. Recurrence of muscle weakness with correction of hypothermia.	If intubated, monitor return of muscle strength, level of consciousness, and ventilation. Maintain patent airway. Monitor respiratory rate and rhythm until patient able to cough and return to previous levels of muscle strength. Ensure availability of nondepolarizing reversal agents (e.g., neostigmine) and emergency respiratory support equipment. Monitor temperature and levels of muscle strength with temperature changes.
Nondepolarizing agents: • atracurium • cisatracurium (Nimbex) • pancuronium • rocuronium • vecuronium	Effects of nondepolarizing agents are usually reversed toward end of surgery by giving anticholinesterase agents (e.g., neostigmine).		
Opioids			
alfentanil (Alfenta) fentanyl (Sublimaze) hydromorphone (Dilaudid) morphine sulfate remifentanil (Ultiva) sufentanil (Sufenta)	Induce and maintain anesthesia, reduce stimuli from sensory nerve endings. Provide analgesia during surgery and recovery in PACU.	Respiratory depression, vomiting, ↓ HR, peripheral vasodilation (when combined with anesthetic). High risk for itching when given regional or IV.	Assess respiratory rate and rhythm, monitor pulse oximetry, protect airway in anticipation of vomiting. Use standing orders for antipruritics, antiemetics. Reverse opioid-induced respiratory depression with naloxone. If used, reversal of analgesic effects also occurs. Monitor closely for recurrent respiratory depression requiring an additional dose of naloxone.
Other Agents			
dexmedetomidine (Precedex)	Induces and maintains sedation before and/or during surgery. Anxiolytic properties.	↓ BP, ↓ HR, sinus arrest, transient ↑ BP during administration of loading dose.	Monitor vital signs.

the direction of the ACP) that contribute to the anesthesia (e.g., ultrasound imaging, nerve stimulator, tourniquets). Monitor vital signs during block delivery and manage oxygen therapy. When a patient is receiving regional anesthesia, have airway equipment, emergency drugs, and a cardiac monitor/defibrillator available to provide advanced airway and cardiopulmonary support if needed.

Spinal and Epidural Anesthesia

Spinal anesthesia and epidural anesthesia are also types of regional anesthesia. **Spinal anesthesia** involves the injection of a local anesthetic into the cerebrospinal fluid in the subarachnoid space, usually below the level of L2 (Fig. 19.6A). The local anesthetic mixes with cerebrospinal fluid. Depending on the extent of its spread, various levels of anesthesia are achieved. Because the local anesthetic is given directly into the cerebrospinal fluid, a spinal anesthetic produces autonomic, sensory, and motor blockade. Patients develop vasodilation and may be hypotensive from the autonomic block. They feel no pain because of the sensory block. They cannot move because of the motor block. The duration of action depends on the drug used and the dose given. A spinal anesthetic may be used for procedures involving the extremities (e.g., joint replacements) and lower gastrointestinal, prostate, and gynecologic surgeries.

An **epidural block** involves injection of a local anesthetic into the epidural space via a thoracic or lumbar approach (Fig. 19.6B). The anesthetic agent binds to nerve roots as they enter

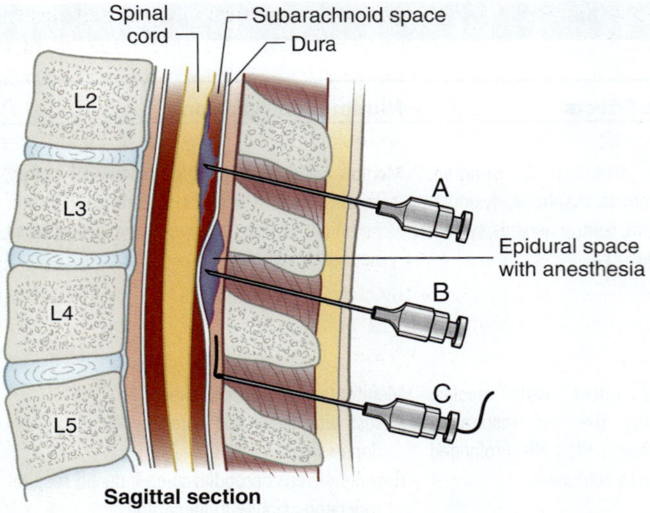

Fig. 19.6 Location of needle point and injected anesthetic relative to dura and spinal cord. (A) Spinal anesthesia. (B) Single-injection epidural. (C) Epidural catheter. (Interspaces most often used are L2–3, L4–5, L3–4.)

and exit the spinal cord. Anesthetic does not enter the cerebrospinal fluid. With the use of a low dose of anesthetic, sensory pathways are blocked but motor fibers are still intact. In higher doses, sensory and motor fibers are blocked. Epidural anesthesia may be the sole anesthetic for a surgical procedure. In addition, a catheter may be placed to allow for intraoperative use and continued analgesia in the postoperative period (Fig. 19.6C). For postoperative analgesia, lower doses of epidural local anesthetic are used, usually in combination with an opioid. Epidural anesthesia is often used for analgesia or in combination with MAC or general anesthesia, in obstetrics, vascular procedures involving the lower extremities, lung resections, and renal and midabdominal surgeries. The desirable effects of vasodilation and analgesia contribute to better surgical outcomes.

With spinal or epidural anesthesia, the patient can stay fully conscious, receive MAC, or choose general anesthesia. The onset of spinal anesthesia is more rapid than that of epidural anesthesia. Both may be extended in duration using indwelling catheters for more doses of anesthetic.

With either anesthesia, closely observe the patient for manifestations of autonomic nervous system blockade. These include hypotension, bradycardia, nausea, and vomiting. There is less autonomic nervous system blockade with epidural anesthesia than with spinal anesthesia. Should "too high" a block be present, the patient may have tingling in the arms and hands, inadequate breathing, or apnea. Other complications include postdural puncture headache, back pain, urinary retention, isolated nerve injury, and meningitis.

Gerontologic Considerations: Patient During Surgery

Aging affects the absorption, distribution, and metabolism of drugs. This results in changes in their onset, peak, and duration independent of the route of administration. Because of this, anesthetic drugs need to be carefully titrated when given to older adults. Physiologic changes with aging may change the patient's response to blood and fluid loss and replacement, hypothermia, pain, tolerance of the procedure, and positioning. Monitor the older adult's response to all anesthetic agents. Postoperative delirium is a common complication and associated with adverse surgical outcomes.[12] Assess the postoperative recovery from anesthesia before the patient is transferred out of the PACU.

Some older adults may have a hard time communicating and following directions because of problems with hearing or vision. This increases the need for clear and concise communication in the OR, especially when the patient is sedated. Because of decreased ability to perceive discomfort or pressure on vulnerable areas and a loss of skin elasticity, the older adult's skin is at risk for injury from tape, electrodes, warming and cooling blankets, and certain types of dressings. Pooled prep solutions in dependent areas can quickly create skin burns or abrasions.

Care and vigilance are needed in preparing and positioning the older patient. The older adult often has osteoporosis and/or osteoarthritis. Misalignment, pressure, or other insults to arthritic joints desensitized from an anesthetic may create long-term injury and disability. Older adults are at a greater risk for perioperative hypothermia. Consider using warming devices. Carefully monitor the patient.

PERIOPERATIVE CRISIS EVENTS

Surgery has inherent risks for an adverse outcome. Some crisis events may be expected (e.g., cardiac arrest in an unstable patient, massive blood loss during trauma surgery). Others occur without warning (e.g., air embolism, hypoxia). Rarer events include anaphylactic reactions and malignant hyperthermia. A crisis demands immediate intervention by all members of the OR team.

Anaphylactic Reactions

Anesthetic agents, antibiotics, blood products, and latex may cause allergic reactions. *Anaphylaxis* is the most severe form of an allergic reaction, with life-threatening pulmonary and circulatory complications. Vigilance and rapid intervention are essential. An anaphylactic reaction causes hypotension, tachycardia, bronchospasm, and pulmonary edema. Anesthesia may mask the initial manifestations of anaphylaxis. Anaphylaxis is discussed in Chapter 13.

Latex allergy has become a concern in the surgical setting. Gloves, catheters, and many devices contain natural rubber latex. Latex allergy protocols in each agency help to provide a latex-safe environment for susceptible patients. Latex allergies are discussed in Chapter 13.

Malignant Hyperthermia

Malignant hyperthermia (MH) is a rare disorder characterized by hyperthermia with skeletal muscle rigidity. It can result in death. MH occurs in genetically susceptible people exposed to certain anesthetic agents.[13] Succinylcholine (Anectine), especially when given with volatile inhalation agents, is the primary trigger of MH. Other factors include stress, trauma, and heat. When MH does occur, it is usually during general anesthesia. It may occur in the recovery period, too.

MH is an autosomal dominant trait. It is variable in its genetic manifestation, so predictions based on family history are important but not reliable. The fundamental defect is hypermetabolism of skeletal muscle resulting from altered control of intracellular calcium. This leads to muscle contracture, hyperthermia, hypoxemia, lactic acidosis, and hemodynamic and cardiac problems. Tachycardia, tachypnea, hypercarbia, and ventricular dysrhythmias may occur but are nonspecific to MH.

MH is diagnosed after ruling out other causes of the hypermetabolism. The rise in body temperature is not an early sign of MH. Unless promptly detected and treated, MH can result in cardiac arrest and death. The definitive treatment of MH is prompt administration of dantrolene (Dantrium, Ryanodex).[14] Dantrolene slows metabolism, reduces muscle contraction, and mediates the catabolic processes associated with MH. Treatment also involves turning off anesthetic agents, providing 100% oxygen, and actively cooling the patient (ice packs in groin, axilla and giving chilled IV fluids). MH can also cause hyperkalemia, disseminated intravascular coagulation, and compartment syndrome.[14] Careful patient monitoring is essential to minimize complications.

To prevent MH, take a careful family history and be alert to the development of MH perioperatively. The patient known or suspected to be at risk for this disorder can receive anesthesia with minimal risk if we take proper precautions. Teach patients with MH about the condition so that family members may consider being genetically tested.

Case Study

Intraoperative Patient

(© wavebreakmedia/iStock.com.)

Patient Profile

G.S., a 23-year-old college student, came to the emergency department with abdominal pain, nausea, and vomiting. He has no medical history. A CT scan shows acute appendicitis. He is scheduled for immediate surgery under general anesthesia.

Subjective Data

- Awake and able to identify himself, his birth date, and surgical procedure
- Rates pain as an 8 on a 0 to 10 scale on arrival to the preoperative holding area

Objective Data

- Peripheral IV catheter in place with LR at 100 mL/hr
- Prescribed cefazolin 1 gm IVPB to be given upon entry into the OR
- Vital signs: heart rate 88, respiratory rate 20, O_2 saturation 99% on room air, BP 124/86, temp 99.3°F (37.4°C)

Interprofessional Care

- Informed consent obtained for the procedure
- Chlorhexidine bath and betadine nasal swabs given for infection prophylaxis

G.S. was taken into the operating room. Induction began with IV medications and inhalation anesthetic followed. G.S. was intubated without difficulty. He is clipped, prepped, and draped for surgery. The surgeon completes the "time out" and begins the surgery. About 10 minutes into surgery, the ACP notices increasing end tidal carbon dioxide level and O_2 consumption. Temperature and heart rate are increased. The ACP suspects malignant hyperthermia and tells the surgical team to begin treatment for malignant hyperthermia.

Discussion Questions

1. ***Recognize:*** What are the usual manifestations of malignant hyperthermia? Explain the pathophysiologic process.
2. ***Analyze:*** What complications is G.S. at risk for if he experiences malignant hyperthermia?
3. ***Plan***: What therapy do you expect?
4. ***Prioritize***: What is the interprofessional team's priority for G.S. at this time?
5. ***Act:*** What activities can you delegate to assistive personnel (AP)?
6. ***Evaluate***: What do you need to continually monitor?
7. ***Safety:*** Describe specific nursing actions you will take to prevent injury and promote patient safety.

Answers available at http://evolve.elsevier.com/Lewis/medsurg.

BRIDGE TO NCLEX EXAMINATION

The number of the questions corresponds to the same-numbered outcome at the beginning of the chapter.

1. Which items would the nurse wear for proper attire in the semirestricted area of the surgery department?
   a. Street clothing
   b. Surgical attire and head cover
   c. Street clothing and shoe covers
   d. Surgical attire, head cover, shoe covers
2. Which activities might the nurse perform in the role of a scrub nurse during surgery? (*select all that apply*)
   a. Checking electrical equipment
   b. Preparing the instrument table
   c. Assisting with draping the patient
   d. Passing instruments to the surgeon and assistants
   e. Documenting activities occurring in the operating room
3. The nurse is caring for a patient undergoing surgery for a knee replacement. Which factors are critical to the patient's safety during the procedure? (*select all that apply*)
   a. Universal protocol is followed.
   b. The ACP is an anesthesiologist.
   c. The patient has adequate health insurance.
   d. The patient's family is in the surgery waiting area.
   e. The patient's allergies are conveyed to the surgical team.
4. Which action is the nurse's *primary* responsibility for the care of the patient undergoing surgery?
   a. Developing a patient-centered plan of nursing care
   b. Carrying out tasks related to surgical policies and procedure
   c. Ensuring that the patient has been assessed for safe administration of anesthesia
   d. Performing a preoperative history and physical assessment to identify patient needs

5. Which action would the nurse take when scrubbing at the scrub sink?
   a. Scrub from elbows to hands
   b. Scrub without mechanical friction
   c. Scrub for a minimum of 10 minutes
   d. Hold the hands higher than the elbows
6. Which factors in positioning a patient for surgery increase the risk of patient injury? *(select all that apply)*
   a. Loss of pain perception
   b. Incorrect musculoskeletal alignment
   c. Vasoconstriction of the peripheral vessels
   d. Hypovolemia contributing to decreased perfusion
   e. Inability to sense pressure over bony prominences
7. Why is IV induction for general anesthesia the method of choice for *most* patients?
   a. The patient is not intubated.
   b. The agents are nonexplosive.
   c. Induction is rapid and controlled.
   d. Emergence is longer but with fewer complications.

1. d; 2. b, c, d; 3. a, e; 4. a; 5. d; 6. a, b, d, e; 7. c.

For rationales to these answers and even more NCLEX review questions, visit http://evolve.elsevier.com/Lewis/medsurg.

EVOLVE WEBSITE/RESOURCES LIST

http://evolve.elsevier.com/Lewis/medsurg
Review Questions (Online Only)
Key Points
Answer Keys for Questions
- Rationales for Bridge to NCLEX Examination Questions

Conceptual Care Map Creator
Audio Glossary
Content Updates

REFERENCES

1. Association of periOperative Registered Nurses (AORN): *2021 Edition: guidelines for perioperative practice*, Denver, 2021, AORN.
2. Rothrock JC: *Alexander's care of the patient in surgery*, ed 16, St. Louis, 2019, Elsevier.
3. Phillips N: *Berry & Kohn's operating room technique*, ed 14, St. Louis, 2020, Elsevier.
4. Competency and Credentialing Institute: CNOR certification. Retrieved from https://www.cc-institute.org/learn/.
5. AORN: AORN position statement on RN first assistants. Retrieved from https://www.aorn.org/-/media/aorn/guidelines/position-statements/aorn_position_statement_rnfa.pdf.
6. American Association of Nurse Anesthetists: Scope of nurse anesthesia practice. Retrieved from. https://www.aana.com/docs/default-source/practice-aana-com-web-documents-(all)/professional-practice-manual/scope-of-nurse-anesthesia-practice.pdf?sfvrsn=250049b1_6.
7. AORN: Guideline update: prevention of retained surgical items. Retrieved from https://www.aorn.org/essentials/retained-surgical-items.
8. Occupational Safety and Health Administration: Bloodborne pathogens and needlestick prevention. Retrieved from https://www.osha.gov/bloodborne-pathogens.
9. Association of periOperative Registered Nurses: Electrosurgery: guideline update 2021. Retrieved from https://www.aorn.org/essentials/electrosurgical-safety.
10. AORN: AORN guideline on team communication. Retrieved from https://www.aorn.org/essentials/team-communication.
11. The Joint Commission: National Patient Safety Goals. Retrieved from https://www.jointcommission.org/-/media/tjc/documents/standards/national-patient-safety-goals/2021/npsg_chapter_hap_jan2021.pdf.
12. Smith G, D'Cruz JR, Rondeau B, et al.: General anesthesia for surgeons. Retrieved from https://www.ncbi.nlm.nih.gov/books/NBK493199/.
13. Macfarlane AJR, Gitman M, Bornstein KJ, et al.: Updates in our understanding of local anaesthetic systemic toxicity: a narrative review, *Anaesthesia* 76:S1, 2021.
14. Hopkins PM, Girard T, Dalay S, et al.: Malignant hyperthermia, *Anaesthesia* 76:655, 2021.

20

Postoperative Care

Diane M. Rudolphi

http://evolve.elsevier.com/Lewis/medsurg/

CONCEPTUAL FOCUS

Gas Exchange
Fluids and Electrolytes
Infection
Pain
Perfusion
Safety
Tissue Integrity

LEARNING OUTCOMES

1. Prioritize nursing responsibilities related to managing patients in the postanesthesia care unit (PACU).
2. Prioritize nursing responsibilities to maintain patient safety and prevent postoperative complications in the PACU and clinical unit.
3. Apply data from the initial nursing assessment to the management of the patient after transfer from the PACU to the clinical unit.
4. Select nursing interventions to manage potential problems during the postoperative period.
5. Distinguish discharge criteria from Phase I and Phase II postanesthesia care.

KEY TERMS

airway obstruction
atelectasis
delayed emergence
emergence delirium
patient-controlled analgesia (PCA)
postoperative ileus (POI)

The postoperative period begins immediately after surgery and continues until the patient is discharged from care. As the nurse, you play a vital role in supporting ventilation and perfusion, maintaining fluid and electrolyte balance, promoting comfort, reducing infection, and promoting safety. This chapter focuses on the concepts central to postoperative nursing. Specific surgeries and their related postoperative care are discussed in other chapters of this text.

POSTOPERATIVE CARE OF SURGICAL PATIENT

The patient's immediate recovery period takes place in a *postanesthesia care unit (PACU)*. It is usually next to the operating room (OR). This location limits transportation of the patient right after surgery and gives ready access to anesthesia and OR staff. The goals of PACU care are to maintain patient safety during recovery from anesthesia, identify actual and potential patient problems that may occur because of anesthesia and surgery, and intervene appropriately. Patients in the PACU need frequent assessment and intervention.

Postanesthesia Care Unit Admission

The patient's initial admission into the PACU is a joint effort among the health care team. This includes the surgeon, anesthesia care provider (ACP), OR nurse, and PACU nurse. This collaboration fosters a smooth transfer of care to the PACU and helps determine which phase of care we provide to the patient.

PACU Progression

There are 3 phases of postanesthesia care. During each phase, we provide different levels of care depending on the patient's needs (Table 20.1).[1,2] Patients move through the phases of care as determined by their condition and the type of anesthesia received. If a patient assigned to Phase I care on admission to the PACU is stable and recovering well, the patient may rapidly progress through Phase I to either Phase II care or an inpatient unit. An accelerated system of care called fast-tracking involves admitting ambulatory surgery patients directly to Phase II care. Although fast-tracking can result in time and cost savings, the patient's safety is the primary factor determining where and at what level we provide postoperative care. Phase III is a phase in

TABLE 20.1 Phases of Postanesthesia Care

Phase I
- Care during the immediate postanesthesia period.
- ECG and more intense monitoring (e.g., arterial BP monitoring, mechanical ventilation). *Goal:* Prepare patient for transfer to Phase II level of care, an inpatient unit, or intensive care setting.

Phase II
- Ambulatory surgery patients.
- Fast-tracking (i.e., patients who have bypassed Phase I level of care). *Goal:* Prepare patient for transfer to extended observation, home, or extended care facility.

Extended Observation
- Extended care or observation after transfer/discharge from Phase I or Phase II levels of care. *Goal:* Prepare patient for self-care.

Blended Levels of Care
- Various levels of care offered in the same environment.

Source: American Society of PeriAnesthesia Nurses: *2015–2017 Perianesthesia nursing standards, practice recommendations and interpretive statements,* Cherry Hill, NJ, 2015, The Society.

which the patient may be delayed from progressing out of the PACU (e.g., if beds are not available on the units).[3]

Phase I Initial Assessment

As the patient is admitted to the PACU, the ACP gives a postanesthesia hand-off report (Table 20.2). Hand-off reports should be standardized and interactive, allowing you to ask questions and clarify information.[1,3] The ACP should stay in the PACU until you accept responsibility for the care of the patient. Potential problems in the postoperative period are shown in Fig. 20.1. Table 20.3 describes key parts of a PACU assessment.

Begin your initial assessment by evaluating the patient's airway, breathing, and circulation (ABC) status. Residual neuromuscular blockade, opioid use, and patient characteristics such as sleep-disordered breathing (e.g., obstructive sleep apnea [OSA], abnormal airway anatomy) affect oxygenation and ventilation. Be alert for signs of inadequate oxygenation and ventilation (Table 20.4). Any sign of respiratory distress needs prompt intervention.

Pulse oximetry (SpO_2) monitoring devices are a noninvasive way of assessing oxygenation and provide an early warning of hypoxemia. They are valuable for assessing the patient who is receiving medications (specifically opioids) that depress respirations. *Transcutaneous carbon dioxide ($PtcCO_2$)* and *end-tidal CO_2 ($PetCO_2$) (capnography) monitoring* are used to detect respiratory depression in high-risk patients.[2] Pulse oximetry, capnography, $PtcCO_2$, and $PetCO_2$ are discussed in Chapter 27. Two acoustic techniques can be used to continuously monitor the patient's respiratory status. Acoustic transducers/sensors placed on the neck measure respiratory rate while pulse oximetry-derived respiratory rate (RR_{oxi}) monitors hemodynamic changes in the respiratory cycle.[4]

Monitor and note any changes in ECG findings from the patient's preoperative baseline. Measure the BP and compare it with baseline readings. Invasive monitoring (e.g., arterial BP) may be needed. Assess temperature, peripheral pulses, capillary refill, and skin condition (e.g., color, moisture). Any signs of inadequate tissue perfusion need prompt intervention.

Focus your initial neurologic assessment on level of consciousness; orientation; sensory and motor status; and size, equality, and reactivity of the pupils. Assess for, note, and report any new asymmetric findings. The patient may be awake, drowsy but arousable, or asleep. Because hearing is the first sense to return in the unconscious patient, explain all activities to the patient from the time of admission to the PACU. If the patient received a regional anesthetic (e.g., spinal, epidural), sensory and motor blockade may still be present. Assess dermatome levels (Fig. 20.2). During recovery from regional anesthesia, sensory and motor function first returns distal to the site where the anesthetic was given. The areas near the site of injections are the last to recover.

TABLE 20.2 PACU Hand-Off Report

General Information
- Patient name and age
- Surgeon and anesthesia care provider
- Surgical procedure
- Presence of tubes, drains, catheters, and IV lines
- Type of anesthesia (e.g., general, regional, monitored anesthesia care)
- Use of any reversal agents
- Airway status (artificial airway and/or interventions to maintain adequate oxygenation)
- Pain management interventions
- NPO status and postoperative orders that need started

Patient History
- Indication for surgery
- Medical history, medications, allergies
- Preoperative or baseline vital signs, laboratory, and diagnostic findings
- Level of consciousness, orientation
- Specific patient characteristics (e.g., hearing, vision, mobility problems)
- Patient preferences (e.g., cultural, personal beliefs/restrictions)
- Patient emotional status on arrival to OR

Intraoperative Management
- Anesthetic agents
- Other drugs received preoperatively or intraoperatively
- Last dose of opioid administration/pain management plan
- Total fluid replacements, including blood transfusions
- Total fluid losses (e.g., blood, nasogastric drainage)
- Urine output

Intraoperative Course
- Unexpected anesthetic events or reactions
- Unexpected surgical events
- Most recent vital signs and monitoring trends
- Results of laboratory tests and x-rays

! SAFETY ALERT

Regional Anesthesia

- Monitor for complications of regional anesthesia.
- Be alert for respiratory distress, hypotension, dysrhythmias, changes in heart rate, bleeding or hematoma at site, headache, neurologic deficit or prolonged block, urinary retention, nausea, and itching.
- Implement treatment protocols and notify the HCP as needed.

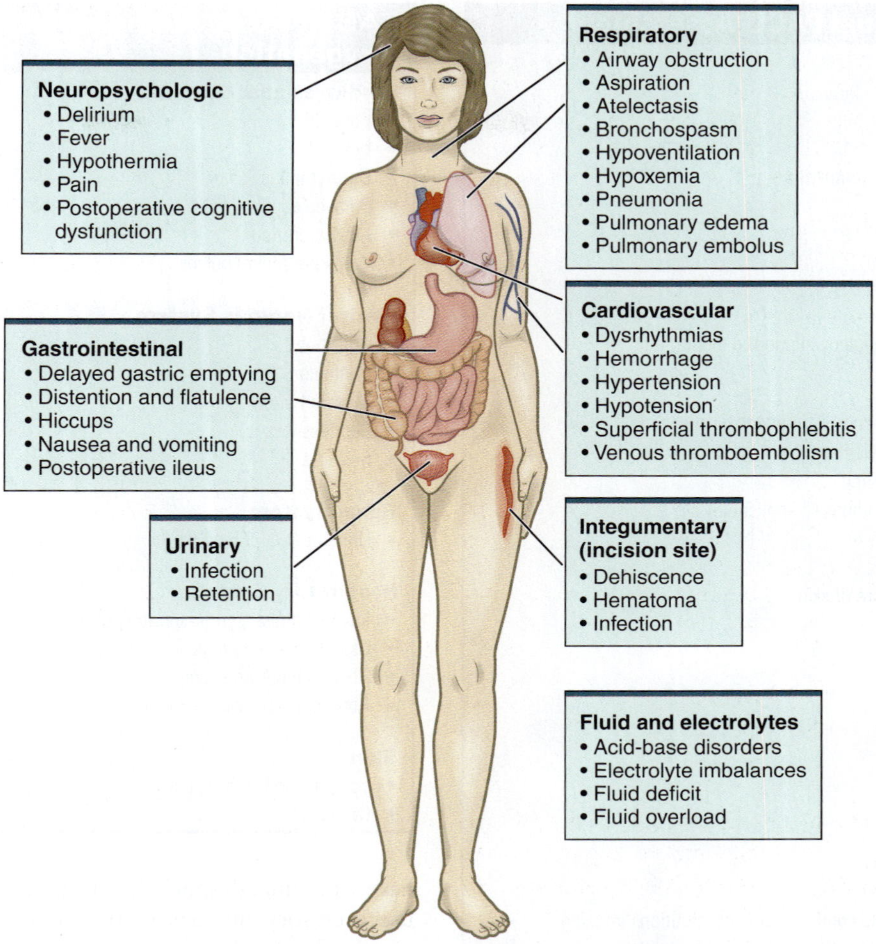

Fig. 20.1 Potential problems in the postoperative period.

Assess the urinary system and fluid balance by measuring intake and output. Intraoperative fluid totals are part of the ACP report. Note the presence of all IV lines, irrigation solutions and infusions, and output devices, including catheters and wound drains. Assess the surgical site. Note the condition of dressings and the type and amount of drainage. Implement orders related to incision care.

The rest of this chapter discusses the nursing management of select problems (Table 20.5). You can apply this information to patients in both the PACU and clinical unit.

RESPIRATORY PROBLEMS

Etiology

PACU

In the immediate postanesthesia period, common causes of airway compromise include obstruction, hypoxemia, and hypoventilation (Table 20.6). Patients at high risk include those who (1) have had general anesthesia; (2) are older than 55 years of age; (3) have a history of tobacco use; (4) have preexisting lung problems and/or sleep-disordered breathing; (5) are obese and/or have an unusual body habitus (e.g., large or short neck); (6) have co-morbidities (e.g., kidney problems, diabetes, hypertension); or (7) have undergone airway, thoracic, or abdominal surgery. Pulmonary complications pose the greatest risk to patients in the postanesthesia and immediate postoperative period. High-risk patients should be monitored in PACU or a critical unit.[1,2]

Airway obstruction is often caused by the patient's tongue blocking the airway (Fig. 20.3). The base of the tongue falls backward against the soft palate and occludes the pharynx. It is most pronounced in the supine position and in the patient who is extremely sleepy after surgery.

Hypoxemia, or a PaO_2 less than 60 mm Hg, is characterized by nonspecific signs and symptoms ranging from agitation to somnolence, hypertension to hypotension, and tachycardia to bradycardia. Pulse oximetry shows low O_2 saturation (less than 90%).

The most common cause of hypoxemia after surgery is atelectasis. **Atelectasis** (alveolar collapse) may be the result of bronchial obstruction caused by retained secretions, decreased respiratory excursion, or general anesthesia. Atelectasis occurs when mucus blocks bronchioles or there is not enough alveolar surfactant to hold the alveoli open (Fig. 20.4). As air becomes trapped beyond the mucus and is absorbed, the alveoli collapse. Atelectasis may affect a part of or an entire lobe of the lung.

Other causes of hypoxemia include pulmonary edema, pulmonary embolism (PE), aspiration, and bronchospasm. An accumulation of fluid in the alveoli can cause *pulmonary edema.*

TABLE 20.3 Initial PACU Assessment

Airway
- Patency
- Oral or nasal airway
- Laryngeal mask airway
- Endotracheal tube with ventilator settings

Breathing
- Respiratory rate and quality
- Auscultate breath sounds
- Pulse oximetry
- Capnography or other technology-supported monitoring
- Supplemental O_2

Circulation
- ECG monitoring: rate and rhythm
- BP: noninvasive or arterial line
- Hemodynamic pressure readings (if applicable)
- Temperature
- Capillary refill
- Color, temperature, moisture of skin
- Apical and peripheral pulses

Neurologic
- Level of consciousness
- Orientation
- Sensory and motor status
- Pupil size and reaction

Surgical Site
- Dressings and visible incisions
- Drains: type, patency, and drainage
- IV assessment: location and condition of sites, solutions infusing

Genitourinary
- Urine output

Gastrointestinal
- Nausea, vomiting
- Intake (fluids, irrigations)
- Output (vomitus)
- Bowel sounds

Pain
- Incision
- Other

Patient Safety Needs
- Patient position
- Fall risk assessment

It may be the result of fluid overload, heart failure, prolonged airway obstruction, sepsis, or aspiration.

Patients are at risk for *aspiration* of gastric contents into the lungs during intubation or after surgery. This can occur with vomiting due to anesthesia depressing the protective airway reflexes. Gastric aspiration may result in laryngospasm, pneumonia, and pulmonary edema. Because of the life-threatening consequences of aspiration, prevention is the goal.

Bronchospasm is the result of an increase in bronchial smooth muscle tone closing small airways. Airway edema develops, causing secretions to build up in the airway. The patient will have wheezing, dyspnea, hypoxemia, and tachypnea. They may use accessory muscles to try to compensate. Bronchospasm may be due to aspiration, endotracheal intubation, pharyngeal suctioning, or an allergic response. (Allergic responses are discussed in Chapter 14.) Bronchospasm may occur in any patient. It occurs more often in patients with a history of smoking, asthma, and chronic obstructive pulmonary disease (COPD).

TABLE 20.4 Signs of Inadequate Oxygenation

Cardiovascular System
- ↑ or ↓ BP
- ↑ or ↓ HR
- Dysrhythmias
- Delayed capillary refill
- ↓ O_2 saturation
- Weak peripheral pulses

Central Nervous System
- Agitation
- Confusion
- Muscle twitching
- Restlessness
- Seizures

Renal System
- Urine output <0.5 mL/kg/hr

Respiratory System
- Increased to absent respiratory effort
- Use of accessory muscles
- Abnormal breath sounds
- Abnormal ABG values

Skin
- Cool, flushed, or moist skin
- Cyanosis

Hypoventilation, a common complication in the PACU, appears as a decreased respiratory rate or effort, hypoxemia, and increasing hypercapnia (increasing $PaCO_2$). It may result from depression of the central respiratory drive (from anesthesia or use of opioids) and/or poor respiratory muscle tone (from neuromuscular blockade or disease).

! SAFETY ALERT

Hypoventilation

- Always assess for a decreased respiratory rate when giving opioids.
- Use a sedation assessment scale (e.g., Richmond Agitation and Sedation Scale, available at www.icudelirium.org/docs/RASS.pdf) to assess for levels of sedation and promote patient safety when giving opioids in the PACU.
- Begin emergency management protocols if hypoventilation is present.

Clinical Unit

Common causes of respiratory problems are atelectasis and pneumonia, especially in patients with co-morbidities (e.g., OSA, COPD, heart failure) and after abdominal or thoracic surgery.[1,2] The development of mucous plugs and decreased

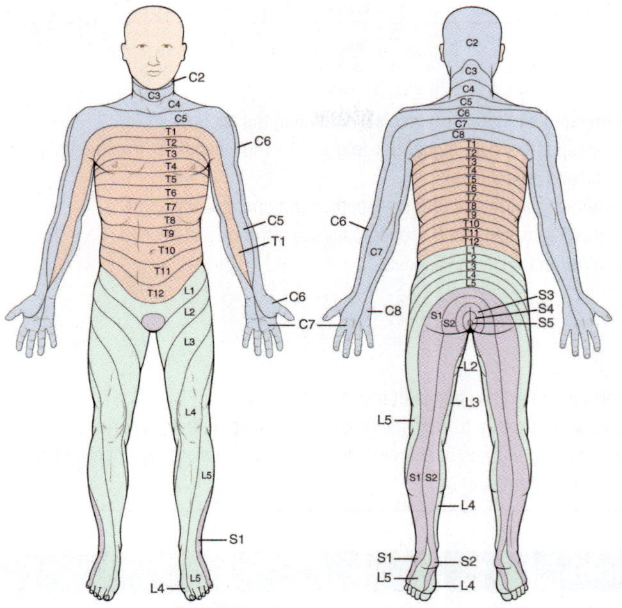

Sensory level anesthesia necessary for surgical procedures

Sensory level	Type of surgery
S2-S5	Hemorrhoidectomy
L2-L3 (knee)	Foot surgery
L1-L3 (inguinal ligament)	Lower extremity surgery
T10 (umbilicus)	Hip surgery Transurethral resection of the prostate Vaginal delivery
T6-T7 (xiphoid process)	Lower abdominal surgery Appendectomy
T4 (nipple)	Upper abdominal surgery Cesarean section

Fig. 20.2 Sensory innervation by spinal nerves and sensory level required for various surgical procedures. (From Pardo M, Miller R: *Basics of anesthesia,* ed 7, St Louis, 2018, Elsevier.)

surfactant production is directly related to hypoventilation, ineffective coughing, history of tobacco use, immobility, and bed rest. Increased bronchial secretions occur when the respiratory passages have been irritated by heavy smoking, COPD, pulmonary infection, or from dry mucous membranes that occurs with intubation, inhalation anesthesia, and dehydration. Without intervention, atelectasis can progress to pneumonia.

NURSING MANAGEMENT: RESPIRATORY PROBLEMS

Assessment

In completing a respiratory assessment, pay close attention to the patient's airway patency, chest symmetry, depth, rate, and character of respirations. Impaired ventilation may first be seen as a decreasing pulse oximetry reading, slowed breathing, and/or reduced chest and abdominal movement during breathing. Abdominal or accessory muscle use may occur with respiratory distress. Auscultating breath sounds will alert you to decreased or absent breath sounds. These findings may mean airflow is diminished or obstructed. You should immediately stimulate and wake patients who show a poor respiratory effort, noisy respirations, or other signs of respiratory distress. Once patients are awake, coach them to take deep breaths.

Regular monitoring of vital signs, including pulse oximetry, capnography, or other technology-supported monitoring (e.g., acoustic monitoring), and a thorough respiratory assessment allow you to recognize early signs of respiratory problems. Manifestations of hypoxemia include tachypnea, gasping, anxiety, restlessness, confusion, and a rapid or thready pulse.

TABLE 20.5 NURSING MANAGEMENT

Caring for the Postoperative Patient

PACU

- Assess patient's initial airway, breathing, and circulation status.
- Evaluate for the return to consciousness, ability to maintain airway and breathing.
- Perform ongoing assessments for postoperative problems (e.g., airway obstruction, hypoventilation, ↑ or ↓ BP, dysrhythmias, emergence delirium).
- Administer and titrate O_2 based on agency protocols.
- Give analgesics and IV fluids.
- Evaluate patient's readiness for transfer to clinical unit or discharge from ambulatory surgery.
- Give hand-off report to RN about patient status when transferring patient to clinical unit.
- Provide discharge teaching for patient and caregiver after ambulatory surgery.
- Supervise AP:
  - Assist with positioning of patients in the lateral recovery position.
  - Obtain vital signs, pulse oximetry, and capillary blood glucose levels (per agency policy). Report abnormal levels to RN.
  - Aid patient with elimination needs.

Clinical Unit

- Assess patient on initial admission to the unit.
- Assess for complications (e.g., atelectasis, hemodynamic instability, cognitive problems, pain, fluid and electrolyte imbalance, fever or hypothermia, nausea and vomiting, urinary retention, wound infection).
- Develop and implement a patient specific plan of care based on identified risk factors and potential complications.
- Titrate O_2 administration according to prescribed parameters.
- Monitor pain level and give prescribed analgesics.
- Give medications.
- Provide wound care, including dressing changes.
- Insert urinary catheter as prescribed for urinary retention.
- Develop and implement patient and caregiver education, including discharge teaching.
- Supervise AP:
  - Record oral intake and output.
  - Obtain vital signs, pulse oximetry and capillary blood glucose levels (per agency policy). Report abnormal levels to RN.
  - Aid patient with nutrition, elimination, and hygienic needs.
  - Reposition and ambulate patient as instructed.
  - Help patient with deep breathing and coughing exercises.

Continued

TABLE 20.5 NURSING MANAGEMENT—cont'd

Caring for the Postoperative Patient

PACU	Clinical Unit
Collaborate With Interprofessional Team	
Respiratory Therapist	
• Provide respiratory care modalities that support patient recovery from anesthesia (e.g., O_2 therapy, nebulizer treatments, pulmonary drainage procedures, mechanical ventilation, and airway support). • Institute extubation protocols. • Monitor pulse oximetry, capnography, or other technology-assisted means of assessing hypoxemia or hypoventilation. • Assist with O_2 and/or ventilation management during patient transport. • Perform ABG sampling in the absence of an arterial line.	• Institute rapid intubation protocols if needed in the absence of ACP. • Provide respiratory care modalities (e.g., O_2 therapy, nebulizer treatments, pulmonary drainage procedures). • Assist with O_2 and/or ventilation support during patient transport. • Monitor pulse oximetry and capnography and titrate O_2 as needed. • Perform ABG sampling as needed.
Physical Therapist	
• Perform initial assessment to determine normal functioning level if surgery was emergent. • Support patient motion and joint mobility.	• Support patient motion and joint mobility. • Support patient return to baseline functional mobility following surgery. • Support nursing staff on best measures for joint positioning, transferring from bed to chair, and/or ambulation.

TABLE 20.6 Postoperative Respiratory Complications

Complications	Mechanisms	Manifestations	Interventions
Airway Obstruction			
Laryngeal edema	Allergic drug reaction Mechanical irritation from intubation Fluid overload	Similar to laryngospasm	O_2 therapy Antihistamines Corticosteroids Sedatives Possible intubation
Laryngospasm	Irritation from endotracheal tube, anesthetic gases, or gastric aspiration Most likely to occur after removal of endotracheal tube	Inspiratory stridor (crowing respirations) Sternal retraction Acute respiratory distress	O_2 therapy Positive pressure ventilation IV muscle relaxant Lidocaine Corticosteroids
Retained thick secretions	Secretion stimulation by anesthetic agents Dehydration of secretions	Noisy respirations Coarse crackles	Suctioning Deep breathing and coughing IV hydration Chest PT
Tongue falling back	Muscular flaccidity associated with ↓ consciousness and muscle relaxants	Use of accessory muscles Snoring respirations ↓ Air movement	Patient stimulation Head tilt, jaw thrust (Fig. 20.3) Artificial airway
Hypoxemia			
Aspiration	Inhalation of gastric contents into lungs	Unexplained tachypnea Bronchospasm ↓ O_2 saturation Atelectasis Interstitial edema Alveolar hemorrhage Respiratory failure	O_2 therapy Cardiopulmonary support Antibiotics
Atelectasis	Bronchial obstruction caused by retained secretions or ↓ lung volumes	↓ Breath sounds ↓ O_2 saturation	Humidified O_2 therapy Deep breathing Incentive spirometry Early mobilization
Bronchospasm	↑ Smooth muscle tone with closure of small airways	Wheezing Dyspnea Tachypnea ↓ O_2 saturation	O_2 therapy Bronchodilators
Pulmonary edema	Fluid overload ↑ Hydrostatic pressure ↓ Interstitial pressure ↑ Capillary permeability	↓ O_2 saturation Crackles Infiltrates on chest x-ray	O_2 therapy Diuretics Fluid restriction

TABLE 20.6 Postoperative Respiratory Complications—cont'd

Complications	Mechanisms	Manifestations	Interventions
Pulmonary embolism	Thrombus dislodged from peripheral venous system and lodged in pulmonary arterial system	Acute tachypnea Dyspnea Tachycardia Hypotension ↓ O_2 saturation Bronchospasm	O_2 therapy Cardiopulmonary support Anticoagulant therapy
Hypoventilation			
Depressed central respiratory drive	Medullary depression from anesthetics, opioids, sedatives	Shallow respirations ↓ Respiratory rate, apnea ↓ PaO_2 ↑ $PaCO_2$	Start capnography or other technology-supported respiratory monitoring Stimulation Reversal of opioids or benzodiazepines Mechanical ventilation
Mechanical restriction	Tight casts, dressings, abdominal binders Positioning and obesity preventing lung expansion	As above	Elevate head of bed Repositioning Loosen dressings
Pain	Shallow breathing to prevent incisional pain	↑ Respiratory rate Hypotension Hypertension ↓ $PaCO_2$ ↓ PaO_2 Reports of pain Guarding behavior	Opioid analgesic drug therapy NSAID therapy Complementary and alternative therapies (e.g., music, imagery)
Poor respiratory muscle tone	Neuromuscular blockade Neuromuscular disease	As above	Reversal of paralysis Mechanical ventilation

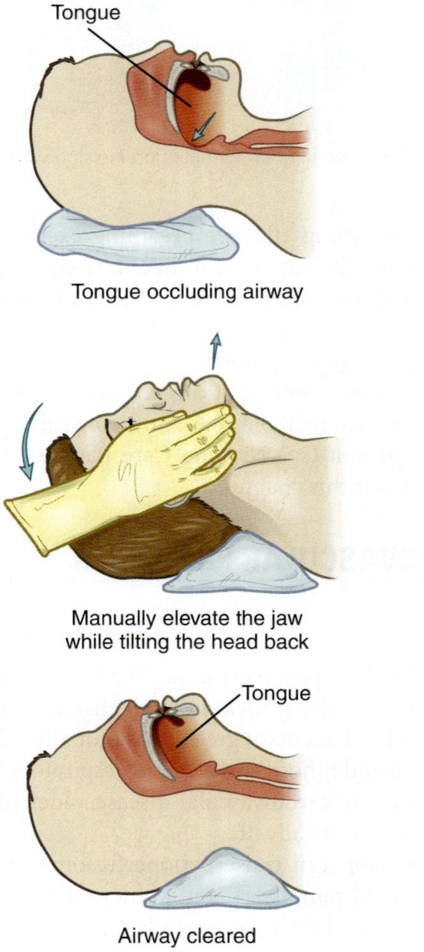

Fig. 20.3 Etiology and relief of airway obstruction.

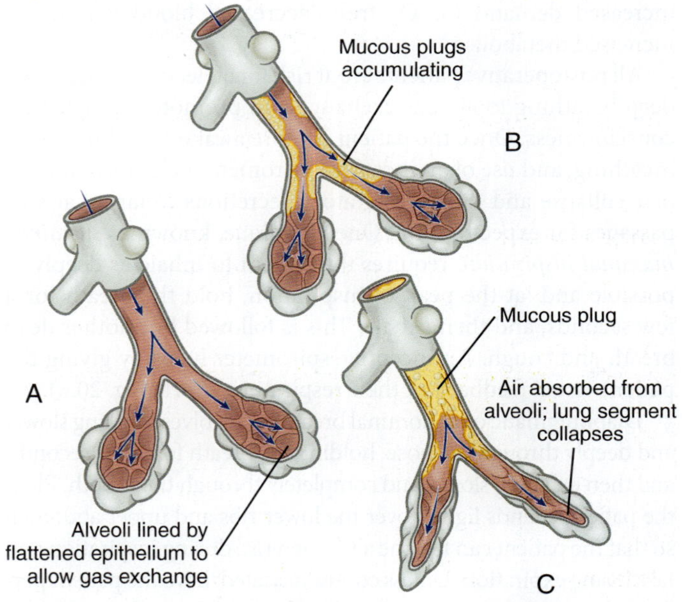

Fig. 20.4 Postoperative atelectasis. (A) Normal bronchiole and alveoli. (B) Mucous plug in bronchiole. (C) Collapse of alveoli resulting from atelectasis after absorption of air.

Note and record the characteristics of sputum or mucus. Mucus from the trachea and throat is normally colorless and thin. Sputum from the lungs and bronchi is normally thick and pale yellow. Changes in sputum color or consistency may indicate a respiratory infection.

◆ Clinical Problems

The main clinical problem related to respiratory issues is impaired respiratory function.

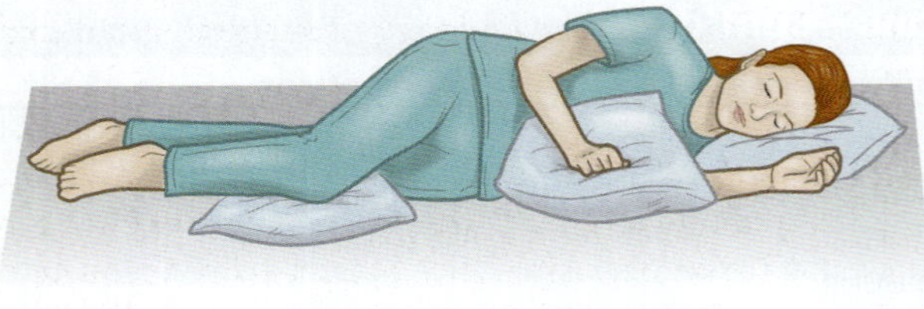

Fig. 20.5 Position of patient during recovery from general anesthesia.

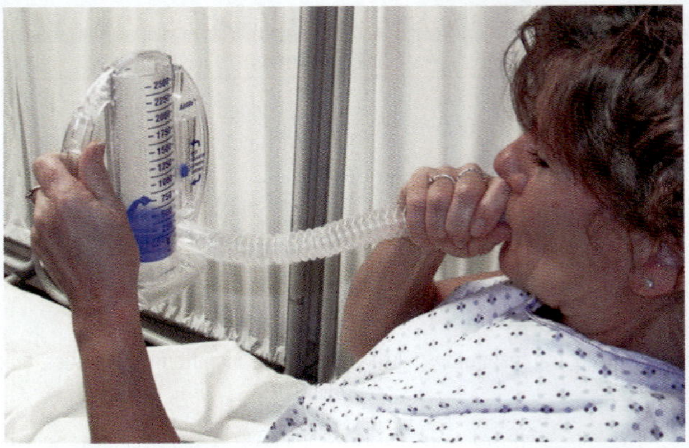

Fig. 20.6 Proper use of an incentive spirometer. (Courtesy Christine R. Hoch, MSN, RN, ACNS-BC, Nursing Instructor, University of Delaware, Newark, DE.)

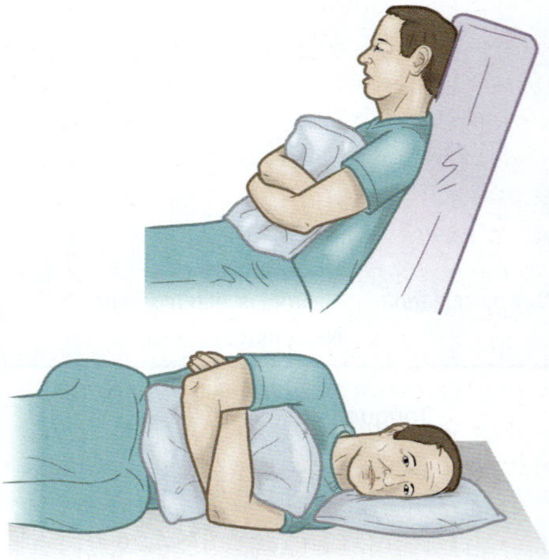

Fig. 20.7 Techniques for splinting incision when coughing.

◆ Implementation

In the PACU, nursing interventions are aimed at preventing and treating respiratory problems. Proper positioning of the patient aids breathing and protects the airway.

! SAFETY ALERT

Postoperative Patient Positioning

- Position the unconscious patient in a lateral "recovery" position (Fig. 20.5).
- This position keeps the airway open and reduces the risk for aspiration if vomiting occurs.

Place the conscious patient in a supine position with the head of the bed elevated. This position maximizes expansion of the thorax by decreasing abdominal pressure on the diaphragm.

Start O_2 therapy via nasal cannula or face mask if ordered. O_2 therapy helps to eliminate anesthetic gases and meet the increased demand for O_2 from decreased blood volume or increased metabolism.

All postoperative patients are at risk for atelectasis. Encourage deep breathing to aid gas exchange and promote the return to consciousness. Once the patient is more awake, coughing, deep breathing, and use of an incentive spirometer help prevent alveolar collapse and move respiratory secretions to larger airway passages for expectoration. One technique, known as *sustained maximal inspiration,* requires the patient to inhale as deeply as possible and, at the peak of inspiration, hold the breath for a few seconds, and then exhale. This is followed by another deep breath and cough. An incentive spirometer helps by giving the patient visual feedback of their respiratory effort (Fig. 20.6).

Diaphragmatic or abdominal breathing involves inhaling slowly and deeply through the nose, holding the breath for a few seconds, and then exhaling slowly and completely through the mouth. Place the patient's hands lightly over the lower ribs and upper abdomen so that the patient can feel the abdomen rise during inspiration and fall during expiration. Unless contraindicated, have the patient perform these maneuvers 10 times every hour while awake.

Effective coughing is essential in mobilizing secretions. If secretions are in the respiratory tract, deep breathing often moves them up and stimulates the cough reflex. Splinting an abdominal incision with a pillow or a rolled blanket supports the incision and aids in coughing and expectorating secretions (Fig. 20.7).

Changing the patient's position every 1 to 2 hours will allow full chest expansion, increase perfusion of both lungs, and prevent pressure injury. Help the patient sit in a chair and ambulate as soon as ordered. Provide adequate and regular pain medication. Incisional pain often is the greatest barrier to the patient performing effective breathing exercises and ambulation. Reassure the patient that these activities will not cause the incision to open. Adequate oral or IV hydration is essential to maintain the integrity of mucous membranes and to thin secretions for easy expectoration.

Other nursing interventions for specific respiratory problems are detailed in Table 20.6. A nursing care plan for the postoperative patient (see Nursing Care Plan 20.1) is available on the website for this chapter.

CARDIOVASCULAR PROBLEMS

Etiology

PACU

In the immediate postanesthesia period, the most common cardiovascular problems include hypotension, hypertension, and dysrhythmias. Patients at greatest risk for altered cardiovascular function include those with altered respiratory function, those with a history of cardiovascular disease, older adults, the debilitated, and the critically ill.

Hypotension can cause hypoperfusion to the vital organs, especially the brain, heart, and kidneys. Disorientation, loss of consciousness, chest pain, and oliguria reflect hypoperfusion, hypoxemia, and the loss of physiologic compensation. Intervention must be prompt to prevent the devastating complications of cardiac ischemia or infarction, cerebral ischemia, renal ischemia, and bowel infarction.

The most common cause of hypotension in the PACU is fluid and blood loss, which may lead to hypovolemic shock. Hemorrhage is always a risk of surgery. Marked blood loss is possible when cauterization or sutures fail. Hemorrhage can occur at the incisional site but most often occurs internally. Assess incisional dressings/sites. Look for changes in level of consciousness and vital signs trends of a decreasing blood pressure with increasing heart rate. The treatment is aimed at restoring circulating volume with fluid administration or blood products. If there is no response to volume administration, you should consider heart dysfunction as a cause of hypotension.

Primary heart dysfunction, which may occur in myocardial infarction, cardiac tamponade, or PE, results in an acute drop in cardiac output. Secondary heart dysfunction occurs because of the negative *chronotropic* (rate of heart contraction) and negative *inotropic* (force of heart contraction) effects of drugs, such as β-adrenergic blockers or opioids. Other causes of hypotension include decreased systemic vascular resistance and dysrhythmias.

Hypertension most often occurs from sympathetic nervous system stimulation. This may be the result of pain, anxiety, bladder distention, or respiratory distress. Hypertension may be related to hypothermia or preexisting hypertension.

Many problems can cause dysrhythmias. These include hypoxemia, hypercapnia, electrolyte and acid-base imbalances, circulatory instability, preexisting heart disease, hypothermia, pain, surgical stress, and many anesthetic agents.

Clinical Unit

On the clinical unit, postoperative fluid and electrolyte imbalances contribute to heart problems. Such imbalances may result from a combination of the body's normal response to the stress of surgery, excessive fluid losses, and IV fluid replacement. Fluid status directly affects cardiac output.

Fluid retention during postoperative days 1 to 3 can result from the stress response, which maintains both blood volume and BP. Fluid retention results from the release of antidiuretic hormone (ADH) and adrenocorticotropic hormone (ACTH) and activation of the renin-angiotensin-aldosterone system (RAAS). ADH release leads to increased water reabsorption and decreased urine output, increasing blood volume. ACTH stimulates the adrenal cortex to secrete cortisol and, to a lesser degree, aldosterone (see Figs. 16.9 and 16.10). Fluid losses resulting from surgery decrease kidney perfusion, stimulating the RAAS and causing marked release of aldosterone. Mechanisms that increase aldosterone lead to significant sodium and fluid retention, thus increasing blood volume.

Fluid overload may occur during this period of fluid retention if we infuse IV fluids too rapidly, when chronic disease (e.g., heart, kidney) exists, or when the patient is an older adult. Fluid deficits from untreated preoperative dehydration, blood loss during surgery, or slow or inadequate fluid replacement can decrease cardiac output and tissue perfusion. Losses from vomiting, bleeding, wound drainage, or suctioning can contribute to fluid deficits.

Hypokalemia can result from urinary and gastrointestinal (GI) tract losses. Low serum potassium levels directly affect the heart's contractility and may contribute to decreases in cardiac output and tissue perfusion. The patient with adequate renal function can receive potassium replacement, usually 40 mEq/day. Urine output of at least 0.5 mL/kg/hr and a normal serum creatinine indicate adequate renal function.

The state of tissue perfusion or blood flow affects cardiovascular status. The stress response contributes to an increase in clotting tendencies by increasing platelet production. A *venous thromboembolism (VTE)* may form in leg veins because of venous stasis, vein injury, or a hypercoagulable state. VTE is especially common in postoperative patients, older adults, obese persons, immobilized patients, and patients with a history of VTE, PE, or predisposition to clotting. It is a potentially life-threatening complication because it may lead to PE. Suspect PE in any patient with tachypnea, chest pain, hypotension, agitation, tachycardia, and dyspnea, especially when the patient is receiving O_2 therapy. Postoperative VTE prophylaxis often includes early ambulation, pneumatic compression devices, and anticoagulation.[5] Superficial thrombophlebitis is an uncomfortable but less serious complication that does not lead to PE. It may develop in a superficial leg or arm vein because of venous stasis, vein trauma, and/or irritation from IV catheters or solutions. PE and VTE are discussed in Chapters 30 and 41, respectively.

Syncope (fainting) may result from decreased cardiac output, volume loss (including fluids and blood), or defects in cerebral perfusion. Syncope often occurs because of postural hypotension when the patient ambulates. Normally when the patient stands up quickly, the arterial baroreceptors respond to the fall in BP with sympathetic nervous system stimulation. This produces vasoconstriction and maintains BP. These sympathetic and vasomotor functions may be diminished in the older adult and the immobile, volume depleted, or postanesthesia patient.

NURSING MANAGEMENT: CARDIOVASCULAR PROBLEMS

Assessment

The most important aspect of the cardiovascular assessment is frequent vital sign monitoring. Plan to obtain vital signs every 15 minutes in Phase I, or more often until stabilized and then less often in Phase II. Compare postoperative vital signs with preoperative and intraoperative findings to determine when the signs are returning to baseline. Notify the ACP or HCP if any of the following occurs:

- Systolic BP <90 mm Hg or >160 mm Hg
- Pulse rate <60 beats/min or >120 beats/min
- Pulse pressure (difference between systolic and diastolic BP) narrows
- BP trends gradually decrease or increase over several consecutive readings
- Change in heart rhythm

Hypotension accompanied by a normal pulse and warm, dry skin is usually from the residual vasodilating effects of anesthesia. Continue to observe the patient. Hypotension accompanied by a rapid or weak pulse and cold, clammy, pale skin may indicate hypovolemic shock and needs immediate treatment.

ECG monitoring is recommended for patients who have a history of heart disease and for older patients who have undergone major surgery. You should assess the apical-radial pulse carefully and report any deficits or irregularities. Valuable information about tissue perfusion is found in assessing peripheral pulses and skin/mucous membrane color, temperature, and moisture.

◆ Clinical Problems

Clinical problems related to cardiovascular issues include:

- Altered blood pressure
- Fluid imbalance
- Impaired cardiac function
- Inadequate tissue perfusion

◆ Implementation

◆ PACU

Begin treatment of hypotension with O_2 therapy to promote oxygenation of hypoperfused organs. The most common cause of hypotension is fluid loss. IV fluid boluses may be ordered to normalize BP. Inspect the surgical area and incision to determine if excess bleeding is the cause of volume loss. Primary heart dysfunction may require drug intervention. Peripheral vasodilation and hypotension may require vasoconstrictive drugs to increase systemic vascular resistance.

Treatment of hypertension centers on removing the cause of sympathetic nervous system stimulation. This may include giving analgesics, assisting with voiding, and correcting respiratory problems. Rewarming corrects hypothermia-induced hypertension. The patient with preexisting hypertension or who has undergone heart or vascular surgery usually needs drug therapy to reduce BP.

Most dysrhythmias seen in the PACU have identifiable causes. Identifying the cause is a critical first step in correcting the dysrhythmia. With life-threatening dysrhythmias (e.g., ventricular tachycardia), follow your agency's protocol for advanced cardiac life support.

◆ Clinical Unit

Continue to monitor vital signs. Keep an accurate intake and output record, monitor laboratory findings (e.g., electrolytes, hematocrit), and manage IV therapy after surgery.

Early ambulation is the most significant general nursing measure to prevent complications. Walking (1) increases muscle tone; (2) stimulates circulation, which prevents venous stasis and VTE, and speeds wound healing; (3) increases vital capacity and supports normal respiratory function; and (4) improves feelings of well-being. Begin progression to ambulation by first raising the head of the patient's bed for 1 to 2 minutes. Then help the patient to sit, with legs dangling, while monitoring the pulse rate. If you do not note changes or problems, help the patient ambulate while monitoring the pulse. If you note changes in the pulse or dizziness occurs, sit the patient in a nearby chair until the BP and pulse are stable. Then help the patient back to the bed. If dizziness occurs, it may be frightening for the patient. Injury can result from a fall, so take measures to ensure patient and staff safety.

> **CHECK YOUR PRACTICE**
>
> You are caring for an older, obese patient who is 1 day post-colon resection with plans for moving out of the bed to a chair. You help the patient to a sitting position while dangling legs at the bedside. The patient reports feeling dizzy. The patient's BP is 108/64 and apical heart rate is 124.
>
> - What should you do?

NEUROLOGIC AND PSYCHOLOGIC PROBLEMS

Etiology

PACU

After surgery, some patients may develop **emergence delirium**. It is a short-term neurologic change manifested by behaviors such as restlessness, agitation, disorientation, thrashing, and shouting. If delirium occurs, first suspect hypoxia. Other causes include anesthetic agents, bladder distention, pain, long duration of preoperative fasting, residual neuromuscular blockade, or the presence of an endotracheal tube.

Delayed emergence can also be a problem. Patients with **delayed emergence** spend longer periods in the PACU and have prolonged hospital courses. Identifying the causative factors is critical for determining appropriate interventions.[6] The most common cause of delayed emergence after anesthesia is drug-related. This includes anesthetic agents as well as drugs used during the perioperative period. Other causes include hypoxia, hypercapnia, hemorrhage, VTE, metabolic problems, electrolyte imbalances, hypertension, liver disease, uremia, central anticholinergic syndrome, and hypothyroidism.

Clinical Unit

Two types of cognitive impairments in surgical patients are *postoperative cognitive dysfunction (POCD)* and *delirium.* POCD is a decline in the patient's cognitive function (e.g., memory, ability to concentrate) for weeks or months after surgery. POCD occurs mainly in the older adult. Preexisting cognitive impairment, duration of anesthesia, complications during surgery, and infection contribute to the development of POCD. Quickly and thoroughly investigate any changes in mental status as the causes may be life threatening.

Postoperative delirium is more common in the older patient. Delirium may result from severe pain, fluid and electrolyte imbalances, hypoxemia, drug effects, sleep deprivation, and sensory deprivation or overload. Signs include cognitive problems, varying levels of consciousness, altered psychomotor activity, and a disturbed sleep/wake cycle. See Chapter 64 for more about delirium.

Alcohol withdrawal delirium results from the patient undergoing alcohol withdrawal. It appears as restlessness, insomnia, nightmares, irritability, and auditory or visual hallucinations.

Chapter 11 discusses the identification and management of alcohol withdrawal delirium.

Mental health and well-being correlate with a decreased likelihood of complications. Psychiatric illnesses such as depression and anxiety are associated with higher treatment costs, and an increased risk of acute and chronic pain.[7]

NURSING MANAGEMENT: NEUROLOGIC AND PSYCHOLOGIC PROBLEMS

Assessment

Assess the patient's level of consciousness, orientation, memory, and ability to follow commands. Determine the size, reactivity, and equality of the pupils. Assess the patient's sleep/wake cycle and sensory and motor status. Determine the possible cause if the patient has an altered neurologic status. If the patient was mentally alert before surgery and becomes cognitively impaired after surgery, do further assessment to rule out hypoxia, delirium, or POCD.

Clinical Problems

Clinical problems related to neurologic and psychologic issues include:

- Impaired sleep
- Neurologic problem
- Risk for injury
- Sensory deficit

Implementation

PACU

The most common cause of agitation in the PACU is hypoxemia. Focus attention on evaluating respiratory function. The most common cause of delayed emergence is prolonged drug action. It usually spontaneously resolves with time. If needed, antagonists can reverse the effects of benzodiazepines and opioids.

Until the patient is awake and able to communicate effectively, you are responsible for patient safety. This includes monitoring physiologic status, having the side rails up and the call bell available, securing equipment (e.g., IV lines, artificial airways), verifying allergies, and using 2 patient identifiers before giving drugs or completing treatments.

Clinical Unit

Interventions to prevent perioperative delirium begin with screening and identification of risk factors. Assistive devices that help promote orientation include clocks, calendars, photos, hearing aids, and eyeglasses. Encourage family to be at the bedside. Choose medications carefully (e.g., avoiding sedatives, antipsychotics, opioids). Assess for agitation, pain, or anxiety.[6] Help the patient achieve fluid and electrolyte balance, adequate nutrition and sleep, proper bowel and bladder function, and early mobilization.

To prevent or limit psychologic problems, provide adequate support for the patient. This includes listening to and talking with the patient, offering explanations and reassurance, and encouraging the presence and aid of the patient's caregiver(s). Evaluate the patient's behavior to distinguish a normal reaction to a stressful situation from one that is becoming abnormal or excessive. Recognizing alcohol withdrawal delirium can be a challenge. Record and report any unusual or disturbed behavior so that a diagnosis can be made and treatment started.

PAIN AND DISCOMFORT

Etiology

Pain is a common problem and a significant fear for patients. Pain is caused by the interaction of physiologic and psychologic factors. The incision and retraction during surgery traumatize the skin and underlying tissues. In addition, there may be reflex muscle spasms around the incision. Anxiety and fear, sometimes related to the anticipation of pain, create tension and further increase muscle tone and spasm. Positioning during surgery and the use of internal devices such as an endotracheal tube or catheters may also cause discomfort. The effort and movement associated with coughing, deep breathing, and ambulating may worsen pain by creating tension on the incision area. Other sources of discomfort include nausea and vomiting, environmental noise, noxious odors, and shivering.

The patient does not feel pain when the internal viscera are cut. However, pain does result from pressure in the internal viscera. Deep visceral pain may signal a complication such as intestinal distention, bleeding, or abscess formation. Pain may limit respiratory movement, increasing the risk for atelectasis.

NURSING MANAGEMENT: PAIN

Assessment

Assess the patient on arrival to the PACU and at frequent intervals. The patient's self-report is the single most reliable indicator of pain. Use a pain scale, such as a numeric or FACES pain scale, to assess the severity or intensity of pain. (Pain scales are discussed in Chapter 9). Assess pain levels at rest and during activities. Verbalization of pain is not always possible in the PACU, so assess the patient for other indications of pain (e.g., restlessness, grimacing, changes in vital signs). Identify the location of the pain. Expect that patients will have incisional pain, especially with movement, and with some procedures (e.g., removal of drains). Other causes of pain, such as a full bladder, may be present.

Involve patients in the assessment and management of their pain. Assessing patients from different cultures or those who do not speak English may be challenging. Take extra time and include family in exploring the pain experience with these patients. Adapt care to meet your patient's unique needs and expectations for pain control.

Clinical Problems

Clinical problems associated with pain include:

- Pain
- Impaired respiratory function
- Musculoskeletal problem
- Impaired sleep

◆ Implementation

Begin before surgery to develop a plan for pain control that includes behavioral modalities and control of anxiety. Evaluate adjustments to or continuation of drugs used to treat chronic pain. Teach patients to report pain and how pain will be managed after surgery. Share pain management plans during the hand-off report.

The acute pain of surgery almost always requires the use of analgesics. Management should include an interprofessional approach.[8] Pain control techniques include the use of single modalities (e.g., opioid drugs, PCA, regional analgesic [local anesthetic infiltration]), or multimodal analgesia. *Multimodal analgesia,* or the use of 2 or more analgesics with different mechanisms of action (e.g., an opioid and a nonsteroidal antiinflammatory drug [NSAID]), is recommended. Medications such as ibuprofen and acetaminophen are routinely used adjunctively as a pain management plan. This has resulted in a reduction in patient's use and requirement of opioids. Many medications can be given via various routes based on patient needs. For example, the IV or rectal route would be most effective if a patient is vomiting. Ultimately, the choice of modalities should be procedure- and patient-specific.

Over-prescribing and over-use of opioids have resulted in an opioid crisis in the United States. Multimodal analgesia can effectively manage pain using fewer opioids. This translates to fewer opioid-related adverse effects and a reduction in the potential for addiction.[9]

The HCP often writes orders for multimodal pain medications and other comfort measures on an as-needed (PRN) basis. Time analgesic doses to ensure that they are in effect during activities that may be painful, such as walking. Although opioid analgesics are often essential for the patient's comfort, there are undesirable side effects. The most common include constipation, nausea and vomiting, respiratory and cough depression, and hypotension.

Before giving any analgesic, first assess the patient's pain, including location, quality, and intensity; vital signs; and level of consciousness. Treat incisional pain as ordered. If the patient reports chest or leg pain, analgesics may mask a complication (e.g., VTE). If it is gas pain, opioids can worsen it. If the analgesic does not relieve the pain or makes the patient lethargic or somnolent, notify the HCP and request a change.

Patient-controlled analgesia (PCA) allows the patient to self-administer preset doses of analgesics. The goals of PCA are to provide immediate analgesia and maintain an acceptable level of pain control. Continuous infusions allow for a steady blood level of analgesia with additional patient doses used prior to painful events (e.g., walking, deep breathing, and coughing) or for breakthrough pain. Some advantages of PCA are early ambulation, better pain management than with as-needed analgesia, and greater patient satisfaction.

The route of PCA delivery may be IV, oral, epidural, or transdermal. The transdermal route is for short-term pain management and may offer advantages over the IV route (e.g., needleless, low infection risk, decreased drug errors from pump malfunction or inaccurate programming). (PCA is discussed in Chapter 8.)

! SAFETY ALERT

PCA

- Carefully check the HCP's order and program the pump for IV or epidural PCA to deliver the ordered dose of analgesic (e.g., continuous rate, bolus dose, maximum dose).
- A patient's death or serious injury from a drug error (e.g., wrong drug, wrong dose, wrong rate) is a serious reportable event (never event).

Epidural analgesia is the infusion of opioid analgesics through a catheter placed into the epidural space surrounding the spinal cord. The goal of epidural analgesia is delivery of the drug directly to opiate receptors in the spinal cord. Administration methods include intermittent bolus dosing, continuous infusion, and epidural PCA. This technique results in a constant circulating level and a reduced total dose of medication. The use of epidural analgesia for managing pain after surgery is increasing.

Perineural local anesthesia, the infiltration of a nonopioid drug into the surgical site, is another way to manage postoperative pain. A disposable or mechanical infusion pump delivers the local anesthetic via a catheter directly to the surgical incision site. A single dose of bupivacaine liposome injectable suspension (Exparel) provides pain relief with reduced opioid needs for up to 72 hours.

Complementary and alternative therapies such as music therapy, guided imagery, relaxation exercises, and aromatherapy are effective adjuncts in pain management. Nondrug approaches such as repositioning, massage, and distraction can enhance pain management.

CHECK YOUR PRACTICE

Although PCA analgesia is infusing as ordered, your postoperative patient reports ongoing pain that is rated 8 on a 0–10 scale.

- What steps would you take next to manage this patient's pain more effectively?

TEMPERATURE CHANGES

Etiology

Knowing your patient's temperature in the postoperative period is important (Table 20.7). Perioperative temperature management can prevent numerous complications.

Hypothermia

Perioperative *hypothermia* is a core body temperature less than 96.8°F (36°C). Hypothermia may be due to skin exposure, use of cold irrigants, skin preparations, and unwarmed inhaled gases. Although all patients are at risk for postoperative hypothermia, patients at high risk should be monitored closely. This includes patients with hypotension or low preoperative core body temperature, older adults, females, and those with pre-existing medical conditions or who undergo prolonged procedures.[10] Long surgical procedures, open cavity procedures (e.g., abdominal or thoracic), and prolonged anesthetic administration can lead to redistribution of body heat from the core to the periphery.

TABLE 20.7 **Postoperative Temperature Changes**

Time After Surgery	Temperature	Possible Causes
Up to 12 hr	Hypothermia: ≤96.8°F (36°C)	Effects of anesthesia, body heat loss during surgical procedure
First 48 hr (postoperative days 1 and 2)	Mild elevation: ≤100.4°F (38°C)	Inflammatory response to surgical stress
	Moderate elevation: >100.4°F (38°C)	Lung congestion, dehydration
After first 48 hr (postoperative day 3 and later)	Elevation >100°F (37.8°C)	Infection (e.g., wound, urinary, respiratory)

This places the patient at an increased risk for hypothermia and complications.[1]

Complications of hypothermia can include vasoconstriction with resulting hypertension, compromised immune function, bleeding, cardiac events, surgical site infection (SSI), altered drug metabolism, increased pain, and shivering. Shivering can increase resting energy expenditure and O_2 consumption up to 500%, causing hypoxemia and myocardial ischemia (angina). Shivering can also increase carbon dioxide production; increase heart rate, BP, and intracranial pressure; and significantly affect the patient's comfort level.[1]

Fever

Fever may occur at any time after surgery (Table 20.7). SSI, particularly from aerobic organisms, is often accompanied by a fever that spikes in the afternoon or evening and returns to near-normal levels in the morning. The respiratory tract may be infected from stasis of secretions with atelectasis. Urinary tract infections (UTIs) may occur from catheterization. Superficial thrombophlebitis may occur at the IV site. A thrombus in the leg veins may raise temperature.

Intermittent high fever accompanied by shaking chills and diaphoresis suggests septicemia. This may occur at any time after surgery. It can result from microorganisms introduced into the bloodstream during surgery, especially in GI or genitourinary (GU) procedures. Septicemia may occur later from a wound or UTI.

Surgical patients who receive broad antibiotic therapy to prevent or treat infection are at risk for *C. difficile* (CDI) infections. Manifestations of CDI may include fever, diarrhea, and abdominal pain.

Malignant hyperthermia (MH) is a rare muscle metabolism disorder triggered by general anesthetic agents. Although often a late sign, it is characterized by a rapid rise in core body temperature and severe muscle rigidity. Other signs include tachycardia, hypercarbia, metabolic and respiratory acidosis, myoglobinuria, and elevated creatine kinase levels. MH is a life-threatening complication. While most cases of MH occur during general anesthesia, the 1-hour period right after surgery (e.g., in the PACU) is a critical time.[1]

❖ NURSING MANAGEMENT: TEMPERATURE CHANGES

◆ Assessment

Take the patient's temperature on arrival to the PACU and every hour if the patient stays normothermic. If the patient is hypothermic, take the temperature every 15 minutes until normothermic. Use the same route to measure temperature during the patient's stay in the PACU.

Assess the color and temperature of the skin. Communicate risk factors for hypothermia or MH to all members of the perioperative team. Observe the patient for early signs of inflammation and infection that may precede a fever so that any complication is treated promptly.

◆ Clinical Problems

The main clinical problem related to temperature regulation is altered temperature.

◆ Implementation

Passive warming measures include the use of warmed cotton blankets, socks, reflective blankets, and limited skin exposure. *Active warming measures* involve the application of external warming devices, including forced air warmers, heated water mattresses, radiant warmers, heated and humidified O_2, and warmed IV fluids. When using any external warming device, record body temperature and the patient's comfort level at 15-minute intervals. Take care to prevent skin injuries.

Apply O_2 therapy via nasal cannula or mask to treat the increased demand for O_2 caused by shivering. Shivering can be treated with opioids. Keep the supplies readily available to manage MH. Treatment for MH includes the administration of dantrolene (Dantrium), cooling measures (e.g., ice packs), and correcting acid-base imbalances.

Use meticulous asepsis with wound and IV site care. Encourage airway clearance with deep breathing, coughing, and use of the incentive spirometer. If fever develops, antipyretic drugs may be given (see Table 12.6). Depending on the suspected cause of the fever, obtain cultures of the wound, sputum, urine, or blood. If a bacterial infection is the source of the fever, start antibiotics as soon as you obtain cultures. Fever above 103°F (39.4°C) may require body-cooling measures.

GASTROINTESTINAL PROBLEMS

Etiology

Postoperative nausea and vomiting (PONV) are common complications, affecting as many as 80% of high-risk patients. Risk factors include being female, history of motion sickness or previous PONV, nonsmoking status, action of anesthetics or opioids, and duration and type of surgery. The most significant risk factors are gastroesophageal reflux and being under 50 years of age.[11] Delayed gastric emptying and slowed peristalsis that result from handling of the bowel during abdominal surgery contribute to PONV, as does starting oral intake too soon after surgery.

Constipation may occur after surgery. It can be due to anesthetics used during surgery that may paralyze the intestine, changes in diet and fluid intake, immobility, and the use of opioids for pain relief. Opioids decrease peristalsis, slow fecal transport, and decrease a patient's urge to defecate.

Postoperative ileus (POI) is the temporary impairment of gastric and bowel motility after surgery. It results from the handling or reconstruction of the intestine during surgery and limited diet intake before and after surgery. POI is normal after abdominal surgery and may occur after nonabdominal surgery. After abdominal surgery, motility in the large intestine may be reduced for 2 to 7 days. Motility in the small intestine resumes within several hours after surgery.

There is some controversy regarding the definition, incidence, and risk factors associated with POI.[12] Risk factors include the use of opioids, immobility, older age, being male, prior abdominal surgery, and early postoperative feeding. Use of opioid analgesia may prolong the duration of POI. Abdominal cramps, increasing abdominal distention, constipation, nausea, vomiting, and dehydration often accompany POI.[2]

Hiccups are intermittent spasms of the diaphragm caused by irritation of the phrenic nerve, which innervates the diaphragm. The phrenic nerve may be irritated by gastric distention, intestinal obstruction, intraabdominal bleeding, or a subphrenic abscess. Indirect irritation of the phrenic nerve may occur with acid-base and electrolyte imbalances. Reflex irritation may be from drinking hot or cold liquids or from the presence of a nasogastric (NG) tube. Hiccups usually last a short time and stop spontaneously.

❖ NURSING MANAGEMENT: GASTROINTESTINAL PROBLEMS

◆ Assessment

Ask the patient about feelings of nausea. If nausea is present, assess the severity using a verbal descriptor or numeric scale. If vomiting occurs, determine the quantity, characteristics, and color of the vomitus. Assess the abdomen for distention and presence of bowel sounds. Because bowel sounds are often absent or diminished right after surgery, auscultate all 4 quadrants to determine the presence, frequency, and characteristics of the sounds. The return of normal bowel motility is usually accompanied by passing gas or stool and the ability to tolerate oral intake without nausea or vomiting.

◆ Clinical Problems

Clinical problems related to GI issues include:

- Electrolyte imbalance
- Fluid imbalance
- Impaired bowel elimination
- Impaired gastrointestinal function

◆ Implementation

When the patient is NPO, give IV fluids to maintain fluid and electrolyte balance. Begin oral fluids as ordered and tolerated. Depending on the type of the surgery, the patient may begin oral intake as soon as the gag reflex returns. Offer clear liquids first and continue the IV fluids, usually at a reduced rate. If the patient tolerates oral intake, the IV fluids are stopped.

Be alert to prevent aspiration if the patient vomits while still lethargic from anesthesia. Position the patient in the lateral recovery position and have suction equipment available. Interventions for PONV include monitoring fluid status and providing antiemetic medications and alternative therapies (see Table 46.1). Prophylactic antiemetic medications are given for patients at high risk for PONV. Consider alternative modalities to avoid medication side effects. Patients using complementary interventions such as aromatherapy (essential oils) require fewer antiemetics.[13] Other interventions for PONV that may help include imagery, music, and acupressure.

Constipation may be prevented using bowel protocols that include the use of a stool softener and laxative. Assess the patient regularly to detect the return of peristalsis. Encourage the patient to expel gas. Gas pains tend to become pronounced on the second or third postoperative day. Ambulation and frequent repositioning may provide relief. Positioning the patient on the right side permits gas to rise along the transverse colon and aids its release. Bisacodyl (Dulcolax) suppositories may stimulate colonic peristalsis and expulsion of gas and stool. Resuming a normal diet after bowel sounds have returned also aids the return of normal peristalsis.

The goal of treatment for POI is the relief of symptoms and return of normal GI function. Management includes bowel rest or the withholding of solid foods with a gradual reintroduction of food. Start with clear liquids and advance the diet to solid food with an ongoing assessment of tolerance.

An NG tube may be needed to decompress the stomach to prevent nausea, vomiting, and abdominal distention. Oral care is critical for comfort and stimulation of salivary glands when the patient is NPO or has an NG tube.

URINARY PROBLEMS

Etiology

Low urine output (800 to 1500 mL) in the first 24 hours after surgery is common regardless of fluid intake. Causes include increased aldosterone and ADH secretion resulting from the stress of surgery; fluid restriction before surgery; and fluid loss through surgery, drainage, and diaphoresis. By the second or third day, the patient will have increased urine output as fluid is mobilized and the immediate stress reaction subsides.

Acute urinary retention can occur for a variety of reasons. Anesthesia depresses the nervous system, including the micturition reflex arc and the higher centers that influence it. The bladder fills more completely than normal before the patient feels the urge to void. Anesthesia also impedes voluntary micturition. Anticholinergic and opioid drugs interfere with the ability to start voiding or to empty the bladder completely.

Urinary retention is more likely to occur after lower abdominal or pelvic surgery because spasms or guarding of the abdominal and pelvic muscles interferes with micturition. Pain may alter perception and interfere with the patient's awareness of bladder filling. Immobility and bed rest impair voiding ability. The supine position reduces the ability to relax the perineal muscles and external sphincter.

Oliguria (diminished output of urine) can be a sign of renal failure and is a serious problem after surgery. It may result from renal ischemia caused by inadequate renal perfusion.

❖ NURSING MANAGEMENT: URINARY PROBLEMS

◆ Assessment

Examine the urine for quantity and quality. Urine output should be at least 0.5 mL/kg/hr. Note the color, amount, and odor. Assess indwelling catheters for patency. To decrease the risk for catheter-associated urinary tract infection (CAUTI), remove the catheter as soon as possible or within 24 hours, unless there is a reason to continue its use. Most patients void within 6 to 8 hours after surgery. If no voiding occurs, bladder scan or percuss the suprapubic area for signs of bladder distention.

◆ Clinical Problems

The main clinical problem related to the urinary system is impaired urinary elimination.

◆ Implementation

You can promote voiding by helping the patient into a normal position. Other helpful techniques include providing privacy, running water, offering water for the patient to drink, or pouring warm water over the perineum. Walking, preferably to the bathroom, and the use of a bedside commode are other measures to help with voiding.

The HCP may leave an order to intermittently catheterize the patient in 6 to 8 hours if voiding has not occurred. Because of the risk for CAUTI, first confirm that the bladder is full. Consider fluid intake during and after surgery and determine bladder fullness (e.g., discomfort with bladder palpation). Scan the bladder with a portable ultrasound to assess volume of urine in the bladder and avoid unnecessary catheterization. If catheterization is needed, an intermittent straight catheterization, as compared to an indwelling catheter, limits the risk for CAUTI.

SKIN PROBLEMS

Etiology

Surgery generally involves an incision through the skin and underlying tissues, disrupting the protective skin barrier. Wound healing is a major concern after surgery. One of the greatest risks during the perioperative period is SSI. SSIs occur in 2% to 5% of patients undergoing surgery. They are associated with prolonged hospitalizations, increased costs, and poor patient outcomes. Most SSIs are preventable using evidence-based strategies. These include hand hygiene; selection, timing, and duration of prophylactic antibiotics; surgical site skin preparation; and maintaining perioperative normothermia. Reducing the incidence of SSIs is a major goal of the surgical care improvement project (SCIP) and prevention of postoperative infections initiative.[2] Research supports that when best practices are used, prolonged postoperative antibiotic use does not provide any additional benefit in preventing SSI and instead may result in antimicrobial resistance.[14]

SSIs may result from wound contamination from 3 major sources: (1) exogenous flora present in the environment and on the skin, (2) oral flora, and (3) intestinal flora. The incidence of SSI is higher in patients who are malnourished, immunosuppressed, older, or who have had a long hospital stay or a lengthy surgical procedure (more than 3 hours). After bowel surgery, particularly after a traumatic injury, patients are at high risk. SSI may involve the entire incision and may extend downward through deeper tissues. A local abscess may spread throughout a body cavity, as in peritonitis.

Evidence of SSI usually does not become clear before the 3rd to 5th postoperative day. Local findings include redness, swelling, and increasing pain and tenderness at the site. Systemic findings are fever and leukocytosis.

Fluid accumulation in a wound may create pressure, impair circulation and wound healing, and predispose the patient to infection. To allow for drainage, the HCP may place a drain in the incision or make a stab wound next to the incision. Drains may be of soft rubber and drain into a dressing, or firm catheters attached to a Hemovac or other source of gentle suction.

Adequate nutrition is essential for wound healing. The patient who is well nourished before surgery can tolerate the lack of intake for several days. However, the patient with nutrition problems due to chronic diseases (e.g., diabetes, ulcerative colitis, alcoholism) is more prone to delayed wound healing. The patient who cannot meet nutrition needs may need enteral or parenteral nutrition to promote healing.

❖ NURSING MANAGEMENT: SURGICAL WOUNDS

◆ Assessment

Assessment of the wound and dressing requires knowledge of the type of wound, the drains inserted, and expected drainage related to the specific type of surgery. Immediately after surgery, check the wound every 15 to 30 minutes or as ordered. When drainage appears on the dressing, record the type, amount, color, and odor of drainage. Assess the effect of position changes on drainage. A small amount of serous drainage is common from any type of wound. If a drain is in place, assess the amount of drainage and compare to what is expected. Expected drainage from tubes is listed in Table 20.8. An abdominal incision drain will likely have a moderate amount of serosanguineous drainage in the first 24 hours. In contrast, an inguinal herniorrhaphy should have only minimal serous drainage.

Expect the drainage to change from sanguineous (red) to serosanguineous (pink) to serous (clear yellow) over hours or days, depending on the type of surgery. Purulent drainage may occur with an SSI. *Wound dehiscence* (separation and disruption of previously joined wound edges) may follow a sudden discharge of brown, pink, or clear drainage. Wound dehiscence is discussed in Chapter 12. Notify the HCP of any excess or abnormal drainage or significant changes in vital signs.

TABLE 20.8 Output From Tubes, Drains, and Catheters

Substance	Daily Amount	Color	Odor	Consistency
Indwelling Catheter				
Urine	800–1500 mL for first 24 hr Minimum expected output: 0.5 mL/kg/hr	Clear, yellow	Ammonia	Watery
Nasogastric Tube or Gastrostomy Tube				
Gastric contents	<1500 mL/day	Pale, yellow-green Bloody after GI surgery	Sour	Watery
Open Drains (e.g., Penrose)				
Wound drainage	Varies with procedure May decrease over hours or days	Varies with procedure Initially may be sanguineous or serosanguineous, changing to serous	Same as wound dressing Foul odor may indicate infection	Thin, watery
Closed Suction Drains (e.g., Hemovac, Jackson-Pratt)				
Wound drainage	Varies with procedure May decrease over hours or days	Varies with procedure Initially may be sanguineous or serosanguineous, changing to serous	Little to no odor Foul odor may indicate infection	Thin, watery
T-Tube				
Bile	500 mL	Bright yellow to dark green	Acid	Thick
Mediastinal Chest Tube				
Wound drainage post cardiothoracic surgery	Varies with procedure Should decrease over several hours after surgery	Sanguineous or serosanguineous	N/A	Thin
Pleural Chest Tube				
Fluid that has collected in the pleural space	Varies with procedure Decreases over hours or days >100 mL/hr is considered excessive	Varies with indication for insertion and fluid collected in the pleural spaces	N/A	Varies with indication for insertion

◆ Clinical Problems

Clinical problems related to surgical wounds include:

- Impaired tissue integrity
- Infection
- Risk for infection

◆ Implementation

The incision may be covered with a dressing after surgery. Many HCPs prefer to change the first postoperative dressing. If the initial operative dressing is saturated, follow agency policy as to changing or simply reinforcing the dressing. Skin graft dressings may stay in place for 3 to 5 days to avoid disturbing the graft site and promote graft acceptance. Specially trained nurses may change these dressings. Skin grafts are discussed in Chapter 25.

When you change a dressing, note the number and type of drains present. Avoid dislodging the drains. Inspect the incision site carefully. The area around the sutures may be slightly reddened and swollen, which is an expected inflammatory response. However, the skin around the incision should be of normal color and temperature. If the wound is healing by primary intention, has little or no drainage, or has no drains in place, use a single-layer dressing or no dressing. Use a multilayer dressing when drains are in place, moderate to heavy drainage is occurring, or healing occurs other than by primary intention. Wound healing and care are discussed in Chapter 11.

DISCHARGE FROM THE PACU

The decision to discharge the patient from the PACU is based on written discharge criteria approved by the agency's anesthesiology and medical staff (Table 20.9). Standardized scoring systems (e.g., *Modified Aldrete Scoring System*) are often used to determine the patient's general condition and readiness for discharge from the PACU. The choice of discharge site is based on patient acuity, access to follow-up care, and the potential for complications.

Discharge to the Clinical Unit

Before discharging the patient from the PACU to the clinical unit, give a hand-off report about the patient to the receiving nurse. The report summarizes the operative and postanesthesia period. It should include information as to where the patient's caregivers are waiting. Nurse-to-nurse communication must

TABLE 20.9 Surgery Discharge Criteria

PACU Discharge Criteria (Phase I)

- Patient awake, easily arousable (or baseline)
- Vital signs at baseline or stable
- No excess bleeding or drainage
- No respiratory depression
- O_2 saturation >90%
- Pain controlled or acceptable
- Nausea and vomiting controlled
- Report given

Ambulatory Surgery Discharge Criteria (Phase II or Extended Observation)

- All PACU discharge criteria (Phase I) met
- No IV opioid drugs for last 30 min
- Voided if appropriate to surgical procedure or orders
- Able to ambulate if not contraindicated
- Responsible adult present to accompany and drive patient home
- Written discharge instructions given and patient and caregiver understanding confirmed

be accurate and allow for questions. The use of a standardized communication tool, such as SBAR *(Situation-Background-Assessment-Recommendation),* enhances a safe transfer of the patient from PACU to the clinical unit (Table 20.10).

When you receive the patient on the clinical unit, assist the PACU transport staff to safely move the patient from the stretcher to the bed. Take care to protect IV lines, drains, and traction devices. Obtain vital signs and compare the patient status with the report provided by the PACU nurse. After this, perform a more focused assessment and initiate postoperative orders and nursing care (Table 20.11).

AMBULATORY SURGERY

Phase II and Extended Observation

Advances in minimally invasive and noninvasive procedures, anesthesia, and analgesia have resulted in an increase in ambulatory surgeries. Ambulatory surgery patients include those patients receiving Phase II and extended observation postoperative care (Table 20.1). PONV and pain are common problems after ambulatory surgery. These can lead to delirium, prolonged PACU stay, delayed discharge, readmission, delayed resumption of usual activities, and decreased patient satisfaction.

Ambulatory Surgery Discharge

The patient leaving an ambulatory surgery setting must be hemodynamically stable, mobile, alert, and able to provide a degree of self-care when discharged to home (Table 20.9). PONV and pain must be under control. Overall, the patient must be stable and near the level of preoperative functioning for discharge from the unit. The patient may not drive and must be accompanied by an adult at the time of discharge. Carefully assess the patient's readiness for discharge and home care needs. Determine availability of caregivers (e.g., family, friends) and access to (1) a pharmacy for prescriptions, (2) a phone in the case of an emergency, and (3) follow-up care.

TABLE 20.10 Postoperative SBAR Hand-Off Communication

Situation

Patient ____________ Date of birth ____________
Transferring to Room # ____________ Surgeon ____________
ACP ____________ Type of Anesthesia ____________
Procedure ____________
Surgical site(s) ____________
Medical history ____________
Code status ____________ Isolation precautions ____________

Background

Allergies ____________
Medications received in PACU ____________
IV site/fluids ____________
Dressings and/or drains ____________
Significant OR events ____________

Assessment

PACU vital signs T ______ P ______ RR ______ BP ______ O_2 Sat ______
O_2 source ____________ FIO_2 ____________
Pain rating at discharge ____________
Method of pain management ____________
Last dose of pain medication ____________
Mental status ____________
Nausea/vomiting at discharge ____________
Intake ____________ Output ____________
Laboratory tests ____________
Recovery comments ____________

Recommendations

Equipment needed ____________
Orders to be completed ____________
Family ____________
Other notes ____________
Transferring RN ____________ Phone # for questions ____________
Receiving RN ____________

Planning for Discharge and Follow-Up Care

Preparation for the patient's discharge is an ongoing process that begins before surgery. Include the patient and caregiver in discharge planning. Provide them with information and support to make informed decisions about ongoing care (Table 20.12). The informed patient is prepared as events unfold and gradually assumes more responsibility for self-care during the postoperative period.

As discharge approaches, assess the needs of the patient. Patients should be given verbal and written instructions. Some may benefit from pictures and/or videos to refer back to upon discharge (e.g., for information about wound care or dressing changes). Many agencies have television systems connected to institutionally approved databases for patient education. Include caregivers in the discharge process. Once the patient and/or caregiver has reviewed the discharge information, they should provide the nurse with a "teach back" demonstration verifying correct technique and understanding.

Common reasons patients seek help after discharge include unrelieved pain, questions about drugs, and wound issues

TABLE 20.11 NURSING ASSESSMENT

Care of Patient on Admission to Clinical Unit

1. Record time of patient's return to unit and assess airway, breathing, and circulation.
2. Obtain baseline vital signs, including O_2 saturation.
3. Assess neurologic status, including level of consciousness and movement of extremities.
4. Assess level of pain:
   - Last dose and type of pain control
   - Current pain rating
5. Assess wound, dressing, and drainage tubes:
   - Type and amount of drainage
   - Tubing connected to gravity or suction drainage (per orders)
6. Assess color, temperature, and appearance of skin.
7. Position for airway maintenance, comfort, and safety (bed in low position, side rails up).
8. Check IV infusion:
   - Type of solution
   - Amount of fluid remaining
   - Patency and flow rate
   - Condition of insertion site and size of catheter
9. Assess urinary status:
   - Time of voiding
   - Presence of catheter, patency, and total output
   - Bladder distention or urge to void
10. Assess for any nausea or vomiting.
    - Availability of emesis basin and tissues
11. Position call bell within reach and orient patient to use of call bell.
12. Determine emotional state and provide support as needed.
13. Check for presence of caregiver.
    - Orient patient and caregiver to immediate environment
14. Check and carry out postoperative orders.

TABLE 20.12 PATIENT & CAREGIVER TEACHING

Surgical Discharge

Include the following information in discharge instructions for the patient and caregiver after surgery.

- Symptoms to report (e.g., discomfort in other parts of the body, fever, increased incisional pain, swelling, redness, bleeding, drainage)
- When and how to take prescribed drugs and possible side effects (reinforce education regarding multimodal pain control)
- Care of wound, incision, drain (e.g., dressing change)
- Personal hygiene and showering recommendations
- Activities allowed and prohibited, when various activities can be resumed safely (e.g., driving, return to work, sexual intercourse, leisure activities, lifting restrictions)
- Diet restrictions or modifications
- Where and when to return for follow-up appointment
- Answers to any questions or concerns
- Who and what phone number to call to report symptoms, ask additional questions, and address concerns after discharge

(e.g., drainage). Attention to complete discharge instructions may prevent needless distress for the patient and caregiver. Standardized, preprinted discharge instructions that are surgery specific and easy to read ensure that information is complete.

Document the discharge teaching in the chart. The postoperative phase of care extends into the recuperative period. Assessment and evaluation of the patient after discharge may be done with a follow-up call or by a visit from a home health nurse, who can address any specific questions and concerns.

Increasingly, patients are discharged from the hospital with many care needs. They may be transferred to transitional care facilities, to long-term care facilities, or directly home. When discharged directly to home, the patient is expected to continue self-care, with help from caregivers or home health care personnel (e.g., nurses, physical therapists). The care may include dressing changes, wound care, catheter or drain care, antibiotic therapy, or physical therapy. Working together with the discharge planner or case manager, ensure the patient's safe transition from hospital-based care to community- or home-based care.

CHECK YOUR PRACTICE

You are caring for a young adult patient who had a laparoscopic appendectomy 18 hours ago. The patient meets the discharge criteria, and the HCP has asked you to provide discharge teaching for the patient.

- What should you cover in the discharge teaching plan?

Gerontologic Considerations: Postoperative Patient

The older surgical patient deserves special consideration. The older adult has decreased respiratory function, including decreased ability to cough and decreased thoracic compliance. These changes lead to an increase in the work of breathing and a decreased ability to eliminate drugs. Carefully monitor reactions to anesthetic drugs. Pneumonia is a common complication in older adults.

Altered vascular function in the older adult is due to atherosclerosis and decreased elasticity in the blood vessels. Circulating blood volume decreases. Hypertension is common. Cardiac function is often compromised with limited compensatory responses to changes in BP and volume. Monitor cardiovascular status closely throughout the postoperative period.

Drug toxicity is a potential problem in the older adult. Renal perfusion normally decreases, along with a reduced ability to remove drugs. Decreased liver function leads to reduced drug metabolism and increased drug activity. Carefully assess renal and liver function to prevent drug overdose and toxicity.

Observe for changes in mental status. Age, alcohol use, poor baseline cognition, hypoxia, metabolic imbalances, hypotension, and polypharmacy can contribute to postoperative delirium. Anesthetics, especially anticholinergic and benzodiazepine drugs, increase the risk for delirium.

Pain control in the older patient is challenging because of possible preexisting cognitive deficits, impaired communication, and physiologic changes that affect drug metabolism. Patients may hesitate to ask for pain medication because they believe pain is inevitable after surgery. Some older patients may fear addiction or be nervous about using PCA machines. Thoroughly assess pain in a surgical patient who does not report any pain. Encourage the use of analgesics as needed. Explain to the patient and caregiver that untreated pain has a negative effect on recovery.

Case Study

Postoperative Patient

(© BananaStock/ BananaStock/ Thinkstock.)

Patient Profile

E.G., a 74-year-old retired college professor, has just undergone a right total hip replacement to repair a right hip fracture. He fell off a ladder while painting his house. His medical history includes type 2 diabetes and COPD. The surgery was done under general anesthesia and lasted 3 hours.

Subjective Data

- Active walker in his home community
- Smokes 1 pack of cigarettes per day × 58 years
- Always had problems sleeping
- Difficulty hearing, wears hearing aid
- Upset with injury and its impact on life
- Widower; no relatives nearby or friends to assist with care
- Reports pain is 8 on a 0 to 10 scale on arrival to PACU

Objective Data

- Abduction pillow between legs
- Peripheral IV catheter
- Jackson-Pratt drain visible at the site of the hip dressing
- Indwelling urinary catheter in place
- O_2 saturation 92% on 4 L nasal cannula

Interprofessional Care

Postoperative Orders

- Vital signs per PACU routine
- Glucose level on arrival and every 4 hours. Call for glucose level <70 mg/dL or >250 mg/dL. Follow protocol for managing hypoglycemia.
- 0.45% normal saline at 100 mL/hr
- Morphine via patient-controlled analgesia 1 mg q10min (20 mg max/4 hr) for pain
- Advance diet as tolerated
- O_2 therapy to keep O_2 saturation >90%
- Albuterol 2.5 mg via nebulizer every 4 hours as needed for wheezing
- Encourage coughing, deep breathing and incentive spirometry q1hr × 10 while awake
- Neurovascular checks q1hr × 4 hr
- Assess, empty and record output of Jackson-Pratt drain every 2 hours × 4 hr
- Maintain strict intake and output
- Pneumatic compression boots while in bed at 40 mm Hg
- Ambulate to chair and in halls 3 times daily

Discussion Questions

1. ***Recognize:*** What should you include when assessing E.G.?
2. ***Recognize:*** What factors predispose E.G. to the following problems: atelectasis, SSI, and VTE?
3. ***Analyze:*** How would you determine E.G. is sufficiently recovered from general anesthesia to be discharged to the clinical unit?
4. ***Analyze:*** What complications is E.G. at risk for developing?
5. ***Plan:*** What referrals may be indicated based on E.G.'s medical history?
6. ***Plan:*** What potential postoperative problems on the clinical unit might you expect?
7. ***Prioritize:*** What priority nursing interventions would be appropriate to prevent postoperative complication such as atelectasis, SSI, and VTE?
8. ***Act:*** Identify activities that can be delegated to assistive personnel (AP).
9. ***Act:*** What teaching will you provide so that E.G. can successfully self-manage care?
10. ***Evaluate:*** What outcomes would indicate that interprofessional care with respiratory therapy was effective?
11. ***Safety:*** What are risk factors for E.G. developing postoperative delirium? What are the signs and symptoms of delirium?
12. ***Safety:*** Identify 2 areas of risk for injury to E.G. What actions can you take to ensure patient safety?

Answers available at http://evolve.elsevier.com/Lewis/medsurg.

BRIDGE TO NCLEX EXAMINATION

The number of the question corresponds to the same-numbered outcome at the beginning of the chapter.

1. Which actions would the nurse prioritize when admitting a patient to the PACU?
   a. Assess the surgical site, noting presence and character of drainage.
   b. Assess the amount of urine output and the presence of bladder distention.
   c. Assess for airway patency and quality of respirations and obtain vital signs.
   d. Review results of intraoperative laboratory values and medications received.

2. A patient is admitted to the PACU after major abdominal surgery. During the initial assessment the patient tells the nurse, "I think I am going to throw up." Which is the *priority* intervention?
   a. Increase the rate of the IV fluids.
   b. Give antiemetic medication as ordered.
   c. Obtain vital signs, including O_2 saturation.
   d. Position patient in lateral recovery position.

3. After admitting a postoperative patient to the clinical unit, which assessment data require attention first?
   a. O_2 saturation of 85%
   b. Respiratory rate of 13/min
   c. Temperature of 100.4°F (38°C)
   d. Blood pressure of 90/60 mm Hg

4. A 70-kg postoperative patient has an average urine output of 25 mL/hr during the first 8 hours. Which interventions would the nurse prioritize? *(Select all that apply.)*
   a. Obtain a bladder ultrasound scan.
   b. Perform a straight catheterization.
   c. Continue to monitor this normal finding.
   d. Evaluate the patient's fluid volume status.

5. Which factors would the nurse include in discharge criteria for a Phase II patient? *(select all that apply)*
   a. Nausea and vomiting controlled.
   b. Ability to drive themselves home.
   c. No respiratory depression present.
   d. Written discharge instructions understood.
   e. Opioid pain medication given 45 minutes ago.

1. c; 2. d; 3. a; 4. a, d; 5. a, c, d, e.

For rationales to these answers and even more NCLEX review questions, visit http://evolve.elsevier.com/Lewis/medsurg.

EVOLVE WEBSITE/RESOURCES LIST

http://evolve.elsevier.com/Lewis/medsurg
Review Questions (Online Only)
Key Points
Answer Keys for Questions
- Rationales for Bridge to NCLEX Examination Questions
- Answer Guidelines for Case Study
- Answer Guidelines for Managing Care of Multiple Patients Case Study (Section 4)

Student Case Study
- Patient Undergoing Surgery

Nursing Care Plan
- eNursing Care Plan 19.1: Postoperative Patient

Conceptual Care Map Creator
Audio Glossary
Content Updates

REFERENCES

1. Schick L, Windle P: In *Perianesthesia nursing core curriculum: Preprocedure, phase I and phase II PACU nursing*, ed 4, St Louis, 2021, Elsevier.
2. Rothrock J: In *Alexander's care of the patient in surgery*, ed 16, St Louis, 2019, Elsevier.
*3. American Association of Nurse Anesthesiology. Postanesthesia care practice considerations. Retrieved from https://www.aana.com/search?keyword=post+anesthesia+care, 2019.
*4. Eisenberg ME, Givony D, Levin R: Acoustic respiration rate and pulse oximetry-derived respiration rate: a clinical comparison study, *J Clin Monit Comput* 34:139, 2020.
*5. Matharu GS, Kunutsor SK, Judge A, Blom AW, Whitehouse MR: Clinical effectiveness and safety of aspirin for venous thromboembolism prophylaxis after total hip and knee replacement, *JAMA Intern Med* 180:376, 2020.
6. American Society of Anesthesiologists. What is the perioperative brain health initiative? Retrieved from https://www.asahq.org/brainhealthinitiative/about.
*7. Pan X, Wang J, Lin Z, Dai W, Shi Z: Depression and anxiety are risk factors for postoperative pain-related symptoms and complications in patients undergoing primary total knee arthroplasty in the United States, *J Arthroplasty* 34:2337, 2019.
8. Harbaugh CM, Suwanabol PA: Optimizing pain control during the opioid epidemic, *Surg Clin North Am* 99:867, 2019.
*9. Sim V, Hawkins S, Gave AA, et al.: How low can you go, *J Trauma Acute Care Surg* 87:100, 2019.
*10. Link T: Guidelines in practice: hypothermia prevention, *AORN J* 111:653, 2020.
*11. Finch C, Parkosewich JA, Perrone D, Weidman KH, Furino L: Incidence, timing, and factors associated with postoperative nausea and vomiting in the ambulatory surgery setting, *J PeriAnesthesia Nurs* 34:1146, 2019.
12. Lee M, Vaughan-Shaw P, Vimalachandran D: A systematic review and meta-analysis of baseline risk factors for the development of postoperative ileus in patients undergoing gastrointestinal surgery, *Ann R Coll Surg Engl* 102:194, 2020.
*13. Fearrington M, Qualls B, Carey M. Essential oils to reduce postoperative nausea and vomiting. Retrieved from https://www.sciencedirect.com/science/article/abs/pii/S1089947219300644.
*14. Jonge SW, Boldingh QJ, Solomkin JS, et al.: Effect of postoperative continuation of antibiotic prophylaxis on the incidence of surgical site infection: a systematic review and meta-analysis, *Lancet Infect Dis*, 2020. Retrieved from https://doi.org/10.1016/s1473-3099(20)30084-0.

*Evidence-based information for clinical practice.

21

Emergency and Disaster Nursing

Samantha J. Bonaduce and Mariann M. Harding

http://evolve.elsevier.com/Lewis/medsurg/

CONCEPTUAL FOCUS

Gas Exchange
Interpersonal Violence
Perfusion
Thermoregulation

LEARNING OUTCOMES

1. Apply the steps in triage, the primary survey, and the secondary survey to a patient with a medical, surgical, or traumatic emergency.
2. Relate the pathophysiology to the assessment and interprofessional care of select environmental emergencies.
3. Relate the pathophysiology to the assessment and interprofessional care of select toxicologic emergencies.
4. Select appropriate nursing interventions for victims of violence.
5. Distinguish among the responsibilities of health care providers, the community, and select federal agencies in emergency and mass casualty incident preparedness.

KEY TERMS

drowning
emergency
frostbite
heat exhaustion
heatstroke
hypothermia
mass casualty incident (MCI)
primary survey
secondary survey
submersion injury
terrorism
triage
violence

Entire books are dedicated to the nursing care of emergency patients. It is a unique specialty that requires a solid understanding of specific nursing concepts and approaches to patient problems. Nurses unaccustomed to the emergency department (ED) often describe the flow as "chaotic" and uncertain. Indeed, it may have this appearance. The challenge of the ED is that the nurse does not know what patient will come through the doors. The ED nurse must be prepared to meet this challenge. This chapter presents an overview of the triage process and care of select emergency patients. Common emergencies discussed include heat- and cold-related emergencies, submersion injuries, bites and stings, and various poisonings. The chapter concludes with a discussion of terrorism, mass casualty incidents, and the methods of response.

The emergency management of various medical, surgical, and traumatic emergencies is discussed throughout this book. Tables outline the emergency management of specific problems. Table 21.1 lists these emergency management tables by title, chapter number, and page.

More than 130 million people visit EDs each year.[1] While the number visiting the ED is down slightly, the number of patients admitted to the hospital is increasing. There are several reasons for this increase. Continued growth in retail clinics, telehealth, and other sources of care for nonemergent problems has resulted in the ED seeing older, sicker patients with more complex needs.[2]

ED nurses care for patients of all ages with a variety of problems. However, some EDs specialize in specific patient populations or conditions, such as pediatric ED or trauma ED. The Emergency Nurses Association (ENA) is the specialty organization aimed at advancing emergency nursing practice. The ENA provides standards of care for nurses working in the ED. They offer a certification process that allows nurses to become certified emergency nurses (CENs).

CARE OF EMERGENCY PATIENT

Recognizing life-threatening illness or injury is one of the most important goals of emergency nursing. Starting interventions

TABLE 21.1 EMERGENCY MANAGEMENT

Emergency Management Tables Throughout the Book

Title	Chapter
Abdominal Trauma	47
Acute Abdominal Pain	47
Acute GI Bleeding	46
Acute Soft Tissue Injury	67
Acute Thyrotoxicosis	54
Anaphylactic Shock	14
Chest Injuries	30
Chest Pain	37
Chest Trauma	30
Depressant Toxicity	11
DKA	53
Dysrhythmias	39
Eye Injury	22
Fractured Extremity	67
Head Injury	61
Hyperthermia	21
Hypoglycemia	53
Hypothermia	21
Inhalation Injury	26
SCI	65
Shock	42
Stimulant Toxicity	11
Stroke	62
Submersion Injuries	21
Tonic-Clonic Seizures	63

to reverse or prevent a crisis is often a priority before making a medical diagnosis. This process begins with your first contact with a patient. Prompt identification of patients who need immediate treatment and determining appropriate interventions are essential nurse competencies.

Triage

Triage refers to the process of rapidly determining patient acuity. It is one of the most important assessment skills needed by ED nurses. ED nurses often confront multiple patients who have a variety of problems. The triage process works on the premise that we must treat patients who have a threat to life before other patients.

A *triage system* identifies and categorizes patients so that the most critically ill are treated first. The ENA and American College of Emergency Physicians support the use of a 5-level triage system.[3] The *Emergency Severity Index* (ESI) is a 5-level triage system that incorporates concepts of illness severity and resource use (e.g., electrocardiogram [ECG], laboratory tests, radiology studies, IV fluids) to determine who we should treat first (Table 21.2). The ESI includes a triage algorithm that directs you to assign an ESI level to patients coming into the ED. The ESI Implementation Handbook details the triage algorithm.[3]

First, assess the patient for any threats to life (ESI-1) (Fig. 21.1). Ask, "Does this patient need lifesaving intervention?" Or, for ESI-2, is this a high-risk patient who cannot wait to be seen? Next, evaluate patients who do not meet the criteria for ESI-1

TABLE 21.2 Examples of Patients at Each ESI Level

ESI Level	Examples
1	Cardiac arrest, intubated trauma patient, overdose with bradypnea, severe respiratory distress, anaphylactic shock, hypoglycemia with change in mental status
2	Chest pain from ischemia, multiple trauma unless responsive, suicidal patient, immunocompromised patient with a fever, acute stroke
3	Abdominal pain or gynecologic disorders unless in severe distress, hip fracture in older patient, vomiting, hypertension
4	Closed extremity trauma, simple laceration, cystitis
5	Cold symptoms, minor burn, poison ivy, recheck (e.g., wound), prescription refill

or ESI-2 for the number of expected resources they may need. Assign patients to ESI-3, ESI-4, or ESI-5 based on this determination. Vital signs are important. Patients assigned to ESI-3 must have normal vital signs. Patients with abnormal vital signs may be reassigned to ESI-2.[3]

CHECK YOUR PRACTICE

You are working in the ED with your preceptor, who is a triage nurse. A 24-year-old man arrives and states, "I think I have food poisoning. I've been vomiting all night, and now I have diarrhea." The patient reports abdominal cramping that he rates as 6/10. He denies fever or chills. Vital signs: T = 97.8°F (36.6°C), HR = 94, RR = 16, BP = 121/74 mm Hg.

- Assign a triage acuity rating using the ESI.

After you complete the initial focused assessment to determine the presence of actual or potential threats to life, proceed with a more detailed assessment. A systematic approach to this assessment decreases the time needed to identify potential threats to life and limits the risk of overlooking a life-threatening problem. A primary and secondary survey is the approach used for all trauma patients. For nontrauma patients, the primary survey is followed by a focused assessment. Focused assessments are discussed in Chapter 3.

Primary Survey

The **primary survey** (Table 21.3) focuses on airway, breathing, circulation (ABC), disability, exposure, full set of vitals and family presence, and getting other monitoring devices. If there is uncontrolled external hemorrhage, the usual ABC assessment format may be reprioritized to <C>ABC. The C stands for catastrophic hemorrhage. If present, it must be controlled first.[4] Apply direct pressure with a sterile dressing followed by a pressure dressing to any obvious bleeding sites.

The primary survey aims to identify life-threatening problems so that we can start appropriate interventions (Table 21.4). You may identify life-threatening problems related to ABCs at any point during the primary survey. When this occurs, start interventions at once before moving to the next step of the survey.

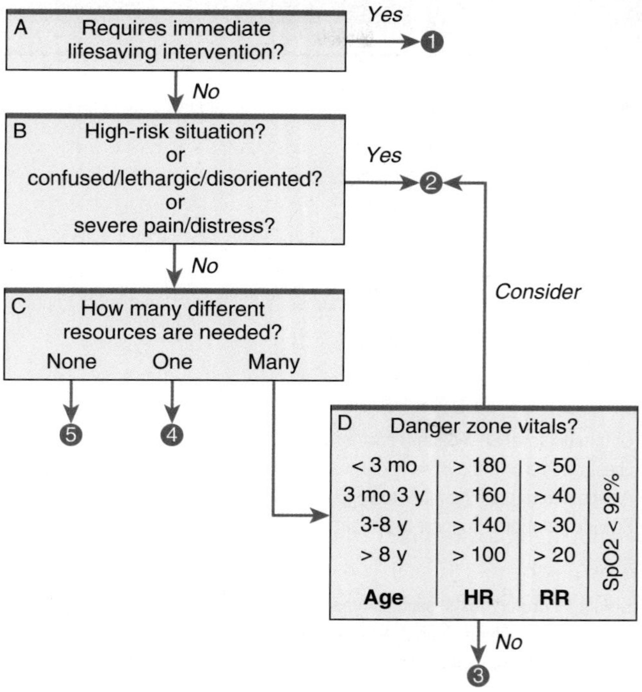

Resources: Count the number of different types of resources, not the individual tests or radiographs (e.g., complete blood count, electrolytes, and coagulants equals one resource, while completed blood count plus chest radiograph equals two resources).

Resources	Not resources
• Labs (blood, urine) • Electrocardiogram, radiographs • Computed tomography, magnetic resonance imaging, ultrasound, angiography	• History and physical exam (including pelvic) • Point-of-care testing
• Intravenous fluids (hydration)	• Saline or heparin lock
• Intravenous, intramuscular, or nebulized medications	• Oral medications • Tetanus immunization • Prescription refills
• Specialty consultation	• Phone call to primary care physician
• Simple procedure = 1 (laceration repair, urinary catheter) • Complex procedure = 2 (procedural sedation)	• Simple wound care (dressings, recheck) • Crutches, splints, slings

Fig. 21.1 ESI Triage Algorithm.

TABLE 21.3 Emergency Assessment

Primary Survey

Assessment	Interventions
Alertness (A_1) and Airway (A_2) With Cervical Spine Stabilization and/or Immobilization	
• Assess alertness (e.g., AVPU). • Assess for respiratory distress. • Determine airway patency. • Check for loose teeth or foreign bodies. • Assess for bleeding, vomitus, or edema.	• Maintain cervical spine stabilization and/or immobilization. • Open airway using jaw-thrust maneuver. • Remove or suction any foreign bodies. • Insert oropharyngeal or nasopharyngeal airway, tracheostomy. • Begin rapid sequence intubation. • Immobilize cervical spine using rigid cervical collar and cervical immobilization device.
Breathing	
• Assess ventilation. • Scan chest for signs of breathing. • Look for paradoxical movement of the chest wall during inspiration and expiration. • Note use of accessory muscles or abdominal muscles. • Observe and count respiratory rate. • Note color of nail beds, mucous membranes. • Auscultate lungs. • Assess for jugular venous distention and trachea position.	• Give supplemental O_2 via appropriate delivery system (e.g., nonrebreather mask). • Ventilate with bag-valve-mask with 100% O_2 if respirations are inadequate or absent. • Prepare to intubate if severe respiratory distress (e.g., agonal breaths) or arrest. • Have suction available. • If absent breath sounds, prepare for needle thoracostomy and chest tube insertion.
Circulation and Control of Hemorrhage	
• Assess for uncontrolled bleeding. • Check carotid or femoral pulse. • Palpate pulse for quality and rate. • Assess skin color, temperature, moisture. • Check capillary refill.	• If absent pulse, start CPR and advanced life support measures. • Control bleeding with direct pressure and pressure dressings. • If shock symptoms or hypotensive, start 2 large-bore (14- to 16-gauge) IVs and start infusions of normal saline or lactated Ringer's solution. • Consider intraosseous or central venous access if IV access cannot be rapidly obtained. • Give blood products if ordered.

Continued

TABLE 21.3 Emergency Assessment—cont'd

Assessment	Interventions
Disability	
• Assess level of consciousness by determining response to verbal and/or painful stimuli (e.g., Glasgow Coma Scale). • Assess pupils for size, shape, equality, and reactivity.	• Periodically reassess level of consciousness, mental status, and pupil size, and reactivity.
Exposure (E_1) and Environmental Control (E_2)	
• Assess full body for determination of other or related injuries. • Assess environment.	• Remove clothing for adequate assessment. • Stabilize any impaled objects. • Keep patient warm with blankets, warmed IV fluids, overhead lights to prevent heat loss, if appropriate. • Maintain privacy.
Full Set of Vitals (F_1) and Family Presence (F_2)	
• Assess vital signs and pulse oximetry. • Determine caregiver's desire to be present during invasive procedures and/or CPR.	• Obtain bilateral BP if patient has sustained or is suspected of having sustained chest trauma or if the BP is abnormal. • Assign health team member to support caregiver(s). • Provide emotional support to patient and caregiver.
Get Monitoring Devices (G_1) and Give Comfort (G_2)	
• Determine need for adjunct measures for monitoring the patient's condition: **L**—Laboratory studies **M**—Monitor cardiac status **N**—Naso or orogastric tube **O**—Oxygen and ventilation assessment **P**—Pain assessment and management	• Obtain laboratory tests, such as type and crossmatch, CBC and metabolic panel, lactate, blood alcohol, toxicology screening, ABGs, coagulation profile, cardiac biomarkers, pregnancy. • Continuously monitor ECG. • Insert NG tube; insert orogastric tube in a patient with significant head or facial trauma. • Monitor oxygenation and ventilation (e.g., continuous pulse oximetry, capnography). • Manage pain with pharmacologic (e.g., NSAIDs, IV opioids) and nonpharmacologic (e.g., distraction, positioning, music) pain management strategies. • Provide comfort measures as appropriate (e.g., ice, position of comfort, warm blanket).

AVPU, A = alert; V = responsive to voice; P= responsive to pain; U = unresponsive.

TABLE 21.4 Potential Life-Threatening Problems Found During Primary Survey

Airway	• Inhalation injury (e.g., fire victim) • Obstruction (partial or complete) from foreign bodies, debris (e.g., vomitus), or tongue • Penetrating wounds and/or blunt trauma to upper airway structures
Breathing	• Anaphylaxis • Flail chest with pulmonary contusion • Hemothorax • Pneumothorax (e.g., open, tension)
Circulation	• Direct cardiac injury (e.g., myocardial infarction, trauma) • Pericardial tamponade • Shock (e.g., massive burns, hypovolemia) • Uncontrolled external hemorrhage • Hypothermia
Disability	• Head injury • Stroke

List is not all-inclusive.

A = Alertness and Airway

Nearly all immediate trauma deaths occur because of airway obstruction. Saliva, bloody secretions, vomitus, laryngeal trauma, dentures, facial trauma, fractures, and the tongue can obstruct the airway. Patients at risk for airway compromise include those who drown or have seizures, anaphylaxis, foreign body obstruction, or cardiopulmonary arrest. If an airway is not maintained, obstruction of airflow, hypoxia, and death will result. Signs of a compromised airway include dyspnea, inability to speak, gasping (agonal) breaths, foreign body in the airway, and trauma to the face or neck. The patient's alertness level is a crucial factor for choosing the right airway interventions. Determine level of consciousness (LOC) by assessing the patient's response to verbal and/or painful stimuli. A simple mnemonic to remember is *AVPU: A* = alert, *V* = responsive to voice, *P* = responsive to pain, and *U* = unresponsive.[5]

Airway maintenance should progress rapidly from the least to the most invasive method. Treatment includes opening the airway using the *jaw-thrust maneuver* (avoiding hyperextension of the neck), suctioning and/or removal of foreign body, inserting a nasopharyngeal or oropharyngeal airway (in unconscious patients only), and endotracheal intubation. If intubation is impossible because of airway obstruction, an emergency cricothyroidotomy or tracheotomy is done (see Chapter 28). Ventilate patients with 100% O_2 using a bag-valve-mask (BVM) device before intubation or cricothyroidotomy.

Rapid-sequence intubation is the preferred procedure for securing an unprotected airway in the ED. It involves the use of sedatives and paralytic drugs. These drugs aid in intubation and reduce the risk for aspiration and airway trauma. See Chapter 28 for more about intubation.

If the patient has a suspected spinal cord injury and is not already immobilized, the cervical spine must be stabilized at the same time as the assessment of the airway. This can be done with manual stabilization or the use of a rigid cervical collar (C collar). Keep the bed flat. Continue to monitor airway patency and breathing effectiveness.

B = Breathing

Adequate airflow through the upper airway does not ensure adequate ventilation. Many problems cause breathing changes. Common ones include fractured ribs, pneumothorax, penetrating injury, allergic reactions, pulmonary emboli, and asthma attacks. Patients with these problems may have a variety of signs and symptoms. There may be dyspnea, paradoxical or asymmetric chest wall movement, decreased or absent breath sounds on the affected side, visible wounds to the chest wall, cyanosis, tachycardia, and hypotension.

Every critically injured or ill patient has increased metabolic and O_2 demand. They should receive supplemental O_2. Give high-flow O_2 (100%) via a nonrebreather mask and monitor the patient's response. Life-threatening problems (e.g., flail chest, tension pneumothorax) can severely and quickly compromise ventilation. Interventions may include BVM ventilation with 100% O_2, needle decompression, intubation, and treatment of the underlying cause.

C = Circulation and Control of Hemorrhage

An effective circulatory system includes the heart, intact blood vessels, and adequate blood volume. Uncontrolled internal or external bleeding places a person at risk for hemorrhagic shock (see Chapter 42). Check either a femoral or carotid pulse. Peripheral pulses may be absent due to direct injury or vasoconstriction. Assess the quality and rate of the pulse if found. Assess the skin for color, temperature, and moisture. Altered mental status and delayed capillary refill (longer than 3 seconds) are common signs of shock. When evaluating capillary refill in cold environments, remember that cold temperature delays refill.

Insert IV lines into the upper extremities unless contraindicated, such as an open fracture or an injury that affects limb circulation. Insert 2 large-bore (14- to 16-gauge) IV catheters. Start aggressive fluid resuscitation using normal saline or lactated Ringer's solution. Consider intraosseous or central venous access if unable to rapidly obtain venous access. See Chapter 42 for more about hypovolemic shock and fluid resuscitation.

The HCP may order type-specific packed red blood cells if needed. In an emergency (life-threatening) situation, give blood that is not cross-matched (e.g., O negative) if immediate transfusion is needed.

D = Disability

Conduct a brief neurologic assessment as part of the primary survey. The patient's LOC is a measure of the degree of disability. Use the Glasgow Coma Scale (GCS) to determine the LOC (see Table 61.5).[6] This allows for consistent communication among the interprofessional care team. Remember! The GCS is not accurate for intubated or aphasic patients. Last, assess the pupils for size, shape, equality, and reactivity.

E = Exposure and Environmental Control

Remove the patient's clothing so you can perform a thorough physical assessment. This often requires cutting off the clothing. Be careful not to cut through any area that is forensic evidence (e.g., bullet hole). Do not remove any impaled objects (e.g., knife). Removing these could cause bleeding and further injury. Once the patient is exposed, use warming blankets, overhead warmers, and warmed IV fluids to limit heat loss, prevent hypothermia, and maintain privacy.

F = Full Set of Vitals and Family Presence

Obtain a full set of vital signs, including BP, heart rate, respiratory rate, O_2 saturation, and temperature after the patient is exposed. If the patient has sustained or is suspected of having sustained chest trauma, or if the BP is abnormally high or low, obtain a BP in both arms.

Research supports the benefits for patients, caregivers, and staff of *family presence* during resuscitation and invasive procedures.[7] Patients and caregivers report that caregivers provide comfort. Patients state caregivers serve as advocates and help remind the care team of their "personhood." Caregivers who are present during invasive procedures and resuscitation view themselves as active participants in the care process. They voice feeling that they receive better information to make decisions. They believe that they comfort the patient and that it is their right to be with the patient. It is essential to assign a health care team member to explain the care being delivered and answer questions if a caregiver is present during resuscitation or invasive procedures.

G = Get Monitoring Devices and Give Comfort

Start adjunct measures for monitoring the patient's condition if not already done. Use the memory aid LMNOP to remember these resuscitation aids:

L: Laboratory tests, such as type and crossmatch, complete blood count (CBC) and metabolic panel, blood alcohol, toxicology screening, arterial blood gases (ABGs), coagulation profile, cardiac biomarkers, pregnancy test, and urinalysis.
M: Monitor ECG for heart rate and rhythm.
N: Nasogastric (NG) tube to decompress and empty the stomach, reduce the risk for aspiration, and test the contents for blood. Place an orogastric tube in a patient with significant head or facial trauma since an NG tube could enter the brain.
O: Oxygenation and ventilation assessment. Continuously monitor O_2 saturation and end-tidal CO_2 ($EtCO_2$) if the patient is receiving mechanical ventilation (see Chapter 28).
P: Pain assessment and management.

Most patients who come to the ED report pain.[8] Providing comfort measures is critical when caring for patients in the ED. Many EDs have pain management protocols for nurses to use to treat pain early, beginning at triage. Pain management should include a combination of pharmacologic and nonpharmacologic measures. You are the advocate in ensuring comfort measures for the patient.

TABLE 21.5 Emergency Assessment

Secondary Survey

Assessment	Interventions
History (H_1) and Head-to-Toe Assessment (H_2)	
History	• Use the mnemonic **MIST** to obtain details of the prehospital report of the incidence or illness: **M**echanism of injury, **I**njuries sustained, **S**igns and symptoms before arrival, and **T**reatment provided before arrival. • Use the mnemonic **SAMPLE** to determine **S**ymptoms from the injury or illness; **A**llergies, including tetanus status; **M**edication history; **P**ast history (e.g., preexisting medical/psychiatric problems, last menstrual period); **L**ast meal/oral intake; and **E**vents/Environment preceding illness or injury.
Head-to-toe assessment	• Note general appearance, including skin color.
Head, neck, and face	• Assess face and scalp for lacerations, bone or soft tissue deformity, tenderness, bleeding, foreign bodies. • Inspect eyes, ears, nose, and mouth for bleeding, foreign bodies, drainage, pain, deformity, bruising, lacerations. • Palpate head for depressions of cranial or facial bones, contusions, hematomas, areas of softness, bony crepitus. • Assess neck for stiffness, pain in cervical vertebrae, tracheal deviation, distended neck veins, bleeding, edema, difficulty swallowing, bruising, subcutaneous emphysema, bony crepitus.
Chest	• Observe rate, depth, and effort of breathing, including chest wall movement and use of accessory muscles. • Palpate for bony crepitus and subcutaneous emphysema. • Auscultate breath sounds. • Obtain 12-lead ECG and chest x-ray. • Inspect for external signs of injury: petechiae, bleeding, cyanosis, bruises, abrasions, lacerations, old scars.
Abdomen and flanks	• Look for symmetry of abdominal wall and bony structures. • Inspect for external signs of injury: bruises, abrasions, lacerations, punctures, old scars. • Auscultate for bowel sounds. • Palpate for masses, guarding, femoral pulses. • Note type and location of pain, rigidity, or distention of abdomen.
Pelvis and perineum	• Gently palpate pelvis. • Assess genitalia for blood at the meatus, priapism, bruising, rectal bleeding, anal sphincter tone. • Determine ability to void.
Extremities	• Inspect for signs of external injury: deformity, bruising, abrasions, lacerations, swelling. • Observe skin color and palpate skin for pain, tenderness, temperature, and crepitus. • Evaluate movement, strength, and sensation in arms and legs. • Assess quality and symmetry of peripheral pulses.
Inspect Posterior Surfaces	• Logroll and inspect and palpate back for deformity, bleeding, lacerations, bruises. Maintain cervical spine immobilization, if appropriate.
Just Keep Reevaluating	• Use the memory aid **VIPP** to reevaluate and assess effectiveness of interventions provided: **V**ital signs, **I**njuries sustained and interventions, **P**rimary survey, and **P**ain level • Document in the health record • Keep the process moving along quickly • More tests may be done, such as bronchoscopy, CT/MRI, angiography

Secondary Survey

The secondary survey begins after addressing each step of the primary survey and starting any lifesaving interventions. The **secondary survey** is a brief, systematic process that aims to identify *all* injuries (Table 21.5). It is helpful for discovering unknown problems in patients with a poor or confusing history.[4,5]

H = History and Head-to-Toe Assessment

Obtain a history and mechanism of the injury or illness. These details provide clues to the cause and guide specific assessments and interventions. The patient may not be able to give a history. However, caregivers, friends, bystanders, and prehospital personnel can often provide the necessary information.

Use the memory aid "MIST" to help you obtain a prehospital report of the incident or illness:

M: Mechanism of injury
I: Injuries sustained
S: Signs and symptoms before arrival
T: Treatment before arrival

Details of the incident are important because the mechanism of injury and injury patterns can predict specific injuries. For example, a restrained front-seat passenger may have knee or femur fractures from hitting the dashboard and a chest injury from the airbag. Those who fell off a ladder or roof may have fractures, spinal cord injury, or head trauma.

SAMPLE is a memory aid that prompts you to ask about a patient's history:

S: Symptoms from the injury or illness
A: Allergies (e.g., drugs, food, latex, environment) and tetanus status
M: Medication history
P: Past history (e.g., preexisting medical or psychiatric problems, surgeries, smoking history, recent use of drugs or alcohol, last menstrual period, baseline mental status)

TABLE 21.6 Tetanus Vaccines and TIG for Wound Management

	TYPE OF WOUND	
Vaccination History	**Clean, Minor Wounds**	**All Other Wounds**
Age 11 and Older[a]		
Unknown or <3 doses of tetanus toxoid-containing vaccine	Tdap and recommend catch-up vaccination	Tdap and recommend catch-up vaccination TIG
≥3 doses of tetanus toxoid-containing vaccine *and* <5 years. since last dose	No indication	No indication
≥3 doses of tetanus toxoid-containing vaccine *and* 5–10 years since last dose	No indication	Tdap preferred (if not yet received) or Td
≥3 doses of tetanus toxoid–containing vaccine *and* >10 years since last dose	Tdap preferred (if not yet received) or Td	Tdap preferred (if not yet received) or Td

Td, Tetanus-diphtheria toxoid absorbed; *Tdap,* tetanus toxoid, reduced diphtheria toxoid, and acellular pertussis vaccine; *TIG,* tetanus immune globulin (human).
Source: Centers for Disease Control and Prevention: Tetanus. Retrieved from www.cdc.gov/tetanus/clinicians.html.

L: Last meal/oral intake
E: Events or environmental factors leading to the illness or injury

After you collect the patient's history, a head-to-toe assessment completes the H part of the secondary survey. Note any abnormalities.

Head, neck, and face. Check eyes for extraocular movements. A disconjugate gaze is a sign of neurologic damage. Battle's sign, or bruising directly behind the ears, may indicate a fracture of the base or posterior part of the skull. "Raccoon eyes," or periorbital bruising, usually occurs with a fracture of the base of the frontal part of the skull. Check the ears for blood and cerebrospinal fluid. Do not block clear drainage from the ear or nose.

Chest. Inspection and palpation of the chest will help detect heart and lung injuries. These may be life-threatening and need immediate intervention.

Abdomen and flanks. Frequent evaluation for subtle changes in the abdomen is essential. Motor vehicle crashes and assaults can cause blunt trauma. Penetrating trauma tends to injure specific organs. Stabilize, but do not remove any impaled objects. They must be removed in a controlled environment, such as the operating room.

If the patient has blunt abdominal trauma or you suspect intraabdominal hemorrhage, perform a *focused abdominal sonography for trauma* (FAST).[9] FAST can identify blood in the peritoneal space and assess cardiac function. It is noninvasive and done quickly at the bedside. However, a FAST cannot rule out a retroperitoneal bleed. If we suspect a bleed, a CT scan is usually done.

Pelvis and perineum. Inspect and gently palpate the pelvis. Do not rock the pelvis. Pain may indicate a pelvic fracture and the need for imaging. Assess for bladder distention, hematuria, dysuria, or inability to void. The HCP may perform a rectal examination to check for blood, prostate gland problems, and loss of sphincter tone (e.g., spinal cord injury).

Extremities. Assess the upper and lower extremities for point tenderness, crepitus, and deformities. If not done prehospital, splint injured extremities above and below the injury to decrease further soft tissue injury and pain. The HCP should realign grossly deformed, pulseless extremities before splinting. Check pulses before and after movement or splinting of an extremity. A pulseless extremity is a time-critical emergency. Immobilize and elevate injured extremities and apply ice packs. Antibiotics are given for open fractures to prevent infection.

Assess extremities for *compartment syndrome.* This occurs over several hours as pressure and swelling increase inside a muscle compartment of an extremity. This compromises the viability of the muscles, nerves, and arteries. Potential causes include crush injuries, fractures, edema, and hemorrhage.

I = Inspect Posterior Surfaces

An often overlooked part of the assessment is the back of the patient. Logroll the trauma patient while protecting the cervical spine. Up to 4 or more people with 1 person supporting the head may be needed to complete this assessment.

J = Just Keep Reevaluating

After you complete the secondary survey, record all findings. Ongoing monitoring and evaluation are critical. Provide appropriate care and assess the patient's response.

Use the memory aid VIPP for the reevaluation process:
V: Vital signs
I: Injuries sustained and interventions
P: Primary survey
P: Pain level

The evaluation of airway patency and the effectiveness of breathing are always the highest priorities. Monitor respiratory rate and rhythm, O_2 saturation, and ABGs (if ordered) to evaluate the patient's respiratory status. A portable chest x-ray can confirm the exact placement of tubes. Give tetanus prophylaxis based on vaccination history and the condition of any wounds (Table 21.6).[10]

Closely monitor LOC and vital signs. Note the quality of peripheral pulses and skin temperature, color, and moisture for information about circulation and perfusion. When indicated, insert an indwelling catheter to decompress the bladder, monitor urine output, and check for hematuria. Notify the HCP of any changes that may occur to the patient during this ongoing assessment process.

Depending on the patient's injuries or illness, the patient may be (1) transported for diagnostic tests (e.g., CT scan, angiography) or to the operating room for immediate surgery, (2) admitted, or (3) transferred to another facility. You may go with critically ill patients on transports. You are responsible for monitoring the patient during transport, notifying the HCP if the patient becomes unstable, and starting life-support measures as needed.

Cardiac Arrest and Targeted Temperature Management

Many patients arrive at the ED in cardiac arrest. Patients with nontraumatic, out-of-hospital cardiac arrest benefit from a combination of good chest compressions and rapid defibrillation (see Appendix A), targeted temperature management (TTM), and supportive care. TTM for at least 24 hours after the return of spontaneous circulation (ROSC) decreases mortality rates and improves neurologic outcomes in many patients.[11] It is recommended for all patients who are comatose or do not follow commands after ROSC.

TTM, also called therapeutic hypothermia, involves three phases: induction, maintenance, and rewarming. The induction phase begins in the ED. The goal core temperature is 89.6°F to 96.8°F (32°C to 36°C). We use a variety of methods to cool patients. These include icepacks, cooling pads, and blankets. We can perform endovascular cooling with a special central venous catheter.[11] Patients need mechanical ventilation and invasive monitoring and require continuous assessment. Protocols often direct the care of these patients.

Death in the Emergency Department

The loss of life in the ED is a stressful event. Death is often sudden and happens after an accident or unexpected illness (e.g., myocardial infarction [MI]). Sudden death is, by its nature, unexpected and thus shocking for family and friends. It is crucial for you to identify and manage your feelings about sudden death so you can help them begin the grieving process (see Chapter 10).

You play a key role in providing comfort. Provide a private area for them to say goodbye and, if appropriate, arrange for a visit from a chaplain. Assist the family by collecting personal belongings and making mortuary arrangements. At times, you may need to contact the medical examiner or coroner. An autopsy may be done at the family's request, or if death occurred within 24 hours of ED admission, from suspected trauma or violence, or in an unusual way.

Some patients who die in the ED are candidates for organ donation after circulatory death. We can harvest certain tissues and organs (e.g., corneas, liver, pancreas, lungs, kidneys).[12] Organ procurement groups aid in screening potential donors, counseling donor families, obtaining informed consent, and harvesting organs from patients on life support or who die in the ED. Approaching caregivers about donation after an unexpected death can be distressing to both the staff and caregivers. However, for many, donation may be the first positive step in the grieving process.

Gerontologic Considerations: Emergency Care

People over age 60 account for 20% of all ED visits.[13] Regardless of a patient's age, aggressive interventions are provided for all injuries or illnesses unless the patient has a preexisting terminal illness, an extremely low chance for survival, or an advance directive indicating a different course of action.

Understanding the physiologic and psychosocial aspects of aging will improve the care delivered to older adults in the ED (see Chapter 5). Many older adults dismiss their symptoms as simply "normal for their age." It is important to fully explore any complaint by an older adult.

The older population is at high risk for injury because of the many changes that occur with aging. Falls are the leading cause of injury.[13] Common causes of falls in older adults include weakness, environmental hazards, syncope, and orthostatic hypotension. When assessing a patient who has fallen, determine whether the physical findings may have caused the fall or are due to the fall itself. For example, a patient may come to the ED with acute confusion. The confusion may be due to a stroke that caused the patient to fall. Or the patient may have a head injury because of a fall from tripping on a rug.

ENVIRONMENTAL EMERGENCIES

Environmental emergencies discussed here include heat and cold-related emergencies, submersion injuries, bites, stings, and envenomation. Increased interest in outdoor activities, such as running, cycling, skiing, and swimming, has increased the number of environmental emergencies seen in the ED. Illness or injury may be caused by the activity, exposure to weather, or attack from animals or humans.

HEAT-RELATED EMERGENCIES

Brief exposure to intense heat or prolonged exposure to less intense heat leads to heat stress. This occurs when thermoregulatory mechanisms, such as sweating, vasodilation, and increased respirations, cannot compensate for exposure to increased ambient temperatures. Ambient temperature is a product of environmental temperature and humidity. Strenuous activities in hot or humid environments, clothing that interferes with perspiration, fever, and preexisting illness predispose people to heat stress (Table 21.7). Table 21.8 presents the management of heat-related emergencies.

Heat Cramps

Heat cramps are severe cramps in large muscle groups fatigued by heavy work.[14] Cramps are brief and intense and tend to occur during rest after exercise or heavy labor. Nausea, tachycardia, pallor, weakness, and profuse sweating are often present. The condition occurs most often in healthy, acclimated athletes with inadequate fluid intake. Cramps resolve rapidly with rest and oral or IV replacement of sodium and water. Elevation, gentle massage, and analgesia minimize pain from heat cramps. Tell the patient to avoid strenuous activity for at least 12 hours. When discharge teaching, emphasize salt replacement during strenuous exercise in hot, humid environments. Recommend the use of commercially prepared electrolyte solutions.

TABLE 21.7 Risk Factors for Heat-Related Emergencies

Alcohol	
Age	• Infants • Older adults
Environmental Conditions	• High humidity • Lack of access to water, shelter, or shade • Lack of acclimatization • Physical exertion, especially during hot weather • Prolonged exposure to high temperature
Preexisting Illness	• Dehydration • Diabetes • Head injury • Heart disease • Obesity • Sickle cell disease • Skin disorders (e.g., large burn scars) • Spinal cord injury • Stroke or other CNS lesion • Thyrotoxicosis
Prescription Drugs	• Anticholinergics • Antihistamines • Antipsychotics • β-Adrenergic blockers • Benzodiazepines • Calcium channel blockers • Diuretics • Phenothiazines • Thyroid agonists • Tricyclic antidepressants
Street Drugs	• Amphetamines • Lysergic acid diethylamide (LSD) • Phencyclidine (PCP) • 3,4-Methylenedioxymethamphetamine (MDMA, Ecstasy)

Heat Exhaustion

Prolonged exposure to heat over hours or days leads to **heat exhaustion**. Symptoms include fatigue, nausea and vomiting, and extreme thirst. Hypotension, tachycardia, elevated body temperature, dilated pupils, mild confusion, ashen color, and profuse sweating are present. Heat exhaustion usually occurs in people engaged in strenuous activity in hot, humid weather.

Provide oral and IV fluid replacement as ordered. Implement evaporative cooling measures. Consider hospital admission for older adults, the chronically ill, or those who do not improve within 3 to 4 hours.

Heatstroke

Heatstroke is the most severe form of heat stress. It is a medical emergency. Heatstroke results from failure of the hypothalamic thermoregulatory processes. Increased sweating, vasodilation, and increased respiratory rate deplete fluids and electrolytes, specifically sodium. Eventually, sweat glands stop functioning. Core temperature increases rapidly, within 10 to 15 minutes. The brain is very sensitive to thermal injuries. Cerebral edema and hemorrhage may occur from direct thermal injury to the brain and decreased cerebral blood flow. Death from heatstroke is directly related to the amount of time that the body temperature is high.[14] Prognosis is related to age, health status, and length of exposure. Older adults and those with diabetes, chronic kidney disease, heart disease, or lung disease are more prone.

Interprofessional Care

Treatment focuses on stabilizing the patient's ABCs, rapidly reducing the core temperature, and monitoring for dysrhythmias. Give 100% O_2 to compensate for the hypermetabolic state. Ventilation with a BVM or intubation and mechanical ventilation may be needed. Place the patient on continuous ECG monitoring and pulse oximetry. Monitor laboratory findings. Correcting electrolyte imbalances and coagulation abnormalities is critical.

The most effective treatment for heatstroke is cold water immersion.[14] You can also place the patient in a cool environment. Other measures to consider include spraying the patient with cool water in front of a large fan, placing a moist sheet over the patient, or applying ice packs to the groin and axillae. In refractory cases, we may perform peritoneal or rectal lavage with iced fluids.

Monitor the patient's temperature and control shivering. Shivering increases core temperature due to the heat generated by muscle activity. This hampers cooling efforts. The HCP may order drugs to control shivering.

Heatstroke places the patient at risk for kidney injury due to *rhabdomyolysis*. It is a serious syndrome caused by the breakdown of skeletal muscle. Carefully monitor the urine for color, amount, pH, and myoglobin.

Discharge teaching focuses on how to avoid future problems. Stress the importance of proper hydration and wearing appropriate clothing. Teach patients the early signs of and interventions for heat-related stress. Encourage caregivers to check on those at risk during periods of high temperatures. They should ensure adequate water intake, verify operable air conditioning, and assess for heat-related illness.

COLD-RELATED EMERGENCIES

Cold injuries may be localized (e.g., frostbite) or systemic (e.g., hypothermia). Contributing factors include age, duration of exposure, ambient temperature, homelessness, preexisting conditions, drugs that suppress shivering, and alcohol intoxication. Smokers have an increased risk for cold-related injury because of the vasoconstrictive effects of nicotine.

Frostbite

Frostbite is true tissue freezing that results in the formation of ice crystals in the tissues and cells. Peripheral vasoconstriction is the first response to cold stress. It results in a decrease in blood flow and vascular stasis. As cell temperature decreases, ice crystals form in intracellular spaces. The organelles are damaged, and the cell membrane is destroyed. This results in edema.

Most (90%) cases involve the hands and feet. The cheeks, nose, ears, and penis are also commonly affected.[5] Frostbite depth depends on ambient temperature, length of exposure,

TABLE 21.8 EMERGENCY MANAGEMENT

Hyperthermia

Cause	Assessment Findings	Interventions
Table 21.7	**Heat Cramps** • Severe muscle contractions in exerted muscles • Thirst **Heat Exhaustion** • Altered mental status (e.g., anxiety) • Ashen, pale skin • ↓ BP • Extreme thirst • Fatigue, weakness • ↑ HR • Profuse sweating • Temperature (99.6°F–105.8°F [37.5°C–41°C]) • Weak, thready pulse **Heatstroke** • Altered mental status (ranging from confusion to coma) • ↓ BP • Hot, dry skin • ↑ HR • Tachypnea • Temperature >105.8°F (41°C) • Weakness	**Initial** • Manage and maintain ABCs. • Provide high-flow O_2 via nonrebreather mask or BVM. • Establish IV access • Begin IV fluid replacement for significant heat injury. • Place patient in a cool environment. • For heatstroke, start rapid cooling measures: remove patient's clothing, place wet sheets over patient, and place in front of fan; immerse in a cool water bath; give cool IV fluids or lavage with cool fluids. • Obtain 12-lead ECG. • Obtain blood for electrolytes and CBC. • Insert urinary catheter. **Ongoing Monitoring** • Monitor ABCs, temperature and vital signs, level of consciousness. • Monitor heart rhythm, O_2 saturation, urine output. • Replace electrolytes as needed. • Monitor urine for myoglobinuria. • Monitor clotting studies for disseminated intravascular coagulation.

type and condition (wet or dry) of clothing, wind chill, and contact with metal surfaces. Other factors that affect severity include previous frostbite injury, exhaustion, and poor peripheral vascular status.

Superficial frostbite involves the skin and subcutaneous tissue, usually the ears, nose, fingers, and toes. The skin appearance ranges from waxy pale yellow to blue to mottled. The skin feels crunchy and frozen. The patient may report tingling, numbness, or a burning sensation. Handle the area carefully and never squeeze, massage, or scrub the injured tissue because it is easily damaged. Swelling will occur with thawing. Remove clothing and jewelry as they may constrict the extremity and decrease circulation.

Immerse the affected area in circulating temperature-controlled water (99.0°F to 102°F) [37.2°C to 38.9°C]).[5] Use warm soaks for the face. The patient often has a warm, stinging sensation as tissue thaws. Blisters form within a few hours (Fig. 21.2). Debride the blisters and apply a sterile dressing. Avoid heavy blankets and clothing because friction and weight can lead to sloughing of damaged tissue. Rewarming is very painful. Residual pain may last weeks or even years. Give analgesia and tetanus prophylaxis as appropriate. Assess the patient for systemic hypothermia.

Deep frostbite involves muscle, bone, and tendon. The skin is white, hard, and insensitive to touch. The area has the appearance of deep thermal injury with mottling, gradually progressing to gangrene (Fig. 21.3). Immerse the affected extremity in a temperature-controlled, circulating water bath (99.0°F to 102°F) [37.2°C to 38.9°C]) until flushing occurs distal to the injured area.[5]

After rewarming, elevate the extremity to reduce edema. Significant edema may begin within 3 hours, with blistering in 6 hours to days. Give IV analgesia to manage the pain from tissue thawing. All patients should start on nonsteroidal antiinflammatory drugs (NSAIDs) because of their dual role as an analgesic and antiinflammatory. Give tetanus prophylaxis. Assess the patient for systemic hypothermia.

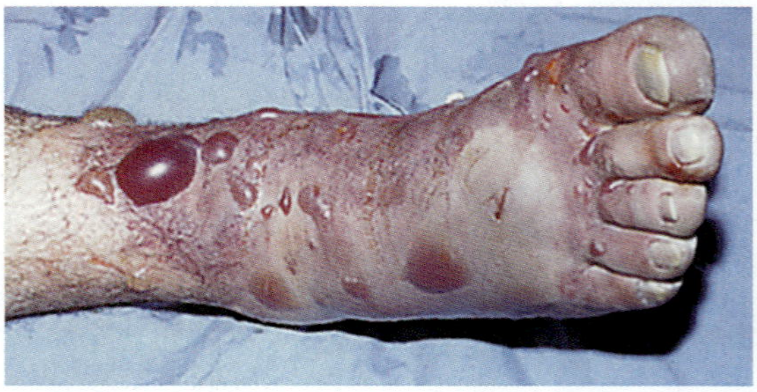

Fig. 21.2 Edema and blister formation 24 hours after frostbite injury occurring in an area covered by a tightly fitted boot. (Courtesy Cameron Bangs, MD. From Auerbach PS, Donner HJ, Weiss EA: *Field guide to wilderness medicine,* ed 2, St Louis, 2003, Mosby.)

Treatment options to reduce tissue damage with severe frostbite include pentoxifylline, anticoagulation, hyperbaric O_2 therapy, and thrombolytic therapy.[15] Amputation may be needed if the injured area is not treated or treatment is unsuccessful. It may take as long as 90 days to determine the final necrotic area. Prophylactic antibiotics are given if the wound is at risk for infection.

Hypothermia

Hypothermia is a core temperature below 95°F (35°C).[5] It occurs when heat produced by the body cannot compensate for

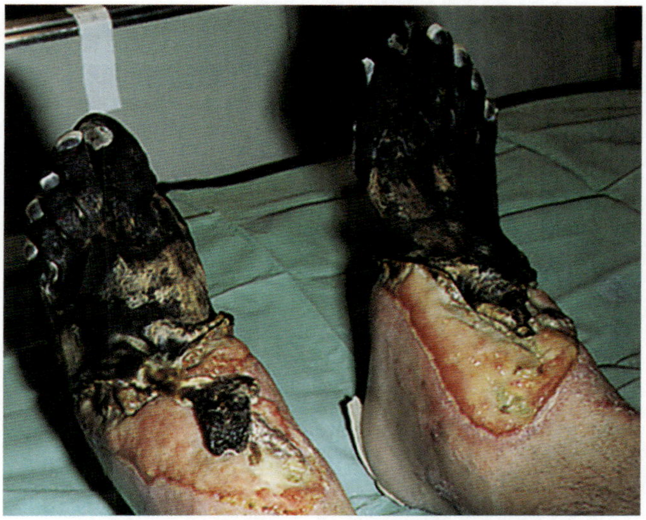

Fig. 21.3 Gangrenous necrosis 6 weeks after the frostbite injury is shown in Fig. 21.2. (Courtesy Cameron Bangs, MD. From Auerbach PS, Donner HJ, Weiss EA: *Field guide to wilderness medicine,* ed 2, St Louis, 2003, Mosby.)

heat lost to the environment. This may occur in a healthy person with environmental exposure (primary) or someone with a specific condition that produces hypothermia (secondary). There are many risk factors for hypothermia. These include exposure to freezing temperatures, cold winds, and wet terrain; medications (e.g., phenothiazines, neuromuscular blocking agents); alcohol use; traumatic injury; shock; and diabetes.[5] Wet clothing, inadequate clothing, and immersion in cold water (e.g., drowning) increase evaporative heat loss. Older adults are more prone because of decreased body fat, decreased energy reserves, decreased basal metabolic rate, decreased shivering response, and chronic medical problems. Peripheral vasoconstriction is the body's first attempt to conserve heat. As cold temperatures persist, shivering and movement are the body's only mechanisms for producing heat.

Assessment findings are variable and depend on core temperature (Table 21.9). Patients with *mild hypothermia* (93°F to 95°F [33.9°C to 35°C]) have shivering, lethargy, confusion, behavior changes, and minor heart rate changes. *Moderate hypothermia* (86°F to 93°F [30°C to 33.9°C]) causes rigidity, bradycardia, slowed respiratory rate, BP obtainable only by Doppler, metabolic and respiratory acidosis, and hypovolemia. Shivering decreases or disappears at core temperatures of 86°F (30°C).[5]

As core temperature drops, metabolic rate decreases 2 to 3 times. The cold myocardium is very irritable, making it vulnerable to dysrhythmias (e.g., atrial and ventricular fibrillation). Decreased renal blood flow decreases glomerular filtration rate, which impairs water reabsorption and leads to dehydration. The hematocrit increases as intravascular volume decreases. Cold

TABLE 21.9 EMERGENCY MANAGEMENT

Hypothermia

<table>
<tr><th>Cause</th><th>Assessment Findings</th><th>Interventions</th></tr>
<tr>
<td>
Environmental
• Inadequate clothing for environmental temperature
• Prolonged exposure to cold
• Prolonged immersion or near-drowning
Health Care Associated
• Administration of neuromuscular blocking agents
• Blood administration
• Cold IV fluids
• Inadequate warming or rewarming in the ED or operating room
Metabolic
• Hypoglycemia
• Hypothyroidism
Other
• Alcohol
• Barbiturates
• Phenothiazines
• Shock
• Trauma
</td>
<td>
• Core body temperature:
  • Mild hypothermia: 93°F–95°F (33.9°C–35°C)
  • Moderate hypothermia: 86°F–93°F (30°C–33.9°C)
  • Severe hypothermia: <86°F (30°C)
• Shivering, ↓ or absent at core body temperatures ≥86°F (30°C)
• Altered mental status (ranging from confusion to coma)
• Areflexia (absence of reflexes)
• Blue, white, or frozen extremities
• ↓BP
• Cyanotic, pale skin
• Dysrhythmias: bradycardia, atrial fibrillation, ventricular fibrillation, asystole
• Fixed, dilated pupils
• Hypoventilation
</td>
<td>
Initial
• Remove patient from cold environment.
• Manage and maintain ABCs.
• Provide high-flow O_2 via nonrebreather mask or BVM.
• Anticipate intubation for decreased or absent gag reflex.
• Establish IV access with 2 large-bore catheters for fluid resuscitation.
• Rewarm patient:
  • Passive: Remove wet clothing, apply dry clothing, and warm blankets, use radiant lights.
  • Active external: Apply heating devices (e.g., air or fluid-filled warming blankets), use warm water immersion.
  • Active internal: Provide warmed IV fluids; heated, humidified O_2. Peritoneal lavage with warmed fluids. Extracorporeal circulation (e.g., cardiopulmonary bypass, rapid fluid infuser, hemodialysis).
• Obtain 12-lead ECG.
• Anticipate need for defibrillation.
• Warm central trunk first in patients with severe hypothermia to limit rewarming shock.
• Assess for other injuries.
• Keep head covered with warm, dry towels or stocking cap to limit loss of heat.
• Treat patient gently to avoid increased cardiac irritability.
Ongoing Monitoring
• Monitor ABCs, temperature, level of consciousness, and vital signs.
• Monitor O_2 saturation, heart rate, and rhythm.
• Monitor electrolytes, glucose.
</td>
</tr>
</table>

blood becomes thick and acts as a thrombus, placing the patient at risk for stroke, MI, pulmonary emboli, and renal failure. Decreased blood flow leads to hypoxia, anaerobic metabolism, lactic acid accumulation, and metabolic acidosis.

Severe hypothermia (below 86°F [30°C]) makes the person appear dead and is a potentially life-threatening situation. Metabolic rate, heart rate, and respirations are so slow that they may be hard to detect. Reflexes are absent. The pupils are fixed and dilated. Profound bradycardia, ventricular fibrillation, or pulseless electrical activity may be present. Effort is made to warm the patient to at least 86°F (30°C) before pronouncing the person dead. The cause of death is usually refractory ventricular fibrillation.

Interprofessional Care

Treatment focuses on managing and maintaining ABCs, rewarming the patient, correcting dehydration and acidosis, and treating dysrhythmias. Mildly hypothermic patients may be rewarmed with passive and active external measures since their risk for dysrhythmia is low. Those with moderate or severe hypothermia need active internal rewarming measures.

Carefully monitor core temperature during rewarming procedures. Rewarming places the patient at risk for *afterdrop,* a further drop in core temperature. This occurs when cold peripheral blood returns to the central circulation. Rewarming shock can produce hypotension and dysrhythmias. Thus, patients with moderate to severe hypothermia should have the core warmed before the extremities. Discontinue active rewarming once the core temperature reaches 90°F to 95° F (32.2°C to 35° C).

Patient teaching focuses on how to avoid future cold-related problems. Essential information includes dressing in layers for cold weather, covering the head, carrying high-carbohydrate foods for extra calories, and developing a survival plan should an injury occur in an extreme environment.

CHECK YOUR PRACTICE

You are working in the ED when the paramedics arrive with a patient who was found lying on the sidewalk outside the bus station. He is wearing only a lightweight shirt and pants. The outdoor temperature is 12°F (–11.1°C). The patient is unresponsive. Initial vital signs are as follows: rectal temperature = 89.5°F (31.9°C), HR = 38, RR = 8, BP (by Doppler) = 86 mm Hg.

- What are your priority interventions?

SUBMERSION INJURIES

Submersion injury results when a person becomes hypoxic from submersion in a liquid, usually water.[5] Around 4000 deaths from drowning occur each year in the United States. Most victims are children younger than 4 years. The main risk factors for submersion injury include the inability to swim, substance use, poor judgment, trauma, seizures, hypothermia, stroke, and child neglect. Aggressive resuscitation efforts (e.g., airway and ventilation management) improve survival, especially in the prehospital phase.

Drowning is the process of experiencing respiratory impairment after submersion in water or other fluid.[16] Submersion in cold water (below 32°F [0°C]) may slow the progression of hypoxic brain injury.

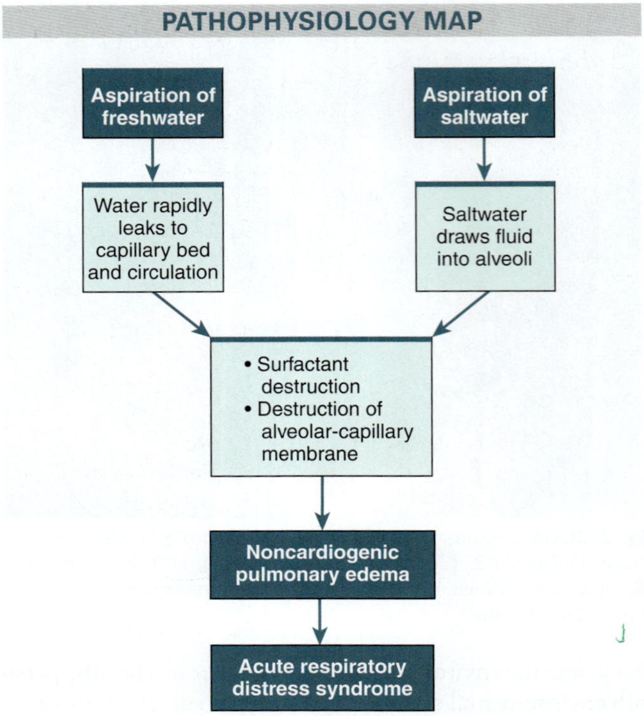

Fig. 21.4 Pathophysiology of submersion injury.

Most drowning victims do not aspirate any liquid due to laryngospasm. If liquid is aspirated, it is in small amounts. Drowning victims who do aspirate water develop pulmonary edema, which can cause acute respiratory distress syndrome (see Chapter 32).

The osmotic gradient caused by aspirated fluid leads to fluid imbalances in the body (Fig. 21.4). Hypotonic freshwater is rapidly absorbed into the circulatory system through the alveoli. Freshwater is often contaminated with chlorine, mud, or algae. This causes the breakdown of lung surfactant, fluid seepage, and pulmonary edema.

Hypertonic saltwater draws fluid from the vascular space into the alveoli, impairing alveolar ventilation and causing hypoxia. The body tries to compensate for hypoxia by shunting blood to the lungs. This results in increased pulmonary pressures and deteriorating respiratory status. More and more blood is shunted through the alveoli. Since the blood is not adequately oxygenated, hypoxemia worsens. This causes cerebral injury, edema, and brain death.

Interprofessional Care

Treatment focuses on correcting hypoxia and fluid imbalances, supporting basic physiologic functions, and rewarming when hypothermia is present. Initial evaluation involves assessing the airway, cervical spine, breathing, and circulation (Table 21.10). Mechanical ventilation with positive end-expiratory pressure or continuous positive airway pressure can improve gas exchange across the alveolar-capillary membrane when pulmonary edema is present (see Chapter 28).

TABLE 21.10 EMERGENCY MANAGEMENT

Submersion Injuries

Cause	Assessment Findings	Interventions
• Entrapment or entanglement with objects in water • Inability to swim or exhaustion while swimming • Loss of ability to move secondary to trauma, stroke, hypothermia, MI • Poor judgment due to alcohol or drugs • Seizure while in water	**Cardiac** • ↓ BP • Bradycardia • Dysrhythmias • ↑HR • Cardiac arrest **Respiratory** • Cough with pink-frothy sputum • Crackles, rhonchi • Cyanosis • Dyspnea • Respiratory distress • Respiratory arrest **Other** • Exhaustion • Coma • Coexisting illness (e.g., MI) or injury (e.g., cervical spine injury) • Core temperature slightly elevated or below normal, depending on water temperature and length of submersion • Panic	**Initial** • Manage and maintain ABCs. • Assume cervical spine injury in all drowning victims and stabilize or immobilize cervical spine. • Provide 100% O_2 via nonrebreather mask or BVM. • Anticipate need for mechanical ventilation if airway is compromised (e.g., absent gag reflex). • Establish IV access with 2 large-bore catheters for fluid resuscitation and infuse warmed fluids, if appropriate. • Obtain 12-lead ECG. • Assess for other injuries. • Remove wet clothing and cover with warm blankets. • Obtain temperature and begin rewarming, if needed. • Obtain cervical spine and chest x-rays. • Insert gastric tube and urinary catheter. **Ongoing Monitoring** • Monitor ABCs, vital signs, level of consciousness. • Monitor O_2 saturation, heart rate, and rhythm. • Monitor temperature and maintain normothermia. • Monitor for signs of acute respiratory failure.

Declining neurologic status suggests cerebral edema, worsening hypoxia, or profound acidosis. Drowning victims may have head and neck injuries that cause changes in the LOC. Complications can develop in patients who are free of symptoms immediately after the drowning episode. Consequently, observe all victims of drowning in a hospital for a minimum of 4 to 8 hours.[16]

Patient teaching focuses on water safety and how to reduce the risks of drowning. Remind patients and caregivers to lock all swimming pool gates; use life jackets on all watercrafts, including inner tubes and rafts; and learn water survival skills. Emphasize the dangers of combining alcohol and drugs with swimming and other water sports.

STINGS AND BITES

Animals, spiders, snakes, and insects cause injury and even death by biting or stinging. Morbidity is a result of either direct tissue damage or lethal toxins. Direct tissue damage is a product of the animal's size, teeth characteristics, and jaw strength. Tissue may be lacerated, crushed, or chewed. Teeth, fangs, stingers, spines, or tentacles release toxins that have local or systemic effects. Death from an animal bite is due to blood loss, allergic reactions, or lethal toxins.

Hymenopteran Stings

The *Hymenoptera* family includes bees, yellow jackets, hornets, wasps, and fire ants. Stings can cause mild discomfort or life-threatening anaphylaxis (see Chapter 42). Venom may be cytotoxic, hemolytic, allergenic, or vasoactive. Symptoms may begin immediately or be delayed up to 48 hours. Reactions are more severe with multiple stings. Most hymenopterans sting repeatedly. However, the domestic honeybee stings only once, usually leaving a barbed stinger with an attached venom sac in the skin so that venom release continues.

African honeybees (killer bees) look like domestic bees. If threatened, these bees aggressively swarm and can repeatedly sting their victims. These attacks can be fatal.

SAFETY ALERT

Hymenopteran Stings

- Remove the stinger using a scraping motion with a thin, flat object, like a fingernail, knife, or credit card.
- Do not use tweezers because they may squeeze the stinger and release more venom.
- Remove rings, watches, or any restrictive clothing around the sting site.

Manifestations of mild reactions include stinging, burning, swelling, and itching. More severe reactions may present with edema, headache, fever, syncope, malaise, nausea, vomiting, wheezing, bronchospasm, laryngeal edema, and hypotension. Treatment depends on the severity of the reaction. Treat mild reactions with elevation, cool compresses, antipruritic lotions, and oral antihistamines. More severe reactions require IM or IV antihistamines, subcutaneous epinephrine, and corticosteroids. Chapter 15 discusses allergic reactions and related patient teaching.

Snake Bites

There are more than 45,000 snakebites each year in the United States. *Envenomation* (poisoning by venom) occurs in about 8000 cases, with only five deaths each year.[17] The two families of venomous snakes found in the United States are Crotalidae or pit vipers (rattlesnakes, copperheads, cottonmouths) and Elapidae (coral snakes). Almost all the venomous bites are from pit vipers.

Snake venom may be hemolytic, neurotoxic, vascular toxic, or any combination of these. When bites occur, you will see fang or puncture marks. The patient often has severe pain at the site. There may be swelling, discoloration, and blistering. If moderate envenomation has occurred, the patient will have paresthesias, lymphadenopathy, and nausea and vomiting. Treatment includes wound care and tetanus prophylaxis. Immobilize the affected extremity. Remove potentially constricting clothing. Most bites are minor and resolve without antivenom therapy. Patients with suspected envenomation are observed for at least 8 hours to ensure no life- or limb-threatening symptoms develop.

Manifestations of severe envenomation include profound edema, tachycardia, blurred vision, headache, chills, paresthesias, hypotension, and muscle twitching. The patient may report a metallic taste in the mouth. As symptoms progress, pulmonary edema, coagulopathy, thrombocytopenia, and hemorrhage may develop.

Snakebites from exotic species are mainly neurotoxic. They cause autonomic dysfunction, paralysis, and dysrhythmias.

Treatment of severe envenomation requires close patient monitoring. The ABCs are most important! Anticipate fluid resuscitation and provide respiratory support. Monitor limb circumference every 30 minutes. Mark any advancing edema. Monitor laboratory results. On rare occasions, the patient will need a fasciotomy.[5] The HCP will discuss the bite with the poison control center. The decision to give antivenom is in consultation with a snake venom expert. There is specific antivenom therapy, often obtained from a zoo, for each species. Antivenom is given only if symptom progression occurs and platelet and coagulation studies are abnormal.

Tick Bites

Ticks live throughout the United States. Specific types are more prevalent in certain regions. Tick-borne pathogens can be passed to humans by the bite of an infected tick. Common tick-borne illnesses include Lyme disease, Rocky Mountain spotted fever, anaplasmosis, Colorado tick fever, tickborne relapsing fever, and tularemia.[18]

Ticks transmit pathogens that cause disease through their feeding process. The infected tick attaches to its host and can slowly feed for up to several days. During this time, saliva from the tick can be transferred to the host. Tick saliva may harbor pathogens acquired by the tick from a prior host. The tick should be removed as soon as possible to stop the flow of saliva. Use forceps or tweezers to grasp the tick close to the point of attachment and pull upward in a steady motion (Fig. 21.5). After you remove the tick, clean the skin with soap and water. Do not use a hot match, petroleum jelly, nail polish, or other products to remove the tick. These measures may cause a tick to salivate, thus increasing the risk for infection.

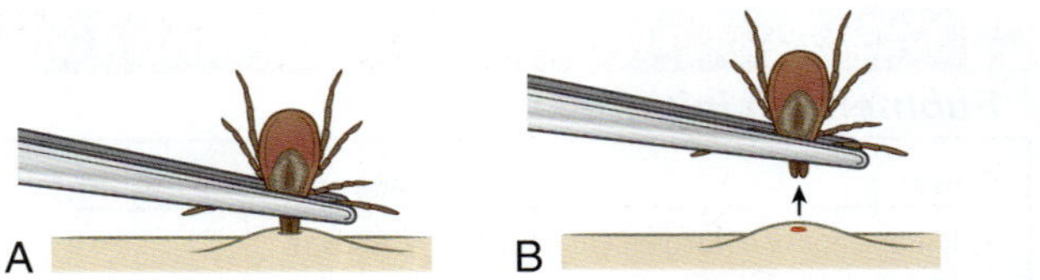

Fig. 21.5 Tick removal. (A) Use tweezers to grasp the tick close to the skin. (B) With a steady motion, pull the tick's body up and away from the skin. Do not be alarmed if the tick's mouthparts stay in the skin. Once the mouthparts are removed from the rest of the tick, it can no longer transmit disease.

Lyme disease is the most common tick-borne disease in the United States.[18] It is caused by the bacterium *Borrelia burgdorferi* that lives on the tick. In most cases, the tick must be attached for at least 36 hours to transmit the bacterium. Symptoms usually appear in about 7 days. The first stage begins with flu-like symptoms (e.g., headache, stiff neck, fatigue). Many patients develop a characteristic bullseye rash. This is a circular area of redness 5 cm or more in diameter. Treatment at this stage includes doxycycline, cefuroxime, or amoxicillin.[18] The rash, if it develops, will disappear even if the patient is not treated.

Monoarticular arthritis, meningitis, and neuropathies occur days or weeks after the initial manifestations. Treatment at this stage involves IV ceftriaxone or penicillin. Chronic arthritis, heart disease, and peripheral nerve problems occur in the later stage of the disease. These illnesses can last several months to years after the initial skin lesion. Chapter 69 discusses more about Lyme disease.

Rocky Mountain spotted fever is the most lethal tick disease.[18] It is caused by *Rickettsia rickettsia,* which is spread to humans by the ixodid tick. The incubation period is 2 to 14 days. A pink macular rash appears on the palms, wrists, soles, feet, and ankles. Other symptoms include fever, chills, malaise, muscle pain, and headache. It is hard to diagnosis in the early stages. Without treatment, the disease can be fatal. Antibiotic therapy with doxycycline is the treatment of choice.

Animal and Human Bites

Every year more than 5 million animal bites are reported in the United States. Animal bites from dogs and cats are most common. Wild or domestic rodents (e.g., squirrels, hamsters) follow as the third most common offenders. The few bite deaths (15 to 20) are mainly from dogs. The greatest problems from animal bites are infection and destruction of skin, muscle, tendons, blood vessels, and bone. The bite may cause a simple laceration or cause a crush injury, puncture wound, or tearing of multiple layers of tissue (Fig. 21.6). The severity of the injury depends on animal size, victim size, and anatomic location of the bite. Children are at greatest risk.[19]

Dog bites usually occur on the extremities. Facial bites are common in small children. Cat bites can cause deep puncture wounds. They can involve tendons and joint capsules. There is a greater risk for infection than with dog bites. Septic arthritis, osteomyelitis, and tenosynovitis can occur. The most common infectious organisms from dog and cat bites are the *Pasteurella*

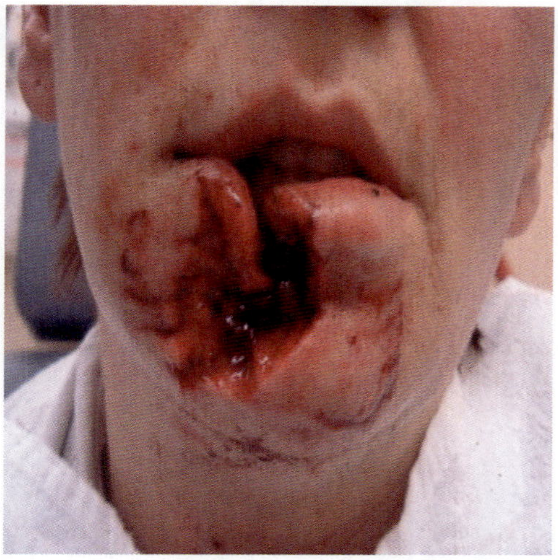

Fig. 21.6 Dog bite wound. (From Mannion C, Kanatas A, Telfer MR: One dog bite too far, *Brit J Oral Max Surg* 49:159, 2011.)

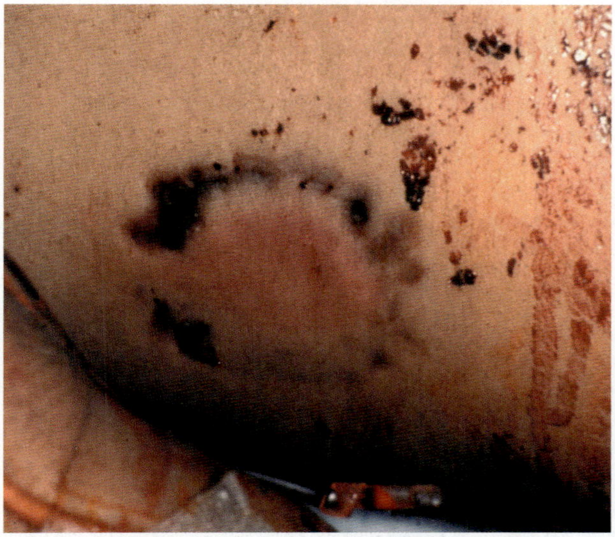

Fig. 21.7 Human bite injury. (From Stevens MR, Emam HA, Cunningham L: *Oral & maxillofacial trauma,* ed 4, St Louis, 2013, Elsevier.)

species (e.g., *Pasteurella multocida*). Most healthy cats and dogs carry this organism in their mouths.

The human jaw has great crushing ability, causing laceration, puncture, crush injury, soft tissue tearing, and even amputation (Fig. 21.7). Hands, fingers, ears, nose, vagina, and penis are the most common sites of human bites. Often these injuries are due to violence or sexual activity. There is a high risk of infection from oral bacterial flora, most often *Staphylococcus aureus, Streptococcus* organisms, and hepatitis virus. Infection risk is influenced by the injury's type, location, and extent; patient comorbidities; and time elapsed from the injury to seeking health care.[19] Initial signs of infection include severe pain, edema, and redness at the injury site.

Interprofessional Care

Obtain a history of the bite injury. Note whether an animal was known to the victim or not (and if not, if it was domestic or wild), the immunization status of the animal and patient, and the patient's comorbidities.[19] Assess the wound. Clean the wound, followed by copious irrigation with sterile saline. Assist the HCP with any debridement or wound closure. We often leave puncture wounds open. Lacerations may be loosely sutured. Plastic surgery consultation may be needed for disfiguring facial wounds. Splint wounds over joints.

Provide tetanus prophylaxis and analgesics as needed. Prophylactic antibiotics are used for bites at risk for infection. These include wounds over joints, those older than 6 to 12 hours, puncture wounds, and bites of the hand or foot. People at greatest risk for infection are infants, older adults, immunosuppressed patients, patients with substance or alcohol use disorder, people with diabetes, or those taking corticosteroids. Report a bite injury to the police as required.

Consider rabies postexposure prophylaxis in the management of all animal bites. Rabies is caused by a neurotoxic virus in the saliva of an infected animal. Most rabies carriers are wild animals, like raccoons, skunks, bats, foxes, and coyotes. Rabies is usually transmitted through the saliva via a bite by the infected animal. If the saliva from the infected animal has come in contact with its claws, theoretically rabies may be transmitted through a scratch. The virus spreads through the central nervous system (CNS) via peripheral nerves. People who develop rabies may have flu-like symptoms, confusion, paresthesias, or numbness, resulting in death.

Consider rabies exposure if an animal attack was not provoked, involves a wild animal, or involves a domestic animal not immunized against rabies. Always provide postexposure vaccinations when the animal is not found, or a wild animal caused the bite. The series of 4 rabies vaccine injections (human diploid cell rabies vaccine [HDCV, Imovax Rabies]) are given on days 0, 3, 7, and 14 to provide active immunity.[20] Give an initial, weight-based dose of rabies immune globulin (RIG [HyperRab S/D]) to provide passive immunity at the same time as the first dose of vaccine.

DRUG ALERT

Rabies Postexposure Prophylaxis

- If possible, give the calculated dose of RIG via infiltration around the wound edges.
- Give any remaining volume of RIG IM at a site distant from the vaccine site (e.g., gluteal site for bite wounds on the arm).
- Give the HDCV IM in the deltoid.

TOXICOLOGIC EMERGENCIES

Toxicologic emergencies include acute poisonings and intake of substances of abuse. A poison is any chemical that harms the body. More than 2 million cases of poisoning occur each year in the United States. Poisonings can be accidental, occupational, recreational, or intentional. Poisoning may be due to toxic plants or contaminated foods. (Chapter 46 discusses food poisoning.) Natural or manufactured toxins can be ingested, inhaled, injected, splashed in the eye, or absorbed through the skin. Chapter 11 discusses emergencies related to substance use.

TABLE 21.11 Common Poisons

Poison	Manifestations	Treatment
acetaminophen (Tylenol)	*Phase 1* (within 24 hr of ingestion): Malaise, diaphoresis, nausea, vomiting *Phase 2* (24–28 hr after ingestion): Right upper quadrant pain, ↓ urine output, ↓ nausea, ↑LFTs *Phase 3* (72–96 hr after ingestion): Nausea, vomiting, malaise, jaundice, hypoglycemia, enlarged liver, possible coagulopathies, including DIC *Phase 4* (7–8 days after ingestion): Recovery, resolution of symptoms or permanent liver damage, LFTs remain high	Activated charcoal, *N*-acetylcysteine (oral form may cause vomiting, IV form can be used)
Acids and Alkalis		
• *Acids:* Toilet bowl cleaners, antirust compounds • *Alkalis:* Drain cleaners, dishwashing detergents, ammonia	Excess salivation, dysphagia, epigastric pain, pneumonitis; burns of mouth, esophagus, and stomach	Immediate dilution (water, milk), corticosteroids (for alkali burns). Do not induce vomiting.
• Aspirin and aspirin-containing drugs	Tachypnea, ↑ HR, fever, seizures, pulmonary edema, occult bleeding or hemorrhage, metabolic acidosis	Activated charcoal, gastric lavage, urine alkalinization, hemodialysis for severe acute ingestion, mechanical ventilation, supportive care
Bleaches	Irritation of lips, mouth, and eyes, superficial injury to esophagus; chemical pneumonia and pulmonary edema	Washing of exposed skin and eyes, dilution with water and milk, gastric lavage. Do not induce vomiting.
Carbon monoxide	Dyspnea, headache, tachypnea, confusion, impaired judgment, cyanosis, respiratory depression	Remove from source, apply 100% O_2 via nonrebreather mask, BVM, or mechanical ventilation; consider hyperbaric O_2 therapy.
Cyanide	*In small amounts*: Almond odor to breath, headache, dizziness, nausea, confusion, weakness, ↑ BP, ↑ HR, tachypnea *In large amounts*: Seizures, ↓ BP, bradypnea and respiratory arrest, ↓ HR, coma	IV hydroxocobalamin, IV sodium nitrate, IV sodium thiosulfate, supportive care
Ethylene glycol (antifreeze)	Sweet aromatic odor to breath, nausea, vomiting, slurred speech, ataxia, lethargy, respiratory depression	Activated charcoal, gastric lavage, supportive care
Iron	Vomiting (often bloody), diarrhea (often bloody), fever, hyperglycemia, lethargy, ↓ BP, seizures, coma	Gastric lavage, chelation therapy (deferoxamine [Desferal])
NSAIDs	Gastroenteritis, abdominal pain, drowsiness, nystagmus, liver and kidney damage	Activated charcoal, gastric lavage, supportive care
Tricyclic antidepressants (e.g., amitriptyline)	*In low doses:* Anticholinergic effects, agitation, ↑ BP, ↑ HR *In high doses:* CNS depression, dysrhythmias, ↓ BP, respiratory depression	Multidose activated charcoal, gastric lavage, serum alkalinization with sodium bicarbonate, mechanical ventilation, supportive care. Do not induce vomiting.
Alcohol, barbiturates, benzodiazepines, cocaine, hallucinogens, stimulants	See Chapter 11	See Chapter 11

The severity of the poisoning depends on the type, concentration, and route of exposure (Table 21.11). Toxins can affect every tissue of the body, so symptoms can be seen in any body system. Specific management of toxins involves decreasing absorption, enhancing elimination, and implementing toxin-specific interventions. Consult the local poison control center (available 24 hours a day) for the most current treatment protocols for specific poisons.[21] Binding agents, such as activated charcoal, cathartics, hemodialysis, urine alkalinization, and antidotes, may be given to increase the elimination of poisons.[21] Chelating agents are indicated for poisonings by some metals, such as lead, arsenic, mercury, and iron.

Decontamination takes priority over all interventions except those needed for life support. Wear personal protective equipment (PPE) for decontamination to prevent secondary exposure. In some cases, decontamination is done by those specially trained in hazardous material decontamination before the patient arrives at the hospital and again at the hospital if needed.

Skin and eye decontamination involve removing the toxins from the skin and eyes using copious amounts of water or saline. Most toxins can be safely removed with water or saline. As a rule, brush dry substances from the skin and clothing before using water. Do not remove powdered lime or mustard gas with water. Just brush lime off. Water mixes with mustard gas and releases chlorine gas.

Focus patient teaching on how the poisoning occurred. Arrange for an evaluation and follow-up by a mental health professional for all patients who have poisoning because of a suicide attempt or substance use.

Many health care workers (e.g., nurses, housekeepers) are at risk for exposure to hazardous materials (e.g., antineoplastic drugs, cleaning agents). Always consult the Material Safety Data Sheet for specific information about hazardous agents in the workplace. OSHA should evaluate all poisoning related to a workplace hazard.

VIOLENCE

Violence is the acting out of the emotions of fear and/or anger to cause harm to someone or something. It may be the result of organic disease (e.g., temporal lobe epilepsy), psychosis (e.g., schizophrenia), or criminal behavior (e.g., assault, murder). The patient cared for in the ED may be the victim or the perpetrator of violence. Violence can take place in a variety of settings, including the home, community, and workplace.

EDs are high-risk areas for *workplace violence.*[22] Measures to protect staff include on-site security personnel, metal detectors, surveillance cameras, staff trained in self-defense, and locked access doors. The ENA recommends every ED have a comprehensive workplace violence prevention program.[22]

An ED nurse must be aware of *family and intimate partner violence* (IPV) or the possibility of a patient being a victim or perpetrator of human trafficking. IPV occurs in all cultures, socioeconomic groups, age groups, and genders. Although men can be victims of family violence and IPV, most victims are women, children, and older adults. IPV and human trafficking are coercive behavior patterns in relationships that involve fear, humiliation, intimidation, neglect, or intentional physical, emotional, financial, or sexual injury. See Chapter 58 for information on sexual assault.

Human trafficking involves using force, fraud, or coercion to force the victim to provide labor, services, or a commercial sex act. Risk factors for being a victim include recent migration or relocation, substance use, mental health problems, involvement with the child welfare system, and being a runaway or homeless youth. Traffickers often identify and use their victims' vulnerabilities to create dependency.

It is likely that the ED nurse will come in contact with either a victim or perpetrator of human trafficking. We believe that over 80% of victims interacted with the health care system while being trafficked.[23] Common reasons victims present to the ED include physical injuries, such as fractures and lacerations, infections, reproductive health problems, toxicologic emergencies, and mental health problems such as suicide. ED nurses are uniquely positioned to help identify and report a trafficking victim or perpetrator to the proper authorities.

In the ED, we must screen for family violence and IPV. Ask questions such as, "Do you feel safe at home? Is anyone hurting you?" Barriers to effective screening include lack of privacy, fear of offending the patient, lack of time, and discomfort with the topic. Developing and implementing policies, procedures, and staff education programs improve screening practices.

Be sensitive when gathering information about suspected abuse and trafficking as it may potentially increase the patient's risk. Start appropriate interventions for patients who you suspect or find are victims of abuse or trafficking. This includes making referrals, notifying appropriate agencies, providing emotional support, and informing victims about their options. The ENA encourages ED nurses to become certified *sexual assault nurse examiners* (SANEs). SANEs provide expert emergency care, collect and document evidence, take part in staff and community education, and advocate for sexual assault and rape victims.

AGENTS OF TERRORISM

Terrorism is the intentional use of violence to cause harm.[24] Terror tactics may include biologic, chemical, nuclear, or explosive events. Prompt recognition and identification of potential health hazards are essential in the preparedness of health care professionals.

Biologic agents include bacteria, fungi, viruses, and toxins. Agents most often used include anthrax, smallpox, botulism, plague, tularemia, and hemorrhagic fever. If enough supplies are available, we can treat anthrax, plague, and tularemia with antibiotics, and the organisms are not resistant.[24] Vaccines are available for some agents.

Chemicals can be weapons of mass destruction. We categorize them by their target organ or effect. Nerve agents are the most toxic and rapidly acting chemical agents. For example, sarin is a highly toxic nerve gas that can cause death within minutes of exposure. Radioactive dust and smoke can spread and cause illness if inhaled. *Ionizing radiation,* such as that from a nuclear bomb or damage to a nuclear reactor, is a serious threat to the safety of victims and the environment. Exposure to ionizing radiation may include skin contamination with radioactive material.

Since radiation cannot be seen, smelled, felt, or tasted, you should start measures to limit contamination and provide for decontamination. Begin decontamination procedures immediately if external radioactive contaminants are present.

Explosive devices cause blast, crush, and/or penetrating injuries. Blast injuries result from the supersonic pressurization shock wave caused by the explosion. This shock wave mainly damages the lungs, GI tract, and middle ear. Crush injuries often result from explosions in confined spaces causing structural collapse. Some explosive devices contain materials that are projected during the explosion, leading to penetrating injuries.

PENETRATING TRAUMA

Penetrating trauma is an injury that occurs when an object pierces the skin and enters the body creating an open wound. When the object goes all the way through, creating an entry and exit wound, it is a perforating injury. The most common causes of penetrating and perforating injuries in the United States are gunshot and stab wounds. The severity of the injury largely depends on the body part involved. Patients with penetrating trauma have the best outcome when they are promptly evaluated and treated. All victims must first have a primary assessment to maintain airway, breathing, and circulation; control bleeding; and evaluate neurologic status.

Penetrating head trauma causes a traumatic brain injury (TBI). It has a high mortality rate. Most deaths from TBI are from gunshot wounds. Other causes include stab wounds, motor vehicle accidents, or occupational accidents. Those who survive penetrating head trauma often have permanent neurologic deficits.

Patients with penetrating neck trauma are at risk for injury to major blood vessels, the airway, and the spinal cord. Anticipate bleeding, respiratory, and neurologic problems. Chest wounds can damage the heart, lungs, esophagus, diaphragm, or trachea. Penetrating wounds to the heart are almost 80% fatal. Lung injury can cause pneumothorax or hemothorax requiring emergent decompression and chest tube insertion (see Chapter 28).

Penetrating wounds to the abdomen often result from gunshot wounds. Severity and prognosis depend on the organs injured. Mortality from abdominal wounds is about 5%. Death usually occurs later due to hemorrhage or infection.

Extremity trauma is usually not life threatening but can cause permanent disability. Blood vessels may be affected, leading to hemorrhage. Angulated fractures can cause penetrating trauma. Nerves, tendons, ligaments, and muscles can be injured. Early interventions include control of bleeding and stabilization of the injured extremity.

EMERGENCY AND MASS CASUALTY INCIDENT PREPAREDNESS

The term **emergency** usually refers to an extraordinary event that requires a rapid and skilled response and that the community's existing resources can manage. An emergency is different from a **mass casualty incident (MCI)**. With an MCI, the number of people killed or injured in a single incident is large enough to strain or overwhelm a community's ability to respond with existing resources. They always need assistance from resources outside the affected community (Fig. 21.8). MCIs can be human made (e.g., involving NBC agents) or natural (e.g., hurricane) events or disasters. MCIs usually involve large numbers of victims, physical and emotional suffering, and permanent changes within a community.

When an emergency or an MCI occurs, first responders go to the scene. Triage of victims of an emergency or an MCI differs from the usual ED triage. Several systems exist. Many use colored tags to designate the seriousness of the injury and the chance for survival. One system uses green for minor injuries and yellow for urgent but not life-threatening injuries. Red means a life-threatening injury requiring immediate intervention. Black indicates those who are expected to die or are deceased.[25]

Triage in an emergency or MCI must be done in less than 15 seconds. Victims need to be treated and stabilized and, if there is known or suspected contamination, decontaminated at the

Fig. 21.8 American Red Cross. (Photo used with the permission of the American Red Cross.)

BOX 21.1 ETHICAL/LEGAL DILEMMAS

Good Samaritan

Situation

You are employed as a charge nurse at a subacute rehabilitation facility. It is midnight, and you are driving home from work when you see a motor vehicle crash with a person at the side of the road waving and yelling for help. You stop and call 911 to report the incident. What do you do next?

Ethical/Legal Points for Consideration

- As a licensed health care professional, you are under no legal obligation to stop and give aid.
- If you stop, you assume an obligation not to leave the scene until sufficiently trained first responders arrive and assume control.
- Many states encourage health care professionals to stop and give aid by having "Good Samaritan" laws. These laws vary somewhat from state to state. They offer immunity from lawsuits for bystanders who provide aid in emergencies except in the case of gross negligence.
- A Good Samaritan must not be in the place of employment or under employment conditions.
- An example of gross negligence may be refusing to help someone who is seriously bleeding in favor of a person with a minor injury because the bleeding person looked old or disheveled.
- If there is a national disaster, an act of terrorism, or a major emergent need for HCPs, you may need to go to an assigned site to offer aid. The Good Samaritan Act would not cover you under these circumstances.

Discussion Questions

1. What factors do you think contribute to a health care professional's decision whether to stop to provide aid?
2. What basic aid would you feel comfortable providing if you do not have an emergency or trauma background?
3. Would your professional liability (malpractice) insurance cover you if someone claimed that you acted negligently while giving aid?

scene. After this, they are moved to hospitals. Many other victims arrive at hospitals on their own. The total number of victims a hospital can expect is estimated by doubling the number of victims who arrive in the first hour.

In addition to the services provided by first responders, many communities have *community emergency response teams* (CERTs). CERTs are recognized by the Federal Emergency Management Agency (FEMA) as important partners in emergency preparedness. CERT training helps citizens understand their responsibility in preparing for a natural or human-made disaster. Participants learn what to expect after a disaster and how to safely help themselves, their family, and their neighbors. Training includes lifesaving skills with emphasis on decision-making and rescuer safety. CERTs are an extension of the first responder services. They can offer immediate help to victims and organize untrained volunteers to assist until professional services arrive.[26]

All health care team members have a role in emergency and MCI preparedness. Knowing your agency's *emergency response plan* is essential. This includes knowing your individual and the response team's roles and responsibilities, plus taking part in emergency/MCI preparedness drills. Drills allow us to become familiar with emergency response procedures. These include hospital disaster drills, computer simulations, and tabletop exercises.

Response to MCIs often requires the aid of a federal agency. The National Incident Management System (NIMS), American Red Cross, FEMA, and National Disaster Medical System (NDMS) are examples of federal resources.

All disasters result in stress to those involved. This stress can persist for an extended period. It is influenced by the nature of the event, age, coping mechanisms, role in the event, and medical and mental health history. Many hospitals have a *critical incident stress management unit.* This unit arranges group discussions to allow people to share their feelings about the experience. This is important for emotional recovery.

Case Study

Trauma

(© Thinkstock.)

Patient Profile

Paramedics bring D.F., a 20-year-old female trauma victim, to the ED by helicopter. She was the driver in a motor vehicle crash and was not wearing a seat belt. Two unrestrained children in the car were pronounced dead at the scene. The paramedics said there was significant damage to the car on the driver's side.

Subjective Data

- Asking, "What happened? Where am I?"
- Reports shortness of breath and leg pain

Objective Data

Physical Assessment

- Vital signs: BP = 85/40 mm Hg, HR = 140 beats/min, RR = 36 breaths/min; O_2 saturation = 85% with 100% nonrebreather mask
- Decreased breath sounds on left side of chest
- Asymmetric chest wall movement
- Glasgow Coma Score = 14; pupils slightly unequal
- Badly deformed left lower leg with significant swelling and a pedal pulse by Doppler only
- 4-cm head laceration, bleeding controlled

Discussion Questions

1. ***Analyze***: What are D.F.'s most likely life-threatening injuries?
2. ***Prioritize:*** What is the priority of care for D.F.?
3. ***Prioritize:*** What interventions does she need immediately?
4. ***Plan***: What other interventions should you consider?
5. ***Plan:*** What are the best practice guidelines for fluid resuscitation in patients with hypovolemic shock?
6. ***Act:*** What activities could you delegate to assistive personnel (AP)?
7. ***Act:*** Several family members have arrived in the ED, including the mother of 1 of the children who died. The second child who died was the patient's child. How should you approach the family?

Answers are available at http://evolve.elsevier.com/Lewis/medsurg.

BRIDGE TO NCLEX EXAMINATION

The number of the question corresponds to the same-numbered outcome at the beginning of the chapter.

1. An older man arrives in triage disoriented and dyspneic. His skin is hot and dry. His wife states that he was fine earlier today. The nurse's next *priority* would be to
   a. assess his vital signs.
   b. obtain a brief medical history from his wife.
   c. start supplemental O_2 and have the provider see him.
   d. determine the kind of insurance he has before treating him.
2. A patient has a core temperature of 90°F (32.2°C). The *most* appropriate rewarming technique would be
   a. passive rewarming with warm blankets.
   b. active internal rewarming using warmed IV fluids.
   c. passive rewarming using air-filled warming blankets.
   d. active external rewarming by submersing in a warm bath.
3. What interventions does the nurse anticipate for a patient with an aspirin overdose? *(select all that apply.)*
   a. Hemodialysis
   b. Corticosteroids
   c. Hyperbaric O_2
   d. Gastric lavage
   e. Activated charcoal

4. An older woman arrives in the ED reporting severe pain in her right shoulder. The nurse notes her clothes are soiled with urine and feces. She tells the nurse that she lives with her son and that she "fell." She is tearful and asks you if she can be admitted. What possibility should the nurse consider?
   a. Dementia
   b. Possible cancer
   c. Family violence
   d. Orthostatic hypotension
5. A chemical explosion occurs at a nearby industrial site. First responders report that victims are decontaminated at the scene, and about 125 workers will need medical evaluation and care. The first action of the nurse receiving this report should be to
   a. issue a code blue alert.
   b. activate the hospital's emergency response plan.
   c. notify the Federal Emergency Management Agency (FEMA).
   d. arrange for the American Red Cross to provide aid to victims.

1. a; 2. b; 3. a, d, e; 4. c; 5. b.

For rationales to these answers and even more NCLEX review questions, visit http://evolve.elsevier.com/Lewis/medsurg.

EVOLVE WEBSITE/RESOURCES LIST

http://evolve.elsevier.com/Lewis/medsurg
Review Questions (Online Only)
Key Points
Answer Keys for Questions
- Rationales for Bridge to NCLEX Examination Questions
- Answer Guidelines for Case Study
- Answer Guidelines for Managing Care of Multiple Patients Case Study (Section 4)

Student Case Study
- Patient with Musculoskeletal Trauma

Conceptual Care Map Creator
Audio Glossary
Content Updates

REFERENCES

1. Centers for Disease Control and Prevention (CDC): Emergency department visits. Retrieved from www.cdc.gov/nchs/fastats/emergency-department.htm.
2. American College of Emergency Physicians: Emergency department usage trends before COVID-19. Retrieved from https://www.acepnow.com/article/emergency-department-usage-trends-before-covid-19/.
3. Emergency Nurses Association: Emergency Severity Index (ESI). Retrieved from https://www.ena.org/education/esi.
4. McQuillan KA, Makic MB: *Trauma nursing: from resuscitation through rehabilitation*, ed 5, St. Louis, 2020, Elsevier.
5. Sweet V: *Emergency nursing core curriculum*, ed 7, St Louis, 2018, Elsevier.

*6. Khoshfetrat M, Yaghoubi MA, Hosseini BM, et al.: The ability of GCS, FOUR, and Apache II in predicting the outcome of patients with traumatic brain injury: a comparative study, *Biomed Res Ther* 7:3614, 2020.

*7. Powers K, Reeve CL: Family presence during resuscitation: medical–surgical nurses' perceptions, self-confidence, and use of invitations, *Am J Nurs* 120:28, 2020.

*8. Varndell W, Fry M, Elliott D: Pain assessment and interventions by nurses in the emergency department: a national survey, *J Clin Nurs* 13:2352, 2020.

9. Bloom BA, Gibbons RC: Focused assessment with sonography for trauma. Retrieved from https://www.ncbi.nlm.nih.gov/books/NBK470479/.

10. CDC: Tetanus: Prevention. Retrieved from www.cdc.gov/tetanus/about/prevention.html.

*11. Walker AC, Johnson NJ: Targeted temperature management and postcardiac arrest care, *Emerg Med Clin* 37:381, 2019.

*12. Badenes R, Monleón B, Martín-Loeches I: Organ recovery procedure in donation after controlled circulatory death with normothermic regional perfusion: state of the art. *Annual Update in Intensive Care and Emergency Medicine* 2020:503, 2020.

13. CDC: Emergency department visits among adults aged 60 and over: United States, 2014–2017. Retrieved from https://www.cdc.gov/nchs/products/databriefs/db367.htm.

14. Gauer R, Meyers BK: Heat-related illnesses, *AFP* 99:482, 2019.

*15. Joshi K, Goyary D, Mazumder B, et al.: Frostbite: current status and advancements in therapeutics, *J Therm Biol* 93:102716, 2020.

16. McCall JD, Sternard BT: Drowning. Retrieved from https://www.ncbi.nlm.nih.gov/books/NBK430833/.

17. CDC: Venomous snakes. Retrieved from www.cdc.gov/niosh/topics/snakes/default.html.

18. Pace EJ, O'Reilly M: Tickborne diseases: diagnosis and management, *AFP* 101:530, 2019.

*19. Greene SE, Fritz SA: Infectious complications of bite injuries, *Infect Dis Clin* 35:219, 2021.

20. CDC: Rabies. Retrieved from www.cdc.gov/vaccines/hcp/vis/vis-statements/rabies.html.

21. National Capital Poison Control Center: Act fast. Retrieved from www.poison.org.

22. Wolf L, Perhats C, Delao A, et al.: Violence and its impact on the emergency nurse, *J Emerg Nurs* 46:354, 2020.

*23. Tortolero GA: *Human trafficking victim identification and response within the United States healthcare system*, International Association for Healthcare Security and Safety Foundation, 2020.

24. Williams M, Armstrong L, Sizemore DC: Biologic, chemical, and radiation terrorism review. Retrieved from https://www.ncbi.nlm.nih.gov/books/NBK493217/.

25. US Department of Health and Human Services: START adult triage algorithm. Retrieved from https://remm.hhs.gov/startadult.htm.

26. Department of Homeland Security: Community emergency response team. Retrieved from www.ready.gov/community-emergency-response-team.

* Evidence-based information for clinical practice.

Case Study

Applying Clinical Judgment With Multiple Patients

You have been called into work at 1100 to cover patients for a nurse who had a family emergency. You take over care for the following 3 patients on a surgical unit. You have 1 AP available who is assigned to help you. 2 other RNs are on the unit.

 (© Ryan Mcvay/ Photodisc/Thinkstock)	F.D., a 66-year-old woman, is scheduled for an abdominal hysterectomy at 1300 today for endometrial cancer. She has type 2 diabetes, hypertension, and a history of atrial fibrillation controlled with drug therapy. She has been NPO since midnight. Capillary blood glucose level at 0730 was 198 mg/dL. She received 4 units of regular insulin at 0800 but no other morning medications. IV of normal saline is infusing at 125 mL/hr. Weight 205 lb, height 5 ft 2 in Vital signs: BP 180/94, 84 and regular, 20.
 (©shironosov/ iStock/Thinkstock)	G.S., a 63-year-old male, had a laparoscopic cholecystectomy yesterday afternoon. His history includes hypertension and type 2 diabetes. His capillary glucose 1 hour ago was 135 mg/dL. He is scheduled for discharge this evening.
 (©BananaStock/ BananaStock/Thinkstock)	E.G., a 74-year-old man, had surgery for a fractured hip yesterday. He is receiving dextrose 5% in 0.45 normal saline at 100 mL/hr, morphine via PCA at 1 mg q10min (20 mg max in 4 hr) for pain, and heparin 5000 units subcutaneous every 12 hr. O_2 to keep O_2 saturation >93%. A self-suction drain is in place at the surgical site. He has good respiratory effort when using his incentive spirometer.

1. Highlight all the findings above that require your follow-up.
2. After receiving report, which patient should you see first?
3. Which tasks should you delegate to the AP? (select all that apply)
   a. Explain discharge instructions to G.S.
   b. Obtain 1200 vital signs on E.G. and F.D.
   c. Measure capillary glucose levels on F.D. and G.S.
   d. Confirm E.G.'s understanding of how to use the PCA pump.
   e. Remind E.G. and G.S. to use their incentive spirometers every hour.
4. When you enter F.D.'s room, you find her somewhat withdrawn and lethargic. Her face is cool and slightly clammy. What initial action would be most appropriate?
   a. Give 1 ampule of D_{50} IV stat.
   b. Increase F.D.'s IV rate to 150 mL/hr.
   c. Obtain a stat capillary glucose level.
   d. Ask the AP to give F.D. a glass of orange juice.

Case Study Progression

F.D.'s capillary glucose reading was 52 mg/dL. You notify her HCP and give 1 ampule of D_{50} IV dextrose as ordered. You then change her IV infusion to D_5 0.9%. You check her capillary glucose within 15 minutes and then monitor her glucose levels each hour.

5. A preoperative checklist for F.D. is used to ensure completion of (select all that apply)
   a. removal of nail polish and jewelry.
   b. signed and witnessed informed consent.
   c. patient understanding of sensory information.
   d. identification of surgical site with surgical skin marker.
   e. notification of family of where to wait for the surgeon afterward.
6. Choose the most likely options for the information missing from the statement, below, by selecting from the list of options provided.

Based on F.D.'s assessment data and history, she is at risk for postoperative complications, including ___________, ___________, ___________, and ___________.

Options:
Atelectasis
Delayed wound healing
Delirium
Paralytic ileus
Pressure injury
VTE
Wound infection

7. The laboratory calls to report that E.G.'s aPTT (activated partial thromboplastin time) is 94 seconds. You assess him and find that the hip dressing is saturated with serosanguinous drainage. The next dose of heparin is due at 2100 this evening; the last dose was at 0900 this morning. Use an X for the nursing actions listed below that are Indicated (appropriate or necessary), Contraindicated (could be harmful), or Nonessential (makes no difference or not necessary) for D.B. at this time.

Nursing Action	Indicated	Contraindicated	Nonessential
Initiate bleeding precautions.			
Remove the hip dressing and leave the wound uncovered.			
Obtain a STAT repeat aPTT.			
Notify the HCP of the aPTT and E.G.'s condition.			
Discontinue the PCA morphine.			
Prepare to administer protamine.			
Obtain a full set of vital signs.			

8. E.G.'s BP is 92/54 with a heart rate of 110 bpm. Respiratory rate is 30 breaths/min, and O_2 saturation is 98% on 2 L of O_2. The priority would be to
   a. notify physical therapy that his session today will have to be postponed until evening.
   b. notify the previous RN that a medication error occurred with the heparin dose at 0900.
   c. send an order for stat CBC and type and screen for 4 units of packed red blood cells.
   d. notify the HCP of the laboratory result and anticipate orders for a reversal agent.
9. Which instructions should you give to the AP who will be assisting E.G. with ADLs? *(select all that apply)*
   a. Use a soft toothbrush for oral care.
   b. Provide an emery board for nail care.
   c. Avoid overinflating blood pressure cuffs.
   d. Use an electric razor to shave the patient.
   e. Offer mouthwash with alcohol for rinsing.
10. When providing discharge instructions to G.S., he tells you that the AP told him that he could do whatever activity he was comfortable doing—to let pain guide his progress. Your initial reaction to this statement should be to

Continued

Case Study—cont'd

a. ask the AP to clarify what was said to G.S.
b. report the AP's actions to the nurse manager.
c. teach G.S. about the reason for activity restrictions.
d. clarify the discharge instructions with the health care provider.

10. Use an X to indicate whether the instructions below are Indicated (appropriate or necessary), Contraindicated (could be harmful), or Nonessential (makes no difference or not necessary) for G.S.'s discharge at this time.

Nursing Action	Indicated	Contraindicated	Nonessential
You can shower tomorrow.			
Notify the HCP if there is any redness, swelling, bile-colored drainage, or pus from any incision			
Weigh yourself every day.			
Remain off work for 4 weeks.			
Take your pain medication as prescribed.			
You need to stay on a full liquid diet for an additional week.			

Answers available at http://evolve.elsevier.com/Lewis/medsurg.

22

Assessment and Management: Visual Problems

Mariann M. Harding

http://evolve.elsevier.com/Lewis/medsurg/

CONCEPTUAL FOCUS

Coping
Functional Ability
Infection
Sensory Perception

LEARNING OUTCOMES

1. Describe the structures and functions of the visual system.
2. Explain the physiologic processes involved in normal vision.
3. Obtain significant subjective and objective assessment data related to the visual system.
4. Perform a physical assessment of the visual system using the appropriate techniques.
5. Distinguish normal from common abnormal findings of a physical assessment of the visual system.
6. Link the age-related changes in the visual system to differences in assessment findings.
7. Describe the purpose, significance of results, and nursing responsibilities related to diagnostic studies of the visual system.
8. Compare and contrast the types of refractive errors and appropriate corrections.
9. Describe the common causes and assistive measures for visual impairment.
10. Discuss nursing measures that promote eye health.
11. Explain the pathophysiology, clinical manifestations, and interprofessional and nursing management of the patient with an eye disorder.
12. Discuss the general nursing care of patients undergoing eye surgery.

KEY TERMS

age-related macular degeneration (AMD)
astigmatism
cataract
conjunctivitis
enucleation
glaucoma
hordeolum
hyperopia
keratitis
myopia
presbyopia
retinal detachment
retinopathy
strabismus

For people to be as independent as possible and take part in fulfilling activities, it is important that the visual system is as functional as possible. The impact of poor vision or blindness can be devastating to activities of daily living (ADLs) and independence. The psychosocial consequences can include decreased quality of life, social isolation, depression, and loss of self-esteem. Vision loss also takes a huge toll on caregivers. This makes our being involved in vision-loss prevention, detection, and treatment measures important.

STRUCTURES AND FUNCTIONS OF VISUAL SYSTEM

The visual system is part of the central nervous system (CNS). It consists of 2 main parts, the eyes, which contain the image receptors, and the brain. The brain functions to process and interpret the information transmitted from the receptors into images. Anatomically, the visual system is made up of the orbit, the ocular adnexa (external tissues and structures surrounding the eye), the eye, and the visual pathway (optic nerve, optic chiasm, lateral geniculate nucleus, and visual cortex).

Periocular Structures

Orbit

The orbits, or eye sockets, are the bony structures that house the eyeballs. 7 bones form the orbit: frontal, zygoma, maxilla, ethmoid, sphenoid, lacrimal, and palatine (Fig. 22.1). The average orbit is 35 mm high and 40 mm wide. In addition to the eye, the orbits contain the associated muscles, nerves, blood vessels, and fat.

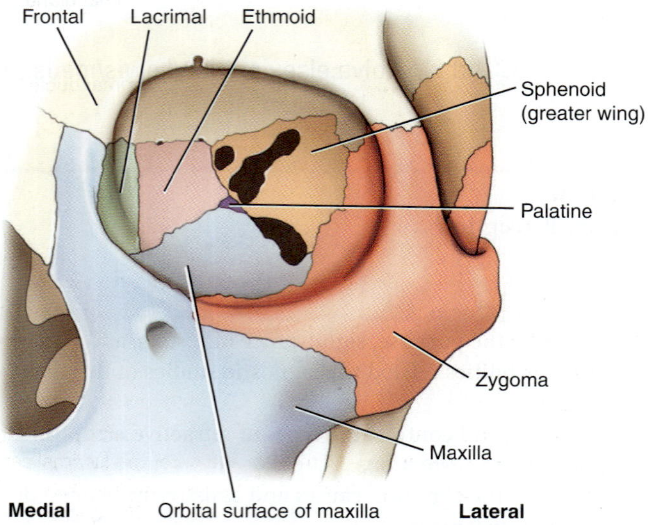

Fig. 22.1 Bones that form the orbit, or eye socket. (From Lampignano J, Kendrick L: *Bontrager's textbook of radiographic positioning and related anatomy*, ed 9, St Louis, 2018, Mosby.)

Within the orbit are 3 main orbital openings, or *fissures:* optic canal, superior orbital fissure, and inferior orbital fissure. They are all important channels for arteries, veins, and nerves. The optic canal is located at the top of the socket. It provides an entry point for the optic nerve (cranial nerve [CN] II). The superior orbital fissure is a small slit in the posterior orbit. It is the main entry point for several other cranial nerves to enter the orbit from the brain. These include the oculomotor nerve (CN III), trochlear nerve (CN IV), trigeminal nerve (CN V), and abducens nerve (CN VI). The inferior orbital fissure is in the floor of the orbit. It holds the zygomatic branch of the maxillary nerve.

There are 6 extraocular muscles: (1) superior and inferior rectus muscles, (2) medial and lateral rectus muscles, and (3) superior and inferior oblique muscles. They emerge from the apex of the orbit and attach to the eye to stabilize and move it (Fig. 22.2). Neuromuscular coordination produces simultaneous movement of the eyes in the same direction.

Ocular Adnexa

The ocular adnexa include the eyebrows, eyelids, eyelashes, and lacrimal system. Eyebrows, eyelids, and eyelashes are vital in protecting the eye. They are a physical barrier to dust and foreign particles. Blinking protects the eye from injury, distributes tears over the anterior surface of the eyeball, and supplies necessary nourishment to surface cells.

The upper and lower eyelids join at the medial and lateral canthi. Eyelid skin is the thinnest skin in the body. It measures less than 1 mm thick. The upper eyelids contain the levator palpebrae superioris muscle. It is innervated by the superior division of CN III. This muscle elevates and retracts the upper eyelid. The eyelids close through the action of the orbicularis muscle. It is innervated by CN VII.

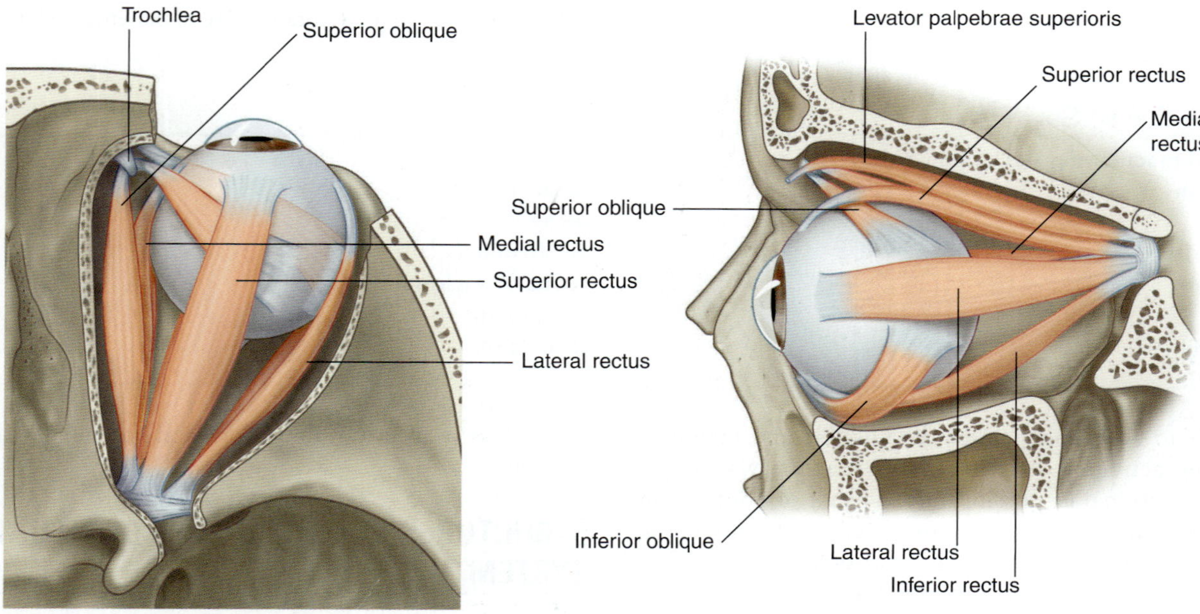

Fig. 22.2 The 6 extraocular muscles. (From Drake R, Vogl AW, Mitchell AWM: *Gray's anatomy for students*, ed 3, Philadelphia, 2015, Churchill Livingstone.)

Lacrimal System

The lacrimal system includes the structures for tear production and drainage. The main lacrimal gland and accessory lacrimal glands make tears. The lacrimal glands, in the superotemporal orbit, are exocrine glands. They make and secrete the aqueous layer of tear film and are responsible for reflex tear production. The tear film moistens the eye and supplies oxygen to the cornea. The accessory lacrimal glands, the *glands of Wolfring* and *glands of Krause,* are found within the conjunctiva of the upper eyelid. They are responsible for baseline tear production. Tears pass over the surface of the eye and then enter the nasolacrimal system. The nasolacrimal drainage system includes the puncta, canaliculi, lacrimal sac, and nasolacrimal duct (Fig. 22.3).

Eyeball

The eyeball, or globe, is composed of 3 layers (Fig. 22.4). The tough outer layer is composed of the cornea, conjunctiva, and sclera. The middle layer consists of the uveal tract (iris, choroid and ciliary body) and the innermost layer, the retina. The *anterior cavity* is divided into the anterior and posterior chambers. The anterior chamber lies between the iris and posterior surface of the cornea. The posterior chamber lies between the anterior surface of the lens and posterior surface of the iris. The *posterior cavity* lies in the large space behind the lens and in front of the retina.

External Ocular Structures

The conjunctiva is a transparent mucous membrane that covers the inner surfaces of the eyelids and extends over the sclera. Glands in the conjunctiva secrete mucus and tears. Tenon capsule, also called the fascia bulbi, is a thin layer of fascia that encases the eyeball behind the conjunctiva. The capsule extends posteriorly, ultimately fusing with the optic nerve.

The cornea allows light to enter the eye. It is transparent and avascular. Its curved shape refracts or bends incoming light rays to help focus them on the retina. The cornea has 6 layers: epithelium, Bowman layer, stroma, Descemet membrane, Dua layer, and endothelium.

The sclera, the white part of the eye, is a fibrous connective tissue layer. It protects the eye and helps the eye to maintain its shape and structure. The sclera extends from the cornea to the optic nerve. We call the junction of the sclera and cornea the limbus.

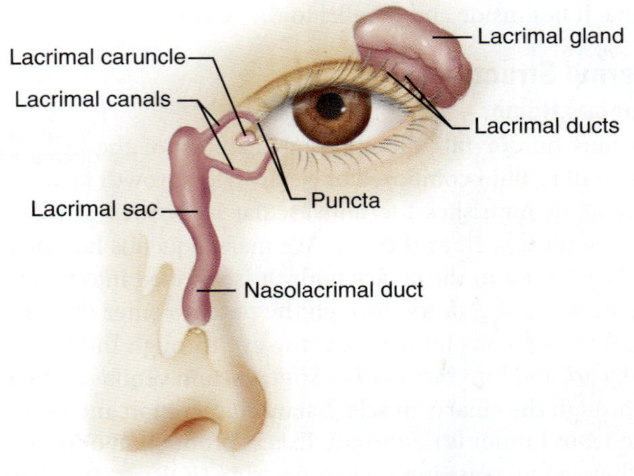

Fig. 22.3 External eye and lacrimal apparatus. Tears made in the lacrimal gland pass over the surface of the eye and enter the lacrimal canal. From there the tears are carried through the nasolacrimal duct to the nasal cavity. (Modified from Patton KT, Thibodeau GA: *Anatomy and physiology,* ed 8, St Louis, 2013, Mosby.)

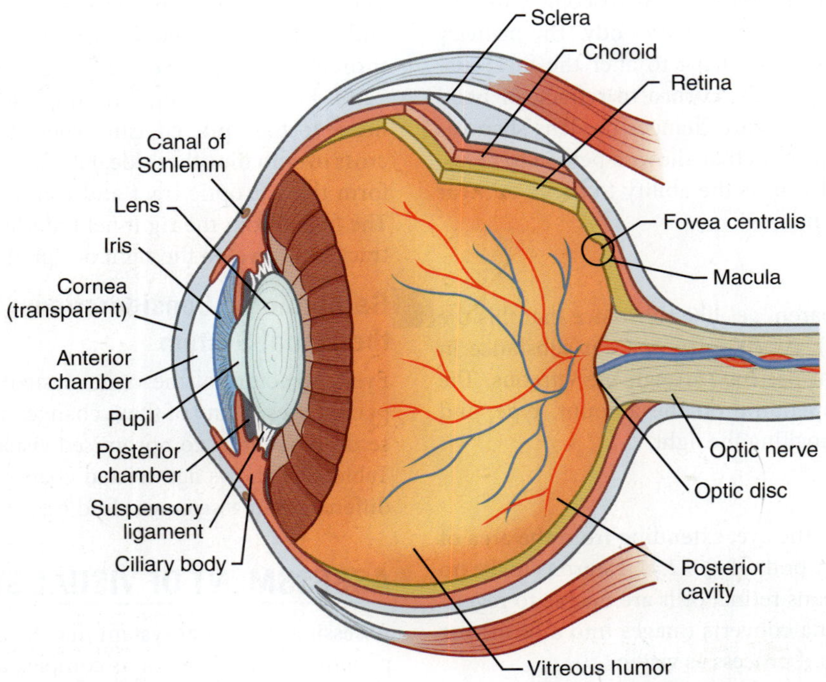

Fig. 22.4 The human eye. (Modified from Patton KT, Thibodeau GA: *Anatomy and physiology,* ed 8, St Louis, 2013, Mosby.)

Middle Ocular Structures

The iris gives the eye its color. It has a small round opening in the center called the *pupil*. The pupil allows light to enter the eye. It constricts by action of the iris sphincter muscle (under parasympathetic control) and dilates by action of the iris dilator muscle (under sympathetic control). This controls the amount of light that enters the eye.

The ciliary body contains the ciliary muscle and ciliary processes. It is behind the iris. The ciliary muscle helps us focus by changing the shape of the lens to refract light onto the retina. The ciliary processes make aqueous humor for both the anterior and posterior chamber. The choroid is a highly vascular structure that nourishes the ciliary body, iris, and outer part of the retina. It lies inside and parallel to the sclera.

Internal Structures

Aqueous Humor

Aqueous humor fills the anterior chamber of the eye. It is a clear watery fluid composed of electrolytes, growth factors, and proteins. It nourishes the nonvascular structures of the anterior chamber, such as the lens. We make aqueous humor from capillary blood in the ciliary body. It is secreted into the posterior chamber and flows through the pupil to enter the anterior chamber. Aqueous humor exits the eye through the *trabecular meshwork* and into the *canal of Schlemm* and venous circulation or through the ciliary muscle. Balanced secretion and excretion of aqueous humor is important. Excess production or decreased outflow can increase intraocular pressure (IOP) greater than the normal 10 to 21 mm Hg. This is called *glaucoma*.

Lens

The lens is a biconvex structure behind the iris. Small fibers collectively called the suspensory ligament, or the zonule, keep the lens in place. The zonule is a series of microscopic wire-like threads that connect the lens to the ciliary body. The primary function of the lens is to change shape to alter the focal distance of the eye. It works with the cornea to refract, or bend light. The action of the ciliary body changes the lens shape as part of accommodation, a process that allows a person to focus. An example of accommodation is the ability to focus on near objects, such as when reading.

Vitreous Humor

Vitreous humor is a transparent gel-like substance that fills the posterior cavity (Fig. 22.4). Any nontransparent substance in the vitreous will block light passing through the vitreous. The effect on vision varies, depending on the amount, type, and location of the substance blocking the light.

Retina

The retina lines the back of the eye, extending from the area of the optic nerve to the ciliary body (Fig. 22.4). Neurons make up most of the retina. This means retinal cells are unable to regenerate if destroyed. The retina converts images into a form that the brain can understand and process as vision.

The retina has 2 main parts, the peripheral retina and central retina. The central retina contains the macula and fovea. The macula is around 6 mm in diameter. It is responsible for the central visual field. The fovea is at the center of the macula. This area provides the sharpest visual acuity, which we need for activities in which detail is important, like reading and driving.

The retina contains light-sensitive structures called photoreceptor cells. There are 2 types of photoreceptors, rods and cones. Rods and cones convert light to neural signals, which the nervous system translates into vision. Rods are mostly found in the peripheral retina. They are responsible for most of our peripheral vision and night vision. Rods perceive only light and dark. They do not contribute to color vision. Cones are in the central retina, condensed mostly in the fovea. They are responsible for central vision and color vision. There are 3 types of cone cells: red, green, and blue. They all work together to create the full color spectrum.

The retina receives oxygen and nutrients from the choroid and the retinal vascular systems. The central retinal artery carries blood and nutrients into the retina. The central retinal vein carries blood away from the retina.

Optic Nerve

The optic nerve, or CN II, transmits vision information from the retina to the brain. The optic nerve begins at the optic disc. That is the region of the retina where the optic nerve and vessels leave the retina. Because there are no photoreceptor cells over the optic disc, there is an anatomic blind spot in this area. In the center of the optic disc is a white, cup-shaped area called the optic cup.

VISUAL PATHWAY

For light to reach the retina, it must pass through many structures: the cornea, aqueous humor, lens, and vitreous humor. These structures must be clear for light to reach the retina and stimulate the photoreceptor cells. Once the image travels through the refractive media, it is focused on the retina (Fig. 22.5). From the retina, the impulses travel through the optic nerve to the optic chiasm, where the nasal fibers of each eye cross over to the other side. Fibers from the left field of both eyes form the left optic tract and travel to the left occipital cortex. The fibers from the right field of both eyes form the right optic tract and travel to the right occipital cortex.

Gerontologic Considerations: Effects of Aging on the Visual System

Every structure of the visual system is subject to changes as a person ages. Many of these changes are not serious. Others may result in severely compromised visual acuity in the older adult. Table 22.1 shows age-related changes in the visual system and differences in assessment findings.

ASSESSMENT OF VISUAL SYSTEM

Assessing the visual system may be as simple as determining a patient's visual acuity or as complex as collecting complete subjective and objective data about the visual system. The patient in a clinic or office setting is often seeking routine eye care or a

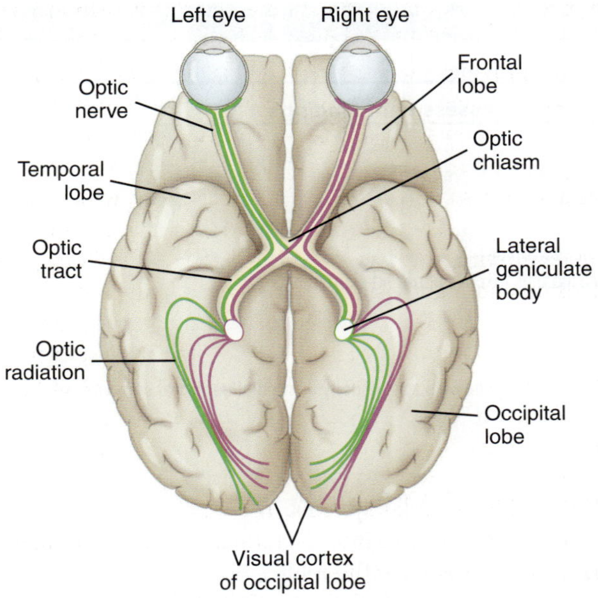

Fig. 22.5 The visual pathway. Fibers from the nasal portion of each retina cross over to the opposite side of the optic chiasma, ending in the lateral geniculate body of the opposite side. Location of a lesion in the visual pathway determines the resulting visual defect.

change in their eyewear prescription. However, the patient may have some underlying concerns that they do not mention or even recognize. To perform an appropriate visual assessment, determine what is necessary for the specific patient. While many of these assessments are within your scope of practice, some require special training.

Case Study

Patient Introduction

(© Jack Hollingsworth/Photodisc/Thinkstock.)

F.M. is an 81-year-old woman who comes to the emergency department with visual changes. F.M. states that her vision "looks like everything is covered with a spider web." She reports seeing periodic light flashes and small white spots "floating" in the air.

Discussion Questions

1. What are some possible causes of F.M.'s vision problems?
2. What type of assessment would be most appropriate for F.M.: comprehensive, focused, or emergency?
3. What assessment questions will you ask her?

You will learn more about F.M. and her condition as you read through this assessment chapter.

Answers available at http://evolve.elsevier.com/Lewis/medsurg.

Subjective Data

Important Health Information

Health history. Take a health history, including the ocular and nonocular history. The patient's nonocular history can be significant in assessing and treating an eye problem. Ask the patient about systemic diseases that may have eye manifestations. These include diabetes, hypertension, cancer, rheumatoid arthritis, syphilis and other sexually transmitted infections (STIs), acquired immunodeficiency syndrome (AIDS), muscular dystrophy, myasthenia gravis, multiple sclerosis, inflammatory bowel disease, and thyroid disease. Include any history of stroke or neurologic problems because these have the potential to result in visual field defects.

Obtain a history of tests for visual acuity. Include the date of the last examination and any change in glasses or contact lenses. Ask the patient about a history of strabismus, amblyopia, cataracts, retinal detachment, refractive surgery, or glaucoma. Note any trauma to the eye, its treatment, and sequelae.

Obtain information about allergies. Allergies often cause eye symptoms, such as itching, burning, watering, drainage, and blurred vision.

Medications. Obtain a complete medication history, including eyedrops. Many drugs effect the eye. For example, many cold preparations contain a form of epinephrine (e.g., pseudoephedrine) that can dilate the pupil. Note the use of any antihistamine or decongestant since these can cause dry eyes. Ask whether the patient uses corticosteroids, thyroid medications, or oral hypoglycemics and insulin. Long-term use of corticosteroid preparations can contribute to the development of glaucoma or cataracts.[1] Note whether the patient is taking any β-blockers, since β-blockers used to treat glaucoma can potentiate their effects. Hydroxychloroquine, which we use to treat rheumatoid arthritis and other autoimmune diseases, has the potential to result in retinal toxicity. It is important that these patients have annual eye examination.

Surgery or other treatments. Obtain a history of both ocular and nonocular surgeries. Include laser-based surgery and invasive treatments, such as retinal injections.

Functional Health Patterns

The focus of the functional health pattern assessment depends on the presence or absence of vision loss and whether the loss is permanent or temporary. Table 22.2 lists suggested health history questions related to the functional health patterns.

Health perception–health management pattern. Patient characteristics, such as gender, ethnicity, and age, are important in assessing eye problems (Box 22.1). Men are more likely to have color blindness. Age-related macular degeneration (AMD) occurs more often in women.

The patient's visual health can affect activities at home or at work. It is important to know how the patient perceives the current health problem. As outlined in Table 22.2, guide the patient in describing the current problem. Assess the patient's ability to perform self-care, especially any eye care related to the patient's eye problem.

The patient may not recognize the importance of eye-safety practices, such as wearing protective eyewear during potentially hazardous activities or avoiding noxious fumes and other eye irritants. Ask about the use of sunglasses in bright light. Prolonged exposure to ultraviolet (UV) light can affect the retina. Ask about night driving habits and any problems encountered. Today, millions of people wear contact lenses, but many do not care for them properly. The type of contact lenses and the patient's wearing and care habits may provide an opportunity for teaching.

Hereditary systemic diseases (e.g., sickle cell anemia) can significantly affect eye health. In addition, many refractive errors and other eye problems are hereditary. Determine whether the patient

TABLE 22.1 GERONTOLOGIC ASSESSMENT DIFFERENCES

Visual System

Changes	Differences in Assessment Findings
Eyebrows and Eyelashes	
Loss of pigment in hair	Graying of eyebrows, eyelashes
Eyelids	
Loss of orbital fat, decreased muscle tone	Entropion, ectropion
Tissue atrophy and stretching, prolapse of fat into eyelid tissue, loosening of the levator palpebrae superioris muscle	Dermatochalasis (excess upper lid skin), ptosis
Conjunctiva	
Tissue damage related to chronic exposure to ultraviolet light or to other chronic environmental exposure	Pinguecula (small yellowish spot usually on medial aspect of conjunctiva)
Sclera	
Lipid deposition	Scleral color yellowish as opposed to bluish
Cornea	
Cholesterol deposits in peripheral cornea	Arcus senilis (milky white-gray ring encircling periphery of cornea) (Fig. 22.6)
Tissue damage related to chronic exposure	Pterygium (thick, triangular bit of pale tissue that extends from inner canthus of eye to nasal border of cornea)
Decrease in water content, atrophy of nerve fibers	Decreased corneal sensitivity and corneal reflex
Epithelial changes	Loss of corneal luster
Accumulation of lipid deposits	Blurred vision
Lacrimal Apparatus	
Decreased tear secretion	Dryness
Malposition of eyelid and punctal eversion resulting in tears overflowing lid margins instead of draining through puncta	Tearing, irritated eyes
Iris	
Increased rigidity of iris	Decreased pupil size
Dilator muscle atrophy or weakness	Slow recovery of pupil size after light stimulation
Loss of pigment	Change of iris color
Ciliary muscle becoming smaller, stiffer	Decrease in near vision and accommodation
Lens	
Biochemical changes in lens proteins, oxidative damage, chronic exposure to ultraviolet light	Cataracts
Increased rigidity of lens	Presbyopia
Opacities in lens (also may be related to opacities in cornea and vitreous)	Reports of glare, night vision impaired
Accumulation of yellow substances	Yellow color of lens
Retina	
Retinal vascular changes related to atherosclerosis and hypertension	Narrowed, pale, straighter arterioles. Acute branching
Decrease in number of cones	Changes in color perception, especially blue and violet
Loss of photoreceptor cells, retinal pigment, epithelial cells, and melanin	Decreased visual acuity
AMD due to vascular changes	Loss of central vision, presence of yellow deposits, atrophy of macular retinal pigment
Vitreous	
Liquefaction and detachment of vitreous	Increased "floaters"

has a family history of eye problems, including cataracts, tumors, glaucoma, refractive errors (especially myopia, hyperopia), and retinal degenerative conditions (e.g., AMD, retinal detachment).

Nutritional-metabolic pattern. High doses of vitamins containing antioxidant, carotenoids, and omega-3 fatty acids (vitamins C and E, beta-carotene, zinc) may be important to eye health. Some patients with AMD may benefit from vitamin supplements.

Elimination pattern. Straining to defecate (Valsalva maneuver) can raise IOP. After eye surgery, many HCPs do not want patients to strain. Assess the patient's usual elimination pattern. Determine whether there is the potential for constipation in the patient who has had eye surgery.

Activity-exercise pattern. Reduced vision, symptoms accompanying an eye problem, or activity restrictions after surgery can affect the patient's usual level of activity or exercise.

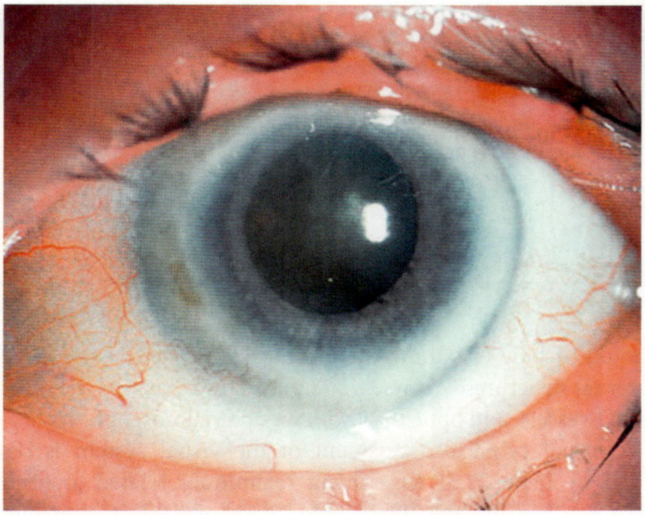

Fig. 22.6 Arcus senilis, or age-related degeneration of the cornea. (From Stein HA: Preliminary evaluation. *Ophthalmic Assistant*, 1:107, 2018.)

Ask about leisure activities during which the patient may incur an eye injury. For example, gardening, woodworking, and other craft activities can result in corneal or conjunctival foreign bodies or even penetrating injuries of the globe. Sports activities, such as racquetball, baseball, and tennis, carry risks for blunt trauma to the eyes. People should wear protection goggles for these sports.

Sleep-rest pattern. In the otherwise healthy person, lack of sleep may cause eye irritation, especially if the patient wears contact lenses. Painful eye problems, such as corneal abrasions, may disrupt normal sleep.

Cognitive-perceptual pattern. Assess for other cognitive or perceptual problems. For example, the functional ability of a patient with a visual deficit will be further compromised if the patient also has hearing problems. The patient who cannot see to read may find it harder to follow discharge instructions if they also have trouble hearing or remembering verbal instructions. Eye pain is always an important symptom to assess. If eye pain is present, ask the patient about treatment and response.

Self-perception–self-concept pattern. The loss of independence that can follow a partial or complete loss of vision, even if the condition is temporary, can have devastating effects on the patient's self-concept. Evaluate the potential effect of vision loss on the patient's self-image. For instance, disabling glare from a cataract may prevent nighttime driving. In today's highly mobile society, losing the ability to drive can represent a significant loss of independence and self-esteem.

Role-relationship pattern. Eye problems can negatively affect the patient's ability to take part in roles and responsibilities in the home, work, and social environments. For example, with decreased visual acuity, the patient may no longer adequately function at work. Many occupations place workers in conditions in which eye injury may occur. For example, factory workers may be at risk from flying metal debris. Eye-safety practices, such as the use of goggles or safety glasses, are now a legal requirement in some workplaces. The patient with diabetes may not be able to see well enough to self-administer insulin. This patient may resent dependence on a caregiver who takes over this function. Sensitively ask if the problem has affected the patient's preferred roles and responsibilities.

TABLE 22.2 HEALTH HISTORY

Visual System

Health Perception–Health Management

- Describe the change in your vision. Describe how this affects your daily life.
- Do you wear protective eyewear (sunglasses, safety goggles, hats)?[a]
- Do you wear contact lenses? If so, how do you take care of them?
- If you use eyedrops, how do you instill them?
- Do you have any allergies that cause eye symptoms?[a]
- Do you have a family history of cataracts, glaucoma, or macular degeneration?[a]

Nutritional-Metabolic

- Do you take any nutrition supplements?[a]
- Describe your diet.
- Does your visual problem affect your ability to obtain and prepare food?[a]

Elimination

- Do you have to strain to void or defecate?[a]

Activity-Exercise

- Are your activities limited in any way by your eye problem?[a]
- Do you take part in any leisure activities that have the potential for eye injury?[a]

Sleep-Rest

- Is your vision affected by the amount of sleep you get?[a]
- Does your eye problem affect your sleep?[a]

Cognitive-Perceptual

- Does your eye problem affect your ability to read?[a]
- Do you have any eye pain?[a]
- Do you have any eye itching, burning, or foreign body sensation?[a]

Self-Perception–Self-Concept

- How does your eye problem make you feel about yourself?

Role-Relationship

- Do you have any problems at work or home because of your eyes?[a]
- Have you made any changes in your social activities because of your eyes?[a]

Sexuality-Reproductive

- Has your eye problem caused a change in your sex life?[a]
- For women: Are you pregnant? Do you use birth control pills?[a]
- For men: Do you use any erectile dysfunction drugs? Any vision problems with their use?[a]

Coping-Stress Tolerance

- Do you feel able to cope with your eye problem?[a]
- How do you feel that your eye problem has affected your life? How do you cope with these changes?[a]

Value-Belief

- Do you have any conflicts about the treatment of your eye problem?[a]

[a] If yes, describe.

Sexuality-reproductive pattern. The patient with severe vision loss may develop such a poor self-image that they lose the ability to be sexually intimate. Assure the patient that low vision or blindness does not affect a person's ability to be sexually expressive. Often touch is more important than vision.

BOX 22.1 PROMOTING HEALTH EQUITY

Visual Problems

- Glaucoma is the leading cause of blindness among Blacks and Hispanics.[2]
- Hispanics, Blacks, and Native Americans have the highest incidence of diabetic retinopathy.
- Whites have the highest incidence of AMD.

Coping–stress tolerance pattern. The patient with temporary or permanent vision problems may have emotional stress. Assess the patient's coping methods and availability of support systems.

Value-belief pattern. Be sensitive to each patient's values and spiritual beliefs as these may guide decisions about eye care. It can be hard to understand why a patient refuses treatment that has potential benefit or wants treatment that may have limited potential benefit.

Case Study

Subjective Data

(© Jack Hollingsworth/Photodisc/Thinkstock.)

A focused subjective assessment of F.M. revealed the following information:

- ***History:*** Extraocular extraction of cataract on right eye with implantation of intraocular lens 2 months ago. Type 2 diabetes, hypothyroidism, and hypertension.
- ***Medications:*** Glucophage 500 mg twice daily, levothyroxine 100 mcg daily, metoprolol 50 mg daily.
- ***Health Perception–Health Management:*** States she used antibiotic and corticosteroid eyedrops after surgery as directed and followed up with surgeon. Recovery was uneventful. Stopping using eyedrops 2 weeks ago. Does not have allergies. Had excellent eyesight until today.
- ***Elimination:*** Has had problems moving bowels with increased straining. Trying prune juice to help.
- ***Activity-Exercise:*** Walks in the mall at least 1/2 mile 3 times a week. No resistance or isotonic exercises.
- ***Cognitive-Perceptual:*** Denies eye pain, itching, or tearing. Having difficulty reading.
- ***Coping–Stress Tolerance:*** Afraid she is having a stroke.

Discussion Questions

1. Which subjective assessment findings most concern you?
2. What should you include in the physical assessment? For what would you be looking?
3. How will you individualize the assessment based on her age and condition?

You will learn more about the physical assessment of the visual system in the next section.

Answers available at http://evolve.elsevier.com/Lewis/medsurg.

Objective Data

Physical Assessment

Physical assessment of the visual system includes inspecting the eye structures and determining the status of their respective functions. Physiologic functional assessment includes (1) assessing the patient's visual acuity, ability to judge closeness and distance, and extraocular muscle function; (2) evaluating visual fields; (3) checking pupil function; and (4) measuring IOP. Assessment should include examining the ocular adnexa, external eye, and internal structures. We assess some structures, such as the retina, blood vessels, and optic disc, with an ophthalmoscope.

TABLE 22.3 Normal Physical Assessment of Visual System

- Visual acuity 20/20 both eyes. No diplopia
- External eye structures symmetric and without lesions or deformities
- Lacrimal apparatus nontender and without drainage
- Conjunctiva clear. Sclera white
- PERRLA (pupils equal, round, reactive to light and accommodation)
- Lens clear
- EOMs intact (extraocular movements intact)

Normal physical assessment of the visual system is outlined in Table 22.3. Assessment techniques related to vision are described in Table 22.4. Table 22.5 shows select assessment abnormalities. We use a *focused assessment* (Box 22.2) to evaluate the status of previously identified vision problems and to monitor for signs of new problems.

Initial observation. Your initial observation of the patient can provide information that will help focus the assessment. A patient dressed in clothing with unusual color combinations may have a color-vision deficit. Note an unusual head position. The patient with diplopia may hold the head in a skewed position to try to see a single image. The patient with a corneal abrasion or photophobia will cover the eyes with the hands to try to block out room light. Make a crude estimate of depth perception by extending a hand for the patient to shake.

During the initial observation, observe the patient's overall facial and eye appearance. The eyes should be symmetric and normally placed on the face. The globes should not have a bulging or sunken appearance.

Assessing functional status

Visual acuity. Always record the patient's visual acuity. When doing your eye assessment, assess the right eye first and then the left eye. Note the patient's visual acuity before the patient receives any eye care.

To assess visual acuity, position the person on a mark exactly 20 feet (6 m) from the Snellen eye chart. If the person wears glasses or contacts, leave them on. Cover 1 eye at a time during the test. Ask the person to read down the lines of the chart to the smallest line of letters and numbers possible. Record the result using the numeric fraction at the end of the last successful line read. Indicate whether any letters were missed and if corrective lenses were worn (e.g., "Right eye, 20/30-2, with contacts"). Next ask the patient to cover the other eye and repeat the process. Normal visual acuity is 20/20. The first number indicates the distance the person is standing or sitting from the chart. The second number gives the distance at which a normal eye can read that line.

If the patient reports near vision problems or is 40 years of age or older, use a hand-held vision screener with varying print sizes (e.g., a Jaeger chart). Hold the card at 14 in (35 cm) from the eye in good light to assess near vision. Examine each eye separately, with glasses on if worn. A normal result is "14/14" in each eye, read without hesitancy and without the patient moving the card. If you must assess near visual acuity without access to a Jaeger eye chart, you can still make an accurate assessment using newsprint

TABLE 22.4 NURSING ASSESSMENT

Assessment Techniques: Visual System

Description	Purpose
Color Vision Testing	
In the Ishihara test, a patient identifies numbers or paths formed by pattern of dots in series of color plates.	Determines ability to distinguish colors
Confrontation Visual Field Test	
Patient faces examiner, covers 1 eye, fixates on examiner's face, and counts number of fingers that examiner brings into patient's field of vision.	Determines if patient has a full field of vision, without obvious blind spots or vision loss
Intraocular Pressure Testing: Tonometry	
Anesthetized corneal surface is gently touched several times with covered end of probe. Examiner records several readings to obtain a mean IOP.	Measures IOP. Normal pressure is 10–21 mm Hg
Keratometry	
Examiner aligns projection and notes readings of corneal curvature. Often done before fitting contact lenses, before refractive surgery, or after corneal transplantation.	Measures corneal curvature
Ophthalmoscopy	
Examiner holds ophthalmoscope close to patient's eye, shining light into back of eye and looking through aperture on ophthalmoscope. Examiner adjusts dial to choose the ophthalmoscope lens that produces desired amount of magnification to inspect retina.	Provides magnified view of retina and optic nerve (Fig. 22.7)
Pupil Function Testing	
Examiner shines light into patient's pupil and checks pupillary response. Each pupil is examined independently. Examiner checks for consensual and accommodative response.	Determines if patient has normal pupillary response
Visual Acuity Testing	
Patient reads from Snellen chart at 20 ft (distance vision test) or Jaeger chart at 14 in (near vision test). Examiner notes smallest print patient can read on each chart.	Determines distance and near visual acuity

or a container label. Record the acuity as "reads newspaper headline at X inches." If the patient is unable to read any of the lines on both the near and distant visual acuity charts, the next step is to assess whether they can see hand motion and light perception.

Extraocular muscle functions. Assess the corneal light reflex to evaluate for weakness or imbalance of the extraocular muscles. In a darkened room, ask the patient to look straight ahead while shining a penlight directly on the cornea. The light reflection should be in the center of both corneas as the patient faces the light source.

To assess eye movement, hold a finger or an object within 10 to 12 inches of the patient's nose. Ask the patient to follow with eyes only the movement of the object or finger in the 6 cardinal positions of gaze. This test can indicate weakness or paralysis in the extraocular muscles and cranial nerves (CN III, CN IV, and CN VI).

Pupil function and intraocular pressure. Pupil function is determined by inspecting the pupils and their reactions to light. We often abbreviate the normal finding as PERRL (pupils are equal [in size], round, and reactive to light). The pupils should react to light directly (pupil constricts when a light shines into the eye) and consensually (pupil constricts when a light shines into the opposite eye). In a small number of people, the pupils are normally unequal in size *(anisocoria)*.

To test for accommodation, ask the person to focus on a distant object. This process dilates the eyes. Then have the person shift the focus to a near object, such as your finger held about 3 inches from the person's nose. A normal response is constriction of the eyes and convergence (inward movement of both eyes toward each other). When you assess accommodation with the pupillary light reflex, a normal response is *PERRLA* (pupils are equal, round, and reactive to light and accommodation).

We measure IOP (Table 22.4) by a variety of methods, including tonometry. Normal IOP ranges from 10 to 21 mm Hg.

Assessing structures. We assess the visual system structures primarily by inspection. The visual system is unique because we can inspect not only the external structures but also many of the internal structures. The iris, lens, vitreous, retina, and optic nerve can be seen directly through the clear cornea and pupil opening. This direct inspection requires special observation equipment, such as the slit lamp microscope or ophthalmoscope. These allow us to examine the conjunctiva, sclera, cornea, anterior chamber, iris, lens, vitreous, and retina under magnification.

The *ophthalmoscope* is a hand-held instrument with a light source and magnifying lenses. It allows us to be able to see the posterior part of the eye. It is used to magnify the retina and optic nerves and bring them into crisp focus (Fig. 22.7). We can get vital information about the vascular system and CNS. Skilled use of this instrument takes practice.

Eyebrows, eyelashes, and eyelids. All structures should be present and symmetric, without deformities, redness, or swelling. Eyelashes extend outward from the lid margins. In normal closing, the upper and lower eyelid margins just touch. The lacrimal puncta should be open and positioned properly against the globe.

Conjunctiva and sclera. We can easily assess the conjunctiva and sclera at the same time. Assess the color and smoothness. Look for lesions or foreign bodies. The conjunctiva covering the sclera is normally clear, with fine blood vessels visible. These blood vessels are more common in the periphery.

The sclera is normally white. A slight yellow cast may be found in some dark-skinned people, such as Blacks and Native Americans, or in the older adult from lipid deposition. A pale blue cast caused by scleral thinning can be normal in older adults.

Cornea. The cornea should be clear, transparent, and shiny. The iris should appear flat and not bulge toward the cornea. The area between the cornea and iris should be clear, with no blood or purulent material visible in the anterior chamber.

Iris. Both irises should be of similar color and shape. However, a color difference between the irises occurs normally in a small number of people.

Retina and optic nerve. Examine the optic nerve or disc for size, color, and abnormalities. The optic disc is creamy yellow

TABLE 22.5 ASSESSMENT ABNORMALITIES

Visual System

Finding	Description	Possible Etiology and Significance
Subjective Data		
Blurred vision	Gradual or sudden inability to see clearly	Refractive errors, corneal opacities, cataracts, migraine aura, retinal changes (detachment, AMD)
Diplopia	Double vision	Abnormal extraocular muscle action related to muscle or cranial nerve pathologic condition
Dryness	Discomfort, sandy, gritty, irritation, burning	Decreased tear formation or changes in tear composition from aging or various systemic diseases
Pain	Foreign body sensation	Superficial corneal erosion or abrasion. Can result from contact lens wear or trauma. Conjunctival or corneal foreign body
	Severe, deep, throbbing	Anterior uveitis, acute glaucoma, infection. Acute glaucoma may cause nausea, vomiting
Photophobia	Persistent abnormal intolerance to light	Inflammation or infection of cornea or anterior uveal tract (iris and ciliary body)
Spots, floaters	Patient describes seeing spots, "spider webs," "curtain," or floaters within the field of vision	Most common cause is vitreous liquefaction (benign phenomenon). Other causes include hemorrhage into the vitreous humor, retinal holes or tears
Objective Data		
Eyelids		
Allergic reactions	Redness, excessive tearing, and itching of lid margins	Many possible allergens. Associated eye trauma can occur from rubbing itchy eyelids
Blepharitis	Redness, swelling, and crusting along lid margins	Bacterial invasion of lid margins. Often chronic
Dermatochalasis	Excess eyelid skin	May eventually obstruct superior and peripheral vision
Ectropion	Outward turning of lower lid margin	Age-related tissue changes, posttraumatic changes, facial paralysis
Entropion	Inward turning of upper or lower lid margin, unilateral or bilateral	Age-related tissue changes, posttraumatic changes, facial paralysis
Hordeolum (sty) (Fig. 22.8)	Small, superficial white nodule along lid margin	Infection of meibomian gland of eyelid. Causative organism is usually bacterial (most often *Staphylococcus aureus*)
Ptosis	Drooping of upper eyelid, unilateral or bilateral	Myasthenia gravis, congenital, or mechanical causes from eyelid tumors or excess skin
Conjunctiva		
Conjunctivitis	Redness, swelling of conjunctiva. May be itchy	Bacterial or viral infection. May be allergic response or inflammatory response to chemical exposure
Subconjunctival hemorrhage	Appearance of blood spot on sclera. May be small or can affect entire sclera	Conjunctival blood vessels rupture, leaking blood into the subconjunctival space.
Cornea		
Corneal abrasion	Localized painful disruption of the epithelial layer of cornea. Can be seen with fluorescein dye	Trauma. Overwear or improper fit of contact lenses
Globe		
Exophthalmos (Fig. 22.9)	Protrusion of globe beyond its normal position within bony orbit. Sclera often visible above iris when eyelids are open	Intraocular or periorbital tumors Hyperthyroidism
Pupil		
Abnormal response to light or accommodation	Pupils respond asymmetrically or abnormally to light stimulus or accommodation	CNS disorders, general anesthesia
Anisocoria	Pupils unequal, constricted	CNS disorders. Slight difference in pupil size is normal in some people
Extraocular Muscles		
Strabismus	Deviation of eye position in 1 or more directions	Overaction or underaction of 1 or more extraocular muscles
Lens		
Cataract	Opacification of lens. Pupil can appear cloudy or white when opacity is visible behind pupil opening	Aging, trauma, diabetes, long-term systemic corticosteroid therapy
Visual Field Defect		
Central	Loss of central vision	Macular disease
Peripheral	Partial or complete loss of peripheral vision	Glaucoma. Interruption of visual pathway (e.g., tumor, stroke). Migraine headache

BOX 22.2 FOCUSED ASSESSMENT

Visual System

Use this checklist to make sure the key assessment steps have been done.

Subjective

Ask the patient about any of the following and note responses.

Changes in vision (e.g., acuity, blurred)	Y	N
Eye redness, itching, discomfort	Y	N
Drainage from eyes	Y	N

Objective: Physical Assessment

Inspect

Eyes for any discoloration or drainage	✓
Conjunctiva and sclera for color and vascularity	✓
Lens for clarity	✓
Eyelid for ptosis	✓
Assess	✓
Vision based on patient looking at nurse or Snellen chart	
Extraocular movements (EOMs)	✓
Peripheral vision	✓
PERRLA	✓

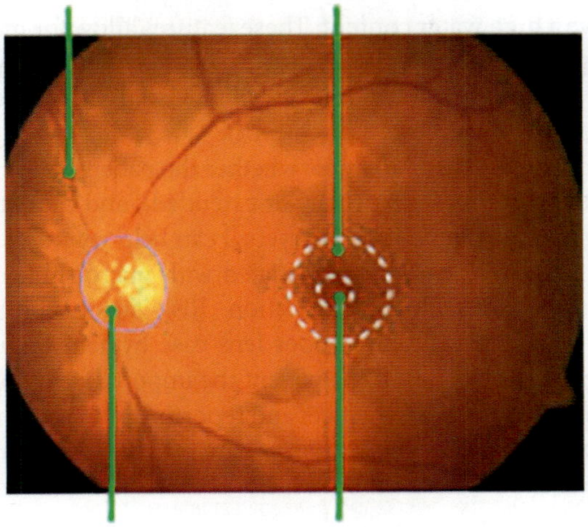

Fig. 22.7 Magnified view of retina. (From Acharya UR, Mookiah MR: Automated screening system for retinal health, *Computers in Biology and Medicine*, 75:54, 2016.)

with distinct margins. A central depression in the disc, called the *physiologic cup,* may be seen. This area is the exit site for the optic nerve. The cup should be less than half the diameter of the disc. Normally, no hemorrhages or exudates are present in the fundus (retinal background). Careful inspection of the fundus can reveal retinal holes, tears, detachments, or lesions. Small hemorrhages can occur with diabetes or hypertension. They can appear in various shapes, such as dots or flames. Finally, examine the macula for shape and appearance. This area normally has no blood vessels.

Special Assessment Techniques

Color vision. Testing the patient's ability to distinguish colors is an important part of the assessment. Some occupations require accurate color discrimination. The Ishihara color test assesses the patient's ability to recognize a pattern of color in a series of color plates.

Stereopsis. Stereoscopic vision allows a patient to see objects in 3 dimensions. An event that causes a patient to have monocular vision (e.g., enucleation, patching) results in the loss of stereoscopic vision. Without stereopsis, the person's ability to judge distances or the height of a step is impaired. This can have profound consequences if the person trips over a step when walking or follows too closely behind another vehicle when driving.

Case Study

Objective Data: Physical Assessment and Diagnostic Studies

(© Jack Hollingsworth/Photodisc/Thinkstock.)

F.M.'s physical assessment findings were as follows:

- PERRL. No abnormalities noted of external eye structures.
- EOMs intact and symmetric.

The HCP performs an ophthalmoscopic examination and finds a partial retinal detachment. Ultrasonography confirms the diagnosis.

Discussion Questions

1. Are these the diagnostic studies that you expected to be ordered?
2. Which diagnostic study results most concern you?

Answers available at http://evolve.elsevier.com/Lewis/medsurg.

DIAGNOSTIC STUDIES OF VISUAL SYSTEM

Diagnostic studies of the visual system provide vital information in monitoring the patient's condition and planning appropriate interventions. Table 22.6 presents common diagnostic studies of the visual system.

VISION PROBLEMS

Refractive Errors

Refraction is the eye's ability to bend light rays so that they fall on the retina. In the normal eye, parallel light rays are focused through the lens into a sharp image on the retina. When the light does not focus properly, we call it a refractive error. This defect prevents light rays from converging into a single focus on the retina. Defects are a result of irregularities of the corneal curvature, focusing power of the lens, or length of the eye.

Refractive errors are the most common vision problem. Blurred vision is the major symptom. In some cases, the patient may have eye discomfort, eyestrain, or headaches. Most refractive errors can be corrected using eyeglasses or contact lenses, refractive eye laser surgery, or surgical implantation of an artificial lens.

Myopia (nearsightedness) is an inability to accommodate for objects at a distance. It causes light rays to be focused in front of the retina. This means the person can see near objects but objects in the distance are blurry. Myopia may occur from excessive light refraction by the cornea or lens or an abnormally long eye. Myopia is the most common refractive error. Around 30% of Americans have myopia.[3] There is strong evidence that many people inherit myopia or the tendency to develop myopia.[3]

Hyperopia (farsightedness) is an inability to accommodate for near objects. It causes the light rays to focus behind the

TABLE 22.6 Diagnostic Studies

Visual System

Study	Purpose	Description and Nursing Responsibility
Amsler grid test	Monitors macular problems	Self-administered test using a hand-held card printed with a grid of lines (like graph paper) (Fig. 22.15). Using 1 eye at a time, patient fixates on center dot and notes any abnormalities of grid lines, such as wavy, missing, or distorted areas.
Fluorescein angiography	Provides information about flow of blood through retinal vessels	Fluorescein injected IV into peripheral vein followed by serial photographs (over 10-min period) of retina through dilated pupils If extravasation occurs, fluorescein is toxic to tissue. Tell patient that dye can sometimes cause transient nausea or vomiting. Yellow-orange discoloration of urine and skin may occur.
Perimetry (visual field) testing	Detects changes in central and peripheral vision	Person sits and looks inside a bowl-shaped instrument called a *perimeter.* While staring at the center of bowl, a light flashes. The person presses a button each time flash is seen. A computer records the results. A printout shows if there are areas where flashes of light were not seen.
Refractometry	Measures refractive error	Patient sits looking through apertures at Snellen acuity chart and lenses are changed. Patient chooses lenses that make acuity sharpest. Eye dilation may help visualize retina and optic nerves. Pupil dilation may last 3–4 hr, making it difficult to focus on near objects.
Ultrasonography	Assesses size and structure of eye	*A-scan* determines the right power of a lens implant before cataract surgery. *B-scan* used to diagnose pathologic conditions, including intraocular foreign bodies or tumors, vitreous opacities, retinal detachments.

retina, and the person must use accommodation to focus the light rays on the retina for near objects. The person with hyperopia can see distant objects clearly. This type of error occurs when the cornea or lens does not have adequate focusing power or the eyeball is too short.

Presbyopia is the loss of accommodation associated with age. One usually starts to notice this condition in the early to mid-40s. As the eye ages, the lens becomes larger, firmer, and less elastic. These changes, which progress with aging, result in an inability to focus on near objects.

Astigmatism is an uneven or irregular curvature of the cornea. The irregularity causes the incoming light rays to be bent unequally. Thus the light rays do not come to a single point of focus on the retina. This results in vision distortion. Astigmatism can occur in conjunction with any of the other refractive errors.

Aphakia is the absence of the lens. Rarely, the lens may be absent congenitally. It may be removed during cataract surgery. A lens that is traumatically injured is removed and replaced with an intraocular lens (IOL) implant. The absence of the lens results in a significant refractive error. Without the focusing ability of the lens, images are projected behind the retina.

Nonsurgical Corrections

Corrective glasses. The right corrective lenses can enhance vision in those with myopia, hyperopia, presbyopia, and astigmatism. Many people call glasses for presbyopia "reading glasses" because they are usually worn only for close work. Presbyopic correction may be combined with a correction for another refractive error, such as myopia or astigmatism. In these combined glasses, the presbyopic correction is in the lower part of the glass lens. A traditional bifocal or trifocal has visible lines. Many lenses that correct vision at various distances do not have visible lines. The prescription varies throughout the lens, allowing distance focusing in the top two-thirds and near focus in the bottom one-third of the lens.

Contact lenses. Contact lenses are another way to correct refractive errors. Contact lenses are made from various plastic and silicone substances. They are highly permeable to oxygen and have a high water content. These features allow for increased wearing time with greater comfort. If the oxygen supply to the cornea is decreased, it becomes swollen, visual acuity decreases, and the patient has severe discomfort.

In general, you need to know whether the patient wears contact lenses, the pattern of wear (daily or extended), and care practices. Shining a light obliquely on the eyeball can help you to see a contact lens. Contact lenses are associated with microbial keratitis, a severe sight-threatening complication. Risk factors for keratitis include poor hand cleaning, poor lens case hygiene, and inadequate lens cleaning. Teach the patient the importance of following recommended cleaning practices and reporting redness, sensitivity, vision problems, and pain to the eye care provider. Tell the patient to remove contact lenses at once if any of these problems occur.

Surgical Therapy

Surgery can eliminate or reduce the need for eyeglasses or contact lenses and correct refractive errors by changing the focus of the eye. Surgical management for refractive errors includes laser surgery and IOL implantation.

Laser. *Laser-assisted in situ keratomileusis* (LASIK) may be considered for patients with low to moderately high myopia or hyperopia, with or without astigmatism. The procedure first involves using a laser or surgical blade to create a flap in the cornea. The flap is folded back, exposing the middle section (stroma) of the cornea. Pulses from a computer-controlled laser vaporize a part of the stroma. The flap is then repositioned, adhering on its own without sutures in a few minutes.[4]

Photorefractive keratectomy (PRK) is indicated for low to moderate myopia or hyperopia, with or without astigmatism. It is a good option for a patient with insufficient corneal thickness for a LASIK flap. In PRK, the epithelium is removed, and the laser sculpts the cornea to correct the refractive error.

TABLE 22.7 Diagnostic Criteria

Classifications of Visual Impairment

Classification is based on the vision in the better eye with the best possible correction.

20/30 to 20/60	Mild vision loss or near-normal vision
20/70 to 20/160	Moderate visual impairment
20/200 or worse	Severe visual impairment
20/500 to 20/1000	Profound visual impairment
Less than 20/1000	Near-total visual impairment
No light perception	Total visual impairment or total blindness

Source: American Optometry Association. Retrieved from https://www.aoa.org/healthy-eyes/caring-for-your-eyes/low-vision-and-vision-rehab?sso=y.

Laser-assisted subepithelial keratomileusis (LASEK) is similar to PRK, except that the epithelium is replaced after surgery.

Implant. *Refractive intraocular lens* (refractive IOL) implantation is an option for patients with a high degree of myopia or hyperopia. Like cataract surgery, it involves removing the patient's natural lens and implanting an IOL. The IOL implant used is a special lens designed to correct the patient's refractive error. Refractive IOLs can correct both myopia and presbyopia.

Phakic intraocular lenses (phakic IOLs) are sometimes called *implantable contact lenses.* They are implanted into the eye without removing the eye's natural lens. They are used for patients with high degrees of myopia or hyperopia. Unlike refractive IOLs, the phakic IOL is placed in front of the eye's natural lens. Leaving the natural lens preserves the eye's ability to focus for reading vision.

VISUAL IMPAIRMENT

Visual impairment describes vision that cannot be fully corrected by corrective lenses, medical treatment, or surgery. Visual impairment includes conditions ranging from low vision to the absence of all vision (total blindness) (Table 22.7).

People with severe visual impairment are unable to read ordinary print even with correction. They may or may not be legally blind. *Legal blindness* is defined as the best-corrected vision in the better eye of 20/200 or less or 20 degrees or less of remaining visual field. Most blindness in the United States is the result of common eye diseases, including cataracts, glaucoma, AMD, and diabetic retinopathy.

NURSING MANAGEMENT: VISUAL IMPAIRMENT

Assessment

It is important to assess how long the patient has had a visual impairment. Recent loss of vision has different implications for nursing care. Determine how the patient's visual impairment affects their functioning. Ask the patient about any problems with doing daily tasks. For example, how hard is it for the patient to read, use their phone, move around in their home, or watch television? Other questions can help to determine the personal meaning that the patient attaches to the visual impairment. Ask how the vision loss has affected specific aspects of the patient's life. Has the patient lost a job? What activities does the patient not engage in because of their vision?

Assess the patient's emotional reactions, coping methods, and support systems. The patient may attach many negative meanings to the impairment because of societal views of blindness. For example, the patient may view the impairment as punishment or view themselves as useless and burdensome.

BOX 22.3 PROMOTING POPULATION HEALTH

Responsible Eye Care

- Regular hand washing prevents the spread of disease from 1 eye to the other.
- Seeking appropriate health care can lead to early detection of disease and prevent further loss of vision in patients with certain types of partial vision loss.
- Wearing sunglasses and practicing proper nutrition may help to prevent cataract development and AMD.
- Wearing eye protection during potentially hazardous work, hobby, and sport activities reduces the risk for eye injuries.

Clinical Problems

Clinical problems for the patient with visual impairment include:

- Sensory deficit
- Difficulty coping
- Impaired role performance

Planning

The overall goals are that the patient with impaired vision will (1) make a successful adjustment to the impairment, (2) discuss feelings related to the loss, (3) identify personal strengths and support systems, and (4) use appropriate coping methods. If the patient has been functioning at an appropriate or acceptable level, the goal is to maintain the current level of function.

Implementation

Health Promotion

Encourage the patient with preventable causes of further visual impairment to seek appropriate health care (Box 22.3). For example, the patient with vision loss from glaucoma may be able to prevent further vision loss with prescribed therapies and eye examinations.

Acute Care

Provide emotional support and direct care to the patient with recent visual impairment. Allow the patient to express fear, anger, and grief. Help the patient identify positive coping methods. Caregivers are intimately involved in the experiences that occur with vision loss. With the patient's knowledge and permission, include caregivers in discussions and encourage them to express their concerns.

TABLE 22.8 Sighted-Guide Technique

- Ask the patient whether they would like help.
- Stand slightly in front and to one side of the patient and offer an elbow for the patient to hold.
- Walk slightly in front of the patient at a pace that's comfortable for them.
- Serve as the sighted guide. As you walk, describe the environment to help orient the patient. For example, "We're going through an open doorway and approaching 2 steps down."
    - Give advance notice of stairs and whether they go up or down.
    - Tell the patient when you approach ground level.
    - Give advance notice of changes in ground surface (e.g., going from hard flooring to a carpeted area).
- Never guide someone into a seat backward. Help the patient sit by placing 1 of their hands on the back of the chair. Then, allow the patient to orient themselves to the chair independently.

Many people are uncomfortable around a person with visual impairment because they are not sure what behaviors are appropriate. Being sensitive to the patient's feelings without being overly worried or smothering the patient's independence is vital in creating a therapeutic nursing presence. Communicate in a normal conversational tone and manner with the patient and address the patient, not the caregiver. Introduce yourself and all people who approach the patient. It is important to say good-bye when leaving the patient's presence. Making eye contact with the patient achieves several goals. It ensures that you are speaking while facing the patient so that the patient has no difficulty hearing. Establishing eye contact ensures that you can observe the patient's facial expressions and reactions. Help the patient using *sighted-guide technique* (Table 22.8).

◆Ambulatory Care

In working with the patient who is visually impaired, remember that a person classified as legally blind may have some useful vision. Rehabilitation after partial or total loss of vision can foster independence, self-esteem, and productivity. Know what services and devices are available and make appropriate referrals. For the legally blind patient the primary resource for services is the appropriate state agency for rehabilitation. Legally blind persons are often eligible for federal and state assistance and income tax benefits. A list of agencies that serve the partially sighted or blind patient is available from the American Foundation for the Blind (www.afb.org).

Braille or audio books for reading and a cane or guide dog for ambulation are examples of vision substitution techniques. These are usually best for the patient with no functional vision. For most patients who have some remaining vision, vision enhancement techniques can help in learning to ambulate, read printed material, and perform ADLs.

Optical devices for vision enhancement. A wide range of technologies are available to help people with low vision. These devices include desktop video magnification/closed circuit units, electronic hand-held magnifiers, text-to-speech scanners (material read aloud to you), E-readers, and computer tablets (material read aloud, magnification, image zooming, brighter screen, voice recognition). Many of these devices require some training by an assistive technology professional. Encourage patients to practice with the device to ensure they can use it successfully.

Nonoptical methods for vision enhancement. *Approach magnification* is a simple way to enhance the patient's residual vision. Recommend that the patient sit closer to the television or hold books closer to the eyes. Contrast enhancement techniques include watching television in black and white, using a black felt-tip marker, and using contrasting colors (e.g., a red stripe at the edge of steps or curbs). Increased lighting can be provided by halogen lamps, direct sunlight, or gooseneck lamps that are aimed directly at the reading material or other near objects. Large type is often helpful, especially when used with other vision enhancements.

Non–24-hour sleep/wake disorder. A common problem that can occur in blind people, especially those who are totally blind, is *non–24-hour sleep/wake disorder (non-24)*. It is a circadian rhythm sleep disorder in which a person's biologic clock does not synchronize to a 24-hour day.[5] It is caused by lack of light input to the circadian clock.

People with non-24 have problems falling asleep or staying asleep at night. During the day, they may have an uncontrollable urge to sleep. This can result in severe sleep issues, including insomnia, excessive sleepiness, changing patterns of when a person sleeps, and social and work consequences.

Taking melatonin can shift the circadian clock earlier (an advance) or later (a delay). Tasimelteon (Hetlioz), a melatonin receptor agonist, also can be used for treatment. It works by targeting receptors in the brain that control the timing of the sleep/wake cycle.

◆ Evaluation

The overall expected outcomes are that the patient with visual impairment will:

- Follow treatment plan to prevent further loss of vision
- Be able to use adaptive coping methods
- Maintain self-esteem and take part in social interactions
- Function safely within their environment

Gerontologic Considerations: Visual Impairment

The older adult is at an increased risk for vision loss caused by eye disease. They may have other deficits, such as limited mobility, that further affect the ability to function in usual ways. Societal devaluation of older adults may compound the self-esteem or isolation issues associated with visual impairment. Financial resources may be inadequate to secure vision services or assistive devices.

The older patient with vision loss is more likely to have cognitive problems.[6] The combination of decreased vision and confusion increases fall risk, which can have serious consequences. Decreased vision may compromise the older patient's ability to function, resulting in concerns about independence and a diminished self-image. Decreased manual dexterity may make instilling prescribed eyedrops hard. Those with low vision are more likely to make medication errors that are potentially dangerous, such as taking too much insulin or mistaking one drug for another.

EYE TRAUMA

Although the eyes are well protected by the bony orbit and fat pads, everyday activities can result in eye trauma. The most common eye injuries in the United States are due to falls and fights. Injuries at home may be caused by cooking cleaning, gardening, power tool use, and home repair work. Sport- and work-related injuries are other causes of eye trauma.[7]

CHECK YOUR PRACTICE

You are working in your garden when your neighbor comes running into your yard. She is screaming and waving her arms. Her husband was using a chain saw to cut down a tree when a wood chip flew into his eye. When you go to your neighbor's yard, the husband is on the ground crying in pain. You assess the wood chip embedded in his eye.

- What should you do next?

Table 22.9 outlines the emergency management of the patient with an eye injury. Chemical burns can be devastating to the eye and need immediate attention. Alkaline chemicals with a pH greater than 7 are the most harmful. They can penetrate the eye and damage the inner components. Acidic chemicals with a pH of less than 7 are unable to penetrate the eye but can damage the cornea. Both types of injury have the potential to result in blindness.

A *Morgan lens* may be used to provide continuous irrigation of an injured eye. It consists of a sterile plastic device resembling a contact lens that floats over the eye (never physically touches it). The device is connected to tubing that delivers irrigating solution. The Morgan lens provides relief for chemical or thermal burns and removes nonembedded foreign materials in the eye.

Trauma is often a preventable cause of vision loss. Many eye injuries could be prevented by wearing protective eyewear. Your role in individual and community education is very important in reducing the incidence of eye trauma.

EXTRAOCULAR INFLAMMATION AND INFECTION

One of the most common eye conditions is inflammation or infection of the external eye. Many external irritants or microorganisms can affect the eye, conjunctiva, and cornea.

An external **hordeolum** (or a *sty*) is an infection of the meibomian glands in the lid margin (Fig. 22.8). The most common bacterial infective agent is *Staphylococcus aureus.* A red, swollen, circumscribed, and acutely tender area develops rapidly.

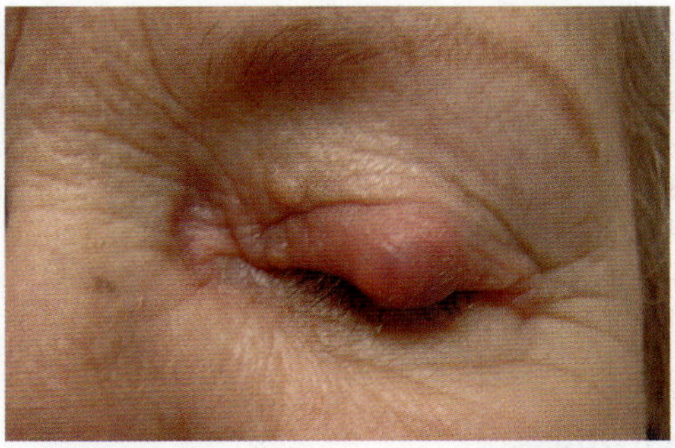

Fig. 22.8 Sty on the upper eyelid caused by staphylococcal infection. (Courtesy Stephen J. Laquis, MD, FACS Ophthalmic Facial Plastic Surgery Specialists, Fort Myers, FL.)

TABLE 22.9 EMERGENCY MANAGEMENT

Eye Injury

Etiology	Assessment Findings	Interventions
Chemical Burn • Acid • Alkaline **Foreign Bodies** • Ceramics • Glass • Metal • Plastic • Wood **Thermal Burn** • Direct burn from hot surface • Indirect burn from UV light (e.g., welding torch, looking directly at sun) **Trauma** • Blunt (e.g., fist) • Penetrating (e.g., glass, metal, or wood fragments; knife, stick, other object)	• Abnormal or decreased vision • Abnormal IOP • Absent eye movements • Blood in the anterior chamber • Fluid drainage from eye (e.g., blood, aqueous humor) • Pain • Photophobia • Prolapsed globe • Redness—diffuse or localized • Swelling • Tearing • Visible foreign body • Visual field defect	**Initial** • Determine mechanism of injury. • Ensure airway, breathing, and circulation. • Assess for other injuries. • Assess for chemical exposure. • Begin eye irrigation *immediately* in case of chemical exposure. Do not stop until emergency personnel arrive to continue irrigation. Use sterile saline or water if saline is unavailable. • Assess visual acuity. • Do not put pressure on the eye. • Tell patient not to blow nose. • Do not try to treat the injury (except as noted above for chemical exposure). • Stabilize foreign objects. • Cover the eye(s) with dry, sterile patches and a protective shield. • Do not give the patient food or fluids. • Elevate head of bed 45 degrees. • Give proper analgesia. **Ongoing Monitoring** • Reassure the patient. • Monitor pain. • Anticipate surgical repair for penetrating injury, globe rupture, or globe avulsion.

Have the patient apply warm, moist compresses at least 4 times a day until it improves. This may be the only treatment needed. If it tends to recur, teach the patient to do lid scrubs daily using eye scrub. On occasion, antibiotic ointments or drops may be needed.

A *chalazion* is a chronic inflammatory granuloma of the meibomian glands in the lid. It may evolve from a sty or occur in response to the material released into the lid when a blocked gland ruptures. The chalazion usually appears on the upper lid as a swollen, tender, reddened area that may be painful. Initial treatment is like that for a sty. If warm, moist compresses are not effective in promoting spontaneous drainage, the HCP may drain the lesion or inject it with corticosteroids.

Blepharitis is a common chronic bilateral inflammation of the lid margins. The lids are red rimmed with many scales or crusts on the lid margins and lashes. The patient mainly has itching. They may also have burning, irritation, and photophobia.

If a staphylococcal infection caused blepharitis, an eye antibiotic ointment must be used. Often blepharitis is caused by both staphylococcal and seborrheal microorganisms. The treatment must be more vigorous to avoid a sty, *keratitis* (inflammation of the cornea), and other eye infections. Emphasize good cleaning practices of the skin and scalp. Gentle cleansing of the lid margins with baby shampoo or lid scrubs can effectively soften and remove crusting.

Conjunctivitis

Conjunctivitis is an infection or inflammation of the conjunctiva. Infections may be bacterial or viral. Conjunctival inflammation may result from exposure to allergens or chemical irritants. Careful hand washing and use of individual or disposable towels help prevent spreading the condition.

Bacterial Infections

Acute bacterial conjunctivitis *(pinkeye)* is a common infection. Although it occurs in every age group, epidemics are common among children. *S. aureus* is the most common cause. The patient with pinkeye may have discomfort, pruritus, redness, and a mucopurulent drainage. Although it typically occurs initially in 1 eye, it generally spreads to the unaffected eye. It is usually self-limiting. Treatment with antibiotic drops may shorten the course. Teach patients the importance of hand washing and avoiding contact with an infected person.

Viral Infections

Many different viruses cause conjunctival infections. The patient with viral conjunctivitis may have tearing, foreign body sensation, redness, and mild photophobia. This condition is usually mild and self-limiting. However, it can be severe, with increased discomfort and subconjunctival hemorrhaging. Adenovirus conjunctivitis may be contracted in contaminated swimming pools and through direct contact with an infected patient.

Epidemic keratoconjunctivitis (EKC) is the most serious ocular adenoviral disease. EKC is spread by direct contact. In the medical setting, contaminated hands and instruments can be the source of spread. The patient may have tearing, redness, photophobia, and foreign body sensation. In most patients, the disease involves only 1 eye. Treatment is primarily palliative and includes ice packs, artificial tears, and dark glasses. Treatment for severe cases can include mild topical corticosteroids to temporarily relieve symptoms and topical antibiotic ointment. Teach the patient the importance of good hygiene practices to avoid spreading the disease.

Chlamydial Infections

Trachoma is a chronic conjunctivitis caused by *Chlamydia trachomatis* (serotypes A through C). It is a major cause of blindness worldwide. Trachoma is most often seen in underdeveloped countries. It is transmitted mainly by the hands and flies. Adult inclusion conjunctivitis (AIC) is caused by *C. trachomatis* (serotypes D through K).[8] AIC is becoming more prevalent in the United States due to the increase in sexually transmitted chlamydial infection. For unknown reasons, AIC does not carry the long-term consequences of trachoma.

Manifestations of both trachoma and AIC are mucopurulent eye discharge, irritation, redness, and lid swelling. Antibiotic therapy is usually effective for trachoma and AIC. Patients with AIC have a high risk for concurrent chlamydial genital infection and STIs that may need treatment.

Allergic Conjunctivitis

Conjunctivitis caused by exposure to an allergen can be mild and transitory, or it can be severe enough to cause significant swelling. The defining symptom of allergic conjunctivitis is itching. The patient may have burning, redness, and tearing. The patient may develop allergic conjunctivitis in response to pollens, animal dander, ocular solutions, and medications. Teach the patient to avoid known allergens if possible. Artificial tears can be effective in diluting the allergen and washing it from the eye. Topical medications include antihistamines and corticosteroids.

Keratitis

Keratitis is an inflammation or infection of the cornea. It is caused by a variety of microorganisms or by other factors. The condition may involve the conjunctiva and/or the cornea. When it involves both, the disorder is termed *keratoconjunctivitis.*

Bacterial Infections

The cornea can become infected by a variety of bacteria. Risk factors include mechanical or chemical corneal epithelial damage, contact lens wear, nutrition deficiencies, immunosuppressed states, and contaminated products (e.g., lens care solutions and cases, topical medications, cosmetics). Treatment includes topical antibiotics. In some cases, the patient may need subconjunctival antibiotic injection or, in severe cases, IV antibiotics.

Viral Infections

Herpes simplex virus keratitis (HSK) is the most common cause of corneal blindness in developed countries. It is a growing problem, especially with immunosuppressed patients. The corneal ulcer has a characteristic dendritic (tree-branching) appearance. Pain and photophobia are common.

Current treatment for HSK includes topical ganciclovir or trifluridine or oral or IV acyclovir or valacyclovir.[9] Treatment may also involve corneal debridement. Topical corticosteroids

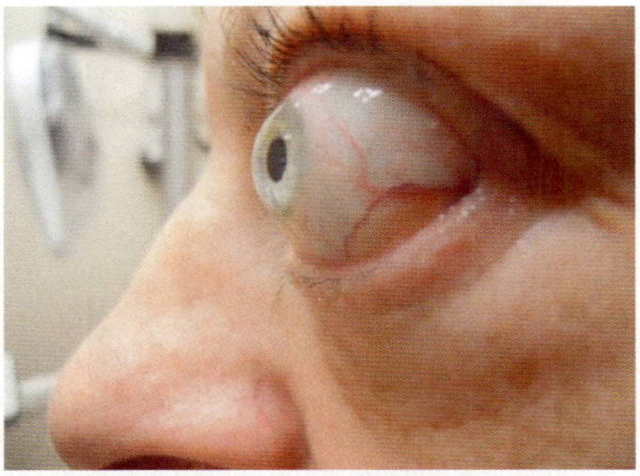

Fig. 22.9 Exophthalmos. (Courtesy Stephen J. Laquis, MD, FACS Ophthalmic Facial Plastic Surgery Specialists, Fort Myers, FL.)

are usually contraindicated because they contribute to a longer course and possible deeper corneal ulceration.

The varicella-zoster virus (VZV) that causes chickenpox can affect the eye. Herpes zoster ophthalmicus (HZO) may occur by reactivation of a latent infection that persisted after an earlier attack of varicella or by contact with a patient with chickenpox or herpes zoster. It occurs most often in the older adult or immunosuppressed patient. Care of the patient with acute HZO includes antiviral agents. Oral antivirals started within 72 hours of symptom onset can reduce disease severity and complications. Other treatment includes analgesics for pain, topical corticosteroids to reduce inflammation, and mydriatic agents to dilate the pupil and relieve pain. The patient may apply warm compresses and povidone-iodine gel to the affected skin.

Other Causes of Keratitis

Keratitis may be caused by fungi, such as *Aspergillus, Candida,* and *Fusarium* species. This is especially true in the case of eye trauma in an outdoor setting where fungi are prevalent in the soil and moist organic matter.

Acanthamoeba keratitis is caused by a parasite that is associated with contact lens wear, usually from contaminated lens care solutions or cases. Homemade saline solution is particularly susceptible to *Acanthamoeba* contamination. Teach the patient who wears contact lenses about good lens care practices. Treatment is difficult because the organism is resistant to most drugs. Antifungal agents (e.g., ketoconazole) may be given. If antimicrobial therapy fails, the patient may need a corneal transplant.

Exposure keratitis occurs when the eyelids cannot adequately close. The patient with *exophthalmos* (protruding eyeball) from thyroid eye disease or masses posterior to the globe is susceptible to exposure keratitis (Fig. 22.9).

Corneal Ulcer

Tissue loss caused by a corneal infection produces a *corneal ulcer* (infectious keratitis) (Fig. 22.10). The infection can be due to bacteria, viruses, or fungi. Corneal ulcers are often painful. The patient may feel as if there is a foreign body in the eye. Other symptoms can include tearing, purulent or watery discharge, redness, and photophobia. Treatment is aggressive to avoid permanent vision loss. Antibiotic, antiviral, or antifungal eyedrops may be given as often as every hour for the first 24 hours. An untreated corneal ulcer can result in corneal scarring and perforation, or hole, in the cornea. A corneal transplant may be needed.

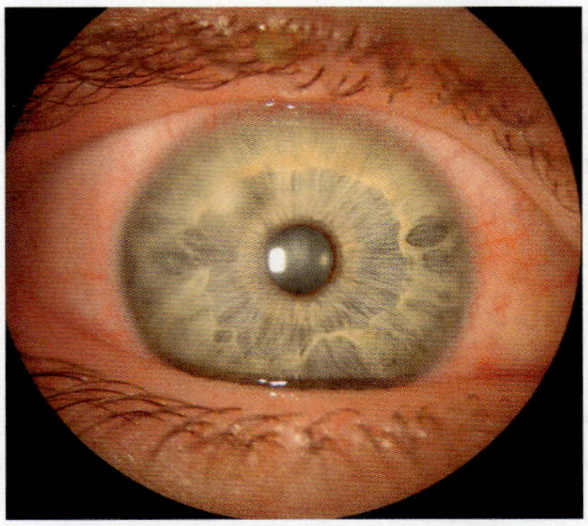

Fig. 22.10 Corneal ulcer. Infection associated with poor contact lens care. (Courtesy Cory J. Bosanko, OD, FAAO, Eye Centers of Tennessee, Crossville, TN.)

❖ NURSING MANAGEMENT: INFLAMMATION AND INFECTION

Assess for ocular changes. This include edema, redness, decreased visual acuity, feelings that a foreign body is present, and discomfort. Consider the psychosocial aspects of the patient's condition, especially when vision is impaired.

The patient's primary need is for information about prescribed care and how to perform that care. Careful asepsis and frequent, thorough hand washing are essential to prevent spreading organisms from 1 eye to the other, to other patients, to caregivers, and to health care team members. Teach the patient and caregivers how to avoid sources of eye irritation or infection and to respond appropriately if an eye problem occurs. The patient with infective disorders that may have a sexual mode of transmission needs specific information about those disorders.

Apply warm or cool compresses as needed. Darkening the room and giving an analgesic are other comfort measures. If the patient's visual acuity is decreased, modify the environment and activities for safety. Suggest alternative ways to perform daily activities and self-care.

The patient may need eyedrops as often as every hour. If the patient receives 2 or more different drops, stagger the eye drops to promote maximum absorption. For example, if 2 different eyedrops are ordered hourly, give 1 drop on the hour and 1 drop on the half hour (unless otherwise prescribed). The patient who needs to instill eyedrops frequently may have sleep deprivation. Review the proper technique for instilling eye drop.

Review the use and care of lenses and lens care products. Teach the patient who wears contact lenses and develops infections to discard all opened or used lens care products and cosmetics. This will decrease the risk for reinfection from contaminated products.

DRY EYE DISORDERS

Keratoconjunctivitis sicca (dry eyes) is a common problem, especially in older adults and people with certain systemic autoimmune diseases. These include scleroderma, systemic lupus erythematosus, and Sjögren syndrome. It is caused by a decrease in the quality or quantity of the tear film. Patients with dry eyes report irritation or "sand in my eye." The sensation typically worsens through the day.

Treatment is aimed at the underlying cause. With decreased tear secretion, the patient may use artificial tears or ointments. Cyclosporine ophthalmic emulsion (Restasis) helps to increase the eyes' natural ability to make tears. In severe cases, closure of the lacrimal puncta may be done.

STRABISMUS

Strabismus is a condition in which a person cannot consistently focus both eyes simultaneously on the same object. One eye may deviate in *(esotropia)*, out *(exotropia)*, up *(hypertropia)*, or down *(hypotropia)*. Strabismus in an adult may be caused by thyroid disease, neuromuscular problems of the eye muscles, retinal detachment repair, or cerebral lesions. The primary problem is double vision.

CORNEAL DISORDERS

Corneal Scars

Any wound (e.g., trauma, infection) to the cornea can cause it to become scarred and opacified, thus decreasing the normal transparency. The treatment is a corneal transplant.

Keratoconus

In *keratoconus,* the anterior cornea thins and bulges forward, taking on a cone shape. It usually occurs bilaterally. There is a familial tendency. Keratoconus usually appears during adolescence and slowly progresses between ages 20 and 60 years. The main symptom is blurred vision. Early treatment involves glasses or rigid contact lenses.

Intacs inserts are an option when contact lenses or glasses no longer help a patient achieve adequate vision. They are clear plastic lenses surgically inserted on the cornea to help flatten the bulge and improve vision. Collagen cross-linking uses UV light and special eye drops to strengthen collagen fibers in the cornea. Doing this helps to flatten or stiffen it, keeping it from bulging further. Sometimes, the cornea can perforate as central corneal thinning progresses. In these cases, a corneal transplant is done before the cornea can perforate.

Corneal Transplant

Around 52,000 corneal transplants (keratoplasty) are done in the United States each year. The surgery is one of the fastest and safest of all tissue or organ transplant surgeries.[10] The common indications involve corneal problems or eye injuries. These include ulceration, keratitis, scarring, and keratoconus. Types of corneal transplants include penetrating (full thickness) and lamellar (partial thickness).

Penetrating (full-thickness) cornea transplant involves transplanting all 3 layers of the cornea. In this procedure, the HCP removes the full thickness of the patient's cornea and replaces it with a donor cornea that is sutured into place (Fig. 22.11). Vision recovery may take up to 12 months.

During a *lamellar cornea transplant,* only some layers of the cornea are replaced with the transplant. This can include the deepest layer, called the *endothelium* (posterior lamellar cornea transplant). Versions of this procedure include Descemet stripping endothelial keratoplasty (DSEK) or Descemet membrane endothelial keratoplasty (DMEK). Lamellar transplants may be better than full penetrating transplants when the disease process is limited to only part of the cornea.

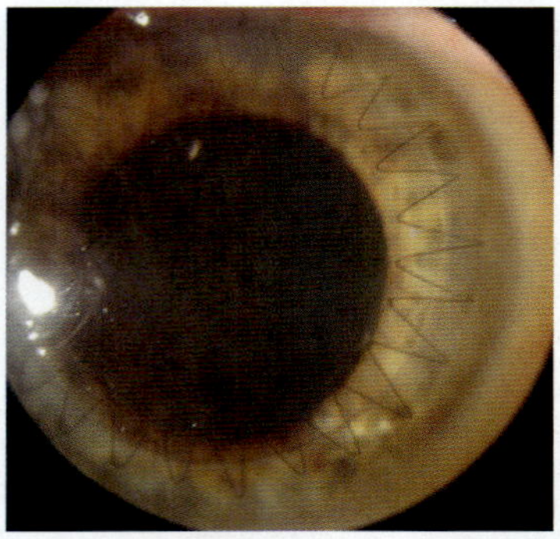

Fig. 22.11 Sutures on a donated cornea after penetrating keratoplasty (corneal transplant). (Courtesy Cory J. Bosanko, OD, FAAO, Eye Centers of Tennessee, Crossville, TN.)

The time between the donor's death and the removal of the tissue should be as short as possible. Eye banks test donors for human immunodeficiency virus (HIV), syphilis, and hepatitis B and C. The tissue is preserved in a special nutritive solution. Improved methods of tissue procurement and preservation, postoperative topical corticosteroids, and careful follow-up have decreased graft rejection. Matching the blood type of the donor and recipient improves the success rate.

INTRAOCULAR DISORDERS

CATARACT

A **cataract** is an opacity within the lens. The patient may have a cataract in 1 or both eyes. If cataracts are present in both eyes, one may affect the patient's vision more than the other. Cataract removal is the most common surgery in the United States.

Etiology and Pathophysiology

Most cataracts are age related *(senile cataracts)*. Other factors include blunt or penetrating trauma, smoking, alcohol use, radiation or UV light exposure, certain drugs (e.g., steroids), and ocular inflammation. The rate of cataract development varies from patient to patient. The patient with diabetes tends to develop cataracts at a younger age.[11]

In senile cataract formation, altered metabolic processes within the lens cause an accumulation of water and changes in the lens fiber structure. These changes affect lens transparency, causing vision changes.

Clinical Manifestations and Diagnostic Studies

The patient with cataracts may have a decrease in vision, abnormal color perception, and glare. Glare is due to light scatter caused by the lens opacities. It may be significantly worse at night when the pupil dilates. Vision decline is gradual.

Diagnosis is based on decreased visual acuity or other vision problem. The opacity is directly observable by ophthalmoscopic or slit lamp microscopic examination. A totally opaque lens creates the appearance of a white pupil. Table 22.6 lists other diagnostic studies that may be helpful in evaluating a cataract.

TABLE 22.10 Interprofessional Care

Cataract

Diagnostic Assessment
- History and physical assessment
- Visual acuity measurement
- Ophthalmoscopy
- Slit lamp microscopy
- Glare testing, potential acuity testing in select patients
- Keratometry and A-scan ultrasound (if surgery is planned)
- Other tests (e.g., visual field perimetry) to determine cause of visual loss

Management

Nonsurgical
- Change in glasses prescription
- Strong reading glasses or magnifiers
- Increased lighting
- Lifestyle adjustment

Acute Care: Surgical Therapy

Preoperative
- Mydriatic, cycloplegic agents
- Nonsteroidal antiinflammatory drugs
- Topical antibiotics
- Antianxiety medications

Surgery
- Removal of lens
- Phacoemulsification
- Extracapsular extraction
- Correction of surgical aphakia
- Intraocular lens implantation (most frequent type of correction)
- Contact lenses

Postoperative
- Topical antibiotic
- Topical corticosteroid or other antiinflammatory agent
- Mild analgesia, if necessary
- Eye patch or shield and activity as prescribed

Interprofessional Care

Interprofessional care for cataracts is outlined in Table 22.10. Currently, no treatment is available to "cure" cataracts other than surgical removal. The presence of a cataract does not necessarily indicate a need for surgery. Often changing the patient's eyewear prescription can improve visual acuity, at least temporarily.

Other vision aids, such as strong reading glasses or magnifiers, may help the patient with near vision. Increasing the amount of light to read or do other near-vision tasks is useful. The patient may be willing to adjust their lifestyle to adjust to vision decline. For example, if glare makes it hard to drive at night, a patient may choose to drive only during daylight hours or to have a someone else drive at night. Sometimes, informing and reassuring the patient about the disease process makes the patient comfortable about choosing nonsurgical measures, at least temporarily.

Surgical therapy

When palliative measures no longer provide an acceptable level of vision function, the patient is a candidate for surgery. The patient's occupational needs and lifestyle changes are also factors affecting the decision to have surgery. In some instances, factors other than the patient's vision may influence the need for surgery. Lens-induced problems, such as increased IOP, may require lens removal. Opacities may prevent the HCP from getting a clear view of the retina in the patient with diabetic retinopathy or other sight-threatening problems. In those cases, the cataract is removed to allow retinal visualization and adequate management of the problem.

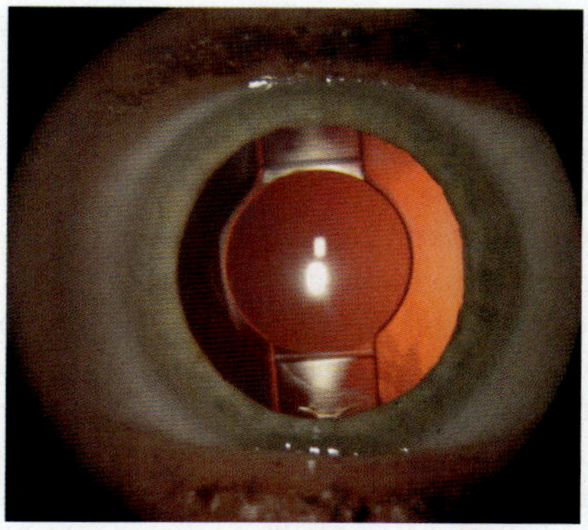

Fig. 22.12 Intraocular lens implant after cataract surgery. (Courtesy Cory J. Bosanko, OD, FAAO, Eye Centers of Tennessee, Crossville, TN.)

DRUG ALERT

Cycloplegics and Mydriatics
- Teach the patient to wear dark glasses to decrease photophobia.
- Monitor for signs of systemic toxicity (e.g., tachycardia, CNS effects).

Preoperative phase. Because most patients have local anesthesia, they do not need an extensive physical assessment. However, most patients with cataracts are older adults who may other medical problems that need evaluated and controlled before surgery. Most patients are admitted on an outpatient basis. The patient normally presents several hours before surgery to allow time for preoperative procedures.

The patient often receives 3 different eye drops before surgery. A *mydriatic* (α-adrenergic agonist) produces pupillary dilation (mydriasis) by contracting the iris dilator muscle. *Cycloplegics*, such as tropicamide (Mydriacyl), are anticholinergic agents. They block the effects of acetylcholine on the ciliary body and iris sphincter muscles. This produces mydriasis and paralysis of accommodation (cycloplegia).[11] Nonsteroidal antiinflammatory eyedrops reduce inflammation and edema. The patient may also receive antianxiety medication before surgery.

Intraoperative phase. The most common form of cataract surgery is *phacoemulsification*. In this procedure, a very small incision is made in the surface of the eye in or near the cornea. A thin ultrasound probe is inserted into the eye and ultrasonic vibrations are used to dissolve the clouded lens into fragments. These pieces are then suctioned out through the same ultrasound probe.[11] The small incisions are self-sealing and usually do not need sutures.

An *extracapsular cataract extraction procedure* is used for very advanced cataracts where the lens is too dense to dissolve into fragments. This technique requires a larger incision so that the cataract can be removed in 1 piece without being fragmented inside the eye. Sutures are needed to close the larger wound. Vision recovery is often slower.

Most patients have an IOL implanted at the time of cataract extraction surgery (Fig. 22.12). The lens of choice is a posterior chamber lens that is placed in the capsular bag behind the iris. At the end of the procedure, other drugs, such as antibiotics and corticosteroids, may be given.

Postoperative phase. Unless complications occur, the patient is usually ready to go home as soon as the effects of sedative agents have worn off. Postoperative medications include antibiotic drops to prevent infection and corticosteroid drops to decrease inflammation. The eyedrops are gradually reduced in frequency and then stopped when the eye has healed.

Recommendations for activity restrictions and nighttime eye shielding vary based on the HCP's preference. Many prefer that the patient avoid activities that increase the IOP. These include bending, stooping, coughing, and lifting.

After surgery, the HCP measures the patient's visual acuity, checks anterior chamber depth, assesses corneal clarity, and measures IOP at each visit. Even on the operative day, the patient's uncorrected visual acuity in the operative eye may be good. However, it is not unusual if the patient's visual acuity is reduced right after surgery. Multifocal IOL can correct for both near and far vision. Some patients may still need glasses or contact lenses to achieve their best visual acuity.

NURSING MANAGEMENT: CATARACTS

Assessment

Before surgery, obtain an appropriate history and physical assessment. Assess the patient's distance and near visual acuity. If the patient is going to have surgery, note the visual acuity in the patient's unoperated eye. Use this information to determine how visually compromised the patient may be while the operative eye is healing. Assess the psychosocial impact of the visual disability and the level of knowledge about the disease process and treatment options.

Planning

Before surgery, the overall goals are that the patient with a cataract will (1) make informed decisions about treatment options and (2) have minimal anxiety. After surgery, the overall goals are that the patient with a cataract will (1) understand and follow discharge instructions, (2) maintain an acceptable level of physical and emotional comfort, and (3) remain free of infection and other complications.

Implementation

Health Promotion

There are no proven measures to prevent cataract development. However, it is wise to suggest that the patient wear sunglasses, avoid unnecessary radiation, and maintain appropriate intake of antioxidant vitamins (e.g., vitamins C, E) and good nutrition. Provide information about vision enhancement techniques for the patient who chooses not to have surgery.

Acute Care

Before surgery, the patient with cataracts needs accurate information about the disease process and treatment options since cataract surgery is considered an elective procedure. Be available to the patient and caregiver to help them make an informed decision about treatment. For the patient having surgery, provide information, support, and reassurance about the surgical and postoperative experience to reduce anxiety. Photophobia is common when receiving pupil dilation medications. Therefore decreasing the room lighting is helpful. These medications produce transient stinging and burning.

TABLE 22.11 PATIENT & CAREGIVER TEACHING

After Eye Surgery

Include the following information in the teaching plan for the patient and caregiver after eye surgery:

- Proper hygiene and eye care techniques to ensure that dressings and/or surgical wound is not contaminated during eye care
- Signs and symptoms of infection (e.g., increased or purulent drainage, increased redness, any decrease in visual acuity) and when and how to report these to allow for early recognition and treatment of possible infection
- Importance of following restrictions on head positioning, bending, coughing, and Valsalva maneuver to optimize visual outcomes and prevent increased IOP
- How to instill eye medications using aseptic technique and adherence with prescribed eye medication routine to prevent infection
- How to take pain medication and report pain not relieved by medication
- Importance of continued follow-up to maximize potential visual outcomes
- Measures to cope with visual loss, such as large screens, audiobooks, and additional lighting, and promote safety

Patients who have cataract surgery remain at the agency for only a few hours. The patient and caregiver are responsible for almost all postoperative care. Give them written and verbal instructions before discharge. Include the caregiver in the instructions because some patients may have difficulty with self-care activities, especially if the vision in the unoperated eye is poor. Table 22.11 outlines patient and caregiver teaching after eye surgery. A nursing care plan for the patient after eye surgery (eNursing Care Plan 22.1) is available on the website for this chapter.

After cataract surgery, the patient usually has little or no pain. Mild analgesics are usually enough to relieve any pain. If the pain is intense, the patient should notify the HCP because this may indicate hemorrhage, infection, or increased IOP. They may have some scratchiness or blurriness in the operative eye. Remind them not to rub or scratch their eyes.

Most patients have little visual impairment after surgery. IOL implants provide immediate visual improvement. Many patients achieve a usable level of visual acuity within a few days after surgery.

A few patients may have significant visual impairment after surgery. They may need several weeks to achieve a usable level of visual acuity. These include patients who do not have an IOL implanted at the time of surgery and those with poor vision in their unoperated eye. For those patients, the time between surgery and receiving glasses or contacts can be a period of significant visual disability. Suggest ways the patient and caregiver can modify activities and the environment to maintain an adequate level of safe functioning. Suggestions may include getting help with steps, removing area rugs and other potential obstacles, preparing meals for freezing before surgery, or obtaining audio books for diversion until visual acuity improves.

If a patch is used, tell patients that they will not have depth perception until the patch is removed. This makes special measures to avoid falls or other injuries necessary. The patient with significant visual impairment in the unoperated eye needs more help while the operative eye is patched. Some patients may need 1 or 2 weeks for the visual acuity in the operated eye to reach an adequate level for most vision needs. These patients need special assistance until the vision improves.

◆ Evaluation

The overall expected outcomes are that the patient after cataract surgery will:

- Have improved vision
- Be better able to take care of self
- Have minimal to no pain
- Be optimistic about expected outcomes

Gerontologic Considerations: Cataracts

Most patients with cataracts are older. When the older patient is visually impaired, even temporarily, the patient may have a loss of independence, lack of control over their life, and a significant change in self-perception. Societal devaluation of the older adult complicates these experiences. The older patient often needs emotional support and encouragement, as well as specific suggestions to allow a maximum level of independent function. Assure the older patient that cataract surgery can be done safely and comfortably with minimal sedation.

RETINOPATHY

Retinopathy is a process of microvascular damage to the retina. It can lead to blurred vision and progressive vision loss. Retinopathy may develop slowly or rapidly. It occurs most often in adults with diabetes or hypertension.

Diabetic retinopathy is a common complication of diabetes, especially in patients with long-standing uncontrolled disease.[12] *Nonproliferative retinopathy* is the most common form of diabetic retinopathy. It is characterized by capillary microaneurysms, retinal swelling, and hard exudates. Macular edema represents a worsening of the retinopathy as plasma leaks from macular blood vessels. As capillary walls weaken, they can rupture, leading to intraretinal "dot or blot" hemorrhaging (Fig. 22.13). A severe loss in central vision can result. As the disease advances, *proliferative retinopathy* may occur. New blood vessels grow, but they are abnormal, fragile, and predisposed to leak, thus causing severe vision loss. Diagnosis and treatment of diabetic retinopathy are discussed in Chapter 53.

Hypertensive retinopathy is caused by blockages in retinal blood vessels from hypertension. These changes may not affect a person's vision at first. On a routine eye examination, retinal hemorrhages, anoxic cotton-wool spots, and macular swelling can be seen. Sustained, severe hypertension can cause sudden vision loss from swelling of the optic disc and nerve

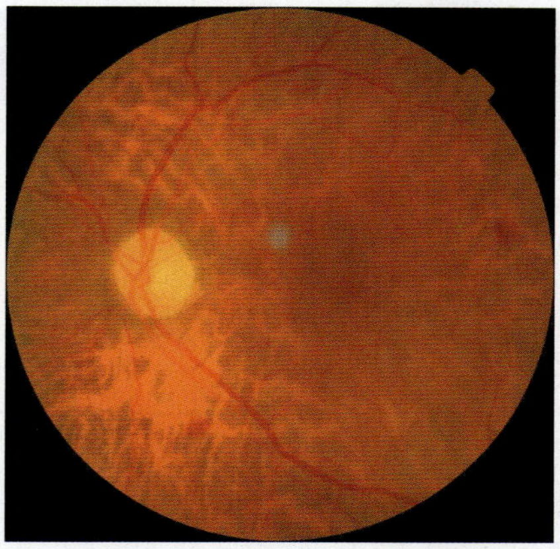

Fig. 22.13 Diabetic retinopathy. Intraretinal dot or blot hemorrhages. (Courtesy Cory J. Bosanko, OD, FAAO, Eye Centers of Tennessee, Crossville, TN.)

(papilledema). Treatment, which may be an emergency, focuses on lowering the BP. Normal vision is usually restored by treating hypertension (see Chapter 36).

RETINAL DETACHMENT

A **retinal detachment** is a separation of the sensory retina and the underlying pigment epithelium, with fluid accumulation between the 2 layers. A retinal detachment is an emergency. If it is not treated quickly, more of the retina can detach. This increases the risk of permanent vision loss or blindness.

Etiology and Pathophysiology

We classify retinal detachments based on the cause. The most common is a retinal break. *Retinal breaks* are an interruption in the full thickness of the retinal tissue. They can be classified as tears or holes. *Retinal holes* are small breaks that occur spontaneously. *Retinal tears* can occur as the vitreous humor shrinks during aging and pulls on the retina. The retina tears when the traction force exceeds the strength of the retina. Once the retina has a break, liquid vitreous can enter the subretinal space between the sensory layer and the retinal pigment epithelium layer. The fluid lifts the retina away from the underlying tissue, causing a *rhegmatogenous* retinal detachment.

Nonrhegmatogenous detachments include tractional and exudative detachments.[13] Tractional detachments are caused by scar tissue that grows on the surface of the retina. It pulls the retina off the back wall of the eye. This may occur from diabetes. Exudative detachments are often caused by AMD, a tumor, blunt injury to the eye, or an inflammatory disorder.[13] Risk factors for retinal detachment are listed in Table 22.12.

Clinical Manifestations and Diagnostic Studies

Patients with a detaching retina describe symptoms that include flashes of light, floaters (small flecks), and a "cobweb," "hairnet," or ring in the field of vision. Once the retina has detached, the patient describes a gradual loss of peripheral or central vision, "like a curtain" coming across the field of vision. There is no pain.

The area of visual loss corresponds inversely to the area of detachment. For example, if the retinal detachment involves the

TABLE 22.12 Risk Factors for Retinal Detachment

- Age
- AMD
- Diabetic retinopathy
- Eye surgery
- Eye trauma
- Family or personal history of retinal detachment
- Severe myopia
- Thinning of the peripheral retina

Source: National Eye Institute, National Institutes of Health: Retinal detachment. Retrieved from https://www.nei.nih.gov/learn-about-eye-health/eye-conditions-and-diseases/retinal-detachment.

superior retina, the defect is seen in the inferior visual field. If the detachment is small or develops slowly, the patient may not be aware of a visual problem.

Visual acuity measurements should be the first diagnostic procedure with any report of vision loss (Table 22.13). The HCP can see a retinal detachment using direct and indirect ophthalmoscopy or slit lamp microscopy in conjunction with a special lens to view the far periphery of the retina. Ultrasound may be useful in finding a retinal detachment if the eye care provider cannot see retina (e.g., when the cornea, lens, or vitreous is hazy or opaque).

TABLE 22.13 Interprofessional Care

Retinal Detachment

Diagnostic Assessment
- History and physical assessment
- Visual acuity measurement
- Ophthalmoscopy
- Slit lamp microscopy
- Ultrasound if cornea, lens, or vitreous is hazy or opaque

Management

Preoperative
- Mydriatic, cycloplegic agents
- Photocoagulation of retinal break that has not progressed to detachment

Surgery
- Laser photocoagulation
- Cryopexy
- Scleral buckling
- Vitrectomy
- Intravitreal bubble

Postoperative
- Topical antibiotics
- Topical corticosteroid
- Analgesia
- Mydriatics
- Positioning and activity as prescribed

Interprofessional Care

Some retinal breaks are not likely to progress to detachment. In these situations, the HCP simply monitors the patient and teaches them to seek immediate evaluation if warning signs and symptoms of impending detachment occur. The goals of treatment are to seal any retinal breaks and reattach the retina.[11] Several techniques are used to meet these goals.

Surgical Therapy

Laser photocoagulation and cryopexy. Retinal tears or holes without accompanying detachment may be treated by sealing the retina to the posterior wall using photocoagulation or cryopexy.[13] Photocoagulation uses a laser to make small burns around the retinal tear. Cryopexy uses a special freezing probe to apply intense cold around the tear. The probe is activated with compressed nitrous oxide gas that temporarily freezes the break. The freeze-thaw reaction creates scarring in the area. In both procedures, the resulting scar tissue seals the retina to prevent a detachment.

For retinal breaks accompanied by significant detachment, photocoagulation or cryopexy may be used with scleral buckling. When used alone, laser photocoagulation and cryopexy therapy are outpatient procedures. They usually require topical anesthesia. The patient may have minimal adverse symptoms during or after the procedure.

Scleral buckling. *Scleral buckling* is an extraocular surgical procedure that involves placing a band around the globe to move the pigment epithelium, choroid, and sclera toward the detached retina. A silicone implant is sutured against the sclera, causing the sclera to buckle inward. An encircling band may be placed over the implant if there are multiple retinal breaks, if suspected breaks cannot be found, or if there is widespread inward traction on the retina (Fig. 22.14). If present, subretinal fluid may be drained using a small-gauge needle. This promotes contact between the retina and buckled sclera. Scleral buckling is usually done as an outpatient procedure.

Intraocular procedures. Intraocular procedures are used on occasion. *Pneumatic retinopexy* is the intravitreal injection of a gas to form a temporary bubble in the vitreous. The bubble closes retinal breaks and provides opposition of the separated retinal layers. Because the intravitreal bubble is temporary, this technique is combined with laser photocoagulation or cryopexy. The patient with an intravitreal bubble must position the head so that the bubble is in contact with the retinal break. The patient may need to maintain this position as much as possible for up to several weeks.

Vitrectomy is the surgical removal of the vitreous. It may relieve traction on the retina, especially when the traction results from proliferative diabetic retinopathy. Vitrectomy may be combined with scleral buckling to provide a dual effect in relieving traction.

Postoperative considerations. Vision prognosis varies. It depends on the extent, length, and area of detachment. After surgery, the patient may be on bed rest and need special positioning to maintain proper position of an intravitreal bubble. The level of activity restriction after retinal detachment surgery varies. Verify the prescribed level of activity with the HCP and help the patient plan for any help needed related to activity restrictions.

The patient may need multiple topical medications, including antibiotics, antiinflammatory agents, or dilating agents. Give prescribed pain medications. Teach the patient to take the medication as prescribed after discharge.

In most cases, retinal detachment is an urgent situation. The patient is suddenly confronted with the need for surgery. The patient needs emotional support, especially during the immediate preoperative period when surgery preparations can lead to more anxiety.

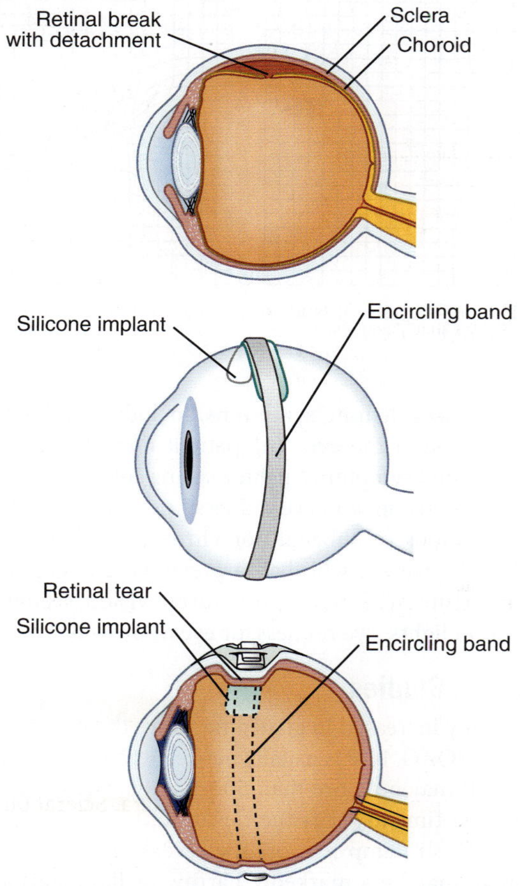

Fig. 22.14 Retinal break with detachment and surgical repair by scleral buckling technique.

The patient may go home within a few hours of surgery or stay in the hospital for several days, depending on the HCP and type of repair. Discharge planning and teaching are important and should begin early. Table 22.11 discusses patient and caregiver teaching after eye surgery. Because the patient is at increased risk for retinal detachment in the other eye, teach the patient the signs and symptoms of retinal detachment. Promote the use of protective eyewear to help avoid damage related to trauma.

AGE-RELATED MACULAR DEGENERATION

Age-related macular degeneration (AMD) is a leading cause of irreversible central vision loss. AMD is classified as dry (nonexudative) or wet (exudative). *Dry AMD* is the more common form, accounting for 90% of all cases. Those with dry AMD often notice that close vision tasks become harder. In dry AMD, the macular cells start to atrophy. This leads to a slowly progressive and painless vision loss.

Wet AMD is the more severe form. It accounts for most cases of AMD-related blindness. Wet AMD has a more rapid onset of vision loss. With wet AMD there is the development of abnormal blood vessels in or near the macula. Many patients with wet AMD have dry AMD first.

Etiology and Pathophysiology

AMD is related to retinal aging. Other risk factors include family history, obesity, hypertension, and being White. Smoking significantly increases the risk of AMD, with a dose response relationship. The risk increases with an increased number of pack-year exposure.[14]

Dry AMD starts with the abnormal accumulation of yellowish extracellular deposits called *drusen* in the retinal pigment epithelium. Over time, atrophy and degeneration of macular cells occur. In wet AMD, vascular endothelial growth factor (VEGF) promotes the growth of new blood vessels in an abnormal location in the retinal epithelium. As the new blood vessels grow, they leak fluid and can bleed. This causes scar tissue to gradually form.

Clinical Manifestations and Diagnostic Studies

The patient may have blurred and darkened vision, *scotomas* (blind spots in the visual field), and *metamorphopsia* (vision distortion). Vision distortion includes the illusion that straight lines, such as the edge of a door or sentences on a page, are wavy or that some objects are smaller than they really are. If only 1 eye is affected, the patient may not notice early changes in vision. Acute vision loss may occur from either form.

In addition to visual acuity measurement, the primary diagnostic procedure is ophthalmoscopy. The HCP looks for drusen and other fundus changes associated with AMD. The Amsler grid test may help define the involved area. It provides a baseline for future comparison (Fig. 22.15). Fundus fluorescein angiography and/or indocyanine green dyes may help to further determine the extent and type of AMD. Retinal anatomy can be analyzed using optical coherence tomography (OCT), which looks at pathology in the macula, or scanning laser ophthalmoscopy.

Interprofessional Care

The goals of care are to reverse or minimize vision loss and improve vision function. Visual prognosis varies greatly. Treatment options for patients with wet AMD include medications that are injected directly into the vitreous cavity. Ranibizumab (Lucentis), bevacizumab (Avastin), aflibercept (Eylea), and pegaptanib (Macugen) inhibit VEGF. This helps to slow vision loss by stopping new vessels from forming.[14] Side effects can include blurred vision, eye irritation, eye pain, and photosensitivity. Injections are given at 4- to 6-week intervals, depending on treatment response. Disease stability is determined by OCT. The findings determine the need for continued intravitreal injections.

Verteporfin (Visudyne) IV is part of photodynamic therapy (PDT) to treat wet AMD. Laser light shone into the eye activates verteporfin and causes it to create blood clots that block the abnormal blood vessels. By sealing the leaky blood vessels, PDT slows down central vision loss. Until the body completely excretes the drug, it can be activated by exposure to sunlight or other high-intensity light, such as halogen. The patient must avoid direct exposure to sunlight and other intense forms of light for 5 days after treatment. Exposing the skin to sunlight could activate the drug in that area, causing a chemical burn.

Taking a supplement of antioxidant vitamins (e.g., vitamin C, vitamin E), lutein, zeaxanthin, and zinc may help slow the progression of AMD.[14] Teach the patient to eat dark green, leafy vegetables containing lutein (e.g., kale, broccoli, spinach) and foods, such as beef, pork, dairy, and whole grains, that are high in zinc. Smoking cessation may help in halting the progression of dry AMD.

The management of the patient with visual impairment is appropriate for the patient with AMD. Many patients with low-vision assistive devices can continue reading and keep a license to drive during the daytime and at lowered speeds. The permanent loss of central vision has significant psychosocial implications for nursing care. Avoid giving the impression that "nothing can be done" about the problem when caring for the patient with AMD. Although treatment may not recover lost vision, much can be done to augment the remaining vision.

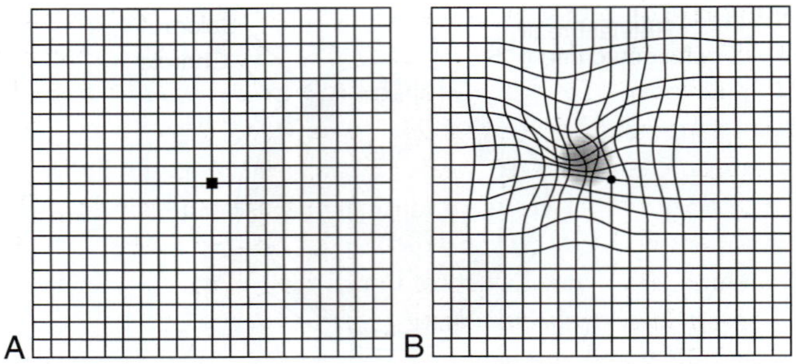

Fig. 22.15 Amsler grid. (A) Normal grid. (B) Abnormal grid as seen by person with AMD.

GLAUCOMA

Glaucoma is a group of disorders characterized by increased IOP and its consequences, optic nerve atrophy, and peripheral visual field loss. Glaucoma is the second leading cause of permanent blindness in the United States and the leading cause of blindness among Blacks.[2] Many people with glaucoma are unaware of their condition. The incidence of glaucoma increases with age. Genetic factors play a role in some types of glaucoma.

Etiology and Pathophysiology

A proper balance between the rate of aqueous production *(inflow)* and the rate of aqueous reabsorption *(outflow)* is essential to maintain the IOP within normal limits. We call the place where the outflow occurs the *angle* because it is the angle where the iris meets the cornea. When the rate of inflow is greater than the rate of outflow, IOP can increase above the normal limits. If IOP stays increased, permanent vision loss may occur.

Primary open-angle glaucoma (POAG) is the most common type of glaucoma. In POAG the outflow of aqueous humor is decreased in the trabecular meshwork. The drainage channels become clogged, like a clogged kitchen sink.[15] Damage to the optic nerve can then result.

Angle-closure glaucoma (ACG) is due to a reduction in the outflow of aqueous humor that results from angle closure. Usually, this is caused by the lens bulging forward from the aging process. Angle closure may also occur due to pupil dilation in the patient with anatomically narrow angles. Acute angle-closure glaucoma (AACG) may be precipitated by situations in which the pupil stays partially dilated long enough to cause an acute and significant rise in the IOP. This may occur with drug-induced mydriasis, emotional excitement, or darkness. Drug-induced mydriasis may occur from topical eye preparations or many systemic medications (both prescription and OTC). Check medication records before giving medications to the patient with ACG. Teach the patient not to take any mydriatic medications.

Clinical Manifestations

POAG develops slowly and without symptoms of pain or pressure. The patient usually does not notice the gradual visual field loss until peripheral vision has been severely compromised.[15] Eventually, the patient with untreated glaucoma has "tunnel vision," with only a small center visual field. All peripheral vision is absent.

AACG causes definite symptoms, including sudden, severe pain in or around the eye. The patient often has nausea and vomiting. Vision symptoms include seeing colored halos around lights, blurred vision, and eye redness.

Manifestations of subacute or chronic ACG appear more gradually. The patient who had a previous, unrecognized episode of subacute ACG may report blurred vision, seeing colored halos around lights, eye redness, or eye or brow pain.

Diagnostic Studies

IOP is usually increased in glaucoma above the normal 10 to 21 mm Hg. In POAG, IOP is usually between 22 and 32 mm Hg. In AACG, IOP may be more than 50 mm Hg. Measurements are repeated over time to verify the elevation.

In POAG, slit lamp microscopy reveals a normal angle. In ACG, there may be a markedly narrow or flat anterior chamber angle, an edematous cornea, a fixed and moderately dilated pupil, and ciliary injection (hyperemia of the ciliary blood vessels produces a red color).

Measures of peripheral and central vision provide more diagnostic information. Perimetry produces a complete map of the patient's visual field. It may reveal subtle changes in peripheral vision early in the disease process. In ACG, central visual acuity is reduced if the patient has corneal edema, and the visual fields may be markedly decreased. Central acuity may remain 20/20 even in the presence of severe peripheral visual field loss. As glaucoma progresses, *optic disc cupping* may be one of the first signs of chronic POAG. The optic disc becomes wider, deeper, and paler (light gray or white). This is visible with direct or indirect ophthalmoscopy (Fig. 22.16).

Interprofessional Care

The primary focus of treatment is to keep the IOP low enough to prevent the patient from developing optic nerve damage. Treatment varies with the type of glaucoma. The diagnostic and interprofessional care of glaucoma is outlined in Table 22.14.

Chronic Open-Angle Glaucoma

Drug therapy is the initial treatment in POAG (Table 22.15). The patient must understand that continued treatment and supervision are needed because the drugs control, but do not cure, glaucoma. Because of their superior efficacy and systemic safety, prostaglandin analogs are the preferred choice for initial treatment.

Many patients with glaucoma have systemic illnesses or take systemic medications that may affect their therapy. The patient taking a β-adrenergic blocking glaucoma agent may have an additive effect if they also take a systemic β-adrenergic blocking drug. All β-adrenergic blocking glaucoma agents are contraindicated in the patient with bradycardia, second- or third-degree heart block, cardiogenic shock, and heart failure. The noncardioselective β-adrenergic blocking glaucoma agents are contraindicated in the patient with chronic obstructive pulmonary disease (COPD) or asthma. They may have profound effects in the older patient.

Argon laser trabeculoplasty (ALT) is a noninvasive way to lower IOP when medications are not successful or when the patient either cannot or will not use the drug therapy as recommended. ALT is an outpatient procedure that uses topical anesthetic. The laser stimulates scarring and contraction of the trabecular meshwork, which opens the outflow channels. ALT reduces IOP most of the time. The patient uses topical corticosteroids for 3 to 5 days after the procedure. The most common complication is an acute rise in IOP. The HCP examines the patient at 1 week and again at 4 to 6 weeks after surgery.

Filtration surgery, also called a *trabeculectomy,* may be used if drug and laser therapy are not successful.

Acute Angle-Closure Glaucoma

AACG is an emergency that needs immediate intervention. Carbonic anhydrase inhibitors (Table 22.15) and oral or IV hyperosmotic agents, including glycerin (Ophthalgan), isosorbide (Ismotic), and mannitol (Osmitrol), are usually successful in immediately lowering IOP. A laser peripheral iridotomy or surgical iridectomy is necessary for long-term treatment and prevention of more episodes. These procedures allow the aqueous humor to flow through a newly created opening in the iris and into normal outflow channels. A procedure may be done on the other eye as a precaution because many patients often have an acute attack in the other eye.

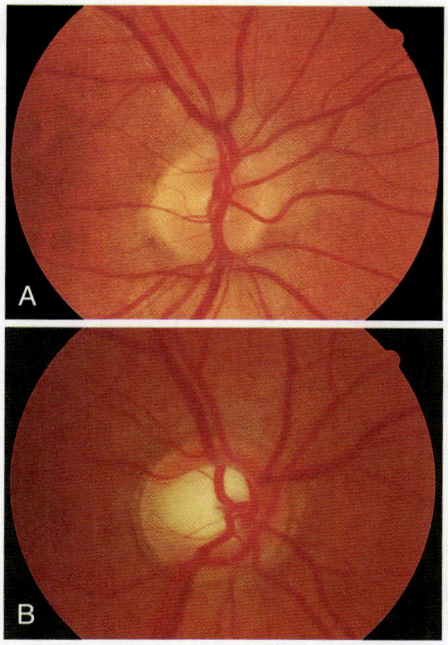

Fig. 22.16 (A) In the normal eye the optic cup is pink with little cupping. (B) In glaucoma the optic cup is bleached, and optic cupping is present. Note the appearance of the retinal vessels, which travel over the edge of the optic cup and appear to dip into it.

TABLE 22.14 Interprofessional Care

Glaucoma

Diagnostic Assessment
- History and physical assessment
- Visual acuity measurement
- Tonometry
- Ophthalmoscopy
- Slit lamp microscopy
- Gonioscopy
- Visual field perimetry

Management

Chronic Open-Angle Glaucoma

Drug Therapy (Table 22.15)
- α-Adrenergic agonists
- β-Adrenergic blockers
- Carbonic anhydrase inhibitors
- Miotics
- Prostaglandin agonists

Surgical Therapy
- Argon laser trabeculoplasty (ALT)
- Trabeculectomy with or without filtering implant

Acute Angle-Closure Glaucoma
- Carbonic anhydrase inhibitors
- Hyperosmotic agent
- Laser peripheral iridotomy
- Surgical iridectomy

NURSING MANAGEMENT: GLAUCOMA

Assessment

Because glaucoma is a chronic condition requiring long-term management, assess the patient's ability to understand and adhere to the treatment plan. Assess the patient's psychologic reaction to the diagnosis of a potentially sight-threatening chronic disorder. Include the patient's caregiver in the assessment because the chronic nature of this disorder also affects them. For example, caregivers may have to administer eyedrops if the patient is unwilling or unable.

Clinical Problems

Clinical problems for the patient with glaucoma include:
- Sensory deficit
- Pain
- Impaired role performance

Planning

The overall goals are that the patient with glaucoma will (1) have no progression of visual impairment, (2) follow the treatment plan, and (3) have no complications.

Implementation

Health Promotion

Loss of vision from glaucoma is preventable. Teach the patient and caregiver about the risk for glaucoma and that it

TABLE 22.15 Drug Therapy

Acute and Chronic Glaucoma

Drug	Action	Side Effects	Nursing Considerations
α-Adrenergic Agonists			
apraclonidine (Iopidine), brimonidine (Alphagan)	↓ Aqueous humor production	Eye redness, irregular heart rate, dry mouth, fatigue	Topical drops Used to control or prevent acute postlaser IOP rise (used before and immediately after ALT and iridotomy, Nd:YAG laser capsulotomy) Teach patient at risk for systemic reactions to occlude puncta
β-Adrenergic Blockers			
betaxolol (Betoptic)	β_1 cardioselective ↓ IOP, ↓ aqueous humor production	Eye discomfort Systemic reactions rare but include bradycardia, heart block, pulmonary distress, headache, depression	Topical drugs Contraindicated in patient with bradycardia, cardiogenic shock, or heart failure Systemic absorption can have additive effect with systemic β_1-blocking agents
carteolol levobunolol (Betagan) optipranolol timolol maleate (Timoptic, Istalol)	β_1 and β_2 noncardioselective blockers ↓ IOP, ↓ aqueous humor production	Same as betaxolol	Topical drops Same as betaxolol Contraindicated in patients with asthma or COPD
Carbonic Anhydrase Inhibitors			
Systemic			
acetazolamide (Diamox) methazolamide	↓ Aqueous humor production	Paresthesias, hearing problems, tinnitus, anorexia, taste changes, GI problems, headache, drowsiness, depression, kidney stones	Sulfa-type allergic reactions may occur in patient allergic to sulfa Diuretic effect can alter fluid and electrolyte balance Do not give to patient on high-dose aspirin therapy May cause gout attacks
Topical			
brinzolamide (Azopt) dorzolamide (Trusopt)	↓ Aqueous humor production	Transient stinging, blurred vision, redness	Sulfa-type allergic reactions may occur in patient allergic to sulfa
Miotics			
pilocarpine (Isopto Carpine, Pilocar)	Parasympathomimetic Stimulates ciliary muscle contraction, causing miosis and opening of trabecular meshwork, ↑ aqueous outflow Partially inhibits cholinesterase	Eye pain and burning, headache, blurred vision, decreased adaptation to the dark, syncope, dysrhythmias, hypotension	Topical drops Caution patient about ↓ visual acuity caused by miosis, particularly in dim light
Prostaglandin Agonists			
bimatoprost (Lumigan) latanoprost (Xalatan) tafluprost (Zioptan) travoprost	↑ Outflow of aqueous humor between the uvea and sclera and the usual exit through the trabecular meshwork	Increased brown iris pigmentation, stinging, redness, dryness, itching, and foreign body sensation	Topical drops Teach patient to only administer 1 drop per day Have patient remove contact lens 15 min before instilling
Rho Kinase Inhibitors			
netarsudil (Rhopressa)	↓ Aqueous humor production and ↑ outflow	Redness, blurred vision, headache	Topical drops Teach patient to only administer 1 drop per day

ALT, Argon laser trabeculoplasty; *Nd:YAG,* neodymium-doped yttrium aluminum garnet (laser).

increases with age. Stress the importance of early detection and treatment in preventing visual impairment. A comprehensive eye examination is important in identifying people with glaucoma or those at risk for developing glaucoma. The current recommendations for an eye examination are (1) every 2 to 4 years between ages 40 to 54 years, (2) every 1 to 3 years between ages 55 to 64 years, and (3) every 1 to 2 years for people age 65 years or older.[16] Those at higher risk for glaucoma and other problems should have their eyes checked more often.

◆ Acute Care

Acute nursing interventions are directed primarily toward the patient with AACG and the surgical patient. The patient with AACG needs medication immediately to lower the IOP. Most surgeries for glaucoma are outpatient procedures. Provide care to relieve any discomfort related to the procedure. Patient and caregiver teaching after eye surgery is discussed in Table 22.11.

Ambulatory care. Because of the chronic nature of glaucoma, teach the patient to follow the treatment plan and follow-up recommendations prescribed by the HCP. Provide accurate information about the disease process and treatment options, including the reason for each option. The patient needs information about the purpose, frequency, and technique for administering antiglaucoma drugs. Encourage adherence by helping the patient set up a medication administration schedule and advocating a change in therapy if the patient reports unacceptable side effects.

◆ Evaluation

The overall expected outcomes are that the patient with glaucoma will:
- Have no further loss of vision
- Adhere to the treatment plan
- Safely function within own environment
- Have relief from pain associated with the disease and surgery

INTRAOCULAR INFLAMMATION AND INFECTION

The term *uveitis* is used to describe inflammation of the uveal tract, retina, vitreous body, or optic nerve. Inflammation may be caused by bacteria, viruses, fungi, or parasites. *Cytomegalovirus retinitis* (CMV retinitis) is an opportunistic infection that occurs in patients with AIDS or immunosuppression. The cause of sterile intraocular inflammation includes autoimmune disorders, AIDS, cancer, or disorders associated with systemic diseases, such as inflammatory bowel disease. Pain and photophobia are common symptoms.

Endophthalmitis is an extensive intraocular inflammation of the vitreous cavity. Bacteria, viruses, fungi, or parasites can induce this serious inflammatory response. The mechanism of infection may be endogenous, in which the infecting agent arrives at the eye through the bloodstream, or exogenous. In that case the infecting agent is introduced through a surgical wound or a penetrating injury. Although rare, endophthalmitis is a devastating complication of intraocular surgery or penetrating eye injury. It can lead to irreversible blindness within hours or days. Manifestations include eye pain, photophobia, decreased visual acuity, headaches, reddened and swollen conjunctiva, and corneal edema.

Treatment depends on the underlying cause. Intraocular infections require antimicrobial agents. They may be delivered topically, subconjunctivally, intravitreally, systemically, or in some combination. Inflammatory responses require antiinflammatory medications (e.g., corticosteroids). The patient is usually uncomfortable and may be anxious and frightened. Provide accurate information and emotional support. In severe cases, the patient may need enucleation. When the patient has lost visual function or even the entire eye, the patient will grieve the loss. Your role includes helping the patient through the grieving process.

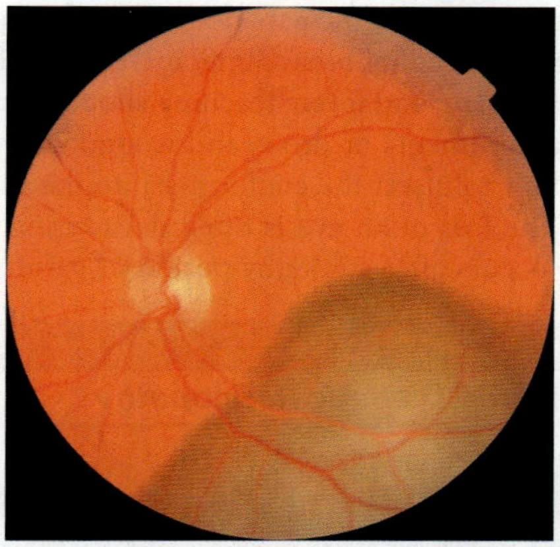

Fig. 22.17 Uveal melanoma. A large tumor in the choroid, the most common location in the eye for melanoma. (Courtesy Cory J. Bosanko, OD, FAAO, Eye Centers of Tennessee, Crossville, TN.)

OCULAR TUMORS

Benign and cancerous tumors can occur in many areas of the eye, including the conjunctiva, retina, and orbit. Eyelid cancers include basal cell and squamous cell cancers (see Chapter 25).

Uveal melanoma is a cancer of the iris, choroid, or ciliary body. It more often occurs in light-skinned people with light eye color, who are over age 60, and have chronic UV exposure.[17] Uveal melanoma can arise from preexisting nevi in the eye. Tumors may be asymptomatic or there may be vision loss. This depends on their size and location and presence of hemorrhage and retinal detachment. As with other cancers, cancer stage and cell type are important variables in the prognosis. Diagnostic testing may include ultrasound, MRI, angiography, and fine-needle aspiration biopsy. Uveal melanoma often appears as a dome-shaped, well-circumscribed, solid brown to golden pigment in the iris, choroid, or ciliary body (Fig. 20.17).

Depending on the status of the involved eye, treatment options can include radiation therapy, photocoagulation, thermotherapy, resection, and eye removal. Many patients do not lose their eye. Some may have good vision after treatment in the affected eye.

ENUCLEATION

Enucleation is the removal of the eye. The primary reason for enucleation is a blind, painful eye. This may result from glaucoma, infection, or trauma. Enucleation may be used to treat ocular cancer. The surgery includes severing the extraocular muscles close to their insertion on the globe, inserting an implant to maintain the intraorbital anatomy, and suturing the ends of the muscles over the implant. The conjunctiva covers the joined muscles. A clear conformer is placed over the conjunctiva until the permanent prosthesis is fitted. A pressure dressing helps prevent bleeding.

After surgery, observe the patient for signs of complications, including excess bleeding or swelling, increased pain, displacement of the implant, and fever. Teaching should include how to instill topical ointments or drops and wound cleansing. Teach the patient how to insert the conformer into the socket in case it falls out. The loss of an eye is often devastating, even when enucleation occurs after a lengthy period of painful blindness. Recognize the patient's emotional response and provide support to the patient and caregivers.

About 6 weeks after surgery, the wound is sufficiently healed for the permanent prosthesis. An ocularist fits the prosthesis and designs it to match the remaining eye. Teach the patient how to remove, cleanse, and insert the prosthesis. Special polishing is needed periodically to remove dried protein secretions.

Case Study

Glaucoma and Diabetic Retinopathy

(© Kevin Peterson/ Stockbyte/Thinkstock.)

Patient Profile

J.K. is a 68-year-old woman with a history of osteoarthritis and type 2 diabetes for the past 15 years. She now has diabetic retinopathy. She returns to the eye clinic with her daughter for continued care of primary open-angle glaucoma (POAG) and reexamination for changes in diabetic retinopathy. Her current drug therapy for POAG includes topical timolol maleate 0.5% extended (Timoptic-XE) and latanoprost (Xalatan) 0.005% once daily in both eyes. At her last examination, she had microaneurysms and hard exudates of the retina.

Subjective Data

- Can no longer read the newspaper and reports that medication labels are difficult to read.
- States she is not always successful in getting the eyedrops instilled because her hands are gnarled and painful from osteoarthritis.

Objective Data

- Distant and near visual acuity: 20/60 (right eye) and 20/50 (left eye), with a reduction from 20/40 (both eyes) at her last visit
- Intraocular pressure (IOP) 20 mm Hg in each eye
- A new blind spot with visual field testing in the left eye
- Fluorescein angiography reveals diabetic macular edema in both eyes

Interprofessional Care

- Brimonidine 0.15% (left eye) 15 min before and immediately after argon laser trabeculoplasty (ALT)
- Argon laser to left eye to seal leaking microaneurysms from macular edema
- Check IOP 1 hr after ALT
- Continue previous glaucoma drop regimen
- Follow-up examination in 2 wk for possible ALT of right eye

Discussion Questions

1. ***Recognize:*** Explain the cause of the new blind spot.
2. ***Recognize:*** What is the cause of the vision loss from diabetic retinopathy?
3. ***Analyze:*** What main complication is J.K. at risk for?
4. ***Plan:*** Why is ALT an appropriate treatment for J.K.?
5. ***Prioritize:*** Based on the assessment data, what are the priority clinical problems?
6. ***Prioritize:*** What are the priority nursing interventions for J.K.?
7. ***Act:*** What is the purpose of the eyedrops before and immediately after ALT?
8. ***Act:*** What teaching will you provide so J.K. can manage her care?
9. ***Evaluate:*** What outcomes would indicate interprofessional care was effective?

Answers available at http://evolve.elsevier.com/Lewis/medsurg.

BRIDGE TO NCLEX EXAMINATION

The number of the question corresponds to the same-numbered outcome at the beginning of the chapter.

1. In a patient with a hemorrhage in the posterior cavity of the eye, the nurse knows that blood is accumulating
   a. in the aqueous humor.
   b. between the lens and retina.
   c. between the cornea and lens.
   d. in the space between the iris and lens.
2. Increased intraocular pressure may occur due to
   a. edema of the corneal stroma.
   b. dilation of the retinal arterioles.
   c. blockage of the lacrimal canals and ducts.
   d. increased aqueous humor production by the ciliary process.
3. Ask patients using eyedrops to treat their glaucoma about
   a. use of corrective lenses.
   b. their usual sleep pattern.
   c. a history of heart or lung disease.
   d. sensitivity to opioids or depressants.
4. Always assess the patient with an eye problem for
   a. visual acuity.
   b. pupillary reactions.
   c. intraocular pressure.
   d. confrontation visual fields.
5. When examining the patient's eyes, which finding would be of *most* concern to the nurse?
   a. Intraocular pressure of 16 mm Hg
   b. Slightly yellowish cast of the sclera
   c. Outward turning of the lower lid margin
   d. Small, white nodule on the upper lid margin
6. Presbyopia occurs in older people because
   a. the eyeball elongates.
   b. the lens becomes inflexible.
   c. the corneal curvature becomes irregular.
   d. light rays are focusing in front of the retina.
7. Before injecting fluorescein for angiography, it is important for the nurse to *(select all that apply)*
   a. obtain an emesis basin.
   b. ask if the patient is fatigued.
   c. administer a topical anesthetic.
   d. inform patient that skin may turn yellow.
   e. assess for allergies to iodine-based contrast media.
8. A patient says she was diagnosed with astigmatism. When she asks what that is, what is the best explanation the nurse can give to the patient?
   a. "It happens because the lens of the eye is absent."
   b. "People with astigmatism have abnormally long eyeballs."

c. "The cornea of the eye is uneven or irregular with astigmatism."
d. "Astigmatism occurs because the eye muscles weaken with age."

9. Which intervention would be part of the plan of care for a patient who has new vision loss?
   a. Allow the patient to express feelings of grief and anger.
   b. Have the AP perform all self-care activities for the patient.
   c. Address any family present first when discussing care concerns.
   d. Speak loudly and clearly, addressing the patient with each contact.
10. Which patient behaviors would the nurse promote for healthy eyes? *(select all that apply)*
   a. Protective sunglasses when bicycling
   b. Taking part in a smoking cessation program
   c. Supplementing diet intake of vitamin C and beta-carotene
   d. Washing hands thoroughly before putting in or taking out contact lenses
   e. A woman avoiding pregnancy for 4 weeks after receiving MMR immunization
11. The *most* important intervention for the patient with epidemic keratoconjunctivitis is
   a. cleansing the affected area with baby shampoo.
   b. monitoring spread of infection to the opposing eye.
   c. regular instillation of artificial tears to the affected eye.
   d. teaching the patient and caregivers good hygiene techniques.
12. What should be included in the discharge teaching for the patient who had cataract surgery? *(Select all that apply.)*
   a. Eye discomfort is often relieved with mild analgesics.
   b. A decline in visual acuity is common for the first month.
   c. Stay on bed rest and limit activity for the first few weeks.
   d. Notify the provider if an increase in redness or drainage occurs.
   e. Following activity restrictions is essential to reduce intraocular pressure.

1. b; 2. d; 3. c; 4. a; 5. d; 6. b; 7. a, d; 8. c; 9. a; 10. a, b, c, d; 11. d; 12. a, d, e.

For rationales to these answers and even more NCLEX review questions, visit http://evolve.elsevier.com/Lewis/medsurg.

EVOLVE WEBSITE/RESOURCES LIST

http://evolve.elsevier.com/Lewis/medsurg
Review Questions (Online Only)
Key Points
Answer Keys for Questions
- Rationales for Bridge to NCLEX Examination Questions
- Answer Guidelines for Case Studies

Student Case Study
- Patient Undergoing Cataract Surgery

eNursing Care Plan
- eNursing Care Plan 22.1: Patient After Eye Surgery

Conceptual Care Map Creator
Audio Glossary

REFERENCES

*1. Roberti G, Oddone F, Agnifili L, Katsanos A, et al.: Steroid-induced glaucoma: epidemiology, pathophysiology, and clinical management, *Surv Ophthalmol* 65:458, 2020.
2. National Eye Institute: Statistics and data. Retrieved from www.nei.nih.gov/eyedata.
3. American Optometric Association: Myopia. Retrieved from www.aoa.org/patients-and-public/eye-and-vision-problems/glossary-of-eye-and-vision-conditions/myopia?sso=y.
4. US Food and Drug Administration: Lasik. Retrieved from https://www.fda.gov/medical-devices/surgery-devices/lasik.
5. Emens J: Non-24-hour sleep-wake rhythm disorder. In *Circadian rhythm sleep-wake disorders*, 2020, Springer.
*6. Saydah S, Gerzoff RB, Taylor CA, Ehrlich JR, Saaddine J: Vision impairment and subjective cognitive decline–related functional limitations—United States, 2015–2017, *MMWR (Morb Mortal Wkly Rep)* 68:453, 2019.
7. American Academy of Ophthalmology: Preventing eye injuries. Retrieved from www.aao.org/eye-health/diseases/preventing-injuries.
*8. Azari AA, Arabi A: Conjunctivitis: a systematic review, *J Ophthalmic Vis Res* 15:372, 2020.
9. Merck manual professional version: herpes simplex keratitis. Retrieved from https://www.merckmanuals.com/professional/eye-disorders/corneal-disorders/herpes-simplex-keratitis.
10. Eye Bank Association of America: Eye banking statistical report. Retrieved from: https://restoresight.org/what-we-do/publications/statistical-report/.
11. Yanoff M, Duker JS: *Ophthalmology*, 5th ed, St. Louis, 2020, Elsevier.
*12. American Academy of Ophthalmology: Diabetic retinopathy. Retrieved from https://www.aao.org/preferred-practice-pattern/diabetic-retinopathy-ppp.
13. Love GH: The black veil: caring for patients with retinal detachments, *Nursing* 49:34, 2019. 2019.
*14. American Academy of Ophthalmology: Age-related macular degeneration. Retrieved from https://www.aao.org/preferred-practice-pattern/age-related-macular-degeneration-ppp.
15. Glaucoma Research Foundation: Glaucoma. Retrieved from www.glaucoma.org/glaucoma/.
16. Mayo Clinic: Eye exam. Retrieved from https://www.mayoclinic.org/tests-procedures/eye-exam/about/pac-20384655.
17. National Cancer Institute: Intraocular melanoma. Retrieved from https://www.cancer.gov/types/eye/hp/intraocular-melanoma-treatment-pdq.

* Evidence-based information for clinical practice.

23

Assessment and Management: Auditory Problems

Mariann M. Harding

http://evolve.elsevier.com/Lewis/medsurg/

CONCEPTUAL FOCUS

Functional Ability
Infection
Sensory Perception
Stress and Coping

LEARNING OUTCOMES

1. Describe the structures and functions of the auditory system.
2. Obtain significant subjective and objective assessment data related to the auditory system from a patient.
3. Perform a physical assessment of the auditory system using the appropriate techniques.
4. Distinguish normal from common abnormal findings of a physical assessment of the auditory system.
5. Link the age-related changes in the auditory system to differences in assessment findings.
6. Describe the purpose, significance of results, and nursing responsibilities related to diagnostic studies of the auditory system.
7. Explain the pathophysiology, clinical manifestations, and nursing and interprofessional management of common ear problems.
8. Compare the common causes, management, and rehabilitative potential of conductive and sensorineural hearing loss.
9. Explain the use, care, and patient teaching related to assistive hearing devices.
10. Describe measures used to assist the patient in adapting to decreased hearing.

KEY TERMS

acoustic neuroma
benign paroxysmal positional vertigo (BPPV)
external otitis
Ménière disease
nystagmus
otosclerosis
presbycusis
tinnitus
vertigo

AUDITORY SYSTEM

Hearing is a complex process that allows us to interact with the environment. It is the basis for social interaction and communication. Having a hearing impairment can lead to major challenges that can adversely affect well-being. Difficulties with related concepts, including functional ability and cognition, may be present with hearing loss. Problems with equilibrium can impair coordination, balance, and orientation. This chapter presents an overview of auditory function and discusses care when problems occur.

STRUCTURES AND FUNCTIONS OF AUDITORY SYSTEM

The auditory system is composed of the peripheral auditory system and central auditory system. The peripheral auditory system includes the structures of the ear itself: external, middle, and inner ear (Fig. 23.1). This system is involved with the reception and perception of sound. The inner ear functions in hearing and balance.

The central auditory system integrates and assigns meaning to what you hear. This system includes the vestibulocochlear

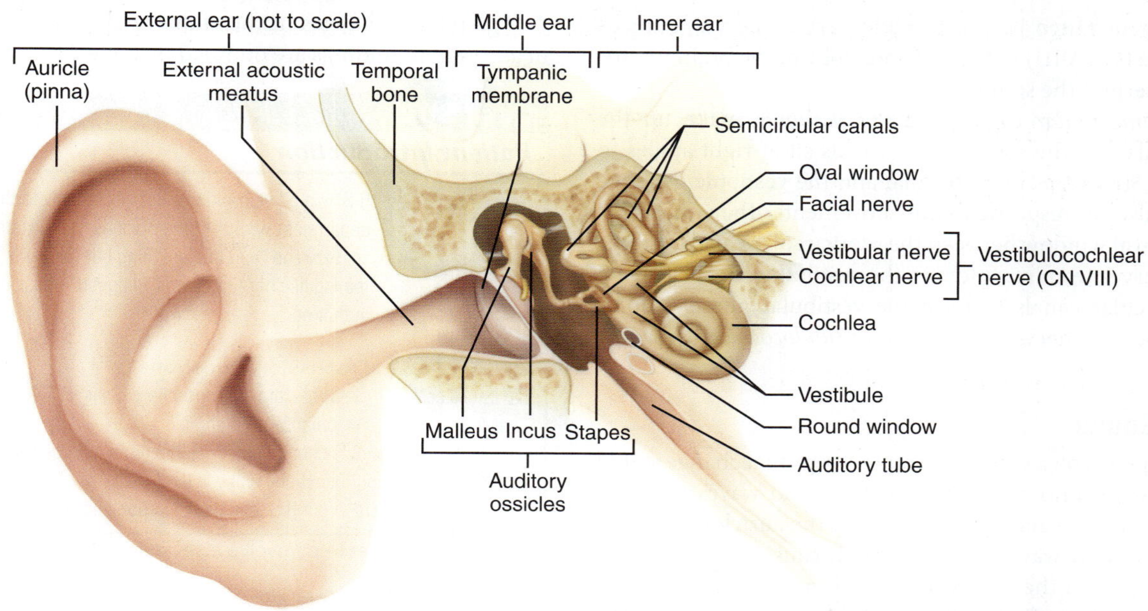

Fig. 23.1 External, middle, and inner ear. (Modified from Patton KT, Thibodeau GA: *Anatomy and physiology,* ed 8, St Louis, 2013, Mosby.)

nerve (cranial nerve [CN] VIII) and auditory cortex of the brain. The brain and its pathways transmit and process sound and sensations that maintain your equilibrium.

The role of the external and middle part of the ear is to conduct and amplify sound waves from the environment. This part of sound conduction is termed *air conduction.* Problems in these parts of the ear may cause *conductive hearing loss,* resulting in a decrease in sound intensity and/or a distortion in sound.

Damage to or a problem of the inner ear or along the nerve pathways results in *sensorineural hearing loss.* Besides causing distortion or faintness of sound, sensorineural hearing loss may affect the ability to understand speech or cause complete hearing loss. Impairment within the auditory pathways of the brain causes *central hearing loss.* Central hearing loss causes difficulty in understanding the meaning of words the person heard. Types of hearing loss are discussed later in this chapter.

External Ear

The external ear consists of the *auricle* (pinna), external auditory canal, and *tympanic membrane (TM),* or eardrum. The auricle is composed of cartilage and connective tissue covered with epithelium, which also lines the external auditory canal (Fig. 23.1). The external auditory canal is a slightly S-shaped tube about 1 inch (2.5 cm) in length in the adult. The lining of the first one-third of the canal contains fine hairs (cilia), sebaceous (oil) glands, and ceruminous (wax) glands. The oil and wax lubricate the ear canal, keep it free from debris, and kill bacteria. Thin epithelium lines the distal two-thirds of the canal. It is over bone and very sensitive.

The function of the external ear and canal is to collect and transmit sound waves to the TM. The TM is a shiny, translucent, pearl-gray membrane. It is made up of epithelial cells, connective tissue, and mucous membrane. It serves as a partition and transmits sounds between the external auditory canal and middle ear.

Middle Ear

The middle ear cavity is an air space in the temporal bone. Mucous membrane lines the middle ear and is continuous from the nasal pharynx via the eustachian (auditory) tube. The eustachian tube equalizes atmospheric air pressure between the middle ear and throat. This allows the TM to move freely. It is normally closed, opening only with yawning, swallowing, and chewing. Blockage of the tube can occur with allergies, nasopharyngeal infections, or enlarged adenoids. A tube that stays open is *patulous.* When this occurs, *autophony,* or hearing your own voice, may be present.

The middle ear contains the *ossicles,* the 3 smallest bones in the body: *malleus, incus,* and *stapes.* Vibrations of the TM cause the ossicles to move and transmit sound waves to the oval window. The superior part of the middle ear is the *epitympanum,* or the attic. It also communicates with air cells within the mastoid bone. The mastoid is the posterior part of the temporal bone. The facial nerve (CN VII) traverses above the oval window of the middle ear. The thin, bony covering of the facial nerve can become damaged by chronic ear infection, skull fracture, or trauma during ear surgery. Problems may occur with voluntary facial movements, eyelid closure, and taste discrimination. Permanent damage to the facial nerve can result.

Inner Ear

The inner ear consists of 3 spaces in the temporal bone, assembled in a system called the bony labyrinth. The space is filled with watery fluid called perilymph. Within the perilymph is the membranous labyrinth. It follows the shape of the bony labyrinth and holds a thicker fluid called *endolymph.*

The inner ear holds the functional organs for hearing and balance. The receptor organ for hearing is the *organ of Corti.* It lies on the basilar membrane in the *cochlea.* Its tiny hair cells transform fluid vibrations from sounds into electrical impulses.

These are transmitted by the acoustic part of the vestibulocochlear nerve (CN VIII) to the temporal lobe of the brain to process and interpret the sound.

Three *semicircular canals* and the *vestibule* make up the organ of balance. The semicircular canals sit at right angles to each other. Structures in each canal and the vestibule generate nerve impulses in response to our movements. The vestibule is beside the oval window between the semicircular canals and the cochlea. Nerves from receptors in the vestibule join those from the semicircular canals to form the vestibular nerve. It joins with the cochlear nerve to form the *vestibulocochlear nerve,* or CN VIII.

Hearing Sound

Hearing depends on a series of complex steps that change sound waves in the air into electrical signals. Sound waves travel by air (air conduction) and are picked up by the auricles and auditory canal. Sound waves strike the TM, causing it to vibrate. The central part of the TM is connected to the malleus, which then starts to vibrate. The malleus transmits the vibration to the incus and then the stapes. As the stapes moves back and forth, it pushes the membrane of the oval window in and out.

Movement of the oval window makes waves in the perilymph. These vibrations are picked up by the tiny sensory hair cells of the cochlea, which initiate nerve impulses. These impulses are carried by nerve fibers to the main branch of the acoustic portion of CN VIII and then to the brain. The bones of the skull can also transmit sound directly to the inner ear (bone conduction).

We measure sound waves in 2 ways, intensity or strength and frequency or pitch. We measure the intensity in terms of decibels (dB). The lowest hearing decibel level is 0 dB, which is nearly total silence and the softest sound that we can hear. Normal speech is around 40 to 65 dB; a soft whisper is 20 dB. Sounds above 90 dB can lead to hearing damage if people are exposed to them every day or all the time. Hearing becomes uncomfortable if the sound pressure level is above 110 dB.

Frequency is the measurement of the number of sound vibrations in 1 second. We measure it in hertz (Hz). The higher the frequency is, the higher the pitch. Normally, a child and a young adult can hear frequencies from about 16 to 20,000 Hz, but hearing is most sensitive between 500 and 4000 Hz. This is similar to normal speech frequencies.

Gerontologic Considerations: Effects of Aging on Auditory System

Presbycusis, or hearing loss due to aging, is the third most common health issue in older adults, after arthritis and heart disease.[1] Calcification of the ossicles diminishes sound transmission. **Tinnitus**, or ringing in the ears, may accompany the hearing loss that results from the aging process. Cerumen glands atrophy, causing cerumen (earwax) to be much drier. The hair in the ear becomes thicker and coarser, trapping the hard, dry earwax in the canal. Accumulation of dry earwax in the external canal can interfere with the transmission of sound. Atrophy of vestibular structures in the inner ear causes a decline in balance, slowing of motor responses, and musculoskeletal limitations.

Age-related changes in the auditory system and differences in assessment findings are outlined in Table 23.1.

Case Study

Patient Introduction

(© iStock.com/EyeMark.)

R.S. is a 57-year-old woman who comes to the emergency department with extreme dizziness. R.S. states that she is so dizzy she "can't do anything but lie down." She reports feeling like her right ear is "plugged" and is having ringing in that ear.

Discussion Questions

1. What are the possible causes of R.M.'s hearing and balance problems?
2. Is her condition stable or an emergency?
3. What assessment questions will you ask?

You will learn more about R.S. and her condition as you read this chapter.

Answers available at http://evolve.elsevier.com/Lewis/medsurg

ASSESSMENT OF AUDITORY SYSTEM

Assessment of the auditory system should include assessment of hearing and equilibrium because the auditory and *vestibular* (balance) systems are closely related. It is often hard to separate symptoms related to these 2 systems. Help the patient describe symptoms and problems to determine the source of the problems. Health history questions to ask a patient with an auditory problem are listed in Table 23.2.

TABLE 23.1 GERONTOLOGIC ASSESSMENT DIFFERENCES

Auditory System

Changes	Differences in Assessment Findings
External Ear	
Increased hair growth	Visible hair, especially in men
Loss of elasticity in cartilage	Collapsed ear canal
Thicker, drier earwax	Impacted earwax, potential hearing loss
Middle Ear	
Atrophy of TM	Conductive hearing loss
Inner Ear	
Hair cell degeneration, neuron degeneration in auditory nerve and central pathways, reduced blood supply to cochlea, calcification of ossicles	Presbycusis, diminished sensitivity to high-pitched sounds, impaired speech reception, tinnitus
Less effective vestibular apparatus in semicircular canals	Alterations in balance and body orientation
Brain	
Decline in ability to filter out unwanted and unnecessary sound	Difficulty hearing in a noisy environment, heightened sensitivity to loud sounds

TABLE 23.2 HEALTH HISTORY

Auditory System

Health Perception–Health Management

Hearing

- Have you had a change in your hearing?[a] If yes, how does this change affect your daily life?
- Do you use any devices to improve your hearing, such as a hearing aid, special volume control, or headphones?[a]
- How do you protect your hearing?
- Do you have any allergies that result in ear problems?[a]

Equilibrium

- When did the dizziness or spinning sensation first occur?
- Does this sensation occur when you first stand up, when you are lying down, or both?
- Have you ever fallen because of the dizziness?[a]
- Can you drive or walk alone? If no, elaborate.
- Are there any times of the day when your symptoms are worse?[a]

Tinnitus

- How long have you had ringing in your ears? Has it changed?[a] Describe the ringing (e.g., buzzing, ringing, roaring). Do you also have a feeling of fullness or pressure?[a]
- When does it bother you the most?
- What things have you tried that help or have not helped?
- What medications are you taking?

Nutritional-Metabolic

- Do you notice any change in symptoms with changes in diet?[a]
- Does your ear problem cause nausea that interferes with your food intake?[a]
- Does chewing or swallowing cause you any ear discomfort?[a]

Elimination

- Does straining during a bowel movement cause ear pain?[a]

Activity-Exercise

- Do you need help with certain activities, like lifting, bending, climbing stairs, driving, or speaking because of symptoms?[a]

Sleep-Rest

- Is your sleep disturbed by noises or ringing in the ears or by a sensation of spinning?[a]

Cognitive-Perceptual

- Do you have ear pain?[a] What relieves the pain? What makes it worse? Does the pain affect your hearing or balance?
- Have you noticed any problem with communicating or understanding what people are saying?[a]

Self-Perception–Self-Concept

- Have changes in your hearing affected how you feel about yourself or your feeling of independence?[a]

Role-Relationship

- What effect has your ear problem had on your work, family, or social life?
- Do you notice any effects of your ear problems on your life?[a]

Sexuality-Reproductive

- Has your ear problem caused a change in your sex life?[a]

Coping–Stress Tolerance

- Do you consider your ear problem a source of stress?[a]
- How do you cope when you are having symptoms?

Value-Belief

- Do you have a conflict between what your HCP would like you to do and what you believe you should do?

[a]If yes, describe.

Problems with balance may manifest as vertigo or nystagmus. **Vertigo** is a sense that the person or objects around the person are moving or spinning. It is usually stimulated by head movement. *Dizziness* is a sensation of being off-balance that occurs when standing or walking. **Nystagmus** is an abnormal eye movement that may be seen as a twitching of the eyeball or described by the patient as a blurring of vision with head or eye movement.

At first, try to determine symptoms that are related to balance and separate them from those related to hearing loss or tinnitus. The symptoms can be combined later in the assessment to help make a diagnosis and care plan for the patient.

Subjective Data

Important Health Information

Many ear problems result from childhood illnesses or problems of adjacent organs. This makes a careful assessment of past health problems important. Ask the patient about previous ear problems, especially during childhood. Note the (1) frequency of acute middle ear infections (otitis media); (2) surgeries (e.g., myringotomy, tonsillectomy, tympanoplasty); (3) TM perforations; (4) drainage; and (5) history of mumps, measles, or scarlet fever. Assess for systemic conditions, including diabetes, rheumatoid arthritis, and multiple sclerosis, that are associated with hearing loss.[2] Note head injury because it may result in hearing loss. Information about food and environment allergies is important because they can cause edema of the eustachian tube and prevent aeration of the middle ear.

Record symptoms such as vertigo, tinnitus, and hearing loss in the patient's words. Ask for specific details of the sensations and situations that cause them or make them worse. Details about family members with hearing loss and type of hearing loss is important. Some congenital hearing loss is hereditary. The age of onset of presbycusis follows a familial pattern. Record the use of and satisfaction with a hearing aid. Note any problems with impacted earwax.

Medications

Obtain information about present or past use of ototoxic drugs. More than 200 drugs that are ototoxic and have the potential to cause hearing loss, tinnitus, and vertigo. These include aspirin, some antibiotics (aminoglycosides, erythromycin, vancomycin), loop diuretics, nonsteroidal antiinflammatory drugs (NSAIDs), antimalarial agents, and certain chemotherapy drugs (e.g., bleomycin, cyclophosphamide, cisplatin). Ask about hearing and balance problems, in patients receiving these drugs. For many, the hearing loss may be reversible if treatment is stopped. Chemicals used in industry (e.g., toluene, carbon disulfide, mercury) may damage the inner ear.

Functional Health Patterns

Hearing and balance problems can affect all aspects of a person's life. To assess the impact of hearing loss, ask health history questions based on a functional health patterns approach (Table 23.2).

Health perception–health management pattern. Note the onset of hearing loss, whether sudden or gradual, and who noted the onset (e.g., patient, family, significant others). Gradual hearing losses are often noted by those who communicate with the patient. The patient often notes sudden losses and those worsened by other problems.

Assess the patient for personal measures used to preserve hearing. The use of protective ear covers or earplugs is good practice for people in high-noise environments. Note if the patient is a swimmer and the frequency and duration of swimming and use of ear protection. Knowing the type of water (pool, lake, ocean) in which the swimming takes place helps identify contact with contaminated water. Assess for the placement of any item in the ear which can cause trauma to the canal and TM.

Nutritional-metabolic pattern. Ask the patient about any ear pain (otalgia) or discomfort when chewing or swallowing. These symptoms may occur with middle ear problems. Note changes in symptoms with food intake. Alcohol, sodium, and diet supplements affect the amount of endolymph in the inner ear system. Patients with Ménière disease may notice some symptom improvement with alcohol restriction and a low-sodium diet.

Clenching or grinding of the teeth helps distinguish problems of the ear from referred pain of the temporomandibular joint (TMJ). Ask about dental problems and dentures. Referred pain from the teeth, gums, or throat can cause ear pain.

Elimination pattern. Elimination patterns are of interest in the patient with perilymph fistula and after surgery. Frequent constipation or straining with bowel or bladder elimination may interfere with healing or repair of a perilymph fistula. After middle ear surgery (stapedectomy), the patient needs to prevent increased intracranial (and consequent inner ear) pressure from straining during bowel movements. Stool softeners may be needed after surgery for the patient who reports chronic problems with constipation.

Activity-exercise pattern. A review of the patient's activity-exercise pattern is essential when assessing for balance problems. Ask about the onset, duration, and frequency of symptoms. Identify activities that relieve or worsen symptoms and how they relate to the time of the day. For example, patients with Ménière disease are less able to compensate as the day progresses.

Sleep-rest pattern. Ask the patient with chronic tinnitus about sleep problems. Find out if they have tried anything to minimize the tinnitus, such as having a fan on or using white noise devices. Assess for snoring. It can be caused by swelling or hypertrophy of tissue in the nasopharynx. This excess tissue can impair eustachian tube function and cause the sensation of ear fullness or pain.

Cognitive-perceptual pattern. Pain occurs with some ear problems, especially those involving the middle ear and auditory canal. If pain is present, ask the patient to describe the pain, any drainage present *(otorrhea),* history of teeth grinding, and treatments used for relief. Note the effect on the pain level when you move the auricle and palpate the tragus.

Note the patient's ability to pay attention and follow directions. Problems with these tasks may be an early sign of hearing loss. The patient may not recognize a gradual hearing loss. Ask caregivers if they have noted any change in the patient's hearing.

Self-perception–self-concept pattern. Ask the patient to describe how the ear problem has affected their personal life and feelings about themselves. Hearing loss and chronic vertigo are particularly distressing for the patient. Hearing loss can result in embarrassing social situations that affect the patient's self-concept. People may think a person with chronic vertigo is intoxicated. Question the patient gently about such situations. Clarify the symptom history with the patient and consider an evaluation with a hearing specialist.

Role-relationship pattern. Ask the patient about the effect that an ear problem or vertigo has had on family life, work responsibilities, and social relationships. Hearing loss can result in strained relationships and misunderstandings.

Ask about employment or contact with environments that have excessive noise levels, such as work with jet engines and machinery and amplified music. Document the use of preventive devices worn in noisy environments. Many jobs rely on the ability to hear accurately and respond appropriately. If hearing loss is present, assess the effect this has on the patient's job. The unpredictability of vertigo attacks can have devastating effects on all aspects of life. Ordinary activities which require balance, such as driving, cooking, and work, all have an element of danger.

Sexuality-reproductive pattern. Determine whether hearing loss or vertigo has interfered with having a satisfactory sex life. Although intimacy does not depend on the ability to hear, hearing loss can interfere with establishing or maintaining a relationship.

Coping–stress tolerance pattern. Ask about coping style, stress management strategies, and available support. If the patient seems unable to manage the situation, outside intervention may be needed. Denial is a common response to a hearing problem and should be assessed.

Value-belief pattern. Ask the patient about any conflicts produced by the problem or treatment related to values or beliefs. Make every effort to resolve the problem so that the patient does not have added stress. Ask about the use of home remedies such as hot oil in the ear.

Objective Data

Physical Assessment

During the interview to obtain a health history, obtain objective data about the patient's ability to hear. Look for cues that a patient cannot hear (Table 23.3). Record these observations. This is important because the patient is often unaware of hearing loss

Case Study

Subjective Data

(© iStock.com/ EyeMark.)

A focused subjective assessment of R.S. revealed the following information:

- ***History:*** Mild osteoarthritis. Hysterectomy 5 years ago. Last saw HCP 6 months ago.
- ***Medications:*** Multivitamin 1 PO daily, ASA 81 mg PO daily, ibuprofen 200 mg PO every 6 hours as needed.
- ***Health Perception–Health Management:*** She says last night she felt like she had the start of a cold. The symptoms were present this morning when she woke up. She tried to clear her ear by blowing her nose and could not use that ear to talk on the phone. Had excellent hearing until today. Denies any syncope. Does not have allergies.
- ***Nutritional-Metabolic:*** States she is nauseous but has not vomited. Has only had a few sips of water since the symptoms started.
- ***Activity-Exercise:*** Dizziness worse when standing. It is still present when lying down but is less. Her husband drove her to the emergency room since she was unable to drive. Normally walks 1–2 miles 5 times a week and attends yoga class 2 times a week.
- ***Cognitive-Perceptual:*** Denies any ear pain, headache.
- ***Coping–Stress Tolerance:*** Concerned she is having a stroke.

Discussion Questions

1. Which subjective assessment findings concern you most?
2. Based on the subjective assessment findings, what should you include in the physical assessment? For what would you be looking?

You will learn more about the physical assessment of the auditory system in the next section.

Answers available at http://evolve.elsevier.com/Lewis/medsurg.

or does not admit to changes in hearing until moderate losses have occurred.

A normal assessment of the auditory system is shown in Table 23.4. Age-related changes of the auditory system and differences in assessment findings are found in Table 23.1.

A *focused assessment* is used to evaluate the status of previously identified auditory problems and monitor for signs of new problems. A focused assessment of the auditory system is shown in Box 23.1.

External ear. Inspect and palpate the external ear before assessing the external canal and TM. Observe the auricle, preauricular area, and mastoid area for symmetry, color of skin, swelling, redness, and lesions. Then palpate the auricle and mastoid areas for tenderness and nodules. Grasping the auricle or pressing on the tragus may cause pain, especially if the external ear or canal is inflamed.

External auditory canal and tympanic membrane. Before inserting an otoscope, inspect the canal opening for patency, palpate the tragus, and gently move the auricle to check for discomfort. Select a speculum slightly smaller than the size of the ear canal. Tip the patient's head to the opposite shoulder. Grasp the top of the auricle and gently pull up and backward to straighten the canal. Hold the otoscope while stabilizing it with your fingers on the patient's cheek, and then insert it slowly. A tight seal of the speculum is essential during this step of the assessment. Observe the canal for size and shape and the color, amount, and type of earwax. Be careful when clearing the canal of earwax. Damage can occur to the middle ear if the TM is perforated.

Inspect the TM for color, fluid behind the membrane, landmarks, contour, and intactness (Fig. 23.2). The TM is normally pearl gray, white, or pink; shiny; and translucent. The handle (manubrium) of the malleus and its short process (umbo) should be visible through the membrane. The position and dome (concave) shape of the TM cause the light from the otoscope to reflect in a cone shape with crisp edges. If the TM is bulging or retracted, the edges of the light reflex will be fuzzy (diffuse) and may spread over the TM. A pneumatic otoscope creates negative pressure to pull at the TM. It is helpful in confirming TM retraction or fluid behind the

TABLE 23.3 Signs of Possible Hearing Loss

- Does not respond to or understand oral communication
- Has excessively loud or soft speech
- Answers questions inappropriately
- Tilts head, leans forward when listening
- Constantly needs to clarify conversation
- States other people mumble all the time
- Increases the volume of radio or TV
- Difficulty hearing over the phone

TABLE 23.4 Normal Physical Assessment of Auditory System

- Ears symmetric in location and shape
- Auricles and tragus nontender, without lesions
- Canal clear, TM intact, landmarks and light reflex intact
- Able to hear low whisper at 30 cm.
- Weber test results, no lateralization. Rinne test results: Air conduction > Bone conduction

BOX 23.1 FOCUSED ASSESSMENT

Auditory System

Use this checklist to make sure the key assessment steps have been done.

Subjective

Ask the patient about any of the following and note responses.

Changes in hearing	Y	N
Ear pain	Y	N
Ear drainage	Y	N
Tinnitus	Y	N

Objective: Physical Assessment

Inspect

Alignment and position of ears on head	✓
Size, shape, symmetry, color, and skin intactness	✓
External auditory meatus for discharge or lesions	✓

Assess

Hearing based on ability to respond to conversation, respond to a whisper, or hear a ticking watch	✓

Case Study
Objective Data: Physical Assessment

(© iStock.com/ EyeMark.)

Physical assessment findings of R.S. were as follows:
- Neurologic and otoscopic assessments normal
- Unable to hear whisper on the right at 30 cm
- Vision normal. PERRLA (pupils equal, round, and reactive to light and accommodation) without nystagmus
- Gait unsteady. No motor weakness
- Skin pale, warm, and dry
- Heart rate 84 beats/min, temperature 97.4°F (36.3°C)

Discussion Questions
1. What physical assessment findings concern you most?
2. What diagnostic studies might you expect to be ordered?

As you continue to read this chapter, consider diagnostic studies that you would expect being performed for R.S.

Answers available at http://evolve.elsevier.com/Lewis/medsurg.

TM. You cannot examine the middle and inner ear with the otoscope.

Table 23.5 summarizes assessment abnormalities of the auditory system.

DIAGNOSTIC STUDIES OF AUDITORY SYSTEM

Table 23.6 describes common diagnostic studies used to assess the auditory system. Several tests are available to determine the cause of certain hearing losses. CT scan and MRI can detect lesions such as a tumor of the auditory nerve.

Audiometry

Audiometry is used as a screening test for hearing acuity and as a diagnostic test to determine the degree and type of hearing loss. The most common test performed by the audiologist is pure-tone audiometry. The audiometer produces pure tones at varying intensities to which the patient can respond. Hearing loss can affect certain sound frequencies. The specific pattern produced on the audiogram by these losses can help diagnose the type of hearing loss. Threshold refers to the signal level at which pure tones are detected (pure-tone thresholds) or the signal level at which the patient correctly hears 50% of the signals (speech detection thresholds).

Case Study
Objective Data: Diagnostic Studies

(© iStock.com/ EyeMark.)

The Weber's test shows lateralization to the left. An audiogram confirms low-frequency, sensorineural hearing loss with normal speech discrimination. An MRI of the head is normal.

Discussion Questions
1. Are these the diagnostic studies that you expected to be ordered?
2. Which diagnostic study results are of most concern to you?

Answers available at http://evolve.elsevier.com/Lewis/medsurg.

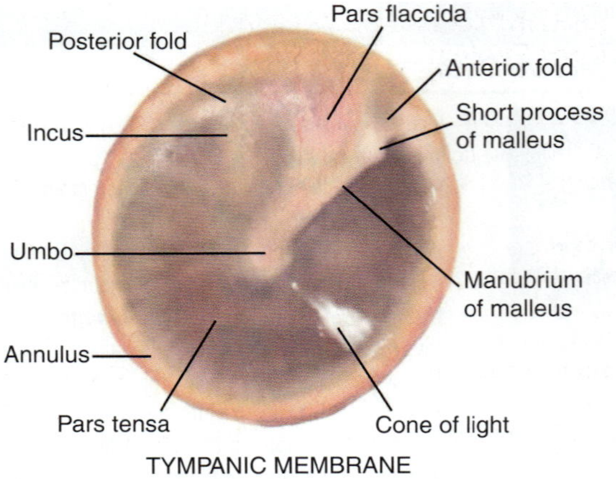

Fig. 23.2 Normal tympanic membrane. (From Jarvis C: *Physical examination and health assessment,* ed 7, St Louis, 2015, Elsevier.)

EXTERNAL EAR AND CANAL PROBLEMS

EXTERNAL OTITIS

The skin of the external ear and canal is subject to the same problems as skin anywhere on the body. **External otitis** involves inflammation or infection of the epithelium of the auricle and ear canal. Swimming may change the flora of the external canal because of chemicals and contaminated water. This can result in an infection often referred to as "swimmer's ear." Trauma from picking the ear or using sharp objects (e.g., hairpins) often causes the initial break in the skin. Piercing of cartilage in the upper part of the auricle increases the risk for infection.

The warm, dark environment of the ear canal provides a good growth medium for microorganisms. Bacteria or fungal infection may cause external otitis. *Staphylococcus aureus* is the most common bacterial cause. Fungi, especially *Candida albicans* and *Aspergillus,* thrive in the warm, moist climate.

Malignant external otitis is a serious infection caused by *P. aeruginosa.* It occurs mainly in older patients with diabetes. The infection, which can spread from the external ear to the parotid gland and temporal bone (osteomyelitis), is usually treated with antibiotics.

Ear pain *(otalgia)* is an early sign of external otitis. Even in mild cases, the patient may have significant pain with chewing, moving the auricle, or pressing on the tragus. Swelling of the ear canal can muffle hearing. There may be serosanguineous (blood-tinged) or purulent (white to thick green) drainage. Fever occurs when the infection spreads to surrounding tissue.

❖ NURSING AND INTERPROFESSIONAL MANAGEMENT: EXTERNAL OTITIS

External otitis is diagnosed by otoscopic examination of the ear canal. Take care to avoid pain when pulling on the pinna to straighten out the canal or when inserting the otoscope speculum. The TM may be hard to see due to swelling in the canal. Culture and sensitivity studies of the drainage may be done. Moist heat, mild analgesics, and topical anesthetic drops usually control the pain. Topical treatments may include

TABLE 23.5 ASSESSMENT ABNORMALITIES

Auditory System

Finding	Description	Possible Cause and Significance
External Ear and Canal		
Discharge	Infection of external ear, usually painful	Swimmer's ear, infection of external ear. Possibly caused by ruptured TM and otitis media
Exostosis	Bony growth extending into canal causing narrowing of canal	May interfere with seeing TM. Usually asymptomatic
Impacted earwax	Wax that was not normally excreted from the ear. Cannot see TM	Decreased hearing possible, pain, sensation of fullness in auditory canal, removal necessary before otoscopic examination
Scaling or lesions	Change in usual appearance of skin	Seborrheic dermatitis, actinic keratosis, basal or squamous cell carcinoma
Sebaceous cyst behind ear	Usually within skin, may see a black dot (opening to sebaceous gland)	Removal or incision and drainage if painful
Swelling of pinna, pain	Infection of glands of skin, hematoma caused by trauma	Aspiration (for hematoma)
Tophi	Hard nodules in the helix or antihelix consisting of uric acid crystals	Occur with gout, metabolic disorders. Further diagnosis needed
Tympanic Membrane (TM)		
Hairline fluid level, yellow-amber bubbles above fluid level	Caused by transudate of blood and serum, meniscus of fluid producing hairline appearance	Serous otitis media
Lack of landmarks, bulging red or blue TM (Fig. 23.3)	Fluid-filled middle ear, pus, blood	Acute otitis media, perforation
Perforated TM	Previous TM perforations that have failed to heal. Thin, transparent layer of epithelium surrounding TM	Chronic otitis media, mastoiditis, drainage
Recruitment	Perception that sounds are getting too loud too fast	Sensorineural hearing loss. Hearing aid hard to use
Retracted TM	Appearance of shorter, more horizontal malleus. Absent or bent cone of light	Vacuum in middle ear, blockage of eustachian tube, negative pressure in middle ear

TABLE 23.6 Diagnostic Studies

Auditory System

Study	Description, Purpose, and Considerations
Auditory	
Audiometry	*Pure-tone audiometry* quantifies hearing loss. Sounds are presented through earphones in soundproof room. Patient responds when sound is heard. Response is recorded on an audiogram. Purpose is to determine patient's hearing range in terms of decibels (dB) and Hertz (Hz) for diagnosing hearing loss. Tinnitus can cause inconsistent results. *Speech audiometry* includes speech reception threshold (measure of intensity at which speech is recognized) and word recognition score (ability to discriminate among various speech sounds).
Auditory brainstem response (ABR)	Measures electrical peaks along auditory pathway of inner ear to brain. Provides information related to acoustic neuromas, brainstem problems, and stroke.
Auditory evoked potential (AEP)	Similar to an electroencephalogram (see Chapter 60 and Table 60.10). Electrodes are placed typically at vertex, mastoid process, and forehead. A computer is used to isolate auditory from other electrical activity of brain. Patient should avoid loud noises for 24 hr before the test.
Electrocochleography	Test records electrical activity in cochlea and auditory nerve. Electrode placed on or through the TM. Used to assess and monitor patients with dizziness.
Tympanometry	Used to check middle ear and mobility of TM. A probe is placed snugly into external ear canal, and positive and negative pressures are applied. Measurements are made of TM movement.
Tuning Fork Tests	
Rinne test	Compares hearing by bone conduction (BC) and air conduction (AC). Stem of vibrating tuning fork held against mastoid bone (for BC of sound) and time noted. When the sound is no longer perceived behind the ear (BC of sound), time is noted once again and the still-vibrating fork is moved close to the pinna (AC of sound). Have the patient report when the sound next to the ear canal (AC) is no longer heard and note time. Normally, sound is heard twice as long in front of the ear as it is on the bone. With conductive hearing loss, the relationship is reversed; BC is longer than AC. With sensorineural hearing loss, both AC and BC are reduced, but AC is longer.
Weber test	Stem of vibrating tuning fork is placed on midline of skull or forehead. Patient asked to indicate where the sound is heard best. In normal auditory function, the patient perceives a midline tone, and the sound is heard equally in both ears. If a patient has conductive hearing loss in 1 ear, the sound will be heard louder (lateralizes) in that ear. If sensorineural loss is present, the sound is louder (lateralizes) in the normal (unaffected) ear.

Continued

TABLE 23.6 Diagnostic Studies—cont'd

Auditory System

Study	Description, Purpose, and Considerations
Vestibular Tests	
Electronystagmography (ENG)	Used to diagnose diseases of vestibular system such as dizziness and balance disorders. Electrodes are placed near patient's eyes. Eye movement (nystagmus) is recorded on graph during specific eye movements and when ear is irrigated. Caloric test may be part of testing to measure responses to warm and cold water circulated into the ear canal. Have patient eat a light meal before test to avoid nausea. Observe patient for vomiting. Ensure patient safety.
Posturography	Balance test that can isolate one semicircular canal from others to determine site of lesion. Done in a boxlike device in which floor moves in response to a correction in balance by patient. Tell patient that test may be uncomfortable. Can be stopped at any time at patient's request.
Rotary chair testing	Evaluates peripheral vestibular system. Patient is seated in a chair driven by a motor under computer control. Test is usually done in the dark. Tell patient to eat light meal before test to avoid nausea. Observe patient for vomiting. Ensure patient safety.

antibiotics for infection and corticosteroids for inflammation. If the surrounding tissue is involved, systemic antibiotics are used. Improvement should occur in 48 hours. The patient needs to adhere to the prescribed therapy for 7 to 14 days for complete resolution (see Table 15.3).

Wash hands before and after applying eardrops (otic drops). The drops should be at room temperature. Cold drops can cause vertigo due to stimulation of the semicircular canals. Heated drops can burn the TM. The tip of the dropper should not touch the ear during application to prevent contamination of the entire bottles. Position the ear so that the drops can run into the canal. The patient should stay in this position for 2 minutes to allow the drops to spread. Sometimes you can place the drops onto a wick of cotton, then place the wick in the canal. Tell the patient not to push the cotton farther into the ear. Careful handling and disposal of material saturated with drainage are important. Teach the patient ways to reduce the risk for external otitis (Table 23.7).

TABLE 23.7 PATIENT & CAREGIVER TEACHING

Preventing External Otitis

Include the following instructions when teaching the patient and caregiver:

1. Do not put anything in your ear canal unless requested by your HCP.
2. Report itching if it becomes a problem.
3. Earwax is normal.
   - It lubricates and protects the canal.
   - Report chronic excess earwax if it impairs your hearing.
4. Keep your ears as dry as possible.
   - Use earplugs if you are prone to swimmer's ear.
   - Turn your head to each side for 30 seconds at a time to help water run out of the ears.
   - Do not dry with cotton-tipped applicators.
   - A hair dryer set to low and held at least 6 inches from the ear can speed water evaporation.

CERUMEN AND FOREIGN BODIES IN EXTERNAL EAR CANAL

The ear canal may be obstructed by cerumen (earwax) or a foreign object. Impacted earwax can cause discomfort and decreased hearing. Other symptoms include tinnitus and vertigo. Remove an impaction by irrigating the canal with body-temperature solutions to soften the earwax. Special syringes may be used. These vary from a simple bulb syringe to special irrigating equipment. Place the patient in a sitting position with an emesis basin under the ear. Pull the auricle up and back, and direct the flow of solution above or below the impaction. Do not completely occlude the ear canal with the syringe tip. If irrigation does not remove the wax, use mild lubricant drops to soften the earwax. The HCP may need to remove severe impactions.

Attempts to remove a foreign object from the ear may result in pushing it farther into the canal. Vegetable matter in the ear tends to swell. This can create a secondary inflammation, making removal more difficult. Mineral oil or lidocaine drops can be used to kill an insect before removal under microscope guidance. The HCP should remove impacted objects.

Cleanse ears with a washcloth and finger. Avoid using cotton-tipped applicators. Penetration of the middle ear by a cotton-tipped applicator can cause serious injury to the TM and ossicles. Their use can also cause earwax to become impacted against the TM and impair hearing.

TRAUMA

Trauma to the external ear can cause injury to the subcutaneous tissue and result in a hematoma. If a hematoma is not aspirated, inflammation of the membranes of the ear cartilage (perichondritis) can result. Blows to the ear can cause conductive hearing loss if the ossicles in the middle ear are damaged or the TM is perforated. Head trauma that injures the temporal lobe of the cerebral cortex can impair the ability to understand the meaning of sounds.

MALIGNANCY OF EXTERNAL EAR

Skin cancers are the only common cancers of the ear. Precancerous actinic keratoses, rough sandpaper-like lesions on the upper border of the auricle, are associated with chronic sun exposure. They are often treated with liquid nitrogen. Cancers in the external ear canal include basal cell carcinoma in the pinna and squamous cell carcinoma in the ear canal. If left untreated,

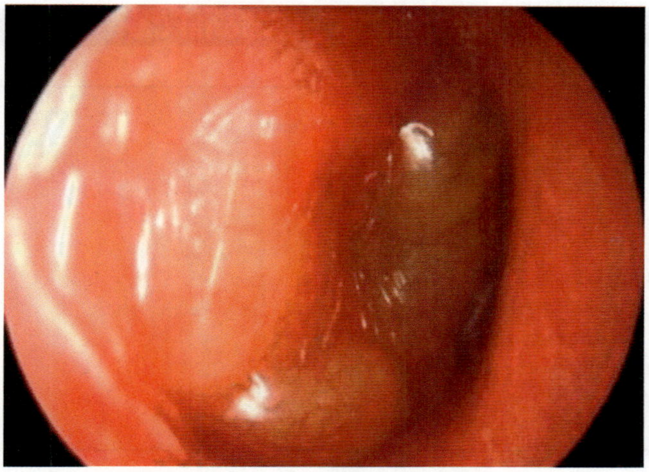

Fig. 23.3 Acute otitis media. (From Bourayou R, et al: Otitis, sinusitis, and related conditions. In Cohen J, et al, editors: *Infectious disease*, ed 4, St Louis, 2017, Mosby.)

they can invade underlying tissue. Teach the patient about the dangers of sun exposure and the importance of using hats and sunscreen when outdoors. See Chapter 25 for more about skin cancer.

MIDDLE EAR AND MASTOID PROBLEMS

OTITIS MEDIA

Acute Otitis Media

Acute otitis media is an infection of the TM, ossicles, and space of the middle ear. Swelling of the auditory tube from colds or allergies can trap bacteria, causing a middle ear infection. Pressure from the inflammation pushes on the TM, causing it to become red, bulging, and painful (Fig. 23.3). Acute otitis media is usually a childhood disease. In children, the auditory tube that normally drains fluid and mucus from the middle ear is shorter and narrower, and its position is flatter than in adults. Infection can be due to viruses or bacteria. Pain, fever, malaise, drainage, and reduced hearing are signs and symptoms of infection.

Oral antibiotics and eardrops are used if an infection is present (see Table 15.3). Surgery is reserved for the patient who does not respond to medical treatment. A *myringotomy* involves an incision in the TM to release the increased pressure and exudate from the middle ear. A tympanostomy tube may be placed short- or long-term for ventilation of the ear. Prompt treatment of acute otitis media can help prevent spontaneous perforation of the TM. If allergies are a causative factor, the patient may receive antihistamines and a nasal corticosteroid spray.

Otitis Media With Effusion

Otitis media with effusion is an inflammation of the middle ear with a collection of fluid in the middle ear space. The fluid may be thin, mucoid, or purulent. If the auditory tube does not open and allow equalization of atmospheric pressure, negative pressure within the middle ear pulls fluid from surrounding tissues. This problem often follows upper respiratory tract or chronic sinus infections, barotrauma (caused by pressure change), or otitis media.

Symptoms include a feeling of fullness of the ear, a "plugged" feeling or popping, and decreased hearing. The patient does not have pain, fever, or discharge from the ear. It is common to have otitis media with effusion for weeks to months after an episode of acute otitis media. It usually resolves without treatment but may recur.

Chronic Otitis Media and Mastoiditis

Repeated attacks of otitis media may lead to chronic otitis media, especially in adults who have a history of recurrent otitis media in childhood. Because the mucous membrane of the middle ear is continuous with the air cells of the mastoid bone, both can be involved in the chronic infectious process.

In *chronic otitis media* there is purulent exudate and inflammation that can involve the ossicles, auditory tube, and mastoid bone. It is often painless. Hearing loss, nausea, and episodes of dizziness can occur. Hearing loss is a complication from inflammatory destruction of the ossicles, TM perforation, or accumulation of fluid in the middle ear space. A mass of epithelial cells and cholesterol in the middle ear *(cholesteatoma)* may develop. As the cholesteatoma enlarges it can destroy the adjacent bones. Unless removed surgically, it can cause extensive damage to the ossicles and impair hearing.

Otoscopic examination of the TM may reveal changes in color and mobility or a perforation. Culture and sensitivity tests of the drainage are necessary to identify the organisms involved so the patient may receive the right antibiotic therapy. The audiogram may show a hearing loss as great as 50 to 60 dB if the ossicles are damaged or separated. Sinus x-rays, MRI, or a CT scan of the temporal bone can assess for bone destruction and the presence of a mass.

❖ NURSING AND INTERPROFESSIONAL MANAGEMENT: CHRONIC OTITIS MEDIA

The goals of treatment are to clear the middle ear of infection, repair any perforations, and preserve hearing (Table 23.8). Otic and systemic (oral, IV) antibiotic therapy is started based on the culture and sensitivity results. In many cases of chronic otitis media, antibiotic resistance is present. The patient may need to have frequent evacuation of drainage and debris in an outpatient setting.

Often chronic TM perforations do not heal with conservative treatment, and surgery is necessary. *Tympanoplasty (myringoplasty)* involves reconstruction of the TM and/or the ossicles. A *mastoidectomy* is often done with a tympanoplasty to remove infected portions of the mastoid bone. Removal of tissue stops at the middle ear structures that appear capable of conducting sound. Sudden pressure changes in the ear and postoperative infections can disrupt healing or cause facial nerve paralysis.

Expect impaired hearing during the postoperative period if there is packing in the ear. A cotton ball dressing is used if an incision was made through the external auditory canal. Teach the patient to change the cotton packing as needed (Table 23.9). If a postauricular (behind the ear) incision was used and a drain is in place, place a dressing over that area. Then, place a soft outer dressing over the top of that dressing. This will prevent putting pressure on the auricle. Monitor the tightness of the

TABLE 23.8 Interprofessional Care

Chronic Otitis Media

Diagnostic Assessment
- History and physical assessment
- Otoscopic examination
- Culture and sensitivity of middle ear drainage
- Audiometry
- Imaging: Mastoid x-ray, CT scan, MRI

Management
- Ear irrigations
- Otic, oral, or IV antibiotics (see Table 15.3)
- Analgesics
- Antiemetics (see Table 46.1)
- Surgery
  - Tympanoplasty
  - Mastoidectomy

TABLE 23.9 PATIENT & CAREGIVER TEACHING

After Ear Surgery

Include the following information in the teaching plan for the patient and caregiver after ear surgery:
1. Sleep on your back or the unoperated ear for 1 week.
2. Avoid air travel and sun exposure for 6 weeks.
3. If you need to cough or sneeze, keep your mouth open.
4. Blow your nose gently, without blocking either nostril.
5. Do not shampoo your hair for 5 days. Wear a shower cap when bathing.
6. No swimming. Keep your ear dry for 6 weeks.
7. You may resume strenuous activity and contact sports in 1 month.
8. Change your ear dressing daily as prescribed.
9. Report excess drainage or severe dizziness to the HCP.

outer dressing to prevent tissue necrosis. Assess the amount and type of drainage. Keep the suture line dry.

OTOSCLEROSIS

Otosclerosis is a hereditary autosomal dominant disease. It is the most common cause of hearing loss in young adults. Spongy bone develops from the bony labyrinth, preventing movement of the footplate of the stapes in the oval window. This reduces the transmission of vibrations to the inner ear fluids and results in conductive hearing loss. Otosclerosis is typically bilateral, though 1 ear may show faster progression of hearing loss. The patient is often unaware of the problem until the loss becomes so severe that communication is difficult.

Otoscopic examination may reveal a reddish blush of the TM (Schwartz sign). It is caused by the vascular and bony changes within the middle ear. Tuning fork tests (e.g., Rinne) and an audiogram show good hearing by bone conduction with poor hearing by air conduction (air-bone gap) (Table 23.6). Usually, a difference of at least 20 to 25 dB between air and bone conduction levels of hearing occurs with otosclerosis.

TABLE 23.10 Interprofessional Care

Otosclerosis

Diagnostic Assessment
- History and physical assessment
- Otoscopic examination
- Rinne test
- Weber test
- Audiometry
- Tympanometry

Management
- Hearing aid
- Surgery (stapedectomy, stapes prosthesis)
- Sodium fluoride drug therapy

Interprofessional care of otosclerosis is outlined in Table 23.10. Microdrill or laser surgical treatment involves opening the footplate (stapedotomy) or replacing the stapes with a metal or Teflon substitute (prosthesis). These procedures are usually done with the patient under conscious sedation. The ear with poorer hearing is repaired first. The other ear may be operated on within a year. Right after surgery the patient often reports a significant improvement in hearing in the operative ear. Because blood and fluid accumulate in the middle ear during the postoperative period, the hearing level decreases somewhat, but it improves gradually with healing.

The hearing loss from otosclerosis may be stabilized by giving oral sodium fluoride supplements. They slow bone resorption and promote the calcification of bony lesions. Amplifying sound with a hearing aid may be helpful in mild disease.

Nursing management of the patient undergoing surgery for otosclerosis is like that of the patient having a tympanoplasty. Place a cotton ball in the ear canal and cover the ear with a small dressing. The patient may have dizziness, nausea, and vomiting because of stimulation of the labyrinth during surgery. Disturbing the perilymph fluid can cause nystagmus. Teach the patient to avoid sudden movements that may bring on or worsen vertigo and actions that increase inner ear pressure. These include coughing, sneezing, lifting, bending, and straining during bowel movements. The patient with nausea and vomiting often needs antiemetic drugs (see Table 46.1).

INNER EAR PROBLEMS

Three manifestations that indicate disease of the inner ear are vertigo, sensorineural hearing loss, and tinnitus. Symptoms of vertigo arise from the vestibular labyrinth, while hearing loss and tinnitus arise from the auditory labyrinth. There is an overlap between manifestations of inner ear problems and central nervous system (CNS) disorders.

MÉNIÈRE DISEASE

Ménière disease is a progressive disorder leading to an accumulation of endolymph in the membranous labyrinth. Although it usually affects only 1 ear, it can affect both. The cause is unknown.

TABLE 23.11 Interprofessional Care

Ménière Disease

Diagnostic Assessment
- History and physical assessment
- Audiometry
- Vestibular tests (including caloric test, positional test)
- Electronystagmography
- Glycerol test

Management

Acute Care

Drug Therapy
- Anticholinergics
- Antihistamines corticosteroids
- Antiemetics (see Table 46.1)
- Benzodiazepines

Surgical Therapy
- Endolymphatic sac decompression
- Endolymphatic shunt
- Labyrinthectomy
- Vestibular nerve section

Ambulatory Care
- Diuretics (see Table 36.7)
- Antihistamines
- Diet restriction of sodium, caffeine, nicotine, alcohol
- Vestibular exercises
- Vestibular rehabilitation

Genetic, immune, and environmental factors may play a role. Symptoms usually begin between 40 and 60 years of age.[3]

The excess fluid and resulting pressure lead to hearing and balance problems, including episodic vertigo, tinnitus, and ear pressure or fullness. Sensorineural hearing loss occurs gradually over time. The patient has significant disability because of sudden, severe attacks of vertigo with nausea, vomiting, and nystagmus. A sense of fullness in the ear, increasing tinnitus, and muffled hearing may precede an attack.[3] The patient may have the feeling of being pulled to the ground ("drop attacks"). Some patients report feeling like they are whirling in space. Attacks may last minutes to hours and may occur several times a year. The clinical course is highly variable.

NURSING AND INTERPROFESSIONAL MANAGEMENT: MÉNIÈRE DISEASE

Interprofessional care of Ménière disease (Table 23.11) includes diagnostic tests to rule out other causes of the symptoms, including CNS disease. Results that suggest Ménière disease include low-frequency sensorineural hearing loss on audiogram, 2 or more spontaneous episodes of vertigo, and abnormal vestibular tests.[3] A glycerol test may aid in diagnosis. The patient receives an oral dose of glycerol, followed by serial audiograms over 3 hours. Improved hearing or speech discrimination supports a diagnosis of Ménière disease. This is attributed to the osmotic effect of glycerol pulling fluid from the inner ear.

No cure exists for Ménière disease. The primary goal is to treat symptoms and reduce the number of attacks. During acute

TABLE 23.12 NURSING MANAGEMENT

Care of the Patient With Acute Ménière Disease

- Administer medications and IV hydration as ordered.
- Keep patient in a quiet, darkened room in a comfortable position.
- Have patient avoid sudden head movements and position changes.
- Teach the patient to close the eyes until vertigo stops.
- Avoid fluorescent or flickering lights and television.
- Implement fall precautions.
- Implement measures to address nausea and vomiting.
- Monitor intake and output and daily weights.
- Help the patient with ambulation as needed.

vertigo attacks, antihistamines (e.g., meclizine, diphenhydramine), anticholinergics (e.g., scopolamine), and benzodiazepines (e.g., lorazepam) can decrease vertigo and lessen nausea and vomiting.[4] Those with severe vomiting may need IV hydration and antiemetics (e.g., ondansetron). Plan nursing interventions to minimize vertigo and maintain patient safety (Table 23.12). Management between attacks may include diuretics and antihistamines. A low-salt diet with limited caffeine and alcohol intake often helps. Vestibular exercises may be recommended.

Frequent and incapacitating attacks are indications for surgical intervention. Decompression of the endolymphatic sac and shunting can reduce the pressure on the cochlear hair cells and prevent further damage and hearing loss. If relief is not achieved, a vestibular nerve section (cutting the nerve) may be done. When involvement is unilateral, surgical ablation of the labyrinth, resulting in the loss of vestibular and hearing cochlear function, is an option. Some patients with severe attacks of vertigo have shown improvement with the injection of gentamicin through the TM. This results in inner ear damage that reduces endolymph production.

Discharge teaching should emphasize ways to protect the patient from injury between attacks. Review with the patient the need to sit or lie down at the onset of any dizziness. Discuss home safety and measures to decrease fall risk. Teach the need to avoid swimming under water and being on high places, like ladders, until vertigo is under control. Encourage the patient to practice any balance therapy exercises daily.

BENIGN PAROXYSMAL POSITIONAL VERTIGO

Benign paroxysmal positional vertigo (BPPV) is a common cause of vertigo. About 50% of the cases of vertigo may be due to BPPV. In BPPV, free-floating debris ("ear rocks") in the semicircular canal causes vertigo with specific head movements, such as getting out of bed, rolling over in bed, and sitting up from lying down. The debris is composed of small crystals of calcium carbonate that come from the utricle in the inner ear. The utricle may have been injured by head trauma, infection, or degeneration from the aging process. However, for many patients, we do not know the cause.

Symptoms of BPPV include nystagmus, vertigo, light-headedness, loss of balance, and nausea. There is no hearing loss. Symptoms tend to be intermittent and may be confused with those of Ménière disease. Diagnosis is based on the results of auditory and vestibular tests.

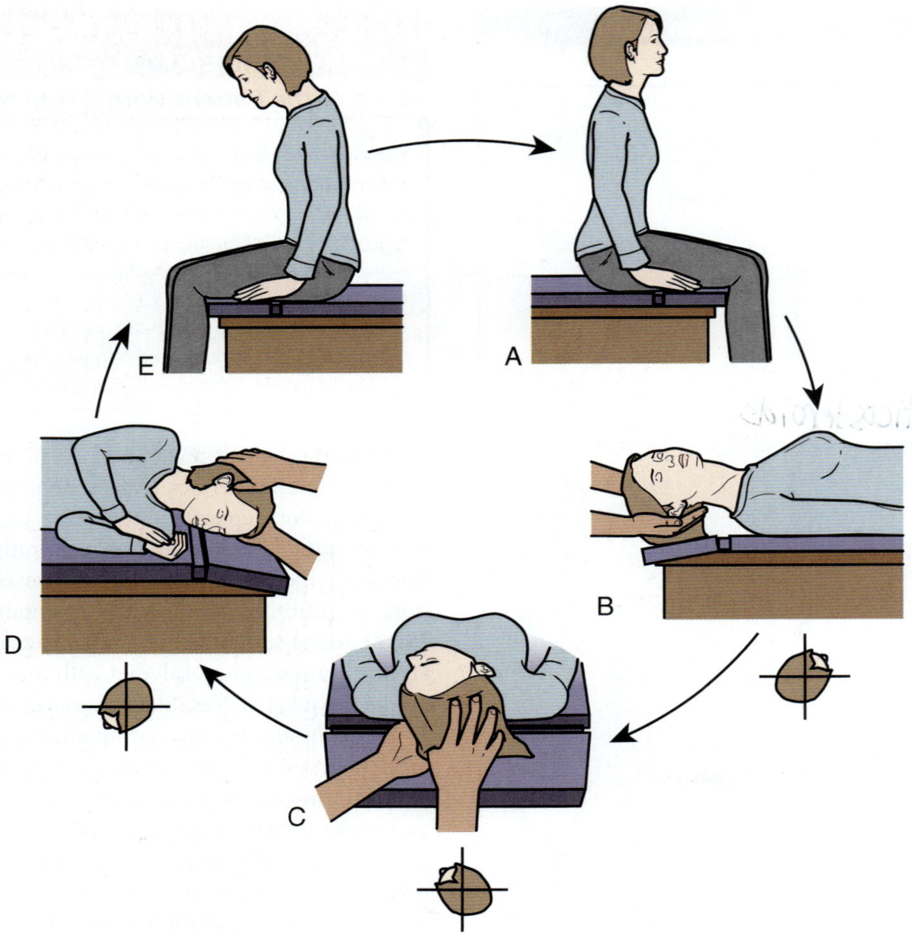

Fig. 23.4 Epley maneuver.

Although BPPV is bothersome, it is rarely serious unless a person falls. The Epley maneuver, or canalith repositioning procedure, is effective in providing symptom relief for many patients. This maneuver does not change the presence of debris but changes the location. It moves ear debris from areas in the inner ear that cause symptoms into less sensitive areas where they do not cause these problems. A trained HCP can teach the patient how to perform the maneuver (Fig. 23.4).

ACOUSTIC NEUROMA

An **acoustic neuroma** is a unilateral benign tumor that occurs where the vestibulocochlear nerve (CN VIII) enters the internal auditory canal. Early diagnosis is important because the tumor can compress the trigeminal and facial nerves and arteries within the internal auditory canal. Symptoms usually begin between 40 and 60 years of age.

Early symptoms are due to CN VIII compression and destruction. They include unilateral, progressive, sensorineural hearing loss, reduced touch sensation in the posterior ear canal, unilateral tinnitus, and mild, intermittent vertigo. Diagnostic tests include neurologic and audiometric tests and MRI.

Radiation therapy for small tumors can preserve hearing and vestibular function. Surgical treatment is effective for all tumors. Surgery on tumors larger than 3 cm can leave the patient with permanent hearing loss and facial paralysis. Stereotactic radiosurgery may slow tumor growth and preserve the facial nerve. Follow-up care after surgery is important to monitor hearing and tumor recurrence. Teach the patient to report any clear, colorless discharge from the nose. This may be cerebrospinal fluid (CSF), which increases the risk for infection.

HEARING LOSS AND DEAFNESS

Hearing disorders are a common cause of disability. Age is the strongest predictor of impaired hearing. In the United States, about 25% of those ages 65 to 74 and 50% of those 75 and older have hearing loss.[5] Causes of hearing loss are shown in Fig. 23.5.

Types of Hearing Loss

Conductive Hearing Loss

Conductive hearing loss occurs when outer or middle ear problems impair the transmission of sound waves to the inner ear. Common causes of conductive hearing loss in adults include impacted earwax, otitis media, TM perforation, otosclerosis, allergies, and benign tumors.[6]

The audiogram shows better hearing through bone than through air (air-bone gap). The patient often speaks softly because hearing their own voice (which is conducted by bone) seems loud. The patient may seem to hear better in a noisy environment. The first step is to identify and treat the cause if

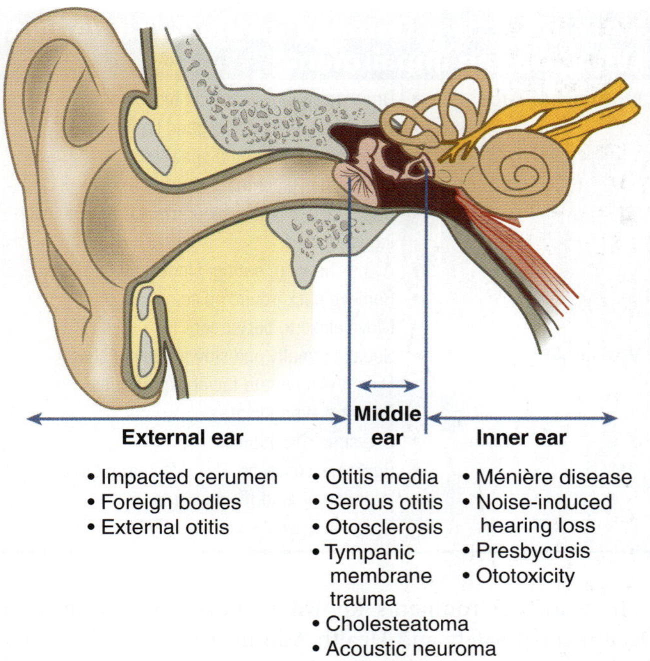

Fig. 23.5 Causes of hearing loss.

possible. If correction of the cause is not possible, a hearing aid may help if the loss is greater than 40 to 50 dB.

Sensorineural Hearing Loss

Sensorineural hearing loss is caused by damage in the inner ear or the vestibulocochlear nerve (CN VIII). Congenital and hereditary factors, noise exposure, aging (presbycusis), Ménière disease, trauma, and ototoxicity can cause sensorineural hearing loss. The main problems are the ability to hear sound but not to understand speech and the lack of understanding of the problem by others. The ability to hear high-pitched sounds (including consonants) diminishes. Sounds become muffled and hard to understand. An audiogram shows a loss in decibel levels of the 4000-Hz range and eventually the 2000-Hz range. A hearing aid may help some patients, but it only makes sounds and speech louder, not clearer.

Mixed Hearing Loss

Mixed hearing loss occurs from a combination of conductive damage in the outer or middle ear and sensorineural damage in the inner ear or auditory nerve. Conductive loss can often be treated surgically. Sensorineural loss is usually treated with hearing aids.

Central and Functional Hearing Loss

Central hearing loss involves an inability to interpret sound, including speech, because of a problem in the brain (CNS). A careful history is helpful because there are usually cases of deafness in the family. Refer the patient to a qualified hearing and speech service if needed.

An emotional or a psychologic factor can cause functional hearing loss. The patient does not seem to hear or respond to pure-tone subjective hearing tests, but no physical reason for hearing loss can be found. Psychologic counseling may help.

Genetic Link

Hereditary hearing loss is labeled non-syndromic or syndromic. Most persons have *non-syndromic hearing impairment,* in which hearing loss is the only problem. *GJB2* gene mutations are one of the most common causes of non-syndromic hearing loss. These result in changes in the production of the protein Connexin 26, which has a role in the cochlear function. Other genetic mutations increase the risk for ototoxicity or result in malformations of structures in the middle and/or inner ear. *Syndromic hearing impairment* is part of a syndrome associated with other problems. These often involve the eye, kidney, musculoskeletal, and nervous systems. There are more than 400 syndromes that include hearing loss.

Clinical Manifestations

Common early signs of hearing loss are answering questions inappropriately and not responding when not looking at the speaker (Table 23.3). Other behaviors that suggest hearing loss include straining to hear, cupping the hand around the ear, reading lips, and an increased sensitivity to slight increases in noise level. Often the patient is unaware of minimal hearing loss. Family and friends who get tired of repeating or talking loudly are often the first to notice the hearing loss. Pressure exerted by significant others is a significant factor in whether the patient seeks help for impaired hearing.

Sudden hearing loss, or sudden deafness, occurs as an unexplained, rapid loss of hearing (usually in 1 ear) either at once or over several days. It is a medical emergency. The patient should see an HCP at once.

Classification of Hearing Loss

We often classify hearing loss by the decibel level or loss as recorded on the audiogram. Normal hearing is in the 0- to 15-dB range at all frequencies. Most people with a hearing loss of 90 dB or greater have been deaf since birth (congenitally deaf). Table 23.13 describes the levels of hearing loss.

Tinnitus

Tinnitus is the perception of sound that originates in the head. It is often called "ringing in the ears" or "head noise." Bilateral tinnitus is sometimes the first symptom of hearing loss, especially in older adults. It may be soft or loud, high pitched or low pitched. Often, tinnitus occurs because of noise exposure. It also can be a drug side effect. More than 200 drugs are known to cause tinnitus. It can also occur with TMJ, stroke, and head and neck injuries.[7]

❖ NURSING AND INTERPROFESSIONAL MANAGEMENT: HEARING LOSS AND DEAFNESS

Deafness is often called an "invisible disability" because you cannot tell someone has hearing loss by looking at them. The disability usually is noted when you communicate with the person. You need to establish good communication so the patient has needed health information and feels included in their care.

TABLE 23.13 **Diagnostic Criteria**

Classification of Hearing Loss

Decibel (dB) Loss	Meaning
0–15	Normal hearing
16–25	Slight hearing loss
26–40	Mild impairment
41–55	Moderate impairment
56–70	Moderately severe impairment
71–90	Severe impairment
>90	Profound deafness

Hearing level, communication style, and language varies greatly. Assess these factors so you are aware of the patient's needs.

Problems with communication and interaction with others can be the source of many problems for the patient and caregiver. Hearing loss can affect the ability to understand and follow the advice of HCPs. You need to confirm the patient's understanding of health teaching. Descriptive visual aids can be helpful. If the patient uses sign language to communicate, the Americans with Disabilities Act requires using an interpreter when presenting significant information, such as consent or discharge teaching. Use and teach verbal and nonverbal communication techniques as described in Table 23.14.

Sometimes the patient refuses to admit or may be unaware of impaired hearing. Irritability is common because the patient must concentrate so hard to understand speech. The loss of clarity of speech in the patient with sensorineural hearing loss is frustrating. The patient may hear what is said but not understand it. Loneliness, depression, and cognitive decline can occur with advanced hearing loss.[8]

CHECK YOUR PRACTICE

Your newly assigned 68-year-old female patient is being discharged today after a hip replacement. Before going to her room, you prepared the materials and information for her discharge. You sit down by her bed and start talking with her. She shakes her head and says, "No, no." You are perplexed until she flashes a bracelet that says *I am deaf*.

- How will you proceed?

Health Promotion

Environmental Noise Control

Noise is the most preventable cause of hearing loss. Fig. 23.6 shows the dB levels of common indoor and outdoor sounds. Sudden severe loud noise (acoustic trauma) and chronic exposure to loud noise (noise-induced hearing loss) can damage hearing. Acoustic trauma causes hearing loss by destroying the hair cells of the organ of Corti. Sensorineural hearing loss from increased and prolonged environmental noise, such as amplified sound, is occurring at an increasing rate. Three factors affect noise-induced hearing loss: how loud the noise is, how close you are to the noise, and how long you hear the noise. Health teaching about avoiding continued exposure to noise levels greater than 70 dB is essential (Box 23.2).

TABLE 23.14 **Communicating With Patients With Hearing Impairment**

Nonverbal Aids	• Draw attention with hand movements. • Have speaker's face in good light. • Avoid light behind the speaker. • Maintain eye contact. • Use a face shield or clear mask if a face covering is needed. • Avoid chewing, eating, smoking while talking. • Remove background noise. • Move close to better ear.
Verbal Aids	• Speak normally and slowly. Do not shout. • Do not exaggerate facial expressions. • Do not overenunciate. • Use simple sentences. • Rephrase sentence. Use different words. • Write name or difficult words. • Speak in normal voice directly into better ear.

In work environments known to have high noise levels, Occupational Safety and Health Administration (OSHA) standards require employers to implement a hearing conservation program. Such programs should include noise exposure analysis, ways to control noise exposure, and employee-employer education. OSHA mandates ear protection for workers in environments where the noise levels consistently exceed 85 dB. Periodic audiometric screening provides baseline data on hearing and a way to measure later hearing loss.

Immunizations

Various viruses can cause deafness because of fetal damage and malformations affecting the ear. Promote childhood and adult immunizations, including the measles, mumps, and rubella (MMR) vaccine. Rubella infection during the first 8 weeks of pregnancy is associated with a high incidence of congenital rubella syndrome, which causes sensorineural deafness. Women of childbearing age should be tested for antibodies to these viral diseases. Women should avoid pregnancy for at least 3 months after being immunized. Immunization must be delayed if a woman is pregnant. Women can be vaccinated safely for rubella during the postpartum period.

Ototoxic Substances

Monitor the patient who is receiving ototoxic drugs or exposed to ototoxic agents for signs and symptoms of ototoxicity. These include tinnitus, diminished hearing, and balance problems. If symptoms develop, stopping the drug may prevent further damage and allow the symptoms to disappear.

Assistive Devices and Techniques

Hearing Aids

Hearing aids are sound-amplifying devices designed to improve hearing in people with hearing loss. The patient with suspected hearing loss should have a hearing assessment by a qualified audiologist. If a hearing aid is needed, it should be fitted by an audiologist or a speech and hearing specialist. Many types of hearing aids are available, each with advantages

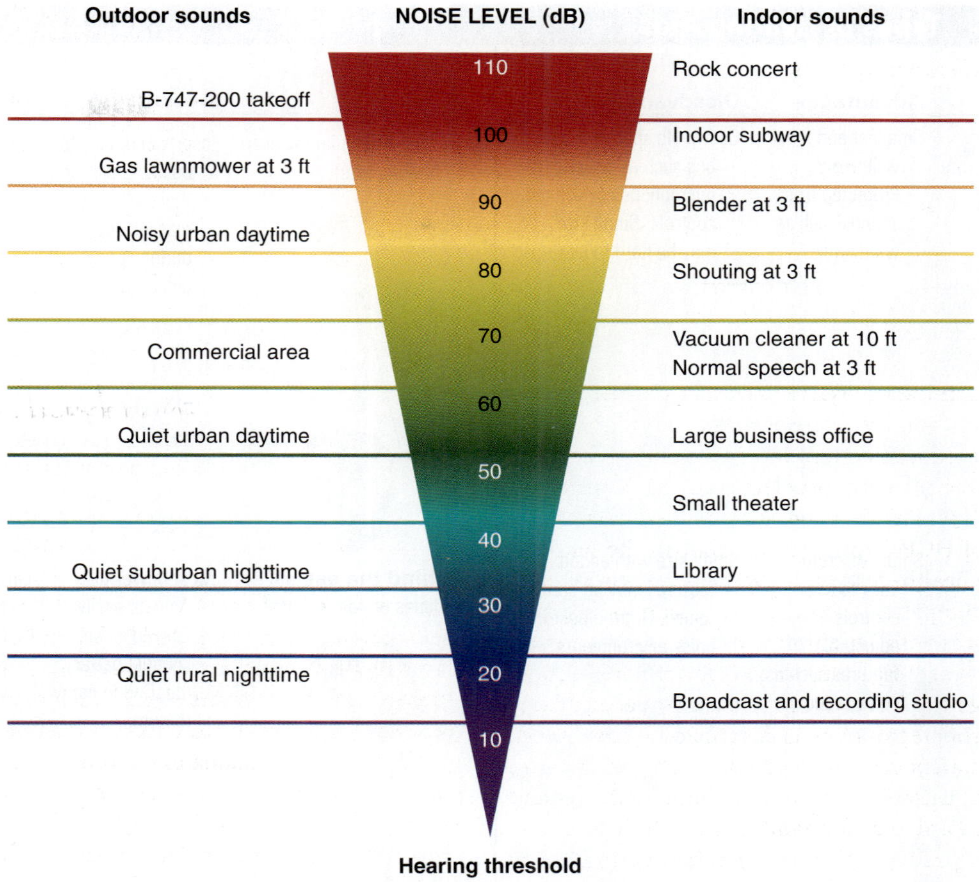

Fig. 23.6 Decibel levels of common sounds.

BOX 23.2 PROMOTING POPULATION HEALTH

Promoting Healthy Hearing

- Wear ear protection during recreational and work activities involving high noise levels.
- Monitor your audio level and how long you use personal listening devices.
- Avoid exposure to excessively loud noise whenever possible.
- Keep amplified music at a reasonable level.
- Undergo audiometric screening to detect hearing loss before it progresses.
- Avoid injury from cotton-tipped applicators and other cleaning materials.

and disadvantages (Table 23.15). The type of hearing aid chosen is based on the type and severity of hearing loss, financial resources, and patient's lifestyle.[9]

Patients who are motivated and optimistic about using a hearing aid are more successful users. Determine the patient's readiness for hearing aid therapy (Box 23.3). Assess their acknowledgment of a hearing problem, their feelings about wearing a hearing aid, the degree to which the hearing loss affects life, and any problems the patient has manipulating small objects, such as putting a battery in a hearing aid.

At first, the patient should wear hearing aids at home or quiet environments. The patient must first adjust to voices (including their own voice) and household sounds. Then, they should try increasing and decreasing the volume as situations require. As the patient adjusts to the increase in sounds and background noise, they can progress to situations in which several people will be talking at once. Next, the environment is expanded to the outdoors and then a shopping mall or grocery store. Adjustment to different environments occurs gradually, depending on the patient.

When a hearing aid is not being worn, it should be placed in a dry, cool area. The battery should be disconnected or removed when not in use. Battery life averages 1 week, depending on the hearing aid, battery, and amount of use. Ear molds should be cleaned weekly or as needed. Toothpicks or pipe cleaners can easily clear a clogged ear tip.

An *implantable hearing device* may be an option for those with mild to severe hearing loss who are unable or do not wish to wear regular hearing aids. There are 2 types: bone-anchored and implantable middle-ear devices. Bone-anchored devices are mainly used for conductive hearing loss or single-sided deafness. They are implanted into the bone of the skull. The sound signal bypasses the middle and outer ear, sending it straight to the cochlea.

Implantable middle-ear hearing devices help increase the transmission of sound vibrations reaching the inner ear. They involve a small prosthesis attached to one of the bones of the middle ear. Rather than amplifying the sound traveling to the TM like a hearing aid, these devices help move the bones directly.

TABLE 23.15 Types of Hearing Aids

Type	Advantages	Disadvantages
Completely in the canal (mild to moderate hearing loss) 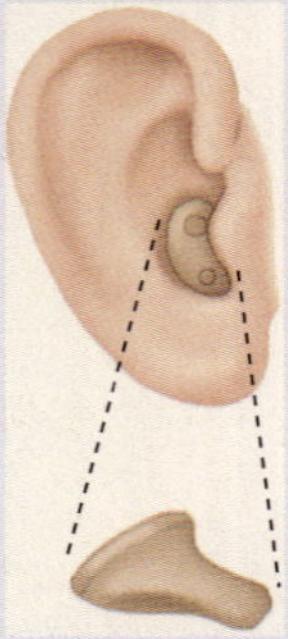	Smallest and least visible aid. Protected from sounds such as wind noise	Costly. No space for add-ons such as directional microphones or volume controls. Small size may be hard to use.
In the canal (mild to severe hearing loss) 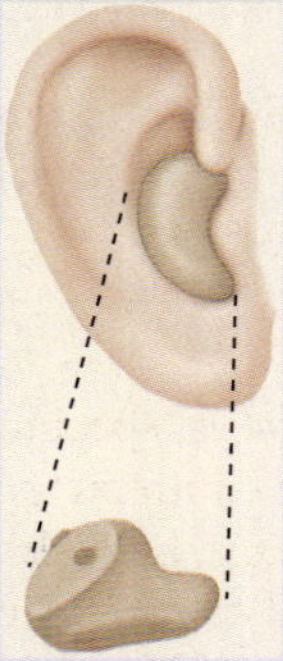	Small, discrete. Easy to use controls. Has adjustable features such as noise reduction	Small size with added features may be hard to use. Not the best in noisy environments.
In the ear (mild to severe hearing loss) 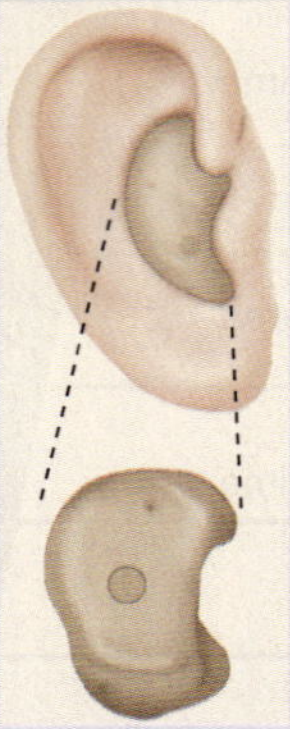	Inserts and adjusts easily. Good for those who wear glasses and during sports and activities.	Visible. May pick up wind noise. Susceptible to moisture.
Behind the ear (all types of hearing loss) 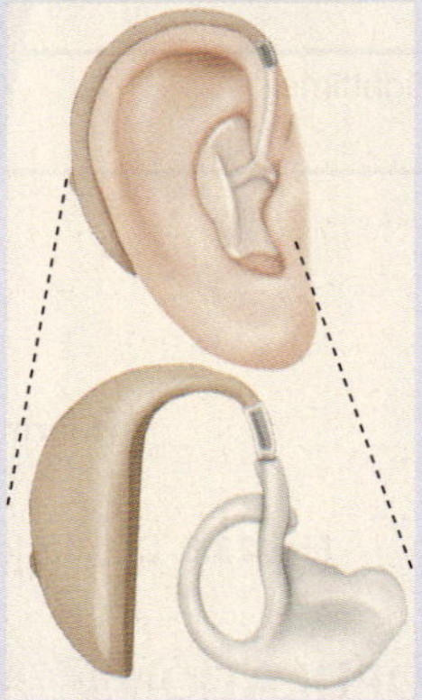	Most powerful. Adjusts easily. Easy to clean. Longest battery life. Can fit many features.	Largest, most visible. Newer models may be smaller and less obvious. May pick up wind.

BOX 23.3 EVIDENCE-BASED PRACTICE

Hearing Aid Rehabilitation

As a nurse in a community-based health clinic, you provide medication education for patients with new prescriptions. S.T. is a 76-year-old patient who has been prescribed a metered dose inhaler for treatment of chronic bronchitis. As you prepare to review medication use with S.T., you quickly discern he has marked bilateral hearing loss. When you ask about the hearing loss, he says he does not use hearing aids.

Making Clinical Decisions

Synthesis of Best Available Evidence

Age-related hearing loss (presbycusis) is one of the most common problems affecting older adults. Research findings suggest the way in which hearing aid use is introduced may have impact on a patient's readiness to adopt hearing aid use. For example, one HCP may recommend hearing aid use as part of their expert opinion based on test results. Another HCP may ask the patient's opinion about hearing aid use, recognizing the patient's responsibility and right in decision making.

Clinician Expertise

While you provide S.T. written materials and use a demonstration inhaler to explain inhaler administration, you realize his hearing loss may affect his ability to get all needed information to use his medications safely and effectively. You ask him to tell you more about how hearing loss has affected his life, especially situations in which he has had problems with his hearing.

Patient Preferences and Values

S.T. tells you he often feels isolated due to his hearing loss. However, he is concerned about the cost because he does not have a hearing health care benefit on his Medicare plan. He states he does not like the visibility of hearing aids. They would "tell everyone that I'm hard of hearing."

Implications for Nursing Practice

1. What options besides hearing aid use could you discuss with S.T. to address his hearing loss?
2. How would you introduce a hearing clinic referral to S.T. to ensure he remains the decision maker about his own health?

Reference for Evidence

Ruusuvuori J, Aaltonen T, Lonka E, et al.: Discussing hearing aid rehabilitation at the hearing clinic: patient involvement in deciding upon the need for a hearing aid, *Health Commun* 35:1146, 2020.

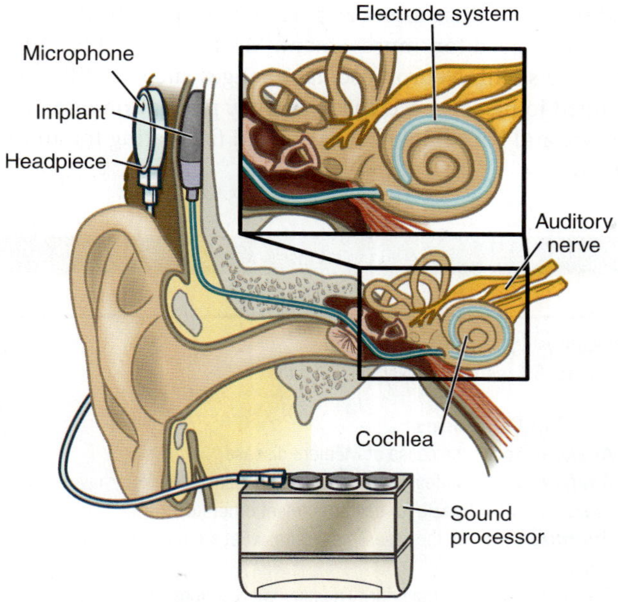

Fig. 23.7 Cochlear implant.

TABLE 23.16 Classification of Presbycusis

Type	Hearing Change and Prognosis
Cochlear	
Stiffening of basilar membrane, which interferes with sound transmission in the cochlea	Hearing loss increases from low to high frequencies. Speech discrimination affected with higher frequency losses. Helped by appropriate forms of amplification
Metabolic	
Atrophy of blood vessels in wall of cochlea with interruption of essential nutrient supply	Uniform loss for all frequencies accompanied by recruitment. Good response to hearing aid
Neural	
Degenerative changes in cochlea and spinal ganglion	Loss of speech discrimination. Amplification alone not sufficient
Sensory	
Atrophy of auditory nerve. Loss of sensory hair cells	Loss of high-pitched sounds. Little effect on speech understanding. Good response to sound amplification

Cochlear Implant

A *cochlear implant* may be used for some people with severe to profound sensorineural hearing loss in one or both ears.[10] The implant bypasses damaged or missing portions of the ear and directly activates CN VIII. The ideal patient is one who became deaf after they acquired speech and language. The system has an external portion consisting of a microphone, sound processor, and transmitter, and an internal portion that includes a receiver and several electrodes (Fig. 23.7). The microphone picks up sounds in the environment. The processor then converts the sounds into electronic signals that are sent to the transmitter. The transmitter forwards these signals to the receiver, where they are passed on to the electrodes. The electrodes stimulate the auditory nerve, which carries the information directly to the brain, where it is interpreted as sound.

Extensive training and rehabilitation are essential to receive the most benefit from an implant. Besides providing sound to the person who heard none, cochlear implants improve speech-reading ability, allow self-monitoring of the loudness of speech, improve the sense of security, and decrease feelings of isolation.

Speech Reading

Speech reading, or *lip reading,* involves trying to understand speech from observing the speaker's lip movements. It can be helpful in increasing communication by supplementing what the patient can hear. It allows for about 40% understanding of the spoken word. The patient uses visual cues associated with speech, such as gestures and facial expressions, to help clarify the spoken message.

Sign Language

Sign language is a visual language for people with profound hearing impairment. It involves specific hand gestures along with facial expressions, head movements, shoulder raises, and other body movements. There are many different sign languages. American Sign Language (ASL) is used in the United States and the English-speaking parts of Canada.

Assistive Listening Devices

Assistive listening devices (ALDs) are helpful in specific situations. Amplified telephones are the most common type of ALDs. Direct amplification devices, FM systems, and television listeners send sound directly to a hearing aid or other receiver. Notification systems take the place of alarms, such as doorbells and smoke detectors. They use amplified sounds, visual light cues, or vibration to notify the patient about their surroundings. People with profound deafness may be helped by text-telephone alerting systems that flash when activated by sound, closed captioning on television, and a specially trained dog. The dogs are trained to alert their owners to specific sounds within the environment, thus increasing the person's safety and independence.

Gerontologic Considerations: Hearing Loss

Presbycusis, hearing loss associated with aging, includes the loss of peripheral auditory sensitivity and a decline in word recognition ability. The person hears vowels but cannot distinguish consonants because they are in the high-frequency range. Because consonants help us recognize spoken words, this causes a decreased ability to understand speech. This may lead to confusion and embarrassment because of the difference in what was said and what was heard. Hearing loss in older adults is also associated with poorer cognitive and physical function and higher healthcare use. It can contribute to feelings of isolation as it becomes harder to enjoy talking to family or friends.

Degenerative changes in the inner ear cause presbycusis. Noise exposure is a common factor. Table 23.16 describes the classification of specific causes and associated hearing changes of presbycusis. Often, a person may have more than one type of presbycusis. The prognosis for hearing depends on the cause of the loss. Sound amplification with the right device is often helpful in improving the understanding of speech. In other situations, an audiologic rehabilitation program can be valuable.

The older adult is often reluctant to use a hearing aid. Reasons cited most often include cost, appearance, lack of knowledge about hearing aids, amplification of competing noise, and unrealistic expectations. Some older adults may tend to accept their losses as part of getting older and believe there is no need for improvement. Most hearing aids and batteries are small. Neuromuscular changes such as stiff fingers, enlarged joints, and decreased sensory perception often make the care and handling of a hearing aid frustrating for an older person.

Case Study

Ménière Disease

(© iStock.com/ EyeMark.)

Patient Profile

While R.S. is in the emergency department, she starts violently vomiting. She tells you that any movement is making her feel like she is "spinning like crazy." The HCP decides to admit her under observation with plans to administer an intratympanic injection of dexamethasone.

Objective Data

- Skin pale, extremely diaphoretic
- Heart rate 112 beats/min, respirations 22 breaths/min, BP 100/64

Interprofessional Care

- 1000 mg sodium diet as tolerated
- Ondansetron 2 mg IV now
- Lorazepam 1 mg IV every 6 hours
- Meclizine 25 mg PO every 6 hours
- Electronystagmogram and glycerol test
- Dextrose 5% with 0.45% NaCl at 75 mL/hr

Discussion Questions

1. ***Analyze:*** Explain the cause of Ménière disease.
2. ***Analyze***: What manifestations of Ménière disease does R.S. have?
3. ***Plan:*** Give the rationale for each treatment ordered.
4. ***Prioritize:*** Based on the assessment data, what are the priority clinical problems?
5. ***Prioritize:*** What are the priority nursing interventions for R.S.?
6. ***Act:*** Identify interventions that you can delegate to assistive personnel.
7. ***Safety:*** Name an area of risk for injury. What actions will you take to ensure patient safety?
8. ***Act:*** What teaching will you provide so R.S. can successfully self-manage her condition after discharge?
9. ***Evaluate:*** What outcomes would indicate care was effective?

Answers available at http://evolve.elsevier.com/Lewis/medsurg.

BRIDGE TO NCLEX EXAMINATION

The number of the question corresponds to the same-numbered outcome at the beginning of the chapter.

1. In a patient with vertigo, the parts of the ear most likely involved are the *(select all that apply)*
   a. cochlea.
   b. ossicles.
   c. vestibule.
   d. semicircular canals.
   e. tympanic membrane.
2. A patient reports tinnitus and balance problems. The medication that may be responsible is
   a. digoxin.
   b. warfarin.
   c. furosemide.
   d. acetaminophen.
3. What assessment technique should the nurse use to assess an adult patient's tympanic membrane?
   a. Have the patient tilt the head toward the nurse.
   b. Stabilize the otoscope with your fingers on the patient's cheek.
   c. Pull the auricle down and back to straighten the auditory canal.
   d. Use a speculum slightly larger than the size of the patient's ear canal.
4. A normal finding the nurse would expect when assessing hearing would be
   a. absent cone of light.
   b. bluish purple tympanic membrane.
   c. midline tone heard equally in both ears.
   d. fluid level at hairline in the tympanic membrane.
5. Common age-related changes in the auditory system include *(select all that apply)*
   a. drier earwax.
   b. tinnitus in both ears.
   c. auditory nerve degeneration.
   d. atrophy of the tympanic membrane.
   e. greater ability to hear high-pitched sounds.
6. The nurse teaches a patient scheduled for an electronystagmography that the test involves
   a. measuring ear drum movement in response to pressure.
   b. recording eye movements associated with ear irrigation.
   c. placing an electrode on the eardrum and assessing for dizziness.
   d. wearing headphones and determining which sounds can be heard.
7. Care of the patient with an acute attack of Ménière disease includes *(select all that apply)*
   a. giving antiemetics as needed.
   b. implementing fall precautions.
   c. keeping the room dark and quiet.
   d. placing the patient on NPO status.
   e. ambulating in the hall independently.

8. The patient who has a conductive hearing loss
  a. hears better in a noisy environment.
  b. hears sound but does not understand speech.
  c. often speaks loudly because their own voice seems low.
  d. has clearer sound with a hearing aid if the loss is less than 30 dB.

9. Teach the patient who is newly fitted with bilateral hearing aids to *(select all that apply)*
  a. replace the batteries monthly.
  b. clean the ear molds weekly or as needed.
  c. clean ears with cotton-tipped applicators daily.
  d. disconnect or remove the batteries when not in use.
  e. initially restrict usage to quiet listening in the home.

10. Which strategies would *best* aid the nurse communicate with a patient who has a hearing loss? *(select all that apply)*
  a. Overenunciate speech.
  b. Speak normally and slowly.
  c. Exaggerate facial expressions.
  d. Raise the voice to a higher pitch.
  e. Write out names or difficult words.

1. c, d; 2. c; 3. b; 4. c; 5. a, b, c, d; 6. b; 7. a, b, c; 8. a; 9. b, d, e; 10. b, e.

For rationales to these answers and even more NCLEX review questions, visit http://evolve.elsevier.com/Lewis/medsurg.

EVOLVE WEBSITE/RESOURCES LIST

http://evolve.elsevier.com/Lewis/medsurg
Review Questions (Online Only)
Key Points
Answer Keys for Questions
- Rationales for Bridge to NCLEX Examination Questions
- Answer Guidelines for Case Studies Conceptual Care Map Creator

Audio Glossary
Content Updates

REFERENCES

1. Hearing Loss Association of America. Retrieved from http://hearingloss.org.

*2. Young YH: Contemporary review of the causes and differential diagnosis of sudden sensorineural hearing loss, *Int J Audiol* 59:243, 2020.

3. Crane BT, Minor L: Peripheral vestibular disorders. In *Cummings Otolaryngology*, ed 7, St. Louis, 2021, Elsevier.

*4. Pfieffer ML, Anthamatten A, Glassford M: Assessment and treatment of dizziness and vertigo, *Nurse Pract* 44:29, 2019.

5. National Institute on Deafness and Other Communication Disorders: Quick statistics about hearing. Retrieved from https://www.nidcd.nih.gov/health/statistics/quick-statistics-hearing#.

6. Hearing Loss Association of America (HLAA): Conductive hearing loss. Retrieved from https://www.hearingloss.org/hearing-help/hearing-loss-basics/types-causes-and-treatment/.

*7. Henry J, McMillan L, Manning C: Multidisciplinary tinnitus care, *J Nurse Pract* 15:671, 2019.

*8. Shukla A, Harper M, Pedersen E, et al.: Hearing loss, loneliness, and social isolation: a systematic review, *Otolaryngol Head Neck Surg* 162:622, 2020.

9. Food and Drug Administration: Types of hearing aids. Retrieved from https://www.fda.gov/medical-devices/hearing-aids/types-hearing-aids.

10. HLAA: Cochlear implants and other implantable devices. Retrieved from https://www.hearingloss.org/hearing-help/technology/cochlear-implantable-devices/.

*Evidence-based information for clinical practice.

24

Assessment: Integumentary System

Margaret R. Rateau

http://evolve.elsevier.com/Lewis/medsurg/

CONCEPTUAL FOCUS

Health Promotion

Tissue Integrity

LEARNING OUTCOMES

1. Describe the structures and functions of the integumentary system.
2. Link the age-related changes in the integumentary system to differences in assessment findings.
3. Obtain significant subjective and objective data related to the integumentary system from a patient.
4. Compare the components for describing primary and secondary lesions.
5. Perform a physical assessment of the integumentary system using appropriate techniques.
6. Specify the structural and assessment differences in light- and dark-skinned persons.
7. Distinguish normal from common abnormal findings of a physical assessment of the integumentary system.
8. Describe the purpose, significance of results, and nursing responsibilities related to diagnostic studies of the integumentary system.

KEY TERMS

alopecia, Table 24.8
dermis
epidermis
erythema, Table 24.8
hirsutism, Table 24.8
intertriginous
keloid
keratinocytes
melanocytes
mole (nevus), Table 24.8
pruritus
sebaceous glands

The integumentary system is the largest organ of the body. It is composed of the skin, hair, nails, and certain glands. The skin has 2 major layers: the epidermis (outer layer) and the dermis (inner layer). The subcutaneous tissue (layer) lies under the dermis (Fig. 24.1). The skin is as complex as any organ, but, unlike the others, it is readily visible. Being able to see and touch the skin helps you assess your patients. You can see abnormalities, understand their significance, and intervene early.

STRUCTURES AND FUNCTIONS OF SKIN AND APPENDAGES

Structures

Epidermis

The **epidermis**, the outer layer of the skin, is relatively thin. Its thickness ranges from 0.5 mm on the eyelids to 1.5 mm on the palms of the hands and soles of the feet.[1] There are no lymphatic or vascular structures in the epidermis. It is supported by passive circulation from the dermis.

The epidermis is divided into 5 distinct but interrelated layers. Two of the layers are the stratum corneum (the surface layer) and the stratum germinativum (deepest, basal layer) (Fig. 24.1).

Most epithelial cells are keratinocytes (90%). The remaining cells are melanocytes, Langerhans' cells, and Merkel cells. **Keratinocytes** form in the basal layer. Initially, they are undifferentiated and shaped like columns. As they mature (keratinize), they move to the surface. There they flatten and die, forming the outer skin layer (stratum corneum). Keratinocytes make a fibrous protein, keratin, which is vital to the skin's protective barrier function. The upward movement of keratinocytes from the basal layer to the outermost levels of the stratum corneum takes about 14 days. The keratinocytes stay there for another 14 days, allowing the epidermis to regenerate every 28 days. Thus, each month you have a new layer of skin.

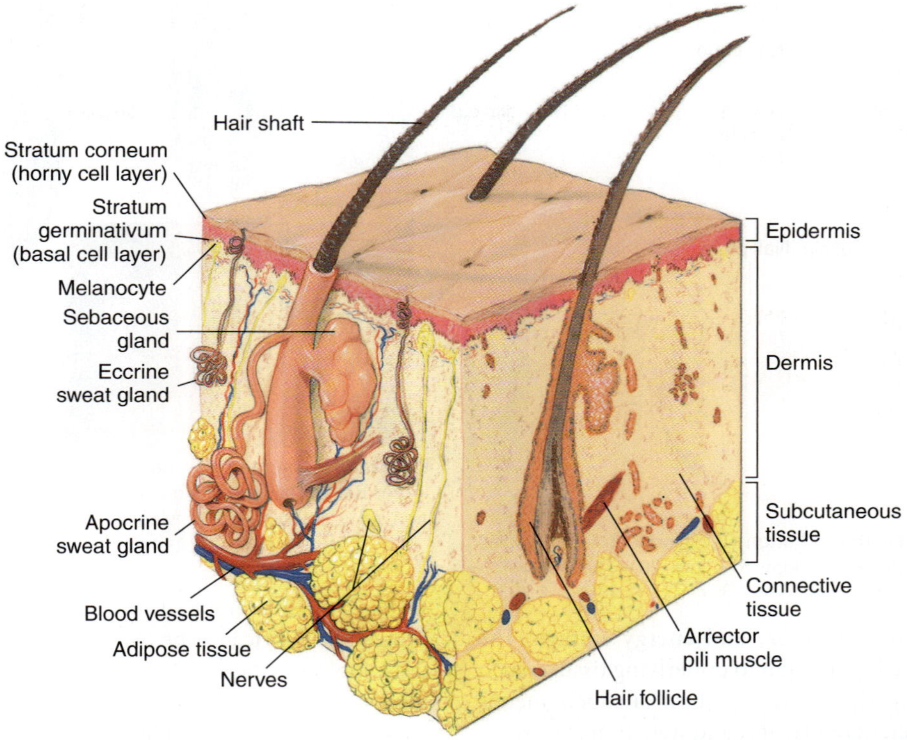

Fig. 24.1 Longitudinal view of the skin. (From Jarvis C: *Physical examination and health assessment,* ed 6, St Louis, 2012, Saunders.)

Many skin problems result from changes in this cell cycle. If dead cells slough off too rapidly, the skin appears thin and eroded. If new cells form faster than you shed old cells, the skin becomes scaly and thickened. The epidermis fails to function normally with skin cancer and psoriasis (discussed in Chapter 25).

Melanocytes are found in the deep, basal layer. They contain melanin, a pigment that gives color to the skin and hair and protects the body from damaging ultraviolet (UV) sunlight. Sunlight and hormones stimulate the melanosome (within the melanocyte) to increase the production of melanin. People of all races have similar numbers of melanocytes. In darker skin, the melanosomes are larger and more numerous. They make more eumelanin, the form of melanin that gives us the coloring of our skin.[2] Increased melanin forms a natural sun shield for dark skin and results in a decreased incidence of skin cancer. The distribution of melanocytes varies from one area of the body to another. For example, the face has more melanocytes than the abdomen.

Langerhans' cells are a type of dendritic cell. They are immunocompetent cells that recognize antigens. When they are depleted, the skin cannot initiate an immune response. The Langerhans cells in bioengineered skin grafts are removed to prevent graft rejection. We find decreased numbers of Langerhans cells with skin diseases such as psoriasis and sarcoidosis. *Merkel cells* are found in the basal layer. They are involved in the sensation of light touch. We use them when feeling the texture of an object and figuring out what it is.

The basement membrane zone is between the epidermis and dermis. It provides for the (1) exchange of fluids between the epidermis and dermis and (2) structural support for the epidermis. The basement membrane helps to secure the 2 layers together. Inflammation and separation of the epidermal and dermal layers result in the blisters seen with problems such as burns, full-thickness wounds, and mechanical trauma.

Dermis

The **dermis** is the connective tissue below the epidermis. Its thickness ranges from 0.6 mm on the eyelid to 3.0 mm on the back, palms of the hands, and soles of the feet.[1] The dermis is very vascular, containing many blood vessels. It also contains nerves, lymphatic vessels, hair follicles, sebaceous glands, and specialized cells such as mast cells and macrophages that protect the body from external stimuli.

The dermis is made of 3 types of connective tissue: collagen, elastic fibers, and reticular fibers. Collagen forms the greatest part of the dermis. It gives the skin toughness and strength. Collagen is critical in wound healing. The primary cell type in the dermis is the *fibroblast,* which makes collagen and elastin.

The dermis has 2 layers: an upper, thin papillary layer and a deeper, thicker reticular layer. The papillary layer is arranged haphazardly in ridges, or papillae, which extend into the outer epidermal layer. These elevated surface ridges form fingerprints and footprints. The reticular layer forms the bulk of the dermis. It is made up of thick collagen bundles arranged parallel to the skin's surface.

Subcutaneous Tissue

The subcutaneous tissue lies below the dermis. It is made of loose connective tissue and fat cells that provide insulation,

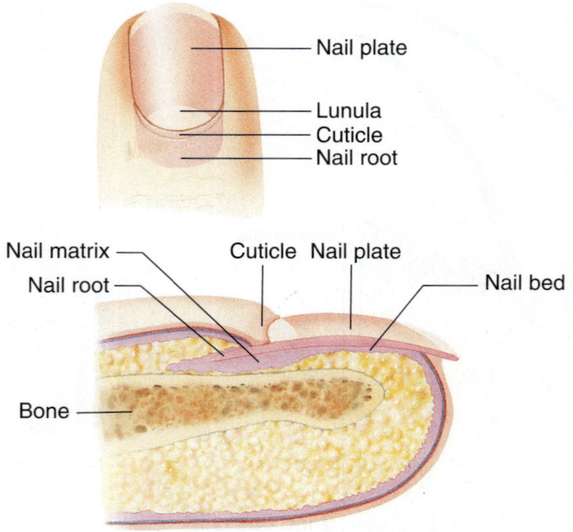

Fig. 24.2 Structure of a nail. (From Patton KT, Thibodeau GA, Douglas M: *Essentials of anatomy and physiology,* St Louis, 2014, Mosby.)

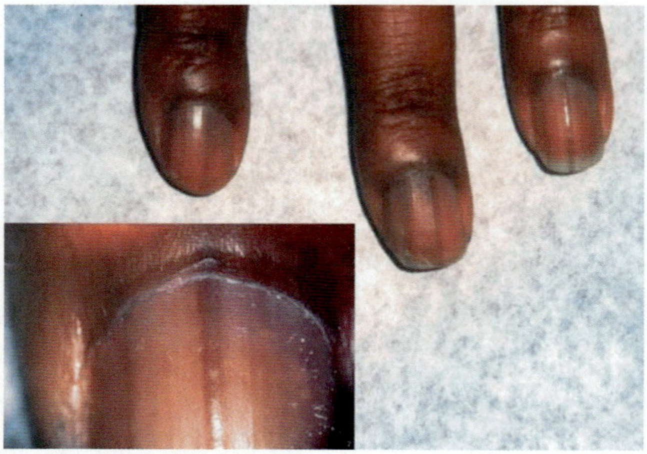

Fig. 24.3 Pigmented nail bands normally seen with dark skin color. (From Ball J, Dains J, Flynn J, et al.: *Seidel's guide to physical examination,* ed 8, St Louis, 2014, Mosby.)

cushioning, temperature regulation, and energy storage. The subcutaneous tissue attaches the skin to underlying tissues, such as muscle and bone. The distribution pattern of subcutaneous tissue varies with gender, heredity, age, and nutrition status.

Skin Appendages

Skin appendages include the hair, nails, and glands (sebaceous, apocrine, and eccrine). These appendages are epidermal extensions that have their roots in the dermis. They receive nutrients, electrolytes, and fluids from the dermis. Hair and nails form from specialized keratin. Systemic diseases can affect the condition and health of both hair and nails.

Hair grows on most of the body except for the lips, palms of the hands, interdigital spaces, portions of the genitalia, and soles of the feet. The density and pattern of distribution varies depending on age, sex, and race. Hair color is a result of heredity. It is determined by the type and amount of melanin in the hair shaft. Hair grows about 1 cm per month. People lose about 50 to 100 hairs each day.[3] Baldness, or **alopecia**, results when we do not replace lost hair.

Nails are made of heavily keratinized cells. The part of the nail that you can see is the nail body. The rest is the nail root. A fold of skin hides most of the nail root. The cuticle borders this skinfold. Nail growth begins in the nail root. The part of the nail root you can see is the *lunula.* This white, crescent-shaped area is the site of mitosis and nail growth (Fig. 24.2). Under the nail is an area of epidermis called the *nail bed.* The nail bed has many blood vessels. Nails grow slowly but continuously. Fingernails grow much faster than toenails, on average of 0.1 mm/day.[4] It takes 3 to 6 months to replace a fingernail. A toenail may take 12 months or longer to replace. Nail color ranges from pink to yellow or brown depending on skin color. Color and texture variations in nails may be normal or represent an abnormal condition. Pigmented longitudinal bands *(melanonychia striata)* occur in the nail bed in 90% or more of people with dark skin (Fig. 24.3).[5]

There are 2 major types of glands in the skin: sebaceous and sweat (apocrine and eccrine) glands. **Sebaceous glands** secrete *sebum,* which is emptied into the hair follicles. Sebum waterproofs and lubricates the skin and promotes the absorption of fat-soluble substances. Sebum is somewhat bacteriostatic and fungistatic. These glands depend on sex hormones, particularly testosterone, to regulate sebum secretion and production. Actual production varies depending on age, sex, and testosterone and estrogen levels. Sebaceous glands are present on all areas of the skin except the palms and soles and dorsum of the feet. These glands are most abundant on the face, scalp, upper chest, and back.

The *apocrine sweat glands* are mainly found in the axillary, genital, and breast areas. They are always connected to a hair follicle. These glands enlarge and become active at puberty because of reproductive hormones. They secrete a thick milky substance that is naturally odorless. Odor occurs when skin surface bacteria alter the secretions.

The *eccrine sweat glands* are found on most of the body, except the lips, ear canals, nail beds, labia minora, glans penis, and prepuce. One square inch of skin has about 3000 eccrine sweat glands. Their main function is to cool the body by evaporation, excrete waste products, and moisturize surface cells. Sweat is a transparent watery solution composed of salts, ammonia, urea, and other wastes. In extreme situations, the body can make 2 to 4 L of sweat per hour or up to 12 L in 24 hours. Heat, certain mental stimuli, and ingesting hot, spicy foods stimulate sweat secretion.

Functions of Integumentary System

The skin's main function is to protect the underlying body tissues by serving as a barrier to the external environment. The skin acts as a barrier against invasion by bacteria and viruses and prevents excess water loss. The fat in the subcutaneous layer insulates the body and provides protection from trauma. Melanin screens and absorbs UV radiation.

The skin with its nerve endings and special receptors collects sensory information from environmental stimuli. These highly specialized nerve endings give information to the brain related to pain, heat and cold, touch, pressure, and vibration.

TABLE 24.1 GERONTOLOGIC ASSESSMENT DIFFERENCES

Integumentary System

Changes	Differences in Assessment Findings
Skin	
↓ Subcutaneous fat, muscle laxity, degeneration of elastic fibers, collagen stiffening	Wrinkling, sagging breasts and abdomen, redundant flesh around eyes, slowness of skin to flatten when pinched (tenting)
↓ Extracellular water, surface lipids, and sebaceous gland activity	Dry, flaking skin
↓ Activity of apocrine and sebaceous glands	Dry skin with minimal to no perspiration, skin color uneven
Increased capillary fragility and permeability	Bruising
Increased focal melanocytes in basal layer with pigment accumulation	Solar lentigines on face and back of hands
↓ Blood supply	↓ In rosy appearance of skin and mucous membranes. Skin cool to touch. ↓ Awareness of pain, touch, temperature, peripheral vibration
↓ Proliferative capacity	Delayed wound healing
↓ Immunocompetence	↑ In skin cancers
Hair	
↓ Melanin and melanocytes	Gray or white hair
↓ Oil	Dry, coarse hair. Scaly scalp
↓ Hair density	Thinning and hair loss
Cumulative androgen effect; decreasing estrogen levels	Facial hirsutism, baldness
Nails	
↓ Peripheral blood supply	Thick, brittle nails, ↓ nail growth
Increased keratin	Longitudinal ridging
↓ Circulation	Prolonged return of blood to nails on blanching

The skin controls heat regulation by responding to changes in internal and external temperature with vasoconstriction or vasodilation. The skin's excretory function and heat regulation are related. We lose between 600 and 900 mL of water daily through insensible water loss (invisible vaporization from the lungs and skin), which helps regulate body temperature. Sebum and sweat lubricate the skin surface. Endogenous synthesis of vitamin D, which is critical to calcium and phosphorus balance, occurs in the epidermis. We make Vitamin D in the epidermis when UV light acts on vitamin D precursor cells.

Gerontologic Considerations: Effects of Aging on Integumentary System

Many skin changes occur with aging. Depending on how you view yourself, the normal, visible effects of aging on the skin and hair may have a profound psychologic effect. Having a youthful look may affect a person's self-image. The appearance of the signs of aging can be a threat to self-concept. Other changes in skin structure related to aging can pose a serious risk. Table 24.1 outlines age-related changes of the integumentary system and differences in assessment findings.

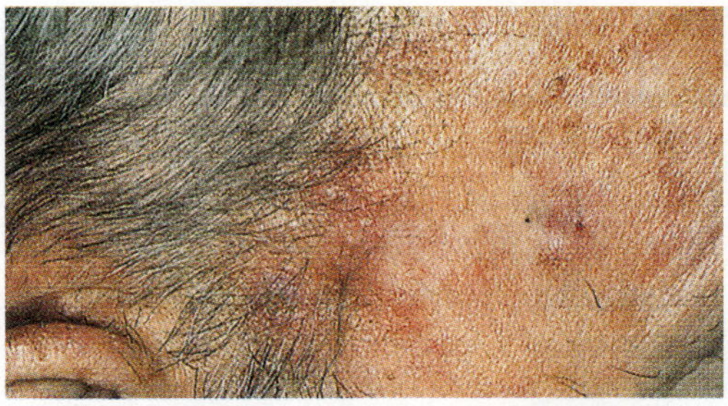

Fig. 24.4 Photoaging. Irregular pigmentation and keratoses occur in sun-damaged skin on forehead. (From Gawkrodger D, Ardern-Jones MR: *Dermatology,* ed 5, Edinburgh, 2012, Churchill Livingstone.)

Chronic UV exposure is the major cause of premature aging or photoaging and wrinkling of skin.[6] Sun damage to the skin is cumulative (Fig. 24.4). The wrinkling of sun-exposed areas such as the face and hands is more marked than in a sun-shielded area, such as the buttocks. A photoaged person is more susceptible to skin cancers because UV exposure decreases the ability to repair cellular damage. Chronic UV exposure from tanning beds causes the same damage as UV from the sun. Other factors that influence skin aging include diabetes, smoking, and alcohol use.

The junction between the dermis and epidermis flattens. This causes the layers to lose their tight bond. Skin tears and other trauma become common as the epidermis slides separately from the dermis. Collagen fibers stiffen, and elastic fibers degenerate. The amount of subcutaneous tissue decreases. These changes, with the added effects of gravity, lead to wrinkling. Fewer free fatty acids in the epidermis result in dry, scaly, itchy skin. Dryness, combined with trauma caused by scratching, increases the risk for cracks in the skin and secondary infections. Decreased subcutaneous fat increases the risk for traumatic injury, hypothermia, and skin shearing, which may lead to a pressure injury.

Fewer melanocytes are present. With decreased levels of melanin, hair color fades. Hormonal and vitamin deficiencies can cause dry, thin hair and alopecia. The growth rate of the hair and nails decreases. The nail plate thins. Nails become brittle and more prone to splitting and yellowing. Nails, especially the toenails, may thicken with age. With aging, the apocrine and eccrine sweat glands atrophy. This causes dry skin and decreased body odor.

Benign neoplasms related to the aging process can occur. These growths include seborrheic keratoses, vascular lesions such as cherry angiomas, and skin tags. *Actinic keratoses* appear on areas of chronic sun exposure, especially in the person who has a fair complexion and light eyes (blue, green, hazel). These premalignant skin lesions place a person at increased risk for squamous and basal cell cancers.

ASSESSMENT OF INTEGUMENTARY SYSTEM

The general skin assessment begins with your first contact with the patient and continues throughout the examination. As you are meeting your patient for the first time, take a moment to note the overall condition of the patient's skin and hair. You will assess specific areas of the skin when examining other body systems unless the chief complaint is a skin problem. Record a general statement about the skin's physical condition (Table 24.2).

TABLE 24.2 Normal Physical Assessment of Integumentary System

Skin	• Evenly pigmented. No petechiae, purpura, lesions, or excoriations • Warm, [redacted] turgor
Nails	• Pink, oval, adhere to nail bed with 160-degree angle
Hair	• Shiny and full; amount and distribution appropriate for age and gender • No flaking of scalp, forehead, or pinna

In addition, ask the health history questions outlined in Table 24.3 when you note a skin problem.

Case Study

Patient Introduction

(© iStockphoto/ Thinkstock.)

D.A. is a 74-year-old woman who comes to the medical clinic with concerns related to "spots" on her face. She says they have been there for a while, and she thought they were just "age spots." She became concerned after her friend was diagnosed with a malignant melanoma.

Discussion Questions

1. Which type of assessment should you perform: comprehensive, focused, or emergency?
2. What are the possible causes of D.A.'s facial lesions?
3. What questions would you ask D.A. to determine the possible causes?

You will learn more about D.A. and her condition as you read this chapter.

Answers available at http://evolve.elsevier.com/Lewis/medsurg.

Subjective Data

Perform the interview using a sensitive and nonjudgmental attitude. The problem may be the result of poor hygiene or unhealthy behaviors. Some problems are highly visible and affect the patient's body image and self-concept. A thorough health history yields information about possible causes and the effect of the problem on the person's life.

Important Health Information

Health history. A health history reveals previous trauma, surgery, or disease that involves the skin. Many diseases have skin manifestations (Table 24.4). Determine if the patient has noticed any problems such as jaundice (liver disease), delayed wound healing (diabetes), cyanosis (respiratory, cardiovascular disorder), or pallor (anemia). Obtain specific information related to food sensitivities, pet or drug allergies, and skin reactions to insect bites and stings. Note any history of chronic or unprotected exposure to UV light, including tanning bed use and radiation treatments.

Medications. A thorough medication history is important. Ask the patient about skin-related problems that occurred because of taking a medication. Many hormones, antibiotics, corticosteroids, and antimetabolites have side effects that manifest in the skin. Medications may contain fragrances and preservatives that can cause skin reactions. Document the use of medications specifically used to treat a primary skin problem, such as acne, or a secondary skin problem, such as itching. Record the drug's name, length of use, method of application, and effectiveness.

TABLE 24.3 HEALTH HISTORY

Integumentary System

Health Perception–Health Management
- Describe your daily hygiene practices.
- What skin products are you now using?
- Describe any current skin problems, including onset, course, and treatment (if any).

Nutritional-Metabolic
- Describe any changes in your skin, hair, nails, and mucous membranes.
- Have you noticed any recent changes in the way sores or wounds heal?[a]
- Have you had any weight loss or dietary changes?[a]

Elimination
- Have you noticed recent changes in your skin related to excess sweating, dryness, or swelling?[a]

Activity-Exercise
- Do your leisure or work activities involve using any chemicals that might irritate your skin?[a]
- Do you do anything to protect yourself from the sun?[a]

Sleep-Rest
- Does your skin problem keep you awake or awaken you from sleep?[a]

Cognitive-Perceptual
- Do you have any unusual sensations of heat, cold, or touch?[a]
- Do you have any pain associated with your skin problem?[a]
- Do you have any joint pain?[a]

Self-Perception–Self-Concept
- How does your skin make you feel about yourself?

Role-Relationship
- Has your skin problem changed your relationships with others?[a]
- Have you changed your lifestyle because of your skin problem?[a]

Sexuality-Reproductive
- Has your skin problem changed your intimate relationships with others?[a]
- Has your birth control method (if used) caused a skin problem?[a]

Coping–Stress Tolerance
- Are you aware of any situation or stressor that changes your skin problem?[a]
- Do you think that stress plays a role in your skin problem?[a]
- How do you handle stress?

Value-Belief
- Are there any cultural beliefs that influence your thinking or feelings about your skin problem?[a]
- Are there any treatment options that you would be opposed to using?

[a] If yes, describe.

Surgery or other treatments. Determine if any surgeries, including cosmetic surgery, were done on the skin. Record any biopsy results. Note any treatments specific for a skin problem (e.g., phototherapy) or for a health problem (e.g., radiation therapy). Document any treatments undergone primarily for cosmetic purposes, such as tanning booth use, laser resurfacing, or cosmetic "peels."

Functional Health Patterns

Health perception–health management pattern. Ask about health practices, such as self-care habits related to daily hygiene. Assess the frequency of use and sun protection factor (SPF) of sunscreen products. Note the use of personal care products (e.g., shampoos, moisturizing agents, cosmetics), including brand name, quantity, and frequency. Record a

TABLE 24.4 **Diseases With Skin Manifestations**

Systemic Problem	Skin Manifestations
Cardiovascular	
Peripheral vascular disease	Loss of hair on hands and feet. Delayed capillary filling. Dependent rubor (redness), pain
Rheumatic heart disease	Petechiae, urticaria, nodules, erythema
Thromboangiitis obliterans (Buerger disease)	Pallor or cyanosis, gangrene, ulceration
Venous ulcers	Leathery, brownish skin on lower leg; itching, concave lesion with edema. Scar tissue with healing
Endocrine	
Addison disease	Loss of body hair (especially axillary), generalized hyperpigmentation (accentuated in folds)
Androgen deficiency	Development of sparse hair. Marked ↓ in sebum production
Androgen excess	Enlarged facial pores, male sex characteristics, acne, acceleration of coarse hair growth
Diabetes	Erythematous plaques of shins, delayed wound healing, neuropathy, acanthosis nigricans (velvety, dark skin on the neck and in skin folds)
Glucocorticoid excess (Cushing syndrome)	Atrophy, striae, epidermal thinning, telangiectasia, acne. ↓ Subcutaneous fat over extremities. Thin, loose dermis. Impaired wound healing. Increased vascular fragility. Mild hirsutism. Excess collection of fat over clavicles, back of neck, abdomen, and face
Hyperpituitarism (acromegaly)	Coarsened skin, deepened lines. ↑ Oiliness and sweating, acne. ↑ Number of nevi, hyperpigmentation; hypertrichosis (excess hair growth)
Hyperthyroidism	↑ Sweating, warm skin with persistent flush, thin nails, alopecia. Fine, soft hair
Hypoparathyroidism	Opaque, brittle nails with transverse ridges. Coarse, sparse hair with patchy alopecia
Hypothyroidism	Cold, dry, pale to yellow skin. Generalized nonpitting edema. Dry, coarse, brittle hair. Brittle, slow-growing nails
Gastrointestinal	
Cystic fibrosis	Abnormal sweat gland function
Deficiency of essential fatty acids	Scaly skin
Inflammatory bowel disease	Mouth ulcers, erythema nodosum
Liver disease and biliary tract obstruction	Jaundice, itching, pigmentary abnormalities, changes in nails and hair, spider angiomas, telangiectasia
Malabsorption syndrome	Acquired ichthyosis (dry, scaly skin)
Hematologic	
Anemia	Pallor, hyperpigmentation, pale mucous membranes, hair loss, nail dystrophy
Clotting disorders	Purpura, petechiae, bruising
Immune	
HIV infection	Kaposi sarcoma, eosinophilic folliculitis
Hodgkin lymphoma	Itching, sensitive skin
Non-Hodgkin lymphoma	Papules, nodules, plaques, itching
Metabolic	
Nicotinic acid (niacin) deficiency	Redness of exposed areas of skin of hand or foot, face, or neck; infected dermatitis
Vitamin B_1 (thiamine) deficiency	Edema, redness of soles of feet
Vitamin B_2 (riboflavin) deficiency	Red fissures at corner of mouth, glossitis
Vitamin C deficiency	Petechiae, purpura, bleeding gums
Musculoskeletal and Connective Tissue	
Dermatomyositis	Edema; purplish-red upper eyelids; scaly, macular erythema over knuckles
Scleroderma	Leathery hardening and stiffness of skin
Systemic lupus erythematosus	Discoid lesions, maculopapular semiconfluent rash (butterfly rash), alopecia, mouth ulcers
Neurologic	
Chronic sensory polyneuropathies, spinal cord trauma	Trophic changes in skin resulting from sensory denervation, pressure injuries, anesthesia, paresthesias
Renal	
Chronic kidney disease	Dry skin, itching, uremic frost, pallor, bruises
Reproductive Organs	
Paget disease	Eczematous patch of nipple and areola
Primary syphilis	Chancre
Secondary syphilis	Generalized skin lesions, alopecia
Tertiary syphilis	Gummas
Respiratory	
↓ Oxygenation due to respiratory disease	Cyanosis

BOX 24.1 GENETIC RISK ALERT

- The primary risk factor leading to skin cancer and melanoma is environmental exposure to UV radiation. UV radiation damages DNA, causing genetic defects. The resulting abnormal skin cells can lead to cancer.[7]
- Inherited genetic factors can increase skin cancer risk. A person has an increased risk for developing melanoma if they have a first-degree relative (e.g., parent, full sibling) who had a melanoma.
- People with a fair complexion (light-colored skin that easily freckles, red or blond hair, and blue or light-colored eyes) have an increased risk for skin cancer.

description of any current skin problem, including onset, symptoms, course, and treatment. Note any medications used for treating hair loss.

Obtain information about the family history of any skin diseases (Box 24.1). Include congenital and familial diseases (e.g., alopecia, psoriasis) and systemic diseases with skin manifestations (e.g., diabetes, thyroid disease, cardiovascular diseases, immune disorders). Note any family and personal history of skin cancer, particularly melanoma.

Nutritional-metabolic pattern. Ask about the condition of skin, hair, nails, and mucous membranes. Have there been any changes related to diet? A diet history reveals the adequacy of nutrients essential to healthy skin and wound healing, such as protein and vitamins A, D, E, and C. Note any food allergies that cause a skin reaction. Ask obese patients if they have areas of chafing or a rash in **intertriginous** areas. This is where skin surfaces overlap and rub on each other (e.g., below the breasts, axillae, groin). Skin in these areas is predisposed to skin tags *(acrochordons)* and candidiasis (yeast), intertrigo (bacteria, fungi, yeast), and erythrasma (bacteria) infections. Note any excess or absent sweating. Ask the patient about poor or delayed wound healing.

Elimination pattern. Ask the patient about skin problems, such as dehydration, edema, and **pruritus** (itching). These can indicate changes in fluid balance. If urinary or fecal incontinence is a problem, ask about the condition of the skin in the anal and perineal areas.

Activity-exercise pattern. Obtain information about environmental hazards in relation to hobbies and recreational activities, including exposure to known carcinogens, chemical irritants, and allergens. Ask the patient if any changes occur in the skin during exercise or other activities.

Sleep-rest pattern. Ask the patient about changes in sleep patterns caused by a skin problem. For example, itching can be distressing and interfere with normal sleep. Poor sleep and resulting tiredness can be reflected in a patient's face by dark circles under the eyes and a decreased firmness in the facial skin.

Cognitive-perceptual pattern. Assess the perception of the sensations of heat, cold, pain, and touch. Note any discomfort associated with a skin problem, especially when observed in intact skin. Are there any reports of unusual skin sensations? Patients with neuropathy may describe numbness, tingling, or crawling sensations in their arms or legs. Ask about joint pain. Assess the mobility of the joints since a skin problem may cause changes in mobility.

Self-perception–self-concept pattern. Assess any feelings related to having a skin problem, such as sadness, anxiety, despair, or altered body image. These feelings can occur with classic signs of aging or visible skin problems such as acne, rosacea, and psoriasis, which alter physical appearance.

Role-relationship pattern. Determine how the skin problem affects relationships with family members, peers, and work associates. Ask the patient about the effect of environmental factors on the skin, such as occupational exposure to irritants, sun, and unusually cold or unhygienic conditions. Contact dermatitis caused by allergens and irritants is a common problem associated with occupation.

Sexuality-reproductive pattern. Assess the effect of the patient's skin problem on sexual activity. Note the reproductive status of the female patient relative to possible therapeutic interventions. For example, isotretinoin used to treat acne, and topical fluorouracil used to treat actinic keratoses, are teratogenic drugs that may cause abnormal fetal development. Pregnant women or women who could become pregnant should not use them.

Coping–stress tolerance pattern. Assess the role that stress may play in creating or worsening a skin problem. Discuss what coping strategies the patient uses to manage the problem.

Value-belief pattern. Assess cultural or religious beliefs that could influence the patient's self-image as related to the skin problem. Values and beliefs that may influence or limit the choice of treatment options.

Case Study

Subjective Data

(© iStockphoto/ Thinkstock.)

A focused subjective assessment of D.A. reveals the following:

- ***History:*** Negative except for an appendectomy at age 16.
- ***Medications:*** None at present. NKA.
- ***Health Perception–Health Management:*** Washes her face with a skin cleanser in the morning and nighttime. After cleansing, she applies a moisturizer with SPF 15. She has used these facial products for the past 3 years since she first started noticing small age spots appearing. Before that, she just used soap and water.
- ***Nutritional:*** D.A. reports that her skin seems drier as she ages but otherwise no changes besides the "age spots" or "whatever they are." Denies any changes in the way cuts or sores heal. No weight loss. Does not take any vitamins or mineral supplements.
- ***Elimination:*** Although skin is a little dry, D.A. does not perceive it to be excessively dry. Denies excess sweating or any swelling.
- ***Activity-Exercise:*** Loves to garden and go for walks outdoors. Reports a history of frequent, sometimes severe, sunburns as a child. No use of sunscreen growing up but does remember her mother making her wear T-shirts over her bathing suits to help prevent sunburn. Has used sunscreen for the past 20 years when outdoors. Reapplies as needed.
- ***Cognitive-Perceptual:*** Denies any pain or discomfort associated with skin lesions.
- ***Coping–Stress Tolerance:*** Fearful that she might have skin cancer.

Discussion Questions

1. Which subjective assessment findings concern you most?
2. What should you include in the physical assessment? What specific characteristics of the skin lesions would you be looking for?

You will learn more about the physical assessment of the skin in the next section.

Answers available at http://evolve.elsevier.com/Lewis/medsurg.

Objective Data

Physical Assessment

The physical assessment begins with a systematic, general inspection and then a more specific assessment of problem areas. A normal range of differences exists in the skin, hair, and nails. Note normal skin changes related to age, genetic factors, and environmental exposures from other changes. Look for changes in the color of the skin, turgor, temperature, dryness, thickness, and vascularity. General principles when assessing the skin are:

- Have a private room of moderate temperature with good lighting. A room with exposure to daylight is preferred.
- Ensure that the patient is comfortable and in a dressing gown that allows easy access to all skin areas.
- Perform a general inspection and then a lesion-specific assessment.
- Use the metric system when taking measurements.
- Use the right terminology when documenting.

Clinical photography. Photographs are an adjunct to documentation and promote communication among the interprofessional team. We use them to assess and monitor skin problems and determine if the problem has improved or declined with treatment. They can be used to track moles and precancerous lesions and detect any changes early. Follow agency protocol for obtaining the patient's consent to photograph lesions.

Inspection. Inspect the skin for general color and pigmentation, vascularity, bruising, lesions, and discolorations. The critical factor in assessing skin color is change. A skin color that is normal for one patient can be a sign of a pathologic problem in another patient. The skin color depends on the amount of melanin (brown), carotene (yellow), oxyhemoglobin (red), and reduced hemoglobin (bluish-red) present at a particular time. The most reliable areas to assess erythema, cyanosis, pallor, and jaundice are the areas of least pigmentation. These include the sclera, conjunctivae, nail beds, lips, and buccal mucosa. We see true skin color best in photo-protected areas such as the buttocks. Activity, sun (UV) exposure, emotions, cigarette smoking, and edema, as well as respiratory, renal, cardiovascular, and hepatic disorders, can directly affect skin color.

Note the presence of body art such as piercings and tattoos. The nose, ears, eyebrows, lips, navel, and nipples are common sites of piercing. Examine tattoos and needle-track marks. Note the location and characteristics of the surrounding skin area. Tattoo pigments deposited in the skin may cause itching, pain, and sensitivity for several weeks after the tattoo is placed.

Examine the skin for problems related to vascularity (see Table 33.6). Is there any bruising? Note vascular and purpuric lesions such as *angioma* (benign tumor of blood or lymph vessels), *petechiae* (tiny, flat, purplish-red pinpoint lesions), or *purpura* (purple or reddish areas with bruising that do not blanche). Note the reaction to direct pressure on the lesion. If a lesion blanches on direct pressure and then refills, the redness is due to dilated blood vessels. If the discoloration stays, it is the result of subcutaneous or intradermal bleeding or a nonvascular lesion. Note any pattern of bruising. Is the discoloration in the shape of the hand or fingers? Are bruises at different stages of resolution? These may indicate other health problems or abuse and need further investigation.

Record the color, size, height, distribution, location, and shape of any lesions. Lesions may be primary or secondary lesions. *Primary skin lesions* develop on previously unaltered skin. The common characteristics of primary skin lesions are shown in Table 24.5. *Secondary skin lesions* are lesions that change with time or occur because of scratching or infection (Table 24.6).

We usually describe skin lesions in terms related to the lesions' configuration (solitary or pattern in relation to other lesions) and distribution (arrangement of lesions over an area of skin) (Table 24.7). Note any unusual odors. Skin sites with lesions, such as rashes, may be colonized with yeast or bacteria, which can cause distinctive odors in areas where skin rubs together (Fig. 24.5).

Inspect all body hair. Note the distribution, texture, and quantity of hair. Changes in the normal distribution of body hair and growth may indicate an endocrine or vascular problem. Inspect the nails, including nail shape, thickness, curvature, and surface. Note any grooves, pitting, ridges, or detachment from the nail bed. Changes in nail smoothness or thickness can occur with anemia, psoriasis, thyroid problems, decreased circulation, and some infections.

Palpation. Palpate the skin to obtain information about temperature, turgor, moisture, and texture. Use the back of your hand to gauge skin temperature. The skin should be warm, not hot; skin temperature increases when blood flow to the dermis increases. A local temperature increase occurs with burns and local inflammation. A general increase occurs when a person has a fever. A decreased body temperature may occur when shock or other circulatory problems, chilling, or infection are present.

Turgor refers to the elasticity of the skin. Assess turgor by gently pinching an area of skin under the clavicle or on the back of the hand. Skin with good turgor should easily move when lifted and immediately return to its original position when released. In older or patients with dehydration, a loss of turgor occurs and can cause tenting of the skin.

Skin moisture (dampness or dryness of the skin) increases in areas where skin rubs together. Skin moisture varies with environmental temperature, muscular activity, body weight, and body temperature. The skin should be intact with no flaking, scaling, or cracking. Skin generally becomes drier with increasing age.

Texture refers to the fineness or coarseness of the skin. The skin should feel smooth and firm, with the surface evenly thin in most areas. Thickened callus areas are normal on the soles and palms and relate to weight bearing. Increased skin thickness is often work related and the result of excess pressure. Excess calluses on the soles of patients with neuropathy or diabetes predispose them to developing lesions.

Use a focused assessment (Box 24.2) to evaluate the status of previously identified skin problems and monitor for signs of new problems. Assessment abnormalities of the skin are described in Table 24.8.

Assessment of Dark Skin

The structures of dark skin are often harder to assess (Table 24.9). Color is easiest to assess in areas where the epidermis is thin, and

TABLE 24.5 Primary Skin Lesions

Lesion	Description
Macule 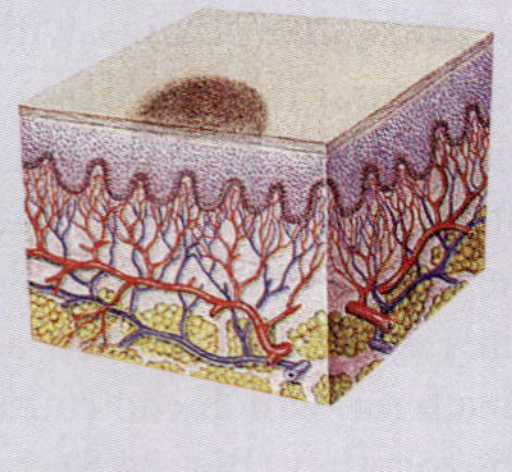	Circumscribed, flat discoloration that is blue, red, brown, or hypopigmented. <0.5 cm in diameter. If lesion >0.5 cm, it is a patch *Examples:* freckles, petechiae, measles, flat mole (nevus), café-au-lait spots, vitiligo (complete depigmentation)
Papule 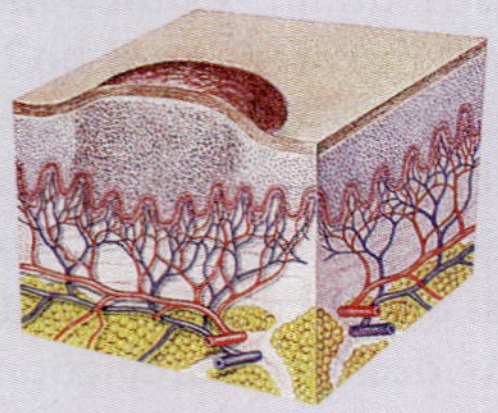	Elevated, solid lesion. <0.5 cm in diameter. Color varies. If lesion is >0.5 cm in diameter, it is a nodule *Examples:* wart (verruca), elevated moles, lipoma, basal cell cancer
Plaque 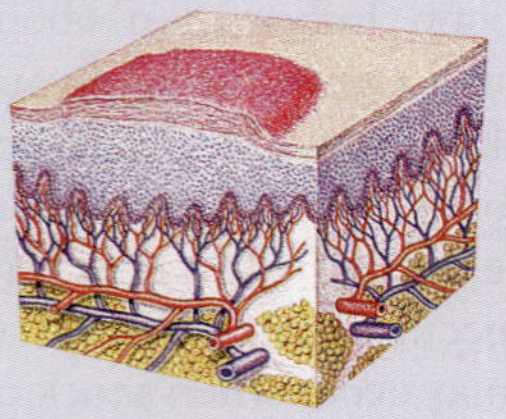	Circumscribed, elevated, superficial, solid lesion. >0.5 cm in diameter *Examples:* psoriasis, seborrheic and actinic keratoses
Pustule 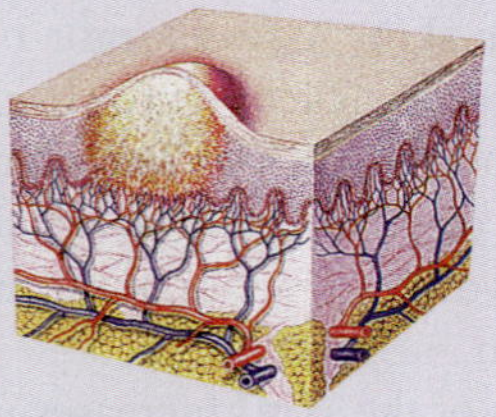	Elevated, superficial lesion filled with purulent fluid *Examples:* acne, impetigo
Vesicle 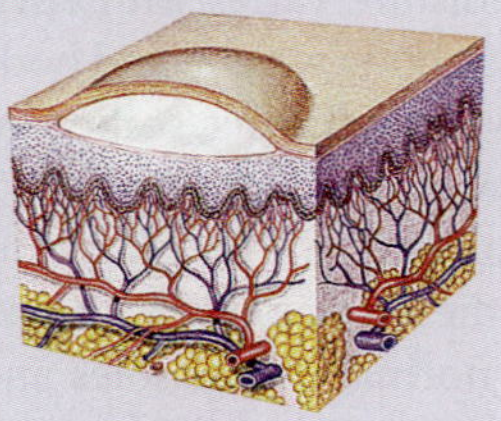	Circumscribed, superficial collection of serous fluid. <0.5 cm in diameter. If lesion >0.5 cm, it is a bulla *Examples:* varicella (chickenpox), herpes zoster (shingles), second-degree burn
Wheal 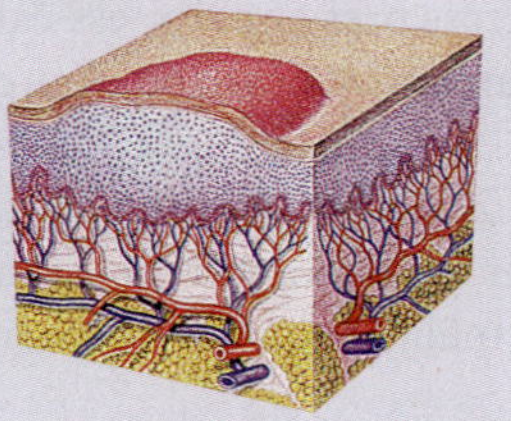	Firm, edematous, irregularly shaped area. Size varies. May last only a few hours *Examples:* insect bite, urticaria, angioedema

TABLE 24.6 Secondary Skin Lesions

	Description
Atrophy 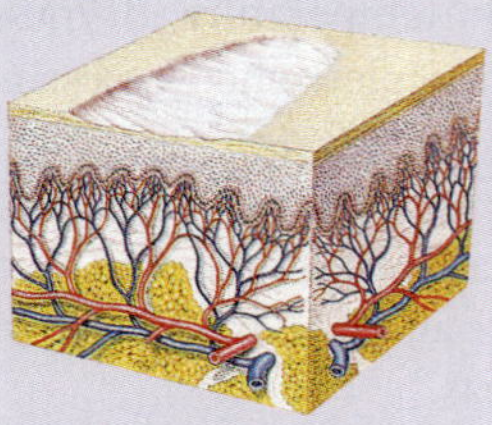	Depression in skin resulting from thinning of the epidermis or dermis *Examples:* aged skin, striae
Excoriation 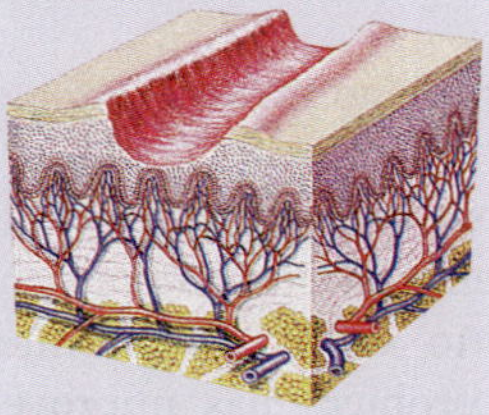	Area in which epidermis is missing, exposing the dermis *Examples:* abrasion, scratch
Fissure 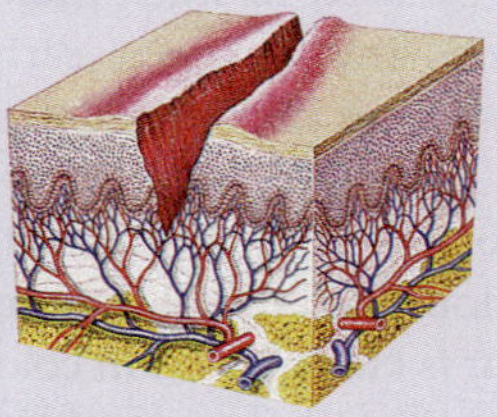	Linear crack or break from the epidermis to the dermis. Dry or moist *Examples:* athlete's foot, chapping, eczema
Scale 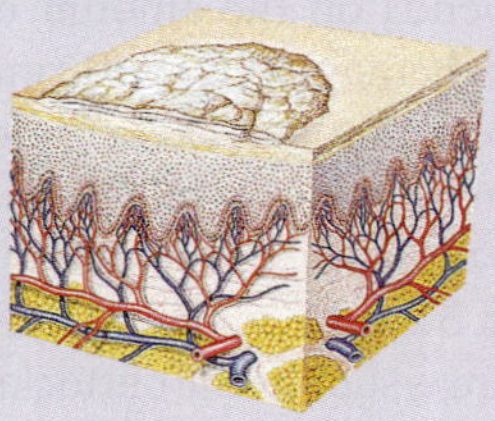	Excess, dead epidermal cells made by abnormal keratinization and shedding *Examples:* flaking of skin after a drug reaction or sunburn
Scar 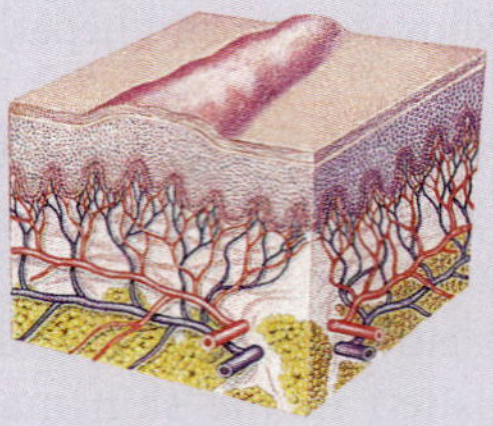	Abnormal formation of connective tissue that replaces normal skin *Examples:* surgical incision, healed wound
Ulcer 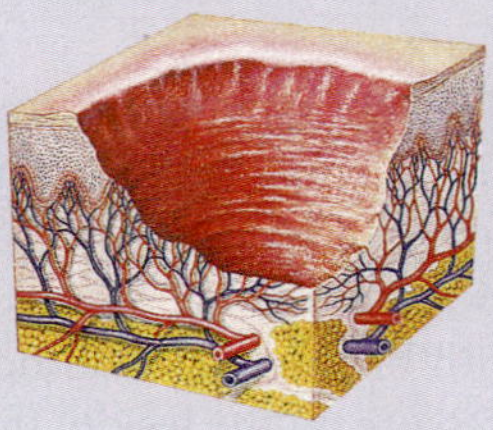	Loss of the epidermis and dermis. Crater-like, irregular shape. Heals with scarring *Examples:* pressure injury, chancre

TABLE 24.7 Lesion Distribution Terminology

Term	Description
Annular	Circular, begins in center and spreads to periphery (e.g., tinea corporis [ringworm])
Asymmetric	Unilateral distribution
Confluent	Merging together (e.g., urticaria [hives])
Discrete	Distinct individual lesions that are separate (e.g., acne)
Gyrate	Twisted, coiled spiral, snakelike
Grouped	Clusters of lesions (e.g., vesicles of contact dermatitis)
Localized	Clearly defined, limited areas of involvement (confined to one area)
Polycyclic	Annular lesions grow together (e.g., psoriasis)
Solitary	Single lesion
Symmetric	Bilateral distribution
Zosteriform	Linear arrangement along a dermatome area (e.g., herpes zoster)

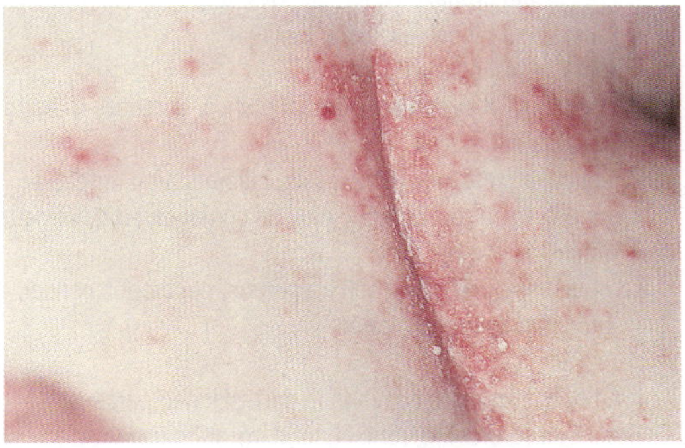

Fig. 24.5 Intertrigo. Rash in body folds with *Candida* infection. (From Graham-Brown R, Bourke J, Cunliffe T: *Dermatology: Fundamentals of practice*, Edinburgh, 2008, Mosby.)

pigmentation is not influenced by sun exposure, such as the lips, mucous membranes, nail beds, and protected areas (e.g., buttocks). Palmar and plantar surfaces are lighter than other skin areas in darker-skinned persons. Rashes are often harder to see and may have to be palpated. Wrinkling is less apparent in those with dark skin.

Persons with dark skin are predisposed to certain skin and hair problems. **Keloid** is an overgrowth of collagenous tissue at the site of a skin injury (e.g., ear piercing) (Fig. 24.6). *Vitiligo* is a total loss of pigment in the affected area (Fig. 24.7). In *dermatosis papulosa nigra,* the person has small, pigmented wart-like papules, often on the face (Fig. 24.8). *Nevus of Ota* is a slate-gray or blue-gray birthmark found on the forehead and face around the eye area. It may involve the sclera. *Traction alopecia* may be the result of trauma from hair rollers or from tight braiding of the hair (Fig. 24.9). The hair loss may be temporary or permanent. *Pseudofolliculitis* is an inflammatory response to ingrown hairs that occurs after shaving too closely in the beard area. The ingrown hairs result in pustules and papules.

Because of the darkness of the skin in some people, color may not be a reliable indicator of systemic conditions (e.g., flushed skin with fever). Cyanosis may be hard to detect because a normal bluish hue occurs in dark-skinned people. Dark skin rarely shows a blanch response, making it harder to identify pressure injuries.

BOX 24.2 FOCUSED ASSESSMENT

Integumentary System

Use this checklist to make sure the key assessment steps have been done.

Subjective

Ask the patient about the following and note responses.

Hair loss (unusual or rapid)	Y	N
Changes in skin (e.g., lesions, bruising)	Y	N
Nail discoloration	Y	N

Objective: Diagnostic

Check the following for results and critical values.

Biopsy results	✓
Albumin	✓

Objective: Physical Assessment

Inspect

Skin for color, integrity, scars, lesions, signs of breakdown	✓
Facial and body hair for distribution, color, quantity, hygiene	✓
Nails for shape, contour, color, thickness, cleanliness	✓
Dressings, if present	✓

Palpate

Skin for temperature, texture, moisture, thickness, turgor, mobility	✓

Case Study

Objective Data: Physical Examination

(© iStockphoto/ Thinkstock.)

Physical assessment findings of D.A.'s skin are as follows:

- Complexion fair. Wrinkles around eyes, above upper lip, and on sides of cheeks bilaterally. Normal skin temperature and turgor.
- Lesions: on upper right forehead measuring 2 × 3 mm; on left forehead near hairline measuring 1 × 2 mm; and on left lower cheek measuring 2 × 2.5 mm.

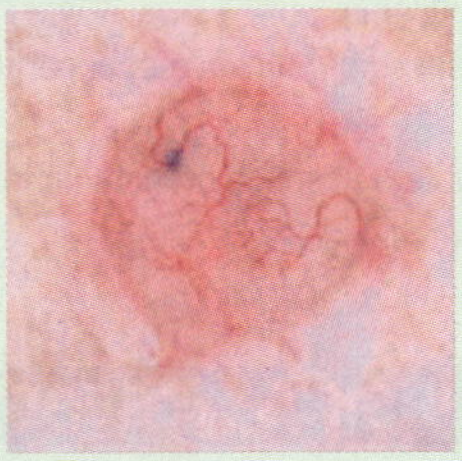

Cheek lesion. (From Bolognia JL, Schaffer JV, Duncan KO, et al: *Dermatology essentials,* Philadelphia, 2014, Saunders.)

- The lesions are slightly erythematous and do not blanch with direct pressure. Borders are distinct. The lesions on the forehead have minimal elevation noted on palpation. The lesion on the cheek is slightly elevated.
- No other skin lesions noted elsewhere.

Discussion Questions

1. Which physical assessment findings concern you most?
2. What diagnostic studies do you think may be ordered for D.A.?

You will learn more about diagnostic studies related to the skin in the next section.

Answers available at http://evolve.elsevier.com/Lewis/medsurg.

TABLE 24.8 ASSESSMENT ABNORMALITIES

Integumentary System

Finding	Description	Possible Etiology and Significance
Alopecia	Hair loss (local or general)	Heredity, friction, rubbing, traction, trauma, stress, infection, inflammation, chemotherapy, pregnancy, emotional shock, tinea capitis, immunologic factors
Angioma	Tumor consisting of blood or lymph vessels	Normal increase in incidence with aging, liver disease, pregnancy, varicose veins
Carotenemia (carotenosis)	Yellow discoloration of skin, no yellowing of sclerae, most noticeable on palms and soles	Vegetables containing carotene (e.g., carrots, squash), hypothyroidism
Comedo (acne lesion)	Enlarged hair follicle plugged with sebum, bacteria, and skin cells; can be open (blackhead) or closed (whitehead)	Heredity, certain drugs, hormonal changes with puberty and pregnancy
Cyanosis	Slightly bluish-gray or dark purple discoloration of the skin and mucous membranes caused by excess amounts of reduced hemoglobin in capillaries	Cardiorespiratory problems, vasoconstriction, asphyxiation, anemia, leukemia, and cancers
Cyst	Sac containing fluid or semisolid material	Obstruction of a duct or gland, parasitic infection
Ecchymosis (bruising)	Large, bruise-like lesion caused by collection of extravascular blood in dermis and subcutaneous tissue	Trauma, bleeding disorders
Erythema	Redness occurring in patches of variable size and shape	Heat, certain drugs, alcohol, UV rays, any problem that causes dilation of blood vessels in the skin
Hematoma	Extravasation of blood of enough size to cause visible swelling	Trauma, bleeding disorders
Hirsutism	Male distribution of hair in women	Abnormality of ovaries or adrenal glands, decrease in estrogen level, familial trait
Hypopigmentation	Loss of pigmentation resulting in lighter patches than the normal skin	Chemical agents, nutrition, burns, inflammation, infection
Intertrigo	Dermatitis of overlying surfaces of the skin (Fig. 24.5)	Moisture, irritation, obesity; may be complicated by *Candida* infection
Jaundice	Yellow (in white patients) or yellowish-brown (in dark-skinned patients) discoloration of the skin, best seen in the sclera, due to increased bilirubin in the blood	Liver disease, red blood cell hemolysis, pancreatic cancer, common bile duct obstruction
Keloid	Hypertrophied scar beyond wound margins (Fig. 24.6)	Predisposition more common in dark-skinned persons
Lichenification	Thickening of the skin with accentuated normal skin markings	Repeated scratching, rubbing, and irritation usually because of itching or neurosis
Mole (nevus)	Benign overgrowth of melanocytes	Defects of development; excess numbers and large, irregular moles; often familial
Petechiae	Pinpoint, discrete deposits of blood <1–2 mm in the extravascular tissues and visible through the skin or mucous membrane	Inflammation, marked vasodilation, blood vessel trauma, blood dyscrasia that results in bleeding tendencies (e.g., thrombocytopenia)
Telangiectasia	Visibly dilated, superficial, small blood vessels, often found on face and thighs	Aging, acne, sun exposure, alcohol, liver failure, corticosteroids, radiation, certain systemic diseases, skin tumors
Tenting	Failure of skin to return immediately to normal position after gentle pinching	Aging, dehydration, cachexia
Varicosity	Increased prominence of superficial veins	Interruption of venous return (e.g., from tumor, incompetent valves, inflammation), often found on lower legs with aging
Vitiligo	Complete absence of melanin (pigment) resulting in chalky-white patch (Fig. 24.7)	Autoimmune, familial, thyroid disease

TABLE 24.9 NURSING ASSESSMENT

Assessment Variations in Light- and Dark-Skinned Persons

Light Skin	Dark Skin
Cyanosis	
Grayish blue tone, especially in nail beds, earlobes, lips, mucous membranes, palms, and soles	Ashen or gray color most easily seen in the conjunctiva of the eye, mucous membranes, and nail beds
Ecchymosis	
Dark red, purple, yellow, or green color, depending on age of bruise	Purple to brownish-black. Hard to see unless occurring in an area of light pigmentation
Erythema	
Reddish tone, increased skin temperature may be present from inflammation	Deeper brown or purple skin tone, increased skin temperature may be present from inflammation

Continued

TABLE 24.9 NURSING ASSESSMENT—cont'd

Assessment Variations in Light- and Dark-Skinned Persons

Light Skin	Dark Skin
Jaundice	
Yellowish color of skin, sclera, fingernails, palms, and oral mucosa	Yellowish green color most obviously seen in sclera of eye (do not confuse with yellow eye pigmentation, which may be seen in patients with dark skin), palms, and soles
Pallor	
Pale skin color that may appear white or ashen; also seen on lips, nail beds, and mucous membranes	Lack of underlying red tone in brown or black skin. In lighter dark-skinned persons, yellowish-brown skin. In darker dark-skinned persons, ashen or gray skin
Petechiae	
Lesions appearing as small, reddish-purple pinpoints, best seen on abdomen and buttocks	Hard to see. May be seen in the buccal mucosa of the mouth or conjunctiva of the eye
Rash	
May be seen and felt with light palpation	Not easily seen. May be felt with light palpation
Scar	
Generally heals, showing narrow scar line	Higher incidence of keloid development, resulting in a thickened, raised scar (Fig. 24.6)

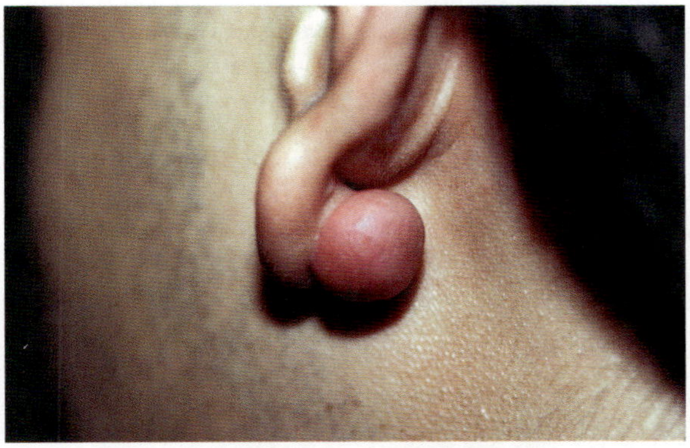

Fig. 24.6 Keloid. Hypertrophic scarring after skin injury, which is more common in dark-skinned persons. (From Kliegman RM et al.: *Nelson textbook of pediatrics,* Philadelphia, 2011, Saunders.)

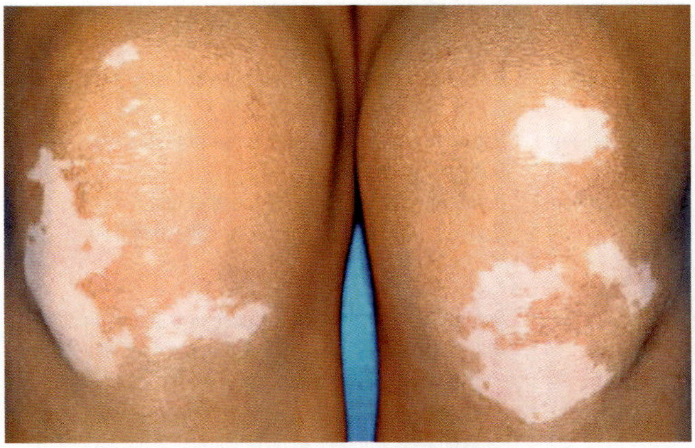

Fig. 24.7 Vitiligo. Total loss of pigment in the affected area. (From Marks JG, Miller JJ: *Principles of dermatology,* St. Louis, 2019, Elsevier.)

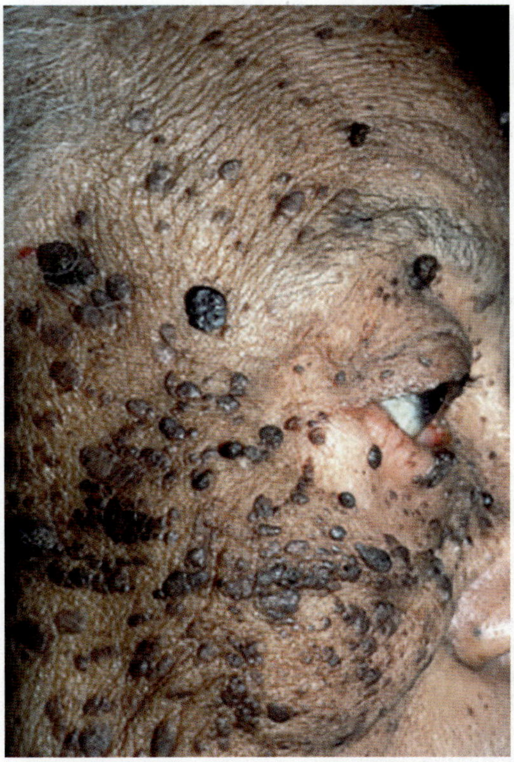

Fig. 24.8 Dermatosis papulosa nigra. Small, pigmented wart-like papules, often on the face. (From James W, Berger T, Elston D: *Andrews' diseases of the skin,* ed 12, Edinburgh, 2016, Elsevier.)

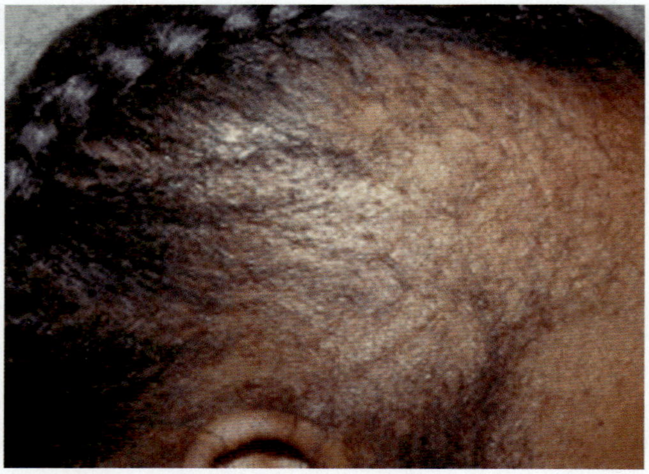

Fig. 24.9 Traction alopecia. Hair loss in scalp because of prolonged tension from hair rollers, braiding, or straightening combs. (From Ahanogbe I, Gavino A: Evaluation and management of the hair loss patient in the primary care setting, *Prim Care* 42:569, 2015.)

DIAGNOSTIC STUDIES OF INTEGUMENTARY SYSTEM

Table 24.10 presents common diagnostic studies used for the integumentary system. The main diagnostic techniques related to skin problems are inspection of an individual lesion and a careful history related to the problem. If we cannot make a definitive diagnosis with these techniques, other tests may be needed. With *dermatoscopy*, the HCP uses a lighted instrument with optical magnification up to 10 times normal to see skin structures and colors not visible to the naked eye.[8] These devices can help the HCP determine if a lesion should be biopsied.

Biopsy is one of the most common diagnostic tests used to evaluate a skin lesion. A biopsy is needed when we suspect cancer or the specific diagnosis is questionable. Techniques include punch, incisional, excisional, and shave biopsies. The method used depends on factors such as the site of the biopsy, cosmetic result desired, and type of tissue needed.

TABLE 24.10 Diagnostic Studies

Integumentary System

Study	Description and Purpose	Nursing Responsibility
Biopsy		
Excisional	Used when good cosmetic results and/or entire lesion removal desired. Skin closed with subcutaneous and skin sutures.	*Before:* Verify that consent form is signed (if needed). *During:* Help with site preparation, anesthesia, procedure, and hemostasis. Properly identify specimen. *After:* Apply dressing, give postprocedure instructions to patient.
Incisional	Wedge-shaped incision made in lesion too large for excisional biopsy. Useful when specimen needed is larger than shave or punch biopsy.	
Punch	Special punch biopsy instrument of appropriate size used. Instrument rotated to appropriate level to include dermis and some fat. Suturing depends on size and site. Provides full-thickness skin for diagnostic purposes.	
Shave	Single-edged razor blade used to shave off superficial lesions or small sample of a large lesion. Provides thin specimen for diagnostic purposes.	
Microscopic Tests		
Culture	Test identifies fungal, bacterial, and viral organisms. For *fungi,* scraping or swab of skin performed. For *bacteria,* material obtained from intact pustules, bullae, or abscesses. For *viruses,* vesicle or bulla and exudate taken from base of lesion.	*Before:* Teach patient the purpose of test. *During:* Properly identify specimen. Follow instructions for storing specimen if not immediately sent to laboratory.
Immunofluorescence studies	Some skin diseases have specific, abnormal antibody proteins that we can identify with fluorescence studies. Can examine both skin tissue and serum.	*Before:* Teach patient the purpose of test. *During:* Help obtain specimen. For punch biopsy, place specimen in special fixative (e.g., Michel's) and not formalin.
Mineral oil slides	To check for infestations, place scrapings on slide with mineral oil and view microscopically.	*Before:* Teach patient the purpose of test. *During:* Prepare slide.
Potassium hydroxide (KOH)	Hair, scales, or nails examined for superficial fungal infection. Put specimen on glass slide and add 10%–20% concentration of KOH.	*Before:* Teach patient the purpose of test. *During:* Prepare slide.
Tzanck test (Wright's and Giemsa's stain)	Fluid and cells from vesicles examined. Used to diagnose herpes infections. Specimen put on slide, stained, and examined microscopically.	*Before:* Teach patient the purpose of test. *During:* Use sterile technique for collecting fluid.
Miscellaneous		
Patch test (Fig. 24.10)	Used to assess for allergic dermatitis and photoallergic reactions. Application of allergens to the patient's skin (usually on the back) for 48 hr. Test sites examined 48 hr later for a reaction, characterized by the presence of erythema, papules, and/or vesicles. May do additional readings beyond 48 hr.	*Before:* Teach patient the purpose of test and procedure. *After:* Tell patient to leave patches in place for 48 hr. During this time, it is important not to wash the area or play vigorous sports because if the adhesive tape peels off, the process will need to be repeated. Do not expose the patches to sunlight or other sources of UV light.
Wood's lamp (blacklight)	Examination of skin with long-wave UV light causes specific substances to fluoresce (e.g., *Pseudomonas* organisms, fungal infections, vitiligo).	*Before:* Teach patient the purpose of test and procedure. Tell patient it is not painful. *During:* Darken room.

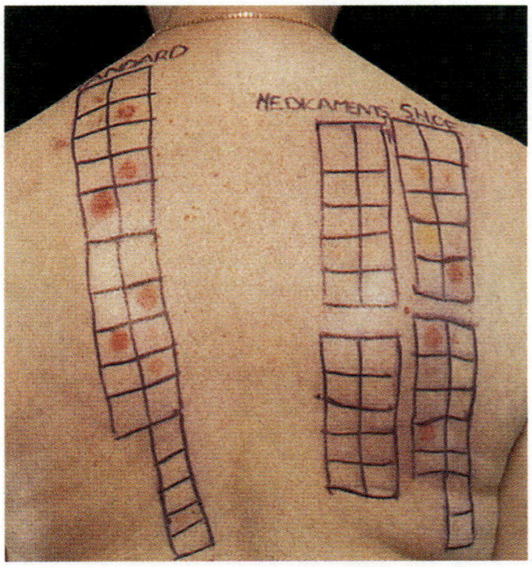

Fig. 24.10 Patch test. Results from applying possible allergens to the skin show positive reactions in the sites labeled "standard" and "shoe." (From Graham-Brown R, Bourke J, Cunliffe T: *Dermatology: Fundamentals of practice,* Edinburgh, 2008, Mosby.)

Other diagnostic procedures include stains and cultures for fungal, bacterial, and viral infections. Direct immunofluorescence is a special diagnostic technique used on biopsy specimens. It may be done in certain conditions such as bullous diseases and systemic lupus erythematosus. Indirect immunofluorescence is done on blood samples.

Case Study

Objective Data: Diagnostic Studies

(© iStockphoto/ Thinkstock.)

The HCP examines the lesion via dermatoscopy and uses a Wood's lamp to rule out a fungal infection. The HCP suspects basal cell cancer.

Discussion Questions

1. Are these the diagnostic tests you expected the HCP to perform?
2. What, if any, other diagnostic studies would you expect the HCP to order?
3. What are the interprofessional team's priorities for D.A. at this time?

Answers available at http://evolve.elsevier.com/Lewis/medsurg.

BRIDGE TO NCLEX EXAMINATION

The number of the question corresponds to the same-numbered outcome at the beginning of the chapter.

1. The nurse provides diligent skincare because the primary function of the skin is
   a. insulation.
   b. protection.
   c. sensation.
   d. absorption.
2. Age-related assessment findings of the hair and nails include *(select all that apply)*
   a. oily scalp.
   b. scaly scalp.
   c. thinner nails.
   d. thicker, brittle nails.
   e. longitudinal nail ridging.
3. When assessing the nutritional-metabolic pattern in relation to the skin, the nurse asks the patient about
   a. joint pain.
   b. the use of moisturizing shampoo.
   c. recent changes in wound healing.
   d. self-care habits related to daily hygiene.
4. The nurse assessed a patient's skin lesions as firm, edematous, and irregularly shaped with a variable diameter. They would be called
   a. wheals.
   b. papules.
   c. fissures.
   d. plaques.
5. During the physical assessment of a patient's skin, the nurse would
   a. use a flashlight in a poorly lit room.
   b. note cool, moist skin as a normal finding.
   c. pinch up a fold of skin to assess for turgor.
   d. perform a lesion-specific assessment and then a general inspection.
6. Patients with dark skin are more likely to develop
   a. keloids.
   b. wrinkles.
   c. skin rashes.
   d. skin cancer.
7. On inspection of a patient's dark skin, the nurse notes a blue-gray birthmark on the forehead and eye area. This assessment finding is called
   a. vitiligo.
   b. intertrigo.
   c. Nevus of Ota.
   d. telangiectasia.
8. Diagnostic testing is recommended for skin lesions when
   a. a health history cannot be obtained.
   b. a more definitive diagnosis is needed.
   c. percussion reveals an abnormal finding.
   d. treatment with prescribed medication has failed.

1. b; 2. b, d, e; 3. c; 4. a; 5. c; 6. a; 7. c; 8. b.

For rationales to these answers and even more NCLEX review questions, visit http://evolve.elsevier.com/Lewis/medsurg.

EVOLVE WEBSITE/RESOURCES LIST

http://evolve.elsevier.com/Lewis/medsurg
Review Questions (Online Only)
Key Points
Answer Keys for Questions
- Rationales for Bridge to NCLEX Examination Questions
- Answer Guidelines for Case Studies

Conceptual Care Map Creator
Audio Glossary
Content Updates

REFERENCES

1. Brannon H: The individual layers of skin and their functions. Retrieved from https://www.verywellhealth.com/skin-anatomy-1068880.
2. Difference Between: Difference between black and white skin. Retrieved from https://www.differencebetween.com/difference-between-black-and-white-skin/.
3. Medical News Today: How much hair loss is normal? Retrieved from https://www.medicalnewstoday.com/articles/327188.
4. Science ABC: How fast do nails grow? Retrieved from https://www.scienceabc.com/humans/fast-nails-grow.html.
5. Health Jade: Melanonychia. Retrieved from https://healthjade.net/melanonychia/.

*6. Huang AH, Chien AL: Photoaging: a review of current literature, *Curr Derm Rep* 9:22, 2020.

*7. Carr S, Smith C, Wernberg J: Epidemiology and risk factors of melanoma, *Surg Clin* 100:1, 2020.

*8. Naderi Z, Radmanesh M: Assessment of sensitivity and specificity of dermoscopy in diagnosis of malignant and premalignant skin lesions, *JCR* 7:9072, 2020.

*Evidence-based information for clinical practice.

25

Integumentary Problems

Mary M. Cameron

http://evolve.elsevier.com/Lewis/medsurg/

CONCEPTUAL FOCUS

Cellular Regulation
Coping
Infection
Pain
Tissue Integrity

LEARNING OUTCOMES

1. Outline health promotion practices related to environmental hazards.
2. Explain the etiology, clinical manifestations, and interprofessional and nursing management of skin cancers.
3. Relate the etiology, clinical manifestations, and interprofessional and nursing management of bacterial, viral, and fungal skin infections.
4. Describe the etiology, clinical manifestations, and interprofessional and nursing management of infestations and insect bites.
5. Discuss the etiology, clinical manifestations, and interprofessional and nursing management of allergic skin disorders.
6. Explain the etiology, clinical manifestations, and interprofessional and nursing management related to benign skin disorders.
7. Select appropriate nursing interventions to manage the patient with a skin problem.
8. Explain the indications and nursing management related to common cosmetic procedures and skin grafts.

KEY TERMS

acne vulgaris, Table 25.10
actinic keratosis
basal cell carcinoma (BCC)
cellulitis, Table 25.5
cryosurgery
curettage
dysplastic nevi (DN)
herpes zoster, Table 25.6
impetigo, Table 25.5
lichenification
melanoma
psoriasis
rosacea, Table 25.10
squamous cell carcinoma (SCC)
sun protection factor (SPF)

This chapter discusses common skin problems and skin cancer. Impaired skin integrity affects many body functions. The skin reflects both physical and psychologic well-being. Many skin problems leave underlying tissues unprotected from infection and chemical dangers. Lesions can be painful because the skin has many sensory nerve endings. Skin problems are often highly visible, potentially affecting body image and causing distress.

ENVIRONMENTAL HAZARDS

Sun exposure comes with serious risk and results in permanent skin damage. Sunlight is made up of visible light and ultraviolet (UV) light. There are 2 types of UV light: UVA and UVB. Specific wavelengths (Table 25.1) have different effects on the skin. UVA light is responsible for tanning, UVB for sunburn. The damage caused by UV rays is cumulative. It results in degenerative changes in the dermis and premature aging (e.g., loss of elasticity, thinning, wrinkling). Prolonged and repeated sun exposure increases risk for actinic keratosis (AK), basal and squamous cell cancers, and melanoma.

Provide teaching on sun protection. People often do not understand the risks of sun exposure. Following sun safety guidelines beginning early in life can help avoid the damaging effects of the sun and prevent skin cancer later in life.

TABLE 25.1 Wavelengths of Sun and Effects on Skin

Wavelength	Effect
Long (ultraviolet A [UVA])	Can cause elastic tissue damage and actinic skin damage Contributes to skin cancer
Middle (ultraviolet B [UVB])	Causes sunburn and cumulative effect of sun damage Major factor in developing skin cancer
Short (ultraviolet C [UVC])	Blocked by the atmosphere and does not reach earth

Fair-skinned persons and those with light-colored eyes should be especially cautious about sun exposure. They have less melanin and thus less natural protection.

Teach the patient ways to avoid the damaging effects of the sun. This includes wearing protective clothing, including sunglasses, a large-brimmed hat, and a darker colored, long-sleeved shirt of a tightly woven fabric or carrying an umbrella. The greatest risk is with midday sun, between the hours of 10:00 a.m. and 2:00 p.m., regardless of the latitude. This is when 80% of UV rays occur. Even on overcast days, serious sunburn can occur because up to 80% of the sun's UV rays can penetrate the clouds. Warn people of the dangers of tanning booths and sun lamps, which emit UVA. Tanning booths increase the risk for sunburn, cataracts, and skin cancer (Box 25.1).[1]

Sunscreens can filter both UVA and UVB wavelengths. The 2 types of topical sunscreens are chemical and physical. Chemical sunscreens absorb into the skin. There they absorb or filter UV light, resulting in decreased UV light penetration. Physical sunscreens sit on top of the skin. They reflect UV radiation away from the skin. Regular sunscreen use decreases the risk for melanoma.

The US Food and Drug Administration (FDA) rates sunscreen products on their **sun protection factor (SPF)**. The SPF measures the effectiveness of a sunscreen in filtering and absorbing UV radiation. All sunscreen labels in the United States must say which rays they protect against. Products labeled with "broad spectrum" block both UVA and UVB.[2] Sunscreens with broad spectrum labeling must have an SPF of at least 15. Sunscreens with an SPF of 15 or more filter 92% of the UVB rays and make sunburn unlikely when applied appropriately.

People need to select the right sunscreen for their needs. The general suggestion is that everyone should use daily sunscreen with a minimum SPF of 15. Teach patients to look for the term *broad spectrum* on sunscreen packaging. People with a history of skin cancer or problems with sun sensitivity should use a product with an SPF of at least 30. Sunscreens should be applied 20 to 30 minutes before going outdoors, even in cloudy weather. The SPF value of all sunscreens decreases with time. Sunscreen should be reapplied every 2 hours. You should apply 1 ounce per total body application. The ears, toes, and lips also need sunscreen. Sunscreens are not "waterproof" and must be reapplied after swimming.

Some drugs potentiate the sun's effects, even with brief exposure. The chemicals in these drugs absorb light when exposed to natural sunlight and release energy that harms cells and tissues. Common photosensitizing drugs are shown in Table 25.2. The

BOX 25.1 EVIDENCE-BASED PRACTICE

Tanning Booths and Skin Cancer

You are a nurse working in a dermatology clinic. D.F., a 30-year-old woman with fair skin and blue eyes, is completing her health history before her annual skin screening. She says she visits an indoor tanning salon every other week. She tells you that being tan makes her feel "healthier and prettier."

Making Clinical Decisions

Best Available Evidence

There is a strong link between exposure to UVA from indoor tanning booth use and increased risk for all skin cancers. Skin damage starts with the 1st visit. 95% of persons with melanoma who are diagnosed before age 30 report having used tanning booths. Melanoma risk increases with the number of years, hours, and sessions of indoor tanning independent of outdoor exposure.

Clinician Expertise

You note that D.F. has several skin cancer risk factors: fair skin, blue eyes, frequent use of tanning booths.

Patient Preferences and Values

After listening, D.F. tells you that she will consider reducing the frequency of her visits—going only when she has an important event to attend.

Implications for Nursing Practice

1. How would you respond to D.F., given the information that she shared with you?
2. What resources can help address her view that a "tan looks healthy?"
3. What sun safety guidelines should she follow to prevent skin cancer?

Reference for Evidence

Alberg AJ, LoConte NK, Foxhall L, et al.: American Society of Clinical Oncology policy statement on skin cancer prevention, *JCO Oncology Practice* 16:490, 2020.

TABLE 25.2 Drug Therapy

Drugs That May Cause Photosensitivity

Categories	Examples
Antidepressants	fluoxetine, paroxetine, venlafaxine
Antidysrhythmics	amiodarone (Cordarone), quinidine
Antihistamines	cetirizine (Zyrtec), chlorpheniramine, clemastine, diphenhydramine, loratadine
Antimicrobials	tetracycline, azithromycin (Zithromax), ciprofloxacin, sulfonamides
Antifungals	griseofulvin, ketoconazole
Antipsychotics	chlorpromazine, haloperidol
Cholesterol-lowering agents	atorvastatin, simvastatin
Diuretics	furosemide (Lasix), thiazides
Hypoglycemics	glipizide, glyburide
Nonsteroidal antiinflammatory drugs	diclofenac (Voltaren), ibuprofen, naproxen, piroxicam (Feldene),

manifestations of drug-induced photosensitivity (Fig. 25.1) are like those of a sunburn. These include swelling, redness, vesicles, and papular, plaque-like lesions. Assess the photosensitivity of each drug. Teach patients who are taking these drugs about their photosensitizing effect and the need to protect the skin from photosensitivity reactions by using sunscreen products.

Teach patients to assess their skin monthly. They should have a periodic professional assessment of areas that are hard to see. The cornerstone of skin assessment is the ABCDE rule. Assess lesions for ***Asymmetry***, ***Border*** irregularity, ***Color*** change and variation, ***Diameter*** of 6 mm or more, and ***Evolving*** in

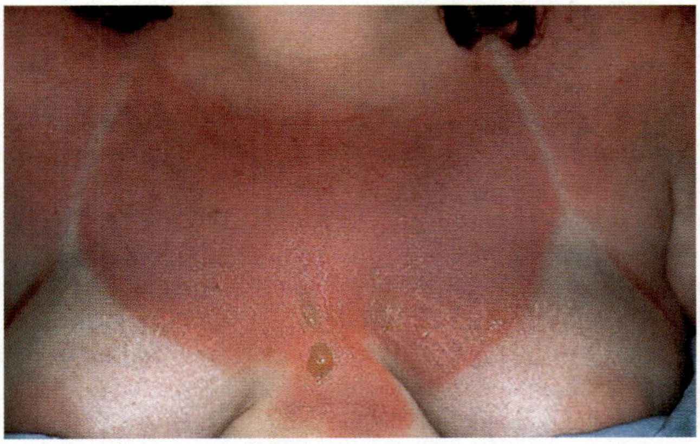

Fig. 25.1 Photosensitivity reaction in a patient taking methotrexate. (From Valeyrie-Allanore L, Obeid O, Revuz J: *Dermatology*, ed 4, St. Louis, 2018, Elsevier.)

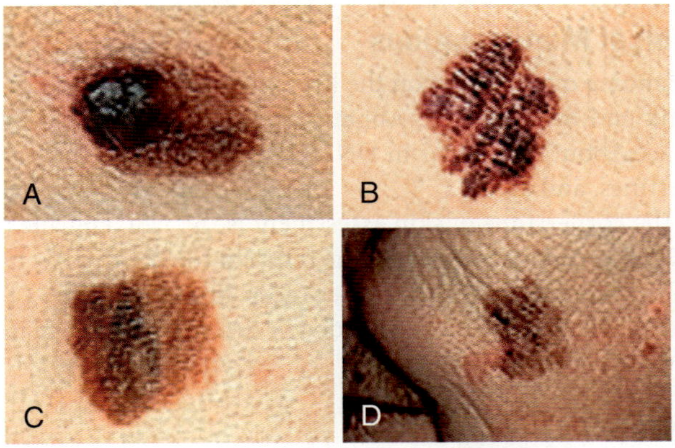

Fig. 25.2 The ABCDEs of melanoma. (A) Asymmetry: one half unlike the other half. (B) Border irregularity: edges are ragged, notched, or blurred. (C) Color: varied pigmentation; shades of tan, brown, and black. (D) Diameter: greater than 6 mm (diameter of a pencil eraser). (E, *not pictured*) Evolving; changing appearance (change in shape, size, color, or other characteristic noted over time). (From The Skin Cancer Foundation, New York, NY.)

appearance (Fig. 25.2). Emphasize that a persistent lesion that does not heal and lesions once flat and now raised, once small and recently growing, or changing in appearance are warning signs. Patients should consult their HCP at once if any lesions or moles show any clinical signs (ABCDEs).

SKIN CANCER

Skin cancer is the most commonly diagnosed cancer.[3] Skin cancers are either nonmelanoma or melanoma. The fact that skin lesions are so visible increases the chance of early detection and diagnosis. This often leads to a highly favorable prognosis.

Risk Factors

Risk factors for skin cancer include (1) having fair skin, blond or red hair with blue eye color; (2) history of outdoor sunbathing; (3) living near the equator or at high altitudes; (4) family or personal history of skin cancer; (5) having an outdoor occupation; (6) spending a lot of time in outdoor recreation activities; and (7) indoor tanning.[3] The Fitzpatrick Classification of Skin Type can help you determine a person's skin complexion and their risk for skin cancer (Table 25.3). Patients treated with oral methoxsalen (psoralen) and psoralen plus ultraviolet A radiation (PUVA) have a higher risk.

Dark-skinned persons are less susceptible to skin cancer because of their increased melanin, which acts like a sunscreen (Box 25.2). However, there is still a risk, and they need to wear sunscreen. They often have melanomas on areas with less melanin, such as the palms, soles, mucous membranes, and under the nails. Since it is common for people with dark skin to have pigmented, longitudinal bands on their nails, assess for nail discoloration.

NONMELANOMA SKIN CANCER

Nonmelanoma skin cancers (basal cell and squamous cell cancers) are the most common forms of skin cancer. More than 5.4 million new cases are diagnosed each year.[3] Nonmelanoma skin cancers do not develop from melanocytes. They develop in the basement membrane of the skin. Although there are few deaths from nonmelanoma skin cancer, they have the potential for severe local destruction, disfigurement, and disability.

Nonmelanoma skin cancers usually develop in sun-exposed areas, such as the face, head, neck, back of the hands, and arms. The most common causative factor is sun exposure. There are some differences between basal and squamous cell cancers. Squamous cell cancers usually occur on the head and neck, where there is the highest degree of UV radiation. Basal cell cancers do not follow that pattern and may occur in sun-protected areas.

Actinic Keratosis

Actinic keratosis (AK), or *solar keratosis,* is the most common precancerous skin lesion. They affect most of the older White population. Sun exposure is a key factor. AKs appear most often on skin that has been exposed to the sun or to artificial UV light. They may spontaneously resolve if a person reduces exposure to sunlight.

TABLE 25.3 Fitzpatrick Classification of Skin Type

Skin Type	Skin Color	Characteristics
I	White, freckles, very fair. Red or blond hair. Blue eyes	Always burns, never tans
II	White, fair. Red or blond hair. Blue, hazel, or green eyes	Usually burns, tans with difficulty
III	Cream white, fair. Any eye or hair color	Sometimes mild burn, gradually tan
IV	Brown, typical Mediterranean skin	Rarely burns, tans with ease
V	Deep brown, Middle Eastern skin types	Very rarely burns, tans very easily
VI	Black	Never burns, tans very easily

BOX 25.2 PROMOTING HEALTH EQUITY

Skin Cancer

- Blacks, Asians, and Hispanics have a lower incidence of skin cancer than Whites.
- Melanoma in dark-skinned persons often goes unrecognized until the advanced stages.

The clinical appearance of AK can be highly varied. The typical lesion is an irregularly shaped, flat, slightly red papule with indistinct borders and an overlying hard keratotic scale or horn (Table 25.4). Because AK is impossible to distinguish from squamous cell cancer, treatment should be aggressive. Nonsurgical procedures are the first-line treatment. Any lesion that persists should be evaluated for a biopsy.

Basal Cell Carcinoma

Basal cell carcinoma (BCC) is a locally invasive cancer arising from epidermal basal cells. It is the most common type of skin cancer but the least deadly. BCC usually occurs in middle-aged to older adults. Most BCCs occur in the head and neck area (e.g., sun-exposed), followed by the trunk and extremities.[4]

Table 25.4 describes manifestations of BCC. Some BCCs are pigmented, with curled borders and an opaque appearance. They may be hard to distinguish from melanoma. A tissue biopsy is needed to confirm the diagnosis. BCCs rarely metastasize (Fig. 25.3). However, untreated BCC may result in massive tissue destruction. Treatment depends on the tumor location and histologic type, size, history of recurrence, and patient characteristics (Table 25.4).

Squamous Cell Carcinoma

Squamous cell carcinoma (SCC) is a cancer arising from keratinizing epidermal cells. SCC can be aggressive and has the potential to metastasize. It may lead to death if not treated early. SCC often occurs at the base of an AK or another lesion. The main risk factors are sun exposure and immunosuppression after an organ transplant.[5] Pipe, cigar, and cigarette smoking contribute to SCC on the mouth and lips. Table 25.4 outlines the manifestations of SCC. A biopsy should always be done when a lesion is thought to be SCC.

MELANOMA

Melanoma is a tumor arising from melanocytes, the cells that make melanin. It causes most skin cancer deaths. The incidence of melanoma is steadily rising.[1] More than 107,000 new cases are diagnosed each year in the United States, and almost 8000 people die from the disease.[6] Melanoma can metastasize to any organ, including the brain and heart.

A combination of environmental and genetic factors is likely involved in the development of melanoma. UV radiation from the sun is the main cause. Artificial sources of UV radiation, such as sunlamps and tanning booths, also play a role. UV radiation damages the deoxyribonucleic acid (DNA) in skin cells, causing "misspellings" (mutations) in their genetic code. This alters the cells. Although anyone can develop melanoma, the risk is greatest for people who have red or blond hair, blue or light-colored eyes, and light-colored skin that freckles easily. These people have less melanin and thus less protection from UV radiation. The use of immunosuppressive drugs and a history of dysplastic nevi (DN) also increase risk.

A person may have a genetic predisposition toward getting melanoma. Of those with melanoma, 5% to 10% have a first-degree relative (e.g., parent, full sibling) who had melanoma.[1] This risk greatly increases if multiple relatives had melanoma. Mutated genes have been found in some families who have a high familial incidence of melanoma.

Cutaneous melanoma begins in the skin. There are 4 subtypes of melanoma: (1) superficial spreading melanoma, (2) nodular melanoma, (3) lentigo maligna melanoma, and (4) acral lentiginous melanoma.

Clinical Manifestations

Melanoma often occurs on the lower legs in women and on the trunk and head in men. About 25% occur in existing nevi or moles. About 20% occur in DN. Rarely, it occurs in the mouth, intestines, and eyes.

The cornerstone of skin assessment is the ABCDE rule (Fig. 25.2). Because most melanoma cells continue to make melanin, melanoma tumors are often deep brown or black (Table 25.4). Lesions showing any sudden or progressive change in the ABCDE rule need evaluated.

Interprofessional Care

One of the first steps in diagnosing a suspicious lesion is dermoscopic examination. Dermoscopy can help the HCP decide if a lesion should be biopsied. Biopsy can determine the type of lesion. A biopsy should be done using an excisional biopsy technique. Shave biopsy, shave excision, or electrocauterization are avoided because they do not measure the depth of the lesion.

The most important prognostic factor is tumor thickness at the time of diagnosis. We assess tumor thickness with the *Breslow measurement*. It indicates tumor depth in millimeters (Fig. 25.4). Melanomas less than 1 mm thick have a small chance of spreading. As the melanoma becomes thicker, it has a greater chance of spreading.

Treatment depends on the site of the original tumor and the stage of the cancer. Melanoma staging (stages 0 to IV) is based on tumor size (thickness), nodal involvement, and metastasis. In stage 0, melanoma is confined to 1 place (in situ) in the epidermis. Melanoma is nearly 100% curable by excision if diagnosed at stage 0. Unfortunately, those with deep tumors or disease that has already spread to lymph nodes often develop metastases. The 5-year survival rate for those with advanced disease is around 27%.[6]

The initial treatment of melanoma is wide surgical excision. Melanoma that has spread to the lymph nodes or nearby sites usually requires additional (adjuvant) therapy with combinations of immunotherapy, targeted therapy, chemotherapy, and/or radiation therapy.

TABLE 25.4 Premalignant and Malignant Skin Problems

Etiology and Pathophysiology	Clinical Manifestations	Treatment
Actinic Keratosis		
• Actinic (sun) damage • Premalignant skin lesions • Common in older Whites • Increase in number with age	• Flat or elevated, dry, hyperkeratotic scaly papule. Often multiple • May be rough or wart-like • Rough adherent scale on red base, which returns when removed • Often on sun-exposed area	• Excision (cryosurgery, laser, chemical peel). Topical fluorouracil, imiquimod, ingenol mebutate. Photodynamic therapy • Recurrence possible even with adequate treatment
Atypical or Dysplastic Nevi		
• Morphologically between common acquired nevi and melanoma • May be precursor of melanoma	• Often >5 mm. Irregular border, possibly notched. Frequently multiple • Varying colors of tan, brown, black, red, or pink within single mole • Central part often raised with flat edges • Most common site on back, but possible in uncommon mole sites such as scalp or buttocks (Fig. 25.5)	• Careful monitoring of those with a familial tendency to melanoma or dysplastic nevi • Excisional biopsy for suspicious lesions
Basal Cell Carcinoma		
• Change in basal cells. • No maturation or normal keratinization • Continuing division of basal cells and formation of enlarging mass • Related to sun exposure, skin type, x-ray radiation, scars, some types of nevi • Slow-growing tumor that invades local tissue • Metastasis rare, 90% cure rate with primary lesions	*Nodular and ulcerative*: • Small, slowly enlarging papule • Borders semitranslucent or "pearly" with overlying telangiectasia • Erosion, ulceration, and depression of center • Normal skin markings lost (Fig. 25.3) *Superficial*: • Red, pearly, sharply defined, barely elevated plaques	• Surgical excision, electrodessication and curettage, cryosurgery, radiation therapy, laser therapy, photodynamic therapy • Vismodegib (Erivedge), sonidegib (Odomzo) for metastatic or recurrent locally invasive lesions • Fluorouracil, imiquimod for superficial lesions
Cutaneous T-Cell Lymphoma		
• Origins in skin. Localized chronic, slowly progressing disease • Possibly related to environmental toxins and chemical exposure • Mycosis fungoides (MF) is most common form • Sézary syndrome is an advanced form of MF • Prevalence twice as high in men • Disease course is unpredictable. 10% have progressive disease	• Classic presentation involves 3 stages: patch (early), plaque, and tumor (advanced) • History of persistent macules followed by gradual appearance of indurated red plaques on trunk • Appears similar to psoriasis • Itching, lymphadenopathy	• Treatment usually controls symptoms but is not curative • Phototherapy, radiation therapy, extracorporeal photopheresis, chemotherapy, biologic therapy (interferon) • Medications include corticosteroids, topical nitrogen mustard, imiquimod, retinoids, romidepsin (Istodax), denileukin diftitox (Ontak), vorinostat (Zolinza)
Melanoma		
• Neoplastic growth of melanocytes anywhere on skin, eyes, or mucous membranes • Classified by major histologic mode of spread • Correlation between survival rate and depth of invasion • Poor prognosis unless diagnosed and treated early • Spreading by local extension, regional lymphatic vessels, and bloodstream	• Irregular color, surface, and border • Variegated color, including red, white, blue, black, gray, brown • Flat or elevated. Eroded or ulcerated • Often <1 cm in size • Most common sites in males are back, then chest. In females are legs, then back (Fig. 25.2)	• Surgical excision and possible sentinel lymph node evaluation • Adjuvant therapy after surgery if lesion >1.5 mm in depth • Key adjuvant therapies include immunotherapy (cytokines, PD-1 inhibitors, CTLA-4 inhibitors), targeted therapy (BRAF and MEK inhibitors)

Continued

TABLE 25.4 Premalignant and Malignant Skin Problems—cont'd

Etiology and Pathophysiology	Clinical Manifestations	Treatment
Squamous Cell Carcinoma (SCC)		
• Often occurs on previously damaged skin (e.g., from sun, radiation, scar) • Cancer of squamous cell of epidermis. Invades dermis, surrounding skin • Most common on sun-exposed areas such as face and hands • High cure rate with early detection and treatment	• *Superficial*: Thin, scaly, red plaque without invasion into the dermis • *Early:* Firm nodules with indistinct borders, scaling, ulceration • *Late:* Covering of lesion with scale or horn from keratinization, ulceration	• Surgical excision, cryosurgery, radiation therapy, electrosurgery, laser therapy, photodynamic therapy • Untreated lesion may metastasize to regional lymph nodes and distant organs • Fluorouracil, imiquimod for noninvasive SCC • Immunotherapy for metastatic lesions

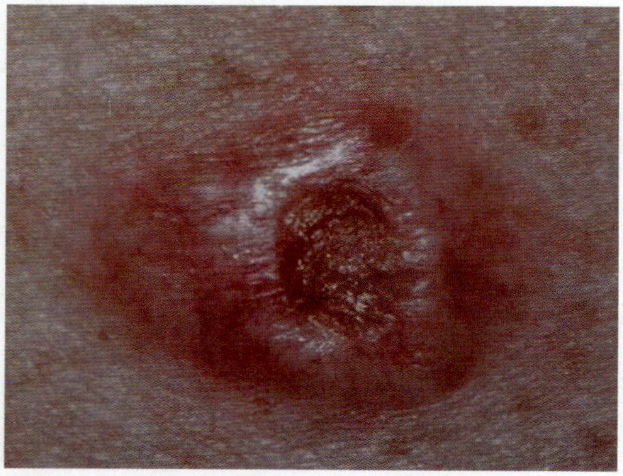

Fig. 25.3 Basal cell carcinoma. Rolled, well-defined border and central erosion. (From Goldman L, Schafer A: *Goldman-Cecil medicine*, ed 25, Philadelphia, 2016, Saunders.)

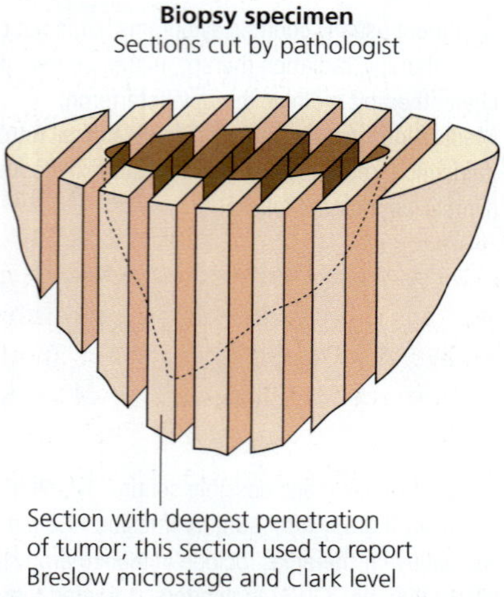

Fig. 25.4 Breslow measurement of tumor thickness. (From Habif TP: *Clinical dermatology: a color guide to diagnosis and therapy*, ed 6, St Louis, 2016, Mosby.)

Immunotherapy can include cytokines (α-interferon, interleukin-2), PD-1 inhibitors, and CTLA-4 inhibitors. Cytokines enhance the production of many immune system cells, including T cells and B cells. Drugs that block PD-1 or CTLA-4 boost the immune response against melanoma cells.[7] Anti–PD-1 agents include nivolumab (Opdivo) and pembrolizumab (Keytruda). They block PD-1, a protein on T cells that keeps T cells from attacking other cells in the body. Atezolizumab (Tecentriq) targets PD-L1, a protein related to PD-1 that is found on some tumor cells. Ipilimumab (Yervoy) blocks the action of CTLA-4, another protein that normally suppresses the action of T cells.

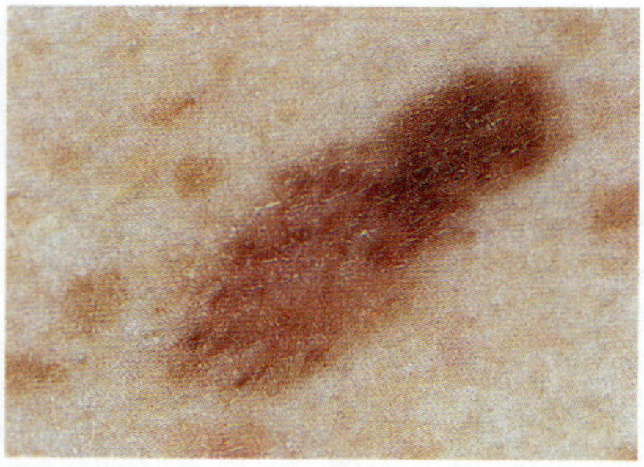

Fig. 25.5 Dysplastic nevus. Irregular border and color. (From Graham-Brown R, Bourke J, Cunliffe T: *Dermatology: fundamentals of practice,* Edinburgh, 2008, Mosby.)

Targeted therapy for melanoma includes BRAF and MEK inhibitors. About half of melanomas have *BRAF* gene mutations, which make an altered BRAF protein that signals melanoma cells to proliferate. Vemurafenib (Zelboraf), dabrafenib (Tafinlar), and encorafenib (Braftovi) directly target BRAF genes. The MEK gene works with the BRAF gene, so drugs that block MEK proteins also help treat melanomas with BRAF gene changes. MEK inhibitors include Trametinib (Mekinist), binimetinib (Mektovi), and cobimetinib (Cotellic).[6,7]

Chemotherapy is not as effective for melanoma as it is for most other cancers. It is usually used only with advanced disease. Drugs used include dacarbazine and temozolomide.[6] Radiation therapy has a role in treating lymph node and brain metastases.

Atypical or Dysplastic Nevus

Dysplastic nevi (DN), or atypical moles, are nevi that are larger than usual (greater than 5 mm across) with irregular borders and various shades of color (Fig. 25.5). DN may have the same ABCDE characteristics as melanoma, but they are less pronounced. About 5% to 17% of the White population have DN.[8] Those with DN have an increased risk for developing melanoma in a mole or elsewhere on the body. The more DN a person has, the higher the risk. Those with 10 or more DN have 12 times the risk for developing melanoma.

> **CHECK YOUR PRACTICE**
>
> You are working in an HCP office, and your next patient is a 64-year-old White man. He is worried about the many "brown" spots on his face and arms. He tells you that they probably happened because he worked outside in construction most of his life.
>
> - How do you distinguish among an age spot (lentigo), normal mole, and melanoma?
> - What risk factors would you assess for in a patient with a suspected cancerous lesion?

SKIN INFECTIONS AND INFESTATIONS

Bacterial Infections

Bacterial infection can occur as a primary infection after a break in the skin. A secondary infection can occur in already damaged skin or as a sign of a systemic disease (Table 25.5). Risk factors include the presence of excess moisture, obesity, having atopic dermatitis, systemic corticosteroid or antibiotic use, and having a chronic disease, such as diabetes.

Staphylococcus aureus and group A β-hemolytic streptococci are the main types of bacteria that cause primary and secondary skin infections. Streptococci cause impetigo, erysipelas, cellulitis, and lymphangitis. *S. aureus* causes impetigo, folliculitis, cellulitis, and furuncles (Fig. 25.6). When an infection is present, the resulting drainage is infectious. Good skin hygiene and infection control practices help prevent the spread of the infection.

Viral Infections

Viral infections of the skin are hard to treat. When a virus infects a cell, a skin lesion may develop. Lesions can also result from an inflammatory response to viral infections. Herpes simplex, herpes zoster (Fig. 25.7), and warts (Fig. 25.8) are the most common viral infections affecting the skin (Table 25.6).

Infestations and Insect Bites

There are many opportunities for exposure to *infestations* (harboring insects or worms) and insect bites (Table 25.7). In many instances, an allergy to the venom plays a key role in the reaction. In other cases, the clinical manifestations are a reaction to the eggs, feces, or body parts of the invading organism. Some people react with a severe hypersensitivity (anaphylaxis), which can be life threatening (see Chapter 14).

Preventing insect bites by avoidance or using repellents is somewhat effective. Meticulous hygiene related to care of personal articles, clothing, bedding, and pets can reduce the incidence of infestations. Prompt, routine skin inspection is necessary in areas where there is a risk for tick bite. Lyme disease, caused by a tick, is discussed in Chapter 69.

Fungal Infections

Because of the large number of fungi that are present everywhere, exposure to some pathologic varieties may occur. Skin, hair, and nails can become infected with fungi, including candidiasis and tinea unguium. Common fungal infections of the skin are described in Table 25.8. Most infections are harmless in healthy adults, but they can cause embarrassment and distress.

Fungal infections are easy to diagnose. A microscopic examination showing the appearance of hyphae (thread-like structures) in a skin scraping mounted in 10% to 20% potassium hydroxide (KOH) indicates a fungal infection. A Wood light examination of hair infected with certain fungi will fluoresce blue to green.

ALLERGIC SKIN PROBLEMS

Patients often seek treatment for irritant or allergic dermatitis, 2 common types of contact dermatitis. *Irritant contact dermatitis* results from direct chemical injury to the skin. *Allergic contact dermatitis* is an antigen-specific, type IV delayed hypersensitivity response. Allergic and contact dermatitis is discussed in Chapter 14. Skin problems from allergies and hypersensitivity reactions can be challenging (Table 25.9). A careful history and discussion of exposure to possible offending agents can provide valuable data. Patch testing can help determine possible causative agents (see Fig. 24.10). The best treatment of allergic dermatitis is to avoid known irritants. The extreme itching and its potential for chronicity make it a frustrating problem for you and the patient, especially if we cannot find the offending agent.

Skin Drug Reactions

Stevens-Johnson syndrome (SJS) and *toxic epidermal necrolysis* (TEN) are rare, life-threatening diseases. They are violent immune responses that often occur as a severe adverse reaction to either a drug or, more rarely, an infection. The result is the acute destruction of the epithelium of the skin and mucous membranes. SJS, SJS-TEN overlap, and TEN represents a spectrum of disease severity. SJS involves less than 10% of total body surface area. SJS-TEN overlap involves 10% to 29%. TEN involves more than 30% of total body surface area.[9]

SJS and TEN typically occur 4 to 21 days after starting use of the offending drug. Systemic symptoms, including fever, cough, headache, anorexia, myalgia, and nausea, precede skin and mucous membrane findings by 1 to 3 days. Skin involvement starts as a red, macular rash with purpuric centers. Over a period of hours to days, the rash merges to form blisters with sheet-like epidermal detachment (Fig. 25.9). The lesions usually start on the palms, soles, and trunk, then spread to the face and extremities. They are very painful. Most people have mucosal lesions in the eye, mouth, and genital areas.

Identifying and stopping the offending drug(s) is the most important action in caring for a patient with SJS/TEN. Common drugs involved include sulfonamides, fluoroquinolones, NSAIDs, allopurinol, antiseizure drugs, and antiretroviral drugs. Immunotherapy may play a role in slowing disease progression and promoting skin repair.

The patient receives supportive care, often in an intensive care unit. Interventions focus on airway management, preserving renal function, maintaining fluid and electrolyte balance, and pain control. Fluid replacement is given to maintain urine output. Proper wound care helps prevent infection and promote healing. Dressing with petrolatum gauze or other nonadhesive material provides a barrier and offers moisture to help the skin repair.

TABLE 25.5 Common Bacterial Skin Infections

Etiology and Pathophysiology	Clinical Manifestations	Treatment and Prognosis
Carbuncle		
• Multiple, interconnecting furuncles	• Many pustules appearing in reddened area • Most common at nape of neck	• Incision and drainage (possibly with packing), antibiotics, meticulous care of involved skin, frequent application of warm, moist compresses • Heal slowly with scar formation
Cellulitis		
• Inflammation of subcutaneous tissues • May be a primary infection or secondary complication • Often following break in skin • *Staphylococcus aureus* and streptococci usual causative agents • Deep inflammation of subcutaneous tissue from enzymes produced by bacteria	• Hot, tender, red, edematous area with diffuse borders • Chills, malaise, fever (Fig. 25.6)	*Topical:* • Moist heat, immobilization, and elevation *Systemic:* • Systemic antibiotic therapy • Hospitalization if severe for IV antibiotic therapy based on culture and sensitivity • Progression to gangrene possible if untreated
Erysipelas		
• Superficial cellulitis mainly involving the dermis • Group A β-hemolytic streptococci	• Red, hot, sharply demarcated plaque, Indurated, painful • Bacteremia possible • Most common on face and extremities • Toxic signs: fever, ↑ WBC count, headache, malaise	• Systemic antibiotics, usually penicillin • Hospitalization often needed
Folliculitis		
• Usually staphylococci • Present in areas subjected to friction, moisture, rubbing, oil • Increased incidence in patients with diabetes	• Small pustule at hair follicle opening with minimal redness • Development of crusting • Most common on scalp, beard, extremities in men • Tender to touch	• Topical antibiotics (e.g., mupirocin) • Cleanse with chlorhexidine • Warm saline compresses • Usually heals without scarring • If lesions extensive and deep, possible scarring, loss of involved hair follicles, and treatment with systemic antibiotics
Furuncle		
• Deep infection with staphylococci around hair follicle • Often occurs with severe acne or seborrheic dermatitis	• Tender, red, painful area around hair follicle • Draining pus and core of necrotic debris on rupture • Most common on face, back of neck, axillae, breasts, buttocks, perineum, thighs	• Same as for carbuncles
Furunculosis		
• Increased incidence in patients who are obese, diabetic, chronically ill, regularly exposed to moisture, pressure	• Lesions as above • Malaise, regional adenopathy, fever	*Topical:* • Incision and drainage of painful nodules • Warm, moist compresses to reddened plaques • Measures to reduce surface staphylococci include antimicrobial cream to nares, armpits, groin and antiseptic to entire skin • Meticulous personal hygiene *Systemic:* • Systemic antibiotic effective against MRSA pending culture and sensitivity results • Often recurrent with scarring
Impetigo		
• Streptococci, staphylococci, or combination of both • Primary or secondary infection. • Contagious	• Vesiculopustular lesions that develop thick, honey-colored crust surrounded by redness • Itches • Most common on face as primary infection	*Topical:* • Wound care with warm saline or aluminum acetate soaks followed by soap-and-water removal of crusts • Topical antibiotic cream or ointment (mupirocin, retapamulin) • Good personal hygiene *Systemic:* • Systemic antibiotics (e.g., cephalexin, doxycycline, dicloxacillin, clindamycin) for widespread infections or systemic manifestations

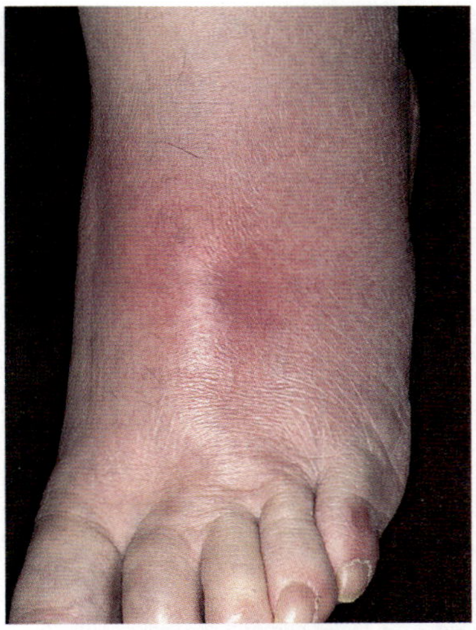

Fig. 25.6 Cellulitis with characteristic redness, tenderness, and edema. (From Habif TP: *Clinical dermatology: a color guide to diagnosis and therapy*, ed 5, St Louis, 2011, Mosby.)

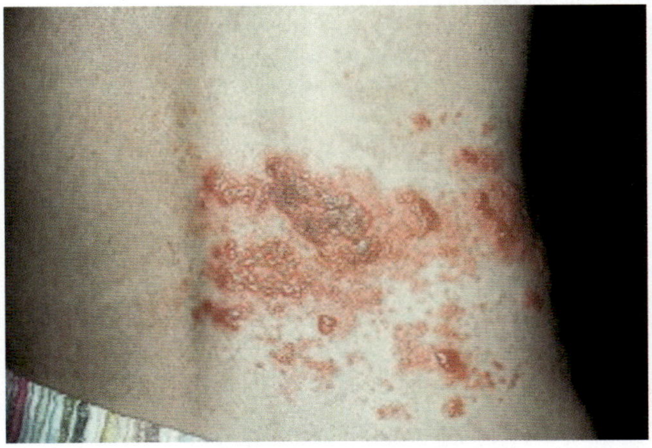

Fig. 25.7 Herpes zoster (shingles) involving the lumbar dermatome. (From Elsevier Point of Care, 2020, Elsevier.)

Because of painful oral lesions, most patients need parenteral or enteral nutrition to meet nutrient needs. Apply eyedrops, lubricating ointment, and antibiotic drops to those with conjunctivitis.

BENIGN SKIN PROBLEMS

The list of benign skin problems is long. Some of the most common and distressing ones include acne (Fig. 25.10), psoriasis, and seborrheic keratoses. Benign skin problems are outlined in Table 25.10.

Psoriasis is a chronic autoimmune disease. It is fairly common, affecting around 7.5 million Americans.[9] Men and women develop psoriasis at equal rates. The rate is highest in Whites.[9] It usually develops in those 15 to 35 years old. One-third of people with psoriasis have at least 1 relative with the disease. Psoriasis is associated with metabolic syndrome, heart disease, and type 2 diabetes. Up to 40% of people also have psoriatic arthritis. Psoriatic arthritis is discussed in Chapter 69.

The diagnosis of plaque psoriasis, the most common form, is based on the skin's appearance (Fig. 25.11). Lesions are distinct

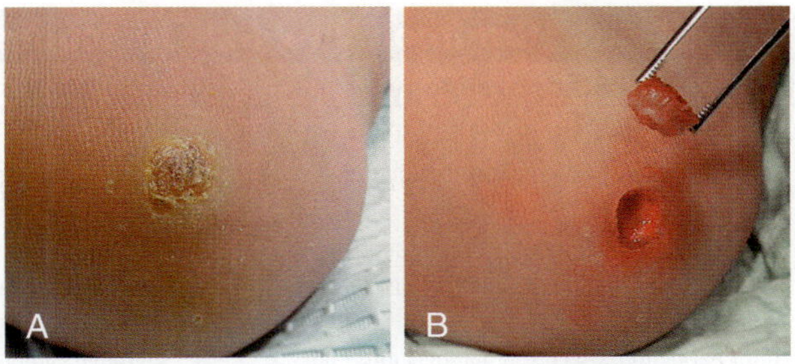

Fig. 25.8 Plantar wart. (A) Keratotic lesion. (B) After excision. (From Swartz MH: *Textbook of physical diagnosis: history and examination*, ed 6, Philadelphia, 2010, Saunders.)

and appear as red, scaling papules that merge to form plaques. The affected area is normally rounded, with adherent silver scales that bleed easily when removed. Plaques are common on the knees, elbows, scalp, hands, feet, and lower back. They are often itchy and may be painful. The extent of the disease varies. Most people have mild disease. Some have psoriasis on much of their skin surface.

We tailor treatment to the person's needs. This varies depending on the location of lesions, severity, patient preferences, and comorbidities. Goals range from improved quality of life to complete disease resolution. Psoriasis for most is more emotionally than physically disabling. It erodes the self-image. The person may be self-conscious and withdraw from social contacts. Quality of life can diminish as people avoid activities. Depression is common.

DRUG ALERT

Isotretinoin

- Used to treat acne (Table 25.10)
- Can cause serious damage to fetus
- Contraindicated in women who are pregnant or want to become pregnant
- Cannot donate blood during treatment and for 1 month after treatment ends
- May cause depression and suicidal ideation

INTERPROFESSIONAL CARE: SKIN PROBLEMS

Many different treatments are used in dermatology. Advances in this field have brought relief to many previously chronic, untreatable problems. Many of the specific treatments require specialized equipment. They are usually used by a dermatologist or specially trained nurse. The history, physical assessment, and diagnostic test results guide therapy.

Phototherapy

UV light therapy is a part of treating many skin problems, including psoriasis, cutaneous T-cell lymphoma, atopic dermatitis, vitiligo, and itching. Light sources available include broadband UVB, narrowband UVB, and long-wave UV (UVA1). One form of phototherapy combines the use of the photosensitizing drug methoxsalen with UVA light (PUVA). With PUVA, patients receive methoxsalen and then are exposed to UVA.

Treatments are generally given 2 to 3 times a week. Side effects include nausea, itching, and redness. Taking methoxsalen with

TABLE 25.6 Common Viral Skin Infections

Etiology and Pathophysiology	Clinical Manifestations	Treatment and Prognosis
Herpes Simplex Virus (HSV) Types 1 and 2		
• Oral or genital HSV infections serotyped as either HSV-1 or HSV-2 • Both are recurrent lifelong viral infections • Worsened by sunlight, trauma, menses, stress, and systemic infection • Contagious to those not previously infected • Transmitted by respiratory droplets or virus-containing fluid (e.g., saliva, cervical secretions) • Infection in one area readily transmitted to another site by contact	*First episode:* • Symptoms occurring 2 days to 2 weeks after contact • Painful local reaction • Single or grouped vesicles on reddened base • Systemic symptoms (e.g., fever, malaise) possible or no symptoms possible *Recurrent:* • Recurrence in similar spot • Characteristic grouped vesicles on reddened base	• Symptomatic • Soothing, moist compresses. Petroleum jelly to lesions • Scarring not usual result • Antiviral agents such as acyclovir (Zovirax), famciclovir, valacyclovir (Valtrex)
Herpes Zoster (Shingles)		
• Activation of the varicella-zoster virus • Incidence increases with age • Potentially contagious to anyone who has not had varicella or who is immunosuppressed	• Linear distribution along a dermatome of grouped vesicles and pustules on reddened base (see Fig. 25.7) • Usually unilateral on trunk, face, and lumbosacral areas • Burning, pain, and neuralgia preceding outbreak • Mild to severe pain during outbreak	*Topical:* • Wet compresses, silver sulfadiazine (Silvadene) to ruptured vesicles *Systemic:* • Antiviral agents (e.g., acyclovir, famciclovir, valacyclovir) within 72 h of onset to prevent postherpetic neuralgia • Analgesia. Mild sedation at bedtime • Gabapentin (Neurontin) to treat postherpetic neuralgia • Usually heals without complications, but scarring and postherpetic neuralgia possible • Vaccine (Zostavax) to prevent shingles one-time dose for adults ≥60 year
Plantar Warts		
• Caused by human papillomavirus (HPV)	• Wart on bottom surface of foot, growing inward because of pressure of walking or standing (Fig. 25.8) • Painful when pressure applied • Interrupted skin markings • Cone shaped with black dots (thrombosed vessels) when wart removed	• Topical immunotherapy (imiquimod), cryosurgery, salicylic acid, duct tape
Verruca Vulgaris		
• Caused by HPV • May disappear spontaneously in 1–2 years • Mildly contagious by autoinoculation • Specific response dependent on body part affected • Prevalence greater in youth and immunosuppressed	• Circumscribed, hypertrophic, flesh-colored papule limited to epidermis • Painful on lateral compression	• Multiple treatments, including surgery using blunt dissection with scissors or curette • Liquid nitrogen therapy • Blistering agent (cantharidin) • Keratolytic agent (salicylic acid) • CO_2 laser destruction

food and milk may reduce nausea. Caution patients about taking methoxsalen and exposure during therapy to UV rays from sunlight or artificial UV light. Because of the risk for cataracts, patients receiving PUVA need to wear prescription goggles that block 100% of UV light. Teach patients to wear the eyewear for 24 hours after taking the medication when outdoors or near a bright window (UVA penetrates glass). Perform frequent skin assessments on all patients receiving phototherapy. The immunosuppressive effects of PUVA increase the risk for SCC, BCC, and melanoma.

Photodynamic therapy is a special type of phototherapy used to treat AK and some skin cancers. This therapy uses a photosensitizing agent in a different way than other phototherapy treatments. The patient receives the photosensitizing agent IV or topically, depending on the area treated. Time is allowed for the drug to be absorbed by the target cells. Light is then applied to the area, causing the drug to react with oxygen. This starts a reaction that kills the cells.

CHECK YOUR PRACTICE

You are working in a dermatology clinic, preparing a 64-year-old woman for phototherapy to treat multiple actinic keratoses on her nose and both cheeks. She says the first lesion appeared a few years ago. She then started to worry about all the time she spent in her garden without sunscreen. She thought the lesions were just "age spots" and was unconcerned until a few started to grow and periodically bleed.

- What teaching will you do to get her ready for the procedure and to take care of herself after?

TABLE 25.7 Common Infestations and Insect Bites

Etiology and Pathophysiology	Clinical Manifestations	Treatment and Prognosis
Bedbugs		
• Cimicidae species • Feeding periodic, usually at night • Present in furniture, walls during day	• Wheal surrounded by vivid flare • Firm hives transforming into persistent lesion • Severe itching • Often grouped in threes appearing on uncovered parts of body	• Lesions usually require no treatment • Severe itching may require use of antihistamines or topical corticosteroids
Bees and Wasps		
• Hymenoptera species	• Intense, burning, local pain • Swelling and itching • Severe hypersensitivity may lead to anaphylaxis	• Cool compresses • Local application of antipruritic lotion • Antihistamines if indicated • Usually uneventful recovery
Pediculosis (Head Lice, Body Lice, Pubic Lice)		
• *Pediculus humanus* var. *capitis, Pediculus humanus* var. *corporis, Phthirus pubis* • Parasites that suck blood, leave excrement and eggs on skin and hair, live in seams of clothing (if body lice) and in hair as nits. Transmission of pubic lice often by sexual contact	• Minute, red, noninflammatory • Points flush with skin. Progression to papular wheal-like lesions • Itching • Secondary excoriation, especially parallel linear excoriations in intrascapular region • Nits and eggs firmly attached to hair shaft in head and body	• γ-Benzene hexachloride or pyrethrins to treat various parts of body • Spinosad (Natroba) topical suspension 0.9% to treat scalp and hair • Screen and treat close contacts (e.g., bed partners and playmates) as needed • Do not share head gear
Scabies		
• *Sarcoptes scabiei* • Mite penetrates stratum corneum, deposits eggs • Allergic reaction to eggs, feces, mite parts • Transmission by direct physical contact, sometimes by shared personal items • Rarely seen in dark-skinned people	• Severe itching, especially at night, usually not on face • Presence of burrows, especially in interdigital webs, flexor surface of wrists, genitalia, and anterior axillary folds • Red papules (may be crusted), possible vesiculation, interdigital web crusting	• 5% permethrin topical lotion, 1 overnight application with second application 1 wk later, may yield 95% eradication • Treat all family members, treat environment with plastic covering for 5 days, launder all clothes and linen with bleach • Treat sexual partner • Antibiotics, if secondary infections present • Possible residual itching up to 4 wk after treatment • Recurrence possible if not adequately treated
Ticks		
• *Borrelia burgdorferi* (spirochete transmitted by ticks in certain areas) causes Lyme disease • Endemic areas include Northeast, Mid-Atlantic states, parts of Midwest and West (see Chapter 69)	• Spreading, ring-like rash 3–4 wk after bite (see Fig. 69.7) • Rash common in groin, buttocks, axillae, trunk, and upper arms and legs • Warm, itchy, or painful rash • Flu-like symptoms • Cardiac, arthritic, and neurologic manifestations possible • Unreliable laboratory test	• Oral antibiotics, such as doxycycline • IV antibiotics for arthritic, neurologic, and cardiac symptoms • Rest and healthy diet • Most patients recover

Radiation Therapy

The use of radiation therapy to treat BCC and SCC varies. The best candidates are those with lesions in challenging locations, such as the ear, nose, scalp, neck, and shin; those who may have trouble with wound healing; or those with medical comorbidities who cannot have surgery.[10] Use is limited in those with melanoma to palliative pain control or treating brain metastases.

Radiation therapy requires multiple visits to a radiology department. It can cause permanent hair loss *(alopecia)* of the irradiated areas. Other adverse effects depend on the location and dose of radiation delivered. They include telangiectasia, atrophy, changes in pigmentation, ulceration, hearing loss, eye damage, atrophy, and mucositis. Shielding is needed to prevent lens damage if the irradiated area is around the eyes. See Chapter 16 for more on radiation therapy.

Total body skin radiation is a treatment for cutaneous T-cell lymphoma. Treatment follows a lengthy course and causes premature skin aging. Patients have varying degrees of permanent alopecia and radiation dermatitis with a transient loss of sweat gland function.

TABLE 25.8 Common Fungal Infections of the Skin and Nails

Etiology and Pathophysiology	Clinical Manifestations	Treatment and Prognosis
Candidiasis		
• Caused by *Candida albicans* • Also known as moniliasis • 50% of adults are symptom-free carriers • Appears in warm, moist areas such as groin area, oral mucosa, and submammary folds • Immunosuppression (e.g., from HIV infection, chemotherapy, radiation, and organ transplantation) allows yeast to become pathogenic	*Mouth:* White, cheesy plaque, resembles milk curds *Vagina:* Vaginitis with red, edematous, painful vaginal wall, white patches. Vaginal discharge. Itching. Pain on urination and intercourse *Skin:* Diffuse, popular, red rash with pinpoint satellite lesions around edges of affected area	• Azole antifungals (e.g., fluconazole, ketoconazole) or other specific medication such as vaginal suppository or oral lozenge • Sexual abstinence or use of condom • Skin hygiene to keep area clean and dry • Powder is effective on nonmucosal surfaces of skin to prevent recurrence
Tinea Corporis		
• Various dermatophytes, often called *ringworm*	• Typical annular (ring-like) scaly appearance, well-defined margins • Reddened	• Cool compresses • Topical antifungals for isolated patches. Creams or solutions of miconazole, ketoconazole, clotrimazole, butenafine
Tinea Cruris		
• Various dermatophytes • Often called *jock itch*	• Well-defined scaly plaque in groin area • Does not affect mucous membranes	• Topical antifungal cream or solution
Tinea Pedis		
• Various dermatophytes • Often called *athlete's foot*	• Interdigital scaling and maceration • Scaly plantar surfaces sometimes with redness and blistering • May be itchy and painful	• Topical antifungal cream, gel, solution, spray, powder
Tinea Unguium (Onychomycosis)		
• Various dermatophytes • Incidence increases with age	• May affect only a few nails on 1 hand • Affects toenails most often • Scaliness under distal nail plate • Brittle, thickened, broken, or crumbling nails with yellowish discoloration	• Oral antifungal (terbinafine [Lamisil], itraconazole [Sporanox]) • Topical antifungal cream or solution (minimal effectiveness) if unable to tolerate systemic treatment • Thinning of toenails if needed • Nail avulsion (removal) is an option

Laser Technology

Laser treatment is expanding rapidly as an efficient treatment for many types of skin problems (Table 25.11). Depending on the type of laser and the wavelength, lasers serve a wide variety of functions. Lasers can make measurable, repeatable, consistent zones of tissue damage. They can cut, coagulate, and vaporize tissue to some degree. Laser light does not accumulate in body cells and cannot cause cumulative cellular changes or damage. With less damage to surrounding tissue, there is a decreased risk for scarring.

The surgical use of laser energy requires a focusing device to produce a small, high-density spot of energy. Several types of lasers are available. The CO_2 laser, the most common, has many applications as a vaporizing and cutting tool for most tissues. The argon laser emits light that is mainly absorbed by hemoglobin. It helps in the treatment of vascular and other pigmented lesions. Other, less common lasers include copper and gold vapors and neodymium:yttrium-aluminum-garnet (Nd:YAG). Those who work with laser equipment must be familiar with agency procedures on laser safety.

Drug Therapy

Antibiotics

We use several topical and systemic antibiotics to treat skin problems. Sometimes they are used concurrently. Common OTC topical antibiotics include bacitracin-neomycin-polymyxin (Neosporin), bacitracin, and polymyxin B. Prescription topical antibiotics include (1) mupirocin (for superficial *Staphylococcus* infections such as impetigo), (2) gentamicin (used for *Staphylococcus,* many gram-negative organisms), and (3) erythromycin (used for gram-positive cocci [staphylococci, streptococci] and gram-negative cocci and bacilli). Metronidazole is a common therapy for rosacea. Topical erythromycin and clindamycin are options for acne.

Systemic infections require systemic antibiotics. They have a role in treating acne and bacterial infections, such as erysipelas, cellulitis, abscesses, and certain wound infections. Frequently used oral drugs include penicillin, erythromycin, doxycycline, clindamycin, and linezolid. Vancomycin is the drug of choice for severe infections.[11]

Corticosteroids

Corticosteroids are effective in treating a wide variety of skin problems. They can be used topically, intralesionally, or systemically. Topical corticosteroids have local antiinflammatory and antipruritic effects. Since corticosteroids may change the manifestations, try to diagnose a skin problem before applying a corticosteroid preparation.

The potency of a preparation depends on the concentration of active drug. With prolonged use, high-potency corticosteroids

TABLE 25.9 **Common Allergic Skin Problems**

Etiology and Pathophysiology	Clinical Manifestations	Treatment and Prognosis
Allergic Contact Dermatitis		
• Type IV delayed hypersensitivity response (see Chapter 14) • Absorbed agent acts as antigen • Sensitization occurs after one or more exposures • Appearance of lesions 2–7 days after contact with allergen	• Red papules and plaques • Sharply circumscribed with occasional vesicles • Itching • Area of dermatitis often takes shape of causative agent (e.g., metal allergy and band-like dermatitis on ring finger).	• Topical or oral corticosteroids, antihistamines • Skin lubrication • Elimination of contact allergen • Avoidance of irritating affected area • Systemic corticosteroids if sensitivity severe
Atopic Dermatitis		
• Type 1 hypersensitivity response (see Chapter 14) • Genetically influenced, chronic, relapsing disease • Exaggerated by a skin response to environmental allergens • Associated with allergic rhinitis and asthma	• Multiple presentations, including acute, subacute, and chronic stages. • *Acute stage:* Redness, oozing vesicles, with extreme itching • *Subacute stage:* Scaly, light red to red-brown plaques. Itching • *Chronic stage:* Thickened skin with accentuation of skin markings (lichenification), possible hypopigmentation or hyperpigmentation. Dry skin. Itching. Common in antecubital and popliteal space	• Lubrication of dry skin • Topical immunomodulators (pimecrolimus [Elidel], tacrolimus [Protopic]) • Stress reduction reduces flares • Corticosteroids, phototherapy for severe inflammation and itching • Antibiotics for secondary infection as needed
Drug Reaction		
• May be caused by any drug that acts as antigen and causes hypersensitivity reaction • Certain drugs (e.g., penicillin) more likely to cause reactions • Not all reactions are allergic, some are intolerance (e.g., gastric upset)	• Rash of any morphology • Often red, macular and papular, semiconfluent, generalized rash with abrupt onset • Appearance as late as 14 days after cessation of drug. May be itchy • Some reactions may be life threatening requiring immediate and intensive care	• Withdrawal of drug if possible • Antihistamines, topical or systemic corticosteroids may be necessary depending on severity of symptoms
Urticaria (Hives)		
• Often an allergic event • Redness and edema in upper dermis resulting from a local increase in permeability of capillaries (usually from histamine release)	• Spontaneously occurring, raised or irregularly shaped wheals, varying size, usually multiple • A single lesion usually resolves in 24 hr • Can occur anywhere on the body	• Removal of triggering agent, if known • Oral antihistamine therapy • Possibly systemic corticosteroids

can cause adrenal suppression, especially if a large surface area is covered and occlusive dressings are used. Other side effects include skin atrophy from impaired cell mitosis, capillary fragility, rosacea, acne, and bruising. In general, atrophy does not occur until a corticosteroid has been in use for 2 to 3 weeks. If drug use is stopped at the first sign of atrophy, recovery usually occurs in several weeks. Rebound dermatitis can occur when therapy is stopped. Tapering the use of high-potency topical corticosteroids when improvement is noted reduces the risk.

Low-potency corticosteroids act more slowly. They can be used for a longer time without producing serious side effects. Low-potency corticosteroids are safe to use on the face and areas where skin may touch or rub together, such as the axillae and groin.

The most potent delivery system for a topical corticosteroid is an ointment. Apply creams and ointments in thin layers and slowly massage into the site 1 to 3 times a day.

Intralesional corticosteroids are injected directly into or just beneath the lesion. This method provides a reservoir of medication with an effect lasting several weeks to months. Intralesional injection is common in the treatment of psoriasis, alopecia areata (patchy hair loss), cystic acne, hypertrophic scars, and keloids. Triamcinolone acetonide (Kenalog) is the most common drug used for intralesional injection.

Systemic corticosteroids can have remarkable results in treating a skin problem. However, they often have undesirable systemic effects (see Chapter 54). Corticosteroids are helpful in short-term therapy for acute problems such as contact dermatitis caused by poison ivy. Long-term therapy is reserved for those with severe disease such as bullous (blistering) disorders.

Antihistamines

Oral antihistamines are helpful in treating urticaria (hives), angioedema, and itching that can occur in problems such as atopic dermatitis, allergic dermatitis, and other allergic skin reactions. Several antihistamines may be tried before getting an acceptable effect. Antihistamines with sedative effects, such as diphenhydramine, may be better with itching because the tranquilizing and sedative effects enhance symptom relief. Warn the patient about sedative effects, a problem when driving or using heavy machinery. Antihistamines, such as loratadine (Claritin), fexofenadine (Allegra), and cetirizine (Zyrtec), bind to peripheral histamine receptors, giving antihistamine action without sedation. They are not effective for controlling itching. Use antihistamines with caution in older adults because of their long half-life and anticholinergic effects.

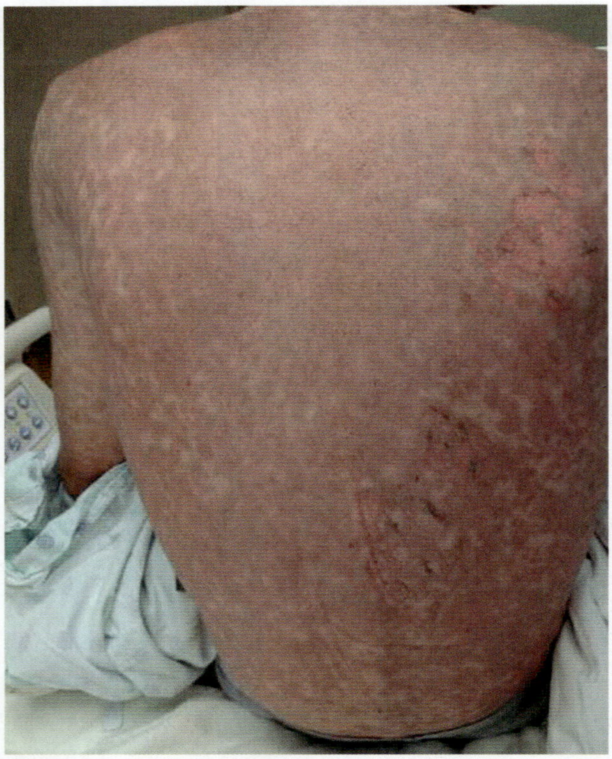

Fig. 25.9 Toxic epidermal necrolysis. (From *Ferri's clinical advisor 2018.* Dabiri, G, Rüenger T. Published January 1, 2018. Page 1282.e2. © 2018.)

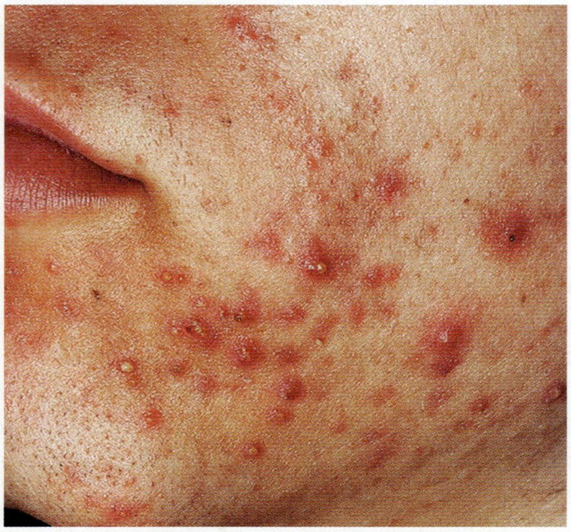

Fig. 25.10 Acne with papules and pustules. (From James WD, Berger T, Elston DMD: *Andrews' diseases of the skin,* ed 11, Philadelphia, 2011, Saunders.)

Topical Fluorouracil

Fluorouracil is a topical cytotoxic agent with selective toxicity for sun-damaged cells. It is used to treat precancerous lesions (especially AK) and some skin cancers. Patient adherence is a consideration in the use of fluorouracil. Use causes redness, burning, and itching within 3 to 5 days. Painful, eroded areas over the damaged skin occur within 1 to 3 weeks, depending on skin thickness at the site. Reduce redness and itching by applying a low-potency topical corticosteroid 20 minutes after dosing. Treatment must continue with applications 1 or 2 times a day for 2 to 4 weeks. Healing may take up to 4 weeks after stopping treatment.

Adherence to therapy depends on your teaching. Tell the patient that they will look worse before they look better. Teach them about the side effects. Because fluorouracil is a photosensitizing drug, tell the patient to avoid sunlight during treatment. After treatment, skin should be smooth and free of AK. AK may recur in treated areas. Multiple courses of therapy may be necessary over the years for those with severely sun-damaged skin.

Immunomodulators

Topical immunomodulators, such as pimecrolimus (Elidel) and tacrolimus (Protopic), are used to treat atopic dermatitis, psoriasis, and rosacea.[12] They work by suppressing an overreactive immune system. The side effects are minimal. They include a transient burning or feeling of heat at the application site. Use may increase the risk for skin cancer and precancerous lesions.

The topical immunomodulator imiquimod (Aldara) is used to treat external genital warts, AK, and superficial BCC. It stimulates the production of α-interferon and other cytokines to enhance cell-mediated immunity. It boosts the immune response only where applied. Most patients using this cream have skin reactions, including redness, swelling, blistering, peeling, itching, and burning. Dosing varies depending on the type of lesion treated and the strength prescribed.

Diagnostic and Surgical Therapy

Skin Scraping

Scraping with a scalpel blade can yield a sample of surface cells (stratum corneum) for microscopic inspection and diagnosis. The most common tests of skin scrapings are mineral oil examination for scabies and 10% to 20% KOH for fungus.

Electrodessication and Electrocoagulation

Electrical energy can be converted to heat that burns and destroys tissue. The major uses of these therapies are coagulation of bleeding vessels to obtain hemostasis and destruction of small *telangiectasias* (dilation of groups of superficial capillaries and venules). *Electrodessication* usually involves more superficial destruction. It uses a monopolar electrode. *Electrocoagulation* uses a bipolar electrode. It has a deeper effect, with better hemostasis, but an increased chance of scarring. While minor electrosurgery on patients with a pacemaker poses minimal risk, the electrical energy can affect both pacemakers and internal defibrillators.

Curettage

Curettage is the removal and scooping away of tissue using an instrument called a *curette.* A curette looks like a small spoon with very sharp edges. A curette can remove many types of small, soft skin tumors and superficial lesions, such as warts, AK, seborrheic keratosis, and small BCCs and SCCs. The area to be curetted is anesthetized before the procedure. The HCP removes the lesion and then cauterizes the skin. The removed tissue is usually sent for biopsy. A dressing may be applied. You will need to teach the patient wound care. A small scar and hypopigmentation can result.

Punch Biopsy

Punch biopsy is a common procedure used to obtain a tissue sample for histologic study or to remove small lesions (Fig. 25.12).

TABLE 25.10 Common Benign Skin Problems

Etiology and Pathophysiology	Clinical Manifestations	Treatment and Prognosis
Acne Vulgaris		
• Inflammatory disorder of sebaceous glands • More common in teenagers • May begin and persist into adulthood • Flare can occur with use of corticosteroids and androgen-dominant birth control pills and before menses.	• Noninflammatory lesions, including open comedones (blackheads) and closed comedones (whiteheads) • Inflammatory lesions, including papules and pustules • Most common on face, neck, and upper back (Fig. 25.10)	*Topical:* • Mechanical removal of multiple lesions with comedo extractor • Topical benzoyl peroxide, retinoids, antimicrobials (clindamycin, minocycline, erythromycin) *Systemic:* • Systemic antibiotics • Use of isotretinoin for severe nodulocystic acne may provide lasting remission. Pregnancy tests, monitor liver function, cholesterol, triglycerides, and for depression • Aim is to suppress new lesions and minimize scarring • Spontaneous remission possible • Often improves with sun exposure
Acrochordons (Skin Tags)		
• Common after midlife • Appearance on neck, axillae, and upper trunk from mechanical friction or redundant skin (associated with obesity)	• Small, skin-colored, soft, pedunculated papules • May become irritated	• No treatment medically necessary • Surgical removal when needed. Usually just snipping without anesthesia
Lentigo		
• Increased number of normal melanocytes in basal layer of epidermis from sun exposure and aging • Also called "liver spots" or "age spots"	• Hyperpigmented, brown to black macule or patch (flat lesion) on sun-exposed areas	• Evaluate carefully for progression • Treatment only for cosmetic purposes: liquid nitrogen, laser resurfacing • May recur • Biopsy when suspicious of melanoma
Lipoma		
• Benign tumor of adipose tissue, often encapsulated • Most common in 40- to 60-year-old age group	• Rubbery, compressible, round mass of adipose tissue • Single or multiple • Variable in size, may be very large • Most common on trunk, back of neck, forearms	• Usually no treatment • Biopsy to distinguish from liposarcoma • Excision usual treatment (when indicated)
Nevi (Moles)		
• Grouping of normal cells derived from melanocyte-like precursor cells	• Hyperpigmented areas that vary in form and color • Flat, slightly elevated, verrucoid, polypoid, dome-shaped, sessile, papillomatous • Preservation of normal skin markings • Hair growth possible	• No treatment necessary except for cosmetic reasons • Skin biopsy for suspicious nevi
Psoriasis		
• Autoimmune chronic dermatitis that involves very rapid turnover of epidermal cells • Family predisposition • Usually develops before age 40	• Sharply demarcated silvery scaling plaques on reddish skin often on the scalp, elbows, knees, palms, soles, and fingernails (Fig. 25.11) • Itching, burning, pain • Localized or general, intermittent or continuous • Symptoms vary in intensity from mild to severe	• Goal to reduce inflammation and suppress rapid turnover of epidermal cells. No cure, but control is possible *Topical treatments:* • Corticosteroids, tazarotene, calcipotriene, anthralin, tacrolimus, halobetasol propionate and tazarotene (Duobrii) • Intralesional injection of corticosteroids for chronic plaques *Systemic treatments:* • Natural or artificial UVB. PUVA (UVA with topical or systemic photosensitizer) • Traditional and oral therapies: methotrexate, retinoid (acitretin), apremilast (Otezla), cyclosporine • Biologic therapies for moderate to severe plaque disease: adalimumab (Humira), brodalumab (Siliq), certolizumab pegol (Cimzia), etanercept (Enbrel), golimumab (Simponi), guselkumab (Tremfya), infliximab (Remicade), ixekizumab (Taltz), risankizumab-rzaa (Skyrizi), secukinumab (Cosentyx), ustekinumab (Stelara)

Continued

TABLE 25.10 Common Benign Skin Problems—cont'd

Etiology and Pathophysiology	Clinical Manifestations	Treatment and Prognosis
Rosacea		
• Common disorder of the central face • Cause is unclear	4 major subtypes: • Erythematotelangiectatic (ETR): Telangiectasia (thread-like red lines or patterns on the skin), redness, flushing. • Papulopustular (PPR): Redness, flushing, papules, pustules. • Phymatous (PHY): Thickening of the skin, hypertrophy of the nose. • Ocular rosacea (OR): Tearing, stinging, itching, dryness of the lids.	• Avoid triggers: sun, extreme heat/cold, heavy exercise, spicy foods, alcohol use, smoking • Ablative laser surgery • Oral treatments: azithromycin, doxycycline, isotretinoin, minocycline, trimethoprim/sulfamethoxazole • Topical treatments: Brimonidine, oxymetazoline hydrochloride cream, azelaic acid, ivermectin, metronidazole, sodium sulfacetamide
Seborrheic Keratoses		
• Benign, familial, exact etiology unknown • Usually occur after age 40, increase in number with age	• Irregularly round or oval, often warty papules or plaques • Well-defined shape, appearance of being stuck on • Increase in pigmentation with time • Usually multiple, may be itchy	• Removal by curettage or cryosurgery for cosmetic reasons or to eliminate source of irritation • Biopsy if unable to distinguish from melanoma

PUVA, Psoralen ultraviolet A; *UVA,* ultraviolet A; *UVB,* ultraviolet B.

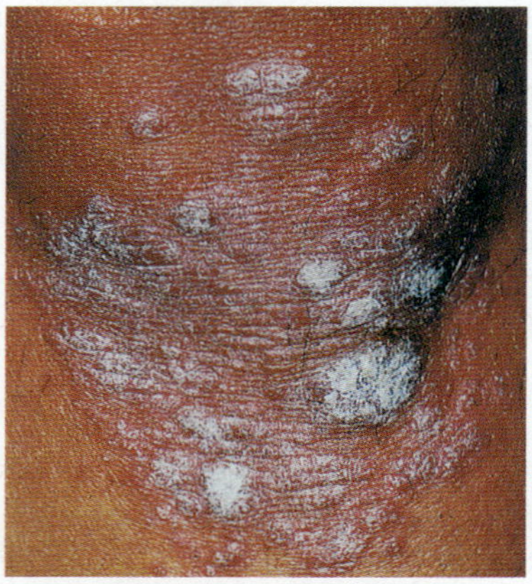

Fig. 25.11 Psoriasis. Characteristic inflammation and scaling. (From Habif TP: *Clinical dermatology: a color guide to diagnosis and therapy,* ed 5, St Louis, 2011, Mosby.)

TABLE 25.11 Skin Problems Treated by Laser

- Acne scars
- Hair removal
- Hemangiomas
- Leg veins
- Pigment discoloration in epidermis
- Pigmented nevi
- Port wine stain
- Psoriasis
- Resurfacing of skin
- Rosacea
- Skin lesions
- Tattoo removal
- Vascular lesions
- Warts
- Wrinkles

The procedure is simple. The HCP marks the biopsy area and then anesthetizes it so that the anesthetic will not obscure the landmarks. The HCP rotates the punch into the skin and removes a small cylinder of skin. Hemostasis is achieved with pressure or absorbable gelatin (Gelfoam) packing. Sites of 4 mm or larger are usually closed with sutures. Punch biopsies are not done below the knee if other sites are available. Circulatory changes can make evaluating the tissue sample difficult.

Cryosurgery

Cryosurgery is the use of subfreezing temperatures to destroy epidermal lesions. Cryosurgery is used to treat common and genital warts, skin tags, thin seborrheic keratoses, AK, BCC, and SCC. Topical liquid nitrogen is the agent most often used for cryosurgery. Damage occurs in treated tissue because of intracellular ice formation. It causes the cell to rupture during thaw, leading to cell death and necrosis. The degree of damage depends on the rate of cooling and the minimum temperature achieved.

Liquid nitrogen is applied topically (directly onto the lesion) with a direct spray or contact probe. Tell patients that they will feel a painful, stinging cold sensation. The lesion first becomes swollen and red. It may blister. A scab forms and falls off in 1 to 3 weeks. The skin lesion sloughs along with the scab. Growth of new skin follows.

The size of an affected area may limit the use of cryotherapy. Other disadvantages include the potential for harming adjacent healthy tissue and the low temperature of liquid nitrogen destroying melanocytes, leaving an area of hypopigmentation resembling a scar.

Excision

Excision is an option if the lesion involves the dermis. Complete closure of the excised area usually results in a good cosmetic result.

A specific type of excision is *Mohs surgery,* the microscopically controlled removal of a skin cancer. In this procedure, the HCP removes tissue sections in thin horizontal layers.

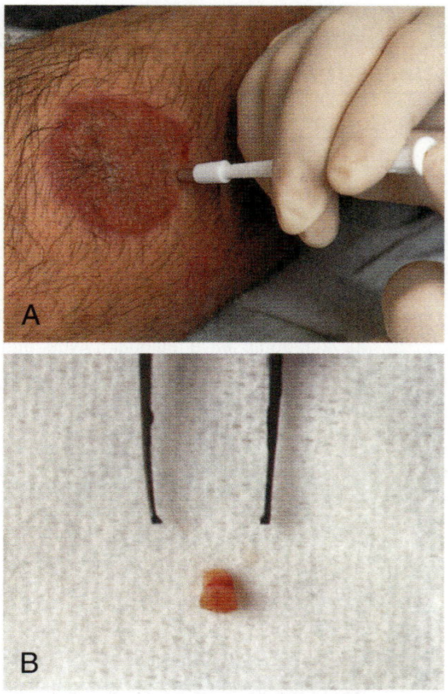

Fig. 25.12 Punch biopsy. (A) Removal of skin for diagnostic purposes. (B) Specimen obtained. (From Graham-Brown R, Bourke J, Cunliffe T: *Dermatology: fundamentals of practice,* Edinburgh, 2008, Mosby.)

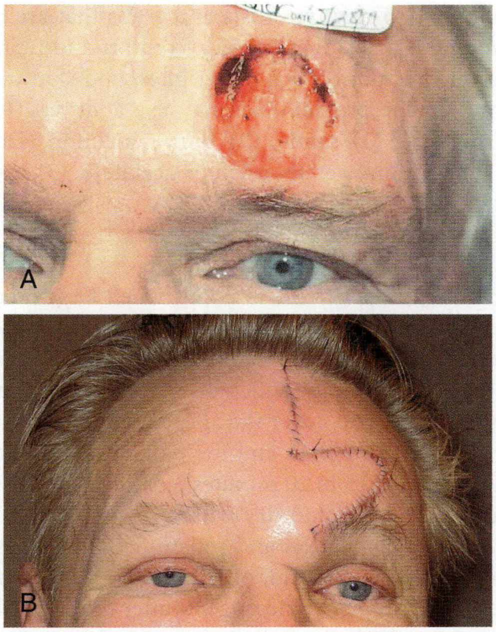

Fig. 25.13 (A) Removal of melanoma by Mohs surgery. (B) After plastic surgery using a skin flap to repair defect. (Courtesy Peter Bonner, Placitas, NM.)

All the specimen's margins are examined to see if any cancer cells remain (Fig. 25.13). Any residual tumor not removed by the first excision is removed in serial excisions done the same day. Benefits of Mohs surgery are that it preserves normal tissue, produces the smallest possible wound, and can completely remove the cancer. Although it can be a lengthy procedure, it is done in an outpatient setting using local anesthesia.

NURSING MANAGEMENT: SKIN PROBLEMS

A careful history is important in diagnosing skin problems. You must be skilled at detecting findings that could lead to finding the cause of many skin problems. After a careful history and physical assessment, inspect the lesions.

Nursing interventions for skin problems fall into broad categories (Table 25.12). They apply to many problems in both inpatient and outpatient settings. A nursing care plan for the patient with chronic skin lesions (eNursing Care Plan 25.1) is available on the website for this chapter.

In your patient teaching, stress the duration of the treatment. Review specific instructions about each therapy. Skin problems may be slow to resolve. Tell the patient to follow package directions when using OTC drugs. If the package insert says use should not exceed 7 days, patients should heed this warning. Teach the patient to stop care and notify the HCP if any systemic signs of inflammation or extensions of the skin problem (e.g., more lesions, increased redness or swelling) develop.

Wet Compresses

It is important to know how to apply a wet compress (Table 25.13). We often apply wet compresses for superficial skin problems that involve inflammation, itching, and infection. They are appropriate for damaged, oozing skin. Wet compresses

TABLE 25.12 NURSING MANAGEMENT

Skin Problems

- Assess patient's skin for acute and chronic skin problems.
- Assess patient's risk factors for skin problems.
- Document skin problems and risk factor assessment and develop a plan of care.
- Determine whether patient is taking drugs that increase photosensitivity.
- Teach about risks associated with sun exposure and methods for decreasing exposure to the sun.
- Administer prescribed therapies such as dressings and oral or topical medications.
- Teach about therapies used for skin disorders, including dressings, baths, and oral or topical medications used on an outpatient basis.
- Evaluate treatment for effectiveness and any adverse effects.

TABLE 25.13 NURSING MANAGEMENT

Applying a Wet Compress

- Select compress material that is 4 to 8 layers thick and slightly larger than the area being treated. Use gauze or any clean material. Do not use gauze sponges with fillers as they retain too much solution.
- Use tap water at room temperature. If drinkable water is not available, use filtered, bottled, or sterile water. Add ordered additives.
- The temperature of the fluid should be tepid. However, when an antiinflammatory effect is desired, the fluid should be cool.
- When using continuous compresses, remove the compress and replace with a new one as needed. Do not add solution to a compress as this can change the fluid's concentration and damage the skin.
- Intermittent compresses are placed for 10–30 min, several times a day.
- Assess the skin at regular intervals. If the skin appears macerated, stop the compresses for 2–3 days.
- Change and wash daily any material used repeatedly throughout the day.
- Protect the patient from discomfort and chilling.
- Use a water-resistant pad to help protect the mattress, linens, and furniture.

are a good way to remove crusts and scabs that are adhering to the wound surface. They provide comfort and treatment of problems such as poison ivy, insect bites, and skin infections. Depending on the problem, we may use additives. Common solutions include (1) saline, (2) Burow solution (Domeboro powder [aluminum acetate; calcium acetate]), (3) acetic acid (vinegar), and (4) silver nitrate.

◆ Baths

Baths are an appropriate intervention when large areas of the body need treatment. Baths may be relaxing and will help decrease itching. Agents such as colloidal oatmeal (Aveeno) and sodium bicarbonate can be added directly to bath water. Fill the tub with tepid water to cover the affected areas. Depending on the severity of the problem and the patient's discomfort, have the patient soak for 15 to 20 minutes 3 or 4 times a day. Tell the patient not to rub the skin dry with a towel but gently pat to prevent increased irritation and inflammation. To sustain the hydrating effect, apply cream, ointment emollients (moisturizers), or other prescribed topical agents after the bath. This helps seal the moisture in the hydrated cells and increases the absorption of any topical agents.

◆ Hygienic Practices

The patient's skin type, lifestyle, culture, age, and gender influence hygienic practices. The normal acidity of the skin and perspiration protect against bacterial overgrowth. Most soaps are alkaline and neutralize the skin surface, leading to a loss of protection. Using mild, moisturizing soaps and lipid-free cleansers and avoiding hot water and vigorous scrubbing can noticeably decrease local skin irritation and inflammation. Skin piercings in which jewelry has been inserted can be cared for with antibacterial soaps that do not contain sulfites.

In general, skin and hair must be washed often enough to remove excess oil and excretions and prevent odor. Older persons should avoid harsh soaps and shampoos and frequent bathing because of the dryness of their skin and scalp. Using moisturizers right after a bath or shower (while the skin is still damp) seals in the moisture.

◆ Topical Medications

Topical medications are often used to treat skin problems. The effectiveness of topical therapy depends on which base the medication is prepared in. Table 25.14 describes common bases for topical preparations and their considerations. The base selected depends on the properties needed.

Apply topical agents as directed. As a rule, apply a topical agent in a thin film to clean skin and spread evenly in a downward motion in the direction of hair growth. Thick creams will spread easier if the skin is still damp. If you are using a secondary dressing, you can apply the agent directly onto a dressing. Teach the patient and caregiver proper dosing, application technique, expected results, and common reactions.

Occlusion with a plastic wrap is an effective way to increase the absorption of topical corticosteroids or simple emollients. The plastic wrap traps perspiration against the outer layer of the epidermis. Applying agents to moist skin increases absorption 10-fold. Use tape or stretch wraps to keep the plastic wrap in place. For lesions on the feet or lower legs, the patient can wear socks over the plastic wrap. Wraps applied multiple times daily are kept in place for 2 to 8 hours. Some patients choose to use the occlusion technique at bedtime. Occlusion is not appropriate in areas prone to infection, such as skin creases.

TABLE 25.14 Drug Therapy

Common Bases for Topical Medications

Agent	Considerations
Cream	Emulsions of oil and water. Most common base for topical medications. Versatile. Lubrication and protection
Gel	Nongreasy combination of propylene glycol and water. May contain alcohol. Work well on the scalp. Good for acute exudative problems (e.g., poison ivy)
Lotion	Emulsions of water, alcohol, and/or oil. Cooling and drying. Some leave residual powder film after evaporation of water. May cause stinging when used in skinfolds. Useful with subacute itching problems
Ointment	Oil with differing amounts of water added in suspension. Lubrication and prevention of dehydration. More lubricating than a cream. May be too occlusive for problems with lots of exudate or in body creases. Petrolatum most common
Paste	Mixture of powder and ointment. Used when drying effect necessary because moisture is absorbed
Powder	Promotion of dryness. Lubricates skinfold areas to prevent irritation. Base for antifungal preparations. Protect patient from inhaling

◆ Control of Pruritus

Many problems cause *pruritus* (itching). This includes dry skin, almost any physical or chemical stimulus to the skin (e.g., drugs or insects), and any scaling skin problem. The itch sensation is carried by the same nonmyelinated nerve fibers as pain and temperature. The patient will have pain rather than an itch if the epidermis is damaged or absent. It is important to figure out if itching preceded a skin lesion. Itching can lead to scratching that results in an excoriated and inflamed lesion.

Certain circumstances make itching worse. Teach the patient ways to help break the itch/scratch cycle. A cool environment may cause vasoconstriction and decrease itching. Hydration, wet compresses, and moisturizers (including antipruritic lotions) are normally helpful. Apply wet compresses for 30 to 60 minutes, pat the skin dry, and apply a lubricant or medication. Topical and injectable corticosteroids are sometimes used. Topically applied menthol, camphor, or phenol numb itch receptors. Systemic antihistamines may give relief. The main side effect of most antihistamines is sedation. This may be desirable because itching is often worse at night and can interfere with sleep. Adequate rest increases the patient's ability to tolerate itching, thereby decreasing skin damage from scratching. Have the patient avoid anything that causes vasodilation, such as heat or rubbing. Dry skin lowers the itch threshold and increases the itch sensation.

Lichenification is a thickening of epidermis with exaggerated markings resembling a washboard. It is caused by chronic scratching or rubbing of the skin. Lichenification often occurs with atopic dermatoses and other itching problems. The hands, forearms, shins, and nape of the neck are common sites. Scratching may become a habit. Persistent scratching can cause excoriations. Treating the cause of the itching is the key to preventing lichenification.

◆ Preventing Spread

Although most skin problems are not contagious, infection control precautions indicate wearing gloves when working with any open wounds or lesions with drainage. Not all infected drainage is purulent. Careful hand washing and properly disposing of soiled dressings are the best means of preventing the spread of infections or infestations. The most common contagious lesions include impetigo, streptococcal infections, staphylococcal infections (e.g., methicillin-resistant *S. aureus* [MRSA]), fungal infections, primary chancre, scabies, and pediculosis.

◆ Preventing Secondary Infections

Open skin lesions are susceptible to invasion by other viral, bacterial, or fungal organisms. Meticulous hygiene, hand washing, and dressing changes are important to minimize the risk for secondary infections. Warn the patient about scratching lesions, which can cause excoriations and create a portal of entry for pathogens. Trim the patient's nails short to minimize trauma from scratching.

◆ Postprocedure Care

Provide teaching about skin care after simple procedures, such as skin biopsy, excision, and cryosurgery. In general, review cleansing, dressing changes, topical agent use, and the signs and symptoms of infection. Teach the patient how to tell normal inflammation from an infection. A slight red border first few days after is normal. Signs and symptoms of infection include redness that persists longer than a week or extends beyond a 1-cm border, a fever greater than 101°F, increased pain, pronounced swelling, and purulent drainage. If these occur, they should be reported to the HCP at once.

After a skin procedure, cleanse any oozing wound with a saline solution twice daily or as ordered by the HCP. Safe drinking water is a safe alternative in some situations. Apply antibiotic or ordered ointment with a nonadherent secondary dressing. Wounds that are kept moist and covered heal more rapidly and with less scarring. The initial crust that forms should be left undisturbed as a protective coating for the damaged skin beneath it. Healing crusts that have been moisturized and protected will separate naturally from healed epidermis.

We can cover a sutured wound with a variety of dressings. Sutures are generally removed in 4 to 14 days, depending on the placement site. Sometimes alternating sutures are removed after the third day. Incision lines may need daily cleansing, usually with plain water. If necessary, a topical antibiotic is applied and the wound either is covered with a dry dressing or left open to air. The patient may have some swelling and discomfort in the first 24 hours. Intermittent application of cold (ice packs) over the dressing may reduce edema. Mild analgesics, such as acetaminophen, should control discomfort.[13]

◆ Psychologic Effects of Chronic Skin Problems

Emotional stress can occur for those who suffer from chronic skin problems, such as psoriasis, atopic dermatitis, or acne. The visibility of skin lesions often presents a real problem to the patient. The sequelae could result in social and employment problems with subsequent financial implications, a poor self-image, and problems with sexuality.

Help the patient to follow the treatment plan. Allow the patient to verbalize the "Why me?" question, even though there is no ready answer. Refer the patient to dermatology support groups. Many are listed on the American Academy of Dermatology website (www.aad.org). These groups are helpful with patient support and education.

The location of lesions and scars is the determining factor with respect to their cosmetic implications. Facial scars are the most damaging psychologically because they are so visible. Creative use of cosmetics can do much to mask lesions and scarring. Consider the patient's sensitivity to product ingredients when selecting cosmetics. Oil-free, hypoallergenic cosmetics may help the patient with allergies. Rehabilitative cosmetics are available to help camouflage and deemphasize such lesions as *vitiligo* (loss of pigmentation), *melasma* (tan to brown patches on the face), and healed wound sites. These commercially available products are opaque, smudge resistant, and water resistant.

COSMETIC PROCEDURES

A vast array of cosmetic procedures is available. Common ones include chemical peels, toxin injections, fillers, laser surgery, breast enlargement and reduction (see Chapter 56), face-lift, eyelid-lift, brow-forehead lift, and liposuction. Common cosmetic topical procedures are outlined in Table 25.15. Other common procedures include the injection of botulinum (e.g., Botox, Dysport) and dermal fillers (e.g., collagen, calcium hydroxyapatite, hyaluronic acid fillers [Restylane, Juvéderm]).[14] Transitory side effects may occur, such as mild redness, pain, swelling, and bruising. Uncommon side effects from cosmetic procedures include allergic reaction, infection, grayish skin discoloration, or lumps at the injection sites. Tell the patient that the procedure will need repeating at prescribed intervals to maintain the desired appearance.

The reasons for undergoing these procedures are as varied as the techniques. The most common reason is to improve body image. If someone feels better about themselves after having cosmetic procedures, they often act more confident and self-assured. Often social position and economic considerations are part of the decision. Maintain a supportive, nonjudgmental attitude. If the patient wishes to change or enhance a body feature perceived as unattractive and has realistic expectations about the outcome, you should support this decision.[15]

Surgical Therapies

Laser Surgery

Laser surgery is used to treat congenital and acquired vascular lesions (cherry angiomas, spider leg veins, hemangiomas,

TABLE 25.15 Common Cosmetic Topical Procedures

Tretinoin (Retin-A, Renova)	Chemical Peels (e.g., Jessner, Trichloroacetic Acid [TCA], Salicylic Acid)	Microdermabrasion	α-Hydroxy Acids (e.g., Glycolic Acid, Lactic Acid)
Indications			
Improves appearance of photodamaged skin, especially fine wrinkling. Reduces actinic keratoses	Improves appearance of photodamaged skin, acne scarring, actinic and seborrheic keratoses	Smooths appearance of photodamaged and wrinkled skin, acne scarring	Smooths appearance of photodamaged and wrinkled skin, acne scarring
Description			
Initially applied every 2–3 days. Treatment stopped if severe inflammation occurs. Maximum response in 8–12 mo	Solution applied in varying amounts to the skin, causing a controlled burn with a loss of melanin	Epidermis and top dermal layer removed by applying aluminum oxide or baking soda crystals. Reepithelialization of abraded surface then occurs	Low concentrations (<10%) in many skin care products consumers can apply to the skin. Higher concentrations (50%–70%) applied only by an HCP
Side Effects			
Redness, swelling, flaking, pigmentation changes. Teratogenic. Increases phototoxicity if taking other photosensitive drugs	Moderate swelling and crusting for 1 wk. Redness for 6–8 wk. Pink tone possible for several mo. Photosensitivity	Light pink tone that resolves within 24 hr. Photosensitivity	Photosensitivity, slight irritation at lower concentrations, severe redness, oozing, and flaking skin possible with higher concentrations
Patient Teaching			
Apply at night since preparation is inactivated by light. Apply emollients, use sunscreen, use sun avoidance measures, avoid abrasive or drying facial cleansers for severe sensitivity (e.g., excess irritation)	Use sunscreen. Avoid sun for 6 mo to prevent hyperpigmentation	Generous application of emollients and sunscreen	Use sunscreen and sun avoidance measures

port-wine stains, and tattoo removal) and for skin resurfacing and hair removal. Lasers can reduce scarring and fine wrinkles around the lips or eyes and remove facial lesions (Table 25.11). Swelling, redness, and bruising are common after treatment. The treated areas usually are kept moist with ointment or occlusive dressings for the first few days. The patient must protect treated skin from the sun.

Face-Lift

A face-lift *(rhytidectomy)* is the lifting and repositioning of the lower two-thirds of the face and neck to improve appearance (Fig. 25.14). Indications for this procedure include:

- Redundant soft tissue or scarring resulting from disease (e.g., acne scarring)
- Asymmetric redundancy of soft tissues (e.g., facial palsy)
- Redundant soft tissue resulting from trauma
- Preauricular lesions
- Redundant soft tissues resulting from *solar elastosis* (sagging of the skin from sun damage), changes in body weight, and the effects of gravity
- Restore body image

The surgical approach and lines of incisions vary according to the desired correction and the position of the hairline. Eyelid-lifts *(blepharoplasty)* can remove redundant tissue and possibly improve the field of vision. Preventing hematoma formation is important after surgery. Ice packs are usually applied for the first 24 to 48 hours to reduce swelling and bruising. The pain is often minimal. Antibiotics are used at the HCP's discretion. Complications can occur if the person smokes or does not follow activity restrictions.

Liposuction

Liposuction is a technique for removing subcutaneous fat to improve facial and body contours. Although not a substitute for diet and exercise, it can be successful in removing areas of fat from almost any body area that is resistant to other techniques.

Liposuction is relatively free of complications. Possible contraindications include the use of anticoagulants, uncontrolled hypertension, diabetes, and poor cardiovascular status. Those younger than 50 years of age with good skin elasticity are the best candidates. However, patients older than 50 can be treated successfully.

The procedure is usually done on an outpatient basis under local anesthesia. One or more sessions may be needed, depending on the size of the area. The HCP inserts a blunt-tipped cannula through a small incision and pushes into the fat to break it loose from the fibrous stroma. Multiple repeated thrusts disrupt the fat and create tunnels. The loosened fat is removed with a powerful suction. Afterward, firm pressure is applied to the wounds until drainage stops. It may take several months for the results to be evident.

❖ NURSING MANAGEMENT: COSMETIC SURGERY

Many cosmetic surgeries are done in well-equipped day-surgery units or in dermatologist or plastic surgeon in-office surgery suites.

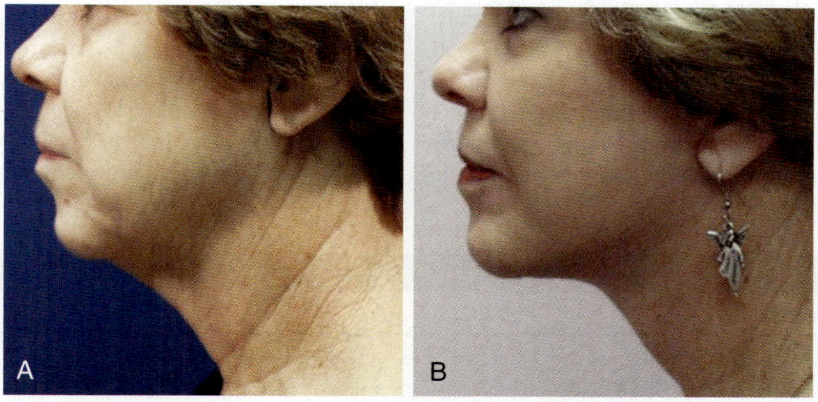

Fig. 25.14 Face-lift. (A) Preoperative. (B) Postoperative. (From Cuzalina A, Copty TV, Khan H: *Current therapy in oral and maxillofacial surgery,* St Louis, 2012, Elsevier.)

◆ Preoperative Management

A major consideration before surgery relates to informed consent and realistic expectations of what cosmetic surgery can accomplish.[15] Although the HCP should provide this information, reinforce as needed and answer questions and concerns. For instance, a face-lift has little or no effect on deep wrinkling of the forehead and temples, deep nasolabial grooves, or vertical lip wrinkles. Before-and-after treatment photographs of similar cases are often useful in helping the patient to set realistic expectations.

Review the timeframe for healing. Explain the oozing, crusting stage of an abrasive procedure so the patient can plan time off from work if necessary. Since wound healing may not be complete for 1 year, the patient should not expect complete results at once. The final result is affected by the patient's age, general health, and skin type and the extent (severity) of the problem being treated. Efforts should be made to correct or control any existing health problem before the procedure.

◆ Postoperative Management

Most cosmetic procedures are not very painful. Usually, mild analgesics are enough to keep the patient comfortable.[13] Although infection is not a common problem after cosmetic surgery, assess the sites for signs of infection. Teach the patient signs and symptoms of infection. Stress that it is important to report them at once so that treatment can be started.

If the surgery involved a change in the skin's circulation, as in a face-lift, carefully monitor for adequate circulation. Warm, pink skin that blanches on pressure shows that adequate circulation is present in the surgical area. Supportive, compressive dressings and ice packs may be applied early in the postoperative period.

SKIN GRAFTS

Uses

Skin grafts may be necessary to protect underlying structures or to reconstruct areas for cosmetic or functional purposes. They may be used to facilitate rapid closure and minimize complications. Ideally, wounds heal by primary intention. However, large wounds, surgically created wounds, trauma, and chronic wounds can result in extensive tissue destruction, making healing by primary intention impossible. In these cases, skin grafting may be necessary to close the defect. Improved surgical techniques make it possible to graft skin, bone, cartilage, fat, fascia, muscles, and nerves. For cosmetically pleasing results, the color, thickness, texture, and hair-growing nature of skin used for grafting should match the recipient site. See Chapter 26 for more about skin grafting for patients with burn injuries.

Types

The 2 types of traditional skin grafts are free grafts and skin flaps. We describe free grafts by how they supply blood to the grafted skin. One method is to transfer the graft (epidermis and part or all the dermis) to the recipient site from the donor site. The *autograft* (from the patient's own body) or *isograft* (from an identical twin) revascularizes and becomes fixed to the new site. The other method of free skin grafting is by *reconstructive microsurgery.* With the use of an operating microscope, the HCP establishes circulation immediately in the graft by connecting blood vessels in the skin flap to vessels in the recipient site.

Skin flaps involve moving a section of skin and subcutaneous tissue from one part of the body to another without terminating the vascular attachment *(pedicle).* Skin flaps are used to cover wounds with a poor vascular bed, provide padding when needed, and cover wounds over cartilage and bone. The patient may need intermediate flap placement if the recipient site is far removed from the donor site. For instance, a skin flap from the thigh to the head would require an intermediate graft. The flap is advanced to the recipient site when circulation is well established at the intermediate site. The patient's needs and the type of defect determine the type of flap and the route of transfer.

Soft tissue expansion is a technique for providing skin (1) for resurfacing of a defect, such as a burn scar; (2) for removal of a disfiguring mark (e.g., a tattoo); or (3) as a preliminary step in breast reconstruction. A subcutaneous tissue expander of a proper size and shape is placed under the skin, usually as an outpatient procedure. Weekly expansion with saline solution can be done in a health care setting or by the patient at home. This expansion procedure is repeated until the skin reaches the size needed for the repair. This may take from several weeks to 3 to 4 months. Once enough skin is available, the old incision is opened, the expander is removed, and the soft tissue is ready to be used as an advancement flap. The tissue expander next to a defect has the primary tissue characteristics, such as color and texture.

Engineered skin substitutes (e.g., Apligraf, Dermagraft, Integra) are gaining popularity. There are several available, each with its own indications and benefits. Some are 2-layered membranes with both dermal and epidermal components. Others are only 1 layer. The skin is engineered from neonatal foreskins and cadavers. Skin substitutes do not contain structures such as blood vessels, hair follicles, sweat glands, or cells such as melanocytes, Langerhans cells, macrophages, and lymphocytes.[16] Engineered skin grafts have an extended shelf life. Some are cryopreserved. Others shipped overnight as they are needed. Advantages include ready availability, no donor site, application in outpatient settings, minimal scarring, and less pain.

Case Study

Melanoma and Dysplastic Nevi

(© Dimedrol68/ iStock/Think stock.)

Patient Profile

G.L. is a 48-year-old White, fair-skinned man who is a long-distance truck driver. In his leisure time, he enjoys swimming and bicycling. He comes to the clinic because of a changing lesion on his left arm.

Subjective Data

- History of a basal cell cancer (BCC) on his left ear in the last 4 years
- Father treated for metastatic melanoma in the past 2 years
- First noted the lesion 1 month ago when it started changing size
- Anxious that removing the lesion will require extensive, disfiguring surgery

Objective Data

Physical Assessment

- Has a 4-mm lesion, deep brown, scalloped with vaguely defined borders
- 5 dysplastic nevi found on back

Diagnostic Studies

- Excisional biopsy confirmed superficial spreading melanoma.
- Sentinel node biopsy results were negative.
- Diagnostic tests indicate melanoma stage I.

Discussion Questions

1. ***Recognize***: What risk factors for melanoma does G.L. have?
2. ***Recognize***: What manifestations of melanoma are present?
3. ***Analyze***: What is the prognosis for a patient with this stage of melanoma?
4. ***Plan***: What treatment options are available for him?
5. ***Prioritize:*** What is the priority of care for G.L.?
6. ***Prioritize:*** Based on the assessment data presented, what are the priority clinical problems?
7. ***Act:*** How would you help G.L. deal with his anxiety over the treatment outcomes?
8. ***Act:*** What would you include in his teaching plan to address future sun exposure?

Answers available at http://evolve.elsevier.com/Lewis/medsurg.

BRIDGE TO NCLEX EXAMINATION

The number of the question corresponds to the same-numbered outcome at the beginning of the chapter.

1. Which safe sun practices would the nurse include in a teaching plan for a patient with photosensitivity? *(select all that apply)*
   - **a.** Wear protective clothing.
   - **b.** Apply sunscreen liberally and often.
   - **c.** Emphasize the short-term use of a tanning booth.
   - **d.** Avoid exposure to the sun, especially during midday.
   - **e.** Wear any sunscreen that is available from the drugstore.

2. When teaching a patient with melanoma, the nurse recognizes that the patient's prognosis is *most* dependent on
   - **a.** the thickness of the lesion.
   - **b.** the degree of asymmetry in the lesion.
   - **c.** the amount of ulceration in the surrounding skin.
   - **d.** how much color variation is present in the lesion.

3. The nurse determines that a patient with which disorder is *most* at risk for spreading the disease?
   - **a.** Tinea pedis
   - **b.** Impetigo on the face
   - **c.** Candidiasis of the nails
   - **d.** Psoriasis on the palms and soles

4. A mother and her children have been diagnosed with pediculosis corporis at a health care center. An appropriate treatment is
   - **a.** applying pyrethrins to the body.
   - **b.** topical application of griseofulvin.
   - **c.** moist compresses applied frequently.
   - **d.** administration of systemic antibiotics.

5. A common site for the lesions caused by atopic dermatitis is the
   - **a.** buttocks.
   - **b.** temporal area.
   - **c.** antecubital space.
   - **d.** plantar surface of the feet.

6. During the assessment of a patient, you note an area of red, sharply defined plaques covered with silvery scales that are mildly itchy on the patient's knees and elbows. You would describe this finding as
   - **a.** lentigo.
   - **b.** psoriasis.
   - **c.** actinic keratosis.
   - **d.** seborrheic keratosis.

7. In teaching a patient who is using topical corticosteroids to treat acute dermatitis, the nurse should tell the patient that *(select all that apply)*
   a. the cream form is the most efficient system of delivery.
   b. short-term topical corticosteroid use usually does not cause systemic side effects.
   c. use a glove to apply a large amount of topical ointment to prevent further infection.
   d. abruptly stopping the use of topical corticosteroids may cause the dermatitis to reappear.
   e. systemic side effects from topical corticosteroids are likely if the patient is malnourished.
8. Important patient teaching after a chemical peel includes
   a. avoidance of sun exposure.
   b. application of firm bandages.
   c. limitation of vigorous exercise.
   d. use of moist heat to relieve discomfort.

1. a, b, d; 2. a; 3. b; 4. a; 5. c; 6. b; 7. b, d; 8. a.

For rationales to these answers and even more NCLEX review questions, visit http://evolve.elsevier.com/Lewis/medsurg.

EVOLVE WEBSITE/RESOURCE LIST

http://evolve.elsevier.com/Lewis/medsurg
Review Questions (Online Only)
Key Points
Answer Keys for Questions
- Rationales for Bridge to NCLEX Examination Questions
- Answer Guidelines for Case Study

Nursing Care Plan
- eNursing Care Plan 25.1: Patient With Chronic Skin Lesions

Conceptual Care Map Creator
Audio Glossary
Content Updates

REFERENCES

1. Medscape: Melanoma. Retrieved from https://emedicine.medscape.com/article/1295718-overview#a2.
2. US Food and Drug Administration: Sunscreen Innovation Act. Retrieved from www.fda.gov/drugs/guidancecomplianceregulatoryinformation/ucm434782.htm.
3. American Cancer Society: Skin cancer facts. Retrieved from www.cancer.org/cancer/skin-cancer.html.

*4. Cameron MC, Lee E, Hibler BP, et al.: Basal cell carcinoma: epidemiology; pathophysiology; clinical and histological subtypes; and disease associations, *J Am Acad Dermatol* 80(2):5, 2019.

*5. Tang CH, Sue YM, Hsieh WT, et al.: Increased risk of cutaneous squamous cell carcinoma in organ transplant recipients and patients on chronic dialysis: a cancer registry-based study in Taiwan, *Acta Derm Venereol* 99:13, 2019.

6. American Cancer Society: Melanoma skin cancer. Retrieved from https://www.cancer.org/cancer/melanoma-skin-cancer.html.

*7. Swetter SM, Tsao H, Bichakjian CK, et al.: Guidelines of care for the management of primary cutaneous melanoma, *J Am Acad Dermatol* 80:1, 2019.

8. Medscape: Atypical mole: Clark nevus or dysplastic nevus. Retrieved from https://emedicine.medscape.com/article/1056283-overview#a6.
9. American Academy of Dermatology: Psoriasis. Retrieved from https://www.aad.org/public/diseases/psoriasis.

*10. Roberto BS, Feliciani G, Del Duca M, et al.: Clinical evidence of abscopal effect in cutaneous squamous cell carcinoma treated with diffusing alpha emitters radiation therapy: a case report, *JCB* 11:5, 2019.

*11. Claeys KC, Zasowski EJ, Trinh TD, et al.: Open-label randomized trial of early clinical outcomes of ceftaroline fosamil versus vancomycin for the treatment of acute bacterial skin and skin structure infections at risk of methicillin-resistant *Staphylococcus aureus, Infect Dis Ther* 8:2, 2019.

12. Medscape: Allergic contact dermatitis treatment and management: topical immunomodulators. Retrieved from https://emedicine.medscape.com/article/1049216-treatment#d9.

*13. McLawhorn JM, Stephany MP, Bruhn WE, et al.: An expert panel consensus on opioid-prescribing guidelines for dermatologic procedures, *J Am Acad Dermatol* 82:700, 2020.

*14. Percec I, Bertucci V, Solish N, et al.: An objective, quantitative, dynamic assessment of hyaluronic acid fillers that adapt to facial movement, *Plast Reconstr Surg* 145:2, 2020.

*15. Jafferany M, Salimi S, Mkhoyan R, et al.: Psychological aspects of aesthetic and cosmetic surgery: clinical and therapeutic implications, *Dermatologic Ther* 33:e13727, 2020.

16. Poinas A, Perrot P, Lorant J, et al.: CICAFAST: comparison of a biological dressing composed of fetal fibroblasts and keratinocytes on a split-thickness skin graft donor site versus a traditional dressing: a randomized controlled trial, *Trials* 20:1, 2019.

*Evidence-based information for clinical practice.

26

Burns

Cecilia Bidigare

http://evolve.elsevier.com/Lewis/medsurg/

CONCEPTUAL FOCUS

Coping
Fluids and Electrolytes
Gas Exchange
Infection
Nutrition
Pain
Perfusion
Tissue Integrity

LEARNING OUTCOMES

1. Relate the causes of burns to prevention strategies for burn injuries.
2. Distinguish between partial-thickness and full-thickness burns.
3. Apply tools used to determine the severity of burns.
4. Compare the pathophysiology, clinical manifestations, complications, and interprofessional care throughout the 3 burn phases.
5. Compare the fluid and electrolyte shifts during the emergent and acute burn phases.
6. Outline the nutrition needs of the burn patient.
7. Compare burn wound care techniques and surgical options for partial-thickness and full-thickness burn wounds.
8. Prioritize nursing interventions in the management of the burn patient's physiologic and psychosocial needs.
9. Examine the physiologic and psychosocial aspects of burn rehabilitation.
10. Develop a plan of care to prepare the burn patient and caregiver for discharge.

KEY TERMS

chemical burns
debridement
electrical burns
eschar
escharotomy
excision
full-thickness burns
inhalation injuries
partial-thickness burns
thermal burns

The focus of this chapter is the nursing care of patients with burn injuries. Heat, chemicals, electric current, or radiation can cause significant burns. Injury severity ranges from mild to life-threatening. Patients with less serious burns are managed in outpatient clinics. Those with major burn injuries will require prolonged hospitalization in a specialty burn center.

A burn injury affects many body systems. A patient exposed to smoke may have problems with gas exchange. Expect to see fluid and electrolyte imbalances. Full-thickness burns can alter perfusion to limbs. Patients with burns are at risk for malnutrition and immobility. Infection is a constant threat. The most common cause of death after a major burn injury is multiple organ dysfunction syndrome as a response to sepsis.

Patients and caregivers often experience overwhelming emotions, including fear, anger, guilt, or depression. Patients often have anxiety when anticipating painful dressing changes. Coping with pain daily can affect the patient physically and mentally. Others fear possible permanent lifestyle changes and disfigurement.

The needs of patients with major burns are extensive. They require the expertise of many health care team members. These include nurses, health care providers (HCP), occupational (OT) and physical (PT) therapists, dietitians, social workers, psychologists, and clergy. Nurses caring for burn patients usually have extensive specialized training. Providing care to burn patients can be emotionally and physically challenging. However, it is very rewarding to work as a burn team member and contribute to the recovery of patients with devastating injuries.

An estimated 486,000 Americans seek medical care each year for burns.[1] Around 40,000 people are hospitalized, with

TABLE 26.1 Common Sources of Burn Injury

Home Hazards

Bathroom and Kitchen

- Water heaters set at 120°F (60°C) or higher
- Microwaved food
- Steam, hot grease, or liquids from cooking

General Household

- Carelessness with cigarettes, matches, candles
- Heat lamps
- Fireplaces (e.g., gas, wood)
- Flammables (e.g., starter fluid, gasoline, kerosene)
- Frayed or defective wiring
- Multiple extension cords per outlet
- Open space heaters
- Outdoor grills (e.g., propane, charcoal)

Occupational Hazards

- Cement
- Chemicals
- Combustible fuels
- Electricity from power lines
- Fertilizers, pesticides
- Hot metals
- Sparks from live electric sources
- Steam pipes
- Tar

TABLE 26.2 PROMOTING POPULATION HEALTH

Strategies to Reduce Burn Injury in Homes

- Install and maintain smoke alarms in your home—on every floor and near all rooms family members sleep in. Test your smoke alarms once a month to make sure they are working properly. Use long-life batteries when possible.
- Create and practice a family fire escape plan. Involve kids in the planning. Make sure everyone knows at least 2 ways out of every room. Identify a central meeting place outside.
- Use safe cooking practices, such as never leaving food unattended on the stove. Supervise or restrict children's use of stoves, ovens, and especially microwaves.
- Set your water heater's thermostat to 120°F or lower.
- Store chemicals in approved, labeled containers
- Replace or repair frayed wiring.
- Avoid outdoor activities during electrical (e.g., lightning) storms.
- Ensure the electrical power source is off before beginning repairs.
- Never use gasoline or other flammable liquids to start a fire.
- Never leave candles unattended or near open windows or curtains.
- Consider a flame-retardant smoking apron for older or "at-risk" people.
- Before placing a child in the bath or getting in the bath yourself, test the water.
- Have a "kid-free zone" of at least 3 feet around the stove and areas where hot food or drink is prepared or carried.
- Never hold a child while you are cooking, drinking a hot liquid, or carrying hot foods or liquids.

60% receiving care in specialized burn centers. About 3275 Americans die each year from their injuries. Worldwide, over 11 million people seek medical attention annually for burn injuries, and about 180,000 die.[2] Although burn injuries in the United States have decreased over the past 20 years, injuries still occur, often to those living in low- and middle-income counties.[3]

Most burn accidents are preventable when safety policies are in place. Coordinated national burn prevention programs in higher-income countries have focused on child-resistant lighters, tap water anti-scald devices, stricter building codes, having smoke detectors, and burn safety education curriculums in schools.[4] As a nurse, you can advocate for and teach about burn prevention strategies (Tables 26.1 and 26.2).

TYPES OF BURN INJURY

Thermal Burns

Thermal burns are due to exposure to external heat sources such as hot metals, scalding liquids, steam, or flames. The severity of the injury depends on the temperature of the burning agent and duration of skin contact. This is the most common type of burn injury. Causes of thermal injury include grease fires when cooking, house fires, smoking, and the use of gasoline for cleaning or incineration.

Chemical Burns

Contact with acids, alkalines, or organic compounds can cause **chemical burns** through absorption, inhalation, or ingestion. Dangerous chemicals are in homes, businesses, and industries. For example, severe injury can occur with exposure to lye and sulfuric acid, common chemicals used to unclog sinks in homes. Exposure to wet cement, oven cleaners, and heavy industrial cleaners can cause chemical burns. Chemicals such as phenols (chemical disinfectants) and petroleum products (creosote and gasoline) cause not only external burns but also systemic toxicity. Acid chemicals cause tissue necrosis. Alkaline chemicals cause liquefaction necrosis, which can be more damaging. Some chemicals will have heat-producing reactions once exposed to the skin, causing superficial blisters or even deep burns.

Electrical Burns

Electrical burns result from the intense heat generated from an electric current. Direct damage to nerves and vessels can cause tissue anoxia and cell death. The severity of an electrical injury depends on the voltage, tissue resistance, current pathways, surface area in contact with the current, and length of time that the current flow was sustained (Fig. 26.1). Current that passes through vital organs (e.g., brain, heart, kidneys) causes more life-threatening sequela when compared to a current passing through other tissues. The severity of an electrical injury can be hard to determine initially since most of the damage is below the skin.

Contact with an electric current can cause muscle contractions strong enough to fracture the long bones and vertebrae. Forceful propulsion of the body from an electrical source can cause injuries such as spinal and limb fractures. For this reason, consider cervical spine injury for all patients with electrical burns.

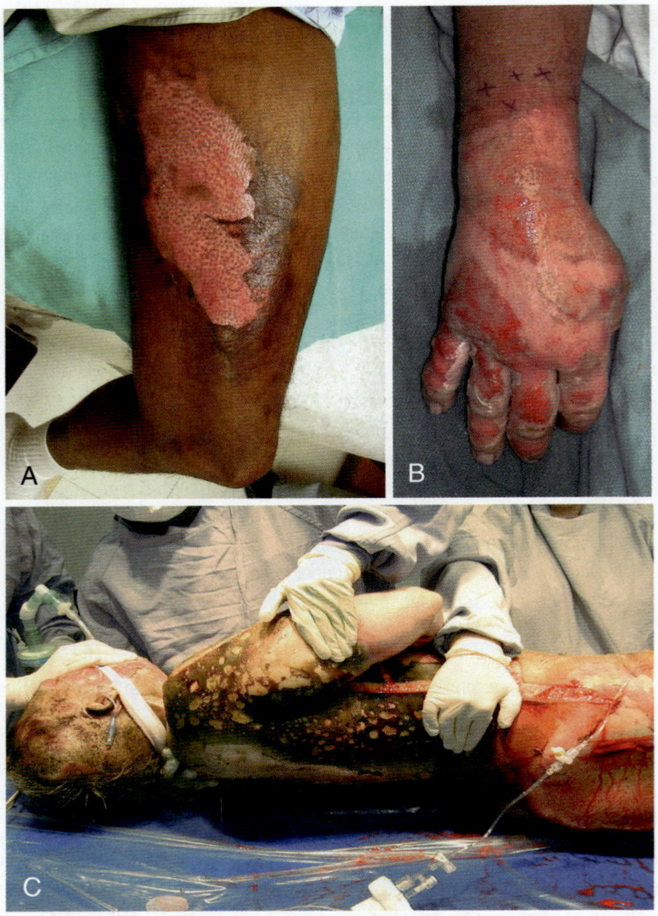

Fig. 26.1 Types of burn injury. (A) Superficial, partial-thickness scald burn to the thigh. (B) Deep, partial-thickness flame burn to the hand. (C) Full-thickness flame burn to posterior chest and arm. (Courtesy Judy Knighton, Toronto, Canada.)

TABLE 26.3 Burn Center Referral Criteria

Burn injuries that should be referred to a burn center include the following:

- Partial-thickness burns greater than 10% total body surface area (TBSA)
- Burns that involve the face, hands, feet, genitalia, perineum, or major joints
- Third-degree burns in any age-group
- Electrical burns, including lightning injury
- Chemical burns
- Inhalation injury
- Injury in patients with preexisting medical disorders that could complicate management, prolong recovery, or affect mortality
- Any patient with burns and concomitant trauma (e.g., fractures) in which the burn injury poses the greatest risk for morbidity or mortality. In such cases, if the trauma poses a greater immediate risk, the patient may be stabilized in a trauma center before being transferred to a burn unit. HCP judgment is necessary in such situations and would be in concert with the regional medical control plan and triage protocols.
- Burned children in hospitals without qualified personnel or equipment for the care of children
- Burn injury in patients who will need special social, emotional, or rehabilitative intervention

Source: American Burn Association: Guidelines for the operation of burn centers. Retrieved from http://ameriburn.org/wp-content/uploads/2017/05/burncenterreferralcriteria.pdf.

Electrical injury puts the patient at risk for respiratory arrest, severe metabolic acidosis, and myoglobinuria. An electric shock can cause immediate cardiac standstill or ventricular fibrillation. Massive muscle and blood vessel damage can release myoglobin from injured muscle and hemoglobin from damaged red blood cells (RBCs). Myoglobin can block the renal tubules resulting in acute kidney injury (AKI; see Chapter 51).

Cold Thermal Injury

Cold thermal injury, or frostbite, is discussed in Chapter 21.

CLASSIFICATION OF BURN INJURY

Severity is determined by (1) depth of burn, (2) extent of burn calculated in percent of total body surface area (TBSA), (3) location of the burn, (4) preexisting health issues, and (5) associated injuries. The American Burn Association (ABA) provides referral criteria based on injury severity to determine which patients need specialized treatment in a burn center (Table 26.3).[5]

Burn Depth Classification

Four factors influence burn depth: (1) temperature of the agent, (2) duration of contact, (3) thickness of the epidermis and dermis, and (4) blood supply to the area. Burn injury is determined according to the extent of injury through the epidermis, dermis, and underlying structures. One method describes an injury as first, second, third, or fourth degree. The ABA recommends using the terms partial-thickness burns and full-thickness burns to classify burns (Figs. 26.2 and 26.3). **Partial-thickness burns** involve the epidermis and sometimes part of the dermis. A **full-thickness injury** occurs if the epidermis and dermis are destroyed. **Eschar** is another name for full-thickness nonviable burn tissue. Burns can extend beyond the skin and involve tendons, ligaments, muscle, and adipose. Table 26.4 compares the various burn classifications according to the depth of injury

Extent of Burn

Nurses are responsible for estimating the extent of burn injury. The *Lund-Browder chart* (Fig. 26.4A) and the *Rule of Nines* (Fig. 26.4B) are common methods used to determine burn TBSA. We often use the Rule of 9's for initial adult triage. Use the Lund-Browder formula for children because it considers the patient's age in proportion to relative body-area size. Electronic tools (e.g., the *Sage Burn Diagram* at www.sagediagram.com) and mobile applications (e.g., BurnMed, Mersey Burns) are available for estimating TBSA.

Location of Burn

The location of the burn injury influences the severity. Face, neck, and circumferential torso burns may interfere with gas exchange. Circumferential leathery eschar can restrict chest movement. Edema from inflammation and fluid resuscitation can narrow the airway.

Hand, foot, and joint burns can limit mobility and function. Full-thickness circumferential extremity burns can impair perfusion distal to the injury. Injured hands and feet are challenging to manage because of the superficial vascular and nerve supplies that require protection. Infection is a risk for patients with ear or nose burns with exposed cartilage since the skin and subcutaneous tissues are thin and there are no blood vessels. Patients with buttocks or perineum burns are at high risk for infection from urine or feces contamination.

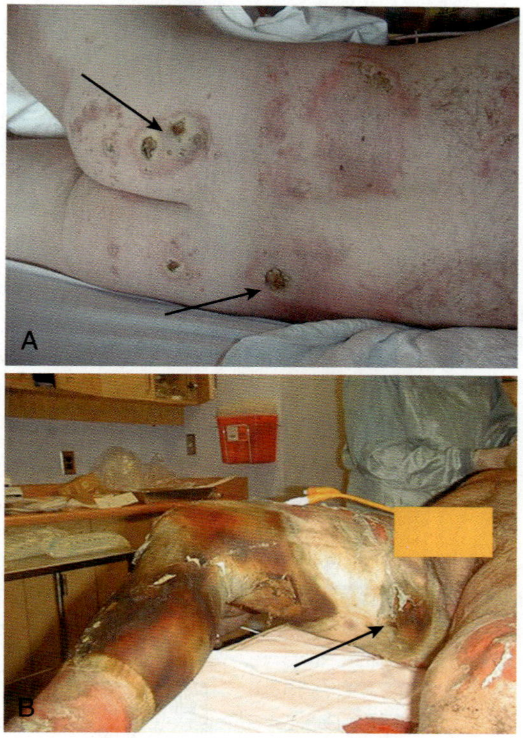

Fig. 26.2 Electrical injury produces heat coagulation of blood supply and contact area as electric current passes through the skin. (A) Back and buttock *(arrows)*. (B) Leg *(arrow)*. (Courtesy Judy Knighton, Toronto, Canada.)

Patient Risk Factors

Patients with preexisting chronic diseases have a poorer prognosis for recovery because of the increased demands placed on the body by burn injury.[6] Patients with diabetes or peripheral vascular disease are at high risk for delayed healing, especially with foot and leg burns.

PREHOSPITAL AND EMERGENCY CARE

Scene safety is a priority at the time of the injury. Once assured, first responders will remove the person from the source of the burn and stop the burning process.[7] The wounds are flushed with copious amounts of water. Cooling the burn tissue helps minimize the depth of the injury. Afterward, wrapping the

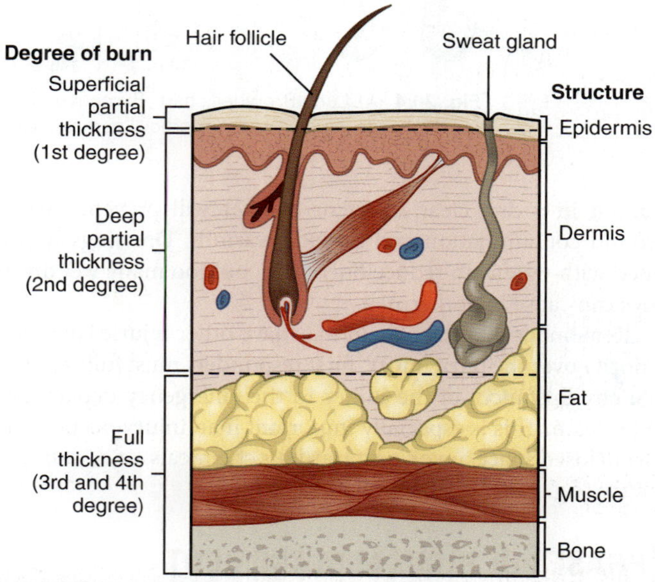

Fig. 26.3 Cross-section of skin showing the depth of burn and structures involved.

TABLE 26.4 Classification of Burn Injury Depth

Classification	Appearance	Possible Cause	Structures Involved
Partial-Thickness Skin Destruction			
Superficial (first-degree) burn	Erythema, blanching on pressure, pain and mild swelling, no vesicles or blisters (although after 24 hr, skin may blister and peel)	Quick heat flash Superficial sunburn	Superficial epidermal damage with hyperemia. Tactile and pain sensation intact
Deep (second-degree) burn	Fluid-filled vesicles that are red, shiny, wet (if vesicles have ruptured). Severe pain caused by nerve injury. Mild to moderate edema	Chemicals Contact burns Electric current Flame Flash Scald Tar, cement	Epidermis and dermis are involved in varying depths. Skin elements, from which epithelial regeneration occurs, remain viable
Full-Thickness Skin Destruction			
Third- and fourth-degree burns	Dry, waxy white, brown or charred, leathery, or hard skin. Visible thrombosed vessels. Insensitivity to pain because of nerve destruction. Possible muscle, tendon, and bone involvement	Chemical Electric current Flame Scald Tar, cement	All skin elements and local nerve endings destroyed. Coagulation necrosis present. Surgical intervention required for healing

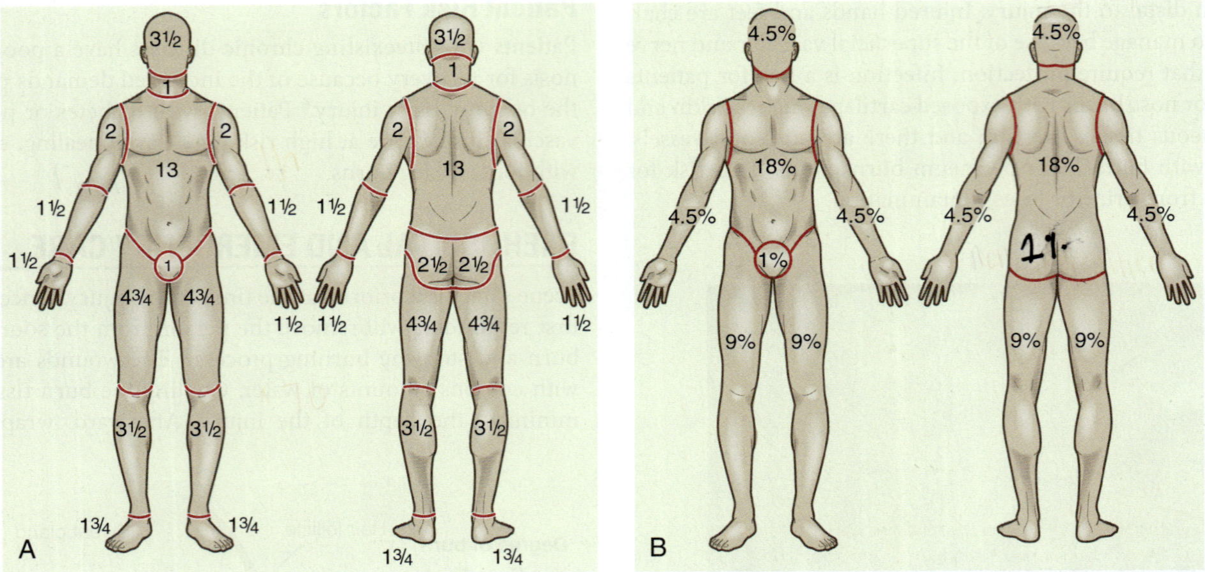

Fig. 26.4 (A) Lund-Browder chart. By convention, areas of partial-thickness injury are in *blue* and areas of full-thickness injury in *red*. Superficial partial-thickness burns are not calculated. (B) Rule of Nines chart.

patient in a dry, clean sheet or blanket will prevent further wound contamination and provide warmth. Dressings moistened with water can reduce burn pain, but too many wet dressings can cause hypothermia.

Remember that the patient may have other injuries that take priority over the burn injury. First responders must fully explain the circumstances of the injury to the emergency department (ED) team. This is especially important if an injury occurred in an enclosed space, involved hazardous chemicals, or a traumatic injury (e.g., fall).

PHASES OF BURN MANAGEMENT

Burn management for those with significant injuries can be organized chronologically into 3 phases: (1) emergent (resuscitative), (2) acute (wound healing), and (3) rehabilitative (restorative). A nursing care plan for the patient with burn injury (eNursing Care Plan 26.1) is available on the website for this chapter.

EMERGENT PHASE

During the emergent (resuscitative) phase, the health care team prioritizes life-threatening problems. This phase usually lasts up to 72 hours after the initial injury for patients with burns extending over 20% of their bodies. The priority nursing concerns are fluid and electrolyte shifts and gas exchange.

Pathophysiology

Fluid and Electrolyte Shifts

Burn shock is a combination of distributive and hypovolemic shock. It is a significant threat to a patient with a major burn (Fig. 26.5). Increased capillary permeability will cause a massive shift of fluids from the intravascular to interstitial spaces. The patient's vital signs will begin to change as water, sodium, and

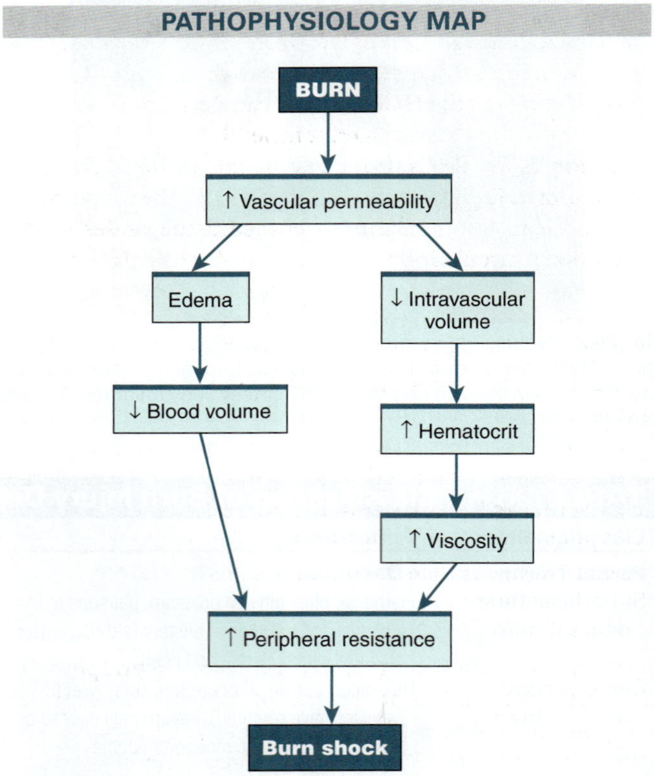

Fig. 26.5 At the time of major burn injury, capillary permeability increases. All fluid components of the blood begin to leak into the interstitium, causing edema and a decreased blood volume. Hematocrit increases. The blood becomes more viscous. The combination of decreased blood volume and increased viscosity increases peripheral resistance. Burn shock, a type of hypovolemic shock, rapidly ensues and, if not corrected, can result in death.

plasma proteins move into the interstitial spaces. The progressive loss of protein from the vascular space will reduce colloidal osmotic pressure. This causes more fluid to shift out of the

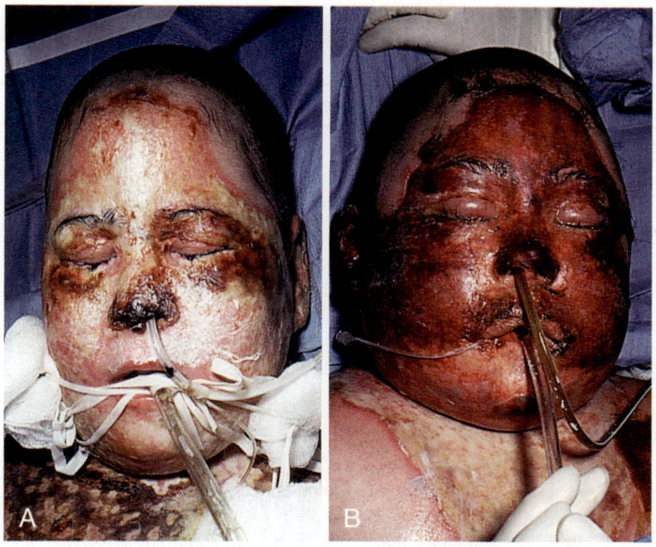

Fig. 26.6 (A) Facial edema before fluid resuscitation. (B) Facial edema after 24 hours. (Courtesy Judy Knighton, Toronto, Canada.)

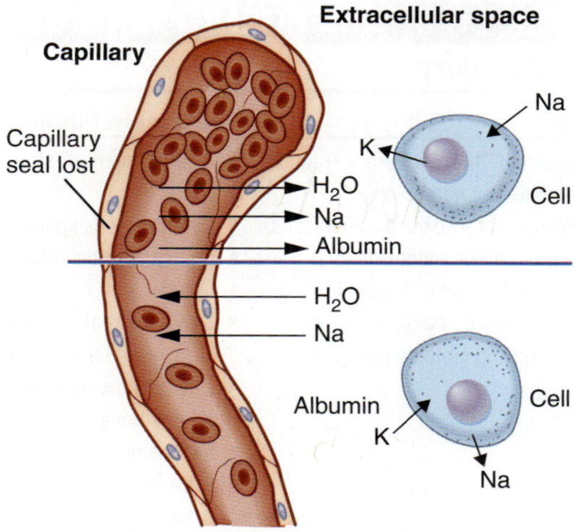

Fig. 26.7 The effects of burn shock are shown above the *purple line*. As the capillary seal is lost, interstitial edema develops. Cellular integrity is altered. Sodium *(Na)* moves into the cell in abnormal amounts and potassium *(K)* leaves the cell. The shifts after the resolution of burn shock are shown below the *blue line*. Water and sodium move back into the circulating volume through the capillary. Albumin stays in the interstitium. Potassium is transported into the cell and sodium is transported out as the cellular integrity returns.

vascular space into the interstitial spaces (Fig. 26.6). We call this *third spacing*. The patient may have massive edema and significant wound drainage. Loss of intravascular fluid can cause burn shock. Monitor for hypotension, tachycardia, and tachypnea. Report changes to the HCP. Patients can develop AKI and ultimately death if not resuscitated sufficiently.

Hemolysis of RBCs from circulating factors released at the time of injury from the burned tissue affects perfusion. Thrombosis in the capillaries of burned tissue causes the loss of additional circulating RBCs. Monitor for a high hematocrit from hemoconcentration due to fluid loss. Hematocrit levels will return to normal after burn shock resolves.

Major electrolyte shifts of sodium and potassium occur during this phase. A potassium shift develops first when injured cells and hemolyzed RBCs release potassium into the circulation. Sodium rapidly moves to the interstitial spaces (Fig. 26.7).

The emergent phase ends once capillary membrane permeability is restored after successful fluid resuscitation. Interstitial fluid gradually returns to the vascular space (Fig. 26.7). Potassium levels decline and sodium levels increase.

Inflammation and Healing

Burn injury causes coagulation necrosis. Neutrophils and monocytes accumulate at the site of injury. Fibroblasts and newly formed collagen fibrils appear and begin wound repair within the first 6 to 12 hours after injury. (The inflammatory response is discussed in Chapter 12.)

Immunologic Changes

A burn injury challenges the body's immune system by altering the skin's barrier to invading organisms. Bone marrow depression occurs and circulating levels of immunoglobulins decrease. Defects occur in white blood cell (WBC) function. The inflammatory cytokine cascade, triggered by tissue damage, impairs the function of lymphocytes, monocytes, and neutrophils. Therefore the patient is at high risk of infection.

Clinical Manifestations

Seeing a patient with major burns can be overwhelming due to the burns and the smell of burned tissue and hair. The patient is normally alert and able to answer questions during admission or until intubated (if there is respiratory compromise). Monitor cognition and report any changes. Unconsciousness or altered mental status usually results from hypoxia due to inhalation injury. Other possibilities include head trauma, substance use, or the side effects of sedation or pain medication. Patients are often frightened and need your calm reassurances. Give the patient simple explanations of what to expect.

Often patients will shiver from heat loss, anxiety, or pain. Provide warm blankets and increase the room temperature or turn on heat lamps. Full thickness burns are painless since nerves in the dermis are destroyed. Partial-thickness burns are very painful.

Complications

The 3 systems most susceptible to complications during the emergent phase of burn injury are the respiratory, cardiovascular, and renal systems.

Respiratory

Inhalation injuries from breathing noxious chemicals or hot air will damage the respiratory tract. Three types of inhalation injuries can occur:

- Injury from exposure to toxic gases, including carbon monoxide and/or cyanide
- Above the glottis injury from direct heat or chemicals causing severe mucosal edema
- Below the glottis injury causing airway inflammation and edema resulting in atelectasis and pneumonia

TABLE 26.5 EMERGENCY MANAGEMENT

Inhalation Injury

Etiology	Assessment Findings	Interventions
• Exposure of the respiratory tract to intense heat or flames • Inhalation of noxious chemicals, smoke, or carbon monoxide (CO) • Occurs with being trapped in an enclosed space, being in an explosion, or having clothing catch fire	• Altered mental status, including confusion, coma • Carbonaceous sputum • Cherry-red skin color (CO levels >20%) • Coughing • Darkened oral or nasal membranes • Decreased O_2 saturation • Difficulty swallowing • Dysrhythmias • Increasing hoarseness • Irritation of upper airways or burning pain in throat or chest • Productive cough with black, gray, or bloody sputum • Rapid, shallow respirations • Restlessness, anxiety • Singed nasal or facial hair • Smoky breath	**Initial** • If unresponsive, assess circulation, airway, and breathing. • If responsive, monitor the airway, breathing, and circulation. • Assess for a thermal burn. • Provide 100% humidified O_2. • Anticipate endotracheal intubation and mechanical ventilation with significant inhalation injury. • Monitor vital signs, level of consciousness, O_2 saturation, and heart rhythm. • Obtain ABGs, carboxyhemoglobin levels, and chest x-ray. • Remove non-adherent clothing, jewelry, glasses, or contact lenses (if the face was exposed). • Establish IV access with 2 large-bore catheters if burn >20% TBSA. • Begin fluid replacement. • Insert indwelling urinary catheter if burn >20% TBSA. • Elevate burned limb(s) above the heart to decrease edema. • Give IV analgesia and assess effectiveness frequently. • Identify and treat other injuries (e.g., fractures, pneumothorax, head injury). • Cover concurrent burned areas with dry dressings or clean sheets. • Anticipate the need for fiberoptic bronchoscopy or intubation. **Ongoing Monitoring** • Monitor airway, breathing, and circulation. • Monitor vital signs, O_2 saturation, heart rhythm, and level of consciousness. • Monitor pain level. • Monitor urine output.

TBSA, Total body surface area.

The severity of inhalation injury ranges from mild to severe (Table 26.5). Rapid initial and ongoing assessment is critical. Airway compromise and pulmonary edema can quickly develop within hours of injury. The patient may need a fiberoptic bronchoscopy and carboxyhemoglobin blood levels to confirm a suspected inhalation injury. Patients exposed to carbon monoxide from smoke will have elevated carboxyhemoglobin levels. Examine sputum for carbon particles. Watch for signs of respiratory distress, such as increased agitation, anxiety, restlessness, or a change in the rate or character of breathing. Symptoms may not be present at first.

Patients with preexisting lung disease are more likely to develop a respiratory infection. Pneumonia, a common complication of major burns, is the leading cause of death in patients with an inhalation injury.

Cardiovascular

Other complications can affect perfusion besides burn shock. Deep circumferential burns and subsequent edema formation can impair blood flow to the extremities. If untreated, ischemia, paresthesia, and necrosis can occur. An **escharotomy** (an incision through the full-thickness eschar) will restore circulation to compromised extremities or improve chest expansion (Fig. 26.8).[8] HCPs perform this procedure.

Burn patients are at risk for venous thromboembolism (VTE), especially if other risk factors are present. These include advanced age, obesity, extensive or lower extremity burns, concomitant lower extremity trauma, and prolonged immobility. It is recommended the patient receive low-molecular-weight heparin (enoxaparin) or low-dose unfractionated heparin if there are no contraindications. Apply intermittent pneumatic compression devices if the patient is immobile.

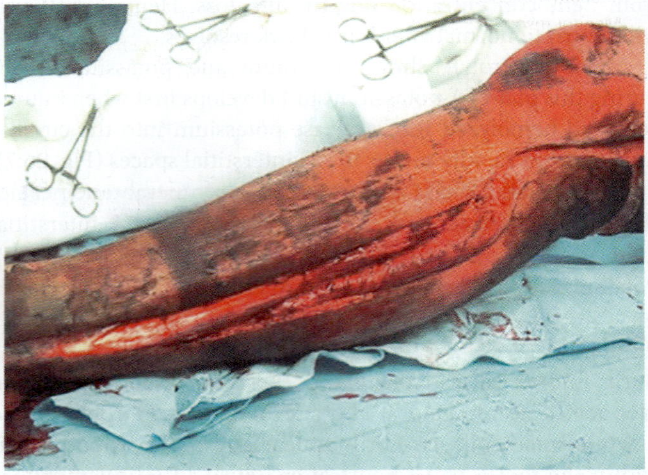

Fig. 26.8 Escharotomies of the lower leg. (Source: Sheridan R: Medical aspects of trauma and burns. In Goldman L, Schafer A [Eds], *Goldman-Cecil medicine*, ed 26, Philadelphia, 2020, Elsevier.)

TABLE 26.6 Interprofessional Care

Burn Injury

Emergent Phase	Acute Phase	Rehabilitation Phase
Fluid Therapy (Table 26.7) • Assess fluid needs. • Begin IV fluid replacement. • Insert an indwelling urinary catheter. • Monitor urine output. **Wound Care** • Start daily shower and wound care. • Debride as needed. • Assess the extent and depth of burns. • Give tetanus toxoid or tetanus antitoxin. **Pain and Anxiety** • Assess and manage pain and anxiety. **Physical and Occupational Therapy** • Place the patient in a position that prevents contracture formation and reduces edema. • Assess the need for splints. **Nutrition Therapy** • Assess nutrition needs and begin feeding patients by the most appropriate route as soon as possible. **Respiratory Therapy** • Assess oxygenation needs. • Provide supplemental O_2 as needed. • Intubate if needed. • Monitor respiratory status. **Psychosocial Care** • Provide support to patients and caregivers during the initial crisis phase.	**Fluid Therapy** • Continue to replace fluids, depending on the patient's clinical response. **Wound Care** • Continue daily shower and wound care. • Continue debridement (if needed). • Assess wound daily and adjust dressing protocols as needed. • Observe for complications (e.g., infection). **Early Excision and Grafting (Table 26.9)** • Provide temporary allografts. • Provide permanent autografts. • Care for donor sites. **Pain and Anxiety** • Continue to assess for and treat pain and anxiety. **Physical and Occupational Therapy** • Begin a daily therapy program for maintenance of a range of motion. • Assess the need for splints and anti-contracture positioning. • Encourage and aid patients with self-care as possible. **Nutrition Therapy** • Continue to assess diet to support wound healing. **Respiratory Therapy** • Continue to assess oxygenation needs. • Continue to monitor respiratory status. • Monitor for signs of complications (e.g., pneumonia). **Psychosocial Care** • Provide ongoing support, counseling, and teaching to patients and caregiver about physical and emotional aspects of care and recovery. • Begin discharge planning. **Drug Therapy (Table 26.8)** • Assess the need for drugs (e.g., antibiotics). • Continue to monitor effectiveness and adjust dosage as needed.	• Continue to teach patients and caregivers about wound care. • Continue to encourage and aid the patient in resuming self-care. • Continue to prevent or minimize contractures. • Assess risk for scarring (surgery, physical and occupational therapy, splinting, pressure garments). • Discuss possible reconstructive surgery. • Prepare for discharge home or transfer to a rehabilitation hospital. • Discuss the possible need for home care nursing.

Renal

The most common renal complication during the emergent phase is AKI.[9] If the patient becomes hypovolemic, blood flow to the kidneys will decrease, causing renal ischemia. If this continues, AKI will develop.

With full-thickness and major electrical burns, released myoglobin (from muscle cell breakdown) and hemoglobin (from RBC breakdown) can block renal tubules. Monitor the adequacy of fluid replacement because this can prevent the tubule obstruction.

NURSING AND INTERPROFESSIONAL MANAGEMENT: EMERGENT PHASE

In the emergent phase, the patient's survival depends on a rapid and thorough assessment, analyzing findings, planning and prioritizing interventions, and evaluating the results. Nurses, HCPs, and other clinicians initially focus on airway management, fluid and electrolyte balance, wound care, and nutrition (Table 26.6).

Airway Management

Work with respiratory therapists to monitor the patient's airway and breathing pattern (Table 26.5). Place the patient in a high Fowler's position unless contraindicated (e.g., spinal injury). The treatment for inhalation injury includes administering 100% O_2 with a non-rebreather mask, aerosolized heparin, N-acetylcysteine, and albuterol. Encourage deep breathing and coughing every hour. Reposition the patient every 1 to 2 hours. Suction if needed. Draw ABGs to assess the adequacy of gas exchange. Make sure to place the patient on telemetry. Monitor pulse oximetry and capnography. Evaluate the patient's response to interventions. Report adverse responses or declines to HCPs.

TABLE 26.7 Fluid Resuscitation Formulas

American Burn Association

2 mL lactated Ringer's solution per kilogram (kg) of body weight per percent of total body surface area (% TBSA) burned = Total fluid requirements for the first 24 hr after burn injury

Application

- ½ of the total in the first 8 hr
- ¼ of the total in the second 8 hr
- ¼ of the total in third 8 hr

Example

For a 70-kg patient with a 50% TBSA burn: mL × 70 × 50 (TBSA burned) = 7000 mL in 24 hr

- ½ of the total in first 8 hr = 3500 mL (438 mL/hr)
- ¼ of the total in second 8 hr = 1750 mL (219 mL/hr)
- ¼ of the total in third 8 hr = 1750 mL (219 mL/hr)

American Burn Association Consensus Fluid Resuscitation

2–4 mL lactated Ringer's solution per kilogram (kg) of body weight per percent of total body surface area (% TBSA) burned = Total fluid requirements for the first 24 hr after burn

In general, the patient with significant face and neck burns needs intubation within 1 to 2 hours after injury. Early intubation prevents the need for an emergency cricothyrotomy. Other patients will need intubation if symptoms of severe respiratory distress (e.g., hoarseness, shortness of breath) develop (see Chapters 28 and 32). Extubation may occur at the end of the emergent phase when airway edema resolves. This is usually 3 to 5 days after the initial injury. Other patients will be intubated for many weeks or months due to extensive lung damage.

! SAFETY ALERT

Pulse CO-Oximetry Monitoring

- Standard pulse oximetry (SpO_2) does not distinguish oxyhemoglobin from carboxyhemoglobin.
- A patient with CO poisoning will have normal SpO_2 readings despite high carboxyhemoglobin levels.
- For patients with suspected or confirmed CO poisoning, use a pulse CO oximetry (SpCO) device.

◆ Fluid Therapy

Nurses have many responsibilities during fluid resuscitation.[10] Insert at least 2 large-bore IVs when burns are greater than 20% TBSA. The HCP may elect to insert a central line. It is critical to select IVs that can handle large volumes of fluid. Central lines are discussed in Chapter 17.

You will need to estimate the TBSA of the burn wounds to calculate the initial IV fluid requirements for resuscitation (Fig. 26.4). Use the ABA formula to calculate the fluid needs for the first 24 hours after injury (Table 26.7 or www.mdcalc.com/parkland-formula-for-burns).[11] For adults with thermal burns, multiplying 2 mL lactated Ringer's/patient's weight in kg/TBSA burned to calculate fluid needs. Remember that formulas are estimates. Fluids are titrated based on the patient's response. Crystalloid solutions and sometimes colloids (albumin) are used for resuscitation. Insert an indwelling catheter for patients with burns greater than 20% TBSA. Monitor the patient for early signs of fluid overload, especially older patients or those with chronic heart, lung, or kidney diseases. Assess for the adequacy of fluid resuscitation hourly using urine output and cardiac parameters:

- *Urine output for adults:* 0.5 to 1 mL/kg/hr; *for children*: 1 to 1.5 mg/kg/hr.
- *Cardiac parameters:* Mean arterial pressure (MAP) greater than 65 mm Hg, systolic BP greater than 90 mm Hg, heart rate less than 120 beats/min. MAP and BP are best measured by an arterial line. Manual BP measurement is often invalid because of edema and vasoconstriction.

Patients with an electrical injury have greater than normal fluid needs to prevent AKI. They often require an osmotic diuretic (mannitol [Osmitrol]) to increase urine output and overcome hemoglobinuria or myoglobinuria. A higher hourly output of 75 to 100 mL/hr is best.

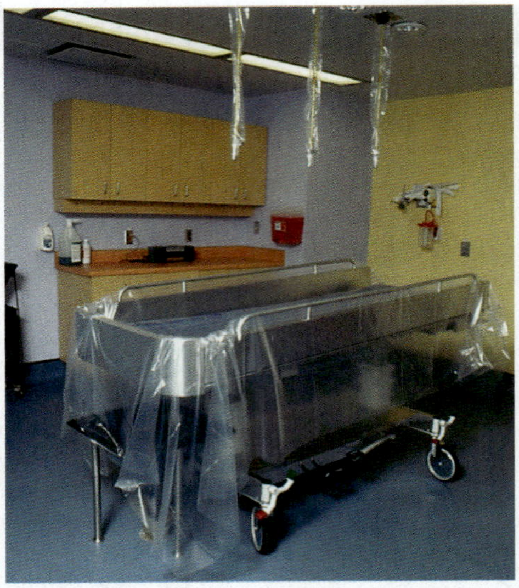

Fig. 26.9 Shower trolley. Showering presents an opportunity for PT and wound care. (Courtesy Judy Knighton, Toronto, Canada.)

CHECK YOUR PRACTICE

You are admitting an adult with thermal burns who weighs 72 kg and has 45% TBSA burn. Calculate the patient's fluid requirements for the first 24 hrs using the ABA Formula (2 mL/kg/% total body surface area burn).

◆ Wound Care

A patient with significant burns is admitted or transferred to a burn unit after being stabilizing in the ED. The patient will shower or receive a trolley bath (Fig. 26.9). Patients can lose body heat through their wounds. Prevent shivering by keeping the room warm (around 85°F [29.4°C]). Always wear personal protective equipment (PPE) (e.g., disposable hats, masks, gowns, gloves) when the patient's burn wounds are exposed. Wear non-sterile disposable gloves when removing contaminated dressings and washing wounds. Patients find wound care

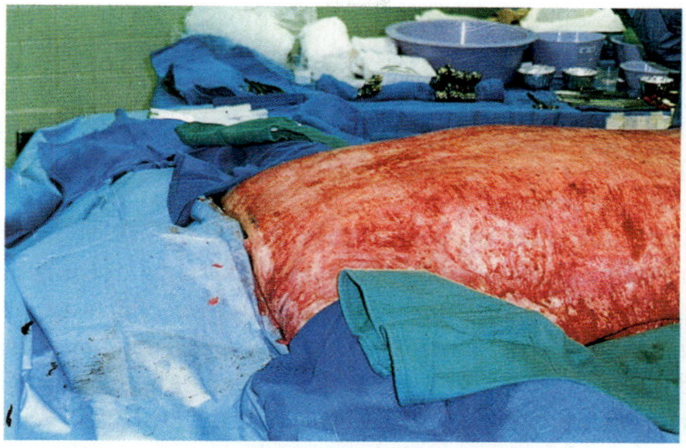

Fig. 26.10 Surgical debridement of full-thickness burns is necessary to prepare the wound for grafting. (Courtesy Judy Knighton, Toronto, Canada.)

Fig. 26.11 Application of silver sulfadiazine cream to saline-moistened gauze. (Courtesy Judy Knighton, Toronto, Canada.)

to be physically and emotionally demanding. Provide emotional support and begin to build trust during this activity.

Partial-thickness burn wounds appear pink to cherry-red and are wet and shiny with serous exudate. These painful wounds may or may not have intact blisters. Most partial thickness burns will heal within several weeks or months. Full-thickness burns can be white, red, brown, or charred. Patients may not have pain since the nerves in the dermis are destroyed. Patients with large full-thickness burns will require skin grafts. Give analgesia to manage pain during wound cleansing, debridement, and dressing application.

Use a mild cleanser and washcloths and perform cleansing and gentle wound debridement. **Debridement** is the removal of necrotic tissue from the wound bed. Skilled nurses will use scissors and forceps to remove loose burn tissue and blisters. Extensive surgical debridement occurs in the operating room (Fig. 26.10). Once the bathing is finished, the skin and burns are dried, and the total burn percentage is re-estimated. Next, we apply dressings.

Many different types of dressings and topical agents are available. These include antimicrobial creams, hydrocolloids, alginates, hydrogels, collagen, and hyaluronic acid (Fig. 26.11).[12] HCPs will prescribe topical agents based on the burn depth, bacterial count, and cost. Some burns are treated with a topical ointment and left open to the air. Others will be dressed with various products and covered with secondary dressings such as gauze. Dressing changes continue once or twice a day depending on the severity of the burn and type of dressings. Patients may have a specific specialty dressing that is changed every 5 to 7 days. Some burn centers use ace wraps or tubular elastic dressings to hold all burn dressings in place and reduce edema.

Silver very good for burns.

! SAFETY ALERT

Drug Allergy Check Sulfa in ABt.

- Check the patient for any allergies to sulfa since many burn antimicrobial creams contain sulfa.

◆ Other Care Measures

Certain parts of the body (e.g., face, eyes, hands, arms, ears, perineum) need vigilant nursing care. The face is vascular and can become very swollen. Facial burns are often covered with ointments and gauze but not wrapped to limit pressure on delicate facial structures. An eye exam should occur soon after admission for all patients with facial burns. Periorbital edema can temporarily prevent eye-opening and is often frightening for the patient. Assure that the swelling is not permanent. Instill artificial tears into the eyes for moisture and comfort.

Keep the ears free from pressure because of their poor vascularization and the tendency to become infected. Do not use pillows for the patient with ear burns. The pressure on the cartilage may cause chondritis. The ear may stick to the pillowcase, causing pain and bleeding. Raise the patient's head using a rolled towel placed under the shoulders to avoid pressure necrosis. Follow the same strategy for the patient with neck burns to hyperextend the neck and prevent neck contracture.

Extend burned hands and arms and raise them on pillows or foam wedges to reduce edema. The PT will evaluate and provide splints to keep burned joints in positions of function. Remove the splints often and inspect the skin and bony prominences to avoid areas of pressure from inappropriate or prolonged application. Collaborate with PT/OT to schedule therapy sessions. Work with PT and OT to provide range-of-motion (ROM) exercises during dressing changes and throughout the day. ROM aids the shift of the interstitial fluid back into the vascular bed, maintains function, and prevents skin and joint contractures.

Keep the patient's perineum clean and dry after voiding or bowel movements. Remove indwelling catheters used for fluid resuscitation as soon as possible. If the patient has frequent, loose stools, consider using a fecal diversion device.

◆ Drug Therapy

◆ Analgesics and Sedatives

Provide analgesics for the patient's comfort. Early in the postburn period, give IV pain medications. The onset of action is fast. Common drugs used for pain control are shown in Table 26.8. Opioids are the drug of choice for severe pain. When given appropriately, these drugs should provide adequate pain relief.

Evaluate the pain management plan often since the patient's needs may change and tolerance to drugs may develop, especially

TABLE 26.8 Drug Therapy

Burns

Drugs	Purpose
Analgesics	
morphine	Relieve pain
sustained-release morphine (MS Contin)	
hydromorphone (Dilaudid)	
sustained-release hydromorphone (Dilaudid CR)	
fentanyl (Sublimaze)	
oxycodone and acetaminophen (Percocet)	
nonsteroidal antiinflammatory (e.g., ketorolac)	
adjuvant analgesics (e.g., gabapentin)	
Anticoagulants	
enoxaparin (Lovenox)	Prevent venous thromboembolism
heparin	
Antidepressants	
citalopram (Celexa)	Reduce depression, improve mood
sertraline (Zoloft)	
Gastrointestinal Support	
aluminum hydroxide and magnesium hydroxide (Maalox)	Neutralize stomach acid
calcium carbonate and magnesium carbonate (Mylanta)	
esomeprazole (Nexium)	Decrease stomach acid and risk for Curling ulcer
cimetidine (Tagamet)	
nystatin	Prevent overgrowth of *Candida albicans* in oral mucosa
Nutrition Support	
Minerals: zinc, iron (ferrous sulfate)	Promote cell integrity and hemoglobin formation
Vitamins A, C, E, and multivitamins	Promote wound healing
Sedatives/Hypnotics	
lorazepam (Ativan)	Reduce anxiety
midazolam (Versed)	Provide short-acting amnesic effects
zolpidem (Ambien)	Promote sleep

during the acute phase. Remember that the patient's pain level may not directly correlate with the extent and depth of the burn. Analgesic needs vary from one patient to another. Consider a multimodal approach to pain control. Sedatives/hypnotics and antidepressants given with analgesics help with anxiety, insomnia, or depression. Include nondrug methods such as digital technology distraction.[13]

◆ Tetanus Immunization

Patients routinely receive tetanus toxoid because of the risk of exposure to clostridium tetani. Tetanus immunoglobulin would be considered if the patient has not received an active immunization within 10 years before the burn injury. Tetanus immunization is discussed in Table 21.6.

◆ Nutrition Therapy

A hypermetabolic state proportional to the size of the wound occurs after a major burn injury. Resting metabolic expenditure may increase by 50% to 100% above normal.[14] The core temperature increases. Catecholamine release stimulates catabolism and heat production. Massive catabolism occurs with protein breakdown and increased gluconeogenesis. Failure to supply adequate calories and protein leads to weight loss, malnutrition, and delayed healing.

Early nutrition support within several hours of the burn injury can reduce complications and mortality, optimize burn wound healing, and minimize the negative effects of hypermetabolism and catabolism. Dietitians will calculate nutrition needs and recommend supplements or enteral nutrition (EN). Non-intubated patients with a burn of less than 20% TBSA will usually be able to consume enough calories to meet their nutrition needs. Work with the dietitian to provide a high protein, high carbohydrate diet. Patients with major burns may develop an ileus and need a gastro-jejunal tube for decompression and EN. Calorie-containing nutrition supplements are given to meet the caloric needs. We may give supplemental vitamins (see Table 26.8).

Intubated patients and those with larger burns need more support. Early EN, usually with smaller bore tubes, preserves GI function, increases intestinal blood flow, and promotes optimal conditions for wound healing. In general, begin the feedings slowly at a rate of 20 to 40 mL/hr and increase to the goal rate within 24 to 48 hours. Assess bowel sounds every 8 hours.

ACUTE PHASE

The acute phase of burn care begins with the mobilization of interstitial fluid and subsequent diuresis and continues until wounds are nearly healed. This may take weeks or months depending on the burn severity and the patient's response to treatment.

Pathophysiology

Oxygenation problems may resolve. However, sometimes inhalation injuries will not resolve for many days, weeks, or months. Vital signs are more stable. Wound healing begins as WBCs surround the burn wound and phagocytosis occurs. Necrotic tissue begins to slough. Unfortunately, many patients with major burns will have complications during this phase. The patient may now become more aware of the enormity of the situation.

Clinical Manifestations

Partial-thickness wounds begin to heal at the wound margins. Epithelial buds, from the hair follicles and glands in the dermal bed, eventually close the wound. Healing is spontaneous and usually occurs within 10 to 21 days. Patients often have more pain during the acute phase due to repeated dressing changes, therapy exercises, opioid tolerance, fatigue, and reduced coping ability. Surgical procedures continue for extensive debridement and skin grafting.

Fluid and Electrolytes

Because the body is trying to reestablish fluid and electrolyte balance in the initial acute phase, it is important to follow serum electrolyte levels closely.

Sodium

Hyponatremia can develop from excess GI suction and diarrhea. Manifestations include headache, irritability, confusion, vomiting, seizures, and even coma. The patient may develop *dilutional hyponatremia* from excess water intake. To avoid this condition, offer the patient fluids other than water, such as juice or nutrition supplements.

Hypernatremia may occur after successful fluid resuscitation if large amounts of hypertonic solutions were given. EN or inappropriate fluid administration can cause hypernatremia. Manifestations include changes in mental status, ranging from drowsiness, restlessness, confusion, and lethargy to seizures and coma. Restricting sodium in IV fluids and EN can reduce levels.

Potassium

Hyperkalemia may occur if the patient has renal failure, adrenocortical insufficiency, or massive deep muscle injury (e.g., electrical burn). Damaged cells release large amounts of potassium. Dysrhythmias and arrest can occur with high potassium levels. The patient may have confusion, tetany, muscle cramps, paresthesia, and weakness.

Hypokalemia occurs with vomiting, diarrhea, prolonged GI suction, and IV therapy without potassium supplementation. The patient loses potassium through their burn wounds. Besides dysrhythmias, the patient may have muscle weakness, paresthesia, decreased GI motility, and decreased reflexes (see Chapter 17).

Complications

Infection

A burn injury destroys the body's first line of defense, the skin. The person's normal flora will quickly colonize the burn wound. The WBCs have functional defects. The patient is immunosuppressed for many months after the burn injury.

Localized inflammation, induration, and sometimes purulent drainage can be seen at the burn wound margins. Watch for signs and symptoms of systemic infection, including hypothermia or hyperthermia, increased heart and respiratory rate, decreased BP, and decreased urine output. The patient may have mild confusion, chills, malaise, and loss of appetite. The WBC count can rise over 20,000/μL (20×10^9/L). The causative organisms of sepsis are usually gram-negative bacteria (e.g., *Pseudomonas, Proteus*), putting the patient at risk for septic shock. Sepsis is a leading cause of death in the patient with major burns. It may lead to multiple organ dysfunction syndrome (see Chapter 42).

Fungal infections may develop in the patient's mucous membranes (mouth, genitalia) due to systemic antibiotic therapy and low resistance. In severe cases, fungal infections spread to the blood. The offending organism is usually *Candida albicans*. Administer antifungals such as nystatin and fluconazole as ordered.

Cardiovascular and Respiratory

The same cardiovascular and respiratory complications present in the emergent phase may continue into the acute phase of care. New problems, such as pneumonia, might arise, requiring prompt intervention.

Neurologic

Neurologic problems may result due to severe hypoxia from respiratory injuries or as a complication from electrical injuries. Other causes of neurologic problems include electrolyte imbalance, stress, cerebral edema, sepsis, sleep problems, and the use of analgesics and antianxiety drugs.

Some patients may become disoriented, withdraw, be combative, hallucinate, or have frequent nightmare-like episodes. Delirium is more acute at night and occurs more often in older patients. Use a screening tool to diagnose delirium (see Table 64.19). Start nursing interventions to prevent delirium. Orient and reassure a patient who is confused or agitated. This state is usually transient, lasting from a day or 2 to several weeks. However, some complications can last for years and be serious.

Musculoskeletal

The musculoskeletal system is especially prone to complications during the acute phase. PT and OT are vitally important. As the burns begin to heal and scar tissue forms, the skin is less supple and pliant. ROM may be affected. Skin and joint contractures can occur. Because of pain, the patient prefers a flexed position for comfort. Have the patient stretch and move the burned body parts as much as possible. Consult with PT or OT about proper positioning and splinting to prevent or reduce contracture formation.

Gastrointestinal

The GI system may develop complications during this phase. Diarrhea may result from the use of EN or antibiotics. Constipation can occur as a side effect of opioids, decreased mobility, and a low-fiber diet. *Curling ulcer* is a type of gastroduodenal ulcer characterized by diffuse superficial lesions (including mucosal erosion). The stress response can decrease blood flow to the GI tract.

Aim to prevent Curling ulcer by feeding the patient as soon as possible after the burn injury. Antacids, H_2-histamine blockers (e.g., cimetidine), and proton pump inhibitors (e.g., omeprazole) are used prophylactically to neutralize stomach acids and inhibit histamine and the secretion of hydrochloric acid (Table 26.8). Patients with major burns may have occult blood in their stools during the acute phase and require close monitoring for bleeding.

Endocrine

Watch for transient increases in the patient's blood glucose levels because of stress-mediated cortisol and catecholamine release. There is increased mobilization of glycogen stores and gluconeogenesis. Subsequently, glucose is produced with an increase in insulin production. However, insulin's effectiveness decreases because of relative insulin insensitivity. This results in a high blood glucose level. The increased caloric intake needed to meet metabolic requirements can increase blood glucose levels. When hyperglycemia occurs, check glucose levels and administer insulin. Monitor blood glucose testing results. This stress-induced condition reverses as metabolic demands are met, and less stress is placed on the entire system.

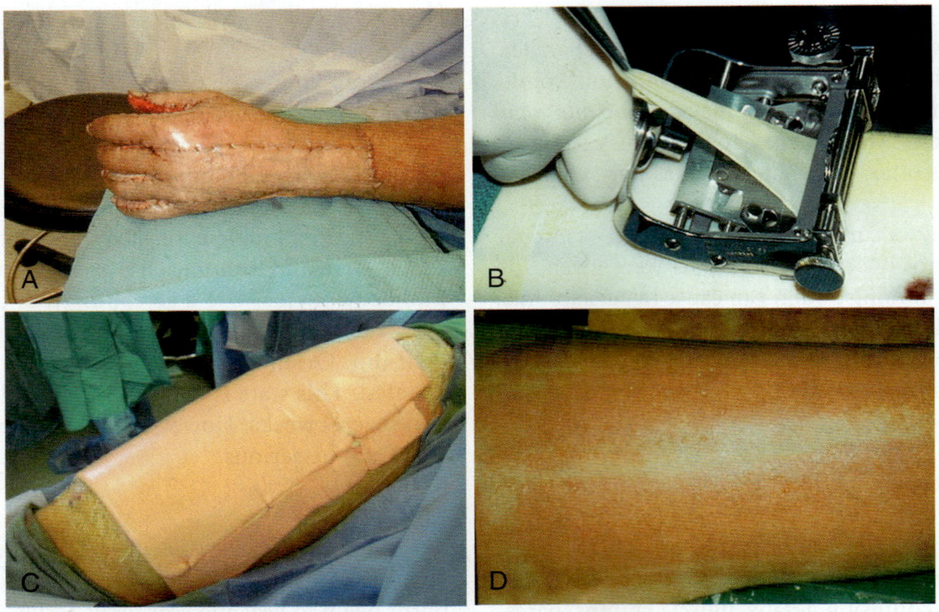

Fig. 26.12 (A) Freshly applied split-thickness sheet skin graft to the hand. (B) Split-thickness skin graft harvested from a patient's thigh using a dermatome. (C) Donor site is covered with a hydrophilic foam dressing after harvesting. (D) Healed donor site. (Courtesy Judy Knighton, Toronto, Canada.)

NURSING AND INTERPROFESSIONAL MANAGEMENT: ACUTE PHASE

The major therapeutic interventions in the acute phase are (1) wound care, (2) excision and grafting, (3) pain management, (4) physical and occupational therapy, and (5) nutrition therapy.

Wound Care

The goals of wound care are to (1) prevent infection by cleansing and debriding the area of necrotic tissue that would promote bacterial growth and (2) promote wound re-epithelialization and/or successful skin grafting.

Wound care consists of ongoing observation, assessment, cleansing, debridement, and dressing reapplication. Dressing changes, topical antimicrobial therapy, graft care, and donor site care is done as often as needed, depending on the topical cream or dressing. Collagenase is used for *enzymatic debridement* of burn wounds. It promotes the removal of nonviable tissue from the healthy wound bed.[15]

Gently cleanse wounds to remove the old antimicrobial agent and any loose necrotic tissue, scabs, or dried blood. After cleansing, cover the wound with topical antimicrobial creams (e.g., silver sulfadiazine) or silver-impregnated dressings. Avoid silver sulfadiazine if the patient has an allergy or sensitivity to sulfa.

Excision and Grafting

Many patients, especially those with major burns, have surgery on day 1 or 2 (emergent phase). With **excision**, devitalized tissue (eschar) is surgically removed down to the subcutaneous tissue or fascia. Surgical excision can result in massive blood loss.

A *dermatome* is used to remove the donor skin for grafting (Fig. 26.12B). An autograft is the patient's skin used for grafting. The abdomen and thighs are common donor sites. The donor skin can be meshed to allow for greater wound coverage. Sometimes it is applied as an unmeshed sheet for a better cosmetic result when grafting the face, neck, and hands. Sometimes wounds are covered with a biologic dressing or allograft for temporary coverage until permanent grafting can occur (Table 26.9).

The graft is placed on clean, viable tissue to achieve good adherence. Grafts can be stapled or sutured into place (Fig. 26.12A). Negative pressure wound therapy dressings are often placed on top of skin grafts to optimize adherence of the graft to the excised wound bed. Outer occlusive dressings apply just enough pressure to promote adherence of the graft to the wound bed and help control bleeding.

The goals of donor site care are to promote rapid, moist wound healing, decrease pain at the site, and prevent infection. The choices of dressings for donor sites include transparent dressings (e.g., OpSite), xenograft, silver sulfadiazine, silver-impregnated dressings, calcium alginate, and hydrophilic foam dressings (Fig. 26.12C).[16] Nursing care of the donor site is specific to the dressing used. Many newer dressings decrease healing time, which allows earlier harvesting of skin at the same site. The average healing time for a donor site is 10 to 14 days (Fig. 26.12D).

Recell is a newer burn treatment product for partial and full-thickness wounds. It uses a small sample of the patient's skin to produce a sprayed-on suspension.[17] Meshed autografts are required with Recell for full-thickness wounds.

Cultured Epidermal Autografts

In the patient with large body burns, only a limited amount of unburned skin may be available as donor sites for grafting, and some of that skin may not be suitable for harvesting. Cultured epidermal autograft (CEA) is a method of getting permanent

TABLE 26.9 Skin Grafts Used for Burn Injury

Graft Type	Source and Description	Coverage
Allograft (or homograft) (same species) Autografts	Cadaveric skin	Temporary (3 days to 2 weeks)
Autograft	Patient's skin	Permanent
Cultured epithelial autograft (CEA)–Epical Recell	Patient's own skin cell cultures	Permanent
Dermal Substitutes		
Allover	Acellular dermal matrix derived from donated human skin	Permanent
Apligraf	Donated neonatal foreskin fibroblasts and keratinocytes in bovine collagen gel	Permanent
Biobrane	Semipermeable silicone membrane bonded to nylon fabric	Temporary (10–21 days)
Integra	Biodegradable dermal layer made of bovine collagen and glycosaminoglycan bonded to silicone membrane	Permanent
Matriderm	Bovine collagen and elastin matrix	Permanent
OrCel	Donated neonatal foreskin fibroblasts and keratinocytes in bovine collagen sponge	Permanent
Xenograft (or heterograft) (different species)	Porcine skin	Temporary (3 days to 2 weeks)

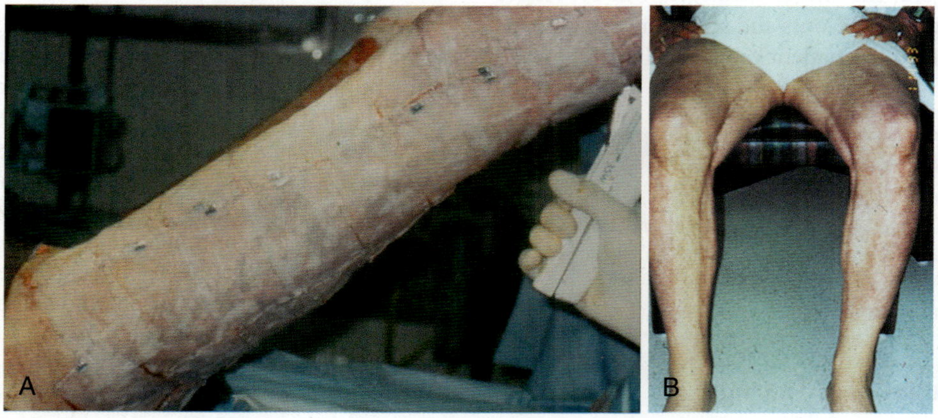

Fig. 26.13 Patient with cultured epithelial autograft (CEA). (A) Intraoperative application of CEA. (B) Healed CEA.

skin from a person with limited skin available for harvesting.[18] CEA is grown from biopsy samples obtained from the patient's unburned skin. The specimens are sent to a commercial laboratory, where the biopsied keratinocytes are grown in a culture medium containing epidermal growth factor. After about 18 to 25 days, the keratinocytes have expanded up to 10,000 times. They form sheets that we can use as skin grafts on excised burn wounds (Fig. 26.13A). CEA grafts generally form a seamless, smooth replacement skin tissue (Fig. 26.13B). However, problems include a poor graft take because of thin epidermal skin, graft loss during healing, infection, and contractures.

Dermal Substitutes

Dermal substitutes act as a synthetic dermis and are covered by a skin graft. The Integra artificial skin dermal regeneration template is an example of a skin replacement system. As with CEA, it is used in the treatment of life-threatening full-thickness or deep partial-thickness burn wounds when a conventional autograft is not available or advisable, as in older or high anesthetic-risk patients. It also is used in reconstructive burn surgery procedures.

Integra artificial skin has a 2-layer membrane composed of acellular dermis and silicone. After the wound is excised, the bilayer membrane is placed dermal layer down, and the wound is wrapped with dressings in the OR. The dermal layer functions as a biodegradable template that induces the organized regeneration of new dermis by the body. The silicone layer stays intact for 3 weeks as the dermal layer degrades and epidermal autograft becomes available. At this point, the silicone is removed during a second surgery and replaced by the patient's epidermal autograft.

Pain Management

Many aspects of burn care cause pain. Eliminating all pain is difficult, but most patients will have acceptable levels of relative comfort if they receive adequate analgesia. To provide effective pain management, you must understand both the physiologic and psychological aspects of pain. Pain management is discussed in Chapter 9.

Burn patients have 2 kinds of pain: (1) *continuous, background pain* that might be present throughout the day and night, and (2) *treatment-induced pain* caused by dressing changes, ambulation, and rehabilitation activities. The first line of treatment is medication (Table 26.8). With background pain, frequent IV administration of an opioid (e.g., hydromorphone) provides a steady, therapeutic level of the drug. If tolerating food, slow-release, twice-daily opioids (e.g., morphine) can be used. Patient-controlled analgesia (PCA) is used in some burn centers. Anxiolytics (e.g., lorazepam, midazolam) and adjuvant analgesics (e.g., gabapentin, pregabalin) can enhance opioid effectiveness. Their use can help reduce opioid dosage and undesirable side effects.

Breakthrough doses of analgesia must be available. Additional doses of opioids are usually given. For treatment-induced pain, pre-medicate with an analgesic, and possibly an anxiolytic, via the IV or oral route.

Some patients respond to complementary therapy. Relaxation breathing, guided imagery, hypnosis, biofeedback, computerized gaming, and music therapy can help patients cope with pain (see Chapter 7).

Remember, the more control the patient has in managing pain, the more successful the chosen strategies will be. Active participation in asking for time-outs and scheduling treatments and rest periods can help the patient reduce feelings of anticipatory pain.

CHECK YOUR PRACTICE

A patient with a burn injury is prescribed fentanyl (Sublimaze) before a dressing change. The patient has multiple IV lines. You are not sure which line to use to give the drug. You know that mixing up IV lines can lead to serious drug errors.

- How would you determine which IV line to use to give the drug?

◆ Physical and Occupational Therapy

Continuous therapy throughout burn recovery is critical if the patient is to regain and maintain muscle strength and optimal joint function. A good time for exercise is during dressing changes when bulky dressings are removed and patients are medicated for pain. Passive and active ROM should be performed on all joints. PT and OT may provide exercises after dressing changes. Maintain the schedule for wearing custom-fitted splints designed to keep joints in a functional position. Check the skin to make sure the splints are not causing excessive pressure.

◆ Nutrition Therapy

The goal of nutrition therapy during the acute burn phase is to provide adequate calories and protein to promote healing. When the wounds are still open, the burn patient is in a hypermetabolic and catabolic state.

The patient may benefit from an antioxidant protocol, which includes selenium, vitamin E, acetylcysteine, ascorbic acid, zinc, and a multivitamin. Meeting daily caloric requirements is crucial and should start within the first 1 to 2 days post-burn. The dietitian regularly calculates the daily caloric requirements and makes adjustments as the patient's condition changes (e.g., wound healing improves, sepsis develops). Monitor laboratory values (e.g., albumin, prealbumin, total protein, transferrin) as available.

Encourage the patient to eat high-protein, high-carbohydrate foods to meet caloric goals. Ask caregivers to bring in their favorite foods from home. Appetite is usually reduced. You will need to reinforce the steps being taken to achieve adequate intake. Ideally, weight loss should not be more than 10% of the pre-burn weight. Record the patient's daily caloric intake using calorie count sheets. Review the sheets with the dietitian. Weigh the patient weekly to evaluate progress.

REHABILITATION PHASE

The formal rehabilitation phase begins when the patient's wounds have nearly healed, and they are engaging in some level of self-care. This may happen as early as 2 weeks or as long as 7 to 8 months after a major burn injury. Goals for the patient now are to (1) work toward resuming a functional role in society and (2) rehabilitate from any functional and cosmetic postburn reconstructive surgery.

Pathophysiologic Changes and Clinical Manifestations

Burn wounds heal by either spontaneous re-epithelialization or skin grafting. Layers of keratinocytes begin rebuilding the tissue structure destroyed by the burn injury. Collagen fibers, present in the new scar tissue, help with healing and add strength to weakened areas. The new skin appears flat and pink. In about 4 to 6 weeks, the area becomes raised and hyperemic. If adequate ROM is not continued, the new tissue will shorten, causing a contracture. Mature healing is reached in about 12 months when suppleness has returned, and the pink or red color has faded to a slightly lighter hue than the surrounding unburned tissue.

Scarring has 2 characteristics: (1) discoloration and (2) contour. Discoloration fades with time. Tell patients with heavily pigmented skin that it will take longer for it to regain tone because of altered melanocytes. Often, the skin does not regain its original tone, though this is impossible to predict. Provide teaching and emotional support to help the patient with grieving about these body changes. Cosmetic camouflage or pigment implantation can help even out unequal skin tones and improve the patient's overall appearance and self-image.

Scar tissue tends to develop altered contours. That is, it is no longer flat or slightly raised but becomes elevated and enlarged above the original burned area. Some HCPs believe that pressure can help keep a scar flat. Gentle pressure is maintained on the healed burn with custom-fitted pressure garments and clear, thermoplastic facemasks.[19] Pressure garments and masks should never be worn over unhealed wounds. Pressure garments are worn up to 23 hours a day for as long as 12 to 18 months.

The patient typically reports discomfort from itching where healing is occurring. Teach the patient that water-based moisturizers and short-term use of oral antihistamines (e.g., hydroxyzine [Atarax]) can help reduce itching. Massage, cooling, emollients, gabapentin, antidepressants, and anesthetic creams also may help.

Skin flaking occurs as the epithelium is replaced by new cells. The newly formed skin is very sensitive to trauma. Blisters and

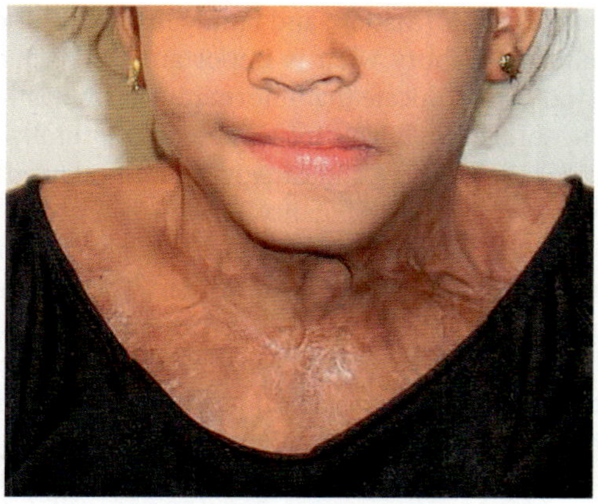

Fig. 26.14 Neck contracture. (Courtesy Linda Bucher, RN, PhD, CEN, CNE, Staff Nurse, Virtua Memorial Hospital, Mt. Holly, NJ.)

skin tears are likely to develop from slight pressure or friction. These newly healed areas can be more or less sensitive to cold, heat, and touch. Grafted areas are more likely to be less sensitive until peripheral nerve regeneration occurs. Have patients protect healed burn areas from direct sunlight for about 3 months to prevent hyperpigmentation and sunburn injury. Tell patients to wear sunscreen when exposing healed skin to the sun.

Complications

The most common complications during the rehabilitation phase are skin and joint contractures and hypertrophic scarring. Joint contractures may develop because of the shortening of scar tissue in the flexor tissues of a joint. Areas that are most susceptible to contractures include the anterior and lateral neck areas, axillae, antecubital fossae, fingers, groin areas, popliteal fossae, knees, and ankles (Fig. 26.14). Some involve ligaments and tendons.

Carefully watch the patient for these potential problems. Encourage proper positioning, splinting, and exercise. Tell the patient to continue with these strategies until the skin matures at around 1-year post healing. Rehabilitative therapy is aimed at the extension of body parts because the flexors are stronger than the extensors.

Burned legs may be wrapped with elastic (e.g., tensor, ACE) bandages to assist with circulation to leg-graft and donor sites before ambulation. Burned arms can be wrapped with a layer of tubular elastic gauze (e.g., Tubigrip). This interim pressure prevents blister formation, promotes venous return, and decreases pain and itchiness. Custom-fitted pressure garments replace the elastic bandages and tubular gauze once the skin is healed.

NURSING AND INTERPROFESSIONAL MANAGEMENT: REHABILITATION PHASE

The first step is to ask the patient about thoughts and feelings about discharge. Encourage both the patient and caregiver to take part in care. The patient and caregiver may need wound care instructions. Tell the patient to take a shower, not a bath, to wash the wounds. Have the patient or caregiver demonstrate a dressing change. Provide advice on scar management, moisturizing, and sun protection. Suggest using water-based creams that penetrate the dermis (e.g., Vaseline Intensive Rescue) on healed areas to keep the skin supple and moisturized. This will decrease itching and flaking. Antihistamines taken at bedtime may help if itching persists.

Make sure they know when to contact the burn team (e.g., signs of infection, increased pain). Stress the need to keep outpatient visits. The need for further reconstructive surgery is reviewed during follow-up appointments. If needed, work with a social worker or discharge manager to arrange home care services to assist with care.

Assess pain management and nutrition needs during each visit. Encourage the patient to perform the PT and OT exercises. Reassure the patient to maintain morale, especially once the patient realizes that recovery can be slow.

Gerontologic Considerations: Burns

Older patients present many challenges for the burn team. They have thinner dermal layers, a loss of elastic fibers, a reduction in subcutaneous adipose tissue, and a decrease in vascularity. As a result, the thinner dermis, with reduced blood flow, sustains deeper burns with poorer rates of healing.

Once injured, the older adult has more complications in the emergent and acute phases of burn resuscitation because of preexisting comorbidities. Older patients with diabetes, heart failure, or COPD have morbidity and mortality rates exceeding those of healthy, younger patients. Burn wounds and donor sites take longer to heal. Recovery from surgical procedures can be more difficult. Weaning from a ventilator can be a challenge and pneumonia is a frequent complication. Although usually self-limiting, delirium, if it develops, maybe distressing. It usually takes longer for these patients to rehabilitate to the point at which they can safely return home. For some, returning home to independent living may not be possible. Working with communities to identify strategies to prevent burn injuries in older adults is a priority.

EMOTIONAL/PSYCHOLOGIC NEEDS OF PATIENTS AND CAREGIVERS

Patients and caregivers have many emotional and psychological needs during the often lengthy, unpredictable, and complex course of care. You have an important supportive and counseling role as patients struggle to get their lives back on track.[20]

To manage the enormous range of emotional responses that the burn patient may have, assess the circumstances of the burn (e.g., cause, people involved), family relationships, and previous ways of coping with stress. At any time, the patient may have a variety of emotions, such as fear, anxiety, anger, guilt, and depression (Table 26.10).

Burn survivors often have thoughts and feelings that are frightening and disturbing. There may be guilt about the incident, reliving the burn experience, fear of dying, concern about future therapy and surgery, frustrations with ongoing discomfort and treatment, and hopelessness about the future. During recovery, new fears may occur: "Can I do this?" "Am I a desirable person?" "How can I go outside looking like this?" These challenges confront patients throughout their recovery and often for years to come.

TABLE 26.10 Common Emotional Responses

Emotion	Possible Verbal Expression
Anger	• Why did this happen to me?
	• The nurses enjoy hurting me.
	• I hope the person who did this to me dies.
Anxiety	• I feel out of control.
	• What is going to happen to me?
	• When will I look normal again?
Depression	• It is no use going on like this.
	• I do not care what happens to me.
	• I wish people would leave me alone.
Fear	• Will I die?
	• What will happen next?
	• Will I be disfigured?
	• Will my family and friends still love me?
Guilt	• If only I had been more careful.
	• I am being punished because I did something wrong.
Hopefulness	• What do I need to do to survive this injury emotionally and return to my life/family/friends?
	• What am I meant to learn from this injury?

A burn injury may adversely affect a person's self-esteem. Some fear the loss of relationships because of perceived or actual physical disfigurement. In a society that values physical beauty, changes in body image can result in psychological distress.

Open and frequent communication among the patient, caregivers, close friends, and burn team members is essential. Because of the tremendous psychologic impact of a burn injury, be sensitive to the patient's emotions and concerns. Encourage the patient to discuss fears about loss of lifestyle, loss of function, temporary or permanent deformity and disfigurement, return to work and home life, and financial burdens resulting from a long and costly hospitalization and rehabilitation.

Encourage independence and an eventual return to pre-burn activities, such as school or work. Peer counseling and informal interactions with other burn survivors may bring comfort and help to restore confidence. Reassure patients that their feelings during this period of adjustment are a normal reaction to an extraordinary life event. Frustration and impatience are expected as they establish a new life. Help patients in adapting to a realistic, yet positive appraisal of their specific situation, emphasizing what they *can* do instead of what they *cannot* do.

Caregivers may share some or all these challenges and feelings. At times, they may feel helpless or too exhausted to help their loved ones. Continued support from trusted and familiar burn team members is essential. Helping caregivers assist with aspects of the patient's care helps them to reconnect with their loved one and eases the transition home. Many burn survivors and their caregivers remark on the powerful learning experience of the burn and a renewed appreciation of life, despite the ongoing challenges of a prolonged recovery. Acknowledge that their feelings are real and common. Most burn survivors speak of satisfaction with their post-burn life and are more empowered as time goes on.

It is important to address spiritual and cultural needs because both have a role in treatment decisions and recovery. Pastoral care may be a helpful resource for the patient and caregiver. The need for support, information, and family involvement may vary among cultures. Identify what is important to the patient and caregiver and communicate that information in the patient's plan of care. Encourage the burn care team to be culturally aware of and sensitive to the patient and caregiver's cultural needs.

The awkward issue of sexuality must be met with honesty. Acceptance of any changes in physical appearance is hard at first for the patient and their significant other. The nature of skin injury can cause modifications in processing sexual stimuli. Touch is an important part of sexuality. Immature scar tissue may make the sensation of touch unpleasant or may dull it. This may be only transient, but the patient and partner need to know that it is normal and receive anticipatory guidance from the burn team to avoid undue emotional strain.

Burn survivors may have preexisting mental health or substance use issues, which may have contributed to the burn incident. The stress of burn injury can precipitate a psychological crisis. Assessment by a psychiatrist who can prescribe appropriate drugs and offer counseling may be needed. Early psychiatric intervention is essential if the patient has a psychiatric illness or if the injury was a suicide attempt. Many burn patients have posttraumatic stress disorder. A history of mental health issues can influence the length of hospitalization and the time needed to prepare for discharge. However, distress and trauma symptoms can act as a catalyst for positive posttraumatic growth. Coping styles and social support assist in these positive changes postburn.

Psychological support begins in the hospital, but links to community resources are needed to ensure continuity of treatment. A referral to a psychiatrist, psychologist, psychiatric advanced practice nurse (APN), mental health counselor, or social worker is discussed if concerns are raised at burn clinic follow-up.

Caregiver and patient support groups may be beneficial in meeting the patient and caregiver's emotional needs at any phase of the recovery process. Speaking with others who have had burn trauma can be beneficial. Similar persons can confirm that the patient's feelings are normal and share helpful advice. The Phoenix Society (www.phoenix-society.org) is an international, highly respected burn survivors' support group. For many years, the society has offered valuable support and resources (e.g., the annual World Burn Congress conference) to burn survivors, caregivers, and burn team staff.

SPECIAL NEEDS OF NURSES

Warm, trusting, and mutually satisfying relationships often develop between burn patients and nursing staff during hospitalization and the long-term rehabilitation period. Sometimes the bond can be so strong that the patient has difficulty separating from the hospital and staff. The frequency and intensity of family contact can be rewarding as well as draining. It may be difficult to cope with the deformities caused by the burn injury, odors, unpleasant sight of wounds, and the reality of the pain that accompanies the burn and its treatment. Do not hesitate to seek help from coworkers, a manager, or the employee assistance program should you feel the need.[21]

In time, you will come to know that specialized burn care provides a critical difference in helping patients not only survive but also cope and triumph over an intense and complex injury. Ongoing support services or critical incident stress debriefings led by a psychiatrist, psychologist, psychiatric APN, or social worker may be helpful. Peer support groups (e.g., ABA, International Society for Burn Injuries) can serve a similar purpose by helping you cope with difficult feelings from caring for burn patients. Attention to yourself is important to maintain a positive attitude and a healthy work-life balance. Time with family and friends and relaxation at home are essential parts of self-care and a balanced life with purpose and meaning.

Case Study

Burn Injury

(© Comstock/Thinkstock.)

Patient Profile

G.M., a 70-year-old man, arrives at the ED with burns to his face, neck, chest, right arm and hand, and right foot. He was burning brush on his farm when the fire went out of control.

Subjective Data

- Reports blurry vision and trouble swallowing
- States his burns are painful. Pain rated 8/10
- Says he is a "diabetic" and has "high blood pressure"
- Allergic to sulfa

Objective Data

Physical Assessment

- Is awake, alert, and oriented, but in some distress
- Eyes are red, irritated
- Voice is hoarse; nasal hair is singed. Frequent nonproductive cough
- Face is reddened with blisters noted on the nose and forehead
- Right arm, right hand, anterior chest, neck, and right foot have shiny, bright red, moist burns
- Shivering
- Vital signs: Temp 96.5, pulse 102/min, respiratory rate 26/min, BP 142/84 mm Hg, O_2 saturation 89% with O_2 nasal cannula 4 L/min
- Scattered wheezing throughout all lung fields

Discussion Questions

1. ***Recognize:*** What subjective and objective findings are you *most* concerned about?
2. ***Recognize:*** What metabolic disturbances would you expect to develop soon? Explain the physiologic basis for these changes.
3. ***Analyze:*** What complication is G.M. at risk for?
4. ***Plan:*** How will you involve other interprofessional team members?
5. ***Prioritize:*** What *priority* interventions do you need to implement in this situation?
6. ***Evaluate:*** What outcomes would indicate initial interprofessional care for the priority problem was effective?
7. ***Plan:*** What analgesics might be considered to relieve his pain?
8. ***Plan:*** Which criteria for burn center referral does G.M. meet for admission to the hospital burn unit?
9. ***Safety:*** What risk factors does G.M have for infection?
10. ***Act:*** What measures would be taken to support G.M.'s caregivers?
11. ***Act:*** What discharge teaching would you provide to G.M. and his family so they can successfully manage his care at home?
12. ***Act:*** What interventions are necessary before discharge to ensure G.M.'s safety at home?

Answers available at http://evolve.elsevier.com/Lewis/medsurg.

BRIDGE TO NCLEX EXAMINATION

The question number corresponds to the same-numbered outcome at the beginning of the chapter.

1. Which instruction would the nurse provide to prevent burn injuries?
   a. Set hot water temperature at 140°F.
   b. Use only hardwired smoke detectors.
   c. Encourage regular home fire exit drills.
   d. Do not allow older adults to cook unattended.
2. Which wound description indicates a need for excision and grafting? *(select all that apply)*
   a. Red, painful blisters
   b. Leathery, brown, exposed tendon
   c. Pearly white color, insensitive to pain, dry
   d. Charred eschar, visible thrombosed blood vessels
   e. Large, fluid-filled vesicles, moderate edema, moist, red
3. Estimate the total body surface area burn injury using the rule of 9's. Burns involve the entire right arm and upper back. _____%
4. A patient is hospitalized with burns to his head, neck, and anterior and posterior chest after an explosion in his garage. The respiratory therapist applied a non-rebreather mask. On assessment, the nurse auscultates wheezes throughout the lung fields. On reassessment, the wheezes are gone, and the breath sounds are greatly decreased. Respiratory rate is 6/min. Oxygen saturation decreases to 88%. The patient is unresponsive. What is the *priority* nursing intervention?
   a. Notify the HCP and get ready for intubation.
   b. Encourage the patient to cough and auscultate the lungs again.
   c. Obtain vital signs, oxygen saturation, and a STAT arterial blood gas.
   d. Document the findings and continue to monitor the patient's breathing.
5. Which lab result supports the need for additional IV fluid to treat burn shock?
   a. Hematocrit 52%
   b. Sodium 137 mEq/L
   c. WBC 12.5×10^9/L
   d. Potassium 3.4 mmol/L
6. What nutrition intervention may promote wound healing for a patient with a 10% burn injury?
   a. Eat a high-protein, high-carbohydrate diet
   b. Increase normal caloric intake by about 4 times
   c. Eat at least 1500 calories/day in small, frequent meals
   d. Eat a lactose-free diet to reduce the potential for diarrhea

7. A patient has 25% TBSA burn from a car fire. His wounds have been debrided and covered with a silver-impregnated dressing. What is the *most* important nursing intervention following surgery?
   a. Wash the wound with soap and water 3 times a day.
   b. Medicate for pain relief in between dressing changes.
   c. Reapply a new dressing without disturbing the wound bed.
   d. Assess the wound for signs of infection during dressing changes.
8. What nursing interventions can be used to manage burn pain? *(select all that apply)*
   a. Suggest pain management options.
   b. Use a pain-rating tool to monitor the patient's level of pain.
   c. Delay painful dressing changes until the patient's pain is completely relieved.
   d. Use a multimodal approach (e.g., sustained-release and short-acting opioids, NSAIDs, adjuvant analgesics).
   e. Provide nonpharmacologic therapies (e.g., music therapy, distraction) to replace opioids in the acute phase of a burn injury.
9. What intervention prevents hypertrophic scarring during the rehabilitation phase of burn recovery?
   a. Applying pressure garments
   b. Repositioning the patient every 2 hours
   c. Performing active ROM at least every 4 hours
   d. Applying a water-based moisturizer to healed skin
10. A patient is recovering from second- and third-degree burns over 30% of his body, and the burn care team is planning for discharge. The *first* action the nurse would take when meeting with the patient would be to
    a. arrange a return-to-clinic appointment and prescription for pain medications.
    b. give the patient written information and websites resources for burn survivors.
    c. teach the patient and the caregiver proper wound care to be performed at home.
    d. review the patient's current health care status and readiness for discharge to home.

1. c; 2. b, c, d; 3. 18%; 4. a; 5. a; 6. a; 7. d; 8. a, b, d; 9. a; 10. d.

For rationales to these answers and even more NCLEX review questions, visit http://evolve.elsevier.com/Lewis/medsurg.

EVOLVE WEBSITE/RESOURCES LIST

http://evolve.elsevier.com/Lewis/medsurg
Review Questions (Online Only)
Key Points
Answer Keys for Questions
- Rationales for Bridge to NCLEX Examination Questions
- Answer Guidelines for Case Study
- Answer Guidelines for Managing Care of Multiple Patients Case Study (Section 5)

Student Case Study
- Patient With Burns

Nursing Care Plan
- eNursing Care Plan 26.1: Patient with a Thermal Burn Injury

Conceptual Care Map Creator
Audio Glossary
Content Updates

REFERENCES

*1. American Burn Association: Burn incidence and treatment in the US: 2016 fact sheet. Retrieved from http://ameriburn.org/who-we-are/media/burn-incidence-fact-sheet/.
2. WHO International: Burns key facts. Retrieved from https://www.who.int/news-room/fact-sheets/detail/burns.
*3. United States Fire Administration: U.S. fire deaths, fire death rates, and risk of dying in a fire. Retrieved from https://www.usfa.fema.gov/data/statistics/fire_death_rates.html.
4. U.S. Fire Administration: Burn and scald prevention outreach materials. Retrieved from https://www.usfa.fema.gov/prevention/outreach/burn_prevention.html.
5. American Burn Association: Burn referral. Retrieved from https://ameriburn.org/public-resources/burn-center-referral-criteria/.
*6. Abhinav A, Ravi KC, Vinayak C, et al.: The role of comorbidities in the prognosis of thermal burns, *Int J Biomath* 27(1), 2019.
7. UpToDate: Emergency care of moderate and severe thermal burns in adults. Retrieved from https://www.uptodate.com/contents/emergency-care-of-moderate-and-severe-thermal-burns-in-adults.
8. Butts CC, Holmes JH, Carter JE: Surgical escharotomy and decompressive therapies in burns, *J Burn Care Res* 41(2), 2020.
*9. Torgeir F, Kjetil GB, Kine MN, et al.: Acute kidney injury in burn patients admitted to the intensive care unit: a systematic review and meta-analysis, *Crit Care* 24(1), 2020.
10. Cooper C, Cochran A, Coffey R: Nurses can resuscitate, *J Burn Care Res* 41(Supp 1), 2020.
11. American Burn Association: *Shock and fluid resuscitation. Advanced burn life support course provider manual*, 2018.
*12. Nímia HH, Carvalho VF, Isaac C, et al.: Comparative study of silver sulfadiazine with other materials for healing and infection prevention in burns: a systematic review and meta-analysis, *Burns* 45(2), 2019.
*13. Gates M, Hartling L, Shulhan-Kilroy J, et al.: Digital technology distraction for acute pain in children: a meta-analysis, *Pediatrics* 145(2), 2020.
14. Houschyar M, Borrelli MR, Tapking C, et al.: Burns: modified metabolism and the nuances of nutrition therapy, *J Wound Care* 29(3), 2020.
*15. Pham CH, Collier ZJ, Fang M, et al.: The role of collagenase ointment in acute burns: a systematic review and meta-analysis, *J Wound Care* 28:S9–15, 2019.
*16. Rapp SJ, Dershem V, Zhang X, et al.: Varying negative pressure wound therapy acute effects on human split-thickness autografts, *J Burn Care Res* 41(1), 2020.
17. Recell. Retrieved from https://recellsystem.com/.
18. Cultured epidermal autographs. Retrieved from https://www.epicel.com/patients/.
*19. DeBruler DM, Baumann ME, Zbinden JC, et al.: Improved scar outcomes with increased daily duration of pressure garment therapy, *Adv Wound Care* 9(8), 2020.
20. Bäckström J, Willebrand PM, Öster C: Identifying the needs of family members in burn care-nurses' different approaches, *J Burn Care Res* 40(3), 2019.
*21. Bayuo J, Agyei Bediako F, Allotey G, et al.: Developing support strategies for burn care nurses through an understanding of their experiences: a meta-ethnographic study, *Int J Nurs Pract* 25(2), 2019.

* Evidence-based information for clinical practice.

Case Study

Applying Clinical Judgment With Multiple Patients

You are working the day shift on a medical-surgical unit. The following 4 patients are among the 7 you are assigned to care for today. You have an AP who is assigned to work with you. There are 15 other patients on the unit being cared for by an additional 2 RNs and 2 APs.

 (© Jack Hollingsworth/Photodisc/Thinkstock.)	J.K., a 68-year-old woman, had pneumatic retinopexy surgery yesterday to repair a partially detached retina. She has a history of type 2 diabetes, diabetic retinopathy, and hypertension. She is scheduled to be discharged today, but the night RN is concerned because her BP is 180/94.
 (© Jack Hollingsworth/Photodisc/Thinkstock.)	R.S., a 57-year-old woman, is under observation with Ménière disease. She continues to have extreme dizziness, tinnitus, and nausea. The HCP plans to give an intratympanic injection of dexamethasone today. Vital signs: 100/64, 112, RR 20.
 (© iStock.com/EyeMark.)	D.A., a 74-year-old woman, is admitted to the hospital with symptoms of chest tightness and shortness of breath. Her history is negative except for a recent diagnosis of basal cell carcinoma (BCC) on her face. She was scheduled to have the BCC surgically removed tomorrow. The HCP suspects D.A.'s symptoms are caused by anxiety but wants to rule out any coronary artery disease before surgery.
 (© Comstock/Thinkstock.)	D.B., a 70-year-old man, was admitted 3 hr ago from the ED with partial-thickness burns on his chest and arms (estimated to be 6% TBSA). Vital signs: 142/84, 102, RR 22, O_2 saturation 94% with O_2 at 6 L/min vis nasal cannula. Scattered wheezing throughout all lung fields.

1. Highlight all the findings above that require your follow-up.
2. After receiving the report, which patient would you see first? Why?
3. Which tasks could you delegate to the AP? *(select all that apply)*
   a. Obtain vital signs on J.K.
   b. Take a BP reading on D.B.
   c. Perform a shift assessment on D.A.
   d. Explain planned diagnostic testing to D.A.
   e. Obtain a 12-lead electrocardiograph on J.K.
4. When you enter D.B.'s room, he tells you he is not feeling well. He says he has a headache, and his legs are "cramping up." He is unaware that he is in the hospital.

Use an X for the nursing actions listed below that are Indicated (appropriate or necessary), Contraindicated (could be harmful), or Nonessential (makes no difference or not necessary) for D.B. at this time.

Nursing Action	Indicated	Contraindicated	Nonessential
Perform a respiratory assessment.			
Direct the AP to stay with D.B. while you contact the HCP.			
Obtain a STAT blood glucose measurement.			
Administer as-needed acetaminophen for headache relief.			
Place the head of the bed flat.			
Have the AP obtain vital signs with O_2 saturation.			
Review recent laboratory results.			

Case Study Progression

D.B.'s vital signs are BP 114/48 mm Hg, heart rate is 112 beats/min, respirations are 18 breaths/min, and the temperature is 98°F (36.8°C). You receive notification that his laboratory results are available. They show the following:

Laboratory Results

Sodium	129 mmol/L
Potassium	5.0 mmol/L
HCO_3	26 mmol/L
BUN	37 mg/dL
Creatinine	2 mg/dL
Glucose	128 mg/dL
Calcium	9.1 mg/dL

5. Choose the most *likely* option for the information missing from statement below by selecting from the lists of options provided.

Based on the assessment findings and laboratory results, the nurse determines the patient is experiencing ______1______. To manage this problem, you expect that the HCP will order _____2_____.

Options for 1	Options for 2
Hyperglycemia	Furosemide
Hyperkalemia	Insulin
Hyponatremia	IV fluids

6. You notify his HCP, who orders a normal saline IV to infuse at 100 mL/hr. Which nursing actions would you include in D.B.'s plan of care at this time?

Use an X to indicate which actions listed in the left column would be included in the plan of care for S.S.

Nursing Actions	Relevant Nursing Actions
Administer IV furosemide.	
Suggest a referral to the dietitian for parenteral nutrition.	
Monitor serum electrolyte values.	
Administer as ordered analgesia.	

Continued

Case Study—cont'd

Nursing Actions	Relevant Nursing Actions
Administer IV fluid replacement therapy as ordered.	
Initiate daily weights and intake and output.	

7. D.B. is thirsty and asks for something to drink. Which fluids would be appropriate to give him? *(select all that apply)*
   a. Gatorade
   b. Tap water
   c. Cola/soda
   d. Apple juice
   e. Orange juice
8. D.A. just returned to the unit following a transesophageal echocardiogram. Which action is the highest priority?
   a. Have the AP assist D.A. to lie flat on her back.
   b. Obtain vital signs and pulse oximetry every 4 hr.
   c. Maintain D.A. on NPO status until her gag reflex returns.
   d. Assess the lower extremities for signs of circulatory compromise.
9. In addition to teaching J.K. how to administer postoperative eye drops, you will also explain
   a. position and activity restrictions.
   b. how to change the dressing on her eye.
   c. the necessity for restricting fluid intake.
   d. that protective eyewear will no longer be needed.
10. Which interventions are appropriate for R.S. at this time?
   a. Inserting a nasogastric tube
   b. Keeping the room dark and quiet
   c. Placing an emesis basin at the bedside
   d. Elevating the head of the bed to the height desired
   e. Raising the side rails and having the bed in a low position

Answers available at http://evolve.elsevier.com/Lewis/medsurg.

27

Assessment: Respiratory System

Samantha J. Bonaduce

http://evolve.elsevier.com/Lewis/medsurg/

CONCEPTUAL FOCUS

Functional Ability

Gas Exchange

LEARNING OUTCOMES

1. Distinguish the structures and functions of the upper respiratory tract, lower respiratory tract, and chest wall.
2. Describe the processes of inspiration and expiration.
3. Describe the process of oxygenation and ventilation.
4. Identify the respiratory defense mechanisms.
5. Discuss the significance of arterial blood gas values in relation to respiratory function.
6. Relate the signs and symptoms of inadequate oxygenation to physical assessment findings.
7. Link age-related changes of the respiratory system to key differences in assessment findings.
8. Obtain significant subjective and objective assessment data related to the respiratory system.
9. Perform a physical assessment of the respiratory system using the appropriate techniques.
10. Distinguish normal from common abnormal findings in a physical assessment of a patient's respiratory system.
11. Describe the purpose, significance of results, and nursing responsibilities related to diagnostic studies of the respiratory system.

KEY TERMS

adventitious breath sounds
chemoreceptor
compliance
crackles, Table 27.6
dyspnea
fremitus
mechanical receptors
oximetry
oxygenation
resistance
surfactant
tidal volume (VT)
ventilation
wheezes, Table 27.6

The primary purpose of the respiratory system is gas exchange. This involves the transfer of oxygen (O_2) and carbon dioxide (CO_2) between the atmosphere and blood. While adequate perfusion is needed to distribute O_2 to the body tissues, adequate oxygenation depends on a healthy, functioning respiratory system.

STRUCTURES AND FUNCTIONS OF RESPIRATORY SYSTEM

The respiratory system is divided into 2 parts: the upper respiratory tract and the lower respiratory tract (Fig. 27.1).

Upper Respiratory Tract

The *upper respiratory tract* includes the nose, mouth, pharynx, epiglottis, larynx, and trachea. Air enters the respiratory tract through the nose. The nose is made of bone and cartilage. It is divided into 2 nares by the nasal septum. The inside of the nose is shaped into 3 passages by projections called *turbinates.* The turbinates increase the surface area of the nasal mucosa that warms and moistens the air as it enters the nose. The internal nose opens directly into the sinuses. The nasal cavity connects with the pharynx. It is a tubular passageway that is subdivided into 3 parts: *nasopharynx, oropharynx,* and *laryngopharynx.*

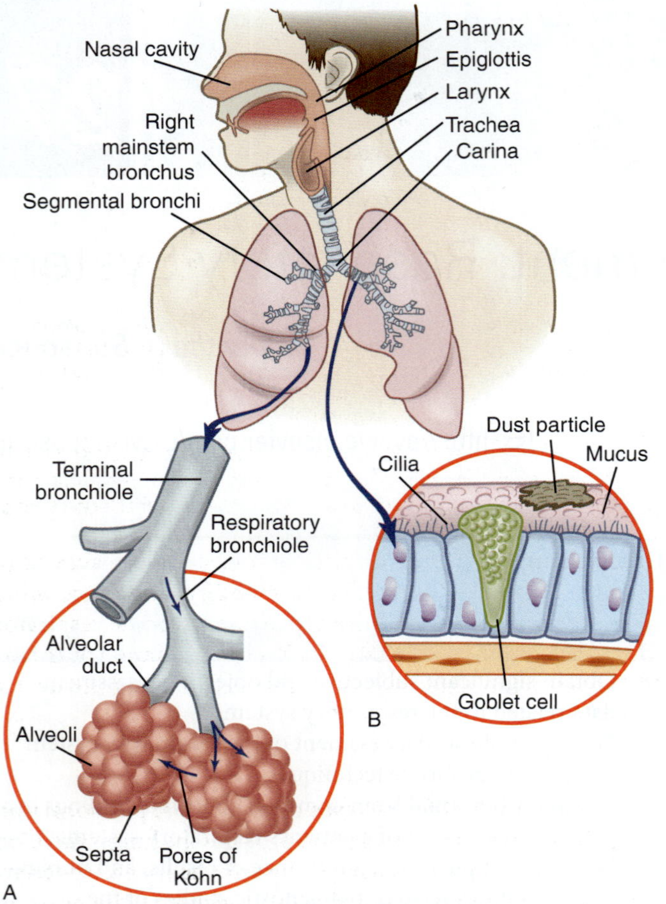

Fig. 27.1 Structures of the respiratory tract. (A) Pulmonary functional unit. (B) Ciliated mucous membrane. (Redrawn from Price SA, Wilson LM: *Pathophysiology: clinical concepts of disease processes,* ed 6, St Louis, 2003, Mosby.)

The nose protects the lower airway by warming and humidifying air and filtering small particles before air enters the lungs. The olfactory nerve, found within the mucosa of the upper part of the nasal cavity, is responsible for the sense of smell.[1]

Air moves through the oropharynx to the laryngopharynx. It then travels through the epiglottis to the larynx before moving into the trachea. The *epiglottis* is a small flap behind the tongue that closes over the larynx during swallowing. This prevents solids and liquids from entering the lungs. The vocal cords are in the larynx. Air passes through the glottis (the opening between the vocal cords) and into the trachea.

The trachea is a cylindrical tube about 5 inches (10 to 12 cm) long and 1 inch (1.5 to 2.5 cm) in diameter. U-Shaped cartilages keep the trachea open but allow the adjacent esophagus to expand for swallowing. The trachea divides into the right and left mainstem bronchi at a point called the *carina.* The carina is located at the *angle of Louis,* which is at the level of the 4th and 5th thoracic vertebrae.[2] The carina is highly sensitive. Stimulation of this area during suctioning causes vigorous coughing.

Lower Respiratory Tract

Once air passes the carina, it is in the lower respiratory tract. The *lower respiratory tract* consists of the bronchi, bronchioles, alveolar ducts, and alveoli. Except for the right and left mainstem bronchi, all lower airway structures are found within the lungs. The right lung is divided into 3 lobes (upper, middle, and lower) and the left lung into 2 lobes (upper and lower) (Fig. 27.2).

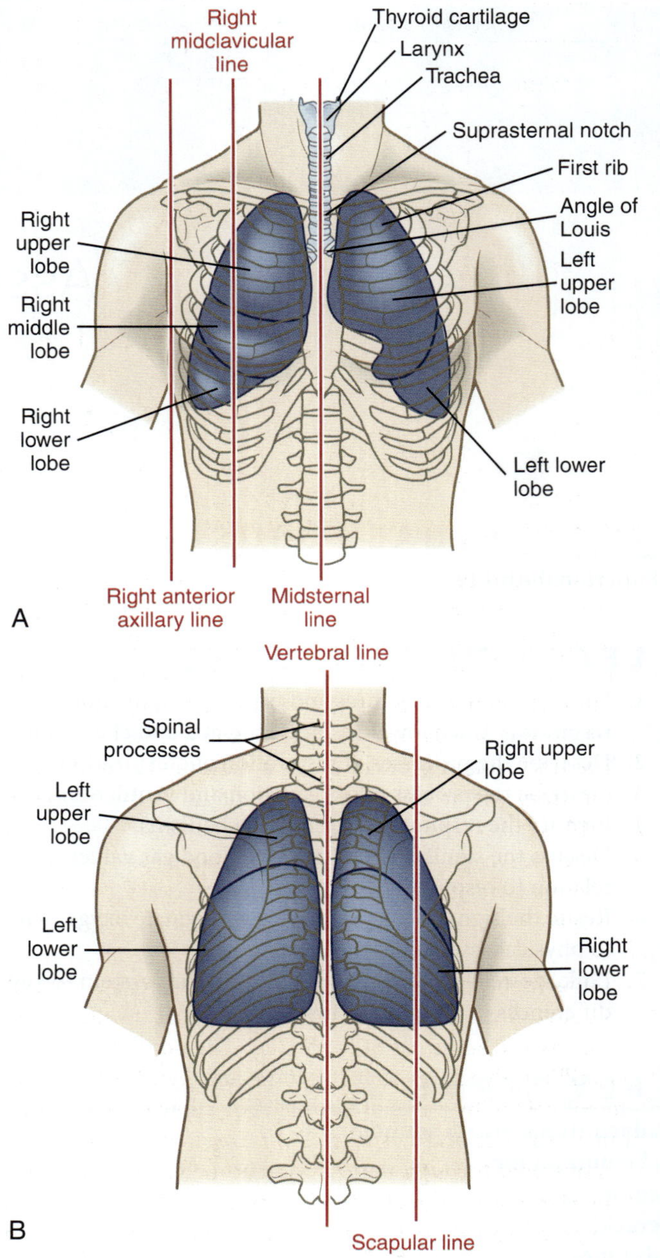

Fig. 27.2 Landmarks and structures of the chest wall. (A) Anterior view. (B) Posterior view. (Redrawn from Thompson JM, McFarland GK, Hirsch JE, et al: *Mosby's clinical nursing,* ed 5, St Louis, 2002, Mosby.)

The mainstem bronchi, pulmonary vessels, and nerves enter the lungs through a slit called the *hilus.* The right mainstem bronchus is shorter, wider, and straighter than the left mainstem bronchus. That is why aspiration is more likely to occur in the right lung than in the left lung.

The mainstem bronchi subdivide several times to form the lobar, segmental, and subsegmental bronchi. Further divisions form the bronchioles. The most distant bronchioles are

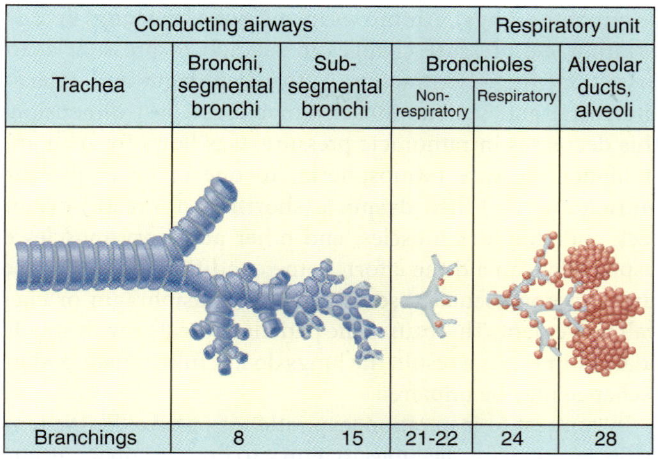

Fig. 27.3 Structures of lower airways. (Redrawn from Thompson JM, McFarland GK, Hirsch JE, et al.: *Mosby's clinical nursing*, ed 5, St Louis, 2002, Mosby.)

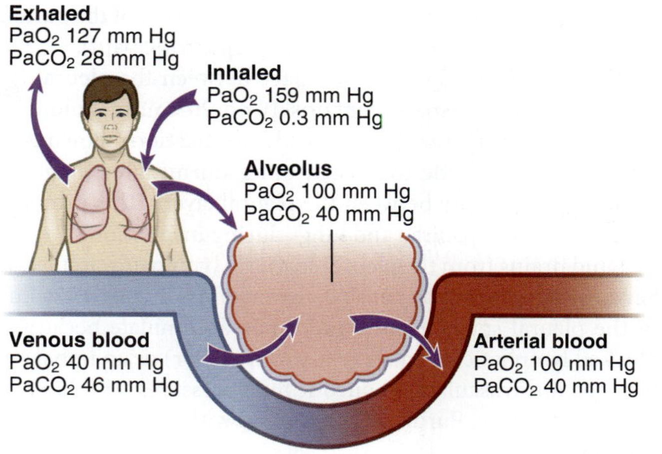

Fig. 27.4 Partial pressure of respiratory gases in normal respiration. The pressures are shown in inhaled and exhaled air from the lungs and at the level of the alveoli and pulmonary venous and arterial blood vessels.

the respiratory bronchioles. The bronchioles are encircled by smooth muscles that constrict and dilate in response to various stimuli. The terms *bronchoconstriction* and *bronchodilation* refer to a decrease or increase in the diameter of the airways caused by contraction or relaxation of these muscles. Beyond the bronchioles lie the alveolar ducts and alveoli (Fig. 27.3).

The trachea and bronchi act as a pathway to conduct gases to and from the alveoli. The volume of air in the trachea and bronchi is called the *anatomic dead space* (VD).[3] This air does not take part in gas exchange. In adults, a normal **tidal volume (V_T)**, or volume of air exchanged with each breath, is about 500 mL (in a 150-lb man). Of each 500 mL inhaled, about 150 mL is VD.

The alveoli are the final part of the respiratory tract (Fig. 27.3). *Alveoli* are small sacs in the lungs that are the primary site of gas exchange for O_2 and CO_2. The adult lung has over 300 million alveoli, each 0.3 mm in diameter. The alveoli are interconnected by pores of Kohn.[4] They allow movement of air from alveolus to alveolus (Fig. 27.1). Deep breathing promotes air movement through these pores and helps move mucus out of the respiratory bronchioles. Bacteria can also move through these pores, spreading infection to previously uninfected areas. Alveoli have a total volume of about 2500 mL, with a surface area for gas exchange that is about the size of a tennis court.

Gases are exchanged across the alveolar-capillary membrane, where the alveoli come in contact with pulmonary capillaries (Fig. 27.4). In conditions such as pulmonary edema, excess fluid fills the interstitial space and alveoli. This reduces gas exchange.

Surfactant

Because alveoli are unstable, they have a natural tendency to collapse. Alveolar cells secrete surfactant. **Surfactant** is a lipoprotein that lowers the surface tension in the alveoli.[5] It reduces the amount of pressure needed to inflate the alveoli and makes them less likely to collapse. Normally, each person takes a slightly larger breath, termed a *sigh,* after every 5 or 6 breaths. This sigh stretches the alveoli and promotes surfactant secretion.

When there is not enough surfactant, the alveoli collapse. The term *atelectasis* refers to collapsed, airless alveoli. The postoperative patient is at risk for atelectasis because of the effects of anesthesia, decreased mobility, and pain, which can alter breathing and lung expansion. In acute respiratory distress syndrome (ARDS), lack of surfactant contributes to widespread atelectasis and collapse of lung tissue (see Chapter 32).

Blood Supply

The lungs have 2 different types of circulation: pulmonary and bronchial. Pulmonary circulation provides the lungs with blood that takes part in gas exchange. The pulmonary artery receives deoxygenated blood from the right ventricle of the heart and delivers it to pulmonary capillaries that lie directly alongside the alveoli. O_2–CO_2 exchange occurs at this point. The pulmonary veins return oxygenated blood to the left atrium, which then delivers it to the left ventricle, and into systemic circulation. Venous blood is collected from capillary networks of the body and returned to the right atrium by way of the superior and inferior vena cava.

Bronchial circulation starts with the bronchial arteries, which arise from the thoracic aorta. Bronchial circulation does not take part in gas exchange but provides O_2 to the bronchi and other lung tissues. Deoxygenated blood returns from the bronchial circulation through the azygos vein into the superior vena cava.[1]

Chest Wall

The chest wall is shaped, supported, and protected by 24 ribs (12 on each side). The thoracic cage, which consists of the ribs and sternum, protect the lungs and the heart from injury. The *mediastinum* is the space in the middle of the thoracic cavity. It contains the major organs of the chest, including the heart, aorta, and esophagus. The mediastinum physically separates the right and left lungs into 2 separate compartments.

The chest cavity is lined with a membrane called the *parietal pleura.* The lungs are lined with a membrane called the *visceral pleura.* The parietal and visceral pleurae join to form one continuous membrane. The visceral pleura does not have any sensory (pain) fibers or nerve endings. The parietal pleura has pain fibers. This is why irritation or inflammation of the parietal pleura can cause pain with each breath (pleuritic pain).

The *intrapleural space* is the space between the pleural layers. Normally this space contains 10 to 20 mL of fluid. This fluid serves 2 purposes: (1) it provides lubrication, allowing the pleural layers to slide over each other during breathing, and (2) it increases unity between the pleural layers. This promotes expansion of the pleurae and lungs during inspiration.

Fluid drains from the pleural space via lymphatic circulation. Several conditions may cause a pleural effusion, or excess fluid in the pleural space. Pleural fluid may accumulate because of blocked lymphatic drainage (e.g., from cancer) or an imbalance between intravascular and oncotic fluid pressures. This happens with heart failure. Purulent pleural fluid with bacterial infection is called *empyema.*

The *diaphragm* is the major muscle of respiration. During inspiration the diaphragm contracts, moves downward, and increases intrathoracic volume. At the same time, the internal intercostals relax and the external intercostal muscles contract. This increases the lateral and anteroposterior (AP) dimension of the chest.[6] The scalene muscles also contract on inspiration, raising the first and second ribs. This causes the size of the thoracic cavity to increase and intrathoracic pressure to decrease, pulling air into the lungs.

The diaphragm is made up of 2 hemidiaphragms, each innervated by the right and left phrenic nerves. The phrenic nerves arise from the spinal cord between C3 and C5, the 3rd and 5th cervical vertebrae. Injury to the phrenic nerve results in hemidiaphragm paralysis on the side of the injury. Complete spinal cord injuries above the level of C3 result in total diaphragm paralysis and dependence on a mechanical ventilator (see Chapter 65).

Physiology of Respiration

Oxygenation

Oxygenation refers to the process of obtaining O_2 from the atmospheric air and making it available to the organs and tissues of the body. The lungs' ability to oxygenate arterial blood adequately is evaluated by partial pressure of O_2 in arterial blood (PaO_2), arterial O_2 saturation (SaO_2), and patient assessment.

O_2 is carried in the blood in 2 forms: dissolved O_2 and hemoglobin-bound O_2. The PaO_2 represents the amount of O_2 dissolved in the plasma. It is expressed in millimeters of mercury (mm Hg). The SaO_2 is the amount of O_2 bound to hemoglobin in comparison with the amount of O_2 the hemoglobin can carry. The SaO_2 is expressed as a percent. For example, if the SaO_2 is 90%, this means that 90% of hemoglobin attachments for O_2 have O_2 bound to them.

O_2 and CO_2 move back and forth across the alveolar-capillary membrane by diffusion. The overall direction of movement is from the area of higher concentration to the area of lower concentration. Thus, O_2 moves from alveolar gas (atmospheric air) into the arterial blood and CO_2 from the arterial blood into the alveolar gas. Diffusion continues until equilibrium is reached.

Ventilation

Ventilation involves *inspiration,* or inhalation (movement of air into the lungs), and *expiration,* or exhalation (movement of air out of the lungs). Air moves in and out of the lungs because intrathoracic pressure changes in relation to pressure at the airway opening. Contraction of the diaphragm and external intercostal and scalene muscles increases chest dimensions. This decreases intrathoracic pressure. Gas flows from an area of higher pressure (atmospheric) to one of lower pressure (intrathoracic). When **dyspnea** (shortness of breath) occurs, neck and shoulder muscles, and other accessory muscles of respiration, can aid the effort. Some conditions (e.g., rib fractures, neuromuscular disease) may limit diaphragm or chest wall movement. This causes the patient to breathe with smaller tidal volumes. As a result, the lungs do not fully inflate, and gas exchange may be impaired.

In contrast to inspiration, expiration is passive. *Elastic recoil* is the tendency for the lungs to return to their original size after being stretched or expanded. The elasticity of lung tissue is due to the elastin fibers found in the alveolar walls and surrounding the bronchioles and capillaries. The elastic recoil of the chest wall and lungs allows the chest to passively decrease in size (volume). When intrathoracic pressure rises, air moves out of the lungs.

Exacerbations of asthma or chronic obstructive pulmonary disease (COPD) cause expiration to become an active, labored process (see Chapter 31). Intercostal, scalene, and accessory muscles (e.g., abdominal, trapezius) help expel air during labored breathing.

Compliance and Resistance

Changes in compliance and/or resistance can affect both oxygenation and ventilation. **Compliance** refers to the ability of the lungs to expand. This is a result of the elasticity of the lungs and elastic recoil of the chest wall.[6] With decreased compliance, it is harder for the lungs to inflate. This occurs with conditions that increase fluid in the lungs (e.g., pulmonary edema, ARDS, pneumonia), make lung tissue less elastic or distensible (e.g., pulmonary fibrosis, sarcoidosis), or restrict lung movement (e.g., pleural effusion). Compliance increases when there is destruction of alveolar walls and loss of tissue elasticity, as in COPD.

Resistance refers to any obstacle to airflow during inspiration and/or expiration. The main factor affecting airway resistance is changes in the diameter (size) of the airways. For example, a patient with an acute asthma attack has narrowed airways, resulting in increased resistance. Giving bronchodilators decreases resistance by increasing the diameter of the bronchi, promoting air entry. The presence of secretions in the bronchi also increases resistance. Secretions can partially occlude airways, making airways narrower. This makes it harder for patients to get air into their lungs. Moving secretions from the airway with mucolytics or expectorants helps decrease resistance.

Control of Respiration

Located in the brainstem, the respiratory center (the medulla) responds to chemical and mechanical signals. The medulla sends impulses to the respiratory muscles through the spinal cord and phrenic nerves.

Chemoreceptors

A **chemoreceptor** is a receptor that responds to a change in the chemical composition ($PaCO_2$ and pH) of the fluid around it. Central chemoreceptors are found in the medulla. They respond to changes in the hydrogen ion (H^+) concentration.[7] An increase in the H^+ concentration *(acidosis)* causes the medulla to increase the respiratory rate and VT. A decrease in H^+ concentration *(alkalosis)* has the opposite effect. Changes in $PaCO_2$ regulate ventilation primarily by their effect on the pH of cerebrospinal fluid. When the $PaCO_2$ level is increased, more CO_2 is available to combine with H_2O and form carbonic acid (H_2CO_3). This lowers the cerebrospinal fluid pH and stimulates an increase in respiratory rate. The opposite process occurs with a decrease in $PaCO_2$ level.

Peripheral chemoreceptors are found in the carotid bodies at the bifurcation of the common carotid arteries and in the aortic bodies above and below the aortic arch.[7] The peripheral chemoreceptors respond to decreases in PaO_2 and pH and increases in $PaCO_2$. These changes also stimulate the respiratory center.

In a healthy person, an increase in $PaCO_2$ or a decrease in pH causes an immediate increase in the respiratory rate. The $PaCO_2$ does not vary more than about 3 mm Hg if lung function is normal. Conditions such as COPD change lung function and may result in chronically elevated $PaCO_2$ levels. In these instances, the patient is not sensitive to further increases in $PaCO_2$ as a stimulus to breathe. They may be maintaining ventilation largely because of a hypoxic drive from the peripheral chemoreceptors (see Chapter 31).

Mechanical Receptors

Mechanical receptors are found in the conducting upper airways, chest wall, diaphragm, and capillaries of the alveoli. They are stimulated by a variety of physiologic factors, such as irritants, muscle stretching, and alveolar wall distortion. The 3 major types of mechanical receptors are irritant, stretch, and juxtacapillary (J) receptors.[5]

Irritant receptors are found in the conducting airways. These receptors are sensitive to inhaled particles and aerosols. When stimulated, they initiate the cough reflex. Signals from stretch receptors, in the smooth muscle of the airways, aid in the control of respiration. As the lungs inflate, stretch receptors activate the inspiratory center to inhibit further lung expansion. This is the *Hering-Breuer reflex*, which prevents overdistention of the lungs. Stimulation of J receptors, found in the capillaries of the alveoli, occurs with increased pulmonary capillary pressure. This causes rapid, shallow respiration (tachypnea) seen in pulmonary edema.

Respiratory Defense Mechanisms

Respiratory defense mechanisms are efficient in protecting the lungs from inhaled particles, microorganisms, and toxic gases. The defense mechanisms include air filtration, mucociliary clearance system, cough reflex, reflex bronchoconstriction, and alveolar macrophages.

Air Filtration

Nasal hairs filter inspired air. In addition, the abrupt changes in direction of airflow that occur as air moves through the nasopharynx and larynx increase air turbulence. This causes particles and bacteria to contact the mucosa lining these structures. Most large particles (greater than 5 μm) are less dangerous because they are removed in the nasopharynx or bronchi and do not reach the alveoli.

The velocity of airflow slows greatly after it passes the larynx, facilitating the deposition of smaller particles (1 to 5 μm). They settle the way that sand does in a river, a process termed *sedimentation.* Particles less than 1 μm in size are too small to settle in this manner and are deposited in the alveoli. An example of small particles that can build up is coal dust, which can lead to pneumoconiosis (see Chapter 30).

Mucociliary Clearance System

Below the larynx, the mucociliary clearance system, also called the *mucociliary escalator*, is responsible for the movement of mucus. Goblet cells and submucosal glands continually secrete mucus at a rate of about 100 mL/day. This mucus forms a blanket that contains the impacted particles and debris from distal lung areas (Fig. 27.1). Secretory immunoglobulin A (IgA) in the mucus helps protect against bacteria and viruses.

Cilia cover the airways from the level of the trachea to the respiratory bronchioles (Fig. 27.1). Each ciliated cell has about 200 cilia. They beat rhythmically about 1000 times per minute in the large airways, moving mucus toward the mouth. We normally swallow the mucus without noticing.

The ciliary beat is slower further down the tracheobronchial tree. As a result, we remove particles that penetrate more deeply into the airways less rapidly. Dehydration, smoking, inhaling high O_2 concentrations, infection, and drugs, such as atropine, anesthetics, alcohol, or cocaine, impair ciliary action. Patients with COPD and cystic fibrosis often have repeated lower respiratory tract infections. These conditions are associated with destroyed cilia, resulting in impaired secretion clearance, a chronic productive cough, and chronic colonization by bacteria. These lead to frequent respiratory tract infections.

Cough Reflex

The cough is a protective reflex that clears the airway by a high-pressure, high-velocity flow of air. It is a backup for mucociliary clearance, especially when this clearance mechanism is overwhelmed or ineffective. Coughing is effective in removing secretions only above the subsegmental level (large or main airways). Secretions below this level must be moved upward by the mucociliary mechanism before we can remove them by coughing.

Reflex Bronchoconstriction

Reflex bronchoconstriction is another defense mechanism. When we inhale large amounts of irritating substances (e.g., dusts, aerosols), the bronchi constrict to prevent entry of the irritants. A person with hyperreactive airways, such as a person with asthma, may have bronchoconstriction after inhalation of triggers, such as cold air, perfume, or other strong odors.

Alveolar Macrophages

Because there are no ciliated cells below the level of the respiratory bronchioles, the primary defense mechanism at the

TABLE 27.1 GERONTOLOGIC ASSESSMENT DIFFERENCES

Respiratory System

Changes	Differences in Assessment Findings
Structures	
↑ Anteroposterior diameter ↓ Chest wall compliance Chest wall stiffening	Barrel chest appearance, kyphotic posture, ↓ chest wall movement, ↓ deep breathing, ↓ cough effectiveness
Costal cartilage calcification ↓ Elastic recoil	↓ Vital capacity, ↑ residual volume, ↑ functional residual capacity
↓ Functioning alveoli	↓ Breath sounds, particularly at lung bases
↓ Respiratory muscle strength	↓ PaO_2 and SaO_2, normal pH and $PaCO_2$
Defense Mechanisms	
↓ Alveolar macrophage function	↓ Cough effectiveness, ↓ secretion clearance, thickened mucus
↓ Cell-mediated immunity ↓ Cilia function	↑ Risk for upper respiratory aspiration, infection, influenza, pneumonia
↓ Cough force ↓ Sensation in pharynx ↓ Specific antibodies	Respiratory infections may be more severe and last longer
Respiratory Control	
↓ Response to hypercapnia ↓ Response to hypoxemia	Slight ↓ PaO_2 and ↑ $PaCO_2$ before respiratory rate changes ↓ Ability to maintain acid-base balance Significant hypoxemia or hypercapnia may develop from relatively small incidents Retained secretions, excessive sedation, or positioning that impairs chest expansion may change PaO_2 or SpO_2 values

alveolar level is alveolar macrophages. *Alveolar macrophages* rapidly phagocytize inhaled foreign particles, such as bacteria. The debris is moved to the level of the bronchioles for removal by the cilia or removed from the lungs by the lymphatic system. Particles (e.g., coal dust, silica) that cannot be adequately phagocytized tend to remain in the lungs for indefinite periods and can stimulate inflammatory responses. Because cigarette smoke impairs alveolar macrophage activity, the smoker who works in an occupation with heavy dust exposure (e.g., mining, foundries) has an especially high risk for lung disease.

Gerontologic Considerations: Effects of Aging on Respiratory System

We consider age-related changes in the respiratory system as alterations in structure, defense mechanisms, and respiratory control (Table 27.1). Structural changes include calcification of the costal cartilages, which can interfere with chest expansion. The outward curvature of the spine is marked, especially with osteoporosis, and the lumbar curve flattens. Therefore, the chest may appear barrel shaped, and the person may need to use accessory muscles to breathe. Respiratory muscle strength progressively declines after age 50. Overall, the lungs in the older adult are harder to inflate.

Within the lung, the number of functional alveoli decreases, and they become less elastic. Small airways in the lung bases close earlier in expiration. Therefore, more inspired air is distributed to the lung apices and ventilation is less well matched to perfusion, lowering the PaO_2. As a result, older adults have less tolerance for exertion, and dyspnea can occur if their activity exceeds their normal exercise.

In older adults, *respiratory defense mechanisms* are less effective because of a decline in immune function and the ability to produce antibodies. The alveolar macrophages are less effective at phagocytosis. An older patient has a less forceful cough and fewer and less functional cilia. Mucous membranes tend to be drier. Retained mucus predisposes the older adult to respiratory tract infections. Formation of secretory IgA, an important defense mechanism, is decreased. Swallowing is slower because of transit time in the pharyngeal area. There is reduced sensation in the pharynx. Consequently, the older adult is at greater risk for aspiration.

The aging process alters respiratory control, resulting in a more gradual response to changes in blood O_2 or CO_2 level. The PaO_2 may drop to a slightly lower than normal level and the $PaCO_2$ may rise to a level slightly higher than normal before the respiratory rate changes.

The extent of these changes in people of the same age varies greatly. For example, the older adult who has a significant smoking history, is obese, and has a chronic illness is at greater risk for adverse outcomes.

ASSESSMENT OF RESPIRATORY SYSTEM

Determining a patient's needs related to the respiratory system requires an accurate health history and a thorough physical assessment. A respiratory assessment can be part of a comprehensive or focused assessment. Use judgment in determining whether all or part of the history and physical assessment are needed, based on your evaluation of the patient's degree of respiratory distress. If respiratory distress is severe, only obtain pertinent information and defer a thorough assessment until the patient's condition stabilizes.

Case Study

Patient Introduction

(© Fuse/ Thinkstock.)

F.T. is a 70-year-old man who comes to the emergency department (ED) with nausea, fatigue, and increased shortness of breath, which started 3 days ago. He says that he started using his albuterol inhaler every 4 hours 2 days ago. While it worked at first, it is no longer helping. He can walk only a few feet in his apartment before he becomes short of breath. He sleeps in a recliner in the living room. He has noticed some swelling to his hands and feet and has been having trouble urinating.

Discussion Questions

1. What are the possible causes of F.T.'s shortness of breath?
2. Does F.T. need to be admitted to the hospital or is his condition stable?
3. What questions would be a priority during the subjective assessment?

You will learn more about F.T. and his condition as you read this assessment chapter.

Answers available at http://evolve.elsevier.com/Lewis/medsurg.

BOX 27.1 GENETIC RISK ALERT

- Respiratory problems with a strong genetic link include cystic fibrosis, COPD from α_1-antitrypsin deficiency, and asthma.
- If people have a family history of these respiratory problems, they have a greater risk for developing them.
- Although cigarette smoking is a major risk factor for COPD, only a minority of cigarette smokers develop symptomatic disease. The risk for COPD related to cigarette smoking is genetically related.

Subjective Data

Important Health Information

Health history. It is important to determine the frequency of upper respiratory problems (e.g., colds, sore throats, sinus problems, allergies). Do seasonal changes influence these problems? Ask about a history of lower respiratory problems, such as asthma, COPD, pneumonia, and tuberculosis (TB).

Ask the patient with allergies about possible precipitating factors or triggers, such as medications, pollen, smoke, mold, or pet exposure. Record the characteristics and severity of the allergic reaction, such as runny nose, wheezing, scratchy throat, or chest tightness. Determine the frequency of asthma exacerbations.

Ask about a history of other health problems (Box 27.1). Respiratory symptoms are often manifestations of problems that involve other body systems. For example, the patient with heart problems may have dyspnea (shortness of breath) because of heart failure. The patient with human immunodeficiency virus (HIV) infection may have frequent respiratory tract infections because of compromised immune function.

Medications. Take a thorough medication history, including the names of prescription and over-the-counter (OTC) medications. Ask about the dose (if known), frequency, length of time taken, side effects, and the reason for taking the medication. Assess for overuse of short-term bronchodilators as a key indicator of symptom control. Cough is a common side effect of angiotensin-converting enzyme (ACE) inhibitors. Encourage the patient to bring all medications and inhalers to each visit with an HCP.

If the patient is using O_2 for a breathing problem, record the fraction of inspired O_2 concentration (FIO_2), flow rate (liters per minute), method of administration, number of hours used per day, and effectiveness of the therapy. Assess safety practices. Include the patient's cognitive and physical ability related to using O_2 and any metered-dose inhalers.

Surgery or other treatments. Find out if the patient has been hospitalized for a respiratory problem. Note the dates, therapy (including surgery), and status of the problem. Determine if the patient has ever been intubated because of a respiratory problem. Ask about the use of and response to respiratory treatments, such as a nebulizer, humidifier, airway clearance modalities (see Chapter 28), high-frequency chest wall oscillation, postural drainage, and percussion.

Functional Health Patterns

Health history questions to ask a patient with a respiratory problem are outlined in Table 27.2.

Health perception–health management pattern. Ask the patient if there has been a perceived change in health status within the last several days, months, or years. In COPD, lung function declines slowly over many years. The patient may not notice this decline because they have been altering activity to accommodate reduced tolerance. If an upper respiratory tract infection is superimposed on a chronic problem, dyspnea and decreased exercise tolerance may occur very quickly. In asthma, symptoms may occur or worsen during exercise, in the presence of mold, or with changes in temperature or air pollution.

Explore common manifestations of respiratory problems (e.g., cough, dyspnea). Describe the course of the patient's illness, including when it began, type of symptoms, and factors that worsen or relieve these symptoms. Because of the chronic nature of respiratory problems, the patient may relate a change in symptoms (rather than the onset of new symptoms) when describing the present illness. For example, increased shortness of breath or increased purulence of sputum may suggest an acute COPD exacerbation.

If a cough is present, assess its quality. For example, a loose-sounding cough occurs with secretions. A dry, hacking cough may mean an airway irritation or obstruction. A harsh, barky cough suggests upper airway obstruction from inhibited vocal cord movement due to subglottic edema. Assess whether the cough is strong enough to clear secretions. Note whether it is productive or nonproductive of secretions. Determine if the cough is acute or chronic (longer than 3 weeks in duration) or if it first began with an upper respiratory tract infection. The pattern and cause of the cough are determined by asking questions such as: What has been the pattern of coughing? Has it been regular or paroxysmal (i.e., sudden, periodic onset) or related to a time of day, the weather, certain activities, talking, or deep breathing? Any change over time? Do you clear your throat a lot? What have you tried to relieve the coughing? Did you try any prescription or OTC drugs?

If the patient has a productive cough, evaluate the characteristics of sputum: amount, color, consistency, and odor. Quantify the amount of sputum per day. Note any recent increases or decreases in the amount. Sputum is normally clear or slightly whitish. If a patient is a cigarette smoker, the sputum is usually clear to gray with occasional specks of brown. The patient with COPD may have clear, whitish, or slightly yellow sputum, especially in the morning on rising. If the patient reports any change from baseline color, suspect pulmonary complications. Note any changes in consistency of sputum to thick, thin, or frothy and pink tinged. These changes may indicate dehydration, postnasal drip or sinus drainage, or possible pulmonary edema. Normally sputum should be odorless. A foul odor or exceptionally bad breath or taste in the mouth suggests an infectious process. Ask the patient if sputum production increases or decreases with changes in position (e.g., increased with lying down) or activity.

When assessing sputum, determine if the patient has a history of spitting or coughing up blood *(hemoptysis)*. Hemoptysis can range from a slight streaking of blood in the sputum to massive coughing up of blood. The patient may not be able to tell between hemoptysis and *hematemesis* (vomiting blood).

TABLE 27.2 HEALTH HISTORY

Respiratory System

Health Perception–Health Management

- Describe your daily activities. Have breathing problems prevented you from doing activities that you used to be able to do?[a] Are your breathing problems better, worse, or about the same compared with 6 months ago?
- How do your breathing problems affect your self-care abilities?
- Have you ever smoked? Do you smoke now? If so, what have you smoked? Cigarettes? Cigars? Pipes? Electronic cigarettes?
- If yes, how many cigarettes each day and for how long? Are you interested in stopping smoking? Are there aids we can tell you about that would assist your quitting? Would you be willing to come back for a visit so that we can explore your quitting? If you stopped smoking, did you do so because of your health?[a] How did you stop?
- Have you ever used chewing tobacco?
- Have you ever smoked street drugs?[a]
- Do you get the flu shot yearly? When was your last flu shot? Have you had a Pneumovax vaccination?
- What equipment helps you manage your respiratory problems? How often do you use it? Does it help? Cause problems?
- Do you feel that your respiratory problem is getting better or worse?

Nutritional-Metabolic

- Have you recently lost weight because of trouble eating related to your respiratory problem? How much weight have you lost? Have you lost this weight voluntarily?
- Do any foods affect your breathing?[a] Sputum production?[a]

Elimination

- Does your breathing problem make it hard for you to get to the toilet?[a]
- Are you inactive because of shortness of breath to the point that you have incontinence?[a] Constipation?[a]

Activity-Exercise

- Are you ever short of breath during exercise?a At rest?[a]
- Do you get too short of breath to do the things you want to do?[a]
- Is your home 1 story? 2 stories? How many steps from the street to your door?
- Can you walk up a flight of steps without stopping?
- Are you able to maintain your typical activities of daily living? If not, what are you able to do independently? What do you need help with? What have you had to give up?
- What do you do when you get short of breath? Does this help? How long does it take you to recover after you have been short of breath?

Sleep-Rest

- Do breathing problems cause you to wake up during the night?[a]
- Can you lie flat at night? If not, how many pillows do you use?
- Do you need to sleep upright in a chair?[a]
- Are you or your partner aware of any snoring?
- Do you awaken in the morning feeling rested?
- Do you ever wake up in the morning with a headache?[a]
- Do you fall asleep easily during the day?[a]

Cognitive-Perceptual

- Do you have any pain with breathing?[a] On a scale from 0 to 10, with 0 being "no pain" and 10 being "the worst pain you can imagine," where would you rate your pain? Does it hurt more on inspiration?[a] Expiration?[a] Or both?[a]
- If you are having pain with breathing, describe the pain.
- Has the pain gotten better, worse, or stayed about the same over the past 6 months?
- Do you ever feel restless, irritable, or confused without a reason?[a]
- Do you have difficulty remembering things?[a]

Self-Perception–Self-Concept

- Describe how your respiratory problems have changed your life.
- If you use O_2, do you ever go out without bringing it with you? How often does this occur? Why?

Role-Relationship

- Has your respiratory problem caused any problems in your work, family, or social relationships?[a]

Sexuality-Reproductive

- Has your respiratory problem caused a change in your sexual activity?[a]
- Have you and your partner talked about ways to minimize your breathing problems during sexual activity?

Coping–Stress Tolerance

- On a daily/weekly basis, how often do you leave your home?
- Do you feel under any stress right now?
- Does stress influence your breathing?[a]
- Do you notice if your emotions have any effect on your respiratory problems?
- Are you aware of any respiratory support groups in your area?

Value-Belief

- What do you think causes/has caused your respiratory problem(s)?
- How are you feeling right now?
- Do you think the things you have been told to do for your respiratory problems help? If not, why?
- What are you looking for/expecting from the HCP today, in terms of your breathing problem(s)?

[a] If answer is "yes" to any of these questions, ask the patient to describe.

Hemoptysis occurs with a variety of conditions such as pneumonia, TB, lung cancer, and severe bronchiectasis.

Assess for a history of any difficulty breathing. For example, *wheezes* are musical sounds that can be audible. Wheezing indicates some degree of airway obstruction, such as asthma, foreign body aspiration, and emphysema. Assess for any history of family exposure to *Mycobacterium tuberculosis.*

Smoking is the most important risk factor for COPD and lung cancer. Ask about cigarette use and find out about the use of any tobacco products. This includes cigars, pipes, chewing tobacco, electronic cigarettes (e-cigarettes), and hookah (instrument for vaporizing and smoking flavored tobacco). Find out about exposure to secondhand smoke. Determine if the patient has tried to quit using tobacco products, including using prescription, OTC, and herbal remedies.

Discuss current and past smoking habits. Quantify smoking habits in *pack-years.* Do this by multiplying the number of packs of cigarettes smoked per day by the number of years smoked. For example, a person who smoked 1 pack (20 cigarettes) per day for 15 years has a 15 pack-year history. If they smoked 2 packs for 15 years, then it would be a 30 pack-year history.

TABLE 27.3 Dyspnea Rating Scale

Modified Borg Rating Scale for Perceived Dyspnea

Rate	Description
0	Nothing at all
0.5	Very, very slight shortness of breath
1	Very mild shortness of breath
2	Mild shortness of breath
3	Mild shortness of breath or breathing difficulty
4	Somewhat severe
5	Strong or hard breathing
6	
7	Severe shortness of breath or very hard breathing
8	
9	Extremely severe
10	Shortness of breath so severe you need to stop

From Hillegass E: *Essentials of cardiopulmonary physical therapy,* ed 4, Philadelphia, 2017, Saunders.

Ask where the patient has lived and traveled. Risk factors for TB include immigrating from an area with high rates of TB or living in a group setting, such as a prison. Other risk factors include exposure to people with high rates of TB transmission, such as the homeless, IV drug users, and people with HIV infection. Risk factors for fungal lung infections include those exposed to bird and rodent feces or polluted water, those working closely with the soil, and immunocompromised patients.

Assess if the patient received immunizations for influenza (flu), COVID, and pneumococcal pneumonia. Ask the patient about the use of equipment to manage respiratory symptoms (e.g., home O_2 equipment, inhalers, devices for sleep apnea). Find out the type of equipment used, cleaning of the device, frequency of use, its effect, and any side effects. Have patients show you the use of their inhalers. Many patients do not use these devices correctly (see Chapter 28).

Nutritional-metabolic pattern. Weight loss can be a symptom of respiratory disease. Determine if weight loss was intentional. If not, was food intake changed by anorexia (from medications), fatigue (from hypoxemia, increased work of breathing), or feeling full quickly (from lung hyperinflation)? Anorexia, weight loss, and chronic malnutrition are common in patients with COPD, lung cancer, TB, and chronic severe infection (bronchiectasis). Assess fluid intake. Dehydration can cause sputum to thicken and obstruct the airway. Rapid weight gain from fluid retention may impair gas exchange.

Elimination pattern. Activity intolerance from dyspnea could result in incontinence, if unable to reach a toilet when needed. Dyspnea can be the cause of limited mobility, which can cause constipation. Ask the patient with dyspnea about frequency, urgency, and elimination patterns (e.g., day vs. night). People with a chronic cough, especially women, may have urinary incontinence during paroxysms of coughing.

Activity-exercise pattern. Determine if dyspnea limits activity. Assess whether the patient's residence (e.g., number of steps, levels) poses any problems. Ask the patient about the perceived degree of the dyspnea (Table 27.3). For example, can the patient walk up 1 flight of stairs without stopping because of dyspnea? Is dyspnea with activity better, worse, or about the same in the last few days or months? Determine if the patient has difficulty breathing in a certain position, or if dyspnea is relieved by assuming a different position (e.g., tripod position in COPD).

Discuss whether the patient can carry out activities of daily living without dyspnea or other respiratory symptoms. If unable, record the amount and type of care the patient needs. Immobility and sedentary habits are risk factors for hypoventilation leading to atelectasis or pneumonia.

Sleep-rest pattern. Determine if the patient wakes up at night because of lung problems. The patient with asthma or COPD may awaken with chest tightness, wheezing, or coughing. This suggests a need for adjunct therapy or other medication changes. The patient with heart disease (e.g., heart failure) may sleep with the head elevated on several pillows to avoid breathing problems brought on by lying flat *(orthopnea).* Excess weight interferes with normal ventilation and may cause sleep apnea (see Chapter 7). Extremely obese persons may hypoventilate while awake or asleep. Manifestations of sleep apnea include snoring, insomnia, abrupt awakenings, daytime drowsiness, and early morning headaches. Night sweats may be a sign of TB.

Cognitive-perceptual pattern. Because hypoxia can cause neurologic symptoms, ask the patient about apprehension, restlessness, irritability, and memory changes. These can indicate inadequate cerebral oxygenation. Assess the patient's cognitive ability to cooperate with treatment. Hypoxemia interferes with the ability to learn and retain information. Failure or inability to take part in needed therapy may result in worsening of respiratory problems. For this reason, teaching may be more effective if the caregiver is present during teaching sessions to provide reinforcement later.

Ask about any discomfort or pain with breathing. Explore reports of chest pain carefully to rule out heart involvement. Problems such as pleurisy, fractured ribs, and costochondritis cause chest pain. Assessment of the patient having pain with breathing, such as onset, exact location of the pain, and factors that make the pain better or worse, can help establish a diagnosis.

Self-perception–self-concept pattern. Dyspnea limits activity, impairs ability to fulfill normal roles, and often alters self-esteem. A patient may be reluctant to appear in public with a highly visible nasal cannula and O_2 equipment. A barrel chest, clubbed fingers, pursed-lip breathing, and frequent expectoration of sputum or throat clearing can be embarrassing and lead to social isolation. Explore with the patient any body image concerns. Referral to a support group or pulmonary rehabilitation program may be beneficial in developing a support system and coping strategies.

Role-relationship pattern. Acute and chronic respiratory problems can seriously affect performance in work or other activities. Discuss the impact of medications, O_2 therapy, and special routines (e.g., pulmonary hygiene for cystic fibrosis) on the patient's family, job, and social life.

Review the nature of the patient's work and frequency and intensity of exposure to fumes, toxins, asbestos, coal, fibers, or silica. Ask whether symptoms are worse in specific situations (e.g., home vs. work environments). Hobbies, such as woodworking (sawdust) or pottery (silica), and animal exposure (allergies) can cause respiratory problems. Because of hyperreactive airways, exposure to fumes, smoke, and other chemicals may trigger an attack in the patient with asthma.

Sexuality-reproductive pattern. Most patients can continue to have satisfactory sexual relationships despite marked physical limitations. In a tactful manner, ask whether breathing difficulties have caused changes in sexual activity. If so, discuss positions that decrease dyspnea during sexual activity and alternative strategies for sexual fulfillment. For example, patients may need to perform good pulmonary hygiene (bronchodilators, coughing, deep breathing) before intimacy. They may need to use O_2 therapy equipment during intercourse just like they would with any strenuous physical activity.

Coping–stress tolerance pattern. Dyspnea causes anxiety, and anxiety worsens dyspnea. The result is a vicious cycle—the patient avoids activities that cause dyspnea, becoming more deconditioned and more dyspneic. The outcome is often physical and leads to social isolation. Assess how often the patient leaves home and interacts with others. Referral to a support group or pulmonary rehabilitation program may be helpful.

The chronic nature of many respiratory problems, such as COPD and asthma, can cause prolonged stress. Ask about the patient's coping strategies to manage this stress.

Value-belief pattern. Determine the patient's adherence to their treatment program. Explore possible reasons for lack of adherence, including conflict with cultural beliefs, financial constraints (e.g., costs of prescriptions), or failure to understand benefit. Correct misinformation and provide up-to-date information about respiratory conditions and medication management. Including the patient and caregiver in the planning of care can improve adherence.

Case Study

Subjective Data

(© Fuse/Thinkstock.)

A focused subjective assessment of F.T. revealed the following information:

- ***History:*** COPD, hypertension, heart failure, benign prostatic hyperplasia. No known allergies.
- ***Medications:*** Metoprolol (Toprol XL) 50 mg daily PO, furosemide 20 mg PO daily, finasteride 5 mg/day PO, Advair inhaler (fluticasone and salmeterol) 2 puffs twice daily, and albuterol inhaler 2 puffs every 4 hr PRN. Uses O_2 @ 3 L/min via nasal cannula at home for the past 10 years.
- ***Health Perception–Health Management:*** States he usually manages his COPD well with the Advair inhaler and occasional use of the albuterol inhaler. He thinks he caught a cold from his granddaughter last week. Increasing difficulty breathing, even with albuterol. Has a history of 30 pack-years of smoking, quitting 5 years ago.
- ***Nutritional-Metabolic Pattern:*** Eating and drinking very little over past 2–3 days.
- ***Elimination:*** Voiding small amounts of dark, concentrated urine (mostly at night).
- ***Activity-Exercise:*** At present, cannot walk 100 feet without feeling short of breath. Cannot walk up 1 flight of stairs (21 steps) to get in or out of his apartment without stopping to catch his breath.
- ***Sleep-Rest:*** Difficulty sleeping. Last night he slept upright in his recliner.
- ***Cognitive-Perceptual:*** Denies any pain with the shortness of breath. Feels slightly irritable because of lack of sleep.
- ***Coping–Stress Tolerance:*** Does not know how he will manage to get groceries or clean his apartment. His daughter lives an hour away and has 3 children in school.

Discussion Questions

1. Of the information provided, which subjective assessment findings concern you most?
2. From the information provided from F.T., what other information would you ask him about his condition (time permitting)?
3. What type of assessment would be most appropriate for F.T.: comprehensive, focused, or emergency?
4. F.T. cannot use his inhaler appropriately while he is talking with you. Is this a good time to teach him about the proper use of his inhaler?
5. What will you include in the physical assessment? What would you think will be priorities in your physical assessment?

You will learn about the physical assessment of the respiratory system in the next section.

Answers available at http://evolve.elsevier.com/Lewis/medsurg.

Objective Data

Physical Assessment

Vital signs are important data to collect before examining the respiratory system (Table 27.4).

Nose. Inspect the nose for patency, inflammation, deformities, symmetry, and discharge. Check each nostril for air patency with respiration while briefly occluding the other nostril. Tilt the patient's head backward and push the tip of the nose upward gently. With a nasal speculum and a good light, inspect the interior of the nose. The mucous membrane should be pink and moist, with no evidence of edema (bogginess), exudate, or bleeding. Inspect the nasal septum for deviation, perforations, and bleeding. Some septal deviation is normal in an adult. Inspect the turbinates for polyps, which are abnormal, fingerlike projections of swollen nasal mucosa. Polyps may result from long-term irritation of the mucosa (e.g., from allergies). Assess any discharge for color and consistency. Purulent and malodorous discharge could occur with a foreign body. Watery discharge could be related to allergies or from cerebrospinal fluid. Bloody discharge could be from trauma or dryness. Thick mucosal discharge could mean an infection.

Mouth and pharynx. Using a good light source, inspect the interior of the mouth for color, lesions, masses, gum retraction, bleeding, and poor dentition. Inspect the tongue for symmetry and lesions. Observe the pharynx by pressing a tongue blade gently against the middle of the back of the tongue. If the oropharynx is tight, have the patient yawn. Yawning usually allows more structures to be visible. The pharynx should be smooth and moist, with no evidence of exudate, ulcerations, swelling, or postnasal drip. Note the color, symmetry, and any enlargement of the tonsils. Stimulate the gag reflex by placing a tongue blade along the side of the pharynx, at the back of the tongue. A normal response (gagging) means that cranial nerves IX (glossopharyngeal) and X (vagus) are intact and that the airway is protected.

Neck. Inspect the neck for symmetry and tender or swollen areas. Palpate the lymph nodes while the patient is sitting erect

TABLE 27.4 Manifestations of Inadequate Oxygenation

Manifestations	ONSET Early	ONSET Late
Cardiovascular		
Cool, clammy skin		X
Cyanosis		X
Dysrhythmias	X	X
Hypertension (mild)	X	
Hypotension		X
Tachycardia	X	
Central Nervous System		
Apprehension	X	
Coma		X
Combativeness		X
Confusion, lethargy	X	X
Restlessness, irritability	X	
Respiratory		
Dyspnea on exertion	X	
Dyspnea at rest		X
Pause for breath between sentences, words		X
Retraction of intercostal spaces on inspiration		X
Tachypnea	X	
Use of accessory muscles		X
Other		
Diaphoresis	X	X
Fatigue	X	X
↓ Urine output	X	X

with the neck slightly flexed. Progression of palpation is from the nodes around the ears, to the nodes at the base of the skull, and then to those under the angles of the mandible to the midline. The patient may have small, mobile, nontender nodes *(shotty nodes),* which are not a sign of a pathologic condition. Tender, hard, or fixed nodes may indicate disease. Describe the location and characteristics of any palpable nodes.

Thorax and lungs. Picture imaginary lines on the chest to help identify abnormalities (Fig. 27.2). Describe abnormalities in terms of their location relative to these lines (e.g., 2 cm lateral from the right midclavicular line).

Chest examination is best done in a well-lit, warm room. Take measures to ensure the patient's privacy. Expose the patient's chest. Perform all physical assessment maneuvers (inspection, palpation, percussion, auscultation) on either the anterior or the posterior chest first rather than moving from anterior to posterior or vice versa with each maneuver. It is best to begin on the posterior chest, particularly with female patients, since you can obtain more information without interference from breast tissue. If the patient tires or you are interrupted, you will obtain baseline data with the most information from examining the posterior chest.

When assessing the *posterior chest,* ask the patient to lean forward with arms folded. This position moves the scapulae away from the spine, exposing more of the area you need to examine. When assessing the *anterior chest,* have the patient sit upright or position the patient supine with the head of the bed elevated to 30 degrees (semi-Fowler's position). The patient may need to lean forward for support on the bedside table to facilitate breathing.

Inspection. First, observe the patient's appearance. Note any evidence of respiratory distress, such as tachypnea or use of accessory muscles. Next, determine the shape and symmetry of the chest. Chest movement should be equal on both sides. The AP diameter should be less than the side-to-side or transverse diameter. Normal AP ratio is 1:2. An increase in AP diameter (e.g., barrel chest) may be due to normal aging or result from lung hyperinflation. Look for abnormalities in the sternum (e.g., *pectus carinatum* [a prominent protrusion of the sternum]) and *pectus excavatum* (an indentation of the lower sternum above the xiphoid process). Note any spinal curvature. Spinal curvatures that affect breathing include kyphosis, scoliosis, and kyphoscoliosis.

Observe the respiratory rate, depth, and rhythm. The normal adult respiratory rate is 12 to 20 breaths/min. Inspiration (I) should take half as long as expiration (E) (I/E ratio = 1:2). Observe for abnormal breathing patterns. Note *Kussmaul* (rapid, deep breathing), *Cheyne-Stokes* (abnormal respirations characterized by alternating periods of apnea and deep, rapid breathing), or *Biot's* (irregular breathing with apnea every 4 to 5 cycles) respirations.

Skin color provides clues to respiratory status. Cyanosis, a late sign of hypoxemia, is best seen in light-skinned patients as a bluish tinge to the mucous membranes, lips, and palms of the hands. In dark-skinned persons, cyanosis may be seen as a gray or white discoloration in the conjunctivae or around the mouth. Causes of cyanosis include hypoxemia or decreased cardiac output. Inspect the fingers for evidence of long-standing hypoxemia, known as *clubbing.* It is an increase in the angle between the base of the nail and the fingernail to 180 degrees or more. Clubbing usually accompanied by an increase in the depth, bulk, and sponginess of the end of the finger.

Palpation. Determine tracheal position by gently placing the index fingers on either side of the trachea just above the suprasternal notch and gently pressing backward. Normal tracheal position is midline; deviation to the left or right is abnormal. Tracheal deviation occurs away from the side of a tension pneumothorax or a neck mass, but toward the side of a pneumonectomy or lobar atelectasis.

Symmetry of chest expansion and extent of movement are determined at the level of the diaphragm. Place your hands over the lower anterior chest wall along the costal margin and move them inward until the thumbs meet at midline. Ask the patient to breathe deeply. Observe the movement of the thumbs away from each other. Normal expansion is 1 inch (2.5 cm). Hand placement on the posterior side of the chest is at the level of the tenth rib. Move the thumbs until they meet over the spine (Fig. 27.5). You can check expansion anteriorly or posteriorly. It is not necessary to check both.

Normal chest movement is equal. Unequal expansion occurs when air entry is limited by conditions involving the lung (e.g., atelectasis, pneumothorax) or the chest wall (e.g., incisional

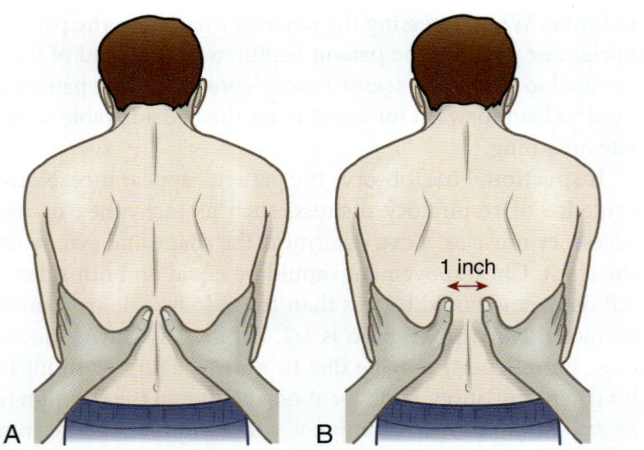

Fig. 27.5 Estimation of thoracic expansion. (A) Exhalation. (B) Maximal inhalation.

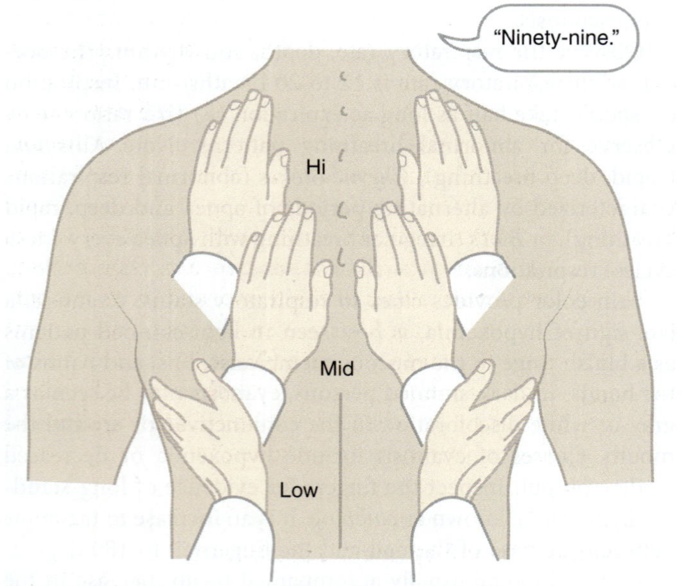

Fig. 27.6 Hand position for tactile fremitus. Place the palms of the hands in the position designated as *"low"* on the right and left sides of the chest. Compare the intensity of vibrations. Continue for all positions in each sequence.

pain). Equal but decreased expansion occurs in conditions that produce a hyperinflated or barrel chest or in neuromuscular diseases (e.g., amyotrophic lateral sclerosis, spinal cord lesions). Movement may be absent or unequal over a pleural effusion, an atelectasis, or a pneumothorax.

Fremitus is the vibration of the chest wall made by vocalization. You can feel tactile fremitus by placing the palmar surface of your hands against the patient's chest with the fingers hyperextended. Ask the patient to repeat a phrase, such as "boy-oh-boy," "toy boat," or "blue balloons," in a deeper, louder-than-normal voice. At the same time, move your hands from top to bottom on the patient's chest (Fig. 27.6). As you palpate, simultaneously compare vibrations (right side vs. left side, from top to bottom). Tactile fremitus is most intense by the sternum and between the scapulae because these areas are closest to the major bronchi. Fremitus is less intense farther away from these areas.

TABLE 27.5 Percussion Sounds

Sound	Description
Dull	Sound with medium-intensity pitch and duration heard over areas of "mixed" solid and lung tissue, such as top area of liver, partially consolidated lung tissue (pneumonia), or fluid-filled pleural space
Flat	Soft, high-pitched sound of short duration heard over very dense tissue where air is not present, such as posterior chest below level of diaphragm
Hyperresonance	Loud, lower pitched sound than normal resonance heard over hyperinflated lungs, such as in chronic obstructive pulmonary disease and acute asthma
Resonance	Low-pitched sound heard over normal lungs
Tympany	Drum-like, loud, empty quality sound heard over pneumothorax

Note any increase, decrease, or absence of fremitus. Increased fremitus occurs when the lung becomes filled with fluid or is denser. As the patient's voice moves through a dense tissue or fluid, you can feel that the vibration is increased. This happens with pneumonia, lung tumors, thick bronchial secretions, and above a pleural effusion (the lung is compressed upward). Fremitus is decreased if the hand is farther from the lung (e.g., pleural effusion) or the lung is hyperinflated (e.g., barrel chest). Absent fremitus may occur with pneumothorax or atelectasis. The anterior chest is harder to palpate for fremitus because of the large muscles and breast tissue.

Percussion. Percussion is used to assess the density or aeration of the lungs. Percussion sounds are described in Table 27.5.

The anterior chest is percussed with the patient in a semi-sitting or supine position. Starting above the clavicles, percuss downward, intercostal space by intercostal space. The area over lung tissue should be resonant, except for the area of cardiac dullness. To percuss the posterior chest, have the patient sit leaning forward with arms folded. The posterior chest should be resonant over lung tissue to the level of the diaphragm.

Auscultation. During chest auscultation, have the patient breathe slowly and a little more deeply than normal through the mouth. Auscultation should proceed from the lung apices to the bases, comparing opposite areas of the chest. If the patient is in mild respiratory distress or you think the patient will tire easily, start at the bases. Place the stethoscope over lung tissue, not over bony prominences. At each placement of the stethoscope, listen to at least 1 cycle of inspiration and expiration. Visualize the location of normal breath sounds (Fig. 27.7).

Lung sounds are heard anteriorly from a line drawn perpendicular from the sternum lateral to the midclavicular line. From the xiphoid process, palpate inferiorly (down) 2 ribs in the midaxillary line and around to the posterior chest. This gives you a fairly accurate and easy way to locate the lung fields. When recording the location of lung sounds, divide the anterior and posterior right lung into thirds (upper, middle, and lower) and the left lung into upper and lower areas. With practice, you will be able to identify which lobes of the lung has particular lung sounds.

The 3 normal breath sounds are bronchial, bronchovesicular, and vesicular (Fig. 27.8). *Bronchial sounds* are loud,

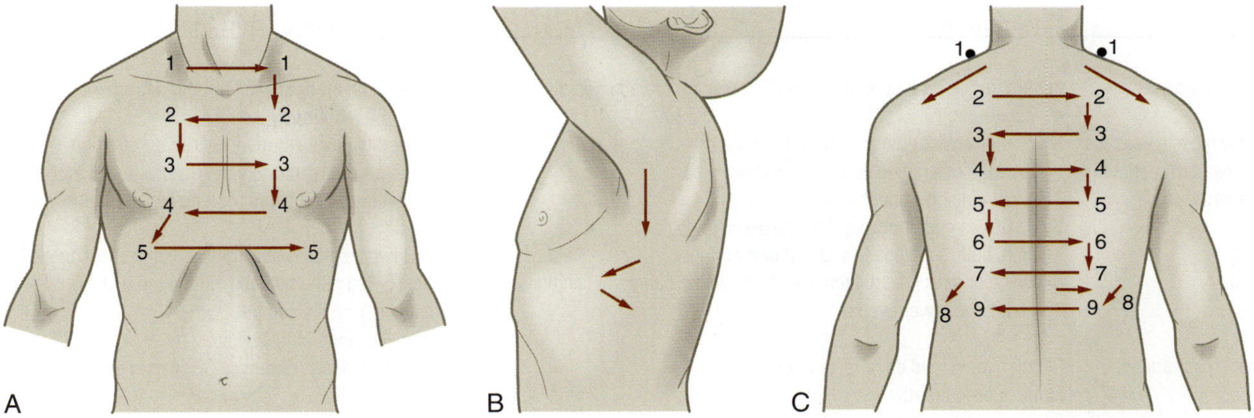

Fig. 27.7 Sequence for auscultation of the chest. (A) Anterior sequence. (B) Lateral sequence. (C) Posterior sequence. Place the stethoscope at each position and listen to at least 1 complete inspiratory and expiratory cycle. Keep in mind that with a female patient the breast tissue will influence the anterior examination.

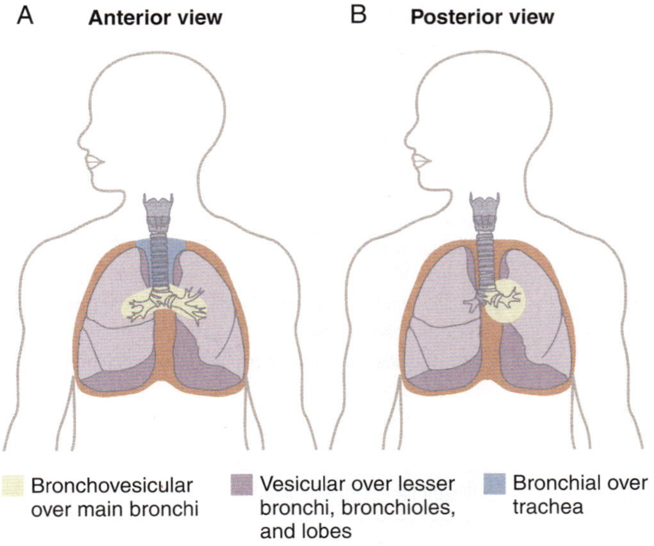

Fig. 27.8 Normal auscultatory sounds. (A) Anterior view. (B) Posterior view.

high-pitched sounds that resemble air blowing through a hollow pipe. Bronchial sounds have an inspiratory to expiratory (I/E) ratio of 2:3, with a gap between inspiration and expiration. To hear bronchial breath sounds, place the stethoscope next to the trachea in the neck. *Bronchovesicular sounds* have a medium pitch and intensity. They are best heard anteriorly between the first and second intercostal space and posteriorly between the scapulae. Bronchovesicular sounds have a 1:1 ratio, with inspiration equal to expiration. *Vesicular sounds* are relatively soft, low-pitched, gentle, rustling sounds. They are heard over all lung areas except the major bronchi. Vesicular sounds have a 3:1 ratio, with inspiration 3 times longer than expiration.

We classify breath sounds into 2 main categories: normal and abnormal (adventitious). There are a variety of terms that we have used inconsistently to describe abnormal breath sounds. **Adventitious breath sounds** include crackles (fine and coarse), wheezes, stridor, and pleural friction rub (Table 27.6). A *focused assessment* is used to evaluate the status of previously identified respiratory problems and to monitor for signs of new problems. Box 27.2 shows a focused assessment of the respiratory system.

As you begin your assessment of lung sounds, first note the air entry, which may be adequate, slightly decreased, or decreased. Absent air entry in any part of the lung is an assessment finding that you should report at once. Next, listen for the breath sounds and the presence of normal and adventitious sounds. Are the normal breath sounds where you would expect to hear them? Focus your assessment on the characteristics of any abnormal sound, including the location, pitch (e.g., high, low), duration of sound, and whether the sound is heard on inspiration, expiration, or both.

Assessment abnormalities of the thorax and lungs are outlined in Table 27.6. A record of the normal physical assessment of the respiratory system is shown in Table 27.7. Chest examination findings in common pulmonary problems are described in Table 27.8. Age-related changes in the respiratory system and assessment findings are outlined in Table 27.1.

Case Study

Objective Data: Physical Assessment

(© Fuse/ Thinkstock.)

Physical assessment findings of F.T. are as follows:

Temp: 38°C (100.4°F), apical pulse 110 (irregular), respiratory rate 30 (regular, shallow, slightly labored), BP 170/90 mm Hg. Sitting on edge of bed with arms resting on bedside table. Skin color normal for race with no signs of cyanosis. Using accessory muscles in neck and shoulders. Trachea midline. Barrel-shaped chest; chest expansion minimal but equal. Prolonged expiration. Slight clubbing noted. Edema: 3+ pitting edema of both lower legs and feet, bilaterally. Lungs: adequate air entry at apices bilaterally with fine crackles; decreased air entry to right middle lobe and both bases with coarse crackles. Slight expiratory wheeze heard throughout all lung fields. Cough: moist, productive, with yellow-tinged sputum.

You decide to check F.T.'s O_2 saturation (SpO_2). His SpO_2 is 87% on room air.

Discussion Questions

1. What physical assessment findings concern you most?
2. Identify 3 interventions that may be implemented immediately.
3. With F.T.'s physical assessment information, what diagnostic studies would you expect to be ordered?

You will learn about diagnostic studies of the respiratory system in the next section.

Answers available at http://evolve.elsevier.com/Lewis/medsurg.

TABLE 27.6 ASSESSMENT ABNORMALITIES

Respiratory System

Finding	Description	Common Etiology and Significance
Inspection		
Abdominal paradox	Inward (rather than normal outward) movement of abdomen during inspiration	Inefficient and ineffective breathing pattern; nonspecific sign of severe respiratory distress
Accessory muscle use. Intercostal retractions	Neck and shoulder muscles used to assist breathing; muscles between ribs pull in during inspiration	COPD, asthma exacerbation, secretion retention Indicates severe respiratory distress/failure, hypoxemia
↑ AP diameter	AP chest diameter equal to lateral. Slope of ribs more horizontal (90 degrees) to spine	COPD, asthma, cystic fibrosis, lung hyperinflation, advanced age
Clubbing	↑ Depth, bulk, sponginess of distal part of finger	Chronic hypoxemia, cystic fibrosis, lung cancer, bronchiectasis
Cyanosis	Bluish color of skin best seen in lips and on the palpebral conjunctiva (inside the lower eyelid)	Reflects 5–6 g of hemoglobin not bound with O_2. ↓ O_2 transfer in lungs, ↓ cardiac output. Nonspecific, unreliable indicator
Kussmaul respirations	Regular, rapid, and deep respirations Fruity odor to breath	Metabolic acidosis. Increases CO_2 excretion
Pursed-lip breathing	Exhalation through mouth with lips pursed together to slow exhalation	COPD, asthma. Suggests ↑ breathlessness Strategy taught to slow expiration, ↓ dyspnea
Splinting	Voluntary ↓ in tidal volume to ↓ pain on chest expansion	Thoracic or abdominal incision, chest trauma, pleurisy
Tachypnea	Rate >20 breaths/min	Fever, anxiety, hypoxemia, restrictive lung disease Magnitude of ↑ above normal rate reflects ↑ work of breathing
Tripod position. Inability to lie flat	Leaning forward with arms and elbows supported on overbed table	COPD, asthma exacerbation, pulmonary edema Indicates moderate to severe respiratory distress
Palpation		
Altered chest movement	Unequal or equal but ↓ movement of 2 sides of chest with inspiration	Unequal movement caused by atelectasis, pneumothorax, pleural effusion, splinting Equal but ↓ movement caused by barrel chest, restrictive disease, neuromuscular disease
Altered tactile fremitus	↑ or ↓ in vibrations	↑ in pneumonia, pulmonary edema. ↓ in pleural effusion, lung hyperinflation. Absent in pneumothorax, atelectasis
Tracheal deviation	Leftward or rightward movement of trachea from normal midline position	Nonspecific sign of change in position of mediastinal structures. Medical emergency if caused by tension pneumothorax (trachea deviates to side opposite collapsed lung)
Percussion		
Dullness	Medium-pitched sound over areas that normally make a resonant sound	↑ Density (pneumonia, large atelectasis), ↑ fluid in pleural space (pleural effusion)
Hyperresonance	Loud, lower pitched sound over areas that normally make a resonant sound	Lung hyperinflation (COPD), lung collapse (pneumothorax), air trapping (asthma)
Auscultation		
Absent breath sounds	No sound heard over entire lung or area of lung	Pneumothorax, pleural effusion, mainstem bronchi obstruction, large atelectasis, pneumonectomy, lobectomy
Bronchophony, whispered pectoriloquy	Spoken or whispered syllable more distinct than normal on auscultation	Pneumonia
Coarse crackles	Louder, discontinuous, low-pitched sounds caused by air passing through airway intermittently occluded by mucus, unstable bronchial wall. May be heard on inspiration, expiration, or both. Similar sound to blowing through straw under water	Excess fluid within the lungs, heart failure, pulmonary edema, pneumonia with severe congestion, COPD
Egophony	Spoken "E" similar to "A" on auscultation because of altered transmission of voice sounds	Pneumonia, pleural effusion
Fine crackles	Short, discontinuous, high-pitched sounds heard just before the end of inspiration. Result of rapid equalization of gas pressure when collapsed alveoli or terminal bronchioles suddenly snap open. Similar sound to that made by rolling hair between fingers	Interstitial edema (early pulmonary edema), alveolar filling (pneumonia), loss of lung volume (atelectasis), early phase of heart failure, idiopathic pulmonary fibrosis
Pleural friction rub	Creaking or grating sound from roughened, inflamed pleural surfaces rubbing together. Evident during inspiration, expiration, or both. No change with coughing. Often uncomfortable, especially on deep inspiration	Pleurisy, pneumonia, pulmonary infarct
Stridor	Continuous musical or crowing sound of constant pitch. Result of partial obstruction of larynx or trachea	Croup, epiglottitis, vocal cord edema after extubation, foreign body
Wheezes	Continuous high-pitched squeaking or musical sound caused by rapid vibration of bronchial walls. First evident on expiration but possibly evident on inspiration as obstruction of airway increases. May be audible without stethoscope	Bronchospasm (caused by asthma), airway obstruction (caused by foreign body, tumor), COPD

BOX 27.2 FOCUSED ASSESSMENT

Respiratory System

Use this checklist to make sure the key assessment steps have been done.

Subjective

Ask the patient about any of the following and note responses.

Shortness of breath	Y	N
Pain with breathing	Y	N
Cough	Y	N
Sputum production (color, quantity)	Y	N
Wheezing	Y	N

Objective: Physical Assessment

Observe

Respirations: Rate, quality, and pattern
Accessory muscle use
Mouth or nose breathing

Inspect

Neck for position of trachea
Shape, symmetry, and movement of chest wall
Skin and nails for integrity and color

Palpate

Chest and back for abnormalities (i.e., masses)

Auscultate

Lung sounds (anterior and posterior)

Objective: Diagnostic

Check the following diagnostic tests for abnormal results.

Arterial blood gases
Chest x-ray
Hemoglobin
Hematocrit

DIAGNOSTIC STUDIES OF RESPIRATORY SYSTEM

Numerous diagnostic studies are available to assess the respiratory system. Select studies are described in more detail here.

Two methods are used to assess the effectiveness of gas transfer in the lung and tissue oxygenation: (1) oximetry and (2) analysis of *arterial blood gases* (ABGs) (Table 27.9). These are primarily used to assess for hypoxia. For the patient with normal or near-normal cardiac function, assessing SaO_2 or PaO_2 is usually enough to determine the level of oxygenation. With either one, we can also use CO_2 monitoring to assess for hypercapnia to determine patient's oxygenation and ventilatory status. The patient with impaired cardiac output or hemodynamic instability (e.g., altered level of consciousness, changes in heart rate and rhythm, low BP) may have inadequate tissue O_2 delivery and/or abnormal O_2 consumption. For these patients, we can evaluate venous O_2 saturation values.

TABLE 27.7 Normal Physical Assessment of the Respiratory System

Nose	• Symmetric with no deformities • Nasal mucosa pink, moist with no edema, exudate, blood, or polyps • Nasal septum straight (slight nasal deviation possible) • Nares patent bilaterally
Oral mucosa	• Light pink, moist, no exudate or ulcerations
Pharynx	• Smooth, moist, and pink
Neck	• Trachea midline
Chest	• AP diameter 1:2 • Respirations nonlabored at 12–20 breaths/min • Breath sounds vesicular without crackles or wheezes • Expansion equal bilaterally with no increase in tactile fremitus

TABLE 27.8 Chest Assessment Findings in Respiratory Problems

Problem	Inspection	Palpation	Percussion	Auscultation
Asthma exacerbation	Prolonged expiration, tripod position, pursed lips	↓ Movement	Hyperresonance	Wheezes, ↓ breath sounds ominous sign (severely decreased air movement)
Atelectasis	No change unless involves entire segment, lobe	If small, no change If large, ↓ movement, ↓ fremitus	Dull over affected area	Fine crackles (may disappear with deep breaths) Absent sounds if large
COPD	Barrel chest, cyanosis, tripod position, use of accessory muscles	↓ Movement	Hyperresonant or dull if consolidation	Crackles, wheezes, distant breath sounds
Pleural effusion	Tachypnea, use of accessory muscles	↑ Movement ↑ Fremitus above effusion Absent fremitus over effusion	Dull	↓ or absent over effusion, egophony above effusion
Pneumonia	Tachypnea, use of accessory muscles, duskiness or cyanosis	↑ Fremitus over affected area	Dull over affected areas	*Early:* Bronchial sounds *Later:* Fine and/or coarse crackles, egophony, whispered pectoriloquy
Pulmonary edema	Tachypnea, labored respirations, cyanosis, pink-tinged sputum	↓ Movement or normal movement	Dull or normal depending on amount of fluid	Fine or coarse crackles
Pulmonary fibrosis	Tachypnea	↓ Movement	Normal	Crackles or sounds like Velcro being pulled apart

TABLE 27.9 Diagnostic Studies

Oxygenation

Study	Description and Purpose	Nursing Responsibility
Arterial blood gases (ABGs)	Arterial blood is obtained through puncture of radial or femoral artery or through arterial catheter. Done to assess acid-base balance, oxygenation/ventilation status, need for and/or change in O_2 therapy, or change in ventilator settings. See Table 27.13 for reference values.	*Before:* Indicate whether patient is using O_2 (flow rate in L/min). Avoid change in O_2 therapy or interventions (e.g., suctioning, position change) for 15 min before obtaining sample. *During:* Assist with positioning (e.g., palm up, wrist slightly hyperextended if radial artery is used). Collect blood in heparinized syringe. To ensure accurate results, expel all air bubbles. *After:* Apply pressure to radial artery for at least 5 min after specimen is obtained to prevent hematoma at the arterial puncture site. Send sample to lab promptly for analysis.
O_2 Monitoring		
Noninvasive oximetry (SpO_2)	Monitors arterial O_2 saturation. Probe attaches to finger, toe, earlobe, bridge of the nose for SpO_2 monitoring. Used for intermittent or continuous monitoring and exercise testing. *Normal SpO2:* >95%	*During:* Apply probe. When interpreting SpO_2 values, first assess patient status and presence of factors that can alter accuracy of pulse oximeter reading. These include motion, low perfusion, cold extremities, bright lights, acrylic nails, dark skin color, carbon monoxide, and anemia.
Invasive oximetry ($ScvO_2$/SvO_2)	Monitors venous O_2 saturation intermittently by obtaining a blood sample from the PA catheter or continuously via a fiberoptic sensor as part of a specific central line and monitor. *Normal ScvO2/SvO2:* 60%–80%	*During:* Make sure the equipment is properly placed and prepped. Changes in these values provide an early warning of a change in cardiac output or tissue O_2 delivery. A decrease suggests that less O_2 is being delivered to the tissues or that more O_2 is being consumed.
CO_2 Monitoring		
End-tidal CO_2 ($PetCO_2$) (capnography) (see Fig. 27.9)	Assesses the level of CO_2 in exhaled air. Graphically displays partial pressure of CO_2. Expired gases are sampled from patient's airway and analyzed by a CO_2 sensor to measure exhaled CO_2. Sensor may be attached to an adaptor on endotracheal or tracheostomy tube. A nasal cannula with a side stream capnometer can be used in patients without an artificial airway. Can be a diagnostic measure to detect lung disease and for monitoring patients. *Normal difference between $PaCO_2$ and $PetCO_2$: 2–5 mm Hg ($PaCO_2$: 35–45 mm Hg; $PetCO_2$: 40–50 mm Hg).*	*Before:* Teach patient and caregiver about purpose of capnography monitoring, emphasizing the benefit of continuous monitoring. *During:* Make sure that sensor is properly attached. Record data per agency policy.

Oximetry

Oximetry is the measurement of the blood's O_2 saturation.[8] We can measure O_2 saturation in both arterial and venous blood. There are noninvasive and invasive means to measure these values.

Arterial

We monitor arterial O_2 saturation (SaO_2) noninvasively and continuously using *pulse oximetry.* We can place the probe on the finger, toe, ear, forehead, or bridge of the nose. The abbreviation SpO_2 is used to indicate the SaO_2. It represents how much O_2 hemoglobin is carrying compared to how much it could carry. SpO_2 and heart rate are displayed on the monitor as digital readings. Normal SpO_2 values are greater than 95% (Table 27.10).[9]

In many agencies, we assess SpO_2 with each routine vital sign check. SpO_2 values are used during exercise testing and when adjusting flow rates during O_2 therapy. Pulse oximetry is especially valuable in perioperative and critical care situations, in which anesthesia, sedation, or decreased consciousness may mask hypoxia. We can detect changes in SpO_2 and treat the patient quickly.

Pulse oximetry values are less accurate when the SpO_2 is less than 70%.[10] At this level, the oximeter may display a value that is ±4% of the actual value. For example, if the SpO_2 reading is 70%, the actual value can range from 66% to 74%. Pulse oximetry is inaccurate if hemoglobin variants (e.g., carboxyhemoglobin, methemoglobin) are present. Other factors that can alter the accuracy of pulse oximetry include motion, anemia, cold extremities, bright fluorescent lights, intravascular dyes, thick acrylic nails, and dark skin color. Accurate SpO_2 measurements may be hard to obtain on patients who are hypothermic, receiving IV vasopressor therapy (e.g., norepinephrine), or have hypoperfusion or vasoconstriction (e.g., shock).[11] If there is doubt about the accuracy of the SpO_2 reading, obtain an ABG analysis to verify the values.

Venous

Invasive O_2 saturation measurements include venous blood analysis (Table 27.11). Measuring the O_2 saturation of hemoglobin in venous blood helps to determine the adequacy of tissue oxygenation. The O_2 saturation of venous blood from a central venous catheter (CVC) is called *central venous O_2 saturation* ($ScvO_2$). The blood received and measured as $ScvO_2$ from

TABLE 27.10 Normal and Critical Values for PaO_2 and SpO_2

PaO_2 (mm Hg)	SpO_2 (%)	Significance	Manifestations	Management
80–100	≥95	Normal value	Asymptomatic	• Routine patient assessment
60–79	90	Mild hypoxemia	Restlessness, tachycardia, dysrhythmias, dyspnea, hypertension	• Assess patient as needed • Supplemental O_2 may be needed
40–59	88	Moderate hypoxemia	Confusion, lethargy, dysrhythmias, hypotension, respiratory distress, accessory muscle use	• O_2 required • Escalate level of care. Obtain critical care consult • Monitor frequently for sudden deterioration in condition
<40	75	Severe hypoxemia	Cyanosis, coma, respiratory and/or cardiac arrest possible	• High FIO_2, intubation, mechanical ventilation • Continuous patient assessment and evaluation

TABLE 27.11 Normal Mixed Venous Blood Gas Values

pH	7.31–7.41
PvO_2	38–42 mm Hg
SvO_2	60%–80%
$PvCO_2$	38–55 mm Hg
HCO_3^-	22–26 mEq/L (mmol/L)

$PvCO_2$, Partial pressure of CO_2 in venous blood; *PvO_2*, partial pressure of O_2 in venous blood; *SvO_2*, mixed venous O_2 saturation.

a CVC is primarily from the superior vena cava (SVC), which supplies the upper body (e.g., brain). The O_2 saturation of blood from a pulmonary artery (PA) catheter is the *mixed venous O_2 saturation* (SvO_2). SvO_2 values measured from the PA catheter are a mixture of blood from the SVC, inferior vena cava (IVC), and coronary return.

$ScvO_2$ and SvO_2 reflect the balance among oxygenation of the arterial blood, tissue perfusion, and tissue O_2 consumption (Table 27.12).[12] This gives a global indicator of the balance between O_2 delivery and O_2 consumption. Normal $ScvO_2$ or SvO_2 at rest is 60% to 80%. Even though these values vary slightly, we use both effectively in the treatment of critically ill patients in the ICU. $ScvO_2$ and SvO_2 are useful in assessing hemodynamic status and response to treatments or activities when considered in conjunction with SaO_2.

Carefully review sustained decreases and increases in $ScvO_2$ or SvO_2. Decreased $ScvO_2$ or SvO_2 may indicate decreased arterial oxygenation, low CO, low hemoglobin level, or increased O_2 consumption or extraction, which is the ability of tissues to take O2 from the blood. If the $ScvO_2$ or SvO_2 falls below 60%, determine which factor has changed. Observe for changes in arterial oxygenation (e.g., monitor pulse oximetry, ABGs) and indirectly assess CO and tissue perfusion. This is done by noting any changes in mental status, strength and quality of peripheral pulses, capillary refill, urine output, and skin color and temperature. If arterial oxygenation, CO, and hemoglobin level are unchanged, a fall in $ScvO_2$ or SvO_2 indicates increased O_2 consumption or extraction. This could represent an increased metabolic rate, pain, movement, fever, or shivering. If O_2 consumption increases without a comparable increase in O_2 delivery, more O_2 is extracted from the blood. $ScvO_2$ and SvO_2 will continue to fall.[12]

Increased $ScvO_2$ or SvO_2 may indicate a clinical improvement (e.g., increased arterial O_2 saturation, improved perfusion, decreased metabolic rate) or problem (e.g., sepsis). In sepsis, O_2 is not extracted properly at the tissue level related to the immune response, leaking vessels, and increased fluid build-up, resulting in increased $ScvO_2$ or SvO_2.

Changes in $ScvO_2$ or SvO_2 guide your interventions. For example, you may note that the patient's HR increased slightly during repositioning but that the $ScvO_2$ remained stable. In this case, you would conclude that the patient tolerated the position change. If the $ScvO_2$ dropped, this would be a sign to stop the activity until the $ScvO_2$ returned to baseline.

In many cases, as activity or metabolism increases, HR and CO increase, and $ScvO_2$ or SvO_2 stays constant or varies slightly. However, critically ill patients often have conditions (e.g., HF, shock) that prevent substantial increases in CO. In these cases, $ScvO_2$ or SvO_2 can be a useful indicator of the balance between O_2 delivery and consumption.

Arterial Blood Gases

ABGs are obtained to determine oxygenation status and acid-base balance. ABG analysis includes measurement of the PaO_2, $PaCO_2$ (the partial pressure of CO_2 in arterial blood), acidity (pH), bicarbonate (HCO_3^-), and SaO_2. Normal values for ABGs are shown in Table 27.13.

Blood for ABG analysis can be obtained by arterial puncture or from an arterial catheter, which is usually inserted into the radial or femoral artery. Both techniques allow for intermittent analysis. An arterial catheter permits ABG sampling without repeated arterial punctures. The normal PaO_2 decreases with advancing age. It varies in relation to the distance above sea level. At higher altitudes, the barometric pressure is lower, resulting in a lower inspired O_2 pressure and a lower PaO_2.

CO_2 Monitoring

CO_2 can be monitored using transcutaneous CO_2 ($PtCO_2$) and end-tidal CO_2 ($PetCO_2$) capnography. Transcutaneous measurement of CO_2 is a noninvasive method of estimating arterial pressure of CO_2 ($PaCO_2$) using an electrode placed on the skin.[13]

$PetCO_2$ is the noninvasive measurement of alveolar CO_2 during exhalation when CO_2 concentration is at its peak

TABLE 27.12 Interpreting $ScvO_2$ and SvO_2 Measurements

$ScvO_2$ and SvO_2 Measurement[a]	Physiologic Basis for Change in $ScvO_2$ or SvO_2	Clinical Diagnosis and Rationale
High $ScvO_2$ or SvO_2 (80%–95%)	↑ O_2 supply ↓ O_2 demand	• Patient receiving more O_2 than needed by clinical condition • Anesthesia, which causes sedation and ↓ muscle movement • Hypothermia, which ↓ metabolic demand (e.g., with cardiopulmonary bypass) • Sepsis caused by ↓ ability of tissues to use O_2 at the cellular level • False high positive because pulmonary artery catheter is wedged in a pulmonary capillary (SvO_2 only)
Normal $ScvO_2$ or SvO_2 (60%–80%)	Normal O_2 supply and metabolic demand	• Balanced O_2 supply and demand
Low $ScvO_2$ or SvO_2 (<60%)	↓ O_2 supply caused by low hemoglobin Low arterial saturation (SaO_2) Low cardiac output ↑ O_2 demand	• Anemia or bleeding with compromised cardiopulmonary system • Hypoxemia resulting from ↓ O_2 supply or lung disease • Cardiogenic shock caused by left ventricular pump failure • Metabolic demand exceeds O_2 supply in conditions that ↑ muscle movement and metabolic rate (e.g., seizures, fever)

[a]$ScvO_2$ values are generally slightly higher than SvO_2 values.
Source: Urden LD, Stacy KM, Lough ME: *Critical care nursing: diagnosis and management,* ed 9, St Louis, 2022, Elsevier.

TABLE 27.13 Normal Arterial Blood Gas Values

Laboratory Value	Sea Level BP 760 mm Hg	1 Mile Above Sea Level BP 629 mm Hg
pH	7.35–7.45	7.35–7.45
PaO_2	80–100 mm Hg	65–75 mm Hg
SaO_2	>95%	>95%
$PaCO_2$	35–45 mm Hg	35–45 mm Hg
HCO_3-	22–26 mEq/L (mmol/L)	22–26 mEq/L (mmol/L)

BP, Barometric pressure; *HCO_3–*, bicarbonate; *PaO_2*, partial pressure of O_2 in arterial blood; *$PaCO_2$*, partial pressure of arterial CO_2; *SaO_2*, arterial O_2 saturation.

(Fig. 27.9). It is used to monitor and assess trends in the patient's ventilatory status. Expired gases are sampled from the patient's airway and are analyzed by a CO_2 sensor that uses infrared light to measure exhaled CO_2. The sensor may be attached to an adaptor on the endotracheal tube or the tracheostomy tube. A nasal cannula with a sidestream capnometer can be used in patients without an artificial airway. Capnography is usually presented as a graph of expiratory CO_2 plotted against time.[14]

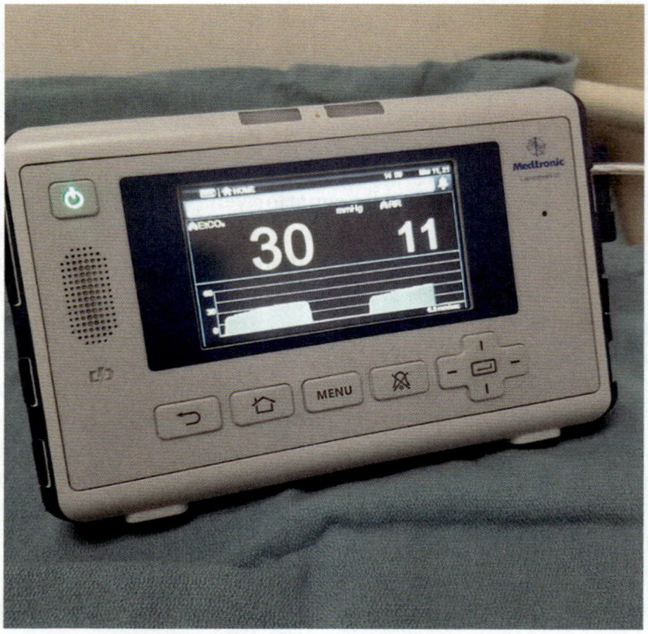

Fig. 27.9 End-tidal CO_2 detector.

Sputum Studies

Observe the patient's sputum for color, volume, viscosity, and presence or absence of blood. We can obtain a sputum sample by expectoration, tracheal suction, or bronchoscopy. When the patient is unable to expectorate spontaneously, sputum may be collected by inhaling an irritating aerosol, usually hypertonic saline. This is called *sputum induction*.

Specimens may be examined for culture and sensitivity to identify an infecting organism (e.g., *Mycobacterium*) or to confirm a diagnosis (e.g., cancer). Table 27.14 describes common sputum tests and our responsibilities when obtaining samples.

Skin Tests

Skin tests may be done to assess for allergies (see Chapter 14) or exposure to TB bacilli or fungi. Skin tests involve the intradermal injection of an antigen. Table 27.15 discusses how to interpret tuberculin skin testing. For example, a positive result on a TB skin test means that the patient has been exposed to the antigen. It does not mean that the patient has TB. A negative result means either no exposure or a depression of cell-mediated immunity, which occurs in HIV infection.

Our responsibilities are similar for all skin tests. First, to prevent a false-negative reaction, be sure that the injection is intradermal and not subcutaneous. After the injection, circle the site(s) and tell the patient not to remove the marks. When charting administration of the antigen, draw a diagram of the forearm and hand, and label the injection site. The diagram is especially helpful when the patient receives more than one test.

When reading test results, use a good light. If an induration is present, use a marking pen to indicate the periphery on all

TABLE 27.14 Sputum Studies

Study	Description and Purpose	Nursing Responsibility
Acid-fast bacteria (AFB) smear and culture	2 different tests used to assess sputum for acid-fast bacilli (e.g., *Mycobacterium tuberculosis*). In AFB smear (a rapid test), sputum sample spread thinly on glass slide, treated with a fluorochrome stain, and examined under a microscope for AFB. Culture for AFB may take up to 6 weeks.	*During:* Obtain specimen in early morning after mouth care because secretions collect during night. Have patient expectorate sputum into container after coughing deeply. If unsuccessful, try increasing oral fluid intake unless fluids are restricted. Can collect sputum in sterile container (sputum trap) during suctioning via endotracheal tube or by aspirating secretions from the trachea. If patient cannot produce specimen, they may need bronchoscopy (Fig. 27.10). *After:* Send specimen to laboratory promptly for analysis.
Culture and sensitivity	Diagnose bacterial infection, select antibiotic, and evaluate treatment. Sputum specimen collected in a sterile container. Takes 48–72 hr for results.	
Cytology	Determines presence of abnormal cells that may indicate cancer. Single sputum specimen collected in special container with fixative solution.	
Gram stain	Sputum staining allows for classification of bacteria into gram-negative and gram-positive types. Results guide therapy until culture and sensitivity results are complete.	

TABLE 27.15 Interpreting TB Skin Testing

Types of Responses	Consider Positive in the Following Groups
Positive Reactions	
≥5-mm induration	• HIV-infected people • People who had recent contact with a person with TB disease • People with fibrotic lesions on chest x-ray consistent with prior TB • Patients with organ transplants • Immunosuppressed persons (e.g., taking the equivalent of ≥15 mg/day of prednisone for ≥1 months)
≥10-mm induration	• Recent immigrants (<5 years) from high-prevalence countries • Injecting drug users • Residents and employees of high-risk congregate settings • Mycobacteriology laboratory personnel • People with clinical conditions (e.g., diabetes mellitus, end-stage kidney disease) that place them at high risk
≥15-mm induration	• Any person (including those with no known risk factors for TB)
False Reactions	**Possible Causes**
False-negative reactions (do not react even though infected)	• Anergy, immunosuppression • Recent TB infection (within 8–10 weeks of exposure) • Overwhelming TB infection • Very old TB infection (many years) • Recent live virus vaccination (e.g., measles, chickenpox)
False-positive reactions (react even though not infected)	• Nontuberculous mycobacteria (e.g., *Mycobacterium avium-intracellulare* [MAI] or *Mycobacterium avium* complex [MAC]) • Previous BCG vaccine

Source: Centers for Disease Control and Prevention: Tuberculosis (TB) fact sheet: tuberculin skin testing. Retrieved from www.cdc.gov/tb/publications/factsheets/testing/skintesting.htm.

4 sides of the induration. As the pen touches the raised area, make a mark. Then determine the diameter of the induration in millimeters. Do not measure reddened, flat areas.

Endoscopy

Bronchoscopy

Bronchoscopy is a procedure in which the bronchi are seen through a fiberoptic tube (Fig. 27.10). Bronchoscopy may be used for diagnostic purposes (obtain biopsy specimens) and for treatment (e.g., to remove mucous plugs, foreign bodies). Laser therapy, electrocautery, cryotherapy, and stents may be placed through a bronchoscope to achieve patency of an airway that has been partially or nearly fully obstructed by tumors (Table 27.16).

Bronchoscopy can be done in an outpatient procedure room, surgery, or at the bedside in the critical care or medical-surgical unit. The patient may be positioned supine, in low-Fowler's, or even be seated. The HCP inserts the bronchoscope through the nose or mouth. Depending on the approach, the nasopharynx or oropharynx is anesthetized with local anesthetic spray. The bronchoscope is coated with water-soluble lubricant and inserted down into the airways. Small amounts (30 mL) of sterile saline may be injected through the scope and withdrawn and examined for cells, a technique termed *bronchoalveolar lavage* (BAL). Bronchoscopy can be done through the endotracheal tube of a mechanically ventilated patient.

Lung Biopsy

Lung biopsy may be done (1) transbronchially, (2) percutaneously or via transthoracic needle aspiration (TTNA), (3) by video-assisted thoracic surgery (VATS), or (4) as an open lung biopsy (Table 27.16). The purpose of a lung biopsy is to obtain tissue, cells, and/or fluid for evaluation. Specimens can be cultured or examined for cancer cells.

Transbronchial biopsy involves passing a forceps or needle through the bronchoscope for a specimen. A combination of transbronchial lung biopsy and BAL is used to distinguish infection and rejection in lung transplant recipients. A percutaneous

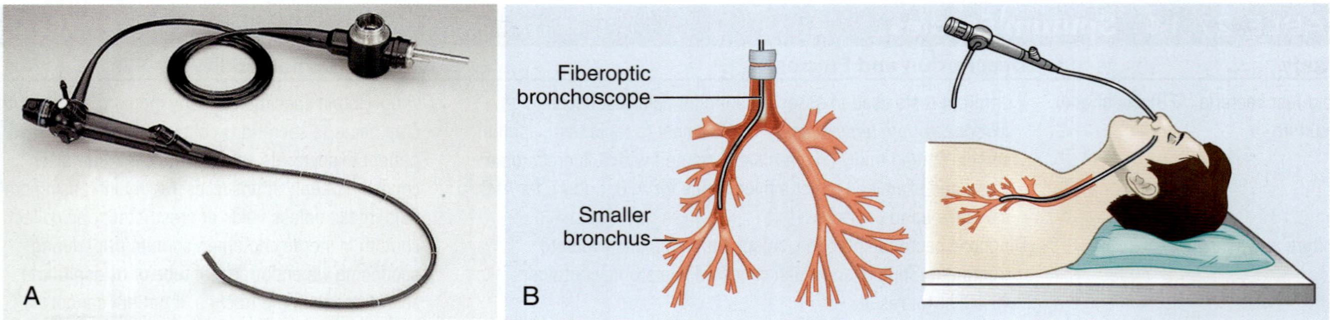

Fig. 27.10 Fiberoptic bronchoscope. (A) The transbronchoscopic balloon-tipped catheter and the flexible fiberoptic bronchoscope. (B) The catheter is introduced into a small airway and the balloon inflated with 1.5 to 2 mL of air to occlude the airway. Bronchoalveolar lavage is done by injecting and withdrawing 30-mL aliquots of sterile saline solution, gently aspirating after each instillation. Specimens are sent to the laboratory for analysis. (A, Courtesy Olympus America Inc, Melville, NY.)

TABLE 27.16 Diagnostic Studies

Respiratory System

Study	Description and Purpose	Nursing Responsibility
Endoscopy		
Bronchoscopy (Fig. 27.10)	Flexible fiberoptic scope used for diagnosis, biopsy, specimen collection, or assessment of changes. May be done to suction mucous plugs, lavage lungs, or remove foreign objects.	*Before:* Obtain signed consent. Have patient be NPO for 6–12 hr before the test. Give sedative as ordered. *After:* Keep patient NPO until gag reflex returns. Monitor for recovery from sedation. Blood-tinged mucus is not abnormal. If biopsy was done, monitor for hemorrhage and pneumothorax.
Lung biopsy	Specimens may be obtained by transbronchial or percutaneous biopsy or via transthoracic needle aspiration (TTNA), video-assisted thoracoscopic surgery (VATS), or open lung biopsy. Transbronchial biopsy and VATS can be done in the bronchoscopy suite. TTNA done under CT guidance in radiology department. Open lung and VATS done in the OR. Tests used to obtain specimens for laboratory analysis.	*Before:* Obtain signed consent. Same as bronchoscopy if procedure done with bronchoscope, and same as thoracotomy if open lung biopsy done. *After TTNA:* Check breath sounds q4hr for 24 hr and report any respiratory distress. Check incision site for bleeding. Chest x-ray should be done after TTNA or transbronchial biopsy to check for pneumothorax. *After VATS:* A chest tube may be placed postprocedure until lung has reexpanded. Monitor breath sounds to follow chest reexpansion. Encourage deep breathing for lung reinflation.
Mediastinoscopy	Scope inserted through a small incision in suprasternal notch and advanced into mediastinum to inspect and biopsy lymph nodes. Used to diagnose lung cancer, non-Hodgkin lymphoma, granulomatous infections, and sarcoidosis.	*Before:* Obtain signed consent. Prepare patient for surgery. Performed in OR using a general anesthetic. *After:* Monitor as for bronchoscopy.
Exercise Testing	Used to diagnose and determine exercise capacity. A *complete test* involves walking on a treadmill while monitoring expired O_2 and CO_2, respiratory rate, heart rate, and heart rhythm. In a *modified test* (desaturation test), only SpO_2 is monitored.	*Before:* Have patient wear comfortable shoes. *During:* Encourage patient to hold handlebars on treadmill and walk as quickly as possible.
Pulmonary Function Tests	Used to evaluate lung function. Involves use of spirometer to assess air movement as patient performs prescribed respiratory maneuvers (Tables 27.17 and 27.18).	*Before:* Avoid scheduling immediately after mealtime. Avoid administration of inhaled bronchodilator 6 hr before. Assess for respiratory distress. *During:* Assess for respiratory distress. *After:* Assess for respiratory distress. Provide rest after procedure.
Radiology		
Chest x-ray	Used to screen, diagnose, and evaluate changes in respiratory system. Most common views are anteroposterior (AP) and lateral.	*Before:* Have patient undress to waist, put on gown, and remove any metal between neck and waist.
Computed tomography (CT) scan	Diagnose suspicious lesions difficult to assess (e.g., mediastinum, hilum, pleura) by conventional x-ray. Common types are helical or spiral CT (contrast medium usually used) and high-resolution CT scan (contrast medium not used). Spiral CT used to diagnose a pulmonary embolism.	*Before:* Before contrast medium used, evaluate renal function. Assess if patient is allergic to shellfish, since the contrast is iodine based. Patient may need to be NPO 4 hr prior to study. *During:* Warn patient that contrast injection may cause a feeling of being warm and flushed. Patient must lie completely still during scan. *After:* Encourage patient to drink fluids to avoid renal problems with any contrast.

TABLE 27.16 **Diagnostic Studies—cont'd**

Respiratory System

Study	Description and Purpose	Nursing Responsibility
Magnetic resonance imaging (MRI)	Used for in-depth diagnosis of lesions difficult to assess by CT scan (e.g., lung apex) and for differentiating vascular from nonvascular structures. An IV contrast agent (gadolinium) may be given.	*Before:* Oral and/or IV contrast injection may be used. Check for pregnancy, allergies, and renal function before test. Have patient remove all metal objects. Remove metallic foil patches. Contraindicated for persons with implanted metallic devices or other metal fragments unless noted to be MRI safe. Ask about any history of surgical insertion of staples, plates, dental bridges, or other metal appliances. Patient may need to be fasting. Assess for claustrophobia and the need for antianxiety medication. *During:* Patient must lie completely still during scan.
Positron emission tomography (PET) scan	Glucose-containing nuclear tracer substance injected and taken up by metabolically active cells. Follow-up scan shows different-colored tissues based on metabolic rate. Because cancer cells have an increased uptake of glucose, "hot spots" reflecting increased glucose consumption indicate the presence of active cancer. Used to distinguish benign and cancerous lung nodules.	*Before:* Obtain IV access to inject the tracer substance. Patients should be NPO, except for water and medications, for at least 4 hr prior. Hold glucose-containing IV solutions and change to normal saline. Check blood glucose levels. The glucose level must be between 60–140 mg/dL (3.3–7.8 μmol/L) for accurate glucose metabolic activity. *During:* Patient must lie completely still during scan. *After:* Encourage fluids to excrete radioactive substance.
Pulmonary angiogram	Visualize pulmonary vasculature and locate obstruction or pathologic conditions (e.g., pulmonary embolus). Contrast medium injected through a catheter threaded into pulmonary artery or right side of heart. Series of x-rays taken after contrast medium is injected into pulmonary artery.	*Before:* Assess for allergies, especially to contrast dye. Have patient fast 6–12 hr before. Give sedative and other drugs, as ordered. *After:* Check pressure dressing site after procedure. Monitor BP, pulse, and circulation distal to injection site. Place compression device over site. Maintain IV and/or oral fluid intake.
Ventilation-perfusion (V/Q) scan	Assesses ventilation and perfusion of lungs. IV radioisotope given to assess perfusion. To assess ventilation, patient inhales a radioactive gas (xenon or krypton) that outlines alveoli. Normal scans show homogeneous radioactivity. ↓ or absent radioactivity suggests lack of perfusion or airflow. Ventilation without perfusion suggests a pulmonary embolus.	Same as for chest x-ray. *After:* No precautions needed afterward because the gas and isotope transmit radioactivity for only a brief interval.
6-Minute Walk Test	Used to measure functional capacity and response to treatment in patients with heart or lung disease. Pulse oximetry usually monitored during walk. Distance walked measured and used to monitor progression of disease or improvement after rehabilitation.	*During:* Patient walks as far as possible during 6 min, stopping when short of breath and continuing when able. Continually assess and observe patient tolerance to test.
Thoracentesis (Fig. 27.11)	Used to obtain specimen of pleural fluid for diagnosis, remove pleural fluid, or instill medication. Obtain chest x-ray after procedure to check for pneumothorax.	*Before:* Explain procedure and obtain signed consent. *During:* Usually done in patient's room. Position patient upright with elbows on an overbed table and feet supported. Tell patient not to talk or cough during procedure. *After:* Observe for signs of hypoxia and pneumothorax, and verify breath sounds in all fields. Encourage deep breaths to expand lungs. Send labeled specimens to laboratory promptly for analysis.

or TTNA biopsy involves inserting a needle through the chest wall, usually under bedside ultrasound or CT guidance. Because of the risk for a pneumothorax, a chest x-ray is done after TTNA.

In VATS, a rigid scope with a lens is passed through a trocar placed into the pleura via 1 or 2 small incisions in the thoracic cavity. The HCP views the lesions in the pleura or peripheral lung on a monitor directly via the scope and can obtain biopsy specimens. A chest tube is kept in place until the lung expands. VATS is much less invasive than open lung biopsy. It is associated with shorter hospital stays and reduced mortality.[15] It is ideal for pleural biopsy and resecting lung nodules.

An open lung biopsy is used when other procedures cannot diagnose pulmonary disease. With the patient under anesthesia, the chest is opened with a thoracotomy incision and a biopsy specimen is obtained. Post-procedure care is the same as after thoracotomy (see Chapter 28).

Thoracentesis

Thoracentesis is the insertion of a large-bore needle through the chest wall into the pleural space to obtain specimens for diagnostic evaluation, remove pleural fluid, or instill medication (see Fig. 27.11). The patient is positioned sitting upright, leaning on an overbed table with feet supported. The skin is cleansed and a local anesthetic (lidocaine) is injected subcutaneously. A percutaneous catheter may be left in to allow further drainage of fluid (Table 27.16).

Pulmonary Function Tests

Pulmonary function tests (PFTs) measure lung volumes and airflow. The results of PFTs can diagnose pulmonary disease, monitor disease progression, assess response to bronchodilators, and evaluate disability. Airflow measurement is obtained by trained personnel using a spirometer. The patient inserts a mouthpiece,

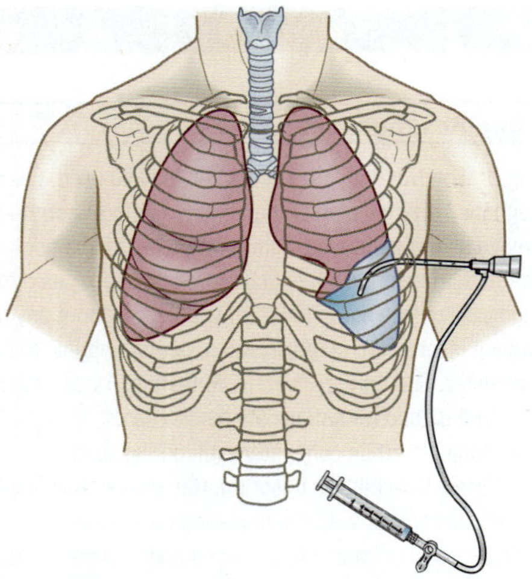

Fig. 27.11 Thoracentesis. A catheter is positioned in the pleural space to remove accumulated fluid.

takes as deep a breath as possible, and exhales as hard, as fast, and for as long as possible. Verbal coaching is given to ensure that the patient continues blowing out until exhalation is complete.

Computer software calculates the patient's percent of predicted values, that is, how well the performance compares with an average based on age, gender, race, and height.[16] Normal values are 80% to 120% of the predicted value. Normal values for PFTs are shown in Tables 27.17 and 27.18.

Spirometry may be done before and after giving a bronchodilator to determine the patient's response. This helps gauge the reversibility of airway obstruction (e.g., asthma). A positive bronchodilator response is an increase of greater than 200 mL or 12% in FEV_1 after administering a bronchodilator.

Home spirometry may be used to monitor lung function in people with asthma, cystic fibrosis, or COPD, as well as before and after lung transplantation or thoracic surgeries. A peak flow meter is the hand-held instrument used at home. The person blows through it forcefully and quickly after taking a deep breath. Spirometry changes can warn of early lung transplant rejection or infection. Data from a peak flow meter provide important feedback to patients with asthma so that they can learn to change activities and medications in response to changes in peak expiratory flow rates.

TABLE 27.17 Lung Volumes and Capacities

Parameter	Definitions	Normal Value (L)[a]
Volumes		
Expiratory reserve volume (ERV)	Additional air that can be forcefully exhaled after normal exhalation is complete	1.0
Inspiratory reserve volume (IRV)	Maximum volume of air that can be inhaled forcefully after normal inhalation	3.0
Residual volume (RV)	Amount of air remaining in lungs after forced expiration. Air available in lungs for gas exchange between breaths	1.5
Tidal volume (V_T)	Volume of air inhaled and exhaled with each breath. Only a small proportion of total capacity of lungs	0.5
Capacities		
Functional residual capacity (FRC)	Volume of air remaining in lungs at end of normal exhalation (FRC = ERV + RV). Increase or decrease possible with lung disease	2.5
Inspiratory capacity (IC)	Maximum volume of air that can be inhaled after normal expiration (IC = V_T + IRV)	3.5
Total lung capacity (TLC)	Maximum volume of air that lungs can contain (TLC = IRV + V_T + ERV + RV)	6.0
Vital capacity (VC)	Maximum volume of air that can be exhaled after maximum inspiration (VC = IRV + V_T + ERV). Higher VC for men (generally)	4.5

[a]Normal values vary with patient's height, weight, age, race, and gender.

TABLE 27.18 Pulmonary Function Airflow

Measure	Description	Normal Value[a]
Forced vital capacity (FVC)	Amount of air that can be quickly and forcefully exhaled after maximum inspiration	>80% of predicted
Forced expiratory volume in first second of expiration (FEV_1)	Amount of air exhaled in first second of FVC. Grades severity of airway obstruction	>80% of predicted
FEV_1/FVC ratio	Dividing value for FEV_1 by value for FVC. Useful in differentiating obstructive and restrictive pulmonary dysfunction	*Age <50:* ≥75% of predicted *Age ≥50:* ≥70% of predicted
Forced midexpiratory flow rate ($FEF_{25\%-75\%}$)	Measurement of airflow rate in middle half of forced expiration. Early indicator of disease of small airways	*Age <50:* ≥75% of predicted *Age ≥50:* ≥70% of predicted
Peak expiratory flow rate (PEFR)	Maximum airflow rate during forced expiration. Aids in monitoring bronchoconstriction in asthma. Can be measured with peak flow meter	Up to 600 L/min
Maximal voluntary ventilation (MVV)	Deep breathing as rapidly as possible for specified period. Fairly nonspecific test that gives information about exercise capacity. Used in conjunction with exercise stress test	About 170 L/min

[a]Normal values vary with patient's height, age, race, and gender.

Case Study

Objective Data: Diagnostic Studies

(© Fuse/ Thinkstock.)

The HCP orders the following diagnostic studies for F.T.:

- Pulse oximetry
- Chest x-ray
- 12-lead electrocardiogram (ECG)
- CBC, basic metabolic panel (electrolytes, BUN, creatinine)
- ABGs
- Sputum for culture and sensitivity

F.T.'s SpO_2 is 87% on O_2 @ 3/L min via nasal cannula. The chest x-ray shows a slightly enlarged heart and bilateral consolidation to both lower lobes. The 12-lead ECG reveals sinus tachycardia, rate 110, with no ST segment elevation or depression and no T-wave inversion. The ABGs show compensated respiratory alkalosis with hypoxemia. The WBC is 17,350/µL and potassium 2.9 mEq/L. Sputum results are pending. F.T. is admitted to the medical nursing unit.

Discussion Questions

1. Which diagnostic test results concern you most?
2. What do you think is the cause of F.T.'s problems?
3. What patient teaching can you do with F.T. as he is waiting to be admitted to the hospital unit?
4. What is the interprofessional team's top priority for F.T. at this time?

Answers available at http://evolve.elsevier.com/Lewis/medsurg.

BRIDGE TO NCLEX EXAMINATION

The number of the question corresponds to the same-numbered learning outcome identified at the beginning of this chapter.

1. The key anatomic landmark that separates the upper respiratory tract from the lower respiratory tract is the
   a. carina.
   b. larynx.
   c. trachea.
   d. epiglottis.
2. A patient asks, "How does air get into my lungs?" The nurse bases their answer on knowledge that air moves into the lungs because of
   a. positive intrathoracic pressure.
   b. contraction of the accessory abdominal muscles.
   c. stimulation of the respiratory muscles by the chemoreceptors.
   d. a decrease in intrathoracic pressure from an increase in thoracic cavity size.
3. The nurse can *best* determine adequate arterial oxygenation of the blood by assessing
   a. heart rate.
   b. hemoglobin level.
   c. arterial oxygen partial pressure.
   d. arterial carbon dioxide partial pressure.
4. Defense mechanisms that help protect the lung from inhaled particles and microorganisms include the *(select all that apply)*
   a. cough reflex.
   b. mucociliary escalator.
   c. alveolar macrophages.
   d. reflex bronchoconstriction.
   e. alveolar capillary membrane.
5. A student nurse asks the RN what can be measured by arterial blood gas (ABG). The RN tells the student that the ABG can measure *(select all that apply)*
   a. acid-base balance.
   b. bicarbonate (HCO_3–).
   c. mixed venous O_2 (SvO_2).
   d. compliance and resistance.
   e. partial pressure of O_2 (PaO_2).
6. To detect early signs or symptoms of inadequate oxygenation, the nurse would examine the patient for
   a. dyspnea and hypotension.
   b. apprehension and restlessness.
   c. cyanosis and cool, clammy skin.
   d. increased urine output and diaphoresis.
7. During the respiratory assessment of an older adult, the nurse would expect to find *(select all that apply)*
   a. a vigorous reflex cough.
   b. increased chest expansion.
   c. increased residual volume.
   d. decreased lung sounds at base of lungs.
   e. increased anteroposterior (AP) chest diameter.
8. When assessing subjective data related to the respiratory health of a patient with emphysema, the nurse would ask about *(select all that apply)*
   a. date of last chest x-ray.
   b. dyspnea during rest or exercise.
   c. pulmonary function test results.
   d. ability to sleep through the entire night.
   e. prescription and over-the-counter medication.
9. When auscultating the chest of an older patient in mild respiratory distress, it is *best* to
   a. begin listening at the apices.
   b. begin listening at the lung bases.
   c. begin listening on the anterior chest.
   d. ask the patient to breathe through the nose with the mouth closed.
10. Which respiratory assessment finding does the nurse interpret as abnormal?
    a. Inspiratory chest expansion of 1 inch
    b. Symmetric chest expansion and contraction
    c. Resonance (to percussion) over the lung bases
    d. Bronchial breath sounds in the lower lung fields
11. The nurse is preparing the patient for a diagnostic procedure to remove pleural fluid for analysis. The nurse would prepare the patient for which test?
    a. Thoracentesis
    b. Bronchoscopy

c. Pulmonary angiography
d. Sputum culture and sensitivity

1. a; 2. d; 3. c; 4. a, b, c, d; 5. a, b, e; 6. b; 7. c, d, e; 8. b, d, e; 9. b; 10. d; 11. a.

For rationales to these answers and even more NCLEX review questions, visit http://evolve.elsevier.com/Lewis/medsurg.

EVOLVE WEBSITE/RESOURCES LIST

http://evolve.elsevier.com/Lewis/medsurg
Review Questions (Online Only)
Key Points
Answer Keys for Questions
- Rationales for Bridge to NCLEX Examination Questions
- Answer Guidelines for Case Study

Conceptual Care Map Creator
Audio Glossary
Content Updates

REFERENCES

1. Patton KT, Thibodeau GA: *Structure and function of the body*, ed 16, St Louis, 2020, Mosby.
2. Tatco V, Smith D: Carina. Retrieved from https://radiopaedia.org/articles/carina.
3. Meriam-Webster Dictionary: Anatomic dead space. Retrieved from https://www.merriam-webster.com/medical/anatomical%20dead%20space.
4. Goel A, Gaillard F: Pores of Kohn. Retrieved from https://radiopaedia.org/articles/pores-of-kohn.
5. Stacy KM: Pulmonary anatomy and physiology. In Urden LD, Stacy KM, Lough ME, editors: *Critical care nursing: diagnosis and management*, ed 9, St Louis, 2022, Mosby.
6. Mortola JP: How to breathe? Respiratory mechanics and breathing pattern, *Respir Physiol Neurobiol* 261:48, 2019.
7. Gao L, Ortega-Saenz P, Lopez-Barneo J: Acute oxygen sensing—role of metabolic specifications in peripheral chemoreceptor cells, *Respir Physiol Neurobiol* 265:100, 2019.
8. Meriam-Webster Dictionary: Oximetry. Retrieved from: https://www.merriam-webster.com/medical/oximetry.
9. Pagana KD, Pagana TJ, Pagana TN: *Mosby's diagnostic and laboratory test reference*, ed 15, St. Louis, 2021, Mosby.
10. Wilson SF, Giddens JF: *Health assessment for nursing practice*, ed 7, St Louis, 2022, Mosby.
11. Mohamed Elhossieny KM: Accuracy of pulse oximetry in comparison with arterial blood gas, *Res Opin Anesth Intensive Care* 7:51, 2020.
12. Sole ML, Goldenberg Klein D, Moseley MJ: *Introduction to critical care nursing*, ed 8, St. Louis, 2021, Saunders.
13. Linz D, Homerg M, van der Velden RMJ, et al.: Sleep apnea, obesity and COPD depress respiration during catheter ablation procedures: implications for transcutaneous carbon dioxide monitoring, *Int J Cardiol* 29052, 2020.
14. Scully K, Rickerby J, Dunn J: Implementation science: incorporating obstructive sleep apnea screening and capnography into everyday practice, *J Perianesth Nurs* 35:7, 2020.
15. Jarrar D: Video-assisted thoracic surgery (VATS). Retrieved from https://emedicine.medscape.com/article/1970013-overview.
16. Mottram CD: *Ruppel's manual of pulmonary function testing*, ed 11, St Louis, 2018, Mosby.

28

Supporting Ventilation

Eugene E. Mondor

http://evolve.elsevier.com/Lewis/medsurg/

CONCEPTUAL FOCUS

Acid-Base Balance
Functional Ability
Gas Exchange
Nutrition
Sleep

LEARNING OUTCOMES

1. Identify airway clearance techniques that promote gas exchange.
2. Describe the indications for O_2 therapy, including delivery methods and complications.
3. Explain the purpose, function, and nursing responsibilities related to chest tubes and chest drainage systems.
4. Identify the types of chest surgery and appropriate perioperative care.
5. Relate the important aspects of care for the patient receiving noninvasive ventilation.
6. Distinguish the indications for and modes of mechanical ventilation.
7. Select appropriate nursing interventions related to the care of an intubated patient.
8. Identify the steps involved in suctioning a patient with an oral endotracheal tube or tracheostomy.
9. Describe complications of mechanical ventilation and corrective actions to ensure optimal ventilation and safe patient care.
10. Describe the process of weaning from mechanical ventilation.
11. Select appropriate nursing interventions related to care of the patient with a new tracheostomy.
12. Outline the essential teaching needed for the patient with a permanent tracheostomy.

KEY TERMS

assist-control (AC) ventilation
chest physical therapy (CPT)
continuous positive airway pressure (CPAP)
decannulation
endotracheal (ET) tube
extubation
intubation
mechanical ventilation
negative pressure ventilation
noninvasive ventilation (NIV)
positive end-expiratory pressure (PEEP)
positive pressure ventilation (PPV)
pressure control (PC) ventilation
pressure support ventilation (PSV)
pressure ventilation
pursed-lip breathing (PLB)
synchronized intermittent mandatory ventilation (SIMV)
thoracotomy
tracheostomy
volume ventilation
weaning

The exchange of O_2 and carbon dioxide (CO_2) is vital for life. The purpose of this chapter is to provide an overview of various strategies we use to promote optimal ventilation and oxygenation. Promoting respiratory function is important for best patient outcomes. Without an optimal route for ventilation, O_2 therapy will not benefit the patient. While providing optimal ventilation is no guarantee that oxygenation will improve, without a patent airway, the patient will die.

RESPIRATORY PHYSIOTHERAPY

Breathing Exercises

Two main types of breathing exercises are diaphragmatic breathing and pursed-lip breathing. *Diaphragmatic (abdominal) breathing* focuses on using the diaphragm instead of the accessory muscles of the chest to achieve maximum inhalation and slow the respiratory rate. Ideal candidates for diaphragmatic breathing instruction are

TABLE 28.1 PATIENT & CAREGIVER TEACHING

Pursed-Lip Breathing

Teach the patient to use PLB before, during, and after any activity that may cause them to be short of breath.

1. Inhale slowly and deeply through the nose.
2. Exhale slowly through pursed lips, as if whistling.
3. Be sure to relax your facial muscles without puffing your cheeks—like whistling—while you are exhaling slowly.
4. Make breathing out (exhalation) 3 times as long as breathing in (inhalation).
5. The following activities can help you get the "feel" of PLB:
   - Blow through a straw in a glass of water, forming small bubbles.
   - Blow a lit candle enough to bend the flame without blowing it out.
   - Steadily blow a table-tennis ball across a table.
   - Blow a tissue held in the hand until it gently flaps.
6. Practice 8–10 repetitions of PLB 3 or 4 times a day.

PLB, Pursed-lip breathing.

TABLE 28.2 PATIENT & CAREGIVER TEACHING

Effective Huff Coughing

Help the patient assume a sitting position with head slightly flexed, shoulders relaxed, knees flexed, forearms supported by pillow, and, if possible, feet on the floor.

Then teach the patient to:

1. Inhale slowly through the mouth while breathing deeply from the diaphragm.
2. Hold the breath for 2–3 sec.
3. Forcefully exhale quickly as if they are fogging up a mirror with their breath (thus creating a "huff"). This helps moves secretions into larger airways.
4. Repeat the "huff" 1 or 2 more times while refraining from a "regular" cough.
5. Cough when mucus is felt in the airways (breathing tubes).
6. Rest for 5–10 regular breaths.
7. Repeat the huffs (3–5 cycles) until you feel you have cleared mucus, or you become tired.

thoracic and abdominal surgery patients. Diaphragmatic breathing in patients with chronic obstructive pulmonary disease (COPD) may increase the work of breathing (WOB) and dyspnea. People with moderate to severe COPD with marked hyperinflation may not tolerate diaphragmatic breathing.

The purpose of **pursed-lip breathing (PLB)** is to prolong exhalation, which prevents bronchiolar collapse and air trapping.[1] PLB is simple, easy to teach, and easy to learn (Table 28.1). It gives the patient more control over breathing, especially during exercise and periods of dyspnea. PLB slows the respiratory rate and is easier than diaphragmatic breathing. Teach the patients to use "just enough" positive pressure with PLB because excessive resistance may increase the WOB. In the patient with extreme acute dyspnea, focus on helping the patient slow the respiratory rate by using PLB.

Airway Clearance Techniques

Many patients with COPD or other respiratory conditions who retain secretions, such as cystic fibrosis (CF) and bronchiectasis, need help to adequately clear their airways. Airway clearance techniques (ACTs) loosen mucus and secretions so they can be cleared by coughing. This helps maintain a patent airway. Techniques include huff coughing, chest physiotherapy, postural drainage, airway clearance devices, and high-frequency chest ventilation. ACTs are often used with other treatments. For example, the patient may receive bronchodilator therapy before ACT. Then the ACT is used, followed by effective coughing (e.g., huff coughing). Respiratory therapists (RTs), physical therapists, and nurses can teach patients and caregivers ACTs.

Huff Coughing

Huff coughing, or *huffing,* is a forced expiratory technique that consists of a series of smaller coughs. You can easily teach the patient huff coughing. Position the patient and ensure they are breathing deeply from the diaphragm. After holding the breath for a few seconds, the patient exhales with several small coughs, then rests for several breaths, and repeats the cycle.[2] Persons with COPD and emphysema benefit from huff coughing. Table 28.2 outlines teaching about huff coughing.

Chest Physical Therapy

Chest physical therapy (CPT) consists of postural drainage, percussion, and vibration. It can be done on spontaneously breathing patients as well as those who are intubated and mechanically ventilated. CPT is used for patients with excessive bronchial secretions who have difficulty clearing them.

CPT should be done by a physiotherapist or other trained person. Complications from improperly performed CPT include fractured ribs, bruising of the chest wall, hypoxemia, and discomfort. CPT may be stressful for some patients. Teaching can help ease fear and anxiety and gain trust and cooperation.

Postural Drainage

Postural drainage is the use of positioning techniques that drain secretions from specific segments of the lungs and bronchi into the trachea. The postural drainage position used depends on the areas of lung that are involved. This is determined by patient assessment, chest x-rays, chest auscultation, and, when possible, patient preference. For example, a patient with left lower lobe involvement needs postural drainage of only the affected region. On the other hand, a person with CF may need postural drainage of all segments.

The purpose of various positions in postural drainage is to drain each segment toward the larger airways. The patient who cannot tolerate a head-down position may use a side-lying position. We usually give aerosolized bronchodilators and hydration therapy before postural drainage. The patient stays in the chosen position for about 5 minutes during percussion and vibration. A common order is to perform postural drainage 2 to 4 times a day. In acute situations, we may do postural drainage as often as every 4 hours.[3] Schedule the procedure at least 1 hour before meals or 3 hours after meals.

Postural drainage is best for patients with atelectasis, CF, COPD, and pneumonia. Some commercially available specialty beds can rotate and percuss the patient in various postural drainage positions. Patients with traumatic brain injury, neck injury, chest trauma, hemoptysis, heart disease, or pulmonary embolus should not receive postural drainage. It is contraindicated in hemorrhage and when the patient is not stable.

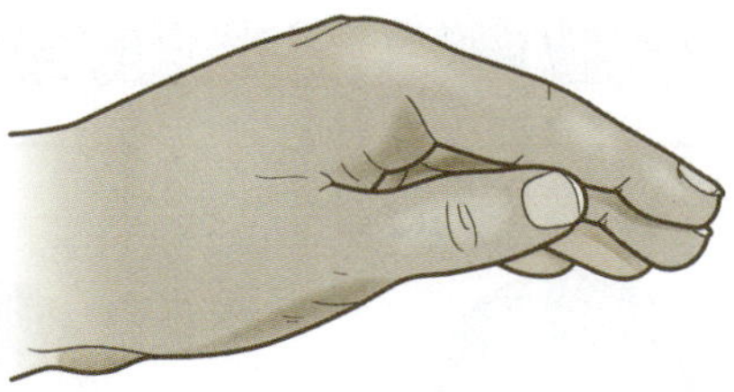

Fig. 28.1 Cupped-hand position for percussion. Cup the hand as though scooping up water.

Percussion

Percussion is done in the appropriate postural drainage position. Place the hands in a cuplike position with the fingers and thumbs closed (Fig. 28.1). The cupped hand should create an air pocket between the patient's chest and the hand. Both hands alternate in a rhythmic fashion. You will hear a hollow sound if done correctly. The air-cushion impact promotes the movement of thick mucus. For patient comfort, place a thin towel over the area you will percuss. The patient may choose to wear a T-shirt or hospital gown.

Vibration

Vibration promotes movement of secretions to the larger airways. We perform vibration by tensing the hand and arm muscles repeatedly and pressing mildly with the flat of the hand on the affected area while the patient slowly exhales a deep breath. Commercially available mechanical chest vibrators are available for hospital and home use.

Airway clearance devices. Airway clearance devices are available to help mobilize secretions. They are sometimes easier to tolerate than CPT and often take less time than CPT sessions. Popular devices include the Flutter, Acapella, and TheraPEP Therapy System.

The Flutter mucus clearance device is a hand-held device. It is shaped like a small, fat pipe. The Flutter has a mouthpiece, a high-density stainless-steel ball, and a cone that holds the ball. To use the Flutter, the patient takes a slightly bigger than normal breath and exhales through the mouth and into the Flutter. As a result, the steel ball moves, which causes vibrations in the airways. The vibration helps loosen mucus in the airways to allow improved expectoration. Flutter use should be followed by huffing and coughing. Clean a Flutter daily in warm, soapy water.

The Acapella is another small hand-held device. It combines positive expired pressure (PEP) and airway vibrations to mobilize secretions. It can be used in any setting. Patients are free to sit, stand, or recline. Prior to use, the resistance dial on the device needs to be set (1=minimal exhalation resistance, 5=high exhalation resistance). The patient takes in a deep breath through the nose or mouth, then seals their lips around the mouthpiece, and exhales through the device. You should hear the gentle noise of the rocker inside the device on exhalation. The Acapella can help deliver aerosolized drugs.

The TheraPEP Therapy System is similar to the Acapella. It uses PEP and can assist with airway clearance and deliver aerosolized drugs. TheraPEP can have either a mouthpiece or mask that is attached to tubing that is connected to a small adjustable resistor and a pressure indicator. The patient inhales through the nose or mouth, holds the breath for a few seconds, then exhales through the resistor. The pressure indicator gives visual feedback about the pressure that the patient needs to hold during exhalation to receive maximal benefit of PEP.

High-frequency chest wall oscillation. High-frequency chest wall oscillation uses an inflatable vest (e.g., Vest System, Smart Vest) with hoses connected to a high-frequency pulse generator. The pulse generator delivers air to the vest, which vibrates the chest. The high-frequency airwaves dislodge mucus from the airways, mobilize the mucus, and move it toward larger airways. The vest is easy to apply. It can be used without the aid of another person. The unit weighs 23 to 30 lbs. (10 to 13 kg), are quiet, come in a suitcase, and are portable.

O_2 THERAPY

O_2 therapy is a common treatment for hypoxemia and hypoxia. O_2 is a colorless, odorless, tasteless gas that constitutes 21% of the atmosphere. Giving supplemental O_2 increases the partial pressure of O_2 (PO_2) in inspired air. O_2 therapy requires an HCP order. The dose of O_2 administered to patients is the *fraction of inspired oxygen (FIO_2).*

We give O_2 to treat hypoxemia caused by many problems, such as shock, pneumonia, and pulmonary emboli. O_2 therapy is tailored to meet each patient's unique circumstances and physiologic needs. For most patients, the goal of O_2 therapy is to keep the SaO_2 greater than 92% during rest, sleep, and activity, or the PaO_2 greater than 60 mm Hg. We may modify these goals depending on the patient's clinical situation. For example, the HCP may accept an SpO_2 an PaO_2 greater than 88% for the patient with longstanding COPD.

DRUG ALERT

O_2

- O_2 is considered a drug.
- Administering high levels of O_2 (FIO_2 greater than 60% for more than 24 hr) to mechanically ventilated patients can lead to O_2 toxicity.
- Target FIO_2 levels are to maintain SpO_2 >92% and PaO_2 between 60 and 100 mm Hg.
- Assess PaO_2 and SpO_2 as needed.
- Monitor for manifestations of O_2 toxicity: blurred vision, coughing, chest pain, dyspnea, seizures.

Methods of O_2 Administration

There are various ways to administer O_2 (Table 28.3). The device used depends on the patient's underlying condition, the FIO_2 the patient needs, advantages and disadvantages of each device, comfort, cost, and financial resources.

We classify O_2 delivery systems as low-flow or high-flow systems. Low-flow O_2 delivery devices are appropriate for patients who are awake, alert, and spontaneously breathing with a stable, intact respiratory drive. These devices provide O_2 in concentrations that do not meet all the patient's inspiratory demands.[4] Low-flow devices pull in a proportion of room air, which makes the exact FIO_2 unknown. We do know the range of FIO_2

TABLE 28.3 Methods of O_2 Administration

Description	Nursing Interventions	
Low-Flow Delivery Devices		
Nasal Cannula		
• Most commonly used. • O_2 delivered through plastic tubing (prongs) that fits in the nares. • Used for a patient requiring low O_2 concentrations. • Achieves O_2 concentrations of 24% (at 1 L/min) to 44% (at 6 L/min). • Safe • Easy to set-up and use • Patient can eat, talk, or cough while wearing device. • Allows some freedom of movement.	• Stabilize nasal cannula when caring for a restless patient. • Amount of O_2 inhaled depends on room air and patient's breathing pattern. • Most patients with COPD can tolerate 2–4 L/min through a cannula. • Assess the nares and ears for skin breakdown. May need to pad tubing where it sits on ears. • If flow rates are >5 L/min, nasal membranes may dry and place patient at risk for nose bleeds.	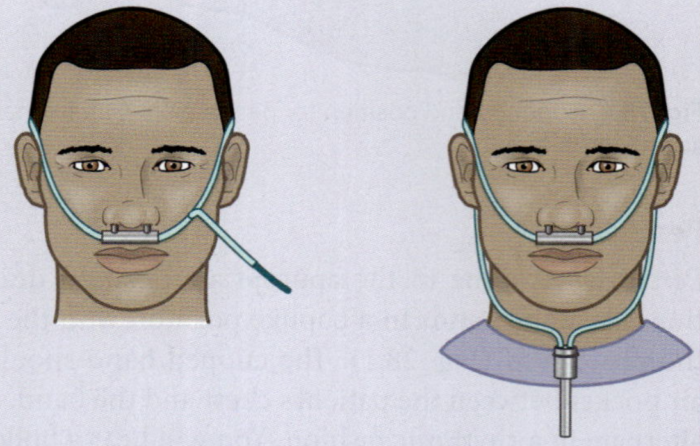
O_2-Conserving Cannula		
• Generally indicated for longer-term O_2 therapy at home (e.g., CF, pulmonary hypertension). • Looks like a "moustache" (Oxymizer) or "pendant" type. • Cannula has a built-in reservoir that ↑ O_2 concentration and allows patient to use lower flow, usually 30%–50%, which increases comfort, lowers cost, and can be increased with activities. • Can deliver O_2 flow rates up to 15 L/min.	• More expensive than standard nasal cannula. • Cannula is highly visible. • Assess the nares and ears for skin breakdown. May need to pad tubing where it sits behind ears. • Cannot clean cannula. Change cannula every week. • May need ABGs and oximetry to determine correct flow rate.	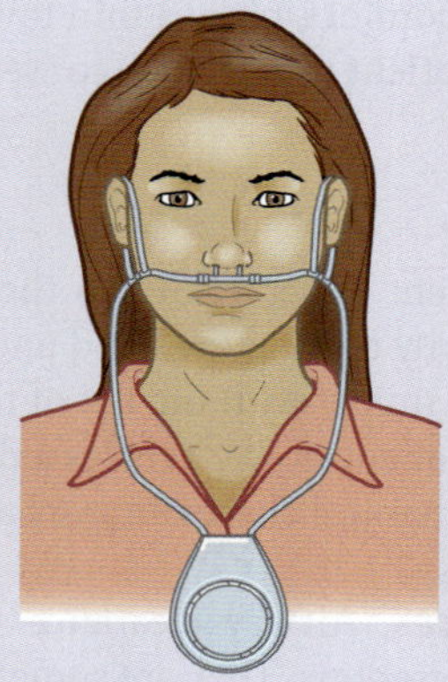 Pendant-type O_2-conserving cannula.
Partial and Non-Rebreather Masks		
• Used for short-term therapy for patients with higher O_2 needs • Achieves O_2 concentrations of 60%–90% (with flow rates of 10–15 L/min). • O_2 flows into reservoir bag and mask during inhalation. • Bag allows patient to rebreathe about first third of exhaled air (rich in O_2) in conjunction with flowing O_2. • Vents stay open on partial mask. Some agencies prefer this over non-rebreather as a safety issue.	• O_2 flow rate must be sufficient to keep bag from deflating during inspiration to avoid CO_2 buildup and rebreathing of CO_2. • If deflation occurs, increase flowrate on flowmeter on wall to keep bag inflated. • Mask should fit snugly. • With non-rebreather masks, make sure valves open during expiration and close during inhalation to prevent decrease in FIO_2 or build-up in CO_2. • Monitor patient closely, since more advanced interventions such as CPAP, Bi-PAP, or intubation with mechanical ventilation may be needed.	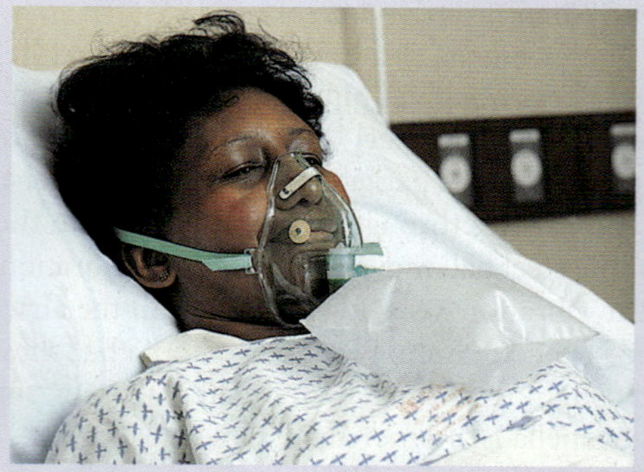
Simple Face Mask		
• Covers the nose and mouth. • Achieves O_2 concentrations of 35%–50% with flow rates of 6–12 L/min. • Mask provides adequate humidification of inspired air. • Safe • Easy to set up and use • Typically used only for short periods.	• Wash and dry under mask q4hr and PRN. • Mask must fit snugly. • Must have flow rates of at least 6 L/min to wash exhaled gases out of mask (if O_2 flow rate not high enough, CO_2 rebreathing is possible) • May change to nasal cannula while patient is eating. • Watch for pressure necrosis at top of ears from elastic straps if patient wears for a longer time. Gauze or other padding may alleviate this problem.	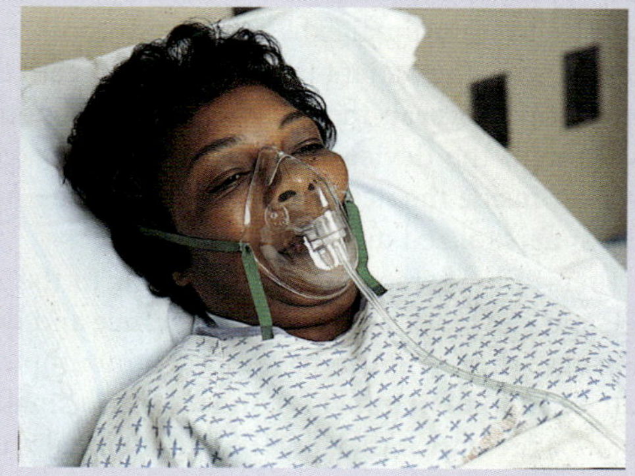

high flow.

TABLE 28.3 Methods of O_2 Administration—cont'd

Description	Nursing Interventions
High-Flow Delivery Devices	
High-Flow Nasal Cannula	
• Blends O_2 with compressed air to generate high FIO_2 • Achieves O_2 concentration up to 100% (at flow rate of up to 60 L/min). • Heated humidifier capable of providing 100% humidity. • Soft and flexible nasal prongs. • More comfortable than mask.	• Nasal cannula must be smaller than 50% of nares to allow flow during exhalation and flush out end-expiratory CO_2. • Well tolerated. • Patients can eat and drink with device in place. • Patient may describe feeling of always having to blow nose ("rainout") due to humidification.
Tracheostomy Collar	
• Collar attaches to neck with elastic strap and can deliver humidity and O_2 through the tracheostomy. • Some O_2 concentration is lost into atmosphere because collar does not fit tightly. • Venturi device can be attached to flowmeter and can deliver exact amounts of O_2 through the collar.	• Secretions collect inside collar and around tracheostomy. • Remove collar and clean at least q4hr and PRN to prevent aspiration of fluid and infection. • Because condensation occurs in tubing, periodically drain tubing distal to tracheostomy.
Tracheostomy T-Piece	
• Almost identical to tracheostomy collar, but it has a T-connector attached to an O_2 blender. • Tight fit allows better O_2 and humidity delivery than tracheostomy collar. • T-piece allows an inline catheter to be connected for suctioning.	• Because T-piece connector can disconnect easily, monitor closely. • T-piece connector may pull on the tracheostomy tube, causing irritation and potential tissue damage. Monitor closely.
Venturi Mask	
• Mask can deliver precise, high-flow rates of O_2. • Lightweight plastic, cone-shaped mask. Masks are available for delivery of 24%, 28%, 31%, 35%, 40%, and 50% O_2. • Method is especially helpful for giving low, constant O_2 concentrations to patients with COPD. • Adaptors can increase humidification.	• Entrainment device on mask must be changed to deliver higher concentrations of O_2. • Air entrainment ports must not be occluded. • Uncomfortable. • Must be removed for eating. • Patient can talk but voice may be muffled.

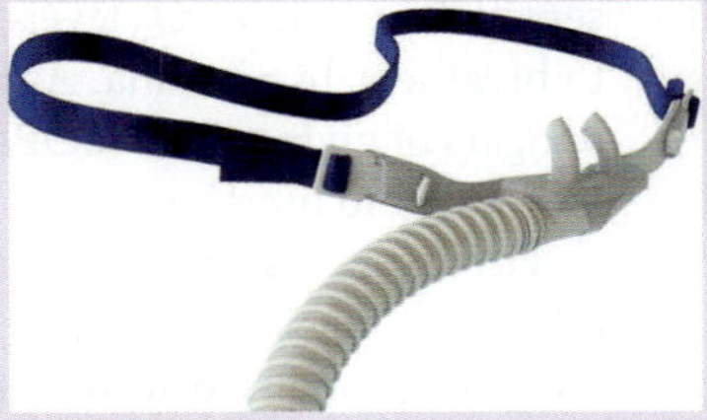

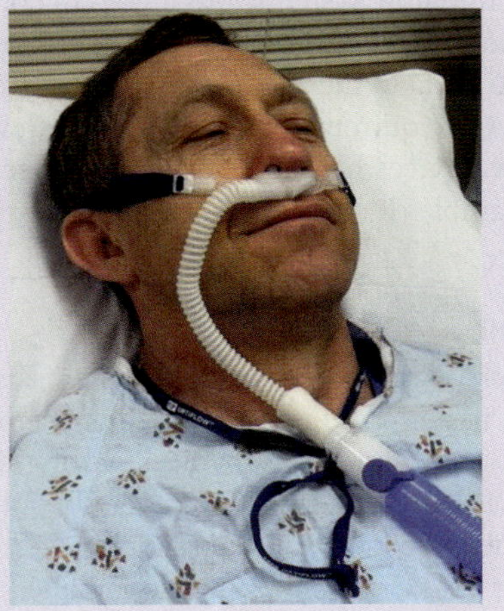

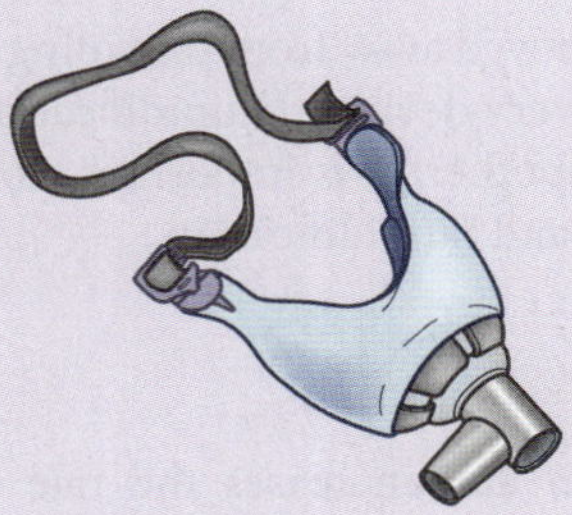

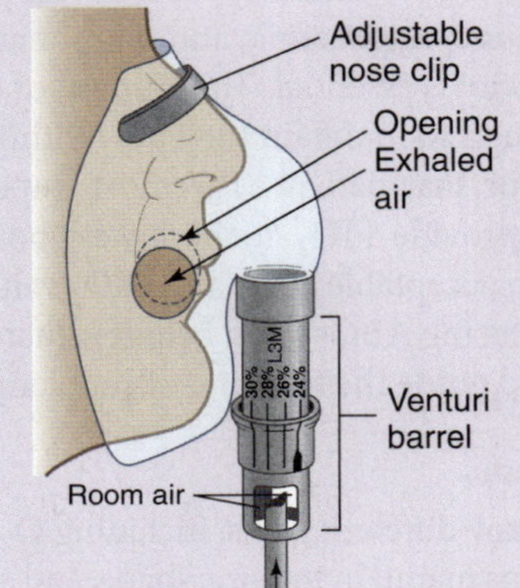

Bi-PAP, Bi-level positive airway pressure; *CF,* cystic fibrosis; *COPD,* chronic obstructive pulmonary disease; *CPAP,* continuous positive airway pressure; *FIO2,* fraction of inspired oxygen.

delivered by each device. Examples include nasal prongs, simple masks, and non-rebreather masks.

High-flow O_2 delivery devices deliver fixed O_2 concentrations (e.g., 28%, 35%) independent of the patient's respiratory rate or pattern. High flow systems provide O_2 in concentrations that meet or exceed the patient's inspiratory demand. These patients are also awake, alert, and spontaneously breathing, but have higher O_2 requirements that low flow devices cannot meet.[4] High flow devices help meet achieving specific PaO_2 or SpO_2 targets. Examples include the Venturi mask and high-flow nasal cannula.

Humidification

O_2 obtained from O_2 cylinders or wall systems is a dry gas. Dry O_2 has an irritating effect on mucous membranes and dries secretions. Humidification involves adding sterile water attached to the O_2 delivery device to prevent breathing dry air. A common device used for humidification when the patient has a cannula or mask is a small plastic jar filled with sterile water called a *bubble-through humidifier.* It is attached to the O_2 source by a flowmeter.

Many agencies have moved away from providing humidification for low flow O_2 delivery devices. Humidification with high flow O_2 devices (e.g., Vapotherm) is important. Follow agency policy about O_2 therapy and humidification.

Complications

Combustion

O_2 supports combustion and increases the rate of burning. Smoking must be prohibited in any patient care area where O_2 is being used. Display a "No Smoking" sign on the patient's door and in any area where O_2 is in use. Caution the patient against smoking with an O_2 cannula in place as it can easily ignite and cause significant burns and life-threatening airway issues.

O_2 Toxicity

O2 toxicity may result from prolonged exposure to a high level of O_2 (FIO_2). High O_2 concentrations can result in a severe inflammatory response because O_2 free radicals damage the alveolar-capillary membrane.[5] This can cause severe pulmonary edema, shunting of blood, hypoxemia, and pulmonary edema.

Preventing O_2 toxicity is essential. The amount of O_2 administered should be enough to maintain the PaO_2 within a normal or acceptable range for that patient. The most important rule you can follow is to provide FIO_2 at the lowest possible level while still maintaining acceptable SpO_2 and PaO_2 values for that specific patient. Monitoring ABGs often helps evaluate the effectiveness of therapy and guide the tapering of supplemental O_2.

Absorption Atelectasis

The alveoli contain many different gases, including O_2, CO_2, and nitrogen. Nitrogen helps maintain the size, shape, and structure of the alveolus. If the bronchial tubes become obstructed (e.g., with mucous), the exchange of O_2 and CO_2 cannot occur. Nitrogen will eventually move out of the alveolus and into the bloodstream. This is a "nitrogen washout." As a result, the alveolus collapses, and absorption atelectasis occurs. This can worsen hypoxemia.

Frequent chest x-rays for patients requiring higher levels of O_2 therapy, monitoring ABGs, suctioning the airway as needed, and giving O_2 at the lowest level possible help avoid this condition.

CO_2 Narcosis

Chemoreceptors control the drive to breathe. They respond to CO_2 and O_2 concentrations in the blood. Normally, an increase in CO_2 in the blood is a major stimulant of the respiratory center. However, some patients (e.g., COPD) develop a tolerance for high CO_2 levels. As a result, the respiratory center loses its sensitivity to high CO_2 levels. For these patients, a major "drive" to breathe is hypoxemia. As a result, there is concern about the dangers of giving O_2 to COPD patients and reducing their drive (stimulus) to breathe.

However, the hypoxic drive is complex and involves many other factors. Not all patients with COPD retain CO_2. Therefore, it is good practice to administer O_2 to any patient who will likely benefit from O_2 therapy, whether they need it or not. The danger of not giving O_2 to a patient far outweighs the risk of administering O_2 when it is not needed.

Infection

Infection is a rare complication of O_2 use. It is often related to the device used and how often the device must be cleaned or changed. Heated nebulizers present the highest risk. The constant use of humidity supports bacterial growth. Whenever possible, use disposable and single patient use equipment. Follow agency policy about the frequency of equipment changes.

NURSING MANAGEMENT: O_2 THERAPY

We use pulse oximetry and/or ABGs to determine the FIO_2 each patient needs. The goal is an O_2 saturation (SpO_2) of at least 92% or a PaO_2 of at least 60 mm Hg. Titrate the O_2 concentration with close monitoring of the PaO_2 and $PaCO_2$. Assess mental status and vital signs before starting O_2 therapy and frequently thereafter. Nursing management of the patient receiving O_2 therapy is outlined in Table 28.4.

TABLE 28.4 NURSING MANAGEMENT

O_2 Administration

- Assess need for adjustments in O_2 flow rate.
- Evaluate response to O_2 therapy, especially when changes are made.
- Provide patient and caregiver teaching about O_2 therapy (see Table 28.5).
- Monitor patient for adverse effects of O_2 therapy.
- Supervise AP:
  - Use pulse oximetry to measure O_2 saturation and report level to RN.
  - Assist patient with adjustment of O_2 delivery devices (e.g., nasal cannula, simple face mask).
  - Report to RN any change in patient condition.

Collaborate With Respiratory Therapist

- Assist with choosing optimal O_2 delivery device.
- Make sure equipment is clean and replaced as needed.
- Check accuracy of O_2 delivery.
- Frequently assess need for adjustments in O_2 flow rate.

O_2 Therapy at Home

Some patients need O_2 therapy at home to treat hypoxemia associated with chronic conditions. The patient with mild to moderate hypoxemia that persists after discharge from the hospital may need short-term therapy. For example, a patient who had COVID pneumonia may need continued O_2 therapy to treat hypoxemia for a few weeks after discharge. Home health personnel can assess the patient's oxygenation status after an acute episode to determine if they still need O_2.

Patients usually rent home O_2 systems. The company then sends a RT to the home. The therapist teaches the patient and caregiver how to use the O_2 system, maintain it, troubleshoot, recognize when the supply is low, and reorder O_2. Table 28.5 shows patient and caregiver teaching guide for using O_2 at home.

Nasal cannulas, including O_2 conservation systems, deliver O_2 from a central source in the home. Sources include a liquid O_2 storage system, compressed O_2 in tanks or cylinders, or an O_2 concentrator or extractor. The one chosen depends on the patient's activity level, environment, insurance coverage, and proximity to an O_2 supply company. To increase mobility in the home, the patient can use extension tubing with some devices without lowering the O_2 flow delivery. The patient who is active outside the home can use a small, portable system, such as liquid O_2.

Patients may need O_2 only during exercise and/or sleep. Evaluate the need for O_2 during these periods with a 6-minute walk test or overnight oximetry. The patient on long-term therapy needs assessed at regular intervals (e.g., every 30 to 90 days during the first year, then each year if they are stable).

Encourage the patient who uses home O_2 to remain active and travel normally. If travel is by car, they can make arrangements for O_2 to be available at their destination. O_2 supply companies can help with these arrangements. If a patient plans to travel by bus, train, or airplane, the patient should inform these agencies when making reservations that they need O_2. O_2 needs for flying can be determined by a pulmonary function test, a 6-minute walk test, hypoxic challenge test, or predictive formula. Portable O_2 concentrators are a ready source of renewable O_2. They can be available by recharging at home or with a direct current (DC) (e.g., auto) power supply. Several are approved by airlines for in-flight use. The patient should contact the airline to determine accommodations and policies for in-flight O_2.

TABLE 28.5 PATIENT & CAREGIVER TEACHING

Home O_2 Use

The company that provides the O_2 and equipment will teach the patient about O_2 delivery and equipment care. The following are some general instructions that you may include when teaching the patient and caregiver about the use of home O_2.

Patient Care

- Set the O_2 flowrate at the rate your HCP told you to set it at. Do not change the rate without first talking to your HCP.
- If you have any shortness of breath, are lightheaded or dizzy, or develop wheezing, call the HCP right away
- Check to make sure you have enough O_2 on hand for weekends and holidays. The company will tell you how to check the O_2 level and when / how you re-order more O_2.

Decreasing Risk for Infection

- Wash hands before and after using your O_2 therapy.
- Wash nasal cannula (prongs) with a liquid soap and thoroughly rinse once or twice a week.
- Brush teeth or use mouthwash several times a day.
- Ask the company providing the equipment how often to change the tubing and filter.
- Replace cannula every 2–4 weeks.
- If you have a cold, replace the cannula after your symptoms pass.

Safety Issues

- Keep O_2 tanks at least 5 feet (1.5 m) away from any source of heat (e.g., gas stoves, fireplaces)
- Post "No Smoking—Oxygen in Use" warning signs on the front and back doors of your home.
- Do not allow smoking in the home, and do not smoke yourself while wearing O_2. Nasal cannulas and masks can catch fire and cause serious burns to face and airways.
- Store O_2 tanks upright.
- Do not use blankets or fabrics that carry a static charge, such as wool or synthetics.
- Do not use flammable liquids such as paint thinners, cleaning fluids, gasoline, kerosene, oil-based paints, or aerosol sprays while using O_2.
- Inform the staff at your electric company if you are using a concentrator. In case of a power failure, they will know the medical urgency of restoring your power.

ARTIFICIAL AIRWAYS

Patients sometimes need help to maintain a patent airway. Inserting a small, plastic tube into the nose, mouth, or trachea, thereby bypassing upper airway and laryngeal structures, creates a route for ventilation to occur. There are 5 artificial airways we commonly use in practice.

Nasopharyngeal Airway

A nasopharyngeal airway (NPA) is a small, flexible plastic tube inserted into the nostril to help maintain a route for ventilation (Fig. 28.2). The NPA can be placed in a conscious or unconscious patient. To measure the length of the tube needed, hold an NPA up to the side of the patient's face. Choose an NPA that correctly measures from the tip of the nose to the tip of the ear. To select the right internal diameter, choose a tube with a slightly smaller diameter than the patent's nostrils.

Choose the nostril of greatest airflow. Lubricate the tube, and gently insert while rotating the tube toward the patient's ear. Stop if you encounter any obstruction or difficulty. When correctly positioned, the flange should rest comfortably against the nostril.

Oropharyngeal Airway

The oropharyngeal airway (OPA) is a smaller, shorter tube of firm, hard plastic. The tube is curved, with a flange on 1 end and blunt opening on the other. Do not insert an OPA in a conscious patient as this will induce vomiting and risk of aspiration. Only insert the OPA into an unconscious patient.

To measure the length of the OPA needed, hold the OPA up to the side of the patient's face. Measure the tube against the corner of the mouth to the angle of the jaw or earlobe. If the tube

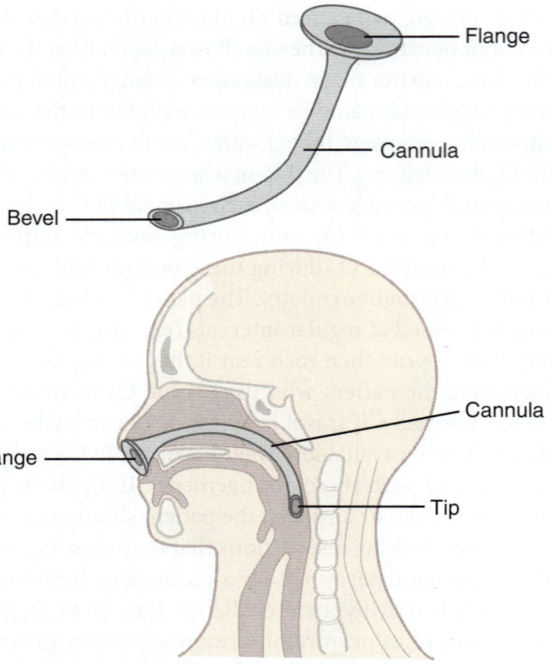

Fig. 28.2 Nasopharyngeal airway.

is too short, you may push the tongue into the oropharynx and occlude the airway. If the tube is too long, you may damage the posterior oropharynx.

To insert the OPA, lubricate the tube with water soluble lubricant. Insert the tube with the bevel pointed towards the roof of the mouth. As the flange reaches the lips, rotate the OPA 90 degrees so that the curvature of the OPA fits the natural curvature of the upper airway. Correctly inserted, the flange will fit comfortably against the lips.

Endotracheal Tube

The **endotracheal (ET) tube** is a long, flexible, plastic tube that secures a patient's airway when they need mechanical ventilation. An ET consists of a standard adaptor (used to attach the bag-valve-mask [BVM] or ventilator), cuff, pilot balloon, and radiopaque markings along the length of the tube. The markings help gauge the distance the tube is inserted. The parts of the oral ET tube are shown in Fig. 28.3.

The most common sizes are 7F and 8F tubes. The size refers to the internal diameter of the tube. Often, females need a 7F tube, and males need an 8F tube. A larger diameter tube can also be used. A larger tube reduces the WOB because of less airway resistance. It is also easier to suction and remove secretions and, if needed, perform bronchoscopy.

In *oral intubation,* the ET tube is passed into the mouth, through the vocal cords, and into the trachea with the aid of a laryngoscope or a bronchoscope. Oral ET intubation is preferred for intubations because the airway can be secured rapidly.

Indications for intubation include (1) acute respiratory distress, (2) apnea, (3) upper airway obstruction (e.g., burns, tumor, bleeding), (4) ineffective clearance of secretions, and (5) high risk for aspiration. ET intubation is done quickly and safely at the bedside by an HCP or RT. ET intubation is common in

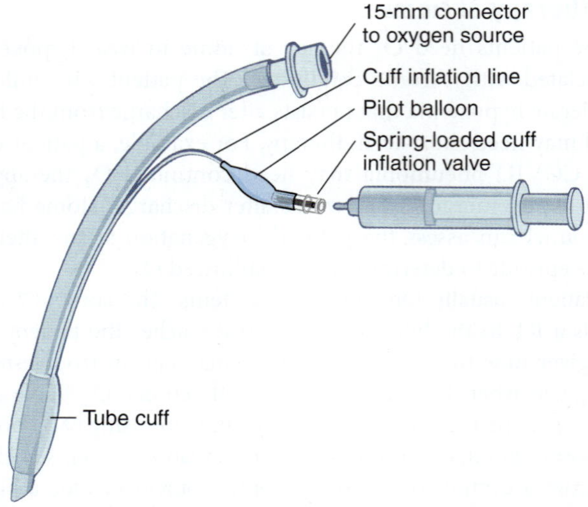

Fig. 28.3 Parts of an endotracheal tube. (From Beare PG, Myers JL: *Adult health nursing,* ed 3, St. Louis, 1998, Mosby.)

ICU patients requiring mechanical ventilation for short periods of time (e.g., less than 2 weeks).

Nasotracheal Tube

When oral intubation through the mouth is not possible (e.g., unstable cervical spine injury, dental abscess, epiglottitis), a nasotracheal (NT) tube can help provide an airway. The NT tube is slightly longer than the oral ET tube. It is inserted through the nostril and placed blindly (without seeing the larynx). We attach the patient to the ventilator via the standard adaptor at the end of the NT tube.

Tracheostomy

The **tracheostomy** is a special type of artificial airway. It is a small, plastic tube that consists of a flange, pilot balloon, balloon inflation port, and a cuff. The tube is placed into the trachea through a surgical incision that is created on the anterior surface of the neck. The tracheostomy may be inserted urgently (when oral and/or nasal intubation is not possible). Tracheostomies and their care are discussed later in this chapter.

PROCEDURES TO SUPPORT VENTILATION

A variety of diagnostic, therapeutic, and surgical strategies are available to assist patients with improving oxygenation and promoting more effective ventilation. Bronchoscopy may be used for diagnostic purposes and treatment (e.g., remove mucous plugs, foreign bodies). It can help achieve patency of an airway that has been partially or nearly obstructed by tumors. A **thoracentesis** can relieve symptoms by draining air or excess fluid from the pleural space. Usually, we remove no more than 1000 to 1200 mL of fluid at one time. Rapid removal of a large volume of pleural fluid can result in hypotension, hypoxemia, or re-expansion pulmonary edema. These procedures are discussed in Chapter 27.

Chest Tubes and Pleural Drainage

If enough fluid or air accumulates in the pleural space, the normally negative subatmospheric pressure becomes positive and 1 or both lungs collapse. Inserting a chest tube into the pleural

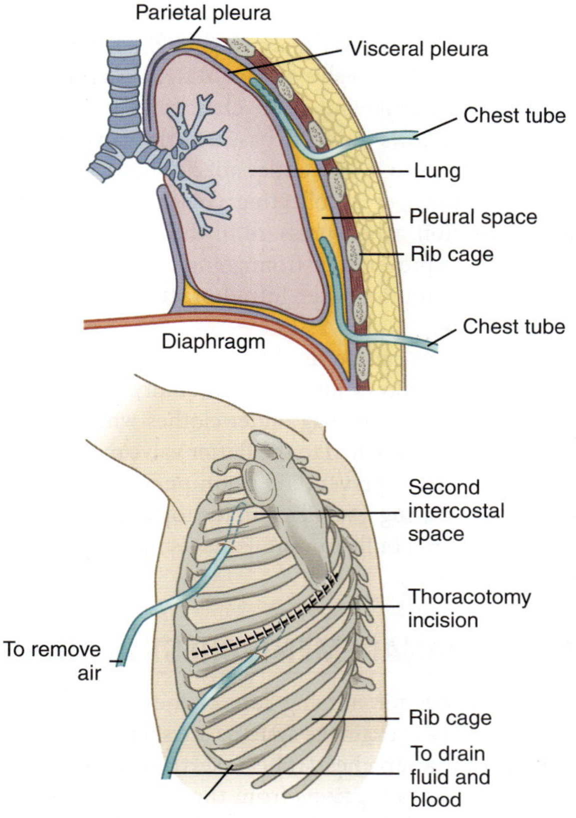

Fig. 28.4 Placement of chest tubes.

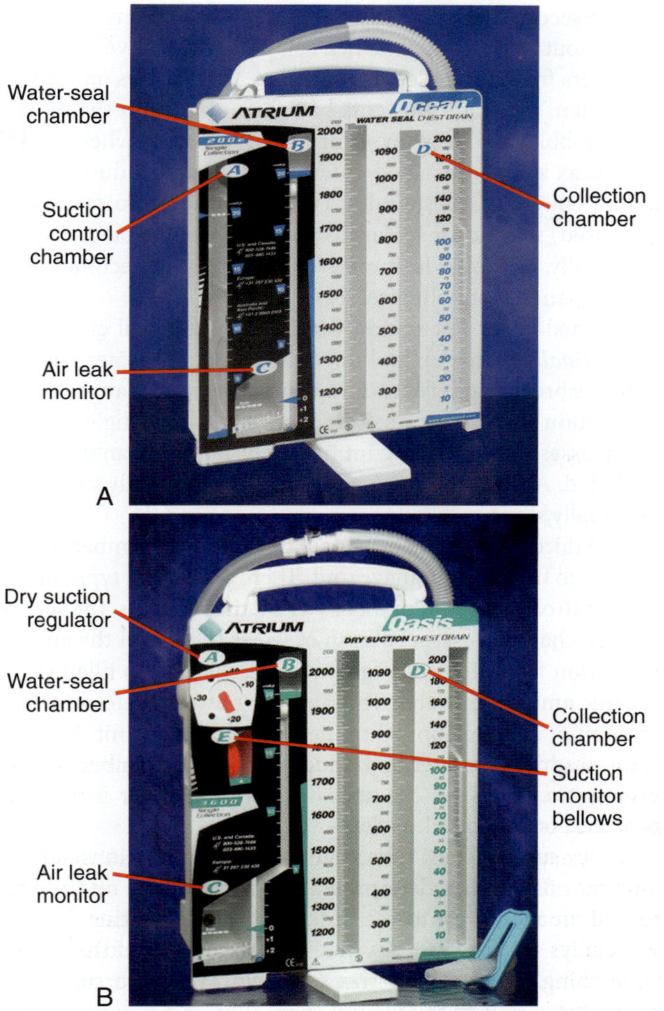

Fig. 28.5 Chest drainage unit. Both units have 3 chambers: (1) collection chamber; (2) water-seal chamber; and (3) suction control chamber. Suction control chamber requires connection to a wall suction source for the suction to work. (A) Water suction. This unit uses water in the suction control chamber to control the suction pressure. (B) Dry suction. This unit controls suction by using a regulator control dial. (From Atrium Medical Corporation, Hudson, NH.)

space can re-establish negative pressure, drain the pleural space, and allow for lung expansion.[6]

Chest tubes are about 20 in (51 cm) long and vary in size from 12F to 40F. The size inserted depends on the reason for the chest tube insertion. Large (36F to 40F) tubes are used to drain blood. Medium (24F to 36F) tubes are used to drain fluid. Small (12F to 24F) tubes are used to drain air. Pigtail catheters are very small (10F to 14F) tubes with a curly end designed to keep them in place.[7] Sometimes, they are a safe and effective alternative to larger-bore chest tubes for treatment of pneumothorax.

Chest Tube Insertion

Insertion of a chest tube can take place in the ED, surgery, or at the bedside. Time permitting, a chest x-ray is done to confirm the affected side. The patient is positioned with the arm raised above the head on the affected side to expose the midaxillary area, the standard site for insertion. Elevate the head (up to 45 degrees when possible) to lower the diaphragm and reduce the risk for injury.

The area is cleansed with an antiseptic solution. The HCP injects a local anesthetic and makes a small incision over a rib. The chest tube is advanced up and over the top of the rib to avoid the intercostal nerves and blood vessels that are behind the rib inferiorly (Fig. 28.4). Once inserted, the HCP sutures the tube in place and closes the incision with sutures. The tube is connected to a pleural drainage system. The wound is covered with an occlusive dressing. Most HCPs prefer to seal the wound around the chest tube with petroleum (airtight) gauze. Tube placement is confirmed by chest x-ray.

Inserting a chest tube is painful. Monitor the patient's comfort frequently and use appropriate pain-relieving interventions.

Pleural Drainage System

A chest tube is usually attached to a drainage device or chamber to collect fluid, air, and/or blood from the chest cavity. Many disposable, plastic chest drainage systems are available. Manufacturers include directions for set-up and use with each unit. Most units have a 2000 mL capacity.

All drainage units have 3 basic compartments (Fig. 28.5). The first compartment, or collection chamber, receives fluid and air from the pleural space. The drained fluid stays in this chamber while expelled air vents to the second compartment.

The second compartment is the water-seal chamber. It contains about 2 cm of water, which acts as a 1-way valve. Incoming air enters from the collection chamber and bubbles up through the water. The water prevents backflow of air into the patient. Brisk bubbling of air often occurs in this chamber when a pneumothorax is first evacuated. Intermittent bubbling during exhalation, coughing, or sneezing (when intrathoracic pressure is increased) may occur as long as there is air in the pleural space. Eventually, as the air leak resolves and the lung becomes more fully expanded, bubbling ceases.

Normal water fluctuation within the water-seal chamber is called *tidaling*. This up and down movement of water with the patient's breathing reflects intrapleural pressure changes during inspiration and expiration. This is normal. If tidaling stops suddenly, assess the chest tube immediately. It may mean the tube is occluded. As the lung re-expands, tidaling gradually slows then eventually stops.

The third compartment, the suction control chamber, applies suction to the chest drainage unit. There are 2 main types of suction control: water and dry. For wet suction systems, the suction control chamber uses a column of water to control the amount of suction from the wall regulator. The chamber is filled with a specific amount of water. This amount of water determines the amount of suction applied to the chest drainage unit. You may need to add more water to the suction control chamber as water evaporates. Problems can arise with this chamber if the chest tube unit is tipped or knocked over.

A dry suction chest tube system does not contain water. The amount of suction is determined by turning a dial on the chest tube drainage device to the ordered amount. Suction pressure is usually −20 cm H_2O. A visual alert shows you if the suction is working. Higher pressures (−40 cm H_2O) are sometimes needed to evacuate the pleural space. Lower pressure (−10 cm H_2O) may be used for frail and older patients at risk for tissue damage.

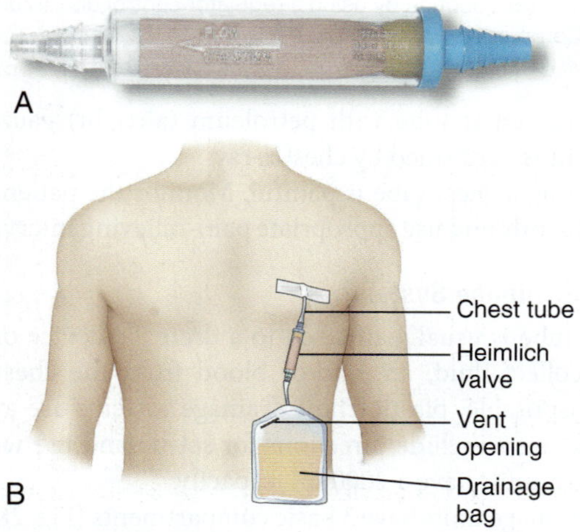

Fig. 28.6 (A) Heimlich chest drain valve is a specially designed valve that is used in place of a chest drainage unit for small uncomplicated pneumothorax. The valve allows for escape of air but prevents the reentry of air into the pleural space. (B) Placement of valve between chest tube and vented drainage bag, which can be worn under a gown or clothes. (A, Courtesy and © Becton, Dickinson and Company.)

A flutter valve (also called the *Heimlich valve*) is used to remove air from the pleural space (Fig. 28.6). This device consists of a 1-way rubber valve within a rigid plastic tube. It is attached to the external end of the chest tube. It has 2 nozzles. The inlet nozzle allows the air to pass into the valve through the chest tube attached to it. The outlet nozzle allows the air to pass to the environment or a collecting device during expiration. During inspiration, when pressure in the chest decreases, the valve closes. This prevents air from going back into the patient's chest. During expiration, when intrathoracic pressure increases, the valve opens.

The flutter valve can be used for a small to moderate-sized pneumothorax. It allows for patient mobility. The patient can hide the smaller drainage bag under clothes when they ambulate. Drainage bags attached to the flutter valve must have a vent to the atmosphere to prevent a tension pneumothorax. This is done by simply cutting a small slit in the top of any drainage bag that does not have a built-in vent. Patients may go home with a flutter valve in place.

NURSING MANAGEMENT: CHEST DRAINAGE

General guidelines for nursing care of the patient with chest tubes and chest tube drainage systems are shown in Table 28.6.

Immediately after chest tube insertion, closely monitor the patient for complications from the chest tube placement and drainage. Monitor vital signs, including respiratory rate and rhythm. If volumes from 1 to 1.5 L of fluid and/or blood are removed rapidly, re-expansion pulmonary edema or severe, symptomatic hypotension may occur. Ask the HCP how much drainage to expect. Notify the HCP if excess drainage occurs.

Inspect the integrity of the system. Monitor the color and amount of drainage hourly in the first few hours after chest tube insertion. Report drainage greater than 200 mL in the first hour, development of subcutaneous emphysema, or any signs and symptoms of respiratory distress to the HCP at once.

Subcutaneous emphysema can occur from air leaking into the tissue surrounding the chest tube insertion site. If present, you will feel a "crackling" sensation when palpating the skin. A small amount of subcutaneous air is harmless and will be reabsorbed. However, severe subcutaneous emphysema around the head and neck can cause swelling with airway compromise.

Sterile technique during dressing changes can reduce infection of the insertion site. Implement measures to reduce the risk for atelectasis and shoulder stiffness. Encourage coughing, deep breathing, incentive spirometer use, and range-of-motion (ROM) exercises.

If a chest tube suddenly becomes disconnected, the immediate priority is to reestablish the water-seal system. In some agencies, when disconnection occurs, the exposed end of the chest tube is immersed in sterile water to act as a water seal until a new system can be set up and chest drainage reestablished. Do not clamp the tube. The danger of rapid accumulation of air in the pleural space, causing tension pneumothorax, is far greater than that of a small amount of atmospheric air that enters the pleural space. We no long "milk" or "strip" chest tubes. Doing so generates large changes in intrathoracic pressure.[8]

You can momentarily clamp a chest tube to change the drainage apparatus or check for air leaks. Appearance of a new air leak warrants assessment of the drainage system to identify whether the air leak is coming from the patient or from the system. Follow your agency policy about specific clinical situations when you may clamp a chest tube.

TABLE 28.6 Chest Tubes and Chest Tube Drainage Units

Set-Up and Insertion

1. Explain procedure to the patient and family/significant others.
2. Gather equipment:
   - Thoracotomy or chest tube insertion tray
   - Disposable chest drainage unit (CDU)
   - Chest tube
   - Bottle of sterile water
   - 1% lidocaine
   - Suction tubing and collection container
   - Occlusive dressing
3. Prepare CDU:
   - *Wet suction:* Add sterile water to 2-cm mark in water-seal chamber and to 20-cm mark (or as ordered) in suction control chamber.
   - *Dry suction:* Add sterile water to the fill line of the air leak meter. Attach suction tubing to wall suction and increase suction until the bellows-like float moves across the display window.
4. Position and support the patient to minimize movement during procedure.

Clinical Status

- Monitor the patient. Assess vital signs, lung sounds, pain and need for analgesia.
- Evaluate for subcutaneous emphysema at insertion site.
- Have the patient breathe deeply periodically to promote lung expansion. Encourage ROM exercises to the shoulder on the affected side. Encourage use of incentive spirometry every hour while awake to prevent atelectasis or pneumonia.
- Assess for complications. Auscultate the lungs (↓ or absent breath sounds may indicate air and/or fluid reaccumulating in chest); observe color and characteristics of chest tube drainage (significant bleeding >100 mL/hr); observe chest tube insertion site daily (infection may be identified by change in color or amount of drainage, erythema at site, patient fever, ↑ WBCs).

Chest Tube Dressings

- Change dressing according to policy and HCP preference.
- Remove old dressing carefully. Assess the site for inflammation or infection and culture site as needed.
- Cleanse the site according to policy, maintaining strict sterile asepsis.
- Redress with occlusive dressing. Some HCPs prefer a petroleum gauze dressing around the tube to prevent air leak. Date the dressing and document dressing change.

General Chest Tube Management

- Keep all connections between chest tubes, drainage tubing, and the drainage collector tight. Tape all connections.
- Keep all tubing loosely coiled below chest level. Position tubing so that drainage flows freely. Never raise the drainage system to the level of the patient's chest because fluid can drain back into the lungs.
- Observe for air fluctuations (tidaling) and bubbling in the water-seal chamber.
- Mark the time of measurement and the fluid level on the drainage unit according to policy. Report any change in the quantity or characteristics of drainage (e.g., clear yellow to bloody) to the HCP. Notify HCP if >100 mL/hr drainage.
- Change the unit if the collection chamber is full. Do not try to empty it.
- Never compress, milk, or strip chest tube tubing.

Wet Suction System (see manufacturer's directions for use)

- Keep the suction control chamber at the right water level by adding sterile water as needed to replace water lost to evaporation.
- After filling the suction control chamber to the ordered suction amount (generally 20 cm H_2O suction), connect the suction tubing to the wall suction.
- Dial the wall suction regulator until there is continuous, gentle bubbling in the suction control chamber (no more than 120 mm Hg). Vigorous bubbling is not necessary and will increase the rate of evaporation.
- If there is no bubbling in the suction control chamber, (1) there is no suction, (2) suction is not high enough, or (3) the pleural air leak is so large that suction is not high enough to evacuate it.

Dry Suction System (see manufacturer's directions for use)

- After connecting patient to system, turn the dial on the chest drainage system to amount ordered (generally −20 cm H_2O), connect suction tubing to wall suction source. Increase the suction until the float appears in the window of the CDU.
- If ordered to decrease suction, turn the dial down and depress the high-negativity vent. Assess for a rise in the water level of the water-seal chamber.

TABLE 28.6 Chest Tubes and Chest Tube Drainage Units—cont'd

Chest Tube Complications

1. Tidaling
   - In the spontaneously breathing patient, if fluid does not rise with inspiration or fall with expiration, the drainage system may be blocked, the lungs have re-expanded, or the system is attached to suction.
   - If the chest tube is connected to suction, disconnect momentarily from wall suction to check for tidaling.
2. Bubbling
   - If bubbling increases, there may be an air leak in the drainage system or a leak from the patient.
   - Suspect a system leak when bubbling is continuous.
   - Retape tubing connections
   - Ensure chest tube dressing is air occlusive
   - If leak persists, briefly clamp the chest tube at the patient's chest. If the leak stops, the air is coming from the patient.
   - If the air leak persists, briefly and methodically move the clamps down the tubing away from the patient until the air leak stops. The leak will then be present between the last 2 clamp points. If the air leak persists all the way to the drainage unit, replace the unit.
3. Drainage System Overturned
   - If the drainage system is overturned and the water seal is disrupted, return it to an upright position and encourage the patient to take a few deep breaths.
4. Inadvertent Disconnection from Patient
   - If the drainage system breaks, place the distal end of the chest tubing (patient-side) in a container of sterile water as an emergency water seal.

CHECK YOUR PRACTICE

You are caring for a 37-year-old male patient who has chest injuries from a motorcycle accident. He has 2 chest tubes in place that are each attached to a chest drainage system. While assisting him to turn in bed, you accidentally disconnect 1 of the chest tubes from the drainage system.

- What is your most immediate priority?

Chest Tube Removal

Chest tubes are removed when the lungs are re-expanded, and fluid drainage has ceased or is minimal. Sometimes, we discontinue the suction and allow the chest tube to drain by gravity for 24 hours before removing the tube.

Give pain medication about 30 to 60 minutes before chest tube removal. Gather dressing supplies, including petroleum gauze and dry gauze dressing. Explain the procedure to the patient. In most settings, the HCP or an advanced practice nurse removes the tube. They cut the suture holding the chest tube in place. With the patient holding their breath or bearing down (Valsalva maneuver), the tube is removed. The site is immediately covered with the airtight, occlusive dressing to prevent air from entering the pleural space. A dry gauze dressing is placed over top. The pleura will seal off, and the wound usually heals in a few days. A chest x-ray is done 30 to 60 minutes after chest tube removal to check for pneumothorax or fluid accumulation.

Observe the wound for drainage and reinforce the dressing if needed. Monitor and record vital signs. Assess the patient for respiratory distress. This may signify a recurrence of the original problem. If respiratory distress occurs, notify the HCP at once.

Chest Surgery

Chest surgery is done for various reasons, including lung, heart, vascular, and esophageal problems. The most common chest surgeries are described in Table 28.7.

Thoracotomy

A **thoracotomy** is a surgical incision into the chest to gain access to the heart, lungs, esophagus, thoracic aorta, or anterior spine. Two common approaches to a thoracotomy are the median sternotomy and lateral thoracotomy.

The median sternotomy involves splitting the sternum. It is mainly used for surgery involving the heart. A lateral thoracotomy can be done using a posterolateral or anterolateral incision. A *posterolateral incision* is used for most surgeries involving the lung. The incision is made from front to back at the level of the 4th, 5th, or 6th intercostal space. Strong mechanical retractors are used to separate the ribs and gain access to the lung. An *anterolateral incision* is made in the 4th or 5th intercostal space from the sternal border to the midaxillary line. This procedure is often done for surgery or trauma victims, mediastinal operations, and wedge resections of the upper and middle lobes of the lung.

Video-Assisted Thoracic Surgery

Video-assisted thoracoscopic surgery (VATS) is a widely used, minimally invasive surgical approach for thoracic procedures. It provides a real-time 2-dimensional video image of the inside of the chest cavity. VATS is used for diagnosis and treatment of pleural disease, masses and nodules, and interstitial lung disease. Through incisions just large enough to insert the instruments, the HCP can inspect the chest cavity, biopsy suspicious areas, obtain fluid samples for analysis, and remove tissue.

VATS is increasingly being used for patients with chest trauma. The HCP can examine, diagnose, and manage injuries in both blunt and penetrating trauma, including injuries to the diaphragm. A chest tube is placed in the pleural space through 1 or more of the incisions at the end of the procedure, secured with sutures, and connected to a drainage unit in the usual manner.

The advantages of VATS include less pain, faster return to normal activity, reduced length of hospital stay, lower postoperative morbidity, and fewer complications. Patients who have low respiratory reserve or are too debilitated to tolerate an open thoracotomy approach may benefit from the VATS procedure.

❖ NURSING MANAGEMENT: CHEST SURGERY

◆ Preoperative Care

Assess cardiopulmonary status to determine their ability to tolerate the surgery and provide a baseline reference for

TABLE 28.7 Chest Surgeries

Type	Description	Indications
Decortication		
Removal or stripping of thick, fibrous membrane from visceral pleura Allows for improved lung expansion	Need chest tubes postoperatively	Empyema or other inflammatory process unresponsive to conservative management
Exploratory Thoracotomy		
Incision into thoracic cavity to look for injured or bleeding tissues	Need chest tubes postoperatively	Chest trauma
Lobectomy		
Removal of 1 lobe of lung	Lung tissue expands to fill up space left by resected lobe Need chest tubes postoperatively	Lung cancer, bronchiectasis, TB, advanced emphysema, benign lung tumors, fungal infections
Lung Volume Reduction Surgery		
Bronchoscopy procedure	Used to place one-way valves in airways leading to the diseased parts of the lung Valves let air out, but not in, thus collapsing a certain segment of lungs	Advanced emphysema, α_1-antitrypsin emphysema
Open surgical procedure	Involves reducing lung volume by multiple wedge excisions or VATS Removes most diseased lung tissue	Emphysema, lung cancer
Pneumonectomy		
Removal of entire lung	When lobectomy or segmental resection will not remove all diseased lung Fluid will gradually fill space where lung was removed May have chest tube postoperatively Position patient on operative side to promote expansion of remaining lung	Lung cancer (most common)
Segmental Resection		
Removal of 1 or more lung segments	Indicated for a patient unable to handle more extensive surgery Remaining lung tissue expands to fill space Need chest tubes postoperatively	Lung cancer, bronchiectasis
Thoracotomy (Not Involving Lungs)		
Incision into thorax for surgery on other organs	Postoperative care related to thoracotomy and reason for surgical procedure Need chest tubes after surgery	Hiatal hernia repair, open heart surgery, esophageal surgery, tracheal resection, thoracic aorta repair
Video-Assisted Thoracic Surgery (VATS)		
Video-assisted technique with a rigid scope with a distal lens inserted into pleura and image shown on a monitor screen	Allows HCP to manipulate instruments passed into pleural space through separate small intercostal incisions Done under general anesthesia in operating room May need chest tube after surgery	Lung biopsy, lobectomy, resection of nodules, fistula repair
Wedge Resection		
Removal of small, localized lesion that occupies only part of a lung segment	Most conservative approach Done to remove small peripheral nodules or for patients unable to handle more extensive surgery Need chest tubes after surgery	Lung biopsy, excision of small nodules

postoperative care. Preoperative evaluation may include chest x-ray, electrocardiogram (ECG), ABGs, pulmonary function studies, CT or MRI. Laboratory studies may include CBC, blood glucose, serum electrolytes, blood urea nitrogen (BUN), serum creatinine, prothrombin time/international normalized ratio (PT/INR), and activated partial thromboplastin time (aPTT).

The patient should be in the best possible health and, if applicable, stop smoking before elective surgery. Anxiety associated with anticipated surgery makes smoking cessation difficult. Provide encouragement, support, and teaching about ways to help stop smoking before surgery (see Chapter 11).

Teach the patient what to expect after surgery. Include the use of O_2, IV fluids, the chance of intubation, blood administration, and the purpose and function of chest tubes. Reassure the patient that they will receive adequate analgesia to reduce pain. Explain how to use patient-controlled analgesia (PCA), if planned.

Preoperative teaching should always include exercises for effective deep breathing and incentive spirometry use. If the patient practices these techniques before surgery, they will be easier to perform after surgery. Teach the patient how to splint the incision with a pillow to promote deep breathing. Have them teach-back ROM exercises on the affected surgical side.

The thought of losing part of a vital organ is often frightening. Reassure the patient that the lungs have a large degree of functional reserve. Even after the removal of 1 lung, there is enough lung tissue left to maintain adequate oxygenation. Answer the patient and caregiver's questions openly and honestly.

◆ Postoperative Care

The thoracotomy incision is the most painful surgical incision for patients and a difficult one for nurses to manage. Pain after a thoracotomy is typically intense because respiratory muscles are cut during surgery. For most chest surgeries, chest tubes are placed in the pleural space to allow for lung re-expansion. In a pneumonectomy, chest tubes may be placed in the space where the lung was removed.

Pain management is a priority to prevent respiratory compromise. A multimodal management approach is best after thoracic surgery. This may include the use of oral, subcutaneous, and/or IV opioids, PCA, epidural infusions, and/or intercostal nerve blocks. Effective pain management allows patients to breathe deeply, cough, move the arm and shoulder on the operative side, and mobilize.

Nursing care priorities include assessing respiratory function, including observing respiratory rate and effort, breath sounds, and sputum volume and color. Monitor chest tube function. Note amount and type of drainage. Daily chest x-rays are often done. Assess pain, monitor temperature, and observe the surgical site as you would for other postoperative patients (see Chapter 20). Care after thoracotomy is described in eNursing Care Plan 27.1 (available on the website for this chapter).

NONINVASIVE VENTILATION

Noninvasive ventilation (NIV) uses a mask instead of an ET tube to help oxygenate and ventilate a patient. The mask can be nasal or full face. NIV is ideal for those who need a higher level of ventilatory support, but their condition is not bad enough to need mechanical ventilation. Good candidates for using NIV are patients with COPD exacerbations and heart failure (HF).[9] The patient with an acute myocardial infarction or gastrointestinal (GI) bleed is not a candidate for NIV. Two common modes are continuous positive airway pressure (CPAP) and bi-level positive airway pressure (Bi-PAP).

Continuous Positive Airway Pressure

Continuous positive airway pressure (CPAP) helps restore functional residual capacity (FRC). It provides 1 level of pressure. That pressure is delivered continuously during both inspiration and expiration. CPAP is a common treatment for obstructive sleep apnea.

CPAP is delivered through a tight-fitting face mask, nasal mask, or nasal pillows. It increases WOB because the patient must forcibly exhale against the CPAP. Therefore, it is used with caution in patients with heart problems. Monitor the patient closely. Report any decline in their condition to the HCP at once.

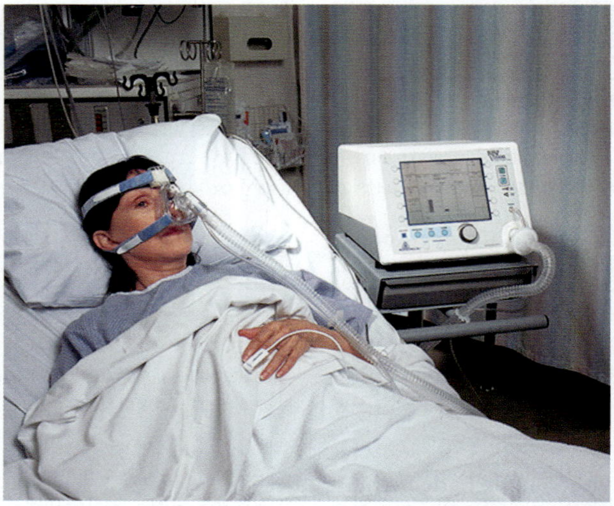

Fig. 28.7 Bi-PAP delivered through a face mask. (Courtesy Respironics Inc., Murrysville, PA.)

Bilevel Positive Airway Pressure

Bilevel positive airway pressure (Bi-PAP) provides 2 levels of positive pressure support: inspiratory positive airway pressure (IPAP) and expiratory positive airway pressure (EPAP) (Fig. 28.7). IPAP is a higher level of pressure than EPAP. It helps with CO_2 removal. EPAP is a lower level of pressure. It helps keep the alveoli open at end expiration, assisting with oxygenation.

The patient must be awake, alert, able to breathe spontaneously, and tolerate the face piece. Bi-PAP is used for COPD patients with acute conditions (e.g., pneumonia) or exacerbation of chronic conditions (e.g., HF, acute respiratory failure [ARF]). Its use after extubation from mechanical ventilation can help prevent reintubation. Patients with shock, altered mental status, or increased airway secretions cannot use Bi-PAP because of the risk for aspiration and the inability to remove the mask.

❖ NURSING MANAGEMENT: NONINVASIVE VENTILATION

Patients with NIV need constant assessment. Assess level of consciousness (LOC), hemodynamic stability, and WOB. Patients who develop a decreased LOC may not be able to maintain a patent airway because they cannot protect their airway or clear secretions. In this situation, they may need intubation and mechanical ventilation. Any degree of hemodynamic instability (e.g., tachycardia, hypotension) warrants immediate re-evaluation of NIV.

Provide mouth, nare, and eye care. Provide measures to protect the skin from breakdown and ulceration. Any degree of redness constitutes a Stage I pressure injury. Attempts to alleviate pressure from the tightfitting mask, including alternating the length of time the mask is on, is important. Using masks of different sizes and styles can help. Collaborate with the RT.

The patient must be able to remove the mask independently due to the risk of vomiting. Elevate the head of the bed 30 to 45 degrees.

MECHANICAL VENTILATION

Mechanical ventilation is the process by which a ventilator is used to deliver O_2 to the lungs. It is a means of supporting patients until they recover the ability to breathe independently. It can serve as a bridge to long-term mechanical ventilation or until a decision is made to stop ventilatory support. Mechanical ventilation is not curative.

Indications for mechanical ventilation include (1) ARF, (2) apnea, (3) inability to breathe or protect the airway, (3) acute respiratory distress, (4) severe hypoxemia and/or hypercarbia, and (5) respiratory muscle fatigue.[10] Other patients who receive mechanical ventilation include those with hemorrhage, trauma, neuromuscular problems, drug overdose, burns, and shock.

Patients with chronic lung disease and their caregivers should discuss mechanical ventilation before a health crisis occurs. Encourage all patients, especially those with chronic illnesses, to discuss the subject of life-sustaining measures, including mechanical ventilation, with their families and HCPs. The patient's wishes about end-of-life treatment should be recorded in an advance directive.

The decision to use, withhold, or stop mechanical ventilation must be made carefully. We must respect the wishes of the patient. When the health care team, patient, and/or caregiver disagree over the treatment that the patient wishes, conferences are essential to keep the lines of communication open and discuss options. Sometimes, you may need to consult the agency's ethics committee for assistance.

Types of Ventilators

Negative Pressure Ventilation

Negative pressure ventilation involves the use of chambers that encase the chest or body and surround it with intermittent subatmospheric (or negative) pressure. It is a form of NIV, as it does not require an artificial invasive airway.

The "iron lung" was the first form of negative pressure ventilation. It was developed in the 1950s during the polio epidemic. Intermittent negative pressure around the chest pulls the chest wall outwards, reducing intrathoracic pressure. Air rushes into the upper airway, which is outside the sealed chamber. Expiration is passive. The machine cycles off, allowing chest retraction. This type of ventilation is like normal ventilation in that decreased intrathoracic pressures produce inspiration, and expiration is passive.

A few portable negative pressure ventilators are available for home use. They are mainly for patients with chronic neuromuscular diseases and central nervous system problems. Some of these patients will have used negative pressure ventilators for years. They are rarely used for acutely ill patients.

Positive Pressure Ventilation

Positive pressure ventilation (PPV) is the main method of mechanical ventilation used with acutely ill patients (Fig. 28.8). During inspiration, the ventilator pushes air into the lungs under positive pressure. Unlike spontaneous ventilation, intrathoracic pressure is increased during lung inflation, not decreased. Expiration is passive, as occurs in normal expiration. Ventilators can deliver positive pressure breaths to the patient by either volume or pressure ventilation.

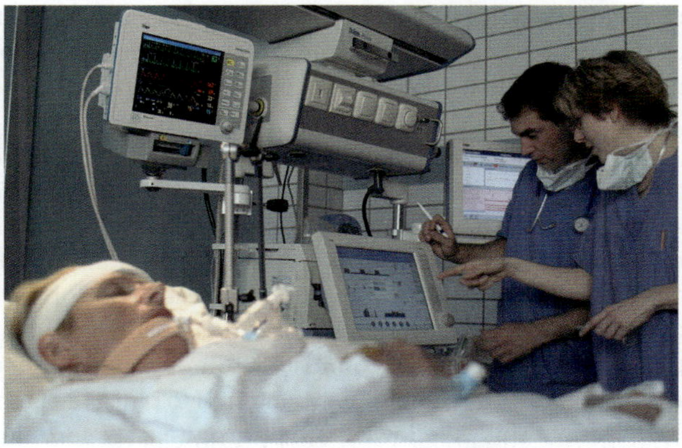

Fig. 28.8 Patient receiving mechanical ventilation. (Courtesy Draeger Medical, Houston, TX.)

Volume ventilation. With **volume ventilation**, a predetermined tidal volume (V_T) is delivered with each inspiration.[11] The amount of pressure needed to deliver the breath varies based on the compliance and resistance of the lungs. The V_T is consistent from breath to breath, but the airway pressures needed to deliver the V_T will vary.

Pressure ventilation. With pressure ventilation, the peak inspiratory pressure (PIP) is predetermined.[11] The VT delivered to the patient will vary, based on the pressure selected and compliance and resistance factors of the lungs. Careful attention must be given to monitoring the exhaled V_T to prevent hypoventilation and hypoxemia.

Endotracheal Intubation Procedure

Intubation is the process of securing the airway with an oral or nasal ET tube, providing an effective route for ventilation. Unless ET intubation is emergent, consent for the procedure is obtained. Tell the patient and caregiver the reason for ET intubation and steps in the procedure. Explain that the patient will not be able to speak while intubated, but that you will provide other means of communication. Tell them that the patient's hands may have removable mitts or wrists may have soft restraints applied to remind them not to touch the ET tube.

Have a self-inflating BVM attached to O_2 and suctioning equipment ready at the bedside. The BVM has a reservoir that is filled with O_2 so that it delivers concentrations of up to 100%. A patent IV is needed to give pre-intubation drugs. Assemble and check the equipment. Remove any dentures or partial plates (for oral intubation) and give drugs as ordered. Premedication varies depending on the patient's LOC (e.g., awake, obtunded), urgency (e.g., emergent, nonemergent), and the HCP's preferences.

For oral intubation, place the patient supine with the head slightly extended and the neck flexed ("sniff position"). This position allows the HCP to see the vocal cords more easily. For nasal intubation, spray the nasal passages with a local anesthetic and vasoconstrictor (e.g., lidocaine with epinephrine) to reduce trauma and bleeding. Before starting intubation, preoxygenate the patient using the BVM and 100% O_2 for at least 2 minutes. Each intubation attempt is limited to less than 30 seconds. Ventilate the patient between successive attempts using the BVM and 100% O_2.

Rapid sequence induction (RSI) is the rapid, concurrent administration of both a sedative and a paralytic drug during emergency airway management to induce unconsciousness for intubation. It decreases the risks for aspiration and injury. RSI is not indicated in patients who are in cardiac arrest or have a known difficult airway. The patient receives a sedative-hypnotic-amnesic (e.g., propofol, etomidate) to induce unconsciousness and a rapid-onset opioid (e.g., fentanyl) to blunt the pain of the procedure. This is followed with a drug (e.g., rocuronium) to produce skeletal muscle paralysis.

During intubation, monitor vital signs, including heart rate and rhythm, signs of visible chest movement, BP, and mean arterial pressure (MAP). Monitor O_2 status with pulse oximetry. Immediately inform the team if the SpO_2 is less than 92%. Monitor the patient's tolerance to the procedure. Follow agency policy about RSI drug administration.

Immediately after intubation, inflate the cuff on the ET tube. Help confirm placement of the ET tube while continuing to manually ventilate the patient using the BVM with 100% O_2. Auscultate the lungs for bilateral breath sounds and the epigastrium for the absence of air sounds. Observe for symmetric chest wall movement. SpO_2 should be stable or improve.

Use an $EtCO_2$ detector to help confirm placement by noting the presence of exhaled CO_2 from the lungs. A portable $EtCO_2$ monitor can help confirm correct placement of the tube (Fig. 28.9). A steadily rising CO_2 value and the presence of a waveform confirms correct placement. Or place a colorimetric CO_2 detector between the BVM and ET tube and look for a color change (indicating the presence of CO_2) or a number. At least 5 or 6 exhalations with a consistent CO_2 level must occur to confirm tube placement in the trachea.

If the findings support ET tube placement, help secure the ET per agency policy. Connect the ET tube to a ventilator and closed suctioning system (Fig. 28.10). Assess the need to suction the ET tube and pharynx. Insert a bite block, if needed. Secure it separately from the ET tube to the patient's face. This will help prevent the patient from biting the ET and preventing O_2 delivery.

Obtain a chest x-ray to confirm tube location (2 to 3 cm above the carina in the adult). This position allows the patient to move the neck without moving the tube or causing it to enter the right mainstem bronchus. Once positioning is confirmed with x-ray, record and mark the position of the oral ET tube at the lip or teeth. For a nasotracheal tube, mark the exit of the tube at the nare.

Obtain ABGs 15 to 30 minutes after intubation to determine baseline oxygenation and ventilation status. ABG values assess oxygenation and ventilation and assist in our determining changes to ventilator settings. Continuous pulse oximetry gives data about arterial oxygenation. $EtCO_2$ monitoring provides data about ventilation.

There are risks with oral ET intubation. It is hard to place the tube with limited head and neck mobility (e.g., spinal cord injury). Teeth can be chipped or accidentally removed during the procedure. Patients can obstruct the ET tube by biting down on the tube. Salivation increases, and swallowing is difficult. Sedation, along with a bite block or oropharyngeal airway, can help prevent obstruction. Mouth care is a challenge because of limited space in the oral cavity.

Ventilator Settings

Ventilator settings include the respiratory rate, V_T, O_2 concentration (FIO_2), positive end expiratory pressure (PEEP), inspiratory:expiratory ratio, and sensitivity (Table 28.8). Settings are based on the patient's condition, LOC, respiratory muscle strength, chest x-ray, and ABGs. Manipulating ventilator settings (Fig. 28.11) can help correct hypoxemia and hypercarbia. As the patient's condition improves, we can adjust the settings to allow them to take more control over their own WOB. Know your responsibility regarding changing ventilator settings. In most settings, this task is the responsibility of the HCP or RT. Always assess the patient's response to any setting changes.

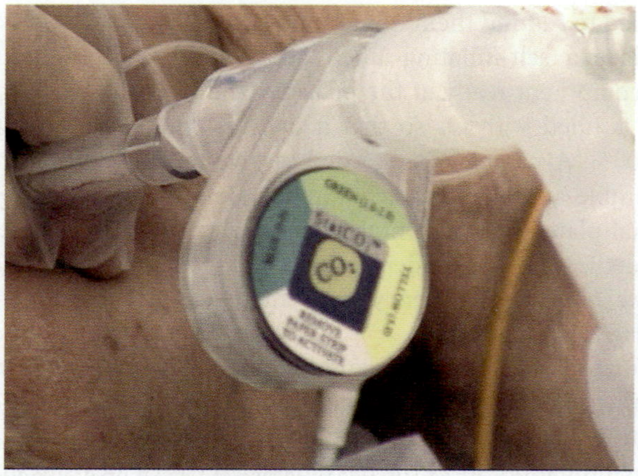

Fig. 28.9 End-tidal CO_2 detector. Used to help confirm placement of an endotracheal tube post-intubation. (From Thomsen TW, Setnik GS: Orotracheal intubation, *Procedures Consult,* 2017.)

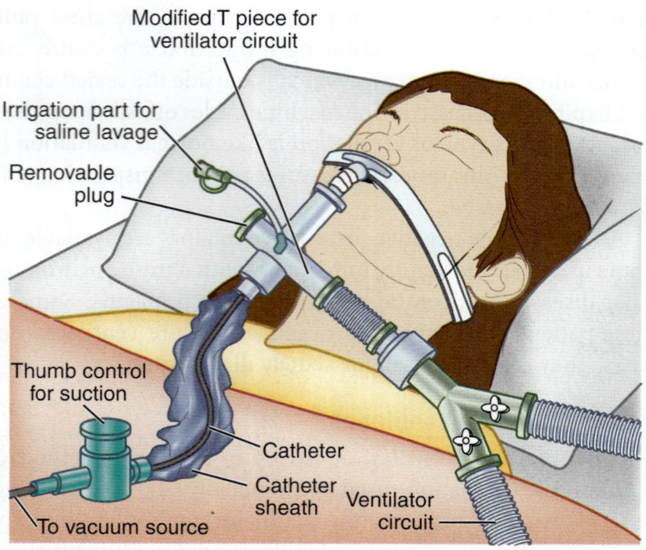

Fig. 28.10 Oral ET tube connected to ventilator circuit and closed tracheal suction system.

TABLE 28.8 Adjustable Ventilator Settings

Parameter	Mode	Description
Respiratory rate	Full support	Number of breaths the ventilator delivers per minute. *Example:* 12–20 breaths/min
Tidal volume (V_T)	Full support	Volume of gas delivered to patient during each ventilator breath. *Example:* 4–8 mL/kg
O_2 concentration (FIO_2)	All modes	Fraction of inspired O_2 (FIO_2) delivered to patient. May be set between 30% and 100%. You would never intubate a patient and place on room air (21%). *Usually adjusted* to maintain PaO_2 level >60 mm Hg or SpO_2 level >92%
Positive end-expiratory pressure (PEEP)	All modes	Positive pressure applied at the end of expiration of ventilator breaths. *Example*: 5 cm H_2O
Pressure support	Spontaneous Breathing Mode	Positive pressure used to augment patient's inspiratory pressure during spontaneous breathing. *Usual setting:* 5–10 cm H_2O
I/E ratio		Duration of inspiration (I) to duration of expiration (E). *Example:* 1:2 (exhalation is twice as long as inspiration)
Inspiratory flow rate and time	Full, partial support	Speed with which the V_T is delivered. *Example:* 40–80 L/min and time is 0.8–1.2 s
Sensitivity	Full, partial support	Determines the amount of effort the patient must generate to initiate a breath from the ventilator. The "trigger" to initiate the breath can be set on the ventilator for either pressure or flow triggering. *Example:* A pressure trigger is set 0.5–1.5 cm H_2O below baseline pressure; a flow trigger is set 1–3 L/min below baseline flow
Peak inspiratory pressure (PIP)	Full support	The maximal pressure the ventilator can generate to deliver the V_T. When the PIP limit is reached, the ventilator ends the breath and spills the undelivered volume into the atmosphere. *Example:* 30 cm H_2O

Positive End-Expiratory Pressure

Positive end-expiratory pressure (PEEP) is a ventilator setting in which positive pressure is applied to the airway during exhalation.[12] During exhalation, airway pressure normally drops to near 0. Exhalation occurs passively. With PEEP, exhalation remains passive, but pressure falls to the preset PEEP level, often set between 5 to 10 cm H_2O. PEEP increases FRC and often improves oxygenation by restoring the lung volume that normally remains at the end of passive exhalation. The mechanisms by which PEEP increases FRC and oxygenation include splinting open of previously collapsed alveoli (increasing the opportunity for O_2 and CO_2 to diffuse across the alveolar capillary membrane) and preventing alveolar collapse throughout the respiratory cycle.

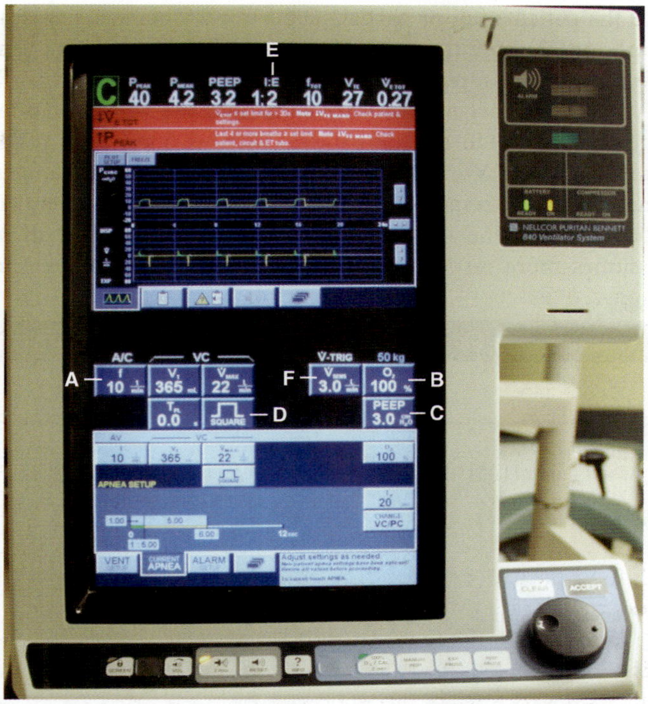

Fig. 28.11 Ventilator control panel. (From Roberts JR: *Roberts and Hedges' clinical procedures in emergency medicine and acute care*, ed 7, St Louis, 2019, Elsevier.)

PEEP is indicated in all patients who are mechanically ventilated. An intubated patient would never be placed on zero PEEP. PEEP is titrated to the point that oxygenation improves without compromising hemodynamics. We call this *optimal PEEP.* Often 5 cm H_2O PEEP (referred to as *physiologic PEEP*) is used to replace the glottic mechanism, which is bypassed when the patient has an oral ET tube.[12] We can often reduce FIO_2 when PEEP is used.

The classic indication for PEEP therapy is ARDS. PEEP is used with caution in patients with traumatic brain injury, increased ICP, low CO, and hypovolemia. In these cases, the adverse effects of high PEEP may outweigh the benefits. During weaning PEEP improves gas exchange, vital capacity, and inspiratory force.

Modes of Volume Ventilation

The way by which the ventilator delivers effective ventilation is called the *ventilator mode.* The selected ventilator mode is based on how much WOB the patient can perform. WOB is the inspiratory effort needed to overcome the elasticity and viscosity of the lungs along with the airway resistance. The ventilator mode is mainly determined by the patient's LOC, respiratory drive, WOB, and ABGs.

Modes of mechanical ventilation can be complex. This is because there are many different manufacturers of ventilators. Similarly, terminology among manufacturers differs as many companies trademark a mode of ventilation with a particular name. To begin to understand mechanical ventilation, focus on 2 key components: (1) how much work the ventilator is doing for the patient (full or partial support or spontaneous breathing) and (2) how the breath is being delivered to the patient (volume or pressure).

In *full support* mechanical ventilation, the ventilator does most of the WOB for the patient. There is often a set respiratory rate, set V_T, and PIP limit. In a *partial support* mode, there is shared responsibility between the patient and ventilator. There may be a set respiratory rate or V_T, but the patient assumes more responsibility for breathing. In a *spontaneous mode* of mechanical ventilation, the patient is intubated or has a tracheostomy. The patient assumes responsibility for almost all breathing. Spontaneous modes are often used just before the patient is extubated from the ventilator.

Let us look at the 5 most common modes of mechanical ventilation in North America. These modes include (1) assist control, (2) pressure control, (3) synchronous intermittent mandatory ventilation, (4) pressure support, and (5) CPAP (Table 28.9).

TABLE 28.9 Modes of Mechanical Ventilation

Mode of Ventilation	Ventilator Settings	Nursing Implications
Full Support		
Assist-control (AC)	• Set respiratory rate, V_T, inspiratory time, and PEEP • Ventilator delivers a pre-set number of breaths with designated V_T • If the patient initiates a spontaneous breath, a full breath with designated V_T is delivered	• V_T is consistent; trend pressure (PIP) • Hyperventilation can occur if patient increases respiratory rate above set rate • To limit spontaneous breaths, sedation may be needed • Example: New surgical patients
Pressure-control (PC)	• Set respiratory rate, peak inspiratory pressure (PIP), inspiratory time, and PEEP • Ventilator delivers a pre-set number of breaths up to a specific PIP (set by HCP) • If the patient initiates a spontaneous breath, a full breath delivered up to the set PIP is delivered	• PIP is never exceeded; trend V_T as will be variable • To limit spontaneous breaths, sedation may be needed • Example: ARDS (decreased compliance, increased resistance)
Pressure regulated volume control (PRVC)	• Set respiratory rate, V_T, PIP, PEEP, and sensitivity • Ventilator attempts to deliver the desired V_T with the least amount of PIP • Ventilator software analyzes resistance and compliance of each breath and continuously makes adjustment	• Trend V_T and PIP • Monitor for increased WOB
Partial Support Modes		
Synchronized intermittent mandatory ventilation (SIMV)	• Set respiratory rate and V_T for all ventilator-delivered breaths (can also be set up with a PIP, but V_T more common) • Inspiratory time, sensitivity, and PEEP also set • Ventilator delivers the pre-set number of breaths with designated V_T in "synchrony" with the patient's own inspirations • Between "ventilator-delivered breaths," patient breathes at their own rate and V_T	• Muscle fatigue may occur due to ↑ WOB
Spontaneous Modes		
Pressure support ventilation (PSV)	• Set inspiratory pressure level, PEEP, and sensitivity • When the patient initiates a breath, a high flow of gas is delivered to the preselected pressure level, and pressure is maintained throughout inspiration • Patient determines V_T, respiratory rate, and inspiratory time • Provides an augmented inspiration to a spontaneously breathing patient	• Patient must be awake and alert and be able to initiate a breath • Observe respiratory rate and V_T • Reduces WOB • Increased ventilator synchrony • Monitor for increased WOB • Monitor for apnea
Proportional assist ventilation (PAV)	• Will increase or decrease airway pressure in response to the patient's own respiratory effort • Provides a level of support at a percentage of patient effort (e.g., 80%); if patient working hard to initiate a breath, ventilator offers more support • Patient determines own inspiratory volume and inspiratory flow rate	• Monitor WOB • PAV is of no use in the patient who is not spontaneously breathing (will give no support)
Continuous positive airway pressure (CPAP)	• One set level of pressure (on inspiration and expiration), PEEP • Patient is spontaneously breathing through the ventilator circuit • There is no set respiratory rate, V_T, or inspiratory time	• Patient must be awake and alert and breathing spontaneously • Observe respiratory rate and V_T • Monitor for increased WOB • Monitor for apnea
Other		
Airway pressure release ventilation (APRV)	• Can be used as a full support or spontaneous mode of ventilation • Set pressure (P-high, P-low) and time (T-high, t-low) • Most of ventilator-delivered breath is spent at P-high and T-high (V_T is not a set variable) • Quick timed release (P-low, T-low) allows for CO_2 elimination • Permits spontaneous breathing at P-high, T-high	• Trend ABGs and acid-base balance • APRV increases venous return to the heart • Hemodynamics improvement may occur

Full support modes

Assist control. In assist-control (AC) ventilation (or volume control), the ventilator delivers a preset V_T at a preset respiratory rate.[12] When the patient initiates a spontaneous breath, the ventilator senses a change in the airflow in the ventilator circuit and then delivers the preset V_T. The patient's respiratory rate on AC ventilation will never be below the set respiratory rate. On AC ventilation, the patient can take a breath whenever they want. If the patient breathes over and above the set respiratory rate, the ventilator will deliver the additional breath with the designated V_T.

AC ventilation is the most common mode of full support mechanical ventilation when the patient is first intubated. It is used in patients with a variety of problems. This includes new postoperative patients and those with neuromuscular disorders and ARF.

With AC, the potential for hyperventilation exists. For example, a patient waking up after anesthesia may begin to take more spontaneous breaths above the set respiratory rate. As a result, the patient will receive all additional breaths with the full V_T. This can easily lead to respiratory alkalosis.

Pressure control. Pressure-control (PC) ventilation provides the patient with a pressure-limited breath.[11] In other words, besides a set respiratory rate, there is a set PIP. When the patient initiates the breath, the ventilator will deliver a volume of gas up to the PIP limit. In PC mode, the PIP limit will never be exceeded but there is no set V_T.

Like AC, PC ventilation permits the patient to take a breath over and above the set rate anytime they like. When the patient takes a breath above the set rate, the ventilator will deliver the breath based on the current ventilator settings.

PC ventilation is good for patients with decreased compliance and increased resistance ("stiff lungs"). This allows us to have control over the amount of pressure going into the patient, thereby decreasing risk of volutrauma and barotrauma.

Partial support modes

Synchronized intermittent mandatory ventilation. In synchronized intermittent mandatory ventilation (SIMV), both the patient and the ventilator do the WOB. The ventilator delivers a preset V_T at a preset respiratory rate, in synchrony with the patient's spontaneous breathing.[11] In between the ventilator-delivered breaths, the patient can breathe spontaneously and achieve whatever V_T they can achieve. In other words, the patient receives the designated V_T for the machine delivered breaths, but during the spontaneous breaths, the patient can breathe at whatever respiratory rate they wish. Their V_T is variable.

SIMV is used when the patient's condition is too good for a full support mode of mechanical ventilation, but they are not yet ready for a spontaneous mode. Sometimes, we combine SIMV with pressure support. Benefits of SIMV include improved patient-ventilator synchrony, lower mean airway pressures, and prevention of respiratory muscle atrophy as the patient takes on more responsibility for the WOB.

Spontaneous breathing modes

Pressure support. With pressure support ventilation (PSV), positive pressure is applied to the airway only during inspiration. The patient must be able to initiate a breath in this mode. The level of positive airway pressure is preset so that the inspiratory flow rate of the gas is greater than the patient's inspiratory flow rate. As the patient starts a breath, the ventilator senses the spontaneous respiratory effort and supplies a rapid flow of gas at the initiation of the breath and then a tapering flow towards the end of inhalation.[11] With PSV, the patient determines their own inspiratory length, V_T, and respiratory rate.

PSV is the most common mode of spontaneous mechanical ventilation in North America. Its purpose is to help facilitate weaning. It may be combined with SIMV during weaning when patients have a less than stable respiratory drive. PSV is not used during ARF because of the risk for hypoventilation and apnea. Advantages include increased patient comfort, decreased WOB (because inspiratory efforts are augmented), decreased O_2 consumption (because inspiratory work is reduced), and increased endurance conditioning (because the patient is exercising respiratory muscles).

Continuous positive airway pressure. CPAP refers to a mode of spontaneous ventilation where the ventilated patient controls almost all aspects of the breath.[11] Do not confuse this with noninvasive CPAP that is used for sleep apnea. With this CPAP, all that is set is the FIO_2 and PEEP. There is one level of pressure on both inspiration and expiration. There is no set respiratory rate, no set V_T, and no set PIP. The patient determines their respiratory rate and V_T.

CPAP is used to assess the patient's respiratory rate and rhythm, WOB, and hemodynamic status after a period of intubation. In most circumstances, this mode will be used for a short period of time, around 30 to 120 minutes. If the patient is stable, respiratory assessment parameters stay with normal limits, and there is no increased WOB or desaturation, the patient is often extubated.

Newer Modes of Mechanical Ventilation

Advances in technology have led to the development of many other modes of mechanical ventilation. These include (1) pressure-regulated volume control (PRVC), (2) airway pressure release ventilation (APRV), and (3) proportional assist ventilation (PAV; Table 28.9).

Pressure-regulated volume control. Pressure-regulated volume control (PRVC) is a full support mode of mechanical ventilation. It combines features of both volume and pressure delivery of the mechanical breath. In this mode, there is a set VT to be achieved and a PIP limit. The ventilator attempts to deliver the targeted VT with the least amount of pressure.11 The ventilator constantly analyzes, breath by breath, resistance and compliance of the lungs, the exhaled VT and PIP. It adjusts the delivery of each breath based on feedback received.

Airway pressure release ventilation. *Airway pressure release ventilation (APRV)* can be used in full support or spontaneous mode, depending on the patient. There are 2 levels of pressure in APRV: pressure-high (p-high) and pressure-low (p-low). There are also 2 time values: time-high (t-high) and time-low (t-low). For most of the ventilator breath (inhalation), the patient is at p-high and t-high (e.g., pressure of 30 cm H_2O for around 6 to 8 seconds).[13] During exhalation, pressure drops to near zero (p-low) for a very short period (t-low, about 0.8 second) to promote CO_2 elimination.

APRV permits spontaneous breathing at any point during the inspiratory respiratory cycle (p-high, t-high). We adjust the pressure levels in APRV to meet oxygenation goals. The timed releases are increased or decreased to meet ventilation goals. V_T is not set. It varies depending on the pressure levels, lung compliance and resistance, and degree of spontaneous breathing effort.

APRV is best for patients who need high pressure levels to open collapsed alveoli. It allows for spontaneous respirations. This may reduce the need for deep sedation or paralysis.

Proportional assist ventilation. *Proportional assist ventilation (PAV)* is a partial support mode of mechanical ventilation. In this mode, the ventilator generates and adjusts inspiratory pressures in proportion to the patient's own respiratory efforts.[11] The patient determines their own inspiratory flow rate and volume. The support that the ventilator provides the patient is a proportion of the patient's effort (e.g., 80%). The ventilator continually monitors compliance and resistance and calculates the degree of support it needs to offer. The patient is an active participant in breathing while receiving PAV. Decreased WOB and less dyssynchrony occur.

NURSING MANAGEMENT: MECHANICALLY VENTILATED PATIENT

Care of the mechanically ventilated patient requires an interprofessional approach (Table 28.10). Nurses and other team members must constantly synthesize large amounts of data about the patient's status, communicate even the smallest changes with one another, and collaborate on needed changes. This section reviews important aspects to be consider when caring for a patient who needs mechanical ventilation.

Artificial Airway Management

Managing an artificial airway is often a shared responsibility between you and the RT. Agency policy dictates which providers perform which task. Nursing responsibilities include (1) maintaining correct tube placement, (2) maintaining proper cuff inflation, (3) maintaining tube patency, and (4) maintaining alarm systems.

Maintaining Correct Tube Placement

Continuously monitor the patient with an ET tube for placement. Note the exit point from the mouth or nare. Assess the integrity of the tape or securement device. Observe for symmetric chest wall movement. Auscultate to confirm bilateral breath sounds.

If the tube moves or is dislodged, it could easily migrate upwards in the pharynx or enter the right or left mainstem bronchus (thus ventilating only 1 lung). This is an airway emergency. Stay with the patient and try to maintain the airway. Support ventilation with a BVM and 100% O_2. Call for the appropriate help to assess or reposition the tube. If a dislodged tube is not repositioned, minimal or no O_2 is delivered to the lungs, or the entire V_T is being delivered to 1 lung. This places the patient at risk for hypoxemia, pneumothorax, and respiratory and/or cardiac arrest.

TABLE 28.10 NURSING MANAGEMENT

Care for the Patient Requiring Mechanical Ventilation

- Monitor LOC, hemodynamic stability, patient-ventilator interaction, patient tolerance to ET or tracheostomy.
- Auscultate breath sounds and respiratory effort, assessing for decreased ventilation or adventitious sounds.
- Monitor ventilator settings and alarms.
- Monitor tube placement and cuff pressure.
- Determine need for ET tube suctioning and suction patients as needed.
- Give sedatives, analgesics, and NMBA drugs as ordered.
- Reposition and re-secure ET tube (per agency policy).
- Provide ordered VTE and GI prophylaxis.
- Develop plan for communication with the patient.
- Monitor oxygenation level and signs of respiratory fatigue during weaning.
- Teach patient and caregiver about mechanical ventilation and weaning.
- Supervise AP:
  - Obtain vital signs and report to RN.
  - Provide personal hygiene, skin care, and oral care.
  - Assist with frequent position changes, including early mobility.
  - Help to perform passive or active ROM exercises.

Collaborate With Respiratory Therapist
- Maintain ventilator system.
- Change ventilator settings as needed or ordered by HCP.
- Maintain correct cuff inflation on ET tube.
- Auscultate breath sounds and respiratory effort, assessing for decreased ventilation or adventitious sounds.
- Determine need for ET tube suctioning and suction patients as needed.
- Reposition and re-secure ET tube (based on agency policy).

Collaborate With Dietitian
- Assess and monitor nutrition status.
- Recommend EN formulas and optimal diet.

Collaborate With Physical and Occupational Therapist
- Perform ROM exercises.
- Assist with early and progressive ambulation.

Collaborate With Speech Language Therapist
- Perform swallowing studies.
- Assess cognitive function and assist with communication.
- Provide teaching for patient with a long-term tracheostomy.

Collaborate With Social Worker
- Work with the patient and caregiver to identify care needs.
- Help the patient with transitions through the health care system.

! SAFETY ALERT

Endotracheal Tube Placement

- Maintain proper ET tube position by recording and marking the position of the tube at the lip or teeth (e.g., 21 cm at the teeth; 23 cm at the lips).
- Assess ET tube position at least once per shift and with changes in patient position, early mobility, and before and after patient transport.

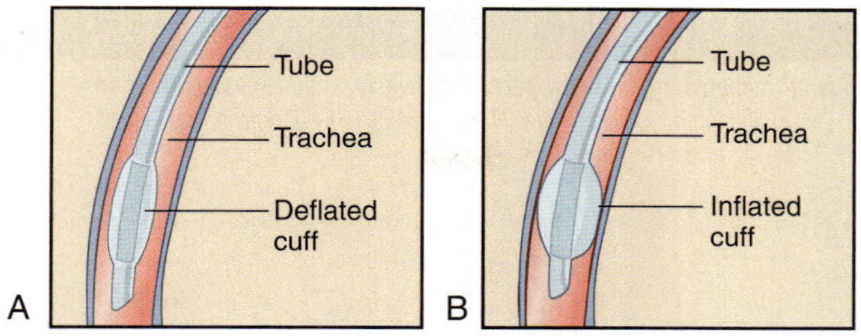

Fig. 28.12 Endotracheal tube cuff. (A) Tube in place with cuff deflated. (B) Tube in place with cuff inflated.

Maintaining Proper Cuff Inflation

The cuff is an inflatable, pliable, plastic sleeve encircling the lower, outer wall of the ET tube (Fig. 28.12). The cuff stabilizes and "seals" the ET tube within the trachea, prevents escape of ventilating gases. It also helps maintain correct tube position and "seals off" the lower airways, thus protecting against aspiration.

Excess volume in the cuff can damage the tracheal mucosa. To prevent this, inflate the cuff with air and measure and monitor the cuff pressure. To ensure adequate tracheal perfusion, maintain cuff pressure at 20 to 30 cm H_2O.[14] Measure and record cuff pressure after intubation and on a routine basis (e.g., every 8 hours) using the *minimal occluding volume* (MOV) *technique.* To perform the MOV technique in the mechanically ventilated patient, place a stethoscope over the trachea and inflate the cuff to MOV by adding air until you hear no air at PIP (end of ventilator inspiration). For the spontaneously breathing intubated patient, you inflate until you hear no sound after a deep breath or after inhalation with a BVM. Second, use a manometer to confirm that cuff pressure is between 20 and 30 cm H_2O. Record cuff pressure in the chart. If adequate cuff pressure cannot be maintained or larger volumes of air are needed to keep the cuff inflated, there could be a leak in the cuff or tracheal dilation at the cuff site. In these situations, notify the HCP.

Maintaining Tube Patency

Suctioning is needed to clear secretions and to maintain airway patency Indications for suctioning include (1) visible secretions in the ET tube, (2) increase in respiratory rate or frequent coughing, (3) sudden decrease in SpO_2, (4) suspected aspiration of secretions. Other signs that indicate the patient needs suctioning include an increase in peak airway pressure and auscultating adventitious breath sounds over the trachea or bronchi.

Assess the need for suctioning hourly. Indications include visible coughing, coarse crackles or wheezes over large airways, moist cough, increase in PIP, and restlessness or agitation. Neurologic patients may not show any signs of the need to be suctioned, so suctioning once per shift (at minimum) is recommended. Do not suction routinely. Suction the patient when needed. Note the color, character, consistency, and amount of sputum suctioned.

Two common ways we suction are the *closed-suction technique* (CST) and the *open-suction technique* (OST). The CST uses a suction catheter that is enclosed in a plastic sleeve connected directly to the patient-ventilator circuit (Fig. 28.10). With CST, exposure to the patient's secretions and infection is reduced for the patient and HCP's safety. The CST is the way we suction most intubated patients (Table 28.11).[15]

TABLE 28.11 Closed Suctioning Technique

The suction technique described here is appropriate for those patients with an oral ET tube or tracheostomy, who are receiving invasive mechanical ventilation. Maintaining a closed circuit at all times is best to reduce the risk for infection and for staff safety.

Before You Begin

1. Gather all equipment.
2. Wash hands and don personal protective equipment and gloves.
3. Explain procedure and patient's role in assisting with secretion removal by coughing.
4. Monitor neurologic and cardiopulmonary status (e.g., LOC, vital signs, ECG, SpO_2) before, during, and after suctioning.
5. Check suction source and regulator. Adjust suction pressure to no greater than 120 mm Hg pressure with tubing occluded.
6. Press [Silence] on the ventilator (to pause the alarms while suctioning).

How to Perform the Closed Suction Technique

7. Connect the suction tubing to the end of the in-line suction catheter.
8. Hyperoxygenate the patient by pressing the [100% FIO_2] button on the ventilator. This is the safest way to hyperoxygenate the patient.
   - Another option is to manually increase the FIO_2 to 100%. NOTE: Remember to return FIO_2 to baseline level when done suctioning, if not done automatically after preset time by ventilator.
   - Least preferred method is to disconnect the ventilator tubing and provide manual ventilation with 100% O_2 using a BVM device. Attach a PEEP valve to the BVM for patients on >5 cm H_2O PEEP. Have a second person give 5 or 6 breaths over 30 sec.
9. Gently but quickly insert the in-line suction catheter into the oral ET tube/tracheostomy, pausing momentarily to pull back on the plastic sleeve containing the catheter. When the patient begins to cough more forcefully, STOP catheter insertion. NOTE: Do NOT insert the catheter until you meet resistance. This means that the end of the suction catheter is hitting the carina (fragile, vascular tissue that separates right and left mainstem bronchus).
10. Apply continuous suction on withdrawal of the catheter over around 10 sec.
11. Observe patient tolerance to procedure.
12. Disconnect the suction tubing from the end of the in-line suction catheter and attach the Yankauer. Gently suction the patient's oral cavity.
13. Ask the patient if they need another suction pass.
14. If the patient does need more suctioning, ensure the ventilator is still providing FIO_2 100%. If not, press the [100% FIO_2] button again.
15. Repeat steps 9 through 13.
16. When the patient does not need more suctioning, ensure the suction tubing is attached to the end of the in-line suction catheter.
17. Rinse the catheter and connecting tubing with the sterile saline solution. Always rinse the tubing away from the patient.
18. Ensure the FIO_2 has returned to its previous setting, or manually return the FIO_2 to the desired value.
19. Reassess the patient for hemodynamic stability and that suctioning was effective. Auscultate to assess changes in lung sounds.
20. Record time, amount, character of secretions and patient's response to suctioning.

We perform OST when we need sterile sputum samples or CST is not available. OST is best performed with 2 persons. One removes the patient from the ventilator and uses the BVM while the second person suctions the patient. Table 28.12 describes the OST method.

TABLE 28.12 Open Suctioning Technique

The suction technique described here is appropriate for those patients with an oral ET tube or tracheostomy, who are receiving invasive mechanical ventilation. Please note that this is best done with 2 people.

Before You Begin

Follow the same steps (steps 1–6) as identified in Closed Suctioning Technique (Table 28.11).

How to Perform the Open Suction Technique

1. Use sterile technique to open catheter package, using the inside of the package as a sterile field.
2. Fill the sterile solution container with sterile normal saline or water.
3. Don sterile gloves. Designate 1 hand as contaminated for connecting and disconnecting the tubing at the suction catheter and operating the suction control.
4. Pick up the sterile suction catheter with dominant hand. Check function of equipment by suctioning a small volume of sterile saline solution from the container.
5. Have the second person hyperoxygenate the patient with 100% FIO_2. Disconnect the ventilator tubing from the ET tube/tracheostomy and provide manual ventilation to the patient with 100% O_2 using a BVM device. Attach a PEEP valve to the BVM for patients on >5 cm H_2O PEEP. Have the second person give 5 or 6 breaths over 30 sec.
6. Once hyperoxygenated, have the second person remove the bagger from the end of the oral ET tube or tracheostomy, and gently but quickly insert the in-line suction catheter *without suction* into the airway. When the patient begins to cough more forcefully, STOP catheter insertion. Do not insert the catheter until you meet resistance. This means that the end of the suction catheter is hitting the carina (fragile, vascular tissue that separates right and left mainstem bronchus).
7. Apply continuous suction on withdrawal of the catheter over around 10 sec.
8. Once the catheter is removed, immediately have the second person reattach the BVM to the oral ET tube/tracheostomy and hyperoxygenate the patient.
9. Observe patient tolerance to procedure. Immediately stop suctioning the patient and remove the in-line suction catheter from the patient if they become bradycardic or hypotensive. A vagal response may have occurred.
10. Ask the patient if they need another suction pass. Wait at least 30 sec (ventilator) or 5–6 breaths (BVM) in between each suctioning pass.
11. Rinse the sterile suction catheter (with sterile saline solution) between suctioning passes.
12. If the patient needs more suctioning, have the second person remove the BVM from the oral ET tube or tracheostomy and repeat steps 8 through 12.
13. When the patient does not need more suctioning, the second person will reattach the patient to the ventilator. Discard all used suctioning supplies. Dispose of the catheter by wrapping it around the fingers of gloved hand and pulling glove over catheter.
14. Reassess the patient for hemodynamic stability and that suctioning was effective. Auscultate to assess changes in lung sounds.
15. Record time, amount, character of secretions, and patient's response to suctioning.

Potential complications from suctioning include hypoxemia, bronchospasm, increased intracranial pressure (ICP), dysrhythmias, hypertension, hypotension, airway trauma (mucosal damage), pulmonary bleeding, pain, and infection.[16] Closely assess the patient, including ECG and SpO_2, before, during, and after suctioning. If the patient does not tolerate suctioning (e.g., decreased SpO_2, increased or decreased BP, sustained coughing, dysrhythmias), stop at once. Continue to reassess the patient until they achieve hemodynamic stability, recover, and/or the situation resolves before trying to suction again. Prevent hypoxemia by always hyperoxygenating the patient before and after each suctioning pass and limiting each pass to 10 seconds or less.

Causes of dysrhythmias during suctioning include (1) hypoxemia resulting in myocardial ischemia; (2) vagal stimulation caused by tracheal irritation; and (3) sympathetic nervous system stimulation caused by anxiety, discomfort, or pain. Dysrhythmias include tachydysrhythmias and bradydysrhythmias, premature beats, and asystole. Stop suctioning if any new dysrhythmias develop. Avoid excess suctioning in patients with severe hypoxemia or bradycardia.

Tracheal mucosal damage may occur due to suction pressures greater than 120 mm Hg, overly vigorous catheter insertion, and the suction catheter itself. Blood streaks or tissue shreds in aspirated secretions may indicate mucosal damage. This increases the risk for infection and bleeding, especially if the patient is receiving anticoagulants.

Secretions may be thick and hard to suction because of inadequate hydration or humidification, or infection. Maintain adequate hydration when indicated (e.g., IV fluids). Provide supplemental humidification of inspired gases through the ventilator to help thin secretions. Turning (e.g., every 2 hours) and early mobilization help move secretions into larger airways. If infection is the cause of thick secretions, give antibiotics as ordered.

◆ Maintaining Alarm Systems

You need to assure that all ventilator alarms are always on. Alarms alert us to potentially dangerous situations, such as patient-ventilator dyssynchrony, ventilator disconnection or malfunction, or unplanned extubation (Table 28.13). On many ventilators, we can temporarily suspend or silence alarms for up to 2 minutes for suctioning. After that time, the alarm system automatically turns back on.

! SAFETY ALERT

Alarm Fatigue

- Alarm fatigue can develop in those who hear an excess number of alarms, resulting in sensory overload.
- This can cause a delayed response to alarms or dismissing them altogether and can lead to serious adverse events (e.g., patient death).
- One way to reduce alarm fatigue includes customizing alarm parameters based on patient specific needs.

TABLE 28.13 NURSING MANAGEMENT
Ventilator Alarms

Alarm	Possible Causes	Interventions
Apnea	• Change in patient condition • Increased WOB • Inappropriate mode of ventilation • Loss of airway • Oversedation • Respiratory arrest	• ↑ Analgesia • ↑ Sedation • Change mode of ventilation • Disconnect patient from ventilator, attach BVM, call for help
High-pressure limit	• ↑ Compliance (e.g., pulmonary edema, ARDS, tension pneumothorax, atelectasis, pneumonia) • Condensate (water) in tubing • Coughing, secretions • Improper alarm setting • Kinked or compressed tubing (e.g., patient biting on ET tube) • Patient fighting ventilator (ventilator dyssynchrony) • ↑ Resistance (e.g., bronchospasm)	• Suction the patient • Reassure patient • Administer analgesia and/or sedation • Unkink tubing • Insert bite block • Give bronchodilator • Remove water from ventilator tubing • Assess breath sounds, obtain chest x-ray
High V_T, minute ventilation, or respiratory rate	• Anxiety, pain • Change in patient condition (e.g., ↑ metabolic demand, fever, hypoxia, hypercapnia, septic shock, patient condition improving) • Excess condensate or secretions in tubing (e.g., false reading)	• Reassure patient • Administer analgesia and/or sedation • Assess and reassess patient for change in condition • Change mode of ventilation • Remove water or secretions from tubing
Low-pressure limit	• Disconnect from ventilator disconnect • ET tube or tracheotomy cuff leak (e.g., patient speaking, grunting) • Loss of airway (e.g., partial or total extubation)	• Check all connections • Confirm adequate V_T • Reinflate cuff PRN • Time permitting, confirm ET tube/tracheostomy position with chest x-ray
Low V_T, minute ventilation, or respiratory rate	• ET tube or tracheotomy cuff leak (e.g., air leak) • Inappropriate mode of ventilation • Insufficient gas flow • Oversedation • Disconnection, loose connection, or leak in circuit	• Reduce sedation • Assess ventilator circuit for leaks • Measure cuff pressure to ensure cuff is adequately inflated • Change mode of ventilation • Based on respiratory rate and patient condition, disconnect patient from ventilator, attach BVM, call for help
Ventilator inoperative	• Internal battery not charged • Malfunction • Power failure	• Plug ventilator into correct power source at all times • Disconnect patient from ventilator, attach BVM, call for help

Analgesia and Sedation

Patients receiving PPV may need analgesia (e.g., fentanyl, hydromorphone) and/or sedation (e.g., propofol) to help with ventilation. Before giving analgesia or sedation, try to identify the cause of distress. Common problems that can result in patient pain, agitation or anxiety include PPV itself, hypoxemia, hypercapnia, drugs, environmental stressors (e.g., fear, sleep deprivation), and the discomfort from intubation.

Assess the effectiveness in achieving an acceptable level of patient comfort by using a valid pain scale, sedation scale (e.g., Richmond Agitation and Sedation Scale [RASS], Sedation Agitation Scale [SAS]), and/or delirium scale. Consider using relaxation techniques (e.g., music therapy) to complement drug therapy. The goal is to have the patient awake, interacting with their environment, and breathing comfortably and in synchrony with the ventilator.

At times, we decide to paralyze the patient with a neuromuscular blocking agent (NMBA). NMBAs paralyze skeletal muscles, including the diaphragm. The purpose is to decrease WOB and provide more effective synchrony with the ventilator, thus improving both oxygenation and ventilation. Remember that the paralyzed patient can hear, see, and feel. It is essential to give IV sedation and analgesia concurrently when the patient is paralyzed. The patient may or may not be aware of their surroundings. Always address them as if they were awake and alert.

Monitoring patients receiving NMBAs is challenging. The nurse giving these drugs often receives additional training. We can assess the depth of paralysis by using the train-of-four (TOF) peripheral nerve stimulation and observing for signs of pain or anxiety (e.g., changes in HR and BP), and ventilator dyssynchrony. The TOF assessment involves using a peripheral nerve stimulator to deliver 4 successive stimulating currents to elicit muscle twitches (Fig. 28.13). The number of twitches varies with the depth of neuromuscular blockade. The usual goal is 1 or 2 twitches out of 4 currents.

Noninvasive electroencephalogram technology (e.g., bispectral index monitoring [BIS]) can also help guide analgesic, sedative, and NMBA therapy.[17] A NMBA should never be given to a patient with a cholinesterase deficiency. Excess administration of NMBAs may predispose the patient to prolonged paralysis and muscle weakness even after the drugs are stopped.

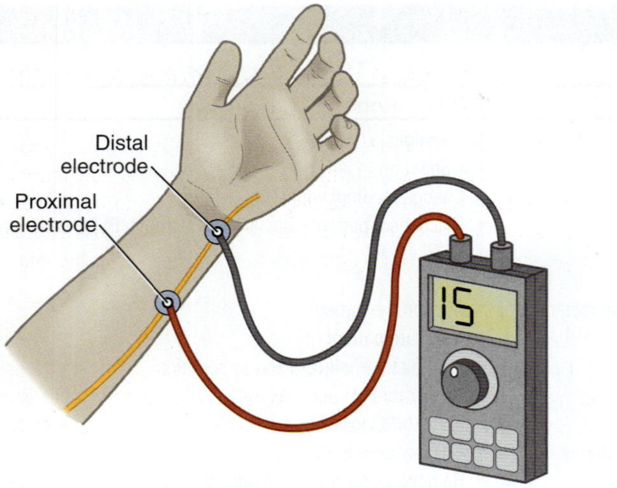

Fig. 28.13 Peripheral nerve stimulator. Placement of electrodes along ulnar nerve.

Hemodynamic Monitoring

The patient receiving invasive mechanical ventilation is hemodynamically monitored. Continuous assessment of the ECG, respiratory rate, synchrony with the ventilator, BP and MAP, and SpO_2 provides vital information. Promptly treat ventilator dyssynchrony, hypertension, hypotension, and decreased O_2 saturations. The patient who cannot maintain heart rate, CO, and BP targets may need IV fluids and drug therapy, such as vasopressors and inotropes.

Oxygenation and Ventilation

Monitoring the respiratory rate and rhythm is important. Is the patient using accessory muscles? Auscultate breath sounds. Assess air entry and breath sound for each lobe, both anteriorly and posteriorly. Is the patient "riding" the ventilator (not taking any breaths over and above the set rate)? Are they initiating some spontaneous breaths? Is there an increase in the WOB? Ensure ordered changes to mechanical ventilation (e.g., respiratory rate, FIO_2, PEEP, V_T, minute ventilation) are made.

Assess for signs of hypoxemia, such as a change in mental status (e.g., confusion), dusky skin, and dysrhythmias. Periodic ABGs and continuous SpO_2 provide objective data about oxygenation. CVP or PA catheters with $ScvO_2$ or SvO_2 capability provide an indirect measure of the tissue oxygenation status.

Indicators of ventilation include $PaCO_2$ and end-tidal carbon dioxide ($EtCO_2$, $PETCO_2$). Changes in $PaCO_2$ reflect alveolar hyperventilation (decreased $PaCO_2$) or hypoventilation (increased $PaCO_2$). $EtCO_2$ monitoring *(capnography)* is done by analyzing exhaled gas directly at the patient-ventilator circuit *(mainstream sampling)* or by transporting a sample of gas through a small-bore tubing to a bedside monitor *(sidestream sampling)*. Continuous $EtCO_2$ monitoring can assess the patency of the airway and presence of breathing. Gradual changes in $EtCO_2$ values may accompany an increase in CO_2 production (e.g., sepsis, hypoventilation), or a decrease in CO_2 production (e.g., hypothermia, decreased CO, metabolic acidosis). $EtCO_2$ is normally 35 to 45 mm Hg.[18]

TABLE 28.14 Oral Care for Patient on a Ventilator

General Measures
1. Gather all equipment.
2. Wash hands and don personal protective equipment and gloves.
3. Explain procedure to the patient and caregiver (if present).
4. Perform oral care every 2–4 hr using toothettes or a suction toothbrush, a Yankauer suction device, and toothpaste or mouthwash (use 0.12% Chlorhexidine oral rinse twice daily).
5. Provide oral care for 1–2 min, suctioning often.
6. Apply a mouth moisturizer to oral mucosa and lips with each cleaning.
7. Suction oral cavity and pharynx only when needed.
8. Dispose of trash and clean equipment. Rinse non-disposable oral suction apparatus with sterile normal saline and place on a dry paper towel.
9. Change all oral suction equipment and suction tubing every 24 hr.

Oral Care

When an oral ET tube is in place, the patient's mouth is always open. Moisten the lips, tongue, and gums with saline or water swabs to prevent mucosal drying. Oral care provides comfort and prevents injury to the gums and plaque formation (Table 28.14). Using Chlorhexidine, either as a mouthwash or toothpaste, at least 3 times per day, can help decrease oral contamination and ventilator-associated pneumonia (VAP). If space is limited in the oral cavity, use smaller or pediatric-sized oral products for providing oral care.

Skin Integrity

Frequent assessment and good care are needed to prevent skin breakdown on the face, lips, tongue, and nares because of pressure from the ET tube or the method used to secure the ET tube. Ongoing assessment is a shared responsibility between the RN and RT. Reposition and re-tape the ET tube (per agency policy) as needed to prevent skin breakdown. Two staff members should always perform repositioning to maintain correct position of the tube and to prevent accidental ET tube dislodgment. Monitor the patient for any signs of respiratory distress throughout the procedure.

For the orally intubated patient, remove the bite block (if present) and the old tape. Provide oral hygiene; then reposition the ET tube to the opposite side of the mouth. Replace the bite block (if used) and reconfirm proper cuff inflation and tube placement. Secure the ET tube again (per agency policy).

We can use a commercial device to secure the ET tube. Some may increase the risk for skin breakdown compared to tape. If you use a commercial device, follow the manufacturer's directions for maintaining tube position, providing skin care, and preventing skin breakdown. Always assess the skin under the ET tube, including upper and lower lips and chin, and underneath any securement devices for redness and skin breakdown.

Nutrition Therapy

Nutrition problems make the patient prone to poor O_2 transport from anemia. They can delay weaning from mechanical ventilation, decrease resistance to infection, and slow extubation and recovery. The presence of an ET tube eliminates the normal route for eating. A nasogastric (NG) or an orogastric (OG) tube is inserted and connected to low, intermittent suction when a patient is intubated.

The main goal of nutrition support is to prevent or correct nutrition problems. This goal is achieved through early enteral (EN), or if not possible, parenteral nutrition. EN preserves the structure and function of the gut mucosa and stops the movement of gut bacteria across the intestinal wall and into the bloodstream.[19] Patients likely to remain intubated for 3 to 5 days should have a nutrition assessment completed on admission and EN started within 24 hours. Consult the dietitian to determine the patient's caloric and nutrient needs.

◆ Venous Thromboembolism and GI Prophylaxis

The intubated patient is often confined to bed, with brief changes of position. As a result of the decreased mobility, stasis of blood in the lower extremities and the risk of venous thromboembolism (VTE) is of real concern. Start VTE prophylaxis as ordered (see Chapter 41). We might assist them to a sitting position in a chair at the bedside.

Patients may be stressed because of the serious illness, immobility, or discomfort from the ventilator. This places them at risk for developing stress ulcers and GI bleeding. Patients with a pre-existing ulcer or those receiving corticosteroids have a higher risk. Any circulatory compromise, including reduced CO caused by PPV, may contribute to ischemia of the gastric and intestinal mucosa and increase the risk for translocation of bacteria from the GI tract. Stress ulcer prophylaxis includes giving histamine (H_2)-receptor blockers (e.g., ranitidine), proton pump inhibitors (PPIs) (e.g., esomeprazole), or EN.

◆ Early Mobility

Maintaining muscle strength and preventing complications from immobility are important. With few exceptions (hemodynamically unstable patient, those receiving NMBA, unstable cervical or thoracic spine fractures medically contraindicated condition), we encourage most patients receiving invasive mechanical ventilation to exercise and mobilize as soon as possible.

Plan for early and progressive mobility (Box 28.1).[20] Collaborate with physical and occupational therapy. Help the patient perform passive and then active exercises to maintain muscle tone. Simple maneuvers, such as leg lifts or arm circles, are appropriate. Prevent contractures and pressure injures by proper positioning and using specialized mattresses or beds. Use a portable ventilator or provide manual ventilation with a BVM and 100% O_2 when ambulating patients who are mechanically ventilated.

◆ Communication

Intubated patients have stress from not being able to talk and communicate their needs. Inability to communicate may be because of analgesia, sedation, the ET tube, or neurologic impairment. This lack of communication can be frustrating for the patient, caregiver, and health care team. To communicate more effectively, use a variety of methods.

Provide the patient with a paper and pencil, a white board, or cellphone for texting. A communication board with pictures of common needs is convenient for patients who may speak other languages. A visual alphabet for spelling words is useful for patients who are weak or have difficulty writing.

As part of every procedure, explain what will happen or is happening to the patient. When the patient cannot speak, use picture boards, notepads, magic slates, or computers. When speaking with the patient, look directly at the patient and use hand gestures as appropriate.

Nonverbal communication is important. High levels of procedure-related touch and lower levels of comfort-related touch often characterize the ICU environment. Patients have different levels of tolerance for touch, usually related to culture and personal history. If appropriate, use comforting touch with ongoing evaluation of the patient's response. Encourage the caregiver to talk to the patient, even if the patient is intubated, is sedated, or appears comatose. Hearing is often the last sense to decrease. Even if the patient cannot respond, they may still be able to hear.

BOX 28.1 EVIDENCE-BASED PRACTICE

The Mechanically Ventilated Patient and Early Mobilization

W.R. is a 72-year-old female patient who has been in the ICU for 3 days. She failed extubation in the PACU after a cholecystectomy, was reintubated, and admitted to the adult ICU. Weaning trials are planned for today. Yesterday, you started passive exercises and dangling with W.R. Today, you and the physical therapist discuss early mobilization with her and her husband.

Making Clinical Decisions

Best Available Evidence

Implementing an early exercise and mobilization protocol for stable, mechanically ventilated patients is safe and well tolerated. Early mobilization improves patient outcomes. Involving patients and caregivers in decision-making around care (e.g., early mobilization) is a priority among this group.

Clinician Expertise

Your unit has successfully implemented an early mobilization protocol for intubated and mechanically ventilated patients in your ICU (part of the ABCDEF bundle). You are aware that patients and their families often worry about ambulating with complex equipment attached to them.

Patient Preferences and Values

W.R. writes on the computer that she does not want to get out of bed until her "breathing tube is out and she has no more IV lines." Her husband tells you she is "afraid of falling."

Implications for Nursing Practice

1. What will you tell W.R. and her husband about the benefits of early mobilization?
2. How will you help reduce W.R.'s concerns about being "afraid of falling"?
3. How will you involve W.R. and her husband in the decision to take part in the early mobilization program?

Reference for Evidence

Schallom M, Tymkew H, Vyers K, et al.: Implementation of an interdisciplinary AACN early mobility protocol, *Crit Care Nurse* 40:e7, 2020.

◆ Psychosocial Concerns

The patient receiving mechanical ventilation often has physical and emotional stress. The patient supported by a ventilator cannot speak, move, or breathe normally. Tubes and machines cause pain and fear. Anxiety is common. There is a loss of independence. They may have feelings of helplessness and hopelessness. Usual activities, such as eating and elimination, are complicated. Many patients and caregivers feel uncomfortable in the ICU with its complex equipment, high noise and light levels, and intense pace of activity. Sleeplessness and loss of control enhance anxiety.

Feeling safe is an overpowering need. Work to strengthen the factors that affect feeling safe. Encourage hope, as appropriate. Build trusting relationships with both the patient and caregiver. Involve them in decision-making as much as possible.

To help reduce anxiety, include patients and caregivers in all conversations. Explain the purpose of equipment and procedures. Encourage them to express concerns, ask questions, and state their needs. Structure the environment in a way that decreases anxiety. For example, encourage caregivers to bring in photographs and personal items. Relaxation techniques (e.g., music therapy) and antianxiety drugs (e.g., lorazepam) may reduce the stress response that anxiety can trigger.

Preventing Delirium

The ABCDEF Bundle is evidence-based practice of providing care that strives to attain an environment in which all patients receiving mechanical ventilation are calm, delirium free, and able to express their needs for pain control, positioning, and reassurance. The ABCDEF Bundle ensures (1) **A**ssessment, (2) **B**reathing trials are done daily, (3) correct **C**hoice of analgesia and sedation, (4) **D**elirium prevention and management, (5) **E**arly mobility, and (6) **F**amily engagement (see Chapter 64).[21]

"Rescue" Therapies

Rescue therapies alleviate hypoxemia in patients who are not able to maintain reasonable oxygenation despite appropriate mechanical ventilation, high FIO_2, and PEEP. Rescue therapies are tailored to each patient's requirements. Three therapies, inhaled pulmonary vasodilators, proning, and extracorporeal membrane oxygenation (ECMO), are briefly discussed here.

Inhaled Pulmonary Vasodilators

Inhaled pulmonary vasodilators, such as nitric oxide (NO) and epoprostenol (Flolan), are gas molecules that take part in the regulation of pulmonary vascular tone. For example, inhibiting NO production results in pulmonary vasoconstriction. Continuous inhaled NO results in pulmonary vasodilation. Giving pulmonary vasodilators by inhalation helps increase pulmonary arterial blood flow and decrease pulmonary pressures. As a result, there may be an improvement in gas exchange and arterial oxygenation.

Prone Positioning

Prone positioning is the repositioning of a patient from a supine or lateral position to a prone (on the stomach, face down) position. Proning improves lung recruitment through various mechanisms (see Fig. 32.11). Gravity reverses the effects of fluid in the dependent parts of the lungs. The heart rests on the sternum, away from the lungs, contributing to an overall uniformity of pleural pressures. The prone position requires increased sedation and is nurse intensive. It is an effective supportive therapy used in critically ill patients with severe ARDS to improve oxygenation. Patients with refractory hypoxemia and ARDS should remain prone for at least 12 hours per day.[22]

Extracorporeal Membrane Oxygenation

Extracorporeal membrane oxygenation is an alternative form of pulmonary support for the patient with severe respiratory failure (Fig. 28.14). Think of ECMO as a modification of cardiac bypass or kidney dialysis. ECMO involves removing blood from a patient through large-bore vascular access catheters. When the blood goes through the ECMO unit, it is infused with O_2. CO_2 is removed at the same time. The newly oxygenated blood is then returned to the patient.

ECMO is very labor intensive. It most often occurs in an ICU, with a skilled team of specialists, including a perfusionist and specially trained nurses. There are specific criteria the patient must meet to receive ECMO. It requires systemic anticoagulation. The risk of bleeding is considered before starting therapy.

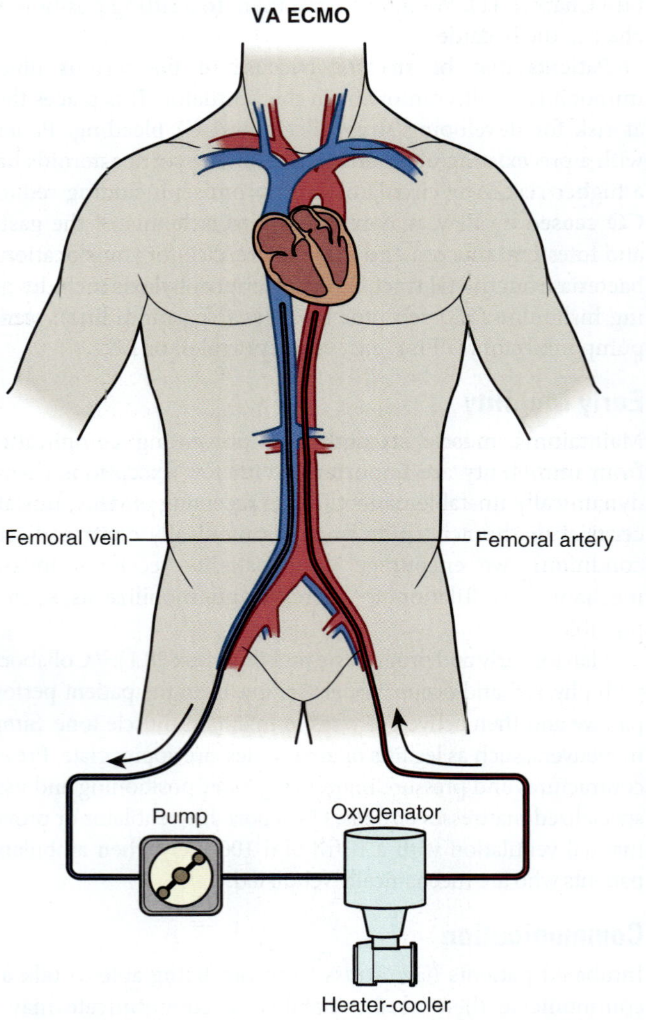

Fig. 28.14 ECMO circuit. The circuit consists of a blood pump, oxygenator, and heating-cooling element. Circulatory access is typically obtained through the femoral vein and artery. Blood is removed from the patient, O_2 is added by the oxygenator, CO_2 is removed, and the blood re-infused back into the patient. (From Mann DL, Zipes DP, Libby P, et al.: *Braunwald's heart disease: a textbook of cardiovascular medicine,* ed 11, St Louis, 2019, Saunders.)

Complications of Mechanical Ventilation

Aspiration

Aspiration is a potential hazard for the patient with an oral ET tube. The ET tube passes through the epiglottis, keeping it in an open position. As a result, the patient cannot protect the airway from aspiration. The high-volume, low-pressure ET cuff cannot totally prevent the trickle of oral or gastric secretions into the trachea. Further, secretions collect above the cuff. When the cuff is deflated, those secretions can move into the lungs.

Oral intubation increases salivation and swallowing is difficult. Suction the patient's mouth often. Use a Yankauer (tonsil-tip) suction catheter or a sterile single-use catheter. Other factors contributing to aspiration include improper cuff inflation, patient positioning, and decreased gastric mobility and bowel function if receiving EN. Even when the cuff is properly inflated, take precautions to prevent vomiting, which can lead to aspiration. Some newer oral ET tubes provide continuous suctioning of secretions above the cuff (Fig. 28.15). Unless contraindicated, keep the head of the bed elevated at least 30 degrees in all intubated patients who are receiving EN.

Sodium and Water Imbalance

Progressive fluid retention can occur 48 to 72 hours after starting PPV, especially with PEEP. Fluid retention is associated with decreased urine output and increased sodium retention. Fluid balance changes may be due to decreased CO, which causes decreased renal perfusion. This stimulates the release of renin with the subsequent production of angiotensin and aldosterone. This results in sodium and water retention.

As a part of the stress response, release of antidiuretic hormone (ADH) and cortisol contributes to sodium and water retention. Less insensible water loss occurs with an artificial airway because ventilated gases delivered to the patient are humidified. Pressure changes in the thorax decrease release of atrial natriuretic peptide, which contributes to sodium and water retention.

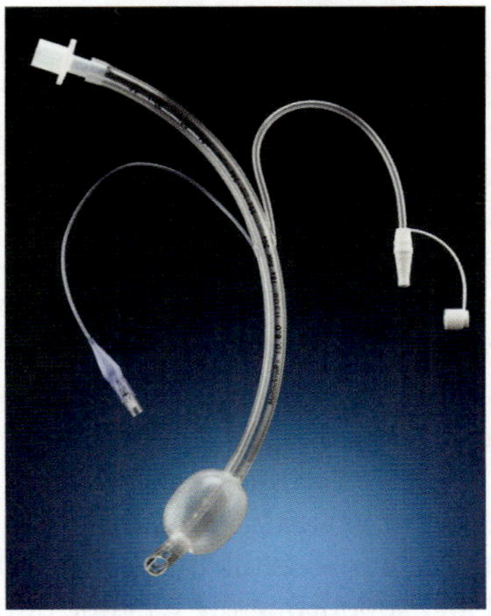

Fig. 28.15 The Hi-Lo Evac Tube. A specialized endotracheal tube with separate side port for aspiration of subglottic secretions. Sideport exits above the cuff. Sideport is attached to continuous low suction (20 mmHg), which allows for suctioning of secretions from the subglottic area. (Reprinted by permission of Nellcor Puritan Bennett Inc, Pleasanton, CA.)

Adverse Hemodynamic Effects

PPV affects circulation because of the transmission of increased mean airway pressure to various structures in the thorax. Increased intrathoracic pressure compresses the thoracic vessels. This compression decreases venous return to the heart, preload, systolic BP, MAP, and CO. Mean airway pressure increases further when more than 5 cm H_2O of PEEP is being used.

Alveolar Ventilation Changes

Alveolar hypoventilation can be caused by inappropriate ventilator settings, air leaking from the ventilator tubing or around the ET tube or tracheostomy cuff, lung secretions or obstruction, and administering too much analgesia or sedation. A low V_T or respiratory rate decreases minute ventilation. This results in hypoventilation, atelectasis, and respiratory acidosis.

Alveolar hyperventilation can occur if the respiratory rate or V_T is too high (mechanical overventilation) or if the patient receiving assisted ventilation is hyperventilating. Hyperventilation leads to respiratory alkalosis. If hyperventilation is spontaneous, it is important to determine the cause and treat it. Common causes include hypoxemia, pain, anxiety, or compensation for metabolic acidosis. Patients who fight the ventilator or breathe out of synchrony may be anxious or in pain. If the patient is anxious and fearful, sitting with them and coaching them to breathe with the ventilator or weaning the ventilator to a more appropriate setting may help.

Barotrauma

Barotrauma results when increased airway pressure distends the lungs and possibly ruptures fragile alveoli or blebs. The risk for barotrauma increases as lung inflation pressures increase. Patients with noncompliant (stiff) lungs are at greatest risk. This includes those with ARDS.

Increasing inflation pressure also places the patient at risk for a pneumothorax. With PPV, a simple pneumothorax can become a life-threatening tension pneumothorax. The mediastinum and contralateral lung are compressed, reducing CO. Immediate treatment is needed.

Volutrauma

Volutrauma can occur if too large a volume of air (V_T) is used to ventilate noncompliant lungs. Volutrauma causes alveolar rupture and movement of fluids and proteins into the alveolar spaces. To minimize volutrauma, we use low-volume ventilation in patients with stiff, noncompliant lungs (e.g., ARDS).

Auto-Positive End-Expiratory Pressure

Auto-PEEP is a result of inadequate exhalation time. Auto-PEEP is PEEP over and above what has been set by the HCP.[11] This added PEEP may result in increased WOB, barotrauma, and hemodynamic instability. Interventions to limit auto-PEEP include sedation and analgesia, large-diameter ET tube, bronchodilators, short inspiratory times, and decreased respiratory rates. Reducing water accumulation in the ventilator circuit by frequent emptying or use of heated circuits limits auto-PEEP.

◆ Alterations in Gastric Motility

Immobility, sedation, impaired circulation, decreased oral intake, opioid use, and stress contribute to decreased peristalsis. The patient's inability to exhale against a closed glottis may make defecation difficult. As a result, the ventilated patient is at risk for constipation. Start a bowel regimen to help with motility.

◆ Ventilator Disconnection and Malfunction

Ventilators may become disconnected from the patient. Most disconnections are discovered by low-pressure alarms. The most frequent site for disconnection is between the tracheal tube and the adapter. Push connections together to secure tightly. Teach the patient the importance of not touching the ET tube. Be certain that alarms are always set and activated. You can pause alarms (not turn off) during suctioning. Make sure you reactivate all alarms before leaving the patient.

Ventilator malfunction has been known to occur. Although most agencies have emergency generators in case of a power failure, and newer ventilators may have battery backup, power failure is always a possibility. Have a plan for manually ventilating all patients who depend on a ventilator. If, at any time, you decide the ventilator is malfunctioning (e.g., failure of O_2 supply), or, if you cannot determine the cause of an alarm and the patient is in respiratory distress, disconnect the patient from the machine and manually ventilate with a BVM and 100% O_2 until help arrives and the ventilator is fixed or replaced.

CHECK YOUR PRACTICE

You are caring for a 75-year-old woman who was orally intubated yesterday for respiratory distress due to pneumonia. She is on AC (full support) ventilation. Her ventilator settings are RR 14 (set), FIO_2 40%, PEEP 5 cm H_2O, V_T 400 mL. You respond to the ventilator alarm. You hear audible air escaping from around her mouth as you suction her. The alarm panel shows "low exhaled tidal volume." She appears anxious. Vital signs: HR 112, RR 26, and SpO_2 89%.

- What would be your next steps?

◆ Ventilator-Associated Pneumonia

Ventilator-associated pneumonia is pneumonia that occurs 48 hours or more after ET intubation. It occurs in as many as 40% of all intubated patients.[23] Patients who develop VAP have significantly longer days mechanically ventilated, longer hospital stays, and higher mortality rates.[23] Most patients develop VAP early, often within 96 hours of starting mechanical ventilation.

The most common organisms that cause VAP are gram-negative bacteria (e.g., *Escherichia coli, Klebsiella, Streptococcus pneumoniae, Haemophilus influenzae*).[23] Others include antibiotic-resistant organisms, such as *Pseudomonas aeruginosa* and oxacillin-resistant *Staphylococcus aureus*.[23] These organisms are abundant in the hospital environment and the patient's GI tract. They can spread in several ways, Examples include contaminated respiratory equipment, inadequate hand washing, adverse environment (e.g., poor room ventilation, high traffic flow), and decreased patient ability to cough and clear secretions. Colonization of the oropharynx tract by gram-negative organisms predisposes the patient to gram-negative pneumonia. Poor nutrition, immobility, and the underlying disease process (e.g., immunosuppression, organ failure) increase risk.

Signs that suggest VAP include a fever, high white blood cell count, change in color and/or amount of sputum, crackles or wheezes on auscultation, and new lung infiltrates observed on chest x-ray. We obtain sputum cultures and start broad-spectrum antibiotics

Guidelines for VAP prevention include (1) minimizing sedation, including daily spontaneous awakening trials (SATs) or daily spontaneous breathing trials (SBTs), (2) early mobilization, (3) use of ET tubes with subglottic secretion drainage ports, (4) elevating the head of the bed a minimum of 30 to 45 degrees unless contraindicated, (5) oral care with chlorhexidine, and (6) no routine changes of the ventilator circuit tubing.[23]

Other preventive measures include strict hand washing before and after suctioning whenever ventilator equipment is touched and after contact with any respiratory secretions. Always wear gloves when in contact with the patient and change gloves between activities (e.g., emptying urinary catheter drainage, hanging an IV drug). As it collects, always drain the water that collects in the ventilator tubing away from the patient.

! SAFETY ALERT

VAP Prevention

- Practice good hand hygiene techniques before and after suctioning and between patient care tasks.
- Keep the head of the bed elevated 30 to 45 degrees.
- Turn patient according to agency policy.
- Begin early mobilization.
- Follow agency policy for limiting sedation with SAT.
- Perform daily SBT unless contraindicated.
- Wear gloves when providing oral hygiene.
- Suction patients as needed for comfort.

◆ Unplanned Extubation

Unplanned extubation can be due to patient self-removal of the ET tube or accidental removal during movement or a procedure. Sometimes the unplanned extubation is obvious (e.g., the patient is holding the ET tube). Other times, the tip of the ET tube is in the hypopharynx or esophagus, and the extubation is not obvious. Signs of unplanned extubation include sounding of the low-pressure ventilator alarm, decreased or absent breath sounds, respiratory distress, or an audible cuff leak. The patient may be talking to you. Sometimes, an unplanned extubation can be an immediate life-threatening event.

Help prevent unplanned extubation by ensuring that the ET tube is secured and supporting the ET tube during repositioning, procedures, and patient transfers. Giving adequate sedation and analgesia and following weaning protocols decrease the incidence of self-extubation.

Using restraints to immobilize the patient's hands is a deterrent to self-extubation. Explain to the patient and caregiver when you use short-term restraints for patient safety and discuss the use of alternatives. Reassess for the continued need of restraints and limit restraint use when possible.

! SAFETY ALERT

Unplanned Extubation

What to do during an unplanned extubation:

- Stay with the patient and call for help.
- Support oxygenation as needed by applying an adjunct therapy, such as a nasal cannula or manually ventilating the patient with a BVM and 100% O_2.
- Immediately notify the HCP and RT.
- Assess for respiratory distress.
- Assess the need for reintubation.
- If the patient cannot protect their airway or is in respiratory distress, prepare for immediate reintubation.
- Provide emotional support and reassure the patient.

◆ Weaning From Positive Pressure Ventilation

Weaning is the process of gradually reducing ventilator support and allowing the patient to assume greater responsibility for breathing spontaneously. The weaning process typically differs for patients on short-term ventilation (3 to 5 days) versus long-term ventilation (longer than 5 days). Those with short-term ventilation (e.g., after heart surgery) have a very straightforward weaning process. Patients with prolonged PPV (e.g., patients with COPD who develop respiratory failure, ARF patients) often have a weaning process that consists of alternating gains and losses. Preparation for weaning begins almost as soon as the patient is intubated and involves a team approach.

Weaning is a complex process. It consists of an assessment of both respiratory and nonrespiratory factors (Table 28.15). First, the primary problem that prompted intubation and mechanical ventilation should be resolving. Second, the lungs should be reasonably clear on auscultation and chest x-ray. Third, the patient needs to be able to breathe spontaneously. The patient who transitions from a full support to a spontaneous mode of mechanical ventilation, is hemodynamically stable, and has acceptable ABGs and SpO_2 shows tolerance of the weaning process.

Nonrespiratory factors include neurologic status, hemodynamic stability, acid-base balance, nutrition status, fluid and electrolyte balance, and hemoglobin. It is important to have an alert, well-rested, and well-informed patient relatively free from pain and anxiety who can cooperate with the weaning plan. This does not mean complete withdrawal from sedatives or analgesics. Instead, drugs should be titrated to achieve comfort without causing excessive drowsiness.

A *spontaneous awakening trial* and a *spontaneous breathing trial* help assess the ability of the patient to maintain a stable respiratory drive and adequate O_2 saturation. An SAT should be done by stopping all sedatives and, in patients without active pain, all opioids. Sedation should be restarted at 50% of the previous dose in patients who "fail" the SAT (increased respiratory

TABLE 28.15 Indicators of Weaning Readiness

Patients receiving mechanical ventilation should have a formal assessment of "readiness for weaning" if the following are satisfied:

1. Awake, alert, easily rousable
2. Reversal of the underlying cause/condition of respiratory failure
3. Hemodynamically stable
   - Absence of dysrhythmias, myocardial ischemia
   - Absence of clinical hypotension (low dose or no vasopressor therapy)
4. Adequate oxygenation
   - PaO_2/FIO_2 >300
   - SpO_2 ≥92%
   - PEEP ≤5–8 cm H_2O
   - FIO_2 ≤40%
   - pH ≥7.35
5. Stable, intact respiratory drive with ability to initiate spontaneous respirations
6. Other Weaning Criteria[a]
   - Hemoglobin ≥7 g/dL
   - Core temperature ≤ 101.3°F (38.5°C)

Weaning Assessment

Measurement	What It Means	Normal Value	Usual Criteria for Extubation
Spontaneous respiratory rate (RR)	Respiratory rate (number of breaths) over 1 min	12–20 breaths/min	>8–10 breaths/min <30 breaths/min
Spontaneous tidal volume (V_T)	Amount of air moved in and out of the lungs during a single breath (at rest)	>5–7 mL/kg	≥5 mL/kg
Minute ventilation (V_E)	Volume of air moved in and out of the lungs during 1 min (at rest) V_T multiplied by respiratory rate over 1 min. *For example:* 0.350 (V_T) × 28 (f) = 9.8 L/min.	3–10 L/min	<15 L/min
Negative inspiratory force or pressure (NIF, NIP)	Amount of negative pressure that a patient can generate Measure of expiratory muscle strength and ability to cough. *Measured by clinician:* A pressure manometer (Nifometer) is attached to airway or mouth and the patient is asked to take a big deep breath. Clinician observes the values on the Nifometer.	<– 20 to –30 cm H_2O	<–20 cm H_2O The more negative the number, the better indication for extubation.
Rapid shallow breathing index, RSBI (f/V_T)	Tobin number Is the spontaneous respiratory rate (over 1 min) divided by V_T (in liters). *For example:* 30 (f)/0.400 (V_T) = 75	<105	<105
Spontaneous breathing trial (SBT)	If patient passes daily weaning screen, assess patient during SBT with little or no ventilator assistance. Trial should be at least 30 min to a maximum of 120 min.		Successful completion of trial is based on assessment (e.g., LOC, vital signs, ABG, chest x-ray, patient WOB).

[a]The decision to use these criteria is made by the HCP and based on agency policy and HCP preference.

rate, decreasing O_2 saturations, low V_T) and remain off in patients who "pass."

An SBT should last at least 30 minutes but no more than 120 minutes. It may be completed with low levels of FIO_2, PEEP, or low levels of PSV.[24] Tolerating the SBT may lead to extubation. Failure to tolerate an SBT should prompt a search for reversible or complicating factors and a return to the previous mode of mechanical ventilation. Unless contraindicated, all patients should have an SBT daily.

There is no "right" way to wean the patient from mechanical ventilation. Most HCPs will attempt weaning early in the morning after the patient had a good night's rest. The patient should be hemodynamically stable and comfortable. Obtain baseline vital signs and respiratory parameters. Place the patient in bed in a semi-recumbent position or sitting in a chair at the bedside.

All health care team members should be familiar with the weaning plan. Weaning approaches include decreasing the number of ventilator-delivered breaths in SIMV. Or we gradually decrease the degree of pressure support daily as ventilatory status permits. PSV provides gentle, slow respiratory muscle conditioning. It may be beneficial for patients who are deconditioned or have heart problems.

During the weaning trial, closely monitor the patient for signs and symptoms that may signal a need to end the trial. These include tachypnea, dyspnea, tachycardia, dysrhythmias, sustained desaturation (SpO_2 less than 92%), hypertension or hypotension, agitation, diaphoresis, anxiety, and changes in mental status. Should the patient not tolerate the weaning trial, allow the patient's respiratory muscles to rest between trials. Once the respiratory muscles become fatigued, they may need 12 to 24 hours to recover.

The patient and caregiver need ongoing emotional support. Explain the weaning process to the patient and family to keep them informed of progress. Record the patient's tolerance throughout the weaning process. Include statements about the patient's and the caregiver's feelings.

◆ Extubation

Extubation is the physical removal of the oral or nasal ET tube. Extubation assessments should include muscle strength (negative inspiratory force) and endurance (spontaneous V_T, vital capacity, minute ventilation, rapid shallow breathing index) (Table 28.15). There should be minimal secretions and the ability to cough and gag.

Before extubation, hyperoxygenate and suction the patient. Have an alternative O_2 delivery device (e.g., nasal prongs) set up. Loosen the ET tapes or commercial holder. Have the patient take a deep breath, and at the peak of inspiration, deflate the ET tube cuff and slowly remove the tube in one smooth motion.

After removal, encourage the patient to deep breath and cough. Suction the oropharynx as needed. Assess their ability to speak. Give supplemental O_2 and provide oral care. Carefully monitor vital signs, respiratory status, and oxygenation immediately after extubation and for the first 2 to 3 hours (per agency policy). If the patient does not tolerate extubation (e.g., decreased SpO_2 levels, tachypnea or bradypnea, tachycardia, decreased LOC, decrease in PaO_2, increase in $PaCO_2$), immediate reintubation or a trial of noninvasive ventilation may be needed.

TRACHEOSTOMY

A **tracheostomy** is a surgically created stoma (opening) in the anterior part of the trachea (Fig. 28.16A). A tracheostomy may be done to (1) establish a patent airway, (2) bypass an upper airway obstruction, (3) simplify removal of secretions, (4) permit long-term mechanical ventilation, and (5) facilitate weaning. When the need for an artificial airway is expected to be prolonged, early tracheotomy (done within 10 to 14 days) appears to have advantages over delayed tracheotomy. These include fewer ventilator dependent days, reduced length of stay, decreased pain, and improved communication.

The tracheostomy tube is shorter in length and slightly wider in diameter than an ET tube. This makes it easier to keep the tube clean and promotes better oral and bronchial hygiene. A tracheostomy (compared to an ET tube) may increase patient comfort because no tube is present in the mouth. There is also less risk of long-term damage to vocal cords.

A variety of tracheostomy tubes are available to meet patient needs (Table 28.16). All tracheostomy tubes have a faceplate, or flange, which rests against the neck and an *obturator.* It is used to help insert the tube. Many tracheostomy tubes have an *outer cannula* (which keeps the airway patent) and an *inner cannula* (which can be disposable or non-disposable and removed for cleaning) (Fig. 28.16B).

Cuffed and *uncuffed* tracheostomy tubes are available. A tracheostomy tube with an inflated cuff is used the most, especially if the patient needs mechanical ventilation. The cuff is inflated through the balloon inflation port on the tracheostomy tube. Cuffs ensure the patient receives the volume of air delivered by the ventilator and decrease the risk of aspiration. Cuffless tubes are often used for patients with longer-term tracheostomies, when mechanical ventilation is not needed, and the risk of aspiration has decreased. With some tracheostomies, talking and eating is possible.

The outer and/or inner cannula may be *fenestrated* or *non-fenestrated.* A *fenestrated tube* has an opening (a hole) on the dorsal surface of the tube. This helps promote spontaneous breathing. With a cuffed, fenestrated tracheostomy tube, when the cuff is deflated and the inner cannula removed, air can pass from the lungs up through the opening in the tracheostomy tube and through the vocal cords (including larynx) and into the upper airway (including the mouth and nose). This allows the patient to breathe spontaneously and speak with the tracheostomy tube in place. When the cuff is reinflated and the inner cannula reinserted, air cannot pass from the lungs through the vocal cords.

Most patients who need mechanical ventilation have an oral ET tube first. The oral ET tube can be quickly inserted in an emergency. When swelling, trauma, or upper airway

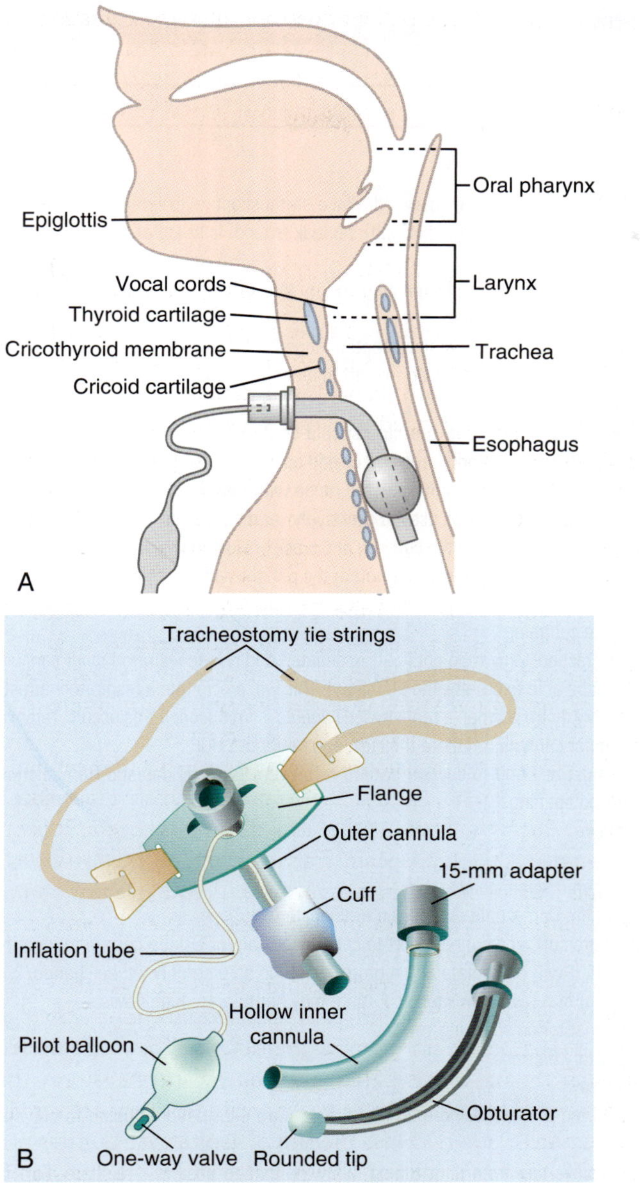

Fig. 28.16 Tracheostomy tube. (A) Placement of a tracheostomy tube. (B) Parts of a tracheostomy tube.

obstruction prevents oral ET intubation, an emergent *surgical cricothyroidotomy* (or cricothyrotomy) is needed. This procedure, which can be completed in minutes, involves making an incision through the skin and cricothyroid membrane on the anterior surface of the neck.

Most surgical tracheostomies are done in the operating room using general anesthesia. They may be done electively on intubated patients who need prolonged mechanical ventilation. A horizontal incision is made on the anterior part of the trachea. The tracheostomy tube is inserted, the incision is sutured, and a sterile dressing applied.

A newer surgical technique is the *percutaneous tracheostomy.* Using local anesthesia, sedation, and under video-assisted guidance, the ET tube is withdrawn up to the level of the glottis. A needle is placed between the second and third tracheal rings, into the middle of the trachea. A dilator is then placed over the top of the needle. The opening is progressively made larger (with increasingly larger dilators) until the hole is big enough for insertion of the tracheostomy tube. Percutaneous tracheostomy approaches have less risk of bleeding and fewer postoperative complications. Surgical and percutaneous tracheostomies may be done at the bedside in the emergency department or ICU.

Preparing the Patient for a Tracheostomy

Preprocedure Care

Before the tracheostomy procedure (and time permitting), explain the purpose of the procedure to both the patient and caregiver. If the patient is having the tracheostomy in the operating room, follow all policies for preparing the patient for surgery (see Chapter 18).

If the procedure is being done at the bedside, ensure all appropriate personnel, including RT, are present. A BVM, suction, and emergency resuscitation equipment should be readily available, functional, and at the bedside.

Record baseline vital signs. Ensure an existing IV line is patent. Help assemble and set up all the equipment. Position the patient supine. Give analgesia and sedation as ordered by the HCP.

During the Procedure

Monitor hemodynamic status. Observe the patient's response to analgesia and/or sedatives. Note the patient's tolerance to the procedure. Observe the SpO_2 and immediately notify the HCP if the SpO_2 is less than 92%.

Postprocedure Care

The tracheostomy cuff is inflated immediately. We use several methods to confirm correct tracheostomy tube placement: (1) auscultation of the patient's chest for air entry, (2) $EtCO_2$ capnography, (3) video-assisted confirmation for percutaneous tracheostomy, and (4) passage of a suction catheter through the tracheostomy tube. After placement is confirmed, the ET tube is removed. The tracheostomy tube is sutured and secured in place with cotton tracheostomy ties, tracheostomy tapes, or Velcro straps.

Monitor vital signs. SpO_2 readings should remain stable. Obtain a chest x-ray. Note and record the ventilator settings, including mode, FIO_2, and PEEP. Complications of a tracheostomy include airway obstruction, bleeding, infection, and potential tube dislodgement (Table 28.17). Observe the amount of blood on the dressing at the insertion site. Notify the HCP if bleeding persists.

❖ NURSING MANAGEMENT: PATIENT WITH A TRACHEOSTOMY

This section highlights general guidelines when caring for a patient with a tracheostomy during the first few days after the procedure (Table 28.18). Considerable variation exists regarding which health care team member is responsible for care activities. In some places, it is the nurse who is responsible. In others, it is a shared responsibility between nursing and RT. Follow your agency policy.

TABLE 28.16 NURSING MANAGEMENT
Specific Types of Tracheostomies

Tube and Characteristics	Nursing Management
Tracheostomy tube with cuff and pilot balloon When properly inflated, low-pressure, high-volume cuff distributes cuff pressure over large area, minimizing pressure on tracheal wall.	**Procedure for cuff inflation:** • Mechanically ventilated patient: • *Minimal occlusion volume (MOV) technique* recommended. Place stethoscope over lateral neck (beside trachea). Inflate cuff by slowly injecting air into the cuff until no leak (sound) is heard at peak inspiratory pressure (end of ventilator inspiration). • *Spontaneously breathing patient:* Inflate cuff by slowly injecting air into the cuff until no sound is heard after deep breath or during inhalation with bag-valve-mask. • *Immediately after cuff inflation:* Confirm pressure is within accepted range 20–30 cm H_2O (15–22 mm Hg) with a manometer. Record cuff pressure and volume of air used for cuff inflation in chart. **Care of patient with an inflated cuff:** • Monitor and record cuff pressure q8hr and PRN. Cuff pressure should be 20–30 cm H_2O (15–22 mm Hg) to allow adequate tracheal capillary perfusion. If needed, remove or add air to the pilot tubing using a syringe and stopcock. Afterward, confirm cuff pressure is within accepted range with manometer. • Report inability to keep the cuff inflated or need to use progressively larger volumes of air to keep cuff inflated. Potential causes include tracheal dilation at the cuff site or a crack or slow leak in the 1-way inflation valve. If the leak is due to tracheal dilation, the HCP may cannulate the patient with a larger tube.
Fenestrated tracheostomy tube (Shiley, Portex) with cuff, inner cannula, and decannulation plug When non-fenestrated inner cannula is removed, cuff deflated, and decannulation plug inserted, air flows around tube, through fenestration in outer cannula, and up over vocal cords. Patient can then speak. A fenestrated inner cannula can be used to facilitate cleaning and weaning from mechanical ventilation.	• If possible, assess risk of aspiration before removing inner cannula. A speech pathologist may be able to assist if available. Deflate cuff. Note coughing. • *Never* insert decannulation plug in tracheostomy tube until cuff is deflated and non-fenestrated inner cannula removed. Otherwise, patient will not be able to breathe (no air inflow). This will precipitate a respiratory arrest. • Assess for dyspnea and/or respiratory distress when a fenestrated cannula is first used. If this occurs, remove the cap, insert a non-fenestrated inner cannula, reinflate the cuff, and notify the HCP. • A non-fenestrated inner cannula must be used to suction patient to prevent tracheal damage from suction catheter passing through fenestrated openings. • Cuff management as described above.
Talking tracheostomy tube (Portex with cuff, 2 external tubings) Has 2 tubings, 1 leading to cuff and 1 to opening above the cuff. When port is connected to air source, air flows out of opening and up over the vocal cords, allowing the patient to speak.	• Patient must be awake, alert, and hemodynamically stable. • Must be able to tolerate cuff deflation. Can exhale around the tracheostomy tube. • When patient wants to speak, deflate cuff, and connect port to compressed air (or O_2). Be certain to identify correct tubing. If gas enters the cuff, it will overinflate and rupture, requiring an emergency tube change. • Use lowest flow (typically 4–6 L/min) that results in speech. Patient may not tolerate high flows. • Give O_2 through tracheal collar or adaptor on speaking valve. • Observe for dyspnea and/or respiratory distress. • Cuff management as described above.
Tracheostomy tube (Bivona, Fome-Cuf) with foam-filled cuff Cuff filled with plastic foam. Before insertion, cuff is deflated. After insertion, cuff self-inflates. Pilot tubing not capped. No cuff pressure monitoring needed. Patient cannot speak with this tube.	• Before insertion, withdraw all air from the cuff using a 20-mL syringe. Cap pilot balloon tubing to prevent reentry of air. • After tracheostomy is inserted, remove cap from pilot tubing, allowing cuff to passively reinflate. Cuff is always inflated on this tube. • Do not inject air into tubing or cap pilot balloon tubing while it is in patient. Air will flow in and out in response to pressure changes (head turning). Place tag on tubing to alert staff not to cap or inflate cuff. • Tube tends to collect moisture and secretions while patient is on the ventilator. • Deflate cuff daily to assess integrity of cuff. Assess ability to easily deflate cuff. Difficulty deflating cuff indicates a need for tube change. If aspirate returns with air, cuff is no longer intact. • Tube can be used for up to 1 month in patients on home mechanical ventilation. • Good choice for patients who need inflated cuff at home since teaching about cuff pressure is simplified.

Much of the management of the patient receiving mechanical ventilation through a tracheostomy is the same as that of the patient with an ET tube. There are some slight differences. At a minimum, you must assess the tracheostomy site and confirm patency of the tracheostomy tube every shift, or more often based on your assessment. Observe the site for any redness, inflammation, edema, ulceration, or signs of infection. Perform sterile dressing changes every 12 to 24 hours. You may need another person to help you with tracheostomy care. Clean around the stoma with normal saline and apply a sterile precut dressing around the tracheostomy tube site. You can complete dressing changes more often if needed. Care of the stoma and cannula for the patient with a tracheostomy is described in Table 28.19.

Because an inflated tracheostomy cuff exerts pressure on the tracheal mucosa, inflate the cuff with the least amount of air needed to obtain an airway seal. Measure cuff inflation pressure with a cuff manometer at least every 8 hours. Cuff inflation

TABLE 28.17 Complications of Tracheostomy

Closely monitor patients with a tracheostomy for the following potential complications:

- Air leak
- Airway obstruction
- Altered body image
- Aspiration
- Bleeding
- Fistula formation
- Impaired cough
- Infection
- Subcutaneous emphysema
- Tracheal necrosis
- Tracheal stenosis
- Tube displacement

TABLE 28.18 NURSING MANAGEMENT

Caring for the Patient With a Tracheostomy

Nursing management of the patient with a tracheostomy includes most of the care provided to the patient who is intubated and mechanically ventilated with an oral ET tube.

- Assess tracheostomy site at least once per shift for any signs of inflammation or infection.
- Suction the tracheostomy as needed.
- Provide tracheostomy care per agency guidelines.
- Maintain appropriate cuff inflation pressure at 20–30 cm H_2O (15–22 mm Hg).
- Teach patient and caregiver about tracheostomy care.

Collaborate With the Respiratory Therapist

- Ensure equipment is available for suctioning and tracheotomy care.
- Measure tracheal cuff pressures.
- Maintain appropriate cuff inflation pressure at 20–30 cm H_2O (15–22 mm Hg).
- Provide tracheostomy care per agency guidelines.
- Replace the tracheostomy tube or ventilate the patient with a BVM device if accidental dislodgment occurs.
- Assist with decannulation.

Supervise the LPN/VN

- Determine the need for suctioning.
- Suction the tracheostomy.
- Assess patient status after suctioning.
- Provide tracheostomy care using sterile technique.
- Notify the RN of any changes in respiratory status.

Collaborate With the Dietitian

- Assess risk for aspiration.
- Recommend a diet to promote nutrition and decrease aspiration risk.

Collaborate With Physical and Occupational Therapy

- Develop a plan for active range of motion and early mobility.
- Help facilitate any adaptation for patients going home with a tracheostomy.

Collaborate With Speech Language Pathology

- Assess swallowing ability and risk for aspiration.
- Develop plan to avoid aspiration.

TABLE 28.19 NURSING MANAGEMENT

Stoma and Cannula Care for a Tracheostomy

The following are general guidelines for basic tracheostomy care. Follow the specific policies in your agency.

Before You Begin

1. Explain procedure to patient.
2. Use tracheostomy care kit or collect sterile equipment (e.g., suction catheter, 1 pair sterile gloves, 1 pair non-sterile gloves, water basin, tracheostomy ties, tube brush or pipe cleaners, 4- × 4-inch gauze pads, sterile water or normal saline, tracheostomy dressing [optional]).
   - Note: Clean technique is used for the patient with a tracheostomy at home.
3. Position patient in semi-Fowler's position.
4. Assemble supplies on bedside table.
5. Wash hands. Put on PPE.

Providing Tracheostomy Care

6. Open sterile equipment. Pour sterile H_2O or normal saline into 2 compartments of sterile container or 2 basins, then apply sterile gloves.
7. If present, unlock and remove inner cannula. Many tracheostomy tubes do not have inner cannulas. Care for these tubes includes all steps listed below, except for inner cannula care.
8. Inner cannula care
   - Disposable: If using a disposable inner cannula, replace with new cannula.
   - Non-disposable:
     - Immerse inner cannula in sterile solution and clean inside and outside of cannula using tube brush or pipe cleaners.
     - Rinse cannula in sterile solution. Remove from solution and shake to dry. Insert inner cannula into outer cannula with the curved part downward, and lock in place.
9. Stoma care:
   - Remove dried secretions from stoma using 4 × 4-inch gauze pad soaked in sterile water or saline. Gently pat area around the stoma dry. Be sure to clean under the tracheostomy flange (faceplate), using cotton swabs to reach this area.

pressure should not exceed 20 to 30 cm H_2O (15 to 22 mm Hg). Higher pressures may compress tracheal capillaries, limit blood flow, and predispose the patient to tracheal necrosis. The minimal occlusion volume (MOV) is one technique used to inflate the tracheostomy cuff (Table 28.16).

Suctioning and tracheostomy care are complex nursing activities. Every nurse who performs suctioning and tracheostomy care must know the scope of practice and policies of the agency for all health care personnel. Collaborate with the RT, who will play a key role in the patient's care.

Suction the tracheostomy tube as needed. Try to avoid suctioning through the newly created tracheostomy in the first few hours after the procedure. This may worsen discomfort and promote bleeding. Suctioning may be done using sterile glove and catheter technique, or an existing in-line suction catheter (Fig. 28.17). Each time you suction the patient, observe the amount, color, and clarity of secretions. Note patient tolerance.

At first, patients should receive humidified air to compensate for the loss of the upper airway to warm and moisturize secretions.[25] Humidification helps keep secretions thin, decrease formation of mucous plugs, and promote comfort.

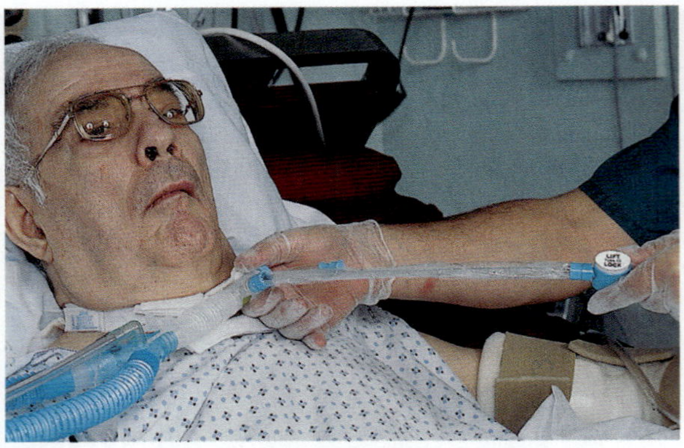

Fig. 28.17 Suctioning a tracheostomy tube with a closed system suction catheter. (From Potter PA, Perry AG: *Basic nursing: essentials for practice,* ed 7, St. Louis, 2011, Mosby.)

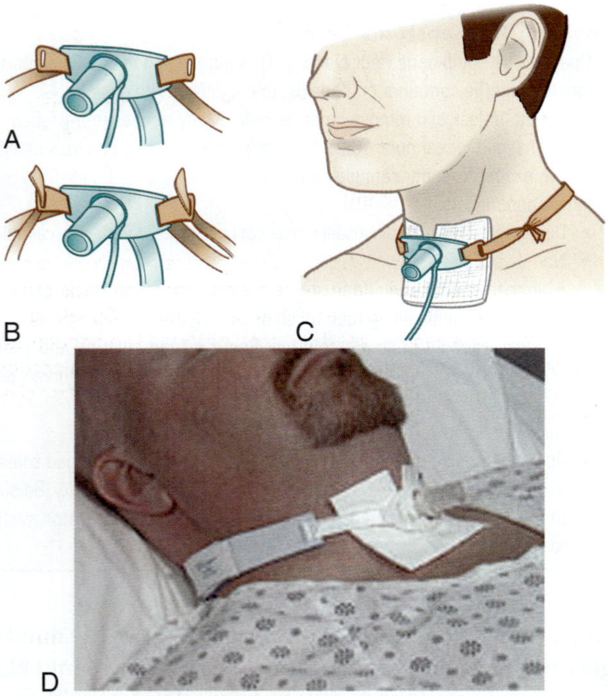

Fig. 28.18 Changing tracheostomy tapes. (A) Cut a small slit about 1 inch (2.5 cm) from the end. Put the slit end into the opening of the cannula. (B) Make a loop with the other end of the tape. (C) Tie the tapes together with a double knot on the side of the neck. (D) A Velcro tracheostomy tube holder. (D, Courtesy Dale Medical Products.)

If the inner cannula is disposable, replace per manufacturer and agency guidelines. If non-disposable, clean the inner cannula at least every shift. Cleaning removes mucus from the inside of the tube to prevent airway obstruction.

Change the tracheostomy tapes after the first 24 hours and then as needed (Fig. 28.18). Using a 2-person technique, 1 person stabilizes the tracheostomy while the other person changes the tapes. During the procedure, apply gentle pressure to the flange. Tie the tracheostomy tapes (or Velcro straps) securely with room for 2 fingers between the tapes and the skin. These steps are considered best practice to ensure that the tracheostomy does not become accidentally dislodged during the procedure. In some centers, the HCP or RT may complete this task.

When turning and repositioning the patient, take care not to dislodge the tracheostomy tube. Because tube may be difficult to reinsert in the immediate postoperative period, several precautions are needed. Keep a replacement tube of equal or smaller size at the bedside, readily available for emergency reinsertion. Do not change tracheostomy tapes for at least 24 hours afterwards. The HCP often performs the first tube change. This happens usually no sooner than 7 days after the tracheotomy.

◆ Accidental Decannulation

If the tracheostomy tube is accidentally dislodged, immediately call for help. While waiting for the HCP or RT to arrive, you have several options. These depend on agency policy.

Quickly assess the patient's LOC, their ability to breathe, and the presence of any respiratory distress. If respiratory distress is present, and it is within your scope of practice, one option is to quickly use a hemostat to spread the opening where the tube was. Insert the obturator in the replacement tube, lubricate with saline, and insert the tube into the stoma. Once the tube is inserted, remove the obturator at once so that air can flow through the tube. Another option is to insert a suction catheter to allow air passage and serve as a guide for insertion. Thread the tracheostomy tube over the catheter and remove the catheter. Trying to reinsert is easier if the stoma tract is mature or more than 1 week old.

If the tube cannot be replaced because of tract immaturity (less than 1 week old) or other circumstances, immediately place the patient in semi-Fowler's position to decrease dyspnea. Cover the stoma with a sterile dressing and ventilate the patient with the BVM over the nose and mouth. If a patient has had a total laryngectomy, there will be complete separation between the upper airway and trachea. Ventilate this patient through the tracheostomy stoma. Severe dyspnea and hypoxemia may progress to respiratory and cardiac arrest.

CHECK YOUR PRACTICE

You are caring for a patient who had a surgically created tracheostomy 6 hours ago. While suctioning the patient, he coughs, dislodging the tracheostomy tube.

- What should you do?

◆ Decannulation

Removal of the tracheostomy from the trachea is called **decannulation**. Removal is possible when the primary condition for which the patient received a tracheostomy has been resolved. The patient also needs to (1) be hemodynamically stable, (2) have a stable, intact respiratory drive, (3) be able to adequately exchange air, and (4) independently expectorate secretions.

Immediately prior to decannulation, explain to the patient what will occur. Monitor vital signs. Suction the patient through the tracheostomy. Clear the mouth of any oral secretions. Loosen and/or cut the tracheostomy tapes. Remove any visible sutures holding the tracheostomy in place. Deflate the tracheostomy cuff. Pull the tracheostomy tube outwards in one smooth motion. Stop if you meet any resistance and notify the HCP immediately.

After removing the tube, apply a sterile occlusive dressing and monitor for bleeding. Change the dressing if it gets soiled or wet. If needed, close the stoma with tape strips. Monitor respiratory status and O_2 saturation for airway compromise or difficulty breathing. Apply an alternate method of O_2 delivery (e.g., nasal prongs) if needed. Teach the patient to splint the stoma with the fingers when coughing, swallowing, or speaking. Epithelial tissue begins to form in 24 to 48 hours, and the opening closes within 4 or 5 days. Surgery to close the tracheostomy is usually not needed.

NURSING MANAGEMENT: CARE OF THE PATIENT WITH A LONG-TERM TRACHEOSTOMY

Some patients have a tracheostomy for life. They may be receiving mechanical ventilation or have a tracheal or laryngeal problem. Care of the patient with a long-term tracheostomy includes all the same care as patients with a new tracheostomy. This includes observing the tracheostomy site, cleaning the inner cannula, suctioning, and changing tracheostomy tapes.

The tracheostomy tube should be changed around 1 month after the first tube change and every 1 to 3 months thereafter. When a tracheostomy has been in place for several months, the healed tract should be well formed. Changing the tracheostomy tube is important as it permits assessment of the stoma and cleaning of the tube. Teach the patient signs and symptoms of infection and how to change the tube at home using a clean technique. Engaging patients to take part in their care helps decrease complications and infection and promotes their feeling of well-being.

Swallowing Problems

An inflated tracheostomy tube cuff may result in swallowing problems by interfering with the normal function of muscles used to swallow. Therefore for long-term tracheostomy patients, we need to evaluate the patient's swallowing ability and risk for aspiration.

A speech language therapist (SLT) should assess the patient's ability to swallow. To assess for aspiration, the patient receives thickened fluids of different consistencies. If the patient can swallow without aspiration when the cuff is deflated, the cuff may be left deflated or a cuffless tube may be inserted. At this time, patients may have varying levels of thickened fluids and soft foods.

Speech With a Tracheostomy Tube

The spontaneously breathing patient may be able to talk with a tracheostomy. Several options are available depending upon the type of tracheostomy (Fig. 28.19). For example, if the patient is at low risk of aspiration, (1) remove the inner cannula (if non-fenestrated), (2) deflate the cuff, and (3) place the cap on the tube. When the tracheostomy cuff is deflated, exhaled air can flow upward over the vocal cords. When a fenestrated cannula is first used, frequently assess the patient for respiratory distress. If the patient cannot tolerate the procedure, remove the cap, insert a non-fenestrated cannula, and reinflate the cuff. Monitor for improvement in patient condition.

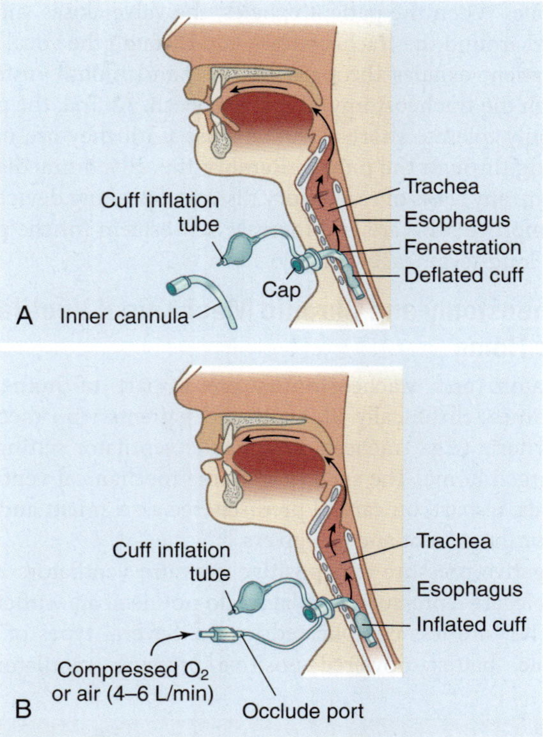

Fig. 28.19 Tracheostomy tubes. (A) Fenestrated tracheostomy tube with cuff deflated, inner cannula removed, and tracheostomy tube capped to allow air to pass over the vocal cords. (B) Speaking tracheostomy tube. One tube is used for cuff inflation. The second tube is connected to a source of compressed air or O_2. When the port on the second tube is occluded, air flows up over the vocal cords, allowing speech with an inflated cuff.

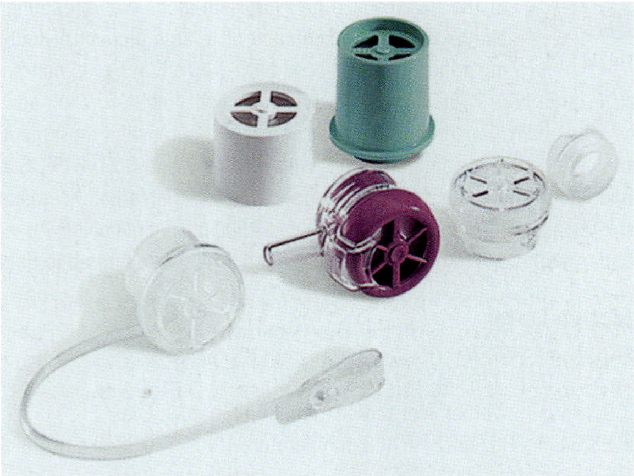

Fig. 28.20 Passy-Muir tracheostomy speaking valve. The valve is placed over the hub of the tracheostomy tube after the cuff is deflated. Multiple options are available for ventilated and nonventilated patients. The 1-way valve allows air to enter the lungs during inspiration and redirects air upward over the vocal cords into the mouth during expiration. (Courtesy Passy-Muir, Inc, Irvine, CA.)

The Passy-Muir valve is a simple device that attaches to the hub of the tracheostomy tube (Fig. 28.20). With the cuff deflated, the valve redirects air flow through the vocal cords. On inspiration, the valve on the device opens, allowing the patient to inhale. When the patient exhales, the valve closes, air flows upward around the tracheostomy, and through the vocal cords. The patient exhales through the nose and mouth instead of through the tracheostomy, allowing speech. At first, the patient may only tolerate short periods of use until they are used to exhaling through the mouth. Remove the valve immediately if there are any signs of respiratory distress. Speaking devices may help improve self-care and increase self-esteem for the patient with a long-term tracheostomy.

◆ Tracheostomy and Chronic Mechanical Ventilation in the Home

Ventilators and tracheostomies are a part of home care. Sometimes, chronically ill, ventilated patients who meet specific criteria (e.g., tracheostomy, stabile ventilator settings) are discharged home. The success of home mechanical ventilation depends, in part, on careful predischarge assessment and planning for the patient and caregivers.[26]

Negative pressure and positive pressure ventilators can be used. Negative pressure ventilators do not need an artificial airway. They are less complicated to use. Several types of small, portable, battery-powered positive pressure ventilators are available. They can be attached to a wheelchair or placed on a bedside table. Settings and alarms on these ventilators are simpler to use than standard ventilators.

Home mechanical ventilation has advantages and disadvantages. Having the patient in the home eliminates the strain that the hospital setting imposes on family dynamics. Caregivers may experience many feelings when they first hear about the need for long-term mechanical ventilation.[27] These feelings are often balanced by the chance to care for the patient. At home, the patient may be more mobile and able to take part in more activities of daily living on a personalized schedule.

Disadvantages include problems related to equipment, reimbursement, and caregiver stress and fatigue. Ventilated patients are often dependent and require extensive nursing care, at least at first. Disposable products may not be reimbursable.

Carefully assess financial resources when arranging home ventilation. Hold a care conference before starting a discharge teaching plan. Caregivers may seem enthusiastic about providing care but may not understand the sacrifices they may have to make financially and in personal time and commitment. Encourage caregivers to consider respite care to periodically relieve their stress and fatigue.

Case Study

Mechanical Ventilation

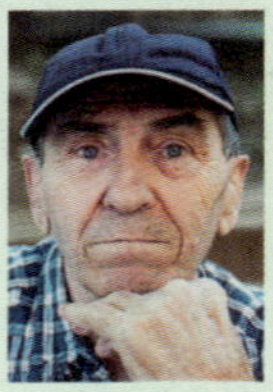

(© Thinkstock.)

Patient Profile

R.K. is a 72-year-old male who collapsed in his home. He was found by the police during a wellness check when his nephew became concerned that he had not heard from him for 2 days. Police activated the emergency response system. On arrival of the paramedics, he was semi-alert, was breathing at 32 beaths/min, and incontinent of a large amount of foul-smelling urine. He was placed on O_2 @ 15 L/min with non-breather mask. A large bore #18G IV was placed in his right lower arm. On admission to the emergency department, R.K. had weak, non-purposeful movement of all 4 limbs. Vital signs became unstable, with BP 84/49 and SpO_2 84%. Suddenly he made no spontaneous respiratory effort. R.K. was immediately intubated. A chest x-ray and ABG were done. He received a 500 mL IV fluid bolus. An indwelling urinary catheter and OG tube were inserted. R.K. was admitted to the ICU.

Objective Data

Physical Assessment

- Weight: 168 lb. (76 kg)
- GCS: Motor: 5; Verbal: Not scored (patient intubated); Eyes: 2.
- BP 85/64 mm Hg (cuff); HR 128; temperature 102° F (39.3° C); SpO_2 is 94%
- ECG shows atrial fibrillation with a rapid ventricular response.
- Breath sounds: coarse crackles bilaterally, decreased breath sounds to the right middle and both lower lobes
- Thick, purulent secretions suctioned from ET tube
- Appears dehydrated (dry mucous membranes, cracked lips)

Diagnostic Studies

- Chest x-ray shows right middle and bilateral lower lung lobe consolidation
- ABGs: pH 7.27; PaO_2 75 mm Hg; $PaCO_2$ 54 mm Hg; HCO_3 25 mEq/L

Interprofessional Care

- Full support positive pressure ventilation: AC. Settings: FIO_2 100%, V_T 500 mL, respiratory rate 14 breaths/min (patient is making no spontaneous respiratory effort), PEEP 5 cm H_2O
- HOB elevated at 30 degrees
- IV 0.9% at 75mL/hr
- EN at 25 mL/hr, increase by 20 mL/hr every 4 hr with a goal of 75 mL/hr
- 12 lead ECG in AM
- Daily chest x-ray for next 3 days
- Chest physiotherapy and mobilize tomorrow
- Urine for culture and sensitivity
- Drug Therapy:
  - Famotidine 10 mg IV q12hr
  - Enoxaparin 40 mg subcutaneous daily
  - Ceftriaxone 1gram IV q24hr
  - Azithromycin 500 mg IV q24hr
  - Fentanyl 50 mcg IV q1hr PRN

Discussion Questions

1. ***Recognize***: Why do you think R.K. collapsed?
2. ***Analyze***: From a respiratory perspective, what findings from the physical assessment and diagnostic studies concern you most? Which need would be addressed first?
3. ***Plan***: Identify 2 reasons for intubating and providing mechanical ventilation for R.K.
4. ***Prioritize*** Based on R.K.'s ABGs, should any ventilator setting(s) be changed? If so, what changes would you suggest?
5. ***Plan***: R.K.'s condition deteriorates. PaO_2 drops to 58 mm Hg, and SpO_2 is 85%. What can be done to help improve oxygenation?
6. ***Act***: R.K.'s caregivers want to know why he is receiving tube feedings. What would you tell them?
7. ***Safety:*** What safety precautions would be implemented for R.K. while he is a patient in the adult ICU?
8. ***Evaluate***: What implications would increasing PEEP have for R.K.'s hemodynamic status?

Answers available at http://evolve.elsevier.com/Lewis/medsurg.

BRIDGE TO NCLEX EXAMINATION

The number of the question corresponds to the same-numbered outcome at the beginning of the chapter.

1. Which technique would be most appropriate for a patient with mild COPD to promote airway clearance?
   a. Huff coughing
   b. Postural drainage
   c. Pursed lip breathing
   d. High-frequency chest wall oscillation
2. The major advantage of a Venturi mask is that it can
   a. deliver up to 80% O_2.
   b. provide continuous 100% humidity.
   c. deliver a precise concentration of O_2.
   d. be used while a patient eats and sleeps.
3. In a spontaneously breathing patient, the nurse notes tidaling of the water level in the water-seal chamber of the chest tube drainage system. The nurse would
   a. continue to monitor the patient.
   b. check all connections for a leak in the system.
   c. raise the collection unit above the level of the heart.
   d. clamp the tubing at a distal point away from the patient.
4. After a left lower lobe lobectomy, an appropriate nursing measure is to
   a. position the patient prone every 2 hours.
   b. monitor the chest tube drainage and functioning.
   c. auscultate lung sounds frequently in the lower left lobe.
   d. administer IV fluid boluses to maintain blood pressure.
5. Which assessment finding concerns you *most* in a patient with pneumonia who is receiving noninvasive ventilation (Bi-PAP)?
   a. New onset of confusion to time and place
   b. Fine crackles on auscultation of affected lobe
   c. Patient asks to remove the mask for oral care
   d. HR: 98, RR: 16 bpm, BP: 110/60, SpO_2: 93%
6. A patient with multiple gunshot wounds returns to the ICU from surgery. Vital signs are stable. They are making no spontaneous respiratory effort. Which mode of ventilation would be most appropriate?
   a. Assist control (AC)
   b. Pressure support (PS)
   c. Bi-level positive airway pressure (Bi-PAP)
   d. Synchronized intermittent mandatory ventilation (SIMV)
7. Nursing management of a patient with an oral ET tube would include
   a. maintaining ET tube cuff pressure at 35 to 40 cm H_2O.
   b. routine suctioning of the ET tube at least every 2 hours.
   c. observing the patient for spontaneous respiratory effort and work of breathing.
   d. preventing ET tube dislodgment by limiting mouth care to lubrication of the lips.
8. Which nursing action would be the *highest priority* when suctioning a patient with an oral ET tube or tracheostomy?
   a. Hyperoxygenate with 100% FIO_2 before suctioning.
   b. Auscultate lung sounds after suctioning is completed.
   c. Instill 5 mL of normal saline into the tube before suctioning.
   d. Give antianxiety medications 30 minutes before suctioning.
9. The nurse monitors the patient with positive pressure mechanical ventilation for
   a. paralytic ileus because pressure on the abdominal contents affects bowel motility.
   b. diuresis and sodium depletion because of increased release of atrial natriuretic peptide.
   c. signs of cardiovascular insufficiency because pressure in the chest impedes venous return.
   d. respiratory acidosis in a patient with COPD because of alveolar hyperventilation and increased PaO_2 levels.
10. Which findings indicate the patient is ready for weaning from mechanical ventilation? *(select all that apply)*
    a. Serum hemoglobin of 15 g/dL
    b. Respirations of 18 breaths/min
    c. Patient is alert and follow commands
    d. Chest x-ray shows large pleural effusion
    e. Mean arterial pressure (MAP) of 55 mm Hg
    f. ABGS: pH 7.38, $PaCO_2$ 37 mm Hg, HCO_3^- 24 mEq/L, PaO_2 94
11. Immediate care priorities in the first few hours for a patient with a new tracheostomy include
    a. encouraging early mobility.
    b. changing the tracheostomy ties.
    c. suctioning the tracheostomy hourly.
    d. observing for bleeding at the insertion site.
12. Appropriate discharge teaching for the patient with a permanent tracheostomy after a total laryngectomy would include (*select all that apply*)
    a. encouraging regular exercise such as swimming.
    b. washing around the stoma daily with a moist washcloth.
    c. emphasizing the importance of regular follow-up appointments
    d. providing pictures and "hands-on" instruction for tracheostomy care.
    e. having a list of emergency contact numbers and where to obtain supplies.

1. a; 2. c; 3. a; 4. b; 5. a; 6. a; 7. c; 8. a; 9. c; 10. a, b, c, f; 11. d; 12. b, c, d, e.

For rationales to these answers and even more NCLEX review questions, visit http://evolve.elsevier.com/Lewis/medsurg.

EVOLVE WEBSITE/RESOURCES LIST

http://evolve.elsevier.com/Lewis/medsurg
Review Questions (Online Only)
Key Points
Answer Keys to Questions
- Rationales for Bridge to NCLEX Examination Questions
- Answer Guidelines for Case Study

Student Case Study
- Patient with Pulmonary Embolism and Respiratory Failure

Nursing Care Plan
- eNursing Care Plan 28.1: Patient on Mechanical Ventilation

Conceptual Care Map Creator
Audio Glossary

REFERENCES

1. Cleveland Clinic: Pursed-lip breathing. Retrieved from https://my.clevelandclinic.org/health/articles/9443-pursed-lip-breathing.
2. Cystic fibrosis Foundation: coughing and huffing. Retrieved from https://www.cff.org.
3. Evans JR: Postural drainage: does it really work?. Retrieved from https://www.healthline.com/health/postural-drainage.
*4. Hardavella G, Karampinis I, Frille A, et al.: Oxygen devices and delivery systems, *Breathe* 15:e108, 2019.
5. Physiopedia: oxygen therapy. Retrieved from https://www.physio-pedia.com/index.php?title=Oxygen_Therapy&oldid=256768.
*6. Sasa RI: Evidence-based update on chest tube management: is your practice current? *Am Nurse Today* 14:10, 2019.
7. Guthrie JM, Azan B, Lim G: Pigtail insertion. Retrieved from https://epmonthly.com/article/pigtail-insertion/.
8. Loughran P: Stripping or milking of chest tubes, *Crit Care Nurse* 39:72, 2019.
9. Soo Hoo GW: Non-invasive ventilation. Retrieved from https://emedicine.medscape.com/article/304235-overview.
10. Chappell, B: How to do noninvasive positive pressure ventilation. Retrieved from https:// www.merckmanuals.com/professional/critical-care-medicine/how-to-do-other-airway-procedures/how-to-do-noninvasive-positive-pressure-ventilation.
11. Hess DR, Kacmarek RM: *Essentials of mechanical ventilation*, ed 4, New York, 2019, McGraw Hill.
*12. Hill B: Principles of mechanical ventilation for non-critical care nurses, *Br J Nurs* 29:470, 2020.
13. Swindin J, Sampson C, Howatson A: Airway pressure release ventilation, *BMJ Education* 20:80, 2020.
14. Kumar CM, Seet E, Van Zundert, TCRV: Measuring endotracheal tube intracuff pressure: No room for complacency, *J Clin Monit Comput* 35(3), 2021.
*15. Lavigne MC: Comparing suctioning techniques used to assist mechanical ventilation: protecting you and your patients. Retrieved from https://www.ijic.info/article/view/15984/10338.
16. Stacy KM: Pulmonary therapeutic management. In Urden LD, Stacy KM, Lough ME, editors: *Priorities in critical care nursing*, ed 8, St. Louis, 2020, Elsevier.
17. Bass S, Vance ML, Reddy A: Bispectral index for titrating sedation in ARDS patients during neuromuscular blockade, *Am J Crit Care* 28:377, 2019.
*18. Duckworth RL: How to read and interpret end-tidal capnography waveforms. Retrieved from https://www.jems.com/patient-care/how-to-read-and-interpret-end-tidal-capnography-waveforms/.
19. Allen K, Hoffman L: Enteral nutrition in the mechanically ventilated patient. Retrieved from https://www.cpncampus.com/biblioteca/files/original/90ae7047639714627102672 81c3ed381.pdf.
20. Escalon M, Lichtenstein AH, Posner E: The effects of early mobilization on patients requiring extended mechanical ventilation across multiple ICUs, *Crit Care Explor* 2:e0119, 2020.
21. Stollings JL, Devlin JW, Lin JC: Best practices for conducting interprofessional team rounds to facilitate performance of the ICU liberation (ABCDEF) bundle, *Crit Care Med* 48:562, 2020.
*22. Guérin C, Albert RK, Beitler J, et al.: Prone position in ARDS patients: why, when, how and for whom, *Intensive Care Med* 46:2385, 2020.
23. Papazian L, Klompas M, Luyt CE: Ventilator-associated pneumonia in adults: a narrative review, *Intensive Care Med* 46:888, 2020.
24. Sethi S: Ventilator associated pneumonia. Retrieved from https://www.merckmanuals.com/professional/pulmonary-disorders/pneumonia/ventilator-associated-pneumonia.
25. Hashimoto DA, Axtell A, Auchincloss HG: Percutaneous tracheostomy, *N Engl J Med* 383:e112, 2020.
*26. Patton J: Tracheostomy care, *Br J Nurs* 28:1060, 2019.
27. Leasa D, Elson S: Building a comprehensive system of services to support adults living with long-term mechanical ventilation. Retrieved from https://www.ncbi.nlm.nih.gov/pmc/articles/PMC4904516/.

*Evidence-based information for clinical practice.

29

Upper Respiratory Problems

Janice A. Sarasnick

http://evolve.elsevier.com/Lewis/medsurg/

CONCEPTUAL FOCUS

Cellular Regulation
Functional Ability
Gas Exchange
Infection
Sensory Perception

LEARNING OUTCOMES

1. Describe the clinical manifestations and nursing and interprofessional management of problems of the nose.
2. Discuss the clinical manifestations and nursing and interprofessional management of problems of the paranasal sinuses.
3. Describe the clinical manifestations, nursing, and interprofessional management of an upper respiratory infection.
4. Describe the clinical manifestations and nursing and interprofessional management of problems of the pharynx and larynx.
5. Outline the risk factors for and clinical manifestations of head and neck cancer.
6. Discuss the nursing and interprofessional management of patients undergoing surgery for head and neck cancer.
7. Explain essential components of discharge teaching for the patient going home with a permanent tracheostomy after total laryngectomy for cancer.

KEY TERMS

acute laryngitis
airway obstruction
allergic rhinitis
epistaxis
influenza
laryngectomy, **Table 29.7**
pharyngitis
rhinoplasty
sinusitis
upper respiratory infections

This chapter discusses problems of the upper respiratory system, which includes the nose, sinuses, pharynx, and larynx, and the care of those undergoing surgery for head and neck cancers. The primary concern with upper respiratory problems is the impact on ventilation and oxygen (O_2) availability. They can negatively affect sleep and impair the ability to obtain and maintain nutrition. Sinus and upper respiratory tract infections, allergies, and oral problems can change the senses of both smell and taste. The patient with head and neck cancer often has depression, changes in body image, and impaired sexuality.

NASAL AND PARANASAL SINUS PROBLEMS

DEVIATED SEPTUM

Deviated septum is a deflection of the normally straight nasal septum. The cause is usually from trauma or is genetic. Up to 80% of adults may have septa that are slightly off-center. The diagnosis of a deviated septum is generally reserved for those whose septa are severely shifted.[1] A deviated septum can interfere with both airflow and sinus drainage due to the narrowed passageway.

Symptoms vary depending on the degree of deviation. Minor septal deviations can range from asymptomatic to nasal congestion and frequent sinus infections. Manifestations of severe septal deviation include facial pain, nosebleeds *(epistaxis),* and obstruction to nasal breathing.

The diagnosis is made during examination with a nasal speculum. The medical management of minor septal deviation focuses on symptom control. For nasal inflammation and congestion, use saline rinses and decongestants to clear nasal passages and analgesics for pain relief. For severe septal deviation, a nasal septoplasty reconstructs and properly aligns the deviated septum.

NASAL FRACTURE

Nasal fracture is the most common facial fracture and the third most common fracture of any bone.[2] They often occur from blunt trauma, including fights, automobile accidents, falls, and sports injuries. Using protective sports equipment and safeguarding against falls can prevent many nasal fractures.

There is no universally accepted classification system for nasal fractures. We can classify nasal fractures by their fracture pattern (e.g., impacted, comminuted) or the direction of injury (e.g., lateral, frontal). *Simple fractures* may be unilateral or bilateral. They typically have little or no displacement. Powerful frontal blows can cause *complex fractures,* which may involve damage to adjacent facial structures, such as the teeth or eyes. Patients with nasal fractures from blunt force trauma should be evaluated for injury to the cervical spine, orbital sockets, and mandible. Complications include airway obstruction, nosebleeds, meningeal tears causing cerebrospinal fluid (CSF) leakage, septal hematoma, and cosmetic deformity.

Diagnosis of a nasal fracture is based on health history and physical assessment. Although facial deformity with a nasal fracture is common, a nosebleed may be the only manifestation. Other manifestations include localized pain, crepitus on palpation, swelling, difficulty breathing out of the nostrils, and bruising.

Assess the patient's ability to breathe through each side of the nose. Note the presence of edema, bleeding, or hematoma. Periorbital bruising involving both eyes is called *raccoon eyes.* It suggests a basilar skull fracture. It increases the chance of CSF leaking into the nasal cavities. Inspect the nose internally for evidence of septal deviation, clear drainage, edema, or bleeding. Clear or pink-tinged persistent drainage after control of bleeding suggests a possible CSF leak. If needed, send a specimen to the laboratory to determine the fluid type.

Goals of nursing care are to maintain a patent airway, reduce edema and pain, prevent complications, and provide emotional support. The best way to maintain the airway is to keep the patient sitting upright. Apply ice to the face and nose in 10- to 20-minute intervals to help reduce edema and bleeding. Tell the patient not to blow their nose once bleeding has stopped so they do not disrupt the clot or cause further trauma. Give analgesia as ordered to control pain. Acetaminophen is preferred over nonsteroidal antiinflammatory drugs (NSAIDs) or aspirin for the first 48 hours to avoid prolonging clotting time and increasing the risk for bleeding. Nasal stuffiness may be relieved with nasal decongestants, saline nasal sprays, and a humidifier. The patient should avoid hot showers and alcohol for the first 48 hours to prevent an increase in swelling. Encourage the patient to quit or decrease smoking to help tissue healing.

When a fracture is confirmed, the goals are to realign the fractured bones using either manual manipulation or surgery.[3] Simple fractures are often reduced with manual manipulation. With complex nasal fractures, considerable swelling of soft tissues occurs. It may be necessary to wait to repair the fracture until after the edema subsides. This may be 5 to 10 days. Antibiotics should be considered for any nasal fracture with disruption to the mucosa.

Surgical options include septoplasty and rhinoplasty. Septoplasty is done to correct a deviated septum. Patients have rhinoplasty for several reasons. Both procedures help maintain a patent airway, restore function of the nose, and help reestablish the patient's cosmetic appearance. The presence of septal hematoma increases the patient's risk for deformity and infection, which may require drainage and antibiotic therapy.

RHINOPLASTY

Rhinoplasty is the surgical reconstruction of the nose. It is done for cosmetic reasons or to improve airway function when trauma or developmental deformities result in nasal obstruction.

Most rhinoplasty is an outpatient procedure using regional or general anesthesia. Nasal tissue is added or removed, and the nose may be lengthened or shortened. Plastic implants are sometimes used to reshape the nose. Incisions are typically inside the nose and hidden. Sonic rhinoplasty employs an ultrasonic device to gently aspirate bone, enabling a refined cosmetic result.[4]

Before surgery, assess the patient's expectations of the surgery. Actual or perceived changes in body image (e.g., deformed or enlarged nose) can affect self-esteem and interactions with others. The HCP can use digital photographs to show patients their projected appearance after surgery. These images can help patients decide whether to undergo rhinoplasty.

Obtain a medication history. Aspirin-containing drugs and NSAIDs may need to be stopped for 5 days to 2 weeks before surgery to reduce the risk of bleeding. Encourage smoking cessation to promote postoperative wound healing.

During the immediate postoperative period, nursing interventions include (1) ensuring patency of the airway, (2) continuous assessment of respiratory status, (3) monitoring for airway obstruction, (4) pain management, and (5) observation of the surgical site for edema, bleeding, and infection.

After surgery, nasal packing may be inserted to apply pressure and prevent bleeding or septal hematoma formation. An external plastic splint protects and supports the new shape of the nose during the healing process. If present, nasal packing is usually removed 1 or 2 days after surgery. The splint may be left in place for 1 to 2 weeks.

Teaching is important because the patient must be able to detect complications at home. The patient typically has temporary nasal and/or facial edema and bruising. Cold compresses and elevating the head can help minimize swelling and discomfort. Teach about activity restrictions aimed at preventing bleeding and injury (no nose blowing, swimming, heavy lifting, strenuous exercise). Sometimes swelling may be slow to resolve, delaying the achievement of a full cosmetic result for up to 1 year.

EPISTAXIS

Epistaxis (nosebleed) most often occurs in adults over age 50. Nosebleeds can be caused by trauma, low humidity, upper respiratory tract infections, allergies, sinusitis, foreign bodies, chemical irritants (e.g., street drugs), overuse of decongestant nasal

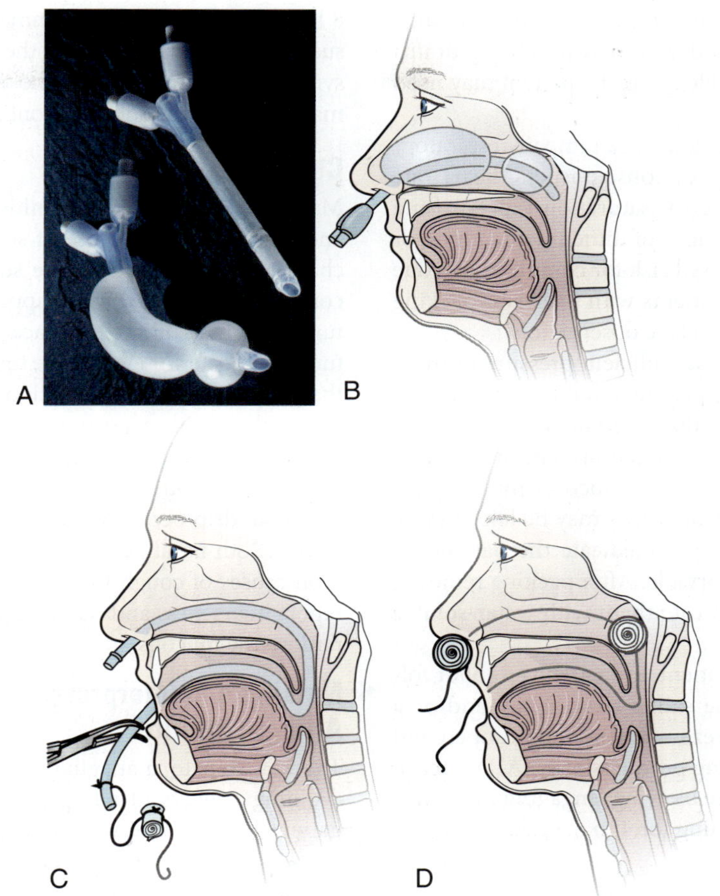

Fig. 29.1 (A) Epistaxis balloon. The balloon is inflated after insertion. (B) Epistaxis balloon properly position in nares. (C) Method for placing posterior nasal pack. A catheter is passed through the bleeding side of the nose and pulled out through the mouth with a hemostat. Strings are tied to the catheter. The pack is pulled up behind the soft palate and into the nasopharynx. (D) Nasal pack in position in the posterior nasopharynx. Dental roll at the nose helps maintain the correct position. (A, Courtesy Boston Medical, Westborough, MA. B, From Roberts JR, Hedges JR: *Clinical procedures in emergency medicine,* ed 5, Philadelphia, 2009, Saunders.)

sprays, facial or nasal surgery, anatomic malformation, and tumors. Conditions that prolong bleeding time or change platelet counts may predispose a patient to nosebleeds.[5] Bleeding time may be prolonged if the patient takes aspirin, NSAIDs, warfarin, or other anticoagulant drugs.

We describe nosebleeds as anterior or posterior. About 90% of nosebleeds occur in the anterior part of the nasal cavity. They are easy to visualize. Anterior bleeding can be self-treated and usually stops spontaneously. Posterior bleeding occurs more often with older adults with other health problems. Since posterior nosebleeds are closer to the throat, it is often hard to determine how much blood loss has occurred. Posterior bleeding may need medical treatment.

Nursing and Interprofessional Management: Epistaxis

Use simple first aid measures to control nosebleeds:

1. Place the patient in a sitting position, leaning slightly forward with head tilted forward.
2. Apply direct pressure by squeezing the entire soft lower part of the nose (nostrils) together for 5 to 15 minutes.
3. If bleeding does not stop within 15 minutes, seek medical assistance.

An anterior bleed may be treated medically by placing a pledget (nasal tampon) impregnated with anesthetic solution (lidocaine) and/or vasoconstrictive agents (epinephrine) into the nasal cavity. Absorbable materials, such as oxidized cellulose (surgical), gelatin foam (Gelfoam), or a gelatin-thrombin combination (Floseal), are another option. Packing for anterior bleeds can stay in place for 48 to 72 hours. Silver nitrate may be used to chemically cauterize a specific bleeding point. Thermal cauterization is reserved for more severe bleeding. It may require the use of local or general anesthesia.[6]

It may be harder to find the location of a posterior bleed. Posterior bleeds often need packing. Packing with compressed nasal sponges (e.g., Merocel) or epistaxis balloons (e.g., Rapid Rhino) is best because of the ease of placement. Packing is inserted into the nares and advanced along the floor of the nasal cavity. The sponge expands with moisture to fill the nasal cavity and tamponade bleeding. An epistaxis balloon inflated with air achieves the same pressure effect (Fig. 29.1). In the absence of a specific nasal device, we may use a size 10F, 12F, or 14F Foley catheter with a 30-mL balloon. A nasal sling (folded 2 × 2–inch gauze pad) may be gently taped under the nares to absorb drainage. If packing does not stop the bleeding, the patient may need arterial embolization.

Nasal sponges, packing, and balloons can impair respiratory status. Closely monitor the level of consciousness, heart rate and rhythm, respiratory rate, and O_2 saturation (SpO_2) using pulse oximetry. Observe for any signs of difficulty breathing or swallowing. Because of the increased risk for complications due to the location of the injury, all patients with posterior packing should be on a monitored unit for close observation.

Nasal packing is painful because sufficient pressure must be applied to stop the bleeding. The patient should receive appropriate analgesia. Nasal packing predisposes patients to infection from bacteria (e.g., *Staphylococcus aureus*) present in the nasal cavity. Antibiotics effective against staphylococci may be prescribed. Nasal packing for posterior bleeds may be left in place for 2 to 3 days. Before removal, pre-medicate the patient for pain as this procedure is uncomfortable. After packing removal, cleanse the nares gently and lubricate them with water-soluble jelly.

Before discharge, teach the patient and caregiver about follow-up care. Review how to use saline nasal spray and/or a humidifier. Have the patient sneeze with the mouth open and avoid the use of aspirin-containing products or NSAIDs. Teach the patient to avoid vigorous nose blowing, engaging in strenuous activity, and lifting and straining for 4 to 6 weeks.

ALLERGIC RHINITIS

Allergic rhinitis is inflammation of the nasal mucosa, often in response to a specific allergen. We usually describe allergic rhinitis by the causative allergen (seasonal or perennial) and the frequency of symptoms (episodic, intermittent, or persistent). *Episodic* refers to symptoms related to sporadic exposure to allergens not typically encountered in the patient's normal environment. An example is exposure to animal dander when visiting another person's home. *Intermittent* means that the symptoms are present less than 4 days a week or less than 4 weeks per year. *Persistent* means that symptoms are present more than 4 days a week and for more than 4 weeks per year.

Seasonal rhinitis usually occurs in the spring and fall. It is caused by an allergy to pollens from trees, flowers, grasses, or weeds. Attacks may last for several weeks during times when pollen counts are high. Then it disappears and often recurs at the same time the next year. *Perennial rhinitis* occurs year-round from exposure to environmental allergens, such as animal dander, dust mites, cockroaches, fungi, and molds. Both seasonal and perennial rhinitis can be classified as episodic, intermittent, or persistent, depending on the duration and frequency of symptoms.

Sensitization to an allergen occurs with initial allergen exposure, which results in the production of antigen-specific immunoglobulin E (IgE) (see Fig. 14.6). After exposure, mast cells and basophils release histamine, cytokines, prostaglandins, and leukotrienes. These cause the early symptoms of sneezing, itching, rhinorrhea (runny nose), and congestion (stuffy nose).[7] Within 4 to 8 hours after exposure, inflammatory cells infiltrate the nasal tissues, causing and maintaining the inflammatory response. Because symptoms of rhinitis are like those of the common cold, the patient may think the condition is a continuous or repeated cold.

Clinical Manifestations

Manifestations of allergic rhinitis are sneezing; watery, itchy eyes and nose; decreased sense of smell; and thin, watery nasal discharge that can lead to more sustained mucus production and congestion. Nasal turbinates appear pale, boggy, and swollen. The turbinates may fill the air space and press against the nasal septum. The posterior ends of the turbinates can become so enlarged that they obstruct sinus aeration or drainage and result in sinusitis. With chronic exposure to allergens, the patient may develop a headache, stuffy nose, nasal congestion, and sinus pressure. Nasal polyps, soft, painless growths in the sinus cavity, may form. Postnasal drip occurs when mucous runs down the back of the throat. Both nasal polyps and postnasal drip are the most common causes of cough for people with allergies. The patient may report hoarseness and the need to frequently clear the throat to remove the mucous.

❖ Nursing and Interprofessional Management: Allergic Rhinitis

The key step to managing allergic rhinitis is identifying and avoiding triggers of allergic reactions (Table 29.1). Teach the patient to take note when allergic reactions occur and keep a diary of activities that precipitate the reaction. Patients are often more aware of intermittent exposure to an allergen, such as pets, than they are of more persistent exposure to allergens, such as dust mites, cockroaches, or mold. Identifying triggers is the first step toward avoiding them.

The goal of drug therapy is to reduce inflammation from allergic rhinitis, reduce nasal symptoms, minimize complications, and maximize quality of life. Appropriate oral medication options include H_1-antihistamines, decongestants, and leukotriene receptor antagonists (LTRAs). Intranasal medications include antihistamines, anticholinergics, corticosteroids, mast-cell stabilizers, and decongestants (Table 29.2).[8,9]

Second-generation antihistamines are used before first-generation antihistamines because of their non-sedating effects. Teach patients taking antihistamines to have adequate fluid intake to reduce adverse symptoms and keep secretions thin. Nasal corticosteroid sprays decrease inflammation with little absorption in the systemic circulation. This makes systemic side effects are rare. If monotherapy does not relieve symptoms, a 2-drug combination, such as an oral H_1-antihistamine and an intranasal corticosteroid, may be helpful.

DRUG ALERT

Antihistamines

- First-generation antihistamines (e.g., diphenhydramine) can cause drowsiness and sedation.
- Warn patients that operating machinery and driving may be dangerous because of the sedative effect.

TABLE 29.1 PATIENT & CAREGIVER TEACHING

Avoiding Allergens in Allergic Rhinitis

Include the following instructions when teaching a patient or caregiver about allergic rhinitis:

What to Avoid	Specific Approaches
House dust	• Focus on the bedroom. Remove carpeting. Limit furniture. • Put the pillows and mattress in airtight vinyl bags. • Limit clothing in the bedroom to items worn often. Place clothing in airtight, zipper-sealed vinyl clothes bags. • Install a high-efficiency particulate air (HEPA) filter. • Close the air-conditioning vent into room. • Use blinds rather than draperies.
House dust mites	• Wash bedding in hot water (140°F [60°C]). • Wear a mask when vacuuming. • Install a filter on the outlet port of vacuum cleaner. • Avoid sleeping or lying on upholstered furniture. • Keep house temperature and conditions cool and dry.
Mold spores	• The 3 *D*s that promote growth of mold spores are darkness, dampness, and drafts. • Ventilate closed rooms and open doors. Consider adding windows to dark rooms and keeping a small light on in closets. • Basement light with a timer that provides light several hours a day may decrease mold growth. • Avoid places with high humidity (e.g., basements, clothes hampers, greenhouses, barns).
Pet allergens	• Remove pets from interior of home. • Clean living area thoroughly. • Do not expect instant relief. Symptoms usually do not improve for 1–2 months after pet removal.
Pollens	• Stay inside with doors and windows closed during high-pollen season. • Install an air conditioner with an air filter. Wash filters weekly during high-pollen season. • Use your car's air conditioner "recirculation" feature (circulates air inside the car while shutting off air coming into the vehicle from the outside). • Avoid having plants, especially in the bedroom.
Smoke	• Encourage family and friends to refrain from smoking (if possible) or to go outdoors to smoke. • Presence of a smoker will sabotage any symptom reduction program.

DRUG ALERT

Pseudoephedrine (Sudafed)

- Large doses may cause tachycardia and palpitations, especially in patients with heart disease.
- Overdose in those over 60 years of age may result in central nervous system depression, seizures, and hallucinations.

Immunotherapy (allergy shots) may be used when a specific, unavoidable allergen is identified, and drugs are not tolerated or are ineffective in controlling symptoms. Immunotherapy involves controlled exposure to small amounts of the known allergen through frequent (at least weekly) injections with the goal of decreasing sensitivity. Sublingual or intranasal administration of allergen immunotherapy may be an option for select patients. Immunotherapy is discussed in Chapter 14.

UPPER RESPIRATORY INFECTIONS

ACUTE VIRAL RHINOPHARYNGITIS

An **upper respiratory infection** (URI) is an infection of the nose, sinuses, and/or throat. Viruses cause most URI. However, bacterial agents may cause a URI as well. *Acute viral rhinopharyngitis* (nasopharyngitis, common cold) is one type of URI. Sinusitis and influenza are examples of other types of URI.[10] There are over 200 viruses that may cause a URI. The most typical viruses are the rhinovirus, coronavirus, influenza, parainfluenza, respiratory syncytial virus (RSV), and enterovirus. The most common bacterium is *Streptococcus pyogenes*. It is a group A streptococcus that causes strep throat.[11] Adults may have an average of 2 to 3 colds per year.

Viruses are contagious. They spread by airborne droplets emitted by the infected person while breathing, talking, sneezing, or coughing. Because the pathogens can survive on inanimate objects for up to 3 days, transmission may occur by directly touching the surface and then touching your eyes, nose, or mouth with contaminated hands. Frequency of infections increases in winter months when people stay indoors, and overcrowding is more common. Other factors that increase susceptibility include fatigue, physical and emotional stress, allergies affecting the nose and throat, and a compromised immune status. Exercise, managing stress, sleeping adequately, and eating a well-balanced diet may reduce the number and or severity of URIs.[12]

Clinical Manifestations

Symptoms typically begin 2 or 3 days after infection. They may include runny nose, watery eyes, nasal congestion, sneezing, cough, sore throat, fever, headache, and fatigue. Patients are contagious 1 to 2 days before symptom onset and remain contagious until symptoms have subsided. Symptoms may last 2 to 14 days, with typical recovery in 7 to 10 days.

❖ Nursing and Interprofessional Management: URI

Interventions are directed at relieving symptoms. Care includes rest, oral fluids, antipyretics, and analgesics. Warm saltwater gargles, ice chips, lozenges, or sprays may help ease a sore throat. Saline nasal spray reduces nasal congestion. Antihistamine and decongestant therapy reduce postnasal drip and decreases the severity of cough, nasal obstruction, and nasal discharge. Caution patients to use intranasal decongestant sprays for no more than 5 days to prevent rebound congestion from occurring. Cough suppressants for irritating, bothersome coughs can be used but may not be effective. Patients may ask about vitamin C, echinacea, and zinc products. There is inconclusive evidence to support treatment with these therapies.

Complications include acute bronchitis, sinusitis, otitis media, tonsillitis, and pneumonia. Antibiotics have no effect on

TABLE 29.2 Drug Therapy
Rhinitis and Sinusitis

Drug	Mechanism of Action	Side Effects	Nursing Actions
Anticholinergic Nasal Spray			
ipratropium bromide	Blocks nasal cholinergic receptors, reducing nasal secretions in the common cold and nonallergic rhinitis.	Nasal dryness and irritation, nosebleeds may occur. Does not cause systemic side effects.	• May reduce the need for other rhinitis medications.
Antihistamines			
First-Generation Oral Agents			
brompheniramine diphenhydramine	Bind with H_1 receptors on target cells, blocking histamine release. Relieve acute symptoms of allergic response (itching, sneezing, rhinorrhea).	Cross blood-brain barrier, often causing sedation and somnolence. Can cause paradoxic stimulation (restlessness, nervousness, insomnia). Anticholinergic side effects (palpitations, dry mouth, constipation, urinary hesitancy).	• Warn patient that operating machinery and driving may be dangerous because of sedative effect. • Teach patient to report palpitations, change in heart rate, change in bowel or bladder habits. • Teach patient not to use alcohol because of additive depressant effect. • Rapid onset of action, no drug tolerance with prolonged use.
Second-Generation Oral Agents			
cetirizine (Zyrtec) desloratadine (Clarinex) fexofenadine (Allegra) levocetirizine (Xyzal) loratadine (Claritin)	Same as above.	Limited affinity for brain H_1 receptors. Cause minimal sedation, few effects on psychomotor activities or bladder function.	• Teach patient to expect few, if any, side effects. • More expensive than traditional antihistamines. • Rapid onset of action, no drug tolerance with prolonged use.
Second-Generation Nasal Sprays			
azelastine (Astelin) olopatadine (Patanase)	Blocks histamine release and reduces nasal congestion.	Headache, bitter taste, somnolence, nasal irritation.	• Longer use increases risk for rebound vasodilation, which can increase congestion.
Corticosteroid Nasal Sprays			
budesonide (Rhinocort) ciclesonide (Omnaris) flunisolide fluticasone (Flonase) fluticasone mometasone (Nasonex) triamcinolone	Inhibits inflammatory response of allergic rhinitis. Decreases mucosal inflammation and facilitates drainage of sinuses. Systemic effects may occur with higher than recommended doses.	At recommended dose, systemic side effects unlikely due to low systemic absorption. Mild transient nasal irritation, mucosal drying, nosebleeds. In rare instances, localized fungal infection with *Candida albicans.*	• Adherence important. Teach patient to use on regular basis and not PRN. • Have patient clear nasal passages before use. • Reinforce that spray acts to decrease inflammation and it may take several days or 1–2 wks to achieve maximum effects. • Stop use if nasal infection develops.
Decongestants			
Oral			
pseudoephedrine (Sudafed)	Stimulates adrenergic receptors and promotes vasoconstriction of superficial vessels in the nose and reduces nasal congestion.	CNS stimulation, causing insomnia, excitation, headache, irritability, increased blood and ocular pressure, dysuria, palpitations, tachycardia.	• Tolerance variable. • Advise patient of adverse reactions. • Patient to inform HCP if preexisting cardiovascular disease, hypertension, diabetes, glaucoma, benign prostatic hyperplasia, liver or kidney disease present before starting therapy. • Rebound nasal congestion may occur with chronic overuse.
Nasal Spray			
oxymetazoline phenylephrine	Same as above.	Same as above.	• Teach not to use for >5 days or >3 or 4 times/day. • Rebound nasal congestion may occur. • Addiction possible.
Leukotriene Receptor Antagonists (LTRAs) and Inhibitors			
Antagonists			
montelukast (Singulair) zafirlukast (Accolate)	Suppress leukotriene activity, thereby inhibiting airway edema, mucus production, bronchoconstriction, and inflammation.	Well tolerated. May cause headaches, dizziness, rash, altered liver function, GI changes. *Zafirlukast and zileuton:* Monitor PT levels if patient is taking warfarin.	• Monitor liver function tests periodically while on therapy. Stop if elevated. • Give on empty stomach. • Do not stop therapy without consulting HCP. • Do not use for acute attacks.
Inhibitors			
zileuton (Zyflo)			

TABLE 29.2 Drug Therapy—cont'd

Rhinitis and Sinusitis

Drug	Mechanism of Action	Side Effects	Nursing Actions
Mast Cell Stabilizer Nasal Spray			
cromolyn spray	Suppresses release of histamine and other inflammatory mediators from mast cells.	Minimal side effects. Occasional nasal irritation.	• Reinforce that spray prevents symptoms. • Begin 1 week before pollen season starts and use throughout pollen season. • For isolated allergy, use prophylactically before exposure to allergen. • When used to treat chronic rhinitis, may use antihistamine and/or nasal decongestant at the same time.

viruses. They are an option only if complications are present. Refer to an HCP if there is no improvement in symptoms within 10 to 14 days.

Teach patients to recognize the manifestations of a secondary bacterial infection. These include a temperature higher than 103°F (39.4°C); tender, swollen glands; severe sinus or ear pain; or significantly worsening symptoms. Green, purulent nasal drainage during the later stages of a cold is not uncommon and not always indicative of bacterial infection. In a patient with lung disease, signs of infection include a change in consistency, color, or volume of the sputum. Because infection can progress rapidly, teach the patient with chronic respiratory disease to immediately report sputum changes, increased shortness of breath, and chest tightness.

During the cold season, teach patients with a chronic illness or a compromised immune system to avoid crowded situations and those with obvious cold symptoms. Frequent hand washing and avoiding hand-to-face contact can help prevent direct spread.

INFLUENZA

Influenza (flu) is a highly contagious respiratory illness that causes significant morbidity and mortality. The flu season begins in September and continues through April of each year, peaking between December to February. Millions of people are infected yearly, causing an increased burden to the community and health care system. Although we do not know the exact number of flu-related deaths, it is thought that it is responsible for up to 49,000 deaths annually, depending on the strain.[13] Vaccination of high-risk groups may help prevent many of these deaths.

Etiology and Pathophysiology

We classify influenza viruses into 4 serotypes (A, B, C, D). Only A and B cause significant illness in humans. Influenza A is subtyped based on the presence of 2 surface proteins: hemagglutinin (H) and neuraminidase (N). The H antigens enable the virus to enter the cell, and the N antigens facilitate cell-to-cell transmission. As a result, we name influenza A viruses by their H and N-type (e.g., H3N2).

Influenza A is the most common and most virulent flu virus. It can infect a variety of animals and humans. More than 100 types of influenza A can occur in birds (avian flu), pigs (swine flu), horses, seals, and dogs. When the virus mutates (changes), this allows it to infect different species. When a new viral strain reaches humans, people do not have immunity. The virus can spread quickly around the globe, causing a *pandemic*. For example, type A H1N1 influenza (swine flu) emerged in 2009. It had never been seen in humans before, resulting in a worldwide pandemic. The reemergence of a strain that has not circulated for many years can also trigger a pandemic. *Epidemics* are more localized outbreaks, often occurring yearly, caused by variants of already circulating strains of the influenza virus.

Influenza B and C viruses only infect humans. We do not divide them into subtypes. Outbreaks of influenza B can cause regional epidemics. The disease it produces is milder than that caused by influenza A. Influenza C causes mild illness and does not cause epidemics or pandemics. Influenza D only occurs in animals.

The flu is communicable between humans mainly through infected droplets, inhalation of aerosolized particles, and, to a lesser extent, through direct contact with contaminated surfaces. The virus has an incubation period of 1 to 4 days, with peak transmission risk starting 1 day before the onset of symptoms and continuing for 5 to 7 days after a person first becomes sick.[14]

Clinical Manifestations

For some patients, it may be hard to tell between the common cold and flu (Table 29.3). The onset of flu is abrupt. There may be chills, fever, and generalized myalgia, often accompanied by a headache, cough, sore throat, and fatigue. Assessment findings are usually minimal, with normal breath sounds on chest auscultation. In uncomplicated cases, symptoms often subside within 7 days.

Common complications include pneumonia, which can be either primary influenza [viral] pneumonia or secondary bacterial pneumonia, and ear or sinus infections. Dyspnea and diffuse crackles are signs of pulmonary complications. Some patients, especially older adults, have weakness or lethargy that may last for weeks. The patient who develops secondary bacterial pneumonia usually has a gradual improvement of flu symptoms, then worsening cough and purulent sputum. Treatment with antibiotics is usually effective if started early.

Diagnostic Studies

The flu is often diagnosed based on the patient's health history, physical assessment, and knowledge of other cases of

TABLE 29.3 Comparison of Common Cold and Influenza

Manifestations and Treatment	Common Cold (Viral Rhinitis)	Influenza
Symptom onset	Appear gradually	Abrupt onset. Within 3–6 hr
Fever	Rare	Characteristically high 102–104°F (38.9–40°C]). Lasts 3–4 days
Headache	Uncommon, but may occur	Common (can be severe)
General aches and pains	Slight	Often severe myalgia
Fatigue and weakness	Sometimes. Usually mild	Usual. Starts early and can last up to 2–3 weeks
Exhaustion	Uncommon	Usual at beginning of illness
Stuffy nose	Common	Sometimes
Sneezing	Common	Sometimes
Sore throat	Common	Sometimes
Chest discomfort, cough	Common. Mild to moderate hacking cough	Common
Complications	Sinus congestion. Earache	Bronchitis, pneumonia, acute respiratory failure, and acute respiratory distress syndrome (ARDS). Can be life-threatening
Prevention	Hand washing. Avoid close contact with anyone who has a cold	Hand washing. Annual vaccination. Antiviral drugs. Avoid close contact with anyone who has the flu
Treatment	Temporary relief of symptoms: rest, hydration, decongestants, acetaminophen or ibuprofen for headache, aches, and pains	Antiviral drugs if given within 24–48 hr of onset. Rest, hydration, acetaminophen, or ibuprofen for headache, aches, and pains

Adapted from Centers for Disease Control and Prevention. Retrieved from www.cdc.gov/flu/about/qa/coldflu.htm.

influenza in the community. Testing can help distinguish the flu from other viral and bacterial infections with similar manifestations that may be serious but are treated differently. Cultures are often done via the nose or throat and may help identify the causative agent. The preferable method of culture collection is from the nasopharyngeal area via a mid-turbinate nasal swab. This should occur within 4 days of symptom onset. Guidelines for testing include those who are high-risk (e.g., immunocompromised) or patients with acute onset respiratory symptoms. In the hospital, we often test those with cardiopulmonary disease whose condition is worsening.[15]

Rapid influenza diagnostic tests (RIDTs) can help detect the virus in secretions from the respiratory tract. Depending on the method, the test may be completed in the HCP's office, with results available in as little as 15 minutes. RIDTs are best used within the first 48 hours of the onset of symptoms. The main disadvantages of RIDTs are that the patient may have a false-negative result, and the test is more sensitive to Influenza A than B.[16]

❖ Nursing and Interprofessional Management: Influenza

The most effective strategy is prevention. Two types of flu vaccines are available: inactivated and live attenuated (Table 29.4). Receiving a flu vaccine results in the production of antibodies against the viruses in the vaccine.

The flu vaccine is changed on a yearly basis. The content depends on the virus strains the Centers for Disease Control and Prevention (CDC) determines as being most likely to cause illness in the upcoming flu season. The best time to receive the vaccine is in September or October (before flu exposure) because it takes 2 weeks for antibodies to form and provide full protection from the flu. However, the vaccine can be given at any time during the flu season.

! SAFETY ALERT

Influenza Vaccination

- Advocate for vaccination of all people older than 6 months of age, especially those at high risk (e.g., health care workers, residents of long-term care facilities).
- Give high priority to groups, such as health care workers, who can transmit the flu to high-risk persons.

Vaccinating healthy people decreases the incidence and risk for transmitting influenza to those who have less ability to cope with the effects of this illness. Current vaccines are highly purified, and reactions are very rare. Soreness at the injection site is the most reported adverse effect. Contraindications are a history of severe allergic reactions to a previous flu vaccine. Patients with anaphylactic hypersensitivity to eggs should discuss the vaccine with their HCP, as alternatives for vaccinating patients with egg allergies are now available.

The primary nursing goals for those with the flu are symptom relief and preventing secondary infection. Unless the patient is at high risk or complications develop, supportive therapy is often all the patient needs. Rest, hydration, analgesics, and antipyretics can provide symptom relief. Older adults and those with a chronic illness may need hospitalized.

There are several antiviral medications we can use that shorten the duration of flu symptoms and reduce the risk for complications. Zanamivir (Relenza), oseltamivir (Tamiflu), and peramivir (Rapivab) are neuraminidase inhibitors that prevent the virus from being released and spreading to other cells.[17] Zanamivir is given using an inhaler. Oseltamivir is available as an oral capsule. Peramivir is given IV. The newest drug is baloxavir marboxil (Xofluza). It is a PA endonuclease inhibitor that works by inhibiting viral replication. Patients receive 1 oral dose. Do not give Xofluza with dairy products or calcium-fortified drinks.

TABLE 29.4 **Types of Influenza Immunization**

Trivalent (TIV) or Quadrivalent (QIV) Inactivated Influenza Vaccine	Live Attenuated Influenza Vaccine (LSIV)
Trivalent: Protects against 3 different types of influenza virus (2-type A; 1-type B) *Quadrivalent:* Protects against 4 different types of influenza virus (2-type A; 2-type B)	Made from weakened influenza virus
Given by injection	Given as an intranasal spray into both nostrils
Approved for use in people ≥6 months of age	Approved for healthy people ages 2–49 years • Children 2–8 years and have not had influenza vaccine before need 2 doses (second dose 4 weeks after first dose) • Children >9 years need 1 dose
Should NOT be used in: • Infants <6 months in age • Serious allergy/reaction to previous influenza vaccine • Guillain-Barré syndrome diagnosed within previous 6 weeks	Should NOT be used in: • Children <2 years or adults >50 years • Pregnant women or women who plan to become pregnant
Can be used in people at increased risk: • People of any age with chronic medical conditions • Residents of nursing homes and long-term care facilities • People who are immunocompromised • Pregnant women	Prior to receiving the vaccination, please inform the HCP if you or the person you are caring for have any of the following: • Immunodeficiency • Children or adolescents receiving aspirin or other salicylates • Medical conditions that increase the risk for complications from influenza (chronic heart, lung, liver, kidney, or CNS problems, diabetes; hemoglobinopathies) • HCPs of high-risk patients because of risk for viral transmission from vaccine (should not care for high-risk patients for 7 days after vaccination)
Most common side effects are injection site reactions, such as pain, redness, and swelling	Adverse effects are rare. When effects do occur, may resemble mild flu with runny nose, nasal congestion, cough, and headache

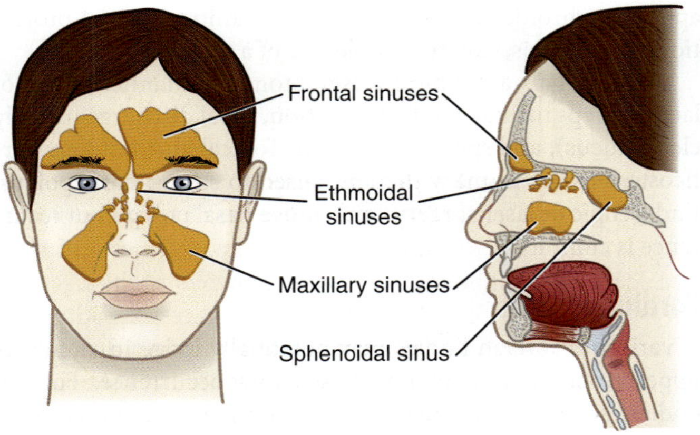

Fig. 29.2 Location of the sinuses.

Treatment with antiviral medication should be started as soon as possible in hospitalized patients with influenza, those with severe or complicated illness, or those at high risk for complications. For maximum benefit in treating the flu, therapy should begin within 2 days of the onset of symptoms. It can be started later based on clinical judgment.

SINUSITIS

Sinusitis affects 1 in every 7 adults. It develops when inflammation or swelling of the mucosa blocks the openings (ostia) in the sinuses, through which mucus drains into the nose (Fig. 29.2). *Rhinosinusitis,* which may accompany sinusitis, is concurrent inflammation or infection of the nasal mucosa. Nasal polyps, foreign bodies, deviated septa, or tumors can cause obstruction of mucus drainage. Secretions that accumulate behind the blocked ostia provide a rich medium for growth of bacteria, viruses, and fungi, all of which may cause infection.

Viral sinusitis may follow a URI in which the virus penetrates the mucous membrane and decreases ciliary function. Viral infections usually resolve without treatment in less than 14 days. If symptoms worsen after 3 to 5 days or last for longer than 10 days, a secondary bacterial infection may be present. Only 5% to 10% of patients with viral sinusitis develop a bacterial infection and need antibiotic therapy.

Sinusitis can be classified as acute, subacute, recurrent acute, or chronic.[18] *Acute sinusitis* typically begins within 1 week of a URI and lasts less than 4 weeks. *Subacute sinusitis* is present when symptoms progress over 4 to 12 weeks. Recurrent acute rhinosinusitis is defined as having 4 or more sinus infections per year, lasting 7 to 10 days, without having continual symptoms. *Chronic sinusitis* (lasting longer than 12 weeks) is a persistent infection usually related to allergies or nasal polyps. It generally results from repeated episodes of acute sinusitis that result in irreversible loss of the normal ciliated epithelium lining the sinus cavity.

Clinical Manifestations

Acute sinusitis causes significant pain over the affected sinus, purulent nasal drainage, nasal obstruction, congestion, fever, and malaise. The patient may appear acutely ill. Inspect the nasal mucosa and palpate the paranasal sinuses for pain. Findings that indicate acute sinusitis include edematous mucosa, discolored purulent nasal drainage, enlarged turbinates, tenderness over the involved frontal and/or maxillary sinuses, and *halitosis* (bad breath). Recurrent headaches are common. They may change in intensity with position changes or when secretions drain.

The symptoms of chronic sinusitis are often nonspecific. The patient is rarely febrile. They may have facial or dental pain, nasal congestion, and increased drainage. Severe pain and purulent drainage are often absent. Some symptoms mimic those seen with allergies. X-rays or CT scans of the sinuses may help confirm the diagnosis. CT scans may show sinuses filled with fluid or a thickened mucous membrane. Nasal endoscopy with a flexible scope may be used to examine the sinuses, obtain a specimen for culture, and restore normal drainage.

As many as 50% of patients with moderate to severe asthma have chronic sinusitis. The exact link between these diseases is unclear. Postnasal drip from sinusitis may trigger asthma by stimulating bronchoconstriction. Gastroesophageal reflux disease (GERD) and smoking may increase the risk for a person with asthma developing sinusitis. Appropriate treatment of sinusitis often causes a reduction in asthma symptoms.

❖ Nursing and Interprofessional Management: Sinusitis

If allergies are the precipitating cause of sinusitis, teach the patient ways to reduce sinus inflammation and infection, including environmental control of allergens and appropriate drug therapy.

Initial treatment for acute sinusitis focuses on symptom relief. Medications include oral or topical decongestants to promote drainage, intranasal corticosteroids to decrease inflammation, analgesics to relieve pain, and saline nasal spray to relieve congestion. Teach patients using topical decongestants to use the medication for no longer than 5 days to prevent rebound congestion caused by vasodilation. Saline irrigation of the nasal cavity can rinse nasal passages, promote drainage, and decrease inflammation. Saline nasal spray is available over the counter.

If symptoms worsen or last longer than 1 week, antibiotic therapy may be prescribed.

With chronic sinusitis, mixed bacterial flora is often present, and infections are hard to eliminate. Broad-spectrum antibiotics may be used for 4 to 6 weeks. Patient and caregiver teaching for acute and chronic sinusitis is shown in Table 29.5.

Medical therapy may not relieve the symptoms of some patients with persistent, recurrent, or chronic sinus illnesses. These patients may need nasal endoscopic surgery to relieve blockage caused by hypertrophy or septal deviation. This is usually an outpatient procedure under local anesthesia. Propel, a self-expanding implant, can be placed directly in the sinus during surgery. Propel helps maintain patency to the sinus cavity after surgery and provides local corticosteroid delivery directly to the sinus lining before dissolving after 30 days.

TABLE 29.5 PATIENT & CAREGIVER TEACHING

Acute or Chronic Sinusitis

Include the following instructions when teaching the patient and caregiver about managing sinusitis:

1. Get plenty of rest to help the body fight infection and promote recovery.
2. Keep well hydrated by drinking 6–8 glasses of water per day to loosen secretions.
3. Take hot showers. Use a steam inhaler (15-min vaporization of boiled water), bedside humidifier, or nasal saline spray to promote secretion drainage.
4. Apply warm, damp towels around nose, cheeks, and eyes to ease facial pain.
5. Sleep with head elevated to help sinuses drain and reduce congestion.
6. Report a temperature of 100.4°F (38°C) or higher, which indicates infection.
7. Follow prescribed medication plan:
   - Take analgesics to relieve pain.
   - Take decongestants/expectorants to relieve swelling.
   - Take antibiotics (as prescribed) for infection. Take the entire prescription and report continued symptoms or a change in symptoms.
   - Use nasal sprays to relieve congestion.
8. Perform nasal saline washes once or twice a day to wash sinuses.
9. Do not smoke and avoid exposure to smoke. It will irritate and worsen symptoms.
10. If allergies predispose to sinusitis, follow instructions about environmental control, drug therapy, and immunotherapy to reduce the inflammation and prevent sinus infection.

NASAL AND SINUS OBSTRUCTION

Nasal Polyps

Nasal polyps are soft, painless, benign (non-cancerous) growths that form slowly in response to repeated inflammation of the sinus or nasal mucosa. They are most common in adults over age 40 and are twice as likely to occur in men.[19] Polyps, which appear as chronic yellow, gray, or pink semitransparent projections in the naris, can exceed the size of a grape.

Small polyps are typically asymptomatic. Manifestations of larger polyps include nasal obstruction, nasal discharge (usually clear mucus), and speech distortion. Topical and systemic corticosteroids are primary therapies used to shrink nasal polyps. Endoscopic or laser surgery can remove nasal polyps, but recurrence is common.

Foreign Bodies

A variety of foreign bodies may potentially lodge in an adult's upper respiratory tract, but it is a rare occurrence. Foreign bodies, such as food, may cause a local inflammatory reaction and nasal discharge. The discharge may become purulent and foul-smelling if the object stays in the nasal cavity for an extended time. Foreign bodies can cause pain, difficulty breathing, and nasal bleeding.

We usually remove foreign bodies from the nose through the route of entry. Sneezing or blowing the nose with the opposite nostril closed may be effective in removing the foreign object. Avoid irrigating the nose or pushing the object backward since these could cause aspiration and airway obstruction. If sneezing or blowing the nose does not remove the object, consult an HCP.

PHARYNGEAL PROBLEMS

ACUTE PHARYNGITIS

Acute **pharyngitis** is an acute inflammation of the pharyngeal walls. It may include the tonsils, palate, and uvula. It can be caused by a viral, bacterial, or fungal infection. Viral pharyngitis accounts for about 90% of cases. Bacterial pharyngitis ("strep throat") usually results from group A β-hemolytic streptococci and accounts for 5% to 10% of cases.

Fungal pharyngitis, such as candidiasis, can develop with the prolonged use of antibiotics or inhaled corticosteroids. It can also occur in immunosuppressed patients, especially those with human immunodeficiency virus (HIV) infection. Other causes of pharyngitis include dry air, smoking, GERD, allergy, postnasal drip, ET intubation, chemical fumes, and cancer.

Clinical Manifestations

Symptoms of acute pharyngitis range in severity from a "scratchy" throat to pain so severe that swallowing is difficult. Because both viral and streptococcal infections appear as a red and edematous pharynx (with or without patchy exudates), it may be hard to tell between them.

Four classic manifestations present in bacterial pharyngitis include (1) fever greater than 100.4°F (38°C); (2) anterior cervical lymph node enlargement; (3) tonsillar or pharyngeal exudate; and (4) absence of cough.[20] However, appearance is not always diagnostic. When 2 or 3 of these criteria are present, a rapid antigen detection test and/or a throat culture can help with the diagnosis. White, irregular patches on the oropharynx suggest fungal infection with *Candida albicans*.

❖ Nursing and Interprofessional Management: Acute Pharyngitis

The goals of treatment are infection control, symptom relief, and prevention of secondary complications.

For viral pharyngitis, antibiotics are not recommended. For bacterial pharyngitis caused by group A β-hemolytic streptococci, penicillin is the drug of choice. This antibiotic must be taken several times a day for a full 10 days to prevent complications, such as rheumatic fever. For patients allergic to penicillin, erythromycin and clindamycin are substitutes.[21] Other antibiotics, such as azithromycin (Zithromax) or a 1st generation cephalosporin, are options. Most people with streptococcal infections are contagious until they have been on antibiotics for 24 to 48 hours. Repeat throat cultures after antibiotic therapy are not needed.

Candida infections are treated with nystatin, an antifungal antibiotic. Teach patients to swish the preparation in their mouths for as long as possible before swallowing it. Treatment should continue until symptoms are gone. Patients taking inhaled corticosteroids are at risk for infection with *Candida* organisms. Thoroughly rinsing the mouth with water after using corticosteroids can prevent this infection.

Teach patients to use ibuprofen or acetaminophen for pain relief. Encourage the patient to increase fluid intake. For symptom relief, have patients gargle with warm salt water (½ tsp of salt in 8 oz of water); drink warm or cold liquids; and suck on popsicles, hard candies, or throat lozenges. Cool, bland liquids and gelatin will not irritate the pharynx. Citrus juices are often irritating. Encourage the patient to use a cool-mist vaporizer or humidifier.

PERITONSILLAR ABSCESS

Peritonsillar abscess is a complication of tonsillitis. It is most often caused by group A β-hemolytic streptococci. The abscess causes pain, swelling, and blockage of the throat (when severe), threatening airway patency. The patient may have a high fever, chills, leukocytosis, difficulty swallowing, and a muffled voice. Treatment consists of IV antibiotic therapy and needle aspiration or incision and drainage of the abscess. In some cases, an emergency tonsillectomy is done. An elective tonsillectomy is scheduled after the infection has subsided.

LARYNGEAL AND TRACHEAL PROBLEMS

LARYNGEAL POLYPS

Laryngeal polyps develop on the vocal cords from vocal abuse (e.g., excessive talking, singing) or irritation (e.g., intubation, cigarette smoking). The most common sign is hoarseness. Conservative treatment involves voice rest and adequate hydration. Large polyps may cause dysphagia, dyspnea, and stridor. They may need surgically removed. Polyps are usually benign but may be removed because they can become cancerous.

ACUTE LARYNGITIS

Acute laryngitis is swelling and inflammation of the voice box (larynx). A virus (e.g., flu, common cold) is the most common cause. Other causes include inflammatory or infectious conditions of the upper respiratory tract (e.g., tonsillitis, acute bronchitis), overuse of one's voice (e.g., yelling loudly at a concert or a sporting event), exposure to smoke, or chemical inhalation.

The classic hallmark signs include a tingling or burning sensation at the back of the throat, a persistent need to clear the throat, and hoarseness, which may be accompanied by complete loss of voice. The patient may have a low-grade fever, persistent cough, or feeling of fullness in the throat. Symptoms will appear suddenly, increase in severity over 2 to 3 days, then gradually subside over the next 7 to 10 days as the condition improves. It usually resolves within 21 days.

Diagnosis of acute laryngitis is made based on the history, physical assessment, and changes in voice. Treatment for acute laryngitis is supportive. The patient is strongly encouraged to limit use of the larynx. This includes no talking or singing, which, realistically, is almost impossible to do. Patients will want to whisper when communicating but whispering places increased strain on the vocal cords that may worsen the pain. Acetaminophen, cough suppressants, throat lozenges, and using a humidifier are helpful for throat discomfort.

Have the patient increase fluid intake. They should avoid caffeine and alcohol, which may worsen a sore throat. Encourage smoking cessation. If a bacterial cause is known, such as acute bronchitis or tonsillitis, antibiotics should help resolve the condition. If symptoms last longer than 3 weeks, patients should return to their HCP for further investigation and treatment.

AIRWAY OBSTRUCTION

Acute airway obstruction is a medical emergency. Airway obstruction can be caused by aspiration of food or a foreign body, allergic reactions, edema and inflammation caused by infections or burns, peritonsillar or retropharyngeal abscesses, cancer, laryngeal or tracheal stenosis, and trauma.

Airway obstruction may be partial or complete. The presentation of an airway obstruction often depends on the cause of the obstruction and/or location of the blockage. For example, objects lodged within the larynx may cause voice hoarseness or complete airway obstruction. Tracheal obstruction may cause wheezing. Objects lodged within the lower respiratory system (e.g., bronchus) may cause a cough or decreased air entry on the affected side.

Manifestations include choking, stridor, flaring nostrils, wheezing, restlessness, tachycardia, cyanosis, and changes in level of consciousness.[22] Prompt assessment and treatment are essential because partial obstruction may quickly progress to complete obstruction. Complete airway obstruction can result in permanent brain damage or death if not corrected within 3 to 5 minutes.

Your immediate priority is to ensure the patient has a patent airway. Interventions to reestablish a patent airway include the obstructed airway (Heimlich) maneuver (see Appendix A), cricothyroidotomy, ET intubation, or tracheostomy. Unexplained partial airway obstruction or recurrent symptoms indicate the need for more tests, including a chest x-ray, laryngoscopy, and rigid bronchoscopy.

HEAD AND NECK CANCER

Head and neck cancer is classified according to the area where it occurs. These cancers may involve the nasal cavity and paranasal sinuses, nasopharynx, oropharynx, larynx, oral cavity, and/or salivary gland. Cancer of the oral cavity is discussed in Chapter 46. Most head and neck cancers arise from squamous cells that line the mucosal surfaces of the head and neck.

More than 53,000 new cases of head and neck cancer are diagnosed each year in the United States.[23] Tobacco use causes 85% of head and neck cancers. Excess alcohol use is another major risk factor. Head and neck cancer most often occurs in people over age 50 and twice as often in men. Head and neck cancers in those younger than 50 years are often related to human papillomavirus (HPV) infection. Other risk factors include exposure to the sun, asbestos, industrial carcinogens, marijuana use, radiation therapy to the head and neck, and poor oral hygiene.[24]

Unfortunately, most patients have locally advanced disease at the time of diagnosis. Disability from both the disease and its treatment is significant because of the potential loss of voice, adverse effects from chemotherapy and/or radiation, disfigurement, and social concerns.

Clinical Manifestations

The early manifestations vary with the location of the tumor. For example, patients with pharyngeal cancer may have what feels like a lump in the throat or a sore throat that does not get better with treatment. Some have white or red patches in the mouth or a change in the quality of the voice. Hoarseness that lasts more than 2 weeks may be a symptom of early laryngeal cancer.

Other manifestations may include ear pain or ringing in the ears, swelling or lumps in the neck, constant coughing, and coughing up blood. Swelling of the jaw can cause dentures to fit poorly or become uncomfortable. Unintentional weight loss and difficulty with chewing, swallowing, moving the tongue or jaw, and breathing are typically late symptoms. A partially or fully obstructed airway is often a late manifestation of head and neck cancer.

TABLE 29.6 Interprofessional Care
Head and Neck Cancer

Diagnostic Assessment
- History and physical assessment
- Indirect pharyngoscopy and laryngoscopy
- Endoscopy
- Biopsy
- Chest x-ray
- Barium swallow

Management
- Surgery (Table 29.7)
- Radiation therapy
- Chemotherapy
- Targeted therapy
- Respiratory therapy
- Physical therapy
- Occupational therapy
- Speech therapy

Diagnostic Studies

Early detection is key to patient survival. Physical assessment involves a focused assessment of the ears, nose, throat, mouth, and neck. Thoroughly examine the mouth, including the area under the tongue and dentures, with a flashlight. There may be thickening of the normally soft and pliable oral mucosa. Inspect the floor of the mouth and tongue. *Leukoplakia* (white patch) or *erythroplakia* (fiery red patch) may be present. Both leukoplakia and carcinoma in situ (localized to a defined area) may precede invasive carcinoma by many years. Palpate the lymph nodes in the neck.

If lesions are suspected, the HCP may examine upper airways using indirect pharyngoscopy and laryngoscopy (which involves using a laryngeal mirror). The larynx and vocal cords are visually inspected for lesions and tissue mobility. Typically, multiple biopsy specimens are obtained to help determine the extent of the disease. A CT scan or MRI may be done to detect local and regional spread. Positron emission tomography (PET) scanning is also used in diagnosis. The interprofessional care of head and neck cancer is outlined in Table 29.6.

Staging of Head and Neck Cancer

Head and neck cancer is staged based on the size of the tumor (T), number and location of involved lymph nodes (N), and extent of metastasis (M). This is referred to as *TNM staging*.[25] Staging is slightly different for each type of cancer. Generally, stage 0 is in situ, or confined to where it began, through stage 4, with more advanced disease. Oral cancer staging considers a patient's HPV status. TNM staging is discussed in Chapter 16.

Interprofessional Care

The choice of treatment for head and neck cancer is based on many factors. These include the tumor location, TNM stage, age and overall general health, urgency of treatment, cosmetic and functional considerations (e.g., ability to talk, swallow, chew), and patient choice. Treatment options include surgery, radiation therapy, chemotherapy, targeted therapy, or any combination of these therapies.

Surgical Therapy

Surgery is often the first-line treatment option for head and neck cancers. Some patients may be treated with surgery alone. For other patients, combining surgery with radiation therapy and/or chemotherapy may be appropriate. Surgical options depend on the location and stage of cancer (Table 29.7). After extensive surgery to remove head and neck cancer, reconstructive operations can help restore both the structure and function of the affected areas.

TABLE 29.7 Surgical Procedures for Head and Neck Cancer

Cordectomy	Removal of part or all the vocal cords May be changes in tone of voice Removing part of a vocal cord may lead to a hoarse voice If both vocal cords are removed, speech will no longer be possible
Laser surgery	An endoscope with a laser is inserted down the throat, and the tumor can be vaporized or removed
Laryngectomy	Removal of part (partial) or all (total) the larynx Total laryngectomy changes airflow in and out of the lungs, and normal voice production will not be possible (Fig. 29.3)
Lymph node removal	Amount of tissue and number of lymph nodes removed depend on how far cancer has spread
Pharyngectomy	Removal of part or all the throat
Tracheostomy	Creates an alternate pathway for breathing by creating a stoma in the trachea
Vocal cord stripping	Removal of outer layers of tissue on the vocal cords May be used for a biopsy or to treat some stage 0 cancers confined to the vocal cords Rarely affects speech
Neck Dissection Surgery	
Modified radical neck dissection	Most common type of neck dissection Removal of all lymph nodes Less neck tissue removed than with radical dissection May spare the nerves in the neck and, sometimes, the blood vessels or muscle
Radical neck dissection	Removal of all the tissue on the side of the neck from the mandible to the clavicle Removes the muscle, nerve, salivary gland, major blood vessels
Selective neck dissection	If cancer has not spread far, fewer lymph nodes are removed May save muscle, nerve, blood vessels in the neck

Radiation Therapy

Radiation therapy can be delivered by either external-beam therapy or internal implants (brachytherapy). Brachytherapy is a concentrated and localized method of delivering radiation that involves placing a radioactive source near or into the tumor. The goal is to deliver high doses of radiation to the target area while limiting the exposure of surrounding tissues. Thin, hollow, plastic needles are inserted into the tumor area, and radioactive seeds are placed in the needles. The seeds emit continuous radiation. Radiation therapy and brachytherapy are discussed in Chapter 16.

Radiation therapy is often preferred for patients with early head and neck cancer because it offers the patient good results with voice preservation. Some patients refuse surgery for advanced lesions because of the extent of the procedure and potential risks involved. In this situation, radiation therapy is used as the sole treatment or in combination with chemotherapy. Other patients may opt for surgery and a combination of either radiation and/or chemotherapy treatments.

Chemotherapy and Targeted Therapy

Chemotherapy is used in combination with radiation therapy for patients with stage 3 or 4 head and neck cancers. Chemotherapy agents currently recommended include cisplatin, 5-fluorouracil, carboplatin, docetaxel (Taxotere), paclitaxel, methotrexate, and bleomycin.[26]

Cetuximab (Erbitux), a targeted therapy, is used with chemotherapy to treat patients with late-stage head and neck cancer. The drug targets epidermal growth factor receptor (EGFR), a specific protein within cancer cells, and stops the cells from growing. Targeted therapy is discussed in Chapter 16 and Table 16.13.

Nutrition Therapy

Many patients with head and neck cancer are malnourished even before treatment begins. Treatment modalities increase the risk for malnutrition. For example, after radical neck surgery, the patient may be unable to consume nutrients orally because of swelling, the location of sutures, or difficulty with swallowing. Side effects from chemotherapy and radiation therapy can impair the patient's ability to maintain adequate nutrition. Painful oral mucositis often leads to breaks in treatment if the patient is relying solely on oral intake for nutrition.

A thorough nutrition assessment and prophylactic placement of a gastrostomy tube in high-risk patients are vital to maintaining adequate nutrition.[27] Enteral nutrition (EN) may be started before treatment to obtain and maintain optimal nutrition needed for tissue repair (see Chapter 44.) Elevate the head of the bed while the patient is eating. Observe for feeding intolerance. Adjust the amount, time, and/or formula if nausea, vomiting, diarrhea, or distention occurs. Teach the patient and caregiver about EN.

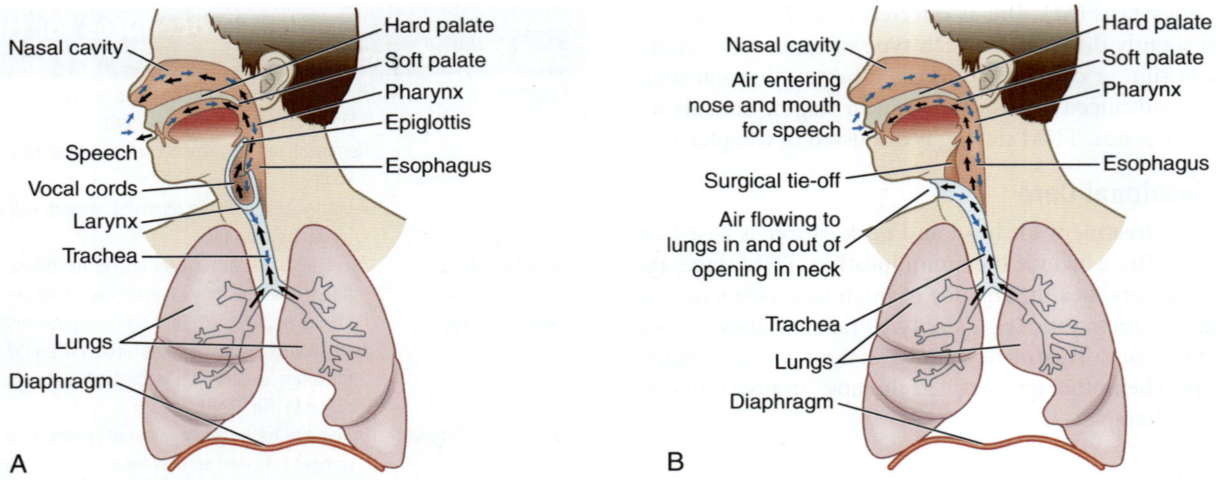

Fig. 29.3 Airflow in and out of the lungs (A) before and (B) after total laryngectomy. There is no anatomic connection between the nose, mouth, and throat. Inhaled and exhaled air enters the lungs through a surgically created stoma (hole) in the neck.

Patients who are not candidates for or who refuse EN need to be monitored closely for weight loss.[27] Antiemetics or analgesics given before meals can reduce nausea and mouth pain. Bland foods are easier for patients to tolerate. Patients can increase caloric intake by adding dry milk to foods during preparation, eating foods high in calories, and using oral supplements. It is helpful to add mild sauces and gravy to food. This adds calories and moistens food so that it is easier to swallow

Expect swallowing problems when the patient resumes eating after surgery. The type and degree of difficulty varies depending on the surgery. A video-fluoroscopic swallowing study may evaluate the safety of swallowing after surgery. When the patient can successfully swallow with low or no risk for aspiration, they may have small amounts of thickened liquids or pureed foods while in high-Fowler's position. Avoid thin, watery fluids because they are hard to swallow and increase the risk for aspiration. Closely monitor and observe for any signs or symptoms of respiratory distress and/or choking when eating resumes. Oral suctioning can help prevent aspiration.

Physical Therapy

After surgery for head and neck cancer, the physical therapist will help teach the patient how to use the upper extremities to assist with support and movement of the head. In the immediate postoperative period, the patient should begin an exercise program to maintain strength and movement in the shoulders and neck. Without exercise, the patient may develop a "frozen" shoulder and limited range of neck motion. The patient should continue the exercise program after discharge to prevent future functional disabilities.

Speech Therapy

Before surgery, a speech therapist should meet with the patient and caregiver to discuss any effect that surgery will have on the voice and potential adaptations or voice restoration options. The International Association of Laryngectomees, a group for laryngectomy patients, focuses on helping patients reestablish speech. Local groups, such as "Lost Chord" or "New Voice," often have volunteers to visit patients before surgery.

We use 3 major approaches to restore oral communication: (1) electrolarynx, (2) tracheoesophageal puncture (TEP) voice restoration, and (3) esophageal speech. An *electrolarynx* is a hand-held, battery-powered device that creates speech with the use of sound waves (Fig. 29.4A). This option allows for speech immediately after surgery. It needs little maintenance and is easy to learn. The primary disadvantage is the mechanical sound quality, which many patients find unacceptable.

In TEP, a fistula is created in the tracheoesophageal wall. It diverts pulmonary air across the pharyngoesophageal mucosa for phonation when the tracheostoma is occluded. A one-way prosthetic valve is placed in the tract. The valve prevents aspiration of food or saliva from the esophagus into the tracheostomy. To speak, the patient manually blocks the stoma with the finger. Air moves from the lungs, through the prosthesis, into the esophagus, and out the mouth. Speech is made by the air vibrating against the esophagus and is formed into words by moving the tongue and lips. A common voice prosthesis is the Blom-Singer prosthesis (Fig. 29.4B). TEP offers the best speech quality with the highest degree of patient satisfaction.

Esophageal speech depends upon air entering the esophagus and then being expelled past the pharyngoesophageal segment, the vibratory source for sound production. The primary disadvantages of developing esophageal speech are the length of time needed to learn the technique and the reduction in voice quality.

❖ NURSING MANAGEMENT: HEAD AND NECK CANCER

◆ Assessment

Table 29.8 presents subjective and objective data to obtain from a person with head and neck cancer.

◆ Clinical Problems

Clinical problems for the patient with head and neck cancer include:

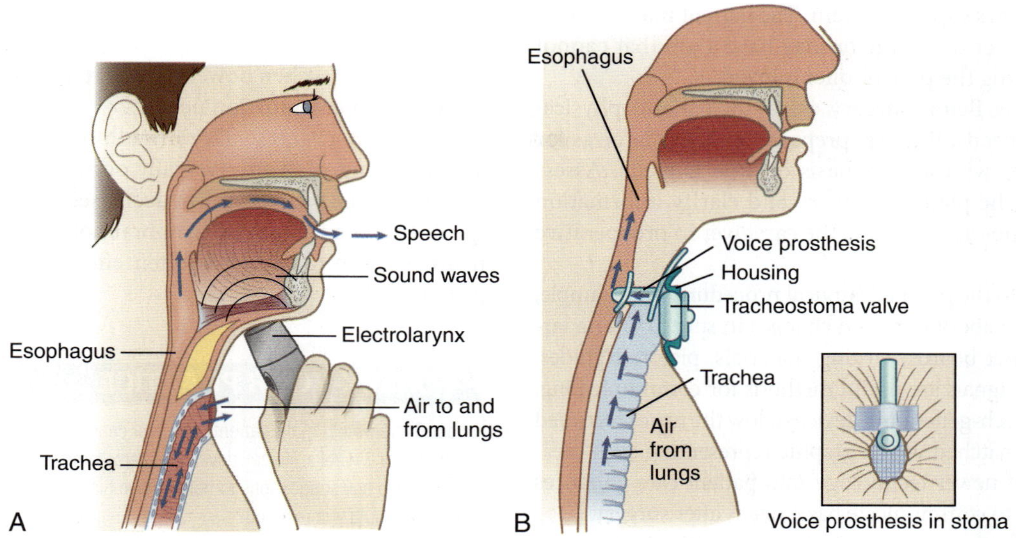

Fig. 29.4 (A) The sound waves created by the electrolarynx allow the person to speak. (B) The Blom-Singer voice prosthesis and valve.

TABLE 29.8 NURSING ASSESSMENT

Head and Neck Cancer

Subjective Data

Important Health Information

Health history: Positive family history; prolonged tobacco use (cigarettes, pipes, cigars, chewing tobacco, smokeless tobacco); prolonged, heavy alcohol use; poor intake of fruits and vegetables

Medications: Prolonged use of over-the-counter medication for sore throat, decongestants

Functional Health Patterns

Health perception–health management: Does not take part in preventive health measures, long history of alcohol and tobacco use

Nutritional-metabolic: Mouth ulcer that does not heal, change in fit of dentures, change in appetite, sudden or unexplained weight loss, swallowing difficulty (e.g., sensation of a lump in throat, pain with swallowing, aspiration when swallowing)

Activity-exercise: Fatigue with minimal exertion

Cognitive-perceptual: Sore throat, pain on swallowing, referred ear pain

Objective Data

Respiratory

Hoarseness, change in voice quality, chronic laryngitis, nasal voice, palpable neck mass and lymph nodes (tender, hard, fixed), tracheal deviation; dyspnea, stridor (late sign)

Gastrointestinal

White (leukoplakia) or red (erythroplakia) patches inside mouth, ulceration of mucosa, asymmetric tongue, exudate in mouth or pharynx, mass or thickening of mucosa

Possible Diagnostic Findings

Mass on direct or indirect laryngoscopy; tumor on soft tissue x-ray, CT scan, or MRI; positive biopsy

- Impaired respiratory function
- Risk for aspiration
- Difficulty coping
- Impaired communication

More information on clinical problems and the care of the patient with head and neck cancer is presented in eNursing Care Plan 26.2 on the website for this chapter.

◆ Planning

The overall goals are that the patient will have (1) a patent airway, (2) an acceptable body image, (3) no complications related to therapy, (4) adequate nutrition intake, (5) minimal to no pain, and (6) the ability to communicate.

◆ Implementation

◆ Health Promotion

Many head and neck cancers can be prevented. Their development is closely related to personal habits, mainly tobacco use and excess alcohol use. Poor oral hygiene and HPV infection are also risk factors for head and neck cancer.

Include information about risk factors in health teaching. Encourage good oral hygiene. Teach patients about safe sex practices to prevent HPV infection (e.g., use condoms, encourage monogamous relationships, choose a partner who has had no or few previous partners). When cancer has been diagnosed, tobacco and alcohol cessation are still important. The chance of a cure, by any treatment modality, for a patient with head and neck cancer who continues to smoke and use alcohol is decreased. Also, the risk for a second primary cancer is significantly increased. Give patients information about smoking cessation and techniques for success. If needed, refer to an alcohol treatment program. Smoking cessation and treatment of alcohol use are discussed in Chapter 11.

◆ Acute Care

Teach the patient and caregiver about the type of treatment, care needed, and reason for treatment and care. Help prepare them to deal with the psychological impact of the diagnosis of cancer, change in physical appearance, possible need for EN, and use of other communication methods because of loss of voice.

Assess the patient's support system. The patient may not have someone to help after discharge or may have a job that cannot be continued, leaving the patient unemployed.

Surgical therapy. Before surgery, assess the patient's physical and psychosocial needs. Physical preparation is the same as for any major surgery, with an emphasis on oral hygiene. Assess understanding of the planned surgery and clarify information as needed. When possible, include the caregiver in preoperative teaching.

Tailor teaching to the planned surgical procedure. For example, include information about expected changes in speech after a laryngectomy. Alphabet boards, writing materials, pictorial guides, laptops, and hand signals are useful methods for communicating. Programmable speech-generating devices allow the use of recorded messages that are matched with a graphic representing each message. Integration of newer technology into patient care enhances the patient's ability to communicate basic needs after surgery.

Immediately after surgery, nursing care priorities include airway management, wound care, nutrition, communication, and psychosocial issues related to body image changes. Maintaining a patent airway is essential. Inflammation in the surgical area may compress the trachea. Keep the patient in a semi-Fowler's position to decrease edema and limit tension on suture lines.

Give analgesic drugs as needed for pain control. Because patients may not be able to speak, have them nonverbally rate their pain (e.g., visual pain scale) to help assess the effectiveness of the medication. Pain management is discussed in Chapter 9. Monitor vital signs frequently. Be alert for hemorrhage, as many of the structures in the head and neck area are very vascular. Pay attention to heart rate, BP, SpO_2, and hemoglobin values.

The patient with a laryngectomy needs frequent suctioning via the tracheostomy tube. Secretions typically change in amount and consistency over time. The patient may initially have a large amount of blood-tinged secretions that gradually diminish and thicken. Maintain adequate fluid intake (IV, enteral) and humidification of inspired gases to keep secretions liquid and mucous membranes moist. Encourage deep breathing and coughing.

Pressure dressings, packing, or drainage tubes may be present, depending on the surgery. Do not change any dressing unless you have a specific order from the HCP. Dressings are typically not present with skin flaps. This allows better visualization of the flap and avoids excess pressure on tissue. Initially, check skin flaps hourly for color and any change in size or edema. We may use doppler ultrasound to determine the presence of a pulse, depending upon the location of the skin flap.

Care for any Hemovac, Jackson-Pratt, and Penrose drains that are in use. Drainage may be bloody at first, then serosanguineous. It should gradually decrease in volume over 24 to 48 hours. Monitor patency of drainage tubes every hour in the first few hours after surgery, then every 4 hours to ensure proper functioning. If tubing becomes obstructed, fluid will accumulate under the skin flap. This predisposes the patient to hematomas or seromas, impaired wound healing, and increased risk for infection. After removal of the drainage tubes, closely monitor the area to detect any swelling. Closely monitor incision sites for signs of infection.

The patient may have a nasogastric (NG) tube inserted during surgery to remove gastric contents via intermittent suction for the first 24 to 48 hours until peristalsis returns. Because the NG tube lies close to internal incision lines, do not manipulate or move the tube. When bowel sounds return, start EN slowly and advance to meet nutrition needs.

Radiation therapy. Dry mouth *(xerostomia)*, a frequent and annoying problem, typically occurs within a few weeks of treatment. The patient's saliva decreases in volume and becomes thick. This change may be temporary or permanent. Pilocarpine hydrochloride (Salagen) is often effective in increasing saliva production.

CHECK YOUR PRACTICE

Your 64-years-old male patient with oral cancer has been receiving radiation therapy for 3 weeks. He has developed xerostomia and oral mucositis. He asks if you have any suggestions to help relieve his symptoms.

- How would you respond?

Once patients can have foods or fluids by mouth, they can get symptom relief by increasing fluid intake, chewing sugarless gum or sugarless candy, using nonalcoholic mouth rinses (baking soda, glycerin solutions), and using artificial saliva. Teach patients to always carry a water bottle with them. Fluoride gels or treatments can help prevent dental deterioration caused by xerostomia.

Oral mucositis can cause irritation, ulceration, and pain. Teach the patient oral care basics, including the use of a soft toothbrush and regular flossing. The patient can wear empty fluoride gel trays, bite blocks, athletic mouth guards, or gauze pads during radiation treatments. This prevents radiation scatter to the tongue and cheek from metal work in the mouth. Warm bland rinses, like those with salt and baking soda, 4 to 6 times daily may be helpful. Sucking on ice chips can help with the pain. Patients should avoid commercial mouthwashes and hot, spicy, or acidic foods because they are irritating.

Skin over the irradiated area often becomes reddened and sensitive to touch. Teach patients to use only prescribed lotions and skin products while undergoing radiation therapy and to not use any lotions within 2 hours before treatment. Skin care for patients having radiation therapy is discussed in Chapter 16.

Fatigue is a common side effect of radiation therapy and chemotherapy. Encourage patients to walk 15 to 30 minutes each day since regular exercise can give them more energy. Teach patients to do activities that are most important to them and to rest during periods of low energy. Identify support systems. Encourage patients to ask for help.

Stoma care. Should the patient have a stoma after surgery, teach the patient proper care of the stoma. The patient should wash the area around the stoma daily with a moist cloth. A nasal wash spray is used every 1 to 2 hours to keep the stoma moist and prevent crusting. Dried secretions can be removed with tweezers. If a laryngectomy tube is in place, the patient must remove the entire tube at least daily and clean it in the same manner as a tracheostomy tube. The inner cannula may have to be removed and cleaned more often. A scarf or loose shirt can hide the stoma.

The patient should cover the stoma when coughing (because mucus may be expectorated) and during any activity (e.g., shaving, applying makeup) that may lead to inhalation of foreign materials. Because water can easily enter the stoma, the patient should wear a plastic collar when taking a shower. Swimming is contraindicated. Humidification is given with mechanical ventilation or after extubation with a tracheostomy mask. After discharge, the patient can use a bedside humidifier.

Psychosocial needs. Psychosocial care of the patient with head and neck cancer is of utmost importance. Issues concerning depression, change in body image, and sexuality are common. Although we discuss changes before surgery, the patient may not be psychologically prepared for the extent of these changes. If the patient has a significant other, this person's reaction to the patient's altered appearance is important. Acceptance by another person can promote an improved self-image.

Depression may occur for many reasons: inability to speak because of surgical procedure and/or presence of ET or tracheostomy tube, altered physical appearance, edema, loss of independence and reliance upon others, and feelings of helplessness and hopelessness. Depression also may be related to concern about the prognosis.

Allow the patient and caregiver to express their feelings and emotions. Convey acceptance to help patients regain positive feelings about their body image and self-concept. Encourage participation in support groups. Provide information about groups available through the local branch of the American Cancer Society. Provide a psychiatric referral for the patient who has prolonged or severe depression.

Surgical devices such as tracheostomy and gastrostomy tubes may dramatically affect body image. Xerostomia and fatigue can physically affect sexuality. It may be hard for the patient to talk about sexual problems because of changes in communication. Help the patient and partner by allowing them to talk about their sexuality and how surgery and treatment may affect their relationship. Helping the patient see that sexuality involves much more than appearance may relieve some anxiety.

◆ Ambulatory Care

The patient may be discharged with a tracheostomy and an NG or gastrostomy feeding tube. Some patients may need a home health care referral and assessment to evaluate the patient's or caregiver's ability to perform self-care activities. Both patient and caregiver need to learn how to manage tubes and whom to call if there are problems. Provide pictorial instructions for tracheostomy care, suctioning, stoma and skin care, and EN as appropriate. Encouraging the patient to take part in self-care is an important part of rehabilitation.

Teach the patient the importance of wearing a Medic Alert bracelet or other identification that alerts emergency personnel of the possible changes in breathing status because of surgery. Because the patient no longer breathes through the nose, they often lose the ability to smell smoke. Teach the patient to install smoke and carbon monoxide detectors in the home. The loss of smell and radiation therapy may lead to decreased taste. Encourage eating food that is colorful, attractive, and nutritious. Refer to a dietitian as needed.

The patient can resume exercise, recreation, and sexual activity when able. Most patients can return to work 1 to 2 months after surgery. However, many never return to a full-time job. The changes that follow a total laryngectomy can be upsetting. Loss of speech, loss of the ability to taste and smell, inability to make audible sounds (including laughing and weeping), and the presence of a permanent tracheal stoma that produces undesirable mucus are often overwhelming to patients.

◆ Evaluation

Expected outcomes for the patient with head and neck cancer who is treated surgically are that the patient will:

- Have effective coughing and secretion clearance
- Swallow oral foods without aspiration
- Uses effective coping strategies
- Use effective communication techniques

Case Study

Laryngeal Cancer

(© iStockphoto/ Thinkstoc.)

Patient Profile

M.R., a 69-years-old retired baker, is on your medical floor with influenza. He told his HCP that he has "a cough that just won't go away," difficulty swallowing, and "a sore throat that really hasn't gotten better" over the past year. His wife passed away 6 years ago. He has 3 adult children. One daughter lives in the same city. He has a history of hypertension, smoking, alcohol use, gastroesophageal reflux disease (GERD), and type 2 diabetes.

Subjective Data

- States that his symptoms worsened in the past 3 months
- Has used various cough and cold remedies over the past 6 months to relieve symptoms without relief
- Has lost weight because of decreased appetite and difficulty swallowing
- Has smoked 3 packs of cigarettes a day for the past 50 years
- Consumes 4 to 6 cans of beer a day

Objective Data

Physical Assessment

- Temp 102.4°F (39.1°C), heart rate 99 beats/min, BP 176/84 mm/Hg
- Respiratory rate 24 breaths/min; respirations short, shallow, slightly labored; SpO_2 87% on room air
- Awake and alert
- Appears gray, malnourished, dehydrated
- Small, irregular white patches on the sides of oral cavity
- Enlarged cervical nodes bilaterally, nontender
- Lung sounds diminished at bases with occasional fine crackles on expiration

Diagnostic Studies

- Chest x-ray: lung fields clear
- Laryngoscopy: mass in subglottic area (requires further evaluation)
- CT scan: subglottic lesion with lymph node involvement
- Diagnosis: laryngeal cancer

Continued

Case Study—cont'd

Laryngeal Cancer

Interprofessional Care

- *Surgery:* Suggests a total laryngectomy
- *Oncology:* Suggests radiation and chemotherapy after surgery
- *Gastroenterology:* Percutaneous gastrostomy tube preoperatively for EN
- *Dietary:* Review nutrition options with/without ET tube/tracheostomy
- *Physical therapy:* Visit pre-surgery to explain postoperative exercise routine
- *Social worker:* Assess social supports available postoperatively

Discussion Questions

1. ***Recognize***: What assessment information suggests M.R. was at risk for laryngeal cancer?
2. ***Recognize***: What factors may affect wound healing after surgery?
3. ***Prioritize:*** What are your priority teaching strategies before his total laryngectomy?
4. ***Act***: How would you explain the gastrostomy tube to M.R.?

Case Progression

M.R. is transferred to the clinical unit after 24 hours in ICU. He is awake, alert, but slightly confused. His BP is 168/94 mm Hg. A tracheostomy tube is in place with O_2 via tracheal mask. Enteral feeding transfusing at 30 mL/hr via gastrostomy tube. The indwelling catheter is patent and draining a moderate amount of amber urine. M.R. is picking at his surgical drains. When you try to reassure him, he just starts waving his hands at you.

5. ***Analyze:*** What information would you want to know from the ICU nurse who has just transported M.R. to the clinical unit?
6. ***Prioritize:*** Based on the assessment data presented, what are your priority clinical problems?
7. ***Act:*** How would you best meet M.R.'s communication needs during the first few postoperative days?
8. ***Act***: Four hours after transfer to the clinical unit, M.R. is tearful and is staring at the wall. What should you do?
9. ***Safety:*** What teaching does M.R. need to help him assume self-care after his surgery? What precautions should he take because of his stoma?

Answers available at http://evolve.elsevier.com/Lewis/medsurg.

BRIDGE TO NCLEX EXAMINATION

The number of the question corresponds to the same-numbered outcome at the beginning of the chapter.

1. A patient is seen in the clinic for a nosebleed, which is controlled by placing anterior nasal packing. During discharge teaching, the nurse teaches the patient to
   a. use aspirin for pain relief.
   b. remove the packing later that day.
   c. avoid vigorous nose blowing and strenuous activity.
   d. insert more packing into the nose if re-bleeding occurs.

2. A patient with allergic rhinitis reports severe nasal congestion; sneezing; and watery, itchy eyes and nose at various times of the year. When teaching the patient about how to control these symptoms, the nurse teaches the patient to
   a. avoid all intranasal sprays and oral antihistamines.
   b. limit the usage of nasal decongestant spray to 10 days.
   c. use oral decongestants at bedtime to prevent symptoms during the night.
   d. keep a diary of when the allergic reaction occurs and what precipitates it.

3. A patient is seen at the clinic with fever, muscle aches, sore throat with yellowish exudate, and headache. The nurse anticipates that the interprofessional management will include *(select all that apply)*
   a. providing antipyretic for fever
   b. immediate treatment with antibiotics.
   c. a throat culture or rapid strep antigen test.
   d. supportive care, including cool, bland liquids.
   e. comprehensive history to determine possible cause.

4. A 19 year-old patient arrives at the clinic with a sore throat and fever of 102.4°F (39.1°C). Assessment findings include enlarged anterior cervical lymph nodes and exudate at the back of the throat. What is the priority nursing action?
   a. Administer morphine 1 mg IV for pain
   b. Administer acetaminophen for pain and fever
   c. Increase hydration by providing oral and IV fluids
   d. Document the assessment findings in the nursing notes.

5. When planning health care teaching to prevent or detect early head and neck cancer, which people would be the *priority* to target? *(select all that apply)*
   a. 65-years-old man who has used chewing tobacco most of his life
   b. 45-years-old rancher who uses chewing tobacco while driving his herds of cattle
   c. 21-years-old college student who drinks beer on weekends with his fraternity brothers
   d. 78-years-old woman who has been drinking liquor since her husband died 15 years ago
   e. 22-years-old woman who has been diagnosed with human papilloma virus of the cervix

6. While in the recovery room, a patient with a total laryngectomy is suctioned and has bloody mucus with some clots. Which nursing interventions would apply? (*select all that apply*)
   a. Notify the health care provider at once.
   b. Place the patient in semi-Fowler's position.
   c. Use a bag-valve-mask (BVM) and begin rescue breathing for the patient
   d. Instill 10 mL of normal saline into the tracheostomy tube to loosen secretions.
   e. Continue patient assessment, including O_2 saturation, respiratory rate, and breath sounds.

7. Appropriate discharge teaching for the patient with a permanent tracheostomy after a total laryngectomy for cancer would include (*select all that apply*)
   a. encouraging regular exercise such as swimming.
   b. washing around the stoma daily with a moist washcloth.
   c. encouraging participation in postlaryngectomy support group.

d. providing pictures and "hands-on" instruction for tracheostomy care.
e. teaching how to hold breath and trying to gag to promote swallowing reflex.

1. c; 2. d; 3. a, c, d, e; 4. b; 5. a, b, d, e; 6. b, e; 7. b, c, d.

For rationales to these answers and even more NCLEX review questions, visit http://evolve.elsevier.com/Lewis/medsurg.

EVOLVE WEBSITE/RESOURCES LIST

http://evolve.elsevier.com/Lewis/medsurg
Review Questions (Online Only)
Key Points
Answer Keys for Questions
- Rationales for Bridge to NCLEX Examination Questions
- Answer Guidelines for Case Study

Student Case Study
- Patient with Head and Neck Cancer/Laryngectomy with Tracheostomy

Nursing Care Plans
- eNursing Care Plan 29.1: Patient Having Total Laryngectomy and/or Radical Neck Surgery

Conceptual Care Map Creator
Audio Glossary
Content Updates

REFERENCES

1. American Academy of Otolaryngology: Deviated septum. Retrieved from https://www.enthealth.org/nose-landing-page/.
2. Haraldson SJ: Nasal fracture. Retrieved from https://emedicine.medscape.com/article/84829-overview.
3. Healthwise Staff: Broken nose (Nasal fracture). Retrieved from https://www.uofmhealth.org/health-library/aa49289spec.
4. Shiffman MA, DiGiuseppe A: *Advanced aesthetic rhinoplasty: Art, science, and new clinical technologies*, New York, 2013, Springer (Classic).
*5. Tunkel DE, Anne S, Payne SC, et al.: Clinical practice guideline: nosebleed (epistaxis), *Otolaryngol Head Neck* 162(S1), 2020.
6. Nguyen QA: Epistaxis treatment and management. Retrieved from https://emedicine.medscape.com/article/863220-treatment.
7. Sheikh J: Allergic rhinitis. Retrieved from https://emedicine.medscape.com/article/134825-overview#a5.
8. InformedHealth.org: Which medications can relieve allergic rhinitis? Retrieved from https://www.ncbi.nlm.nih.gov/books/NBK279486/.
9. American Academy of Asthma, Allergy, and Immunology: Hay fever and allergy medications. Retrieved from www.aaaai.org/conditions-and-treatments/library/allergy-library/hay-fever-medications.
10. Kaiser Permanente: Upper respiratory infection (cold): care instructions. Retrieved from https://healthy.kaiserpermanente.org/health-wellness/health-encyclopedia/he.upper-respiratory-infection-cold-care-instructions.uf7165.
11. Thomas M, Koutsothanasis GA, Bomar PA: Upper respiratory tract infection. Retrieved from https://www.ncbi.nlm.nih.gov/books/NBK532961/.
12. Centers for Disease Control and Prevention (CDC): Healthy habits to help prevent flu. Retrieved from https://www.cdc.gov/flu/prevent/actions-prevent-flu.html.
13. CDC: Disease burden of influenza. Retrieved from https://www.cdc.gov/flu/about/burden/index.html.
14. CDC: How flu spreads. Retrieved from https://www.cdc.gov/flu/about/disease/spread.htm#:~:text=People%20with%20flu%20are%20most,7%20days%20after%20becoming%20sick.
15. Medscape: Influenza clinical practice guidelines. Retrieved from https://reference.medscape.com/viewarticle/908552.
16. CDC: Rapid influenza diagnostic tests. Retrieved from https://www.cdc.gov/flu/professionals/diagnosis/clinician_guidance_ridt.htm.
17. US Food and Drug Administration: Influenza (flu) antiviral drugs and related information. Retrieved from www.fda.gov/drugs/drugsafety/informationbydrugclass/ucm100228.htm.
18. Sharma GK, Lofgren DH, Taliaferro HG: Recurrent acute rhinosinusitis. Retrieved from https://www.ncbi.nlm.nih.gov/books/NBK459372/.
19. del Toro E, Portela J: Nasal polyps. Retrieved from https://www.ncbi.nlm.nih.gov/books/NBK560746/.
20. Sykes EA, Wu V, Beyea MM, et al.: Pharyngitis: approach to diagnosis and treatment, *Can Fam Physician* 66:251, 2020.
*21. Mustafa Z, Ghaffari M: Diagnostic methods, Clinical guidelines, and antibiotic treatment for Group A Streptococcal pharyngitis, *Front Cell Infect Microbiol* 10:644, 2020.
22. Heller J, Zieve D, Conaway B: Blockage of upper airway. Retrieved from https://medlineplus.gov/ency/article/000067.htm.
23. American Cancer Society: Key statistics for oral and oropharyngeal cancers. Retrieved from www.cancer.org/cancer/oral-cavity-and-oropharyngeal-cancer/about/key-statistics.html.
24. American Society of Clinical Oncology Cancer: Net: head and neck cancer: risk factors and prevention. Retrieved from www.cancer.net/cancer-types/head-and-neck-cancer/risk-factors-and-prevention.
*25. Chow LQ: Head and neck cancer, *N Engl J Med* 382:60, 2020.
26. Cancer Treatment Centers of America: Head and neck cancer drug information. Retrieved from www.cancercenter.com/head-and-neck-cancer/diagnostics-and-treatments/tab/drug-information/.
*27. Kristensen MB, Isenring E, Brown B: Nutrition and swallowing therapy strategies for patients with head and neck cancer, *Nutrition* 69:110548, 2020.

*Evidence-based information for clinical practice.

30

Lower Respiratory Problems

Eugene E. Mondor

http://evolve.elsevier.com/Lewis/medsurg/

CONCEPTUAL FOCUS

Cellular Regulation
Clotting
Functional Ability
Gas Exchange
Infection

LEARNING OUTCOMES

1. Compare and contrast the clinical manifestations and nursing and interprofessional management of patients with acute bronchitis and pertussis.
2. Distinguish among the types of pneumonia and their etiology.
3. Describe the pathophysiology, clinical manifestations, diagnostic studies, and interprofessional and nursing management of patients with pneumonia.
4. Explain the pathophysiology, classification, clinical manifestations, complications, diagnostic abnormalities, and interprofessional and nursing management of patients with tuberculosis.
5. Describe the pathophysiology, clinical manifestations, and nursing and interprofessional management of a patient with a lung abscess.
6. Identify the etiology, clinical manifestations, and nursing and interprofessional management of a patient with a pleural effusion.
7. Compare and contrast the pathophysiology, clinical manifestations, and nursing and interprofessional management of fractured ribs, flail chest, and pneumothorax.
8. Describe the pathophysiology, clinical manifestations, and nursing and interprofessional management of pulmonary embolism, pulmonary hypertension, and cor pulmonale.
9. Identify the causative factors, clinical manifestations, and nursing and interprofessional management of patients with environmental lung diseases.
10. State lung disorders in which lung transplantation may be a treatment option, explaining the nursing and interprofessional management of the transplant patient.
11. Describe the etiology, risk factors, pathophysiology, clinical manifestations, and interprofessional and nursing management of the patient with lung cancer.

KEY TERMS

acute bronchitis
community-acquired pneumonia (CAP)
cor pulmonale
empyema
flail chest
hemothorax
hospital-acquired pneumonia (HAP)
lung abscess
pertussis
pleural effusion
pleurisy (pleuritis)
pneumoconiosis
pneumonia
pneumothorax
pulmonary edema
pulmonary embolism (PE)
pulmonary hypertension
tension pneumothorax
tuberculosis (TB)

A variety of problems affect the lower respiratory system. This chapter discusses lower respiratory tract diseases that influence gas exchange. We will focus on infectious, restrictive, traumatic, vascular, environmental, and oncologic problems that have the potential to impair gas exchange. Left untreated, many of these conditions will have profound consequences for the patient, as adequate oxygenation and ventilation are both essential for life.

LOWER RESPIRATORY TRACT INFECTIONS

Lower respiratory tract infection is a common and serious problem. It is the reason for thousands of clinic and emergency department (ED) visits and hospital admissions each year. In the United States, pneumonia and influenza cause around 50,000 deaths each year.[1]

ACUTE BRONCHITIS

Acute bronchitis is a self-limiting inflammation of the bronchi in the lower respiratory tract. It is the reason for 2.7 million outpatient clinic visits and 4 million ED visits per year. Viruses cause most acute bronchial infections. Air pollution, dust, inhalation of chemicals, smoking, chronic sinusitis, and asthma are other triggers.

Cough is the most common symptom. It may last for up to 3 weeks and is the main reason for seeking medical care. Coughing is more frequent at night. When present, sputum is often clear, although some patients have purulent sputum. Other symptoms may include headache, fever, malaise, hoarseness, myalgias, dyspnea, and chest pain.

Diagnosis is based on the assessment. Assessment may reveal normal breath sounds or crackles or wheezes, usually on expiration and with exertion. *Consolidation* (when fluid accumulates in the lungs), suggestive of pneumonia, is absent with bronchitis. Chest x-rays are normal and not needed unless we suspect pneumonia or some other lung problem.

The goal of treatment is to relieve symptoms and prevent pneumonia. Treatment is supportive. It includes cough suppressants (e.g., dextromethorphan), encouraging oral fluid intake, and using a humidifier. Throat lozenges, hot tea, and honey may help relieve cough. β_2-agonist (bronchodilator) inhalers are useful for patients with wheezes or underlying lung problems. We do not prescribe antibiotics for viral infections because they are not effective against viruses and giving them promotes antibiotic resistance. Antibiotics may be given to patients with underlying chronic conditions who are at risk for or have a prolonged infection with systemic symptoms.

Encourage patients to not smoke, avoid secondhand smoke, and wash their hands often (Box 30.1). If acute bronchitis is due to influenza, we may start treatment with antiviral drugs. If patients with acute bronchitis develop a fever, have trouble breathing, or have symptoms last longer than 4 weeks, they should see their HCP.

BOX 30.1 PROMOTING POPULATION HEALTH

Preventing Respiratory Diseases

- Wash hands often to prevent and avoid spreading infections.
- Get a Tdap, pneumococcal, COVID, and flu vaccines as directed by the HCP.
- Avoid smoking and exposure to environmental smoke.
- Wear proper personal protective equipment (PPE) when working in an occupation with prolonged exposure to dust, fumes, or gases.
- Avoid exposure to allergens, indoor pollutants, and ambient air pollutants.

PERTUSSIS

Pertussis is a highly contagious respiratory tract infection. It is caused by the gram-negative bacillus *Bordetella pertussis*. The bacteria attach to the cilia of the respiratory tract and release toxins that damage the cilia, causing inflammation and swelling. Cases of pertussis have been steadily increasing in the United States since the 1980s.[2] The largest increase is in teens and adults. We think that immunity from childhood tetanus, diphtheria, and pertussis vaccine (Tdap) vaccination may decrease over time, allowing a milder (but still contagious) infection to occur. The Centers for Disease Control and Prevention (CDC) currently recommends that all adolescents (11 years and older) and adults who have not received a dose of Tdap receive a one-time vaccination as soon as possible.[3]

Manifestations of pertussis occur in stages. The 1st stage, lasting 1 to 2 weeks, manifests as a mild upper respiratory tract infection (URI) with a low-grade or no fever, runny nose, watery eyes, malaise, and mild, nonproductive cough. The 2nd stage, from the 2nd to 10th weeks of infection, is characterized by paroxysms of cough. The last stage lasts 2 to 3 weeks. The cough is less severe. The patient may still be weak.

The hallmark characteristic of pertussis is uncontrollable, violent coughing. Inspiration after each cough produces the typical "whooping" sound as the patient tries to breathe in air against an obstructed glottis. The "whoop" is often not present in teens and adults (especially those who are vaccinated). Coughing is more frequent at night. Vomiting may occur with coughing. Unlike acute bronchitis, the cough with pertussis may last from 6 to 10 weeks.

In the community, diagnosis is mainly by history and assessment. In the acute care setting, the CDC recommends nasopharyngeal cultures, polymerase chain reaction (PCR) of nasopharyngeal secretions, or serology testing.[4] The treatment is macrolide (erythromycin, azithromycin) antibiotics to minimize symptoms and prevent disease spread (see Table 15.8). For the patient who cannot take macrolides, trimethoprim/sulfamethoxazole is used.

The patient is infectious from the beginning of the 1st stage through the 3rd week after onset of symptoms or until 5 days after starting antibiotic therapy. Place hospitalized patients on droplet precautions. Patients should not use cough suppressants and antihistamines as they are ineffective and may cause coughing. Corticosteroids and bronchodilators are also not helpful. The CDC recommends antibiotic therapy for those who had close contact with the patient.

PNEUMONIA

Pneumonia is an acute infection of the lung parenchyma. Despite progress in antibiotic therapy to treat pneumonia, pneumonia still has significant morbidity and mortality. Pneumonia and lower respiratory tract infections were the 4th leading cause of death worldwide in 2019.[5]

Etiology

Normally, various defense mechanisms protect the airway distal to the larynx from infection. Mechanisms that create a mechanical barrier to microorganisms entering the tracheobronchial tree include air filtration, epiglottis closure over the trachea, cough reflex, mucociliary escalator mechanism, and reflex bronchoconstriction. Immune defense mechanisms include secretion of immunoglobulins A and G and alveolar macrophages.

Pneumonia is more likely to occur when defense mechanisms become incompetent or are overwhelmed by the virulence or quantity of infectious agents. A weakened cough or epiglottal reflex may allow aspiration of oropharyngeal contents into the lungs. Tracheal intubation bypasses normal filtration processes and interferes with the cough reflex and mucociliary escalator mechanism. Air pollution, smoking, viral URIs, and normal changes that occur with aging can impair the mucociliary mechanism. Chronic diseases can suppress the immune system's ability to inhibit bacterial growth. Risk factors for pneumonia are listed in Table 30.1.

Pathogens that cause pneumonia reach the lung in 3 ways:

1. *Aspiration* of normal flora from the nasopharynx or oropharynx. Many organisms that cause pneumonia are normal inhabitants of the mouth and pharynx in healthy adults.
2. *Inhalation* of microbes present in the air. Examples include *Mycoplasma pneumoniae* and fungal pneumonias.
3. *Hematogenous spread* from a primary infection elsewhere in the body. One example is *Staphylococcus aureus* from infective endocarditis.

Classifications of Pneumonia

There is no universally accepted classification system for pneumonia. Some classify pneumonia by the causative pathogens (e.g., bacterial, viral, fungal), disease characteristics, or appearance on chest x-ray. The most widely recognized and effective way to classify pneumonia is as either *community-acquired* or *hospital-acquired* pneumonia. This classification helps the HCP identify the most likely cause (Table 30.2) and the choice of antimicrobial therapy.

Community-Acquired Pneumonia

Community-acquired pneumonia (CAP) is an acute lung infection that occurs in patients who have not been hospitalized or lived in a long-term care facility within 14 days of symptom onset. The decision to treat the patient at home or admit to a hospital is based on several factors. These include the patient's age, vital signs, mental status, presence of co-morbid conditions, and condition. We can use various tools (Table 30.3) to support clinical judgment.

Hospital-Acquired Pneumonia

Hospital-acquired pneumonia (HAP), or nosocomial pneumonia, is pneumonia in a non-intubated patient that begins 48 hours or longer after admission to hospital and was not present when they were admitted. *Ventilator-associated pneumonia*

TABLE 30.1 Risk Factors for Pneumonia

- Abdominal or chest surgery
- Age >65 years
- Air pollution
- Altered level of consciousness (e.g., head injury, seizures, anesthesia, drug overdose, stroke)
- Bed rest and prolonged immobility
- Chronic diseases: chronic lung and liver disease, diabetes, heart disease, cancer, chronic kidney disease
- Debilitating illness
- Enteral feedings via naso- or orogastric or intestinal tubes
- Exposure to bats, birds, rabbits, and farm animal feces
- Immunosuppressive conditions and/or therapy (e.g., corticosteroids, cancer chemotherapy, HIV infection, immunosuppressive therapy after organ transplant)
- Inhalation or aspiration of noxious substances
- IV drug use
- Malnutrition
- Resident of a long-term care facility
- Smoking
- Tracheal intubation (endotracheal intubation, tracheostomy)
- URI

TABLE 30.2 Organisms Causing Pneumonia

Community-Acquired Pneumonia (CAP)

Typical

- *Escherichia coli*
- *Haemophilus influenzae*[a]
- *Klebsiella pneumoniae*[a]
- *Methicillin resistant staphylococcus aureus* (MRSA)
- *Moraxella catarrhalis*
- *Pseudomonas*
- *Staphylococcus aureus*[a]
- *Streptococcus pneumoniae*[a]

Atypical

- Chlamydophila pneumoniae
- Coxiella burnettii
- Influenza A and B
- Legionella pneumophilia
- Mycoplasma pneumoniae
- Mycobacterium tuberculosis

Respiratory Viruses

- Parainfluenza virus
- Respiratory syncytial virus
- Rhinovirus

Other Causes of CAP

- Fungi
- Oral anaerobes

Hospital-Acquired Pneumonia (HAP)

- *Escherichia coli*[b]
- *Haemophilus influenzae*
- *Klebsiella pneumoniae*[b]
- Microaspiration of bacteria that colonize the mouth, oropharynx
- *Pseudomonas aeruginosa*[b]
- *Proteus* species
- *Serratia marcescens*
- *Staphylococcus aureus*
- *Streptococcus pneumoniae*[a]

[a]Most common cause of CAP.
[b]Most common causes of HAP.

TABLE 30.3 Pneumonia Severity Index (PSI)

The PSI can supplement clinical judgment to determine the severity of pneumonia and if patients need to be hospitalized.

Factor	Points
Demographics	
Age in years	
Women	– 10
Extended care resident	+10
Other Conditions	
Stroke, kidney disease, heart failure	+10 each
Active cancer	+30
Liver disease	+20
Assessment	
Respiratory rate ≥30/min, BP < 90, altered mental status	+20 each
Pulse 125/min	+10
Temperature <95°F (35°C) or ≥104°F (40°C)	+15
Pleural effusion	+10
Laboratory Results	
pH < 7.35	+30
BUN ≥30 mg/dL, Sodium <130 mEq/L	+20 each
Glucose 250 mg/dL, Hematocrit < 30%, pAO_2 <60 mm Hg or O_2 <90 percent	+10 each
Scoring:	
<70 points	Outpatient
71-90 points	Outpatient vs. Observation
>91 points	Inpatient

Source: Community-acquired pneumonia severity index (PSI) for adults. Retrieved from https://www.clinicalkey.com/#!/tools/calculators/calculator/77-s2.0-99.

(VAP), a type of HAP, refers to pneumonia that occurs more than 48 hours after endotracheal intubation.[6] VAP is discussed in Chapter 28. Both HAP and VAP are associated with longer hospital stays, increased associated costs, sicker patients, and increased mortality.

Once the diagnosis of CAP, HAP, or VAP is made, treatment is started based on risk factors, speed of onset, clinical presentation, underlying medical conditions, hemodynamic stability, and the most likely causative pathogen. *Empiric antibiotic therapy,* the initiation of treatment before a definitive diagnosis or causative agent is made, should be started as soon as pneumonia is suspected. Empiric antibiotic therapy is based on the drugs known to be effective for the most likely cause. Antibiotic therapy is adjusted once the results of sputum cultures identify the exact pathogen causing the infection.

Types of Pneumonia

There are several types of pneumonia. *Viral pneumonia* is the most common type. It occurs in one third of all pneumonia cases. It may be mild and self-limiting or cause potentially life-threatening problems, such as acute respiratory failure (ARF) in influenza. Patients with *bacterial pneumonia* may be extremely unwell and need hospital admission. *Mycoplasma pneumonia,* which has traits of both bacteria and viruses, is often called "atypical" pneumonia. It is mild and occurs in persons younger than 40 years of age.

Aspiration Pneumonia

Aspiration pneumonia results from the abnormal entry of material from the mouth or stomach into the trachea and lungs. Conditions that increase the risk for aspiration include decreased level of consciousness (e.g., seizure, anesthesia, head injury, stroke, alcohol use), swallowing problems, and having a nasogastric (NG) tube with or without enteral feeding. With loss of consciousness, the gag and cough reflexes are depressed, making aspiration more likely.

The aspirated material (food, water, vomitus, oropharyngeal secretions) triggers an inflammatory response. The most common form of aspiration pneumonia is a primary bacterial infection. Typically, the sputum culture shows more than 1 organism, including aerobes and anaerobes, since they both make up the flora of the oropharynx.

Until cultures are done and results obtained, initial antibiotic therapy is based on an assessment of probable cause, severity of illness, and patient factors (e.g., malnutrition, current use of antibiotic therapy). For patients who aspirate in hospitals, antibiotic coverage should include both gram-negative organisms and methicillin-resistant *Staphylococcus aureus* (MRSA). Aspiration of acidic gastric contents can cause *chemical (noninfectious) pneumonitis,* which may not need antibiotic therapy. However, secondary bacterial infection can occur in these patients 48 to 72 hours later.

Necrotizing Pneumonia

Necrotizing pneumonia is a rare complication of bacterial lung infection. It causes the lung tissue to turn into a thick, liquid mass. Cavitation and lung abscesses can occur. This sometimes happens with CAP. We do not know the exact mechanisms involved. Common causative organisms include *Staphylococcus, Klebsiella,* and *Streptococcus.* Signs and symptoms include respiratory insufficiency and/or failure, leukocytosis, and abnormalities on chest imaging.[7] Treatment includes long-term antibiotic therapy and possible surgery.

Opportunistic Pneumonia

Opportunistic pneumonia is inflammation and infection of the lower respiratory tract in immunocompromised patients. Persons at risk include those with altered immune responses. This can include people with severe protein-calorie malnutrition or immunodeficiencies (e.g., human immunodeficiency virus [HIV] infection) and those receiving radiation therapy, chemotherapy, and any immunosuppressive therapy, including long-term corticosteroid therapy. In addition to the risk for bacterial and viral pneumonia, the immunocompromised person may develop an infection from organisms that do not normally cause disease, such as *Pneumocystis jiroveci* pneumonia (PJP) or cytomegalovirus (CMV).[8]

PJP is occurring with greater frequency in HIV-negative, immunocompromised persons.[8] The onset is slow and subtle. Symptoms include fever, tachypnea, tachycardia, dyspnea,

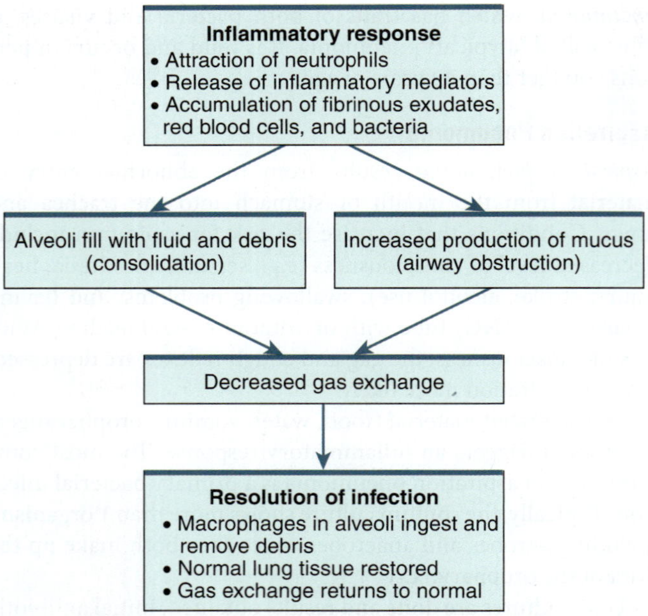

Fig. 30.1 Pathophysiologic course of pneumonia.

nonproductive cough, and hypoxemia. The chest x-ray usually shows diffuse bilateral infiltrates. In widespread disease, the lungs have massive consolidation.

PJP can be life-threatening, causing ARF and death. Infection can spread to other organs, including the liver, bone marrow, lymph nodes, spleen, and thyroid. Bacterial and viral pneumonias first must be ruled out because of the vague presentation of PJP. Although the causative agent is fungal, PJP does not respond to antifungal agents. Treatment consists of IV or oral trimethoprim/sulfamethoxazole, depending on the severity of disease, overall clinical condition, and the patient's response.

CMV, a herpes virus, can cause viral pneumonia. Most CMV infections are asymptomatic or mild. Severe disease can occur in people with an impaired immune response. CMV is one of the most important life-threatening infectious complications after hematopoietic stem cell transplant.[9] Antiviral medications (e.g., ganciclovir, cidofovir) and high-dose immunoglobulin are part of treatment.

Pathophysiology

Specific pathophysiologic changes related to pneumonia vary depending on the offending pathogen. Almost all pathogens trigger an inflammatory response in the lungs (Fig. 30.1). Inflammation, characterized by an increase in blood flow and vascular permeability, activates neutrophils to engulf and kill the offending pathogens. As a result, the inflammatory process attracts more neutrophils, airway edema occurs, and fluid leaks from the capillaries and tissues into alveoli. Normal O_2 transport is affected, leading to manifestations of hypoxia (e.g., tachypnea, dyspnea, tachycardia).

Atelectasis, the absence of gas or air in 1 or more areas of the lung, may occur with pneumonia (Fig. 30.2). Atelectasis may be asymptomatic. Some patients have extreme shortness of breath and severe chest pain. *Consolidation,* a feature typical of bacterial pneumonia, occurs when the normally air-filled

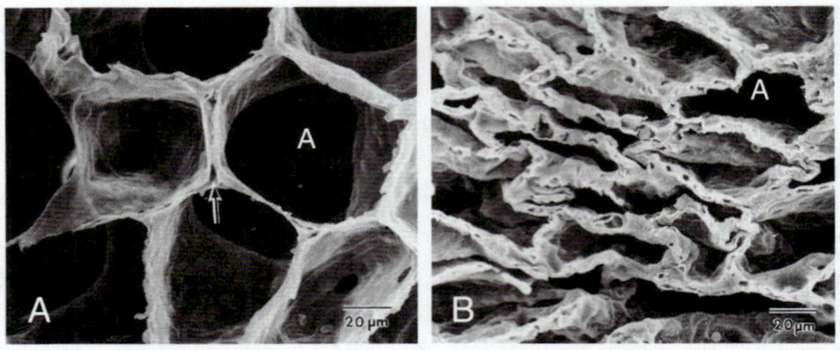

Fig. 30.2 Atelectasis. Scanning electron micrograph of lung parenchyma. (A) Alveoli *(A)* and alveolar-capillary membrane *(arrow).* (B) Effects of atelectasis. Alveoli *(A)* are partially or totally collapsed. (A, From Dantzker DR, Bone RC, George RB, editors: *Pulmonary and critical care medicine,* vol 1, St Louis, 1993, Mosby. B, From Albertine KH, Williams MC, Hyde DM: Anatomy of the lungs. In RJ Mason, VC Broaddus, JF Murray, et al., editors: *Murray and Nadel's textbook of respiratory medicine,* ed 4, Philadelphia, 2005, Saunders.)

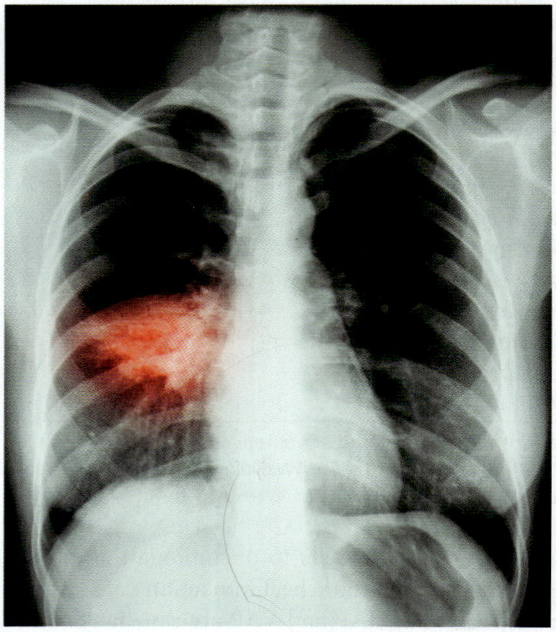

Fig. 30.3 Chest x-ray of a patient with acute bacterial pneumonia. (© iStock.com/stockdevil.)

alveoli become filled with water, fluid, and/or debris (Fig. 30.3). This can potentially obstruct airflow, impair gas exchange, and cause significant respiratory insufficiency. Over time and with appropriate antibiotic therapy, macrophages lyse and process the debris. This allows lung tissue to recover and gas exchange to return to normal.

Clinical Manifestations

The most common presenting symptoms of pneumonia are cough, fever, chills, dyspnea, tachypnea, and pleuritic chest pain. The cough may or may not be productive. Sputum may be green, yellow, or even rust colored (bloody). Viral pneumonia may initially be seen as influenza, with respiratory symptoms appearing and/or worsening 12 to 36 hours after onset.

The older or debilitated patient may not have classic symptoms of pneumonia. Confusion or stupor (possibly related to hypoxia) may be the only finding. The older adult may have hypothermia, rather than fever. Nonspecific manifestations include diaphoresis, anorexia, fatigue, myalgias, and headache.

Fine or coarse crackles may be auscultated over the affected region. If consolidation is present, bronchial breath sounds, egophony (an increase in the sound of the patient's voice), and increased fremitus (chest wall vibrations made by vocalization) may be present. Patients with pleural effusion may have dullness to percussion over the affected area.

Complications

A major problem today is pneumonia caused by multidrug-resistant (MDR) pathogens. Common culprits include MRSA and gram-negative bacilli. Risk factors for MDR pneumonia include advanced age, immunosuppression, history of antibiotic use, and prolonged mechanical ventilation. Antibiotic susceptibility tests can identify MDR pathogens. The virulence of these pathogens can severely limit the available and appropriate antimicrobial therapy. MDR pathogens increase mortality from pneumonia.

Other complications from pneumonia develop more often in older adults and those with underlying chronic diseases. These include:

- *Pleurisy,* inflammation of the pleura.
- *Pleural effusion,* or fluid in the pleural space. In most cases, the effusion is sterile and reabsorbed in 1 to 2 weeks. Sometimes, effusions require aspiration by thoracentesis.
- *Bacteremia,* bacterial infection in the blood, is more likely to occur in infections with *Streptococcus pneumoniae* and *Haemophilus influenzae.*
- *Pneumothorax* can occur when air collects in the pleural space, causing the lungs to collapse.
- *ARF* is a leading cause of death in patients with severe pneumonia. ARF occurs when pneumonia damages the lungs' ability to exchange O_2 and CO_2 across the alveolar-capillary membrane.
- *Sepsis* can occur when bacteria within alveoli enter the bloodstream. Severe sepsis can lead to shock and multisystem organ dysfunction syndrome (MODS) (see Chapter 42).

Lung abscess is not a common complication of pneumonia. It may occur with pneumonia caused by *S. aureus* and gram-negative organisms. *Empyema,* the accumulation of purulent exudate in the pleural cavity, may occur in up to 20% of cases. It requires antibiotic therapy and drainage of the exudate by a chest tube or open surgical drainage. Pleurisy, pleural effusion, and lung abscess are discussed later in this chapter.

Diagnostic Studies

The common diagnostic procedures for pneumonia are outlined in Table 30.4. History, physical assessment, and chest x-ray often give enough information to make immediate decisions about early treatment. Chest x-ray often shows patterns characteristic of the infecting pathogen and is important in diagnosing pneumonia. X-ray may also show pleural effusions. Bronchoscopy with bronchial washings or thoracentesis may be done to obtain cell and fluid samples from patients not responding to initial therapy.

Arterial blood gases (ABGs) may show hypoxemia, hypercapnia, and acidosis. Leukocytosis occurs in most patients with bacterial pneumonia. The white blood cell (WBC) count is usually greater than 15,000/μL (15×10^9/L) with the presence of bands (immature neutrophils). Ideally, we should obtain a sputum specimen for culture and Gram stain to identify the organism before starting antibiotic therapy. However, we should not delay starting antibiotic therapy if we cannot obtain a specimen. Delays in antibiotic therapy can increase the risk for mortality. Blood cultures are done for patients who are seriously ill.

C-reactive protein (CRP), procalcitonin, and interleukin 6 (IL-6) are currently being explored as ways to help tell pneumonia from other types of heart and respiratory failure.[10]

TABLE 30.4 Interprofessional Care

Pneumonia

Diagnostic Assessment
- History and physical assessment
- Chest x-ray
- Sputum: Gram stain, culture and sensitivity test
- Pulse oximetry and/or ABGs
- CBC, white blood cell differential, and routine blood chemistries
- Blood cultures (if indicated)

Management
- O_2 therapy
- Critical care management, with mechanical ventilation as needed
- Increased fluid intake (at least 2–3 L/day), IV fluids
- VTE prophylaxis
- Physiotherapy, early mobility
- Balance between activity and rest

Drug Therapy
- Appropriate antibiotic therapy (Table 30.6)
- Antipyretics
- Analgesics
- NSAIDs (if no contraindications)

Interprofessional Care

Prompt treatment with the appropriate antibiotic is essential. Antibiotics are highly effective for both bacterial and mycoplasma pneumonia. In uncomplicated cases, the patient responds to drug therapy within 48 to 72 hours. Signs of improvement include decreased temperature, improved breathing, and less chest discomfort. Abnormal physical findings can last more than 7 days.

Pneumococcal vaccine is used to prevent *S. pneumoniae* infection (Table 30.5). Although cough suppressants, mucolytics, bronchodilators, and corticosteroids are often prescribed as adjunctive therapy, the use of these drugs is debatable. However, they may be prescribed for patients with underlying chronic conditions.

Currently, there is no definitive treatment for most viral pneumonias. Care is generally supportive. In most circumstances, viral pneumonia is self-limiting and will often resolve in 3 to 4 days. Antiviral therapy may be used to treat pneumonia caused by influenza (e.g., oseltamivir, zanamivir) or a few other viruses (e.g., acyclovir for herpes simplex virus).

Drug Therapy

The HCP selects empiric therapy based on the likely pathogen. Table 30.6 presents the drug therapy for bacterial CAP.

TABLE 30.5 Pneumococcal Vaccines

Vaccine[a]	Recommendations for Use
Pneumococcal conjugate vaccine (PCV13, Prevnar 13): Protect against 13 types of pneumococcal bacteria	• Children <2 years • Adults ≥65 years • Anyone 2–64 years old with certain medical conditions (e.g., sickle cell disease, asplenia, immunodeficiencies, HIV infection, chronic kidney disease, leukemia, cancer, long-term immunosuppressive therapy)
Pneumococcal polysaccharide vaccine (PPSV23, Pneumovax 23): Protect against 23 types of pneumococcal bacteria	• Adults ≥50 years • Adults 19–64 years old who smoke • Anyone 2–64 years old who have high risk of pneumococcal disease (e.g., heart disease, lung disease, diabetes, alcohol use, cirrhosis, sickle cell disease, immunocompromised, cancer)

[a]For more details on scheduling of pneumococcal vaccinations, see https:www.cdc.gov/pneumococcal/vaccination.html.

TABLE 30.6 Drug Therapy

Bacterial Community-Acquired Pneumonia

Patient Variable	Treatment Options
Outpatient	
Healthy No comorbidities or risk factors for antibiotic-resistant infection	Beta lactam *OR* Macrolide *OR* doxycycline
Co-Morbidities COPD; diabetes; chronic liver, lung, heart, or renal disease; cancer; alcohol use; no spleen	Respiratory fluoroquinolone *OR* β-Lactam plus macrolide (doxycycline may be substituted for macrolide) OR Beta lactam plus doxycycline plus macrolide
Inpatient	
Medical Unit	Respiratory fluoroquinolone *OR* β-Lactam plus macrolide (doxycycline may be substituted for macrolide)
ICU	β-Lactam plus either azithromycin or respiratory fluoroquinolone
Special Considerations	
• Community-acquired methicillin-resistant *Staphylococcus aureus* (CA-MRSA)	Vancomycin or linezolid (Zyvox)
• *Pseudomonas* infection	Antipneumococcal and antipseudomonal β-lactam *OR* Antipneumococcal, antipseudomonal β-lactam plus either respiratory fluoroquinolone or ciprofloxacin or levofloxacin *OR* Antipneumococcal, antipseudomonal β-lactam plus aminoglycoside plus either ciprofloxacin or levofloxacin
• *Pseudomonas* infection in patient with penicillin allergy	Substitute aztreonam for the above β-lactam

Source: Community acquired pneumonia in adults. Retrieved from https://www.clinicalkey.com/#!/content/clinical_overview/67-s2.0-77188ebd-e5b9-49a1-88a0-0211995a4b85#treatment-options-heading-35.

For all types of pneumonia, empiric antibiotic therapy is based on whether the patient has risk factors for MDR pathogens. The prevalence and resistance patterns of MDR pathogens vary among localities and agencies. Therefore, antibiotic therapy must be adapted to local patterns of antibiotic resistance. Multiple regimens exist. All treatment should initially include antibiotics that are effective against both resistant gram-negative and resistant gram-positive organisms.

Clinical improvement usually occurs in 3 to 5 days. Patients who do not respond to therapy or deteriorate need aggressive re-evaluation to assess for noninfectious causes, complications, coexisting infectious processes, or pneumonia caused by an MDR pathogen.

We switch the patient from IV to oral antibiotic therapy as soon as they are improving clinically and able to take oral medication. Stable patients can be discharged on oral antibiotics. Total treatment time for patients with CAP should be a minimum of 5 days. The patient should be afebrile for 48 to 72 hours before stopping treatment. Stress the importance of completing the full course of antibiotic treatment. Longer treatment time may be needed if initial therapy was not active against the identified pathogen or complications occur.

Nutrition Therapy

Hydration is important to prevent dehydration and thin and loosen secretions. Carefully monitor fluid intake. If the patient is an older adult, has heart failure (HF), or has a known preexisting respiratory condition, administer IV fluids carefully to avoid fluid overload. Pay close attention to intake and output. Monitor and replace electrolytes as needed.

Weight loss may occur in patients with pneumonia because of increased metabolic needs, difficulty eating due to dyspnea, nonspecific abdominal symptoms, and activity intolerance. Small, frequent meals are easier for dyspneic patients to tolerate. Offer foods high in calories and nutrients. A nutrition assessment by a dietitian may be done on admission to acute care.

❖ NURSING MANAGEMENT: PNEUMONIA

◆ Assessment

Table 30.7 presents subjective and objective data to obtain from a patient with pneumonia.

◆ Clinical Problems

Clinical problems for the patient with pneumonia may include:

- Impaired respiratory function
- Infection
- Fluid imbalance
- Activity intolerance
- Altered body temperature

Additional information on clinical problems and interventions for the patient with pneumonia is shown in eNursing Care Plan 30.1 on the website for this chapter.

◆ Planning

The overall goals are that the patient with pneumonia will have (1) no signs of hypoxemia, (2) normal breathing patterns, (3) clear breath sounds, (4) normal chest x-ray, (5) normal WBC count, and (6) no complications.

TABLE 30.7 NURSING ASSESSMENT

Pneumonia

Subjective Data

Important Health Information

Health history: Lung cancer, COPD, diabetes, chronic debilitating disease, malnutrition, immunosuppression, exposure to chemical toxins, dust, or allergens

Medications: Antibiotics, corticosteroids, chemotherapy, or any immunosuppressants

Surgery or other treatments: Recent abdominal or chest surgery, splenectomy, endotracheal intubation, enteral feedings, or any surgery with general anesthesia.

Functional Health Patterns

Health perception–health management: Smoking, alcohol use, illicit drug use, recent tract URI, malaise

Nutritional-metabolic: Anorexia, nausea, vomiting

Activity-exercise: Prolonged bed rest or immobility. Fatigue, weakness. Dyspnea, cough.

Cognitive-perceptual: Pain with breathing, nasal congestion, chest pain, sore throat, headache, abdominal pain, muscle aches

Objective Data

Cardiovascular

- Tachycardia

General

- Fever, restlessness, or lethargy. Splinting of thoracic cavity

Neurologic

- Changes in mental status, ranging from confusion to delirium

Respiratory

- Tachypnea, pharyngitis
- Asymmetric chest movements or retraction, decreased excursion
- Nasal flaring, use of accessory muscles (neck, abdomen)
- Crackles, friction rub on auscultation, dullness on percussion over consolidated areas, ↑ tactile fremitus on palpation
- Pink, rusty, purulent, green, yellow, or white sputum (amount may be scant to copious)

Possible Diagnostic Findings

- Leukocytosis, positive sputum on Gram stain and culture, Patchy or diffuse infiltrates, abscesses, pleural effusion, or pneumothorax on chest x-ray
- leftAbnormal ABGs with ↓ or normal PaO_2, ↓ or normal $PaCO_2$, and ↑ or normal pH initially, and later ↓ PaO_2, ↑ $PaCO_2$, and ↓ pH

◆ Implementation

◆ Health Promotion

To reduce the risk for pneumonia, teach patients to practice good health habits, such as frequent hand washing, good nutrition, adequate rest, regular exercise, and coughing or sneezing into the elbow rather than hands. Avoiding smoking is one of the most important health-promoting behaviors. If possible, avoid exposure to people with URIs. If a URI occurs, it requires prompt attention with supportive measures (e.g., rest, fluids). If symptoms persist for longer than 7 days, the person should seek medical care. Identifying patients at risk and taking measures to prevent pneumonia are important. Encourage those at risk for pneumonia (e.g., chronically ill, older adult) to obtain needed vaccines.

TABLE 30.8 NURSING MANAGEMENT

Care of the Patient With Pneumonia

- Monitor respiratory status:
  - Breath sounds, noting areas of decreased or absent ventilation, and presence of adventitious sounds.
  - Rate, rhythm, depth, and effort of respirations.
  - Characteristics of any secretions.
  - Ability to cough effectively and presence of fatigue.
- Assess for signs of hypoxemia.
- Administer antibiotic and IV fluid therapy as ordered.
- Administer medications (e.g., bronchodilators and inhalers) to promote airway patency and gas exchange.
- Keep the head of the bed elevated at least 30 degrees.
- Turn and reposition the patient every 2 hrs to promote lung expansion and mobilize secretions.
- Encourage the patient to cough, deep breathe, and use the incentive spirometer.
- Implement measures to manage fever (see Table 12.5).
- Administer analgesics as ordered to relieve pain.
- Provide ordered VTE and GI prophylaxis.
- Monitor intake and output.
- Supervise AP:
  - Obtain vital signs and report to RN.
  - Provide personal hygiene, skin care, and oral care
  - Assist with frequent position changes, including early mobility
  - Report to RN any change in patient condition.

Collaborate With Respiratory Therapist

- Apply O_2 therapy as ordered.
- Perform chest physiotherapy (e.g., percussion, postural drainage).

Collaborate With Dietitian

- Assess and monitor nutrition status.
- Recommend optimal diet.

Collaborate With Physical and Occupational Therapist

- Perform ROM exercises.
- Assist with early and progressive ambulation.

◆ Acute Care

Nursing care for the patient with pneumonia is outlined in Table 30.8. Although many patients with pneumonia are treated on an outpatient basis, the nursing care plan for a patient with pneumonia (see eNursing Care Plan 30.1) applies to both patients at home and hospitalized.

Essential nursing care for hospitalized patients with pneumonia includes monitoring assessment findings and the response to therapy. We provide supportive measures according to the patient's needs. These may include O_2 therapy to treat hypoxemia and analgesics to relieve chest pain. Implement measures to reduce fever (see Table 12.5). Prompt collection of specimens and timely administration of antibiotics is critical. Hydration, nutrition support, and positioning are part of the care plan. Work with the respiratory therapist to monitor the patient's condition and provide chest physiotherapy.

Balance rest and activity to each patient's tolerance. Benefits of early mobility include improved lung and chest expansion, mobilization of secretions, and prevention of venous stasis.

Practice strict medical asepsis and adherence to infection control guidelines to reduce the incidence of possible transmission between staff and patients. Staff and visitors should wash their hands when entering and leaving the patient's room. Staff must wash hands or use hand sanitizer before and after providing care and on removing gloves.

Implement measures to reduce the incidence of pneumonia in patients at higher risk. To prevent aspiration in the patient who has problems swallowing, elevate the head-of-bed to at least 30 degrees. Assess for presence of a gag reflex before giving food or fluids. Patients who have an orogastric or NG tube are at risk for aspiration pneumonia. Although feeding tubes are small, any interruption in the integrity of the lower esophageal sphincter can allow reflux of gastric contents. Elevating the head of the bed can help prevent this complication.

After surgery, treat pain to a comfort level that permits the patient to deep breathe and cough yet remain awake and alert and achieve optimum mobility. Twice-daily oral hygiene with chlorhexidine swabs reduces the risk of pneumonia in postoperative patients.[11]

In the ICU, strictly adhere to the ventilator bundle (see Table 28.10), a group of interventions aimed at reducing the risk for VAP. Maintain sterile aseptic technique when suctioning the patient's trachea. Use caution when handling ventilator circuits, tracheostomy tubing, and nebulizer circuits that can become contaminated from patient secretions.

◆ Ambulatory Care

Teach the patient about the importance of taking every dose of the prescribed antibiotic (see Table 15.9). Review any drug-drug and food-drug interactions. Explain the need for adequate rest to promote recovery. Tell the patient to drink plenty of liquids (at least 6 to 10 glasses/day, unless contraindicated) and avoid alcohol and smoking. A cool mist humidifier or warm bath may help the patient breathe easier. Tell them that it may be several weeks before their usual sense of well-being returns. Explain that a follow-up chest x-ray may be done in 6 to 8 weeks to evaluate resolution of pneumonia. The older adult or chronically ill patient may have a prolonged period of convalescence.

Teaching should include information about available influenza and pneumococcal vaccines. Patients can receive the pneumococcal vaccine and influenza vaccine at the same time but not in the exact same location. The vaccines cannot be mixed into 1 injection.

◆ Evaluation

The expected outcomes are that the patient with pneumonia will have:

- Effective respiratory rate, rhythm, and depth of respirations
- Lungs clear to auscultation
- No complications

TUBERCULOSIS

Tuberculosis (TB) is an infectious disease caused by *Mycobacterium tuberculosis*. It usually involves the lungs, but can infect any organ, including the brain, kidneys, and bones.

BOX 30.2 PROMOTING HEALTH EQUITY

Tuberculosis

- 88% of TB cases in the United States occur in racial and ethnic minorities. 71.4% of these persons were born outside of the United States.
- Asians have the highest TB rate, followed by Hispanics (30%) and Blacks (20%).
- American Indian/Alaska Natives, and Native Hawaiian/Pacific Islanders have the lowest TB rates amongst all ethnic groups (1%).

Source: Centers for Disease Control and Prevention: Health disparities in TB. Retrieved from https://www.cdc.gov/tb/topic/treatment/default.htm.

About 25% of the world's population is infected with TB.[12] The incidence of TB worldwide declined until the mid-1980s. We are now seeing increasing rates of TB. This is attributed to HIV disease and the emergence of drug-resistant strains of *M. tuberculosis*. TB is the leading cause of mortality in patients with HIV infection.

TB occurs disproportionately in the poor, underserved, and minorities (Box 30.2). People most at risk include the homeless, residents of inner-city neighborhoods, foreign-born people, those living or working in institutions (long-term care facilities, prisons, shelters, hospitals), IV drug users, overcrowded living conditions, less than optimal sanitation, and those with poor access to health care. Immunosuppression from any cause (e.g., HIV infection, cancer, long-term corticosteroid use) increases the risk for active TB infection.

Etiology and Pathophysiology

M. tuberculosis is a gram-positive, aerobic, acid-fast bacillus (AFB). It is usually spread from person to person by airborne droplets expectorated when breathing, talking, singing, sneezing, and coughing. A process of evaporation leaves small droplet nuclei, 1 to 5 μm in size, suspended in the air for minutes to hours. Another person then inhales the bacteria. Humans are the only known reservoir for TB. TB is not highly infectious. Transmission requires close contact and frequent or prolonged exposure. TB does not spread by touching, sharing food utensils, kissing, or any other physical contact.

Factors that influence transmission include the (1) number of organisms expelled into the air, (2) concentration of organisms (small spaces with limited ventilation would mean higher concentration), (3) length of time of exposure, and (4) immune system of the exposed person. Once inhaled, these small droplets lodge in bronchioles and alveoli. A local inflammatory reaction occurs, and the infection is established. This is called the *Ghon lesion* or *focus*. It represents a calcified TB granuloma, the hallmark of a primary TB infection. The formation of a granuloma is a defense mechanism aimed at walling off the infection and preventing further spread. Bacillus replication is inhibited, stopping the infection.

Most immunocompetent adults infected with TB can completely kill the mycobacteria. Some people have the mycobacteria in a non-replicating dormant state. Of these persons, 5% to 10% develop active TB infection when the bacteria begin to

TABLE 30.9 Classification of Tuberculosis

Class	Exposure or Infection	Description
0	No TB exposure	No TB exposure, not infected (no history of exposure, negative tuberculin skin test)
1	TB exposure, no infection	TB exposure, no evidence of infection (history of exposure, negative tuberculin skin test)
2	Latent TB infection, no disease	TB infection without disease (positive reaction to tuberculin skin test, negative bacteriologic studies, no x-ray findings compatible with TB, no clinical evidence of TB)
3	TB, clinically active	TB infection with clinically active disease (positive bacteriologic studies or both a significant reaction to tuberculin skin test and clinical or x-ray evidence of current disease)
4	TB, but not clinically active	No current disease (history of previous episode of TB or abnormal, stable x-ray findings in a person with a positive reaction to tuberculin skin test. Negative bacteriologic studies if done. No clinical or x-ray evidence of current disease)
5	TB suspect	TB suspect (diagnosis pending). Person should not be in this classification for >3 months

TABLE 30.10 Latent Tuberculosis Infection (LTBI) Compared to Tuberculosis Disease

LTBI	TB Disease
Has no symptoms	Has symptoms that may include: • Bad cough that lasts ≥3 week • Pain in the chest • Coughing up blood or sputum • Weakness or fatigue • Weight loss, no appetite • Chills • Fever • Sweating at night
Does not feel sick	Usually feels sick
Cannot spread TB bacteria to others	May spread TB bacteria to others
Usually has a positive TST or blood test result showing TB infection	Usually has a positive TST or blood test result showing TB infection
Has a normal chest x-ray and a negative sputum smear	May have an abnormal chest x-ray or positive sputum smear or culture
Needs treatment for latent TB infection to prevent active TB disease	Needs treatment for active TB disease

Source: Centers for Disease Control and Prevention. Tuberculosis (TB) fact sheets: the difference between latent TB infection and TB disease. Retrieved from https://www.cdc.gov/tb/publications/factsheets/general/ltbiandactivetb.htm.

multiply months or years later. While *M. tuberculosis* is aerophilic (O_2 loving) and has an affinity for the lungs, the infection can spread through the lymphatic system and find good environments for growth in other organs. These include the cerebral cortex, spine, bone epiphyses, liver, kidneys, lymph nodes, and adrenal glands.

Once a strain of *M. tuberculosis* develops resistance to the first-line drug therapy (isoniazid and rifampin), it is defined as *multidrug-resistant tuberculosis (MDR-TB).*[13] Extensively drug-resistant TB (XDR-TB) is a rare type of MDR-TB. XDR-TB is also resistant to any fluoroquinolone and at least 1 second-line drug.[13] Resistance results from several problems, including incorrect prescribing, lack of case management, and nonadherence to the prescribed regimen.

Classification

We use several systems to classify TB. The American Thoracic Society classifies TB based on disease development (Table 30.9). We also classify TB by (1) its presentation (primary, latent, reactivated) and (2) whether it is pulmonary or extrapulmonary.

Primary TB infection starts when the bacteria are inhaled and trigger an inflammatory reaction. Most people have effective immune responses that encapsulate the organisms for the rest of their lives, preventing the initial infection from progressing to disease. If the initial immune response is not adequate, the body cannot contain the organism. As a result, the bacteria replicate and *active TB disease* results. When active disease develops within the first 2 years of infection, it is called *primary TB.* People co-infected with HIV are at greatest risk for developing active TB.

Post-primary TB, or *reactivation TB,* is defined as TB disease occurring 2 or more years after the initial infection. If the site of TB is pulmonary or laryngeal, the person is infectious and can transmit the disease to others.

Latent TB infection (LTBI) occurs in a person who does not have active TB disease (Table 30.10). People with LTBI have a positive skin test but are asymptomatic. They cannot transmit the TB bacteria to others but can develop active TB disease later. Immunosuppression, diabetes, poor nutrition, HIV, glucocorticoid therapy, pregnancy, stress, and chronic disease can reactivate the disease. Treatment of LTBI is as important as primary TB.

Clinical Manifestations

Symptoms of pulmonary TB usually do not develop until 2 to 3 weeks after infection or reactivation. The primary manifestation is an initial dry cough. It often becomes productive with mucoid or mucopurulent sputum. Active TB disease may initially present with constitutional symptoms (e.g., fatigue, malaise, anorexia, unexplained weight loss, low-grade fevers, night sweats). Dyspnea is a late symptom that may signify considerable pulmonary disease or a pleural effusion. Hemoptysis is also a late symptom.

Sometimes, TB has a more acute, sudden presentation. The patient may have a high fever, chills, flu-like symptoms, pleuritic pain, a productive cough, and ARF. Lung auscultation may be normal or reveal adventitious sounds, such as crackles. Hypotension and hypoxemia may be present.

Immunosuppressed (e.g., HIV-infected) people and older adults are less likely to have fever and other signs of an infection. In patients with HIV, classic manifestations of TB, such as fever, cough, and weight loss, may be wrongly attributed to PJP or other HIV-associated opportunistic diseases. Respiratory problems in patients with HIV are assessed to determine the cause. A change in cognitive function may be the only initial presenting sign of TB in an older person.

The manifestations of extrapulmonary TB depend on the organs infected. For example, renal TB can cause dysuria and hematuria. Bone and joint TB may cause severe pain. Headaches, vomiting, and lymphadenopathy may be present with TB meningitis.

Complications

Properly treated, pulmonary TB typically heals without complications, except for scarring and residual cavitation within the lung. Significant lung damage, although rare, can occur in patients who are poorly treated or who do not respond to TB treatment.

Miliary TB is widespread dissemination of the mycobacterium through the bloodstream to several distant organs. The infection is characterized by a large amount of TB bacilli and may be fatal if untreated. It can occur with primary disease or reactivation of LTBI. Manifestations slowly progress over a period of days, weeks, or even months. Symptoms vary depending on the organs that are affected. Fever, cough, and lymphadenopathy are present. Hepatomegaly and splenomegaly may occur.

Pleural TB, a specific type of extrapulmonary TB, can result from either primary disease or reactivation of a latent infection. Chest pain, fever, cough, and a unilateral pleural effusion are common. A pleural effusion is caused by bacteria in the pleural space, which trigger an inflammatory reaction and a pleural exudate of protein-rich fluid. Empyema is less common than effusion but may occur from large numbers of TB organisms in the pleural space. Diagnosis is confirmed by AFB cultures and a pleural biopsy.

Because TB can infect organs throughout the body, other acute and long-term complications can result. TB in the spine (Pott disease) can lead to destruction of the intervertebral disc and adjacent vertebrae. Central nervous system (CNS) TB can cause bacterial meningitis. Abdominal TB can lead to peritonitis, especially in HIV-positive patients. The kidneys, adrenal glands, lymph nodes, and urogenital tract can be affected.

Diagnostic Studies

Tuberculin Skin Test

The tuberculin skin test (TST) (Mantoux test) using purified protein derivative (PPD) is the standard method to screen people for *M. tuberculosis*. The test is given by injecting 0.1 mL of PPD intradermally on the ventral surface of the forearm. We read the test by inspection and palpation 48 to 72 hours later for the presence or absence of induration. Induration, a palpable, raised, hardened area or swelling (not redness) at the injection site means the person has been exposed to TB and has developed antibodies. Antibody formation occurs 2 to 12 weeks after initial exposure to the bacteria. Any indurated area present is measured and recorded in millimeters. Based on the size of the induration and risk factors, we make an interpretation based on CDC standards for determining a positive test (see Table 27.15).

Two-step testing with the Mantoux test is recommended for baseline or initial screening for health care workers and those who have a decreased response to allergens. If the 1st test is positive, the person does not need the 2nd test. They do, however, need further evaluation for active disease. If the 1st test is negative, a 2nd test is done 1 to 3 weeks later. Some people with LTBI or who were previously infected with TB may have a false-negative result with the 1st test. Repeating the test may stimulate (boost) the body's ability to react in future tests.[14] A positive reaction to a subsequent test could be a new infection or the result of the boosted reaction to an old infection. A previously negative 2 step test ensures that any future positive results can be accurately interpreted as being caused by a new infection.

Interferon-γ Release Assays

Interferon-γ (INF-γ) release assays (IGRAs) are another screening tool for TB. IGRAs are blood tests that detect INF-γ release from T cells in response to *M. tuberculosis*.[15] Examples of IGRAs include QuantiFERON-TB Gold In-Tube test (QFT-GIT) and the T-SPOT.TB test. Test results are available in a few hours.

IGRAs have several advantages over the TST. IGRAs require only 1 patient visit, are not subject to reader bias, have no "booster" phenomenon, and are not affected by bacillus Calmette-Guérin (BCG) vaccination. The cost of an IGRA is much higher than the TST. Guidelines suggest that both tests are viable options. The choice should be based on context and reasons for testing. Neither IGRAs nor TST can tell between LTBI and active TB infection. LTBI can only be diagnosed by excluding active TB.

Chest X-Ray

Although the chest x-ray findings are important, it is not possible to make a diagnosis of TB based solely on chest x-ray findings. The chest x-ray may appear normal in a patient with TB. Findings suggestive of TB include upper lobe infiltrates, cavitary infiltrates, lymph node involvement, and pleural and/or pericardial effusion. Other diseases, such as sarcoidosis, can mimic the appearance of TB.

Bacteriologic Studies

Sputum culture is the gold standard for diagnosing TB. We need 3 consecutive sputum specimens, each collected at 8- to 24-hour intervals, with at least 1 early morning specimen. The initial test involves microscopic examination of stained sputum smears for AFB. A definitive diagnosis of TB requires mycobacterial growth, which can take up to 6 weeks. For patients in whom suspicion of TB is high, treatment is started while waiting for culture results. Samples for other suspected TB sites can be collected from gastric washings, cerebrospinal fluid (CSF), or fluid from an effusion or abscess.

Interprofessional Care

Most patients with TB are treated on an outpatient basis (Table 30.11). Many people can continue to work and maintain their lifestyles with few changes. Patients with sputum smear–positive TB are considered infectious for the first 2 weeks after starting treatment. Advise these patients to restrict visitors, and avoid travel, public transportation, and trips to public places. Teach them the importance of good hand washing and oral

TABLE 30.11 Interprofessional Care

Pulmonary Tuberculosis

Diagnostic Assessment
- History and physical assessment
- Tuberculin skin test (TST)
- QuantiFERON-TB Gold In-Tube test (QFT-GIT) or T-SPOT.TB test
- Chest x-ray
- Bacteriologic studies
- Sputum smear for acid-fast bacilli (AFB)
- Sputum culture

Management
- Long-term treatment with antimicrobial drugs (Tables 30.12 and 30.13)
- Follow-up AFB smears, cultures, and chest x-rays
- Follow-up care, addressing needs and concerns of patient and close contacts, and involving community health care workers and social workers

hygiene. Hospitalization may be needed for the severely ill or debilitated patient.

Drug Therapy

Active disease. The mainstay of TB treatment is drug therapy (Table 30.12). Because of the growing prevalence of MDR-TB, it is important to manage the patient with active TB aggressively. Drug therapy is divided into 2 phases: intensive and continuation (Table 30.13). In most circumstances the treatment regimen for patients with previously untreated TB consists of a plan with 4 drugs (isoniazid, rifampin, pyrazinamide, and ethambutol). If drug susceptibility test results show that the bacteria are susceptible to all drugs, ethambutol may be stopped. If the patient develops a toxic reaction to the primary drugs, other drugs can be used, including rifabutin and rifapentine (Priftin). If pyrazinamide is not included in the initial phase (e.g., liver disease, pregnancy), the remaining 3 drugs are used for the initial phase.

DRUG ALERT

Isoniazid

- Alcohol may increase risk for liver toxicity.
- Teach patient to avoid drinking alcohol during treatment.
- Monitor for signs of hepatitis before and while taking drug.

Sensitivity testing guides the treatment for MDR-TB. MDR-TB therapy in the initial phase typically includes 5 drugs: 1 or 2 first-line agents, a fluoroquinolone, an injectable antibiotic, and 1 or more second-line agents, for at least 6 months after sputum culture is negative. This is followed by at least 4 drugs, minus the injectable antibiotic, for 18 to 24 months. Two newer drugs, bedaquiline (Sirturo) and Delamanid (Deltyba), are used in combination with other drugs to treat MDR-TB and XDR-TB.

Many people do not adhere to the treatment program and complete the full course of therapy (Box 30.3). Nonadherence is a major factor in the emergence of MDR-TB and treatment failures. *Directly observed therapy* (DOT) involves providing the antitubercular drugs directly to patients and watching as they swallow the drugs. It is the preferred way to ensure adherence for all patients with TB, especially for those at risk

TABLE 30.12 Drug Therapy

Tuberculosis

Drug	Common Side Effects
For Active TB	
ethambutol (Myambutol)	Headache, blurred vision, ocular toxicity (decreased red-green color discrimination)
isoniazid	Liver toxicity, asymptomatic elevation of aminotransferases (ALT, AST) Vomiting, confusion, headache
pyrazinamide	Liver toxicity, joint pain, hyperuricemia
rifampin	Liver toxicity, thrombocytopenia Orange discoloration of bodily fluids (sputum, urine, sweat, tears) Anorexia, nausea, abdominal discomfort
For Drug Resistant TB	
Fluoroquinolones • levofloxacin • moxifloxacin	GI problems, neurologic effects (dizziness, headache), rash
Injectable antibiotics	Hepatitis, GI toxicity
Aminoglycosides	Prolonged QT interval
• amikacin	Ototoxicity, kidney toxicity
• capreomycin (Capastat)	Liver toxicity, nausea
• kanamycin	
bedaquiline (Sirturo)	Joint and muscle pain Nausea, vomiting, liver problems
pretomanid	Peripheral neuropathy Vision problems Nausea, vomiting, liver problems
streptomycin	Ototoxicity, neurotoxicity, kidney toxicity
Other Drugs Used in TB	
rifabutin (Mycobutin) (for TB and co-existing HIV infection)	Liver toxicity, thrombocytopenia, neutropenia Orange discoloration of bodily fluids (sputum, urine, sweat, tears) Nausea, vomiting, anorexia
rifapentine (Priftin) (as an alternate to rifampin)	Like those of rifampin

ALT, Alanine transaminase; *AST,* aspartate aminotransferase.

for nonadherence.[16] DOT is an expensive but essential public health measure. In many areas, the public health nurse administers DOT at a clinic site.

Fixed-dose combination drugs may enhance adherence. Combinations of isoniazid and rifampin and of isoniazid, rifampin, and pyrazinamide are available to simplify therapy. The therapy for people with HIV uses the same medications as outlined in Table 30.13, but in a slightly different schedule. In the intensive phase, HIV patients take isoniazid, ethambutol, pyrazinamide, and a rifamycin for the 1st 2 months, then isoniazid and a rifamycin for the last 4 months.[17]

Teach patients about the adverse effects of drug therapy and when to seek medical care. The major side effect of isoniazid, rifampin, and pyrazinamide is nonviral hepatitis. Baseline liver function tests (LFTs) are done at the start of treatment and monitored closely (e.g., every 2 to 4 weeks), especially if results are abnormal.

Latent tuberculosis infection. In people with LTBI, drug therapy helps prevent a TB infection from developing into active

TABLE 30.13 Drug Therapy

Tuberculosis Treatment Regimens

Intensive TB Medication Phase (2 Months)		Continuation TB Medication Phase (4 or 7 Months)	
Option #1: Preferred Method			
4 drugs: isoniazid, rifampin, pyrazinamide, ethambutol[a]	Daily for 8 weeks (40–56 doses)	2 drugs: isoniazid, rifampin	Daily for 18 weeks (90–126 doses) OR 3 times weekly for 18 weeks (54 doses)[b]
Alternative TB Drug Dosing—Option #1			
4 drugs: isoniazid, rifampin, pyrazinamide, ethambutol[a]	Daily for 2 weeks (14 doses), then 3 times per week for 6 weeks (18 doses)[b]	2 drugs: isoniazid, rifampin	3 times weekly for 18 weeks (54 doses)[b]
Alternative TB Drug Dosing—Option #2			
4 drugs: isoniazid, rifampin, pyrazinamide, ethambutol[a]	3 times weekly for 8 weeks (24 doses)[b]	2 drugs: isoniazid, rifampin	3 times weekly for 18 weeks (54 doses)[b]

[a]Ethambutol may be stopped if drug tests confirm susceptibility to first line drugs

[b]Any patient receiving TB medication less than 7 days/week must receive directly observed therapy (DOT).

Source: Centers for Disease Control and Prevention: Tuberculosis (TB) fact sheet: general considerations for treatment of TB disease. Retrieved from https://www. cdc.gov/tb/publications/factsheets/treatment/treatmenthivnegative.htm.

TB disease. Because a person with LTBI has fewer bacteria, treatment is much easier. Usually only 1 drug is needed. Drug regimens for LTBI are outlined in Table 30.14.

The standard treatment regimen for LTBI is 9 months of daily isoniazid. It is an effective and inexpensive drug that the patient can take orally. This plan is also recommended for patients with HIV and those with fibrotic lesions on chest x-ray. While the 9-month plan is more effective, adherence issues may make a 6-month plan preferable. An alternative 3-month regimen of isoniazid and rifapentine may be used for otherwise healthy patients who we presume are not infected with MDR bacilli. Patients who are resistant to isoniazid may receive 4-month therapy with rifampin. Because of severe liver injury and deaths, the CDC does not recommend the combination of rifampin and pyrazinamide for treatment of LTBI.

Bacille Calmette-Guérin vaccine. Bacille Calmette-Guérin (BCG) vaccine is a live, attenuated strain of *Mycobacterium bovis.* The vaccine is given to infants in parts of the world with a high prevalence of TB. In the United States, it is t rarely used because of the low risk for infection, the vaccine's variable effectiveness against adult pulmonary TB, and potential interference with TST reactivity. The BCG vaccination can result in a false-positive TST. IGRA results are not affected. The BCG

BOX 30.3 ETHICAL/LEGAL DILEMMAS

Patient Adherence

Situation

While working at a health clinic at a homeless shelter, you discover that F.C., a 64-year-old man with tuberculosis (TB), has not been taking his drug therapy. He tells you that it is hard for him to get to the clinic to obtain his medications, much less to keep on a schedule. You are concerned about F.C. and the risk he poses for the other people at the shelter, in the park, and at the meal sites where he often visits.

Ethical/Legal Points for Consideration

- Adherence is a complex issue involving a person's culture, values, and beliefs, perceived risk for disease, access to treatment, availability of resources, and perceived consequences of failure to adhere to treatment.
- State emergency detention laws provide public health officials with the legal authority to take action to apprehend and hold a person with TB who we believe to be a threat to public health.
- The federal government and many states have provisions for quarantine, detention, and treatment of patients with TB who do not adhere to treatment.
- Advocacy for both the patient and the community obliges you to involve other health care team members, such as social services, to aid in obtaining resources or support for the patient to complete a course of treatment.
- With the threats of bioterrorism and the globalization of infectious disease, it seems unlikely that the government's power to detain will change anytime soon.

Discussion Questions

1. How would you begin your initial conversation with F.C. about your concerns?
2. What alternatives of care can we offer to F.C.?
3. Under what circumstances, if any, are HCPs justified in overriding a patient's autonomy or decision making?

Source: Kavanagh MM, Gostin LO, Stephens J: Tuberculosis, human rights, and law reform: addressing the lack of progress in the global tuberculosis response. Retrieved from https://journals.plos.org/plosmedicine/article?id=10.1371/journal.pmed.1003324.

TABLE 30.14 Drug Therapy

LTBI Regimens

Drug	Duration (Months/Weeks)	Interval	Number of Doses (Minimum)
isoniazid and rifapentine (preferred method)	3 months (12 weeks)	Once weekly[a]	12
rifampin	4 months (16 weeks)	Daily	112
isoniazid and rifampin	3 months (12 weeks)	Daily	84
isoniazid	6 months (24 weeks)	Daily	168
isoniazid	9 months (36 weeks)	Daily	252

[a]Use directly observed therapy (DOT).

Source: Centers for Disease Control and Prevention. Tuberculosis (TB): treatment regimens for latent tuberculosis infections (LTBI). Retrieved from https://www.cdc.gov/tb/topic/treatment/ltbi.htm.

vaccine should be considered only for select persons who meet specific criteria (e.g., health care workers who are continually exposed to patients with MDR-TB and when infection control precautions are not successful).

NURSING MANAGEMENT: TUBERCULOSIS

Assessment

Ask the patient about a previous history of TB, chronic illness, or any immunosuppressive disease or medications. Obtain a social and occupational history to determine risk factors for TB transmission. Assess the patient for productive cough, night sweats, fever, weight loss, pleuritic chest pain, and abnormal lung sounds. If the patient has a productive cough, early morning is the best time to collect sputum specimens for an AFB smear.

Clinical Problems

Clinical problems for the patient with TB may include:

- Impaired respiratory function
- Infection
- Deficient knowledge
- Lack of knowledge

Planning

The overall goals are that the patient with TB will (1) have normal lung function, (2) adhere to the treatment plan, (3) take measures to prevent the spread of TB, and (4) have no recurrence.

Implementation

Health Promotion

The goal is to eradicate TB worldwide. Screening programs in known risk groups are valuable in detecting persons with TB. For example, the person with a positive TST should have a chest x-ray to assess for active TB disease. Report people diagnosed with TB to public health authorities for identification and assessment of contacts and risk to the community. Treatment of LTBI reduces the number of TB carriers in the community.

Programs to address the social determinants of TB are needed to decrease TB transmission. Reducing HIV infection, poverty, overcrowded living conditions, malnutrition, smoking, and drug and alcohol use can help minimize TB infection rates. Improving access to health care and education are important.

Acute Care

Patients admitted to the ED or directly to the unit with respiratory symptoms should be assessed for the possibility of TB. Those strongly suspected of having TB should (1) be placed on airborne isolation; (2) receive a medical workup, including chest x-ray, sputum smear and culture; and (3) start appropriate drug therapy. Airborne infection isolation is needed for the patient with pulmonary or laryngeal TB until the patient is not infectious. Patients should be placed in a single-occupancy room with negative pressure and airflow of 6 to 12 exchanges per hour. Everyone entering the room should wear a high-efficiency particulate air (HEPA) or N95 mask.

Teach patients to cover the nose and mouth with paper tissues every time they cough, sneeze, or produce sputum. The tissues should be thrown into a paper bag and disposed of with the trash or flushed down the toilet. Emphasize careful hand washing after handling sputum and soiled tissues. If patients need to be out of the negative-pressure room, they must wear a standard surgical mask to prevent exposure to others. Minimize prolonged visitation to other parts of the hospital.

Identify and screen close contacts of the person with TB. Anyone testing positive for TB infection needs further evaluation and treatment for either LTBI or active TB disease.

Ambulatory Care

Patients who respond clinically are discharged home if their household contacts have already been exposed and the patient is not posing a risk to others. A sputum specimen for AFB smear and culture should be done monthly until 2 consecutive specimen cultures are negative. More frequent AFB smears may be done to assess the early response to treatment and determine infectiousness. Negative cultures are needed to declare the patient not infectious.

Teach the patient how to minimize exposure to close contacts and household members. Homes should be well ventilated, especially the areas where the infected person spends a lot of time. While still infectious, the patient should sleep alone and spend as much time as possible outdoors. Teach them to minimize time in congregate settings and public transportation.

Teach the patient and caregiver about adherence with the treatment plan. Most treatment failures occur because the patient does not take the drug, stops taking it too soon, or takes it irregularly. Strategies to improve adherence include teaching and counseling, reminder systems, incentives or rewards, contracts, and DOT.

Notify the public health department. They are responsible for follow-up on household contacts and assessing the patient for adherence. If adherence is an issue, the public health department may be responsible for DOT (Box 30.4). Most patients are considered adequately treated when drug therapy has been completed, cultures are negative, there is improvement in their condition, and improvement on chest x-ray.

Because about 5% of patients have relapses, teach the patient to recognize the symptoms that occur with recurrent TB. If these symptoms occur, the patient should seek immediate medical attention. Teach the patient about factors that could reactivate TB, such as immunosuppressive therapy, cancer, and prolonged debilitating illness. If the patient has any of these, we must notify the HCP so that the patient can be monitored for TB reactivation. In some situations, it is necessary to put the patient on anti-TB therapy. Because smoking is associated with poor outcomes, encourage patients who smoke to quit. Provide patients with teaching and resources to help them stop smoking.

Evaluation

The expected outcomes are that the patient with TB will have:

- Resolution of the disease
- Normal lung function
- Absence of any complications
- No further transmission of TB

BOX 30.4 EVIDENCE-BASED PRACTICE

Adherence to TB Treatment Program

You are a nurse working in an outpatient health clinic with C.J., a 42-year-old woman diagnosed 2 months ago with active TB. She is on directly observed therapy (DOT). You notice C.J. has started to miss and has been late for her appointments. She tells you it is hard to make her appointments as a new job requires long work hours. She asks if she needs to continue with her visits to get her drugs. She says she is "feeling better" and does not understand what all the fuss over the drugs is about. She adds that she is "perfectly capable of taking my own pills."

Making Clinical Decisions

Best Available Evidence

Guidelines for effective case management of patients with TB include education, home visits, patient reminders, and incentives. TB clinic attendance and treatment completion rates are higher when patients take part in DOT compared to self-administered therapy. When appointments are missed, phone calls, Web-based videos, or home visits will engage patients, resulting in improved attendance and treatment completion.

Clinician Expertise

You are aware that patient-centered care includes being responsive to patients' changing needs. You know that patients may stop attending appointments and taking their drugs when feeling well again. This can lead to treatment failure, the need to restart therapy, and multidrug resistance.

Patient Preferences and Values

C.J. tells you she has a busy job and does not always remember her appointments. She stated that she would like to be responsible for taking her drugs.

Implications for Nursing Practice

1. What information you want to obtain from C.J.?
2. What teaching would you provide to C.J. about taking her own medications?
3. How will you determine if C.J. is adhering to the drug treatment plan?

Source: Pradipta IS, Houtsma D, van Boven JFM, et al.: Interventions to improve medication adherence in tuberculosis patients: A systematic review of randomized controlled studies, *NPJ Prim Care Respir Med* 30:21, 2020.

ATYPICAL MYCOBACTERIA

There are more than 30 acid-fast mycobacteria that cause diseases other than TB. These include lung disease, lymphadenitis, skin or soft tissue disease, and disseminated disease. Atypical mycobacteria are not airborne or transmitted by droplets. They can be found in tap water, soil, bird feces, and house dust.

People who are immunosuppressed (e.g., HIV/AIDS) or have chronic lung disease are most susceptible to infection. Pulmonary symptoms include cough, shortness of breath, weight loss, fatigue, and blood-tinged sputum.

Diagnosis is challenging and differs based on the site of the infection. We cannot tell this type of lung disease from TB either clinically or radiologically. Diagnostic studies done include a chest x-ray and 3 sputum specimens tested for AFB. Treatment may include a prolonged course of antibiotics, depending on the organism cultured and patient's condition.

PULMONARY FUNGAL INFECTIONS

Pulmonary fungal pneumonia is an infectious process in the lungs caused by endemic (native and common) or opportunistic fungi (Table 30.15). *Endemic* fungal pathogens cause infection in healthy people and immunocompromised people in certain areas. For example, *Coccidioides,* which causes coccidioidomycosis, is a fungus found in the soil of dry, low-rainfall areas.[18] It is endemic in many areas of the southwestern United States. *Opportunistic* fungal infections occur in immunocompromised patients (e.g., those receiving chemotherapy, immunosuppressive drugs) and in patients with HIV and cystic fibrosis. Pulmonary fungal infections can be life-threatening.

TABLE 30.15 Fungal Lung Infections

Infection	Organism
Endemic Fungal Infections	
Blastomycosis	*Blastomyces dermatitidis*
Coccidioidomycosis	*Coccidioides immitis*
Histoplasmosis	*Histoplasma capsulatum*
Opportunistic Fungal Infections	
Aspergillosis	*Aspergillus niger, Aspergillus fumigatus*
Candidiasis	*Candida albicans*
Cryptococcosis	*Cryptococcus neoformans*

Pulmonary fungal infections are acquired by inhaling spores. They are not transmitted from person to person. The patient does not have to be placed in isolation. The manifestations are like those of bacterial pneumonia. Skin testing, serology, and biopsy methods help identify the infecting organism.

The choice of antifungal agent is based on the pathogen identified on culture or most likely suspected. Amphotericin B is the standard therapy for treating serious systemic fungal infections. It must be given IV to achieve adequate blood and tissue levels because the GI tract does not absorb it well. Less serious infections can be treated with oral antifungals, such as ketoconazole, fluconazole (Diflucan), voriconazole (Vfend), and itraconazole (Sporanox). We monitor therapy effectiveness with fungal serology titers.

LUNG ABSCESS

Etiology and Pathophysiology

A **lung abscess** is necrosis of lung tissue. It typically results from bacteria aspirated from the oral cavity in patients with periodontal disease. Lung abscess can also result from IV drug use, cancer, pulmonary emboli, TB, and various parasitic and fungal diseases. The abscess usually develops slowly, beginning with an enlarging area of infection that becomes necrotic and eventually forms a cavity filled with purulent material. Abscesses usually contain more than 1 type of microbe, most often anaerobic flora of the mouth and pharynx.

The lung area most often affected due to aspiration is the posterior segment of the upper lobes. The abscess may erode into the bronchial system, causing foul-smelling or sour-tasting sputum. It may grow toward the pleura and cause pleuritic pain. Multiple small abscesses, sometimes referred to as *necrotizing pneumonia*, can occur within the lung.

Clinical Manifestations and Complications

Manifestations usually occur slowly over a period of weeks to months, especially if anaerobic organisms are the cause. Symptoms of abscess caused by aerobic bacteria develop more acutely and resemble bacterial pneumonia. The most common is cough-producing purulent sputum (often dark brown) that is foul smelling and foul tasting. Hemoptysis is common, especially when an abscess ruptures into a bronchus. Other manifestations include fever, chills, weakness, night sweats, pleuritic pain, dyspnea, anorexia, and weight loss.

Assessment reveals decreased breath sounds on auscultation over the involved segment of lung. Bronchial breath sounds may be transmitted to the periphery if the communicating bronchus becomes patent, and the segment begins to drain. Crackles may be present in the later stages as the abscess drains.

The infection can spread through the bloodstream and cause several possible complications. Pulmonary abscess, bronchopleural fistula, bronchiectasis, and empyema from perforation of the abscess into the pleural cavity can occur.[19]

Diagnostic Studies

A chest x-ray is often the only test needed to diagnose a lung abscess. The presence of a single cavitary lesion with an air-fluid level and local infiltrate confirms the diagnosis. CT scanning may be helpful if the abscess is not clear on chest x-ray. If there is drainage via the bronchus, sputum will contain the microorganisms that are present in the abscess. However, expectorated sputum samples are often contaminated with oral flora, making it hard to determine the responsible organism(s).

Bronchoscopy may be used to (1) avoid oropharyngeal contamination, (2) collect a specimen if drainage is delayed, or (3) assess for underlying cancer. Pleural fluid and blood cultures may be used to identify the offending organisms. Although nonspecific, an elevated neutrophil count may indicate an infection. Necrotic pulmonary lesions also can be caused by lung infarction, pulmonary embolism, and sarcoidosis.

Interprofessional and Nursing Care

Monitor the patient's vital signs, LOC, and respiratory rate and rhythm. Note any signs and symptoms of respiratory distress. Observe for any signs of hypoxemia. Apply O_2 as needed.

Teach the patient how to cough effectively. Chest physiotherapy and postural drainage are not recommended because they may promote movement of microorganisms into adjacent bronchi and other lobes of the lungs, extending infection. Rest, optimal nutrition, and adequate fluid intake promote recovery. If dentition is poor or dental hygiene is not adequate, encourage the patient to obtain dental care. Collaborate with the social worker to evaluate options for dental care if the patient has limited resources.

IV antibiotic therapy should be started immediately. Clindamycin is first-line therapy for its effectiveness against *Staphylococcus* and anaerobic organisms. IV antibiotics are switched to oral antibiotics once the patient shows clinical and chest x-ray signs of improvement.

Because of the need for prolonged antibiotic therapy, teach the patient to take antibiotics as directed for the entire prescribed period (see Table 15.9). Sometimes the patient must return periodically during the course of antibiotic therapy for repeat cultures and sensitivity tests to ensure that the infecting organism is not becoming resistant to the antibiotic. When antibiotic therapy is complete, the patient is re-evaluated.

If the patient does not adequately respond to antibiotic treatment, percutaneous drainage of the abscess may be done. A small catheter, guided by CT or ultrasound, may be placed to drain the abscess. Surgery is sometimes done when reinfection of a large cavitary lesion occurs, when an empyema develops, or to establish a diagnosis when there is evidence of an underlying problem, such as cancer. The usual procedure in such cases is a lobectomy. A pneumonectomy may be needed for multiple abscesses.

RESTRICTIVE RESPIRATORY DISORDERS

Disorders that impair the ability of the chest wall and diaphragm to move with respiration are called *restrictive respiratory disorders*. There are 2 categories: *extrapulmonary conditions*, in which the lung tissue is normal, and *intrapulmonary conditions*, in which the primary cause is the lung or pleura. Examples of extrapulmonary and intrapulmonary conditions are listed in Table 30.16.

The hallmark characteristic of a restrictive lung disorder is a reduced total lung capacity (TLC). The hallmark characteristic of an obstructive disorder is reduced forced expiratory volume (FEV_1). Mixed obstructive and restrictive disorders sometimes occur together. For example, a patient may have both asthma

TABLE 30.16 Common Causes of Restrictive Lung Disease

Intrapulmonary Causes

Parenchymal Disorders
- Acute respiratory distress syndrome (ARDS)
- Atelectasis
- Chronic empyema
- Interstitial lung diseases
- Pneumonia

Pleural Disorders
- Pleural effusion
- Pleurisy (pleuritis)
- Pneumothorax

Extrapulmonary Causes

Central Nervous System
- Head injury, central nervous system lesion (e.g., tumor, stroke)
- Opioid and barbiturate overdose

Chest Wall
- Kyphoscoliosis
- Obesity-hypoventilation syndrome

Neuromuscular System
- Amyotrophic lateral sclerosis
- Guillain-Barré syndrome
- Muscular dystrophy
- Myasthenia gravis

(an obstructive problem) and pulmonary fibrosis (a restrictive problem). Pulmonary function tests are the best way to distinguish between restrictive and obstructive respiratory disorders.

ATELECTASIS

Atelectasis is a lung condition characterized by collapsed, airless alveoli. There may be decreased or absent breath sounds and dullness to percussion over the affected area. The most common cause is obstruction of the small airways with secretions. This is common in patients on bedrest and in almost all postoperative surgery patients. Normally, the pores of Kohn provide collateral passage of air from one alveolus to another. Deep inspiration opens the pores effectively. For this reason, deep-breathing exercises, coughing, incentive spirometry, and early mobility are important to prevent atelectasis and treat the patient at risk (see Chapter 20).

PLEURISY

Pleurisy (pleuritis) is an inflammation of the pleura. It can be caused by infectious diseases, cancer, autoimmune disorders, chest trauma, GI disease, and some drugs. The inflammation usually subsides once we treat the cause. The pain of pleurisy is typically abrupt, sharp in onset, and worse with inspiration. The patient's breathing is short, shallow, and rapid to avoid unnecessary pleura and chest wall movement. A pleural friction rub may occur. This is the sound heard over areas where inflamed visceral pleura and parietal pleura rub together during inspiration. This sound, like a squeaking door, is usually loudest at peak inspiration.

Treatment is directed at the underlying cause and providing pain relief. Teach the patient to splint the rib cage when coughing. If the pain is severe, intercostal nerve blocks may be considered.

PLEURAL EFFUSION

A **pleural effusion** is an abnormal collection of fluid in the pleural space. It is not a disease, but a sign of another condition. A balance among hydrostatic pressure, oncotic pressure, and capillary membrane permeability governs movement of fluid in and out of the pleural space. Fluid accumulation can be due to increased pulmonary capillary pressure, decreased oncotic pressure, increased pleural membrane permeability, or obstruction of lymphatic flow.

Types of Pleural Effusions

We classify pleural effusions as transudative or exudative depending on the protein content. A *transudate effusion* occurs mainly in non-inflammatory conditions. It is an accumulation of protein-poor, cell-poor fluid. The fluid is usually clear, pale yellow. Causes include (1) increased hydrostatic pressure found in HF or (2) decreased oncotic pressure from hypoalbuminemia (e.g., with chronic liver or renal disease). An *exudative effusion* results from increased capillary permeability due to an inflammatory reaction. The fluid is rich in protein. They most often occur with an infection or cancer (called a malignant effusion).

An **empyema** is a collection of purulent fluid in the pleural space. Common causes include pneumonia, TB, lung abscess, and infected surgical chest wounds.

Clinical Manifestations

Common manifestations are dyspnea, cough, and occasional sharp, non-radiating chest pain that may be worse on inhalation. Breath sounds may be decreased over the affected area. A chest x-ray may show decreased chest movement on the affected side. A chest x-ray and CT reveal the volume and location of the effusion. Additional manifestations seen with empyema include fever, night sweats, cough, and weight loss.

Interprofessional and Nursing Care

The management of pleural effusions is to treat the underlying cause. For example, adequate treatment of HF with diuretics and sodium restriction may result in a decreased incidence of pleural effusion. The treatment of malignant effusions is more difficult. These effusions often re-occur and re-accumulate quickly after thoracentesis.

Treatment options for an empyema include antibiotic therapy (to eradicate the causative organism), percutaneous drainage, chest tube insertion, and intrapleural fibrinolytic therapy (instilled through the chest tube to dissolve fibrous adhesions). Some patients may need surgery. Surgical options include drainage, decortication, or an open window thoracostomy.

Chemical pleurodesis is done to obliterate the pleural space and prevent re-accumulation of effusion fluid. This procedure first requires chest tube drainage of the effusion. Once the fluid is drained, a chemical slurry is instilled into the pleural space. Talc is the most effective agent used. Other agents we use include doxycycline and bleomycin. The chest tube is clamped for 8 hours while the patient is turned in different positions. This allows the chemical to contact the entire pleural space. After 8 hours, the chest tube is unclamped and attached to a drainage unit. Chest tubes are left in place until fluid drainage is less than 150 mL/day and no air leaks are noted. Fever and chest pain are common side effects after pleurodesis.

We provide supportive nursing care according to the patient's needs. This may include O_2 therapy to treat hypoxemia and analgesics to relieve chest pain. Implement measures to manage fever (see Table 12.5). Hydration, nutrition support, and positioning are part of the care plan. Work with the respiratory therapist to monitor the patient's condition and provide chest physiotherapy. Care of the patient with a chest tube is described in Chapter 28.

INTERSTITIAL LUNG DISEASES

Interstitial lung disease (ILD), or *diffuse parenchymal lung disease,* refers to more than 200 lung disorders in which the tissue between the air sacs of the lungs (the interstitium) is affected by inflammation or scarring (fibrosis).[20] Most ILDs are rare.

Many times, the cause of an ILD is unknown. Known causes are inhalation of occupational and environmental toxins, certain drugs, radiation therapy, connective tissue disorders, infection, and cancer. Treatment is aimed at reducing exposure to the causative agent or treating the underlying disease process. While scarring is not reversible, treatment with corticosteroids and immunosuppressant drugs can minimize progression. A lung transplant may be an option for some patients.

IDIOPATHIC PULMONARY FIBROSIS

Idiopathic pulmonary fibrosis (IPF) is a progressive disorder characterized by chronic inflammation and formation of scar tissue in the connective tissue.[21] Risk factors include smoking and exposure to wood and metal dust. IPF affects more men. It typically first appears between the ages of 50 and 70 years. We do not know the cause of IPF.

Manifestations include exertional dyspnea, a dry, nonproductive cough, clubbing of the fingers, and inspiratory crackles. Fatigue, weakness, anorexia, and weight loss may occur as the disease progresses. Chest x-ray findings are generally nonspecific. Pulmonary function tests may be abnormal, with reduced vital capacity and impaired gas exchange. Open lung biopsy using video-assisted thoracic surgery (VATS) often helps to confirm the pathology. It is the gold standard for diagnosis.

The course is variable, and the prognosis is poor. The median survival rate is 2.5 to 3.5 years after diagnosis. There is no known cure for IPF. Many people diagnosed with IPF are first treated with a corticosteroid, sometimes in combination with other drugs that suppress the immune system (e.g., methotrexate, cyclosporine). Kinase inhibitor drugs, which block multiple pathways that are involved with scarring, include nintedanib (Ofev) and pirfenidone (Esbriet).

O_2 therapy and pulmonary rehabilitation should be prescribed for all patients. A lung transplant may be an option for those who meet criteria.

SARCOIDOSIS

Sarcoidosis is a chronic, multisystem granulomatous disease of unknown cause that mainly affects the lungs. The disease may also involve the skin, eyes, liver, kidney, heart, and lymph nodes. Signs and symptoms vary depending on what organs are affected. Pulmonary symptoms include dyspnea, cough, and chest pain. Many patients do not have symptoms.

Staging and treatment decisions are based on chest x-ray, pulmonary function tests, and severity of symptoms. Some patients have a spontaneous remission. Treatment is aimed at suppressing the inflammatory response. Patients are followed every 3 to 6 months with pulmonary function tests, chest x-ray, and CT scan to monitor disease progression.

CHEST TRAUMA AND THORACIC INJURIES

Traumatic injuries to the chest contribute to many deaths. Chest injuries range from simple rib fractures to cardiorespiratory arrest. We classify the primary mechanisms of injury as either blunt trauma or penetrating trauma.

Blunt trauma occurs when the chest strikes or is struck by an object. The impact can cause shearing and compression of chest structures. The external injury may appear minor, but internally, organs may be severely damaged. Rib and sternal fractures can easily tear lung tissue. In a high-velocity impact, shearing forces can result in tearing of the aorta. Compression of the chest may result in heart or lung contusion, crush injury, and organ rupture.

In *penetrating trauma,* a foreign object impales or passes through the body tissues, creating an open wound. Examples include knife wounds, gunshot wounds, and injuries with other sharp objects. Emergency care of the patient with a chest injury is outlined in Table 30.17. The most common chest emergencies and their management are described in Table 30.18.

FRACTURED RIBS

Rib fractures are the most common type of chest injury from blunt trauma. Ribs 5 through 9 are most often fractured because they are the least protected by chest muscles. A splintered or displaced fractured rib can damage the pleura, lungs, heart, and other internal organs.

Manifestations include pain at the site of injury, especially during inspiration and with coughing. The patient splints the affected area. They take shallow breaths to try to decrease the discomfort. Atelectasis and pneumonia may develop because of pain, decreased chest wall movement, and retained secretions.

The goal of treatment is to decrease pain so that the patient can breathe adequately and clear secretions. Strapping the chest with tape or using a thoracic binder is not recommended. These limit chest expansion and predispose the person to atelectasis and hypoxemia. NSAIDs, opioids, and thoracic nerve blocks can be used to reduce pain and assist with deep breathing and coughing. Surgical plating of fractured ribs may be done for those patients with extreme chest wall deformity. Teaching should emphasize deep breathing, coughing, incentive spirometry, appropriate use of pain medications, and when appropriate, early mobility.

FLAIL CHEST

Flail chest results from the fracture of 3 or more consecutive ribs, in 2 or more separate places, causing an unstable segment (Fig. 30.4). It also can be caused by fracture of the sternum and several consecutive ribs. The resulting chest wall instability causes paradoxical movement during breathing. During inspiration, the affected part is sucked in, and during expiration, it bulges out. In other words, the affected (flail) area moves in the opposite direction with respect to the intact part of the chest. This paradoxical chest movement may prevent adequate ventilation and increase the work of breathing.

A flail chest is usually apparent on assessment. The patient has rapid, shallow respirations and tachycardia. Movement of the thorax is asymmetric and uncoordinated. The patient may ventilate poorly and try to splint the chest to assist with breathing. Abnormal chest cavity movement, crepitus near the rib fractures, and chest x-ray all assist in the diagnosis.

Initial therapy consists of ensuring adequate ventilation and supplemental O_2 therapy. The goal is to promote lung expansion and ensure adequate oxygenation. The underlying injured

TABLE 30.17 EMERGENCY MANAGEMENT

Chest Trauma

Etiology	Assessment Findings	Interventions
Blunt • Assault with blunt object • Crush injury • Explosion • Fall • Motor vehicle collision • Pedestrian accident • Sports injury **Penetrating** • Arrow • Gunshot • Knife • Stick	**Respiratory** • Audible air escaping from chest wound • ↓ Breath sounds on side of injury • Cough with or without hemoptysis • Cyanosis of mouth, face, nail beds, mucous membranes • Dyspnea, respiratory distress • Frothy secretions • ↓ O_2 saturation • Tracheal deviation **Cardiovascular** • Asymmetric BP values in arms • ↓ BP • Chest pain • Distended neck veins • Dysrhythmias • Muffled heart sounds • Narrowed pulse pressure • Rapid, thready pulse **Surface Findings** • Abrasions • Asymmetric chest movement • Bruising • Contusions • Lacerations • Open chest wound • Subcutaneous emphysema	**Initial** • If unresponsive, immediately assess circulation, airway, and breathing. • If responsive, monitor airway, breathing, and circulation. • Apply high-flow O_2 to keep SpO_2 >90%. • Establish IV access with 2 large-bore catheters. Begin IV fluid resuscitation as appropriate. • Remove clothing to assess injury. • Cover sucking chest wound with nonporous dressing taped on 3 sides (vent dressing). • Stabilize impaled objects with bulky dressings. *Do not remove object.* • Assess for life-threatening injuries and treat appropriately. • Place patient in a semi-Fowler's position if breathing is easier *after* cervical spine injury has been ruled out. • Give small amounts of analgesia as needed for pain and to help with breathing. • Prepare for emergency needle decompression if tension pneumothorax or cardiac tamponade present. **Ongoing Monitoring** • Monitor LOC, vital signs, O_2 saturation, cardiac rhythm, respiratory rate and rhythm, urine output. • Anticipate intubation for respiratory distress. • Release vent dressing if tension pneumothorax develops after sucking chest wound is covered.

TABLE 30.18 EMERGENCY MANAGEMENT

Chest Injuries

Injury and Description	Manifestations	Intervention
Cardiac Tamponade Blood rapidly collects in pericardial sac, compresses myocardium because pericardium does not stretch, and prevents ventricles from filling.	Muffled, distant heart sounds, hypotension, neck vein distention, ↑ central venous pressure	Medical emergency. Pericardiocentesis with surgical repair as appropriate.
Flail Chest Fracture of 2 or more adjacent ribs in 2 or more places with loss of chest wall stability (see Fig. 30.4).	Paradoxical movement of chest wall, respiratory distress. May be associated hemothorax, pneumothorax, pulmonary contusion	O_2 as needed to maintain O_2 saturation, analgesia. Positive pressure mechanical ventilation for acute respiratory distress; will also help stabilize flail segment. Treat associated injuries. Possible surgical fixation for severe damage to chest wall.
Hemothorax Blood in the pleural space, may or may not occur in conjunction with pneumothorax.	Dyspnea, decreased or absent breath sounds, dullness to percussion, ↓ Hgb, shock (depending on blood volume lost)	Chest tube insertion with chest drainage system. Autotransfusion of collected blood, treatment of hypovolemia as needed with IV fluid, packed red blood cells.
Pneumothorax Air in pleural space (see Fig. 30.5).	Dyspnea, ↓ movement of involved chest wall, decreased or absent breath sounds on the affected side, hyperresonance to percussion	Chest tube insertion with chest drainage system.
Tension Pneumothorax Air in pleural space that does not escape. Increased air in the pleural space shifts organs and increases intrathoracic pressure (see Fig. 30.6).	Cyanosis, air hunger, extreme agitation, subcutaneous emphysema, neck vein distention, hyperresonance to percussion, tracheal deviation away from affected side (late sign)	Medical emergency: needle decompression followed by chest tube insertion with chest drainage system.

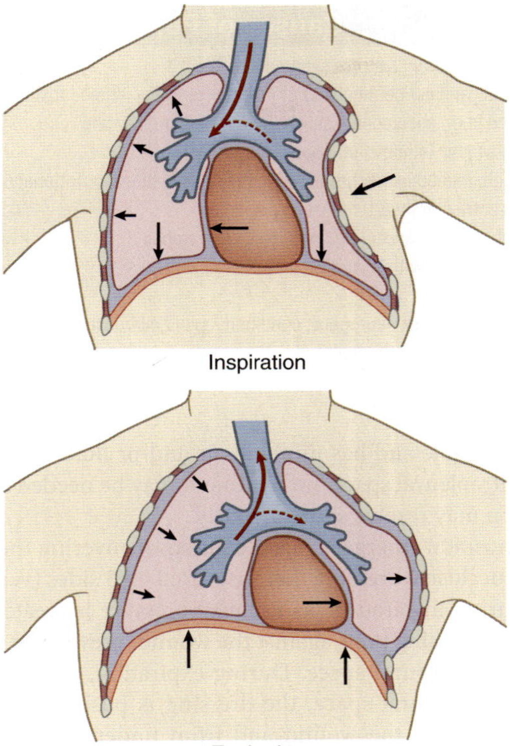

Fig. 30.4 Flail chest causes paradoxical respiration. On inspiration, the flail section moves inward with mediastinal shift to the uninjured side. On expiration, the flail section bulges outward with mediastinal shift to the injured side.

lung may be contused, worsening hypoxemia. Analgesia can help promote adequate respiration. Some patients may need mechanical ventilation. In cases of extreme deformity, surgical fixation of the flail segment may be done. The lung parenchyma and fractured ribs heal with time. Some patients continue to have intercostal pain several weeks after the flail chest has resolved.

PNEUMOTHORAX

A **pneumothorax** is caused by air entering the pleural cavity. Normally, negative (subatmospheric) pressure exists between the visceral pleura (surrounding the lung) and parietal pleura (lining the chest cavity), known as the *pleural space.* The pleural space has a few milliliters of lubricating fluid to reduce friction when the tissues move. When the volume of air that enters this normally subatmospheric space increases, lung volume decreases. As a result, the change to positive pressure causes a partial or complete lung collapse.

We can describe a pneumothorax as *open* (air entering through an opening in the chest wall) or *closed* (no external wound). Penetrating trauma allows air to enter the pleural space through an opening in the chest wall (Fig. 30.5). A penetrating chest wound may be called a *sucking chest wound,* since air enters the pleural space through the chest wall during inspiration. A pneumothorax should be suspected after any trauma to the chest wall.

If a pneumothorax is small, mild tachycardia and dyspnea may be the only manifestations. With a larger pneumothorax,

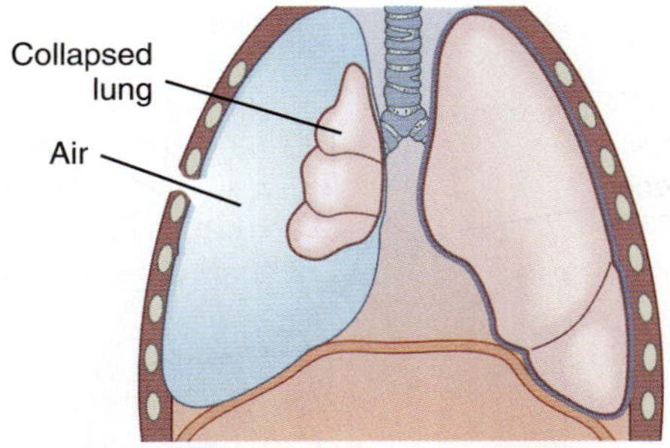

Fig. 30.5 Open pneumothorax. Collapse of lung results from disruption of chest wall and outside air entering the thoracic cavity.

respiratory distress may be present, including short, shallow, rapid respirations, dyspnea, and low O_2 saturation. On auscultation, breath sounds are absent over the affected area. A chest x-ray will show air or fluid in the pleural space and reduced lung volume.

Types of Pneumothoraxes

Spontaneous Pneumothorax

A spontaneous pneumothorax typically occurs due to the rupture of small blebs (air-filled sacs) on the surface of the lung. These blebs can occur in healthy, young people or from lung disease, such as COPD, asthma, cystic fibrosis, and pneumonia. Smoking increases the risk for bleb formation. Other risk factors include being tall and thin, male gender, family history, and previous spontaneous pneumothorax.

Iatrogenic Pneumothorax

Iatrogenic pneumothorax can occur due to laceration or puncture of the lung during medical procedures. For example, transthoracic needle aspiration, subclavian catheter insertion, pleural biopsy, and transbronchial lung biopsy all have the potential to injure the lung. Barotrauma from excessive ventilatory pressure during manual or mechanical ventilation can rupture alveoli, creating a pneumothorax. Esophageal procedures may result in a pneumothorax. For example, tearing of the esophageal wall during insertion of a gastric tube can allow air from the esophagus to enter the mediastinum and pleural space.

Tension Pneumothorax

Tension pneumothorax occurs when air enters the pleural space but cannot escape. The continued accumulation of air in the pleural space causes increasingly elevated intrapleural pressures. This results in compression of the lung on the affected side and pressure on the heart and great vessels, pushing them away from the affected side (Fig. 30.6). The mediastinum shifts toward the unaffected side, compressing the "good" lung, which further compromises oxygenation and ventilation. As the pressure increases, venous return decreases and cardiac output falls.

Tension pneumothorax may result from either an open or a closed pneumothorax. In an open chest wound, a flap may act as a one-way valve. Thus, air can enter on inspiration but cannot escape. Tension pneumothorax can occur with mechanical ventilation and resuscitative efforts. It can also occur if chest tubes are clamped or become blocked in a patient with a

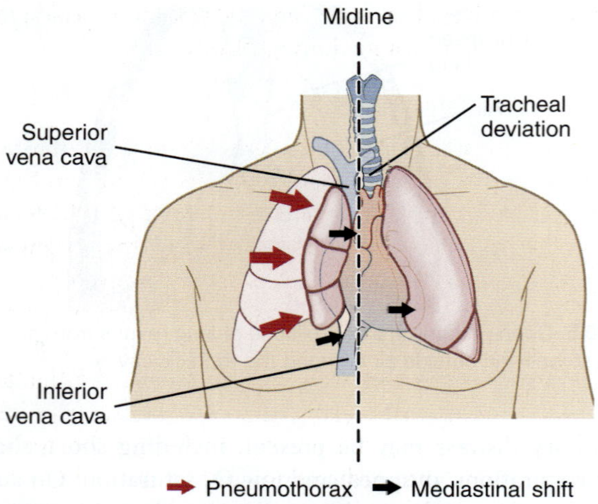

Fig. 30.6 Tension pneumothorax. As pleural pressure on the affected side increases, mediastinal displacement occurs, causing respiratory and cardiovascular compromise. Tracheal deviation is an external (but late) sign of mediastinal shift.

pneumothorax. Unclamping the tube or relieving the obstruction may correct this situation.

Tension pneumothorax is a medical emergency. It affects both the respiratory and cardiovascular systems. Manifestations include severe dyspnea, marked tachycardia, neck vein distention, and profuse diaphoresis. Decreased or absent breath sounds will be present on the affected side. Tracheal deviation is a very late sign. If the problem is not quickly identified and tension in the pleural space is not relieved (needle compression), the patient is likely to die from inadequate cardiac output and severe hypoxemia.

Hemothorax

Hemothorax is an accumulation of blood in the pleural space from injury to the chest wall, diaphragm, lung, blood vessels, or mediastinum. When it occurs with pneumothorax, it is called a *hemopneumothorax*. The patient with a traumatic hemothorax needs immediate insertion of a chest tube for evacuation of the blood. Sometimes, blood drained from a chest tube can be reinfused back into the patient (autotransfusion) after the injury. However, this requires special equipment and set-up prior to chest tube insertion.

Chylothorax

Chylothorax is the presence of lymphatic fluid in the pleural space. The thoracic duct is disrupted either traumatically or from cancer, allowing lymphatic fluid to fill the pleural space. This milky white fluid is high in lipids. Normal lymphatic flow through the thoracic duct is 1500 to 2500 mL/day. This amount can increase up to 10-fold after ingesting fats. Some cases heal with conservative treatment (chest drainage, bowel rest, diet). Octreotide may reduce the flow of lymphatic fluid. Surgery (thoracic duct ligation) and pleurodesis (the artificial production of adhesions between the parietal and visceral pleura) are options for some persons.

Interprofessional Care

Treatment of a pneumothorax depends on its severity, underlying cause, and hemodynamic stability of the patient. If the patient is stable and has minimal air and/or fluid accumulated in the intrapleural space, no treatment may be needed since the condition may resolve spontaneously.

Pre-hospital emergency care consists of covering the wound with an occlusive dressing that is secured on 3 sides (vent dressing). During inspiration, as negative pressure is created in the chest, the dressing pulls against the wound, preventing air from entering the pleural space. During expiration, as the pressure rises in the pleural space, the dressing is pushed out and air escapes through the wound and from under the dressing. If the object that caused the open chest wound is still in place, pre-hospital care providers will not remove it. They will stabilize the impaled object with a bulky dressing and arrange transport to the nearest medical facility.

In acute care, the most definitive and common treatment of pneumothorax and hemothorax is to insert a chest tube and connect it to water-seal drainage. Repeated spontaneous pneumothorax may need surgical treatment with a partial pleurectomy, stapling, or pleurodesis to promote adherence of the pleurae to one another. Tension pneumothorax is a medical emergency, requiring urgent needle decompression followed by chest tube insertion to water-seal drainage. Care of the patient with chest tubes is described in Chapter 28.

TABLE 30.19 Causes of Pulmonary Edema

- Acute respiratory distress syndrome (ARDS)
- Altered capillary permeability of lungs: aspiration, inhaled toxins, inflammation (e.g., pneumonia), severe hypoxia, near-drowning
- Anaphylactic (allergic) reaction
- Hypoalbuminemia: nephrotic syndrome, liver disease, nutritional disorders
- Left ventricular (heart) failure
- Lymph system cancer (e.g., non-Hodgkin lymphoma)
- Overhydration with IV fluids
- O_2 toxicity
- Unknown causes: neurogenic condition, opioid overdose, reexpansion pulmonary edema, high altitude

VASCULAR LUNG DISORDERS

PULMONARY EDEMA

Pulmonary edema is an abnormal accumulation of fluid in the alveoli and interstitial spaces of the lungs. It is a complication of various heart and lung problems (Table 30.19). In severe cases, pulmonary edema can be a life-threatening medical emergency. The most common cause of pulmonary edema is left-sided HF.

The patient often presents with varying degrees of dyspnea, diaphoresis, and wheezing, depending upon the severity of pulmonary edema and underlying medical condition. A 3rd heart sound may be present. Sputum may be blood-tinged and frothy sputum. A chest x-ray is the best option for confirming the diagnosis.

Treatment is often directed towards finding the underlying cause of the edema and reducing the amount of fluid in the lungs. Goals include simultaneously improving oxygenation, ventilation, and cardiac output.

Place the patient in a semi or high Fowler's position. Administer O_2 to keep SpO_2 greater than 90%. This may require low or high flow O_2 delivery devices, non-invasive ventilation (e.g., Bi-PAP), or mechanical ventilation. Preload reduction may be accomplished by giving IV diuretics (e.g., furosemide) or nitroglycerine. Small amounts of IV morphine can reduce afterload. Cardiac output can be supported with IV Dobutamine. Monitor the patient's vital signs, work of breathing, breath sounds, urinary output, electrolyte balance, and response to treatment.

PULMONARY EMBOLISM

Etiology and Pathophysiology

Pulmonary embolism (PE) is the blockage of 1 or more pulmonary arteries by a thrombus, fat or air embolus, or tumor tissue. A PE consists of material that gains access to the venous system and then to the pulmonary circulation. The PE travels with blood flow through ever-smaller blood vessels until it lodges and obstructs perfusion of the alveoli. The lower lobes are most often affected.

Most PEs arise from deep vein thrombosis (DVT) in the deep veins of the legs. *Venous thromboembolism (VTE)* is the preferred term to describe the spectrum from DVT to PE. Other sites of origin of PE include femoral or iliac veins, right side of the heart (atrial fibrillation), and pelvic veins (especially after surgery or childbirth). Upper extremity DVT sometimes occurs in the presence of central venous catheters or arterial lines. These cases may resolve with removal of the catheter. A *saddle embolus* refers to a large thrombus lodged at an arterial bifurcation (Fig. 30.7).

Less common causes include fat emboli (from fractured long bones), air emboli (from improperly administered IV therapy), bacterial vegetation on heart valves, amniotic fluid, and cancer.[22] Risk factors for PE include immobility or reduced mobility, surgery within the last 3 months (especially pelvic and lower extremity surgery), history of VTE, cancer, obesity, oral contraceptives, hormone therapy, smoking, prolonged air travel, HF, pregnancy, and clotting disorders.

Clinical Manifestations

The signs and symptoms of PE are varied and nonspecific, making diagnosis difficult. Manifestations depend on the type, size, and extent of emboli. Small emboli may go undetected or cause vague, transient symptoms. Symptoms may begin slowly or appear suddenly. Dyspnea is the most common presenting symptom in patients with PE. Mild to moderate hypoxemia may occur. Other manifestations include tachypnea, cough, chest pain, hemoptysis, crackles, wheezing, fever, accentuation of pulmonic heart sound, tachycardia, and syncope. Massive PE may cause a sudden change in mental status, hypotension, feelings of impending doom, and cardiorespiratory arrest.

Complications

About 10% of patients with massive PE die within the 1st hour. Identifying the patient "at-risk" for VTE is essential. Treatment with anticoagulants significantly reduces mortality.

Complications include pulmonary infarction and pulmonary hypertension. *Pulmonary infarction* (death of lung tissue) is most likely when there is (1) occlusion of a large or medium-sized pulmonary vessel (more than 2 mm in diameter), (2) insufficient collateral blood flow from the bronchial circulation, or (3) pre-existing lung disease. Infarction results in alveolar necrosis and hemorrhage. Sometimes the necrotic tissue becomes infected, and an abscess may develop. Pleural effusions are common.

Pulmonary hypertension results from hypoxemia or from involvement of a large surface area of the pulmonary bed. As a single event, a PE rarely causes pulmonary hypertension. Recurrent PEs or PEs that do not completely resolve gradually reduce capillary bed blood flow over time. This may eventually cause *chronic thromboembolic pulmonary hypertension*.[23] Dilation and hypertrophy of the right ventricle occurs. Depending on the severity of pulmonary hypertension and how

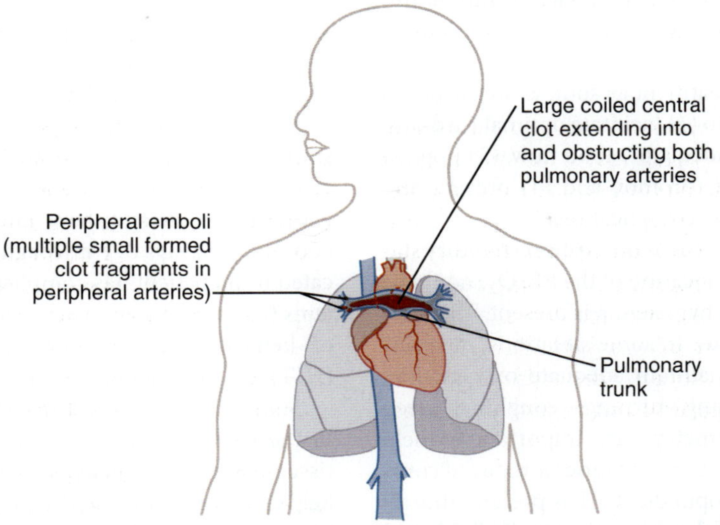

Fig. 30.7 Saddle pulmonary embolus. This embolus straddles the bifurcation of a major artery, with the clot extending down into both right and left branches of the major vessel.

quickly it develops, outcomes can vary. Some patients dying within months while and others live for decades.

Diagnostic Studies

ABG analysis is important but does not diagnose a PE. The PaO_2 may be low because of inadequate oxygenation from occluded pulmonary vessels preventing matching of perfusion to ventilation. The pH is often normal unless respiratory alkalosis develops because of prolonged hyperventilation or to compensate for lactic acidosis caused by shock.

Abnormal findings may be seen on a chest x-ray (atelectasis, pleural effusion) and ECG (nonspecific ST segment and T wave changes), but they are not diagnostic for PE. Serum troponin levels and b-type natriuretic peptide (BNP) levels are often high.

D-dimer is a laboratory test that measures the amount of cross-linked fibrin fragments. These fragments are the result of clot degradation. The disadvantage of D-dimer testing is that it is neither specific (many other conditions cause increases) nor sensitive, because up to 50% of patients with a small PE have normal results. Patients with suspected PE and an elevated D-dimer level but normal venous ultrasound may need a spiral CT or lung scan.

A *spiral (helical) CT scan* (CT angiography or CTA) is the most common test to diagnose PE. An IV injection of contrast media is needed to view the pulmonary blood vessels. The scanner continuously rotates around the patient while obtaining views (slices) of the pulmonary vasculature. This allows us to see all anatomic regions of the lungs. Computer reconstruction gives a 3-D picture and assists in seeing PEs.

If a patient cannot have contrast media, a ventilation-perfusion (V/Q) scan is done. The V/Q scan has 2 parts. It is most accurate when both are done:

1. *Perfusion scanning* involves IV injection of a radioisotope. A scanning device images the pulmonary circulation.
2. *Ventilation scanning* involves inhalation of a radioactive gas, such as xenon. Scanning reflects the distribution of gas through the lung. The ventilation portion requires the patient's cooperation. It may not be possible to perform in the critically ill patient, especially if the patient is intubated.

Interprofessional Care

To reduce mortality, we start treatment as soon as we suspect a PE (Table 30.20). The goals are to (1) facilitate optimal cardiorespiratory function, (2) ensure adequate blood flow, (3) prevent further growth or extension of thrombi, and (4) prevent and avoid further recurrence and any complications.

Immediate assessment should focus on cardiorespiratory status, which varies by the size and location of the PE. O_2 should be given by mask or cannula when hypoxemia is present. The FIO_2 is titrated based on ABG analysis. In some situations, mechanical ventilation is needed to maintain adequate oxygenation. Respiratory measures—including turning, coughing, deep breathing, and incentive spirometry—are important to help prevent atelectasis. Pain from pleural irritation or reduced coronary blood flow is treated with opioids. If HF is present, diuretics are used. If manifestations of shock are present, IV fluids and vasopressor agents are given as needed to support circulation.

TABLE 30.20 Interprofessional Care

Acute Pulmonary Embolism

Diagnostic Assessment

- History and physical assessment
- Chest x-ray
- Continuous ECG monitoring
- Pulse oximetry, ABGs
- Spiral (helical) CT scan (gold standard for ventilated or non-ventilated patient); if unavailable, computed tomography angiography (CTA) or pulmonary angiography
- Ventilation-perfusion (V/Q) lung scan (best for non-ventilated patient)
- Potentially useful lab tests (but not diagnostic); D-dimer level, troponin level, b-natriuretic peptide level
- Ultrasound of upper or lower extremities (based on likely source)

Management

- Supplemental O_2, intubation if needed
- Monitor hemoglobin, assess patient for bleeding
- Monitor activated partial thromboplastin time and international normalized ratio levels
- Balance activity and rest
- Inferior vena cava filter
- Pulmonary embolectomy in life-threatening situation

Drug Therapy

- Unfractionated heparin IV
- Low-molecular-weight heparin (e.g., enoxaparin [Lovenox])
- Factor Xa Inhibitors (e.g., apixaban [Eliquis], edoxaban)
- Thrombin Inhibitors (e.g., dabigatran [Pradaxa])
- Warfarin (Coumadin) for long-term therapy
- Fibrinolytics (e.g., activase) for life-threatening situation
- Analgesia

Drug Therapy

Immediate anticoagulation is required for patients with PE. Drug therapy for patients with acute PE occurs in 3 phases: initial (for the first 7 days), longer (up to 6 weeks), and extended (6 months and beyond). Subcutaneous low-molecular-weight heparin (LMWH) (e.g., enoxaparin, fragmin, fondaparinux) is the recommended treatment for patients with acute PE. LMWH is safer and more effective than unfractionated heparin. Monitoring the aPTT is not necessary or useful with LMWH. Unfractionated IV heparin is effective but hard to titrate to therapeutic levels.

Warfarin (Coumadin), an oral anticoagulant, should be started at the time of diagnosis. Warfarin should be given for at least 3 to 6 months and then reevaluated. Alternatives to warfarin include apixaban (Eliquis), dabigatran (Pradaxa), and edoxaban (Savaysa). Anticoagulant therapy may be contraindicated if the patient has complicating factors, such as liver problems (causing changes in the clotting), overt bleeding, a history of hemorrhagic stroke, heparin-induced thrombocytopenia (HIT), or other blood dyscrasias.

Some HCPs use direct thrombin inhibitors (see Table 41.10) in the treatment of PE. Similarly, fibrinolytic agents, such as tissue plasminogen activator (tPA) or alteplase (Activase), may help dissolve the PE and the source of the thrombus in the pelvis or deep leg veins, thus, decreasing the risk for recurrent emboli. Fibrinolytic therapy is discussed in Chapter 37.

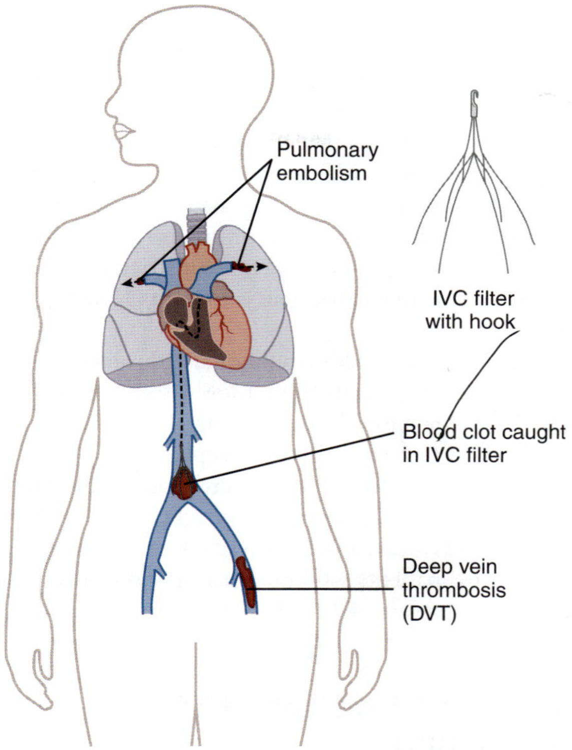

Fig. 30.8 Inferior vena cava *(IVC)* filter. This small device is placed in the inferior vena cava. It helps trap blood clots that may travel from the lower extremities up towards the brain and heart.

Surgical Therapy

Hemodynamically unstable patients with massive PE in whom thrombolytic therapy is contraindicated may be candidates for pulmonary embolectomy. Embolectomy, the removal of emboli, can be achieved through a diagnostic imaging (vascular catheter) or surgical approach. It can help decrease right ventricular afterload. Surgical outcomes have improved in recent years, in part due to rapid diagnosis and enhanced surgical procedures.

Percutaneous interventional techniques, surgical embolectomy, ultrasound-guided catheter thrombolysis, and aspiration thrombectomy are newer, moderately invasive procedures for PE. In patients who are at high risk and for whom anticoagulation is contraindicated, an inferior vena cava (IVC) filter may be the treatment of choice (Fig. 30.8). This device, inserted through the femoral vein, is placed at the level of the renal veins in the inferior vena cava. Once inserted, the filter expands and prevents the movement of large clots upwards and into the pulmonary system. Complications are rare but include misplacement, migration, and perforation.

NURSING MANAGEMENT: PULMONARY EMBOLISM

Prevention of PE begins with prevention of DVT. Identifying the "at risk" patient is essential. Nursing measures aimed at prevention of PE are similar to those for prophylaxis of VTE. These include the use of intermittent pneumatic compression devices, early ambulation, and anticoagulant medications.

Initially, keep the patient on bed rest in a semi-Fowler's position to facilitate breathing. Assess cardiopulmonary status with careful monitoring of vital signs, cardiac rhythm, pulse oximetry, ABGs, and lung sounds. Apply O_2 therapy as directed. Maintain a patent IV line for medications and fluid therapy. Monitor laboratory results to ensure therapeutic ranges of INR (for warfarin) and aPTT (for IV heparin). Monitor platelet counts for thrombocytopenia and the development of HIT. Observe the patient for complications of anticoagulant and fibrinolytic therapy (e.g., bleeding, bruising). Implement fall precautions once the patient can be out of bed.

The patient may be anxious because of pain, inability to breathe, and fear of death. Provide emotional support and reassurance to help relieve the patient's anxiety.

Teaching about long-term anticoagulant therapy is essential. Anticoagulant therapy continues for at least 3 months. Patients with large or recurrent emboli may be treated indefinitely with anticoagulants. INR levels are drawn at intervals and warfarin dosage is adjusted. Some patients are monitored by nurses in an anticoagulation clinic.

Long-term management of PE is similar to that for the patient with VTE (see more about VTE in Chapter 41). Discharge planning is aimed at preventing worsening of the current condition and avoiding complications and recurrence. Reinforce the need for the patient to return to the HCP for regular follow-up care.

PULMONARY HYPERTENSION

In **pulmonary hypertension** there is an elevated pulmonary artery pressure (greater than 20 mm Hg) from an increase in resistance to blood flow through the pulmonary circulation. Normally, the pulmonary circulation is characterized by low resistance and low-pressure vessels. In pulmonary hypertension, the pulmonary pressures are high.

There are 5 classes of pulmonary hypertension.[24] Each class (group) is based on cause:

Group 1: Attributed to medication, specific diseases, genetic (inherited) link, or idiopathic
Group 2: Related to left-sided HF
Group 3: Related to the lungs and hypoxia
Group 4: Related to the cardiovascular system and thromboembolism
Group 5: Multifactorial (and often unclear) origins (e.g., hematologic, metabolic, renal involvement)

Pulmonary hypertension can occur as a primary disease *(idiopathic pulmonary arterial hypertension)* or as a secondary complication of a respiratory, heart, autoimmune, liver, or connective tissue problem *(secondary pulmonary arterial hypertension).*

IDIOPATHIC PULMONARY ARTERIAL HYPERTENSION

Etiology and Pathophysiology

Idiopathic pulmonary arterial hypertension (IPAH) was previously known as *primary pulmonary hypertension* (PPH). The cause of IPAH is unknown. It is related to connective tissue diseases, cirrhosis, and HIV. The exact relationship between these

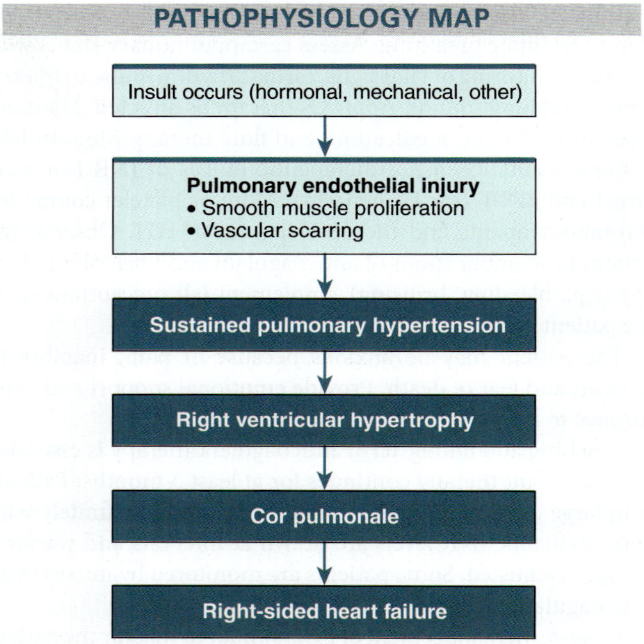

Fig. 30.9 Pathogenesis of pulmonary hypertension and cor pulmonale.

disorders and IPAH is unclear. Similarly, the pathophysiology of IPAH is poorly understood. We believe that some type of insult (e.g., hormonal, mechanical) to the pulmonary endothelium may occur, causing a cascade of events leading to vascular scarring, endothelial dysfunction, and smooth muscle proliferation (Fig. 30.9). IPAH affects more females.

Clinical Manifestations and Diagnostic Studies

The classic symptoms are dyspnea on exertion and fatigue. Exertional chest pain, dizziness, and syncope may occur. These are related to the inability of cardiac output to increase in response to increased O_2 demand. Abnormal heart sounds may be heard, including an S_3. Eventually, as the disease progresses, dyspnea occurs at rest. Pulmonary hypertension increases the workload of the right ventricle and causes right ventricular hypertrophy (a condition called *cor pulmonale*) and, eventually, HF.

Right-sided cardiac catheterization is the definitive test to diagnose any type of pulmonary hypertension. It gives an accurate measurement of pulmonary artery pressures, cardiac output, and pulmonary vascular resistance. Diagnostic evaluation often includes ECG, chest x-ray, pulmonary function tests, echocardiogram, and CT scan. Confirmation of IPAH requires a workup to exclude conditions that may cause secondary pulmonary hypertension.

The mean time between onset of symptoms and the diagnosis is about 2 years. By the time patients become symptomatic, the disease is already in the advanced stages and the pulmonary artery pressure is 2 to 3 times normal values.

Interprofessional and Nursing Care

Early recognition is essential to interrupt the vicious cycle responsible for disease progression. Encourage patients to report unexplained shortness of breath, syncope, chest discomfort, and feet and ankle edema to their HCP.

Although IPAH has no cure, treatment can relieve symptoms, improve quality of life, and prolong life. If untreated, IPAH can rapidly progress, causing right-sided HF and death within a few years. New drug therapy has greatly improved survival. Drug therapy consists of agents that dilate the pulmonary blood vessels, reduce right ventricular overload, and reverse remodeling (Table 30.21). Diuretics are used to manage peripheral edema. Anticoagulants reduce the risk of thrombus formation. Because hypoxia is a potent pulmonary vasoconstrictor, low-flow O_2 gives symptomatic relief. The goal is to keep O_2 saturation 90% or greater.

Surgical therapy includes pulmonary thromboendarterectomy (PTE), in which clots are removed from the pulmonary arteries. It is a technically demanding, high risk procedure, done only at certain centers. Atrial septostomy (AS) is a palliative procedure that involves the creation of an intra-atrial right-to-left shunt to decompress the right ventricle. It is used for some patients awaiting a lung transplant. A lung transplant is an option for patients who do not respond to drug therapy and progress to severe right-sided HF. Disease recurrence has not been reported in persons who had a lung transplant.

SECONDARY PULMONARY ARTERIAL HYPERTENSION

Secondary pulmonary arterial hypertension (SPAH) occurs when another disease causes a chronic increase in pulmonary artery pressures. The primary disease can cause anatomic or vascular changes that result in the pulmonary hypertension. SPAH can develop due to parenchymal lung disease, left ventricular dysfunction, intracardiac shunts, chronic PE, or systemic connective tissue disease.[25]

The symptoms can reflect the underlying disease, but some are directly related to SPAH. These include dyspnea, fatigue, lethargy, and chest pain. Initial physical findings can include right ventricular hypertrophy and signs of right-sided HF (increased pulmonic heart sound, S_4 heart sound, peripheral edema, hepatomegaly).

Diagnosis of SPAH is like that of IPAH. With SPAH, we treat the underlying primary disorder. When irreversible pulmonary vascular damage has occurred, therapies for IPAH are started. A PTE may offer a cure for patients with chronic pulmonary hypertension caused by PE.

COR PULMONALE

Cor pulmonale is enlargement of the right ventricle caused by a primary respiratory disorder. Almost any disorder that affects the respiratory system can cause cor pulmonale. The most common cause is COPD. Pulmonary hypertension is usually a pre-existing condition in the person with cor pulmonale. Overt HF may be present. Fig. 30.9 outlines the cause and pathogenesis of pulmonary hypertension and cor pulmonale.

Clinical Manifestations and Diagnostic Studies

Manifestations are subtle and often masked by symptoms of the lung problem. Common symptoms include exertional dyspnea,

TABLE 30.21 Drug Therapy
Pulmonary Hypertension

Drug	Mechanism of Action	Considerations
Calcium Channel Blockers		
diltiazem (Cardizem, cardizem LA) nifedipine (Procardia)	• ↓ BP • Act on vascular smooth muscle, causing dilation • Lower pulmonary artery pressure	• Successful in a very small number of patients • Only used in patients who do not have right-sided HF • Used at high doses in comparison to other uses of calcium channel blockers
Endothelin Receptor Antagonists		
ambrisentan (Letairis) bosentan (Tracleer) macitentan (Opsumit)	• Binds to endothelin-1 receptors and blocks the constriction of pulmonary arteries • Promotes relaxation of pulmonary arteries • ↓ Pulmonary artery pressure	• Given orally • For patients with New York Heart Association (NYHA) class II to IV symptoms • Hepatotoxic • Monitor liver function tests monthly
Phosphodiesterase (Type 5) Enzyme Inhibitors		
sildenafil (Revatio) tadalafil (Adcirca)	• Promote smooth muscle relaxation in lung vasculature	• Given orally • Contraindicated in patients taking nitroglycerin, since may cause refractory hypotension
Vasodilators		
iloprost (Ventavis) treprostinil (Tyvaso)	• Synthetic analogs of prostacyclin (PGI_2) • Dilate systemic and pulmonary arterial vasculature • Help relieve dyspnea	• Given by inhalation • For patients with NYHA class III or IV HF • Given 6–9 times a day using a disk inserted into a nebulizer • Can cause orthostatic hypotension. Do not give to patients with systolic BP <85 mm Hg.
Vasodilators		
epoprostenol (Flolan, Veletri) treprostinil (Remodulin)	• Promote pulmonary vasodilation and reduce pulmonary vascular resistance • Relieves dyspnea and chest congestion	• For patients who do not respond to calcium channel blockers or have NYHA class III or IV right-sided HF • Given by continuous IV (central line) or continuous subcutaneous route • Half-life of epoprostenol is short. Potential clinical deterioration from abrupt withdrawal if infusion disrupted

tachypnea, cough, and fatigue. Physical signs include evidence of right ventricular hypertrophy on ECG and an increase in intensity of S_2. Chronic hypoxemia leads to polycythemia and increased total blood volume and viscosity. Polycythemia is often present in cor pulmonale from COPD.

If HF accompanies cor pulmonale, peripheral edema, weight gain, distended neck veins, full, bounding pulse, and enlarged liver may occur. Various laboratory tests and imaging studies are used to confirm the diagnosis of cor pulmonale (Table 30.22).

Interprofessional and Nursing Care

Early identification is essential before changes to the heart occur that may be irreversible. Management is directed at determining the cause and treating the underlying problem.

Long-term O_2 therapy, the mainstay of treatment to correct the hypoxemia, reduces vasoconstriction and pulmonary hypertension. All other interventions are tailored for each patient. If fluid, electrolyte, and/or acid-base imbalances are present, they must be corrected. Diuretics may help decrease plasma volume and reduce the workload on the heart but must be used with caution. In some cases, decreases in fluid volume from diuresis can worsen heart function. Bronchodilator therapy is needed if the underlying respiratory problem is due to an obstructive disorder.

Other treatments may include vasodilator therapy, calcium channel blockers, anticoagulants, digitalis, and phlebotomy. All have varying degrees of success. Chronic management of cor pulmonale from COPD is like that described for COPD (see Chapter 31).

ENVIRONMENTAL LUNG DISEASES

Environmental or occupational lung diseases result from inhaled dust or chemicals. The extent of lung damage is influenced by the toxicity of the inhaled substance, amount and duration of exposure, and individual susceptibility. Environmentally induced lung disease includes pneumoconiosis, chemical pneumonitis, and hypersensitivity pneumonitis.

Pneumoconiosis is a general term for a group of lung diseases caused by inhalation and retention of mineral or metal dust particles. The literal meaning of *pneumoconiosis* is "dust in the lungs." We classify these diseases by the origin of the dust (e.g., silicosis, asbestosis, berylliosis). For example, silicosis occurs from inhaling silica from sand and rock. Coal worker's pneumoconiosis (CWP), or *black lung*, is caused by inhaling large amounts of coal dust. It is a hazard for underground coal miners. The inhaled substance is ingested by macrophages, which releases substances that cause cell injury and death.

TABLE 30.22 Interprofessional Care

Cor Pulmonale

Diagnostic Assessment
- History and physical assessment
- ABGs, SpO_2
- Serum and urine electrolytes
- b-Type natriuretic peptide (BNP)
- ECG
- Chest x-ray
- Echocardiography
- CT scan, MRI
- Cardiac catheterization

Management
- Treat the cause (which may be difficult, often involves improving O_2 delivery to the patient and right ventricular function)
- O_2 therapy
- Low-sodium diet

Drug Therapy (Depending on the Primary Cause)
- Bronchodilators
- Diuretics (use with caution)
- Pulmonary vasodilators
- Calcium channel blockers
- Inotropic agents
- Digitalis
- Anticoagulation therapy

Fibrosis occurs from tissue repair after inflammation. Breathing problems become evident after many years of repeated exposure, resulting in diffuse *pulmonary fibrosis* (excess connective tissue).

Asbestos is a group of minerals composed of microscopic fibers. For many years, asbestos was used for insulation and to help fireproof buildings. When disturbed, asbestos releases tiny filament particles into the air. Once inhaled, the tiny fibers become deposited within the lung. Asbestosis causes chronic lung inflammation. People with repeated exposure are at a greater risk for disease. Lung cancer, either squamous cell carcinoma or adenocarcinoma, is the most frequent cancer from asbestos exposure. There is a lapse of at least 15 to 19 years between first exposure and development of lung cancer. Mesothelioma, both pleural and peritoneal, is associated with asbestos exposure.[26]

Chemical pneumonitis results from exposures to toxic chemical fumes. There are 2 types of chemical pneumonitis: acute and chronic. In the acute form, there is diffuse lung injury characterized by pulmonary edema. Chronically, the clinical picture is that of *bronchiolitis obliterans* (obstruction of the bronchioles due to inflammation and fibrosis). The chest x-ray is normal or shows hyperinflation.

Hypersensitivity pneumonitis, or extrinsic allergic alveolitis, is a form of parenchymal lung disease seen when a person inhales an antigen to which they are allergic. There are acute, subacute, and chronic forms. Examples include bird fancier's lung (exposure to particles in feathers and droppings of birds) and farmer's lung (inhalation of hay dust particles).

Clinical Manifestations

Symptoms of many environmental lung diseases may not occur until at least 10 to 15 years after the initial exposure to the inhaled irritant. Manifestations common to all pneumoconiosis include dyspnea, cough, wheezing, and weight loss. Pulmonary function studies often show reduced vital capacity. A chest x-ray often shows lung involvement specific to the primary problem. CT scans have been useful in detecting early lung involvement.

COPD is the most common complication of environmental lung disease. Other associated problems include acute pulmonary edema, lung cancer, mesothelioma, and TB. Appearance of these symptoms and complications are often the reason the patient seeks medical care. Cor pulmonale is a late complication. It is more common in conditions where there is diffuse pulmonary fibrosis.

Interprofessional and Nursing Care

The best approach to managing environmental lung diseases is to prevent or decrease environmental and occupational exposure. Teach those at risk about the use of appropriate PPE. Wearing masks and ensuring well-designed, effective ventilation systems are in place are appropriate for some occupations. Smoke inhalation by nonsmokers has led to laws requiring a smoke-free workplace. Periodic inspections and monitoring of workplaces by agencies such as the Occupational Safety and Health Administration (OSHA) and the National Institute for Occupational Safety and Health (NIOSH) reinforce employers' obligations to provide a safe work environment. NIOSH is responsible for workplace safety and health regulations in the United States.

Encourage regular medical check-ups for those in high-risk occupations. Early diagnosis is essential to halting the disease process. Care is directed toward preventing disease progression and monitoring, improving, or controlling respiratory symptoms. Treatment depends on the cause and severity of the condition. Acute care may include O_2 therapy, IV fluid, percussion therapy, inhaled bronchodilators, corticosteroids, and NSAIDs. Some patients need mechanical ventilation. Longer term care includes pulmonary rehabilitation. Patients should be immunized against pneumococcal pneumonia and influenza. Discontinuing exposure to the offending inhalant and smoking cessation may or may not be effective in stopping disease progression.

LUNG TRANSPLANTATION

Lung transplantation has become an important alternative option for patients with end-stage lung disease. Unfortunately, the limiting factor is the lack of donors. A variety of pulmonary problems are potentially treatable with a lung transplant (Table 30.23). Better patient selection criteria, improvements in surgical techniques, enhanced immunosuppression, and excellent postoperative care have resulted in improved survival rates.

Preoperative Care

Patients being considered for a lung transplant have an extensive evaluation. Absolute contraindications include cancer

TABLE 30.23 Common Indications for a Lung Transplant

- Progressive lung disease and greater than 50% chance of death in the next 2 years without a lung transplant
- Chronic obstructive pulmonary disease (COPD)
- Cystic fibrosis
- Emphysema with α_1-antitrypsin deficiency
- Idiopathic pulmonary fibrosis
- Interstitial lung disease
- Pulmonary arterial hypertension

within the past 2 years (excluding some types of skin cancer), untreatable advanced dysfunction of another major organ system (e.g., heart, liver, renal failure), uncorrectable bleeding condition, *mycobacterium tuberculosis,* severe obesity (BMI >35kg/m²), and significant psychosocial problems.[27] The patient and family must be able to cope with complex postoperative care (e.g., adherence to immunosuppressive therapy, monitoring for infection). Many transplant centers require outpatient pulmonary rehabilitation before surgery to maximize physical conditioning.

In the United States, the United Network for Organ Sharing (UNOS) designates recipients of donor lungs based on a lung allocation score (LAS). The LAS helps prioritize waiting list recipients based on the urgency of need and expected post-transplant survival expectations.

Patients who are accepted as transplant candidates must always carry a pager in case a donor organ becomes available. They must be prepared to be at their transplant center at a moment's notice. Patients may have to limit their travel in case they need to quickly return to the transplant center.

Surgical Procedure

Four types of lung transplant procedures are available: single-lung, bilateral lung, heart-lung, and transplantation of lobes from a living-related donor.

A *single-lung transplant* involves a thoracotomy incision on the affected side of the chest. The opposite lung is ventilated while the diseased lung is excised, and the donor lung implanted. There are 3 anastomoses: bronchus, pulmonary artery, and pulmonary veins. In a *bilateral lung transplant,* the incision is made across the sternum and the donor lungs are implanted separately. A median sternotomy incision is used for a *heart-lung transplant* procedure. *Lobar transplantation* from living donors is reserved for those who urgently need a transplant and are unlikely to survive until a donor becomes available. Most of these recipients are patients with cystic fibrosis. The donors are their parents or relatives. Once anastomosis is complete, the lung is gently reinflated, perfusion is re-established, chest tubes are inserted, and the surgical incision is closed.

Postoperative Care

Immediate postoperative care often includes mechanical ventilation and hemodynamic monitoring in the ICU. IV therapy, immunosuppression, nutrition support, detection of early rejection, and preventing or treating complications, including infection, are priorities. Once hemodynamic stability has been achieved and mechanical ventilation discontinued, the patient is transferred to a high-acuity observation or surgical unit.

Lung transplant recipients are at high risk for multiple complications. Infections are the leading cause of death, especially within the 1st year after transplant.[28] Bacterial bronchitis and pneumonia are the most common infections. CMV, fungi, viruses, and mycobacteria are also causative agents. Noninfectious issues may include VTE, diaphragmatic dysfunction, and cancer.

Immunosuppressive therapy usually includes a 3 drug regimen of tacrolimus, mycophenolate mofetil (CellCept), and prednisone. (The mechanisms of action of these drugs are discussed in Table 14.17.) Drug levels are monitored on a regular basis. Lung transplant recipients usually receive higher levels of immunosuppressive therapy than other organ recipients.

Acute rejection is fairly common. Between 28% and 64% of patients will have 1 episode of acute rejection in the 1st year after their transplant.[29] When acute rejection occurs, it typically occurs in the first 5 to 10 days after the transplant. Signs include low-grade fever, fatigue, dyspnea, dry cough, and O_2 desaturation. Accurate diagnosis of rejection is by transbronchial biopsy completed via bronchoscopy. Treatment consists of high doses of IV corticosteroids for 3 days, followed by high doses of oral prednisone. In patients with persistent or recurrent acute rejection, antilymphocyte therapy may be useful.

Bronchiolitis obliterans (BOS) is a manifestation of chronic rejection in lung transplant patients. BOS is characterized by airflow obstruction that progresses over time. The onset is often subacute, with gradual development of exertional dyspnea, nonproductive cough, wheezing, and/or low-grade fever. Airway obstruction is not responsive to bronchodilators and corticosteroid therapy. Additional immunosuppressive agents may be used to treat chronic rejection. Because acute rejection is a major risk factor for BOS, preventing acute rejection is key to decreasing chronic rejection.

Before discharge, the patient needs to be able to perform self-care activities, including managing their medication plan, and know when to call the transplant team. Patients are taught pulmonary clearance measures, including chest physiotherapy and deep-breathing and coughing techniques to help minimize complications. Home spirometry is used to monitor trends in lung function. Teach patients to keep medication logs, laboratory results, and spirometry records. An outpatient rehabilitation program can improve physical endurance.

After discharge, the transplant team follows the patient for transplant-related issues. Patients return to their HCP for health maintenance and routine illnesses. Care coordination among the transplant team, inpatient team, and primary care team is essential for ongoing successful management. Information about organ transplants, histocompatibility, rejection, and immunosuppressive therapy is found in Chapter 14.

LUNG CANCER

Lung cancer is the leading cause of cancer-related deaths in the United States.[30] Lung cancer accounts for 25% of all cancer deaths, more than those caused by breast, prostate, and colon cancer combined. In 2021, around 235,000 new cases of lung cancer will be diagnosed, and 131,000 Americans will die.[30] Although lung cancer has a high mortality and low cure rate, advances in medical treatment are improving the response to treatment.

Etiology

Smoking causes 80% to 90% of all lung cancers.[31] There is no safe form of tobacco or tobacco product. Using smokeless tobacco, pipes and cigars, hookah and waterpipe, bidis, and kreteks all pose significant risk for lung cancer.

Tobacco smoke contains over 7000 chemicals, of which 250 are harmful. Of the harmful substances in tobacco smoke, 69 interfere with normal cell development and are linked to lung cancer. Exposure to tobacco smoke causes changes in the bronchial epithelium. These changes usually return to normal with smoking cessation. The risk for lung cancer gradually decreases with smoking cessation, reaching that of nonsmokers within 10 to 15 years of quitting.

The risk for developing lung cancer is directly related to total exposure to tobacco smoke. Measures of exposure include the total number of cigarettes smoked in a lifetime, age of smoking onset, depth of inhalation, tar and nicotine content, and the use of unfiltered cigarettes. Nonsmokers can also develop lung cancer. Sidestream smoke (smoke from burning cigarettes, cigars) has the same carcinogens found in mainstream smoke (smoke inhaled and exhaled by the smoker). This exposure to secondhand smoke creates a health risk for nonsmoking adults and children.

Other risk factors include exposure to high levels of pollution, radiation (especially radon exposure), and asbestos. Heavy or prolonged exposure to industrial agents, such as radon, coal dust, asbestos, chromium, silica, arsenic, and diesel exhaust, increases risk, especially in smokers.[31]

Marked variations exist in a person's tendency to develop lung cancer. Differences in incidence, risk factors, and survival exist between men and women (Box 30.5). Genetic, hormonal, and molecular influences may contribute to these differences. At the same time, the incidence and survivability vary between racial and ethnic populations (Box 30.6).

Pathophysiology

We think most primary lung tumors arise from mutated epithelial cells. The growth of mutations, which are caused by carcinogens, is influenced by various genetic factors. Once underway, epidermal growth factor promotes tumor development. Tumor cells grow slowly, taking 8 to 10 years for a tumor to reach 1 cm in size, the smallest lesion detectable on x-ray. Lung cancers occur mainly in the segmental bronchi or beyond and usually occur in the upper lobes.

There are 2 broad subtypes of primary lung cancer: non-small cell lung cancer (NSCLC) (84%) and small cell lung cancer (SCLC) (13%) (Table 30.24).[32] Lung cancers metastasize mainly by direct extension and through the blood and lymph system. The common sites for metastasis are the lymph nodes, liver, brain, bones, and adrenal glands.

BOX 30.5 BIOLOGIC SEX CONSIDERATIONS

Lung Cancer

Men

- Have a 1 in 15 chance of developing lung cancer (smokers and nonsmokers)
- Diagnosed with lung cancer more than women
- Die from lung cancer more than women
- Male smokers are 10 times more likely to develop lung cancer than nonsmokers
- Lung cancer incidence and deaths are decreasing in men

Women

- Have a 1 in 17 chance of developing lung cancer (smokers and nonsmokers)
- Lung cancer incidence and deaths are increasing in women.
- Develop lung cancer after fewer years of smoking than men
- Develop lung cancer at a younger age than men
- Nonsmoking women are at greater risk for developing lung cancer than nonsmoking men
- Women with lung cancer live, on the average, 12 months longer than men

BOX 30.6 PROMOTING HEALTH EQUITY

Lung Cancer

Blacks

- Have the highest incidence of lung cancer
- Are more likely to die from lung cancer than any other ethnic group
- Have a higher rate of lung cancer among men than in other ethnic groups

Whites

- Have the 2nd highest death rate from lung cancer
- Have a higher rate of lung cancer among women than in other ethnic groups

Asians/Pacific Islanders and Hispanics

- Have the lowest rates of lung cancer in both men and women

Source: American Lung Association: Lung cancer fact sheet. Retrieved from https://www. lung.org/lung-health-diseases/lung-disease-lookup/lung-cancer/resource-library/lung-cancer-fact-sheet.

Other Types of Lung Tumors

SCLC and NSCLC account for 97% of lung tumors. The other 3% include:

- *Hamartomas,* the most common benign tumor, is a slow-growing congenital tumor composed of fibrous tissue, fat, and blood vessels.
- *Mucous gland adenoma* is a benign tumor arising in the bronchi. It consists of columnar cystic spaces.
- *Mesotheliomas* are either malignant or benign. They start in the visceral pleura. Malignant mesotheliomas are related to asbestos exposure. Benign lesions are localized.

Secondary metastases from other cancers can occur. Cancer cells from another part of the body reach the lungs through the pulmonary capillaries or lymphatic network. The main cancers that spread to the lungs often start in the breast, GI, or genitourinary tract.

Paraneoplastic Syndrome

Lung cancer can cause *paraneoplastic syndrome.* Paraneoplastic syndrome may be initiated by hormones, cytokines, enzymes (secreted by tumor cells), or antibodies (made by the body in

TABLE 30.24 Types of Primary Lung Cancer

Type	Growth Rate	Characteristics	Response to Therapy
Non–Small Cell Lung Cancer (NSCLC)			
Adenocarcinoma	Moderate	• Accounts for 40% of lung cancers • Most common lung cancer in United States • Most common cancer in people who have not smoked • Found in peripheral areas of lung • Often has no manifestations until widespread metastasis is present	• Surgical resection may be tried depending on staging • Does not respond well to chemotherapy
Large cell (undifferentiated) cancer	Rapid	• Accounts for 10% of lung cancers • Composed of large cells that are anaplastic • Often arise in bronchi • Is highly metastatic via lymphatics and blood	• Surgery is not usually done because of high rate of metastases • Tumor may be radiosensitive but often recur
Squamous cell cancer	Slow	• Accounts for 25%–30% of lung cancers • Centrally located • Causes early symptoms of nonproductive cough and hemoptysis • Does not have a strong tendency to metastasize	• Surgical resection may be tried • Adjuvant chemotherapy and radiation • Depending on the staging, life expectancy is better than for SCLC
Small Cell Lung Cancer (SCLC)			
Small cell cancer	Very rapid	• Accounts for about 10%–15% of lung cancers • Very aggressive form of lung cancer • Spreads early via lymphatics and bloodstream • Frequent metastasis to brain • Associated with endocrine problems	• Chemotherapy mainstay of treatment; more responsive to chemotherapy than NSCLC • Radiation used as adjuvant therapy and palliative measure • Overall poor prognosis

response to the tumor) that destroy healthy cells. Sometimes, paraneoplastic syndrome manifests before the cancer is diagnosed.

Examples of paraneoplastic syndrome include hypercalcemia, syndrome of inappropriate antidiuretic hormone secretion (SIADH), adrenal hypersecretion, polycythemia, and Cushing syndrome. SCLCs are most often associated with paraneoplastic syndrome. The conditions may stabilize with treatment of the underlying cancer. SIADH, adrenal hypersecretion, and Cushing syndrome are discussed in Chapter 54.

Clinical Manifestations

The manifestations of lung cancer are usually nonspecific. They may appear late in the disease process. Symptoms may be masked by a chronic cough attributed to smoking or smoking-related lung disease. Manifestations depend on the type of primary lung cancer, its location, and extent of metastatic spread. Lung cancer often presents as a lobar pneumonia that does not respond to treatment.

The most common symptom and often the one that is reported first is a persistent cough. The patient may have dyspnea or wheezing. Blood-tinged sputum may be present because of bleeding caused by the cancer. Chest pain, if present, may be localized or unilateral, ranging from mild to severe.

Later manifestations include nonspecific systemic symptoms, such as anorexia, nausea and vomiting, fatigue, and weight loss. Hoarseness may be present due to laryngeal nerve involvement. Dysphagia, unilateral paralysis of the diaphragm, and superior vena cava obstruction may occur because of intrathoracic spread of the cancer. Lymph nodes are often palpable in the neck or axillae. Mediastinal involvement may lead to pericardial effusion, cardiac tamponade, and dysrhythmias.

Diagnostic Studies

A chest x-ray is the first diagnostic test done for patients with suspected lung cancer. The x-ray may be normal or identify a

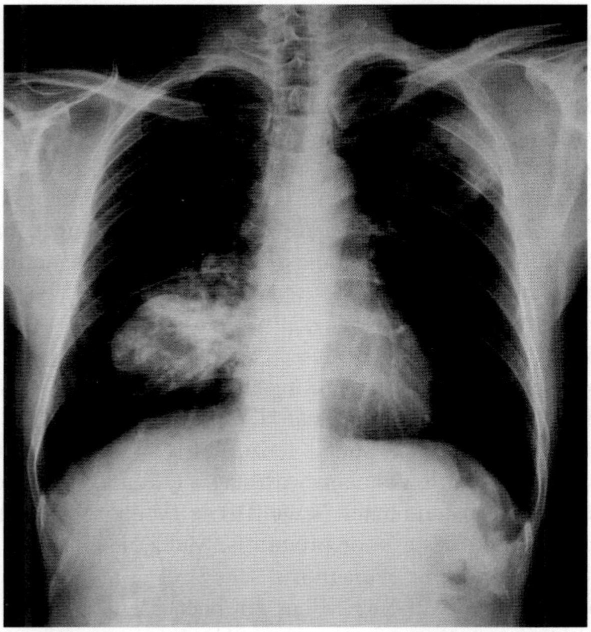

Fig. 30.10 Lung cancer lesion. (© iStock.com/Sutthaburawonk.)

lung mass or infiltrate (Fig. 30.10). Evidence of metastasis to the ribs or vertebrae and a pleural effusion may be seen on chest x-ray. CT scanning is used to further evaluate the lung mass. CT scans can identify the location and extent of masses in the chest, any mediastinal involvement, and lymph node enlargement.

Sputum cytology can identify cancer cells, but sputum samples are rarely used in diagnosing lung cancer because cancer cells are not always present in the sputum. A definitive diagnosis requires a biopsy. Cells for biopsy can be obtained by CT-guided needle aspiration, bronchoscopy, mediastinoscopy, or VATS. If a thoracentesis is done to relieve a pleural effusion, the fluid is analyzed for cancer cells.

TABLE 30.25 Interprofessional Care

Lung Cancer

Diagnostic Assessment

- History and physical assessment
- Chest x-ray
- Bronchoscopy
- Cytologic study of bronchial washings or pleural space fluid
- Transbronchial or percutaneous fine-needle aspiration
- CT scan, MRI, PET
- Mediastinoscopy
- Video-assisted thoracoscopic surgery (VATS)
- Laboratory tests: CBC, electrolytes, BUN, creatinine, WBC and differential, liver function tests, calcium chemistries

Management

- Surgery (segmental or wedge resection, lobectomy, pneumonectomy)
- Radiation therapy
- Chemotherapy
- Targeted therapy and immunotherapy
- Prophylactic cranial radiation
- Bronchoscopic laser therapy
- Photodynamic therapy
- Airway stenting
- Radiofrequency ablation

Accurate assessment of lung cancer is critical for staging and determining appropriate treatment. Bone scans and CT scans of the brain, pelvis, and abdomen assess for metastases. A CBC with differential, electrolyte panel, and liver and renal function tests are done. Sometimes pulmonary function tests may be done. MRI and/or positron emission tomography (PET) may be used to evaluate and stage lung cancer. Table 30.25 outlines the diagnostic assessment and management of lung cancer.

Staging

Staging of NSCLC is done using the TNM staging system.[33] Under the TNM system, cancer is grouped into 4 stages with A or B subtypes. A simplified version of staging of NSCLC is shown in Table 30.26. Patients with stages I, II, and IIIA disease may be surgical candidates. Stage IIIB or IV disease is usually inoperable and has a poor prognosis. Many NSCLCs are not resectable at the time of diagnosis.

Staging of SCLC by TNM has not been useful because this cancer is aggressive and always considered systemic. The stages of SCLC are *limited* and *extensive*. *Limited* means that the tumor is only on 1 side of the chest and regional lymph nodes. *Extensive* SCLC means that the cancer extends beyond the limited stage. Unfortunately, most patients with SCLC have extensive disease at time of diagnosis.

Screening for Lung Cancer

Many medical groups recommend cancer screening for high-risk patients. Adults ages 50 to 80 with a history of smoking (20 pack-year smoking history or currently smoke) or who quit smoking but less than 15 years ago should have annual screening for lung cancer.[34] Screening is done using low-dose CT.

TABLE 30.26 Staging of Non–Small Cell Lung Cancer

Stages	Characteristics
0	Cancer cells found in first layer of cells in the respiratory airway or alveoli
I	Tumor is small and localized to lung. No lymph node involvement
A	Tumor <3 cm, minimally invasive
B	Tumor 3–4 cm and invading main airway (but not into right or left bronchi), visceral pleura.
II	Increased tumor size, some lymph node involvement
A	Tumor 4–5 cm with invasion of main airway (but not right or left bronchi), visceral pleura
B	Tumor 5–7 cm involving the bronchus and lymph nodes near bronchi on same side of chest; tumor 5–7 cm with visceral and parietal pleura, diaphragm, phrenic nerve involvement; 2 or more tumors in same lobe of lung
III	Increased spread of tumor
A	1 or more tumors ≤5 cm or smaller spread to the nearby (same side) structures (chest wall, pleura, pericardium), or metastases into diaphragm, hear, bone, and regional lymph nodes below carina
B	1 or more tumors >5 cm in the same lung, involving heart, trachea, esophagus, mediastinum; lymph node involvement (same side or opposite side, or below carina),
C	Tumor >5 cm and more than 1 tumor in a different lobe of the lung; lymph nodes on opposite side involved
IV	Distant metastasis (to the other lung)
A	Metastases to the other lung, pleura, pericardium; 1 new tumor outside of chest
B	Metastases widespread and 2 or more tumors outside of the chest

Interprofessional Care

Surgical Therapy

Surgical resection is the treatment of choice in NSCLC stages I to IIIA without mediastinal involvement. Resection gives the best chance for a cure. Factors that affect survival include the size of the primary tumor and preexisting co-morbidities. For other NSCLC stages, patients may have surgery in conjunction with radiation therapy, chemotherapy, and targeted therapy.

Surgical procedures include segmental or wedge resection procedures, lobectomy (removal of 1 or more lobes of the lung), or pneumonectomy (removal of 1 entire lung). VATS may be used to treat lung cancers near the outside of the lung. Surgery is generally not done for SCLC because of its rapid growth and dissemination at the time of diagnosis.

When the tumor is operable, the patient's cardiopulmonary status must be evaluated to determine the ability to have surgery. Pulmonary function studies, ABGs, and anesthesia and critical care consults are often done to assess the patient's cardiopulmonary status and overall surgical risk.

Radiation Therapy

Radiation therapy may be used as treatment for both NSCLC and SCLC. Radiation therapy may be given as curative, palliative, or adjuvant therapy in combination with surgery, chemotherapy, or targeted therapy.

Radiation therapy may be the primary therapy in the person who cannot undergo surgical resection because of co-morbidities. Radiation therapy relieves dyspnea and hemoptysis from bronchial obstructive tumors and treats superior vena cava syndrome. It can treat pain from metastatic bone lesions or brain metastasis. Radiation before surgery can reduce the tumor mass before surgical resection. Complications of radiation therapy include esophagitis, skin irritation, nausea and vomiting, anorexia, and radiation pneumonitis (see Chapter 16).

Stereotactic body radiotherapy (SBRT), or *stereotactic radiosurgery (SRS),* is a type of radiation therapy that uses high doses of radiation delivered to tumors outside the CNS. SBRT uses special positioning procedures and radiology techniques to deliver a higher dose of radiation to the tumor and expose only a small part of healthy lung. It does not destroy the tumor, but damages tumor DNA. Therapy is given over 1 to 3 days. SBRT is an option for patients with early-stage lung cancers who cannot have surgery.

Chemotherapy

Chemotherapy is the main treatment for SCLC. In NSCLC, chemotherapy may be used to treat nonresectable tumors or as adjuvant therapy to surgery. A variety of chemotherapy drugs and multidrug protocols are used. Chemotherapy for lung cancer typically consists of combinations of 2 of these drugs: etoposide, carboplatin, cisplatin, paclitaxel, vinorelbine, docetaxel, gemcitabine, and pemetrexed (Alimta).

Targeted Therapy

Targeted therapy uses drugs that block the growth of molecules involved in specific aspects of tumor growth (see Chapter 16). Because this therapy inhibits growth rather than directly killing cancer cells, targeted therapy may be less toxic than chemotherapy. One targeted therapy for NSCLC is tyrosine kinase inhibitors. They block signals for growth in the cancer cells. Agents include cetuximab (Erbitux), erlotinib (Tarceva), afatinib (Gilotrif), gefitinib (Iressa), osimertinib (Tagrisso), and necitumumab (Portrazza).

Another type of kinase inhibitor is used to treat patients with NSCLC who have an abnormal *anaplastic lymphoma kinase (ALK)* gene. Drugs in this class include crizotinib (Xalkori), brigatinib (Alunbrig), and ceritinib (Zykadia). These drugs directly inhibit the kinase protein made by the ALK gene that is responsible for cancer development and growth.

Another targeted therapy used to treat lung cancer inhibits the growth of new blood vessels (angiogenesis) by targeting vascular endothelial growth factor. Bevacizumab (Avastin) is an angiogenesis inhibitor.

Immunotherapy

Nivolumab (Opdivo), atezolizumab (Tecentriq), and pembrolizumab (Keytruda) are drugs that target PD-1, a protein on T cells that normally helps keep these cells from attacking other cells in the body. By blocking PD-1, these drugs boost the immune response against cancer cells. This can shrink some tumors or slow their growth. Nivolumab and pembrolizumab can be used in people with metastatic NSCLC whose cancer has progressed after other treatments and with tumors that express PD-1.

Other Therapies

Prophylactic cranial irradiation. Patients with SCLC have early metastases, especially to the CNS. Most chemotherapy does not penetrate the blood-brain barrier. As a result, after successful systemic treatment, the patient is at risk for brain metastases. Prophylactic radiation can decrease the incidence of brain metastases and may improve survival rates in patients with limited SCLC.

Bronchoscopic laser therapy. Bronchoscopic laser therapy makes it possible to remove obstructing bronchial lesions. The laser's thermal energy is transmitted to the target tissue. It is a safe and effective treatment of endobronchial obstructions from tumors. Symptoms of airway obstruction are relieved due to thermal necrosis and tumor shrinkage. The procedure may be repeated as needed.

Photodynamic therapy. Photodynamic therapy (PDT) is a form of treatment for early-stage lung cancers that uses a combination of a drug and a specific type of light. Cancer cells are killed when the drug, known as a photosynthesizer, is exposed to a specific wavelength of light. Porfimer (Photofrin) is the most used photosynthesizer. After an IV injection, it selectively concentrates in tumor cells in the esophagus and outer layers of the airways. After a set time (usually 48 hours), the tumor is exposed to laser light via bronchoscopy, activating the drug and causing cell death. Necrotic tissue is removed with bronchoscopy a few days later. This process can be repeated as needed. PDT can affect nutrient delivery to cancer cells and stimulate the immune system to attack the cancer cells.

Airway stenting. Stents are used alone or in combination with other techniques for relief of dyspnea, cough, or respiratory insufficiency. The stent is inserted during a bronchoscopy. The advantage of a stent is that it supports the airway wall against collapse or external compression and can delay extension of tumor into the airway lumen. At this time, we do not know which patients will benefit most from airway stents.

Radiofrequency ablation. Radiofrequency ablation therapy is used to treat small NSCLC lung tumors that are near the outer edge of the lungs. This therapy is an alternative to surgery in patients who cannot or choose not to have surgery. A thin, needle-like probe is inserted through the skin into the tumor. CT scans are used to guide placement. An electric current is then passed through the probe, which heats and destroys cancer cells. Local anesthesia is used for this outpatient procedure.

❖ NURSING MANAGEMENT: LUNG CANCER

◆ Assessment

It is important to determine the patient and caregiver's understanding of the condition, diagnostic tests (those completed as well as those planned), treatment options, and prognosis. Assess the patient's anxiety level and support available from family and significant others. Subjective and objective data that you should obtain are described in Table 30.27.

◆ Clinical Problems

Clinical problems for the patient with lung cancer may include:

- Impaired respiratory function
- Difficulty coping
- Pain
- Deficient knowledge

TABLE 30.27 NURSING ASSESSMENT
Lung Cancer

Subjective Data

Important Health Information

Health history: Exposure to secondhand smoke, airborne carcinogens (e.g., asbestos, radon, hydrocarbons), other pollutants. Urban living environment. Chronic lung disease (e.g., TB, COPD, bronchiectasis). History of cancer.

Medications: Cough medicines, bronchodilators, expectorants, other respiratory medications

Functional Health Patterns

Health perception–health management: Smoking history, including what was smoked, amount per day, and number of years. Family history of lung cancer. Frequent respiratory tract infections

Activity-exercise: Fatigue. Persistent cough (productive or nonproductive). Dyspnea at rest or with exertion, hemoptysis (late symptom)

Cognitive-perceptual: Chest pain or tightness, shoulder and arm pain, headache, bone pain (late symptom)

Objective Data

Cardiovascular

- Pericardial effusion, cardiac tamponade, dysrhythmias (late signs)

General

Fever, nose and/or throat infection, neck and axillary lymphadenopathy, paraneoplastic syndrome (e.g., syndrome of inappropriate ADH secretion)

GI

- Anorexia, nausea, vomiting, weight loss, dysphagia (late)

Musculoskeletal

- Pathologic fractures, muscle wasting (late)

Neurologic

- Confusion, disorientation, unsteady gait (brain metastasis)

Respiratory

- Wheezing, hoarseness, stridor, dyspnea on exertion (unilateral diaphragm paralysis), pleural effusions (late signs)

Skin

- Edema of neck and face (superior vena cava syndrome), digital clubbing. Jaundice (liver metastasis)

Other Possible Diagnostic Findings

- Lesions and any metastases found on chest x-ray, CT scan, MRI, PET scan
- Positive sputum or bronchial washings for cytologic studies.
- Positive fiberoptic bronchoscopy and biopsy findings

◆ Planning

The overall goals are that the patient with lung cancer will have a (1) patent airway, (2) adequate tissue oxygenation, (3) minimal discomfort, and (4) understanding about the type of lung cancer, and (5) a realistic outlook about treatment and prognosis.

◆ Implementation

◆ Health Promotion

The best way to halt the epidemic of lung cancer is to prevent people from smoking, help smokers stop smoking, and decrease exposure to environmental pollutants. Because most smokers start in the teenage years, prevention of teen smoking has the most significant role in reducing the incidence of lung cancer. A wealth of material is available to the smoker who is interested in smoking cessation.

Modeling healthy behavior by not smoking, promoting smoking cessation programs, and actively supporting education and policy changes related to smoking are important nursing activities. Many changes have occurred because we know that secondhand smoke is a health hazard. Laws prohibit smoking in most public places and limit public smoking to designated areas.

◆ Acute Care

Care of the patient with lung cancer initially involves support and reassurance during diagnostic evaluation. It is important to recognize the multiple stressors that occur when someone receives a lung cancer diagnosis. The stress response is a normal and adaptive response but can become detrimental when stress is overwhelming and intense. Patients have the stress of their symptoms, including dyspnea and cough. Diagnostic and therapeutic interventions provide more stress by placing patients in unfamiliar environments with unusual and perhaps painful procedures. Emotional stressors include waiting for test results and awareness of the high mortality rate from lung cancer. Worries about role performance and ability to care for their family while undergoing cancer treatment provide further stress. Assess every patient since each will have unique stressors. The insight gained will help the patient and caregiver cope with the stress of both illness and treatment.

Patient-centered care depends on the diagnosis and plan for treatment. Teach signs and symptoms to report (e.g., hemoptysis, dysphagia, chest pain, hoarseness). Provide comfort, teach ways to reduce pain, and monitor for drug side effects. Teach the patient to recognize signs and symptoms that may indicate progression or recurrence of disease. Be available to listen to the patient and their families. Encourage them to share their thoughts, fears, and concerns. Foster appropriate coping strategies for both the patient and caregiver and help them access resources to deal with the illness.

Care of the patient undergoing radiation therapy and chemotherapy is discussed in Chapter 16.

CHECK YOUR PRACTICE

You are completing discharge teaching with E.S., a 72- year-old patient who had a lobectomy for NSCLC. She tells you, "I'm not going to give up smoking my cigarettes because I am just going to die anyhow. I might as well enjoy smoking while I can."

- How would you respond?

◆ Ambulatory Care

Counseling patients on smoking cessation and prevention is essential in decreasing mortality from lung cancer. Assess smoking cessation readiness. Some patients may not perceive value in quitting smoking once they have a diagnosis of lung cancer. As nurses, however, we can encourage the patient to perhaps quit or decrease the number of cigarettes smoked per day. We might be able to gain support from family members who may wish to quit smoking with the patient. Explain the importance of maintaining a smoke-free environment in the home, particularly if O_2 will be in use. If the treatment plan includes home O_2, the teaching plan must include the safe use of O_2.

For many patients with lung cancer, little can be done to significantly prolong their lives. Radiation therapy and chemotherapy can provide palliative relief from distressing symptoms. Constant pain may become a major problem. Measures used to relieve pain are discussed in Chapter 9. Care of the patient with cancer is discussed in Chapter 16. The palliative care team should be involved as the patient and family move toward the end of life (see Chapter 10). Social workers and spiritual care advisors are invaluable in end-of-life situations. The team can provide information about disability, financial planning, and community resources for end-of-life care, such as hospice and home care.

◆ Evaluation

The expected outcomes are that the patient with lung cancer will:
- Have adequate breathing patterns
- Maintain adequate oxygenation
- Have minimal to no pain
- Convey feelings openly and honestly, with a realistic attitude about prognosis

Case Study

Pneumonia and Lung Cancer

(©iStockphoto/Thinkstock.)

Patient Profile

J.H. is a 52-year-old male who comes to the ED with shortness of breath. He says it has really increased over the past several months. J.H. has not been to a doctor for many years, as he is often "too busy with work." His wife told him to get his "cough checked out."

Subjective Data
- 38 pack-year history of cigarette smoking
- Has had 25-lb weight loss despite a normal appetite in the past few months
- Admits to a "smoker's cough" for the past 2 to 3 years
- Recently started coughing up a small amount of blood-tinged sputum
- Married and the father of 3 adult children

Objective Data

Physical Assessment
- Thin, pale man who looks older than stated age
- Height 6 ft (182.9 cm); weight 135 lb (61.2 kg)
- Intermittently confused and anxious
- Vital signs: temperature 102.6°F (39.2°C), heart rate 120, respiratory rate 36 (shallow, slightly labored), BP 98/54
- Lung auscultation: Coarse crackles (left upper and left lower lobes) that clear with cough; decreased breath sounds (right middle lobe and right lower lobe)
- Chest wall has limited excursion on right side

Diagnostic Studies
- ABGs: pH 7.51, PaO_2 62 mm Hg, $PaCO_2$ 30 mm Hg, HCO_3^- 22 mEq/L
- SpO_2 saturation 88% (room air)
- Chest x-ray: Right lung (RML, RLL) consolidation, with visible mass around right bronchus; small pleural effusion (<150mL) on the right side
- Bronchoscopy: Biopsy of mass reveals small cell lung cancer (SCLC)

Interprofessional Care
- Diagnosis: Pneumonia with SCLC
- Follow-up and discuss with patient and family appropriate treatment options

Discussion Questions
1. ***Recognize:*** How would you classify J.H.'s pneumonia? Why is this important?
2. ***Analyze:*** Which findings concern you?
3. ***Analyze:*** What is your analysis of J.H.'s ABG results?
4. ***Plan:*** How would you expect other health care team members to be involved in J.H.'s care?
5. ***Prioritize:*** Based on the assessment data presented, what are the priority clinical problems?
6. ***Prioritize:*** What are the priority nursing interventions for J.H.?
7. ***Act:*** Identify activities that you can delegate to assistive personnel (AP).
8. ***Act:*** You are planning a meeting with J.H. and his family at 1400 hours to discuss their needs. The morning of the meeting, the HCP informs you that J.H. is terminally ill. Who will you include in this meeting?
9. ***Act:*** J.H.'s children tell you that they are worried they will get lung cancer, since their father has it and they grew up around his secondhand smoke. They want to know what kind of screening is available for them. How will you respond?
10. ***Evaluate:*** How would radiation therapy help J.H.?

Answers available at http://evolve.elsevier.com/Lewis/medsurg.

BRIDGE TO NCLEX EXAMINATION

The number of the question corresponds to the same-numbered outcome at the beginning of the chapter.

1. When caring for a patient with acute bronchitis, the nurse will *prioritize* interventions by
   a. auscultating lung sounds.
   b. encouraging fluid restriction.
   c. administering antibiotic therapy.
   d. teaching the patient to avoid cough suppressants.
2. Which patient(s) have the greatest risk for aspiration pneumonia? *(select all that apply)*
   a. Patient who had thoracic surgery
   b. Patient with acute opioid overdose
   c. Patient who had a myocardial infarction
   d. Patient who is receiving nasogastric enteral feeding
   e. Patient who has a traumatic brain injury from blunt trauma

3. An appropriate nursing intervention to help a patient with pneumonia manage thick, purulent secretions would be to
   a. perform postural drainage every hour.
   b. provide analgesics every 3 hours to promote comfort.
   c. administer O_2 as prescribed to maintain optimal O_2 levels.
   d. teach them how to cough effectively and expectorate secretions.
4. A patient with TB is admitted to the hospital and placed in a single patient room on airborne precautions. What should the nurse teach the patient? *(select all that apply)*
   a. No visitors will be allowed while in airborne isolation.
   b. Expect regular TB skin testing to evaluate for infection.
   c. Adherence to precautions includes coughing into a paper tissue.
   d. Take all medications for full length of time to prevent multidrug-resistant TB.
   e. Wear a standard isolation mask if leaving the airborne infection isolation room.
5. When caring for a patient with a lung abscess, what is the nurse's *priority* intervention?
   a. Postural drainage
   b. Antibiotic administration
   c. Obtaining a sputum specimen
   d. Asking the patient about a family history of lung cancer
6. The patient with a right-side pleural effusion has stable vital signs and O_2 at 6 L/min via nasal cannula. A right-side chest tube is attached to straight drainage. Which actions would the nurse include in the plan of care? *(select all that apply)*
   a. Placing the patient on NPO status
   b. Administering analgesia as ordered
   c. Maintaining high-Fowler's position
   d. Encouraging deep breathing and coughing
   e. Monitoring color and amount of chest tube drainage
7. You are caring for a patient with several traumatic injuries after a multiple-vehicle accident. Which assessment finding would lead you to suspect a flail chest?
   a. Chest-tube is draining bright red blood
   b. Tracheal deviation to the unaffected side
   c. Paradoxical chest movement during respiration
   d. Little to no movement of the involved chest wall
8. When planning care for a patient at high risk for pulmonary embolism, the nurse prioritizes
   a. maintaining the patient on strict bed rest.
   b. using intermittent pneumatic compression devices.
   c. encouraging the patient to cough and deep breathe.
   d. encouraging a fluid intake of 2000 mL per 8-hour shift.
9. The nurse would closely monitor patients exposed to a chlorine leak from a local factory for
   a. pulmonary edema.
   b. anaphylactic shock.
   c. respiratory acidosis.
   d. acute tubular necrosis.
10. Management of a patient after a lung transplant includes which measures? *(select all that apply)*
   a. Mechanical ventilation in the early postoperative period
   b. Assisting with a lung biopsy if acute rejection is suspected
   c. IV fluid therapy accompanied by accurate intake and output
   d. Immunosuppressant therapy, which usually involves a 3 drug regimen
   e. Pulmonary clearance measures, including deep-breathing and coughing
11. Nursing care of a patient with Stage 4 lung cancer would include
   a. Coordinating a referral to palliative care
   b. Limiting visitors to decrease infection risk
   c. NPO status and starting parenteral nutrition
   d. Avoiding talking about the cancer diagnosis

1. a; 2. b, d, e; 3. d; 4. c, d, e; 5. b; 6. b, c, d, e; 7. c; 8. b; 9. a; 10. a, b, c, d, e; 11. a.

For rationales to these answers and even more NCLEX review questions, visit http://evolve.elsevier.com/Lewis/medsurg.

EVOLVE WEBSITE/RESOURCES LIST

http://evolve.elsevier.com/Lewis/medsurg
Review Questions (Online Only)
Key Points
Answer Keys for Questions
- Rationales for Bridge to NCLEX Examination Questions
- Answer Guidelines for Case Study

Student Case Studies
- Patient With Lung Cancer
- Patient With Pulmonary Embolism and Respiratory Failure

Nursing Care Plans
- eNursing Care Plan 30.1: Patient With Pneumonia

Conceptual Care Map Creator
Audio Glossary
Content Updates

REFERENCES

1. Centers for Disease Control and Prevention (CDC), National Center for Health Statistics: Deaths and mortality. Retrieved from https://www.cdc.gov/nchs/fastats/deaths.htm.
2. CDC: Fast facts: pertussis. Retrieved from http://www.cdc.gov/pertussis/fast-facts.html.
3. CDC: Vaccine information statement (VIS)-Tdap: tetanus, diphtheria, and pertussis. Retrieved from http://www.cdc.gov/vaccines/hcp/vis/vis-statements/tdap.html.
4. CDC: Pertussis (whooping cough): diagnosis confirmation. Retrieved from https://www.cdc.gov/pertussis/clinical/diagnostic-testing/diagnosis-confirmation.html.
*5. World Health Organization (WHO): WHO reveals leading causes of death and disability worldwide: 2000-2019. Retrieved from https://www. www.who.int/news/item/09-12-2020-who-reveals-leading-causes-of-death-and-disability-worldwide-2000-2019.
*6. Modi AR, Kovacs CS: Hospital-acquired and ventilator-associated pneumonia: diagnosis, management, and prevention, *Clev Clin J of Med* 87:633, 2020.

7. Saha BK: Rapidly progressive necrotizing pneumonia: remember the streptococcus anginous group! Retrieved from https://www.ncbi.nlm.nih.gov/pmc/articles/PMC7406454/.
*8. Salzer HJF, Schafer G, Hoenigl M, et al: Clinical, diagnostic, and treatment disparities between HIV-infected and non-HIV-infected immunocompromised patients with pneumocystis jirovecii pneumonia. Retrieved from https://www.karger.com/Article/Pdf/487713.
9. Einsele H, Ljungman P, Boeckh M: How I treat CMV reactivation after allogeneic hematopoietic stem cell transplantation, *Blood* 135:1619, 2020.
*10. Karakioulaki M, Stolz D: Biomarkers in pneumonia-beyond procalcitonin, *Int J Mol Sci* 20:2019, 2004.
*11. Warren C, Medei MK, Wood B, et al.: A nurse-driven oral care protocol to reduce hospital-acquired pneumonia, *AJN* 119:44, 2019.
12. WHO: Tuberculosis. Retrieved from https:// www.who.int/news-room/fact-sheets/detail/tuberculosis.
13. CDC: Fact sheet: Multi-drug resistant tuberculosis (MDR-TB). Retrieved from: https://www.cdc.gov/tb/publications/factsheets/drtb/mdrtb.htm.
14. Massachusetts Department of Public Health: Booster or recall effect and two-stage tuberculin skin testing. Retrieved from https://www.mass.gov/service-details/booster-or-recall-effect-and-two-stage-tuberculin-skin-testing.
*15. Zhou G, Luo Q, Luo S, et al.: Interferon-γ release assays or tuberculin skin test for detection and management of latent tuberculosis infection: a systematic review and meta-analysis, *Lancet Infect Dis* 20:1457, 2020.
*16. Pradipta IS, Houtsma D, van Boven JFM, et al: Interventions to improve medication adherence in tuberculosis patients: a systematic review of randomized controlled studies. Retrieved from https://www.nature.com/articles/s41533-020-0179-x.
17. CDC: Tuberculosis fact sheet: special considerations for treatment of TB disease in persons infected with HIV. Retrieved from https://www.cdc.gov/tb/publications/factsheets/treatment/treatmenthivpositive.htm.
18. CDC: Fungal diseases: where valley fever comes from. Retrieved from https://www.cdc.gov/fungal/diseases/coccidioidomycosis/causes.html.
19. Kamangar N: Lung abscess clinical presentation. Retrieved from https://emedicine.medscape.com/article/299425-clinical.
20. Wong AW, Ryerson CJ, Guler SA: Progression of fibrosing interstitial lung disease. Retrieved from https://respiratory-research.biomedcentral.com/articles/10.1186/s12931-020-1296-3.
21. Lee J: Idiopathic pulmonary fibrosis. Retrieved from https://www.merckmanuals.com/en-ca/professional/pulmonary-disorders/interstitial-lung-diseases/idiopathic-pulmonary-fibrosis.
22. Duffett L, Castellucci LA, Forgie MA: Pulmonary embolism: update on management and controversies. Retrieved from https://www.bmj.com/content/bmj/370/bmj.m2177.full.pdf
23. Kim NH, Delcroix M, Jais X, et al: Chronic thromboembolic pulmonary hypertension. Retrieved from https:// erj.ersjournals.com/content/53/1/1801915.
24. Yaghi S, Novikov A, Trandafirescu T: Clinical update on pulmonary hypertension, *J Invest Med* 68:821, 2020.
25. University of Wisconsin School of Medicine and Public Health Primary and secondary pulmonary hypertension. Retrieved from https://www.uwhealth.org/thoracic-surgery/primary-and-secondary-pulmonary-hypertension/11358#.
26. American Cancer Society: Risk factors for malignant mesothelioma. Retrieved from https://www.cancer.org/cancer/malignant-mesothelioma/causes-risks-prevention/risk-factors.html.
27. Cheronis N, Rabold E, Singh A, et al.: Lung transplantation in COPD, *Crit Care Nurs Q* 44:61, 2021.
28. Bos S, Vos R, Van Raemdonck DE, et al.: Survival in adult lung transplantation: where are we in 2020? *Curr Opin Organ Transplant* 25:268, 2020.
*29. Parulekar AD, Kao CC: Detection, classification, and management of rejection after lung transplantation, *J Thorac Dis* 11:S1732, 2019.
30. American Cancer Society: Key statistics for lung cancer. Retrieved from https://www.cancer.org/cancer/lung-cancer/about/key-statistics.html
31. CDC: Lung cancer: what are the risk factors for lung cancer? Retrieved from https://www.cdc.gov/cancer/lung/basic_info/risk_factors.htm.
32. Bohnenkamp S, Lacovara J: Non-small cell lung cancer: Part 1, *Med-Surg Nursing* 29:411, 2020.
33. Lababede O, Meziane MA: The eighth edition of TNM staging of lung cancer: Reference chart and diagrams, *Oncologist* 23:844, 2018.
*34. US Preventive Services Task Force: Screening for lung cancer: US Preventive Services Task Force recommendation statement, *JAMA* 325:962, 2021.

*Evidence-based information for clinical practice.

31

Obstructive Pulmonary Diseases

Eugene E. Mondor

http://evolve.elsevier.com/Lewis/medsurg/

CONCEPTUAL FOCUS

Fatigue
Functional Ability
Gas Exchange
Infection
Self-Management

LEARNING OUTCOMES

1. Describe the pathophysiology, clinical manifestations, and interprofessional and nursing management of the patient with bronchiectasis.
2. Describe the pathophysiology, clinical manifestations, and interprofessional and nursing management of the patient with cystic fibrosis.
3. Describe the etiology, pathophysiology, and clinical manifestations of asthma.
4. Explain the difference between an acute asthma exacerbation and status asthmaticus.
5. Describe the interprofessional care and nursing management of the patient with asthma.
6. Identify the classes of drugs used in the treatment of asthma and chronic obstructive pulmonary disease (COPD).
7. Describe the etiology, pathophysiology, clinical manifestations, and interprofessional care of the patient with COPD.
8. Explain the nursing management of the patient with COPD.

KEY TERMS

α_1-antitrypsin deficiency (AATD)
asthma
bronchiectasis
chronic bronchitis
chronic obstructive pulmonary disease (COPD)
cor pulmonale
cystic fibrosis (CF)
emphysema
peak expiratory flow rate
status asthmaticus

Imagine needing to consciously think about every breath that you take each minute, each hour, and every day of your life. Many people with obstructive lung disease have this experience. Obstructive pulmonary diseases are the most common chronic lung diseases. They have in common increased resistance to airflow because of airway obstruction or airway narrowing.

The 4 obstructive lung diseases discussed in this chapter are bronchiectasis, cystic fibrosis (CF), asthma, and chronic obstructive pulmonary disease (COPD). Drug therapy plays a key role in managing these conditions. Knowing common terms used in discussing respiratory care will help you better understand this content (Table 31.1).

BRONCHIECTASIS

In **bronchiectasis**, the bronchioles are dilated, making it hard to clear secretions. It most often results from poorly treated or untreated lung infections, immune system problems, or genetic factors. Bronchiectasis affects more than 500,000 people in the US.[1] It is more common in women. It affects 1 in every 150 people over age 75.[2]

Etiology and Pathophysiology

The hallmark characteristic of bronchiectasis is permanent, abnormal dilation of medium-sized bronchi. It results from inflammatory changes that destroy elastic and muscular structures supporting the bronchial wall. There is a continuing cycle of inflammation, airway damage, and remodeling, enhanced by the accumulation of neutrophils in the airways. Airways can become colonized with microorganisms (e.g., *Pseudomonas*), causing the bronchial walls to weaken and pockets of infection to form (Fig. 31.1).

When the walls of the bronchial system are injured, the mucociliary mechanism is damaged. This allows bacteria and mucus to accumulate within the pockets. Bacteria attract neutrophils, which enhances inflammation and causes edema.

TABLE 31.1 Common Terms Used in Respiratory Care

Respiratory Terms	
FeNO	Fractional concentration of exhaled nitric oxide (NO)
FEV1	Forced expired volume in 1 second
FEV1/FVC	Volume of air exhaled during the 1st second of a forced exhalation, expressed as a percentage (%) of FVC
FVC	Forced vital capacity
Pharmacologic Terms	
ICS	Inhaled corticosteroid
LABA	Long-acting B2 agonist
LAMA	Long-acting muscarinic antagonist
SABA	Short-acting B2 agonist
SAMA	Short-acting muscarinic antagonist

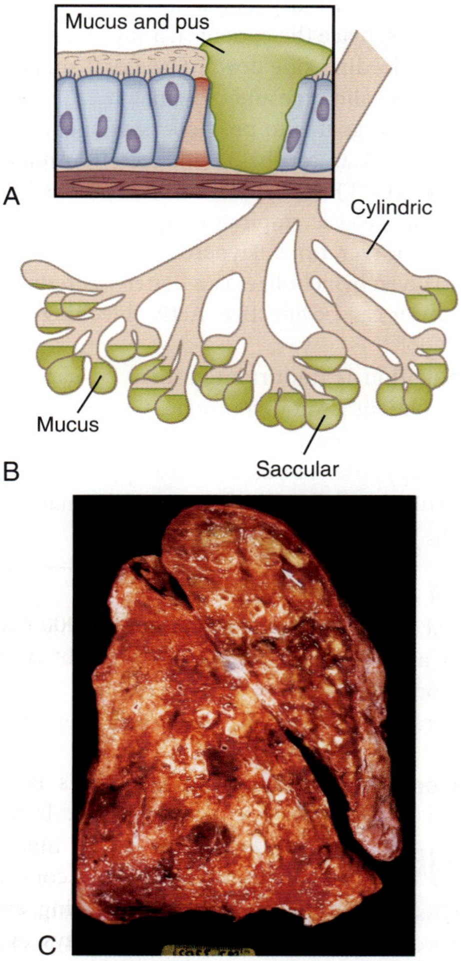

Fig. 31.1 Pathologic changes in bronchiectasis. (A) Longitudinal section of bronchial wall where chronic infection has caused damage. (B) Collection of purulent material in dilated bronchioles, leading to persistent infection. (C) Bronchiectasis in a patient with CF who underwent lung transplantation. Cut surfaces of the lung show markedly distended peripheral bronchi filled with mucopurulent secretions. (*C,* From Kumar V, Abbas AK, Aster JC: *Robbins and Cotran pathologic basis of disease,* ed 10, Philadelphia, 2021, Saunders.)

Impaired clearance of mucus by the cilia leads to stasis of thick mucus. This results in a reduced ability to clear mucus from the lungs and decreased expiratory airflow.

Around 40% of cases have no known cause.[1] CF is the main cause of bronchiectasis in children. Bacterial infection of the lungs is the main cause in adults. It can follow a single episode of severe pneumonia or infection that was either not treated or received inadequate or delayed treatment. Other risk factors include airway obstruction with mucus plugs, impaired pulmonary defenses, and repeated aspiration. Several systemic problems, such as diabetes, inflammatory bowel disease, rheumatoid arthritis, immune disorders (e.g., acquired immunodeficiency syndrome [AIDS]), and α-1 antitrypsin deficiency (AATD), are risk factors.[3]

Clinical Manifestations

The key sign is a persistent cough with consistent production of thick, tenacious, purulent sputum. In rare situations, some patients with severe disease and upper lobe involvement may have no sputum production and little cough. Recurrent infections injure blood vessels. Large connections (anastomoses) may develop between blood vessels in the lungs, and hemoptysis may occur. In severe cases, bleeding can be life-threatening. Other manifestations include pleuritic chest pain, dyspnea, wheezing, clubbing, weight loss, and anemia. Adventitious sounds are heard (e.g., crackles, wheezes) over the lung fields.

Complications

Complications include pulmonary hypertension and repeated exacerbations of the condition, often accompanied by chronic inflammation and hypoxemia. Colonization with multi-drug resistant organisms can occur, especially if the patient has received antibiotic therapy over long periods of time.

Neovascularization (development of new blood vessels after injury) of the bronchial arteries is a significant complication.[4] This can lead to hemoptysis and in some situations hemorrhage. Massive hemoptysis is a life-threatening emergency.

Diagnostic Studies

A person who presents with a chronic productive cough with copious purulent sputum (which may be blood streaked) should be suspected of having bronchiectasis. A CT scan is the gold standard for diagnosing bronchiectasis.

Chest x-rays may show nonspecific abnormalities. Spirometry usually shows an obstructive pattern, including decreases in FEV_1 and FEV_1/FVC (see Table 27.18). Sputum cultures may confirm the presence of infection. Patients often have *Hemophilus influenzae, Staphylococcus aureus,* or *Pseudomonas aeruginosa.*[4] *P. aeruginosa* leads to frequent exacerbations and rapid decline in lung function. A complete blood cell count and AAT level may be done.

INTERPROFESSIONAL CARE

There is no cure for bronchiectasis. Most patients are safely managed on an outpatient basis. Contact with the health care system is often related to an exacerbation. When the patient is not responding to care, hospitalization may be needed for monitoring and further treatment.

Therapy is aimed at treating acute flare-ups and preventing a decline in lung function. Antibiotics are the mainstay of treatment. They are often given for a minimum of 14 days. Antibiotics may be given orally, IV, or inhaled (nebulizer). Choice of antibiotic mainly depends on culture results or the most likely organism. Long-term antibiotic therapy is given to patients who have symptoms that recur a few days after stopping antibiotics.

Bronchodilator therapy with short-acting β-2 agonists (SABAs), long-acting β-2 agonists (LABAs), or anticholinergics can prevent bronchospasm and stimulate mucus clearance. Patients may receive oral or inhaled corticosteroids (ICS) depending on the severity of the condition.

Surgical resection of parts of the lungs was common in the past. It has largely been replaced by more effective supportive therapy and antibiotic treatment. For select patients who are disabled despite maximal therapy, a lung transplant may be an option.

NURSING MANAGEMENT: BRONCHIECTASIS

Assessment

When the patient in immediate distress, priorities include maintaining a patent airway, ensuring an adequate route for ventilation, and stable vital signs. Notify the HCP, especially if the patient is expectorating large amounts of blood.

For the patient not in immediate distress, obtain a patient and family history. If possible, identify onset, risk factors, and any past complications. Review the current drug therapy and treatments the patient is receiving.

Clinical Problems

Clinical problems for the patient with bronchiectasis may include:

- Impaired respiratory function
- Activity intolerance
- Deficient knowledge

Planning

The overall goals for the patient with bronchiectasis include (1) maintain a patent airway; (2) have slow, steady, and unlabored breathing; and (3) develop a routine that permits as much functional independence as possible with activities of daily living (ADLs).

Implementation

Health Promotion

Patient teaching is important. Encourage them to follow as healthy a lifestyle as possible. Stress the need to quit smoking or, at minimum, reduce the amount smoked. Stress the need to follow a healthy diet. Encourage the patient to engage in some type of regular exercise (within the comfort and safety of their condition). Discuss how to prevent exacerbations and review airway clearance techniques (ACTs).

Maintaining hydration is important to liquefy secretions. Unless contraindicated, the patient should drink at least 2 to 3 L of fluid daily. To achieve this, tell the patient to increase intake by 1 glass per day until they reach that goal. Have the patient use low-sodium fluids to avoid fluid retention. Rest is important to prevent overexertion.

Teach the patient and caregiver signs and symptoms to report to the HCP. These include increased work of breathing (WOB), sputum production, or dyspnea. Fever, chills, and chest pain may or may not occur with an exacerbation. Teach patients when to contact the HCP if hemoptysis occurs. Some patients expectorate a "spot" of blood at times. This is usual for them and does not require urgent attention. However, if the patient expectorates a moderate to large amount of blood, they should contact the HCP at once.

Acute Care

In the acute care setting, elevate the head of the bed to at least 30 degrees. Monitor vital signs and respiratory status, including rate, rhythm, and SpO_2. Apply O_2 therapy via a low-flow delivery device (e.g., nasal cannula) if O_2 saturation is less than 90% on room air. If you suspect that the patient may be bleeding from the airways, place the patient in a side-lying position with the suspected bleeding side down. Have oral suction available. Ensure there is a valid type and crossmatch.

One important goal is to promote drainage and removal of mucus. Various ACTs can help with secretion removal. Chest physiotherapy (CPT) with postural drainage is widely used. Direct hydration of the respiratory system may help with the expectoration of secretions. Hyperosmolar agents (e.g., hypertonic saline) given by nebulizer can liquefy secretions. At home, a steamy shower can be effective. Active bleeding is a contraindication to CPT.

Good nutrition is important. It may be hard to maintain because the patient is often anorexic. Oral hygiene to cleanse the mouth and remove dried sputum crusts may improve the patient's appetite. Foods that are appealing, provided in smaller quantities, and offered more often may increase the desire to eat.

Evaluation

The expected outcomes of a patient with bronchiectasis include:

- Maintain a patent airway
- Have a normal respiratory rate and rhythm
- Demonstrate a health balance between activity and rest with ADLs
- Perform optimal self-management

CYSTIC FIBROSIS

Cystic fibrosis (CF) is an inherited, autosomal recessive genetic disorder, characterized by altered transport of sodium and chloride ions in and out of epithelial cells. Airway obstruction occurs because of changes in exocrine glandular secretions, resulting in increased mucus production. This defect also affects the gastrointestinal (GI) system (pancreas and biliary tract) and reproductive organs. There are about 30,000 people in the US living with CF. More than 50% of the CF population are adults.[5]

BOX 31.1 GENETICS IN CLINICAL PRACTICE

Cystic Fibrosis

Genetic Basis

- Autosomal recessive disorder
- Caused by mutations in CF transmembrane regulator *(CFTR)* gene
- *CFTR* gene provides the instructions for making the protein that controls the channel that transports sodium and chloride
- There are more than 1,700 different mutations of the *CFTR* gene
- Mutations in the *CFTR* gene disrupt the function of the channels, preventing them from regulating the flow of sodium, chloride, and water across cell membranes
- The most common mutation is 2 copies (homozygous) of the *F508* mutation in the *CFTR* gene

Incidence

- In the US, 1 in 2500–3000 White births
- One in 25–30 Whites are carriers of the gene
- 10,000 new cases diagnosed each year, most before 1 year of age

Clinical Implications

- Most people who have a child with CF are not aware of a family history of CF.
- We should offer CF screening to all people of reproductive age regardless of family history.

Genetic Testing

- Can identify if a person is a carrier of the mutation for the *CFTR* gene
- Blood-based DNA testing is available for disease and carrier states
- All 50 states require newborn CF screening
- Testing is usually done in children if CF is suspected or if parents are possible carriers
- In parents who are known carriers, amniocentesis between 15 and 20 weeks or chorionic villus sampling between 10 and 13 weeks of pregnancy can be done (although testing can also occur in pregnant women beyond these dates)

The median age at diagnosis is 6 to 8 months of age. Two-thirds of patients are diagnosed in the first year of life.[5] Some are not diagnosed until they are adults. The severity and progression of CF vary. With early diagnosis and improvements in therapy, the prognosis of patients with CF has significantly improved. The median predicted survival in 1970 was 16 years of age. Today it has increased to more than 46 years.[6] There are many persons with CF who have lived beyond this age.

Genetic Link

CF is an autosomal recessive disorder (Box 31.1). The CF gene is found on chromosome 7, which makes a protein called *CF transmembrane conductance regulator (CFTR).*[7] The CFTR protein localizes to the epithelial surface of the airways, GI tract, and ducts of the liver, pancreas, and sweat glands. Under normal conditions, CFTR regulates sodium and chloride movement in and out of epithelial cells.

Mutations in the *CFTR* gene change this protein so that the channels are blocked. As a result, cells that line the passageways of the lungs, pancreas, intestines, and other organs make secretions that are low in sodium chloride content (thus low in water content), making them abnormally thick and sticky

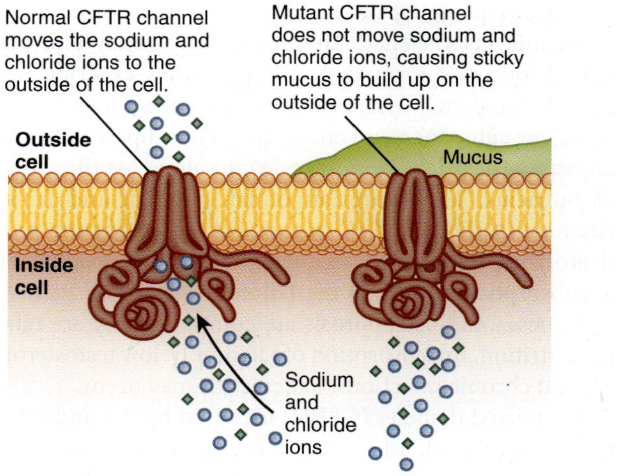

Fig. 31.2 Cystic fibrosis transmembrane conductance regulator *(CFTR)* is a protein of the cell membrane that normally helps sodium and chloride move in and out of cells. People with CF inherit a defective gene. As a result, movement of sodium and chloride is blocked. Abnormally thick sticky mucus is produced on the outside of the cell.

(Fig. 31.2). The thick secretions plug up the ducts in these organs. This causes scarring in the organs and results in organ failure. The high concentrations of sodium and chloride in the sweat of the patient with CF result from decreased chloride reabsorption in the sweat duct.

Pathophysiology

CF has a significant effect on the airways. It can affect both the upper and lower respiratory tracts. CF progresses from being a disease of the small airways to involving the larger airways with destruction of lung tissue. The mucus lining the airways becomes dehydrated and tenacious due to defects in chloride secretion and sodium absorption. Cilia become overwhelmed with thick secretions. As a result, cilia motility is decreased, allowing mucus to adhere to the airways. At the same time, the bronchioles become obstructed with the thick mucus, leading to scarring of the airways, air trapping, and hyperinflation of the lungs.

With CF, there is a persistent, chronic airway infection that cannot be cured. *Pseudomonas* is the most common organism in adults.[7] Antibiotic resistance can develop after multiple exposures to antibiotics. Lung inflammation is associated with chronic infection. It can narrow airways and cause a decrease in lung function. An increase in inflammatory mediators (e.g., interleukins, oxidants, proteases released by neutrophils) contributes to disease progression.

Lung disorders that initially occur are chronic bronchiolitis and bronchiectasis. Over a long period, pulmonary vascular remodeling occurs because of local hypoxia and arteriolar vasoconstriction. Enlarged pulmonary arteries, pulmonary hypertension, and cor pulmonale occur in the later phases of the disease. Blebs and large cysts are severe manifestations of lung destruction. Pneumothorax may occur. There is a proliferation of capillaries in response to chronic infection. During exacerbations, there may be erosion of these capillaries and hemoptysis can occur. Hemoptysis may range from scant streaking to major bleeding, which can be fatal.

Mucous plugging of the pancreatic exocrine ducts causes pancreatic insufficiency. This results in atrophy and progressive fibrotic cyst formation. The pancreas's exocrine function may be completely lost. Because of this, the pancreas does not make enough pancreatic enzymes, such as lipase, amylase, and proteases (trypsin, chymotrypsin), to allow for the absorption of nutrients. Malabsorption of fat, protein, and fat-soluble vitamins (A, D, E, and K) occurs. Fat malabsorption results in steatorrhea (large, oily, frequent bowel movements). Protein malabsorption results in the failure to grow and gain weight. Osteopenia and osteoporosis are common. They are related to malnutrition, malabsorption of vitamin D, low testosterone levels, and chronic infections. Pancreatitis may occur.

CF-related diabetes (CFRD) is caused by the underdevelopment of pancreatic islet cells (in utero) and destruction of islet cells over the person's lifetime. CFRD is unique because it has characteristics of both type 1 and type 2 diabetes. The pancreas in people with CF makes insulin, but they make it too late to fully respond to carbohydrate intake.

Persons with CF often have other GI problems, including gastroesophageal reflux disease GERD, gallstones, and cirrhosis. Mucus deposits in the ducts can damage the liver and gall bladder. Liver enzymes may become chronically increased. Cirrhosis develops over time. Portal hypertension can occur. *Distal intestinal obstruction syndrome (DIOS)* results from an intermittent obstruction, often in the terminal ileum at the point of the ileocecal junction. It is caused by thickened, dehydrated stool and mucus. DIOS develops because of chronic malabsorption related to exocrine dysfunction, under- or over-dosing of pancreatic replacement enzyme supplements, dehydration, and swallowing of mucus. The patient may appear to have a small bowel obstruction.

Clinical Manifestations

The manifestations vary depending on the severity of the disease. Severity may vary greatly, both within families and among different families. Carriers do not have symptoms.

Meconium ileus in a newborn prompts the diagnosis in 20% of people. Other signs that suggest a CF diagnosis in childhood are acute or persistent respiratory symptoms (wheezing, coughing, frequent pneumonia), failure to thrive, malnutrition, steatorrhea, bronchiectasis, and family history. Without treatment, a large, protuberant abdomen may develop with an emaciated appearance of the extremities.

In adults, patients often present with atypical symptoms, such as new-onset diabetes or infertility problems. A common symptom of CF in the adult is a frequent cough. With time, the cough becomes persistent and produces thick, purulent sputum. URI manifestations may include chronic sinusitis and nasal polyposis. Other lung problems include recurring lung infections, such as bronchiolitis, bronchitis, and pneumonia. With advanced lung disease, clubbing occurs. As the disease progresses, periods of clinical stability are interspersed by exacerbations characterized by increased cough, weight loss, increased sputum production, and decreased lung function. Over time, exacerbations become more frequent, bronchiectasis worsens, and the recovery of lost lung function is less complete. These changes may lead to respiratory failure.

Patients with DIOS may have right lower quadrant pain (the area of the ileocecal valve), nausea, vomiting, and a palpable mass. Insufficient pancreatic enzyme release causes the typical pattern of protein and fat malabsorption. Many persons are thin with a low body mass index (BMI). They may have frequent bulky, foul-smelling stools.

Both males and females have delayed puberty. Some women have difficulty conceiving. The cervical mucus may be thick. During exacerbations, menstrual irregularities and secondary amenorrhea are common. Most women with CF can become pregnant. Most pregnancies result in viable infants.

Nearly all men with CF have reproductive issues. Because the vas deferens fails to develop in utero, there is no transport of sperm from storage in the testes to the penile urethra. However, they make sperm normally and can father a child with assisted reproductive technology.

Complications

Complications include CFRD and bone, sinus, and liver disease. Respiratory failure and cor pulmonale caused by pulmonary hypertension are late complications of CF. Pneumothorax, a rare but serious complication, is caused by the formation of bullae and blebs on the surface of the lung. A small amount of blood in sputum is common because of chronic lung infection. Massive hemoptysis, though rare, can be life-threatening. Liver failure and bowel obstruction may occur in severe CF.

Diagnostic Studies

The diagnostic criteria for CF include a combination of clinical presentation, family history, and laboratory and genetic testing. The sweat glands of patients with CF secrete normal volumes of sweat. They do not absorb sodium chloride from their sweat as it moves through the sweat duct. As a result, they excrete 4 times the normal amount of sodium and chloride in sweat. This problem usually does not directly affect the person's health but helps confirm a diagnosis of CF.

The sweat chloride test is the gold standard for diagnosing CF. It is done with the pilocarpine iontophoresis method.[8] Pilocarpine is placed on the skin and carried by a small electric current to stimulate sweat production. This part of the process takes about 5 minutes. Explain to the patient they may feel a slight tingling or warmth. Next, the area (usually an arm) is wrapped in plastic to promote sweating. The sweat is collected on filter paper or gauze and then analyzed for sweat chloride concentrations. The test takes about 1 hour. Sweat chloride values above 60 mmol/L are considered positive for the diagnosis of CF.[8] A second sweat chloride test is done at the same time (1 test in each arm) to confirm the diagnosis.

Genetic testing is often done if the results from a sweat chloride test are uncertain. We can send a blood or cell sample to a laboratory that specializes in genetic testing. Most laboratories test for only the most common mutations of the CF gene. Because more than 1700 mutations cause CF, screening for all mutations is difficult and done only at specialized laboratories.

Interprofessional Care

An interprofessional team should be involved in the care of a patient with CF. The Cystic Fibrosis Foundation funds more than 120 CF care centers nationwide. The high quality of specialized care from the care center network has led to the improved length and quality of life for people with CF. These care centers offer the best care, treatments, and support for those with CF. The teams at these care centers include a nurse, physician, respiratory therapist, physical therapist, dietitian, social worker, and often a nurse practitioner.

Management of lung problems aims at relieving airway obstruction and controlling infection. Aerosol and nebulizer treatments promote drainage of thick bronchial mucus. The drugs we use dilate the airways, liquefy mucus, and promote clearance.

The abnormal viscosity of secretions is increased by concentrated DNA from neutrophils involved in chronic infection. Drugs that degrade the DNA in CF sputum (e.g., inhaled dornase alfa [Pulmozyme]) increase airflow and reduce the number of acute exacerbations. Inhaled hypertonic saline (7%) increases osmolality, allowing water to collect on airway surfaces. It is effective in clearing mucus and decreases the frequency of exacerbations. Some patients need bronchodilators (e.g., β_2-adrenergic agonists) to control bronchospasm, but the long-term benefit is not known.

ACTs are critical since the normal ciliary motion in CF airways is impaired. CPT (including postural drainage with percussion and vibration) and high-frequency chest wall oscillation loosen mucus. Specialized expiratory techniques that use airflow to remove the loosened secretions help clear secretions. Examples include breathing exercises, pursed-lip breathing, and huff coughing (see Chapter 28). Patients may prefer a certain technique or device that works well for them in their daily routine. No ACT is better than the others.

Most patients with CF die of complications from lung infection. Thus, early intervention with antibiotics is key when infection is present. Antibiotic choice should be based on sputum culture results. The usual treatment is 2 antibiotics with different mechanisms of action (e.g., cephalosporin and an aminoglycoside). They may be given for 10 days to 3 weeks or longer. Prolonged high-dose therapy (larger doses, more frequent dosing) may be needed because many drugs are abnormally metabolized and rapidly excreted in the patient with CF. Some need chronic suppressive therapy. If home support and resources are adequate, the patient and caregiver may be able to administer IV antibiotic therapy at home independently.

Oral agents used for mild exacerbations (e.g., increased cough and sputum) include a semisynthetic penicillin, trimethoprim/sulfamethoxazole (to treat *S. aureus*), or oral quinolones, especially ciprofloxacin (to treat *Pseudomonas*). Quinolones are used with caution because of the rapid development of resistant strains.

Most patients have *Pseudomonas* infection, which can be hard to treat over time because the organism develops resistance to antibiotics. *Pseudomonas* can form a biofilm that protects the organism from antibiotics. A common antibiotic used to treat patients with chronic *Pseudomonas* infection is aerosolized tobramycin. It is given twice a day, every day, every other month. Azithromycin used longer than 6 months decreases the frequency of exacerbations, especially in those infected with *Pseudomonas*. We also think it acts as an antiinflammatory.

The patient with cor pulmonale or hypoxemia may need home O_2 therapy. Those with a large pneumothorax need chest tube drainage, sometimes repeatedly. Sclerosing of the pleural space or partial pleural stripping and pleural abrasion may be done for recurrent episodes of pneumothorax. With massive hemoptysis, bronchial artery embolization is done. CF has become a leading reason for lung transplantation.

The management of pancreatic insufficiency includes pancreatic enzyme replacement of lipase, protease, and amylase (e.g., pancrelipase [Pancreaze, Creon, Zenpep]) taken before each meal and snack. Adequate intake of fat, calories, protein, and vitamins is important. Fat-soluble vitamins (A, D, E, and K) must be supplemented since they are malabsorbed. Caloric supplements improve nutrition status. Extra salt is needed when sweating is increased, such as during hot weather, with a fever, or from intense physical activity. Hyperglycemia may need insulin treatment.

If the patient develops DIOS with partial or complete bowel obstruction, we make every attempt to manage the condition medically. Options include prokinetic agents (e.g., macrolide antibiotics, metoclopramide), mucolytics (oral N-acetylcysteine [NAC]), stimulant laxatives, lactulose, and polyethylene glycol (PEG) electrolyte solution.[9] Careful monitoring of bowel habits and patterns is essential for CF patients. If DIOS does not resolve with medical treatment, surgery may be done to prevent ischemic bowel.

All patients with CF should have CFTR genotyping. This will help see if they carry a mutation that is a target of CFTR modulator therapy. Drugs, such as ivacaftor/lumacaftor (Orkambi) and Ivacaftor (Kalydeco), are used to treat patients with specific *CFTR* gene mutations.[10]

NURSING MANAGEMENT: CYSTIC FIBROSIS

Assessment

Subjective and objective data you should obtain from the patient with CF are shown in Table 31.2.

Clinical Problems

Clinical problems for the patient with CF may include:

- Impaired respiratory function
- Nutritionally compromised
- Deficient knowledge

Planning

The overall goals are that the patient with CF will have (1) adequate airway clearance, (2) absence of respiratory infection, (3) adequate nutrition to maintain appropriate weight, (4) ability to independently (or with assist) perform ADLs, (5) recognize and treat complications related to CF, and (6) actively take part in planning and implementing the treatment plan.

Implementation

Acute Care

Acute care for the patient with CF includes relief of bronchoconstriction, airway obstruction, and airflow limitation. Interventions include aggressive CPT, antibiotics, and O_2

TABLE 31.2 NURSING ASSESSMENT
Cystic Fibrosis

Subjective Data	Objective Data
Important Health Information • *Health history:* Recurrent respiratory and sinus infections, persistent cough with excess sputum production • *Medications:* Use of and compliance with bronchodilators, antibiotics	**Cardiovascular** • ↑ Heart rate **Eyes** • Scleral icterus **General** • Restlessness, failure to thrive
Functional Health Patterns • *Health perception–health maintenance:* Family history of CF, when diagnosed, genetic testing • *Nutritional-metabolic:* Diet intolerances, voracious appetite, weight loss, heartburn • *Elimination:* Intestinal gas. Large, frequent bowel movements, constipation • *Activity-exercise:* Fatigue, ↓ exercise tolerance, amount and type of exercise. Dyspnea, cough, excess mucus or sputum production, coughing up blood, ACTs • *Cognitive-perceptual:* Abdominal pain • *Sexuality-reproductive:* Delayed menarche, menstrual problem, infertility • *Coping–stress tolerance:* Anxiety, depression, difficulty coping	**GI** • Protuberant abdomen; abdominal distention; foul, fatty stools **Respiratory** • Sinus congestion, postnasal drip, persistent runny nose • Decreased breath sounds, adventitious breath sounds (crackles, wheezes) • Sputum (thick, tenacious) • ↑ WOB, accessory muscle use, barrel chest **Skin** • Salty skin; clubbing; cyanosis (circumoral, nail bed) **Possible Diagnostic Findings** • Abnormal sweat chloride test, abnormal ABGs and pulmonary function tests • Abnormal chest x-ray, fecal fat analysis

therapy in severe disease. Measures to optimize nutrition are important.

In severe cases, patients may be cared for in the intensive care unit (ICU). Reasons for ICU admission include acute respiratory insufficiency or failure and hemoptysis. The patient may need mechanical ventilation and hemodynamic monitoring.

◆ Ambulatory Care

A focus on ACTs, treatment of infection with antibiotic therapy, nutrition support (including pancreatic enzymes), and psychosocial support are important components of care. This may involve many members of the health care team, including physician, nursing, dietary, pharmacy, physiotherapy, occupational therapy, and psychology.

We should encourage the patient to take part in aerobic exercise. It is effective in clearing the airways. Considerations when planning an exercise program include (1) meeting increased nutrition demands of exercise, (2) observing for dehydration, (3) drinking large amounts of fluid, and (4) replacing salt losses.

As these persons continue into adulthood, you can help them achieve greater independence by allowing them to assume more responsibility for their care and life goals. One issue to discuss with the patient is sexuality. Delayed development of secondary sex characteristics and irregular menses are common. The issue of marrying and having children is complicated. Genetic counseling is appropriate when the patient is considering having children. Another concern is uncertainty surrounding the shortened life span of the parent with CF.

Other crises and life transitions that must be dealt with in the young adult include identifying employment goals, developing motivation, learning to cope with the treatment, and adjusting to the need for dependence if health fails. Disclosing the CF diagnosis to friends, potential spouses, and/or employers may pose significant emotional, social, and financial challenges. Referral to counseling may help depending on the patient's ability to cope with the condition and availability of support networks.

CF imposes a significant emotional and financial burden on the patient and family. In many situations, the cost of drugs, special equipment, and health care poses financial hardship. The burden of living with a chronic disease at a young age can be emotionally overwhelming. There is a higher incidence of anxiety and depression among persons with CF than their unaffected peers.[11] Issues related to costs of health care, burden of self-care, career choices, fertility, and decreased life expectancy may lead to depression. Community resources are available to help patients and caregivers. The Cystic Fibrosis Foundation can be a source of information and support.

ASTHMA

Asthma is a diverse disease characterized by bronchial hyperreactivity with reversible expiratory airflow limitation, either spontaneously or with treatment. Signs and symptoms can be variable. For example, there may be mild shortness of breath and chest tightness with a minor asthma attack. A major asthma attack may include severe shortness of breath, accessory muscle use, stridor, and severe hypoxemia. If left untreated, respiratory and/or cardiac arrest can occur.

Asthma affects around 25 million adult Americans.[12] It is a major public health concern. There are more than 2 million emergency department (ED) visits, 10 million outpatient visits, and 500,000 hospitalizations each year.[13] The clinical course of asthma is unpredictable. It ranges from periods of adequate control to frequent attacks with poor control of symptoms. The mortality for asthma has decreased over the past 10 years. Unfortunately, more than 4000 people still die each year from asthma.[13]

Risk Factors and Triggers

Risk factors for asthma and triggers of asthma attacks are related to the patient (e.g., genetic factors) or the environment (e.g., pollen) (Table 31.3 and Box 31.2). We discuss the most important risk factors and triggers of asthma attacks here.

Nose and Sinus Problems

Most patients have a history of allergic rhinitis. Treatment of allergic rhinitis usually improves asthma symptoms. Acute and chronic sinusitis, especially bacterial rhinosinusitis, may worsen

TABLE 31.3 Triggers of Asthma Attacks

Air Pollutants	• Aerosol sprays • Cigarette smoke • Exhaust fumes • Oxidants • Perfumes • Sulfur dioxides
Allergen Inhalation	• Animal dander (e.g., dogs, cats, mice, guinea pigs) • Cockroaches • House dust mite • Molds • Pollens
Drugs	• Aspirin • β-Adrenergic blockers • NSAIDs
Food Additives	• Beer, wine, dried fruit, shrimp, processed potatoes • Monosodium glutamate • Sulfites (bisulfites and metabisulfites) • Tartrazine
Occupational Exposure	• Agriculture, farming • Industrial chemicals and plastics • Laundry detergents • Metal salts • Paints, solvents • Wood and vegetable dusts
Pulmonary	• Sinusitis, allergic rhinitis • Viral URI
Other Factors	• Exercise and cold, dry air • GERD • Hormones, menses • Stress

BOX 31.2 BIOLOGIC SEX CONSIDERATIONS

Asthma

Men

- Before puberty, asthma affects more boys.
- Boys most likely to have less severe symptoms by late teen years.

Women

- In adulthood, asthma affects more women.
- Between 40 and 60 years of age, have a higher incidence and severity.
- Women who present to the emergency department are more likely to need hospitalization.
- Have a higher overall mortality.

asthma. Patients often have chronic sinus problems that cause inflammation of the mucous membranes and can trigger an asthma attack. Sinusitis must be treated and large nasal polyps removed for the patient to have good control of their asthma.

Allergens

Allergens cause varying degrees of allergic reactions in susceptible persons. Indoor and outdoor allergens, such as cockroaches, furry animals, fungi, pollen, and molds, can trigger asthma attacks. However, we are not clear about their role in the development of asthma.

Cigarette Smoke

The Centers for Disease Control and Prevention (CDC) estimates that 21% of persons with asthma smoke.[14] In a person with asthma, smoking is associated with a faster decline of lung function, increased severity, more frequent HCP visits, and a decreased response to treatment. *Passive smoking* is the exposure of non-smokers to cigarette smoke. It is also known as *environmental tobacco smoke* (ETS) or secondhand smoke. It is also a risk factor.

Air Pollutants

Various air pollutants, such as wood smoke or vehicle exhaust, can trigger asthma attacks. In heavily industrialized or densely populated areas, climate conditions often lead to concentrated pollution in the atmosphere, especially with thermal inversions and stagnant air masses. News sources often report ozone alert days. Patients with breathing problems should minimize outdoor activity during these times.

Respiratory Tract Infections

Respiratory tract infections are often a major trigger of an acute asthma attack. Acute URIs can decrease the diameter of the airways and induce airway hyperresponsiveness. Viral-induced changes in epithelial cells, the accumulation of cells that enhance inflammation, and edema of airway walls contribute to altered respiratory function. These changes may worsen asthma.

Immune Response

People who have a lower incidence of asthma were exposed to certain infections early in life. They received fewer antibiotics, were around other children (e.g., siblings, day care), or lived in rural settings or with pets. The *hygiene hypothesis* suggests that in extremely clean environments, a newborn and child's immune system will not fully mature and develop. In other words, exposure to different germs and various infections during infancy and childhood helps strengthen your immune system. However, we know that this view does not tell the full story. The link between respiratory problems and the predisposition to develop certain conditions, like asthma, is complicated.

Genetics

The genetics of asthma are complex. Many genes may be involved. They are likely responsible for different responses to triggers and asthma drugs. Atopy, the genetic predisposition to develop an allergic (immunoglobulin E [IgE]–mediated) response to common allergens, is a major risk factor.

Gastroesophageal Reflux Disease

GERD is more common in people with asthma. GERD can worsen asthma symptoms because reflux may trigger bronchoconstriction and cause aspiration. Asthma drugs can also worsen GERD symptoms. β_2-Agonists used to treat asthma (especially when given orally) relax the lower esophageal sphincter. This allows stomach contents to reflux into the esophagus and potentially be aspirated. GERD treatment can improve nocturnal asthma control, improve quality of life, and prevent asthma symptoms in some patients. GERD is discussed in Chapter 46.

Drugs and Food Additives

Some people with asthma have what we call the *asthma triad:* nasal polyps, asthma, and sensitivity to aspirin and nonsteroidal antiinflammatory drugs (NSAIDs).[15] Some persons with asthma who use salicylic acid (e.g., aspirin) or NSAIDs can develop wheezing within 2 hours. In addition, there is usually profound rhinorrhea, congestion, and tearing. Angioedema can occur. These patients must avoid salicylic acid and NSAIDs. Teach the patient the importance of reading labels. Salicylic acid is in many OTC drugs and some foods, beverages, and flavorings. Under the care of an allergist, daily administration of the drug can desensitize some patients.

β-Adrenergic blockers in oral form (e.g., metoprolol) or topical eye drops (e.g., timolol) may trigger an asthma attack because they can cause bronchospasm. ACE inhibitors (e.g., lisinopril) may cause a dry, hacking cough, making asthma symptoms worse. Asthma attacks can occur after the use of sulfite-containing preservatives found in topical ophthalmic solutions, IV corticosteroids, and some inhaled bronchodilator solutions.

Food and drug additives that may trigger asthma include tartrazine (yellow dye no. 5) and sulfiting agents. They are common preservatives and sanitizing agents. Sulfiting agents are in fruits, beer, and wine. They are used in salad bars to protect vegetables from oxidation. Food allergies triggering asthma reactions in adults are rare.

Exercise

We call asthma that is induced or becomes worse during physical exertion exercise-induced asthma (EIA) or exercise-induced bronchoconstriction (EIB).[16] Typically, symptoms of EIA or EIB are worse during activities in which there is exposure to cold, dry air. For example, swimming in an indoor heated pool is less likely to cause symptoms than skiing.

Varying degrees of airway obstruction may occur due to changes in airway mucosa caused by hyperventilation during exercise. Inhaling either cool or re-warmed air and airway edema from capillary leakage in the airway wall contributes to this condition. EIB often occurs after less than 10 minutes of vigorous exercise. It most often resolves within 60 minutes.[16]

Occupational Factors

Occupational asthma is the most common job-related respiratory problem. Occupational irritants cause a change in the responsiveness of the airways. The development of symptoms may not occur until the patient has had months to years of exposure. These agents are diverse and include wood dusts, laundry detergents, metal salts, chemicals, paints, solvents, and plastics. Often, people with occupational asthma give a history of arriving at work feeling well but gradually develop symptoms, which may become progressively worse, by the end of the day.

Psychologic Factors

Many people report that symptoms worsen with stress. An asthma attack caused by any trigger can cause panic, stress, and anxiety. These emotions, and other psychologic factors, can lead to bronchoconstriction through stimulation of the cholinergic reflex pathways. Extreme behavioral expressions (e.g., crying, laughing, anger, fear) can lead to hyperventilation and hypocapnia, which can cause airway narrowing and an asthma attack.

Pathophysiology

The main pathophysiologic process in asthma is persistent but variable inflammation of the airways. Airflow is limited because inflammation results in bronchoconstriction, airway hyperresponsiveness (hyperreactivity), and edema of the airways. Exposure to allergens or irritants starts the inflammatory cascade (Fig. 31.3). A variety of inflammatory cells are involved, including mast cells, macrophages, eosinophils, neutrophils, T and B lymphocytes, and epithelial cells of the airways.

As the inflammatory process begins, mast cells (found beneath the basement membrane of the bronchial wall) degranulate and release multiple inflammatory mediators. IgE antibodies are linked to mast cells, and the allergen cross-links the IgE. As a result, inflammatory mediators, such as leukotrienes, histamine, cytokines, prostaglandins, and nitric oxide, are released (Fig. 31.4). Inflammatory mediators have effects on the (1) blood vessels, causing vasodilation and increasing capillary permeability (runny nose); (2) nerve cells, causing itching; (3) smooth muscle cells, causing bronchial spasms and airway narrowing; and (4) goblet cells, causing mucus production. As a result, edema of airway mucosa, muscle spasm, and accumulation of secretions produce varying degrees of expiratory airflow obstruction (Fig. 31.5).

This process is the *early-phase response* of asthma. Clinically, it occurs within minutes after exposure to an allergen or irritant. It generally resolves within 1 to 2 hours. Symptoms can recur 4 to 6 hours after the early response because of the influx of inflammatory cells, which are set in motion by the initial response. At this later time, the patient may develop symptoms again or worsening of symptoms.

We call this the *late-phase response.* It occurs in about 50% of people with asthma. In the late-phase response, the body activates more inflammatory cells, with continuing airway inflammation. Bronchoconstriction with symptoms can last for 24 hours or more. Corticosteroids are often effective in treating inflammation in this late phase. Chronic inflammation may cause structural changes in the bronchial wall, known as *remodeling.* Over time, a progressive loss of lung function occurs that therapy cannot fully reverse. Structural changes include fibrosis of the subepithelium, hypertrophy of the smooth muscle of the airways, mucus hypersecretion, continued inflammation, and angiogenesis. Remodeling and genetic factors may explain why some persons have persistent asthma and limited response to therapy.

Clinical Manifestations

The characteristic manifestations of an asthma attack are wheezing, cough, dyspnea, and chest tightness after exposure to a risk factor or trigger. Normally, the bronchioles constrict during expiration. However, in asthma, the airways become narrower than usual because of bronchospasm, edema, and mucus. As a

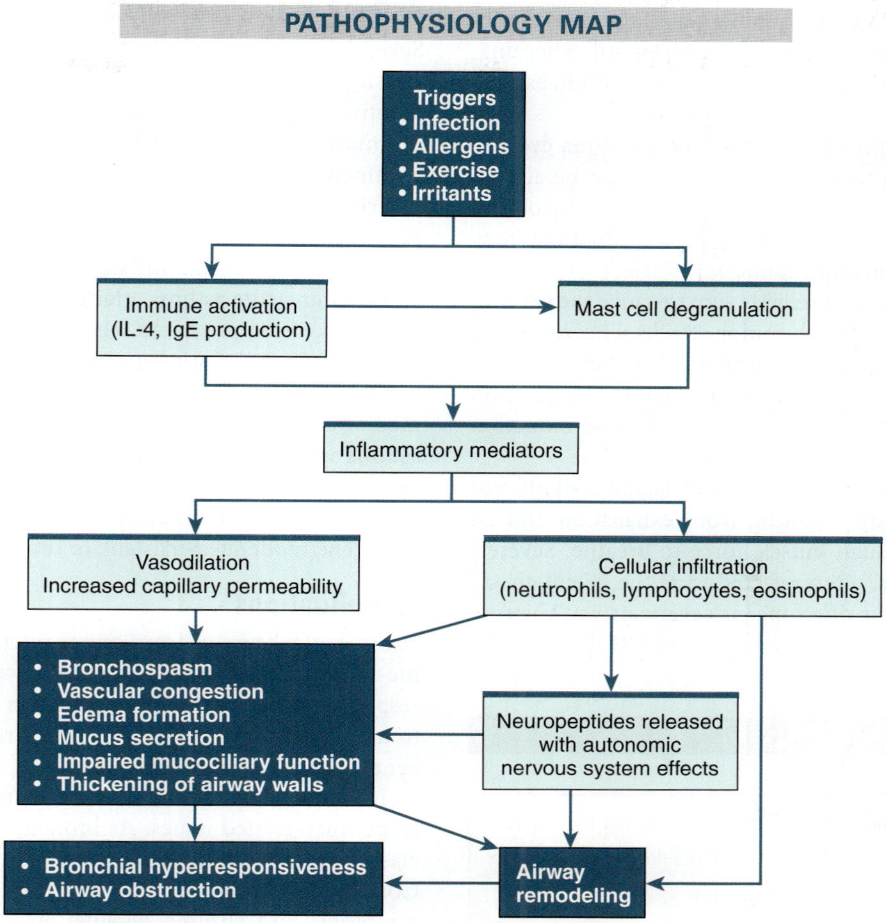

Fig. 31.3 Pathophysiology of asthma. *IL,* Interleukin; *IgE,* immunoglobulin E. (Adapted from McCance KL, Huether SE: *Pathophysiology: the biologic basis for disease in adults and children*, ed 7, St. Louis, 2015, Elsevier.)

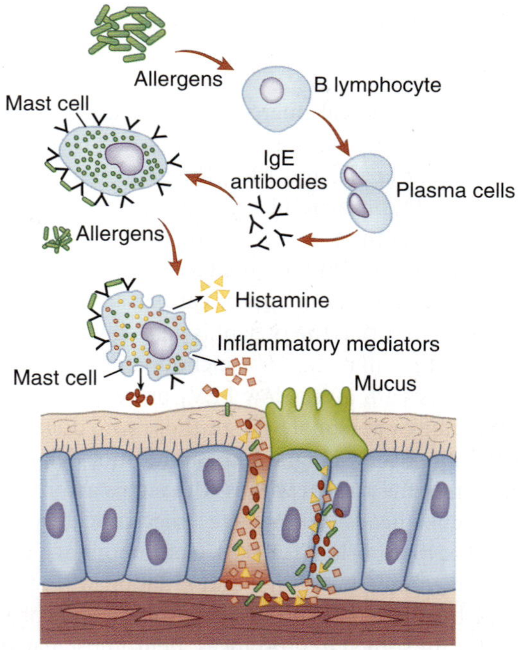

Fig. 31.4 Allergic asthma is triggered when an allergen cross-links immunoglobulin E *(IgE)* receptors on mast cells, which are then activated to release histamine and other inflammatory mediators (early-phase response). A late-phase response may occur due to further inflammation and edema.

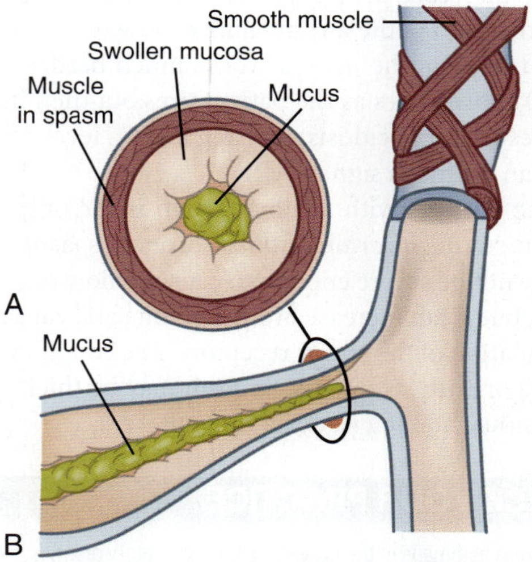

Fig. 31.5 Factors causing expiratory obstruction in asthma. (A) Cross section of a bronchiole occluded by muscle spasm, edema of mucosa, and mucus in the lumen. (B) Longitudinal section of a bronchiole. (Redrawn from Price SA, Wilson SM: *Pathophysiology: clinical concepts of disease processes*, ed 6, St. Louis, 2003, Mosby.)

result, it takes longer for the air to move out of the bronchioles (airflow obstruction). This causes the characteristic wheezing, air trapping, and hyperinflation of the lungs. As a result, expiration may be prolonged.

The most common finding during an acute asthma event is wheezing. For wheezing to occur, the patient must be able to move enough air to make the sound. Wheezing usually occurs first on exhalation. As asthma progresses, the patient may wheeze during inspiration and expiration.

However, wheezing is an unreliable sign to gauge the severity of an attack. Many patients with minor attacks wheeze loudly. Others with severe attacks do not wheeze. The patient with a severe asthma attack may wheeze only during forced expiration or have no audible wheezing because of the marked reduction in airflow.

Decreased or absent breath sounds may signal a significant decrease in air movement resulting from exhaustion and an inability to generate enough muscle force to breathe. Severely decreased breath sounds, often referred to as the "silent chest," are an ominous sign. This often means severe airway obstruction and impending acute respiratory failure (ARF).

! SAFETY ALERT

Silent Chest

- If the patient with asthma has been wheezing, followed by a sudden absence of a wheeze (e.g., silent chest) and the patient struggling to breathe, this is a life-threatening emergency.
- Call for help immediately.
- The patient may need mechanical ventilation.

Hyperventilation occurs during an asthma attack as lung receptors respond to the increase in lung volume from trapped air and airflow limitation. Decreased alveolar perfusion and ventilation and increased alveolar gas pressure lead to V/Q mismatch. The patient may be hypoxemic early with decreased $PaCO_2$ and increased pH (respiratory alkalosis) because they are hyperventilating. As the airflow limitation worsens with subsequent air trapping, the patient works much harder to breathe. The $PaCO_2$ normalizes as the patient tires but then increases to produce respiratory acidosis. A rising $PaCO_2$ level and decreasing pH is an ominous sign of ARF.

In some patients with asthma, cough is the only symptom. This is termed *cough variant asthma.* Bronchospasm is not present or may not be severe enough to cause airflow obstruction or wheezing, but it can increase bronchial tone and cause irritation with stimulation of the cough receptors. The cough may be nonproductive or with secretions. Sputum may be thick, tenacious, and gelatinous, making removal difficult.

CHECK YOUR PRACTICE

A patient with asthma is in the ED with acute respiratory distress. He has been receiving therapy and seems to be responding. You suddenly notice he is no longer wheezing.

- Should you consider this finding a sign that he is doing better?

Asthma Classifications

Several sets of national and international guidelines exist for classifying asthma. Each guideline has a slightly different perspective about asthma and how to classify the severity of an asthma attack. The severity of an asthma attack is used to guide treatment decisions. All the guidelines focus on assessing the severity of the disease at diagnosis and initial treatment and periodic monitoring to control the disease. All groups endorse the use of "stepping up" or "stepping down" medications during and after an acute asthma attack and having an "action plan" to help prevent future attacks. They promote patient teaching and adherence to the treatment plan.

The Global Initiative for Asthma (GINA) guidelines are the most widely recognized evidence-based strategies for addressing asthma worldwide.[17] Many HCPs use the 2012 National Heart, Lung, and Blood Institute (NIH) guidelines for classifying asthma severity (Table 31.4). They describe asthma as intermittent, mild persistent, moderate persistent, or severe persistent.[18]

Complications

Asthma attacks range from minor interferences in breathing to life-threatening episodes. Depending on a person's physiologic response, asthma can rapidly progress from normal breathing to an acute, severe attack or a life-threatening medical emergency within a few minutes.

In some people, airway remodeling predisposes them to respiratory-related issues. As bronchi become thicker and less elastic and airways become narrower, this may increase WOB. Compromised lung function may lead to a state of continuous symptoms and chronic debilitation, including fatigue, headaches, and lack of activity. Asthma predisposes patients to pneumonia, worse episodes of the flu, and in rare situations, tension pneumothorax. ARF and status asthmaticus are the most severe complications of an asthma attack.

Status Asthmaticus

A life-threatening medical emergency, **status asthmaticus** is the most extreme form of an acute asthma attack. It is characterized by hypoxia, hypercapnia, and ARF. The patient is unresponsive to treatment with bronchodilators and corticosteroids. They may have chest tightness, a severely marked increase in shortness of breath, or suddenly be unable to speak. Hypotension, bradycardia, and respiratory and/or cardiac arrest may occur if we do not recognize that the patient is getting worse.

IV magnesium sulfate has a bronchodilator effect. It may be given to patients with a very low FEV_1 or peak flow (less than 40% of predicted or personal best) or those who do not respond to initial treatment. IV magnesium should not delay the need for intubation of the patient who is with status asthmaticus.

The patient needs immediate mechanical ventilation. Hemodynamic monitoring is critical. Continuous analgesic infusions (e.g., ketamine, morphine) and sedation with drugs such as propofol help decrease WOB and promote synchrony with the ventilator. In some circumstances, neuromuscular blocking agents (e.g., rocuronium) may be used. Inhaled anesthetics, such as isoflurane, are an option for those not responding to conventional treatment. These patients are cared for in the ICU.

TABLE 31.4 Diagnostic Criteria

Asthma Severity Classification

	ASTHMA SEVERITY			
		PERSISTENT		
Components of Severity	**Intermittent**	**Mild**	**Moderate**	**Severe**
Impairment				
Symptoms	>2 days/week	>2 days/week, not daily	Daily	Continuous
Flare-ups	Brief, vary in intensity	Noticeable	More frequent	Daily
Interference with ADLs	Usually none	May affect ADLs	Some limitations, may affect ADLs	Often restricts ADLs
Nighttime awakenings	>2/month	3–4/month	>1/week, but not nightly	Every night (7/week)
Lung function[a]	FEV_1 >80% (normal FEV_1 between attacks); FEV_1/FVC normal	FEV_1 >80% predicted; FEV_1/FVC normal	FEV_1 60%–80% predicted; FEV_1/FVC reduced by 5%	FEV_1 <60% predicted; FEV_1/FVC reduced by >5%
Risk	Consider severity and interval since last attack. →			
	Frequency and severity may fluctuate over time. →			
	Relative annual risk for exacerbation may be related to FEV_1. →			
Recommended Step for Initiating Treatment	**Step 1**	**Step 2**	**Step 3**	**Step 4 or 5**
	Reevaluate asthma control in 2–6 weeks and adjust therapy as needed			

Guidelines for Using Table

- This stepwise approach is meant to help guide the HCP. It is not a substitute for patient assessment and clinical decision making.
- Assign patients to the most severe step in which any feature occurs.
- Clinical features may overlap across steps. Determine level of severity by assessing impairment and risk. Assess impairment by recall of previous 2 to 4 weeks spirometry results.
- A person's classification should change over time with treatment. After treatment, the focus switches to the level of control, not the classification of severity.

[a]Percent predicted values for FEV_1 or ratio of FEV_1/FVC. Normal FEV_1/FVC: 8–19 years, 85%; 20–39 years, 80%; 40–59 years, 75%; 60–80 years, 70%.
Source: Adapted from National Asthma Education and Prevention Program, National Heart, Lung, and Blood Institute: *Expert Panel report 3: guidelines for the diagnosis and management of asthma,* NIH pub no 08-4051, Bethesda, MD, 2007, National Institutes of Health.

Diagnostic Studies

Tests used to diagnose asthma are shown in Table 31.5. In general, the HCP should consider a diagnosis of asthma if various indicators (e.g., manifestations, health history, peak flow variability, spirometry) are positive.

Under-diagnosis of asthma is common. The history is important to determine if a person has had similar attacks, which are often precipitated by a known trigger. Because wheezing and cough occur with a variety of disorders (e.g., COPD, GERD, vocal cord problems, heart failure [HF]), it is important to determine if asthma or another disease is causing these problems. Table 31.6 shows a comparison of asthma and COPD.

The **peak expiratory flow rate** (PEFR) measured by the peak flow meter (at home or in a health care setting) is a test of lung function. PEFR measures the maximum rate of airflow after a forceful exhalation. When monitored routinely, PEFR measurements can provide a baseline of the patient's health status. PEFR can help predict an asthma attack or monitor the severity of disease. Test results depend on the patient's age, gender, and height. Since peak flow meters vary, PEFR should be compared with the patient's previous best measurements using their meter.

Spirometry is usually normal between asthma attacks if the patient has no other underlying lung disease. The patient may show an obstructive pattern including a decrease in forced vital capacity (FVC), PEFR, FEV_1, and FEV_1/FVC ratio.

When a spirometry test is scheduled, the patient must stop taking any bronchodilator drugs for 6 to 12 hours before the test. Spirometry can be done before and after the administration of a bronchodilator to assess the degree of the response. This helps determine the reversibility of airway obstruction, which is important in diagnosing asthma. A positive (favorable) response to the bronchodilator is an increase of more than 200 mL and an increase of more than 12% between pre-administration and post-administration values.[19]

A hand-held, point-of-care device to measure fractional exhaled nitric oxide (FeNO) can help determine asthma severity. FeNO levels are increased in people with asthma from eosinophilic-induced airway inflammation. FeNO can gauge loss of asthma control and attacks, adherence to therapy, or if more inhaled or oral antiinflammatory medication is needed.[20]

Increased serum eosinophil counts and IgE levels suggest an allergen or genetic link with asthma. Allergy skin testing can assess sensitivity to specific allergens. A positive skin test does not necessarily mean that the allergen is causing the asthma attack. On the other hand, a negative allergy test does not mean that the asthma event is not allergy related.

TABLE 31.5 Interprofessional Care

Asthma

Diagnostic Assessment

- History and physical assessment
- Spirometry, including response to bronchodilator therapy
- Peak expiratory flow rate (PEFR)
- Chest x-ray
- Pulse oximetry
- Allergy skin testing (if indicated)
- Blood level of eosinophils and IgE (if indicated)

Management

- Identify and avoid or eliminate triggers
- Patient and caregiver teaching
- Drug therapy (Tables 31.8 and 31.9 and Figs. 31.6 and 31.7)
- Asthma action plan (Fig. 31.11)
- Desensitization (immunotherapy) if indicated
- Assess for control (e.g., Asthma Control Test [ACT])

Acute Attacks

- Inhaled corticosteroids (alternatives: IV or oral corticosteroids)
- Inhaled β_2-adrenergic agonists
- Inhaled anticholinergics
- Position upright (semi to high-Fowler's)
- O_2 by nasal cannula or mask
- SpO_2 monitoring
- ABGs
- IV fluids
- IV magnesium
- As required: Mechanical ventilation

A chest x-ray in an asymptomatic patient with asthma is usually normal. Chest x-rays are usually not done unless other manifestations, such as fever or chills, are present. It can show if something else is causing symptoms similar to those of asthma (e.g., pneumonia, foreign body in the airway). A sputum specimen for culture may be done to rule out bacterial infection, especially if the patient has purulent sputum, a history of URI, a fever, or an increased white blood cell (WBC) count.

Interprofessional Care

The goal of care is to achieve and maintain control of the asthma. Guidelines provide direction about medications (based on steps) the patient needs (Figs. 31.6 and 31.7). The HCP will step up medication therapy as asthma symptoms worsen and step down the medication as the patient achieves control (Table 31.7). The level of control is determined by the patient's medication use, symptoms, and PEFR or FEV_1.

Drug Therapy

Drug therapy for asthma can be complex. Asthma drugs are divided into 2 general types: (1) *short-term controller*, ("rescue") agents, to treat attacks, and (2) *preferred reliever* agents (Table 31.8). You need to understand the different classes of drugs used to treat asthma and asthma attacks, their desired effects, side effects, and when to use different drugs.

The history, drug therapy, and frequency and severity of attacks help the HCP decide which types of drugs are best suited to control asthma symptoms. Current guidelines all suggest a stepwise approach to drug therapy. Common drugs used in asthma therapy are discussed in Table 31.9.

TABLE 31.6 Comparison of Asthma and COPD[a]

	Asthma	COPD
Clinical Features		
Age	Usually <40 years (onset)	Usually 30–45 years (onset)
Smoking history	No causal relationship	Causal relationship: Often long history (>10–20 pack-years)
Health and family history	Presence of allergy, rhinitis, eczema. Family history of asthma	Infrequent allergies. May have exposure to environment pollutants. With AATD, family history of lung or liver disease without smoking
Clinical symptoms	Intermittent, vary day to day. May be worse at night or early morning	Slowly progressive, persistent. Worsening of condition over time
Dyspnea	Absent except in attacks or poor control	Dyspnea during exercise and/or ADL's
Sputum	Infrequent	Often
Disease course	Often stable (with varying number and severity of attacks each year)	Progressive worsening (with increasingly more frequent exacerbations)
Diagnostic Study Results		
ABGs	Normal between or during attacks	Between exacerbations in advanced COPD • Often low-normal pH and PaO_2 • High-normal $PaCO_2$ with normal to high HCO_3^- (may be fully or partially compensated respiratory acidosis)
pH	↑ Early in attack, then ↓ if prolonged or severe attack	Normal →↓
PaO_2	↓	N→↓
$PaCO_2$	↓ Early in attack, then ↑ if prolonged or severe attack	N→↑
Chest x-ray	May be normal or show some degree of hyperinflation	Hyperinflation, flattened diaphragm. May have cardiac enlargement
Lung volumes	Often normal	Usually not normal as disease progresses
• Total lung capacity	↑	↑
• Residual volume	↑	↑
• FEV_1	↓→ N	↓
• FEV_1/FVC	N→↓	↓ (<70%)

[a]Patients may have features of both asthma and COPD.

Corticosteroids

All guidelines recommend using ICS as first-line agents in an acute asthma attack and as the first step in acute asthma management.[21] They are the most effective short-term controller drugs for asthma. Corticosteroids are antiinflammatory drugs. They reduce bronchial hyperresponsiveness, block the

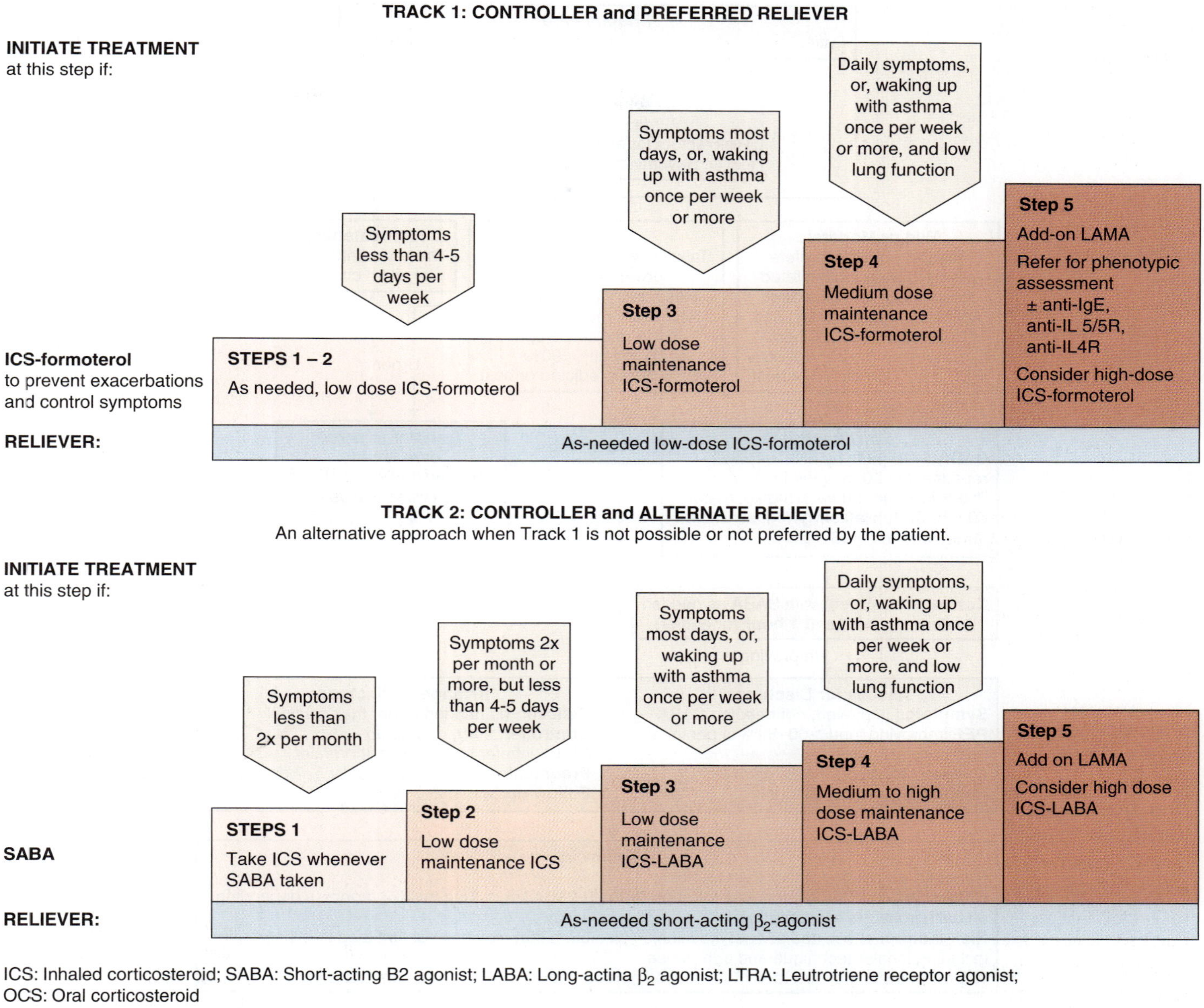

Fig. 31.6 Stepwise approach to asthma treatment. *IL,* Interleukin; *LABA,* long-acting β-2 agonist; *OCS,* oral corticosteroid.

late-phase response, and inhibit the migration of inflammatory cells. They are more effective in improving asthma control than any other drug.

ICSs side effects include easy bruising and decreased bone mineral density. Oropharyngeal candidiasis, hoarseness, and dry cough are local side effects. These problems can be reduced or prevented by using a spacer with the metered-dose inhaler (MDI) and by gargling with water or mouthwash after each use. Using a spacer or holding device can help get more drug into the lungs.

Bronchodilators

The 3 classes of bronchodilator drugs used in asthma therapy are β_2-adrenergic agonists (also referred to as β_2-agonists), methylxanthines, and anticholinergics.

β_2-Adrenergic agonist drugs. β_2-Adrenergic agonists may be SABAs or LABAs. While inhaled SABAs remain effective drugs for relieving acute bronchospasm (as seen in an acute asthma attack), they are no longer first-line therapy. They do play a key role in asthma management. These drugs have an onset of action within minutes and are effective for 4 to 8 hours. They stimulate β-adrenergic receptors in the bronchioles, producing bronchodilation. They also increase mucociliary clearance.

β_2-Adrenergic agonists can prevent bronchospasm caused by different triggers because they prevent the release of inflammatory mediators from mast cells. They do not inhibit the late-phase response of asthma or have antiinflammatory effects. If used often, inhaled β_2-adrenergic agonists may cause tremors, anxiety, nausea, tachycardia, and palpitations.[22]

Too frequent use of β_2-adrenergic agonists indicates poor asthma control, may mask the severity of the condition, and lead to reduced drug effectiveness. SABAs should not be used alone for recurrent, repeated asthma attacks, or for long-term control. Guidelines suggest that they may be an alternate

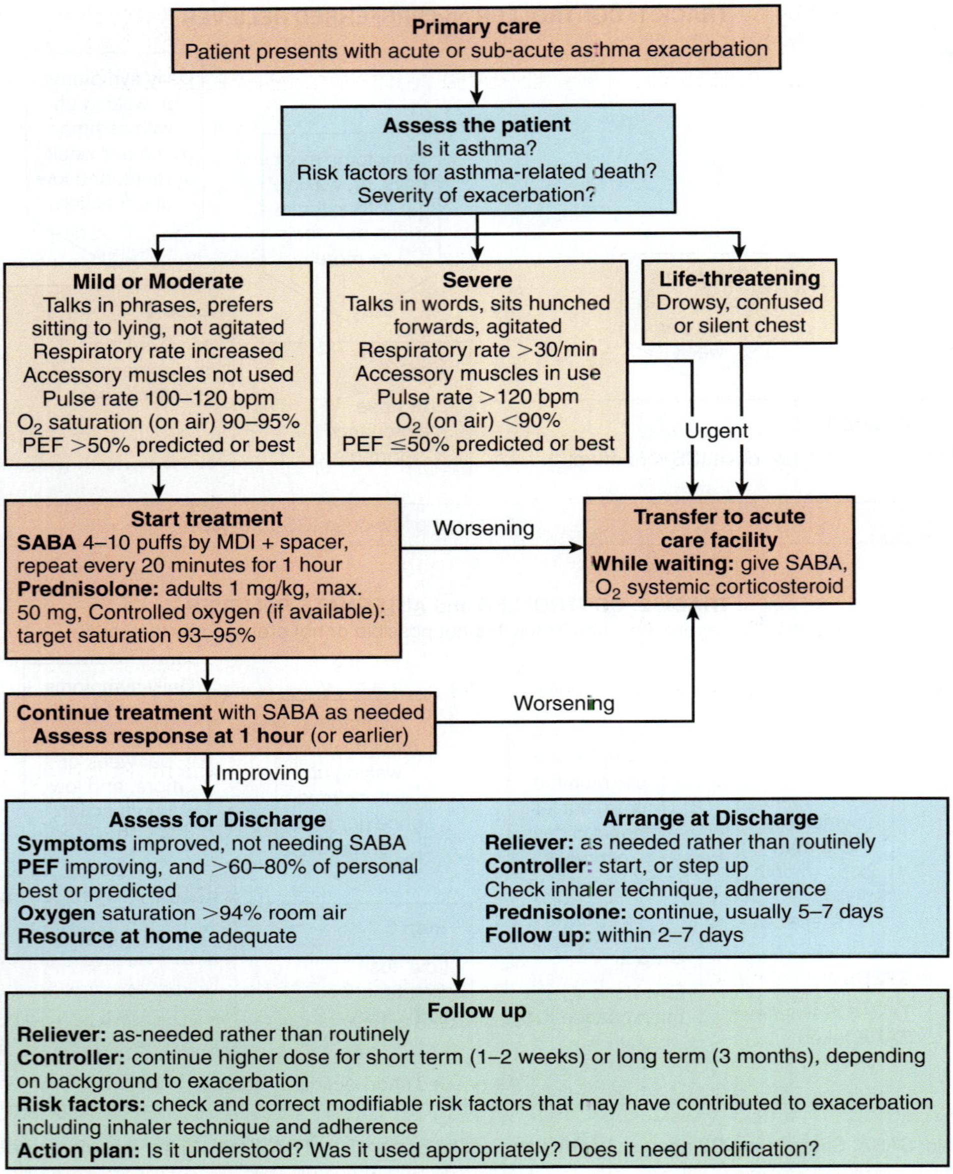

O_2: oxygen; PEF: peak expiratory flow; SABA: short-acting beta$_2$-agonist (doses are for salbutamol)

Fig. 31.7 Management of patient with acute asthma attack. (Modified from GINA evidence-based strategy document, 2021. Retrieved from https://ginasthma.org.)

reliever medication when the patient does not respond to low-dose ICS.

Like SABAs, LABAs should not be used alone as primary treatment. They should only be used only if the patient does not respond to medium-dose ICS. In other words, LABAs can be used as an adjunct to treatment. Examples of LABAs used in the treatment of asthma attacks include salmeterol and formoterol.

LABAs are effective for 12 hours. Tell patients that LABAs should not be used to treat acute symptoms or to obtain quick relief from bronchospasm. Teach the patient that these drugs are used only once every 12 hours. Combination therapy using an ICS and a LABA is available in several inhalers (e.g., fluticasone/salmeterol [Advair], budesonide/formoterol [Symbicort]). Combinations are more convenient, improve adherence, and ensure that patients receive the LABA with an ICS.

DRUG ALERT

β_2-Adrenergic Agonists

- Use with caution in patients with heart problems.
- Both SABAs and LABAs may cause increased BP and heart rate, central nervous system stimulation, and dysrhythmias.

DRUG ALERT

Long-Acting β_2-Adrenergic Agonists (LABAs)

- Should not be the first or only drug used to treat asthma.
- Should be added to the treatment plan only if other drugs do not control asthma.
- Do not use to treat wheezing that is getting worse.

TABLE 31.7 Components of Asthma Control

Components of Control	CLASSIFICATION OF ASTHMA CONTROL: Well Controlled	Not Well Controlled	Poorly Controlled
Impairment			
Symptoms	≤2 days/week	>2 days/week	Throughout the day
Nighttime awakenings	≤2/months	1–3/weeks	≥4/weeks
Interference with normal activity	None	Some limitation	Extremely limited
FEV_1 or PEFR	>80% predicted/personal best	60%–80% predicted/personal best	<60% predicted/personal best
Risk			
Attacks requiring additional pharmacologic management	0–1/year	≥2/years	≥2/years
Progressive loss of lung function	Evaluation requires long-term follow-up. →		
Treatment-related adverse effects	Can vary in intensity from none to very troublesome and worrisome. Level of intensity does not correlate to specific levels of control but should be considered in the overall assessment of risk. →		
Recommended Action for Treatment (based on assessment of control)	• Maintain current step. • Regular follow-up every 1–6 months to maintain control. • Consider step down if well controlled for at least 3 months.	• Step up 1 step. • Reevaluate in 2–6 weeks. • For side effects, consider alternative treatment options.	• Consider oral corticosteroids. • Step up 1 or 2 steps and reevaluate in 2 weeks. • For side effects, consider alternative treatment options.

Source: Adapted from National Asthma Education and Prevention Program, National Heart, Lung, and Blood Institute: *Expert Panel report 3: guidelines for the diagnosis and management of asthma,* NIH pub no 08-4051, Bethesda, MD, 2007, National Institutes of Health.

TABLE 31.8 Drug Therapy

Asthma

Types of Drugs	Drug Class
Controller Drugs	Corticosteroids Short-acting β_2 adrenergic agonists (SABA)
Maintenance, Reliever and Alternate Reliever Drugs (MART)	Anticholinergics • Short-acting muscarinic antagonist (SAMA) • Long-acting muscarinic antagonist (LAMA) β_2 adrenergic agonists • Short-acting β-adrenergic agonist (SABA) • Long-acting β-adrenergic agonist (LABA) Corticosteroids Leukotriene modifiers • Leukotriene receptor antagonist • Leukotriene inhibitor Methylxanthines Monoclonal antibodies • Anti-IgE • Anti-interleukin 5 Phosphodiesterase inhibitors Combination preparations • SAMA/SABA • ICS/LABA • LAMA/LABA

Methylxanthines. Sustained-release methylxanthine preparations are not a first-line controller medication. They are used only as an alternative therapy. One example is theophylline, a methylxanthine that is a weak bronchodilator with mild anti-inflammatory effects. Theophylline use has been replaced by newer drugs, namely inhaled ICS and β_2-adrenergic agonists. GINA no longer recommends theophylline as part of its treatment guidelines.

There are several problems with theophylline. First, there are many side effects. Second, there is well interactions with many other drugs. Third, because theophylline has a very narrow margin of safety, we must check serum blood levels regularly to see if drug levels are within therapeutic range.

Anticholinergic drugs. Anticholinergic drugs affect the muscles around the bronchi (large airways). When the lungs are irritated, these bands of muscle can tighten, causing bronchoconstriction via the parasympathetic nervous system. Anticholinergics work by preventing these muscles from tightening. Consequently, these drugs promote bronchodilation.

Anticholinergic drugs are less effective than equivalent doses of SABAs. Therefore, short-acting anticholinergic drugs are not used except for in severe acute asthma attacks. Examples include ipratropium and tiotropium.

Leukotriene Modifiers

Leukotrienes are inflammatory mediators produced from arachidonic acid metabolism. They are potent bronchoconstrictors. Some leukotrienes cause airway edema and inflammation, contributing to the worsening symptoms of an acute asthma attack.

Leukotriene receptor antagonists (LTRAs) block the release of some substances from mast cells and eosinophils, producing bronchodilator and antiinflammatory effects. LTRAs do not reverse bronchospasm in acute asthma attacks. They are less effective than corticosteroids and used only as adjunct therapy for those patients who do not respond to treatment with ICS. LTRAs include zafirlukast (Accolate), montelukast (Singulair), and zileuton (Zyflo CR).

Monoclonal Antibodies

Anti-immunoglobulin E. Omalizumab (Xolair) is a monoclonal antibody to IgE that decreases circulating free IgE levels. Omalizumab prevents IgE from attaching to mast cells, thus

TABLE 31.9 Drug Therapy

Asthma and COPD

Drug	Use	Route	Considerations
Anticholinergics			
Short Acting (SAMA)			
ipratropium (Atrovent HFA)	Asthma, COPD	Nebulizer, MDI	Can be monotherapy. Produces bronchodilation within minutes. Side effects: Headache, dry mouth, dizziness, palpitations.
Long Acting (LAMA)			
aclidinium bromide (Tudorza Pressair)	COPD	DPI	Side effects: Headache, cough, cold symptoms. Do not take with other anticholinergics.
revefenacin (Yupelri)	COPD	Nebulizer	Dosed once daily as maintenance treatment. Does not cause usual side effects of other anticholinergics. Do not take with other anticholinergics.
tiotropium bromide (Spiriva Handi-Haler)	COPD	DPI	Side effects: Headache, dry mouth, dizziness, palpitations. Dosed once daily as maintenance treatment. Do not take with other anticholinergics. Blurred vision if powder comes in contact with eyes. Maximum effect 1 week after starting drug.
umeclidinium (Incruse Ellipta)	COPD	DPI	Dosed once daily as maintenance treatment. Side effects: Cough, cold symptoms, arthralgia
β_2-Adrenergic Agonists			
Inhaled: Short Acting (SABA)			
albuterol (Proventil HFA, Ventolin HFA, Proair HFA)	Asthma COPD	Nebulizer, MDI Oral	Produces bronchodilation within 5 minutes; effects last 2–5 hr. Oral tablets (long-acting, extended release) not for acute situation. Side effects: Tremors, headache, tachycardia, nausea. MDI may be more effective than nebulizer as drug delivered more quickly to the lungs. Use with caution in patients with cardiac disorders because of ↑ BP and heart rate, CNS stimulation, and ↑ risk for dysrhythmias.
Epinephrine (Primatene Mist HFA)	Asthma	MDI	Sold OTC. Side effects: tachycardia, ↑ BP. Do not take with MAO inhibitors.
levalbuterol (Xopenex, Xopenex HFA)	Asthma COPD	Nebulizer, MDI	Response occurs within 15 minutes of administration, and peak effect in 90 min. Do not use if solution discolored. Side effects: Tremors, headache, rash
Inhaled: Long Acting (LABA) In asthma: Never use as monotherapy. Use in combination with ICSs. In COPD: Some drugs used as monotherapy. Not used for rapid relief of dyspnea.			
arformoterol (Brovana)	COPD	Nebulizer	Monitor for paradoxical bronchospasm at high doses. Side effects: GI distress, edema, leg cramps.
formoterol (Foradil Perforomist)	Asthma	DPI, nebulizer (Perforomist)	Side effects: Tremors, tachycardia, GI distress. Use with caution in diabetes, can increase glucose levels.
indacaterol	COPD	DPI	Once daily use. Use with caution in diabetes, can increase glucose levels. Side effects: Nausea, headache, sore throat.
olodaterol (Stiolto, Striverdi Respimat)	COPD	MDI	Once daily use. Side effects: Dizziness, cold symptoms.
salmeterol (Serevent Diskus)	COPD	DPI	Do not use more than twice daily. Side effects: Tremors, tachycardia, muscle pain, cold symptoms. Helps prevent exercise-induced asthma in those with persistent asthma.
Corticosteroids			
hydrocortisone (Solu-Cortef)	Asthma	IV	Oral preferred over IV.
methylprednisolone (Medrol, Solu-Medrol)	Asthma	Oral, IV	Side effects: hyperglycemia, fluid retention. May take 2 weeks for results to be seen in severe COPD exacerbation.
prednisone	Asthma COPD	Oral	Take oral dose in morning with food or milk. High dose may cause GI distress. Long-term therapy requires vitamin D and calcium supplements to prevent osteoporosis. Long-term steroid therapy: discontinue gradually to prevent adrenal insufficiency.

TABLE 31.9 **Drug Therapy—cont'd**

Asthma and COPD

Drug	Use	Route	Considerations
Inhaled			
beclomethasone dipropionate (Qvar)	Asthma	MDI	Do not use in acute attack. May not see effects until after at least 2 weeks of regular treatment. Side effects: Headache, hoarseness.
budesonide (Pulmicort Flexhaler)	Asthma	DPI	Do not use in acute attack. May not see effects until after at least 2 weeks of regular treatment. Side effects: Headache cold symptoms.
ciclesonide (Alvesco)	Asthma	MDI	Do not use in acute attack. Side effects: Cold symptoms, nose bleeds.
fluticasone (Flovent HFA, Flovent Diskus)	Asthma	MDI, DPI	Do not use in acute attack. Rinse mouth with water or mouthwash after use to prevent oral fungal infections. Side effects: Headache, cold symptoms. Spacer device with MDI may decrease incidence of oral candidiasis. May not see effects until after at least 2 weeks of regular treatment.
mometasone (Asmanex HFA, Asmanex Twisthaler)	Asthma	DPI	Do not use in acute attack. May not see effects until after at least 2 weeks of regular treatment.
Leukotriene Modifiers			
Leukotriene Receptor Antagonists			
montelukast (Singulair)	Asthma	Oral	Do not use in acute attack. Can be used to prevent wheezing and SOB caused by asthma during exercise. Side effects: Headache, fatigue, dizziness, GI distress.
zafirlukast (Accolate)	Asthma	Oral	Do not use in acute attack. No specific side effects. Take at least 1 hr before or 2 hr after meals. Contraindicated in cirrhosis. Affects metabolism of oral warfarin (drug ↑ prothrombin time).
Leukotriene Inhibitor			
zileuton (Zyflo, Zyflo CR)	Asthma	Oral tablets	Do not use in acute attack. Do not crush, chew, or cut tablets. Monitor liver enzymes. May interfere with metabolism of warfarin and theophylline. Changes in sleep pattern and behavioral abnormalities reported.
Methylxanthines			
IV agent: aminophylline (second-line therapy) *Oral:* theophylline	Asthma COPD	IV, oral	Side effects: CNS stimulation, headache, tachycardia, dysrhythmias, nausea, vomiting, altered glucose levels. Nicotine ↑ metabolism of methylxanthines in liver (dosage increase needed for those who smoke). Many drug interactions. Taking drug with food or antacids may help GI effects. Very limited use.
Monoclonal Antibodies			
Anti-IgE			
omalizumab (Xolair)	Asthma	Subcutaneous	Dose and frequency based on total IgE levels and pre-treatment weight. Total IgE levels elevated up to 1 year after therapy stopped; do not use as a guide for dosing drug. Side effects: Dizziness, joint pain, fatigue Pain, burning at injection site, anaphylactic reaction possible. Give only under direct medical supervision every 2–4 weeks.
Anti-Interleukin 5			
mepolizumab (Nucala)	Asthma	Subcutaneous	Add-on therapy in patients with severe asthma attacks despite receiving other asthma drugs. Give only under direct medical supervision every 4 weeks. Side effects: Headache, back pain. Hypersensitivity reactions have been known to occur hours and days later.
reslizumab (Cinqair)	Asthma	IV	Add-on therapy in patients receiving other asthma drugs. Given every 4 weeks as an IV infusion over 1 hr. Risk for anaphylactic reactions.
Phosphodiesterase Inhibitor Type 4 (PDE-4)			
roflumilast (Daliresp)	COPD	Oral	Do not use in acute attack. Used in severe COPD to reduce exacerbation frequency. Side effects: GI distress, headache, suicidal thoughts, insomnia. Do not take with theophylline, phenytoin.

Continued

TABLE 31.9 Drug Therapy—cont'd

Asthma and COPD

Drug	Use	Route	Considerations
Combination Agents			
These are a few of the many combination drugs available for long-term management of asthma and COPD.			
SAMA/SABA			
ipratropium/albuterol (Combivent Respimat)	COPD	Nebulizer, MDI	Do not use in acute attack. Long-term therapy only.
ICS/LABA			
budesonide/formoterol (Symbicort)	Asthma	MDI	Do not use in acute attacks.
fluticasone/salmeterol (Advair Diskus or HFA)	Asthma COPD	DPI, MDI	Long-term therapy only. Side effects: Headache, cold symptoms.
fluticasone/vilanterol (Breo Ellipta)	COPD	DPI	Rinse mouth after using.
mometasone furoate/formoterol fumarate (Dulera)	Asthma	MDI	
LAMA/LABA			
umeclidinium/vilanterol (Anoro Ellipta)	COPD	DPI	Do not use in acute attacks. Long-term therapy only. Side effects: Sore throat, cold symptoms.

preventing the release of chemical mediators. It is given to patients with moderate to severe asthma or those not controlled with ICSs alone. There is a risk for anaphylaxis, so patients must receive the injection in a setting where this emergency can be treated.

Anti-interleukin 5. Interleukin (IL)-5 is a cytokine involved in the inflammatory response in asthma by promoting eosinophil activity.[23] By inhibiting IL-5, monoclonal antibodies inhibit the production and survival of eosinophils. As a result, inflammation and edema of the airway subside. They are mainly used for patients with a history of severe asthma attacks and as an adjunct with other asthma medication. These drugs include mepolizumab (Nucala), reslizumab (Cinqair), and benralizumab (Fasenra).

Nonprescription Combination Drugs

Several combination drugs are available OTC. They are usually combinations of a bronchodilator (ephedrine) and an expectorant (guaifenesin). Often, patients seek OTC drugs because they are less expensive than prescription drugs. Many people consider these drugs safe because they can be obtained without a prescription. In general, they should be avoided due to their potential side effects.

Inhalers containing epinephrine may be available. These agents are advertised as relieving bronchospasm. Those containing ephedrine and epinephrine are potentially dangerous because they stimulate the central nervous and cardiovascular systems. Side effects include nervousness, palpitations, dysrhythmias, tremors, insomnia, and increased BP. Teach patients about the dangers of OTC combination drugs. They are possibly unsafe to a patient with underlying heart problems For the patient who insists on taking these drugs, encourage them to discuss their use with the HCP. Caution them to read and follow the directions on the label. They should notify their HCP if an untoward reaction occurs.

Inhalation Devices for Drug Delivery

Many asthma drugs are given by inhalation because the onset of action is faster and systemic side effects are reduced. Inhalation devices include MDIs, dry powder inhalers (DPIs), and nebulizers.

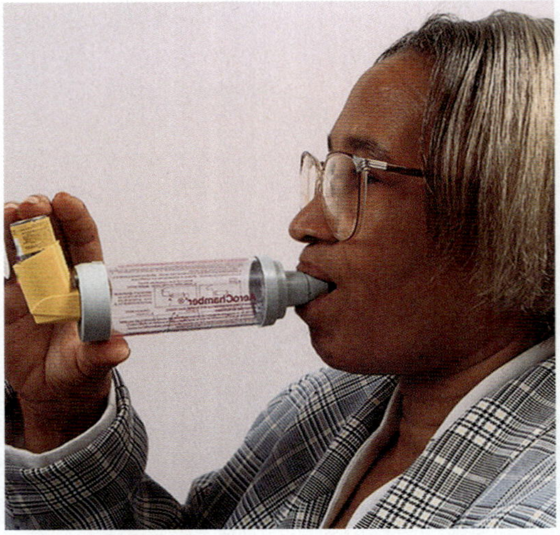

Fig. 31.8 Example of an AeroChamber spacer used with a metered-dose inhaler. (From Potter PA, Perry AG, Stockert P, et al.: *Fundamentals of nursing,* ed 9, St Louis, 2017, Mosby.)

Inhalers. MDIs are small, hand-held, pressurized devices that deliver a measured dose of drug with each activation. The dose is usually 1 or 2 puffs. Depending on the specific MDI, a spacer or holding chamber is used to reduce the amount of drug delivered to the oropharynx and improve the amount of drug delivered to the lungs. Examples include AeroChamber and InspirEase (Fig. 31.8). Spacers help people who have hand-breath coordination problems. The number of times and frequency that an MDI must be primed vary widely. Follow the package insert.

The patient who needs to use several MDIs is often unclear about the order in which to use them. In most circumstances, a quick-acting drug (e.g., ICS) is used, followed by reliever medications (as needed) for clinical conditions that do not improve. Teach the patient about the different drugs used to treat asthma, how they work, and the indications for use. Review the order in which the patient should take their medications.

Using an inhaler seems simple, but most patients do not use it the right way. When you use your inhaler the wrong way, less medicine gets to your lungs. (Your physician may give you other types of inhalers.)

For the next 2 weeks, read these steps aloud as you do them or ask someone to read them to you. Ask your physician or nurse to check how well you are using your inhaler.

Use your inhaler in one of the three ways pictured below (**A** or **B** is best, but **C** can be used if you have trouble with **A** or **B**).

Steps for Using Your Inhaler

Getting ready
1. Take off the cap and shake the inhaler.
2. Breathe out all the way.
3. Hold your inhaler the way your doctor said (**A, B,** or **C** below).

Breathe in slowly
4. As you start breathing in **slowly** through your mouth, press down on the inhaler **one** time. (If you use a holding chamber, first press down on the inhaler. Within 5 seconds, begin to breathe in slowly.)
5. Keep breathing in **slowly,** as deeply as you can.

Hold your breath
6. Hold your breath as you count to 10 slowly, if you can.
7. For inhaled quick-relief medicine (β_2-agonists), wait about 1 minute between puffs. There is no need to wait between puffs for other medicines.

A. Hold inhaler 1 to 2 inches in front of your mouth (about the width of two fingers).

B. Use a spacer/holding chamber. These come in many shapes and can be useful to any patient.

C. Put the inhaler in your mouth.

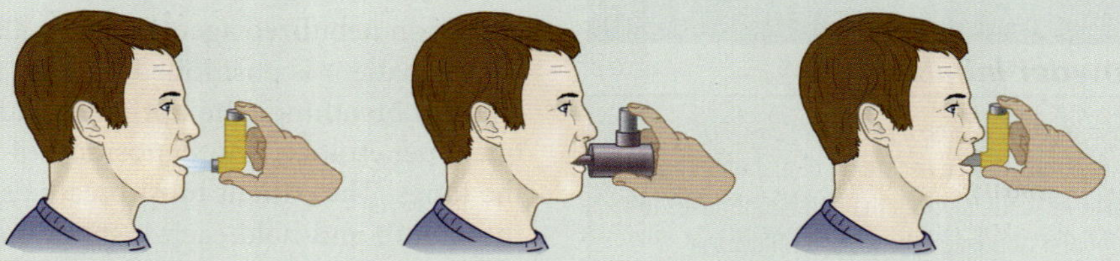

Clean Your Inhaler as Needed

Look at the hole where the medicine sprays out from your inhaler. If you see "powder" in or around the hole, clean the inhaler. Remove the metal canister from the L-shaped plastic mouthpiece. Rinse only the mouthpiece and cap in warm water. Let them dry overnight. In the morning, put the canister back inside. Put the cap on.

Know When to Replace Your Inhaler

For medicines you take each day (an example): Say your new canister has 200 puffs (number of puffs is listed on canister) and you are told to take 8 puffs per day.

25 days
8 puffs per day) 200 puffs in canister

So this canister will last 25 days. If you started using this inhaler on May 1, replace it on or before May 25.

You can write the date on your canister.

For **quick-relief medicine take as needed** and count each puff.

Do not put your canister in water to see if it is empty as water may enter MDI and impair inhaler.

Fig. 31.9 How to use your metered-dose inhaler.

Another potential problem is patient technique when using drug delivery devices. An MDI drug is effective only if taken properly. Review MDI technique during each visit. The patient needs to know how to use the MDI correctly (Fig. 31.9), how to determine whether the MDI is empty, and how to effectively clean and care for the device. Problems using an MDI are listed in Table 31.10.

Dry powder inhalers. DPIs are simpler to use than MDIs. The DPI contains dry, powdered medication and is breath activated (Fig. 31.10). DPIs have several advantages over MDIs. They require less manual dexterity. There is no need to coordinate device puffs with inhalation. Some disadvantages are that some common drugs are not available in DPIs. The medication may clump if exposed to humidity. Since the medicine is delivered only by the patient's inspiratory effort, patients with a low FEV_1

TABLE 31.10 Problems Using a Metered-Dose Inhaler (MDI)

- Not coordinating activation with inspiration
- Activating MDI in the mouth while breathing through nose
- Inhaling too rapidly
- Not holding the breath for 10 sec (or as close to 10 sec as possible)
- Holding MDI upside down or sideways
- Inhaling more than 1 puff with each inspiration
- Not shaking MDI before use (if indicated)
- Not waiting enough time between each puff
- Not opening mouth wide enough (if using open mouth technique), causing medication to bounce off teeth, tongue, or palate
- Not having adequate strength to activate MDI
- Not being able to understand and follow directions
- Inadvertently using an empty container

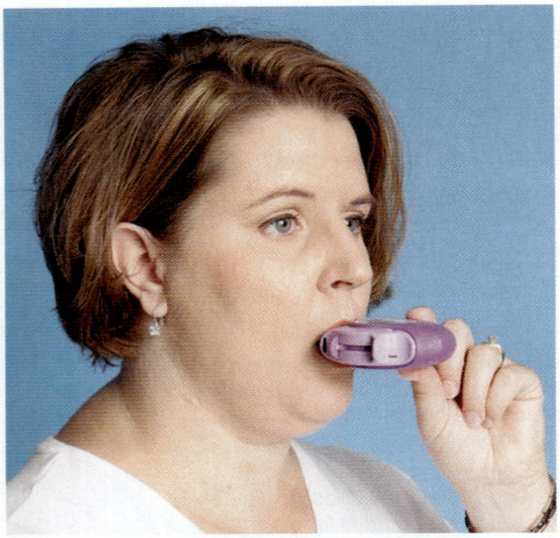

Fig. 31.10 Example of a dry powder inhaler (DPI). (From Potter PA, Perry AG, Stockert P, Hall A: *Fundamentals of nursing,* ed 9, St Louis, 2017, Mosby.)

TABLE 31.11 **PATIENT & CAREGIVER TEACHING**

How to Use a Dry Powder Inhaler (DPI)

Include the following instructions when teaching a patient to use a DPI:

1. Remove mouthpiece cap or open the device according to manufacturer's instructions. If there is an external counter, note the number of doses left.
2. Load the medicine into the inhaler or engage the lever to allow the medicine to become available. Some DPIs are held upright while loading. Others are held sideways or in a horizontal position.
3. Do not shake your medicine.
4. Tilt your head back slightly and breathe out, getting as much air out of your lungs as you can. Do not breathe into your inhaler because this could affect the dose.
5. Close your lips tightly around the mouthpiece of the inhaler.
6. Breathe in deeply and quickly. This will ensure that the medicine moves down deeply into your lungs. You may not taste or sense the medicine going into your lungs.
7. Hold your breath for 10 sec or as long as you can to disperse the medicine into your lungs.
8. If there is an external counter, note the number of doses left. It should be 1 less than the number in step 1 above.
9. Do not keep your DPI in a humid place, such as a shower room, because the medicine may clump.

(less than 1 L) may not be able to inspire the medication. Table 31.11 describes how to use a DPI.

Differences between MDIs and DPIs are described in Table 31.12. Both systems when used with comparable drug doses provide equal efficacy. Costs vary widely. Therefore, patients should use the device best suited to their needs.

Nebulizers. Nebulizers are small machines used to convert drug solutions into mists. The mist can be inhaled through a face mask or mouthpiece held between the teeth with the lips closed around the device. Nebulizers are usually used for those who have severe asthma or difficulty with the MDI inhalation. They do not provide better delivery of medication than a spacer with an inhaler.

TABLE 31.12 **Comparison of Metered-Dose and Dry Powder Inhalers**

	Metered-Dose Inhaler (MDI)	Dry Powder Inhaler (DPI)
Shake before use	May be needed for some (e.g., albuterol), but not for others (read package insert)	No
Inspiration	Slow	Rapid
Spacer	May be used with ICS or for more effective delivery	Not used
Counting device	Many have an external device (some devices do not)	Most preloaded forms include counter
Inhalations/dose	Often 2/dose	Often 1/dose

Nebulizers are usually powered by a compressed air or O_2 generator. At home, the patient may have an air-powered compressor. In the hospital, wall O_2 or compressed air powers the nebulizer.

Aerosolized medication orders must include the drug, dose, diluent, and whether it is to be nebulized with O_2 or compressed air. The advantage of nebulized therapy is that it is easy to use. Common nebulized agents include albuterol and ipratropium.

The patient is positioned upright, as this position allows for efficient breathing. The upright position also helps ensure adequate penetration and deposition of the aerosolized drug into the lungs. The patient must breathe slowly and deeply through the mouth and hold each inspiration for 2 to 3 seconds. Deep diaphragmatic breathing helps ensure delivery of the drug. Tell the patient to breathe normally in between large, inhaled breaths. After treatment, have the patient cough effectively.

To reduce the potential for bacterial growth, review cleaning procedures for respiratory equipment. An effective home-cleaning method is to wash the nebulizer daily in soap and water, rinse it with water, and soak it for 20 to 30 minutes in a 1:1 white vinegar–water solution, followed by a water rinse and air drying.

NURSING MANAGEMENT: ASTHMA

Assessment

If a patient is not in acute distress, obtain a detailed health history. Include information about when the condition was first diagnosed, triggers, and what helped relieve past asthma attacks. Assessment of the patient with asthma may be normal, especially between attacks. Subjective and objective data you should obtain from a patient with asthma are outlined in Table 31.13.

Clinical Problems

Clinical problems for the patient with asthma may include:

- Impaired respiratory function
- Activity intolerance
- Anxiety
- Deficient knowledge

Additional information on clinical problems and interventions is presented in eNursing Care Plan 31.1 on the website for this chapter.

TABLE 31.13 NURSING ASSESSMENT
Asthma

Subjective Data	Objective Data
Important Health Information *Health history:* Allergic rhinitis, sinusitis, or skin allergies. Previous asthma attacks (frequency, severity) and required hospitalization. Symptoms worsened by triggers in the environment. GERD. Occupational exposure to chemical irritants (e.g., paints, dust) *Medications:* Use of medications. Adherence, inhaler technique. Use of antibiotics. Pattern and amount of "controller" and "preferred reliever" (or "alternate" reliever) used per week. Drugs that may trigger an attack in susceptible persons, such as aspirin, NSAIDs, β-adrenergic blockers **Functional Health Patterns** *Health perception–health management:* Family history of allergies and/or asthma. Recent URI or sinus infection *Activity-exercise:* Fatigue, decreased or absent exercise tolerance. Dyspnea, cough (especially at night), productive cough with yellow or green sputum or sticky sputum. Chest tightness, feelings of suffocation, air hunger, talking in short sentences or words or phrases, sitting upright to breathe *Sleep-rest:* Awakened from sleep because of cough or breathing difficulties, insomnia *Coping–stress tolerance:* Emotional distress, stress in work environment or home	**Cardiovascular** Tachycardia, pulsus paradoxus, jugular venous distention, hypertension or hypotension, premature ventricular contractions **General** Restlessness or exhaustion, confusion, upright or forward-leaning body position **Respiratory** Nasal discharge, nasal polyps, mucosal swelling Crackles, decreased or absent breath sounds, and wheezes (inspiratory, expiratory, or both) on auscultation Hyperresonance on percussion Sputum (thick, white, tenacious) ↑ work of breathing with use of accessory muscles. Intercostal and supraclavicular retractions. Tachypnea with hyperventilation. Prolonged expiration Skin Diaphoresis, cyanosis (circumoral, nail bed), eczema **Possible Diagnostic Findings** Abnormal pulmonary function tests: ↓ flow rates; FVC, FEV_1, PEFR, and FEV_1/FVC ratio (often improve between attacks with drug therapy). Abnormal ABGs during attacks, ↓ O_2 saturation, serum and sputum eosinophilia, ↑ serum IgE, chest x-ray showing hyperinflation with attacks.

◆ Planning

The overall goals are that the patient with asthma will achieve asthma control, as evidenced by (1) minimal symptoms during the day and night, (2) acceptable activity levels (including exercise), (3) maintaining greater than 80% of personal best PEFR, (4) few or no adverse effects of drug therapy, (5) no acute asthma attacks, and (6) adequate knowledge to carry out the treatment plan.

◆ Implementation

◆ Health Promotion

Your role in preventing asthma attacks or decreasing their severity focuses mainly on teaching the patient and caregiver. Teach the patient to identify and avoid known personal triggers for asthma (e.g., cigarette smoke, pet dander) and irritants (e.g., cold air, aspirin, foods, cats, indoor air pollution) (Table 31.3). Washing bedclothes in hot water or cooler water with detergent and bleach has some effect on allergen levels.

When cold air cannot be avoided, dressing properly with scarves or using a mask helps reduce the risk for an asthma attack. Aspirin and NSAIDs should be avoided if they are known to trigger an attack. Many OTC drugs contain aspirin. Teach the patient to read the labels carefully. Nonselective β-blockers (e.g., propranolol) are contraindicated because they inhibit bronchodilation. Selective β-blockers (e.g., atenolol) should be used with caution. Desensitization (immunotherapy) may be partially effective in decreasing the patient's sensitivity to known allergens.

Prompt diagnosis and treatment of URIs and sinusitis may help prevent an asthma attack. If occupational irritants are involved, the patient may need to consider changing jobs. Those who are obese often find that weight loss improves asthma control. If exercise is planned or if the patient had an asthma attack before with exercise, the HCP can suggest a pre-treatment or long-term control plan to prevent bronchospasm.

◆ Acute Care

During an acute attack, signs and symptoms, medication use, and PEFR or FEV_1 measurements can be used to help identify the severity of an asthma attack and guide health care teams in providing the most appropriate treatment. The goal is to achieve rapid control of the symptoms and return the patient to their previous level of functioning as quickly as possible. Therapy is tailored to patient history, severity of symptoms, frequency of exacerbations, and patient response.

Patients with mild or moderate asthma attacks may be seen in an outpatient clinic or ED. These attacks occur no more than twice per week, with minimal interference in day-to-day activity. The patient is alert, oriented, and speaks in sentences. The patient may describe chest tightness, varying degrees of difficulty breathing, and a slight increase in the use of asthma drugs. O_2 saturation is usually greater than 90% on room air and PEFR greater than 50% of predicted or personal best.

ICS are the mainstays of treatment for mild to moderate asthma attacks. Monitor vital signs. Most patients improve shortly after receiving medication. When the patient improves, review the asthma action plan with them. Teach the patient the importance of a follow-up appointment with the HCP. If the patient's condition is slow to respond, does not respond, or the

HCP suspects another condition may be occurring or contributing to the acute attack, we should transfer the outpatient to an acute care facility.

A severe acute attack is usually frightening enough for most patients to go to the ED. In many cases, a severe attack will call for hospital admission. Managing the patient with a severe attack focuses on correcting hypoxemia and continually observing and/or improving ventilation.

In a severe attack, continuously monitor vital signs and WOB. The patient may be tachycardic, tachypneic, and solely focused on breathing. Respiratory rates greater than 30 breaths/min may be present. They may use accessory muscles. The patient may be agitated, restless, or confused from hypoxemia. The patient often sits forward to maximize diaphragmatic movement.

Bedside PEFR may be used to monitor airflow obstruction. Serial PEFR results, oximetry, and measurement of arterial blood gases (ABGs) give information about the severity of the attack and the response to therapy. Obtaining a PEFR during a severe asthma attack is usually not possible. However, if it can be obtained, PEFR less than 200 L/min or 50% or less of predicted or of personal best indicates severe obstruction.

$O_{2\,\text{therapy}}$ is given to achieve a PaO_2 of at least 60 mm Hg or O_2 saturation greater than 90%. O_2 monitoring should be continuous with pulse oximetry. Give drugs as ordered. If the patient can swallow, oral corticosteroids will be part of the treatment plan. Otherwise, IV steroids will be given. SABAs may be part of a patient's asthma plan. Symptoms may gradually diminish after medication therapy but often re-occur.

Auscultate lung sounds. If not immediately audible, auscultation may reveal inspiratory or expiratory wheezing. Louder wheezing may occur in airways that are responding to therapy as airflow increases. As improvement continues and airflow increases, breath sounds increase and wheezing decreases. The "silent chest" is an ominous clinical finding. It often signals impending ARF. Immediately notify the HCP.

The disappearance of most bronchospasm, resolution of edema and cellular infiltration of airway mucosa, and elimination of mucous plugs may take several days to improve after a severe attack. As a result, therapy must be continued even after clinical improvement. Always evaluate the patient's response to therapy.

An important nursing goal during an acute attack is to decrease the patient's anxiety and sense of panic. Assess the patient's level of anxiety. Position the patient comfortably (usually sitting, in semi- to high-Fowler's position) to maximize chest expansion. A calm, quiet, reassuring attitude may help the patient relax. A technique called "talking down" can help the patient remain calm. In talking down, you gain eye contact with the patient. In a firm, calm voice, coach the patient to use pursed-lip breathing. Pursed-lip breathing keeps the airways open by maintaining positive pressure (see Table 28.1). Stay with the patient until the respiratory rate has slowed.

When the acute attack subsides, encourage rest. Provide a quiet, calm environment. When the patient is less exhausted, can breathe easier, and is beginning to recover, try to obtain a history and do a physical assessment. If caregivers are present, they may be able to provide information about the patient's health history. This information is important in planning and implementing a patient-centered plan of care.

◆ Ambulatory Care

A major goal in asthma care is to maximize the patient's ability to safely manage an acute asthma episode using an asthma action plan (Fig. 31.11). Action plans are important for all people with asthma, especially those who have frequent, acute attacks. They are based on the patient's asthma symptoms and PEFR. The action plan dictates what symptoms or PEFR necessitate a change in asthma drug therapy to gain control.

The patient must measure PEFR at least daily. PEFR monitoring, when done correctly, is a reliable, objective measure of asthma control (Table 31.14). Some patients may not perceive minimal but important changes in their breathing. They may have a significant decrease in lung function without any noticeable symptoms other than a change in PEFR.

If a patient's PEFR is in the green zone (usually 80% to 100% of the patient's personal best), the patient should take their usual medications. A PEFR within the yellow zone (usually 50% to 80% of personal best) indicates caution. A PEFR in the red zone (50% or less of personal best) indicates a serious problem. In other words, something is triggering the patient's asthma (e.g., viral infection). The patient should seek out their HCP as soon as possible.

The written asthma action plan needs to clearly identify the "step-up" increase in medications during the acute phase of an infection. For example, the patient can use different strategies, such as using the low dose ICS more often. Although it may happen, it is unusual for a patient's PEFR to drop from the green zone to the red zone quickly. Usually, the patient has time to make changes in medications, avoid triggers, and notify the HCP. The dose is "stepped down" once the symptoms subside.

Involve caregivers in asthma action plans. They should know where to find the patient's medications. Teach them how to decrease the patient's anxiety if an asthma attack occurs. When the patient is stabilized or controlled, the caregiver can gently remind the patient about monitoring daily PEFR by asking questions, such as "What zone are you in?" or "How's your peak flow today?" A patient and caregiver teaching guide for the patient with asthma is shown in Table 31.15.

Exercise (e.g., swimming, walking, cycling) within the patient's limit of tolerance is beneficial. It may require pre-treatment with medication. Good nutrition and uninterrupted sleep are important. If a patient with asthma reports poor sleep because of symptoms, their asthma is not under good control and their plan should be re-evaluated. Encourage the patient to maintain a fluid intake of 2 to 3 L/day.

Validated questionnaires (e.g., Asthma Control Test [ACT] available at www.asthmacontroltest.com) can be used to assess quality-of-life. Patients may have frequent absences from school or work. They may have psychologic issues, such as stress, anxiety, and depression. Asthma support groups are available online and around the country. Relaxation therapies (e.g., yoga, meditation, breathing techniques) may help a patient lessen respiratory muscle workload and decrease the respiratory rate.

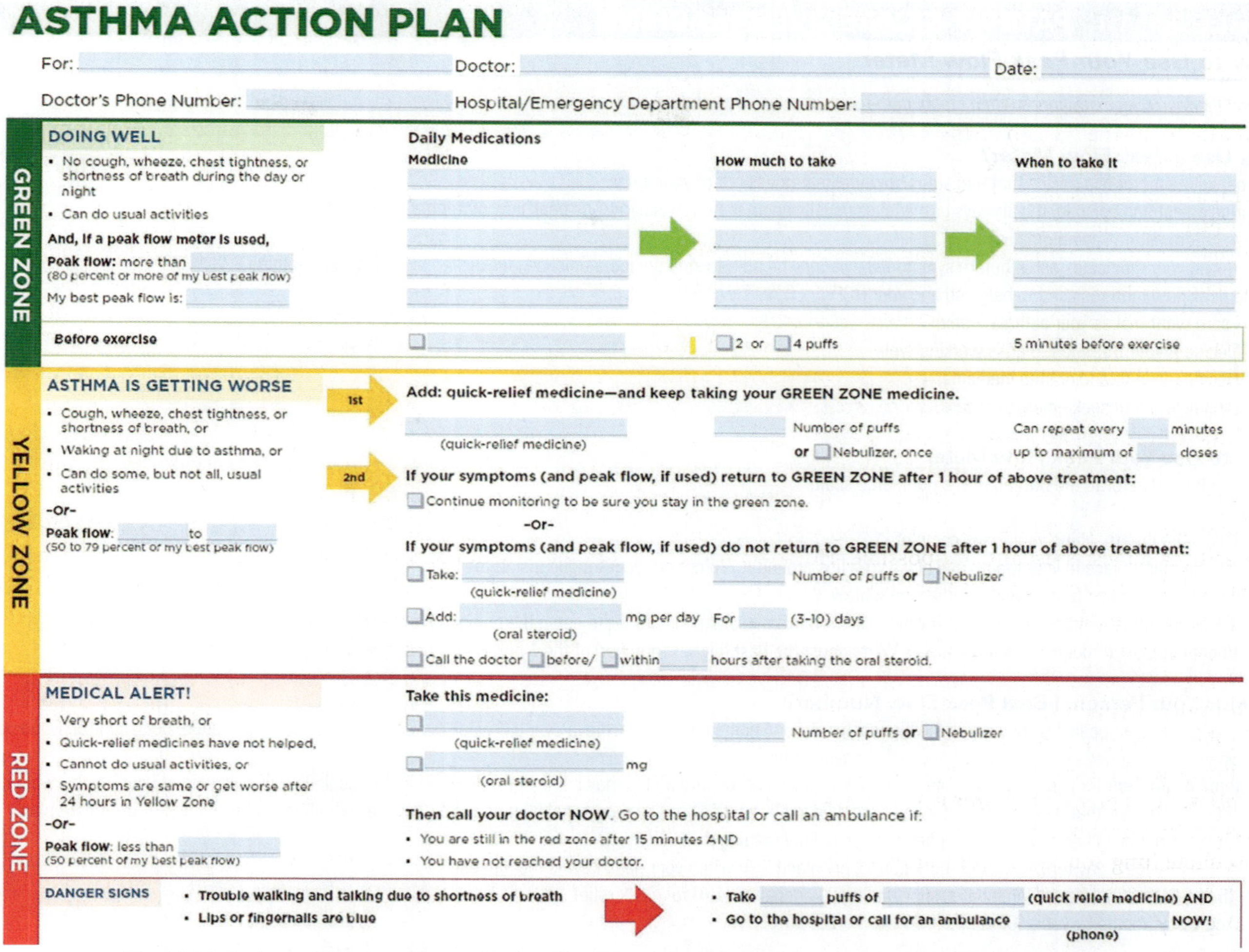

ASTHMA ACTION PLAN

For: Doctor: Date:

Doctor's Phone Number: Hospital/Emergency Department Phone Number:

GREEN ZONE

DOING WELL
- No cough, wheeze, chest tightness, or shortness of breath during the day or night
- Can do usual activities

And, if a peak flow meter is used,
Peak flow: more than (80 percent or more of my best peak flow)
My best peak flow is:

Daily Medications
Medicine | How much to take | When to take it

Before exercise | 2 or 4 puffs | 5 minutes before exercise

YELLOW ZONE

ASTHMA IS GETTING WORSE
- Cough, wheeze, chest tightness, or shortness of breath, or
- Waking at night due to asthma, or
- Can do some, but not all, usual activities

-Or-
Peak flow: to (50 to 79 percent of my best peak flow)

1st Add: quick-relief medicine—and keep taking your GREEN ZONE medicine.
(quick-relief medicine) Number of puffs or Nebulizer, once Can repeat every minutes up to maximum of doses

2nd If your symptoms (and peak flow, if used) return to GREEN ZONE after 1 hour of above treatment:
Continue monitoring to be sure you stay in the green zone.
-Or-
If your symptoms (and peak flow, if used) do not return to GREEN ZONE after 1 hour of above treatment:
Take: (quick-relief medicine) Number of puffs or Nebulizer
Add: (oral steroid) mg per day For (3-10) days
Call the doctor before/ within hours after taking the oral steroid.

RED ZONE

MEDICAL ALERT!
- Very short of breath, or
- Quick-relief medicines have not helped,
- Cannot do usual activities, or
- Symptoms are same or get worse after 24 hours in Yellow Zone

-Or-
Peak flow: less than (50 percent of my best peak flow)

Take this medicine:
(quick-relief medicine) Number of puffs or Nebulizer
(oral steroid) mg

Then call your doctor NOW. Go to the hospital or call an ambulance if:
- You are still in the red zone after 15 minutes AND
- You have not reached your doctor.

DANGER SIGNS
- Trouble walking and talking due to shortness of breath
- Lips or fingernails are blue

- Take puffs of (quick relief medicine) AND
- Go to the hospital or call for an ambulance (phone) NOW!

Fig. 31.11 Asthma action plan. (Source: National Heart, Lung, and Blood Institute, 2021, Bethesda, MD. Retrieved from https://www.nhlbi.nih.gov/health-topics/all-publications-and-resources/asthma-action-plan-2020.)

Disparities in socioeconomic status and access to health care may be part of the reason some people have poorly controlled asthma. Explore and try to eliminate any potential barriers to health care. Use culturally appropriate resources and educational material in languages other than English to help improve knowledge about asthma.

◆ Patient Teaching Related to Drug Therapy

Two factors that promote successful asthma management include knowing about asthma drugs and taking them correctly. The drug regimen for asthma can be confusing and complex. Reinforcement and frequent repetition of key learning points are often needed.

Teach patients about their medications. Include the name, purpose, dose, method of administration, and when to use. Help the patient understand the differences between "controller," "preferred reliever," and "alternate reliever" drugs. They need to be able to monitor their response to therapy and know when symptoms are not improving and they need help. Review side effects and what to do if they occur. Teach patients about how to properly prime, use, and clean devices. Some patients may benefit from keeping a diary to record medication use, wheezing, or coughing, PEFR, side effects of drugs, and activity level. This information will help the HCP adjust the medication if needed.

Several factors can affect the correct use of inhalation devices. These include advanced age, changes in dexterity (e.g., arthritis in hands, coordination), cognition, affordability, convenience, and administration time and preference. A social service referral can help lower-income patients obtain access to care.

Make sure that patients understand how to use their inhaler device. Review package inserts with the patient. Give the patient printed instructions. At every visit, reassess their inhaler and device techniques and asthma action plan.

Adherence with drug therapy is a major challenge in the management of chronic asthma. Lack of adherence often occurs when the patient is symptom free and does not use drug therapy regularly because they do not feel an immediate benefit. The patient does not realize that the medications treat the ongoing inflammation that accompanies asthma. Explain the importance and purpose of taking the long-term agents. Stress that maximum improvement may take some time. Tell them that

TABLE 31.14 PATIENT & CAREGIVER TEACHING

How to Use Your Peak Flow Meter

Include the following instructions when teaching the patient to use a peak flow meter:

Why Use a Peak Flow Meter?

- A peak flow meter is a device that measures how well air moves out of your lungs.
- During an asthma episode, the airways of the lungs usually begin to narrow slowly. The peak flow meter may tell you if there is narrowing in the airways, sometimes even before asthma symptoms occur.
- By taking your medicines early (before symptoms), you may be able to stop an acute episode quickly and avoid a severe asthma attack.
- The peak flow meter is used to help you and your HCP:
  - Learn what makes your asthma worse.
  - Decide if your treatment plan is working well.
  - Decide when to add or stop medicine.
  - Decide when to seek emergency care.

How to Use Your Peak Flow Meter

1. Move the indicator to the bottom of the numbered scale.
2. Stand up.
3. Take a deep breath, filling your lungs completely.
4. Place the mouthpiece in your mouth and close your lips around it. Do not put your tongue inside the hole.
5. Blow out as hard and fast as you can in a single blow.
   - Write down the number you get. But if you cough or make a mistake, do not write down the number. Perform the action again.
   - Repeat steps 1 through 5 two more times. Write down the best (highest number) of the 3 blows in your asthma diary.

What is Your Personal Best Peak Flow Number?

- Your personal best peak flow number is the highest (peak flow) number you can achieve over a 2-week period when your asthma is under good control. Good control is when you feel good and do not have any asthma symptoms.
- Asthma is different for every patient. Your best peak expiratory flow rate (PEFR) may be higher or lower than the peak flow of someone of your height, weight, and gender. This means that it is important for you to test yourself and find your own personal best peak flow number, which is the basis for your treatment plan.
- To find your personal best peak flow number, take peak flow readings:
  - At least twice a day for 2–3 weeks, between 12 noon and 2 PM when your peak flow is the highest
  - 15 to 20 minutes after taking inhaled short-acting β_2-agonist (SABA) for quick relief
  - And as instructed by your HCP

The Peak Flow Zone System

Once you know your personal best peak flow number, your HCP will help you place the peak flow numbers into zones. Zones are set up like a traffic light (red, yellow, green). As you trend your peak flow numbers over time, this will help you know what to do when the number changes. For example:

- *Green Zone* (more than __L/min [80% of your personal best number]) signals good control. No asthma symptoms are present. Take your medicines as usual.
- *Yellow Zone* (between __ and __L/min [50% to <80% of your personal best number]) signals caution. If you stay in the yellow zone after several measures of peak flow, follow your plan, including taking any reliever medications. If you continue to register peak flow readings in the yellow zone, your asthma may not be under good control. Contact your HCP and ask if you need to change or increase your daily medicines.
- *Red Zone* (<__L/min [<50% of your personal best number]) signals a medical alert. Take your reliever medication right away. Call your HCP and ask what to do or go directly to the ED.

Use a Logbook to Keep Track of Your Peak Flow

- Record your personal best peak flow number and peak flow zones in your asthma logbook.
- Measure your peak flow when you wake up, *before* taking medicine. Write down your peak flow number in the diary every day, or as instructed by your HCP.

without regular use, swelling in the airways may progress and asthma will likely worsen over time.

◆ Evaluation

The expected outcomes are that the patient with asthma will

- Maintain patent airway with removal of secretions
- Have normal respiratory rate, unlabored breathing, and adequate breath sounds
- Report decreased anxiety with increased control of breathing
- Correctly use medications
- Manage asthma and acute asthma attacks with a written asthma action plan

CHRONIC OBSTRUCTIVE PULMONARY DISEASE

Chronic obstructive pulmonary disease (COPD) is a progressive lung disease characterized by persistent airflow limitation. COPD is associated with an enhanced chronic inflammatory response in the airways and lungs. The main causes are cigarette smoking and other noxious particles and gases. Exacerbations and other coexisting problems may contribute to the severity of the disease.

Previous definitions of COPD have included such terms as *chronic bronchitis* and *emphysema*. Each condition has features of COPD, but neither by itself is COPD. **Chronic bronchitis**

TABLE 31.15 PATIENT & CAREGIVER TEACHING

Asthma

Include the following information in a teaching plan for the patient with asthma and the caregiver to help to improve the patient's quality of life and promote lifestyle changes that support successful living with asthma:

What Is Asthma?
- Basic anatomy and physiology of lung
- Pathophysiology of asthma
- Relationship of pathophysiology to signs and symptoms
- Measurement and correlation of spirometry and peak expiratory flow rate

What Is Good Asthma Control?
- Personal ideas of good control
- Use the Asthma Control Test available at www.asthmacontroltest.com

Obstacles to Asthma Treatment and Control
- Discuss with patient and caregiver possible obstacles (e.g., denial, poor perception of asthma severity by patient, cost of medications)

Environment and Trigger Control
- Identify triggers and preventive measures (use trigger diary)
- Avoiding allergens and other triggers
- Need to maintain good hydration

Medications
- Classes (include mechanism of action)
- Terms: Controller, reliever, and alternate reliever
- Correct use of inhalers, spacer, and nebulizer
- Write out a medication list, identify schedule
- Asthma Action Plan (Fig. 31.11)

Pursed-Lip Breathing (see Chapter 28)
Correct Use of Peak Flow Meter (Table 31.14)
Asthma Action Plan (Fig. 31.11)
- Peak flow zones
- Patient-centered care asthma action plan with HCP and patient
- Early recognition of infection
- Building a partnership with the HCP

For more information, visit the American Lung Association website at www.lung.org/lung-disease/asthma.

is the presence of cough and sputum production for at least 3 months in each of 2 consecutive years. It is an independent disease that may precede or follow the development of airflow limitation. **Emphysema**, the destruction of alveoli without fibrosis, describes one of several structural abnormalities in COPD.

Around 16 million adults in the US have COPD.[24] The number of people with COPD is underestimated because the disease is usually not diagnosed until it is moderately advanced. COPD is the 3rd leading cause of death in the US, causing more than 140,000 deaths each year.[25]

Risk Factors

Many factors affect the development and progression of COPD (Box 31.3). Next, we discuss the most common risk factors.

BOX 31.3 BIOLOGIC SEX CONSIDERATIONS

COPD

Men
- COPD is slightly more common in men
- Have a poorer response to O_2 therapy

Women
- Prevalence of COPD is increasing
- The increase is likely due to more women smoking and increased susceptibility (e.g., smaller lungs and airways)
- Women who smoke are 50% more likely to develop COPD compared to men who smoke
- Women with COPD have a lower quality of life, more exacerbations, less phlegm, and increased dyspnea

TABLE 31.16 Effects of Tobacco Smoke on the Respiratory System

Area of Defect	Acute Effects	Long-Term Effects
Respiratory mucosa		
• Nasopharyngeal	↓ Sense of smell	Cancer
• Tongue	↓ Sense of taste	Cancer
• Vocal cords	Hoarseness	Chronic cough, cancer
• Bronchus and bronchioles	Bronchospasm, cough	Chronic bronchitis, asthma, cancer
Cilia	Paralysis, sputum accumulation, cough	Chronic bronchitis, cancer
Mucous glands	↑ Secretions, ↑ cough	Hyperplasia and hypertrophy of glands, chronic bronchitis
Alveolar macrophages	↓ Function	↑ Incidence of infection
Elastin and collagen fibers	↑ Destruction by proteases ↓ Function of antiproteases (α_1-antitrypsin) ↓ Synthesis and repair of elastin	Emphysema

Cigarette Smoking

The major risk factor for developing COPD is cigarette smoking. Of the 16 million people in the US who have COPD, around 38% report that they currently smoke.[26] COPD should be considered in any person who is over the age of 40 with a smoking history of 10 or more pack-years.

Cigarette smoke has several direct effects on the respiratory tract (Table 31.16). The irritating effect of smoke causes hyperplasia of cells, including goblet cells, increasing mucus production. Hyperplasia reduces airway diameter and makes it harder to clear secretions. Smoking reduces ciliary activity and may cause actual loss of cilia. Smoking causes abnormal dilation of the distal air space and destruction of alveolar walls. Many cells develop large, atypical nuclei, which we consider pre-cancerous. Smoking is the source of chronic, enhanced inflammation of various parts of the lung with structural changes and repair (*remodeling*) over time.

Cigarette smoking causes oxidative stress and an imbalance between proteases that break down connective tissue in the lung and antiproteases that protect the lungs. These changes increase with more severe disease and persist even after the patient has stopped smoking. In adults, ETS can cause decreased lung function, increased respiratory symptoms, and severe lower respiratory tract infections (e.g., pneumonia). ETS increases the risk for nasal sinus and lung cancer.

Infection

Severe recurring respiratory tract infections in childhood are associated with reduced lung function and increased respiratory symptoms in adulthood. We are not sure if COPD is related to recurrent infections in adults. People who smoke and have human immunodeficiency virus (HIV) infection have faster development of COPD.[27] Tuberculosis is also a risk factor.

Asthma

Patients with COPD may have asthma. Asthma may be a risk factor for COPD. There is a considerable pathologic and functional overlap between asthma and COPD, especially among older adults, who may have components of both. We call this *asthma-COPD overlap syndrome.*

Air Pollution

High levels of urban air pollution are harmful to people with existing lung disease. The effect of outdoor air pollution as a risk factor for developing COPD is unclear. Another risk factor is exposure to coal and other biomass fuels people use for indoor heating and cooking. Many people who have never smoked are at increased risk because of cooking with these fuels in poorly ventilated areas.

Occupational Chemicals and Dusts

If a person has intense or prolonged exposure to various dusts, vapors, irritants, or fumes in the workplace, symptoms of lung impairment consistent with COPD can develop. If a person has occupational exposure and smokes, the risk for COPD increases significantly.

Aging

Many believe aging is a risk factor for COPD, but the research is not clear. Does the aging process lead to COPD? Or is COPD a result of cumulative exposures that occur over a lifetime?

Normal aging results in stiffening of the chest wall and decrease in exercise tolerance. The lungs gradually lose their elastic recoil. The thoracic cage becomes stiff and rigid, and the ribs are less mobile. The shape of the rib cage gradually changes because of the increased residual volume (RV), causing it to enlarge and become more rounded. Decreased chest compliance and loss of elastic recoil together affect the mechanical aspects of ventilation and increase the WOB. The number of functional alveoli decreases as peripheral airways lose supporting tissues. Over time, the surface area for gas exchange decreases and the PaO_2 decreases. Changes in the elasticity of the lungs reduce the ventilatory reserve. These age-related changes are similar to those seen in the patient with COPD.

BOX 31.4 GENETICS IN CLINICAL PRACTICE

α_1-Antitrypsin Deficiency

Genetic Basis
- Autosomal recessive disorder
- Gene provides instructions for the liver to make the protein α_1-*Antitrypsin* (AAT), which protects the lungs and liver from proteolytic enzymes
- Mutations in *SERPINA1* gene cause α_1-antitrypsin deficiency (AATD)
- Without enough functional AAT, proteolytic enzymes destroy alveoli and cause lung disease

Incidence
- Occurs in 1 in 3000–5000 live births in the US
- People of northern European and Iberian descent most affected

Clinical Implications
- AATD can cause lung and liver disease
- Disease onset and first diagnosis usually occurs between ages 30 to 45 years of age
- Disease predisposes to early-onset emphysema
- Purified AAT replacement therapy helps prevent worsening of the condition

Genetic Testing
- DNA testing is available
- Serum assay is available to measure the amount of AAT

Genetics

An intriguing question is why some smokers develop COPD and others do not. The fact that a small number of smokers get COPD suggests genetic factors may play a role in who develops COPD. Because of genetic-environment interaction, 2 people may have the same smoking history, but only 1 develops COPD. Genetics may play a role in why people who never smoked but were exposed to ETS over long periods of time develop COPD. We have identified 1 genetic factor: "Z" allele of the AAT protein.[28]

Alpha-1 Antitrypsin Deficiency

Alpha-1 (α1) antitrypsin deficiency (AATD) is an autosomal recessive disorder that may eventually affect the lungs and liver (Box 31.4). AAT is a protein made by the liver and normally found in the lungs. The main function of AAT is to protect lung tissue from attack by proteases during inflammation related to smoking and infections. Unfortunately, few people are tested for AATD until symptoms are present and they are seeking medical care. About 2% of all people diagnosed with COPD in the US have undetected AATD.[29] Smoking speeds the disease process in these patients. Genetic counseling may be appropriate for the patient with AATD who is planning to have children.

Pathophysiology

COPD is characterized by chronic inflammation of the airways, lung parenchyma (respiratory bronchioles and alveoli), and pulmonary blood vessels (Fig. 31.12). The pathophysiology of COPD is complex and involves many mechanisms. The defining feature of COPD is airflow limitation not fully reversible during

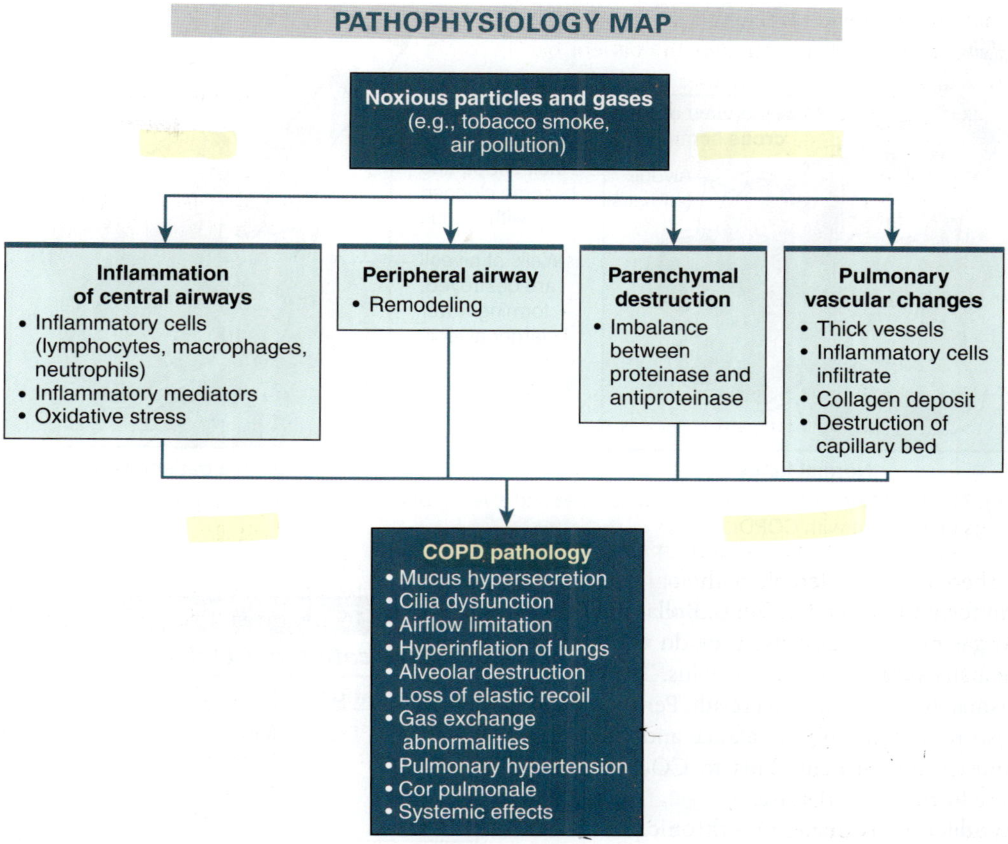

Fig. 31.12 Pathophysiology of COPD.

forced exhalation. The main cause is the loss of elastic recoil and airflow obstruction, from mucus hypersecretion, mucosal edema, and bronchospasm.

As the disease progresses, abnormalities in airflow limitation, air trapping, and gas exchange worsen. In severe COPD, pulmonary hypertension and systemic manifestations occur. COPD has an uneven distribution of pathologic changes. Severely impaired and/or destroyed areas of lung tissue exist alongside areas of relatively normal lung.

The inflammatory process most often starts with inhaling noxious particles and gases (e.g., cigarette smoke). With repeated exposure, chronic inflammation causes tissue destruction and disrupts the normal defense mechanisms and repair process of the lung. We do not clearly understand the exact mechanisms for the enhanced inflammatory response. In some people, it may be genetically determined.

The predominant inflammatory cells in COPD are neutrophils, macrophages, and lymphocytes. This is different from that of asthma, in which eosinophils, mast cells, neutrophils, lymphocytes, and macrophages are the main culprits. Inflammatory cells attract other inflammatory mediators (e.g., leukotrienes) and proinflammatory cytokines (e.g., tumor necrosis factor).

The inflammatory process may be increased by the oxidants made by cigarette smoke and other inhaled particles and released from the inflammatory cells. Oxidants adversely affect the lungs as they inactivate antiproteases (which prevent the natural destruction of the lungs), stimulate mucus secretion, and increase fluid in the lungs. A result of the inflammatory process is structural changes in the lungs.

After inhaling oxidants in tobacco or air pollution, the activity of proteases (which break down connective tissue of the lungs) increases and antiproteases (which protect against breakdown) are inhibited. So, the natural balance of protease/antiprotease is tipped in favor of alveolar destruction and loss of the lungs' elastic recoil.

Inability to expire air is a main characteristic of COPD. The main site of the airflow limitation is in the smaller airways. As the peripheral airways become obstructed, air is progressively trapped during expiration. The volume of residual air that is in the lungs at end expiration becomes greatly increased in severe COPD. As air is trapped in the lungs, the chest hyper-expands and becomes barrel shaped because the respiratory muscles cannot function effectively. As a result, functional residual capacity (FRC) is increased. The residual air, combined with the loss of elastic recoil, makes passive expiration of air difficult. The patient must now inhale when the lungs are in an "overinflated" state. As a result, the patient becomes dyspneic with limited exercise capacity.

Typically, the patient does not have problems with hypoxemia at rest until late in the disease. At first, hypoxemia may develop during exercise and the patient may benefit from supplemental O_2. Gas exchange problems result in hypoxemia and hypercapnia (increased CO_2) as the disease worsens. As the air trapping increases, walls of alveoli are destroyed (Fig. 31.13). Bullae (large air spaces in the parenchyma) and blebs (air spaces

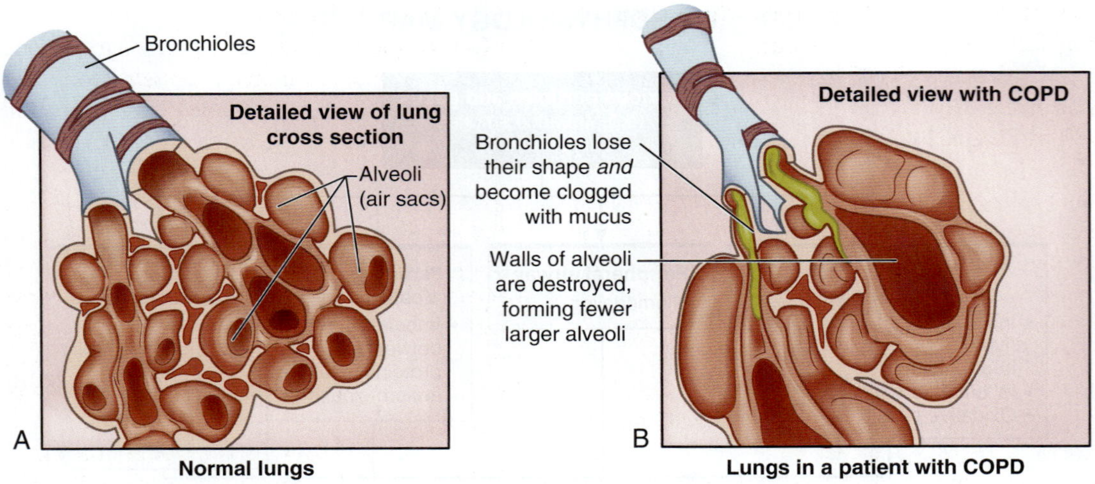

Fig. 31.13 (A) Normal lungs showing bronchioles and alveoli. (B) Changes in the bronchioles and alveoli in the lungs of a patient with COPD.

next to pleurae) can form in and on the lungs. Bullae and blebs are not effective in gas exchange because they do not contain a capillary that normally surrounds each alveolus. Therefore, a significant V/Q mismatch and hypoxemia result. Peripheral airway obstruction also results in V/Q imbalance and combined with respiratory muscle impairment leads to CO_2 retention, particularly in severe forms of the disease.

Excess mucus production, resulting in a chronic productive cough, is a feature of persons with predominant chronic bronchitis. However, not all COPD patients have sputum production. When present, excess mucus production results from an increased number of mucus-secreting goblet cells, enlarged submucosal glands, cilia dysfunction, and stimulation from inflammatory mediators.

Pulmonary vascular changes causing mild to moderate pulmonary hypertension may occur late in the course of COPD. The small pulmonary arteries vasoconstrict due to hypoxia. As the disease advances, the structure of the pulmonary arteries changes, resulting in thickening of the vascular smooth muscle. Because of the loss of alveolar walls and the capillaries surrounding them, pressure in the pulmonary circulation increases. Pulmonary hypertension may progress and lead to hypertrophy of the right ventricle. The right ventricle dilates and may lead to right HF.

Chronic inflammation is an underlying problem for many COPD patients. Common diseases, including osteoporosis and diabetes, have occurred.

Classification of COPD

We classify COPD as mild, moderate, severe, and very severe (Table 31.17). An FEV_1/FVC ratio of less than 70% establishes the diagnosis of COPD. The severity of obstruction (as shown by FEV_1) determines the stage of COPD. Management of COPD is based on the patient's symptoms, classification, and exacerbation history.

Clinical Manifestations

The manifestations of COPD typically develop slowly. A clinical diagnosis of COPD should be considered in any patient who has chronic cough or sputum production, dyspnea, and a history of exposure to risk factors for the disease (e.g., tobacco smoke, occupational dusts). It is sometimes hard to tell COPD from asthma, especially if the person has a history of smoking.

A chronic intermittent cough is often the first symptom. Patients often dismiss the cough as they associate it with smoking or environmental exposure. The cough may be productive. Significant airflow limitation may exist without cough or sputum. Typically, dyspnea is progressive, usually occurs with exertion, and is present every day.

Patients may report chest heaviness, not being able to take a deep breath, gasping, increased effort to breathe, and air hunger. They tend to ignore symptoms and rationalize that "I'm getting older" or "I'm out of shape." Some change behaviors to avoid dyspnea, such as taking the elevator instead of the stairs. Patients will seek medical care when dyspnea becomes severe or impairs their ability to complete ADLs.

In late stages of COPD, dyspnea may be present at rest. The patient must work harder to breathe. As more alveoli become overdistended, increasing amounts of air are trapped. This causes the diaphragm to flatten. Effective abdominal breathing is decreased because of the flattened diaphragm. As a result, the patient becomes more of a chest breather, relying on the intercostal and accessory muscles. Chest breathing is not particularly efficient, especially over long periods.

Wheezing and chest tightness may be present. These symptoms may vary by time of the day or from day to day, especially

TABLE 31.17 Diagnostic Criteria

Classification of COPD Severity

Classification	Level of Severity	FEV_1 Results
GOLD 1	Mild	$FEV_1 \geq 80\%$ predicted
GOLD 2	Moderate	FEV_1 50%–80% predicted
GOLD 3	Severe	FEV_1 30%–50% predicted
GOLD 4	Very severe	$FEV_1 < 30\%$ predicted

Adapted from Global strategy for diagnosis, management and prevention of COPD 2021. Retrieved from www.goldcopd.org. © Global Initiative for Chronic Obstructive Pulmonary Disease.

in those with severe disease. Chest tightness, which often follows activity, may feel like muscle contractions.

The person with advanced COPD often has fatigue, weight loss, and anorexia. Even with adequate caloric intake, the patient may still lose weight. Fatigue is a highly prevalent symptom that affects ADLs.

The expiratory phase is often prolonged. We may hear decreased breath sounds and/or wheezes in all lung fields. Because the anteroposterior diameter of the chest increases ("barrel chest") from the chronic air trapping, the patient may need to breathe louder than normal for us to hear breath sounds with a stethoscope. The patient may sit upright with arms supported on a fixed surface, such as an overbed table *(tripod position)*. They may naturally purse lips on expiration (pursed-lip breathing).

Over time, hypoxemia (PaO_2 less than 60 mm Hg or O_2 saturation less than 88% on room air) may develop with hypercapnia ($PaCO_2$ over 45 mm Hg). A bluish-red skin color results from polycythemia and cyanosis. Polycythemia develops from the increased production of red blood cells as the body tries to compensate for chronic hypoxemia. Hemoglobin concentrations may reach 20 g/dL (200 g/L) or more. Some persons, though, have low hemoglobin and hematocrit because of chronic anemia.

Complications

Primary complications of COPD include pulmonary hypertension, cor pulmonale, acute exacerbations, and ARF.

Pulmonary Hypertension and Cor Pulmonale

In COPD, the main cause of pulmonary hypertension is constriction of the pulmonary vessels from alveolar hypoxia. Chronic hypoxia stimulates red blood cell production, which causes polycythemia. This results in increased viscosity of the blood. These patients have increased pulmonary vascular resistance, and, as a result, develop pulmonary hypertension.

Normally, the right ventricle and pulmonary circulatory system are low-pressure systems compared with the left ventricle and systemic circulation. With pulmonary hypertension (pressure within the lungs increases), the pressures on the right side of the heart must increase to push blood into the lungs. Eventually, because the pressure in the lungs is so high, right HF develops.

Cor pulmonale results from pulmonary hypertension (Fig. 31.14). It is a late manifestation of COPD. Once the patient develops cor pulmonale, the prognosis worsens. Not all patients with COPD develop cor pulmonale.

Dyspnea is the most common symptom of chronic cor pulmonale. Lung sounds are normal, or crackles may be present in the bases. Heart sounds may include S_3, S_4, and systolic murmurs. Other manifestations of right HF may develop. These include distended neck veins, hepatomegaly with right upper quadrant tenderness, peripheral edema, and weight gain.

Typically, the patient has large pulmonary vessels on chest x-ray and increased pressure on the right heart.

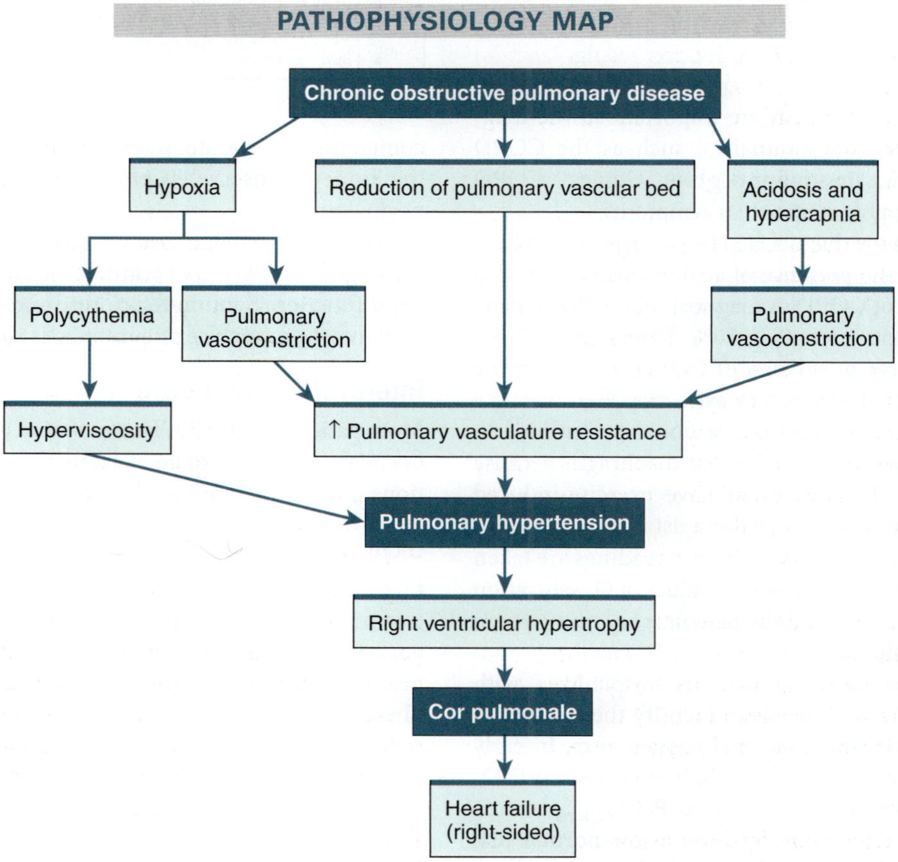

Fig. 31.14 Mechanisms involved in the pathophysiology of pulmonary hypertension and cor pulmonale from COPD.

The initial treatment of cor pulmonale is aimed at managing the underlying cause, including COPD. Continuous, long-term, low-flow O_2 therapy is often part of care. Diuretics may be given if left HF or pulmonary edema are present but must be used with caution. In some cases, decreases in fluid volume from diuresis can worsen heart function. Long-term anticoagulation therapy is started to help decrease the risk for venous thromboembolism (VTE). HF is the focus of Chapter 38.

Acute Exacerbations

An exacerbation of COPD is an acute event characterized by a worsening of the patient's respiratory symptoms. Exacerbations are signaled by a sudden change in the patient's usual dyspnea, cough, and/or sputum (e.g., something different from the usual daily patterns). Respiratory infections are a common cause.[30] Exacerbations are common and increase in frequency (on average 1 or 2 per year) as the disease progresses. As the severity of COPD increases, exacerbations are associated with poorer outcomes.

Acute Respiratory Failure

Patients with severe COPD who have severe exacerbations are at risk for ARF. Suddenly stopping a medication may cause ARF. All too often, COPD patients wait too long to contact their HCP when they first develop symptoms suggestive of an exacerbation. By the time the patient seeks out medical attention, their condition has worsened to the point that they need mechanical ventilation and ICU admission. ARF is discussed in Chapter 32.

Diagnostic Studies

A history and physical assessment are important in the diagnostic workup. Validated questionnaires, such as the COPD Assessment Test (www.catestonline.org) or Clinical COPD Questionnaire (www.ccq.nl), help assess symptoms.

Spirometry confirms the diagnosis in those suspected of having COPD. It confirms the presence of airflow obstruction and determines the severity of COPD. A diagnosis of COPD is made when the FEV_1/FVC ratio is less than 70%.[31] The FEV_1 value is a guideline for the degree of severity of COPD. The lower the FEV_1, the more obstructed are the airways.

Other diagnostic studies that may be done are outlined in Table 31.18. Chest x-rays often show a flat diaphragm because of hyperinflated lungs. Patients often have exercise-induced hypoxemia. A physical or respiratory therapist may do a 6-minute walk test. During this test, pulse oximetry readings are taken when the patient is walking and at rest. If values of O_2 saturation are 88% or lower when at rest and the patient is breathing room air, they qualify for O_2 therapy.

We usually monitor ABGs in patients hospitalized with acute COPD exacerbations. ABGs help identify the severity of the exacerbation by assessing abnormal oxygenation. In early stages, there may be a normal or only slightly decreased PaO_2 and usually a normal or slightly increased $PaCO_{2\ level}$. In the later stages of COPD, typical findings are a low-normal pH, high-normal or above-normal $PaCO_2$, and high-normal bicarbonate (HCO_3^-). This may indicate either partially or fully compensated respiratory acidosis. In a fully compensated state, the kidneys conserve HCO_3^- to increase the pH to within the normal range.

TABLE 31.18 Interprofessional Care

COPD

Diagnostic Assessment
- History and physical assessment
- Chest x-ray
- Spirometry
- ABGs
- 6-Min walk test
- Serum α_1-antitrypsin levels
- COPD Assessment Test (CAT) or Clinical COPD Questionnaire (CCQ)

Management
- Smoking cessation
- Drug therapies (Tables 31.9 and 31.19)
- Airway clearance techniques
- Breathing exercises and retraining
- Hydration of 2–3 L/day (if not contraindicated)
- Immunizations: Influenza, pneumococcal, COVID-19
- Long-term O_2 (if indicated)
- Progressive exercise plan, especially walking and upper body strengthening
- Pulmonary rehabilitation program
- Nutrition supplements
- Treatment of complications
  - Pulmonary hypertension
  - Cor pulmonale
  - Acute exacerbations
  - ARF
- Surgical therapy (if suitable candidate, based on age, medical history, severity and stage of COPD)
  - Lung volume reduction
  - Bullectomy
  - Lung transplant

An ECG may be normal or show signs of right HF. An echocardiogram or (MUGA) (cardiac blood pool) scan can evaluate heart function. Sputum for culture and sensitivity may be done if an infection, such as pneumonia, is suspected.

Interprofessional Care

Most patients with COPD are treated as outpatients. They are hospitalized for an acute exacerbation of COPD or complications, such as pneumonia, HF, or ARF.

Oxygen Therapy

O_2 therapy is often part of the treatment of COPD. It is the only treatment linked to improved survival.[32] For most patients, the goal of O_2 therapy is to keep the SaO_2 greater than 90% during rest, sleep, and exertion or the PaO_2 greater than 60 mm Hg. These goals may be modified for the patient with moderate to severe COPD. For example, based upon the patient's condition, the HCP may accept a SaO_2 or PaO_2 greater than 88%.

Drug Therapy

Drug therapy for COPD can reduce symptoms, increase exercise capacity, and improve overall health. This will hopefully

TABLE 31.19 Drug Therapy

Suggested Options for COPD Treatment

	Fewer Daily Symptoms	More Daily Symptoms
Less than 2 exacerbations, no hospitalizations	Short-acting β-2 agonist (SABA) OR Long-acting β-2 agonist (LABA)	LAMA or LABA
More than 2 exacerbations, 1 hospitalization	Long-acting muscarinic agents (LAMA)	LAMA or LABA and LAMA or LABA and ICS

reduce the number and severity of exacerbations. Choice of drug therapy is based on several factors. These include the patient's symptoms, how quickly they occur, FEV_1 results, the perceived risk of or number of exacerbations, and the ability to maintain spontaneous ventilation.[33] Table 31.19 shows suggestions for drug therapy.

Like asthma, medications are given in a stepwise fashion. In COPD, they are usually stepped up. Stepping down is rare because continual symptoms are present. The inhaled route is preferred. Changes in therapy are usually based on symptoms and repeated exacerbations.[33]

Bronchodilator drug therapy relaxes bronchial smooth muscle in the airway and improves the ventilation of the lungs, thus reducing the degree of breathlessness. Bronchodilator therapy is the first-line treatment for most patients. They do not respond as dramatically to bronchodilator therapy as those with asthma. However, bronchodilator therapy reduces dyspnea and increases FEV_1.

Bronchodilator drugs commonly used are β_2-adrenergic agonists, anticholinergics, and, to a much lesser extent, methylxanthines (Table 31.8). The choice of bronchodilator depends on the patient's response. These drugs are given on a scheduled or as-needed basis.

A short-acting β_2-adrenergic agonist (SABA) is a mainstay of COPD treatment. The most common SABA is albuterol. LABAs are often can be used as monotherapy. Salmeterol and formoterol are widely used LABAs.

Anticholinergics block the action of acetylcholine on the muscarinic receptors in the smooth muscle of the bronchotracheal tree. The most common short-acting muscarinic agent (SAMAs) is ipratropium bromide. For the patient who needs a drug with a more prolonged effect, long-acting muscarinic agents (LAMAs) such as tiotropium are an option.

Combining short-acting bronchodilators with anticholinergic medications into 1 "combination" drug may help improve bronchodilation of the airways and potentially decrease the risk for side effects. Albuterol and ipratropium can be nebulized together or delivered by inhalation spray (Combivent Respimat).

Depending upon the severity of symptoms and stage of COPD, regular treatment with ICS may be prescribed. However, unlike asthma, an ICS is not used as monotherapy in COPD because of the side effects. An ICS is often combined with a LABA for enhanced effect. Examples of combinations of ICSs with LABAs are fluticasone/salmeterol (Advair) and budesonide/formoterol (Symbicort). Oral corticosteroids should not be used for long-term therapy in COPD but are effective for short-term use to treat acute exacerbations.

We rarely use methylxanthines such as theophylline because of the development of newer drugs. The methylxanthines have serious side effects. Careful monitoring is needed. Theophylline interacts with many drugs and has a very narrow therapeutic window. A low dose of theophylline with an ICS may help a few patients who do not respond to other inhaled medications.

Roflumilast (Daliresp) is an oral agent used to decrease exacerbations in patients with severe COPD and chronic bronchitis. It is an antiinflammatory drug used for long-term therapy. It does not treat acute problems.

Mucolytic agents, such as NAC, may be used for COPD patients who have an acute exacerbation. They have antiinflammatory and mucolytic properties. NAC may help improve overall health and quality of life in some patients.

Inhaled long-acting anticholinergics, LABAs, and ICSs all help reduce COPD exacerbations. Some patients with COPD are on "triple therapy," which includes a LABA, LAMA, and ICS. Fluticasone/umeclidinium/vilanterol is one example of a "triple therapy" agent. New drugs and delivery devices are becoming available at a rapid pace for the treatment of patients with COPD.

Respiratory Care

Teaching the patient with COPD breathing retraining exercises is important. The 2 main types of breathing retraining exercises are (1) pursed-lip breathing and (2) diaphragmatic breathing (see Table 28.1). Diaphragmatic breathing in some patients with COPD may increase the WOB and dyspnea.

Many patients have ineffective coughing patterns that do not clear their airways of sputum. We can teach the patient ways to cough effectively to bring the secretions to the central airways to expectorate them. Effective coughing techniques are discussed in Chapter 28.

ACTs loosen mucus and secretions so they can be cleared by coughing (see Chapter 28). ACTs are especially helpful in patients who have a COPD exacerbation. They are often used in conjunction with other treatments. Typically, the patient receives bronchodilator therapy through an inhaler device (e.g., nebulizer) before ACT. Then, the ACT is used, followed by effective coughing (e.g., huff coughing). Airway clearance devices can also help mobilize secretions (see Chapter 28).

Nutrition Therapy

Many COPD patients with advanced disease are underweight with loss of muscle mass and cachexia. Weight loss, malnutrition, and muscle dysfunction can affect quality of life and contribute to increased mortality.[34] Factors that contribute to malnutrition include increased inflammatory mediators, increased metabolic rate from ventilatory effort, and lack of appetite. Other factors include taste changes caused by chronic mouth breathing, excess sputum, fatigue, anxiety, depression, and drug side effects.

There is no specific diet for the patient with COPD. Consensus is that a well-balanced diet that includes fresh fruits, whole grains, and vegetables is best.[34] A diet high in protein, moderate in carbohydrates, and moderate to high in fat is recommended for most patients. Meals can be divided into 5 or 6 small portions a day. Offer high-protein and moderate calorie nutrition supplements between meals. The dietitian is an excellent resource for what combination of nutrients and supplements are best.

Underweight patients need extra protein and calories. They may need 25 to 45 kcal/kg body weight and more than 1.5 g of protein/kg body weight to maintain their weight. The patient with malnutrition may need up to 2.5 g of protein/kg of body weight to maintain muscle mass.

To decrease dyspnea and conserve energy, the patient should rest for at least 30 minutes before eating and use a bronchodilator before meals. Teach the patient to avoid exercise and treatments for at least 1 hour before and after eating. If a patient desaturates while eating, O_2 therapy by nasal cannula may help. Encourage activity, such as walking, to stimulate appetite.

Getting the patient to eat adequate amounts of nutritionally sound foods may be difficult. Teach the patient or those responsible for meal preparation ways to make mealtime easier and more nutritious by increasing calories and protein without increasing the amount of food eaten (Table 31.20).

Surgical Therapy

Various surgical procedures can help manage severe COPD. However, it is important to remember that many patients with severe COPD are not candidates for surgery.

One type of surgery is *lung volume reduction surgery* (LVRS). The goal of LVRS is to reduce the size of the lungs by removing some of the diseased lung tissue so that the remaining healthy lung tissue can perform better. Reducing the diseased lung tissue by about 30% results in decreased airway obstruction and increased room for the remaining normal alveoli (small air sacs at the end of each bronchiole) to expand and function.[35] Besides improving lung and chest wall mechanics, LVRS can allow the diaphragm to return to its normal shape. This allows the patient to breathe more efficiently.

Another surgical procedure is *bronchoscopic lung volume reduction (BLVR)*. It involves placing multiple 1-way valves, by bronchoscopy, in the airways leading to the diseased parts of the lung. The valves allow air to leave the lung during exhalation and prevent air from entering during inspiration. By completely occluding a specific area of the lung, this collapses that area. BLVR produces a result similar to LVRS.[36] Pneumothorax is a common complication.

In a *bullectomy*, 1 or more very large bullae are removed. Removal of bullae helps decrease WOB. A lung transplant helps a very small number of patients with advanced COPD. Although single-lung transplant is most common because of a shortage of donors, a bilateral transplant can be done. Lung transplants are discussed in Chapter 28.

TABLE 31.20 NUTRITION THERAPY

Maximizing Food Intake in COPD

- Eat high-calorie foods first.
- Limit liquids at mealtimes.
- Rest before meals.
- Try more frequent meals and snacks.
- Try cold foods, which can make you feel less full than hot foods.
- Keep ready-prepared meals available for times when you have increased shortness of breath.

NURSING MANAGEMENT: COPD

Assessment

Subjective and objective data that you should obtain from a person with COPD are outlined in Table 31.21.

Clinical Problems

Clinical problems for the patient with COPD may include:

- Impaired respiratory function
- Activity intolerance
- Nutritionally compromised
- Ineffective coping

Additional information on clinical problems and interventions is presented in eNursing Care Plan 31.2 available on the website for this chapter.

Planning

The overall goals are that the patient with COPD will have (1) relief from symptoms, (2) ability to perform ADLs and improved exercise tolerance, (3) no complications related to COPD, (4) knowledge and ability to implement a long-term treatment plan, (5) prevention of disease progression, and (6) overall improved quality of life.

Implementation

Health Promotion

The incidence of COPD would decrease dramatically if people would not begin smoking or would stop smoking. Counseling the patient in smoking cessation is vital. It is the only way to slow the progression of the disease. After a person stops smoking, the fast decline in lung function found with smoking slows to almost non-smoking levels. The sooner the smoker stops, the less lung function is lost and the sooner the symptoms decrease, especially cough and sputum production. Smoking cessation is discussed in Chapter 11.

Nurses who smoke should evaluate their own smoking behavior and its relationship to their health. Nurses and other HCPs who smoke should be aware that the odor of smoke is obvious on their clothes and hair. It can be offensive or tempting to patients.

People with COPD should avoid others who are sick, practice good hand-washing techniques, take drugs as prescribed, exercise regularly, and maintain a healthy weight. The patient is very susceptible to lung infections. Early treatment of respiratory tract infections and COPD exacerbations helps prevent progression and complications of COPD. They should receive influenza and COVID-19 vaccinations. The pneumococcal

TABLE 31.21 NURSING ASSESSMENT
COPD

Subjective Data
Important Health Information

Health history: Long-term exposure to chemical pollutants, respiratory irritants, occupational fumes, dust; recurrent respiratory tract infections; previous hospitalizations

Medications: Use of O_2 (include frequency and duration of O_2 use), bronchodilators, corticosteroids, antibiotics, anticholinergics, OTC drugs, illicit substances

Functional Health Patterns

Health perception–health management: Smoking (pack-years, including passive smoking, willingness to stop smoking, and previous attempts); what was smoked (e.g., cigarettes, pipes, cigars, e-cigarettes); family history of respiratory disease (especially α_1-antitrypsin deficiency [AATD])

Nutritional-metabolic: Anorexia, weight loss or gain

Activity-exercise: Increasing dyspnea and/or increase in sputum volume or purulence; fatigue, ability to perform ADLs; swelling of feet; progressive dyspnea, especially on exertion; ability to walk up 1 flight of stairs without stopping; wheezing; recurrent cough; sputum production (especially in the morning); orthopnea

Elimination: Constipation, gas, bloating

Sleep-rest: Insomnia; sitting up position for sleeping, paroxysmal nocturnal dyspnea

Cognitive-perceptual: Headache, chest or abdominal soreness

Coping–stress tolerance: Anxiety, depression

Objective Data

Cardiovascular

Tachycardia, dysrhythmias, jugular venous distention, distant heart tones, right HF, S_3 (cor pulmonale), pedal edema

General

Debilitation, restlessness, upright position

GI

Ascites, hepatomegaly (cor pulmonale)

Musculoskeletal

Muscle atrophy, ↑ anteroposterior diameter (barrel chest)

Respiratory

Rapid, shallow breathing
Prolonged expiratory phase; pursed-lip breathing
Use of accessory muscles
↓ Chest excursion and diaphragm movement
Wheezing, crackles, decreased or bronchial breath sounds inability to speak

Skin

Cyanosis (bronchitis), pallor or ruddy color, digital clubbing, poor skin turgor, thin skin, easy bruising; peripheral edema (cor pulmonale)

Possible Diagnostic Findings

Abnormal ABGs (compensated respiratory acidosis, ↓ PaO_2 or SaO_2, ↑ $PaCO_2$), pulmonary function tests showing expiratory airflow obstruction (e.g., low FEV_1, low FEV_1/FVC. Chest x-ray: flattened diaphragm and hyperinflation with/without infiltrates. Echocardiogram: Large right ventricle. Polycythemia

vaccine is recommended for all smokers ages 19 or older and all patients with COPD.

Avoiding or controlling exposure to occupational and environmental pollutants and irritants is another preventive measure to maintain healthy lungs. Assess exposure to environmental or occupational irritants. Determine ways to control or avoid them. For example, teach the patient to avoid smoke-filled rooms and air pollutants.

◆ Acute Care

The patient with COPD may need hospitalization for other complications, such as cor pulmonale or ARF or an acute exacerbation. Exacerbations may be treated at home or in the hospital, depending on severity. The severity is determined by the patient's history leading up to the exacerbation, symptoms, hemodynamic stability, O_2 requirements, WOB, ABGs, and the presence of co-existing diseases. The presence of other problems often complicates exacerbations.

The nursing management of the patient with an acute COPD exacerbation is outlined in Table 31.22. Assess patients for manifestations of exacerbation, including increased dyspnea, increased sputum volume, or increased sputum purulence. They may have malaise, insomnia, fatigue, depression, confusion, decreased exercise tolerance, increased wheezing, or fever.

Are these new symptoms or worsening of usual symptoms? Be alert for signs of severity, such as using accessory muscles, central cyanosis, edema in the lower extremities, unstable BP, right HF, and altered alertness. Assess ABGs for respiratory acidosis and worsening hypoxemia, indicating an "acute-on-chronic" respiratory failure. Ask about the number of exacerbations per year and if treatment occurred in the home or hospital.

SABAs and oral systemic corticosteroids are the usual treatments for exacerbations. SABAs with short-acting anticholinergics are an option. Drug administration by MDI or nebulizer works equally well. Sicker patients often prefer the nebulizer. Antibiotics are given if the exacerbation is caused by a bacterial infection (e.g., pneumonia). Patients with HF may receive small doses of diuretics.

In the hospital, most patients receive O_2 therapy. We try to use non-invasive mechanical methods (e.g., bi-level positive airway pressure [Bi-PAP]) to support ventilation rather than invasive ventilatory support. If needed, the patient will receive mechanical ventilation.

Once the immediate crisis has resolved, reassess the degree and severity of any underlying problems. The information obtained will help in planning care going forward and assist with changes in the treatment plan that may be needed after discharge.

◆ Ambulatory Care

The health care team works together to formulate a patient-centered treatment plan. The most important aspect in the long-term care of the patient with COPD is teaching. A large part of your role is to help the patient self-manage their disease. A patient and caregiver teaching guide is shown in Table 31.23.

TABLE 31.22 NURSING MANAGEMENT
Acute COPD Exacerbation

Regularly monitor indicators of respiratory function:
- Vital signs with SpO_2
- Auscultate lung sounds; note respiratory rhythm and WOB
- ABGs (as needed)
- Manifestations of hypoxia

Give drug therapy as ordered, included bronchodilators, diuretics, and/or antibiotics

Place the patient in high-Fowler's or other position to optimize respiratory function

Give IV fluids as ordered and encourage fluids as tolerated

Promote adequate rest periods, such as 90 minutes of undisturbed sleep and limited visitors, as needed.

Ensure adequate nutrition with small frequent meals and supplements

Provide measures to promote comfort and reduce anxiety

Evaluate the patient's response to treatment

Be prepared to institute resuscitation protocols and respiratory support

Notify the HCP should the patient's condition worsen

Provide patient and caregiver teaching about COPD (Table 31.23)

Supervise AP
- Assist with hygiene and ADLs as needed
- Provide frequent oral hygiene and encourage oral fluids
- Obtain daily weights, vital signs, and intake and output

Collaborate With Interprofessional Team Members

Respiratory Therapist
- Administer O_2 therapy
- Provide chest physiotherapy
- Monitor respiratory status

Dietitian
- Assess nutrition status
- Recommend interventions to meet patient's nutrition needs
- Provide instructions for diet changes as needed

Physical Therapist
- Assess current level of fitness
- Assist with ambulation and exercise

Social Worker
- Assist with obtaining medical equipment after discharge
- Assist with financial resources

Stress the importance of regular follow-up appointments. Regular follow-ups help us monitor response to treatment and see if any changes must be made. Each visit is an opportunity for you to discuss nonpharmacologic approaches to manage COPD to further enhance the treatment plan. Teach the patient and caregiver early recognition of the 3 main manifestations of exacerbations (increased dyspnea, increased sputum volume, increased sputum purulence) to promote early treatment. This may prevent hospitalization and ARF.

Pulmonary rehabilitation. Pulmonary rehabilitation can be done in an inpatient or outpatient setting or in the home.

TABLE 31.23 PATIENT & CAREGIVER TEACHING
COPD

Include the following information in the teaching plan to assist the patient with COPD and the caregiver to improve quality of life through promoting lifestyle practices that support successful living with COPD:

What Is COPD?
- Basic anatomy and physiology of lung
- Basic pathophysiology of COPD
- Signs and symptoms of COPD, acute exacerbation
- How to tell COPD from the common cold, flu, pneumonia
- Tests to assess breathing

Breathing and Airway Clearance Exercises
- Pursed-lip breathing (see Chapter 28)
- Airway clearance technique: huff cough (see Chapter 28)

Energy Conservation Techniques
- Daily activities (e.g., waking up, bathing, grooming, shopping, traveling)
- Consult with physical therapist and occupational therapist

Medications
- Types (include class, mechanism of action, types of devices)
- Establishing medication schedule
- Correct use of inhalers, spacer, and nebulizer
- Reason for use of O_2 equipment
- Guide for home O_2 use and equipment

Psychosocial Support

Allow opportunity for open discussion (with patient and/or caregiver, depending on patient comfort level)
- Worries about dependency
- Problems with emotions (e.g., depression, anxiety, panic)
- Concerns about interpersonal relationships (e.g., intimacy)
- Worry about chronic condition and fear of dying
- Treatment decisions and end-of-life issues
- Support and rehabilitation groups

COPD Management Plan

Nurse, patient, and other health care team members, as necessary develop and write up COPD management plan that meets patient needs.
- Focus on self-management
- Reduce risk factors, especially smoking cessation
- Exercise program of walking and arm strengthening
- Recognition of signs and symptoms of respiratory infection, HF
- Need to report changes in condition
- Cause of acute exacerbations
- Importance of annual flu vaccinations
- Importance of yearly follow-up

Nutrition Support (Table 31.20)
- Ways to lose weight (if overweight)
- Ways to gain weight (if underweight)
- Dietitian consult

For more information, see American Lung Association at www.lung.org/lung-disease/copd.

Components vary. They usually include exercise training, smoking cessation, nutrition counseling, and teaching. Physical therapists or nurses with experience in respiratory care are often responsible for managing pulmonary rehabilitation. Pulmonary rehabilitation is generally indicated for any degree of airway obstruction or GOLD classification. It works best if the patient starts when COPD is in a moderate stage, but even patients who have advanced COPD can benefit. Outcomes include relief of dyspnea and fatigue, improved emotional function, and enhanced sense of control that people have over their COPD.

Pulmonary rehabilitation may be inaccessible to some because of location, cost, disability, or transportation. One alternative program to in-person rehabilitation uses the Internet or gaming technology. The HCP must assess each patient and approve the program to ensure patient safety.

Activity. The patient with severe COPD typically uses upper thoracic and neck muscles to breathe rather than the diaphragm. Thus, the patient may have difficulty with upper extremity activities, especially those that require raising the arm above the head. Exercise training may improve muscle function and help to reduce dyspnea. It also leads to energy conservation, which is an important part of COPD rehabilitation.

Often, the patient is already using some alternative energy-saving practices for ADL. Ask about and explore alternative methods of hair care, shaving, showering, and reaching. In severe COPD, the patient should try to sit as much as possible when performing activities. If the patient uses home O_2 therapy, O_2 should be used during hygiene because these tasks are energy consuming. The occupational therapist is an excellent resource for activity suggestions.

Encourage the patient to make a schedule and plan daily and weekly activities, leaving plenty of time for rest periods. Another energy-saving tip is to exhale when pushing, pulling, or exerting effort during an activity and inhale during rest.

Regular exercise is important (Box 31.5). To ensure long-term adherence, the exercise plan must be appropriate and safe for the patient and easy to perform. Walking or other endurance exercises (e.g., stationary cycling, treadmills at a slow rate) combined with strength training are the best ways to strengthen muscles and improve endurance. Many patients with moderate or severe COPD are anxious and fearful of walking or performing exercise. Teach the patient coordinated walking with slow, pursed-lip breathing. Both patients and caregivers need support while they build the confidence they need to walk, perform daily exercises, or help with these activities.

Developing exercise endurance is important. If it takes longer than 5 minutes to return to baseline, the patient has most likely "overdone it." They should go at a slower pace during the next exercise period. Keeping a diary or log of the exercise program may help.

Patients often ask whether moving to a warmer or drier climate will help. In general, such moves are generally not beneficial. Discourage moves to places with an elevation of 4000 ft or more because of the lower partial pressure of O_2 found in the air at higher elevations. Other disadvantages of moving may be that a person leaves a job, friends, and familiar environment, which could be stressful. This may outweigh any advantage gained from being in a different climate.

BOX 31.5 EVIDENCE-BASED PRACTICE

Physical Activity and Chronic Obstructive Pulmonary Disease

You are working as a nurse in a pulmonary clinic with N.T., a 71-year-old man who was just discharged from the hospital with a new diagnosis of COPD. He tells you he has been inactive for most of the past 8 months because "my breathing seems to worsen with any type of activity."

Making Clinical Decisions

Best Available Evidence

Patients with COPD who take part in regular moderate activity (e.g., brisk walking) have fewer severe flare-ups and are less likely to be admitted or re-admitted to the hospital. Activity improves lung function and lessens depressive symptoms. The season of the year and temperature can be barriers to outdoor exercise.

Clinician Expertise

Physical inactivity is common in patients with COPD. You are aware that inactivity may place N.T. at a greater risk for functional decline and readmission.

Patient Preference and Values

N.T. tells you that he misses taking walks every day with his wife and dog. He is wondering if he would be able to resume this activity at a slower pace.

Implications for Practice

1. What factors will you discuss with N.T. about activity and COPD?
2. How would you assess N.T.'s willingness and motivation to engage in activity?
3. How would you involve interprofessional team members to assist N.T. in regular activity?

Reference

da Silva MMC, Arcuri JF, Di Lorenzo VAP: Individualized, low-cost and accessible pulmonary rehabilitation program based on functional clinical tests for individuals with COPD, *Trials* 22:367, 2021.

Psychosocial care. Coping is a challenge for the patient and family. As COPD progresses, patients are often confronted with many lifestyle changes that may involve decreased ability to care for themselves, decreased energy for social activities, and loss or change in a job.

When a patient is first diagnosed or has complications that require hospitalization, expect a variety of responses. Emotions often expressed include denial, anger, frustration from perceived or real increased dependence, and loneliness from social isolation. Guilt may result if the disease is related to smoking.

Patients experience losses as the disease progresses. Because many patients have depression and anxiety, assess for both. Ask patients if they "feel down" or "feel blue." Do they appear anxious about being able to control their breathlessness? Do they know what to do if they have an exacerbation? Are they showing concern over more difficulty in self-care activities, such as preparing meals and bathing? How is the family coping?

It is important to convey a sense of understanding and caring. Teach patients about COPD and their treatment, which can help provide a sense of control. The patient may benefit from stress management techniques (e.g., massage, muscle relaxation). Include caregivers so they can help the patient cope. Support groups at local American Lung Association chapters (e.g., the Better Breathers Club), hospitals, and clinics can be helpful.

A mental health referral may be needed for proper screening and diagnosis of depression or other problems. Cognitive and behavioral therapy may improve quality of life. Drugs may be used to treat both depression and anxiety. When the patient becomes anxious because of dyspnea, pursed-lip breathing and SABAs may be appropriate.

Sexuality and sexual activity. Modifying sexual activity can contribute to well-being. First, assess if the patient has any concerns related to sexuality and functioning. Ask open-ended questions to assess if the patient wants or is willing to discuss their concerns with you. For example, you could ask, "How does your shortness of breath affect your desire for intimacy with your partner?" This type of general, open-ended question gives the patient an opportunity to discuss concerns with you.

Dyspnea, the predominant symptom in COPD, should not be a major problem in sexual activity, except for patients in severe late stages. Generally, if the patient can walk up 2 flights of stairs or walk briskly, they should have enough energy for sexual activity. The patient with heart disease should discuss appropriate levels of activity with their HCP. Using an inhaled bronchodilator before sexual activity can help ventilation. Other suggestions that may be helpful: (1) plan sexual activity during the part of the day when breathing is best, which is usually late morning or early afternoon; (2) use slow pursed-lip breathing; (3) refrain from sexual activity after eating or drinking alcohol; (4) choose less stressful positions (e.g., side-lying); and (5) use O_2 if prescribed.

Most patients with COPD are older. Their sexual performance issues may be related to aging. This is a good opportunity to teach the patient about the normalcy of age-related changes. Encourage open communication between partners about their needs, expectations, and any problems they encounter.

Sleep. Adequate sleep is important to maintain quality of life and productivity. Most patients with COPD have sleep problems. Current tobacco use, depression, and anxiety are all common in COPD and lead to more trouble sleeping. β_2-Agonists may cause restlessness and insomnia. Postnasal drip or nasal congestion may cause coughing and wheezing at night.

Hyperinflation of the lungs and reduction in ventilation can result in severe drops in O_2 saturation (down to 60% or less) during sleep. This leads to an increased workload on the heart. Hypercapnia may contribute to more frequent awakening. The net result is sleeping poorly and waking up unrefreshed and fatigued.

Nasal saline sprays or rinses before sleep and in the morning may help. If the patient is prescribed O_2 therapy, using it at night may decrease insomnia. If the patient is a restless sleeper, snores, stops breathing while asleep, and tends to fall asleep during the day, the patient may need testing for sleep apnea (see Chapter 8).

End-of-life considerations. The trajectory of COPD is a gradual decline in health characterized by increasing exacerbations with an increased risk of death. In the later, severe stages of this disease, palliative, end-of-life, and hospice care are important components of care for the patient with advanced COPD.

Patients need to know that symptoms can be managed, but COPD cannot be cured. End-of-life issues and advance directives are important topics for discussion in the latter stages of COPD. This may be hard for the patient and family to consider because of the uncertainty of the disease.

◆ Evaluation

The expected outcomes are that the patient with COPD will

- Maintain a patent airway by effectively coughing
- Maintain an effective rate, rhythm, and depth of respirations
- Have clear breath sounds
- Return to pre-exacerbation baseline respiratory function
- Have $PaCO_2$ and PaO_2 values within normal for the patient
- State ways to promote an optimal level of functioning with ADLs

Gerontologic Considerations: COPD

Older adults have physiologic changes, including reduced lean body mass, decreased respiratory muscle strength, increased dyspnea, and lower exercise tolerance that may increase the burden of disease from COPD. This may lead to a higher incidence of acute exacerbations, which require hospitalization. Smoking cessation is a key intervention but may be hard to achieve. Older adults may have difficulty handling increased secretions during an exacerbation.

COPD is often complicated by the presence of other problems, such as diabetes, heart disease, hypertension, osteoporosis, impaired cognition, and lung cancer. These problems can make it harder for patients to cope with the stress of an exacerbation. Some drugs used to treat common problems, such as hypertension, can worsen COPD symptoms. If possible, we avoid using nonspecific β-blockers since they can block the β_2 receptors in the airway and cause bronchoconstriction. ACE inhibitors may cause a dry cough or worsen a present cough.

Drugs used to manage an exacerbation can complicate disease management and increase the chance of adverse events. Assess for potential drug-drug interactions, especially in patients being treated for other problems.

Cognitive impairment and complex medication plans can contribute to nonadherence. Writing action plans in large font and setting reminders can help patients with poor memory and vision problems. Arthritis can hinder the person from using proper techniques for MDIs. Review MDI technique during visits. Have DPI or spacers prescribed (if possible) because they are easier to use.

Older patients with COPD often have impaired quality of life. An important role for us is to focus on ways to improve quality of life. Psychologic support becomes imperative to help patients achieve successful outcomes. In the later stages of COPD, palliative and hospice care can help manage symptoms and improve the quality of the rest of their lives (Box 31.6).

BOX 31.6 ETHICAL/LEGAL DILEMMAS

Advance Directives

Situation

L.H., an 84-year-old man with end-stage COPD, is admitted to the hospital in ARF. He is placed on full support mechanical ventilation and transferred to the ICU. L.H. is making no spontaneous breaths. He infrequently responds by opening his eyes, sometimes to the sound of voice, and other times only to painful stimuli. A chest x-ray shows pneumonia in both lungs. Antibiotics are ordered. A Foley drains a small amount of cloudy, dark amber urine.

L.H. had his advance directives (AD) drawn up 5 years ago. Copies were given to his wife and HCP at that time. His wife brings the documents to the ICU and tells you that the hospital must stop treating her husband. She insists that per his AD, the health care team should allow him to die. However, their oldest son, who lives out of state and is currently on his way to see his dad, tells you over the telephone that he will file a lawsuit against the hospital if they do not provide full care to his father.

Ethical/Legal Points for Consideration

- A living will permits persons to share their preferences and refusals should they become terminally ill or be in a situation in which there is no hope of recovery and they cannot speak for themselves.
- The durable power of attorney for health care permits persons to name a proxy to make health care decisions in the event the person is incapacitated.
- AD laws vary from state to state concerning the need for witnesses and naming the proxy.
- Families may be divided about decisions for their loved ones. Conflicts often arise when feelings of remorse or guilt and money and/or property are involved. This situation requires you to notify the HCP, engage social work and spiritual care, and ask for a family conference. In some circumstances, a consult from the ethics committee may be needed.
- HCPs are obligated to follow the patient's AD when a patient is no longer able to speak for themselves.
- In your scope of nursing practice, you may need to (1) teach patients and families about ADs; (2) make AD documents available to patients; (3) determine if all involved HCPs are aware of the patient's AD; (4) assist the patient and family in communicating with the HCP when a "no code" or "DNR" (do not resuscitate) order is requested; and (5) assist the conflicted family in obtaining appropriate counseling when needed.
- You need to be aware and informed about the decision-making laws and regulations in your state about ADs and your role with respect to ADs.

Discussion Questions

1. What should you do with the information provided by L.H.'s wife?
2. The HCP asks that you organize a family conference. How would you address the family's needs at the conference?
3. What other health care team members could you invite to the meeting to help facilitate discussion and decision making?
4. The family conference does not go well. While L.H.'s wife accepts her husband's end-stage COPD diagnosis, the son does not. The wife and son have different views on how L.H.is to be managed. What would be your approach to L.H.'s plan of care? How might you involve the family members in L.H.'s plan of care?

Case Study

COPD

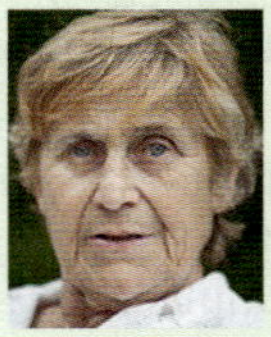

(© iStockphoto/ Thinkstock.)

Patient Profile

H.M. a 68-year-old female patient, has been in the hospital for 6 days with an acute COPD exacerbation (GOLD 3 [severe]). She was admitted after 4 days of increasing shortness of breath. She noted an increased volume of sputum. It was initially white but turned "greenish." H.M. is scheduled for discharge tomorrow. Her 73-year-old husband will care for her at home.

Subjective Data

Preadmission

- Husband said her skin tone looked "bluish"
- Increased Ventolin HFA use at home to 5 or 6 times a day for dyspnea
- Described having "jitters" and "racing heart"

Medical History

- Had 3 or 4 COPD exacerbations in the past year that were managed at home
- 30 pack-year history of smoking; smokes half a pack per day now to "clear out lungs" in the morning
- Eats a regular diet but "gets full fast"
- Cannot climb 1 flight of stairs without stopping; is able to walk down the flat driveway about 20 ft (6 m) without difficulty
- Awakens 2–3 times per night coughing and short of breath
- Sleeping in the recliner sitting upright
- Last spirometry: decreased FEV_1 (48%) and FEV_1/FVC (62%)

Objective Data

Emergency Department

Physical Assessment

- Weight 129 lb (58.5kg), height 5 ft 8 in (172cm), BMI 20 kg/m^2
- Temp 100°F (37.8°C), pulse 86 (regular), respiratory rate 28 (shallow, slightly labored), BP 136/76 mm Hg
- Increased anteroposterior diameter of chest
- Slight use of accessory neck muscles with breathing
- Distant breath sounds with occasional expiratory wheezes
- 2+ non-pitting pedal edema

Diagnostic Studies

- ABG: pH 7.34, $PaCO_2$ 59 mm Hg, HCO_3^- 27 mEq/L, PaO_2 68 mm Hg
- WBC: 16,500/μL
- Chest x-ray: hyperinflation, flat diaphragm, no sign of pneumonia
- Sputum: negative (no organisms present)

24.Hours Post-Admission to Hospital

- ABG: pH 7.30, $PaCO_2$ 63 mm Hg, HCO_3^- 29 mEq/L, PaO_2 64 mm Hg

Interprofessional Care

- O_2 @ 4 L/min via nasal catheter
- Prednisone 40 mg/day PO for 5 days
- Doxycycline 100 mg/day PO for 10 days

Answers available at http://evolve.elsevier.com/Lewis/medsurg.

Continued

Case Study—cont'd

COPD

- Ipratropium HFA MDI 2 puffs 4 times a day
- Lasix 10 mg po twice daily
- At discharge: Advair Diskus 250/50 one inhalation q12hr

Discussion Questions

1. ***Recognize:*** What manifestations show H.M. had a COPD exacerbation?
2. ***Analyze:*** What is the most likely cause of her exacerbation?
3. ***Analyze:*** Why would H.M. "feel full fast" when eating? What could you do to address this issue?
4. ***Analyze:*** What symptoms indicate overuse of inhalers? Which drug would cause the symptoms described?
5. ***Analyze:*** Interpret the ABG on admission and 24 hours post-admission. In comparing both ABGs, do you see a pattern?
6. ***Prioritize:*** Based on the assessment data presented, what are the priority clinical problems?
7. ***Act:*** What is one suggestion you could make to H.M. that could halt the progression of her COPD?
8. ***Act:*** What should you include in her discharge planning and teaching?
9. Develop a conceptual care map for H.M.

BRIDGE TO NCLEX EXAMINATION

The number of the question corresponds to the same-numbered outcome at the beginning of the chapter.

1. The nurse teaches a patient with bronchiectasis that which problem would warrant a call to the clinic?"
   - **a.** Blood clots in the sputum
   - **b.** Sticky sputum on a hot day
   - **c.** Producing large amounts of sputum daily
   - **d.** Increased shortness of breath after eating a large meal
2. Which treatment(s) would the nurse expect to implement in the management plan of an adult patient with cystic fibrosis? *(select all that apply)*
   - **a.** Airway clearance techniques
   - **b.** Bronchodilators and mucolytics
   - **c.** Pancreatic enzyme replacement
   - **d.** IV corticosteroids on a chronic basis
   - **e.** Inhaled tobramycin to combat *Pseudomonas* infection
3. A 37-year-old patient is concerned they have asthma. Of the symptoms they describe to you, which ones suggest asthma or risk factors for asthma? *(select all that apply)*
   - **a.** Prolonged inhalation
   - **b.** Gastric reflux or heartburn
   - **c.** Cough worse at night or early in the morning
   - **d.** History of allergic rhinitis or chronic sinusitis
   - **e.** Chest pain and syncope after exercising with a stationary bicycle for 5 minutes
4. Which finding indicate that a patient with asthma is developing status asthmaticus? *(select all that apply)*
   - **a.** Anxiety and panic
   - **b.** Positive sputum culture
   - **c.** Unable to speak in complete sentences
   - **d.** Chest x-ray shows hyperinflated lungs
   - **e.** Lack of response to conventional treatment
5. Which statement indicates the patient with asthma requires further teaching about self-care?
   - **a.** "I use my corticosteroid inhaler every time I feel short of breath."
   - **b.** "I get a flu shot every year and see my HCP if I have an upper respiratory tract infection."
   - **c.** "I use my inhaler before I visit my aunt who has a cat, but I only visit for a few minutes because of my allergies."
   - **d.** "I walk 30 minutes every day, but sometimes I have to use my bronchodilator inhaler before walking to prevent me from getting short of breath."
6. Which medication would be appropriate to administer to a patient experiencing an acute asthma attack?
   - **a.** IV theophylline
   - **b.** Montelukast (Singulair)
   - **c.** Inhaled hypertonic saline
   - **d.** Albuterol (Proventil HFA)
7. The plan of care for the patient with chronic obstructive pulmonary disease (COPD) would include *(select all that apply)*
   - **a.** exercise such as walking.
   - **b.** high flow rate of O_2 administration.
   - **c.** low-dose oral corticosteroid therapy.
   - **d.** use of monthly chest x-rays to monitor the progression of COPD.
   - **e.** breathing exercises, such as pursed-lip breathing that focus on exhalation.
8. What would the nurse include when teaching a patient how to use a metered-dose inhaler (MDI)?
   - **a.** After activating the MDI, breathe in as quickly as you can.
   - **b.** Estimate the amount of remaining medicine in the MDI by floating the canister in water.
   - **c.** Disassemble the plastic canister from the inhaler and rinse both pieces under running water every week.
   - **d.** To determine how long the canister will last, divide the total number of puffs in the canister by the puffs needed per day.

1. a; 2. a, b, c, e; 3. b, c, d; 4. a, c, e; 5. a; 6. d; 7. a, c, e; 8. d.

For rationales to these answers and even more NCLEX review questions, visit http://evolve.elsevier.com/Lewis/medsurg.

EVOLVE WEBSITE/RESOURCES LIST

http://evolve.elsevier.com/Lewis/medsurg
Review Questions (Online Only)
Key Points
Answer Keys for Questions
- Rationales for Bridge to NCLEX Examination Questions
- Answer Guidelines for Case Study

Student Case Studies
- Patient With Asthma
- Patient With Chronic Obstructive Pulmonary Disease
- Patient With Cystic Fibrosis

Nursing Care Plans
- eNursing Care Plan 31.1: Patient With Asthma
- eNursing Care Plan 31.2: Patient With Chronic Obstructive Pulmonary Disease

Conceptual Care Map Creator
- Conceptual Care Map for Case Study

Audio Glossary
Content Updates

REFERENCES

1. American Lung Association: Learn about bronchiectasis. Retrieved from https://www.lung.org.
2. My Cleveland Clinic: Bronchiectasis. Retrieved from https://my-clevelandclinic.org.
3. Emmons EE: Bronchiectasis. Retrieved from https://emedicine.medscape.com/article/296961-overview#a4.
4. Coruh B, Niven AS: Bronchiectasis. Retrieved from https://www.merckmanuals.com/en-ca/professional/pulmonary-disorders/bronchiectasis-and-atelectasis/bronchiectasis.
5. Cystic Fibrosis Foundation: About cystic fibrosis. Retrieved from https://www.cff.org/What-is-CF/About-Cystic-Fibrosis/.

*6. Leonard J: Average life expectancies for cystic fibrosis. Retrieved from https://www.medicalnewstoday.com/articles/326316.

7. Turcios N: Cystic fibrosis lung disease: an overview, *Respir Care* 65:233, 2020.
8. Schmidt H, Sharma G: Sweat testing. Retrieved from https://www.ncbi.nlm.nih.gov/books/NBK547728/.

*9. Green J, Carroll W, Gilchrist FJ: Interventions for treating distal intestinal obstruction syndrome (DIOS) in cystic fibrosis. Retrieved from https://www.ncbi.nlm.nih.gov/pmc/articles/PMC6513219/pdf/CD012798.pdf.

10. Cystic Fibrosis News Today: Kalydeco (ivacaftor). Retrieved from https://cysticfibrosisnewstoday.com/kalydeco-ivacaftor/.

*11. Havermans T, Willem L: Prevention of anxiety and depression in cystic fibrosis, *Curr Opin Pulm Med* 25:654, 2019.

12. Asthma and Allergy Foundation of America: Asthma facts and figures. Retrieved from https://www.aafa.org/asthma-facts/.
13. Asthma MD: Asthma statistics. Retrieved from: https://www.asthmamd.org/asthma-statistics/#_ftn2.
14. Centers for Disease Control and Prevention (CDC): Percentage of people with asthma who smoke. Retrieved from https://www.cdc.gov/asthma/asthma_stats/people_who_smoke.htm.
15. Morris MJ: What is the triad of asthma, aspirin sensitivity, and nasal polyps? Retrieved from https://www.medscape.com/answers/296301-7932/what-is-the-triad-of-asthma-aspirin-sensitivity-and-nasal-polyps.
16. Rodriguez T: Exercise-induced bronchoconstriction with or without asthma: a unique challenge. Retrieved from https://www.pulmonologyadvisor.com/home/topics/asthma/exercise-induced-bronchoconstriction-with-or-without-asthma-management/.

*17. Global Initiative for Asthma (GINA): Global strategy for asthma management and prevention (2021 update). Retrieved from https://ginasthma.org.

18. National Asthma Education and Prevention Program: Asthma care quick reference: diagnosing and managing asthma. Retrieved from https://www.nhlbi.nih.gov/files/docs/guidelines/asthma_qrg.pdf.
19. Nevstruev YV, Dem'yanenko AV, Semernik IV: Non-invasive methods for diagnosing diseases of the bronchopulmonary system, *RSEMW* 24:484, 2019.
20. Asthma and Allergy Foundation of America: FeNo tests to monitor FeNo levels. Retrieved from https://www.aafa.org/media/1640/feno-tests-to-monitor-feno-levels.pdf.
21. Larsson K, Kankaanranta H, Janson C, et al.: Bringing asthma care into the twenty-first century, *NPJ Prim Care Respir Med* 30:25, 2020.
22. Hsu E, Bajaj T: Beta-2 agonists. Retrieved from https://www.ncbi.nlm.nih.gov/books/NBK542249/.
23. Mayo Clinic: Anti-interleukin-5 therapy for severe asthma. Retrieved from https://www.mayoclinic.org/medical-professionals/pulmonary-medicine/news/anti-interleukin-5-therapy-for-severe-asthma-a-new-therapeutic-option/mac-20451437.
24. CDC: Copd. Retrieved from https://www.cdc.gov/copd/index.html.
25. CDC: Disease or condition of the week: COPD. Retrieved from https://www.cdc.gov/dotw/copd/index.html.
26. CDC: Tips from former smokers: smoking and COPD. Retrieved from https://www.cdc.gov/tobacco/campaign/tips/diseases/copd.html.

*27. Cribbs SK, Crothers K, Morris A: Pathogenesis of HIV-related lung disease: immunity, infection, and inflammation, *Physiol Rev* 100:603, 2020.

28. Strange C: Alpha-1 antitrypsin deficiency associated with COPD, *Clin Chest Med* 41:339, 2020.

*29. da Costa CH, Noronha Filho AJ, Marques e Silva RMF, et al.: Alpha 1-antitrypsin deficiency in patients with COPD patients: is systematic screening necessary? *BMC Res Notes* 12:4043, 2019.

30. Baqdunes MW, Leap J, Young M, et al.: Acute exacerbation of COPD, *Crit Care Nurs Q* 44:74, 2021.
31. Gundry S: COPD 1-Pathophysiology, diagnosis and prognosis, *Nurs Times* 116:27, 2020.
32. Daher A, Dreher M: Oxygen therapy and noninvasive ventilation in COPD, *Clin Chest Med* 41:529, 2020.
33. Global Initiative for COPD (GOLD): Pocket guide to diagnosis, management and prevention: a guide for health care professionals: 2020 report. Retrieved from https://goldcopd.org/wp-content/uploads/2020/03/GOLD-2020-POCKET-GUIDE-ver1.0_FINAL-WMV.pdf.
34. Scoditti E, Massaro M, Garbarino S, et al.: Role of diet in COPD prevention and treatment. Retrieved from https://www.ncbi.nlm.nih.gov/pmc/articles/PMC6627281/#__ffn_sectitle.
35. Cleveland Clinic: Lung volume reduction surgery. Retrieved from https://my.clevelandclinic.org/health/treatments/13794-lung-volume-reduction-surgery-lvrs.

*36. Abia-Trujillo D, Johnson MM, Patel NM, et al.: Bronchoscopic lung volume reduction: a new hope for patients with severe emphysema and air trapping, *Mayo Clin Proc* 96:464, 2021.

*Evidence-based information for clinical practice.

32

Acute Respiratory Failure and Acute Respiratory Distress Syndrome

Eugene E. Mondor

http://evolve.elsevier.com/Lewis/medsurg/

CONCEPTUAL FOCUS

Acid-Base Balance
Anxiety
Gas Exchange

LEARNING OUTCOMES

1. Discuss the etiology, pathophysiology, and clinical manifestations of hypoxemic and hypercapnic acute respiratory failure (ARF).
2. Describe the nursing and interprofessional management of hypoxemic and hypercapnic respiratory failure.
3. Discuss the pathophysiology and clinical manifestations of acute respiratory distress syndrome (ARDS).
4. Describe the nursing and interprofessional management of ARDS.
5. Identify interventions to prevent and manage complications of ARF and ARDS.

KEY TERMS

acute respiratory distress syndrome (ARDS)
acute respiratory failure (ARF)
alveolar hypoventilation
chronic respiratory failure (CRF)
hypercapnic respiratory failure
hypoxemia
hypoxemic respiratory failure
hypoxia
PaO_2/FIO_2 (P/F) ratio
permissive hypercapnia
refractory hypoxemia
shunt
V/Q mismatch
work of breathing (WOB)

This chapter discusses acute respiratory failure (ARF) and acute respiratory distress syndrome (ARDS). The management of patients with ARF and ARDS focuses on interventions to promote adequate oxygenation, ensure effective ventilation, identify and treat the underlying causes, and prevent complications. When respiratory function is insufficient, it affects all body systems.

ACUTE RESPIRATORY FAILURE

The major function of the respiratory system is gas exchange. **Acute respiratory failure (ARF)** occurs when oxygenation, ventilation, or both are inadequate. ARF is not a disease. It is a symptom that reflects insufficient lung function (Fig. 32.1). In ARF, not enough O_2 is transferred to the blood, or inadequate CO_2 is removed from the lungs. ARF occurs with problems involving the lungs or other body systems (Table 32.1).

Conditions that interfere with diffusion of O_2 result in **hypoxemia**. This causes a decrease in arterial O_2 (PaO_2) and saturation (SaO_2) to less than the normal values. Insufficient CO_2 removal results in hypercapnia. This causes an increase in arterial CO_2 ($PaCO_2$). We use arterial blood gases (ABGs) to assess changes in pH, PaO_2, $PaCO_2$, bicarbonate, and SaO_2. We use pulse oximetry to assess arterial O_2 saturation (SpO_2).

We classify ARF as hypoxemic or hypercapnic (Fig. 32.2). **Hypoxemic respiratory failure** is a PaO_2 less than 60 mm Hg (on room air and at sea level) with either normal or slightly subnormal $PaCO_2$ levels.[1] In hypoxemic respiratory failure (also called *oxygenation failure*), the main problem is the inadequate exchange of O_2 between the alveoli and pulmonary capillaries. The PaO_2 level shows an inadequate amount of oxygen in arterial blood (O_2 saturation). This low PaO_2 level may exist despite supplemental O_2.

Hypercapnic respiratory failure (or *ventilatory failure*) is a $PaCO_2$ greater than 50 mm Hg, which may be accompanied by hypoxemia and/or acidemia (arterial pH less than 7.35).[2] The main problem is insufficient CO_2 removal. This causes the

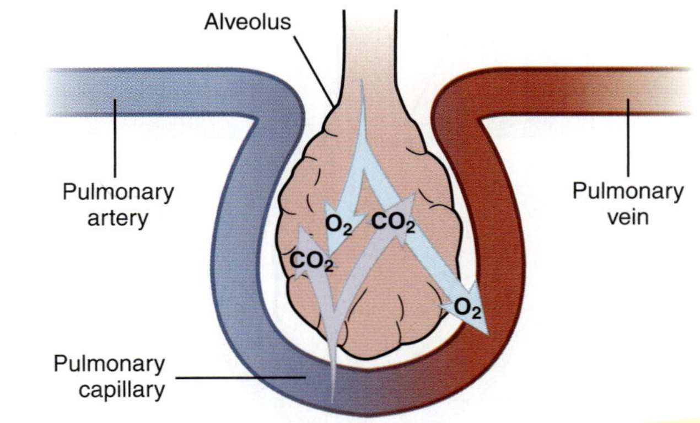

Fig. 32.1 Normal gas exchange unit in the lung: the alveolus and pulmonary capillary.

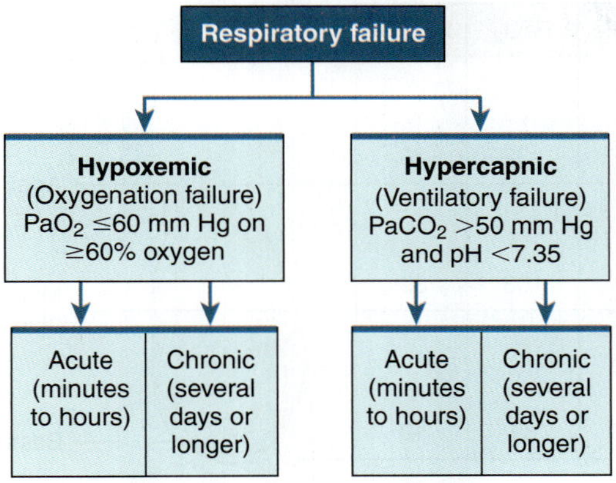

Fig. 32.2 Classification of ARF.

TABLE 32.1 Common Causes of ARF

Hypoxemic Respiratory Failure	Hypercapnic Respiratory Failure
ARDS	**ARDS**
Asthma	**Asthma**
Chronic bronchitis	**Chronic bronchitis**
Emphysema	**Emphysema**
Pulmonary edema	**Pulmonary edema**
Respiratory system	**Respiratory system**
• Bronchiectasis	• COPD
• Hepatopulmonary syndrome (e.g., low-resistance flow state, V/Q mismatch)	• Cystic fibrosis
• Pneumonia	• Hypoventilation syndrome (causes include CNS, obesity, chest wall, and neuromuscular)
• Pneumothorax	• Upper airway obstruction
• Pulmonary embolism (e.g., thrombus emboli, fat emboli)	**Chest wall**
• Pulmonary Fibrosis	• Kyphoscoliosis
• Toxic inhalation (e.g., smoke inhalation)	• Pain
	• Severe obesity
	• Thoracic trauma (e.g., flail chest)
Cardiac	**CNS**
• Anatomic shunt (e.g., ventricular septal defect)	• Brainstem injury or infarction
• Cardiogenic pulmonary edema	• Sedative and opioid overdose
• Cardiogenic shock (decreasing blood flow through pulmonary vasculature)	• Severe head injury
• High CO states: diffusion limitation	• Spinal cord injury
	Neuromuscular
	• Amyotrophic lateral sclerosis
	• Critical illness polyneuropathy
	• Guillain-Barré syndrome
	• Muscular dystrophy
	• Multiple sclerosis
	• Myasthenia gravis
	• Phrenic nerve injury
	• Poliomyelitis
	• Toxin exposure or ingestion

$PaCO_2$ to be higher than normal. As the $PaCO_2$ level climbs, the body will eventually be unable to compensate for the increase. This causes acidemia to worsen.

Significant changes in PaO_2 and $PaCO_2$ may occur with ARF. These develop over several minutes to a few hours to 1 or 2 days. The patient may have hemodynamic instability (e.g., tachycardia, hypotension), increased respiratory effort, and decreased level of consciousness. Urgent intervention is needed. On the other hand, **chronic respiratory failure** (CRF) develops more slowly, over days to weeks. The patient is usually more stable as the body had time to compensate for the small but subtle changes. CRF does not typically present as an immediate, life-threatening condition.

Patients may have both types of respiratory failure at the same time. For example, a patient with chronic obstructive pulmonary disease (COPD) who has pneumonia can have "acute-on-chronic" respiratory failure. Here, the patient has an underlying chronic respiratory problem. The new infection, when added to the chronic problem, results in the "acute-on-chronic" clinical picture.

Etiology and Pathophysiology

Hypoxemic Respiratory Failure

Four physiologic mechanisms may cause hypoxemia and hypoxemic respiratory failure: (1) mismatch between ventilation (V) and perfusion (Q), referred to as **V/Q mismatch**; (2) shunt; (3) diffusion limitation; and (4) alveolar hypoventilation. The most common causes are V/Q mismatch and shunt.

Ventilation-perfusion mismatch. In normal lungs, the volume of blood perfusing the lungs and the amount of gas reaching the alveoli are almost identical. So, when you compare normal alveolar ventilation (4 to 6 L/min) to pulmonary blood flow (4 to 6 L/min), you have a V/Q ratio of 0.8 to 1.2.[3] In a perfect match, ventilation and perfusion yield a V/Q ratio of 1:1, expressed as V/Q = 1. When the match is not 1:1, a V/Q mismatch occurs.

This example implies that ventilation and perfusion are perfectly matched in all areas of the lung. This situation does not normally exist. In reality, some regional mismatch occurs. For example, at the apex of the lung, V/Q ratios are greater than 1 (more ventilation than perfusion). At the base of the lung, V/Q ratios are less than 1 (less ventilation than perfusion). Because changes at the lung apex balance changes at the base, the net effect is a close overall match (Fig. 32.3).

Many problems can cause a V/Q mismatch (Fig. 32.4). The most common are those in which increased secretions are present in the airways (e.g., COPD) or alveoli (e.g., pneumonia) or bronchospasm is present (e.g., asthma). V/Q mismatch may result from pain, alveolar collapse (atelectasis), or pulmonary emboli.

V/Q	PaO_2	$PaCO_2$
3.3	132	28
1.0	108	39
0.63	89	42

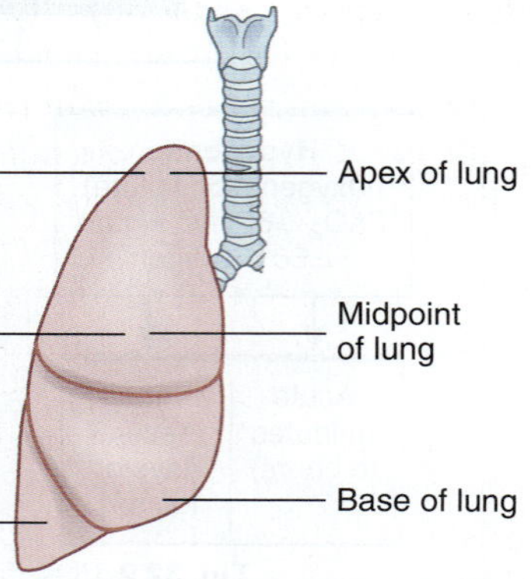

Fig. 32.3 Regional V/Q differences in the normal lung. The PaO_2 is higher at the apex of the lung and lower at the base. Values for $PaCO_2$ are the opposite (i.e., lower at the apex and higher at the base). Blood that exits the lung is a mixture of these values.

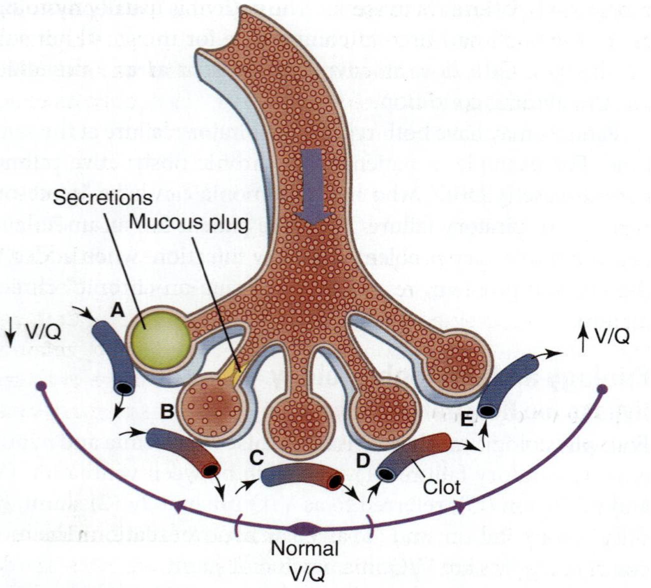

Fig. 32.4 Causes of V/Q mismatch. (A) Absolute shunt: no ventilation occurs because of fluid filling the alveoli. (B) Ventilation partially compromised by secretions in the airway. (C) Normal lung unit. (D) Perfusion partially compromised by emboli obstructing blood flow. (E) Dead space, no perfusion because of obstruction of the pulmonary capillary.

Pain interferes with chest and abdominal wall movement and increases muscle tension. This can compromise ventilation. The patient may be unwilling to take big, deep breaths. As a result, short, shallow respirations contribute to the development of atelectasis. This is the beginning of a V/Q mismatch. At the same time, pain activates the stress response, increasing baseline metabolic state. O_2 consumption and CO_2 production (as a by-product of cell and tissue metabolism) increase. The increased O_2 demand, increased CO_2 levels, and decreased O_2 supply all increase ventilation demands. Since there is no effect on blood flow to the lungs, the V/Q mismatch worsens.

Pulmonary emboli affect perfusion. When a pulmonary embolus occurs, it limits blood flow distal to the occlusion. Some areas of normal lung ventilation remain, but there is decreased perfusion to other parts from the vessel occlusion. This results in a V/Q mismatch. If the embolus is large enough to block a major pulmonary artery, it can cause severe hemodynamic instability.

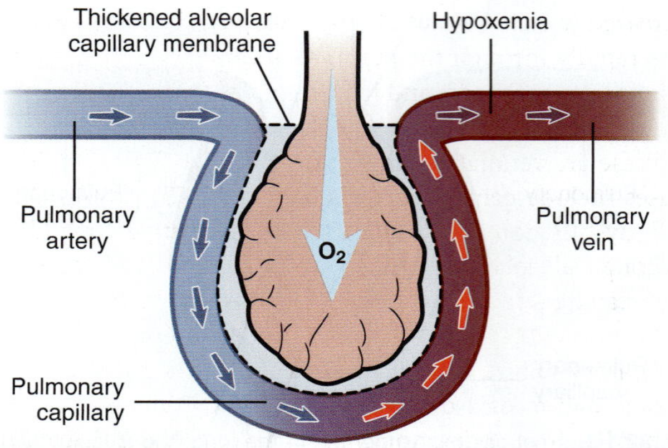

Fig. 32.5 Diffusion impairment. Reduced exchange of CO_2 and O_2 because of the thickened alveolar-capillary membrane.

The best way to treat hypoxemia caused by a V/Q mismatch is to treat the cause. O_2 therapy is an appropriate first step to reverse hypoxemia. Most patients with a hypoxemic V/Q mismatch will respond to O_2 therapy. Frequent ABG analysis, pulse oximetry, and continuous assessment of level of consciousness, respiratory rate and rhythm, and response to O_2 therapy are important.

Shunt. A **shunt** occurs when blood exits the heart without having taken part in gas exchange. A shunt is an extreme V/Q mismatch. There are 2 types of shunt: anatomic and capillary. An *anatomic shunt* occurs when blood passes through an anatomic channel in the heart (e.g., a ventricular septal defect) and bypasses the lungs.[4] A *capillary shunt* occurs when blood flows through the pulmonary capillaries without taking part in gas exchange.[4] It occurs in conditions where the alveoli fill with fluid (e.g., pneumonia) and gas exchange is severely impaired at the alveolar-capillary membrane.

O_2 therapy alone is not effective at increasing the PaO_2 if hypoxemia is due to shunt. Patients with a shunt are usually more hypoxemic than patients with V/Q mismatch. They often need mechanical ventilation with a high fraction of inspired O_2 (FIO_2) to improve gas exchange.

Diffusion impairment. *Diffusion impairment* occurs when gas exchange across the alveolar-capillary membrane is compromised by a process that damages or destroys the alveolar membrane or affects blood flow through the pulmonary capillaries (Fig. 32.5).[5] Conditions that cause the alveolar-capillary membrane to become thicker (fibrotic) slow gas transport. These include pulmonary fibrosis, interstitial lung disease, and ARDS. The accumulation of fluid, white blood cells, or protein in the alveoli contributes to a decrease in gas exchange between the alveolus and capillary bed. This occurs with pulmonary edema.

The classic sign of diffusion impairment is hypoxemia that worsens with exercise but not at rest. With exercise, blood moves quickly through the lungs. This decreases the time for O_2 diffusion across the alveolar-capillary membrane. Diffusion impairment can occur in conditions where CO is markedly increased (e.g., high-output heart failure [HF]). As blood circulates rapidly through the pulmonary capillary bed, there is less time for gas exchange, and hypoxemia occurs.

Alveolar hypoventilation. Alveolar hypoventilation is a decrease in ventilation that increases the $PaCO_2$. Common causes include central nervous system (CNS) problems, chest wall dysfunction, acute asthma, or restrictive lung disease. Although alveolar hypoventilation is mainly a mechanism of hypercapnic respiratory failure, it contributes to hypoxemia.

Interrelationship of mechanisms. Rarely is acute hypoxemic respiratory failure caused by a single factor. More often, it is a combination of 2 or more factors. For example, the patient with ARF from pneumonia may have a V/Q mismatch and shunt. Inflammation, edema, and exudate obstruct the airways (V/Q mismatch) and fill the alveoli with exudate (shunt). Contributing factors include increases in O_2 demand from anxiety and unrelieved pain.

Consequences of Hypoxemia

Hypoxemia can lead to hypoxia if not corrected. Hypoxia, a decrease in O_2 supply at the cellular level, occurs when the PaO_2 falls enough to cause signs and symptoms of inadequate oxygenation. If hypoxia is severe, the cells shift from aerobic to anaerobic metabolism. Anaerobic metabolism uses more fuel, produces less energy, and is less efficient than aerobic metabolism. The waste product of anaerobic metabolism is lactic acid. Lactic acid is harder to remove from the body than CO_2 because it must be buffered with sodium bicarbonate. When the body does not have enough sodium bicarbonate to buffer the lactic acid, metabolic acidosis occurs. Left uncorrected, tissue and cell dysfunction, and ultimately cell death, occurs.

Hypercapnic Respiratory Failure

In acute hypercapnic respiratory failure, or *ventilatory failure*, the respiratory system cannot maintain CO_2 levels within normal limits. This condition occurs from either an increase in CO_2 production or a decrease in alveolar ventilation. Hypercapnic respiratory failure can be acute or chronic.

Many problems can cause hypercapnic respiratory failure. We group these into 4 categories: (1) CNS problems, (2) neuromuscular problems, (3) chest wall abnormalities, and (4) problems affecting the airways and/or alveoli. Hypercapnic ARF due to CNS problems, neuromuscular problems, and/or chest wall abnormalities can occur in the presence of normal lungs.

Central nervous system problems. Several CNS problems can suppress the drive to breathe. An example is an overdose of a respiratory depressant drug (e.g., opioid). In a dose-related manner, CNS depressants decrease CO_2 reactivity in the brainstem. This allows arterial CO_2 levels to rise. Brainstem infarction or traumatic brain injury (TBI) may interfere with the function of the respiratory center in the medulla. The medulla does not sense a change in $PaCO_2$, and as a result, an increase in respiratory rate does not occur.

TBI with a decreased level of consciousness can hinder the patient's ability to protect the airway, breathe, or manage secretions. High-level spinal cord injuries (SCI) can affect nerve supply to the respiratory muscles of the chest wall and diaphragm.

Neuromuscular problems. Various neuromuscular problems place patients at risk for respiratory failure. For example, patients with Guillain-Barré syndrome and multiple sclerosis have respiratory muscle weakness or paralysis. As a result, they cannot eliminate CO_2 and maintain normal $PaCO_2$ levels. Exposure to toxins (e.g., carbamate/organophosphate pesticides, chemical nerve agents) can interfere with the nerve supply to muscles and lung ventilation. Respiratory muscle weakness can occur from muscle wasting during critical illness or peripheral nerve damage.

Chest wall abnormalities. Several conditions can prevent normal chest wall or diaphragm movement and limit lung expansion. With severe obesity, the weight of the chest and abdominal contents limit lung expansion. In patients with flail chest, fractures prevent the rib cage from expanding normally. With kyphosis, the change in spinal configuration compresses the lungs and prevents normal chest wall expansion.

Problems of the airway and alveoli. Patients with COPD, asthma, and cystic fibrosis are at higher risk for hypercapnic respiratory failure because the underlying pathophysiology results in airflow obstruction and air trapping. Respiratory muscle fatigue and ventilatory failure occur from the added work of breathing (WOB) needed to inspire air against increased airway resistance and air trapped within the alveoli.

Consequences of hypercapnia. The body can tolerate increased CO_2 levels better than low O_2 levels. This is because with slow changes in $PaCO_2$, the body may have time to compensate. For example, consider the patient with COPD who develops an upper respiratory tract infection. Because a slow, steady increase in $PaCO_2$ level occurred over several days, there was time for the kidneys to compensate (e.g., by retaining bicarbonate). This will initially minimize the change in arterial pH. However, unless we identify and correct the primary cause, the patient will likely get worse.

Clinical Manifestations

Respiratory failure may develop suddenly (acute, minutes or hours) or gradually (chronic, several days or weeks). A sudden decrease in PaO_2 and/or a rapid rise in $PaCO_2$ implies a severe respiratory problem, which can quickly become a life-threatening emergency. An example is a patient with asthma who develops severe bronchospasm and a marked decrease in airflow. This results in respiratory muscle fatigue, acidemia, and ARF.

Signs of respiratory failure are related to the extent of change in PaO_2 or $PaCO_2$, the speed of change (acute versus chronic), and the patient's ability to compensate for this change. When the patient's compensatory mechanisms fail, respiratory failure occurs. Because clinical signs vary, frequent patient assessment is a priority.

A lack of O_2 affects all body systems (Table 32.2). For example, a decreased level of consciousness may occur without enough blood, O_2, and glucose supplied to the brain. Permanent brain damage can result if hypoxia is severe and prolonged. Gastrointestinal (GI) system changes include tissue ischemia and increased intestinal wall permeability. Bacteria can migrate from the GI tract into systemic circulation. Renal function may be impaired. Sodium retention, peripheral edema, and acute kidney injury (AKI) may occur.

TABLE 32.2 Common Manifestations of Hypoxemia and Hypercapnia

Specific	Nonspecific
Hypoxemia	
Respiratory	Cardiovascular
Accessory muscle use	↑ BP (early), ↓ BP (late)
Dyspnea	Dysrhythmias (late)
Intercostal muscle retraction	↑ HR
Nasal flaring	Skin cool, clammy, and diaphoretic
Paradoxical chest or abdominal wall movement with respiratory cycle (late)	CNS
	Agitation
	Confusion
Prolonged expiration	Disorientation
↓ SpO_2 (<90%)	↓ Level of consciousness
Tachypnea	Restless, combative behavior
Cyanosis (late)	Coma (late)
	Other
	Fatigue
	Inability to speak in complete sentences without pausing to breathe
Hypercapnia	
Respiratory	Cardiovascular
Dyspnea	↑ BP
Limited chest wall movement	Dysrhythmias
Pursed-lip breathing	↑ HR
Tripod position	CNS
↓ Respiratory rate or rapid rate with shallow respirations	Agitation
	Confusion, disorientation
↓ Tidal volume	Morning headache
↓ Minute ventilation	Progressive somnolence
	↑ ICP
	Coma (late)
	Neuromuscular
	↓ Deep tendon reflexes
	Muscle weakness
	Tremors, seizures (late)

One of the first signs of hypoxemic ARF is a change in mental status. Mental status changes occur early because the brain is sensitive to changes in O_2 (and to a lesser degree CO_2) levels and acid-base balance. Restlessness, confusion, and agitation suggest inadequate O_2 delivery to the brain. A morning headache and low respiratory rate with a decreased level of consciousness may indicate problems with CO_2 removal.

Tachycardia, tachypnea, pallor, and a mild increase in WOB are early signs of ARF.[6] These changes indicate attempts by the heart and lungs to compensate for decreased O_2 delivery and rising CO_2 levels. It is important to understand that cyanosis is an unreliable indicator of hypoxemia. It is a late sign in ARF. It often does not occur until deoxygenated hemoglobin concentration in the capillaries is around 5 g/dL.[7]

Observing the patient's position helps assess the effort associated with the **work of breathing (WOB)**. WOB is the effort needed by the respiratory muscles to inhale air into the lungs. Patients with mild respiratory distress may be able to lie down. In moderate distress, patients may prefer to sit. With severe distress, they may be unable to breathe unless sitting upright. The tripod position helps decrease the WOB in patients with moderate to severe COPD and ARF. The patient sits with the arms propped on the overbed table or the knees. Propping the arms increases the anteroposterior diameter of the chest and changes pressure in the thorax.

The patient in ARF may have a rapid, shallow breathing pattern or a slower respiratory rate. Both predispose the patient to hypoxemia and insufficient CO_2 removal (hypercarbia). Increased respiratory rates require a substantial amount of work and can lead to respiratory muscle fatigue. A change from a rapid rate to a slower rate in a patient in respiratory distress, such as that seen with acute asthma, suggests severe respiratory muscle fatigue. There is an increased chance of respiratory arrest.

The patient's ability to speak is related to the severity of dyspnea. The dyspneic patient may be able to speak only a few words at a time between breaths. For example, the patient may have "2-word" or "3-word" dyspnea. This means the patient can say only 2 or 3 words before pausing to breathe.

You may see dyspneic patients using pursed-lip breathing. This technique increases SaO_2 by slowing respirations, increasing time for expiration, and preventing small bronchioles from collapsing. You may see *retraction* (inward movement) of the intercostal spaces or supraclavicular area and accessory muscle use (e.g., sternocleidomastoid) during inspiration or expiration. Using accessory muscles often signifies a moderate degree of respiratory distress.

Paradoxical breathing occurs with severe respiratory distress. Normally, the thorax and abdomen move outward on inspiration and inward on exhalation. With paradoxical breathing, the abdomen and chest each move in the opposite direction. Paradoxical breathing results from maximal use of the accessory muscles of respiration. The patient may be diaphoretic from the increased WOB.

Auscultate breath sounds. Note the presence and location of any abnormal breath sounds. Fine crackles may occur with pulmonary edema. Coarse crackles heard on expiration indicate fluid in the airways. This may be a sign of pneumonia or some degree of HF. Absent or decreased breath sounds occur with atelectasis, pleural effusion, or hypoventilation. Bronchial breath sounds over the lung periphery occur with lung consolidation from pneumonia. You may hear a pleural friction rub if pneumonia involves the pleura.

Diagnostic Studies

The most common diagnostic studies used to evaluate ARF are chest x-ray and ABG analysis. A chest x-ray helps identify possible causes of respiratory failure (e.g., atelectasis, pneumonia). ABGs evaluate oxygenation (PaO_2) and ventilation ($PaCO_2$) status and acid-base (pH, bicarbonate) balance. Pulse oximetry monitors oxygenation status indirectly.

Other diagnostic studies that may be done include a complete blood cell count, serum electrolytes, urinalysis, and 12-lead ECG. Blood and sputum cultures (Gram stain, culture, and sensitivity) may reveal infection. A CT scan or V/Q lung scan may be done if a pulmonary embolus is suspected. For the patient in severe ARF who needs mechanical ventilation, end-tidal CO_2 ($EtCO_2$) can assess trends in ventilation.[8]

NURSING AND INTERPROFESSIONAL MANAGEMENT: ARF

Because many different problems cause ARF, initial management and specific care vary. Factors considered include patient age, underlying comorbidities, severity of onset, and suspected or most likely cause of the respiratory failure. We then tailor management strategies to what best meets the patient's unique needs. In acute care settings, collaboration among the health care team (e.g., nurses, physicians, respiratory therapists, pharmacists) is essential.

For mild to moderate ARF, O_2 administration via a high-flow O_2 delivery device (e.g., Optiflow) may be started. Non-invasive ventilation, such as bi-level positive airway pressure (Bi-PAP), may be an option for patients who are awake, alert, able to maintain a patent airway and clear their own secretions.

In severe ARF, the patient will receive care in an intensive care unit (ICU). ICU care will include mechanical ventilation. Continuous pulse oximetry and arterial BP monitoring will occur. ABGs will be performed often. Central or mixed venous O_2 saturation [$ScvO_2$ or SvO_2] data help determine the adequacy of tissue perfusion and the patient's response to treatment. Central venous pressure (CVP) monitoring may be ordered. The patient may need advanced hemodynamic monitoring to evaluate parameters such as ejection fraction, CO, and pulmonary capillary wedge pressure (PCWP).

Assessment

Table 32.3 presents subjective and objective data that you should obtain from the patient with ARF. A thorough assessment may result in the early detection of respiratory insufficiency. This allows us to intervene sooner and may prevent worsening respiratory failure. Monitor patients with preexisting cardiac and/or respiratory disease closely. Any change in their overall condition may cause significant respiratory and hemodynamic decompensation.

The priority is immediately assessing the patient's ability to maintain a patent airway and breathe (ventilate). Observe trends in ABGs, pulse oximetry, and assessment findings. Remain alert to subtle changes that can occur in your patient's condition from hypoxemia or hypercarbia. Your ability to detect problems, notify the HCP, implement appropriate treatment, and evaluate response to therapy is essential.

Clinical Problems

Clinical problems for the patient with ARF may include:

- Impaired respiratory system function
- Inadequate tissue perfusion
- Acid-base imbalance

Additional information on clinical problems and interventions for the patient with ARF is presented in eNursing Care Plan 32.1 (available on the website for this chapter).

Planning

The overall goals for the patient with ARF include (1) independently maintain a patent airway, (2) absence of dyspnea or

TABLE 32.3 NURSING ASSESSMENT

ARF

Subjective Data

Important Health Information

Health history: Age, weight, level of consciousness, tobacco use, alcohol or drug use, hospitalizations related to lung disease, thoracic or spinal cord trauma, occupational exposures to lung toxins

Medications: Use of home O_2, inhalers (bronchodilators), home nebulization, immunosuppressant (e.g., corticosteroid) therapy, CNS depressants, illicit substances

Surgery or other treatments: Past intubation and mechanical ventilation, recent thoracic or abdominal surgery

Functional Health Patterns

Health perception–health management: Exercise, self-care activities, immunizations (flu, pneumonia, hepatitis)

Nutritional-metabolic: Eating habits; history of bloating, indigestion; recent weight gain or loss, change in appetite. Use of vitamins or herbal supplements

Activity-exercise: Fatigue, dizziness, dyspnea at rest or with activity, wheezing, cough (productive or nonproductive), sputum (volume, color, viscosity), palpitations, swollen feet, change in exercise tolerance

Sleep-rest: Changes in sleep pattern, use of CPAP

Cognitive-perceptual: Headache, chest pain or tightness, chronic pain

Coping–stress tolerance: Anxiety, depression, feelings of hopelessness. Risk for drug and/or alcohol use, nicotine withdrawal

Objective Data

Cardiovascular

Tachycardia progressing to bradycardia, dysrhythmias, extra heart sounds (S_3, S_4). Bounding pulse. Hypertension progressing to hypotension. Pulsus paradoxus, jugular venous distention, pedal edema

GI

Abdominal distention, ascites, epigastric tenderness, hepatojugular reflex

Neurologic

Somnolence, confusion, slurred speech, restlessness, delirium, agitation, tremors, seizures, coma, asterixis, ↓ deep tendon reflexes, papilledema

Respiratory

Increased respiratory rate (shallow, labored, increased WOB). Accessory muscle use with retractions, increased diaphragmatic excursion or asymmetric chest expansion, paradoxical chest and abdominal wall movement. Tactile fremitus, crepitus, or deviated trachea (late sign) on palpation. Absent, decreased, or adventitious breath sounds. Pleural friction rub. Bronchial or bronchovesicular sounds heard in other than normal location, inspiratory stridor

Skin

Pale, cool, clammy skin or warm, flushed skin. Peripheral and/or central cyanosis. Peripheral dependent edema

Possible Diagnostic Findings

↓/↑ pH, ↑/↓ $PaCO_2$, ↑/↓ bicarbonate, ↓ PaO_2, ↓ SaO_2, abnormal hemoglobin, ↑ WBC count, changes in serum electrolytes. Abnormal chest x-ray. Abnormal CVP or pulmonary artery pressures. Initially, CO may be ↑ due to the stress response. As hypoxemia, hypercapnia, and acidosis become more severe, CO will ↓.

recovery to baseline breathing patterns, (3) effectively cough and able to clear secretions, (4) normal ABG values or values within the patient's baseline, and (5) breath sounds within the patient's baseline.

◆ Implementation

◆ Prevention

For the patient at risk for ARF, prevention and early recognition of respiratory problems is important. This is especially important for patients with neuromuscular, cardiac, or respiratory problems (e.g., COPD). Do a thorough history and physical assessment to identify risk factors. Preventing atelectasis, pneumonia, and complications of immobility and optimizing hydration and nutrition can decrease the risk for ARF. Assess patients at high risk more often and implement preventive measures. Early strategies may include teaching patients about deep breathing and coughing, incentive spirometry, and early ambulation.

◆ Acute Care

Interventions to improve the patient's oxygenation and ventilation status are essential to improving O_2 delivery and patient outcomes. The primary aim is to identify and treat the underlying cause of the ARF. Patients with V/Q mismatch, shunting, or diffusion impairment may be managed slightly differently, depending on the underlying cause. We monitor patients continuously for their response to therapy, including changes in respiratory status, trends in ABGs, and signs of clinical improvement.

◆ Respiratory Therapy

The goals of respiratory care include maintaining adequate oxygenation and ventilation and correcting acid-base imbalance. Interventions include O_2 therapy, mobilizing secretions, and positive pressure ventilation (PPV) (Table 32.4).

◆ Oxygen Therapy

The primary goal of O_2 therapy is to correct hypoxemia. This requires O_2 administration. Never withhold O_2 from a patient. Always administer O_2 at the lowest possible FIO_2 (O_2 concentration) needed to keep the PaO_2, SpO_2, and SaO_2 within patient-specific goals. Observe the patient's response to O_2 therapy. Closely monitor for changes in mental status, respiratory rate, and ABGs. A trend towards a normal PaO_2 level lets you know that the patient is responsive to O_2.

Several methods are available to provide O_2. Chapter 28 and Table 28.3 discuss O_2 delivery devices. The device selected depends upon the patient's overall condition, degree of respiratory failure, ability to maintain a patent airway, the amount of FIO_2 the device delivers, and the patient's ability to breathe spontaneously. The selected O_2 delivery device must help maintain PaO_2 at 60 mm Hg or higher and SaO_2 at 90% or higher.

The patient with hypoxemia is often agitated, disoriented, and restless. A face mask, though appropriate, may cause anxiety. Anxiety can cause dyspnea and increase O_2 consumption and CO_2 production. The patient may try to remove the mask. In this case, you need to explore other O_2 therapy options.

TABLE 32.4 Interprofessional Care

ARF

Diagnostic Assessment

- Vital signs with pulse oximetry (SpO_2)
- History and physical assessment
- Arterial blood gases (ABGs)
- Chest x-ray
- CBC with differential
- Serum electrolytes
- 12-Lead ECG
- Blood, sputum, and/or urine cultures (if indicated)
- Hemodynamic monitoring (if indicated)

Management

Respiratory Therapy

- O_2 therapy
- Mobilization of secretions
  - Positioning (unless contraindicated, head of bed elevated)
  - Effective coughing
  - Chest physiotherapy
  - Suctioning of the airway
  - Oral and/or IV hydration
  - Humidification (of O_2)
  - Ambulation (early mobility)
- Positive pressure ventilation (PPV)
  - Noninvasive positive pressure ventilation (e.g., BiPAP)
  - Intubation with positive pressure ventilation

Drug Therapy

- Reduce pain, anxiety, restlessness (e.g., fentanyl, morphine, hydromorphone, lorazepam)
- Relieve bronchospasm (e.g., albuterol)
- Reduce pulmonary congestion (e.g., furosemide, morphine)
- Treat pulmonary infections (e.g., antibiotics)
- Reduce airway inflammation (e.g., corticosteroids)

Supportive Therapy

- Manage the underlying cause of ARF
- Monitor hemodynamic status
- Optimize balance between activity and rest
- Monitor for deterioration in patient condition
- Be vigilant in avoiding and preventing complications

Breathing high O_2 concentrations for prolonged periods is not without potential adverse effects. Exposure to higher FIO_2 (greater than 60%) for longer than 48 hours poses a risk for *O_2 toxicity.* In this situation, oxygen-free radicals from the high O_2 levels cause inflammation and cell death by disrupting the alveolar-capillary membrane. *Absorption atelectasis* is another risk. O_2 can replace nitrogen and other gases normally present in the alveoli. Without nitrogen to help maintain the size and shape of the alveolus, structural support is lost, and the alveolus collapses. Other effects of prolonged exposure to high O_2 levels include increased pulmonary capillary permeability, decreased surfactant production, surfactant inactivation, and fibrotic changes in the alveoli.[9]

Another risk of O_2 therapy is specific to patients with chronic hypercapnia (e.g., patients with COPD). Chronic hypercapnia blunts the response of chemoreceptors to high CO_2 levels as a respiratory stimulant. Initial O_2 therapy may be provided through a low-flow device, such as a nasal cannula at 1 to 2 L/min or a Venturi mask at 24% to 28%. Those who do not respond to O_2 therapy or other interventions may need mechanical ventilation with higher FIO_2.

◆ Mobilizing Secretions

Retained pulmonary secretions may cause or worsen ARF. This occurs because the movement of O_2 into the alveoli and the removal of CO_2 is severely limited or blocked. Secretions can be mobilized by proper positioning, effective coughing, chest physiotherapy, suctioning, humidification, hydration, and, when possible, early ambulation.

Patient positioning. Position the patient with ARF upright. Elevate the head of the bed at least 30 degrees or use a reclining chair or chair bed. This helps maximize respiratory expansion, decrease dyspnea, and mobilize secretions. A sitting position improves pulmonary function by promoting the downward movement of the lungs. When lungs are upright, ventilation and perfusion are best in the lung bases. If there is a chance for aspiration, position the patient side-lying.

We may place a patient with a 1-sided lung problem in a lateral or side-lying position. This position, called *good lung down,* allows for improved V/Q matching in the affected lung. Pulmonary blood flow and ventilation are better in dependent lung areas. Secretions can drain out of the affected lung so they can be removed with suctioning. For example, place a patient with right-sided pneumonia on the left side. This will maximize ventilation and perfusion in the "good" lung and aid in secretion removal from the affected lung (postural drainage). Patients with ARF often have problems with both lungs. They may need repositioning at regular intervals on both sides to optimize air movement and drainage of secretions.

Effective coughing. When secretions are present, encourage the patient to cough. Unfortunately, not all patients will have enough strength or force to produce a cough that will clear the airway of secretions. *Augmented coughing (quad coughing)* may benefit some patients. To aid with augmented coughing, place 1 or both hands at the anterolateral base of the patient's lungs (Fig. 32.6). As you observe deep inspiration end and expiration begin, move your hands forcefully upward. This increases abdominal pressure and helps the patient cough. It increases expiratory flow and promotes secretion clearance.

Huff coughing is a series of coughs performed while saying the word "huff." This technique prevents the glottis from closing, forcing air and mucous from the airways.[10] The patient takes a deep breath, holds the breath for 2 or 3 seconds, and then forcefully exhales. COPD patients generate higher flow rates with a huff cough than a normal cough, which is less tiring.

The *staged cough* also helps clear secretions. To perform a staged cough, the patient assumes a sitting position. They breathe in and out 3 or 4 times through the mouth, then cough while bending forward and pressing a pillow inward against the diaphragm.

Chest physiotherapy. Chest physiotherapy is indicated for all patients producing sputum or have severe atelectasis

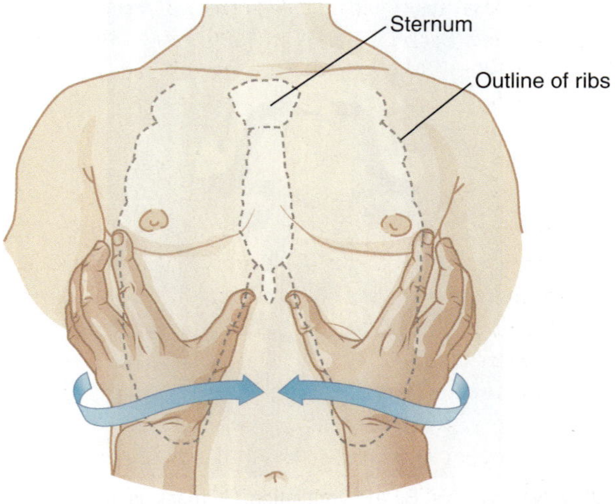

Fig. 32.6 Augmented coughing is performed by placing 1 or both hands on the anterolateral base of the lungs. After the patient takes a deep inspiration and at the beginning of expiration, move the hand(s) forcefully upward. This increases abdominal pressure and helps produce a forceful cough. (From American Association of Critical Care Nurses: *AACN advanced critical care nursing,* St Louis, 2009, Mosby.)

or pulmonary infiltrates on chest x-ray. Postural drainage, percussion, and vibration to the affected lung segments help move secretions to the larger airways. Then, they can be removed by coughing or suctioning. Contraindications include TBI and increased intracranial pressure (ICP), unstable orthopedic injuries (e.g., spinal fractures, fractured ribs, fractured sternum), and recent hemoptysis.[11] See more about chest physiotherapy in Chapter 28.

Suctioning. Suctioning may be needed if the patient is unable to expectorate secretions. Inserting a soft-tip suction catheter through a nasopharyngeal tube in the awake, non-intubated patient may help remove secretions at the back of the throat. Perform suctioning with caution, as stimulating the gag reflex may induce vomiting. We only suction through an artificial airway (e.g., endotracheal tube [ET], tracheostomy) as needed (see Chapter 28).

Humidification. Humidification is an adjunct in secretion management. We can thin secretions with aerosols of sterile normal saline or mucolytic drugs (e.g., acetylcysteine mixed with a bronchodilator) given by nebulizer. O_2 given by aerosol mask can thin secretions and promote their removal. Be aware that aerosol therapy may cause bronchospasm and severe coughing, causing a decrease in PaO_2. Frequent assessment of the patient's tolerance to therapy is critical.

Hydration. Thick, viscous secretions are hard to expel. Unless contraindicated, adequate fluid intake (2 to 3 L/day) keeps secretions thin and easier to remove. This may not be possible in the patient with ARF. The patient who is unable to take enough fluids orally needs IV hydration. Assess cardiac and renal status to determine whether the patient can tolerate the IV fluid volume and avoid HF and pulmonary edema. Regularly assess for signs of fluid overload (e.g., crackles, dyspnea, weight gain, increased CVP).

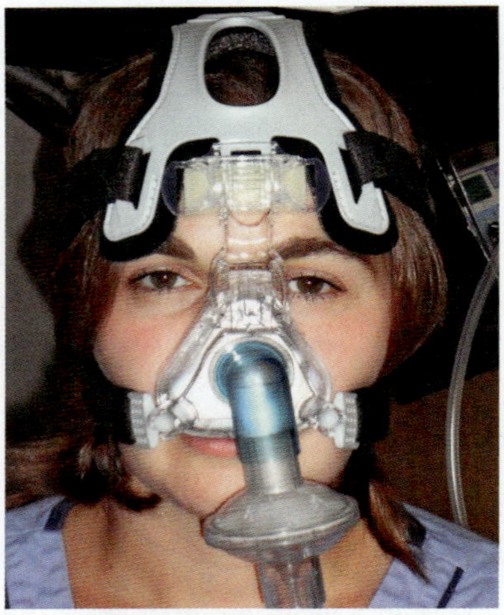

Fig. 32.7 Noninvasive BiPAP ventilation. A mask is placed over the nose or nose and mouth. Positive pressure from a mechanical ventilator aids the patient's breathing efforts, decreasing the work of breathing. (Courtesy Richard Arbour, RN, MSN, CCRN, CNRN, CCNS, FAAN, and Anna Kirk, RN, MSN.)

CHECK YOUR PRACTICE

You are caring for a 72-year-old male patient with hypoxemic ARF. He has a history of atrial flutter and COPD. A chest x-ray shows left-sided pneumonia. Your patient is awake but mildly confused. He has a productive cough with thick, yellow-green purulent sputum.

- What respiratory interventions would you expect to be ordered?

◆ Positive Pressure Ventilation

If initial measures do not improve oxygenation and ventilation, the patient may need enhanced ventilatory assistance. Noninvasive positive pressure ventilation (NIPPV) is one option. With NIPPV, a mask is placed tightly over the patient's nose or nose and mouth (Fig. 32.7). When the patient breathes spontaneously, a mechanical ventilator or table-top unit delivers PPV to the patient. With NIPPV, it is possible to provide O_2 and decrease WOB, avoiding the need for intubation.

NIPPV is most useful in managing CRF in those with chest wall or neuromuscular problems. It may help patients with a chronic respiratory problem that is worse due to cardiac problems or infection. It is an option for patients who refuse intubation but still want some degree of ventilatory support (e.g., patients with end-stage COPD). NIPPV is not appropriate for patients with a decreased level of consciousness, high O_2 requirements, facial trauma, hemodynamic instability, or excessive secretions. NIPPV after extubation can help avoid reintubation.

There are 2 forms of NIPPV used for patients with ARF. Continuous positive airway pressure (CPAP) delivers 1 level of pressure—a constant pressure—to the patient's airway during inspiration and expiration. BiPAP uses 2 different levels of positive pressure (one on inspiration, another on expiration). With both CPAP and BiPAP, the patient must be awake and alert, have stable vital signs, and maintain spontaneous ventilation.

The most frequently used NIPPV for ARF is BiPAP.[12] BiPAP provides O_2 therapy and humidification, decreases WOB, and reduces respiratory muscle fatigue. It helps open collapsed airways and decrease shunt. If respiratory status worsens with NIPPV, PPV via mechanical ventilation with higher O_2 concentrations is needed. Chapter 28 discusses mechanical ventilation.

◆ Drug Therapy

Drug therapy depends on several factors. These include the cause of ARF, the patient's comorbidities, and whether an infection is present. Goals of drug therapy include (1) reduce airway inflammation and bronchospasm, (2) relieve pulmonary congestion, (3) treat infection, and (4) reduce anxiety, pain, and restlessness.

◆ Reduce Airway Inflammation and Bronchospasm

Relief of bronchospasm increases alveolar ventilation. In acute bronchospasm, short-acting bronchodilators (e.g., albuterol) may be given at 15- to 30-minute intervals until a response occurs. Give these drugs using a hand-held nebulizer or a metered-dose inhaler with a spacer. Side effects include tachycardia and hypertension. Prolonged use can increase the risk for dysrhythmias and cardiac ischemia. Monitor the patient's vital signs and ECG for any changes.

Corticosteroids (e.g., IV methylprednisolone) may be used in combination with other drugs, such as bronchodilators, to relieve inflammation and bronchospasm. It may take several hours to see their effects. Inhaled corticosteroids may take 4 to 5 days for optimum therapeutic effects, so they will not relieve dyspnea and increased WOB quickly.

DRUG ALERT

IV Corticosteroids

- Monitor potassium levels. Corticosteroids worsen hypokalemia caused by diuretics.
- Prolonged use causes adrenal insufficiency.
- Hyperglycemia, especially in those with diabetes, is common.

◆ Relieve Pulmonary Congestion

Interstitial fluid can accumulate in the lungs because of injury to the alveolar capillary membrane from HF or fluid overload. IV diuretics (e.g., furosemide), morphine, or nitroglycerin can decrease pulmonary congestion caused by HF. Use caution when giving these drugs. Changes in heart rate and rhythm and significant decreases in BP are common.

◆ Treat Infection

Lung infections (e.g., pneumonia, acute bronchitis) can result in excessive mucus production, fever, increased O_2 consumption, and inflamed, fluid-filled, and/or collapsed alveoli. Alveoli that are fluid filled or collapsed cannot take part in gas exchange. Consequently, pulmonary infections can either cause or worsen ARF. IV antibiotics are given to treat infection. Chest x-rays can show the location and extent of infection. Sputum cultures help identify the organisms causing the infection and their sensitivity to antimicrobial drugs.

◆ Reduce Anxiety, Pain, and Restlessness

Anxiety, pain, and restlessness may result from hypoxemia and dyspnea. They increase O_2 consumption and CO_2 production (from an increased metabolic rate) and increase WOB. For the non-intubated patient, this may cause tachypnea and ineffective ventilation. They may cause ventilator dyssynchrony for the intubated patient and increase the risk for unplanned extubation (see Chapter 28).

We promote patient comfort in several ways. Frequently turn and reposition the patient. Provide reassurance and emotional support to the patient and caregiver. IV benzodiazepines (e.g., lorazepam, midazolam) and opioids (e.g., morphine, fentanyl) may decrease anxiety, restlessness, and pain. We should start these drugs at the lowest dose possible. Assess for treatable causes of restlessness (e.g., hypoxemia, pain, delirium) and manage as needed. Often, restlessness and mental status changes are the first signs of hypoxemia or patient-ventilator dyssynchrony. You should address the causes and not depend solely on the use of analgesics and sedatives.

! SAFETY ALERT

Managing Restlessness and Sedation

- Pain, hypoxemia, delirium, electrolyte imbalance, TBI, and drug reactions can cause restlessness.
- Assess and treat all reversible causes of restlessness.
- Monitor patients closely for CNS, cardiac, and respiratory depression when giving sedative and analgesic drugs, especially in the non-intubated patient.
- Sedative and analgesic drugs may have a prolonged effect in critically ill and older adult patients. This can delay weaning from mechanical ventilation and increase length of stay.

◆ Nutrition Therapy

Maintaining protein and energy stores is especially important. The hypermetabolic state in critical illness increases the calories needed to maintain a stable body weight and muscle mass. Nutrition depletion causes a loss of muscle mass, including the respiratory muscles, which may delay recovery. The dietitian often determines the best method of feeding and optimal calorie and fluid requirements. Ideally, enteral nutrition (EN) should be started within 24 to 48 hours (see Chapter 44).

◆ Evaluation

The expected outcomes are that the patient with ARF will

- Independently maintain a patent airway
- Maintain adequate oxygenation
- Have hemodynamic stability
- Achieve a return to baseline respiratory system function

Gerontologic Considerations: Acute Respiratory Failure

Many factors contribute to an increased risk for ARF in older adults. The reduced ventilatory capacity that accompanies aging increases the risk for ARF. Physiologic changes in the lungs include alveolar dilation, larger air spaces, and loss of surface area for gas exchange. Decreased elastic recoil within the airways, decreased chest wall compliance, and decreased respiratory muscle strength occur.[13]

In older adults, the PaO_2 falls further, and the $PaCO_2$ rises to a higher level before the respiratory system is stimulated to change the rate and depth of breathing. This delayed response contributes to the development of respiratory insufficiency. A history of tobacco use can accelerate age-related respiratory changes. Poor nutrition status and less physiologic reserve in the cardiopulmonary system increase the risk for further compromising respiratory function and ARF.

ACUTE RESPIRATORY DISTRESS SYNDROME

Acute respiratory distress syndrome (ARDS) is a sudden and progressive form of ARF in which the alveolar-capillary membrane becomes damaged and more permeable to intravascular fluid (Fig. 32.8). Next to septic shock, ARDS is one of the most common conditions seen in the adult ICU. ARDS accounts for about 10% of all adult ICU admissions.[14] The incidence of ARDS in the United States is more than 200,000 cases each year. Despite supportive therapy, the mortality rate is around 35%.[15]

Etiology

Table 32.5 lists conditions that predispose patients to ARDS. The most common cause is sepsis. ARDS may also develop because of multisystem organ dysfunction syndrome (MODS).

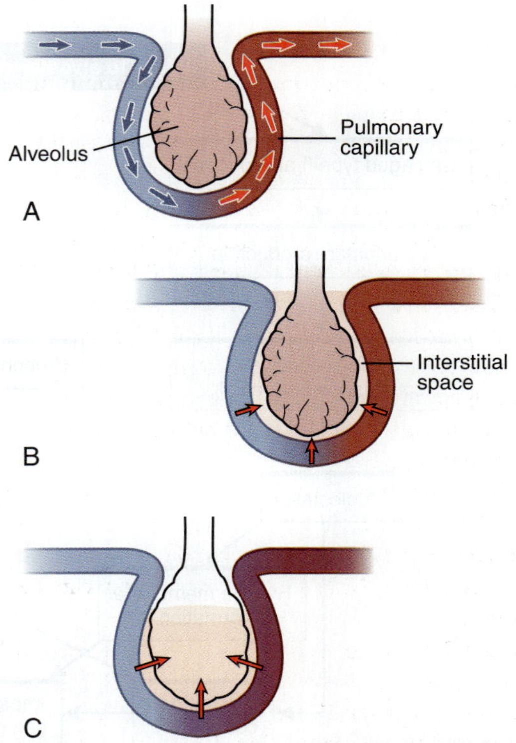

Fig. 32.8 Stages of edema formation in ARDS. (A) Normal alveolus and pulmonary capillary. (B) Interstitial edema occurs with accumulation of and increased flow of fluid into the interstitial space. (C) Alveolar edema occurs when the fluid crosses the alveolar-capillary membrane, causing severe impairment in gas exchange.

Patients with multiple risk factors are 3 or 4 times more likely to develop ARDS.

Either a direct or indirect lung injury causes ARDS. In direct lung injury, the pathogen comes into contact with the lung tissue. For example, aspiration of gastric contents into the lung immediately initiates the inflammatory response. In an indirect injury, ARDS develops due to a problem somewhere else in the body. For example, necrotizing pancreatitis or bowel obstruction with perforation causes widespread inflammation and infection. As a result, septic mediators gain entrance to the bloodstream and often move toward the lungs, which provide a favorable, dark, moist environment for their proliferation. This can be the beginning of ARF, which, left untreated, can progress to ARDS.

TABLE 32.5 Predisposing Conditions to ARDS

Direct Lung Injury	Indirect Lung Injury
Common Causes	
• Aspiration (gastric contents or other substances) • Bacterial or viral pneumonia • Sepsis	• Massive trauma • Sepsis and septic shock (especially gram-negative infection) • Severe TBI • Shock states (hypovolemic, cardiogenic)
Less Common Causes	
• Chest trauma (blunt or penetrating) • Embolism: fat, air, amniotic fluid, thrombus • Inhalation of toxic substances • Near-drowning • O_2 toxicity • Radiation pneumonitis	• Acute pancreatitis • Cardiopulmonary bypass • Disseminated intravascular coagulation • Opioid drug overdose • Transfusion-related acute lung injury (e.g., multiple blood transfusions) • Urosepsis

Pathophysiology

The pathophysiologic changes in ARDS are divided into 3 phases: (1) injury or exudative phase, (2) reparative or proliferative phase, and (3) fibrotic or fibroproliferative phase. The pathophysiology of ARDS is shown in Fig. 32.9.

Injury or Exudative Phase

The *injury or exudative phase* usually occurs 24 to 72 hours after the initial insult (direct or indirect).[16] It generally lasts 7 to 10 days. Engorgement of the peribronchial and perivascular interstitial space causes interstitial edema. Fluid in the parenchyma of the lung surrounding the alveoli crosses the alveolar membrane and enters the alveolar space. V/Q mismatch and shunt develop because the alveoli fill with fluid. Blood in the capillary network cannot be oxygenated.

We do not know the exact cause of the alveolar-capillary membrane damage. Some think it is caused by stimulation of the inflammatory and immune systems. This stimulation attracts neutrophils to the pulmonary interstitium. The neutrophils

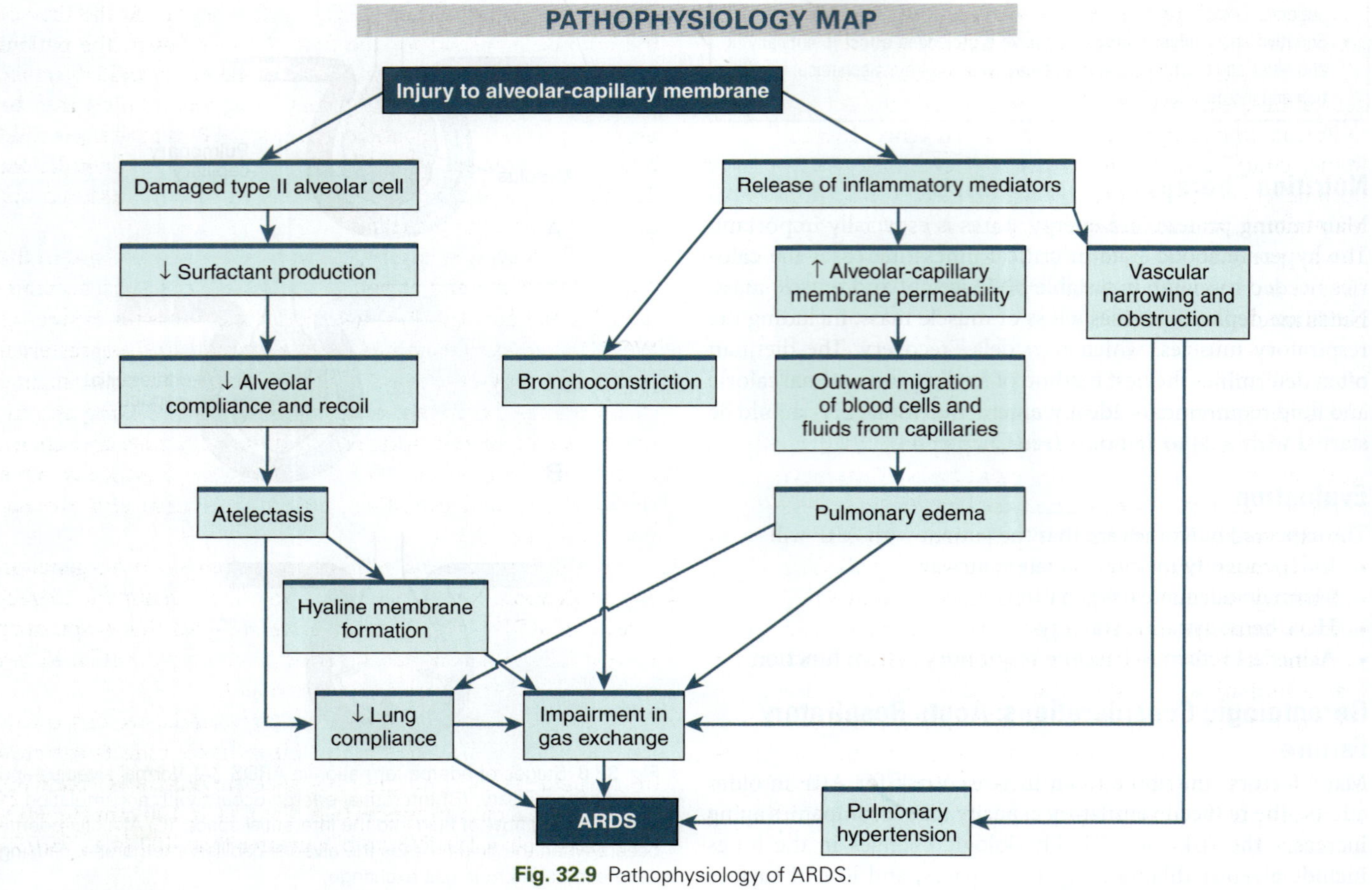

Fig. 32.9 Pathophysiology of ARDS.

release biochemical, humoral, and cellular mediators that produce changes in the lung. These changes include increased pulmonary capillary membrane permeability, destruction of collagen, formation of pulmonary microemboli, and pulmonary artery vasoconstriction.

Hypoxemia and the stimulation of juxtacapillary receptors in the parenchyma of the stiff lung *(J reflex)* initially cause an increase in respiratory rate and a decrease in tidal volume (V_T). This breathing pattern increases CO_2 removal, causing respiratory alkalosis. CO increases in response to hypoxemia, a compensatory effort to increase pulmonary blood flow. As atelectasis, pulmonary edema, and pulmonary shunt increase, compensation fails. Hypoventilation, decreased CO, and decreased tissue O_2 perfusion occur.

The changes caused by ARDS damage both alveolar type I cells and alveolar type II cells (which make surfactant). This damage, in addition to fluid and protein accumulation, results in surfactant dysfunction. The function of surfactant is to maintain alveolar stability and prevent alveolar collapse. When surfactant synthesis is decreased, or surfactant becomes inactivated, alveoli become unstable and collapse *(atelectasis).* Widespread atelectasis further decreases lung compliance, compromises gas exchange, and contributes to hypoxemia.

Necrotic cells, protein, and fibrin form hyaline membranes that line the inside of each alveolus. In ARDS, the hyaline membrane thickens. This causes more atelectasis, further impairing gas exchange and reducing lung compliance.

Severe V/Q mismatch and shunting of pulmonary capillary blood result in hypoxemia unresponsive to increasing O_2 concentrations. This classic sign of ARDS is called **refractory hypoxemia**. In other words, despite receiving higher O_2 concentrations, the patient's condition continues to get worse. Diffusion impairment, caused by a thickened hyaline membrane, contributes to and worsens hypoxemia. As the lungs become less compliant because of decreased surfactant, pulmonary edema, and atelectasis, the patient must generate higher airway pressures to inflate "stiff" lungs. Reduced lung compliance increases the patient's WOB. At this point, the patient needs mechanical ventilation.

Reparative or Proliferative Phase

The *reparative* or *proliferative phase* of ARDS begins 1 to 2 weeks after the initial lung injury.[17] During this phase, there continues to be an influx of neutrophils, monocytes, lymphocytes, and fibroblasts as part of the inflammatory response. Increased pulmonary vascular resistance and pulmonary hypertension may occur because fibroblasts and inflammatory cells destroy the pulmonary vasculature. Lung compliance continues to decrease due to interstitial fibrosis. Hypoxemia continues because of the thickened alveolar membrane. This causes V/Q mismatch, diffusion limitation, and shunting. Fluid in the lungs and secretions in the airways increase airway resistance. The proliferative phase is complete when dense, fibrous tissue replaces the diseased lung. If the reparative phase persists, widespread fibrosis results. If the reparative phase stops, the lesions will often resolve.

Fibrotic or Fibroproliferative Phase

The *fibrotic phase* (*chronic* or *late phase*) of ARDS may start as early as 24 hours after the initial lung injury.[18] Not all patients who develop ARDS enter the fibrotic stage. For those who do, it is associated with a poorer prognosis. Collagenous and fibrous tissues remodel the lung. Diffuse scarring of the lungs, interstitial fibrosis, and alveolar duct fibrosis result in decreased lung compliance.[18] This reduces the surface area for gas exchange because the interstitium is fibrotic, and hypoxemia continues. Varying degrees of pulmonary hypertension may result from pulmonary vascular destruction and fibrosis.

Clinical Progression

Progression of ARDS varies among patients. Some survive the acute phase of lung injury. Pulmonary edema resolves, and complete recovery occurs within a week or so. The chance for survival is poorer in those who enter the fibrotic stage. Patients may need several weeks of long-term mechanical ventilation. It is not known why injured lungs repair and recover in some patients and worsen in others. Several factors are essential in determining the clinical course and outcome of ARDS. These include the nature of the initial injury, extent, and severity of comorbidities, how quickly the patient received medical care, and additional pulmonary complications (e.g., pneumothorax). Genetics may be a factor for a person's predisposition to developing ARDS.[19]

Clinical Manifestations and Diagnostic Studies

The initial presentation of ARDS is often subtle. At the time of the initial injury, and for the first 24 to 72 hours, the patient may not have respiratory symptoms or have only mild dyspnea, tachypnea, cough, and restlessness. Lung auscultation may be normal or reveal fine, scattered crackles. ABGs may show mild hypoxemia and respiratory alkalosis caused by hyperventilation. The chest x-ray may be normal or reveal diffusely scattered, but minimal interstitial infiltrates.

As ARDS evolves, symptoms worsen because of fluid in the lung parenchyma and alveoli and increased secretion accumulation in the airways. Respiratory distress becomes evident as WOB increases. Tachypnea and intercostal and suprasternal retractions may be present. Tachycardia, diaphoresis, mental status changes, cyanosis, and pallor may occur. Lung auscultation usually reveals scattered to diffuse crackles and coarse crackles on expiration. After 72 hours, the chest x-ray often shows diffuse and extensive bilateral interstitial and alveolar infiltrates (Fig. 32.10).

As ARDS progresses, ABGs reflect changes in oxygenation and ventilation. Refractory hypoxemia is the hallmark characteristic of ARDS. Hypercapnia often signifies that respiratory muscle fatigue and hypoventilation have severely affected gas exchange. Respiratory failure is imminent.

To help evaluate the severity of hypoxemia, we can calculate the **PaO2/FIO2** (P/F) ratio. This measure reflects the ratio of the patient's PaO_2 to the FIO_2 that the patient is receiving. Under normal circumstances (e.g., PaO_2 80 to 100 mm Hg; FIO_2 0.21 [room air]), the P/F ratio is greater than 400 (e.g., 95/0.21

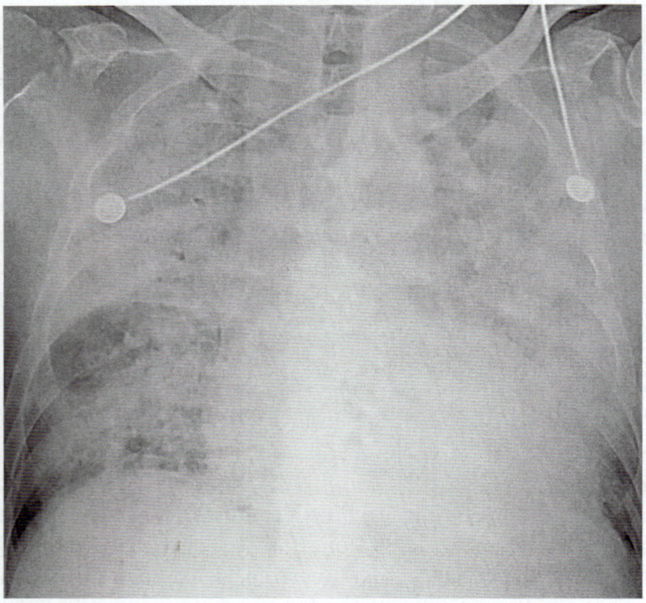

Fig. 32.10 Chest x-ray of a patient with ARDS. The x-ray shows extensive areas of consolidation. (From Walker CM, Chung JH: *Muller's imaging of the chest*, ed 2, St Louis, 2019, Elsevier.)

TABLE 32.6 Diagnostic Criteria

Berlin Definition of ARDS

Timing

Within 1 week of a known clinical insult or new or worsening respiratory symptoms

Chest X-Ray

Bilateral opacities: not fully explained by effusions, lobar/lung collapse, or nodules

Oxygenation

Mild ARDS: PaO_2/FIO_2 ratio ≥300 with PEEP or CPAP ≤5 cm H_2O
Moderate ARDS: PaO_2/FIO_2 ratio ≥200 with PEEP or CPAP ≤5 cm H_2O
Severe ARDS: PaO_2/FIO_2 ratio <100 with PEEP or CPAP ≤5 cm H_2O

Modified from Bellani G, Pham T, Laffey JG: Missed or delayed diagnosis of ARDS: A common and serious problem, *Intensive Care Med* 46:1180, 2020.

= 452). With the onset and progression of lung injury and impaired O_2 delivery through the alveolar-capillary membrane, the PaO_2 often remains lower than expected despite increased FIO_2. The P/F ratio distinguishes among mild (<300), moderate (<200), and severe (<100) ARDS (Table 32.6).

CHECK YOUR PRACTICE

You are caring for a 26-year-old woman with ARDS who experienced near-drowning 4 days ago. She is mechanically ventilated and receiving continuous IV sedation. The ventilator settings are full support (control mode), FIO_2 = 0.90 (90%), PEEP = +15 cm H_2O, V_T = 350 mL, respiratory rate 12 breaths/min (patient taking no breaths above the set rate on the ventilator), peak pressure = 35 cm H_2O. The patient's PaO_2 is 83 mm Hg.

- Calculate and interpret the PaO_2/FIO_2 (P/F) ratio.

TABLE 32.7 Complications of ARDS

Cardiovascular
- ↑ CO
- Dysrhythmias
- Hypotension

CNS and Psychologic
- Delirium
- PTSD

GI
- Hypermetabolic state, ↑ nutrient requirements
- Paralytic ileus
- Pneumoperitoneum
- Ulceration and GI bleeding

Hematologic
- Anemia
- Disseminated intravascular coagulation
- Thrombocytopenia
- VTE

Infection
- Catheter-related infection (e.g., central and peripheral IV catheters, urinary catheters)
- Sepsis

Renal
- AKI

Respiratory
- Pulmonary emboli
- Pulmonary fibrosis
- Ventilator-associated volutrauma, barotrauma
- Ventilator-associated pneumonia (VAP)

The decrease in lung compliance and increase in pulmonary resistance are associated with profound dyspnea, hypoxemia, increased WOB, and respiratory distress. We often refer to the chest x-ray as a "whiteout" because consolidation and infiltrates are widespread throughout the lungs, leaving few recognizable air spaces (Fig. 32.10). Pleural effusions may be present. Severe hypoxemia, hypercapnia, metabolic acidosis, and organ failure often accompany ARDS.

Complications

Complications may develop because of ARDS itself or its treatment (Table 32.7). Besides the lungs, the vital organs most often involved are the kidneys, liver, and heart. The main cause of death in ARDS is MODS, often accompanied by sepsis.

Abnormal Lung Function

Most patients will recover from ARDS within a year. Many will have normal to near normal lung function. However, not all patients regain normal lung function. Sometimes, abnormal lung function can persist for years or the rest of the patient's life. The severity of scarring and changes within the lungs are key factors. Mechanical ventilation, duration of time ventilated, and use of extracorporeal life support may be contributing factors.

Patients may report fatigue, chest pain, shortness of breath after minimal activity, and persistent dyspnea post-ARDS.

Ventilator-Associated Pneumonia

Risk factors for ventilator-associated pneumonia (VAP) include impaired host defenses, invasive monitoring devices, aspiration (e.g., patients receiving EN), and prolonged mechanical ventilation. Implementing a ventilator bundle protocol reduces the incidence of VAP in mechanically ventilated patients (Table 32.8).[20]

Barotrauma

Barotrauma occurs when fragile alveoli are overdistended with excess pressure during mechanical ventilation. The high peak airway pressures needed to ventilate the lungs predispose patients with ARDS to barotrauma. It results in alveolar air escaping from ruptured alveoli. This can lead to pulmonary interstitial emphysema, pneumothorax, subcutaneous emphysema, pneumopericardium, and tension pneumothorax. Providing ventilation with a smaller V_T (e.g., 4 to 8 mL/kg) and varying amounts of PEEP minimizes the risk for barotrauma.

GI Ulcers

Patients with ARF and ARDS are at high risk for GI ulcers because the blood is diverted from the GI to the respiratory system to help meet the body's demand for O_2. Management strategies include correcting predisposing conditions, such as hypotension, shock, and acidosis. Prophylactic management includes antiulcer drugs, such as proton pump inhibitors (e.g., pantoprazole) and mucosal-protecting drugs (e.g., sucralfate). Early EN helps prevent mucosal damage.

Venous Thromboembolism (VTE)

ARDS patients are susceptible to the effects of immobility and venous stasis. They are at risk for deep vein thrombosis (DVT) and pulmonary emboli. Prophylactic management may include intermittent pneumatic compression stockings, anticoagulation, and, when possible, early ambulation.

Acute Kidney Injury

AKI can occur from decreased renal perfusion and subsequent decreased O_2 delivery to the kidneys. This most often occurs because of hypotension in septic shock. It may also result from hypoxemia or nephrotoxic drugs (e.g., vancomycin) used to treat ARDS-related infections. Monitor intake and output, daily weight, and daily creatinine and urea levels.

Patients in ARDS often receive continuous renal replacement therapy (CRRT). They are frequently hemodynamically unstable and need vasopressors and/or inotropes to maintain heart rate and BP. They cannot tolerate the large volumes of fluid that traditional hemodialysis would remove. CRRT is slow, gentle, and continuous. The patient can receive CRRT 24 hours a day. The overall mortality rate for ARDS patients is higher in those who need CRRT.[21]

Psychological Issues

Recovery is far from complete for the patient who survives ARDS. Survivors may have anxiety, issues with memory and attention, inability to focus, nightmares, depression, and in some instances, various degrees of posttraumatic stress disorder (PTSD). PTSD can occur in ARDS survivors up to 5 years later.[22]

NURSING AND INTERPROFESSIONAL MANAGEMENT: ARDS

Management of a patient with ARF (Table 32.4) and the nursing care plan for ARF (eNursing Care Plan 32.1 available on the website for this chapter) apply to patients with ARDS. The next section discusses additional care for the patient with ARDS (Table 32.9).

TABLE 32.8 Components of a Ventilator Bundle

- Good handwashing before, during (as needed), and after delivery of patient care
- Elevate head of the bed 30–45 degrees
- Daily assessment of readiness for extubation (see Chapter 28)
- GI ulcer prophylaxis (see Chapter 46)
- VTE prophylaxis (see Chapter 41)
- Daily oral care with chlorhexidine (0.12%) solution
- Strict infection control measures

Source: Institute for Healthcare Improvement: How-to guide: prevent VAP. Retrieved from www.ihi.org/resources/Pages/Tools/HowtoGuide-PreventVAP.aspx.

TABLE 32.9 Interprofessional Care

ARDS

General Care
- Hemodynamic monitoring
- Identify and treat underlying cause

Respiratory Therapy (see Chapter 28)
- O_2 administration
- Mechanical ventilation
  - Low V_T ventilation
  - Permissive hypercapnia
  - PEEP
- Positioning strategies (e.g., prone)
- Extracorporeal membrane oxygenation (ECMO)

Supportive Care
- Analgesia and sedation
- Neuromuscular blocking agents
- IV fluid administration (keep on the "dry" side)
- Inotropic and vasopressor drugs
  - norepinephrine
  - vasopressin
  - dopamine
  - dobutamine
- VAP prophylaxis
- Nutrition therapy
- VTE prophylaxis

◆ Assessment

Because ARDS is the most severe form of ARF, the subjective and objective data you should obtain from someone with ARDS are the same as those for ARF (Table 32.3). Patient information may not be possible to obtain on admission due to the urgent need to protect the airway (intubation), initiate mechanical ventilation, monitor vital signs, and assist with urgent treatments and procedures (e.g., inserting an arterial and/or central line, initiating vasopressors to maintain BP).

◆ Planning

With appropriate therapy, overall patient goals include a PaO_2 of 60 mm Hg or higher and adequate lung ventilation to help correct any acid-base imbalance. Longer-term goals include (1) PaO_2 within normal limits for age or at baseline on room air, (2) SaO_2 greater than 90%, (3) resolution of the cause(s), and (4) clear lungs on auscultation.

◆ Implementation

Patients with moderate to severe ARDS receive care in an ICU. The entire health care team has important roles in the care of the patient with ARDS.

Even with appropriate therapy, the clinical course of ARDS is complex and unpredictable. Patients often need several days of mechanical ventilation to allow time for the overwhelming inflammation and fluid accumulation in the lungs to begin resolving. All mechanically ventilated patients with ARDS in the ICU will have continuous heart rate, respiratory rate, BP, and SpO_2 monitoring. $EtCO_2$ monitoring is standard. Best practices for care of the patient with ARDS include (1) O_2 administration, (2) mechanical ventilation, (3) low V_T ventilation, (4) permissive hypercapnia, (5) PEEP, (6) prone positioning, and (7) extracorporeal membrane oxygenation (ECMO).[23]

◆ Respiratory Therapy

◆ Oxygen Administration

The primary goal of O_2 therapy is to correct hypoxemia. Initially, using a high-flow system that delivers higher O_2 concentrations to maximize O_2 delivery may be all that is needed. Continuously monitor SpO_2 to assess the effectiveness of O_2 therapy. However, for most patients diagnosed with ARDS, high-flow O_2 delivery, including BiPAP, is temporary. As respiratory failure worsens, high-flow O_2 will not be able to keep the PaO_2 within acceptable ranges. Patients with moderate to severe ARDS and refractory hypoxemia need mechanical ventilation to maintain an acceptable PaO_2. Even with mechanical ventilation, the patient may need an FIO_2 of 70% or higher to keep the PaO_2 at least 60 mm Hg. Most HCPs agree that in the injury and reparative phases, they may have to accept a lower-than-normal PaO_2 (e.g., PaO_2 55 to 80 mm Hg) and SpO_2 (88% to 95%).

◆ Mechanical Ventilation

Mechanical ventilation is required for the patient with moderate to severe ARDS. Pressure-control ventilation helps to keep the inspiratory and plateau pressures from becoming too high. This prevents alveolar overdistention and rupture. By reducing the amount of pressure going into the stiff, noncompliant lungs, we can help prevent further lung injury. However, no mode of mechanical ventilation is superior to the others.[23]

Low tidal volume (V_T) ventilation. Patients with ARDS are ventilated with a low V_T of 4 to 8 mL/kg.[24] Delivering a large V_T into stiff lungs can cause volutrauma and barotrauma. Volutrauma causes *alveolar fractures* (damage or tears in the alveolar capillary membrane) and the movement of fluids and protein into the alveolar spaces. Low V_T ventilation reduces mortality and the risk for volutrauma.

Permissive hypercapnia. As a result of delivering a lower-than-normal V_T to the patient with ARDS, the $PaCO_2$ level will slowly rise above normal limits. This is known as **permissive hypercapnia**. It is a consequence of low V_T ventilation, not a specific strategy. A $PaCO_2$ of up to 60 mm Hg is acceptable in the early phase of ARDS. The patient usually tolerates this rise in $PaCO_2$ if it is gradual, allowing the brain and systemic circulation to compensate. We do not use permissive hypercapnia with pregnant patients or those with TBI or increased ICP.

Frequent ABG samples are needed with careful monitoring of the pH, PaO_2, and $PaCO_2$ values. The pH is kept between 7.30 and 7.45. Acidosis and rising CO_2 levels are powerful stimulants to breathe. As a result, when permissive hypercapnia occurs, the patient usually receives continuous IV analgesia and sedation.

Positive end-expiratory pressure (PEEP). During PPV, it is common to apply PEEP at 5 cm H_2O to compensate for the loss of glottic function with an ET. PEEP increases functional residual capacity or the volume of air left in the lungs at the end of a normal expiration. PEEP helps open ("recruit") collapsed alveoli.

We typically apply PEEP in increments of 3 to 5 cm H_2O until oxygenation is adequate, with an FIO_2 of 60% or less (if possible). PEEP may improve ventilation in respiratory units that collapse at low airway pressures, thus allowing the FIO_2 to be lowered. Patients with ARDS may need higher levels of PEEP (e.g., 10 to 20 cm H_2O). There is no identified optimal level of PEEP for patients with ARDS.

PEEP is not without complications. The added intrathoracic and intrapulmonic pressures generated by positive pressure remaining in the lungs and transmitted to surrounding structures (e.g., inferior vena cava, heart) at end expiration can compromise venous return. This compromise can decrease the amount of blood returning to both the right and left sides of the heart. Dramatic reductions in preload, CO, and BP can occur. High levels of PEEP or excess inspiratory pressures can cause barotrauma and volutrauma.

◆ Prone Positioning

Prone positioning is an option for patients with refractory hypoxemia and ARDS who do not respond to other strategies to increase PaO_2. By turning the patient prone, perfusion may be better matched to ventilation (Fig. 32.11). Air-filled alveoli in the anterior part of the lung become dependent. Alveoli in the posterior part of the lungs are "recruited" (given the opportunity to re-expand), improving oxygenation.

Placing a patient prone requires an ICU intensivist, respiratory therapist, and at least 3 nurses. Special attention must be given to securing and maintaining the airway before, during, and after proning. Once prone, the patient needs reattached to hemodynamic monitoring equipment and positioned in a side-lying position.

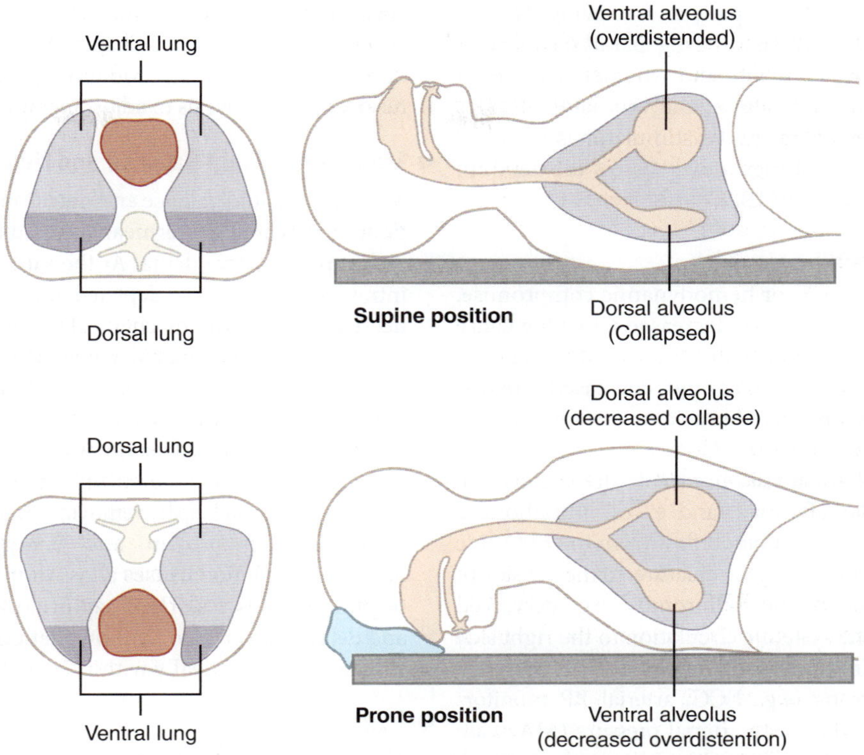

Fig. 32.11 Changes in the lung that occur because of prone positioning.

Some patients will have a big improvement in PaO_2 when prone. The improvement in oxygenation may be enough to allow a reduction in FIO_2 or PEEP. You may see hemodynamic instability (dysrhythmias, a decrease in BP) from fluid shifts while the patient is prone. There may be more need for airway suctioning as secretions are mobilized. Research suggests that patients be proned early in the course of ARDS. They can stay in the prone position for up to 16 hours per day.[25] We do not know the optimal length of time that a patient should be prone.

Alternatives to prone positioning include continuous lateral rotation therapy (CLRT) and kinetic therapy. CLRT provides continuous, slow, side-to-side turning by rotating the actual bed frame less than 40°. The bed moves laterally for 18 of every 24 hours to simulate postural drainage and help mobilize pulmonary secretions. Some beds have a vibration feature that provides chest physiotherapy. This assists with secretion mobilization and removal. Kinetic therapy is like CLRT, in that patients rotate side-to-side 40° or more. Obtain baseline assessments of the patient's pulmonary status (e.g., respiratory rate and rhythm, breath sounds, ABGs, SpO_2) and continue to monitor the patient throughout the therapy.

◆ Extracorporeal Membrane Oxygenation (ECMO)

ECMO is used most often in specialized ICUs in major cities. Like hemodialysis, a large blood vessel is cannulated (most often the internal jugular, femoral artery, or femoral vein), and a catheter is inserted. Blood exits the body through the catheter and enters the ECMO unit. There, O_2 is delivered into the blood, and CO_2 is removed. Oxygenated blood is returned to the patient. $ECCO_2R$ is like ECMO. It does not require as high blood flow rates. It is only used to enhance oxygenation. Both ECMO and $ECCO_2R$ are expensive and require specially trained nurses and other personnel.

◆ Supportive Therapy

◆ Analgesia and Sedation

Analgesia and sedation, either by direct IV or continuous IV infusion, are essential. Analgesia and sedation decrease the discomfort from having an ET tube, help reduce WOB, and prevent ventilator dyssynchrony.

Patients who breathe asynchronously with mechanical ventilation may benefit from adjusting ventilator inspiratory flow rates or other settings. Patients who stay asynchronous with mechanical ventilation despite aggressive analgesia and sedation may need a neuromuscular blocking agent (NMBA). These drugs, such as vecuronium or pancuronium, relax skeletal muscles and promote synchrony with mechanical ventilation. Remember that a patient receiving neuromuscular blockade can appear to be asleep but still be awake and in pain. For this reason, simultaneous administration of analgesia and sedation with NMBAs is essential.

! SAFETY ALERT

Neuromuscular Blockade

- Always give concurrent analgesia and sedation to patients receiving an NMBA. This eliminates patient awareness, ensures patient comfort, and avoids the terrifying experience of being awake and in pain while paralyzed.
- Use an NMBA for the shortest duration and at the lowest dose possible to avoid complications.

Monitoring sedation levels in patients receiving NMBA is challenging. We monitor levels of drug paralysis through assessment. Note the respiratory rate and whether the patient is taking breaths above the set rate on the ventilator. Besides $ETCO_2$ monitoring, a peripheral nerve stimulator is an additional adjunct used in some settings to help assess the depth of paralysis in a patient receiving NMBA.

◆ Promoting Tissue Perfusion

Patients with ARDS are at risk for hemodynamic compromise. Those on PPV and PEEP often have decreased CO. One cause is decreased venous return from the PEEP-induced increase in intrathoracic pressure. Dysrhythmias and decreased preload can decrease CO. Changes in intrathoracic or intrapulmonary pressures from PPV can also decrease CO.

Patients receiving PPV are at risk for alveolar hyperinflation, increased right ventricular afterload, and excess intrathoracic pressures. These changes can limit blood flow from the right side of the heart, through the pulmonary vasculature, to the left side of the heart and cause hemodynamic compromise (e.g., decreased CO). Blood return from the systemic circulation to the right side of the heart may be impaired, decreasing preload and CO.

Hemodynamic monitoring (e.g., ECG, arterial BP monitoring, SpO_2) is essential. BP and mean arterial pressure (MAP) are important indicators of the adequacy of CO. CVP may be ordered. Newer technologies permit us to monitor stroke volume variation, CO, and mixed venous oxygen saturation ($ScvO_2$ or SvO_2) non-invasively. Closely monitor BP and indicators of CO and tissue perfusion (SaO_2, mixed venous O_2 saturation) with the start of or changes in mechanical ventilation. A decrease in CO is treated with IV fluids, drugs, or both. Chapter 42 discusses drugs used to treat decreased CO and shock. Monitoring trends in hemodynamic status over time allows us to adjust therapy as needed.

◆ Maintaining Fluid Balance and Nutrition

Maintaining fluid balance and nutrition is challenging. Increasing pulmonary capillary permeability results in fluid in the lungs and causes pulmonary edema. At the same time, the patient may be intravascularly volume depleted and at risk for hypotension and decreased CO (from mechanical ventilation and PEEP).

Monitor hemodynamic parameters, urine output, and daily weights to assess fluid volume status. Monitor intake and output hourly. Keep the ARDS patient on the "dry" side. In other words, avoid aggressive resuscitation with IV fluids. Since ARDS is an inflammatory process, diuretics play a minimal role. Dialysis therapy, such as CRRT, can help by removing small amounts of fluid hourly.

Maintaining protein and energy stores is important. Nutrition depletion causes a loss of muscle mass, including the respiratory muscles. This may prolong mechanical ventilation and delay recovery. Consult the dietician. We should start EN as soon as possible, ideally within 24 to 48 hours.[26]

◆ Evaluation

The expected outcomes for the patient with ARDS are similar to those for a patient with ARF. The patient with ARDS should be able to maintain and sustain adequate oxygenation and ventilation with decreasing amounts of O_2, be hemodynamically stable, and be free of complications.

Case Study

Acute Respiratory Distress Syndrome

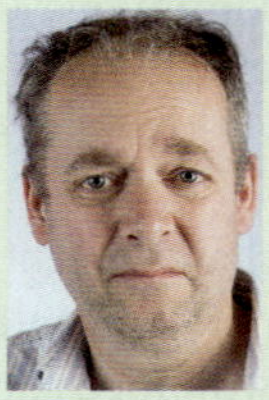

(© Thinkstock.)

Patient Profile

J.N., a 67-year-old male patient, was admitted 36 hours ago to the surgical ICU after emergent surgery for a small bowel obstruction, acute ischemic bowel, and perforated colon. He is intubated and mechanically ventilated.

Health History

- Mild obesity, hypertension, type 2 diabetes
- Lumbar spine surgery 5 years ago
- Chronic back pain controlled with ibuprofen 400 mg po q4–6hr as needed

Operative Procedure

- Surgery relieved small bowel obstruction, resected 2 feet of intestine, repaired the perforated colon, irrigated the abdominal cavity
- HR was 102 to 135, BP dropped to 70 mm Hg for 6 minutes, SpO_2 was greater than 90% for the duration of surgery
- Received 4 units of packed red blood cells and 5 L of 0.9% saline

Postoperative Status

J.N.'s condition worsened over the first 24 hours in the ICU. He became more tachycardic and hypotensive. J.N. continued to have declining SaO_2 levels, increased WOB, and worsening hemodynamic status. Despite direct IV analgesia and sedation, his respiratory rate increased. He was often "out-of-sync" with the ventilator and required progressively higher FIO_2. A chest x-ray showed bilateral pleural effusions and a right-sided pneumothorax, requiring chest tube placement. J.N. stayed dyssynchronous with the ventilator, so continuous IV analgesia and sedation infusions were ordered. NMBA was started to decrease his WOB and achieve ventilator synchrony.

Current Status

J.N. remains hemodynamically unstable, requiring IV norepinephrine to support his BP. He is still mechanically ventilated and is receiving 100% FIO_2 with PEEP 15 cm H_2O. His oxygenation continues to worsen. Urine output has greatly decreased over the past 6 hours. He was diagnosed with AKI, and CRRT is being considered. His wife has brought in a copy of his advance directives. They state he does not want to be kept alive by artificial means. J.N.'s wife and adult children are at the bedside and voicing concerns about his condition.

Objective Data

Physical Assessment

- *CNS:* Sedated, paralyzed. Head of bed elevated 30 degrees. Temperature 101°F (38.3°C) rectally
- *Cardiovascular:* BP 96/54 mm Hg. 2+ carotid, radial, and femoral pulses; 1+ dorsalis pedis pulses. Skin cool, slow capillary refill. ECG shows:

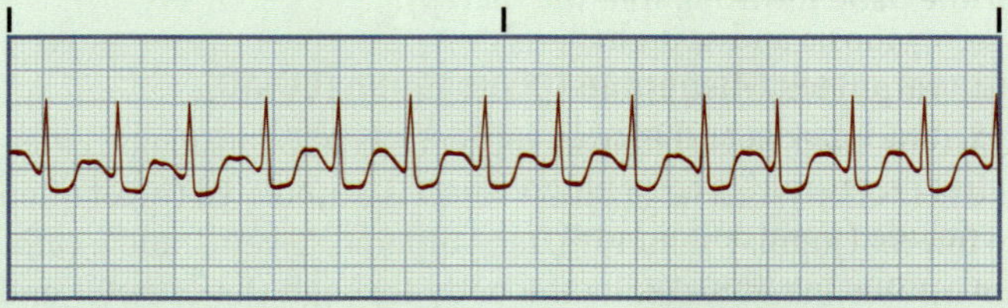

- *Respiratory:* Intubated, mechanically ventilated. No accessory muscle use or retractions. Respiratory rate 18 breaths/min and in sync with ventilator. SpO_2 88%, coarse crackles bilaterally throughout all lung fields. Ventilator settings: V_T 350 mL, FIO_2 100%, rate 18/min, PEEP 15 cm H_2O, peak inspiratory pressure 35 cm H_2O

Case Study—cont'd

Acute Respiratory Distress Syndrome

- *GI:* Surgical dressing dry and intact; colostomy draining a moderate amount of serosanguineous drainage. NG tube draining a small amount of dark brown fluid. Receiving EN at 50 mL/hr via small-bore feeding tube.
- *Renal:* Indwelling bladder catheter draining concentrated, dark amber urine less than 30 mL/hr.

Diagnostic Findings

- Chest x-ray: Bilateral, scattered interstitial infiltrates compatible with ARDS
- Current ABG: pH 7.23, PaO_2 59 mm Hg, $PaCO_2$ 57 mm Hg, HCO_3 16 mEq/L, O_2 saturation 88%.
- Hemoglobin 6.9 g/dL (69 g/L), WBC 20.6/μL (20.6×10^9/L)
- Increased BUN and creatinine values

Discussion Questions

1. ***Recognize:*** What is the cause of ARDS for J.N? Is this a direct or indirect cause?
2. ***Recognize:*** How does the pathophysiology of ARDS predispose him to refractory hypoxemia?
3. ***Analyze:*** What manifestations does J.N. have that support a diagnosis of ARDS?
4. ***Analyze:*** Calculate the PaO_2/FIO_2 ratio. What does this value tell you about the seriousness of his condition?
5. ***Analyze:*** What other complications is J.N. at risk for developing from ARDS?
6. ***Plan:*** You are orienting a new nurse who asks you why you allowed J.N.'s family to stay at the bedside during your physical assessment and morning rounds with the ICU team. How would you respond?
7. ***Prioritize:*** What priority interventions should be implemented to improve J.N.'s respiratory status and hypoxemia?
8. ***Act:*** What information would you give to J.N.'s family about his status?
9. ***Act:*** Given the patient's advance directives, what ethical/legal issues could you encounter?

Answers available at http://evolve.elsevier.com/Lewis/medsurg.

BRIDGE TO NCLEX EXAMINATION

The number of the question corresponds to the same-numbered outcome at the beginning of the chapter.

1. Which signs and symptoms lead the nurse to suspect hypoxemic rather than hypercapnic respiratory failure? *(select all that apply)*
   - **a.** Cyanosis
   - **b.** Tachypnea
   - **c.** Morning headache
   - **d.** Paradoxical breathing
   - **e.** Use of pursed-lip breathing
2. An important consideration in selecting an O_2 delivery device for the patient with acute hypoxemic respiratory failure is to
   - **a.** always start with noninvasive positive pressure ventilation.
   - **b.** apply a low-flow device, such as a nasal cannula or face mask.
   - **c.** be able to correct the PaO_2 to a normal level as quickly as possible.
   - **d.** base the selection on the patient's condition and amount of FIO_2 needed.
3. The *most* common early manifestations of ARDS that the nurse may see are
   - **a.** dyspnea and tachypnea.
   - **b.** cyanosis and apprehension.
   - **c.** respiratory distress and frothy sputum.
   - **d.** bradycardia and increased work of breathing.
4. Interventions used in managing the patient with ARDS include *(select all that apply)*
   - **a.** prone positioning.
   - **b.** IV injection of surfactant.
   - **c.** low tidal volume ventilation.
   - **d.** aggressive IV fluid resuscitation.
   - **e.** positive end expiratory pressure (PEEP).
5. Which intervention is *most* likely to prevent or limit volutrauma in the patient with ARDS who is mechanically ventilated?
   - **a.** Increasing PEEP
   - **b.** Increasing the inspiratory flow rate
   - **c.** Use of low tidal volume ventilation
   - **d.** Suctioning the patient via endotracheal tube hourly

1. a, b, d; 2. d; 3. a; 4. a, c, e; 5. c.

For rationales to these answers and even more NCLEX review questions, visit http://evolve.elsevier.com/Lewis/medsurg.

EVOLVE WEBSITE/RESOURCES LIST

http://evolve.elsevier.com/Lewis/medsurg
Review Questions (Online Only)
Key Points
Answer Keys to Questions
- Rationales for Bridge to NCLEX Examination Questions
- Answer Guidelines for Case Study

Student Case Studies
- Patient With Acute Respiratory Failure and Ventilatory Management
- Patient With Pulmonary Embolism and Respiratory Failure

Nursing Care Plans
- eNursing Care Plan 32.1: Patient With Acute Respiratory Failure

Conceptual Care Map Creator
Audio Glossary
Content Updates

REFERENCES

1. Stratton SJ: Acute respiratory failure. *BMJ Best Practice.* Retrieved from: https://bestpractice.bmj.com/topics/en-us/853.
2. Shebl E, Burns B: Respiratory failure. Retrieved from: https://www.ncbi.nlm.nih.gov/books/NBK526127/.
3. Stacy KM: Pulmonary anatomy and physiology. In Urden LD, Stacy KM, Lough ME, editors: *Critical care nursing: diagnosis and management*, ed 9, St. Louis, 2021, Elsevier.
4. Hess DR, Kacmarek RM: *Essentials of mechanical ventilation*, ed 4, New York, 2019, McGraw Hill.
5. Powers KA, Dhamoon AS: Physiology, pulmonary ventilation, and perfusion. Retrieved from: https://www.ncbi.nlm.nih.gov/books/NBK539907/.
6. Davis TM, Olff C: Acute respiratory failure and acute lung injury. In Good VS, Kirkwood PL, editors: *Advanced critical care Nursing*, ed 2, St. Louis, 2018, Elsevier.
7. Kayner AM: Respiratory failure clinical presentation. Retrieved from: https://emedicine.medscape.com/article/167981-clinical#b2.
8. Rackley CR: Monitoring during mechanical ventilation, *Resp Care* 65:832, 2020.
9. Kacmarek RM, Stoller JK, Heuer AJ: *Egan's fundamentals of respiratory care*, ed 12, St Louis, 2021, Elsevier.
10. Stang D, Case-Lo C: COPD and cough: How they're related and what you need to know. Retrieved from https://www.healthline.com/health/copd/coughing.
11. Levine AR, Stankiewicz J: Chest physiotherapy. Retrieved from: https://www.merckmanuals.com/professional/pulmonary-disorders/pulmonary-rehabilitation/chest-physiotherapy.
12. Fung C, Hackenson D: Acute respiratory failure: non-invasive ventilation and high flow nasal cannula. In Hyzy RC, McSparron J, editors: *Evidence-based critical care: a case study approach*, ed 2, Switzerland, 2020, Springer Nature.
13. Tran D, Rajwani K, Berlin DA: Pulmonary effects of aging, *Curr Opin Anaesthesiol* 31:19, 2018.
14. *Matthay MA, Zemans RL, Zimmerman GA, et al.: Ards, *Nat Rev Dis Primers* 5:18, 2019.
15. *Kaku S, Nguyen CD, Htet NN, et al.: ARDS: etiology, pathogenesis, and summary on management, *J Intens Care Med* 35:723, 2020.
16. *Saguil A, Fargo MV: ARDS: diagnosis and management, *Am Fam Physician* 101, 2020. 730.
17. *Gibson J, Loddenkemper R, Sibille Y, Lundback B, eds: ARDS. *European Lung White Book*. Retrieved from: https://www.erswhitebook.org/files/public/Chapters/20_ARDS.pdf.
18. *Kamo T, Tasaka S, Suzuki T, et al.: Prognostic values of the Berlin definition criteria, blood lactate level, and fibroproliferative changes on high-resolution computed tomography in ARDS patients, *BMC Pulm Med* 19:37, 2019.
19. Odeyemi Y, Moraes AGD, Gajic O: What factors predispose patients to ARDS?. In Deutschman CS, Neligan PJ, editors: *Evidence-based practice of critical care*, ed 3, St. Louis, 2020, Elsevier.
20. Kallet RH: Ventilator bundles in transition: from prevention of ventilator-associated pneumonia to prevention of ventilator-associated events, *Resp Care* 64:994, 2019.
21. *Panitchote A, Mehkri O, Hastings A, et al.: Clinical predictors of renal non-recovery in acute respiratory distress syndrome, *BMC Nephrol* 20:255, 2019.
22. Bein T, Bienvenu OJ, Hopkins RO: Focus on long-term cognitive, psychological and physical impairments after critical illness, *Intensive Care Med* 45:1466, 2019.
23. *Papazian L, Aubron C, Brochard L, et al.: Formal guidelines: management of acute respiratory distress syndrome, *Ann Intensive Care* 9:69, 2019.
24. Harmon EM: ARDS treatment and management. Retrieved from: https://emedicine.medscape.com/article/165139-treatment#d10.
25. *Lucchini A, Bambi S, Mattiussi E, et al.: Prone position in ARDS patients, *Dimen Crit Care Nursing* 39:39, 2020.
26. *Kopp Lugli A, de Watteville A, Hollinger A, et al.: Medical nutrition therapy in critically ill patients treated on intensive and intermediate care units: a literature review, *J Clin Med* 8:1395, 2019.

*Evidence-based information for clinical practice.

Case Study

Applying Clinical Judgment With Multiple Patients

You are assigned to care for the following 4 patients on a medical-surgical unit. You are sharing 1 AP with another RN.

(© Fuse/Thinkstock.)

F.T., a 70-year-old man with COPD, was admitted 2 days ago with bilateral lower lobe pneumonia. He is receiving IV antibiotics. Vital signs: 150/70, 94, RR 24, 99.4°F (37.4°C), O_2 saturation 96% on O_2 at 3 L/min via nasal cannula.

(© iStockphoto/Thinkstock.)

M.R., a 69-year-old man, is 6 days postoperative after a total laryngectomy with tracheostomy for laryngeal cancer. He developed pneumonia after surgery. He transferred from ICU at 0200 to accommodate a new patient. His last pain medication was 4 hours ago. He is awake, alert, but slightly confused. A tracheostomy tube is in place with O_2 via tracheal mask. Enteral feeding running at 30 mL/h via gastrostomy tube. Vital signs: 168/94, 84, RR 22, O_2 saturation 96%.

(© iStockphoto/Thinkstock.)

J.H. is a 52-year-old man with right lower lobe pneumonia and small cell lung cancer. He and his family are currently considering his treatment options. He is intermittently confused and anxious. Vital signs: 118/62, 106, RR 28 and shallow, 102.6°F (39.2°C), O_2 saturation 92% on O_2 at 4 L/min via nasal cannula.

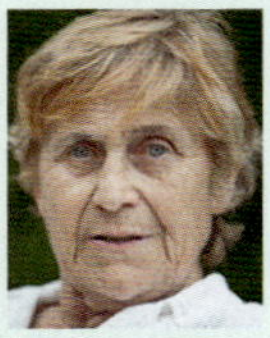

(© iStockphoto/Thinkstock.)

H.M. is a 68-year-old woman admitted 6 days ago with a COPD exacerbation. She has not been able to ambulate much because of her shortness of breath. She is on oral prednisone and ipratropium. She is being discharged later today. She is starting Advair Diskus and O_2 therapy at home.

1. Highlight all the findings above that require your follow-up.
2. After receiving report, which patient should you see first?

Case Study—cont'd

3. Which morning tasks can you delegate to the AP? *(select all that apply)*
   a. Take vital signs and a pulse oximetry reading on F.T.
   b. Assess M.R.'s pain level and show him how to administer his feeding.
   c. Assist H.M. with AM care and gather belongings in anticipation of discharge.
   d. Provide coffee for J.H.'s family as they await a family meeting with the HCP.
   e. Teach F.T. how to do pursed-lip breathing and titrate O_2 to maintain saturation >95%.
4. While you are assessing J.H., the AP tells you that H.M. is reporting chest pain and worsening shortness of breath. M.R. is requesting pain medication. What should you do *first*?
   a. Ask the AP to get H.M.'s vital signs while you give M.R. pain medication.
   b. Ask the AP to increase H.M.'s O_2 to L/min while you assess M.R.'s pain.
   c. Ask the AP to obtain a stat 12-lead ECG on H.M. while you perform a focused cardiac and respiratory assessment.
   d. Ask the AP to have another RN give M.R. his pain medication while you go directly to H.M.'s room.

Case Study Progression

After assessing H.M., you notify her HCP. A stat 12-lead ECG is done, and a blood sample is drawn to check cardiac enzymes. H.M.'s chest pain is not relieved by sublingual nitroglycerin. You then give 1 mg IV morphine. H.M. states that her pain is "a little better" but continues to report dyspnea. The 12-lead ECG and cardiac enzyme results are all within normal limits.

5. Based on these findings, you recognize that H.M. may be experiencing ______1______ and anticipate the HCP will order ______2______ to determine the cause of her symptoms.

Options for 1	Options for 2
Acute heart failure	BNP and echocardiogram
Pneumothorax	D-dimer and spiral CT scan
Pulmonary embolism	ABGs and chest x-ray

6. While the transport nurse goes with H.M. to the radiology department, you turn your attention back to your remaining 3 patients. You see that you need to complete M.R.'s medication reconciliation after his transfer and prepare his morning medications. Choose the most likely options for the information missing from the table below by selecting from the lists of options provided.

Medication	Dose, Route, Frequency	Drug Class	Indication
acetaminophen	1	Analgesic; antipyretic	Reduce pain and fever
2	40 mg subcut daily	Anticoagulant	VTE prophylaxis
ceftriaxone	1 gram IV q12hr	Cephalosporin	3
albuterol nebulizer	2.5 mg q6hr as needed	4	Bronchodilation

Medication	Dose, Route, Frequency	Drug Class	Indication
Options for 1	***Options for 2***	***Options for 3***	***Options for 4***
325 mg rectal q 4 hr as needed 650 mg PEG q 6 hr as needed 1000 mg PEG q 6hr as needed	Enoxaparin Heparin Warfarin	Chemotherapy for laryngeal cancer Relieve dry mouth Treat postoperative pneumonia	β_2-adrenergic agonist Corticosteroid Leukotriene modifier

7. Before giving M.R.'s 0900 enteral feeding, you find his PEG tube clogged. Which action would you take *next*?
   a. Flush the tube with warm water, using a back-and-forth motion.
   b. Obtain an x-ray to confirm the tube is still placed in the stomach.
   c. Notify the HCP so that surgery to insert new tube can be scheduled.
   d. Instill 30 mL of cranberry juice into the tube and recheck in 1 hour.
8. You perform F.T.'s assessment and update his plan of care.
   For each assessment finding, use an X to indicate whether the interventions were Effective (helped to meet expected outcomes), Ineffective (did not help to meet expected outcomes), or Unrelated (not related to the expected outcomes).

Assessment Finding	Effective	Ineffective	Unrelated
Lungs have bibasilar coarse crackles			
Peripheral edema is 3+ bilaterally			
Can perform active range of motion without dyspnea			
Heart rate 80/min, regular			
Restlessness, slightly confused			
Afebrile			
Normal bowel sounds			
Clear sputum			

9. J.H.'s son calls you on the telephone to ask about his father's current condition and long-term prognosis. Which initial response would be most appropriate?
   a. Ask the person what the code word is to identify himself as family.
   b. Empathize with the son's need to know his father's long-term prognosis.
   c. Tell him you are not allowed to discuss any information over the telephone.
   d. Ask J.H.'s son what the HCP has told him to clarify his understanding of the situation.

Answers available at http://evolve.elsevier.com/Lewis/medsurg.

33

Assessment: Hematologic System

Sandra Irene Rome

http: //evolve.elsevier.com/Lewis/medsurg/

CONCEPTUAL FOCUS

Clotting
Functional Ability
Gas Exchange
Infection
Perfusion

LEARNING OUTCOMES

1. Describe the structures and functions of the hematologic system.
2. Distinguish between the different types of blood cells and their functions.
3. Explain the process of hemostasis.
4. Link the age-related changes in the hematologic system to differences in findings of hematologic studies.
5. Obtain subjective and objective assessment data related to the hematologic system from a patient.
6. Perform a physical assessment of the hematologic system using the appropriate techniques.
7. Distinguish normal from common abnormal findings of a physical assessment of the hematologic system.
8. Describe the purpose, significance of results, and nursing responsibilities related to diagnostic studies of the hematologic system.

KEY TERMS

ecchymoses
erythropoiesis
fibrinolysis
hematopoiesis
hemolysis
leukopenia
neutropenia
pancytopenia
petechiae
reticulocyte
thrombocytopenia
thrombocytosis

Hematology is the study of blood and blood-forming tissues. This includes the bone marrow, blood, spleen, and lymph system. You need a basic knowledge of hematology to be able to evaluate several important concepts in the clinical setting. A functioning hematologic system supports our ability to transport oxygen (O_2), carbon dioxide (CO_2), nutrients, wastes, and electrolytes. It maintains intravascular volume, coagulates blood, and combats infections.[1]

STRUCTURES AND FUNCTIONS OF HEMATOLOGIC SYSTEM

Bone Marrow

Blood cell production (**hematopoiesis**) occurs within the bone marrow. *Bone marrow* is the soft material that fills the central core of bones. There are 2 types of bone marrow, yellow (adipose) and red (hematopoietic). Red marrow actively makes blood cells. In adults, we find red marrow mainly in the flat and irregular bones. These include the ends of long bones, pelvic bones, vertebrae, sacrum, sternum, ribs, flat cranial bones, and scapulae.

All 3 types of blood cells (red blood cells [RBCs], white blood cells [WBCs], platelets) develop from a common hematopoietic stem cell in the bone marrow. The hematopoietic *stem cell* is best described as an immature blood cell that can self-renew and differentiate into hematopoietic precursor cells. Several types of blood cells form as the cells mature and differentiate (Fig. 33.1).

The bone marrow responds by a negative feedback system to the need for specific blood cells by increasing that cell's

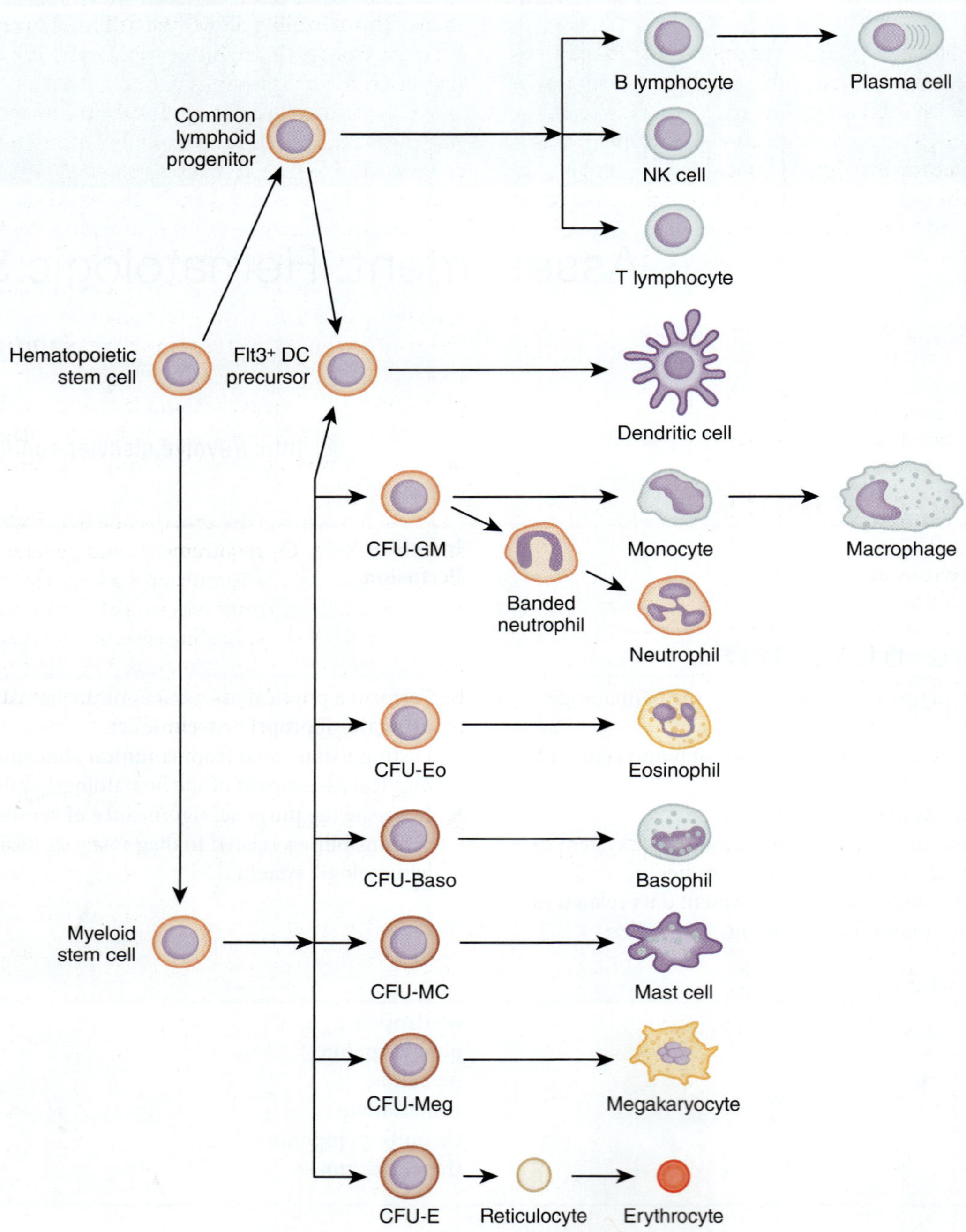

Fig. 33.1 Development of blood cells.

production. Various factors or cytokines (e.g., erythropoietin, granulocyte colony-stimulating factor [G-CSF], stem cell factor, thrombopoietin) stimulate the bone marrow. This results in stem cells differentiating into one of the committed hematopoietic cells (e.g., RBC). For example, when tissue hypoxia occurs, the kidney secretes erythropoietin. It circulates to the bone marrow and causes proerythroblasts to differentiate in the bone marrow.[1]

Blood

Blood is a type of connective tissue. It has 3 major functions: transportation, regulation, and protection (Table 33.1). Blood has 2 major components: plasma and blood cells. In an adult weighing between 150 and 180 lb, the volume of blood is between 4.7 and 5.5 L (5 to 6 quarts).

Plasma

About 55% of blood is plasma (Fig. 33.2).[1] Plasma is composed mainly of water. It also contains proteins, electrolytes, gases, nutrients (e.g., glucose, amino acids, lipids), and waste. The term *serum* refers to plasma minus its clotting factors. Plasma proteins include albumin, globulin, and clotting factors (mostly fibrinogen). Albumin is a protein that helps maintain oncotic pressure in the blood.[1] The liver makes most plasma proteins. The exception is antibodies (immunoglobulins). They are made by plasma cells.

Blood Cells

About 45% of the blood (Fig. 33.2) is composed of formed elements, or blood cells. The 3 types of blood cells are *erythrocytes* (RBCs), *leukocytes* (WBCs), and *thrombocytes* (platelets). The main function of RBCs is O_2 transportation. WBCs help protect the body from infection. Platelets promote blood coagulation.

Erythrocytes. The main functions of RBCs include transport of gases (both O_2 and CO_2) and assistance in maintaining acid-base balance. RBCs are flexible cells with a unique biconcave shape. This flexibility allows the cell to change its shape so that it can easily pass through tiny capillaries. The cell membrane is thin to promote diffusion of gases.

RBCs are mainly composed of a large molecule called *hemoglobin.* Hemoglobin is a complex protein-iron compound composed of heme (an iron compound) and globin (a simple protein). It binds with O_2 and CO_2. As RBCs circulate through the capillaries surrounding alveoli within the lung, O_2 attaches to iron on the hemoglobin. We refer to this O_2-bound hemoglobin as *oxyhemoglobin.* It gives arterial blood its bright red appearance. As RBCs flow to body tissues, O_2 detaches from the hemoglobin and diffuses from the capillary into tissue cells. CO_2 diffuses from tissue cells into the capillary, attaches to the globin part of hemoglobin, and is transported to the lungs for removal. Hemoglobin acts as a buffer and plays a role in maintaining acid-base balance. This buffering function is described in Chapter 17.

Erythropoiesis is the process of RBC production. It is regulated by cellular O_2 requirements and general metabolic activity. Erythropoiesis is stimulated by hypoxia and controlled by *erythropoietin,* a glycoprotein growth factor made and released mainly by the kidney. Erythropoietin stimulates the bone marrow to increase RBC production. We make about 2.5 million RBCs per second. The normal life span of RBCs is about 120 days. We need many essential nutrients for erythropoiesis.

TABLE 33.1 Functions of Blood

Function	Examples
Protection	• Homeostasis of blood coagulation • Combating invasion of pathogens and other foreign substances
Regulation	• Fluid and electrolyte balance • Acid-base balance • Body temperature • Intravascular oncotic pressure
Transportation	• O_2 from lungs to cells • Nutrients from GI tract to cells • Hormones from endocrine glands to tissues and cells • Metabolic waste products (e.g., CO_2, NH_3, urea) from cells to lungs, liver, kidneys

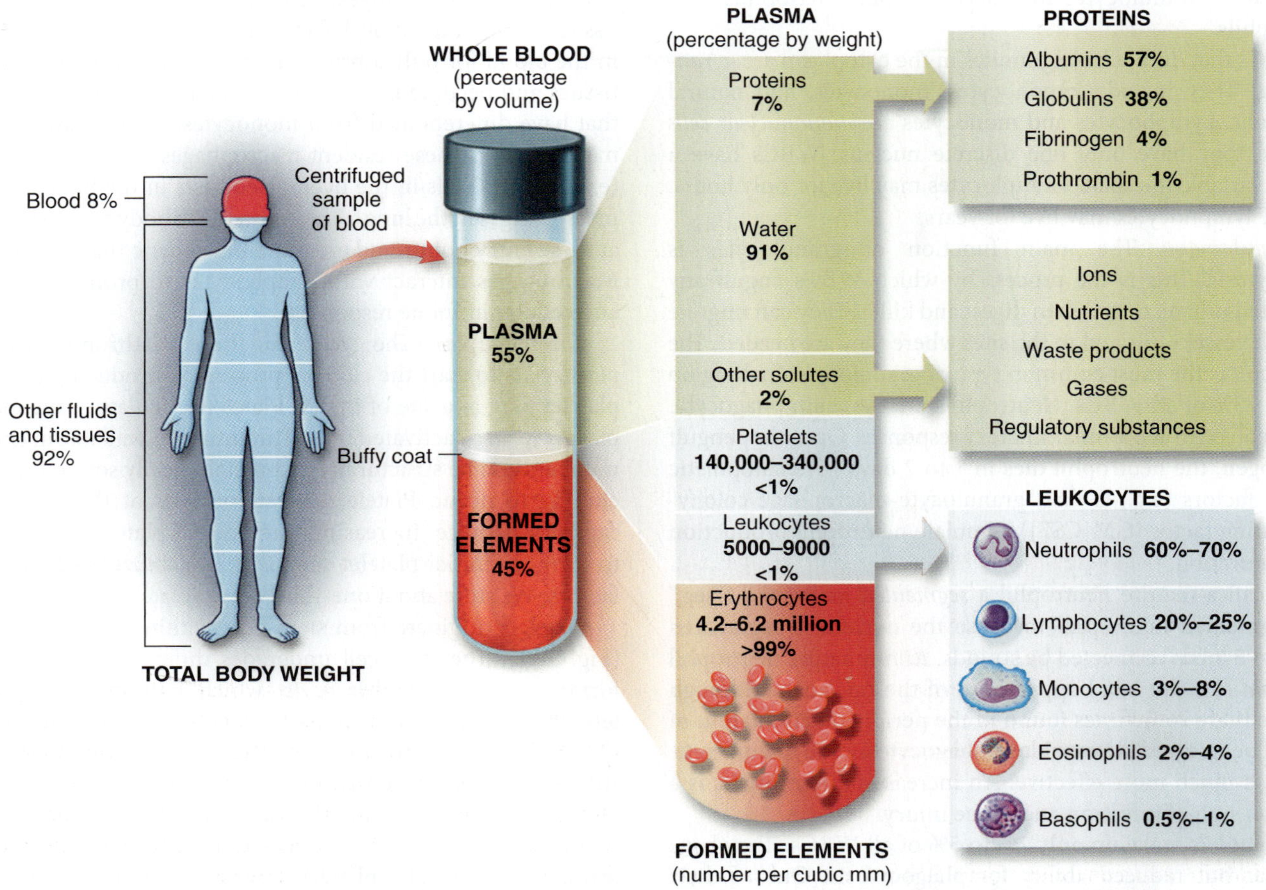

Fig. 33.2 Blood components in a healthy adult. Normally, 45% of the blood is composed of blood cells and 55% is composed of plasma. (From Patton KT, Thibodeau GA: *The human body in health and disease,* ed 7, St Louis, 2018, Mosby.)

These include protein, iron, folate (folic acid), cobalamin (vitamin B_{12}), riboflavin (vitamin B_2), pyridoxine (vitamin B_6), pantothenic acid, niacin, ascorbic acid (vitamin C), copper, and vitamin E. Endocrine hormones, such as thyroxine, corticosteroids, and testosterone, affect RBC production. For example, hypothyroidism may cause anemia.[2]

Several distinct cell types evolve during RBC maturation (Fig. 33.1). The **reticulocyte** is an immature RBC. Reticulocytes can develop into mature RBCs within 48 hours of release into the circulation. A mature RBC lacks a nucleus and cannot undergo mitotic division. Assessing the number of reticulocytes is a useful way to evaluate the rate and adequacy of RBC production.[1]

Hemolysis (destruction of RBCs) by monocytes and macrophages removes abnormal, defective, damaged, and old RBCs from circulation. Hemolysis normally occurs in the bone marrow, liver, and spleen. Because bilirubin is a component of RBCs, hemolysis results in increased bilirubin that our body must process. When hemolysis occurs by normal mechanisms, the liver conjugates and excretes all the bilirubin in bile.

Leukocytes. *Leukocytes* (WBCs) appear white when separated from blood. Like the RBCs, WBCs originate from stem cells within the bone marrow (Fig. 33.1). They may eventually reside in the thymus or secondary lymphoid tissues, such as the spleen, lymph nodes, and Peyer patches. There are several types of WBCs. Each has a different function. WBCs that have granules in the cytoplasm are *granulocytes* (or *polymorphonuclear leukocytes*). Granulocytes include neutrophils, basophils, and eosinophils.

WBCs that do not have granules in the cytoplasm are *agranulocytes.* They include lymphocytes, monocytes, and natural killer cells. Lymphocytes and monocytes are *mononuclear cells* because they have only one discrete nucleus. WBCs have a widely variable life span. Granulocytes may live for only hours. Some T lymphocytes may live for years.

Granulocytes. The main function of granulocytes is *phagocytosis.* This is the process by which WBCs engulf any unwanted organism and then digest and kill it. They can migrate through vessel walls and to the sites where they are needed. The *neutrophil* is the most common type of granulocyte, making up 65% to 75% of all WBCs. Neutrophils are the main phagocytic cells involved in acute inflammatory responses. Once they engulf a pathogen, the neutrophil dies in 1 to 2 days.[1] Hematopoietic growth factors (e.g., G-CSF, granulocyte-macrophage colony-stimulating factor [GM-CSF]) stimulate neutrophil production and maturation.

We call a mature neutrophil a *segmented neutrophil* ("seg," polysegmented neutrophil) because the nucleus is segmented into 2 to 5 lobes connected by strands. An immature neutrophil is a *band* (for the band appearance of the nucleus). Although band cells are sometimes found in the peripheral circulation of normal people and are capable of phagocytosis, the mature neutrophil is much more effective. An increase in neutrophils is a common sign of infection and tissue injury.

Eosinophils make up only 2% to 5% of all WBCs. They have a similar but reduced ability for phagocytosis. One of their main functions is to engulf antigen-antibody complexes formed during an allergic response. High eosinophil levels occur with some cancers, such as Hodgkin lymphoma, in parasitic infections, and in various skin diseases and connective tissue disorders.[1]

Basophils make up less than 1% of all WBCs. They have cytoplasmic granules that contain chemical mediators, such as heparin and histamine. A basophil responds to stimulation by an antigen or by tissue injury by releasing substances from the granules. This is part of the response seen in allergic and inflammatory reactions. *Mast cells* are like basophils, but they reside in connective tissues. They play a key role in inflammation, blood vessel permeability, and smooth muscle contraction.[1]

Lymphocytes. Lymphocytes make up 20% to 25% of the WBCs in the blood.[1] They form the basis of cellular and humoral immune responses. Two lymphocyte subtypes are B cells and T cells. T-cell precursors originate in the bone marrow. They migrate to the thymus gland for further differentiation into T cells. *Natural killer (NK) cells* are lymphocytes that kill virus-infected cells and activate T cells and phagocytes. They do not need prior exposure to antigens. Dendritic cells are the main phagocytic cells in the peripheral organs and skin. Most lymphocytes briefly circulate in the blood and reside in lymphoid and other tissues. See Chapter 14 for more about lymphocyte function.

Monocytes. Monocytes, the other type of agranular WBC, make up about 3% to 8% of the total WBCs.[1] They are potent phagocytic cells that ingest matter, such as bacteria, dead cells, tissue debris, and old or defective RBCs. These cells are present in the blood for only a brief time before they migrate into the tissues and become macrophages. In addition to macrophages that have differentiated from monocytes, tissues have resident macrophages. These resident macrophages have special names (e.g., Kupffer cells in the liver, osteoclasts in the bone, alveolar macrophages in the lung). They protect the body from pathogens at these entry points and are more phagocytic than monocytes. Macrophages interact with lymphocytes to promote humoral and cellular immune responses.

Thrombocytes. The main function of thrombocytes, or *platelets,* is to start the clotting process by producing an initial platelet plug at a site of injury. Platelets circulate suspended in plasma in an unactivated state. They must be available in enough numbers and be structurally and metabolically sound for blood clotting to occur. Platelet activation starts at the site of any capillary damage. Increasing numbers of platelets accumulate to form an initial platelet plug that is stabilized with clotting factors. We store about one-third of our platelets in the spleen.

Platelets originate from stem cells within the bone marrow (Fig. 33.1). The stem cell undergoes differentiation by transforming into a *megakaryocyte,* which fragments into platelets. Platelet production is partly regulated by *thrombopoietin* (TPO). TPO is a growth factor that acts on bone marrow to stimulate platelet production. It is mainly made in the liver. During inflammation, interleukin 6 (IL-6) causes us to make more TPO, which increases platelet production and potential thrombosis. Typically, platelets have a life span of only 8 to 11 days.

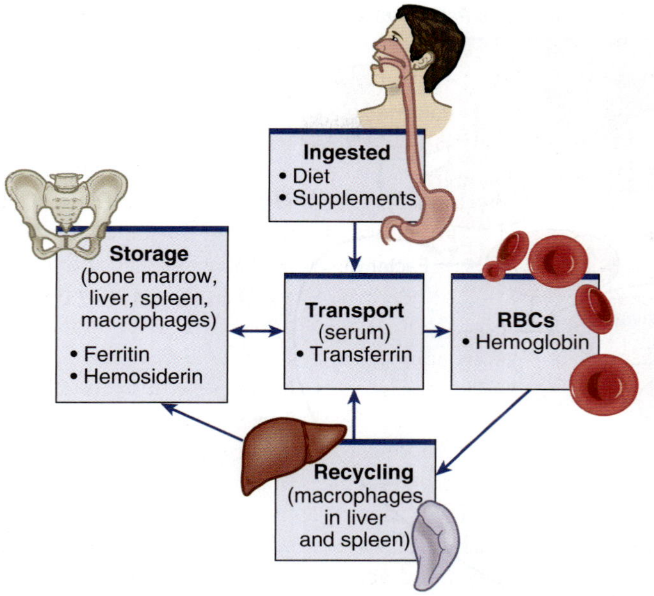

Fig. 33.3 Normal iron metabolism. Iron is ingested in the diet or from supplements. Macrophages break down ingested RBCs. Iron is returned to blood bound to transferrin or stored as ferritin or hemosiderin.

Normal Iron Metabolism

Our iron requirement is 25 mg daily. We get iron from food and supplements. Our body absorbs only 1 to 2 mg of iron from our diet. The rest comes from the continued recycling of iron from RBCs.[1] As part of normal iron metabolism, iron is recycled after macrophages in the liver and spleen phagocytize, or ingest and destroy, old and damaged RBCs.

After dietary iron is absorbed in the duodenum and proximal jejunum, transferrin transports it through the plasma (Fig. 33.3). Transferrin is made in the liver. How much iron is bound to transferrin is a reliable indicator of the iron supply for developing RBCs.

About two-thirds of total body iron is bound to heme in RBCs (hemoglobin) and muscle cells (myoglobin). We store the other one-third as ferritin and hemosiderin (degraded form of ferritin) in the bone marrow, spleen, liver, and macrophages (Fig. 33.3). When we do not replace stored iron, hemoglobin production is reduced. Normally, there is very little iron loss except from blood loss. We lose about 3% daily in urine, sweat, bile, and epithelial cells in the gastrointestinal (GI) tract.

Normal Clotting Mechanisms

Hemostasis describes the arrest of bleeding. This process is important in minimizing blood loss when body structures are injured. The sequence of events includes (1) vascular injury, vasoconstriction, and subendothelial exposure; (2) adhesion; (3) activation of the clotting cascade; (4) formation of a blood clot; and (5) clot retraction and dissolution.[1]

Vascular Injury, Vasoconstriction, and Subendothelial Exposure

When a blood vessel is injured, an immediate local vasoconstrictive response occurs. Vasoconstriction reduces blood leakage from the vessel by restricting the vessel size and pressing the endothelial surfaces together. The latter reaction enhances vessel wall stickiness and keeps the vessel closed after vasoconstriction subsides. Vascular spasm may last for 20 to 30 minutes. This allows time for the body to activate the platelet response and plasma clotting factors. The platelet response and plasma clotting factors are triggered by endothelial injury and the release of substances such as thromboxane A_2 (TXA_2) von Willebrand factor (vWF) and clotting factor VIII. Platelets begin to fill endothelial gaps.[1]

Adhesion

The loss of endothelial cells exposes adhesive glycoproteins, such as collagen and vWF, to which more platelets adhere. The stickiness is termed *adhesiveness.* The formation of clumps is termed *aggregation* or *agglutination.*

Clotting Cascade Activation

The interactions thus far cause the platelets to undergo an activation process. This leads to changes in platelet shape. The platelets then can bind adhesive proteins, including fibrinogen and vWF. Release of various platelet granules (including adenosine phosphate [ADP]) recruits and activates other platelets, clotting factors, and growth factors. As Fig. 33.4 shows, platelet lipoproteins stimulate necessary conversions in the clotting process.

Blood Clot Formation

Platelet aggregation is stimulated by TXA_2 and ADP, which induce fibrinogen receptors on the platelet. The formation of a visible fibrin clot on the platelet plug is the conclusion of a complex series of reactions involving different clotting (coagulation) factors. We label plasma clotting factors with both names and Roman numerals (Table 33.2).[3] Most are glycoproteins made in the liver. Monocytes, endothelial cells, and megakaryocytes make a few clotting factors. Some are enzymes that circulate in an inactive form (zymogens).[3]

Plasma proteins circulate in inactive forms until stimulated to start clotting through the intrinsic or extrinsic pathway (Fig. 33.4). The *intrinsic pathway* is activated by collagen exposure from endothelial injury when the blood vessel is damaged. The *extrinsic pathway* is activated when tissue factor or tissue thromboplastin is released from injured tissues.

Regardless of how we begin to clot, coagulation ultimately follows the same final common pathway of the clotting cascade. Thrombin, in the common pathway, is the most powerful enzyme in the coagulation process (Fig. 33.4). It converts fibrinogen to fibrin, which is an essential part of a blood clot. The final blood clot is a meshwork of protein strands that stabilizes the platelet plug and traps other cells, such as RBCs, phagocytes, and microorganisms.

Clot Retraction and Dissolution

Just as some blood elements foster coagulation *(procoagulants),* others interfere with clotting *(anticoagulants).* This counter mechanism to blood clotting keeps blood in its fluid state.

Antithrombin activity, vessel and platelet activity, and fibrinolysis contribute to anticoagulation. As the name implies, antithrombins keep blood in a fluid state by antagonizing thrombin,

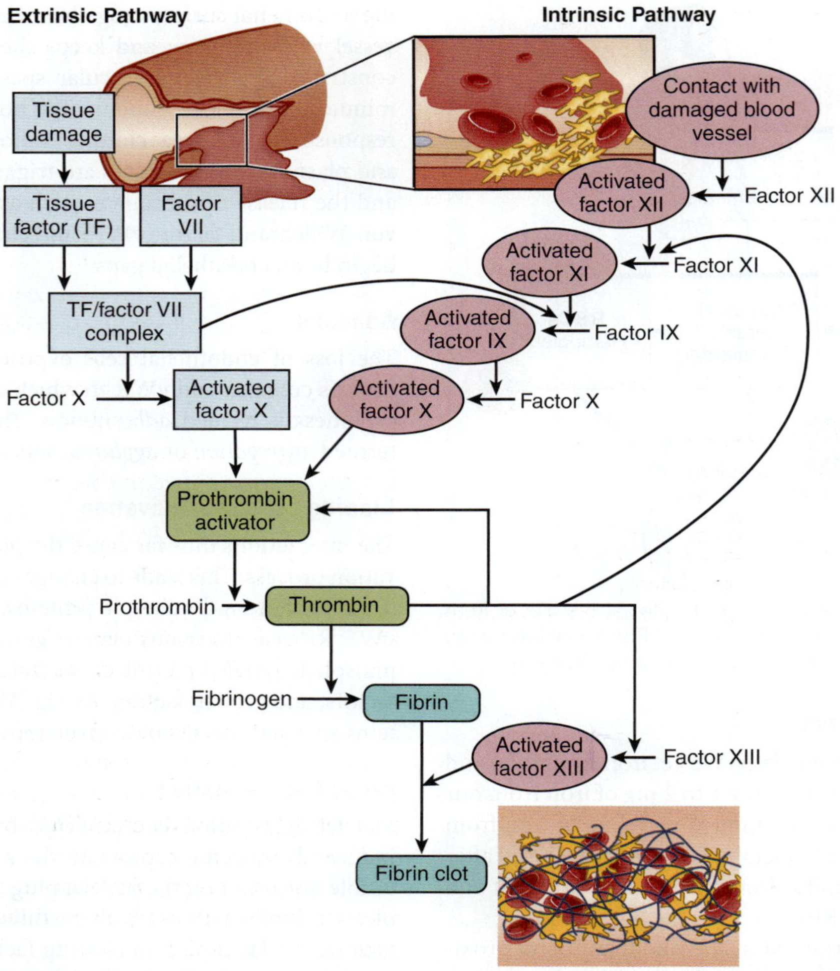

Fig. 33.4 Coagulation mechanism showing steps in the intrinsic pathway and extrinsic pathway as they would occur in the test tube.

a powerful coagulant. Endogenous heparin, antithrombin III, protein C, and protein S are examples of anticoagulants.

The second way we keep blood in its fluid form is **fibrinolysis**, a process resulting in the dissolution of the fibrin clot. The fibrinolytic system starts when plasminogen is activated by substances such as tissue plasminogen activator (t-PA) and urokinase-like plasminogen activator (u-PA) to plasmin (Fig. 33.5). Thrombin can activate the conversion of plasminogen to plasmin, promoting fibrinolysis. Plasmin attacks either fibrin or fibrinogen by splitting the molecules into smaller elements called *fibrin split products* (FSPs) or *fibrin degradation products* (FDPs). You can find more about FSPs in Table 33.8 and in the section on disseminated intravascular coagulation (DIC) in Chapter 34.

Excessive fibrinolysis predisposes the patient to bleeding. In this situation, bleeding results from the destruction of fibrin in platelet plugs or from the anticoagulation effects of increased FSPs. Increased FSPs lead to impaired platelet aggregation, reduced prothrombin, and an inability to stabilize fibrin.

Spleen

The spleen is the largest lymphoid organ. It is found in the upper left quadrant of the abdomen. The spleen has 4 major functions: hematopoietic, filtration, immunologic, and storage. The hematopoietic function is shown by the spleen's ability to make RBCs during fetal development. Through filtration, the mononuclear phagocyte system in the spleen removes old and defective RBCs from the circulation. The spleen can catabolize hemoglobin released by hemolysis and return the iron part of the hemoglobin to the bone marrow for reuse. The spleen filters circulating bacteria, especially encapsulated organisms such as gram-positive cocci. The spleen's rich supply of lymphocytes, monocytes, and stored immunoglobulins plays a role in immunologic function. The spleen is a storage site for RBCs and platelets. It can store more than 300 mL of blood. We store about one-third of platelets in the spleen.

Lymph System

The lymph system, consisting of lymph, lymphatic capillaries, ducts, and lymph nodes, carries fluid from the interstitial spaces to the blood. It is through the lymph that proteins and fat from the GI tract and certain hormones can return to the circulatory system. The lymph system also returns excess interstitial fluid to the blood.

Lymph is pale yellow interstitial fluid that has diffused through lymphatic capillary walls. The lymph vessels collect interstitial fluid from the tissues and transport it as lymph through vessels. Eventually, lymph enters the thoracic duct,

TABLE 33.2 Coagulation Factors

Coagulation Factor	Action
I Fibrinogen	Source of fibrin to form a clot
II Prothrombin	Converted to thrombin, which then activates fibrinogen into fibrin as well as factors V, VII, VIII, XI, XIII, protein C, for clot stabilization
III Tissue factor, tissue thromboplastin	Released from damaged endothelial cells and activates the extrinsic pathway by reacting with factor VII
IV Calcium	Required cofactor at several points in the coagulation cascade
V Proaccelerin (labile) factor	Binds with factor X to activate prothrombin
VII Stable factor, proconvertin	Forms a complex with factor III (tissue factor) and activates factors IX and X
VIII Antihemophilic factor	Works with factor IX and calcium to activate factor X
IX Christmas factor	Together with factor VIII, activates factor X
X Stuart factor	Activates conversion of factor II (prothrombin) to thrombin
XI Plasma thromboplastin antecedent	Activates factor IX when calcium is present
XII Hageman factor	Activates factor XI, which starts the intrinsic pathway
XIII Fibrin-stabilizing factor	Cross-links fibrin strands and stabilizes fibrin clot

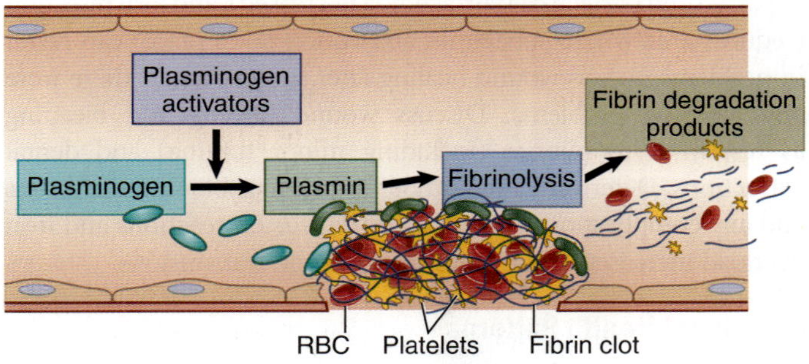

Fig. 33.5 Fibrinolytic system.

which drains into the superior vena cava. Lymph formation increases when interstitial fluid increases. This forces more fluid into the lymph system. When too much interstitial fluid develops or when something interferes with the reabsorption of lymph, *lymphedema* develops. Lymphedema may occur as a complication of mastectomy or lumpectomy with dissection of axillary nodes. In this case, lymphedema is caused by the obstruction of lymph flow from the removal of lymph nodes.

The lymphatic capillaries are thin-walled vessels that have an irregular diameter. They are larger than blood capillaries and do not have valves.

The *lymph nodes* are also part of the lymph system. Their main function is to filter pathogens and foreign particles that are carried by lymph to the nodes. They are round, oval, or bean shaped. Structurally, the nodes are small clumps of lymph tissue. They are found in groups along lymph vessels at various sites. There are more than 200 lymph nodes throughout the body. The greatest number is in the abdomen surrounding the GI tract. They vary in size according to their location. We have both superficial and deep lymph nodes. We can palpate superficial nodes. Evaluating deep nodes requires radiologic examination.[4]

Liver

The liver has metabolic, secretory, vascular, immune, and storage functions.[1,3] It makes all the procoagulants we need for hemostasis and blood coagulation and secretes bilirubin and bile. It stores iron that exceeds tissue needs, which can occur with blood transfusions or diseases that cause iron overload. *Hepcidin,* made by the liver, is a key regulator of iron balance. Iron overload or inflammation stimulates hepcidin synthesis. Hepcidin inhibits the release of stored iron from enterocytes (in the intestines) and macrophages. So, when iron is deficient, hepatocytes make less hepcidin. This results in the release of stored iron and an increase in dietary absorption. Other liver functions are described in Chapters 43 and 48.

Gerontologic Considerations: Effects of Aging on Hematologic System

Aging leads to a decrease in bone marrow mass and cellularity and an increase in bone marrow fat.[5] At birth, hematopoietic tissue occupies 80% to 100% of the marrow space. This is reduced to 50% at age 30 and 30% at age 70.[5] Although the older adult can still maintain adequate blood cell levels, the reduced reserve capacity leaves them more vulnerable to possible problems with clotting, transporting O_2, and fighting infection, especially during periods of increased demand. This contributes to their having a decreased ability to compensate for an acute or chronic illness.

Hemoglobin levels may begin to decrease in both men and women after middle age. Low-normal levels occur in most older people. Total serum iron, total iron-binding capacity, and intestinal iron absorption are all decreased. The RBC plasma membranes are more fragile. This may account for a slight increase in mean corpuscular volume (MCV) and a slight decrease in mean corpuscular hemoglobin concentration (MCHC) of RBCs in some older adults. While iron deficiency may cause low hemoglobin levels, other factors, such as GI bleeding, renal disease, testosterone deficiency, or bone marrow dysfunction, should be ruled out.[3] In 30% to 40% of cases, there is no specific cause of anemia. We call this "unexplained anemia."[6] Healthy older patients are not able to make reticulocytes in response to hemorrhage or hypoxemia as well as younger adults. This is likely due to a blunted response to erythropoietin.[3]

Aging generally does not affect the total WBC count and differential. There may be a slight increase in neutrophils and a decrease in lymphocytes. The function of lymphocytes decreases, blunting the response to infection.[3] During an infection, the older adult may have only a minimal elevation in the total WBC count. This suggests decreased bone marrow reserve of granulocytes and reflects possible impaired stimulation of hematopoiesis and neutrophil function.[3]

The number of platelets is unaffected by the aging process. Functionally, they may have increased adhesiveness. Clotting factors increase with age. Thus, aging is associated with an increased chance of clotting problems, such as venous thromboembolism.[3] Changes in vascular integrity related to aging can manifest as easy bruising.

Table 33.3 outlines the effects of aging on hematologic studies. Immune changes related to aging are detailed in Chapter 14.

ASSESSMENT OF HEMATOLOGIC SYSTEM

Much of the evaluation of the hematologic system is based on the health history and presenting signs and symptoms.

Case Study

Patient Introduction

(© Lisa F. Young/iStock.)

A.J. is a 63-year-old woman who presents to the emergency department with her husband. He came home from work and found his wife at home, weak and in bed after she work. She says she has been slowly getting more "cold and tired," but "that is what happens when you work at my age." Her husband states that she has become more tired over the last couple of weeks and "she looks pale." She has been having trouble working all day and even gets short of breath when doing simple errands. She recently had a "bad cold and sinus infection" that only improved after 2 courses of antibiotics. A.J. says, "I've noticed I've had a lot of bruising lately."

Discussion Questions

1. What are the possible causes of A.J.'s weakness, pallor, and shortness of breath?
2. Is her condition stable or an emergency?
3. What type of assessment is most appropriate for A.J.: comprehensive, focused, or emergency? On what basis did you make that decision?
4. What assessment questions would you ask A.J.?

You will learn more about A.J. and her condition as you read this chapter.

Answers available at http://evolve.elsevier.com/Lewis/medsurg.

TABLE 33.3 GERONTOLOGIC ASSESSMENT DIFFERENCES

Effects of Aging on Hematologic Studies

Study	Changes
CBC Studies	
Hemoglobin (Hgb)	Usually normal in women; possibly slight ↓ in men
Mean corpuscular hemoglobin concentration (MCHC)	May be slightly ↓
Mean corpuscular volume (MCV)	May be slightly ↑
Platelets	May be slightly ↓; possible ↑ in adhesiveness
White blood cell (WBC) count	Decreased response to infection
Clotting Studies	
D-dimers	↑
Erythrocyte sedimentation rate (ESR)	↑ Significantly
Factors V, VII, IX	May be ↑
Fibrinogen	May be ↑
Partial thromboplastin time	May be ↓
Iron Studies	
Erythropoietin	May be ↑
Ferritin	↑
Serum iron	↓
Total iron-binding capacity	↓

Subjective Data

Important Health Information

Health history. Determine if the patient has had prior hematologic problems. Ask about anemia, bleeding problems, and blood disorders. Are there related medical conditions, such as malabsorption or liver (e.g., hepatitis, cirrhosis), kidney, or spleen problems? A solid organ transplant, loss of the spleen to traumatic injury, or a history of IV drug or alcohol use affects the risk for hematologic problems. A history of recent or recurrent infections or blood clotting problems is important to note.

Medications. A complete medication history is important. Ask about the use of vitamins, herbal products, or diet supplements. Many medications may interfere with normal hematologic function.[3] Those on long-term anticoagulant therapy, such as warfarin, are at risk for bleeding problems. Chemotherapy drugs and antiretroviral agents used to treat human immunodeficiency virus (HIV) infection may cause bone marrow depression. A patient previously treated with chemotherapy agents, particularly alkylating agents, has a higher risk for developing a secondary cancer of leukemia or lymphoma.

Surgery or other treatments. Obtain a surgical history. This includes splenectomy, tumor removal, prosthetic heart valve placement, and GI surgeries. A partial or total gastrectomy removes parietal cells, thus reducing intrinsic factor needed for the absorption of cobalamin (vitamin B_{12}). Duodenal excision (where iron absorption occurs), gastric bypass (the duodenum may be bypassed and parietal cell surface area decreased), and ileal resection (reduces area where cobalamin absorption takes place) can result in problems. Assess wound healing after surgery and if there were any bleeding problems. Discuss wound healing and bleeding as responses to injuries (including minor trauma) and dental extractions. Determine the number of previous blood transfusions and any complications. The risk for transfusion reactions and iron overload increases with the number of blood transfusions.

Functional Health Patterns

Key questions to ask a patient with a hematologic problem are outlined in Table 33.4.

Health perception–health management pattern. Ask the patient to describe the usual and present state of health. Gather demographic data, including age, gender, race, and ethnic background. Ask if there is any family history of hematologic problems (Box 33.1). Ask about anemia, cancer, RBC disorders, such as sickle cell disease, and bleeding disorders, such as hemophilia and clotting problems.

Assess risk factors, such as alcohol and cigarette use, which may disrupt the hematologic function. Alcohol is caustic to the GI mucosa and can cause damage that results in GI bleeding, esophageal varices, and decreased absorption of cobalamin and other nutrients.

Chronic alcohol users often have vitamin deficiencies. Alcohol exerts a damaging effect on platelet function and the liver, where we make clotting factors. Consequently, bleeding problems can develop and should be expected with chronic alcohol use. Illicit drug use is important to determine since many of these drugs may affect hematopoiesis.

Cigarette smoking increases low-density lipoprotein (LDL) cholesterol and levels of CO_2. This leads to hypoxia and

TABLE 33.4 HEALTH HISTORY

Hematologic System

Health Perception–Health Management

- Do you have any problem performing daily activities because of a lack of energy?*
- Do you smoke cigarettes or drink alcohol?[a]
- Do you take any prescribed or over-the-counter medications?[a]
- Are you taking any herbs?[a] Home remedies?[a]
- Have you in the past or are you currently consuming illegal drugs? What agents? What route? How often? When did you last use?
- Have you ever received a blood transfusion?[a]
- Is there any family history of anemia, cancer, bleeding, or clotting problems?[a]
- Have you had any surgeries?[a]

Nutritional-Metabolic

- Do you have any problems with eating, chewing, or swallowing?[a]
- Have you had any mouth sores, sore tongue, swollen or sore gums, oral bleeding?[a]
- What kind of diet do you follow? If a vegetarian, do you eat eggs, milk products, fish?
- How has your appetite been?
- Have you had any changes in your weight in the past year?[a]
- Do you take any vitamins, nutrition supplements, or iron?[a]
- Is nausea and vomiting a problem for you?[a]
- Have you ever had any unusual bleeding or bruising?[a]
- Have there been recent changes in the condition or color of your skin?[a]
- Have you had night sweats or cold intolerance?[a]
- Have you noticed any swelling in your armpits, neck, or groin?[a]

Elimination

- Have you had black or tarry stools?[a] Have you had light, clay-colored stools?[a]
- Have you noticed any blood or dark "tea color" in your urine?[a]
- Has your urine had a foul odor or cloudiness?
- Have you had any decrease in urine output?[a]
- Do you ever have diarrhea or change in bowel patterns?[a]

Activity-Exercise

- Do you have any shortness of breath at rest? With activity?[a]
- Do you have any limitations in joint motion?[a] Have any of your joints been swollen?[a]
- Do you have a problem with unsteady gait? Have you fallen recently?[a]
- Do you exercise regularly? What type and how often?[a]
- After activity, do you ever notice bleeding or bruising?[a]

Sleep-Rest

- Have you had excessive fatigue recently?[a]
- Are you more tired than usual?[a]
- Do you feel rested on awakening? If no, explain.

Cognitive-Perceptual

- Have you had any numbness or tingling?[a]
- Have you had any problems with your vision, hearing, or taste?[a]
- Have you noticed any changes in your mental function?[a]
- Do you have any pain, such as bone, joint, or abdominal pain, or abdominal fullness?[a]
- Do you have pain when moving your joints?[a]
- Have your muscles been sore or achy recently?[a]

Self-Perception–Self-Concept

- Does your health problem make you feel differently about yourself?[a]
- Do you have any physical changes that cause you distress?[a]

Role-Relationship

- Does your occupation bring you into contact with hazardous substances?[a]
- Has your present illness caused a change in your roles and relationships?[a]

Sexuality-Reproductive

- Has your problem caused any sexual or intimacy problems that concern you?[a]
- *Women:* When was your last menses? Do you consider your cycle normal? How long does your bleeding usually last? Have you had any increase in cramping or clotting?[a] Have there been any changes in the amount of flow?[a]
- *Men:* Do you ever have impotence?[a]
- Have you had unprotected sex in the past 6 months?[a] Was your partner someone new or a person with whom you have had a long-term sexual relationship?

Coping–Stress Tolerance

- Do you have a support system to help you when needed?
- What coping strategies do you use when your symptoms are worse?
- Do you have any specific symptoms when you feel stressed?[a]

Value-Belief

- Do you have any personal or religious objection to receiving blood or blood products?[a]
- Do you have any conflicts between your planned therapy and your value-belief system?[a]

[a]If yes, describe.

BOX 33.1 GENETIC RISK ALERT

- Hematologic problems with a strong genetic link include sickle cell anemia, hemophilia, thalassemia, and hemochromatosis.
- People with a family history of these problems have a greater risk for developing them.
- Leukemia, pernicious anemia, and clotting disorders may have a genetic predisposition.

changing the anticoagulant properties of the endothelium. Smoking increases platelet reactivity, plasma fibrinogen, hematocrit, and blood viscosity.

Nutritional-metabolic pattern. Determine if the patient has had anorexia, nausea, vomiting, or oral discomfort. A diet history may give clues about the cause of anemia. We need iron, cobalamin, and folic acid for RBC development. Iron and folic acid deficiencies are related to inadequate intake of foods such as meat, fish, eggs, leafy green vegetables, legumes, citrus fruits, and whole-grain and enriched breads, cereals, and rice.[7]

Hematemesis (bright red, brown, or black vomitus) is a manifestation of an underlying problem and always needs investigating. Peptic ulcer disease is a common cause of hematemesis.

Explore any changes in the skin's texture, color, or temperature. Ask about bleeding gum tissue or bleeding from anywhere on the body. Ask about any lumps or swelling in the neck, armpits, or groin. Specifically, ask what the lumps feel like (i.e., hard or soft, tender or nontender). Are they mobile or fixed? Primary lymph tumors are usually not painful. A nontender, consistently swollen lymph node may be a sign of a cancer, such as Hodgkin or non-Hodgkin lymphoma. An acute infection may cause enlarged, tender lymph nodes.[4] Explore any reports of fever. Determine if the patient currently has a fever, recurring fevers, chills, or night sweats.

Ask patients if they have a history of heart or lung diseases. Cardiovascular problems, such as valvular disease or hypertension, may predispose patients to hemolysis. Many medications used to treat cardiovascular disease can cause problems with hematopoietic cell production or coagulation. Lung problems that lead to hypoxemia may cause chronic stimulation of erythropoietin and result in *polycythemia* (excess RBCs).

Elimination pattern. Ask if there has been blood in the urine or stool or if black, tarry stools have occurred. Ask the patient if they have had a recent stool tested for occult blood or colonoscopy.

Activity-exercise pattern. Because fatigue is a prominent symptom in many hematologic problems, ask about feelings of tiredness. Determine any weakness or feelings of heavy extremities. Assess for apathy, malaise, dyspnea, or palpitations. Note any change in the patient's ability to perform regular exercise and/or activities of daily living (ADLs), especially as they relate to a history of falling.

Sleep-rest pattern. Determine whether the patient feels rested after a night's sleep. Fatigue from a hematologic problem often does not resolve after sleep.

Cognitive-perceptual pattern. Assess for any joint pain that may be caused by a hematologic problem. Pain in the joint may occur with an autoimmune disorder, such as rheumatoid arthritis. It may occur with gout from increased uric acid production due to hematologic cancer or hemolytic anemia. Aching bones may result from pressure of expanding bone marrow with diseases such as leukemia. *Hemarthrosis* (blood in a joint) occurs in the patient with bleeding disorders and can be painful.

Note any paresthesias, numbness, and tingling as they may be related to a hematologic disorder. Assess for any changes in vision, hearing, taste, or mental status.

Self-perception–Self-concept pattern. Determine the effect of the health problem on the patient's perception of self and personal abilities. Assess the effect of certain problems, such as bruising, petechiae, and lymph node swelling, on the patient's personal appearance.

Role-relationship pattern. Ask the patient about any past or present occupational or household exposures to radiation or chemicals. If such exposure has occurred, determine the type, amount, and duration of the exposure. A person who was exposed to radiation, as a treatment modality or by accident, has a higher incidence of certain hematologic problems. The same is true of a person who was exposed to certain chemicals (e.g., benzene, vinyl chloride, pesticides). These chemicals are often used by mechanics and petroleum industry works, farmers, construction and transportation workers, or those in the military. Assess the effect of the present illness on the patient's usual roles and responsibilities.

Sexuality-reproductive pattern. Take a careful menstrual history from women. Include the age at which menarche and menopause began, duration and amount of bleeding, incidence of clotting and cramping, and any associated problems. Ask men if they have any erectile problems. Ask the patient about sexual behavior that may increase the risk for HIV infection.

Coping–stress tolerance pattern. The patient with a hematologic problem often needs help with ADLs. Ask the patient if adequate support is available to meet daily needs. Determine the patient's usual methods of handling stress. In the patient with platelet disorders or hemophilia, the potential for hemorrhage can be so frightening that usual life patterns may be drastically curtailed, affecting the person's quality of life.

Value-belief pattern. Treatment for some hematologic problems involves blood transfusions or a bone marrow transplant. Determine if these treatments conflict with the patient's value-belief system, including the patient's cultural and

Case Study

Subjective Data

(© Lisa F. Young/iStock.)

A focused subjective assessment of A.J. revealed the following information:

Medical History: History of mild osteoarthritis. No surgical history. Prefers to take care of self with "natural therapy" and has not seen an HCP for 5 years, except for the recent sinus infection.

Medications: Metamucil 1 Tbsp/day PO; vitamins C, E, and D with calcium.

Health Perception–Health Management: Denies family or personal history of anemia, cancer, or bleeding disorders. Believes she comes from a family with great genes for longevity because they "eat organic foods." Drinks 1 glass of red wine with her evening meal "because it's good for your heart." Reporting a gradual increase in shortness of breath with exertion. Says she really cannot do anything anymore without having to stop and catch her breath. Says, "It's tough getting old."

Nutritional-Metabolic: Eat a lot of pasta "because it is cheap." Uses a lot of garlic for flavoring and the "health benefit of it." Although not a vegetarian, eats little meat.

Elimination: Denies black or tarry stool. Occasional constipation. No problems with urination. Urine without odor.

Activity-Exercise: Having a hard time performing ADLs without having to stop and catch her breath. Denies dyspnea at rest. States joints are stiff on arising in morning and after sitting but able to get around OK and work at her secretarial job. States her walking is steady but weak. No history of falling.

Sleep-Rest: Typically sleeps 8–9 hr per night with no trouble falling asleep. Still feels tired and needs to nap during her lunch break and during her days off.

Cognitive-Perceptual: Denies any numbness or tingling. Admits to being a little hard-of-hearing but can still see "pretty good."

Value-Belief: Prefers natural therapies over traditional medication.

Discussion Questions

1. What subjective assessment findings concern you most?
2. Based on these subjective assessment findings, what type of physical assessment should you perform?
3. What should you include in the physical assessment? For what would you be looking?
4. How will you individualize the physical assessment based on the information from A.J. and her husband?

You will learn more about the physical assessment of the hematologic system in the next section.

Answers available at http://evolve.elsevier.com/Lewis/medsurg.

religious beliefs related to blood and blood transfusions. Notify the HCP if you identify any conflicts.

Objective Data

Physical Assessment

A complete physical assessment is needed to examine all systems that affect or are affected by the hematologic system. A patient's presenting symptoms may not immediately point to a hematologic problem (Table 33.5). For example, paresthesias of the lower extremities may not appear to be a hematologic problem. But when combined with other findings and risk factors, it may indicate cobalamin deficiency and resulting pernicious anemia. Certain aspects of the assessment are specifically relevant. These include skin, lymph nodes, spleen, and liver.

Lymph node assessment. Assess lymph nodes symmetrically. Note location, size (in centimeters), degree of fixation (e.g., movable, fixed), tenderness, and texture. Lightly palpate the superficial lymph nodes using the pads of the fingers (Fig. 33.6). Then gently roll the skin over the area and feel for lymph node enlargement. We cannot palpate deep lymph nodes. They are evaluated by radiologic examination.

Ordinarily, lymph nodes are not palpable in adults. If a node is palpable, it should be small (0.5 to 1 cm), mobile, firm, and nontender to be considered a normal finding. A node that is tender, hard, fixed, or enlarged (whether it is tender or not) is an abnormal finding and needs further investigation. Tender nodes are usually a result of inflammation. Hard or fixed nodes suggest cancer.[4]

TABLE 33.5 ASSESSMENT ABNORMALITIES

Hematologic System

Finding	Description	Possible Cause and Significance
Abdomen		
Distended abdomen	A larger than normal abdominal profile. May be soft or firm, tender or nontender, and accompanied by other symptoms, such as nausea, vomiting, or rebound tenderness	Lymphoma may manifest as abdominal adenopathy, mass(es), or bowel obstruction
Hepatomegaly	Palpable liver	Leukemia, cirrhosis, or fibrosis due to iron overload from sickle cell disease or thalassemia
Splenomegaly	Palpable spleen	Anemia, thrombocytopenia, leukemia, lymphomas, leukopenia, mononucleosis, malaria, cirrhosis, trauma, portal hypertension
Eyes		
Blurred vision, diplopia, visual field cuts	Decreased visual acuity or areas of blindness (field cuts)	Anemia, extreme leukocytosis, polycythemia, hyperviscosity may cause vision problems. Thrombocytopenia may cause intraocular hemorrhage with vision changes. Excessive clotting may cause thromboses in circulation to the brain that cause visual field cuts
Conjunctival pallor	Paleness. Decreased or absence of coloration in the conjunctiva	Low Hgb level (anemia)
Jaundiced sclera	Yellow appearance of sclera	Accumulation of bile pigment resulting from rapid or excessive hemolysis or liver disease or infiltration
Heart and Chest		
Altered blood pressure	*Hypertension:* >140/90 mm Hg	May occur initially as a compensatory mechanism for anemia
	Hypotension: <90 mm Hg systolic or >40 mm Hg drop from baseline	Infectious process, blood loss, compromised cardiovascular compensatory mechanisms
	Orthostasis: heart rate >20 beats/min increase or blood pressure >20 mm Hg decrease from baseline when moving from a lying position to either sitting or standing	Common with anemia, especially if also accompanied by low blood volume
Low O_2 saturation	O_2-carrying capacity as reflected by O_2 saturation by pulse oximetry	O_2 saturation may be decreased in cases of severe anemia
Palpitations	Feeling the heartbeat, flutter, or pound in chest	Anemia, fluid volume overload, hypotension with impending syncope, hypertension, dysrhythmias
Sternal tenderness	Abnormal sensitivity to touch or pressure on sternum	Leukemia resulting from increased bone marrow cellularity, causing increase in pressure and bone erosion. Multiple myeloma because of lytic bone lesions
Tachycardia	Heart rate >100 beats/min	Compensatory mechanism in anemia to increase cardiac output
Lymph Nodes		
Lymphadenopathy	Lymph nodes enlarged (>1 cm). May be tender to touch	Infection, foreign infiltrations, systemic disease such as leukemia, lymphoma, Hodgkin lymphoma, metastatic cancer
Mouth		
Gingival and mucous membrane changes	Pallor, gingival and mucosal ulceration or infection, swelling, or bleeding	Low Hgb level (anemia), neutropenia thrombocytopenia. Inability of impaired leukocytes to combat oral infections. Gingival hyperplasia may be present with some types of leukemia

Continued

TABLE 33.5 ASSESSMENT ABNORMALITIES—cont'd

Hematologic System

Finding	Description	Possible Cause and Significance
Smooth tongue	Tongue surface smooth and shiny. Mucosa thin and red from decreased papillae	Pernicious anemia, iron-deficiency anemia
Musculoskeletal System		
Arthralgia	Joint pain	Bleeding into joints from sickle cell disease, hemophilia
Bone pain	Pain in pelvis, ribs, spine, sternum	Multiple myeloma related to lytic bone lesions. Bone invasion by leukemia cells, bone demineralization resulting from various cancers, sickle cell disease
Joint swelling	Fluid-filled spaces surrounding joints	Occurs with hemophilia and sickle cell anemia as hemarthrosis causes inflammation
Nervous System		
Headache, nuchal rigidity	Pain in the cranium, potentially involving one area or extending from frontal area to back of neck	Generalized headache is a common manifestation of mild to moderate anemia. Severe headache with or without vision changes may signal intracranial hemorrhage due to thrombocytopenia. CNS disease with acute lymphoblastic leukemia, CNS lymphoma
Paresthesias of feet and hands, ataxia	Numbness sensation and extreme sensitivity in central and peripheral nerves. Impaired muscle movement	Cobalamin (vitamin B_{12}) deficiency or folate deficiency
Weakness	Lacking physical strength or energy	Low Hgb level (anemia)
Nose		
Nosebleeds	Spontaneous bleeding from nares	May occur with low platelet counts, especially if patient bends down for a long time, tries to lift a heavy item, or performs an intense Valsalva maneuver
Skin		
Chloroma	A tumor arising from myeloid tissue and containing a pale green pigment	Acute myelogenous leukemia that has infiltrated the skin, rare forms of lymphoma
Cyanosis	Bluish discoloration of skin and mucous membranes	Anemia, excess concentration of deoxyhemoglobin in blood
Excoriation	Scratch or abrasion of skin	Scratching from intense pruritus
Flushing	Transient, episodic redness of skin (usually around face and neck)	Increase in Hgb (polycythemia), congestion of capillaries. Flushing of palms of hands or soles of feet sign of anemia
Jaundice	Yellow appearance of skin and mucous membranes	Accumulation of bile pigment caused by rapid or excessive hemolysis or liver damage
Leg ulcers	Prominent on the malleoli on the ankles	Sickle cell disease
Pallor of skin or nail beds	Paleness. Decreased or absence of skin coloration	Low Hgb level (anemia)
Plasmacytoma	Tumor arising from abnormal plasma cells	Multiple myeloma that has infiltrated tissue
Pruritus	Unpleasant cutaneous sensation that provokes the desire to rub or scratch skin	Hodgkin lymphoma, cutaneous lymphomas, infiltrative leukemias, increased bilirubin

Develop a sequence when examining the lymph nodes. A convenient sequence is to start at the head and neck. First, palpate the preauricular, posterior auricular, occipital, tonsillar, submandibular, submental, superficial cervical, posterior cervical chain, deep cervical chain, and supraclavicular nodes. Next, palpate the axillary lymph nodes and pectoral, subscapular, and lateral groups of nodes. Then examine the epitrochlear nodes found in the antecubital fossa between the biceps and triceps muscles. Last, palpate the inguinal lymph nodes found in the groin.

Palpation of liver or spleen. The liver and spleen are normally not detectable by palpating the abdomen. An enlarged liver or spleen may be detectable by percussion or palpation. Measure the degree of liver enlargement by the number of fingerbreadths it extends below the rib border. The spleen may be harder to detect because of its deep location in the left abdomen. Techniques for palpating the liver and spleen are described in Chapter 43.

Skin assessment. Examine the skin over the entire body in a systematic manner. In patients with RBC disorders, the skin may be pale or pasty. It may have a cyanotic tinge in severe anemia. Erythrocytosis often causes small vessel occlusions, causing a purple, mottled appearance of the face, nose, fingers, or toes. You can best assess color changes in persons with dark skin in the sclera, conjunctiva, buccal mucosa, tongue, lips, nail beds, and palms.[4] *Clubbing of the fingers* (discussed in Chapter 27) can be seen with chronic anemia. Skin assessment is discussed in Chapter 24.

WBC disorders may cause infectious or cancerous skin lesions. These may occur anywhere and have a variable distribution pattern.

Look for findings that can indicate bleeding disorders. Assess for **petechiae** (small purplish red pinpoint lesions), **ecchymoses** (bruising), and *spider nevus* (a form of *telangiectasia*) (Table 33.6). The location of petechiae can indicate an accumulation of blood in the skin or mucous membranes. Small vessels leak under pressure, and the platelet numbers are not enough to stop the bleeding. Petechiae are more likely to occur where clothing constricts the circulation. In general, skin and mucosal bleeding means a platelet disorder. Spontaneous bleeding into joints or muscles means a coagulation factor problem.

A *focused assessment* is used to assess the status of previously identified hematologic problems and to monitor for signs of new problems. A focused assessment of the hematologic system is shown in Box 33.2.

Case Study

Objective Data: Physical Assessment

(© Lisa F. Young/ iStock.)

Physical assessment findings of A.J. are as follows:

BP 100/70 (lying), 88/60 (standing); apical pulse 110 (lying), 124 (standing), regular. Respiratory rate 26, temp 96.8°F (36°C), O_2 saturation 90% on room air. No jugular venous distention. Weight 106 lb (48 kg). Height 5 ft 1 in. Skin pale. 2 ecchymoses on her arms; 1 on the left lower leg. A few scattered petechiae on both ankles. No jaundice noted. Conjunctivae pale. Tongue smooth and shiny. Lungs clear with diminished breath sounds in the bases bilaterally. No visible bleeding. No enlarged lymph nodes, spleen, or liver noted. General weakness with dyspnea on exertion. No numbness or tingling or peripheral edema.

Discussion Questions

1. Which physical assessment findings are of most concern to you?
2. Based on the results of the assessment findings, what diagnostic studies do you think may be ordered for A.J.?

You will learn more about diagnostic studies in relation to the hematologic system in the next section.

Answers available at http://evolve.elsevier.com/Lewis/medsurg.

DIAGNOSTIC STUDIES OF HEMATOLOGIC SYSTEM

The most direct means of evaluating the hematologic system is through laboratory analysis. Select studies are described in more detail here.

Laboratory Studies

Complete Blood Count

The complete blood count (CBC) involves several laboratory tests (Table 33.7). In addition to the CBC, a *peripheral smear* may be done. The smear is used to look at the *morphology* (shape and appearance) of the blood cells and may help with the diagnosis. For example, many immature blast WBCs may indicate acute leukemia. Diseases or treatments can disrupt the entire system. When the entire CBC is suppressed, a condition termed **pancytopenia** (marked decrease in the number of RBCs, WBCs, and platelets) exists.

Red blood cells. The total RBC count is reported as RBC $\times 10^6/\mu L$. However, the total RBC count is not fully reliable in determining the adequacy of RBC function. We must evaluate other data, such as hemoglobin, hematocrit, and RBC indices. Normal values of some RBC tests are different for men and women because normal values are based on body mass. Men usually have a larger body mass than women.

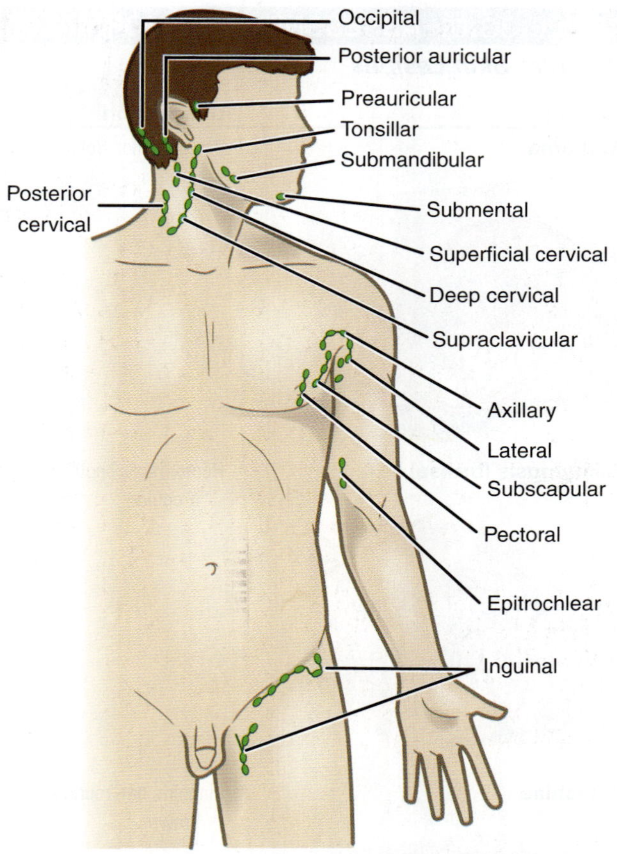

Fig. 33.6 Palpable superficial lymph nodes.

The *hemoglobin (Hgb) value* is reduced with anemia, hemorrhage, and hemodilution, such as that occurring with excess fluid volume. Increased hemoglobin occurs in polycythemia or hemoconcentration, which can develop from volume depletion (dehydration). Increases and decreases of the hematocrit value and RBC count occur with the same conditions that raise and lower the hemoglobin value.

The *hematocrit (Hct) value* is determined by spinning blood in a centrifuge. This causes RBCs and plasma to separate. The RBCs, being the heavier elements, settle to the bottom (Fig. 33.2). The hematocrit value is the percent of RBCs compared with the total blood volume. The hematocrit value generally is 3 times the hemoglobin value. *RBC indices* are special indicators that reflect RBC volume, color, and hemoglobin saturation (Table 33.7).[8] These parameters give insight into the cause of anemia.

White blood cells. The WBC count gives 2 sets of information. The first is a total count of WBCs in 1 μL of peripheral blood. A WBC count over 10,000/μL occurs with infection, inflammation, tissue injury or death, and cancer (e.g., leukemia, lymphoma). Although the degree of WBC elevation does not necessarily predict the severity of illness, it can give clues to the cause. Extremely high WBC counts (e.g., greater than 25,000/μL) occur with certain types of leukemia. A WBC count less than 5000/μL (**leukopenia**) occurs with bone marrow depression, severe or chronic illness, and other types of leukemia.

The second aspect of the WBC count, the *differential count,* measures the percent of each type of WBC. The WBC

TABLE 33.6 ASSESSMENT ABNORMALITIES

Vascular Skin Lesions

Finding	Description	Possible Cause and Significance
Angioma 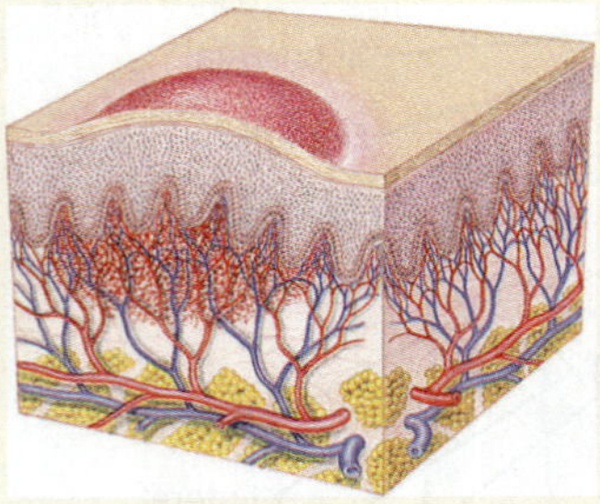	Benign tumor. Consists consisting of blood or lymph vessels	Most are congenital. May disappear spontaneously
Ecchymosis (bruise) 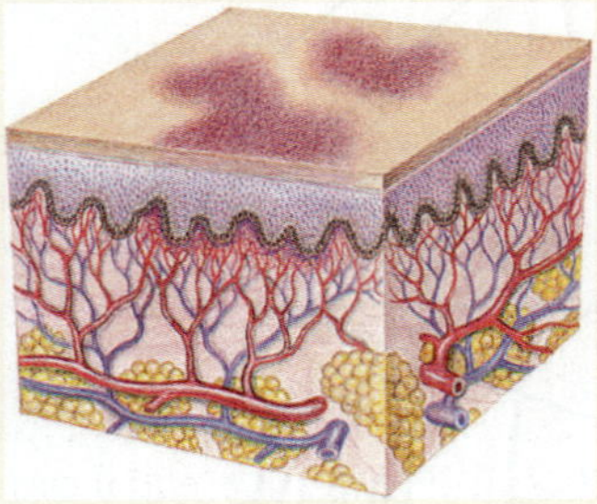	Hemorrhagic spots of varied size. Flat. Round or irregular	Decreased platelets or clotting factors resulting in hemorrhage into skin. Vascular abnormalities. Break in blood vessel walls from trauma
Petechiae 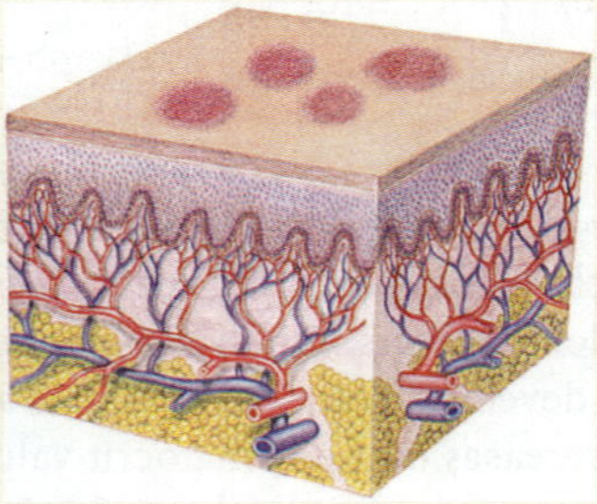	Pinpoint, flat, round area >2 mm. Purple, dark red, or brown	Same as above
Purpura 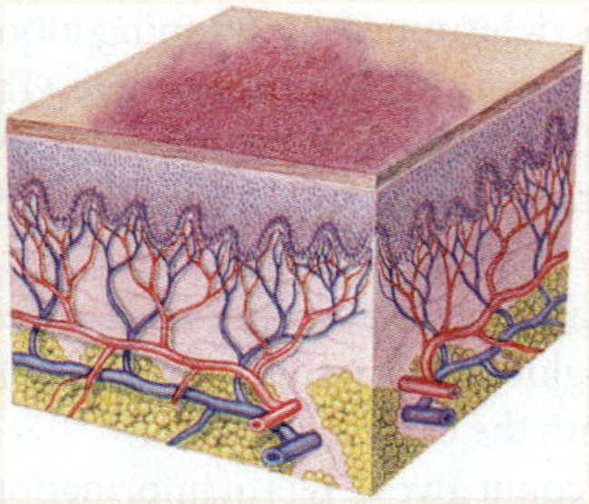	Flat purple or reddish discoloration. <5 mm. Do not blanche.	Same as above
Spider nevus (spider angioma) 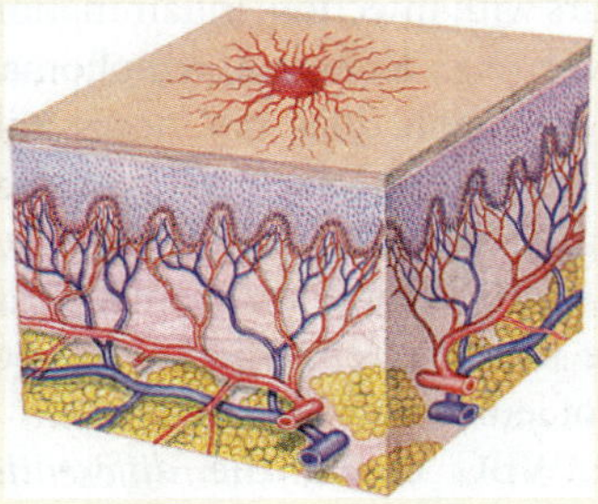	Has a round, red, central part and branching radiations resembling a spider's web. Usually found on face, neck, or chest	High estrogen levels as in pregnancy or liver disease

TABLE 33.6 ASSESSMENT ABNORMALITIES—cont'd

Vascular Skin Lesions

Finding	Description	Possible Cause and Significance
Telangiectasia 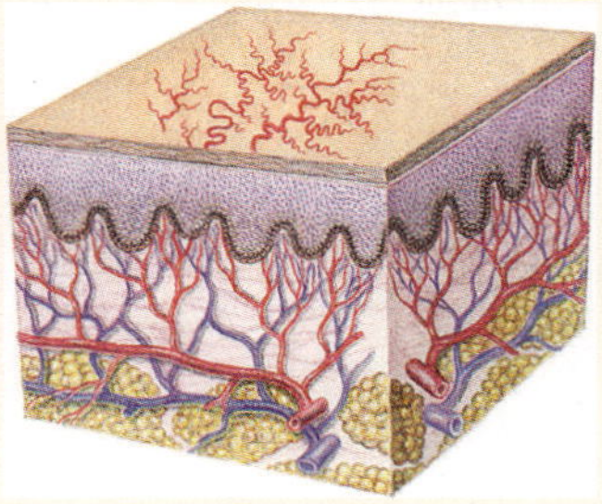	Fine, irregular red lines	Permanently dilated small blood vessels. Usually caused by sun damage or aging. May be seen with varicose veins, scleroderma, rosacea.

Figures from Ball JW, et al.: *Seidel's guide to physical examination,* ed 9, St Louis, 2019, Mosby.

BOX 33.2 FOCUSED ASSESSMENT

Hematologic System

Use this checklist to make sure the key assessment steps have been done.

Subjective

Ask the patient about any of the following and note responses.

Unusual bleeding or bruising	Y	N
Black, tarry stool	Y	N
Blood in vomitus	Y	N
Swelling in neck, armpits, or groin	Y	N
Dark-colored or blood in urine	Y	N
Fatigue	Y	N
Heart palpitations	Y	N

Objective: Diagnostic

Check the following laboratory results for critical values.

CBC	✓
WBC count with differential	✓
Clotting: PT, INR, aPTT, platelets	✓
Hgb, Hct	✓

Objective: Physical Assessment

Inspect

Skin for lesions or color changes	✓

Auscultate

BP for change or orthostasis	✓

Palpate

Pulse for tachycardia	✓
Liver and spleen for enlargement	✓
Lymph nodes for lymphadenopathy	✓

differential gives valuable clues in determining the cause of illness. When infections are severe, we release more granulocytes from the bone marrow as a compensatory mechanism. To meet the increased demand, many young, immature polymorphonuclear neutrophils *(bands)* are released into circulation. More mature neutrophils are called *polymorphonuclear segmented neutrophils (segs)*. Together, bands and segs make up the *absolute neutrophil count* (ANC).

The WBC differential is very important because it is possible for the total WBC count to be essentially normal despite a marked change in one type of WBC. For example, a patient may have a normal WBC count of 8800/μL, but the differential count may show that the proportion of lymphocytes is only 10%. This is an abnormal finding that needs investigation.

When the bone marrow does not make enough neutrophils, neutropenia occurs. **Neutropenia** is a condition in which the ANC is less than 1000 cells/μL. You calculate the ANC by multiplying the total WBC count by the percentage of neutrophils. Neutropenia results from many disease processes, such as leukemia, or from bone marrow suppression. Severe neutropenia is associated with an ANC of less than 500 cells/μL. It is associated with a high risk for infection and death from sepsis.

Platelet count. The platelet count is the number of platelets per microliter of blood. Normal platelet counts are between 150,000 and 400,000/μL. Counts below 100,000/μL signify a condition termed **thrombocytopenia**. Bleeding may occur with thrombocytopenia. Spontaneous hemorrhage is possible once platelet counts fall below 10,000/μL, depending on the clinical situation.[6] A more extensive description of clotting studies is given in Table 33.8.[3,8]

Thrombocytosis is too many platelets. It occurs with inflammation and some cancers (see Chapter 34). The most likely complication of thrombocytosis is excessive clotting.

Blood Typing and Rh Factor

Blood group antigens (A and B) are found only on RBC membranes. They form the basis for the ABO blood typing system (Table 33.9). The presence or absence of 1 or both inherited antigens is the basis for the 4 blood groups: A, B, AB, and O. Blood group A has A antigens, group B has B antigens, group AB has both antigens, and group O has neither A nor B antigens. Each person has antibodies in the serum termed *anti-A* and *anti-B* that react with A or B antigens. These antibodies are

TABLE 33.7 Diagnostic Studies

CBC Studies

Study	Description and Purpose	Reference Intervals
Hemoglobin (Hgb)	Measures gas-carrying capacity of RBC	*Female:* 12–16 g/dL (120–160 g/L) *Male:* 14–18 g/dL (140–180 g/L)
Hematocrit (Hct)	Measures packed cell volume of RBCs. Expressed as a percentage of the total blood volume	*Female:* 37%–47% (0.37–0.47) *Male:* 42%–52% (0.42–0.52)
Platelet count	Number of circulating platelets	150,000–400,000 × 10^3/L (150–400 × 10^9/L)
Total RBC count (erythrocyte count)	Number of circulating RBCs per volume of blood	*Female:* 4.2–5.4 × 10^6/μL (4.2–5.4 × 10^{12}/L) *Male:* 4.7–6.1 × 10^6/μL (4.7–6.1 × 10^{12}/L)
Red cell indices		
Mean corpuscular volume (MCV) $MSV = \frac{Hct \times 10}{RBC \times 10^6}$	Determines relative size of RBCs. Low MCV reflection of microcytosis. High MCV reflection of macrocytosis	80–95 fL
Mean corpuscular hemoglobin (MCH) $MCH = \frac{Hgb \times 10}{RBC \times 10^6}$	Measures average weight of Hgb/RBCs. Low MCH indicates microcytosis or hypochromia. High MCH indicates macrocytosis	27–31 pg
Mean corpuscular hemoglobin concentration (MCHC) $MCHC = \frac{Hgb \times 100}{Hct}$	Evaluates RBC saturation with Hgb. Low MCHC indicates hypochromia. High MCHC occurs with spherocytosis	32%–36% (0.32–0.36)
RBC morphology	Examines shape and size of RBCs	No variation in RBC morphology
Reticulocyte count	Number of immature RBCs released from the bone marrow into the blood	0.5%–2.0% of RBC
WBC count	Total number of WBCs	5000–10,000/μL (5–10 × 10^9/L)
WBC differential	Determines whether each kind of WBC is present in proper proportion. Determines absolute value of each type of WBC by multiplying the percentage of cell type by total WBC count and dividing by 10	*Segmented neutrophils:* 55%–70% (0.55–0.70) *Banded neutrophils:* 0%–8% (0–0.08) *Eosinophils:* 1%–5% (0.01–0.04) *Basophils:* 0.5%–1% (0.005–0.01) *Lymphocytes:* 20%–40% (0.20–0.40) *Monocytes:* 2%–8% (0.02–0.08)

TABLE 33.8 Diagnostic Studies

Clotting Studies

Study	Description and Purpose	Reference Intervals
Activated clotting time (ACT)	Evaluates intrinsic coagulation status. More accurate than aPTT. Used during dialysis, coronary artery bypass procedure, arteriograms	70–120 s
Activated partial thromboplastin time (aPTT)	Assesses intrinsic coagulation by measuring factors I, II, V, VIII, IX, X, XI, XII. Higher in patients receiving heparin	30–40 s
Antithrombin (antithrombin III)	Naturally occurring protein made by liver that inhibits coagulation by inactivating thrombin and other factors. Lower in DIC and hypercoagulable disorders	17–30 mg/dL (170–300 mg/L) or 80%–120% of standard
Bleeding time	Duration of bleeding after a standardized superficial puncture wound of the skin. Measures the integrity of the platelet plug	1–9 min
D-dimer	Assay to measure a fragment of fibrin that forms because of fibrin degradation and clot lysis. Used as an adjunctive measure in diagnosis of hypercoagulable conditions (e.g., DIC, pulmonary embolism)	<250 ng/mL (<250 mcg/L)
Fibrin split products (FSPs) or fibrin degradation products (FDPs)	Reflects degree of fibrinolysis and predisposition to bleed (if present). Screening test for DIC. High levels occur with DIC, advanced cancer, severe inflammation	<10 mcg/mL (<10 mg/L)
Fibrinogen (factor I)	Reflects fibrinogen level. Increase is a possible sign of enhancement of fibrin formation, making patient hypercoagulable. Decrease means patient may be predisposed to bleeding.	200–400 mg/dL (2–4 g/L)
International normalized ratio (INR)	Standardized system of reporting prothrombin time (PT) based on a reference calibration model. Calculated by comparing patient's PT with a control value	0.8–1.1
Plasminogen	Assesses for plasminogen deficiency in patients who have multiple thromboembolic episodes	2.4–4.4 units/mL
Platelet count	Number of circulating platelets	150,000–400,000 × 10^3/L (150–400 × 10^9/L)
Prothrombin time (PT)	Assesses extrinsic coagulation by measuring factors I, II, V, VII, X	11–12.5 sec
Thrombin time	Reflects adequacy of thrombin and time to clot. Prolonged thrombin time means that coagulation is inadequate due to decreased thrombin activity	<21 sec

TABLE 33.9 **ABO and Rh Blood Groups**

	ANTIGENS PRESENT ON RBC		ANTIBODIES POSSIBLY PRESENT IN PLASMA		
Blood Type	**A or B**	**Rh (D)**	**A or B**	**Rh (D)**	**Percent of General Population**
0	—	—	A, B	Rh	7
0+	—	Rh	A, B	—	38
A	A	—	B	Rh	6
A+	A	Rh	B	—	34
B	B	—	A	Rh	2
B+	B	Rh	A	—	9
AB	A, B	—	—	Rh	1
AB+	A, B	Rh	—	—	3

found when the corresponding antigen is absent from the RBC surface. For example, there are B antibodies in the serum of people with blood group A.[8]

Blood reactions based on ABO incompatibilities result from RBC hemolysis. RBCs *agglutinate* (or clump) when a serum antibody is present to react with the antigens on the RBC membrane. For example, agglutination will occur in the blood of a person with type A blood if they receive blood transfused from a person with B antigens (i.e., type B or AB). The anti-B antibodies in the type A blood would react with the B antigens, starting the process that results in RBC hemolysis. Blood component compatibilities for transfusions are outlined in Table 34.33.

The *Rh system* is based on a third antigen, D. It is also on the RBC membrane. Rh-positive people have the D antigen, while Rh-negative people do not. Rh-positive blood is indicated with a "+" after the ABO group (e.g., AB+). Rh status is determined by a Coombs test (Table 33.10).

Because of transfusion therapy or during childbirth, a Rh-negative person may be exposed to Rh-positive blood. After exposure during childbirth, a Rh-negative mother forms an antibody, anti-D, which acts against Rh antigens (Rh-positive people normally have no anti-D). In future pregnancies, the mother's anti-D antibodies can cross the placenta and attack the RBCs of a Rh-positive fetus, causing hemolysis of the RBCs. A pregnant Rh-negative woman should receive Rho(D) immune globulin (RhoGAM) injections to prevent anti-D antibodies from forming.

Iron Metabolism

The laboratory tests used to evaluate iron metabolism include serum iron, transferrin saturation, serum ferritin, and total iron-binding capacity. We may do tests for nutrition deficiencies, leading to defective RBC production (Table 33.10).[8]

Serum iron is a measurement of the amount of protein-bound iron circulating in the serum. *Transferrin saturation* is a better indicator of iron available for erythropoiesis than serum iron. Unlike serum iron, the iron bound to transferrin is readily available for the body to use. You calculate transferrin saturation by dividing serum iron by total iron binding capacity (TIBC) and multiplying by 100. For example, a patient with a serum iron level of 100 mcg/dL and a TIBC of 300 mcg/dL would have a transferrin saturation of about 33%.

Under normal conditions, the serum ferritin concentration correlates closely with body iron stores. In normal patients, 1 ng/mL of ferritin corresponds to 8 to 10 mg of stored iron.

TIBC gives an indirect measure of all proteins that bind or transport iron between the tissues and bone marrow. However, it overestimates transferrin levels by 16% to 20% because it measures other proteins that can bind iron. These other proteins only bind iron when transferrin is more than half saturated. TIBC varies inversely with tissue iron stores. It is higher when iron stores are low and lower when iron stores are high.

Biopsies

Biopsy procedures specific to hematologic assessment are bone marrow examination and lymph node biopsy. A biopsy provides information needed for diagnosis and treatment planning. In general, these procedures are done when a peripheral blood smear is nonspecific.

Bone Marrow Examination

Bone marrow examination is important in evaluating many hematologic problems. It may involve aspiration only or aspiration with biopsy (Table 33.11).[8] The benefits gained from bone marrow examination are (1) a full evaluation of hematopoiesis and (2) the ability to get specimens for cytopathologic and chromosomal analysis. The preferred site for both aspiration and biopsy of bone marrow is the posterior iliac crest. A physician, nurse practitioner, or physician's assistant can perform the procedure. The patient may receive local anesthesia and sedation to minimize anxiety and pain.

For bone marrow aspiration, the skin over the puncture site is cleansed with a bactericidal agent. The skin, subcutaneous tissue, and periosteum are injected with a local anesthetic agent. Once the area is anesthetized, a bone marrow needle is inserted through the cortex of the bone (Fig. 33.7). The stylet of the needle is removed. The hub is attached to a 10-mL syringe, and 0.2 to 0.5 mL of the fluid marrow is aspirated. The patient will have pain when the periosteum is penetrated and with aspiration. Although the pain will last only a few seconds, it can be quite uncomfortable. After the marrow aspiration, the

TABLE 33.10 Diagnostic Studies

Miscellaneous Blood Studies

Study	Description and Purpose	Normal Values
Bilirubin	Measures degree of RBC hemolysis or liver's inability to excrete normal quantities of bilirubin. Increase in indirect bilirubin with hemolysis. Increase in direct bilirubin with obstructive problems (e.g., gallstones, liver tumor)	*Total:* 0.3–1.0 mg/dL (5.1–17.0 μmol/L) *Direct:* 0.1–0.3 mg/dL (1.7–5.1 μmol/L) *Indirect:* 0.2–0.8 mg/dL (3.4–12.0 μmol/L)
Blood smear (peripheral blood smear)	Reviews color, size, shape, quantity of cells in peripheral blood. Provides information about problems affecting RBCs, WBCs, or platelets	Normal quantity of each cell type, normal size, shape and color of RBCs, normal WBC differential count and platelets
Coombs test	Differentiates among types of hemolytic anemias. Detects immune antibodies and Rh factor	Negative
• Direct	Detects antibodies that are attached to RBCs	Negative
• Indirect	Detects circulating antibodies against red cells in serum	Negative
Cobalamin (vitamin B_{12})	Level of cobalamin available for production of new RBCs	160–950 pg/mL (118–701 pmol/L)
Erythrocyte sedimentation rate (ESR)	Measures sedimentation or settling of RBCs in 1 hr. Inflammatory process causes a change in plasma proteins, resulting in aggregation of RBCs and making them heavier. The faster the sedimentation rate, the higher the ESR	<20 mm/h (some gender variation)
Erythropoietin	Measures degree of hormonal stimulation to bone marrow to stimulate the release of RBCs	5–35 IU/mL (5–30 U/L)
Ferritin	Major iron storage protein. Is normally present in blood in concentrations directly related to iron storage	10–300 ng/mL (10–300 mcg/L)
Folic acid (folate)	Amount of folic acid (folate) available for RBC production	5–25 ng/mL (11–57 nmol/L)
Haptoglobin	A serum glycoprotein that binds to Hgb released into the bloodstream by hemolysis. Decreased with red cell hemolysis. Increased with infection, inflammation, cancer	50–220 mg/dL
Hemoglobin (Hgb) electrophoresis	Proteins involved in development of Hgb molecule have a definitive pattern of separation on electrophoresis. This pattern is changed with abnormal Hgb synthesis (e.g., thalassemia) or sickle cell anemia (where Hgb S is increased)	Normal Hb A1: >95% Hb A2: 2%–3% Hb F: 0.8%–2% Hb S: 0 Hb C: 0
Homocysteine	An intermediate amino acid formed during the metabolism of the essential amino acid methionine. Rapidly metabolized through pathways that require cobalamin (vitamin B_{12}) and folic acid. Increased in cobalamin and folic acid deficiency	*Normal:* 4–14 μmol/L
Iron		
• Iron total	Reflects amount of iron combined with proteins in serum. Indicates status of iron storage and use	*Male:* 80–180 mcg/dL (14–32 μmol/L) *Female:* 60–160 mcg/dL (11–29 μmol/L)
• (Total) iron-binding capacity (TIBC)	Measures all proteins available for binding iron. Transferrin represents the largest quantity of iron-binding proteins. Thus, TIBC is an indirect measure of transferrin, an evaluation of the amount of extra iron that can be carried	250–460 mcg/dL (45–82 μmol/L)
Lactic dehydrogenase (LDH)	Intracellular enzyme present in almost all body tissues. Levels rise in response to cell damage. Increased levels confirm diagnosis of injury or disease. Used as a nonspecific marker of hematologic cancer growth and response to treatment	100–190 U/L
Methylmalonic acid (MMA)	Indirect test for cobalamin (vitamin B_{12}). MMA metabolism requires cobalamin. Decreased levels with cobalamin deficiency. Helps distinguish cobalamin deficiency from folic acid deficiency	<3.6 μmol/mmol creatinine
Microglobulin ($beta_2$ microglobulin)	Protein found on the surface of all cells. Increased in cancers such as lymphoma, leukemia, or multiple myeloma. May be used as a tumor marker	*Blood:* 0.7–1.8 mcg/mL *Urine:* ≤300 mcg/L Spinal fluid: ≤2.4 mg/L
Serum protein electrophoresis (SPEP)	Separates proteins in blood on basis of electric charge. Helps detect hyperglobulinemic states, such as in multiple myeloma or some lymphomas	Normal banding pattern of albumin and globulins. Increase in any protein *(protein spike)* is abnormal
Transferrin	Largest of proteins that bind to iron. Increased in most people with iron-deficiency anemia	*Male:* 215–365 mg/dL (2.15–3.65 g/L) *Female:* 250–380 mg/dL (2.5–3.8 g/L)
Transferrin saturation (%)	Decreased in iron-deficiency anemia. Increased in hemolytic and megaloblastic anemia	*Male:* 20%–50% *Female:* 15%–50%

needle is removed. Pressure is applied over the aspiration site to ensure hemostasis. We then cover the site with a sterile pressure dressing.

Complications of bone marrow aspiration are minimal. There is a chance of damaging underlying structures. Other complications include infection if the patient is neutropenic. Hemorrhage may occur in the patient with severe thrombocytopenia.

Monitor the patient's vital signs until stable. Assess the site for excess drainage or bleeding. If bleeding is present, have the

TABLE 33.11 Diagnostic Studies

Hematologic System

Study	Description and Purpose	Nursing Responsibility
Molecular, Cytogenetic, and Gene Analysis Studies		
Cancer genomics (genotyping) **Cell surface immunophenotyping (flow cytometry)** **Chromosomal karyotyping, (PCR)** **Fluorescence in situ hybridization (FISH)**	Assesses for genetic or chromosomal abnormalities of cancer cells. Uses peripheral blood (e.g., leukemia), biopsy specimen (bone marrow, lymph node, tissue), or CSF. Used to confirm diagnosis and determine treatment, prognosis, and response to therapy	*Before:* Explain purpose of testing to patient. HCP will provide specific significance.
Procedures		
Bone marrow biopsy (Fig. 33.7)	Removal of bone marrow through a locally anesthetized site to evaluate status of blood-forming tissue. Used to diagnose and monitor aplastic anemia, multiple myeloma, myelodysplastic syndromes, leukemia, and some lymphomas	*Before:* Explain procedure to patient. Obtain signed consent form. Perform a surgical time-out before procedure. Analgesics may be given to enhance patient comfort and cooperation. *After:* Apply pressure dressing. Assess biopsy site for bleeding and apply pressure as needed. Tenderness at the puncture site for a few days may be normal. Assess for infection.
Lumbar puncture (LP)	Done to obtain CSF for testing for cancer, infection, and degenerative brain diseases. May be used to give chemotherapy to the central nervous system	*During:* Help position patient and provide support. *After:* Watch site for bleeding and signs of infection. Spinal headaches may occur. Follow postprocedure orders for how long the patient should lie flat. Encourage the patient to drink fluids.
Lymph node biopsy	Used to obtain lymph tissue for histologic examination to determine diagnosis and therapy	*Before:* Explain procedure to patient. Obtain signed consent form. *After:* Watch site for bleeding and monitor vital signs, especially if platelet count is low. Change sterile dressing as ordered. Inspect wound for healing and infection.
• Closed (needle) or fine needle	Done at the bedside or in an outpatient area. A very small needle is used to reduce risk for tracking cancer cells through normal subcutaneous tissue	
• Open	Done in operating room or procedure area using either local or general anesthesia. After making an incision, the lymph node and surrounding tissue are excised whenever possible	
Radioisotope Studies		
Bone scan	Radioactive isotope is injected IV and taken up by the bones. Uniform uptake is normal. Increased uptake seen in osteomyelitis, certain fractures, and bone cancer	*Before:* Patient may be asked to drink 4–6 glasses of water and then void before imaging (to see pelvic bones). Obtain IV access for injection of isotope.
SPECT scan (single-photon emission computed tomography)	Radioactive isotope is injected IV. Images from radioactive emissions used to evaluate the structures, such as spleen, liver, bone, and possible tumors. Patient is not a source of radioactivity	*Before:* Obtain IV access for injection of isotope. *After:* Have the patient drink fluids to aid in the excretion of the isotope.
Radiologic Studies		
Computed tomography (CT) scan	Noninvasive radiologic examination using computer-assisted x-ray evaluates the lymph nodes. Contrast medium used in abdominal studies of liver or spleen. Spiral (helical) CT scans used to evaluate lymph nodes	*Before:* Assess for iodine sensitivity if contrast medium used. IV and/or oral contrast may be given prior to procedure, depending on the area being studied. Patient may need to be NPO for 4 hr. *After:* Have patient drink fluids to avoid renal problems with any contrast.
Magnetic resonance imaging (MRI)	Noninvasive procedure produces sensitive images of soft tissue (central nervous system, neck and back, bones and joints, heart, breasts). An IV contrast agent (gadolinium) may be given. Provides a better contrast between normal tissue and pathologic tissue than CT.	*Before:* Oral and/or IV contrast injection may be used. Check for pregnancy, allergies, and renal function before test. Have patient remove all metal objects. Ask about any history of surgical insertion of staples, plates, dental bridges, or other metal appliances. Remove metallic foil patches. Patient may need to be fasting. Assess for claustrophobia and the need for antianxiety medication. *During:* Patient must lie completely still during scan.

Continued

TABLE 33.11 Diagnostic Studies—cont'd

Hematologic System

Study	Description and Purpose	Nursing Responsibility
Positron emission tomography (PET)	Glucose-containing nuclear tracer substance is injected and taken up by metabolically active cells. Follow-up scan shows different-colored tissues based on metabolic rate. Because cancer cells have an increased uptake of glucose, "hot spots" reflecting increased glucose consumption indicate the presence of active cancer. CT scanning may be done in conjunction or images fused.	*Before:* Obtain IV access to inject the tracer substance. Patients should be NPO, except for water and medications, for at least 4 hr prior. Hold glucose-containing IV solutions and change to normal saline. Check the blood glucose levels as high levels may interfere with test. May need bowel preparation depending on area being studied. *After:* Encourage fluids to excrete radioactive substance.
Skeletal x-ray	X-rays done to detect lytic lesions from multiple myeloma.	No specific nursing responsibilities.
Ultrasound (abdominal, liver, spleen)	Noninvasive probe is lubricated and slid across the abdomen to detect density and borders of the abdominal organs. Can detect irregular borders, masses, vascular structure, fluid collections, and biliary tree	*During:* Patients must be comfortable lying flat and having probe compress abdomen.
Urine Studies		
Bence Jones protein (free kappa and lambda light chains)	An electrophoretic measurement used to detect Bence Jones protein, which is found in most cases of multiple myeloma. May be present in some other hematologic disorders and metastatic cancers. Negative finding is normal.	*During:* Obtain random urine specimen early in the morning. If a 24-hr urine collection is done, discard first specimen, and collect all urine voided during the 24 hr, keeping on ice or refrigerated. Remind patient not to put toilet paper in urine collection container.

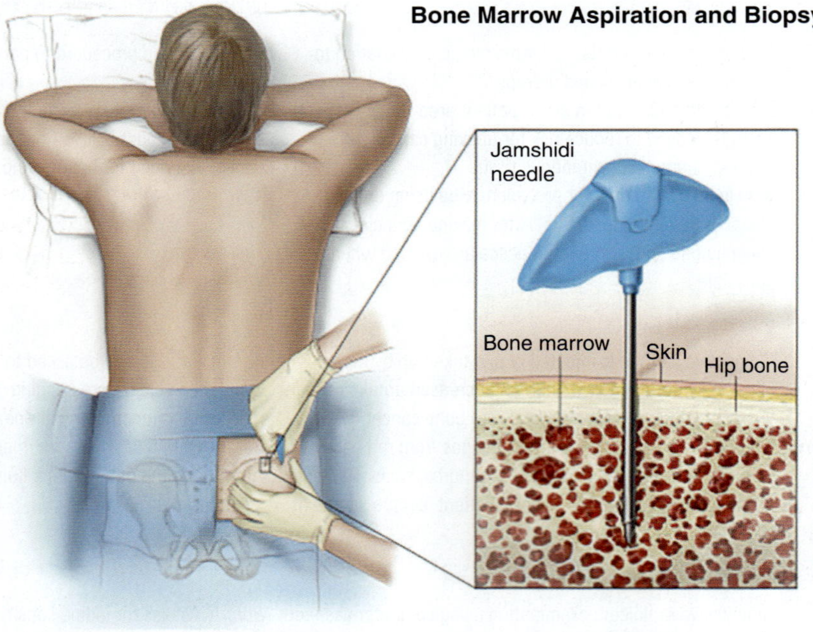

Fig. 33.7 Bone marrow aspiration from the posterior iliac crest.

patient lie supine for 30 to 60 minutes to keep pressure on the site. If the bed is too soft, have the patient lie on a rolled towel to provide more pressure. Notify the HCP if bleeding continues. You may give analgesics for postprocedure pain. Soreness over the puncture site for 3 to 4 days after the procedure is normal.

Lymph Node Biopsy

Lymph node biopsy involves obtaining lymph tissue for histologic examination to determine the diagnosis and help plan therapy. This may be done by either an open or a closed (needle) biopsy.

If the results from a needle biopsy are negative, it may only mean that the cancer cells were not part of the tissue in the biopsy specimen. However, a positive finding may be enough evidence to confirm a diagnosis. This technique is rarely used to confirm an initial diagnosis because larger specimens, such as excisional biopsies, are usually needed to perform cytopathologic tests.

Molecular Cytogenetics and Gene Analysis

Testing for specific chromosomal variations with hematologic problems is essential in diagnosis (Table 33.11). Results determine treatment options, prognosis, and response to therapy. If a large number of abnormal cells are circulating in the blood, such as in acute leukemia, these tests may be done on peripheral blood. However, testing is usually done on samples from bone marrow, lymph node biopsies, and sometimes cerebrospinal fluid (CSF).[3,8]

There are a number of molecular tests. Flow cytometry can detect specific cell populations and their cell surface antigens.[3] Fluorescence in situ hybridization (FISH) identifies genetic defects using nucleic probes that are complementary to a targeted region of deoxyribonucleic acid (DNA). FISH can identify an abnormal extra chromosome 8, which is common in certain leukemias.[3] Reverse transcription polymerase chain reaction (PCR) is another way to detect specific mutations and amount. PCR can detect the Philadelphia chromosome translocation t(9;22) seen in chronic myeloid leukemia and some cases of acute lymphoblastic leukemia.[3]

Case Study

Objective Data: Diagnostic Studies

(© Lisa F. Young/iStock.)

The HCP orders the following diagnostic studies for A.J.:

- CBC, basic metabolic panel (electrolytes, BUN, creatinine), PT/PTT
- Arterial blood gases
- Chest x-ray

A.J.'s CBC reveals an Hgb of 5.9 g/dL, Hct of 18.2%, WBC of 2600/μL (2.6×10^9/L), platelet count of 72,000/μL, PT = 18 seconds, aPTT = 37. Arterial blood gases and chest x-ray are normal. The HCP orders more blood work, including a WBC differential and RBC indices and admits her to the hospital for further evaluation and potential treatment.

Discussion Questions

1. Are these the diagnostic studies that you expected to be ordered?
2. Which diagnostic study results are abnormal?
3. Which diagnostic study results concern you most? What other studies may be ordered on admission?

This case study is continued in Chapter 34.

Answers available at http://evolve.elsevier.com/Lewis/medsurg.

BRIDGE TO NCLEX EXAMINATION

The number of the question corresponds to the same-numbered outcome at the beginning of the chapter.

1. A person who lives at a high altitude may normally have an increased Hgb and RBC count because
- **a.** high altitudes cause vascular fluid loss, leading to hemoconcentration.
- **b.** hypoxia caused by decreased atmospheric O_2 stimulates erythropoiesis.
- **c.** the function of the spleen in removing old RBCs is impaired at high altitudes.
- **d.** impaired production of platelets leads to proportionally higher red cell counts.

2. A patient with cancer arising from granulocytic cells in the bone marrow will have
- **a.** a risk for bleeding.
- **b.** altered oxygenation.
- **c.** decreased production of antibodies.
- **d.** decreased phagocytosis of bacteria.

3. An anticoagulant such as warfarin that interferes with prothrombin production will alter the clotting mechanism during
- **a.** platelet aggregation.
- **b.** activation of thrombin.
- **c.** the release of tissue thromboplastin.
- **d.** stimulation of factor activation complex.

4. When reviewing laboratory results of an older patient with an infection, the nurse would expect to find
- **a.** mild leukocytosis.
- **b.** decreased platelet count.
- **c.** increased hemoglobin and hematocrit levels.
- **d.** decreased erythrocyte sedimentation rate (ESR).

5. Key information from the patient's health history that relates to the hematologic system includes
- **a.** jaundice.
- **b.** bladder surgery.
- **c.** early menopause.
- **d.** multiple pregnancies.

6. While assessing the lymph nodes, the nurse should
- **a.** apply gentle, firm pressure to deep lymph nodes.
- **b.** palpate the deep cervical and supraclavicular nodes last.
- **c.** lightly palpate superficial lymph nodes with the pads of the fingers.
- **d.** use the tips of the second, third, and fourth fingers to apply deep palpation.

7. If a lymph node is palpated, what is a normal finding?
- **a.** Hard, fixed nodes
- **b.** Firm, mobile nodes
- **c.** Enlarged, tender nodes
- **d.** Hard, nontender nodes

8. Nursing care for a patient after a bone marrow biopsy and aspiration includes *(select all that apply)*
- **a.** giving analgesics as needed.
- **b.** preparing to start a blood transfusion.
- **c.** keeping the sterile pressure dressing intact.
- **d.** giving preprocedure and postprocedure antibiotic medications.
- **e.** monitoring vital signs and assessing the site for excess drainage or bleeding.

1. b; 2. d; 3. b; 4. a; 5. a; 6. c; 7. b; 8. a, c, e.

For rationales to these answers and even more NCLEX review questions, visit http://evolve.elsevier.com/Lewis/medsurg.

EVOLVE WEBSITE/RESOURCES LIST

http://evolve.elsevier.com/Lewis/medsurg
Review Questions (Online Only)
Key Points
Answer Keys for Questions
- Rationales for Bridge to NCLEX Examination Questions
- Answer Guidelines for Case Studies

Conceptual Care Map Creator
Audio Glossary
Content Updates

REFERENCES

1. Huether SE, McCance KL, Brashers VL: *Understanding pathophysiology*, ed 7, St Louis, 2020, Elsevier.
*2. Ahmed SS, Mohammed AA: Effects of thyroid dysfunction on hematological parameters: case controlled study, *Ann Med Surg* 57:52, 2020.
3. Keohane EM, Otto CN, Walenga JM: *Rodak's hematology: clinical principles and applications*, ed 6, St. Louis, 2020, Elsevier.
4. Ball JW, Dains JE, Flynn JA, et al.: *Seidel's guide to physical examination: an interprofessional approach*, ed 9, St. Louis, 2019.
*5. Groarke EM, Young NS: Aging and hematopoiesis, *Clin Geriatr Med* 35:285, 2019.
6. Hoffman R, Benz EJ, Silberstein LE, et al.: *Hematology: basic principles and practice*, ed 7, Philadelphia, 2018, Elsevier.
7. Academy of Nutrition and Dietetics: Food and nutrition topics. Retrieved from www.eatright.org.
8. Pagana KD, Pagana TJ, Pagana TN: *Mosby's diagnostic and laboratory test reference*, ed 15, St Louis, 2021, Mosby.

*Evidence-based information for clinical practice

34

Hematologic Problems

Sandra Irene Rome

http://evolve.elsevier.com/Lewis/medsurg/

CONCEPTUAL FOCUS

Cellular Regulation
Clotting
Fatigue
Functional Ability
Gas Exchange
Immunity
Infection
Pain
Perfusion

LEARNING OUTCOMES

1. Describe the general clinical manifestations and complications of anemia.
2. Distinguish the etiologies, clinical manifestations, diagnostic findings, and interprofessional and nursing management of iron deficiency, megaloblastic, and aplastic anemias.
3. Explain the nursing management of anemia from blood loss.
4. Describe the pathophysiology, clinical manifestations, and interprofessional and nursing management of anemia from increased erythrocyte destruction.
5. Describe the pathophysiology and nursing and interprofessional management of polycythemia.
6. Explain the pathophysiology, clinical manifestations, and interprofessional and nursing management of various types of thrombocytopenia.
7. Describe the types, clinical manifestations, diagnostic findings, and interprofessional and nursing management of hemophilia and von Willebrand disease.
8. Explain the pathophysiology, diagnostic findings, and interprofessional and nursing management of disseminated intravascular coagulation.
9. Describe the etiology, clinical manifestations, and interprofessional and nursing management of neutropenia.
10. Describe the pathophysiology, clinical manifestations, and interprofessional and nursing management of myelodysplastic syndromes.
11. Compare and contrast the clinical and laboratory findings of the major types of leukemia.
12. Explain the nursing and interprofessional management of acute and chronic leukemias.
13. Compare Hodgkin lymphoma and non-Hodgkin lymphomas in terms of clinical manifestations, staging, and interprofessional and nursing management.
14. Describe the pathophysiology, clinical manifestations, and interprofessional and nursing management of multiple myeloma.
15. Describe the spleen disorders and related interprofessional care.
16. Describe the nursing management of the patient receiving transfusions of blood and blood components.

KEY TERMS

anemia
aplastic anemia
disseminated intravascular coagulation (DIC)
hemochromatosis
hemolytic anemia
hemophilia
Hodgkin lymphoma
iron deficiency anemia
leukemia
lymphomas
megaloblastic anemias
multiple myeloma
myelodysplastic syndromes (MDS)
neutropenia
non-Hodgkin lymphomas (NHLs)
pernicious anemia
polycythemia
sickle cell disease (SCD)
thalassemia
thrombocytopenia

This chapter discusses common hematologic problems and their associated concepts.

There are a wide range of blood conditions and cancers. Because blood has so many essential functions, hematologic problems affect the patient in many ways. Patients with anemia and hematologic cancer may have to cope with fatigue. Compromised immunity and the risk for infection is a concern among patients with hematologic cancer and a common side effect of therapy. Pain is common with cancer and sickle cell disease (SCD). Clotting is an important protective mechanism that supports homeostasis when injury occurs. Excessive clotting can impair perfusion. Inadequate clotting can lead to blood loss and fluid volume deficit.

ANEMIA

Definition and Classification

Anemia is a deficiency in the number of erythrocytes (red blood cells [RBCs]), the quantity or quality of hemoglobin (Hgb), and/or volume of packed RBCs (hematocrit). It is not a specific disease. Anemia is a manifestation of a pathologic process. It is a common condition with many diverse causes. These include blood loss, impaired RBC production, or increased RBC destruction (Fig. 34.1). The diagnosis of anemia is based on a complete blood count (CBC), reticulocyte count, and peripheral blood smear. Once identified, further research is done to find the specific cause.[1]

Anemia can result from primary hematologic problems or develop because of diseases or disorders of other body systems. We classify the types of anemia by either *morphology* (cell characteristic) or *etiology* (cause). Morphologic classification is based on RBC size and color (Table 34.1). Etiologic classification is based on the clinical condition causing the anemia (Table 34.2).[1] Although the morphologic system is the most accurate way to classify anemia, it is easier to discuss patient care by focusing on the cause of the anemia.

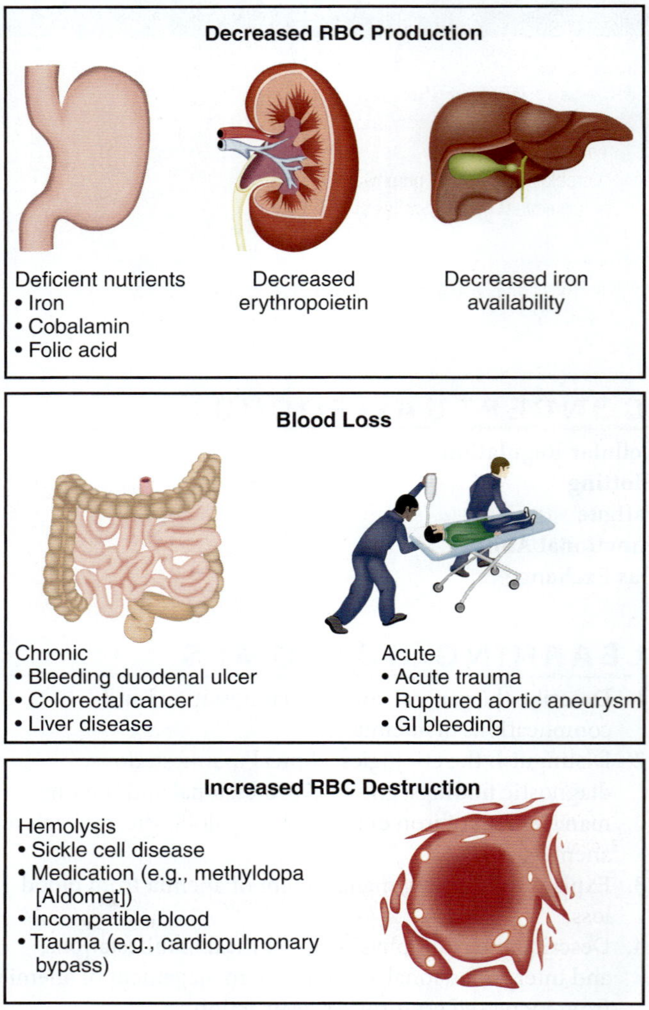

Fig. 34.1 Causes of anemia.

TABLE 34.1 Morphologic Classification of Anemia

Morphology	Etiology
Normocytic, normochromic (normal size and color) MCV 80–95 fL, MCH 27–31 pg	Acute blood loss, hemolysis, chronic kidney disease, chronic disease, cancer, endocrine problems, starvation, aplastic anemia, sickle cell anemia, pregnancy
Microcytic, hypochromic (small size, pale color) MCV <80 fL, MCH <27 pg	Iron deficiency anemia, vitamin B_6 deficiency, copper deficiency, thalassemia, lead poisoning
Macrocytic (megaloblastic), normochromic (large size, normal color) MCV >95 fL, MCH >31 pg	Cobalamin (vitamin B_{12}) deficiency, folic acid deficiency, liver disease (including effects of alcohol use)

MCH, Mean corpuscular hemoglobin; *MCV,* mean corpuscular volume.

Clinical Manifestations

Because RBCs transport O_2, RBC disorders can lead to tissue hypoxia. The manifestations of anemia result from the body's response to the hypoxia. Specific manifestations vary depending on how fast the anemia has evolved, its severity, and any coexisting disease. We often use Hgb levels to determine the severity of anemia.

Mild anemia (Hgb 10 to 12 g/dL [100 to 120 g/L]) may exist without causing symptoms. If symptoms develop, it is because the patient has an underlying disease or has a compensatory response to heavy exercise. Symptoms include palpitations, dyspnea, and mild fatigue.

In moderate anemia (Hgb 6 to 10 g/dL [60 to 100 g/L]), there is an increase in cardiopulmonary symptoms. The patient may have them while resting as well as with activity.

In severe anemia (Hgb less than 6 g/dL [60 g/L]), the patient has many manifestations involving multiple body systems (Table 34.3).

Integumentary. Skin manifestations include pallor, jaundice, and itching. Pallor results from low Hgb levels and reduced blood flow to the skin. Jaundice occurs when RBC hemolysis increases the serum bilirubin concentration. Hemolysis also causes itching from the increased serum and skin bile concentrations.

Cardiopulmonary. Cardiopulmonary manifestations of severe anemia result from the heart and lungs trying

TABLE 34.2 Etiologic Classification of Anemia

Decreased RBC Production

Decreased Hemoglobin Synthesis
- Iron deficiency
- Sideroblastic anemia (↓ porphyrin)
- Thalassemia (↓ globin synthesis)

Decreased Number of RBC Precursors
- Aplastic anemia and inherited disorders (e.g., Fanconi syndrome)
- Anemia of myeloproliferative diseases (e.g., leukemia) and myelodysplasia
- Chronic diseases or disorders
- Medications and chemicals (e.g., chemotherapy, lead)
- Radiation

Defective DNA Synthesis
- Cobalamin (vitamin B_{12}) deficiency
- Folic acid deficiency

Blood Loss

Acute
- Blood vessel rupture
- Splenic sequestration crisis
- Trauma

Chronic
- Gastritis
- Hemorrhoids
- Menstrual flow

Increased RBC Destruction (Hemolytic Anemias)

Acquired (Extrinsic)
- Antibodies against RBCs
- Cancer
- DIC
- Extracorporeal circulation
- HELLP syndrome (hemolysis, ↑ liver enzymes, ↓ platelets associated with pregnancy)
- Infectious agents (e.g., malaria) and toxins
- Physical destruction
- Prosthetic heart valves
- Thrombotic thrombocytopenic purpura (TTP)

Hereditary (Intrinsic)
- Abnormal hemoglobin (sickle cell disease)
- Enzyme deficiency (glucose-6-phosphate dehydrogenase [G6PD])
- Membrane abnormalities (paroxysmal nocturnal hemoglobinuria, hereditary spherocytosis)

to provide adequate amounts of O_2 to the tissues. Cardiac output is maintained by increasing the heart rate (HR) and stroke volume. The low blood viscosity contributes to systolic murmurs and bruits. In extreme cases or when heart disease is present, angina pectoris and myocardial infarction (MI) may occur if myocardial O_2 needs are not met. Heart failure (HF), cardiomegaly, pulmonary and systemic congestion, ascites, and peripheral edema may develop if the heart is overworked for an extended period.

NURSING AND INTERPROFESSIONAL MANAGEMENT: ANEMIA

This section discusses general management of anemia. Specific care for various types of anemia is discussed later in this chapter. More information on the nursing care of the patient with anemia is discussed in eNursing Care Plan 34.1.

Assessment

Table 34.4 outlines the subjective and objective data you should obtain from a patient with anemia. Assess the patient's knowledge about proper nutrition and adherence to safety precautions to prevent cardiopulmonary stress, falls, and injury.

Clinical Problems

Clinical problems for the patient with anemia include:
- Fatigue
- Nutritionally compromised
- Inadequate tissue perfusion

Planning

The overall goals are that the patient with anemia will (1) assume normal activities of daily living, (2) maintain adequate nutrition, and (3) develop no complications from anemia.

Implementation

Correcting the cause of the anemia is the goal of therapy. Implement nursing interventions specific to the patient's needs and type of anemia. Acute interventions may include blood transfusions, drug therapy (e.g., iron supplements), and O_2 therapy to stabilize the patient. Diet and lifestyle changes (described in sections on specific types of anemia) can reverse some anemias.

For the patient with fatigue, encourage alternate rest and activity periods. Help the patient to prioritize activities according to energy levels. Arrange activities (e.g., avoid activity right after meals) to reduce competition for O_2 supply to vital functions. Aid with regular activities (e.g., ambulation, transfers, personal care) to minimize fatigue and risk for injury from falls. Monitor the patient's cardiorespiratory response to activity (e.g., tachycardia, dysrhythmias, dyspnea, diaphoresis, pallor, tachypnea).

Collaborate with the dietitian to determine the number of calories and type of nutrients needed to meet nutrition requirements. Provide information about nutrient needs and how to increase intake of essential nutrients. Encourage increased intake of foods listed in Table 34.5 that are high in the nutrients needed for RBC production.[2]

Gerontologic Considerations: Anemia

Modest changes in RBC mass occur in older adults. Healthy older adults have a modest decline in Hgb of about 1 g/dL after age 70. This is partly due to the decreased production of testosterone in men and estrogen in women.[1]

Anemia is not a normal finding in older adults. For many, anemia is due to an underlying cause, such as iron deficiency, bleeding, chronic disease, renal problems, or a hematologic

TABLE 34.3 Manifestations of Anemia

	SEVERITY OF ANEMIA		
Body System	**Mild (Hgb 10–12 g/dL [100–120 g/L])**	**Moderate (Hgb 6–10 g/dL [60–100 g/L])**	**Severe (Hgb <6 g/dL [<60 g/L])**
Cardiovascular	Palpitations	↑ Palpitations, bounding pulse	↑ HR, ↑ pulse pressure, systolic murmurs, intermittent claudication, angina, HF, MI
Eyes	None	None	Icteric conjunctiva and sclera, retinal hemorrhage, blurred vision
GI	None	None	Anorexia, hepatomegaly, splenomegaly, problems swallowing, sore mouth
General	None or mild fatigue	Fatigue	Sensitivity to cold, weight loss, lethargy
Mouth	None	None	Glossitis, smooth tongue
Musculoskeletal	None	None	Bone pain
Pulmonary	Exertional dyspnea	Dyspnea	Tachypnea, orthopnea, dyspnea at rest
Neurologic	None	"Roaring in the ears"	Headache, vertigo, irritability, depression, impaired thought processes
Skin	None	None	Pallor, jaundice, itching

TABLE 34.4 NURSING ASSESSMENT
Anemia

Subjective Data

Important Health Information

Health history: Recent blood loss or trauma; chronic liver, endocrine, or renal disease (including dialysis); GI disease (malabsorption syndrome, ulcers, gastritis, hemorrhoids); inflammatory disorders (especially Crohn disease); smoking, exposure to radiation or chemical toxins (arsenic, lead, benzenes, copper); infectious diseases; recent travel with possible exposure to infection; angina, MI; history of falling

Medications: Use of vitamin and iron supplements; aspirin, anticoagulants, oral contraceptives, phenobarbital, penicillins, NSAIDs, omeprazole, phenytoin, sulfonamides, herbal products

Surgery or other treatments: Recent surgery, small bowel resection, gastrectomy, prosthetic heart valves, chemotherapy, radiation therapy

Diet history: General diet patterns, alcohol use

Functional Health Patterns

Health perception–health management: Family history of anemia; malaise

Nutritional-metabolic: Nausea, vomiting, anorexia, weight loss; dysphagia, dyspepsia, heartburn; night sweats, cold intolerance

Elimination: Hematuria, ↓ urine output; diarrhea, constipation, flatulence, tarry stools, bloody stools

Activity-exercise: Fatigue, muscle weakness, ↓ strength; dyspnea, orthopnea, cough, hemoptysis; palpitations; shortness of breath with activity

Cognitive-perceptual: Headache; abdominal, chest, and bone pain; painful tongue; paresthesias of feet and hands; itching; changes in vision, taste, or hearing; vertigo; hypersensitivity to cold; dizziness

Sexuality-reproductive: Menorrhagia, metrorrhagia; recent or current pregnancy; male impotence

Objective Data

General

Lethargy, apathy, general lymphadenopathy, fever

Cardiovascular

↑ HR, systolic murmur, dysrhythmias; postural hypotension, widened pulse pressure, bruits (especially carotid); intermittent claudication, ankle edema

GI

Hepatosplenomegaly; glossitis; beefy, red tongue; stomatitis; abdominal distention; anorexia

Neurologic

Headache, roaring in the ears, confusion, impaired judgment, irritability, ataxia, unsteady gait, paralysis, loss of vibration sense

Respiratory

Tachypnea

Skin

Pale skin and mucous membranes; blue, pale white, or icteric sclera; cheilitis (inflammation of the lips); poor skin turgor; brittle, spoon-shaped fingernails; jaundice; petechiae; bruising; nose or gingival bleeding; poor healing; dry, brittle, thinning hair

Possible Diagnostic Findings

↓ RBCs, ↓ Hgb; ↓ Hct; ↑ or ↓ reticulocytes, ↑ or ↓ MCV; possible ↓ serum iron, ferritin, folate, or cobalamin (vitamin B_{12}); heme-positive stools; ↓ serum EPO level; ↑ or ↓ LDH, bilirubin, transferrin (Table 34.6)

problem. For those with no identifiable cause, it may be due to cytokine dysregulation with aging.[1]

Manifestations of anemia in older adults may include pallor, confusion, ataxia, fatigue, and worsening cardiovascular and respiratory problems. Unfortunately, anemia may go unrecognized in older adults because we mistake the manifestations for normal aging changes or overlook them because of another health problem. By recognizing signs of anemia, you can play a key role in the care of older adults with anemia.

ANEMIA CAUSED BY DECREASED RBC PRODUCTION

Normally RBC production (termed *erythropoiesis*) is in equilibrium with RBC destruction and loss. This balance ensures that an adequate number of RBCs is always available. The normal life span of an RBC is 120 days. There are 3 problems that lead to decreased RBC production: (1) decreased Hgb synthesis from iron deficiency anemia,

TABLE 34.5 NUTRITION THERAPY

Nutrients for RBC Production

Role in RBC Production	Food Sources
Amino Acids (Protein)	
Heme and plasma membrane synthesis and structure	Eggs, meat, milk and milk products (cheese, ice cream), poultry, fish, legumes, nuts, soy
Cobalamin (Vitamin B_{12})	
Synthesis of DNA, RBC maturation, facilitates folate metabolism	Meat, eggs, enriched grain products, milk and dairy foods, fish (especially salmon)
Copper	
Mobilizes iron from tissues to plasma	Shellfish, whole grains, beans, nuts, potatoes, organ meats, dark leafy greens, dried fruits
Folic Acid	
Synthesis of DNA and RNA, RBC maturation	Green leafy vegetables, enriched grain products and breakfast cereals, orange juice, peanuts, avocado
Iron	
Hemoglobin synthesis	Lean beef, turkey, pork and chicken, fish, legumes, dark green leafy vegetables, whole-grain and enriched bread and cereals, beans
Niacin	
RBC maturation	Peanut butter, beef, poultry, fish, avocado; enriched and fortified grains
Pantothenic Acid (Vitamin B_5)	
Heme synthesis	Sweet potato, yogurt, avocado, cereal grains, legumes, eggs, milk
Pyridoxine (Vitamin B_6)	
Heme synthesis	Beef, pork, chicken, fish, fortified cereals, potatoes, bananas, nuts, beans
Riboflavin (Vitamin B_2)	
Oxidative reactions	Milk and dairy foods, enriched bread and other grain products, lean meats, eggs, green leafy vegetables
Vitamin C (Ascorbic Acid)	
Maintains iron in its ferrous form, aids in iron absorption	Citrus fruits, green leafy vegetables, strawberries, potatoes, kiwi fruit, tomatoes, green and red bell peppers
Vitamin E	
Heme synthesis. Protection against oxidative damage to RBCs	Vegetable oils, salad dressings, margarine, wheat germ, whole-grain products, seeds, nuts, peanut butter

thalassemia, and sideroblastic anemia; (2) defective deoxyribonucleic acid (DNA) synthesis in RBCs (e.g., cobalamin deficiency, folic acid deficiency) may lead to megaloblastic anemias; and (3) diminished availability of RBC precursors may result in aplastic anemia and anemia of chronic disease (Table 34.2).

IRON DEFICIENCY ANEMIA

Iron deficiency anemia is the most common nutrition disorder in the world. Those most susceptible to iron deficiency anemia are the very young, those on poor diets, and women in their reproductive years.[1] Normally, we lose 1 mg of iron daily in urine, bile, sweat, sloughing of epithelial cells from the skin and intestinal mucosa, and minor bleeding.[3]

Etiology

Iron deficiency anemia may develop from inadequate diet intake, malabsorption, blood loss, or hemolysis. Normal iron intake is usually enough to meet the needs of men and older women. It may be inadequate for people with higher iron needs (e.g., menstruating or pregnant women).

Iron malabsorption may occur after certain types of gastrointestinal (GI) surgery and in malabsorption syndromes. Iron absorption occurs in the duodenum. Thus malabsorption may occur after surgery that involves removal or bypass of the duodenum. It may occur if duodenal disease alters or destroys the absorption surface.

Blood loss is a major cause of iron deficiency in adults. The major sources of chronic blood loss are from the GI and genitourinary (GU) systems. GI bleeding is often not obvious. It may exist for a long time before the problem is found. Loss of 50 to 75 mL of blood from the upper GI tract is enough for stools to appear black *(melena).* The black color results from the iron in the RBCs.

Common causes of GI blood loss are peptic ulcer, gastritis, esophagitis, diverticula, hemorrhoids, and cancer. GU blood loss occurs mainly from menstrual bleeding. Postmenopausal bleeding can contribute to anemia in susceptible older women. In addition to anemia of chronic kidney disease, dialysis treatment may cause iron deficiency anemia because of the blood lost in the dialysis equipment and frequent blood sampling.

Clinical Manifestations

In the early course of iron deficiency anemia, the patient may not have any symptoms. As the disease becomes chronic, any of the general manifestations of anemia may develop (Table 34.3). Specific manifestations may occur with iron deficiency anemia. Pallor is the most common finding. *Glossitis* (inflammation of the tongue) is the second most common. Another finding is *cheilitis* (inflammation of the lips). The patient may report headache, paresthesias, and a burning sensation of the tongue.

Diagnostic Studies

Laboratory values seen with iron deficiency anemia are shown in Table 34.6.[1,6] Other diagnostic studies (e.g., stool occult blood test) are done to find the cause of the iron deficiency. Endoscopy and colonoscopy may detect GI bleeding. A bone marrow biopsy may be done if other tests are inconclusive.

Interprofessional and Nursing Management

The main goal is to treat the underlying problem that is causing iron loss, reduced intake (e.g., malnutrition, alcohol use), or poor iron absorption. We also direct efforts toward replacing iron (Table

TABLE 34.6 Laboratory Results in Anemia

Etiology of Anemia	Hgb/Hct	MCV	Reticulocytes	Serum Iron	TIBC	Transferrin	Ferritin	Bilirubin	Serum B_{12}	Folate
Acute blood loss	↓	N or ↓	N or ↑	N	N	N	N	N	N	N
Aplastic anemia	↓	N or slight ↑	↓	N or ↑	N or ↑	N	N	N	N	N
Chronic blood loss	↓	↓	N or ↑	↓	↓	N	N	N or ↓	N	N
Chronic disease	↓	N or ↓	N or ↓	↓	↓	N or ↓	N or ↑	N	N	N
Cobalamin deficiency	↓	↑	N or ↓	N or ↑	N	Slight ↑	↑	N or slight ↑	↓	N
Folic acid deficiency	↓	↑	N or ↓	N or ↑	N	Slight ↑	↑	N or slight ↑	N	↓
Hemolytic anemia	↓	N or ↑	↑	N or ↑	N or ↓	N	N or ↑	↑	N	N
Iron deficiency	↓	↓	N or slight ↓ or ↑	↓	↑	N or ↓	↓	N or ↓	N	N
Sickle cell anemia	↓	N	↑	N or ↑	N or ↓	N	N	↑	N	↓
Thalassemia major	↓	N or ↓	↑	↑	↓	↓	N or ↑	↑	N	↓

N, Normal.

TABLE 34.7 Interprofessional Care

Iron Deficiency Anemia

Diagnostic Assessment
- History and physical assessment
- Hgb and Hct (hematocrit) levels
- RBC count, including morphology
- Reticulocyte count
- Serum iron
- Serum ferritin
- Serum transferrin
- Total iron-binding capacity (TIBC)
- Stool examination for occult blood

Management
- Identify and treat underlying cause
- Drug therapy
  - Oral: ferrous sulfate or ferrous gluconate
  - IM or IV: iron dextran, sodium ferrous gluconate, iron sucrose
- Nutrition therapy (Table 34.5)
- Packed RBC transfusion

34.7). Teach the patient which foods are good sources of iron (Table 34.5). If nutrition is already adequate, increasing iron intake through diet may not be enough. The patient may need oral, or occasionally, IV iron supplements. If the iron deficiency is from acute blood loss, the patient may need a packed RBC transfusion.

Drug Therapy

Many oral iron preparations are available. When giving iron, consider the following factors:

1. Iron is absorbed best from the duodenum and proximal jejunum. Enteric coated or sustained-release capsules, which release iron farther down in the GI tract, are counterproductive and expensive.
2. The daily dose should provide 100 to 200 mg of elemental iron. This can be taken in 3 or 4 daily doses, with each tablet or capsule containing 60 to 70 mg of iron.[2]
3. Iron is best absorbed in an acidic environment. For this reason and to avoid binding the iron with food, iron should be taken an hour before meals, when the duodenal mucosa is most acidic. Taking iron with vitamin C (ascorbic acid) or orange juice enhances iron absorption. Iron may be taken with meals if absolutely needed to decrease GI side effects.
4. Undiluted liquid iron may stain the teeth. Dilute liquid iron, and have the patient drink it through a straw.
5. GI side effects may occur, including heartburn, constipation, and diarrhea. Have the patient stay upright for 30 minutes after taking oral forms. If side effects develop, the dose and type of supplement may need adjusted. For example, someone may not be able to tolerate ferrous sulfate because of the effects of the sulfate base. Ferrous gluconate may be a better for them. Tell patients that iron will cause their stools to become black because the GI tract excretes excess iron. Constipation is common. The patient should start on stool softeners and laxatives, if needed, when started on iron.

DRUG ALERT

Iron

- Some IV and IM iron preparations have a risk for an allergic reaction, so monitor the patient accordingly.
- Oral iron should be taken 1 hour before meals.
- Vitamin C (ascorbic acid) enhances iron absorption.

In some situations, we many need to give iron parenterally. Parenteral iron is indicated for malabsorption, intolerance of oral iron, a need for iron beyond oral limits, or poor patient adherence in taking oral iron. Parenteral iron can be given IM or IV. We give a test dose of IV iron dextran then observe the patient for 1 hour before giving the rest of dose so we can monitor for anaphylaxis.[4,5]

Because IM iron solutions may stain the skin, use separate needles for withdrawing the solution and injecting the medication. Use a Z-track injection technique.

Assess the Hgb and RBC count to evaluate the response to therapy. Stress adherence with diet and drug therapy. To replenish the body's iron stores, the patient needs to take iron therapy for 2 to 3 months after the Hgb level returns to normal. Monitor patients who need lifelong iron therapy for potential liver problems from the iron storage.

THALASSEMIA

Etiology

Thalassemia is a group of diseases involving inadequate production of normal Hgb, which decreases RBC production. Thalassemia is due to an absent or reduced globulin protein. α-Globin chains are absent or reduced in α-thalassemia. β-Globin chains are absent or reduced in β-thalassemia. Hemolysis occurs as mononuclear phagocytes in the marrow destroy most erythroblasts. Those released into the blood are rapidly destroyed by macrophages in the spleen.[1] Thalassemia is commonly found in persons whose ethnic origins are near the Mediterranean Sea and equatorial or near-equatorial regions of Southeastern Asia, the Middle East, India, Pakistan, China, Southern Russia, and Africa.[1]

Genetic Link

Thalassemia has an autosomal recessive genetic basis (see Fig. 13.4 and Table 13.2). A person with thalassemia may have a heterozygous or homozygous form of the disease. A person who is heterozygous has 1 thalassemic gene and 1 normal gene. They have *thalassemia minor* (or thalassemic trait), which is a mild form of the disease. A homozygous person has 2 thalassemic genes. This causes the more severe form known as *thalassemia major.*[1]

Clinical Manifestations and Diagnostic Studies

The patient with thalassemia minor is often asymptomatic. They have mild to moderate anemia with *microcytosis* (small cells) and *hypochromia* (pale cells), mild splenomegaly, bronzed skin color, and bone marrow hyperplasia.[3]

Thalassemia major is a life-threatening disease. Symptoms develop in childhood by age 2 and can cause growth and development deficits. The person is pale and has other general symptoms of anemia (Table 34.3). Jaundice from RBC hemolysis is prominent. There is pronounced splenomegaly because the spleen continuously tries to remove the damaged RBCs. Hepatomegaly and cardiomyopathy occur from iron deposition.

The bone marrow responds to the reduced O_2-carrying capacity of the blood by increasing RBC production. The marrow becomes packed with immature erythroid precursors that die. This stimulates further RBC production, leading to chronic bone marrow hyperplasia and expansion of the marrow space. This may cause thickening of the cranium and maxillary cavity. Thrombocytosis after spleen dysfunction and/or removal may occur.

Cardiac complications from iron overload, lung disease, and hypertension also contribute to early death. Endocrine problems (diabetes, growth retardation, hypogonadism), osteoporosis, pulmonary hypertension, and thrombosis may occur.[1,2]

Laboratory values seen with thalassemia major are shown in Table 34.6.

Interprofessional Care

Thalassemia minor does not need treatment because the body adapts to the reduction of normal Hgb. Treatment of thalassemia major includes blood transfusions or exchange transfusions in conjunction with chelating agents that bind to iron. Transfusions are generally given when the Hgb drops to less than 7 g/dL (100 g/L), depending on the manifestations.[1] Chelating agents reduce the iron overloading that occurs with chronic transfusion therapy. Drugs used include oral deferasirox (Exjade, JadeNu) or deferiprone (Ferriprox), or IV or subcutaneous deferoxamine (Desferal).[1] A new therapy, luspatercept-aamt (Reblozyl), may be given subcutaneously every 21 days. It improves Hgb levels and reduces transfusion needs. It blocks inhibitors of late-stage RBC production.[6]

Because an enlarged spleen sequesters RBCs, the patient may need a splenectomy. Monitor liver, heart, and lung function and provide treatment as needed.

Hematopoietic stem cell transplantation (HSCT) is the only cure for thalassemia. However, the risks of this procedure may outweigh its benefits. With iron chelation therapy, patients are living longer. We are researching gene transfer therapy to correct the globin gene expression.

TABLE 34.8 Causes of Megaloblastic Anemia

Cobalamin (Vitamin B_{12}) Deficiency
- Chronic alcohol use
- Diet deficiency
- Deficiency of gastric intrinsic factor
  - Celiac disease
  - Gastrectomy
  - Gastric bypass
  - *Helicobacter pylori*
  - Pernicious anemia
- Increased requirement (pregnancy)
- Intestinal malabsorption

Folic Acid Deficiency
- Chronic alcohol use
- Chronic hemodialysis (folic acid lost during dialysis)
- Diet deficiency (e.g., leafy green vegetables, citrus fruits)
- Drugs interfering with absorption or use of folic acid (e.g., metformin phenytoin)
- Increased requirement (pregnancy)
- Malabsorption syndromes
  - Celiac disease
  - Crohn disease
  - Small bowel resection

Drug-Induced Suppression of DNA Synthesis
- Alkylating agents
- Folate antagonists
- Metabolic inhibitors

Inherited Defects
- Defective folate metabolism
- Defective transport of cobalamin

Myelodysplastic Syndromes

MEGALOBLASTIC ANEMIAS

Megaloblastic anemias are characterized by the presence of abnormally large *(macrocytic)* RBCs. We call them *megaloblasts.* Macrocytic RBCs are easily destroyed because they have fragile cell membranes. Megaloblastic anemias are caused by impaired DNA synthesis, which results in defective RBC maturation. Most result from cobalamin (vitamin B_{12}) and folic acid deficiencies. They can also occur with congenital disorders, suppression of DNA synthesis by drugs, inborn errors of cobalamin and folic acid metabolism, and *erythroleukemia* (malignant blood disorder characterized by a proliferation of erythropoietic cells in bone marrow) (Table 34.8).[1]

COBALAMIN DEFICIENCY

The most common cause of cobalamin deficiency is **pernicious anemia**. It is caused by an absence of *intrinsic factor* (IF). Pernicious anemia is a disease of insidious onset. It begins in middle age or later (usually after age 40), with 60 years being the most common age at diagnosis. Pernicious anemia occurs most often in persons of Northern European descent (especially Scandinavians) and Blacks.[1,4]

Etiology

Normally, the parietal cells of the gastric mucosa secrete IF. IF is required for cobalamin (extrinsic factor) absorption. We absorb cobalamin in the distal ileum. Without IF, we do not absorb cobalamin. In pernicious anemia, the gastric mucosa does not secrete IF because of either gastric mucosal atrophy or autoimmune destruction of parietal cells. In the autoimmune process, antibodies are directed against the gastric parietal cells and/or IF itself. Because parietal cells also secrete hydrochloric acid (HCl), in pernicious anemia there is a decrease in HCl in the stomach. An acid environment in the stomach is needed for IF secretion.

Cobalamin deficiency can occur in patients who had GI surgery (e.g., gastrectomy, gastric bypass) or a small bowel resection involving the ileum. Others at risk include those with Crohn disease, ileitis, celiac disease, diverticula of the small intestine, or chronic atrophic gastritis (see Table 34.8). In these cases, cobalamin deficiency results from the loss of IF-secreting gastric mucosal cells or impaired absorption of cobalamin in the distal ileum. Cobalamin deficiency also occurs with excess alcohol or hot tea ingestion, smoking, long-term users of H_2-histamine receptor blockers and proton pump inhibitors, and those who are strict vegetarians.[1]

There is a familial predisposition for pernicious anemia. Assess patients who have a positive family history of pernicious anemia for symptoms. Although the disease cannot be prevented, early detection and treatment can lead to reversal of symptoms.

Clinical Manifestations

General manifestations of anemia due to cobalamin deficiency develop due to tissue hypoxia (Table 34.3). GI manifestations include a sore, red, beefy, and shiny tongue; anorexia, nausea, and vomiting; and abdominal pain. Typical neuromuscular manifestations include weakness, paresthesias of the feet and hands, reduced vibratory and position senses, ataxia, muscle weakness, and impaired cognition. Because cobalamin deficiency–related anemia has an insidious onset, it may take several months or years for manifestations to develop.[1]

Diagnostic Studies

Laboratory data reflective of cobalamin deficiency anemia are shown in Table 34.6. The RBCs appear large (macrocytic) and have abnormal shapes. This structure contributes to RBC destruction because the cell membrane is fragile. Serum cobalamin levels are low.

Normal serum folate levels and low cobalamin levels suggest megaloblastic anemia due to cobalamin deficiency. A serum test for anti-IF antibodies is specific for pernicious anemia. Patients with pernicious anemia have an increased risk for gastric cancer. They may have an upper GI endoscopy and biopsy of the gastric mucosa at the time of diagnosis and at appropriate intervals afterward.

Serum methylmalonic acid (MMA) (high in cobalamin deficiency) and serum homocysteine (high in both cobalamin and folic acid deficiencies) help determine the cause of the anemia.

❖ Interprofessional and Nursing Management

Without cobalamin administration, the patient will die in 1 to 3 years. Most patients need parenteral vitamin B_{12} (cyanocobalamin, hydroxocobalamin) or intranasal cyanocobalamin (Nascobal). A typical treatment schedule consists of 1000 mcg/day of cobalamin IM for 2 weeks, then weekly until the Hgb is normal, and then monthly for life.

The nursing measures discussed in eNursing Care Plan 34.1 for the patient with anemia are appropriate for the patient with cobalamin deficiency anemia. In addition to these measures, assess for neurologic problems that are not corrected by replacement therapy. Implement measures to reduce the risk for injury from the decreased sensitivity to heat and pain. Protect the patient from falling, burns, and trauma. In some people, the neuromuscular problems may not be reversible. They may need physical therapy.

FOLIC ACID DEFICIENCY

Folic acid (folate) deficiency can cause megaloblastic anemia. Folic acid is needed for DNA synthesis leading to RBC formation and maturation. Common causes of folic acid deficiency are shown in Table 34.8.

The manifestations of folic acid deficiency are similar to cobalamin deficiency. It develops insidiously. Symptoms may be attributed to other coexisting problems (e.g., cirrhosis, esophageal varices). GI problems may include stomatitis, cheilosis, dysphagia, flatulence, and diarrhea. Thiamine deficiency, which is often present with folate deficiency, can cause neurologic symptoms.[3]

The diagnostic findings for folic acid deficiency are shown in Table 34.6. The serum folate level is low (normal is 5 to 25 ng/mL [11 to 57 nmol/L]), with a normal serum cobalamin level.

We treat folic acid deficiency with replacement therapy. The usual dosage is 1 to 5 mg/day by mouth.[2,4] The duration of treatment depends on the reason for the deficiency. Teach the patient to eat foods high in folic acid (Table 34.5). The nursing measures discussed in eNursing Care Plan 34.1 for the patient with anemia are appropriate for the patient with folic acid deficiency anemia.

ANEMIA OF CHRONIC DISEASE

Anemia of chronic disease (also called *anemia of inflammation*) usually develops after 1 to 2 months of disease activity. Causes include cancer, autoimmune and infectious disorders (human immunodeficiency virus [HIV], hepatitis, malaria), HF, or chronic inflammation. Bleeding episodes can contribute to anemia of chronic disease.

TABLE 34.9 Causes of Aplastic Anemia

- Chemical agents and toxins (e.g., benzene, insecticides)
- Drugs (e.g., alkylating agents, antiseizure drugs, antimetabolites, antimicrobials, gold, NSAIDs, antithyroid medications, allopurinol)
- Immune suppression of stem cells by autoreactive T lymphocytes
- Inherited stem cell defect (e.g., Fanconi anemia)
- Radiation
- Toxic injury to bone marrow stem cells
- Viral and bacterial infections

Anemia of chronic disease is associated with an underproduction of RBCs and mild shortening of RBC survival. The RBCs are usually normocytic, normochromic, and hypoproliferative. The anemia is usually mild. It can become more severe if the underlying disorder is not treated.

This type of anemia has an immune basis. The cytokines released in these problems, especially interleukin-6 (IL-6), cause an increased uptake and retention of iron within macrophages (see Fig. 33.3). This leads to a diversion of iron from circulation into storage sites, limiting the iron available for RBC production. There is reduced RBC life span, decreased erythropoietin (EPO) production, and an ineffective bone marrow response to EPO.

Anemia of chronic disease must be recognized and distinguished from anemia of other causes. High serum ferritin and increased iron stores distinguish it from iron deficiency anemia. Unlike megaloblastic anemia, there are normal folate and cobalamin blood levels.

The best treatment is to correct the underlying problem. If the anemia is severe, blood transfusions may be needed. They are not recommended for long-term treatment. EPO therapy is used for anemia from renal disease (see Chapter 51) and cancer and its therapies (see Chapter 16). Its use is limited because of the increased risk for thromboembolism and death in some patients.

APLASTIC ANEMIA

Aplastic anemia is a disease in which the patient has peripheral blood *pancytopenia* (decrease of all blood cell types—RBCs, white blood cells [WBCs], platelets) and hypocellular bone marrow. The spectrum can range from a moderate condition managed with EPO or blood transfusions to very severe with potentially fatal bleeding and sepsis. The incidence of aplastic anemia is rare, with an annual rate of 2 new cases per million people in the United States per year.[7]

Etiology

About 70% of aplastic anemias are due to autoimmune activity by autoreactive T lymphocytes.[1] The cytotoxic T cells target and destroy the patient's own hematopoietic stem cells. Other causes include toxic injury to bone marrow stem cells or an inherited stem cell defect (Table 34.9).

Clinical Manifestations

Aplastic anemia can manifest abruptly (over days) or insidiously over weeks to months. It can vary from mild to very severe. The patient may have symptoms caused by suppression of any or all bone marrow elements. General manifestations of anemia, such as fatigue and dyspnea, as well as cardiovascular and cerebral responses, may occur (Table 34.3). The patient with neutropenia (low neutrophil count) is susceptible to infection. They are at risk for septic shock and death. Thrombocytopenia can lead to bleeding (e.g., petechiae, bruising, nosebleeds).

Diagnostic Studies

Laboratory studies confirm the diagnosis. Because aplastic anemia affects all marrow elements, Hgb, WBC, and platelet values are decreased. Other RBC indices are generally normal (Table 34.6). Thus we classify the condition as a normocytic, normochromic anemia. The reticulocyte count is low. Serum iron and total iron-binding capacity (TIBC) may be high as initial signs of decreased RBC production. Bone marrow biopsy, aspiration, and pathologic examination will be done to confirm the laboratory findings. The marrow in aplastic anemia is hypocellular with increased yellow marrow (fat content).

❖ Interprofessional and Nursing Management

Management is based on identifying and removing the causative agent (when possible) and providing supportive care until the pancytopenia resolves. Nursing interventions appropriate for the patient with pancytopenia from aplastic anemia are discussed in eNursing Care Plan 34.1 for anemia, eNursing Care Plan 34.2 for thrombocytopenia, and eNursing Care Plan 34.3 for neutropenia (available on the website for this chapter). Nursing actions are aimed at preventing complications from infection and bleeding.

The prognosis of severe untreated aplastic anemia is poor. Early consideration of an HSCT is critical. The best treatment outcomes for those who receive an HSCT occur in younger patients who have had limited blood transfusions. Prior transfusions increase the risk for HSCT graft rejection. HSCT is discussed in Chapter 16.

Those in the interim or ineligible for HSCT may receive immunosuppressive therapy with antithymocyte globulin (ATG) and cyclosporine.[1] Eltrombopag (Promacta), an oral thrombopoietin receptor agonist, can increase platelet counts. High-dose cyclophosphamide, alemtuzumab, or androgens may be helpful in select patients who do not respond to other treatments.[4] Non-HSCT patients who need ongoing supportive blood transfusion should receive an iron-binding agent to prevent iron overload.

ANEMIA CAUSED BY BLOOD LOSS

An acute or chronic problem can cause anemia from blood loss.

ACUTE BLOOD LOSS

Acute blood loss occurs with sudden bleeding. Causes of acute blood loss include trauma, surgery complications, and problems that disrupt vascular integrity. There are 2 clinical concerns in such situations. First, a sudden reduction in the total blood volume can lead to hypovolemic shock. Second, if the acute loss is

TABLE 34.10 Manifestations of Acute Blood Loss

VOLUME LOST[a]		
%	mL	Manifestations
10	500	None or rare vasovagal syncope
20	1000	No detectable signs or symptoms at rest. ↑ HR with exercise and slight postural hypotension
30	1500	Normal supine BP and pulse at rest. Postural hypotension and ↑ HR with exercise
40	2000	BP, central venous pressure, and cardiac output below normal at rest; air hunger; rapid, thready pulse and cold, clammy skin
50	2500	Shock, lactic acidosis, and potential death

[a]Based on an adult with a total blood volume of 5 L.

more gradual, the body maintains its blood volume by slowly increasing the plasma volume. While this preserves circulating fluid volume, the number of RBCs available to carry O_2 is significantly decreased.

Clinical Manifestations

The manifestations of anemia from acute blood loss are caused by the body's attempts to maintain an adequate blood volume and meet O_2 requirements. Table 34.10 outlines the manifestations of patients with varying degrees of blood volume loss. The signs and symptoms the patient has are more important than the laboratory values. For example, an adult with a bleeding peptic ulcer who had a 750-mL hematemesis (15% of a normal total blood volume) within the past 30 minutes may have postural hypotension and normal Hgb and hematocrit values. Over the next 36 to 48 hours, fluid moving from the extravascular into the intravascular space will replace most of the blood volume deficit. Only then will the Hgb and hematocrit reflect the blood loss.

Assess the patient for pain. Internal bleeding may cause pain due to tissue distention, organ displacement, and nerve compression. Pain may be localized or referred. In the case of retroperitoneal bleeding, the patient may not have abdominal pain. Instead, there may be numbness and pain in a lower extremity from compression of the lateral cutaneous nerve (in the region of the 1st to 3rd lumbar vertebrae). The major complication is shock (see Chapter 42).

Diagnostic Studies

When blood volume loss is sudden, plasma volume has not yet had a chance to increase. Laboratory data do not reflect the RBC loss. Values may seem normal or high for 2 to 3 days. However, once the plasma volume is replaced, the RBC mass is less concentrated. Then, RBC, Hgb, and hematocrit levels are low and reflect the actual blood loss.

❖ Interprofessional and Nursing Management

Interprofessional care is initially concerned with (1) replacing blood volume to prevent shock; (2) promoting coagulation to prevent further bleeding; and (3) finding the source of the bleeding and stopping the blood loss. Blood transfusions (packed RBCs) can be used depending on the volume lost. If a large volume of blood is lost, whole blood, platelets, plasma, and cryoprecipitate may be given because large volumes of RBCs dilute the coagulation system. IV fluids used in emergencies include volume replacement fluids (e.g., 0.9% NaCl, lactated Ringer) or colloids that pull fluids into the vascular space (e.g., dextran, hetastarch, albumin).[8] The amount of infusion varies with the solution used.

The body needs 2 to 5 days to make more RBCs in response to increased EPO. The patient may need iron supplements because iron availability affects the marrow production of RBCs. When anemia exists after acute blood loss, diet iron may not be enough to maintain iron stores. We may need to give oral or parenteral iron preparations.

In the case of trauma, it may be impossible to prevent blood loss. For the postoperative patient, carefully monitor the blood loss from various drainage tubes and dressings and implement appropriate actions.

The anemia should begin to correct itself once we find the source of bleeding, control the blood loss, and replace fluid and blood volumes. There should be no need for long-term treatment of this type of anemia.

CHRONIC BLOOD LOSS

The sources of chronic blood loss are similar to those of iron deficiency anemia (e.g., bleeding ulcer, hemorrhoids, menstrual and postmenopausal blood loss). The effects of chronic blood loss are usually due to depleted iron stores. We consider it an iron deficiency anemia. Management of chronic blood loss anemia involves identifying the source and stopping the bleeding. The patient may need iron supplements.

ANEMIA CAUSED BY INCREASED RBC DESTRUCTION

The third major cause of anemia is **hemolytic anemia**. It is a condition caused by the destruction or hemolysis of RBCs at a rate that exceeds production. Hemolysis can occur with problems intrinsic or extrinsic to the RBCs. *Intrinsic hemolytic anemias,* which are usually hereditary, result from defects in the RBCs themselves (Table 34.2).

More common are the *acquired hemolytic anemias*. In this type of anemia, the RBCs are normal but external factors are causing damage (Table 34.2). Macrophages, particularly those in the spleen, liver, and bone marrow, destroy RBCs that are old, defective, or moderately damaged. Fig. 34.2 shows the sequence of events involved in extravascular hemolysis.

The patient with hemolytic anemia has the general manifestations of anemia with some specific manifestations (Table 34.3). Jaundice occurs because the increased RBC destruction causes increased bilirubin levels. The spleen and liver may enlarge from hyperactivity, which is due to macrophage phagocytosis of the defective RBCs.

A major focus of treatment is to maintain renal function. When RBCs are hemolyzed, the Hgb molecule is released and filtered by the kidneys. The accumulation of Hgb molecules can

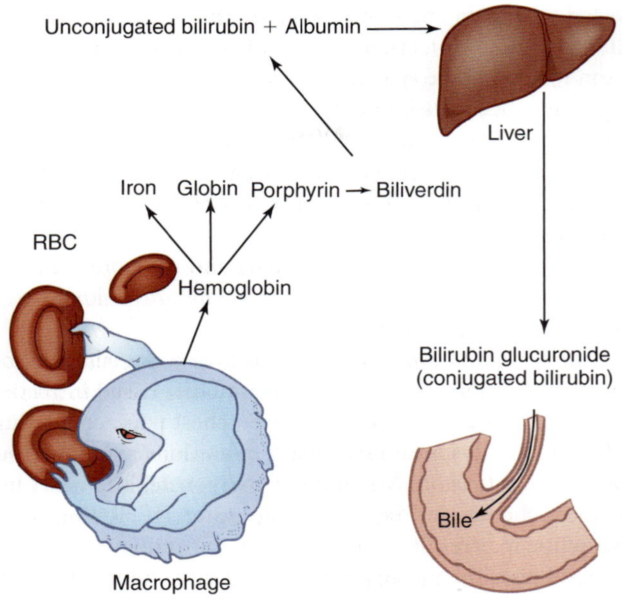

Fig. 34.2 Sequence of events in extravascular hemolysis.

obstruct the renal tubules and lead to acute tubular necrosis (see Chapter 51).

SICKLE CELL DISEASE

Sickle cell disease (SCD) is a group of inherited, autosomal recessive disorders characterized by an abnormal form of Hgb in the RBC. Because this is a genetic disorder, SCD is usually found during routine neonatal screening. Although median survival can now exceed 50 years old, SCD often results in irreversible damage of the lungs, kidneys, brain, retina, or bones that significantly affects patients' quality of life.[1]

Etiology and Pathophysiology

Genetic Link

In SCD, the abnormal Hgb, *hemoglobin S* (Hgb S), results from the substitution of valine for glutamic acid on the β-globin chain of Hgb (see Fig. 13.3). Hgb S causes the RBC to stiffen and elongate, taking on a sickle shape in response to low O_2 levels (Fig. 34.3).

Types of SCD disorders include sickle cell anemia, sickle cell–thalassemia, sickle cell Hgb C disease, and sickle cell trait (Box 34.1).[9] *Sickle cell anemia* is the most severe of the SCD syndromes. It occurs when a person is homozygous for hemoglobin S (Hgb SS), meaning the person has inherited Hgb S from both parents. *Sickle cell–thalassemia* and *sickle cell Hgb C* occur when a person inherits Hgb S from 1 parent and another type of abnormal Hgb (e.g., thalassemia or Hgb C) from the other parent. Both these forms of SCD are less common and less severe than sickle cell anemia. *Sickle cell trait* occurs when a person is heterozygous for hemoglobin S (Hgb AS). This means the person has inherited Hgb S from 1 parent and normal hemoglobin (Hgb A) from the other parent. Sickle cell trait is typically a mild to asymptomatic condition.

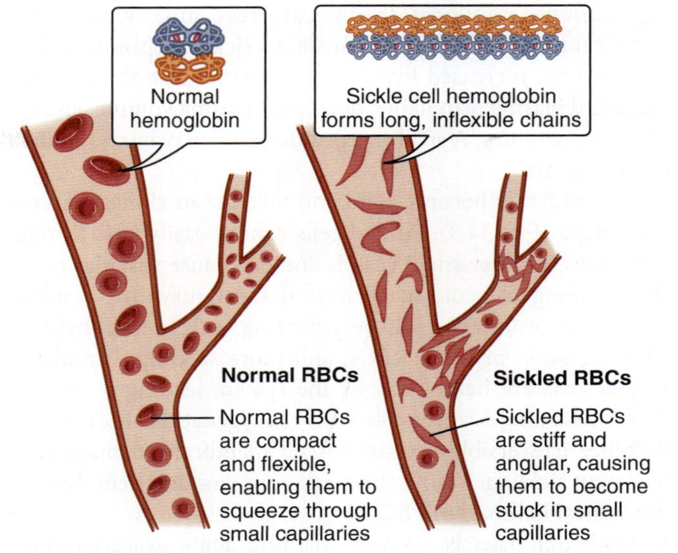

Fig. 34.3 In sickle cell, the hemoglobin forms long inflexible chains and alters the shape of the red blood cells *(RBCs)*. The sickled RBCs can become stuck in the capillaries and occlude the blood flow.

BOX 34.1 GENETICS IN CLINICAL PRACTICE

Sickle Cell Disease

Genetic Basis
- Autosomal recessive disorder
- Mutation in β-globin *(HBB)* gene found on chromosome 11
- Various versions of β-globin result from different mutations in the *HBB* gene
- Hgb S variant involves substitution of valine for glutamic acid in the β-globin gene

Incidence
- Most common inherited blood disorder in the United States
- Affects around 100,000 Americans
- Occurs in about 1 of every 365 African American births
- Occurs in about 1 of every 16,300 Hispanic American births
- Affects people of Mediterranean, Caribbean, Arabian, and East Indian descent
- 1 in 13 African American babies is born with sickle cell trait

Genetic Testing
- DNA testing is available
- Electrophoresis of hemoglobin and sickling screening test are common

Clinical Implications
- Sickle cell trait is the carrier state for sickle cell disease (SCD) and is a mild type of SCD
- If both parents have the trait, there is a 1 in 4 chance that their baby will have SCD
- Genetic counseling is recommended for people with a family history of SCD so they can understand the risks for transmitting the genetic mutation

Sickling Episodes

The major pathophysiologic event of SCD is the sickling of RBCs (Fig. 34.3). The main trigger of sickling episodes is low O_2 tension in the blood. Infection is the most common cause of hypoxia or deoxygenation of the RBCs. Other causes include high altitude, emotional or physical stress, surgery, and blood loss. Events that can trigger or sustain a sickling episode include dehydration, increased hydrogen ion concentration (acidosis), increased plasma osmolality, decreased plasma volume, and low body temperature. A sickling episode can also occur without an obvious cause.

Sickled RBCs become rigid and take on an elongated, crescent shape (Fig. 34.3). Sickled cells cannot easily pass through capillaries or other small vessels and can cause vascular occlusion, leading to acute or chronic tissue injury. The resulting hemostasis promotes a self-perpetuating cycle of local hypoxia, deoxygenation of more RBCs, and more sickling. Circulating sickled cells are hemolyzed by the spleen, leading to anemia. At first, sickling is reversible with reoxygenation. It eventually becomes irreversible because of cell membrane damage from recurrent sickling. Vasoocclusive phenomena and hemolysis are the clinical hallmarks of SCD.

Sickle cell crisis is a severe, painful, acute exacerbation of RBC sickling, causing a vasoocclusive crisis. As sickled cells impair blood flow, vasospasm occurs, further restricting blood flow. Severe capillary hypoxia causes changes in membrane permeability, leading to plasma loss, hemoconcentration, thrombi, and further circulatory stagnation. Tissue ischemia, infarction, and necrosis eventually occur from lack of O_2. Shock is a possible life-threatening consequence because of severe O_2 depletion of the tissues and decreased circulating fluid volume. Sickle cell crisis can begin suddenly and persist for days to weeks.

The frequency, extent, and severity of sickling episodes are highly variable and unpredictable. They depend on the percent of Hgb S present. People with sickle cell anemia have the most severe form because the RBCs have a high percentage of Hgb S.

Clinical Manifestations

The effects of SCD vary from person to person. The severity may be due to genetic variants. Many people with sickle cell anemia are in fairly good health most of the time. However, they may have chronic health problems and pain from organ tissue hypoxia and damage (e.g., involving the kidneys or liver).

The typical patient is anemic but asymptomatic except during sickling episodes. Because most people with sickle cell anemia have dark skin, pallor is easier to detect by examining the mucous membranes. The skin may have a grayish cast. Because of the hemolysis, jaundice is common. Patients are prone to gallstones.

The main symptom associated with sickling is pain. The pain severity can range from minor to excruciating. During sickle cell crisis, the pain is severe because of tissue ischemia. The episodes can affect any area of the body or several sites simultaneously. The back, chest, extremities, and abdomen are affected most often. Pain episodes are often accompanied by other manifestations, such as fever, tachypnea, hypertension, nausea, and vomiting.

Complications

With repeated episodes of sickling, there is gradual involvement of all body systems, especially the spleen, lungs, kidneys, and brain. Organs that need large amounts of O_2 are most often affected and form the basis for many of the complications of SCD (Fig. 34.4). Infection is a major cause of mortality. One reason for this is the spleen does not phagocytize foreign substances as it becomes infarcted and dysfunctional (usually by 2 to 4 years of age) from the sickled RBCs. The spleen becomes small from the repeated scarring, termed *autosplenectomy.*

Pneumonia is the most common infection. It often is of pneumococcal origin. Infections can be so severe that they cause an aplastic and hemolytic crisis and gallstones. *Aplastic crisis* can be so severe that it causes a temporary shutdown of RBC production in the bone marrow.

Acute chest syndrome is a term used to describe acute pulmonary complications that include pneumonia, tissue infarction, and fat embolism. There may be fever, chest pain, cough, lung infiltrates, and dyspnea. Pulmonary infarctions may cause pulmonary hypertension, MI, and cor pulmonale. The heart may become ischemic and enlarged, leading to HF. Retinal vessel obstruction may result in bleeding, scarring, retinal detachment, and blindness. The increased blood viscosity and the lack of O_2 can injure the kidneys. Renal failure may occur. Pulmonary embolism or stroke can result from thrombosis and infarction of cerebral blood vessels. Bone changes may include osteoporosis and osteosclerosis after infarction. Chronic leg ulcers can result from the hypoxia and are especially prevalent around the ankles. *Priapism* (persistent penile erection) may occur if penile veins become occluded.

Diagnostic Studies

A peripheral blood smear may reveal sickled cells and increased, abnormal reticulocytes. Hgb electrophoresis can determine the amount of Hgb S and SCD from other variants.

The accelerated RBC breakdown gives the patient the characteristic findings of hemolysis (jaundice, high serum bilirubin levels) and abnormal laboratory test results (Table 34.6). Skeletal x-rays show bone and joint deformities and flattening. MRI can diagnose a stroke caused by blocked cerebral vessels from sickled cells. Doppler studies can assess for deep vein thromboses (DVTs). A chest x-ray can diagnose infection.

❖ Interprofessional and Nursing Management

Goals of interprofessional care include (1) preventing sequelae from SCD; (2) alleviating the manifestations from complications of SCD; (3) minimizing end-organ damage; and (4) continuously assessing for and promptly treating serious sequelae, such as acute chest syndrome, which can lead to immediate death.[1]

A patient in sickle cell crisis may need to be hospitalized. O_2 therapy treats hypoxia and controls sickling. Assess for any changes in respiratory status. Encourage incentive spirometry. Rest can reduce metabolic requirements. Provide DVT prophylaxis. Fluids will reduce blood viscosity and maintain renal function. Priapism is managed with pain medication and fluids. If it does not resolve within a few hours, a urologist may be called.[2]

Transfusion therapy is needed with an aplastic crisis. Patients who have frequent crises or serious complications, such as acute chest syndrome, may need aggressive RBC exchange transfusion

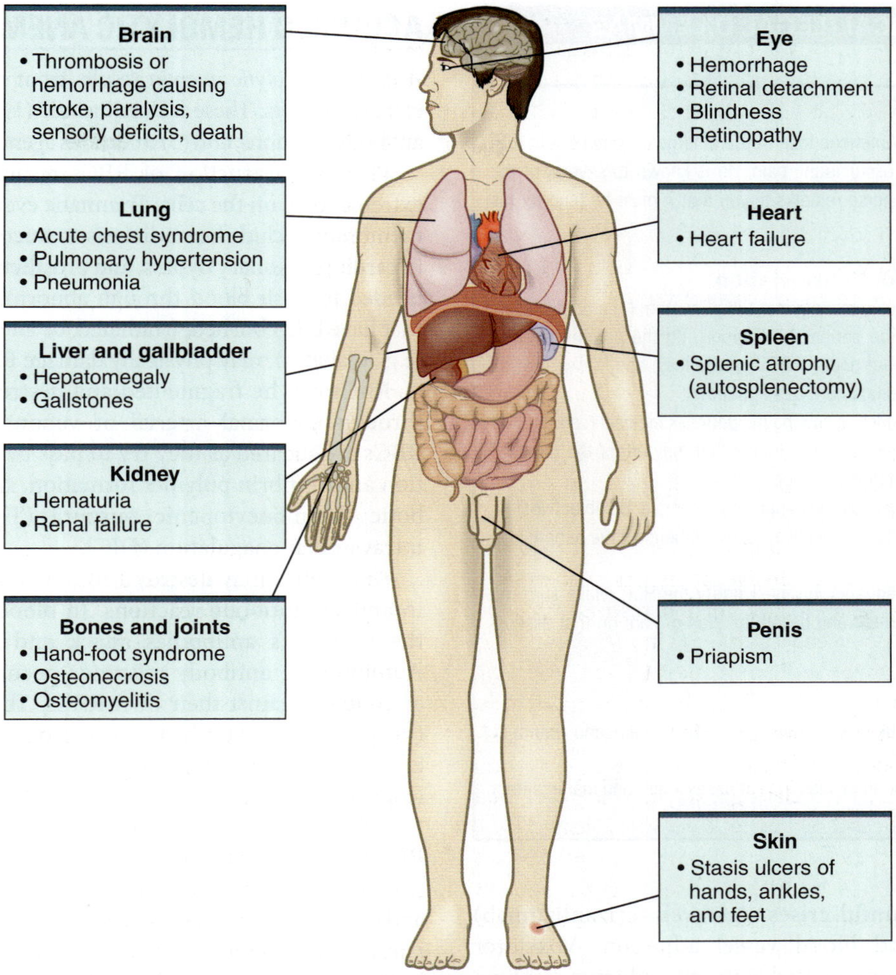

Fig. 34.4 Clinical manifestations and complications of sickle cell disease. (Modified from Huether SE, McCance KL, Brashers VL: *Understanding pathophysiology*, ed 7, St Louis, 2020, Elsevier.)

programs. These patients, like those with thalassemia major, may need iron chelation therapy to reduce transfusion-produced iron overload.

CHECK YOUR PRACTICE

A 21-year-old Black woman presents to the emergency department (ED) after a ski trip to Colorado. She is in excruciating pain in her chest and abdomen. She is short of breath, and her O_2 saturation is 86%. Vital signs show her heart rate is 110 beats/min and respiratory rate 28/min. She has crackles in the lungs. You note 6 previous ED admissions for sickle cell crises.

- What are your priorities for her nursing care?

Use a holistic approach to address the pain and its impact on the patient's quality of life (see Chapter 9).[1] Patients may have different types and sites of pain, as well as acute and chronic pain. Undertreatment of sickle cell pain is a major problem (Box 34.2). SCD patients may develop tolerance. They may need larger doses of pain medication to reduce pain to an acceptable level. Pain can cause patients to have central sensitization, hyperalgesia, and altered opioid metabolism. This can cause mood and emotional problems.

During an acute crisis, optimal pain control usually includes large doses of continuous opioid analgesics, along with breakthrough analgesia, often in the form of patient-controlled analgesia (PCA). Adjunctive measures include nonsteroidal antiinflammatory drugs (NSAIDs), antineuropathic pain drugs (e.g., antidepressants, antiseizure drugs), local anesthetics, or nerve blocks. Occupational and physical therapy can optimize functioning. Social and chaplain services can help to address social, emotional, and spiritual needs.

Infection is a frequent complication. Any febrile illness in a patient with SCD is an emergency. Wound infections, such as chronic leg ulcers, may be treated with rest, antibiotics, and proper wound care (see Chapter 12). Patients with acute chest syndrome receive broad-spectrum antibiotics, O_2 therapy, fluid therapy, and exchange transfusion. Blood transfusions are done sparingly between crises because patients develop antibodies to RBCs and iron overload. Because chronic hemolysis results decreased folic acid stores, the patient should take an oral folic acid supplement.

Various drugs can reduce sickling episodes.[10] Hydroxyurea (Hydrea) increases the production of Hgb F (fetal hemoglobin) and alters the adhesion of sickled RBCs to the endothelium. The increase in Hgb F is accompanied by a reduction in hemolysis, an increase in Hgb concentration, and a decrease

BOX 34.2 ETHICAL/LEGAL DILEMMAS

Pain Management

Situation

N.C., a 21-year-old African American man in the emergency department (ED) in sickle cell crisis, reports excruciating pain. He is known to several of the staff members in the ED. A nurse remarks to you that it must be time for his "fix" of pain drugs.

Ethical/Legal Points for Consideration

- The standard of care for pain management requires that (1) a pain assessment is done based on the patient's self-report, (2) the patient receives the best possible pain relief under the circumstances, and (3) we provide competent and compassionate care to all patients.
- The pain assessment includes reviewing the patient's medical record to see if there are health care issues or conditions that may affect the patient's response to pain and pain management.
- Document patient behaviors related to pain management. Be objective (factual observations) rather than subjective, such as labeling ("the patient is in withdrawal").
- When pain relief is inadequate, you must notify the HCP. Make sure the HCP has assessed the patient and based the plan of care on that assessment.

Discussion Questions

1. How can you teach your peers about pain assessment and management?
2. What factors do you need to include in your assessment and management of N.C.?

in sickled cells and painful crises. Adakveo (crizanlizumab) reduces sickle cell and blood vessel adhesion. Voxelotor (Oxbryta) stabilizes an oxygenated Hgb cell, reducing sickling. Oral glutamine, an amino acid, decreases endothelial adhesion and can reduce the number and frequency of pain crises and hospitalizations.[10]

HSCT is the only available treatment that can cure some patients with SCD. It is not widely available. The selection of appropriate recipients, scarcity of appropriate donors, risk, and cost-effectiveness limit its use. We are researching gene therapy.[10]

Patient teaching and support are important in the long-term care of the patient with SCD. The patient and caregiver must understand the basis of SCD and the reasons for supportive care and ongoing screening tailored to SCD manifestations. Teach the patient ways to avoid crises. Review steps to avoid dehydration and hypoxia, such as avoiding high altitudes and seeking medical attention quickly to counteract problems, such as upper respiratory tract infections. Teach patients to maintain adequate fluid intake. Encourage routine immunizations, such as pneumococcal, influenza, and hepatitis. Screening for retinopathy should begin at age 10. Each person with SCD should have a reproductive life plan.[1] Provide teaching about pain control because the pain during a crisis may be severe and often requires considerable analgesia. Minor pain episodes that are not associated with infection or other symptoms that need medical attention can sometimes be managed at home.

ACQUIRED HEMOLYTIC ANEMIA

Acquired hemolytic anemia results from hemolysis of RBCs from extrinsic factors. These factors include (1) physical destruction, (2) antibody reactions, and (3) infectious agents and toxins (Table 34.2).[1]

Physical destruction of RBCs results from the exertion of extreme force on the cells. Traumatic events that disrupt the RBC membrane include hemodialysis, extracorporeal circulation used in cardiopulmonary bypass, and prosthetic heart valves. The force needed to push blood through abnormal vessels, such as those that have been burned, irradiated, or affected by vascular disease (e.g., diabetes), may physically damage RBCs.

RBCs can be fragmented and destroyed as they try to pass through abnormal arterial or venous microcirculation. The RBCs are sheared as they try to pass by excess platelet aggregation and/or fibrin polymer formation, such as is seen in thrombotic thrombocytopenic purpura (TTP) and disseminated intravascular coagulation (DIC).

Antibodies may destroy RBCs by the mechanisms involved in antigen-antibody reactions. In blood transfusion reactions, the recipient's antibodies attack and hemolyze donor cells. Autoimmune antibody reactions occur when people develop antibodies against their own RBCs. This can be an idiopathic (no prior hemolytic history) or from other autoimmune diseases (e.g., systemic lupus erythematosus [SLE]) or medications (aspirin, clopidogrel, tacrolimus).[2,6]

Infectious agents cause hemolysis in 3 ways: (1) invading the RBC and destroying its contents (e.g., parasites, such as in malaria), (2) releasing hemolytic substances (e.g., *Clostridium perfringens*), and (3) generating an antigen-antibody reaction (e.g., *Mycoplasma pneumoniae*). Various agents may be toxic to RBCs and cause hemolysis. Hemolytic toxins include chemicals, such as oxidative drugs, arsenic, lead, copper, and bee stings or spider bites.

Laboratory findings in hemolytic anemia are shown in Table 34.6. Treatment and management involve general supportive care until the causative agent can be eliminated or at least made less injurious to the RBCs. Because a hemolytic crisis is a potential consequence, be ready to institute appropriate emergency therapy. This includes aggressive hydration and electrolyte replacement to reduce the risk for kidney injury caused by Hgb (from RBC lysis) clogging the kidney tubules and subsequent shock. Supportive care may include giving corticosteroids and blood products or removing the spleen.

The patient with chronic hemolytic anemia may need folate replacement. To suppress the RBC destruction, immunosuppressive agents may be used, such as glucocorticoids or rituximab (Rituxan), a monoclonal antibody to B-cell CD20. For severe cases associated with hemolysis, thrombocytopenia, and acute kidney injury, additional immunosuppressants (e.g., cyclosporine) may be used. Plasma exchange and eculizumab (Soliris), a monoclonal antibody to complement protein C5, are options.[2,4]

OTHER RED BLOOD CELL DISORDERS

HEMOCHROMATOSIS

Hemochromatosis is an iron overload disorder characterized by increased intestinal iron absorption. A genetic defect is the

BOX 34.3 GENETICS IN CLINICAL PRACTICE

Hemochromatosis

Genetic Basis
- Autosomal recessive disorder
- Caused by mutations in the *HFE (C282Y or H63D), HAMP, SLC40A1, FTH1,* and *TFR2* genes
- These genes play a key role in regulating iron absorption, transport, and storage
- Mutations in these genes impair the control of iron absorption during digestion and change iron distribution to other parts of the body, causing iron accumulation in tissues and organs

Incidence
- Most common genetic disease in people of European ancestry
- The C282Y mutation of the *HFE* gene is the most common
- About 1 in 15 people of Northern European ancestry have at least 1 copy of the *C282Y* mutation in the *HFE* gene
- Affects 1 in 300 non-Hispanic whites in the United States

Genetic Testing
- DNA testing is available and recommended for all first-degree relatives of people with the disease
- American Hemochromatosis Society recommends genetic testing regardless of family history

Clinical Implications
- Many people who have the gene mutation do not know it until diseases becomes apparent
- Clinical expression is variable and depends on diet iron, blood loss, and other modifying factors
- Early treatment can prevent serious complications

most common cause (Box 34.3).[11] It may occur with diseases such as sideroblastic anemia and liver disease, and the chronic blood transfusions used to treat thalassemia and SCD.

The normal range for total body iron is 40 mg/kg in women and 50 mg/kg in men. People with hemochromatosis accumulate iron at an increased rate. They may exceed total iron concentrations of 50 g.[2]

Symptoms usually do not develop until after age 40 years in men and after 50 years in women.[11] Early symptoms are nonspecific. They include fatigue, arthralgia, impotence, abdominal pain, and weight loss. Later, the excess iron accumulates in the liver and causes liver enlargement and cirrhosis. Excess iron deposits in the liver, pancreas, heart, joints, and endocrine glands cause diabetes, skin pigment changes (bronzing), heart problems (e.g., cardiomyopathy), arthritis, and testicular atrophy. There may be an enlarged liver and spleen and skin pigmentation changes.

Laboratory values show a high serum iron, TIBC, and serum ferritin. Testing for known genetic mutations confirms the diagnosis. MRI can measure liver and cardiac iron.[4] Liver biopsy can quantify the amount of iron and establish the degree of organ damage.

The goal of treatment is to remove excess iron from the body and minimize any symptoms the patient may have. Iron removal is achieved by removing 500 mL of blood each week until the iron stores are depleted. Then blood is removed less often to maintain iron levels within normal limits.

Iron-chelating drugs may be used. They form a complex with iron and promote its excretion from the body. [4] Deferoxamine chelates and removes iron via the kidneys. It is given IV or subcutaneously. Deferasirox and deferiprone are oral drugs. Diet changes include avoiding vitamin C and iron supplements, uncooked seafood, and iron-rich foods.

We manage problems from organ involvement (e.g., diabetes, HF) with the usual treatment for these problems. The most common causes of death are cirrhosis, liver failure, liver cancer, and HF. With early diagnosis and treatment, life expectancy is normal. However, many cases go undetected and untreated.

POLYCYTHEMIA

Polycythemia is the production and presence of increased numbers of RBCs. The increase in RBCs can be so great that blood circulation is impaired because of the increased blood viscosity *(hyperviscosity)* and volume *(hypervolemia).*

Etiology and Pathophysiology

The 2 types of polycythemia are primary polycythemia, or polycythemia vera, and secondary polycythemia (Fig. 34.5). Their causes and pathogenesis differ, although their complications and manifestations are similar.

Primary Polycythemia

Polycythemia vera is a chronic myeloproliferative disorder. It involves increased production not only of RBCs but also WBCs and platelets. This leads to enhanced blood viscosity and blood volume and congestion of organs and tissues with blood. Splenomegaly and hepatomegaly are common. Patients have hypercoagulopathies that predispose them to clotting. The disease develops insidiously and follows a chronic, vacillating course. The median age at diagnosis is 60 years old, with a slight male predominance.[1]

Genetic Link

Polycythemia vera begins with 1 or more DNA mutations of a single hematopoietic stem cell. Most cases are not inherited, but a familial predisposition may exist.[1] It is associated with mutations in the Janus kinase-2 *(JAK2)* gene. The *JAK2* gene provides instructions for making a protein that promotes cell proliferation, especially blood cells from hematopoietic stem cells.

Secondary Polycythemia

Secondary polycythemia can be either hypoxia driven or hypoxia independent. In hypoxia-driven secondary polycythemia, hypoxia stimulates the kidneys to make EPO, which stimulates RBC production. The need for O_2 may result from high altitude, lung disease, cardiovascular disease, alveolar hypoventilation, defective O_2 transport, or tissue hypoxia.

EPO levels may return to normal once the Hgb stabilizes at a higher level. In this situation, secondary polycythemia is a physiologic response in which the body tries to compensate

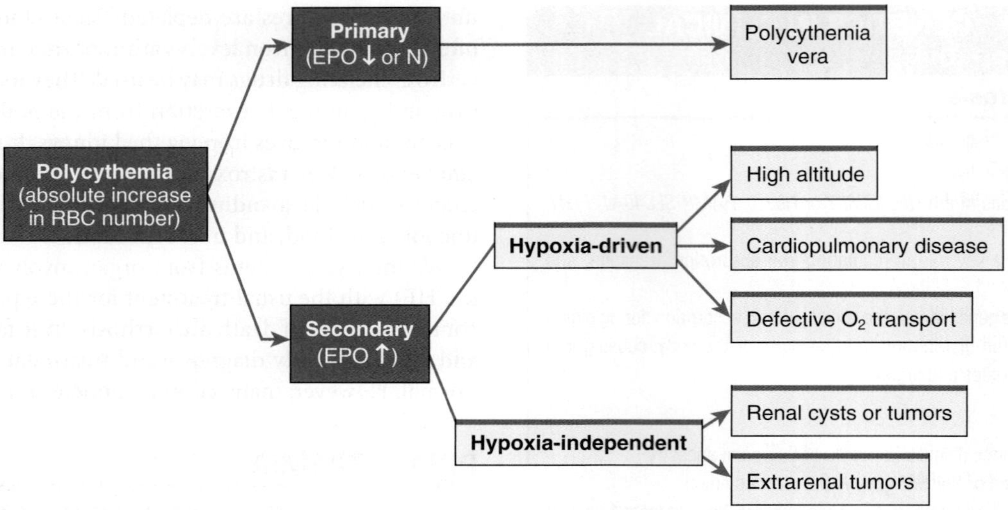

Fig. 34.5 Differentiating between primary and secondary polycythemia. *EPO,* Erythropoietin; *N,* normal.

for a problem, rather than a pathologic response. Chapter 31 discusses hypoxia-driven secondary polycythemia in COPD.

In hypoxia-independent secondary polycythemia, cancer or benign tumor tissue makes EPO. Serum EPO levels often stay increased in these situations. Splenomegaly does not occur with secondary polycythemia.

Clinical Manifestations and Complications

Circulatory manifestations occur due to the hypertension caused by hypervolemia and hyperviscosity. They are often the first manifestations and include headache, vertigo, dizziness, tinnitus, and visual changes. Generalized itching (often exacerbated by a hot bath) may be a striking symptom. It is related to histamine release from an increased number of basophils. Paresthesias and *erythromelalgia* (painful burning and redness of the hands and feet) may be present. The patient may have angina, HF, intermittent claudication, and thrombophlebitis, which may be complicated by embolization. These manifestations are caused by blood vessel distention, impaired blood flow, circulatory stasis, thrombosis, and tissue hypoxia from the hypervolemia and hyperviscosity. The most common acute complication and major cause of mortality is stroke from a thrombosis.

Hemorrhagic phenomena caused by either vessel rupture from overdistention or inadequate platelet function may result in petechiae, bruising, nosebleeds, or GI bleeding. Bleeding can be acute and catastrophic. Hepatomegaly and splenomegaly from organ engorgement may contribute to satiety and fullness. The patient may have pain from peptic ulcers caused either by increased gastric secretions or liver and spleen engorgement. *Plethora* (ruddy complexion) may be present. Uric acid is 1 of the products of RBC destruction. As RBC destruction increases, uric acid production increases. This leads to hyperuricemia and gout.

Although the incidence is low, myelofibrosis and leukemia develop in some patients with polycythemia vera. These disorders may be caused by the chemotherapy drugs used to treat the disease or by a disorder in the stem cells that progresses to erythroleukemia.

Diagnostic Studies

The major diagnostic criteria for polycythemia vera include (1) high Hgb, hematocrit, and RBC mass; (2) bone marrow examination showing hypercellularity of RBCs, WBCs, and platelets; and (3) presence of *JAK2* V617F or *JAK2* exon 12 mutation.[12] Other studies show low EPO level (secondary polycythemia has a high level); (3) high WBC count with basophilia and neutrophilia; (4) high platelet count and platelet dysfunction; and (5) normal or high leukocyte alkaline phosphatase, uric acid, and cobalamin levels.

❖ Interprofessional and Nursing Management

Treatment aims to reduce blood volume and viscosity and bone marrow activity. Phlebotomy is the mainstay of treatment. The aim of phlebotomy is to reduce the hematocrit and keep it less than 45%.[13] At the time of diagnosis, 300 to 500 mL of blood may be removed every few days until the hematocrit is reduced to acceptable levels.[13] Phlebotomy then may be needed every 2 to 3 months, reducing the blood volume by about 500 mL each time. A person managed with repeated phlebotomies eventually becomes iron deficient, although they are rarely symptomatic. Hydration therapy can reduce the blood's viscosity. Low-dose aspirin can prevent clotting.[13]

Myelosuppressive agents, such as hydroxyurea, or busulfan (Myleran), may be given.[13] Ruxolitinib (Jakafi), which inhibits expression of the *JAK2* mutation, is given to those who do not respond to hydroxyurea. α-Interferon (α-IFN)-2b and pegylated IFN alfa-2a are options for women of childbearing age or those with intractable itching.[13]

When acute exacerbations of polycythemia vera develop, you have several nursing responsibilities. Depending on your agency, you may either assist with or perform the phlebotomy. Assess intake and output during hydration therapy to avoid fluid overload (which worsens circulatory congestion) or fluid deficit (which makes the blood more viscous). Give myelosuppressive agents as ordered. Observe the patient and teach them about drug side effects.

Assess the patient's nutrition status. Inadequate food intake can result from GI symptoms of fullness, pain, and dyspepsia.

TABLE 34.11 Causes of Acquired Thrombocytopenia

Impaired Platelet Production
- Cancers and other disorders
  - Aplastic anemia
  - Leukemia, lymphoma, myeloma, myelodysplastic disorders
  - Marrow metastases by solid tumors
- Drugs (chemotherapy, others)
- Immune thrombocytopenia (ITP)
- Infections, bacterial, fungal, viral (hepatitis C virus, HIV, cytomegalovirus)
- Nutrition deficiencies, alcohol use
- Radiation

Increased Platelet Destruction
- Artificial surfaces (e.g., cardiopulmonary bypass, hemodialysis)
- Disseminated intravascular coagulation (DIC)
- Heparin-induced thrombocytopenia (HIT)
- Pregnancy-related
- Thrombotic microangiopathy
  - Atypical hemolytic uremic syndromes (aHUSs)
  - Thrombotic thrombocytopenic purpura (TTP)

Abnormal Platelet Distribution
- Dilution (massive blood transfusion, fluids)
- Splenic sequestration

Begin activities and any drug therapy to decrease thrombus formation.

Because of its chronic nature, polycythemia vera requires ongoing evaluation. Assess the patient for complications with each encounter.

PROBLEMS OF HEMOSTASIS

Hemostasis involves the vascular endothelium, platelets, and coagulation factors. They normally work together to stop bleeding and repair vascular injury. These mechanisms are described in Chapter 33. Disruption in any component may result in bleeding or thrombotic disorders.

Three major disorders of hemostasis discussed in this section are (1) thrombocytopenia (low platelet count), (2) hemophilia and von Willebrand disease (inherited disorders of specific clotting factors), and (3) DIC.

THROMBOCYTOPENIA

Etiology and Pathophysiology

Thrombocytopenia is a reduction of platelets to less than 150,000/μL (150×10^9/L). Acute, severe, or prolonged decreases from normal can result in abnormal hemostasis that presents as prolonged bleeding from minor trauma or spontaneous bleeding without injury.

Platelet disorders occur from impaired production, increased destruction, or abnormal distribution (Table 34.11).[1] While they can be inherited (e.g., Wiskott-Aldrich syndrome), most are acquired. Drugs are a common cause of acquired disorders.[1] Although some drugs are directly myelosuppressive (e.g., chemotherapy, ganciclovir), the usual mechanism of drug-related thrombocytopenia is accelerated platelet destruction caused by antibodies. Antibodies attack the platelets when the drug binds to the platelet surface.

Some drugs affect platelet aggregation. Aspirin doses as low as 81 mg can alter platelet aggregation. Normal function is restored when new platelets are made.

Immune Thrombocytopenia

The most common acquired thrombocytopenia is *immune thrombocytopenia* (ITP). ITP is an acquired immune disorder where there is abnormal platelet destruction. In general, ITP presents as an acute condition in children and a chronic condition in adults.

Thrombocytopenia results from antiplatelet antibodies, impaired platelet production, and T cell–mediated destruction of platelets.[1] In ITP, antibodies coat the platelets. These platelets function normally. When they reach the spleen, these antibody-coated platelets are mistaken as foreign and destroyed by macrophages. Decreased platelet production contributes to ITP. Sometimes autoimmune disease (e.g., SLE) or infection, such as *Helicobacter pylori* or viral infection (HIV), contributes to ITP.[1,14] Platelets normally survive 8 to 10 days. However, in ITP, platelet survival is shortened.

Thrombotic Thrombocytopenic Purpura

TTP is an uncommon syndrome characterized by microangiopathic hemolytic anemia (MAHA), thrombocytopenia, neurologic changes, fever (in the absence of infection), and renal problemss.[1] Not all features are present in all patients. Because it is almost always associated with hemolytic-uremic syndrome (HUS), TTP is often referred to as *TTP-HUS*. The disease is associated with enhanced platelet aggregation, which form microthrombi that deposit in arterioles and capillaries.

In most cases, TTP is caused by the deficiency of a plasma enzyme (ADAMTS13) that breaks down the von Willebrand clotting factor (von Willebrand factor [vWF]) into normal size. vWF is the most important factor that mediates platelet adhesion to damaged endothelial cells. Without the enzyme, unusually large amounts of vWF attach to activated platelets, promoting platelet aggregation. TTP is a medical emergency because bleeding and clotting occur at the same time.

TTP occurs mainly in previously healthy adults, with a slight female predominance. The syndrome may be idiopathic (thought to be due to an autoimmune disorder against ADAMTS13). It may occur due to certain drug toxicities (e.g., chemotherapy, cyclosporine, oral contraceptives, valacyclovir, clopidogrel) pregnancy or preeclampsia, infection, or a known autoimmune disorder, such as SLE or scleroderma.[1]

Heparin-Induced Thrombocytopenia

One of the risks associated with heparin is the life-threatening condition called *heparin-induced thrombocytopenia* (HIT), or *heparin-induced thrombocytopenia and thrombosis syndrome* (HITTS). Typically, patients develop thrombocytopenia 5 to 14 days after the onset of heparin therapy. We suspect HIT if the platelet count decreases by more than 50% or is less than

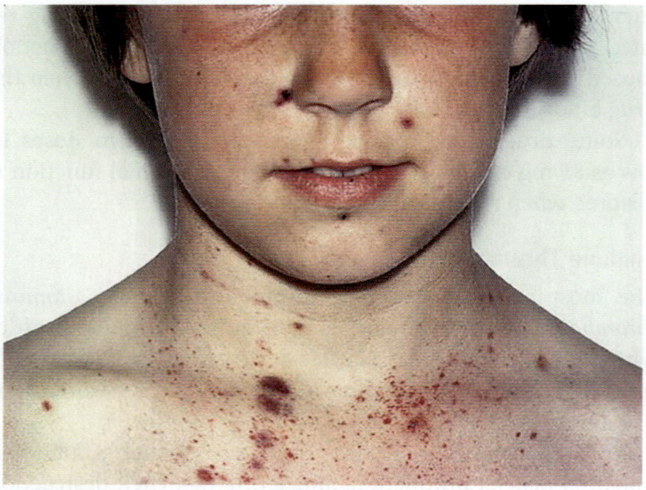

Fig. 34.6 Acute immune thrombocytopenic purpura often presents with purpuric lesions. (From Howard MH, Hamilton PJ: *Hematology*, ed 4, London, 2013, Mosby.)

150,000/μL. As many as 5% of patients on IV heparin therapy develop HIT.[14]

In HIT, platelet destruction and vascular endothelial injury are the 2 major responses to an immune-mediated response to heparin. Platelet factor 4 (PF4) (a protein made and released by platelets) binds to heparin. This PF4-heparin complex then binds to the platelet surface, leading to further platelet activation and release of more PF4, thus creating a positive feedback loop. The body makes antibodies against the PF4-heparin-platelet complex. They are removed prematurely from circulation, leading to thrombocytopenia and platelet-fibrin thrombi.

Although the major problem of HIT is venous thrombosis, arterial thrombosis can occur. DVT and pulmonary emboli most often result as a complication of the thromboses. Other complications include arterial vascular infarcts, causing skin necrosis, stroke, and end-organ damage (e.g., kidneys). Bleeding symptoms are unusual because the platelet count is rarely less than 20,000/μL.

Clinical Manifestations

Many patients with thrombocytopenia are asymptomatic. The most common symptom is bleeding, usually mucosal or cutaneous. Mucosal bleeding may manifest as nosebleeds and gingival bleeding. Large bullous hemorrhages may appear on the buccal mucosa due to the lack of vessel protection by the submucosal tissue. Bleeding into the skin is seen as petechiae, purpura, or bruising. *Petechiae* are small, flat, red or reddish brown microhemorrhages (see Table 33.6). When the platelet count is low, RBCs may leak out of the blood vessels and into the skin to cause petechiae. When there are many petechiae, we call the resulting reddish skin *purpura* (Fig. 34.6). Pain and tenderness are sometimes present.

The major complication of thrombocytopenia is bleeding. Bleeding may be insidious or acute and internal or external. It may occur in any area of the body, including the joints, retina, and brain. Prolonged bleeding from trauma or injury does not usually occur until platelet counts are under 50,000/μL (50×10^9/L).[1] When the count is under 20,000/μL (20×10^9/L),

TABLE 34.12 Laboratory Results in Thrombocytopenia and DIC

Laboratory Test	ITP	TTP	HIT	DIC
Platelets	↓↓↓↓	↓↓↓	↓↓	↓↓↓
Hemolysis				
Haptoglobin	N	↓	N	↓
Hgb	N	↓↓	N	N or ↓
Indirect bilirubin	N	↑	N	N or ↑
LDH	N	↑↑↑	N	↑
Reticulocytes	N	↑	N	N or ↑
Schistocytes	N	↑↑↑	N or ↑	N or ↑
Coagulopathy				
PT	N	N	N	Prolonged
aPTT	N	N	N	Prolonged
D dimer	N	N or ↑	↑	↑↑
Other tests	ITP IgG assay, platelet activation/function assay, *Helicobacter pylori*, hepatitis C, HIV, bone marrow biopsy	ADAMTS13 Urinalysis (for proteinuria, hematuria), Creatinine	Platelet activation/function assay, PF4-heparin complex (antigen assay)	Fibrin split products (FSPs)

spontaneous, life-threatening bleeding (e.g., intracranial bleeding) can occur.

Insidious bleeding may be first detected by discovering the anemia from the blood loss. Be aware of manifestations of internal blood loss, including weakness, fainting, dizziness, tachycardia, abdominal pain, and hypotension. Prolonged bleeding after routine procedures, such as venipuncture or IM injection, may indicate thrombocytopenia.

Because vascular thromboses may occur with thrombocytopenia (e.g., TTP, HIT), assess for signs and symptoms of vascular ischemic problems (see Chapter 41).

Diagnostic Studies

Thrombocytopenia exists when the platelet count is under 150,000/μL (150×10^9/L). The patient's history and assessment, along with laboratory studies, help to determine the cause of the thrombocytopenia. Table 34.12 compares results for types of thrombocytopenia.

Laboratory tests that assess secondary hemostasis or coagulation, such as the prothrombin time (PT) and activated partial thromboplastin time (aPTT), can be normal even in severe thrombocytopenia. If they are increased, this may point toward DIC.

Specific assays, such as ITP antigen-specific assay, platelet activation/function assay, or PF4-heparin complex for HIT, can help with the diagnosis. In TTP, testing for ADAMTS13 deficiency is not always diagnostic. Thrombocytopenia may be severe in TTP, but coagulation studies are normal. Lactate dehydrogenase (LDH) may be increased. With TTP, altered RBC morphology, including *spherocytes* (small, globular, completely hemoglobinated RBCs), fragmented cells (schistocytes), and pronounced reticulocytosis, may be present. These findings are partially a result of intravascular fibrin deposition causing a "slicing" of RBCs.

Bone marrow examination may be done to see if production problems (e.g., leukemia, aplastic anemia, other myeloproliferative disorders) are the cause of thrombocytopenia or when other tests are inconclusive. When destruction of circulating platelets is the cause, bone marrow analysis shows *megakaryocytes* (precursors of platelets) to be normal or increased, even though circulating platelets are reduced. The absence or decreased number of megakaryocytes on bone marrow biopsy is consistent with thrombocytopenia caused by decreased bone marrow production (e.g., aplastic anemia).

Interprofessional Care

Interprofessional care of thrombocytopenia differs based on the cause. Removal or treatment of the underlying cause is sometimes sufficient. The patient with thrombocytopenia should avoid aspirin and other drugs that affect platelet function or production. The following sections discuss management strategies for the different causes of thrombocytopenia (Table 34.13).

Immune Thrombocytopenic Purpura

Multiple therapies are part of managing the patient with ITP. If the patient is asymptomatic, they may not be treated unless the platelet count is under 30,000/µL.[14] Corticosteroids are used initially to treat ITP because they suppress the phagocytic response of splenic macrophages. [14] This alters the spleen's recognition of platelets and increases the platelets' life span. Corticosteroids depress antibody formation and reduce capillary leakage.

Romiplostim (Nplate) and eltrombopag (Promacta) are used for patients with chronic ITP who have an insufficient response to steroids. These drugs are thrombopoietin receptor agonists that increase platelet production. [14] Rituximab (Rituxan) lyses activated B cells, thus reducing the immune recognition of platelets. High doses of IV immunoglobulin (IVIG) and a component of IVIG, anti-Rh_0(D) (anti-D, WinRho), may be given to a patient who does not respond to other treatments. These agents compete with antiplatelet antibodies for macrophage receptors in the spleen.

Immunosuppressive therapy (e.g., azathioprine, cyclosporine A) may be used in refractory cases (Table 34.13).[14] Platelet transfusions can increase platelet counts in cases of life-threatening bleeding, a platelet count less than 10,000/µL, or with bleeding before a procedure.[15] Platelets should not be given prophylactically because of the risk for antibody formation.

The patient may need a splenectomy if they do not respond to treatment. The effectiveness of splenectomy is based on 4 factors. First, the spleen has an abundance of the macrophages that sequester and destroy platelets. Second, structural features of the spleen enhance the interaction between antibody-coated platelets and macrophages. Third, some antibody synthesis occurs in the spleen, so antiplatelet antibodies decrease after splenectomy. Fourth, the spleen normally sequesters about one third of the platelets, so its removal increases the number of platelets in circulation.

TABLE 34.13 Interprofessional Care
Thrombocytopenia

Diagnostic Assessment
- History and physical assessment
- Bone marrow aspiration and biopsy
- CBC, including platelet count
- Specific laboratory studies (Table 34.12)

Management

Immune Thrombocytopenic Purpura
- Corticosteroids
- Romiplostim (Nplate)
- Eltrombopag (Promacta)
- Rituximab (Rituxan)
- Splenectomy
- IV immunoglobulin (IVIG)
- Anti-Rh_0(D)
- Immunosuppressives (e.g., Azathioprine, cyclophosphamide)

Thrombotic Thrombocytopenic Purpura
- Identify and treat or remove of cause
- Plasmapheresis (plasma exchange)
- Corticosteroids
- Rituximab (Rituxan)
- Caplacizumab
- Immunosuppressives (e.g., cyclophosphamide, cyclosporine)
- Splenectomy

Heparin-Induced Thrombocytopenia
- Direct thrombin inhibitor (argatroban [Acova])
- Indirect thrombin inhibitor (fondaparinux [Arixtra])
- Synthetic thrombin inhibitor (bivalirudin)
- Plasmapheresis (plasma exchange)
- Warfarin (Coumadin)
- Direct oral anticoagulants (e.g., apixaban, rivaroxaban)
- Thrombolytic agents

Decreased Platelet Production
- Identify and treat or remove of cause
- Immune therapies (corticosteroids, danazol, cyclosporine)
- Avatrombopag
- Platelet transfusions

Thrombotic Thrombocytopenic Purpura

We treat TTP in a variety of ways. The first step is to treat the underlying disorder or remove the causative agent, if known. If untreated, TTP usually results in irreversible renal failure and death. Plasma exchange (plasmapheresis) (see Chapter 14) can reverse platelet consumption by supplying the right vWF and enzyme (ADAMTS13) and removing the large vWF molecules that bind with platelets. Treatment should continue daily until the patient's platelet counts normalize and hemolysis has ceased. Corticosteroids are used with this treatment.[16]

Rituximab is given to patients who are refractory to plasma exchange. It decreases the level of inhibitory ADAMTS13 immunoglobulin G (IgG) antibodies. Caplacizumab, an anti-VWF antibody, blocks VWF binding to platelets. This can reduce platelet aggregation and thrombosis and normalize the platelet count.[16] Other immunosuppressants, such as cyclosporine or cyclophosphamide, are options. Splenectomy is an option in patients who are refractory to plasma exchange or immunosuppression. Platelet administration is contraindicated because this may lead to new vWF-platelet complexes and increased clotting.[4]

Heparin-Induced Thrombocytopenia

We stop all forms of heparin when HIT is present. This includes heparin flushes for vascular catheters. To maintain anticoagulation, the patient should receive a direct thrombin inhibitor, such as argatroban. Other options are fondaparinux (Arixtra), a factor Xa inhibitor (indirect thrombin inhibitor), or bivalirudin (a synthetic thrombin inhibitor).[17] Warfarin should be started only when the platelet count reaches 150,000/μL. If clotting is severe, the most common treatments are plasmapheresis to clear the platelet-aggregating IgG from the blood, thrombolytic agents to treat the thromboembolic events, and surgery to remove clots. Platelet transfusions are not given because they may enhance thromboembolic events.

Patients who have had HIT should never receive heparin or low-molecular-weight heparin (LMWH) again. This should be noted in the patient's medical record.

Thrombocytopenia From Decreased Platelet Production

The management of acquired thrombocytopenia is based on finding the cause and treating the disease or removing the causative agent. Platelet transfusions are given if life-threatening bleeding develops. Platelet transfusions are generally not done unless the count is under 10,000/μL (10×10^9/L) or the patient is actively bleeding, has an active infection, or is having an invasive procedure.[6]

Acquired thrombocytopenia is often caused by another underlying condition (e.g., aplastic anemia, leukemia) or therapy used to treat another problem.[1,6] For example, in acute leukemia all blood cell types may be depressed. Plus, the patient may receive chemotherapy drugs that cause bone marrow suppression. If the patient can be supported throughout the course of chemotherapy-induced thrombocytopenia, the thrombocytopenia will resolve. If we do not find a cause, we may try immune therapies.[4]

NURSING MANAGEMENT: THROMBOCYTOPENIA

Assessment

Subjective and objective data that you should obtain from a patient with thrombocytopenia are outlined in Table 34.14.

Clinical Problems

The main clinical problem for the patient with thrombocytopenia is impaired tissue perfusion.

Planning

The overall goals are that the patient with thrombocytopenia will (1) have no bleeding, (2) maintain vascular integrity, and (3) manage self-care related to an increased risk for bleeding.

TABLE 34.14 NURSING ASSESSMENT
Thrombocytopenia

Subjective Data

Important Health Information

Health history: Recent or excessive bleeding; viral illness; HIV infection; cancer (especially leukemia or lymphoma); aplastic anemia; SLE; cirrhosis; exposure to radiation or toxic chemicals; DIC

Medications: Many medications, including chemotherapy agents, valproic acid (Depakote), furosemide, gold, NSAIDs, penicillin

Functional Health Patterns

Health perception–health management: Family history of bleeding problems; malaise

Nutritional-metabolic: Bleeding gingiva; coffee-ground or bloody vomitus; easy bruising

Elimination: Hematuria, dark or bloody stools

Activity-exercise: Fatigue, weakness, fainting; nosebleeds, hemoptysis; dyspnea

Cognitive-perceptual: Pain and tenderness in bleeding areas (e.g., abdomen, head, extremities); headache

Sexuality-reproductive: Menorrhagia, metrorrhagia

Objective Data

General

Fever, lethargy

GI

Splenomegaly, abdominal distention; heme-positive stools

Skin

Petechiae, bruising, purpura

Possible Diagnostic Findings

Platelet count <150,000/μL (150×10^9/L), prolonged bleeding time, ↓ Hgb and Hct; normal or ↑ megakaryocytes in bone marrow examination

Implementation

Health Promotion

Discourage using over-the-counter (OTC) medications known to be causes of acquired thrombocytopenia and reduced platelet function. Some have aspirin as an ingredient. Aspirin reduces platelet adhesiveness, thus contributing to bleeding.

Encourage persons to seek care if manifestations of bleeding (e.g., prolonged nosebleeds, petechiae) develop. Observe for early signs of thrombocytopenia in the patient receiving chemotherapy drugs.

Acute Care

The goal during acute episodes of thrombocytopenia is to prevent or control bleeding (see eNursing Care Plan 34.2 on the website for this chapter). Bleeding is usually from superficial sites. Deep bleeding (into muscles, joints, and abdomen) usually occurs only when clotting factors are decreased. Stress that a minor nosebleed or new petechiae may indicate potential bleeding and to notify the HCP.

Bleeding from the posterior nasopharynx may be hard to detect because the person swallows the blood. If you cannot avoid a subcutaneous injection, use a small-gauge needle. Apply direct pressure for at least 5 to 10 minutes after the injection. An

TABLE 34.15 PATIENT & CAREGIVER TEACHING

Thrombocytopenia

Include the following instructions when teaching a patient or caregiver the precautions to take when the platelet count is low:

1. Notify your HCP of any symptoms of bleeding. These include:
   - Black, tarry, or bloody bowel movements
   - Black or bloody vomit, sputum, or urine
   - Bleeding from the mouth or anywhere in the body
   - Bruising or small red or purple spots on the skin
   - Difficulty talking, sudden weakness of an arm or leg, confusion
   - Headache or changes in how well you can see
2. Ask your HCP about restrictions in your normal activities, such as vigorous exercise or lifting weights. In general, walking is safe. Wear sturdy shoes or slippers. If you are weak and at risk for falling, get help or supervision when getting out of bed or chair.
3. Do not blow your nose forcefully; gently pat it with a tissue if needed. For a nosebleed, keep your head up and apply firm pressure to the nostrils and bridge of your nose. If bleeding continues, place an ice bag over the bridge of your nose and the nape of your neck. If you are unable to stop a nosebleed after 10 min, call your HCP.
4. Do not bend down with your head lower than your waist.
5. Prevent constipation by drinking plenty of fluids. Do not strain when having a bowel movement. Your HCP may prescribe a stool softener. Do not use a suppository, an enema, or a rectal thermometer without the permission of your HCP.
6. Shave only with an electric razor. Do not use blades.
7. Do not tweeze your eyebrows or other body hair.
8. Do not puncture your skin, such as getting tattoos or body piercing.
9. Do not use any medication that can prolong bleeding, such as aspirin. If you are unsure about a medication, ask your HCP or pharmacist about it in relation to your thrombocytopenia.
10. Use a soft-bristle toothbrush to prevent injuring the gums. Flossing is usually safe if done gently using the thin tape floss. Do not use alcohol-based mouthwashes because they can dry your gums and increase bleeding.
11. Women who are menstruating should keep track of the number of pads used per day. When you start using more pads per day than usual or bleed more days, notify your HCP. Do not use tampons; only use sanitary pads.
12. Ask your HCP before you have any invasive procedures done, such as a dental cleaning, manicure, or pedicure.

ice pack may be helpful. Avoid IM injections. Help the patient to understand the importance of adhering to self-care measures that reduce the risk for bleeding (Table 34.15).

Note that many of these disorders may be accompanied by vascular clotting, and appropriate assessment and management should be taken. As bleeding occurs, RBCs and coagulation factors are consumed along with platelets. Monitor all blood cell and coagulation studies. In a woman with thrombocytopenia, menstrual blood loss may exceed the usual amount and duration. Suppressing menses with hormonal agents may be needed during predictable periods of thrombocytopenia (e.g., during chemotherapy and HSCT) to reduce menstrual blood loss. Administering platelet transfusions is an important nursing role.

TABLE 34.16 Types of Hemophilia

Type	Inheritance Pattern
Hemophilia A	
Factor VIII	Recessive sex-linked (transmitted by female carriers, occurs almost exclusively in men)
Hemophilia B	
Factor IX	Recessive sex-linked (transmitted by female carriers, occurs almost exclusively in men)
von Willebrand Disease	
vWF, variable factor VIII deficiencies and platelet dysfunction	Autosomal dominant, seen in both genders Recessive (in severe forms of the disease)

◆ Ambulatory Care

Monitor the patient with ITP who is receiving treatment for their response to therapy. Teach the person with acquired thrombocytopenia to avoid causative agents when possible (Table 34.11). If the patient cannot avoid causative agents (e.g., chemotherapy), teach them to avoid injury or trauma during these periods and the signs and symptoms of bleeding (Table 34.15).

Patients with either ITP or acquired thrombocytopenia should have planned periodic medical evaluations to assess and treat situations in which exacerbations and bleeding are likely to occur. Address the impact of the condition on the patient's quality of life.

◆ Evaluation

The expected outcomes are that the patient with thrombocytopenia will

- Have no evidence of bleeding or bruising
- State needed knowledge and skills to manage disease process

HEMOPHILIA AND VON WILLEBRAND DISEASE

Hemophilia is an X-linked recessive genetic disorder caused by a defective or deficient coagulation factor. The 2 major types of hemophilia: *hemophilia A* (classic hemophilia, factor VIII deficiency) and *hemophilia B* (Christmas disease, factor IX deficiency). *von Willebrand disease* is a related disorder involving a deficiency of the von Willebrand coagulation protein. Factor VIII is made in the liver and circulates as a complex with vWF.

Hemophilia A is 4 times as common as hemophilia B.[18] Although rare, there are cases of *acquired hemophilia A* that are due to the body developing antibodies against its own factor VIII. von Willebrand disease is the most common congenital bleeding disorder.

Genetic Link

The inheritance patterns of hemophilia and von Willebrand disease are discussed in Table 34.16 and Box 34.4.

Clinical Manifestations and Complications

The manifestations of hemophilia A and B are similar. All manifestations relate to bleeding. Any bleeding episode in persons with hemophilia may be life threatening. Manifestations

BOX 34.4 GENETICS IN CLINICAL PRACTICE

Hemophilia A and B

Genetic Basis

- X-linked recessive disorder
- *Hemophilia A:* Caused by mutations in the *F8* gene that provides instructions for making coagulation factor VIII
- *Hemophilia B:* Caused by mutations in the *F9* gene that provides instructions for making coagulation factor IX
- Mutations in the *F8* or *F9* gene lead to the production of an abnormal version or reduced amounts of coagulation factors

Incidence

- *Hemophilia A:* 1 in 5,600 male births
- *Hemophilia B:* 1 in 1,400 male births

Genetic Testing

- DNA testing is available

Clinical Implications

- Female carriers transmit the genetic defect to 50% of their sons, 50% of their daughters are carriers
- Males with hemophilia do not transmit the genetic defect to their sons, but all their daughters are carriers
- While rare, female hemophilia can occur if a male with hemophilia mates with a female carrier

include (1) slow, persistent, prolonged bleeding from minor trauma and small cuts; (2) delayed bleeding after minor injuries (the delay may be several hours or days); (3) uncontrollable bleeding after dental extractions or gingival irritation with a hard-bristle toothbrush; (4) nosebleeds, especially after a blow to the face; (5) GI bleeding from ulcers and gastritis; (6) hematuria and potential renal failure from GU trauma; (7) splenic rupture from falls or abdominal trauma; (8) bruising and subcutaneous hematomas (Fig. 34.7) and possible compartment syndrome; (9) neurologic signs, such as pain, anesthesia, and paralysis, which may develop from nerve compression caused by hematoma formation; and (10) hemarthrosis (bleeding into the joints) (Fig. 34.8), which may lead to joint injury and deformity severe enough to cause crippling.[1]

In children, these manifestations may lead to the diagnosis. In adults, these may be the first sign of a mild form of the disease that escaped detection through a childhood free of major injuries, dental procedures, or surgeries.

Diagnostic Studies

Laboratory studies determine the type of hemophilia present. Any factor deficiency within the intrinsic system (factor VIII, IX, XI, or XII or vWF) will yield the laboratory results outlined in Table 34.17.

Interprofessional Care

The goals of interprofessional care are to prevent and treat bleeding. Care for persons with hemophilia or von Willebrand disease requires (1) preventive care, (2) replacement therapy during acute bleeding episodes and as prophylaxis, and (3) treating complications of the disease and its therapy. Most patients can expect almost normal life spans free of bloodborne illnesses because of improvements in the blood donation process and the use of recombinant replacement factors. Designated treatment

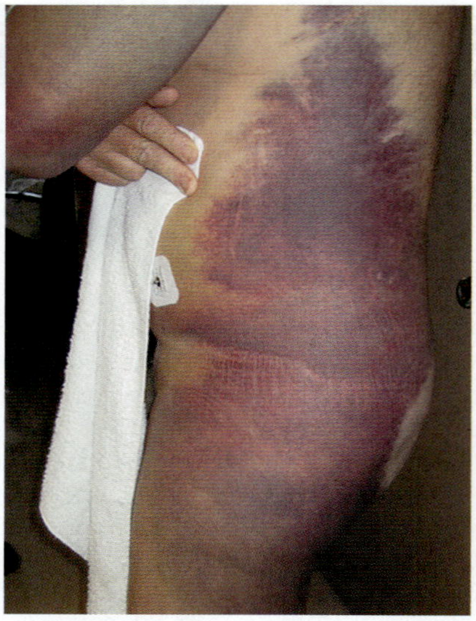

Fig. 34.7 Severe bruising in a person with hemophilia after a fall. (Courtesy Peter Bonner.)

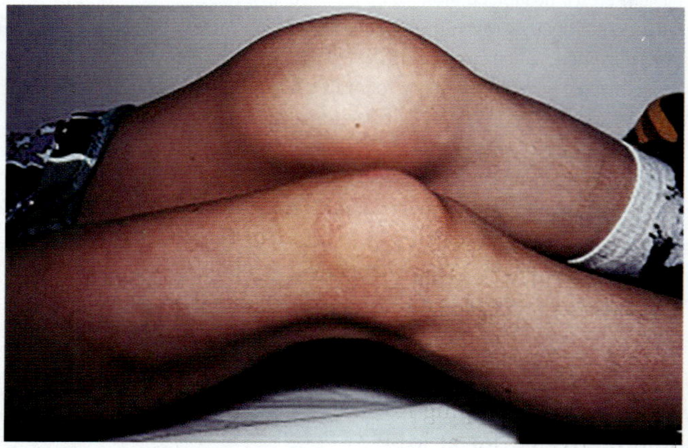

Fig. 34.8 Acute hemarthrosis of the knee is a common complication of hemophilia. (From Lissauer T, Carroll W: *Illustrated textbook of pediatrics*, ed 5, London, 2018, Mosby.)

TABLE 34.17 Laboratory Results in Hemophilia

Test	Results
Bleeding time	Prolonged in von Willebrand disease due to structurally defective platelets. Normal in hemophilia A and B because platelets not affected
Factor assays	Reductions of factor VIII in hemophilia A, factor IX in hemophilia B, vWF in von Willebrand disease
Partial thromboplastin time	Prolonged due to deficiency in intrinsic clotting system factor
Platelet count	Normal. Adequate platelet production
Prothrombin time	Normal. No involvement of extrinsic system
Thrombin time	Normal. No impairment of thrombin-fibrinogen reaction

TABLE 34.18 Drug Therapy

Replacement Factors for Hemophilia

Factor VIII	Factor IX	Von Willebrand	For Patients Who Have Inhibitors
Advate	Alphanine	Alphanate	NovoSeven (factor VIIa)
Adynovate	Alprolix	HumateP	Autoplex T
Afstyla	Bebulin VH	Vonvendi	FEIBA (factor VIII inhibitor bypassing activity)
Alphanate	BeneFIX	Wilate	Emicizumab
Eloctate	Idelvion		
Esperoct	Immunine		
Hemofil M	Ixinity		
Humate-P	Mononine		
Jivi	Profilnine SD		
Koāte-DVI	Rixubis		
Kogenate FS			
Kovaltry			
Monoclate			
NovoEight			
Obizur[a]			
ReFacto			
Wilate			
Xyntha			

[a]For acquired hemophilia A.

centers provide interprofessional care of hemophilia and related disorders.

Replacement of deficient clotting factors is the primary means of supporting a patient with hemophilia. Regular prophylaxis is preferred over on-demand treatment. The most common problem with acute management is starting factor replacement therapy too late and stopping it too soon. Minor bleeding episodes should be treated for at least 72 hours. Surgery and traumatic injuries may need longer therapy. The patient may need prophylactic replacement therapy before surgery and dental care. Table 34.18 lists examples of replacement therapy.[18]

For mild hemophilia A and certain subtypes of von Willebrand disease, desmopressin acetate (DDAVP), a synthetic analog of vasopressin, can stimulate an increase in factor VIII and vWF.[19] This drug acts on platelets and endothelial cells to cause the release of vWF. vWF then binds with factor VIII, thus increasing its concentration. DDAVP can be given IV, subcutaneously, or by intranasal spray. Beneficial effects (e.g., decreased bleeding time) are seen within 30 minutes when given IV and can last for more than 12 hours. Because the drug's effect is short lived, the patient must be closely monitored. They may need repeated doses. It is an appropriate therapy for minor bleeding episodes and dental procedures. The intranasal form may be used as home therapy for some patients with mild to moderate forms of the disease.

Antifibrinolytic therapy (tranexamic acid [Cyklokapron]) reduces fibrinolysis by inhibiting plasminogen activation in the fibrin clot, thus enhancing clot stability.[19] These agents stabilize clots in areas of increased fibrinolysis, such as the oral cavity, and in patients with difficult episodes of nosebleeds and menorrhagia. Topical thrombin and fibrin sealants can treat mucosal bleeding.

Complications of hemophilia treatment include development of inhibitors to factors VIII or IX, allergic reactions, and thrombotic complications with using factor IX because it contains activated coagulation factors. Patients with vWF may develop antibodies against vWF concentrates, the infusion of which could cause life-threatening anaphylaxis. Thus replacement factors for these patients should not contain vWF. Chronically, the development of inhibitors to the factor products can occur and needs expert management. Emicizumab is an option to address the problem of inhibitors for hemophilia A. It is a monoclonal antibody that binds factors IX and X, causing activation of factor X. This leads to thrombin generation, bypassing the need for Factor VIII.[1,4] Gene transfer therapy is an experimental treatment.

❖ NURSING MANAGEMENT: HEMOPHILIA

◆ Implementation

◆ Health Promotion

Because of the hereditary nature of hemophilia, refer affected persons for genetic counseling before reproduction. This is especially important because many persons with hemophilia live into adulthood. Include reproductive concerns and long-term effects in the care plan.

◆ Acute Care

We implement measures to control bleeding. They include the following:

1. Stop the topical bleeding as quickly as possible. Apply direct pressure or ice, pack the area with Gelfoam or fibrin foam, and apply topical hemostatic agents, such as thrombin.
2. Give the specific coagulation factor to raise the level of the deficient coagulation factor. Monitor the patient for signs and symptoms, such as hypersensitivity.
3. When joint bleeding occurs, in addition to giving replacement factors, use the "RICE" protocol: Rest the involved joint to prevent crippling deformities from hemarthrosis, ice the joint for 20 minutes every 3 to 4 hours, compress/wrap the joint, and elevate.[2] Give analgesics to reduce severe pain. Do not use aspirin and aspirin-containing compounds. As soon as bleeding stops, encourage mobilization of the affected area through range of motion exercises and physical therapy. Avoid weight bearing until all swelling has resolved and muscle strength has returned. Orthotics may be prescribed.
4. Manage any life-threatening complications that may develop from bleeding or side effects from coagulation factors. Examples include measures to prevent or treat airway obstruction from bleeding into the neck and pharynx, recognizing compartment syndrome in an extremity, and early assessment and treatment of intracranial bleeding.

◆ Ambulatory Care

Home management is a primary consideration because the disease follows a progressive, chronic course. The patient's knowledge of the illness and how to live with it influences their quality

BOX 34.5 EVIDENCE-BASED PRACTICE

Depression in Patients With Hemophilia

K.S. is a 47-year-old female admitted with hematuria and hypertension. She was diagnosed with hemophilia A as an infant. She describes a history of chronic joint disease and pain from bleeding into joints. You note in her health record that she has been identified as an "inhibitor." In discussion with the clinical nurse specialist, you learn that inhibitors are people with hemophilia A who develop antibodies to attack clotting factors provided in disease treatment. Their management becomes more complex because their immune system resists standard treatments. When you perform your admission interview, you identify behaviors suggesting anxiety and depression. K.S. seems apathetic, responding briefly to questions about her history and symptoms. Then she unexpectedly asks, "Do we have to do this again? After all these trips to the hospital, I've had it with all these questions."

Making Clinical Decisions

Synthesis of Best Available Evidence

Persons with hemophilia often experience pain and impaired function, leading to a decreased quality of life and depression. Anxiety also can be related to the risk of bleeding.

Clinician Expertise

You realize an appropriate approach to the admission interview is to slow the interaction with the patient, speak in a low tone and demonstrate empathy about the repeated hospitalizations. If she continues to show irritability or expresses anger, you will remain calm and supportive. Assure K.S. you are interested in understanding her health concerns so you can provide the best possible care and support her in her disease management efforts. Encourage K. S. to share her feelings about the chronic nature of hemophilia and the years of living with its uncertainty. Ask questions about pain management, disability, and social support with empathy. Allow K. S. to steer the conversation as much as possible.

Patient Preferences and Values

K. S. expresses concern about past failed treatments and tells you she will soon begin treatment with emicizumab.

Implications for Nursing Practice

1. How should you discuss treatment with emicizumab with K.S.?
2. What else would you want to know about her depression and anxiety?
3. What strategies can you suggest to improve her quality of life?

Reference for Evidence

Batt K, Boggio L, Neff A, et al.: Patient-reported outcomes and joint status across subgroups of US adults with hemophilia with varying characteristics: results from the Pain, Functional Impairment, and Quality of Life (P-FiQ) study, *European Journal of Haematology* 100:12, 2018.

and length of life (Box 34.5). Refer the patient and caregiver to a local chapter of the National Hemophilia Foundation to encourage networking with others who are dealing with hemophilia.[18] Provide ongoing assessment of the patient's adaptation to the illness. Psychosocial support and assistance should be readily available as needed.

Most of the long-term care measures are related to patient teaching. Teach the patient to recognize disease-related problems and which problems can be treated at home and which require hospitalization. Immediate medical attention is needed for severe pain or swelling of a muscle or joint that restricts movement or inhibits sleep and for a head injury, swelling in the neck or mouth, abdominal pain, hematuria, melena, and skin wounds in need of suturing.

Teach the patient to perform daily oral hygiene without causing trauma. Understanding how to prevent injuries is another consideration. Teach the patient to take part only in noncontact sports (e.g., golf) and to wear gloves when doing household chores to prevent cuts or abrasions from knives, hammers, and other tools. The patient should wear a Medic Alert tag to ensure that HCPs know about the hemophilia in case of an accident. You can teach many patients or caregivers to self-administer the factor replacement therapies at home.

◆ Evaluation

The overall expected outcomes are similar to those for the patient with thrombocytopenia.

DISSEMINATED INTRAVASCULAR COAGULATION

Disseminated intravascular coagulation (DIC) is a serious bleeding and thrombotic disorder that results from abnormally initiated and accelerated clotting. Subsequent decreases in clotting factors and platelets ensue, which may lead to uncontrollable bleeding. The term DIC can be misleading because it suggests that blood is only clotting. However, there is profuse bleeding that results from the aggregation of platelets and clotting factors. DIC is not a disease. It is always caused by an underlying disease or condition. That underlying problem must be treated for DIC to resolve.

Etiology and Pathophysiology

DIC is an abnormal response of the normal clotting cascade stimulated by a disease process or disorder.[3] Table 34.19 lists diseases and disorders known to predispose a patient to DIC. DIC can occur as an acute, catastrophic condition, or it may exist at a subacute or chronic level. Chronic and subacute DIC is most often seen in patients with long-standing illnesses, such as cancer or autoimmune disease. Occasionally these patients have subclinical disease manifested only by laboratory abnormalities.

Each condition may have 1 or multiple triggering mechanisms to start the clotting cascade. For example, tumors and traumatized or necrotic tissue release tissue factors into circulation. Endotoxin from gram-negative bacteria activates several steps in the coagulation cascade.

The manifestations of DIC result from consumption and depletion of platelets and coagulation factors, as well as clot lysis and formation of fibrin split products (FSPs) that have anticoagulant properties (Fig. 34.9). Tissue factor is released at the site of tissue injury and by some cancers, such as leukemia. It enhances normal coagulation mechanisms. Abundant intravascular thrombin, the most powerful coagulant, is made. It speeds the conversion of fibrinogen to fibrin and enhances platelet aggregation. There is widespread fibrin and platelet deposition in capillaries and arterioles, causing thrombosis. This process can lead to multiorgan failure.

Clotting inhibitory mechanisms, such as antithrombin III (AT III) and protein C, are depressed. Excess clotting activates the fibrinolytic system, which in turn breaks down the newly formed clot, creating FSPs. FSPs have anticoagulant properties. They inhibit normal blood clotting by (1) coating the platelets and interfering with platelet function; (2) interfering with thrombin and thus disrupting coagulation; and (3) attaching to fibrinogen, which interferes with the process needed to form a stable clot. As FSPs accumulate and clotting factors are depleted, the blood loses its ability to clot. A stable clot cannot form at injury sites, which predisposes the patient to bleeding.

TABLE 34.19 Risk Factors for DIC

Acute DIC

Cancers
- Acute leukemia
- Metastatic solid tumors

Hemolytic Processes
- Acute hemolysis from infection or immunologic disorders
- Transfusion of mismatched blood

Obstetric Conditions
- Abruptio placentae
- Amniotic fluid embolism
- HELLP syndrome (hemolysis, ↑ liver enzymes, ↓ platelets associated with pregnancy)
- Septic abortion or pregnancy

Septicemia (Bacterial, Viral, Fungal, Parasitic)

Shock
- Anaphylactic
- Cardiogenic
- Hemorrhagic

Tissue Damage
- Acute anoxia (e.g., after cardiac arrest)
- Extensive burns and trauma
- Heatstroke
- Hepatitis
- Postoperative damage, especially after extracorporeal membrane oxygenation
- Prosthetic devices
- Severe head injury
- Snakebites
- Transplant rejections
- Vascular disorders (e.g., aortic aneurism)

Subacute DIC

Cancer
- Metastatic cancer
- Myeloproliferative/lymphoproliferative cancers

Obstetric
- Retained dead fetus

Chronic DIC
- Cancer
- Liver disease
- SLE

Clinical Manifestations

DIC has both bleeding and thrombotic manifestations. Question bleeding in a person with no history or obvious cause because it may be 1 of the first manifestations of acute DIC.

Bleeding manifestations include manifestations in the (1) skin, such as pallor, petechiae, purpura, oozing blood, venipuncture site bleeding, hematomas, and occult bleeding; (2) respiratory system (e.g., tachypnea, hemoptysis); (3) cardiovascular system, such as tachycardia and hypotension; (4) GI tract, such as upper and lower GI bleeding, abdominal distention, bloody stools; (5) GU tract (e.g., hematuria); (6) neurologic system, such as vision changes, dizziness, headache, and mental status changes; and (7) musculoskeletal system (e.g., bone and joint pain).

Thrombotic manifestations are a result of fibrin or platelet deposition in the microvasculature (Fig. 34.9). These manifestations affect the (1) skin (e.g., cyanosis, ischemic tissue necrosis, hemorrhagic necrosis) (Fig. 34.10); (2) respiratory system (e.g., tachypnea, dyspnea, pulmonary emboli); (3) cardiovascular system (e.g., ECG changes, venous distention); (4) GI tract (e.g., abdominal pain, paralytic ileus); (5) kidney damage and oliguria, leading to failure; and (6) neurologic (e.g., delirium, coma).

Diagnostic Studies

Table 34.20 lists tests used to diagnose acute DIC. D dimer, a polymer resulting from the breakdown of fibrin, is a specific marker for the degree of fibrinolysis. In general, tests that measure raw materials needed for coagulation (e.g., platelets, fibrinogen) are reduced and values that measure clotting times are prolonged. Fragmented RBCs (schistocytes), indicative of partial occlusion of small vessels by fibrin thrombi, may be found on blood smears.

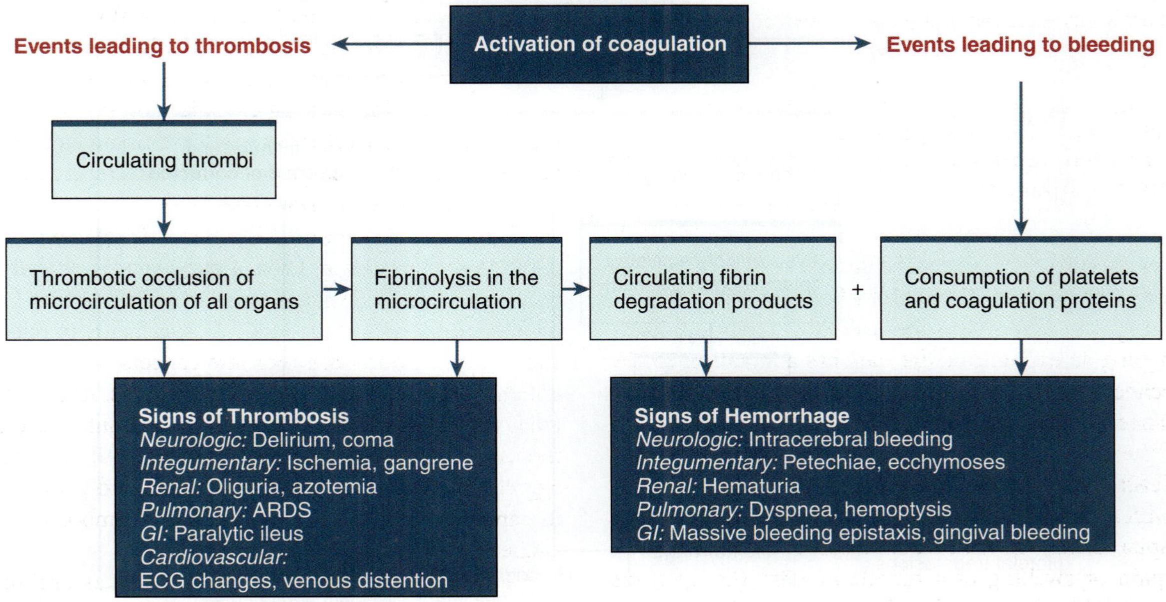

Fig. 34.9 Sequence of events that occur during DIC.

Interprofessional Care

It is important to diagnose DIC quickly, stabilize the patient (e.g., oxygenation, volume replacement), treat the underlying causative disease or problem, and control the ongoing thrombosis and bleeding. Depending on its severity, we use a variety of measures to manage DIC (Fig. 34.11). First, if chronic DIC is diagnosed in a patient who is not bleeding, no treatment for DIC is needed. Treating the underlying disease may be enough

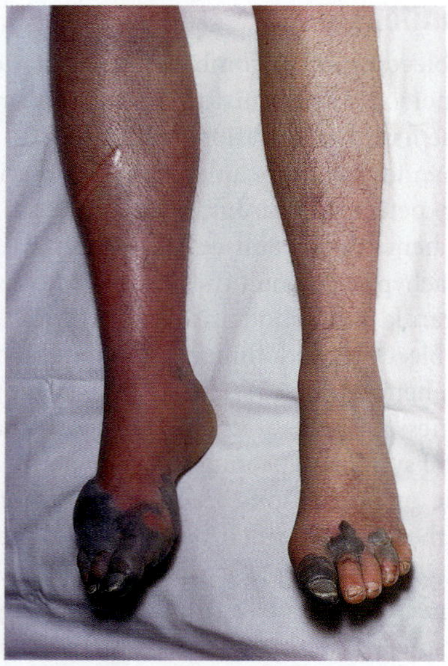

Fig. 34.10 Gangrene from severe DIC. (From Howard MR, Hamilton PJ: *Haematology: an illustrated colour atlas,* ed 4, London, 2013, Churchill Livingstone.)

TABLE 34.20 Laboratory Results in Acute DIC

Test	Finding in Acute DIC
Screening Tests	
Prothrombin time (PT)	Prolonged
Partial thromboplastin time (PTT)	Prolonged
Activated partial thromboplastin time (aPTT)	Prolonged
Fibrinogen	↓
Platelets	↓
Thrombin time	Prolonged
Special Tests	
Antithrombin III (AT III)	↓
D dimers (cross-linked fibrin fragments)	↑
Factor assays (prothrombin and factors V, VIII, X, XIII)	↓ but may be misleading because V and VIII ↑ with inflammation
Fibrin split products (FSPs)	↑
Peripheral blood smear	Schistocytes present
Plasminogen, tissue plasminogen activator	↓
Proteins C and S	↓

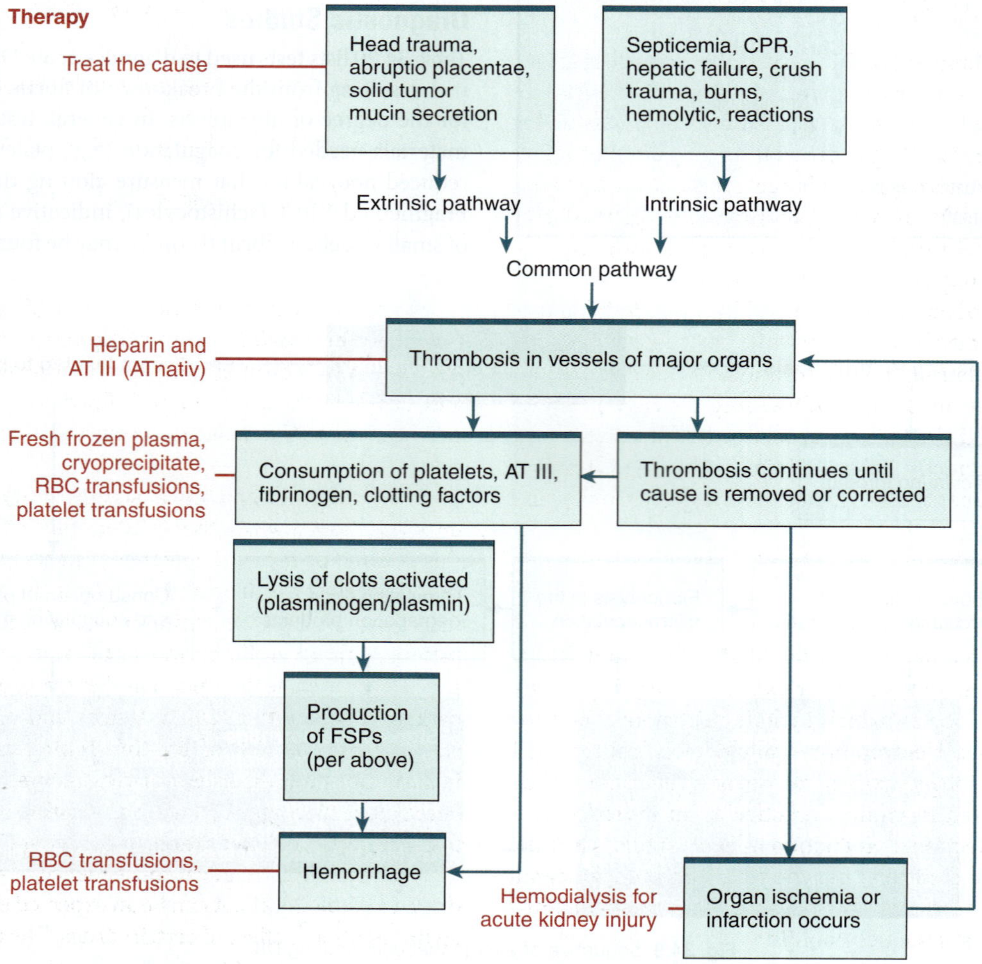

Fig. 34.11 Sites of action for therapies in DIC. *AT III,* Antithrombin III; *FSP,* fibrin split product.

to reverse the DIC (e.g., chemotherapy with DIC caused by cancer). Second, when the patient with DIC is bleeding, therapy is directed toward providing support with needed blood products while treating the primary disorder.

Blood products are given cautiously based on specific component deficiencies to patients who have serious bleeding, are at high risk for bleeding (e.g., surgery), or require invasive procedures. Blood product support with platelets, cryoprecipitate, and fresh frozen plasma (FFP) is usually reserved for a patient with life-threatening bleeding.[1] Therapy stabilizes a patient, prevents severe blood loss or massive thrombosis, and gives time to treat the underlying cause. Cryoprecipitate replaces factor VIII and fibrinogen. It may be given if the fibrinogen level is low and there is potentially dangerous or active bleeding.[4] FFP is given only to patients with significant bleeding and a prolonged PT and aPTT. It replaces all clotting factors except platelets and is a source of antithrombin.

A patient with thrombosis is often treated by anticoagulation with heparin or LMWH. Heparin is used to treat DIC only when the benefit (reduce clotting) outweighs the risk (further bleeding). AT III (ATnativ) may be useful in severe DIC, although it increases the risk for bleeding. Chronic DIC does not respond to oral anticoagulants. It is controlled with long-term use of heparin.

NURSING MANAGEMENT: DISSEMINATED INTRAVASCULAR COAGULATION

Be alert to the development of DIC, especially with the risk factors listed in Table 34.19. Early detection of bleeding and clotting, both occult and overt, must be a primary goal. Assess for signs of external bleeding (e.g., petechiae, oozing at IV or injection sites), signs of internal bleeding (e.g., increased heart rate, changes in mental status, increasing abdominal girth, pain), and any signs that microthrombi may be causing clinically significant organ damage (e.g., decreased renal output).

Remember that because DIC is caused by an underlying disease, that problem must be managed while providing supportive care for the manifestations of DIC. Minimize tissue damage and protect the patient from sources of bleeding. Prompt administration of prescribed therapies is crucial. Give blood products and medications correctly. Table 34.14 and eNursing Care Plan 34.2 provide assessments and interventions appropriate for the patient with DIC.

NEUTROPENIA

Leukopenia refers to a decrease in the total WBC count (granulocytes, monocytes, and lymphocytes). *Granulocytopenia* is a deficiency of granulocytes, which include neutrophils, eosinophils, and basophils. Neutrophilic granulocytes (neutrophils) play a key role in phagocytizing pathogenic microbes. They are closely monitored in clinical practice as an indicator of a patient's risk for infection. A reduction in neutrophils is termed **neutropenia**. Some clinicians use the terms granulocytopenia and neutropenia interchangeably because the largest constituency of granulocytes is the neutrophils.

TABLE 34.21 Common Causes of Neutropenia

Autoimmune Disorders
- Felty syndrome
- SLE

Drugs
- Anticancer agents (busulfan, methotrexate, mercaptopurine, cytarabine, combination therapies)
- Antiinflammatory drugs (indomethacin)
- Antimicrobial agents (ganciclovir, penicillin G, trimethoprim/sulfamethoxazole)
- Cardiovascular drugs (captopril, procainamide)
- Diuretics (hydrochlorothiazide)
- Miscellaneous (ticlopidine, amitriptyline)

Hematologic Disorders
- Addison disease
- Aplastic anemia
- Congenital (cyclic neutropenia)
- Idiopathic neutropenia
- Leukemia
- Myelodysplastic syndrome

Infections
- Fulminant bacterial infection (e.g., typhoid fever, miliary tuberculosis)
- Parasitic
- Rickettsial
- Viral (e.g., hepatitis, influenza, HIV, measles)

Others
- Bone marrow infiltration (e.g., cancer, tuberculosis, lymphoma)
- Hemodialysis
- Hypersplenism (e.g., portal hypertension, storage diseases [e.g., Gaucher disease])
- Nutrition deficiencies (cobalamin, folic acid)
- Severe sepsis

Normally, neutrophils range from 2500 to 8000 cells/μL. Calculate the *absolute neutrophil count* (ANC) by multiplying the total WBC count by the percent of neutrophils (segmented and banded). *Neutropenia* is defined as ANC less than 1000 cells/μL (1×10^9/L). *Severe neutropenia* is an ANC less than 500 cells/μL.[12]

In considering the clinical significance of neutropenia, it is important to know whether the decrease in the neutrophil count was gradual or rapid, the degree of neutropenia, and the duration. The faster the drop and the longer the duration, the greater the chance of life-threatening infection, sepsis, and death. The patient with an ANC between 500 and 1000/μL is at moderate risk for a bacterial infection. Severe neutropenia places the patient at severe risk. Other factors and comorbid conditions can increase the risk of life-threatening consequences. These include immune disorders or treatments (e.g., SLE, steroids), being older than age 60, having an existing infection or previous fungal infection, dehydration, and having COPD.[20]

Neutropenia is a clinical consequence of several conditions or diseases (Table 34.21). It can be an expected effect, a side effect, or an unintentional effect of certain drugs. The most common cause of neutropenia is chemotherapy and immunosuppressive therapy for the treatment of cancer and autoimmune disease. A term we use to describe the lowest point of neutropenia (and other blood cells) in a patient treated with chemotherapy is *nadir.*

Clinical Manifestations

The patient with neutropenia is predisposed to infection with opportunistic pathogens and nonpathogenic organisms from the normal body flora. When the WBC count is low or immature WBCs are present, normal phagocytic mechanisms are impaired. The classic manifestations of inflammation—redness, heat, and swelling—may not occur. WBCs are the major component of pus. Therefore, in the patient with neutropenia, pus formation (e.g., as a visible skin lesion or as lung infiltrates on a chest x-ray) is absent.

! SAFETY ALERT

Neutropenia

- A low-grade fever in neutropenic patients is of great significance. It may indicate infection and lead to septic shock and death unless treated promptly.
- Neutropenic fever (≥100.4°F [38°C] and/or new signs or symptoms suggesting infection and a neutrophil count <500/μL) is a medical emergency.
- Blood cultures should be drawn STAT (within 1 hr) and antibiotics started within 1 hr.

Assume that fever in a neutropenic patient is caused by infection. It requires immediate attention. The immunocompromised, neutropenic patient has little or no ability to fight infection. A minor infection can lead rapidly to sepsis and death. The mucous membranes of the throat and mouth, skin, perineal area, and pulmonary system are common entry points for pathogenic organisms in susceptible hosts.

Manifestations related to infection at these sites include sore throat and dysphagia, ulcerative lesions of the pharyngeal and buccal mucosa, diarrhea, rectal tenderness, vaginal itching or discharge, shortness of breath, and nonproductive cough. Any report of minor pain or any other symptom by the patient may be significant and should be reported to the HCP at once. Minor problems can progress to fever, chills, sepsis, septic shock, and death if not recognized and treated early.

Systemic infections caused by bacterial, fungal, and viral organisms are common in patients with neutropenia. The patient's own flora (normally nonpathogenic) contributes significantly to life-threatening infections. Organisms known to be common sources of infection include gram-positive coagulase-negative *Staphylococcus* and *Staphylococcus aureus,* viridans streptococci and gram-negative *Escherichia coli, Klebsiella, Enterobacter,* and *Pseudomonas aeruginosa.*[20] Fungi involved include *Candida* (usually *C. albicans*) and *Aspergillus* organisms. Viral infections caused by reactivation of herpes simplex and zoster are common after prolonged periods of neutropenia, such as in HSCT patients.[20]

Diagnostic Studies

The primary diagnostic tests for assessing neutropenia are the peripheral WBC count and bone marrow aspiration and biopsy (Table 34.22). A total WBC count of less than 4000/μL (4×10^9/L) reflects leukopenia. However, only a differential count can confirm the presence of neutropenia (neutrophil count less than 1000/μL [1×10^9/L]). Patients with acute leukemia who present with a high WBC may in fact have neutropenia, because most of the WBCs are ineffective leukemia blasts cells.

A peripheral blood smear assesses for immature forms of WBCs (e.g., bands). The hematocrit level, reticulocyte count, and platelet count are done to evaluate bone marrow function. Review the patient's recent past and current drug history. If the cause of neutropenia is unknown, a bone marrow aspiration and biopsy is done to examine cell numbers and morphology. Other studies assess spleen and liver function.

TABLE 34.22 Interprofessional Care

Neutropenia

Diagnostic Assessment

- History and physical assessment
- Risk assessment for severity and duration of neutropenia
- WBC count with differential count
- WBC morphology
- Hgb and Hct
- Reticulocyte and platelet count
- Bone marrow aspiration and biopsy
- Cultures of nose, throat, sputum, urine, stool, obvious lesions, blood (as indicated)
- Chest x-ray, liver function tests, and other diagnostic tests

Management

- Identify and remove cause of neutropenia (if possible)
- Identification of site of infection (if present) and causative organism
- Blood cultures drawn STAT, before antibiotics
- Antimicrobial therapy STAT (within 1 hr)
- Prophylactic hematopoietic myeloid growth factors after myelosuppressive chemotherapy
- Strict hand hygiene
- Single-patient room, positive-pressure or high-efficiency particulate air (HEPA) filtration, depending on risk
- Community isolation and home precautions (if outpatient)
- Safe activity and ambulation to maintain physical and pulmonary function

G-CSF, Granulocyte colony-stimulating factor; *GM-CSF,* granulocyte-macrophage colony-stimulating factor.

❖ Interprofessional and Nursing Management

The nursing and interprofessional care of neutropenia includes (1) determining the cause of the neutropenia, (2) instituting antibiotic therapy promptly, (3) identifying the offending organisms if an infection has developed, (4) giving hematopoietic growth factors prophylactically after chemotherapy, and (5) implementing protective practices (e.g., strict hand washing, skin and oral hygiene) (Tables 34.22 and 34.23).[21] Often patients can be managed on an outpatient basis if the patient and caregiver can monitor for fever and other signs of infection and seek care promptly if needed (Table 34.24).

Sometimes, the cause of the neutropenia can be easily treated (e.g., nutrition deficiencies). However, neutropenia can be a side effect that must be tolerated as a necessary step in therapy (e.g.,

TABLE 34.23 NURSING MANAGEMENT

Caring for the Patient With Neutropenia

- Make sure that hand hygiene is done before, during, and after patient care by everyone caring for the patient.
- Assess patient for signs and symptoms of infection.
- Screen visitors for infectious diseases.
- Place the patient on a diet that observes food safety guidelines (well washed fruits and vegetables; keep hot foods hot and cold foods cold, no undercooked eggs, meats) to protect them from bacteria found in some foods.
- Obtain cultures of sputum, throat, lesions, wounds, urine, and feces.
- Give antibiotics and hematopoietic growth factors.
- Implement measures to manage fever (see Table 12.5).
- Provide daily skin care and frequent oral hygiene.
- Teach patient and caregivers about
  - Hand hygiene.
  - How to avoid infection, including the need for skin care and oral hygiene (Table 34.24).
  - Signs and symptoms of infection and what to do if they occur.

TABLE 34.24 PATIENT & CAREGIVER TEACHING

Neutropenia

Include the following instructions when teaching a patient or caregiver the precautions to take when the neutrophil count is low:

1. Clean your hands often with soap and water. Make sure those around you wash their hands often, especially if they help with your care. You may also use an antibacterial hand gel.
2. Notify your nurse or HCP if you have any of the following:
   Fever ≥100.4°F (38°C)[a]
   Chills or feeling hot
   Redness, swelling, discharge, or new pain on or in your body
   Changes in urination or bowel movements
   Cough, sore throat, mouth sores, or blisters
3. If you are at home, take your temperature as directed and follow instructions on what to do if you have a fever.
4. Avoid crowds and people with colds, flu, or infections. If you are in a public area, wear a mask and use hand sanitizing gel frequently.
5. Avoid uncooked meats, seafood, or eggs and unwashed fruits and vegetables. Ask your HCP about your specific diet guidelines.
6. Avoid prolonged contact with soil, such as gardening, and household renovation.
7. Bathe or shower daily. Use a moisturizer to prevent skin from drying and cracking.
8. Maintain some daily activity as instructed by your health care team. This may include walking and moderate exercise while avoiding crowds.
9. Brush your teeth with a soft toothbrush 4 times daily. You may floss once daily if it does not cause excessive pain or bleeding. Avoid alcohol-based mouthwashes.
10. Do not clean up after pets. You may feed and pet your dog or cat if you wash your hands well after handling.

[a]Confirm the cut-off temperature with the HCP.

chemotherapy, radiation therapy). In some situations, the neutropenia resolves when the primary problem is treated (Table 34.21). Myeloid growth factors (see Table 16.15) can be used to prevent neutropenia or to reduce its severity and duration.[5] Once neutropenia has occurred, these agents are generally not as effective.

Ongoing monitoring is essential. Early identification and appropriate management can prevent death from sepsis.[3] Monitor the neutropenic patient for signs and symptoms of infection (e.g., any fever 100.4°F [38°C] or greater) and early septic shock. Frequent vital signs (e.g., every 15 minutes to 1 hour) and assessing mental status are essential. See Chapter 42 for more information on signs of septic shock. Identifying the infective organism depends on obtaining cultures from various sites. Serial blood cultures (at least 2) or 1 from a peripheral site and 1 from a venous access device should be done promptly and antibiotics started within 1 hour.

Prophylactic antibiotic, antiviral, and antifungal medications may be started, then switched to treatment doses depending on the risk of specific infections and diagnostic results.[20] We usually give broad-spectrum antibiotics by the IV route because of the rapidly lethal effects of infection. However, some oral antibiotics are highly effective. We may give them to patients who do not have a severe or prolonged neutropenia.[20] Using a third- or fourth-generation cephalosporin with broad microorganism coverage (e.g., cefepime, ceftazidime) or a carbapenem (e.g., imipenem/cilastatin) depends on the patient's response and diagnostic tests.

Begin therapy promptly and observe for side effects of antimicrobial agents. Ongoing febrile episodes or a change in the patient's assessment requires a call to the HCP for assessment, or more cultures, diagnostic tests, or antimicrobial therapies. The longer the neutropenia, the greater the risk is for a fungal infection. Antifungal therapy is started whenever a culture is positive or in patients who do not become afebrile with broad-spectrum antibiotic coverage.

Sputum, throat, lesions, wounds, urine, and fecal cultures may be part of surveillance. Depending on the clinical situation, the patient may need CT scans, bronchoscopy with bronchial brushings, or lung biopsy to diagnose the cause of pneumonic infiltrates. Invasive diagnostic studies are often contraindicated because of the concern of introducing infection and the fact that patients are often thrombocytopenic. Despite these many tests, we find the causative organism in only 40% to 50% of neutropenic patients. Thus the priority is to obtain the blood cultures and begin the antibiotic at once.

Keep the following principles in mind: (1) the patient's normal flora is the most common source of microbial colonization and infection; (2) transmission of organisms from humans most often occurs by direct contact with the hands; (3) air, food, water, and equipment provide opportunities for infection transmission; and (4) HCPs, visitors, and other patients with infections can be sources of infection transmission under certain conditions.

Hand hygiene is the single most important preventive measure to minimize the risk for infection in the neutropenic patient. Strict hand hygiene by staff and visitors using an antiseptic hand wash or sanitizing gel before and after contact is the major method to prevent transmission of harmful pathogens.

Separate immunocompromised patients from those who are infected or have conditions that increase the probability of transmitting infections (e.g., respiratory infections). Place the hospitalized patient in a private room. High-efficiency particulate air (HEPA) filtration is an air-handling method with a high-flow filtering system that can reduce or eliminate the number of aerosolized pathogens (especially molds) in the environment for those with prolonged neutropenia.[20] Teach the patient and caregiver to avoid potentially hazardous foods, such as raw and undercooked meats and eggs, and to make sure fruits and vegetables are well-washed before eating.

The nursing measures discussed in eNursing Care Plan 34.3 (available on the website for this chapter) are important in treating the patient with neutropenia. Do not overlook quality-of-life issues for the patient with neutropenia. Fatigue, malaise, a decrease in functioning, and social isolation require coaching on safe activity.

MYELODYSPLASTIC SYNDROME

Myelodysplastic syndrome (MDS) is a group of hematopoietic stem cell disorders that results in peripheral blood cytopenia, abnormal cell morphology in 1 or more cell lines, and increased risk of acute myeloid leukemia (AML).[22] The incidence is 4.5 per 100,000 people per year in the United States. Although it can occur in all age-groups, the highest prevalence is in people older than 80 years of age, at which point the rate increases to 55.4 per 100,000.[23]

Etiology and Pathophysiology

The cause of MDS is unknown. Persons at risk are those who had radiation therapy, had chemotherapy with alkylating agents (e.g., chlorambucil, cyclophosphamide, melphalan), or were exposed to industrial solvents (e.g., benzene, vinyl chloride). Around 50% of MDS patients have an acquired chromosome abndormality.[4] Rarely, genetic disorders cause the disease.

We refer to MDS as a *clonal disorder* because some bone marrow stem cells continue to function normally, while others do not. The abnormal clone of the stem cells is usually found in the bone marrow. Eventually, it may be found in the circulation.

Sometimes, 1 type of MDS transforms into another. Depending on the subtype, MDS may progress to AML.[23] In contrast to AML, in which the leukemic cells show little normal maturation, the clonal cells in MDS always have some degree of maturity. Disease progression is slower than in AML, and sometimes treatment is not needed.

Clinical Manifestations

Manifestations result from neoplastic transformation of the immature hematopoietic stem cells in the bone marrow. MDS often presents as infection and bleeding caused by inadequate numbers of ineffectively functioning circulating granulocytes or platelets. It may be found in the older adult during testing for the symptoms of anemia, thrombocytopenia, or neutropenia. It may be diagnosed incidentally from a routine CBC. During the advanced stage of MDS, life-threatening anemia, thrombocytopenia, and neutropenia occur.

Diagnostic Studies

Bone marrow biopsy with aspirate analysis is essential for both the diagnosis and classification of the specific type of MDS. The patient has peripheral cytopenia and changes in the bone marrow (hypocellular or hypercellular). Laboratory data and bone marrow studies rule out other causes of the dysplasia, such as nonmalignant disorders, cobalamin and folate deficiencies, and infection.

❖ Interprofessional and Nursing Management

Treatment of MDS is based on the premise that treatment aggressiveness of treatment should match disease aggressiveness. This is based on the amount and type of dysplasia in the bone marrow, specific genetic mutations, anticipated patient tolerance, and patient preference.[23] Supportive treatment consists of hematologic monitoring (serial bone marrow and peripheral blood examinations), antibiotic therapy, or transfusions with blood products along with chelators to prevent iron overload. Aminocaproic acid or other antifibrinolytic drugs may be used for patients who are refractory to platelet transfusions.[23]

Low-risk patients may be treated with EPO, myeloid growth factors, thrombopoietin-receptor agonists, or lenalidomide.[23] Azacitidine (Vidaza) and decitabine (Dacogen) are drugs that help to restore normal growth control and differentiation of hematopoietic cells. They reduce the frequency of transformation of MDS to acute leukemia. Side effects include myelosuppression, nausea, vomiting, constipation or diarrhea, and renal problems.

Other treatments for MDS include cytarabine with or without antitumor antibiotics (anthracyclines), ATG, and cyclosporine.[23] Chemotherapy and allogeneic HSCT are used in appropriate patients to treat bone marrow dysfunction of MDS and restore it with normal hematopoiesis.

Nursing care of a patient with MDS is like that of a patient with manifestations of anemia, thrombocytopenia, and neutropenia. See eNursing Care Plan 34.1 for the patient with anemia, eNursing Care Plan 34.2 for the patient with thrombocytopenia, and eNursing Care Plan 34.3 for the patient with neutropenia. The eNursing Care Plans are available on the website for this chapter.

LEUKEMIA

Leukemia is the general term used to describe a group of cancers affecting the blood and blood-forming tissues of the bone marrow, lymph system, and spleen. Leukemia occurs in all age-groups. It results in an accumulation of dysfunctional cells because of a loss of regulation in cell division. An estimated 60,530 new cases are diagnosed each year. Leukemias account for 28% of all childhood cancers. Of those, 75% are lymphoid leukemias.[24] Leukemia follows a progressive course that is eventually fatal if untreated. However, progress in successful cancer treatments has been rapid for hematopoietic and lymphoid cancers in the past 30 years.[24]

Etiology and Pathophysiology

Leukemia has no single cause. All cancers, including leukemia, begin as a mutation in the DNA of certain cells. Most leukemias result from a combination of factors, including genetic and environmental influences. Abnormal genes *(oncogenes)* can cause

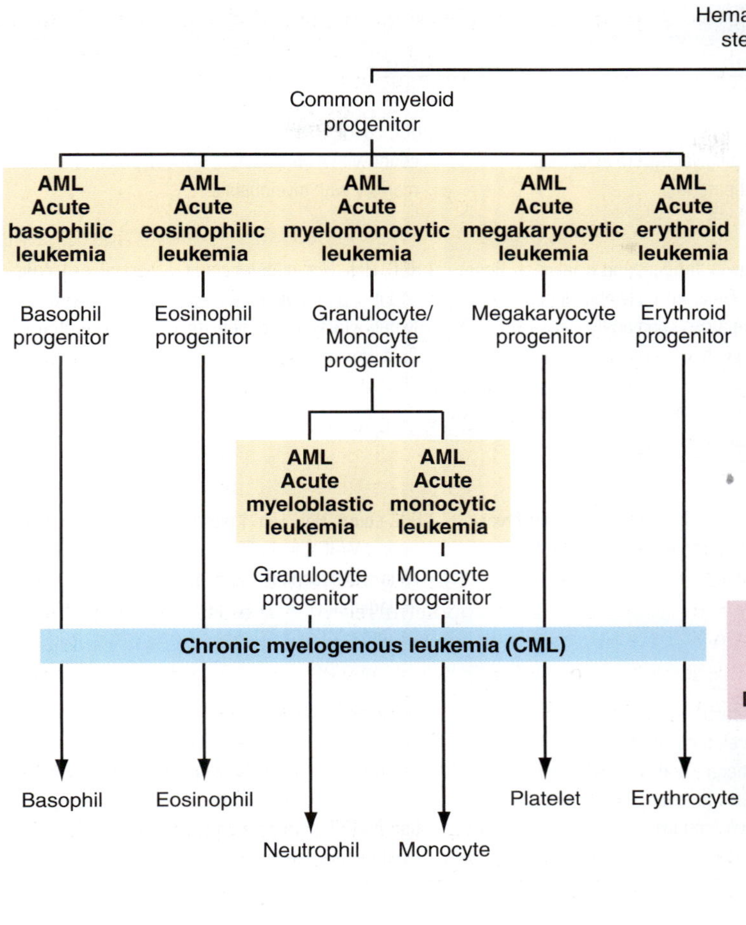

Fig. 34.12 Origins of leukemias, lymphomas, and myeloma. Differentiation pathways of blood-forming cells and the point at which the malignant clone originates. *AML,* Acute myeloid leukemia; *CLL,* chronic lymphocytic leukemia; *NK,* natural killer. (Modified from Huether SE, McCance KL, editors: *Understanding pathophysiology,* ed 7, St Louis, 2017, Elsevier.)

leukemia (see Chapter 16). Chemical agents (e.g., benzene), chemotherapy drugs (e.g., alkylating agents, topoisomerase II inhibitors), viruses, radiation, and immunologic deficiencies increase the risk of leukemia. Depending on the type of leukemia, other potential causes are exposure to pesticides (farmworkers) and smoking. Leukemia occurs more often in those with certain congenital or inherited abnormalities (e.g., Down syndrome).[2]

Classification

We classify leukemia based on acute versus chronic disease and the type of WBC involved. The terms *acute* and *chronic* refer to cell maturity and nature of disease onset. With acute leukemia, there is clonal proliferation of immature hematopoietic cells. The leukemia develops after malignant transformation of a single type of immature hematopoietic cell, followed by cellular replication and expansion of that malignant clone (Fig. 34.12). Chronic leukemias involve more mature forms of the WBC. The disease onset is more gradual.

Leukemia classified by the type of leukocyte involved is either myelogenous or lymphocytic origin. By combining the acute and chronic categories with the cell type involved, 1 can identify 4 major types of leukemia: acute lymphocytic leukemia (ALL), AML, chronic myelogenous (granulocytic) leukemia (CML), and chronic lymphocytic leukemia (CLL). Table 34.25 shows other defining features of these subtypes.

Acute Myeloid Leukemia

AML represents about one third of all leukemias. It makes up about 80% of the acute leukemias in adults.[24] With AML there is uncontrolled proliferation of myeloblasts, the precursors of granulocytes. There is hyperplasia of the bone marrow. The manifestations are usually related to replacement of normal hematopoietic cells in the marrow by leukemic myeloblasts and, to a lesser extent, to infiltration of other organs and tissue (Table 34.25). Its onset is often abrupt and dramatic. A patient may have serious infections and abnormal bleeding from the onset of the disease.

Acute Lymphocytic Leukemia

ALL is the most common type of leukemia in children. It accounts for around 20% of acute leukemia cases in adults.[24] In ALL, immature small lymphocytes proliferate in the bone marrow. Most are of B-cell origin. Most patients have fever

TABLE 34.25 Types of Leukemia

Age of Onset	Clinical Manifestations	Diagnostic Findings
Acute Myeloid Leukemia (AML)		
Accounts for 80% of acute leukemias in adults. Increase in incidence with advancing age after 60 years.	Fatigue and weakness, headache, mouth sores, anemia, bleeding, fever, infection; gingival hyperplasia, mild splenomegaly in some patients	↓ RBC count, Hgb, Hct, platelet count. ↓ to ↑ WBC count with myeloblasts. ↑ LDH. Hypercellular bone marrow with myeloblasts.
Acute Lymphocytic Leukemia (ALL)		
Accounts for 20% of acute leukemias in adults. Most adult patients older than 50 years of age.	Fever, pallor, bleeding, anorexia, fatigue, and weakness. Bone, joint, and abdominal pain. Generalized lymphadenopathy, infections, weight loss, hepatosplenomegaly, headache, mouth sores, neurologic manifestations: CNS involvement, ↑ intracranial pressure (nausea, vomiting, lethargy, cranial nerve dysfunction) from meningeal infiltration. Men may have painless enlargement of the scrotum.	↓ RBC, Hgb, Hct, platelet count. ↓, normal, or ↑ WBC count. ↑ LDH. Hypercellular bone marrow with lymphoblasts. Lymphoblasts may be in cerebrospinal fluid. Presence of Philadelphia chromosome (up to 25% of patients).
Chronic Myelogenous Leukemia (CML)		
Increase in incidence with advancing age. Median age at diagnosis of 67. Rare in children.	No symptoms early in disease. Fatigue and weakness, fever, night sweats, sternal tenderness, weight loss, joint pain, bone pain, massive splenomegaly.	↓ RBC count, Hgb, Hct. ↑ platelet count early, ↓ count later. ↑ WBCs, including a wide variety of myeloid cells and basophils. Nucleated RBCs common. Philadelphia chromosome present in ≈98% of patients.
Chronic Lymphocytic Leukemia (CLL)		
Most common form of leukemia in adults. Increase in incidence with advancing age. Average onset is 72 years of age, with predominance in men.	Frequently no symptoms. Detection of disease often during examination for unrelated condition, chronic fatigue, anorexia, splenomegaly and lymphadenopathy, hepatomegaly. May progress to fever, night sweats, weight loss, fatigue, and frequent infections.	Mild anemia and thrombocytopenia with disease progression. Total WBC count >100,000/μL. ↑ in peripheral lymphocytes and lymphocytes in bone marrow. May have autoimmune hemolytic anemia, idiopathic thrombocytopenic purpura, hypogammaglobulinemia.

at the time of diagnosis. Signs and symptoms may appear abruptly with bleeding or fever, or they may be insidious with progressive weakness, fatigue, bone and/or joint pain, and bleeding. Central nervous system (CNS) infiltration is especially common. Infiltration into other tissues and lymph nodes can occur.[1]

Chronic Myelogenous Leukemia

CML is caused by excessive development of neoplastic granulocytes in the bone marrow. These granulocytes are in all stages of development. They move into the peripheral blood in massive numbers and infiltrate the liver and spleen.[1]

The natural history of CML is a chronic stable phase followed by a more acute, aggressive phase called the *blastic phase*. The chronic phase of CML can last for several years with current therapies. Once CML transforms to an acute or blastic phase, it must be treated more aggressively, similar to an acute leukemia. For younger patients and those that stop responding to maintenance therapies, an HSCT is done.[4]

Genetic Link

The *Philadelphia chromosome* originates from the translocation between the *BCR* gene on chromosome 22 and the *ABL* gene on chromosome 9. The protein that is encoded by the newly created *BCR-ABL* gene on the Philadelphia chromosome interferes with normal cell cycle events, such as the regulation of cell proliferation.

The Philadelphia chromosome is present in about 98% or more of patients with CML. It is a diagnostic hallmark of CML and an important indicator of residual disease or relapse after treatment. However, the presence of the Philadelphia chromosome is not specific to diagnose CML. It is also found in ALL and occasionally in AML.

Chronic Lymphocytic Leukemia

CLL is the most common leukemia in adults in the United States.[24] With CLL there is production and accumulation of functionally inactive but long-lived, small, mature-appearing lymphocytes. B cells are usually involved. The lymphocytes infiltrate the bone marrow, spleen, and liver. Lymph node enlargement (lymphadenopathy) is present throughout the body.

Complications are rare in early-stage CLL but may develop as the disease advances. Pressure on nerves from enlarged lymph nodes causes pain and even paralysis. Mediastinal node enlargement leads to pulmonary symptoms. Because CLL is usually a disease of older adults, treatment decisions must consider disease progression and treatment side effects. Many patients in the early stages of CLL do not need treatment. Others are followed closely and receive treatment only when the disease progresses.

Other Leukemias

Occasionally we cannot determine the subtype of leukemia. The leukemic cells may have lymphoid, myeloid, or mixed characteristics. Often these patients do not respond to treatment and

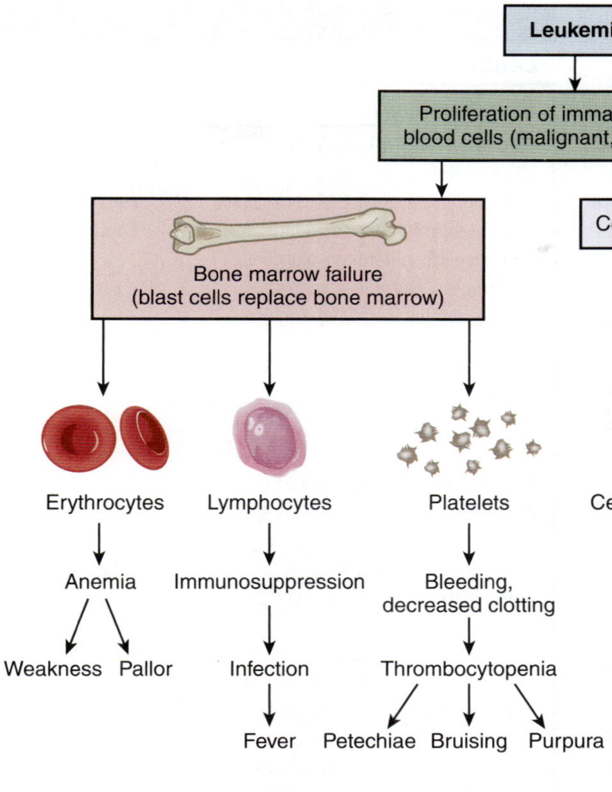

Fig. 34.13 Pathophysiology of leukemia. (Modified from McKinney ES, James SR, Murray SS, et al.: *Maternal-child nursing,* Philadelphia, 2000, Saunders.)

have a poor prognosis. Other rare types include hairy cell and biphenotypic (both abnormal myeloid and lymphoid clones) leukemias.

Overlap Between Leukemia and Lymphoma

Overlap exists between leukemia and non-Hodgkin lymphoma (NHL) because both involve proliferation of lymphocytes or their precursors (Fig. 34.12). A leukemia-like picture with peripheral lymphocytosis and bone marrow involvement may be present in some types of NHL.[1] Patients with more extensive nodal involvement (especially mediastinal), fewer circulating abnormal cells, and fewer blast forms in the marrow are considered to have lymphoma.

Clinical Manifestations

The manifestations of leukemia vary (Table 34.25). They relate to problems caused by bone marrow failure and, sometimes, leukemic infiltrates in tissues (Fig. 34.13). Bone marrow failure results from (1) bone marrow overcrowding by abnormal cells and (2) inadequate production of normal marrow elements. The patient is predisposed to anemia, thrombocytopenia, and decreased number and function of WBCs.

As leukemia progresses, the body makes fewer normal blood cells. The abnormal WBCs continue to accumulate because they do not go through the normal cell life cycle to death *(apoptosis)*. The leukemic cells may infiltrate the patient's organs, leading to splenomegaly, hepatomegaly, lymphadenopathy, bone pain, meningeal irritation, and oral lesions. Solid masses from collections of leukemic cells, called *chloromas,* can occur. A high leukemic white count in the peripheral blood (more than 100,000 cells/μL) can cause the blood to thicken and potentially block circulatory pathways. This is called *leukostasis.* It can be life threatening.

Diagnostic Studies

Peripheral blood evaluation and bone marrow examination are the primary methods used to diagnose and classify the type of leukemia. We use various morphologic, histochemical, immunologic, and cytogenetic methods to identify leukemic cell types, stage of development, and genetic mutations. Knowing the type of leukemia is important because each type has a different prognosis and treatment options. For example, in CML, the finding of the Philadelphia chromosome is an important diagnostic indicator. It is also sometimes present in ALL and affects the treatment.[25,26] Other studies, such as lumbar puncture and PET/CT scans, can detect leukemic cells outside of the blood and bone marrow.

Interprofessional Care

For some patients, cure is a realistic goal. For others, the goal is to attain remission or disease control. In *complete remission,* there is no evidence of disease on physical assessment, the bone marrow and peripheral blood appear normal, and molecular analysis shows no residual problems.[1] *Minimal residual disease* is when tumor cells cannot be detected by morphologic examination but can be identified by molecular testing. With *partial remission,* there is a lack of symptoms and a normal peripheral blood smear, but there is still evidence of disease in the bone marrow. *Molecular remission* means that all molecular studies are negative for residual leukemia.

The patient's prognosis is directly related to the ability to maintain remission. The prognosis becomes more unfavorable with each relapse. After each relapse, the succeeding remission may be harder to achieve and shorter in duration.

Age and cytogenetic analysis are part of treatment decisions. Because chemotherapy is the mainstay of the treatment, you need to understand the principles of cancer chemotherapy (see Chapter 16). Radiation and biologic therapies may be used. Sometimes patients have such a high WBC count (e.g., 100,000 cells/μL or more) that initial emergent treatment may include leukapheresis and hydroxyurea. The purpose of these treatments is to reduce the WBC count and risk for leukemia cell–induced thrombosis. In some cases, such as nonsymptomatic patients with CLL, watchful waiting with active supportive care may be appropriate.

Chemotherapy Stages

We often think about chemotherapy as 3 stages: induction, postinduction or postremission (consolidation), and maintenance.

Induction therapy. The first stage, *induction therapy,* is the attempt to bring about a remission. Induction is aggressive treatment that seeks to destroy leukemic cells in the tissues, peripheral blood, and bone marrow to eventually restore normal hematopoiesis on bone marrow recovery. During induction therapy, a patient may become critically ill because the bone marrow is severely depressed by the chemotherapy. Nursing interventions focus on neutropenia, thrombocytopenia, and anemia. Common chemotherapy drugs for induction of AML include cytarabine and an antitumor antibiotic (anthracycline), such as daunorubicin or idarubicin.[27] After 1 course of induction therapy, around 70% of newly diagnosed patients younger than age 50 achieve complete remission. We assume that leukemic cells persist undetected after induction therapy. This could lead to relapse within a few months without further therapy.[27]

Postinduction or postremission therapy. Terms used to describe postinduction or postremission chemotherapy include *intensification* and *consolidation. Intensification therapy,* or high-dose therapy, may start immediately after induction therapy and last for several months. Other drugs that target the cell in a different way than those given during induction may be added.

Consolidation therapy is started after a remission is achieved. It may consist of 1 or 2 more courses of the same drugs given during induction or involve high-dose therapy (intensive consolidation). The purpose of consolidation therapy is to eliminate remaining leukemic cells that may not be clinically or pathologically evident.

Maintenance therapy. The goal of maintenance therapy is to keep the body free of leukemic cells. It may also be used for acute leukemia, depending on the presence of specific cytogenetic markers and therapies that can target them.[25,27]

Drug Therapy Regimens

Combination drug therapy is the mainstay of treatment for leukemia. The 3 purposes for using multiple drugs are to (1) decrease drug resistance, (2) minimize the drug toxicity by using multiple drugs with varying toxicities, and (3) interrupt cell growth at multiple points in the cell cycle. The drugs used vary. Table 34.26 gives examples of treatment regimens used in various types of leukemia.

Some drugs target small molecules that promote the growth and differentiation of leukemic cells. For example, all-*trans* retinoic acid is used to treat acute promyelocytic leukemia (a type of AML). It causes normal differentiation of the promyelocytes, which has arrested in this type of leukemia by the translocation of the *PML* gene on chromosome 15 to the *RARA* gene on chromosome 17 (t15;17).[27] Midostaurin, a multikinase inhibitor, inhibits this growth pathway in AML patients with the *FLT3* mutation.[27] Imatinib (Gleevec) and other tyrosine-kinase inhibitors target the BCR-ABL protein that is present in nearly

TABLE 34.26 Drug Therapy

Leukemia

Drug Therapy	Other Therapy
Acute Myeloid Leukemia (AML)	
arsenic trioxide, azacitidine, cytarabine, daunorubicin, decitabine, enasidenib, etoposide, fludarabine, gemtuzumab ozogamicin, gilteritinib, glasdegib, idarubicin, ivosidenib, midostaurin, mitoxantrone, sorafenib, tretinoin, venetoclax Combination chemotherapy of cytarabine and antitumor antibiotic (most common initial therapy)	Allogeneic hematopoietic stem cell transplant (HSCT) (see Chapter 16)
Acute Lymphocytic Leukemia (ALL)	
asparaginase, blinatumomab, bosutinib, clofarabine, cyclophosphamide, cytarabine, dasatinib, daunorubicin, dexamethasone, doxorubicin, etoposide, fludarabine, imatinib, inotuzumab ozogamicin, 6-mercaptopurine, methotrexate, nelarabine, nilotinib, pegaspargase, ponatinib, prednisone, rituximab, vincristine Combination chemotherapy of several agents is common over a prolonged time	Cranial radiation therapy, intrathecal methotrexate or cytarabine, allogeneic HSCT, Tisagenlecleucel (CAR-T cell therapy) (see Chapter 16)
Chronic Myelogenous Leukemia	
bosutinib, dasatinib, imatinib, nilotinib, omacetaxine, ponatinib Combination chemotherapy for progression to acute phase as per either AML or ALL therapy	HSCT, α-interferon, leukapheresis
Chronic Lymphocytic Leukemia	
Acalabrutinib, alemtuzumab, chlorambucil, bendamustine, cyclophosphamide, duvelisib, fludarabine, ibrutinib, idelalisib, lenalidomide, obinutuzumab, ofatumumab, prednisone, rituximab, venetoclax, zanubrutinib	Radiation, splenectomy, colony-stimulating factors, allogeneic HSCT

all patients with CML and some patients with ALL.[26] This drug kills only cancer cells, leaving healthy cells alone.

Specific targeted therapy in the form of monoclonal antibodies is an important treatment for hematopoietic cancers. However, cures with these therapies alone are rare. Rituximab binds to the B-cell antigen (CD20) and is a treatment for ALL and CLL.[28] Alemtuzumab (Campath), a treatment for CLL, binds to CD52, a panlymphocyte antigen present on both T and B cells.[28]

Other Treatments

In addition to chemotherapy, corticosteroids and radiation therapy have a role in treating the patient with leukemia. Total body radiation can prepare a patient for bone marrow transplantation. Radiation may be restricted to certain areas, such as the liver and spleen, or other organs affected by infiltrates. In ALL, prophylactic intrathecal methotrexate or cytarabine is given to decrease the CNS involvement which is common in this type of leukemia. When CNS leukemia does occur, cranial radiation is an option. Immunotherapy and targeted therapy, such as monoclonal antibodies and chimeric antigen receptor (CAR) T cells, may be indicated for specific leukemias. These therapies are discussed in Chapter 16.

Hematopoietic Stem Cell Transplantation

HSCT is another option for treating leukemia. The goal of HSCT is to eliminate all leukemic cells from the body using combinations of chemotherapy with or without total body irradiation. This treatment eradicates the patient's hematopoietic stem cells, which are then replaced with those of an HLA-matched sibling, HLA-half-matched relative, volunteer donor *(allogeneic)*, or identical twin *(syngeneic)*. HSCT is discussed in Chapter 16.

The primary complications for patients with allogeneic HSCT are graft-versus-host disease (GVHD), relapse of leukemia, and infection and sepsis. Because HSCT has serious associated risks, the patient must weigh the significant risks for treatment-related death or treatment failure (relapse) with the hope of cure.

NURSING MANAGEMENT: LEUKEMIA

Assessment

Subjective and objective data that you should obtain from a patient with leukemia are outlined in Table 34.27.

TABLE 34.27 NURSING ASSESSMENT
Leukemia

Subjective Data

Important Health Information

Health history: Exposure to chemical toxins (e.g., benzene, arsenic), radiation, or viruses (HTLV-1); chromosome abnormalities (Down syndrome, Klinefelter syndrome, Fanconi syndrome), immunologic deficiencies; organ transplantation; frequent infections; bleeding tendencies

Medications: Chemotherapy

Surgery or other treatments: Radiation exposure; prior radiation and chemotherapy for cancer

Functional Health Patterns

Health perception–health management: Family history of leukemia; malaise

Nutritional-metabolic: Mouth sores, weight loss; chills, night sweats; nausea, vomiting, anorexia, dysphagia, early satiety; easy bruising

Elimination: Hematuria, ↓ urine output; diarrhea, dark or bloody stools

Activity-exercise: Fatigue with progressive weakness; dyspnea, nosebleeds, cough

Cognitive-perceptual: Headache; muscle cramps; sore throat; generalized sternal tenderness, bone, joint, abdominal pain; paresthesias, numbness, tingling, visual changes

Sexuality-reproductive: Prolonged menses, menorrhagia, metrorrhagia, impotence

Objective Data

General

Fever, generalized lymphadenopathy, lethargy

Cardiovascular

↑ HR, systolic murmurs

GI

Gingival bleeding and hyperplasia; oral ulcerations, herpes and *Candida* infections; perirectal irritation and infection; hepatomegaly, splenomegaly

Musculoskeletal

Muscle wasting, bone pain, joint pain

Neurologic

Seizures, disorientation, confusion, impaired coordination, cranial nerve palsies, papilledema

Skin

Pallor or jaundice; petechiae, bruising, purpura, reddish brown to purple cutaneous infiltrates, macules, and papules

Possible Diagnostic Findings

↓, normal, or ↑ WBC count with shift to the left (↑ blast cells) and neutropenia; anemia, ↓ hematocrit and hemoglobin, thrombocytopenia, specific chromosome abnormalities; hypercellular bone marrow aspirate or biopsy with myeloblasts, lymphoblasts, and markedly ↓ normal cells

Clinical Problems

Clinical problems for the patient with leukemia include those for anemia, thrombocytopenia, and neutropenia (see eNursing Care Plan 34.3, available on the website).

Planning

The overall goals are that the patient with leukemia will (1) understand and adhere to the treatment plan; (2) have minimal side effects and complications associated with both the disease and its treatment; and (3) establish realistic hope and goals, feeling supported during periods of treatment, relapse, or remission.

Implementation

Acute Care

The nursing role during acute phases of leukemia is challenging because the patient has many physical and psychosocial needs. As with other forms of cancer, the diagnosis of leukemia can evoke great fear and be equated with death. It may be viewed as a hopeless, horrible disease with many painful and undesirable consequences. The treatment and prognosis are driven by many factors, such as age and type of leukemia. You must understand the patient's type of leukemia, prognosis, treatment plan, and goals. By doing this, you can help the patient to realize that, although the future may be uncertain, one can have a meaningful quality of life while in remission or with disease control and that, in some cases, there is reasonable hope for cure.

The family needs help adjusting to the stress of this abrupt onset of serious illness and the losses imposed by the sick role (e.g., dependence, withdrawal, changes in role responsibilities, changes in body image). The diagnosis of leukemia often brings with it the need to make difficult decisions at a time of profound stress for the patient and family.

Patients may have comorbid conditions that affect treatment decisions. Important nursing interventions include (1) maximizing the patient's physical functioning, (2) teaching patients that acute side effects of treatment are usually temporary, and (3) encouraging patients to discuss their quality-of-life issues.

You are an important advocate in helping the patient and family understand the complexities of treatment decisions and manage the side effects and toxicities. This may include making sure the HCP addresses fertility concerns. A patient may need a long hospitalization or to temporarily relocate to an appropriate treatment center. This can lead a patient to feeling deserted and isolated at a time when support is most needed. You can help to reverse feelings of abandonment and loneliness by balancing the demanding technical needs with a humanistic, caring approach. The patient's needs are best met by care from an interprofessional team (e.g., psychiatric and oncology clinical nurse specialists, case managers, dietitians, chaplains, and social workers).

Quality nursing care significantly affects patient survival and comfort during aggressive chemotherapy. You need to make astute assessments and plan care to help the patient manage the severe side effects. Life-threatening results of bone marrow suppression (neutropenia, thrombocytopenia, and anemia) require prompt nursing interventions. Other critical aspects of care include anticipating, monitoring for, and helping to treat emergencies, such as DIC, tumor lysis syndrome, and leukostasis. Complications of chemotherapy may affect the patient's GI tract, nutrition status, skin and mucosa, cardiopulmonary status, liver, kidneys, and neurologic system. Nursing interventions related to chemotherapy are discussed in Chapter 16.

Review all drugs being given, including the mechanism of action, purpose, routes of administration, doses, potential side effects, safe handling considerations, and toxic effects. Assess laboratory data reflecting drug effects and sequelae of the disease. Unlike treatments for solid tumors, patients with leukemia receive chemotherapy even if they have severe myelosuppression since the underlying disorder is causing the problem and will not resolve unless treated.

◆ Ambulatory Care

Ongoing care is needed to monitor for signs and symptoms of disease control or relapse. For a patient receiving long-term or maintenance chemotherapy, the fatigue of long-term chronic disease management can become discouraging. Teach the patient and caregiver the importance of continued diligence in disease management and the need for follow-up care. Review drug information, self-care measures, and when to seek medical care.

TABLE 34.28 Comparison of Hodgkin and Non-Hodgkin Lymphoma

	Hodgkin Lymphoma	Non-Hodgkin Lymphoma
Cellular origin	B lymphocytes	B lymphocytes (85%) T or natural killer lymphocytes (15%)
Extent of disease	Localized to regional but may be more widespread. Spreads to adjacent tissues	Disseminated, can spread to other areas of the body
B symptoms (fever, drenching night sweats, weight loss)	Common	Uncommon
Extranodal involvement	Rare	Common

The goals of rehabilitation for long-term survivors of leukemia are to manage the physical, psychologic, social, and spiritual consequences and delayed effects from the disease and its treatment. Involving the patient in survivor networks and support groups or services may help the patient to adapt to living after a life-threatening illness. Exploring national and community resources (e.g., American Cancer Society, Leukemia & Lymphoma Society) may reduce the financial burden and the feelings of dependence. Provide resources for spiritual support.

Vigilant follow-up care helps to ensure that we recognize and treat the survivor's unique needs. Often these needs may need a referral or consultation. For example, physical therapy personnel may develop an exercise program to address posttreatment deficits from drug-induced peripheral neuropathy. Patients should follow the advice of their HCP about receiving vaccines.

◆ Evaluation

The expected outcomes are that the patient with leukemia will

- Cope effectively with the diagnosis, treatment regimen, and prognosis
- Have no complications related to the disease or treatment
- Feel supported throughout treatment

LYMPHOMAS

Lymphomas are cancers originating in the bone marrow and lymphatic structures resulting in the proliferation of lymphocytes. Lymphomas make up 4% to 5% of all cancers in the United States.[24] Two major types of lymphoma are Hodgkin lymphoma and NHL. A comparison of these 2 types of lymphoma is shown in Table 34.28.[4]

HODGKIN LYMPHOMA

Hodgkin lymphoma, or *Hodgkin disease,* makes up about 10% of all lymphomas. There is a proliferation of abnormal giant, multinucleated cells, called *Reed-Sternberg cells,* or its variant, *Hodgkin cells* (mononucleated), which proliferate in the lymph nodes.[4] The disease has a bimodal age-specific incidence, occurring most frequently in persons from 15 to 30 years of age and

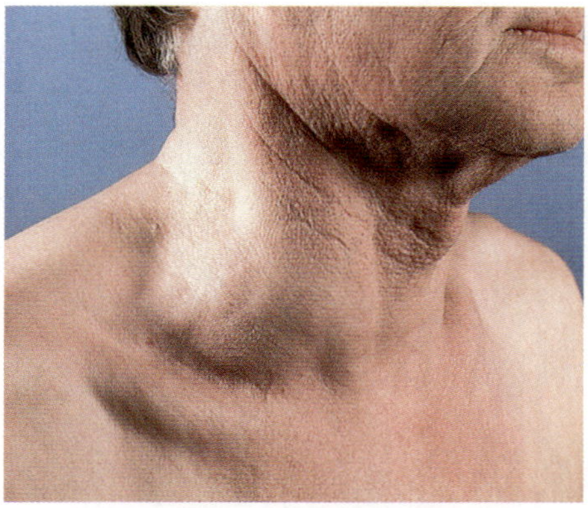

Fig. 34.14 Enlarged cervical lymph node in the neck of a man with Hodgkin lymphoma. (From Howard MR, Hamilton PJ: *Haematology: an illustrated colour atlas,* ed 4, London, 2013, Churchill Livingston.)

older than 55 years of age.[29] Males are affected almost twice as often as females.[4] Each year, about 8480 new cases of Hodgkin's lymphoma are diagnosed, with around 970 deaths.[24] About 85% of all patients are cured.[4]

Etiology and Pathophysiology

Although the cause of Hodgkin lymphoma is unknown, several key factors play a role in its development. The main interacting factors include infection with Epstein-Barr virus (EBV), genetic predisposition, and exposure to occupational toxins. The incidence of Hodgkin lymphoma is increased in those with HIV infection.[29]

The disease likely starts in a single location and then spreads along adjacent lymphatics. However, in recurrent disease, it may spread more diffusely. It eventually infiltrates other organs, especially lungs, spleen, and liver. When the disease begins above the diaphragm, it stays confined to lymph nodes for a variable time. Disease originating below the diaphragm often spreads to extra lymphoid sites, such as the liver. There are 5 histologic subtypes. Nodular sclerosis is the most common.

Clinical Manifestations

The onset of symptoms is usually gradual. The initial sign is often enlargement of cervical, axillary, or inguinal lymph nodes (Fig. 34.14). Subsequent lymph node involvement is generally by spread to adjacent lymph nodes. The nodes are movable and nontender. Enlarged nodes are not painful unless they exert pressure on adjacent nerves.

The patient may have weight loss, fatigue, weakness, fever, chills, tachycardia, or night sweats. A group of initial findings, including fever (>100.4°F [38°C]), drenching night sweats, and weight loss (exceeding 10% in 6 months), are termed *B symptoms.* They correlate with a worse prognosis. After having even small amounts of alcohol, patients with Hodgkin lymphoma may have a rapid onset of pain at the site of disease. The cause for the alcohol-induced pain is unknown. Generalized itching without skin lesions may develop. Cough, dyspnea, stridor, and dysphagia may occur with mediastinal node involvement.

In more advanced disease, there may be hepatomegaly and splenomegaly. Anemia results from increased destruction and decreased production of RBCs. Other signs vary depending on the site of disease. For example, intrathoracic involvement may lead to superior vena cava syndrome. Enlarged retroperitoneal nodes may cause palpable abdominal masses or interfere with renal function. Jaundice may occur from liver involvement. Spinal cord compression leading to paraplegia may occur with extradural involvement. Bone pain occurs from bone involvement.

Diagnostic and Staging Studies

Peripheral blood analysis, lymph node biopsy, bone marrow examination, and radiologic studies are important in evaluating Hodgkin lymphoma. Abnormalities in the CBC, such as a microcytic hypochromic anemia, are variable and not diagnostic. Leukopenia and thrombocytopenia may develop, but they are usually a consequence of treatment, advanced disease, or hypersplenism. Other blood studies may show increased erythrocyte sedimentation rate and LDH, high leukocyte alkaline phosphatase from liver and bone involvement, hypercalcemia from bone involvement, and hypoalbuminemia from liver involvement.

Radiologic evaluation can help define all sites and determine the clinical stage of the disease. PET and CT scans are used to stage and then assess the response to therapy and to distinguish residual tumor from fibrotic masses after treatment. Scans can show masses, such as renal displacement caused by retroperitoneal node enlargement, abdominal or mediastinal lymph node enlargement, and liver, spleen, bone, and brain infiltration.

Using all the information from the various diagnostic studies, HCPs determine a clinical stage of disease (Fig. 34.15). The final staging is based on the clinical stage (extent of the disease), presence of B symptoms, and other unfavorable prognostic features. The terms used in staging involve an A or B classification, depending on whether systemic symptoms are present at diagnosis, and a Roman numeral (I to IV) that reflects the location and extent of the disease.[29]

❖ Interprofessional and Nursing Management

Treatment depends on the nature and extent of the disease. Combination chemotherapy works well because, as in leukemia, the drugs used have an additive antitumor effect without increasing side effects. As with leukemia, therapy must be aggressive. The standard for chemotherapy is the ABVD regimen: doxorubicin (**A**driamycin), **b**leomycin, **v**inblastine, and **d**acarbazine. Patients with favorable early-stage disease receive 2 to 4 cycles of chemotherapy.[29] Patients with early-stage disease but unfavorable prognostic features (e.g., B symptoms) or intermediate-stage disease receive 4 to 6 cycles of chemotherapy. Advanced-stage Hodgkin lymphoma is treated more aggressively using 6 to 8 cycles of chemotherapy. A common regimen is BEACOPP (**b**leomycin, **e**toposide, doxorubicin [**A**driamycin], **c**yclophosphamide, vincristine [**O**ncovin], **pro**carbazine, and **p**rednisone).[29]

The role of involved-site radiation as a supplement to chemotherapy varies depending on the extent of disease and the presence of resistant disease after chemotherapy. Response to therapy is determined by PET and CT scans and other diagnostic tests (e.g., bone marrow biopsy).

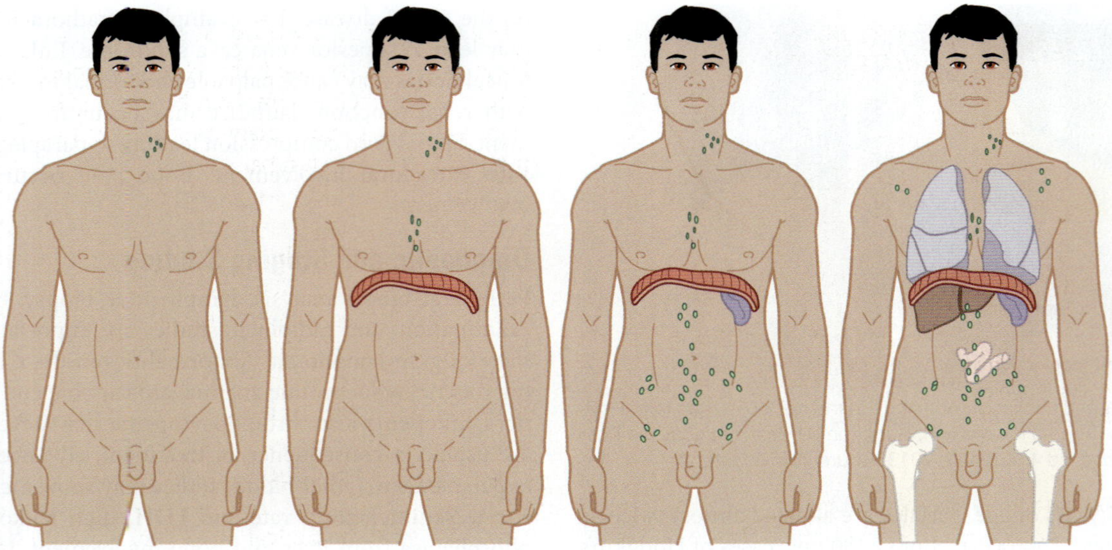

Fig. 34.15 Staging system for Hodgkin lymphoma and non-Hodgkin lymphoma. *Stage I,* Involvement of single lymph node (e.g., cervical node). *Stage II,* Involvement of 2 or more lymph nodes on 1 side of diaphragm. *Stage III,* Lymph node involvement above and below the diaphragm. *Stage IV,* Involvement outside of diaphragm (e.g., liver, bone marrow). The stage is followed by the letter *A* (absence) or *B* (presence) to indicate significant systemic symptoms (e.g., fever, night sweats, weight loss).

A variety of chemotherapy regimens and newer agents, such as brentuximab vedotin, nivolumab, bendamustine, everolimus, or pembrolizumab, are options for patients who have relapsed or refractory disease. Sometimes we give a single drug palliatively to someone who cannot tolerate intensive combination therapy. Ideally, once in remission, a curative option may be intensive chemotherapy with autologous or allogeneic HSCT.[29] HSCT has allowed patients to receive higher, potentially curative doses of chemotherapy while reducing life-threatening leukopenia. Maintenance chemotherapy does not contribute to increased survival after achieving complete remission.

A serious consequence of treatment is the later development of secondary cancers and potential long-term treatment toxicities, such as endocrine, heart, and lung problems. Secondary solid tumor cancers may occur 10 years after ending treatment. The most common secondary cancers are lung and breast cancer, especially with radiation therapy. Patients should have close follow-up and screening for early detection of these problems.

Nursing care focuses on managing problems related to the disease (e.g., pain caused by a tumor, superior vena cava syndrome), pancytopenia, and other side effects of therapy. Because patient survival depends on their response to treatment, supporting the patient through the consequences of treatment is important.

Psychosocial considerations are as important as they are with leukemia. However, the prognosis for Hodgkin lymphoma is better than that for many forms of cancer. Address the physical and spiritual consequences. Fertility issues may be of concern because this disease occurs in adolescents and young adults. Help to ensure that these issues are addressed soon after diagnosis.

NON-HODGKIN LYMPHOMA

Non-Hodgkin lymphomas (NHLs) are a broad group of cancers of primarily B, T, and natural killer (NK) cells. They affect persons of all ages. There are more than 75 types. We classify NHL by the level of differentiation (maturity), cell of origin, immunophenotype (cell surface antigens, CD20, CD52), and genetic and clinical features.[30] The most common subtypes are diffuse large B-cell lymphoma and follicular lymphoma.[4] Burkitt lymphoma is the most aggressive form. A simplified example of the classification system is shown in Table 34.29.[30,31]

A variety of presentations and courses occur, from indolent (slowly developing) to rapidly progressive disease. NHL is the

TABLE 34.29 Classification of Non-Hodgkin Lymphoma[a]

B-Cell Lymphomas
- Burkitt lymphoma
- Diffuse large B-cell lymphoma (DLBCL)
- Follicular lymphoma
- Mantle cell lymphoma
- Marginal zone B-cell lymphoma (MALT)
- Plasmablastic lymphoma
- Small lymphocytic lymphoma/chronic lymphocytic leukemia

T-Cell and Natural Killer (NK)-Cell Lymphomas
- Anaplastic large T-cell lymphoma
- Extranodal NK/T cell lymphoma
- Mycosis fungoides and Sézary syndrome
- Peripheral T-cell lymphoma, not otherwise specified (NOS)

Posttransplant Lymphoproliferative Disorders (PTLD)
- Infectious mononucleosis-like PTLD

Histiocytic and Dendritic Cell Tumors
- Langerhans cell histiocytosis

[a]This is only a partial list.

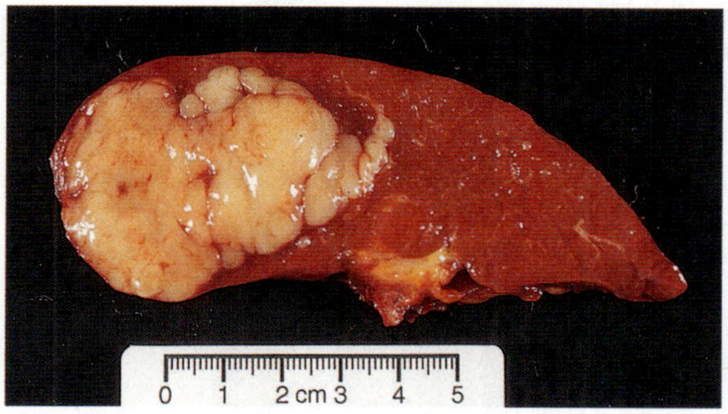

Fig. 34.16 Non-Hodgkin lymphoma involving the spleen. The presence of an isolated mass is typical. (From Cotran RS, Kumar V, Abbas AK: *Robbins pathologic basis of disease,* ed 6, Philadelphia, 1999, Saunders.)

most common hematologic cancer. Each year about 77,240 new cases of NHL are diagnosed and 19,940 deaths occur.[24]

Etiology and Pathophysiology

The cause of NHL is usually unknown. NHLs may result from chromosomal translocations, infections, environmental factors, and immunodeficiency states. Chromosomal translocations have a key role in the pathogenesis of many NHLs. Viruses and bacteria implicated in the pathogenesis of NHL include human T-cell leukemia virus, type 1 (HTLV-1), EBV, human herpesvirus 8, hepatitis C, *H. pylori,* and *Chlamydia trachomatisi*.[4] Chemicals linked to NHL include pesticides, herbicides, solvents, and organic chemicals. NHL is more common in people who have inherited immunodeficiency syndromes, have used immunosuppressive agents (e.g., to prevent rejection after an organ transplant or to treat autoimmune disorders), or received chemotherapy or radiation therapy.

NHL does not have a hallmark feature that parallels the Hodgkin or Reed-Sternberg cell of Hodgkin lymphoma. All NHLs involve lymphocytes arrested in various stages of development and may mimic a leukemia. For example, small lymphocytic lymphoma (SLL) and CLL result from malignant proliferation of small B lymphocytes, with most CLL disease within the bone marrow versus the lymph nodes. Some NHLs can begin outside the lymph nodes. Diffuse large B-cell lymphoma, the most common aggressive lymphoma, is usually found in lymph nodes in the neck or abdomen.

Clinical Manifestations

The method of spread can be unpredictable. Most patients have widespread disease at the time of diagnosis (Fig. 34.16). The primary manifestation is painless lymph node enlargement. The lymphadenopathy can wax and wane in indolent disease. Because the disease has usually spread, other symptoms are present depending on where the disease is present (e.g., hepatomegaly with liver involvement, neurologic symptoms with CNS disease). NHL can manifest in nonspecific ways, such as an airway obstruction, hyperuricemia and renal failure from tumor lysis syndrome, pericardial tamponade, and GI symptoms. Patients with high-grade lymphomas may have lymphadenopathy and B symptoms, such as fever, night sweats, and weight loss.

Diagnostic and Staging Studies

Diagnostic studies used for NHL resemble those used for Hodgkin lymphoma. However, because NHL is more often in extranodal sites, more diagnostic studies may be done. These include an MRI or lumbar puncture to rule out CNS disease, a bone marrow biopsy to determine bone marrow infiltration, or a barium enema or upper endoscopy to look for GI involvement. In early NHL, the CBC may be normal, but some lymphomas manifest in a "leukemic" phase.

Clinical staging, as described for Hodgkin lymphoma, helps to guide therapy (Fig. 34.15). Establishing the precise histologic subtype through biopsy is important. Treatment is guided by the cell type, cytogenetic studies, and clinical behavior: *indolent* (low grade), aggressive (high grade), or *highly aggressive* (very high grade). Other factors, known as the International Prognostic Index (IPI), may be considered for each subtype. These include the clinical stage, number of extranodal sites, serum LDH, WBC count, and patient's age and performance status.[30,31] Immunologic, cytogenetic, and molecular studies are used for making therapeutic decisions and assessing prognosis. Other studies might include blood tests for tumor lysis; screening for hepatitis, HIV, and other infections; skin biopsies; bone marrow biopsies; and lumbar punctures. The prognosis for NHL is based on the histopathology.

❖ Interprofessional and Nursing Management

Treatment involves chemotherapy, biotherapy, radiation, and sometimes phototherapy and topical therapy (Table 34.30).[30,31] More aggressive lymphomas (diffuse large B cell) are generally more responsive to treatment. In contrast, indolent lymphomas (e.g., follicular lymphomas) have a naturally long course but are hard to effectively treat.[30]

Patients with low-grade (indolent) lymphoma may live 10 years or more without treatment. However, some early therapies can be well tolerated and may reduce the time to progression of the disease. Those that have an infectious basis, such as *H. pylori* gastric lymphomas, may be treated with antibiotic or antiviral therapy. HSCT may help in certain subtypes of aggressive or refractory lymphomas. CAR T-cell immunotherapy may be used.

Rituximab, a monoclonal antibody against the CD20 antigen on the surface of normal and malignant B cells, treats NHL in combination with other agents. Once bound to the cells, rituximab causes lysis and cell death. Numerous chemotherapy combinations are used to try to overcome the resistant nature of this disease. Targeted therapies are becoming more prevalent (Table 34.30).

DRUG ALERT

Rituximab (Rituxan)

- Monitor for signs of severe hypersensitivity infusion reactions, especially with first infusion.
- Manifestations may include hypotension, bronchospasm, dysrhythmias, angioedema, and cardiogenic shock.
- Screen for history of hepatitis because the drug may reactivate hepatitis.

TABLE 34.30 Treatment of Non-Hodgkin Lymphoma[a]

Recommended Therapies	Common Chemotherapy Combinations
Indolent (Low-Grade) Follicular Lymphoma, Marginal Zone B-Cell Lymphoma, Mucosa-Associated Lymphoid Tissue (MALT)	
• External beam irradiation for local, limited disease • Single-agent rituximab, obinutuzumab • Rituximab or obinutuzumab with another agent (bendamustine, chlorambucil, cyclophosphamide, lenalidomide) • Combination chemotherapy (R-CHOP or other) • Targeted therapies (duvelisib, tazemetostat) • Radioimmunotherapy • Hematopoietic stem cell transplant (HSCT) • Anti-CD19 CAR-T cell therapy	**R-CHOP:** rituximab, **c**yclophosphamide, doxorubicin **h**ydrochloride, vincristine (**O**ncovin), **p**rednisone **R-CVP:** **r**ituximab, **c**yclophosphamide, **v**incristine, **p**rednisone
Aggressive (Intermediate- or High-Grade) Mantle Cell, Diffuse Large B-Cell, T-Cell, Natural Killer–Cell Lymphomas	
• Combination chemotherapy with localized radiation if needed • Aggressive combination chemotherapy for 3–8 cycles with local radiation if needed • Intrathecal chemotherapy if needed • Single agent or other combination treatment, depending on subtype and response (e.g., acalabrutinib, alemtuzumab, asparaginase, belinostat, bendamustine, bortezomib, brentuximab vedotin, gemcitabine, ibrutinib, lenalidomide, nivolumab, oxaliplatin, pembrolizumab, polatuzumab vedotin, romidepsin, venetoclax, vinorelbine, zanubrutinib) • HSCT (autologous or allogeneic) • Anti-CD19 CAR T-cell therapy	**CHOP** ± rituximab (see above) **ICE** ± rituximab: **i**fosfamide, **c**yclophosphamide, **e**toposide **R-EPOCH:** **r**ituximab, **e**toposide, **p**rednisone, vincristine (**O**ncovin), **c**yclophosphamide, doxorubicin **h**ydrochloride **ESHAP ± R:** **e**toposide, methylprednisolone (**S**olu-Medrol), **h**igh-dose cytarabine (**A**ra-C), cisplatin (**P**latinol), with or without **r**ituximab **Hyper-CVAD ± R:** hyperfractionated **c**yclophosphamide, **v**incristine, doxorubicin (**A**driamycin), **d**examethasone alternating with high-dose methotrexate and cytarabine with or without rituximab **DHAP ± R:** **d**examethasone, **h**igh-dose cytarabine (**A**ra-C), cisplatin (**P**latinol), with or without **r**ituximab
Highly Aggressive (e.g., Burkitt Lymphoma)	
• Aggressive combination chemotherapy for 3–8 cycles • HSCT	**R-EPOCH:** **r**ituximab, **e**toposide, **p**rednisone, vincristine (**O**ncovin), **c**yclophosphamide, doxorubicin **h**ydrochloride **Hyper-CVAD ± R** (see above) **CODOX-M:** **c**yclophosphamide, vincristine (**O**ncovin), **dox**orubicin, high-dose **m**ethotrexate, with or without rituximab (includes intrathecal methotrexate) **ICE** ± rituximab (see above)

[a]The acronym for some drug regimens use the trade name of chemotherapy drugs. In some cases, the trade name drug has been discontinued, and the drug currently used is the generic version.

Another therapy for some types of NHL is the monoclonal antibody ibritumomab tiuxetan (Zevalin). It contains a radioactive particle that can kill cancer cells. The therapy targets the CD20 antigen, which is on the surface of mature B cells and B-cell tumors. Targeting allows for the delivery of the radiation directly to the cancer cells. Side effects include pancytopenia. Use radiation precautions in caring for these patients. Teach patients about safety issues and how to minimize the risk for radiation exposure to staff and others.

In general, T-cell lymphomas are harder to cure. We treat them aggressively up front, often followed by an HSCT. Treatment of cutaneous T-cell lymphomas includes topical corticosteroids or topical chemotherapy for limited-stage disease. For more diffuse disease, treatment may include more aggressive combination therapies.[31]

The nursing care for NHL is similar to that for Hodgkin lymphoma. It is based on managing problems related to the disease (e.g., pain caused by the tumor, spinal cord compression, tumor lysis syndrome), pancytopenia, and other side effects of therapy. However, because NHL can be more extensive and involve specific organs (e.g., CNS, spleen, liver, GI tract, bone marrow), it is important to understand the subtype and extent of the disease. For example, a patient with colon involvement may have acute abdominal pain, guarding, and an enlarged abdomen. A patient with a Burkitt NHL beginning chemotherapy is at high risk for tumor lysis syndrome and needs frequent laboratory monitoring. See Chapter 16 for more on cancer therapies and their effects.

The patient undergoing external beam radiation therapy has special nursing needs. The skin in the radiation field needs special care. Concepts related to safety issues with radiation therapy are important to include in the plan of care (see Chapter 16).

Psychosocial considerations are important. Help the patient and family to understand the disease, treatment, and expected and potential side effects. Some aggressive treatments need close follow-up and even inpatient admission. Fertility issues may be of concern in young patients. As in Hodgkin lymphoma, evaluating patients with NHL for long-term effects of therapy is important because the delayed consequences of disease and treatment may not become apparent for many years.

MULTIPLE MYELOMA

Multiple myeloma, or *plasma cell myeloma,* is a condition in which cancerous plasma cells proliferate in the bone marrow and destroy bone. Multiple myeloma accounts for about 1.8%

of all cancers and 18% of hematologic cancers.[32] The disease is more common in men and in Blacks.[1,4] It generally occurs between the ages of 65 and 74 years old, with an average onset age of 69 years.[32] Most patients need therapy off and on during the course of the disease. About 10% of patients who undergo stem cell transplant may be cured.

Etiology and Pathophysiology

The cause of multiple myeloma is unknown. It is possible that exposure to organic chemicals (e.g., benzene), herbicides, and insecticides plays a role. Viral infections, such as HIV, may increase the risk.

The disease process involves excess production of plasma cells. Normal plasma cells are activated B cells, which make immunoglobulins (antibodies) that protect the body. In multiple myeloma, instead of a variety of plasma cells making antibodies to fight different infections, myeloma tumors make monoclonal antibodies. *Monoclonal* means they are all of 1 kind, making them ineffective and even harmful. Not only do they not fight infections, but they infiltrate the bone marrow. These monoclonal proteins (called *M proteins*) are made up of 2 light chains and 2 heavy chains. *Bence Jones proteins* are the light chain part of these monoclonal antibodies. They may show up in the urine in many patients with multiple myeloma.

The cancerous plasma cells build up in the bone marrow. They produce nuclear factor-κβ (NF- κβ) ligand (RANKL), which binds to RANK receptors on the osteoclast surface, causing activation and osteolytic lesions.[4] As myeloma protein increases, normal plasma cells are reduced. This further compromises the body's normal immune response. Proliferation of cancerous plasma cells and the overproduction of immunoglobulin and proteins may result in the end-organ effects of myeloma on the bone marrow, bone, and kidneys and possibly the spleen, lymph nodes, liver, and heart.

Clinical Manifestations

Multiple myeloma develops slowly and insidiously. The patient often does not have symptoms until the disease is advanced. Skeletal pain is the major manifestation. Pain in the pelvis, spine, and ribs is common and triggered by movement. Diffuse osteoporosis develops as the myeloma protein destroys bone. Osteolytic lesions occur in the skull, vertebrae, long bones, and ribs. Vertebral destruction can lead to vertebral collapse of vertebrae with spinal cord compression. Loss of bone integrity can lead to pathologic fractures.

Bony degeneration causes calcium loss from bones, eventually causing hypercalcemia. Hypercalcemia may cause renal, GI, or neurologic problems, such as polyuria, anorexia, confusion, and heart problems. A serum *hyperviscosity syndrome* leading to cerebral, lung, renal, and other organ dysfunction can occur in some patients. High protein levels caused by the myeloma protein can result in renal tubular obstruction, interstitial nephritis, and renal failure. The patient may have anemia, thrombocytopenia, neutropenia, and immune dysfunction from the replacement of normal bone marrow with plasma cells. Neurologic problems may be caused by regional myeloma cell growth compressing the spinal cord or cranial nerves or by perineuronal or perivascular deposition of the abnormal protein.[4]

Diagnostic Studies

Evaluating multiple myeloma involves laboratory, radiologic, and bone marrow examination. M protein is often found in the blood and urine. Possible findings include pancytopenia, hypercalcemia, Bence Jones protein in the urine, and a high serum creatinine. Bone marrow analysis shows significantly increased numbers of plasma cells in the bone marrow. Skeletal bone surveys, MRI, and/or PET and CT scans show distinct areas of destroyed bone; generalized thinning of the bones; or fractures, especially in the vertebrae, ribs, pelvis, and bones of the thigh and upper arms.

The simplest measure of staging and prognosis in multiple myeloma is based on blood levels of 2 markers: β_2-microglobulin and albumin. Higher levels of β_2-microglobulin and lower levels of albumin are associated with a poorer prognosis.[32] Cytogenetic studies of the bone marrow also play a role in prognostic stratification. For example, deletion of chromosome 17p13 is a high-risk (poor prognostic) feature.

❖ Interprofessional and Nursing Management

Interprofessional care involves managing both the disease and its symptoms. The current treatment options include corticosteroids, chemotherapy, immunotherapy, targeted therapy, and HSCT.[32] Multiple myeloma is seldom cured. Treatment can relieve symptoms, produce remission, and prolong life. Pain control of pain and preventing pathologic fractures are goals of management.

Zoledronic acid and denosumab inhibit bone breakdown. They are given for skeletal pain and hypercalcemia. They inhibit bone resorption without inhibiting bone formation and mineralization. A major focus of nursing care relates to patient safety due to the bone involvement and sequelae from bone breakdown. Because of the potential for pathologic fractures, use caution when moving and ambulating the patient. A slight twist or strain in the wrong area (e.g., a weak area in the patient's bones) may cause a fracture.

DRUG ALERT

Zoledronic Acid (Zometa)

- Make sure the patient is hydrated before giving drug.
- Renal toxicity may occur if IV infusion is given in less than 15 min.
- Patients should have a dental exam prior to first dose and ongoing monitoring for osteonecrosis of the jaw.

Kyphoplasty may be used to control spine vertebral disease. It is a minimally invasive procedure in which cement is injected to stabilize the vertebral compression.

Chemotherapy includes a corticosteroid plus 2 chemotherapy agents, such as bortezomib and lenalidomide or bortezomib and cyclophosphamide. The goal is to reduce the number of plasma cells. Initial treatment depends on whether the patient is a future stem cell transplant candidate and predicted tolerance of therapy. High-dose chemotherapy followed by HSCT has evolved as the standard of care in eligible patients.[32]

Immunotherapy and targeted therapy are options. Immunomodulator drugs (described in Chapter 16) include thalidomide, lenalidomide, and pomalidomide. Proteosome inhibitors include bortezomib, carfilzomib, and ixazomib. Panobinostat is a drug that affects enzymes that promote cancer cell growth. Daratumumab is a monoclonal antibody against CD38, a protein found on the surface of myeloma cells.

Other drugs can treat some complications of multiple myeloma. For example, IV furosemide promotes renal excretion of calcium. Although tumor lysis is rare, once chemotherapy is started, allopurinol may be given to prevent any renal damage from uric acid accumulation (from cell breakdown). Because of the myeloma proteins, the patient is at risk for renal problems and electrolyte and fluid imbalances.

Ambulation and adequate hydration are used to treat hypercalcemia, dehydration, and potential renal damage. Weight bearing helps the bones resorb some calcium. Maintaining adequate hydration helps minimize problems from hypercalcemia and prevent protein precipitates from causing renal tubular obstruction. IV fluids are given to maintain a urine output of 1.5 to 2 L/day if the patient does not already have renal compromise.

In some patients, the levels of plasma proteins are so high that it causes a hyperviscosity of the blood leading to neurologic changes, renal insufficiency, and other problems related to lack of blood flow. In this instance, plasmapheresis is used.

As in any pain management situation, assess the patient and implement measures to control pain (see Chapter 9). Analgesics, such as NSAIDs, acetaminophen, or an acetaminophen/opioid combination, may be more effective than opioids alone in diminishing bone pain. Braces, especially for the spine, may help control pain. Peripheral neuropathy is common with several therapies for multiple myeloma. It contributes to discomfort, the inability to do basic activities of daily living, and the risk for injury from falling.

Patients are at risk for DVT related to chemotherapy and immobility and should receive preventive measures unless their platelet count is low.[32]

Assessment and prompt treatment of infection are important. Recurrent infections may be due to a decrease in the production of normal immunoglobulins, the ineffectiveness of the overproduced and abnormal immunoglobulins, corticosteroids, and/or neutropenia from bone marrow infiltration or side effects of treatment.

The patient's psychosocial needs require sensitive, skilled management. Help the patient and significant others adapt to changes fostered by chronic illness and adjust to the losses related to the disease process, while helping to maximize functioning and quality of life. The patient may have remissions and exacerbations. Patients may be on dialysis because of myeloma-induced renal failure. Acute care is needed at various times during the illness.

The final, acute phase is unresponsive to treatment and usually short in duration. Help the patient and family navigate needed resources, such as palliative or hospice care, social services, and spiritual care, as appropriate.

DISORDERS OF THE SPLEEN

Many illnesses can affect the spleen. Most can cause some degree of *splenomegaly* (enlarged spleen) (Table 34.31). However, an enlarged spleen may be present in some people without any evidence of disease. The term *hypersplenism* refers to the presence of splenomegaly and peripheral cytopenias (anemia, leukopenia, thrombocytopenia) with normal bone marrow. The degree of splenic enlargement varies with the disease. For example, massive splenic enlargement may occur with mononucleosis, chronic myelogenous leukemia, and thalassemia major. Mild splenic enlargement occurs with HF and SLE.

TABLE 34.31 Common Causes of Splenomegaly

Congestion
- Acquired hemolytic anemia
- Cirrhosis of the liver
- HF (portal hypertension)
- Portal or splenic vein thrombosis
- Sickle cell disease
- Thalassemia

Infections and Inflammation
- Autoimmune diseases: SLE, rheumatoid arthritis
- Bacterial infections: brucellosis, endocarditis, salmonella, syphilis, tuberculosis, typhoid fever
- Fungal infections: histoplasmosis, systemic candidiasis
- Parasitic infections: malaria, schistosomiasis, leishmaniasis
- Viral infections: cytomegalovirus, hepatitis, mononucleosis

Infiltrative Diseases and Tumors or Cysts
- Acute and chronic leukemia
- Amyloidosis
- Gaucher disease
- Lymphomas
- Polycythemia vera
- Other primary or secondary tumors and cysts
- Sarcoidosis

The normal spleen holds 350 mL of blood. It stores about one third of our platelet mass. When the spleen enlarges, its normal filtering and storage capacity increases. Consequently, there is often a reduction in the number of circulating blood cells as they engorge the spleen. In addition, there are unusual findings in the peripheral smear. These include abnormally shaped RBCs, Howell-Jolly bodies (a dark purple granule in the RBC), and siderotic granules (Pappenheimer bodies) clustering near the edge of the RBC.[1,4] These findings aid in diagnosing a malfunctioning spleen. A slight to moderate enlargement of the spleen is usually asymptomatic and found during routine abdominal assessment. While massive splenomegaly can be well tolerated, the patient may have abdominal discomfort and early satiety. Other ways we assess the size of the spleen include ultrasound, CT or PET scan, MRI, and liver/spleen nuclear scan.

Sometimes a splenectomy is part of the evaluation or treatment of splenomegaly. Another major reason for splenectomy is splenic rupture. The spleen may rupture from trauma; inadvertent tearing during another surgery; and diseases, such as mononucleosis, malaria, and lymphoid tumors. After a splenectomy, there can be a dramatic increase in peripheral RBC, WBC, and platelet counts.

BOX 34.6 ETHICAL/LEGAL DILEMMAS

Religious Beliefs

Situation

W.D., an 81-year-old woman with dementia, comes to the hospital from long-term care with lower gastrointestinal (GI) bleeding. During colonoscopy, the HCP cauterized the source of the bleed; however, her Hgb is 5.4 g/dL. Her family tells you that she is a Jehovah's Witness and must not receive blood products. If she does not have transfusions, her HCP is concerned she will have cardiopulmonary failure.

Ethical/Legal Points for Consideration

- Competent adults have the right to make health care decisions, including the right to refuse treatment, based on their religious beliefs.
- If the patient is determined to be incompetent and a guardian is appointed, the guardian has the legal right to make the consent or refusal.
- If the HCP believes that the treatment is essential to preserve life and health and there is no legal decision maker, a request is made for a legal determination of whether the patient is incapable of consent or refusal. If the judge agrees, the patient is made a ward of the court for this issue. Usually, the HCP is directed to make a decision based on the patient's best interests.

Discussion Questions

1. What resources do you have available to consult about religious practices?
2. How could you determine if the family were acting in W.D.'s best interest or their own?
3. What nonblood alternatives are available for Jehovah's Witnesses?

Nursing responsibilities for patients with spleen disorders vary depending on the problem. Splenomegaly may be painful. The patient may need analgesics; care in moving, turning, and positioning; and evaluation of lung expansion because spleen enlargement may impair diaphragmatic expansion. If anemia, thrombocytopenia, or leukopenia develops from splenic enlargement, institute nursing measures to support the patient and prevent life-threatening complications.

After a splenectomy, observe the patient for bleeding and shock. Immune deficiencies may develop, such as low IgG levels. Patients have a lifelong risk for infection, especially from encapsulated organisms, such as *Pneumococcus* species. Pneumococcal vaccination reduces this risk.

BLOOD COMPONENT THERAPY

Blood component therapy is often used to manage hematologic diseases. Many therapeutic and surgical procedures depend on blood product support. However, blood component therapy only temporarily supports the patient until the underlying problem is resolved. Because transfusions are not free from hazards, they should be used only if needed. Make sure that the HCP has discussed the risks, benefits, and alternatives with the patient and that this is recorded in the medical record (Box 34.6).

Traditionally, the term *blood transfusion* meant the administration of whole blood. Blood transfusion now has a broader meaning because of the ability to give specific components of blood, such as platelets, packed RBCs, or plasma. Usually, a specific component is ordered. Whole blood may be used in cases of massive bleeding, severe coagulopathy, or shock or in military settings (Table 34.32).[4]

Administration Procedure

In general, we use 18- to 20-gauge IV catheters to give blood components to adults. Smaller gauges, such as 25 gauge, may be used in neonates.[15] Larger sizes (e.g., 16 or 18 gauge) in adults may be preferred when giving rapid transfusions or if the infusion is sluggish. Smaller needles can be used for platelets, albumin, and clotting factor replacement. In emergencies when we cannot establish IV access, we may use the intraosseous route. [15] Verify the patency of the access before requesting the blood component from the blood bank. Most blood product administration tubing is of a "Y type" with a macroaggregate filter (170 to 260 μm; filters out particulate). One arm of the Y is for the isotonic saline solution, and the other arm of the Y for the blood product. You may use infusion pumps or syringes approved for blood administration by your agency. [15]

! SAFETY ALERT

Blood Transfusions

- Do not use dextrose solutions, lactated Ringer solution, or any other solution other than 0.9% sodium chloride for giving blood because they will cause RBC hemolysis.
- Exceptions to these restrictions may be appropriate, such as in trauma situations. These solutions include ABO-compatible plasma and 5% albumin. Follow agency policy.[15]
- Do not give any additives, including medications, in the same tubing as the blood unless you first clear the tubing with saline solution.

After obtaining the blood or blood components from the blood bank, make a positive identification of the blood product and recipient. Improper product-to-patient identification is the most common cause of hemolytic transfusion reactions. This places a great responsibility on nurses to conduct the identification procedure appropriately. Follow the procedures at your agency. Most have a dual-checking system with 2 licensed persons checking the patient identification with the labeled blood component and/or a bar-code scanning system. The blood bank does the typing and crossmatching the donor's blood with the recipient's blood. The result of any needed compatibility testing should be on the product bag or tag.

Table 34.33 outlines blood component compatibilities for transfusions. ABO compatibility is not a prerequisite for platelet transfusions. However, after multiple platelet transfusions, a patient may develop anti-HLA antibodies to the transfused platelets. With the use of lymphocyte typing to match HLA types of the donor and recipient, multiple platelet transfusions can be given with fewer complications to those who develop antibodies to platelets. The patient may be premedicated with an antihistamine and hydrocortisone to decrease the chance of reacting to platelet transfusions if there is a history of reactions.[15]

Take the patient's vital signs before beginning the transfusion so that you have a baseline in case an acute reaction occurs (Table 34.34). If the patient has abnormal vital signs (e.g., high fever), call the HCP to clarify if you should give the blood component. Start the blood as soon as you have it.

TABLE 34.32 Common Blood Products

Description	Special Considerations	Indications for Use
Albumin		
Prepared from plasma. Can be stored for 5 years. Available in 5% or 25% solution. Heat treated. Does not transmit viruses.	Albumin 25% expands the blood volume by ≈3.5 times. Hyperosmolar solution acts by moving water from extravascular to intravascular space.	Hypovolemic shock, hypoalbuminemia, after large-volume paracentesis, replacement in plasmapheresis.
Cryoprecipitates and Commercial Concentrates		
Prepared from fresh frozen plasma. 10–15 mL/bag. Can be stored for 1 year. Once thawed, must be used within 4–6 hr.	See also Table 34.18.	Replacement for fibrinogen deficiency, usually due to DIC, severe liver disease, or massive transfusion. Has other clotting factors, especially factor VIII, factor XIII, and von Willebrand factor.
Fresh Frozen Plasma		
Liquid part of whole blood is separated from cells and frozen. 1 unit is ≈250 mL. Rich in clotting factors but has no platelets. Can be stored for up to 1 year, depending on storage. Must be used within 24 hr after thawing.	Use in treating hemorrhagic shock is being replaced by pure preparations, such as albumin and plasma expanders.	Bleeding caused by deficiency in clotting factors (e.g., DIC, bleeding, massive transfusion, liver disease, vitamin K deficiency, excess warfarin).
Frozen RBCs		
Prepared from RBCs using glycerol for protection and frozen. Can be stored for up to 10 years.	Successive washings with saline solution remove most WBCs and plasma proteins.	Autotransfusion. Stockpiling or rare donors for patients with alloantibodies.
Packed RBCs		
Prepared from whole blood by sedimentation or centrifugation. 1 unit is 250–350 mL. Can be stored up to 42 days depending on processing (anticoagulants and preservatives).	Use of RBCs for treatment allows remaining components of blood (e.g., platelets, albumin, plasma) to be used for other purposes. Less risk of fluid overload. Preferred RBC source because they are more component specific. Leukocyte depletion (leukoreduction) by filtration, washing is frequently used. Decreases non-hemolytic febrile or mild allergic reactions in patients who receive frequent transfusions. Reduces transmission of viruses. Irradiation prevents graft-versus-host disease in immunocompromised patients.	Severe or symptomatic anemia, acute blood loss. 1 unit of RBCs can be expected to ↑ Hgb by 1 g/dL or Hct by 3% in a typical adult. 1 unit can replace a blood loss of 500 mL.
Platelets		
Prepared from fresh whole blood. An apheresed single donation is usually 200–400 mL in volume. May be pooled from multiple donors.	Can obtain multiple units from 1 donor by plateletpheresis. Can be kept at room temperature in the blood bank under gentle agitation for 1–5 days depending on type of collection and storage. For patients who receive frequent transfusions and become refractory, may give leukocyte reduced, HLA, or type specific to prevent alloimmunization to HLA antigens.	Bleeding caused by thrombocytopenia. May be contraindicated in TTP and HITT except in life-threatening hemorrhage. Average corrected count increment is 10×10^9/L. Failure to have an increase may be due to fever, sepsis, splenomegaly, or DIC or development of antibodies *(refractory)*.

TABLE 34.33 Blood Component Compatibilities for Transfusions

	DONOR PRODUCT			
Recipient's Type	**Packed Red Blood Cells**	**Plasma**	**Platelets**	**Cryoprecipitate**
O+	O+, O−	All groups	O, B, A, AB	Any group is safe to transfuse
O−	O−			
A+	A+, A−, O+, O−	A, AB	A, AB, B, O	
A−	A−, O−			
B+	B+, B−, O+, O−	B, AB	B, AB, A, O	
B−	B−, O−			
AB+	All groups	Only AB	Any group	
AB−	AB−, B−, A−, O−			

TABLE 34.34 NURSING MANAGEMENT

Blood Transfusions

- Complete a baseline physical assessment as a basis to assess changes during and after the transfusion.
- Ensure that the IV line is appropriate and patent.
- Double-check patient identification and blood product identification data with another licensed nurse (consider state nurse practice act and agency policy).
- Adjust the transfusion rate according to the HCP orders and agency policy.
- Assess for signs of transfusion reactions.
- Delegate AP to take vital signs as directed.
- Evaluate for therapeutic effect of blood product (improvement in CBC, ↑ BP, ↓ bleeding).
- Monitor for circulatory overload (e.g., shortness of breath) if the transfusion is given rapidly.

Collaborate With Other Team Members

Blood Bank Personnel

- Perform type and crossmatch of the donor's blood with the recipient's blood.
- Note the result of the compatibility testing on the product bag or tag.
- When handing off the blood or blood component to nursing personnel, ensure that a positive identification is made with product and patient's information.
- Assist the HCP in evaluation of transfusion reactions.

Do not refrigerate it on the nursing unit. If you do not start the blood within 30 minutes, return it to the blood bank for storage. During the first 15 minutes or 50 mL of blood infusion, stay with the patient. Reactions are most likely to occur during this time. The infusion rate during this period should be no more than 2 mL/min. Do not infuse packed RBCs quickly except in an emergency. Rapid infusion of cold blood may cause the patient to become chilled. If rapid replacement of large amounts of blood is needed, you might use a blood-warming device. Other blood components, such as FFP and platelets, may be given over 15 to 30 minutes. Refer to your agency's policy and the HCPs orders.

After the first 15 minutes, retake vital signs to assess patient tolerance. The rate of the rest of the infusion is determined by the HCP's orders, the patient's clinical condition, and the product being infused. Observe the patient periodically throughout the transfusion (e.g., every 30 minutes) and up to 1 hour after the transfusion. Most patients not at risk of fluid overload can tolerate the infusion of 1 unit of packed RBCs over 2 hours. The transfusion should not take more than 4 hours to give because of the increased risk for bacterial growth in the product once it is out of refrigeration.

Blood Transfusion Reactions

A *blood transfusion reaction* is an adverse reaction to blood transfusion therapy. It can range in severity from mild symptoms to a life-threatening condition. Because reactions can be significant, perform a careful patient assessment. Common signs and symptoms are associated with more than 1 type of adverse reaction. We describe blood transfusion reactions as acute or delayed (Tables 34.35 and 34.36).[4,15] The HCP and blood bank HCPs are responsible for identifying the type of reaction. A transfusion reaction is a *serious reportable event* (SRE) and a *sentinel event* (see Chapter 1).

Acute Transfusion Reactions

The most common cause of hemolytic reactions is transfusion of ABO-incompatible blood (Table 34.35). This is an example of a type II cytotoxic hypersensitivity reaction (see Chapter 14). Severe hemolytic reactions are rare. Mislabeling specimens and giving blood to the wrong person cause most acute hemolytic reactions. This points to the importance of using proper patient identifiers when drawing blood samples and when giving medications and blood products.

! SAFETY ALERT

Transfusion Reaction

If a transfusion reaction occurs, take the following steps:

1. Stop the transfusion and stay with the patient.
2. Maintain a patent IV line with saline solution.
3. Notify the blood bank and the HCP.
4. Recheck identifying tags and numbers.
5. Monitor vital signs and urine output.
6. Treat symptoms per HCP order.
7. Save the blood bag and tubing and send them to the blood bank.
8. Collect required blood and other specimens as ordered to evaluate for the reaction.
9. Document according to agency policy.

Delayed Transfusion Reactions

Delayed transfusion reactions include delayed hemolytic reactions, infections, GVHD, and iron overload (Table 34.36).

CHECK YOUR PRACTICE

Your 82-year-old male patient with severe iron deficiency anemia is receiving his second unit of packed RBCs. He received the first transfusion without any problems. He is now reporting chills and feels like his heart is racing.

- What should you do?

Autotransfusion

Autotransfusion, or autologous transfusion, involves removing whole blood from a person and transfusing that blood back into the same person. This avoids problems of incompatibility, allergic reactions, and disease transmission. Methods of autotransfusion include:

- *Autologous donation* or *elective phlebotomy* (predeposit transfusion). A person donates blood before a planned surgery. The blood can be frozen and stored for up to 10 years. Usually, the blood is stored without being frozen and given to the person within a few weeks of donation. This technique is beneficial to the patient with a rare blood type or for any patient who may need limited blood product support during a major surgery (e.g., elective orthopedic surgery).
- *Autotransfusion.* A method for replacing blood volume that involves safely and aseptically collecting, filtering, and returning the patient's own blood lost during a major surgery or from a traumatic injury. Autotransfusion collection devices are most often used in surgery. Some allow blood to be automatically and continuously reinfused. Others require collecting the blood for a time (usually no longer than 4 hours) and then reinfusing it. Drainage after the first 24 hours or drainage that may contain pathogens is generally not reinfused. Anticoagulants may be added before reinfusion.

TABLE 34.35 Acute Transfusion Reactions

Cause	Manifestations	Management	Prevention
Acute Hemolytic Reaction			
Infusion of ABO-incompatible whole blood, RBCs, or components containing as little as 10 mL of RBCs. Antibodies in the recipient's plasma attach to antigens on transfused RBCs, causing RBC destruction.	Reactions usually develop in first 15 min. May occur up to 2 hr after. Fever with or without chills; back, abdominal, chest, or flank pain; infusion site pain, ↑ HR, dyspnea, tachypnea, ↓ BP, hemoglobinuria, acute jaundice, dark urine, bleeding, acute kidney injury, shock, cardiac arrest, DIC, death.	• Monitor and maintain BP with IV fluids as ordered. • Treat shock and DIC if present. • Draw blood samples for serologic testing slowly to avoid hemolysis from the procedure. Send other specimens as ordered. • Give diuretics as prescribed to maintain urine flow. • Insert indwelling urinary catheter or measure voided amounts to monitor hourly urine output. Dialysis may be needed if renal failure occurs. • Do not transfuse more RBC-containing components until blood bank has provided newly crossmatched units.	Verify and document patient identification from sample collection to component infusion (e.g., visually compare label on sample collection and blood component with patient identification).
Allergic Reaction (Mild)			
Sensitivity to foreign plasma proteins. More common in people with history of allergies.	Flushing, itching, hives.	• Give antihistamine, corticosteroid, epinephrine, as ordered. • If symptoms are mild and transient, transfusion may be restarted slowly with HCP's order. • Do not restart transfusion if fever or pulmonary symptoms develop.	Treat prophylactically with antihistamines or steroids. Consider washed RBCs and platelets.
Anaphylactic and Severe Allergic Reaction			
Sensitivity to donor plasma proteins. Infusion of IgA proteins to IgA-deficient recipient who has developed IgA antibody.	Anxiety, abdominal pain, hives, dyspnea, wheezing, progressing to bronchospasm, ↓ BP, shock, and possible cardiac arrest.	• Monitor VS frequently. • Start CPR, if indicated. • Administer O_2. • Have epinephrine ready for injection. • Antihistamines, corticosteroids, β_2-agonists may be given. • Do not restart transfusion.	Transfuse extensively washed RBC products from which all plasma has been removed. Use blood from IgA-deficient donor. Use autologous components.
Circulatory Overload Reaction			
Fluid given faster than the circulation can accommodate. People with cardiac or renal disease at risk.	Cough, dyspnea, pulmonary congestion, adventitious breath sounds, headache, hypertension, ↑ HR, distended neck veins.	• Monitor VS. • Place patient upright with feet in dependent position. • Obtain chest x-ray if ordered. • Administer prescribed diuretics, O_2.	Adjust transfusion volume and flow rate based on patient size and clinical status. Have blood bank divide future units into smaller aliquots for better spacing of fluid infused.
Febrile, Nonhemolytic Reaction			
Sensitization to donor WBCs (most common), platelets, or plasma proteins.	Sudden chills, rigors, and fever (rise in temperature of >1°C), headache, vomiting.	Give antipyretics as prescribed (acetaminophen). Do not restart transfusion unless HCP orders.	Consider leukocyte-reduced blood products. Give acetaminophen or diphenhydramine 30 min before transfusion.
Massive Blood Transfusion Reaction			
Can occur with replacement of 10 or more RBC units within 24 hr. RBC transfusions do not contain clotting factors, albumin, and platelets.	Hypothermia and dysrhythmias (from rapid infusion of large quantities of cold blood). Citrate toxicity and hypocalcemia (from the citrate, a storage solution). Hypocalcemia (citrate binds calcium). Hyperkalemia or hypokalemia.	Monitor the patient with frequent vital signs. Draw labs to monitor clotting status and electrolyte levels. Monitor ECG for changes from electrolyte problems	Use blood-warming equipment. Infuse 10% calcium gluconate as ordered. Adjust infusion rate as ordered. Because of dilution effect on coagulation due to massive RBC transfusion, platelets and plasma will also be given.

TABLE 34.35 Acute Transfusion Reactions—cont'd

Cause	Manifestations	Management	Prevention
Sepsis			
Transfusion of bacterially infected blood components.	Rapid onset of chills, rigors, fever, vomiting, diarrhea, marked ↓ BP, shock.	• Monitor VS. • Obtain culture of patient's blood. Other tests may be ordered to discern from a hemolytic reaction. • Treat septicemia as directed—antibiotics, IV fluids, vasopressors,	Collect, process, store, and transfuse blood products according to blood banking standards and complete the transfusion within 4 hr of starting time.
Transfusion-Related Acute Lung Injury (TRALI) Reaction			
Reaction between transfused antileukocyte antibodies and recipient's leukocytes, causing pulmonary inflammation and capillary leak.	Fever, chills, hypotension, tachypnea, frothy sputum, dyspnea, hypoxemia, respiratory failure. Noncardiogenic pulmonary edema. Leading cause of transfusion-related deaths. Arises within 1–6 hr of transfusion.	• Monitor VS frequently • Provide O_2 and administer corticosteroids as ordered. • Start CPR if needed and provide ventilatory and BP support if needed. • Draw blood for arterial blood gases and HLA or antileukocyte antibodies and other tests to discern from hemolysis or circulatory overload. • Obtain chest x-ray.	Provide leukocyte-reduced products. Blood bank personnel will identify donors who are implicated in TRALI reactions and will not allow them to donate.

TABLE 34.36 Delayed Transfusion Reactions

Manifestations	Prevention and Management
Delayed Hemolytic	
Fever, mild jaundice, ↓ hemoglobin. Occurs as early as 3 days or as late as several months posttransfusion as the result of destruction of transfused RBCs by alloantibodies not detected during crossmatch.	Monitor patients with supportive care. Hemolysis may be severe enough to warrant further transfusions with antigen-negative RBCs. Eculizumab may be beneficial.
Graft-Versus-Host Disease	
Rash, diarrhea, hepatitis, fever	Irradiation of blood products to reduce the risk of donor lymphocytes attacking an immunocompromised patient
Infection	
Specific product testing has greatly reduced the risk of infection Potential risk of infection includes: *Babesia* species (babesiosis), Creutzfeldt-Jakob disease ("mad cow disease"), Cytomegalovirus (CMV), dengue fever virus, hepatitis B and C, herpesvirus type 6 (HSV-6), HIV, human herpesvirus 8 (KS virus), Epstein-Barr virus (EBV), HTLV-I/II, malaria, *Trypanosoma cruzi* (Chagas' disease), West Nile virus, Zika virus,	Treatment based on the cause. Ways of detecting some infectious agents prior to product release are now used, such as surface antigen testing and nucleic acid tests for Babesia, hepatitis, HIV, HTLV, treponema pallidum, and *T. cruzi.* West Nile virus, and Zika virus, Donor screening is the only available method to reduce the risk for donor-contaminated blood for malaria and Creutzfeldt-Jakob disease. Leukocyte-reduced components or processing may reduce virus transmission. Patients may be monitored serologically (e.g., CMV titers after allogeneic stem cell transplant).
Iron Overload	
Excess iron is deposited in heart, liver, pancreas, and joints, causing dysfunction. HF, dysrhythmias, impaired thyroid and gonadal function, diabetes, arthritis, cirrhosis. Occurs in patients receiving ≥20 units for chronic anemia (e.g., sickle cell anemia, β-thalassemia) over time.	May be prevented by deferoxamine, which chelates and removes accumulated iron via the kidneys, given IV or subcutaneously. Deferasirox and deferiprone, oral agents that chelate iron, may be used. Phlebotomy may be used.

Case Study

Leukemia

(© Lisa F. Young/ iStock.)

Patient Profile

A.J. is a 63-year-old woman who is brought to the ED by her husband (see the Chapter 33 case study). She has become progressively weaker and was admitted for further evaluation.

Subjective Data

- Progressive weakness over the last couple of weeks
- Had a recent sinus infection that resolved after 2 courses of antibiotics
- Reports periodic shortness of breath
- Has noticed a lot of bruising lately

Objective Data

Physical Assessment

- Scattered petechiae on both ankles and 2 bruises on her arms and 3 on her left lower leg
- Skin is very pale
- BP 100/70 (lying), 88/60 (standing), temperature 96.8°F (36°C), respiratory rate 26/min, apical pulse 110/min (lying), 124/min (standing), O_2 saturation 90% on room air

Laboratory Results

- Hct 18.2%
- Hgb 5.9 g/dL, WBC count 2600/μL (2.6×10^9/L)
- Platelet count 72,000/μL (72×10^9/L)
- Peripheral blood smear shows that 80% of the WBCs are blasts
- PT 18 s, aPTT 37 s
- LDH 560 units/L

Bone Marrow Biopsy

- Multiple myeloblasts (>50%)

Interprofessional Care

- Consultation with a hematologist-oncologist
- 2 units of packed red blood cells
- *Diagnosis:* acute myeloid leukemia (AML)

Discussion Questions

1. ***Recognize***: What laboratory and bone marrow biopsy results suggest AML?
2. ***Recognize***: How is AML treated?
3. ***Analyze***: What is A.J.'s prognosis?
4. ***Plan***: What life-threatening problems can with AML and its treatment? How can you anticipate and assess for these problems?
5. ***Prioritize:*** Based on the assessment data presented, what are the priority clinical problems?
6. ***Prioritize:*** What are the priority nursing interventions for A.J.?
7. ***Prioritize:*** What are the patient teaching priorities for an adult newly diagnosed with AML?
8. ***Act***: What interprofessional team members are likely to be involved in A.J.'s care?
9. ***Act:*** A.J. becomes fatigued after starting chemotherapy. She wants to know if she can still work and do household chores even if she is so fatigued. What is your best advice for her?
10. Develop a conceptual care map for A.J.

Answers available at http://evolve.elsevier.com/Lewis/medsurg.

BRIDGE TO NCLEX EXAMINATION

The number of the question corresponds to the same-numbered outcome at the beginning of the chapter.

1. In a severely anemic patient, the nurse would expect to find
   a. cyanosis and hypertension.
   b. pulmonary edema and fibrosis.
   c. dyspnea and increased heart rate.
   d. dysrhythmias and expiratory wheezing.
2. When obtaining assessment data from a patient with a microcytic, hypochromic anemia, the nurse would ask the patient about
   a. folic acid intake.
   b. diet intake of iron.
   c. a history of gastric surgery.
   d. a history of sickle cell anemia.
3. Nursing interventions for a patient with severe anemia from peptic ulcer disease include *(select all that apply)*
   a. instructions for high-iron diet.
   b. taking vital signs every 8 hours.
   c. monitoring stools for occult blood.
   d. teaching self-injection of erythropoietin.
   e. administration of cobalamin (vitamin B_{12}) injections.
4. The nursing management of a patient in sickle cell crisis includes *(select all that apply)*
   a. monitoring CBC.
   b. optimal pain management and O_2 therapy.
   c. blood transfusions if needed and iron chelation.
   d. rest as needed and deep vein thrombosis prophylaxis.
   e. administration of IV iron and diet high in iron content.
5. A complication of the hyperviscosity of polycythemia is
   a. thrombosis.
   b. cardiomyopathy.
   c. pulmonary edema.
   d. disseminated intravascular coagulation (DIC).
6. When caring for a patient with thrombocytopenia, the nurse instructs the patient to
   a. dab their nose instead of blowing.
   b. be careful when shaving with a safety razor.
   c. continue with physical activities to stimulate thrombopoiesis.
   d. avoid aspirin because it may mask the fever that occurs with thrombocytopenia.
7. The nurse would expect that a patient with von Willebrand disease undergoing surgery would be treated with administration of vWF and
   a. thrombin.
   b. factor VI.
   c. factor VII.
   d. factor VIII.

8. A patient with a head injury develops petechiae across the chest and abdomen and oozing from venipuncture sites. Which measures would the nurse include in the patient's care?
   a. Avoid other venipunctures.
   b. Apply dressings to the sites.
   c. Use an electric razor for shaving.
   d. Provide oral care with glycerin swabs.
   e. Administer warfarin sodium as ordered.
9. Priority nursing actions when caring for a hospitalized patient with a new-onset temperature of 102.2°F (39°C) and severe neutropenia include *(select all that apply)*
   a. starting the prescribed antibiotic STAT.
   b. drawing peripheral and central line blood cultures.
   c. ongoing monitoring of the patient's vital signs for septic shock.
   d. taking a full set of vital signs and notifying the physician immediately.
   e. administering transfusions of WBCs treated to decrease immunogenicity.
10. Because myelodysplastic syndrome arises from immature hematopoietic stem cells in the bone marrow, laboratory results the nurse would expect to find include a(n)
   a. excess of T cells.
   b. excess of platelets.
   c. deficiency of granulocytes.
   d. deficiency of all cellular blood components.
11. Which laboratory findings support the patient's new diagnosis of acute myelocytic leukemia?
   a. Increased WBC, RBC, and LDH
   b. Increased LDH and platelet count
   c. Decreased RBC, hemoglobin, and hematocrit
   d. Decreased RBC, presence of Philadelphia chromosome
12. Multiple drugs are often used in combination to treat leukemia and lymphoma because
   a. there are fewer toxic and side effects.
   b. the chance that 1 drug will be effective is increased.
   c. the drugs are more effective without causing side effects.
   d. the drugs work by different mechanisms to maximize killing of cancer cells.
13. The nurse is aware that a major difference between Hodgkin lymphoma and non-Hodgkin's lymphoma is that
   a. Hodgkin lymphoma occurs only in young adults.
   b. Hodgkin lymphoma is considered potentially curable.
   c. non-Hodgkin's lymphoma can manifest in multiple areas.
   d. non-Hodgkin's lymphoma is treated only with radiation therapy.
14. A patient with multiple myeloma becomes confused with an increased urine output. The laboratory finding that may explain these findings is:
   a. hyperkalemia.
   b. hyperuricemia.
   c. hypercalcemia.
   d. hypocalcemia.
15. When reviewing a patient's hematologic laboratory values after a splenectomy, the nurse would expect to find
   a. RBC abnormalities.
   b. increased WBC count.
   c. decreased hemoglobin.
   d. decreased platelet count.
16. Transfusion complications that can be decreased with leukocyte depletion or reduction of RBC transfusion are
   a. chills and hemolysis.
   b. leukostasis and neutrophilia.
   c. fluid overload and pulmonary edema.
   d. transmission of cytomegalovirus and fever.

1. c; 2. b; 3. a, c; 4. a, b, c, d; 5. a; 6. a; 7. d; 8. a, b, c; 9. a, b, c, d; 10. d; 11. c; 12. d; 13. c; 14. c; 15. b; 16. d.

For rationales to these answers and even more NCLEX review questions, visit http://evolve.elsevier.com/Lewis/medsurg.

EVOLVE WEBSITE/RESOURCES LIST

http://evolve.elsevier.com/Lewis/medsurg
Review Questions (Online Only)
Key Points
Answer Keys for Review Questions
- Rationales for Bridge to NCLEX Examination Questions
- Answer Guidelines for Case Study
- Answer Guidelines for Managing Care of Multiple Patients Case Study (Section 7)

Student Case Studies
- Patient with Chronic Myelogenous Leukemia Including End-of-life Care
- Patient With Sickle Cell Anemia

Nursing Care Plans
- eNursing Care Plan 34.1: Patient With Anemia
- eNursing Care Plan 34.2: Patient With Thrombocytopenia
- eNursing Care Plan 34.3: Patient With Neutropenia

Conceptual Care Map Creator
- Conceptual Care Map for Case Study

Audio Glossary
Content Updates

REFERENCES

1. Keohane EM, Otto CN, Walenga JM: *Rodak's hematology, clinical principles and applications*, ed 6, St. Louis, 2020, Elsevier.
2. Hoffman R, Benz EJ, Silberstein LE, et al.: *Hematology: basic principles and practice*, ed 7, Philadelphia, 2018, Elsevier.
3. Huether SE, McCance KL, Brashers VL: *Understanding pathophysiology*, ed 7, St Louis, 2020, Elsevier.
4. Hoffbrand AV, Steensma DP: *Hoffbrand's essential haematology*, ed 8, Hoboken, 2020, John Wiley & Sons Ltd.
*5. Becker PS, Griffiths EA: Hematopoietic growth factors. NCCN clinical practice guidelines, version 2.2020. Retrieved from www.nccn.org.

*6. Piga A, Perrotta S, Gamberini MR: Lispatercept improves hemoglobin levels and blood transfusion requirements in a study of patients with β-thalassemia, *Blood* 133:1279, 2019.

7. National Institutes of Health: Aplastic anemia. Retrieved from: https://www.niddk.nih.gov/health-information/blood-diseases/aplastic-anemia-myelodysplastic-syndromes/definition-facts.

8. Sweet V, Foley A: *Sheehy's emergency nursing: principles and practice* ed 7, Missouri, 2020, Elsevier.

9. Centers for Disease Control: Sickle cell disease. Retrieved from www.cdc.gov/ncbddd/sicklecell/data.html.

*10. Cisneros GS, Thein SL: Recent advances in the treatment of sickle cell disease, *Front Physiol* 11:435, 2020.

11. The National Institute of Diabetes and Digestive and Kidney Diseases: Hemochromatosis. Retrieved from www.niddk.nih.gov/health-information/liver-disease/hemochromatosis.

12. Pagana KD, Pagana TJ, Pagana TN: *Mosby's diagnostic and laboratory test reference*, ed 15, St. Louis, 2021, Elsevier.

*13. Gerds AT, Gotlib J, Bose P, et al.: Myeloproliferative neoplasms. NCCN clinical practice guidelines, version 1.2020. Retrieved from www.nccn.org.

*14. Neunert C, Terrell DR, Arnold DM, et al.: American Society of Hematology 2019 guidelines for immune thrombocytopenia, *Blood Adv* 3:3829, 2019.

15*. Cohn CS, Delaney M, Johnson ST, et al.: *Technical manual: standards for blood banks and transfusion services*, ed 20, Bethesda, MD, 2020, AABB.

16. Kucukyurt S, Eskazan AE: Assessment and monitoring of patients with immune-mediated thrombotic thrombocytopenic purpura: strategies to improve outcomes, *J Blood Med* 11:319, 2020.

*17. Morgan RL, Ashoorion V, Cuker V, et al.: Management of heparin-induced thrombocytopenia: systemic reviews and meta-analyses, *Blood Adv* 4:5184, 2020.

18. National Hemophilia Foundation. Retrieved from www.hemophilia.org.

*19. Connell NT, Flood VH, Brignardello-Petersen R, et al.: ASH ISTH NHG WFH 2021 guidelines on the management of von Willebrand disease, *Blood Adv* 5:301, 2021.

20*. Baden LR, Swaminathan S: Prevention and treatment of cancer-related infections. NCCN clinical practice guidelines, version 2.2020. Retrieved from www.nccn.org.

*21. Taplitz RA, Kennedy EB, Bow EJ, et al.: Antimicrobial prophylaxis for adult patients with cancer-related immunosuppression: ASCO and IDSA clinical practice guideline update, *J Clin Oncol* 36:3043, 2018.

22. Bewersdort JP, Carraway H, Prebet T: Emerging treatment options for patients with high-risk myelodysplastic syndrome, *Therap Adv Hematol* 11:1, 2020.

*23. Greenberg PL, Stone RM: Myelodysplastic syndromes. NCCN clinical practice guidelines, version 1.2021. Retrieved from www.nccn.org.

24. Siegel RL, Miller KD, Jemal A: Cancer statistics, 2020, *CA Cancer J Clin* 70:7, 2020.

*25. Brown PA, Shah B: Acute lymphoblastic leukemia. NCCN clinical practice guidelines, version 2.2020. Retrieved from www.nccn.org.

*26. Deininger MW, Shah NP: Chronic myeloid leukemia. NCCN clinical practice guidelines, version 2.2021. Retrieved from www.nccn.org.

*27. Tallman MS, Pollyea DA: Acute myeloid leukemia. NCCN clinical practice guidelines, version 2.2021. Retrieved from www.nccn.org.

*28. Wierda WG, Byrd JC: Chronic lymphocytic leukemia/small lymphocytic lymphoma. NCCN clinical practice guidelines, version 2.2021. Retrieved from www.nccn.org.

*29. Hoppe RT, Advani RH: Hodgkin lymphoma. NCCN clinical practice guidelines, version 1.2021. Retrieved from www.nccn.org.

*30. Zelenetz AD, Gordon LI: B-cell lymphomas. NCCN clinical practice guidelines, version 4.2020. Retrieved from www.nccn.org.

*31. Horwitz SM, Ansell S: T-cell lymphomas. NCCN clinical practice guidelines, version 1.2021. Retrieved from www.nccn.org.

*32. Kumar SK, Callander NS: Multiple myeloma. NCCN clinical practice guidelines, version 4.2021. Retrieved from www.nccn.org.

*Evidence-based information for clinical practice.

Case Study

Applying Clinical Judgment With Multiple Patients

You are working on the oncology unit and have been assigned to care for the following 4 patients. You have 1 AP who is assigned to help you, and there are 2 other RNs on your clinical unit.

(© Lisa F. Young/ iStock.)

A.J. is a 63-year-old woman admitted with severe anemia (Hgb 5.9 g/dL and Hct 18.2%) and acute myelocytic leukemia (AML). Her WBC count is 2600/μL, and platelet count is 72,000/μL. A.J. has dyspnea on exertion. She received 2 units of RBCs. Vital signs: 102/60, 100, RR 22, temp 96.8°F (36°C), O_2 saturation 94% with O_2 2 L/min via nasal cannula. She starts chemotherapy tomorrow.

(© g-stockstudio/ iStock/Thinkstock.)

J.J. is a 52-year-old white man newly diagnosed with acute lymphocytic leukemia (ALL). Laboratory results reveal Hgb 6.9 g/dL, Hct 20%, WBC count 120,000/μL (120×10^9/L), and platelet count 9,000/μL (25×10^9/L). Vital signs: 100/70, 110, RR 26, temperature 102.2°F (39°C). He is having a port placed today after he receives platelet transfusions.

(© Studio Grand Ouest/iStock/Thinkstock.)

P.H. is a 45-year-old woman who is receiving chemotherapy for ovarian cancer. She was admitted with fever and chills. Her WBC count is 2200/μL (2.2×10^9/L), with an absolute neutrophil count (ANC) of 400/μL (0.4×10^9/L). She will begin IV antibiotic therapy. Vital signs: 118/60, 98, RR 20, temperature 99.2°F (37.3°C).

(© Ridofranz/ iStock.)

G.L. is a 67-year-old man who came to the ED yesterday with abdominal pain. A CT scan of the abdomen showed several lymphatic masses. The HCP suspects non-Hodgkin lymphoma and admits him for a diagnostic workup. He currently rates his pain as a 3 on a scale of 0 to 10.

1. Highlight all the findings above that require your follow-up.
2. After receiving report, which patient should you see first?
3. Which tasks could you delegate to the AP *(select all that apply)*?

Case Study—cont'd

a. Assist A.J. to a chair after completing her AM care.
b. Obtain the first unit of platelets for J.J. from the blood bank.
c. Explain the importance of isolation to P.H. and her family.
d. Ask A.J. why she has not received regular medical care for 5 years.
e. Assess G.L. for other clinical manifestations of non-Hodgkin lymphoma.

4. When you enter J.J.'s room, you find him somewhat confused and lethargic. His family states he had just had a severe coughing episode.

Use an X for the following nursing actions that are Indicated (appropriate or necessary), Contraindicated (could be harmful), or Nonessential (makes no difference or not necessary) for J.J. at this time.

Nursing Action	Indicated	Contraindicated	Nonessential
Perform a focused neurologic assessment.			
Direct the AP to stay with J.J. while you contact the HCP.			
Ask family members for a copy of his living will.			
Call respiratory therapy to give him a breathing treatment.			
Place him flat, in a side-lying position.			
Obtain vital signs with O_2 saturation.			
Initiate NPO status.			

Case Study Progression

J.J.'s HCP orders a repeat CBC and an emergency CT scan of the head. Your supervisor arranges for another RN to accompany J.J. to the CT scan while you prepare to administer his platelets.

5. Based on P.H.'s condition, the priority need will be prevention of ____1____. To reduce this risk, the most important intervention is to ____2____.

Options for 1	Options for 2
Bleeding	encourage ambulation as tolerated
Infection	initiate bleeding precautions
VTE	perform hand hygiene
	wear a mask in the patient's room

6. While waiting for J.J.'s platelets, you complete A.J.'s assessment and begin to develop her plan of care. Indicate which nursing action listed in the far-left column is appropriate for each potential complication. Note that not all actions will be used.

Nursing Action	Complication	Appropriate Nursing Action for Each Complication
a. Implement neutropenic precautions	Anemia	
b. Administer ferrous sulfate 325 mg TID.	Dehydration	
c. Provide a nutrition supplement with each meal.	Fatigue	
d. Administer O_2 therapy.	Inadequate tissue perfusion	
e. Initiate daily weights.	Infection	
f. Reposition every 2 hours while in bed.		
g. Alternate rest and activity periods.		
h. Monitor laboratory results as available.		

7. An RN from the float pool arrives to accompany J.J. to CT scan at the same time the AP arrives with the platelets. Which intervention would be *most* appropriate?
   a. Put the unit platelets in the refrigerator to start when J.J. returns to the floor.
   b. Ask the RN to verify the correct unit of platelets with you and start the infusion.
   c. Give the RN an SBAR report and ask her to start the platelets on the way to CT scan.
   d. Ask the RN if she would prefer to give the platelets or hold it for J.J.'s return to the unit.
8. G.L. asks you to explain the diagnostic testing he can expect to undergo related to the suspected lymphoma. Which tests will you explain to him? *(select all that apply)*
   a. PET scan
   b. Bone marrow biopsy
   c. Peripheral blood smear
   d. Excisional lymph node biopsy
   e. Lymphangiography of internal lymph nodes
9. The HCP orders ferrous sulfate 325 mg TID for A.J. You teach A.J. to take her iron *(select all that apply)*
   a. at breakfast time in the morning.
   b. with orange juice to increase absorption.
   c. 1 hour before meals to facilitate absorption.
   d. 2 hours after eating to minimize side effects.
   e. whenever she feels tired or is short of breath with activity.

Answers available at http://evolve.elsevier.com/Lewis/medsurg.

35

Assessment: Cardiovascular System

Debra Hagler and Diana Rabbani Hagler

http://evolve.elsevier.com/Lewis/medsurg/

CONCEPTUAL FOCUS

Health Promotion
Nutrition
Perfusion

LEARNING OUTCOMES

1. Discern the anatomic location and function of the pericardial layers, atria, ventricles, and valves.
2. Relate the coronary circulation to the areas of heart muscle supplied by the major coronary arteries.
3. Distinguish the structure and function of arteries, veins, capillaries, and endothelium.
4. Describe the mechanisms involved in the regulation of blood pressure.
5. Relate the various waveforms on a normal electrocardiogram to the associated cardiac events.
6. Obtain significant subjective and objective assessment data related to the cardiovascular system from a patient and/or caregiver.
7. Perform a physical assessment of the cardiovascular system using the appropriate techniques.
8. Distinguish normal from abnormal findings of a physical assessment of the cardiovascular system.
9. Link the age-related changes of the cardiovascular system to the differences in assessment findings.
10. Apply the principles of hemodynamic monitoring to the nursing and interprofessional management of patients.
11. Describe the purpose, significance of results, and nursing responsibilities related to diagnostic studies of the cardiovascular system.

KEY TERMS

action potential
afterload
arterial blood pressure
arterial pressure–based cardiac output (APCO)
cardiac index (CI)
cardiac output (CO)
cardiac reserve
coronary angiography
diastole
diastolic blood pressure (DBP)
ejection fraction (EF)
heaves
hemodynamic monitoring
Korotkoff sounds
mean arterial pressure (MAP)
murmur
point of maximal impulse (PMI)
preload
pulse pressure
systole
systolic blood pressure (SBP)

STRUCTURES AND FUNCTIONS OF CARDIOVASCULAR SYSTEM

Heart

Structure

The heart is a 4-chambered hollow muscular organ normally about the size of a fist. It lies within the thorax, in the mediastinal space that separates the right and left pleural cavities. The heart is composed of 3 layers: a thin inner lining, the *endocardium;* a layer of muscle, the *myocardium;* and an outer layer, the *epicardium.* A fibroserous sac called the *pericardium* covers the heart. The pericardium consists of 2 layers: the inner *(visceral)* layer (part of the epicardium) and the outer *(parietal)* layer. A small amount of pericardial fluid (around 10 to 15 mL) lubricates the space between the pericardial layers *(pericardial space)* and prevents friction between the surfaces as the heart contracts.

The septum vertically divides the heart. The interatrial septum creates a right and left atrium. The interventricular septum creates a right and left ventricle. The wall thickness of each heart chamber is different. The atrial myocardium is thinner than that of the ventricles. The left ventricular wall is 2 to 3 times thicker than the right ventricular wall. The thickness of the left ventricle is needed for the strength to pump the blood into the systemic circulation.[1]

Blood Flow Through Heart

Fig. 35.1 shows the blood flow through the heart.

Heart valves. The 4 valves of the heart keep blood flowing in a forward direction. The cusps of the mitral and tricuspid valves are attached to thin strands of fibrous tissue called *chordae tendineae* (Fig. 35.2). Chordae are anchored in the papillary muscles of the ventricles. This support prevents the eversion of the valve leaflets into the atria during ventricular contraction. The pulmonic and aortic valves (also known as *semilunar valves*) prevent blood from regurgitating back into the ventricles at the end of each ventricular contraction.

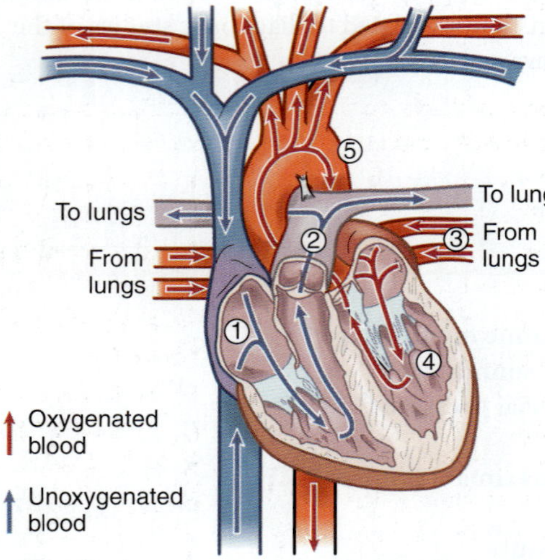

Fig. 35.1 Diagram of blood flow through the heart. *Arrows* show direction of flow. *1,* The right atrium receives venous blood from the inferior and superior venae cava and the coronary sinus. The blood then passes through the tricuspid valve into the right ventricle. *2,* With each contraction, the right ventricle pumps blood through the pulmonic valve into the pulmonary artery and to the lungs. *3,* Oxygenated blood flows from the lungs to the left atrium by way of the pulmonary veins. *4,* It then passes through the mitral valve and into the left ventricle. *5,* As the heart contracts, blood is ejected through the aortic valve into the aorta and enters the systemic circulation.

Blood Supply to Myocardium

The myocardium has its own blood supply, the *coronary circulation* (Fig. 35.3). Blood flow into the 2 major coronary arteries occurs primarily during **diastole** (relaxation of the myocardium). The left coronary artery arises from the aorta and divides into 2 main branches: the left anterior descending artery and left circumflex artery. These arteries supply the left atrium, left ventricle, interventricular septum, and part of the right ventricle. The right coronary artery also arises from the aorta, and its branches supply the right atrium, right ventricle, and part of the posterior wall of the left ventricle. In 90% of people, the atrioventricular (AV) node and the bundle of His receive blood supply from the right coronary artery. For this reason, blockage of this artery often causes serious defects in cardiac conduction.

The divisions of coronary veins parallel the coronary arteries. Most of the blood from the coronary system drains into the coronary sinus (a large channel). It empties into the right atrium, near the entrance of the inferior vena cava.[1]

Conduction System

The conduction system consists of specialized tissue that creates and transports the electrical impulse, or **action potential**. This impulse starts depolarization of the heart cells, leading to heart muscle contraction (Fig. 35.4A). The electrical impulse normally begins in the sinoatrial (SA) node (pacemaker of the heart). Impulses from the SA node travel through interatrial pathways to depolarize the atria, resulting in a contraction.

The electrical impulse travels from the atria to the AV node through internodal pathways. The signal then moves through the bundle of His and the left and right bundle branches. The left bundle branch has 2 divisions: anterior and posterior. The

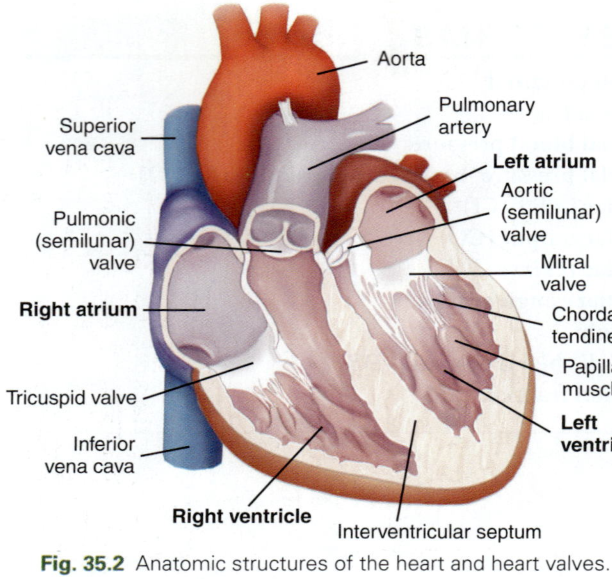

Fig. 35.2 Anatomic structures of the heart and heart valves.

action potential moves through the walls of both ventricles via *Purkinje fibers*. The ventricular conduction system delivers the impulse within 0.12 second. This triggers a synchronized right and left ventricular contraction and ejection of blood into the pulmonary and systemic circulations.

Last, repolarization occurs when the contractile and conduction pathway cells regain their resting polarized condition. Heart muscle cells have a compensatory mechanism that makes them unresponsive or *refractory* to restimulation during the action potential. During ventricular contraction, there is an *absolute refractory period* when heart muscle does not respond to any new stimuli. After this period, heart muscle gradually recovers its excitability, and a *relative refractory period* occurs by early diastole.[2]

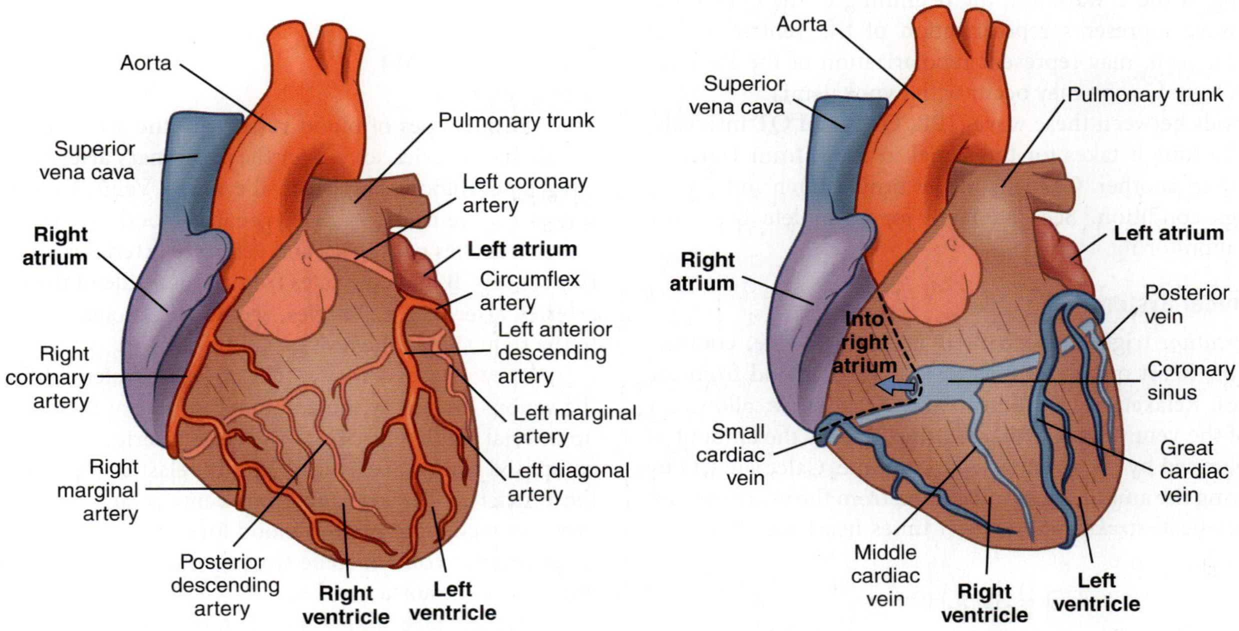

Fig. 35.3 Coronary arteries and veins.

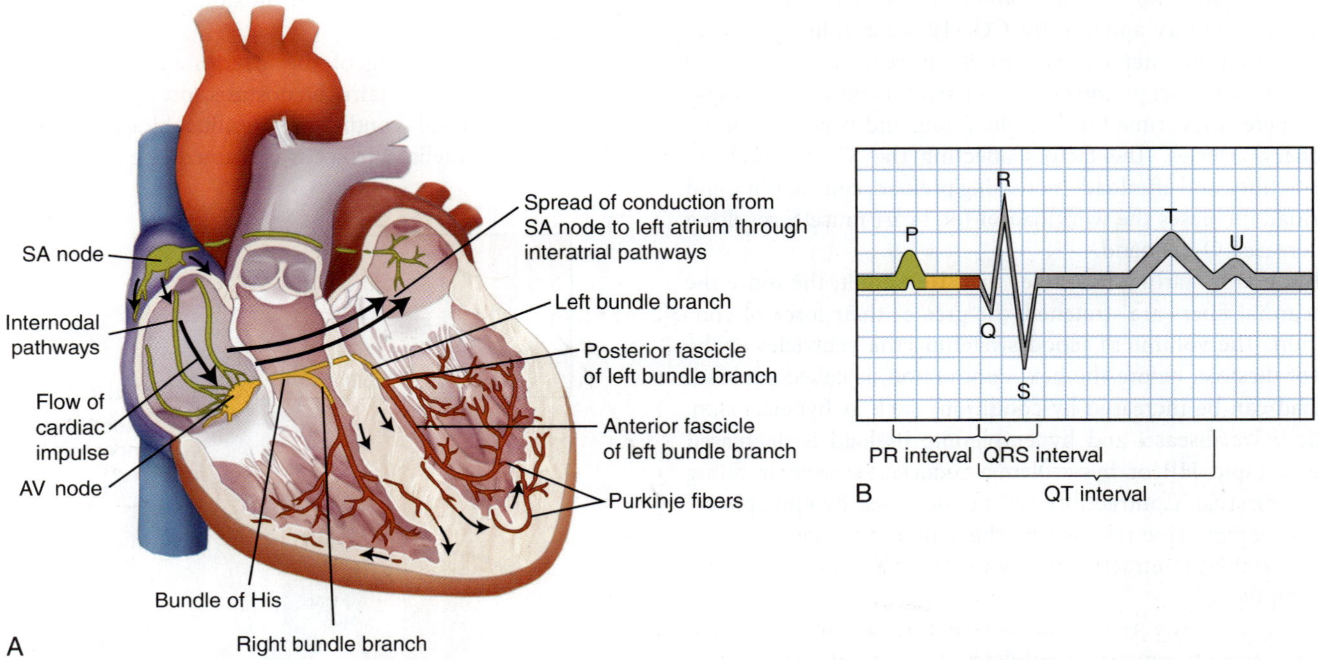

Fig. 35.4 (A) Conduction system of the heart. *AV*, Atrioventricular; *SA*, sinoatrial. (B) The normal ECG pattern. The *P* wave represents depolarization of the atria. The *QRS* complex indicates depolarization of the ventricles. The *T* wave represents repolarization of the ventricles. The *U* wave, if present, may represent repolarization of the Purkinje fibers or be associated with hypokalemia. The PR, QRS, and QT intervals reflect the time it takes for the impulse to travel from one area of the heart to another.

Electrocardiogram. The electrical activity of the heart can be detected using electrodes and recorded on an electrocardiogram (ECG). We use the letters *P, QRS, T,* and *U* to name the separate waveforms (Fig. 35.4B). The first waveform, the P wave, begins with the firing of the SA node. It represents depolarization of the atria. The QRS complex represents depolarization from the AV node throughout the ventricles. A delay of impulse transmission through the AV node accounts for the time between the beginning of the P wave and the beginning of the QRS wave. The T wave represents repolarization of the ventricles. The U wave, if seen, may represent repolarization of the Purkinje fibers. A large U wave may occur with hypokalemia.

Intervals between these waves (PR, QRS, and QT intervals) reflect the time it takes for the signal to travel from 1 area of the heart to another. Changes in the timing often indicates a pathologic condition.[3] See Chapter 39 for a complete discussion of ECG monitoring.

Mechanical System

Depolarization triggers mechanical activity. **Systole**, contraction of the heart muscle, results in ejection of blood from the ventricles. Relaxation of the heart muscle, *diastole*, allows for filling of the ventricles. **Cardiac output (CO)** is the amount of blood pumped by each ventricle in 1 minute. Calculate CO by multiplying the amount of blood ejected from the ventricle with each heartbeat: *stroke volume* (SV) times heart rate (HR) per minute:

$$CO = SV \times HR$$

For the normal adult at rest, CO is maintained in the range of 4 to 8 L/min.

Factors affecting cardiac output. Many factors can affect either the HR or SV and thus the CO. HR is controlled primarily by the autonomic nervous system. It can reach as high as 180 beats/min for short periods without harmful effects. With rapid HRs, there is less time for diastolic filling and perfusion of the coronary arteries. The factors affecting the SV are preload, contractility, and afterload. Increasing preload, contractility, and afterload increases the workload of the heart muscle, resulting in increased O_2 demand.

The Frank-Starling law states that, to a point, the more the myocardial fibers are stretched, the greater their force of contraction. The volume of blood stretching the ventricles at the end of diastole, before the next contraction, is called **preload**. Preload can be increased by conditions such as hypertension, aortic valve disease, and hypervolemia. Preload is decreased when a rapid HR or hypovolemia reduces ventricular filling during diastole. Contractility can be increased by epinephrine and norepinephrine released by the sympathetic nervous system. Increasing contractility raises the SV by increasing ventricular emptying.[1]

Afterload is the peripheral resistance against which the left ventricle must pump. Afterload depends on the size of the ventricle, wall tension, and arterial BP. If the arterial BP is elevated, the ventricles meet increased resistance to ejection of blood, increasing the work demand. Eventually this results in *ventricular hypertrophy,* an enlargement of the heart muscle without an increase in CO or the size of chambers. Both right and left ventricles work against resistance. The right ventricle pumps against the afterload of pulmonary arterial resistance.[2]

Cardiac Reserve

The cardiovascular system must respond to many situations in health and illness (e.g., exercise, stress, hypovolemia). The ability to respond to these demands by maintaining or increasing CO is the **cardiac reserve**.

Vascular System

Blood Vessels

The 3 major types of blood vessels are the arteries, veins, and capillaries. Arteries, except for the pulmonary artery (PA), carry oxygenated blood away from the heart. Veins, except for the pulmonary veins, carry deoxygenated blood toward the heart. Small branches of arteries and veins are arterioles and venules, respectively. Blood circulates from the left side of the heart into arteries, arterioles, capillaries, venules, and veins and then back to the right side of the heart.

Arteries and arterioles. The arterial system differs from the venous system by the amount and type of tissue that make up arterial walls (Fig. 35.5). The large arteries have thick walls composed mainly of elastic tissue. This elastic property cushions the impact of the pressure from ventricular contraction and provides recoil that propels blood forward into the circulation. Large arteries contain some smooth muscle. Examples of large arteries are the aorta and PA.

Arterioles have more smooth muscle and little elastic tissue. Arterioles control arterial BP and distribution of blood flow. They respond readily to local conditions such as low O_2 and increasing levels of carbon dioxide (CO_2) by dilating or constricting.

The innermost lining of the arteries is the endothelium. The endothelium maintains hemostasis, promotes blood flow, and, under normal conditions, inhibits blood coagulation. When the endothelial surface is disrupted (e.g., rupture of an

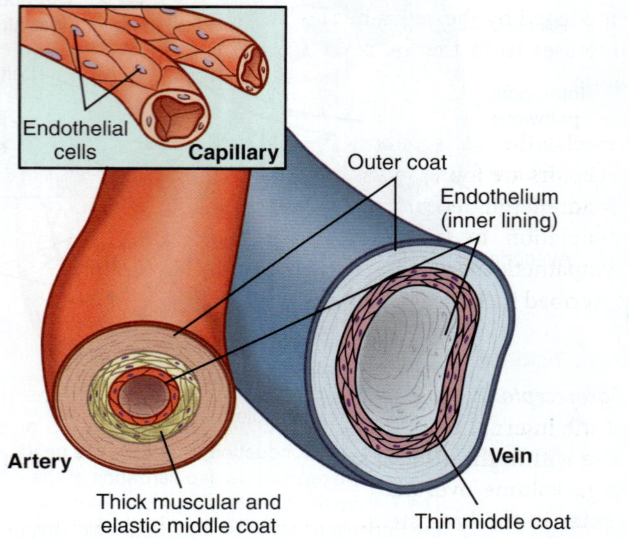

Fig. 35.5 Comparative thickness of layers of the artery, vein, and capillary.

atherosclerotic plaque), the coagulation cascade results in the formation of a fibrin clot.

Capillaries. The thin capillary wall made up of endothelial cells has no elastic or muscle tissue (Fig. 35.5). Exchange of cellular nutrients and metabolic end products takes place through these thin-walled vessels. Capillaries connect the arterioles and venules.

Veins and venules. Venules are small vessels with a minor amount of muscle and connective tissue. Venules collect blood from the capillary beds and channel it to the larger veins.

Veins are large-diameter, thin-walled vessels that return blood to the right atrium (Fig. 35.5). The venous system is a low-pressure, high-volume system. The larger veins have semilunar valves at intervals to maintain the blood flow toward the heart and to prevent backward flow. Several factors affect the amount of blood in the venous system. These include arterial flow, compression of veins by skeletal muscles, changes in thoracic and abdominal pressures, and right atrial pressure.

The largest veins are the *superior vena cava,* which returns blood to the heart from the head, neck, and arms, and the *inferior vena cava.* It returns blood to the heart from the lower part of the body. Pressure in the right side of the heart affects these large vessels. Elevated right atrial pressure can cause distended neck veins or liver engorgement because of resistance to blood flow.[1]

Regulation of Cardiovascular System

Autonomic Nervous System

The autonomic nervous system consists of the sympathetic nervous system and parasympathetic nervous system (see Chapter 60).

Effect on heart. Stimulation of the sympathetic nervous system increases the HR, speed of impulse conduction through the AV node, and force of atrial and ventricular contractions. This effect is mediated by specific sites in the heart called *beta (β)-adrenergic receptors.* They are receptors for norepinephrine and epinephrine.

In contrast, stimulation of the parasympathetic system (mediated by the vagus nerve) slows the HR by decreasing the impulses from the SA node and conduction through the AV node.

Effect on blood vessels. The source of neural control of blood vessels is the sympathetic nervous system. Alpha$_1$ (α_1)-adrenergic receptors are found in vascular smooth muscles. Stimulation of α_1-adrenergic receptors results in vasoconstriction. Decreased stimulation to α_1-adrenergic receptors causes vasodilation. Sympathetic nervous system receptors that influence BP are described in Table 36.1.

Baroreceptors

Baroreceptors in the aortic arch and carotid sinus (at the origin of the internal carotid artery) are sensitive to stretch or pressure within the arterial system. Stimulation of these receptors (e.g., volume overload) sends information to the vasomotor center in the brainstem. This results in temporary inhibition of the sympathetic nervous system and enhancement of the parasympathetic influence. The result is a decreased HR and peripheral vasodilation. Decreased arterial pressure has the opposite effect.

Chemoreceptors

Chemoreceptors are found in the aortic and carotid bodies and the medulla. They can cause changes in respiratory rate and BP in response to increased arterial CO_2 pressure (hypercapnia) and, to less degree, decreased plasma pH (acidosis) and arterial O_2 pressure (hypoxia). Chemoreceptors in the medulla stimulate the vasomotor center to increase BP.[2]

Blood Pressure

The **arterial blood pressure** is a measure of the force exerted by blood against the walls of the arterial system. The **systolic blood pressure (SBP)** is the peak pressure exerted against the arteries when the heart contracts. The **diastolic blood pressure (DBP)** is the residual pressure in the arterial system during ventricular relaxation (or filling).

The main factors influencing BP are CO and *systemic vascular resistance* (SVR):

$$BP = CO \times SVR$$

SVR is the force opposing the movement of blood. This force is created primarily in small arteries and arterioles. Normal BP is SBP less than 120 mm Hg and DBP less than 80 mm Hg (see Chapter 36).[4]

Measurement of Arterial Blood Pressure

We can measure BP with invasive or noninvasive techniques. The invasive technique consists of catheter insertion into an artery. The catheter is attached to a transducer, and the pressure is measured directly. Invasive arterial BP monitoring is discussed later in this chapter.

Noninvasive, indirect measurement of BP is done with a sphygmomanometer and stethoscope. The sphygmomanometer consists of an inflatable cuff and a pressure gauge. We measure BP by auscultating for sounds of turbulent blood flow through a compressed artery (termed **Korotkoff sounds**). The brachial artery is the recommended site for taking a BP.

After placing the right sized cuff on the upper arm, inflate the cuff to a pressure 20 to 30 mm Hg above the patient's usual SBP. This stops blood flow in the artery. If the SBP is not known, estimate the pressure by palpating the brachial pulse and inflating the cuff until the pulse ceases. The pressure noted at this time is the estimated SBP. Inflate the BP cuff 20 to 30 mm Hg above this number.

As you lower the pressure in the cuff, listen over the brachial artery for Korotkoff sounds. There are 5 phases of Korotkoff sounds. The first phase is a tapping sound caused by the spurt of blood into the constricted artery as the pressure in the cuff is gradually deflated. This sound is the SBP. The fifth phase occurs when the sound disappears, which is the DBP.

BP is recorded as the ratio of SBP to DBP (e.g., 120/80 mm Hg). Sometimes, an *auscultatory gap* occurs, which is a loss of sound between the SBP and DBP. Proper BP technique, such as using the correct cuff and positioning arm at heart level, is essential for correct readings (see Table 36.11).

Another noninvasive way to measure BP indirectly is with an automated device that uses oscillometric measurements to assess BP. Although this method does not involve auscultation, attention to proper technique is essential for accuracy.

We can assess SBP and pulse using a Doppler ultrasonic flowmeter. The hand-held transducer is positioned over the artery (identified by audible, pulsatile sounds). The cuff is applied above the artery, inflated until the sounds disappear, and then inflated another 20 to 30 mm Hg beyond that point. The cuff is then slowly deflated. The point where sounds return is the SBP.[4]

Pulse Pressure and Mean Arterial Pressure

Pulse pressure is the difference between the SBP and DBP. It is normally about one-third of the SBP. If the BP is 120/80 mm Hg, the pulse pressure is 40 mm Hg. An increased pulse pressure and SBP may occur when a person exercises or has atherosclerosis of the larger arteries. A decreased pulse pressure may occur with heart failure (HF) or hypovolemia.

Another measurement related to BP is **mean arterial pressure (MAP)**. The MAP refers to the average pressure within the arterial system. It is not the average of the DBP and SBP, because the length of diastole is about twice that of systole at normal HRs. MAP is calculated as follows:

$$\text{MAP} = (\text{SBP} + 2\ \text{DBP}) \div 3$$

A person with a BP of 120/60 mm Hg has an estimated MAP of 80 mm Hg. The MAP must be greater than 60 mm Hg to perfuse the vital organs under most conditions. When the MAP is low for a period of time, vital organs become ischemic.

Gerontologic Considerations: Effects of Aging on the Cardiovascular System

One of the greatest risk factors for cardiovascular disease (CVD) is age. CVD is the leading cause of death in adults older than age 65. The most common problem is coronary artery disease (CAD) due to atherosclerosis. Many of the changes in the cardiovascular system of older adults are a result of the combined effects of the aging process, disease, environmental factors, and lifetime health behaviors.

Age-related changes in the cardiovascular system and differences in assessment findings are found in Table 35.1. With increased age, collagen in the heart increases and elastin decreases. These changes affect the heart muscle's ability to stretch and contract. The older adult has a decreased cardiovascular response to physical and emotional stress and is less sensitive to β-adrenergic agonist drugs. Exercise results in a much smaller increase in CO for older adults than for younger adults.[5]

Heart valves thicken and stiffen from lipid accumulation, collagen degeneration, and fibrosis. The aortic and mitral valves are most often affected. These changes result in either regurgitation of blood when the valve should be closed or narrowing of the orifice of the valve *(stenosis)* when the valve should be open. Turbulent blood flow across the affected valve is heard as a whooshing sound or **murmur** between heartbeats.

TABLE 35.1 GERONTOLOGIC ASSESSMENT DIFFERENCES

Cardiovascular System

Changes	Differences in Assessment Findings
Chest Wall	
Kyphosis	Altered chest landmarks for palpation, percussion, and auscultation. Distant heart sounds
Heart	
Myocardial hypertrophy, ↑ collagen and scarring, ↓ elastin	↓ Cardiac reserve, HF. S_4 may be present
Downward displacement	Difficulty in isolating apical pulse.
↓ CO, HR, SV in response to exercise or stress	↓ Response to exercise and stress. Slowed recovery from activity
Cellular aging and fibrosis of conduction system	↓ Amplitude of QRS complex and slight lengthening of PR, QRS, and QT intervals. Irregular rhythms, ↓ maximal HR, ↓ HR variability
Valvular rigidity from calcification, sclerosis, or fibrosis, impeding complete closure of valves	Systolic murmur (aortic or mitral) possible without a sign of cardiovascular disease
Blood Vessels	
Arterial stiffening caused by loss of elastin in arterial walls, thickening of intima of arteries, and progressive fibrosis of media	↑ In SBP and possible ↑ or ↓ in DBP. Possible widened pulse pressure. ↓ Pedal pulses. Intermittent claudication
↑ Venous tortuosity	Inflamed, painful, or cord-like varicosities. Dependent edema

The number of pacemaker cells in the SA node and conduction cells in the internodal tracts, bundle of His, and bundle branches decreases with age. The decrease contributes to the development of sinus and atrial dysrhythmias and heart blocks. Many older adults have an abnormal resting ECG that shows increases in the PR and/or QT intervals.[6] The number and function of β-adrenergic receptors in the heart decrease with age.[7]

With age, arteries and veins thicken and become less elastic. Arteries become more sensitive to vasopressin (antidiuretic hormone). Both changes increase SBP and pulse pressure with a decreased or unchanged DBP. Valves in the large leg veins return the blood to the heart less effectively, often resulting in dependent edema.

When an older adult changes position (e.g., sits upright), the sympathetic nerve pathway produces a blunted (reduced) HR response, which may lead to a drop in BP and sense of lightheadedness on arising (orthostatic hypotension). *Postprandial hypotension* (decrease in BP of at least 20 mm Hg that occurs within 75 minutes after eating) may occur in otherwise healthy older adults. Both orthostatic and postprandial hypotension may increase fall risk in older adults.

Case Study

Patient Introduction

(©Jupiterimages/ Banana-Stock/ Thinkstock.)

L.P., a 63-year-old man, is brought to the hospital by ambulance at 0600 after reporting chest tightness, shortness of breath (SOB), and "heart pounding" (palpitations). The paramedics started an IV and O_2 at 2 L/min via nasal cannula. They obtained a 12-lead ECG and gave him 4 low-dose ASA and a nitroglycerin tablet. L.P. is pain free on arrival to the emergency department but still has palpitations.

Discussion Questions

1. What are the possible causes of L.P.'s symptoms?
2. Is L.P.'s condition stable or unstable?

You will learn more about L.P. and his condition as you read this assessment chapter.

Answers available at http://evolve.elsevier.com/Lewis/medsurg.

ASSESSMENT OF CARDIOVASCULAR SYSTEM

Subjective Data

A careful health history and physical assessment will help you distinguish symptoms of a cardiovascular problem from problems of other body systems. Explore and record all cues that alert you to the possibility of underlying CVD.

Important Health Information

History of present illness. Ask the patient what problem has led to seeking health care. Fully explore all symptoms the patient reports.

Health history. Many illnesses affect the cardiovascular system directly or indirectly. Ask the patient about a history of angina, diabetes, alcohol and tobacco use, anemia, rheumatic fever, streptococcal throat infections, congenital heart disease, stroke, hypertension, thrombophlebitis, dysrhythmias, and varicosities. Fully explore any symptoms the patient reports. Ask about dyspnea, fatigue, dizziness with position changes, syncope, edema, intermittent claudication, and palpitations.

Assess for allergies to drugs, food, or the environment. Determine whether the patient has ever had a drug reaction or an allergic or anaphylactic reaction. Ask specifically about any allergic reaction to contrast media.

Medications. Assess the patient's current and past use of medications. Record the dose and time last taken for each. Include over-the-counter (OTC) and prescription drugs and herbal supplements. For example, aspirin prolongs the blood clotting time. It is found in some drugs used to treat cold symptoms. Assess for use of noncardiac drugs that can adversely affect the cardiovascular system (Table 35.2).

Surgery or other treatments. Ask the patient about specific treatments, surgeries, or hospital admissions related to cardiovascular problems. Explore any admissions or procedures performed for cardiovascular symptoms. Note whether the patient has had an ECG or a chest x-ray done.

Functional Health Patterns

The strong correlation between lifestyle and cardiovascular health supports the need to review each functional health pattern. Key questions to ask a person with a cardiovascular problem are listed in Table 35.3.

TABLE 35.2 Potential Cardiovascular Effects of Select Noncardiac Drugs

Drug Classification	Examples	Cardiovascular Effects
Anticancer agents	daunorubicin doxorubicin	Dysrhythmias, cardiomyopathy
Antipsychotics	chlorpromazine haloperidol	Dysrhythmias, orthostatic hypotension
Antirheumatics	hydroxychloroquine	Dysrhythmias, cardiomyopathy, heart block, prolonged QT interval,
Corticosteroids	cortisone prednisone	Hypotension, edema, potassium depletion
Hormone therapy, oral contraceptives	estrogen + progestin (Prempro)	MI, thromboembolism, stroke, hypertension
Nonsteroidal antiinflammatory drugs (NSAIDs)	celecoxib (Celebrex) diclofenac ibuprofen	MI, stroke, hypertension, HF
Psychostimulants	amphetamines cocaine	Tachycardia, angina, MI, hypertension, dysrhythmias
Tricyclic antidepressants	amitriptyline doxepin (Silenor)	Dysrhythmias, orthostatic hypotension

Health perception–health management pattern. Ask the patient about the presence of major cardiovascular risk factors. These include abnormal serum lipids, hypertension, sedentary lifestyle, diabetes, obesity, and tobacco use. Estimate the number of pack-years of tobacco use (number of packs smoked per day multiplied by the number of years the patient has smoked). Note the patient's attitude about tobacco use and attempts and methods used to stop. Record the type of alcohol used, amount, and frequency. Note any use of habit-forming or recreational substances.

Confirmed illnesses of blood relatives can highlight any genetic or familial tendencies toward CAD, hypertension, varicosities, bleeding, diabetes, atherosclerosis, and stroke (Box 35.1). Note any family members who had heart disease at an early age (<50 years of age for men; <55 years of age for women). Last, assess for family health history of noncardiac problems that affect the cardiovascular system such as obesity and lung, kidney, or liver disease.

Nutritional-metabolic pattern. Being underweight or overweight may indicate potential cardiovascular problems. Assess the patient's weight history (e.g., over the past year) in relation to height. Determine the amount of salt and saturated fats in the patient's typical diet. In addition to food habits, which are influenced by culture, explore the patient's attitudes and plans about diet and weight management.

Elimination pattern. The patient taking diuretics may report increased voiding and/or nocturia. Ask about incontinence or constipation, including use of prescribed and OTC drugs for constipation. Teach patients with heart problems to avoid straining *(Valsalva maneuver)* during a bowel movement. Ask patients if they have swelling of the lower extremities and if it resolves when their feet are elevated.

TABLE 35.3 HEALTH HISTORY

Cardiovascular System

Health Perception–Health Management

- Do you practice any measures to decrease risk factors for heart disease?[a]
- Have you noticed an increase in heart symptoms such as chest pain or dyspnea?[a]
- Does your heart problem cause you to be less able to care for yourself?[a]
- Do you foresee any potential self-care problems because of your heart problem?[a]
- Have you ever used tobacco? If yes, in what form, how much, and for how long? Have you tried to quit? If yes, what methods have you tried? Are you interested in learning about quitting?
- How often and how much alcohol do you drink?

Nutritional-Metabolic

- Describe your usual daily diet, including salt, fat, and liquid intake.
- What is your present weight? What was your weight 1 year ago? If different, explain.
- Does eating cause fatigue or shortness of breath?[a]

Elimination

- Do your feet or ankles ever swell?[a] If yes, how far up your legs? Does it go away after sleeping all night?
- Have you ever taken drugs to help you get rid of excess fluid or to relieve constipation?[a]
- Are you having any problems related to urination?[a]
- Do you ever strain to have a bowel movement?

Activity-Exercise

- Are your daily activities or exercise limited because of your heart problem?[a]
- When were you last able to comfortably perform your usual activities or exercise?
- Do you have any discomfort or symptoms because of exercise or any activity?[a]
- Can you comfortably walk and talk at the same time?
- How often do you attend activities outside your home?
- What was your most strenuous activity in the past few weeks compared with 6 months ago?

Sleep-Rest

- How many pillows do you sleep on at night? Has this changed recently?[a]
- Do you ever wake up suddenly and feel as if you cannot catch your breath?[a]
- Do you have a history of sleep apnea?[a]
- Do you ever sleep in a chair at night? Is yes, how often?
- How many times a night do you awaken to urinate?

Cognitive-Perceptual

- Do you ever have dizziness or fainting?[a]
- Do you ever find it hard to express yourself or to remember things?[a]
- Do you have any pain (e.g., chest pain, leg pain with activity) because of your heart problem?[a]

Self-Perception–Self-Concept

- Have your perceptions of yourself changed since you were diagnosed with heart disease?[a]
- How has your heart disease affected the quality of your life?

Role-Relationship

- Has this illness affected any of the roles that you play in your daily life?[a]
- How has your heart disease affected your significant others?

Sexuality-Reproductive

- Has your heart disease caused a change in your sexual activity?[a]
- Do you have any heart-related symptoms during sexual activity?[a]
- Do any of your drugs affect your ability to take part in sexual activities?[a]
- *Females:* Are you currently taking oral contraceptives, hormonal therapy, or drug therapy for breast cancer?
- *Males:* Are you taking any drugs to treat erectile dysfunction?

Coping–Stress Tolerance

- Describe your normal coping mechanisms during times of stress or anxiety.
- To whom or where would you turn during a time of stress? Are these people or services helping you now?[a]
- Do you practice any stress reduction techniques?[a]
- Do you have a history of depression?[a]
- Do you feel capable of handling your present health situation?
- Do you have any heart symptoms (e.g., chest pain, palpitations) during times of stress or anger?[a]

Values-Beliefs

- What influence have your values or beliefs had during your illness?
- Do you feel any conflicts between your values or beliefs and the plan of care?[a]
- Describe any cultural or spiritual beliefs that may influence managing your heart problem.

[a]If yes, describe.

Activity-exercise pattern. The benefit of exercise for cardiovascular health is clear, with aerobic exercise being most beneficial. Record the types, duration, intensity, and frequency of exercise. Ask about symptoms during exercise (e.g., chest pain, dyspnea, claudication) that may indicate a cardiovascular problem.

Sleep-rest pattern. Cardiovascular problems often disrupt sleep. *Paroxysmal nocturnal dyspnea* (attacks of shortness of breath, especially at night that awaken the patient) and *Cheyne-Stokes respiration* (periods of very shallow breaths to alternating periods of apnea and deep, rapid breathing) are associated with HF. Note the number of pillows needed to sleep or the need to sleep upright in a chair *(orthopnea)*.

Sleep apnea is associated with an increased risk for life-threatening dysrhythmias, especially in patients with HF. Nocturia, a common finding in CVD, interrupts normal sleep patterns.

Cognitive-perceptual pattern. Ask both the patient and caregiver about cognitive-perceptual problems. Cardiovascular problems such as dysrhythmias, hypertension, and stroke may cause difficulties with syncope, language, and memory. Report pain associated with the cardiovascular system (e.g., chest pain, claudication).

Self-perception–self-concept pattern. Acute cardiovascular events may affect the patient's self-perception. Invasive diagnostic procedures often lead to body image concerns. The patient with chronic CVD may describe an inability to "keep up" previous levels of activity, affecting quality of life.

Role-relationship pattern. Gender, race, and age are related to cardiovascular health. The patient's marital status, role in the household, employment status, number of children and their ages, living environment, and caregivers help you to identify

BOX 35.1 GENETIC RISK ALERT

Coronary Artery Disease (CAD)

- More than 50 genetic links, especially related to lipoprotein genes, have been found in some families with CAD.[5]
- The clustering of CAD in families is strong if early age of onset affected several relatives.

Cardiomyopathy

- Autosomal dominant mutations can cause hypertrophic cardiomyopathy.
- X-linked and autosomal dominant mutations can cause dilated cardiomyopathy.

Hypertension

- Hypertension results from a complex interplay of genetic and environmental factors.
- Lifestyle choices (e.g., smoking, lack of exercise) may trigger genetic tendencies to hypertension.

strengths and support systems in the patient's life. Assess the patient's satisfaction with life roles.

Sexuality-reproductive pattern. Ask the patient about the effect of the cardiovascular problem on sexual activity. Because some patients fear sudden death during sexual intercourse, they may change their sexual behavior. Fatigue, chest pain, or dyspnea may limit activity. Erectile dysfunction (ED) may be a symptom of peripheral vascular disease (PVD) and/or a side effect of some drugs used to treat CVD (e.g., β-blockers, diuretics). Ask male patients about the use of drugs such as phosphodiesterase inhibitors for ED. These drugs are contraindicated if the patient is taking a nitrate because the combination can cause significant hypotension.[6]

Ask female patients if they use oral contraceptives, hormone therapy (HT) for symptoms of menopause, or drug therapy for breast cancer. Women who smoke tobacco and use oral contraceptives are at increased risk for blood clots (e.g., venous thromboembolism). Similarly, there is an increased risk for CVD with the use of HT and selective estrogen-receptor modulators (e.g., tamoxifen).[6]

Coping–stress tolerance pattern. Ask the patient to identify sources of stress and the usual methods of coping with stress. Potentially stressful areas include health concerns, marital relationships, family and friends, occupation, and finances.

Work-related stress, depression, and inadequate social support are risk factors for CVD and heart events. Ask the patient about these factors. Information about the patient's support systems such as family, extended family and friends, counselors, or religious groups is useful in planning care.

Values-belief pattern. Individual values and beliefs, which are greatly affected by culture, may play a key role in the real or potential conflict that a patient faces when dealing with CVD. Some patients may attribute their illness to punishment; others may think that a "higher power" can help them. Information about a patient's values and beliefs will help you to provide support during periods of crisis.

Objective Data

Physical Assessment

Vital signs. Observe the patient's general appearance and obtain vital signs. Measure BP bilaterally. Readings can vary from 5 to 15 mm Hg between arms. Use the arm with the highest BP for later measurements. Obtain an orthostatic (postural) BP and HR while the patient is supine, sitting with legs dangling, and standing. SBP should not decrease more than 20 mm Hg from the supine to the standing position. HR should not increase more than 20 beats/min from the supine to the standing position.

Case Study

Subjective Data

(@ Jupiterimages/ Banana-Stock/ Thinkstock.)

A focused subjective assessment of L.P. revealed the following:

- ***Medical History:*** History of hypertension, mitral valve prolapse with mild regurgitation, HF, and type 2 diabetes.
- ***Oral Medications:*** Lisinopril (Prinivil) 10 mg/day, metoprolol (Lopressor) 50 mg twice daily, aspirin 81 mg/day, furosemide 40 mg/day, and glipizide 5 mg/day.
- ***Health Perception–Health Management:*** L.P. denies any history of chest pain or coronary artery disease. He reports feeling fine until this morning when he awoke and developed shortness of breath (SOB), chest tightness, and palpitations while walking to the bathroom. He thought he was having a heart attack, so his wife called 911. Denies smoking or alcohol intake. SOB and chest tightness are now gone, but he continues to feel palpitations.
- ***Elimination:*** Denies edema or nocturia. States he takes furosemide in the morning and typically "passes urine until lunchtime."

Discussion Questions

1. Which subjective assessment findings most concern you?
2. How will you conduct a patient-centered assessment?
3. Is this a good time to teach him about how to use nitroglycerin tablets?
4. What should you include in the physical assessment? What cues would you be looking for?

You will learn more about the physical assessment of the cardiovascular system in the next section.

Answers available at http://evolve.elsevier.com/Lewis/medsurg.

Peripheral vascular system

Inspection. Inspect the skin for color, hair distribution, and venous pattern. Check the extremities for edema, dependent rubor, clubbing of the nail beds, varicosities, and lesions such as stasis ulcers. Edema in the legs can be caused by gravity, varicosities, or right-sided HF.

Inspect the large neck veins (internal and external jugular) while gradually moving the patient from a supine position to an upright (30 to 45 degrees) position. Right-sided HF can cause distention and prominent pulsations of the neck veins referred to as *jugular venous distention* (JVD).

Palpation. Palpate the upper and lower extremities for temperature, moisture, pulses, and edema bilaterally to assess for symmetry. Look for edema by depressing the skin over the tibia or medial malleolus for 5 seconds. Normally, there is no depression after you release pressure. If pitting edema is present, grade it from 1+ (mild pitting, slight brief indentation) to 4+ (very deep pitting, indentation that lasts a long time).

Palpate the pulses in the neck and extremities for rhythm and force of arterial blood flow. Palpate each carotid pulse separately to avoid vagal stimulation and dysrhythmias. Compare the characteristics of the arteries in the right and left extremities simultaneously to determine symmetry.

When palpating the arteries identified in Fig. 35.6, rate the force of the pulse using the following scale:

0 = Absent
1+ = Weak
2+ = Normal
3+ = Increased, full, bounding

Note the rigidity (hardness) of the artery. The normal pulse feels like a tap, but a narrowed or bulging vessel wall vibrates. The term for a palpable vibration is *thrill.*

We use *capillary refill* to assess arterial flow to the extremities. Position the patient's hands near the level of the heart and squeeze a nail bed briefly to produce blanching. Color should return to the nail bed in less than 2 seconds after release.

Auscultation. An artery that is narrowed or has a bulging wall may create turbulent blood flow. This abnormal flow can cause a buzzing or humming termed a *bruit*. We can hear it with the bell of the stethoscope over the vessel. Auscultate the carotid arteries, abdominal aorta, and femoral arteries as part of the initial cardiovascular assessment. Abnormalities of the cardiovascular system are described in Table 35.4.

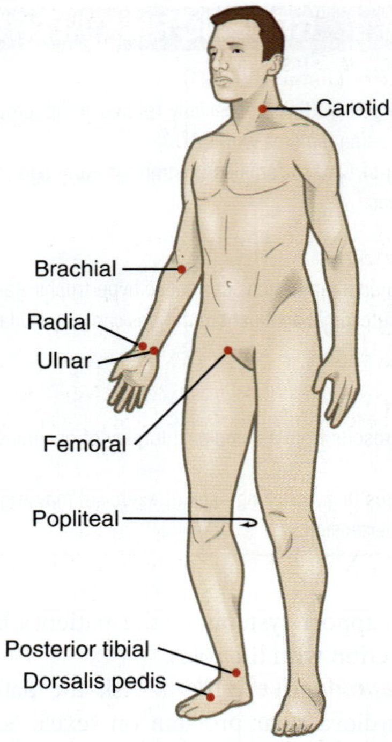

Fig. 35.6 Common sites for palpating arteries.

TABLE 35.4 ASSESSMENT ABNORMALITIES

Cardiovascular System

Finding[a]	Description	Possible Etiology[a] and Significance
Inspection		
Central cyanosis	Bluish or purplish tinge in tongue, conjunctivae, inner surface of lips	Inadequate O_2 saturation of arterial blood because of pulmonary or cardiac disorders
Clubbing of nail beds	Loss of normal angle between base of nail and skin	Endocarditis, congenital defects, prolonged O_2 deficiency
Color changes in extremities with postural change	Pallor, cyanosis, mottling of skin after limb elevation. Dependent rubor (reddish blue discoloration). Glossy skin	Chronic decreased arterial perfusion
Jugular venous distention (JVD)	Distended neck (jugular) veins with patient sitting at 30- to 45-degree angle	↑ Right atrial pressure, right-sided HF
Peripheral cyanosis	Bluish or purplish tinge in extremities or in nose and ears	↓ Blood flow from HF, vasoconstriction, cold environment
Splinter hemorrhages	Small red to black streaks under fingernails	Infective endocarditis
Ulcers	*Venous:* Necrotic crater-like lesion, usually at medial malleolus. Slowly healing wound.	Poor venous return, varicose veins, incompetent venous valves
	Arterial: Pale ischemic base, well-defined edges usually found on toes, heels, lateral malleoli	Arteriosclerosis, diabetes
Varicose veins	Visible dilated, discolored, tortuous vessels in legs	Incompetent valves in vein
Palpation		
Pulse		
<60 beats/min	Bradycardia	Rest, sleep, athletic conditioning, SA or AV node damage, side effect of drugs (e.g., β-blockers), hypothyroidism
>100 beats/min	Tachycardia	Exercise, anxiety, hypovolemia, shock, need for increased CO, hyperthyroidism
Absent	Lack of pulse	Local atherosclerosis, trauma, embolus
Bounding	Sharp, brisk, pounding pulse	Hyperkinetic states (e.g., anxiety, fever), anemia, hyperthyroidism
Displaced point of maximal impulse (apical pulse)	Palpate (or auscultate) the point of maximal impulse below the 5th ICS and to the left of the MCL	Cardiac enlargement because of coronary artery disease, HF, cardiomyopathy
Irregular	Regularly irregular or irregularly irregular. Skipped beats	Dysrhythmias
Pulsus alternans	Regular rhythm, but strength of pulse varies with each beat	HF, cardiac tamponade
Rigidity	Stiffness or inflexibility of vessel wall	Atherosclerosis
Thready	Weak, slowly rising pulse easily obliterated by pressure	Blood loss, ↓ CO, aortic valve disease, peripheral arterial disease
Thrill	Vibration of vessel or chest wall	Aneurysm, aortic regurgitation, arteriovenous fistula

TABLE 35.4 ASSESSMENT ABNORMALITIES—cont'd

Cardiovascular System

Finding[a]	Description	Possible Etiology[a] and Significance
Extremities		
Asymmetry in limb circumference	Measurable swelling of involved limb	Venous thromboembolism, varicose veins, lymphedema
Cold extremities	Hands and/or feet cold to touch. External covering needed for comfort	Peripheral arterial disease, ↓ CO, severe anemia
Delayed capillary refill	Blanching of nail bed for ≥2 sec after release of pressure	↓ Perfusion, anemia
Pitting edema of lower extremities or sacral area	Visible finger indentation after firm pressure, weight gain, tightening of clothing (including shoes), marks or indentations from constricting garments	Interruption of venous return to heart, right-sided HF
Unusually warm extremities	Hands and feet warmer than normal	Thyrotoxicosis
Auscultation		
3rd heart sound (S_3)	Extra heart sound, low pitched, heard in early diastole. Similar to sound of a gallop	Left ventricular failure. Volume overload. Mitral, aortic, or tricuspid regurgitation. Hypertension
4th heart sound (S4)	Extra heart sound, low pitched, heard in late diastole. Similar to sound of a gallop	Forceful atrial contraction from resistance to ventricular filling (e.g., in left ventricular hypertrophy, aortic stenosis, hypertension, coronary artery disease)
Arterial bruit	Turbulent flow sound in peripheral artery	Arterial obstruction or aneurysm
Heart murmurs	Turbulent sounds between normal heart sounds. Note loudness, pitch, shape, quality, duration, timing	Heart valve disorder, abnormal blood flow patterns
Pericardial friction rub	High-pitched, scratchy sound during S_1 and/or S_2 at the apex. Heard best with patient sitting and leaning forward while holding breath at end expiration	Pericarditis
Pulse deficit	Apical HR exceeding peripheral pulse rate	Dysrhythmias, most often atrial fibrillation/flutter or premature ventricular contractions

[a]Limited to common abnormal assessment findings and etiologic factors. (Further discussion of conditions listed is found in Chapters 36 to 42).

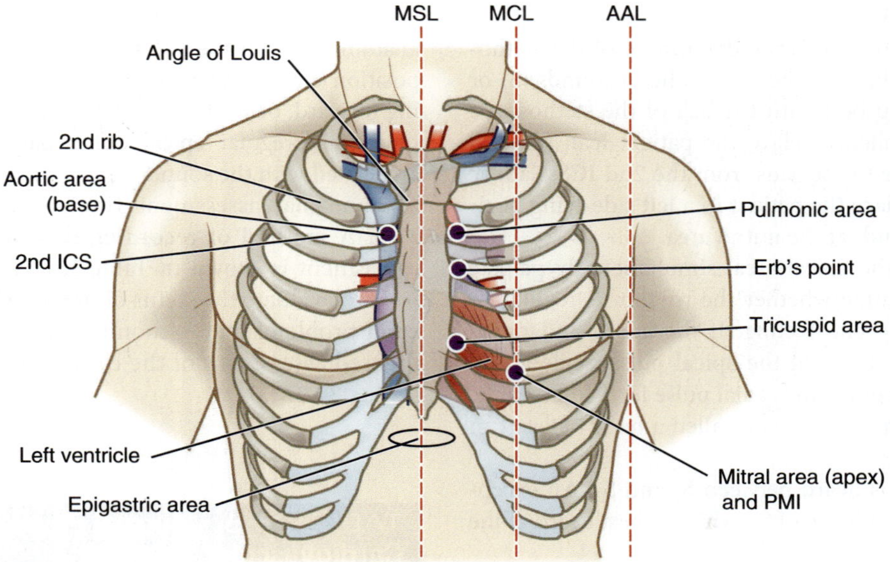

Fig. 35.7 Orientation of the heart within the thorax and cardiac auscultatory areas. *Red lines* indicate the midsternal line *(MSL)*, midclavicular line *(MCL)*, and anterior axillary line *(AAL)*. *ICS*, Intercostal space; *PMI*, point of maximal impulse.

Thorax

Inspection and palpation. Begin examining the thorax with a general inspection and palpation. Next, inspect and palpate the areas where the heart valves project their sounds by finding the intercostal spaces (ICSs). The raised notch, the *angle of Louis,* is where the manubrium and body of the sternum join at the level of the 2nd rib. It is palpable in the midline of the sternum. Palpate for the 2nd ICS, then count each ICSs to find specific auscultatory areas (Fig. 35.7).

Locate the following auscultatory areas: aortic area in the 2nd ICS to the right of the sternum, pulmonic area in the 2nd ICS to the left of the sternum, tricuspid area in the 5th left ICS close to the sternum, and mitral area in the left midclavicular line at the 5th ICS. A 5th auscultatory area is the *Erb point,* located at the 3rd left ICS near the sternum. Normally, we cannot feel pulsations in these areas unless the patient has a thin chest wall. A heart valve disorder may be present if you feel abnormal pulsations or thrills.

Next, inspect and palpate the epigastric area on either side of the midline just below the xiphoid process. In a thin person, you may see abdominal aortic pulsations. Normally, you can palpate the aorta here. Next, inspect the precordium, which is over the heart, for heaves. **Heaves** are sustained lifts of the chest wall in the precordial area that you can see or palpate. They may be caused by left ventricular hypertrophy.

When the patient is supine, palpate the mitral valve area for the **point of maximal impulse (PMI)** (also called the *apical pulse*). This reflects the pulsation of the apex of the heart. The PMI lies medial to the midclavicular line in the 4th or 5th ICS. If you can palpate the PMI, record its position in relation to the midclavicular line and ICSs. If the PMI is below the 5th ICS and left of the midclavicular line, the heart may be enlarged.

Auscultation. Normal heart sounds are made by the movement of blood through the heart valves. We can hear these sounds through a stethoscope placed on the chest wall. The first heart sound (S_1) represents closure of the tricuspid and mitral valves. It has a soft lubb sound. The second heart sound (S_2) represents closure of the aortic and pulmonic valves. It has a sharp dupp sound. S_1 signals the beginning of systole. S_2 signals the beginning of diastole (Fig. 35.8). Listen to the auscultatory areas in sequence (Fig. 35.7).

S_1 and S_2 are heard best with the diaphragm of the stethoscope because they are high pitched. Extra heart sounds (S_3 or S_4), if present, are heard best with the bell of the stethoscope because they are low pitched. Have the patient lean forward while sitting to enhance the sounds from the 2nd ICSs (aortic and pulmonic areas). Place the patient in a left side-lying position to enhance the sounds at the mitral area.

When auscultating the apical area, simultaneously palpate the radial pulse. Determine whether the rhythm is regular or irregular while listening and feeling. If the apical and radial pulses are not equivalent, count the apical pulse while a 2nd person simultaneously counts the radial pulse for 1 full minute. A difference between the 2 numbers, called a *pulse deficit,* can indicate dysrhythmias.

Normally no sound is heard between S_1 and S_2. An exception to this is a normal splitting of S_2, which is best heard at the pulmonic area during inspiration. Splitting of S_2 can be abnormal if it is heard during expiration or if it is constant (fixed) during the respiratory cycle. Describe any sounds heard in addition to S_1 and S_2.

The S_3 heart sound is a low-intensity vibration of the ventricular walls usually from decreased compliance of the ventricles during filling. An S_3 heart sound may be normal (physiologic) in young adults. It is pathologic in patients with left-sided HF or mitral valve regurgitation. S_3 is heard closely after S_2. It is known as a ventricular gallop.

The S_4 heart sound is a low-frequency vibration caused by atrial contraction. It precedes S_1 of the next cycle and is known as an atrial gallop. An S_4 heart sound may be normal in older adults with no evidence of heart disease. It is pathologic in patients with CAD, cardiomyopathy, left ventricular hypertrophy, or aortic stenosis.

Murmurs, if heard, are graded on a 6-point Roman numeral scale based on loudness and recorded as a ratio. I/VI means a murmur that is barely audible with the stethoscope, heard only in a quiet room and then not easily. VI/VI means a murmur that you can hear with the stethoscope lifted just off the chest wall.

Pericardial friction rubs are sounds that occur when inflamed surfaces of the pericardium (pericarditis) move against each other. They are high-pitched, scratchy sounds that may be intermittent and may last several hours to days. Friction rubs are heard best at the apex with patients upright, leaning forward, and holding their breath after expiration.[5]

Record the characteristics of any abnormal sounds. This includes the timing (during systole or diastole), location (the anatomic site on the chest where it is heard the loudest), and position (heard best when the patient is supine, sitting and leaning forward, or in the left side-lying position).[5] Note any other findings (irregular apical pulse, palpable chest wall heaves) associated with the sound.

Abnormal assessment findings are described in Table 35.4. A method of recording data from the cardiovascular assessment is shown in Table 35.5. A focused assessment is used to evaluate the status of previously identified cardiovascular problems and to monitor for signs of new problems. A focused assessment of the cardiovascular system is outlined in Box 35.2.

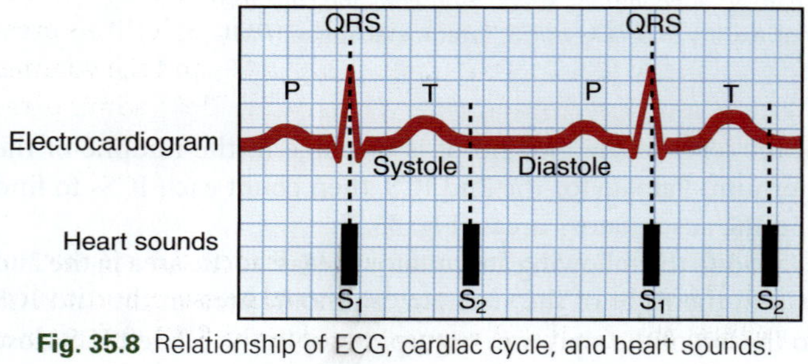

Fig. 35.8 Relationship of ECG, cardiac cycle, and heart sounds.

TABLE 35.5 Normal Physical Assessment of Cardiovascular System

Inspection	No pallor or cyanosis. PMI not visible. No JVD with patient at 45-degree angle
Palpation	Skin warm. Capillary refill <2 sec. PMI palpable in 4th ICS at left MCL. No thrills or heaves. Slight palpable pulsations of abdominal aorta in epigastric area. Carotid and extremity pulses 2+ and equal bilaterally. No pedal or sacral edema
Auscultation	S_1 and S_2 heard. Apical-radial pulse rate equal, 72, and regular. No murmurs or extra heart sounds

MCL, Midclavicular line; *PMI,* point of maximal impulse.

Case Study

Objective Data: Physical Assessment

(© Jupiterimages/ Banana-Stock/ Thinkstock.)

Physical assessment findings of L.P. are as follows:

- BP 100/54, apical pulse rate 154 and irregular, respiratory rate 20, temperature 98.2°F (36.8°C), O_2 saturation 94% on room air
- Awake, alert, and oriented ×3
- Lungs clear on auscultation; systolic murmur present
- Heart monitor shows atrial fibrillation with a rapid ventricular response
- +1 pedal pulses bilaterally
- No peripheral edema, JVD, or heaves noted

Discussion Questions

1. Which physical assessment findings most concern you?
2. Based on the results of the subjective and physical assessment findings, what diagnostic studies do you think will be ordered for L.P.?

You will learn more about diagnostic studies related to the cardiovascular system in the next section.

Answers available at http://evolve.elsevier.com/Lewis/medsurg.

HEMODYNAMIC MONITORING

Hemodynamic monitoring is the measurement of pressure, flow, and oxygenation within the cardiovascular system. The purpose of hemodynamic monitoring is to assess heart function, fluid balance, and the effects of fluids and drugs on CO. Both invasive (internally placed) and noninvasive (externally placed) devices measure hemodynamic parameters (values). These include systemic and pulmonary arterial pressures, central venous pressure (CVP), pulmonary artery wedge pressure (PAWP) (also called pulmonary artery occlusive pressure [PAOP]), CO/cardiac index (CI), SV/SV index (SVI), O_2 saturation of the hemoglobin of arterial blood (SaO_2), and mixed venous O_2 saturation (SvO_2).

From these measurements, you can calculate other values. These include the resistance of the systemic and pulmonary arterial vasculature and O_2 content, delivery, and consumption. The combined data provide a picture of the patient's hemodynamic status and the effects of therapy over time (trends). Pay attention to accuracy of measurement to help guide effective treatment.

BOX 35.2 FOCUSED ASSESSMENT

Cardiovascular System

Use this checklist to remind you of the key assessment steps.

Subjective

Ask the patient about the following and note responses.

Chest pain, discomfort	Y	N
Palpitations	Y	N
Shortness of breath (especially when lying down or at rest)	Y	N
Edema in legs or any part of body	Y	N
Leg pain during exercise	Y	N
Excess urination at night	Y	N

Objective: Diagnostic

Check the following for critical values or changes.

Cardiac biomarkers	✓
Hematocrit, hemoglobin, platelets	✓
Glucose, electrolytes, BUN, creatinine	✓
ECG	✓
Chest x-ray	✓

Objective: Physical Assessment

Inspect and Palpate

Anterior chest wall for pulsations and heaves	✓
Pulses for symmetry, quality, and rhythm	✓

Auscultate

Bilateral BP	✓
Heart for rate, rhythm, and sounds	✓

Hemodynamic Measurements

Cardiac Output and Cardiac Index

CO is the volume of blood in liters pumped by the heart in 1 minute. **Cardiac index** (CI) is the measurement of CO adjusted for body surface area (BSA). CI reflects the relative CO for the body size. The normal CI is 2.8 to 4.2 L per minute per meter squared (L/min/m^2).[13] The volume ejected with each heartbeat is the SV. Like CI, *stroke volume index* (SVI) is the measurement of SV adjusted for BSA.

CO and the forces opposing blood flow determine BP. SVR (opposition encountered by the left ventricle) or *pulmonary vascular resistance* (PVR) (opposition encountered by the right ventricle) is the resistance to blood flow by the vessels. Preload, afterload, and contractility determine SV and thus CO. Table 35.6 presents the formulas and values for common hemodynamic parameters.

Preload

Preload is the volume in the ventricle at the end of diastole. Chamber volume measurements are hard to obtain so we use pressure measurements to estimate the volume. Left ventricular preload is the *left ventricular end-diastolic pressure.* PAWP reflects left ventricular end-diastolic pressure under normal conditions (i.e., when there is no mitral valve dysfunction, intracardiac defect, or dysrhythmia). CVP is measured in the right atrium or in the vena cava close to the heart. It is the right ventricular preload or right ventricular end-diastolic pressure when there is no tricuspid valve dysfunction, intracardiac defect, or dysrhythmia.

The clinical measurement of preload is not a direct measurement of the muscle stretch. The measurement is of the pressure at the time of the peak stretch (end diastole). This pressure indirectly indicates the amount of stretch and the volume. Diuresis and vasodilation decrease preload. Fluid administration increases preload.

Afterload

Afterload refers to the forces opposing ventricular ejection of blood. These forces include systemic arterial pressure, aortic valve resistance, and the blood volume and density. SVR and arterial

TABLE 35.6 Resting Hemodynamic Parameters

Indicators	Normal Range
Preload	
Pulmonary artery diastolic pressure (PADP)	4–12 mm Hg
Pulmonary artery wedge pressure (PAWP) or left atrial pressure (LAP)	6–12 mm Hg
Right atrial pressure (RAP) or central venous pressure (CVP)	2–8 mm Hg
Right ventricular end-diastolic volume (RVEDV) = $\frac{\text{Stroke volume (SV)}}{\text{Right ventricular ejection fraction (RVEF)}}$	100–160 mL
Afterload	
$\text{MAP} = \frac{\text{Systolic blood pressure} + 2\text{ (Diastolic blood pressure)}}{3^a}$	70–105 mm Hg
$\text{PAMP} = \frac{\text{Pulmonary artery systolic pressure (PASP)} + 2\text{PADP}}{3^a}$	10–20 mm Hg
Pulmonary vascular resistance (PVR) = $\frac{\text{(Pulmonary artery pressure [PAMP]} - \text{PAWP)} \times 80}{\text{Cardiac output (CO)}}$	<250 dynes/sec/cm^{-5}
Pulmonary vascular resistance index (PVRI) = $\frac{\text{[PAMP} - \text{PAWP]} \times 80}{\text{Cardiac index (CI)}}$	160–380 dynes/sec/cm^{-5}/m^2
Systemic vascular resistance (SVR) = $\frac{\text{(Mean arterial pressure [MAP]} - \text{CVP)} \times 80}{\text{CO}}$	800–1200 dynes/sec/cm^{-5}
Systemic vascular resistance index (SVRI) = $\frac{\text{(MAP} - \text{CVP)} \times 80}{\text{CI}}$	1970–2390 dynes/sec/cm^{-5}/m^2
Other	
$\text{CI} = \frac{\text{CO}}{\text{Body surface area (BSA)}}$	2.2–4 L/min/m^2
CO = SV × HR	4–8 L/min
Heart rate	60–100 beats/min
$\text{RVEF} = \frac{\text{SV}}{\text{RVEDV} \times \text{V100}}$	40%–60%
$\text{Stoke volume} = \frac{\text{CO}}{\text{Heart rate}}$	60–150 mL/beat
Stoke volume index (SVI) = $\frac{\text{CI}}{\text{Heart rate}}$	30–65 mL/beat/m^2
Stoke volume variation (SVV) = $\frac{SV_{max} - SV_{min}}{SV_{mean}}$	<13%
Oxygenation	
Arterial hemoglobin O_2 saturation	95%–100%
Mixed venous hemoglobin O_2 saturation	60%–80%
Venous hemoglobin O_2 saturation	70%

[a]This formula is an approximation because it does not take the heart rate into consideration. The monitor measures the area under the pressure curve and HR to calculate MAP and PAMP.

pressure are indices of left ventricular afterload, but they do not include all the components of afterload. SVR is the resistance of the systemic vascular bed. Similarly, PVR and pulmonary arterial pressure are indices of right ventricular afterload. PVR is the resistance of the pulmonary vascular bed (Table 35.6).

Increased afterload often results in a decreased CO and increased O_2 demand. CO can be improved and myocardial O_2 needs reduced by decreasing afterload (i.e., decreasing forces opposing contraction). For example, vasodilator drug therapy (e.g., milrinone) can reduce afterload.

Contractility

Contractility describes the strength of contraction. Epinephrine, norepinephrine, isoproterenol (Isuprel), dopamine, dobutamine, digitalis-like drugs, calcium, and milrinone increase or improve contractility. We call these drugs *positive inotropes.* Increased contractility results in increased SV and increased myocardial O_2 needs. *Negative inotropes* reduce contractility. These include certain drugs (e.g., calcium channel blockers, β-adrenergic blockers) and clinical conditions (e.g., acidosis).

There are no direct clinical measures of cardiac contractility. Measuring the patient's preload (PAWP) and CO and graphing the results indirectly indicate contractility. If preload, HR, and afterload remain constant and CO changes, then contractility changed. Contractility is reduced in the failing heart and with cardiac ischemia.[7]

Noninvasive Hemodynamic Monitoring

Methods to estimate CO noninvasively include pulse wave analysis, thoracic electrical bioimpedance or bioreactance, and pulse wave transit time. Noninvasive finger cuff devices or a sensor over the radial artery provides a method of continuous monitoring through pulse wave analysis. CO and BP are calculated from pulsation and pressure waveform analysis in the digital arteries. Bioimpedance methods use electrodes to sense changes in electrical conductivity of the blood and estimate SV. Pulse wave transit time is the time the pulse wave needs to travel from the heart to the peripheral arteries. It can be measured with a device that includes electrodes and pulse oximetry.[8]

CO also can be measured noninvasively and reliably using ultrasound (US) technology. Both transesophageal echocardiography (TEE) and ultrasonic CO monitoring have provided consistent values similar to the standard method of thermodilution CO. Noninvasive CO measurement is less reliable when the patient has structural changes in the heart anatomy.[9]

Major uses of noninvasive hemodynamic monitoring include (1) detecting early signs and symptoms of pulmonary or cardiac problems, (2) determining cardiac or pulmonary cause of dyspnea, (3) evaluating the cause and managing hypotension, (4) monitoring after removing a PA catheter or justifying insertion of a PA catheter, (5) evaluating drug therapy, and (6) diagnosing rejection after heart transplantation. Some noninvasive methods of measuring hemodynamic parameters are less accurate than invasive methods. However, noninvasive methods decrease the patient's risks (i.e., sepsis) from invasive methods.[10]

Principles of Invasive Pressure Monitoring

Invasive lines are used in the ICU to measure systemic and pulmonary BPs. Fig. 35.9 shows the parts of a typical invasive arterial BP monitoring system. The catheter, pressure tubing, flush system, and transducer are disposable.

Pressure monitoring equipment is referenced and zero-balanced to the environment, and dynamic response characteristics are optimized for accuracy. *Referencing* means placing the transducer so that the zero-reference point is at the level of the atria of the heart. The stopcock nearest the transducer is used for the zero reference. To place this level with the atria, use an external landmark, the phlebostatic axis. To find the *phlebostatic axis,* draw 2 imaginary lines with the patient supine (Fig. 35.10A). Draw a horizontal line from the axilla, midway between the anterior and posterior chest walls. Draw a vertical line laterally through the 4th ICS along the chest wall. The phlebostatic axis is the intersection of the 2 imaginary lines. Mark this location on the patient's chest with a permanent marker. Position the port of the stopcock nearest the transducer level at the phlebostatic axis. Tape the transducer to the patient's chest at the phlebostatic axis, or ideally mount it on a bedside pole (Fig. 35.10B).

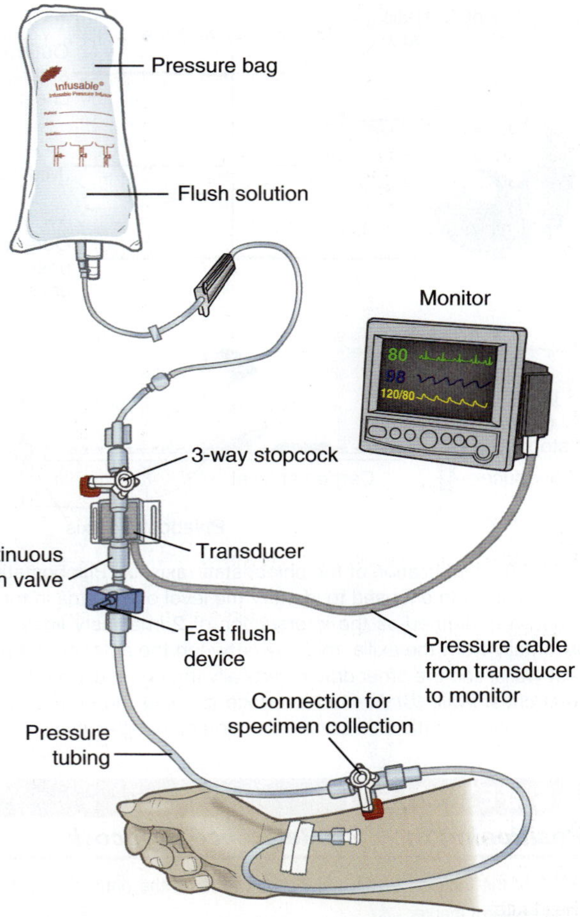

Fig. 35.9 Parts of a pressure monitoring system. The cannula, shown entering the radial artery, is connected via pressure (nondistensible) tubing to the transducer. The transducer converts the pressure wave into an electronic signal. The transducer is wired to the electronic monitoring system, which amplifies, conditions, displays, and records the signal. Stopcocks allow for specimen withdrawal and referencing and zero-balancing procedures. A flush system, consisting of a pressurized bag of IV fluid, tubing, and a flush device, is connected to the system. The flush system provides continuous slow (~3 mL/hr) flushing and a mechanism for fast flushing of lines.

Zeroing confirms that when pressure within the system is zero, the monitor reads 0. To do this, open the reference stopcock to room air (off to the patient) and observe the monitor for a reading of 0. This allows the monitor to use the atmospheric pressure as a reference for 0. Zero the transducer during the initial setup, immediately after insertion of the arterial line, when the transducer has been disconnected from the pressure cable or the pressure cable has been disconnected from the monitor and when the accuracy of the measurements is questioned. Always follow the manufacturer's guidelines.

Optimizing dynamic response characteristics involves checking that the equipment reproduces, without distortion, a signal that changes rapidly. Perform a *dynamic response test (square wave test)* every 8 to 12 hours, when the system is opened to air, or when you question the accuracy of the measurements. It involves activating the fast flush and checking that the equipment reproduces a distortion-free signal (Fig. 35.11).[7]

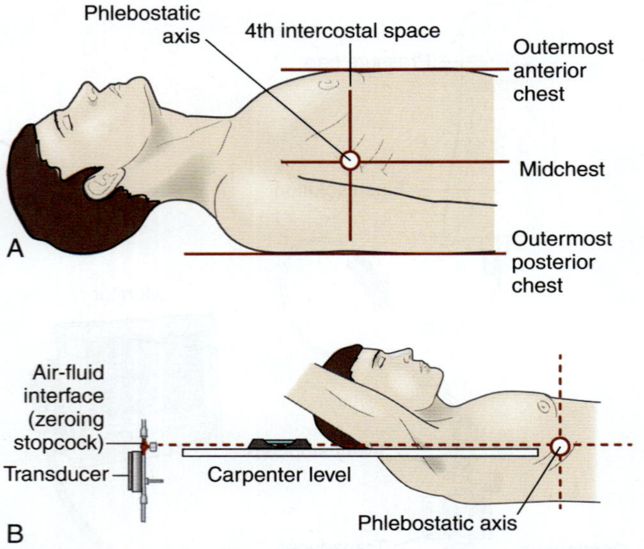

Fig. 35.10 Identification of the phlebostatic axis. (A) Phlebostatic axis is an external landmark used to identify the level of the atria in the supine patient. It is defined as the intersection of 2 imaginary lines: 1 drawn horizontally from the axilla, midway between the anterior and posterior chest walls, and the other drawn vertically through the 4th ICS along the lateral chest wall. (B) Air-fluid interface (zeroing the stopcock) is level with the phlebostatic axis using a carpenter's or laser level.

! SAFETY ALERT

Positioning the Zero Reference Stopcock

- Mark the location of the phlebostatic axis on the patient's chest with a permanent marker.
- Recheck the leveling of the zero-reference stopcock to the phlebostatic axis with any change in the patient's position.
- Transducers higher than the phlebostatic axis will produce falsely low BP readings.
- Transducers lower than the phlebostatic axis will produce falsely high BP readings.

Types of Invasive Pressure Monitoring

Arterial BP

Continuous arterial BP monitoring is indicated for patients in many situations. These include acute hypotension and hypertension, respiratory failure, shock, neurologic injury, coronary interventional procedures, continuous infusion of vasoactive drugs (e.g., norepinephrine), and frequent arterial blood gas (ABG) sampling. A nontapered Teflon catheter is typically used to cannulate an artery (e.g., radial, femoral) using a percutaneous approach. After insertion, the HCP usually sutures the catheter in place. Immobilize the insertion site to prevent dislodging or kinking the catheter line.

Measurements. Use the arterial line to obtain systolic, diastolic, and mean arterial pressure (MAP) (Fig. 35.12). Table 35.7 outlines the steps in obtaining BP measurements with an invasive line. Values with the head of the bed elevated up to 45 degrees are generally equal to measurements with the patient supine unless the patient's BP is extremely sensitive to orthostatic changes. It is important to keep the zero-reference stopcock level with the phlebostatic axis to ensure accurate continuous measurements.

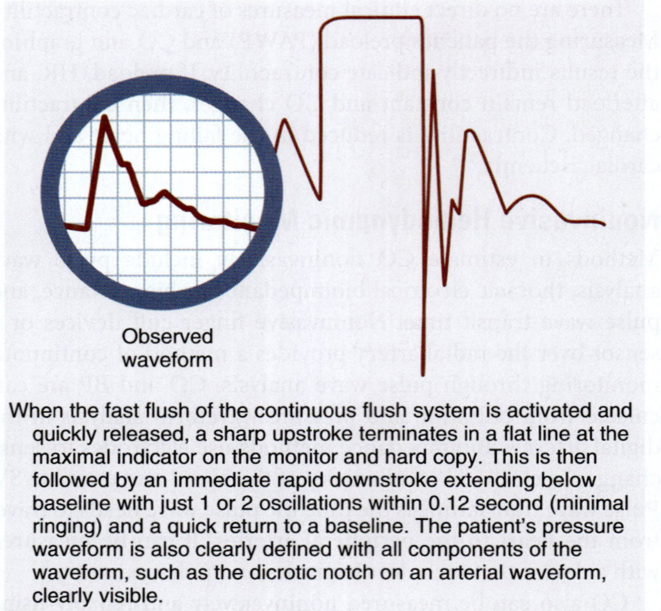

Fig. 35.11 Optimally damped system. Dynamic response test using the fast flush system: normal response. No adjustment in the monitoring system is needed. (From Darovic GO, Vanriper S, Vanriper J: Fluid-filled monitoring systems. In Darovic GO, editor: *Hemodynamic monitoring*, ed 2, Philadelphia, 1995, Saunders.)

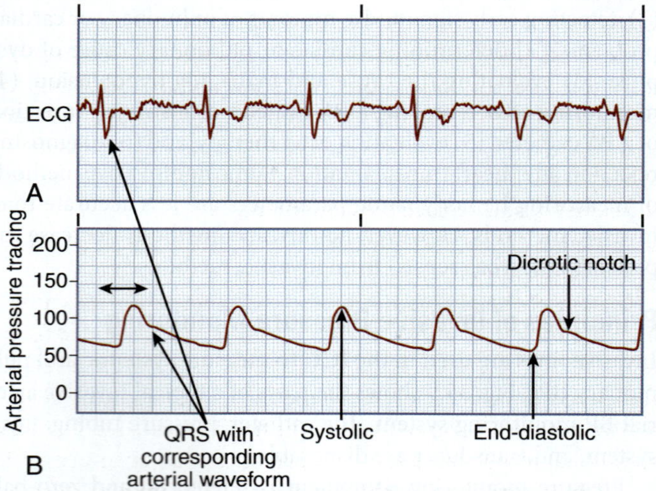

Fig. 35.12 (A) Simultaneously recorded ECG tracing. (B) Systemic arterial pressure tracing. Systolic pressure is the peak pressure. The *dicrotic notch* indicates aortic valve closure. Diastolic pressure is the lowest value before contraction. Mean pressure is the average pressure over time calculated by the monitoring equipment. (Modified from Urden LD, Stacy KM, Lough ME: *Critical care nursing: diagnosis and management*, ed 6, St Louis, 2010, Mosby.)

Set the high- and low-pressure alarms based on the patient's status. Various patient conditions will change the pressure tracings. In HF, the systolic upstroke may be slower. In volume depletion, systolic pressure varies with mechanical ventilation, decreasing during inspiration. Tracings of the arterial wave may be documented in the health record. Observe simultaneous ECG and pressure tracings with dysrhythmias. Urgently address dysrhythmias that significantly decrease arterial BP.

TABLE 35.7 Invasive Arterial Blood Pressure Measurement

1. Explain the procedure to the patient.
2. Position the patient supine and flat or, if appropriate, with the head of the bed less than 45 degrees or prone.
3. Confirm that the zero reference (port of the stopcock nearest the transducer) is at the level of the phlebostatic axis (Fig. 35.10). If the reference stopcock is not taped to the patient's chest, use a leveling device to position the stopcock on a bedside pole at the point level with the phlebostatic axis.
4. Observe the monitor tracing, and assess the quality of the tracing. Perform a dynamic response test (Fig. 35.11).
5. Obtain an analog printout (if available), and measure the systolic and diastolic pressures at end expiration (Fig. 35.12). If no printout is available, freeze the tracing on the oscilloscope screen. Use the cursor to measure the pressures at end expiration.
6. Record the pressure measurements promptly. Include (if available) the printout marked to identify the points read.

Complications. Arterial lines carry the risk for hemorrhage, infection, thrombus formation, neurovascular impairment, and loss of limb. Hemorrhage is most likely to occur if the catheter dislodges or the line disconnects. To avoid this complication, use Luer-Lok connections, monitor the arterial waveform, and activate alarms. If the pressure in the line falls (e.g., when the line is disconnected), the low-pressure alarm sounds immediately, notifying you to promptly correct the problem.

To limit the risk for catheter-related infection, inspect the insertion site for local signs of inflammation. Monitor the patient for signs of systemic infection. Change the pressure tubing, flush bag, and transducer every 96 hours or according to agency policy. If you suspect infection, notify the HCP, remove the catheter, and replace the equipment.

Circulatory impairment can result from formation of a thrombus around the catheter, release of an embolus, spasm, or occlusion of the circulation by the catheter. Before inserting a line into the radial artery, perform an *Allen test* to confirm that ulnar circulation to the hand is adequate. Apply pressure to the radial and ulnar arteries simultaneously. If the patient is able, ask the patient to open and close the hand repeatedly. The hand should blanch. Release the pressure on the ulnar artery while maintaining pressure on the radial artery. If pinkness does not return within 6 seconds, the ulnar artery is not adequate. You should not use the radial artery on that limb for line insertion.

Once the catheter is inserted, assess the neurovascular status distal to the arterial insertion site hourly. The limb with compromised arterial flow will be cool and pale, with capillary refill time longer than 3 seconds. The patient may have symptoms of neurovascular impairment (e.g., paresthesia, pain, paralysis). This is an emergency and must be reported to the HCP at once to avoid the loss of a limb.

To maintain line patency and limit thrombus formation, assess the flush system every 1 to 4 hours to determine that the (1) pressure bag is inflated to 300 mm Hg, (2) flush bag contains fluid, and (3) system is delivering a continuous slow (1 to 3 mL/hr) flush. Follow agency policy for adding heparin to the flush solution.[7]

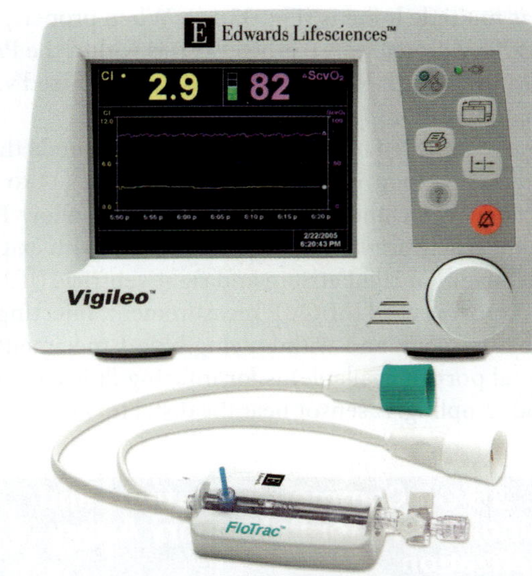

Fig. 35.13 FloTrac sensor and Vigileo monitor. (Courtesy Edwards Lifesciences, Irvine, CA.)

Arterial Pressure-Based Cardiac Output

Arterial pressure–based cardiac output (APCO) measurement is a minimally invasive technique to determine *continuous CO* (CCO)/*continuous CI* (CCI). This technology uses a sensor attached to a standard invasive arterial pressure line and a monitor (Fig. 35.13).

APCO can assess a patient's ability to increase SV in response to fluids *(preload responsiveness)* (Table 35.6). This is determined by using stroke volume variation (SVV) or measuring the percent increase in SV after a fluid bolus. SVV is the variation of the arterial pulsation caused by the heart-lung interaction. It is a sensitive indicator of preload responsiveness in some patients. SVV helps predict if a patient would benefit from additional IV fluid boluses.[11]

Measurements. *Arterial pressure* is the force generated by the ejection of blood from the left ventricle into the arterial circulation. The heart's contractions (systole) produce pulsatile pressure waves. The sensor measures the arterial pulse pressure, which is proportional to SV. APCO monitoring uses the arterial waveform characteristics, along with demographic data (e.g., gender, age, height, weight) to calculate SV, and HR to calculate CCO/CCI and SV/SVI every 20 seconds. CO is calculated by multiplying the HR and calculated SV. It is displayed on a continuous basis. APCO monitoring is often used with a central venous oximetry catheter. Together, these allow for continuous monitoring of central venous O_2 saturation ($ScvO_2$) and SVR that is derived from the CVP.

Pulmonary Artery Flow-Directed Catheter

PA pressure monitoring guides the management of patients with select complicated heart and lung problems (Table 35.8). Pulmonary artery diastolic pressure (PADP) and PAWP are sensitive indicators of heart function and fluid volume status. PADP and PAWP increase in HF and fluid volume overload. They decrease with volume depletion. PA pressures can guide fluid therapy while limiting overcorrection or undercorrection.

A PA flow-directed catheter (e.g., Swan-Ganz) is used to measure PA pressures, including PAWP. The standard PA catheter has multiple lumens (Fig. 35.14). When properly positioned, the distal lumen port (catheter tip) is within the PA. We use this port to monitor PA pressures and sample mixed venous blood (e.g., to monitor O_2 saturation).

A balloon connected to an external valve surrounds the distal lumen port. Balloon inflation has 2 purposes: (1) to allow blood to "float" the catheter forward and (2) to allow PAWP measurement. There are 1 or 2 proximal lumens, with exit ports in the right atrium or right atrium and right ventricle (if 2). The right atrium port is used for CVP measurement, injecting fluid for CO measurement, and withdrawing blood specimens. The 2nd proximal port (if available) is for infusing fluids and drugs or for blood sampling. A sensor near the distal tip monitors core temperature and is used for the thermodilution method of measuring CO.

An advanced technology PA catheter can continuously monitor the patient's SvO_2. CCO and right ventricular ejection fraction (RVEF) can be measured using advanced thermodilution technology. RVEF gives information about right ventricular function and helps to assess right heart contractility. Right ventricular end-diastolic volume, a key indicator of preload, is assessed by dividing SV by RVEF (Table 35.6).

The use of PA pressure monitoring has decreased dramatically. This is due, in part, to risks associated with this invasive technology (e.g., dysrhythmias, infection) and the development of less invasive techniques.[11]

The HCP often inserts a PA catheter at the bedside. Preparation includes arranging the monitor, cables, and infusion and pressurized flush solutions. The system is leveled and zero-referenced to the phlebostatic axis. Note the patient's electrolyte, acid-base, oxygenation, and coagulation status. Imbalances such as hypokalemia, hypomagnesemia, hypoxemia, or acidosis can make the heart more irritable. This can increase the risk for ventricular dysrhythmia during catheter insertion. Coagulopathy increases the risk for hemorrhage.

During insertion, a key nursing role is to observe the characteristic waveforms on the monitor as the HCP moves the catheter through the heart to the PA Fig. 35.15. Monitor the ECG continuously because of the risk for dysrhythmias, especially when the catheter reaches the right ventricle. After insertion and before using the PA catheter, obtain a chest x-ray to confirm catheter placement. Note and record the measurement at the exit point. Apply an occlusive sterile dressing and change it according to agency policy.[7]

TABLE 35.8 Common Indications and Contraindications for Pulmonary Artery Catheterization

Indications
- Assessment of response to therapy in mixed types of shock
- Cardiogenic shock
- Differential diagnosis and response to therapy in pulmonary hypertension
- MI with complications (e.g., HF, cardiogenic shock)
- Potentially reversible systolic HF
- Severe chronic HF requiring vasoactive drug therapy
- Transplantation workup

Contraindications
- Coagulopathy
- Endocardial pacemaker
- Endocarditis
- Mechanical tricuspid or pulmonic valve
- Right heart mass (e.g., thrombus, tumor)

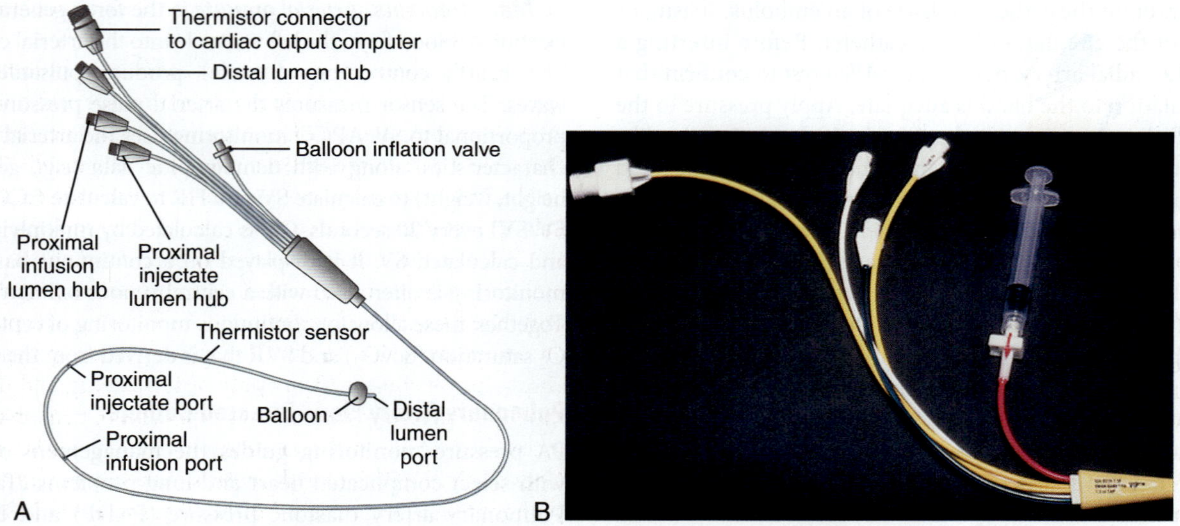

Fig. 35.14 Pulmonary artery (PA) catheter. (A) Catheter with 5 lumens. When properly positioned, the distal lumen exit port is in the PA and the proximal lumen ports are in the right atrium and right ventricle. The distal and 1 of the proximal ports are used to measure PA and CVP, respectively. A balloon surrounds the catheter near the distal end. The balloon inflation valve is used to inflate the balloon with air to allow reading of the PAWP. A thermistor near the distal tip senses PA temperature and measures thermodilution cardiac output when solution cooler than body temperature is injected into a proximal port. (B) Photo of an actual catheter. (B, Courtesy Edwards Critical Care Division, Baxter Healthcare Corporation, Santa Ana, CA.)

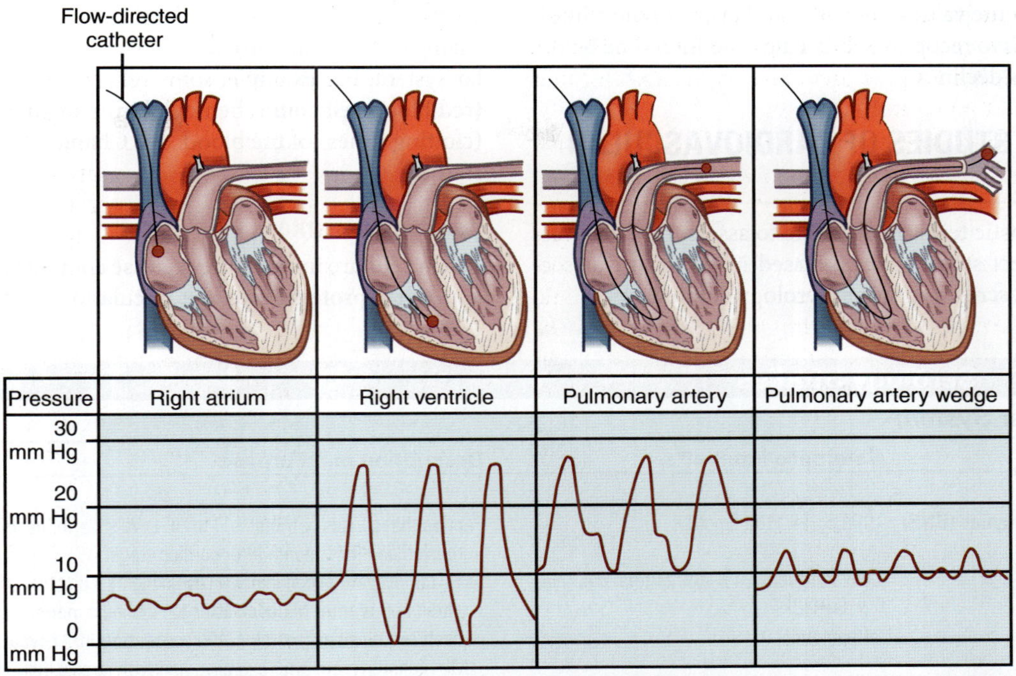

Fig. 35.15 Position of the pulmonary artery flow-directed catheter during progressive stages of insertion with corresponding pressure waveforms. (Modified from Urden LD, Stacy KM, Lough ME: *Critical care nursing: diagnosis and management,* ed 6, St Louis, 2010, Mosby.)

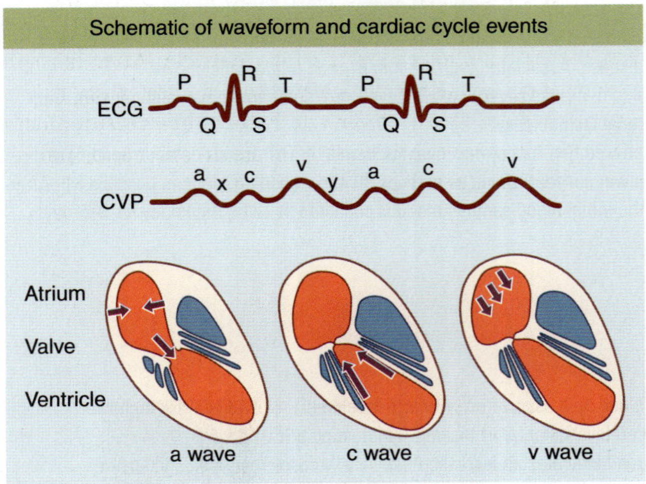

Fig. 35.16 Cardiac events that produce the CVP waveform with *a, c,* and *v* waves. The *a* wave represents atrial contraction. The *x* descent represents atrial relaxation. The *c* wave represents the bulging of the closed tricuspid valve into the right atrium during ventricular systole. The *v* wave represents atrial filling. The *y* descent represents opening of the tricuspid valve and filling of the ventricle. (Modified from Urden LD, Stacy KM, Lough ME: *Critical care nursing: diagnosis and management,* ed 6, St Louis, 2010, Mosby.)

Central Venous or Right Atrial Pressure Measurement

CVP is a measurement of right ventricular preload and reflects fluid volume status. We most often measure it with a central venous catheter placed in the internal jugular or subclavian vein. It can be measured with a PA catheter using the proximal lumen in the right atrium. CVP waveforms (Fig. 35.16) are similar to PAWP waveforms. CVP is measured as a mean pressure at the end of expiration. A high CVP indicates right ventricular failure or volume overload. A low CVP indicates hypovolemia.[11]

❖ NURSING MANAGEMENT: HEMODYNAMIC MONITORING

Assessment of hemodynamic status requires integrating data from many sources and trending data over time. Comprehensive nursing observations give important clues about the patient's hemodynamic status.

Begin by obtaining baseline data about the patient's general appearance, level of consciousness, skin color and temperature, vital signs, peripheral pulses, capillary refill, and urine output. Does the patient appear tired, weak, or exhausted? There may be too little cardiac reserve to sustain even minimum activity. Pallor, cool skin, and decreased pulses may indicate decreased CO. Changes in mental status may reflect problems with cerebral perfusion or oxygenation. Monitor urine output to determine the adequacy of perfusion to the kidneys. The patient with decreased perfusion to the GI tract may develop hypoactive or absent bowel sounds. If the patient is bleeding and developing shock, the BP may be stable at first. The patient may become increasingly pale and cool from peripheral vasoconstriction. Conversely, the patient with septic shock may be warm and pink yet have tachycardia and BP instability. Increased HRs are common in stressed, compromised, critically ill patients. However, sustained tachycardia increases myocardial O_2 demand and can result in decreased CO.

Always correlate your observations of the patient with data obtained from technology (e.g., ECG, arterial and PA pressures, $ScvO_2$, SvO_2). Single hemodynamic values are rarely helpful.

Monitor trends in the values over time and evaluate the clinical picture. The goal is to recognize early clues and intervene before the patient's status declines.[7]

DIAGNOSTIC STUDIES OF CARDIOVASCULAR SYSTEM

Numerous diagnostic tests are available to assess the cardiovascular system. Select studies are discussed in detail in this section. Table 35.9 describes common serology studies.

Blood Studies

Many blood studies provide information about the cardiovascular system. For example, some reflect the O_2-carrying capacity (red blood cell count, hemoglobin) and coagulation properties (clotting times) of the blood. See Chapter 33 about hematology studies.

Cardiac Biomarkers

When cells are injured, they release contents including enzymes and other proteins into the circulation. These *biomarkers* are

TABLE 35.9 Serology Studies

Cardiovascular System

Study	Reference Interval[a]	Description and Purpose
Biomarkers		
b-Type natriuretic peptide (BNP)	<100 pg/mL (100 pmol/L)	Peptide that causes natriuresis. ↑ in HF. Levels ↑ after nesiritide (Natrecor) infusion and for 1 month after cardiac surgery.
CK-MB	Concentrations <4%–6% of total creatine kinase (CK)	Tests for myocardial cell injury. ↑ Levels highly indicative of MI. Serum levels ↑ within 3–6 hr after MI, peak after 12–24 hours, normalize within 48 hours.
Copeptin	<10 pmol/L	Reflects arginine vasopressin (AVP) concentration. ↑ Levels highly indicative of MI. Higher in men, after exercise, and with stress. Influenced by fasting and water load.
C-reactive protein (CRP)	High-sensitivity CRP assay. *Lowest risk:* <1 mg/dL *Moderate risk:* 1–3 mg/dL *High risk:* >3 mg/dL	Marker of inflammation. May help predict risk for cardiac disease and cardiac events such as an acute MI. ↑ in bacterial infections and inflammatory disorders.
Homocysteine	4–14 μmol/L Levels may ↑ with age	Amino acid made during protein catabolism. Risk factor for cardiovascular disease. Associated with vitamin B_{12} and folate deficiencies.
N-terminal (NT)-Pro-BNP	*≤74 years:* 124 pg/mL *>75 years:* 449 pg/mL	Helps to assess severity of HF. Levels are higher in women and patients with renal insufficiency.
Troponin (cardiac)	*Troponin T (cTnT)* <0.1 ng/mL (<0.1 mcg/L) *High sensitivity Troponin T (hsTnT):* <14 ng/L for women <22 ng/L for men *Troponin I (cTnI)* *Negative:* <0.03 ng/mL (<0.03 mcg/L)	Preferred test for cardiac injury/ischemia: hsTnT assays detect troponins at lower concentrations as early as 90 min, speeding triage in possible MI. After the initial blood sample, blood is collected at 12 hr, then daily for 3–5 days.
Lipids		
Cholesterol	<200 mg/dL (<5.2 mmol/L) (varies with age and gender)	A blood lipid associated with arteriosclerosis. ↑ Level is a risk factor for cardiovascular heart disease. Nonfasting or fasting.
Lipoprotein (a) (Lp[a])	<30 mg/dL (<0.3 g/L)	↑ Level indicates an increased risk for atherosclerosis, MI, and stroke. Nonfasting or fasting.
Lipoprotein-associated phospholipase A_2 (Lp-PLA_2)	*Low risk:* ≤151 ng/mL *Moderate risk:* 152–194 ng/mL *High risk:* ≥195 ng/mL	Indicates inflammation and increased risk for CAD. Nonfasting or fasting.
Lipoproteins (HDL, LDL)	HDL Recommended *Male:* >45 mg/dL *Female:* >55 mg/dL *Low risk for CAD:* ≥60 mg/dL *High risk for CAD:* <40 mg/dL LDL <130 mg/dL *Moderate risk for CAD:* 130–159 mg/dL *High risk for CAD:* >160 mg/dL	There are marked day-to-day fluctuations, so more than 1 level is needed for accurate diagnosis. Nonfasting or fasting. Assess risk for heart disease by dividing the total cholesterol level by the HDL level and obtaining a ratio. *Low risk:* Ratio <3 *Average risk:* Ratio 3–5 *Increased risk:* Ratio >5
Triglycerides	*Male:* 40–160 mg/dL *Female:* 35–135 mg/dL	Mixtures of fatty acids. Elevations are associated with cardiovascular disease and diabetes. Avoid alcohol for 24 hr before testing. Nonfasting or fasting.

[a]Reference ranges for the laboratory tests vary by agency because of differences in equipment and reagents used.

useful in diagnosing acute coronary syndrome (ACS) (Table 35.9). Interpreting biomarker level results requires you to consider the time elapsed from the onset of symptoms. Other data (patient symptoms, history, and ECG changes) complete the diagnostic picture for the patient with suspected ACS.

Cardiac-specific troponin is a heart muscle protein released into circulation after injury or infarction. Two subtypes, cardiac-specific troponin T (cTnT) and cardiac-specific troponin I (cTnI), are specific to heart muscle. Normally the troponin level in the blood is very low. A rise in level is diagnostic of myocardial infarction (MI) or injury. cTnT and cTnI are detectable within hours (on average 4 to 6 hours) of MI or injury, peak at 10 to 24 hours, and can be detected for up to 10 to 14 days. Troponin is the biomarker of choice in diagnosing ACS. High-sensitivity troponin (hs-cTnT, hs-cTnI) assays provide even earlier detection of a heart event, within 1 to 3 hours.[12]

Copeptin, a substitute marker for arginine vasopressin (AVP), can be detected in patients with an acute MI, ischemic stroke, or HF. Considering both troponin and copeptin levels together may provide increased sensitivity for rapidly diagnosing acute MI. High copeptin levels are associated with increased mortality in patients with acute MI.[13]

Creatine kinase (CK) enzymes are found in a variety of organs and tissues and occur as 3 isoenzymes. These isoenzymes are specific to skeletal muscle (CK-MM), brain and nervous tissue (CK-BB), and the heart (CK-MB). CK-MB rise is specific for MI or cardiac injury. Levels begin to increase 3 to 6 hours after symptom onset, peak in 12 to 24 hours, and return to baseline within 12 to 48 hours after MI. CK is rarely used for diagnosis of acute MI.

C-Reactive Protein

C-reactive protein (CRP) is made by the liver during periods of acute inflammation. Increased CRP levels are linked with atherosclerosis and the first occurrence of a heart event. The CRP level may predict the risk for future heart events in patients with MI.

Homocysteine

Homocysteine (Hcy) is an amino acid made during protein catabolism. High Hcy levels can be either hereditary or from diet deficiencies of vitamin B_6, vitamin B_{12}, or folate. They are linked to a higher risk for CVD, PVD, and stroke. Hcy testing is recommended for patients with a family history of early CVD or a history of CVD in the absence of common risk factors.

Cardiac Natriuretic Peptide Markers

There are 3 natriuretic peptides: (1) atrial natriuretic peptide (ANP) from the atrium, (2) b-type natriuretic peptide (BNP) from the ventricles, and (3) c-type natriuretic peptide from endothelial and renal epithelial cells. BNP is the marker of choice for distinguishing between a cardiac or respiratory cause of dyspnea. N-terminal pro-brain natriuretic peptide (NT-pro-BNP) is secreted in the ventricles and is more sensitive but less specific than BNP as a diagnostic marker of HF. When DBP increases (e.g., HF), BNP and NT-pro-BNP are released and increase natriuresis (excretion of sodium in the urine). ANP and BNP are discussed in Chapter 36 and Chapter 38.

Serum Lipids

Serum lipids consist of triglycerides, cholesterol, and phospholipids (Table 35.9). These *lipoproteins* circulate in the blood bound to protein. A lipid panel usually measures cholesterol, triglyceride, low-density lipoprotein (LDL), and high-density lipoprotein (HDL).

Triglycerides, the main storage form of lipids, make up about 95% of fatty tissue. Cholesterol, a structural part of cell membranes and plasma lipoproteins, is a precursor of corticosteroids, sex hormones, and bile salts. It is absorbed from food in the gastrointestinal tract and synthesized in the liver. Phospholipids contain glycerol, fatty acids, phosphates, and a nitrogenous compound. Although formed in most cells, phospholipids usually enter the circulation as lipoproteins synthesized by the liver. Apoproteins are water-soluble proteins that combine with most lipids to form lipoproteins.

Different classes of lipoproteins contain varying amounts of the naturally occurring lipids. These include:

1. *Chylomicrons:* primarily exogenous triglycerides from fat intake
2. *Low-density lipoproteins (LDLs):* mostly cholesterol with moderate amounts of phospholipids
3. *High-density lipoproteins (HDLs):* about 50% protein and 50% phospholipids and cholesterol
4. *Very-low-density lipoproteins (VLDLs):* primarily endogenous triglycerides with moderate amounts of phospholipids and cholesterol

Increases in triglycerides and LDL are strongly associated with CAD. An increased HDL level is associated with a decreased risk of CAD. HDLs serve a protective role by mobilizing cholesterol from tissues.

Although a relationship exists between high serum cholesterol levels and CAD, a measure of total cholesterol alone is not enough for an assessment of CAD. A risk assessment is calculated by comparing the total cholesterol to HDL ratio over time. An increase in the ratio means increased risk.

Plasma levels of apolipoprotein A-I (apo A-I) (the major HDL protein) and the ratio of apo A-I to apolipoprotein B (apo B) (the major LDL protein) are stronger predictors of CAD than the HDL cholesterol level alone. Measurements of these lipoproteins can be useful in identifying patients at risk for CAD.

Lipoprotein (a), or Lp(a), has been studied for its role as a risk factor for CAD. Increased levels of Lp(a), especially with increased levels of lactate dehydrogenase (LDH), have been linked with atherosclerosis, especially in women.

Lipoprotein-associated phospholipase A_2 (Lp-PLA_2) is an inflammatory enzyme expressed in atherosclerotic plaques. High levels of Lp-PLA_2 are related to an increased risk for CAD.[14]

Diagnostic Studies

A number of tests provide information about the structure and function of the heart and cardiovascular system (Table 35.10).

TABLE 35.10 Diagnostic Studies

Cardiovascular System

Study	Description and Purpose	Nursing Responsibility
Electrocardiography (ECG)		
12-Lead ECG	Electrodes on the chest and extremities record cardiac electrical activity from 12 different views. A resting 12-lead ECG can identify conduction problems, dysrhythmias, position of heart, cardiac hypertrophy, pericarditis, myocardial ischemia or infarction, pacemaker activity, and effectiveness of drug therapy at 1 point in time.	*Before:* Prepare skin. Apply electrodes and leads. Place patient supine (or with head of bed elevated, if short of breath). Tell patient that no discomfort is involved and to lie still to decrease motion artifact. *During:* Ensure the patient lies still to decrease motion artifact.
ECG Event monitor or loop recorder	Records rhythm changes that are not frequent enough to be recorded in 1 24-hr period. Can aid in diagnosing the cause of chest pain, palpitations, dyspnea, and syncope. It allows more freedom than a regular Holter monitor. Some units have electrodes that attach to the chest and have a loop of memory that captures the onset and end of an event. Other types are placed directly on patient's wrist, chest, or fingers and record the patient's ECG in real time. Recordings may be transmitted over the phone to a receiving unit.	*Before:* Teach how to use equipment for recording and transmitting events. Teach patient about skin preparation for lead placement or steady skin contact to ensure quality tracings. Tell patient to start recording when symptoms begin or as soon after as possible.
ECG Holter monitoring	Recording of ECG rhythm for 24–48 hr to correlate with symptoms and activities recorded in diary. Encourage normal patient activity to simulate conditions that produce symptoms. Electrodes are placed on chest. A recorder stores information until it is recalled, printed, and analyzed for any rhythm changes.	*Before:* Prepare skin. Apply electrodes and leads. Explain importance of keeping an accurate diary of activities and symptoms. Tell patient there is no bathing and showering during monitoring. Skin irritation may develop from electrodes. If device has an event marker, teach patient to push that button when having symptoms.
Signal-averaged ECG (SAECG)	A high-resolution ECG that can identify electrical activity called late potentials. Their presence indicates a patient is at risk for developing ventricular dysrhythmias (e.g., ventricular tachycardia).	Same as for 12-lead ECG.
Functional		
6-Minute walk test	Distance patient can walk on a flat surface in 6 min. Measures response to treatments and determines functional capacity for activities of daily living. Useful in those who are debilitated or unable to perform treadmill or exercise bike testing. May be a better measure of fitness for older adults than exercise testing.	*Before:* Tell patient to wear comfortable shoes. Inform patient to carry or pull O_2 if used routinely. *During:* Encourage patient to walk as quickly as possible.
Exercise or stress testing	Provides information on cardiac function and exercise tolerance. A common protocol uses 3-min stages at set speeds and elevation of treadmill belt. The patient can exercise to either predicted peak HR (calculated by subtracting the person's age from 220) or peak exercise tolerance, at which time the test is ended. The test is end ed for chest discomfort, significant changes in vital signs from baseline, or significant ECG changes (e.g., ischemia, dysrhythmias). The ECG is monitored after exercise for ischemia and rhythm changes or, if ECG changes occurred with exercise, for return to baseline. Important diagnosing CAD. An exercise bike may be used if the patient is unable to walk on the treadmill.	*Before:* Tell patient to wear comfortable clothes and shoes fit for walking or running. Tell patient to report any symptoms. β-Blockers may be held 24 hr before the test because they blunt the HR and limit the patient's ability to achieve maximal HR. Caffeine is held for 24 hr. Patients must refrain from smoking and strenuous exercise for 3 hr before test. Obtain baseline vital signs and 12-lead-ECG. *During:* Monitor vital signs and ECG during each stage of exercise and after until all vital signs and ECG changes have returned to normal or baseline. Monitor patient's response throughout procedure for any signs of distress (e.g., angina, dyspnea).
Noninvasive hemodynamic monitoring	Obtained using a continuous finger cuff or by thoracic bioreactance/bioimpedance methods. Possible to obtain repeated measurements of SV, CO, and systemic BP.	Minimal to no risk. Patients who need hemodynamic monitoring are likely to be in perioperative settings, critical care units, and emergency departments.
Imaging		
Chest x-ray	Patient is placed in lateral and posteroanterior (PA) positions to examine lung fields and heart size (Fig. 35.17). Helps diagnosis HF and pulmonary edema and visualize heart size and contour.	*Before:* Ask about frequency of recent x-rays and chance of pregnancy. Provide lead shielding to areas not being viewed. Remove jewelry or metal objects that may obstruct the view of heart and lungs.
Cardiac computed tomography (CT); electron beam CT (EBCT)	Heart-specific imaging technology with or without IV contrast medium. Used to evaluate heart anatomy, coronary circulation, and blood vessels. EBCT, or ultrafast CT, uses a scanning electron beam to quantify calcification in coronary arteries and heart valves (Fig. 35.19). IV contrast may be used if calcium scoring is below threshold level. Primarily used for risk assessment in asymptomatic patients and to assess for heart disease in patients with atypical symptoms potentially related to cardiac causes.	*Before:* Assess for contrast allergy. Explain that patient may feel a warm sensation, salty taste after IV contrast injection, nausea. *During:* Patient must lie still during test.

TABLE 35.10 Diagnostic Studies—cont'd

Cardiovascular System

Study	Description and Purpose	Nursing Responsibility
Cardiovascular magnetic resonance imaging (CMRI)	Noninvasive imaging technique obtains information about heart tissue, EF, aneurysms, CO, and patency of proximal coronary arteries. Measures regurgitant fraction that may determine valve repair or replacement. It does not involve ionizing radiation. Is a very safe procedure. Provides images in multiple planes with uniformly good resolution.	*Before:* Check for pregnancy, allergies, and renal function before test. Have patient remove all metal objects. Remove metallic foil patches. Patient may need to be fasting. Assess for claustrophobia and need for antianxiety medication Contraindicated for persons with implanted metallic devices or other metal fragments unless noted to be MRI safe. Ask about the presence of staples, plates, dental bridges, or other metal appliances. *During:* Patient must lie completely still during test.
Coronary CT angiography (CTA)	Use of CT with injected IV contrast medium to obtain images of coronary vessels and diagnose CAD. Used to evaluate chest pain and monitor the progression of coronary vascular disease.	*Before:* Assess for contrast allergy. Obtain IV access. Remove metal objects before test. The patient may need to fast for several hours prior. A β-blocker may be given before the test to control HR. *During:* Patients must have a regular heart rhythm for accurate testing.
Echocardiogram • Contrast • M-mode • 2-dimensional • Color-flow imaging (duplex) • Real-time 3-dimensional • Pharmacologic echocardiogram	Ultrasound transducer is placed in 4 positions on the chest to record sound waves bounced off the heart. Records direction and flow of blood through the heart and transforms it to audio and graphic data. Measures valve abnormalities, congenital heart defects, wall motion, EF, and heart function. IV contrast agent may be used to enhance images (Fig. 35.18). Pharmacologic echocardiogram is a substitute for the exercise stress test in persons unable to exercise. IV adenosine, dobutamine, or dipyridamole is given over several minutes or regadenoson (Lexiscan) is given as a single bolus over 10 sec while echocardiogram is performed to detect wall motion abnormalities.	*Before:* Place patient in a left side-lying position. Tell patient about procedure and sensations (pressure and mechanical movement from head of transducer). May be difficult to obtain in patients with COPD due to large amount of air between heart and chest cavity. Pharmacologic echocardiogram: *Before:* Obtain baseline vital signs and IV access for injection of drugs. *During:* Monitor vital signs until baseline achieved. Monitor patient for signs and symptoms of distress or side effects (e.g., dyspnea, dizziness, nausea). Aminophylline may be given to prevent or reverse side effects of dipyridamole.
Exercise (stress) nuclear imaging	Identifies cardiac symptoms and rhythm changes and simulate in a safe environment. Nuclear imaging images are taken at rest. Injection is given at maximum HR (usually 85% of age-predicted maximum) on bicycle or treadmill. Patient then continues exercise for 1 min to circulate the radioactive isotope. Scanning is done 15–60 min after exercise. A resting scan is done 60–90 min after initial infusion or 24 hr later.	*Before:* Tell patient to eat only a light meal between scans. Some drugs may need to be held for 1–2 days before the scan. Patients should not have caffeine 12 hr prior. Obtain IV access. *During:* If targeted maximum HR is not achieved with exercise, test may be changed to pharmacologic imaging.
Magnetic resonance angiography (MRA)	Used for imaging vascular occlusive disease and abdominal aortic aneurysms. Same as MRI but with use of gadolinium as IV contrast medium.	*Before:* Contraindications include allergies to contrast medium and implanted metallic devices or other metal fragments unless noted to be MRA safe. Discuss any implants before scan. Obtain IV access.
Multigated acquisition (MUGA) (cardiac blood pool) scan	Small amount of the patient's blood is removed, mixed with a radioactive isotope (e.g., Technetium-99m [^{99m}Tc sestamibi]), and reinjected IV. With the ECG used for timing, images are obtained during the cardiac cycle. Indicated for patients with MI, HF, or valve disease. Can evaluate the effect of various cardiac or cardiotoxic drugs on the heart and the cardiac EF.	*Before:* Explain procedure to patient. Obtain IV access for removal of blood sample and reinjection of isotope. Start ECG monitoring.
Nuclear imaging	Study involves IV injection of radioactive isotopes (^{99m}Tc sestamibi [Cardiolite]). Radioactive uptake is counted over the heart by scintillation camera. Gives information about heart contractility, myocardial perfusion, and acute injury.	*Before:* Remove bra to decrease artifact. Obtain IV access for injection of isotopes. Explain that radioactive isotope used is a small, diagnostic amount and will lose most of its radioactivity in a few hours. Tell patient that they will be lying still on back with arms extended overhead for 20 min. *During:* Repeat scans are done within a few minutes to hours after the injection.
Pharmacologic nuclear imaging	Regadenoson, dipyridamole, or adenosine are given to produce vasodilation for patients unable to tolerate exercise. Vasodilation increases blood flow to well-perfused coronary arteries. Scanning procedure is same. Aminophylline may be given to prevent or reverse side effects of dipyridamole (e.g., dyspnea, dizziness, nausea). Dobutamine is used if vasodilators are contraindicated.	*Before:* Tell patient to avoid caffeine products and theophylline (for regadenoson or dipyridamole testing) for 12 hr before procedure. Hold calcium channel blockers and β-blockers for 24 hr before the test. *During:* Observe patient for any side effects (dyspnea, dizziness, nausea).

Continued

TABLE 35.10 Diagnostic Studies—cont'd

Cardiovascular System

Study	Description and Purpose	Nursing Responsibility
Positron emission tomography (PET)	Highly sensitive in distinguishing viable and nonviable heart tissue. Uses 2 radionuclides. Nitrogen-13-ammonia is injected IV first and scanned to evaluate myocardial perfusion. A second radioactive isotope, fluoro-18-deoxyglucose, is then injected and scanned to show myocardial metabolic function. In the normal heart, both scans match, but in an ischemic or damaged heart, they differ. The patient may or may not be stressed. A baseline resting scan is usually done for comparison.	*Before:* Obtain IV access to inject the tracer substance. Patients should be NPO, except for water and medications, for at least 4 hr prior. If exercise is part of testing, patient needs to fast and refrain from tobacco and caffeine for 24 hr before test. Hold glucose-containing IV solutions and change to normal saline. Check blood glucose levels. The glucose level must be between 60 and 140 mg/dL (3.3–7.8 μmol/L) for accurate glucose metabolic activity. *During:* Patient must lie completely still during scan. *After:* Encourage fluids to excrete radioactive substance.
Single-photon emission computed tomography (SPECT)	Used to determine size or risk for infarction and to determine infarction size. Small amounts of a radioactive isotope (e.g., ^{99m}Tc tetrofosmin [Myoview], thallium-201) are injected IV, and recordings are made of the radioactivity emitted over a specific area of the body. Circulation of the isotope can detect coronary artery blood flow, intracardiac shunts, motion of ventricles, EF, and size of the heart chambers.	*Before:* Short fasting period may be needed. Obtain IV access for injection of isotope. Remove all jewelry from chest wall. Start ECG monitoring. *During:* Patient must lie completely still during scan. *After:* Encourage fluids to excrete radioactive substance.
Stress echocardiogram	Combination of exercise test and echocardiogram. Evaluates differences in left ventricular wall motion and thickening before and after exercise with ultrasound. Postexercise images taken within 1 min of stopping exercise.	*Before:* Prepare patient for treadmill or exercise bicycle. Tell patient of importance of timely return to examination table for imaging after exercise.
Transesophageal echocardiogram (TEE)	A probe with an ultrasound transducer at the tip is swallowed while the HCP controls angle and depth. As it passes down the esophagus, it sends back clear images of heart size, wall motion, valve abnormalities, endocarditis vegetation, and possible source of thrombi without interference from lungs or chest ribs. A contrast medium may be injected IV for evaluating direction of blood flow if an atrial or ventricular septal defect is suspected. Doppler ultrasound and color flow imaging can be used concurrently.	*Before:* Tell patient to fast for at least 6 hr before test. Remove dentures. *During:* IV sedation is given and throat locally anesthetized. A bite block is placed in the mouth. Monitor vital signs, specifically O_2 saturation and BP. Perform suctioning as needed during procedure. *After:* Patient may not eat or drink until gag reflex returns. Monitor patient until sedation resolves. Sore throat is temporary. A designated driver is needed if test is done in the outpatient department.

Electrocardiography

Electrocardiogram

The basic P, QRS, and T waveforms (Fig. 35.4B) are used to assess heart activity. Deviations from the normal sinus rhythm can indicate problems in heart function. There are many types of ECG monitoring, including a resting 12-lead ECG, ambulatory ECG monitoring, and exercise or stress testing (Table 35.10). Continuous ambulatory ECG (Holter monitoring) provides diagnostic information over a period of time. See Chapter 39 for a complete discussion of ECG monitoring.

Event Monitor

An event monitor is used to record less-frequent ECG events. An event monitor is a portable unit that uses electrodes to store and/or send ECG data. There are 2 types, external and implantable. External event recorders are worn for 2 to 4 weeks. They require electrodes continuously attached to the skin. The patient pushes a button to activate a notation when symptoms occur. The electrocardiographic activity can be sent in real time to an HCP or analyzed at the end of the wearing period. These devices also can perform a routine pacemaker check over the phone.

An implantable loop recorder is used for patients who may have serious yet infrequent dysrhythmias. This small recorder is implanted through a small incision into the chest wall to continuously monitor heart activity.

ECG applications are available for use from a smartphone. By touching special sensors or applying a smartphone watch, patients can see and record their cardiac rhythms for routine monitoring or for later discussion with the HCP.

Functional Studies

Exercise or Stress Testing

Heart symptoms often occur only with activity because of the demand on the coronary arteries to supply more O_2 to the heart muscle. Exercise testing can evaluate the heart's response to physical stress. This helps to assess CVD and set limits for exercise programs. Exercise testing is used for persons who can walk unassisted or use a bicycle. It is also helpful for those with ECGs that limit diagnostic interpretation (e.g., pacemakers) (Table 35.10). ECG and BP are monitored throughout the exercise period for signs of cardiac stress.

6-Minute walk test. A general test of cardiac fitness, often used with older adults, is measuring the distance the patient can walk on a flat surface in 6 minutes. The test can provide a baseline for determining response to treatment and physical therapy.

Imaging

Chest X-Ray

A radiographic picture of the chest can show heart shape and size and anatomic changes in individual chambers (Fig. 35.17). A chest x-ray records any displacement or enlargement of the

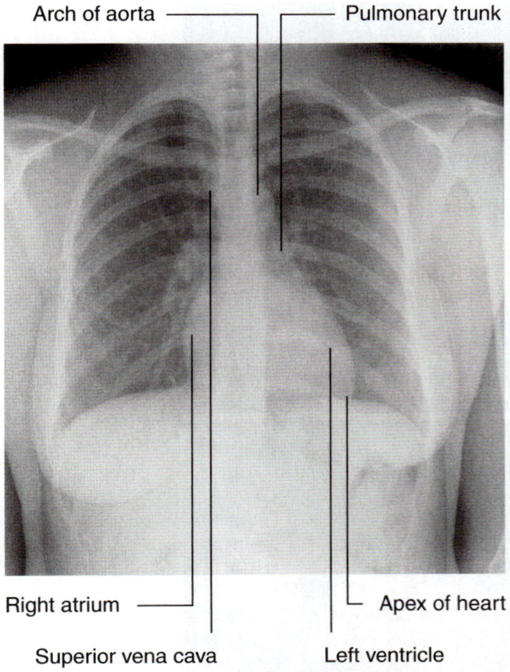

Fig. 35.17 Chest x-ray: standard posterior-anterior view. (From Drake RL, Vogl AW, Mitchell AWM: *Gray's anatomy for students*, ed 2, Philadelphia, 2010, Churchill Livingstone.)

heart, extra fluid around the heart (pericardial effusion), and pulmonary congestion (Table 35.10).

Echocardiography

The echocardiogram uses US waves to record the movement of the structures of the heart. In the normal heart, US waves directed at the heart are reflected back in typical patterns. *Contrast echocardiography* involves the addition of an IV contrast agent (e.g., agitated saline) to help define the images, especially in patients with increased body mass.

The echocardiogram provides information about abnormalities of (1) valvular structures and motion, (2) heart chamber size and contents, (3) ventricular and septal motion and thickness, (4) pericardial sac, and (5) ascending aorta. The **ejection fraction (EF),** or the percentage of end-diastolic blood volume that is ejected during systole, can be measured. The EF provides information about the function of the left ventricle during systole.

Two common types of echocardiograms are the *motion-mode (M-mode) echocardiogram* and the *2-dimensional (2D) echocardiogram.* In the M-mode, a single US beam is directed toward the heart, recording the motion of the intracardiac structures and detecting wall thickness and chamber size. The 2D echocardiogram sweeps the US beam through an arc, producing a cross-sectional view. This shows correct spatial relationships among the structures.

Doppler technology allows for sound evaluation of the flow or motion of the scanned object (heart valves, ventricular walls, blood flow). *Color-flow imaging (duplex)* is the combination of 2D echocardiography and Doppler technology (Fig. 35.18). It uses color changes to show the speed and direction of blood flow. This helps to diagnose pathologic conditions, such as valvular leaks and congenital defects, more effectively.

Real-time 3D ultrasound is a technology that uses multiple 2D echo images with computer technology to provide a reconstruction of the heart. This technique gives information about the structures of the heart and how these structures change during the cardiac cycle.

Stress echocardiography combines the information from a stress test with the information from an echocardiogram. A digital computer compares images before and after exercise, showing wall motion and function. For those persons unable to exercise, IV drugs are used. These include dobutamine, which produces pharmacologic stress on the heart and dipyridamole, which vasodilates healthy arteries. Unhealthy arteries do not respond as well, which is seen on the echocardiogram.

A *bubble study* is a type of contrast echocardiography used to check for a defect in the wall between the 2 upper chambers of the heart, such as a patent foramen ovale (PFO). Tiny bubbles in sterile solution are injected into a vein while an echocardiogram scans to detect any passage of the bubbles from the right to left heart. The bubbles are very small, and the bubble solution is absorbed into the bloodstream without endangering the patient.

TEE provides more precise echocardiography of the heart than surface 2D echocardiography. It removes interference from the chest wall and lungs (Table 35.10). The TEE uses a flexible endoscope with a US transducer in the tip to image the heart and great vessels. The scope is passed into the esophagus to the level of the heart. M-mode, 2D, Doppler, and color flow imaging can be obtained.

TEE is used often in an outpatient setting for evaluation of mitral valve disease and for identification of endocarditis vegetation, thrombus before cardioversion, or the source of heart emboli. In addition, TEE is used in the operating room to assess intraoperative heart function and in the emergency department to detect suspected aortic dissection.

The risks of TEE are low. However, complications include perforation or tearing of the esophagus, hemorrhage, dysrhythmias, vasovagal reactions, and transient hypoxemia. TEE is contraindicated if the patient has a history of esophageal disorders, dysphagia, or radiation therapy to the chest wall. Patients need sedation during a TEE.

Cardiac Computed Tomography (CT)

Cardiac CT is a heart-imaging test that uses CT technology with or without IV contrast (dye) to see the heart anatomy, coronary circulation, and great blood vessels (e.g., aorta, pulmonary veins, artery). This technology may be called *multidetector CT (MDCT) scanning.* Types of CT scans used to diagnose heart disease include coronary CT angiography (CTA) and calcium-scoring CT scan (Table 35.10).

Coronary CTA is a noninvasive test. It is faster, is less risky, and requires less radiation exposure than a cardiac catheterization. Patients must have a normal sinus rhythm for this test. Although the use of coronary CTA is increasing, cardiac catheterization is the gold standard to diagnose CAD. During a cardiac catheterization, procedures (e.g., angioplasty, stent placement) can be done if coronary blockages are found.

The calcium-scoring CT scan is used to find calcium deposits in plaque in the coronary arteries. The most common method used is the electron beam CT (EBCT) (Fig. 35.19). It can detect early coronary calcification before symptoms develop and confirm suspected CAD. The amount of coronary calcium predicts the risk of future cardiac events.

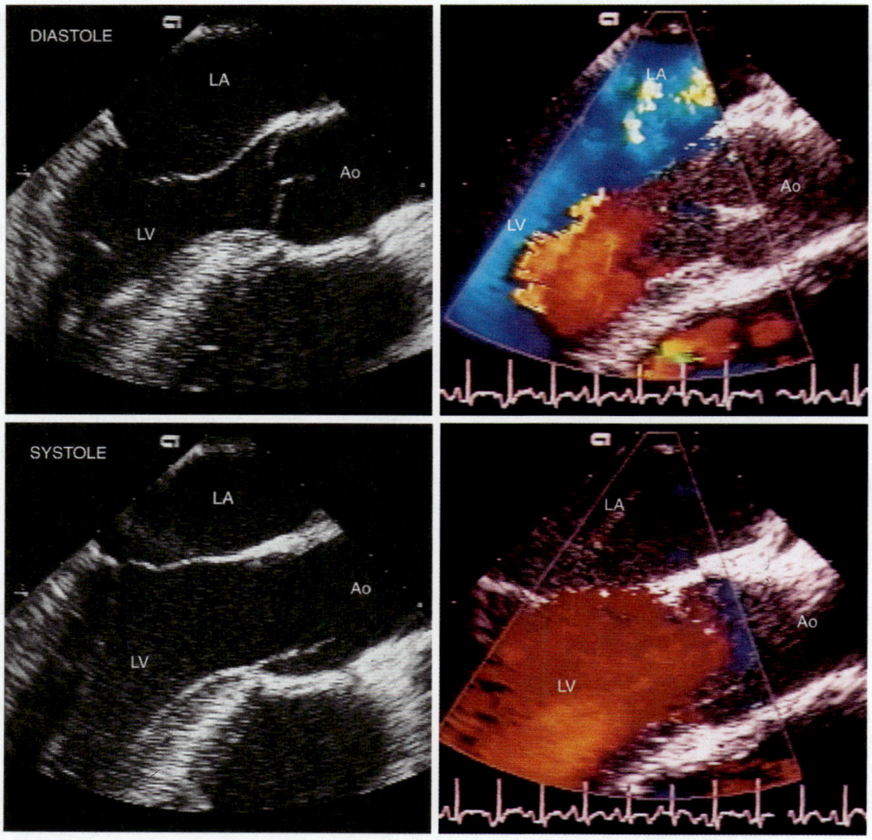

Fig. 35.18 Long-axis images of the aortic and mitral valve with the depth adjusted to optimize evaluation of valve anatomy and motion. The 2-D images *(left)* in diastole *(top)* and systole *(bottom)* show normal aortic and mitral opening and closure. The color flow images *(right)* show normal left ventricular inflow with no aortic regurgitation in diastole *(top)* and normal antegrade flow in the left ventricular outflow tract and no mitral regurgitation in systole *(bottom)*. *Ao,* Aorta; *LA,* left atrium; *LV,* left ventricular. (From Otto C: *Textbook of clinical echocardiography,* ed 3, St Louis, 2004, Saunders.)

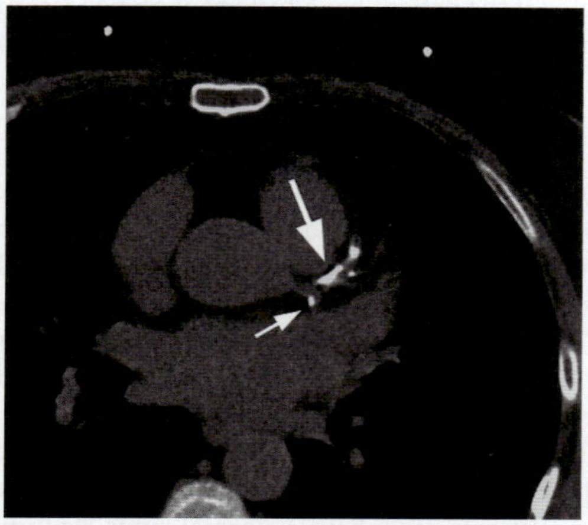

Fig. 35.19 Examples of coronary calcification of the left anterior descending coronary artery *(large arrow)* and left circumflex artery *(small arrow)* as seen on electron beam computed tomography. (From Libby P, Bonow R, Zipes D, et al.: *Braunwald's heart disease: a textbook of cardiovascular medicine,* ed 8, St Louis, 2008, Saunders.)

Cardiovascular Magnetic Resonance Imaging

Cardiovascular magnetic resonance imaging (CMRI) can detect and find areas of MI in a 3D view. It is sensitive enough to find even small MIs that are not apparent with single-photon emission computed tomography (SPECT). CMRI aids in the final diagnosis of MI and the assessment of EF. It plays a role in predicting recovery from MI and diagnosing congenital heart and aortic disorders and CAD. One major advantage of CMRI is that it does not require any radiation to the patient.

Patients with coronary stents can undergo CMRI 6 weeks after stent placement. CMRI is discouraged in those with older model pacemakers and implantable cardioverter defibrillator (ICDs) because the magnets can change the function of the devices. However, when there is a strong clinical need and the benefits outweigh the risks, CMRI can be done at centers experienced in this procedure. Many newer models of pacemakers and ICDs are approved for use with MRI.

Nuclear Cardiology

One of the most common nuclear imaging tests is the multigated acquisition (MUGA) or cardiac blood pool scan. This test provides information on wall motion during systole and diastole, heart valves, and EF (Table 35.10).

Perfusion imaging is used with exercise testing to determine whether the coronary blood flow changes with increased activity. Stress perfusion imaging may show an abnormality even when a resting image is normal. This procedure is used to diagnose CAD, make a prognosis in existing CAD, distinguish viable heart muscle from scar tissue, and determine the potential for success of various interventions (e.g., coronary artery bypass surgery, percutaneous coronary intervention) (see Chapter 37).

Exercise stress perfusion imaging is an option if a patient cannot exercise. IV regadenoson, dipyridamole, or adenosine can be given to dilate the coronary arteries and simulate the effect of exercise. After the drug takes effect, the isotope is injected, and the imaging is done.

SPECT uses technetium, thallium, or sestamibi as an imaging agent (isotope). Patients who are obese or have large breasts may have false-positive results. Patients with severe multivessel coronary disease or blockages in their left main coronary artery may have false-negative results.

Positron emission tomography (PET) stress testing is increasingly being used due to its high sensitivity for revealing myocardial ischemia and viability. This type of myocardial perfusion imaging is often done using rubidium-82.

Interventional Studies

Cardiac Catheterization

Cardiac catheterization provides information about CAD, coronary spasm, congenital and valvular heart disease, and ventricular function. Cardiac catheterization is used to measure intracardiac pressures and O_2 levels, as well as CO and EF (Fig. 35.20). With injection of contrast media and fluoroscopy, the coronary arteries can be seen, chambers of the heart can be outlined, and wall motion assessed (Table 35.11).

Cardiac catheterization is done by inserting a radiopaque catheter into the right and/or left side of the heart. For the right

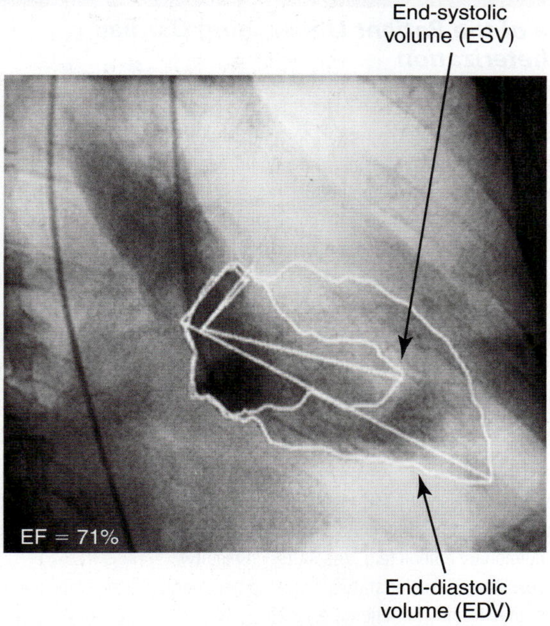

Fig. 35.20 Cardiac catheterization. End-diastolic volume and end-systolic volume used to determine ejection fraction *(EF)*. (From Lough M: *Hemodynamic monitoring: evolving technologies and clinical practice.* St Louis, 2016, Elsevier.)

TABLE 35.11 Interventional Studies

Cardiovascular System

Study	Description and Purpose	Nursing Responsibility
Cardiac catheterization; coronary angiography	Involves insertion of catheter into heart via a vein (for right side of heart) and/or an artery (for left side of heart). Procedure is done to evaluate chest pain and obtain information about the heart and major vessels. Measures pressures within the heart chambers. Contrast medium is injected to help see structures and motion of heart. With coronary angiography, contrast medium is injected directly into coronary arteries to evaluate patency and collateral circulation.	See Table 35.12.
Electrophysiology study (EPS)	Invasive study to record intracardiac electrical activity using catheters (with multiple electrodes) inserted via the femoral or jugular veins into right side of heart. Catheter electrodes record the electrical activity in different heart structures. Can induce and stop dysrhythmias. Insertion of a pacemaker or implantable cardioverter defibrillator (ICD) or ablation of a dysrhythmia pathway may be done during or right after the EPS. See Chapter 34 for more details.	*Before:* Antidysrhythmic drugs may be stopped several days before study. Keep patient NPO 6–8 hr before test. Give premedication to promote relaxation if ordered. Obtain IV access. IV sedation often used during procedure. *After:* Assess vital signs often. Monitor ECG continuously per agency protocol. Patient will be on bedrest for 6–8 hr after procedure.
Fractional flow reserve (FFR)	During cardiac catheterization, a specialized wire is inserted into coronary arteries to measure pressure and flow. Information is used to determine need for angioplasty or stenting on nonsignificant blockages.	Same as for cardiac catheterization.
Intravascular ultrasound (IVUS)	During cardiac catheterization a small ultrasound probe is introduced into coronary arteries. Used to assess blood vessel patency, size and consistency of plaque, arterial walls, and effectiveness of intracoronary artery treatment.	Same as for cardiac catheterization.
Peripheral arteriography and venography	Peripheral vessel blood flow is assessed by injecting contrast media into appropriate arteries or veins (arteriography and venography). Serial x-ray studies done to detect atherosclerotic plaques, occlusion, aneurysms, venous abnormalities, or traumatic injury. See Table 41.9 for more peripheral vascular diagnostic studies.	*Before:* Assess for contrast allergy. Explain that patient may feel a warm sensation, salty taste after contrast injection. Patient may have nausea. Give mild sedative, if ordered. *During:* Observe patient for allergic reaction to contrast media. *After:* Inspect insertion site for bleeding or swelling. Check extremity with puncture site for pulsation, warmth, color, and motion. Encourage fluids to excrete radioactive substance.

TABLE 35.12 NURSING MANAGEMENT

Care of the Patient Undergoing Cardiac Catheterization

Preprocedure

- Assess for allergies, especially to contrast dye.
- Perform baseline assessment, including vital signs, pulse oximetry, heart and breath sounds, neurovascular assessment of extremities (e.g., distal pulses, skin temperature, skin color, sensation).
- Withhold food and fluids for 6 hours before the procedure.
- Assess baseline laboratory values (e.g., cardiac biomarkers, creatinine).
- Teach patient and caregiver about procedure and postprocedure care. Explain the use of local anesthesia at insertion site. Describe the flushed feeling when dye is injected and possible fluttering sensation of heart as catheter is passed.
- Give sedative and other drugs, as ordered.

Postprocedure

- Perform assessment and compare to baseline: vital signs, pulse oximetry, and heart and breath sounds. Note hypotension or hypertension and signs of pulmonary emboli (e.g., respiratory difficulty).
- Assess neurovascular status, including peripheral pulses, color, and sensation, of extremity per agency protocol.
- Place compression device over arterial site to achieve hemostasis, if indicated.
- Observe insertion site for hematoma and bleeding every 15 min for the first hour, then according to agency policy.
- Monitor ECG for dysrhythmias or other changes (e.g., ST segment elevation).
- Monitor patient for chest pain and other sources of pain or discomfort.
- Maintain bedrest as prescribed after femoral access, depending on hemostasis method.
- Maintain IV and/or oral fluid intake and monitor urine output.
- Teach patient and caregiver about discharge care, including signs and symptoms to report to HCP (e.g., site complications, return of chest pain), and any activity restrictions.

side of the heart, the HCP inserts a catheter into the femoral, internal jugular, subclavian, or antecubital vein. Pressures are recorded as the catheter is moved into the vena cava, right atrium, right ventricle, and PA. The catheter is then moved until it is wedged or lodged in position. This blocks the blood flow and pressure from the right side of the heart and detects pressure through the pulmonary capillary bed to the left side of the heart (PAWP).

Left-sided heart catheterization is done by inserting a catheter into a radial, femoral, or brachial artery. The catheter is passed in a retrograde manner up to the aorta, across the aortic valve, and into the left ventricle.

Coronary angiography is done with a left-sided heart catheterization. The catheter is positioned at the origin of the coronary arteries (Fig. 35.3), and contrast medium is injected into the arteries. Patients often feel a temporary flushed sensation with dye injection. The images show the location and severity of any coronary blockages (see Figs. 35.21 and 37.15).

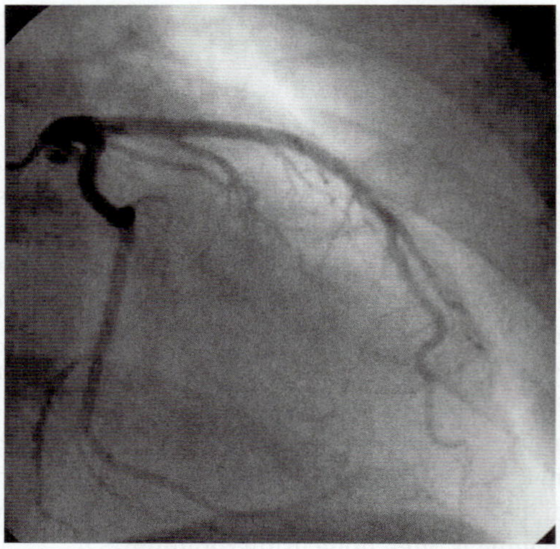

Fig. 35.21 Angiogram showing a normal left coronary and circumflex artery. (From Drake RL, Vogl AW, Mitchell AWM: *Gray's anatomy for students,* ed 2, Philadelphia, 2010, Churchill Livingstone.)

Complications of cardiac catheterization include bleeding or hematoma at the puncture site; allergic reactions to the contrast media; looping or kinking of the catheter; infection; thrombus formation; aortic dissection; dysrhythmias; MI; stroke; and puncture of the ventricles, septum, or lung tissue.[11,15]

Intravascular Ultrasound

Intravascular ultrasound (IVUS), or intracoronary ultrasound (ICUS), is an invasive procedure done in the catheterization laboratory with coronary angiography. The 2D or 3D US images provide a cross-sectional view of the arterial walls of the coronary arteries. In IVUS, a miniature transducer attached to a small catheter is moved to the artery to be studied. Once it is in the artery, US images are obtained. The health of the arterial layers is assessed, including the composition, location, and thickness of any plaque. IVUS can evaluate vessel response to treatments such as stent placement and atherectomy.[15] Patients often have IVUS in addition to angiography or a coronary intervention. Nursing care after IVUS is similar to that of patient after a cardiac catheterization.

Electrophysiology Study

The electrophysiology study (EPS) records and manipulates the heart's electrical activity using electrodes placed inside the heart chambers. It provides information on SA node, AV node, and ventricular conduction. It is particularly helpful in determining the source and treatment of dysrhythmias. Patients with symptomatic tachydysrhythmias are at risk for sudden cardiac death. Information from an EPS helps to make a correct diagnosis and guides treatment decisions (Table 35.11). In EPS, catheters are inserted like a right-sided heart catheterization. Nursing care after EPS is similar to that of a patient after a cardiac catheterization.[15]

Case Study

Objective Data: Diagnostic Studies

(©Jupiterimages/ Banana-Stock/ Thinkstock.)

The HCP orders the following initial diagnostic studies for L.P.:

- 12-lead ECG
- CBC, basic metabolic panel (glucose, electrolytes, BUN, creatinine)
- PTT, PT, INR
- Pro-BNP
- Troponin, CK-MB
- TSH, free T_4
- Chest x-ray

The ECG shows atrial fibrillation with a rapid ventricular response. L.P.'s initial troponin and CK-MB levels are within normal limits. Chest x-ray, CBC, and coagulation studies are all within normal limits. The potassium level is 3.1 mEq/L and pro-BNP is high (1204 pg/mL). The HCP orders 250 mL NSS IV bolus; an oral dose of potassium, a loading dose of IV diltiazem followed by a continuous infusion, and weight-based heparin to be started in the emergency department. L.P. will be admitted to the progressive care unit and have a consult with a cardiologist.

Discussion Questions

1. Are these the diagnostic studies that you expected to be ordered?
2. Which diagnostic study results are abnormal?
3. Which diagnostic study results most concern you?

Answers available at http://evolve.elsevier.com/Lewis/medsurg.

BRIDGE TO NCLEX EXAMINATION

The number of the question corresponds to the same-numbered outcome at the beginning of the chapter.

1. Where is the blood flow altered when a patient has a tricuspid valve problem?
   - **a.** Vena cava and right atrium
   - **b.** Left atrium and left ventricle
   - **c.** Right atrium and right ventricle
   - **d.** Right ventricle and pulmonary artery
2. A patient has a severe blockage in his right coronary artery. Which heart structures would the nurse expect to be affected by this blockage? *(select all that apply)*
   - **a.** AV node
   - **b.** Left ventricle
   - **c.** Coronary sinus
   - **d.** Right ventricle
   - **e.** Pulmonic valve
3. Which part of the vascular system provides hemostasis?
   - **a.** Thin capillary vessels
   - **b.** Endothelial layer of the arteries
   - **c.** Elastic middle layer of the veins
   - **d.** Smooth muscle of the arterial wall
4. Which homeostatic mechanism is stimulated to compensate for a rise in blood pressure?
   - **a.** Baroreceptors that inhibit the sympathetic nervous system, causing vasodilation
   - **b.** Chemoreceptors that inhibit the sympathetic nervous system, causing vasodilation
   - **c.** Baroreceptors that inhibit the parasympathetic nervous system, causing vasodilation
   - **d.** Chemoreceptors that stimulate the sympathetic nervous system, causing an increased heart rate
5. Which action does the P wave on an ECG represent?
   - **a.** Firing of the SA node and repolarizing the atria
   - **b.** Firing of the SA node and depolarizing the atria
   - **c.** Conduction through the AV node and depolarizing the atria
   - **d.** Conduction through the AV node and spreading to the bundle of His
6. Which subjective data related to the cardiovascular system would the nurse plan to obtain? *(select all that apply)*
   - **a.** Annual income
   - **b.** Smoking history
   - **c.** Spiritual preferences
   - **d.** Number of pillows used to sleep
   - **e.** Blood for basic laboratory studies
7. Which heart valve sound is heard best at the left midclavicular line at the level of the 5th ICS?
   - **a.** Aortic
   - **b.** Mitral
   - **c.** Tricuspid
   - **d.** Pulmonic
8. Which condition is likely to cause a pulse deficit of 23 beats?
   - **a.** Dysrhythmia
   - **b.** Heart murmur
   - **c.** Gallop rhythm
   - **d.** Pericardial friction rub
9. Which finding is expected in the assessment of an 81-year-old patient?
   - **a.** Narrowed pulse pressure
   - **b.** Diminished carotid artery pulses
   - **c.** Difficulty isolating the apical pulse
   - **d.** Increased heart rate in response to stress
10. Which item would the nurse zero to establish accurate hemodynamic monitoring for a patient?
    - **a.** Pressure monitoring system to phlebostatic axis
    - **b.** Pressure monitoring system to the level of the midclavicular line
    - **c.** Cardiac output monitoring system to the level of the left ventricle
    - **d.** Pressure monitoring system to the level of the catheter tip in the patient
11. Which nursing responsibilities are priorities when caring for a patient returning from a cardiac catheterization? *(select all that apply)*
    - **a.** Monitoring vital signs and ECG

b. Checking the catheter insertion site and distal pulses
c. Helping the patient to ambulate to the bathroom to void
d. Telling the patient that he will be sleepy from the general anesthesia
e. Teaching the patient about the risks of the radioactive isotope injection

1. c; 2. a, b, d; 3. b; 4. a; 5. b; 6. b, c, d; 7. b; 8. a; 9. c; 10. a; 11. a, b.

For rationales to these answers and even more NCLEX review questions, visit http://evolve.elsevier.com/Lewis/medsurg.

EVOLVE WEBSITE/RESOURCES LIST

http://evolve.elsevier.com/Lewis/medsurg
Review Questions (Online Only)
Key Points
Answer Keys for Questions
Rationales for Bridge to NCLEX Examination Questions
Answer Guidelines for Case Studies
Conceptual Care Map Creator
Audio Glossary
Supporting Media
Animations
- Auscultation of Heart Valves
- Blood Flow: Circulatory System
- Cardiac Cycle During Systole and Diastole
- Pulse Variations

Content Updates

REFERENCES

1. Huether S, McCance K: *Understanding pathophysiology*, ed 7, St Louis, 2020, Elsevier.
2. Pappano AJ, Wier W: *Cardiovascular physiology*, ed 11, St Louis, 2019, Elsevier.
3. Wesley K: *Huszar' ECG and 12-lead interpretation*, ed 5, St Louis, 2017, Elsevier.
4. Potter P, Perry A, Stockert P, Hall A: *Fundamentals of nursing*, ed 10, St Louis, 2021, Elsevier.
5. Jarvis C, Eckhardt A: *Physical examination and health assessment*, ed 8, St Louis, 2020, Elsevier.
6. McCuistion L, DiMaggio K, Winton B, Yeager J: *Pharmacology: a patient-centered nursing process approach*, ed 10, St Louis, 2020, Elsevier.
7. Urden L, Stacey K, Lough M: *Critical care nursing: diagnosis and management*, St Louis, 2018, Elsevier.

*8. Saugel B, Cecconi M, Hajjar LA: Noninvasive cardiac output monitoring in cardiothoracic surgery patients: available methods and future directions, *J Cardiothorac Vasc Anesth* 33:1742, 2020.

*9. Zhang Y, Wang Y, Shi J, Hua Z, Xu J: Cardiac output measurements via echocardiography versus thermodilution: a systematic review and meta-analysis, *PLoS ONE* 14:e0222105, 2019.

*10. Pour-Ghaz I, Manolukas T, Foray N, Raja J, Rawal A, Ibebuogu U, Khouzam R: Accuracy of non-invasive and minimally invasive hemodynamic monitoring: where do we stand? *Ann Transl Med* 7:421, 2019.

11. Parrillo J, Dellinger RP: *Critical care medicine: principles of diagnosis and management in the adult*, ed 5, Philadelphia, 2019, Elsevier.

*12. Tveit SH, Myhre PL, et al.: Superiority of high sensitivity cardiac troponin T vs. I for long-term prognostic value in patients with chest pain: data from the Akershus Cardiac Examination (ACE) 3 study, *Clin Biochem* 78(10), 2020.

*13. Lattuca B, Sy V, et al.: Copeptin as a prognostic biomarker in acute myocardial infarction, *Int J Cardiol* 274:337, 2019.

14. Pagana K, Pagana TJ, Pagana TN: *Mosby's diagnostic and laboratory test reference*, ed 15, St Louis, 2021, Elsevier.
15. Zipes D, Libby P, Bonow R, Mann D, Tomaselli G, Braunwald E: *Braunwald's heart disease: a textbook of cardiovascular medicine*, ed 11, Philadelphia, 2019, Elsevier.

*Evidence-based information for clinical practice.

Hypertension

Rita Wermers

http://evolve.elsevier.com/Lewis/medsurg/

CONCEPTUAL FOCUS

Adherence
Fluids and Electrolytes
Perfusion
Self-Management

LEARNING OUTCOMES

1. Relate the pathophysiology of primary hypertension to the clinical manifestations and complications.
2. Choose appropriate strategies for the prevention of primary hypertension.
3. Describe the interprofessional care for primary hypertension.
4. Explain the interprofessional care of the older adult with primary hypertension.
5. Prioritize the nursing management of the patient with primary hypertension.
6. Describe the nursing and interprofessional care of a patient with a hypertensive crisis.

KEY TERMS

blood pressure (BP)
elevated blood pressure, Table 36.2
hypertension
hypertensive crisis
orthostatic hypotension
primary hypertension
secondary hypertension
systemic vascular resistance (SVR)

Hypertension, or high blood pressure (BP), is one of the most important modifiable risk factors for the development of cardiovascular disease (CVD). As BP increases, so does the risk for myocardial infarction (MI), heart failure (HF), stroke, renal disease, and vision loss. This chapter discusses the nursing and interprofessional care of patients with or at risk for hypertension. Providing comprehensive care will require you to collaborate with many members of the health care team. Patient education is key to hypertension management. Proper nutrition and exercise are important health promotion behaviors.

Current guidelines reveal that around 45% of adults in the United States meet the criteria for the diagnosis of hypertension. Heart disease, often directly related to hypertension, accounts for 23.7% of all deaths each year in the United States.[1,2]

Most people with high BP need a combination of medication and lifestyle modifications.[3] Of the 108 million US adults with hypertension, 71% do not have their BP in control. Of those with uncontrolled BP, 49% are untreated.

The American College of Cardiology Foundation and the American Heart Association (AHA) provides performance measures for hypertension management. Target goals are based on the evidence-based Guideline for the Prevention, Detection, Evaluation, and Management of High Blood Pressure in Adults: A Report of the American College of Cardiology/AHA Task Force on Clinical Practice Guidelines and the Systolic Blood Pressure Intervention Trial (SPRINT). Target goals take age and comorbidities into consideration when recommending treatment options.[4,5]

National guidelines are designed to apply to all racial and ethnic groups. However, specific groups have higher incidences of risk factors (Boxes 36.1 and 36.2). BP control is strongly impacted by social determinants of health. These include lack of access to health care, poverty, and chronic stress.[6] Emerging research highlights the need to include underrepresented populations in clinical and genetic studies.[6,7]

NORMAL REGULATION OF BLOOD PRESSURE

Blood pressure (BP) is the force exerted by the blood against the walls of the blood vessel. It must be adequate to maintain tissue perfusion during activity and rest. Maintaining normal BP and tissue perfusion requires the integration of both systemic factors and local peripheral vascular effects. BP is mainly a function of cardiac output (CO) and systemic vascular resistance (Fig. 36.1).

CO is the total blood flow through the systemic or pulmonary circulation per minute. It is determined by the stroke volume (SV) or the amount of blood pumped out of the left ventricle per beat (about 70 mL) multiplied by the heart rate (HR).

Systemic vascular resistance (SVR) is the force opposing the movement of blood within the blood vessels. The radius of the small arteries and arterioles is the principal factor determining SVR. As arteries narrow, resistance to blood flow increases.

BOX 36.1 PROMOTING HEALTH EQUITY

Hypertension

Blacks

- Have the highest prevalence of hypertension in the world
- Are more likely to have resistant hypertension
- Develop hypertension at a younger age than other ethnicities with higher average BP
- Have a higher incidence of hypertension among women than among men
- Have more nocturnal nondipping BP than Whites, which increases risk for CVD
- Hypertension is more aggressive and results in more severe end-organ damage
- Have the highest death rate from hypertension

Hispanics

- Are less likely to receive treatment for hypertension than Whites and non-Hispanic Blacks
- Have lowest rates of BP control
- Have lowest levels of awareness of hypertension and its treatment

BOX 36.2 BIOLOGIC SEX CONSIDERATIONS

Hypertension

Men

- Before early middle age, hypertension is more common in men

Women

- Hypertension is 2 to 3 times more common in women who take oral contraceptives
- A history of preeclampsia may be an early sign of risk for CVD
- After age 64, hypertension is more common in women. This is due in part to menopause-related factors, such as estrogen withdrawal, overproduction of pituitary hormones, and weight gain
- Harder to control hypertension in older women (ages 70–79) than in women ages 50–69, despite similar treatment

As arteries dilate, resistance to blood flow decreases. A small change in the radius of the arterioles creates a significant change in the SVR. If SVR is increased and CO stays constant or increases, arterial BP will increase.

The mechanisms that regulate BP can affect either CO or SVR or both. Regulation of BP is a complex process involving both short-term (seconds to hours) and long-term (days to weeks) mechanisms. Short-term mechanisms, including the sympathetic nervous system (SNS) and vascular endothelium, are active within a few seconds. Long-term mechanisms include renal and hormonal processes that regulate arteriolar resistance and blood volume. In a healthy person, these regulatory mechanisms work in response to the body's demands.

Sympathetic Nervous System

The nervous system, which reacts within seconds after a drop in BP, increases BP by activating the SNS. Increased SNS activity increases HR and cardiac contractility. It causes widespread vasoconstriction in the peripheral arterioles and promotes the release of renin from the kidneys. The net effect of SNS activation is to increase BP by increasing both CO and SVR.

Specialized nerve cells called *baroreceptors* are found in the carotid arteries and arch of the aorta. These cells sense changes in BP and send this information to the vasomotor centers in the brainstem. The brainstem sends this information through complex networks of neurons that excite or inhibit efferent nerves. SNS efferent nerves innervate cardiac and vascular smooth muscle cells. Under normal conditions, a low level of continuous SNS activity maintains vascular tone. BP may be reduced by the withdrawal of SNS activity or by stimulation of the parasympathetic nervous system (PNS). The PNS decreases the HR (via the vagus nerve) and thereby decreases CO.

The neurotransmitter norepinephrine (NE) is released from SNS nerve endings. NE activates receptors in the sinoatrial node, myocardium, and vascular smooth muscle. The response to NE depends on the type of receptors present. SNS receptors are classified as α_1, α_2, β_1, and β_2 (Table 36.1). The smooth muscle of the blood vessels has α-adrenergic and β_2-adrenergic receptors. α-Adrenergic receptors found in the peripheral vasculature cause vasoconstriction when stimulated by NE.

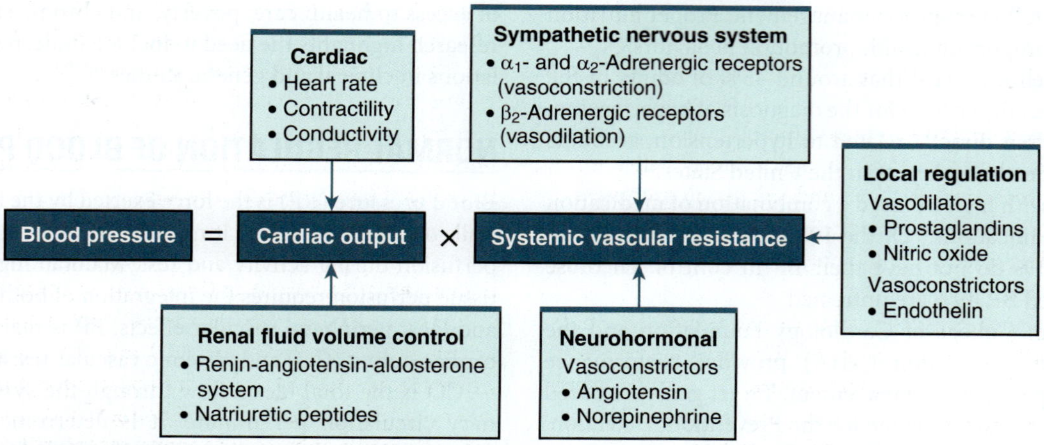

Fig. 36.1 Factors influencing BP. Hypertension develops when one or more of the BP-regulating mechanisms are defective.

TABLE 36.1 Sympathetic Nervous System Receptors Affecting BP

Receptor	Location	Response When Activated
α_1	Vascular smooth muscle	Vasoconstriction
	Heart	↑ Contractility (positive inotropic effect)
α_2	Presynaptic nerve terminals	Inhibition of norepinephrine release
	Vascular smooth muscle	Vasoconstriction
β_1	Heart	↑ Contractility (positive inotropic effect)
		↑ Heart rate (positive chronotropic effect)
		↑ Conduction (positive dromotropic effect)
	Juxtaglomerular cells of the kidney	↑ Renin secretion
β_2	Smooth muscle of blood vessels in heart (e.g., coronary arteries), lungs (e.g., bronchi), and skeletal muscle	Vasodilation
Dopamine receptors	Primarily renal blood vessels	Vasodilation

β_1-Adrenergic receptors in the heart respond to NE and epinephrine with increased HR (chronotropic), increased force of contraction (inotropic), and increased speed of conduction (dromotropic). β_2-Adrenergic receptors are activated mainly by epinephrine released from the adrenal medulla. They cause vasodilation (see Fig. 36.1).

The sympathetic vasomotor center interacts with many areas of the brain to maintain normal BP under various conditions. It is activated during times of pain, stress, and exercise. The SNS response causes an appropriate increase in CO and BP to adjust to the body's increased O_2 demands. During the postural change from lying to standing, there is a transient decrease in BP. The vasomotor center is stimulated. The SNS response causes peripheral vasoconstriction and increased venous return to the heart. If this reaction did not occur, blood flow to the brain would be inadequate, resulting in dizziness or syncope.

Baroreceptors

Baroreceptors have a vital role in maintaining BP stability during normal activities. They are sensitive to stretching. When stimulated by an increase in BP, they send inhibitory impulses to the sympathetic vasomotor center. SNS inhibition results in decreased HR, decreased force of contraction, and vasodilation in peripheral arterioles.

When baroreceptors sense a fall in BP, the SNS is activated. The result is constriction of the peripheral arterioles, increased HR, and increased contractility of the heart. In long-standing hypertension, the baroreceptors become adjusted to increased BP levels and recognize this level as their new "normal."

Vascular Endothelium

The vascular endothelium is a single-cell layer that lines the blood vessels. The endothelium is responsible for several critical functions. These include platelet adhesion, coagulation regulation, immune function, and regulating fluid control within the vessel and extravascular space. The endothelium can cause adhesion and aggregation of neutrophils and stimulate smooth muscle growth.

The endothelium is essential to the regulation and maintenance of vasodilating and vasoconstricting substances. Endothelium-derived vasoactive substances include *nitric oxide* (NO) and *prostacyclin*. Both are vasodilators. Another product of the endothelium is *endothelin* (ET). It is a potent vasoconstrictor (Fig. 36.1). Cardiovascular risk factors, such as smoking and diabetes, can reduce functional endothelial cells. This can cause arterial tone changes (excessive constriction or dilation), which are early warning signals of CVD.

Renal System

The kidneys contribute to BP regulation by controlling sodium excretion and extracellular fluid (ECF) volume (see Chapter 49). Sodium retention results in water retention, which increases ECF volume. This action increases venous return to the heart and SV. Together, these increase CO and BP.

The renin-angiotensin-aldosterone system (RAAS) plays an essential role in BP regulation (Fig. 36.1). The juxtaglomerular apparatus in the kidney secretes renin in response to SNS stimulation, decreased blood flow through the kidneys, or decreased serum sodium concentration. Renin is an enzyme that converts angiotensinogen to angiotensin I. Angiotensin I is then converted to angiotensin II (A-II) by angiotensin-converting enzyme (ACE). A-II increases BP by 2 different mechanisms (see Fig. 49.4). First, A-II is a potent vasoconstrictor and increases SVR. This results in an immediate increase in BP. Second, over a period of hours or days, A-II increases BP indirectly by stimulating the adrenal cortex to secrete aldosterone.

A-II acts at a local level within the heart and blood vessels. These effects include vasoconstriction and tissue growth that result in remodeling of the vessel walls. These changes are linked to the development of primary hypertension and the long-term effects of hypertension (e.g., atherosclerosis, renal disease, cardiac hypertrophy).

Prostaglandins (PGE_2 and PGI_2) secreted by the renal medulla have a vasodilator effect on the systemic circulation. This results in decreased SVR and lower BP. Heart cells secrete the natriuretic peptides (atrial natriuretic peptide [ANP] and b-type natriuretic peptide [BNP]). They oppose the effects of antidiuretic hormone (ADH) and aldosterone. This results in *natriuresis* (excretion of sodium in urine) and diuresis, resulting in reduced blood volume and BP.

Endocrine System

SNS stimulation results in the release of epinephrine along with a small fraction of NE by the adrenal medulla. Epinephrine increases CO by increasing HR and myocardial contractility. Epinephrine activates β_2-adrenergic receptors in peripheral arterioles of skeletal muscle, causing vasodilation. In peripheral arterioles with only α_1-adrenergic receptors (skin and kidneys), epinephrine causes vasoconstriction.

TABLE 36.2 Diagnostic Criteria

Classification of Hypertension

Category	Systolic BP (mm Hg)		Diastolic BP (mm Hg)
Normal	<120	and	<80
Elevated	120–129	and	<80
Hypertension, stage 1	130–139	or	80–89
Hypertension, stage 2	≥140	or	≥90

Source: Whelton PK, Carey RM, Aronow WS, et al.: 2017 ACC/AHA/AAPA/ABC/ACPM/AGS/APhA/ASH/ASPC/NMA/PCNA guideline for the prevention, detection, evaluation, and management of high blood pressure in adults: a report of the American College of Cardiology/AHA Task Force on Clinical Practice Guidelines, *J Am Coll Cardiol* 71:e127, 2018.

A-II stimulates the adrenal cortex to release aldosterone. Aldosterone stimulates the kidneys to retain sodium and water, which increases blood volume and CO (see Fig. 49.4).

Increased blood sodium and osmolarity levels stimulates the release of ADH from the posterior pituitary gland. ADH increases the ECF volume by promoting water reabsorption in the distal and collecting tubules of the kidneys. The resulting increase in blood volume causes an increase in CO and BP.

HYPERTENSION

Classification of Hypertension

Table 36.2 shows the BP classifications for people 18 years of age and older.[5] If either the systolic BP (SBP) or diastolic BP (DBP) is outside of a range, the higher measurement determines the classification. For example, 115/86 would be classified as hypertension stage 1 even though the SBP is within normal limits. SBP increases with age. DBP rises until around 55 years old and then declines. BP classification is based on 2 or more readings, accurately performed on both arms, on 2 separate occasions.

Etiology

Hypertension can result from either primary or secondary causes.

Primary Hypertension

Primary hypertension *(essential* or *idiopathic)* is elevated BP without an identified cause. It accounts for 90% to 95% of all cases of hypertension. Although we do not know the exact cause for primary hypertension, there are many contributing factors. These include changes in endothelial function related to either vasoconstricting or vasodilating agents, increased SNS activity, overproduction of sodium-retaining hormones, increased sodium intake, greater than ideal body weight, age, family history, ethnicity, diabetes, tobacco use, and excess alcohol use.

Secondary Hypertension

Secondary hypertension is elevated BP with a specific cause that often can be identified and corrected (Table 36.3). It accounts for 5% to 10% of hypertension in adults. Secondary hypertension should be suspected in people who suddenly develop high BP, especially if it is severe. Findings that suggest secondary hypertension relate to the underlying cause. For example, an abdominal bruit heard over the renal arteries may indicate renal disease. It is often present in patients with obstructive sleep apnea. Treatment is aimed at removing or treating the underlying cause. Secondary hypertension is a contributing factor to hypertensive crisis.

TABLE 36.3 Common Causes of Secondary Hypertension

- Cirrhosis
- Coarctation or congenital narrowing of the aorta
- Drug-related: estrogen replacement therapy, oral contraceptives, corticosteroids, nonsteroidal antiinflammatory drugs (e.g., COX-2 inhibitors), sympathetic nervous system stimulants (e.g., cocaine, monoamine oxidase)
- Endocrine problems (e.g., pheochromocytoma, Cushing syndrome, thyroid disease)
- Neurologic problems (e.g., brain tumors, stroke, traumatic brain injury)
- Pregnancy-induced hypertension
- Renal disease (e.g., renal artery stenosis, glomerulonephritis)
- Sleep apnea

Pathophysiology of Primary Hypertension

BP rises with any increase in CO or SVR. As hypertension progresses from elevated to stage 1, increases in both blood volume and CO are often present, leading to an increase in SVR. As hypertension progresses, SVR rises, and CO returns to normal. The hemodynamic hallmark of hypertension is a persistently increased SVR. This persistent increase in SVR may occur in several ways. Table 36.4 shows factors that relate to the development of primary hypertension or contribute to its consequences. Abnormalities of any of the mechanisms involved in maintaining normal BP can result in hypertension (Fig. 36.1).

Genetic Link

Genetic variations are associated with the development of hypertension. For example, genetic abnormalities can cause a rare form of hypertension characterized by excess potassium levels. Several genetic variants of substances on the endothelium affect BP and the development of hypertension by influencing the body's sensitivity to salt. When endothelial surface proteins are activated, proinflammatory properties are stimulated. This impairs the endothelial cells' ability to activate vasodilatory effects, leading to hypertension.

Research is currently ongoing to understand the complicated role that endothelial dysfunction and genetics play in the formation and progression of hypertension. We recommend screening children and siblings of persons with hypertension and advising them to adopt healthy lifestyles to minimize their risk for developing hypertension.

Water and Sodium Retention

Excess sodium intake is linked to the development of hypertension. Although most people consume a high-sodium diet, only 1 in 3 will develop hypertension. When sodium is restricted in people with hypertension, their BP usually falls. This suggests that some degree of sodium sensitivity may exist for high sodium intake to trigger the development of hypertension. A high sodium intake may activate a number of systemic mechanisms.

TABLE 36.4 Risk Factors for Primary Hypertension

Risk Factor	Description
Age	• Systolic BP rises progressively with age • After age 50, SBP >140 mm Hg is a more important cardiovascular risk factor than diastolic BP
Alcohol	• Excess alcohol use is associated with hypertension • Moderate alcohol use has cardioprotective properties; males should limit their daily intake of alcohol to 2 drinks per day, and 1 drink per day for females
Diabetes	• Hypertension is more common in patients with diabetes • When hypertension and diabetes coexist, complications (e.g., target organ disease) are more severe
Ethnicity	• Incidence of hypertension is higher in Blacks (Box 36.1)

Excess sodium intake	• High sodium intake can
	  • Contribute to hypertension in salt-sensitive patients
	  • ↓ Effectiveness of certain antihypertensive drugs

Family history	• History of a close blood relative (e.g., parents, sibling) with hypertension ↑risk for developing hypertension
Gender	• More prevalent in men in young adulthood and early middle age • After age 64, hypertension is more prevalent in women (Box 36.2)
Increased serum lipids	• ↑ Cholesterol and triglyceride levels are primary risk factors for atherosclerosis • Hyperlipidemia is more common in people with hypertension
Obesity	• Weight gain ↑ frequency of hypertension • Risk increases with central abdominal obesity
Sedentary lifestyle	• Regular physical activity can help control weight and reduce cardiovascular risk • Physical activity may ↓ BP
Socioeconomic status	• More prevalent in lower socioeconomic groups and among the less educated
Stress	• People exposed to repeated stress may develop hypertension more often • People who develop hypertension may respond differently to stress than those who do not develop hypertension
Tobacco use	• Smoking tobacco greatly↑ risk for CVD • People with hypertension who smoke tobacco are at even greater risk for CVD

Fig. 36.2 shows the relationships among salt intake, BP, and changes in heart structure.

In clinical practice, there is not an easy or straightforward test to identify people whose BP will rise with even a small increase in salt intake *(salt sensitive)* versus those who can ingest large amounts of sodium without much change in BP *(salt resistant)*. The effect of sodium on BP has a strong genetic component. The effect of sodium is more significant in Blacks and middle-aged and older adults. This can increase the risk of renal problems, endothelial dysfunction, and HF in these persons.[7,8]

Altered Renin-Angiotensin-Aldosterone Mechanism

High plasma renin activity (PRA) increases the conversion of angiotensinogen to angiotensin I (see Fig. 49.4). This change in the RAAS may contribute to the development of hypertension. Any rise in BP inhibits the release of renin from the renal juxtaglomerular cells. Based on this feedback loop, we would expect low levels of PRA in patients with primary hypertension. However, only about 30% have low PRA, 50% have normal levels, and 20% have high PRA. These normal or high PRA levels may be related to excess renin secretion from ischemic nephrons.

Stress and Increased Sympathetic Nervous System Activity

Factors such as anger, fear, and pain influence BP. Physiologic responses to stress, which are typically protective, may persist to a pathologic degree, resulting in a prolonged increase in SNS activity. Increased SNS stimulation causes increased vasoconstriction, increased HR, and increased renin release. Increased renin activates the RAAS, leading to elevated BP. People with high levels of repeated psychological stress develop hypertension more than those who have less stress.

Insulin Resistance and Hyperinsulinemia

Defects in glucose, insulin, and lipoprotein metabolism are common in primary hypertension. These defects are not present in secondary hypertension and do not improve when primary hypertension is treated. Insulin resistance is a risk factor in the development of hypertension and CVD. High insulin levels stimulate SNS activity, impair nitrous oxide-mediated vasodilation, promote vascular hypertrophy, and increase renal sodium reabsorption.

Endothelial Dysfunction

Hypertension can manifest as a prolonged vasoconstriction response or as a reduced vasodilator response. High levels of ET may cause prolonged vasoconstriction. Vasodilation effects can be altered by oxygen free radicals, which impair the bioavailability of NO. This leads to cellular dysfunction and an imbalance of the vasodilation and vasoconstriction mechanisms in the endothelium.

Clinical Manifestations

Hypertension is called the "silent killer" because it is often asymptomatic until it becomes severe and target organ disease occurs. A patient with severe hypertension may have a variety of symptoms from the effects on blood vessels in the various organs and tissues or to the increased workload of the heart. These secondary symptoms include fatigue, dizziness, palpitations, angina, and dyspnea.

In the past, we thought headaches and nosebleeds were symptoms of hypertension. They are no more frequent in people with hypertension than in the general population. However, patients with hypertensive crisis may have severe headaches, dyspnea, and nosebleeds.[9]

Complications

The most common complications of hypertension are *target organ diseases* occurring in the heart (hypertensive heart disease), brain (cerebrovascular disease), peripheral vessels (peripheral vascular disease [PVD]), kidneys (nephrosclerosis), and eyes (retinal damage) (Fig. 36.3).

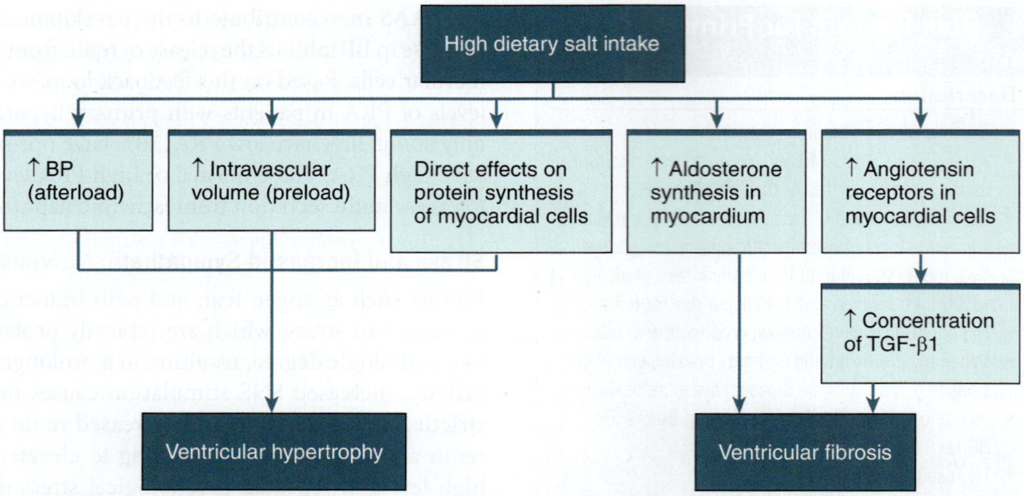

Fig. 36.2 Proposed link among salt intake, BP, and changes in the heart. High diet salt intake exerts hypertrophic effects on the left (and potentially the right) ventricle. Ventricular fibrosis can also result from the high salt intake through mechanisms mediated by the renin-angiotensin-aldosterone system (RAAS). Transforming growth factor-β1 *(TGF-β1)* is a multifunctional cytokine with fibrogenic properties. Overproduction of TGF-β1 (in part mediated by angiotensin II) results in fibrosis and ventricular dysfunction. (Modified from Frisoli TM, Schmieder RE, Grodzicki T, et al.: Salt and hypertension: is salt dietary reduction worth the effort? *Am J Med* 125:433, 2012.)

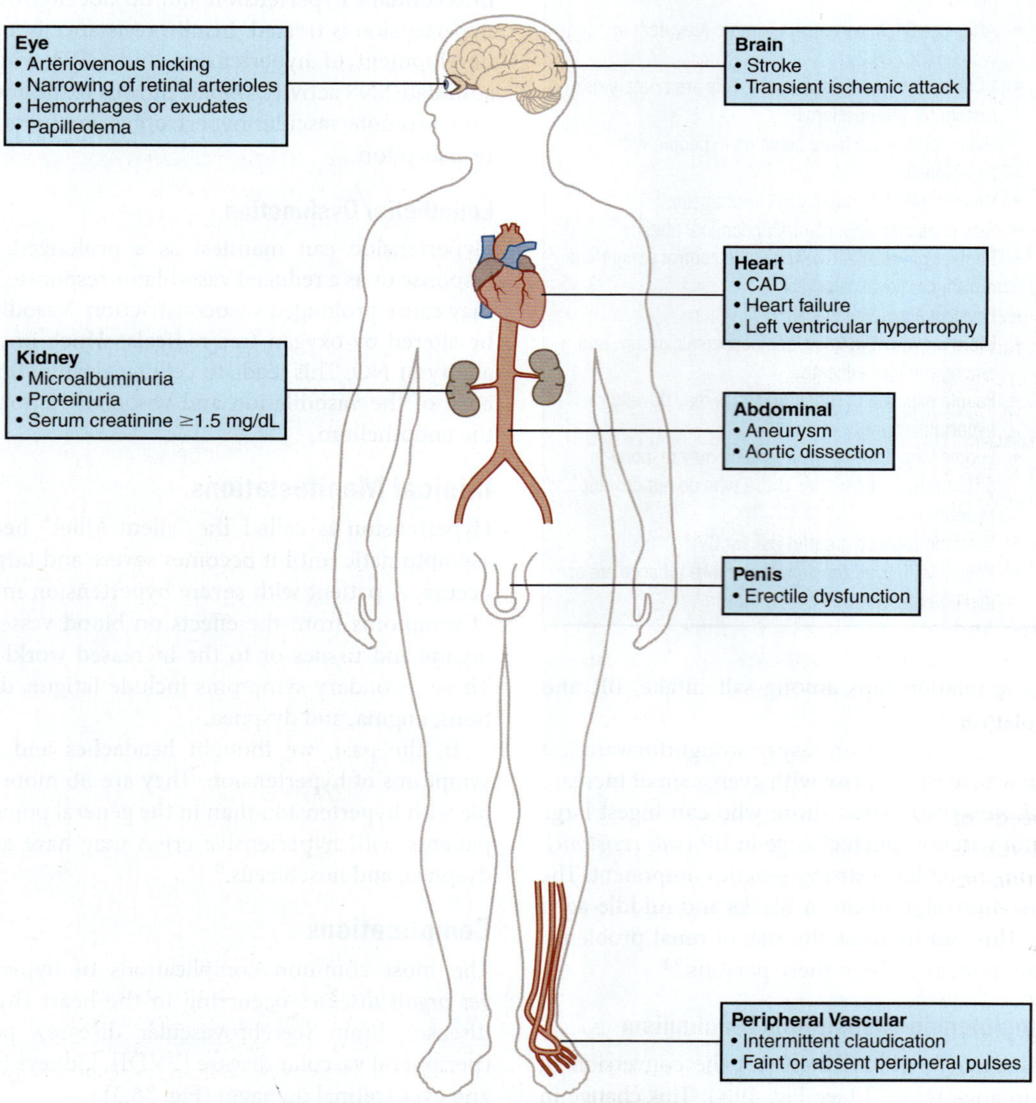

Fig. 36.3 Common complications of hypertension.

Hypertensive Heart Disease

Coronary artery disease. Hypertension is a significant risk factor for coronary artery disease (CAD). The "response-to-injury" theory of atherogenesis suggests that hypertension disrupts the coronary artery endothelium (see Fig. 37.1). This results in a rigid arterial wall with a narrowed lumen and may account for the high rate of CAD, angina, and MI.

Left ventricular hypertrophy. Sustained high BP increases the cardiac workload and causes left ventricular hypertrophy (LVH) (Fig. 36.4). Initially, LVH is a compensatory mechanism that strengthens cardiac contraction and increases CO. However, increased contractility increases myocardial work and O_2 demand. Progressive LVH, especially in the presence of CAD, can cause HF.

Heart failure. HF occurs when the heart's compensatory mechanisms are overwhelmed, and the heart can no longer pump enough blood to meet the body's demands (see Chapter 38). Contractility is depressed. SV and CO are decreased. The patient may have shortness of breath on exertion, paroxysmal nocturnal dyspnea, and fatigue.

Cerebrovascular Disease

Atherosclerosis is the most common cause of cerebrovascular disease. Hypertension is a significant risk factor for cerebral atherosclerosis and stroke. Even in mildly hypertensive people, the risk for stroke is 4 times higher than in normotensive people. Adequate BP control decreases the risk for stroke.

Atherosclerotic plaques are often found at the bifurcation of the common carotid artery and in the internal and external carotid arteries. Portions of the atherosclerotic plaque or the blood clot that forms with disruption of the plaque may break off and travel to cerebral vessels, producing thromboembolism. The patient may have transient ischemic attacks or a stroke. These conditions are discussed in Chapter 62.

Hypertensive encephalopathy may occur after a marked rise in BP if autoregulation does not decrease the cerebral blood flow. *Autoregulation* is a physiologic process that keeps cerebral blood flow constant despite fluctuations in BP. Typically, as pressure in the cerebral blood vessels rises, the vessels constrict to maintain constant flow. When BP exceeds the body's ability to autoregulate, the cerebral vessels suddenly dilate, capillary permeability increases, and cerebral edema develops. This causes a rise in intracranial pressure. If left untreated, patients can die quickly from brain damage. Chapter 60 reviews cerebral blood flow and autoregulation.

Peripheral Vascular Disease

Hypertension speeds up the process of atherosclerosis in the peripheral blood vessels. This leads to PVD, aortic aneurysm, and aortic dissection (see Chapter 41). *Intermittent claudication* (ischemic leg pain precipitated by activity and relieved by rest) is a classic symptom of PVD.

Nephrosclerosis

Hypertension is one of the leading causes of chronic kidney disease (CKD). Some degree of renal disease is usually present even with mild hypertension. Renal disease results from ischemia caused by the narrowing of the renal blood vessels. This leads to atrophy of the tubules, destruction of the glomeruli, and eventual death of nephrons. The remaining intact nephrons can compensate, but changes may eventually lead to renal failure. Laboratory signs of renal disease are albuminuria, proteinuria, microscopic hematuria, and high serum creatinine and blood urea nitrogen (BUN) levels. Nocturia is an early symptom of renal disease (see Chapter 50).

Retinal Damage

Damage to the retinal vessels seen with an ophthalmoscope indicates similar vessel damage in the heart, brain, and kidneys. Manifestations of severe retinal damage include blurred vision, retinal hemorrhage, and vision loss.

Diagnostic Studies

Measurement of BP is essential in assessing and monitoring hypertension. Chapter 35 and the Nursing Management section later in this chapter discuss BP measurement.

Table 36.5 lists diagnostic studies performed in a person with hypertension. Basic laboratory studies may be done to (1) identify or rule out causes of secondary hypertension, (2) evaluate target organ disease, (3) determine overall cardiovascular risk, or (4) establish baseline levels before starting therapy. Routine urinalysis, BUN, and serum creatinine levels are used to screen for renal involvement and provide baseline information about kidney function. Creatinine clearance reflects the glomerular filtration rate. Decreases in creatinine clearance indicate renal insufficiency. Chapter 49 discusses serum creatinine and creatinine clearance.

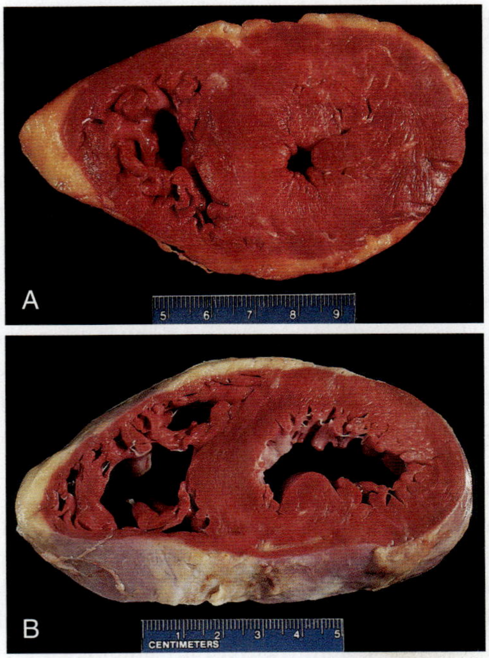

Fig. 36.4 (A) Massively enlarged heart caused by hypertrophy of the muscle in the left ventricle. (B) Compare with the thickness of the normal left ventricle. The patient had severe hypertension. (From Kumar V, Cotran RS, Robbins SL: *Robbins basic pathology*, ed 8, Philadelphia, 2007, Saunders.)

TABLE 36.5 Interprofessional Care

Hypertension

Diagnostic Assessment

- History and physical assessment, including an ophthalmic examination
- Fasting blood glucose
- Routine urinalysis
- Basic metabolic panel with estimated glomerular filtration rate (eGFR)
- Complete blood count
- Serum lipid profile (total lipids, triglycerides, HDL and LDL cholesterol, total-to-HDL cholesterol ratio)
- Serum uric acid, calcium, and magnesium
- 12-Lead ECG

Optional

- 24-hour urinary creatinine clearance
- Echocardiography
- Liver function studies
- Serum thyroid-stimulating hormone (TSH)

Management

- Periodic BP monitoring
  - Home BP monitoring
  - Ambulatory BP monitoring
  - Every 3–6 months by an HCP once goal BP is achieved and stabilized
- Nutrition therapy
  - Restrict salt and sodium
  - Restrict cholesterol and saturated fats
  - Maintain adequate potassium and calcium intake
  - Weight management
- Regular, moderate physical activity
- Tobacco cessation (see Tables 11.3 through 11.5)
- Moderate alcohol use
- Stress management techniques (see Chapter 7)
- Antihypertensive drugs (see Tables 36.7–36.9)
- Patient and caregiver teaching

Measurement of serum electrolytes, especially potassium, is essential to detect hyperaldosteronism, a cause of secondary hypertension. Blood glucose levels aid in the diagnosis of diabetes. A lipid profile gives information about risk factors related to atherosclerosis and CVD. Uric acid levels establish a baseline since the levels often rise with diuretic therapy. An ECG can identify the presence of LVH, cardiac ischemia, or previous MI. If LVH is suspected, echocardiography is often done. If the patient's age, history, physical assessment, or severity of hypertension points to a secondary cause, further diagnostic testing is needed.

Ambulatory Blood Pressure Monitoring

Some patients have high BP readings in a clinical setting and normal readings when BP is measured elsewhere. This phenomenon is referred to as *"white coat"* hypertension. Ambulatory BP monitoring (ABPM) is one method for diagnosing white coat hypertension. It is a noninvasive, fully automated system that measures BP at preset intervals over a 12- to 24-hour period. The equipment is worn continuously for 24 hours, and results are reviewed by the provider. The monitoring equipment includes a BP cuff and a microprocessing unit that fits into a pouch worn on a shoulder strap or belt. Tell patients to hold their arm still by their side when the device is taking a reading. Have them keep a diary of activities that may affect BP. Other applications for ABPM include suspected antihypertensive drug resistance, hypotensive symptoms with antihypertensive therapy, episodic hypertension, or SNS dysfunction.

BP has diurnal variability expressed as sleep-wakefulness difference. For day-active people, BP is highest in the early morning, decreases during the day, and is lowest at night. BP at night (during sleep) usually drops by 10% or more from daytime (awake) BP.[5] ABPM verifies the presence of diurnal variability.

Some patients with hypertension do not show a typical nocturnal dip in BP. They are referred to as "nondippers." Patients at highest risk for CVD are "reverse dippers." They have an increase in nighttime SBP. Current research is focused on using drugs to optimize cardioprotective effects and convert nondippers and reverse dippers to dippers.

Interprofessional Care

The 2019 ACC/AHA guidelines recommend team-based care for the control of risk factors for atherosclerotic cardiovascular disease (ASCVD).[7] Table 36.5 summarizes the interprofessional care for a patient with hypertension. Goals include achieving and maintaining goal BP and reducing cardiovascular risk and target organ disease. Lifestyle modifications are a part of therapy for all patients with elevated BP and hypertension.

Lifestyle Modifications

Lifestyle modifications are directed toward reducing the patient's BP and overall cardiovascular risk. The AHA's "Life's Simple 7" steps support ways to modify and improve health. These are (1) manage BP, (2) control cholesterol, (3) reduce glucose, (4) get active, (5) eat better, (6) lose weight, and (7) stop smoking. Other modifications by the taskforce on hypertension address sodium restrictions and alcohol use. Assess social determinants of health as part of lifestyle modifications (see Chapter 2).[7]

Weight loss. Persons who are overweight have an increased incidence of hypertension and increased risk for CVD. Weight loss can have a significant effect on lowering BP. The effect is seen with even moderate weight loss. A rule of thumb is for every 1 kg of weight lost, BP will decrease by 1 mm Hg. When a person decreases caloric intake, sodium and fat intake are usually also reduced. Although reducing diet fat content has not shown any sustained benefits in BP control, it may slow the progress of atherosclerosis and reduce overall CVD risk (see Chapter 37). Weight loss through a combination of calorie restriction and moderate physical activity is recommended for overweight patients with hypertension.

Nutrition and diet. Plant-based and Mediterranean diets with increased fruit, nut, vegetable, legumes, and lean proteins from fish and vegetables decreases BP and mortality rates from CVD.[7,10] The Dietary Approaches to Stop Hypertension (DASH) eating plan has also been shown to significantly decrease BP.[11]

Sodium reduction. The average adult sodium intake is around 4200 mg/day in men and 3300 mg/day in women. Healthy adults should restrict sodium intake to 2300 mg/day or less.[8] Adults who consume less than 1500 mg of sodium lower their BP even further.[7]

The patient and caregiver, especially the person who prepares the meals, need to learn about low-sodium diets. Review the patient's typical diet to identify foods high in sodium. The AHA calls 6 food groups that are the highest sodium sources in the United States the "Salty Six." They recommend not adding salt and reducing intake of foods in these groups: bread products, lunch meat and cured meats, pizza, soup, sandwiches, and poultry (see Table 38.8). Teaching should include reading labels of over-the-counter (OTC) drugs, prepared and packaged foods, and health products (e.g., toothpaste containing baking soda) to identify hidden sources of sodium.

Sodium restriction may be enough to control BP or allow for lower drug dosages in some patients. Further, moderate sodium restriction lessens the risk for hypokalemia from diuretic therapy. However, the response differs between patients who are salt sensitive or salt resistant.

The significance of other diet elements for the control of hypertension is not certain. Increased diet intake potassium and calcium are associated with lower BP. People with hypertension should receive adequate intake of these from food sources. Calcium supplements are not recommended to lower BP.

Moderate alcohol use. Excess alcohol use is strongly associated with hypertension. Drinking 3 or more alcoholic drinks a day is a risk factor for CVD and stroke. Men should limit their intake of alcohol to no more than 2 drinks per day and women and lighter-weight men to no more than 1 drink per day; 1 drink is defined as 12 oz of regular beer, 5 oz of wine (12% alcohol), or 1.5 oz of 80-proof distilled spirits. Excess alcohol use that results in cirrhosis is a frequent cause of secondary hypertension.

Physical activity. A physically active lifestyle is essential to promote good health. Adults should perform a minimum of 150 minutes of moderate exercise or 75 minutes of vigorous exercise per week. For those unable to do the minimum recommendation, even some exercise improves BP.[7,12,13]

Physical activity guidelines are different for adults age 18 to 65 years, adults over 65 years, and adults age 50 to 64 years with functional limitations. The differences relate to the definition of moderate and vigorous aerobic activity. For adults ages 18 to 65, walking briskly at a pace that noticeably increases the pulse defines moderate-intensity aerobic activity. Jogging at a pace that substantially increases the pulse and causes rapid breathing is an example of vigorous activity for this age group. For all other adults, individual fitness levels guide aerobic intensity.[12]

All adults should perform muscle-strengthening activities using the major muscles of the body at least twice a week. This helps to maintain or increase muscle strength and endurance. Flexibility and balance exercises are recommended at least twice a week for older adults, especially for those at risk for falls.[13] Moderate-intensity activities can lower BP, promote relaxation, and decrease or control body weight. Regular activity of this type can reduce SBP by 4 to 9 mm Hg.[5,7]

Physical activity is more likely to become a habit if it is safe and enjoyable, fits easily into one's daily schedule, and is inexpensive. Many shopping malls open early in the morning, offering a warm, safe, flat area for walking. Some health clubs offer special "off-peak" rates to encourage physical activity among older adults. Some health insurance carriers offer health club discounts as a benefit to encourage member fitness. Cardiac rehabilitation programs offer supervised exercise and education about reducing cardiovascular risk factors.

Help people with hypertension to increase their physical activity by explaining the need for physical activity, describing the types of physical activities, and aiding in starting an exercise plan. Tell sedentary people to increase activity levels gradually. Those with CVD or other serious health problems need a thorough examination and possibly a stress test before beginning an exercise program.

Avoiding tobacco products. Nicotine contained in tobacco causes vasoconstriction and increases BP, especially in people with hypertension. Smoking tobacco is a major risk factor for CVD. Strongly encourage everyone, especially patients with hypertension, to avoid tobacco use. We see the cardiovascular benefits of stopping tobacco use within a year. Teach those who continue to use tobacco products to monitor their BP regularly. Chapter 11 discusses tobacco use and smoking cessation.

Other risk factors. Risk factors can be related to social determinants of health and psychosocial risk factors. These factors can contribute to the risk for developing CVD and to a poorer prognosis and clinical course in those with CVD. Social determinants of health are the conditions in which people are born, grow, live, work, and age and the wider set of forces and systems shaping the conditions of daily life.[14] These factors include socioeconomic status, resources to meet daily needs, support systems, stress at work and in family life, education, health care access, safe housing, and exposure to violence. These risk factors have direct effects on the cardiovascular system by activating the SNS and stress hormones. They can contribute to CVD indirectly by their impact on lifestyle behaviors and choices.

Screening is essential so appropriate referrals can be given to help the patient and family. Referrals might include counseling, behavioral interventions such as community or religious support systems, social work assistance for finding resources such as fresh fruits and vegetables, or information on housing assistance. Once basic needs are met, beneficial options might include relaxation training, stress management, support groups, and exercise training.[6,15]

Drug Therapy

These are the current recommendations for antihypertensive drug therapy[5]:

- In patients 65 years or older with an average SBP of more than 130 mm Hg who are ambulatory and living in a community setting, rather than living in a skilled agency, treatment goals should be to obtain an SBP less than 130 mm Hg.
- In patients 65 years or older with an average SBP of more than 130 mm Hg who live in a skilled agency, and/or have multiple comorbidities or limited life expectancy, treatment should be based on patient preference, clinical experiences, and team input.

TABLE 36.6 Drug Therapy

Antihypertensive Agents

Drug	Mechanism of Action	Nursing Considerations
Adrenergic Inhibitors		
Central-Acting α-Adrenergic Agonists		
clonidine (Catapres) clonidine patch (Catapres-TTS)	↓ Sympathetic outflow from central nervous system ↓ Peripheral sympathetic tone, produces vasodilation, ↓ SVR and BP	Sudden discontinuation may cause withdrawal syndrome, including rebound hypertension, tachycardia, headache, tremors, apprehension, sweating Chewing gum or hard candy may relieve dry mouth Alcohol and sedatives ↑ sedation Transdermal patch may be related to fewer side effects and better adherence
guanfacine	Same as clonidine	Same as clonidine, but not available in the transdermal formulation
methyldopa	Same as clonidine	Teach patient about daytime sedation and avoiding hazardous activities Taking a single daily dose at bedtime minimizes the sedative effect
α_1-Adrenergic Blockers		
doxazosin (Cardura) prazosin (Minipress) terazosin	Block α_1-adrenergic effects, producing peripheral vasodilation (↓ SVR and BP) Beneficial effects on lipid profile	↓ Resistance to the outflow of urine in benign prostatic hyperplasia Take at bedtime to reduce risk associated with orthostatic hypotension
phentolamine	Blocks α_1-adrenergic receptors, resulting in peripheral vasodilation (↓ SVR and BP)	Used in the short-term management of pheochromocytoma Used locally to prevent necrosis of skin and subcutaneous tissue after extravasation of adrenergic drug No oral formulation
β-Adrenergic Blockers		
Cardioselective Blockers		
acebutolol atenolol (Tenormin) betaxolol bisoprolol esmolol (Brevibloc) metoprolol (Lopressor)	Block β_1-adrenergic receptors (Table 36.1) ↓ BP by blocking β-adrenergic effects ↓ CO and sympathetic vasoconstrictor tone ↓ Renin secretion by kidneys	Monitor pulse and BP regularly Use with caution in patients with diabetes because may depress the tachycardia associated with hypoglycemia and adversely affect glucose metabolism Drug of choice for patients with a history of an MI or HF Less effective BP reduction in black patients Esmolol is for IV use only Lose cardioselectivity at higher doses
Non-Cardioselective Blockers		
nadolol (Corgard) pindolol propranolol (Inderal)	Block β_1- and β_2-adrenergic receptors (Table 36.1) ↓ BP by blocking β_1- and β_2-adrenergic effects	Same as cardioselective, except may cause bronchospasm, especially in patients with a history of asthma
Mixed α- and β-Blockers		
carvedilol (Coreg) labetalol	α_1-, β_1-, and β_2-adrenergic blocking properties producing peripheral vasodilation and ↓ heart rate (Table 36.1) ↓ CO, SVR, and BP	Same as β-blockers IV form is available for hypertensive crisis in hospitalized patients Keep patient supine during IV administration Assess patient tolerance of upright position (severe orthostatic hypotension) before allowing upright activities (e.g., commode)
Angiotensin Inhibitors		
Angiotensin-Converting Enzyme (ACE) Inhibitors		
benazepril (Lotensin) captopril enalapril (Vasotec) fosinopril lisinopril (Zestril) moexipril perindopril quinapril (Accupril) ramipril (Altace) trandolapril	Inhibit ACE, ↓ conversion of angiotensin I to angiotensin II (A-II) Inhibit A-II–mediated vasoconstriction	Aspirin and NSAIDs may ↓ effectiveness Adding a diuretic enhances effect, but should not be used with potassium-sparing diuretics Can ↑ serum creatinine Inhibit breakdown of bradykinin, which may cause a dry, hacking cough that can occur at any point during treatment, even years later Captopril may be given orally for hypertensive crisis

TABLE 36.6 Drug Therapy—cont'd

Antihypertensive Agents

Drug	Mechanism of Action	Nursing Considerations
Angiotensin II Receptor Blockers (ARBs)		
azilsartan (Edarbi) candesartan (Atacand) irbesartan (Avapro) losartan (Cozaar) olmesartan (Benicar) telmisartan (Micardis) valsartan (Diovan)	Prevent action of A-II Produce vasodilation ↑ Na^+ and water excretion	Full effect on BP may not be seen for 3–6 weeks Do not affect bradykinin levels, therefore an acceptable alternative to ACE inhibitors in people who develop a dry cough In patients with kidney disease, ACE inhibitors and ARBs should not be used together due to adverse renal effects
Calcium Channel Blockers (CCB)		
Non-Dihydropyridines		
diltiazem extended release (Cardizem LA) verapamil intermediate release (Calan SR) verapamil timed-release (Verelan PM)	Inhibit movement of Ca^{++} across cell membrane, resulting in vasodilation Cardioselective resulting in a ↓ in heart rate and slowing of AV conduction	Use with caution in patients with HF Grapefruit juice may ↑ serum concentrations and toxicity of certain CCBs; avoid concurrent use Used for supraventricular tachydysrhythmias Avoid in patients with second- or third-degree AV block or left ventricular systolic dysfunction
Dihydropyridines		
amlodipine (Norvasc) clevidipine (Cleviprex) felodipine isradipine nicardipine sustained release nifedipine long acting (Procardia XL) nisoldipine (Sular)	Cause vascular smooth muscle relaxation resulting in ↓ SVR and arterial BP	More potent peripheral vasodilators Clevidipine is for IV use only; solution must be changed every 12 hr Use of sublingual short-acting nifedipine in hypertensive emergencies is unsafe and not effective Serious adverse events (e.g., stroke, acute MI) have occurred IV nicardipine is available for hypertensive crisis in hospitalized patients; change peripheral IV infusion sites every 12 hr
Direct Vasodilators		
fenoldopam (Corlopam)	Activates dopamine receptors, resulting in systemic and renal vasodilation	IV use only for hypertensive crisis in hospitalized patients Use cautiously in patients with glaucoma Patient should remain flat for 1 hr after administration
hydralazine	↓ SVR and BP by direct arterial vasodilation	IV use for hypertensive crisis in hospitalized patients Twice-daily oral dosage Not used as monotherapy because of side effects Contraindicated in patients with CAD
minoxidil	↓ SVR and BP by direct arterial vasodilation	Reserved for treatment of severe hypertension associated with renal failure and resistant to other therapy Once- or twice-daily dosage
nitroglycerin	Relaxes arterial and venous smooth muscle, reducing preload and SVR At a low dose, venous dilation predominates; at a higher dose, arterial dilation is present	IV use for hypertensive crisis in hospitalized patients with myocardial ischemia Given by continuous IV infusion with pump or control device
sodium nitroprusside	Direct arterial vasodilation ↓ SVR and BP	IV use for hypertensive crisis in hospitalized patients Given by continuous IV infusion with pump or control device Arterial BP monitoring BP recommended Wrap IV solutions with an opaque material to protect from light Stable for 24 hr then metabolized to cyanide, then thiocyanate Monitor thiocyanate levels with prolonged use (>3 days) or doses ≥4 mcg/kg/min

- In patients over 18 years old with hypertension, known CVD or other risk factors, a BP of 130/80 mm Hg is the goal of treatment.
- In all other patients without CVD or other risk factors, a BP of less than 130/80 mm Hg may be reasonable.

Drugs currently available for treating hypertension have 2 primary actions: (1) decrease the volume of circulating blood and (2) reduce SVR (Tables 36.6, 36.7, and 36.8).[5] Fig. 36.5 shows the various sites and methods of action of antihypertensive agents. Drugs used in the treatment of hypertension include:

- *Adrenergic-inhibiting agents* act by decreasing SNS effects-centrally on the vasomotor center and peripherally to inhibit

TABLE 36.7 Drug Therapy

Diuretic Agents

Drug	Mechanism of Action	Nursing Considerations
Aldosterone Receptor Blockers		
eplerenone (Inspra) spironolactone (Aldactone)	Inhibit the Na^+-retaining and K^+-excreting effects of aldosterone in the distal and collecting tubules	Monitor for orthostatic hypotension and hyperkalemia Do not combine with potassium-sparing diuretics or potassium supplements Use with caution in patients on ACE inhibitors or angiotensin II blockers Classified as potassium-sparing diuretics
Loop Diuretics		
bumetanide (Bumex) furosemide (Lasix) torsemide	Inhibit NaCl reabsorption in the ascending limb of the loop of Henle ↑ Excretion of Na^+ and Cl^- More potent diuretic effect than thiazides, but shorter duration of action	Monitor for orthostatic hypotension and electrolyte abnormalities Remain effective despite renal insufficiency ↑ Diuretic effect at higher doses Less effective for hypertension
Potassium-Sparing Diuretics		
amiloride (Midamor) triamterene (Dyrenium)	↓ K^+ and Na^+ exchange in the distal and collecting tubules ↓ Excretion of K^+, H^+, Ca^{++}, and Mg^{++}	Monitor for orthostatic hypotension and hyperkalemia Contraindicated in patients with renal failure Use with caution in patients on ACE inhibitors or angiotensin II blockers Avoid potassium supplements
Renin Inhibitors		
Aliskiren hemifumarate (Tekturna)	Directly inhibits renin, thus reducing the conversion of angiotensinogen to angiotensin I	May cause angioedema of the face, extremities, lips, tongue, glottis, and/or larynx Not to be used in pregnancy
Thiazide and Related Diuretics		
chlorothiazide chlorthalidone hydrochlorothiazide indapamide metolazone (Zaroxolyn)	Inhibit NaCl reabsorption in the distal convoluted tubule ↑ Excretion of Na^+ and Cl^- Initial ↓ in ECF Sustained ↓ in SVR Lower BP moderately in 2–4 weeks	Monitor for orthostatic hypotension, hypokalemia, and alkalosis May potentiate cardiotoxicity of digoxin by producing hypokalemia Sodium restriction ↓ the risk for hypokalemia NSAIDs can ↓ diuretic and antihypertensive effect and potentially cause renal problems Teach patient to supplement with potassium-rich foods

NE release or to block the adrenergic receptors on blood vessels.

- *ACE inhibitors* prevent the conversion of angiotensin I to angiotensin II and reduce angiotensin II (A-II)–mediated vasoconstriction and sodium and water retention.
- *A-II receptor blockers (ARBs)* prevent angiotensin II from binding to its receptors in the walls of the blood vessels.
- *Calcium channel blockers* (*CCB*) increase sodium excretion and cause arteriolar vasodilation by preventing the movement of calcium into cells.
- *Direct vasodilators* decrease the BP by relaxing the vascular smooth muscle and reducing SVR.
- *Diuretics* promote sodium and water excretion, reduce plasma volume, and reduce the vascular response to catecholamines.

The preferred first-line therapy for patients with stage 1 hypertension includes nonpharmacologic treatment and one first-line drug. The preferred first-line drug classes are a thiazide diuretic, a CCB, and an ACE inhibitor or ARB. For most patients, a diuretic should be the first drug ordered.[5,7] Patients with stage 2 hypertension receive nonpharmacologic treatment and 2 antihypertensive agents from different classifications. If a drug is not tolerated or is contraindicated, then a drug from another class is used.

Once antihypertensive therapy begins, patients should return for follow-up and dosage adjustments monthly until the goal BP is reached. More frequent visits are needed for patients with stage 2 hypertension or with comorbidities. After BP is at goal and stable, follow-up visits can usually be at 3- to 6-month intervals. Comorbidities (e.g., HF), associated diseases (e.g., diabetes), and the need for ongoing monitoring (e.g., laboratory testing) influence the frequency of visits.

DRUG ALERT

Doxazosin (Cardura)

- Use caution when giving the first dose. It is best to give the first dose at bedtime to reduce the first dose BP drop.
- Syncope occasionally occurs 30–90 min after the first dose, a too-rapid increase in dose, or addition of another antihypertensive agent to therapy.
- Severe hypotension can occur with patients taking phosphodiesterase inhibitors, such as sildenafil (Viagra) or tadalafil (Cialis).

TABLE 36.8 Drug Therapy

Combination Therapy for Hypertension

Combinations	Trade Names
ACE Inhibitors and Diuretics	
benazepril/hydrochlorothiazide	Lotensin HCT
enalapril/hydrochlorothiazide	Vaseretic
lisinopril/hydrochlorothiazide	Zestoretic
Angiotensin II Receptor Blockers and CCBs	
olmesartan/amlodipine	Azor
telmisartan/amlodipine	Twynsta
valsartan/amlodipine	Exforge
Angiotensin II Receptor Blockers and Diuretics	
candesartan/hydrochlorothiazide	Atacand HCT
losartan/hydrochlorothiazide	Hyzaar
olmesartan medoxomil/hydrochlorothiazide	Benicar HCT
valsartan/hydrochlorothiazide	Diovan HCT
Angiotensin II Receptor Blocker, Diuretic, and CCB	
amlodipine/hydrochlorothiazide/valsartan	Exforge HCT
β-Blockers and Diuretics	
metoprolol/hydrochlorothiazide	Lopressor HCT
nadolol/bendroflumethiazide	Corzide
olmesartan medoxomil/amlodipine/hydrochlorothiazide	Tribenzor
CCB and ACE Inhibitor	
amlodipine/benazepril	Lotrel
Diuretics and Diuretics	
spironolactone/hydrochlorothiazide	Aldactazide
triamterene/hydrochlorothiazide	Dyazide, Maxzide

Resistant hypertension. Carefully explore all reasons why a patient may not be at goal BP (Table 36.9). *Resistant hypertension* is the failure to reach goal BP in patients who are taking full doses of an appropriate 3-drug therapy regimen that includes a diuretic. Resistant hypertension carries a 2- to 6-fold increase in complications including MI and stroke over other hypertensive patients. Treatments focus on identifying risk factors that could contribute to hypertension, assessing adherence, and evaluating alternative drug therapies. Overactive renal nerves can be a cause of resistant hypertension. Percutaneous catheter-based radiofrequency ablation of the renal nerves (known as *renal denervation*) may be used to help lower BP and SNS activity in patients with resistant hypertension.

❖ NURSING MANAGEMENT: PRIMARY HYPERTENSION

◆ Assessment

Table 36.10 presents subjective and objective data to obtain from a patient with hypertension.

◆ Clinical Problems

Clinical problems for the patient with hypertension include:

- Altered blood pressure
- Body weight problem
- Difficulty coping
- Health maintenance alteration
- Impaired cardiac function
- Impaired sexual function
- Inadequate tissue perfusion
- Nutritionally compromised

◆ Planning

Nursing care focuses on the priority problems of maintaining BP at a level that decreases complications and supporting the patient to manage what may be a complicated drug regimen with many side effects. The overall goals for the patient with hypertension are that the patient will (1) achieve and maintain the goal BP; (2) have minimal side effects of therapy; and (3) manage and cope with this condition.

◆ Implementation

◆ Health Promotion

Primary prevention of hypertension is a cost-effective approach. Current recommendations for primary prevention include lifestyle modifications that avoid or delay the rise in BP in at-risk people. Following the Mediterranean or DASH diet and reducing sodium can lower BP. Changes by the food industry, such as reducing the amount of salt in processed foods, may be useful.

The National Heart, Lung, and Blood Institute provides Web-based educational materials in several languages for HCPs, patients, and the public to raise awareness about the dangers of high BP. Search available publications at https://catalog.nhlbi.nih.gov/.

Patient evaluation. Hypertension is usually discovered through routine screening for insurance, employment, and military physical examinations. You are in an ideal position to assess for the presence of hypertension, identify the risk factors for hypertension and CAD, and teach patients about these conditions. In addition to BP measurement, a health assessment should include such factors as age; gender; diet history (including salt and alcohol intake); weight patterns; tobacco use; and family history of CVD, stroke, renal disease, and diabetes. Note all drugs taken, prescribed, OTC, and recreational. Ask the patient about a history of high BP and the results of any treatment.

Blood pressure measurement. Proper size and correct placement of the BP cuff are critical for accurate measurement (Table 36.11). Place the cuff snugly around the patient's bare upper arm with the midline of the bladder of the cuff (usually marked on the cuff by the manufacturer) placed in line with the brachial artery. Place the patient's arm at the level of the heart during BP measurement. For BP measurements taken in the sitting position, raise and support the arm at the level of the heart. For measurements taken in a supine position, raise and support (e.g., with a small pillow) the arm at heart level. If the arm is resting on the bed, it will be below heart level.

BP can be measured using the auscultatory (oscillatory) method.[16] Note any differences in measurements between each

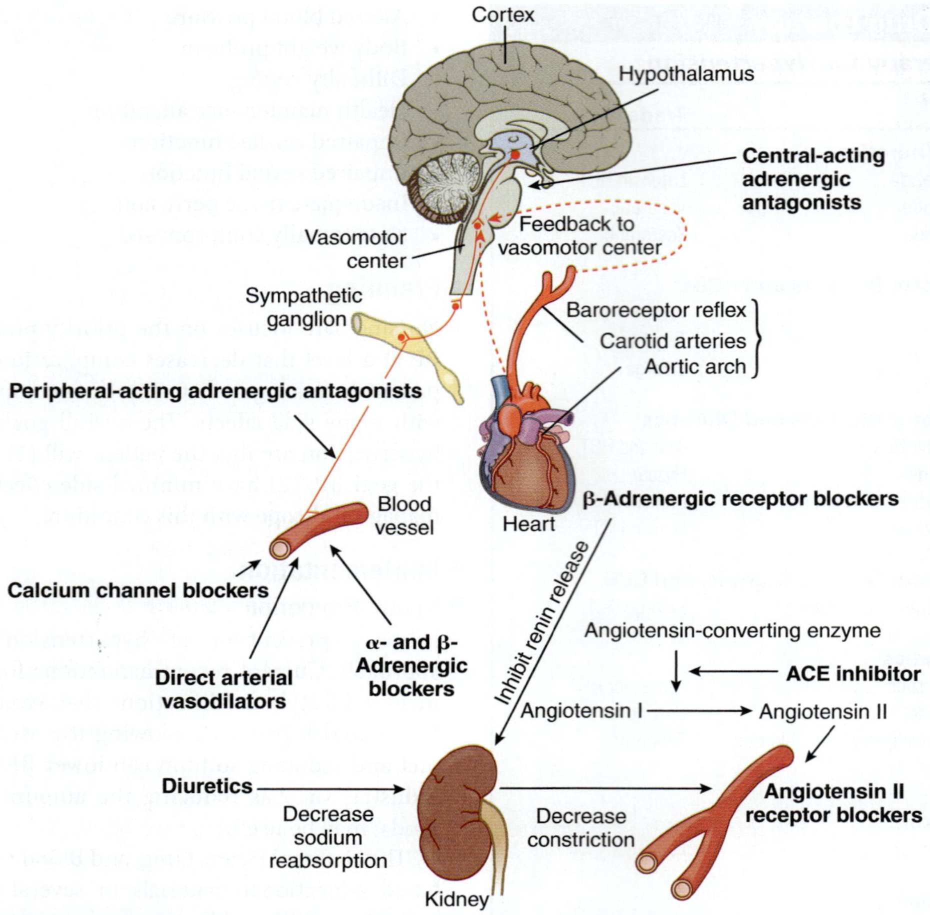

Fig. 36.5 Site and method of action of various antihypertensive drugs *(bold type).* (From US Department of Health and Human Services: *Seventh report of the Joint National Committee on Prevention, Detection, Evaluation, and Treatment of High Blood Pressure* [JNC 7], Washington, DC, 2003, National Institutes of Health.)

arm. Atherosclerosis in the subclavian artery can cause a falsely low reading on the side where the narrowing occurs.

If neither upper arm can be used to measure the BP (e.g., the presence of IV lines, fistula), or if a maximum size BP cuff does not fit the upper arm, use the forearm. In this case, position the proper size cuff midway between the elbow and the wrist. Auscultate Korotkoff sounds over the radial artery or use a Doppler device to note SBP. Use of an oscillometric device on the forearm is acceptable. Forearm and upper arm BPs are not interchangeable.

SAFETY ALERT

BP Measurement

- If using the forearm rather than the upper arm for BP measurement, document the site.
- BP cuffs that are too small or too large will result in readings that are falsely high or low, respectively.
- If bilateral BP measurements are not equal, record this finding and use the arm with the highest BP for all future measurements.

Assess for orthostatic (or postural) changes in BP and HR in older adults, people taking antihypertensive drugs, and patients who report symptoms consistent with reduced BP on standing (e.g., lightheadedness, dizziness, syncope). Start by having the person rest in the supine position for 3 minutes. Take baseline readings for BP and pulse. Have the patient sit and repeat the BP and pulse. Then have the patient stand and assess BP and pulse. After the patient has been standing for 3 minutes, measure BP and pulse again. Usually, the SBP decreases slightly (less than 10 mm Hg) on standing, while the DBP and pulse increase slightly.[17]

Orthostatic hypotension occurs when a patient moves from a supine to standing position, and there is a decrease of 20 mm Hg or more in SBP, a decrease of 10 mm Hg or more in DBP, and/or an increase in the HR of 20 beats/min. Note any lightheadedness or dizziness during the procedure, which is considered an abnormal finding. Common causes include dehydration and inadequate vasoconstrictor mechanisms related to disease or drug therapy.

Some people have a wide gap between the first Korotkoff sound and subsequent beats. This is called the *auscultatory gap.* Failure to inflate the cuff high enough may result in an inaccurate SBP, a reading lower than the patient's actual BP.

Trends in BP are more important than a single value. In acute care settings, BP measurement is usually done to assess volume status and effects of drugs rather than diagnose hypertension. Inform the HCP of any patient with a persistent elevated BP. They should be evaluated for hypertension.[5]

TABLE 36.9 Causes of Resistant Hypertension

Causes of Pseudoresistant Hypertension
- Improper BP measurements (i.e., inappropriate BP cuff size)
- Inadequate drug doses
- Inappropriate drug therapy
- Poor adherence to drug regimen (e.g., due to side effects, finances)
- White coat syndrome

Volume Overload
- Drug-induced
- Corticosteroids
- Cyclosporine and tacrolimus (Prograf)
- Erythropoietin
- Nonsteroidal antiinflammatory drugs
- Oral contraceptives
- Sympathomimetics (e.g., decongestants, diet pills)
- Excess salt intake
- Herbal supplements (e.g., ma huang, bitter orange)
- Inadequate diuretic therapy
- Illegal drugs (e.g., cocaine, amphetamines)
- Licorice
- Volume retention from kidney disease

Associated Conditions
- Excess alcohol use
- Increasing obesity
- Obstructive sleep apnea

Source: Brandani L: Resistant hypertension: a therapeutic challenge, *J Clin Hypertens* 20:76, 2018.

Verifying how BP is obtained at home is important when assessing for potential hypertension. Ensure that the home machine has been validated for accuracy and the patient records measurements at the same time of day for consistency. Confirming office BP readings with BP readings obtained at home can help determine average BP.

Screening programs. Screening programs in the community are widely used to identify persons who have a high BP. At the time of the BP measurement, give each person a written, numeric value of the reading. Explain why further evaluation is needed.

TABLE 36.10 NURSING ASSESSMENT

Hypertension

Subjective Data

Important Health Information
- *Health history:* Known duration and past workup of high BP; cardiovascular, cerebrovascular, renal, or thyroid disease; diabetes; pituitary disorders; obesity; dyslipidemia; menopause or hormone replacement status
- *Medications:* Use of any prescription, OTC, recreational, or herbal products; use of antihypertensive drug therapy

Functional Health Patterns
- *Health perception–health management:* Family history of hypertension or CVD; tobacco use, alcohol use; sedentary lifestyle; health literacy; readiness for change
- *Nutritional-metabolic:* Usual salt and fat intake; weight gain or loss
- *Elimination:* Nocturia
- *Activity-exercise:* Fatigue; dyspnea on exertion, palpitations, exertional chest pain; intermittent claudication, muscle cramps; usual pattern and type of exercise
- *Cognitive-perceptual:* Dizziness; blurred vision; paresthesias
- *Sexual-reproductive:* Erectile dysfunction, decreased libido
- *Coping–stress tolerance:* Stressful life events

Objective Data

Cardiovascular
- SBP consistently >130 mm Hg or DBP >80 mm Hg; orthostatic changes in BP and HR; bilateral BPs significantly different; abnormal heart sounds; laterally displaced apical pulse; decreased or absent peripheral pulses; carotid, renal, or femoral bruits; peripheral edema

Gastrointestinal
- Obesity (BMI ≥30 kg/m^2); abnormal waist-hip ratio

Neurologic
- Mental status changes

Possible Diagnostic Findings
- Abnormal serum electrolytes (especially potassium); ↑ BUN, creatinine, glucose, cholesterol, and triglyceride levels; proteinuria, albuminuria, microscopic hematuria; evidence of ischemic heart disease and left ventricular hypertrophy on ECG; evidence of structural heart disease and left ventricular hypertrophy on echocardiogram; evidence of arteriovenous nicking, retinal hemorrhages, and papilledema on funduscopic examination

◆ Ambulatory Care

Your primary role in the long-term management of hypertension is to assist the patient to reach the goal BP and adhere to the treatment plan (Table 36.12). Your actions include evaluating therapeutic effectiveness, detecting and reporting any adverse treatment effects, assessing and enhancing adherence, and teaching patients and caregivers.

Cardiovascular risk factor modification. Teaching about CVD risk factors is appropriate for all persons. Modifiable CVD risk factors include hypertension, obesity, diabetes, tobacco use, and physical inactivity. Discuss lifestyle modifications based on identified risk factors. Table 36.13 contains general information and health-promoting behaviors for patients with hypertension.

Teaching related to drug therapy. Side effects of antihypertensive therapy are common. They may be so severe or undesirable that the patient does not adhere to the therapy.[5,7] Telling the patient about side effects that may reduce with time may help the person to continue with therapy. The number or severity of side effects may relate to the dose. It may be necessary to change the drug or decrease the dose. Teach the patient to report all side effects to the HCP.

A common side effect of several of the antihypertensive drugs is orthostatic hypotension. It results from a change in the autonomic nervous system's mechanisms for regulating BP during position changes. Consequently, the patient may feel dizzy and faint when assuming an upright position after sitting or lying down. Table 36.13 presents specific measures to teach the patient to control or decrease orthostatic hypotension.

Sexual problems may occur with many antihypertensive drugs. This can be a significant reason that patients do not adhere to the treatment plan. Problems can range from reduced

TABLE 36.11 Blood Pressure Measurement

The patient should not have smoked, exercised, or ingested caffeine within 30 min before measurement.

1. Seat patient with legs uncrossed, feet on the floor, and back supported. Bare the patient's arm and support it at heart level.
2. Begin measurement after the patient has rested quietly for 5 min. Ask the patient to relax as much as possible and not to talk during the measurement.
3. Use the right cuff size. Follow instructions for fit and placement according to manufacturer's recommendations.
4. Measure and record BP in both arms initially and note any differences. There are conditions when an extremity should not be used to measure BP. These exclusions include deep venous thrombosis, arteriovenous fistula or graft, peripherally inserted central line (PICC), lymphedema, and limb ischemia. Use the arm with the highest BP and verify the reference point is at the heart.
5. BP should preferably be taken with an oscillometric device, rather than manually. The accuracy of oscillometric devices may be limited if patients are hypertensive, hypotensive, or have heart dysrhythmias (e.g., atrial fibrillation).
6. Patients with atrial fibrillation may have HR variations causing variations in BP, so it is recommended to take 3 different measurements over several minutes to confirm the BP.
7. For auscultatory measurement, estimate SBP by palpating the radial pulse and inflating the cuff until the pulse disappears. Inflate the cuff 20–30 mm Hg above this level.
8. Deflate the cuff at a rate of 2–3 mm Hg/sec.
9. Record the SBP and DBP. Note the SBP when the first of 2 or more Korotkoff sounds are heard and the DBP when sound disappears.
10. Provide the patient (verbally and in writing) with the BP reading, BP goal, and recommendations for follow-up.
11. Clean BP cuffs between patients according to the agency's policy for reusable medical equipment cleaning.

Source: Whelton PK, Carey RM, Aronow WS, et al: 2017 ACC/AHA/AAPA/ABC/ACPM/AGS/APhA/ASH/ASPC/NMA/PCNA guideline for the prevention, detection, evaluation, and management of high blood pressure in adults: A report of the American College of Cardiology/AHA Task Force on Clinical Practice Guidelines, *J Am Coll Cardiol* 71:e127, 2018.

libido to erectile dysfunction. Rather than discussing a sexual problem with an HCP, the patient may decide to stop therapy. Approach the patient on this sensitive subject and encourage discussion. The sexual problems may be easier for the patient to discuss once you explain that the drug may be the source of the problem.

Changing to another antihypertensive drug can decrease or relieve these side effects. Encourage the patient to discuss sexual issues with the HCP. If the patient is reluctant to do so, offer to alert the HCP to the side effects that the patient has. There are many options for treating hypertension. A plan that is acceptable to the patient should be the goal.

Some unpleasant side effects result from a drug's therapeutic effect, but these can be decreased. For example, diuretics cause dry mouth and frequent voiding. Sugarless gum or hard candy may help ease the dry mouth. Taking diuretics earlier in the day may limit frequent voiding during the night and preserve sleep.

Home blood pressure monitoring. Most patients with known or suspected hypertension should monitor their BP at home. The readings are often lower than those taken in the office setting and are a better predictor of CVD risk. Home BP readings may help achieve patient adherence by reinforcing the need for therapy. However, some patients become overly concerned with the BP readings. Provide information that will help patients understand what their goal or target BP is and why.

CHECK YOUR PRACTICE

You are making a home visit for a 78-year-old woman who is recovering from a hip replacement after she fractured her femur. She currently takes a combination of lisinopril/hydrochlorothiazide. The patient's daughter (her caregiver) tells you that her BP that morning was 150/88. She took it 2 more times, and it was the same. They are both worried and anxious that something is wrong because they heard that a BP over 120/80 is very bad.

- What should you do? What teaching would you provide?

Patient teaching is critical to ensure accuracy. Tell patients to buy an oscillometric BP monitor that uses a cuff for the upper arm or wrist. The patient should bring the BP monitor to the office to verify proper cuff size, the accuracy of the device, and the patient's technique.

Teach the patient to obtain a BP according to the steps in Table 36.11. Tell the patient to measure BP in the nondominant arm, or arm with the higher BP if there is a known difference between arms. Tell the patient to measure BP first thing in the morning (if possible, before taking any drugs) and at night before going to bed. Have the patient record all BP measurements and bring the record to office visits.

For clinical decision making (e.g., changes in dosage, starting a new drug), tell patients to take BP readings as described for 1 week. Stable, normotensive patients should measure morning and evening BP for at least 1 week every 3 months. Devices that have memory or printouts of the readings are convenient for reporting.[5]

Patient adherence. A significant problem in the long-term management of the patient with hypertension is poor adherence to the treatment plan (Box 36.3). The reasons for nonadherence are complicated. They can include inadequate patient teaching, low health literacy, unpleasant drug side effects, the BP returning to normal range with the therapy, the high cost of drugs, and lack of insurance.

It is important to determine the reasons why a patient is not adhering to treatment. Assess the patient's diet, activity level, and lifestyle as other indicators of adherence. Develop a plan with the patient and caregiver to improve adherence. The plan should be compatible with the patient's habits, cultural beliefs, and lifestyle. Active patient participation increases the chance of adherence to the plan. Measures include involving the patient in choosing drugs that are affordable and involving caregivers to help increase patient adherence.

Substituting combination drugs for multiple drugs once the BP is stable may promote adherence. Combination drugs are shown in Table 36.8. They reduce the number of pills that the patient must take each day and may reduce costs.

It is important to help the patient and caregiver understand that primary hypertension is a chronic illness that cannot be cured. Stress that it can be controlled with drug therapy, diet changes, physical activity, periodic follow-up, and other relevant lifestyle modifications.

TABLE 36.12 NURSING MANAGEMENT

Caring for the Patient With Hypertension

You will need to collaborate with many health care team members to deliver, delegate, and coordinate care based on the patient's status.

- Develop and conduct hypertension screening programs.
- Assess patients for hypertension risk factors and develop risk modification plans.
- Teach patients about lifestyle management and drug therapy.
- Monitor for adverse effects of antihypertensive drugs.
- Evaluate the effectiveness of lifestyle management and drug therapy in decreasing BP to acceptable levels.
- Teach about home BP monitoring, including the correct use of automatic BP monitors. Check that the device chosen by the patient meets the Association for the Advancement of Medical Instrumentation Standards (www.dableducational.org/sphygmomanometers/devices_1_clinical.html#ClinTable).
- Make appropriate referrals to other HCPs, such as dietitians or stress management programs.
- Monitor for complications of hypertension, such as CAD, HF, cerebrovascular disease, PVD, and renal disease.
- Assess the patient with a hypertensive crisis for evidence of target organ disease (e.g., encephalopathy, renal insufficiency, cardiac decompensation).
- Manage the patient with hypertensive urgency or emergency, including giving drugs and evaluating for resolution of the crisis.
- Supervise AP in measuring BP.
  - Obtain accurate BP readings in outpatient and inpatient settings.
  - Report high or low BP readings at once to RN.
  - Check postural BPs as directed.

Collaborate With Other Team Members

Dietitian

- Obtain a diet history from the patient.
- Teach the components of the DASH diet.
- Provide instructions for any diet changes needed.

Physical Therapist

- Assess current fitness level.
- Develop an exercise plan with the patient.

DASH, Dietary Approaches to Stop Hypertension.

◆ Evaluation

The overall expected outcomes are that the patient with hypertension will

- Achieve and maintain goal BP as defined for the person
- Understand, accept, and implement the treatment plan
- Report minimal side effects of drug therapy

Gerontologic Considerations: Hypertension

The prevalence of hypertension increases with age. The lifetime risk for developing hypertension is around 90% for normotensive men and women over age 55. Older adults are more likely to have white coat hypertension.[5]

The pathophysiology of hypertension in the older adult involves several age-related physical changes: (1) loss of elasticity in large arteries from atherosclerosis, (2) increased collagen content and stiffness of the myocardium, (3) increased peripheral vascular resistance, (4) decreased adrenergic receptor sensitivity, (5) blunting of baroreceptor reflexes, (6) decreased renal function, and (7) decreased renin response to sodium and water depletion.

In the older adult who is taking antihypertensive drugs, absorption of some agents may be altered because of decreased blood flow to the gut. Metabolism and excretion may be prolonged. Care should be taken to assess for orthostatic

TABLE 36.13 PATIENT & CAREGIVER TEACHING

Hypertension

When teaching the patient and/or caregiver about hypertension, include the following:

General Instructions

- Give the patient the BP reading and explain what it means (e.g., high, low, goal, borderline).
- Encourage the patient to monitor BP at home and teach the patient to call the HCP if BP exceeds high or low limits set by HCP.
- Hypertension is usually asymptomatic, and symptoms (e.g., nosebleeds) do not reliably indicate BP levels.
- Long-term therapy and follow-up care are necessary to treat hypertension. Therapy involves lifestyle changes (e.g., weight management, sodium reduction, smoking cessation, regular physical activity) and, in most cases, drugs to regulate the BP.
- Therapy will not cure but should control, hypertension.
- Controlled hypertension usually results in an excellent prognosis.
- Explain the potential dangers of uncontrolled hypertension (e.g., stroke, heart attack).

Instructions Related to Medication Therapy

- Be specific about the names, actions, dosages, and side effects of prescribed drugs.
- Help the patient plan regular and convenient times for taking medications and measuring BP.
- Do not stop drugs abruptly since withdrawal may cause a severe hypertensive reaction.
- Do not double up on a dose when a dose is missed.
- If BP increases or decreases, do not change the dose of the drug without consulting the HCP.
- Do not take any drugs belonging to someone else.
- Supplement diet with foods high in potassium (e.g., citrus fruits, green leafy vegetables) if taking potassium-wasting diuretics.
- Avoid hot baths, excess amounts of alcohol, and strenuous exercise within 3 hr of taking drugs that promote vasodilation.
- Many drugs cause orthostatic hypotension. Reduce the effects of orthostatic hypotension by rising slowly from the bed, sitting on the side of the bed for a few minutes, standing slowly, and beginning to move if no symptoms develop (e.g., dizziness, lightheadedness).
- Do not stand still for prolonged periods, do leg exercises to increase venous return, or sleep with the head of the bed raised. Do lie or sit down when dizziness occurs.
- Some drugs cause sexual problems (e.g., erectile dysfunction, decreased libido). Consult with the HCP about changing drugs or dosages if sexual problems develop.
- Some side effects may decrease with time (e.g., fatigue, diarrhea).
- Be careful about taking potentially high-risk OTC drugs, such as high-sodium antacids, NSAIDs, appetite suppressants, and cold and sinus medications. Read warning labels and consult with a pharmacist.

BOX 36.3 EVIDENCE-BASED PRACTICE

Medication Adherence in Hypertension

T.B. is a 67-year-old male admitted to the surgery unit after a partial bowel resection for diverticulitis. The health record shows he has a history of stage 2 hypertension. The cardiologist has noted T.B. has repeated nonadherence to the antihypertensive medication plan. T.B.'s BP on arrival to the unit is 160/84 mm/Hg. The current prescribed daily oral medications include hydrochlorothiazide and lisinopril. He is tolerating clear liquids. The HCP prescribed liquid forms of antihypertensive agents. T.B. is refusing to take them.

Making Clinical Decisions

Synthesis of Best Available Evidence

Medication adherence is based on multiple factors. Identifying and understanding those factors represents the first step in developing interventions to improve adherence and facilitate hypertension management.

Clinician Expertise

Several hours later, you realize T.B. has had no visitors since his arrival. You ask him if he is expecting family or friends to come to visit that evening after work, and he responds abruptly, "No one's coming." During the next scheduled postoperative assessment, you ask gently T. B. about his discharge plan and if someone will be available to assist him at home. He said, "I don't know any of the neighbors. We moved to a new community just a month before my wife died late last year. Our 2 kids live up north and couldn't get away from work for this surgery."

The gastroenterology nurse practitioner visits T.B. on rounds. The NP expresses concern about T.B.'s BP, which has consistently remained high. Recognizing the importance of social support, you tell the NP that the patient's wife died late last year, and the adult children live far away. You discuss with the NP about this possible influence on his medication adherence.

Patient Preferences and Values

T.B. tells you, "I used to take my meds like clockwork with my wife over breakfast. After she died, and the diverticulitis got worse, I didn't want to bother most of the time."

Implications for Nursing Practice

1. What other elements of social support could you explore?
2. Besides social support, what other factors could influence his nonadherence to the medication plan?
3. How would you confirm T.B.'s understanding of his medication plan?

Reference for Evidence

Thuy LT, Monkong S, Pookboonmees R, et al.: Factors explaining medication adherence of older adults with hypertension: a cross-sectional study, *PRIJNR* 24:306–320, 2020.

hypotension and acute kidney injury in patients over 65 years old. Older adults who have multiple comorbidities and do not live independently (i.e., skilled agency) should have gradual dosage changes to minimize complications.[5]

Orthostatic hypotension often occurs in older adults because of impaired baroreceptor reflexes. Orthostatic hypotension in this age group is often related to volume depletion or chronic disease states, such as decreased renal and liver function or electrolyte imbalance.

Older adults may have drops in BP after meals. The most significant decrease occurs about 1 hour after eating. BP returns to preprandial levels 3 to 4 hours after eating. Drugs should be started at low doses and increased slowly to reduce the chance of orthostatic hypotension. Measure BP and HR in the supine, sitting, and standing positions at every visit.

After CVD, arthritis is the second most prevalent disease in older adults. Older adults often take prescription and OTC nonsteroidal antiinflammatory drugs (NSAIDs). Nonselective NSAIDs (e.g., ibuprofen) and selective NSAIDs (e.g., celecoxib) can cause loss of BP control and HF. There is the risk for adverse renal effects and/or hyperkalemia when NSAIDs are used with ACE inhibitors, ARBs, or aldosterone antagonists.

HYPERTENSIVE CRISIS

Hypertensive crisis is a term that indicates either a hypertensive urgency or emergency. A hypertensive crisis occurs at systolic BP greater than 180 mm Hg and/or DBP greater than 120 mm Hg. BPs often can be greater than 220/140 mm Hg. The differences between hypertensive urgency and emergency are the presence of target organ damage and the type of treatment the patient will receive.

Hypertensive emergencies have evidence of target organ disease. They most often require hospitalization for immediate, controlled BP reduction. Without prompt treatment, complications include encephalopathy, intracranial or subarachnoid hemorrhage, HF, MI, renal failure, dissecting aortic aneurysm, and retinopathy.[18] Untreated hypertensive emergencies have a 1-year mortality rate of more than 79%. Prompt recognition and treatment are essential to decrease the threat to organ function and life.

Hypertensive urgency is more common. There is no clinical evidence of target organ disease. Hospitalization may not be needed. It may be associated with chronic, stable complications such as stable angina, chronic HF, or prior MI or cerebrovascular accident with no threat of an acute event.

A hypertensive crisis occurs more often in patients with a history of hypertension who have not adhered to their medication regimens or who have been undermedicated. Rapidly increasing BP can cause shearing of the endothelial surface due to turbulent blood flow within the vessels leading to further vascular damage and the release of more vasoconstricting substances. A vicious cycle of increased BP follows, leading to life-threatening damage to target organs.

Hypertensive crisis related to cocaine or crack use is a frequent problem. Other drugs, such as amphetamines, phencyclidine (PCP), and lysergic acid diethylamide (LSD), can cause a hypertensive crisis that may be complicated by drug-induced seizures, stroke, MI, or encephalopathy. Table 36.14 lists common causes of hypertensive crisis.

Clinical Manifestations

A hypertensive emergency often presents as *hypertensive encephalopathy*. This is a syndrome in which a sudden rise in BP is associated with a severe headache, nausea, vomiting, seizures, confusion, and coma (Table 36.14). The manifestations of encephalopathy are the result of increased cerebral capillary permeability, which can lead to cerebral edema and disruption in cerebral function. Retinal examination shows exudates, hemorrhages, and/or papilledema (Fig. 36.6).

Renal insufficiency ranging from minor injury to complete renal failure can occur. Rapid cardiac decompensation ranges from unstable angina to MI and pulmonary edema. Patients can have chest pain and dyspnea. Aortic dissection can cause

TABLE 36.14 EMERGENCY MANAGEMENT

Hypertensive Crisis

Etiology	Assessment Findings	Interventions
• Acute aortic dissection • Drug use (cocaine, amphetamines) • Exacerbation of chronic hypertension • Head injury • Monoamine oxidase inhibitors are taken with tyramine-containing foods • Pheochromocytoma • Preeclampsia, eclampsia • Rebound hypertension (from abrupt withdrawal of some antihypertensive drugs, such as clonidine or β-blockers)	• Systolic BP greater than 180 mm Hg and/or diastolic BP greater than 120 mm Hg • Blurred vision • Chest pain • Confusion • Dyspnea • Headache • Nausea and vomiting • Nosebleeds • Seizures	• Obtain baseline vital signs, including O_2 saturation. • Start continuous BP and ECG monitoring. • Auscultate heart and breath sounds. • Insert IV. • Administer IV antihypertensive medications as ordered (e.g., sodium nitroprusside). • Obtain baseline blood work. • Give O_2 per agency protocol. **Ongoing Monitoring** • Monitor vital signs, level of consciousness, heart and breath sounds, neurologic function, heart rhythm, and O_2 saturation. • Titrate the drug according to MAP or SBP as ordered. • Assess and record response to drugs (e.g., decrease in chest pain). • Measure urine output hourly. • Maintain the patient on bed rest. • Provide reassurance and emotional support to patient and caregiver. • Explain all interventions to patient and caregiver.

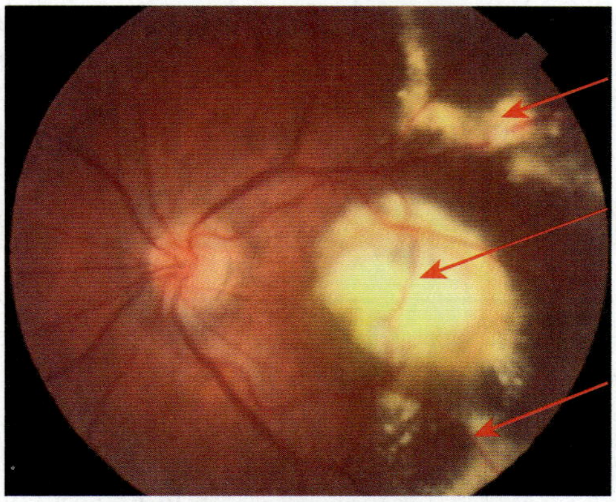

Fig. 36.6 Massive retinal exudates (indicated by *arrows*) from hypertensive retinopathy. To see what a normal retina looks like on ophthalmoscopic examination, see Fig. 22.7. (From Kliegman RM, Behrman RE, Jenson HB, et al.: *Nelson textbook of pediatrics,* ed 18, Philadelphia, 2011, Saunders.)

sudden, severe chest and back pain with reduced or absent pulses in the extremities.

◆ Interprofessional and Nursing Management

Hypertensive emergencies require hospitalization, IV administration of antihypertensive drugs, and intensive monitoring. BP level alone is not the major factor in deciding treatment. The link between elevated BP and signs of new or progressive target organ disease determines the seriousness of the situation.

When treating hypertensive emergencies, we often use the mean arterial pressure (MAP) instead of BP readings to guide and evaluate therapy. Calculate the MAP as follows:

$$MAP = (SBP + 2DBP) \div 3$$

The initial goal is to decrease MAP by no more than 20% to 25% or to decrease MAP to 110 to 115 mm Hg. If the patient is clinically stable, drugs can be titrated to gradually lower BP over the next 24 hours. Lowering the BP too quickly or too much may decrease cerebral, coronary, or renal perfusion. A rapid decrease could cause a stroke, MI, or renal failure.

CHECK YOUR PRACTICE

A 68-year-old male patient presents to the emergency department with a BP 210/118. He reports a severe headache and vomiting. You know that his BP is dangerously high and must be lowered.

- Calculate his MAP.
- What treatments would you expect to be ordered for this patient?

Patients with aortic dissection require special consideration. They should have their SBP lowered to less than 100 to 120 mm Hg as soon as possible (if tolerated). Another exception is the patient with acute ischemic stroke whose BP is lowered to allow the use of thrombolytic agents. Last, an elevated BP in the immediate poststroke period may be a compensatory response to improve cerebral perfusion to ischemic brain tissue. There is no evidence supporting the use of antihypertensive drugs in these patients (see Chapter 62).[5]

IV agents used for hypertensive emergencies include vasodilators (e.g., sodium nitroprusside, fenoldopam, nicardipine), adrenergic inhibitors (e.g., phentolamine, labetalol, esmolol), and the CCB clevidipine (Cleviprex). Sodium nitroprusside is the most effective IV drug to treat hypertensive emergencies. Oral agents may be given along with IV drugs to help make an earlier transition to long-term therapy.

Antihypertensive drugs given IV have a rapid (within seconds to minutes) onset of action. Assess the patient's BP and HR every 2 to 3 minutes during their initial administration. Use an arterial line (see Chapter 35) or an automated, noninvasive BP

DRUG ALERT
Labetalol

- Teach the patient not to stop the drug abruptly.
- Abrupt cessation may precipitate angina or HF.

machine to monitor the BP. Titrate the drug according to MAP or SBP as ordered. Monitor the ECG for dysrhythmias and signs of ischemia or MI. Use extreme caution in treating the patient with CAD or cerebrovascular disease. Measure urine output hourly to assess renal perfusion. Patients receiving IV agents may be kept on bed rest. Getting up (e.g., to use the commode) may cause severe cerebral ischemia and fainting.

Ongoing assessment is essential to evaluate the effectiveness of and the patient's response to therapy. Monitor cardiac, lung, and renal systems for decompensation caused by the severe increase in BP (e.g., angina, pulmonary edema, renal failure).

Frequent neurologic checks, including the level of consciousness, pupillary size and reaction, and movement of extremities, help detect any changes in the patient's condition. The neurologic changes of a hypertensive crisis are often like those of a stroke but without the focal or lateralizing signs often seen with a stroke. In a stroke, impairments affect a specific region or side of the body.

Hypertensive urgencies usually can be managed with oral agents and outpatient follow-up care within 24 hours. The initial decision for oral antihypertensive agents should be made based on the underlying cause of the hypertensive urgency, the patient characteristics, and comorbidities. A disadvantage of oral drugs is the inability to regulate the dosage moment to moment, as can be done with IV therapy. Some of the most commonly used oral drugs are captopril, labetalol, clonidine (Catapres), and amlodipine (Norvasc) (Table 36.6).[18]

Once the hypertensive crisis is resolved, it is essential to determine the cause. The patient will need appropriate management and teaching to avoid future crises.

DRUG ALERT
Clonidine (Catapres)

- Teach the patient to change positions slowly to limit orthostatic hypotension.
- Avoid hazardous activities since the drug may cause drowsiness.
- Do not stop abruptly as this may cause a rebound increase in BP.

Not every patient with an elevated BP will need emergent drug therapy or hospitalization. Allowing the patient to sit for 20 or 30 minutes in a quiet environment may significantly reduce BP. Oral drugs may be started or adjusted. Other interventions include encouraging the patient to share any concerns or fears, answering questions about hypertension, and reducing any adverse stimuli (e.g., excess noise) in the environment.

Case Study
Primary Hypertension

(© Ridofranz/iStock.com)

Patient Profile

R.L. is a 45-years-old Black man with no history of hypertension. At a screening clinic 2 months ago, his BP was 150/95 mm Hg. His HCP has followed him for the past month. During this time, he has been taking hydrochlorothiazide 12.5 mg/day. He is here today for a follow-up visit.

Subjective Data

- Father died of a stroke at age 60
- Mother is alive but has hypertension and a history of MI
- States that he feels fine
- Smokes 1 pack of cigarettes daily for the past 28 years
- Drinks 5–6 beers on most Friday and Saturday nights with work colleagues.
- Has heard that BP drugs "make you impotent"

Objective Data

Physical Assessment

- Mild retinopathy (retinal arteriolar narrowing on ophthalmoscopic examination)
- BP: 166/108 mm Hg (highest of 2 readings, 2 min apart)
- Sustained apical impulse palpable in the 4th intercostal space just lateral to the midclavicular line
- Heart rate is regular with a pulse of 84

Diagnostic Studies

- ECG: mild left ventricular hypertrophy
- Urinalysis: protein 30 mg/dL (0.3 g/L)
- Serum creatinine level: 1.6 mg/dL (141 mmol/L)

Interprofessional Care

- Low-sodium, DASH diet
- Hydrochlorothiazide 25 mg/day oral (dose increase)
- Lisinopril 5 mg once daily (second drug added)

Discussion Questions

1. ***Recognize***: What risk factors does R.L. have for hypertension?
2. ***Recognize***: What stage of hypertension does R.L. have?
3. ***Analyze***: What are the abnormal findings in the objective data?
4. ***Analyze***: Based on the assessment, what target organ disease may be present?
5. ***Analyze***: What additional assessment would be done for this patient?
6. ***Plan***: What medications would you expect to see ordered for this patient?
7. ***Plan***: What referrals may be indicated for R.L.?
8. ***Prioritize***: Based on your assessment, which teaching points about hypertension are the most important?
9. ***Prioritize***: What is the most important problem to manage for R.L. right now?
10. ***Act***: What would you teach this patient about the medications he is prescribed?
11. ***Act***: What other teaching is needed for this patient?
12. ***Evaluate***: What follow-up is needed for this patient to assess his response to your plan?

Answers available at http://evolve.elsevier.com/Lewis/medsurg.

BRIDGE TO NCLEX EXAMINATION

The number of the question corresponds to the same-numbered outcome at the beginning of the chapter.

1. A defect in which BP-regulating mechanisms can result in the development of hypertension? *(select all that apply)*
   a. Release of norepinephrine
   b. Secretion of prostaglandins
   c. Stimulation of the sympathetic nervous system
   d. Stimulation of the parasympathetic nervous system
   e. Activation of the renin-angiotensin-aldosterone system
2. Which item in a patient history would the nurse recognize as a modifiable risk factor for the development of hypertension?
   a. Low-calcium diet
   b. Excess alcohol use
   c. Family history of hypertension
   d. Consumption of a high-protein diet
3. Which information would the nurse apply to a teaching plan for a patient with hypertension?
   a. All patients with elevated BP need drug therapy
   b. Obese persons must achieve a normal weight to lower BP.
   c. It is not necessary to limit salt in the diet if taking a diuretic.
   d. Lifestyle modifications are needed for persons with elevated BP.
4. Which consideration would the nurse include in the management of the older adult with hypertension?
   a. Preventing primary hypertension from converting to secondary hypertension
   b. Recognizing that the older adult is less likely to adhere to the drug therapy regimen than a younger adult
   c. Ensuring that the patient receives larger initial doses of antihypertensive drugs because of impaired absorption
   d. Using a precise technique in assessing the BP of the patient because of the possible presence of orthostatic hypertension
5. A patient with newly discovered high BP has an average reading of 158/98 mm Hg after 3 months of exercise and diet modifications. Which management strategy would the nurse expect?
   a. Drug therapy will be needed because the BP has not reached the goal.
   b. BP monitoring should continue for 3 months to confirm a diagnosis of hypertension.
   c. Lifestyle changes are less important since they were not effective, and drugs will be started.
   d. More changes in the patient's lifestyle are needed for a longer time before starting drug therapy.
6. A patient is admitted to the hospital in a hypertensive emergency (BP 244/142 mm Hg). Sodium nitroprusside is started to treat the elevated BP. Which management strategies would the nurse anticipate? *(select all that apply)*
   a. Measuring hourly urine output
   b. Continuous BP monitoring with an arterial line
   c. Decreasing the MAP by 50% within the first hour
   d. Maintaining bed rest and giving tranquilizers to lower the BP
   e. Assessing the patient for signs of heart failure and changes in mental status

1. a, c, e; 2. b; 3. d; 4. d; 5. a; 6. a, b, e.

For rationales to these answers and even more NCLEX review questions, visit http://evolve.elsevier.com/Lewis/medsurg.

EVOLVE WEBSITE/RESOURCES LIST

http://evolve.elsevier.com/Lewis/medsurg
Review Questions (Online Only)
Key Points
Answer Keys for Questions
- Rationales for Bridge to NCLEX Examination Questions
- Answer Guidelines for Case Study

Student Case Study
- Patient With Hypertension and Stroke

Conceptual Care Map Creator
Audio Glossary
Content Updates

REFERENCES

1. Centers for Disease Control and Prevention: High blood pressure facts. Retrieved from www.cdc.gov/bloodpressure/facts.htm.

*2. Ostchega Y, Fryar CD, Nwankwo T, Nguyen DT: *Hypertension prevalence among adults aged 18 and over: United States, 2017–2018.* NCHS Data Brief, no 364, Hyattsville, MD, 2020, National Center for Health Statistics.

*3. Centers for Disease Control and Prevention (CDC): *Hypertension cascade: hypertension prevalence, treatment and control estimates among US adults aged 18 years and older applying the criteria from the American College of Cardiology and American Heart Association's 2017 hypertension guideline—NHANES 2013–2016*, Atlanta, 2019, US Department of Health and Human Services.

*4. Centers for Disease Control and Prevention: National Health and Nutrition Examination Survey (NHANES). Retrieved from www.cdc.gov/nchs/nhanes/index.htm.

*5. Whelton PK, Carey RM, Aronow WS, et al: 2017 ACC/AHA/AAPA/ABC/ACPM/AGS/APhA/ASH/ASPC/NMA/PCNA guideline for the prevention, detection, evaluation, and management of high blood pressure in adults: a report of the American College of Cardiology/AHA Task Force on Clinical Practice Guidelines, *J Am Coll of Cardiol* 71:e127, 2018.

6. Deere B, Ferdinand K: Hypertension and race/ethnicity, *Curr Opin Cardiol* 35:342, 2020.

*7. Arnett DK, Blumenthal RS, Albert MA, et al.: 2019 ACC/AHA guideline on the primary prevention of cardiovascular disease, *J Am Coll of Cardiol* 74:1376, 2019.

8. Ferguson JF, Aden LA, Barbaro NR, et al.: High dietary salt–induced DC activation underlies microbial dysbiosis-associated hypertension, *JCI Insight* 4:e126241, 2019.
9. American Heart Association: What are the symptoms of high blood pressure? Retrieved from http://www.heart.org/HEARTORG/Conditions/HighBloodPressure/SymptomsDiagnosisMonitoringofHighBloodPressure/What-are-the-Symptoms-of-High-Blood-Pressure_UCM_301871_Article.jsp
*10. Vargas G, Azarbal J, Tota-Maharaj R: A comparative review of established diets for prevention of cardiovascular disease and newer dietary strategies, *Curr Prob Cardiol* 19:100582, 2020. 100582.
11. National Heart, Lung, and Blood Institute: DASH eating plan. Retrieved from www.nhlbi.nih.gov/health-topics/dash-eating-plan.
*12. Haskell WL, Lee IM, Pate RR, et al.: Physical activity and public health: updated recommendations for adults from the American College of Sports Medicine and the American Heart Association. *Circ* 116:1081, 2007. (Classic).
*13. Nelson ME, Rejeski WJ, Blair SN, et al.: Physical activity and public health in older adults: recommendation from the American College of Sports Medicine and the American Heart Association. *Circ* 116:1094, 2007. (Classic)
14. Office of Disease Prevention and Health Promotion: Social determinants of health. Healthy People 2030. Retrieved from: https://health.gov/healthypeople/objectives-and-data/social-determinants-health.
15. Rozanski A, Blumenthal JA, Davidson K,W, et al.: The epidemiology, pathophysiology, and management of psychosocial risk factors in cardiac practice, *J Am Coll Cardiol* 45:637, 2005. (Classic).
16. AACN Clinical Resources Task Force: AACN practice alert: non-invasive blood pressure monitoring. Retrieved from www.aacn.org/~/media/aacn-website/clincial-resources/practice-alerts/nibpadult2016pa.pdf.
17. Jarvis C: *Physical exam and health assessment*, ed 8, Philadelphia, 2019, Elsevier.
*18. Allgaier J, Emmich M, Rastegar V, et al.: Hypertensive urgency or emergency? The use of intravenous medications in hospitalized hypertensive patients without organ dysfunction, *Heart & Lung* 49:824, 2020.

*Evidence-based information for clinical practice.

37

Coronary Artery Disease and Acute Coronary Syndrome

Rose B. Shaffer

http://evolve.elsevier.com/Lewis/medsurg/

CONCEPTUAL FOCUS

Adherence
Fatigue
Glucose Regulation
Pain
Perfusion
Sexuality

LEARNING OUTCOMES

1. Relate the etiology and pathophysiology of coronary artery disease (CAD), chronic stable angina, and acute coronary syndrome (ACS) to the clinical manifestations of each disorder.
2. Describe the nursing role in promoting therapeutic lifestyle changes in patients at risk for CAD.
3. Distinguish the precipitating factors, clinical manifestations, and interprofessional and nursing care of the patient with CAD and chronic stable angina.
4. Explain the clinical manifestations, diagnostic studies, complications, and interprofessional and nursing care of the patient with ACS.
5. Outline drug therapy used to treat patients with CAD, chronic stable angina, and ACS.
6. Prioritize key components to include in the rehabilitation of patients recovering from ACS and coronary revascularization procedures.
7. Distinguish the precipitating factors, manifestations, and interprofessional and nursing care of patients who are at risk for or have had sudden cardiac death.

KEY TERMS

acute coronary syndrome (ACS)
angina
atherosclerosis
chronic stable angina
collateral circulation
coronary artery disease (CAD)
coronary revascularization
metabolic equivalent (MET)
myocardial infarction (MI)
percutaneous coronary intervention (PCI)
Prinzmetal's angina
stent
sudden cardiac death (SCD)
unstable angina (UA)

Cardiovascular disease (CVD) is the leading cause of death worldwide. It is expected to account for more than 22.2 million deaths by 2030.[1] CVD encompasses several disorders of the heart and blood vessels, including coronary artery disease (CAD), cerebrovascular disease, and peripheral artery disease.[2] CAD is the most common type of CVD and the leading cause of death in the United States.[1] Patients with CAD may be asymptomatic or develop chronic stable angina (chest pain). CAD may evolve to more serious conditions of unstable angina (UA) and myocardial infarction (MI), which we refer to as acute coronary syndrome (ACS).

The process of perfusion depends on the heart's ability to generate enough cardiac output (CO) to distribute blood to all body tissues. Significant CAD negatively affects heart function, resulting in impaired CO and decreased perfusion. This chapter discusses the care of patients with CAD, chronic stable angina, and ACS along with measures to promote optimal perfusion.

CORONARY ARTERY DISEASE

Coronary artery disease (CAD) is a type of blood vessel disorder in the general category of atherosclerosis. The term atherosclerosis comes from 2 Greek words: *athere*, meaning "gruel or fatty mush," and *skleros*, meaning "hard."[3] Atherosclerosis begins as soft deposits of fat that harden with age, often referred to as "hardening of the arteries." Atherosclerosis can occur in any artery in the body. When the *atheromas* (fatty deposits) form in the coronary arteries, the disease is called CAD. *Arteriosclerotic heart disease (ASHD), cardiovascular heart disease (CVHD), ischemic heart disease (IHD), coronary heart disease (CHD)* are other terms used to describe CAD.

Etiology and Pathophysiology

Atherosclerosis is characterized by lipid deposits within the intima, the innermost layer of the arterial wall. A layer of endothelial cells lines the intima to provide a barrier between blood and the arterial wall. The endothelium is normally nonreactive to platelets and leukocytes, as well as coagulation, fibrinolytic, and complement factors. Endothelial injury and inflammation play a key role in developing atherosclerosis. Damage to the endothelial lining can result from tobacco use, hyperlipidemia, hypertension, toxins, diabetes, inflammation, and infection (Fig. 37.1A).[3]

C-reactive protein (CRP) is a nonspecific marker of inflammation made by the liver. CRP levels rise when there is systemic inflammation, such as rheumatoid arthritis or inflammatory bowel disease. It may also be increased in CAD. Lipoprotein(a) is a type of low-density lipoprotein (LDL) attached to a protein called apo(a). Homocysteine is made by the breakdown of the essential amino acid methionine, found in diet protein. High lipoprotein(a) and homocysteine levels may contribute to atherosclerosis by (1) damaging the inner lining of blood vessels, (2) promoting plaque buildup, and (3) changing the clotting mechanism to make clots more likely to occur. Although elevation of any of these levels may increase the risk for development of CAD, they are not part of a routine risk assessment for CAD. They can be used in patients with an intermediate or high-risk suspicion of CAD.[4]

Developmental Stages

CAD is a progressive disease that develops in stages over many years. By the time the patient becomes symptomatic, the disease process usually is well advanced. The stages of development in atherosclerosis are (1) fatty streak, (2) fibrous plaque, and (3) complicated lesion.

Fatty streak. *Fatty streaks,* the earliest lesions of atherosclerosis, are lipid-filled smooth muscle cells. As streaks of fat develop within the smooth muscle cells, a yellow tinge appears. Fatty streaks appear in the coronary arteries by age 20. They involve more surface area as one ages. Treatment that lowers LDL cholesterol may slow this process (Fig. 37.1B).

Fibrous plaque. The *fibrous plaque* stage is the beginning of progressive changes in the endothelium of the arterial wall. These changes can appear in the coronary arteries by age 30 and increase with age.

Normally, the endothelium repairs itself immediately. This does not occur in the person with CAD. LDLs and growth factors from platelets stimulate smooth muscle proliferation and thickening of the arterial wall. Once endothelial injury has taken place, lipoproteins (carrier proteins within the bloodstream) transport cholesterol and other lipids into the arterial intima. Collagen covers the fatty streak and forms a fibrous plaque with a grayish or whitish appearance. These plaques can form on one side of the artery or in a circular fashion involving the entire lumen. The borders can be smooth or irregular with rough, jagged edges. The result is a narrowing of the vessel lumen and reduced blood flow to the distal tissue (Fig. 37.1C).

Complicated lesion. The last stage in the development of the atherosclerotic lesion is the most dangerous. As the fibrous plaque grows, continued inflammation can result in plaque instability, ulceration, and rupture. Once the integrity of the artery's inner wall is compromised (plaque rupture), platelets accumulate in large numbers, leading to a thrombus (platelet aggregation and adhesion is the body's attempt to "heal" the ruptured area). The thrombus may adhere to the wall of the artery, leading to further narrowing or total occlusion of the artery. Activation of the exposed platelets causes expression of glycoprotein IIb/IIIa (GP IIb/IIIa) receptors that bind fibrinogen. This, in turn, leads to more platelet aggregation and

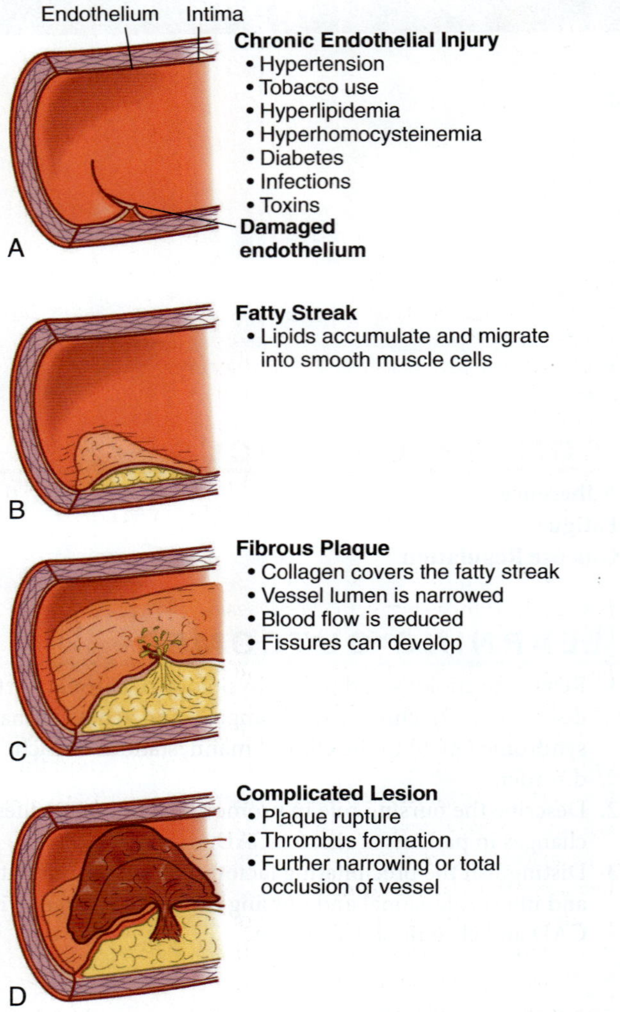

Fig. 37.1 Pathogenesis of atherosclerosis. (A) Damaged endothelium. (B) Fatty streak and lipid core formation. (C) Fibrous plaque covers the lipid core. (D) Complicated lesion: Plaque rupture with thrombus formation.

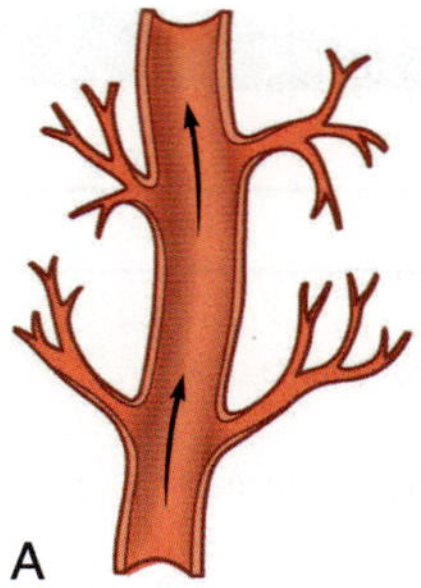

Fig. 37.2 Vessel occlusion with collateral circulation. (A) Open, functioning coronary artery. (B) Partial coronary artery closure with collateral circulation being established. (C) Total coronary artery occlusion with collateral circulation bypassing the occlusion to supply blood to the myocardium.

adhesion, further enlarging the thrombus. At this stage, the plaque is termed a *complicated lesion* (Fig. 37.1D).

Collateral Circulation

Normally, some arterial anastomoses or connections, called **collateral circulation**, exist within the coronary circulation. Two factors contribute to the growth and extent of collateral circulation: (1) inherited predisposition to develop new blood vessels *(angiogenesis)* and (2) presence of chronic ischemia (poor blood flow). When plaque blocks the normal flow of blood through a coronary artery and the resulting *ischemia* is chronic, collateral circulation may develop (Fig. 37.2). When blockages in coronary arteries occur slowly over a long time, collateral circulation has a greater chance to develop, so the heart muscle may still receive an adequate amount of blood and oxygen (O_2) except during increased workload on the heart, such as exercise.

However, with acute coronary occlusion or acute severe coronary spasm, collateral circulation does not have enough time to develop. When this happens, reduced blood flow results in more severe ischemia or infarction.

Risk Factors for Coronary Artery Disease

Nonmodifiable and modifiable risk factors are associated with CAD (Table 37.1). *Nonmodifiable risk factors* include age, gender, ethnicity, family history, and genetics. The *modifiable risk factors* are high serum lipids, high blood pressure (BP), tobacco use, physical inactivity, obesity, diabetes, and metabolic syndrome. *Contributing modifiable risk factors* include psychological states, substance use, and increased levels of CRP, lipoprotein(a), and homocysteine.

Nonmodifiable Risk Factors

Age, gender, ethnicity, and genetics. The incidence of CAD is highest among middle-aged men (Box 37.1). However, the risk for CAD increases for men over age 45 and women over age 55.[4] Heart disease often is diagnosed about 10 years later in women than men (Box 37.2). One possible reason may be the cardioprotective effects of estrogen. Interestingly, hormone replacement therapy does not protect women after menopause and may be harmful.[4] Because women are older at the time of CAD diagnosis, they are more likely to have co-morbidities (e.g., hypertension, diabetes). Women are more likely than men to die after their first MI. CAD is present in Black women at rates higher than White or Hispanic women.[4]

Most women do not consider CAD their greatest health risk.[4] Despite efforts to increase awareness that more women die from heart disease than from breast cancer (e.g., the American Heart Association's [AHA] Go Red for Women campaign), heart disease kills almost 10 times more women than breast cancer. It is the leading cause of death in women. When women present to the HCP, their symptoms may be unrecognized as heart-related because the symptoms are often atypical. These symptoms include fatigue, shortness of breath, upper back pain, indigestion, memory problems, palpitations, and anxiety.[4] These atypical symptoms can relate to many different diseases and syndromes. This lack of recognition of symptoms as a heart

TABLE 37.1 Risk Factors for Coronary Artery Disease

Nonmodifiable Risk Factors	Modifiable Risk Factors

• Increasing age
• Ethnicity (Box 37.1)
• Gender (Box 37.2)
• Genetic predisposition and family history of heart disease (Box 37.3)
	Major
	• BP >120/80 mm Hg
	• Diabetes
	• Lipid levels:
	  • Total cholesterol >200 mg/dL
	  • Triglycerides ≥150 mg/dL
	  • LDL cholesterol >130 mg/dL
	  • HDL cholesterol <40 mg/dL in men or <50 mg/dL in women
	• Metabolic syndrome
	• Obesity (see Chapter 45)
	Physical inactivity
	Tobacco use
	Contributing Risk Factors
	• ↑ Homocysteine, CRP, lipoprotein (a) levels
	• Psychosocial risk factors (e.g., depression, hostility)
	• Substance use

BOX 37.1 PROMOTING HEALTH EQUITY

Coronary Artery Disease

Whites
- White males have the highest incidence of CAD
- Have the highest mortality from CAD

Blacks
- Males have a higher incidence of CAD compared to Hispanic and Asian males

Hispanics
- Have slightly lower rates of CAD than either non-Hispanic Whites or Blacks
- Have lower death rates from CAD than non-Hispanic Whites and Blacks

Native Americans
- Die from heart disease earlier than expected
- Mortality rates for those under age 65 are twice as high as those of other Americans

BOX 37.2 BIOLOGIC SEX CONSIDERATIONS

Coronary Artery Disease and Acute Coronary Syndrome

Men

- First heart event is more often MI than angina
- Report more typical signs and symptoms of angina and MI
- Receive more evidence-based therapies (e.g., diagnostic catheterization, PCI) when acutely ill from CAD (e.g., MI)
- Mortality rates from CAD have decreased more rapidly for men than women
- Have larger diameter coronary arteries. Vessel diameter is inversely related to risk for restenosis after interventions
- After age 55, the incidence of MI in men and women equalizes
- Develop more collateral circulation
- Standard screening for risk for sudden cardiac death is more predictive in men

Women

- First heart event is more often UA than MI
- Fewer women have the "classic" signs and symptoms of angina or MI
- Fatigue is often the first symptom of ACS
- Experience the onset of heart disease about 10 years later than men
- More often have non-obstructive CAD causing angina
- Before menopause, have higher HDL cholesterol levels and lower LDL cholesterol levels. After menopause LDL levels and risk for MI increase
- Report more disability after a heart event
- Seek medical care later in the CAD process, most likely because of lack of recognition of atypical symptoms
- Have more "silent" MIs
- Those who have an MI are more likely to have a fatal heart event within 5 years than men
- Women who have coronary artery bypass graft surgery have a higher mortality rate and more complications after surgery
- Are undertreated with guideline-based recommendations, leading to worse outcomes and increased rates of readmission, reinfarction, and death in the first year after MI

BOX 37.3 GENETICS IN CLINICAL PRACTICE

Familial Hypercholesterolemia

Genetic Basis

- Autosomal dominant disorder
- Heterozygous (most common) and homozygous forms
- Mutation in low-density lipoprotein receptor (LDLR) gene
- Gene codes for low-density lipoprotein (LDL) receptor that binds to LDLs
- High cholesterol levels are a result of defective function of the LDL receptors
- Person has high serum LDLs throughout life

Incidence

- Heterozygotes: 1 in 500
- Homozygotes: rare

Genetic Testing

- DNA testing is available

Clinical Implications

- Develop severe atherosclerosis in early to middle years
- A baseline serum lipid profile that measures total cholesterol, triglycerides, LDLs, and high-density lipoproteins (HDLs) should be done early if there is a history of familial hypercholesterolemia
- Homozygous familial hypercholesterolemia is much more severe. Cholesterol levels may exceed 600 mg/dL
- Develop xanthomas (fatty growths on the skin [e.g., around eyes, over joints])
- Treatment includes low-fat diet, exercise, and lipid-lowering drugs (e.g., PCSK9 inhibitors)

problem leads to delays in women seeking treatment and HCPs recognizing the symptoms.

Genetic Link

Genetic predisposition is a key factor in the occurrence of CAD (Box 37.3). Family history is a risk factor for CAD and MI. Often patients with angina or MI can name a parent or sibling who has CAD or died from CAD. A family history of premature CAD (under age 55) puts the patient at even greater risk for developing CAD.[1]

The genetic basis of CAD/MI is complex and poorly understood. We estimate that the genetic contribution to CAD is as high as 40% to 60%. This proportion relates mainly to genes that control known risk factors (e.g., lipid metabolism). Work is being conducted using genetic risk stratification to determine one's risk for CAD.[5]

Major Modifiable Risk Factors

High serum lipids. High serum lipid levels are a major risk factor for CAD (see Table 35.9). The increased risk for CAD is associated with a total serum cholesterol level greater than 200 mg/dL (5.2 mmol/L), an LDL greater than 130 mg/dL (3.4 mmol/L), a high-density lipoprotein (HDL) level less than 40 mg/dL (1.0 mmol/L) in men and less than 50 mg/dL (1.3 mmol/L) in women, and/or a fasting triglyceride level greater than 150 mg/dL (1.7 mmol/L). Most refer to HDL as the "good cholesterol" and LDL as the "bad cholesterol." Studies in the United States reveal that adults with a total cholesterol in the range of 150 mg/dL, which corresponds to an LDL level of about 100 mg/dL, have low rates of CAD.[6] Drugs used to treat high serum lipids focus mostly on lowering LDL cholesterol.

For the body to be able to use and transport lipids, they must become soluble in blood by combining with proteins. Lipids combine with proteins to form lipoproteins. Lipoproteins are vehicles for fat mobilization and transport. They vary in composition. The 3 main lipoproteins are HDLs, LDLs, and very-low-density lipoproteins (VLDLs).

HDLs contain more protein by weight and fewer lipids than any other lipoprotein. HDLs carry lipids away from arteries to the liver for metabolism through a process called reverse cholesterol transport. This process of HDL transport helps prevent lipid accumulation within the arterial walls.[3] This is why high serum HDL levels are desirable and lower the risk for CAD. Although there are a few medications that help raise HDL (e.g., niacin), research has shown that taking niacin does not reduce the risk of CAD and MI.

Premenopausal women usually have higher HDL levels than men. This may be related to the protective effects of natural estrogen. After menopause, women's HDL levels decrease to levels near those of men. In general, HDL levels are higher in women, decrease with age, and are low in those with CAD. Physical activity, eating more healthy fats, losing excess weight, moderate alcohol use, and quitting smoking help increase HDL levels.

LDLs contain more cholesterol than any of the lipoproteins and have an attraction for arterial walls. High LDL levels correlate closely with an increased incidence of atherosclerosis and CAD. This is why low serum LDL levels are desirable. We cannot routinely calculate LDL if the triglycerides are higher than 400 mg/dL (>4.35 mmol/L). Remember, drugs used to treat high lipid levels focus mostly on lowering LDL. VLDLs have a higher concentration of triglycerides and can deposit cholesterol directly on the walls of arteries.

Triglycerides are the most common type of fat in the blood. High triglyceride levels increase the risk for CAD. Certain diseases (e.g., type 2 diabetes, chronic kidney disease [CKD]), drugs (e.g., corticosteroids, hormone therapy), and genetic disorders are associated with high triglyceride levels. Lifestyle factors that can contribute to high levels include high alcohol intake, high intake of refined carbohydrates and simple sugars, and physical inactivity. When a high triglyceride level is combined with a high LDL level, a smaller, denser LDL particle is formed, which favors deposition on arterial walls. People with insulin resistance often have this pattern.

Guidelines for treating high LDL levels are based on known risk factors and a person's 10-year risk for having heart disease or stroke. The 10-year risk calculator is used for people between the ages of 40 to 79 who have not been diagnosed with CAD, MI, or stroke. The following data generate a risk score: (1) age, (2) gender, (3) race, (4) use of tobacco, (5) diabetes, (6) systolic BP, (7) diastolic BP, (8) use of BP drugs, (9) total cholesterol level, and (10) HDL cholesterol level. A score of less than 5% puts you at a low risk for developing CAD. A 10-year risk calculator is available at www.cvriskcalculator.com.

Hypertension. Hypertension increases the risk for CAD, stroke, peripheral vascular disease, heart failure (HF), and death. In postmenopausal women, hypertension is associated with a higher incidence of CAD than in men and premenopausal women.

According to the most recent published hypertension guidelines, a normal BP is defined as less than 120/80 mm Hg. BP is classified as elevated (BP 120 to 129 mm Hg/<80 mm Hg); stage 1 hypertension (BP 130 to 139/80 to 89 mm Hg); or stage 2 hypertension (BP ≥140/90 mm Hg).[7]

Elevated BP and hypertension are controlled with lifestyle changes and medications. Those with stage 1 or 2 hypertension often need more than 1 drug to reach therapeutic goals (see Tables 36.6, 36.7, and 36.8).[7] Teach patients the importance of achieving and maintaining target BP goals.

The shearing stress of an elevated BP causes endothelial injury that increases the rate of atherosclerosis. Atherosclerosis, in turn, causes narrowed, thickened arterial walls, and decreases the distensibility and elasticity of vessels. More force is needed to pump blood through diseased arteries. This increased force is reflected in a higher BP. This added workload can result in left ventricular (LV) hypertrophy and decreased stroke volume with each contraction. See Chapter 36 for a complete discussion of hypertension.

Tobacco use. Tobacco use is a major CAD risk factor. The risk for developing CAD is much higher in those who smoke tobacco or use smokeless tobacco than in those who do not. Further, tobacco smoking decreases estrogen levels, placing premenopausal women who smoke at greater risk for CAD.

Nicotine in tobacco smoke causes catecholamine (i.e., epinephrine, norepinephrine) release. These neurohormones cause an increased heart rate (HR), peripheral vasoconstriction, and increased BP. These changes increase the heart's workload. Tobacco smoke is related to an increase in LDL levels, a decrease in HDL levels, and release of toxic O_2 radicals. All of these add to vessel inflammation and thrombosis.

Carbon monoxide, found in tobacco smoke, reduces the numbers of hemoglobin sites available for O_2 transport. Thus, the effects of an increased cardiac workload and the O_2-depleting effect of carbon monoxide significantly decrease the O_2 available to the heart muscle. In addition, carbon monoxide is a toxin that injures the endothelium.

At any age, the benefits of smoking cessation are dramatic. CAD risk and mortality rates drop within weeks to months after quitting. The risk goes down even further the longer the time goes by without smoking.[1] However, nicotine is highly addictive. People usually need intensive intervention to quit. Individual and group counseling, nicotine replacement therapy, and smoking cessation drugs (e.g., bupropion, varenicline) are examples of smoking cessation strategies. See Chapter 11, Tables 11.3, 11.4, and 11.5 for information on smoking cessation.

Although the rate of cigarette smoking has decreased in the United States, the rate of using new tobacco products such as electronic cigarettes has increased. Using any tobacco product (e.g., electronic cigarettes, cigars, pipes, smokeless tobacco) carries a potential cardiovascular risk. We need more long-term studies to determine the impact of electronic cigarettes on CAD.[8]

Nonsmokers exposed to secondhand tobacco smoke increase their risk for CAD by 25% to 30%.[1] People who live in the same house as the person who smokes should encourage that person to quit or smoke outside to decrease others' exposure to environmental smoke.

Diabetes. Diabetes is a major modifiable risk factor for CAD. The incidence of CAD is 2 to 4 times greater among people who have diabetes, even with well-controlled glucose levels. Both male and female patients with diabetes manifest CAD at an earlier age than those without diabetes.

Undiagnosed diabetes is often discovered when a person has an MI. An increased tendency toward endothelial dysfunction may cause the development of fatty streaks in the arteries. Patients with diabetes also have changes in lipid metabolism and tend to have high cholesterol and triglyceride levels. Management of diabetes should include lifestyle changes and drug therapy to achieve a glycosylated hemoglobin (A1C or Hb A1C) level of less than 7%.[9]

Metabolic syndrome. *Metabolic syndrome* refers to a cluster of risk factors for CAD whose underlying pathophysiology may be related to insulin resistance. These risk factors include central obesity, hypertension, abnormal serum lipids, and a high fasting glucose level (see Table 45.11). Chapter 45 discusses metabolic syndrome.

Physical inactivity. Physical inactivity increases risk for CAD. Physical inactivity implies a lack of adequate physical exercise on a regular basis. Exercise training for those who are physically inactive reduces the risk for CAD through more efficient lipid metabolism, increased HDL production, a decreased risk of thrombus formation, and more efficient O_2 extraction by the muscles. This decreases the heart's workload. For people with CAD, regular physical activity may reduce symptoms, improve functional capacity, and improve other risk factors, such as insulin resistance, glucose intolerance, and obesity.

Obesity. The death rate from CAD is higher in obese persons. *Obesity* is defined as a body mass index (BMI) of greater than 30 kg/m^2 and a waist circumference more than 40 inches for men and more than 35 inches for women. We calculate BMI by dividing a person's weight (in kilograms) by the square of the height in meters (see Fig. 45.7).

The degree of obesity affects the risk for CAD. Obese persons may have increased levels of LDLs and triglycerides, which are strongly related to atherosclerosis. Obesity is often linked with hypertension and insulin resistance. People who tend to store fat in the abdomen (an "apple" figure) rather than in the hips and buttocks (a "pear" figure) have a higher incidence of CAD (see Table 45.5).

Contributing Modifiable Risk Factors

Psychologic states. Certain behaviors and lifestyles may contribute to the development of CAD. One type of behavior, referred to as type A, includes perfectionism and a hardworking, driven personality. The person with a type A personality often suppresses anger and hostility, has a sense of time urgency, is impatient, and creates stress and tension. This person may be more prone to MIs than one with a type B personality. Type Bs are more easygoing, take upsets in stride, know personal limitations, take time to relax, and are not an overachievers. However, the relationship between behaviors and the risk for CAD/MI is controversial and complex.

Psychologic risk factors include depression, acute and chronic stress (e.g., poverty, serving as a caregiver), anxiety, hostility and anger, and lack of social support. Stressful states contribute to the development and progression of CAD through sympathetic nervous system (SNS) stimulation. An increased release of catecholamines (i.e., epinephrine, norepinephrine) with SNS stimulation increases BP and may contribute to endothelial injury, inflammation, and platelet activation. SNS stimulation increases HR and the force of myocardial contraction, which increases myocardial O_2 demand. Stress-induced mechanisms can cause increased lipid and glucose levels and changes in blood coagulation, which contribute to atherosclerosis.

Substance use. The use of illegal drugs such as cocaine and methamphetamine can produce coronary artery spasm resulting in myocardial ischemia and chest pain. Initially, we cannot distinguish drug-induced chest pain from CAD. Patients often have sinus tachycardia, high BP, and chest pain. Chest pain occurs because of increased myocardial O_2 demand from the increased HR and contractility and coronary vasoconstriction.[10] An MI can occur because of coronary spasm. Serum cardiac biomarkers and an electrocardiogram (ECG) help determine if the patient is experiencing ACS. A drug screen may be helpful to identify if illegal drugs precipitated the cardiac event.

CRP, lipoprotein(a), homocysteine, levels. Increased levels of CRP, lipoprotein(a), and homocysteine increase the risk of CAD. Folic acid deficiency can cause high homocysteine levels, but lowering homocysteine levels through folic acid supplements does not lower the risk of CAD.[11]

❖ INTERPROFESSIONAL AND NURSING MANAGEMENT: CORONARY ARTERY DISEASE

◆ Health Promotion

Management of CAD risk factors may prevent, modify, or slow disease progression. In the United States, CAD-related deaths have gradually declined. This decline relates to our efforts to become healthier and research advances in the treatment of CAD. Prevention and early treatment of heart disease involves a multifaceted approach throughout the life span. In fact, healthy lifestyle behaviors should begin in childhood.

◆ Identifying High-Risk Persons

Clinical signs of CAD are not apparent in the early stages of the disease. Therefore, it is critical to identify people at risk for CAD. Risk screening involves obtaining a thorough health history. Ask the patient about a family history of heart disease in parents and siblings, especially a premature history of CAD (under age 55).[1] Note the presence of any cardiovascular symptoms. Assess environmental factors, such as eating habits, type of diet, and level of exercise, to elicit lifestyle patterns. Include a psychosocial history to determine tobacco use, alcohol intake, recent stressful events (e.g., loss of a spouse), and psychologic state (e.g., anxiety, depression, anger). The place and type of employment provide vital information on the kind of activity performed, exposure to pollutants or toxins, and degree of stress associated with work.

Assess the patient's attitudes and beliefs about health and illness. The patient's attitude gives insight to how disease and lifestyle changes may affect the patient. It can reveal misconceptions about heart disease. Knowing the patient's educational background and health literacy helps determine teaching needs. If the patient has prescribed drugs, you need to assess their knowledge of their medications and adherence to their drug regimen. If the patient is unable to tell you, you can get the information from the patient's HCP or pharmacy.

TABLE 37.2 PATIENT & CAREGIVER TEACHING

Reducing Risk Factors for Coronary Artery Disease

Include the following instructions when teaching risk reduction for coronary artery disease:

Risk Factor	Health-Promoting Behaviors
Hypertension	• Monitor home-based BP and obtain regular check-ups. • Take prescribed drugs for BP control. • Reduce salt intake. • Stop tobacco use. Avoid exposure to environmental tobacco (secondhand) smoke. • Control or reduce weight. • Perform physical activity daily.
High serum lipids	• Reduce total fat intake. • Reduce saturated fat intake. • Take prescribed drugs for lipid reduction. • Adjust total caloric intake to achieve and maintain ideal body weight. • Engage in daily physical activity. • Increase amount of complex carbohydrates, fiber, and vegetable proteins in diet. • Follow-up with HCP for regular lipid panel assessments.
Tobacco use (see Chapter 11)	• Begin a tobacco cessation program. • Change daily routines associated with tobacco use to reduce desire to smoke. • Substitute other activities for smoking. • Ask caregivers to support efforts to stop smoking. • Avoid exposure to environmental tobacco smoke.
Physical inactivity	• Develop and maintain at least 30 min of moderate physical activity daily (minimum 5 days a week). • Increase activities to a fitness level.
Psychologic state	• Increase awareness of behaviors that are harmful to health. • Change patterns that add to stress (e.g., get up 30 min earlier so that breakfast is not eaten on way to work). • Set realistic goals for self. • Reassess priorities considering identified risk factors. • Learn effective stress management strategies (see Chapter 7). • Seek professional help if feeling depressed, angry, or anxious. • Plan time for adequate rest and sleep (see Chapter 8).
Obesity (see Chapter 45)	• Change eating patterns and habits. • Reduce caloric intake to achieve body mass index of 18.5–24.9 kg/m^2. • Increase physical activity to increase caloric expenditure. • Avoid fad and crash diets, which are not effective over time. • Avoid large, heavy meals. Consider smaller, more frequent meals.
Diabetes (see Chapter 53)	• Follow the recommended diet. • Control or reduce weight. • Take prescribed drugs for diabetes. • Monitor glucose levels regularly and follow up with HCP regularly.

Managing High-Risk Persons

Recommend preventive measures for all persons at risk for CAD. The person with non-modifiable risk factors (e.g., age, gender, ethnicity) can still reduce the risk for CAD by controlling other modifiable risk factors. For example, a young person with a family history of premature heart disease can decrease the risk for CAD by maintaining an ideal body weight, getting adequate physical exercise, reducing intake of saturated fats, and avoiding tobacco and illicit drug use.

Encourage people who have modifiable risk factors to make lifestyle changes to reduce their risk for CAD. You play a key role in teaching health-promoting behaviors (Table 37.2). For highly motivated persons, just knowing how to reduce their risk may be all the information they need to start.

For people who are less motivated to take charge of their health, the idea of reducing risk factors may be so remote that they are unable to perceive a threat of CAD. Few people want to make lifestyle changes, especially in the absence of symptoms. First, help them to clarify their personal values. Then, discuss risk factors and have them identify their individual risks. Help them set realistic goals and choose which risk factor(s) to change first. Trying to change too many things at once can be a set-up for failure, so recommend working on one risk factor at a time. Some people are reluctant to change until they have symptoms or have an MI. Others, having had an MI, may find the idea of changing lifelong habits still unacceptable. Help them review options and respect their decisions.

Physical Activity

A regular physical activity program should be designed and implemented following the FITT formula (Table 37.3): Frequency (how often), Intensity (how hard), Type (isotonic), and Time (how long). Everyone should aim for at least 150 minutes (30 minutes at least 5 days per week) of moderate aerobic activity per week. Examples of moderate physical activity include brisk walking, biking, and recreational swimming. Another option is to do 75 minutes of vigorous aerobic activity each week such as jogging, singles tennis, or swimming laps.[12]

The AHA encourages increasing daily physical activity and lowering the chance of developing heart disease simply by walking. Adding weight training to an exercise program 2 days a week can help treat metabolic syndrome and improve muscle strength. Regular physical activity helps with weight reduction, reduces systolic BP, and can help increase HDL cholesterol.

TABLE 37.3 PATIENT & CAREGIVER TEACHING

FITT Activity Guidelines for CAD, Chronic Stable Angina, and ACS

Include the following information in the teaching plan for the patient with chronic stable angina and acute coronary syndrome and the caregiver:

Warm-Up/Cool-Down

Perform mild stretching for 3–5 min before the physical activity and 5 min after the activity. Do not start or stop activity abruptly.

Frequency

Perform physical activity on most days of the week.

Intensity

The patient's HR determines the activity intensity. If an exercise stress test has not been done, the HR of the patient recovering from an MI should not exceed 20 beats/min over the resting HR. Patients taking β-blockers may not be able to achieve the same HR with exercise as those not taking β-blockers. They should discuss specific HR targets with their HCP.

Type of Physical Activity

Select physical activity that is regular, rhythmic, and repetitive, using large muscles to build up endurance (e.g., walking, cycling, swimming, rowing).

Time

Physical activity sessions should be at least 30 min long. Begin slowly at personal tolerance (perhaps only 5–10 min) and build up to 30 min.

TABLE 37.4 NUTRITION THERAPY

Therapeutic Lifestyle Changes to Diet

Diet Recommendations	Recommended Daily Intake

Combined total fat calories from:
• *Saturated fats:* Limit fats that are usually solid at room and refrigerator temperature (e.g., lard, butter, whole-milk products, fatty cuts of meat, bacon)
• *Trans fats:* Mainly in foods made with hydrogenated vegetable oils, such as many hard margarines and shortenings
• *Unsaturated fats*: In oils that are usually liquid at room and refrigerator temperature (e.g., olive, corn, sunflower, soybean). There are 2 types of unsaturated fats:
  • *Monounsaturated fats:* In greatest amounts in foods from plants, including olives, avocadoes, and canola, sunflower, and peanut oils.
  • *Polyunsaturated fats:* Found mostly in nuts, seeds, fish, seed oils, and oysters. Omega-3 fatty acid is a type of polyunsaturated fat that may help reduce the risk of CAD.
	25%–35% of total daily calories (including <7% from saturated fat)

Cholesterol	<200 mg
Plant stanols or sterols (e.g., margarines, nuts, seeds, legumes, vegetable oils)[a]	2 g
Diet soluble fiber[a]	10–25 g of soluble fiber
Total calories	Only enough calories to reach or maintain a healthy weight

[a]Diet options for additional lowering of low-density lipoprotein (LDL).

◆ Nutrition Therapy

Diet recommendations focus on lowering LDL cholesterol through a decreasing saturated fat and cholesterol intake and increasing complex carbohydrates (e.g., whole grains, fruit, vegetables) and fiber (Tables 37.4 and 37.5). Fat intake should be about 25% to 35% of total calories, with most coming from monounsaturated and polyunsaturated fats. Red meat, egg yolks, and whole milk products are major sources of saturated fat and cholesterol. They should be reduced or eliminated from diets. Foods high in unsaturated fat include unsalted nuts (e.g., walnuts, peanuts, almonds) and avocado. Examples of oils low in saturated fat include canola, olive, and avocado. The patient with a high serum triglyceride level should reduce or eliminate alcohol and simple sugars.

Omega-3 fatty acids reduce triglyceride levels and can slow the progression of CAD. They do not affect LDL levels. The AHA recommends eating fatty fish twice a week because it is high in omega-3 fatty acids. Examples of fatty fish include salmon, albacore tuna, and mackerel. Omega-3 fatty acids can be hard to get by diet alone. The HCP may recommend medication supplements to assist in lowering triglycerides. The AHA has a website entitled "4 Ways to Get Good Fats" at https://www.heart.org/en/healthy-living/healthy-eating/eat-smart/fats/4-ways-to-get-good-fats-infographic.

◆ Lipid-Lowering Drug Therapy

The prevalence of total cholesterol levels of 240 mg/dL (6.2 mmol/L) has decreased. This decrease is likely due to increased use of statins rather than to diet changes.[1] The treatment of high cholesterol focuses mostly on lowering LDL cholesterol. A complete lipid profile should be done every 5 years beginning at age 20.[13] Middle-aged adults should be screened every 1 to 2 years. If multiple risk factors are present, more frequent testing is recommended.[13]

The 2019 AHA/ACC cholesterol guideline recommends patients with the following receive statin therapy:

- Known CAD
- At very high risk for CAD with an LDL greater than 70 mg/dL
- Primary elevations of LDL cholesterol levels of ≥190 mg/dL (e.g., familial hypercholesterolemia)
- 40 to 75 years of age with diabetes and LDL cholesterol levels greater than 70 mg/dL
- 40 to 75 years of age without diabetes, with LDL cholesterol levels ≥70 mg/dL plus a 10-year risk for CAD of 7.5% or greater

Guideline details include (1) treating patients with known CAD but no clinical events with a high-dose statin (e.g., atorvastatin 80 mg) to reduce the LDL by 50%, (2) treating very high-risk patients (patients with a history of 1 or more major events and multiple high-risk conditions) with a high dose statin to

TABLE 37.5 NUTRITION THERAPY

Tips to Make Diet and Lifestyle Changes

General Tips

1. Know your calorie needs to achieve and maintain a healthy weight.
2. Know the calorie content of the foods and beverages you eat.
3. Track your weight, physical activity, and calorie intake.
4. Prepare and eat smaller, more frequent meals.
5. Track your activities and, whenever possible, decrease sedentary activities (e.g., watching television, computer time).
6. Incorporate physical movement into daily activities (e.g., take stairs and extra steps whenever possible).
7. Do not smoke or use tobacco products.
8. If you drink alcohol, do so in moderation (i.e., no more than 1 drink for women or 2 drinks for men a day).

Tips Related to Food Choices and Preparation

1. Use the Nutrition Facts panel on food labels and ingredients list when choosing foods to buy.
2. Use fresh or frozen vegetables and fruits in place of canned vegetables and fruits.
3. Replace high-calorie foods with fresh fruits and vegetables.
4. Increase fiber intake by eating beans (legumes), whole-grain products, fruits, and vegetables.
5. Use liquid vegetable oils in place of solid fats.
6. Limit beverages and foods high in added sugars (e.g., sucrose, glucose, fructose, maltose, dextrose, corn syrups, concentrated fruit juice, honey).
7. Choose foods made with whole grains (e.g., whole wheat, oats, rye, barley, brown rice, wild rice, buckwheat).
8. Avoid pastries and high-calorie bakery products (e.g., muffins, doughnuts).
9. Select milk and dairy products that are either fat free or low fat.
10. Reduce salt intake by
    - Comparing the sodium content of similar products (e.g., different brands of tomato sauce) and choosing products with less sodium.
    - Choosing versions of processed foods with reduced salt, including cereals, canned products, and baked goods.
    - Limiting condiments (e.g., soy sauce, ketchup).
11. Use lean cuts of meat and remove skin from poultry before cooking or eating.
12. Avoid processed meats that are high in saturated fat and sodium (e.g., deli meats).
13. Grill, bake, or broil fish, meat, and poultry.
14. Incorporate plant-based meat substitutes into recipes (e.g., soy, tofu, quinoa).
15. Consume whole vegetables and fruits in place of juices.

Source: US Department of Health and Human Services: Your guide to lowering your cholesterol with TLC. Retrieved from www.nhlbi.nih.gov/files/docs/public/heart/chol_tlc.pdf.

lower the LDL to less than 70 mg/dL. For primary prevention (people without known CAD) in adults 40 to 75 years of age, the guideline recommends having a discussion with the HCP to determine their 10-year risk before starting a statin. In contrast, the 2017 American Association of Clinical Endocrinologists (AACE) guideline is more specific because it endorses treating LDL to specific target goals. The AACE guideline states that the LDL goal is less than 130 mg/dL for those with no cardiac risk factors considered at low risk for the development of CAD.[13] Those with 2 or fewer risk factors and a 10-year risk of less than 10% (moderate risk) should be treated to an LDL target of less than 100 mg/dL. Those at high risk (>2 risk factors and a 10-year risk of 10% to 20%; or diabetes or CKD stage 3 to 4 with no other risk factors) should be treated to an LDL of less than 100 mg/dL. Those at very high risk for developing CAD (recent hospitalization for ACS, established CAD, carotid disease, or peripheral vascular disease; diabetes, CKD stage 3 to 4 with 1 or more risk factors) should be treated to an LDL target of less than 70 mg/dL.

Drug therapy continues for a lifetime. If the patient becomes intolerant, we may change the drug. Intolerance to one statin does not mean intolerance to all statins. The patient must fully understand the rationale and goals of treatment, as well as the safety and side effects of lipid-lowering drugs.

Concurrent diet change reduces the need for drug therapy. Treatment also includes weight loss, if overweight, and increased physical activity. Serum lipid levels should be reassessed after 4 to 12 weeks of therapy.[6] If levels are still high, drug therapy may be changed.

◆ Drugs That Restrict Lipoprotein Production

HMG-CoA reductase inhibitors (statins). The statin drugs are the most widely used lipid-lowering drugs (Table 37.6). They inhibit the synthesis of cholesterol in the liver and increase the numbers of hepatic LDL receptors, removing more LDL from the blood. Statins also cause a minor increase in HDL. Rosuvastatin (Crestor) is the most potent statin currently available. Serious adverse effects are rare. They include liver damage and myalgia (muscle ache or weakness without breakdown of skeletal muscle) that can progress to rhabdomyolysis (breakdown of skeletal muscle).

DRUG ALERT
Simvastatin (Zocor)

- Increased risk for rhabdomyolysis when used with fibric acid derivatives (e.g., gemfibrozil), niacin, or erythromycin.
- Prothrombin times may increase in patients taking warfarin (Coumadin).
- Dose should not exceed 40 mg daily.
- Use with caution in patients on amiodarone because it can increase the risk of myopathy.

Niacin. Niacin, a water-soluble B vitamin, is effective in lowering triglyceride levels and mildly lowering LDL levels (Table 37.6). At high doses, niacin increases HDL levels, but it does not correlate to a decreased risk of CAD or MI. Unfortunately, common side effects include severe flushing, itching, gastrointestinal (GI) symptoms, and orthostatic hypotension.

DRUG ALERT
Niacin

- Teach the patient that flushing (especially of face and neck) may occur within 20 min after taking drug and last for 30–60 min.
- Premedicate with aspirin 30 min before taking to reduce flushing.
- Use of extended-release niacin may decrease side effects.

TABLE 37.6 Drug Therapy

Hyperlipidemia

Drug	Mechanism of Action	Side Effects	Nursing Considerations
Restrict Lipoprotein Production			
ATP-Citrate Lyase Inhibitor			
bempedoic acid (Nexletol)	↓ Hepatic synthesis of cholesterol ↓ LDL	Diarrhea Fatigue Muscle pain Upper respiratory tract infection	Monitor uric acid levels due to increased risk of gout. Use in caution with patients who have had a previous tendon rupture.
Fibric Acid Derivatives			
fenofibrate (Tricor) gemfibrozil (Lopid)	↓ Hepatic synthesis and secretion of VLDL ↓ VLDL ↓ Triglycerides ↓ LDL ↑ HDL	Rashes GI problems (e.g., nausea, diarrhea) ↑ Liver enzymes	May ↑ effects of warfarin (Coumadin) and some antihyperglycemic drugs. When used in combination with statins, may increase adverse effects of statins, especially myopathy.
HMG-CoA Reductase Inhibitors (Statins)			
atorvastatin (Lipitor) fluvastatin (Lescol XL) lovastatin pitavastatin (Livalo) pravastatin (Pravachol) rosuvastatin (Crestor) simvastatin (Zocor)	Block synthesis of cholesterol and increase LDL receptors in liver ↓ LDL ↓ Triglycerides ↑ HDL (small amount)	Rash GI problems ↑ Liver enzymes Myopathy, rhabdomyolysis	Well tolerated with few side effects. Monitor liver enzymes and recheck them after any increase in dosage. Assess CK-MM if symptoms of myopathy (e.g., muscle aches, weakness) occur.
Niacin			
niacin (Niaspan)	Inhibits synthesis and secretion of VLDL and LDL ↓ LDL ↓ Triglycerides ↑ HDL	Flushing and itching in upper torso and face GI problems (e.g., nausea, vomiting, dyspepsia, diarrhea) Orthostatic hypotension	Most side effects subside with time. Taking aspirin or ibuprofen 30 min before drug may reduce flushing. Take drug with food. Decreased liver function may occur with high doses.
Omega-3 Fatty Acid			
icosapent ethyl (Vascepa) (eicosapentaenoic acid [EPA])	Inhibits synthesis and/or secretion of triglycerides	Arthralgia	Used for patients with severe hypertriglyceridemia (levels ≥ 500 mg/dL). Used with statin therapy for patients with CAD who have high triglyceride levels. High incidence of bleeding when taken with drugs that increase the risk of bleeding, such as aspirin or warfarin.
omega-3 acid ethyl esters (Lovaza) (eicosapentaenoic acid [EPA] and docosahexaenoic acid [DHA])	↓ Triglycerides ↑ HDL	Anaphylaxis Rash Taste changes GI problems (e.g., constipation, vomiting)	Used for patients with high triglycerides. Give with meals and do not open or dissolve capsules.
Increase Lipoprotein Removal			
Bile-Acid Sequestrants			
colesevelam (Welchol) colestipol (Colestid) cholestyramine (Prevalite)	Binds with bile acids in intestine, forming insoluble complex and excreted in feces Binding results in removal of LDL and cholesterol ↓ LDL	Unpleasant quality to taste GI problems (e.g., indigestion, constipation, bloating)	Effective and safe for long-term use. Side effects lessen with time. Interferes with absorption of many drugs (e.g., digoxin, thiazide diuretics, warfarin, some antibiotics [e.g., penicillin]). Teach patient to take other drugs 1 hour before or 3–4 hr after bile-acid sequestrants.
Proprotein Convertase Subtilisin/Kexin 9 (PCSK9) Inhibitors			
alirocumab (Praluent) evolocumab (Repatha)	Inactivate PCSK9 protein ↓ LDL	Injection-site reactions Muscle pain, limb pain, and fatigue	Used with diet and maximum statin therapy to treat familial hypercholesterolemia, those who need further LDL lowering, or are statin intolerant. Given by injection every 2 wk or every 4 wk at a higher dose.

TABLE 37.6 Drug Therapy—cont'd

Hyperlipidemia

Drug	Mechanism of Action	Side Effects	Nursing Considerations
Decrease Cholesterol Absorption			
Cholesterol Absorption Inhibitor			
ezetimibe (Zetia)	Inhibits the intestinal absorption of cholesterol ↓ LDL ↑ HDL	Infrequent, but may include headache and mild GI distress	When used with a statin, further reduces LDL. Avoid use by patients with liver problems.

Fibric acid derivatives. *Fibric acid derivatives* (Table 37.6) increase HDL levels. They lower triglyceride levels by reducing the liver's production of VLDL and speeding up the removal of triglycerides from the blood. They indirectly lower LDL through their effect on HDL and triglycerides Although most patients tolerate the drugs well, GI irritability is common. They should be used with caution when combined with statins due to increased risk for myopathy.

DRUG ALERT

Gemfibrozil (Lopid)

- May increase the risk for bleeding in patients taking warfarin (Coumadin).
- Use cautiously in patients taking statins due to an increased risk of myopathy.

ATP-citrate lyase inhibitor. Bempedoic acid (Nexletol) helps lower LDL in patients with heterozygous familial hypercholesterolemia or patients with CAD who do not have adequate LDL lowering. We should monitor uric acid levels as the drug increases the risk of gout. Tendon rupture may occur, so use in caution with patients who have had a previous tendon rupture.[14]

Drugs That Increase Lipoprotein Removal

Bile acid sequestrants. Bile-acid sequestrants increase conversion of cholesterol to bile acids in the liver (Table 37.6). The primary effect is a decrease in total cholesterol and LDL levels. Bile-acid sequestrants decrease absorption of many other drugs (e.g., warfarin, thiazides, thyroid hormones, β-adrenergic blockers). Tell patients to take those drugs 1 hour before or 3 to 4 hours after bile-acid sequestrants to decrease this adverse effect.[3]

Proprotein convertase subtilisin/kexin 9 (PCSK9) inhibitors. PCSK9 inhibitors reduce the number of receptors in the liver that remove LDL cholesterol from the blood (Table 37.6). By blocking PCSK9's ability to work, more receptors are available and can get rid of LDL. This decreases circulating LDL levels. Evolocumab (Repatha) and alirocumab (Praluent) are PCSK9 inhibitors. They are not a first-line therapy. They are used with diet and maximum statin therapy for adults with familial hypercholesterolemia, those intolerant of statin drugs, or those with CAD who have an inadequate response to statins.[6] Patients receive subcutaneous injections every 2 weeks or every 4 weeks at a higher dose, depending on patient preference.

Drugs That Decrease Cholesterol Absorption

Ezetimibe (Zetia) selectively inhibits the absorption of diet and biliary cholesterol across the intestinal wall (Table 37.6). When combined with a statin as a combination drug (e.g., ezetimibe and simvastatin [Vytorin]) or as 2 separate drugs (ezetimibe and a statin), even greater reductions in LDLs occur.

Antiplatelet Therapy

We recommended low-dose aspirin (81 mg) to prevent CAD for years. However, its use in primary prevention (people without known CAD) is controversial due to the potential risk for bleeding. Low-dose aspirin may be used for primary prevention in adults age 40 to 59 years who are higher risk of CAD but do not have an increased risk for bleeding. Low-dose aspirin should not be started as primary prevention in adults over age 60.[10] Recommend taking coated aspirin to help with GI protection.

Gerontologic Considerations: Coronary Artery Disease

Heart disease is the leading cause of death in older persons. In the older adult, CAD is often a result of the complex interaction of nonmodifiable risk factors (e.g., age) and lifelong modifiable risk behaviors (e.g., inactivity, tobacco use).

Strategies to reduce CAD risk and treat CAD are effective in this age group. Aggressive treatment of hypertension and hyperlipidemia helps stabilize plaques in the coronary arteries. Tobacco cessation helps to decrease the risk for CAD at any age. Physical activity improves activity performance, endurance, and ability to tolerate stress. It can increase self-esteem, enhance emotional well-being, and improve body image. For the older adult who is obese, making modest diet changes and slowly increasing physical activity (e.g., walking) results in more positive benefits than aiming for a significant weight loss.

The older adult should exercise a minimum of 30 minutes on most days of the week as able. Teach the patient to avoid physical activity in temperature extremes and maintain a moderate pace. Heat intolerance results from a decreased ability to sweat efficiently. When planning a physical activity program, recommend (1) longer warm-up periods, (2) longer periods of low-level activity, and/or (3) longer rest periods between sessions.

TABLE 37.7 Select Conditions Influencing Myocardial O_2 Needs

Decreased O_2 Supply	Increased O_2 Demand or Consumption
Cardiac	
• Coronary artery atherosclerosis	• Aortic stenosis
• Coronary artery spasm	• Cardiomyopathy
• Coronary artery thrombosis	• Dysrhythmias
• Dysrhythmias	• Left ventricular hypertrophy
• Heart failure	• Tachycardia
• Valve disorders	
Noncardiac	
• Anemia	• Anxiety
• Asthma	• Hypertension
• Chronic obstructive pulmonary disease	• Hyperthermia
	• Hyperthyroidism
• Hypovolemia	• Physical exertion
• Hypoxemia	• Substance (stimulant) use (e.g., cocaine, amphetamines)
• Pneumonia	
• Substance (stimulant) use (e.g., cocaine, amphetamines)	

TABLE 37.8 PQRST Assessment of Angina

Use the following memory aid to obtain information from the patient who has chest pain:

	Factor	Questions to Ask Patient
P	Precipitating events	What events or activities precipitated the pain or discomfort (e.g., argument, exercise, resting)?
Q	Quality of pain	What does the pain or discomfort feel like (e.g., pressure, dull, aching, tight, squeezing, heaviness)?
R	Region (location) and radiation of pain	Can you point to where the pain or discomfort is located? Does the pain or discomfort radiate to other areas (e.g., back, neck, arms, jaw, shoulder, elbow)?
S	Severity of pain	On a scale of 0 to 10, with 0 indicating no pain and 10 being the most severe pain you could imagine, what number would you give the pain or discomfort?
T	Timing	When did the pain or discomfort begin? Has it changed since this time? Have you had pain/discomfort like this before?

Encouraging the older patient to adopt a healthy lifestyle may increase the quality of life and reduce the risk for CAD and fatal heart events. Older adults face many of the same challenges as younger persons related to making lifestyle changes. Older adults are more likely to consider change either (1) when hospitalized or (2) when symptoms (e.g., chest pain) are the result of CAD and not normal aging (see Table 35.1). First, assess for health literacy and the readiness to change. Then, help the patient select the lifestyle changes most likely to produce the greatest reduction in risk for CAD.

CHRONIC STABLE ANGINA

CAD is a chronic and progressive disease. Patients who are asymptomatic for many years may eventually develop chronic stable chest pain. When the demand for myocardial O_2 exceeds the ability of the coronary arteries to supply the heart with O_2, *myocardial ischemia* occurs. **Angina**, or chest pain, is the clinical manifestation of myocardial ischemia. It is caused by either an increased demand for O_2 or a decreased supply of O_2 (Table 37.7). The most common reason for angina to develop is significant narrowing of 1 or more coronary arteries by atherosclerosis. This leads to insufficient blood flow to the heart muscle. When ischemia occurs from an atherosclerotic plaque, the artery is usually blocked (stenosed) 70% or more (50% or more for the left main coronary artery).[15]

Chronic stable angina refers to chest pain that occurs intermittently over a long period of time with a similar pattern of onset, duration, and intensity of symptoms. It is often provoked by physical exertion, stress, or emotional upset. It is important to get an accurate assessment of angina symptoms (Table 37.8). Some patients deny feeling pain. They may describe a pressure, heaviness, or discomfort in the chest as a squeezing, heavy, tight, or suffocating sensation. Other symptoms, such as dyspnea or fatigue, may occur. Chronic angina pain usually does not change with position or breathing.

Most angina pain is substernal. It may radiate to the jaw, neck, shoulders, and/or arms. Many people with angina describe a feeling of indigestion or a burning sensation in the epigastric region. The sensation may be felt between the shoulder blades (Fig. 37.3). Often, people who describe pain between the shoulder blades or indigestion type pain dismiss it as not being heart related. Some patients, especially women and older adults, report atypical symptoms of angina, including dyspnea, nausea, mid-epigastric discomfort, and/or fatigue.[4,9] We refer to this as an *angina equivalent*.

The pain of chronic stable angina usually lasts for only a few minutes. It often subsides when the precipitating factor is resolved (e.g., by resting, calming down, using sublingual nitroglycerin [SL NTG]) (Table 37.9). Pain at rest is unusual. It may indicate UA. With ischemia, the 12-lead ECG often shows ST segment depression and/or T wave inversion. These changes represent an inadequate supply of blood and O_2 to the heart muscle. In the normal ECG, the ST segments should be isoelectric or flat (on the isoelectric line) (Fig. 37.4A). ST depression is significant if it is at least 1 mm (1 small box) below the isoelectric line in at least 2 contiguous leads (2 leads that look at the same wall of the heart). The ECG changes return to baseline when adequate blood flow is restored, and pain is relieved.

We treat patients with chronic stable angina with drug therapy. Because chronic stable angina is often predictable, drugs are timed to provide peak effects during the time of day when angina is likely to occur. For example, if angina occurs when rising, the patient can take medication as soon as awakening and wait 30 minutes to 1 hour before engaging in activity. A comparison of the major types of angina is shown in Table 37.10.

Silent ischemia refers to ischemia that occurs in the absence of any subjective symptoms. Patients with diabetes have an increased prevalence of silent ischemia. This is likely due to

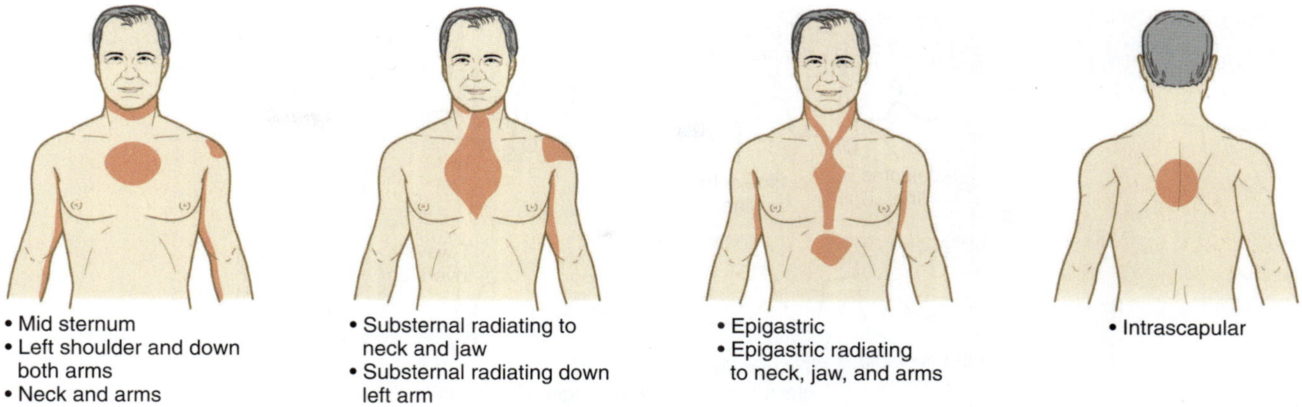

Fig. 37.3 Common locations and patterns of pain during angina or MI.

TABLE 37.9 Precipitating Factors of Angina

Circadian Rhythm Patterns
- Manifestations of CAD tend to occur in the early morning and within the first few hours after awakening

Consumption of Heavy Meal (e.g., holiday meals)
- Can increase the workload of the heart
- During the digestive process, blood is diverted to the GI system, reducing blood flow in the coronary arteries

Physical Exertion
- Increases HR, reducing the time the heart spends in diastole (the time of greatest coronary blood flow), resulting in an increase in myocardial O_2 demand
- Isometric exercise of the arms (e.g., raking, lifting heavy objects, snow shoveling) can cause exertional angina

Sexual Activity
- Increases the cardiac workload and sympathetic stimulation
- In a person with CAD, the extra cardiac workload may precipitate angina

Stimulants (e.g., cocaine, amphetamines)
- Increase HR and BP and increases myocardial O_2 demand
- Stimulate vasoconstriction and decreases myocardial O_2 supply
- May precipitate dysrhythmias

Strong Emotions
- Stimulate the sympathetic nervous system, activating the stress response
- Increase the workload of the heart

Temperature Extremes
- Increase the workload of the heart
- Blood vessels constrict in response to a cold stimulus
- Blood vessels dilate and blood pools in the skin in response to a hot stimulus

Tobacco Use and Environmental Tobacco Smoke
- Decrease available O_2 by increasing the level of carbon monoxide
- Nicotine stimulates catecholamine release, causing vasoconstriction and an increased HR

diabetic neuropathy affecting the nerves that innervate the cardiovascular system. When silent ischemia occurs in a monitored patient, we can see ECG changes (e.g., ST depression and/or T wave inversion) (Fig. 37.4A). Ischemia with pain or without pain has the same prognosis.

Prinzmetal's Angina

Prinzmetal's angina *(variant angina, vasospastic angina)* is a rare form of angina that often occurs at rest without increased physical demand. Risk factors include a history of migraine headaches, Raynaud's phenomenon, and heavy smoking. It is usually due to hyperreactivity of the smooth muscle of a major coronary artery resulting in strong contraction (spasm) of the vessel. Coronary spasm is more common in Asians than whites.[16] The spasm may occur in the presence or absence of CAD.

Factors contributing to coronary artery spasm include increased levels of certain substances (e.g., alcohol, cocaine), exposure to medications that narrow blood vessels (e.g., sumatriptan), or cold weather exposure. When spasm occurs, the patient has angina and transient ST segment elevation (not usually from an MI) (Fig. 37.4B). The pain may occur during rapid-eye-movement (REM) sleep when myocardial O_2 consumption increases between midnight and early morning or at rest. The pain may be relieved by moderate exercise, with SL NTG, or it may disappear spontaneously. Cyclic, short bursts of pain at the same time each day may occur with this type of angina. Treatment includes calcium channel blockers and/or nitrates. The patient should stop the use of any offending substances.

Microvascular Angina

In *microvascular angina,* chest pain occurs in the absence of significant CAD or coronary spasm of a major coronary artery. In these patients, chest pain is related to myocardial ischemia from atherosclerosis or spasm of the small distal branch vessels of the coronary microcirculation. This is known as *coronary microvascular disease or dysfunction* (MVD). It is more common in women.[9,16] Often the angina is prolonged and brought on by physical exertion. These patients usually have a positive stress test. With cardiac catheterization, no obstructive coronary disease is present in the major coronary arteries. Prevention and treatment of coronary MVD follow the same recommendations as for CAD.

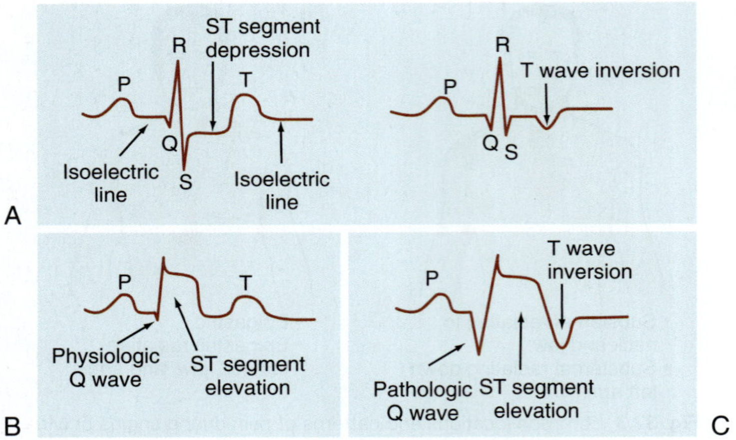

Fig. 37.4 ST segment, T wave, and Q wave changes associated with myocardial ischemia (A), injury coronary spasm (B), and infarction (C). (From Bucher L, Melander S: *Critical care nursing,* Philadelphia, 1999, Saunders.)

TABLE 37.10 Comparison of Major Types of Angina

Type	Etiology	Characteristics
Chronic stable angina	Myocardial ischemia (usually from CAD) caused by an O_2 supply/demand mismatch	• Episodic pain lasting a few minutes • Provoked by exertion or stress • Relieved by rest or nitroglycerin
Microvascular angina	Myocardial ischemia from microvascular disease affecting the small, distal branches of coronary arteries	• More common in women • Triggered by activities of daily living (e.g., shopping, work) vs. physical exercise (exertion) • Treatment may include nitroglycerin (long- and short-acting forms)
Prinzmetal's angina	Coronary vasospasm	• Occurs primarily at rest • Triggered by smoking and increased levels of some substances (e.g., histamine, epinephrine, cocaine) • May occur in presence or absence of CAD • Treatment may include long-acting nitrates and/or calcium channel blockers
Unstable angina	Rupture of unstable plaque, exposing thrombogenic surface	• New-onset angina • Chronic stable angina that increases in frequency, duration, or severity • Occurs at rest or with minimal exertion • Lasts more than 10 min

INTERPROFESSIONAL AND NURSING CARE: CHRONIC STABLE ANGINA

Chronic stable angina can progress or develop into ACS (UA or MI). Therefore, any change in the usual pattern of angina should be evaluated. A patient with chronic stable angina may be admitted with a change in the angina pattern. Until an assessment and diagnostic studies are completed, it may be unclear if the patient is having typical chronic stable angina, UA, or an MI.

The goal of treatment for a patient admitted with angina is to decrease O_2 demand and/or increase O_2 supply. Nursing care focuses on the priority problems of managing acute pain and anxiety while increasing O_2 delivery to the myocardium. The overall goals for a patient who presents with angina include (1) pain relief, (2) immediate and appropriate treatment, (3) preservation of heart muscle if an MI is suspected, (4) effective coping with illness-associated anxiety, (5) participation in a rehabilitation plan, and (6) reduction of risk factors.

Acute Care

If your patient has chest pain, but you are unsure if the pain is from chronic stable angina, UA, or an MI, plan to perform the following measures: (1) position patient upright unless contraindicated and apply supplemental O_2, (2) assess vital signs, (3) apply a continuous ECG monitor, (4) obtain a 12-lead ECG, (5) provide prompt pain relief, first with SL or IV NTG, followed by an IV opioid analgesic, if needed, (6) obtain cardiac biomarkers, (7) assess heart and breath sounds, and (8) obtain a chest x-ray. The patient may be anxious and may have pale, cool, clammy skin. The BP and HR may be high. There may be an atrial (S_4) or a ventricular (S_3) gallop. A new systolic murmur heard during an angina attack may indicate ischemia of a papillary muscle of the mitral valve, causing mitral regurgitation (the mitral valve does not close properly, and blood leaks back into the left atrium). The murmur may be transient and disappear when symptoms resolve.

Ask the patient to describe the pain and rate it on a scale of 0 to 10 before and after treatment to evaluate the effectiveness

TABLE 37.11 Treatment of Chronic Stable Angina and Acute Coronary Syndrome

Strategies for the patient with chronic stable angina should address all the treatment elements and related patient teaching in the following mnemonic:

Element	Treatment
A	Antiplatelet/anticoagulant therapy Antianginal therapy ACE inhibitor/angiotensin receptor blocker
B	β-Blocker BP control
C	Cigarette smoking cessation Cholesterol (lipid) management Calcium channel blockers Cardiac rehabilitation
D	Diet (weight management) Diabetes management Depression screening
E	Education Exercise
F	Flu vaccination

Modified from Smith SC, Benjamin EJ, Bonow RO, et al.: AHA/ACCF secondary prevention and risk reduction therapy for patients with coronary and other atherosclerotic vascular disease: 2011 update, *J Am Coll Cardiol* 58:2432, 2011.

of the interventions. Use the same words the patient used to describe the symptoms (e.g., tightness, pressure). Assess for other signs of pain, such as restlessness; ECG changes; high HR, respiratory rate, or BP; clutching the chest or bed linens; or other nonverbal cues. Support and reassure the patient. Use a calm approach to help reduce the patient's anxiety during an angina attack. If the chest pain is not related to an ACS, the patient may be discharged within 1 or 2 days. Further testing may be done during the hospitalization or as an outpatient.

CHECK YOUR PRACTICE

A visitor finds you in the hallway and tells you that her parent is having chest pain. The patient is not assigned to you.

- How would you proceed?

Patient Teaching

Reassure the patient with a history of angina that a long, active life is possible. Preventing or at least reducing the frequency of angina is key, so teaching is essential. Emphasize risk factor modification to slow the progression of CAD. Help the patient to identify their risk factors for CAD and ways to reduce modifiable risk factors (Tables 37.1 and 37.2). Give the patient information about CAD, angina, precipitating factors for angina (Table 37.9), and medications to treat angina (Tables 37.11 and 37.12 and Fig.37.5).

Teach the patient and caregiver about diets low in salt and saturated fats (Tables 37.4 and 37.5). Maintaining ideal body weight is important in controlling angina because excess weight increases the heart's workload. Give the patient a regular, individualized program of physical activity that conditions rather than stresses the heart. An example includes brisk walking on a flat surface at least 30 minutes a day on most days of the week.[10]

You can provide patient teaching in a variety of ways. One-on-one contact between you and the patient is often the most effective approach. Time during daily care (e.g., assessment, giving drugs) offers many teachable moments. Teaching aids, such as videos, heart models, and printed information, are important resources for patients and caregivers (see Chapter 4).

Help the patient to identify and avoid factors that precipitate angina (Table 37.9). For example, teach the patient to avoid exposure to extremes of weather and eating large, heavy meals. Tell the patient to rest for 1 to 2 hours after a heavy meal because blood shifts to the GI tract.

If needed, arrange for counseling to assess the psychologic adjustment of the patient and caregiver to the diagnosis of CAD and the resulting angina. Many patients feel a threat to identity, self-esteem, and their usual roles in society.

Drug Therapy

Drug therapy for chronic stable angina aims to reduce angina symptoms and the risk for MI and death. The most common medications to optimize myocardial perfusion in chronic stable angina include nitrates, angiotensin-converting enzyme (ACE) inhibitors, β-blockers, and calcium channel blockers (Tables 37.11 and 37.12 and Fig. 37.5). Aspirin is given for secondary prevention (for patients with diagnosed CAD) in the absence of contraindications (e.g., a true aspirin allergy) (Table 37.12).

Nitrates

Short-acting nitrates are first-line therapy for an acute episode of angina. Nitrates produce their principal effects by the following mechanisms:

Dilating peripheral blood vessels: This results in decreased systemic vascular resistance (SVR), venous pooling, and decreased venous blood return to the heart (preload). Myocardial O_2 demand then decreases because of the reduced cardiac workload.

Dilating coronary arteries and collateral vessels: This may increase blood flow to the ischemic areas of the heart. However, when the coronary arteries are severely atherosclerotic, coronary dilation is hard to achieve.

Orthostatic hypotension is common with all nitrates. Monitor BP after the first dose, since venous dilation may cause a drop in BP, especially in volume-depleted patients.

Short-acting nitroglycerin preparations. SL NTG tablets or translingual spray (Nitrolingual) usually relieve pain in about 5 minutes and last about 30 to 40 minutes. The recommended dose of SL NTG is 1 tablet sublingually (SL) or 1 to 2 metered sprays of translingual NTG on or under the tongue. If symptoms are unchanged or worse after 5 minutes, the patient should contact the emergency response system (e.g., 911).

Teach the patient and caregiver the proper storage and use of NTG. It should always be easily accessible to the patient. Store the tablets away from light and heat sources, including body heat, to protect them from degradation. Keep tablets in their

TABLE 37.12 Drug Therapy

Chronic Stable Angina and Acute Coronary Syndrome

Drug	Mechanism of Action and Considerations
Angiotensin-Converting Enzyme (ACE) Inhibitors (see Table 36.6)	
benazepril (Lotensin) captopril enalapril (Vasotec) fosinopril (Monopril) lisinopril (Zestril) quinapril (Accupril) ramipril (Altace)	• Prevents conversion of angiotensin I to angiotensin II, resulting in vasodilation • May prevent or limit ventricular remodeling • Decreases endothelial dysfunction • Useful with HF, decreased LV function, tachycardia, MI, hypertension, diabetes, and chronic kidney disease
Angiotensin II Receptor Blockers (see Table 36.6)	
candesartan (Atacand) irbesartan (Avapro) losartan (Cozaar) olmesartan (Benicar) telmisartan (Micardis) valsartan (Diovan)	• Inhibits binding of angiotensin II to angiotensin I receptors, resulting in vasodilation • Used for patients intolerant of ACE inhibitors
Anticoagulant Agents (see Table 41.10)	
Direct Thrombin Inhibitors	
bivalirudin (Angiomax) argatroban	• Direct inhibition of the clotting factor thrombin • Both drugs can be used during PCI • Argatroban is used mainly for patients with or at risk for heparin-induced thrombocytopenia
Low-Molecular-Weight Heparin[a]	
dalteparin (Fragmin) enoxaparin (Lovenox)	• Binds to antithrombin III, enhancing its effect • Heparin–antithrombin III complex inactivates activated factor X and thrombin • Prevents conversion of fibrinogen to fibrin
Unfractionated Heparin[a]	
heparin	• Prevents conversion of fibrinogen to fibrin and prothrombin to thrombin
Vitamin K Antagonist[a]	
warfarin (Coumadin)	• Interferes with hepatic synthesis of vitamin K–dependent clotting factors • Used for patients with atrial fibrillation or those at risk for thromboembolism (large anterior wall infarctions or ventricular aneurysms) • Closely monitor for bleeding when taking with antiplatelet drugs
Factor Xa Inhibitors	
apixaban (Eliquis) fondaparinux (Arixtra) rivorixaban (Xarelto)	• Block the clotting activity of Factor Xa to prevent clot formation • Apixaban and rivorixaban are used to prevent stroke in patients with non-valvular atrial fibrillation but are not FDA approved to prevent thromboembolism (large anterior wall infarctions or ventricular aneurysms) or for use in patients with mechanical heart valves • Fondaparinux may be used for patients with UA or NSTEMI
Antiplatelet Agents	
aspirin	• Inhibits cyclooxygenase, which in turn produces thromboxane A_2, a potent platelet activator • Given as soon as ACS is suspected, unless truly allergic
cangrelor (Kengreal)	• Inhibits platelet aggregation • Given IV • Approved for use in patients during a PCI procedure
clopidogrel (Plavix)	• Inhibits platelet aggregation • Used in combination with low-dose aspirin to treat ACS with or without PCI and after elective PCI for CAD • An alternative for patients who cannot take aspirin
prasugrel (Effient)	• Inhibits platelet aggregation • Used as an alternative to clopidogrel in combination with aspirin for patients with ACS who had PCI • Not indicated to treat patients with ACS not undergoing PCI • Not for use after elective PCI
ticagrelor (Brilinta)	• Inhibits platelet aggregation • Used in combination with low-dose aspirin to treat ACS with or without PCI • Effectiveness may be decreased by aspirin dosages >100 mg/day
vorapaxar (Zontivity)	• Inhibits platelet aggregation • Increases risk for bleeding, including life-threatening and fatal bleeding (boxed warning) • Must not be used in people who have had a stroke, transient ischemic attack (TIA), or bleeding in the head, because the risk for bleeding in the head is too great
Glycoprotein IIb/IIIa Inhibitors	
abciximab (ReoPro) eptifibatide (Integrilin) tirofiban (Aggrastat)	• Prevents the binding of fibrinogen to platelets, thereby blocking platelet aggregation • May be used in combination with aspirin for patients with ACS or during PCI
β-Adrenergic Blockers (see Table 36.6)	
atenolol (Tenormin) carvedilol (Coreg) metoprolol (Lopressor) nadolol (Corgard)	• Inhibits sympathetic nervous stimulation of the heart • Reduces heart rate, contractility, and BP • Reduces ischemia • Decreases afterload • Cardioselective β-blockers include atenolol, bisoprolol, and metoprolol

TABLE 37.12 Drug Therapy—cont'd

Chronic Stable Angina and Acute Coronary Syndrome

Drug	Mechanism of Action and Considerations
Calcium Channel Blockers (see Table 36.6)	
amlodipine (Norvasc) diltiazem (Cardizem) felodipine nicardipine (Cardene) verapamil (Calan) nifedipine (Procardia)	• Prevents calcium entry into vascular smooth muscle cells and myocytes (cardiac cells) • May prevent or control coronary vasospasm • Promotes coronary and peripheral vasodilation • Reduces HR, contractility, and BP • Dihydropyridines (e.g., nifedipine, amlodipine) are more potent vasodilators • Non-dihydropyridines (e.g., diltiazem, verapamil) have greater effect on reducing heart rate and contractility
Nitrates (see Table 36.6)	
isosorbide dinitrate (Isordil) isosorbide mononitrate (Imdur) Sublingual nitroglycerin (Nitrostat) Translingual spray nitroglycerin (Nitrolingual) Nitroglycerin ointment Transdermal nitroglycerin IV nitroglycerin	• Promotes peripheral vasodilation, decreasing preload and afterload • Promotes coronary artery vasodilation • May prevent or control coronary vasospasm
Opioid	
morphine	• Functions as an analgesic and sedative • Acts as a vasodilator to reduce preload and myocardial O_2 consumption
Sodium Current Inhibitor	
ranolazine (Ranexa)	• Treats chronic angina in patients who have not had an adequate response with other antianginal medications • Does not affect the BP or HR
Thrombolytic Agents	
reteplase (Retavase) alteplase (Activase) tenecteplase (TNKase)	• Breaks up fibrin meshwork in clots • Used only in STEMI when access to a hospital with PCI capability is not available or too far away

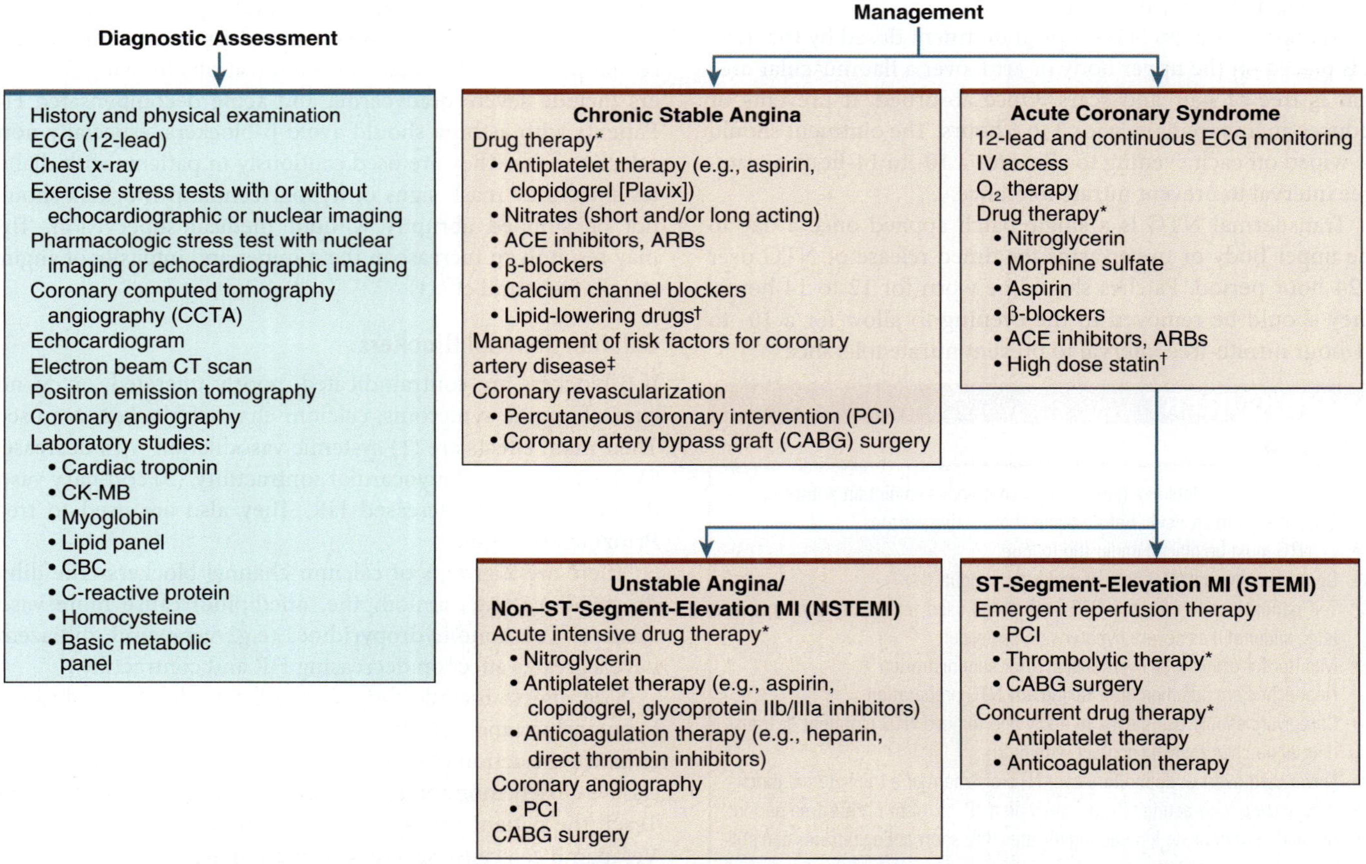

Fig. 37.5 Interprofessional care: chronic stable angina and acute coronary syndrome. *Table 37.12. †Table 37.6. ‡Tables 37.2, 37.4, and 37.5.

original bottles. Once opened, the tablets lose potency. They should be replaced every 6 months.

Tell the patient to sit down and place the NTG tablet under the tongue and allow it to dissolve. If using the spray, the patient should direct it on or under the tongue, not inhale it. SL NTG tablets should cause a tingling sensation when taken; if not, they may be outdated. Warn the patient that a headache, dizziness, or flushing may occur. Caution the patient to change positions slowly after NTG use because orthostatic hypotension may occur.

Patients can use NTG prophylactically before starting an activity that is known to cause angina (e.g., emotionally stressful situation, sexual intercourse). In these cases, the patient can take a tablet or spray 5 to 10 minutes before beginning the activity. Tell the patient to report any changes in the usual pattern of pain, such as increasing frequency, nighttime angina, or angina at rest.

Long-Acting Nitrates

Tolerance to long-acting NTG can develop. To limit this, schedule your patients for a 10- to 14-hour nitrate-free period every day. Remind patients that taking a long-acting NTG preparation should not keep them from using translingual or SL NTG if chest pain develops.

Oral nitrates, such as isosorbide dinitrate (e.g., Isordil) and isosorbide mononitrate (e.g., Imdur), are longer acting than SL or translingual NTG. They can reduce the frequency of angina attacks and treat Prinzmetal's angina. The main side effect is headache from the dilation of cerebral blood vessels. Tell patients to take acetaminophen to relieve the headache. Over time, headaches may decrease.

Nitropaste is a 2% NTG topical ointment dosed by the inch. It is placed on the upper body or arm, over a flat muscular area that is free of hair and scars. Once absorbed, it prevents or reduces angina frequency for 3 to 6 hours. The ointment should be wiped off each evening to allow for a 10- to 14-hour nitrate-free interval to prevent nitrate tolerance.

Transdermal NTG is a single patch applied once a day to the upper body or upper arms for timed release of NTG over a 24-hour period. Patches should be worn for 12 to 14 hours. They should be removed in the evening to allow for a 10- to 14-hour nitrate-free interval to prevent nitrate tolerance.

DRUG ALERT

Nitrates

- Keep SL NTG tablets in a dark, airtight container to maintain potency.
- Tell patients to sit down before using short-acting nitrates.
- SL NTG must be placed under the tongue.
- Spray translingual NTG onto or under the tongue.
- Tell patient not to combine NTG with drugs used for erectile dysfunction (e.g., sildenafil) as severe hypotension can occur.
- Monitor for orthostatic hypotension after administration.
- Headaches are common after taking any NTG preparation.
- Caregivers should use gloves to apply and remove NTG ointment or transdermal patches to avoid contact with drug.
- Never cardiovert or defibrillate over NTG ointment or a transdermal patch.
- When using long-acting nitrates, provide a 10- to 14-hr nitrate-free period.
- Remind patient using long-acting nitrates that short acting nitrates can still be used when needed.

Angiotensin-Converting Enzyme (ACE) Inhibitors and Angiotensin Receptor Blockers (ARBs)

Patients with chronic stable angina who have an ejection fraction (EF) of 40% or less, diabetes, hypertension, or CKD should take an ACE inhibitor (e.g., lisinopril) indefinitely, unless contraindicated. Patients with chronic stable angina and a normal EF, diabetes, and one other CAD risk factor also should take an ACE inhibitor to decrease the risk for MI, stroke, and death.[17]

These drugs result in vasodilation and reduced blood volume. Most important, they can prevent or reverse ventricular remodeling in patients who have had an MI. For patients who are intolerant of ACE inhibitors (e.g., cough, angioedema), angiotensin receptor blockers (ARBs) (e.g., losartan) are used. ACE inhibitors and ARBs are discussed in Chapter 36 and Table 36.6.

β-Adrenergic Blockers

Beta (β)-Blockers are used to relieve angina symptoms in patients with chronic stable angina. Patients who have LV dysfunction, an elevated BP, or had an MI should start and continue β-blockers indefinitely, unless contraindicated due to asthma or severe bradycardia. These drugs decrease myocardial contractility, HR, SVR, and BP, to reduce the myocardial O_2 demand and relieve angina symptoms. β-Blockers that reduce the risk for death in patients with LV dysfunction, HF, or MI include carvedilol (Coreg), metoprolol succinate (Toprol XL), and bisoprolol (Zebeta).[9]

β-Blockers have many side effects. These include bradycardia, hypotension, wheezing from bronchospasm, and GI effects. Many patients report weight gain, depression, fatigue, and sexual problems. Absolute contraindications to using β-blockers include severe bradycardia and acute decompensated HF. Patients with asthma should avoid β-blockers, especially nonselective ones. They are used cautiously in patients with diabetes since they mask signs of hypoglycemia. β-Blockers should not be stopped abruptly without medical supervision. This may result in an increase in the number and intensity of angina attacks (rebound effect).

Calcium Channel Blockers

If β-blockers are contraindicated, poorly tolerated, or do not control angina symptoms, calcium channel blockers are used. Their main effects are (1) systemic vasodilation with decreased SVR, (2) decreased myocardial contractility, (3) coronary vasodilation, and (4) decreased HR. They also are used to treat Prinzmetal's angina.

There are 2 groups of calcium channel blockers. The dihydropyridines (e.g., amlodipine, nifedipine) cause more vasodilation. The nondihydropyridines (e.g., verapamil, diltiazem) have a greater effect on decreasing HR and contractility.

Side effects include fatigue, headache, dizziness, flushing, hypotension, and peripheral edema. The nondihydropyridines enhance the action of digoxin by increasing serum digoxin levels. We closely monitor digoxin levels after starting these agents. Teach the patient the signs and symptoms of digoxin toxicity. Verapamil can cause severe constipation by relaxing GI smooth muscle and slowing peristalsis, especially in older adults.

Lipid-Lowering Drugs

A moderate or high dose of a lipid-lowering drug is given, unless contraindicated (Table 37.6). Patients with chronic stable angina should follow a diet low in saturated fat and cholesterol.

Sodium Current Inhibitor

Ranolazine (Ranexa), a sodium current inhibitor, is used to treat chronic angina in patients who have not had an adequate response with other antianginal medications. Although it is not a first-line agent, it is usually added only when the angina is not well controlled. Ranolazine does not affect the BP or HR. It can prolong the QT interval. Use it very cautiously in patients with a long QT interval or who are taking other QT-prolonging drugs (e.g., fluoxetine [Prozac]). Common side effects include dizziness, nausea, constipation, and headache.

Diagnostic and Intervention Studies

When a patient describes new-onset chest pain, and we suspect CAD or when a patient with chronic stable angina has a change in the angina pattern, a variety of studies are done (Fig. 37.5). After a detailed health history and physical assessment, we compare a 12-lead ECG with a previous ECG for changes that may indicate an ACS. Laboratory tests (e.g., cardiac biomarkers) can determine if the patient has an ACS. Other laboratory tests (e.g., lipid profile, CRP) can identify risk factors for CAD. A chest x-ray may show heart enlargement, aortic calcifications, and pulmonary congestion. An echocardiogram can detect resting LV wall motion abnormalities, which may suggest CAD.

If the ECG and cardiac biomarkers are negative, the patient may have an exercise stress test with or without imaging (echocardiography to look for wall motion abnormalities or nuclear imaging to look for perfusion abnormalities). This may occur during the hospitalization or as an outpatient. For those with physical limitations in walking, a pharmacologic (e.g., adenosine) or dipyridamole stress test with nuclear imaging or a pharmacologic (dobutamine) stress echocardiogram are options. Stress testing with imaging will be abnormal if coronary blockages are greater than 50% in the left main coronary artery or 70% in other vessels. Electron beam computed tomography (EBCT) or coronary computed tomography angiography (CCTA, CTA) testing may be done if there is no evidence of ACS and the patient remains free of chest pain. See Table 35.10 for more about these studies.

Cardiac Catheterization

For patients with increasing angina symptoms, cardiac catheterization is the gold standard test. It can identify and localize CAD, especially when the ECG shows ST depression and/or T wave inversion or cardiac biomarkers are positive. It may be done for a patient with chest discomfort who has a normal ECG and biomarkers but has an abnormal stress test. This procedure should be done only if the patient is a candidate for percutaneous or surgical coronary revascularization.

If a coronary blockage is amenable to treatment, **coronary revascularization** with **percutaneous coronary intervention (PCI)** may be recommended. PCI may be done at the same time as the cardiac catheterization. During PCI, a catheter with a deflated balloon tip is inserted into the blocked coronary artery. The deflated balloon is positioned inside the blockage and inflated. This compresses the plaque against the artery wall, resulting in vessel dilation and a larger vessel diameter. This procedure is called *balloon angioplasty.*

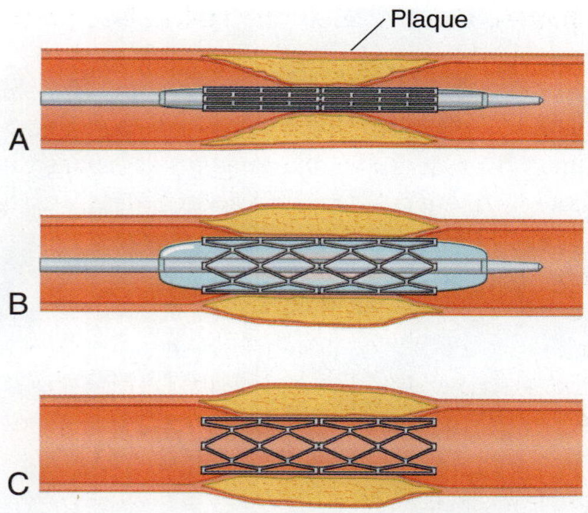

Fig. 37.6 Placement of a coronary artery stent. (A) The stent is placed at the site of the lesion. (B) The balloon is inflated, expanding the stent. The balloon is then deflated and removed. (C) The implanted stent is left in place.

Intracoronary stents are usually placed after a balloon angioplasty. A **stent** is an expandable mesh-like structure designed to keep the vessel open by supporting the arterial wall (Figs. 37.6 and 37.7). There are 2 types of stents: bare metal (BMS) and drug-eluting (DES). A DES is coated with a drug (e.g., everolimus, zotarolimus) to reduce the risk for overgrowth of the intimal lining *(neointimal hyperplasia)* within the stent. This overgrowth, called in-stent restenosis (ISR), is the build-up of scar tissue inside the stent. ISR may occur within a few months to a year after stent placement. The risk of ISR is lower with the use of a DES.

Because stents are thrombogenic, drugs are used to prevent platelet aggregation and thrombosis within the stent. Drugs commonly used during PCI are unfractionated heparin (UH) or low-molecular-weight heparin (LMWH), a direct thrombin inhibitor (e.g., bivalirudin [Angiomax]), and/or a GP IIb/IIIa inhibitor (e.g., eptifibatide [Integrilin]) (Table 37.12). After PCI for stable coronary disease, the patient receives dual antiplatelet therapy (DAPT) (e.g., aspirin plus clopidogrel [Plavix]) until the intimal lining grows over the metal stent and provides a smooth vascular surface.

After DES placement, DAPT is used for a minimum of 12 months to prevent thrombosis inside the stent. With the newer generation DESs, 3 to 6 months of DAPT is enough to prevent stent thrombosis. The duration of DAPT for patients with a BMS is a minimum of 1 month after PCI. Aspirin continues forever with either type of stent.[18]

Potential complications from cardiac catheterization with PCI include (1) abrupt closure from coronary artery dissection or rupture, (2) vascular injury at the artery access site (e.g., femoral, radial), (3) acute MI from acute stent thrombosis or from plaque dislodging and blocking the vessel distal to the original blockage, (4) stent embolization, (5) failure to cross the

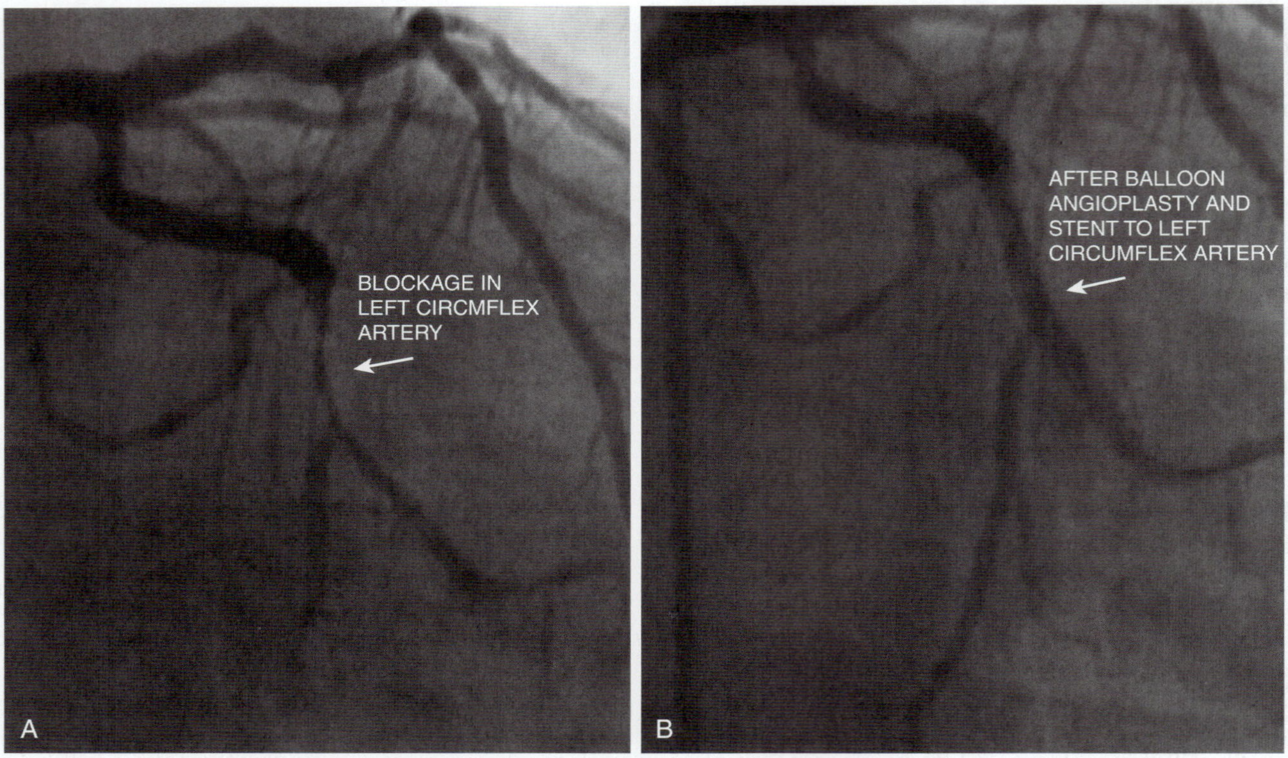

Fig. 37.7 (A) 90% occlusion of the left circumflex artery *(arrow)*. (B) Left circumflex artery is opened following balloon angioplasty and DES placement.

blockage with a balloon or stent, (6) coronary spasm, (7) dye allergy, (8) renal problems, (9) bleeding (e.g., retroperitoneal bleeding when the femoral artery is used or vascular access-site bleeding), (10) infection, (11) stroke, and (12) need for emergent coronary artery bypass graft (CABG) surgery. The risk for dysrhythmias during and after PCI is high, so monitor the ECG afterwards. Before and after catheterization and PCI, patients need frequent interventions (Table 35.12 and Table 37.13).

More PCIs than CABGs are done in the United States.[1] PCI may not be feasible for all patients (e.g., patients with 3-vessel CAD [3 different coronary arteries] and/or significant left main CAD).[19] Coronary revascularization with CABG surgery may be recommended after cardiac catheterization.

Surgical Coronary Revascularization

In patients with chronic stable angina, coronary revascularization with CABG surgery is recommended for patients who (1) do not respond well to medical management, (2) have left main coronary artery or 3-vessel disease, (3) are not candidates for PCI (e.g., blockages are long or difficult to access), or (4) continue to have chest pain after PCI. CABG may be an option for patients with diabetes, LV dysfunction, and/or CKD.[19] CABG surgery and PCI are palliative treatment for CAD and not a cure. Lifestyle changes and medications may help slow the progression of CAD and reduce the risk for recurrent events. Even after CABG, the bypass grafts are subject to the same progressive disease process as native coronary arteries.

CABG surgery consists of placing 1 or more arterial or venous graft(s) to provide blood to the heart muscle distal to the blocked coronary artery. Vessels used as grafts include the (1) saphenous vein from the leg, (2) radial artery from the forearm, and (3) internal mammary artery (IMA), also known as the internal thoracic artery (ITA). It is a branch of the subclavian artery (Fig. 37.8). The gastroepiploic artery is a rarely used option due to the time and difficulty in harvesting it.

Conventional Coronary Artery Bypass Graft Surgery

Traditional CABG surgery requires a sternotomy (opening of the chest cavity) and *cardiopulmonary bypass* (CPB). During CPB, blood is diverted from the patient's heart to a machine. There it is oxygenated and returned (via a pump) to the patient. This allows the HCP to operate on a quiet, non-beating, bloodless heart while vital organs are perfused. CPB can cause postoperative neurologic problems, renal problems, dysrhythmias (especially atrial fibrillation.), and systemic inflammatory response syndrome (SIRS).[19]

The left IMA (LIMA) is the most common artery used for a bypass graft. The proximal part remains attached to its origin (the left subclavian artery). The distal end of the LIMA is dissected from the chest wall. Next, it is sutured to the coronary artery distal to the blockage. It usually is used to bypass the left anterior descending (LAD) artery because the LAD supplies blood to the largest part of the heart muscle (anterior wall). IMAs also tend to have longer patency rates than saphenous veins (Fig. 37.8). Using the right IMA and LIMA carries an increased risk of sternal wound infection, especially in patients with diabetes or obesity.[19,20]

Saphenous veins can be used for bypass grafts. The HCP endoscopically removes the saphenous vein from 1 or both legs. A section is sutured into the ascending aorta near the opening

TABLE 37.13 NURSING MANAGEMENT

Percutaneous Coronary Intervention

Preprocedure

- Assess for allergies, especially to contrast dye.
- Perform baseline assessment, including vital signs, pulse oximetry, heart and breath sounds, neurovascular assessment of extremities (e.g., distal pulses, skin temperature, skin color, sensation).
- Withhold food and fluids for 6–12 hr before planned procedures.
- Assess baseline laboratory values (e.g., cardiac biomarkers, creatinine).
- Give ordered drugs before the procedure and stop drugs not needed for the procedure.
- Teach patient and caregiver about procedure and postprocedure care.

Postprocedure

- Perform assessment and compare to baseline: vital signs, pulse oximetry, heart and breath sounds, neurovascular assessment of extremity used for procedure, assessment of catheter insertion site for hematoma, bleeding, and bruit.
- Assess neurovascular status of involved extremity every 15 min for the first hour, then according to agency policy.
- Place compression device over arterial site to achieve hemostasis, per agency policy.
- Check for bleeding or hematoma at catheter insertion site every 15 min for the first hour, then according to agency policy.
- Report changes in neurovascular status of involved extremity or any bleeding.
- Monitor ECG for dysrhythmias or other changes (e.g., ST segment elevation or depression).
- Monitor patient for chest pain and other sources of pain or discomfort (e.g., back, vascular access site).
- Monitor IV infusions of antianginals (e.g., nitroglycerin) and antiplatelet medications (e.g., eptifibatide).
- Maintain bedrest as prescribed after femoral artery access.
- Teach patient and caregiver about discharge drugs (e.g., aspirin, clopidogrel, lipid lowering drugs).
- Teach patient and caregiver about discharge care, including signs and symptoms to report to HCP (e.g., access site complications, return of chest pain).

Assistive Personnel (AP)

- Supervise AP:
  - Take vital signs and report increases or decreases in HR or BP to RN.
  - Report patient descriptions of chest pain, shortness of breath, and/or any other discomfort or distress to RN.
  - Report changes in neurovascular status of the involved extremity or any bleeding to the RN.
  - Help with oral hygiene and hydration, meals, and toileting.
  - Record oral intake and urine output as ordered.

of the native coronary artery and then anastomosed to the coronary artery distal to the blockage (Fig. 37.8). Saphenous vein grafts are more prone to develop diffuse intimal hyperplasia, future stenosis, and graft occlusion.

The radial artery, another potential graft, is a thick muscular artery prone to spasm. Perioperative calcium channel blockers and long-acting nitrates are used to control the spasms.[20] Patency rates are not as good as the IMA but are better than saphenous veins. Serious extremity complications (e.g., hand

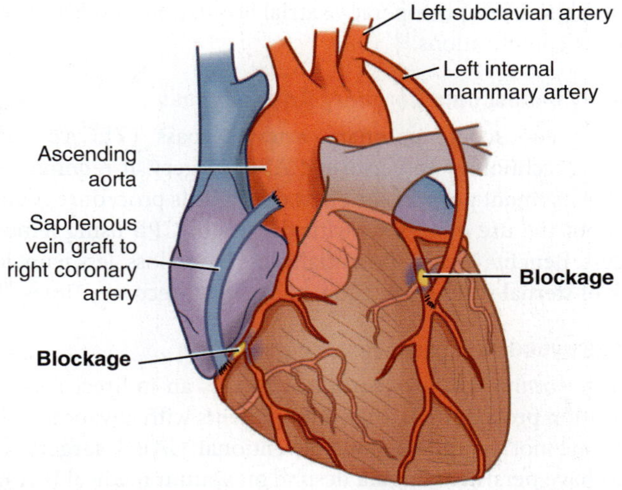

Fig. 37.8 Proximal end of the left internal mammary artery (LIMA) is left attached to the subclavian artery, and the distal end of the LIMA is sutured into the LAD artery below the blockage. Proximal end of the saphenous vein is sutured to the aorta. The distal end is sutured into the right coronary artery below the area of blockage.

ischemia, wound infection) are rare after removal of the radial artery. Patients may have paresthesias and impaired sensation after radial artery harvest.

All bypass grafts are subject to the fat and cholesterol build-up that occurs in the native coronary arteries. Controlling risk factors as well as antiplatelet and statin therapy after CABG surgery helps maintain vein graft patency.

Women have higher periprocedural mortality and morbidity rates than men. We attribute this to the late treatment of CAD. Women first present with CAD at an older age and have more co-morbidities at the time of surgery. Other factors include smaller diameter coronary vessels, smaller body surface area, and the fact that women are less likely to be referred for catheterization.[19]

Minimally Invasive Direct Coronary Artery Bypass

Minimally invasive direct coronary artery bypass (MIDCAB) offers patients an approach to surgical treatment that does not involve a sternotomy and CPB. The technique requires several small incisions between the ribs or a mini-thoracotomy. The LIMA is dissected away from the chest wall by direct visualization.[20] The right IMA is more difficult to access with the thoracotomy approach.[20] A mechanical stabilizer immobilizes the operative site.

In the early days of MIDCAB, we only used the IMA as a graft to the LAD or right coronary artery. Today, MIDCAB can be used for multivessel revascularization in select patients. Some patients have hybrid procedures in which they have a MIDCAB for the LAD artery and undergo a PCI of a second or third artery later.

Off-Pump Coronary Artery Bypass

The *off-pump coronary artery bypass* (OPCAB) procedure uses a median sternotomy to access all coronary vessels. OPCAB is performed on a beating heart (no CPB) using mechanical stabilizers. OPCAB is associated with less blood loss, less renal dysfunction, less postoperative atrial fibrillation, and fewer neurologic complications.[19]

Totally Endoscopic Coronary Artery Bypass

Totally endoscopic coronary artery bypass (TECAB) uses robotic technology to perform CABG surgery. It requires several instrument ports in the chest cavity. This procedure is done without the use of CPB or with the use of CPB using femoral access. Benefits include potentially less blood loss, less pain, less risk of sternal wound infection, and shorter recovery times.[20]

Transmyocardial Laser Revascularization

Transmyocardial laser revascularization is an indirect revascularization procedure. It is used for patients with advanced CAD who are not candidates for conventional CABG surgery and who have persistent angina despite maximum medical therapy. Using a left thoracotomy approach, a high-energy laser creates channels in the heart muscle to allow blood flow to ischemic areas. It is an adjunctive therapy when bypass grafts cannot be placed or in combination with CABG surgery.[20]

Postoperative Care After CABG Surgery

Care after CABG surgery is provided in the intensive care unit (ICU) for the first 24 to 48 hours. Ongoing intensive monitoring of the patient's hemodynamic status is critical. The patient will have many invasive lines for monitoring heart status and other vital functions (see Chapter 35). These include (1) hemodynamic monitoring (e.g., CO), (2) an arterial line for continuous BP monitoring, (3) pleural and mediastinal chest tubes for chest drainage, (4) continuous ECG monitoring, (5) an endotracheal tube connected to mechanical ventilation, (6) epicardial pacing wires for emergency pacing of the heart, (7) a urinary catheter to monitor urine output, and (8) a nasogastric tube for gastric decompression. Most patients are extubated within 6 hours and transferred to a step-down unit within 24 to 48 hours for continued monitoring.

Many of the complications that develop after CABG surgery relate to the use of CPB. Major complications of CPB are systemic inflammation, bleeding and anemia from damage to red blood cells and platelets, fluid and electrolyte imbalances, infections, and hypothermia from CPB. Focus your care on assessing the patient for bleeding (e.g., chest tube drainage, incision sites), monitoring hemodynamics, checking fluid status, replacing blood and electrolytes as needed, and restoring temperature (e.g., warming blankets).

Postoperative dysrhythmias, especially atrial fibrillation (e.g., AF), are common. The incidence of AF after CABG surgery is 20% to 50%.[19] β-Blockers should be started at least 24 hours before CABG surgery and restarted as soon as possible after surgery (unless contraindicated) to reduce the incidence of AF.[19] Discharge may be delayed in patients who develop AF so we can control the HR and start anticoagulation therapy. See Chapter 39 for information on treating AF.

You must also provide wound care for the patient's surgical sites (e.g., leg, chest, arm). Chest incisions often do not need dressings after 24 hours. Management of the chest wound is like that of other chest surgeries (see Chapter 28). Care of the leg incision is minimal since endoscopy is used to harvest the vein.

Care of a radial artery harvest site includes monitoring sensory and motor function of the hand. The patient with radial artery harvest should take a calcium channel blocker and/or a long-acting nitrate after surgery to reduce the incidence of arterial spasm at the arm or anastomosis site.[20]

Other nursing interventions include strategies to manage pain and prevent venous thromboembolism (e.g., early ambulation, sequential compression device) and respiratory complications (e.g., incentive spirometry, splinting during coughing and deep-breathing exercises). Chapter 20 details care of the postoperative patient.

Postoperative cognitive dysfunction (POCD) can manifest days to weeks after surgery. It usually improves within a few months after surgery. For some, POCD becomes a chronic problem. This includes impairment of memory, concentration, language comprehension, and social integration. Depression and anxiety are common. Patients may cry or become teary. POCD is discussed in Chapter 20.

The older patient (> age 80) can often undergo elective CABG with good results. Many have multiple preoperative co-morbidities, so the incidence of postoperative complications (e.g., dysrhythmias, stroke, POCD, infection) is higher. Although the treatment benefits may outweigh risks in this group, morbidity and mortality are higher than in younger persons.[19]

Postoperative nursing care of the patient with a MIDCAB, OPCAB, or TECAB procedure is similar to that for conventional CABG surgery patients. The recovery time usually is shorter. Patients often resume routine activities sooner than patients who have conventional CABG surgery. Pain control is important regardless of the procedure. Patients often report higher levels of pain with a thoracotomy incision than a sternotomy incision.

Alternative Therapies for Refractory Chronic Stable Angina

For patients with refractory angina, *enhanced external counterpulsation* (EECP) may be used. EECP consists of placing inflatable BP cuffs around the legs. The cuffs sequentially inflate during diastole and deflate during systole from the calves to the thighs. This action increases venous return and augments diastolic BP. This increases coronary perfusion, improves LV diastolic filling, and helps with collateral circulation. Patients get treatments 5 days a week for a total of 35 treatments. EECP is contraindicated in patients with decompensated HF, severe peripheral arterial disease, and severe aortic insufficiency.[9]

ACUTE CORONARY SYNDROME

When chest pain from ischemia is prolonged and not immediately reversible, **acute coronary syndrome (ACS)** may develop. ACS includes the spectrum of non-ST elevation ACS (*UA and non–ST-segment-elevation myocardial infarction* (NSTEMI)) and *ST-segment-elevation myocardial infarction* (STEMI) (Fig. 37.9). When patients first present with chest pain, compare the ECG to a previous ECG whenever possible. ST-elevations on the

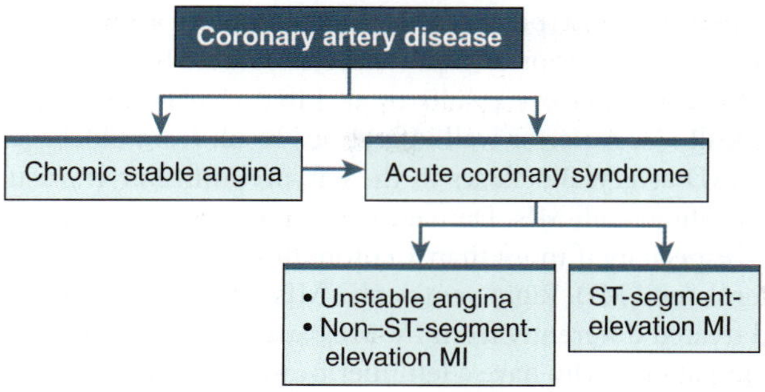

Fig. 37.9 Relationships among coronary artery disease, chronic stable angina, and acute coronary syndrome.

12-lead ECG likely indicate a STEMI (Fig. 37.4B). ST elevation represents myocardial injury that is potentially reversible, but, if not treated, will likely evolve to permanent necrosis (tissue death) of the myocardium. Patients with UA or NSTEMI may or may not have ST segment depression and/or T wave inversion on the ECG. For these patients, it is difficult to tell between UA and NSTEMI until we evaluate serum cardiac biomarkers.[12]

Heart muscle cells become hypoxic within the first 10 seconds of a total coronary occlusion as they are deprived of O_2 and glucose needed for aerobic metabolism and contractility. Anaerobic metabolism begins, and lactic acid accumulates. In ischemic conditions, heart cells are viable for about 20 minutes. Irreversible heart damage starts after 20 minutes if there is no collateral circulation (Fig. 37.2).[21] With restoration of blood flow (reperfusion), aerobic metabolism resumes, contractility is restored. Cellular repair begins.

ACS occurs when a previously stable atherosclerotic plaque ruptures, releasing the lipid core into the vessel. This causes platelet aggregation and thrombus formation. The vessel may be partially blocked by a thrombus (manifesting as UA or NSTEMI) or totally blocked by a thrombus (manifesting as STEMI). It is unclear what causes the plaque to suddenly become unstable. Systemic inflammation (described earlier) may play a role. Patients with suspected ACS need immediate hospitalization.

UNSTABLE ANGINA

Unstable angina (UA) is chest pain that is new in onset, occurs at rest, or occurs with increasing frequency, duration, or less effort than the patient's chronic stable angina pattern. The pain usually lasts 10 minutes or more.

The patient with chronic stable angina may develop UA, or UA may be the first clinical sign of CAD. Unlike chronic stable angina, UA is unpredictable. It must be treated immediately. The patient with previously diagnosed chronic stable angina describes a significant change in the pattern of angina. It occurs with increasing frequency and with less exertion than previously. It may occur during sleep or even at rest. The patient without previously diagnosed angina describes chest pain that has progressed rapidly in the past few hours, days, or weeks, often ending in pain at rest. ECG changes that may occur with UA include ST depression and/or T wave inversion (Fig. 37.4A). We refer to these changes as ischemic changes.

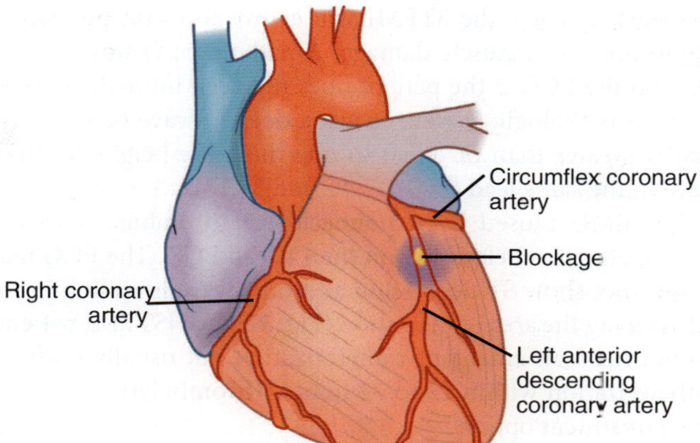

Fig. 37.10 Occlusion of the LAD coronary artery, resulting in acute MI.

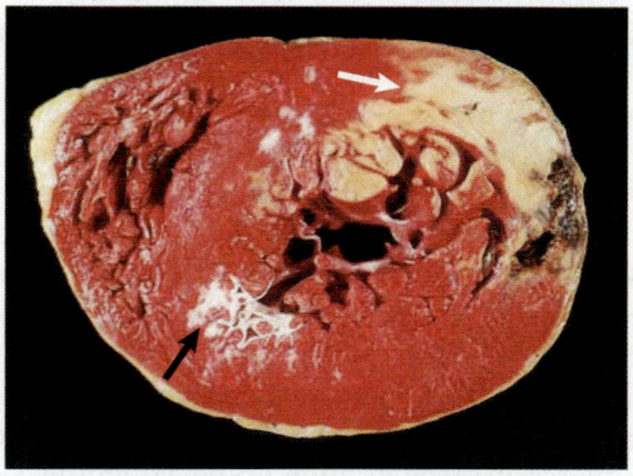

Fig. 37.11 Acute MI in the posterolateral wall of the left ventricle. Note the absence of staining in the areas of necrosis *(white arrow)*. Note the scarring from a previous anterior wall MI *(black arrow)*. (From Kumar V, Abbas AK, Aster JC, et al.: *Robbins and Cotran pathologic basis of disease,* ed 8, Philadelphia, 2010, Saunders.)

ST-ELEVATION AND NON–ST-ELEVATION MYOCARDIAL INFARCTION

A **myocardial infarction (MI)** occurs because of an abrupt stoppage of blood flow through a coronary artery with a thrombus caused by platelet aggregation. This causes irreversible myocardial cell death (necrosis) in the heart muscle beyond the blockage (Figs. 37.10 and 37.11). Serum cardiac biomarkers are released into the blood. Most MIs occur in the person with preexisting CAD.

A STEMI, caused by an occlusive thrombus, results in ST-elevation in the ECG leads facing the area of infarction (Figs. 37.4B; 37.12 and 37.13). ST segment elevation is significant if it is 1 mm (1 small block) or more above the isoelectric line in at least 2 contiguous leads (2 leads that look at the same wall of the heart) except in V_2 and V_3. There the ST elevation must be 2 mm (2 small blocks) or more.[22]

A STEMI is an emergency. To limit the infarct size, the artery must be opened within 90 minutes of presentation to restore blood and O_2 to the heart muscle and limit the infarct size. This can be done either by PCI or with thrombolytic (fibrinolytic) therapy. PCI is the first-line treatment, if available (Fig. 37.6). Thrombolytic therapy is done in hospitals that do not have a catheterization laboratory for PCI. If the patient does not seek treatment quickly, the STEMI will evolve to cause potentially significant heart muscle damage. A pathologic Q wave will be seen on the ECG if the patient does not seek immediate treatment. A pathologic Q wave is just a deep Q wave or a Q wave that is greater than or equal to one-third the height of the R wave in the same lead (Figs. 37.4C and 37.13).

NSTEMI, caused by a nonocclusive thrombus, does not cause ST segment elevation on the 12-lead ECG. The ECG may or may not show ST depression and/or T wave inversion in the leads facing the area of infarction (Fig. 37.12). NSTEMI patients do not need an emergent catheterization but usually undergo catheterization within 12 to 72 hours. Thrombolytic therapy is not a treatment option.

With either NSTEMI or STEMI, an echocardiogram may show *hypokinesis* (worsening myocardial contractility) or *akinesis* (absent myocardial contractility) in the infarcted area(s). The degree of LV dysfunction depends on the area of the heart involved and size of the infarction.

The acute MI process evolves over hours to a few days. The earliest tissue to become ischemic is the subendocardium (the innermost layer of tissue in the heart muscle). If ischemia persists, it takes around 4 to 6 hours for the entire thickness of the heart muscle to necrose. If the thrombus is not completely blocking the artery, the time to complete necrosis may be as long as 12 hours.

Most MIs affect the LV and are described based on the location of damage (e.g., anterior, inferior, lateral, septal, or posterior wall infarction). The location of the MI and ECG changes correlate with the involved coronary artery (Table 37.14). For

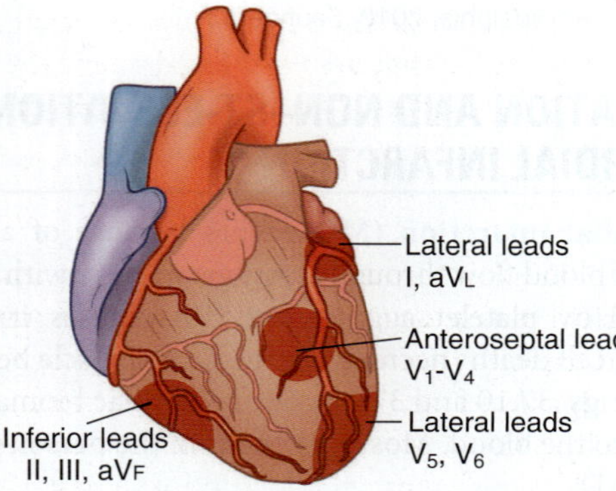

Fig. 37.12 Definitive ECG changes occur in leads that face the area of ischemia, injury, or infarction. Reciprocal changes may occur in leads facing opposite the area of ischemia, injury, or infarction.

example, in most people, the right coronary artery supplies blood to the inferior and posterior LV walls. Blockage of the right coronary artery results in an inferior wall and/or posterior wall MI. Anterior wall infarctions result from blockages in the LAD artery. Blockages in the left circumflex artery usually cause lateral wall MIs. Damage can occur in more than 1 location, especially if more than 1 coronary artery is involved (e.g., anterolateral MI). Right ventricular MIs are much less common and treated differently from LV MIs. Suspect a right ventricular MI in patients who have a left inferior wall STEMI.[23]

The degree of collateral circulation influences the severity of the MI (Fig. 37.2). Not everyone develops collateral circulation. A person with a long history of CAD may develop good collateral circulation to provide the tissue around the evolving infarction with an adequate blood supply. This is one reason a younger person may have a more serious first MI than an older person with the same degree of blockage.

Clinical Manifestations

Pain

Chest pain with an MI is often worse than with previous episodes of angina. Persistent and unlike any other pain, it is usually described as a heavy, pressure, tight, burning, constricted, or crushing feeling. Common locations are the substernal or epigastric area. The pain may radiate to the neck, lower jaw, and arms or to the back (Fig. 37.3). When epigastric pain is present, the patient may relate it to indigestion, take antacids without relief, and therefore delay seeking treatment. It may occur while the patient is active or at rest, asleep, or awake. Pain often occurs in the early morning hours. It usually lasts for 20 minutes or longer.

Not everyone who has an MI has classic symptoms. Some patients may not have pain but may have "discomfort," weakness, nausea, indigestion, or shortness of breath. Some women may have atypical discomfort, shortness of breath, or fatigue. Patients with diabetes may have silent (asymptomatic) MIs because of cardiac neuropathy or have atypical symptoms (e.g., shortness of breath). An older patient may have a change in mental status (e.g., confusion), shortness of breath, pulmonary edema, dizziness, or a dysrhythmia.

Sympathetic Nervous System Stimulation

During the initial phase of MI, the ischemic heart cells release catecholamines (norepinephrine and epinephrine). This results in diaphoresis, increased HR and BP, and vasoconstriction

TABLE 37.14 ECG Evidence in Acute Coronary Syndrome

	ECG EVIDENCE		
Left Ventricle Involvement	**Leads Facing Area**	**Leads Opposite Area (Reciprocal Changes)**	**Associated Coronary Artery**
Septal wall	V_1, V_2	II, III, aVF	Left anterior descending (LAD)
Anterior wall	V_3, V_4	II, III, aVF	LAD
Lateral wall, low	V_5, V_6	II, III, aVF	LAD or circumflex
Lateral wall, high	I, aVL	II, III, aVF	Circumflex
Inferior wall	II, III, aVF	I, aVL, V_5, V_6	Right coronary artery, posterior descending coronary artery

of peripheral blood vessels. The patient's skin may be ashen, clammy, and cool to touch.

Cardiovascular Manifestations

In response to the release of catecholamines, BP and HR may be high initially. Later, the BP may drop because of decreased CO. If severe enough, this may result in decreased renal perfusion and urine output. Crackles, if present, may persist for several hours to several days, suggesting LV dysfunction. Jugular venous distention (JVD), hepatic engorgement, and peripheral edema may mean right ventricular dysfunction.

Your patient may have abnormally distant heart sounds. Other abnormal sounds suggesting LV dysfunction are S_3 and S_4. A loud holosystolic murmur may occur with a ventricular septal defect or papillary muscle rupture resulting in mitral regurgitation (the valve does not close properly allowing blood to leak back into the left atrium).

Nausea and Vomiting

Your patient may have nausea and vomiting. These symptoms can result from reflex stimulation of the vomiting center by the severe pain. They can also result from vasovagal reflexes initiated in the area of the infarcted heart muscle, especially with inferior wall MIs.

Fever

The temperature may increase to 100.4°F (38°C) within 24 to 48 hours. Fever may last 4 to 5 days. This increase is due to a systemic inflammatory process caused by the death of myocardial cells.

Healing Process

The body's response to cell death is the inflammatory process (see Chapter 12). Within 24 hours, leukocytes infiltrate the area. The dead heart cells release enzymes that are important diagnostic indicators of MI. The proteolytic enzymes of the neutrophils and macrophages begin to remove necrotic tissue by the fourth day. During this time, the necrotic muscle wall is thin.

Once infarction takes place, catecholamine-mediated lipolysis and glycogenolysis occur. These processes allow the increased plasma glucose and free fatty acids to be used by the O_2-depleted myocardium for anaerobic metabolism. This is why glucose levels are often high after MI.

The necrotic zone of a STEMI is identified by ECG changes (e.g., lowering of the initially elevated ST segments, T wave inversion and/or a pathologic Q wave) within 1 or 2 days. At this point, the neutrophils and monocytes have cleared the necrotic debris from the injured area. The collagen matrix that will eventually form scar tissue is laid down.

At 10 to 14 days after MI, the new scar tissue is still weak. The heart muscle is vulnerable to increased stress during this time. At the same time, the patient's activity level may be increasing, so special caution and assessment are necessary. By 6 weeks after MI, scar tissue has replaced necrotic tissue and the injured area is considered healed. Often the scarred area is less compliant than the surrounding area. This may be manifested by abnormal wall motion on an echocardiogram or nuclear imaging (e.g., hypokinesis, akinesis), LV dysfunction, altered conduction patterns, dysrhythmias, or HF. Years later, the scarred area may become an irritable focus for life-threatening dysrhythmias causing sudden cardiac death (SCD).

These changes in the infarcted heart muscle also cause changes in the unaffected areas. To try to compensate for the damaged muscle, the normal myocardium hypertrophies and dilates. This process is called *ventricular remodeling*. Remodeling of normal myocardium can lead to the development of late HF, especially in the person with atherosclerosis of other coronary arteries and/or an anterior MI. ACE inhibitor drugs are given to limit ventricular remodeling.

Complications of Myocardial Infarction

Dysrhythmias

Any condition that affects the heart cells' sensitivity to nerve impulses (e.g., ischemia, electrolyte imbalances, SNS stimulation) can cause dysrhythmias. Dysrhythmias are the most common complication after an MI. They occur in 80% to 90% of patients. Ventricular tachycardia (VT) and ventricular fibrillation (VF) are the most common cause of death in patients in the prehospital period. VT or VF most often occur within the first 4 hours after the onset of pain. Premature ventricular contractions (PVCs) may precede VT and VF.

Bradycardias (e.g., complete heart block) can develop when key areas of the conduction system are destroyed (e.g., infarction involves the sinus or atrioventricular node). A patient who is symptomatic with bradycardia may require an external pacemaker or a temporary transvenous pacemaker.

With reperfusion (thrombolytic therapy or PCI), it is common to see PVCs, asymptomatic nonsustained VT, and idioventricular rhythms. These rhythms are not associated with an increased risk for SCD. They are not treated unless the patient is symptomatic.[23] See Chapter 39 for information about dysrhythmias and their management.

Heart Failure

Heart failure (HF) is a complication that occurs when the right or left ventricle's pumping action is reduced. Depending on the severity and extent of the injury, left-sided HF occurs initially with subtle signs, such as mild dyspnea, restlessness, agitation, or slight tachycardia. Other signs indicating the onset of left-sided HF include pulmonary congestion on chest x-ray, an S_3 heart sound, crackles on auscultation of the lungs, paroxysmal nocturnal dyspnea (PND), and orthopnea. Signs of right-sided HF include JVD, hepatic congestion, abdominal distention, or lower extremity edema. See Chapter 38 for information about the treatment of acute decompensated HF.

Cardiogenic Shock

Cardiogenic shock occurs when O_2 and nutrients supplied to the tissues are inadequate because of severe LV failure, papillary muscle rupture, ventricular septal rupture, LV free wall rupture, or right ventricular infarction.[23] This occurs less often when STEMI is treated early and rapidly with PCI or thrombolytic therapy. Cardiogenic shock, which has a high death rate, requires aggressive management. This includes control of dysrhythmias, mechanical circulatory devices (e.g., intraaortic balloon pump [IABP], extracorporeal membrane oxygenation [ECMO]), and support of contractility with vasoactive drugs (e.g., dobutamine). Goals of therapy are to maximize O_2 delivery, reduce O_2 demand, and prevent complications (e.g., acute kidney injury). See more about cardiogenic shock in Chapter 42.

Papillary Muscle Dysfunction or Rupture

Papillary muscle dysfunction may occur if the infarcted area includes or is near the papillary muscle that attaches to the mitral valve (see Fig. 35.2). Suspect papillary muscle dysfunction if you hear a new systolic murmur suggestive of mitral regurgitation at the heart apex. An echocardiogram confirms the diagnosis.

Papillary muscle rupture is a rare and life-threatening complication. It causes acute and massive mitral valve regurgitation with no time for the heart to compensate. Dyspnea, pulmonary edema, and decreased CO result from the backup of blood in the left atrium. This condition aggravates an already damaged LV by reducing CO even further. The patient undergoes rapid clinical decline. Treatment includes afterload reduction with nitroprusside (Nipride) and/or IABP therapy and immediate surgery with mitral valve repair or replacement. See Chapter 40 for information on valve disorders.

Left Ventricular Aneurysm

Left ventricular aneurysm results when the infarcted heart wall thins and bulges out during contraction. This can develop within a few days, weeks, or months. It is more common with anterior MIs.[23] The patient with a ventricular aneurysm may develop HF, dysrhythmias, and angina. Besides ventricular rupture, which is usually fatal, ventricular aneurysms can hide thrombi that can lead to an embolic stroke. Anticoagulation therapy is recommended unless contraindicated.

Ventricular Septal Wall Rupture and Left Ventricular Free Wall Rupture

A new loud systolic murmur heard in patients with acute MI may signal ventricular septal wall rupture. Depending on the size of the defect and degree of right and LV dysfunction, HF and cardiogenic shock may occur. The patient must undergo emergency repair, either surgically or percutaneously. The defect can quickly expand and lead to hemodynamic compromise.[23]

LV free wall rupture is an emergent clinical situation. Rapid hemodynamic compromise and death ensues if not treated immediately. Although this is a rare complication, death rates are high. Free wall rupture occurs more often in patients after their first MI, patients with anterior MIs, older adults, and women.[23]

Pericarditis

Acute pericarditis, an inflammation of the visceral and/or parietal pericardium, may occur 2 or 3 days after an acute MI. The key sign is mild to severe chest pain that increases with inspiration, coughing, and movement of the upper body. Sitting in a forward position often relieves the pain. The pain is usually different from pain due to an MI.

If you suspect pericarditis, assess for the presence of a friction rub over the pericardium. You can hear the sound best with the diaphragm of the stethoscope at the mid to lower left sternal border. It may be persistent or intermittent. Fever may be present. The patient may have hypotension and/or a narrow pulse pressure if there is significant pericardial effusion or cardiac tamponade. Asymptomatic pericardial effusions are common after STEMI.[23]

Besides physical findings, a 12-lead ECG is helpful in making a diagnosis. Typical ECG changes include diffuse ST segment elevations in many unrelated leads (with STEMI, ST elevation occurs in the leads facing the infarcted wall). This reflects the inflammation of the pericardium. Treatment includes pain relief with high doses of aspirin (e.g., 650 mg every 4 to 6 hours). Nonsteroidal antiinflammatory drugs (NSAIDs) and corticosteroids are avoided in the first 4 weeks after MI because they can interfere with myocardial scar formation.[21,23] Pericarditis is discussed in Chapter 40.

Dressler Syndrome

Dressler syndrome is pericarditis and fever that develop 1 to 8 weeks after MI. Although the cause is unclear, it may be an autoimmune reaction to the necrotic heart muscle. The patient has chest pain, fever, malaise, and arthralgia. A pericardial friction rub may be heard. A pericardial effusion may be present on echocardiogram. Laboratory findings include a high white blood cell count and sedimentation rate. High-dose aspirin is the treatment of choice.

Diagnostic Studies

In addition to the patient's history of pain, risk factors, and health history, the primary diagnostic studies used to determine whether a person has UA or MI (STEMI or NSTEMI) include a 12-lead ECG and serum cardiac biomarkers.

Electrocardiogram Findings

The ECG is one of the primary tools to diagnose UA or an MI (STEMI or NSTEMI). Whenever possible, we should compare a new ECG to a previous ECG. Changes in the QRS complex, ST segment, and T wave caused by injury, ischemia, and infarction can develop slowly or quickly with UA and MI. The pattern of ECG changes among the 12 leads provides information on the coronary artery involved in ACS (Table 37.14).

The ECG must be read carefully since changes can be absent or subtle at first. For this reason, we do serial 12-lead ECGs. For diagnostic and treatment purposes, it is important to distinguish between STEMI and NSTEMI/UA. STEMI patients usually have a complete coronary occlusion and must go to the catheterization laboratory emergently. You will see ST elevation in the leads facing the infarcted wall on the 12-lead ECG (Figs. 37.4B, 37.12, and 37.13 and Table 37.14). ST segment elevation is significant if it is 1 mm or more above the isoelectric line (2 mm or more in V2 and V3) in at least 2 contiguous leads.[22] Within a few hours to days, the ST segments begin to lower, with T wave inversion and pathologic Q waves developing in the same leads if reperfusion is delayed or not done (Fig. 37.4C; Fig. 37.13).[37] The pathologic Q wave will remain

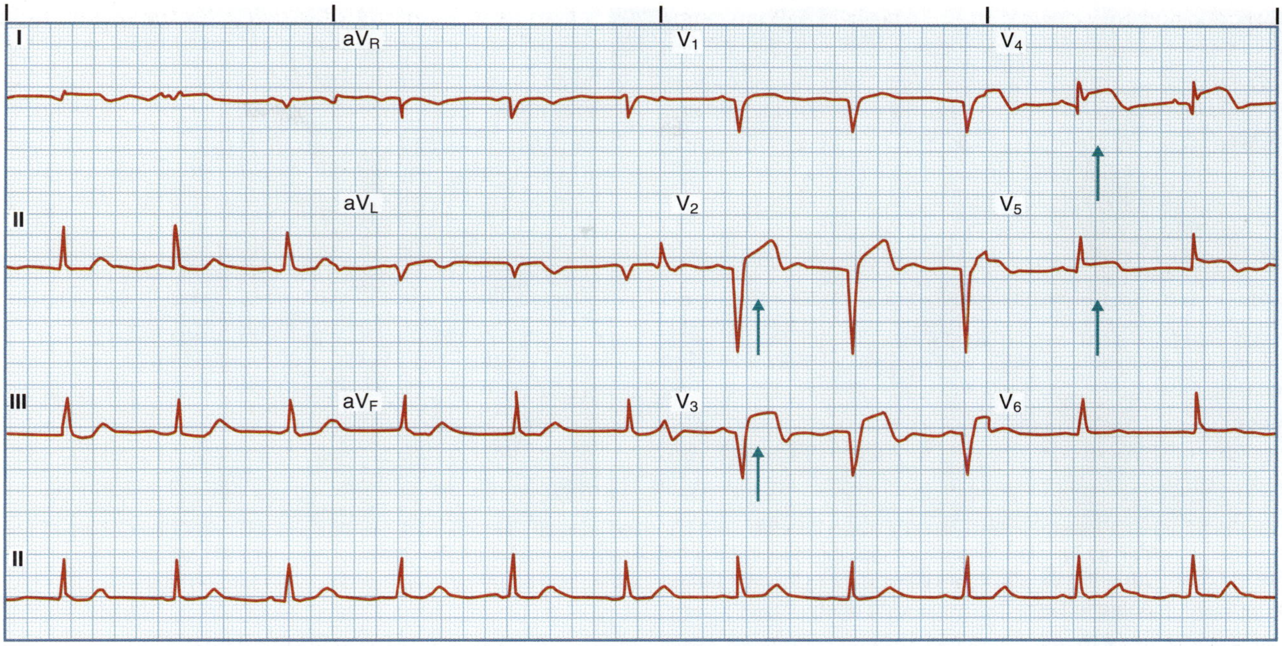

Fig. 37.13 ECG findings with anteroseptal lateral wall MI. Normally, leads I, aVL, and V_1 to V_3 have a positive R wave. Note the pathologic Q waves in these leads and the ST segment elevation in leads V_2 to V_6 *(arrows)*.

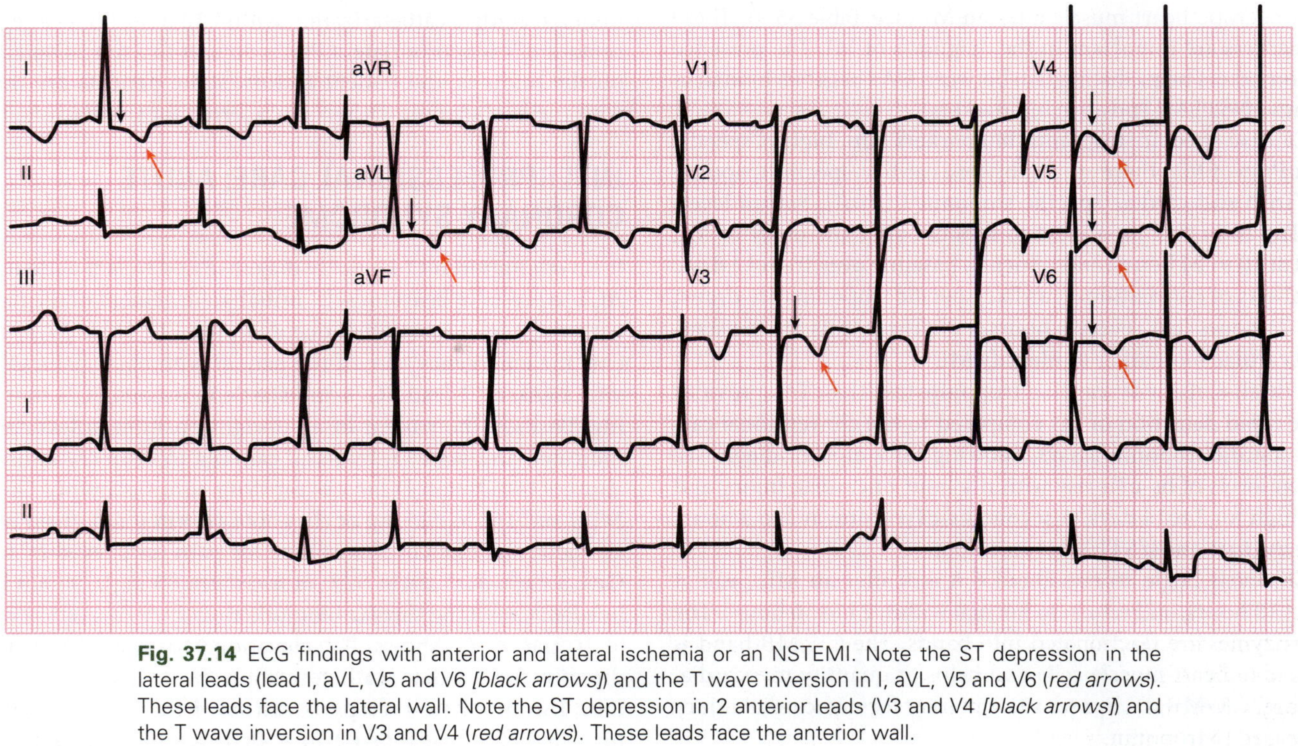

Fig. 37.14 ECG findings with anterior and lateral ischemia or an NSTEMI. Note the ST depression in the lateral leads (lead I, aVL, V5 and V6 *[black arrows]*) and the T wave inversion in I, aVL, V5 and V6 (*red arrows*). These leads face the lateral wall. Note the ST depression in 2 anterior leads (V3 and V4 *[black arrows]*) and the T wave inversion in V3 and V4 (*red arrows*). These leads face the anterior wall.

on the ECG forever. With early reperfusion, Q waves may not develop. T wave inversion may persist for months after a STEMI.

Patients with NSTEMI or UA usually have transient thrombosis or incomplete coronary occlusion. ECG changes with UA or an NSTEMI include ST depression and/or T wave inversion in the leads facing the area of ischemia or infarction (Figs. 37.4 A,37.12, 37.14, and Table 37.14). Both groups may present with angina and have the same ECG changes. The only way to tell if the patient is having an NSTEMI or UA is by drawing cardiac biomarkers. The biomarkers will be high in the NSTEMI patient but normal in the patient with UA. NSTEMI patients do not develop pathologic Q waves on the ECG.

Because MI is a dynamic process that evolves over time, serial ECGs are done to show the evolution of ischemia, injury, infarction, and resolution of the infarction.

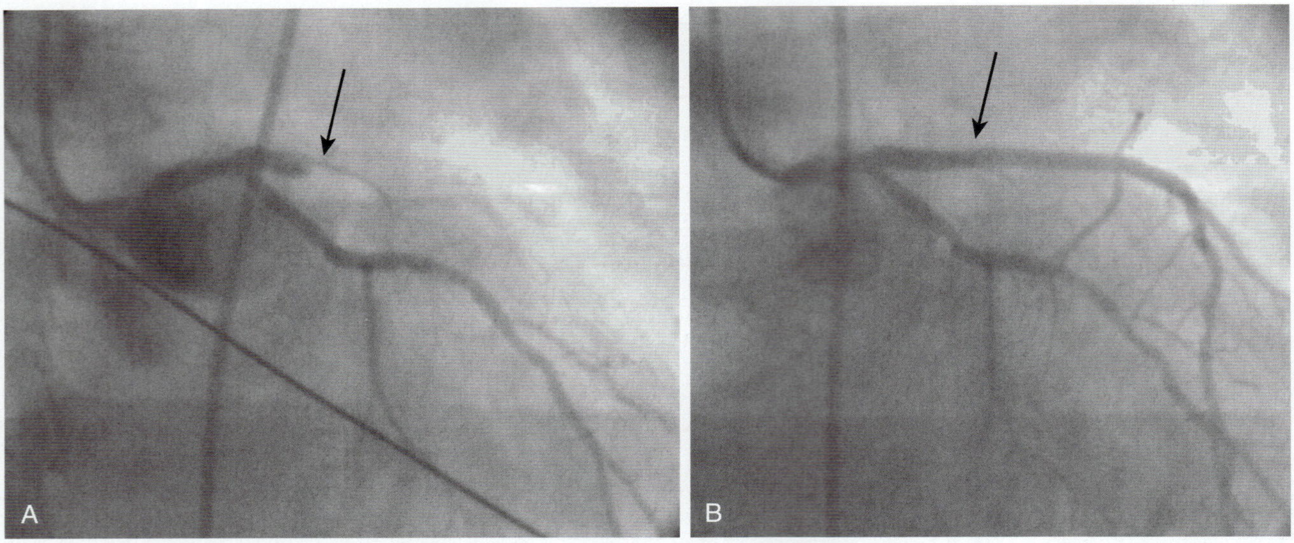

Fig. 37.15 (A) 100% thrombotic occlusion of the left anterior descending artery *(arrow)* causing a STEMI. (B), After PCI with a drug-coated stent to the left anterior descending artery *(arrow)*. Blood flow is restored to the entire left anterior descending artery.

Serum Cardiac Biomarkers

Serum cardiac biomarkers are proteins released into the blood from necrotic heart muscle after an MI (see Table 35.9). These biomarkers are important in the diagnosis of MI. The presence of biomarkers helps distinguish between UA (negative biomarkers) and NSTEMI (positive biomarkers).

Cardiac-specific troponin biomarkers are highly specific indicators of MI. There are 2 subtypes: cardiac-specific troponin T (cTnT) and cardiac-specific troponin I (cTnI). Serum levels of cTnI and cTnT increase 4 to 6 hours after the onset of MI, peak at 10 to 24 hours, and return to baseline over 10 to 14 days. Serial sets of conventional cardiac-specific troponins are drawn over 24 hours (e.g., every 6 hours × 3). These tests are the standard cardiac biomarker to identify MI.

A high-sensitivity cardiac troponin test (hs-cTn) provides more rapid detection of MI compared to the conventional cardiac-specific troponin assays, allowing for a quicker diagnosis. Serum levels of hs-cTn rise within 1 hour of cardiac injury and stay high for 7 to14 days. A second hs-cTn is drawn 2 to 3 hours after the first one if STEMI is ruled out.

CK levels begin to rise about 6 hours after an MI, peak at about 18 hours, and return to normal within 24 to 36 hours. The CK enzymes are fractionated into bands. The CK-MB band is specific to heart muscle cells and helps to quantify myocardial damage. CK-MB is a less sensitive marker for myocardial injury compared to troponin.[12]

Cardiac Catheterization

The patient with a STEMI must undergo cardiac catheterization within 90 minutes of presentation to the emergency department (ED) or receive thrombolytic therapy within 30 minutes in agencies without PCI capability. The goal is to open the totally occluded artery and limit the infarction size (Fig. 37.15). The patient with UA or NSTEMI usually undergoes cardiac catheterization during the hospitalization to diagnose and evaluate the extent of the disease. They do not need an emergent catheterization. Guidelines suggest that it is reasonable for them to undergo cardiac catheterization within 12 to 72 hours after presentation.[12] If appropriate, a PCI is done at this time. Depending on the findings and patient factors, some patients are treated with medical therapy. Others are referred for CABG surgery.

INTERPROFESSIONAL CARE: ACUTE CORONARY SYNDROME

It is very important to quickly diagnose and treat a patient with ACS to preserve heart muscle. Initial management of the patient with chest pain most often occurs in the ED. Table 37.15 presents the emergency care of the patient with chest pain. Obtain vital signs, a 12-lead ECG, and start continuous ECG monitoring. Position the patient in an upright position unless contraindicated and start O_2 by nasal cannula to keep O_2 saturation above 93%. Obtain IV access for drug administration. Give SL NTG and 162 to 325 mg of chewable aspirin if not given before arrival at the ED. Give morphine for pain unrelieved by NTG. Give a high-dose statin (e.g., atorvastatin 80 mg). Obtain baseline labs including cardiac biomarkers.

If the ECG shows ST elevation, the patient is taken directly for cardiac catheterization in PCI-capable hospitals. Thrombolytic therapy is started if the patient is unable to be quickly transported to a PCI-capable hospital. If the ECG shows ST depression and/or T wave inversion, we admit the patient to an ICU or telemetry unit for ongoing care. Dysrhythmias are treated according to agency protocols. Serial cardiac biomarkers are drawn until the peak level drops off. UA and NSTEMI patients start on heparin or GP IIb/IIIa inhibitors (e.g., eptifibatide [Integrilin]) either before catheterization or at the time of PCI. GP IIb/IIIa inhibitors may be used during PCI for STEMI patients. Fig. 37.5 shows the interprofessional care of ACS.

TABLE 37.15 EMERGENCY MANAGEMENT

Chest Pain

Etiology	Assessment Findings	Interventions
Cardiovascular • Aortic aneurysm • Aortic valve disease • Dysrhythmia • MI • Myocardial ischemia • Pericarditis ***Respiratory*** • Costochondritis • Pleurisy • Pneumonia • Pneumothorax, hemothorax • Pulmonary edema • Pulmonary embolus ***Chest Trauma*** • Cardiac tamponade • Flail chest • Great vessel injury • Hemothorax • Pulmonary contusion • Rib/sternal fracture ***Gastrointestinal*** • Cholecystitis • Esophagitis • GERD • Hiatal hernia • Peptic ulcer ***Others*** • Acute anxiety • Drugs (e.g., cocaine) • Strenuous exercise • Stress	• Angina, pain in chest, neck, jaw, arm, or shoulder • Anxiety • Decreased or increased BP • Cold, clammy skin • Decreased O_2 saturation • Diaphoresis • Dyspnea, tachypnea • Dysrhythmias • Epigastric pain • Feeling of impending doom • Indigestion, heartburn • Irregular HR, murmurs • Narrowed pulse pressure • Nausea and vomiting • Palpitations • Pericardial friction rub • Syncope, loss of consciousness • Tachycardia, bradycardia • Unequal BP readings in upper extremities • Weakness	***Initial*** • If unresponsive, assess circulation, airway, and breathing. • If responsive, monitor airway, breathing, and circulation (ABC). • Position patient upright unless contraindicated. • Give O_2 by nasal cannula or nonrebreather mask. • Obtain baseline vital signs, including O_2 saturation. • Auscultate heart and breath sounds. • Obtain 12-lead ECG. • Insert 2 IV catheters. • Assess pain using PQRST mnemonic (Table 37.8). • Medicate for pain as ordered (e.g., nitroglycerin, morphine). • Start continuous ECG monitoring and identify underlying rhythm. • Obtain baseline blood work (e.g., cardiac biomarkers, CBC, basic metabolic panel, coagulation studies). • Obtain portable chest x-ray. • Assess for contraindications for antiplatelet, anticoagulant, or thrombolytic therapy, or percutaneous coronary intervention as appropriate. • Give aspirin for heart-related chest pain unless contraindicated. • Give a high-dose statin. • Give antidysrhythmic drugs for life-threatening dysrhythmias. ***Ongoing Monitoring*** • Monitor ABCs, vital signs, level of consciousness, heart and breath sounds, heart rhythm, and O_2 saturation. • Assess and record response to drugs (e.g., decrease in chest pain) and remedicate or titrate drugs (e.g., nitroglycerin) as needed. • Provide reassurance and emotional support to patient and caregiver. • Explain all interventions and procedures to patient and caregiver in simple terms. • Anticipate need for intubation if respiratory distress is evident. • Prepare for CPR and defibrillation if cardiac arrest is evident. • Anticipate need for transcutaneous pacing for symptomatic bradycardia or heart block.

Emergent Percutaneous Coronary Intervention

Emergent PCI is the first line of treatment for patients with confirmed STEMI (i.e., ST-elevation and positive cardiac biomarkers). The goal is to open the blocked artery within 90 minutes of arrival to an agency that has interventional cardiac catheterization to limit the infarction size. In this case, the patient undergoes a cardiac catheterization to locate and assess the severity of the blockage(s), determine the presence of collateral circulation, and evaluate LV function. During the procedure, BMS or DES is inserted into the blocked coronary artery (Figs. 37.6 and 37.15). If other coronary arteries are found to have significant blockage during the emergent catheterization, PCI may be done at the same time on the noninfarct arteries if the patient is hemodynamically stable.[15] Often STEMI patients with other coronary artery blockages are discharged and brought back later for an elective PCI unless they have ongoing symptoms. After PCI for ACS, DAPT (low-dose aspirin plus ticagrelor [Brilinta] or prasugrel [Effient]) is continued for 1 year. Aspirin is continued forever. Patients with severe LV dysfunction may require VAD therapy and/or inotropes (e.g., dobutamine). A few patients need emergent CABG surgery.

The advantages of PCI (compared to CABG surgery) include (1) faster reperfusion to limit infarction size; (2) it is performed with IV sedation and local anesthesia; (3) the patient is ambulatory shortly after the procedure; (4) the length of stay is about 3 to 4 days after an uncomplicated MI with PCI compared with the 4 to 6 days with CABG surgery, thus reducing hospital costs; and (5) the patient can return to work several weeks sooner after PCI, compared with a 6- to 8-week convalescence after CABG.

Complications of PCI that may lead to emergent CABG include dissection or rupture of the coronary artery, abrupt artery closure, acute stent thrombosis, and failure to cross the blockage with a balloon or stent. There is a risk that the infarction could be extended if a part of the plaque dislodges and blocks the vessel distal to the catheter.

Thrombolytic Therapy

Thrombolytic (fibrinolytic) therapy is indicated only for patients with a STEMI in agencies that do not have an interventional

CHECK YOUR PRACTICE

Your patient had an emergent PCI 2 days ago for a STEMI. You are about to give him his morning medications, which include clopidogrel and aspirin. The patient asks you if he will need to take these medications forever.

- What would you tell the patient?

cardiac catheterization laboratory or when one is too far away to transfer the patient quickly. Patients admitted to non–PCI-capable hospitals can be moved to a PCI-capable hospital if the first medical contact to balloon inflation (PCI) time can be done within 120 minutes.[23] Treatment of STEMI with thrombolytic therapy aims to limit the infarction size by dissolving the thrombus in the coronary artery to reperfuse the heart muscle. The goal is to give the thrombolytic within 30 minutes of the patient's arrival to the ED.

Indications and Contraindications

All thrombolytics (e.g., tenecteplase, alteplase) are given IV (Table 37.12). The cost, efficacy, and ease of administration guide the choice of a thrombolytic agent. Although they have different pharmacokinetics, they all open the blocked artery by lysis of the thrombus. Because thrombolytics lyse the pathologic clot, they may also lyse other clots (e.g., a postoperative site). Patient selection is important because minor or major bleeding can be a complication of therapy.

Inclusion criteria for thrombolytic therapy are (1) chest pain less than 12 hours with 12-lead ECG findings consistent with a STEMI and (2) no absolute contraindications (Table 37.16). Patients with chest pain lasting 12 to 24 hours with ECG changes supporting STEMI may be considered for thrombolytic therapy.[23]

Procedure

Each hospital has a protocol for giving thrombolytic therapy. We complete 2 common steps before starting thrombolytic therapy: (1) draw blood to obtain baseline laboratory values and (2) start 2 or 3 lines for IV therapy. Perform all other invasive procedures before giving the thrombolytic agent to reduce the risk of bleeding.

Depending on the drug selected, therapy is given either by an IV bolus or via an infusion over up to 3 hours. Note the time when therapy begins. Monitor the patient during and after the thrombolytic. Assess heart rhythm, vital signs, and pulse oximetry. Assess the heart and lungs often to evaluate the patient's response to therapy. Regularly assess for changes in neurologic status that may indicate cerebral bleeding.

When reperfusion occurs (e.g., a blocked coronary artery is opened and blood flow is restored to the heart muscle), several clinical signs can be seen. The most reliable sign is the return of the ST segment to baseline on the ECG. Other signs include resolution of chest pain and an early, rapid rise of the serum cardiac biomarkers. These levels increase as the necrotic heart cells release proteins into the circulation after perfusion is restored to the area. The presence of *reperfusion dysrhythmias* (e.g., accelerated idioventricular rhythm) is a less reliable sign of reperfusion. These dysrhythmias are generally self-limiting and do not require aggressive treatment.

A major concern with thrombolytic therapy is reocclusion of the artery. The site of the thrombus is unstable, and another clot may form. Therefore, IV heparin therapy is started. If another clot forms, the patient will describe similar chest pain symptoms, and ECG changes will return. Patients receiving thrombolytic therapy should be moved to an agency with PCI capabilities as soon as possible so PCI can be done if thrombolytic therapy fails.

The main complication with thrombolytic therapy is bleeding. Ongoing nursing assessment is essential. Minor bleeding (e.g., surface bleeding from IV sites or gingival bleeding) is expected. Control bleeding by applying manual pressure followed by a pressure dressing or ice packs.

TABLE 37.16 Contraindications for Thrombolytic Therapy

Absolute Contraindications

- Active internal bleeding
- History of intracranial hemorrhage
- Intracranial or intraspinal surgery within 2 months
- Known structural or vascular abnormality (e.g., arteriovenous malformation)
- Known intracranial cancer (primary or metastatic)
- Recent (within past 3 months) ischemic stroke
- Severe uncontrolled hypertension
- Significant closed-head or facial trauma within past 3 months
- Suspected aortic dissection
- For streptokinase, prior treatment within the past 6 months

Relative Contraindications

- Active peptic ulcer disease
- Current use of oral anticoagulants
- Dementia
- History of chronic, severe, poorly controlled hypertension
- Known intracranial pathology not covered in absolute contraindications
- Major surgery (<3 weeks)
- Noncompressible vascular punctures
- Pregnancy
- Prior ischemic stroke (>3 months ago)
- Recent (within 2–4 weeks) internal bleeding
- Significant hypertension on presentation (SBP >180 mm Hg or DBP >110 mm Hg)
- Traumatic or prolonged (>10 min) cardiopulmonary resuscitation

Source: O'Gara PT, Kushner FG, Ascheim DD, et al: 2013 ACCF/AHA guideline for the management of ST-elevation myocardial infarction: a report of the ACC/AHA Task Force on Practice Guidelines, *Circ* 127:e362, 2013.

SAFETY ALERT

Thrombolytic Therapy

- Minor or major bleeding can occur with thrombolytic drugs.
- Place 2 or 3 IV lines before starting thrombolytic therapy.
- If signs and symptoms of major bleeding occur (e.g., drop in BP, increase in HR, sudden change in the patient's mental status, blood in the urine or stool), stop the drug and notify the HCP.

Drug Therapy

See Table 37.12 and Fig. 37.5 present drug therapy for patients with chronic stable angina and ACS. When a patient presents with suspected ACS, antiplatelet therapy (e.g., chewable aspirin for UA patients plus ticagrelor for STEMI and NSTEMI patients), IV NTG, and high-dose atorvastatin (80 mg) are drug treatments of choice. Since STEMI patients go directly to cardiac catheterization, systemic anticoagulation with either subcutaneous LMWH or IV UH is used only for UA and NSTEMI patients. GP IIb/IIIa inhibitors may be used for NSTEMI patients or during PCI for STEMI patients. DAPT should continue for 1 year after a STEMI or NSTEMI whether the patient receives a stent or not. Aspirin should never be stopped. Oral β-blockers are started within the first 24 hours if there are no contraindications (e.g., HF, heart block, hypotension). Calcium channel blockers are used if the patient cannot tolerate β-blockers. They are used cautiously after MI because they can decrease contractility. ACE inhibitors are added after an MI if there are no contraindications. Nitrates may be used for persistent chest pain.

IV Nitroglycerin

IV NTG is used in the initial treatment of the patient with ACS. SL NTG can be used until the IV NTG is prepared. The goal of therapy is to reduce angina pain and improve coronary blood flow. IV NTG decreases preload and afterload while increasing the myocardial O_2 supply. The onset of action is immediate. Titrate NTG to eliminate chest pain. Because hypotension is a common side effect, closely monitor BP. Patients who become hypotensive may be volume depleted and may benefit from an IV fluid bolus. Closely assess for volume overload after the bolus (e.g., crackles on lung auscultation).

Morphine

Morphine is the drug of choice for chest pain that is unrelieved by NTG. As a vasodilator, it decreases cardiac workload by lowering myocardial O_2 consumption, reducing contractility, and decreasing BP and HR. Morphine can help reduce anxiety and fear. In rare situations, morphine can depress respirations. Monitor patients for signs of bradypnea or hypotension, which are conditions to avoid in myocardial ischemia and infarction.

β-Adrenergic Blockers

β-blockers decrease myocardial O_2 demand by reducing HR, BP, and contractility. They are given to patients who are not at risk for complications of MI (e.g., cardiogenic shock, bradycardia, hypotension). They reduce the risk for reinfarction and HF. Therapy continues indefinitely.

Angiotensin-Converting Enzyme Inhibitors and Angiotensin Receptor Blockers

ACE inhibitors should be started within the first 24 hours if the BP is stable and there are no contraindications. They are taken indefinitely in patients after STEMI or NSTEMI, with HF, or an EF of 40% or less. ACE inhibitors can help prevent ventricular remodeling and prevent or slow the progression of HF. ARBs are an option if patients cannot tolerate ACE inhibitors (e.g., angioedema, cough).

Antidysrhythmic Drugs

Dysrhythmias are the most common complications after an MI. In general, they are self-limiting and not treated aggressively unless they are life threatening (e.g., sustained VT). Chapter 39 discusses the drugs used in the treatment of dysrhythmias.

Lipid-Lowering Drugs

All patients with ACS need a lipid panel. Patients with ACS or CAD should receive lipid-lowering drugs indefinitely, unless contraindicated (Table 37.6). Patients on a lipid lowering drug at the time of the MI should have the dose maximized or switched to a more potent statin.

Aldosterone Antagonists

Aldosterone antagonists (e.g., spironolactone, eplerenone) can decrease mortality after a STEMI regardless of the LV function.[24] One of these drugs should be added if there are no contraindications (e.g., hyperkalemia, increased creatinine).

Stool Softeners

After an MI, the patient may be predisposed to constipation because of bed rest and opioid drugs. Stool softeners (e.g., docusate sodium) prevent straining and the resultant vagal stimulation from the *Valsalva maneuver*. Vagal stimulation produces bradycardia and can provoke dysrhythmias. A laxative may be used, if needed.

Nutrition Therapy

Initially, patients may be NPO (nothing by mouth) except for water until stable (e.g., pain free, nausea resolved). Advance the diet as tolerated to a low-salt, low-saturated-fat, and low-cholesterol diet (Tables 37.4 and 37.5).

❖ NURSING MANAGEMENT: ACUTE CORONARY SYNDROME

◆ Assessment

Table 37.17 presents the subjective and objective data to obtain from a patient with ACS.

◆ Clinical Problems

Clinical problems for the patient with ACS may include

- Impaired cardiac function
- Pain
- Anxiety
- Activity intolerance

More information on clinical problems of patients with ACS is in eNursing Care Plan 37.1 available on the website for this chapter.

◆ Planning

Nursing care focuses on the priority problems of pain and impaired cardiac function. The immediate goals for a patient

TABLE 37.17 NURSING ASSESSMENT
Acute Coronary Syndrome

Subjective Data

Important Health Information

Health history: Previous history of CAD, chest pain/angina, MI, valve disease (e.g., aortic stenosis), heart failure, or cardiomyopathy. History of hypertension, diabetes, anemia, lung disease, hyperlipidemia. History of premature CAD in a family member

Medications: Use of antiplatelets, anticoagulants, nitrates, ACE inhibitors, β-blockers, calcium channel blockers, antihypertensive drugs, lipid-lowering drugs, over-the-counter drugs (e.g., vitamin and herbal supplements)

History of present illness: Description of events related to current illness (Table 37.9), including any self-treatments and response

Functional Health Patterns

Health perception–health management: Sedentary lifestyle, tobacco use, exposure to environmental smoke, drug use

Nutritional-metabolic: Indigestion, heartburn, nausea, belching, vomiting

Elimination: Urinary urgency or frequency, straining at stool

Activity-exercise: Palpitations, dyspnea, dizziness, weakness

Cognitive-perceptual: Substernal chest pain or pressure (squeezing, constricting, aching, sharp, tingling), radiation to jaw, neck, shoulders, back, or arms (Table 37.8)

Coping–stress tolerance: Stressful lifestyle, depression, anger, anxiety, feeling of impending doom

Objective Data

General

Anxious, fearful, restless, distressed

Cardiovascular

Tachycardia or bradycardia, pulsus alternans (alternating weak and strong heartbeats), pulse deficit, dysrhythmias (especially ventricular), murmur, S_3, S_4, ↑ or ↓ BP

Skin

Cool, clammy, pale skin

Possible Diagnostic Findings

Positive serum cardiac biomarkers, ↑ serum lipids; ↑ WBC count. Pathologic Q wave, ST segment elevation, and/or ST-T wave abnormalities on ECG. Heart enlargement, calcifications, or pulmonary congestion on chest x-ray. Abnormal wall motion with stress echocardiogram or resting echocardiogram. Positive findings on cardiac catheterization.

with ACS include (1) pain relief, (2) quick and appropriate treatment, and (3) preservation of heart muscle. During the hospitalization, the overall goals include (1) effective coping with illness-associated anxiety, (2) participation in a rehabilitation plan, and (3) reduce risk factors.

◆ Implementation

◆ Acute Care

Monitor vital signs and pulse oximetry frequently (e.g., every hour) during the first few hours after admission to the ICU or telemetry unit and closely thereafter, according to agency protocol. Start continuous ECG monitoring. Obtain serial 12-lead ECGs and draw serial cardiac biomarkers. Maintain bed rest according to agency policy and gradually increase activity unless contraindicated.

For patients with UA and NSTEMI, heparin (UH or LMWH) is used to prevent microemboli from forming and causing further chest pain. DAPT (e.g., aspirin and ticagrelor) is recommended for STEMI and NSTEMI patients (with or without a stent) (Table 37.12). UA patients receive aspirin. If they have a stent placed, they receive DAPT. Cardiac catheterization is an option for patients with UA and NSTEMI after being stabilized or if angina returns or increases in severity. Depending on the results, options include risk factor reduction with medical management, PCI, or CABG surgery.

For patients with STEMI, reperfusion therapy begins as soon as possible. *Reperfusion therapy* includes emergent PCI (preferred, for PCI-capable hospitals) or thrombolytic therapy (in hospitals not capable of performing PCI). The goal in the treatment of STEMI is to save as much heart muscle as possible. Technical advances in PCI technology have almost eliminated CABG surgery as the primary treatment for patients with STEMI unless there is another reason to perform surgery (e.g., ventricular septal rupture, papillary muscle rupture).

◆ Pain

Provide NTG, morphine, and supplemental O_2 as needed to eliminate or reduce chest pain. Ongoing evaluation and documentation of the effectiveness of the interventions is important. Once pain is relieved, some patients interpret the absence of pain as an absence of heart disease. Provide information about the importance of continued therapy to limit myocardial damage.

◆ Monitoring

Maintain continuous ECG monitoring. Treat life-threatening dysrhythmias quickly. During the initial period after MI, sustained VT and VF are the most common lethal dysrhythmias.[23] In many patients, PVCs precede these dysrhythmias. We usually do not treat isolated PVCs. VT is treated if it is sustained VT. Treatment of nonsustained VT depends on the patient's hemodynamic status.

Using the bedside ST segment monitor, assess the patient's ST segments for shifts above or below the baseline of the ECG (signals reinfarction or ischemia). Silent ischemia, noted only by ST segment depression and/or T wave inversion, occurs without subjective symptoms (e.g., chest pain). Notify the HCP if you see ST segment changes with or without clinical symptoms.

Perform a physical assessment to detect changes from the patient's baseline findings. Assess for signs and symptoms of early HF (e.g., dyspnea, tachycardia, crackles, distended neck veins, an S3 heart sound). Monitor intake and output. If a nasal cannula is being used, check the nares for irritation or dryness, which can cause considerable discomfort.

◆ Rest and Comfort

Promoting rest and comfort for the patient with any degree of heart damage is important. There is no evidence for prolonged bed rest for the patient with an uncomplicated MI (e.g., angina resolved, no signs of complications). Their activity should slowly increase. A patient with an uncomplicated STEMI may sit in a chair within a few hours after the event, especially if the radial

TABLE 37.18 Phases of Rehabilitation After Acute Coronary Syndrome

Phase I: Hospital
- Occurs while the patient is still hospitalized
- Activity level depends on severity of angina or MI
- Patient may first sit up in bed or chair, perform range-of-motion exercises and self-care (e.g., washing, shaving), and progress to walking in hallway and limited stair climbing
- Attention focuses on management of chest pain, anxiety, dysrhythmias, and complications

Phase II: Early Recovery
- Begins after the patient is discharged
- Usually lasts from 2 to 12 weeks and is held in an outpatient facility but may be done in the home
- Activity level is gradually increased under the supervision of the cardiac rehabilitation team and with ECG monitoring
- Team may suggest that physical activity (e.g., walking program) be started at home
- Information about risk factor reduction is provided at this time

Phase III: Late Recovery
- Long-term maintenance program
- Individual physical activity programs are designed and implemented at home, a local gym, or the rehabilitation center
- Patient and caregiver restructure lifestyles and roles
- Therapeutic lifestyle changes should become lifelong habits
- Medical supervision recommended

artery was used for the PCI. A period of bed rest may be ordered after a large STEMI. The use of the bathroom, a commode, or a bedpan is based on patient preference and hemodynamic status. UA and NSTEMI patients may sit in a chair when angina is resolved if there are no complications.

When sleeping or resting, the body requires less work from the heart than it does when active. It is important to plan nursing and other interventions to ensure adequate rest periods free from interruption. Comfort measures that can promote rest include a quiet environment, use of relaxation techniques (e.g., music therapy, guided imagery), and assurance that staff is nearby and responsive to the patient's needs.

The patient must understand the reasons why activity is limited. Gradually increase the patient's heart workload through more demanding physical tasks. Before discharge, it is important that the patient achieve an activity level adequate for home care. Discuss and encourage outpatient cardiac rehabilitation. Table 37.18 outlines the phases of cardiac rehabilitation.

◆ Anxiety

A degree of anxiety is present in all patients with ACS. Your role is to identify the source of anxiety and assist the patient in reducing it. If the patient is afraid of being alone, allow a caregiver to sit by quietly and check the patient frequently. If a source of anxiety is the unknown, explore these concerns with the patient. For anxiety caused by lack of information, provide teaching based on the patient's stated need and level of understanding. Answer the patient's questions with clear, simple explanations.

CHECK YOUR PRACTICE

You are walking in the hallway with a 64-year-old woman who had an MI 3 days ago. She is being discharged tomorrow. She is visibly anxious and irritable, wringing her hands, and talking very fast. She tells you, "My heart is pounding." You do not know if she is anxious or about to have another MI.
- What should you do?

Begin teaching at the patient's level. For example, many patients are not ready to learn about the pathology of CAD. The earliest questions usually relate to how the disease affects perceived control and independence. Examples include
- When will I leave the ICU?
- When can I be out of bed?
- When will I be discharged?
- When can I return to work?
- How many changes will I have to make in my life?
- Will this happen again?

Tell the patient that more complete teaching will begin once they are feeling stronger. Often the patient may not be able to ask the most serious concern of ACS patients: Am I going to die? Even if a patient denies this concern, it is helpful for you to start a conversation by remarking that fear of dying is a common concern among most patients who have had ACS. This gives the patient "permission" to talk about an uncomfortable and fearful topic.

◆ Emotional and Behavioral Reactions

Patients' emotional and behavioral reactions vary, but often follow a predictable pattern (Table 37.19). Your role is to understand what the patient is currently experiencing and to support the use of constructive coping styles.

Assess the support structure of the patient and caregiver. Determine how you can help maximize the support system. Often the patient is separated from their support system at the time of hospitalization. With patient permission, you can talk with the caregiver(s) about the patient's progress and support the caregivers who will provide the necessary assistance to the patient. Open visitation is helpful in decreasing anxiety and increasing support for the patient with ACS.[25] Help the patient identify additional support systems (e.g., spiritual care, Mended Hearts) that can assist during the hospital stay and/or after discharge.

◆ Patient Teaching

Patient teaching is needed at every stage of the patient's hospitalization and recovery (e.g., ED, telemetry unit, home). Give patients and caregivers the tools they need to make informed decisions about their health. For teaching to be meaningful, the patient must be aware of the need to learn. Careful assessment of the patient's health literacy and learning needs helps you set realistic goals (see Chapter 4).

The timing of the teaching is important. When patients and caregivers are in crisis, they may not be ready to learn new information. Answer the patient's questions in simple, brief terms. The answers often need repetition. When the shock accompanying a crisis subsides, the patient and caregiver are better able to focus on new and more detailed information.

TABLE 37.19 Psychosocial Responses to Acute Coronary Syndrome

Anger and Hostility
- Often expressed as, "Why did this happen to me?"
- May be directed at family, staff, or medical regimen

Anxiety and Fear
- Fears long-term disability and death
- Overtly displays apprehension, restlessness, insomnia, tachycardia
- Less overtly displays increased verbalization, projection of feelings to others, hypochondriasis
- Fears activity
- Fears recurrent chest pain, heart attacks, and sudden death

Denial
- May have history of ignoring signs and symptoms related to heart disease
- Minimizes severity of health condition
- Ignores activity restrictions
- Avoids discussing illness or its significance

Dependency
- Totally reliant on staff
- Unwilling to perform tasks or activities unless approved by HCP
- Wants ECG monitoring to continue
- Hesitant to leave the ICU, telemetry unit, or hospital

Depression
- Mourns loss of health, altered body function, and changes in lifestyle
- Realizes seriousness of situation
- Begins to worry about future implications of health problem
- Shows manifestations of withdrawal, crying, apathy
- May be more evident after discharge

Realistic Acceptance
- Focuses on optimum rehabilitation
- Plans changes compatible with altered cardiac function
- Actively engages in lifestyle changes to address modifiable risk factors

Limit your use of medical terms. For example, you are caring for a patient with UA who asks you why he has chest tightness when he climbs stairs. Begin by explaining that the heart is a muscle that works as a pump. Like all muscles, it needs O_2 to work (or pump) properly. When fat and cholesterol block the blood vessels supplying the heart muscle with O_2, less O_2 is available to the muscle. As a result, the pump cannot work well. Tell the patient that the chest tightness (angina) is the heart's message that it is having trouble doing its work. Use a model of the heart to support what you are explaining.

Anticipatory guidance involves preparing the patient and caregiver for what to expect during recovery and rehabilitation. By learning what to expect, the patient gains a sense of control.

The idea of perceived control is operationalized as the process by which the patient makes decisions by cutting back. Cutting back is one way of reducing the psychologic and physiologic losses after ACS (or any other life-changing event). For example, a middle-aged man who smokes 2 packs of cigarettes a day, is 20 lb. overweight, and gets no physical exercise may feel overwhelmed. He may decide that he can live with a weight reduction plan and will get more exercise (though not daily) but that it is not possible for him to quit smoking. He believes that because he is changing 2 of his 3 risk factors, he will be healthier. Ideally, the tobacco risk factor should be a priority for this patient. If the patient does not accept information about risks and effects of tobacco use, you must respect their choices.

In addition to teaching the patient and caregiver what they wish to know, several types of information are essential in achieving optimal health. Table 37.20 presents a teaching guide for the patient with ACS and the caregiver.

TABLE 37.20 PATIENT & CAREGIVER TEACHING

Acute Coronary Syndrome

Include the following information in the teaching plan for the patient with acute coronary syndrome and the caregiver:
- Signs and symptoms of angina and MI and what to do should they occur (e.g., how to take nitroglycerin)*
- When and how to seek help (e.g., contact 911)[a]
- Anatomy and physiology of the heart and coronary arteries
- Cause and effect of CAD
- Definition of terms (e.g., CAD, angina, MI, heart failure)
- Identification of and plan to decrease risk factors[a] (Tables 37.1, 37.2, 37.3, 37.4, and 37.5)
- Reasons for tests and treatments (e.g., ECG monitoring, blood work, cardiac catheterization), activity limitations and rest, diet, and drugs[a]
- Appropriate expectations about recovery (anticipatory guidance)
- Resumption of work, physical activity, sexual activity
- Measures to promote recovery and health (e.g., cardiac rehabilitation)
- Importance of the gradual, progressive resumption of activity[a]

[a] Identified by patients as important to learn before discharge.

Physical Activity

Physical activity, an integral part of rehabilitation, is necessary for optimal physiologic functioning and psychologic well-being. It has a direct, positive effect on maximal O_2 uptake, increasing CO, decreasing blood lipids, decreasing BP, increasing blood flow through the coronary arteries, increasing muscle mass and flexibility, improving the psychologic state, and assisting in weight loss and control. A regular schedule of physical activity, even after many years of sedentary living, is beneficial.

One method of identifying levels of physical activity is by using **metabolic equivalent (MET)** units: 1 MET is the amount of O_2 needed by the body at rest—3.5 mL of O_2 per kilogram per minute, or 1.4 cal/kg of body weight per minute. The MET determines the energy costs of various exercises (Table 37.21).

In the hospital, we gradually increase the activity level so that by the time of discharge the patient can tolerate moderate-energy activities of 3 to 6 METs. Many patients with UA or an uncomplicated MI are in the hospital for 3 or 4 days. By day 2, the patient can walk in the hallway and begin climbing a few steps. Because of the short hospital stay, it is critical to give the patient specific guidelines for physical activity so that overexertion will not occur. Tell the patient to always "listen to what your body is saying"—the most important aspect of recovery.

Teach patients that the AHA recommends 30 minutes of moderate-intensity aerobic activity (e.g., brisk walking) at least 5 days a week.[10] For patients who have been hospitalized for

TABLE 37.21 Energy Expenditure in Metabolic Equivalents (METs)

Low-Energy Activities (<3 METs or <3 cal/min)

Activities in Hospital

- Eating
- Resting supine
- Washing hands, face

Activities Outside Hospital

- Driving a car
- Painting, seated
- Sewing by machine
- Sweeping floor

Moderate-Energy Activities (3–6 METs or 3–5 cal/min)

Activities in Hospital

- Showering
- Sitting on bedside commode
- Using bedpan
- Walking at 3–4 mph

Activities Outside Hospital

- Cycling at 5.5 mph on level ground
- Going up a flight of stairs
- Golfing
- General gardening
- Ironing, standing
- Painting, standing

High Energy Activities (6–8 METs or 6–8 cal/min)

- Mowing lawn using walking mower
- Performing carpentry
- Walking 5 mph

Very-High-Energy Activities (>9 METs or >9 cal/min)

- Cross-country skiing
- Cycling at >13 mph
- Running at >6 mph
- Shoveling heavy snow (not recommended for any patient with CAD)

a coronary event (e.g., PCI, UA, NSTEMI, STEMI), they must "work up" to 30 minutes of exercise per day. An exercise stress test may be done after hospitalization to assess for chest pain with activity and help guide physical activity. The patient who has been physically inactive and just starting an exercise program should do so under supervision whenever possible. Cardiac rehabilitation, either in a group or home setting, is recommended.[10,12,23,26]

Teach patients to check their HR. Some patients may use technology (e.g., cell phone applications, fitness trackers) to check their HR. The patient should know the limits within which to exercise. Tell the patient that the HR should return to the resting HR within a few minutes of stopping the exercise. Tell the patient to stop exercising and rest if chest pain or shortness of breath occurs. The key factor is the patient's response to physical activity in terms of symptoms rather than absolute HR, especially since many patients are taking β-blockers and may not be able to reach a target HR. You cannot overstress this point. Basic physical activity guidelines for patients after ACS follow the FITT formula (Table 37.3).

The basic categories of physical activity are isometric (static) and isotonic (dynamic). Most daily activities are a mixture of the two. *Isometric activities* involve the development of tension during muscular contraction but produce little or no change in muscle length or joint movement. Lifting, carrying, and pushing heavy objects are isometric activities. These activities are associated with the Valsalva maneuver and may cause a vasovagal response. Because the HR and BP change rapidly during isometric work, they should limit isometric exercises.

Isotonic activities involve changes in muscle length and joint movement with rhythmic contractions at relatively low muscular tension. Walking, jogging, swimming, bicycling, and jumping rope are examples of activities that are mostly isotonic. Isotonic exercise can put a safe, steady load on the heart and lungs and improve the circulation to other organs.

Women who have an MI often have poor adherence to a regular physical activity program.[4] Women often are caregivers for everyone but themselves. They may prioritize a physical activity program as less important than caring for others. Often women describe continued fatigue.

Another factor linked to poor adherence to a physical activity program after MI is depression. Depression is common among patients with CAD, especially in women.[4] Routinely screen for depression and recommend referral for treatment as appropriate. Many patients recover physically from ACS or CABG surgery but do not attain psychologic well-being.

◆ Cardiac Rehabilitation

Cardiac rehabilitation is the restoration of a person to an optimal state of function in 6 areas: (1) physiologic, (2) psychologic, (3) mental, (4) spiritual, (5) economic, and (6) vocational. All patients who have had UA, an MI, a PCI, or CABG surgery should receive a referral for outpatient or home-based cardiac rehabilitation (Table 37.18). Exercise-based cardiac rehabilitation is a Class I recommendation from the AHA for any patient with HF or a cardiac event.[9,12,15]

Unfortunately, cardiac rehabilitation is often not recommended, and participation is less than optimal. Outpatient programs are helpful, but not all patients are able to take part in them due to cost, location, and travel limitations (Box 37.4). Home-based cardiac rehabilitation programs then provide an alternative.[26] Maintaining contact (e.g., telehealth, exercise logs, Internet) with the patient is a key to the success of these programs.

In considering rehabilitation, the patient must recognize that CAD is a chronic disease. It is not curable. Therefore, they may need basic lifestyle changes to promote recovery and future health. Tell patients that recovery takes time, and resuming physical activity after ACS or heart surgery is slow and gradual. However, with appropriate and adequate supportive care, recovery is more likely.

◆ Resuming Sexual Activity

It is important to include sexual counseling for heart patients and their partners. This often-neglected area of discussion may be difficult for both the patient and HCP to approach. However, the patient's concern about resumption of sexual activity after

BOX 37.4 EVIDENCE-BASED PRACTICE

Participating in Cardiac Rehabilitation

You are caring for M.M., a 79-year-old male who had a NSTEMI and PCI with stent placement 3 days ago. The HCP prescribed cardiac rehabilitation 3 times per week for 12 weeks, to begin in 4 weeks. M.M. and his wife live in a rural area and express concern that it will be hard for M.M. to travel to attend the nearest center-based program 40 min from their home. They ask you if M.M. needs to take part in the rehabilitation program or if there are other options they can pursue.

Making Clinical Decisions

Synthesis of Best Available Evidence

Cardiac rehabilitation programs help to aid in recovery and prevent further cardiac events. They typically include exercise, healthy lifestyle education, and/or psychologic interventions, such as stress reduction counseling. Programs are available in supervised centers or in the home. Home-based programs are an option to increase access and participation in cardiac rehabilitation. The programs are similar in terms of outcomes of mortality, exercise capacity, and health-related quality of life.

Clinician Expertise

You know that taking part in a home-based or center-based cardiac rehabilitation program will help to aid in recovery and prevent further cardiac events after a NSTEMI.

Patient Preferences and Values

M.M. and his wife want him to take part in cardiac rehabilitation but express concern about attending a hospital-based program.

Implications for Nursing Practice

1. What strategies may be useful in encouraging M.M. to take part in a program?
2. Why is it important to reinforce the benefits of adhering to a recommended exercise program?
3. What would you suggest since they are concerned about not being able to travel to a center-based program?

Reference for Evidence

Thomas RJ, Beatty AL, Beckie TM, et al.: Home-based cardiac rehabilitation: a scientific statement from the American association of cardiovascular and pulmonary rehabilitation, the AHA, and the ACC, *Circulation* 140:e69, 2019.

hospitalization for ACS often produces more stress than the physiologic act. Most patients change their sexual behavior because they are concerned about sexual inadequacy, death during intercourse, and impotence. A concerned and knowledgeable HCP can clarify any misconceptions with specific counseling.

Before providing guidelines on resumption of sexual activity, it is important to know the patient's physiologic status, physiologic effects of sexual activity, and psychologic effects of having an MI. Sexual activity for most middle-aged men and women with their usual partners is a moderate-energy activity equivalent to climbing 2 flights of steps or walking briskly.[27]

You may be uncertain of how and when to begin counseling about resumption of sex. It is helpful to consider sex as a physical activity and to discuss or explore feelings in this area when discussing other physical activities. One helpful approach is, "Many people who have had a heart attack wonder when they will be able to resume sexual activity. Has this been of concern to you?" You may also state, "Sexual activity, like other forms of activity, should be gradually resumed after MI. If your ability to perform sexually is concerning you, the energy you use is likely no more than climbing 2 flights of steps or walking briskly." Facilitate discussion by providing the patient with reading material on resumption of sexual activity. Say something such as, "If resuming sexual activity has been of concern to you, this information should be helpful." This type of nonthreatening statement brings up the topic, allows the patient to explore personal feelings, and gives the patient an opportunity to raise questions with you or another HCP. Table 37.22 outlines common guidelines.

TABLE 37.22 PATIENT & CAREGIVER TEACHING

Sexual Activity After Acute Coronary Syndrome

Include the following information in the teaching plan for the patient and their partner after acute coronary syndrome:

- Resume sexual activity at a level that relates to sexual activity before experiencing ACS.
- Physical training may improve the physiologic response to intercourse. Encourage daily physical activity during recovery.
- Reduce the consumption of food and alcohol before intercourse is anticipated (e.g., waiting 3–4 hr after eating a large meal before engaging in sexual activity).
- Familiar surroundings and a familiar partner reduce anxiety.
- Masturbation may be a useful sexual outlet and may reassure the patient that sexual activity is still possible.
- Avoid hot or cold showers just before and after intercourse.
- Foreplay is desirable because it allows a gradual increase in HR before orgasm.
- Positions during intercourse are a matter of personal choice.
- Orogenital sex places no undue strain on the heart.
- A relaxed atmosphere free of fatigue and stress is optimal.
- Prophylactic use of nitrates to decrease chest pain during sexual activity may be needed.
- Use of erectile agents (e.g., sildenafil) within 48 hr is contraindicated if taking nitrates in any form.
- Avoid anal intercourse because of the chance of inducing a vasovagal response.

Tell the patient that the inability to perform sexually after MI is common and that sexual problems usually disappear after several attempts. Reinforce the idea that patience and understanding usually solve the problem. However, many male patients may be interested in using drugs to correct erectile dysfunction. Warn the patient not to use these drugs with nitrates because severe hypotension, and even death, has been reported. Tell patients to discuss the use of these drugs with their HCP.

It is common for a patient who has chest pain on physical exertion to have some angina during sexual stimulation or intercourse. The patient may take NTG prophylactically if he is not using erectile dysfunction medications. Tell the patient to delay sex after a heavy meal or excess alcohol intake, when extremely tired or stressed, or with unfamiliar partners. Patients should avoid anal intercourse because of the chance of eliciting a vasovagal response.

Tell the patient that resumption of sex depends on the patient and partner's emotional readiness and on the HCP's assessment of the extent of recovery. It is generally safe to resume sexual activity when patients can exercise ≥3 to 5 METS (e.g., walking up a flight of steps) without chest pain or excessive shortness of breath.[27]

◆ Evaluation

The expected outcomes are that the patient with ACS will

- Maintain stable signs of adequate cardiac output
- Have relief of pain and/or shortness of breath
- Report decreased anxiety and increased sense of self-control
- Achieve a realistic program of activity that balances physical activity with energy-conserving activities
- Describe the disease process, measures to reduce risk factors, and rehabilitation activities necessary to manage the therapeutic regimen

SUDDEN CARDIAC DEATH

Sudden cardiac death (SCD) is an abrupt, unexpected death resulting from a variety of cardiac causes. Over 350,000 adults have an out-of-hospital cardiac arrest every year.[1]

Etiology and Pathophysiology

SCD is the sudden unexpected death occurring within 1 hour of symptom onset. In SCD, a sudden disruption in heart function from a life-threatening dysrhythmia causes an abrupt loss of CO and cerebral blood flow. The affected person may or may not have a known history of heart disease. SCD is the first manifestation of CAD or structural heart disease in up to 50% of people. However, SCD can occur without evidence of CAD.[28] CAD is the main cause of SCD in the United States, especially in adults over 35 years of age.[29]

Acute ventricular dysrhythmias (e.g., VT or VF) cause most cases of SCD and may or may not be associated with an acute MI. Many SCD survivors have a history of a prior (old) MI that caused LV dysfunction and a reduced LVEF. These dysrhythmias have a high rate of recurrence. It is difficult to know who is at high risk for SCD. However, LV dysfunction (EF <30%) is the most common criterion to help guide decisions about implantable cardioverter-defibrillators (ICD) implantation. The use of ICDs for primary and secondary prevention has significantly reduced the incidence of SCD from VT and VF.[28,29]

Structural heart disease (e.g., hypertrophic cardiomyopathy) is a risk factor for SCD, especially in young, athletic people. Some cases of SCD (especially in people less than age 45) involve changes in the conduction system. These include prolonged QT syndrome, Wolff-Parkinson-White syndrome complicated by atrial fibrillation, and Brugada syndrome.

Clinical Manifestations

Some people have symptoms within 1 hour of an SCD event, such as angina, palpitations, dizziness, or lightheadedness. People who experience SCD because of CAD fall into 2 groups: (1) those who had a prior (old) MI and (2) those who had an acute MI. SCD is more common in people who had a prior (old) MI. Those who had a prior MI and survive SCD are at risk for another SCD event because of the continued electrical instability from the scarred heart muscle. They are usually referred for an ICD for secondary prevention. Patients who have SCD from an acute MI should undergo at least 40 days of maximal medical therapy to see if there is recovery in the EF before an ICD is implanted.[29]

Interprofessional and Nursing Care

People who survive an SCD event need a diagnostic workup to determine whether they also had an acute MI. Serial analysis of cardiac biomarkers and ECGs are done to rule out ACS. Because some people with SCD have undiagnosed CAD, cardiac catheterization can identify if significant CAD (e.g., greater than 70% stenosis in multiple coronary arteries) was the cause of the SCD event. PCI or CABG surgery may be needed because significant CAD may be a reversible cause of SCD.

If no reversible cause is identified and the EF is low normal, it is useful to know if these patients are likely to have a recurrence. Assessment of dysrhythmias in these patients may include obtaining an electrophysiology study (EPS).[29] EPS is done under fluoroscopy. Pacing electrodes are placed in various intracardiac areas and stimuli are selectively used to reproduce life-threatening dysrhythmias. See Chapters 35 and 39 for a discussion of EPS.

For patients with syncope suspected to be caused by ventricular dysrhythmias, an outpatient wearable cardiac monitor (e.g., Holter monitor) can be used for up to 48 hours or a Mobile Cardiac Outpatient Telemetry (MCOT) (e.g., CardioNet) may be worn up to 30 days. An implantable cardiac loop recorder (e.g., LINQ) may be implanted and left in place up to 3 years.

The most common approach to preventing a recurrence of SCD and improving survival is the use of an ICD.[28,29] See Chapter 39 for a discussion of ICDs. Drug therapy with an antiarrhythmic such as amiodarone may be used with an ICD to decrease episodes of ventricular dysrhythmias if the patient is receiving multiple ICD shocks due to the dysrhythmias.

Some patients at risk for SCD (e.g., during the time when a patient with an MI and low EF must wait at least 40 days on maximum medical therapy to see if there is improvement in LV function) may use a wearable cardioverter-defibrillator (e.g., LifeVest) as a bridge to ICD or heart transplantation.[30] The wearable cardioverter-defibrillator is a personal external defibrillator that has 2 main parts: a garment and monitor. The garment is worn under clothing. It has electrodes that continuously record the patient's ECG and deliver a shock, if needed. If the patient has VT or VF, the device sounds an alarm to confirm that the patient is unresponsive. If the patient is conscious, the patient can press a button to stop the shock. If the patient does not respond, the device sounds an alarm to notify bystanders that a shock is about to be delivered. If the dysrhythmia continues and the patient still does not respond, a treatment shock is delivered through the electrodes.[30] The patient wears the device except when bathing or showering.

Teach people about the care of SCD victims and the needed actions to save lives. Rapid CPR and defibrillation with an automatic external defibrillator (AED), combined with early advanced cardiac life support, has improved long-term survival rates for a witnessed arrest due to ventricular dysrhythmias.

Be alert to the patient's psychosocial adaptation to this sudden "brush with death." Many patients develop a "time bomb" mentality. They and their caregivers fear the recurrence of cardiac arrest. They may become anxious, angry, and depressed. The grief response varies. Patients and caregivers may need to deal with other issues, such as driving restrictions, role reversal, and change in occupation. Be attuned to the specific needs of the patient and caregiver. Provide information and emotional support.

Case Study

Myocardial Infarction

(© iStockphoto/ Thinkstock.)

Patient Profile

D.M., a 51-year-old, white, small business owner, is rushed to the ED by ambulance with crushing, substernal chest pain that radiates down his left arm. He reports dizziness and nausea.

Subjective Data

- Short of breath, nauseous
- History of chronic stable angina and hypertension
- States he is "borderline diabetic"
- Overweight, but recently lost 10 lb.
- Does not exercise
- Has 3 teenage children who are causing "problems"
- Recently lost his best friend and business partner, who died from cancer

Objective Data

Physical Assessment

- Diaphoretic
- BP 165/100 mm Hg, pulse rate 120/min, respiratory rate 26/min

Diagnostic Studies

- 12-lead ECG shows sinus tachycardia with occasional PVCs and ST elevation in leads II, III, aVF, V_5, V_6 consistent with an inferolateral wall MI
- High troponin level
- Total cholesterol 350 mg/dL (9.1 mmol/L)
- Hb A1C 9.0%

Interprofessional Care

- ED: Notify the cardiac catheterization laboratory of patient with STEMI
- O_2 2 L/min via nasal cannula, titrate to keep O_2 saturation above 93%
- Continuous ECG monitoring
- 2 IV access sites
- Aspirin 325 mg (chewable) now
- Atorvastatin 80 mg PO
- Eptifibatide IV (this should *not* delay the patient getting to the cardiac catheterization laboratory)
- Weight-based heparin IV (only used if the patient does not go directly to cardiac catheterization)
- SL NTG until an IV line is placed, then titrate nitroglycerin IV to relieve chest pain; hold for systolic BP below 100 mm Hg
- Morphine 2 mg IV q5–15 min as needed for chest pain unrelieved by NTG
- Vital signs (including pulse oximetry) every 10 min
- Prepare patient for cardiac catheterization with possible PCI

Discussion Questions

1. ***Recognize:*** Explain the pathogenesis of CAD. What risk factors contribute to its development? What risk factors were present in D.M.'s life?
2. ***Analyze***: Which coronary artery(ies) is (are) most likely occluded in D.M.'s coronary circulation?
3. ***Analyze***: Explain the significance of the results of the laboratory tests and the 12-lead ECG finding.
4. ***Plan***: Give a rationale for each treatment measure ordered for D.M.
5. ***Prioritize:*** What are the priority nursing interventions for D.M. before PCI? Immediately after PCI?
6. ***Act***: Identify activities you can delegate to assistive personnel (AP).
7. ***Evaluate***: What outcomes would show that interprofessional care was successful?

Answers and a corresponding conceptual care map available at http://evolve.elsevier.com/Lewis/medsurg.

BRIDGE TO NCLEX EXAMINATION

The number of the question corresponds to the same-numbered outcome at the beginning of the chapter.

1. Which information would the nurse include in teaching a patient about CAD? *(select all that apply)*
   a. Diffuse involvement of plaque formation in coronary veins
   b. Abnormal levels of cholesterol, especially low-density lipoproteins
   c. Accumulation of lipid and fibrous tissue within the coronary arteries
   d. Development of angina due to a decreased blood supply to the heart muscle
   e. Chronic vasoconstriction of coronary arteries leading to permanent vasospasm
2. After teaching a patient about ways to decrease risk factors for CAD, which patient statement indicates to the nurse that further instruction is needed?
   a. "I can keep my blood pressure normal with medication."
   b. "I would like to add weightlifting to my exercise program."
   c. "I can change my diet to decrease my intake of saturated fats."
   d. "I will change my lifestyle to reduce activities that increase my stress."
3. A hospitalized patient with a history of chronic stable angina tells the nurse they are having chest pain. Which information about ischemia would the nurse use as a basis for planning care?
   a. It will always progress to myocardial infarction.
   b. It can be relieved by rest, nitroglycerin, or both.

c. It is often associated with vomiting and extreme fatigue.
d. It indicates that irreversible myocardial damage is occurring.

4. The nurse is caring for a patient who is 2 days post MI. The patient reports that chest pain when taking a deep breath. Which action would be a *priority*?
a. Notify the provider STAT and obtain a 12-lead ECG.
b. Obtain vital signs and auscultate for a pericardial friction rub.
c. Apply high-flow O_2 by face mask and auscultate breath sounds.
d. Medicate the patient with an opiate analgesic and reevaluate in 30 minutes.

5. A patient is in the ICU with a diagnosis of NSTEMI. Which drugs would the nurse expect the patient to receive? *(select all that apply)*
a. Oral statin therapy
b. Antiplatelet therapy
c. Thrombolytic therapy
d. Prophylactic antibiotics
e. Intravenous nitroglycerin

6. A patient is recovering from an uncomplicated MI. Which rehabilitation guideline is a *priority* to include in the teaching plan?
a. Refrain from sexual activity for a minimum of 3 weeks.
b. Plan a diet program that aims for a 1- to 2-lb. weight loss per week.
c. Begin an exercise program that aims for at least 5 30-minute sessions per week.
d. Consider the use of erectile agents and prophylactic NTG before sexual activity.

7. Which finding is the strongest predictor of risk for sudden cardiac death?
a. Aortic valve disease
b. Mitral valve disease
c. Left ventricular dysfunction
d. Atherosclerotic heart disease

1. b, c, d; 2. b; 3. b; 4. b; 5. a, b, e; 6. c; 7. c.

For rationales to these answers and even more NCLEX review questions, visit http://evolve.elsevier.com/Lewis/medsurg.

EVOLVE WEBSITE/RESOURCES LIST

http://evolve.elsevier.com/Lewis/medsurg
Review Questions (Online Only)
Key Points
Answer Keys for Questions
- Rationales for Bridge to NCLEX Examination Questions
- Answer Guidelines for Case Study

Student Case Study
- Patient With Coronary Artery Disease and Acute Coronary Syndrome

Nursing Care Plan
- eNursing Care Plan 37.1: Patient With Acute Coronary Syndrome

Conceptual Care Map Creator
- Conceptual Care Map for Case Study

Audio Glossary
Content Updates

REFERENCES

*1. Virani SS, Alonso A, Benjamin EJ, et al.: Heart disease and stroke statistics---2020 update: a report from the AHA, *Circulation* 141:e139, 2020.
2. World Health Organization: Cardiovascular diseases: key facts. Retrieved from https://www.who.int/news-room/fact-sheets/detail/cardiovascular-diseases-(cvds).
3. Lilly LS: *Pathophysiology of heart disease: a collaborative project of medical students and faculty*, ed 6, Philadelphia, 2016, Wolters Kluwer.
*4. McSweeney JC, Rosenfeld AG, Abel WM, et al.: Preventing and experiencing ischemic heart disease as a woman: state of the science: a scientific statement from the AHA, *Circulation* 137:1302, 2016.
*5. Roberts R, Campillo A: Genetic stratification for primary prevention of coronary artery disease, *Curr Opin Cardiol* 37:529, 2018.
*6. Grundy SM, Stone NJ, Bailey AL, et al.: 2018 AHA/ACC/AACVPR/AAPA/ABC/ACPM/ADA/AGS/ APhA/ASPC/NLA/PCNA guideline on the management of blood cholesterol: a report of the ACC/AHA Task Force on Clinical Practice Guidelines, *Circulation* 39:e1082, 2019.
*7. Whelton PK, Carey RM, Aronow WS, et al.: 2017 ACC/AHA/AAPA/ABC/ACPM/AGS/APhA/ASH/ ASPC/NMA/PCNA guideline for the prevention, detection, evaluation, and management of high blood pressure in adults: a report of the ACC/AHA Task Force on Clinical Practice Guidelines, *Hypertension* 71:e13, 2018.
*8. Bhatnagar A, Whitsel LP, Blaha MJ, et al.: New and emerging tobacco products and the nicotine endgame: the role of robust regulation and comprehensive tobacco control and prevention, *Circulation* 139:e937, 2019.
*9. Fihn SD, Blankenship JC, Alexander KP, et al.: ACC/AHA/AATS/PCNA/SCAI/STS focused update of the guideline for the diagnosis and management of patients with stable ischemic heart disease: a report of the ACC/AHA Task Force on Practice Guidelines and the American College of Physicians, AATS, PCNA, SCAI, and STS, *Circulation* 130:1749, 2014.
10. Kim ST, Park T: Acute and chronic effects of cocaine on cardiovascular health, *Int J Mol Sci* 20:584, 2019.
*11. Amsterdam EA, Wenger NK, Brindis RG, et al.: 2014 ACC/AHA guideline for the management of patients with non–ST-elevation acute coronary syndromes: a report of the ACC/AHA Task Force on Practice Guidelines, *Circulation* 130:e344, 2014.
*12. Arnett DK, Blumenthal RS, Albert MA, et al.: 2019 ACC/AHA guideline on the primary prevention of cardiovascular disease: a report of the ACC/AHA Task Force on Clinical Practice Guidelines, *Circulation* 140:e596, 2019.
*13. Jellinger PS, Handelsman Y, Rosenblit PD, et al.: American Association of Clinical Endocrinologist and American College of Endocrinology guidelines for management of dyslipidemia and prevention of cardiovascular disease, *Endocr Pract* 23(S1), 2017.

14. NEJM Journal Watch: FDA approves new cholesterol-lowering drug. Retrieved from https://www.jwatch.org/fw116376/2020/02/24/fda-approves-new-cholesterol-lowering-drug.
*15. Levine GN, O'Gara PT, Bates ER, et al.: 2015 ACC/AHA/SCAI focused update on primary PCI for patients with ST-elevation myocardial infarction: an update of the 2011 ACCF/AHA/SCAI guideline for PCI and the 2013 ACCF/AHA guideline for the management of ST-elevation myocardial infarction, *Circulation* 137:1135, 2016.
*16. Tamis-Holland JE, Jneid H, Reynolds HR, et al.: Contemporary diagnosis and management of patients with myocardial infarction in the absence of obstructive coronary artery disease, *Circulation* 139:e891, 2019.
*17. The Heart Outcomes Prevention Evaluation (HOPE) Study Investigators: Effects of an angiotensin-converting-enzyme inhibitor, ramipril, on cardiovascular events in high-risk patients, *N Engl J Med* 342:145, 2000. (Classic).
*18. Levine GN, Bates ER, Bittl JA, et al.: 2016 ACC/AHA guideline focused update on duration of dual antiplatelet therapy in patients with coronary artery disease: a report of the ACC/AHA Task Force on Clinical Practice Guidelines, *Circulation* 134:e123, 2016.
19. Hillis LD, Smith PK, Anderson JL, et al.: 2011 ACCF/AHA guideline for coronary artery bypass graft surgery: a report of the ACC/AHA Task Force on Practice Guidelines, *Circulation* 124:e652, 2011. (Classic).
20. Raja SG: *Cardiac surgery: a complete guide*, Switzerland, 2020, Springer.
21. Zipes DP, Libby P, Bonow RO, et al.: *Braunwald's heart disease: a textbook of cardiovascular medicine*, ed 11, St Louis, 2019, Elsevier.
*22. Thygesen K, Alpert JS, Jaffe AS, et al.: Fourth universal definition of myocardial infarction (2018), *Circulation* 138:e618, 2018.
*23. O'Gara PT, Kushner FG, Ascheim DD, et al.: 2013 ACCF/AHA guideline for the management of ST-elevation myocardial infarction: a report of the ACC/AHA Task Force on Practice Guidelines, *Circulation* 127:e362, 2013.
*24. Dahal K, Hendrani A, Sharma SP, et al.: Aldosterone antagonist therapy and mortality in patients with ST-segment elevation myocardial infarction without heart failure: a systematic review and meta-analysis, *JAMA Intern Med* 178:913, 2018.
25. American Association of Critical Care Nurses: Family presence: visitation in the adult ICU. Retrieved from www.aacn.org/clinical-resources/practice-alerts/family-presence-visitation-in-the-adult-icu.
*26. Thomas RJ, Beatty AL, Beckie TM, et al.: Home-based cardiac rehabilitation: a scientific statement from the American Association of Cardiovascular and Pulmonary Rehabilitation, the AHA, and the ACC, *Circulation* 140:e69, 2019.
27. Levine GN, Steinke EE, Bakaeen FG, et al.: Sexual activity and cardiovascular disease: a scientific statement from the AHA, *Circulation* 125:1058, 2012. (Classic).
28. Mitrani RD, Myerburg RJ: Ten advances defining sudden cardiac death, *Trends Cardiovasc Med* 26:23, 2016.
*29. Al-Khatib SM, Stevenson WG, Ackerman MJ, et al.: 2017 AHA/ACC/HRS guideline for management of patients with ventricular arrhythmias and the prevention of sudden cardiac death: a report of the ACC/AHA Task Force on Clinical Practice Guidelines and the Heart Rhythm Society, *Circulation* 138:e272, 2018.
30. Kachur S, Morin DP: Who should receive a wearable defibrillator vest at hospital discharge? *Curr Cardiol Rep* 21:125, 2019.

*Evidence-based information for clinical practice.

38

Heart Failure

Vera Barton-Maxwell

http://evolve.elsevier.com/Lewis/medsurg/

CONCEPTUAL FOCUS

Fatigue
Fluids and Electrolytes
Functional Ability
Gas Exchange
Perfusion
Self-Management

LEARNING OUTCOMES

1. Compare the pathophysiology of heart failure with reduced ejection fraction (HFrEF) and heart failure with preserved ejection fraction (HFpEF).
2. Relate the compensatory mechanisms involved in heart failure (HF) to the development of acute decompensated heart failure (ADHF) and chronic HF.
3. Describe appropriate nursing and interprofessional care to manage the patient with ADHF.
4. Describe appropriate nursing and interprofessional care to manage the patient with chronic HF.
5. Discuss advanced therapeutic options for patients with stage D HF.
6. Discuss the nursing and interprofessional care of a patient with a circulatory assist device.
7. Describe the indications for heart transplantation and the nursing care of heart transplant recipients.

KEY TERMS

acute decompensated heart failure
cardiac resynchronization therapy
heart failure (HF)
heart failure with preserved ejection fraction (HFpEF)
heart failure with reduced ejection fraction (HFrEF)
heart transplantation
intraaortic balloon pump (IABP)
orthopnea
paroxysmal nocturnal dyspnea (PND)
pulmonary edema
ventricular assist device (VAD)

HEART FAILURE

Heart failure (HF) is a complex clinical syndrome that develops in response to myocardial insult. It results in the inability of the heart to provide sufficient blood to meet the oxygen (O_2) needs of tissues and organs. The decreased cardiac output (CO) leads to decreased tissue perfusion, impaired gas exchange, fluid volume imbalance, and decreased functional ability. This chapter describes the nursing and interprofessional care of patients with HF.

The *percentage* of the total blood volume in the left ventricle (LV) at the end of diastole that is pumped out of the LV with the next systole is the left ventricular ejection fraction (LVEF). HF involves a defect in either ventricular systolic function/LV contraction (**heart failure with reduced ejection fraction [HFrEF]**) and/or a defect in ventricular diastolic function/filling (**heart failure with preserved ejection fraction [HFpEF]**).[1]

HF is associated with many cardiovascular diseases (CVDs). These include hypertension (HTN), coronary artery disease (CAD), and myocardial infarction (MI). HF is increasing in incidence and prevalence. This is partially due to better survival after cardiac events and the aging population. HF is primarily a disease of older adults. The incidence is similar in men and women.[2]

HF is a major health problem in the United States. The number of people with HF has increased from 5.7 million (2009–2012) to 6.2 million (2013–2016). That number is projected to rise to over 8 million adults with HF by 2030.[2] HF is the most common reason for hospital admission in adults over the age of 65. This places a significant economic burden on the health care system.[1] The complex, progressive nature of HF often results in poor outcomes, such as hospital readmissions. Around 25% of patients discharged with a primary diagnosis of HF are readmitted within 30 days. Overall survival after the onset of HF has improved. This is likely due to evidence-based risk and management

BOX 38.1 PROMOTING HEALTH EQUITY

Heart Failure

- Blacks and Hispanics develop HF at an earlier age, are admitted to the hospital more often, and have higher mortality rates related to HF as compared to Whites.
- Hispanics have more CVD risk factors but are 25% less likely to die of heart disease than Whites.[4]

TABLE 38.1 Primary Causes of Heart Failure

- Cardiomyopathy (e.g., viral, postpartum, substance use)
- Congenital heart defects (e.g., ventricular septal defect)
- CAD, including MI
- HTN, including hypertensive crisis
- Hyperthyroidism
- Myocarditis
- Pulmonary HTN
- Rheumatic heart disease
- Valve disorders (e.g., mitral stenosis)

TABLE 38.2 Common Precipitating Causes of Heart Failure

Cause	Mechanism
Anemia	↓ O_2-carrying capacity of the blood stimulating ↑ in CO to meet tissue demands, leading to increase in cardiac workload and increase in size of LV
Bacterial endocarditis	*Infection:* ↑ metabolic demands and O_2 requirements *Valve dysfunction:* causes stenosis or regurgitation
Dysrhythmias	May ↓ CO and ↑ workload and O_2 requirements of myocardial tissue
Fluid overload	↑ Preload causing volume overload on the RV
Hypothyroidism	Indirectly predisposes to ↑ atherosclerosis. Severe hypothyroidism decreases myocardial contractility
Infection	↑ O_2 demand of tissues, stimulating ↑ CO
Nutrition deficiencies	May ↓ cardiac function by ↑ myocardial muscle mass and myocardial contractility
Obstructive sleep apnea	Frequent nighttime apnea results in ↑ afterload, intermittent hypoxia, and ↑ sympathetic nervous system activity.
Paget's disease	↑ Workload of the heart by ↑ vascular bed in the skeletal muscle
Pulmonary embolism	↑ Pulmonary pressure resulting from obstruction leads to pulmonary HTN, ↓ CO
Thyrotoxicosis	Changes the tissue metabolic rate, ↑ HR and workload of the heart

approaches.[2] Still, 1 in 8 US adult deaths is associated with an HF diagnosis. The total cost of HF care exceeds $30 billion annually, with over half of these costs spent on hospitalizations.[2]

Etiology

HTN and CAD are the primary risk factors for HF. HTN is a modifiable risk factor that should be aggressively treated and managed (Box 38.1). Long-term treatment of HTN reduces the incidence of HF by 50%.[1] Co-morbidities, such as diabetes, metabolic syndrome, advanced age, tobacco use, and vascular disease, contribute to the development of HF. Other causes include congenital abnormalities (e.g., septal defects), infiltrative cardiomyopathies (e.g., sarcoidosis), infections and inflammatory processes (e.g., viral myocarditis), persistent dysrhythmias, and toxins (e.g., alcohol, drug use, chemotherapy).[3]

Any interference with the normal mechanisms regulating CO may cause HF. CO depends on (1) preload, (2) afterload, (3) myocardial contractility, and (4) HR. These factors affect stroke volume (SV), which is the amount of blood pumped per heartbeat. Thus, the equation: $CO = SV \times HR$. Any changes in these factors can lead to decreased ventricular function and HF. Preload and afterload are discussed in Chapter 31.

The major causes of HF are divided into primary causes (Table 38.1) and precipitating causes (Table 38.2). Precipitating causes increase the workload of the heart, causing acutely decreased heart function.

Genetic Link

Cardiomyopathies, diseases that weaken the heart muscle and cause HF, can be acquired or inherited. The inherited forms involve autosomal dominant traits with variable genetic expression. Such mutations are typically found in genes encoding sarcomeric proteins.[5] The body's largest known protein, *titin,* responds to such a mutated gene. Titin mutations impair sarcomere function and disrupt chemical signaling, which weakens ventricular structure and stability.[6]

Identifying pathogenic genetic variants has important value for disease prediction and therapy. Post-viral myocarditis, which can cause HF, is thought to be caused by an interaction between a virus and a genetic predisposition.[5] Specific genes and gene mutations are linked to the development of HTN and CAD, known risk factors for HF (see Chapters 36 and 37).

Pathophysiology

HF develops in response to myocardial injury and results in decreased heart function. Manifestations of HF are the result of neurohormonal compensatory mechanisms activated in response to myocardial dysfunction, leading to *remodeling* of myocardial structure and changes in function (Fig. 38.1).

Left-Sided Heart Failure

The most common form of HF, left-sided HF, results from the inability of the LV to either (1) empty adequately during systole or (2) fill adequately during diastole. We can further classify left-sided HF as HFrEF (systolic HF), HFpEF (diastolic HF), or a combination of the two.

Heart failure with reduced EF (systolic failure). HFrEF results from an inability of the heart to pump blood effectively (e.g., MI), increased afterload (e.g., HTN), cardiomyopathy, and mechanical problems (e.g., heart valve disease).[3] The hallmark of HFrEF is a decrease in the LVEF. Normal LVEF is 55% to 65%. Patients with HFrEF generally have an LVEF less than 40%. It can be as low as 5% to 10%.

The LV in HFrEF does not generate enough pressure to eject blood forward through the aorta. Over time, the LV dilates and hypertrophies. The weakened heart muscle cannot generate adequate SV, which impairs CO. Because the LV cannot effectively

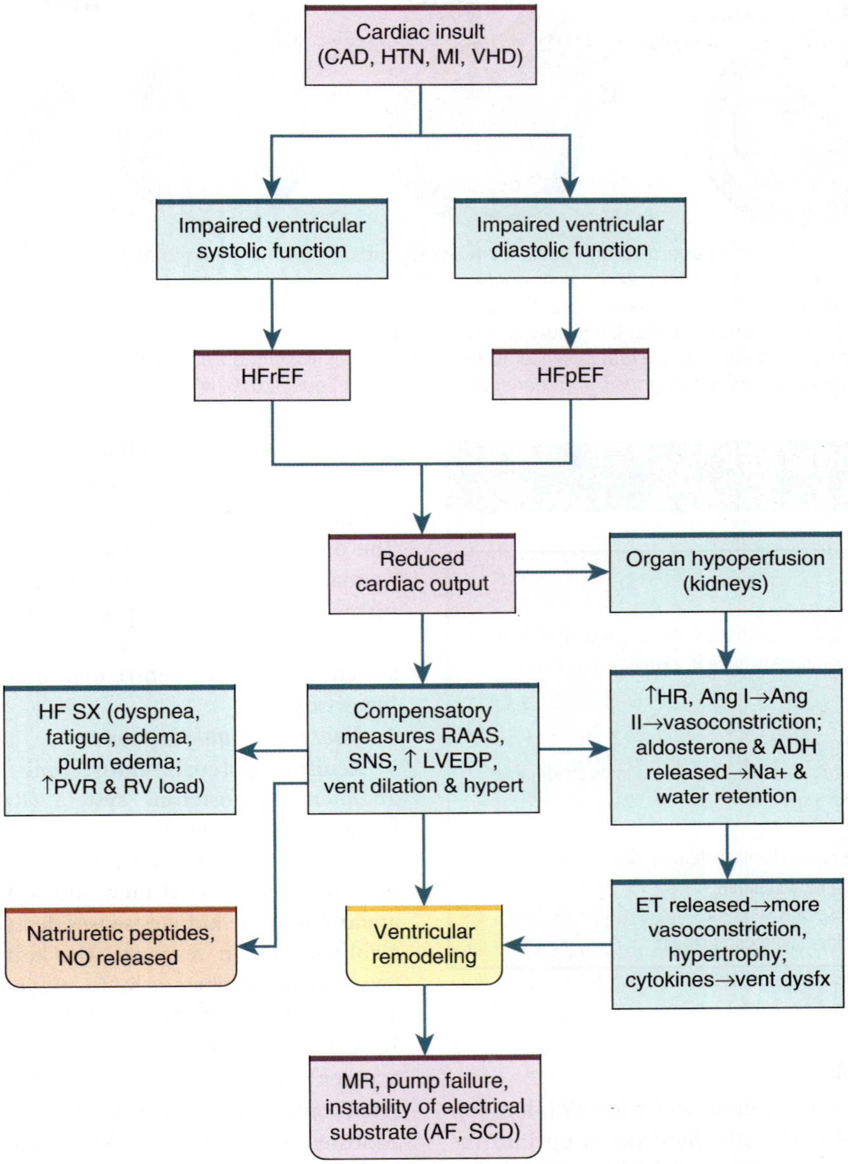

Fig. 38.1 Pathophysiology of HF. *Ang I,* Angiotensin I; *Ang II,* angiotensin II; *ADH,* Antidiuretic hormone; *ET,* endothelin; *HFpEF,* HF with preserved ejection fraction; *HFrEF,* HF with reduced ejection fraction; *LVEDP,* left ventricular end-diastolic pressure; *MR,* mitral regurgitation; *NO,* nitric oxide; *PVR,* pulmonary vascular resistance; *RAAS,* renin-angiotensin-aldosterone system; *SCD,* sudden cardiac death; *SNS,* sympathetic nervous system; *VHD,* valvular heart disease.

push blood forward, end diastolic volumes and pressures in the LV increase. When the LV fails, blood backs up into the left atrium (LA). This causes fluid accumulation in the lungs. The increased pulmonary hydrostatic pressure causes fluid leakage from the pulmonary capillary bed into the interstitium and then the alveoli. This results in pulmonary congestion and edema (Fig. 38.2A–D). Fortunately, therapies can reduce morbidity and mortality in HFrEF.

Heart failure with preserved EF (diastolic failure). HFpEF results from the inability of the ventricles to relax and fill during diastole. About 50% of patients with HF have HFpEF. HTN is the primary cause of HFpEF.[1] Other risk factors include older age, female gender, diabetes, and obesity (Box 38.2). In HFpEF, the LV is generally stiff and noncompliant, causing high filling pressures. Decreased filling volume in the ventricles results in decreased SV. The eventual result of HFpEF is the same as that of HFrEF, a reduced CO leading to fluid congestion. The diagnosis of HFpEF is based on (1) signs and symptoms of HF, (2) normal LVEF, and (3) evidence of LV diastolic dysfunction by echocardiography or cardiac catheterization. Therapies are aimed at reducing underlying risk factors, treating co-morbidities, and reducing symptoms.[7]

Patients with borderline HFpEF (LVEF 41% to 49%) have similar characteristics and receive similar therapies to those for patients with HFpEF.[1] The patient with ventricular failure of any type may have low BP, low CO, and poor renal perfusion. Poor exercise tolerance and dysrhythmias are common. The patient may present acutely from an MI or chronically from worsening cardiomyopathy or HTN. In both acute and chronic causes of HF, the body's response is to use compensatory mechanisms to try to maintain CO and BP.[3]

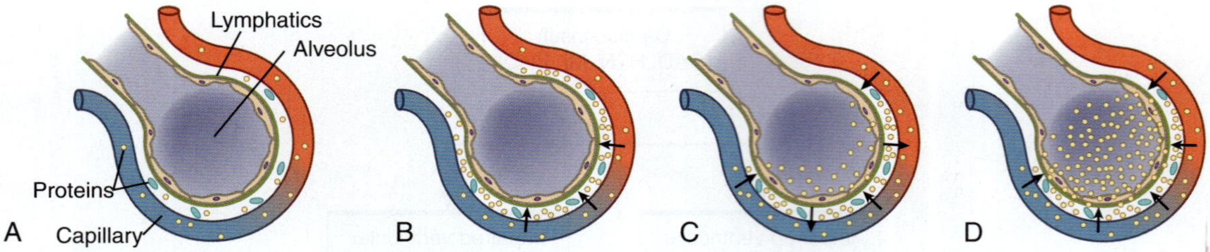

Fig. 38.2 As pulmonary edema progresses, it inhibits O_2 and CO_2 exchange at the alveolar-capillary interface. (A) Normal relationship. (B) Increased pulmonary capillary hydrostatic pressure causes fluid to move from the vascular space into the pulmonary interstitial space. (C) Lymphatic flow increases to try to pull fluid back into the vascular or lymphatic space. (D) Failure of lymphatic flow and worsening of left-sided HF result in further movement of fluid into the interstitial space and into the alveoli. (Modified from Urden LD, Stacy KM, Lough ME: *Critical care nursing: diagnosis and management,* ed 6, St Louis, 2010, Mosby.)

BOX 38.2 BIOLOGIC SEX CONSIDERATIONS

Heart Failure

Men

- Have HFrEF more often
- Ischemic heart disease (MI, CAD) is the most common cause of HF in men
- ACE inhibitor therapy reduces mortality more in asymptomatic HFrEF

Women

- Make up 50% of people living with HF
- Are often misdiagnosed due to perceptions of HF as a male condition
- Underrepresented in major HF trials
- Have HFpEF more often
- With HFrEF, more often have non-ischemic cardiomyopathy
- Often present with greater symptom burden
- HTN is the most common cause of HF
- Women with HF tend to be older compared to men[4]

Right-Sided Heart Failure

Right-sided HF occurs when the right ventricle (RV) does not pump effectively. When the RV fails, fluid backs up into the venous system. This causes movement of fluid into the tissues and organs (e.g., peripheral edema, abdominal ascites, hepatomegaly, jugular venous distention [JVD]).

The most common cause of right-sided HF is left-sided HF. As the LV fails, fluid backs up into the pulmonary system, increasing pressures in the lungs. The RV works harder to push blood to the pulmonary system. Over time, this increased workload weakens the RV, and gradually it fails. Other causes of right-sided HF (independent of the function of the LV) include RV infarction, pulmonary embolism, and *cor pulmonale* (RV dilation and hypertrophy caused by pulmonary disease) (see Chapter 31).

Biventricular Failure

Biventricular failure includes both LV and RV dysfunction. There is an inability of both ventricles to pump effectively. Because of decreased contractility, fluid build-up and systemic venous engorgement occur. Inadequate CO results in decreased perfusion to vital organs.[3]

Compensatory Mechanisms

HF can have an abrupt onset as with acute MI, or it can be a subtle process resulting from slow, progressive changes. The overloaded heart uses compensatory mechanisms to try to maintain adequate CO. The main compensatory mechanisms include (1) neurohormonal responses: renin-angiotensin-aldosterone system (RAAS) and the sympathetic nervous system (SNS); (2) ventricular dilation; and (3) ventricular hypertrophy.

Neurohormonal response

Renin-angiotensin-aldosterone system. The renin-angiotensin-aldosterone system (RAAS) works to maintain homeostasis. The goal of RAAS activation is increased preload and ventricular contractility to maintain CO. RAAS activation promotes retention of fluid and sodium. The juxtaglomerular apparatus in the kidneys senses decreased renal perfusion from a falling CO. In response, the kidneys release renin, which converts angiotensinogen to angiotensin I (see Chapter 49 and Fig. 49.1). Angiotensin I is next converted to angiotensin II by a converting enzyme made in the lungs. Angiotensin II, a potent vasoconstrictor, stimulates renal water and sodium retention and the release of aldosterone from the adrenal gland. Aldosterone acts in the nephron to stimulate sodium retention and potassium excretion and promotes myocardial fibrosis in the failing heart.

Continuous activation of the RAAS and SNS in HF leads to increased levels of antidiuretic hormone (ADH). ADH regulates water retention by stimulating renal tubular reabsorption. It is released via baroreceptor signals in response to arterial low pressure/under filling. ADH causes vasoconstriction and increases BP and central venous pressure (CVP). The consequences are fluid congestion and hyponatremia.[8] Chronic activation of the RAAS can cause harmful effects, such as cardiac myocyte apoptosis (programmed cell death), hypertrophy, and fibrosis. These cause the burdensome signs and symptoms that develop with HF.[9]

Sympathetic nervous system. Baroreceptors sense low arterial pressure, stimulating the sympathetic nervous system (SNS) to try to maintain CO. Catecholamines (epinephrine and norepinephrine) are released. Stimulation of β-adrenergic receptors increases HR *(chronotropy)* and ventricular contractility *(inotropy)*. Chronic SNS stimulation increases myocardial O_2 demand on the already weakened heart.

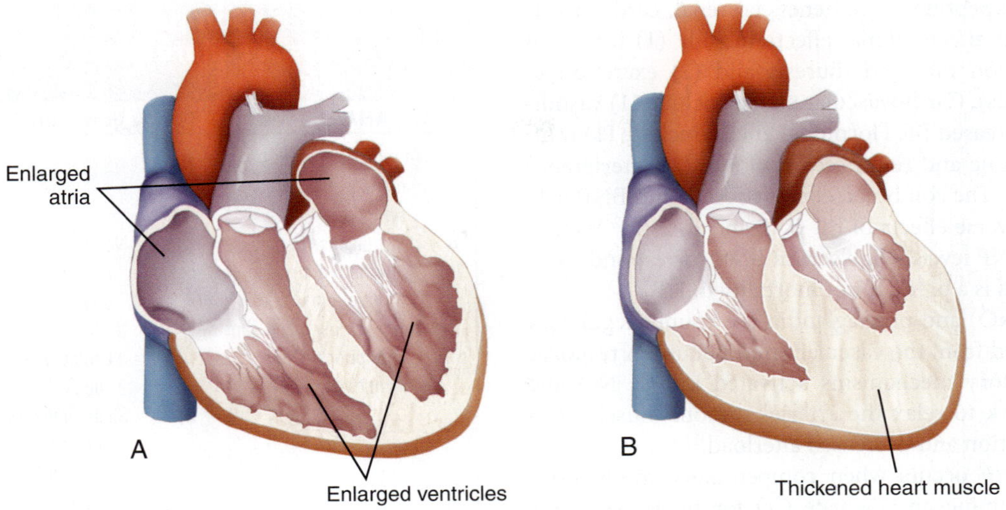

Fig. 38.3 (A) Dilated heart chambers. (B) Hypertrophied heart chambers.

Continuous activation of the neurohormonal responses (RAAS and SNS) in HF leads to high levels of ADH, endothelin, and proinflammatory cytokines. Together, these factors further increase the heart's workload, intensify ventricular dysfunction, and force ventricular remodeling.[8]

Peptides and cytokines. Endothelin, a vasoconstrictor peptide made by the vascular endothelial cells, is stimulated by hypoxia, ischemia, neurohormones, and inflammatory cytokines. Although endothelin stimulates contraction in most smooth muscles, it has the opposite effect on the heart, acting as a negative inotrope. This decreases ventricular contractility in the failing heart.

Myocytes release proinflammatory cytokines in response to heart injury (e.g., MI, HF). Two cytokines, tumor necrosis factor (TNF) and interleukin-1 (IL-1), further depress heart function through a negative inotropic effect, causing myocyte hypertrophy and apoptosis. Over time, a systemic inflammatory response occurs.[10] High levels of endothelin and proinflammatory cytokines increase the heart's workload, progressive LV dysfunction, myocyte hypertrophy, and ventricular remodeling.[9]

Ventricular adaptations

Dilation. *Dilation* is an enlargement of the heart chambers (Fig. 38.3A). It occurs when pressure in the heart chambers (usually the LV) is elevated over time. The heart muscle fibers stretch in response to the volume of blood in the heart at the end of diastole. According to the *Frank-Starling Law,* the strength of the heart's contraction is directly proportional to its diastolic stretch. The implication is that increased preload (a greater influx of blood into the ventricle during diastole) will cause a more forceful contraction. This increased contraction initially leads to increased CO and maintains BP and perfusion. Dilation starts as an adaptive mechanism to cope with increasing blood volume. However, excessive preload exhausts the Frank-Starling mechanism, and overstretched cardiac muscle fibers no longer increase CO.

Hypertrophy. *Hypertrophy* is an adaptive increase in the heart muscle thickness as a slow response to overwork and strain (Fig. 38.3B). It takes time for this increased muscle tissue to develop. Initially, the increased contractile power of the muscle fibers leads to increased CO and maintains tissue perfusion. Over time, hypertrophic heart muscle has poor contractility, needs more O_2 to perform work, has poor coronary artery circulation, becomes ischemic more easily, and is prone to dysrhythmias.

Remodeling. Pathologic *ventricular remodeling* is a change in the structure (dimensions, mass, shape) of the heart. Ventricular remodeling in HF occurs over time in response to pressure or volume overload and/or cardiac injury and compensatory mechanisms. These include neurohormonal, ET, cytokine activation, and ventricular adaptations, including dilation and hypertrophy. This altered shape of the ventricles eventually leads to increased ventricular mass, increased wall tension, increased O_2 consumption, and impaired contractility. The shape of the heart becomes less elliptical and more spherical. The ventricles become larger but less effective pumps. The LVEF further declines due to loss of mechanical advantage from all these changes in the ventricle. Increases in angiotensin II, aldosterone, and cytokines stimulate collagen synthesis leading to fibrosis and further impaired pumping ability.[11] Ventricular remodeling is associated with sudden cardiac death and a worse prognosis in HF. Therapies that reverse remodeling can improve symptoms and quality of life while decreasing hospitalizations and mortality.[11] Evidence-based therapies to prevent or reverse remodeling include ACE inhibitors, angiotensin receptor neprilysin inhibitors, β-adrenergic blockers, aldosterone antagonists, and cardiac resynchronization therapy.

Beneficial Counterregulatory Mechanisms

The body tries to maintain balance through several counterregulatory processes. Natriuretic peptides (atrial natriuretic peptide [ANP] and brain [b-type] natriuretic peptide [BNP]) are hormones made by the heart muscle. ANP is released from the atria and BNP is released from the ventricles in response to increased blood volume and cardiac wall stretching.[12]

The natriuretic peptides have beneficial renal, cardiovascular, and hormonal effects. Renal effects include (1) increased glomerular filtration rate and diuresis and (2) excretion of sodium (natriuresis). Cardiovascular effects include (1) vasodilation and (2) decreased BP. Hormonal effects include (1) inhibition of aldosterone and renin secretion and (2) interference with ADH release. The combined effects of ANP and BNP help to counter the adverse effects of the SNS and RAAS.[12] We can measure serum BNP levels. High serum BNP corresponds with fluid retention and is a predictor of mortality in HF.

Nitric oxide (NO) and prostaglandin are counterregulatory substances released from the vascular endothelium in response to the compensatory mechanisms activated in HF. NO and prostaglandin work to relax the arterial smooth muscle. This results in vasodilation and decreased afterload.[11]

Compensated HF occurs when compensatory mechanisms succeed in maintaining an adequate CO for tissue perfusion. *Decompensated HF* occurs when these mechanisms can no longer maintain adequate CO and inadequate tissue perfusion results.

Classifications of Heart Failure

New York Heart Association Classes of Heart Failure

The New York Heart Association (NYHA) Functional Classification places patients in 1 of 4 categories (I–IV) based on physical activity limitation due to symptom burden.[1] NYHA class designation changes based on worsening or improving symptoms.

The Stages of Heart Failure

The American College of Cardiology Foundation and the American Heart Association (ACCF/AHA) developed a staging system (A–D) that emphasizes the evolution and progression of HF as well as treatment strategies.[1] This system identifies people at risk for developing HF who do not currently have heart disease (stage A). This classification encourages addressing the patient's risk factors and treating existing conditions to prevent disease progression. This staging system is progressive and unidirectional. Patients advance to a higher (worse) stage as the disease progresses. Table 38.3 compares the NYHA classification and ACC/AHA staging system.

TABLE 38.3 Comparison of ACCF/AHA Stage of Heart Failure and NYHA Functional Classification

ACCF/AHA Stages		NYHA Functional Classification	
A	At high risk for HF, but no heart disease or symptoms	**None**	
B	Heart disease is present but there are no signs or symptoms	**I**	No limitation of physical activity. Ordinary physical activity does not cause symptoms of HF.
C	Heart disease is present with prior or current symptoms	**I**	No limitation of physical activity. Ordinary physical activity does not cause symptoms of HF.
		II	Slight limitation of physical activity. Comfortable at rest, but ordinary physical activity results in symptoms of HF.
		III	Marked limitation of physical activity. Comfortable at rest, but less than ordinary activity causes symptoms of HF.
		IV	Inability to carry out any physical activity without discomfort. Symptoms may be present at rest.
D	Advanced heart disease with continued HF requiring specialized therapy	**IV**	Inability to carry out any physical activity without discomfort. Symptoms may be present at rest.

ACCF, American College of Cardiology Foundation; *AHA,* American Heart Association; *NYHA,* New York Heart Association.

Clinical Manifestations: Acute Decompensated Heart Failure

Acute decompensated heart failure (ADHF) is an increase (usually sudden) in symptoms of HF with a decrease in functional status, often requiring rapid escalation of therapy and hospital admission. ADHF is the most common cause of hospitalization for older Americans.[13] The presentation of ADHF typically includes symptoms and signs related to pulmonary congestion and volume overload. Neurohormonal activation leads to impaired regulation of sodium excretion through the kidneys that results in sodium and fluid accumulation. To help compensate, the lymphatic system increases its flow to help maintain a constant volume of the pulmonary extravascular fluid (Fig. 38.2A and B). The lungs become less compliant. There is increased resistance in the small airways. This early stage is associated with a mild increase in the respiratory rate (RR) and a decrease in partial pressure of O_2 in arterial blood (PaO_2).

If pulmonary venous pressure continues to increase, more fluid moves into the interstitial space than the lymphatics can remove, causing *interstitial edema* (Fig. 38.2C). Tachypnea develops, and the patient becomes symptomatic (e.g., short of breath). If the pulmonary venous pressure increases further, the alveolar lining is disrupted. Fluid moves into the alveoli *(alveolar edema)*. This is accompanied by a worsening of the arterial blood gas values (lower PaO_2, increased $PaCO_2$, progressive respiratory acidosis).

ADHF can manifest as **pulmonary edema**. This is an acute, life-threatening situation, in which the lung alveoli become filled with serosanguineous fluid (Fig. 38.2D). The most common cause of pulmonary edema is left-sided HF. Other causes of pulmonary edema are listed in Table 30.19.

Clinical findings of pulmonary edema include acute manifestations of left HF, such as dyspnea, *orthopnea*, and *paroxysmal nocturnal dyspnea*. JVD is often present as the most sensitive and specific sign for elevated LV filling pressures. Coughing provides an early clue to developing pulmonary edema in patients with chronic HF. The patient is usually anxious and pale and may be cyanotic. The RR is often over 30 breaths per minute. You may see use of accessory respiratory muscles. Pink, frothy sputum may be present in patients with severe disease. Auscultation of the lungs may reveal crackles and wheezes throughout. However, the absence of crackles does not rule out ADHF, as many patients with a history of chronic HF develop increased lymphatic drainage of the alveolar edema. The patient's HR is

TABLE 38.4 Clinical Profile in Acute Decompensated Heart Failure

		CONGESTION (WET)	
		No	**Yes**
LOW PERFUSION (COLD)	**No**	**Dry-Warm** • PAWP normal • CO normal • Signs and symptoms: none	**Wet-Warm** • PAWP ↑ • CO normal • Signs and symptoms: dyspnea, edema, orthopnea
	Yes	**Dry-Cold** • PAWP ↓ or normal • CO ↓ • Signs and symptoms: edema, hypotension, cool extremities	**Wet-Cold** • PAWP ↑ • CO ↓ • Signs and symptoms: altered mental status, decreased O_2 saturation, reduced urine output, shock

PAWP, Pulmonary artery wedge pressure.

often rapid with an abnormal S_3 or S_4 heart sound (Table 35.4). BP may be high or decreased depending on the severity of the HF. Hypotension indicates severe LV systolic dysfunction and possible cardiogenic shock. Cool extremities occur with low CO and poor perfusion. Skin pallor, ashy color, or mottling may be present from peripheral vasoconstriction. Sometimes, hoarseness may be present because of compression of the recurrent laryngeal nerve from an enlarged LA (Ortner sign).

We categorize patients with ADHF into 1 of 4 groups based on hemodynamic and clinical status: dry-warm, dry-cold, wet-warm, and wet-cold (Table 38.4).[1] The most common presentation in patients with ADHF is the wet and warm patient. A patient is "wet" due to volume overload (e.g., congestion, dyspnea) but "warm" due to maintaining adequate perfusion (warm skin, positive pulses).

CHECK YOUR PRACTICE

You are assigned to a patient with ADHF who was admitted to the HF unit. The patient has bilateral crackles in the mid-lower lung fields and dyspnea on exertion (e.g., moving from the bed to the commode). Their skin is warm, and pulses are present in all extremities. Your preceptor asks you to categorize your patient based on the classification systems in Tables 38.3 and 38.4.

- In what NYHA class would you place your patient?
- In what ACCF/AHA stage would you place your patient?
- What ADHF clinical profile does your patient best fit?

Clinical Manifestations: Chronic Heart Failure

Chronic HF is a progressive syndrome of reduced CO and increased venous pressure associated with the death of cardiac muscle cells. Neurohormonal and hemodynamic mechanisms to compensate for reduced CO include vasoconstriction and SNS stimulation, an inflammatory response involving cytokines, and ventricular remodeling. These physiologic responses are responsible for the manifestations of chronic HF. Many therapies for chronic HF work by counteracting these mechanisms. Table 38.5 lists the manifestations of right-sided and left-sided chronic HF.

TABLE 38.5 Manifestations of Heart Failure

Right-Sided Heart Failure	Left-Sided Heart Failure
Signs	
• Right ventricular heaves • ↑ HR • Anasarca (massive generalized edema) • Ascites • Edema (e.g., pedal, scrotum) • Hepatomegaly • JVD • Murmurs • Weight gain	• Left ventricular heaves • ↑ HR • S_3 and S_4 heart sounds • ABGs: ↓ PaO_2, slight ↑ $PaCO_2$ • Confusion, restlessness • Dry, hacking cough • Crackles (pulmonary edema) • Pleural effusion • PMI displaced inferiorly and left of the midclavicular line (LV hypertrophy) • Pulsus alternans (alternating pulses: strong, weak) • Shallow respirations up to 32–40/min • Frothy, pink-tinged sputum (advanced pulmonary edema)
Symptoms	
• Anorexia and GI bloating • Anxiety, depression • Fatigue • Nausea • RUQ pain	• Anxiety, depression • Dyspnea • Fatigue, weakness • Nocturia • Orthopnea • Paroxysmal nocturnal dyspnea

Fatigue

Fatigue from usual daily activities can be an early symptom of chronic HF. As CO decreases, fatigue eventually limits activities. Anemia is another potential cause of fatigue in HF.

Dyspnea

Dyspnea is the most common manifestation of chronic HF. It is caused by increased pulmonary pressures from interstitial and alveolar edema. Dyspnea can occur early in the HF disease process with mild exertion. As HF progresses, dyspnea develops with less exertion or at rest.

Orthopnea, or dyspnea in the recumbent position, suggests HF. Orthopnea occurs due to redistribution of fluid from the legs into the lungs while lying down. The dyspnea is usually relieved with sitting up. Ask the patient about the number of pillows used under the head while sleeping or about sleeping in a recliner to aid breathing.

Paroxysmal nocturnal dyspnea (PND) is episodic, sudden dyspnea that wakes a patient at night. PND is caused by fluid accumulation in the pulmonary vessels entering the alveoli while the patient is supine. The patient awakens in a panic with feelings of suffocation and a strong desire to sit or stand to aid breathing.

Cough

A chronic, nonproductive cough that is worse when lying down is often from pulmonary congestion and can be a sign of HF. Other potential causes of cough include gastric conditions, medications (e.g., ACE inhibitors due to increased bradykinin levels), and pulmonary conditions.

Tachycardia

Tachycardia is an early sign of HF. One of the body's first responses to compensate for a reduced CO is to increase the HR via activation of the SNS. Over time, persistent tachycardia is harmful and may worsen HF symptoms. Adequate HR control in patients with chronic HF has been associated with better clinical outcomes, including decreased hospitalizations and mortality.[1]

Palpitations

Palpitations, or an irregular heartbeat, can occur due to dysrhythmias with chronic HF. Atrial fibrillation (AF) is the most common of these dysrhythmias. Patients may report a fast or irregular heartbeat, a fluttering sensation, or "skipped beats" that may be intermittent. Palpitations may be accompanied by dyspnea, lightheadedness, or near syncope if the dysrhythmia further decreases CO.

Edema

Edema is a common sign of HF. Common sites include dependent body areas (peripheral edema), liver (hepatomegaly), abdominal cavity (ascites), and lungs (pulmonary edema, pleural effusion). If the patient is in bed, dependent sacral and scrotal edema may develop. Pressing the edematous skin with the finger may leave a depression *(pitting edema).* Edema can indicate volume overload and be a sign of ADHF. It is important to note that not all lower extremity edema is a result of HF. Hypoproteinemia, renal insufficiency, cellulitis, venous stasis, cirrhosis, and certain drugs can cause peripheral edema.

Changes in Urine Output

Urine output may be decreased because of decreased renal perfusion. HF patients often develop resistance to diuretics, which can result in a drop in urinary output. *Nocturia* is the tendency to urinate excessively during the night. It is due to increased renal perfusion in the supine position.

Skin Changes

A low CO can result in decreased perfusion to the extremities, causing *mottling,* a blue or gray skin coloring. The skin may appear dusky because tissue capillary O_2 extraction is increased with chronic HF. Chronic edema can result in pigment changes. A coolness or clammy feeling to touch can occur with poor perfusion. The skin can become dry from over diuresis. It is important to recognize skin signs of other conditions, such as venous stasis, peripheral arterial disease, and cellulitis.

Neurologic Manifestations

Dizziness, lightheadedness, near syncope, or syncope from hypoperfusion to the brain can occur due to reduced CO and/or dysrhythmias. Hypotension from HF medications and hypovolemia are also common causes of neurologic symptoms in chronic HF.

Mental Status and Behavior Changes

Cerebral hypoperfusion may occur because of hypoxia to the brain from decreased CO. The patient or caregiver may report confusion, forgetfulness, inattentiveness, and restlessness. Assess for possible confounding conditions, including neurologic problems, such as stroke or transient ischemic attack (TIA) and psychologic disorders (especially depression and anxiety). About 1 in 5 patients with HF have clinical depression. This doubles the risk of mortality and readmissions.[14] Patients with psychologic disorders have poorer adherence to treatment plans. Screen all HF patients for depression or coexisting mental health conditions.

Sleep Problems

Snoring and daytime sleepiness can indicate sleep apnea, a common condition with chronic HF. Sleep apnea screening questions include those about daytime sleepiness and falling asleep, feeling rested in the morning, frequent nighttime awakenings, and results of a sleep study. Alternatively, insomnia could be due to psychologic issues, including anxiety or depression, or excessive daytime napping. Nocturia may disturb the patient's rest.

Chest Pain

Chest pain or angina can be the result of the reduced CO associated with HF compounded with CAD. Chest pain in HF can also occur due to myocardial stretch from volume overload. Careful questioning and assessment will help distinguish among potential causes for chest pain in the patient with chronic HF.

Weight Changes

Many factors contribute to weight changes. Progressive weight gain in the patient with chronic HF may indicate fluid retention. Renal failure may contribute to fluid retention. Abdominal fullness from ascites and hepatomegaly often causes anorexia and nausea. As HF advances, cardiac *cachexia* with muscle wasting and fat loss can be masked by edema.

Complications of Heart Failure

Pleural Effusion

Pleural effusion, fluid between the 2 tissue layers (pleura) that cover the lung and line the chest wall, is a common complication in HF. Increased capillary hydrostatic pressure in the circulation causes fluid leakage into the pleural space. Pleural effusions may cause dyspnea, cough, and chest pain. Pleural effusion is discussed in Chapter 30.

Dysrhythmias and Dyssynchronous Contraction

Both atrial and ventricular dysrhythmias are common in HF. Structural changes, including myocardial stretch, fibrosis, and chamber dilation, alter the electrical paths of the heart. Early or delayed depolarizations common in HF can trigger dysrhythmias. AF is quite common in patients with HF. The prevalence increases as the severity of HF increases. AF occurs when numerous sites in the atria fire spontaneously and rapidly, and organized atrial depolarization with contraction no longer occurs. Loss of "atrial kick" during systole may contribute to decreased CO and worsening HF symptoms.

AF promotes thrombus formation within the atria. Thrombi can break loose and form emboli, placing patients at significant risk for stroke. Treatment with anticoagulation is a priority if there are no significant contraindications. Treatment with drugs to achieve HR control is important. Other options include cardioversion and ablation. Atrial fibrillation is discussed in Chapter 39.

An enlarged LV and very low LVEF increase the risk for thrombus formation in the LV. Anticoagulant therapy may be considered.

Patients with HF are at risk for dangerous ventricular dysrhythmias (e.g., ventricular tachycardia [VT], ventricular fibrillation [VF]). SCD (sudden loss of cardiac function due to a fatal ventricular tachyarrhythmia) is a major cause of death in those with HF. Patients with HFrEF are at greatest risk for SCD. Guidelines recommend implanting a prophylactic implantable cardioverter-defibrillator (ICD) for patients with an LVEF less than 35%, who are NYHA Class II or III.[1] SCD is discussed in Chapter 37. Dysrhythmias are discussed in Chapter 39.

Ventricular remodeling can lead to dyssynchrony in ventricular contractions. One ventricle may contract before the other ventricle, leading to poor ventricular filling (preload), reduced force of ventricular contraction (systole), and severe mitral regurgitation (MR). This worsens HF symptoms. **Cardiac resynchronization therapy (CRT),** with implantable cardiac devices, can significantly improve patient morbidity and mortality. Many HF patients receive a combination ICD and CRT device, discussed later in the chapter.

Hepatomegaly

HF can lead to severe hepatomegaly as the liver becomes congested with venous blood. The hepatic congestion can lead to impaired liver function. Eventually liver cells die, fibrosis occurs, and cirrhosis can develop (see Chapter 48).

Cardiorenal Syndrome

Reduction in CO results in decreased renal perfusion, decreased glomerular filtration rate, and increased serum creatinine. Neurohormonal activation causes sodium and water retention, worsening HF symptoms and renal function. Impaired renal function with HF is an independent risk factor for HF morbidity and mortality.[1]

Anemia

The primary cause of anemia in chronic HF is chronic kidney insufficiency. Renal vasoconstriction results in the kidney producing less erythropoietin, leading to anemia. Excessive cytokine production also can reduce erythropoietin secretion. The anemia itself can worsen cardiac function due to increased cardiac workload through tachycardia, fluid retention, and increased SV. Because anemia further reduces renal blood flow, it adds stress to the heart and worsens fatigue and other manifestations of chronic HF.

Diagnostic Studies

Diagnosing HF can be challenging. Signs and symptoms may mimic many other medical conditions (e.g., anemia, lung disease). Diagnostic tests for ADHF and chronic HF are outlined in Table 38.6. A primary goal in diagnosis is to find the underlying cause of HF.

An echocardiogram is a valuable, noninvasive diagnostic tool used in patients with HF. The echocardiogram gives information about chamber size and function, LVEF, heart valve function, wall thickness and motion, presence of effusion or thrombus, and intracardiac and pulmonary pressures. This test helps to distinguish between HFrEF and HFpEF. Other useful tests include 12-lead ECG, ambulatory heart monitors, chest x-ray, 6-minute walk test, multigated acquisition (MUGA) scan, cardiopulmonary exercise stress test, cardiac MRI, and cardiac catheterization/angiogram. Polysomnography studies may help

TABLE 38.6 Interprofessional Care

Heart Failure

Both ADHF and Chronic HF	ADHF	Chronic HF
Diagnostic Assessment		
• History and physical assessment • Determine underlying cause • Serum chemistries, cardiac biomarkers, BNP or NT-proBNP level (see Table 35.9), liver function tests, thyroid function tests, CBC, lipid profile, kidney function tests, urinalysis • Chest x-ray • 12-lead ECG • 2-Dimensional echocardiogram (see Table 35.10) • Nuclear imaging studies (see Table 35.10) • Cardiac catheterization (see Table 35.11)	• Measure LV function • Hemodynamic monitoring • Endomyocardial biopsy in select patients	• Cardiopulmonary exercise stress test • 6-min walk test • Sleep studies in select patients
Management		
• Treatment of underlying cause • Drug therapy (Table 38.7) • Circulatory assist devices (e.g., ventricular assist device) • Daily weights • Sodium- and possibly fluid-restricted diet • O_2 by mask or nasal cannula if indicated	• High-Fowler's position • Noninvasive positive pressure ventilation • Circulatory assist device: IABP, ECMO, LVAD • Endotracheal intubation and mechanical ventilation • Vital signs, urine output at least q1hr until stable • Continuous ECG and pulse oximetry monitoring • Hemodynamic monitoring (e.g., intraarterial BP, PAWP, CO) • Cardioversion (e.g., atrial fibrillation) • Ultrafiltration	• Cardiac resynchronization therapy with biventricular pacing and internal cardioverter-defibrillator • Heart transplantation • Rest-activity periods • Dietitian consult • Physical/occupational therapy consult • Cardiac rehabilitation • Home health nursing care (e.g., telehealth monitoring) • Palliative and end-of-life care

identify obstructive sleep apnea. An endomyocardial biopsy may be done during heart catheterization to evaluate for infective or infiltrative disease in patients who develop unexplained, new-onset HF.

Laboratory studies aid in the diagnosis of HF. In general, BNP and N-terminal prohormone of BNP (NT-proBNP) levels correlate positively with the degree of LV failure.[12] Levels are temporarily higher in patients receiving nesiritide (Natrecor) and may remain high in patients with chronic, stable HF. So, it is important to know baseline levels. Increases in BNP or NT-proBNP levels can be caused by conditions other than HF, including pulmonary embolism, renal failure, and acute coronary syndrome.

Interprofessional Care: Acute Decompensated Heart Failure

Mortality and readmission rates for ADHF remain unacceptably high. Professional HF organizations have developed quality improvement initiatives, such as "Get with the Guidelines" and the Acute Decompensated HF Registry (ADHERE), to help HCPs and agencies improve HF outcomes.[1]

Goals of therapy for the patient hospitalized with ADHF include (1) relieving symptoms; (2) optimizing volume status; (3) supporting oxygenation, ventilation, CO, and end organ perfusion; (4) identifying and addressing the cause of the ADHF; (5) avoiding complications; (6) providing patient teaching addressing factors that precipitated HF exacerbation; and (7) planning discharge.

Patients with ADHF need ongoing monitoring and assessment of vital signs, O_2 saturation, weight, mentation, ECGs, and indicators of volume overload and decreased organ perfusion. Findings indicating fluid volume overload include edema, ascites, JVD, a positive hepatojugular reflux test, an S_3 heart sound, crackles, hypoxia, and worsening renal function.

Stable patients with ADHF may be treated in the emergency department (ED) or admitted to a telemetry unit. Assess these patients at least every 4 hours (e.g., vital signs, pulse oximetry) for adequate oxygenation. Record intake, output, and daily weights to evaluate fluid status. If the patient has dyspnea, place in a high-Fowler's position with the feet horizontal in the bed or dangling at the bedside. This position helps decrease venous return by pooling the blood in the extremities and increases the thoracic capacity for breathing.

If unstable, patients are managed in an intensive care unit (ICU). In addition to continual ECG and O_2 saturation monitoring, we assess vital signs and urine output at least hourly. Signs of decreased perfusion include hypotension, decreased urine output, cool extremities, altered mentation, heart murmur, dysrhythmias, and worsening renal and liver function tests. The patient may have hemodynamic monitoring, including arterial BP and pulmonary artery pressures. If a pulmonary artery (PA) catheter is placed, we monitor CO and pulmonary artery wedge pressure (PAWP). PAWP is an indirect measurement of LA filling pressure. A normal PAWP is 6 to 15 mm Hg. Patients with ADHF may have a PAWP as high as 30 mm Hg. Therapies are adjusted to maximize CO and reduce PAWP. Hemodynamic monitoring is discussed in Chapter 35.

Supplemental O_2 helps increase the PaO_2. In severe pulmonary edema, the patient may need noninvasive positive pressure ventilation (e.g., bilevel positive airway pressure [BiPAP]) or intubation and mechanical ventilation. BiPAP also decreases preload. O_2 therapy and ventilatory support is discussed in Chapter 28.

Nonpharmacologic Therapies

Ultrafiltration, or *aquapheresis,* is an option for the patient with volume overload when diuretics have not been effective.[1] It can rapidly remove intravascular fluid volume and excess sodium from the patient's blood while maintaining hemodynamic stability. Hemodialysis can be used for volume overload with renal failure. These treatments are discussed in Chapter 51.

Implantation of CRT, a biventricular pacemaker, may be done in patients with ADHF who meet specific criteria and do not respond to more traditional therapies.

In the ICU, *mechanical cardiac assist devices* are used temporarily to manage worsening HF. An intraaortic balloon pump (IABP) can increase coronary blood flow to the heart muscle and decrease the heart's workload through *counterpulsation.* The IABP is useful in hemodynamically unstable patients because it can decrease PA pressures and systemic vascular resistance (SVR), leading to improved CO. Ventricular assist devices (VADs) can help maintain the pumping action of a weakened heart.

Extracorporeal membrane oxygenation (ECMO) can offer short-term mechanical circulatory support for refractory HF and cardiogenic shock or as a bridge to heart transplant.[15] ECMO requires an ICU setting and an interprofessional team.

Drug Therapy

Drug therapy is essential in treating ADHF (Table 38.7).

Diuretics. Diuretics are the first line for treating patients with volume overload. They decrease sodium reabsorption at various sites within the kidneys, enhancing sodium and water loss. Decreasing intravascular volume with diuretics reduces fluid returning to the LV (preload). This allows for more efficient LV pumping, decreased pulmonary vascular pressures, and improved alveolar gas exchange. IV loop diuretics (e.g., furosemide) by bolus or infusion is preferred. Increased urine output, decreased symptoms, and fluid weight loss indicate effective diuretic therapy. Serum potassium and magnesium levels are continually monitored.

Vasodilators. Patient with ADHF who are not hypotensive receive vasodilators. IV nitroglycerin (NTG) is a primary venodilator that reduces blood return to the right side of the heart. It also improves coronary artery blood flow by dilating the coronary arteries. So, NTG reduces preload, slightly reduces afterload (in high doses), and increases myocardial O_2 supply. Tolerance often develops with continued IV use, requiring higher doses. When titrating IV NTG, monitor BP often (every 5 to 10 minutes) to avoid hypotension. Patients on IV vasodilators may have an indwelling arterial line or continuous noninvasive blood pressure monitoring.

Sodium nitroprusside (Nitropress) is a potent IV arterial vasodilator that reduces both preload and afterload, thus improving myocardial contraction, increasing CO, and reducing pulmonary congestion. Complications of therapy include hypotension and, at high doses, thiocyanate (cyanide) toxicity. It is given in an ICU.

TABLE 38.7 Drug Therapy
Heart Failure

Drug	Mechanism of Action
Anticoagulants (see Table 37.10)	• Prevent thromboembolism • Recommended for patients with an ejection fraction <20% and/or atrial fibrillation
Antidysrhythmic Drugs (see Table 39.9)	• Prevent or treat dysrhythmias
β-Adrenergic Blockers (see Table 36.6) bisoprolol carvedilol (Coreg) metoprolol succinate (Toprol-XL)	• Promote reverse remodeling • ↓ Afterload • Inhibit SNS • Reverse cardiac remodeling • Reduce mortality in patients with chronic HF
Diuretics (see Table 36.7)	
Loop Diuretics bumetanide (Bumex) furosemide (Lasix)	• Block absorption of sodium and chloride in the kidneys at the loop of Henle • ↑ Urine output • ↓ Fluid volume • ↓ Preload • ↓ Pulmonary venous pressure • Relieve symptoms of fluid congestion
Thiazide Diuretics hydrochlorothiazide metolazone (Zaroxolyn)	• Affect electrolyte reabsorption at the distal renal tubule causing sodium and chloride excretion • ↑ Urine output (milder diuretic effect than loop diuretics) • ↓ BP
Aldosterone Antagonists (Potassium-Sparing Diuretics) eplerenone (Inspra) spironolactone (Aldactone)	• Inhibit aldosterone that causes sodium and water retention and antiinflammatory responses in HF • Prevent potassium loss by inhibiting sodium and potassium exchange in the distal tubule • Mild diuretic effect • Reduce mortality and hospitalizations in patients with chronic HF
Osmotic Diuretics dapagliflozin (Farxiga)	• Inhibit SGLT2 activity and modulate reabsorption of glucose in the kidneys, causing glucose excretion in the urine • Osmotic diuretic in HF • Reduces risk of CV death and hospitalization in those with HFrEF
Morphine morphine (MS Contin, Duramorph)	• Bind to opioid receptors • May decrease the chemoreceptor response to hypoxia, and/or cause vasodilation reducing pulmonary congestion • Reduce anxiety
Neprilysin-Angiotensin Receptor Inhibitors sacubitril/valsartan (Entresto)	• Sacubitril inhibits neprilysin, decreasing natriuretic degradation which promotes diuresis, natriuresis • Valsartan selectively blocks angiotensin II receptors • ↓ BP • Dilate venules and arterioles • ↑ Renal blood flow • May decrease mortality and hospitalizations in patients with chronic HF
Positive Inotropes	
β-Adrenergic Agonists[a] dobutamine dopamine	• ↑ Contractility (positive inotropic effect) • ↑ CO • May reduce PAWP • May cause dysrhythmias • ↑ Myocardial O_2 demand
Digitalis Glycoside digoxin	• Weak positive inotrope mostly at higher doses • Reduce effects of RAAS and SNS • May reduce HF symptoms and hospitalization if added to standard therapy for chronic HF
Phosphodiesterase Inhibitor[a] milrinone	• Produce mild vasodilation • ↑ SV and CO • Promote vasodilation
Renin-Angiotensin-Aldosterone System Inhibitors (see Table 36.6)	
ACE Inhibitors benazepril (Lotensin) captopril enalapril (Vasotec) ***Angiotensin II Receptor Blockers*** losartan (Cozaar) valsartan (Diovan)	• Dilate venules and arterioles • ↓ Afterload and SVR • ↑ Renal blood flow • May relieve HF symptoms • Promote reverse remodeling • May reduce mortality and hospitalizations in patients with chronic HF
Selective SA Node Inhibitor ivabradine (Corlanor)	• Selectively inhibits the I *f*-current in the SA node • ↓ HR • May reduce CVD death and hospitalizations in patients with HFrEF in sinus rhythm with a HR ≥70 bpm • Used only for patients with chronic HF
Vasodilators isosorbide dinitrate/hydralazine (BiDil) nitrates (e.g., nitroglycerin, isosorbide dinitrate [Isordil]) nitroprusside (Nitropress)[a]	• ↓ Afterload • Dilate the arterioles of the kidneys, leading to increased renal perfusion and fluid loss • ↓ BP • ↓ Preload • Nesiritide may reduce PAWP • May relieve HF symptoms (e.g., dyspnea) • Isosorbide dinitrate/hydralazine, fixed dose, may reduce morbidity and mortality in Blacks with HFrEF and NYHA Class III–IV symptoms

[a]Used for ADHF only.

DRUG ALERT

Sodium Nitroprusside (Nitropress)

- Record baseline BP and continuously monitor during administration.
- Arterial BP monitoring is recommended during drug infusion.
- Too rapid rate of IV infusion can reduce BP too quickly and cause hypotension.
- Headache, dizziness, nausea, agitation, and restlessness can occur.
- Monitor for toxic thiocyanate (drug by-product) levels if infusion is greater than 3 mcg/kg/min.

IV nesiritide is a recombinant form of BNP used for short-term treatment of ADHF after a failed response to IV diuretics.[1] As a venous and arterial vasodilator, its main effects include a reduction in PAWP and decrease in dyspnea. The primary adverse effect is symptomatic hypotension, so we carefully monitor BP.

Morphine. Morphine dilates pulmonary and systemic blood vessels, reducing preload and afterload. It is often given in small IV boluses to relieve the dyspnea associated with ADHF. Monitor the patient closely. Morphine has serious adverse effects, including respiratory depression requiring mechanical ventilation.

Positive inotropes. Inotropic drugs increase myocardial contractility and are used for patients with low CO despite adequate or high fluid volume. Drugs include β-agonists (e.g., dopamine, dobutamine, norepinephrine [Levophed]) and phosphodiesterase inhibitors (milrinone). β-Agonists are used as a short-term treatment of ADHF. In addition to increasing myocardial contractility and SVR, dopamine dilates the renal blood vessels and enhances urine output. Unlike dopamine, dobutamine is a selective β-agonist that works mainly on the β_1-receptors in the heart. It does not increase SVR. Effectiveness of inotropes is evaluated by assessing for improved CO, BP, urine output, and reduced filling pressures.

DRUG ALERT

Dopamine and Dobutamine

- Monitor IV site. Tissue necrosis and sloughing can occur with drug extravasation.
- High doses may cause ventricular dysrhythmias.

Milrinone has both inotropic and vasodilator properties. Milrinone improves myocardial contractility, increases CO, decreases afterload, and reduces BP. Like dopamine and dobutamine, this drug is available only for IV use. Adverse effects include dysrhythmias, thrombocytopenia, and liver toxicity.

Digitalis is a weaker positive inotrope that can be added if symptoms persist after other medications have been started. Digoxin can mildly increase contractility but also increases myocardial O_2 consumption. It can reduce heart rate, especially in those with atrial fibrillation. We monitor digoxin levels if toxicity is suspected and make dose adjustments based on renal function. Serum potassium and magnesium levels must be maintained.

Current evidence recommends the use of inotropic therapy only for the short-term management of patients with ADHF who have not responded to conventional drug therapy (e.g., diuretics, vasodilators, morphine).[1] Use continuous cardiac monitoring with all positive inotropic drugs as they can cause life-threatening dysrhythmias.

! SAFETY ALERT

Infusion Pumps

- To control the rate and assist with titration, use an infusion pump whenever you are giving IV vasodilators and inotropes.
- Ideally, pumps with drug libraries can help to avoid rates and doses that are out of the safe range for the drug.

Interprofessional Care: Chronic Heart Failure

The evolution of evidence-based medication and device therapies has dramatically improved the potential for better patient outcomes with chronic HF. The Heart Failure Society of America (HFSA) and the AHA have regularly published and updated guidelines on therapies for HF. Specialized inpatient, transitional, and ambulatory HF units are staffed with interprofessional HF teams (Table 38.6).

Chronic HF therapies are tailored to the patient based on co-morbid conditions. The goals of chronic HF therapies include (1) optimal symptom management, (2) decreased mortality and morbidity, and (3) minimizing side effects. Specifically, these therapies treat the underlying cause and contributing factors, maximize CO, improve ventricular function, improve quality of life (QOL), and preserve target organ function.

In a person with HF, the blood may not be adequately oxygenated, reducing O_2 saturation. The use of supplemental O_2 improves saturation and helps meet tissue O_2 needs. This helps to relieve patient dyspnea and fatigue. Ongoing pulse oximetry monitors the need for and effectiveness of O_2 therapy.

Physical and emotional rest allows the patient to conserve energy and decreases the need for more O_2. The degree of rest recommended depends on the severity of HF. A patient with severe HF may be on bed rest. A patient with mild to moderate HF can be ambulatory with restricted activity. Urge the patient to take part in prescribed activities with adequate recovery periods. Consider a structured exercise program, such as cardiac rehabilitation, for all patients with chronic HF. These programs are associated with decreased hospitalizations, reduced mortality, improved QOL, and less depression.[16]

Drug Therapy

The cornerstone of drug therapy in chronic HF is neurohormonal blockade. The results of neurohormonal blockade include decreased plasma aldosterone levels, decreased SNS activity, vasodilation, and sodium and water excretion. Drug therapy for chronic HF is outlined in Table 38.7.

Evidence-based drug therapy for HFrEF

ACE inhibitors. ACE inhibitors are first-line drugs to decrease mortality, hospitalizations, and symptoms in patients with HFrEF.[1] ACE inhibitors block the RAAS by inhibiting the conversion of angiotensin I to angiotensin II. They reduce afterload and SVR and slow ventricular remodeling by inhibiting ventricular hypertrophy.

Major side effects include symptomatic hypotension, persistent dry cough, hyperkalemia, angioedema (allergic reaction involving edema of the face and airways), and renal insufficiency (in high doses). Aging and renal insufficiency slow the metabolism of ACE inhibitors and may lead to increased serum drug levels. We monitor renal function and serum potassium levels. Examples of ACE inhibitors are shown in Table 38.7. More information about ACE inhibitors is found in Chapter 36.

DRUG ALERT

Captopril

- May cause severe hypotension and hyperkalemia.
- Monitor patient for first-dose hypotension (first-dose syncope).
- Skipping doses or stopping the drug can result in rebound HTN.
- Angioedema, a rare adverse effect, can be sudden and life-threatening.

Angiotensin II receptor blockers. For patients who are unable to tolerate ACE inhibitors, angiotensin II receptor blockers (ARBs) are recommended.[1] They prevent the vasoconstrictor and aldosterone-secreting effects of angiotensin II by binding to the angiotensin II receptor sites. ARBs promote afterload reduction and vasodilation. The side effects are similar to those of ACE inhibitors except that ARBs do not typically cause a cough. Angioedema is less common. Monitoring is similar to that for ACE inhibitors.

Neprilysin-angiotensin receptor inhibitors. Sacubitril/valsartan (Entresto) is a combination of a neprilysin inhibitor (sacubitril) and an ARB (valsartan). This drug provides dual blockade of the RAAS and the natriuretic peptide system. Sacubitril, a recombinant form of BNP, inhibits neprilysin, an enzyme that degrades natriuretic peptides. Sacubitril inhibition allows for more available circulating BNP. This results in decreased SVR, afterload, and CVP and increased natriuresis and diuresis. This drug is an alternative to ACE inhibitors and ARBs in patients meeting criteria with symptomatic HFrEF. It reduces death and hospitalization. Monitor patients for hypotension, renal insufficiency, and angioedema.[17]

Aldosterone antagonists. Spironolactone (Aldactone) and eplerenone (Inspra) are potassium-sparing diuretics that inhibit aldosterone activation. They work by binding to receptors at the aldosterone-dependent sodium-potassium exchange site in the distal renal tubule, where they have a mild diuretic effect. They may prolong survival in patients with HFrEF.[1] Carefully monitor serum potassium levels and renal function.

DRUG ALERT

Spironolactone (Aldactone)

- Monitor potassium levels during treatment.
- Use with caution in patients taking digoxin, since hyperkalemia may reduce the effects of digoxin.
- Teach patient to avoid foods high in potassium (e.g., bananas, oranges).
- Assess male patients for gynecomastia, a common side effect of long-term use.

β-Adrenergic blockers. β-Blockers directly block the negative effects of the SNS (e.g., increased HR) on the failing heart. Three β-blockers decrease mortality in patients with HFrEF: metoprolol succinate (Toprol-XL), bisoprolol, and carvedilol (Coreg). They may also increase LVEF. The improvement in LVEF is dose-related, so we give the highest tolerated dose.[1] However, because β-blockers can reduce myocardial contractility, care must be taken in patients with volume overload. After a low starting dose, the dose is increased every 2 weeks as tolerated. Major side effects include worsening of HF symptoms, hypotension, fatigue, and bradycardia.

DRUG ALERT

Carvedilol (Coreg)

- Obtain standing BP 1 hr after dosing to assess tolerance.
- Overdose can cause profound bradycardia, hypotension, bronchospasm, and cardiogenic shock.
- Abrupt withdrawal may result in sweating, palpitations, and headaches.

Ivabradine (Corlanor). Ivabradine selectively inhibits a particular sodium/potassium current in the SA node, causing a decreased HR. Patients with HFrEF who are in sinus rhythm with an HR greater than 70 bpm and have symptoms despite optimal doses of other medications may have fewer hospitalizations when taking Ivabradine. Monitor patients for bradycardia and lightheadedness.[17]

Hydralazine/isosorbide dinitrate combination (Bidil). This drug is a combination of 2 vasodilators: hydralazine and isosorbide dinitrate. It can significantly reduce mortality and improve LVEF and exercise tolerance by reducing afterload through vasodilation. The drug is specifically effective in Black persons with HFrEF already receiving optimal doses of other evidence-based medications.[1] Major side effects include hypotension and headache. Like other nitrates, it should not be used with phosphodiesterase inhibitors, such as sildenafil (Viagra).

Digitalis. Digitalis (digoxin), a weak positive inotrope, acts mainly as a neurohormonal modulator that reduces the effects of the SNS and suppresses renin secretion from the kidneys. Low-dose digitalis decreases HF hospitalizations and symptoms in patients who are still symptomatic despite standard HF therapies.[1,13] There is no mortality benefit. Better outcomes occur with digoxin serum levels under 0.9 ng/mL. Higher serum levels are associated with increased mortality and digoxin toxicity. Dose should be based on body mass, renal function, and concomitant medications. The usual daily dose in HF is 0.125 mg. Monitor renal function and serum potassium levels.

Dapagliflozin (Farxiga). Dapagliflozin, a sodium-glucose cotransporter-2 (SGLT-2) inhibitor, reduces the risk of CV death and hospitalization for patients with HFrEF. This medication was developed to treat type 2 diabetes by stopping absorption of extra glucose from the urine. The drug's effects in HF appear to be related to the unique osmotic diuretic properties. Side effects include dehydration and serious urinary tract and yeast infections. Use with caution in older adults and those with kidney disease, low BP, or taking diuretics. Monitor volume status and kidney function.

Medications for symptom management

Diuretics. Diuretics reduce symptoms of fluid overload in both HFrEF and HFpEF. They reduce edema, pulmonary venous pressure, and preload by promoting renal excretion of sodium and water (see Table 36.7). Loop diuretics (e.g., furosemide [Lasix], bumetanide [Bumex]) act on the ascending loop of Henle to promote sodium, chloride, and water excretion. Potential problems include low serum potassium levels, ototoxicity, and possible allergic reaction in patients sensitive to sulfa-type drugs. Thiazide diuretics inhibit sodium reabsorption in the distal tubule, promoting excretion of sodium and water. They can severely lower potassium levels.

In chronic HF, the patient receives the lowest effective dose of diuretic. Side effects of diuretics include dehydration, hypotension, orthostasis, renal problems, and electrolyte imbalances. Diuretic resistance in HF patients may require increasing doses and adding different types of diuretics.

Device Therapy

Patients with HFrEF may benefit from implantable cardiac devices. HF patients must be on appropriate therapies before becoming a candidate for device therapy. In patients with an LVEF less than 35%, neurohormonal effects and cardiac remodeling can result in dyssynchronous contraction of the LV and RV, contributing to poor ventricular filling and reduced CO. CRT (biventricular pacing) is recommended for these patients.[1] With CRT, an extra pacing lead is placed through the coronary sinus to a coronary vein of the LV to coordinate right and left ventricular contractions (Fig. 38.4). They are also at significant risk for SCD. An ICD is recommended for primary prevention of SCD.[1] Patients with symptomatic HFrEF often need both CRT and an ICD. Combination implantable devices are available. Pacemakers and defibrillators are discussed in Chapter 39. Mechanical assist devices available to sustain HF patients with deteriorating function and those awaiting cardiac transplant are discussed later in the chapter.

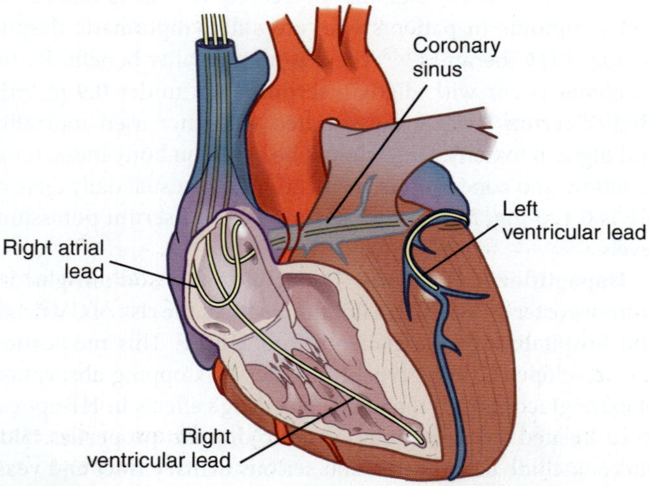

Fig. 38.4 Placement of pacing leads in cardiac resynchronization therapy.

> **CHECK YOUR PRACTICE**
>
> Your patient is scheduled for a biventricular pacemaker for worsening HF. She currently has a demand pacemaker and asks you why she needs this new one.
>
> - How would you respond to her question?

Remote Monitoring of Physiologic Data

Implanted ICD and CRT devices can be used to remotely monitor patients. Information from these devices can predict HF decompensation and help with clinical decision making. Parameters monitored remotely include BP, weight, HR trends (can evaluate adequacy of beta blockade, increasing HR can indicate worsening HF), HR variability (HRV, a reduction is associated with higher risk for exacerbation and hospitalization), patient activity level, dysrhythmias, and intrathoracic impedance (an indicator of intrathoracic fluid level providing early detection of impending ADHF).[18] Implantable remote hemodynamic monitoring is also possible. A PA sensor can be implanted during a right heart catheterization. It can provide information about HR, systolic, diastolic, and mean pulmonary artery pressures (PAP). Early detection of increases in intracardiac pressures, PAP, and fluid status in patients with both HFrEF and HFpEF allows for proactive management and decreased hospitalizations.[19]

Nutrition Therapy

A high-sodium diet and not taking prescribed medications as directed are common reasons HF patients are readmitted to the hospital. Take a detailed diet history. Review what foods the patient eats, and when, where, and how often the patient dines out. Assess the cultural value of food. Use this information to help the patient and caregiver in making diet choices within an individualized and culturally sensitive diet plan. The AHA website has helpful diet guidelines for patients with HF.

HF guidelines vary on sodium restriction. There is agreement that excess sodium may worsen HF symptoms and lead to an exacerbation. A low sodium intake may lead to adverse events in later stages of HFrEF. The degree of sodium restriction depends on the severity of the HF and the effectiveness of diuretic therapy. Generally, sodium intake is restricted to 2 grams per day (Table 38.8). Teach the patient what foods are low and high in sodium content and how to read labels. Review how to find sodium content per serving and the number of servings per package (Fig. 38.5). Teach ways to enhance food flavors without the use of salt (e.g., adding lemon juice, spices). Discuss the high sodium content of most restaurant foods.

The patient with mild to moderate HF usually does not need fluid restrictions. Fluid restrictions may be needed for stage D HF patients with persistent fluid retention despite appropriate sodium restriction.

To monitor fluid status, tell patients to weigh themselves at the same time each day. To ensure valid trending, this should be before breakfast, using the same scale, and wearing the same type of clothing. For patients with visual limitations, suggest scales with large numbers or an audible response. Tell patients to call the HCP about a weight gain of 3 lb (1.4 kg) over 2 days or a 3- to 5-lb (2.3-kg) gain over a week.[13]

TABLE 38.8 Nutrition Therapy

Low-Sodium Diets

General Principles

- Do not add salt or seasonings containing sodium when preparing food.[a]
- Do not use salt at the table.[a]
- 1 tsp of salt equals 2.3 g of sodium.
- Avoid high-sodium foods (e.g., canned soups, processed meats, cheese, frozen meals).
- Limit milk products to 2 cups daily.

Sample Menu Plans for 2400-mg Sodium Diet

Breakfast	Sodium (mg)
⅔ cup bran cereal	161
(⅔ cup Shredded Wheat cereal)[b]	3
1 slice whole-wheat bread	149
1 medium banana	1
6 oz fruit yogurt, fat free	85
1 cup fat-free milk	126
2 Tbsp jelly	5
Coffee, 8 oz	5
Lunch	
Chicken breast sandwich	
2 slices (3 oz) chicken breast, skinless	65
2 slices whole wheat bread	299
1 slice (¾ oz) American cheese	328
(1 slice [¾ oz] Swiss cheese, natural)[b]	54
Large-leaf romaine lettuce	1
2 slices tomato	90
1 Tbsp mayonnaise, low fat	90
1 medium peach	7
Dinner	
¾ cup vegetarian spaghetti sauce	459
(6 oz no-salt-added tomato paste)[b]	260
1 cup spaghetti	1
3 Tbsp parmesan cheese	389
Spinach salad	
1 cup fresh spinach leaves	24
¼ cup fresh carrots (grated)	10
¼ cup fresh mushrooms (sliced)	1
2 Tbsp vinaigrette dressing	0
½ cup canned pears, juice pack	4
½ cup corn, cooked from frozen	4
Snack	
⅓ cup almonds	4
¼ cup dried apricots	3
6 oz fruit yogurt, fat free	85

[a]1 tsp of salt equals 2.3 g of sodium.
[b]Substitutes to reduce to 1500-mg sodium diet.

NURSING MANAGEMENT: HEART FAILURE

Assessment

Subjective and objective data that you should obtain from a patient with HF are shown in Table 38.9. Carefully review the patient's current prescription and over-the-counter (OTC) drugs. Patients with chronic HF often take multiple other medications for coexisting conditions and underlying CVD. OTC medications known to pose significant risk to people with HF include nonsteroidal antiinflammatory drugs (NSAIDs), high-dose aspirin, ephedrine, pseudoephedrine, and diet pills. NSAIDs can increase sodium retention and worsen HF.

Review the patient's diet to assess issues related to HF. Explore the patient's chronic health problems as they may exacerbate HF, affecting the plan of care and the timing and choice of therapies. For example, a patient with sleep apnea may minimize some HF symptoms by using a continuous positive airway pressure device at night.

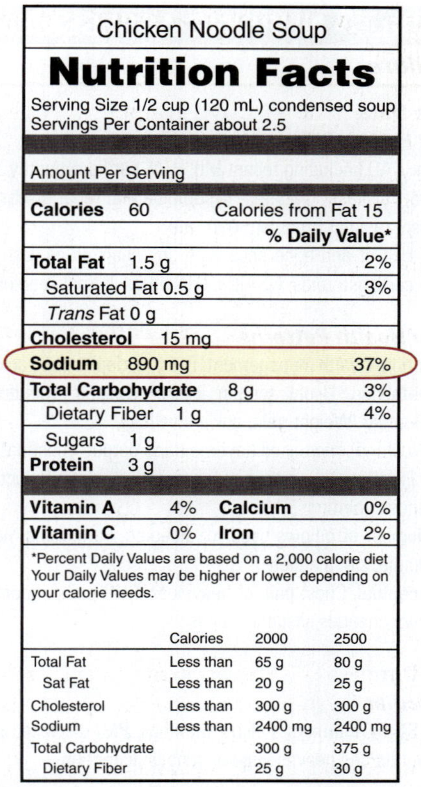
Chicken Noodle Soup

Nutrition Facts

Serving Size 1/2 cup (120 mL) condensed soup
Servings Per Container about 2.5

Amount Per Serving

Calories 60 Calories from Fat 15

% Daily Value*

Total Fat 1.5 g	2%
Saturated Fat 0.5 g	3%
Trans Fat 0 g	
Cholesterol 15 mg	
Sodium 890 mg	37%
Total Carbohydrate 8 g	3%
Dietary Fiber 1 g	4%
Sugars 1 g	
Protein 3 g	
Vitamin A 4%	Calcium 0%
Vitamin C 0%	Iron 2%

*Percent Daily Values are based on a 2,000 calorie diet Your Daily Values may be higher or lower depending on your calorie needs.

	Calories	2000	2500
Total Fat	Less than	65 g	80 g
Sat Fat	Less than	20 g	25 g
Cholesterol	Less than	300 g	300 g
Sodium	Less than	2400 mg	2400 mg
Total Carbohydrate		300 g	375 g
Dietary Fiber		25 g	30 g

Fig. 38.5 Typical nutrition label. Note that a single serving (½ cup) provides more than one third of the daily recommended intake of sodium.

Clinical Problems

Clinical problems for the patient with HF include:

- Activity intolerance
- Fatigue
- Fluid imbalance
- Health maintenance alteration
- Impaired cardiac function
- Impaired respiratory function
- Inadequate tissue perfusion

More information on clinical problems and interventions for the patient with HF is presented in eNursing Care Plan 38.1 on the website for this chapter.

Planning

Nursing care focuses on the priority problems of decreased CO, impaired oxygenation, fluid overload, intolerance of physical activity, and managing a complex medication regimen.

TABLE 38.9 NURSING ASSESSMENT

Heart Failure

Subjective Data

Important Health Information

Health history: CAD (including recent MI), HTN, cardiomyopathy, valve or congenital heart disease, diabetes, hyperlipidemia, renal disease, thyroid or lung disease, rapid or irregular heart rate

Medications: Use of and adherence with any heart drugs. Use of diuretics, estrogens, corticosteroids, NSAIDs, OTC drugs, herbal supplements

Functional Health Patterns

Health perception–health management: Fatigue, depression, anxiety

Nutritional-metabolic: Usual sodium intake. Nausea, vomiting, anorexia, stomach bloating. Weight gain, ankle swelling

Elimination: Nocturia, decreased daytime urine output, constipation

Activity-exercise: Dyspnea, orthopnea, cough (e.g., dry, productive). Palpitations, dizziness, fainting

Sleep-rest: Number of pillows used for sleeping. Paroxysmal nocturnal dyspnea, insomnia, sleep apnea

Cognitive-perceptual: Chest pain or heaviness. RUQ pain, abdominal discomfort. Behavior changes, visual changes

Objective Data

Cardiovascular

Tachycardia, S_3, S_4, murmurs. Pulsus alternans. PMI displaced inferiorly and posteriorly, lifts and heaves, jugular venous distention

Gastrointestinal

Abdominal distention, hepatosplenomegaly, ascites

Neurologic

Restlessness, confusion, decreased attention or memory

Respiratory

Tachypnea, crackles, wheezes. Frothy, blood-tinged sputum

Skin

Cool, diaphoretic skin. Cyanosis or pallor. Peripheral edema (right-sided HF)

Possible Diagnostic Findings

Altered serum electrolytes (especially Na^+ and K^+), ↑ BUN, creatinine, or liver function tests. ↑ NT-proBNP or BNP. Chest x-ray showing cardiomegaly, pulmonary congestion, and interstitial pulmonary edema. Echocardiogram showing increased chamber size, decreased wall motion, decreased LVEF or normal LVEF with evidence of diastolic dysfunction (abnormal relaxation/filling). Atrial and ventricular enlargement on ECG. ↓ O_2 saturation

The overall goals for the patient with HF include (1) decrease in symptoms (e.g., shortness of breath, fatigue); (2) decrease in peripheral edema; (3) increase in exercise tolerance; (4) adherence with the treatment plan, including appropriate evidence-based medication and device therapies; and (5) no complications related to HF.

◆ Implementation

Health Promotion

Communication and joint decision making that includes the patient, caregiver, and interprofessional team promotes high-quality, patient-centered care. Aggressively identify and treat risk factors in the patient with stage A HF in order to prevent or slow the progression to symptomatic HF.[20] Patients with obesity, metabolic syndrome, diabetes, HTN, and hyperlipidemia are already at stage A HF. Recommended lifestyle modifications begin with weight management, diet, and regular exercise. Often, medications are needed. Encourage patients to get recommended vaccinations. Patients with valve disease contributing to HF should be evaluated for valve repair or replacement. Coronary revascularization should be considered in patients with CAD. Antidysrhythmic drugs or pacing therapy may be indicated for patients with serious dysrhythmias or conduction disturbances.

◆ Acute Care

Many persons with HF have 1 or more episodes of ADHF. Common precipitating factors include respiratory infections, dysrhythmias, acute coronary syndrome, uncontrolled HTN, and nonadherence to medications and/or diet. Patients with ADHF are usually stabilized in the ED, then admitted to an ICU, intermediate care unit, or specialized HF unit with continuous ECG monitoring.

Successful HF care depends on several important principles: (1) HF is a progressive disease; (2) treatment plans are established with QOL goals; (3) symptom management depends heavily on adherence to self-management protocols (e.g., daily weights, diet, exercise, recognizing signs and symptoms of decompensation) and drug and device therapies; (4) precipitating factors, etiologies, and contributing conditions must be addressed; (5) complex care needs often require care across settings, increasing risk for fragmented care; and (6) support systems are essential to the success of the treatment plan.

◆ Ambulatory Care

Transitional care programs and protocols help to ensure coordination and continuity of health care as patients transfer between settings. Intensive disease management programs that include extensive patient education on self-management and exercise and close home surveillance follow-up by nurses can reduce short-term readmission rates in the highest risk patients.[21]

Goals of ambulatory HF care include symptom management, QOL maintenance, identifying and mitigating factors precipitating ADHF and hospitalization, and closely monitoring responses to and potential side effects of therapies. HF is a chronic and progressive condition that requires lifelong therapies. Include the patient and caregivers in the overall care plan (Boxes 38.3 and 38.4). Help them develop a clear action plan for response to signs and symptoms of impending exacerbation. A patient and caregiver guide for the patient with HF is shown in Table 38.10.

Home health (HH) professionals can be a vital part of the ambulatory and transitional care HF team. HH nurses often use individualized care protocols coordinated with the patient and HCP to identify worsening HF (e.g., weight gain, increased dyspnea). Many HH agencies offer specialized HF programs. Telehealth and device remote monitoring technology (e.g., electronic scale, BP cuff, pulse oximeter) can collect physiologic and

BOX 38.3 ETHICAL/LEGAL DILEMMAS

Competence

Situation

M.T., a 60-year-old man, has been waiting for a heart transplant for 6 months. He has been in the intensive care unit (ICU) for 1 month with a ventricular assist device (VAD). He recently had a stroke, which is a complication of the device. It left him paralyzed on his right side. He is only able to answer yes/no questions by shaking his head. He has needed mechanical ventilation since his stroke. For the past 2 weeks, he has needed hemodialysis because of renal failure. Recently, when you suction him, he turns his head away from you and bites down on the endotracheal tube. Although he does not have an advance directive, his wife and daughter tell you that, on many occasions before these events, he expressed that he would not want to live if he lost his independence. His wife and daughter request to have the mechanical ventilator withdrawn.

Ethical/Legal Points for Consideration

- Decisional capacity for informed consent related to treatment decisions involves 4 elements: (1) information provided about possible treatment options must be understood by patients, (2) patients must have the capacity to deliberate about the treatment choices and their consequences, (3) patients' treatment decisions must be freely chosen and made without coercion, and (4) patients must be able to communicate their decisions.
- Legal competence, as determined by the courts, has a low threshold. The ability to respond to questions by signaling a yes or no may be enough to prove understanding of the questions, ability to discriminate between choices, and ability to communicate choices, providing that the answers make sense and are appropriate. Review how your state defines legal competence.
- Next of kin are the legal decision makers in the absence of advance directives if the patient is unable to make decisions for himself. Decisional capacity should be tested without assuming it is absent.
- Some courts have accepted past assertions of preferences, past behavior, and assertions of their parties as evidence to support end-of-life preferences in the absence of advance directives.
- Know your agency's policies and local laws and regulations about informed consent and end-of-life decision making.

Discussion Questions

1. What would you do next given M.T.'s behavior and the information from his wife?
2. What are your feelings and concerns about caring for a patient for whom withdrawal of treatment will result in death?

symptom data (Fig. 38.6).[17,18] Results can be sent to the HCP via telephone or secure website. In response to collected data, therapeutic interventions, such as a temporary increase in diuretic therapy, can be implemented to improve function and prevent hospitalization.

Teach the patient the basic mechanism of action of medications and signs of drug toxicity in easily understood terms. Effective self-care includes proper technique in taking a pulse (for a full minute) and use of home monitoring equipment. The patient should understand when to hold heart rate–lowering medications, such as β-blockers and digoxin. If patients are taking diuretic and/or potassium supplement medications, teach them the signs and symptoms of hypokalemia and hyperkalemia. These include weakness, fatigue, constipation, and muscle cramping.

BOX 38.4 EVIDENCE-BASED PRACTICE

Decreasing Readmissions for Heart Failure

N.C. is an 82-year-old female admitted to the cardiac unit with acute HF. Her medical record shows she had an MI 2 years ago. She has been admitted to the hospital 6 times in the last 18 months. N.C. is slightly short of breath when she speaks but has no dyspnea at rest. Her ankles have 1+ edema. Per report of the ED nurse, she received IV furosemide and had an output of 1200 mL before her transfer to the cardiac unit. Her current prescribed daily medications include metoprolol and lisinopril. N.C. is unable to confirm this information but tells you she takes 2 white pills when she remembers. She says she lives alone but her daughter sometimes stops by, but she cannot recall when her daughter last visited. The daughter arrives after she gets off work and tells you she sees her mother several times a week.

Making Clinical Decisions

Synthesis of Best Available Evidence

Readmission for HF is a quality measure. Health care agencies devote extensive resources to trying to minimize the need for patient readmission. Patients with HF who have unrecognized cognitive impairment have higher readmission rates and mortality than persons with intact cognition.

Clinician Expertise

As part of your unit's admission protocol for patients over 70, you complete a Mini-Cog screening for cognitive impairment. N.C. recalls only 1 of the 3 words; she draws the clock face but cannot place the hands for 11:10. You report these findings to the HCP during admission rounds. The patient's daughter, who was present for this screening, asks the HCP about the meaning of the results. The HCP says the findings suggest cognitive impairment and tells her additional measures may be needed to address N.C.'s living situation and her ability to manage her HF. After the HCP leaves, her daughter asks you what can be done to keep her mother out of the hospital. After determining the daughter's understanding of the effects of HF, you suggest including her in all education provided to her mother. You explain that caregiver engagement in education has shown to support better outcomes for patients like N.C. with HF. You confirm with the HF nurse navigator the daughter's interest in being involved in disease management education.

Patient Preferences and Values

N.C.'s daughter tells you, "I thought the heart attack was going to be the end of her. I want to learn everything I can to help her manage the heart failure."

Implications for Nursing Practice

1. What are important topics related to HF management that should be discussed with N.C.'s daughter?
2. How can you continue to involve N.C. in HF self-management despite her cognitive impairment?
3. What other resources can you offer to N.C. and her daughter?

Reference for Evidence

Agarwal KS, Bhimaraj A, Xu J, et al.: Decreasing heart failure readmissions among older patients with cognitive impairment by engaging caregivers, *J Cardiovasc Nurs* 35:253–261, 2020.

Exercise training (e.g., CR) can improve symptoms of chronic HF. Exercise for patients with HF is safe and improves overall sense of well-being. It has been associated with reduced mortality.[16] Tailor exercise programs based on what the patient most enjoys doing. Teach the patient about the importance of rest periods, especially after exertion, and energy-conserving behaviors. Changes may be needed if the environment involves

TABLE 38.10 PATIENT & CAREGIVER TEACHING

Heart Failure

Include the following instructions when teaching the patient and caregiver about the management of heart failure:

Diet Therapy

- Consult the diet plan and list of permitted and restricted foods.
- Adhere to specific sodium restriction guidelines outlined by your HCP.
- Read labels to assess sodium content. Check the labels of over-the-counter drugs, such as laxatives, cough medicines, and antacids for sodium content.
- Avoid using salt when preparing foods or adding salt to foods.
- Weigh yourself at the same time each day, preferably in the morning, using the same scale and wearing similar clothes.
- Eat small, frequent meals.

Activity Program

- Increase walking and other activities gradually, provided they do not cause fatigue or dyspnea.
- Consider a cardiac rehabilitation program.
- Avoid extremes of heat and cold.

Ongoing Monitoring

- Know the signs and symptoms of worsening HF. These include increasing dyspnea, cough, orthopnea, PND, weight gain, edema, fluid retention, fatigue, and tiredness with physical activity.
- Recall the symptoms when illness began. Reappearance of previous symptoms may indicate a recurrence.
- Report at once any of the following to the HCP:
  - Weight gain of 3 lb (1.4 kg) in 2 days, or 3–5 lb (2.3 kg) in a week
  - Difficulty breathing, especially with activity or when lying flat
  - Waking up breathless at night
  - Frequent dry, hacking cough, especially when lying down
  - Fatigue, weakness
  - Swelling of ankles, feet, or abdomen. Swelling of face or difficulty breathing (if taking ACE inhibitors)
  - Nausea with abdominal swelling, pain, and tenderness
  - Dizziness or fainting
- Follow up with HCP on regular basis.
- Consider joining a local support group with your family members and/or caregiver(s).

Health Promotion

- Obtain annual influenza vaccination.
- Obtain pneumococcal and COVID-19 vaccines.
- Develop plan to reduce risk factors (e.g., BP control, tobacco cessation, blood glucose/Hb A1C control, weight reduction).

Rest

- Plan a regular daily rest and activity program.
- After exertion, such as exercise and ADLs, plan a rest period.
- Consider shorter working hours or schedule rest period during working hours.
- Avoid emotional upsets. Share any concerns, fears, feelings of depression, with HCP.

Drug Therapy

- Take each drug as prescribed.
- Develop a system (e.g., daily chart, weekly pillbox) to ensure drugs are taken.
- Count pulse rate each day before taking drugs (if appropriate). Know the limits that your HCP wants for your pulse rate.
- Take BP at determined intervals (if appropriate). Know your target BP limits.
- Know signs and symptoms of orthostatic hypotension and how to prevent them.
- If taking anticoagulants, know signs and symptoms of internal bleeding (bleeding gums, increased bruises, blood in stool or urine) and what to do.
- Know your INR and target range if taking warfarin (Coumadin) and how often to have blood checked.

Fig. 38.6 Home-based telehealth monitoring unit. (Used with permission from Honeywell HomMed.)

an increased cardiac workload (e.g., frequent climbing of stairs). Consult with a physical therapist or occupational therapist as needed.

◆ End-Stage Heart Failure Therapy

Therapeutic options for stage D HF patients include (1) chronic inotropic therapy, (2) mechanical circulatory support (MCS) devices, (3) palliative care and hospice (with or without ICD deactivation), and (4) heart transplant. Patients who are not eligible for heart transplant may be candidates for lifelong MCS. MCS devices have significantly improved outcomes and QOL for patients with end-stage HF. MCS started before onset of severe right HF and systemic organ failure reduces mortality.[13]

◆ Palliative and End-of-Life Care

HF mortality rates remain high. One in 5 persons with HF dies within a year of diagnosis. The estimated 5-year survival rate is worse than for most types of cancer. Repeated hospitalizations and ED visits for ADHF predict end-stage HF.[1,17]

The ACCF and AHA provide guidelines for patients with end-stage HF (stage D).[1] End-of-life discussions and management include advanced directives and information about advanced HF therapies (e.g., VADs, heart transplants), palliative care, and hospice.

Palliative care may be appropriate early in the course of HF in conjunction with other therapies intended to prolong life. Palliative nursing care emphasizes (1) unifying the patient, family, and health care team in formulating a plan of care; (2) aggressive symptom management; (3) avoiding therapies that are not effective and may prolong suffering; (4) integrating emotional and spiritual support for patient and family; and (5) determining when a patient may be ready to consider hospice care.

Patients with advanced CVD are eligible for hospice when (1) an HCP certifies that a life expectancy of 6 months or less is expected assuming the disease takes its normal course, (2) the patient has received optimal medical treatment and is not a candidate for further invasive procedures, and (3) the patient is assessed at NYHA Class IV. End-stage HF patients who meet hospice criteria are often referred late or not at all. Challenges in referring these patients to hospice include (1) difficulties with accurate life expectancy prediction, (2) reluctance to accept a DNR order due to multiple resuscitation survivals and implantable devices, and (3) a lack of patient and family understanding as to the chronic and terminal nature of HF.[22]

End-of-life nursing care of HF patients includes ongoing assessment and evaluation of interventions for effectiveness. Strategies include patient and caregiver support, drug therapies, and nondrug therapies. Palliative and end-of-life care are discussed in Chapter 10.

◆ Evaluation

The expected outcomes are that the patient with HF will:

- Maintain adequate O_2/CO_2 exchange at the alveolar-capillary membrane to meet O_2 needs of the body
- Maintain adequate blood pumped by the heart to meet metabolic demands of the body
- Have a reduction or absence of edema and stable baseline weight
- Achieve a realistic program of activity that balances physical activity with energy-conserving activities

MECHANICAL CIRCULATORY SUPPORT DEVICES

MCS devices decrease cardiac work and improve organ perfusion in patients with HF when conventional drug therapy is no longer adequate. MCS devices can help carefully selected patients for short-term management, long-term and bridge-to-transplant management, or as destination therapy.[13] Short-term MCS include IABPs, extracorporeal membrane oxygenation (ECMO), and continual flow pumps. The limitations of bed rest and the risk for infection and vascular complications prevent long-term use of these devices. Long-term MCS ventricular assist devices (VADs) include percutaneous devices (PVADs) and transplanted devices (LVADs, BiVADs). VADs provide highly effective long-term support as standard care in many heart transplant centers.

The type of device used depends on the extent and nature of the heart problem. They provide support in 3 situations: (1) the left, right, or both ventricles require support while recovering from acute injury (e.g., postcardiotomy); (2) the patient must be stabilized before heart surgery (e.g., a ruptured septum); and (3) the heart has failed, and the patient is awaiting heart transplantation. All MCS devices decrease cardiac workload, increase myocardial perfusion, and augment circulation.

Intraaortic Balloon Pump

The **intraaortic balloon pump (IABP)** provides temporary circulatory assistance by reducing afterload (through reducing systolic pressure) and augmenting the aortic diastolic pressure. This improves coronary blood flow. Table 38.11 lists common indications for an IABP.

The IABP consists of a sausage-shaped balloon, a pump that inflates and deflates the balloon, a control panel for synchronizing the balloon inflation to the cardiac cycle, and fail-safe features. The balloon is inserted percutaneously or surgically into the femoral artery. It is moved toward the heart and placed in the descending thoracic aorta just below the left subclavian artery and above the renal arteries (Fig. 38.7). After placement, an x-ray confirms the position.

A pneumatic device fills the balloon with helium at the start of diastole (immediately after aortic valve closure) and deflates it just before the next systole. The ECG is the trigger used to start the deflation on the upstroke of the R wave (of the QRS) and inflation on the T wave. The dicrotic notch of the arterial pressure tracing is used to refine timing (Fig. 38.8).

IABP therapy is known as *counterpulsation* because the timing of balloon inflation is opposite the ventricular contraction. The

TABLE 38.11 Common Indications and Contraindications for IABP Therapy

Indications

- Acute MI with any of the following[a]:
  - Ventricular aneurysm accompanied by ventricular dysrhythmias
  - Acute ventricular septal defect
  - Acute mitral valve dysfunction
  - Cardiogenic shock
  - Refractory chest pain with or without ventricular dysrhythmias
  - Short-term bridge to heart transplantation
  - Unstable angina unresponsive to drug therapy
  - High-risk interventional cardiology procedures
  - Cardiac surgery (e.g., prophylaxis before surgery, failure to wean from cardiopulmonary bypass [CPB], left ventricular failure after CPB)

Contraindications

- Irreversible brain damage
- Moderate to severe aortic insufficiency
- Abdominal aortic and thoracic aneurysms
- Terminal or untreatable diseases of any major organ system
- Generalized peripheral vascular disease (e.g., aortoiliac disease)[b]
- Major coagulopathy (e.g., disseminated intravascular coagulation [DIC])

[a]Allows time for emergent angiography and corrective heart surgery to be done.
[b]May inhibit balloon placement and is a relative contraindication; sheathless insertion may be used.

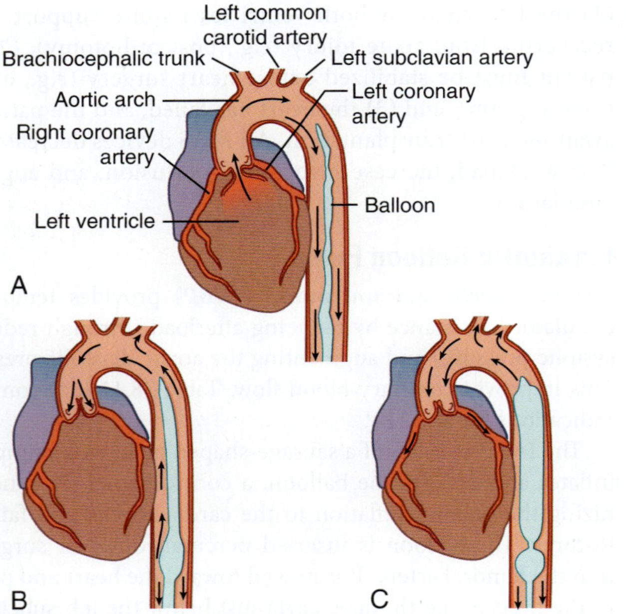

Fig. 38.7 IABP. (A) During systole the balloon is deflated, which helps with ejection of blood into the periphery. (B) In early diastole, the balloon begins to inflate. (C) In late diastole, the balloon is totally inflated, which augments aortic pressure and increases the coronary perfusion pressure. This increases coronary and cerebral blood flow.

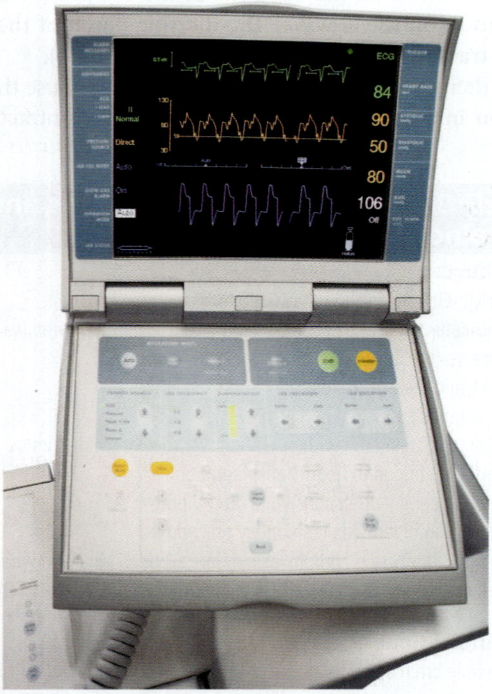

Fig. 38.8 Monitoring on an IABP machine. (© beerkoff/iStock.com.)

IABP assist ratio is 1:1 in the acute phase of treatment, meaning that 1 IABP cycle of inflation and deflation occurs for every heartbeat.

Effects of Counterpulsation

In late diastole when the balloon is totally inflated, blood is forcibly displaced distal to the extremities and proximal to the coronary arteries and main branches of the aortic arch. Diastolic arterial pressure rises (diastolic augmentation). This increases coronary artery perfusion pressure and perfusion of vital organs. The rise in coronary artery perfusion pressure increases blood flow to the myocardium. The balloon is rapidly deflated just before systole. This creates a vacuum that causes aortic pressure to drop. When aortic resistance to left ventricular ejection is reduced (reduced afterload), the left ventricle empties more easily and completely. SV increases while myocardial O_2 consumption decreases. Table 38.12 describes the hemodynamic effects of IABP therapy.

TABLE 38.12 Hemodynamic Effects of Counterpulsation

Effects of Inflation During Diastole

- ↑ Diastolic pressure (may exceed systolic pressure)
- ↑ Pressure in the aortic root during diastole
- ↑ Coronary artery perfusion pressure
- Improved O_2 delivery to the myocardium
- ↓ Angina
- ↓ ECG evidence of ischemia
- ↓ Ventricular ectopy

Effects of Deflation During Systole

- ↓ Afterload
- ↓ Peak systolic pressure
- ↓ Myocardial O_2 consumption
- ↑ Stroke volume, possibly associated with:
- Improved mentation
- Warm skin
- ↑ Urine output
- ↓ HR
- ↑ Forward flow of blood, ↓ preload
- ↓ Pulmonary artery pressures
- ↓ Crackles

Complications of IABP Therapy

Vascular injuries, such as aortic dissection and compromised distal circulation, are common with IABP therapy. Thrombus and embolus formation add to the risk for circulatory compromise to the extremity. The action of the IABP can destroy platelets and cause thrombocytopenia. Movement of the balloon can block the left subclavian, renal, or mesenteric arteries. This can result in a weak or absent radial pulse, decreased urine output, and reduced or absent bowel sounds. Patients receiving IABP therapy are prone to infection. Local or systemic signs of infection require catheter removal. To reduce these complications, perform cardiovascular, neurovascular, and hemodynamic assessments every 15 to 60 minutes, depending on the patient's status (Table 38.13).

Mechanical complications from IABP are rare but can occur. Improper timing of balloon inflation may cause increased afterload, decreased CO, myocardial ischemia, and increased myocardial O_2 demand. If the balloon develops a leak, the pump will automatically stop. The catheter must be promptly removed to avoid an embolus. Signs of a leak include less effective augmentation, repeated alarms for gas loss, and blood backing up into the catheter. A malfunction of the balloon or console triggers fail-safe alarms and automatically shuts down the unit. You must be able to recognize complications immediately and report them to the HCP.

TABLE 38.13 NURSING MANAGEMENT

Complications of IABP Therapy

Potential Complication	Nursing Interventions
Arterial trauma caused by insertion or displacement of balloon	• Assess and mark peripheral pulses before inserting balloon to use as baseline for assessing pulses after insertion. • Assess perfusion to both upper and lower extremities at least every hour. • Measure urine output at least every hour (occlusion of renal arteries causes severe ↓ in urine output). • Observe arterial waveforms for sudden changes. • Keep head of bed no higher than 45 degrees. • Do not flex cannulated leg at the hip. • Immobilize cannulated leg to prevent flexion using a draw sheet tucked under the mattress, soft ankle restraint, or knee immobilizer.
Balloon leak or rupture	• Prepare for emergent removal and possible reinsertion.
Hematologic problems due to platelet aggregation along the balloon (e.g., thrombocytopenia)	• Monitor coagulation profiles, hematocrit, and platelet count.
Hemorrhage from insertion site	• Check site for bleeding at least every hour. • Monitor vital signs for signs of hypovolemia with each check.
Infection at site	• Use strict aseptic technique for insertion and dressing changes for all lines. • Cover all insertion sites with occlusive dressings. • Give prescribed prophylactic antibiotic for entire course of therapy.
Issues related to immobilization (e.g., pressure injuries)	• Reposition patient at least q2hr, being careful to maintain proper positioning. • Use appropriate pressure-relieving devices.
VTE caused by trauma, balloon obstruction of blood flow distal to catheter	• Give prophylactic heparin therapy (if ordered). • Assess pulses, urine output, and level of consciousness at least every hour. • Check circulation, sensation, and movement in both legs at least every hour.

The patient with an IABP is relatively immobile. They are limited to side-lying or supine positions with the head of bed elevated less than 45 degrees. The patient may be receiving mechanical ventilation and often has multiple invasive lines. All of this increases the risk for pressure injury and makes it hard to find a comfortable position. The patient may have sleep problems and anxiety. Adequate sedation, pain relief, skin care, and comfort measures are essential.

As the patient improves, circulatory support provided by the IABP is gradually reduced. Weaning involves reducing the IABP assist ratio from 1:1 to 1:2 and assessing the patient's response. If the patient stays stable, the ratio is changed from 1:2 to 1:3 until the IABP catheter is removed. Pumping must continue until the line is removed even if the patient is stable. This reduces the risk for clot formation around the catheter.

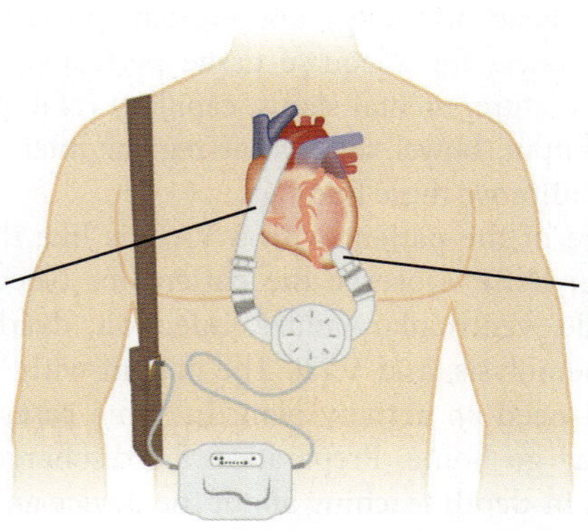

Fig. 38.9 Schematic diagram of a biventricular assist device (BVAD). (From Urden LD, Stacy KM, Lough ME: *Critical care nursing: diagnosis and management,* ed 8, St Louis, 2018, Mosby.)

Ventricular Assist Devices

A **ventricular assist device (VAD)** provides short- and long-term support for the failing heart. VADs are inserted into the path of flowing blood to augment or replace the action of the ventricle. Some VADs are implanted internally (e.g., peritoneum). Others are placed externally. A typical VAD shunts blood from the left atrium or ventricle to the device and then to the aorta. Some VADs provide right or biventricular support (Fig. 38.9). VADs operate on AC current or batteries. They allow for more mobility than the IABP.

Appropriate patient selection for VAD therapy is critical. Failure to wean from cardiopulmonary bypass (CPB) after surgery is a key indicator for VAD support. Other indications include (1) postcardiotomy cardiogenic shock, (2) a bridge to recovery or heart transplantation, and (3) patients with New York Heart Association Class IV heart disease who have failed medical therapy. Relative contraindications for VAD therapy include (1) BSA less than manufacturer's limit (e.g., 1.2 m^2), (2) irreversible end-stage organ damage, and (3) co-morbidities that would limit life expectancy to less than 3 years.

Implantable Artificial Heart

A fully implantable artificial heart can sustain the body's circulatory system. This device can provide a bridge to transplantation or replace the hearts of patients who are not eligible for a transplant and have no other treatment options. A major advantage of the artificial heart is that patients do not need immunosuppression therapy and thus avoid its inevitable, long-term effects. Risks include infection, thrombus, and stroke. Patients need lifelong anticoagulation and ongoing care from the interprofessional team.

NURSING AND INTERPROFESSIONAL MANAGEMENT: MECHANICAL CIRCULATORY SUPPORT

The patient with an IABP needs highly skilled care. Perform frequent and thorough cardiovascular assessments. These include measuring hemodynamic parameters (e.g., arterial BP, CO, SVR), auscultating the heart and lungs, and evaluating the ECG (e.g., rate, rhythm). Assess for adequate tissue perfusion (e.g., skin color and temperature, mental status, capillary refill, peripheral pulses, urine output, bowel sounds) at regular intervals. IABP therapy should improve these findings.

Nursing care of the patient with a VAD is like that of the patient with an IABP. Observe the patient for bleeding, cardiac tamponade, ventricular failure, infection, dysrhythmias, renal failure, hemolysis, and VTE. The patient with VAD may be mobile and need an activity plan. In some cases, patients with VADs may go home. Preparation for discharge is complex and needs in-depth teaching about the device and support equipment (e.g., battery chargers). A competent caregiver must always be present.

Ideally, patients with MCS will recover, receive an artificial heart, or undergo heart transplantation. However, many patients die, or make the decision to no longer seek treatment, and death follows. Both the patient and caregiver need emotional support. Consult other team members, such as social workers or clergy, as needed.

HEART TRANSPLANTATION

Heart transplantation is the transfer of a healthy donor heart to a patient with a diseased heart. It is done to treat a variety of terminal or end-stage heart conditions (Table 38.14). In the United States, more than 3500 patients are awaiting heart transplants. Although the number of end-stage HF patients in need of a transplant has increased, the number of donors has remained about the same. The 1-year heart transplant survival rate is close to 90%. Despite an increasingly complex patient population, half of the recipients are alive 13 years after transplant.[23]

Criteria for Selection

A careful selection process ensures that hearts are distributed fairly and to those who will benefit most. The United Network for Organ Sharing (UNOS) manages a system to assign donor organs. UNOS and transplantation are discussed in Chapter 14.

Indications and contraindications for a heart transplant are outlined in Table 38.14. Once a person meets the criteria for a transplant, an exhaustive physical examination and diagnostic workup are done. We assess heart function and vascular and immune systems. The patient and caregiver undergo a comprehensive psychologic evaluation of coping skills, support systems, and commitment to follow a rigorous life-long regimen. The complexity of the transplant process may be overwhelming to a patient without an adequate support system and understanding of the needed lifestyle changes.

Donor and recipient matching is based on body and heart size and an immunologic assessment. That assessment includes ABO blood type, antibody screen, panel of reactive antibody (PRA) level, and human leukocyte antigen typing.

A person accepted as a transplant candidate is placed on a transplant list. This may happen quickly during an acute illness or after a longer period. Stable patients may wait at home and receive ongoing medical care. If unstable, a patient may be hospitalized for more intensive therapy. Unfortunately, the overall waiting period for a new heart is long. Many patients die while waiting for a transplant.

TABLE 38.14 Common Indications and Contraindications for Heart Transplantation

Indications
- End-stage HF refractory to medical care
- Severe, decompensated, inoperable, heart valve disease
- Recurrent life-threatening dysrhythmias not responsive to maximal interventions, including defibrillators
- Any other heart problems that severely limit normal function and/or have a mortality risk of more than 50% within 2 years

Absolute Contraindications
- Active infection, including HIV infection
- Chronologic age over 70 years or physiologic age over 65 years
- Advanced cerebral or peripheral vascular disease not amenable to correction
- Life-threatening illness (e.g., cancer) that will limit survival to <5 years despite therapy
- Severe lung disease that will likely result in the patient being ventilator-dependent after transplant

Relative Contraindications
- Severe obesity
- Psychologic impairment
- Evidence of noncompliance with medical therapy
- Active substance use (e.g., alcohol, drugs, tobacco)
- Irreversible liver or kidney failure not explained by HF
- Uncontrolled diabetes with vascular and neurologic complications
- Lack of social support network that can make long-term commitment for patient's welfare
- Unrealistic expectations by the patient or caregiver about transplant, its risks, and its benefits

Surgical Procedure

The transplant donor is someone who has irreversible brain injury. A surgical team goes to the hospital of the donor to remove donated organs after the declaration of brain death. The retrieved organs are transported on ice until they can be implanted. For the heart, this is optimally less than 4 hours. Often the donor heart is flown to the recipient's hospital. The donor heart is then implanted into the recipient using 1 of 2 approaches. In the biatrial approach, the recipient's damaged heart is removed at the midatrial level, and the donor heart connected at the LA, PA, aorta, and RA. In the bicaval approach, the RA of the recipient's heart (with the SA node and atrial conduction intact) is preserved and then the donor heart is connected. CPB during the surgery maintains oxygenation and perfusion to vital organs.

Post-Transplantation

After cardiac transplant, a variety of complications can occur. In the first year after transplantation, the major causes of death are infection and acute rejection. There is a risk for SCD.

Immunosuppressive therapy is the key in posttransplant management. Most immunosuppressive regimens include corticosteroids, calcineurin inhibitors (tacrolimus), and antiproliferative drugs (mycophenolate mofetil). The mechanisms of action and side effects of these and other immunosuppressants are discussed in Chapter 14. Because of the use of immunosuppressive therapy, infection is a primary concern after transplant surgery. Long-term immunosuppressive therapy increases the risk for cancers, especially lymphomas, and cardiac vasculopathy (accelerated CAD).

To detect rejection, an endomyocardial biopsy is done weekly for the first month, monthly for the next 6 months, and yearly thereafter. In this procedure, the HCP inserts a catheter into the jugular vein and moves it into the RV. The catheter uses a bioptome, a device with 2 small cups that can be closed, to remove small samples of heart muscle for analysis.

Nursing care throughout the posttransplant period focuses on promoting patient adaptation to the transplant process, monitoring heart function, managing lifestyle changes, and ongoing teaching and support of the patient and caregiver.

Case Study

Heart Failure

(© iStockphoto/ Thinkstock.)

Patient Profile

J.E. is a 70-year-old Hispanic woman who was admitted to the intermediate care unit with increasing shortness of breath, fatigue, and weight gain.

Subjective Data

- HTN for 20 years
- MI at 58 years of age
- Has increasing shortness of breath, fatigue, and an unexplained 11-lb weight gain during the past 2 weeks
- Had a respiratory tract infection 2 weeks ago; has persistent cough and edema in legs
- Cannot climb a flight of stairs without getting short of breath
- Sleeps with head elevated on 3 pillows
- Lives alone, does not always remember to take medication

Objective Data

Physical Assessment

- Moderate respiratory distress, use of accessory muscles, respiratory rate 36 breaths/min
- Systolic heart murmur
- Bilateral crackles in all lung fields
- Cyanotic lips and extremities
- Skin cool and diaphoretic

Diagnostic Studies

- Chest x-ray results: cardiomegaly with right and left ventricular hypertrophy; fluid in lower lung fields
- Echocardiogram results: ejection fraction 20%

Interprofessional Care

- Furosemide 40 mg IV twice daily
- Potassium 40 mEq PO twice daily
- Sacubitril/valsartan (Entresto) 97 mg/103 mg PO twice daily
- Nitroglycerine IV drip starting at 5 mcg/min
- Continuous ECG monitoring
- Diet: 2-gram sodium diet
- Titrate O_2 to keep O_2 saturation >93%
- Monitor intake and output, and daily weights
- Serum electrolytes; cardiac biomarkers q8h × 3

Discussion Questions

1. ***Recognize:*** What clinical manifestations of ADHF did J.E. exhibit?
2. ***Analyze:*** How would a serum NT-proBNP be beneficial in the diagnosis of ADHF?
3. ***Plan:*** Give the rationale for each of the HCP's orders prescribed for J.E.
4. ***Prioritize:*** What are your priority nursing interventions for J.E.?
5. ***Act:*** Which interventions can you delegate to AP or other members of the interprofessional team?
6. ***Evaluate:*** What outcomes would indicate nursing interventions were successful?

Answers and a corresponding concept map available at http://evolve.elsevier.com/Lewis/medsurg.

BRIDGE TO NCLEX EXAMINATION

The number of the question corresponds to the same-numbered outcome at the beginning of the chapter.

1. Which statements accurately describe heart failure with preserved ejection fraction (HFpEF)? *(select all that apply)*
   a. Uncontrolled hypertension is a primary cause.
   b. Left ventricular ejection fraction may be within normal limits.
   c. The pathophysiology involves ventricular relaxation and filling.
   d. Multiple evidence-based therapies have been shown to decrease mortality.
   e. Therapies focus on symptom control and treatment of underlying conditions.
2. Which compensatory mechanism involved in both chronic heart failure and acute decompensated heart failure leads to fluid retention and edema?
   a. Ventricular dilation
   b. Ventricular hypertrophy
   c. Increased systemic blood pressure
   d. Renin-angiotensin-aldosterone activation
3. The nurse is caring for a patient with acute decompensated heart failure who is receiving IV dobutamine. Which drug action is expected? *(select all that apply)*
   a. Raises the heart rate
   b. Dilates renal blood vessels
   c. Increases heart contractility
   d. Acts as a selective β-agonist
   e. Increases systemic vascular resistance

4. A patient with chronic heart failure and atrial fibrillation is treated with low-dose digitalis and a loop diuretic. Which actions would the nurse take to prevent complications of this drug combination? *(select all that apply)*
   a. Monitor serum potassium levels.
   b. Teach the patient how to take a pulse rate.
   c. Keep an accurate measure of intake and output.
   d. Withhold digitalis if the pulse rhythm is irregular.
   e. Teach the patient about diet potassium restrictions.
5. Which factor is a significant barrier to hospice referrals for patients with stage D heart failure?
   a. Family member refusal
   b. Scarcity of hospice care
   c. History of pacemaker placement
   d. Difficulty in estimating prognosis
6. The hemodynamic changes the nurse expects to find after successful initiation of intraaortic balloon pump therapy include *(select all that apply)*
   a. decreased SV.
   b. decreased SVR.
   c. decreased PAWP.
   d. increased diastolic BP.
   e. decreased myocardial O_2 consumption.
7. Which are the greatest risks for patients in the **first** year after heart transplantation? *(select all that apply)*
   a. Cancer
   b. Infection
   c. Rejection
   d. Vasculopathy
   e. Sudden cardiac death

1. a, b, c, e; 2. d; 3. c, d; 4. a, b; 5. d; 6. b, c, d, e; 7. b, c, e.

For rationales to these answers and even more NCLEX review questions, visit http://evolve.elsevier.com/Lewis/medsurg.

EVOLVE WEBSITE/RESOURCES LIST

http://evolve.elsevier.com/Lewis/medsurg
Review Questions (Online Only)
Key Points
Answer Keys for Questions
- Rationales for Bridge to NCLEX Examination Questions
- Answer Guidelines for Case Study

Student Case Study
- Patient With Heart Failure

Nursing Care Plan
- eNursing Care Plan 34.1: Patient With Heart Failure

Conceptual Care Map Creator
- Conceptual Care Map for Case Study

Audio Glossary
Content Updates

REFERENCES

1. Yancy CW, Jessup M, Bozkurt B, et al.: 2013 ACCF/AHA guideline for the management of heart failure: executive summary: a report of the American College of Cardiology Foundation/AHA Task Force on Practice Guidelines, *Circulation* 128:1810, 2013. (Classic).
*2. Virani SS, Alonso A Benjamin EJ, et al.: Heart disease and stroke statistics—2020 update: a report from the AHA, *Circulation* 141:e139, 2020.
3. Reddy Y, Lewis G, Shoh S, et al.: Heart failure pathophysiology, *Circ Heart Fail* 10:e003862, 2017. (Classic).
*4. Eisenberg E, Dipalo K, Pina IL: Sex differences in heart failure, *Clin Card* 41:211, 2018.
5. Rosenbaum AN, Agre KA, Pereira NL: Genetics of dilated cardiomyopathy: practical implications for heart failure management, *Nat Rev Cardiol* 17:286, 2020.
6. Reza N, Owens AT: Advances in the genetics and genomics of heart failure, *Curr Cardiol Rep* 22, 2020.
7. Pagel PS, Tawil JN, Boettcher BT, et al.: Heart failure with preserved ejection fraction: a comprehensive review and update of diagnosis, pathophysiology, treatment, and perioperative implications, *J Cardiothorac Vasc Anesth*, 2020.
8. Chaikijurajai T, Tang WW: Reappraisal of inflammatory biomarkers in heart failure, *Curr Heart Fail Rep* 17:9, 2020.
9. Díaz HS, Toledo C, Andrade DC, Marcus NJ, Del Rio R: Neuroinflammation in heart failure: new insights for an old disease, *J Physiol* 598:33, 2020.
10. Riehle C, Bauersachs J: Key inflammatory mechanisms underlying heart failure, *Herz* 44:96, 2019.
*11. Aimo A, Gaggin HK, Barison A, et al.: Imaging, biomarkers, and clinical predictors of cardiac remodeling in heart failure with reduced ejection fraction, *J Am Col Card* 7:782, 2019.
12. Silver MA, Maisal A, Yancy CW, et al.: BNP Consensus Panel 2004: a clinical approach for the diagnostic, prognostic, screening, treatment monitoring, and therapeutic roles of natriuretic peptides in cardiovascular diseases, *Conges Heart Fail* 10:1, 2004 (Classic).
*13. Lindenfeld J, Albert N, Boehmer JP, et al.: HFSA 2010 comprehensive heart failure practice guidelines, *J Card Fail* 16:e1, 2010 (Classic).
14. Iordani MM: Depression in heart failure, *Health Res J* 6:53, 2020.
*15. Russo JJ, Akeksova N, Pitcher E, et al.: Left ventricular unloading during extracorporeal membrane oxygenation in patients with cardiogenic shock, *J Am Col Card* 73:654, 2019.
*16. Taylor RS, Long L, Mordi IR, et al.: Exercise-based rehabilitation for heart failure: Cochrane systematic review, meta-analysis, and trial sequential analysis, *J Am Col Card* 7:691, 2019.
*17. Yancy CW, Jessup M, Bozkurt B, et al.: 2017 ACC/AHA/HFSA focused update of the 2013 ACCF/AHA guidelines for the management of heart failure: a report of the ACC/AHA Task Force on Clinical Practice Guidelines, *Circ* 136:e137, 2017. (Classic).
18. Faragli A, Abawi D, Quinn C, Cvetkovic M, et al.: The role of non-invasive devices for the telemonitoring of heart failure patients, *Heart Fail Rev* 27:1, 2020.

*19. Abraham WT, Adamson PB, Bourge RC, et al.: Wireless PA hemodynamic monitoring in chronic heart failure: a randomized controlled trial, *Lancet* 377:658, 2011. (Classic).

*20. Schocken DD, Benjamin EJ, Fonarow G, et al.: Prevention of heart failure: a scientific statement from the AHA Councils on Epidemiology and Prevention, Clinical Cardiology, Cardiovascular Nursing, and High Blood Pressure Research, *Circ* 117:2544, 2008. (Classic).

*21. Quan LH, Whitmore K, Negishi K, et al.: Influence of risk reduction of readmission and death by disease management programs in heart failure, *J Card Fail* 25:330, 2019.

*22. Singh GK, Ivynian SE, Ferguson C, Davidson PM, Newton PJ: Palliative care in chronic heart failure: a theoretically guided, qualitative meta-synthesis of decision-making, *Heart Fail Rev* 25:457, 2020.

*23. Lund LH, Edwards LB, Dipchard AL, et al.: The registry of the International Society of Heart and Lung Transplantation: 36th adult heart transplant report—2019, *J Heart Lung Tran* 38:1056, 2019.

*Evidence-based information for clinical practice.

39

Dysrhythmias

Kimberly Day

http://evolve.elsevier.com/Lewis/medsurg/

CONCEPTUAL FOCUS

Fluids and Electrolytes

Perfusion

LEARNING OUTCOMES

1. Examine the nursing care of patients needing continuous electrocardiographic monitoring.
2. Distinguish the clinical characteristics and ECG patterns of normal sinus rhythm, common dysrhythmias, and pacemaker rhythms.
3. Describe the nursing and interprofessional management of patients with common dysrhythmias.
4. Compare and contrast defibrillation and cardioversion.
5. Describe the nursing and interprofessional management of patients with pacemakers and implantable cardioverter-defibrillators.
6. Select appropriate interventions for patients undergoing electrophysiologic testing and radiofrequency catheter ablation therapy.

KEY TERMS

asystole
atrial fibrillation
atrial flutter
automatic external defibrillator (AED)
cardiac pacemaker
complete heart block
dysrhythmias
premature atrial contraction (PAC)
premature ventricular contraction (PVC)
telemetry monitoring
ventricular fibrillation (VF)
ventricular tachycardia (VT)

This chapter describes basic principles of electrocardiographic monitoring and the recognition and treatment of common dysrhythmias. Adequate perfusion requires the heart to generate sufficient cardiac output (CO) to distribute blood to the body tissues. Abnormal heart rhythms, called **dysrhythmias**, can directly decrease CO by changing stroke volume and heart rate (HR). For example, tachycardia from a fever may decrease CO and cause hypotension. Your ability to recognize normal heart rhythms and dysrhythmias is an essential nursing skill.[1] Prompt recognition of a dysrhythmia and assessing the patient's response to the rhythm is critical to maintaining adequate perfusion.

RHYTHM IDENTIFICATION AND TREATMENT

Conduction System

Four properties of heart cells allow the conduction system to start an electrical impulse, send it through the heart tissue, and stimulate muscle contraction (Table 39.1). The heart's conduction system consists of specialized neuromuscular tissue found throughout the heart (see Fig. 35.4A). A normal impulse starts in the sinoatrial (SA) node in the upper right atrium near the entrance of the vena cava. It spreads over the atrial myocardium via interatrial and internodal pathways, causing atrial contraction. The impulse then travels to the atrioventricular (AV) node, through the bundle of His, and down the left and right bundle branches to the Purkinje fibers in the ventricles, causing ventricular contraction.[2]

Nervous Control of the Heart

The autonomic nervous system plays a vital role in the rate of impulse formation, speed of conduction, and strength of cardiac contraction. The parts of the autonomic nervous system that affect the heart are the vagus nerve fibers of the parasympathetic nervous system and the nerve fibers of the sympathetic nervous system.

Stimulation of the vagus nerve slows firing of the SA node and slows impulse conduction of the AV node. This decreases HR. Stimulation of the sympathetic nerves increases SA node firing, AV node impulse conduction, and cardiac contractility. This increases HR.[2]

Electrocardiographic Monitoring

The *electrocardiogram* (ECG) is a graphic tracing of the electrical impulses in the heart. The waveforms on the ECG represent the electrical activity of depolarization and repolarization produced by the movement of ions across the membranes of heart cells (see Fig. 35.4B).

The membrane of a heart cell is semipermeable. This allows it to maintain a high concentration of potassium and a low concentration of sodium inside the cell. Outside the cell, a high concentration of sodium and a low concentration of potassium exist. The inside of the cell, when at rest or in the polarized state, is negatively charged compared with the outside. When a cell or groups of cells are stimulated, the cell membrane changes its permeability. This change allows sodium to move rapidly into the cell. The inside of the cell is then positively charged compared with the outside *(depolarization)*. A slower movement of ions across the membrane restores the cell to the polarized state, called *repolarization*. Fig. 39.1 describes the phases of the cardiac action potential.[2]

A 12-lead ECG view of the heart is helpful in assessing dysrhythmias. Six of the leads measure electrical forces in the frontal plane. These are bipolar (positive and negative) leads I, II, and III and unipolar (positive) leads aVR, aVL, and aVF (Fig. 39.2A and B). The 6 unipolar leads (V_1 through V_6) measure the electrical forces in the horizontal plane (precordial leads) (Fig. 39.2C). The 12-lead ECG may show changes suggesting structural changes, conduction changes, damage (e.g., ischemia, infarction), electrolyte imbalance, or drug toxicity. Fig. 39.3 is an example of a normal 12-lead ECG.

We can use 1 or more ECG leads to continuously monitor a patient. The most common leads used are leads II and V_1 (Fig. 39.4). We use a modified chest lead (MCL_1) when only 3 leads are available for monitoring. MCL_1 is similar to V_1. Accurate ECG interpretation depends on the correct placement of the leads on the patient. The monitoring leads used are determined by the patient's clinical status.[3]

The ECG monitor continuously displays the heart rhythm. Paper attached to the monitor records the ECG (rhythm strip)

TABLE 39.1 Properties of Heart Cells	
Property	**Definition**
Automaticity	Ability to initiate an impulse spontaneously and continuously
Excitability	Ability to be electrically stimulated
Conductivity	Ability to transmit an impulse along a membrane in an orderly manner
Contractility	Ability to respond mechanically to an impulse

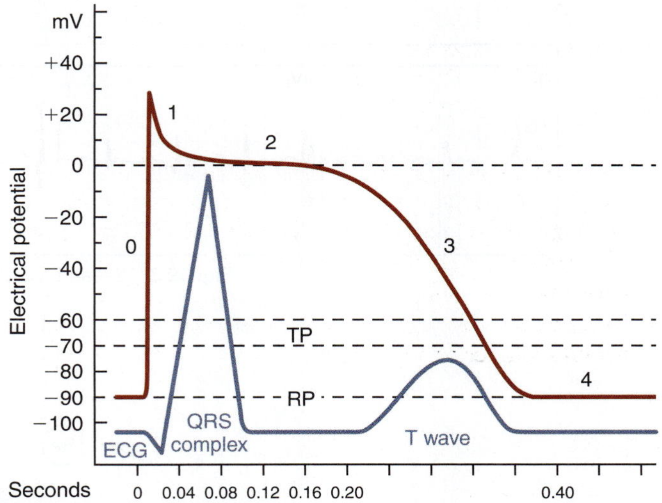

Fig. 39.1 Phases of the cardiac action potential. The electrical potential, measured in millivolts *(mV)*, is indicated along the vertical axis of the graph. Time, measured in seconds (sec), is indicated along the horizontal axis. The action potential has 5 phases, labeled *0* through *4*. Each phase represents a specific electrical event or combination of electrical events. Phase 0 is the upstroke of rapid depolarization and corresponds with ventricular contraction. Phases 1, 2, and 3 represent repolarization. Phase 4 is known as complete repolarization (or the polarized state) and corresponds to diastole. *RP,* Resting membrane potential; *TP,* threshold membrane potential.

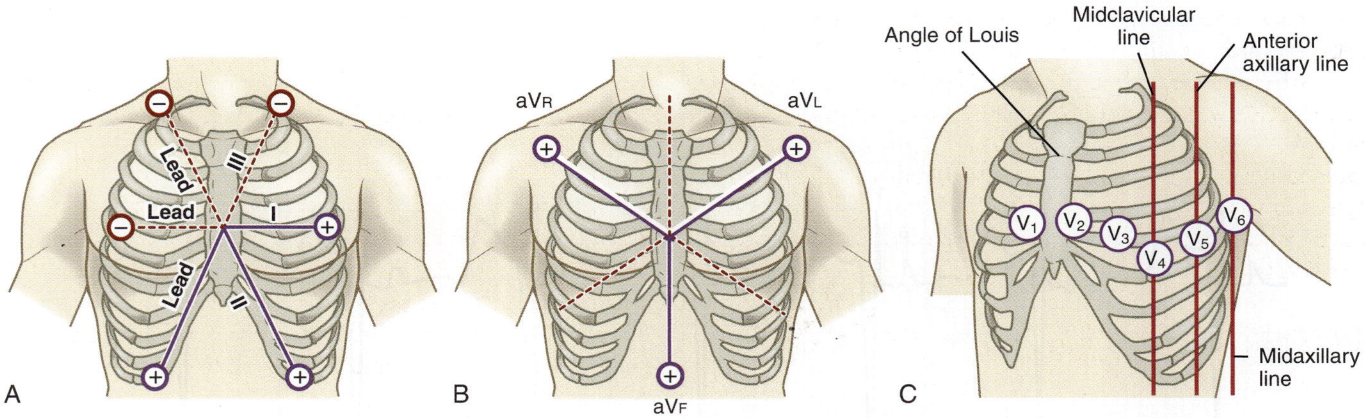

Fig. 39.2 (A) Limb leads I, II, and III. These bipolar leads are placed on the extremities. Shown are the angles from which these leads view the heart. (B) Limb leads aVR, aVL, and aVF. These unipolar leads use the center of the heart as their negative electrode. (C) Placement for the unipolar chest leads: *V_1*, 4th intercostal space at the right sternal border; *V_2*, 4th intercostal space at the left sternal border; *V_3*, halfway between V_2 and V_4; *V_4*, 5th intercostal space at the left midclavicular line; *V_5*, 5th intercostal space at the left anterior axillary line; *V_6*, 5th intercostal space at the left midaxillary line.

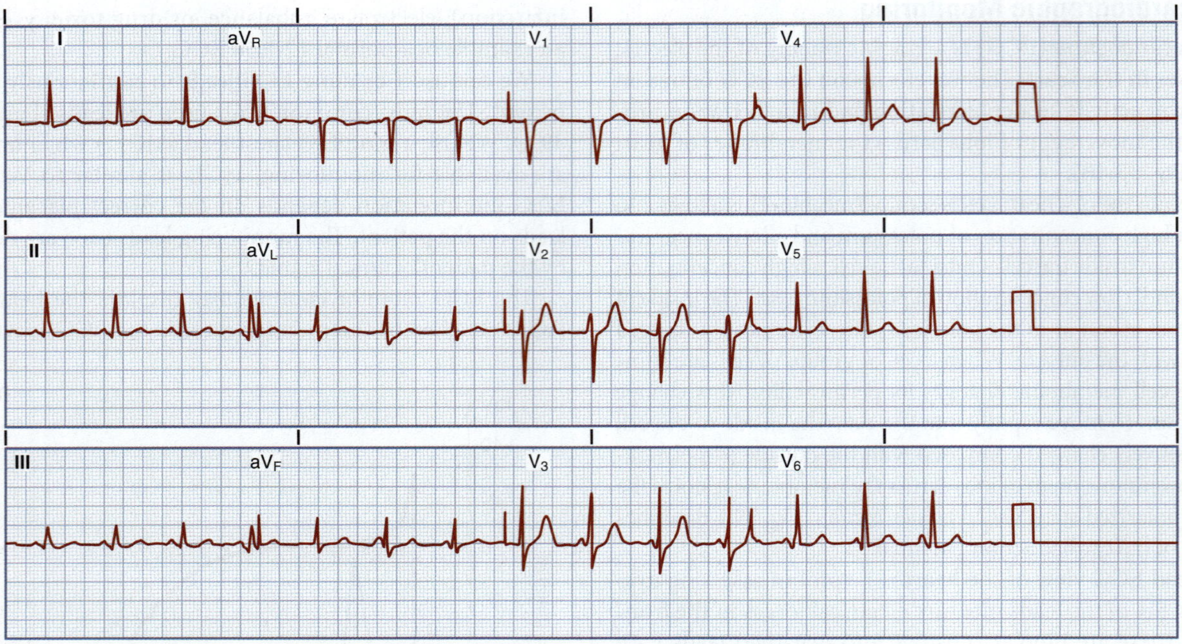

Fig. 39.3 12-lead ECG showing a normal sinus rhythm.

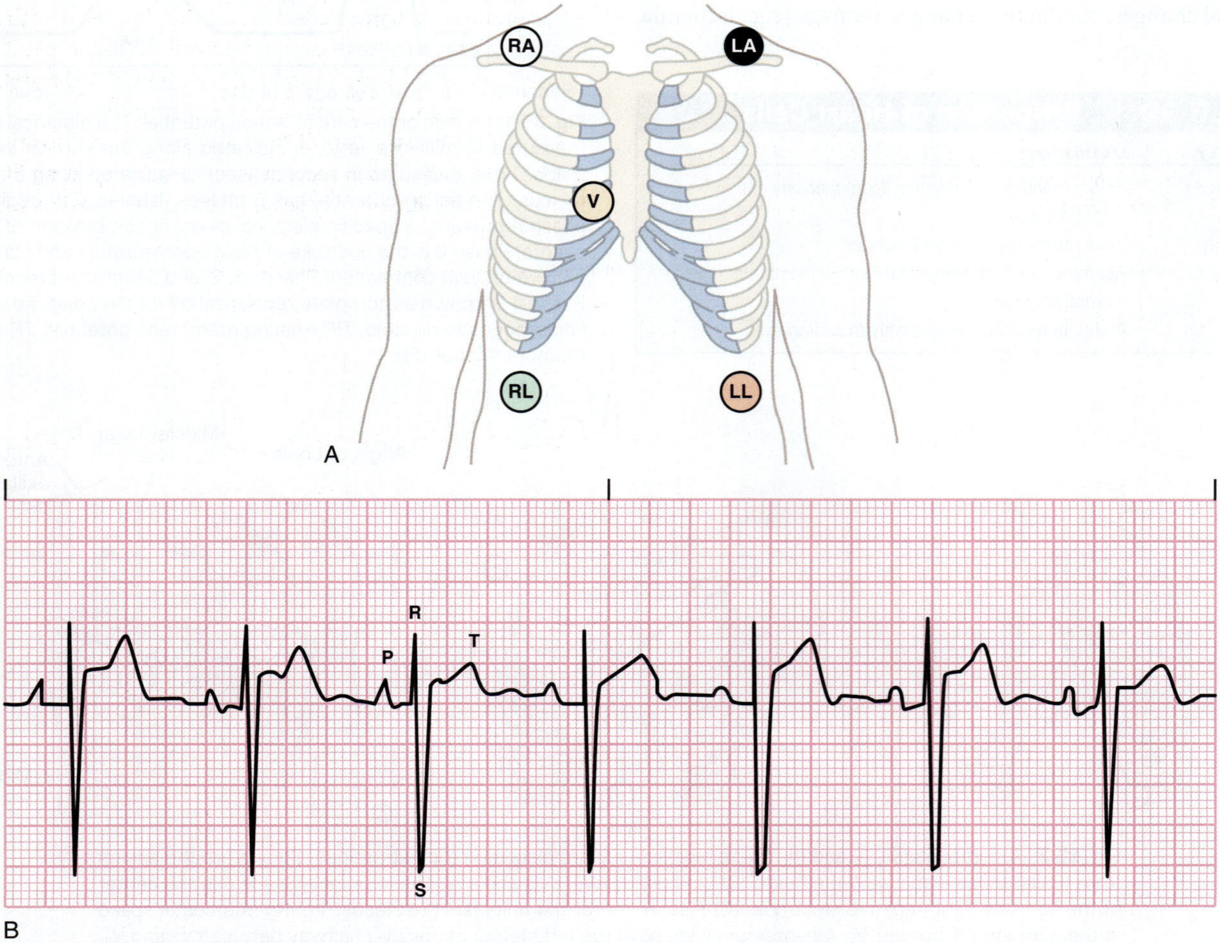

Fig. 39.4 (A) Lead placement for V_1 using a 5-lead system. (B) Typical ECG tracing in lead V_1. *LA,* Left arm; *LL,* left leg; *RA,* right arm; *RL,* right leg; *V,* chest lead.

to provide a record of the patient's rhythm. It allows for measurement of complexes and intervals and assessment of dysrhythmias.

To correctly interpret an ECG, measure time and voltage on the ECG paper. ECG paper consists of large (heavy lines) and small (light lines) squares (Fig. 39.5). Each large square consists of 25 smaller squares (5 horizontal and 5 vertical). Horizontally, each small square (1 mm) represents 0.04 second. This means that 1 large square equals 0.20 second and that 300 large squares equal 1 minute. Vertically, each small square (1 mm) represents 0.1 millivolt (mV). This means that 1 large square equals 0.5 mV. Use these squares to calculate the HR and measure time intervals for the different ECG complexes.

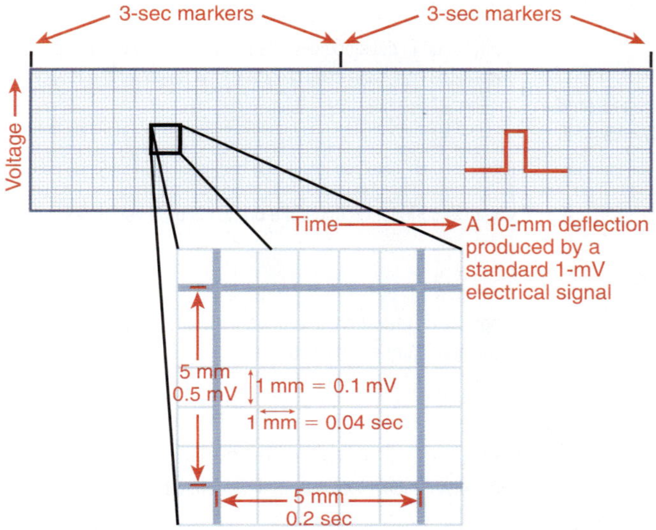

Fig. 39.5 Time and voltage on the ECG; 6-sec strip. (Modified from Wesley K: *Basic dysrhythmias and acute coronary syndromes,* ed 4, St Louis, 2011, Mosby JEMS.)

You can use a variety of methods to calculate the HR from an ECG. The most accurate way is to count the number of QRS complexes in 1 minute. A simpler way is to note that every 3 seconds, a marker appears on the ECG paper (Fig. 39.5). Count the number of QRS complexes in 6 seconds and multiply that number by 10. This is the estimated number of beats per minute (Fig. 39.6).

Another method to calculate the HR is to count the number of small squares between 1 R-R interval. Divide this number into 1500 to get the HR. Last, you can count the number of large squares between 1 R-R interval and divide this number into 300 to get the HR (Fig. 39.6). All these methods are more accurate when the rhythm is regular.

Another way to measure distances on the ECG strip is to use calipers. Often a P or R wave will not fall directly on a light or heavy line. Place the fine points of the calipers exactly on the parts you need to measure and then move to another part of the strip for a more precise time measurement.

Fig. 39.7 shows the components of a normal ECG tracing. Table 39.2 describes ECG waveforms and intervals, normal durations, and possible sources of changes. Table 39.3 presents a systematic approach to assessing a heart rhythm.

ECG leads consist of an electrode pad fixed with electrical conductive gel. Before placing these on the patient, properly prepare the skin. Clip excess hair on the chest wall with scissors. Gently rub the skin with dry gauze until slightly pink. If the skin is oily, wipe with alcohol first. If the patient is diaphoretic, apply a skin protectant before placing the electrode.

Artifact is a distortion of the baseline and waveforms seen on the ECG (Fig. 39.8). It is hard to accurately interpret an ECG when artifact is present. You may see artifact on the monitor when leads

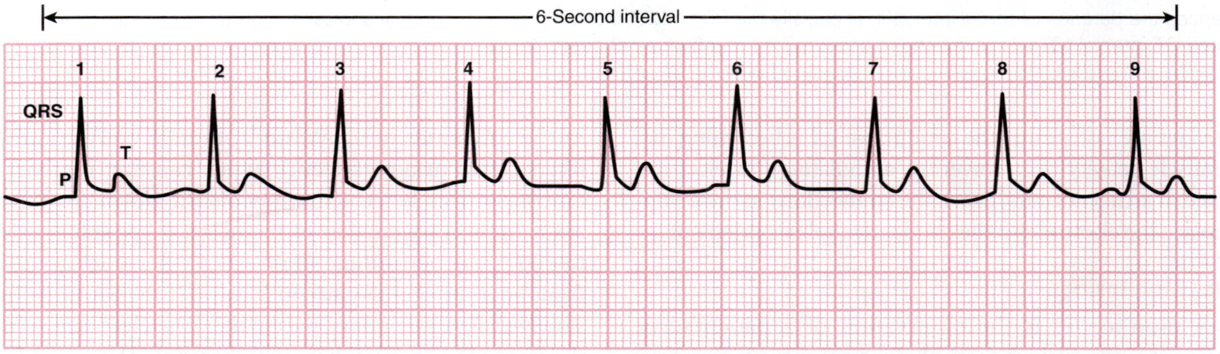

Fig. 39.6 When the rhythm is regular, heart rate can be easily determined by counting the number of "R" waves. The estimated heart rate is 90 beats/min. NOTE: Recorded from lead II.

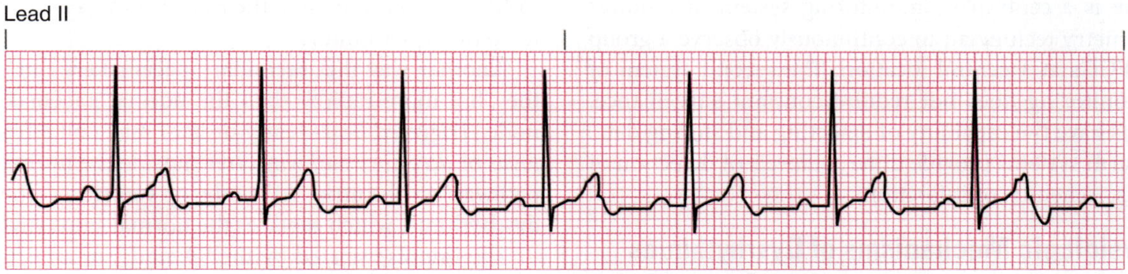

Fig. 39.7 Normal sinus rhythm. NOTE: Recorded from lead II.

TABLE 39.2 ECG Waveforms and Intervals[a]

Description	Normal Duration (sec)	Source of Possible Variation
P Wave		
Represents time for the passage of the electrical impulse through the atrium causing atrial depolarization (contraction). Should be upright	0.06–0.12	Problem in conduction within atria
PR Interval		
Measured from beginning of P wave to beginning of QRS complex. Represents time taken for impulse to spread through the atria, AV node and bundle of His, bundle branches, and Purkinje fibers to a point immediately before ventricular contraction	0.12–0.20	Problem in conduction usually in AV node, bundle of His, or bundle branches but can be in atria as well
QRS Complex		
Q wave: First negative (downward) deflection after the P wave, short and narrow, not present in several leads	<0.03	MI may result in development of a pathologic Q wave that is wide (≥0.03 sec) and deep (≥25% of the height of the R wave)
R wave: First positive (upward) deflection in the QRS complex	Not usually measured	
S wave: First negative (downward) deflection after the R wave	Not usually measured	
QRS Interval		
Measured from beginning to end of QRS complex. Represents time taken for depolarization (contraction) of both ventricles (systole)	<0.12	Problem in conduction in bundle branches or in ventricles
ST Segment		
Measured from the S wave of the QRS complex to the beginning of the T wave. Represents the time between ventricular depolarization and repolarization (diastole). Should be isoelectric (flat)	0.12	Changes (e.g., elevation, depression) usually caused by ischemia, injury, or infarction
T Wave		
Represents time for ventricular repolarization. Should be upright	0.16	Changes (e.g., tall, peaked; inverted) usually caused by electrolyte imbalances, ischemia, infarction
QT Interval[b]		
Measured from beginning of QRS complex to end of T wave. Represents time taken for entire electrical depolarization and repolarization of the ventricles. Normal adult women have slightly longer QT intervals than men.	0.34–0.43	Problems usually affecting repolarization more than depolarization and caused by drugs, electrolyte imbalances, and changes in heart rate

[a]HR influences the duration of these intervals, especially the PR and QT intervals (e.g., QT interval shortens in duration as heart rate increases).
[b]A corrected QT interval (QTc) is calculated to account for the influence of heart rate.

and electrodes are not secure, the conductive gel is becoming dry, there is muscle activity (e.g., shivering, ambulating), or electrical interference. If artifact occurs, check the connections in the equipment. Replace the electrodes if the conductive gel has dried out.

Telemetry Monitoring

Telemetry monitoring is the observation of a patient's HR and rhythm at a site distant from the patient. This technology can help rapidly identify dysrhythmias, ischemia, or infarction. There are 2 types of systems for telemetry monitoring. The first type is a centralized monitoring system. It requires you or a telemetry technician to continuously observe a group of patients' ECGs at a central location. The second system of telemetry monitoring does not require constant surveillance. These systems have the capability of detecting and storing data. Advanced alarm systems provide different levels of detection of dysrhythmias, ischemia, or infarction.

Electrophysiologic Mechanisms of Dysrhythmias

Dysrhythmias result from disorders of impulse formation, impulse conductions, or both. The heart has specialized cells in the SA node, atria, AV node, bundle of His, and Purkinje fibers (His-Purkinje system), which can fire (discharge) spontaneously. This is termed *automaticity.* Normally, the SA node is the natural pacemaker of the heart. It spontaneously fires 60 to 100 times per minute (Table 39.4). A secondary pacemaker from another site may fire in 2 ways. If the SA node fires more slowly than a secondary pacemaker, the electrical signals from the secondary pacemaker may "escape." The secondary pacemaker will then fire automatically at its intrinsic rate. These secondary pacemakers may start from the AV node at a rate of 40 to 60 times per minute or the His-Purkinje system at a rate of 20 to 40 times per minute.

Another way that secondary pacemakers can start is when they fire more rapidly than the normal pacemaker of the SA node. *Triggered beats* (early or late) may come from an *ectopic focus* or *accessory pathway* (area outside the normal conduction pathway) in the atria, AV node, or ventricles. This results in a dysrhythmia, which replaces the normal sinus rhythm.

The impulse started by the SA node, or an ectopic focus, is conducted to the heart cells. The property of myocardial tissue that allows it to be depolarized by a stimulus is called *excitability.*

TABLE 39.3 Approach to Assessing Heart Rhythm

When assessing a heart rhythm, use a consistent and systematic approach. One such approach includes the following:

1. Look for the P wave. Is it upright or inverted? Is there 1 for every QRS complex or more than 1? Are atrial fibrillatory or flutter waves present?
2. Evaluate the atrial rhythm. Is it regular or irregular?
3. Calculate the atrial rate.
4. Measure the duration of the PR interval. Is it normal duration or prolonged? Is the duration consistent before each QRS?
5. Evaluate the ventricular rhythm. Is it regular or irregular?
6. Calculate the ventricular rate.
7. Measure the duration of the QRS complex. Is it normal duration or prolonged?
8. Assess the ST segment. Is it isoelectric (flat), elevated, or depressed?
9. Measure the duration of the QT interval. Correct for heart rate (cQT) to determine if it is normal or prolonged.*
10. Note the T wave. Is it upright or inverted?

Other questions to consider include:

1. What is the dominant or underlying rhythm and/or dysrhythmia?
2. What is the clinical significance of your findings?
3. What is the treatment for the particular rhythm?

*A website for calculating the cQT interval for heart rate can be found at www.mdcalc.com/corrected-qt-interval-qtc.

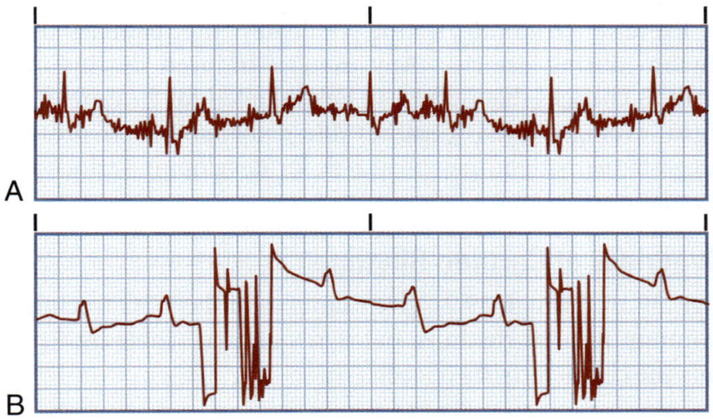

Fig. 39.8 Artifact. (A) Muscle tremor. (B) Loose electrodes.

TABLE 39.4 Intrinsic Rates of the Conduction System

Part of Conduction System	Rate
SA node and atria	60–100 times/min
AV node and bundle of His	40–60 times/min
Bundle branches and Purkinje fibers	20–40 times/min

The level of excitability is determined by the length of time after depolarization before the tissues can be restimulated. The recovery period after stimulation is the *refractory phase* or period. The *absolute refractory phase* or period occurs when excitability is zero, and the heart cannot be stimulated. The *relative refractory period* occurs slightly later in the cycle, and excitability is more likely. In states of *full excitability,* the heart is completely recovered. Fig. 39.9 shows the relationship between the refractory period and ECG.

If conduction is depressed and some areas of the heart are blocked (e.g., by infarction), the unblocked areas are activated

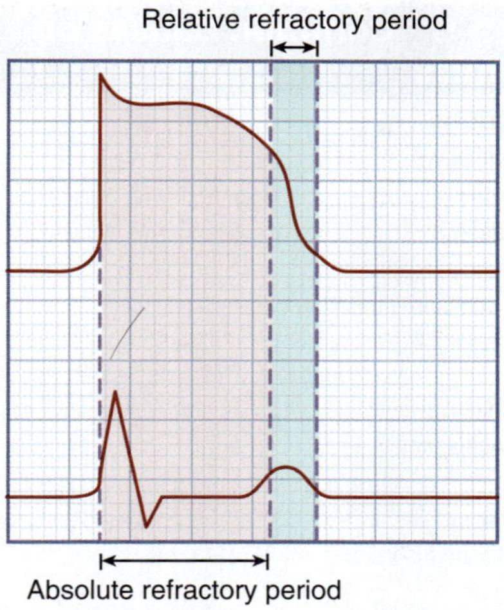

Fig. 39.9 Absolute and relative refractory periods correlated with the heart muscle's action potential and with an ECG tracing. (Modified from Urden LD, Stacy KM, Lough ME: *Critical care nursing: diagnosis and management,* ed 6, St Louis, 2010, Mosby.)

earlier than the blocked areas. When the block is unidirectional, this uneven conduction may allow the initial impulse to reenter areas that were previously not excitable but have recovered. The reentering impulse may be able to depolarize the atria and ventricles, causing a premature beat or rapid rhythm.

Evaluating Dysrhythmias

Dysrhythmias occur as the result of various abnormalities and disease states. Assess the heart rhythm, any changes in rhythm, and the patient's clinical status. Determining the cause of dysrhythmias is a priority. The cause influences the patient's treatment. Table 39.5 presents common causes of dysrhythmias.

Dysrhythmias occurring in nonmonitored settings present management challenges. If the patient becomes symptomatic (e.g., chest pain, syncope), determining the rhythm by heart monitoring is a high priority. Activate the emergency response system (ERS). Table 39.6 outlines the emergency care of the patient with a dysrhythmia.

In addition to continuous ECG monitoring during hospitalization, several other tests can assess dysrhythmias and the effectiveness of antidysrhythmic drug therapy. These include an electrophysiologic study (EPS), Holter monitoring, event monitoring (or loop recorder), exercise treadmill testing, and signal-averaged ECG. They can be done on an inpatient or outpatient basis. See Tables 35.10 and 35.11 for nursing care related to these tests.

An *electrophysiologic study* can identify the causes of heart blocks, tachydysrhythmias (dysrhythmias with rates greater than 100 beats/min), bradydysrhythmias (dysrhythmias with rates less than 60 beats/min), and syncope. An EPS study can locate accessory pathways and determine the effectiveness of antidysrhythmic drugs.

The Holter monitor continuously records the ECG while the patient is ambulatory and performing daily activities. The patient keeps a diary and records activities and any symptoms. Events in the diary are correlated with any dysrhythmias seen on the ECG. Use of event monitors has improved

TABLE 39.5 Common Causes of Dysrhythmias

Heart Conditions
- Accessory pathways
- Cardiomyopathy
- Conduction defects
- Heart failure
- Myocardial ischemia, infarction
- Valve disease

Other Conditions
- Acid-base imbalances
- Alcohol
- Caffeine, tobacco
- Connective tissue disorders
- Drowning
- Drug effects (e.g., antidysrhythmic drugs, stimulants, β-blockers) or toxicity
- Electric shock
- Electrolyte imbalances (e.g., hyperkalemia, hypocalcemia)
- Emotional crisis
- Herbal supplements (e.g., areca nut, wahoo root bark, yerba maté)
- Hypoxia
- Metabolic conditions (e.g., thyroid problems)
- Sepsis, shock
- Toxins

TABLE 39.6 EMERGENCY MANAGEMENT

Dysrhythmias

Assessment Findings	Interventions
• Irregular rate and rhythm; ↑ HR, bradycardia • Chest, neck, shoulder, back, jaw, or arm pain • Cold, clammy skin • ↓ Level of consciousness, confusion • ↓ or ↑ BP • ↓ O_2 saturation • ↓ Peripheral pulses • Diaphoresis • Dizziness, syncope • Dyspnea • Extreme restlessness, anxiety • Feeling of impending doom • Nausea and vomiting • Numbness, tingling of arms • Pallor • Palpitations • Weakness and fatigue	**Initial** • If unresponsive, assess circulation, airway, and breathing (CAB). • If responsive, monitor airway, breathing, and circulation (ABC). • Apply O_2 via nasal cannula or nonrebreather mask. • Take baseline vital signs with O_2 saturation. • Obtain 12-lead ECG. • Begin continuous ECG monitoring. • Identify underlying rate and rhythm. • Identify dysrhythmia. • Establish IV access. • Obtain baseline laboratory studies (e.g., CBC, electrolytes). **Ongoing Monitoring** • Monitor ABCs, vital signs, level of consciousness, O_2 saturation, and heart rhythm. • Anticipate need for antidysrhythmic drugs and analgesics. • Anticipate need for intubation if respiratory distress occurs. • Anticipate need to begin advanced cardiovascular life support (e.g., CPR, defibrillation, transcutaneous pacing).

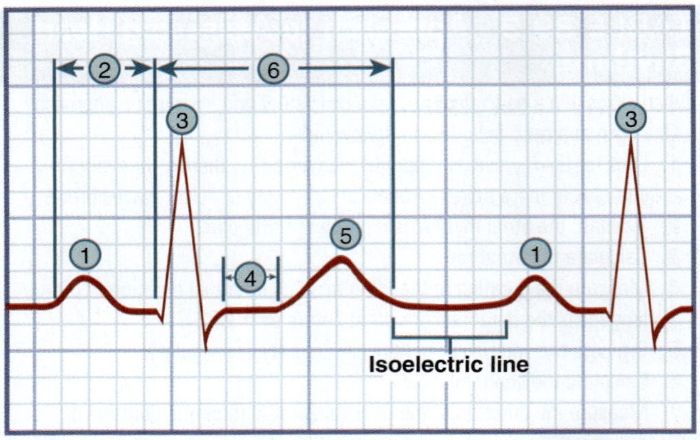

Fig. 39.10 The ECG tracing as seen in normal sinus rhythm. *1,* P wave; *2,* PR interval; *3,* QRS complex: Q wave, R wave, S wave; *4,* ST segment; *5,* T wave; *6,* QT interval. Isoelectric (flat) line or baseline represents the absence of electrical activity in the heart cells. (See Table 35.2 for timing of intervals.)

the evaluation of dysrhythmias in outpatients. Event monitors are recorders that the patient activates only when they have symptoms. New technology using smartphone apps can obtain and save ECG recordings and even detect some dysrhythmias. See an example of KardiaMobile at https://www.alivecor.com/kardiamobile.

Exercise treadmill testing evaluates the patient's heart rhythm during exercise. Any exercise-induced dysrhythmias or ECG changes that occur can be evaluated for treatment. The signal-averaged ECG identifies *late potentials.* Their presence suggests the patient may be at risk for developing serious ventricular dysrhythmias.

Overview of Cardiac Rhythms

Figs. 39.10 through 39.21 give examples of the ECG tracings of common normal rhythms and dysrhythmias. Table 39.7 presents the characteristics of each.

Normal Cardiac Rhythms

Normal sinus rhythm. *Normal sinus rhythm* refers to a rhythm that starts in the SA node at a rate of 60 to 100 beats/min and follows the normal conduction pathway (Fig. 39.10). The P wave is normal, precedes each QRS complex, and has a normal shape and duration. The PR interval is normal. The QRS complex has a normal shape and duration. Normal sinus rhythm implies that cardiac electrical activity is normal.

Sinus arrhythmia. In *sinus arrhythmia,* the conduction pathway is the same as that in sinus rhythm, but the SA node fires irregularly. This often results from changes in intrathoracic pressure during breathing. The HR increases slightly during inspiration and decreases slightly during exhalation. It remains 60 to 100 beats/min. It is common in healthy adults.

Types of Dysrhythmias

Sinus Bradycardia

In *sinus bradycardia,* the conduction pathway is the same as that in sinus rhythm, but the SA node fires at a rate less than 60 beats/min (Fig. 39.11A). *Symptomatic bradycardia* refers to a HR that is less

TABLE 39.7 Characteristics of Common Dysrhythmias

Pattern	Rate and Rhythm	P Wave	PR Interval	QRS Complex
Normal sinus rhythm (NSR)	60–100 beats/min and regular	Normal	Normal	Normal
Sinus bradycardia	<60 beats/min and regular	Normal	Normal	Normal
Sinus tachycardia	101–180 beats/min and regular	Normal	Normal	Normal
Premature atrial contraction (PAC)		Abnormal shape	Normal	Normal (usually)
Paroxysmal supraventricular tachycardia (PSVT)	151–220 beats/min and regular	Abnormal shape, may be hidden in the preceding T wave	Normal or shortened	Normal (usually)
Atrial flutter	*Atrial:* 200–350 beats/min and regular *Ventricular:* > or <100 beats/min and may be regular or irregular	Flutter (F) waves (saw-toothed pattern); more flutter waves than QRS complexes. May occur in a 2:1, 3:1, 4:1, etc., pattern	Not measurable	Normal (usually)
Atrial fibrillation	*Atrial:* 350–600 beats/min and irregular *Ventricular:* > or <100 beats/min and irregular	Fibrillatory (f) waves	Not measurable	Normal (usually)
Junctional dysrhythmias	40–180 beats/min and regular	Inverted, may be hidden in QRS complex or behind the S wave	Shortened, if present	Normal (usually)
First-degree AV block	Normal and regular	Normal	>0.20 sec	Normal
Second-degree AV block				
• **Type I** (Mobitz I, Wenckebach heart block)	*Atrial:* Normal and regular *Ventricular:* Slower and irregular	Normal	Progressive lengthening (longer, longer, longer, drop, now you have a Wenckebach)	Normal QRS width, with pattern of 1 non-conducted (blocked) QRS complex
• **Type II** (Mobitz II heart block)	*Atrial:* Usually normal and regular *Ventricular:* Slower and regular or irregular	More P waves than QRS complexes (e.g., 2:1, 3:1)	Normal or prolonged but consistent for every QRS	Widened QRS, preceded by ≥2 P waves, with non-conducted (blocked) QRS complex
Third-degree AV block (complete heart block)	*Atrial:* Regular but may appear irregular due to P waves hidden in QRS complexes *Ventricular:* 20–60 beats/min and regular	Normal, but no connection with QRS complex	Inconsistent	Normal or widened, no relationship with P waves
Premature ventricular contraction (PVC)	Underlying rhythm can be any rate, regular or irregular rhythm, PVCs occur at variable rates	Not usually visible, hidden in the PVC	Not measurable	Wide and distorted
Ventricular tachycardia (VT)	150–250 beats/min and regular or irregular	Not usually visible	Not measurable	Wide and distorted
Accelerated idioventricular rhythm	40–100 beats/min and regular	Not usually visible	Not measurable	Wide and distorted
Ventricular fibrillation (VF)	Not measurable and irregular	Absent	Not measurable	Not measurable

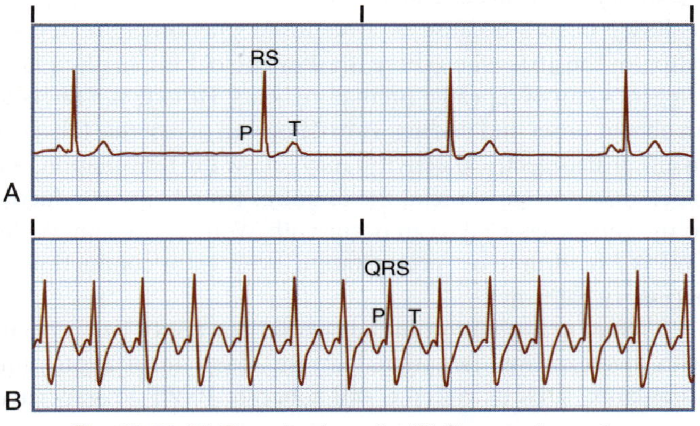

Fig. 39.11 (A) Sinus bradycardia. (B) Sinus tachycardia.

than 60 beats/min and causes the patient to have symptoms of inadequate perfusion (e.g., fatigue, dizziness, chest pain, syncope).[4,5]

Clinical associations. Sinus bradycardia may be a normal sinus rhythm in aerobically trained athletes and in some people during sleep. It also occurs in response to a Valsalva maneuver, hypothermia, increased intraocular pressure, vagal stimulation, and certain drugs (e.g., β-blockers, calcium channel blockers). Common disease states associated with sinus bradycardia are hypothyroidism, increased intracranial pressure, and inferior myocardial infarction (MI).

ECG characteristics. In sinus bradycardia, the HR is less than 60 beats/min, and rhythm is regular. The P wave precedes each QRS complex and has a normal shape and duration. The

PR interval is normal. The QRS complex has a normal shape and duration.

Clinical significance. The significance of sinus bradycardia depends on how the patient tolerates it. Manifestations of symptomatic bradycardia include pale, cool skin, hypotension, weakness, angina, dizziness, confusion, and shortness of breath.

Treatment. If bradycardia is due to drugs, these may have to be held, stopped, or reduced. For the patient with symptoms, treatment consists of giving IV atropine (anticholinergic drug).[6] If atropine is ineffective, transcutaneous pacing or a dopamine or epinephrine infusion are options. The patient may need a permanent pacemaker.

Sinus Tachycardia

The conduction pathway is the same in *sinus tachycardia* as in normal sinus rhythm. The discharge rate from the sinus node increases because of vagal inhibition or sympathetic stimulation. The sinus rate is 101 to 180 beats/min (Fig. 39.11B).[7]

Clinical associations. Sinus tachycardia is associated with many physiologic and psychologic stressors. Stressors include exercise, fever, pain, hypotension, hypovolemia, anemia, hypoxia, hypoglycemia, myocardial ischemia, heart failure (HF), hyperthyroidism, anxiety, and fear. It can be an effect of drugs, such as epinephrine, norepinephrine (Levophed), atropine, caffeine, theophylline, or hydralazine. Many over-the-counter cold remedies have active ingredients (e.g., pseudoephedrine) that can cause tachycardia.

ECG characteristics. In sinus tachycardia, the HR is 101 to 180 beats/min, and rhythm is regular. The P wave is normal and precedes each QRS complex. The PR interval is normal. The QRS complex has a normal shape and duration.

Clinical significance. The clinical significance of sinus tachycardia depends on the patient's tolerance of the increased HR. The patient may have dizziness, dyspnea, and hypotension because of decreased CO. An increased HR increases myocardial oxygen (O_2) consumption. Angina or an increase in infarction size may occur with sinus tachycardia in those with coronary artery disease (CAD) or an acute MI.

Treatment. The underlying cause guides the treatment. For example, if the patient has tachycardia from pain, effective pain management is important to treat the tachycardia. In clinically stable patients, we may try vagal maneuvers. IV β-blockers (e.g., metoprolol), adenosine (Adenocard), or calcium channel blockers (e.g., diltiazem) can reduce HR and decrease myocardial O_2 consumption.[5] Clinically unstable patients may need synchronized cardioversion.

Premature Atrial Contraction

A **premature atrial contraction (PAC)** is a contraction starting from an ectopic focus in the atrium (a location other than the SA node) sooner than the next expected sinus beat. The ectopic signal starts in the left or right atrium and travels across the atria by an abnormal pathway. This creates a distorted P wave (Fig. 39.12). At the AV node, the ectopic signal may be stopped (non-conducted PAC), delayed (lengthened PR interval), or conducted normally. If the signal moves through the AV node, in most cases, it is conducted normally through the ventricles.

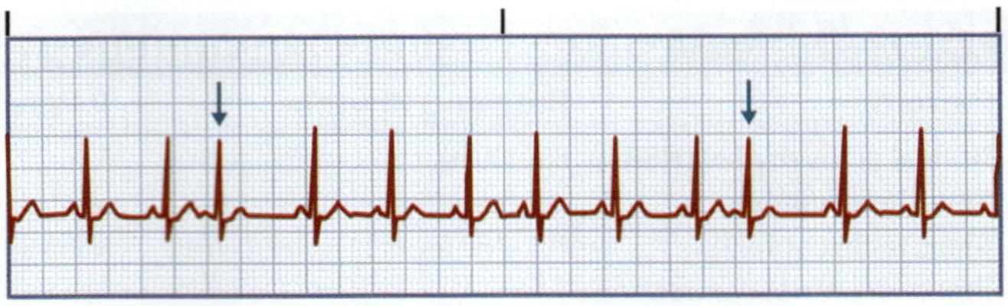

Fig. 39.12 Premature atrial contractions *(arrows)*.

Clinical associations. In a normal heart, a PAC can result from emotional stress, fatigue, or from caffeine, tobacco, or alcohol use. A PAC can also result from hypoxia, electrolyte imbalances, hyperthyroidism, chronic obstructive pulmonary disease (COPD), and heart disease, including CAD and valvular disease.

ECG characteristics. HR varies with the underlying rate and frequency of the PAC. The rhythm is irregular. The P wave has a different shape from that of a P wave originating in the SA node. It may be hidden in the preceding T wave. The PR interval may be shorter or longer than the PR interval coming from the SA node but is within normal limits. The QRS complex is usually normal. If the QRS interval is 0.12 second or more, abnormal conduction through the ventricles is occurring.

Clinical significance. In a person with a healthy heart, isolated PACs are not significant. Patients may report palpitations or a sense that the heart "skipped a beat." In a person with heart disease, frequent PACs may indicate enhanced automaticity of the atria or a reentry mechanism. Such PACs may warn of or start more serious dysrhythmias (e.g., supraventricular tachycardia [SVT]).

Treatment. Treatment depends on the patient's symptoms. Sources of stimulation, such as caffeine or sympathomimetic drugs (e.g., epinephrine, dopamine), may be withdrawn. β-Blockers may be used to decrease PACs.

Paroxysmal Supraventricular Tachycardia

Paroxysmal supraventricular tachycardia (PSVT), also known as supraventricular tachycardia or atrial tachycardia, is a dysrhythmia starting in an ectopic focus anywhere above the bifurcation of the bundle of His (Fig. 39.13).[6] Identifying the ectopic focus is often hard even with a 12-lead ECG since it requires recording the dysrhythmia as it starts.

PSVT occurs because of a reentrant phenomenon (reexcitation of the atria when there is a 1-way block). Usually, a PAC triggers a run of repeated premature beats. *Paroxysmal* refers to an abrupt onset and ending. A brief period of *asystole* (absence of all cardiac electrical activity) may follow the termination. AV block may prevent some of the impulses from being conducted to the ventricles. PSVT can occur with Wolff-Parkinson-White (WPW) syndrome or "preexcitation" with extra conduction or accessory pathways.

Clinical associations. In the normal heart, PSVT may occur with overexertion, emotional stress, deep inspiration, and stimulants, such as caffeine and tobacco. PSVT is associated

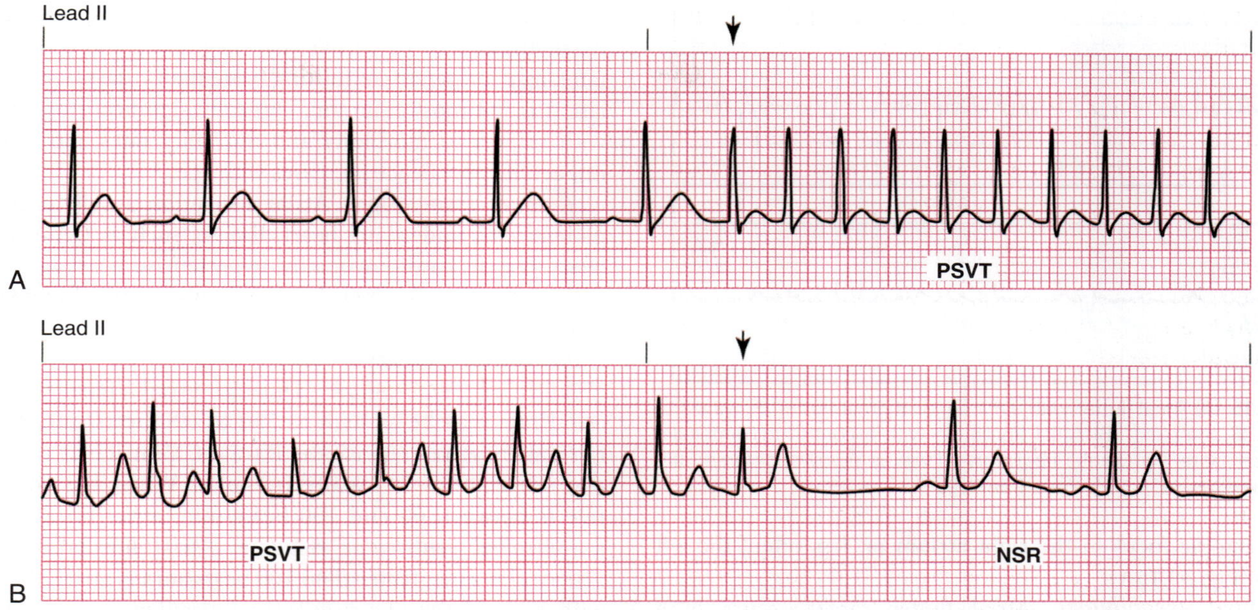

Fig. 39.13 Paroxysmal supraventricular tachycardia (PSVT). *Arrows* indicate beginning and ending of PSVT.

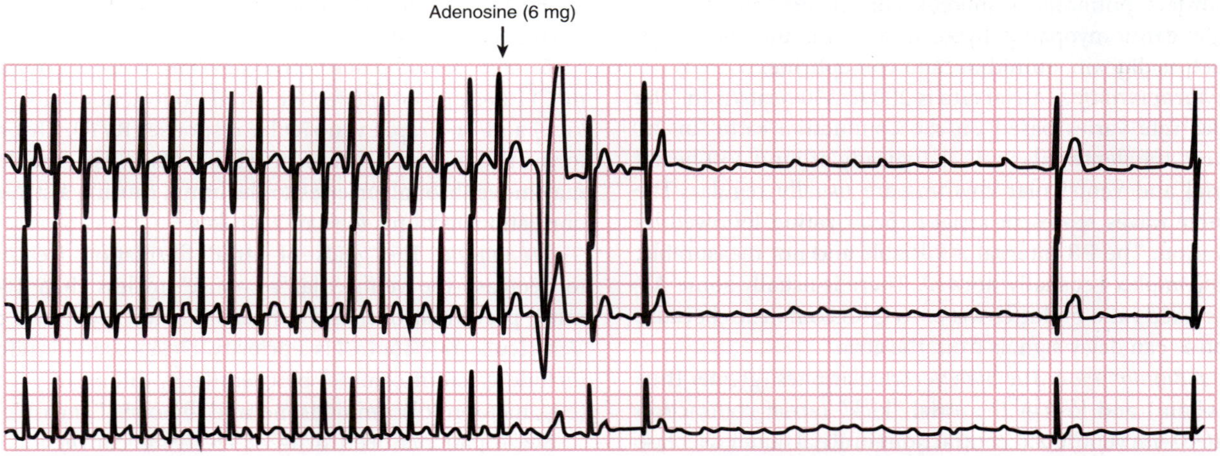

Fig. 39.14 Administration of adenosine rapid IV push. Note that SVT is followed by a brief period of asystole before the return to normal sinus rhythm. This is a common occurrence after adenosine.

with rheumatic heart disease, digitalis toxicity, CAD, and cor pulmonale.

ECG characteristics. In PSVT, the HR is 151 to 220 beats/min. The rhythm is regular or slightly irregular. The P wave may have an abnormal shape or be hidden in the preceding T wave. The PR interval may be shortened or normal. The QRS complex is usually normal.

Clinical significance. The significance of PSVT depends on the associated symptoms. A prolonged episode and HR greater than 180 beats/min will cause decreased CO because of reduced stroke volume. Manifestations include hypotension, palpitations, dyspnea, and angina.

Treatment. Treatment for PSVT includes vagal stimulation and drug therapy. Common vagal maneuvers include Valsalva and coughing. IV adenosine is the drug of choice to convert PSVT to a normal sinus rhythm (Fig. 39.14).[7] This drug has a short half-life (10 seconds) and is well tolerated. IV β-blockers and calcium channel blockers (e.g., diltiazem, verapamil) are options. The patient who becomes hemodynamically unstable undergoes synchronized cardioversion.

DRUG ALERT

Adenosine (Adenocard)

- Explain that the patient may feel chest pressure after receiving the medication.
- Injection site should be as close to the heart as possible (e.g., antecubital area).
- Give IV dose rapidly (over 1 to 2 sec) and follow with a rapid 20-mL normal saline flush. Use a stopcock setup to make sure adenosine gets to the heart quickly.
- Monitor patient's ECG continuously. Brief period of asystole is common (Fig. 39.14).
- Assess the patient for flushing, dizziness, chest pain, or palpitations.

Treatment of recurring PSVT and PSVT in patients with WPW syndrome includes radiofrequency catheter ablation of the accessory pathway.

Atrial Flutter

Atrial flutter is an atrial tachydysrhythmia identified by recurring, regular, sawtooth-shaped flutter waves originating from a

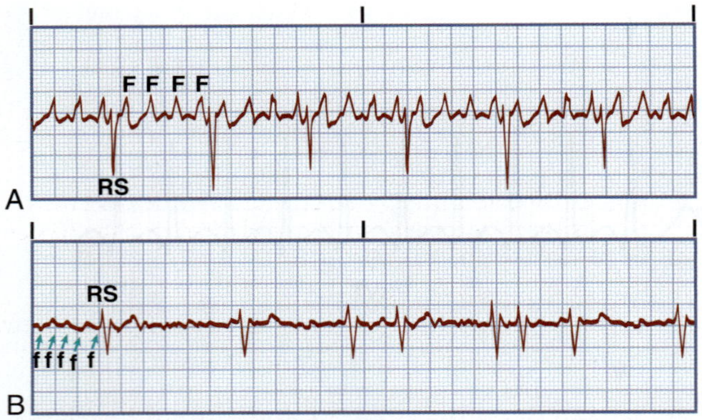

Fig. 39.15 (A) Atrial flutter with a 4:1 conduction (4 flutter *[F]* waves to each QRS complex). (B) Atrial fibrillation with a controlled ventricular response. Note the chaotic fibrillatory *(f)* waves *(arrows)* between the RS complexes. Note: Recorded from lead V_1.

single ectopic focus in the right atrium or, less often, the left atrium (Fig. 39.15A).

Clinical associations. Atrial flutter rarely occurs in a healthy heart. It is associated with CAD, hypertension, mitral valve disorders, pulmonary embolus, chronic lung disease, cor pulmonale, cardiomyopathy, hyperthyroidism, and the use of drugs, such as digoxin, quinidine, and epinephrine.

ECG characteristics. Atrial rate is 200 to 350 beats/min. The ventricular rate varies based on the conduction ratio. In 2:1 conduction, the ventricular rate is typically around 150 beats/min. Atrial and ventricular rhythms are usually regular. The atrial flutter waves represent atrial depolarization followed by repolarization. The PR interval is variable and not measurable. The QRS complex is usually normal. There is usually some AV block in a fixed ratio of flutter waves to QRS complexes because the AV node can delay signals from the atria.

Clinical significance. The high ventricular rates (greater than 100 beats/min) and loss of the atrial "kick" (atrial contraction coordinated with ventricular contraction) in atrial flutter decrease CO. This can cause serious problems, such as HF, especially in the patient with underlying heart disease. Patients with atrial flutter have an increased risk for stroke because thrombi (clots) can form in the atria from the stasis of blood. Patients receive warfarin or another anticoagulant to prevent stroke.[5,8] See Chapter 41 for discussion of anticoagulation therapy.

Treatment. The primary goal in treatment of atrial flutter is to slow the ventricular response by increasing AV block. Drugs used to control ventricular rate include calcium channel blockers and β-blockers.[5] Electrical cardioversion may convert the atrial flutter to sinus rhythm in an emergency (e.g., when the patient is clinically unstable) or electively. Antidysrhythmic drugs can convert atrial flutter to sinus rhythm (e.g., ibutilide [Corvert]) or maintain sinus rhythm (e.g., amiodarone, flecainide).

Radiofrequency catheter ablation in an EPS laboratory is the treatment of choice for atrial flutter. Low-voltage, high-frequency electrical energy is used to ablate (or destroy) the ectopic foci through a catheter in the right atrium. This should restore normal sinus rhythm.

Atrial Fibrillation

Atrial fibrillation is characterized by total disorganization of atrial electrical activity because of multiple ectopic foci. It results in loss of effective atrial contraction (Fig. 39.15B). The dysrhythmia may be paroxysmal (beginning and ending spontaneously) or persistent (lasting more than 7 days). Atrial fibrillation is the most common, clinically significant dysrhythmia with respect to morbidity and mortality rates and economic impact. Its prevalence increases with age.

Clinical associations. Atrial fibrillation usually occurs in a patient with underlying heart disease, such as CAD, valvular heart disease, cardiomyopathy, hypertensive heart disease, HF, and pericarditis. It often develops acutely with thyrotoxicosis, alcohol intoxication, caffeine use, electrolyte problems, stress, and after heart surgery.

ECG characteristics. During atrial fibrillation, the atrial rate may be as high as 350 to 600 beats/min. Chaotic, fibrillatory waves replace the P waves. Ventricular rate varies, and the rhythm is usually irregular. When the ventricular rate is between 60 and 100 beats/min, atrial fibrillation has a *controlled ventricular response.* Atrial fibrillation with a ventricular rate greater than 100 beats/min is atrial fibrillation with a *rapid (or uncontrolled) ventricular response.* The PR interval is not measurable. The QRS complex usually has a normal shape and duration. At times, atrial flutter and atrial fibrillation coexist.

Clinical significance. Atrial fibrillation results in a decrease in CO because of ineffective atrial contractions (loss of atrial kick) and/or a rapid ventricular response (RVR). Thrombi may form in the atria because of blood stasis. An embolized clot may move through arteries to the brain, causing a stroke. Atrial fibrillation accounts for 1 in 7 strokes.[9]

Treatment. The goals of atrial fibrillation treatment are to decrease the ventricular response (to less than 100 beats/min), prevent stroke, and convert to sinus rhythm, if possible. Ventricular rate control is a priority. Drugs used for rate control include calcium channel blockers (e.g., diltiazem), β-blockers (e.g., metoprolol), amiodarone, and digoxin (Lanoxin).

Some patients need drug or electrical conversion of atrial fibrillation to a normal sinus rhythm (e.g., reduced exercise tolerance with rate control drugs, contraindications to warfarin). The most common antidysrhythmic drug used for conversion to and maintenance of sinus rhythm is amiodarone.[6]

Electrical cardioversion may convert atrial fibrillation to a normal sinus rhythm. If a patient is in atrial fibrillation for longer than 48 hours, anticoagulation therapy with warfarin is needed for 3 to 4 weeks before the cardioversion.[8] Anticoagulation therapy continues for several weeks because the procedure can cause the clots to dislodge, placing the patient at risk for stroke. A transesophageal echocardiogram may be done to rule out clots in the atria. If no clots are present, anticoagulation therapy may not be needed before the cardioversion.

If drugs or cardioversion does not convert atrial fibrillation to normal sinus rhythm, the patient needs long-term anticoagulation therapy (Table 39.8). Warfarin requires monitoring for therapeutic levels (e.g., international normalized ratio [INR]). Alternatives to warfarin are available that do not require routine laboratory testing. Examples include dabigatran (Pradaxa), apixaban (Eliquis), and rivaroxaban (Xarelto).[8] See Chapter 41 for more on anticoagulation therapy.

TABLE 39.8 **Drug Therapy**

Antithrombotic Therapy for Atrial Fibrillation and Atrial Flutter

Risk Category	Recommended Therapy
Mechanical heart valve	Warfarin (target INR 2.5–3.5)
CHA_2DS_2-VASc[a] score of 0	No therapy recommended
CHA_2DS_2-VASc score of 1	No therapy recommended. An oral anticoagulant or aspirin (e.g., 81–325 mg/day) may be considered
CHA_2DS_2-VASc score of ≥2 or a history of prior stroke or transient ischemia attack (TIA)	Warfarin (target INR 2.0–3.0) Apixaban (Eliquis) Dabigatran (Pradaxa) Edoxaban (Savaysa) Rivaroxaban (Xarelto)
CHA_2DS_2-VASc score of ≥2 and end-stage kidney disease or on hemodialysis	Warfarin (INR 2.0–3.0) Apixaban (Eliquis)

[a]The CHA_2DS_2-VASc score for nonvalvular atrial fibrillation stroke risk can be calculated at www.mdcalc.com/cha2ds2-vasc-score-for-atrial-fibrillation-stroke-risk/.

CHA_2DS_2-VASc, Congestive heart failure; hypertension; age ≥75 (doubled); diabetes; prior stroke, transient ischemic attack, thromboembolism (doubled); vascular disease; age 65 to 74; sex; *INR,* international normalized ratio.

Modified from January CT, Wann LS, Calkins H, et al.: 2019 AHA/ACC/HRS focused update on the 2014 AHA/ACC/HRS guideline for the management of patients with atrial fibrillation, *Circulation* 140:e125, 2019.

For symptomatic patients with atrial fibrillation refractory to drugs or electrical conversion, radiofrequency catheter ablation, AV nodal ablation, and the Maze procedure are further options. AV nodal ablation involves destruction of the AV node and insertion of a permanent ventricular pacemaker.

The Maze procedure stops atrial fibrillation by interrupting the ectopic foci that are causing the dysrhythmia. Incisions are made in both atria, and *cryoablation* (cold therapy) is used to stop the formation and conduction of ectopic signals and restore normal sinus rhythm.[5]

Left atrial appendage occlusion. The left atrial appendage (LAA) is a pouch that extends off the left atrium. The LAA is a common source of blood clots in patients with atrial fibrillation. LAA occlusion is a treatment strategy to prevent blood clot formation in patients who have atrial fibrillation. Removing or occluding the LAA can decrease the incidence of strokes.

A special stapler can be used to remove the LAA, or the LAA can be occluded manually with sutures or an LAA occlusion device (e.g., Amplatzer Amulet Occluder).[5] These devices are positioned around the LAA and then closed like a clamp that is used to shut off the blood supply. This prevents blood from flowing into and out of the LAA. LAA occlusion is an alternative for patients who cannot use oral anticoagulants.[5]

CHECK YOUR PRACTICE

You are caring for a 72-year-old female patient who was admitted with chest pain. She has continuous EGG monitoring. You are concerned because you think the ECG tracing is hard to interpret, and she may be in atrial fibrillation. Your preceptor tells you that a lot of artifact is present.

- What can you do to improve the ECG tracing?
- How would you determine the patient's rhythm?

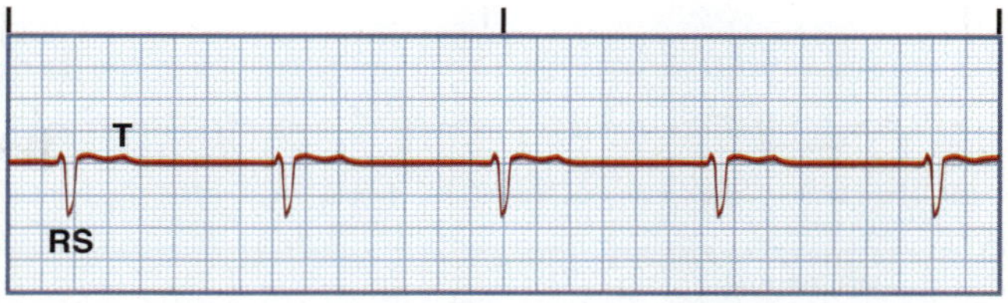

Fig. 39.16 Junctional escape rhythm. P wave is hidden in the RS complex. NOTE: Recorded from lead V_1.

Junctional Dysrhythmias

Junctional dysrhythmias start in the area of the AV node to the bundle of His known as the AV junction. They result because the SA node does not fire, or the signal is blocked. When this occurs, the AV node becomes the pacemaker of the heart. The impulse from the AV node usually moves in a retrograde (backward) fashion. This produces an abnormal P wave that occurs just before or after the QRS complex or is hidden in the QRS complex. The impulse usually moves normally through the ventricles. Junctional premature beats may occur. They are treated like PACs. Other junctional dysrhythmias include junctional escape rhythm (Fig. 39.16), accelerated junctional rhythm, and junctional tachycardia. Their treatment depends on the patient's tolerance of the rhythm and the patient's clinical condition.

Clinical associations. Junctional dysrhythmias are often associated with CAD, HF, cardiomyopathy, electrolyte imbalances, inferior MI, and rheumatic heart disease. Certain drugs (e.g., digoxin, nicotine, amphetamines, caffeine) can also cause junctional dysrhythmias.

ECG characteristics. In junctional escape rhythm, the HR is 40 to 60 beats/min. HR is 61 to 100 beats/min in accelerated junctional rhythm and 101 to 180 beats/min in junctional tachycardia. The rhythm is regular. The P wave is abnormal in shape and inverted. It hidden in the QRS complex (Fig. 35.16). The PR interval is less than 0.12 second when the P wave precedes the QRS complex. The QRS complex is usually normal.

Clinical significance. Junctional escape rhythms serve as a safety mechanism when the SA node has not been effective. Escape rhythms should not be suppressed. Accelerated junctional rhythm is due to sympathetic stimulation to improve CO. Junctional tachycardia indicates a more serious problem. This rhythm may reduce CO, causing the patient to become hemodynamically unstable (e.g., hypotensive).

Treatment. Treatment varies by the type of junctional dysrhythmia. If a patient has symptoms with a junctional escape rhythm, atropine can be used. If accelerated junctional rhythm or junctional tachycardia are caused by drug toxicity, the drug is stopped. In the absence of digitalis toxicity, β-blockers, calcium channel blockers, and amiodarone are used for rate control.

First-Degree AV Block

First-degree AV block is a type of AV block in which every impulse is conducted to the ventricles, but the time of AV conduction is prolonged (Fig. 39.17A). After the impulse moves through the AV node, the ventricles usually respond normally.

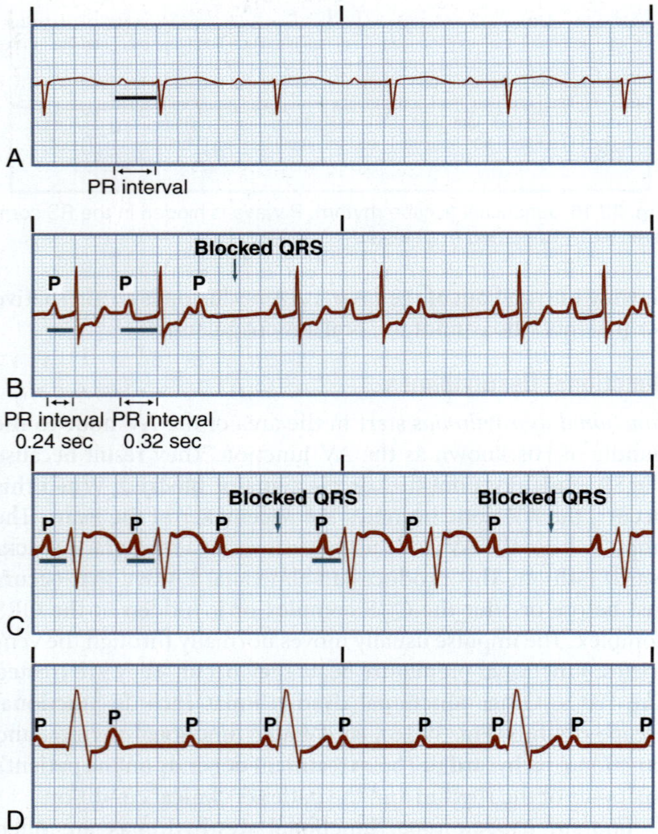

Fig. 39.17 Heart block. (A) First-degree AV block with a PR interval of 0.40 sec. (B) Second-degree AV block, type I, with progressive lengthening of the PR interval until a QRS complex is blocked. (C) Second-degree AV block, type II, with constant PR intervals and variable blocked QRS complexes. (D) Third-degree AV block. Note that there is no relationship between P waves and QRS complexes.

Clinical associations. First-degree AV block is associated with increasing age, MI, CAD, rheumatic fever, hyperthyroidism, electrolyte imbalances (e.g., hypokalemia), vagal stimulation, and drugs, such as digoxin, β-blockers, calcium channel blockers, and flecainide.

ECG characteristics. In first-degree AV block, the HR is normal. The rhythm is regular. The P wave is normal. The PR interval is prolonged (greater than 0.20 second). The QRS complex usually has a normal shape and duration.

Clinical significance. First-degree AV block is usually not serious. Patients are asymptomatic.

Treatment. There is no treatment for first-degree AV block. Treatment of associated conditions may be considered. Monitor patients for changes in heart rhythm (e.g., more serious AV block).

Second-Degree AV Block, Type I

Type I second-degree AV block (Mobitz I or *Wenckebach heart block)* includes a gradual lengthening of the PR interval. AV conduction time is increasingly prolonged until an atrial impulse is not conducted and a QRS complex is blocked (missing) (Fig. 39.17B). Type I AV block most often occurs in the AV node, but it can occur in the His-Purkinje system.

Clinical associations. Type I AV block may result from drugs, such as digoxin or β-blockers. It may be associated with CAD and other diseases that can slow AV conduction.

ECG characteristics. Atrial rate is regular, but ventricular rate may be slower because of non-conducted or blocked QRS complexes resulting in bradycardia. Once a ventricular beat is blocked, the cycle repeats itself with progressive lengthening of the PR intervals until another QRS complex is blocked. Think of the phrase, "longer, longer, longer, drop, now you have a Wenckebach." The rhythm appears on the ECG in a pattern of grouped beats. Ventricular rhythm is irregular. The P wave has a normal shape. The QRS complex has a normal shape and duration.

Clinical significance. Type I AV block is usually a result of myocardial ischemia or inferior MI. It is generally transient and well-tolerated. However, in some patients (e.g., acute MI), it may be a warning sign of a more serious AV conduction problem (e.g., complete heart block).

Treatment. A symptomatic patient may need atropine or a temporary pacemaker to increase HR, especially if the patient has had an MI. If the patient is asymptomatic, observe the rhythm closely. Have a transcutaneous pacemaker (TCP) on standby. Bradycardia is more likely to become symptomatic when hypotension, HF, or shock is already present.

Second-Degree AV Block, Type II

In *type II second-degree AV block (Mobitz II heart block),* a P wave is non-conducted without progressive PR lengthening. This usually occurs when a block in 1 of the bundle branches is present (Fig. 39.17C). On conducted beats, the PR interval is constant. Type II second-degree AV block is a more serious type of block because a certain number of impulses from the SA node are not conducted to the ventricles. This occurs in ratios of 2:1, 3:1, and so on (e.g., 2 P waves to one QRS complex, 3 P waves to 1 QRS complex). It may occur with varying ratios.[5]

Clinical associations. Type II AV block is associated with rheumatic heart disease, CAD, anterior MI, and drug toxicity.

ECG characteristics. Atrial rate is usually normal. Ventricular rate depends on the degree of AV block. Atrial rhythm is regular, but ventricular rhythm may be irregular. The P wave has a normal shape. The PR interval may be normal or prolonged in duration and remains constant on conducted beats. The QRS complex is usually greater than 0.12 second because of bundle branch block.

Clinical significance. Type II AV block often progresses to third-degree AV block. It is associated with a poor prognosis. The reduced HR often results in decreased CO with subsequent hypotension and myocardial ischemia. Type II AV block is an indication for a permanent pacemaker.

Treatment. Transcutaneous pacing or the insertion of a temporary pacemaker may be needed before inserting a permanent pacemaker if the patient is symptomatic (e.g., hypotension, angina).[5,6]

Third-Degree AV Block

Third-degree AV block, or **complete heart block**, is a form of AV dissociation in which no impulses from the atria are conducted to the ventricles (Fig. 39.17D). The atria are stimulated and contract independently of the ventricles. The ventricular rhythm is an escape rhythm. The ectopic pacemaker may be above or below the bifurcation of the bundle of His.

Clinical associations. Third-degree AV block is associated with severe heart disease, including CAD, MI, myocarditis, cardiomyopathy, and some systemic diseases, such as scleroderma. Some drugs can cause third-degree AV block, such as digoxin, β-blockers, and calcium channel blockers.

ECG characteristics. The atrial rate is usually a sinus rate of 60 to 100 beats/min. The ventricular rate depends on the site of the block. If it is in the AV node, the rate is 40 to 60 beats/min. If it is in the His-Purkinje system, it is 20 to 40 beats/min. Atrial and ventricular rhythms are regular but unrelated to each other. The P wave has a normal shape. The PR interval is variable. There is no relationship between the P wave and the QRS complex. The QRS complex is normal if the escape rhythm starts at the bundle of His or above. It is widened if the escape rhythm starts below the bundle of His.

Clinical significance. Third-degree AV block usually results in reduced CO with subsequent ischemia, HF, and shock. Syncope from third-degree AV block may result from severe bradycardia or even periods of asystole.

Treatment. Symptomatic patients need a TCP until a temporary transvenous pacemaker can be inserted.[5,6] Drugs such as dopamine and epinephrine are interim measures to increase HR and support BP until temporary pacing is started. Patients need a permanent pacemaker as soon as possible. Atropine is not an effective treatment.

Premature Ventricular Contractions

A **premature ventricular contraction (PVC)** is a contraction coming from an ectopic focus in the ventricles. It is the premature (early) occurrence of a QRS complex. A PVC is wide and distorted in shape compared with a QRS complex coming down the normal conduction pathway (Fig. 39.18). PVCs that have the same shape are *unifocal* PVCs. PVCs that arise from different foci appear different in shape from each other. These are *multifocal* PVCs. When every other beat is a PVC, the rhythm is *ventricular bigeminy.* When every third beat is a PVC, it is *ventricular trigeminy.* We call 2 consecutive PVCs a *couplet.*

Ventricular tachycardia (VT) occurs when there are 3 or more consecutive PVCs. *R-on-T phenomenon* occurs when a PVC falls on the T wave of a preceding beat (Fig. 39.19). This is especially dangerous because the PVC is firing during the relative refractory phase of ventricular repolarization. Excitability of the heart cells increases during this time. The risk for the PVC to start VT or ventricular fibrillation (VF) is great.

Clinical associations. PVCs are associated with stimulants, such as caffeine, alcohol, nicotine, aminophylline, epinephrine, and isoproterenol. They can occur with electrolyte imbalances, hypoxia, fever, exercise, and emotional stress. Disease states associated with PVCs include MI, mitral valve prolapse, HF, cardiomyopathy, and CAD.

ECG characteristics. HR varies according to intrinsic rate and number of PVCs. Rhythm is irregular because of premature beats. The P wave is rarely visible. It is usually lost in the QRS complex of the PVC. Retrograde conduction may occur with the P wave seen after the ectopic beat. The PR interval is not measurable. The QRS complex is wide and distorted in shape, lasting more than 0.12 second. The T wave is generally large and opposite in direction to the major direction of the QRS complex.

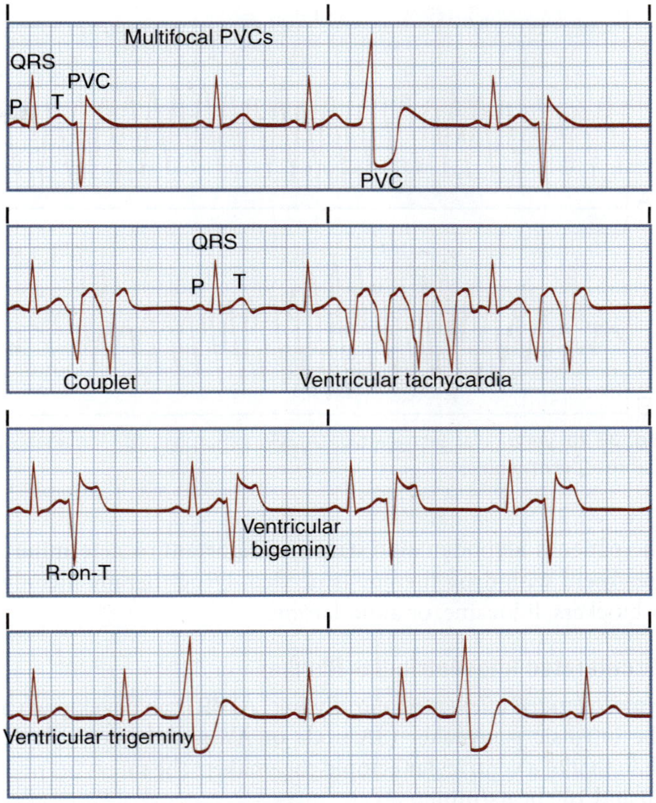

Fig. 39.18 Various types of premature ventricular contractions *(PVCs).*

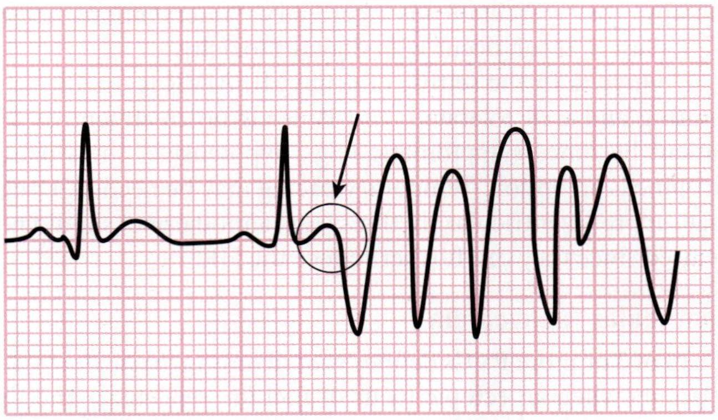

Fig. 39.19 R-on-T phenomenon. The "shock" occurred on the T wave leading to ventricular tachycardia.

Clinical significance. PVCs are usually not harmful in a patient with a normal heart. PVCs in CAD or acute MI indicate ventricular irritability. PVCs may reduce the CO and lead to angina and HF for those with heart disease, so assess the patient's physiologic response. Take the patient's apical-radial pulse rate and determine the pulse deficit since PVCs often do not generate a sufficient ventricular contraction to result in a peripheral pulse.

Treatment. Treatment relates to the cause of the PVCs (e.g., O_2 therapy for hypoxia, electrolyte replacement). Assessing

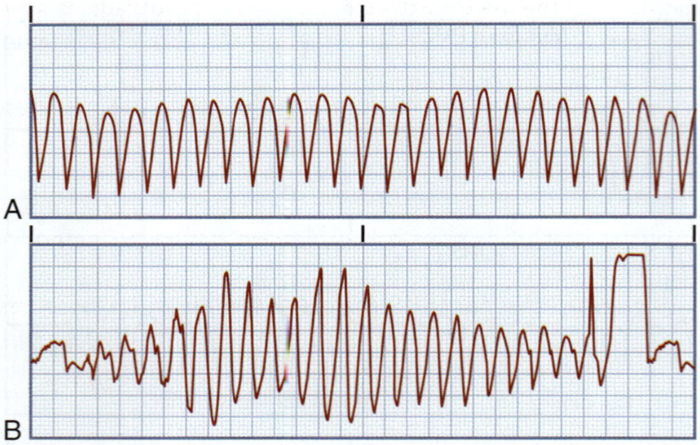

Fig. 39.20 Ventricular tachycardia. (A) Monomorphic. (B) Torsades de pointes (polymorphic).

the patient's hemodynamic status is important to determine if treatment with drug therapy is needed. Drug therapy includes β-blockers, lidocaine, or amiodarone.

Accelerated Idioventricular Rhythm

An *accelerated idioventricular rhythm* (AIVR) can develop when the intrinsic pacemaker (SA node or AV node) rate is slower than that of a ventricular ectopic pacemaker. The rate is between 40 and 100 beats/min.

Clinical associations. It is most often associated with acute MI and reperfusion of the myocardium after thrombolytic therapy or percutaneous coronary interventions (e.g., angioplasty). It can occur with digitalis toxicity.

Treatment. In the setting of acute MI, AIVR is usually self-limiting and well tolerated, and it needs no treatment. If the patient becomes symptomatic (e.g., hypotensive, chest pain), atropine is an option. Temporary pacing may be needed. Drugs that suppress ventricular rhythms (e.g., amiodarone) should not be used since they can further reduce the HR.

Ventricular Tachycardia

A run of 3 or more PVCs defines **ventricular tachycardia (VT)**. It occurs when an ectopic focus or foci fire repeatedly and the ventricle takes control as the pacemaker. Different forms of VT exist, depending on QRS configuration. *Monomorphic* VT (Fig. 39.20A) has QRS complexes that are the same in shape, size, and direction. *Polymorphic* VT occurs when the QRS complexes gradually change back and forth from one shape, size, and direction to another over a series of beats. *Torsades de pointes* (French for "twisting of the points") is polymorphic VT associated with a prolonged QT interval of the underlying rhythm (Fig. 39.20B).

We describe VT as sustained (longer than 30 seconds) or nonsustained (less than 30 seconds). The development of VT is an ominous sign. It is a life-threatening dysrhythmia because of decreased CO and the possible development of VF, which is lethal.

Clinical associations. VT is associated with MI, CAD, significant electrolyte imbalances, cardiomyopathy, long QT syndrome, drug toxicity, and central nervous system disorders. It can occur in patients who have no evidence of heart disease.

ECG characteristics. Ventricular rate is 150 to 250 beats/min. Rhythm may be regular or irregular. AV dissociation may be present, with P waves occurring independently of the QRS complex. The ventricles may depolarize the atria in a retrograde fashion. The P wave is usually buried in the QRS complex. The PR interval is not measurable. The QRS complex appears distorted and wide (greater than 0.12 second in duration). The T wave is in the opposite direction of the QRS complex (Fig. 39.20).

Clinical significance. VT can be stable (patient has a pulse) or unstable (patient is pulseless). Sustained VT causes a severe decrease in CO because of decreased ventricular diastolic filling times and loss of atrial contraction. This results in hypotension, pulmonary edema, decreased cerebral blood flow, and cardiopulmonary arrest. VT must be treated quickly, even if it occurs only briefly and stops abruptly. Episodes may recur if prophylactic treatment is not started. VF may develop.

Treatment. Precipitating causes (e.g., electrolyte imbalances, ischemia) must be identified and treated. If the VT is monomorphic and the patient is clinically stable (e.g., pulse is present) with preserved left ventricular function, options include IV procainamide, lidocaine, or amiodarone.[6] These drugs can be given if VT is polymorphic with a normal baseline QT interval.

Treatment for polymorphic VT with a prolonged baseline QT interval includes IV magnesium, isoproterenol, phenytoin, or antitachycardia pacing (discussed later in this chapter). Drugs that prolong the QT interval (e.g., dofetilide [Tikosyn]) should be stopped. Cardioversion is used if drug therapy is ineffective.

VT without a pulse is a lethal dysrhythmia. It is treated the same as VF. Cardiopulmonary resuscitation (CPR) and rapid defibrillation are the first lines of treatment (Box 39.1). This is followed by administering vasopressors (e.g., epinephrine) and antidysrhythmics (e.g., amiodarone) if defibrillation is unsuccessful.[6]

> **CHECK YOUR PRACTICE**
>
> You are assigned to a 69-year-old male patient on a telemetry unit who is recovering from colon surgery. He has a history of 2 MIs, and he has 3 coronary stents in place. You hear his ECG monitor alarm and see what looks like ventricular tachycardia.
>
> • What should you do?

Ventricular Fibrillation

Ventricular fibrillation (VF) is a severe derangement of the heart rhythm characterized on ECG by irregular waveforms of varying shapes and amplitude (Fig. 39.21). This represents the firing of multiple ectopic foci in the ventricle. Mechanically, the ventricle is simply "quivering," with no effective contraction, so no CO occurs. VF is a lethal dysrhythmia.

Clinical associations. VF occurs in acute MI, myocardial ischemia, and chronic diseases such as HF and cardiomyopathy. It may occur during cardiac pacing or cardiac catheterization procedures because of catheter stimulation of the ventricle. It may happen with coronary reperfusion after thrombolytic

BOX 39.1 ETHICAL/LEGAL DILEMMAS

Scope and Standards of Practice

Situation

A young woman with a history of viral cardiomyopathy is admitted to the intensive care unit (ICU) after having several episodes of nonsustained ventricular tachycardia (VT). While she is being stabilized, she codes (pulseless VT) and needs intubation. A nurse anesthetist tries to intubate her 3 times unsuccessfully. There is an unforeseen delay in the arrival of the anesthesiologist. P.F., an ICU nurse who is a paramedic certified in advanced trauma life support (ATLS) and advanced cardiovascular life support (ACLS), intubates the patient. The next day the nursing supervisor questions P.F. about intubating the patient since this is not within the scope of practice for an ICU nurse in that agency.

Ethical/Legal Points for Consideration

- Each state board of nursing defines their own RN *Scope of Practice,* including rules and regulations that guide practice. They can vary from state to state.
- Individual agencies have policies and procedures that describe the scope of practice for nurses. These can be more restrictive than those of the state.
- P.F. has had training, education, and certification beyond the usual nursing role.
- The life-threatening situation is an extenuating circumstance.
- Negligence may have been a factor if P.F., who is a nurse with training and experience, had not acted.

Discussion Questions

1. What would you have done in this situation?
2. How would you respond to the nursing supervisor?
3. What are the legal ramifications for P.F. in this situation?
4. What are the ethical issues in this situation?

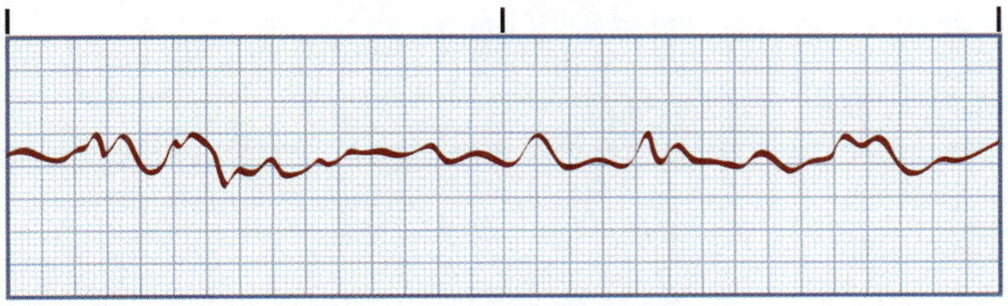

Fig. 39.21 Ventricular fibrillation.

therapy. Other causes are electric shock, hyperkalemia, hypoxemia, acidosis, and drug toxicity.

ECG characteristics. HR is not measurable. Rhythm is irregular and chaotic. The P wave is not visible. The PR interval and the QRS interval are not measurable.

Clinical significance. VF results in an unresponsive, pulseless, and apneic state. If VF is not treated quickly, the patient will not recover.

Treatment. Treatment consists of immediate initiation of CPR and ACLS with the use of defibrillation and definitive drug therapy (e.g., epinephrine, amiodarone). There should be no delay in starting chest compressions and using a defibrillator once available.

Asystole

Asystole is the total absence of ventricular electrical activity. Occasionally, P waves are seen. No ventricular contraction occurs because depolarization does not occur. Patients are unresponsive, pulseless, and apneic. Asystole is a lethal dysrhythmia that needs immediate treatment. VF may masquerade as asystole. Always assess the rhythm in more than 1 lead. The prognosis of a patient with asystole is very poor.

Clinical associations. Asystole is usually a result of advanced heart disease, a severe cardiac conduction system problem, or end-stage HF.

Clinical significance. Generally, the patient with asystole has end-stage heart disease or had prolonged arrest and cannot be resuscitated.

Treatment. Treatment consists of CPR with ACLS measures. These include definitive drug therapy with epinephrine, intubation, and efforts to determine the underlying cause.

Pulseless Electrical Activity

Pulseless electrical activity (PEA) is a situation in which organized electrical activity is seen on the ECG, but there is no mechanical heart activity, and the patient has no pulse. It is the most common dysrhythmia seen after defibrillation. Prognosis is poor unless we quickly identify and treat the underlying cause. Common causes of PEA include hypovolemia, hypoxia, metabolic acidosis, hyperkalemia, hypokalemia, hypoglycemia, hypothermia, toxins (e.g., drug overdose), cardiac tamponade, thrombosis (e.g., MI, pulmonary embolus), tension pneumothorax, and trauma. Treatment begins with CPR, followed by drug therapy (e.g., epinephrine) and intubation. Correcting the underlying cause is critical to prognosis.

Sudden Cardiac Death

The term *sudden cardiac death* (SCD) refers to death from a cardiac cause. Most SCDs result from ventricular dysrhythmias, specifically VT or VF. SCD is discussed in Chapter 37.

INTERPROFESSIONAL AND NURSING MANAGEMENT: DYSRHYTHMIAS

Antidysrhythmic Drug Therapy

Table 39.9 shows antidysrhythmic drugs by their primary effects on the heart cells and the ECG.

Before giving any *antidysrhythmic drug,* perform a thorough assessment with a complete physical assessment, health history, medication allergies, and medication history. Assess for contraindications, cautions, and drug interactions. Obtain a baseline ECG. Assess vital signs, heart and lung sounds, and pulse rate, rhythm, and quality. Assess for signs and symptoms associated with decreased CO because of the dysrhythmia, such as restlessness, syncope, chest pain, dyspnea, and crackles. Review laboratory studies, including electrolytes and liver and kidney function tests.

When giving antidysrhythmics, closely monitor the ECG and vital signs, especially BP and pulse rate. Continue to perform an ongoing physical assessment. Monitor laboratory studies as needed. Give specific instructions for each drug. Teach the patient that oral forms are often better tolerated if taken with food to help decrease GI upset. Tell patients to avoid alcohol, caffeine, and tobacco.

Defibrillation

Defibrillation is the treatment of choice to end VF and pulseless VT. It is most effective when the myocardial cells are not

TABLE 39.9 Drug Therapy

Antidysrhythmic Drugs

Drug	Effects on the Action Potential	Effects on ECG
Class I: Sodium Channel Blockers	Decrease impulse conduction in the atria, ventricles, and His-Purkinje system	
Class IA disopyramide (Norpace) procainamide quinidine	Delay repolarization	Widened QRS and prolonged QT interval
Class IB lidocaine mexiletine phenytoin (Dilantin)	Accelerate repolarization	Little or no effect on ECG
Class IC flecainide propafenone (Rythmol SR)	Decrease impulse conduction	Pronounced prodysrhythmic actions, widened QRS, prolonged QT interval
Class II: β-Adrenergic Blockers esmolol (Brevibloc) metoprolol (Lopressor) propranolol (Inderal)	Decrease automaticity of the SA node, slow impulse conduction in AV node, reduce atrial and ventricular contractility	Bradycardia, prolonged PR interval, AV block
Class III: Potassium Channel Blockers amiodarone dofetilide (Tikosyn) ibutilide (Corvert) sotalol[a] (Betapace)	Delay repolarization, resulting in prolonged duration of action potential and refractory period	Prolonged PR and QT intervals, widened QRS, bradycardia
Class IV: Calcium Channel Blockers diltiazem (Cardizem) verapamil	Decrease automaticity of SA node, delay AV node conduction. Reduce myocardial contractility	Bradycardia, prolonged PR interval, AV block
Other Agents		
adenosine digoxin (Lanoxin)	Decrease conduction through AV node, reduce automaticity of SA node	Prolonged PR interval, AV block
dronedarone (Multaq)[b]	Suppress atrial dysrhythmias though mechanism is unknown	Prolonged QT interval
magnesium	Decrease impulse conduction through AV node	AV block

[a]Sotalol has both class II and class III properties.
[b]Dronedarone has class I through IV properties.

yet anoxic or acidotic. Rapid defibrillation (within 2 minutes) is critical to a successful patient outcome. Defibrillation involves the passage of an electric shock through the heart to depolarize the myocardial cells. The goal is that after repolarization, the SA node will be able to resume the role of pacemaker.

Defibrillators deliver energy using a monophasic or biphasic waveform. Monophasic defibrillators deliver energy in 1 direction. Biphasic defibrillators deliver energy in 2 directions (Fig. 39.22). The shocks delivered are at lower energies and with fewer post-shock dysrhythmias than monophasic defibrillators.

We measure the output of a defibrillator in *joules,* or watts per second. The recommended energy for initial shocks in defibrillation depends on the type of defibrillator. Biphasic defibrillators deliver the first and any successive shocks using 120 to 200 joules. Recommendations for monophasic defibrillators include an initial shock at 360 joules. After the first shock, start CPR immediately, beginning with chest compressions.

We can perform rapid defibrillation using a manual or automatic device (Fig. 39.23). Manual defibrillators require you to interpret heart rhythms, determine the need for a shock, and deliver a shock. An **automatic external defibrillator (AED)** can detect heart rhythms and tell the user to deliver a shock using hands-free defibrillator pads. Proficiency in AED use is part of the basic life support course for health care professionals. Be familiar with the operation of the type of defibrillator used in your clinical setting.

The general steps taken for defibrillation are listed in Table 39.10.

! SAFETY ALERT

Defibrillation and Cardioversion

- Check that the synchronizer switch is OFF for defibrillation.
- Turn the synchronizer switch ON for a cardioversion.
- Never apply defibrillator pads over a pacemaker or implantable cardiovert-er-defibrillator.
- Be certain that personnel and O_2 equipment are "all clear" before discharging the device.

Synchronized Cardioversion

Synchronized cardioversion is the therapy of choice for the patient with ventricular tachydysrhythmias (e.g., VT with a pulse) or supraventricular tachydysrhythmias (e.g., atrial flutter with a RVR). A synchronized circuit in the defibrillator delivers a shock on the R wave of the QRS complex of the ECG.

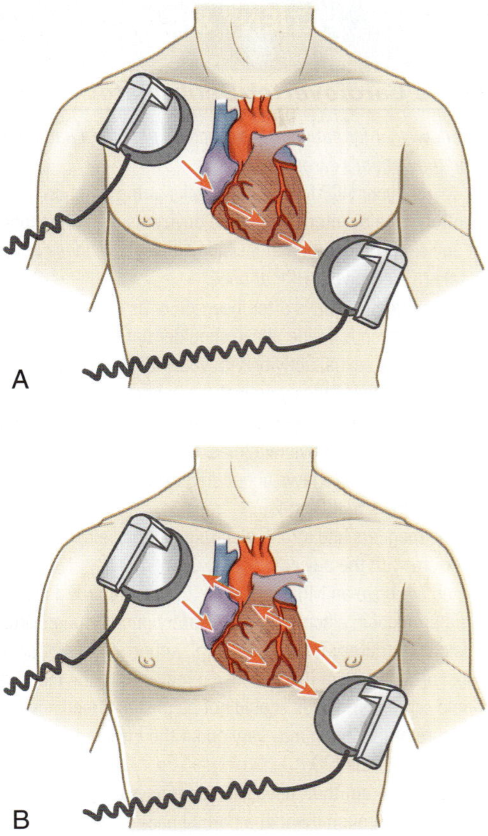

Fig. 39.22 Paddle placement and current flow in monophasic defibrillation (A) and biphasic defibrillation (B).

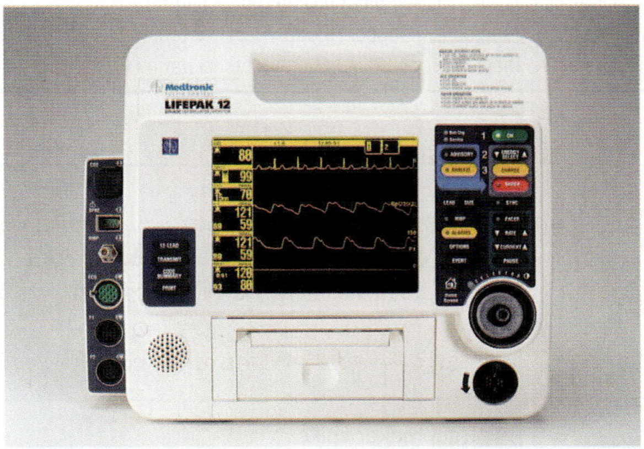

Fig. 39.23 LifePak contains a monitor, defibrillator, and transcutaneous pacemaker. (Courtesy Medtronic Physio-Control, Redmond, WA.)

The synchronizer switch must be turned on when performing cardioversion.

The procedure for synchronized cardioversion is the same as for defibrillation with a few exceptions (Table 39.11). If synchronized cardioversion is done on a nonemergency basis (e.g., the patient is awake and hemodynamically stable), we sedate the patient with IV agents (e.g., midazolam, fentanyl) beforehand. Strict attention to maintaining the patient's airway is critical. If a patient with SVT or VT with a pulse becomes hemodynamically unstable, synchronized cardioversion should be done as quickly as possible. Start the initial energy for synchronized cardioversion at 50 to 100 joules (biphasic defibrillator) and 100 joules (monophasic defibrillator) and increase if needed. Atrial fibrillation requires a higher starting energy level in joules than SVT or VT with a pulse. If the patient becomes pulseless or the rhythm changes to VF, turn the synchronizer switch off and perform defibrillation.

TABLE 39.10 Defibrillation

The following general steps are taken for defibrillation:

1. Continue CPR until the defibrillator is charged.
2. Apply hands-free defibrillator pads to the chest, one on the upper right chest above the nipple and the other on the left side below the breast tissue. If hands-free pads are not immediately available, apply conductive material (e.g., gel pads) to the chest.
3. Turn the defibrillator on and select the proper energy level.
4. Make sure the synchronizer switch is turned off.
5. Charge the defibrillator using the button on the defibrillator.
6. Call and look to see that everyone is "all clear." Ensure staff are not touching the patient or the bed at the time of discharge, and the O_2 source is away from the patient
7. Deliver the charge by depressing the shock button on the defibrillator or the buttons on the paddles simultaneously while pushing down with at least 15 pounds of pressure (7.5 kg).

TABLE 39.11 NURSING MANAGEMENT

Assisting With Cardioversion

Preprocedure

- Obtain 12-lead ECG and initiate ECG monitoring.
- Perform baseline assessment, including vital signs, pulse oximetry. Note any manifestations of the dysrhythmia.
- Withhold food and fluids per institution policy.
- Assess baseline laboratory values (e.g., cardiac biomarkers, electrolytes).
- Teach patient and caregiver about procedure and postprocedure care.
- Remove all metallic objects, dentures, and transdermal patches. You may need to clip or remove chest hair.
- Establish IV access.
- Give sedative and other drugs, as ordered.

Postprocedure

- Maintain patent airway and administer O_2 as needed.
- Monitor ECG for dysrhythmias or other changes (e.g., ST segment elevation).
- Perform assessment and compare to baseline: vital signs, pulse oximetry, and heart and breath sounds.
- Assess level of consciousness and reorient as needed.
- Administer IV dysrhythmic and analgesic medications as ordered.
- Assess for burns and provide skin care.

Implantable Cardioverter-Defibrillator

The *implantable cardioverter-defibrillator* (ICD) is an important technology for patients who (1) have survived SCD, (2) have spontaneous sustained VT, (3) have syncope with inducible VT or VF during EPS, or (4) are at high risk for future life-threatening dysrhythmias (e.g., have cardiomyopathy). The use of ICDs has significantly decreased mortality rates in these patients.[5,10]

The ICD consists of a lead system placed via a subclavian vein to the endocardium. A battery-powered pulse generator is implanted subcutaneously, usually over the pectoral muscle on the patient's nondominant side. The pulse generator is similar in size to a pacemaker. Most systems are single-lead

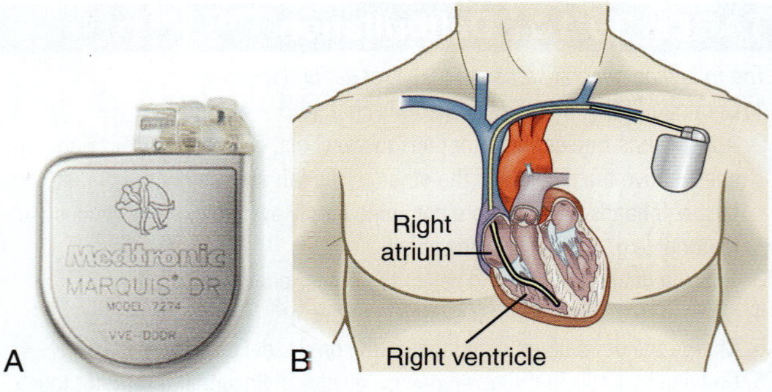

Fig. 39.24 (A) The implantable cardioverter-defibrillator (ICD) pulse generator from Medtronic, Inc. (B) The ICD is placed in a subcutaneous pocket over the pectoral muscle. A single-lead system is placed transvenously from the pulse generator to the endocardium. The single lead detects dysrhythmias and delivers an electric shock to the heart muscle. (Courtesy Medtronic, Inc., Minneapolis, MN.)

systems (Fig. 39.24). The ICD sensing system monitors the HR and rhythm and identifies VT or VF. After the sensing system detects a lethal dysrhythmia, the device delivers a 25-joule or lower shock to the patient's heart. If the first shock is unsuccessful, the device recycles and can continue to deliver shocks.

In addition to defibrillation capabilities, ICDs have *antitachycardia* and *antibradycardia pacing* capabilities. These devices use algorithms that detect dysrhythmias and determine the appropriate response. They can start *overdrive pacing* of SVT and VT, sparing the patient painful defibrillator shocks. They can provide backup pacing for bradydysrhythmias that may occur after defibrillation. Nursing care of the patient undergoing ICD placement is similar to the care of a patient undergoing permanent pacemaker implantation.

Patients with structural or congenital cardiac anomalies may receive a subcutaneous ICD (S-ICD).[11] The S-ICD pulse generator is placed under the skin on the left side of the chest with the electrode under the skin above the sternum. The system delivers a shock if it detects VT or VF. Since the S-ICD does not have any electrodes implanted in the heart, it has no pacing capability.

Teaching the patient who is receiving an ICD and the caregiver is important. Patients may have a variety of emotions. These include fear of body image change, fear of recurrent dysrhythmias, expectation of pain with ICD discharge (described as a feeling of a blow to the chest), and anxiety about going home. Encourage patients and caregivers to take part in local or online ICD support groups. Table 39.12 presents a teaching guide for the patient with an ICD and the caregiver.

◆ Pacemakers

The artificial **cardiac pacemaker** is an electronic device used to pace the heart when the normal conduction pathway is damaged. The basic pacing circuit consists of a power source (battery-powered pulse generator) with programmable circuitry, 1 or more pacing leads, and the myocardium. The electrical signal (stimulus) travels from the pulse generator, through the leads, to the wall of the myocardium. The heart muscle is "captured" and stimulated to contract (Fig. 39.25).

Current pacemakers are small, sophisticated, and precise. They pace the atrium and/or 1 or both ventricles. Most pacemakers are *demand pacemakers*. This means that they sense the heart's electrical activity and fire only when the HR drops below a preset rate. Demand pacemakers have 2 distinct features: (1) a sensing device that inhibits the pacemaker when the HR is adequate and (2) a pacing device that triggers the pacemaker when no QRS complexes occur within a preset time.

In addition to antibradycardia pacing, devices now include antitachycardia and overdrive pacing. *Antitachycardia pacing* involves the delivery of a stimulus to the ventricle to end tachydysrhythmias (e.g., VT). Overdrive pacing involves pacing the

TABLE 39.12 PATIENT & CAREGIVER TEACHING

Implantable Cardioverter-Defibrillator (ICD)

Include the following information in the teaching plan for a patient receiving an ICD and the patient's caregiver:

1. Follow up with your HCP for routine checks of the function of the ICD. This is often done by interrogating the device using a telephone.
2. Report any signs of infection at incision site (e.g., redness, swelling, drainage) or fever to your HCP at once.
3. Keep incision dry for 4 days after insertion or as instructed.
4. Avoid lifting arm on ICD side above shoulder until approved.
5. Discuss resuming sexual activity with your HCP. It is usually safe to resume sexual activity once your incision is healed.
6. Do not drive until cleared by your HCP. This decision is usually based on the ongoing presence of dysrhythmias, the frequency of ICD firings, your overall health, and state laws about drivers with ICDs.
7. Avoid direct blows to ICD site.
8. Avoid large magnets and strong electromagnetic fields because these may interfere with the device.
9. You should not have an MRI unless the ICD is approved as MRI safe or there is a protocol in place for patient safety during the procedure.
10. Travel is not restricted. Tell security (e.g., airport, train station, public buildings) of presence of ICD because it may set off the metal detector. Hand-held screening wands should not be placed directly over the ICD. Manufacturer information may vary about the effect of metal detectors on the function of the ICD.
11. Do not stand near antitheft devices in doorways of stores and public buildings. Walk through them at a normal pace.
12. If your ICD fires once, call your HCP right away. If you feel sick or if it fires more than once, contact the emergency response system.
13. Always wear a Medic Alert ID device.
14. Always carry the ICD identification card and a current list of your drugs.
15. Consider joining an ICD support group
16. Caregivers should learn cardiopulmonary resuscitation (CPR).

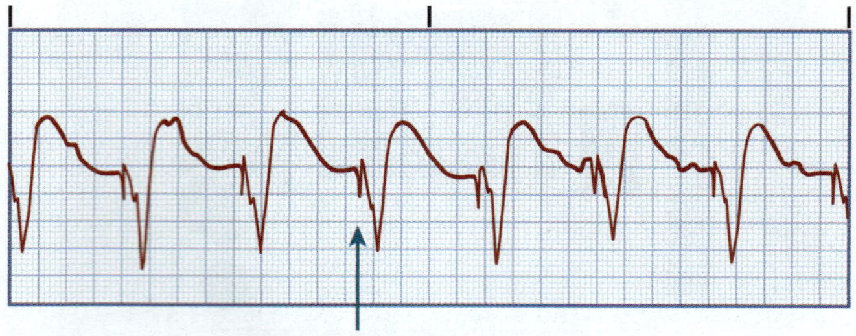

Fig. 39.25 Ventricular capture (depolarization) from signal *(pacemaker spike)* from pacemaker lead in the right ventricle.

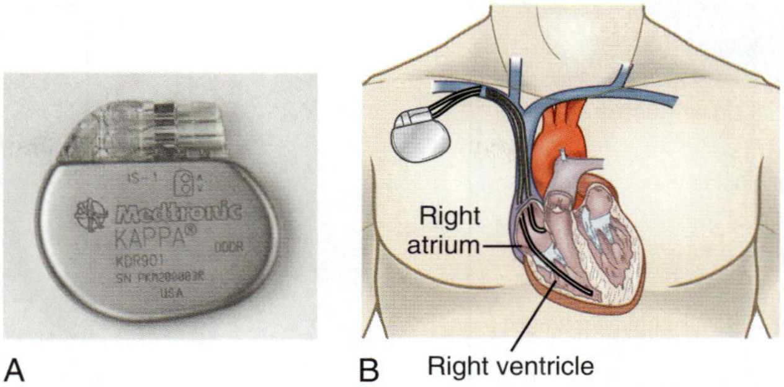

Fig. 39.26 (A) A dual-chamber rate-responsive pacemaker from Medtronic, Inc., is designed to treat patients with chronic heart problems in which the heart beats too slowly to support the body's circulation needs. (B) Pacing leads in both the atrium and the ventricle enable a dual-chamber pacemaker to sense and pace in both heart chambers. (Courtesy Medtronic, Inc., Minneapolis, MN.)

TABLE 39.13 Indications for Permanent Pacemakers

- Acquired AV block
- Second-degree AV block
- Third-degree AV block
- Atrial fibrillation with a slow ventricular response
- Bundle branch block
- Cardiomyopathy
  - Dilated
  - Hypertrophic
- HF
- SA node dysfunction
- Symptomatic bradycardia with unknown cause
- Tachydysrhythmias (e.g., ventricular tachycardia)

atrium at rates of 200 to 500 impulses per minute to try to stop atrial tachycardias (e.g., atrial flutter with an RVR).

◆ Permanent Pacemaker

A *permanent pacemaker* is totally implanted within the body (Fig. 39.26). The power source is placed subcutaneously, usually over the pectoral muscle on the patient's nondominant side. The pacing leads are placed transvenously to the right atrium and/or 1 or both ventricles and attached to the power source. Common reasons for insertion of a permanent pacemaker are found in Table 39.13.

New technology and research are focused on miniaturized, leadless permanent pacemakers. Single-component devices have the battery, sensors, electronics, and stimulating electrodes in a small capsule that is placed in the ventricle using a deflatable sheath. A multicomponent device has a small "seed" that is placed in a cardiac chamber. It acts as an energy transducer while an outside piece beams ultrasound (or radio waves) to the seed. The seed converts the energy to a pacing pulse. The lack of a transvenous lead and subcutaneous pulse generator is a major shift in cardiac pacing.[5,11] Other research is focusing on making permanent pacemakers without batteries.

◆ Cardiac Resynchronization Therapy

Cardiac resynchronization therapy (CRT) is a pacing technique that resynchronizes the heart cycle by pacing both ventricles *(biventricular pacing)*. This promotes improvement in ventricular function (Fig. 38.4). Most HF patients have intraventricular conduction delays causing abnormal ventricular contraction. This causes dyssynchrony between the right and left ventricles and results in reduced systolic function, pump inefficiency, and worsened HF. Patients with severe left ventricular dysfunction may have devices that combine CRT with an ICD.[11]

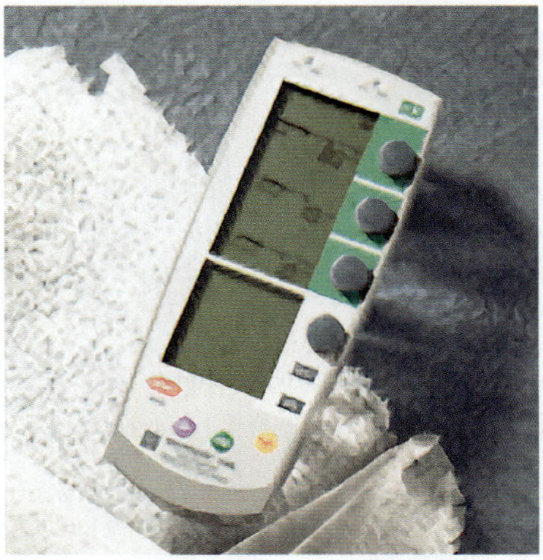

Fig. 39.27 Temporary external, dual-chamber demand pacemaker. (Courtesy Medtronic, Inc., Minneapolis, MN.)

◆ Temporary Pacemaker

A *temporary pacemaker* is one that has the power source outside the body (Fig. 39.27). There are 3 types of temporary pacemakers: transvenous, epicardial, and transcutaneous. Table 39.14 lists common reasons for temporary pacing.

A *transvenous pacemaker* consists of a lead or leads that are threaded transvenously to the right atrium and/or right ventricle and attached to the external power source (Fig. 39.28). Most of these pacemakers are inserted in the ED or ICU in emergency situations. They provide a bridge to inserting a permanent pacemaker or resolving the underlying cause of the dysrhythmia.

Epicardial pacing involves attaching an atrial and a ventricular pacing lead to the epicardium during heart surgery. The leads are passed through the chest wall and attached to the external power source. Epicardial pacing leads are placed in case a bradydysrhythmia or tachydysrhythmia occurs in the early postoperative period.

TABLE 39.14 Common Indications for Temporary Pacemakers

- Maintain adequate HR and rhythm during special circumstances
  - During surgery and postoperative recovery
  - During cardiac catheterization or coronary angioplasty
  - With drug therapy that may cause bradycardia
  - Before implantation of a permanent pacemaker
- Prophylaxis after open heart surgery
- Acute anterior MI with second- or third-degree AV block or bundle branch block
- Acute inferior MI with symptomatic bradycardia and AV block
- EPS to evaluate patient with bradydysrhythmias and tachydysrhythmias

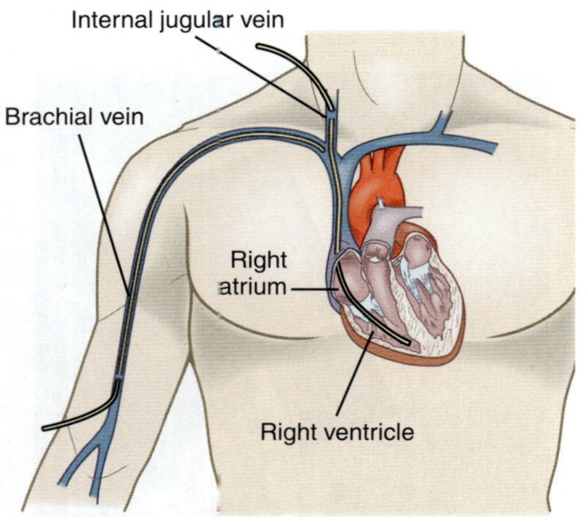

Fig. 39.28 Temporary transvenous pacemaker catheter insertion. A single lead is positioned in the right ventricle through the brachial, subclavian, jugular, or femoral vein.

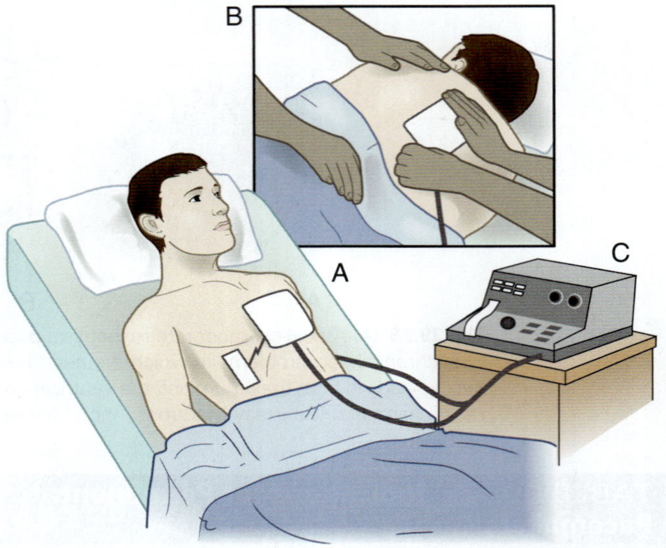

Fig. 39.29 Transcutaneous pacemaker. Pacing electrodes are placed on the patient's anterior (A) and posterior (B) chest walls and attached to an external pacing unit (C).

A *transcutaneous pacemaker* can provide adequate HR and rhythm to the patient in an emergency. Placement of a TCP is a noninvasive, temporary procedure used until a transvenous pacemaker is inserted or more definitive therapy is available.[6]

The TCP consists of a power source and a rate- and voltage-control device that attaches to 2 large, multifunction electrode pads. Position 1 pad on the anterior part of the chest, usually on the V_4 lead position. Place the other pad on the back between the spine and left scapula at the level of the heart (Fig. 39.29). When programming the TCP, use the lowest current that results in a ventricular contraction (capture) to minimize patient discomfort.

Before starting TCP therapy, it is important to tell the patient what to expect. Explain that the muscle contractions created by the pacemaker when the current passes through the chest wall are uncomfortable. Reassure the patient that the TCP is temporary and that it will be replaced by a transvenous or permanent pacemaker as soon as possible. If possible, provide analgesia and/or sedation while the TCP is in use.

◆ Monitoring of Patients With Pacemakers

Patients with temporary or permanent pacemakers are ECG monitored to evaluate the status of the pacemaker. Pacemaker malfunction involves a failure to sense, a failure to capture, or a failure to pace. *Failure to sense* occurs when the pacemaker does not recognize spontaneous atrial or ventricular activity, and it fires inappropriately (Fig. 39.30A). This can result in the pacemaker firing during the excitable period of the cardiac cycle and the potential for VT. Causes of failure to sense include fibrosis around the tip of the pacing lead, battery failure, sensing set too high, or dislodgment of the electrode.

Failure to capture occurs when the electrical charge to the myocardium is insufficient to produce atrial or ventricular contraction (Fig. 39.30B). This can result in serious bradycardia or asystole. Common causes include pacer lead damage, battery failure, dislodgment of the electrode, electrical charge set too low, or fibrosis at the electrode tip.

Failure to pace occurs when the pacemaker does not initiate an electrical stimulus when it should fire (Fig. 39.30C). This can happen from a wire fracture, lead displacement, oversensing, or electrical interference. Table 39.15 describes pacemaker troubleshooting.

Complications of invasive temporary (e.g., transvenous) or permanent pacemaker insertion include infection and hematoma formation at the insertion site, pneumothorax, failure to sense or capture, perforation of the atrial or ventricular septum by the pacing lead, and appearance of "end-of-life" battery power on testing the pacemaker. Several measures can prevent or assess for complications. These include prophylactic IV antibiotic therapy before and after insertion, postinsertion chest x-ray to check lead placement and to rule out a pneumothorax, careful observation of insertion site, and continuous ECG monitoring of the patient's rhythm.

After pacemaker insertion, the patient can be out of bed once stable. Have the patient limit arm and shoulder activity on the operative side to prevent dislodging the newly implanted pacing leads. Observe the insertion site for signs of bleeding and check that the incision is intact. Note any temperature elevation or pain at the insertion site and treat as ordered. Most patients are discharged by the next day if stable.

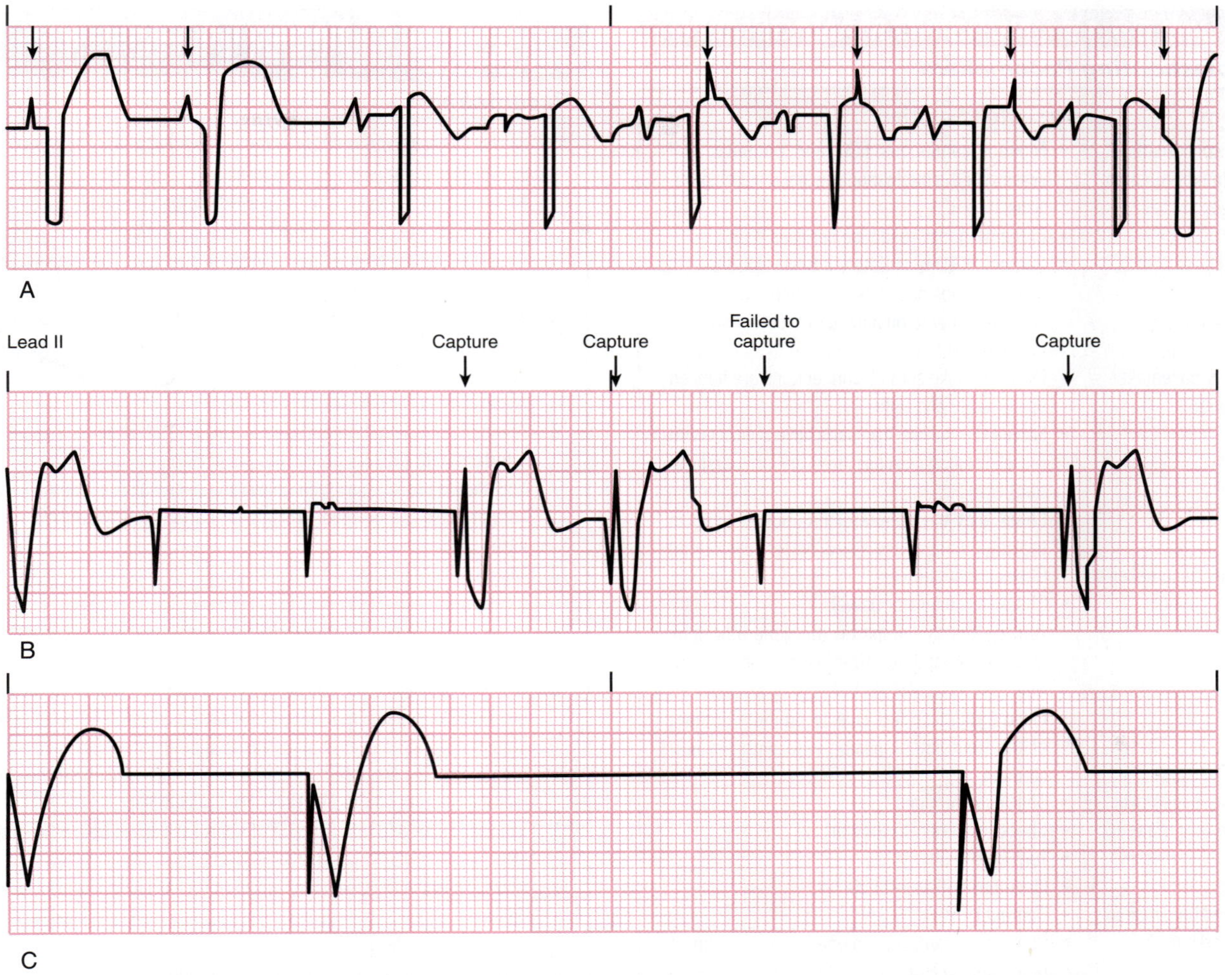

Fig. 39.30 Causes of pacemaker malfunction. (A) Failure to sense: the pacemaker does not sense the patient's own cardiac rhythm and initiates an electrical impulse. Failure to sense manifests as pacer spikes that fall too closely to the patient's own rhythm, earlier than the programmed rate (see *arrows*). (B) Failure to capture: a pacer spike is noted but is not followed by a P wave (atrial pacemaker) or a QRS complex (ventricular pacemaker). (C) Failure to pace: the pacemaker fails to initiate an electrical stimulus when it should fire.

Table 39.16 outlines patient and caregiver teaching for the patient with a pacemaker. The patient with a newly implanted pacemaker and the caregiver may have questions about activity restrictions and concerns about body image. The goals of pacemaker therapy include enhancing physiologic functioning and quality of life. Emphasize this to the patient and caregiver and provide specific advice on activity restrictions.

After discharge, patients need to check pacemaker function on a regular basis. This can include outpatient visits to a pacemaker clinic or home monitoring using telephone transmitter devices. Another method to evaluate pacemaker performance is noninvasive program stimulation. This procedure is done on an outpatient basis in the EPS laboratory.

◆ Radiofrequency Catheter Ablation Therapy

Radiofrequency catheter ablation therapy uses electrical energy to "burn" or ablate areas of the conduction system. Ablation therapy is done after EPS has identified the source of the dysrhythmia. An electrode-tipped ablation catheter ablates accessory pathways or ectopic sites in the atria, AV node, and ventricles. Catheter ablation is a definitive treatment for tachydysrhythmias. It is the nonpharmacologic treatment of choice for atrial dysrhythmias resulting in rapid ventricular rates and AV nodal reentrant tachycardia refractory to drug therapy.[5]

The ablation procedure is an effective treatment with a low complication rate. Nursing care of the patient after ablation therapy is similar to that of a patient undergoing cardiac catheterization (see Chapter 35 and Table 35.11).

SYNCOPE

Syncope is a brief lapse in consciousness accompanied by a loss in postural tone (fainting). The causes of syncope can be cardiovascular or noncardiovascular. The most common cause of syncope is cardioneurogenic syncope, or "vasovagal" syncope (e.g., carotid sinus sensitivity). Other cardiovascular causes relate to dysrhythmias (e.g., tachycardias, bradycardias), prosthetic valve malfunction, pulmonary emboli, and HF. Noncardiovascular causes vary and include stress, hypoglycemia, dehydration, stroke, and seizure.[12]

TABLE 39.15 NURSING MANAGEMENT
Troubleshooting Pacemakers

Problem	Potential Solution
General concern about pacemaker function	• Monitor continuous ECG and patient's vital signs while troubleshooting pacemaker problems • Call emergency response services if needed • Contact HCP immediately if basic troubleshooting does not work, as patient could have a lead wire displaced or a defective lead wire
Temporary pacemaker not firing	• Check to make sure all connections are hooked up correctly and tight • Ensure that hands-free pads have contact with the skin (shave excess hair, dry off perspiration) • Check that the generator has power (plug in the equipment or use a new battery each time)
Temporary pacemaker not capturing	• Check connections • Check for generator power • Turn up the milliamps on the generator, look for capture, and set 10 milliamps above capture • Place patient on left side to promote contact of the transvenous pacing wire with the epicardium
Temporary pacemaker not sensing patient's underlying rhythm	• Check connections • Check for generator power • Turn up sensitivity • Place patient on left side
Permanent pacemaker not working	• Contact HCP • Contact pacemaker company for service if requested by HCP

TABLE 39.16 PATIENT & CAREGIVER TEACHING
Pacemaker

Include the following information in the teaching plan for a patient with a pacemaker and the patient's caregiver:

1. Maintain follow-up care with your HCP to begin regular pacemaker function checks. This is often done by checking the device using a telephone.
2. Report any signs of infection at incision site (e.g., redness, swelling, drainage) or fever to your HCP at once.
3. Keep incision dry for 4 days after implantation, or as ordered.
4. Avoid lifting arm on pacemaker side above shoulder until approved by your cardiologist.
5. Avoid direct blows to pacemaker site.
6. Avoid proximity to high-output electric generators since these can interfere with the function of the pacemaker.
7. You should not have an MRI unless the pacemaker is approved as MRI safe or there is a protocol in place for patient safety during the procedure.
8. Microwave ovens are safe to use and do not interfere with pacemaker function.
9. Avoid standing near antitheft devices in doorways of department stores and public libraries. Walk through them at a normal pace.
10. Travel is not restricted. Tell security (e.g., airport, train station, public buildings) of presence of pacemaker because it may set off the metal detector. Hand-held screening wands should not be placed directly over the pacemaker. Manufacturer information may vary about the effect of metal detectors on the function of the pacemaker.
11. Monitor pulse and tell your HCP if heart rate drops below predetermined rate.
12. Always carry your pacemaker information card and a current list of drugs.
13. Always wear a Medic Alert ID device.
14. Consider joining a pacemaker support group (e.g., www.pacemakerclub.com/).

A diagnostic workup for a patient with syncope from a suspected heart cause begins with ruling out structural and ischemic heart disease. This is done with echocardiography and stress testing. EPS is used to diagnose atrial and ventricular tachydysrhythmias and conduction problems causing bradydysrhythmias, all of which can cause syncope. These problems can be treated with antidysrhythmic drug therapy, pacemakers, ICDs, and/or catheter ablation therapy.

A patient without structural heart disease or in whom EPS testing is not diagnostic may have a *head-up tilt-test*. Normally, an upright position results in gravity displacing 300 to 800 mL of blood to the lower extremities. Specialized nerve fibers called mechanoreceptors are found throughout the vascular system. These respond to the increased blood volume with a reflex increase in sympathetic stimulation and decrease in parasympathetic output. The end results are a slight increase in HR and diastolic BP and a slight decrease in systolic BP.

In cardioneurogenic syncope, the increased venous pooling in the upright position reduces venous return to the heart. This results in a sudden, compensatory increase in ventricular contraction. The brain mistakenly thinks this is a hypertensive state and stops sympathetic stimulation. This produces a paradoxical vasodilation and bradycardia (vasovagal response). The end results are bradycardia, hypotension, cerebral hypoperfusion, and syncope.

In the head-up tilt-test, the patient is placed on a table supported by a belt across the torso and feet. We obtain baseline ECG, BP, and HR with the patient in the horizontal position. Next, the table is tilted 60 to 80 degrees. The patient stays in this upright position for 20 to 60 minutes. We record ECG and HR continuously.[5] BP is measured every 3 minutes throughout the test.

If the patient's BP and HR responses are abnormal and clinical symptoms occur (e.g., faintness), the test is positive. If after 30 minutes there is no response, the table is returned to the horizontal position, and an IV infusion of low-dose isoproterenol may be given to test for a response.

Other diagnostic tests for syncope use recording devices (e.g., Holter monitor or event monitor/loop recorder, see Table 35.10), blood volume determination, hemodynamic testing, and autonomic reflex testing. About 30% of those who have 1 episode of syncope have a recurrence. The underlying cause of syncope and the patient's age and co-morbidities affect the treatment and prognosis.[12]

Case Study

Dysrhythmia: Ventricular Tachycardia

(© iStockphoto/ Thinkstock.)

Patient Profile

J.M, a 54-year-old school teacher, came to the emergency department with shortness of breath, chest discomfort, and a "racing heart." J.M. is alert and oriented and able to answer all your questions with short responses.

Subjective Data

- History of hypertension, diabetes type II
- No known drug allergies
- Takes 500 mg Metformin twice daily
- States this has never happened before, and he is scared
- Reports 7/10 midsternal chest pain

Objective Data

Physical Assessment

- Appears anxious, scared, diaphoretic
- BP 86/54 mm Hg, HR 230 beats/min, respirations 24/min,
- Lungs clear bilaterally
- Heart: no murmurs or gallops, regular

Diagnostic Studies

- 12-Lead ECG shows wide complex ventricular tachycardia
- Serum cardiac biomarkers negative
- Serum potassium 2.8 mEq/L (2.8 mmol/L)
- Glucose 162 mg/dL
- One hour after arrival, J.M. suddenly becomes unresponsive with no heart rate or respirations.

Continuous ECG Monitoring

1. ***Recognize***: Interpret the rhythm J.M. is currently in.
2. ***Analyze***: What are the important findings from J.M.'s history?
3. ***Plan***: What treatment would you expect based on J.M.'s condition?
4. ***Prioritize***: What is the most important intervention that needs done immediately for J.M.?
5. ***Act***: What other interventions would you need to you implement for J.M.?
6. ***Evaluate***: What outcome would indicate that the immediate interventions were successful?
7. ***Safety***: What safety precautions would be needed when performing needed interventions?

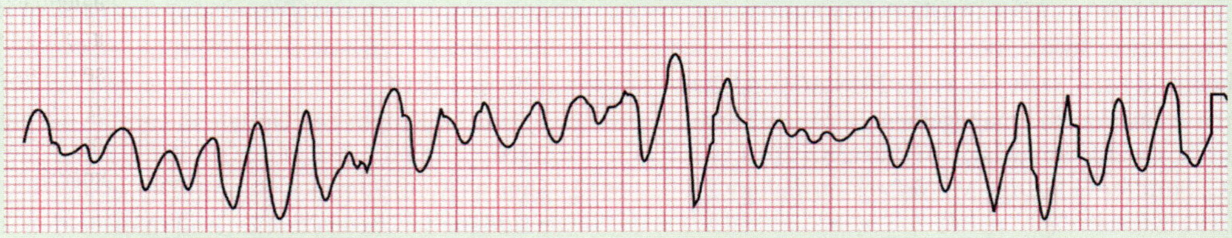

Answers available at http://evolve.elsevier.com/Lewis/medsurg.

BRIDGE TO NCLEX EXAMINATION

The number of the question corresponds to the same-numbered outcome at the beginning of the chapter.

1. A patient with syncope has continuous ECG monitoring. The rhythm strip shows: Atrial rate 74 beats/min and regular; ventricular rate 62 beats/min and irregular; P wave normal shape; PR interval lengthens progressively until a P wave is not conducted; QRS normal shape. Which intervention would the nurse *prioritize?*
   a. Administer epinephrine 1 mg IV push.
   b. Prepare the patient for synchronized cardioversion.
   c. Observe for symptoms of hypotension and angina.
   d. Apply transcutaneous pacemaker pads on the patient.
2. The ECG monitor of a patient in the cardiac care unit after an MI shows ventricular bigeminy with a rate of 50 beats/min. Which action would the nurse take?
   a. Perform defibrillation.
   b. Administer IV amiodarone.
   c. Prepare for pacemaker insertion.
   d. Assess the patient's response.
3. In the patient with supraventricular tachycardia, which assessment indicates decreased cardiac output?
   a. Hypertension and dyspnea
   b. Chest pain and palpitations
   c. Abdominal distention and tachypnea
   d. Bounding pulses and a systolic murmur
4. The nurse prepares a patient for elective synchronized cardioversion. Which information would the nurse consider in planning for the procedure?
   a. Defibrillation delivers a lower dose of electrical energy.
   b. Cardioversion is a treatment for atrial bradydysrhythmias.
   c. Defibrillation delivers a shock during the QRS complex.
   d. Cardioversion is painful for an awake patient.
5. Which patient teaching points would the nurse include when providing discharge instructions to a patient with a new permanent pacemaker? *(select all that apply)*
   a. Avoid or limit air travel.
   b. Take and record a daily pulse rate.
   c. Obtain and wear a Medic Alert ID device at all times.
   d. Avoid lifting arm on the side of the pacemaker above shoulder.
   e. Do not use a microwave oven because it interferes with pacemaker function.
6. Which information would the nurse teach the patient scheduled for a radiofrequency catheter ablation procedure?
   a. Ventricular bradycardia may be induced and treated during the procedure.
   b. A catheter will be placed in both femoral arteries to allow double-catheter intervention.
   c. The procedure will destroy areas of the conduction system that are causing rapid heart rhythms.

d. General anesthetic will be given to prevent the awareness of any "sudden cardiac death" experiences.

1. c; 2. d; 3. b; 4. d; 5. b, c, d; 6. c.

For rationales to these answers and even more NCLEX review questions, visit http://evolve.elsevier.com/Lewis/medsurg.

EVOLVE WEBSITE/RESOURCES LIST

http://evolve.elsevier.com/Lewis/medsurg
Review Questions (Online Only)
Key Points
Answer Keys for Questions
- Rationales for Bridge to NCLEX Examination Questions
- Answer Guidelines for Case Study

Conceptual Care Map Creator
Audio Glossary
Content Updates

REFERENCES

1. American Association of Critical Care Nurses (AACN): AACN scope and standards for progressive and critical care nursing practice, 2019. Retrieved from https://www.aacn.org/~/media/aacn-website/nursing-excellence/standards/aacn-scope-and-standards-for-progressive-and-critical-care-nursing-practice.pdf.
2. Pappano AJ, Wier WG: *Cardiovascular physiology*, ed 11, Philadelphia, 2019, Elsevier.
3. AACN: AACN practice alert: accurate dysrhythmia monitoring in adults, *Critical Care Nurse* 36(6), 2016.

*4. Kusumoto FM, Schoenfeld MH, Barrett C, et al.: 2018 ACC/AHA/HRS guideline on the evaluation and management of patients with bradycardia and cardiac conduction delay, *Circ* 140:e382, 2019.

5. Rossi J, Patterson C, Stouffer G, Runge M: *Netter's cardiology*, ed 3, Philadelphia, 2019, Elsevier.
6. Sinz E, Navarro K, Soderberg ES: *Advanced cardiovascular life support: provider manual 2015*, Dallas, 2015, American Heart Association. (Classic).

*7. Page RL, Joglar JA, Caldwell MA, et al.: 2015 ACC/AHA/HRS guideline for the management of adult patients with supraventricular tachycardia, *Circ* 133:e506, 2016.

*8. January CT, Wann LS, Calkins H, et al.: 2019 AHA/ACC/HRS focused update on the 2014 AHA/ACC/HRS guideline for the management of patients with atrial fibrillation, *Circ* 140:e125, 2019.

9. Centers for Disease Control: Atrial fibrillation. Retrieved from https://www.cdc.gov/heartdisease/atrial_fibrillation.htm.

*10. Winkler A, Jagus-Jamiola A, Uzieblo-Zyczkowska B: Predictors of appropriate interventions and mortality in patients with implantable cardioverter-defibrillators, *Pol Arch Intern Med* 129:667, 2019.

11. Verma N, Knight BP: Update in cardiac pacing, *AER* 8:228, 2019.

*12. Shen WK, Sheldon RS, Benditt DG, et al.: 2017 ACC/AHA/HRS guideline for the evaluation and management of patients with syncope, *Circ* 136:e25, 2017. (Classic).

*Evidence-based information for clinical practice.

40

Inflammatory and Structural Heart Disorders

Patricia Keegan

http://evolve.elsevier.com/Lewis/medsurg/

CONCEPTUAL FOCUS

Functional Ability
Infection
Inflammation
Perfusion

LEARNING OUTCOMES

1. Describe the pathophysiology, clinical manifestations, and interprofessional and nursing management of the patient with infective endocarditis or pericarditis.
2. Describe the pathophysiology, clinical manifestations, and interprofessional and nursing management of the patient with myocarditis.
3. Distinguish the etiology, pathophysiology, and clinical manifestations of rheumatic fever and rheumatic heart disease.
4. Describe the interprofessional and nursing management of the patient with rheumatic heart disease.
5. Describe the pathophysiology, clinical manifestations, and interprofessional and nursing management of patients with various types of valvular heart disease.
6. Relate the pathophysiology, clinical manifestations, and interprofessional and nursing management of patients with different types of cardiomyopathy.

KEY TERMS

aortic regurgitation (AR)
aortic stenosis (AS)
cardiac tamponade
cardiomyopathy (CMP)
dilated cardiomyopathy
hypertrophic cardiomyopathy
infective endocarditis (IE)
mitral valve prolapse (MVP)
myocarditis
pericardiocentesis
pericarditis
regurgitation
rheumatic fever (RF)
rheumatic heart disease
stenosis

This chapter focuses on patients with select inflammatory and structural heart problems. Conceptually, these problems can adversely affect perfusion. Inflammatory, infectious, and structural problems impair cardiac output (CO), which leads to decreased tissue perfusion. The patient may have pain, hyperthermia, and decreased functional and cognitive ability. The nurse plays a key role in providing patients with the education needed to manage problems and their effects.

INFLAMMATORY HEART DISORDERS

INFECTIVE ENDOCARDITIS

Infective endocarditis (IE) is a disease of the *endocardium* (the innermost layer of the heart) and the heart valves (Fig. 40.1). IE is associated with a poor prognosis and a decreased life expectancy.[1] There has been an increase in the number of cases of IE. This is largely related to an increase in IV drug use.[2]

Classification

We often classify IE based on the cause (e.g., IV drug use IE [IVDA IE], fungal IE) or site of involvement (e.g., prosthetic valve endocarditis [PVE]). We also describe IE as subacute or acute. The *subacute form* affects those with preexisting valve disease over a period of months. In contrast, the *acute form* affects those with healthy valves and appears as a rapidly progressive illness.

Etiology and Pathophysiology

IE occurs when blood flow allows organisms to contact and infect previously damaged heart valves or other endothelial surfaces.

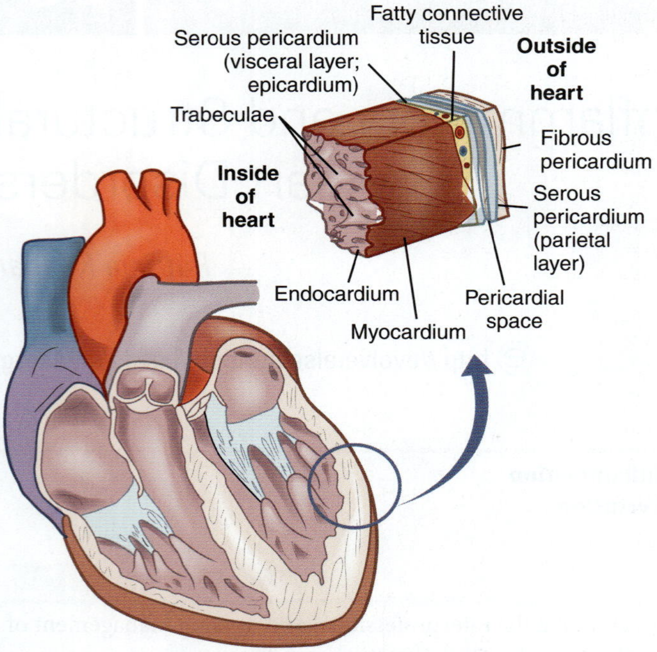

Fig. 40.1 Layers of the heart muscle and pericardium. The section of the heart wall shows the fibrous pericardium, the parietal and visceral layers of the serous pericardium (with the pericardial sac between them), the myocardium, and the endocardium. (Modified from Patton KT, Thibodeau GA: *The human body in health and disease,* ed 5, St Louis, 2010, Mosby.)

TABLE 40.1 Common Risk Factors for Endocarditis

Cardiac Conditions
- Acquired valve disease (e.g., MVP with regurgitation, calcified AS)
- CMP
- Congenital heart disease
- Heart lesions (e.g., ventricular septal defect, asymmetric septal hypertrophy)
- Marfan's syndrome
- Pacemaker
- Prior IE
- Prosthetic heart valve(s)
- Rheumatic heart disease (e.g., mitral valve regurgitation)

Noncardiac Conditions
- Hospital-acquired bacteremia
- IV drug use

Procedure-Associated Risks
- Intravascular devices (e.g., central venous catheter)
- Procedures listed in Table 40.2

About 50% of cases are caused by *Staphylococcus aureus.*[1] Other bacterial causes include *Streptococcus viridans* and coagulase-negative staphylococci. Besides streptococci, other colonizers of the oropharynx, such as the HACEK organisms (*Haemophilus, Actinobacillus, Cardiobacterium, Eikenella, Kingella*) can cause IE.[3] The organisms make biofilms, which protect the organisms from immune defenses and make antimicrobials less effective.[1]

Persons with a variety of underlying cardiac and noncardiac conditions can develop IE (Table 40.1). Patients are categorized into high, moderate, or low risk for developing IE or having a

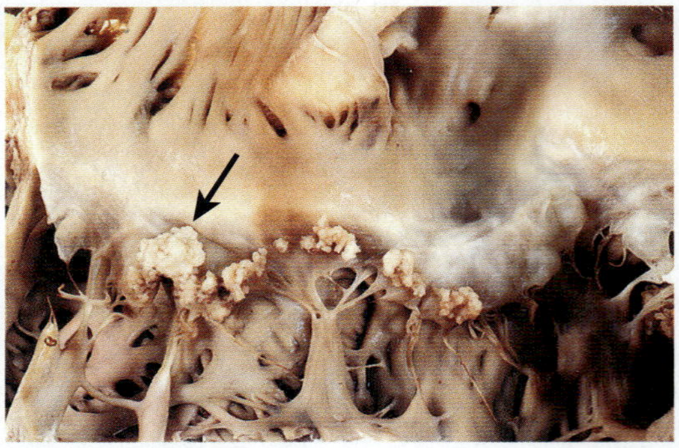

Fig. 40.2 Bacterial IE of the mitral valve. Note the large, irregular vegetations *(arrow)* covering the valve. (From Damjanov I, Linder J: *Pathology: a color atlas,* St Louis, 2000, Mosby.)

poor outcome.[2] The main risk factors for IE include (1) history of IE, (2) IV drug use, (3) having a prosthetic valve, (4) health care–associated infection from use of an intravascular device (e.g., methicillin-resistant *S. aureus* [MRSA]), and (5) renal dialysis.[4]

IE typically develops in 3 stages: (1) bacteremia, (2) adhesion, and (3) vegetation. *Vegetations,* the primary lesions of IE, consist of fibrin, leukocytes, platelets, and microbes that stick to the valve surface or endocardium (Fig. 40.2). The loss of parts of these fragile vegetations into the circulation results in *emboli.* Up to 10.5% of persons with IE develop embolization.[5] Left-sided heart vegetations move to various organs (e.g., brain, kidneys, spleen) and the extremities, causing limb infarction. Right-sided heart lesions move to the lungs, causing pulmonary emboli.

The infection may spread locally and damage the valves or their supporting structures. This can cause dysrhythmias and valve dysfunction. Invasion of the myocardium can lead to heart failure (HF), sepsis, and heart block (Fig. 40.3).

Clinical Manifestations

The manifestations of IE are nonspecific and involve multiple organ systems. Most patients present with fever.[5] Fever may be low grade or absent in older adults or those who are immunocompromised. Other symptoms include chills, weakness, malaise, fatigue, and anorexia.

Vascular signs include *splinter hemorrhages* (black longitudinal streaks) in the nail beds. Petechiae from microembolization of vegetative lesions can occur on the conjunctivae, lips, buccal mucosa, and palate and over the ankles, feet, and antecubital and popliteal areas. *Osler's nodes* (painful, tender, red or purple, pea-size lesions) are found on the fingertips or toes. *Janeway's lesions* (flat, painless, small, red spots) may be seen on the fingertips, palms, soles of feet, and toes. Eye examination may show hemorrhagic retinal lesions called *Roth's spots.*

Most patients have a new or worsening systolic murmur. Murmurs are usually absent in tricuspid IE because right-sided heart sounds are too low to be heard. HF is common. It occurs in up to 80% of patients with aortic valve IE and 50% of those with mitral valve IE.[5]

Diagnostic Studies

The health history is important in assessing IE. Ask patients if they have had any recent (within the past 3 to 6 months) dental,

PATHOPHYSIOLOGY MAP

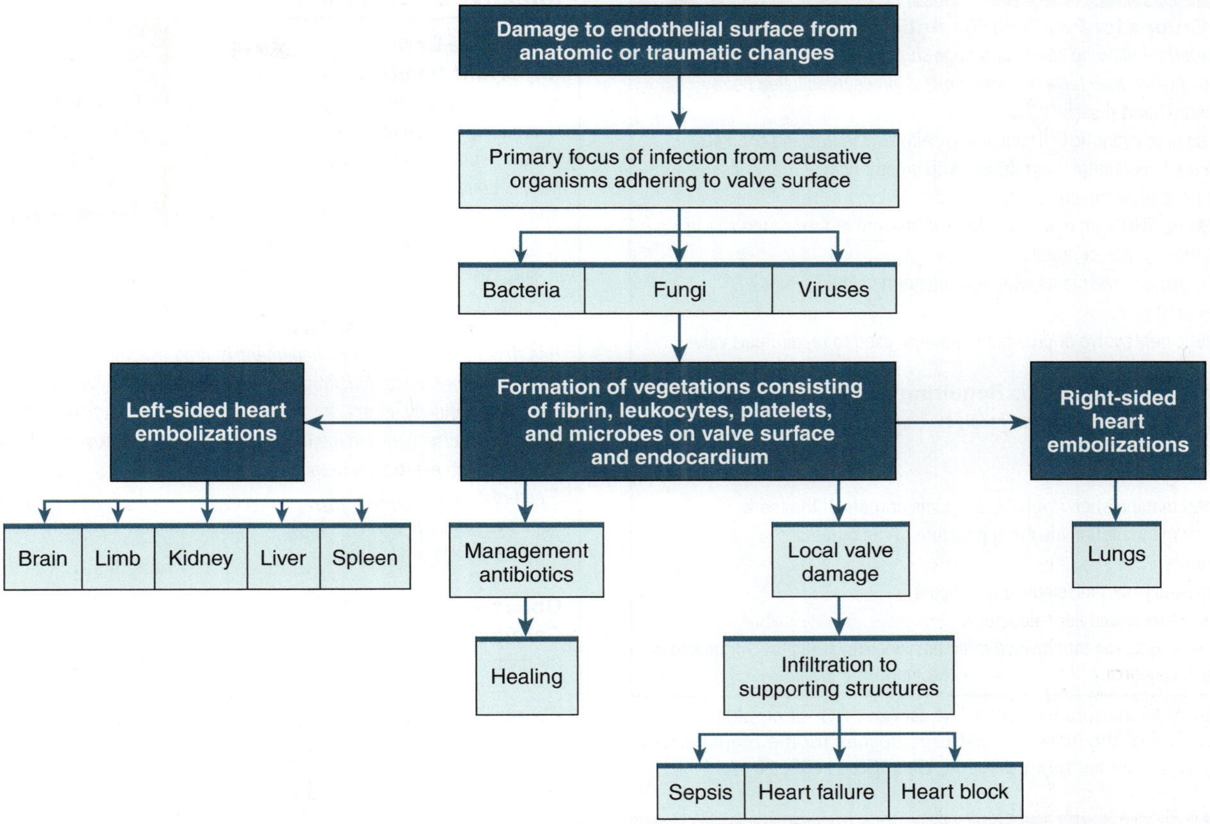

Fig. 40.3 Pathogenesis of IE.

urologic, surgical, or gynecologic procedures, including childbirth. Note any history of IVDA, heart disease, or infections (e.g., skin, respiratory, urinary tract). Have they had a heart catheterization, heart surgery, intravascular device placement, or renal dialysis?

Three blood cultures drawn over a period of 1 hour from 3 different venipuncture sites will be positive in most patients with IE.[6] Culture-negative IE is associated with antibiotic usage within the previous 2 weeks or results from a pathogen not easily detected by standard cultures. Mild leukocytosis occurs in acute IE. The erythrocyte sedimentation rate (ESR) and C-reactive protein (CRP) levels may be increased. Echocardiography can show vegetations.

Guidelines for the diagnosis of IE are based on the Duke Criteria. The patient must have 2 major criteria and 1 minor criterion, or 1 major and 3 minor, or 5 minor criteria. Major criteria include positive blood cultures, typical microorganism for IE from 2 separate blood cultures, evidence of endocardial involvement, and new valvular vegetation. Minor criteria include predisposing heart condition or IV drug use, vascular phenomena, immunologic phenomena, microbiologic evidence, or echocardiographic findings consistent with IE but not meeting major criteria.[7]

Interprofessional Care

Prophylactic Treatment

Situations and conditions that require antibiotic prophylaxis are detailed in Table 40.2.

Drug Therapy

Accurately identifying the causative organism is the key to successful treatment of IE. Long-term treatment is needed to kill dormant bacteria within the valvular vegetations. Complete removal of the organism generally takes weeks. Relapses are common.[1]

Antibiotic therapy is based on blood culture results. The effectiveness of therapy is assessed with subsequent blood cultures. Cultures that stay positive indicate inadequate or inappropriate antibiotics, an aortic root or myocardial abscess, or the wrong diagnosis (e.g., an infection elsewhere). It is reasonable to obtain 2 sets of blood cultures every 24 to 48 hours until the infection is cleared.[5] After completion of antibiotics, follow-up echocardiogram and inflammatory markers are done at 1, 3, 6, and 12 months.[6]

Fungal IE and PVE respond poorly to antibiotic therapy alone. Early valve replacement followed by prolonged (6 weeks or more) antibiotics is needed in these situations. Valve replacement surgery is done in 50% to 60% of cases of IE. Three reasons to perform surgery are for valve dysfunction causing HF, to prevent embolization, or for uncontrolled infection.[6]

Fever that persists after treatment has been started is managed with aspirin, acetaminophen, fluids, and rest (see Table 12.5). Complete bed rest is usually not needed unless the fever continues or there are signs of HF. IE with HF responds poorly to drug therapy and valve replacement, so it can be life-threatening.

TABLE 40.2 Antibiotic Prophylaxis to Prevent Endocarditis

Target Groups for Prophylactic Antibiotics

People with the following heart conditions should receive prophylactic antibiotics when they have the conditions or procedures listed below:

- Congenital heart disease (CHD)
  - Unrepaired cyanotic CHD (including palliative shunts and conduits)
  - Repaired congenital heart defect with prosthetic material or device for 6 months after the procedure
  - Repaired CHD with residual defects at the site or next to the site of prosthetic patch or prosthetic device
- Heart transplant recipients who develop heart valve disease
- History of IE
- Prosthetic heart valve or prosthetic material used to repair heart valve

Conditions or Procedures Requiring Antibiotic Prophylaxis

When the target groups have the following conditions or procedures, they need prophylactic antibiotics:

- Oral
  - Dental manipulation involving the gums or roots of the teeth
  - Dental manipulation involving puncture of the oral mucosa
- Respiratory
  - Respiratory tract incisions (e.g., biopsy)
  - Tonsillectomy and adenoidectomy
- Surgical procedures that involve infected skin, skin structures, or musculoskeletal tissue

Modified from Nishimura RA, Otto CM, Bonow RO, et al.: 2017 Focused update of the 2014 AHA/ACC guidelines for the management of patients with valvular heart disease, *Circ* 135:e1159, 2017.

SAFETY ALERT
Communicating Test Results

- If blood culture results for a patient diagnosed with IE show that the organism is not susceptible to the ordered antibiotic, immediately notify the HCP.
- A National Patient Safety Goal stresses the importance of communicating critical test results to the right HCP in a timely manner.

NURSING MANAGEMENT: INFECTIVE ENDOCARDITIS

Assessment

Subjective and objective data to obtain from a patient with IE are found in Table 40.3. Assess vital signs together with heart sounds to detect a new murmur, a change in a preexisting murmur, and extra sounds (e.g., S_3).

Arthralgia (joint pain) and myalgias are common. Assess the patient for joint or muscle tenderness and decreased range of motion (ROM). Examine the patient for petechiae, splinter hemorrhages, and Osler's nodes. Complete a general systems assessment for hemodynamic or embolic complications.

Clinical Problems

Clinical problems for the patient with IE may include:

- Impaired cardiac output
- Infection
- Fatigue
- Substance use

TABLE 40.3 NURSING ASSESSMENT
Infective Endocarditis (IE)

Subjective Data

Important Health Information

Health history: Valvular, congenital, or syphilitic heart disease, including valve repair or replacement. Previous IE, childbirth, staphylococcal or streptococcal infections, hospital-acquired bacteremia

Medications: Immunosuppressive therapy

Surgery or other treatments: Recent obstetric or gynecologic procedures. Invasive procedures, including catheterization, cystoscopy. Recent dental or surgical procedures, GI procedures (e.g., endoscopy)

Functional Health Patterns

Health perception–health management: IV drug use, alcohol use. Malaise

Nutritional-metabolic: Weight gain or loss, anorexia. Chills, diaphoresis

Elimination: Bloody urine

Activity-exercise: Exercise intolerance, generalized weakness, fatigue. Cough, dyspnea on exertion, orthopnea, palpitations

Sleep-rest: Night sweats

Cognitive-perceptual: Chest, back, or abdominal pain. Headache, joint tenderness, muscle tenderness

Objective Data

Cardiovascular

Dysrhythmia, tachycardia, new murmurs, S_3, S_4. Retinal hemorrhages

General

Fever

Respiratory

Tachypnea, crackles

Skin

Osler's nodes on extremities, splinter hemorrhages under nail beds, Janeway's lesions on fingertips, palms, soles of feet, and toes. Petechiae of skin, mucous membranes, or conjunctivae. Purpura, peripheral edema, finger clubbing

Possible Diagnostic Findings

Leukocytosis, anemia, ↑ ESR, ↑ CRP and cardiac biomarkers. Positive blood cultures, hematuria. Echocardiogram showing chamber enlargement, valvular dysfunction, and vegetations. Chest x-ray showing cardiomegaly and pulmonary infiltrates. ECG showing ischemia and conduction defects. Signs of systemic embolization or pulmonary embolism

More information on clinical problems and interventions for the patient with IE is in eNursing Care Plan 40.1 on the website for this chapter.

Planning

The overall goals for the patient with IE include (1) normal or baseline cardiac function, (2) ability to perform activities of daily living (ADLs) without fatigue, and (3) an understanding of the treatment plan to prevent recurrence.

Implementation

Health Promotion

Teaching the patient at high risk for IE (Tables 40.1 and 40.2) helps reduce the incidence and recurrence of IE. Tell the patient to avoid people with infections, especially upper respiratory tract infections, and to report cold, flu, and cough symptoms. Stress the importance of avoiding fatigue, planning rest periods, using good oral hygiene, and scheduling regular dental visits.[5]

Tell the patient to inform HCPs scheduling invasive procedures about the history of IE. Prophylactic antibiotic therapy may be needed. Refer the patient with a history of IVDA for drug rehabilitation.

◆ Ambulatory Care

A patient with IE has many problems that need nursing management. IE generally requires treatment with antibiotics for 4 to 6 weeks. After initial treatment in the hospital, the patient may continue treatment at home if hemodynamically stable and adherent. Assess the home setting for adequate support. Patients who receive outpatient IV antibiotics need vigilant home nursing care.

Assessment findings are often nonspecific (Table 40.3). Tell the patient and caregiver about the importance of monitoring body temperature. Persistent temperature elevations may mean that the antibiotic is ineffective. Patients are at risk for life-threatening complications, such as stroke, pulmonary edema, and HF. Teach patients and caregivers to recognize signs and symptoms of these complications (e.g., change in mental status, dyspnea, chest pain, unexplained weight gain).

The patient needs adequate periods of physical and emotional rest. Bed rest may be needed when the patient has fever or complications (e.g., heart damage). Otherwise, the patient may perform moderate activity. To prevent problems related to decreased mobility, have the patient wear elastic compression stockings, perform ROM exercises, and deep breathe and cough every 2 hours. The patient may have anxiety and fear. Recognize this and begin strategies to help the patient cope with the illness.

Monitor laboratory data, including blood cultures, to determine antibiotic effectiveness. Assess IV lines for patency and signs of complications (e.g., phlebitis). Give antibiotics as prescribed. Monitor the patient for any adverse drug reactions.

Teach the patient and caregiver the nature of the disease and how to reduce the risk for reinfection. Explain the relationship between follow-up care, good nutrition and dental care, and prompt treatment of common infections (e.g., colds) to stay healthy. Teach the patient about symptoms to report that may indicate another infection (e.g., fever, fatigue, chills). Finally, explain the importance of prophylactic antibiotic therapy before certain invasive procedures (see Table 40.2).

◆ Evaluation

The expected outcomes are that the patient with IE will

- Maintain adequate tissue and organ perfusion
- Maintain normal body temperature
- Report an increase in physical and emotional comfort

ACUTE PERICARDITIS

Pericarditis is a condition caused by inflammation of the pericardial sac (pericardium), often with fluid accumulation. The pericardium is composed of the inner serous membrane (visceral pericardium) and the outer fibrous (parietal) layer (Fig. 40.1). The pericardial space between these 2 layers normally holds 10 to 15 mL of serous fluid. The pericardium anchors the heart, provides lubrication to decrease friction between heart contractions, and helps to prevent excess dilation of the heart during diastole.

TABLE 40.4 Common Causes of Pericarditis

Infectious
- Bacterial: Pneumococci, staphylococci, streptococci, *Neisseria gonorrhoeae, Legionella pneumophila, Mycobacterium tuberculosis,* septicemia from gram-negative organisms
- Fungal: Histoplasma, *Candida* species
- Viral: Coxsackie A and B virus, echovirus, adenovirus, mumps, hepatitis, Epstein-Barr, varicella-zoster, human immunodeficiency virus
- Others: Toxoplasmosis, Lyme disease

Noninfectious
- Acute MI
- Cancers: Lung, breast, leukemia, Hodgkin lymphoma, non-Hodgkin lymphoma
- Dissecting aortic aneurysm
- Myxedema
- Radiation
- Renal failure
- Trauma: Thoracic surgery, pacemaker insertion, cardiac diagnostic procedures

Hypersensitive or Autoimmune
- Dressler syndrome
- Drug reactions (e.g., procainamide, hydralazine)
- Postpericardiotomy syndrome
- Rheumatic fever
- Rheumatologic diseases: Rheumatoid arthritis, systemic lupus erythematosus, systemic sclerosis (scleroderma), ankylosing spondylitis

Etiology and Pathophysiology

Common causes of acute pericarditis are listed in Table 40.4. Most often, the cause of acute pericarditis is *idiopathic* (unknown) or viral. About 20% of cases are due to post-cardiac injury.[8]

There are 3 types of pericarditis: acute, subacute, and chronic. Acute pericarditis develops rapidly, causing the pericardial sac to become inflamed and leak fluid (pericardial effusion). The characteristic pathologic finding in acute pericarditis is inflammation. There is an influx of neutrophils, increased pericardial vascularity, and, eventually, fibrin deposition on the epicardium (Fig. 40.4). Subacute pericarditis occurs weeks to months after an event. Pericarditis lasting more than 6 months is considered chronic.[9]

Post-MI syndrome (Dressler syndrome) pericarditis can occur 4 to 6 weeks after transmural MI (see Chapter 37). This syndrome is more common after a large anterior infarct. Viral pericarditis is often seen after respiratory or GI illness.[10]

Clinical Manifestations

Symptoms include progressive, severe, sharp chest pain.[10] The pain is often worse with deep inspiration and when lying flat. Sitting up and leaning forward relieves the pain. The pain may radiate to the neck, arms, or left shoulder, making it hard to distinguish from angina. One distinction is that the pain from pericarditis can be referred to the trapezius muscle (shoulder, upper back). Dyspnea is related to the patient's breathing in rapid, shallow breaths to avoid chest pain. Fever and anxiety may worsen dyspnea.

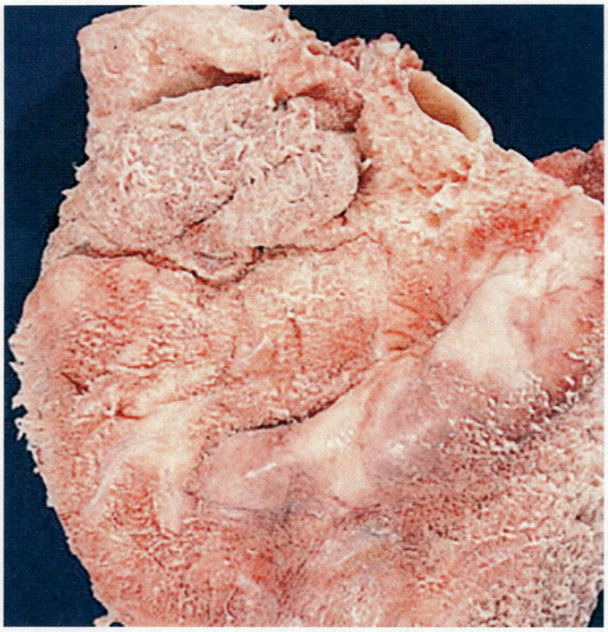

Fig. 40.4 Acute pericarditis. Note shaggy coat of fibers covering surface of heart. (From Carter T, Riegel B: *Cardiac nursing: a companion to Braunwald's heart disease*, St Louis, 2008, Mosby.)

The hallmark finding in acute pericarditis is a *pericardial friction rub*. The rub is a scratching, grating, high-pitched sound believed to result from friction between the roughened pericardial and epicardial surfaces. It is best heard with the stethoscope at the lower left sternal border of the chest with the patient leaning forward. Since it is hard to tell a pericardial friction rub from a pleural friction rub, ask the patient to hold their breath. If you still hear the rub, it is cardiac. Pericardial friction rubs may be hard to identify because they are often intermittent.

Complications

The major complications are pericardial effusion and cardiac tamponade. *Pericardial effusion* is a build-up of fluid in the pericardium. It can occur rapidly (e.g., chest trauma) or slowly (e.g., tuberculosis pericarditis). Large effusions compress nearby structures. Pulmonary tissue compression can cause cough, dyspnea, and tachypnea. Phrenic nerve compression can cause hiccups. Compression of the laryngeal nerve may cause hoarseness. Heart sounds are distant and muffled. BP is usually maintained.

Cardiac tamponade develops as the pericardial effusion volume increases and compresses the heart. The speed of fluid accumulation affects the severity of clinical signs. Tamponade can occur acutely (e.g., rupture of heart, trauma) or subacutely (e.g., from renal failure, cancer).

The patient may report chest pain. They are often confused, anxious, and restless. As the compression of the heart increases, there is decreased CO, muffled heart sounds, narrowed pulse pressure, tachypnea, and tachycardia. Increased jugular venous pressure causes neck vein distention. *Pulsus paradoxus,* if present, is a large decrease in systolic BP during inspiration (Table 40.5). In a patient with a slow onset of a tamponade, dyspnea may be the only sign.

TABLE 40.5 Measuring Pulsus Paradoxus

1. Position the patient in a semirecumbent position.
2. Have patient breathe normally.
3. Using a manually operated BP cuff, measure systolic BP.
4. Inflate BP cuff at least 20 mm Hg above systolic BP.
5. Deflate cuff slowly until you hear sounds throughout the respiratory cycle (inspiration and expiration) and note the pressure.
6. Determine the difference between the measurements taken in steps 3 and 5. This will equal the amount of paradox:

Sounds heard on expiration at	110 mm Hg
Sounds heard throughout cycle at	–82 mm Hg
Amount of paradox	28 mm Hg

The difference is normally <10 mm Hg. If the difference is >10 mm Hg, cardiac tamponade may be present.

Diagnostic Studies

The ECG is useful in diagnosing acute pericarditis, with changes noted in 90% of cases. The most sensitive ECG changes include diffuse (widespread) ST segment elevations. This reflects the abnormal repolarization from the pericardial inflammation. These changes are different from the ST changes seen in MI. In myocardial ischemia, there are usually localized ST segment changes. In acute pericarditis, serial ECGs do not show evolving changes, such as those with MI.

An echocardiogram can determine the presence of a pericardial effusion or cardiac tamponade. Doppler imaging and color M-mode can assess diastolic function and diagnose constrictive pericarditis. A CT scan and MRI can visualize the pericardium and pericardial space. Chest x-ray findings are generally normal, but a large pericardial effusion may appear as cardiomegaly (Fig. 40.5).

Common laboratory findings include leukocytosis and increased CRP and ESR. Troponin levels may be increased in patients with ST segment elevation and acute pericarditis, which could indicate concurrent heart damage. Fluid obtained during pericardiocentesis or tissue from a pericardial biopsy may be studied to determine the cause of the pericarditis.

Interprofessional Care

Management is aimed at identifying and treating the underlying problem and symptoms (Table 40.6). Antibiotics treat bacterial pericarditis. Nonsteroidal antiinflammatory drugs (NSAIDs) control the pain and inflammation. Corticosteroids are used for patients with pericarditis from systemic lupus erythematosus, patients already taking corticosteroids for autoimmune conditions, or patients who do not respond to NSAIDs. They are used cautiously because of their many side effects. Aspirin is recommended for treatment of pericarditis after ST elevation.[10] Colchicine, an antiinflammatory drug used for gout, may help patients with pericarditis present more than 10 days or who have recurrent pericarditis.[10]

Pericardiocentesis is usually done for pericardial effusion with acute cardiac tamponade, purulent pericarditis, or suspected cancer. Hemodynamic support for the patient before the procedure may include giving volume expanders and inotropic agents (e.g., dopamine) and stopping any anticoagulants. The procedure is done rapidly and safely using a percutaneous

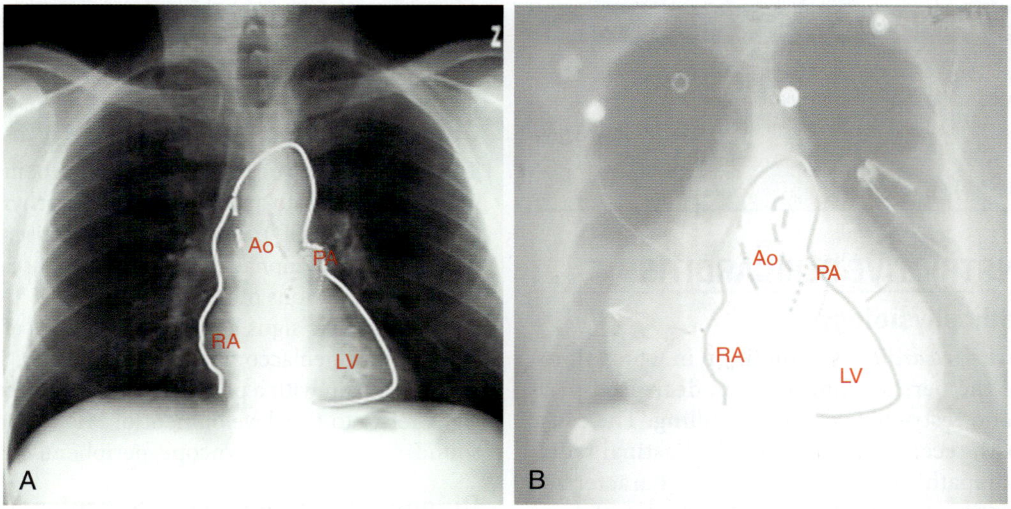

Fig. 40.5 (A) X-ray of a normal chest. (B) Pericardial effusion is present. Note the classic "water bottle shape" heart *(arrows)*. Select structures and great vessels are labeled: *Ao,* ascending aorta; *LV,* left ventricle; *PA,* pulmonary artery; *RA,* right atrium. (From Appleton C, Gilliam L: Cardiac tamponade, *Cardiol Clin* 35:525, 2017.)

TABLE 40.6 Interprofessional Care

Acute Pericarditis

Diagnostic Assessment

- History and physical assessment (note pericardial friction rub, pulsus paradoxus)
- Laboratory: CRP, ESR, white blood cell count
- ECG
- Chest x-ray
- Echocardiogram
- CT scan
- MRI
- Pericardiocentesis, pericardial window
- Pericardial biopsy

Management

- Treatment of underlying disease
- Bed rest
- Drug therapy
  - NSAIDs
  - Corticosteroids
  - Antibiotics (for bacterial infection)
- Pericardiocentesis (for tamponade)
- Pericardial window (for tamponade or ongoing pericardial effusion)

approach guided by echocardiography (Fig. 40.6). A needle is inserted into the pericardial space to remove fluid for analysis and relieve heart pressure. Complications include dysrhythmias, further cardiac tamponade, pneumomediastinum, pneumothorax, myocardial laceration, and coronary artery laceration.

A *pericardial window* is a surgical procedure for diagnosis or drainage of excess fluid. Cutting a "window," or part of the pericardium, allows the fluid to drain continuously into the peritoneum or chest.

NURSING MANAGEMENT: ACUTE PERICARDITIS

Managing the patient's pain and anxiety during acute pericarditis is your key nursing consideration. Assess the pain to distinguish angina (myocardial ischemia) (see Table 37.8) from the pain of pericarditis. Pericarditis pain is usually found in the precordium or left trapezius region. It has a sharp quality that increases with inspiration. Pain is often relieved when the patient sits up or leans forward and is worse when lying flat.

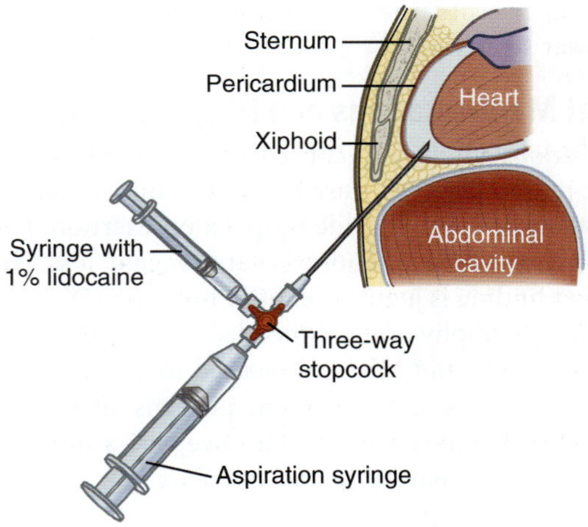

Fig. 40.6 Pericardiocentesis performed under sterile conditions in conjunction with ECG and hemodynamic measurements.

Pain relief measures include keeping the patient on bed rest with the head of the bed raised to 45 degrees and providing an overbed table for support. Antiinflammatory drugs can help control the pain. Give these drugs with food or milk. Tell the patient to avoid alcohol because of the risk of GI bleeding. Other drugs, such as a proton pump inhibitor (e.g., pantoprazole, omeprazole), can reduce stomach acid.

Provide simple, complete explanations of procedures and possible causes of the pain to help reduce anxiety. These explanations are particularly important when the patient is undergoing testing and for the patient who has previously had angina or an MI.

The patient with acute pericarditis is at risk for cardiac tamponade and decreased CO. Monitor for signs of tamponade and prepare for possible pericardiocentesis.

CHECK YOUR PRACTICE

You are assigned to a 58-year-old male patient who had an MI 3 days ago. He has now developed pericarditis. When you are making rounds, you assess that the patient is slightly confused and has prominent neck veins. His heart rate is 118 beats/min.

- What should you do next?

CHRONIC CONSTRICTIVE PERICARDITIS

Etiology and Pathophysiology

Chronic constrictive pericarditis is a condition in which fibrosis and rigidity of the pericardium result in decreased pericardial elasticity and restricted ventricular filling. The cause may be tuberculosis, recent heart surgery, mediastinal radiation therapy, or idiopathic.[11] The condition is characterized by pericardial effusion that is slowly reabsorbed with progression to fibrous scarring, thickening of the pericardium from calcium deposits, and eventual destruction of the pericardial space. The fibrotic, thickened, and adherent pericardium encases the heart and prevents adequate atrial and ventricular stretch.

Clinical Manifestations and Diagnostic Studies

Manifestations of chronic constrictive pericarditis mimic HF and cor pulmonale. Decreased CO accounts for many of the manifestations. These include dyspnea on exertion, peripheral edema, ascites, fatigue, anorexia, and weight loss. The most prominent finding is jugular venous distention (JVD).

Echocardiography is recommended to diagnose constrictive pericarditis.[11] CT and MRI can be used to measure pericardial thickness and assess diastolic filling patterns. ECG changes are often nonspecific in chronic constrictive pericarditis. The heart on the chest x-ray may be normal or enlarged.

◆ Interprofessional Care

The treatment of choice for symptomatic chronic constrictive pericarditis is a *pericardiectomy.* This involves complete resection of the pericardium through a median sternotomy with the use of cardiopulmonary bypass (see Chapter 37). Some patients show immediate improvement. Others may take weeks. The prognosis improves when the patient has surgery before becoming clinically unstable. Diuretics are used in patients who are not surgical candidates.[11]

MYOCARDITIS

Etiology and Pathophysiology

Myocarditis is a focal or diffuse inflammation of the myocardium. Causes include viruses, bacteria, fungi, radiation therapy, and pharmacologic and chemical factors. Coxsackie A and B viruses are the most common causative agents. Autoimmune disorders (e.g., polymyositis) have been linked with the development of myocarditis. It also may be idiopathic.

When the myocardium becomes infected, the causative agent invades the myocytes and causes cellular damage and necrosis. This activates the immune response. Cytokines and O_2 free radicals are released. As the infection progresses, an autoimmune response is activated. This causes further destruction of myocytes and heart dysfunction.

Clinical Manifestations

The features of myocarditis vary from a benign course without overt symptoms to progressive HF, dysrhythmias, or sudden cardiac death (SCD). Fever, fatigue, malaise, myalgias, pharyngitis, dyspnea, lymphadenopathy, and nausea and vomiting are early manifestations of the viral illness.

Early cardiac signs appear 7 to 10 days after viral infection. Pericarditis often accompanies myocarditis. Signs include pleuritic chest pain with a pericardial friction rub and effusion. Late signs relate to the development of HF and include an S_3 heart sound, crackles, JVD, syncope, peripheral edema, and angina.

Diagnostic Studies and Interprofessional Care

The ECG changes with myocarditis are often nonspecific but reflect pericardial involvement (e.g., diffuse ST segment changes). Dysrhythmias and conduction problems may be present. Laboratory findings are often inconclusive. They may include mild to moderate leukocytosis and atypical lymphocytes, high viral titers, and increased ESR, CRP levels, and levels of cardiac biomarkers, such as troponin. The virus is generally present in tissue and pericardial fluid samples only during the first 8 to 10 days of illness.

Endomyocardial biopsy provides histologic confirmation of myocarditis.[12] A biopsy is most diagnostic during the first 6 weeks of acute illness, when lymphocytic infiltration and myocyte damage are present. Nuclear scans, echocardiography, and MRI are used to assess heart function.

Treatment consists of managing symptoms. Angiotensin-converting enzyme (ACE) inhibitors and β-adrenergic receptor blockers (β-blockers) are used if the heart is enlarged or to treat HF (see Chapter 38). Diuretics reduce fluid volume and preload. If the patient is not hypotensive, IV drugs such as nitroprusside and milrinone reduce afterload and improve CO by decreasing systemic vascular resistance. Digoxin improves heart contractility and reduces HR. It is used with caution because of increased sensitivity to the adverse effects (e.g., dysrhythmias) and the potential toxicity. Anticoagulation reduces the risk for clot formation from blood stasis in patients with a low ejection fraction (EF).

DRUG ALERT

Digoxin (Lanoxin)

1. Use cautiously in patients with myocarditis.
2. Myocarditis predisposes to drug-related dysrhythmias and toxicity.

Myocarditis with an autoimmune basis is treated with immunosuppressive agents to reduce heart inflammation and damage. Antivirals may be used as adjunct therapy.

General supportive measures include O_2 therapy, bed rest, and restricted activity. In cases of severe HF, intraaortic balloon pump therapy and ventricular assist devices (VAD) may be needed (see Chapters 35 and 38).

❖ NURSING MANAGEMENT: MYOCARDITIS

Focus your interventions on improving CO and managing the signs and symptoms of HF. Select nursing measures to decrease cardiac workload. These include placing the patient in a semi-Fowler's position, spacing activity and rest periods, and providing a quiet environment. Carefully monitor drugs that increase the heart's contractility and decrease preload, afterload, or both. Evaluate the effectiveness of your interventions on an ongoing basis.

The patient may be anxious about the diagnosis. Assess the level of anxiety, take measures to decrease anxiety, and keep the patient and caregiver informed about the therapeutic plan.

The patient who receives immunosuppressive therapy is at increased risk for infection. Monitor for complications and provide the patient with proper infection control procedures.

Although most patients recover spontaneously, some develop dilated cardiomyopathy. If severe HF occurs, the patient may need a heart transplant.

RHEUMATIC FEVER AND RHEUMATIC HEART DISEASE

Rheumatic fever (RF) is an acute inflammatory disease that can involve all the heart layers. **Rheumatic heart disease** is chronic scarring and deformity of the heart valves resulting from RF. Over 15 million people worldwide have evidence of RHD.[13]

Etiology and Pathophysiology

RF occurs as a complication 2-3 weeks after a group A streptococcal pharyngitis. RHD is the result of valve damage from an abnormal immune response to Streptococcus.[13] RF affects the heart, skin, joints, and CNS. Rheumatic heart disease, caused by RF, mainly affects children and young adults.

Cardiac Lesions and Valve Deformities

About 50% of RF episodes are *rheumatic pancarditis,* involving all layers of the heart (endocardium, myocardium, and pericardium) (see Fig. 40.1).[14]

Rheumatic IE is found mainly in the valves, with swelling and erosion of the valve leaflets. Vegetation forms from deposits of fibrin and blood cells in areas of erosion. The lesions initially create a thickening of the valve leaflets, fusion of commissures and chordae tendineae, and fibrosis of the papillary muscle. Valve leaflets may become calcified, resulting in stenosis. The less mobile valve leaflets may not close properly, resulting in regurgitation. The mitral and aortic valves are most often affected.

Nodules, called *Aschoff's bodies,* are formed by a reaction to inflammation with swelling and destruction of collagen fibers. As Aschoff's bodies age, they become more fibrous, and scar tissue forms in the myocardium. Rheumatic pericarditis develops and affects both layers of the pericardium. The layers become thick and covered with fibrinous exudate. A serosanguineous pericardial effusion may develop. When healing occurs, fibrosis and adhesions develop that partially or completely destroy the pericardial sac. Damage to the heart begins during the first attack of RF. Recurrent infections cause further structural damage.

TABLE 40.7 Diagnostic Criteria

Revised Jones Criteria for Rheumatic Fever

These criteria apply to the initial episode of rheumatic fever in moderate- or high-risk populations.

Major Criteria
- Carditis: Clinical and/or subclinical
- Arthritis
  - Monoarthritis or polyarthritis
  - Polyarthralgia
- Erythema marginatum
- Subcutaneous nodules
- Sydenham's chorea

Minor Criteria
- Monoarthralgia
- Fever
- Laboratory findings: ↑ ESR and/or ↑ CRP
- ECG findings: Prolonged PR interval after accounting for age variability (unless carditis is a major criterion)

Evidence of Group A Streptococcal Infection
- Laboratory findings
  - ↑ Antistreptolysin-O titer, positive throat culture, or positive rapid antigen test for group A streptococci

Modified from Gewitz MH, Baltimore RS, Tani LY, et al.: Revision of the Jones criteria for the diagnosis of acute rheumatic fever in the era of Doppler echocardiography: A scientific statement from the AHA, *Circ* 131:1806, 2015.

Extracardiac Lesions

The systemic lesions of RF involve the skin, joints, and CNS. Painless subcutaneous nodules, arthralgias or arthritis, and chorea may develop.

Clinical Manifestations

Jones criteria are used to diagnose acute RF.[14] The presence of 2 major criteria or 1 major and 2 minor criteria plus evidence of a preceding group A streptococcal infection indicate a high probability of acute RF (Table 40.7).

Major Criteria

Carditis is the most important manifestation of RF. It results in 3 signs: (1) heart murmur or murmurs of mitral or aortic regurgitation, or mitral stenosis; (2) heart enlargement and HF from myocarditis; and (3) pericarditis resulting in muffled heart sounds, chest pain, pericardial friction rub, or signs of effusion.

Monoarthritis or *polyarthritis* is the most common finding in RF. It occurs in up to 75% of patients.[14] The inflammatory process affects the synovial membranes of the joints. This causes swelling, heat, redness, tenderness, and limitation of motion. The larger joints, particularly the knees, ankles, elbows, and wrists, are most often affected.

Sydenham's chorea is the major CNS manifestation.[14] It is characterized by involuntary movements, especially of the face and limbs, muscle weakness, and speech and gait problems.

Erythema marginatum lesions are a less common feature of RF. They occur in less than 10% of RF patients.[15] The

TABLE 40.8 Interprofessional Care

Rheumatic Fever

Diagnostic Assessment
- History and physical assessment
- Laboratory studies (Table 40.7)
  - Chest x-ray
  - Echocardiogram
  - ECG

Management
- Bed rest or limited activity
- Drug therapy
  - Antibiotics
  - NSAIDs
  - Salicylates
  - Corticosteroids

bright pink, nonpruritic, maplike macular lesions occur mainly on the trunk and proximal extremities. They intensify with heat (e.g., warm bath). *Subcutaneous nodules* associated with severe carditis are small, hard, painless swellings found over extensor surfaces of joints, particularly the knees, wrists, and elbows.

Minor Criteria

Minor clinical manifestations (Table 40.7) are helpful in diagnosing the disease. The minor criteria confirm the presence of RF when only 1 major criterion is present.

Evidence of Infection

In addition to the major and minor criteria, there must be evidence of a preceding group A streptococcal infection. Table 40.7 lists the various laboratory tests used to confirm evidence of infection.

Complications

Chronic rheumatic carditis results from changes in valve structure months to years after an episode of RF. Rheumatic IE can result in fibrous tissue growth in valve leaflets and chordae tendineae with scarring and contractures. The mitral valve is most often involved. The aortic and tricuspid valves may be affected.

Diagnostic Studies and Interprofessional Care

No single diagnostic test exists for RF. An echocardiogram may show valvular insufficiency and pericardial fluid or thickening.[15] A chest x-ray may show an enlarged heart. The most consistent ECG change is a prolonged PR interval from delayed AV conduction.

Treatment consists of drug therapy and supportive measures (Table 40.8). Antibiotic therapy does not change the course of the acute disease or the development of carditis. It eliminates residual group A streptococci in the tonsils and pharynx and prevents the spread of organisms through close contact. Salicylates, NSAIDs, and corticosteroids are the 3 inflammatory agents most widely used to control fever and joint manifestations.[15]

TABLE 40.9 NURSING ASSESSMENT

Rheumatic Fever and Rheumatic Heart Disease

Subjective Data

Important Health Information

Health history: Recent streptococcal infection, history of RF or rheumatic heart disease

Functional Health Patterns

Health perception–health management: Family history of RF. Malaise

Nutritional-metabolic: Anorexia, weight loss

Activity-exercise: Palpitations, generalized weakness, fatigue, impaired coordination

Cognitive-perceptual: Chest pain, widespread joint pain, and tenderness (especially large joints)

Objective Data

Cardiovascular

Tachycardia, pericardial friction rub, muffled heart sounds, murmurs, peripheral edema

General

Fever

Musculoskeletal

Signs of monoarthritis or polyarthritis, including swelling, heat, redness, limitation of motion (especially of knees, ankles, elbows, shoulders, wrists)

Neurologic

Chorea (involuntary, purposeless, rapid motions; facial grimaces)

Skin

- Subcutaneous nodules and erythema marginatum

Possible Diagnostic Findings

Cardiomegaly on chest x-ray. Prolonged PR interval on ECG. Valve abnormalities, chamber dilation, and pericardial effusion on echocardiogram. ↑ Antistreptolysin-O titer, positive throat culture, positive rapid antigen test for group A streptococci, ↑ ESR, ↑ CRP, leukocytosis.

❖ NURSING MANAGEMENT: RHEUMATIC FEVER AND RHEUMATIC HEART DISEASE

◆ Assessment

Table 40.9 presents the subjective and objective data to obtain from a patient with RF and rheumatic heart disease.

Inspect the skin for subcutaneous nodules and erythema marginatum. Palpate for subcutaneous nodules over all bony surfaces and along extensor tendons of the hands and feet. The nodules range in size from 1 to 4 cm and are hard, painless, and freely movable. Erythema marginatum can occur on the trunk and inner aspects of the upper arm and thigh. Assess for these bright pink maculae in good light because the rash is hard to see, especially in patients with dark skin.

◆ Clinical Problems

Clinical problems for the patient with RF and rheumatic heart disease include:

- Fatigue

- Impaired cardiac function
- Infection

◆ Planning

The goals for a patient with RF and rheumatic heart disease include (1) normal or baseline heart function, (2) resumption of daily activities without joint pain, and (3) ability to manage the long-term antibiotic therapy.

◆ Implementation

◆ Health Promotion

Early detection and immediate treatment of group A streptococcal pharyngitis can prevent RF. Treatment with an initial dose of intramuscular Benzathine Penicillin G is the most widely used antibiotic to treat RHD.[14] If the patient is allergic to penicillin, a narrow-spectrum cephalosporin (e.g., cephalexin), clindamycin (Cleocin), or azithromycin (Zithromax) is used.[16] Therapy requires strict adherence to the full course of treatment. Teach people in the community to seek prompt medical care for symptoms of streptococcal pharyngitis.

◆ Acute Care

Give antibiotics as prescribed to treat the streptococcal infection. Teach the patient that completing the full course of antibiotics is vital to successful treatment (see Table 15.9).

Promote optimal rest. This reduces cardiac workload and metabolic needs. Position painful joints for proper alignment and apply heat for comfort. Give salicylates, NSAIDs, and corticosteroids as prescribed for joint pain. Implement measures to manage fever (see Table 12.5). Stress the importance of gentle activities during recovery.

> **CHECK YOUR PRACTICE**
>
> Your 28-year-old male patient is recovering from carditis after RF. As you are preparing him for discharge from the hospital, he is pacing the floor and seems quite upset. You ask him to sit down so you can talk. He tells you, "I'm a heart cripple. I will never be able to play ball with my sons or go skiing again. I might as well just go to bed and stay there."
>
> - What are the key elements to include in your teaching plan?

◆ Ambulatory Care

The aim of secondary prevention is to stop a recurrence of RF. Prior history of RF makes the patient more susceptible to a second attack after a streptococcal infection. The best prevention is treatment with prophylactic antibiotics. Patients with RF without carditis need prophylaxis until age 20 and for a minimum of 5 years. Patients with rheumatic carditis and residual heart disease (e.g., persistent valve disease) need lifelong prophylaxis.[16]

Teach the patient with a history of RF about the disease process and the need for ongoing antibiotic prophylaxis. Teach the patient about good nutrition, hygienic practices, and adequate rest. Caution the patient about the possible development of heart valve disease. Tell the patient to seek medical care for symptoms, such as excessive fatigue, dizziness, palpitations, unexplained weight gain, or exertional dyspnea.[16]

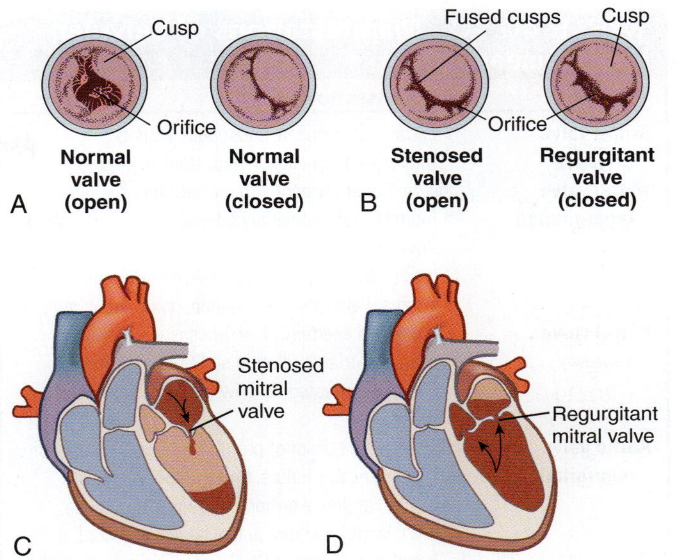

Fig. 40.7 Valvular stenosis and regurgitation. (A) Normal position of the valve leaflets when the valve is open and closed. (B) Open position of a stenosed valve *(left)* and closed position of regurgitant valve *(right)*. (C) Hemodynamic effect of mitral stenosis. The stenosed valve is unable to open sufficiently during left atrial systole, inhibiting left ventricular filling. (D) Hemodynamic effect of MR. The mitral valve does not close completely during left ventricular systole, letting blood reenter the left atrium. At the same time, blood is moving forward through the aortic valve. (From McCance KL, Huether SE: *Pathophysiology: the biologic basis for disease in adults and children*, ed 6, St Louis, 2010, Mosby.)

◆ Evaluation

The expected outcomes are that the patient with RF and rheumatic heart disease will

- Be able to perform ADLs with minimal fatigue and pain
- Adhere to the treatment plan
- Express confidence in managing disease
- Use measures to prevent complications

VALVULAR HEART DISEASE

Two AV valves (mitral and tricuspid) and 2 semilunar valves (aortic and pulmonic) control blood flow through the heart (see Fig. 35.1). The pressure on either side of an open valve is normally equal. However, in a stenotic valve, the valve opening is smaller due to limited leaflet opening. The forward flow of blood is impaired. This creates a difference in pressure on the 2 sides of the open valve. The amount of **stenosis** (constriction or narrowing) is seen in the pressure differences (the higher the difference, the greater the stenosis). When **regurgitation** occurs (referred to as *incompetence* or *insufficiency*), there is incomplete closure of the valve and backward flow of blood (Fig. 40.7).

Congenital heart conditions are the most common cause of valve disorders in children and teens. Aortic stenosis and mitral regurgitation (MR) often occur in older adults who have some form of heart disease. Other causes of valve disease in adults are related to endocarditis, rheumatic heart disease, hypertension, and autoimmune disorders.

TABLE 40.10 Manifestations of Valvular Heart Disease

Type	Manifestations
Mitral valve prolapse	Palpitations, dyspnea, chest pain, activity intolerance, syncope, holosystolic murmur
Mitral valve regurgitation	*Acute:* Generally poorly tolerated. New systolic murmur with pulmonary edema. Cardiogenic shock develops rapidly *Chronic:* Weakness, fatigue, exertional dyspnea, edema. Palpitations, S_3 gallop, holosystolic murmur
Mitral valve stenosis	Dyspnea on exertion. Hoarseness, hemoptysis, fatigue. Atrial fibrillation on ECG. Palpitations. Loud, accentuated S_1. Low-pitched, diastolic murmur
Aortic valve regurgitation	*Acute:* Abrupt onset of profound dyspnea, chest pain, left ventricular failure, and cardiogenic shock *Chronic:* Fatigue, exertional dyspnea, orthopnea, PND. Water-hammer pulse, heaving precordial impulse, ↓ or absent S_1, S_3, or S_4. Soft, high-pitched diastolic murmur, Austin Flint murmur
Aortic valve stenosis	Angina, syncope, dyspnea on exertion, HF, normal or soft S_1, ↓ or absent S_2, systolic murmur, prominent S_4
Tricuspid and pulmonic stenosis	*Tricuspid:* Peripheral edema, ascites, hepatomegaly. Diastolic low-pitched murmur with increased intensity during inspiration *Pulmonic:* Fatigue, loud midsystolic murmur

PND, Paroxysmal nocturnal dyspnea.

MITRAL VALVE STENOSIS

Etiology and Pathophysiology

Worldwide, the most common cause of mitral stenosis is rheumatic heart disease.[17] Rheumatic mitral stenosis is widespread in developing countries. Less common causes are congenital mitral stenosis, rheumatoid arthritis, radiation exposure, and systemic lupus erythematosus. Rheumatic IE causes scarring of the valve leaflets and the chordae tendineae. Contractures and adhesions develop between the commissures (the junctional areas). The stenotic mitral valve takes on a "fish mouth" shape because of the thickening and shortening of the mitral valve structures. Severe mitral annular calcification can cause stenosis in older adults.

These deformities block the blood flow and create a pressure difference between the left atrium and left ventricle during diastole. As a result, left atrial pressure and volume increase. This causes higher pulmonary vasculature pressure. The overloaded left atrium places the patient at risk for atrial fibrillation. In chronic mitral stenosis, pressure overload occurs in the left atrium, pulmonary bed, and right ventricle.

Clinical Manifestations

The main symptom is exertional dyspnea from reduced lung compliance (Table 40.10). Heart sounds include a loud 1st heart sound and a low-pitched, diastolic murmur (best heard at the apex with the stethoscope). Less often, patients may have hoarseness (from atrial enlargement pressing on the laryngeal nerve), hemoptysis (from pulmonary hypertension), and chest pain (from decreased CO and coronary perfusion). Emboli can form in the left atrium from atrial fibrillation and cause a stroke. Fatigue and palpitations from atrial fibrillation may occur.

MITRAL VALVE REGURGITATION

Etiology and Pathophysiology

Mitral valve function depends on intact mitral leaflets, mitral annulus, chordae tendineae, papillary muscles, left atrium, and left ventricle. A defect in any of these structures can cause regurgitation. MR may result from problems with the leaflets or from the surrounding structures. In primary (degenerative) MR, a problem with the leaflets causes the regurgitation. In secondary (functional) MR, myocardial disease causes the regurgitation.[17] Most cases are caused by MI, chronic rheumatic heart disease, mitral valve prolapse, ischemic papillary muscle dysfunction, and IE. MI with left ventricular failure increases the risk for rupture of the chordae tendineae and acute MR.

MR allows blood to flow backward from the left ventricle to the left atrium because of incomplete valve closure during systole. Both the left ventricle and left atrium must work harder to preserve an adequate CO. In acute MR, the sudden increase in pressure and volume transmits back to the pulmonary bed. This results in pulmonary edema and, if not treated, cardiogenic shock. In chronic MR, the added volume results in left atrial enlargement, left ventricular dilation and hypertrophy, and, finally, a decrease in CO.

Clinical Manifestations

The nature of its onset determines the clinical course of MR (Table 40.10). Patients with acute MR have thready peripheral pulses and cool, clammy extremities. A low CO may mask a new systolic murmur. Rapid assessment (e.g., heart catheterization) and intervention (e.g., valve repair or replacement) are critical.

Patients with chronic MR may remain asymptomatic for many years. Early symptoms of left ventricular failure may include weakness, fatigue, palpitations, and dyspnea. These gradually progress to orthopnea, paroxysmal nocturnal dyspnea, and peripheral edema. Increased left ventricular volume leads to an audible 3rd heart sound (S_3), even with normal left ventricular function. The murmur is a loud holosystolic murmur at the apex radiating to the left axilla. Patients with asymptomatic MR must be monitored carefully.

Treatment for MR depends on the cause of the regurgitation. Primary MR typically requires valve repair or replacement before significant left ventricular failure or pulmonary hypertension develops.[17] Medical management includes guideline-directed medical therapy (GDMT).

MITRAL VALVE PROLAPSE

Etiology and Pathophysiology

Mitral valve prolapse (MVP) is an abnormality of the mitral valve leaflets and the papillary muscles or chordae that allows the leaflets to prolapse, or buckle, back into the left atrium during systole (Fig. 40.8). MVP affects 2% to 3% of the general population.

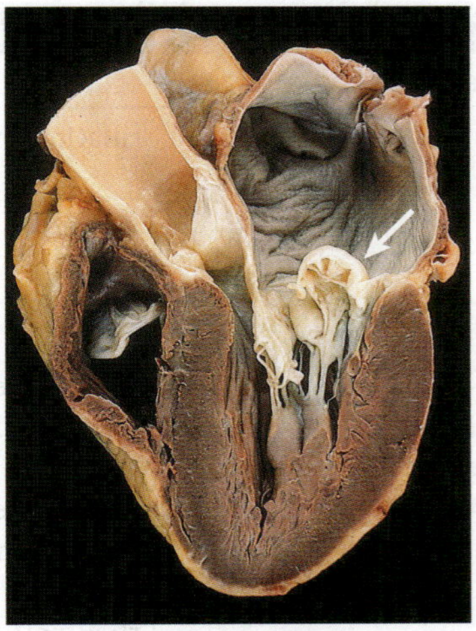

Fig. 40.8 MVP. In this valvular abnormality, the mitral leaflets have prolapsed back into the left atrium. There is hooding *(arrow)*. The left ventricle is on the right. (From Kumar V, Abbas AK, Aster JC, et al.: *Robbins and Cotran pathologic basis of disease,* ed 8, Philadelphia, 2010, Saunders.)

The use of the term *prolapse* can be misleading because it is used even when the valve is working normally. MVP is usually benign, but serious complications can occur, including MR, IE, SCD, HF, and cerebral ischemia.

Genetic Link

Although the cause of MVP is unknown, there is an increased familial incidence. The genetic inheritance is often autosomal dominant (see Chapter 13). MVP in this group results from a connective tissue defect affecting only the valve, as part of Marfan's syndrome, or another hereditary condition that affects collagen structure.

Clinical Manifestations

MVP has a broad range of severity. Most patients are asymptomatic for their entire lives. About 10% of those with MVP become symptomatic. A characteristic of MVP is a regurgitation murmur that is louder during systole. MVP does not alter S_1 or S_2 heart sounds. Severe MR is an uncommon but serious complication of MVP.

M-mode and 2-D echocardiography can confirm MVP. Dysrhythmias, such as premature ventricular contractions, paroxysmal supraventricular tachycardia, and ventricular tachycardia, may cause palpitations, lightheadedness, and syncope. IE may occur in patients with MR associated with MVP.

Patients may have chest discomfort caused by abnormal tension on the papillary muscles.[18] Chest pain episodes tend to occur in clusters, especially during periods of stress. Dyspnea, palpitations, and syncope sometimes accompany the chest pain and do not respond to antianginal treatment (e.g., nitrates). β-Blockers may control palpitations and chest pain. Encourage the patient to stay hydrated, exercise regularly, and avoid caffeine.

Most patients with MVP have a benign, manageable course. For those who do develop symptomatic MR, no current therapy delays the need for valve surgery. A teaching plan for patients with MVP is outlined in Table 40.11.

TABLE 40.11 PATIENT & CAREGIVER TEACHING

Mitral Valve Prolapse (MVP)

Include the following information in the teaching plan for a patient with MVP and the patient's caregiver:

- Take drugs as prescribed (e.g., β-blockers to control palpitations, chest pain).
- Adopt healthy eating habits.
- Avoid caffeine. It is a stimulant and may worsen symptoms.
- If you use diet pills or other over-the-counter drugs, check for common ingredients that are stimulants (e.g., caffeine, ephedrine) since these can worsen symptoms.
- Begin, or maintain, an exercise program to achieve optimal health.
- Contact the HCP or emergency response system (ERS) if symptoms develop or worsen (e.g., palpitations, fatigue, shortness of breath, anxiety).

AORTIC VALVE STENOSIS

Etiology and Pathophysiology

Congenital **aortic stenosis (AS)** is generally found in childhood, adolescence, or young adulthood. In older adults, AS is a result of RF or degeneration, similar to coronary artery disease. AS is the most frequent degenerative valve disorder, affecting 3% of people over 65 years of age.[19] In rheumatic valve disease, fusion and calcification cause the valve leaflets to stiffen and retract, resulting in stenosis. AS due to rheumatic heart disease accompanies mitral valve disease. Isolated AS is usually nonrheumatic.

AS causes obstruction of blood flow from the left ventricle to the aorta during systole. The result is left ventricular hypertrophy and increased myocardial O_2 consumption because of the increased myocardial mass. As the disease progresses and compensation fails, reduced CO leads to decreased tissue perfusion, pulmonary hypertension, and HF. Left untreated, severe AS has a poor prognosis.

Clinical Manifestations

Manifestations (Table 40.10) develop when the valve orifice becomes about one-third of its normal size. They include the classic triad of angina, syncope, and exertional dyspnea, reflecting left ventricular failure.[19] Auscultation often reveals a crescendo-decrescendo, holosystolic murmur that may radiate to the carotids.

Some patients may be asymptomatic. The prognosis is poorer for patients with symptoms and those whose valve obstruction is not fixed. Nitroglycerin is used cautiously to treat angina in patients with AS. It can significantly reduce BP and worsen chest pain.

DRUG ALERT

Nitroglycerin

- Use cautiously in patients with AS since significant hypotension may occur.
- The drug can worsen chest pain due to the decrease in preload and drop in BP.

AORTIC VALVE REGURGITATION

Etiology and Pathophysiology

Aortic regurgitation (AR) may be the result of primary disease of the aortic valve leaflets, the aortic root, or both.[20] Trauma, IE, or aortic dissection can cause acute AR, which is a life-threatening emergency. Chronic AR generally results from rheumatic heart disease, a congenital bicuspid aortic valve, syphilis, a connective tissue problem, or a postsurgical cause.[20]

AR causes retrograde (backward) blood flow from the ascending aorta into the left ventricle during diastole. This results in volume overload. The left ventricle initially compensates for chronic AR by dilation and hypertrophy. Myocardial contractility eventually declines, and blood volume in the left atrium and pulmonary bed increases. This leads to pulmonary hypertension and right ventricular (RV) failure.

Clinical Manifestations

Patients with acute AR have sudden signs of cardiovascular collapse (Table 40.10). The patient develops severe dyspnea, chest pain, and hypotension, indicating left ventricular failure and cardiogenic shock, a life-threatening emergency.

Patients with chronic, severe AR develop a *water-hammer pulse* (strong, quick beat that collapses immediately). Heart sounds may include a soft or absent S_1, S_3, or S_4 and a soft, high-pitched diastolic murmur.

The patient with chronic AR generally is asymptomatic for years.[20] Exertional dyspnea, orthopnea, and paroxysmal nocturnal dyspnea develop only after considerable heart dysfunction has occurred (Table 40.10). Angina occurs less often than in AS.

TRICUSPID AND PULMONIC VALVE DISEASE

Etiology and Pathophysiology

Tricuspid regurgitation (TR) can be primary or secondary. Primary TR is less common. It is typically due to IE or congenital malformation. Secondary TR is caused by RV dilatation from pulmonary hypertension, cor pulmonale, or pulmonary outflow tract obstruction. The patient does not show JVD, enlarged liver, and peripheral edema until regurgitation is severe. Diagnosis is made by history, physical, and echocardiogram. The prognosis is poor for severe TR.

Tricuspid stenosis is usually caused by RF. Signs and symptoms include a fluttering discomfort in the neck, fatigue, and possible right upper quadrant pain.

Pulmonary regurgitation is often asymptomatic. A crescendo-decrescendo murmur is present. Potential causes include pulmonary hypertension, surgical repair of tetralogy of Fallot (TOF), or congenital valve disease. It can cause RV dilation.

Pulmonic stenosis is often due to congenital heart disease. It results in RV hypertension and hypertrophy (Table 40.10). It is largely asymptomatic. When symptoms develop, they are similar to those of AS (syncope, dyspnea, angina). Symptoms typically do not present until adulthood.

TABLE 40.12 Interprofessional Care

Valvular Heart Disease

Diagnostic Assessment
- History and physical assessment
- Chest x-ray
- Complete blood count
- ECG
- Echocardiography (Doppler, transesophageal)
- Heart catheterization

Management

Conservative Therapy
- Prophylactic antibiotic therapy (Table 40.2)
  - RF
  - IE
- Sodium restriction
- Drug therapy to treat or control HF
  - Vasodilators (e.g., nitrates, ACE inhibitors)[a]
  - Positive inotropes (e.g., digoxin)
  - Diuretics
  - β-Blockers
- Anticoagulation therapy (see Table 41.10)
- Antidysrhythmic drugs (see Table 39.9)
- Percutaneous transluminal balloon valvuloplasty
- Percutaneous valve replacement

Surgical Therapy
- Valve repair
  - Annuloplasty
  - Commissurotomy (valvulotomy)
  - Valvuloplasty
- Valve replacement

[a]Use cautiously in patients with aortic stenosis.

DIAGNOSTIC STUDIES: VALVULAR HEART DISEASE

Diagnosis of valvular heart disease includes information from the history and physical assessment and a variety of tests (Table 40.12). An echocardiogram shows valve structure, function, and heart chamber size. Transesophageal echocardiography and Doppler color-flow imaging help diagnose and monitor valvular heart disease progression. Real-time 3D echocardiography can help assess mitral valve and congenital heart disease.

Chest x-ray shows the heart size, altered pulmonary circulation, and valve calcification. An ECG identifies HR, rhythm, and any ischemia or ventricular hypertrophy. Heart catheterization detects pressure changes in the heart chambers, records pressure differences across the valves, and measures the size of valve openings.

INTERPROFESSIONAL CARE: VALVULAR HEART DISEASE

Conservative Therapy

Overall treatment focuses on preventing exacerbations of HF, acute pulmonary edema, thromboembolism, and recurrent RF and IE (Table 40.12). HF is treated with vasodilators, positive

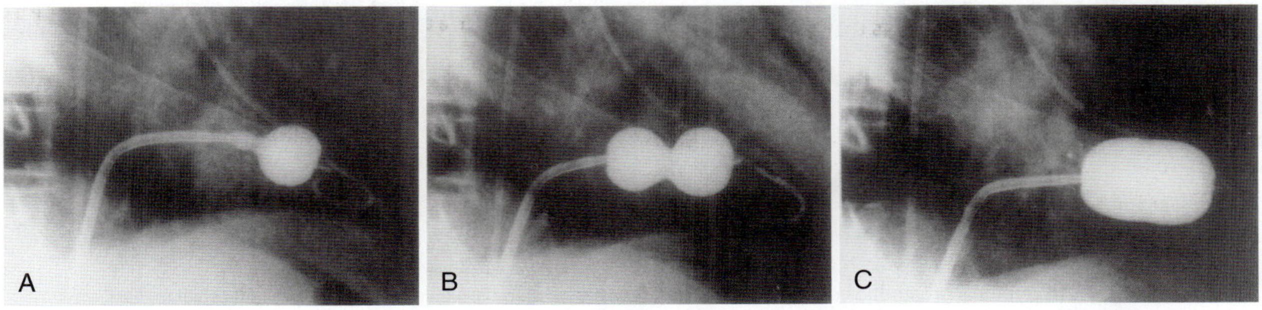

Fig. 40.9 Mitral valvuloplasty performed by the Inoue technique. The catheter is placed in the mitral valve and the distal part of the Inoue balloon inflated (A). The balloon is then pulled back in the mitral valve and inflated for 10 to 15 seconds under fluoroscopic control (B) until the waist of the balloon is no longer visible (C) and the balloon falls back into the left atrium. (From Crawford MH, DiMarco JP, Paulus WJ: *Cardiology,* ed 3, Edinburgh, 2010, Mosby.)

inotropes, β-blockers, diuretics, and a low-sodium diet (see Chapter 38).

Atrial dysrhythmias are common. They are treated with calcium channel blockers, β-blockers, antidysrhythmic drugs, or electrical cardioversion (see Chapter 39). Anticoagulant therapy is used in patients with atrial fibrillation to prevent systemic or pulmonary emboli.

Percutaneous Transluminal Balloon Valvuloplasty

An alternative treatment for some patients with valvular heart disease is *percutaneous transluminal balloon valvuloplasty* (PTBV). During PTBV, the fused commissures are split open. Balloon valvuloplasty treats mitral, tricuspid, pulmonic, and AS.[20]

The PTBV procedure is typically done in the cardiac catheterization laboratory. It involves threading a balloon-tipped catheter from the femoral artery or vein to the stenotic valve. The balloon is inflated to separate the valve leaflets. A single- or double-balloon technique may be used. Using a single Inoue balloon with an hourglass shape allows sequential inflation. This technique is the most popular because it is easy and has good results with few complications. It is not a permanent fix for stenosis (Fig. 40.9).

Surgical Therapy

The decision for valve repair or replacement depends on the patient's symptoms using the New York Heart Association classification system for functional disability (see Table 38.3).[20] The procedure used depends on the (1) valves involved, (2) pathology and severity of the disease, and (3) patient's clinical condition (Box 40.1).

Valve Repair

Valve repair is preferred over replacement when clinically appropriate. Repair has a lower operative mortality rate than valve replacement. It is often used in mitral or tricuspid valve disease.[20] Although repair avoids the risks of replacement, it may not restore total valve function.

Open surgical *valvuloplasty* involves repair of the valve by suturing the torn leaflets, chordae tendineae, or papillary muscles. It is mainly used to treat mitral or TR.

Minimally invasive valve surgery involves a mini-sternotomy or parasternal approach. It may include robotic and thoracoscopic surgical systems. Advantages include shorter lengths of stay, fewer blood transfusions, less pain, and lower risk for sternal infection and postoperative atrial fibrillation.

For patients with mitral or TR, further valve repair or reconstruction using annuloplasty is an option. *Annuloplasty* involves reconstruction of the annulus, with or without the aid of prosthetic rings.

BOX 40.1 ETHICAL/LEGAL DILEMMAS

Do Not Resuscitate

Situation

J.L., a 68-year-old man, is admitted for a second mitral valve repair and coronary artery bypass graft surgery. He did not adhere to the treatment plan after his original surgery 7 years ago. You are worried about his future adherence to drugs, diet, and exercise. He is now on dialysis, making him a high-risk open surgical patient. J.L. and his caregiver request all treatment and decline to discuss advance directives (ADs) or do-not-resuscitate (DNR) orders.

Ethical/Legal Points for Consideration

- Patient adherence to past treatment plans is not a factor when considering DNR decisions. Many circumstances related to nonadherence are outside the patient's control, such as finances, transportation, availability of help, and declining physical and medical capabilities.
- Based on their expertise, HCPs have the right to refuse to provide treatment that offers no benefit to the patient.
- ADs do not include a DNR order. If the patient is unable to speak for himself or herself, the HCP can start a DNR order only after a conversation with the health care proxy and/or nearest kin. The decision usually depends on evidence of the patient's preferences (substituted judgment standard) or what is thought to be in the best interest of the patient.
- If there is an AD refusing resuscitation, the HCP is required to act accordingly but is not compelled to enact a DNR without clear direction from the patient or proxy.
- If the involved parties disagree about the patient's treatment plan, a referral can be made to an ethics committee, they can seek treatment from another HCP, or they may seek legal intervention by way of a court order.

Discussion Questions

- How can a lack of understanding or limited financial resources contribute to nonadherence with the plan of care?
- What type of information should be given to a patient and caregiver in discussions about ADs and DNR orders? Who should provide this information?
- Who can initiate a referral to an ethics committee?

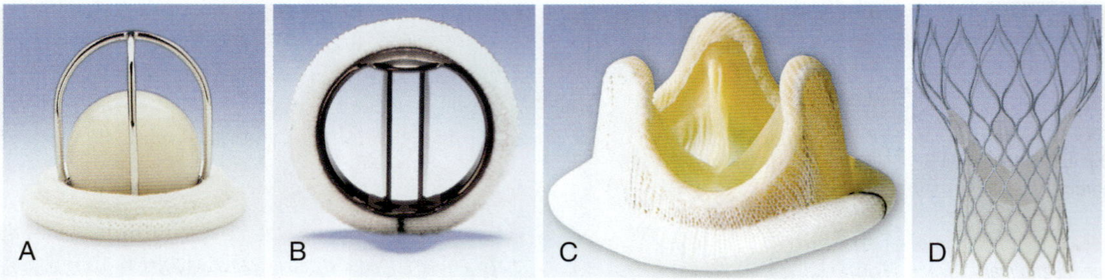

Fig. 40.10 Types of prosthetic heart valves. (A) Starr-Edwards caged ball valve. (B) St. Jude bi-leaflet valve. (C) Carpentier-Edwards porcine valve. (D) CoreValve transcatheter aortic valve (CV26 Hero), Medtronic 2015. (*A, B, and C,* From Bonow RO, Mann DL, Zipes DP, et al.: *Braunwald's heart disease: a textbook of cardiovascular medicine,* ed 9, Philadelphia, 2012, Saunders.)

Valve Replacement

Valve replacement may be needed for mitral, aortic, tricuspid, and pulmonic valve disease. Desirable valves are nonthrombogenic, durable, and create minimal stenosis. A wide variety of prosthetic mechanical or biologic (tissue) valves are available. (Fig. 40.10).

Mechanical valves are made from artificial materials. They consist of combinations of metal alloys, pyrolytic carbon, and Dacron. *Biologic valves* are made from bovine, porcine, or human (cadaver) heart tissue. They usually contain some human-made materials. A "decellularizing" process allows for decreased calcification of the bioprosthetic valve. They produce a more natural pattern of blood flow compared with mechanical valves.

Mechanical valves are more durable and last longer than biologic valves. However, they have an increased risk for thromboembolism. Patients need long-term anticoagulation therapy, which increases the risk of bleeding. Anticoagulation therapy is not needed with biologic valves because of their low thrombogenicity. However, they are less durable and tend to cause early calcification, tissue degeneration, and stiffening of the leaflets. Both valve types are subject to leaking and risk of IE.

Transcatheter therapies are another option for treating valvular heart disease. They are used to treat patients at high risk for surgery who have aortic or mitral bioprosthetic valve failure. Transcatheter edge-to-edge repair is available for patients with severe MR who are very high risk for open surgery. Transcatheter pulmonary valve replacement is approved for use in pediatric and adult patients with pulmonary valve disease caused by congenital heart disease.

Transcatheter aortic valve replacement (TAVR) is an option for patients with severe, symptomatic AS. In over 90% of patients, the procedure is done using a transfemoral approach. The evaluation for TAVR includes an echocardiogram, coronary CT angiogram, and potentially a heart catheterization.[17] Imaging can determine valve size and help in planning the procedure. Currently, there are 3 commercially available TAVR valves in the United States. The Edwards Sapien 3 valve is made of bovine pericardial tissue. It is a balloon-expandable valve (Fig. 40.11).[21] The CoreValve transcatheter aortic valve is a self-expanding valve made of porcine pericardial tissue (Fig. 40.10D).[22] The 3rd valve, Lotus, is available for use in patients deemed high risk for open surgery. It is currently in clinical trials for patients at a lower surgical risk.

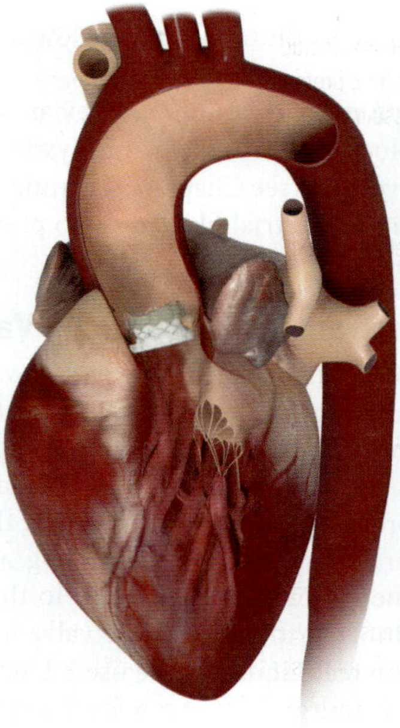

Fig. 40.11 Edwards Sapien 3 Transcatheter Heart Valve. (Courtesy Edwards Lifesciences LLC, Irvine, CA.)

Patients with biologic valves who have atrial fibrillation need long-term anticoagulation. Some patients with biologic valves or annuloplasty with prosthetic rings may need anticoagulation the first few months after surgery until endothelial cells cover the suture lines (endothelialized).

The choice of valves depends on many factors. A mechanical valve may be best for a younger patient because it is more durable. If a patient cannot take an anticoagulant (e.g., women of childbearing age), a biologic valve is an option. Frail patients with co-morbidities need to be evaluated by a qualified heart team for a full evaluation before considering surgery.[23] Encourage patients to discuss short- and long-term consequences of valve choices with their HCPs.

NURSING MANAGEMENT: VALVULAR DISORDERS

Assessment

Table 40.13 presents the subjective and objective data to obtain from a patient with valve disease.

TABLE 40.13 NURSING ASSESSMENT

Valvular Heart Disease

Subjective Data

Important Health Information

Health history: RF, IE; congenital defects, MI, chest trauma, CMP; syphilis, Marfan's syndrome, streptococcal infections

Functional Health Patterns

Health perception–health management: IV drug use, fatigue

Activity-exercise: Palpitations, generalized weakness, activity intolerance, dizziness, fainting, dyspnea on exertion, cough, hemoptysis, orthopnea

Sleep-rest: Paroxysmal nocturnal dyspnea

Cognitive-perceptual: Angina or atypical chest pain

Objective Data

Cardiovascular

Abnormal heart sounds, including murmurs, S_3, and S_4. Dysrhythmias, including atrial fibrillation, premature ventricular contractions. Tachycardia. ↑ or ↓ in pulse pressure, hypotension, water-hammer or thready peripheral pulses

Gastrointestinal

Ascites, hepatomegaly, unexplained weight gain

General

Fever

Respiratory

Crackles, wheezes, hoarseness

Skin

Diaphoresis, flushing, cyanosis, clubbing, peripheral edema

Possible Diagnostic Findings

Cardiomegaly on chest x-ray. ECG abnormalities specific to involved valve. Echocardiogram (valve disorders, chamber dilation), heart catheterization (abnormal valves, chamber pressures, CO, and blood flow, depending on involved valve)

◆ Clinical Problems

Clinical problems for the patient with valvular heart disease include:

1. Impaired cardiac function
2. Fatigue
3. Fluid imbalance

More information on clinical problems and interventions is in eNursing Care Plan 40.2, available on the website for this chapter.

◆ Planning

The overall goals for the patient with valve disease include (1) normal heart function, (2) improved activity tolerance, and (3) an understanding of the disease process and health maintenance measures.

◆ Implementation

◆ Health Promotion

Encouraging early treatment of streptococcal infections and providing prophylactic antibiotics for patients with a history of RF are critical in preventing acquired rheumatic valve disease. The patient at risk for IE and any patient with certain heart conditions must receive prophylactic antibiotics (Table 40.2). Teach the person with a history of RF, IE, or congenital heart disease to report symptoms of valvular heart disease.

◆ Acute Care and Ambulatory Care

A patient with progressive valvular heart disease may need outpatient care or hospitalization for management of HF, IE, embolic disease, or dysrhythmias. HF is the most common reason for ongoing medical care.

Design activities considering the patient's limitations. An appropriate exercise plan can increase cardiac tolerance. The patient should limit activities that cause fatigue and dyspnea. They need to avoid strenuous physical exercise because damaged valves may not handle the increased CO. Develop your patient's care plan to emphasize conserving energy, setting priorities, and taking planned rest periods. Discourage tobacco use. Consider a referral to a vocational counselor if the patient has a physically or emotionally demanding job.

Perform ongoing cardiac assessments to monitor the effectiveness of drugs. Teach the actions and side effects of drugs to increase adherence. The patient must understand the importance of prophylactic antibiotic therapy to prevent IE (Table 40.2).

When valvular heart disease can no longer be managed medically, surgery is needed. See Chapter 37 for the care of a patient having heart surgery. The patient on anticoagulants (e.g., warfarin) after surgery for valve replacement must have the international normalized ratio (INR) checked regularly to determine proper dosage and adequacy of therapy. INR values of 2.5 to 3.5 are therapeutic for patients with most mechanical valves.

Table 41.15 outlines teaching related to anticoagulant therapy. Teach the patient to follow up with an HCP regularly and when to seek urgent medical care. Tell the patient to notify the HCP of any signs of infection, HF, or bleeding and any planned invasive or dental work. Last, encourage patients to wear a Medic Alert device or bracelet and carry the manufacturer's valve information card.

◆ Evaluation

The expected outcomes are that a patient with valvular heart disease will

1. Maintain adequate tissue and organ perfusion
2. Achieve fluid balance
3. Achieve an optimal level of activity
4. Describe disease process and measures to prevent complications

CARDIOMYOPATHY

Cardiomyopathy (CMP) is a group of diseases that directly affect myocardial structure or function. We classify CMP as primary or secondary. *Primary CMP* refers to idiopathic conditions involving only the heart muscle. In *secondary CMP,*

TABLE 40.14 Causes of Cardiomyopathy

Dilated CMP
- Cardiotoxic agents: alcohol, cocaine, doxorubicin
- Coronary artery disease
- Genetic (autosomal dominant)
- Hypertension
- Metabolic problems
- Muscular dystrophy
- Myocarditis
- Pregnancy
- Valve disease

Hypertrophic CMP
- AS
- Genetic (autosomal dominant)
- Hypertension

Restrictive CMP
- Amyloidosis
- Cancer
- Endomyocardial fibrosis
- Post-radiation therapy
- Sarcoidosis
- Ventricular thrombus

another disease process causes myocardial disease. Common causes of secondary CMP are shown in Table 40.14.

Three major types of CMP are dilated, hypertrophic, and restrictive. Each type has its own pathogenesis, clinical presentation, and treatment protocols (Tables 40.15 and 40.16). CMP that leads to cardiomegaly and HF is the main reason for heart transplants.

Takotsubo cardiomyopathy is a transient heart syndrome that causes apical akinesis and mimics acute coronary syndrome.[24] Patients often have chest pain, ST segment elevation on ECG, and elevated cardiac biomarkers consistent with an MI. However, when the patient undergoes heart catheterization, there is no significant coronary artery disease. It is an acute, stress-related syndrome that is more common in postmenopausal women. Treatment is largely supportive. Around 5% of patients need anticoagulation.[24]

TABLE 40.15 Types of CMP

Dilated	Hypertrophic	Restrictive
Cardiac Output		
↓	Normal or decreased	Normal or ↓
Cardiomegaly		
Moderate to severe	Mild to moderate	Mild
Contractility		
↓	↑ or ↓	Normal or ↓
Dysrhythmias		
Sinus tachycardia, atrial and ventricular dysrhythmias	Atrial and ventricular dysrhythmias	Atrial and ventricular dysrhythmias
Major Manifestations		
Fatigue, weakness, palpitations, dyspnea	Exertional dyspnea, fatigue, angina, syncope, palpitations	Dyspnea, fatigue
Outflow Tract Obstruction		
None	↑	None
Valvular Incompetence		
Atrioventricular (AV) valves, especially mitral	Mitral valve	AV valves

TABLE 40.16 Interprofessional Care
Cardiomyopathy

Diagnostic Assessment
- History and physical assessment
- ECG
- b-Type natriuretic peptide (BNP)
- Chest x-ray
- Echocardiogram
- Nuclear imaging studies
- Heart catheterization
- Endomyocardial biopsy

Management
- Drug therapy
  - Nitrates (except in hypertrophic cardiomyopathy)
  - β-Blockers
  - Antidysrhythmics
  - ACE inhibitors
  - Calcium channel blockers
  - Diuretics
  - Digitalis (except in hypertrophic CMP unless used to treat atrial fibrillation)
  - Anticoagulants (if indicated)
- VAD
- Cardiac resynchronization therapy
- Implantable cardioverter-defibrillator
- Surgical repair
- Heart transplant
- Cardiac rehabilitation
- Palliative and hospice care

DILATED CARDIOMYOPATHY

Etiology and Pathophysiology

Dilated cardiomyopathy is the most common type of CMP, with a prevalence of 5 to 8 cases per 100,000 people in the United States. It causes HF in 20% to 45% of cases.[25] Dilated CMP is a primary myocardial disorder with genetic or acquired origins. Alcohol-related dilated CMP has its own unique presentation and treatment. Other common causes of dilated CMP are shown in Table 40.14.

Dilated CMP appears with diffuse inflammation and rapid degeneration of heart fibers. This results in ventricular dilation, impaired systolic function, atrial enlargement, and blood stasis in the left ventricle. SCD from dysrhythmias is a leading cause of death in idiopathic dilated CMP. Ventricular dilation causes *cardiomegaly* (Fig. 40.12) and contractile dysfunction. In contrast to HF, the walls of the ventricles do not hypertrophy.

Clinical Manifestations

The signs and symptoms of dilated CMP may develop acutely after an infection or slowly over time. Symptoms can include decreased exercise capacity, fatigue, dyspnea at rest, paroxysmal nocturnal dyspnea, and orthopnea. As the disease progresses, the patient may have a dry cough, palpitations, abdominal bloating, nausea, vomiting, and anorexia. Signs can include an abnormal S_3 and/or S_4, dysrhythmias, heart murmurs, pulmonary crackles, edema, weak peripheral pulses, pallor, hepatomegaly, and JVD. Decreased blood flow through an enlarged heart promotes stasis and blood clot formation and may lead to systemic embolization.

Diagnostic Studies

The diagnosis of dilated CMP is based on the patient's history and exclusion of other causes of HF. Echocardiography is usually the basis for diagnosing dilated CMP. EF less than 20% has a 50% mortality rate within 1 year. The chest x-ray may show cardiomegaly with signs of pulmonary venous hypertension and pleural effusion. The ECG may show tachycardia, bradycardia, and dysrhythmias with conduction problems. Laboratory studies may show increased b-type natriuretic peptide (BNP) levels if HF is present.

Heart catheterization evaluates the patient for coronary artery disease. An endomyocardial biopsy done at the time of the right-sided heart catheterization can identify any infectious organisms or other causes of disease.

❖ Interprofessional and Nursing Care

Interventions focus on controlling HF by enhancing heart contractility and decreasing preload and afterload. This is similar to how we manage chronic HF. Treatment guidelines are based on the specific stage of disease progression (see Table 38.3). Treatment of patients with Class IV (stage D) HF is more palliative than curative.

Several different types of drugs are available to manage HF (see Table 38.7). Nitrates (e.g., nitroglycerin) and diuretics (e.g., furosemide) decrease preload. ACE inhibitors reduce afterload. β-Blockers (e.g., metoprolol) and aldosterone antagonists (e.g., spironolactone) control the neurohormonal stimulation that occurs in HF. Dysrhythmias are treated with the appropriate antidysrhythmic (see Chapter 39). Anticoagulation therapy reduces the risk for systemic embolization from clots that form in the heart chambers.

Drug and nutrition therapy and cardiac rehabilitation may help lessen symptoms of HF and improve CO and quality of life. A patient with secondary dilated CMP is treated for the underlying disease process. For example, teach the patient with alcohol-related dilated CMP to abstain from alcohol. See Chapter 11 for more on alcohol use.

Unfortunately, dilated CMP does not respond well to therapy, and patients have multiple episodes of HF. Patients may be hospitalized for infusions of dobutamine or milrinone, followed by aggressive diuresis. Sometimes these treatments are done in an outpatient setting or in the home under nursing supervision. After treatment, many patients see an improvement in symptoms for several weeks. Medical management is based on clinical guidelines for HF. Statins may be helpful (see Table 37.6).

Patients may benefit from nondrug therapies. A VAD allows the heart to rest and recover from acute HF or serves as a bridge to a heart transplant. Other options include cardiac resynchronization therapy and an implantable cardioverter-defibrillator (ICD) (see Chapter 38).

A heart transplant may be considered in the patient with terminal or end-stage CMP. A permanent, implantable VAD, known as *destination therapy,* is an option for patients with advanced disease who are not candidates for a heart transplant (see Chapter 38). Currently, about 50% of heart transplants are done to treat CMP. Heart transplant recipients have a good prognosis. However, donor hearts are scarce. Many patients with dilated CMP die before receiving a heart.

Patients with dilated CMP are very ill and have a grave prognosis. Your expert nursing care is critical. Observe for signs and symptoms of worsening HF, dysrhythmias, embolus formation, and drug effectiveness. The goals of therapy are to keep the patient at an optimal level of functioning and out of the hospital. Always include caregivers when planning a patient's care. Encourage caregivers to learn cardiopulmonary resuscitation (CPR). Teach them when and how to access emergency care.

Home health and hospice nursing can provide the patient and caregiver with palliative care. This includes strategies to maximize and maintain functional status or end-of-life care to prepare for a peaceful death.

HYPERTROPHIC CARDIOMYOPATHY

Etiology and Pathophysiology

Hypertrophic cardiomyopathy is a genetic disorder that causes asymmetric left ventricular hypertrophy without ventricular dilation.[25] In one form of the disease, the septum between the 2 ventricles becomes enlarged and blocks the blood flow from the left ventricle. We call this *hypertrophic obstructive cardiomyopathy* (HOCMP) or *asymmetric septal hypertrophy* (ASH).

Hypertrophic CMP occurs less often than dilated CMP. It is more common in men than in women. It is usually diagnosed in young adults and, most often, in active, athletic persons. Hypertrophic CMP is the most common cause of SCD in otherwise healthy young people. It accounts for 3% of deaths in young competitive athletes. 1st-degree relatives of patients with HOCMP need to be screened for the disease.

Early identification is important (Table 40.14). The 4 main characteristics of hypertrophic CMP are (1) massive ventricular hypertrophy; (2) rapid, forceful contraction of the left ventricle; (3) impaired relaxation (diastole); and (4) obstruction to aortic outflow (not present in all patients).[25] Ventricular hypertrophy is associated with a thickened intraventricular septum and ventricular wall (Fig. 40.12). The result is poor filling of the stiff ventricle. Decreased ventricular filling and obstruction to outflow decreases CO, especially during exertion.

Clinical Manifestations

Some patients with hypertrophic CMP may be asymptomatic. Others have exertional dyspnea, fatigue, angina, and syncope. The most common symptom is dyspnea caused by an elevated left ventricular diastolic pressure. Fatigue

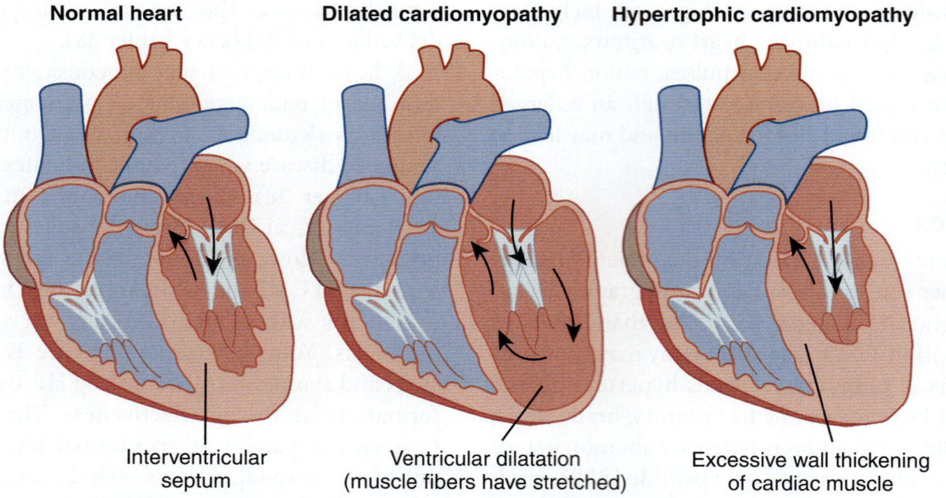

Fig. 40.12 The normal heart, compared with dilated CMP and hypertrophic CMP.

occurs because of the resulting decrease in CO and in exercise-induced flow obstruction. Angina can be caused by the increased left ventricular mass or compression of the small coronary arteries by the hypertrophic ventricular myocardium. The patient may have syncope from obstruction to aortic outflow during increased activity. This results in decreased CO and cerebrovascular circulation. Syncope also can be caused by dysrhythmias, such as supraventricular tachycardia, atrial fibrillation, ventricular tachycardia, and ventricular fibrillation (see Chapter 39).

Diagnostic Studies

Clinical findings may be unremarkable. On chest palpation, the apical impulse can be exaggerated and displaced to the left. Auscultation may reveal an S_4 and a systolic murmur between the apex and sternal border at the 4th intercostal space. ECG findings usually show ventricular hypertrophy, ST-T wave abnormalities, prominent Q waves in the inferior or precordial leads, and dysrhythmias (see Chapter 39).

The echocardiogram is the main diagnostic tool used to confirm hypertrophic CMP. It may show wall motion abnormalities and diastolic dysfunction. Heart catheterization and nuclear stress testing may help diagnose and guide the treatment of hypertrophic CMP.

❖ Interprofessional and Nursing Care

The goals of care are to improve ventricular filling by reducing ventricular contractility and relieving left ventricular outflow obstruction. These can be achieved with β-blocker (e.g., metoprolol) or calcium channel blocker (e.g., verapamil) therapy.[25] Amiodarone or sotalol (Betapace) are effective antidysrhythmic drugs but do not prevent SCD. Patients at risk for SCD need a cardioverter-defibrillator (see Chapter 39).

AV pacing is helpful for patients with hypertrophic CMP and outflow obstruction. When the ventricles are paced from the apex of the right ventricle, septal depolarization occurs first. This allows the septum to move away from the left ventricular wall and reduces the degree of obstruction of the outflow tract.

Some patients with severe symptoms unresponsive to therapy may be candidates for surgical treatment of their hypertrophied septum. A *ventriculomyotomy and myectomy* involve cutting into the thickened septal muscle and removing some of the ventricular muscle. Most patients have an improvement in symptoms and exercise tolerance after surgery.

An alternative nonsurgical procedure to reduce symptoms and the left ventricular outflow obstruction is *percutaneous transluminal septal myocardial ablation* (PTSMA). This procedure consists of injecting alcohol into the first septal artery branching off the left anterior descending artery to cause ischemia and septal wall infarction. Ablation of the septal wall decreases the obstruction to flow, and the patient's symptoms decrease. The procedure can improve HF symptoms and exercise capacity. Potential complications of PTSMA include conduction problems (e.g., heart block) and MI.

Interventions for hypertrophic CMP focus on relieving symptoms, observing for and preventing complications, and providing emotional support. Focus your teaching on helping patients plan to avoid strenuous activity and dehydration. Any activity that causes an increase in systemic vascular resistance (thus increasing the obstruction to forward flow) is dangerous. Rest and elevation of the feet to improve venous return to the heart can help manage chest pain. Vasodilators, such as nitroglycerin, may worsen the chest pain by decreasing venous return and further increasing obstruction of blood flow from the heart.

RESTRICTIVE CARDIOMYOPATHY

Etiology and Pathophysiology

Restrictive cardiomyopathy is the least common type of CMP. It is a disease of the myocardium that impairs diastolic filling and stretch. Systolic function stays unchanged. The specific cause of restrictive CMP is unknown, but several pathologic processes may be involved. Myocardial fibrosis, hypertrophy, and infiltration stiffen the ventricular wall with loss of ventricular compliance. Secondary causes of restrictive CMP include amyloidosis, endocardial fibrosis, sarcoidosis, and radiation to the thorax. With restrictive CMP, the ventricles are resistant to filling and require high diastolic filling pressures to maintain CO.

Clinical Manifestations and Diagnostic Studies

Classic manifestations of restrictive CMP are fatigue, exercise intolerance, and dyspnea. These occur because the heart cannot increase CO by increasing the HR without further compromising ventricular filling. Other symptoms may include angina, orthopnea, syncope, and palpitations. The patient may have signs of HF, including dyspnea, peripheral edema, weight gain, ascites, hepatomegaly, and JVD.

The chest x-ray may be normal, or it may show cardiomegaly from atrial enlargement. Pleural effusions and pulmonary congestion may occur as the patient progresses to HF. The most common dysrhythmias are supraventricular (atrial fibrillation) or AV block. Echocardiography may show a left ventricle that is normal size with a thickened wall, slightly dilated right ventricle, and dilated atria. Endomyocardial biopsy, CT scan, and nuclear imaging may help in the diagnosis.

Interprofessional and Nursing Care

There is no specific treatment for restrictive CMP. Treatments aim to improve diastolic filling and the underlying disease process. Treatment includes conventional therapy for HF and dysrhythmias. A heart transplant may be an option. Nursing care is similar to the care of a patient with HF. As in the treatment of patients with hypertrophic CMP, teach the patient to avoid situations that impair ventricular filling and increase systemic vascular resistance, such as strenuous activity and dehydration.

Nursing care of a patient with CMP includes patient-specific teaching based on their manifestations. All patients with CMP are at risk for IE from any procedure that may cause bacteremia. Teach the patient about the need for prophylactic antibiotics (see Table 40.2). A guide for patient and caregiver teaching is outlined in Table 40.17.

TABLE 40.17 PATIENT & CAREGIVER TEACHING

Cardiomyopathy

Include the following information in the teaching plan for a patient with cardiomyopathy and the patient's caregiver.

- Take all drugs as prescribed and regularly follow up with HCP.
- Follow a low-sodium diet (if prescribed) and read all product labels (food and over-the-counter drugs) for sodium content.
- Drink 6 to 8 glasses of water a day unless fluids are restricted.
- Achieve and maintain a reasonable weight and avoid large meals.
- Avoid alcohol, caffeine, diet pills, and over-the-counter cold medicines that may contain stimulants.
- Balance activity and rest periods.
- Avoid heavy lifting or vigorous isometric exercises and check with HCP for exercise guidelines.
- Use stress management techniques: relaxation breathing, guided imagery.
- Report any signs of HF to HCP, including weight gain, edema, shortness of breath, and increased fatigue.
- Encourage caregivers to learn CPR because of the potential for cardiac arrest (see Appendix A).
- Access emergency response system (ERS) according to the HCP's instructions.

Case Study

Valvular Heart Disease

(© JennaDub/iStock/Thinkstock.)

Patient Profile

R.B. is a 50-year-old man admitted to the hospital for acute decompensated HF due to valvular heart disease.

Subjective Data

- History of IV drug use
- Reports regular alcohol use of 1 pint of whiskey per day
- States, "I'm short of breath all the time. I can't sleep when I lay down."
- Describes chest pain with minimal exertion
- Recently unemployed
- States, "I'm always tired."
- States, "The prescribed drugs are too expensive. I can't afford them."
- 35 pack year history

Objective Data

Physical Assessment

- 3rd heart sound (S_3)
- Loud holosystolic murmur of mitral regurgitation
- Missing all teeth from periodontal disease
- Vital signs: Temp 99.0°F (37.2°C); apical-radial pulse equal at 110 beats/min, irregular; respirations 24; BP 104/58 mm Hg

Diagnostic Studies

- ECG shows atrial fibrillation with a rapid ventricular response
- Chest x-ray shows pulmonary congestion and cardiomegaly
- Transesophageal echocardiography shows left atrial and ventricular hypertrophy and mitral and aortic regurgitation. EF 30%

Discussion Questions

1. ***Recognize:*** Distinguish between mitral and aortic regurgitation.
2. ***Analyze***: Identify the cause and course of R.B.'s disease based on his history and current assessment.
3. ***Plan:*** What medical treatments or surgical procedures will R.B. need as his condition worsens?
4. ***Prioritize:*** Identify the priority interventions for R.B.
5. ***Act***: Identify the tasks that you would delegate to assistive personnel (AP).
6. ***Evaluate:*** What information would indicate that R.B. understands why he will need to continue taking anticoagulants after the valve replacement surgery?
7. ***Safety***: What safety precautions would we initiate for R.B.?

Answers available at http://evolve.elsevier.com/Lewis/medsurg.

BRIDGE TO NCLEX EXAMINATION

The number of the question corresponds to the same-numbered outcome at the beginning of the chapter.

1. Which findings would the nurse expect when assessing a patient with infective endocarditis? *(select all that apply)*
   a. Retinal hemorrhages
   b. Splinter hemorrhages
   c. Presence of Osler's nodes
   d. Painless nodules over bony prominences
   e. Erythematous macules on the palms and soles
2. Which intervention is *a priority* in nursing management of a patient with myocarditis?
   a. Providing meticulous skincare
   b. Assuring tight glycemic control
   c. Administering antibiotic prophylaxis
   d. Monitoring oxygenation and ventilation
3. Which condition would the nurse teach the patient is a possible long-term consequence of rheumatic fever?
   a. Valvular heart disease
   b. Pulmonary hypertension
   c. Superior vena cava syndrome
   d. Hypertrophy of the right ventricle
4. Which is a *priority* intervention for a patient during the acute phase of rheumatic fever?
   a. Giving IV antibiotics as prescribed
   b. Managing pain with opioid analgesics
   c. Encouraging fluid intake for hydration
   d. Performing frequent active range-of-motion exercises
5. A patient is diagnosed with mitral stenosis and new-onset atrial fibrillation. Which interventions could the nurse delegate to assistive personnel (AP)? *(select all that apply)*
   a. Obtain and record daily weight.
   b. Determine apical-radial pulse rate.
   c. Observe for overt signs of bleeding.
   d. Teach the patient how to avoid bruising and bleeding.
   e. Obtain and record vital signs, including pulse oximetry.
6. The nurse is caring for a patient newly admitted with heart failure secondary to dilated cardiomyopathy. Which intervention would be a *priority*?
   a. Encourage caregivers to learn CPR.
   b. Consider a consultation with hospice for palliative care.
   c. Monitor the patient's response to prescribed medications.
   d. Arrange for the patient to enter a cardiac rehabilitation program.

1. a, b, c, e; 2. d; 3. a; 4. a; 5. a, c, e; 6. c.

For rationales to these answers and even more NCLEX review questions, visit http://evolve.elsevier.com/Lewis/medsurg.

EVOLVE WEBSITE/RESOURCES LIST

http://evolve.elsevier.com/Lewis/medsurg
Review Questions (Online Only)
Key Points
Answer Keys for Questions
- Rationales for Bridge to NCLEX Examination Questions
- Answer Guidelines for Case Study

Student Case Study
- Patient With Rheumatic Fever and Heart Disease

Nursing Care Plans
- eNursing Care Plan 40.1: Patient With Infective Endocarditis
- eNursing Care Plan 40.2: Patient With Valvular Heart Disease

Conceptual Care Map Creator
Audio Glossary
Content Updates

REFERENCES

*1. Di Domenico EG, Rimoldi SG, Cavallo I, et al.: Microbial biofilm correlates with an increased antibiotic tolerance and poor therapeutic outcome in infective endocarditis, *BMC Microbiol* 19:228, 2019.
*2. Kadri AN, Wilner B, Hernandez AV, et al.: Geographic trends, patient characteristics, and outcomes of infective endocarditis associated with drug abuse in the United States from 2002 to 2016, *J Am Heart Assoc* 8:e012969, 2019.
3. Yallowitz AW, Decker LC: Infectious endocarditis. Retrieved from https://www.ncbi.nlm.nih.gov/books/NBK557641/.
4. Rajani R, Klein JL: Infective endocarditis: a contemporary update, *Clin Med* 20:31, 2020.
5. Elsaghir H, Al Khalili Y: Septic Emboli. Retrieved from https://www.ncbi.nlm.nih.gov/books/NBK549827/.
6. Lung B, Duval X: Infective endocarditis: innovations in the management of an old disease, *Nat Rev Cardiol* 16:623, 2019.
*7. Hubers SA, DeSimone DC, Gersh BJ, Anavekar NS: Infective endocarditis: a contemporary review, *Mayo Clin Proc* 95:982, 2020.
*8. Chiabrando JG, Bonaventura A, Vecchie A, et al.: Management of acute and recurrent pericarditis: JACC State-of-the-Art Review, *J Am Coll Cardiol* 75:76, 2020.
9. Ismail TF: Acute pericarditis: update on diagnosis and management, *Clin Med* 20:48, 2020.
10. Spangler, S: Acute pericarditis medication. Retrieved from https://emedicine.medscape.com/article/156951-medication.
11. Yadav NK, Siddique MS: Constrictive pericarditis. Retrieved from https://www.ncbi.nlm.nih.gov/books/NBK459314/.
12. Razzano D, Fallon JT: Myocarditis: somethings old and something new, *Cardiovasc Pathol* 44:107155, 2020.
13. Dass C, Kanmanthareddy A: Rheumatic heart disease. Retrieved from https://www.ncbi.nlm.nih.gov/books/NBK538286/.
*14. Gewitz MH, Baltimore RS, Tani LY, et al.: Revision of the Jones criteria for the diagnosis of acute rheumatic fever in the era of Doppler echocardiography: a scientific statement from the AHA, *Circ* 131:1806, 2015. (Classic).
15. Sika-Paotonu D, Beaton A, Raghu A, et al.: *Acute rheumatic fever and rheumatic heart disease*, Oklahoma City, 2017, University of Oklahoma Press.
16. Wallace M: Antibiotics for rheumatic fever. Retrieved from https://emedicine.medscape.com/article/240582-medication.
17. Zipes DP, Libby P, Bonow RO, et al.: *Braunwald's heart disease: a textbook of cardiovascular medicine*, ed 11, St Louis, 2019, Elsevier.

18. Shah SN, Gangwani MK, Oliver TI. Mitral valve prolapse. Retrieved from https://www.ncbi.nlm.nih.gov/books/NBK470288/.
19. Ren, X: Aortic stenosis treatment and management. Retrieved from https://emedicine.medscape.com/article/150638-treatment.
20. Wang SS: Aortic regurgitation. Retrieved from https://emedicine.medscape.com/article 150490.
21. Edwards Lifesciences: TAVR with the Sapien 3 Valve. Retrieved from https://tavrbyedwards.com/.
22. Medtronic; Evolut TAVR Platform, CoreValve® Transcatheter Aortic Valve Implantation (TAVI) platform. Retrieved from www.medtronic.com/us-en/healthcare-professionals/therapies-procedures/cardiovascular/transcatheter-aortic-valve-replacement.html.
*23. Nishimura RA, Otto CM, Bonow RO, et al.: 2017 ACC/AHA focused update of the 2014 guidelines for the management of patients with valvular heart disease, *Circ* 135:e1159, 2017. (Classic).
24. Tomich, E: Takotsubo (stress) cardiomyopathy (broken heart syndrome). Retrieved from https://emedicine.medscape.com/article/1513631-overview.
*25. Ommen SR, Mital S, Burke MA, et al.: AHA/ACC guideline for the diagnosis and treatment of patients with hypertrophic cardiomyopathy: a report of the ACC/AHA Joint Committee on Clinical Practice Guidelines, *Circ* 142, 2020. 2020.

*Evidence-based information for clinical practice.

41

Vascular Disorders

Kimberly Day

http://evolve.elsevier.com/Lewis/medsurg/

CONCEPTUAL FOCUS

Glucose Regulation
Perfusion
Tissue Integrity

LEARNING OUTCOMES

1. Relate the etiology and pathophysiology of peripheral artery disease (PAD) to the major risk factors.
2. Describe the clinical manifestations and interprofessional and nursing management of the patient with PAD of the lower extremities
3. Plan appropriate nursing and interprofessional management for the patient with acute arterial ischemic disorders
4. Distinguish the pathophysiology, clinical manifestations, and nursing and interprofessional management of the patient with thromboangiitis obliterans (Buerger disease) and Raynaud phenomenon.
5. Distinguish the pathophysiology, clinical manifestations, and interprofessional and nursing management of patients with different types of aortic aneurysms.
6. Select appropriate nursing interventions for a patient undergoing an aortic aneurysm repair.
7. Describe the pathophysiology, clinical manifestations, and interprofessional and nursing management of the patient with aortic dissection.
8. Evaluate the patient's risk factors for developing superficial vein thrombosis or venous thromboembolism (VTE).
9. Distinguish between the clinical characteristics of superficial vein thrombosis and VTE.
10. Outline the interprofessional and nursing management of patients with superficial vein thrombosis and VTE.
11. Prioritize the key aspects of nursing management for the patient receiving anticoagulant therapy.
12. Relate the pathophysiology and clinical manifestations to the interprofessional care of patients with varicose veins, chronic venous insufficiency, and venous leg ulcers.

KEY TERMS

acute arterial ischemia
aneurysm
aortic dissection
chronic venous insufficiency (CVI)
critical limb ischemia
deep vein thrombosis (DVT)
intermittent claudication
peripheral artery disease (PAD)
post-thrombotic syndrome (PTS)
superficial vein thrombosis
thromboangiitis obliterans (Buerger disease)
varicose veins
venous thromboembolism (VTE)
venous thrombosis
Virchow's triad

Vascular system problems include disorders of the arteries, veins, and lymphatic vessels. These problems can result in decreased perfusion and ischemia of the peripheral tissues. Patients often have pain and difficulties with mobility and activities of daily living. Education is a key part of management. Proper nutrition, smoking cessation, and exercise are important health promotion behaviors. Following measures to promote safety, especially for those on anticoagulant therapy, is critical.

We classify arterial disorders as atherosclerotic, aneurysmal, and nonatherosclerotic vascular diseases. Atherosclerotic vascular disease is divided into coronary, cerebral, peripheral, mesenteric, and renal artery disease.[1] This chapter discusses peripheral artery disease, aortic aneurysm and dissection, and venous diseases.

PERIPHERAL ARTERY DISEASE

Peripheral artery disease (PAD) involves thickening of artery walls. This results in a progressive narrowing of the arteries of the upper and lower extremities. PAD prevalence increases with age. It typically becomes symptomatic between ages 50 and 70 years. In people with diabetes, PAD occurs earlier. In the United States, about 8.5 million people over age 40 have PAD. The prevalence is highest in Blacks.[2,3]

PAD is strongly related to other types of cardiovascular disease (CVD) and their risk factors. Patients with PAD have a significantly higher risk for general mortality, CVD mortality, major coronary events, and stroke.[3] PAD is a marker of advanced systemic atherosclerosis. Patients with PAD are more likely to have coronary artery disease (CAD) and/or cerebral artery disease.

Unfortunately, many people in the United States are unaware of PAD and its risk factors. PAD remains underdiagnosed and undertreated.

Etiology and Pathophysiology

The leading cause of PAD is *atherosclerosis*. It is a gradual thickening of the *intima* (the innermost layer of the arterial wall) and *media* (middle layer of the arterial wall). This results from cholesterol and lipids deposited within the vessel walls, leading to narrowing of the artery (see Fig. 37.1). Although we do not know the exact cause of atherosclerosis, inflammation and endothelial injury play a major role (see Chapter 37). Atherosclerosis often affects certain segments of the arterial tree. These include the coronary, carotid (see Chapter 62), and lower extremity arteries. Symptoms occur when vessels are 60% to 75% blocked.

Other risk factors for PAD are similar, but not identical, to those for CAD. Key risk factors for PAD are tobacco use (most important), diabetes, hypertension, high cholesterol, and age over 60 (Box 41.1).[2] Having multiple risk factors dramatically increases the risk for PAD.

BOX 41.1 BIOLOGIC SEX CONSIDERATIONS

Vascular Disorders

Men

- Thromboangiitis obliterans (Buerger disease) occurs most often in men younger than 40 years of age
- Abdominal aortic aneurysms (AAAs) and aortic dissections are more common in men
- Men with AAAs are more likely to undergo endovascular aneurysm repair or open aneurysm repair
- Sexual problems are common after aortic surgery.

Women

- Women with PAD have poorer social functioning and higher rates of depression than men with PAD[4]
- Women with PAD have faster functional decline and greater mobility loss than men with PAD
- Raynaud's phenomenon occurs mainly in women between 15 and 40 years of age.
- Risk for VTE is greater in women over age 35 who use tobacco and oral contraceptives or oral hormone therapy, are pregnant or postpartum, or have a family history of VTE
- Primary varicose veins are more common and more symptomatic in women
- Women with AAAs are at higher risk for rupture
- In-hospital mortality is higher in women undergoing revascularization
- Women have more graft thrombosis and amputation after lower extremity bypass surgery

PERIPHERAL ARTERY DISEASE OF THE LOWER EXTREMITIES

Lower extremity PAD may affect the iliac, femoral, popliteal, tibial, or peroneal arteries, or any combination of these arteries (Fig. 41.1). The femoral popliteal area is the most common site in patients without diabetes. Those with diabetes tend to develop PAD in the arteries below the knee. Those with advanced PAD often have multiple arterial occlusions.

Clinical Manifestations

The severity of PAD symptoms depends on the site and extent of the blockage and the amount of collateral circulation. The classic symptom of lower extremity PAD is **intermittent claudication.** This ischemic muscle pain is caused by exercise, resolves within 10 minutes or less with rest, and is reproducible. The pain is due to the buildup of lactic acid from anaerobic metabolism. Once the patient stops exercising, the lactic acid clears, and the pain subsides. PAD of the iliac arteries causes pain in the buttocks and thighs. Calf pain occurs with femoral or popliteal artery involvement.

As many as one-third of patients with PAD have classic symptoms. Others have no symptoms or present with atypical leg symptoms (e.g., burning, heaviness, pressure, soreness, tightness, weakness) in atypical locations (e.g., ankle, foot, hamstring, hip, knee, shin). PAD involving the internal iliac arteries may result in erectile dysfunction.

Paresthesia (numbness or tingling) in the toes or feet may result from nerve tissue ischemia. True peripheral neuropathy occurs more often in patients with diabetes and in those with long-standing ischemia. Neuropathy causes severe shooting

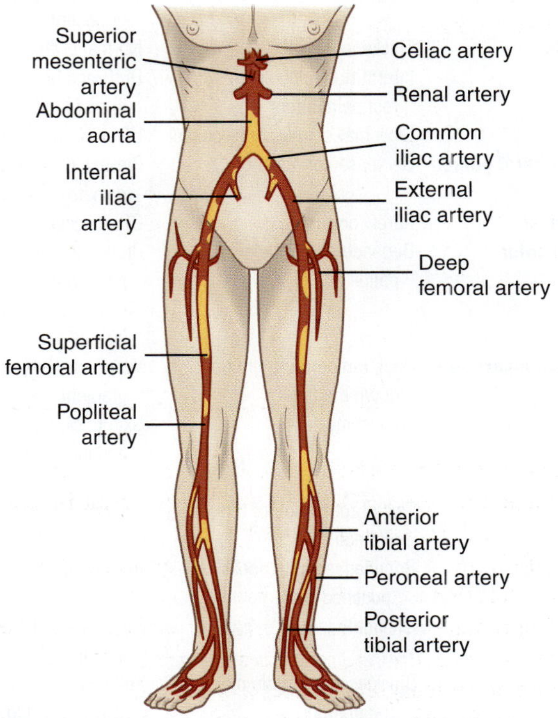

Fig. 41.1 Common anatomic locations of atherosclerotic lesions (shown in *yellow*) of the abdominal aorta and lower extremities.

or burning pain in the extremity. It does not follow particular nerve roots and may be present near ulcerated areas. Gradual, reduced blood flow to neurons causes loss of sensation to pressure and deep pain. So, patients may not notice lower extremity injuries.

The limb's appearance gives vital information about reduced blood flow. The skin becomes thin, shiny, and taut. The lower legs lose their hair. Pedal, popliteal, or femoral pulses are decreased or absent. Pallor (blanching of the foot) develops when the leg is elevated *(elevation pallor)*. Conversely, *reactive hyperemia* (redness of the foot) develops when the limb is in a dependent position *(dependent rubor)* (Table 41.1).

As PAD progresses and involves multiple arterial segments, continuous pain develops at rest. *Rest pain* most often occurs in the foot or toes. It is worse with limb elevation. Rest pain occurs when blood flow does not meet basic metabolic needs of the distal tissues. It occurs more often at night because cardiac output tends to drop during sleep and the limbs are at heart level. Patients often try to relieve pain by gravity. They dangle the leg over the side of the bed or sleep in a chair.

TABLE 41.1 Comparison of Peripheral Artery and Venous Disease

Characteristic	Peripheral Artery Disease	Venous Disease
Ankle-brachial index	≤0.90	>0.90
Capillary refill	>3 sec	<3 sec
Dermatitis	Rarely occurs	Often occurs
Edema	Absent unless leg constantly in dependent position	Lower leg edema
Hair	Loss of hair on legs, feet, toes	Hair may be present or absent
Nails	Thickened, brittle	Normal or thickened
Pain	Intermittent claudication or rest pain in foot Ulcer may or may not be painful	Dull ache or heaviness in calf or thigh Ulcer often painful
Peripheral pulses	Decreased or absent	Present, may be hard to palpate with edema
Pruritus	Rarely occurs	Often occurs
Skin color	Dependent rubor, elevation pallor	Bronze-brown pigmentation Varicose veins may be visible
Skin temperature	Cool, temperature gradient down the leg	Warm, no temperature gradient
Skin texture	Thin, shiny, taut	Skin thick, hardened, and indurated
Ulcer		
• Location	Tips of toes, foot, or lateral malleolus	Near medial malleolus
• Margin	Rounded, smooth, looks "punched out"	Irregularly shaped
• Drainage	Minimal	Moderate to large amount
• Tissue	Black eschar or pale pink granulation	Yellow slough or dark red, "ruddy" granulation

Critical limb ischemia (CLI) is a condition characterized by chronic ischemic rest pain lasting more than 2 weeks, nonhealing arterial leg ulcers, or gangrene of the leg from PAD. Patients with PAD who have diabetes, heart failure (HF), and a history of a stroke have a higher risk for CLI.[3]

Complications

Lower extremity PAD progresses slowly. Prolonged ischemia leads to atrophy of the skin and underlying muscles. Minor trauma to the feet (e.g., stubbing one's toe, blister from shoes) can result in delayed healing, wound infection, and tissue necrosis, especially in the patient with diabetes. Arterial (ischemic) ulcers most often occur over bony prominences on the toes, feet, and lower legs (Table 41.1). Nonhealing arterial ulcers and gangrene are the most serious complications. If PAD develops over an extended period, collateral circulation may prevent gangrene.

Amputation may be needed if adequate blood flow is not restored or if severe infection occurs. Uncontrolled pain and severe, spreading infection are indicators for amputation in people who are not candidates for revascularization.

Diagnostic Studies

Various tests assess blood flow and the vascular system (Table 41.2). Doppler ultrasound with duplex imaging maps blood flow throughout an entire arterial region. It can determine the degree of blood flow when we have difficulty palpating a peripheral pulse due to severe PAD.

Segmental BPs are obtained using Doppler ultrasound and a sphygmomanometer at the thigh, below the knee, and at ankle level while the patient is supine. A drop in segmental BP of greater than 30 mm Hg suggests PAD. Angiography and magnetic resonance angiography show the location and extent of PAD (see Table 35.10).

The *ankle-brachial index* (ABI) is a PAD screening tool. It is done using a hand-held Doppler. Calculate the ABI for each leg by dividing the ankle systolic BP (SBP) by the higher of the brachial SBPs. PAD guidelines recommend uniform reporting of ABI results (Table 41.3).[3] Calcified and stiff arteries in patients who are older or have diabetes often show a falsely elevated ABI.

Interprofessional Care

Table 41.2 outlines the interprofessional care for a patient with PAD.

Risk Factor Modification

The first treatment goal for patients with PAD is to reduce CVD risk factors. This may require both lifestyle changes and drug therapy (see Tables 37.2 to 37.6). Hypertension is a well-known risk factor for PAD progression. Encourage reducing sodium intake and following the dietary approaches to stop hypertension (DASH) or Mediterranean diet. Chapter 36 discusses hypertension.

Tobacco cessation is essential to reduce the risk for CVD events, PAD progression, and death. This is a difficult process with a high incidence of relapse. Suggest tobacco cessation strategies (see Tables 11.3–11.6).

TABLE 41.2 Interprofessional Care

Peripheral Artery Disease

Diagnostic Assessment

- Health history and physical assessment, including palpation of peripheral pulses
- Doppler ultrasound studies
- Segmental BPs
- ABI (Table 41.3)
- Duplex imaging
- Angiography
- Magnetic resonance angiography

Management

- CVD risk factor modification
  - Tobacco cessation
  - Regular physical exercise
  - Achieve or maintain ideal body weight
  - Follow Dietary Approaches to Stop Hypertension (DASH) diet or Mediterranean diet
  - Tight glucose control with diabetes, including Hb A1C monitoring
  - Tight BP control
  - Treatment of hyperlipidemia and hypertriglyceridemia (see Table 37.6)
  - Antiplatelet agent (aspirin, clopidogrel [Plavix])
  - ACE inhibitors (see Table 36.6)
- Treatment of claudication symptoms
  - Structured walking or exercise program
  - Cilostazol or pentoxifylline
- Nutrition therapy
- Physical/occupational therapy
- Proper foot care (see Table 53.23)

Surgical Therapy

- Percutaneous transluminal balloon angioplasty with or without stent
- Percutaneous transluminal atherectomy
- Percutaneous transluminal cryoplasty
- Peripheral artery bypass surgery
- Patch graft angioplasty, often in conjunction with bypass surgery
- Endarterectomy (for localized stenosis; rarely done as a stand-alone procedure)
- Thrombolytic therapy or mechanical clot extraction therapy (for acute ischemia only)
- Sympathectomy (for pain management only)
- Amputation

TABLE 41.3 Interpreting Ankle-Brachial Index Results

(ABI	Clinical Significance
>1.30	Noncompressible arteries
1.00–1.30	Normal ABI
0.91–0.99	Borderline ABI
≤0.90	Abnormal ABI
Classification of PAD Severity	
0.90–0.71	Mild PAD
0.70–0.41	Moderate PAD
≤0.40	Severe PAD

Diabetes is a major risk factor for PAD. It increases the risk for amputation. Patients with diabetes should maintain a glycosylated hemoglobin (A1C) below 7.0%.[5] Chapter 53 discusses diabetes.

Support aggressive lipid management for all patients with PAD. Both diet interventions and drug therapy are needed. Statins (e.g., simvastatin) and a fibric acid derivative (gemfibrozil) may be used (see Table 37.6).

Drug Therapy

Angiotensin-converting enzyme (ACE) inhibitors (e.g., ramipril) can reduce PAD symptoms. Antiplatelet agents are critical to reduce the risks for CVD events and death. Oral antiplatelet therapy should include low-dose aspirin therapy. Aspirin-intolerant patients may take clopidogrel (Plavix) daily. Combination antiplatelet therapy with aspirin and clopidogrel may be used by select high-risk patients. Anticoagulants (e.g., warfarin) are not recommended for preventing CVD events in patients with PAD.

DRUG ALERT

Clopidogrel (Plavix) and Omeprazole (Prilosec)

- Taking omeprazole with clopidogrel reduces the antiplatelet effect by half.
- This reduced effect increases the risk for myocardial infarction (MI) and stroke.

Two drugs are available to treat intermittent claudication: cilostazol and pentoxifylline. Cilostazol—a phosphodiesterase inhibitor—inhibits platelet aggregation and increases vasodilation. Pentoxifylline—a synthetic dimethylxanthine derivative—improves the flexibility of RBCs and decreases fibrinogen concentration, platelet adhesiveness, and blood viscosity. It is not as effective as cilostazol. Most take cilostazol less than 3 months due to side effects.[3]

DRUG ALERT

Cilostazol

- Contraindicated in patients with HF.

Exercise Therapy

A supervised exercise program is recommended as part of the initial treatment for all patients with intermittent claudication. The patient should exercise for 30 to 45 min/day, at least 3 times/week, for a minimum of 3 months. Although we most often prescribe walking, other modes of exercise (e.g., cycling) improve walking ability and quality of life.[3]

Encouraging exercise is especially important for women, because they have faster functional decline and greater mobility loss than men with PAD. Overall, patients with PAD who have higher levels of daily physical activity have better survival rates.[3,4]

Nutrition Therapy

Teach patients with PAD to maintain a body mass index (BMI) less than 25 kg/m^2 and a waist circumference less than 40 inches for men and less than 35 inches for women. Even modest, sustained weight loss of 3% to 5% yields important reductions in triglycerides, glucose, A1C, and the risk for developing type 2 diabetes. Greater weight loss has greater benefits. Recommend a diet reduced in calories and salt for obese or overweight persons.

Care of the Patient With Critical Limb Ischemia

Optimal therapy for the patient with CLI is revascularization via bypass surgery using an *autogenous* (native) vein. An alternative is percutaneous transluminal angioplasty (PTA).[3] Patients with CLI who are not candidates for surgery or PTA may receive IV prostanoids (e.g., iloprost [Ventavis]).[6,7] However, the FDA has not approved this drug for CLI treatment. Patients with CLI should continue optimal drug therapy (e.g., statin, antiplatelet, ACE inhibitor, β-blocker) to reduce the risk for a CVD event.

Conservative management includes protecting the extremity from trauma, decreasing ischemic pain, preventing and controlling infection, and improving perfusion. Carefully inspect, cleanse, and lubricate feet to prevent skin cracking and infection. Avoid lubrication between the toes and soaking the patient's feet to prevent skin *maceration* (or breakdown). Keep the affected foot clean and dry. Cover any ulcers with a dry, sterile dressing. We use a variety of wound care products to treat deep ulcers. Healing is unlikely without increasing the blood flow.

Encourage the patient to wear soft, roomy, and protective footwear and avoid extremes of heat and cold. Keep the patient's heels free of pressure. Place a pillow under the calves so that the heels are off the mattress or use a heel protection device. Giving analgesics and placing the bed in the reverse Trendelenburg position may control pain and increase perfusion to the lower extremities.

Spinal cord stimulation may help manage pain for patients with CLI. Other promising strategies include growth factors and gene and stem cell therapy to stimulate blood vessel growth *(angiogenesis)*. Unfortunately, almost half of the patients with CLI will die within 5 years.[7]

Interventional Radiology Catheter-Based Procedures

Interventional radiology catheter-based procedures are alternatives to surgery for treating lower extremity PAD. These procedures take place in a catheterization. They are similar to angiography in that they involve inserting a specialized catheter into the femoral artery. The PTA procedure uses a catheter with a balloon at the tip. The tip of the catheter is moved to the narrowed (stenotic) area of the artery. The balloon is then inflated, compressing the atherosclerotic intimal lining.[3]

Stents—expandable metallic devices—are placed within the artery after the balloon angioplasty. The stent holds the artery open. Angioplasty balloons and peripheral stents may be coated with a drug (e.g., paclitaxel) to limit new tissue growth in the treated area and improve long-term patency rates.[3]

Atherectomy is the removal of the obstructing plaque. A directional atherectomy device uses a high-speed cutting disk that cuts long strips of the atheroma. Laser atherectomy uses ultraviolet energy to break up the atheroma. Another type of atherectomy catheter has a diamond-coated tip that rotates at a high speed like a drill.

Cryoplasty combines PTA and cold therapy. A specialized balloon is filled with liquid nitrous oxide, which changes to gas as it enters the balloon. Expansion of the gas results in cooling to 14°F (−10°C). The cold temperature limits restenosis by reducing smooth muscle cell activity.

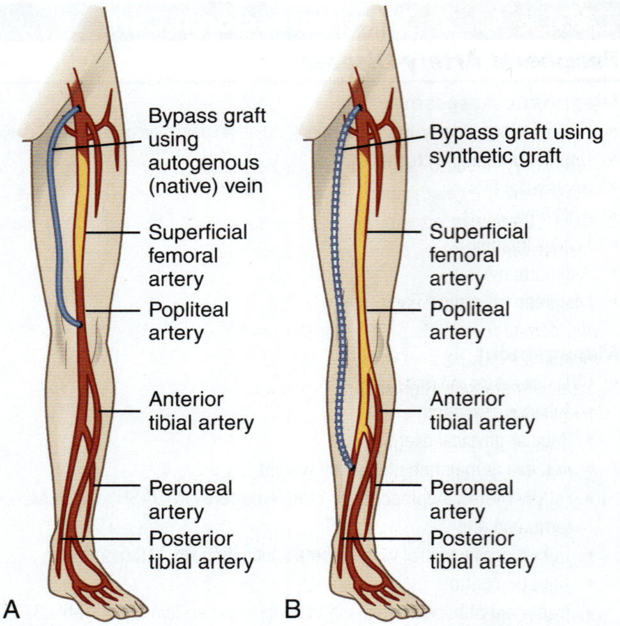

Fig. 41.2 (A) Femoral-popliteal bypass graft around an occluded superficial femoral artery. (B) Femoral–posterior tibial bypass graft around occluded superficial femoral, popliteal, and proximal tibial arteries.

Nursing care is the same as for diagnostic angiography (see Tables 35.10 and 35.12). Antiplatelet agents are given afterwards to reduce the risk for restenosis. Long-term, low-dose aspirin therapy or clopidogrel is recommended.

Surgical Therapy

Various surgical approaches are used to improve blood flow beyond a blocked artery. When possible, peripheral artery bypass surgery is done with an autogenous vein to bypass (carry blood around) the lesion (Fig. 41.2). Synthetic grafts are used for long routes, such as an axillary-femoral bypass. When a person's own vein is not available, a human umbilical vein or a composite sequential bypass graft (native vein plus synthetic graft) can be used.[3] PTA with stenting may be done in combination with bypass surgery.

Other options include *endarterectomy* (opening the artery and removing the obstructing plaque) and *patch graft angioplasty* (opening the artery, removing plaque, and sewing a patch to the opening to widen the lumen). In-hospital mortality is higher in women undergoing revascularization than men, regardless of disease severity or surgical procedure.[4]

Amputation may be needed if tissue necrosis is extensive, gangrene or osteomyelitis develops, or all major arteries in the limb are blocked. Preserving as much of the limb as possible improves rehabilitation potential. Amputation is discussed in Chapter 67.

❖ NURSING MANAGEMENT: LOWER EXTREMITY PERIPHERAL ARTERY DISEASE

◆ Assessment

Table 41.4 presents subjective and objective data that you should obtain from a patient with PAD.

TABLE 41.4 NURSING ASSESSMENT

Peripheral Artery Disease

Subjective Data

Important Health Information

Health history: Tobacco use, diabetes, hypertension, hyperlipidemia, hypertriglyceridemia, hyperuricemia, impaired renal function, obesity. ↑ High-sensitivity C-reactive protein, homocysteine, or lipoprotein (a) [Lp(a)] levels. Positive family history, sedentary lifestyle, stress

Functional Health Patterns

Health perception–health management: Family history of CVD. Tobacco use, including exposure to environmental smoke

Nutritional-metabolic: High sodium, saturated fat, and cholesterol intake. Elevated Hb A1C

Activity-exercise: Exercise intolerance

Cognitive-perceptual: Buttock, thigh, or calf pain that is precipitated by exercise and that subsides with rest (intermittent claudication) or progresses to pain at rest. Burning pain in feet and toes at rest. Numbness, tingling, sensation of cold in legs or feet. Progressive loss of sensation and deep pain in extremities

Sexuality-reproductive: Erectile dysfunction

Objective Data

Cardiovascular

Decreased or absent peripheral pulses. Feet cool to touch. Capillary refill >3 s. Bruits may be present at pulse sites

Neurologic

Impaired mobility or sensation

Skin

Loss of hair on legs and feet. Thick toenails. Pallor with elevation. Dependent rubor. Thin, cool, shiny skin with muscle atrophy. Skin breakdown and arterial ulcers, especially over bony areas. Gangrene

Possible Diagnostic Findings

Arterial stenosis evident with duplex imaging, ↓ Doppler pressures, ↓ ABI, angiography shows peripheral atherosclerosis

◆ Clinical Problems

Clinical problems for the patient with PAD may include:

- Activity intolerance
- Impaired tissue integrity
- Inadequate tissue perfusion
- Musculoskeletal problem
- Pain

Additional information on clinical problems and interventions for the patient with PAD of the lower extremities is presented in eNursing Care Plan 41.1 on the website for this chapter.

◆ Planning

Nursing care focuses on the priority problems of poor tissue perfusion and pain. The overall goals for the patient who has lower extremity PAD include (1) adequate tissue perfusion; (2) pain relief; (3) increased exercise tolerance; (4) intact, healthy skin on the extremities; and (5) knowledge of disease and treatment plan.

◆ Implementation

◆ Health Promotion

Assess the patient for and provide instructions on how to control CVD risk factors (see Table 37.2). Teach diet modification to reduce cholesterol, saturated fat, and salt (see Tables 37.4 and 37.5). Teach proper foot care and injury prevention. Encourage patients with positive family histories of cardiac, diabetes, or vascular disease to obtain regular follow-up care.

◆ Acute Care

After surgical or radiologic intervention, observe the patient in a recovery area. Check the operative extremity every 15 minutes initially and then hourly. Assess color, temperature, capillary refill, peripheral pulses, and sensation and movement. Immediately notify the HCP of any loss of palpable pulses or change in the Doppler sound over a pulse. We do not obtain postoperative ABI measurements as they place the patient at risk for graft thrombosis. Compare assessment findings with the patient's baseline and with findings in the opposite limb.

PAD patients with a history of chronic ischemic rest pain may have tolerance to opioids. Thus, aggressive pain management may be needed after surgery.

After the patient leaves the recovery area, continue to monitor extremity perfusion. Assess for complications, such as bleeding, hematoma, thrombosis, embolization, and compartment syndrome. A dramatic increase in pain, loss of previously palpable pulses, extremity pallor or cyanosis, numbness or tingling, or a cold extremity suggests graft or stent blockage. Report these findings to the HCP at once.

CHECK YOUR PRACTICE

You are caring for a 74-year-old male patient who is recovering from left femoral-popliteal bypass graft surgery. When you respond to the patient's call bell, the patient reports severe pain in the operative leg. On assessment, you cannot palpate the dorsalis pedis and posterior tibial pulses. The foot is cold to touch.

- What are your next actions?

Do not place the patient in a knee-flexed position except for exercise. Turn the patient and position frequently with pillows to support the incision. On postoperative day 1, assist the patient out of bed several times. Walking even short distances is desirable. A walker may be helpful, especially for frail, older patients. Discourage prolonged sitting with legs lowered, since it may cause pain and edema, increase the risk for venous thrombosis, and place stress on the suture lines. Graduated compression stockings may help control leg edema. If edema develops, position the patient supine, and elevate the leg above heart level.

Surgical site infection (SSI) is a serious complication. Careful postoperative assessment and wound care are important. SSIs are associated with early graft loss, longer hospitalization, reoperation, and sepsis.

◆ Ambulatory Care

Assess for CVD risk factors and teach health promotion strategies. Continued tobacco use dramatically decreases the patency rates of grafts and stents and increases the risk for an MI or stroke.

Long-term antiplatelet therapy with aspirin or clopidogrel is used after surgery. Patients having distal peripheral bypass surgery (i.e., below the knee) using synthetic graft materials receive dual antiplatelet therapy (clopidogrel plus aspirin) for 1 to 3 months, followed by lifelong single antiplatelet therapy.

Encourage supervised exercise training after revascularization. Explain that exercise decreases CVD risk factors, including hypertension, hyperlipidemia, obesity, and glucose levels. Foot care is especially important in the patient with diabetes and PAD (see Table 53.21). Diabetic neuropathy increases the patient's risk for injury. Tell patients to inspect their legs and feet daily for changes in skin color or texture. Show patients how to palpate pulses and check skin temperature and capillary refill. Stress reporting any changes or the presence of ulceration or inflammation to the HCP.

Thick or overgrown toenails and calluses are potentially serious and need regular attention by an HCP (e.g., podiatrist). Patients who have poor eyesight, back problems, obesity, or arthritis may need help with foot care. Encourage patients to wear clean, all-cotton or all-wool socks and comfortable shoes with rounded (not pointed) toes and soft insoles. Tell patients to lace shoes loosely and to break in new shoes gradually (Table 41.5).

TABLE 41.5 PATIENT & CAREGIVER TEACHING

Peripheral Artery Bypass Surgery

Include the following information in the teaching plan for a patient undergoing peripheral artery bypass surgery and the patient's caregiver:

1. Reduce risk factors by stopping tobacco use, controlling blood glucose levels with diabetes, controlling BP, lowering cholesterol and triglyceride levels, achieving or maintaining ideal body weight, and exercising regularly.
2. Provide teaching about the basic mechanism of action (why prescribed for patient), side effects, and safety precautions for drugs such as antiplatelets, antihypertensives, lipid-lowering therapy, and pain medication.
3. Eat healthy—it is essential to recovery. Drink plenty of fluids, eat a well-balanced diet (e.g., foods high in protein, vitamins C and A, and zinc; high-fiber foods; fresh fruits and vegetables), eat fewer high-fat foods, and reduce salt intake.
4. Take part in a supervised exercise program or take a daily walk. In the beginning, take several short walks a day and rest between activities. Gradually increase your walking to 30 to 40 min/day, 3 to 5 days/week.
5. Care for feet and legs. Inspect feet and wash them daily. Wear clean cotton or wool socks and well-fitting shoes. File toenails straight across. Avoid sitting with legs crossed, extreme hot and cold temperatures, and prolonged standing.
6. Follow routine postoperative wound care that includes keeping incision clean and dry; do not disturb Steri-Strips (if present).
7. Monitor for signs and symptoms of impaired healing or infection of the leg incision, and notify HCP if any of the following occur:
   - Prolonged drainage or pus from the incision
   - Increased redness, warmth, pain, or hardness along incision
   - Separation of wound edges
   - Temperature >100°F (37.8°C)
8. Keep all follow-up appointments with HCP.
9. Notify HCP at once of increased leg or foot pain or a change in the color or temperature of leg or foot.

◆ Evaluation

The expected outcomes are that a patient with PAD of the lower extremities will have

- Adequate peripheral tissue perfusion
- Increased activity tolerance
- Effective pain management
- Knowledge of disease and treatment plan

ACUTE ARTERIAL ISCHEMIC DISORDERS

Etiology and Pathophysiology

Acute arterial ischemia is a sudden interruption in the arterial blood supply to a tissue, an organ, or an extremity that—if left untreated—can result in tissue death. It is caused by embolism, thrombosis of an atherosclerotic artery, or trauma. *Embolization* of a thrombus from the heart is the most frequent cause of acute arterial occlusion. Heart conditions in which thrombi can develop include infective endocarditis, mitral valve disease, atrial fibrillation, cardiomyopathies, and prosthetic heart valves. Noncardiac sources of emboli include aneurysms, ulcerated atherosclerotic plaque, recent endovascular procedures, and venous thrombi.

Thrombi that originate in the left side of the heart may dislodge and travel anywhere in the systemic circulation. Most emboli block an artery of the leg where vessels branch (e.g., iliofemoral, popliteal, tibial) or narrow. Sudden local thrombosis may occur at the site of an atherosclerotic plaque. Hypovolemia (e.g., shock), hyperviscosity (e.g., polycythemia), and hypercoagulability (e.g., chemotherapy) predispose a person to thrombotic arterial occlusion.

Traumatic injury to an extremity may cause partial or total arterial blockage. Acute arterial occlusion may develop from arterial dissection in the carotid artery or aorta or from a procedure-related arterial injury (e.g., after angiography).

Clinical Manifestations

Manifestations of acute arterial ischemia include the *6 Ps: pain, pallor, pulselessness, paresthesia, paralysis,* and *poikilothermia* (adaptation of the limb to the environmental temperature, most often cool). If you detect these signs, immediately notify the HCP. Without immediate intervention, ischemia may progress to tissue necrosis and gangrene within a few hours.

Paralysis is a late sign of acute arterial ischemia and signals the death of nerves supplying the extremity. Foot drop occurs from nerve damage. Because nerve tissue is very sensitive to hypoxia, limb paralysis or ischemic neuropathy may persist even after revascularization.

Interprofessional Care

Early diagnosis and treatment are essential to keep the affected limb viable during acute arterial ischemia. Anticoagulant therapy with IV unfractionated heparin (UH) is started to prevent thrombus growth and inhibit further embolization. In patients undergoing embolectomy, UH should be followed by long-term anticoagulation.

To restore blood flow, the thrombus is removed as soon as possible. Options consist of surgical thrombectomy (recommended procedure), percutaneous catheter-directed thrombolytic therapy, percutaneous mechanical thrombectomy with or without thrombolytic therapy, or surgical bypass.[7]

Percutaneous catheter-directed thrombolytic therapy using alteplase or urokinase is recommended for acute arterial ischemia of less than 14 days. The HCP inserts a catheter into the femoral artery and moves it to the site of the clot. The thrombolytic drug is continuously infused. Thrombolytics work by directly dissolving the clot over a period of 24 to 48 hours. (Chapter 37 discusses thrombolytic therapy.) Close monitoring is required to make sure the catheter does not move and the patient does not bleed from the catheter insertion site.

Surgical revascularization may be used in a patient with trauma (e.g., lacerated artery) or with significant arterial blockage. Amputation is done for patients with ischemic rest pain and tissue loss in those whom limb salvage is not possible. If the patient is at risk for further embolization from a persistent source (e.g., chronic atrial fibrillation), long-term anticoagulation is recommended.

THROMBOANGIITIS OBLITERANS

Thromboangiitis obliterans (Buerger's disease) is a non-atherosclerotic, segmental, recurrent inflammatory disorder of the small and medium arteries and veins of the arms and legs. Cerebral, coronary, mesenteric, pulmonary, and/or renal arteries are rarely involved. The disease occurs mostly in men younger than 45 years of age with a long history of tobacco and/or marijuana use without other CVD risk factors (e.g., hypertension, hyperlipidemia, diabetes).[8]

In the acute phase of Buerger disease, an inflammatory thrombus blocks the vessel. Over time, the thrombus becomes more organized and the inflammation in the vessel wall subsides.[8] During the chronic phase, thrombosis and fibrosis in the vessel cause tissue ischemia.

The symptoms of Buerger disease often are confused with PAD and other autoimmune diseases (e.g., scleroderma). Patients may have intermittent claudication of the feet, hands, or arms. As the disease progresses, rest pain and ischemic ulcerations develop. Other signs and symptoms may include color and temperature changes of the limbs, paresthesia, superficial vein thrombosis, and cold sensitivity.

There are no laboratory or diagnostic tests specific to Buerger disease. The diagnosis is based on age of onset; history; symptoms; involvement of distal vessels; presence of ischemic ulcerations; and exclusion of autoimmune disease, diabetes, thrombophilia (inherited tendency to clot) and other sources of emboli, such as atherosclerosis and aneurysm.[8]

The main treatment is the complete cessation of tobacco and marijuana use in any form. Use of nicotine replacement products is contraindicated. Conservative management includes avoiding limb exposure to cold temperatures, a supervised walking program, antibiotics to treat any infected ulcers, and analgesics to manage the ischemic pain. Teach patients to avoid trauma to the extremities.

IV iloprost (Ventavis)—a prostaglandin analog that promotes vasodilation—is used to manage rest pain, promote healing of ischemic ulcers, and decrease the need for amputation.[8] Surgical options include lumbar sympathectomy (transection of a nerve, ganglion, and/or plexus of the sympathetic nervous system), implanting a spinal cord stimulator, and bypass surgery.[8] Sympathectomy and a spinal cord stimulator can improve distal blood flow, reduce pain, and decrease the rate of amputation. Neither alters the inflammatory process. Bypass surgery may be used in select patients with severe ischemia. Stem cell therapy promotes ulcer healing, new blood vessel formation, and nerve cell regeneration.[8]

Painful ulcerations may require finger or toe amputations. Amputation below the knee may be needed in severe cases. The rate of amputation in those who continue tobacco or marijuana use after diagnosis is much higher than in those who stop.

RAYNAUD'S PHENOMENON

Raynaud's phenomenon is an episodic vasospastic disorder of small cutaneous arteries, most often involving the fingers and toes. It occurs more often in women, especially those between 15 and 40 years of age. The pathogenesis of Raynaud phenomenon is due to abnormalities in the vascular, intravascular, and neuronal mechanisms that cause vasodilation.[9,10]

Raynaud's phenomenon may occur in isolation (primary Raynaud phenomenon) or with an underlying disease (e.g., thyroid conditions, scleroderma, systemic lupus erythematosus) (secondary Raynaud phenomenon). Other contributing factors include the use of vibrating machinery or work in cold environments, exposure to heavy metals (e.g., lead), and high homocysteine levels.

Diagnosis is based on persistent symptoms for at least 2 years. Patients with Raynaud phenomenon should have routine follow-up to monitor for development of connective tissue or autoimmune diseases.

Raynaud phenomenon is characterized by vasospasm-induced color changes (white, blue, and red) of fingers, toes, ears, and nose. Decreased perfusion results in pallor (white). The digits then appear cyanotic (bluish purple) (Fig. 41.3). These changes are followed by rubor (red), a hyperemic response when blood flow is restored. The patient usually describes coldness

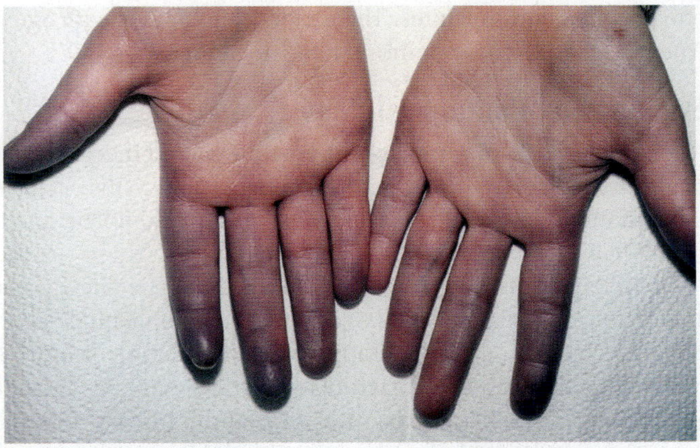

Fig. 41.3 Raynaud's phenomenon. (From James WD, Elston DM, Dirk M: *Andrews' diseases of the skin clinical atlas*, St Louis, 2018, Elsevier.)

and numbness in the vasoconstrictive phase. This is followed by throbbing, aching pain, tingling, and swelling in the hyperemic phase. An episode usually lasts only minutes but may last for several hours. Triggers include cold exposure, emotional upsets, tobacco use, and caffeine.

After frequent, prolonged attacks, the skin may become thickened and the nails brittle. Complications include *punctate* (small hole) lesions of the fingertips and superficial gangrenous ulcers.

Patient teaching about preventing episodes is the focus of nursing care. Tell patients to avoid temperature extremes and wear loose, warm clothing as protection from the cold, including gloves when handling cold objects. Immersing hands in warm water often decreases the vasospasm. The patient should stop using all tobacco products and avoid caffeine and other drugs that have vasoconstrictive effects (e.g., amphetamines, ergotamine, pseudoephedrine). Suggest appropriate stress management strategies.

Sustained-release calcium channel blockers (e.g., nifedipine [Procardia]) are the first-line drug therapy. They relax smooth muscles of the arterioles by blocking the influx of calcium into the cells. This reduces the frequency and severity of vasospastic attacks. If symptoms persist, other vasodilators (e.g., phosphodiesterase-5 inhibitors [sildenafil]) or topical nitroglycerin 2% ointment may be used.[10] Calcium channel blockers can be taken with nitroglycerin topical ointment. Phosphodiesterase-5 inhibitors are not used with topical nitroglycerin due to risk for hypotension.

Prompt intervention is needed for patients with digital ulceration or critical ischemia. Treatment options include prostacyclin infusion therapy (e.g., iloprost), antibiotics, analgesics, and surgical debridement of necrotic tissue. Botulinum toxin A and statins may lessen the severity of Raynaud phenomenon.[9] Sympathectomy is done only in severe cases refractory to medical treatment when digit survival is threatened.

AORTIC ANEURYSMS

The aorta is the largest artery. It supplies O_2, nutrients, and blood to all vital organs. One of the most common problems affecting the aorta is an **aneurysm,** which is a permanent, localized outpouching or dilation of the vessel wall. Aneurysms occur more often in men and in whites. The incidence increases with age.[11] Aneurysms may occur in more than 1 location.

Etiology and Pathophysiology

Aortic aneurysms may involve the aortic arch and thoracic and/or abdominal aorta. Three-fourths of aortic aneurysms occur in the abdominal aorta (Fig. 41.4). Most abdominal aortic aneurysms (AAAs) occur below the renal arteries.

A variety of disorders are associated with aortic aneurysms. The main causes are classified as degenerative, congenital, infectious, mechanical (e.g., penetrating or blunt trauma), or inflammatory (e.g., aortitis). Risk factors for aortic aneurysms include age, male gender, hypertension, CAD, family history, tobacco use, high cholesterol, lower extremity PAD, carotid artery disease, previous stroke, and obesity. Tobacco use is the most important modifiable risk factor.[11] The larger the aneurysm, the greater is the risk for rupture.

Genetic Link

Both aortic aneurysm and aortic dissection have a strong genetic component. The familial tendency is related to several congenital anomalies. Examples include bicuspid aortic valve, coarctation of the aorta, Turner syndrome, autosomal dominant polycystic kidney disease, specific collagen defects (e.g., Ehlers-Danlos syndrome), and premature breakdown of vascular elastic tissue (e.g., Marfan syndrome).[11]

Classification

Aneurysms are classified as true or false aneurysms (Fig. 41.5A–C). A *true aneurysm* is one in which the wall of the artery forms the aneurysm, with at least 1 vessel layer still intact. True aneurysms are subdivided into fusiform and saccular types. A *fusiform aneurysm* is circumferential and relatively uniform in shape. A *saccular aneurysm* is pouchlike with a narrow neck connecting the bulge to 1 side of the arterial wall.

A *false aneurysm,* or *pseudoaneurysm,* is not an aneurysm. It is a disruption of all arterial wall layers with bleeding that is contained by surrounding anatomic structures. False aneurysms may result from trauma, infection, peripheral artery bypass graft surgery (at the site of the graft-to-artery anastomosis), or arterial leakage after removal of a cannula (e.g., femoral artery catheter, intraaortic balloon pump).

Clinical Manifestations

Thoracic aortic aneurysms (TAAs) are often asymptomatic. When present, symptoms include deep, diffuse chest pain that may extend to the interscapular area. Ascending aorta and aortic arch aneurysms can cause (1) angina from decreased blood flow to the coronary arteries; (2) transient ischemic attacks from decreased blood flow to the carotid arteries; and (3) coughing,

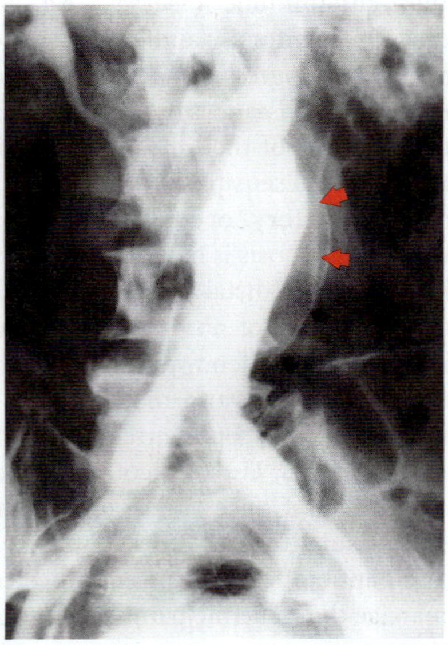

Fig. 41.4 Angiography showing fusiform abdominal aortic aneurysm. Note calcification of the aortic wall *(arrows)* and extension of the aneurysm into the common iliac arteries. (Courtesy Jo Menzoian, Boston, MA.)

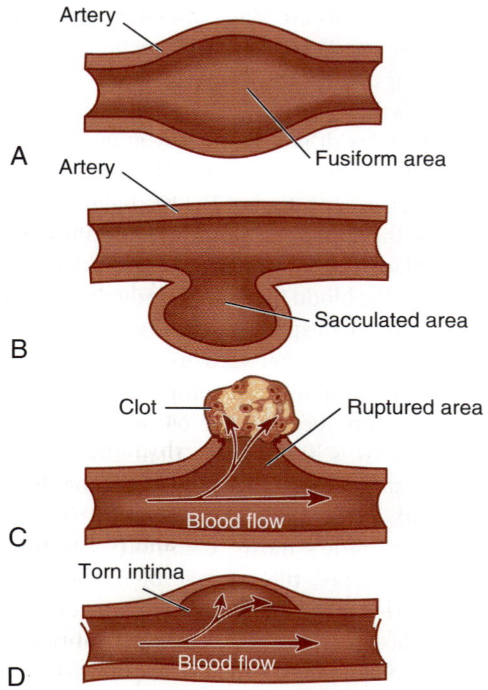

Fig. 41.5 (A) True fusiform abdominal aortic aneurysm. (B) True saccular aortic aneurysm. (C) False aneurysm, or pseudoaneurysm. (D) Aortic dissection.

shortness of breath, hoarseness, and/or difficulty swallowing from pressure on the laryngeal nerve. If the aneurysm presses on the superior vena cava, decreased venous return can result in jugular venous distention and edema of the face and arms.

AAAs are often asymptomatic. They are often found during routine physical assessment or evaluation for another problem (e.g., abdominal x-ray, CT scan). A pulsatile mass in the periumbilical area slightly to the left of the midline may be present. Bruits may be auscultated over the aneurysm. Physical findings may be hard to detect in obese persons.

AAA symptoms may mimic pain associated with abdominal or back disorders. Compression of nearby anatomic structures and nerves may cause symptoms, such as back pain, epigastric discomfort, altered bowel elimination, and intermittent claudication. Sometimes, aneurysms spontaneously embolize plaque, causing "blue toe syndrome" (patchy mottling of the feet and toes in the presence of palpable pedal pulses).

Complications

Aneurysm rupture is more likely to occur in people who smoke tobacco.[11] If rupture occurs into the retroperitoneal space, bleeding may be controlled by surrounding anatomic structures, preventing exsanguination and death. In this case, the patient often has severe back pain. Back or flank bruising *(Grey Turner sign)* may be present.

If rupture occurs into the thoracic or abdominal cavity, patients can die from massive hemorrhage. The patient who reaches the hospital will be in hypovolemic shock with tachycardia, hypotension, pale clammy skin, decreased urine output, altered level of consciousness, and abdominal tenderness. Shock is discussed in Chapter 42. In this situation, simultaneous resuscitation and immediate surgical repair are needed. For patients admitted to the hospital with a ruptured AAA, in-hospital mortality is high at 53%.[11]

Diagnostic Studies

Chest x-rays may reveal abnormal widening of the thoracic aorta. An abdominal x-ray may show calcification within the aortic wall. An ECG may rule out MI, since thoracic aneurysm or dissection symptoms can mimic angina. Echocardiography assesses the function of the aortic valve. Ultrasound is useful for aneurysm screening and to monitor aneurysm size. A CT scan or MRI can diagnose and assess the location and severity of aneurysms. Angiography gives helpful information by using contrast imaging to map the entire aortic system (see Table 35.10).

Interprofessional Care

The main goal of care is to prevent the rupture of an aneurysm. Early detection and prompt treatment are essential. Conservative medical therapy of small, asymptomatic AAAs (less than 5.4 cm) is the best practice.[11] This consists of risk factor modification (ceasing tobacco use, decreasing BP, optimizing lipid profile, gradually increasing physical activity).[11] Patients should receive management for hypertension, hyperlipidemia, diabetes, and other CVD risk factors. A statin and an ACE inhibitor may be prescribed. Those with small aneurysms—4.0 to 5.4 cm—should have monitoring of aneurysm size using ultrasound or CT every 6 to 12 months. Ultrasound monitoring every 3 years is done for patients with AAAs smaller than 4.0 cm in diameter.

Surgical repair is recommended in patients with asymptomatic aneurysms 5.5 cm in diameter or larger. Surgical intervention may occur sooner if the patient has a genetic disorder (e.g., Marfan, Ehlers-Danlos syndrome), the aneurysm expands rapidly, the patient becomes symptomatic, or the risk for rupture is high. A careful review of body systems is needed to identify any comorbidities that affect the patient's surgical risk. Existing carotid or coronary artery blockages may be corrected before aneurysm repair.

Surgical Therapy

For elective aneurysm repair surgery, the patient should be well hydrated with normal electrolytes, coagulation, and hematocrit. If the aneurysm ruptures, emergent surgery is required.

Open aneurysm repair (OAR) involves a large abdominal incision through which the surgeon (1) cuts into the diseased aortic segment, (2) removes any thrombus or plaque, (3) sutures a synthetic graft to the aorta proximal and distal to the aneurysm, and (4) sutures the native aortic wall around the graft to act as a protective cover (Fig. 41.6). For iliac artery aneurysms, a bifurcated graft replaces the entire diseased segment. With saccular aneurysms, it may be possible to excise only the bulbous lesion and repair the artery by primary closure (suturing the artery together) or applying an autogenous or synthetic patch graft.

All OARs require aortic cross-clamping proximal and distal to the aneurysm. Most resections are done in 30 to 45 minutes. Then the clamps are removed, and blood flow is restored.

The risk for postoperative complications, such as acute kidney injury, increases in patients who have OAR of AAAs above the level of the renal arteries.

Endovascular graft procedure. Minimally invasive endovascular aneurysm repair (EVAR) is an alternative to OAR for select patients. EVAR involves the placement of a sutureless aortic graft into the abdominal aorta inside the aneurysm via the femoral artery. Grafts are made of various materials, such as a Dacron cylinder consisting of several sections, and supported with multiple rings of flexible wire. Eligibility criteria include iliofemoral vessels that allow for safe graft insertion and vessels of sufficient length and width to support the graft.[11]

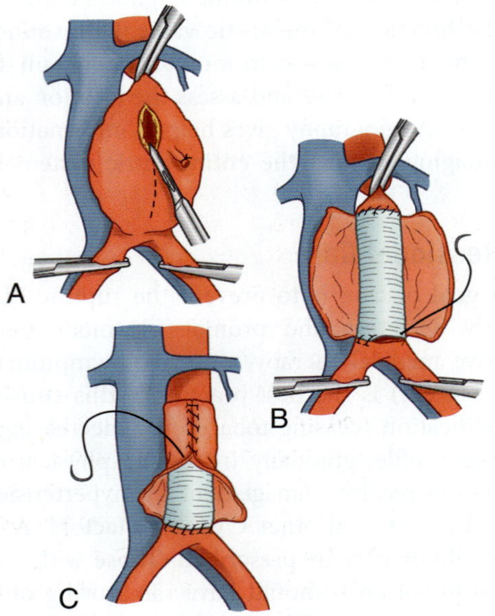

Fig. 41.6 Surgical repair of an abdominal aortic aneurysm. (A) Incising the aneurysmal sac. (B) Insertion of synthetic graft. (C) Suturing native aortic wall over synthetic graft.

The main section of the graft is bifurcated. It is delivered through a femoral artery catheter. The second part of the graft is inserted through the opposite femoral artery. When all graft components are in place, they are deployed against the vessel wall by balloon inflation. The blood then flows through the endovascular graft, preventing further expansion of the aneurysm (Fig. 41.7).

Angiography is done afterward to check for leaks and to confirm patency of all stent-graft components. The aneurysmal wall shrinks over time because the blood is diverted through the endograft. EVAR is less invasive than OAR and requires a shorter hospital stay. EVAR also has fewer complications, such as paraplegia and death.

Complications. The most common complication of AAA repair is *endoleak*, the seepage of blood back into the old aneurysm. This may result from an inadequate seal at either graft end, a tear through the graft fabric, or leakage between overlapping graft segments. Repair may require coil embolization (insertion of beads) for hemostasis.

Other complications include aneurysm growth above or below the graft, aneurysm rupture, aortic dissection, bleeding, renal artery occlusion caused by stent migration, graft thrombosis, incisional site hematoma, and incisional infection. Patients undergoing EVAR need periodic imaging for the rest of their lives to monitor for an endoleak, assess stability of the aneurysm, and determine the need for surgery.

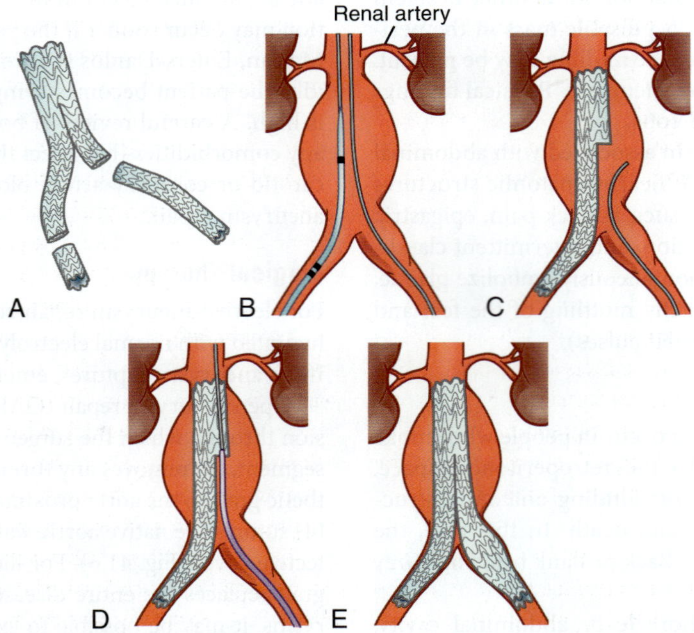

Fig. 41.7 Bifurcated (2-branched) endovascular stent grafting of an aneurysm. (A) Insertion of a woven polyester graft covered by a tubular metal web (stent). (B) The stent graft is inserted through a large blood vessel (e.g., femoral artery) using a delivery catheter. The catheter is positioned below the renal arteries in the area of the aneurysm. (C) The stent graft is slowly released into the blood vessel. When the stent comes in contact with the blood vessel, it expands to a preset size. (D) A second stent graft can be inserted in the opposite vessel, if needed. (E) Fully deployed bifurcated stent graft.

A potentially lethal complication in an emergency repair of a ruptured AAA is the development of *intraabdominal hypertension* (IAH) with associated *abdominal compartment syndrome*. Persistent IAH reduces blood flow to the viscera. Abdominal compartment syndrome refers to the impaired organ perfusion caused by IAH and resulting multisystem organ failure. IAH is confirmed by measuring the patient's intraabdominal pressure indirectly through a catheter and transducer system.

Treatment goals include controlling situations that lead to IAH. Interventions include open (surgical) decompression, percutaneous drainage, and percutaneous drainage combined with a thrombolytic infusion. Conservative measures, such as intubation, ventilation, patient positioning, gastric decompression, cautious fluid resuscitation, pain management, and temporary hemofiltration, are used.

NURSING MANAGEMENT: AORTIC ANEURYSMS

Assessment

Begin by doing a thorough history and physical assessment. Because atherosclerosis is a systemic disease, look for signs of coexisting cardiac, pulmonary, cerebral, and lower extremity vascular problems. Monitor the patient for signs of aneurysm rupture. These include diaphoresis; pallor; weakness; tachycardia; hypotension; abdominal, back, groin, or periumbilical pain; changes in level of consciousness; or a pulsating abdominal mass.

Obtain baseline data to compare with later assessments. Pay special attention to the character and quality of the patient's peripheral pulses and renal and neurologic status. Before surgery, mark pedal pulse sites (dorsalis pedis, posterior tibial) with a marker. Note any skin lesions on the lower extremities.

Planning

The overall goals for a patient undergoing aortic surgery include (1) normal tissue perfusion; (2) intact motor and sensory function; and (3) no complications related to surgical repair, such as thrombosis, infection, or rupture.

Implementation

Health Promotion

To promote overall health, encourage the patient to reduce CVD risk factors (see Table 37.2). These include controlling BP, ceasing tobacco use (see Chapter 11), and maintaining normal body weight and serum lipid levels. These measures also help ensure continued graft patency after surgical repair. Counsel the patient about taking part in moderate physical activity.

Acute Care

Before surgery, provide emotional support and teaching to the patient and caregiver (see Chapter 18). In general, aortic surgery patients have a bowel preparation and skin cleansing with an antimicrobial agent the day before surgery. They are NPO after midnight the day of surgery and receive IV antibiotics before the first incision. Patients with a history of CVD should receive a β-blocker (e.g., metoprolol).

After surgery, patients typically go to an ICU for 24 to 48 hours for close monitoring. When the patient arrives in the ICU, various devices are in place. These include an endotracheal tube for mechanical ventilation, an arterial line, a central venous pressure (CVP) catheter, peripheral IV lines, an indwelling urinary catheter, and a nasogastric (NG) tube. The patient needs continuous ECG and pulse oximetry monitoring. If the thorax is opened during surgery, chest tubes will be in place. The patient may have a lumbar catheter draining cerebrospinal fluid to prevent neurologic problems. Pain medication is given via subcutaneous infusion into incision site (e.g., On-Q pain pump), epidural catheters, or IV patient-controlled analgesia (PCA).

In addition to the usual goals of care for a postoperative patient (e.g., maintaining adequate respiratory function, fluid and electrolyte balance, and pain control [see Chapter 20]), check for graft patency and renal perfusion. Watch for and intervene to limit or treat cardiac ischemia, dysrhythmias, infections, VTE, and neurologic complications. eNursing Care Plan 41.2 for the patient with an aneurysm repair or other aortic surgery is available on the website for this chapter.

Graft patency. An adequate BP is important to maintain graft patency. Prolonged low BP may result in graft thrombosis. Give IV fluids and blood components as ordered to maintain adequate blood flow. Monitor CVP or PA pressures and urine output hourly in the immediate postoperative period to assess the patient's hydration and perfusion status.

Avoid severe hypertension which may stress the arterial anastomoses. This can result in leakage of blood or rupture at the suture lines. Drug therapy with IV diuretics (e.g., furosemide) or IV antihypertensive agents (e.g., labetalol, hydralazine, sodium nitroprusside) may be indicated.

Cardiovascular status. Myocardial ischemia or infarction may occur in the perioperative period from decreased myocardial O_2 supply or increased myocardial O_2 demands. Dysrhythmias may occur because of electrolyte imbalances, hypoxemia, hypothermia, or myocardial ischemia. Maintain continuous ECG monitoring. Administer O_2 per protocol. Other care includes frequent electrolyte and arterial blood gas determinations and giving IV antidysrhythmics, antihypertensives, and electrolytes as needed. Provide adequate pain control.

Infection. A prosthetic vascular graft infection is a rare but potentially life-threatening complication. Nursing interventions to prevent infection include giving a broad-spectrum antibiotic as prescribed (see Table 15.8). Assess temperature regularly, and promptly report fever. Monitor laboratory results for a high WBC count, which may be the first sign of an infection. Ensure adequate nutrition. Assess the surgical incision for signs of infection (e.g., redness, swelling, drainage). Keep surgical incisions clean and dry and perform wound care as prescribed.

Use good hand-washing and strict aseptic technique in the care of all peripheral, arterial, and CVP catheter insertion sites. These are ports of entry for bacteria. Meticulous perineal care for the patient with an indwelling urinary catheter and early catheter removal are essential to minimize the risk for urinary tract infection.

Gastrointestinal status. After OAR, postoperative ileus may develop because of anesthesia and the handling of the bowel during surgery. The intestines may become swollen and bruised. Peristalsis ceases for variable intervals. A retroperitoneal surgical approach decreases the risk for bowel complications.

An NG tube may be present and connected to low, intermittent suction to decompress the stomach, prevent aspiration of stomach contents, and decrease pressure on suture lines. Record the amount and character of the NG output. While the patient is NPO, provide frequent oral care. Ice chips or lozenges can help soothe a dry or irritated throat. Assess for bowel sounds every 4 hours. Note the passing of flatus as it signals returning bowel function. Encourage early ambulation to help the return of bowel function. A postoperative ileus rarely lasts beyond the fourth postoperative day.

If the blood supply to the bowel is disrupted during surgery, ischemia or infarction (death) of intestinal tissue may result. Manifestations of this rare, but serious, complication include absent bowel sounds, fever, abdominal distention and pain, diarrhea, and bloody stools. If bowel infarction occurs, immediate reoperation is needed to restore blood flow and resect the infarcted area of bowel.

Neurologic status. Neurologic complications can occur after aortic surgery. When the ascending aorta and aortic arch are involved, assess the patient's level of consciousness, pupil size and response to light, facial symmetry, tongue position, speech, upper extremity movement, and quality of hand grasps. When the descending aorta is involved, perform a neurovascular assessment of the lower extremities. Record all assessments and report changes from baseline to the HCP immediately.

Peripheral perfusion status. The location of the aneurysm determines the type of peripheral perfusion assessment. Check and record all peripheral pulses hourly for several hours and then routinely (based on agency policy). When the ascending aorta and aortic arch are involved, assess the carotid, radial, and temporal artery pulses. For surgery of the descending aorta, assess the femoral, popliteal, posterior tibial, and dorsalis pedis pulses (see Fig. 35.6). You may need a Doppler to assess peripheral pulses. Check skin temperature and color, capillary refill time, and sensation and movement of the extremities.

Sometimes, lower extremity pulses may be absent for a short time after surgery because of vasospasm and hypothermia. A decreased or absent pulse together with a cool, pale, mottled, or painful extremity may indicate embolization or graft occlusion. Report these findings to the HCP at once. Graft occlusion requires reoperation if identified early. It is essential to compare your findings with the preoperative status to determine the cause of a decreased or absent pulse and the proper treatment. In some patients, pulses may have been absent before surgery because of coexistent PAD.

Renal perfusion status. The patient will have an indwelling urinary catheter after surgery. In the immediate postoperative period, record hourly urine output. Further evaluate renal function by monitoring daily BUN and serum creatinine levels. CVP pressures give vital information about hydration status. Maintain accurate fluid intake and output and record daily weights until the patient resumes a regular diet.

Decreased renal perfusion can occur from embolization of an aortic thrombus or plaque to either or both renal arteries. Hypotension, dehydration, prolonged aortic clamping during surgery, or blood loss can lead to kidney ischemia. Irreversible renal failure may occur after surgery, particularly in high-risk people (e.g., patients with diabetes).

◆ Ambulatory Care

Teach the patient and caregiver to gradually increase activities. They should avoid heavy lifting for 6 weeks. Fatigue, poor appetite, and irregular bowel patterns are common.

Teach the patient and caregiver to look for changes in color or warmth of the extremities. They can learn to palpate peripheral pulses to assess changes in pulse quality. Report any redness, swelling, increased pain, drainage from incisions, or fever greater than 100°F (37.8°C) to the HCP.

Sexual problems in male patients are common after aortic surgery. A referral to a urologist and counseling may be useful if erectile dysfunction occurs.

◆ Evaluation

Expected outcomes are that the patient who undergoes aortic surgery will have:

- Patent arterial graft with adequate distal perfusion
- Adequate urine output
- No signs of infection

AORTIC DISSECTION

Aortic dissection, often called *"dissecting aneurysm,"* is not a type of aneurysm. Rather, dissection results from the creation of a false lumen between the intima (inner lining) and the media (middle layer) of arterial wall (Figs. 41.5D and 41.8). We classify aortic dissection based on the location of the dissection and duration of onset. *Type A dissection* affects the ascending

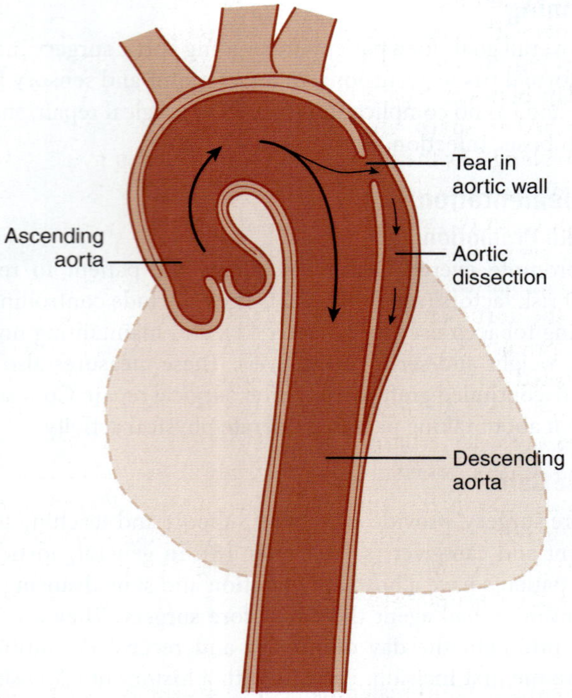

Fig. 41.8 Aortic dissection.

aorta and arch, requiring emergency surgery. *Type B dissection* begins in the descending aorta, allowing for potential conservative management.[12] Dissections are acute (first 14 days), subacute (14 to 90 days), or chronic (greater than 90 days) based on symptom onset.

Etiology and Pathophysiology

Nontraumatic aortic dissection is caused by weakened elastic fibers in the arterial wall. Chronic hypertension hastens this process. In aortic dissection, a tear develops in the inner layer of the aorta. Blood surges through this tear into the middle layer of the aorta, causing the inner and middle layers to separate (dissect). If the blood-filled channel ruptures through the outside aortic wall, aortic dissection is often fatal.

As the heart contracts, each pulsation increases the pressure on the damaged area and worsens the dissection. Extension of the dissection may cut off blood supply to the brain, kidneys, spinal cord, and extremities. The false lumen may remain patent, become thrombosed (clotted), rejoin the true lumen by way of a distal tear, or rupture.

Men have a higher risk for developing aortic dissection than women.[13] Women who develop aortic dissection are older and more likely than men to present with HF, coma, or altered mental status.[13] Hypertension is the most important risk factor for aortic dissection.[12,13] Other risk factors include age, aortic diseases (e.g., aortitis, coarctation, arch hypoplasia), atherosclerosis, blunt trauma, tobacco use, cocaine or methamphetamine use, congenital heart disease (e.g., bicuspid aortic valve), connective tissue disorders (e.g., Marfan's syndrome), family history, history of heart surgery, and pregnancy.

Clinical Manifestations

About 80% of patients with an acute type A aortic dissection report an abrupt onset of severe anterior chest or back pain. Patients with acute type B aortic dissection are more likely to report pain in their back, abdomen, or legs. Pain location may overlap between type A and B dissections. The pain may be described as "sharp" and "worst ever," or as "tearing," "ripping," or "stabbing." As the dissection progresses, pain may follow the path of the dissection. Older patients are less likely to have an abrupt onset of pain and more likely to have hypotension and vague symptoms. Some patients have a painless aortic dissection, emphasizing the importance of the physical assessment.

If the aortic arch is involved, the patient may have neurologic problems. These include altered level of consciousness, weakened or absent carotid and temporal pulses, dizziness, and syncope. Type A aortic dissection usually disrupts blood flow in the coronary arteries and causes aortic valve insufficiency. When either subclavian artery is involved, the radial, ulnar, and brachial pulse quality and BP readings may be different between the left and right arms. As the dissection progresses down the aorta, the abdominal organs and lower extremities show evidence of decreased tissue perfusion.

Complications

A severe and life-threatening complication of an acute ascending aortic dissection is *cardiac tamponade.* This occurs when blood from the dissection leaks into the pericardial sac.

TABLE 41.6 Interprofessional Care

Aortic Dissection

Diagnostic Assessment
- Health history and physical assessment
- ECG
- Chest x-ray
- CT scan
- Transesophageal echocardiogram
- MRI

Management
- Bed rest
- Pain relief with opioids
- Blood transfusion (if needed)

Drug Therapy (see Table 36.6)
- IV β-blockers
- IV calcium channel blockers
- ACE inhibitors

Surgical Therapy
- Endovascular aortic dissection repair
- Open surgical repair

Manifestations of tamponade include hypotension, narrowed pulse pressure, jugular venous distention, muffled heart sounds, and pulsus paradoxus (see Chapter 40).

An aorta weakened by dissection may rupture. Hemorrhage may occur into the mediastinal, pleural, or abdominal cavities. Aortic rupture typically results in exsanguination and death.

Aortic dissection can lead to occlusion of the blood supply to vital organs. Spinal cord ischemia leads to weakness and decreased sensation. Rarely, lower extremity paralysis may occur. Renal ischemia can lead to renal failure. Abdominal (mesenteric) ischemia can occur and cause abdominal pain, decreased bowel sounds, altered bowel function, and bowel necrosis.

Diagnostic Studies

Diagnostic studies to detect aortic dissection are similar to those for suspected aneurysms (Table 41.6). An ECG can help rule out cardiac ischemia. A chest x-ray may show a widening of the mediastinum and pleural effusion. MRI, 3D CT scanning, and transesophageal echocardiography (TEE) are equally reliable for diagnosing acute aortic dissection. A CT scan or MRI can give detailed information on the severity of the dissection and related complications (e.g., pericardial effusions, carotid dissection). TEE is preferred in very unstable patients or those with contraindications to CT or MRI (e.g., those with metal implants, allergies to contrast material).

Interprofessional Care

Patients with acute aortic dissection are managed in the ICU. The initial goals of therapy for acute aortic dissection without complications are heart rate (HR) and BP control and pain management. Lowering HR and BP reduces aortic wall stress by decreasing SBP and myocardial contractility (Table 41.6). This limits extension of the dissection. An IV β-blocker (e.g., esmolol) is titrated to a target HR under 60 beats/min or SBP between 100 and 110 mm Hg. A calcium channel blocker (e.g., diltiazem) can be used to lower HR if a β-blocker is contraindicated. Morphine decreases sympathetic nervous system stimulation and relieves pain. Supportive treatment for an acute aortic dissection is a bridge to surgery.

Conservative Therapy

The patient with an acute or chronic Type B aortic dissection without complications can be treated conservatively. Treatment includes pain relief, HR and BP control, and CVD risk factor modification with close surveillance imaging with CT or MRI.

Endovascular Dissection Repair

Endovascular repair is a treatment option for acute type B aortic dissections with complications (e.g., hemodynamic instability) and chronic type B aortic dissection with complications (e.g., peripheral ischemia).[14] Thoracic endovascular aortic repair (TEVAR) is similar to EVAR. Fewer postsurgical complications occur with TEVAR. However, TEVAR does not prevent the risk for renal failure, paraplegia, or stroke.[14] If a lumbar spinal drain is inserted to help decrease or prevent neurologic complications, strict aseptic technique is used to prevent infection.

Surgical Therapy

An acute type A aortic dissection is a surgical emergency. Mortality rate is 50% within 48 hours of symptom onset. Otherwise, surgery is indicated when conservative therapy is ineffective or when complications (e.g., HF) occur. Open surgical repair is recommended for patients with a chronic dissection who have a connective tissue disorder or an aneurysm greater than 5.5 cm.[12,14]

The aorta is fragile after dissection. Surgery is delayed, when possible, to allow time for edema to decrease and to permit blood clotting in the false lumen. Surgery involves resection of the aortic segment with the intimal tear and replacement with a synthetic graft. Even with prompt surgical intervention, the in-hospital mortality is high.[14] Causes of death include aortic rupture, mesenteric ischemia, MI, sepsis, stroke, and multiorgan failure.

❖ NURSING MANAGEMENT: AORTIC DISSECTION

Preoperatively, keep the patient in bed in a semi-Fowler's position and maintain a quiet environment. Manage pain and anxiety, giving opioids and sedatives as prescribed. These measures help to keep the HR and SBP at the lowest possible level that maintains vital organ perfusion (typically HR less than 60 beats/min; SBP between 100 and 120 mm Hg).

Titrating IV antihypertensive agents requires careful supervision. Maintain continuous ECG and arterial BP monitoring. Monitor vital signs frequently, sometimes as often as every 2 to 3 minutes, until target HR and BP are reached. Look for changes in peripheral pulses and signs of increasing pain, restlessness, and anxiety.

Postoperative care is similar to that after OAR. In preparation for discharge, focus on patient and caregiver teaching. Help patients understand that they need to take antihypertensive drugs daily for the rest of their lives. β-Blockers are used to control HR and BP and decrease myocardial contractility. ACE inhibitors (e.g., lisinopril) are given if the patient cannot tolerate β-blockers. It is important that patients understand the drug regimen and side effects (e.g., dizziness, depression, fatigue, erectile dysfunction). Tell the patient to discuss any side effects with the HCP before stopping any medication.

Follow up with regularly scheduled MRIs or CTs is essential. The most common cause of death in long-term survivors is aortic rupture from redissection or aneurysm formation. Tell patients that if the pain or other symptoms return, they should activate the emergency response system (ERS) for immediate care.

ACUTE AND CHRONIC VENOUS DISORDERS

PHLEBITIS

Phlebitis is an acute inflammation of the walls of small, cannulated veins. Manifestations include pain, tenderness, warmth, redness, swelling, and a palpable cord. Risk factors are mechanical irritation from an IV catheter, infusion of irritating drugs, and IV catheter location in an area of flexion (e.g., wrist and antecubital area). Avoid IV catheter insertion in these areas whenever possible.

Phlebitis is rarely infectious. It usually resolves quickly after catheter removal. If edema is present, elevate the extremity to promote fluid reabsorption. Apply warm, moist heat and give oral NSAIDs (e.g., ibuprofen) or topical NSAIDs (e.g., diclofenac gel) to relieve pain and inflammation.

VENOUS THROMBOSIS

Venous thrombosis involves the formation of a *thrombus* (blood clot) with vein inflammation. It is the most common disorder of the veins. We classify it as either superficial vein thrombosis or deep vein thrombosis. **Superficial vein thrombosis** is the formation of a thrombus in a superficial vein, usually the greater or lesser saphenous vein. **Deep vein thrombosis (DVT)** involves a thrombus in a deep vein, most often the iliac and/or femoral veins. **Venous thromboembolism (VTE)** is the preferred terminology. It represents the spectrum from DVT to pulmonary embolism (PE) (Table 41.7). Chapter 30 discusses PE.

Superficial vein thrombosis is serious. Nearly 25% of patients with superficial vein thrombosis have a DVT or PE at the time of diagnosis.[15] These patients are at risk for developing recurrent VTE.

Etiology

The 3 key factors (called **Virchow triad**) that cause venous thrombosis are (1) venous stasis, (2) damage of the endothelium (inner lining of the vein), and (3) hypercoagulability (Fig. 41.9). The patient at risk for developing VTE usually has predisposing conditions to these 3 factors (Table 41.8).

Venous Stasis

Normal venous blood flow depends on the action of muscles in the extremities and the function of venous valves, which allow flow in one direction. *Venous stasis* occurs when the valves are dysfunctional or the muscles of the extremities are inactive. Venous stasis occurs most often in people who are obese or pregnant, have chronic HF or atrial fibrillation, have been traveling on long trips without regular exercise, have a prolonged surgical procedure, or are immobile for long periods (e.g., spinal cord injury, fractured hip, limb paralysis).

TABLE 41.7 Comparison of Superficial Vein Thrombosis and Venous Thromboembolism

	Superficial Vein Thrombosis	Venous Thromboembolism (VTE)
Usual location	Typically, superficial leg veins (e.g., varicosities). Sometimes superficial arm veins.	Deep veins of arms (e.g., axillary, subclavian), legs (e.g., femoral), pelvis (e.g., iliac), vena cava, and pulmonary system.
Clinical findings	Tenderness, itchiness, redness, warmth, pain, inflammation, and induration along the course of superficial vein. Vein appears as a palpable cord. Edema rarely occurs.	Tenderness to pressure over involved vein, induration of overlying muscle, venous distention. Edema. May have mild to moderate pain, deep reddish color to area caused by venous congestion. Some have no obvious physical changes in the affected extremity.
Sequelae	If untreated, clot may extend to deeper veins and VTE may occur.	Embolization to lungs (PE) may occur and may result in death. Pulmonary hypertension and post-thrombotic syndrome with or without venous leg ulceration may develop.

Endothelial Damage

Damage to the endothelium may be caused by direct (e.g., surgery, intravascular catheterization, trauma, burns, prior VTE) or indirect (chemotherapy, diabetes, sepsis) injury. Damaged endothelium stimulates platelet activation and starts the coagulation cascade. This predisposes the patient to thrombus development.

Hypercoagulability of Blood

Blood hypercoagulability occurs with many problems. These include severe anemias, polycythemia, cancers (e.g., breast, brain, pancreas, GI tract); nephrotic syndrome; high homocysteine levels; and protein C, protein S, and antithrombin deficiency. A patient with sepsis is predisposed to hypercoagulability because of endotoxins released from bacteria. Some drugs (e.g., corticosteroids, estrogens) predispose a patient to thrombus formation.

Women who use tobacco, take estrogen-based oral contraceptives, are postmenopausal on oral hormone therapy, are over 35 years old, and have a family history of VTE have a very high risk for VTE.[15] Women who take oral contraceptives and use tobacco double their risk. Smoking causes hypercoagulability by increasing plasma fibrinogen and homocysteine levels and activating the intrinsic coagulation pathway.

Pathophysiology

Localized platelet aggregation and fibrin entrap RBCs, WBCs, and more platelets to form a thrombus. A frequent site of thrombus formation is the valve cusp of a vein, where venous stasis occurs. As a thrombus enlarges, increased numbers of blood cells and fibrin collect behind it. This makes a larger clot with a "tail" that eventually blocks the lumen of the vein.

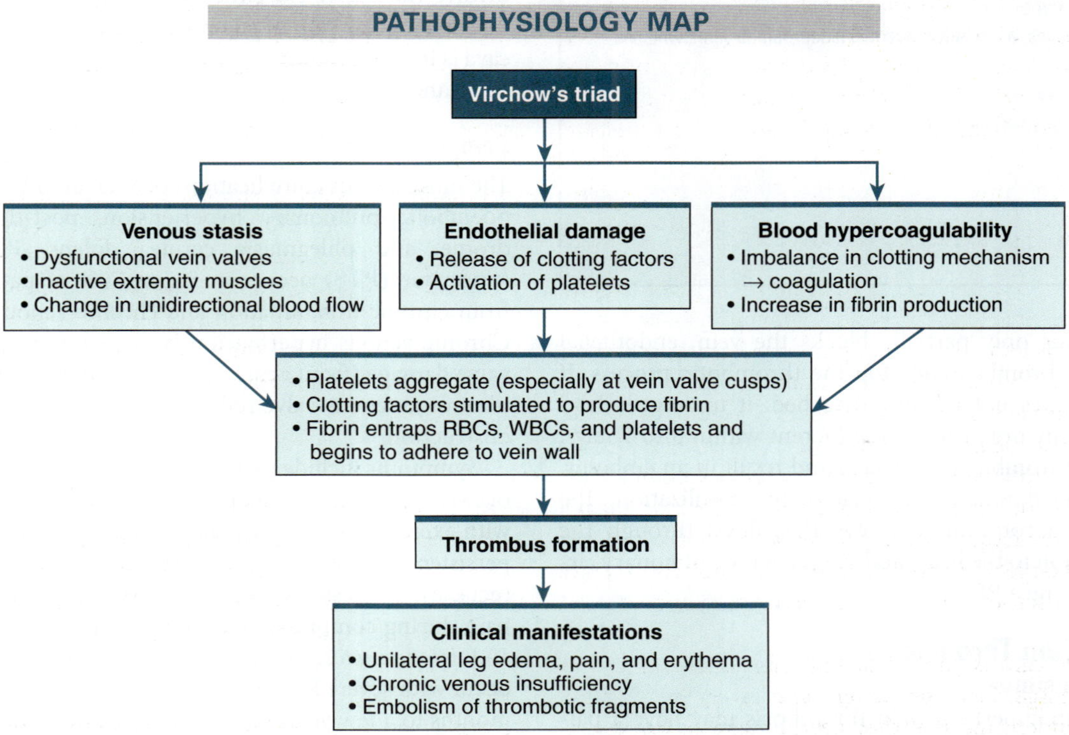

Fig. 41.9 Pathophysiology of VTE.

TABLE 41.8 Risk Factors for VTE

Endothelial Damage
- Abdominal and pelvic surgery (e.g., gynecologic, urologic surgery)
- Caustic or hypertonic IV drugs
- Pelvis, hip, or leg fractures
- History of VTE
- Indwelling, peripherally inserted central vein catheter
- IV drug use
- Trauma

Venous Stasis
- Advanced age
- Atrial fibrillation
- Bed rest
- Chronic heart failure
- Fractured leg or hip
- Long trips without adequate exercise
- Obesity
- Orthopedic surgery (especially hip or lower extremity)
- Pregnancy and postpartum period
- Prolonged immobility
- Spinal cord injury or limb paralysis
- Stroke
- Varicose veins

Hypercoagulability of Blood
- Antiphospholipid antibody syndrome
- Antithrombin III deficiency
- Cancer (especially breast, brain, hepatic, pancreatic, GI)
- Dehydration or malnutrition
- Elevated (clotting) factor VIII or lipoprotein (a)
- Erythropoiesis-stimulating drugs (e.g., epoetin alfa [Procrit])
- High altitudes
- Hormone therapy
- High homocysteine levels
- Nephrotic syndrome
- Oral contraceptives, especially in women older than 35 years who use tobacco
- Polycythemia vera
- Pregnancy and postpartum period
- Protein C deficiency
- Protein S deficiency
- Sepsis
- Severe anemias
- Tobacco use

If a thrombus only partially blocks the vein, endothelial cells cover the thrombus and stop the thrombotic process. If the thrombus does not become detached, it undergoes lysis or becomes firmly organized and adherent within 5 to 7 days. The organized thrombus may detach and result in an embolus. Turbulent blood flow is a major factor in embolization. The thrombus can become an embolus that flows through the venous circulation to the heart and lodges in the pulmonary circulation, becoming a PE.

Superficial Vein Thrombosis

Clinical Manifestations

The patient with superficial vein thrombosis may have a palpable, firm, subcutaneous cordlike vein (Table 41.7). The area surrounding the vein may be itchy, painful to the touch, reddened, and warm. A mild temperature elevation and leukocytosis may be present. Extremity edema may occur. Lower extremity superficial vein thrombosis often involves varicose veins.

Risk factors include increased age, pregnancy, obesity, cancer, recent fracture(s), estrogen therapy, recent sclerotherapy (e.g., treatment for varicose veins), recent surgery or long-distance travel, hypercoagulability, and a history of chronic venous insufficiency (CVI), superficial vein thrombosis, or VTE. It can occur in people with endothelial problems (e.g., Buerger disease).

Interprofessional Care

Ultrasound can confirm the diagnosis (clot 5 cm or larger) and rule out clot extension to a deep vein. If the superficial vein thrombosis affects a very short vein segment (less than 5 cm) and is not near the saphenofemoral junction, anticoagulants may not be needed. Oral NSAIDs can ease symptoms. Other interventions include telling the patient to wear graduated compression stockings or bandages, apply warm compresses, elevate the affected limb above the level of the heart, apply topical NSAIDS, and perform mild exercise, such as walking.

Venous Thromboembolism

Clinical Manifestations

The patient with lower extremity VTE may have unilateral leg edema, pain, tenderness with palpation, dilated superficial veins, a sense of fullness in the thigh or the calf, paresthesias, warm skin, redness, or a systemic temperature greater than 100.4°F (38°C) (Table 41.7). If the inferior vena cava is involved, both legs may be edematous and cyanotic. About 10% of VTEs involve the upper extremity veins. They may extend into the internal jugular vein or superior vena cava. If the superior vena cava is involved, similar symptoms may occur in the arms, neck, back, and face.

Complications

The most serious complications of VTE are PE, chronic thromboembolic pulmonary hypertension, post-thrombotic syndrome, and phlegmasia cerulea dolens. **Post-thrombotic syndrome (PTS)** occurs in 8% to 70% of patients. It results from chronic inflammation and chronic venous hypertension. Chronic venous hypertension is caused by vein wall and vein valve damage (from acute inflammation and thrombus reorganization), venous valve reflux, and persistent venous (outflow) obstruction.

Symptoms include pain, aching, fatigue, heaviness, sensation of swelling, cramps, pruritus, tingling, paresthesia, bursting pain with exercise, and venous claudication. Manifestations include persistent edema, spider veins (telangiectasia), venous dilation (ectasia), redness, cyanosis, increased pigmentation, eczema, pain during compression, atrophie blanche (white scar tissue), and *lipodermatosclerosis* (Fig. 41.10). Venous ulceration can occur with severe PTS. Signs of PTS typically begin within a few months to a few years of a VTE. Risk factors include persistent leg symptoms 1 month after VTE, proximal VTE location (e.g.,

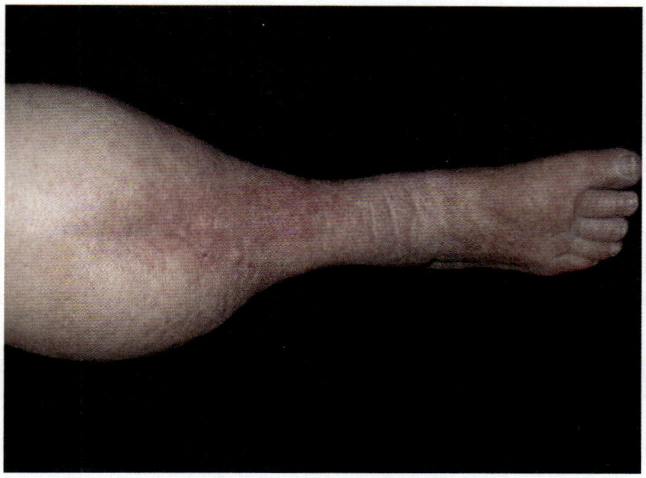

Fig. 41.10 Lipodermatosclerosis. The leg becomes tapered like an "inverted bottle." Skin becomes scarred and leathery with brown discoloration and changes in pigmentation. (From Larocca C, Phillips TJ, et al: *Treatment of skin disease: comprehensive therapeutic strategies*, St Louis, 2018, Elsevier.)

near the iliofemoral junction), extensive VTE, recurrent VTE on the same side, asymptomatic VTE, and residual thrombus. Other factors include obesity, older age, poor INR control, daily tobacco use before pregnancy, increased D-dimer levels, elevated inflammatory markers, and varicose veins.

Phlegmasia cerulea dolens (swollen, blue, painful leg) is a rare complication of severe lower extremity VTE. It involves the major leg veins, causing near-total occlusion of venous outflow. Patients typically have sudden, massive swelling; deep pain; and intense cyanosis of the extremity. If untreated, the venous obstruction causes arterial occlusion and gangrene, requiring amputation.

Diagnostic Studies

Diagnosis of an initial VTE is based on the assessment combined with D-dimer testing and/or ultrasound. Table 41.9 presents the diagnostic studies used to determine the site or location and extent of a VTE.

Interprofessional Care

Prevention. All health care team members have important roles in VTE prevention. VTE prevention is a core measure of high-quality health care in high-risk hospitalized patients developed by The Joint Commission (TJC) and the National Quality Forum. TJC recommends that hospitals have a policy that addresses VTE prevention on admission of all adult patients. In patients at risk for VTE, interventions used are based on bleeding and thrombosis risk, medical history, current drugs, medical diagnoses, scheduled procedures, and patient preferences.

Early and aggressive mobilization is the easiest and most cost-effective method to decrease VTE risk. Patients on bed rest should change position at least every 2 hours. Unless contraindicated, teach patients to flex and extend their feet, knees, and hips at least every 2 to 4 hours while awake. Patients who are able should be out of bed in a chair for meals and walk at least 4 to 6 times per day. Teach the patient and caregiver about the importance of these measures. Early and frequent ambulation is sufficient prophylaxis for patients at very low risk for VTE who had minor surgical procedures. Anticoagulation and mechanical prophylaxis are not recommended for acutely ill medical patients at low risk for VTE.

Graduated compression stockings (e.g., thromboembolic deterrent [TED] hose) are a part of VTE prevention in hospitalized patients. VTE prevention is enhanced if the stockings are used along with anticoagulation. Proper stocking use means any toe hole is under the toes, the heel patch is over the heel, a thigh gusset is on the inner thigh (thigh length only), and there are no wrinkles. The stockings should not be rolled down, cut, or otherwise altered. Stockings that are not fitted and worn correctly impede venous return. This can cause arterial ischemia, edema, skin breakdown, and VTE. Stockings are not recommended if the patient already has a VTE.[15]

TABLE 41.9 Diagnostic Studies

VTE

Study	Description and Abnormal Findings
Blood Laboratory Studies	
ACT, aPTT, INR, bleeding time, Hgb, Hct, platelet count	Altered if patient has underlying blood dyscrasia (e.g., increased Hgb and Hct in patient with polycythemia).
D-dimer	Fragment of fibrin formed from fibrin degradation and clot lysis. High results suggest VTE. *Normal results:* <250 ng/mL (<250 mcg/L)
Fibrin monomer complex	Forms when concentration of thrombin exceeds that of antithrombin. Presence is evidence of thrombus formation and suggests VTE. *Normal results:* <6.1 mg/L
Noninvasive Venous Studies	
Duplex ultrasound	Combination of compression ultrasound with spectral and color flow Doppler. Veins examined for compressibility and intraluminal filling defects to help determine location and extent of thrombus (most widely used test to diagnose VTE).
Venous compression ultrasound	Evaluation of deep femoral, popliteal, and posterior tibial veins *Normal finding:* Veins collapse with application of external pressure. *Abnormal finding:* Veins do not collapse with application of external pressure. Failure to collapse suggests a thrombus.
Invasive Venous Studies	
Computed tomography venography (CTV)	Uses spiral CT to evaluate veins in the pelvis, thighs, and calves after injection of contrast material. May be done simultaneously with CT angiography of pulmonary vessels for patients being evaluated for VTE.
Contrast venography (phlebogram)	X-ray determination of location and extent of clot using contrast media to outline filling defects. Identifies the presence of collateral circulation. Once the gold standard, but now rarely done.
Magnetic resonance venography	Uses MRI with specialized software to evaluate blood flow through veins. Can be done with or without contrast. Highly accurate for pelvic and proximal veins. Less accurate for calf veins. Can distinguish acute and chronic thrombus.

ACT, Activated clotting time.

Intermittent pneumatic compression devices (IPCs) use inflatable sleeves or boots to compress the calf and thigh and/or foot and ankle to improve venous return. The sleeves apply external pressure through an electric pump. IPCs may be used with graduated compression stockings. Ensure correct fit of IPCs by accurately measuring the extremities. IPCs will not be effective if they are not applied correctly, if the fit is incorrect, or if the patient does not wear the device continuously while at rest. The IPCs can be removed for bathing, skin assessment, and ambulation. IPCs are not worn when a patient has an active VTE because of the risk for PE.

Drug therapy. Anticoagulants are used routinely for VTE prevention and treatment. The regimen depends on the patient's VTE risk. The goal of anticoagulant therapy for VTE prevention is to prevent clot formation. The goals for treatment of a confirmed VTE are to prevent new clot development, spread of the clot, and embolization.

The 3 major classes of anticoagulants available are (1) vitamin K antagonists (VKAs), (2) thrombin inhibitors (both indirect and direct), and (3) factor Xa inhibitors (Table 41.10).[15,16] Anticoagulant therapy does not dissolve the clot. Clot lysis

TABLE 41.10 Drug Therapy
Anticoagulant Therapy

Drug	Route of Administration	Considerations
Thrombin Inhibitors: Indirect		
Low-Molecular-Weight Heparin (LMWH)		
dalteparin (Fragmin) enoxaparin (Lovenox)	Subcutaneous	Routine coagulation tests typically not needed. Monitor CBC count at regular intervals. Do not expel air bubble from prefilled syringe. If giving subcutaneously, inject deep into subcutaneous tissue (preferably into the abdominal fatty tissue or above the iliac crest), inserting the entire length of the needle. Hold skinfold during injection but release before removing needle. Do not aspirate. Do not inject IM. Do not rub site after injection. Rotate sites. Reduced dosage needed in patients with renal problems. Use extreme caution in patients with a history of HIT. *Antidote:* Protamine reverses the effects of LMWH.
Unfractionated Heparin (UH)		
heparin sodium	Continuous IV Intermittent IV Subcutaneous	Therapeutic effects measured at regular intervals by the aPTT or ACT. Monitor CBC counts at regular intervals and titrate according to parameters. Follow administration guidelines for LMWH if giving subcutaneously. IV given as an adjunct for existing blood clots. SQ given prophylactically to prevent the development of clots. *Antidote:* Protamine reverses the effect of UH.
Factor Xa Inhibitors		
apixaban (Eliquis) betrixaban (Bevyxxa) edoxaban (Savaysa) fondaparinux (Arixtra) rivaroxaban (Xarelto)	PO PO PO Subcutaneous PO	All approved for VTE prevention and treatment. Routine coagulation tests not needed. Monitor CBC and creatinine at regular intervals. May cause thrombocytopenia. Do not expel air bubble before giving fondaparinux. Follow administration guidelines as described for subcutaneous LMWHs. *Antidote:* Andexanet alfa (Andexxa) reverses the effects of all Factor Xa inhibitors.
Thrombin Inhibitors: Direct		
Hirudin Derivatives		
bivalirudin (Angiomax) desirudin (Iprivask)	IV Subcutaneous	Therapeutic effect measured by ACT or aPTT. Used in patients with HIT who need anticoagulation. *Antidote:* None.
Synthetic Thrombin Inhibitors		
argatroban (Acova) dabigatran (Pradaxa)	IV PO	Argatroban therapeutic effect measured by aPTT. No routine coagulation tests needed for dabigatran. Used in patients at risk for or with HIT, for VTE prevention in joint replacement surgery, stroke prevention in nonvalvular atrial fibrillation. *Antidote:* Idarucizumab (Praxbind) reverses the effect of dabigatran only.
Vitamin K Antagonists (VKA)		
warfarin (Coumadin)	PO	INR used to monitor therapeutic levels. Give at the same time each day. Variations of certain genes (e.g., *CYP2CP, VKORC1*) may influence response to drug. *Antidote:* Vitamin K. For VKA-related bleeding, treatment with prothrombin complex concentrate (human) (Kcentra), IV vitamin K and/or fresh frozen plasma is recommended.

ACT, Activated clotting time; *HIT,* heparin-induced thrombocytopenia.

TABLE 41.11 Blood Coagulation Tests

Test and Drugs Monitored	Normal Value	Therapeutic Value
Activated Clotting Time (ACT)	70–120 sec*	>300 sec
• Hirudin derivatives (e.g., bivalirudin [Angiomax])		
• Synthetic thrombin inhibitors (e.g., argatroban [Acova])		
• Unfractionated heparin (e.g., heparin [Hep-Lock])		
Activated Partial Thromboplastin Time (aPTT)	30–40 sec	46–70 sec
• Hirudin derivatives		
• Synthetic thrombin inhibitors		
• Unfractionated heparin		
Anti-Factor Xa		
• Factor Xa inhibitors (e.g., fondaparinux	0 units/mL	0.6–1.0 units/mL
[Arixtra], rivaroxaban [Xarelto])	0 units/mL	0.2
• Low-molecular-weight heparin (e.g., enoxaparin [Lovenox])		1.5 units/mL
International Normalized Ratio (INR)	0.75–1.25	2–3
• Vitamin K antagonists (e.g., warfarin [Coumadin])		

[a]Varies based on type of system and test reagent or activator used.

begins naturally through the body's intrinsic fibrinolytic system (see Chapter 33).

Vitamin K antagonists. The oral anticoagulant for long-term or extended anticoagulation is warfarin, a VKA. Warfarin inhibits activation of the vitamin K–dependent coagulation factors II, VII, IX, and X and the anticoagulant proteins C and S. See the list of clotting factors in Table 33.2. Fig. 33.4 shows the clotting pathways. Warfarin begins to take effect in 48 to 72 hours and achieves maximum effect several days later. Thus, an overlap of a parenteral anticoagulant (e.g., UH or low-molecular-weight heparin [LMWH]) and warfarin typically is required for 5 days. We monitor the level of anticoagulation daily using the INR. The INR is a standardized system of reporting prothrombin time (PT) (Table 41.11).

Take a careful history before starting warfarin. Do not give antiplatelet drugs or NSAIDs with warfarin as these increase bleeding risk.[16] Many other drugs, vitamins, minerals, and herbal supplements interact with warfarin. A diet that varies in vitamin K intake (e.g., green leafy vegetables) can make it hard to achieve and maintain a target INR level. Genetic variants in the genes *VKORC1* and cytochrome P450 2C9 *(CYP2C9)* may influence how some people respond to warfarin. See Table 13.5 and Fig. 13.7.

Thrombin inhibitors. There are 2 major classes of *indirect thrombin inhibitors*: UH and LMWHs. UH (e.g., heparin) affects both the intrinsic and common pathways of blood coagulation by way of the plasma antithrombin. Antithrombin inhibits thrombin-mediated conversion of fibrinogen to fibrin by affecting factors II (prothrombin), IX, X, XI, and XII (see Fig. 33.4).

Heparin can be given subcutaneously for VTE prevention or by continuous IV infusion for VTE treatment. IV heparin use requires frequent monitoring of clotting status by measuring activated partial thromboplastin time (aPTT) (Table 41.11).

One serious side effect of heparin is *heparin-induced thrombocytopenia* (HIT). An immune reaction to heparin causes a severe, sudden decrease in the platelet count along with a paradoxical increase in venous or arterial thrombosis. We diagnose HIT by measuring the presence of heparin antibodies in the blood. Treatment includes immediately stopping heparin therapy. If further anticoagulation is needed, we give a non-heparin anticoagulant (e.g., fondaparinux).[16] Another side effect of long-term heparin therapy is osteoporosis.

LMWHs (e.g., enoxaparin [Lovenox]) are derived from UH. They have more predictable dose responses, longer half-lives, and fewer bleeding complications than UH. LMWHs are less likely to cause HIT and osteoporosis. LMWHs typically do not require ongoing anticoagulant monitoring and dose adjustment. Their antiinflammatory properties may help prevent PTS and venous ulcer development. Protamine reverses the effect of LMWH.

Direct thrombin inhibitors are classified as hirudin derivatives or synthetic thrombin inhibitors. Hirudin is made using recombinant deoxyribonucleic acid (DNA) technology. It binds specifically with thrombin and directly inhibits its function without causing plasma protein and platelet interactions. Hirudin derivatives (e.g., bivalirudin [Angiomax]) are given by continuous IV infusion. Bivalirudin is given to patients with or at risk for HIT having a percutaneous coronary intervention. Anticoagulant activity is monitored using aPTT or activated clotting time (ACT) (Table 41.11). If bleeding occurs, there is no antidote for hirudin derivatives.

Argatroban—a synthetic direct thrombin inhibitor—hinders thrombin. Like bivalirudin, it is an alternative to heparin for the prevention and treatment of HIT and for patients with or at risk for HIT needing percutaneous coronary interventions. The effect of argatroban is not reversible. Its anticoagulant effect is monitored using aPTT or ACT.

Dabigatran (Pradaxa) is an oral direct thrombin inhibitor. It is used for VTE prevention after elective joint replacement, for stroke prevention in nonvalvular atrial fibrillation, and as a treatment for VTE. Dabigatran has 5 major advantages compared to warfarin: rapid onset, no need to monitor anticoagulation, few drug-food interactions, lower risk for major bleeding, and predictable dose response.

Factor Xa inhibitors. *Factor Xa inhibitors* inhibit factor Xa directly or indirectly, producing rapid anticoagulation. These include fondaparinux (Arixtra), rivaroxaban (Xarelto), apixaban (Eliquis), and edoxaban (Savaysa). All are used for both VTE prevention and treatment. Fondaparinux is contraindicated in patients with severe renal disease. Although coagulation monitoring or dose adjustment is not needed, anticoagulant activity can be measured using anti-Xa assays (Table 41.11).

Anticoagulant therapy for VTE prevention. For VTE prevention in the hospitalized medical patient at risk for thrombosis who is not bleeding, low-dose UH, LMWH, or fondaparinux is used. If the patient is at low VTE risk, drug prophylaxis is not needed. Patients with moderate VTE risk (e.g., general, gynecologic, urologic surgery) should receive either UH or LMWH. Patients with high VTE risk (e.g., trauma) should receive UH or LMWH until discharge. Patients having abdominal or pelvic surgery for cancer or major orthopedic surgery (e.g., total knee or hip replacement) should receive VTE prophylaxis.[15]

Anticoagulant therapy for VTE treatment. Patients with confirmed VTE should receive initial treatment with either LMWH, UH, or an oral factor Xa drug. Oral VKA therapy may be an option. A therapeutic INR is maintained between 2.0 and 3.0 if VKA therapy is used. Active treatment of VTE should continue for at least 3 months.

Patients with multiple co-morbidities, complex medical issues, or a very large VTE usually are hospitalized for parenteral UH administration. Depending on the presentation and home situation, patients may be safely managed as outpatients.

Thrombolytic therapy for VTE treatment. Another treatment option for patients with a thrombus is catheter-directed administration of a thrombolytic drug (e.g., urokinase, tPA). It dissolves the clot(s), reduces the acute symptoms, improves deep venous flow, reduces valvular reflux, and may help to decrease the incidence of PTS. Catheter-directed thrombolysis is an option for patients who have a low risk of bleeding and present with an acute, extensive, symptomatic, proximal VTE. Systemic anticoagulation is needed before, during, and after catheter-directed thrombolysis. (Chapter 37 discusses thrombolytic therapy.)

CHECK YOUR PRACTICE

Your 55-year-old female patient is admitted with an extensive VTE in her right leg. She is receiving weight-based IV heparin per agency protocol: 18 units/kg/hr. You receive the following critical laboratory result: aPTT 122 s.

- Describe your next actions.

Surgical and interventional radiology therapies. A few patients with extensive, acute, proximal VTE who are not candidates for catheter-directed thrombolysis and/or interventional radiology therapies (due to bleeding risk) may have surgery.[3,15] Surgical options include open venous thrombectomy and inferior vena cava interruption. *Venous thrombectomy* involves the removal of a clot through a vein incision. Anticoagulant therapy is used after venous thrombectomy.

Vena cava interruption devices (e.g., Greenfield, Vena Tech, TrapEase filters) can be placed percutaneously through the right femoral or right internal jugular veins. The filter device is opened, and the spokes penetrate the vessel walls (Fig. 41.11). The filters act as a "sieve-type" device. They filter clots without interrupting blood flow. Complications after the insertion are rare but include air embolism, improper placement, migration of the filter, and perforation of the vena cava with retroperitoneal bleeding. Over time, clots can clog the filter and completely block the vena cava, requiring filter removal and replacement. A filter device is recommended with acute PE or proximal VTE of the leg in patients with active bleeding or if anticoagulant therapy is contraindicated or ineffective.

Percutaneous endovascular interventional radiology procedures can be used along with catheter-directed thrombolytic therapy, especially for severely symptomatic patients with iliocaval or iliofemoral obstruction. The procedures are like those used in the treatment of lower extremity PAD. The difference is accessing an occluded vein instead of an artery. Options include mechanical thrombectomy, pharmacomechanical devices, post-thrombus extraction, angioplasty, and/or stenting.[15] Anticoagulation therapy is recommended after an iliofemoral interventional radiology procedure. Post procedure nursing care focuses on (1) maintaining catheter systems (if continuous infusions); (2) monitoring for bleeding, embolization, and impaired perfusion; and (3) VTE prevention teaching.

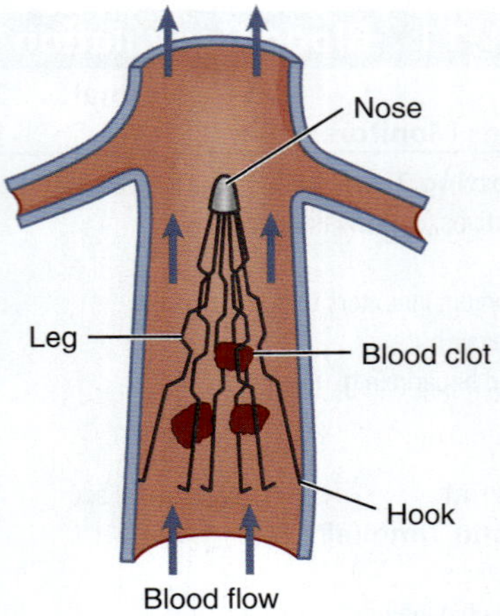

Fig. 41.11 Inferior vena cava interruption technique using Greenfield stainless-steel filter to prevent pulmonary embolism. As blood travels up the vena cava, clots are trapped in the filter.

NURSING MANAGEMENT: VENOUS THROMBOEMBOLISM

Assessment

Table 41.12 presents the subjective and objective data to obtain from a patient with VTE.

Clinical Problems

Clinical problems for the patient with VTE include:

- Inadequate tissue perfusion
- Pain
- Impaired tissue integrity
- Impaired respiratory function
- Musculoskeletal problem

Planning

The overall goals for the patient with VTE include (1) pain relief, (2) decreased edema, (3) increased knowledge of disorder and treatment plan, (4) no skin ulceration, (5) no bleeding complications, and (6) no evidence of PE.

Nursing Implementation

Acute Care

Focus your nursing care for the patient with VTE on preventing thrombi and reducing inflammation (Table 41.13). Review with the patient any drugs, vitamins, minerals, and herbal supplements that may interfere with anticoagulant therapy. Depending on the anticoagulant ordered, monitor INR, aPTT, ACT, anti-factor Xa levels, complete blood count (CBC), creatinine, factor X levels, hemoglobin, hematocrit, platelet levels, and/or liver enzymes. Monitor platelet counts for patients getting UH

TABLE 41.12 NURSING ASSESSMENT

VTE

Subjective Data

Important Health Information (Table 41.8)

Health history: Trauma to vein, intravascular catheter (e.g., peripherally inserted central catheter), varicose veins, pregnancy or recent childbirth, bacteremia, obesity, prolonged bed rest, irregular heartbeat (e.g., atrial fibrillation), COPD, HF, cancer, coagulation disorders and hypercoagulable states, systemic lupus erythematosus, MI, spinal cord injury, stroke, prolonged travel, recent bone fracture, dehydration

Medications: Use of estrogens (including oral contraceptives, hormone therapy), tamoxifen, raloxifene (Evista), corticosteroids, excessive amounts of vitamin E, erythropoiesis-stimulating drugs

Surgery or other treatments: Any recent surgery, especially orthopedic, gynecologic, GI, or urologic. Previous surgery involving veins. Central venous catheter

Functional Health Patterns

Health perception–health management: IV drug abuse, tobacco use, obesity

Activity-exercise: Inactivity

Cognitive-perceptual: Pain in area on palpation or ambulation

Objective Data

Cardiovascular

Distention and warmth of superficial veins in affected area. Edema and cyanosis of extremities, neck, back, and face (if superior vena cava involvement)

General

Fever, anxiety, pain

Skin

Increased size of extremity when compared with other side. Taut, shiny, warm skin, redness, tender to palpation. No physical changes in the affected extremity in some patients

Possible Diagnostic Findings

Leukocytosis, abnormal coagulation, anemia or ↑ hematocrit and RBC count, ↑ D-dimer level, positive venous compression on duplex ultrasound study; positive CT venogram, magnetic resonance venogram, or contrast venogram study

or LMWH to assess for HIT. Direct thrombin inhibitors may need adjustment for patients with renal or liver disease. Check the results of pertinent tests before starting, giving, or changing anticoagulant therapy.

Monitor for and reduce the risk for bleeding with anticoagulant therapy (Table 41.14). Bleeding risk is greater in people receiving LMWH or UH with an active gastroduodenal ulcer, prior bleeding history, low platelet count, hepatic or renal failure, rheumatic disease, cancer, or age greater than 85 years. Patients receiving warfarin with an INR of 5.0 or more have a higher risk for bleeding. In case of anticoagulation above target goals, give reversal agents (e.g., protamine, vitamin K) or make dosage adjustments as prescribed.

Early ambulation does not increase the short-term risk of a PE in patients with VTE. In addition, early ambulation after acute VTE results in a more rapid decrease in edema and limb pain, fewer PTS symptoms, and better quality of life. Teach the patient and caregiver the importance of physical activity. Help the patient ambulate several times a day. For patients with acute VTE with severe edema and limb pain, bed rest with limb elevation may initially be prescribed.

TABLE 41.13 NURSING MANAGEMENT

Caring for the Patient With VTE

- Assess patients for VTE risk and monitor for VTE in at-risk patients (see Table 41.8).
- Teach patients at risk for VTE about preventive measures, including leg exercise and ambulation, using graduated compression stockings and intermittent pneumatic compression devices (IPCs), avoiding nicotine, and taking anticoagulant drugs.
- Measure patients for graduated compression stockings and/or IPCs.
- Assess for the use of medications and substances that may affect the coagulation status.
- Give prescribed oral, subcutaneous, and IV anticoagulants.
- Evaluate the effect of anticoagulant drugs by monitoring appropriate laboratory results and side effects of therapy (Table 41.11).
- Titrate doses of unfractionated heparin (UH), warfarin, and direct thrombin inhibitors based on results of blood studies and agency protocols.
- Assess for complications of VTE, including PE and chronic venous insufficiency.
- Teach the patient and caregiver the manifestations of PE and the need to contact the emergency response system if these occur.
- Provide discharge teaching about use of graduated compression stockings, diet, laboratory testing, and anticoagulant therapy (Table 41.15).
- Supervise the AP:
  - Reposition patients who are on bed rest at least every 2 hr.
  - Remind patients about the need to flex and extend the legs and feet at least every 2 hr while in bed.
  - Help ambulatory patients to walk at least 4 to 6 times daily.
  - Help patients with putting on graduated compression stockings.
  - Apply IPCs.
- Collaborate with the physical therapist:
  - Assess patient's mobility status.
  - Develop exercise/muscle strengthening program as needed.
- Collaborate with the dietitian:
  - Assess patient's diet and nutrition status.
  - Provide diet teaching as needed.

DRUG ALERT

Anticoagulant Therapy

- Observe closely for any signs of bleeding: hypotension, tachycardia, hematuria, melena, hematemesis, petechiae, bruising, oozing or visible bleeding from trauma site or surgical incision.
- Tell patients to report bleeding: black or bloody stools, bleeding gums, bloody urine or sputum, coffee-ground or bloody vomit, excessive bruising, nosebleeds, excessive menstrual bleeding.
- Assess for mental status changes, especially in the older patient, since this may indicate cerebral bleeding.
- Tell patients to avoid taking aspirin, NSAIDs, fish oil supplements, garlic supplements, ginkgo biloba, and certain antibiotics (e.g., sulfamethoxazole and trimethoprim [Bactrim]).

◆ Ambulatory Care

Focus discharge teaching on modifying VTE risk factors, monitoring laboratory values, diet and drug instructions, and

TABLE 41.14 NURSING MANAGEMENT

Patient Receiving Anticoagulants

Assessment

- Monitor vital signs as indicated.
- Examine urine and stool for overt and occult signs of blood.
- Inspect skin often, especially under any splinting devices.
- Evaluate platelet count for signs of heparin-induced thrombocytopenia.
- Evaluate appropriate laboratory coagulation tests for target therapeutic levels.
- Evaluate lower extremity for bruising or hematoma development if intermittent pneumatic compression device used.
- Perform assessments frequently for signs and symptoms of bleeding (e.g., hypotension, tachycardia) or clotting.
- Notify the HCP of any abnormalities in assessments, vital signs, or laboratory values.

Injections

- Avoid IM injections.
- Minimize venipunctures.
- Use small-gauge needles for venipunctures, unless therapy requires a larger gauge.
- Apply manual pressure for at least 10 min (or longer if needed) on venipuncture sites.

Patient Care

- Avoid restrictive clothing.
- Humidify any supplemental O_2.
- Apply moisturizing lotion to skin.
- Use electric razors, not straight razors.
- Perform physical care in a gentle manner.
- Tell patient not to forcefully blow nose.
- Avoid removing or disrupting established clots.
- Use soft toothbrushes or foam swabs for oral care.
- Reposition the patient carefully at regular intervals.
- Limit tape application. Use paper tape as appropriate.
- Give stool softeners to avoid hard stools and straining.
- Use support pads, mattresses, bed cradles, and therapeutic beds as indicated.
- Apply graduated compression stockings or intermittent pneumatic compression devices (if ordered) with attention to proper size, application, and use.
- Perform risk for fall and skin breakdown assessments per agency policy and implement safety and preventive measures as needed.

guidelines for follow-up. Recommend the patient stop smoking and avoid all nicotine products. Teach the patient to avoid constrictive clothing. Tell women with a history of VTE to stop oral contraceptives or hormone therapy. Teach patients to limit standing or sitting in a motionless, leg-dependent position.

When traveling long distances, tell patients to frequently exercise the calf muscles, take short walks, and maintain hydration with nonalcoholic, noncaffeinated beverages. For those at high risk for VTE who are planning a long trip, recommend properly fitted, knee-high graduated compression stockings during travel to decrease edema and VTE risk. Aspirin or anticoagulant use is not suggested for long-distance travelers. Teach the patient and caregiver to contact ERS for signs and symptoms of PE, such as sudden onset of dyspnea, tachypnea, and pleuritic chest pain.

Review drug dosage, actions, and side effects, the need for routine blood tests, and what symptoms need immediate medical

TABLE 41.15 PATIENT & CAREGIVER TEACHING

Anticoagulant Therapy

Include the following information in the teaching plan for a patient receiving anticoagulant therapy and the patient's caregiver:

1. Give reasons for and action of anticoagulant drug and how long therapy will last.
2. Take drug at the same time each day (preferably in afternoon or evening).
3. Depending on drug prescribed, obtain blood tests to assess therapeutic effect and whether change in dosage is needed.
4. Contact emergency response system immediately for any of the following adverse side effects of drug therapy:
   - Blood in urine or stool; or black, tarry stools
   - Vomiting blood, coffee-grounds emesis
   - Unusual bleeding from gums, skin, or nose, or heavy menstrual bleeding
   - Severe headaches or stomach pain
   - Chest pain, shortness of breath, palpitations (heart racing)
   - Weakness, dizziness, mental status changes
   - Cold, blue, or painful feet
5. Avoid activities with a high risk for injury that may cause bleeding (e.g., vigorous brushing of teeth, contact sports, rollerblading, use of straight razor).
6. Avoid all aspirin-containing drugs and NSAIDs.
7. Limit alcohol intake to small to moderate amounts (12 oz beer, 4 oz wine, 1 oz hard liquor/day).
8. Wear a Medic Alert device saying the anticoagulant drug being taken.
9. If taking warfarin (Coumadin), avoid frequent or dramatic changes in eating foods high in vitamin K (e.g., broccoli, spinach, kale, greens). Do not take supplemental vitamin K.
10. Consult with HCP before beginning or stopping any drug, vitamin, mineral, or dietary or herbal supplement.
11. Inform all HCPs, including dentist, of anticoagulant therapy.
12. Correct dosing is essential. Provide supervision if patient has confusion or cognitive problems.
13. Implement safety precautions to prevent falls (e.g., avoid use of throw rugs).
14. Apply pressure for 10 to 15 min if bleeding occurs (e.g., nosebleed).

attention (Table 41.15). Devices are available for home monitoring of INR. Teach patients taking LMWH or fondaparinux and their caregivers how to give the drug subcutaneously. A well-balanced diet is important. Teach patients taking warfarin to follow a consistent diet of foods containing vitamin K. They should avoid any supplements containing vitamin K (e.g., vitamins, green tea). Tell the patient to avoid excess amounts of vitamin E and alcohol. Encourage proper hydration to prevent hypercoagulability of the blood, which may occur with dehydration.

The overweight patient needs implement a diet plan and increase physical activity to achieve and maintain desired weight. Exercise may help patients with VTE and PTS and improves the patient's quality of life. Help the patient develop an exercise program with an emphasis on leg strength training and aerobic activity.

Graduated compression stockings reduce swelling in patients with a proximal VTE.[15] Alternatively, IPCs may be used for patients with significant edema and moderate to severe PTS.

The long-term use of graduated compression stockings may not prevent PTS development.

◆ Evaluation

The expected outcomes are that the patient with VTE will have:

- Minimal to no pain
- Intact skin
- Increased knowledge of disorder and treatment plan
- No signs of hemorrhage or occult bleeding

VARICOSE VEINS

Varicose veins, or *varicosities,* are dilated (3 mm or larger in diameter), tortuous superficial veins. They are often found in the saphenous vein system. Varicosities may be small and harmless or large and bulging. *Primary varicose veins* (idiopathic) due to a weakness of the vein walls are more common in women. *Secondary varicose veins* result from direct injury, a previous VTE, or excessive vein distention. Secondary varicose veins may occur in the esophagus (esophageal varices), vulva, spermatic cords (varicoceles), and anorectal area (hemorrhoids), and as abnormal arteriovenous (AV) connections.

Congenital varicose veins result from chromosomal defects that cause abnormal development of the venous system. *Reticular veins* are smaller varicose veins that appear flat, less tortuous, and blue-green in color. *Telangiectasias* (often called spider veins) are small visible vessels (generally less than 1 mm in diameter) that appear bluish black, purple, or red.

Etiology and Pathophysiology

Superficial veins in the lower extremities become dilated and tortuous in response to backward (retrograde) blood flow and increased venous pressure. Risk factors include family history of chronic venous disease, weak vein structure, female gender, tobacco use, increasing age, obesity, multiparity, history of VTE, venous obstruction resulting from extrinsic pressure by tumors, thrombophilia, phlebitis, previous leg injury, and occupations that require prolonged standing or sitting.

In primary varicose veins, weak vein walls allow the vein valve ring to enlarge, so the leaflets no longer fit together properly (incompetent). Incompetent vein valves allow backward blood flow, particularly when the patient is standing. This results in increased venous pressure and further venous distention. High pressure in the superficial veins can be caused by vein valve dysfunction in the deep veins or perforator veins (veins that perforate the deep fascia of muscles to connect the superficial veins to the deep veins).

Clinical Manifestations and Complications

Discomfort from varicose veins varies among people. It tends to be worse after episodes of superficial vein thrombosis. Symptoms affect women more often than men. The most common symptoms include a heavy, achy feeling or pain after prolonged standing or sitting. Walking or limb elevation relieves pain. Some patients feel pressure or an itchy, burning, tingling, throbbing, or cramp-like leg sensation. Swelling, restless or tired legs, fatigue, and nocturnal leg cramps may occur.

Superficial venous thrombosis is the most frequent complication of varicose veins. It may occur spontaneously or after trauma, surgery, or pregnancy. Rare complications include rupture of the varicose veins resulting in external bleeding and skin ulcerations.

Diagnostic Studies and Interprofessional Care

Superficial varicose veins often can be diagnosed by physical assessment. Duplex ultrasound imaging is the gold standard to evaluate venous anatomy, valvular competence, and venous obstruction.[17] Conservative treatment involves rest with limb elevation; graduated compression stockings; leg strengthening exercise, such as walking; and weight loss, if indicated.

Drug Therapy

Venoactive drugs work by stimulating release of chemicals within the vein walls to strengthen the circulation and reduce inflammation and edema. Several natural and synthetic venoactive agents have been used to treat varicose veins and advanced chronic venous disease. These include micronized purified flavonoid fraction, rutosides (e.g., horse chestnut seed extract [*Aesculus hippocastanum*]), proanthocyanidins (from grapes and apples), and *Ruscus* (butcher's broom).[16]

Therapeutic benefits of venoactive drugs include pain relief, edema reduction, and decreased leg cramping and restless legs. These drugs are widely used in Europe. They are not approved by the FDA. However, many are available over the counter as diet or herbal supplements.

DRUG ALERT

***Horse Chestnut Seed Extract* (Aesculus hippocastanum)**

- May interact with lithium and antidiabetic, antiplatelet, and anticoagulant drugs.
- Should not be taken by persons with liver or kidney disease or with a latex allergy.

Interventional and Surgical Therapies

Sclerotherapy involves the direct IV injection of a liquid or foam sclerosing substance (e.g., hypertonic saline, polidocanol, glycerin) that chemically ablates (destroys) the treated veins. Sclerotherapy can be used on telangiectasias, perforator veins, reticular veins, smaller varicose veins, and venous malformations (Fig. 41.12). This procedure is done in an office setting and causes minimal discomfort.

The most common complications of sclerotherapy are residual pigmentation, matting (new telangiectasias develop in the area), thrombophlebitis, and ulcers.[17] After injection, a graduated compression stocking or bandage is worn. Patients should not travel long distances during the first week after sclerotherapy to minimize the risk for a VTE.

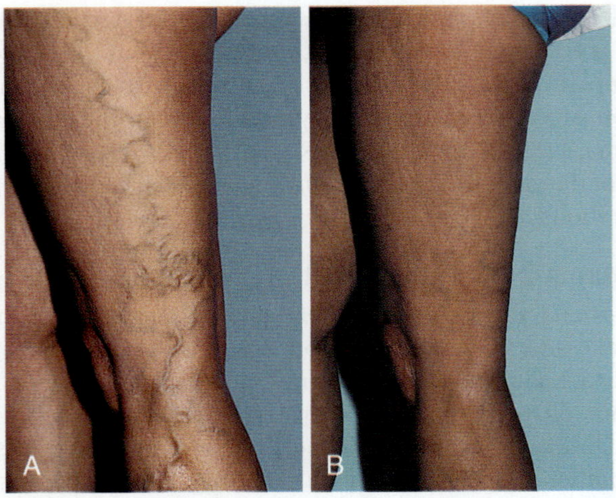

Fig. 41.12 (A) Lateral aspect of varicose veins before treatment. (B) Lateral aspect of varicose veins 2 years after initial treatment with sclerotherapy. (From Goldman MP, Guex JJ, Weiss RA: *Sclerotherapy: treatment of varicose and telangiectatic leg veins,* ed 5, Philadelphia, 2011, Mosby.)

Other noninvasive options include transcutaneous laser therapy for telangiectasias and high-intensity pulsed-light therapy for reticular veins. Transcutaneous laser or light therapy is used for patients in whom sclerotherapy is contraindicated or has been ineffective. Vascular lasers work by heating the hemoglobin in the vessels, resulting in vessel sclerosis. Complications of these therapies include pain, blistering, hyperpigmentation, and superficial erosions.

A minimally invasive treatment option for saphenous vein reflux is endovenous ablation using thermal energy from radiofrequency or laser therapy. The HCP inserts a catheter into the vein to heat the vein wall, which then causes the vein to collapse. Complications include bruising, skin burns, hyperpigmentation, infection, paresthesia, superficial or deep vein thrombosis, and PE. Graduated compression stockings or bandages are worn afterwards. Endovenous thermal ablation may be done in combination with surgical ligation or phlebectomy.

Surgical intervention is needed for recurrent superficial venous thrombosis or when symptoms cannot be controlled with other therapy. The traditional surgical intervention involves ligation of the entire vein (usually the greater saphenous vein) and removal of its incompetent branches. An alternative but time-consuming technique is *ambulatory phlebectomy*. This involves pulling the varicosity through a "stab" incision followed by excision of the vein. *Transilluminated powered phlebectomy* involves the use of a tissue resector to destroy clusters of varicosities and removes the pieces via aspiration. Complications include bleeding, bruising, and infection.

❖ NURSING MANAGEMENT: VARICOSE VEINS

Prevention is a key factor related to varicose veins. Tell the patient to avoid sitting or standing for long periods, maintain ideal body weight, take precautions against injury to the extremities, avoid wearing constrictive clothing, and walk daily.

After vein ligation surgery, encourage the patient to deep breathe, which promotes venous return. Check the extremities regularly for color, movement, sensation, temperature, edema, and quality of pedal pulses. Some bruising and discoloration are normal. Elevate the legs 15 degrees to limit edema. Remove graduated compression stockings or bandages every 8 hours for short periods and then reapply them.

Long-term management is directed toward improving circulation and appearance, relieving discomfort, and avoiding complications. Varicosities can recur in other veins after surgery. Teach the patient the proper use and care of custom-fitted graduated compression stockings. The patient should apply stockings in bed before rising in the morning.

Emphasize the importance of periodic positioning of the legs above the heart. The overweight patient may need help with weight loss. The patient with a job that requires long periods of standing or sitting needs to frequently flex and extend the hips, legs, and ankles and change positions.

CHRONIC VENOUS INSUFFICIENCY AND VENOUS LEG ULCERS

Chronic venous insufficiency (CVI) describes abnormalities of the venous system that result in advanced signs and symptoms, such as edema, skin changes, and/or venous leg ulcers.[17] CVI can lead to *venous leg ulcers* (also called *venous stasis ulcers* or *varicose ulcers*). Although CVI and venous leg ulcers are not life-threatening diseases, they are painful, slow to heal, debilitating, and costly conditions that adversely affect patients' quality of life. They are a common problem in older adults.

Etiology and Pathophysiology

Both long-standing primary varicose veins and PTS can progress to CVI. *Ambulatory venous hypertension* causes serous fluid and RBCs to leak from the capillaries and venules into the tissue. This causes edema and chronic inflammatory changes. Enzymes in the tissue eventually break down RBCs. This releases *hemosiderin,* which causes a brownish skin discoloration. Over time, fibrous tissue replaces the skin and subcutaneous tissue around the ankle. This results in thick, hardened, contracted skin. Although the causes of CVI are known, the exact pathophysiology of venous leg ulcers is unknown.

Clinical Manifestations and Complications

In patients with CVI, the skin of the lower leg is leathery, with a characteristic brownish or "brawny" appearance from the hemosiderin deposition. Edema usually has been persistent for a prolonged period. Eczema with itching and scratching is often present (see Table 41.1).

Venous ulcers classically occur above the medial malleolus (Fig. 41.13). The ulcer is often quite painful, particularly when edema or infection is present. Pain may be worse when the leg is in a dependent position. If the venous ulcer is untreated, the wound becomes wider and deeper, increasing the risk for infection.

Interprofessional and Nursing Care

Compression is essential for venous ulcer healing and preventing venous ulcer recurrence. A variety of options are available for compression therapy. These include custom-fitted graduated compression stockings, elastic tubular support bandages, a Velcro wrap (CircAid), IPCs, and multilayer (3 or 4) bandage systems (e.g., Profore). Evaluate the patient when choosing a compression method. Before starting compression therapy, assess the arterial status to make sure that PAD is not present. An ABI of 0.4 or less suggests severe PAD, and the patient should not have any type of compression therapy.[3] Show how to correctly apply the compression therapy and have the patient "show back" the skill. Stockings should be worn daily to prevent recurrent leg ulcers. Tell the patient to replace stockings every 4 to 6 months.

Discuss activity guidelines and proper limb positioning. Tell patients with CVI to avoid standing or sitting for long periods, which decreases blood return from the lower extremities. Teach patients to frequently elevate their legs above the level of the heart to reduce edema. Encourage patients to begin a daily walking program once an ulcer heals. Tell the patient and caregiver to avoid trauma to the limbs. Teach proper foot and leg care to avoid more skin trauma.

Moist environment dressings are the basis of wound care. A variety of dressings are available. These include transparent film dressings, hydrocolloids, hydrogels, foams, alginates, gauze, and combination dressings. Dressing decisions should be based on wound characteristics, cost, best evidence, and clinician judgment. Chapter 12 and Table 12.14 discuss dressings.

Evaluate the patient's nutrition status. A balanced diet with adequate protein, calories, and nutrients is essential. Foods high in protein (e.g., meat, beans, cheese, tofu), vitamin A (green leafy vegetables), vitamin C (citrus fruits, tomatoes, cantaloupe), and zinc (meat, seafood) are most important for healing. For patients with diabetes, maintaining normal blood glucose levels aids the healing process.

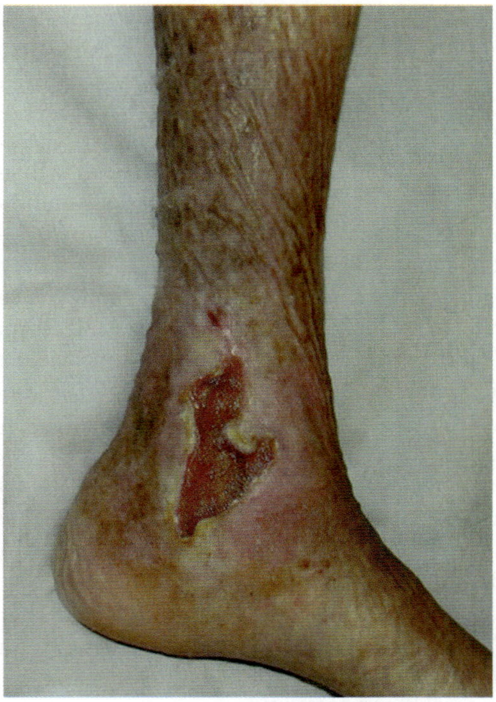

Fig. 41.13 Venous leg ulcer. (From Quick C, Biers SM: *Essential surgery: problems, diagnosis, and management*, St Louis, 2020, Elsevier.)

Though venous leg ulcers are colonized by bacteria, routine use of antibiotics is not indicated. Signs of infection include change in quantity, color, or odor of the drainage; pus; redness of the wound edges; change in sensation around the wound; and warmth around the wound. There may be increased local pain, edema, or both; dark-colored granulation tissue; induration around the wound; delayed healing; and cellulitis. If signs of infection occur, obtain a wound culture. Culture results guide antibiotic therapy. The usual treatment for infection is wound debridement, wound excision, and systemic antibiotics.

If the ulcer does not heal with conservative therapy, drug therapy should be considered. Pentoxifylline is recommended with compression therapy to improve healing. Pentoxifylline minimizes WBC activation and adhesion to capillary endothelium and decreases oxidative stress.

Other treatments are considered for large venous leg ulcers that do not respond to standard therapy after 4 to 6 weeks. These include coverage with a skin replacement or substitute, such as split-thickness skin grafts or artificial bioengineered skin. Chapter 26 discusses skin grafting. Although grafts help with healing, they do not replace the need for lifelong compression therapy.

Patients with CVI have dry, flaky, itchy skin. Daily moisturizing decreases itching and prevents skin cracking. Contact dermatitis may result from contact with sensitizing products. These include such as topical antimicrobial agents (e.g., gentamicin); additives in bandages or dressings (e.g., adhesives); ointments containing lanolin, alcohols, or benzocaine; and over-the-counter creams or lotions with fragrance or preservatives. Assess wounds for signs of infection with each dressing change (Table 41.16).

TABLE 41.16 NURSING MANAGEMENT

Caring for the Patient With Chronic Venous Insufficiency

- Assess the patient for increases in edema, eczema, and venous leg ulcers.
- Assess diet and nutrition status and make referrals as needed.
- Assess for the use of venoactive diet supplements or herbs that may adversely affect co-morbid conditions and/or prescription drugs.
- Choose best options for compression therapy and wound care.
- Give prescribed analgesics, antibiotics, or other drugs.
- Apply compression therapy.
- Provide wound care for venous leg ulcers.
- Evaluate for the effectiveness of therapies and need for alternative approaches.
- Teach patient and caregiver about the manifestations, complications, and treatment of venous insufficiency.
- Supervise the AP:
  - Aid patients in elevating legs to reduce edema and pain.
  - Apply graduated compression stockings.
- Collaborate with the dietitian:
  - Assess diet and nutrition status.
  - Provide diet education as needed.

Case Study

Peripheral Artery Disease

(© IPGGutenbergUKLtd/iStock/Thinkstock.)

Patient Profile

S.J., a 73-year-old man, is admitted to the hospital with rest pain in both legs and a nonhealing ulcer of the big toe on the right foot.

Subjective Data

- History of a MI, stroke, hypertension, HF, type 1 diabetes
- Underwent a left femoral-popliteal bypass 5 years ago
- Has a 45-pack-year history of tobacco use
- Has been using insulin for 30 years
- Reports sudden, intense increase in right foot pain for past 2 hr
- Has slept in recliner with right leg in dependent position for several months to decrease leg pain

Current Medications

- Furosemide (Lasix) 40 mg/day PO
- Isosorbide dinitrate/hydralazine hydrochloride (BiDil) 1 tablet every 8 hr
- Aspart (NovoLog) insulin with meals (sliding scale)
- Glargine insulin 50 units/day subcutaneously
- Diltiazem sustained release (Cardizem LA) 240 mg/day PO
- Aspirin 325 mg/day PO
- Fish oil daily (self-prescribed)

Objective Data

Physical Assessment

- BP 148/92 mm Hg, irregular apical HR 90/min, respiratory rate 22/min, temp 97.9°F (36.6°C)
- Alert and oriented, anxious, with no apparent physical or mental deficits from stroke
- Has 1+ right femoral pulse, popliteal pulse by Doppler only, posterior tibial pulse by Doppler only, and dorsalis pedis pulse absent (not palpable or present by Doppler). Left leg pulses are 1+
- Right leg ABI: 0.20. Left leg ABI: 0.68
- Has a 2-cm necrotic ulcer on tip of right big toe
- Has thickened toenails. Shiny, thin skin on legs. No hair on both lower legs
- Right foot is very cool, pale, and mottled in color with decreased sensation
- No peripheral edema
- Bedside glucose measurement 298 mg/dL (last meal 4 hr before admission)

Discussion Questions

1. ***Recognize***: What risk factors do you identify that led to S.J. having PAD?
2. ***Analyze***: What are the important findings from S.J.'s assessment?
3. ***Plan***: What treatment options are possible?
4. ***Prioritize***: What is the important thing the team can do for S.J.?
5. ***Act***: What role do APs have in providing care?
6. ***Evaluate***: What do you need to continually monitor?
7. ***Safety***: What safety precautions should we consider?

Answers available at http://evolve.elsevier.com/Lewis/medsurg.

BRIDGE TO NCLEX EXAMINATION

The number of the question corresponds to the same-numbered outcome at the beginning of the chapter.

1. A 50-year-old woman who weighs 95 kg has a history of high blood pressure, high sodium intake, tobacco use, and sedentary lifestyle. Which is the *most important* risk factor for peripheral artery disease (PAD) to address in the nursing plan of care?
   a. Salt intake
   b. Tobacco use
   c. Excess weight
   d. Sedentary lifestyle
2. Which information would the nurse include when explaining the cause of rest pain with PAD?
   a. Vasospasm of cutaneous arteries in the feet
   b. Decrease in blood flow to the nerves of the feet
   c. Increase in retrograde venous perfusion to the lower legs
   d. Constriction in blood flow to leg muscles during exercise
3. A patient with infective endocarditis develops sudden left leg pain with pallor, paresthesia, and a loss of peripheral pulses. Which action would the nurse take *first*?
   a. Notify the HCP of the change in perfusion.
   b. Start anticoagulant therapy with IV heparin.
   c. Elevate the leg to improve the venous return.
   d. Position the patient in reverse Trendelenburg.
4. Which clinical manifestations can the nurse expect to see in both patients with Buerger disease and patients with Raynaud phenomenon? *(select all that apply)*
   a. Intermittent low-grade fevers
   b. Sensitivity to cold temperatures
   c. Gangrenous ulcers on fingertips
   d. Color changes of fingers and toes
   e. Episodes of superficial vein thrombosis
5. A patient is admitted to the hospital with a diagnosis of abdominal aortic aneurysm. Which signs and symptoms would suggest that the aneurysm has ruptured?
   a. Rapid onset of shortness of breath and hemoptysis
   b. Sudden low back pain and bruising along the flank
   c. Patchy blue mottling on feet and toes and rest pain
   d. Gradually increasing substernal chest pain and diaphoresis
6. Which nursing interventions are the *priority* 8 hours after an abdominal aortic aneurysm repair?
   a. Assessing nutrition status and diet preferences
   b. Starting IV heparin and monitoring anticoagulation
   c. Administering IV fluids and watching kidney function
   d. Elevating the legs and applying compression stockings
7. Which goal is the *first* priority of interprofessional care for a patient with a suspected acute aortic dissection?
   a. Reduce anxiety
   b. Monitor chest pain
   c. Control blood pressure
   d. Increase myocardial contractility

8. Which patient is at *highest* risk for venous thromboembolism (VTE)?
   a. a. A 62-year-old man with spider veins who is having arthroscopic knee surgery
   b. b. A 32-year-old woman who smokes, takes oral contraceptives, and is planning a long flight
   c. A 26-year-old woman who is 3 days postpartum and received maintenance IV fluids for 12 hours during her labor
   d. d. An active 72-year-old man at home recovering from transurethral resection of the prostate for benign prostatic hyperplasia
9. Which clinical findings would the nurse expect in a person with an acute lower extremity VTE? *(select all that apply)*
   a. Pallor and coolness of foot and calf
   b. Mild to moderate calf pain and tenderness
   c. Grossly decreased or absent pedal pulses
   d. Unilateral edema and induration of the thigh
   e. Palpable cord along a superficial varicose vein
10. Which treatment would the nurse anticipate for an otherwise healthy person with an initial VTE?
   a. IV argatroban as an inpatient
   b. IV unfractionated heparin as an inpatient
   c. Subcutaneous unfractionated heparin as an outpatient
   d. Subcutaneous low-molecular-weight heparin as an outpatient
11. Which instruction is a *key* aspect of teaching for the patient on anticoagulant therapy?
   a. Monitor for and report any signs of bleeding.
   b. Do not take acetaminophen (Tylenol) for a headache.
   c. Decrease your dietary intake of foods containing vitamin K.
   d. Arrange to have blood drawn twice a week to check drug effects.
12. The nurse is planning care and teaching for a patient with venous leg ulcers. Which patient action is the *most* important in healing and control of this condition?
   a. Following activity guidelines.
   b. Using moist environment dressings.
   c. Taking horse chestnut seed extract daily.
   d. Applying graduated compression stockings.

1. b; 2. b; 3. a; 4. b, c, d; 5. b; 6. c; 7. c; 8. b; 9. b, d; 10. d; 11. a; 12. d.

For rationales to these answers and even more NCLEX review questions, visit http://evolve.elsevier.com/Lewis/medsurg.

EVOLVE WEBSITE/RESOURCES LIST

http://evolve.elsevier.com/Lewis/medsurg
Review Questions (Online Only)
Key Points
Answer Keys for Questions
- Rationales for Bridge to NCLEX Examination Questions
- Answer Guidelines for Case Study

Student Case Studies
- Patient With Abdominal Aortic Aneurysm
- Patient With Chronic Peripheral Artery Disease

Nursing Care Plans
- eNursing Care Plan 41.1: Patient With Peripheral Artery Disease of the Lower Extremities
- eNursing Care Plan 41.2: Patient After Surgical Repair of the Aorta

Conceptual Care Map Creator
Audio Glossary
Content Updates

REFERENCES

* 1. Creager MA, Belkin B, Bluth EI, et al.: 2012 ACCF/AHA/ACR/SCAI/SIR/STS/SVM/SVN/SVS key data elements and definitions for peripheral atherosclerotic vascular disease: a report of the ACCF/AHA Task Force on Clinical Data Standards, *Circ* 125:395, 2012. (Classic).
2. Centers for Disease Control and Prevention: Peripheral arterial disease (PAD) fact sheet. Retrieved from https://www.cdc.gov/heartdisease/pad.htm.
*3. Gerhard-Herman M, Gornick H, Barrett C, et al.: 2016 AHA/ACC guideline on the management of patients with lower extremity peripheral artery disease: Executive summary, *Circ* 135:e686, 2017. (Classic).
*4. Patel T, Baydoun H, Patel NK, et al.: Peripheral arterial disease in women: the gender effect, *CRM* 21:404, 2019.
*5. Fan Y, Shen Y, Zhou J, et al.: Visit-to-visit hemoglobin A1c variability is associated with the risk of lower-extremity amputation in patients with Type 2 diabetes, *Diabetes Care* 43:e178, 2020.
*6. Meini S, Dentali F, Melillo E: Prostanoids for critical limb ischemia: a clinical review and consideration of current guideline recommendations, *Angioplasty* 7:226, 2020.
* 7. Haghighat L, Ionescu C, Regan C, et al.: Review of the current basic science strategies to treat critical limb ischemia, *Vasc Endovasc Surg* 53:316, 2019.
8. Qaja E, Muco E, Hashmi M: Buerger disease. Retrieved from https://www.ncbi.nlm.nih.gov/books/NBK430858/.
9. Herrick A, Wigley F: Raynaud's phenomenon, *Best Pract Res Clin Rheumatol* 34, 2020.
10. Pauling J, Hughes M, Pope J: Raynaud's phenomenon: an update on diagnosis, classification and management, *Clin Rheumatol* 38:3317, 2019.
*11. Chaikof EL, Dalman RL, Eskandari MK, et al.: The Society of Vascular Surgery practice guidelines on the care of patients with an abdominal aortic aneurysm, *J Vasc Surg* 67:2, 2018.
12. Kaji S: Acute medical management of aortic dissection, *Gen Thorac Cardiovasc Surg* 67:203, 2019.
*13. Rylski B, Georgieva N, Beyersdorf F, et al.: Gender-related differences in patients with acute aortic dissection type A, *J Thorac Cardiovasc Surg*, 2019.
*14. Boufi M, Patterson B, Loundou A, et al.: Endovascular versus open repair for chronic type B dissection treatment: a meta-analysis, *Ann Thorac Surg* 107:1559, 2019.
*15. Ortel T, Neuman I, Ageno W, et al.: American Society of Hematology 2020 guidelines for management of venous thrombo-

embolism: treatment of deep vein thrombosis and pulmonary embolism, *Blood Adv* 4:4693, 2020.
16. Burcham JR, Rosenthal LD: *Lehne's pharmacology for nursing care*, ed 10, St. Louis, 2019, Elsevier.
17. Youn Y, Lee J: Chronic venous insufficiency and varicose veins of the lower extremities, *Korean J Intern Med* 34:269, 2019.

*Evidence-based information for clinical practice.

42

Shock, Sepsis, and Multiple Organ Dysfunction Syndrome

Helen Miley

http://evolve.elsevier.com/Lewis/medsurg/

CONCEPTUAL FOCUS

Fluid and Electrolytes
Gas Exchange
Inflammation
Perfusion

LEARNING OUTCOMES

1. Relate the pathophysiology to the clinical manifestations of the different types of shock.
2. Compare the effects of shock, sepsis, systemic inflammatory response syndrome, and multiple organ dysfunction syndrome (MODS) on the major body systems.
3. Compare the interprofessional care, drug therapy, and nursing management of patients with different types of shock.
4. Describe the interprofessional care and nursing management of a patient with MODS.

KEY TERMS

cardiogenic shock
hypovolemic shock
multiple organ dysfunction syndrome (MODS)
neurogenic shock
obstructive shock
sepsis
septic shock
shock
systemic inflammatory response syndrome (SIRS)

Shock, systemic inflammatory response syndrome (SIRS), sepsis, and multiple organ dysfunction syndrome (MODS) are serious and interrelated problems (Fig. 42.1). **Shock** is a syndrome characterized by decreased tissue perfusion and impaired cellular metabolism. This results in an imbalance between the supply of and demand for O_2 and nutrients. The exchange of O_2 and nutrients at the cellular level is essential to life. When cells are hypoperfused, the demand for O_2 and nutrients exceeds the supply at the microcirculatory level. Ischemia can occur, leading to cell injury and death. Thus shock is life-threatening. This chapter gives an overview of the different types of shock, SIRS, sepsis, and MODS and their related management.

SHOCK

Classification of Shock

The 4 main categories of shock are cardiogenic, hypovolemic, distributive, and obstructive (Table 42.1). Although the cause, initial presentation, and management vary for each type, the physiologic responses of cells to hypoperfusion are similar.

Cardiogenic Shock

Cardiogenic shock occurs when either systolic or diastolic dysfunction of the heart's pumping action results in reduced cardiac output (CO), stroke volume (SV), and BP. These changes compromise myocardial perfusion, further depress myocardial function, and decrease CO and perfusion. Causes of cardiogenic shock are shown in Table 42.1. It is the leading cause of death from acute myocardial infarction (MI). Although the in-hospital mortality has improved due to aggressive intervention, the 6- to 12-month mortality remains 50%.[1]

Fig. 42.2 shows the pathophysiology of cardiogenic shock. The heart's inability to pump the blood forward is called *systolic dysfunction.* This inability results in a low CO (less than 4 L/min) and *cardiac index* (less than 2.5 L/min/m^2). Systolic dysfunction primarily affects the left ventricle because systolic pressure is greater on the left side of the heart. The most common cause of systolic dysfunction is acute MI. When systolic dysfunction affects the right side of the heart, blood flow through the pulmonary circulation is reduced. Decreased filling of the heart results in decreased SV. Table 42.1 lists causes of diastolic dysfunction.

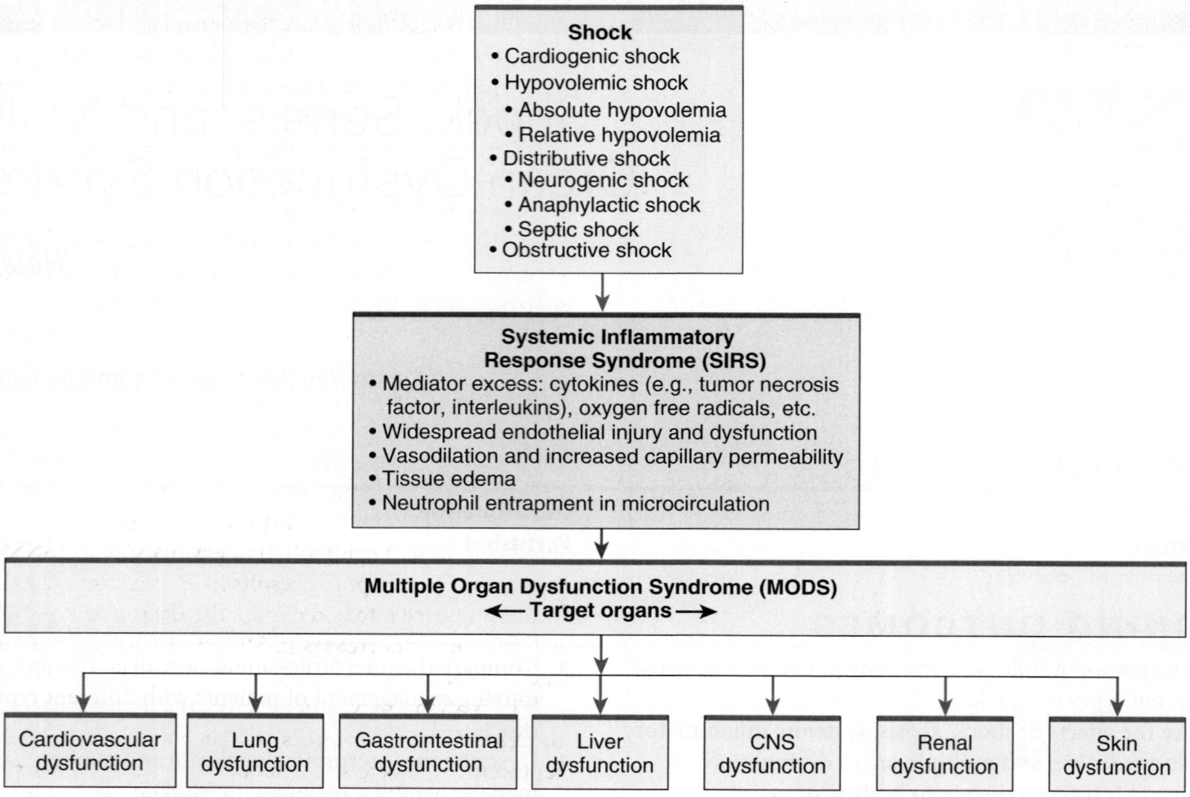

Fig. 42.1 Relationship of shock, systemic inflammatory response syndrome, and multiple organ dysfunction syndrome.

TABLE 42.1 Classification of Shock States

Types and Causes	Associated Conditions
Cardiogenic Shock	
• Diastolic dysfunction: inability of the heart to fill	Cardiac tamponade, ventricular hypertrophy, cardiomyopathy
• Dysrhythmias	Bradydysrhythmias, tachydysrhythmias
• Structural factors	Valvular stenosis or regurgitation, ventricular septal rupture, tension pneumothorax
• Systolic dysfunction: inability of the heart to pump blood forward	MI, cardiomyopathy, blunt cardiac injury, severe systemic or pulmonary hypertension, myocardial depression from metabolic problems
Hypovolemic Shock	
Absolute Hypovolemia	
• External loss of whole blood	Hemorrhage from trauma, surgery, GI bleeding
• Loss of other body fluids	Vomiting, diarrhea, excessive diuresis, diabetes insipidus, diabetes
Relative Hypovolemia	
• Fluid shifts	Burn injuries, ascites
• Internal bleeding	Fracture of long bones, ruptured spleen, hemothorax, severe pancreatitis
• Massive vasodilation	Sepsis
• Pooling of blood or fluids	Bowel obstruction

Types and Causes	Associated Conditions
Distributive Shock	
Anaphylactic Shock	
• Hypersensitivity (allergic) reaction to a sensitizing substance	Contrast media, blood or blood products, drugs, insect bites, anesthetic agents, food or food additives, vaccines, environmental agents, latex
Neurogenic Shock	
• Hemodynamic consequence of spinal cord injury and/or disease at or above T5	Severe pain, drugs, hypoglycemia, injury
• Spinal anesthesia	
• Vasomotor center depression	
Septic Shock	
• At-risk patients	Older adults, patients with chronic diseases (e.g., diabetes, chronic kidney disease, HF), patients receiving immunosuppressive therapy or who are malnourished or debilitated
• Infection	Pneumonia, peritonitis, urinary tract, invasive procedures, indwelling lines and catheters
Obstructive Shock	
• Physical obstruction impeding the filling or outflow of blood resulting in reduced CO	Cardiac tamponade, tension pneumothorax, superior vena cava syndrome, abdominal compartment syndrome, pulmonary embolism

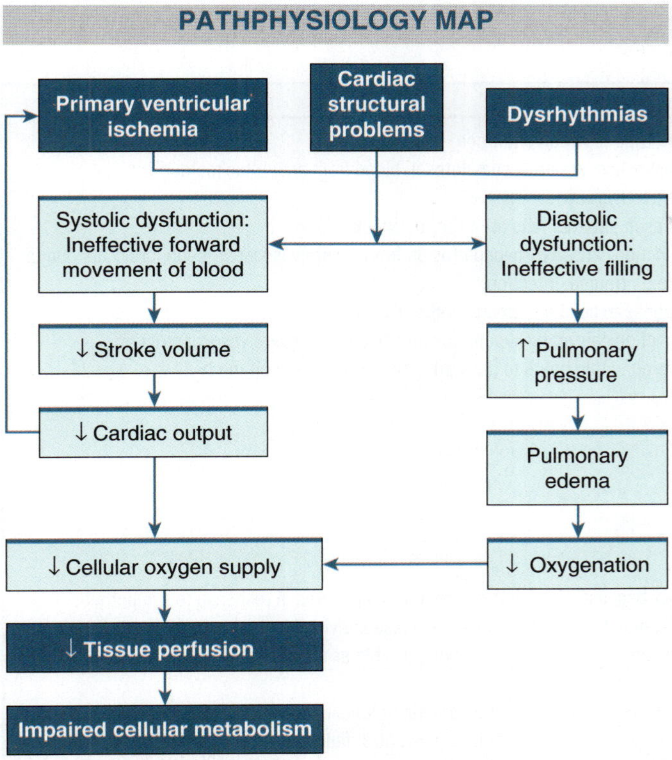

Fig. 42.2 The pathophysiology of cardiogenic shock.

The early presentation of a patient with cardiogenic shock is similar to that of a patient with acute decompensated heart failure (HF) (see Chapter 38). The patient may have tachycardia and hypotension. Pulse pressure may be narrowed due to the heart's inability to pump blood forward during systole and increased volume during diastole. An increase in systemic vascular resistance (SVR) increases the workload of the heart. This increases myocardial O_2 consumption.

On assessment, the patient is tachypneic. There are crackles on auscultation of breath sounds because of pulmonary congestion. The hemodynamic profile shows an increase in the pulmonary artery (PA) wedge pressure (PAWP), stroke volume variation (SVV), and pulmonary vascular resistance.

Signs of peripheral hypoperfusion (e.g., cyanosis, pallor, weak peripheral pulses, cool and clammy skin, delayed capillary refill) occur. Decreased renal blood flow results in sodium and water retention and decreased urine output. Anxiety, confusion, and agitation may develop with impaired cerebral perfusion. Tables 42.2 and 42.3 describe the laboratory findings and clinical presentation of a patient with cardiogenic shock.

Hypovolemic Shock

Hypovolemic shock occurs from inadequate fluid volume in the intravascular space to support adequate perfusion (Table 42.1).[2] The volume loss may be either an absolute or a relative volume loss. *Absolute hypovolemia* results when fluid is lost through hemorrhage, gastrointestinal (GI) loss (e.g., vomiting, diarrhea), fistula drainage, diabetes insipidus, or diuresis. In *relative hypovolemia,* fluid volume moves out of the vascular space into the extravascular space (e.g., intracavitary space). We call this type of fluid shift *third spacing.* One example of relative volume loss is fluid leaking from the vascular space to the interstitial space from increased capillary permeability, as seen in burns (see Chapter 26).

Whether the intravascular volume loss is absolute or relative, the consequences are similar. The reduced intravascular volume results in a decreased venous return to the heart, decreased preload, decreased SV, and decreased CO. A cascade of events results in decreased tissue perfusion and impaired cellular metabolism, the hallmarks of shock (Fig. 42.3).

The patient's response to acute volume loss depends on several factors, including extent of injury, age, and general state of health. The clinical presentation of hypovolemic shock is consistent (Table 42.3). An overall assessment of physiologic reserves may indicate the patient's ability to compensate. A patient may compensate for a loss of up to 15% of the total blood volume (approximately 750 mL). Further loss of volume (15% to 30%) results in a sympathetic nervous system (SNS)-mediated response.[2] This response results in an increase in heart rate, CO, and respiratory rate and depth. The decreased circulating blood volume causes decreases in SV, central venous pressure (CVP), and PAWP.

The patient may appear anxious. Urine output begins to decrease. If hypovolemia is quickly corrected by crystalloid fluid replacement, tissue dysfunction is generally reversible. If volume loss is greater than 30%, compensatory mechanisms may fail and immediate replacement with blood products should be started. Loss of autoregulation in the microcirculation and irreversible tissue destruction occur with loss of more than 40% of the total blood volume. Common laboratory studies and assessments that are done include serial measurements of hemoglobin and hematocrit levels, electrolytes, lactate, blood gases, mixed central venous O_2 saturation (SvO_2), and hourly urine outputs (Table 42.2).

Distributive Shock

Distributive shock has many causes. It is a condition of relative hypovolemia due to intravascular volume redistribution from loss of vascular tone or disordered permeability. The 3 subsets are neurogenic, anaphylactic, and septic.[3]

Neurogenic shock. **Neurogenic shock** is a hemodynamic phenomenon that can occur within 30 minutes of a spinal cord injury and last up to 6 weeks. Neurogenic shock related to spinal cord injuries is generally associated with a cervical or high thoracic injury. The injury results in a massive vasodilation without compensation because of the loss of SNS vasoconstrictor tone.[4] This massive vasodilation leads to a pooling of blood in the blood vessels, tissue hypoperfusion, and impaired cellular metabolism (Fig. 42.4).

In addition to spinal cord injury, spinal anesthesia can block transmission of impulses from the SNS. Depression of the vasomotor center of the medulla from drugs (e.g., opioids, benzodiazepines) can decrease vasoconstrictor tone of the peripheral blood vessels, resulting in neurogenic shock (Table 42.1).

The classic manifestations are hypotension (from the massive vasodilation) and bradycardia (from unopposed parasympathetic stimulation).[4] The patient may not be able to regulate

TABLE 42.2 Diagnostic Studies

Shock

Study	Finding	Significance of Finding
Arterial blood gases	Respiratory alkalosis	Found in early shock due to hyperventilation
	Metabolic acidosis	Occurs later in shock when lactate accumulates in blood from anaerobic metabolism
Base deficit	>–6	Acid production due to hypoxia
Blood cultures	Growth of organisms	May grow organisms in patients who are in septic shock
BUN	↑	Impaired kidney function caused by hypoperfusion from severe vasoconstriction, or occurs due to cell catabolism (e.g., trauma, infection)
Creatine kinase	↑	Trauma, MI in response to cellular damage and/or hypoxia
Creatinine	↑	Impaired kidney function caused by hypoperfusion because of severe vasoconstriction
DIC screen		Acute DIC can develop within hours to days after an initial assault on the body (e.g., shock)
• D-dimer	↑	
• Fibrin split products (FSPs)	↑	
• Fibrinogen level	↓	
• INR	↑	
• Platelet count	↓	
• PTT and PT	↑	
• Thrombin time	↑	
Glucose	↑	Found in early shock because of release of liver glycogen stores in response to sympathetic nervous system stimulation and cortisol. Insulin insensitivity develops
	↓	Depleted glycogen stores with liver dysfunction possible as shock progresses
Electrolytes (serum)		
• Sodium	↑	Found in early shock because of ↑ secretion of aldosterone, causing renal retention of sodium
	↓	May be iatrogenic if excess hypotonic fluid is given after fluid loss
• Potassium	↑	Results when dead cells release potassium. Occurs in acute kidney injury and acidosis
	↓	Found in early shock because of ↑ secretion of aldosterone, causing renal excretion of potassium
Lactate level	↑	Usually ↑ once significant hypoperfusion and impaired O_2 use at the cellular level have occurred. By-product of anaerobic metabolism
Liver enzymes (ALT, AST, GGT)	↑	Liver cell destruction in progressive stage of shock
Procalcitonin (PCT)	↑	Biomarker released in response to bacterial infections
RBC count, hematocrit, hemoglobin	Normal	Remains within normal limits in shock because of relative hypovolemia and pump failure and in hemorrhagic shock before fluid resuscitation
	↓	Hemorrhagic shock after fluid resuscitation when fluids other than blood are used
	↑	Nonhemorrhagic shock caused by actual hypovolemia and hemoconcentration
Troponin	↑	MI
White blood cell count	↑, ↓	Infection, septic shock

ALT, Alanine aminotransferase; *AST,* aspartate aminotransferase; *BUN,* blood urea nitrogen; *DIC,* disseminated intravascular coagulation; *GGT,* γ-glutamyl transferase; *INR,* international normalized ratio; *PT,* prothrombin time; *PTT,* partial thromboplastin time.

body temperature. Combined with massive vasodilation, the inability to regulate temperature promotes heat loss. At first, the patient's skin is warm due to the massive vasodilation. As the heat disperses, the patient is at risk for hypothermia. Later, the patient's skin may be cool or warm depending on the ambient temperature (*poikilothermia,* taking on the temperature of the environment). The skin is usually dry. Tables 42.2 and 42.3 further describe the laboratory findings and clinical presentation of a patient with neurogenic shock.

Although spinal shock and neurogenic shock often occur in the same patient, they are not the same disorder. *Spinal shock* is a transient condition that is present after an acute spinal cord injury (see Chapter 65). The patient with spinal shock has an absence of all voluntary and reflex neurologic activity below the level of the injury.

Anaphylactic shock. *Anaphylactic shock* is an acute, life-threatening hypersensitivity (allergic) reaction to a sensitizing substance (e.g., drug, chemical, vaccine, food, insect venom).[5] The reaction quickly causes massive vasodilation, release of vasoactive mediators, and an increase in capillary permeability. As capillary permeability increases, fluid leaks from the vascular space into the interstitial space.

Anaphylactic shock can lead to respiratory distress due to laryngeal edema or severe bronchospasm and circulatory failure from the massive vasodilation. The patient has a sudden onset of symptoms, including dizziness, chest pain, incontinence, swelling of the lips and tongue, wheezing, and stridor. Skin changes include flushing, pruritus, urticaria, and angioedema. The patient may be anxious and confused and have a sense of impending doom.

A patient can have a severe allergic reaction, leading to anaphylactic shock, after contact, inhalation, ingestion, or injection with an antigen (allergen) to which the person has previously been sensitized (Table 42.1). IV administration of the antigen (allergen) is the route most likely to cause anaphylaxis. However, oral, topical, and inhalation routes can cause

TABLE 42.3 Clinical Presentation of Types of Shock

Cardiogenic Shock	Hypovolemic Shock	Neurogenic Shock	Anaphylactic Shock	Septic Shock	Obstructive Shock
Cardiovascular System					
Tachycardia ↓ BP ↓ SV, CO ↑ SVR, PAWP, CVP ↓ Capillary refill	Tachycardia ↓ Preload ↓ CO, CVP, PAWP ↑ SVR ↓ Capillary refill	Bradycardia ↓ BP ↓ CO, CVP, SVR ↓/↑ Temperature	Tachycardia ↓ CO ↓ CVP, PAWP Chest pain Third spacing of fluid	Tachycardia ↓/↑ Temperature Myocardial dysfunction Biventricular dilation ↓ Ejection fraction	Tachycardia ↓↓ BP ↓ Preload ↓ CO ↑ SVR, CVP
Gastrointestinal System					
↓ Bowel sounds Nausea, vomiting	Absent bowel sounds	Bowel dysfunction	Abdominal pain Cramping Diarrhea Nausea Vomiting	GI bleeding Paralytic ileus	↓ To absent bowel sounds
Neurologic System					
↓ Cerebral perfusion: • Anxiety • Confusion • Agitation	↓ Cerebral perfusion: • Anxiety • Confusion • Agitation	Flaccid paralysis below the level of the lesion Loss of reflex activity	Anxiety Feeling of impending doom Confusion ↓ LOC Metallic taste	Change in mental status (e.g., confusion) Agitation Coma (late)	↓ Cerebral perfusion: Anxiety Confusion Agitation
Renal System					
↑ Na^+ and H_2O retention ↓ Renal blood flow ↓ Urine output	↓ Urine output	Bladder dysfunction	Incontinence	↓ Urine output	↓ Urine output
Respiratory System					
Tachypnea Crackles Cyanosis	Tachypnea → bradypnea (late)	Dysfunction related to level of injury	Shortness of breath Edema of larynx and epiglottis Stridor Wheezing	Hyperventilation Crackles Respiratory alkalosis → respiratory acidosis Hypoxemia Respiratory failure ARDS Pulmonary hypertension	Tachypnea → bradypnea (late) Shortness of breath
Skin					
Pallor Cool, clammy	Pallor Cool, clammy	↓ Skin perfusion Cool or warm Dry	Flushing Pruritus Urticaria Angioedema	Warm and flushed → cool and mottled (late)	Pallor Cool, clammy
Diagnostic Findings (see Table 42.2)					
↑ b-Type natriuretic peptide (BNP) ↑ Blood glucose ↑ BUN ↑ Cardiac biomarkers Chest x-ray (e.g., pulmonary infiltrates) ECG (e.g., dysrhythmias) Echocardiogram (e.g., left ventricular dysfunction	Electrolyte changes ↓ Hematocrit ↓ Hemoglobin ↑ Lactate ↑ Urine specific gravity		History of allergies Exposure to contrast media	↑ Blood glucose ↑ Lactate ↓ Platelets Positive blood cultures ↑ Procalcitonin ↑ Urine specific gravity ↓ Urine Na^+ ↑/↓ WBC	Specific to cause of obstruction

PATHOPHYSIOLOGY MAP

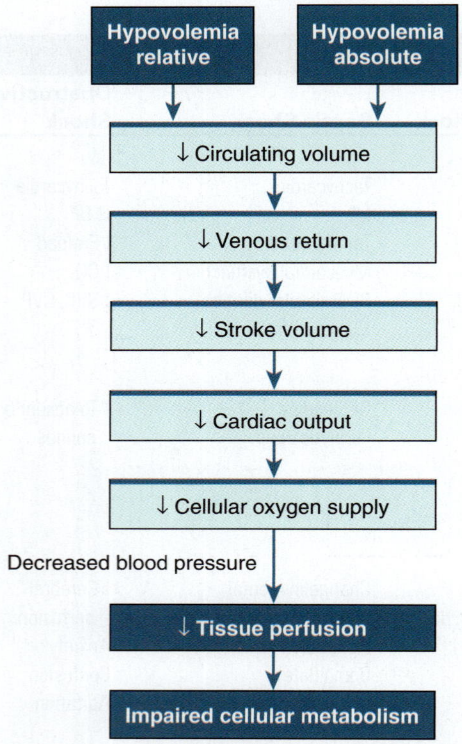

Fig. 42.3 The pathophysiology of hypovolemic shock.

PATHOPHYSIOLOGY MAP

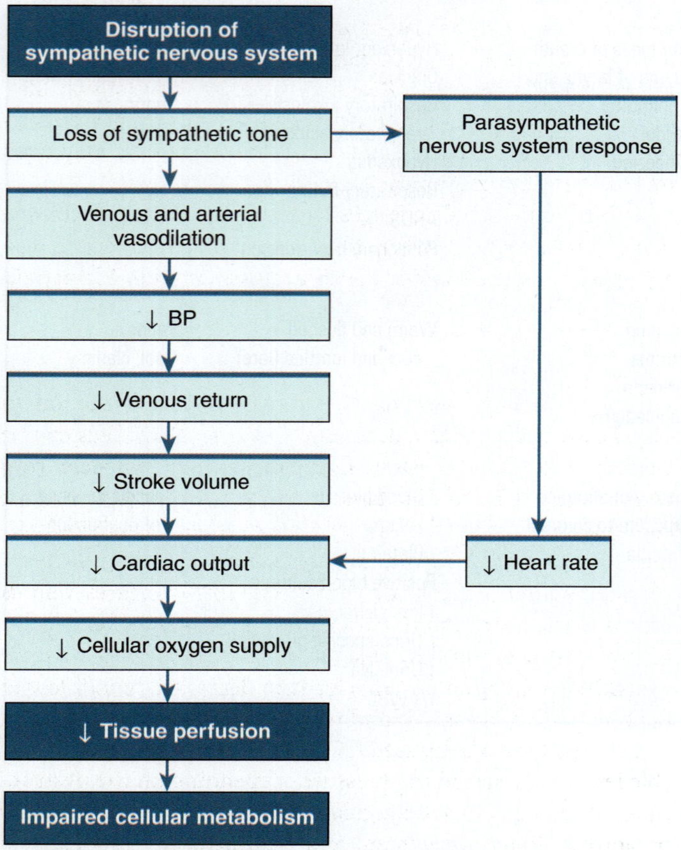

Fig. 42.4 The pathophysiology of neurogenic shock.

TABLE 42.4 Diagnostic Criteria

Sepsis

Infection, documented or suspected, and some of the following:

General Variables

- Altered mental status
- Fever (temperature >100.9°F [38.3°C])
- Heart rate >90 beats/min
- Hyperglycemia (blood glucose >140 mg/dL) in the absence of diabetes
- Hypothermia (core temperature <97.0°F [36°C])
- SBP ≤100 mm Hg
- Significant edema or positive fluid balance (>20 mL/kg over 24 hr)
- Tachypnea (respiratory rate ≥22/min)

Inflammatory Variables

- ↑ C-reactive protein
- Leukocytosis (WBC count >12,000/μL)
- Leukopenia (WBC count <4000/μL)
- Normal WBC count with >10% immature forms (bands)
- ↑ Procalcitonin

Hemodynamic Variables

- Arterial hypotension (SBP <90 mm Hg, MAP <70 mm Hg, or a decrease in SBP >40 mm Hg)

Organ Dysfunction Variables

- Acute oliguria (urine output <0.5 mL/kg/hr for at least 2 hr despite adequate fluid resuscitation)
- Arterial hypoxemia (PaO_2/FIO_2 <300)
- Coagulation abnormalities (INR >1.5 or PTT >60 s)
- Hyperbilirubinemia (total bilirubin >4 mg/dL)
- Ileus (absent bowel sounds)
- Serum creatinine increase >0.5 mg/dL
- Thrombocytopenia (platelet count <100,000/μL)

Tissue Perfusion Variables

- Hyperlactatemia (>1 mmol/L)
- Mottling, ↓ capillary refill

FIO_2, Fraction of inspired O_2; *INR*, international normalized ratio; *PaO_2*, partial pressure of arterial O_2; *PTT*, partial thromboplastin time.
Source: Singer M, Deutschman CS, Seymour CW, et al.: The third international consensus definitions for sepsis and septic shock (Sepsis-3), *JAMA* 315:801, 2016.

anaphylactic reactions. Tables 42.2 and 42.3 describe the laboratory findings and clinical presentation of a patient in anaphylactic shock. Quick action is critical to prevent an allergic reaction from progressing to anaphylactic shock. Anaphylaxis is discussed in Chapter 14.

Septic shock. **Sepsis** is a life-threatening syndrome in response to infection. It is characterized by a dysregulated patient response along with new organ dysfunction related to the infection (Table 42.4).[6] In as many as 30% of patients with sepsis, we never identify the causative agent. Sepsis and septic shock have a high incidence worldwide, with a mortality rate of 25% or higher.[7]

Septic shock is a subset of sepsis. It has an increased mortality risk due to profound circulatory, cellular, and metabolic abnormalities. Septic shock is characterized by persistent hypotension, despite adequate fluid resuscitation, and inadequate tissue perfusion that results in tissue hypoxia.[8] The main organisms that cause sepsis are gram-negative and gram-positive bacteria. Parasites,

PATHOPHYSIOLOGY MAP

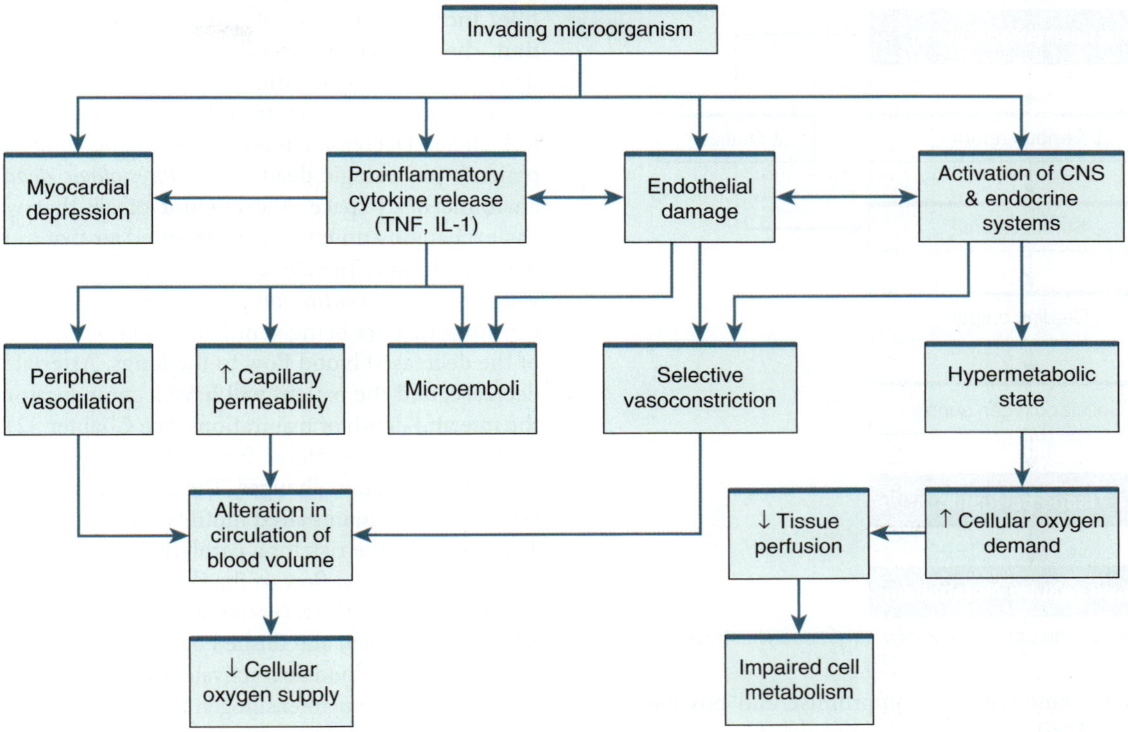

Fig. 42.5 The pathophysiology of septic shock. *IL,* Interleukin; *TNF,* tumor necrosis factor.

fungi, and viruses can also cause sepsis and septic shock.[8] Fig. 42.5 presents the pathophysiology of septic shock.

When a microorganism enters the body, this triggers normal immune and inflammatory responses. However, in sepsis and septic shock, the body's response to the microorganism is exaggerated. Both proinflammatory and antiinflammatory responses are activated. Coagulation increases, and fibrinolysis decreases.[6] Endotoxins from the microorganism cell wall stimulate the release of cytokines. These include tumor necrosis factor (TNF), interleukin-1 (IL-1), and other proinflammatory mediators that act through secondary mediators, such as platelet-activating factor, IL-6, and IL-8.[9] (See Chapter 12 for more about the inflammatory response.) The release of platelet-activating factor results in the formation of microthrombi and microvasculature obstruction. The combined effects of the mediators result in endothelial damage, vasodilation, increased capillary permeability, and neutrophil and platelet aggregation and adhesion to the endothelium.

Septic shock has 3 major pathophysiologic effects: vasodilation, maldistribution of blood flow, and myocardial depression. Patients may be euvolemic, but because of acute vasodilation and shifting of fluids out of the intravascular space, relative hypovolemia and hypotension occur. Blood flow in the microcirculation is decreased, causing poor O_2 delivery and tissue hypoxia. We think the combination of TNF and IL-1 has a role in sepsis-induced myocardial dysfunction. The ejection fraction (EF) is decreased for the first few days after the initial insult. Because of a decreased EF, the ventricles dilate to maintain the SV. The EF typically improves, and ventricular dilation resolves over 7 to 10 days. Persistent high CO and a low SVR beyond 24 hours is an ominous finding. It is often associated with hypotension and MODS. Coronary artery perfusion and myocardial O_2 metabolism are not primarily altered in septic shock.

Respiratory failure is common. The patient initially hyperventilates as a compensatory mechanism, causing respiratory alkalosis. Once the patient can no longer compensate, respiratory acidosis develops. Respiratory failure develops in 85% of patients with sepsis; 40% develop acute respiratory distress syndrome (ARDS) (see Chapter 32). These patients may need intubation with mechanical ventilation.

Other signs include changes in neurologic status, decreased urine output, and GI dysfunction, such as GI bleeding and paralytic ileus. Table 42.3 gives the clinical presentation of a patient with septic shock.

Obstructive Shock

Obstructive shock develops when a physical obstruction to blood flow occurs with a decreased CO (Fig. 42.6). This can be caused by restricted diastolic filling of the right ventricle from compression (e.g., cardiac tamponade, tension pneumothorax, superior vena cava syndrome).[10] Other causes include *abdominal compartment syndrome,* in which increased abdominal pressures compress the inferior vena cava. This decreases venous return to the heart. Pulmonary embolism and right ventricular thrombi cause an outflow obstruction as blood leaves the right ventricle through the PA. This leads to decreased blood flow to the lungs and decreased blood return to the left atrium.

Patients have a decreased CO, increased afterload, and variable left ventricular filling pressures depending on the obstruction. Other signs include jugular venous distention and pulsus paradoxus. Rapid assessment and treatment are important to

PATHOPHYSIOLOGY MAP

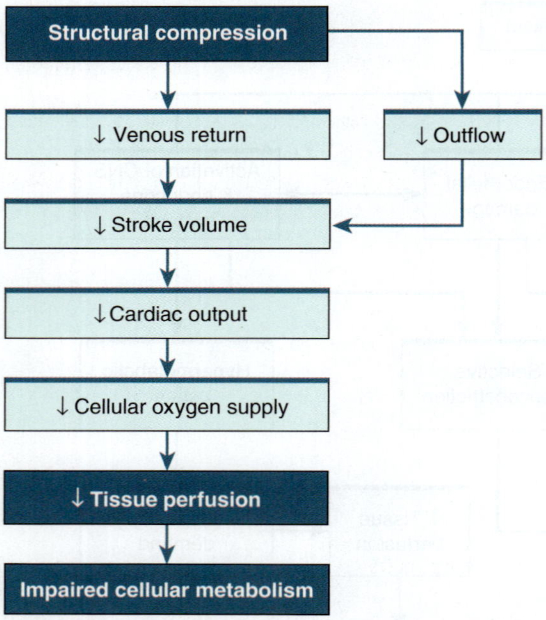

Fig. 42.6 The pathophysiology of obstructive shock.

prevent further hemodynamic compromise and possible cardiac arrest (Fig. 42.6).

Stages of Shock

In addition to understanding the underlying pathogenesis of the type of shock the patient has, management is guided by knowing where the patient is on the shock "continuum." We categorize shock into 4 overlapping stages: (1) initial stage, (2) compensatory stage, (3) progressive stage, and (4) refractory stage.[5]

Initial Stage

The *initial stage* of shock occurs at a cellular level. This stage is usually not clinically apparent. Metabolism changes at the cellular level from aerobic to anaerobic, causing lactic acid buildup. Lactic acid is a waste product that is removed by the liver.[7] However, this process requires O_2, which is unavailable because of the decrease in tissue perfusion.

Compensatory Stage

In the *compensatory stage* the body activates neural, hormonal, and biochemical compensatory mechanisms to try to overcome the increasing consequences of anaerobic metabolism and maintain homeostasis. The patient's clinical presentation begins to reflect the body's responses to the imbalance in O_2 supply and demand (Table 42.5).

A classic sign of shock is a drop in BP. This occurs because of a decrease in CO and a narrowing of the pulse pressure. The baroreceptors in the carotid and aortic bodies immediately respond by activating the SNS. The SNS stimulates vasoconstriction and the release of the potent vasoconstrictors epinephrine and norepinephrine. Blood flow to the heart and brain is maintained. Blood flow to the nonvital organs, such as kidneys, GI tract, skin, and lungs, is diverted or shunted.

The myocardium responds to the SNS stimulation and the increased O_2 demand by increasing the heart rate and contractility. Increased contractility increases myocardial O_2 consumption. The coronary arteries dilate to try to meet the increased O_2 demands of the myocardium.

Shunting blood away from the lungs has an important clinical effect. Decreased blood flow to the lungs increases the patient's physiologic dead space. *Physiologic dead space* is the anatomic dead space (the amount of air that will not reach gas-exchanging units) and any inspired air that cannot take part in gas exchange. The clinical result of an increase in dead space ventilation is a *ventilation-perfusion mismatch.* Some areas of the lungs that are being ventilated will not be perfused because of the decreased blood flow to the lungs. Arterial O_2 levels will decrease, and the patient will have a compensatory increase in the rate and depth of respirations (see Chapter 32).

The shunting of blood from other organ systems results in clinically important changes. The decrease in blood flow to the GI tract results in impaired motility and a slowing of peristalsis. This increases the risk for a paralytic ileus.

Decreased blood flow to the skin results in the patient feeling cool and clammy. The exception is the patient in early septic shock who may feel warm and flushed because of a hyperdynamic state. Decreased renal blood flow activates the renin-angiotensin system. Renin stimulates angiotensinogen to make angiotensin I, which is then converted to angiotensin II. Angiotensin II is a potent vasoconstrictor that causes both arterial and venous vasoconstriction. The net result is an increase in venous return to the heart and an increase in BP. Angiotensin II stimulates the adrenal cortex to release aldosterone. This results in sodium and water reabsorption and potassium excretion by the kidneys. The increase in sodium reabsorption raises the serum osmolality and stimulates the release of antidiuretic hormone (ADH). ADH increases water reabsorption by the kidneys, further increasing blood volume. The increase in total circulating volume results in an increase in CO and BP.

A multisystem response to decreasing tissue perfusion starts during the compensatory stage of shock. At this stage, the body can compensate for the changes in tissue perfusion. If the cause of the shock is corrected, the patient will recover with little or no residual effects. If the cause of the shock is not corrected and the body is unable to compensate, the patient enters the progressive stage of shock.

Progressive Stage

The *progressive stage* of shock begins as compensatory mechanisms fail. Changes in the patient's mental status are important findings in this stage. Patients must be moved to the intensive care unit (ICU), if not already there, for advanced monitoring and treatment.

The cardiovascular system is now profoundly affected. CO begins to fall, causing a decrease in BP and coronary artery, cerebral, and peripheral perfusion. Decreased cellular perfusion continues. Altered capillary permeability occurs, allowing fluid and protein to leak out of the vascular space into the surrounding interstitial space. Circulating volume decreases with an increase in systemic interstitial edema. The patient may have *anasarca* (diffuse profound edema). Fluid leakage from the vascular space affects the solid organs (e.g., liver, GI tract, lungs) and peripheral tissues by further decreasing perfusion.

TABLE 42.5 **Manifestations of Stages of Shock**

Compensatory Stage	Progressive Stage	Refractory Stage
Cardiovascular System		
Sympathetic nervous system response: • Epinephrine/norepinephrine (vasoconstriction) release • ↑ Myocardial O_2 consumption • ↑ Contractility • ↑ HR • Coronary artery dilation • Narrowed pulse pressure • ↓ BP	↑ Capillary permeability → systemic interstitial edema ↓ CO → ↓ BP and ↑ HR MAP <60 mm Hg (or 40 mm Hg drop in BP from baseline) ↓ Coronary perfusion → dysrhythmias, myocardial ischemia, MI ↓ Peripheral perfusion → ischemia of distal extremities, ↓ pulses, ↓ capillary refill	Profound hypotension ↓ CO Bradycardia, irregular rhythm ↓ BP inadequate to perfuse vital organs
Gastrointestinal System		
↓ Blood supply ↓ GI motility Hypoactive bowel sounds ↑ Risk for paralytic ileus	Vasoconstriction and ↓ perfusion → ischemic gut (e.g., stomach, intestines, gallbladder, pancreas): • Erosive ulcers • GI bleeding • Translocation of GI bacteria • Impaired absorption of nutrients	Ischemic gut
Hepatic System		
	Failure to metabolize drugs and waste products Cell death (↑ liver enzymes) Jaundice (↓ clearance of bilirubin) ↑ NH_3 (ammonia) and lactate	Metabolic changes from accumulation of waste products (e.g., NH_3, lactate, CO_2)
Hematologic System		
	DIC: • Thrombin clots in microcirculation • Consumption of platelets and clotting factors	DIC progresses
Neurologic System		
Oriented to person, place, time Restless, apprehensive, confused Change in level of consciousness	↓ Cerebral perfusion pressure ↓ Cerebral blood flow ↓ Responsiveness to stimuli Delirium	Unresponsive Areflexia (loss of reflexes) Pupils nonreactive and dilated
Renal System		
↓ Renal blood flow ↑ Renin resulting in release of angiotensin (vasoconstrictor) ↑ Aldosterone causing Na^+ and H_2O reabsorption ↑ Antidiuretic hormone causing H_2O reabsorption	Renal tubules become ischemic → acute tubular necrosis ↓ Urine output ↑ BUN-to-creatinine ratio ↑ Urine sodium ↓ Urine osmolality and specific gravity ↓ Urine potassium Metabolic acidosis	Anuria
Respiratory System		
• ↓ Blood flow to the lungs: • ↑ Physiologic dead space • ↑ Ventilation-perfusion mismatch • Hyperventilation • ↑ Minute ventilation (V_E) • Tachypnea	ARDS: • ↑ Capillary permeability • Pulmonary vasoconstriction • Pulmonary interstitial edema • Alveolar edema • Diffuse infiltrates • Tachypnea • ↓ Compliance • Moist crackles	Severe refractory hypoxemia Respiratory failure
Skin		
Pale and cool Warm and flushed	Cold and clammy	Mottled, cyanotic
Temperature		
Normal or abnormal	Hypothermia or hyperthermia	Hypothermia

Sustained hypoperfusion results in weak peripheral pulses. Ischemia of the distal extremities eventually occurs. Myocardial dysfunction from decreased perfusion results in dysrhythmias, myocardial ischemia, and possibly MI. The result is complete deterioration of the cardiovascular system.

The pulmonary system is often the first system to show signs of critical dysfunction. Blood flow to the lungs is reduced. In response to the decreased blood flow and SNS stimulation, the pulmonary arterioles constrict. This increases PA pressure. As the pressure within the pulmonary vasculature increases, blood flow to the pulmonary capillaries decreases and ventilation-perfusion mismatch worsens.

Another key response in the lungs is fluid movement from the pulmonary vasculature into the interstitial space. As capillary permeability increases, fluid moving into the interstitial spaces results in interstitial edema, bronchoconstriction, and decreased functional residual capacity. With further increases in capillary permeability, fluid moves into the alveoli, causing alveolar edema and a decrease in surfactant production. The combined effects of pulmonary vasoconstriction and bronchoconstriction are impaired gas exchange, decreased compliance, and worsening ventilation-perfusion mismatch. Clinically, the patient has tachypnea, crackles, and an overall increased work of breathing.

The GI system is affected by prolonged decreased tissue perfusion. As the blood supply to the GI tract is decreased, the normally protective mucosal barrier becomes ischemic. This ischemia predisposes the patient to ulcers and GI bleeding (see Chapter 46). It increases the risk for bacterial migration from the GI tract to the blood and lungs. There is a decreased ability to absorb nutrients.

The loss of the liver's functional ability leads to a failure of the liver to metabolize drugs and waste products (e.g., lactate, ammonia). Jaundice results from the accumulation of bilirubin. As the liver cells die, liver enzymes increase. The liver loses its ability to function as an immune organ. Kupffer cells no longer destroy bacteria from the GI tract. Instead, they are released into the bloodstream, increasing the risk of bacteremia.

Prolonged hypoperfusion on the kidneys causes renal tubular ischemia. The resulting acute tubular necrosis may lead to acute kidney injury (AKI). This can be worsened by nephrotoxic drugs (e.g., certain antibiotics, anesthetics, diuretics) (see Chapter 51). The patient has decreased urine output and increased blood urea nitrogen (BUN) and serum creatinine. Metabolic acidosis occurs from the kidneys' inability to excrete acids (especially lactic acid) and reabsorb bicarbonate.

Hematologic dysfunction adds to the complexity of the clinical picture. The patient is at risk for disseminated intravascular coagulation (DIC). The consumption of platelets and clotting factors with secondary fibrinolysis results in clinically significant bleeding from many orifices. These include the GI tract, lungs, and puncture sites (see Chapter 34). Table 42.3 shows laboratory values in DIC.

In this stage, aggressive interventions are needed to prevent the development of MODS.

Refractory Stage

In this last stage of shock, decreased perfusion from peripheral vasoconstriction and decreased CO worsen anaerobic metabolism. Lactic acid accumulation contributes to increased capillary permeability and dilation. Increased capillary permeability allows fluid and plasma proteins to leave the vascular space and move to the interstitial space. Blood pools in the capillary beds due to the constricted venules and dilated arterioles. The loss of intravascular volume worsens hypotension and tachycardia and decreases coronary blood flow. Decreased coronary blood flow leads to worsening myocardial depression and a further decline in CO. Cerebral blood flow cannot be maintained and cerebral ischemia results.

The patient now has profound hypotension and hypoxemia. The failure of the liver, lungs, and kidneys results in an accumulation of waste products, such as lactate, urea, ammonia, and CO_2. The failure of an organ system affects several other organ systems. Recovery is unlikely in this stage. The organs are in failure, and the body's compensatory mechanisms are overwhelmed (Table 42.5).

Diagnostic Studies

There is no single diagnostic study to determine whether a patient is in shock. The diagnosis starts with a history and physical assessment. A thorough medical and surgical history and a history of recent events (e.g., surgery, chest pain, trauma) give valuable data.

Decreased tissue perfusion in shock leads to an increased lactate with a base deficit (the amount needed to bring the pH back to normal). These laboratory changes reflect an increase in anaerobic metabolism.[7] Table 42.2 outlines laboratory findings seen in shock.

Other diagnostic studies include a 12-lead electrocardiogram (ECG), continuous ECG monitoring, chest x-ray, continuous pulse oximetry, and hemodynamic monitoring. Chapter 35 discusses hemodynamic monitoring.

Interprofessional Care

Successful management of a patient in shock depends on the early recognition and treatment of shock. Prompt intervention in the early stages of shock may prevent the decline to the progressive or irreversible stage. Successful management includes (1) identifying patients at risk for developing shock; (2) integrating the patient's history, physical assessment, and clinical findings to establish a diagnosis; (3) interventions to control or eliminate the cause; (4) protecting target and distal organs from dysfunction; and (5) providing multisystem supportive care.

Table 42.6 provides an overview of the initial assessment findings and interventions for the emergency care of patients in shock. General management strategies begin with ensuring that the patient is responsive and has a patent airway. Once the airway is established, either naturally or with an endotracheal tube, O_2 delivery must be optimized. Supplemental O_2 and mechanical ventilation may be needed to maintain an arterial O_2 saturation of 90% or more (PaO_2 greater than 60 mm Hg) to avoid hypoxemia (see Chapter 28). The mean arterial pressure (MAP) and circulating blood volume are optimized with fluid replacement and drug therapy.

TABLE 42.6 EMERGENCY MANAGEMENT

Shock

Common Causes	Assessment Findings	Interventions
Medical • Addisonian crisis • Dehydration • Diabetes • Diabetes insipidus • MI • Pulmonary embolus • Sepsis **Surgical** • Aortic dissection • GI bleeding • Postoperative bleeding • Ruptured ectopic pregnancy or ovarian cyst • Ruptured organ or vessel • Vaginal bleeding **Trauma** • Fractures, spinal injury • Multiorgan injury • Ruptured or lacerated vessel or organ (e.g., spleen)	• Anxiety • Chills • Confusion • Cool, clammy skin (warm skin in early onset of septic and neurogenic shock) • Cyanosis • Dysrhythmias • Extreme thirst • Feeling of impending doom • Hypotension • ↓ Level of consciousness • Narrowed pulse pressure • Nausea and vomiting • Obvious hemorrhage or injury • ↓ O_2 saturation • Pallor • Rapid, weak, thready pulses • Restlessness • Tachypnea, dyspnea, or shallow, irregular respirations • Temperature dysregulation • Weakness	**Initial** • If unresponsive, assess circulation, airway, and breathing (CAB). • If responsive, monitor airway, breathing, and circulation (ABC). • Stabilize cervical spine as appropriate. • Control any external bleeding with direct pressure or pressure dressing. • Give high-flow O_2 (100%) by nonrebreather mask or bag-valve-mask. • Anticipate need for intubation and mechanical ventilation. • Establish IV access with 2 large-bore catheters (14- to 16-gauge) or an intraosseous access device; aid with central line insertion. • Begin fluid resuscitation with crystalloids (e.g., 30 mL/kg repeated until hemodynamic improvement is seen). • Draw blood for laboratory studies (e.g., blood cultures, lactate, WBC). • Assess for life-threatening injuries (e.g., cardiac tamponade, liver laceration, tension pneumothorax). • Consider vasopressor therapy if hypotension persists after fluid resuscitation. • Insert an indwelling urinary catheter and nasogastric tube. • Start antibiotic therapy after blood cultures if sepsis is suspected. • Obtain 12-lead ECG and treat dysrhythmias. **Ongoing Monitoring** • ABCs • Level of consciousness • Vital signs, including pulse oximetry; peripheral pulses, capillary refill, skin color and temperature • Respiratory status • Heart rate and rhythm • Urine output

Oxygen and Ventilation

O_2 delivery depends on CO, available hemoglobin, and arterial O_2 saturation (SaO_2). Methods to optimize O_2 delivery are directed at increasing supply and decreasing demand. Supply is increased by (1) optimizing the CO with fluid replacement and/or drug therapy, (2) increasing the hemoglobin through blood transfusions, and/or (3) increasing the arterial O_2 saturation with supplemental O_2 and mechanical ventilation.

Plan care to avoid disrupting the balance of O_2 supply and demand. Space activities that increase O_2 consumption (e.g., endotracheal suctioning, position changes) appropriately for O_2 conservation. Intermittent or continuous monitoring of $ScvO_2$ by a central venous catheter or mixed venous O_2 saturation (SvO_2) may be helpful. Both reflect the dynamic balance between O_2 supply and demand. Assess these values along with related hemodynamic measures (e.g., arterial pressure–based cardiac output [APCO], O_2 consumption, hemoglobin) to evaluate the patient's response to treatments and activities (see Chapters 28 and 35).

Fluid Resuscitation

The cornerstone of therapy for septic, hypovolemic, and anaphylactic shock is volume expansion with fluid administration (Table 42.7).[8] The goal for fluid resuscitation is to restore tissue perfusion. Fluid resuscitation should start using 1 or 2 large-bore (e.g., 14- to 16-gauge) IV catheters, an intraosseous (IO) access device, or a central venous catheter.

SAFETY ALERT

Intraosseous (IO) Access

- Use an IO access device for emergency resuscitation when IV access cannot be obtained.
- Insertion sites include the sternum, proximal and distal tibia, and proximal and distal humerus.
- Remove IO devices within 24 hr of insertion or as soon as possible after peripheral or central IV access is obtained.
- Monitor for complications: extravasation of drugs and fluids into the soft tissue, fractures caused during insertion, and osteomyelitis.

The choice of fluid is based on the type and volume of fluid lost and the patient's clinical status. The ideal choice of fluid is controversial.[11–13] Currently, normal saline is most often used in the initial resuscitation of shock. Large-volume resuscitation with normal saline can lead to hyperchloremic metabolic acidosis. Lactated Ringer solution can cause serum lactate levels to increase because the failing liver cannot convert lactate to bicarbonate.[13] Transfusions of RBCs may be given to treat hypovolemic shock due to bleeding. Colloids (4% to 5%) have not been shown to improve patient outcomes.[12,13]

Fluid responsiveness is determined by clinical assessment. Although BP helps to determine whether the patient's CO is adequate, an assessment of end-organ perfusion (e.g., urine output, neurologic function, peripheral pulses) provides more

TABLE 42.7 Fluid Therapy in Shock

Fluid Type	Mechanism of Action	Type of Shock	Nursing Implications
Crystalloids			
Isotonic			
• 0.9% NaCl, normal saline solution (NSS) • Lactated Ringer (LR) solution	Fluid primarily stays in the intravascular space, ↑ intravascular volume.	Used for initial volume replacement in most types of shock.	Monitor patient closely for circulatory overload. Do not use LR in patients with liver failure. LR may be used if hyperchloremic acidosis develops from use of NSS in fluid resuscitation.
Hypertonic			
• 1.8%, 3%, 5% NaCl	Fluid stays in the intravascular space, increases serum osmolarity, shifts fluid volume from intracellular space to extracellular space to intravascular space.	May be used for initial volume expansion in hypovolemic shock.	Monitor patient closely for signs of hypernatremia (e.g., disorientation, seizures). Central line preferred for infusing saline solutions ≥3%, since these may damage veins.
Blood or Blood Products			
Packed red blood cells Fresh frozen plasma Platelets	Replaces blood loss, increases O_2-carrying capability. Replaces coagulation factors. Helps control bleeding caused by thrombocytopenia.	All types.	Same precautions as any blood administration (see Chapter 34).
Colloids			
Human serum albumin (5% or 25%)	Can increase plasma colloid osmotic pressure. Rapid volume expansion.	All types except cardiogenic and neurogenic shock.	Use 5% solution in hypovolemic patients. Use 25% solution in patients with fluid and sodium restrictions. Monitor for circulatory overload. Mild side effects of chills, fever, and urticaria may develop. More expensive than crystalloids.
dextran (dextran 40)	Hyperosmotic glucose polymer.	Limited use because of side effects, including reducing platelet adhesion, diluting clotting factors.	Increases risk for bleeding. Monitor patient for allergic reactions and acute kidney injury. Has maximum volume recommendations per manufacturer.

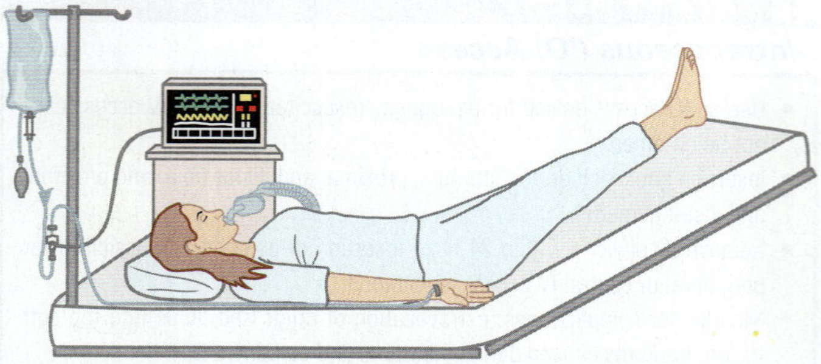

Fig. 42.7 Passive leg raise challenge in a patient with septic shock.

relevant data. Monitor vital signs, cerebral and abdominal perfusion pressures, capillary refill, neurologic status, and skin temperature. Evaluate trends in BP with an automatic BP cuff or an arterial catheter. Use an indwelling urinary catheter to monitor urine output during resuscitation. Hemodynamic parameters, such as SVV or CO, are also used.

Other interventions we use to monitor fluid response include a passive leg raise (PLR) challenge and inferior vena cava evaluation.[14,15] A PLR challenge provides a transient increase in fluid volume of 150 to 500 mL by placing the patient supine and raising the legs to 45 degrees (Fig. 42.7). Response is monitored within 1 to 2 minutes by measuring CO, CI, SV, SVV, or other parameters for improvement. If the response is positive, the patient is fluid responsive and should receive more fluids.

! SAFETY ALERT

Complications of Fluid Resuscitation

- Warm crystalloid and colloid solutions during massive fluid resuscitation to prevent hypothermia.
- When giving large volumes of packed RBCs, remember that they do not contain clotting factors.
- Assess for hypocalcemia and disseminated intravascular coagulation (DIC).
- Replace clotting factors based on the clinical status and laboratory studies.

Drug Therapy

The goal of drug therapy is to correct decreased tissue perfusion. Decisions on which drug to use should be based on the physiologic goal. We give IV drugs used to improve perfusion via an infusion pump and central venous line. Many of these drugs have vasoconstrictor properties that are harmful if the drug leaks into the tissues while being infused peripherally (Table 42.8).

Sympathomimetic drugs. Drugs that mimic the action of the SNS are called *sympathomimetic*. Their effects are mediated through their binding to α- or β-adrenergic receptors. They differ in their relative α- and β-adrenergic effects.[16]

Many of these drugs cause peripheral vasoconstriction and are called *vasopressor drugs* (e.g., norepinephrine, dopamine, phenylephrine). These drugs can cause severe peripheral vasoconstriction and an increase in SVR, further risking

TABLE 42.8 Drug Therapy

Shock

Drug[a]	Mechanism of Action	Type of Shock	Nursing Implications
angiotensin II (Giapreza)	↑ BP, ↑ MAP ↑ SVR	Septic and other distributive shock	Give via central line. Monitor for thromboembolic events. Provide VTE prophylaxis.
dobutamine	↑ Myocardial contractility ↓ Ventricular filling pressures ↓ SVR, PAWP ↑ CO, SV, CVP ↑/↓ HR	Used in cardiogenic shock with severe systolic dysfunction Used in septic shock to increase O_2 delivery and raise $ScvO_2$ or SvO_2 to 70% if Hgb >7 g/dL or Hct ≥30%	Give via central line (infiltration leads to tissue sloughing). Do not give in same line with $NaHCO_3$. Monitor HR, BP (hypotension may worsen, requiring addition of a vasopressor). Stop infusion if tachydysrhythmias develop.
dopamine	Positive inotropic effects: ↑ Myocardial contractility ↑ Automaticity ↑ Atrioventricular conduction ↑ HR, CO ↑ BP, ↑ MAP ↑ MVO_2 Can cause progressive vasoconstriction at high doses	Cardiogenic shock	Give via central line (infiltration leads to tissue sloughing). Do not give in same line with $NaHCO_3$. Monitor for tachydysrhythmias. Monitor for peripheral vasoconstriction (e.g., paresthesias, coldness in extremities) at moderate to high doses.
epinephrine (Adrenalin)	*Low doses:* β-Adrenergic agonist (cardiac stimulation, bronchodilation, peripheral vasodilation) ↑ HR, contractility, CO ↓ SVR *High doses:* α-Adrenergic agonist (peripheral vasoconstriction) ↑ SV, SVR ↑ Systolic/↓ diastolic BP, widened pulse pressure ↑ CVP, PAWP	Cardiogenic shock Anaphylactic shock Septic shock, if 2nd agent needed after norepinephrine Cardiac arrest, pulseless ventricular tachycardia, ventricular fibrillation, asystole	Monitor for HR >110 beats/min. Monitor for dyspnea, pulmonary edema. Monitor for chest pain, dysrhythmias from ↑ MVO_2. Monitor for renal failure due to ischemia.
hydrocortisone (Solu-Cortef)	↓ Inflammation, reverses ↑ capillary permeability ↑ BP, HR	Septic shock requiring vasopressor therapy (despite fluid resuscitation) to maintain adequate BP Anaphylactic shock if hypotension persists after initial therapy	Monitor for hypokalemia, hyperglycemia. Consider use as continuous infusion.
nitroglycerin	Venous dilation Dilates coronary arteries ↓ Preload, MVO_2, SVR, BP	Cardiogenic shock	Continuously monitor BP and HR, since reflex tachycardia may occur. Glass bottle recommended for infusion.
norepinephrine (Levophed)	β_1-Adrenergic agonist (cardiac stimulation) α-Adrenergic agonist (peripheral vasoconstriction) Renal and splanchnic vasoconstriction ↑ BP, MAP, CVP, PAWP, SVR ↑/↓ CO	Cardiogenic shock after MI Septic shock—first drug of choice for BP unresponsive to adequate fluid resuscitation	Give via central line (infiltration leads to tissue sloughing). Monitor for dysrhythmias due to ↑ MVO_2 requirements.
phenylephrine	α-Adrenergic agonist (peripheral vasoconstriction) Renal, mesenteric, splanchnic, cutaneous, and pulmonary blood vessel constriction ↑ HR, BP, SVR ↑/↓ CO	Neurogenic shock	Monitor for reflex bradycardia, headache, restlessness. Monitor for renal failure from ↓ renal blood flow. Give via central line (infiltration leads to tissue sloughing).
sodium nitroprusside	Arterial and venous vasodilation ↓ Preload, afterload ↓ CVP, PAWP ↑/↓ CO ↓ BP	Cardiogenic shock with ↑ SVR	Continuously monitor BP. Protect solution from light. Wrap infusion bottle with opaque covering. Give with D_5W only. Monitor serum cyanide levels and for signs of cyanide toxicity (e.g., metabolic acidosis, tachycardia, altered level of consciousness, seizures, coma, almond smell on breath).
vasopressin	Antidiuretic hormone Nonadrenergic vasoconstrictor ↑ MAP ↑ Urine output	Shock states (most often septic shock) refractory to other vasopressors	Given with norepinephrine and in low doses. Infusions are not titrated. Monitor hemodynamic pressures and urine output.

[a]Consult agency guidelines, pharmacist, pharmacology references, and drug manufacturer's materials for more information and dosing recommendations.

CVP, Central venous pressure; *MVO_2,* myocardial O_2 consumption; *PAWP,* pulmonary artery wedge pressure; *SVR,* systemic vascular resistance.

tissue perfusion. The increased SVR increases the workload of the heart and myocardial O_2 demand. It can harm a patient in cardiogenic shock by causing further myocardial damage and increasing the risk for dysrhythmias.[17] Use of vasopressor drugs is limited to patients who do not respond to fluid resuscitation. Adequate fluid resuscitation must be achieved before starting vasopressors because the vasoconstrictor effects in patients with low blood volume will further reduce tissue perfusion. Typically, if hypotension persists after adequate fluid resuscitation, we then give a vasopressor (e.g., norepinephrine, dopamine) and/or an inotrope (e.g., dobutamine).

The goal of vasopressor therapy is to achieve and maintain a MAP of greater than 65 mm Hg.[16] Continuously monitor end-organ perfusion (e.g., urine output, level of consciousness) and serum lactate levels (e.g., every 3 hours for the first 6 hours) to ensure that tissue perfusion is adequate.

Vasodilator drugs. Patients in cardiogenic shock have decreased myocardial contractility. Vasodilators may be needed to decrease afterload. This reduces myocardial workload and O_2 requirements. Although generalized sympathetic vasoconstriction is a useful compensatory mechanism for maintaining BP, excessive constriction can reduce tissue blood flow and increase the workload of the heart. The reason for using vasodilator therapy is to break the harmful cycle of widespread vasoconstriction causing a decrease in CO and BP, resulting in further sympathetic-induced vasoconstriction.

The goal of vasodilator therapy, as in vasopressor therapy, is to maintain the MAP greater than 65 mm Hg. Monitor hemodynamic parameters (e.g., CVP, CO, $ScvO_2/SvO_2$, SV, PA pressures) and assessment findings so that fluids can be increased, or vasodilator therapy decreased if a serious fall in CO or BP occurs. The vasodilator agent most often used for the patient in cardiogenic shock is nitroglycerin. Vasodilation may be enhanced with nitroprusside or nitroglycerin in noncardiogenic shock.

Nutrition Therapy

Protein-calorie malnutrition is common because of hypermetabolism. Nutrition is vital to reducing mortality.[18] Enteral nutrition (EN) should be started within the first 24 hours. However, full calorie replacement is not recommended for previously well-nourished adults early in a critical illness.[18] Start the patient on a *trophic feeding*. This is a small amount of EN (e.g., 10 mL/hr). Early EN enhances perfusion of the GI tract and helps maintain the integrity of the gut mucosa. Advance feedings as tolerated and as prescribed. We use parenteral nutrition (PN) only if EN is contraindicated. Chapter 44 discusses EN and PN.

Weigh the patient daily on the same scale at the same time of day. If the patient has a significant weight loss, rule out dehydration before adding more calories. Large weight gains are common because of third spacing of fluids. Monitor serum protein, total albumin, prealbumin, BUN, serum glucose, and serum electrolytes to assess nutrition status.

Measures Specific to Type of Shock

Cardiogenic Shock

For a patient in cardiogenic shock, the overall goal is to restore heart function and the balance between O_2 supply and demand in the myocardium. Cardiac catheterization is done as soon as possible after the initial insult.[1] Specific measures to restore blood flow include angioplasty with stenting, emergency revascularization, and valve replacement. Until these interventions are done, we must support the heart to optimize SV and CO to achieve optimal perfusion (Tables 42.8 and 42.9).[12]

Hemodynamic management aims to reduce the workload of the heart through drug therapy and/or mechanical interventions. Drug choice is based on the clinical goal. Drugs can decrease the workload of the heart by dilating coronary arteries (e.g., nitrates) and reducing preload (e.g., diuretics), afterload (e.g., vasodilators), and heart rate and contractility (e.g., β-adrenergic blockers).

The patient may benefit from a circulatory assist device (e.g., intraaortic balloon pump, ventricular assist device [VAD]) (see Chapter 39). The goals are to decrease SVR and left ventricular workload so that the heart can heal. A VAD may be used as a temporary measure for the patient in cardiogenic shock who is awaiting heart transplantation. Heart transplantation is an option for a small, select group of patients with cardiogenic shock.

Hypovolemic Shock

The underlying principles of managing hypovolemic shock focus on stopping the fluid loss and restoring circulating volume. We often calculate the initial fluid resuscitation using a 3:1 rule (3 mL of isotonic crystalloid for every 1 mL of estimated blood loss). Table 42.7 describes fluids used for volume resuscitation, their mechanism of action, and specific nursing implications.

Septic Shock

Patients in septic shock need large amounts of fluid replacement (Fig. 42.8). The overall goal of fluid resuscitation is to restore the intravascular volume and organ perfusion. We achieve initial volume resuscitation by giving 30 mL/kg of an isotonic crystalloid solution. Albumin 4% to 5% is an option when patients need substantial volume.

A fluid challenge technique (e.g., a minimum of 30 mL/kg of crystalloids) may be done and repeated until hemodynamic improvement (e.g., increase in MAP and/or CVP) is seen. To optimize and evaluate large-volume fluid resuscitation, hemodynamic monitoring is needed. Table 42.9 shows predetermined end points of fluid resuscitation along with methods to reassess volume status.

If the patient is hypotensive after initial volume resuscitation and no longer fluid responsive, we may add vasopressors. The first drug of choice is norepinephrine.[16] Vasodilation and low CO, or vasodilation alone, can cause low BP despite adequate fluid resuscitation. Vasopressin may be added for those who are refractory to initial vasopressor therapy.[17] Exogenous vasopressin can replace the stores of physiologic vasopressin that are often depleted in septic shock.

DRUG ALERT

Vasopressin

- Given along with norepinephrine.
- Infuse at low doses (e.g., 0.03 units/min) using an IV pump.
- Do not titrate infusion.
- Use cautiously in patients with coronary artery disease.

TABLE 42.9 Interprofessional Care

Shock

Oxygenation	Circulation	Drug Therapies	Supportive Therapies
Cardiogenic Shock			
• Provide supplemental O_2 (e.g., nasal cannula, nonrebreather mask) • Intubation and mechanical ventilation, if needed • Monitor $ScvO_2$ or SvO_2	• Restore blood flow with angioplasty with stenting, emergent coronary revascularization • Reduce workload of heart with circulatory assist devices: IABP, VAD	• Nitrates (e.g., nitroglycerin) • Inotropes (e.g., dobutamine) • Diuretics (e.g., furosemide) • β-Adrenergic blockers (contraindicated with ↓ ejection fraction)	• Treat dysrhythmias
Hypovolemic Shock			
• Provide supplemental O_2 • Monitor $ScvO_2$ or $ScvO_2$	• Rapid fluid replacement using 2 large-bore (14–16 gauge) peripheral IV lines, an intraosseous access device, or central venous catheter • Restore fluid volume (e.g., blood or blood products, crystalloids) • End points of fluid resuscitation: • CVP 15 mm Hg • PAWP 10–12 mm Hg	• No specific drug therapy	• Correct the cause (e.g., stop bleeding, GI losses) • Use warmed IV fluids, including blood products (if appropriate)
Septic Shock			
• Provide supplemental O_2 • Intubation and mechanical ventilation, if needed • Monitor $ScvO_2$ or SvO_2	• Aggressive fluid resuscitation (e.g., 30 mL/kg of crystalloids repeated if hemodynamic improvement is noted) • End points of fluid resuscitation are based on: • Focused physical assessment including vital signs, cardiopulmonary assessment, capillary refill, peripheral pulses, and skin or any 2 of the following: • $ScvO_2$ >70 or SvO_2 >65 • CVP 8–12 mm Hg • Cardiovascular ultrasound • Fluid responsiveness with passive leg raise or fluid challenge	• Antibiotics as ordered • Vasopressors (e.g., norepinephrine) • Inotropes (e.g., dobutamine) • Anticoagulants (e.g., low-molecular-weight heparin)	• Obtain cultures (e.g., blood, wound) before beginning antibiotics • Monitor temperature • Control blood glucose • Stress ulcer prophylaxis
Neurogenic Shock			
• Maintain patent airway • Provide supplemental O_2 • Intubation and mechanical ventilation (if needed)	• Cautious administration of fluids	• Vasopressors (e.g., phenylephrine) • Atropine (for bradycardia)	• Minimize spinal cord trauma with stabilization • Monitor temperature
Anaphylactic Shock			
• Maintain patent airway • Optimize oxygenation with supplemental O_2 • Intubation and mechanical ventilation, if needed	• Aggressive fluid resuscitation with colloids	• Epinephrine (IM or IV) • Antihistamines (e.g., diphenhydramine) • Histamine (H_2)-receptor blockers • Bronchodilators: nebulized (e.g., albuterol) • Corticosteroids (if hypotension persists)	• Identify and remove offending cause • Prevent via avoidance of known allergens • Premedicate with history of prior sensitivity (e.g., contrast media)
Obstructive Shock			
• Maintain patent airway • Provide supplemental O_2 • Intubation and mechanical ventilation, if needed	• Restore circulation by treating cause of obstruction • Fluid resuscitation may provide temporary improvement in CO and BP	• No specific drug therapy	• Treat cause of obstruction (e.g., pericardiocentesis for cardiac tamponade, needle decompression or chest tube insertion for tension pneumothorax, embolectomy for pulmonary embolism)

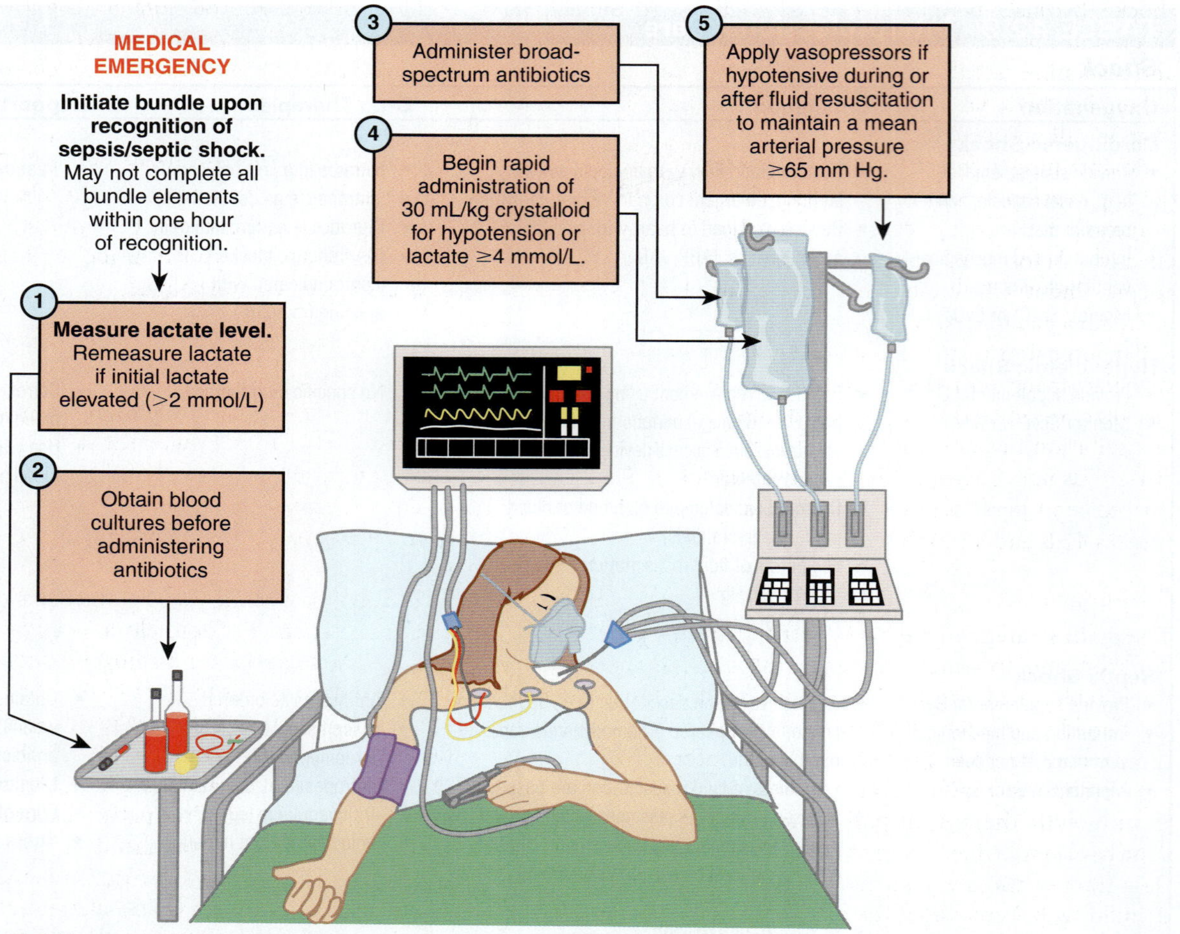

Fig. 42.8 Hour-1 bundle for sepsis and septic shock. (From Institute for Healthcare Improvement: Surviving Sepsis campaign.)

Vasopressor drugs may increase BP but can decrease SV. Giving an inotropic agent (e.g., dobutamine) can offset the decrease in SV and increase tissue perfusion (Table 42.8). IV corticosteroids may be considered for patients in septic shock who cannot maintain an adequate BP despite vasopressor therapy and fluid resuscitation.

To try to meet the increasing tissue demands coupled with a low SVR, the patient initially has a normal or high CO. If the patient is unable to achieve and maintain an adequate CO and has unmet tissue O_2 demands, CO may have to be increased using drug therapy (e.g., dopamine). $ScvO_2$ or SvO_2 monitoring is used to assess the balance between O_2 delivery and consumption, and adequacy of the CO (see Chapter 35). If balance is maintained, tissue demands will be met.

Broad-spectrum antibiotics are an important and early part of therapy. They should be started within the first hour of sepsis or septic shock.[19] Obtain cultures (e.g., blood, wound, urine, stool, sputum) before starting antibiotics. However, this should not delay the start of antibiotics within the first hour. Specific antibiotics may be ordered after we identify the organism.

Glucose levels should be maintained below 180 mg/dL (10.0 mmol/L) for patients in shock.[7] Monitor glucose levels according to agency policy. Stress ulcer prophylaxis with proton pump inhibitors (e.g., pantoprazole) and VTE prophylaxis (e.g., heparin, enoxaparin [Lovenox]) are recommended.[7]

Neurogenic Shock

The specific treatment of neurogenic shock is based on the cause. If the cause is spinal cord injury, we use general measures to promote spinal stability (e.g., spinal precautions, cervical stabilization with a collar). Once the spine is stabilized, treating hypotension and bradycardia are essential to prevent further spinal cord damage. Treatment involves vasopressors (e.g., phenylephrine) to maintain BP and organ perfusion (Table 42.8). Bradycardia may be treated with atropine. Infuse fluids cautiously because hypotension is not related to fluid loss. The patient with a spinal cord injury is monitored for hypothermia caused by hypothalamic dysfunction (Table 42.9).

Anaphylactic Shock

The first strategy in managing patients at risk for anaphylactic shock is prevention. A thorough history is key to avoiding risk factors for anaphylaxis (Table 42.1). The clinical presentation of anaphylactic shock is dramatic. Immediate intervention is required. Epinephrine is the drug of choice to treat anaphylactic shock.[6] It causes peripheral vasoconstriction and bronchodilation and opposes the effect of histamine. Diphenhydramine and histamine receptor blockers (e.g., famotidine) are given as adjunctive therapies to block the ongoing release of histamine from the allergic reaction.

Maintaining a patent airway is important. The patient can quickly develop airway compromise from laryngeal edema or bronchoconstriction. Nebulized bronchodilators are highly effective. Aerosolized epinephrine can reduce treat laryngeal edema. Endotracheal intubation may be needed to secure and maintain a patent airway.

Hypotension results from fluid leaking out of the intravascular space into the interstitial space due to increased vascular permeability and vasodilation. Aggressive fluid resuscitation, usually with crystalloids, is needed. IV corticosteroids may be helpful in anaphylactic shock if significant hypotension persists after 1 to 2 hours of aggressive therapy (Tables 42.8 and 42.9).

Obstructive Shock

The main strategy in treating obstructive shock is early recognition and treatment to relieve or manage the obstruction (Table 42.1). Mechanical decompression for pericardial tamponade, tension pneumothorax, and hemopneumothorax may be done by needle or tube insertion. A pulmonary embolism requires immediate anticoagulation therapy, thrombolytic therapy, or pulmonary embolectomy. Superior vena cava syndrome, a compression or obstruction of the outflow tract of the mediastinum, may be treated by radiation, debulking, or removal of the mass or cause. A decompressive laparotomy may be done for abdominal compartment syndrome for patients with high intraabdominal pressures and hemodynamic instability.

NURSING MANAGEMENT: SHOCK

Assessment

Focus your assessment on the ABCs: airway, breathing, and circulation. Next, assess for tissue perfusion. This includes evaluating vital signs, level of consciousness, peripheral pulses, capillary refill, skin (e.g., temperature, color, moisture), and urine output. As shock progresses, the patient's neurologic status declines, urine output decreases, skin becomes cooler and mottled, and peripheral pulses decrease.

To understand the complexity of the patient's clinical status, integrate all the assessment data. Obtain a brief history from the patient or caregiver. Include a description of the events leading to the shock state, time of onset and duration of symptoms, and health history (e.g., medications, allergies). Obtain details about any care the patient received before hospitalization.

Clinical Problems

Clinical problems for the patient in shock may include:

- Impaired cardiac function
- Impaired respiratory function
- Altered BP

More information on nursing diagnoses and interventions for the patient with shock is presented in eNursing Care Plan 42.1 (available on the website for this chapter).

Planning

The overall goals for a patient in shock include (1) adequate tissue perfusion, (2) restoration of normal or baseline BP, (3) recovery of organ function, (4) avoiding complications from prolonged states of hypoperfusion, and (5) preventing health care–associated complications.

Implementation

Health Promotion

You play a key role in the prevention of shock by identifying patients at risk. In general, patients who are older, are immunocompromised, or have chronic illnesses are at an increased risk. Any person who has surgery or trauma is at risk for shock from hemorrhage, spinal cord injury, sepsis, and other problems (Table 42.1).

Planning is essential to help prevent shock after you identify an at-risk patient. For example, a patient with an acute anterior wall MI is at high risk for cardiogenic shock.[1] The main goal for this patient is to limit the infarct size. This is done by restoring coronary blood flow. Rest, analgesics, and sedation can reduce the myocardial demand for O_2. Modify the ICU environment to provide care at intervals that will not increase the patient's O_2 demand. For example, if the patient becomes tired with bathing, perform this care at a time that does not interfere with tests or other activities that may increase O_2 demand.

A person with certain severe allergies, such as to drugs, shellfish, insect bites, and latex, is at increased risk for anaphylactic shock. This risk can be decreased by carefully assessing the patient for allergies.

> **SAFETY ALERT**
>
> ***Preventing Allergic Reactions***
>
> - Always confirm the patient's allergies before giving drugs or starting diagnostic procedures (e.g., CT scan with contrast media).
> - Premedicate (e.g., diphenhydramine, methylprednisolone) patients who need a drug to which they are at high risk for an allergic reaction (e.g., contrast media).
> - Encourage patients with allergies to obtain and wear a medical alert device and report all allergies to their HCPs.
> - Teach patients about kits that contain equipment and drugs (e.g., epinephrine) for the treatment of acute allergic reactions.

Careful monitoring of fluid balance can help prevent hypovolemic shock. Ongoing monitoring of intake and output and daily weights is important. Identifying trends in the patient's condition is more meaningful than any single piece of clinical information.

Carefully monitor all patients for infection. Progression from an infection to sepsis and septic shock depends on the patient's defense mechanisms. Patients who are immunocompromised are at high risk for opportunistic infections. Strategies to decrease the risk for health care–associated infections (HAIs) include decreasing the number of invasive catheters (e.g., central lines, bladder catheters), using aseptic technique during invasive procedures, and paying strict attention to hand washing. Change equipment per agency policy. Thoroughly sanitize or discard (if disposable) equipment between patient use.

Evidence-based guidelines are available to reduce the risk for HAIs (e.g., ventilator-associated pneumonia, central line infections, catheter-associated urinary tract infections). These guidelines, called *care bundles,* outline key interventions aimed at reducing infections.[18]

◆ Acute Care

Your role in shock involves (1) monitoring the patient's ongoing status, (2) identifying trends to detect changes in the patient's condition, (3) planning and implementing nursing interventions and therapy, (4) evaluating the patient's response to therapy, (5) providing emotional support to the patient and caregiver, and (6) collaborating with other health care team members to coordinate care.

Neurologic status. Assess the patient's neurologic status, including orientation and level of consciousness using a valid tool, at least every 1 to 2 hours. Neurologic status is the best indicator of cerebral blood flow. Be aware of the manifestations of neurologic involvement (e.g., changes in behavior, restlessness, blurred vision, confusion, paresthesias). Note any subtle changes in the patient's mental status (e.g., mild agitation) and report them to the HCP.

Orient the patient to person, place, time, and events on a regular basis. Orientation to the ICU environment is especially important. Reduce noise and light levels to control sensory input. Keep a day-night cycle of activity, and rest as much as possible. Sensory overload and disruption of the patient's diurnal cycle may contribute to delirium (see Chapter 64).

Cardiovascular status. We base most of the therapy for shock on information about cardiovascular status. If the patient is unstable, continuously assess heart rate and rhythm, BP, CVP, and PA pressures, including CO, SVR, SV, and SVV (if available). Monitoring trends in hemodynamic parameters provides more important information than single values. Integrating hemodynamic with physical assessment data is essential in planning strategies to manage the patient with shock. Chapter 35 discusses cardiovascular monitoring.

Continuously monitor the patient's ECG. Dysrhythmias may result from the cardiovascular and metabolic problems. Assess heart sounds for an S_3 or S_4 sound or new murmurs. An S_3 sound usually indicates HF. Monitor the patient's skin for signs of adequate perfusion. Changes in temperature, pallor, flushing, cyanosis, diaphoresis, and piloerection may indicate hypoperfusion.

Give the prescribed therapy to correct cardiovascular problems. Assess the patient's response to fluid and drug administration as often as every 5 to 10 minutes. Make adjustments (e.g., drug titration) as needed. Once tissue perfusion is restored and the patient is stabilized, you can decrease the frequency of monitoring and slowly wean the patient off drugs to support BP and tissue perfusion.

CHECK YOUR PRACTICE

You are admitting a 69-year-old male patient to the ICU with a diagnosis of sepsis. Your findings show that he is confused, with weak peripheral pulses and a BP of 84/50.

- What fluids would you expect to be ordered?
- How much fluid would you expect to infuse to improve his BP?
- Despite aggressive fluid resuscitation, the patient is still hypotensive. What drug would you expect to give to improve tissue perfusion?

Respiratory status. Frequently assess respiratory status to ensure adequate oxygenation, detect complications, and provide data about acid-base status. At first, monitor the rate, depth, and rhythm of respirations as often as every 15 to 30 minutes. Increased rate and depth provide information about the patient's attempts to correct metabolic acidosis. Assess breath sounds every 1 to 2 hours and as needed for any changes that may indicate fluid overload or accumulation of secretions.

Use pulse oximetry to continuously monitor O_2 saturation. Pulse oximetry using a patient's finger may not be accurate in a shock state because of poor peripheral circulation. Instead, attach the probe to the ear, nose, or forehead (according to the manufacturer's guidelines). Arterial blood gases (ABGs) give definitive information on ventilation and oxygenation status and acid-base balance. Initial interpretation of ABGs is often your responsibility. A PaO_2 less than 60 mm Hg (in the absence of chronic lung disease) indicates hypoxemia and the need for higher O_2 concentrations or for a different mode of O_2 administration. Low $PaCO_2$ with a low pH and low bicarbonate level may mean that the patient is trying to compensate for metabolic acidosis from increasing lactate levels.

A rising $PaCO_2$ with a persistently low pH and PaO_2 indicates the need for advanced pulmonary management. Many patients in shock are intubated and on mechanical ventilation. Maintaining a patent airway and monitoring for ventilator-related complications are critical. Chapter 28 discusses mechanical ventilation.

Renal status. At first, measure urine output every 1 to 2 hours to assess the adequacy of renal perfusion. Inserting an indwelling urinary catheter helps to measure during resuscitation. Urine output less than 0.5 mL/kg/hr may indicate inadequate renal perfusion. Use trends in serum creatinine values to assess renal function. Serum creatinine is a better indicator of renal function than BUN levels because the patient's catabolic state affects BUN levels.

Body temperature. Monitor temperature every 4 hours if normal. In the presence of a high or subnormal temperature, obtain hourly core temperatures (e.g., urinary, esophageal, PA catheter). Use light covers and control the room temperature to keep the patient comfortably warm. If the patient's temperature increases to greater than 101.5°F (38.6°C) and the patient becomes uncomfortable or shows cardiovascular compromise, treat the fever with antipyretic drugs (e.g., ibuprofen) and remove some of the patient's covers. Consider a cooling device if fever persists despite treatment (see Table 12.5).

Gastrointestinal status. Auscultate bowel sounds at least every 4 hours. Monitor for abdominal distention. If a nasogastric tube is present, measure drainage and check for occult blood. Check all stools for occult blood.

Skin integrity. Hygiene is especially important because impaired tissue perfusion predisposes the patient to skin breakdown and infection. Perform bathing and other nursing measures carefully because a patient in shock has problems with O_2 delivery to tissues. Use clinical judgment in determining priorities of care to limit the demands for increased O_2. Monitor trends in O_2 consumption (e.g., SpO_2, $ScvO_2/SvO_2$) during all interventions to assess the patient's tolerance of activity.

The increased O_2 demand that occurs with repositioning those with limited O_2 reserves makes preventing pressure injuries challenging. Turn the patient at least every 1 to 2 hours. Maintain good body alignment. Use a pressure-relieving or pressure-reducing mattress or a specialty bed as needed. Perform passive range of motion 3 or 4 times a day to maintain joint mobility and help to prevent breakdown.

Oral care is essential because mucous membranes may become dry and fragile in the volume-depleted patient. The intubated patient usually has difficulty swallowing, causing pooled secretions in the mouth. Apply a water-soluble lubricant to the lips to prevent drying and cracking. Brush the patient's teeth or gums with a soft toothbrush every 12 hours. Swab the lips and oral mucosa with a moisturizing solution every 2 to 4 hours.

Emotional support. Do not underestimate the effects of fear and anxiety when the patient and caregiver are faced with a life-threatening situation. Fear, anxiety, and pain may worsen respiratory distress and increase catecholamine release. When implementing care, monitor the patient's mental state and pain level. Give drugs to decrease anxiety and pain as needed. Continuous infusions of a benzodiazepine (e.g., lorazepam) and an opioid or sedative (e.g., morphine, propofol) are helpful in decreasing anxiety and pain.[20]

Do not overlook the patient's spiritual needs. Patients may want a visit from a spiritual or religious leader. One way to provide support is to offer to call the leader rather than wait for the patient or caregiver to express a wish for counseling.

CHECK YOUR PRACTICE

Your patient is a 74-year-old man recovering from septic shock after a perforated diverticulum. He has been in the ICU for 7 days. His condition has finally stabilized. His wife has been at his bedside for his entire ICU stay. While caring for him, you suggest that she take a brief walk and get some coffee. She bursts out with tears, "I can't leave him. You know that he almost died."

- How can you support this caregiver?

Caregivers need to be informed of the patient's condition. Give the patient and caregiver simple explanations of all procedures before you carry them out and information about the plan of care. If they ask questions about progress and prognosis, give simple and honest answers.

If possible, the same nurses should care for the patient. This decreases anxiety, limits conflicting information, and increases trust. If the prognosis becomes grave, support the caregiver when making tough decisions, such as withdrawing life support. The health care team must promote realistic expectations and outcomes. Remember, compassion is as essential as scientific and technical expertise in providing care.

Ensure that the caregiver can spend time with the patient, provided the patient perceives this time as comforting.[20] Explain in simple terms the purpose of any tubes and equipment attached to or surrounding the patient. Tell them what they may and may not touch. If possible, place the patient's hands and arms outside the sheets to encourage therapeutic touch. Encourage caregivers to perform simple comfort measures if desired. Provide privacy as much as possible while assuring them that help is readily available should it be needed. Always position the call light in reach of the patient or caregiver.

◆ Ambulatory Care

Rehabilitation of the patient who had a critical illness requires prevention or early treatment of complications and teaching focused on disease management or prevention of recurrence based on the initial cause of shock. Continue to monitor the patient for complications throughout the recovery period. These may include decreased range of motion, muscle weakness, decreased physical endurance, AKI (see Chapter 51), and fibrotic lung disease (from ARDS) (see Chapter 32). Patients recovering from shock often need diverse services after discharge. These can include admission to transitional care units (e.g., for mechanical ventilation weaning), rehabilitation centers (inpatient or outpatient), or home health care agencies. Start planning for a safe transition from hospital to home as soon as the patient is admitted to the hospital.

◆ Evaluation

The expected outcomes are that the patient who has shock will have:

- Adequate tissue perfusion with restoration of normal or baseline BP
- Normal organ function with no complications from hypoperfusion
- Decreased fear and anxiety

SYSTEMIC INFLAMMATORY RESPONSE SYNDROME AND MULTIPLE ORGAN DYSFUNCTION SYNDROME

Etiology and Pathophysiology

Systemic inflammatory response syndrome (SIRS) is a systemic inflammatory response to a variety of insults, including infection (sepsis), ischemia, infarction, and injury.[20] Generalized inflammation in organs remote from the initial insult characterizes SIRS. Many different mechanisms can trigger SIRS. These include:

- Mechanical tissue trauma: burns, crush injuries, surgery
- Abscess formation: intraabdominal, extremities
- Ischemic or necrotic tissue: pancreatitis, vascular disease, MI
- Microbial invasion: bacteria, viruses, fungi, parasites
- Endotoxin release: gram-negative and gram-positive bacteria
- Global perfusion deficits: postcardiac resuscitation, shock states
- Regional perfusion deficits: distal perfusion deficits

Multiple organ dysfunction syndrome (MODS) is the failure of 2 or more organ systems in an acutely ill patient such that homeostasis cannot be maintained without intervention.[21] MODS results from SIRS. These 2 syndromes represent the ends of a continuum. Transition from SIRS to MODS does not occur in a clear-cut manner (Fig. 42.1).

Organ and Metabolic Dysfunction

When the inflammatory response is activated, consequences include the release of mediators, direct damage to the endothelium, and hypermetabolism. Vascular permeability increases. This allows mediators and protein to leak out of the endothelium and into the interstitial space. White blood cells begin to digest the foreign debris, and the coagulation cascade is activated (see Chapter 33). Hypotension, decreased perfusion, microemboli, and redistributed or shunted blood flow eventually compromise organ perfusion.

The respiratory system is often the first system to show signs of dysfunction in SIRS and MODS.[21] Inflammatory mediators have a direct effect on the pulmonary vasculature. The endothelial damage from the release of inflammatory mediators causes increased capillary permeability. This causes movement of fluid from the pulmonary vasculature into the pulmonary interstitial spaces. The fluid then moves to the alveoli, causing alveolar edema. Type I pneumocytes (alveolar cells) are destroyed. Type II pneumocytes are damaged. Surfactant production is decreased. The alveoli collapse. This creates an increase in *shunt* (blood flow to the lungs that does not take part in gas exchange) and worsening ventilation-perfusion mismatch. The result is ARDS. Patients with ARDS need aggressive pulmonary management with mechanical ventilation. See Chapter 32 for a discussion of ARDS.

Cardiovascular changes include myocardial depression and massive vasodilation in response to increasing tissue demands. Vasodilation results in decreased SVR and BP. The baroreceptor reflex causes release of *inotropic* (increasing force of contraction) and *chronotropic* (increasing heart rate) factors that enhance CO. To compensate for hypotension, CO increases by an increase in heart rate and SV. Increases in capillary permeability cause a shift of albumin and fluid out of the vascular space. This further reduces venous return and thus preload. The patient becomes warm and tachycardic with a high CO and a low SVR. Other signs include decreased capillary refill, skin mottling, increased CVP and PAWP, and dysrhythmias. $ScvO_2$ or SvO_2 may be abnormally high because the patient is perfusing areas not consuming much O_2 (e.g., skin, nonworking muscle). Other areas may have blood shunted away from them. Eventually, either perfusion of vital organs becomes insufficient or the cells are unable to use O_2 and their function is further compromised.

Neurologic dysfunction in SIRS and MODS often presents as mental status changes. These acute changes can be an early sign of SIRS or MODS. The patient may be confused and agitated, combative, disoriented, lethargic, or comatose. These changes are due to hypoxemia, the effects of inflammatory mediators, and impaired perfusion.

AKI from hypoperfusion and the effects of the mediators are common. Decreased renal perfusion activates the SNS and the renin-angiotensin system. Stimulating the renin-angiotensin system causes systemic vasoconstriction and aldosterone-mediated sodium and water reabsorption. Another risk factor for AKI is the use of nephrotoxic drugs. Many antibiotics used to treat gram-negative bacteria (e.g., aminoglycosides) can be nephrotoxic. Careful monitoring of drug levels is essential to avoid nephrotoxic effects.

The GI tract plays a key role in the development of MODS. GI motility is often decreased in critical illness, causing abdominal distention and paralytic ileus. In the early stages of SIRS and MODS, blood is shunted away from the GI mucosa. This makes it highly vulnerable to ischemic injury. Decreased perfusion leads to a breakdown of the normally protective mucosal barrier. This increases the risk for ulceration, GI bleeding, and bacterial movement from the GI tract into circulation.

Metabolic changes are pronounced. Both SIRS and MODS trigger a hypermetabolic response. Glycogen stores are rapidly converted to glucose (glycogenolysis). Once glycogen is depleted, amino acids are converted to glucose (gluconeogenesis), reducing protein stores. Fatty acids are mobilized for fuel. Catecholamines and glucocorticoids are released and cause hyperglycemia and insulin resistance. The net result is a catabolic state with a loss of lean body mass (muscle).

Hypermetabolism may last for several days and cause liver dysfunction. Liver dysfunction in MODS may begin long before clinical evidence of it is present. Protein synthesis is impaired. The liver cannot make albumin, a key protein in maintaining plasma oncotic pressure. This changes plasma oncotic pressure, causing fluid and protein to leak from the vascular spaces to the interstitial space. At this point, giving albumin does not normalize oncotic pressure.

As hypermetabolism persists, the patient cannot convert lactate to glucose and lactate accumulates (lactic acidosis). Despite increases in glycogenolysis and gluconeogenesis, eventually the liver cannot maintain an adequate glucose level and the patient becomes hypoglycemic. Hypoglycemia can also develop due to acute adrenal insufficiency.

DIC may result from dysfunction of the coagulation system. DIC causes microvascular clotting and bleeding at the same time because of the depletion of clotting factors and excessive fibrinolysis. Chapter 34 discusses DIC.

Electrolyte imbalances are common. They result from the hormonal and metabolic changes and fluid shifts. These changes worsen mental status changes, neuromuscular problems, and dysrhythmias. ADH and aldosterone release results in sodium and water retention. Aldosterone increases urinary potassium loss. Catecholamines cause potassium to move into the cell, causing hypokalemia. Hypokalemia can cause dysrhythmias and muscle weakness. Metabolic acidosis results from impaired tissue perfusion, hypoxia, and the shift to anaerobic metabolism. This increases lactate levels. Progressive renal dysfunction contributes to metabolic acidosis. Hypocalcemia, hypomagnesemia, and hypophosphatemia are common.

Clinical Manifestations of SIRS and MODS

The clinical manifestations of SIRS and MODS are described in Table 42.10.

❖ NURSING AND INTERPROFESSIONAL MANAGEMENT: SIRS AND MODS

The prognosis for the patient with MODS is poor, with mortality rates of 40% to 60%.[21] Mortality increases as more organ systems fail. The most common cause of death is sepsis. Survival improves with early, goal-directed therapy. So, the most important goal is to prevent SIRS from progressing to MODS.

Your key role is vigilant assessment and ongoing monitoring to detect early signs of deterioration or organ dysfunction. Interprofessional care for patients with SIRS and MODS focuses on (1) preventing and treating infection, (2) maintaining tissue oxygenation, (3) nutrition and metabolic support, and (4) appropriate support of individual failing organs. Table 42.10 outlines the management for patients with SIRS and MODS.

TABLE 42.10 Manifestations and Management of SIRS and MODS

Manifestations	Management
Cardiovascular System	
Biventricular failure ↓ BP, MAP, SVR ↑ HR, CO, SV Massive vasodilation Myocardial depression Systolic, diastolic dysfunction	Volume management to ↑ preload Hemodynamic monitoring Arterial pressure monitoring to maintain MAP >65 mm Hg Vasopressors Intermittent or continuous $ScvO_2$ or SvO_2 monitoring Balance O_2 supply and demand Continuous ECG monitoring Circulatory assist devices VTE prophylaxis
Central Nervous System	
Acute change in neurologic status Confusion, disorientation, delirium Fever Hepatic encephalopathy Seizures	Evaluate for hepatic or metabolic encephalopathy Optimize cerebral blood flow ↓ Cerebral O_2 requirements Prevent secondary tissue ischemia Calcium channel blockers (reduce cerebral vasospasm)
Endocrine System	
Hyperglycemia → hypoglycemia	Provide continuous insulin infusion and glucose to maintain blood glucose 140–180 mg/dL (7.77–10.0 mmol/L)
Gastrointestinal System	
GI bleeding Hypoperfusion → ↓ peristalsis, paralytic ileus Mucosal ischemia • ↓ Intramucosal pH • Potential translocation of gut bacteria • Potential abdominal compartment syndrome Mucosal ulceration on endoscopy	Stress ulcer prophylaxis • Antacids (e.g., Maalox) • Proton pump inhibitors (e.g., omeprazole) • sucralfate (Carafate) Monitor abdominal distention, intraabdominal pressures Dietitian consult Enteral nutrition Stimulate mucosal activity Provide essential nutrients and optimal calories
Hepatic System	
Bilirubin >2 mg/dL (34 μmol/L) Hepatic encephalopathy Jaundice ↑ Liver enzymes (ALT, AST, GGT) ↓ Serum albumin, prealbumin, transferrin ↑ Serum NH_3 (ammonia)	Maintain adequate tissue perfusion Provide nutrition support (e.g., enteral nutrition) Careful use of drugs metabolized by liver
Hematologic System	
↑ Bleeding times, ↑ PT, ↑ PTT ↑ D-dimer ↑ Fibrin split products ↓ Platelet count (thrombocytopenia)	Observe for bleeding from obvious and/or occult sites Replace factors being lost (e.g., platelets) Minimize traumatic interventions (e.g., IM injections, multiple venipunctures)
Renal System	
Prerenal: renal hypoperfusion • BUN/creatinine ratio >20:1 • ↓ Urine Na^+ <20 mEq/L • ↑ Urine osmolality • Urine specific gravity >1.020	Diuretics • Loop diuretics (e.g., furosemide) • May need to ↑ dosage due to ↓ glomerular filtration rate
Intrarenal: acute tubular necrosis • BUN/creatinine ratio <10:1–15:1 • ↑ Urine Na^+ >20 mEq/L • ↓ Urine osmolality • Urine specific gravity ~1.010	Continuous renal replacement therapy (see Chapter 51)
Respiratory System	

• Development of ARDS (see Chapter 32):
  • Bilateral fluffy infiltrates on chest x-ray
  • ↓ Compliance
  • Dyspnea (severe)
• ↑ C-reactive protein
  • Minute ventilation
  • PaO_2/FIO_2 ratio <200
  • PAWP <18 mm Hg
  • Pulmonary hypertension
  • Refractory hypoxemia
  • Tachypnea
  • Ventilation-perfusion (V/Q) mismatch
	Optimize O_2 delivery and minimize O_2 consumption
	Mechanical ventilation (see Chapter 28)
	• Positive end-expiratory pressure
	• Lung protective modes (e.g., pressure-control inverse ratio ventilation, low tidal volumes)
	• Permissive hypercapnia
	• Positioning (e.g., continuous lateral rotation therapy, prone positioning)

ALT, Alanine aminotransferase; *AST,* aspartate aminotransferase; *GGT,* γ-glutamyl transferase; *PA,* pulmonary artery; *PAWP,* pulmonary artery wedge pressure; *PT,* prothrombin time; *PTT,* partial thromboplastin time; *$ScvO_2$,* O_2 saturation in venous blood; *SvO_2,* O_2 saturation in mixed venous blood; *SVR,* systemic vascular resistance.

◆ Preventing and Treating Infection

Aggressive infection control strategies are essential to decrease the risk for HAIs. Early, aggressive surgery is recommended to remove necrotic tissue (e.g., early debridement of burn tissue) that can provide a culture medium for microorganisms. Aggressive pulmonary management, including early mobilization, can reduce the risk for infection. Strict asepsis can decrease infections related to intraarterial lines, endotracheal tubes, indwelling urinary catheters, IV lines, and other invasive devices or procedures. Daily assessment of the ongoing need for invasive lines and other devices is an important strategy to prevent or limit HAIs.

Despite aggressive strategies, infection may develop. Once an infection is suspected, begin interventions to treat the cause. Send appropriate cultures and start broad-spectrum antibiotic therapy, as ordered. Adjust therapy based on the culture results, if needed.

◆ Maintaining Tissue Oxygenation

Hypoxemia often occurs because patients have greater O_2 needs and decreased O_2 supply to the tissues. Interventions that decrease O_2 demand and increase O_2 delivery are essential. Sedation, mechanical ventilation, analgesia, and rest may decrease O_2 demand and should be considered. Treating fever, chills, and pain decreases O_2 demand. O_2 delivery may be optimized by individualizing tidal volumes with positive end-expiratory pressure, increasing preload (e.g., fluids) or myocardial contractility to enhance CO, or reducing afterload to increase CO.

◆ Nutrition and Metabolic Needs

Hypermetabolism can result in profound weight loss, cachexia, and further organ failure. Protein-calorie malnutrition is a key sign of hypermetabolism. Total energy expenditure is often increased 1.5 to 2.0 times the normal metabolic rate. Because of their short half-life, monitor plasma transferrin and prealbumin levels to assess hepatic protein synthesis.

The goal of nutrition support is to preserve organ function. Providing early and optimal nutrition decreases morbidity and mortality rates. EN is preferred. If we cannot use EN, then consider PN (see Chapter 44). Provide glycemic control with insulin with a goal of 180 mg/dL or less.[6]

◆ Support of Failing Organs

Support of any failing organ is a goal of therapy. For example, the patient with ARDS requires aggressive O_2 therapy and mechanical ventilation (see Chapter 28). DIC should be treated appropriately (e.g., blood products) (see Chapter 34). Renal failure may require dialysis. Continuous renal replacement therapy is better tolerated than hemodialysis, especially in a patient with hemodynamic instability (see Chapter 51).

A final consideration may be that further interventions are futile. It is important to maintain communication between the health care team and the patient's caregiver about realistic goals and outcomes for the patient with MODS. Withdrawing life support and starting end-of-life care may be the best options for the patient.

Case Study

Shock

(© Thinkstock.)

Patient Profile

K.L., a 25-year-old Korean American male, was not wearing his seat belt when he was driving a motor vehicle involved in a crash. K.L. was ejected through the windshield and found 10 ft from his car. He was face down, conscious, and moaning. His wife and daughter were in the car with their seat belts on. They sustained minor injuries and are very frightened and upset. All passengers were taken to the ED. This information pertains to K.L.

Subjective Data

- States, "I can't breathe"
- Cries out when abdomen is palpated

Objective Data

Physical Assessment

- *Cardiovascular:* BP 80/56 mm Hg; apical pulse 138 but no palpable radial or pedal pulses; carotid pulse 1+. ECG shows:

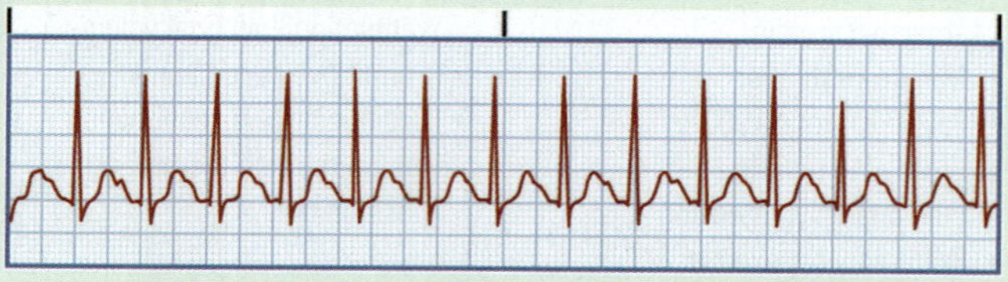

- *Respiratory:* respiratory rate 35 breaths/min; labored breathing with shallow respirations; asymmetric chest wall movement; absence of breath sounds on left side. Trachea deviated slightly to the right
- *Abdomen:* slightly distended and left upper quadrant painful on palpation
- *Musculoskeletal:* open compound fracture of the lower left leg

Diagnostic Studies

- Chest x-ray: hemothorax with 6 rib fractures
- Hematocrit: 28%

Interprofessional Care (in the ED)

- Intraosseous access in right proximal tibia placed prehospital
- Left chest tube placed, draining bright red blood
- Fluid resuscitation started with crystalloids
- High-flow O_2 via nonrebreather mask

Emergency Surgical Procedures

- Splenectomy
- Repair of torn intercostal artery
- Repair of compound fracture

Discussion Questions

- ***Recognize***: What types of shock is K.L. experiencing? What clinical manifestations of this type does he display?
- ***Recognize***: What were the causes of K.L.'s shock states?
- ***Analyze***: What are his potential complications?
- ***Plan:*** What ongoing nursing assessment parameters are essential?
- ***Prioritize:*** Based on the assessment data presented, what are the priority clinical problems?
- ***Prioritize:*** What are the priority nursing responsibilities for K.L.?
- ***Act:*** K.L.'s parents arrive. English is their second language. They are very anxious and asking about their son. What can you do to provide culturally competent family-centered care?
- ***Act:*** Identify the tasks that could be delegated to assistive personnel (AP).

Answers available at http://evolve.elsevier.com/Lewis/medsurg.

BRIDGE TO NCLEX EXAMINATION

The number of the question corresponds to the same-numbered outcome at the beginning of the chapter.

1. A patient has a spinal cord injury at T4. Vital signs include falling blood pressure with bradycardia. The nurse recognizes that the patient is experiencing
   - **a.** a relative hypervolemia.
   - **b.** an absolute hypovolemia.
   - **c.** neurogenic shock from low blood flow.
   - **d.** neurogenic shock from massive vasodilation.
2. A 78-year-old man with a history of diabetes has confusion and temperature of 104°F (40°C). There is a wound on his right heel with purulent drainage. After an infusion of 3 L of normal saline solution, his assessment findings are BP 84/40 mm Hg; heart rate 110; respiratory rate 42 and shallow; CO 8 L/min; and PAWP 4 mm Hg. This patient's symptoms are *most* likely indicative of
   - **a.** sepsis.
   - **b.** septic shock.
   - **c.** multiple organ dysfunction syndrome.
   - **d.** systemic inflammatory response syndrome.
3. Treatment for cardiogenic shock includes *(select all that apply)*
   - **a.** dobutamine to increase myocardial contractility.
   - **b.** vasopressors to increase systemic vascular resistance.
   - **c.** circulatory assist devices such as an intraaortic balloon pump.
   - **d.** corticosteroids to stabilize the cell wall in the infarcted myocardium.
   - **e.** Trendelenburg positioning to facilitate venous return and increase preload.
4. The *most* accurate assessment parameters for the nurse to use to determine adequate tissue perfusion in the patient with MODS are
   - **a.** blood pressure, pulse, and respirations.
   - **b.** breath sounds, blood pressure, and body temperature.
   - **c.** pulse pressure, level of consciousness, and pupillary response.
   - **d.** level of consciousness, urine output, and skin color and temperature.

1. d; 2. b; 3. a, c; 4. d.

For rationales to these answers and even more NCLEX review questions, visit http://evolve.elsevier.com/Lewis/medsurg.

EVOLVE WEBSITE/RESOURCES LIST

http://evolve.elsevier.com/Lewis/medsurg
Review Questions (Online Only)
Key Points
Answer Keys to Questions
- Rationales for Bridge to NCLEX Examination Questions
- Answer Guidelines for Case Study
- Answer Guidelines for Managing Care of Multiple Patients Case Study (Section 8)

Student Case Studies
- Patient With Acute Pancreatitis and Septic Shock
- Patient With Cardiogenic Shock
- Patient With Sepsis

Nursing Care Plan
- eNursing Care Plan 42.1: Patient in Shock

Conceptual Care Map Creator
Audio Glossary
Content Updates

REFERENCES

1. Vahdatour C, Collins D, Goldberg G: Cardiogenic shock, *J Am Heart Assoc* 8:8, 2019.
2. Pepe M, Bortone AS, Giordano A, et al.: Cardiogenic shock following acute myocardial infarction: what's new? *Shock* 53:391, 2020.
3. Smith N, Lopez RA, Silberman M: Distributive shock. Retrieved from https://www.ncbi.nlm.nih.gov/books/NBK470316/.
4. Dave S, Cho J: Neurogenic shock. Retrieved from https://www.ncbi.nlm.nih.gov/books/NBK459361.
*5. Shaker M, Wallace D, Golden D, et al.: Anaphylaxis—a 2020 practice parameter update, systematic review and Grading of Recommendations, Assessment, Development, and Evaluation (GRADE) analysis, *J Allergy Clin Immunol* 145:1082, 2020.
*6. Rhodes A, Evans L, Alhazzani W, et al.: Surviving Sepsis Campaign: international guidelines for management of sepsis and septic shock: 2016, *Crit Care Med* 45:3, 2017. (Classic).
7. Center for Disease Control: Sepsis. Retrieved from https://www.cdc.gov/sepsis/what-is-sepsis.html.
8. Rhee C, Strich J, Klompas M, et al.: SEP-1 has brought much needed attention to improving sepsis care...but now is the time to improve SEP-1, *Crit Care Med* 48:779, 2020.
9. Maggio PM: Sepsis and septic shock. Retrieved from https://www.merckmanuals.com/professional/critical-care-medicine/sepsis-and-septic-shock/sepsis-and-septic-shock.
*10. Konstantinides SV, Meyer G, Becattini C, et al.: ESC Guidelines for the diagnosis and management of acute pulmonary embolism developed in collaboration with the European Respiratory Society: the Task Force for the Diagnosis and Management of Acute Pulmonary Embolism of the European Society of Cardiology, *Eur Respir J* 54, 2019.
11. Truong TN, Dunn AS, McCardle K, et al.: Adherence to fluid resuscitation guidelines and outcomes in patients with septic shock: reassessing the "one-size-fits-all" approach, *J Crit Care* 51:94, 2019.
*12. Silversides JA, Perner A, Malbrain ML: Liberal versus restrictive fluid therapy in critically ill patients, *Intensive Care Med* 45:1440, 2019.
*13. Brown RM: SMART trial: balanced crystalloids vs saline in sepsis, *Am J Respir Crit Care Med* 200:1487, 2019.
*14. Pickett JD, Bridges E, Kritek PA: Passive leg-raising and prediction of fluid responsiveness: systematic review, *Crit Care Nurse* 37:32, 2017. (Classic).

*15. Gonzalez J, Ortega J, Crenshaw N: Rapid ultrasound for shock and hypotension: a clinical update for the advanced practice provider: part 1, *Adv Emerg Nurs J* 42:270, 2020.

16. Scheeren T, Bakker J, DeBacke D, et al.: Current use of vasopressors in septic shock, *Ann Intensive Care* 9:20, 2019.

*17. Nagendran M, Russell JA, Walley KR, et al.: Vasopressin in septic shock: an individual patient data meta-analysis of randomised controlled trials, *Intensive Care Med* 45:844, 2019.

18. Singer P: Preserving the quality of life: nutrition in the ICU, *Crit Care* 23:139, 2019.

*19. Pelton ID, Brown SM, Bledsoe J, et al.: ED door-to-antibiotic time and long-term mortality in sepsis, *Chest* 155:938, 2019.

*20. Ungarian J, Rankin J, Then K: Delirium in the ICU: is dexmedetomidine effective? *Crit Care Nurse* 39:8, 2019.

21. Chakraborty R, Burns B: Systemic inflammatory response syndrome. Retrieved from https://www.ncbi.nlm.nih.gov/books/NBK547429.

*Evidence-based information for clinical practice.

Case Study

Applying Clinical Judgment With Multiple Patients

You are working on the cardiovascular stepdown unit and have been assigned to care for the following 5 patients. You have 1 AP assigned to help you.

 (© Jupiterimages/ Banana-Stock/ Thinkstock)	L.P. is a 63-year-old man who came to the ED with chest pain, dyspnea, and palpitations. Cardiac enzymes were normal. ECG showed atrial fibrillation with a rapid ventricular response. He has been on IV diltiazem and IV heparin for 24 hr. Although his heart rate has decreased, the atrial fibrillation persists. Vital signs: 124/72, 102, RR 18, O_2 saturation 98% on 2 L/min via nasal cannula.
 (© iStockphoto/ Thinkstock.)	J.E. is a 70-year-old woman admitted with shortness of breath, fatigue, and weight gain. She has a systolic murmur and bilateral crackles. Her ejection fraction is 20%. She is receiving IV furosemide, PO potassium and enalapril, and IV nesiritide infusion. Cardiac enzymes are normal. Vital signs: 108/62, 92, RR 22, O_2 saturation 94% on 6 L/min via nasal cannula.
 (© iStockphoto/ Thinkstock.)	D.M. is a 51-year-old man who was admitted 2 days ago with a suspected inferolateral wall MI. Cardiac catheterization showed a 90% blockage of his left anterior descending (LAD) artery. Angioplasty was done, and 2 stents inserted. During his admission, he has been diagnosed with diabetes and hypertension. He is now 2 days post-PTCA, has had no recurrence of his chest pain, and is to be discharged today.
 (© iStockphoto/ Thinkstock.)	J.M. is a 68-year-old man admitted 5 days ago with acute decompensated HF. He had electrophysiology studies and implantation of an implantable cardiodefibrillator (ICD). He now is being treated for HF. Discharge is expected tomorrow.
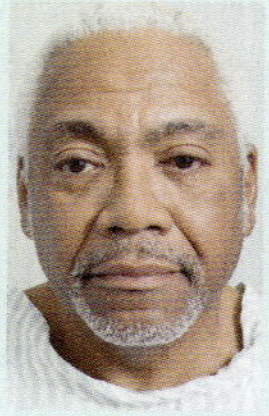 (© iStockphoto/ Thinkstock.)	S.J. is a 73-year-old man admitted with rest pain in both legs and a nonhealing ulcer of the big toe on the right foot. He has history of MI, stroke, hypertension, and type 1 diabetes. He had a left femoral-popliteal bypass 5 years ago. Right foot is cool, pale, and mottled with decreased sensation. He has a 1+ right femoral pulse, right posterior tibial pulse only obtained by Doppler. Right dorsalis pedis pulse absent by Doppler. Left leg pulses are 1+. Vital signs: 148/92, 90 and irregular, RR 22.

1. Highlight all the findings above that require your follow-up.
2. After receiving report, which patient should you see first? Second?
3. Which tasks could you delegate to the AP? *(select all that apply)*
   a. Calculating intake for L.P.'s heparin infusion.
   b. Report changes in pain or sensation of S.J.'s legs.
   c. Teach D.M. about activity restriction after PTCA.
   d. Obtain vital signs and O_2 saturation for to L.P. and J.M.
   e. Hook up J.M. to 12-lead ECG and monitor for dysrhythmias.
4. As you are assessing L.P., the AP tells you that S.J. is diaphoretic and reports chest pain. Use an X for the nursing actions listed below that are Indicated (appropriate or necessary), Contraindicated (could be harmful), or Nonessential (makes no difference or not necessary) for S.J. at this time.

Nursing Action	Indicated	Contraindicated	Nonessential
Administer prescribed as-needed nitroglycerin.			
Change the right foot dressing and perform a peripheral vascular assessment.			
Obtain a 12-lead ECG and start continuous ECG monitoring per protocol.			
Call respiratory therapy to give him a breathing treatment.			
Perform focused heart and lung assessments.			
Apply O_2 per nasal cannula per protocol.			
Obtain vital signs with O_2 saturation.			

Case Study Progression

S.J. rates his chest pain as a 9/10. His blood pressure is 110/70, heart rate 110, respiratory rate 26, and O_2 saturation 93% on room air. You obtain a 12-lead ECG and administer 0.4 mg SL nitroglycerin with minimal pain relief after 5 minutes. The 12-lead ECG shows new ST elevation in leads II, III, and aVF.

5. Which interventions would you expect the HCP to order for S.J.? *(select all that apply)*
   a. Cardiac biomarkers
   b. IV morphine sulfate
   c. Emergent cardiac catheterization
   d. Furosemide 40 mg IV push STAT
   e. Increase the O_2 flow rate to 12 L/min
6. Choose the most *likely* option for the information missing from statement below by selecting from the lists of options provided.

Case Study—cont'd

Because J.E is receiving nesiritide, he is at risk for experiencing ________1______. To detect this complication, you will need to monitor _____2_____.

Options for 1	Options for 2
Hypokalemia	Blood pressure
Hypotension	Respiratory rate
respiratory depression	Serum potassium levels

7. You are preparing to give morning medications. Which patient's medication should be given first?
   a. Oral potassium and enalapril to J.E.
   b. Oral metoprolol, aspirin, and clopidogrel to D.M.
   c. IV furosemide, oral enalapril and metoprolol to J.M.
   d. Subcut Novolog, oral diltiazem and furosemide to S.J.
8. What would you include in teaching about ICDs with J.M. and his family?
   a. Avoid air travel.
   b. Avoid driving for 6 weeks.
   c. Avoid any sexual activity in case the ICD discharges.
   d. Avoid standing near antitheft devices in stores and public buildings.
9. You are reviewing J.M.'s assessment findings in preparation for his discharge tomorrow. For each assessment finding, use an X to indicate whether the interventions were Effective (helped to meet expected outcomes), Ineffective (did not help to meet expected outcomes), or Unrelated (not related to the expected outcomes).

Assessment Finding	Effective	Ineffective	Unrelated
Peripheral edema is 3+ bilaterally			
Can walk to the bathroom and back without becoming fatigued and short of breath			
Heart rate 101/min, regular			
Restlessness, inattentive			
Weight has decreased by 12 lb in 5 days			
Normal bowel sounds			
Reports no chest pain after walking in hall			

10. You ask the AP to take D.M.'s vital signs before and after having him walk 300 feet. When reviewing the patient's chart, you note record of the patient's walk but not his vital signs. What is your initial action?
    a. Report the incident to the charge nurse for follow-up.
    b. Talk to the AP about why the vital signs were not recorded.
    c. Walk D.M. yourself again and take his vital signs pre- and post-activity.
    d. Ask the AP to ambulate D.M. again and obtain his vital signs before and after.

43

Assessment: Gastrointestinal System

Kara Ann Ventura

http://evolve.elsevier.com/Lewis/medsurg/

CONCEPTUAL FOCUS

Elimination
Fluids and Electrolytes
Nutrition

LEARNING OUTCOMES

1. Describe the structures and functions of the organs of the gastrointestinal tract.
2. Describe the structures and functions of the liver, gallbladder, biliary tract, and pancreas.
3. Distinguish the processes of ingestion, digestion, absorption, and elimination.
4. Explain the processes of biliary metabolism, bile production, and bile excretion.
5. Link the age-related changes of the gastrointestinal system to the differences in assessment findings.
6. Obtain significant subjective and objective assessment data related to the gastrointestinal system from a patient.
7. Perform a physical assessment of the gastrointestinal system using appropriate techniques.
8. Distinguish normal from abnormal findings of a physical assessment of the gastrointestinal system.
9. Describe the purpose, significance of results, and nursing responsibilities related to diagnostic studies of the gastrointestinal system.

KEY TERMS

absorption
bilirubin
borborygmi, Table 43.10
cheilosis, Table 43.10
digestion
endoscopy
hematemesis, Table 43.10
ingestion
Kupffer cells
melena, Table 43.10
pyrosis, Table 43.10
pyorrhea
steatorrhea, Table 43.10
tenesmus, Table 43.10
Valsalva maneuver

The gastrointestinal (GI) system, also called the *digestive system,* consists of the GI tract and its associated organs and glands. Included in the GI tract are the mouth, esophagus, stomach, small intestine, large intestine, rectum, and anus. The associated organs are the liver, pancreas, and gallbladder (Fig. 43.1). Problems that change physiologic processes or associated organs affect a person's ability to maintain nutrition status and eliminate waste.

STRUCTURES AND FUNCTIONS OF GASTROINTESTINAL SYSTEM

The GI tract extends around 30 ft (9 m) from the mouth to the anus. The GI tract is essentially a tube composed of 4 layers. From the inside to the outside, these layers are (1) mucosa lining; (2) submucosa connective tissue, which contains glands, blood vessels, and lymph nodes; (3) muscle; and (4) serosa.

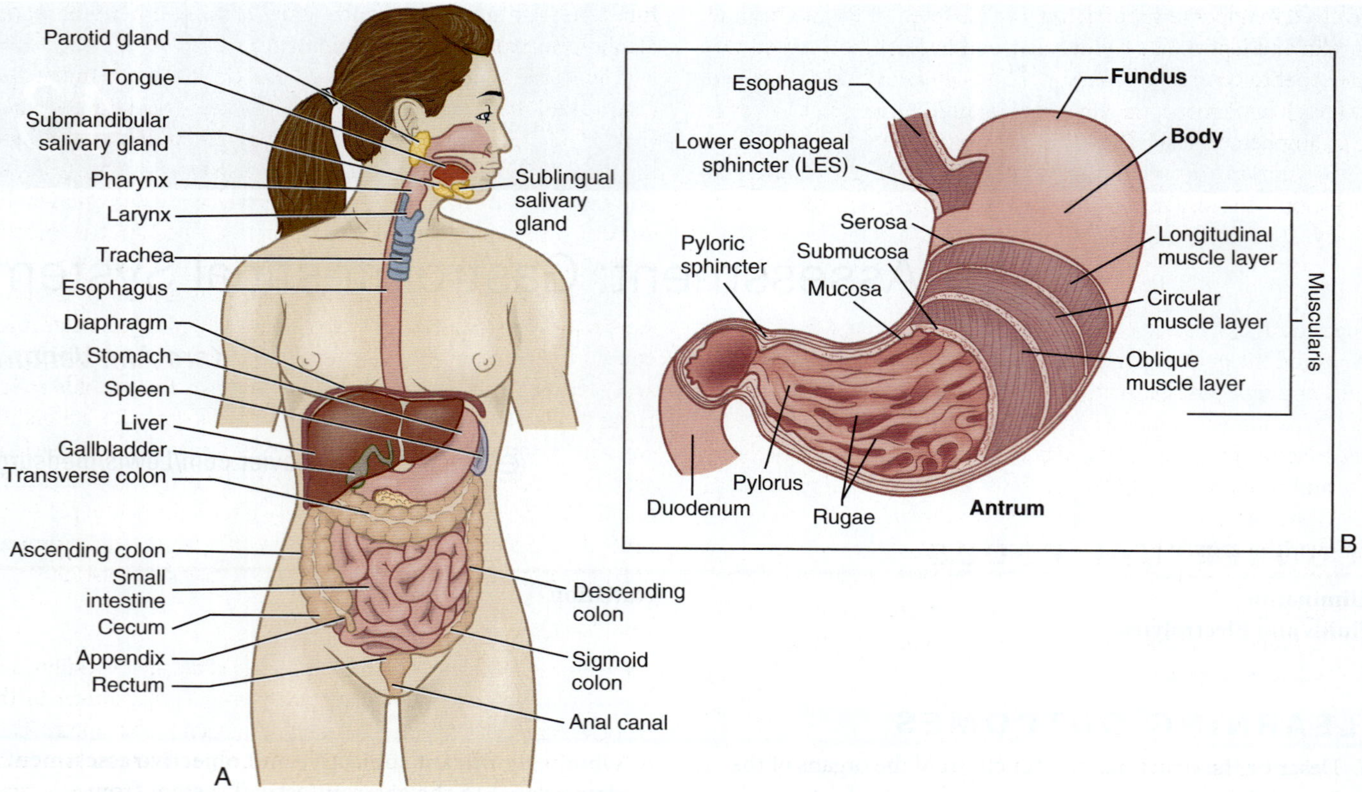

Fig. 43.1 (A) Location of organs of the GI system. (B) Parts of the stomach.

There are 3 smooth muscle layers: the oblique (inner) layer, circular (middle) layer, and longitudinal (outer) layer.

Parasympathetic and sympathetic branches of the autonomic nervous system (ANS) innervate the GI tract. The parasympathetic (cholinergic) system is mainly excitatory. The sympathetic (adrenergic) system is mainly inhibitory. For example, parasympathetic stimulation increases peristalsis, and sympathetic stimulation decreases it. Both sympathetic and parasympathetic afferent fibers relay sensory information.

The GI tract has its own nervous system: the enteric nervous system (ENS) or intrinsic nervous system. The ENS system regulates motility and secretion along the entire GI tract. The ENS is composed of 2 networks: (1) Meissner plexus in the submucosa and (2) Auerbach (myenteric) plexus between the muscle layers. The submucosal plexus controls secretion and is involved in many sensory functions. The myenteric plexus is the major nerve supply to the GI tract and controls GI movements. Although the ENS receives innervation from the ANS, it functions independently of the brain and spinal cord.

Circulation in the GI system is unique in that venous blood draining the GI tract organs empties into the portal vein, which then perfuses the liver. This allows the liver to clean the blood of bacteria and toxins from the GI tract. The celiac artery, superior mesenteric artery (SMA), and the inferior mesenteric artery (IMA) supply arterial blood to the GI tract. The stomach and duodenum receive their blood supply from the celiac axis. The distal small intestine to mid large intestine receives its blood supply from branches of the hepatic and SMA. The distal large intestine through the anus receives its blood supply from the IMA. The GI tract and accessory organs receive 25% to 30% of the cardiac output at rest and 35% or more after eating. Because such a large percent of the cardiac output perfuses these organs, the GI tract is a major source from which to divert blood flow during exercise, stress, or injury.

The peritoneum almost completely covers the abdominal organs. The 2 layers of the peritoneum are the *parietal layer,* which lines the abdominal cavity wall, and the *visceral layer*. It covers the abdominal organs. The peritoneal cavity is the potential space between the parietal and visceral layers. The 2 folds of the peritoneum are the mesentery and omentum. The mesentery attaches the small intestine and part of the large intestine to the posterior abdominal wall. It contains blood and lymph vessels. The omentum hangs like an apron from the stomach to the intestines. It contains fat and lymph nodes.

The main function of the GI system is to supply nutrients to body cells. This is accomplished through the processes of (1) *ingestion* (taking in food), (2) *digestion* (breaking down food), and (3) *absorption* (transferring food products into circulation). *Elimination* is the process of excreting the waste products of digestion.

Ingestion

Ingestion is the intake of food. *Appetite,* the desire to ingest food, influences how much food a person eats. We have an appetite center in the hypothalamus. Several factors, including hypoglycemia, an empty stomach, and a decrease in body temperature, stimulate appetite. The hormone *ghrelin* released from the stomach mucosa plays a role in appetite stimulation. Another hormone, *leptin,* is involved in appetite suppression. See Chapter 48 for more about ghrelin and leptin. The sight, smell, and taste of food can stimulate appetite. Stomach distention, illness (especially accompanied by fever), hyperglycemia, nausea and vomiting, and certain drugs (e.g., amphetamines) inhibit appetite.

Deglutition, or swallowing, is the mechanical portion of ingestion. The organs involved in deglutition are the mouth, pharynx, and esophagus.

Mouth

The mouth consists of the lips and oral (buccal) cavity. The lips surround the opening of the mouth and function in speech. The hard and soft palates form the roof of the oral cavity. The oral cavity contains the teeth, used in *mastication* (chewing), and the tongue. The tongue is a solid muscle mass. It aids in chewing and moving food to the back of the throat for swallowing. The taste receptors (taste buds) are on the sides and tip of the tongue. The tongue is also important in speech.

Within the oral cavity are 3 pairs of salivary glands: parotid, submaxillary, and sublingual glands. These glands produce saliva. Saliva consists of water, protein, mucin, inorganic salts, and salivary amylase.

Pharynx

The pharynx is a muscular tube lined with mucous membrane. It has 3 divisions: nasopharynx, oropharynx, and laryngeal pharynx. The mucous membrane is continuous with the nasal cavity, mouth, auditory tubes, and larynx. During ingestion, the oropharynx is the route for food from the mouth to the esophagus. Food or liquid stimulates receptors in the oropharynx, initiating the swallowing reflex. During swallowing, the epiglottis closes over the opening to the larynx and prevents food from entering the respiratory tract. The tonsils and adenoids, composed of lymphoid tissue, help the body prevent infection.

Esophagus

The esophagus is a hollow, muscular tube that receives food from the pharynx and moves it to the stomach. It is 7 to 10 in (18 to 25 cm) long and 0.8 in (2 cm) in diameter. The esophagus is in the thoracic cavity. It is structurally composed of 4 layers: inner mucosa, submucosa, muscularis propria, and outermost adventitia. The upper third of the esophagus is composed of striated skeletal muscle. The distal two thirds are composed of smooth muscle.

Between swallows, the esophagus is collapsed and the *upper esophageal sphincter* (UES) closed. With swallowing, the UES relaxes, and a peristaltic wave moves the bolus into the esophagus. The muscular layers contract *(peristalsis)* and propel the food to the stomach. The *lower esophageal sphincter* (LES) at the distal end of the esophagus controls the opening of the esophagus into the stomach. It stays contracted except during swallowing, belching, or vomiting. The LES is an important barrier that normally prevents reflux of acidic gastric contents into the esophagus.

Digestion and Absorption

Stomach

The stomach's functions are to store food, mix food with gastric secretions, and empty contents in small boluses into the small intestine. The stomach absorbs only small amounts of water, alcohol, electrolytes, and certain drugs.

The stomach is usually J shaped and lies obliquely in the epigastric, umbilical, and left hypochondriac regions of the abdomen (Fig. 43.5, later in the chapter). It always contains gastric fluid and mucus. The 3 main parts of the stomach are the fundus (cardia), body, and antrum (Fig. 43.1). The pylorus is a small portion of the antrum proximal to the pyloric sphincter. The LES and pyloric sphincter guard the entrance to and exit from the stomach.

The stomach wall has 4 layers. The serous (outer) layer of the stomach is continuous with the peritoneum. The muscular layer consists of the longitudinal (outer) layer, circular (middle) layer, and oblique (inner) layer. The mucosal layer forms folds called rugae that have many small glands. In the fundus, the glands contain (1) chief cells, which secrete pepsinogen, and (2) parietal cells, which secrete hydrochloric (HCl) acid, water, and intrinsic factor. HCl acid makes gastric juice acidic. This acidic pH helps protect us against ingested organisms. Intrinsic factor promotes cobalamin (vitamin B_{12}) absorption in the small intestine.

Small Intestine

The primary functions of the small intestine are digestion and **absorption**, the uptake of nutrients from the gut lumen to the bloodstream. The small intestine is a coiled tube about 23 ft (7 m) in length and 1 to 1.1 in (2.5 to 2.8 cm) in diameter. It extends from the pylorus to the ileocecal valve. The small intestine is composed of the duodenum, jejunum, and ileum. The ileocecal valve prevents reflux of large intestine contents into the small intestine.

The mucosa of the small intestine is thick, vascular, and glandular. The functional units of the small intestine are *villi.* They are minute, fingerlike projections in the mucous membrane. Villi contain epithelial cells that produce the intestinal digestive enzymes. The epithelial cells on the villi also have *microvilli.* The circular folds in the mucous and submucous layers, along with the villi and microvilli, increase the surface area for digestion and absorption.

The digestive enzymes on the brush border of the microvilli chemically break down nutrients for absorption. Between the bases of the villi lie the crypts of Lieberkühn, which contain the multipotent stem cells. These are the precursors for the other epithelial cell types. Brunner's glands in the submucosa of the duodenum secrete an alkaline fluid containing bicarbonate that neutralizes acidic fluids and protects the mucosa. Intestinal goblet cells secrete mucus that protects the mucosa.

Physiology of Digestion

Digestion is the physical and chemical breakdown of food into absorbable substances. The timely movement of food through the GI tract and the secretion of specific enzymes promote digestion. These enzymes break down food to particles of appropriate size for absorption (Table 43.1).

The process of digestion begins in the mouth, where food is chewed, mechanically broken down, and mixed with saliva. Saliva helps us swallow by lubricating food. Saliva contains amylase, which breaks down starches to maltose. Chewing and the sight, smell, thought, and taste of food stimulate the release of saliva. A person makes about 1 L of saliva each day. After

TABLE 43.1 GI Secretions

Daily Amount (mL)	Secretions/ Enzymes	Action
Salivary Glands		
1000–1500	Salivary amylase	Initiates starch digestion
Stomach		
2500	HCl acid	Activation of pepsinogen to pepsin
	Intrinsic factor	Essential for cobalamin absorption in ileum
	Lipase	Fat digestion
	Pepsinogen	Protein digestion
Small Intestine		
3000	Aminopeptidases	Protein digestion
	Amylase	Carbohydrate digestion
	Enterokinase	Activation of trypsinogen to trypsin
	Lactase	Lactose to glucose and galactose
	Lipase	Fat digestion
	Maltase	Maltose to 2 glucose molecules
	Peptidases	Protein digestion
	Sucrase	Sucrose to glucose and fructose
Pancreas		
700	Amylase	Starch to disaccharides
	Chymotrypsin	Protein digestion
	Lipase	Fat digestion
	Trypsinogen	Protein digestion
Liver and Gallbladder		
1000	Bile	Emulsifies fats and aids in absorption of fatty acids and fat-soluble vitamins (A, D, E, K)

TABLE 43.2 Phases of Gastric Secretion

Stimulus to Secretion	Secretion
Cephalic (nervous)	
Sight, smell, taste of food (before food enters stomach). Initiated in the CNS and mediated by the vagus nerve.	HCl acid, pepsinogen, mucus
Gastric (hormonal and nervous)	
Food in antrum of stomach, vagal stimulation.	Release of gastrin from antrum into circulation to stimulate gastric secretions and motility
Intestinal (hormonal)	
Presence of chyme in small intestine.	*Acidic chyme* (pH <2): Release of secretin, gastric inhibitory polypeptide, cholecystokinin into circulation to decrease HCl acid secretion *Chyme* (pH >3): Release of gastrin from duodenum to increase acid secretion

swallowing, food moves through the esophagus to the stomach. No digestion or absorption occurs in the esophagus.

Both GI secretion and motility are under neural and hormonal control. Food entering the stomach and small intestine triggers the release of hormones into the bloodstream (Tables 43.2 and 43.3). These hormones play important roles in the control of HCl acid secretion, production and release of digestive enzymes, and motility.

In the stomach, muscle action mixes the food with gastric secretions to form *chyme,* which is now ready for absorption. Protein digestion begins with the release of pepsinogen from chief cells. The stomach's acidic environment results in the conversion of pepsinogen to its active form, pepsin. Pepsin begins the breakdown of proteins. There is minimal digestion of starches and fats. The stomach also serves as a reservoir for food, releasing it slowly into the small intestine. The length of time that food stays in the stomach depends on the composition of the food. The average meal stays in the stomach for 3 to 4 hours.

In the small intestine, the physical presence and chemical nature of chyme stimulates motility and secretion. Secretions involved in digestion include enzymes from the pancreas, bile from the liver, and enzymes from the small intestine (Table 43.1). Carbohydrates are broken down to monosaccharides, fats to glycerol and fatty acids, and proteins to amino acids. Enzymes on the brush border of the microvilli complete the digestion process. These enzymes break down disaccharides to monosaccharides and peptides to amino acids for absorption.

The absorption of most of the end products of digestion occurs in the small intestine. The movement of the villi enables these end products to come in contact with the absorbing membrane. Monosaccharides, fatty acids, amino acids, water, electrolytes, vitamins, and minerals are absorbed.

Elimination

Large Intestine

The large intestine is a hollow, muscular tube around 5 to 6 ft (1.5 to 1.8 m) long and 2 in (5 cm) in diameter. The 4 parts of the large intestine are shown in Fig. 43.2.

The most important functions of the large intestine are water and electrolyte absorption. The large intestine also forms feces and serves as a reservoir for the fecal mass until defecation occurs. Feces are composed of water (75%), bacteria, unabsorbed minerals, undigested foodstuffs, bile pigments, and desquamated (shed) epithelial cells. The large intestine secretes mucus, which acts as a lubricant and protects the mucosa.

Microorganisms in the colon contribute to digestion by (1) producing vitamin K and some B vitamins and (2) breaking down proteins that are not digested or absorbed in the small intestine into amino acids. Bacteria deaminate the amino acids, resulting in ammonia. Ammonia is carried to the liver, where it is converted to urea. Urea is excreted by the kidneys. Bacteria produce gas that escapes the colon through the anus as *flatulence* or *flatus.* If an infection or antibiotics alter the normal microbiome, an overgrowth of pathogenic bacteria can occur and cause disease.

The movements of the large intestine are usually slow. However, propulsive (mass movements) peristalsis does occur. Food entering the stomach and duodenum triggers gastrocolic and duodenocolic reflexes, resulting in peristalsis in the colon. These reflexes are more active after the first daily meal and often result in bowel evacuation.

TABLE 43.3 Hormones Controlling GI Secretion and Motility

Hormone	Source	Activating Stimuli	Function
Gastrin	Gastric and duodenal mucosa	Stomach distention, partially digested proteins in pylorus	Stimulates gastric acid secretion and motility. Maintains LES tone.
Cholecystokinin	Duodenal mucosa	Fatty acids and amino acids in small intestine	Contracts gallbladder and relaxes sphincter of Oddi. Allows increased flow of bile into duodenum. Release of pancreatic digestive enzymes.
Gastric inhibitory peptide	Duodenal mucosa	Fatty acids and lipids in small intestine	Inhibits gastric acid secretion and motility.
Secretin	Duodenal mucosa	Acid entering small intestine	Inhibits gastric motility and acid secretion. Stimulates pancreatic bicarbonate secretion.

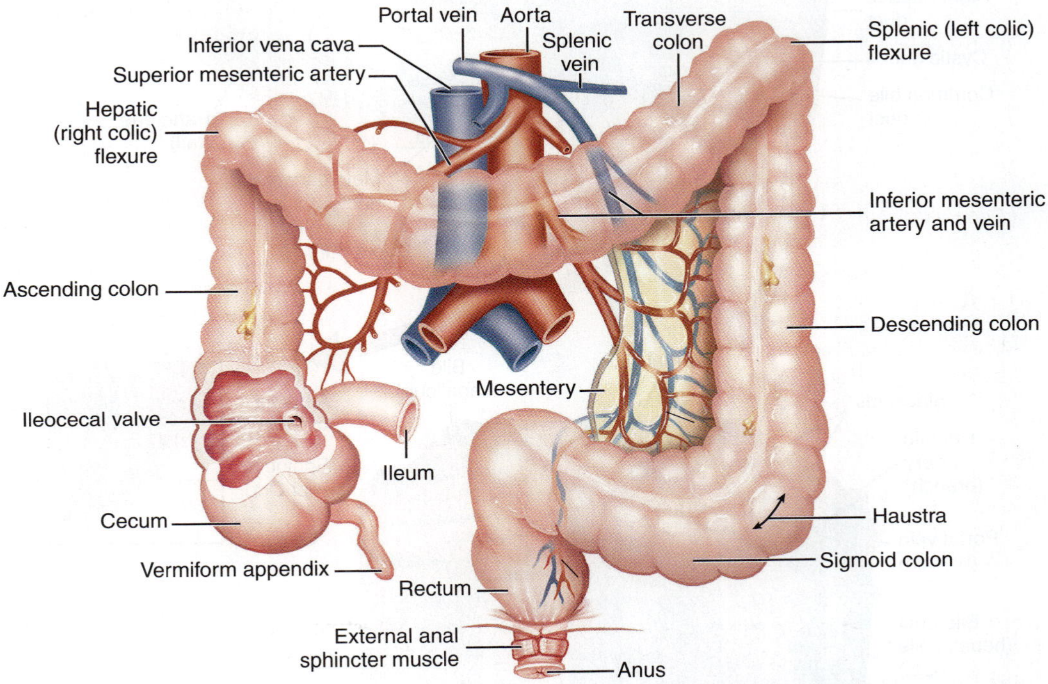

Fig. 43.2 Anatomic locations of the large intestine. (From Patton KT, Thibodeau GA: *Anatomy and physiology,* ed 7, St Louis, 2018, Mosby.)

Defecation is a reflex action involving voluntary and involuntary control. Feces in the rectum stimulate sensory nerve endings that produce the desire to defecate. The reflex center for defecation is in the parasympathetic nerve fibers in the sacral part of the spinal cord. These fibers produce contraction of the rectum and relaxation of the internal anal sphincter. When a person feels the desire to defecate, they can voluntarily relax the external anal sphincter. An acceptable environment for defecation is usually needed or the urge to defecate will be ignored. If you suppress defecation for long periods, problems can occur, such as constipation or fecal impaction.

The **Valsalva maneuver**, often referred to as "bearing down," can promote defecation. During this maneuver, the person inspires deeply and holds the breath, closing the airway, while contracting abdominal muscles and bearing down. This increases both intraabdominal and intrathoracic pressures and reduces venous return to the heart. The heart rate temporarily decreases along with a decrease in cardiac output. This results in a transient drop in BP. When the patient relaxes, thoracic pressure falls, resulting in a sudden flow of blood into the heart, increased heart rate, and an immediate rise in BP. The Valsalva maneuver may be contraindicated in the patient with a head injury, eye surgery, heart problems, hemorrhoids, abdominal surgery, or liver cirrhosis with portal hypertension.

Liver, Biliary Tract, and Pancreas

Liver

The liver is the largest internal organ in the body, weighing around 3 lb (1.36 kg). It lies in the right epigastric region (Fig. 43.5 later in the chapter). Most of the liver is enclosed in peritoneum. It has a fibrous capsule that divides it into right and left lobes (Fig. 43.3).

The functional units of the liver are lobules. A lobule consists of rows of hepatic cells *(hepatocytes)* arranged in cords that radiate out from a central vein. Capillaries called *sinusoids* lie between the rows of hepatocytes. Sinusoids are lined with **Kupffer cells**. They carry out phagocytic activity, removing bacteria and toxins from the blood. The hepatic cells secrete bile into tiny canals called *canaliculi*. These merge with other canals to form larger, interlobular bile ducts, which unite into the 2 main left and right hepatic ducts.

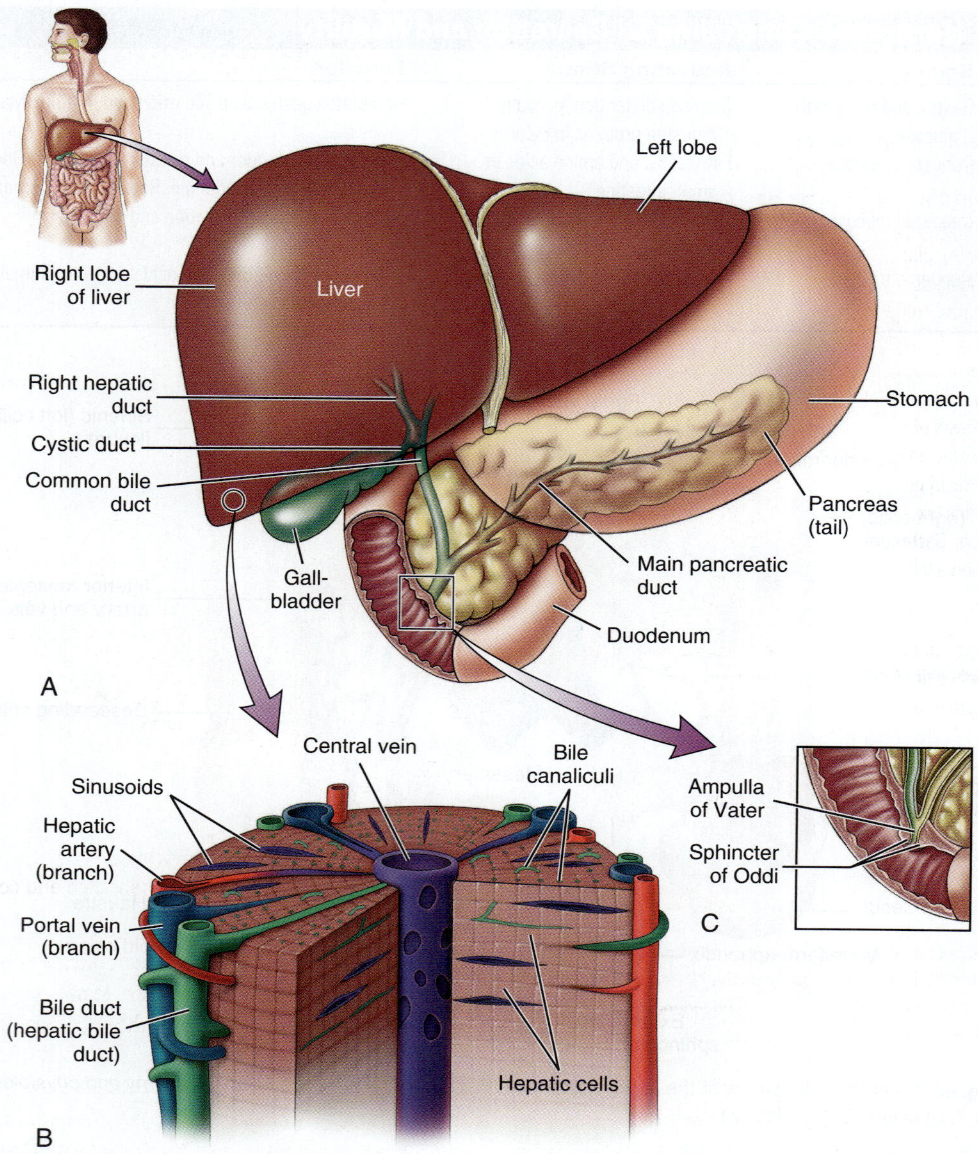

Fig. 43.3 (A) Gross structure of the liver, gallbladder, pancreas, and duct system. (B) Liver lobule. (C) Entrance of the common bile duct into the duodenum.

The liver has a rich blood supply. The portal circulatory system brings blood to the liver from the stomach, intestines, spleen, and pancreas. About 25% of the blood supply comes from the hepatic artery, a branch of the celiac artery. The other 75% comes from the portal vein. The portal vein carries absorbed products of digestion directly to the liver. Once in the liver, the portal vein branches and comes in contact with each lobule.

The liver performs many functions and is essential for life. It has metabolic, secretory, vascular, and storage functions (Table 43.4). The hepatic cells constantly make bile. Bile consists of water, cholesterol, bile salts, electrolytes, fatty acids, and bilirubin. It provides the alkaline medium needed for the action of pancreatic lipase. Bile salts are needed for fat emulsification and digestion.

Bilirubin metabolism. The liver constantly makes **bilirubin**, a pigment derived from the breakdown of hemoglobin (Fig. 43.4). When released into the bloodstream, it binds to albumin. This form of bilirubin is called *unconjugated.* It is insoluble in water and transported to the liver. In the liver, unconjugated bilirubin is conjugated with glucuronic acid and excreted in bile into the intestine. *Conjugated* bilirubin is soluble in water. In the intestines, bacterial action reduces bilirubin to stercobilinogen and urobilinogen. Stercobilinogen accounts for the brown color of stool. A small amount of urobilinogen is reabsorbed into the blood. It then is returned to the liver through the portal circulation. There, it is excreted again in the bile or entered into circulation and excreted by the kidneys.

Biliary Tract

The biliary tract consists of the gallbladder and ducts that connect the liver, gallbladder, and duodenum. The gallbladder is a pear-shaped sac found below the liver. Its function is to concentrate and store bile. It holds around 45 mL of bile. The presence of fat in the upper duodenum triggers the release of cholecystokinin, which causes the gallbladder to contract and release bile.

The hepatic ducts receive bile from the canaliculi in the liver lobules. The left and right hepatic ducts merge with the cystic

TABLE 43.4 Liver Functions

Function	Description
Metabolic Functions	
Blood clotting	Synthesis of prothrombin (factor I), fibrinogen (factor II) and factors V, VII, IX, and X.
Carbohydrate metabolism	Performs glycogenesis (conversion of glucose to glycogen), glycogenolysis (process of breaking down glycogen to glucose), gluconeogenesis (formation of glucose from amino acids and fatty acids).
Detoxification	Inactivates drugs and harmful substances and excretes their breakdown products.
Fat metabolism	Synthesis of lipoproteins, breakdown of triglycerides into fatty acids and glycerol, formation of ketone bodies, synthesis of fatty acids from amino acids and glucose, synthesis and breakdown of cholesterol.
Protein metabolism	Synthesis of nonessential amino acids, synthesis of plasma proteins (except gamma globulin), synthesis of clotting factors. Bacteria in colon deaminate amino acids to form ammonia (NH_3), which is then changed to urea (NH_4).
Secretory Functions	
Bile production	Formation of bile, which contains bile salts, bile pigments (mainly bilirubin), and cholesterol.
Bilirubin	Conjugation and secretion of bilirubin.
Vascular Functions	
Blood filtration	Breakdown of old RBCs, WBCs, bacteria, and other particles. Breakdown of hemoglobin from old RBCs to bilirubin and biliverdin.
Blood reservoir	Serves as temporary storage for blood within general circulation.
Storage Functions	
Storage	Stores glucose in form of glycogen; vitamins, including fat-soluble (A, D, E, K) and water-soluble (B_1, B_2, cobalamin, folic acid); fatty acids; minerals (iron, copper); and amino acids in form of albumin and β-globulins.

duct from the gallbladder to form the common bile duct. Bile moves down the common bile duct to enter the duodenum at the ampulla of Vater (Fig. 43.3). The pancreatic duct also enters the duodenum at this point.

Pancreas

The pancreas is a long, slender gland lying behind the stomach and in front of the first and second lumbar vertebrae. It consists of a head, body, and tail. The peritoneum covers the anterior surface of the pancreas. The pancreas has lobes and lobules. The pancreatic duct extends along the gland and enters the duodenum through the common bile duct at the ampulla of Vater (Fig. 43.3).

The pancreas has both exocrine and endocrine functions. The exocrine function contributes to digestion through the production and release of enzymes (Table 43.1). The endocrine function occurs in the islets of Langerhans, whose β cells secrete insulin and amylin; α cells secrete glucagon; δ cells secrete somatostatin; and F cells secrete pancreatic polypeptide.

Gerontologic Considerations: Effects of Aging on GI System

The process of aging changes the functional ability of the GI system. Diet, alcohol intake, and obesity affect organs of the GI

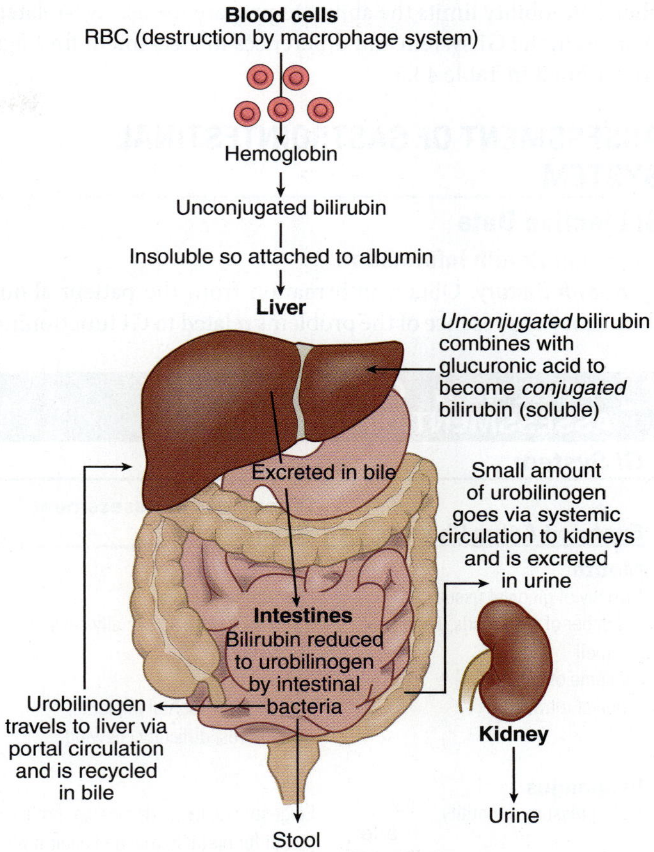

Fig. 43.4 Bilirubin metabolism and conjugation.

system, making it a challenge to separate the sole effects of aging from lifestyle. Many factors can lead to a decrease in appetite and make eating less pleasurable. Caries and periodontal disease can lead to loss of teeth. Taste buds decline in number and the sense of smell lessens, leading to decreased ability to taste. With less saliva, a very dry mouth *(xerostomia)* is common.[1]

Age-related changes in the esophagus include delayed emptying, resulting from smooth muscle weakness; reduced UES opening; and an incompetent LES. Although GI motility decreases with age, secretion and absorption are less affected. The older adult often has a decrease in intrinsic acid and HCl acid secretion *(hypochlorhydria)*.[2]

Chronic constipation affects 30% to 40% of adults over age 60.[3] Factors that may increase the risk for constipation include slower peristalsis, anorectal dysfunction, inactivity, decreased fiber intake, inadequate fluid intake, and constipating medications. Neurologic, cognitive, and metabolic problems may play a role. See Chapter 47 for more about constipation.

The liver size decreases after 50 years of age, but results of liver function tests (LFTs) stay within normal ranges. Age-related enzyme changes in the liver decrease the liver's ability to metabolize drugs and hormones. The size of the pancreas is unaffected by aging. It does undergo structural changes, such as fibrosis, fatty acid deposits, and atrophy. Gallbladder diseases increase with age.[4]

Older adults, especially those over 85, are at risk for decreased food intake. The inability to obtain food affects nutrition intake. Economic constraints may reduce the number of fresh fruits and vegetables consumed and, thus, the amount of fiber. Immobility limits the ability to prepare meals. Age-related changes in the GI system and differences in assessment findings are outlined in Table 43.5.

ASSESSMENT OF GASTROINTESTINAL SYSTEM

Subjective Data

Important Health Information

Health history. Obtain information from the patient about the history or presence of the problems related to GI functioning and fully explore any symptoms. Ask about any abdominal pain, nausea, vomiting, abdominal distention, jaundice, heartburn, dyspepsia, changes in appetite, hematemesis, indigestion, bloating, and trouble swallowing. Review the patient's bowel habits. Ask about diarrhea, constipation, melena, rectal bleeding, and excessive gas. Assess for related conditions, such as food intolerance or allergies, lactose intolerance, and anemia. Ask the patient about a history or presence of problems, such as reflux, gastritis, hepatitis, colitis, gallstones, hemorrhoids, peptic ulcer, cancer, diverticuli, or hernias.

TABLE 43.5 GERONTOLOGIC ASSESSMENT DIFFERENCES

GI System

Expected Aging Changes	Differences in Assessment Findings
Mouth	
Atrophy of gingival tissue	Poor-fitting dentures
↓ Number of taste buds, ↓ sense of smell	↓ Sense of taste (especially salty and sweet)
↓ Volume of saliva	Dry oral mucosa
Gingival retraction	Loss of teeth, dental implants, dentures, difficulty chewing
Esophagus	
↓ LES pressure, ↓ motility	Epigastric distress, dysphagia, potential for hiatal hernia and aspiration
Abdominal Wall	
↓ Number and sensitivity of sensory receptors	Less sensitivity to surface pain
Thinner and less taut	More visible peristalsis, easier palpation of organs
Stomach	
Atrophy of gastric mucosa, ↓ blood flow	Food intolerances, signs of anemia from cobalamin malabsorption, slower gastric emptying
Small Intestines	
Slightly ↓ motility and secretion of most digestive enzymes	Indigestion, slowed intestinal transit, delayed absorption of fat-soluble vitamins
Liver	
↓ Protein synthesis, ↓ ability to regenerate	↓ Drug and hormone metabolism
↓ Size and lowered position	Easier palpation because of lower border extending past costal margin
Large Intestine, Anus, Rectum	
↓ Anal sphincter tone and nerve supply to rectal area	Fecal incontinence
↓ Muscular tone, ↓ motility	Flatulence, abdominal distention, relaxed perineal musculature
↓ Transit time, ↓ sensation to defecation	Constipation, fecal impaction
Pancreas	
Pancreatic ducts distended, ↓ lipase production, ↓ pancreatic reserve	Impaired fat absorption, ↓ glucose tolerance

Ask the patient about weight history. Explore in detail any unexplained or unplanned weight loss or gain within the past 6 to 12 months. Discuss any history of chronic dieting and repeated weight loss and gain.

Medications. Assess the patient's past and current use of medications. Ask about the reason for taking the medication, the dose and frequency, length of time taken, route, its effect, and any side effects. Include information about probiotics and nutrition supplements. Many medications cause side effects in the GI system. GI problems can affect drug absorption and effectiveness. Antacids and laxatives may affect medication absorption. Ask the patient about laxative or antacid use, including the kind and frequency.

Many chemicals, herbal supplements, and drugs may be hepatotoxic (see *livertox.nih.gov*). They can result in significant harm unless monitored closely. Examples include chronic high doses of acetaminophen and nonsteroidal antiinflammatory drugs (NSAIDs). NSAIDs may also cause upper GI bleeding, with an increasing risk as the person ages. Other medications, such as antibiotics, may change the normal bacterial composition in the GI tract, resulting in diarrhea.

Case Study

Patient Introduction

(© iStockphoto/ Thinkstock.)

Patient Profile

L.C. is a 58-year-old Native American man from a Pueblo tribe in northern New Mexico. L.C.'s wife and family drove 50 miles to take him to the Indian Health Service hospital. He comes into the emergency department (ED) doubled over with abdominal pain. He is grimacing and holding his abdomen with both arms. You are working as the triage nurse that morning.

Discussion Questions

1. What are the possible causes for L.C.'s acute abdominal pain?
2. Is his condition stable or is it an emergency?
3. What type of assessment should you do: comprehensive, focused, or emergency?
4. What assessment questions will you ask him?
5. How will you individualize the assessment based on his ethnic/cultural background?

You will learn more about L.C. and his condition as you read this assessment chapter.

Answers available at http://evolve.elsevier.com/Lewis/medsurg.

Surgery or other treatments. Obtain information about hospitalizations for any problems related to the GI system. Record any abdominal or rectal surgery, including the year, reason for surgery, postoperative course, and blood transfusions. Terms related to common GI surgeries are listed in Table 43.6.

Functional Health Patterns

Key questions to ask a patient with a GI problem are outlined in Table 43.7.

Health perception–health management pattern. Ask about the patient's health practices related to the GI system. This includes maintaining normal body weight, proper dental care, adequate nutrition, and effective elimination habits.

Ask about recent foreign travel with possible exposure to hepatitis or parasitic infestation. Explore any sexual and drug use behaviors that may increase risk for hepatitis exposure. Determine whether the patient has received hepatitis A and B vaccination.

Assess the patient for habits that directly affect GI functioning. High rates of binge drinking alcohol and the intake of alcohol in large quantities or for long periods have harmful effects on the stomach mucosa.[5] Chronic alcohol exposure causes fatty infiltration of the liver and can cause damage, leading to cirrhosis and hepatocellular cancer. Obtain a history of cigarette smoking. Nicotine is irritating to the GI tract mucosa. Cigarette

TABLE 43.6 GI Surgeries

Procedure	Description
Appendectomy	Removal of appendix
Cholecystectomy	Removal of gallbladder
Choledochojejunostomy	Opening between common bile duct and jejunum
Choledocholithotomy	Opening into common bile duct for removal of stones
Colectomy	Removal of colon
Colostomy	Opening into colon
Esophagoenterostomy	Removal of part of esophagus with segment of colon attached to remaining part
Esophagogastrostomy	Removal of esophagus and anastomosis of remaining part to stomach
Gastrectomy	Removal of stomach
Gastrostomy	Opening into stomach
Glossectomy	Removal of tongue
Hemiglossectomy	Removal of half of tongue
Herniorrhaphy	Repair of a hernia
Ileostomy	Opening into ileum
Mandibulectomy	Removal of mandible
Pyloroplasty	Enlargement and repair of pyloric sphincter area
Vagotomy	Resection of branch of vagus nerve

TABLE 43.7 HEALTH HISTORY

GI System

Health Perception–Health Management
- Describe any measures used to treat GI symptoms such as diarrhea or constipation.
- Do you smoke?[a] Do you drink alcohol?[a]
- Are you exposed to any chemicals on a regular basis?[a] Have you been exposed in the past?[a]
- Have you recently traveled outside the United States?[a]

Nutritional-Metabolic
- Describe your usual daily food and fluid intake.
- Do you take any supplemental vitamins or minerals?[a]
- Have you had any changes in appetite or food tolerance?[a]
- Has there been any weight change in the past 6–12 months?[a]
- Are you allergic to any foods?[a]

Elimination
- Describe the frequency and time of day you have bowel movements. What is the consistency of the bowel movement?
- Do you use laxatives or enemas?[a] If so, how often?
- Have there been any recent changes in your bowel pattern?[a]
- Do you have any pain with bowel movements or pain relieved by bowel movements?
- Describe any skin problems caused by GI problems.
- Do you need any assistive equipment, such as ostomy equipment, raised toilet seat, commode?

Activity-Exercise
- Do you have limitations in mobility that make it hard for you to obtain and prepare food?[a]
- Sleep-Rest
- Do you have any problem sleeping because of a GI problem?[a]
- Are you awakened by symptoms such as gas, abdominal pain, diarrhea, or heartburn?[a]

Cognitive-Perceptual
- Have you had any change in taste or smell that have affected your appetite?[a]
- Do you have any heat or cold sensitivity that affects eating?[a]
- Does pain interfere with food preparation, appetite, or chewing?[a]
- Do pain medications cause constipation, diarrhea, or appetite suppression?[a]

Self-Perception–Self-Concept
- Describe any changes in your weight that have affected how you feel about yourself.
- Have you had any changes in normal elimination that have affected how you feel about yourself?[a]
- Do you have any symptoms of GI disease caused physical changes that are a problem for you?[a]

Role-Relationship
- Describe the impact of any GI problem on your usual roles and relationships.
- Have any changes in elimination affected your relationships?[a]
- Do you live alone? Describe how your family or others assist you with your GI problems.

Sexuality-Reproductive
- Describe the effect of your GI problem on your sexual activity.
- Coping–Stress Tolerance
- Do you have GI symptoms in response to stressful or emotional situations?[a]
- Describe how you deal with any GI symptoms that result.

Value-Belief
- Describe any cultural or religious beliefs about food and food preparation that may influence the treatment of your GI problem.

[a]If yes, describe.

BOX 43.1 GENETIC RISK ALERT

Colorectal Cancer (CRC)

- CRC may run in families if first-degree relatives (parents, siblings) or many other family members (grandparents, aunts, uncles) had CRC. This is especially true when family members are diagnosed with CRC before age 50
- Genetic conditions associated with an increased risk for CRC include:
  - Hereditary nonpolyposis colorectal cancer (HNPCC). It is caused by mutations in several different genes.
  - Familial adenomatous polyposis (FAP). FAP is characterized by multiple polyps that are noncancerous at first but eventually develop into cancer if not treated. Most cases of FAP are due to mutations of the adenomatous polyposis coli *(APC)* gene.

Inflammatory Bowel Disease (IBD)

- People with IBD have a genetic predisposition or susceptibility to the disease.
- First-degree relatives have a 5- to 20-fold increased risk for developing IBD.

smoking is related to GI cancers (especially mouth and esophageal cancers), esophagitis, and ulcers. Smoking delays the healing of ulcers.

Family history is an important part of this health pattern. About one third of cases of colorectal cancer (CRC) occur in patients with a family history. Because of the relationship between CRC and breast cancer, ask about a history of either type of cancer in the family (Box 43.1).

Nutritional-metabolic pattern. A thorough nutrition assessment is essential. Take a diet history and ask about both content and amount or portion size. Food preferences and preparation may vary by culture and religion. Open-ended questions allow the patient to express beliefs and feelings about the diet. For example, you can say, "Please tell me about your food and beverage intake over the past 24 hours." You can use a 24-hour diet recall to analyze the adequacy of the diet. Help the patient recall the preceding day's food intake, including early morning and nighttime intake, snacks, and liquids. Then evaluate the diet in relation to recommended servings for diet intake using a guide such as MyPlate *(www.choosemyplate.gov)*. A 1-week recall may provide more information on usual diet patterns. Compare weekday and weekend diet intake patterns in relation to both the quality and quantity of food.

Ask the patient about the use of sugar and salt substitutes, caffeine intake, and amount of fluid and fiber intake. Note any changes in appetite, food tolerance, and weight. Anorexia and weight loss may indicate cancer or inflammation. Decreased food intake can be the consequence of economic problems or depression.

Ask about food allergies and intolerances, including lactose and gluten. Have the patient describe the allergic response and any GI symptoms.

Elimination pattern. Elicit a detailed account of the patient's bowel elimination pattern. Note the frequency, time of day, and usual stool consistency. Ask about the presence of pain with bowel movements, if bowel movements relieve pain, and any recent changes in bowel patterns. Explore the use of laxatives and enemas, including type, frequency, and results.

Document the amount and type of fluid and fiber intake. These influence the frequency and consistency of stools. Inadequate fiber intake can be associated with constipation. Look for any association between a skin and GI problem. Food allergies can cause skin lesions, pruritus, and edema. Diarrhea can result in redness, irritation, and pain in the perianal area. External drainage systems, such as an ileostomy or ileal conduit, may cause local skin irritation.

Activity-exercise pattern. Activity and exercise affect GI motility. Immobility is a risk factor for constipation. Assess ambulatory status to determine if the patient can secure and prepare food. If the patient is unable to do these tasks, see if a family member or an outside agency is meeting this need. Note any limitation in the ability to feed oneself. Assess for access to a toilet. Identify the use of and access to supplies such as a commode or ostomy supplies.

Sleep-rest pattern. GI symptoms can interfere with the quality of sleep. Nausea, vomiting, diarrhea, indigestion, and bloating can produce sleep problems. Ask the patient if GI symptoms affect sleep or rest. For example, a patient with gastroesophageal reflux disease (GERD) may wake with burning epigastric pain.

A patient may have a bedtime ritual that involves a specific food or beverage. Herbal teas may be sleep inducing. Document individual routines and comply with these whenever possible to avoid sleeplessness. Hunger can prevent sleep. A light, easily digested snack may be helpful.

Cognitive-perceptual pattern. Sensory changes can result in problems related to acquiring, preparing, and ingesting food. Changes in taste or smell can affect appetite and eating pleasure. Vertigo can make shopping or standing at a stove difficult and dangerous. Heat or cold sensitivity can make some foods painful to eat. Problems in expressive communication limit the patient's ability to state personal food preferences.

Both acute and chronic pain influence intake. Behaviors associated with pain include avoiding activity, fatigue, and disrupted eating patterns. For patients receiving opioid medications, assess for decreased appetite, constipation, nausea, and sedation.

Self-perception–self-concept pattern. Many GI and nutrition problems affect the patient's self-perception. Overweight and underweight persons may have problems related to self-esteem and body image. Repeated attempts to achieve a personally acceptable weight can be discouraging and depressing for some people. The way a person recounts a weight history can alert you to potential problems in this area.

The need for external devices to manage elimination, such as a colostomy or an ileostomy, may be challenging for some patients. The patient's willingness to engage in self-care and to discuss this situation provides you with valuable information related to body image and self-esteem.

The altered physical changes from advanced liver disease can be disturbing for the patient. Jaundice, muscle wasting, and ascites cause significant changes in external appearance. Assess the patient's attitude about these changes.

Role-relationship pattern. Problems related to the GI system, such as cirrhosis, hepatitis, ostomies, obesity, and cancer, may affect the patient's ability to maintain usual roles and relationships. A person may need to leave a job or reduce work hours. Changes in body image and self-esteem can affect relationships.

Sexuality-reproductive pattern. Changes related to sexuality and reproductive status can result from problems of the GI system. For example, obesity, jaundice, and ascites could decrease the acceptance of a potential sexual partner. An ostomy can affect the patient's confidence related to sexual activity. Your sensitive questioning can identify potential problems.

Anorexia can affect the reproductive status of a female patient. Obesity leads to reduced fertility and increased miscarriage rates in women.

Coping–stress tolerance pattern. Determine what is stressful for the patient and what coping mechanisms the patient uses. Factors outside the GI tract can influence its functioning. Both psychologic and emotional factors, such as stress and anxiety, influence GI functioning in many people. Stress can manifest as anorexia, nausea, epigastric and abdominal pain, or diarrhea. It can worsen some GI problems, such as peptic ulcer disease, irritable bowel syndrome, and IBD. However, never attribute GI symptoms solely to psychologic factors.

Value-belief pattern. Assess the patient's spiritual, religious, and cultural beliefs about food and food preparation. Whenever possible, respect these preferences. Determine if any value or belief could interfere with planned interventions. For example, if the patient with anemia is a vegetarian, you will need to consider how to increase their intake of iron-rich foods other than meat. Thoughtful assessment and consideration of the patient's beliefs and values usually increase adherence and satisfaction.

Case Study

Subjective Data

(© iStockphoto/Thinkstock.)

A focused subjective assessment of L.C. revealed the following information:

- ***Health History:*** Negative history for medical or surgical problems.
- ***Medications:*** None.
- ***Health Perception–Health Management:*** L.C. states he has not been feeling well for the past several weeks. He feels weak and fatigues easily. Denies exposure to chemicals. No recent travel outside of the United States. Smokes 1 pack of cigarettes per day for 20 years. Drinks 3–4 bottles of beer per day.
- ***Nutritional-Metabolic:*** L.C. is 5 ft, 9 in tall and weighs 140 lb (BMI: 20.7 kg/m^2). States has been losing weight over the past several months and does not have an appetite. No food allergies.
- ***Elimination:*** Reports alternating episodes of constipation and diarrhea. He noticed some bright red blood in stools. Has not had a bowel movement for 4 days.
- ***Cognitive-Perceptual:*** Rates pain as a 9 on a scale of 0 to 10. States pain comes and goes in waves. Prefers to lie still with knees flexed and drawn into his abdomen.

Discussion Questions

1. Which subjective assessment findings concern you most?
2. Based on these subjective assessment findings, what should you include in the physical assessment? What would you be looking for?
3. What would be your priority assessment?

You will learn more about physical assessment of the GI system in the next section.

Answers available at http://evolve.elsevier.com/Lewis/medsurg.

Objective Data

Physical Assessment

Mouth

Inspection. Inspect the mouth for symmetry, color, and size. Observe for abnormalities, such as pallor or cyanosis, cracking, ulcers, or fissures. The dorsum (top) of the tongue should have a thin white coating. The undersurface should be smooth. Observe for any lesions. Using a tongue blade, inspect the buccal mucosa. Note the color, any areas of pigmentation, and any lesions. Dark-skinned persons normally have patchy areas of pigmentation. In assessing the teeth and gums, look for caries, loose teeth, abnormal shape and position of teeth, and swelling, bleeding, discoloration, or gingival inflammation. Note any distinctive breath odor.

Inspect the pharynx by tilting the patient's head back and depressing the tongue with a tongue blade. Observe the tonsils, uvula, soft palate, and anterior and posterior pillars. Tell the patient to say "ah." The uvula and soft palate should rise and remain in the midline.

Palpation. Palpate any suspicious areas in the mouth. Note ulcers, nodules, indurations, and areas of tenderness. The mouth of the older adult needs careful assessment. Pay attention to dentures (e.g., fit, condition), the ability to swallow, and the tongue. Note any lesions. Ask the patient with dentures to remove them during an oral exam to allow for good visualization and palpation of the area.

Abdomen. We use 2 systems to anatomically describe the surface of the abdomen. One system divides the abdomen into 4 quadrants by a perpendicular line from the sternum to the pubic bone and a horizontal line across the abdomen at the umbilicus (Fig. 43.5A and Table 43.8). The other system divides the abdomen into 9 regions (Fig. 43.5B). We often assess only the epigastric, umbilical, and suprapubic or hypogastric regions.

For the abdominal assessment, good lighting should shine across the abdomen. The patient should be in the supine position and as relaxed as possible. To help relax the abdominal muscles, have the patient slightly flex the knees and raise the head of the bed slightly. The patient should have an empty bladder. Use warm hands when doing the abdominal assessment to avoid eliciting muscle guarding. Ask the patient to breathe slowly through the mouth.

The standard approach for examining the abdomen is appropriate for an older adult. The abdomen may be thinner and laxer unless the patient is obese.

Inspection. Assess the abdomen for skin changes (color, texture, scars, striae, dilated veins, rashes, lesions), umbilicus (location and contour), symmetry, and contour (flat, rounded [convex], concave, protuberant, distended). Note observable hernias or masses. Is there any movement (pulsations, peristalsis)? A normal aortic pulsation may be seen in the epigastric area. Look across the abdomen tangentially (across the abdomen in a line) for peristalsis. Peristalsis is not normally visible in an adult but may be visible in a thin person.

Auscultation. When you examine the abdomen, auscultate before percussion and palpation because these latter procedures may alter the bowel sounds. Use the diaphragm of the stethoscope to auscultate bowel sounds because they are high pitched. Use the bell of the stethoscope to detect lower pitched sounds. Warm the stethoscope in your hands before auscultating to help prevent abdominal muscle contraction. Listen in the epigastrium and in all 4 quadrants. Start in the right lower quadrant because bowel sounds are normally present there. Listen for bowel sounds for at least 2 minutes. Do not count bowel sounds. Determine if they are normal, hypoactive, or hyperactive.

The frequency and intensity of bowel sounds vary depending on the phase of digestion. Normal sounds are high pitched and gurgling. Stomach growling or loud gurgles *(borborygmi)* indicate hyperperistalsis. The bowel sounds are high pitched (rushes and tinkling) when the intestines are under tension, as in intestinal obstruction. Listen for decreased or absent bowel sounds. If you are patient and listen for several minutes, you will often find the bowel sounds are not absent but are hypoactive. If you do not hear bowel sounds, note the amount of time you listened in each quadrant without hearing bowel sounds.

Listen for vascular sounds. A *bruit,* best heard with the bell of the stethoscope, is a swishing or buzzing sound and indicates turbulent blood flow. Normally, you should not hear aortic bruits.

Percussion. The purpose of percussing the abdomen is to estimate the size of the liver and spleen and determine the presence of fluid, distention, and masses. Sound waves vary according to the density of underlying tissues. Air produces a higher pitched, hollow sound termed *tympany.* Fluid or masses produce a short, high-pitched sound with little resonance termed *dullness.* Lightly percuss all 4 quadrants of the abdomen and assess the distribution of tympany and dullness (Fig. 43.6). Tympany is the predominant percussion sound of the abdomen.

To percuss the liver, start below the umbilicus in the right midclavicular line and percuss lightly upward until you hear dullness. This is the lower border of the liver. Next, start at the nipple line in the right midclavicular line and percuss downward between ribs to the area of dullness indicating the upper border of the liver. Measure the height or vertical space between the 2 borders to determine the size of the liver. The normal range of liver height in the right midclavicular line is 2.4 to 5 in (6 to 12.7 cm).

Palpation. Use palpation to assess the abdominal organs and detect any tenderness, distention, masses, or fluid. Palpation is important because it may reveal a tumor. Begin with light palpation. Palpate any areas in which the patient reports tenderness last.

Use *light palpation* to detect tenderness or cutaneous hypersensitivity, muscular resistance, masses, and swelling. Help the patient relax for deeper palpation. Keep your fingers together and press gently with the pads of the fingertips, depressing the abdominal wall about 0.4 in (1 cm). Use smooth movements and palpate all quadrants (Fig. 43.7A).

Use *deep palpation* to delineate abdominal organs and masses (Fig. 43.7B). Use the palmar surfaces of your fingers to press more deeply. Again, palpate all quadrants. Note the location, size, and shape of masses, as well as the presence of tenderness. During these maneuvers, observe the patient's facial expression because it will provide nonverbal cues of discomfort or pain.

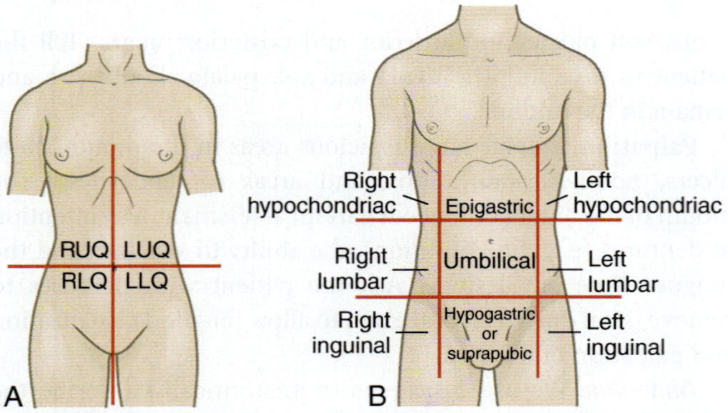

Fig. 43.5 (A) Abdominal quadrants. (B) Abdominal regions. *LLQ,* Left lower quadrant; *LUQ,* left upper quadrant; *RLQ,* right lower quadrant; *RUQ,* right upper quadrant.

TABLE 43.8 Structures Located in Abdominal Regions

Right Upper Quadrant	Left Upper Quadrant	Right Lower Quadrant	Left Lower Quadrant
• Liver and gallbladder	• Left lobe of liver	• Lower pole of right kidney	• Lower pole of left kidney
• Pylorus	• Spleen	• Cecum and appendix	• Sigmoid flexure
• Duodenum	• Stomach	• Portion of ascending colon	• Part of descending colon
• Head of pancreas	• Body of pancreas	• Bladder (if distended)	• Bladder (if distended)
• Right adrenal gland	• Left adrenal gland	• Right ovary and fallopian tube	• Left ovary and fallopian tube
• Portion of right kidney	• Portion of left kidney	• Uterus (if enlarged)	• Uterus (if enlarged)
• Hepatic flexure of colon	• Splenic flexure of colon	• Right spermatic cord	• Left spermatic cord
• Portion of ascending and transverse colon	• Portion of transverse and descending colon	• Right ureter	• Left ureter

Another method for deep abdominal palpation is the 2-hand method. Place one hand on top of the other and apply pressure to the bottom hand with the fingers of the top hand. With the fingers of the bottom hand, feel for organs and masses. Practice both methods of palpation to determine which is most effective.

Check a problem area on the abdomen for rebound tenderness by pressing in slowly and firmly over the painful site. Withdraw the palpating fingers quickly. Pain on withdrawal of the fingers indicates peritoneal inflammation. Because assessing for rebound tenderness may produce pain and severe muscle spasm, it should be done at the end of the assessment and only by an experienced practitioner.

To palpate the liver, place your left hand behind the patient to support the right eleventh and twelfth ribs (Fig. 43.8). The patient may relax on your hand. Press the left hand forward and place the right hand on the patient's right abdomen lateral to the rectus muscle. The fingertips should be below the lower border of liver dullness and pointed toward the right costal margin. Gently press in and up. The patient should take a deep breath with the abdomen so that the liver drops and is in a better position for palpation. Try to feel the liver edge as it comes down to the fingertips. During inspiration, the liver edge should feel firm, sharp, and smooth. Describe the surface and contour and any tenderness. If the patient has chronic obstructive pulmonary disease, large lungs, or a low diaphragm, the liver may be palpated 0.4 to 0.8 in (1 to 2 cm) below the right costal margin.

To palpate the spleen, move to the patient's left side. Place your right hand under the patient, and support and press the patient's left lower rib cage forward. Place your left hand below the left costal margin and press it in toward the spleen. Ask the patient to breathe deeply. The fingertips can feel the tip or edge of an enlarged spleen. The normal spleen size range is about 5 in long (12.7 cm), 3 in wide (7.6 cm), and 1.5 in (3.8 cm) thick. It is normally not palpable. If it is palpable, do not continue, because manual compression of an enlarged spleen may cause it to rupture.

Rectum and anus. Inspect perianal and anal areas for color, texture, masses, rashes, scars, erythema, fissures, and external hemorrhoids. Palpate any masses or unusual areas with a gloved hand.

For the digital examination of the rectum, place a gloved, lubricated index finger against the anus while having the patient gently bear down (Valsalva maneuver). Then, as the sphincter relaxes, insert the finger. Point the finger toward the umbilicus. Try to get the patient to relax. Insert the finger into the rectum as far as possible and palpate all surfaces. Assess any nodules, tenderness, or irregularities. Use the gloved finger to remove a stool sample and check it for occult blood. However, a single

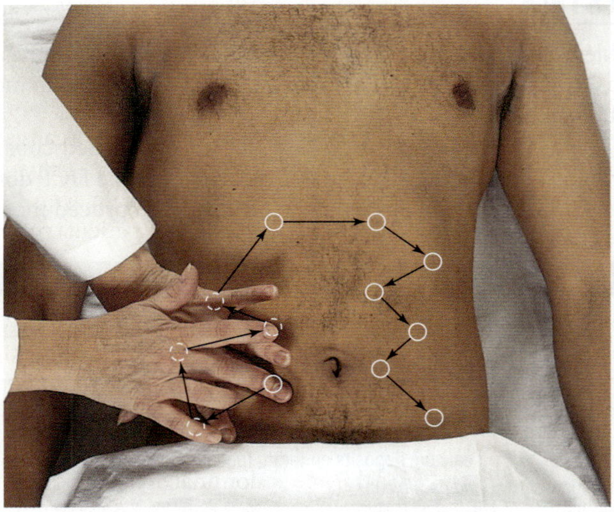

Fig. 43.6 Technique for percussion of the abdomen. Moving clockwise, percuss lightly in all 4 quadrants. (From Jarvis C: *Physical examination and health assessment,* ed 8, St Louis, 2020, Saunders.)

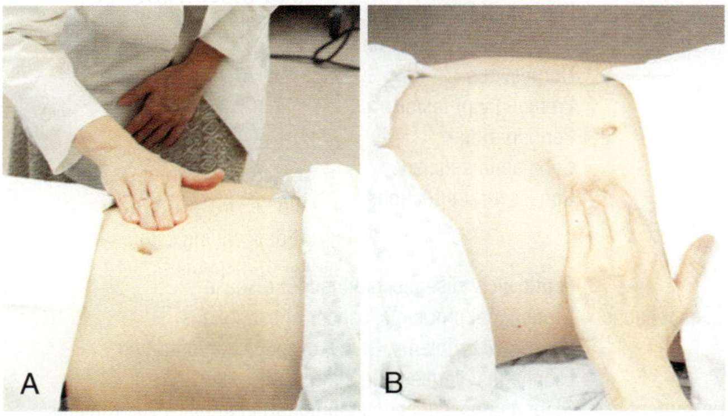

Fig. 43.7 (A) Technique for light palpation of the abdomen. (B) Technique for deep palpation.

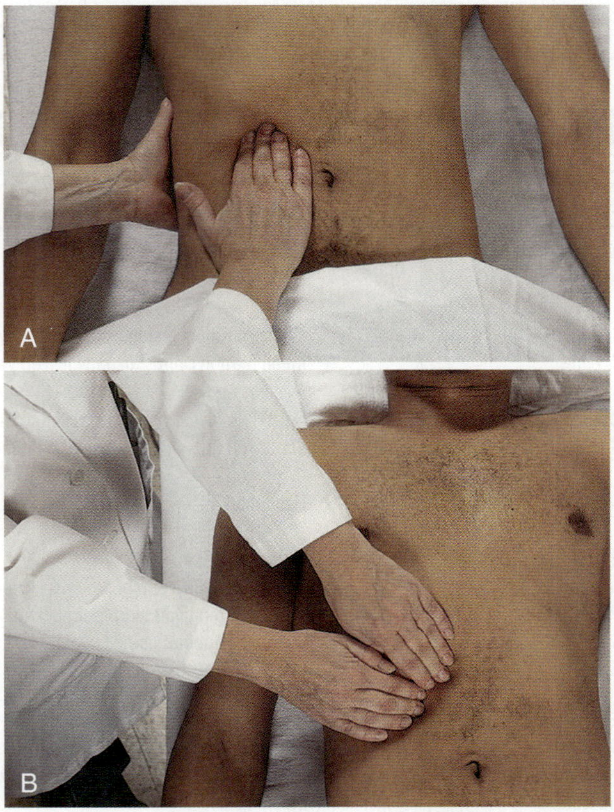

Fig. 43.8 (A) Technique for liver palpation. (B) Alternative technique to palpate liver with fingers hooked over the costal region. (From Jarvis C: *Physical examination and health assessment,* ed 8, St Louis, 2020, Saunders.)

guaiac-based fecal occult blood test has limited sensitivity in detecting CRC.

Findings of a normal physical assessment of the GI system are shown in Table 43.9. Table 43.10 outlines assessment abnormalities. Gerontologic differences in the GI system and differences in assessment findings are described in Table 43.5. A *focused assessment* (Box 43.2) evaluates the status of previously identified GI problems and monitors for signs of new problems.

TABLE 43.9 Normal Physical Assessment of GI System

Mouth
- Moist and pink lips
- Pink and moist buccal mucosa and gingivae without plaques or lesions
- Teeth in good repair
- Protrusion of tongue in midline without deviation or twitches
- Pink uvula (in midline), soft palate, tonsils, and posterior pharynx
- Swallows smoothly without coughing or gagging

Abdomen
- Flat without masses or scars. No bruises
- Bowel sounds in all quadrants
- No abdominal tenderness; nonpalpable liver and spleen
- Liver 10 cm in right midclavicular line
- Generalized tympany

Anus
- Absence of lesions, fissures, and hemorrhoids
- Good sphincter tone
- Rectal walls smooth and soft
- No masses
- Stool soft, brown, and heme negative

Case Study

Objective Data: Physical Assessment

(© iStockphoto/ Thinkstock.)

A focused assessment of L.C. reveals the following: BP 120/74, heart rate 110, respiratory rate 24, temperature 100.4°F (43°C). Abdomen firm and slightly distended. High-pitched bowel sounds in upper quadrants. No bowel sounds auscultated in left lower quadrant. Mild abdominal palpation elicits pain.

Discussion Questions

1. Which physical assessment findings concern you most?
2. Based upon the assessment data presented so far, what would be 3 priority clinical problems?
3. What diagnostic studies do you think may be ordered for L.C.?

You will learn more about diagnostic studies related to the GI system in the next section.

Answers available at http://evolve.elsevier.com/Lewis/medsurg.

DIAGNOSTIC STUDIES OF GASTROINTESTINAL SYSTEM

Tables 43.11 and 43.12 present common diagnostic studies of the GI system. Selected diagnostic studies are described in more detail here.

For most diagnostic studies, make sure the signed consent form for the procedure is in the medical record. The HCP doing the procedure is responsible for explaining the procedure and

TABLE 43.10 ASSESSMENT ABNORMALITIES

GI System

Finding	Description	Possible Etiology and Significance
Mouth		
Acute marginal gingivitis	Friable, edematous, painful, bleeding gingivae	Irritation from ill-fitting dentures or orthodontic appliances, calcium deposits on teeth, food impaction
Candidiasis	White, curdlike lesions surrounded by erythematous mucosa	*Candida albicans*
Cheilitis	Inflammation of lips (usually lower) with fissuring, scaling, crusting	Often unknown
Cheilosis	Softening, fissuring, and cracking of lips at angles of mouth	Riboflavin deficiency
Geographic tongue	Scattered red, smooth (loss of papillae) areas on dorsum of tongue	Unknown
Glossitis	Reddened, ulcerated, swollen tongue	Exposure to streptococci, irritation, injury, vitamin B deficiencies, anemia
Herpes simplex	Vesicular lesion	Herpesvirus
Leukoplakia	Thickened white patches	Premalignant lesion
Pyorrhea	Recessed gingivae, purulent pockets	Periodontitis
Smooth tongue	Red, slick appearance	Cobalamin deficiency
Ulcer, plaque on lips or in mouth	Sore or lesion	Cancer, viral infections
Esophagus and Stomach		
Dyspepsia	Burning or indigestion	Peptic ulcer disease, gallbladder disease
Dysphagia	Difficulty swallowing, sensation of food sticking in esophagus	Esophageal problems, cancer of esophagus
Eructation	Belching	Various GI problems, GERD, dyspepsia, rumination
Hematemesis	Vomiting of blood	Esophageal varices, bleeding peptic ulcer
Nausea and vomiting	Feeling of impending vomiting, expulsion of gastric contents through mouth	GI infections, common manifestation of many GI problems, stress, fear, and pathologic conditions

TABLE 43.10 ASSESSMENT ABNORMALITIES—cont'd

GI System

Finding	Description	Possible Etiology and Significance
Odynophagia	Painful swallowing	Cancer of esophagus, esophagitis
Pyrosis	Heartburn, burning in epigastric or substernal area	Hiatal hernia, esophagitis, incompetent LES
Abdomen		
Absence of liver dullness	Tympany on percussion	Air from viscus (e.g., perforated ulcer)
Absent bowel sounds	No bowel sounds on auscultation	Peritonitis, paralytic ileus, obstruction
Ascites	Accumulated fluid within abdominal cavity, eversion of umbilicus (usually)	Peritoneal inflammation, heart failure, metastatic cancer, cirrhosis
Borborygmi	Waves of loud, gurgling sounds	Hyperactive bowel from eating
Bruit	Humming or swishing sound heard through stethoscope over vessel	Partial arterial obstruction (narrowing of vessel), turbulent flow (aneurysm)
Distention	Excessive gas accumulation, enlarged abdomen, generalized tympany	Obstruction, paralytic ileus
Hepatomegaly	Enlargement of liver, liver edge >1–2 cm below costal margin	Metastatic cancer, hepatitis, venous congestion, cardiac congestion
Hernia	Bulge or nodule in abdomen, usually appearing on straining	Inguinal (in inguinal canal), femoral (in femoral canal), umbilical (herniation of umbilicus), diastasis rectus (deformity) or incisional (defect in muscles after surgery)
Hyperresonance	Loud, tinkling rushes	Intestinal obstruction
Masses	Lump on palpation	Tumors, cysts
Nodular liver	Enlarged, hard liver with irregular edge or surface	Cirrhosis, focal nodular hyperplasia, cancer
Rebound tenderness	Sudden pain when fingers withdrawn quickly	Peritoneal inflammation, appendicitis
Splenomegaly	Enlarged spleen	Chronic leukemia, hemolytic states, portal hypertension, some infections
Rectum and Anus		
Fissure	Ulceration in anal canal	Straining, irritation
Hemorrhoids	Thrombosed veins in rectum and anus (internal or external)	Portal hypertension, chronic constipation, prolonged sitting or standing, pregnancy
Mass	Firm, nodular edge	Tumor, cancer
Melena	Abnormal, black, tarry stool containing digested blood	Cancer, bleeding in upper GI tract from ulcers, varices
Pilonidal cyst	Opening of sinus tract, cyst in midline just above coccyx	Probably congenital
Steatorrhea	Fatty, frothy, foul-smelling stool	Chronic pancreatitis, biliary obstruction, malabsorption problems
Tenesmus	Painful and ineffective straining, Sense of incomplete evacuation	Inflammatory bowel disease, irritable bowel syndrome, diarrhea from GI infection (e.g., food poisoning)

obtaining written consent. You have a key role in teaching patients about the procedures. When preparing the patient, it is important to ask about any known allergies to drugs, iodine, shellfish, or contrast media.

Many GI system diagnostic procedures require (1) measures to cleanse the GI tract and (2) ingestion or injection of a contrast medium or a radiopaque tracer. Often, the patient has a series of GI diagnostic tests done. Monitor the patient closely to ensure adequate hydration and nutrition during the testing period.

Some diagnostic studies are especially difficult and uncomfortable for the older adult. Adjustments may be needed during the preparation, especially for those with certain health conditions (e.g., diabetes).[6] Consider any physical limitations and pressure points when positioning the older patient during testing. Monitor the patient closely to avoid problems, such as dehydration from prolonged fluid restriction and diarrhea from bowel-cleansing procedures.

Radiologic Studies

Upper GI Series

An upper GI series with small bowel follow-through provides visualization of the oropharyngeal area, esophagus, stomach, and small intestine. The procedure consists of the patient swallowing contrast medium (a thick barium solution or gastrografin) and then assuming different positions on the x-ray table. The movement of the contrast medium is observed with fluoroscopy, and a series of x-rays are taken. An upper GI series is useful in identifying esophageal strictures, polyps, tumors, hiatal hernias, foreign bodies, and ulcers.

Lower GI Series

The purpose of a lower GI series, or a barium enema, is to observe (using fluoroscopy) the colon filling with contrast medium and to observe (by x-ray) the filled colon. The patient receives an enema of contrast medium. This procedure identifies polyps,

BOX 43.2 FOCUSED ASSESSMENT
GI System

Use this checklist to make sure the key assessment steps have been done.

Subjective

Ask the patient about any of the following and note responses.

Loss of appetite	Y	N
Abdominal pain	Y	N
Changes in stools (color, blood, consistency, frequency, pain)	Y	N
Nausea, vomiting	Y	N
Painful swallowing	Y	N

Objective: Diagnostic

Check the following results for critical values.

Endoscopy: colonoscopy, sigmoidoscopy, esophagogastroduodenoscopy	✓
CT scan	✓
Radiologic series: upper GI, lower GI	✓
Stool for occult blood or ova and parasites	✓
Liver function tests	✓

Objective: Physical Assessment

Inspect

Skin for color, scars, petechiae, and other lesions.	✓
Abdominal contour for symmetry and distention	✓
Perianal area for intact skin, hemorrhoids	✓

Auscultate

Bowel sounds	✓

Palpate

Abdominal quadrants using light touch	✓
Abdominal quadrants using a deep technique	✓

tumors, and other lesions in the colon. Adding air contrast after the barium provides better visualization (Fig. 43.9). Because the patient must retain the barium, an older or immobile patient may not tolerate it very well.

Virtual Colonoscopy

Virtual colonoscopy combines CT scanning or MRI to produce images of the colon and rectum less invasively. It requires radiation and prior cleansing of the colon but no sedation.

Compared to conventional colonoscopy, virtual colonoscopy provides a better view inside the colon that is narrow from inflammation or a growth.[7] If a polyp is found, it will have to be removed by conventional colonoscopy. Virtual colonoscopy may be less sensitive in obtaining information on the details and color of the mucosa and in detecting small (less than 10 mm) or flat polyps.

Endoscopy

Endoscopy refers to the direct visualization of a body structure through an endoscope. An endoscope is a fiberoptic instrument with a light and camera attached, allowing the ability to take video and still pictures (Fig. 43.10). Some endoscopes have a channel through which to pass instruments, such as biopsy forceps and cytology brushes.

Endoscopy can examine the esophagus, stomach, duodenum, and colon. *Endoscopic retrograde cholangiopancreatography* (ERCP) visualizes the pancreatic, hepatic, and common bile ducts. Endoscopy is often combined with diagnostic procedures, including biopsy, cytologic studies, invasive, and therapeutic procedures. Examples include polypectomy, sclerosis or banding of varices, cauterization of bleeding sites, common bile duct stone removal, and balloon dilation.

TABLE 43.11 Diagnostic Studies
GI System

Study	Description and Purpose	Nursing Responsibility
Endoscopy		
Colonoscopy	Directly visualizes entire colon up to ileocecal valve with flexible fiberoptic scope. Patient's position is changed frequently during procedure to assist with advancement of scope to cecum. Used to diagnose or detect inflammatory bowel disease, polyps, tumors, and diverticulosis and dilate strictures. Procedure allows for biopsy and removal of polyps without laparotomy	*Before:* Bowel preparation prior varies depending on HCP. Patient should avoid fiber for up to 72 hr prior, then either a clear or full liquid diet 24 hr before. Bowel cleansing should follow a split-dose regimen. The evening before the procedure, the patient should use a cleansing solution. The second dose should begin 4–6 hr before the procedure. A split-dose regimen started early morning the day of a procedure provides better cleansing for patients scheduled in the afternoon. Encourage the patient to drink all the solution. Stools will be clear or clear yellow liquid when the colon is clean. Bisacodyl tablets or suppositories may be given before the cleansing solution to remove the bulk of the stool. Explain to patient that a flexible scope will be inserted while patient in side-lying position and sedation will be given. *After:* Patient may have abdominal cramps caused by stimulation of peristalsis because the bowel is constantly inflated with air during procedure. Teach patients about pain post-colonoscopy and the characteristics of this pain. Tell patients if pain lasts longer than 24 hr to notify HCP. Check vital signs. Observe for rectal bleeding and manifestations of perforation (e.g., malaise, abdominal distention, tenesmus)

TABLE 43.11 Diagnostic Studies—cont'd

GI System

Study	Description and Purpose	Nursing Responsibility
Endoscopic retrograde cholangiopan-creatography (ERCP)	Fiberoptic endoscope (using fluoroscopy) is orally inserted into descending duodenum. Then common bile and pancreatic ducts are cannulated. Contrast medium is injected into ducts to allow for direct visualization of structures. Can be used to retrieve a gallstone from distal common bile duct, dilate strictures, biopsy, and diagnose pseudocysts	*Before:* Explain procedure. Keep patient NPO 8 hr before. Ensure consent form is signed. Give sedation immediately before and during procedure. Give antibiotics if ordered. *After:* Check vital signs. Assess for perforation or infection. Pancreatitis is most common complication. Check for return of gag reflex
Esophagoga-stroduodenoscopy (EGD)	Directly visualizes mucosal lining of esophagus, stomach, and duodenum with flexible endoscope. Test may use video imaging to visualize stomach motility. Detects inflammation, ulcerations, tumors, varices, or Mallory-Weiss tears. Biopsies may be taken. Varices can be treated with band ligation or sclerotherapy	*Before:* Keep patient NPO for 8 hr. Ensure consent form is signed. Give preoperative medication if ordered. Explain to patient that local anesthesia may be sprayed on throat before insertion of scope and that patient will be sedated during procedure. *After:* Keep patient NPO until gag reflex returns. Gently tickle back of throat to determine reflex. Use warm saline gargles for relief of sore throat. Check temperature q15–30 min for 1–2 hr (sudden temperature spike is sign of perforation). Asses for pain which may be a sign of perforation
Laparoscopy (peritoneoscopy)	Visualize peritoneal cavity and contents with laparoscope. Double-puncture peritoneoscopy permits better visualization of abdominal cavity, especially liver. Done in operating room. Can obtain biopsy specimen	*Before:* Ensure consent form is signed. Keep patient NPO 8 hr. Give preoperative sedative medication. Ensure bladder and bowels are emptied. *After:* Observe for complications of bleeding and bowel perforation after the procedure
Sigmoidoscopy	Directly visualizes rectum and sigmoid colon with lighted flexible endoscope. Sometimes a special table is used to tilt patient into knee-chest position. Used to detect tumors, polyps, inflammatory and infectious diseases, fissures, hemorrhoids	*Before:* Bowel preparation similar to colonoscopy. Explain to patient knee-chest position, need to take deep breaths during insertion of scope, and possible urge to defecate as scope is passed. Encourage patient to relax and let abdomen go limp. *After:* Observe for rectal bleeding after polypectomy or biopsy
Video capsule endoscopy	Patient swallows a vitamin-sized capsule with camera, which provides endoscopic visualization of GI tract (Fig. 43.11). Camera takes >50,000 images during test, relaying them to monitoring device that patient wears on a belt. Images then downloaded to computer. Used to look at areas of GI tract not accessible by upper and lower endoscopy	*Before:* Keep patient NPO for 8 hr. May have bowel preparation similar to colonoscopy. After swallowing capsule, clear liquids resumed in 2 hr and food in 4 hr. *After:* 8 hr after swallowing device, patient returns to have monitoring device removed. Tell patient that capsule is disposable and will be present in a bowel movement
Radiology		
Cholangiography		
• Magnetic resonance cholangiopancrea-tography (MRCP)	Use of MRI technology to obtain images of biliary and pancreatic ducts	Same as MRI
• Percutaneous tran-shepatic catheter (PTC)	Under local anesthesia and monitored anesthesia care, a long needle is passed into liver (under fluoroscopy) and into bile duct. Bile is removed. Radiopaque contrast medium directly injected into biliary system. Used to determine filling of hepatic and biliary ducts	*Before:* Assess patient's medications for contraindications, precautions, or complications with use of contrast medium. Keep patient NPO for 8–12 hr before test. Start prophylactic IV antibiotics 1 hr prior *After:* Observe patient for signs of hemorrhage, bile leakage, and infection. Observe safety precautions until sedation wears off. Maintain bed rest for 6 hr
• Surgical cholangio-gram	Contrast medium is injected into common bile duct during surgery on biliary structures	*Before:* Explain that anesthetic will be used. Assess patient's medications for contraindications or precautions with use of contrast medium
Computed tomography (CT) scan	Noninvasive radiologic examination allows for exposures at different depths. Using oral and IV contrast medium accentuates density differences. Detects biliary tract, liver, and pancreatic disorders	*Before:* Before contrast medium used, evaluate renal function. Assess if patient is allergic to shellfish since the contrast is iodine based. Patient may need to be NPO prior. *During:* Warn patient that contrast injection may cause a feeling of being warm and flushed. Patient must lie completely still during scan. *After:* Encourage patient to drink fluids to avoid renal problems with any contrast
Defecography	Uses fluoroscopy or MRI to assess the shape and position of the rectum during defecation. Using a lubricated small plastic tip, fill rectum and anus with barium. Oral barium allows small bowel to be visualized. The person then sits on a toilet-like seat attached to the x-ray table and is asked to push and empty the rectum. Images are taken while person is sitting at rest, straining, squeezing, and during defecation. Detects pelvic floor abnormalities	*Before:* Keep patient NPO for 2 hr. 2 enemas are given 2 hr before, 15 min apart. Oral barium is given 1 hr before.

Continued

TABLE 43.11 Diagnostic Studies—cont'd

GI System

Study	Description and Purpose	Nursing Responsibility
Gastric emptying breath test (GEBT)	Noninvasive test that measures CO_2 in a patient's breath. Used to diagnose delayed gastric emptying. Baseline breath test done. Then patient eats a special test meal that includes a scrambled egg mix and *Spirulina platensis,* a protein enriched with carbon-13. It is measured in breath samples collected at multiple time points after the meal	*Before:* Teach patient to be NPO after midnight and that the test takes 4 hr. *During:* Can be done in any clinical setting. It does not require special training or special precautions related to radiation
Lower GI or barium enema	Fluoroscopic x-ray examination of colon using contrast medium given rectally (enema) (Fig. 43.9). Double-contrast or air-contrast barium enema is test of choice. Air is infused after the barium flows through transverse colon. Used to detect the presence of tumors, diverticula, and polyps	*Before:* Give laxatives and enemas until colon is clear of stool evening before. Follow clear liquid diet evening before. Keep patient NPO for 8 hr before test. Teach patient that cramping and urge to defecate may occur during procedure and patient may be placed in various positions on tilt table. *After:* Give fluids, laxatives, or suppositories to help in expelling barium. Observe stool for passage of contrast medium. Tell patient that stool may be white for up to 72 hr.
Magnetic resonance imaging (MRI)	Noninvasive procedure using radiofrequency waves and a magnetic field. IV contrast medium (gadolinium) may be used. Used to detect hepatobiliary disease, hepatic lesions, and sources of GI bleeding and stage colorectal and other cancers	*Before:* Check for pregnancy, allergies, and renal function. Have patient remove all metal objects. Ask about any staples, plates, dental bridges, or other metal appliances. Remove metallic foil patches. Patient may need to be fasting. Assess for claustrophobia and the need for antianxiety medication. *During:* Patient must lie completely still during scan
Nuclear imaging scans (scintigraphy)	Tracer doses of a radioactive isotope are injected IV, and a scanning device picks up radioactive emission, which is recorded on paper. Shows size, shape, and position of organ. Identifies functional disorders and structural defects	*Before:* Tell patient that the substance used contains only traces of radioactivity and poses little to no danger. Schedule no more than 1 radionuclide test a day. Explain to patient need to lie flat during scanning
• Gastric emptying studies	Assesses ability of stomach to empty solids. Patient eats cooked egg containing ^{99m}Tc and toast with water. Images are obtained at 0, 1, 2, and 4 hr later. Used to study gastric emptying disorders caused by ulcers, ulcer surgery, diabetes, cancer, or functional disorders	Same as above
• Hepatobiliary scintigraphy (HIDA)	Patient is given IV injection of ^{99m}Tc and positioned under camera to record distribution of tracer dose in liver, biliary tree, gallbladder, and proximal small intestine. Used to identify obstructions of bile ducts (gallstones, tumors), gallbladder disease, and bile leaks	Same as above
• Scintigraphy of GI bleeding	^{99m}Tc–labeled sulfur colloid or ^{99m}Tc labeling of the patient's own RBCs to determine the site of active GI blood loss. Sulfur colloid or patient's RBCs are injected, then images of abdomen taken at intermittent intervals	Same as above
Small bowel series	Contrast medium is ingested, and films taken every 30 min until medium reaches terminal ileum	*Before:* Explain procedure, including the need to drink contrast medium and assume various positions on x-ray table. Keep patient NPO for at least 8 hr. Tell patient to avoid smoking after midnight. *After:* Take measures to prevent contrast medium impaction (fluids, laxatives). Tell patient that stool may be white for up to 72 hr.
Upper GI or barium swallow	Fluoroscopic x-ray study using contrast medium. Used to diagnose structural abnormalities of esophagus, stomach, and duodenum	Same as for small bowel series
Ultrasound	Noninvasive procedure. High-frequency ultrasound waves are passed into body structures and recorded as they are reflected. Used to show size and shape of an organ	

TABLE 43.11 Diagnostic Studies—cont'd

GI System

Study	Description and Purpose	Nursing Responsibility
• Abdominal ultrasound	A conductive gel is applied to skin, and a transducer is placed on the area. Detects abdominal masses (tumors, cysts), gallstones, biliary and liver disease, ascites	*Before:* Teach patient to be NPO for 8–12 hr. Air or gas can reduce quality of images. Food intake can cause gallbladder contraction, resulting in suboptimal study
• Endoscopic ultrasound (EUS)	Small ultrasound transducer is installed on tip of endoscope. Because EUS transducer gets close to the organ(s) being examined, images obtained are more accurate and detailed than those provided by traditional ultrasound. Detects and stages esophageal, gastric, rectal, biliary, and pancreatic tumors and abnormalities	Same as EGD
• Ultrasound elastography (Fibroscan)	Transient elastography uses an ultrasound transducer to assess level of liver fibrosis. Used to monitor patients with chronic liver disease	*Before:* Explain the need to lie in dorsal decubitus position with right arm in extreme abduction
Virtual colonoscopy	Combines CT scanning or MRI with computer virtual reality software. Air is introduced via a tube placed in rectum to enlarge colon to enhance visualization. Images obtained while patient is on back and abdomen. Computer combines images to form 2D and 3D pictures that are viewed on monitor. Detects intestine and colon diseases, including polyps, cancer, diverticulosis, and lower GI bleeding	*Before:* Bowel preparation similar to colonoscopy

TABLE 43.12 Laboratory Studies

GI System

Test	Reference Interval	Description and Purpose
Blood Studies		
Amylase	60–120 U/L (30–220 U/L)	Enzyme secreted by pancreas. Important in diagnosing acute pancreatitis. Level peaks in 24 hr and then returns to normal in 48–72 hr
Gastrin	25–100 pg/mL when fasting	Hormone secreted by cells of the antrum of the stomach, the duodenum, and the pancreatic islets of Langerhans
Lipase	0–160 U/L	Enzyme secreted by pancreas. Important in diagnosing pancreatitis. Level stays higher longer than serum amylase in acute pancreatitis
Fecal Tests		
Fecal analysis	Note form, consistency, and color. Specimen examined for mucus, blood, pus, parasites, and fat content	Teach patient to keep diet free of red meat for 24–48 hr before occult blood test
Fecal DNA testing	Negative	Detects shredded cell debris from polyps, adenomas, and cancers
Fecal occult blood	Negative	Detects blood in stool related to the presence of inflammatory bowel disease, diverticulosis, ulcers, cancer, and other GI problems
Stool culture	Normal intestinal flora	Tests for the presence of bacteria, including *Clostridium difficile*

The major complication of GI endoscopy is perforation through the structure being studied. Many endoscopic procedures require short-acting IV sedation. All endoscopic procedures require informed, written consent. Specific endoscopy procedures are discussed in Table 43.11.

Capsule endoscopy is a noninvasive approach to visualize the GI tract (Fig. 43.11). Colon capsule endoscopy is useful in diagnosing small bowel disease and monitoring inflammation in patients with IBD. Its sensitivity in detecting small lesions, colonic polyps, and CRC is being researched.[7]

Liver Function Studies

LFTs are serologic (blood) studies that reflect hepatic disease. Table 43.13 describes the most common LFTs.

Liver Biopsy

The purpose of a liver biopsy is to obtain hepatic tissue. The tissue is used to establish a diagnosis of cancer or liver disease or assess and stage fibrosis and cirrhosis. It may be done to follow the progression of liver disease.

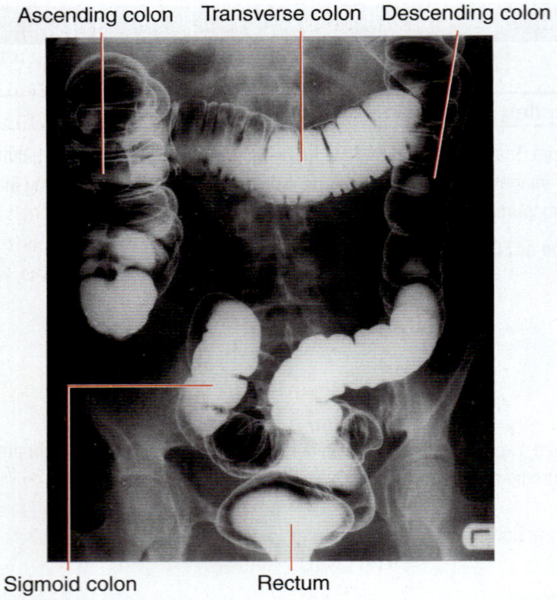

Fig. 43.9 Barium enema x-ray showing the large intestine. (From Drake RL, Vogl W, Mitchell AWM: *Gray's anatomy for students*, ed 4, St Louis, 2020, Elsevier.)

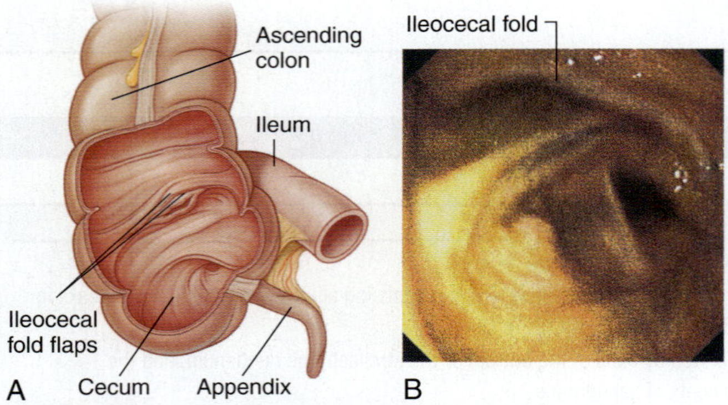

Fig. 43.10 (A) Illustration showing the ileocecal junction and the ileocecal fold. (B) Endoscopic image of the ileocecal fold. (From Drake RL, Vogl W, Mitchell AWM: *Gray's anatomy for students*, ed 4, 2020, Elsevier.)

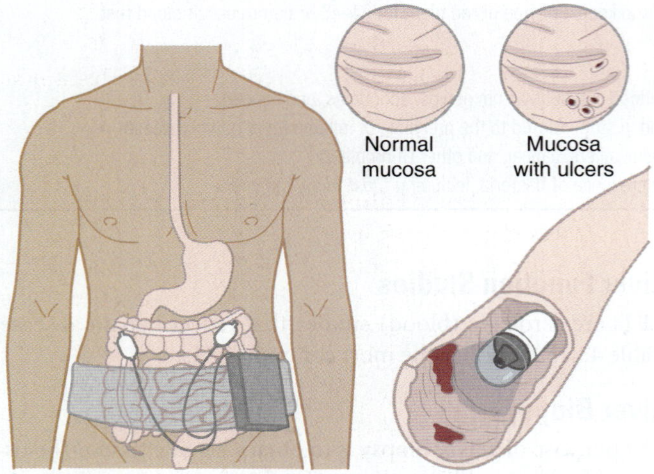

Fig. 43.11 Capsule endoscopy. The pill-sized video capsule has its own camera and light source. As it travels through the GI tract, it sends messages through sensing electrodes placed on the chest and abdomen to a data recorder worn on a waist belt. After the test, the images are viewed on a computer.

TABLE 43.13 Liver Function Tests

Test	Reference Interval	Description and Purpose
Bile Formation and Excretion		
Serum bilirubin		Measures liver's ability to conjugate and excrete bilirubin, distinguishing between unconjugated (indirect) and conjugated (direct) bilirubin in plasma
• Total	0.3–1.0 mg/dL (5.1–17 μmol/L)	Measures direct and indirect total bilirubin
• Direct	0.1–0.3 mg/dL (1.7–5.1 μmol/L)	Measures conjugated bilirubin. High in obstructive jaundice
• Indirect	0.2–0.8 mg/dL (3.4–12 μmol/L)	Measures unconjugated bilirubin. High in hepatocellular and hemolytic conditions
Urinary bilirubin	0 or negative	Measures urinary excretion of conjugated bilirubin
Hemostatic Function		
Prothrombin time (PT)	11–12.5 s	Determination of prothrombin activity
Vitamin K	0.1–2.2 ng/mL (0.22–4.88 nmol/L)	Essential cofactor for many clotting factors
Lipid Metabolism		
Cholesterol (serum)	200 mg/dL (<5.2 mmol/L), varying with age	Synthesized and excreted by liver. High in biliary obstruction. Low in cirrhosis and malnutrition
Protein Metabolism		
α-Fetoprotein	<10 ng/mL (<10 mcg/L)	Sign of hepatocellular cancer
Ammonia	10–80 mcg/dL (6–47 μmol N/L)	Conversion of ammonia to urea normally occurs in liver. Increase can result in hepatic encephalopathy due to liver cirrhosis
Protein (serum)	*Albumin:* 3.5–5.0 g/dL (35–50 g/L) *Globulin:* 2.3–3.4 g/dL (23–34 g/L) *Total protein:* 6.4–8.3 g/dL (64–83 g/L)	Measures serum proteins made by liver
Serum Enzymes		
Alanine aminotransferase (ALT)	4–36 U/L	High in liver damage and inflammation
Alkaline phosphatase (ALP)	30–120 U/L (0.5–2.0 μkat/L)	Originates from bone and liver. Serum levels rise when excretion is impaired because of biliary tract obstruction
γ-Glutamyl transpeptidase (GGT)	Male and Female >45: 8–38 U/L Female <45: 5–27 U/L	Present in biliary tract, not in skeletal or heart muscle. High in hepatitis, cholestatic liver diseases and alcoholic liver diseases. More sensitive for liver dysfunction than ALP
Aspartate aminotransferase (AST)	0–35 U/L (0.0–0.58 μkat/L)	High in liver damage and inflammation

TABLE 43.14 NURSING MANAGEMENT

Care of the Patient Undergoing Closed Liver Biopsy

Preprocedure

- Perform baseline assessment, including vital signs, pulse oximetry.
- Withhold food and fluids for 8–12 hr before.
- Check patient's coagulation status (prothrombin time, clotting or bleeding time).
- Give sedative and other drugs, as ordered.
- Obtain type and crossmatch (In event patient bleeds and requires blood).
- Teach patient and caregiver about procedure and postprocedure care. Explain need to hold breath after expiration when needle is inserted.
- Ensure informed consent has been signed.

Postprocedure

- Check vital signs to detect internal bleeding q15min × 2, q30min × 4, q1hr × 4.
- Notify HCP of dyspnea, cyanosis, and restlessness, which may occur with pneumothorax.
- Keep patient lying on right side for minimum of 2 hr to splint puncture site. Then maintain bed rest for 12–14 hr, as ordered.
- Apply a small dressing over the needle insertion site.
- Teach patient and caregiver about discharge care, including signs and symptoms to report to HCP (e.g., site complications) and any activity restrictions. Tell patient to avoid straining or coughing, which increase intraabdominal pressure.

A liver biopsy can be open and closed. The *open method* involves making an incision and removing a wedge of tissue. It is done in the operating room with the patient under general anesthesia, often with another surgical procedure. The *closed,* or *needle, biopsy* can be done 2 ways. A percutaneous procedure is often done with ultrasound or CT guidance. The HCP administers a local anesthetic, then inserts a needle between 6th and 7th or 8th and 9th intercostal spaces on the right side to obtain specimen of hepatic tissue. Table 43.14 outlines the nursing management of a patient undergoing a liver biopsy. A liver biopsy done in interventional radiology can be obtained through a transjugular approach. The HCP enters the jugular vein and advances a small sheath into the hepatic vein. A biopsy needle is passed through the sheath, into the vein wall, then into the liver tissue.

Case Study

Objective Data: Diagnostic Studies

(© iStockphoto/ Thinkstock.)

The ED physician performs a rectal examination and finds a palpable mass. The following diagnostic tests are ordered:

- CBC
- Electrolytes
- Liver function tests
- Urinalysis
- CT scan of the abdomen
- Colonoscopy

The CBC reveals an Hgb of 6.8 g/dL and Hct of 20%. The WBC count is normal. The electrolytes, liver function tests, and urinalysis are within normal limits. The CT scan reveals pockets of gas and fluid in the ascending colon and 2 medium-sized tumors in the transverse colon.

Discussion Questions

1. Which diagnostic study results concern you most?
2. With this information, what other diagnostic studies would you expect to be ordered for L.C.?
3. What are the interprofessional team's priorities for L.C. at this time?

Case study continued in Chapter 47.

Answers available at http://evolve.elsevier.com/Lewis/medsurg.

BRIDGE TO NCLEX EXAMINATION

The number of the question corresponds to the same-numbered outcome at the beginning of the chapter.

1. A patient is admitted to the hospital with diarrhea and dehydration. The nurse recognizes that increased peristalsis resulting in diarrhea can be related to
   a. sympathetic inhibition.
   b. mixing and propulsion.
   c. sympathetic stimulation.
   d. parasympathetic stimulation.
2. A patient has a high blood level of indirect (unconjugated) bilirubin. One cause of this finding is that
   a. the gallbladder is unable to contract to release stored bile.
   b. bilirubin is not being conjugated and excreted into the bile by the liver.
   c. the Kupffer cells in the liver are unable to remove bilirubin from the blood.
   d. there is an obstruction in the biliary tract preventing flow of bile into the small intestine.
3. As gastric contents move into the small intestine, the bowel is normally protected from the acidity of gastric contents by the
   a. inhibition of secretin release.
   b. secretion of mucus by goblet cells.
   c. release of pancreatic digestive enzymes.
   d. release of gastrin by the duodenal mucosa.
4. A patient has jaundice with pale colored stools. This is *most* likely related to
   a. decreased bile flow into the intestine.
   b. increased production of urobilinogen.
   c. increased bile and bilirubin in the blood.
   d. increased production of cholecystokinin.
5. An 80-year-old man states that, although he adds a lot of salt to his food, it still does not have much taste. The nurse's response is based on the knowledge that the older adult
   a. should not have any changes in taste.
   b. has a loss of taste buds, especially for sweet and salt.
   c. has some loss of taste but no problems chewing food.
   d. loses some sense of taste related to the increased ability to smell.
6. When the nurse is assessing the health perception–health maintenance pattern as related to gastrointestinal function, an appropriate question to ask is

a. "What is your usual bowel elimination pattern?"
b. "What percentage of your income is spent on food?"
c. "Have you traveled to a foreign country in the last year?"
d. "Do you have diarrhea when you are under a lot of stress?"

7. When assessing the abdomen, the nurse should
a. position the patient in the supine position with the bed flat and knees straight.
b. listen for bowel sounds in the epigastrium and all 4 quadrants for 2 minutes.
c. describe bowel sounds as absent if no sound is heard in a quadrant after 2 minutes.
d. use the following order of techniques: inspection, palpation, percussion, auscultation.

8. Normal physical assessment findings of the gastrointestinal system are *(select all that apply)*
a. nonpalpable spleen.
b. borborygmi in upper right quadrant.
c. tympany on percussion of the abdomen.
d. liver edge 2 to 4 cm below the costal margin.
e. finding of a firm, nodular edge on the rectal examination.

9. In preparing a patient for a colonoscopy, the nurse explains that
a. a signed permit is not needed.
b. sedation will be used during the procedure.
c. one cleansing enema part of the required preparation.
d. light meals should be eaten for 3 days before the procedure.

1. d; 2. b; 3. b; 4. a; 5. b; 6. c; 7. b; 8. a, c; 9. b

For rationales to these answers and even more NCLEX review questions, visit http://evolve.elsevier.com/Lewis/medsurg.

EVOLVE WEBSITE/RESOURCES LIST

http://evolve.elsevier.com/Lewis/medsurg
Review Questions (Online Only)
Key Points
Answer Keys for Questions
- Rationales for Bridge to NCLEX Examination Questions
- Answer Guidelines for Case Studies

Conceptual Care Map Creator
Audio Glossary

REFERENCES

*1. Seo K, Kim HN: Effects of oral health programs on xerostomia in community-dwelling elderly: a systematic review and meta-analysis, *Int J Dent Hyg* 18:1, 2020.
2. Rawish F, Muhammad A: Achlorhydria. Retrieved from https://www.ncbi.nlm.nih.gov/books/NBK507793/.
3. Amir M, Mahmud M, Hana A, Fadi A, Afif Y: Chronic constipation in the elderly patient: updates in evaluation and management, *Korean J Fam Med* 41:3, 2020.
*4. Qiyun G, Guoqing Z, Tao X: Risk factors for gallstone disease in Shanghai: an observational study, *Medicine (Baltimore)* 99:3, 2020.
*5. Stadlbauer V, Horvath A, Komarova I, et al.: A single alcohol binge impacts on neutrophil function without changes in gut barrier function and gut microbiome composition in healthy volunteers, *PLoS One* 1:14, 2019.
*6. Valentine OM, Nabil M: Bowel preparation for colonoscopy in 2020, *Curr Gastroenterol Rep* 6:22, 2020.
7. Timo R, Nadine M, Francesco V, Raja A, Markus FN: Advanced endoscopic imaging in colonic neoplasia, *Visc Med* 36:1, 2020.

*Evidence-based information for clinical practice.

Nutrition Problems

Mariann M. Harding

http://evolve.elsevier.com/Lewis/medsurg/

CONCEPTUAL FOCUS

Functional Ability
Health Promotion
Nutrition

LEARNING OUTCOMES

1. Relate the components of a well-balanced diet to their impact on health outcomes.
2. Describe the etiology, clinical manifestations, and interprofessional and nursing management of malnutrition.
3. Describe the components of a nutrition assessment.
4. Explain the indications, complications, and nursing management related to the use of enteral nutrition.
5. Explain the indications, complications, and nursing management related to the use of parenteral nutrition.
6. Compare the etiology, clinical manifestations, and nursing management of eating disorders.

KEY TERMS

anorexia nervosa (AN)
bulimia nervosa (BN)
enteral nutrition (EN)
malabsorption syndrome
malnutrition
parenteral nutrition (PN)
refeeding syndrome
tube feeding

This chapter focuses on problems related to nutrition. A review of normal nutrition provides a basis for evaluating nutrition status. We need sufficient energy, protein, and other nutrients to maintain health. Many problems affect nutrition by changing the way we ingest, absorb, digest, and metabolize nutrients. These changes can lead to malnutrition and health problems that affect functional status and quality of life. This makes assessment and interventions aimed at promoting optimal nutrition important nursing roles.

NUTRITION PROBLEMS

Nutrition is the sum of processes by which one takes in and uses nutrients. We view nutrition status on a continuum from undernutrition to normal nutrition to overnutrition. Any change in nutrient intake or use can cause nutrition problems. Nutrition problems occur in all ages, cultures, ethnic groups, and socioeconomic classes and across all educational levels.

Many factors influence nutrition. We establish our attitudes toward food and eating habits early. Diet intake often reflects cultural or religious practices. Financial status and community resources affect the food someone can buy.

NORMAL NUTRITION

Nutrition is important for energy, growth, and maintaining and repairing body tissues. Optimal nutrition, in the absence of any underlying disease process, results from eating a balanced diet (Box 44.1). The major components of the basic food groups are macronutrients (carbohydrates, fats, proteins), micronutrients (vitamins, minerals, electrolytes), and water. Optimal nutrition and daily physical activity are essential for health.

Body type, age, gender, medications, physical activity, and the presence of disease influence a person's daily caloric requirements. Adjustments in caloric intake are necessary depending on changes in health status and daily activity level. There are several ways to estimate caloric needs. The Mifflin–St. Jeor equation calculates daily adult energy (calorie) requirements based on resting metabolic rate (Table 44.1).[1] A simple way to estimate daily calories needed is by kilocalories per kilogram (kcal/kg). An average adult should consume 20 to 25 cal/kg body weight to

BOX 44.1 PROMOTING POPULATION HEALTH

Health Impact of a Well-Balanced Diet

- Reduces risk for anemia
- Maintains normal body weight and prevents obesity
- Maintains good bone health and reduces risk for osteoporosis
- Lowers the risk for developing high cholesterol and type 2 diabetes
- Decreases the risk for heart disease, hypertension, and some cancers

TABLE 44.1 Estimating Daily Energy (Calorie) Requirements

Mifflin–St. Jeor Equation

For each gender, use the formula below to calculate energy expenditure:

Men: 10 × weight (kg) + 6.25 × height (cm) – 5 × age (year) + 5

Women: 10 × weight (kg) + 6.25 × height (cm) – 5 × age (year) – 161

To determine total daily calorie needs, the energy expenditure is multiplied by the appropriate activity factor, as follows:

1.200 = sedentary (little or no exercise)
1.375 = lightly active (light exercise/sports 1–3 days/week)
1.550 = moderately active (moderate exercise/sports 3–5 days/week)
1.725 = very active (hard exercise/sports 6–7 days a week)
1.900 = extra active (very hard exercise/sports and physical job)

Example

Man: Weight 180 lb (82 kg); height 5 ft, 10 in (178 cm); age 50, very active

Energy expenditure = 10 (82) + 6.25 (178) – 5 (50) + 5 × 1.725 = 2911

Woman: Weight 150 lb (68 kg); height 5 ft, 6 in (168 cm); age 60; lightly active

Energy expenditure = 10 (68) + 6.25 (168) – 5 (60) –161 × 1.375 = 1745

lose weight and 25 to 30 cal/kg to maintain weight. Those with injury or illness may need at least 30 to 35 cal/kg.

Carbohydrates, the body's main source of energy, yield about 4 cal/g. We classify them as either simple or complex depending on the number of sugars they have. Simple carbohydrates come in 2 forms: monosaccharides, such as glucose and fructose, which are found in fruits and honey, and disaccharides, such as sucrose, maltose, and lactose. They are found in foods such as table sugar, malted cereal, and milk. Complex carbohydrates (polysaccharides) include starches, such as cereal grains, potatoes, and legumes.

Carbohydrates are the chief protein-sparing ingredient in a nutritionally sound diet. The Dietary Reference Intake (DRI) recommendations are that 45% to 65% of total calories should come from carbohydrates.[2] A person should take around 14 g of fiber per 1000 calories eaten per day from fruits, vegetables, and whole grains. This equals roughly 28 to 30 g for a typical 2000-calorie diet. We should choose food and beverages with little added sugar or caloric sweeteners.

Fats are a major source of energy for the body. One gram of fat yields 9 calories. Fats are stored in adipose tissue and the abdominal cavity. They act as carriers of essential fatty acids and fat-soluble vitamins. Fats give us a feeling of satiety after eating. Fat intake should be no more than 20% to 35% of total calories.[2]

Fats can be divided into (1) potentially harmful (saturated fat and *trans* fat) and (2) healthier diet fat (monounsaturated and polyunsaturated fat). One type of polyunsaturated fat, omega-3 fatty acids, may be especially beneficial to your heart. Omega-3 fatty acids (found in some types of fatty fish) may decrease the risk for coronary artery disease.[3]

Diets high in excess calories, usually in the form of fats, contribute to obesity. We should consume less than 10% of calories from saturated fatty acids (about 20 g of saturated fat per day in a 2000-calorie diet) and choose foods with no *trans*-fatty acids.[2]

Proteins are an essential part of a well-balanced diet. They are needed for tissue growth, repair, and maintenance; body regulatory functions; and energy production. Ideally, 10% to 35% of daily caloric needs should come from protein.[2] The recommended daily protein intake is 0.8 to 1 g/kg of body weight. For the normal healthy person of average body size, this equals about 45 to 65 g of protein daily. One gram of protein yields 4 calories. Amino acids are the basic units of protein structure. We classify the 22 amino acids as essential or nonessential. The body can make nonessential amino acids if an adequate supply of protein is available. The body cannot make the 9 essential amino acids. Their availability depends totally on one's diet. We obtain them from both animal and plant sources. *Complete proteins* contain all the essential amino acids. Proteins that lack one or more of the essential amino acids are *incomplete proteins.* Table 44.2 lists foods high in protein.

TABLE 44.2 NUTRITION THERAPY

Foods High in Protein

Complete Proteins

- Eggs
- Fish
- Meats
- Milk and milk products (e.g., cheese)
- Poultry

Incomplete Proteins

- Grains (e.g., corn)
- Legumes (e.g., navy beans, soybeans, peas)
- Nuts (e.g., peanuts)
- Seeds (e.g., sesame seeds, sunflower seeds)

Vitamins are organic compounds needed in small amounts for normal metabolism. Vitamins function in enzyme reactions that facilitate amino acid, fat, and carbohydrate metabolism. A diet consisting of foods from the 5 basic food groups is essential for obtaining the recommended intake of essential vitamins. Vitamins are divided into 2 categories: *water-soluble* vitamins (vitamin C and the B-complex vitamins) and *fat-soluble* vitamins (vitamins A, D, E, and K). Since the body stores excess fat-soluble vitamins, consuming too much can result in toxicity. There are upper limits for vitamins A, D, and E.

Mineral salts (e.g., magnesium, iron, calcium) make up about 4% of the total body weight. The body needs minerals to build and repair tissues, regulate body fluids, and assist in various functions. Minerals needed in amounts greater than 100 mg/day are *major minerals.* Minerals present in minute amounts are *trace elements.* Table 44.3 lists the major minerals and trace elements. Some minerals are stored and can be toxic if taken in excess amounts. The amount of minerals needed daily varies

TABLE 44.3 Major Minerals and Trace Elements

Major Minerals
- Calcium
- Chloride
- Magnesium
- Phosphorus
- Potassium
- Sodium
- Sulfur

Trace Elements
- Chromium
- Copper
- Fluoride
- Iodine
- Iron
- Manganese
- Molybdenum
- Selenium
- Zinc

from a few micrograms of trace minerals to 1 g or more of the major minerals, such as calcium, phosphorus, and sodium. A well-balanced diet usually meets the daily requirements of minerals. However, deficiency and excess states can occur.

VEGETARIAN DIET

There are many types of vegetarians and no strict definition of the word "vegetarian." The common element among all vegetarians is the exclusion of red meat from the diet. Many vegetarians are *vegans,* who are pure or total vegetarians and eat only plants, or *lacto-ovo-vegetarians.* They eat plants, dairy products, and eggs.

Without a well-planned diet, vegetarians can have vitamin or protein deficiencies. Plant protein, although of lesser quality than animal protein, fulfills most protein requirements. Combinations of vegetable protein foods (e.g., cornmeal, kidney beans) can increase the nutritional value. Milk made from soybeans or almonds is an excellent protein source and should be calcium fortified. Vegans and lacto-ovo-vegetarians are also at risk for iron deficiency. Table 44.4 lists examples of foods high in iron.

The main deficiency for a strict vegan is a lack of cobalamin (vitamin B_{12}).[2] We obtain cobalamin from animal protein, special supplements, or foods fortified with the vitamin. Vegans not using cobalamin supplements can develop megaloblastic anemia and the neurologic signs of cobalamin deficiency. Other deficiencies that may be present include calcium, zinc, and vitamins A and D.

TABLE 44.4 NUTRITION THERAPY

Foods High in Iron

These foods provide 25%–39% of the Dietary Reference Intake (DRI) of iron.

Food	Selected Serving Size
Breads, Cereals, and Grain Products	
Farina, regular or quick cooked (enriched)	⅔ cup
Oatmeal, instant, fortified, prepared (enriched)	⅔ cup
Ready-to-eat cereals, fortified (enriched)	1 oz
Meat, Poultry, Fish, and Alternatives	
Beef liver, braised	3 oz
Chicken or turkey liver, braised	½ cup diced
Clams: steamed, boiled, or canned (drained)	3 oz
Oysters: baked, broiled, steamed, or canned (undrained)	3 oz
Pork liver, braised	3 oz
Soybeans, cooked	½ cup

Culturally Competent Care: Nutrition

People have unique cultural heritages that may affect eating customs and nutrition status. Each culture has its own beliefs and behaviors related to food and the role that food plays in the cause and treatment of disease. Culture and religion can influence which foods are considered edible, how they are prepared, when they are eaten, and how and who prepares them. Some religions, such as Judaism and Islam, have specific laws about food.

Assess the patient's diet history and the extent to which they adhere to diet practices. Avoid cultural stereotyping. Do not make assumptions or generalizations about diet based on a person's cultural background. Diet habits differ within and among ethnic groups. Acculturation, the process by which a person adopts the lifestyle of a new culture, can affect diet practices.

Implement needed changes to ensure that we serve proper meals. A Jewish patient who eats only Kosher food may find comfort in knowing that an enteral feeding formula is Kosher. Another example is adjusting meal plans for the Muslim patient observing Ramadan (the Islamic month of *fasting,* in which Muslims refrain from eating and drinking during daylight hours).

MALNUTRITION

Malnutrition is a deficit, excess, or imbalance in a person's intake of energy and/or nutrients.[4] It may occur with or without inflammation. Malnutrition affects body composition and functional status. Other terms we use to describe malnutrition are *undernutrition* and *overnutrition.*

Overnutrition refers to the ingestion of more food than is required for body needs, as in obesity. See Chapter 45 for information about obesity. *Undernutrition* occurs when nutrition reserves are depleted and nutrient and energy intake are not sufficient to meet daily needs or added metabolic stress. Most use the term malnutrition to refer to undernutrition. We use the terms interchangeably here.

Malnutrition is a problem worldwide across the care continuum (community, hospital, long-term care). Rates for malnutrition in the hospital setting range from 30% to 50%.[5] The prevalence of malnutrition in older adults ranges from about 6% (community-dwelling older adults) to 50% (rehabilitation settings).[6]

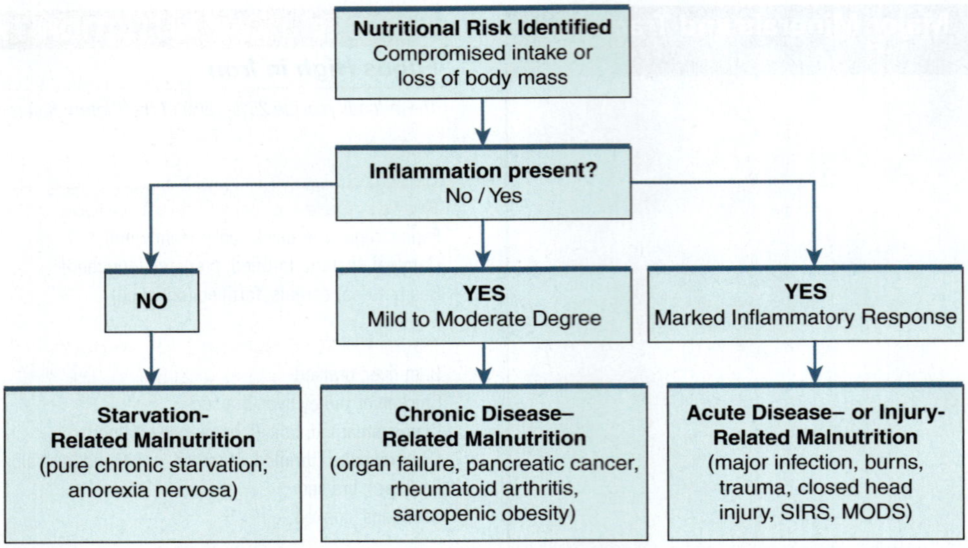

Fig. 44.1 Definitions of malnutrition. *MODS,* Multiple organ dysfunction syndrome; *SIRS,* systemic inflammatory response syndrome. (From Nix S: *Williams' basic nutrition and diet therapy,* ed 15, St Louis, 2018, Elsevier.)

Etiology

Several terms describe the types and causes of adult malnutrition. There are 3 cause-based terms used in clinical settings. They stress the interaction and importance of inflammation on nutrition status (Fig. 44.1).[7]

- *Starvation-related malnutrition,* or primary PCM, occurs when nutrition needs are not met. In primary PCM, there is chronic starvation without inflammation (e.g., anorexia nervosa).
- *Chronic disease-related malnutrition,* or secondary PCM, occurs when diet intake does not meet tissue needs, although it would under normal conditions. It is related to conditions that have sustained mild to moderate inflammation. Examples of conditions associated with secondary PCM include organ failure, cancer, rheumatoid arthritis, and obesity.
- *Acute disease-related or injury-related malnutrition* is related to acute disease or injury states with marked inflammatory response (e.g., major infection, burns, trauma, surgery).

Contributing Factors

Many factors contribute to malnutrition. These include socioeconomic factors, physical illnesses, incomplete diets, and drug-nutrient interactions. Table 44.5 lists conditions that increase the risk for malnutrition.

Socioeconomic Factors

Those with limited financial resources may have *food insecurity* (inadequate access). Food insecurity is a major public health problem. It affects the overall quality of food that is available in both quantity and nutritional value. Those with food insecurity usually choose less expensive "filling" foods. They tend to be more energy dense (high fat) and lack nutritional value. This type of diet increases the risk for nutrition problems.

To help obtain food, people may use "safety net programs." These include food assistance programs; housing and energy subsidies; and in-kind contributions from relatives, friends, food pantries, or charitable organizations. Consult with social workers to help patients gain access to government and local programs, such as Meals on Wheels, that deliver nutritious meals to homebound people.

TABLE 44.5 Conditions That Increase the Risk for Malnutrition

- Chronic alcohol use
- Decreased mobility that limits access to food or its preparation
- Dementia
- Depression
- Drugs with antinutrient or catabolic properties (e.g., corticosteroids, antibiotics)
- Excess dieting to lose weight
- Need for increased nutrients because of hypermetabolism or stress (e.g., infection, trauma, fever)
- No oral intake and/or receiving standard IV solutions for 10 days (adults) or for 5 days (older adults)
- Nutrient losses from malabsorption, dialysis, diarrhea, or wounds
- Swallowing problems (e.g., head and neck cancer, stroke)

The "heat or eat" phenomenon is problematic. Those with limited economic resources may struggle to pay bills or put food on the table. Older adults on a fixed income have an added burden of deciding on whether to pay for medications or food. You and the dietitian can help patients in making food choices that meet nutrition requirements while staying within their limited resources.

Physical Illnesses

Malnutrition is a common consequence of illness, surgery, injury, or hospitalization. The hospitalized patient, especially the older adult, is at risk for becoming malnourished. Prolonged illness, major surgery, sepsis, draining wounds, burns, hemorrhage, fractures, and immobilization can contribute to malnutrition. Undernutrition can worsen a pathologic condition. An

TABLE 44.6 **Recommended Daily Vitamin Intake and Manifestations of Deficiencies**

Vitamin	Dietary Reference Intake	Manifestations of Deficiencies
Fat Soluble		
A (retinol)	*Men:* 900 mcg/retinol equivalents[a] *Women:* 700 mcg/retinol equivalents	Dry, scaly skin. Increased susceptibility to infection, night blindness, anorexia, eye irritation, keratinization of respiratory and GI mucosa, bladder stones, anemia, retarded growth
D	*Adults ages 19–70:* 600 IU *Adults age >70:* 800 IU	Muscular weakness, excessive sweating, diarrhea and other GI problems, bone pain, active or healed rickets, osteomalacia
E	*Adults:* 15 mg	Neurologic deficits
K	*Men:* 120 mcg *Women:* 90 mcg	Blood coagulation problems
Water Soluble		
B_1 (thiamine)	*Men:* 1.2 mg *Women:* 1.1 mg	Anorexia, fatigue, nervous irritability, constipation, paresthesias, insomnia
B_6 (pyridoxine)	*Men ages 19–50:* 1.3–1.7 mg *Men age >51:* 1.7 mg *Women ages 19–50:* 1.3–1.5 mg *Women age >51:* 1.5 mg	Seizures, dermatitis, anemia, neuropathy with motor weakness, anorexia
B_{12} (cobalamin)	*Adults:* 2.4 mcg	Megaloblastic anemia, anorexia, glossitis, sore mouth and tongue, pallor, neurologic problems (e.g., depression, dizziness), weight loss, nausea, constipation
C	*Men:* 90 mg *Women:* 75 mg	Bleeding gums, loose teeth, easy bruising, poor wound healing, scurvy, dry, itchy skin
Folate (folic acid)	*Adults:* 400 mcg	Impaired cell division and protein synthesis, megaloblastic anemia, anorexia, fatigue, sore tongue, diarrhea, forgetfulness

[a]1 retinol equivalent = 10 international units vitamin A activity from β-carotene or 3.33 international units vitamin A activity from retinol.

existing deficiency state is likely to become more severe during illness.

Anorexia, nausea, vomiting, diarrhea, abdominal distention, and abdominal cramping may accompany gastrointestinal (GI) disease. Any combination of these symptoms interferes with normal food intake and metabolism. In addition, a patient may restrict intake to a few foods or fluids that may not be nutritious out of fear of worsening an existing GI problem.

Malabsorption syndrome is the impaired absorption of nutrients from the GI tract. Decreases in digestive enzymes or in bowel surface area can quickly lead to a deficiency state. Many drugs have GI side effects and alter normal digestive and absorptive processes. For example, antibiotics can change the normal flora of the intestines. This decreases the body's ability to make biotin, a B-complex vitamin whose production depends on that gut flora.

Fever, which accompanies many illnesses, injuries, and infections, increases basal metabolic rate (BMR) and nitrogen loss. Each degree of temperature increase on the Fahrenheit scale raises the BMR by about 7%. Without an increase in caloric intake, the body uses protein stores to supply calories and protein depletion develops. After the body temperature returns to normal, the rate of protein breakdown and resynthesis may stay increased for several weeks.

Consider the nutrition requirements of a patient who is not overtly ill but having diagnostic studies. This patient may be nutritionally fit on entering the hospital but can become malnourished because of diet restrictions imposed by multiple diagnostic studies.

Incomplete Diets

Vitamin deficiencies are rare in most developed countries. When vitamin imbalances do occur, they usually involve several vitamins rather than a single one. This may happen with a person with a pattern of alcohol and drug use, those who are chronically ill, and those who follow poor diet practices. Persons who had surgery on the GI tract may be at risk for vitamin deficiencies. For example, resection of the terminal ileum poses a risk for deficiencies of fat-soluble vitamins. After a gastrectomy, patients need cobalamin supplements. Because intrinsic factor (normally made in the stomach) is not available to bind with cobalamin, cobalamin cannot be absorbed in the ileum. Followers of fad diets or poorly planned vegetarian diets are at risk.

Manifestations of vitamin imbalances range from skin problems to neurologic signs. The recommended dietary allowances for essential vitamins and manifestations of imbalances are outlined in Table 44.6.

Drug-Nutrient Interactions

A *drug-nutrient interaction* occurs when a drug affects the use of nutrients in the body. Many drug and food or beverage interactions may occur. Potential adverse interactions include incompatibilities, altered drug effectiveness, and impaired nutrition. Many drugs have side effects, such as changes in taste, appetite, and nausea. Grapefruit juice can increase the absorption of some drugs, enhancing their effect. Drug-nutrient interactions can occur with the use of herbs and diet supplements. Monitor and prevent these potential interactions for patients in the hospital and at home.

Pathophysiology of Starvation

Knowing the pathophysiology of the starvation process will help you understand the physiologic changes that occur in malnutrition. Initially, the body selectively uses carbohydrates (glycogen) rather than fat and protein to meet metabolic needs. These carbohydrate stores, found in the liver and muscles, are minimal. They may be totally depleted within 18 hours. During the early phase of starvation, the body uses protein only in its normal role in cellular metabolism.

Once carbohydrate stores are depleted, the body converts skeletal protein to glucose for energy. Alanine and glutamine are the first amino acids used in *gluconeogenesis,* the process by which the liver forms glucose. The resulting plasma glucose allows metabolic processes to continue. When these amino acids are used as energy sources, the person may be in negative nitrogen balance (nitrogen excretion exceeds nitrogen intake).

Within 5 to 9 days, the body uses fat to supply much of the needed energy. In prolonged starvation, fat provides up to 97% of calories, conserving protein. Depletion of fat stores depends on the amount available. Fat stores are generally used up in 4 to 6 weeks. Once fat stores are gone, the body uses visceral and body proteins, including those in internal organs and plasma. They rapidly decrease because they are the only remaining body source of energy available.

If a malnourished patient has surgery, physical trauma, or an infection, the stress response is superimposed on the starvation response. The body uses protein stores for energy to meet the increased metabolic energy expenditure.

As protein depletion continues, liver function becomes impaired and protein synthesis decreases. The decrease in protein synthesis lowers plasma oncotic pressure. A major function of plasma proteins, primarily albumin, is to maintain the osmotic pressure of blood. When the oncotic pressure decreases, body fluids shift from the vascular space into the interstitial compartment. Eventually, albumin leaks into the interstitial space along with the fluid. Edema becomes observable. Edema in the patient's face and legs can mask underlying muscle wasting.

As the total blood volume decreases, the skin appears dry and wrinkled. As fluids shift to the interstitial space, ions also move. Sodium (the main extracellular ion) concentration increases in the cell. Potassium (the main intracellular ion) and magnesium shift to the extracellular space. The sodium-potassium exchange pump has high-energy needs, using 20% to 50% of all calories ingested. When the diet is extremely deficient in calories and essential proteins, the pump will fail. This leaves sodium inside the cell (along with water), and the cell expands.

The liver is the body organ that loses the most mass during protein deprivation. Fat gradually infiltrates the liver due to decreased synthesis of lipoproteins. Death will rapidly ensue if the person does not receive protein and necessary nutrients.

Impact of Inflammation

Inflammation affects nutrient metabolism and is an important part of nutrition status. During the starvation process, there is a decreased BMR, sparing of skeletal muscle, and decreased protein breakdown. In inflammatory states, there are changes in the expression of proinflammatory (e.g., interleukin-6 [IL-6]) and antiinflammatory cytokines (e.g., IL-10). Cytokine changes result in increased protein and skeletal muscle breakdown, increased BMR, decreased insulin secretion, decreased negative acute phase protein (albumin, prealbumin) production, and increased positive acute phase protein (e.g., C-reactive protein [CRP]) production.

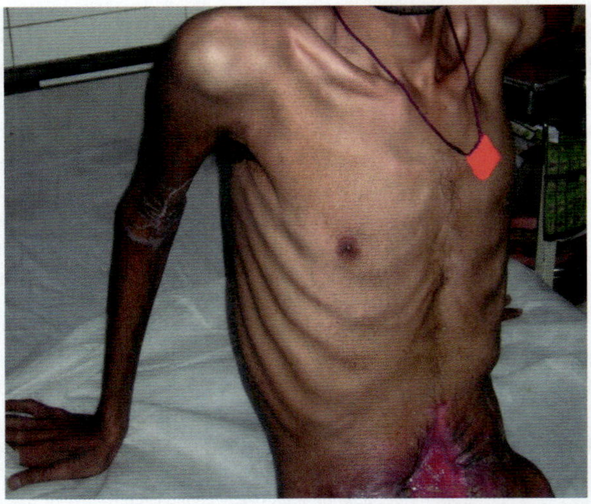

Fig. 44.2 Severe malnutrition with muscle wasting and loss subcutaneous tissue. (From Carlson GL, Fearon K: *Principles and practice of surgery*, ed 7, St Louis, 2018, Elsevier.)

Clinical Manifestations and Diagnostic Studies

The manifestations of malnutrition range from mild to emaciation and death (Fig. 44.2). The most obvious signs are seen in the skin (dry and scaly skin, brittle nails, rashes, hair loss), mouth (crusting and ulceration, changes in tongue), muscles (decreased mass, weakness), and CNS (mental changes, such as confusion, irritability). The speed at which malnutrition develops depends on the quantity and quality of the protein intake, caloric value, illness, and person's age.

The manifestations result from numerous interactions at the cellular level. As protein intake declines, the muscles (the largest store of protein in the body) become wasted and flabby. This leads to weakness and fatigability. Decreased protein is available for tissue repair, causing delayed wound healing. The person is more susceptible to infections. Both humoral and cell-mediated immunity are deficient. Leukocytes decrease in the peripheral blood. Impaired phagocytosis occurs because of the lack of energy needed to drive the process. The lack of iron and folic acid (necessary building blocks for red blood cells [RBCs]) causes anemia.

The diagnosis of malnutrition is best determined by nutrient intake, functional status, and body composition, including a thorough history of weight loss. Obtain vital signs, height, and weight. Perform a complete physical assessment. Table 44.7 outlines the assessment and findings of the patient with malnutrition.

There are no specific laboratory tests for malnutrition. Serum electrolyte levels reflect changes taking place between the intracellular and extracellular spaces. The serum potassium level often increases. The RBC count and hemoglobin level indicate the presence and degree of anemia. The total lymphocyte count decreases with malnutrition. Calculate it by multiplying the percent of lymphocytes times the total white blood cell (WBC)

TABLE 44.7 NURSING ASSESSMENT

Malnutrition

Subjective Data

Important Health Information

Health history: Severe burns, major trauma, hemorrhage, draining wounds, bone fractures with prolonged immobility, chronic renal or liver disease, cancer, malabsorption syndromes, GI obstruction, infectious diseases, acute (e.g., trauma, sepsis) or chronic inflammatory condition (e.g., rheumatoid arthritis)

Medications: Corticosteroids, chemotherapy, diet pills, diet supplements, herbs

Surgery or other treatments: Recent surgery, radiation

Functional Health Patterns

Health perception–health management: Alcohol or drug use. Malaise, apathy

Nutritional-metabolic: Increase or decrease in weight, weight problems. Increase or decrease in appetite, typical diet intake, food preferences and aversions, food allergies or intolerance. Ill-fitting or absent dentures. Dry mouth, problems chewing or swallowing, bloating, or gas. ↑ Sensitivity to cold, delayed wound healing

Elimination: Constipation, diarrhea, nocturia, decreased urine output

Activity-exercise: Increase or decrease in activity. Weakness, fatigue, decreased endurance

Cognitive-perceptual: Pain in mouth. Paresthesias, loss of position, and vibratory sense

Role-relationship: Change in family (e.g., loss of a spouse), financial resources, food availability

Sexual-reproductive: Amenorrhea, impotence, decreased libido

Objective Data

General

Listless, cachectic, underweight for height

Cardiovascular

↑ or ↓ heart rate, ↓ BP, dysrhythmias, peripheral edema

Eyes

Pale or red conjunctivae, gray keratinized epithelium on conjunctiva (Bitot spots). Dryness and dull appearance of conjunctivae and cornea, soft cornea. Blood vessel growth in cornea. Redness and fissuring of eyelid corners

GI

Swollen, smooth, raw, beefy red tongue (glossitis), hypertrophic or atrophic papillae. Dental cavities, absent or loose teeth, discolored tooth enamel. Spongy, pale, receded gums with a tendency to bleed easily, periodontal disease. Ulcerations, white patches, or plaques. Redness, swelling of oral mucosa. Distended, tympanic abdomen. Ascites, hepatomegaly, decreased bowel sounds, steatorrhea

Musculoskeletal

Decreased muscle mass with poor tone, "wasted" appearance, bowlegs, knock-knees, beaded ribs, chest deformity, prominent bony structures

Neurologic

Decreased or loss of reflexes, tremor; irritability, confusion, syncope, peripheral neuropathy

Respiratory

↓ Respiratory rate, ↓ vital capacity, crackles, weak cough, slight cyanosis

Skin

Dry, brittle, sparse hair with color changes and lack of luster, alopecia. Dry, scaly lips. Fever blisters, angular crusts, and lesions at corners of mouth (cheilosis). Brittle, ridged nails. Decreased tone and elasticity of skin. Cool, rough, dry, scaly skin with brown-gray pigment changes. Reddened, scaly dermatitis, scrotal dermatitis.

Possible Diagnostic Findings

↓ Hemoglobin and hematocrit, ↓ mean corpuscular volume (MCV), mean corpuscular hemoglobin (MCH), or mean corpuscular hemoglobin concentration (MCHC). Altered serum electrolyte levels, especially hyperkalemia. ↓ BUN and creatinine, ↓ serum albumin, transferrin, and prealbumin. ↑ C-reactive protein, ↓ lymphocytes, ↑ liver enzymes, ↓ serum vitamin levels

count. Liver enzyme levels may increase. Serum levels of both fat-soluble and water-soluble vitamins usually decrease. Low serum levels of fat-soluble vitamins correlate with the presence of *steatorrhea* (fatty stools).

Albumin and prealbumin are *negative acute phase proteins.* This means that during an inflammatory response, the liver decreases synthesis of these proteins. Low or below normal levels indicate the presence of inflammation. Because of the strong relationship between inflammation and malnutrition, they are useful in identifying patients at risk for poor outcomes.[8]

NURSING AND INTERPROFESSIONAL MANAGEMENT: MALNUTRITION

Assessment

As a nurse, you are responsible for nutrition screening across care settings. Nutrition screening identifies those who are malnourished or at risk for malnutrition. The Joint Commission requires nutrition screening for all patients within 24 hours of admission with a detailed nutrition assessment if a patient is at risk. Following a standard approach to nutrition screening using valid and reliable tools will accurately identify those at risk. Many screening and assessment tools are available. Hospital-specific screening tools review common admission assessment data, including a history of weight loss, intake before admission, use of nutrition support, chewing or swallowing issues, and skin breakdown.

The Malnutrition Universal Screening Tool (Fig. 44.3) and Nutrition Risk Screening are common tools used with adults in acute care. The MNA assesses nutrition status in older adults. In long-term care, we use the Minimum Data Set (MDS) form to obtain nutrition information. In home care settings, the Outcome and Assessment Information Set (OASIS) is used to collect information on diet, oral intake, dental health, swallowing problems, and any need for meal assistance.

If screening identifies a person at risk, perform a full nutrition assessment. A nutrition assessment is a comprehensive approach that includes medical, nutrition, and medication histories; physical assessment; anthropometric measurements; and

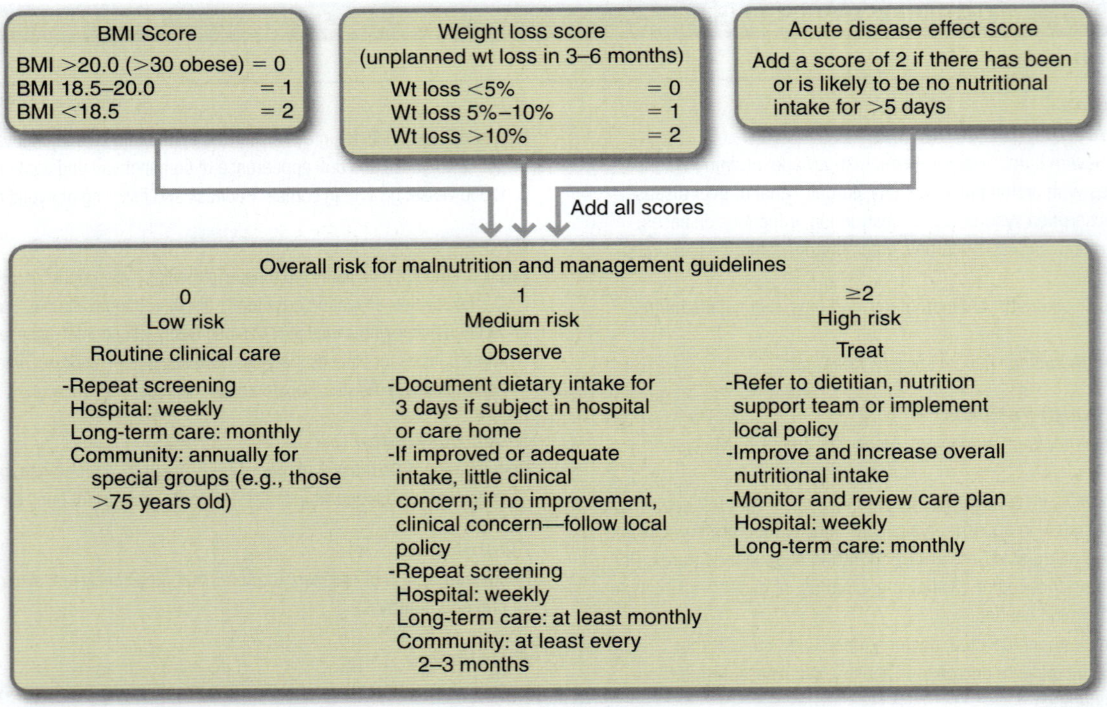

Fig. 44.3 The Malnutrition Universal Screening Tool (MUST) for adults. (Adapted from Mahan LK, Raymond JL: *Krause's food & the nutrition care process,* ed 14, St Louis, 2016, Saunders.)

TABLE 44.8 Nutrition Physical Assessment

Anthropometric Measurements
- Height and weight
- Body mass index (BMI)
- Rate of weight change
- Amount of weight loss

Physical Assessment
- Physical appearance
- Muscle mass and strength
- Dental and oral health

Laboratory Data
- Glucose
- Electrolytes
- Lipid profile
- Blood urea nitrogen (BUN)
- Albumin, prealbumin, C-reactive protein

Functional Status
- Ability to perform basic and instrumental activities of daily living
- Handgrip strength
- Performance tests (e.g., timed walk tests)

laboratory data (Table 44.8). A nutrition assessment provides the basis for nutrition intervention.

Obtain a complete diet history from the patient or caregiver. Assessing the foods eaten over the past week reveals a great deal about the patient's diet habits and knowledge of good nutrition. Often, the patient's nutrition state is not the reason for seeking medical care. However, it may be a contributing factor to the problem and have an impact on management and recovery.

◆ Anthropometric Measurements

Obtain height, weight, and girth measurements. Calculate the body mass index (BMI). We often use waist circumference and hip-to-waist ratio to assess nutrition status (see Chapter 45). Obtaining accurate measures of weight and height are critical. When possible, measure the patient's actual height rather than using the patient's self-report. Alternatives to standing height (stature) measurements include arm demi-span and knee-height measurements. The *arm demi-span* is the distance from a point on the midline at the suprasternal notch to the web between the middle and ring fingers with the arm horizontally outstretched. For persons confined to bed, using a Luft ruler is an alternative to standing height.

When assessing weight, obtain a detailed weight history, noting weight loss. Ask whether the weight loss was intentional and the period over which it took place. A loss of more than 5% of usual body weight over 6 months (whether intentional or unintentional) is a critical indicator for further assessment, especially in the older adult.[9] If an involuntary weight loss exceeds 10% of the usual weight, determine the reason. Unintentional weight loss is important to consider in the obese person. Malnutrition can be present despite excess body weight. Determine the patient's current weight in relation to ideal body weight.

Body mass index is a measure of weight for height (see Fig. 45.7). A BMI of less than 18.5 kg/m^2 is considered underweight, normal weight is a BMI between 18.5 and 24.9 kg/m^2, and overweight is a BMI between 25 and 29.9 kg/m^2. A BMI of 30 kg/m^2

or greater is obese. BMIs outside the normal weight range are associated with increased mortality.

Measure skinfold thickness at various sites (indicators of subcutaneous fat stores) and midarm muscle circumference (indicator of protein stores). The sites most reflective of body fat are those over the biceps and triceps, below the scapula, above the iliac crest, and over the upper thigh. Compare the measures obtained with standards for healthy persons of the same age and gender. Both skinfold thickness and midarm circumference may decrease in malnutrition. Shifts in hydration status influence these measurements. These measurements are most beneficial when done serially and by persons trained in anthropometry.

◆ Functional Measurements

Functional assessment focuses on performance of activities of daily living (ADLs) tools. The tools used most often are the Katz Index and Lawton Scale. Measuring muscle strength can assess physical functional status, an important outcome of nutrition status.[9] We can measure handgrip strength with a hand dynamometer. Timed gait and chair stands are markers of lower extremity strength.

◆ Clinical Problems

Clinical problems for the patient with malnutrition include:

- Nutritionally compromised
- Body weight problem
- Risk for impaired tissue integrity
- Inadequate community resources

◆ Planning

The overall goals are that the patient with malnutrition will (1) achieve an appropriate weight, (2) consume a specified number of calories per day on an individualized diet, and (3) have no adverse consequences related to malnutrition or nutrition therapies.

◆ Implementation

◆ Health Promotion

It is part of your role to teach and reinforce healthy eating habits. Use MyPlate, the Dietary Guidelines for Americans, and Nutrition Facts food labels to promote healthy nutrition. The MyPlate approach is a visual guide for sensible meal planning. It helps Americans eat healthfully and make good food choices. MyPlate focuses on the proportions of 5 food groups (grains, protein, fruits, vegetables, and dairy) that you should eat at each meal (Fig. 44.4 and Table 44.9). At the health professionals' link at www.myplate.gov, you can download daily food plans, sample menus, and tips for how to be physically active. These materials are valuable to use in patient teaching. MyPlate materials for older adults are available at https://hnrca.tufts.edu/myplate/.

There are many resources to help people eat a nutritious diet and maintain a healthy weight. Electronic and print sources are available for determining nutrition information in commonly consumed foods. Many food products have Nutrition Facts labels (Fig. 44.5). Consumer and health professional education materials on Nutrition Facts labels are available on the US Food and Drug Administration (FDA) website (www.fda.gov/Food/LabelingNutrition/ucm20026097.htm).

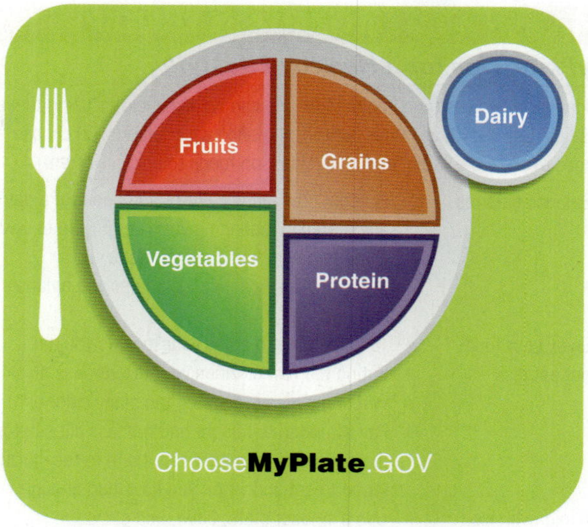

Fig. 44.4 MyPlate is the primary food group symbol that serves as a reminder to make healthy food choices and to build a healthy plate at mealtimes. It is a visual cue that shows the 5 food groups from which to select healthy foods. The plate is divided into 4 slightly different-sized quadrants. Fruits and vegetables take up half the space. Grains and protein make up the other half. The vegetables and grains portions are the largest portion. Next to the plate is a blue circle for dairy, which could be a glass of milk or food, such as cheese or yogurt. For more information, see www.myplate.gov. (From US Department of Agriculture, Center for Nutrition Policy and Promotion: *Guidance on use of USDA's MyPlate and statements about amounts of food groups contributed by foods on food product labels*, Washington, DC.)

Help the patient find reliable Internet sources that provide evidence-based food and nutrition recommendations. Interactive web-based programs and mobile device applications are available to track physical activity, calories, nutrients, and foods eaten. Mobile device applications help with making healthy eating choices easier. Some use built-in barcode scanners to scan foods quickly and give their nutrition facts. Users can compare items for their nutrition benefit and cost. Other applications give information on portion sizes and adjustments needed to reduce calories, sodium, or fat in the diet based on the user's height, weight, and activity level.

◆ Acute Care

Collaborate with the HCP and dietitian to identify patients with malnutrition and implement appropriate interventions to meet the patient's nutrition needs. Assess nutrition during your assessment of the patient's other physical problems. Identify risk factors for malnutrition and why they exist. With increased stress, such as surgery, severe trauma, and sepsis, the patient needs more calories and protein. Wound healing requires increased protein synthesis. The patient having major surgery who is malnourished or is at risk for malnutrition needs several weeks of increased protein and calorie intake preoperatively to promote healing after surgery.

Teach the patient and caregiver the importance of good nutrition. Discuss the reason for daily weights, intake, and output. Measure weight and height on admission. Daily weights give an

TABLE 44.9 NUTRITION THERAPY

MyPlate Tips for a Healthy Lifestyle

Making food choices for a healthy lifestyle can be as simple as using these 10 tips. Use the ideas in this list to (1) balance your calories, (2) choose foods to eat more often, and (3) cut back on foods to eat less often.

1. Balance calories	• Find out how many calories you need for a day as a first step in managing your weight. Go to www.myplate.gov to find your calorie level. • Being physically active also helps you balance calories.
2. Enjoy your food, but eat less	• Take the time to enjoy your food as you eat it. • Eating too fast or when your attention is elsewhere may lead to eating too many calories. • Pay attention to hunger and fullness cues before, during, and after meals. Use them to recognize when to eat and when you have had enough.
3. Avoid oversized portions	• Use a smaller plate, bowl, and glass. • Portion out foods before you eat. • When eating out, choose a smaller size portion, share a dish, or take home part of your meal.
4. Foods to eat more often	• Eat more vegetables, fruits, whole grains, and fat-free or 1% milk and dairy products. • These foods have the nutrients you need for health, including potassium, calcium, vitamin D, and fiber. • Make them the basis for meals and snacks.
5. Make half your plate fruits and vegetables	• Choose red, orange, and dark-green vegetables such as tomatoes, sweet potatoes, and broccoli, along with other vegetables, for your meals. • Add fruit to meals as part of main or side dishes or as dessert.
6. Switch to fat-free or low-fat (1%) milk	• They have the same amount of calcium and other essential nutrients as whole milk. • They have fewer calories and less saturated fat.
7. Make half your grains whole grains	• To eat more whole grains, substitute a whole-grain product for a refined product. • For example, eat whole-wheat bread instead of white bread, or brown rice instead of white rice.
8. Foods to eat less often	• Cut back on foods high in solid fats, added sugars, and salt. • Limit cakes, cookies, ice cream, candies, sweetened drinks, pizza, and fatty meats such as ribs, sausages, bacon, and hot dogs. • Use these foods as occasional treats, not everyday foods.
9. Compare sodium in foods	• Use the Nutrition Facts label (Fig. 44.4) to choose lower sodium versions of foods, such as soup, bread, and frozen meals. • Select foods labeled "low sodium," "reduced sodium," or "no salt added."
10. Drink water instead of sugary drinks	• Cut calories by drinking water or unsweetened beverages. • Soda, energy drinks, and sports drinks are a major source of added sugar and calories in American diets.

Source: US Department of Agriculture Center for Nutrition Policy and Promotion: Nutrition education series, DG tips sheet no 1, June 2011. Retrieved from www.myplate.gov and www.health.gov/dietaryguidelines.

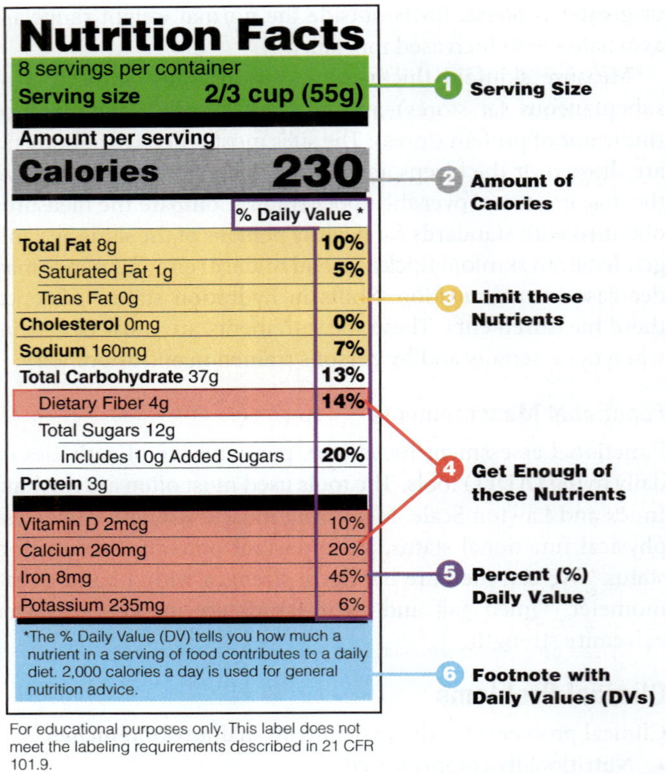

Fig. 44.5 Sample of a Nutrition Facts label. (From US Department of Health and Human Services, *Nutrition facts label,* Silver Spring, MD.)

ongoing record of body weight gain or loss. Rapid gains and losses are usually the result of shifts in fluid balance. In conjunction with accurate recording of food and fluid intake, body weight gives a clear picture of the patient's fluid and nutrition state.

If the patient can take food by mouth, obtain a daily calorie count and diet diary to give an accurate record of food intake. Help the patient and caregiver select high-calorie and high-protein foods (unless medically contraindicated). Table 44.10 gives examples of high-calorie, high-protein foods. Offering foods preferred by the patient enhances intake. You may have caregivers bring the patient's favorite foods from home.

Make sure the environment is conducive to eating. Provide a quiet environment. Offer oral hygiene and hand hygiene. Help the patient to a comfortable position and place the bedside table at the right height. Clear the bedside table of clutter. Place urinals, bedpans, and emesis basins out of sight. If needed, open cartons and packages. Protect mealtime from unnecessary interruptions by performing nonurgent care before or after mealtime.

The undernourished patient usually needs to have between-meal supplements. These may consist of items prepared in the dietary department or commercially prepared products. Eating these items provides extra calories, proteins, fluids, and nutrients. If the patient is unable to consume enough nutrition with a high-calorie, high-protein diet, consider adding oral liquid supplements.

Oral liquid supplements are widely used as an adjunct to meals and fluid intake in the patient whose intake is deficient.

TABLE 44.10 NUTRITION THERAPY

High-Calorie, High-Protein Diet

Suggestions for foods for a high calorie, high protein diet include:

Breads and Cereals
- Buttermilk biscuits, muffins, banana bread, zucchini bread
- Granola and other cereals with dried fruit
- Hot cereals (oatmeal, cream of wheat) prepared with milk, added fat (butter or margarine), and sugar
- Potatoes prepared with added fat (butter and whole milk)

Vegetables
- Fried vegetables
- Vegetables prepared with added fat (margarine, butter)

Fruits
- Canned fruit in heavy syrup
- Dried fruit

Meat
- Casseroles
- Fried meats
- Meats covered in cream sauces or gravy
- Peanut butter

Milk and Milk Products
- Ice cream
- Milkshakes
- Whipping cream, heavy cream
- Whole milk and milk products (yogurt, ice cream, cheese)
- Whole milk with added nutrition supplements

They provide advanced nutrition and calories and are inexpensive. These include milkshakes, puddings, or commercially available products (e.g., Carnation Instant Breakfast, Ensure, Boost). In long-term care, using these instead of water for oral medication administration increases caloric intake.

Some patients may benefit from appetite stimulants, such as megestrol acetate or dronabinol (Marinol), to improve intake. Enteral nutrition (EN) may be an option in the patient who is still unable to take in enough calories (Fig. 44.6). If EN is not possible, consider starting parenteral nutrition (PN).

◆ Refeeding Syndrome

Refeeding syndrome is the body's response to the switch from starvation to a fed state in the initial phase of nutrition therapy in patients who are severely malnourished.[10] Conditions that predispose patients to refeeding syndrome include chronic alcohol use, cancer, trauma, inflammatory bowel disease, and major surgery. Hypophosphatemia is the hallmark of refeeding syndrome. Other manifestations include hyperglycemia, fluid retention, hypokalemia, and hypomagnesemia. Serious outcomes include dysrhythmias and respiratory arrest.

In the at-risk patient, we should start feeding rates at no more than 50% of their usual energy requirements and gradually increase. Monitor electrolyte values and maintain ECG monitoring. Many receive phosphate, potassium, magnesium, and B vitamin supplements.

◆ Ambulatory Care

Many patients are discharged on a therapeutic diet. Discharge preparation for both the patient and caregiver is essential. Teach them about the cause of the undernourished state and ways to avoid the problem in the future. They need to be aware that undernourishment, whatever the cause, can recur and that adhering to their diet for a few weeks cannot fully restore a normal nutrition state. It may take many months to reach this goal.

Assess their ability to follow the diet instructions considering past eating habits, religious and ethnic preferences, age, income, resources, and state of health. Emphasize the need for continual follow-up care to achieve and maintain rehabilitation. In your discharge planning, ensure proper follow-up, such as visits by the home health nurse and outpatient dietitian referrals.

Determine the need for nutritious meals and snacks after discharge from the hospital. If access to a dietitian is limited, you may be the main source of nutrition information. In your assessment, consider the availability and acceptability of community resources that provide meals, such as Meals on Wheels, senior congregate feeding sites, and the Supplemental Nutrition Assistance Program (SNAP). SNAP allows low-income households, regardless of age, to buy more food of a greater variety.

Keeping a diet diary for 3 days at a time is one way to analyze and reinforce healthful eating patterns. These records are helpful in follow-up care. Encourage self-assessment of progress by having the patient weigh themselves once or twice a week and keep a weight record.

◆ Evaluation

The expected outcomes are that the patient who is malnourished will:

- Achieve and maintain optimal body weight
- Consume a well-balanced diet
- Have no adverse outcomes related to malnutrition
- Maintain optimal physical functioning

Gerontologic Considerations: Malnutrition

Nutrition affects quality of life, functional status, and health in older adults. They are particularly vulnerable to malnutrition across care settings. Older hospitalized adults with malnutrition are more likely to have poor wound healing, pressure injuries, infections, decreased muscle strength, postoperative complications, and increased mortality. They are less able to regain body weight lost after illness or surgery.

You play a key role in performing a complete assessment of factors related to their nutrition risk. Older adults may report little or no appetite, problems with eating or swallowing, inadequate servings of nutrients, and fewer than 2 meals per day. Limited incomes may cause them to restrict the number of meals or the nutrient quality of meals eaten. Social isolation is a problem in older adults. Those who live alone may lose their desire to cook and report decreased appetite. Functional limitations may affect the ability to feed oneself, buy food, or cook and prepare meals. Some may lack transportation to buy food.[6]

Chronic illnesses associated with aging can affect nutrition status. For example, depression and dysphagia (from a stroke) can affect intake. Poor oral health from gum disease, missing

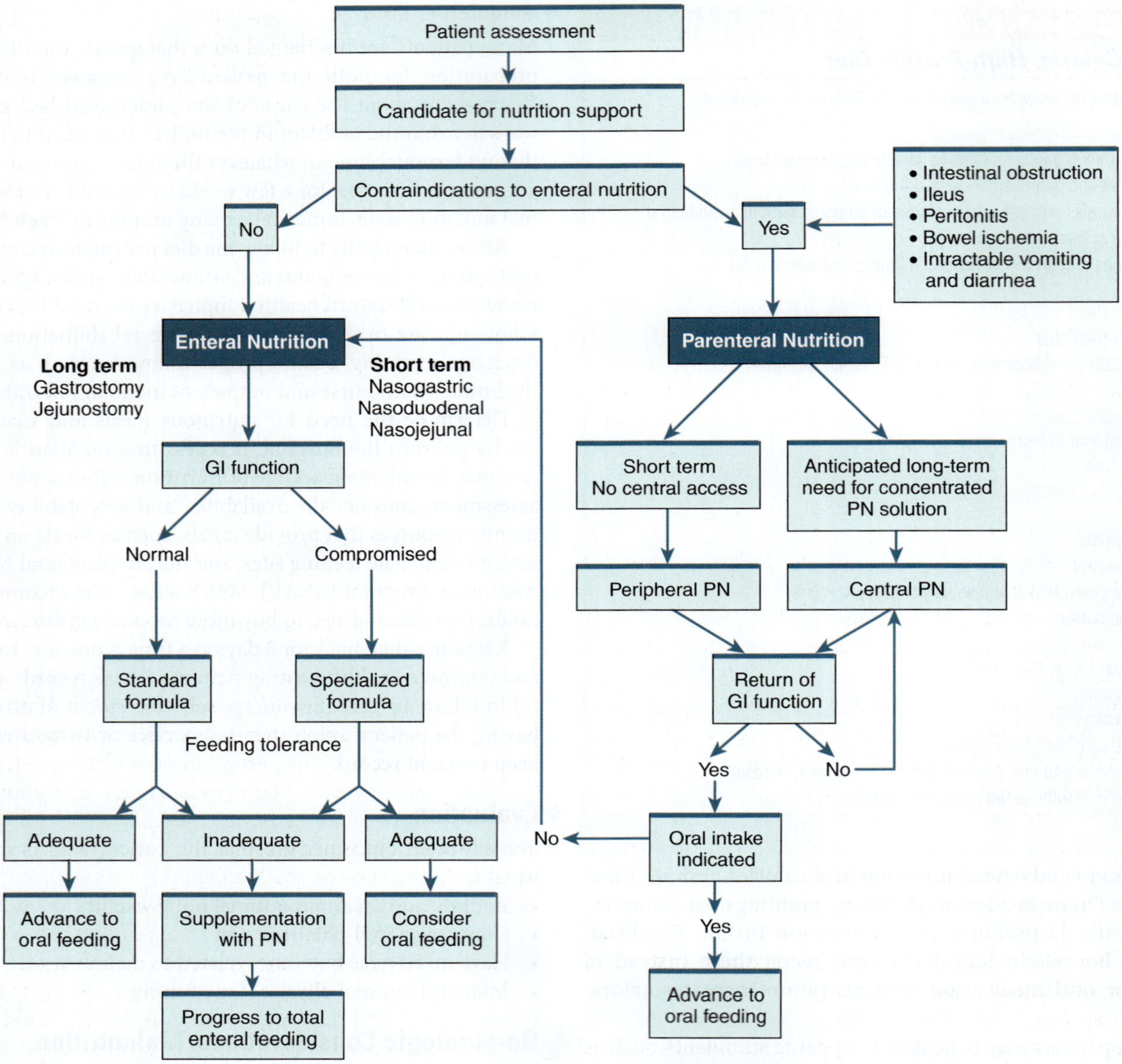

Fig. 44.6 Nutrition support algorithm. (Adapted from Ukleja A, Freeman KL, Gilbert K, ASPEN Board of Directors: Standards for nutrition support: adult hospitalized patients, *Nutr Clin Pract* 25:403, 2010.)

teeth, or dry mouth can impair the ability to chew and swallow food.[6] Medications can cause dry mouth, change the taste of food, or decrease appetite. Older adults with dementia (see Chapter 64) or a stroke (see Chapter 62) present unique challenges regarding eating and feeding.

Physiologic changes associated with aging include a decrease in lean body mass and redistribution of fat around internal organs, which can decrease caloric requirements. Sarcopenia (loss of lean body mass with aging) affects muscle strength and function. Older adults on bed rest or prolonged inactivity lose more lean body mass than younger adults. Changes in smell and taste (from medications, nutrient deficiencies, taste-bud atrophy) affect appetite.

General nutrition guidelines apply to older adults. Their requirements may vary depending on the degree of malnutrition and physiologic stress. To prevent loss of muscle mass and maintain function, older adults may need to increase their protein intake and ingest a moderate amount of high-quality protein at each meal.[11] Daily vitamin D requirements are higher for older adults (Table 44.6).[2]

Focus your initial care strategies on improving oral intake and providing a pleasant, social environment for meals. Special strategies, such as using adaptive devices and proper positioning, may be needed to help increase intake.[11] Some older adults may need nutrition support therapies until their strength and general health improve. Before starting any nutrition support therapy (e.g., EN, PN) for an older patient unable to give consent, review their advance directives about artificial nutrition and hydration.

Malnourished or nutritionally at-risk older adults are vulnerable when discharged from the hospital to the home. They may not be able to shop for or prepare foods during their initial recovery period. Consult with the social worker and dietitian to ensure there is access to food on discharge. Home-delivered meals or groceries or senior congregate feeding programs are an appropriate referral. Community nutrition programs can make mealtime a pleasant, social event. Improving the social setting of a meal often improves intake.

SPECIALIZED NUTRITION SUPPORT

If patients are unable to maintain or achieve adequate nutrition status, nutrition support may be needed. Fig. 44.6 shows a decision-making tree for nutrition support.

Some agencies have nutrition support teams. The team's function is to manage the nutrition support of select patients. The nutrition support nurse on that team is a key resource for issues about patients' nutrition and nutrition access. Other team members often include the HCP, dietitian, and pharmacist.

Enteral Nutrition

Enteral nutrition (EN), also known as **tube feeding**, is nutrition (e.g., a nutritionally balanced liquefied food or formula) delivered through a tube, catheter, or stoma directly into the GI tract. EN is used with the patient who has a functioning GI tract but is unable to take any or enough oral nourishment or when it is unsafe to do so.

Indications for EN include persons with anorexia, orofacial fractures, head and neck cancer, neurologic or psychiatric conditions that prevent oral intake, extensive burns, or critical illness (especially if mechanical ventilation is needed), and those receiving chemotherapy or radiation therapy. Contraindications for EN include GI obstruction, prolonged ileus, severe diarrhea or vomiting, and enterocutaneous fistula. EN is easily administered, safer, more physiologically efficient, and less expensive than PN.

There is a wide variety of EN formulas. Their concentration, flavor, osmolality, and amounts of protein, sodium, and fat vary. There are special formulas for patients with diabetes and liver, kidney, or lung disease. Most are lactose free. Concentrations range from 1 to 2 cal/mL. Most standard formulas provide between 1 and 1.5 cal/mL. The more calorically dense the formula, the less water it has. The number and size of particles in the formula determine its osmolality. The more hydrolyzed or broken down the nutrients, the greater the osmolality.

A formula with a high sodium content is contraindicated in the patient with cardiovascular problems, such as heart failure. Those with short bowel syndrome or ileocecal resection should not receive one with a high fat content because of impaired fat absorption.

Common delivery options are continuous infusion or intermittent (bolus) feedings by infusion pump, bolus feedings by gravity, and bolus feedings by syringe. Critically ill patients often receive EN by continuous infusion. Bolus feeding may be an option if the patient improves or is receiving EN at home.

The type of EN access depends on the (1) anticipated length of time EN will be needed, (2) risk for aspiration, (3) patient's clinical status, (4) adequacy of digestion and absorption, and (5) patient's anatomy (e.g., extreme obesity). Fig. 44.7 shows the locations of commonly used enteral feeding tubes.

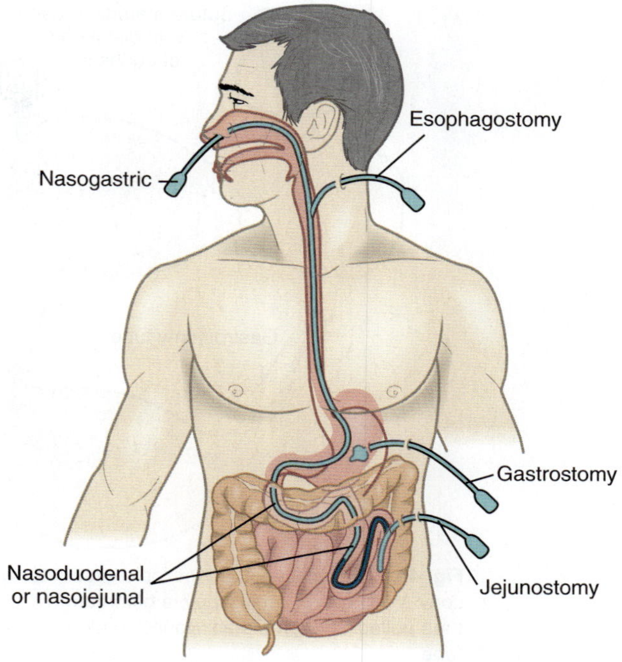

Fig. 44.7 Common enteral feeding tube placement locations.

Orogastric, Nasogastric, and Nasointestinal Tubes

Nasally and orally placed tubes (orogastric, nasogastric [NG], nasoduodenal, nasojejunal) are appropriate for short-term feeding (less than 4 weeks). Nasoduodenal and nasojejunal tubes are transpyloric tubes. They are used when pathophysiologic conditions call for feeding the patient below the pyloric sphincter. Placement into the small intestine decreases the chance of regurgitating gastric contents into the esophagus and aspiration. However, the patient can still aspirate gastric secretions if the stomach is not emptying properly.

Polyurethane or silicone feeding tubes are long, small in diameter, soft, and flexible. This design decreases the risk for mucosal damage from prolonged placement. These tubes are radiopaque, making their position readily identified by x-ray. A stylet is used for tube placement in a comatose patient because the ability to swallow is not essential during insertion. A complication that can result from using a stylet is perforation.

While smaller feeding tubes have many advantages over tubes with wider lumens, such as the standard NG tube, there are some disadvantages. Because of the small diameter and length, these tubes clog easily. They are harder to use for checking residual volume (RV). They are particularly prone to occlusion if you do not thoroughly crush and dissolve oral drugs before administration. Failure to flush the tubing before and after giving drugs or checking RV can cause tube occlusion. Vomiting or coughing can dislodge the tube. They can become knotted or kinked. Problems with a tube may require removal and insertion of a new tube, adding to cost and patient discomfort.

Gastrostomy and Jejunostomy Tubes

If feedings are needed for an extended time, tubes can be placed in the stomach (gastrostomy) or small bowel (jejunostomy). A gastrostomy tube can be placed surgically, radiologically,

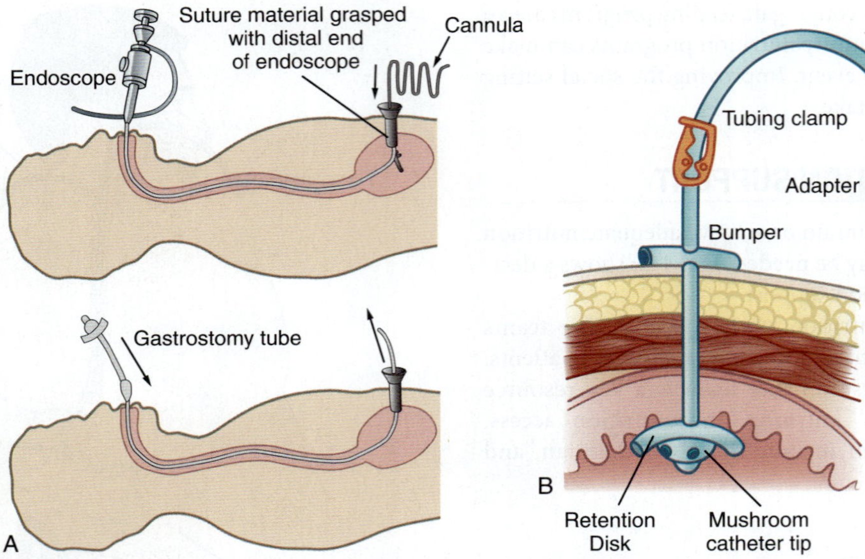

Fig. 44.8 Percutaneous endoscopic gastrostomy. (A) Gastrostomy tube placement via percutaneous endoscopy. With use of endoscopy, a gastrostomy tube is inserted through the esophagus into the stomach and then pulled through a stab wound made in the abdominal wall. (B) A retention disk and bumper secure the tube.

or endoscopically (Fig. 44.7). The patient must have an intact, unobstructed GI tract. The esophageal lumen must be wide enough to pass the endoscope for percutaneous endoscopic gastrostomy (PEG) tube placement (Fig. 44.8). PEG tube and radiologically placed gastrostomy tube procedures have fewer risks than surgical placement. The procedure requires IV sedation and local anesthesia. IV antibiotics are given before the procedure.

For the patient with chronic reflux, feeding through a jejunostomy (J-tube) may be necessary to reduce the risk for aspiration. Jejunostomy tubes are placed either endoscopically or with open or laparoscopic surgery. Combination gastrojejunostomy (G-J) tubes allow for simultaneous gastric decompression and small bowel feeding. When a patient has a G-J tube, it is important to know which port is the gastric and which is the jejunal.

The tube is either premarked or marked at the skin insertion site. Feedings can start within 24 hours after a surgically placed gastrostomy or jejunostomy tube without waiting for flatus or a bowel movement. Most other PEG tube feedings can start within 4 hours of insertion, although agency policies may vary.

EN and Safety

You have a critical role in ensuring that EN is administered safely. Aspiration and dislodged tubes are important safety concerns. Nursing management of EN is addressed in Table 44.11.

Accidental tube removal can result in delayed feedings and potential discomfort with tube replacement. The management of common problems in patients receiving EN is outlined in Table 44.12. A nursing care plan for the patient receiving EN (eNursing Care Plan 44.1) is available on the website for this chapter.

Specific care and teaching related to feeding tubes and EN are discussed in the following section. Remember it is important to teach the patient and caregiver how to care for the feeding tube and properly administer EN.

Tube position. Obtain x-ray confirmation of newly inserted nasal or orogastric tubes to confirm proper position before starting feedings or medications.[12] Smaller feeding tubes can pass directly into the bronchus on insertion without any obvious respiratory manifestations. Do not use the auscultation method to determine tube placement. Placing a tube under electromagnetic guidance reduces the risk for misplacement during blind insertion. Capnography, a direct monitor of breath-to-breath CO_2 level, can help determine tube placement in the respiratory tract.[12]

Maintain proper placement of the tube after starting feedings. To determine if a tube is still in the proper position, mark the exit site of the tube at the time of the initial x-ray and check the tube external length at regular intervals.[13] Consider applying a nasal bridle in patients who try to pull out a tube or for whom taping the nose is difficult.

A small bowel tube may dislocate upward into the stomach, or the tube's tip can dislocate upward into the esophagus. If you see a significant increase in the external length, use other bedside tests to help determine whether the tube has become dislocated. These measures include assessing aspirate color and pH. Because each measure has limitations, confirm placement with more than one test. If you are checking VR, watch for unexpected changes in volume. An increase in VR may indicate displacement of a small intestine tube into the stomach.

Aspiration risk. Evaluate all enterally fed patients for risk for aspiration. Before starting feedings, ensure the tube is in the right position. Proper patient positioning decreases the risk for aspiration. To prevent aspiration, always keep the head of the bed elevated 30 to 45 degrees. If the patient does not tolerate a backrest elevation, use a reverse Trendelenburg position to elevate the head of the bed, unless contraindicated. If you need

TABLE 44.11 NURSING MANAGEMENT

EN

Maintaining EN Infusions

- Check tube placement before feeding and before each medication administration.
- Assess for bowel sounds before feeding.
- Flush NG or gastrostomy tube as needed.
- Evaluate nutrition status of patient receiving enteral feedings.

Ensuring Patient Safety

- Give medications in the safest form possible.
    - Dilute viscous liquid medications.
    - Use liquid medications only if they are designated safe for enteral use.
    - Do not add medications to enteral feeding formula.
    - If using tablets, only use immediate-release forms.
    - Crush drugs to a fine powder and dissolve in 30–60 mL of purified water.
- Employ measures to decrease aspiration risk.
- Keep head of bed elevated to 30- to 45-degree angle.
- Check for RV per agency policy.
- Assess regularly for complications related to tubes and enteral feedings (e.g., aspiration, diarrhea, abdominal distention, hyperglycemia, fecal impaction).
- Teach patient and caregiver about home EN and tube care.

Delegate to Licensed Practical/Vocational Nurse (LPN/VN)

- Insert NG tube for stable patient.
- Flush NG and gastrostomy tubes.
- Give bolus or continuous enteral feeding for stable patient.
- Remove NG tube.
- Give medications through NG or gastrostomy tube to stable patient.
- Provide skin care around gastrostomy or jejunostomy tubes.

Supervise Assistive Personnel (AP)

- Provide oral care to patient with NG, gastrostomy, or jejunostomy tube.
- Weigh patient who is receiving EN.
- Keep the head of bed elevated 30–45 degrees.
- Report patient symptoms (e.g., nausea, diarrhea) that may indicate problems with EN to RN or LPN.
- Alert RN or LPN about infusion pump alarms.
- Empty drainage devices and measure output.

Collaborate With Dietitian

- Evaluate nutrition status of patient receiving EN.
- Select appropriate EN formula.
- Monitor for and manage complications related to EN.
- Teach patient and caregiver about home EN.

Collaborate With Pharmacist

- Select appropriate form of each medication being given enterally.
- Determine if medication must be given separately.

to lower the head of the bed for a procedure, quickly returning the patient to at least 30 degrees is critical. Follow agency policy for stopping feeding while the patient is supine. With bolus feedings, keep the head elevated for 30 to 60 minutes after feeding.

There is much disagreement about whether to check RV when giving feedings into the stomach. Some think an increased RV increases the risk for aspiration. Other research does not support the practice. Follow your agency policy for checking RV. Common protocols call for checking RV every 6 to 8 hours in non-critically ill patients and before each bolus feeding.

TABLE 44.12 NURSING MANAGEMENT

EN Problems

Problems and Causes	Management
Constipation	
Decreased fluid intake	• Increase fluid intake if not contraindicated. • Give total fluid intake of 30 mL/kg body weight.
Formula	• Change formula to one with more fiber content. • Give as-needed laxative.
Inactivity	• Encourage ambulation unless contraindicated. • Collaborate with physical therapy to promote activity.
Dehydration	
Diarrhea, vomiting	• Decrease rate or change formula. • Check drugs that patient is receiving, especially antibiotics. • Avoid bacterial contamination of formula and equipment.
Fluid intake	• Increase intake and check amount and number of feedings. • Administer supplemental tube, oral, or IV fluid intake if appropriate.
High-protein formula	• Change formula to one with less protein.
Hyperosmotic diuresis	• Check blood glucose levels often. • Change formula to one with less glucose.
Diarrhea	
Contaminated formula	• Refrigerate unused formula and record date opened. • Discard outdated formula. • Discard formula left standing for longer than manufacturer's guidelines. • 8 hr for ready-to-feed formulas (cans). • 4 hr for reconstituted formula. • 24 hr for closed-system enteral formulas. • Use a closed system.
Feeding too fast	• Dilute or decrease rate of feeding. • Change to continuous feedings. • Stop excess water boluses.
Formula	• Change to a formula that has more fiber or is less hypertonic. • Change to continuous feedings.
Infection	• Obtain stool culture for fecal leukocyte determination, *C. difficile*, and/or toxin assay.
Medications	• Check for drugs that may cause diarrhea (e.g., sorbitol in liquid medications, antibiotics).
Tube moving distally	• Properly secure tube before beginning feeding. • Check placement before each bolus feeding or at least every 4 hr if continuous feedings.
Vomiting	
Delayed gastric emptying	• Consult with HCP about a prokinetic drug. • Follow agency policy to manage RV.
Improper tube placement	• Replace tube in proper position. • Check tube position before each bolus feeding and every 4 hr if continuous feedings.

Other measures to decrease aspiration risk include giving feedings continuously, minimizing the use of sedation, and performing frequent oral suctioning, if needed. Promotility drugs, such as erythromycin or metoclopramide, improve gastric emptying and may reduce aspiration risk.

Site care. Skin care around gastrostomy and jejunostomy tube sites is important because the action of digestive juices irritates the skin. Assess the skin around the feeding tube daily for signs of redness and maceration. Monitor bumper tension and routinely check for pressure injury.

To keep the skin clean and dry, initially rinse it with sterile water and dry it. Apply a dressing until the site is healed. After that, wash with mild soap and water. A protective ointment (zinc oxide, petroleum gauze) or a skin barrier (Karaya, Stomahesive) may be used on the skin around the tube. If the skin is irritated, consider using other types of drain or tube pouches. Consult a wound, ostomy, and continence nurse (WOCN) if problems occur.

Tube patency. All enteral feedings require routine flushing. Flush feeding tubes in adults with 30 mL of warm tap water every 4 hours during continuous feedings or before and after each bolus feeding. Use sterile water in immunocompromised and critically ill patients. Always flush tubes between each medication and after all medications are given. Flush clogged tubes with warm water, using a back-and-forth motion. If that does not work, a pancreatic enzyme solution, an enzymatic declogging kit, or mechanical devices for clearing feeding tubes are options.[13]

Misconnection. An *enteral feeding misconnection* is an inadvertent connection between an enteral feeding system and a nonenteral system, such as an IV line, a peritoneal dialysis catheter, or a tracheostomy tube cuff. With an enteral feeding misconnection, EN formula intended for the GI tract is given IV or into the respiratory tract. Severe patient injury and death can result from tubing misconnection. Table 44.13 gives tips to decrease the risk for enteral feeding misconnections.

Gerontologic Considerations: Enteral Nutrition

EN can improve nutrition status in the older patient. Because of physiologic changes, the older adult is more vulnerable to complications from EN, especially fluid and electrolyte imbalances. Complications such as diarrhea can leave the patient dehydrated. Decreased thirst perception or impaired cognitive function decreases the patient's ability to seek needed fluids.

With aging, there is an increased risk for glucose intolerance. As a result, the older patient may be more susceptible to hyperglycemia from the high carbohydrate load of some EN formulas. The older adult with compromised cardiovascular function (e.g., heart failure) will have a decreased ability to handle large volumes of formula. If this happens, the patient may need a more concentrated formula (2.0 cal/mL). The older adult has an increased risk for aspiration caused by gastroesophageal reflux disease (GERD), delayed gastric emptying, hiatal hernia, or decreased gag reflex. Physical mobility, fine motor movement, and visual changes may contribute to problems managing EN in the home setting.

TABLE 44.13 NURSING MANAGEMENT

Decreasing Enteral Feeding Misconnections

The following are tips to help you decrease your risk for making an enteral feeding misconnection:

1. Teach visitors, LPN/VNs, and AP to notify the nurse if an enteral feeding line becomes disconnected and not to reconnect any line.
2. Do not change or adapt IV or feeding devices because it may compromise the safety features that are part of the design.
3. Do not use an IV pump or IV tubing to deliver an enteral feeding.
4. When making a reconnection or connecting any new device or infusion, trace lines back to their origins and ensure connections are secure.
5. When patient arrives on a new unit or setting or during shift handoff, recheck connections and trace all tubes.
6. Route tubes and catheters that have different purposes in unique and standardized directions (e.g., route IV lines toward the patient's head and enteral lines toward the feet).
7. Label or color-code feeding tubes and connectors.
8. When there are multiple access points and/or several bags hanging, place proximal and distal labels on all tubings.
9. Check the patient's vital signs after making any connection.
10. Identify and confirm a solution's label, since a 3-in-1 PN solution can look like an enteral nutrition formulation bag. Label the bags with large, bold statements such as "WARNING! For Enteral Use Only—NOT for IV Use."
11. Make all connections under proper lighting conditions.

TABLE 44.14 Common Indications for PN

- Chronic severe diarrhea and vomiting
- Complicated surgery or trauma
- GI obstruction
- GI tract anomalies and fistulae
- Intractable diarrhea
- Severe anorexia nervosa
- Severe malabsorption
- Short bowel syndrome

Parenteral Nutrition

Parenteral nutrition (PN) is the administration of nutrients directly into the bloodstream. PN is used when the GI tract cannot be used for the ingestion, digestion, and absorption of essential nutrients. Table 44.14 lists common reasons for PN.

Composition

PN is customized to meet the needs of each patient. The composition is reformulated as the patient's condition changes. This requires you to collaborate with the health care team in delivering PN to the patient.

Different commercially prepared PN base solutions are available. Some contain dextrose and protein in the form of amino acids. A 3-in-1 or total nutrient admixture containing an IV fat emulsion, dextrose, and amino acids is widely used.[14] Standard electrolytes (sodium, potassium, chloride, calcium, magnesium, phosphate) are available in some premixed solutions or added by pharmacy. The pharmacy also adds prescribed vitamins and trace elements (zinc, copper, chromium, selenium, manganese) to meet the patient's needs.

Calories

Calories in PN mainly come from carbohydrates in the form of dextrose and fat in the form of fat emulsion. Dextrose 100 to 150 g/day (1 g provides about 3.4 calories, as opposed to oral carbohydrates, which provide 4 calories) has a protein-sparing effect. Providing adequate nonprotein calories in the form of glucose and fat allows the use of amino acids for wound healing and not for energy. However, overfeeding can lead to metabolic complications. To minimize these problems, the recommended energy intake is 20 to 30 cal/kg/day in a nonobese patient.[15]

Fat-emulsion solutions of 10%, 20%, and 30% are available. Fat emulsions supply about 1 cal/mL (10% solution) or 2 cal/mL (20% solution). Fat emulsions primarily contain soybean or safflower triglycerides with egg phospholipids added as an emulsifier.[16] They supply a large number of calories in a small amount of fluid. This is beneficial when the patient is at risk for fluid overload.

IV fat emulsions should provide up to 20% to 30% of total calories of PN.[15,16] Most stable patients receive 1 g/kg/day. Critically ill patients may not tolerate this dose and may receive less than 1 g/kg/day. Serum triglyceride levels are done at the beginning of PN and then closely monitored. Give IV fat emulsions administered separately over a minimum of 12 hours. The initial infusion rate should not exceed 0.5 mL/kg/hr. If no reactions occur, the rate can increase to 1 mL/hr.

Fat emulsions are contraindicated in the patient with a problem with fat metabolism, such as hyperlipidemia. They are used cautiously in the patient at risk for fat embolism (e.g., fractured femur) and the patient with an allergy to eggs or soybeans.

Protein

Protein is provided at the rate of 0.8 to 1.5 g/kg/day depending on the patient's needs. Protein requirements can exceed 150 g/day (2 g/kg/day) to ensure a positive nitrogen balance in septic, critically ill, burn, or multiple trauma patients.[14] Protein needs may be lower than 1 g/kg in those with acute kidney injury or end-stage renal disease who are not on dialysis.

Electrolytes

The exact amount of electrolytes needed depends on the patient's health problem and on serum electrolyte levels. Assess individual requirements daily at the beginning of therapy and then several times a week as the treatment progresses. The following are ranges for average daily electrolyte requirements for adult patients without renal or liver impairment:

- Sodium: 1 to 2 mEq/kg
- Potassium: 1 to 2 mEq/kg
- Magnesium: 8 to 20 mEq
- Calcium: 10 to 15 mEq
- Phosphate: 20 to 40 mmol

Trace Elements and Vitamins

Zinc, copper, manganese, selenium, and chromium are added according to the patient's condition and needs. Monitor levels of these elements. The daily addition of a multivitamin preparation to the PN generally meets the vitamin requirements. The HCP may order additional amounts.

Methods of Administration

PN is given as central PN or peripheral parenteral nutrition (PPN). Central PN and PPN differ in nutrient content and tonicity, which is measured in milliosmoles (mOsm; the concentration of particles in a fluid).

Central parenteral nutrition. *Central PN* is indicated when long-term support is needed or when the patient has high protein and caloric requirements. We give central PN through a central venous catheter or a peripherally inserted central catheter (PICC) whose tip lies in the superior vena cava (see Chapter 17). Central PN solutions are hypertonic, measuring at least 1600 mOsm/L. The high glucose content ranges from 20% to 50%. Central PN must be infused in a large central vein so that rapid dilution can occur. The use of a peripheral vein for hypertonic, central PN solutions would cause irritation and thrombophlebitis.

Peripheral parenteral nutrition. PPN is given through a peripherally inserted catheter or vascular access device into a large vein. PPN is used when (1) nutrition support is needed for only a short time, (2) protein and caloric requirements are not high, (3) the risk for a central catheter is too great, or (4) to supplement inadequate oral intake.

Compared with central PN, PPN has fewer nutrients. While this makes PPN less hypertonic, it still has an osmolality of up to 800 mOsm/L. This increases the risk for phlebitis. Another potential complication is fluid overload. PPN requires large volumes of fluid, which many patients cannot tolerate.

NURSING MANAGEMENT: PARENTERAL NUTRITION

Nursing management of patients receiving PN is outlined in Table 44.15 and eNursing Care Plan 44.2, available on the website for this chapter. Complications from PN are related to either the catheter or the PN infusion itself (Table 44.16).

Home Nutrition Support

Home PN or EN is an accepted mode of nutrition therapy for patients who are at risk for or are malnourished and need continued nutrition support. Some patients receive home therapy for many months, even years. It is important to teach the patient and caregiver about catheter or tube care, proper technique in mixing and handling of the solutions and tubing, and side effects and complications.

Home nutrition therapies are expensive. Specific criteria must be met for expenses to be reimbursed. The discharge planning team must be involved early to help plan for such issues. Home nutrition support may be a burden for the patient and caregivers and affect the quality of life. Tell the family about support groups, such as the Oley Foundation (*www.oley.org*), that provide peer support and advocacy.

EATING DISORDERS

Eating disorders are psychiatric conditions associated with physiologic alterations and risk for death. The manifestations of eating disorders vary across gender, age, socioeconomic status, and race and ethnicity. Patients with eating disorders may be

TABLE 44.15 NURSING MANAGEMENT

PN Infusions

Preparation of PN Solutions

- All PN solutions must be prepared by a pharmacist or trained technician using strict aseptic techniques under a laminar flow hood.
- Add nothing to PN solutions after they are prepared in the pharmacy.
- Limit number of people involved in preparing and administering PN to reduce risk for infection.
- PN solutions are ordered daily to adjust to the patient's current needs.
- PN solution label shows the nutrient content, all additives, time mixed, and expiration date and time.
- Solutions must be refrigerated until 30 min before use and are good for 24 hr at room temperature.

Maintaining PN Infusions

- Follow proper aseptic techniques to reduce infection risk.
- Use a 0.22-micron filter with parenteral solutions not containing fat emulsion and a 1.2-micron filter with solutions containing fat emulsion.
- Change filters and IV tubing with each new PN container or every 24 hr.
- Label tubing and filter with date and time they are put into use.
- If a multilumen catheter is present, use a dedicated line for PN.
- Do not draw blood from a line dedicated for PN unless absolutely necessary.
- Control the infusion rate. Give PN using an infusion pump.
- Set an alarm to alert for tubing obstruction.
- Periodically check the volume infused because pump malfunctions can change the rate.

Ensuring Patient Safety

- Before starting PN, check label and ingredients in solution to make sure they match what the HCP ordered.
- A second RN should verify infusion pump settings before beginning PN.
- Trace the administration tubing to the point of origin in the body at the start of the infusion and at all handoffs.
- Check the solution for leaks, color changes, particulate matter, clarity, and fat emulsions separating. If present, promptly return it to the pharmacy for replacement.
- Discontinue a PN solution and replace it with a new solution if bag is not empty at the end of 24 hr. At room temperature, the solution (especially when containing fat emulsion) is a good medium for microorganism growth.
- If fat emulsions are infused separately from the PN solution, the preferred delivery method is a continuous low volume delivered over 12 hr.

Hyperglycemia

- Check glucose levels at bedside q4–6hr.
- Maintain a glucose range of 140–180 mg/dL. Give sliding scale doses of insulin to keep the glucose level in the normal range.

Hypoglycemia

- If a PN formula bag should empty before the next solution is available, a 10% or 20% dextrose solution (based on the amount of dextrose in the central PN solution) or 5% dextrose solution (based on the amount of dextrose in the peripheral PN solution) can be given to prevent hypoglycemia.

Catheter-Related Infections

- Carefully assess the catheter site for signs of inflammation and infection. Phlebitis can readily occur because of the hypertonic infusion. Catheter-related infection and septicemia can occur:
  - Local manifestations: redness, tenderness, and exudate at the catheter insertion site
  - Systemic manifestations: fever, chills, nausea, vomiting, and malaise
- Immunosuppressed patients are at high risk for infection. Note subtle signs in patients receiving chemotherapy, corticosteroids, or antibiotics, which can mask signs of infection.
- To reduce the risk for infection, catheters with antibiotic or antiseptic surfaces may be used.
- Follow agency policy for changing catheter dressings and other central line infection prevention measures (see Chapter 17).
- If you suspect an infection during a dressing change, send a culture specimen of the site and drainage and notify the HCP at once.
- If a catheter-related infection is suspected, blood cultures are drawn. A chest x-ray is taken to detect changes in pulmonary status.

Transitioning to Oral Nutrition

- Encourage oral nourishment and keep a careful record of intake. A general rule is that 60% of caloric needs should be met orally or through EN before discontinuing PN.
- Begin with clear liquids and advance as tolerated to a soft diet.

Assessing Effectiveness

- Monitor initial vital signs q4–8hr.
- Weigh patient daily as a measure of the patient's hydration status.
- Maintain accurate intake and output record.
- Determine the cause of any weight changes (e.g., fluid gained from edema, actual increase or decrease in tissue weight).
- Assess blood levels of glucose, electrolytes, and urea nitrogen.
- CBC and hepatic enzyme studies are obtained a minimum of 3 times per week until stable and then weekly as the patient's condition warrants.

hospitalized for fluid and electrolyte problems; dysrhythmias; and nutrition, endocrine, and metabolic problems. Menstrual problems may occur in women of childbearing age. Many of the nutrition problems associated with these disorders require you to implement a nutrition plan of care.

The 3 most common types of eating disorders are anorexia nervosa, bulimia nervosa, and binge-eating disorder. *Binge-eating disorder* is less severe than bulimia nervosa and anorexia nervosa. Those with binge-eating disorder do not have a distorted body image. They are often overweight or obese. Risk factors for eating disorders involve a range of biologic, psychologic, and sociocultural issues. Some persons report a history of anxiety, perfectionism, and social problems, such as bullying or a limited social network.[17]

Eating disorders also occur in some who are health conscious. For example, men with *bigorexia* or muscle dysmorphia (an extreme concern with becoming more muscular) may use steroids or other drugs to increase muscle mass. They may also use supplements and protein shakes to increase their body weight and mass.

The *female athlete triad* is a syndrome in which eating disorders, amenorrhea, and osteoporosis are present. The triad occurs in females taking part in sports that emphasize leanness and low body weight.

TABLE 44.16 Complications of PN

Catheter-Related Problems
- Air embolus
- Catheter-related sepsis
- Dislodgment
- Hemorrhage
- Occlusion
- Phlebitis
- Pneumothorax, hemothorax, and hydrothorax
- Thrombosis of vein

Metabolic Problems
- Altered renal function
- Essential fatty acid deficiency
- Hyperglycemia, hypoglycemia
- Hyperlipidemia
- Liver dysfunction
- Refeeding syndrome

Education and emotional support for the patient and family are vital. Support groups, such as the National Association of Anorexia Nervosa and Associated Disorders (ANAD) (www.anad.org), are helpful to those affected by these disorders.

ANOREXIA NERVOSA

Anorexia nervosa (AN) is characterized by restricting energy intake, difficulty maintaining an appropriate weight, an intense fear of gaining weight or being fat, and distorted body image.[18] AN most often occurs between the ages of 13 and 19. Up to 90% are female. Those with AN generally restrict the number of calories and the types of food they eat. Some exercise compulsively, purge via vomiting and laxatives, and/or binge eat. There may be an unwillingness to maintain a healthy weight, refusal to eat, continuous dieting, detailed food rituals, and avoiding social situations. They often go to great lengths to conceal their eating habits.

Common assessment findings include signs of malnutrition, significant weight loss or low BMI (under 17), hypothermia, and muscle weakness (Fig. 44.9). Diagnostic studies often show osteopenia or osteoporosis, iron-deficiency anemia, a high blood urea nitrogen level from marked intravascular volume depletion, and abnormal renal function. A lack of potassium intake and urinary potassium loss leads to decreased potassium. Manifestations of decreased potassium include muscle weakness, dysrhythmias, and renal failure. Leukopenia; hypoglycemia; and decreased sodium, magnesium, and phosphorus may be present.

Many patients with AN are anxious about treatment due to their fear of gaining weight. Therefore, building rapport with the patient is essential.[18] Treatment involves a combination of nutrition support and psychiatric care. Nutrition care focuses on reaching and maintaining a healthy weight and having normal eating patterns. A specialist closely supervises nutrition repletion to ensure consistent and ongoing weight gains. The patient may be hospitalized if there are complications that cannot be managed in an outpatient therapy program. Refeeding syndrome is a rare but serious complication of refeeding programs. The patient may need EN or PN. Family-based therapy is recommended in addition to behavior- and emotion-focused therapy.

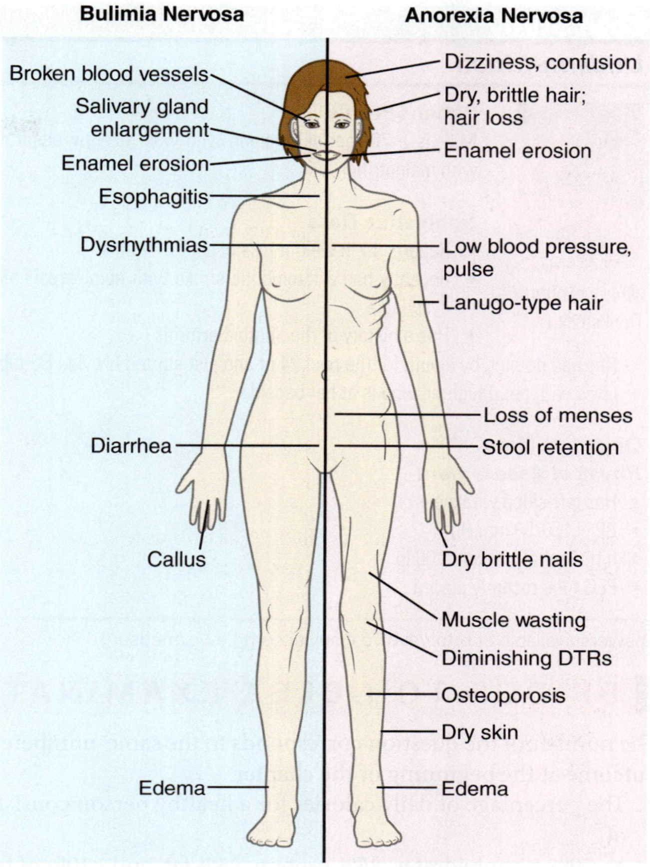

Fig. 44.9 Manifestations of anorexia nervosa and bulimia nervosa. (Modified from Mahan LK, Raymond JL: *Krause's food & the nutrition care process,* ed 14, St Louis, 2016, Saunders.)

BULIMIA NERVOSA

Bulimia nervosa (BN) is characterized by recurrent episodes of binge eating. To prevent weight gain, the person then engages in inappropriate compensatory behaviors (vomiting, laxative or diuretic misuse, overexercise). Like those with AN, the person with BN is concerned with body image. They may have normal weight for height, or their weight may fluctuate with bingeing and purging. There may have signs of frequent vomiting, such as macerated knuckles, swollen salivary glands, broken blood vessels in the eyes, and dental problems (Fig. 44.9). Abnormal laboratory values, including hypokalemia, metabolic alkalosis, and increased serum amylase, may occur from frequent vomiting.

Over time, problems associated with BN become increasingly hard to deal with effectively. A treatment combination of psychologic counseling (cognitive behavioral and family therapy) and nutrition counseling is essential. Fluoxetine (Prozac) is the only FDA-approved antidepressant for treating BN.

Case Study

Undernutrition

(© iStockphoto/ Thinkstock.)

Patient Profile

M.S. is a 70-year-old woman who was recently admitted with malnutrition.

Subjective Data

- Reports 30-lb weight loss in past 2 months
- Recently had a thrombotic stroke with hemiparesis and dysphagia
- Has a history of rheumatoid arthritis
- Has had nothing by mouth for the past 24 hr and just started EN via PEG tube
- Lives with her daughter, who is at her bedside

Objective Data

Physical Assessment

- Has left-sided weakness
- BP is 150/90 mm Hg
- 5 ft, 4 in tall, weight 100 lb
- PEG tube recently placed

Laboratory Results

- Serum albumin 2.9 g/dL
- Prealbumin 11.0 mg/dL
- C-reactive protein 0.9 mg/L

Discussion Questions

1. ***Recognize***: What are M.S.'s risk factors for malnutrition?
2. ***Recognize:*** Calculate and interpret her BMI.
3. ***Analyze***: Which complications of EN is M.S. at risk for?
4. ***Plan:*** What should we include in a nutrition program for M.S.?
5. ***Prioritize:*** What is the nursing care priority for M.S.?
6. ***Prioritize:*** Based on the assessment data presented, what are the priority clinical problems?
7. ***Act:*** Which interventions can you delegate to assistive personnel (AP)?
8. ***Act:*** To ensure M.S.'s safety, what nursing interventions are needed considering M.S.'s recent weight loss?
9. ***Evaluate:*** What assessment data would you need to collect to decide if care was effective?

Answers available at http://evolve.elsevier.com/Lewis/medsurg.

BRIDGE TO NCLEX EXAMINATION

The number of the question corresponds to the same-numbered outcome at the beginning of the chapter.

1. The percentage of daily calories for a healthy person consists of
   a. 50% carbohydrates, 25% protein, 25% fat, and <10% of fat from saturated fatty acids.
   b. 65% carbohydrates, 25% protein, 25% fat, and >10% of fat from saturated fatty acids.
   c. 50% carbohydrates, 40% protein, 10% fat, and <10% of fat from saturated fatty acids.
   d. 40% carbohydrates, 30% protein, 30% fat, and >10% of fat from saturated fatty acids.
2. Place in order the substrates the body uses for energy during starvation, beginning with 1 for the first component and ending with 4 for the last component.
   a. Skeletal protein
   b. Glycogen
   c. Visceral protein
   d. Fat stores
3. A complete nutrition assessment including anthropometric measurements is *most* important for the patient who
   a. has a BMI of 25.5 kg/m^2.
   b. reports episodes of nightly nocturia.
   c. reports a 5-year history of chronic constipation.
   d. reports unintentional weight loss of 10 lb in 2 months.
4. Which method is *best* to use when confirming initial placement of a blindly inserted small-bore NG feeding tube?
   a. X-ray
   b. Air insertion
   c. Observing patient for coughing
   d. pH measurement of gastric aspirate
5. A patient is receiving peripheral parenteral nutrition. The solution is completed before the new solution arrives on the unit. The nurse gives
   a. 20% intralipids.
   b. 5% dextrose solution.
   c. 0.45% normal saline solution.
   d. 5% lactated Ringer's solution.
6. A patient with anorexia nervosa shows signs of malnutrition. During initial refeeding, the nurse carefully assesses the patient for *(select all that apply)*
   a. hypokalemia.
   b. hypoglycemia.
   c. hypercalcemia.
   d. hypomagnesemia.
   e. hypophosphatemia.

1. a; 2. b, a, d, c; 3. d; 4. a; 5. b; 6. a, d, e.

For rationales to these answers and even more NCLEX review questions, visit http://evolve.elsevier.com/Lewis/medsurg.

EVOLVE WEBSITE/RESOURCES LIST

http://evolve.elsevier.com/Lewis/medsurg
Review Questions (Online Only)
Key Points
Answer Keys for Questions
- Rationales for Bridge to NCLEX Examination Questions
- Answer Guidelines for Case Study

Nursing Care Plans
- eNursing Care Plan 44.1: Patient Receiving Enteral Nutrition
- eNursing Care Plan 44.2: Patient Receiving Parenteral Nutrition

Conceptual Care Map Creator
Audio Glossary
Content Updates

REFERENCES

1. Mifflin MD, St Jeor ST, Hill LA, et al.: A new predictive equation for resting energy expenditure in healthy individuals, *Am J Clin Nutr* 51:242, 1990. (Classic).
2. US Department of Health and Human Services, US Department of Agriculture: 2020-2025 Dietary guidelines for Americans, ed 9. Retrieved from https://www.dietaryguidelines.gov/sites/default/files/2020-12/Dietary_Guidelines_for_Americans_2020-2025.pdf.
*3. Bernasconi AA, Wiest MM, Lavie CJ, et al.: Effect of omega-3 dosage on cardiovascular outcomes: an updated meta-analysis and meta-regression of interventional trials, *Mayo Clin Proc*, 2020.
4. World Health Organization: Malnutrition. Retrieved from https://www.who.int/news-room/fact-sheets/detail/malnutrition.
*5. Cortes R, Bennasar-Veny M, Castro-Sanchez E, et al.: Nutrition screening tools for risk of malnutrition among hospitalized patients: a protocol for systematic review and meta-analysis, *Medicine* 99:e22601, 2020.
*6. Saffel-Shrier S, Johnson MA, Francis SL: Position of the academy of nutrition and dietetics and the society for nutrition education and behavior: food and nutrition programs for community-residing older adults, *J Nutr Educ Behav* 51:781, 2019.
*7. White JV, Guenter P, Jensen G, et al.: Consensus statement of the Academy of Nutrition and Dietetics/ASPEN: characteristics recommended for the identification and documentation of adult malnutrition, *J Acad Nutr Diet* 112:730, 2012. (Classic).
*8. Evans DC, Corkins MR, ASPEN Malnutrition Committee, et al.: The use of visceral proteins as nutrition markers: an ASPEN position paper, *Nutr Clin Pract*, 2020.
*9. Jensen GL, Cederholm T, Correia MI, et al.: GLIM criteria for the diagnosis of malnutrition: a consensus report from the global clinical nutrition community, *JPEN* 43:32, 2019.
10. Reber E, Friedli N, Vasiloglou MF, Schuetz P, Stanga Z: Management of refeeding syndrome in medical inpatients, *J Clin Med* 8:2202, 2019.
*11. Volkert D, Beck AM, Cederholm T, et al.: ESPEN guideline on clinical nutrition and hydration in geriatrics, *Clin Nutr* 38:10, 2019.
*12. Judd M: Confirming nasogastric tube placement in adults, *Nursing2020* 50:43, 2020.
*13. Boullata JI, Carrera AL, Harvey L, et al.: ASPEN safe practices for enteral nutrition therapy, *JPEN* 41:15, 2017. (Classic).
14. Hellerman Itzhaki M, Singer P: Advances in medical nutrition therapy: parenteral nutrition, *Nutrients* 12:717, 2020.
15. ASPEN: Appropriate dosing for parenteral nutrition. Retrieved from http://www.nutritioncare.org/uploadedFiles/Documents/Guidelines_and_Clinical_Resources/PN%20Dosing%201-Sheet-FINAL.pdf.
*16. Mayer K, Klek S, García-de-Lorenzo A, et al.: Lipid use in hospitalized adults requiring parenteral nutrition, *JPEN* 44:S28, 2020.
17. National Eating Disorders Association: Learn. Retrieved from www.nationaleatingdisorders.org/.
18. Komar E, Kameg B: Anorexia nervosa: an overview for primary care providers, *Nurse Pract* 45(8), 2020.

*Evidence-based information for clinical practice.

45

Obesity

Mariann M. Harding

http://evolve.elsevier.com/Lewis/medsurg/

CONCEPTUAL FOCUS

Functional Ability
Health Promotion
Nutrition
Self-Management

LEARNING OUTCOMES

1. Discuss the epidemiology and etiology of obesity.
2. Explain the health risks associated with obesity.
3. Use classification systems to determine body size.
4. Discuss comprehensive therapy for the patient with obesity.
5. Distinguish among the bariatric surgical procedures used to treat obesity.
6. Describe the nursing and interprofessional management related to surgical therapies for obesity.
7. Describe the etiology, clinical manifestations, and nursing and interprofessional management of metabolic syndrome.

KEY TERMS

bariatric surgery
body mass index (BMI)
extreme obesity
lipectomy
metabolic syndrome
obese
obesity
overweight
waist-to-hip ratio (WHR)

OBESITY

Obesity is an excessively high amount of body fat or adipose tissue. Obesity is a global problem because it is a major risk factor for leading causes of death, including type 2 diabetes, heart disease, and certain cancers. Those who are overweight often have other problems, such as problems with mobility and sleeping, that affect health.

The consequences of obesity extend beyond the physical changes. Social stigma can take an emotional toll on a person's psychologic well-being. Many struggle with altered body image, depression, and low self-esteem and withdraw from social interaction. Attitudes about obesity can create biases and discrimination against people who are obese. Obesity should be viewed and treated as a chronic disease, just like other chronic diseases, such as diabetes and hypertension.

Epidemiology of Obesity

Obesity is a major public health issue in the United States (Fig. 45.1). Currently, about 43% of adults in the United States are obese. Significant geographic, racial and ethnic, and income disparities exist. Obesity rates are highest in the South and Midwest (Fig. 45.2), among Blacks and Hispanics (Fig. 45.3, Box 45.1), and among lower-income, less-educated Americans.[1]

Obesity in adulthood is often a problem that begins in childhood or adolescence. More than 1 in 10 children becomes obese as early as age 2 to 5.[1] Reversing the childhood obesity crisis is a key part of addressing the obesity epidemic.

Etiology and Pathophysiology

Obesity is a complex, multifactorial disease. It is the result of an energy imbalance where one takes in more calories than one needs for the body's physical and metabolic functions. This results in an abnormal increase and accumulation of fat cells. Many factors, including genetic and environmental influences, can contribute to obesity. Personal decisions about food choices, portion sizes, and exercise also are factors.

In obesity, there is an increase in the number of adipocytes, or fat cells, and an increase in their size *(hypertrophy)*. Adipocyte *hypertrophy* is a process by which fat cells can increase their volume several thousand times to accommodate large increases in lipid storage. When storage of existing fat cells is exceeded, preadipocytes are triggered to become adipocytes. This process occurs mainly in the visceral (intraabdominal) and subcutaneous tissues. The greatest increase in the number of fat cells occurs from infancy through adolescence.

Most obese persons have *primary obesity,* which is excess calorie intake over energy expenditure for the body's metabolic demands. Others have *secondary obesity*, in which a medical problem caused the weight gain. These problems include some congenital conditions, endocrine disorders, central nervous system (CNS) lesions and disorders, or drugs (e.g., corticosteroids, antipsychotics).

Fig. 45.1 The obesity epidemic has taken its toll on both adults and children in the United States. (© iStock.com/IPGGutenbergUKLtd.)

Genetic Link

We have linked over 400 genes to obesity. Having one or more of these genes means the person is more predisposed to obesity than people without these genes, but it does not mean that they will become obese. Genes contribute to obesity in many ways. They affect appetite, satiety (the sense of fullness), food cravings, body-fat distribution, and how we store calories. Having a family history of obesity increases a person's chance of developing obesity.[2]

Several rare forms of obesity result from mutations in a single gene. Obesity is also part of several genetic syndromes caused by mutation or chromosomal abnormalities, such as Prader–Willi syndrome.[2] The best link is with a gene known as *FTO* (fat mass and obesity-associated gene). People with a certain allele of the *FTO* gene appear to have an increased appetite and reduced satiety, with a higher calorie intake.

Physiologic Regulatory Mechanisms in Obesity

Knowing how appetite is triggered and energy is spent is important for understanding obesity and specific targets for drug therapy. The hypothalamus, gut, and adipose tissue synthesize hormones and peptides that stimulate or inhibit appetite (Fig. 45.4). The hypothalamus is a major site for regulating appetite. Neuropeptide Y, made in the hypothalamus, is a powerful appetite stimulant. When it is imbalanced, it leads to overeating and obesity. Hormones and peptides made in the gut and adipocyte cells affect the hypothalamus and have a critical role in appetite and energy balance

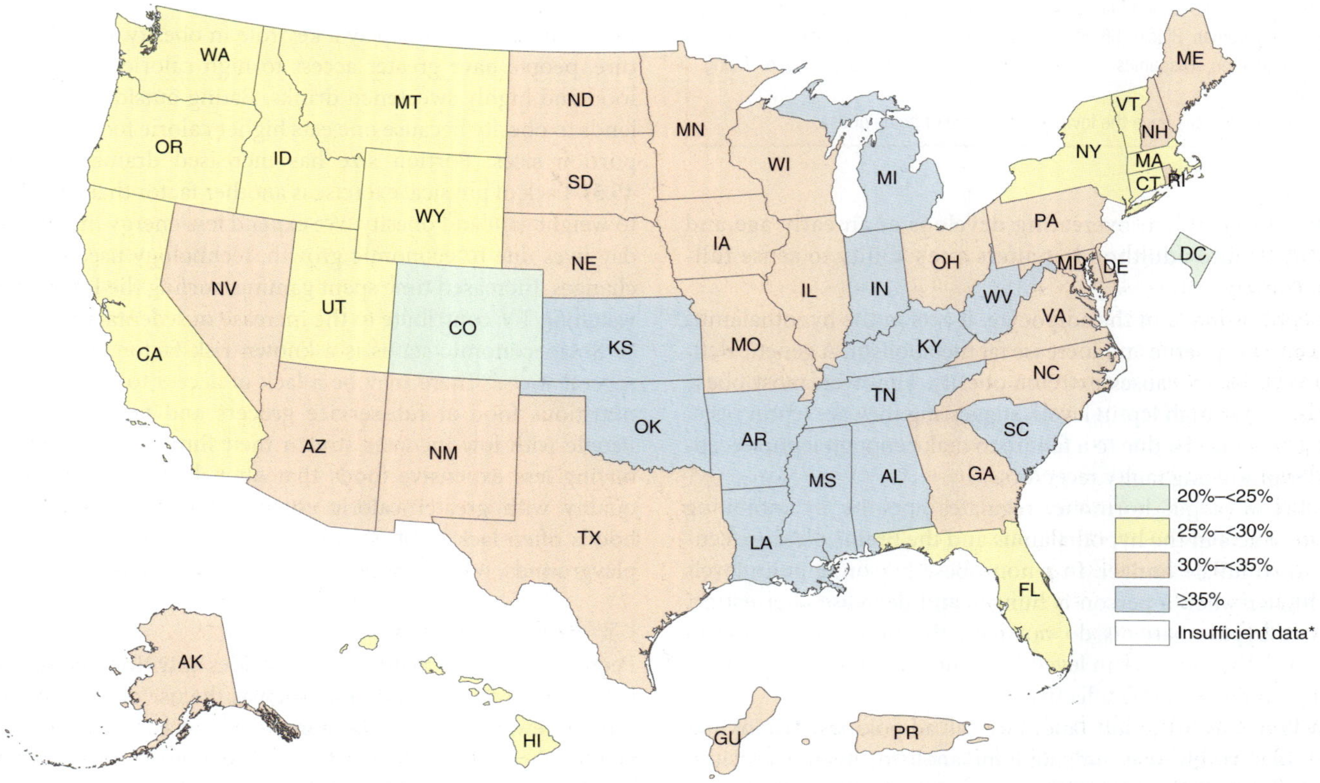

Fig. 45.2 Prevalence of obesity among US adults by state and territory. (Source: Behavioral Risk Factor Surveillance System. Retrieved from https://www.cdc.gov/obesity/data/prevalence-maps.html.)

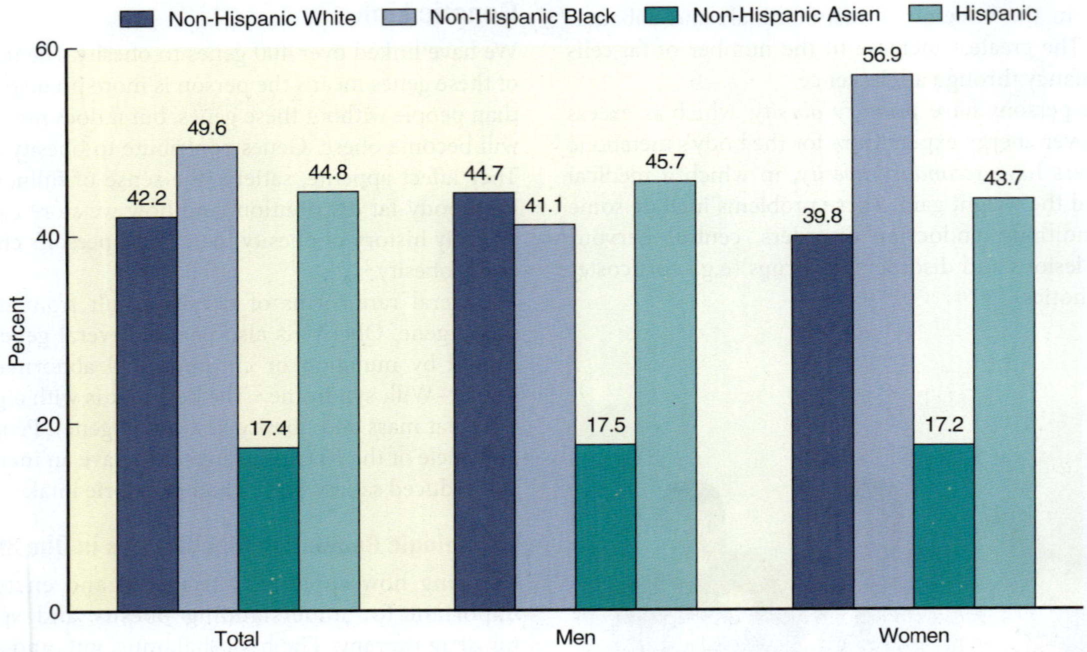

Fig. 45.3 Obesity affects some groups disproportionately. Among US adults, Black and Hispanic populations have the highest rates of obesity. (Source: Centers for Disease Control and Prevention: Prevalence of obesity and severe obesity among adults: US, 2017–2018. Retrieved from https://www.cdc.gov/nchs/products/databriefs/db360.htm.)

BOX 45.1 PROMOTING HEALTH EQUITY

Obesity

- Hispanics (44.8%) and Blacks (49.6%) have the highest rates of obesity.
- Among women, Blacks (56.9%) have the highest prevalence of being obese.
- Among men, Hispanics (45.7%) have the highest prevalence of being obese.
- Asian Americans have the lowest prevalence of being obese.

(Table 45.1). When overeating develops at an early age and continues into adulthood, it alters one's ability to sense fullness *(satiety)*.

Leptin is made in the adipocyte. It acts in the hypothalamus to suppress appetite and increase fat metabolism. A genetic deficiency of leptin causes extreme obesity. However, most obese persons have high leptin levels, suggesting they are leptin resistant.[3] This may be due to a failure to make enough leptin receptors or producing faulty receptors.

Ghrelin, a gut hormone, regulates appetite by inhibiting leptin. It acts in the hypothalamus and the brain's pleasure centers to stimulate hunger. In a non-obese person, ghrelin levels are higher when a person is hungry and decrease after eating. Gastric bypass patients do not have the premeal increase in ghrelin.[2] The low ghrelin levels help suppress appetite and contribute to the surgery's effectiveness.

Adipocytes make substances we call adipokines. Adipokines play roles in glucose and lipid metabolism, insulin sensitivity, energy homeostasis, inflammation, immunity, and vascular function. Excess visceral fat is associated with adipokine dysfunction, which leads to insulin resistance, dyslipidemia, and high blood pressure.[4] This causes people with abdominal (android) obesity more complications of obesity.

Environmental Factors

Environmental factors play a key role in obesity. In today's culture, people have greater access to high-calorie, energy-dense food and highly sweetened drinks. Eating outside of the home lends to obesity because one eats higher calorie foods with large portion sizes. Portion size has increased dramatically (Fig. 45.5). Lack of physical exercise is another factor that contributes to weight gain and obesity. We expend less energy in our everyday lives due to economic growth, technology use, and social changes. Increased time spent gaming, surfing the Internet, and watching TV contribute to the increase in sedentary habits.

Socioeconomic status is a known risk factor for obesity in several ways.[5] There may be a lack of access to affordable and nutritious food at full-service grocers and farmer's markets. People with low incomes stretch their limited food dollars by buying less expensive foods that often have poor nutritional quality with greater caloric content. Low-income neighborhoods often lack locations for healthy exercise, such as parks, playgrounds, walking trails, and swimming pools.

Psychosocial Factors

People use food for many reasons besides nutrition. Associations with food begin in childhood, such as the use of food for comfort or rewards. The social component of eating begins early in life when food is associated with pleasure and fun at such events as birthday parties and holidays. Stress, sadness, anxiety, and other emotions can lead people to eat too much. Eating

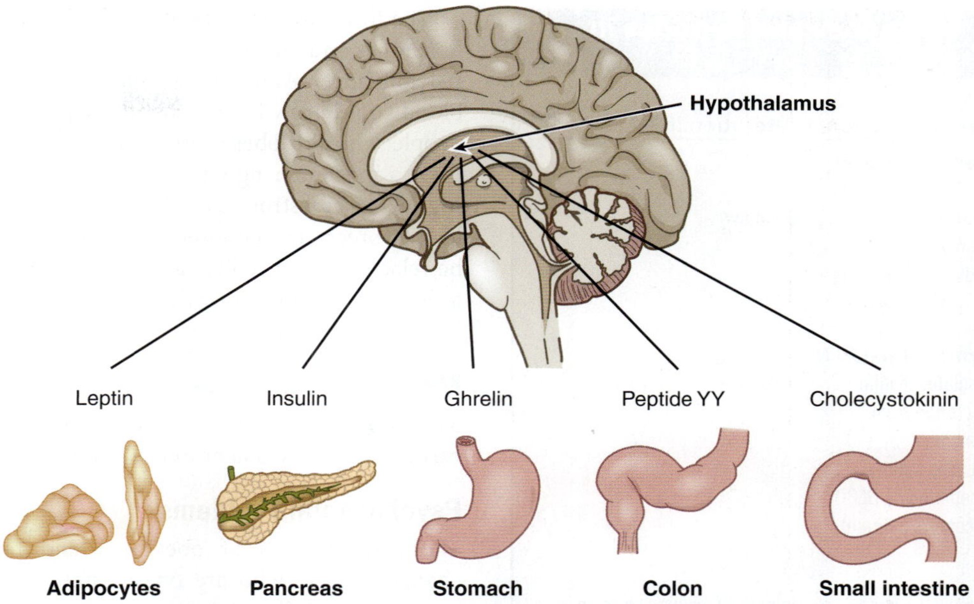

Fig. 45.4 Common hormones and peptides that interact with the hypothalamus to control and influence eating patterns, metabolic activities, and digestion. Obesity disrupts this balance (Table 45.3).

while watching television, working, studying, or browsing the Internet can lead to consuming unnecessary calories and an increase in weight.

HEALTH RISKS ASSOCIATED WITH OBESITY

Many problems occur at a higher rate in people who are obese than in people of normal weight (Fig. 45.6). Mortality rates rise as obesity increases, especially when obesity is primarily visceral fat.[4] In addition to health problems, many persons have a reduced quality of life (Box 45.2). Fortunately, most of these conditions can improve if a person loses weight.

Cardiovascular Problems

Obesity is a significant risk factor for cardiovascular disease (CVD) and stroke in both men and women. Android obesity is the best predictor of these risks. It is linked with increased low-density lipoproteins (LDLs), high triglycerides, and decreased high-density lipoproteins (HDLs).[6] Hypertension can occur because of increased circulating blood volume, abnormal vasoconstriction, increased inflammation (damaging blood vessels), and increased risk for sleep apnea (raises BP). Excess body fat can lead to chronic inflammation throughout the body, especially in blood vessels, thus increasing the risk for heart disease.

Diabetes

Obesity is the greatest risk factor for developing type 2 diabetes. Hyperinsulinemia and insulin resistance, common features of type 2 diabetes, are found in obesity.

Excess weight decreases the effectiveness of insulin. When insulin does not work effectively, too much glucose stays in the bloodstream. The body then makes more insulin to compensate. Pancreatic beta cells (cells that make insulin) may get overworked and become worn out. Over time, the pancreas is no longer able to keep glucose in the normal range.

Obesity complicates the management of type 2 diabetes by increasing insulin resistance and glucose intolerance. Adiponectin, an adipokine that increases insulin sensitivity, is decreased in those who are obese. These factors make drug treatment for diabetes less effective.

Gastrointestinal and Liver Problems

Gastroesophageal reflux disease (GERD) and gallstones are more prevalent. Gallstones occur due to the supersaturation of the bile with cholesterol. Nonalcoholic steatohepatitis (NASH) is a condition in which lipids are deposited in the liver, resulting in a fatty liver. NASH may increase hepatic glucose production. NASH can eventually progress to cirrhosis and can be fatal. Weight loss can improve NASH.

Respiratory and Sleep Problems

The increased fat mass from obesity may lead to sleep apnea and obesity hypoventilation syndrome. Sleep apnea results from increased fat around the neck, leading to snoring and hypoventilation while sleeping. The increased distribution of fat around the diaphragm causes reduced chest wall compliance, increased work of breathing, and decreased total lung capacity. Weight loss can improve lung function.

Poor sleep and sleep deprivation may increase appetite. Sleep deprivation can occur with obesity. Building up a sleep debt over a matter of days can impair metabolism and disrupt hormone levels. Leptin levels fall in people who are sleep deprived, thus increasing appetite.

Musculoskeletal Problems

Obesity is associated with an increased incidence of osteoarthritis because of the stress put on weight-bearing joints, especially

TABLE 45.1 Hormones and Peptides in Obesity

Where Produced	Normal Function	Alteration in Obesity
Anorexins (Suppress Appetite)		
Cholecystokinin		
Small intestine	Inhibits gastric emptying Sends satiety signals to hypothalamus	Unknown
Glucagon-Like Peptide-1 (GLP-1)		
Small intestine	Stimulates insulin secretion from pancreas Increases satiety (mediated by GLP-1 receptors in brain)	Unknown
Insulin		
Pancreas	Decreases appetite	Increased insulin secretion, which stimulates ↑ liver synthesis of triglycerides and ↓ HDL production
Leptin		
Adipocytes	Suppresses appetite and hunger Regulates eating behavior	Obesity is associated with high levels Leptin resistance develops so people who are obese may lose the effect of appetite suppression
Peptide YY		
Colon	Inhibits appetite by slowing GI motility and gastric emptying	Circulating levels are decreased. ↓ Release after eating
Orexins (Stimulate Appetite)		
Ghrelin		
Stomach (primarily)	Stimulates appetite ↑ After food deprivation ↓ In response to food in the stomach	Normal postprandial decline does not occur, which can lead to increased appetite and overeating
Neuropeptide Y		
Hypothalamus	Stimulates appetite	Imbalance causes increased appetite

the knees and hips. Increased body fat also triggers inflammatory mediators and contributes to cartilage deterioration. Hyperuricemia and gout often occur in people who are obese and in those who have metabolic syndrome (discussed later in this chapter).

Cancer

Obesity is one of the most important preventable causes of cancer. The cancers most strongly linked to excess body fat are breast, colorectal, endometrial, esophagus, gallbladder, kidney, liver, ovarian, stomach, and thyroid cancer.[7]

The links between obesity and cancer are complex. Several hormones and factors often present in obese states increase the risk for cancer. Adipokines from fat cells may stimulate cell and blood vessel growth. For example, leptin, which is increased in people who are obese, promotes cell proliferation. Fat tissue plays a role in changing androgens into estrogens. The resulting increased estrogen levels, especially after menopause, may lead to breast and endometrial cancer. Esophageal cancer may be related to acid reflux caused by abdominal obesity. Insulin, a powerful cellular growth factor, is increased in obesity and linked to colorectal cancer.

Metabolic Syndrome

Metabolic syndrome is a growing obesity-related health concern. It is discussed later in this chapter.

Psychosocial Problems

The consequences of obesity extend beyond the physical changes. Those who are obese often experience stigma, and in some cases discrimination, in 3 important areas of living: employment, education, and health care. The social stigma associated with obesity has an emotional toll on a person's psychologic well-being. Many obese persons have low self-esteem, are lonely, and have major depression.[8]

NURSING AND INTERPROFESSIONAL MANAGEMENT: OBESITY

Assessment

The first step in the treatment of obesity is to determine whether any physical conditions are present that may be causing or contributing to obesity. This requires a thorough history and physical assessment (Table 45.2). Before you begin, examine your own personal beliefs and any potential biases related to obesity. If you associate obesity with a lack of willpower and overindulgence, you may convey your attitude to patients. They may experience shame in a setting that claims to be a caring one.

When assessing a person who is overweight or obese, be sensitive and nonjudgmental in asking specific and leading questions about weight, diet, and exercise (Table 45.3). In doing so, you can often obtain information that the patient may have withheld out of embarrassment or shyness. Patients need to understand the reason for questions asked about weight or diet habits. You must be ready to respond to their concerns.

CHECK YOUR PRACTICE

You are working in the hypertension clinic, and the provider has asked you to do an assessment on a 54-year-old man for referral to a weight loss program. He is 5 ft, 9 in and weighs 242 lb. His BP has been hard to control with drugs and diet. While you are trying to do an assessment, he interrupts you and asks you if he can leave. He angrily tells you, "I am not going to give up my favorite foods, quit drinking, or exercise. Do you understand that?"

- How would you respond?

Assess a patient's willingness to change and potential for change. If people are not ready for change, offer them the

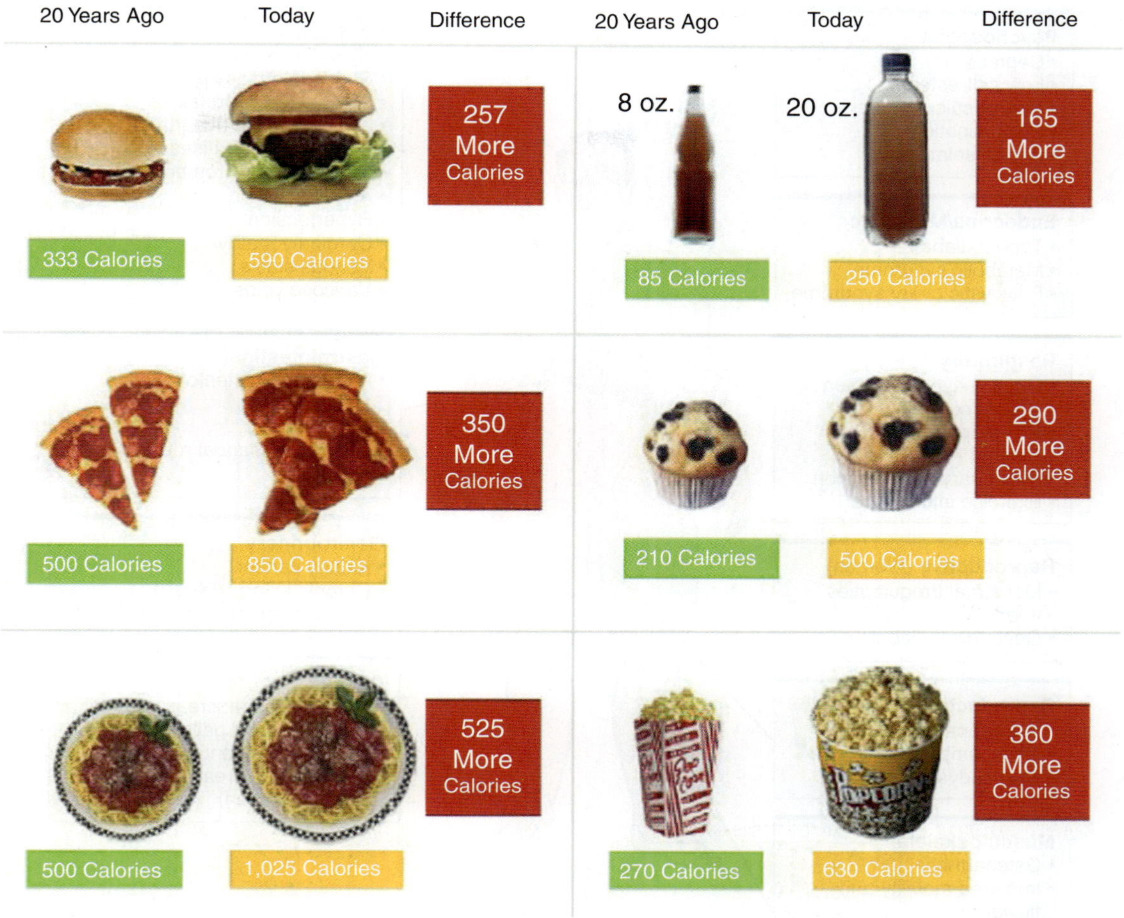

Fig. 45.5 Changes in portion size over the years. (Adapted from https://www.nhlbi.nih.gov/health/educational/wecan/portion/documents/PD1.pdf.)

opportunity to return for further discussion when they are ready to discuss their weight again and make lifestyle changes.

When obtaining the history, explore genetic and endocrine factors, such as hypothyroidism, hypothalamic tumors, Cushing syndrome, hypogonadism in men, and polycystic ovary syndrome in women. Laboratory tests of liver function and thyroid function, a fasting glucose level, and a lipid panel (triglyceride level, LDL and HDL cholesterol levels) aid in evaluating the cause and effects of obesity. Assess for any comorbid diseases related to obesity, such as hypertension, sleep apnea, and diabetes. These problems will require special treatment.

Assess each body system with particular attention to any areas in which the patient has expressed a problem or concern. Measurements may include height (without shoes), weight (obtain in a private location and in a gown, if possible), waist circumference, and BMI. Have the right equipment to take these measurements. Provide special chairs, examination tables, and scales that can accommodate an obese person.

◆ Classifications of Body Weight and Obesity

An important part of the assessment is to determine and classify a patient's body weight. Common assessment methods include BMI, waist circumference, waist-to-hip ratio (WHR), and body shape. The most widely used and endorsed measures are BMI and waist circumference. These measures are cost-effective, reliable, and easily used in all practice settings.

◆ Body Mass Index

The most common way we classify weight is the **body mass index (BMI).** We calculate BMI by dividing a person's weight (in kilograms) by the square of the height in meters (Fig. 45.7). Table 45.4 shows the classification of overweight and obesity by BMI. Persons with a BMI less than 18.5 kg/m^2 are considered underweight. A BMI between 18.5 and 24.9 kg/m^2 reflects a normal body weight. A BMI of 25 to 29.9 kg/m^2 is classified as being **overweight**. Those with a BMI of 30 kg/m^2 or above are considered **obese**. The term **extreme obesity** *(morbid* or *severe obesity)* is used for those with a BMI greater than 40 kg/m^2.

There are some limitations to using BMI. You need to consider BMI in relation to the patient's age, gender, and body build. For example, an athlete may have a high BMI, but because of a high muscle mass, the BMI is not an accurate assessment. In contrast, in those who have lost body mass (e.g., older adults), the BMI would underestimate the degree of obesity. For this reason, we combine other measures with the BMI for an accurate evaluation of a person's weight.

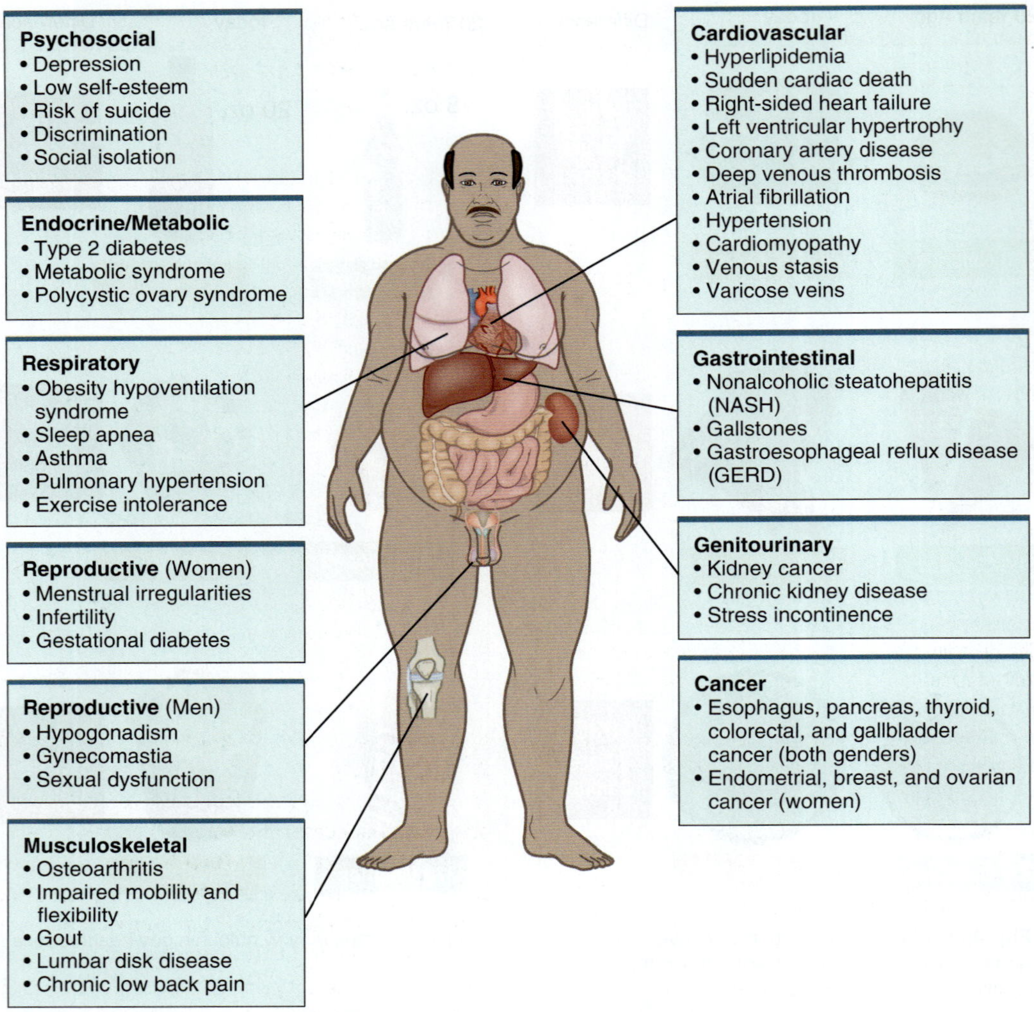

Fig. 45.6 Health risks associated with obesity.

BOX 45.2 PROMOTING POPULATION HEALTH

Health Impact of Maintaining a Healthy Weight

- Lowers the risk for hypertension and high cholesterol
- Increases chance for longevity and better quality of life
- Reduces the risk for developing type 2 diabetes
- Reduces the risk for heart disease, stroke, and gallbladder disease
- Reduces the risk for breathing problems, including sleep apnea and asthma
- Decreases the risk for developing osteoarthritis, low back pain, and some types of cancers

Waist Circumference

Waist circumference is another way to assess and classify a person's weight. It is measured just above the iliac crest after the patient has exhaled. Health risks increase if the waist circumference is greater than 40 inches in men and greater than 35 inches in women.[9] People who have visceral fat with android obesity have an increased risk for CVD and metabolic syndrome.

Waist-to-Hip Ratio

The **waist-to-hip ratio (WHR)** is another way to assess obesity. Calculate the WHR by dividing the waist measurement by the hip measurement. In women, the ratio should be 0.8 or less, and in men, it should be 1.0 or less. This means that in women the waist should be narrower than the hips, and in men, the waist should be narrower or the same as the hips. A higher WHR indicates abdominal obesity, which puts a person at a greater risk for health complications.

Body Shape

Body shape is another way we can identify those who are at a higher risk for health problems (Table 45.5). People with fat mainly in the abdominal area and an *apple-shaped body* have *android obesity.* Those with fat distribution in the upper legs with a *pear-shaped body* have *gynoid obesity.* Genetics plays an important role in determining a person's body shape and weight.

Clinical Problems

Clinical problems for the patient with obesity may include:

- Bodyweight problem
- Altered blood glucose level

TABLE 45.2 NURSING ASSESSMENT

Patient With Obesity

Subjective Data

Important Health Information

Health history: Obesity onset; diseases related to metabolism and obesity, including hypertension, CVD, stroke, cancer, chronic joint pain, respiratory problems, diabetes, cholelithiasis, metabolic syndrome

Medications: Endocrine preparations, diet pills, herbal products

Surgery or other treatments: Prior weight-loss procedures (bariatric surgery)

Functional Health Patterns

Health perception–health management: Family history of obesity; perception of problem; methods of weight loss tried

Nutritional-metabolic: Table 45.3

Elimination: Constipation

Activity-exercise: Typical exercise; drowsiness, somnolence; dyspnea on exertion, orthopnea, paroxysmal nocturnal dyspnea

Sleep-rest: Sleep apnea, CPAP use

Cognitive-perceptual: Feelings of rejection, depression, isolation, guilt, or shame; meaning or value of food; adherence to prescribed reducing diets, degree of long-term commitment to a weight loss program

Role-relationship: Change in financial status or family relationships; personal, social, and financial resources to support a reducing diet; food environment, including who prepares food

Sexuality-reproductive: Menstrual irregularity, heavy menstrual flow in women, birth control practices, infertility; effect of obesity on sexual activity and attractiveness to significant other

Objective Data

General

Body mass index ≥30 kg/m^2; waist circumference: woman >35 in (89 cm), man >40 in (102 cm)

Respiratory

Increased work of breathing; wheezing; rapid, shallow breathing

Cardiovascular

Hypertension, tachycardia, dysrhythmias

Musculoskeletal

Decreased joint mobility and flexibility; knee, hip, and low back pain

Reproductive

Gynecomastia and hypogonadism in men

Possible Diagnostic Findings

Increased serum glucose, cholesterol, triglycerides; chest x-ray showing enlarged heart; ECG showing dysrhythmia; abnormal liver function tests

- Musculoskeletal problem
- Risk for disease
- Negative self-image

◆ Planning

The overall goals are that the patient with obesity will (1) modify eating patterns, (2) take part in regular exercise, (3) achieve and maintain weight loss to a specified level, and (4) minimize or prevent health problems related to obesity.

◆ Implementation

Obesity is one of the most challenging health problems. Despite knowing the benefits of weight loss, most people find the process tough. Successful weight management will be a hard, lifelong commitment. Obesity treatment begins with patients understanding their weight history and deciding on a plan that is best for them. It is rare to find an obese person who has not tried to lose weight. Some people have met with limited and temporary success, and others have met only with failure.

TABLE 45.3 Nutrition Assessment

Patient With Obesity

When assessing the patient with obesity and before selecting a weight loss strategy, ask the following questions:

- What is your history with weight gain and weight loss?
- Are other family members overweight?
- How has your body weight affected your health?
- What do you think contributes to your weight?
- What does food mean to you? How do you use food, such as stress relief, provide comfort, boredom?
- Describe your normal diet. What types of foods do you usually eat? What types of beverages and how much are you drinking?
- Describe your motivation for losing weight.
- What have you already tried to lose weight? Was it successful? If not, why not?
- Would you like to manage your weight differently? If so, how?
- What sort of barriers do you think impede your weight loss efforts?
- Are there any major stresses that will make it hard to focus on weight control?
- How much time can you devote to exercise on a daily or weekly basis?
- Describe the support you have from family and/or friends for losing weight.

Achieving an "ideal" BMI is not necessary and may not be a realistic goal. Modest weight loss of even 5% of starting weight can have health benefits.[10] Greater weight losses produce greater benefits. In general, the average weight loss program (except for bariatric surgery) results in a 10% loss of body weight. This average should not be considered a failure since it is associated with significant health benefits.

Effective treatment requires continuous attention and reinforcement from the health care team. Barriers to counseling patients about obesity include (1) time constraints, (2) not wanting to cause the patient embarrassment, and (3) lack of reimbursement for weight management services. Other barriers are bias from low patient adherence to treatment plans and patients having a "quick fix" mentality. This can make team members feel that treating obesity is not worth the long-term effort needed.[11]

Together with other members of the health care team, you have a key role in planning for and managing the care of a patient with obesity. You can help patients by building their motivation and being a source of information. Using motivational interviewing (see Chapter 4) helps patients understand why they want to lose weight and helps them gain confidence in their ability to do so. Focusing on the reasons for wanting to lose weight may help patients develop strategies for a weight loss program. While teaching patients, stress healthy eating habits and adequate exercise as lifestyle patterns to develop and maintain (Box 45.3).

A weekly check of body weight is a good method of monitoring progress. Daily weighing is not recommended because of fluctuations that result from retained water (including urine) and feces. Teach the patient to record the weight at the same time of the day, wearing the same type of clothing.

TABLE 45.4 Diagnostic Criteria

Classification of Overweight and Obesity

	BMI (kg/m²)	Obesity Class	DISEASE RISK RELATIVE TO NORMAL WEIGHT AND WAIST CIRCUMFERENCE: Men ≤40 in (102 cm) Women ≤35 in (89 cm)	DISEASE RISK RELATIVE TO NORMAL WEIGHT AND WAIST CIRCUMFERENCE: Men >40 in (102 cm) Women >35 in (89 cm)
Underweight	<18.5	—	—	—
Normal	18.5–24.9	—	—	—
Overweight	25.0–29.9	—	Increased	High
Obesity	30.0–34.9	Class I	High	Very high
	35.0–39.9	Class II	Very high	Very high
Extreme obesity	≥40.0	Class III	Extremely high	Extremely high

Source: National Heart, Lung, and Blood Institute: Classification of overweight and obesity by BMI, waist circumference, and associated disease risks. Retrieved from www.nhlbi.nih.gov/health/public/heart/obesity/lose_wt/bmi_dis.htm.

$$\text{BMI (kg/m}^2\text{)} = \frac{\text{Weight (pounds)} \times 703}{\text{Height (inches)}^2}$$

Weight in Pounds

Height in Feet and Inches	120	130	140	150	160	170	180	190	200	210	220	230	240	250
4'6	29	31	34	36	39	41	43	46	48	51	53	56	58	60
4'8	27	29	31	34	36	38	40	43	45	47	49	52	54	56
4'10	25	27	29	31	34	36	38	40	42	44	46	48	50	52
5'0	23	25	27	29	31	33	35	37	39	41	43	45	47	49
5'2	22	24	26	27	29	31	33	35	37	38	40	42	44	46
5'4	21	22	24	26	28	29	31	33	34	36	38	40	41	43
5'6	19	21	23	24	26	27	29	31	32	34	36	37	39	40
5'8	18	20	21	23	24	26	27	29	30	32	34	35	37	38
5'10	17	19	20	22	23	24	26	27	29	30	32	33	35	36
6'0	16	18	19	20	22	23	24	26	27	28	30	31	33	34
6'2	15	17	18	19	21	22	23	24	26	27	28	30	31	32
6'4	15	16	17	18	20	21	22	23	24	26	27	28	29	30
6'6	14	15	16	17	19	20	21	22	23	24	25	27	28	29
6'8	13	14	15	17	18	19	20	21	22	23	24	25	26	28

Underweight · Normal weight · Overweight · Obese · Extreme obesity

Fig. 45.7 Body mass index *(BMI)* chart. Healthy weight: BMI 18 to 24.9 kg/m²; overweight: BMI 25 to 29.9 kg/m²; obesity: BMI 30 kg/m². BMI = weight (kg)/height (m²).

A holistic approach to weight loss is most effective. This includes nutrition therapy, exercise, behavior therapy, and, for some, drugs or surgical intervention (Table 45.6). Combining more than one aspect supports more effective weight loss and weight control efforts. Any supervised plan of care must be directed at 2 different processes: (1) successful weight loss, which requires a short-term energy deficit, and (2) successful weight control, which requires long-term behavior changes.

Setting a realistic and healthy goal, such as losing 1 to 2 lb per week, should be mutually agreed on at the beginning of a weight loss program. Trying to lose too much too fast usually results in a sense of frustration and failure for the patient. You can help

TABLE 45.5 Relationship Between Body Shape and Health Risks

Body Shape	Characteristics	Health Risks
Android (apple) 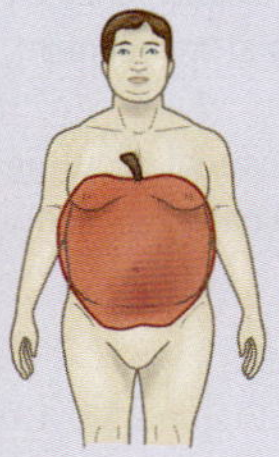	• Fat mainly in abdominal area • Fat also found over upper body (neck, arms, shoulders) • Greater risk for obesity-related complications	• Breast, endometrial cancer • Diabetes • ↓ HDL cholesterol • Heart disease • Hypertension • ↑ Triglycerides • Visceral fat more active, causing ↓ insulin sensitivity
Gynoid (pear) 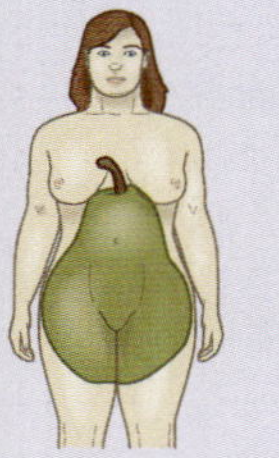	• Fat mainly in the upper legs • Has a better prognosis but hard to treat	• Cellulite • Osteoporosis • Varicose veins • Subcutaneous fat traps and stores fat • Trapped fatty acids stored as triglycerides

BOX 45.3 PROMOTING POPULATION HEALTH

Maintaining a Healthy Weight

- Weigh yourself regularly.
- Eat 5 or more servings of fruits and vegetables daily.
- Choose whole-grain foods, such as brown rice and whole-wheat bread.
- Avoid highly processed foods made with refined white sugar, flour, and saturated fat.
- Avoid foods that are high in "energy density" or have a lot of calories in a small amount of food.
- Take part in exercise:
  - 150 min of moderate-intensity aerobic activity (i.e., brisk walking) every week
  - Muscle-strengthening activities on 2 or more days a week

TABLE 45.6 Interprofessional Care

Obesity

Diagnostic Assessment

- History and physical assessment
- Family history
- BMI, waist circumference, waist-to-hip ratio
- Assessment of health risks and comorbidities

Management

- Manage comorbidities
- Lifestyle interventions
  - Behavior therapy
  - Comprehensive therapy
  - Diet plan
  - Drug therapy (Table 45.8)
  - Exercise
  - Support groups
  - Surgical therapy (Table 45.9)

patients understand that losing large amounts of weight in a short period causes skin and underlying tissue to lose elasticity and tone. Slower weight loss offers better cosmetic results.

Inevitably, the patient reaches plateau periods during which they lose no weight. These plateaus may last from several days to several weeks. Remind the patient that plateaus are normal occurrences during weight loss.

Encourage the patient to keep an electronic or paper journal. Have them record their daily food and drink consumption and exercise. They should note where they eat and with who. This can give insight into factors that influence eating habits that the patient can control or change. Reviewing the journal can help find relationships among food intake, exercise, and weight loss. Apps can give immediate access to nutrition information and track nutrient intake.

Nutrition Therapy

Restricting diet intake so that it is below energy requirements is a cornerstone for any weight loss or maintenance program. There is no best diet for weight loss. Any diet can work if it reduces caloric intake compared to expenditure and is one to which the patient will adhere.[12] The ability to adhere to a diet depends on food preferences, cultural traditions, food availability, and motivation.

It is best to recommend a diet in which calorie restriction includes a variety of healthy foods. Table 45.7 shows an example of a 1200-calorie diet. In general, the diet should emphasize fruits, vegetables, whole grains, and fat-free or low-fat dairy products. Lean meat, fish, poultry, beans, and eggs provide sufficient protein and the B-complex vitamins. The patient should limit the intake of saturated fats, cholesterol, salt, and added sugars. Encourage the appropriate fluid intake in the form of water. Have them limit or avoid alcoholic and sugary beverages. They increase caloric intake and are low in nutrition value.

Restrictive diets are hard to maintain on a long-term basis. The more restrictive the diet, the greater the demand for discipline in the face of an intense desire to eat foods not allowed on the diet. Patients will find it easier to fit a diet with a variety

TABLE 45.7 NUTRITION THERAPY

1200-Calorie–Restricted Weight-Loss Diet

General Principles

1. Eat regularly. Do not skip meals.
2. Measure foods to determine the correct portion size.
3. Avoid concentrated sweets, such as sugar, candy, honey, pies, cakes, cookies, and regular sodas.
4. Reduce fat intake by baking, broiling, or steaming foods.

Sample Meal Plan

Meal	Exchanges	Menu Plan
Breakfast	1 starch	½ cup cooked oatmeal
	1 fat	6 almonds, chopped
	1 fruit	¾ cup blueberries
	1 dairy	1 cup fat-free milk
	Beverage	Coffee
Lunch	2 starches	1 pita, 6 inches across
	2 meats	2 oz tuna fish in water
	1 fat	1 Tbsp reduced fat mayonnaise
	1 vegetable	1 cup raw carrots
	Beverage	Diet soda
Snack	1 fruit	1 small apple
Dinner	3 meats	3 oz grilled chicken
	2 starches	⅔ cup brown rice
	2 vegetables	1 cup sautéed spinach
	2 fats	2 tsp olive oil
	Free	1 cup tossed salad greens with 1 Tbsp fat-free dressing
	Beverage	Decaffeinated iced tea
Snack	1 milk	6 oz low-fat yogurt

of foods into their lifestyle and not become as bored with their food options. A list of healthy or low-calorie foods serves as a good reference and allows the patient to dine out on occasion.

There is no clear consensus on the number of meals a person on a diet should eat. Some advocate several small meals per day because the body's metabolic rate temporarily increases right after eating. However, patients eating several small meals a day might consume more calories unless they carefully adhere to portion sizes and total daily calorie allotment.

A very low-calorie diet plan that limits calories to a total of 800 or less per day may be prescribed if rapid weight loss is needed. These diets are not sustainable on a long-term basis. They should be provided only by trained HCPs in a medical setting. Persons on very low-calorie diets need frequent monitoring because the severe energy restriction places them at risk for multiple health complications.

Many people try to lose weight by following a fad diet. A *fad diet* promises fast weight loss with minimal effort and quick results. They are often promoted widely on social media and on television to gain publicity. Often, fad diets advocate eliminating one category of foods, such as carbohydrates. People who follow a fad diet may lose a large amount of weight in a short time, but it is not sustainable. Most regain the weight they lost, if not more. Therefore, discourage using a fad diet.

The degree of success of any diet depends in part on the amount of weight to lose. A moderately obese person will obviously reach a weight goal more easily than a person with extreme obesity. Because men have a higher percentage of lean body mass, they are often able to lose weight more quickly than women. Women have a higher percent of body fat, which is metabolically less active than muscle tissue. Postmenopausal women are particularly prone to weight gain, especially increased abdominal fat.

When a person first starts a weight loss program, food portion sizes must be carefully determined to stay within diet guidelines. Food portions can be weighed using a scale. Everyday objects can be used as a visual cue to determine portion sizes. The size of a woman's fist or a baseball is equivalent to a serving of vegetables or fruit. The recommended portion size of meat is 3 oz. This is about the size of a person's palm or a deck of cards. A serving of cheese is about the size of a thumb or 6 dice. The standard size for chopped vegetables is ½ cup. A portion size quiz is available at www.nhlbi.nih.gov/health/educational/wecan/eat-right/portion-distortion.htm.

Exercise

Exercise plays a key role in losing and maintaining a healthy weight. Patients should aim for at least 150 minutes of moderate exercise or 75 minutes a week of vigorous exercise per week. That works out to 30 minutes of brisk walking or 15 minutes of running for 5 days a week. The type of exercise (high vs. low intensity) does not seem to affect overall weight loss. More intensive exercise may result in weight loss with a reduced time commitment, making it preferable to some people. 200 to 300 minutes per week of moderate exercise is recommended to maintain weight loss or prevent weight regain after weight loss.[11]

Explore ways to incorporate exercise in daily routines. It may be as simple as parking farther from entry doors or taking the stairs versus an elevator. Encourage the person to use a tracker to monitor progress towards their goals. Patients can swim and cycle, which both have long-term benefits. Joining a health club can help with getting exercise. Stress to patients that engaging in weekend exercise only or in spurts of strenuous exercise is not helpful and can be dangerous.

Behavior Therapy

The assumptions behind behavior therapy are (1) persons who are obese have maladaptive eating and exercise patterns, and (2) these habits can be modified with specific interventions. Behavior therapy provides the person with tools to help change eating and physical activity patterns. It should include counseling sessions with a trained interventionist. The interventionist and patient should mutually set specific, attainable goals that identify the behavior to be modified and how goals will be achieved. Persons who are in behavior therapy are more successful in maintaining weight loss over an extended time than those who do not take part in such training.[13]

Behavior techniques include (1) self-monitoring, (2) stimulus control, and (3) rewards. *Self-monitoring* involves keeping a record of food and calorie intake, physical activity, and body weight. Record-keeping helps the patient see behavior patterns and areas for change. Regular review of self-monitoring records helps us evaluate progress toward goals.

Stimulus control is aimed at eliminating cues that trigger eating. By looking at the cues and events before eating, the person can identify areas in which to make behavior changes to break the chain and prevent overeating. For example, if the patient overeats while watching television, limiting eating to a certain area (e.g., kitchen table) can be an effective way to weaken the link between eating and television watching. The more often the person does not eat in front of the television, the less likely television watching will trigger overeating.

Rewards may be incentives for weight loss. Short- and long-term goals are useful benchmarks for earning rewards. It is important that the reward for a specified weight loss not be related to food, such as dinner out or a favorite treat. Reward items do not need to cost money. For example, time for a hot bath or an hour of pleasure reading would be an enjoyable reward for many people. Changing existing behaviors is hard. Praise your patient's successes, even small ones, at every opportunity.

Support Groups

People who are on a weight management plan are often encouraged to join a group in which others are also trying to change their eating habits. Many self-help groups offer support, tips, and information on dieting. For example, Take Off Pounds Sensibly (TOPS) (www.tops.org) is the oldest organization of this type. Behavior therapy and nutrition education are key parts of the program. WW (www.weightwatchers.com) offers a food plan that is nutritionally balanced and practical to follow. Group leaders, all of whom have successfully lost weight, support members in following their weight loss plan and achieving their weight goals.

Jenny Craig (www.jennycraig.com) and Nutrisystem (www.nutrisystem.com) are other popular weight-loss group programs. They offer special prepackaged foods and supplements that a person buys as part of their weight loss plan. The person only consumes the program's foods and drinks until they lose an agreed-on amount of weight. The person is encouraged to buy the same type of foods for the maintenance phase of the program, lasting from 6 months to 1 year. Behavior modification training is part of these programs. People must learn how to adjust their diet once they are no longer using commercial products. This can be challenging for many, and they may regain the weight they lost. A downside is these centers are cost-prohibitive for those with limited financial resources.

In recent years, many employers have begun workplace weight loss programs. The reason for such programs is that better health repays the cost of the programs through improved work performance, decreased absenteeism, less hospitalization, and lower insurance costs. Both employees and employers report benefiting from such programs.

Drug Therapy

Drug therapy should be part of a holistic weight loss program that includes a reduced-calorie diet, exercise, and behavior therapy. Drug therapy is reserved for adults with a BMI of 30 kg/m^2 or greater (obese) or adults with a BMI of 27 kg/m^2 or greater (overweight) who have at least 1 weight-related condition, such as hypertension, type 2 diabetes, or dyslipidemia.[14] The FDA-approved drugs for weight loss are shown in Table 45.8.

TABLE 45.8 **Drug Therapy**

Obesity

Drug	Mechanism of Action	Nursing Considerations
bupropion/naltrexone (Contrave)	• *bupropion:* antidepressant • *naltrexone:* opioid antagonist	• Side effects: nausea, constipation, headache, dizziness, insomnia, dry mouth • Monitor for suicidal thoughts and behaviors and neuropsychiatric reactions • Can increase BP and heart rate. Should not be used in patients with uncontrolled hypertension • Can cause seizures. Must not be used in patients who have seizure disorder
liraglutide (Saxenda)	• Glucagon-like peptide 1 (GLP-1) agonist • Induces satiety	• Used to treat type 2 diabetes • Injected • Side effects: nausea, diarrhea, headache, fatigue, dizziness • Monitor for suicidal ideation, pancreatitis
orlistat (Xenical, Allī [low-dose form available over the counter])	• Inhibits gastrointestinal (GI) lipase • Blocks fat breakdown and absorption in intestine • Results in undigested fat excreted in feces	• Side effects: stool leakage, flatulence, diarrhea, abdominal bloating, especially if a high-fat diet is consumed • Liver injury, kidney stones may occur • May need daily multivitamin supplement • Taken with each main meal containing fat
phentermine/topiramate ER (Qsmyia)	• *phentermine*: Sympathomimetic • *topiramate:* Decreases appetite	• Side effects: dizziness, insomnia, dry mouth, headache, high blood pressure • Do not use in patients with glaucoma or hyperthyroidism • Must avoid pregnancy • Can increase heart rate. Should not be used in patients with uncontrolled hypertension or heart disease
Plenity	• Gel pieces increase the volume of stomach and small intestine contents • Induces satiety	• Side effects: abdominal pain, constipation • Taken twice a day orally, 20 min before lunch and dinner, with 16 oz of water • Should not be used in patients with GI disease
semaglutide (Wegovy)	• Mimics GLP-1 • Induces satiety	• Side effects: GI distress • Subcut injection once weekly • Can cause hypoglycemia in persons with type 2 diabetes

Your role related to drug therapy is to teach the patient about proper administration, side effects, and how the drugs fit into the overall weight loss plan. Drugs will not cure obesity. People must understand that without substantial changes in food intake and increased exercise, they will gain weight when they stop drug therapy. Careful evaluation for other medical conditions can help determine which drug, if any, is best for the patient.

Review with the patient their insurance coverage for weight loss treatments. Many insurance companies do not pay for weight-loss drugs. Tell the patient not to change drug dosages without consulting with the HCP. Finally, discourage patients from buying over-the-counter diet aids unless recommended by an HCP.

BARIATRIC SURGERY

Bariatric surgery involves surgery on the stomach and/or intestines to help a person with extreme obesity lose weight. Surgery is currently the only treatment that has a successful and lasting impact for sustained weight loss for those with extreme obesity.[15]

Criteria for bariatric surgery include having a BMI of 40 kg/m^2 or more or a BMI of 35 kg/m^2 or more with at least 1 weight-related comorbidity, such as type 2 diabetes, hypertension, sleep apnea, heart failure, or liver failure. Most people who have bariatric surgery successfully improve their overall quality of life. In addition to losing weight, outcomes include better glucose control with improvement or reversal of diabetes, normalization of BP, decreased total cholesterol and triglycerides, decreased GERD, and decreased sleep apnea.[16]

Insurance coverage for bariatric surgery varies. Those who cover surgery often require extensive documentation. This often includes taking part in a supervised weight loss program for at least 6 months and a psychologic evaluation.

Because of the risks and costs of surgery, surgical candidates are screened for psychologic, physical, and behavioral problems that are associated with poor surgical outcomes. These include mood disorders, binge eating disorders, and substance use that may interfere with a commitment to lifelong behavior changes. Other contraindications include illnesses that are known to reduce life expectancy and are not likely to improve with weight loss. These include advanced cancer; end-stage kidney, liver, heart, and lung disease; or inability to comply with medical care.

Bariatric surgeries fall into 1 of 3 broad categories: restrictive, malabsorptive, or a combination of malabsorptive and restrictive (Table 45.9 and Fig. 45.8). *Restrictive procedures* reduce the size of the stomach, so less food is eaten. In *malabsorptive procedures,* the small intestine is shortened or bypassed, so less food is absorbed. Most procedures are done laparoscopically. This results in fewer wound infections, shorter hospital stays, and a faster recovery period.

Restrictive Surgeries

Restrictive bariatric surgery reduces either the size of the stomach, which causes the patient to feel full more quickly, or the

TABLE 45.9 Surgical Therapy for Obesity

Description	Advantages	Disadvantages
Restrictive Surgery		
Adjustable Gastric Banding (AGB) (Lap-Band, Realize Band) (Fig. 45.8A)		
• Inflatable band encircles stomach • Creation of gastric pouch with about 30 mL (1 oz) capacity • Later stretches to 60–90 mL (2–3 oz) • Upper gastric pouch connected by very narrow channel to lower section of stomach	• Food digestion occurs normally • Band can be adjusted to ↑ or ↓ restriction • Can be reversed • No dumping syndrome • No malabsorption • Low complication rate	• Some nausea and vomiting initially (eating too much too quickly) • May have food intolerance, gastric dysmotility, regurgitation • Problems with adjusting device • Band may slip or erode into stomach wall • Gastric perforation or obstruction may occur, requiring surgery • Weight loss may be more limited than with other types of surgery
Sleeve Gastrectomy (Gastric Sleeve) (Fig. 45.8B)		
• About 75% of stomach removed • Creation of sleeve-shaped stomach with 60–150 mL (2–5 oz) capacity	• Preserves stomach function • Does not bypass intestines • Weight loss can occur rapidly	• Leakage related to stapling • Not reversible • Nutrition problems common
Gastric Plication		
• Adapted version of sleeve gastrectomy (gastric sleeve) • Sleeve created by suturing rather than removing stomach	• Minimal surgery compared to sleeve gastrectomy • Does not bypass intestines	• Requires hospital stay of 24–48 hr • Nausea common after procedure • Risks include stomach leakage from sutured areas, blockage of stomach from swelling or fold too tight
Intragastric Balloon		
• Involves placing a deflated balloon into stomach • Balloon then filled with saline and occupies space in stomach	• Most are placed endoscopically as an outpatient procedure	• Left in place up to 6 months • Once device is in stomach, nausea, vomiting, abdominal pain, indigestion, gastric ulcers can occur
Malabsorptive Surgery		
Biliopancreatic Diversion (BPD) With or Without Duodenal Switch (Fig. 45.8C)		
• 70% of the stomach removed horizontally • Anastomosis between stomach and intestine • Decreases the amount of small intestine available for nutrient absorption • Duodenal switch cuts the stomach vertically and is shaped like a tube	• Able to eat larger meals than with gastric bypass or banding procedures • Less food intolerance • Rapid weight loss • Greater long-term weight loss	• Abdominal bloating, foul-smelling gas (steatorrhea) common • Often have 3 or 4 loose bowel movements a day • Nutrition problems include malabsorption of fat-soluble vitamins, iron deficiency anemia, protein-calorie malnutrition • Dumping syndrome common • Most complicated of weight loss surgeries
Combination of Restrictive and Malabsorptive Surgery		
Roux-en-Y Gastric Bypass (RYGB) (Fig. 45.8D)		
• Surgery on stomach to create a pouch (restrictive) • Small gastric pouch connected to jejunum • Remaining stomach and first segment of small intestine are bypassed (malabsorptive)	• Better weight loss results than with restrictive procedures • Lower incidence of malnutrition and diarrhea • Rapid improvement of weight-related co-morbidities • Good long-term results	• Leak at site of anastomosis can occur • Nutrition problems include anemia (iron deficiency, cobalamin deficiency, folic acid deficiency); calcium deficiency • Dumping syndrome common • Not reversible
Other		
Gastric Pacemaker (Gastric Electrical Stimulation Device) (Fig. 45.9)		
• Device implanted into abdomen • Works like a pacemaker to deliver electrical impulses to vagus nerve, which tells brain when stomach is full	• Least invasive of weight loss surgeries • Procedure done on outpatient basis	• Must charge device 1–2 times/week • If battery completely drained, device must be reprogrammed • Side effects include nausea, vomiting, heartburn, belching, swallowing problems

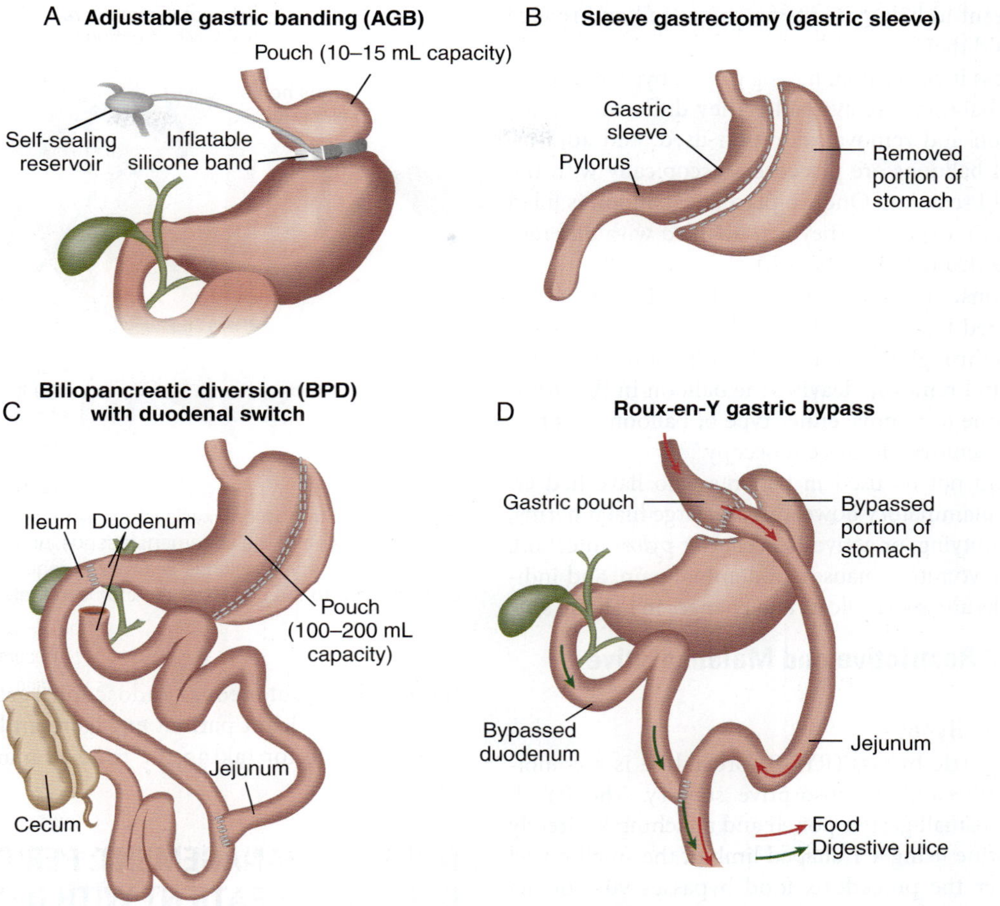

Fig. 45.8 Bariatric surgical procedures. (A) Adjustable gastric banding (AGB) uses a band to create a gastric pouch. (B) Sleeve gastrectomy involves creating a sleeve-shaped stomach by removing about 75% of the stomach. (C) Biliopancreatic diversion *(BPD)* with duodenal switch procedure creates an anastomosis between the stomach and intestine. (D) Roux-en-Y gastric bypass procedure involves constructing a gastric pouch whose outlet is a Y-shaped limb of small intestine.

amount allowed to enter the stomach. Digestion is not altered, so the risk for anemia or cobalamin deficiency is low. The most common restrictive surgeries include adjustable gastric banding and sleeve gastrectomy.

Adjustable Gastric Banding

Adjustable gastric banding (AGB) involves limiting the stomach size with an inflatable band placed around the fundus of the stomach (Fig. 45.8A). The band is connected to a subcutaneous port that can be inflated or deflated (by fluid injection in the HCP's office) to meet the patient's needs. The band divides the stomach into 2 unequal parts. The upper part acts as the new stomach. Because it holds much less, the patient feels full more quickly. The band also causes a delay in stomach emptying, providing patients with further satiety.

AGB can be either modified or reversed at a later date if needed. AGB is the preferred option for patients who are surgical risks because it is done laparoscopically. Risks include the band slipping and some food intolerance. Because it is restrictive only, patients must follow a strict diet to lose, and not regain, the weight.

Sleeve Gastrectomy (Gastric Sleeve)

In the sleeve gastrectomy (gastric sleeve), about 75% of the stomach is removed, leaving a sleeve-shaped stomach (Fig. 45.8B). While the stomach is drastically reduced in size, its function is preserved. Removing most of the stomach eliminates hormones made in the stomach that stimulate hunger, such as ghrelin.

An *endoscopic sleeve gastroplasty* is a minimally invasive procedure that requires no resection or bypass of the GI tract. The HCP places sutures endoscopically in the stomach, making it smaller and changing its shape.

Gastric Plication

Gastric plication is similar to a gastric sleeve in that it reduces the size of the stomach. It is done by folding the stomach wall inward and then placing sutures to secure the folded stomach wall. An advantage is reversibility since there is no gastric resection.

Intragastric Balloons

Intragastric balloon systems use an inflated balloon to occupy space in the stomach. The balloon does not change the stomach's anatomy. It is meant to help patients feel more full and reduce the amount of food they can eat.

Balloons are less invasive than having gastric bypass surgery. Several different balloons are available. They differ in volume, means of insertion and removal, duration used, and adjustability. Fluid-filled balloons are placed endoscopically with the patient under mild sedation. Once in place, the balloon is filled with saline so that it expands. They can be filled with different amounts of saline (from 400 to 700 mL).

With air balloons, the patient swallows the balloon in a capsule that is attached to a thin catheter. The balloon is inflated with nitrogen gas through the catheter. After inflation, the catheter is detached and removed, leaving the balloon in the stomach. When it is time to remove either type of balloon, it is first deflated and then removed under endoscopy.

Balloons should not be used in patients who have had GI surgery or have inflammatory bowel disease, large hiatal hernia, delayed gastric emptying, or active *Helicobacter pylori* infection. Patients may have vomiting, nausea, abdominal pain, and indigestion. Other risks are gastric ulcers and changes in balloon size.

Combination of Restrictive and Malabsorptive Surgery

Roux-en-Y Gastric Bypass

The Roux-en-Y gastric bypass (RYGB) procedure is a combination of restrictive and malabsorptive surgery. The RYGB involves creating a small gastric pouch and attaching it directly to the small intestine using a Y-shaped limb of the small bowel (Fig. 45.8D). After the procedure, food bypasses 90% of the stomach, the duodenum, and a small segment of the jejunum.

Many complications can occur, including GI tract leaks, gastric remnant distention, ulcers, gallstones, and hernias. Because sections of the small intestine are bypassed, poor iron absorption can cause iron deficiency anemia. Patients need to take a multivitamin with iron and calcium supplements. Chronic anemia caused by cobalamin deficiency may occur. This problem can usually be managed with parenteral or intranasal cobalamin.

Another complication is *dumping syndrome,* in which gastric contents empty too rapidly into the small intestine, overwhelming its ability to digest nutrients. Symptoms can include vomiting, nausea, weakness, sweating, faintness, and, on occasion, diarrhea. Patients are discouraged from eating sugary foods after surgery to avoid dumping syndrome.

Other Bariatric Procedures

A gastric pacemaker, or gastric electrical stimulation, controls nerve impulses from the brain to the stomach. It is an implantable pacemaker-like device surgically placed under the skin in the abdomen with lead wires around the vagus nerve just above the stomach (Fig. 45.9). The device sends signals to block vagus nerve impulses, resulting in decreased hunger and increased satiety. External controllers allow the patient to charge the device and HCPs to adjust the device's settings.

Aspiration therapy involves removing a portion of gastric contents 20 to 30 minutes after each meal through a

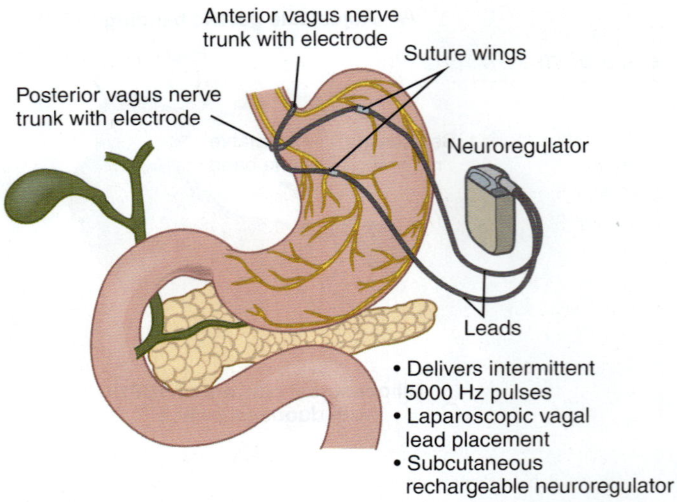

Fig. 45.9 Gastric pacemaker system. An electrical stimulator is surgically implanted into the abdomen. It sends intermittent electrical pulses to the vagus nerve, which is involved in regulating stomach emptying and signaling to the brain that the stomach feels empty or full.

modified percutaneous endoscopic gastrostomy tube. It requires significant patient engagement because the patient is responsible for taking the time to manually perform the procedure.

❖ NURSING MANAGEMENT: PERIOPERATIVE CARE OF THE PATIENT WITH OBESITY

This section discusses general nursing considerations for the care of a patient with obesity who is having surgery. Special nursing considerations are described for the patient who is having bariatric surgery (Table 45.10). See Chapters 18 through 20 for more on the care of the surgical patient.

◆ Preoperative Care

Special considerations are needed for the patient with obesity, especially extreme obesity, who is having surgery. Before surgery, interview the patient to obtain past and current health information and any assistive devices currently in use (e.g., continuous positive airway pressure [CPAP] for sleep apnea). Focus on identifying comorbidities that increase the risk for complications in the perioperative period. You may need to coordinate care with the patient's specialists.

Have a plan in place before the patients arrive so that they receive optimal care and do not feel embarrassed. You must have available appropriately sized hospital gowns, beds, and commodes that accommodate an increased body size and necessary patient transfer equipment. Use a larger BP cuff size to avoid measurement errors. Ensure that the cuff is available and placed in the patient's room.

Consider how the patient will be weighed and transported throughout the hospital. A wheelchair with removable arms that is large enough to safely accommodate the patient and pass easily through doorways should be available.

TABLE 45.10 NURSING MANAGEMENT

Care of the Patient Undergoing Bariatric Surgery

Preoperative

- Assess for use of assistive devices. Note any physical limitations or mobility issues.
- Perform baseline assessment, including vital signs, pulse oximetry, height, weight, BMI, skin condition, nutrition status, and heart, lung, and bowel sounds.
- Assess baseline laboratory values and diagnostic test results (e.g., pulmonary function tests).
- Teach patient and caregiver about the procedure and postoperative care. Review coughing and deep breathing techniques, incentive spirometer use, and methods of turning and positioning to prevent pulmonary complications.
- Explain the need for frequent assessment and interventions to prevent VTE.
- Have available proper-sized hospital gowns, beds, BP cuffs, and transfer equipment.

Immediate Postoperative

- Perform assessment and compare to baseline: vital signs, pulse oximetry, and heart and lung sounds.
- Assess abdominal wound for the amount and type of drainage, condition of the incision, and signs of infection.
- Observe for anastomosis leak (tachycardia, fever, tachypnea, chest and abdominal pain).
- Help patient turn, cough and deep breath, and use incentive spirometer at least every 2 hr.
- Protect the incision against any straining that accompanies turning and coughing.
- Give pain medications as needed.
- Position the patient upright at a minimum of a 45-degree angle.
- Maintain IV and/or oral fluid intake and monitor urine output.
- Institute measures to prevent VTE.
- Nutrition
    - Start with room temperature water and low-sugar clear liquids.
    - Teach the patient to avoid drinking with a straw.
    - Begin with 15 mL every 10–15 min, gradually increase to 90 mL every 30 min.
    - Move to a low-fat, full-liquid diet after 48 hr if tolerating clear liquids.
    - Observe for dehydration (thirst, decreased urine output, headache, dizziness).

You may need to use different assessment techniques to assess heart, lung, and bowel sounds. For example, because of the large chest wall, breath and heart sounds are often distant. You can use an electronic stethoscope to amplify lung, heart, and bowel sounds. Excess adipose tissue may make obtaining venous access difficult. A longer IV catheter is helpful (longer than 1 in) to go through the overlying tissue to the vein. It is important that the cannula is far enough into the vein, so it does not dislodge or infiltrate.

Teach the patient coughing and deep breathing techniques and methods of turning and positioning to prevent pulmonary complications after surgery. If possible, show how to use a spirometer before surgery. Spirometer use helps prevent and treat postoperative lung congestion. Practicing these strategies beforehand can help the patient perform them correctly after surgery. If the patient uses CPAP at home for sleep apnea, arrange for CPAP use while the patient is hospitalized.

◆ Special Considerations for Bariatric Surgery

Ensure that the patient scheduled for bariatric surgery understands the surgical procedure. Your teaching depends on the type of procedure and surgical approach (Table 45.9). Stress that we will frequently assess vital signs and general assessment to monitor for complications. Tell the patient that we will help them with ambulation soon after surgery. They will be encouraged to cough and deep breathe to prevent pulmonary complications.

◆ Postoperative Care

The initial postoperative care focuses on careful assessment and immediate intervention for cardiopulmonary complications. The transfer from surgery may require many staff members. During the transfer, keep the patient's airway stabilized.

The body stores anesthetics in adipose tissue. This places the patient with excess adipose tissue at risk for resedation. As adipose cells release anesthetics back into the bloodstream, the patient may become sedated after surgery. If this happens, be prepared to perform a head-tilt or jaw-thrust maneuver. Keep the patient's oral and nasal airways open.

Obesity can cause a patient's breathing to become shallow and rapid. The extra adipose tissue in the chest and abdomen compresses the diaphragm, thoracic, and abdominal structures. This compression restricts the chest's ability to expand, preventing the lungs from working as efficiently as they would otherwise. The patient retains more CO_2 with less O_2 delivered to the lungs. This results in hypoxemia. Keep the head of the bed elevated to reduce abdominal pressure and increase lung expansion.[17] Administer O_2 therapy as needed.

Implement venous thromboembolism (VTE) precautions. Diligence in turning and ambulation postoperatively will help prevent complications. The patient will typically begin walking the evening after surgery and then at least 3 or 4 times each day. Help the patient as needed. The patient may be reluctant to move or may not have the stamina to walk even a short distance. Have proper help and equipment when moving the patient.

Wound infection, dehiscence, and delayed healing are potential problems. Assess the patient's skin often. Keep skin folds clean and dry to prevent dermatitis and bacterial or fungal infections. Implement measures to reduce the risk of pressure injury.

◆ Special Considerations for Bariatric Surgery

Patients have significant abdominal pain after bariatric surgery (Table 45.10). Give pain medications as needed. Be aware that pain could be from an anastomosis leak rather than typical surgical pain. Abdominal wounds require frequent observation for the amount and type of drainage, condition of the incision, and signs of infection. Monitor vital signs to help identify problems, such as infection or anastomosis leak.

The patient usually starts a low-sugar, clear-liquid diet within 24 hours after surgery. Begin with 15-mL increments every 10 to 15 minutes. If the patient does not have any nausea or other problems, gradually increase intake to a goal of 90 mL every 30 minutes. Teach the patient to avoid gulping fluids or drinking with a straw to reduce the incidence of air swallowing. Avoid drinks with caffeine. The patient who tolerates clear liquids is advanced to a low-calorie, full-liquid diet.

◆ Ambulatory and Home Care

The patient who is having bariatric surgery has not been successful in the past in following or maintaining a prescribed diet. Now the patient must reduce oral intake because of the anatomic changes from their surgery. The patient must clearly understand their diet. A dietitian is usually part of the bariatric team and helps the patient with the transition to the new diet.

Patients usually are discharged on a full liquid diet. Within 10 to 14 days after surgery, depending on tolerance, the patient may begin a pureed or soft foods diet with vitamin supplementation.[18] Most patients transition to the usual diet 4 to 6 weeks after surgery.

The usual diet is high in protein with some carbohydrates and fiber. It should consist of 6 small feedings daily. Many need a protein supplement once or twice a day for the first few months after surgery to meet their protein needs. Patients should not consume fluids with meals. Fluids and foods high in carbohydrates tend to promote diarrhea and dumping syndrome. Calorie-dense foods should be avoided to permit more nutritious food to be consumed. Teach the patient to eat slowly and stop eating when feeling full. The person cannot overeat or binge eat without consequences, such as vomiting and abdominal pain.

Stress the importance of long-term follow-up care, in part because of potential complications. Teach patients to inform the HCP of any changes in their physical or emotional condition. Nutrition deficiencies are expected after malabsorptive bariatric surgery, including anemia, vitamin deficiencies, and diarrhea. Patients should take multivitamins with folate, calcium, vitamin D, iron, and vitamin B_{12} for life.[18] Peptic ulcer formation, dumping syndrome, and small bowel obstruction may be seen late in the recovery and rehabilitation stage.

Several potential psychologic problems may arise after surgery. Assess social functioning, self-esteem, sexual life, and activities of daily living in follow-up care. Some patients feel guilty that they had to achieve weight loss by having surgery rather than the "willpower" of reduced diet intake and exercise. Be ready to provide support and assist the patient in moving away from such negative feelings.

By 6 to 8 months after surgery, most patients have lost considerable weight and are able to see how much their appearance has changed. Help the patient adjust to a new body image. Massive weight loss may leave the patient with large quantities of flabby skin that can result in problems related to altered body image (Fig. 45.10). Discuss this possible outcome with the patient before surgery and again during the rehabilitation phase. Cosmetic surgery may help with this situation. Do not hesitate to encourage counseling for unresolved psychologic issues.

Often one result of bariatric surgery is the return of fertility in women. Women must carefully consider the risk for pregnancy after bariatric surgery. Pregnancy complications can result from anemia and nutrition deficiencies. Depending on the type of surgery, intestinal obstructions and hernias may occur with pregnancy. In general, encourage women to postpone pregnancy for 12 to 18 months after bariatric surgery.

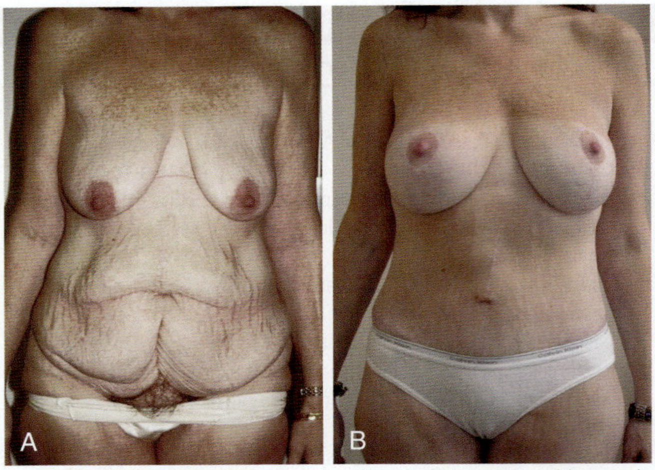

Fig. 45.10 (A) Preoperative view of a 37-year-old woman with massive weight loss who had gastric bypass surgery. (B) View 2½ years after abdominoplasty. She had breast surgery, thigh lift, back lift with excision of excess skin of the lower back and upper buttocks, and upper arm surgery. (From Shermak MA: Contouring the epigastrium, *Aesthet Surg J.* 25:506, 2005.)

CHECK YOUR PRACTICE

You are working in the bariatric surgery outpatient clinic. When you walk into the clinic room where a 36-year-old woman is waiting for her follow-up visit, you find her distraught and crying. You ask her what is wrong. She responds, "I am a total failure. I have been fat all my life, and I had to have this horrible surgery to help me. Why couldn't I do it on my own?"

- How can you handle this situation?

◆ Evaluation

The expected outcomes are that the patient with obesity will:

- Achieve and maintain optimal weight
- Have improvement in obesity-related comorbidities
- Integrate healthy practices into daily routines
- Be free from adverse side effects of surgery
- Have an improved self-image

Gerontologic Considerations: Obesity in Older Adults

The prevalence of obesity is increasing in older people. The number of obese older persons has markedly risen because of increases in both the total number of older persons and the percent of the older adults who are obese. Obesity is more common in older women than in older men. A decrease in energy expenditure is an important contributor to a gradual increase in body fat with age.

Obesity in older adults can worsen age-related declines in physical function and lead to frailty and disability. Obesity is associated with decreased survival. Those who are obese live 6 to 7 years less than people of normal weight.

Obesity worsens many changes associated with aging. Excess body weight places more demands on arthritic joints. The mechanical strain on weight-bearing joints can lead to premature immobility. Excess intraabdominal weight can cause problems with urinary incontinence. Excess weight may contribute to hypoventilation and sleep apnea.

Obesity affects the quality of life for older adults. Weight loss can improve physical functioning and obesity-related health complications. The same therapeutic approaches for obesity discussed earlier also apply to older adults.

COSMETIC SURGERY

Lipectomy

A **lipectomy** (adipectomy) is the surgical removal of excess skin and adipose tissue. It is often done on the abdomen of people who are obese or have lost a lot of weight to remove flabby folds of tissue (Fig. 45.10). Other areas such as the waist, hips, back, buttocks, breasts, and arms may also be targeted. Body image and self-esteem usually improve after surgery. A lipectomy is not without complications. Monitor afterward for the effects of anesthesia and the potential for poor wound healing and infection. Stress to the patient that tissue removal does not prevent obesity from recurring, especially if eating habits stay the same.

Liposuction

Another cosmetic surgical procedure is liposuction, a suction-assisted lipectomy. This surgery helps improve facial appearance or body contours. A good candidate is a person who has excess fat under the chin, along the jawline, in the nasolabial folds, over the abdomen, or around the waist and upper thighs. A long, hollow, stainless steel cannula is inserted through a small incision over the fatty tissue to be suctioned. This procedure is not usually recommended for an older person because the skin is less elastic and will not accommodate the new underlying shape.

METABOLIC SYNDROME

Metabolic syndrome is a group of metabolic risk factors that increase a person's chance of developing CVD, stroke, and diabetes. Just over 1 in 3 adults have metabolic syndrome. The prevalence is 50% for those 60 years of age and older. We are seeing the number of persons aged 20 to 39 years with metabolic syndrome steadily increasing.[19] Metabolic syndrome is diagnosed if a person has 3 or more of the conditions listed in Table 45.11. These include obesity, hypertension, abnormal lipid levels, and high glucose.

Etiology and Pathophysiology

The main underlying risk factor for metabolic syndrome is insulin resistance related to excess visceral fat (Fig. 45.11). Insulin resistance is the decreased ability of the body's cells to respond to the action of insulin. The pancreas compensates by secreting more insulin, resulting in hyperinsulinemia.

Other characteristics include hypertension, increased risk for clotting, and abnormal cholesterol levels. The net effect of these states is an increased prevalence of coronary artery disease.

Clinical Manifestations

The signs of metabolic syndrome are impaired fasting glucose, hypertension, abnormal cholesterol levels, and obesity. Medical problems develop over time if the condition is not addressed.

TABLE 45.11 Diagnostic Criteria

Metabolic Syndrome

Any 3 of the 5 measures are needed to diagnose metabolic syndrome:

Measure	Criteria
Waist circumference	≥40 in (102 cm) in men ≥35 in (89 cm) in women
Triglycerides	>150 mg/dL (1.7 mmol/L) *OR* Drug treatment for high triglycerides
HDL cholesterol	<40 mg/dL (0.9 mmol/L) in men <50 mg/dL (1.1 mmol/L) in women *OR* Drug treatment for high cholesterol
BP	≥130 mm Hg systolic BP *OR* ≥85 mm Hg diastolic BP *OR* Drug treatment for hypertension
Fasting glucose	≥100 mg/dL *OR* Drug treatment for elevated glucose

Source: National Heart, Lung, and Blood Institute: How is metabolic syndrome diagnosed? Retrieved from www.nhlbi.nih.gov/health/health-topics/topics/ms/diagnosis.

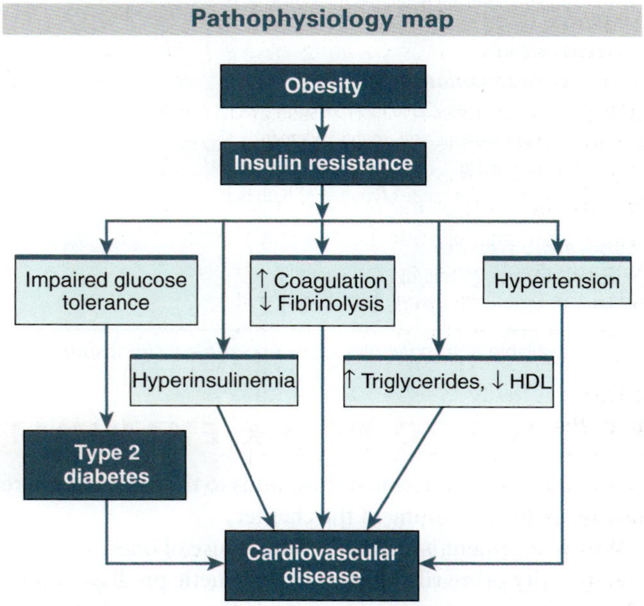

Fig. 45.11 Relationship among insulin resistance, obesity, diabetes, and CVD.

Patients are at a higher risk for heart disease, stroke, diabetes, renal disease, and polycystic ovary syndrome. Patients who have metabolic syndrome and smoke are at an even higher risk.

NURSING AND INTERPROFESSIONAL MANAGEMENT: METABOLIC SYNDROME

There is no specific management of metabolic syndrome. The adoption of a healthy lifestyle is the cornerstone of treatment. Other interventions focus on weight loss and controlling risk factors for CVD and type 2 diabetes. The person needs to maintain a healthy weight, increase exercise, and follow healthy diet habits.

You can help patients by giving information on healthy diets, exercise, and smoking cessation. The diet, which should be low in saturated fats, should promote weight loss. Weight loss and maintaining a lower weight are a priority in those with abdominal obesity and metabolic syndrome.

Because sedentary lifestyles contribute to metabolic syndrome, increasing regular exercise will lower a patient's risk factors. In addition to helping with weight loss, regular exercise decreases triglyceride levels and increases HDL cholesterol levels in those with metabolic syndrome.

There are no specific medications for metabolic syndrome. Patients may receive drugs to lower cholesterol and BP as needed. Metformin (Glucophage) can lower glucose levels and enhance the cells' sensitivity to insulin. Patients with obesity may be candidates for bariatric surgery.

Case Study

Obesity

(© Thinkstock.)

Patient Profile

S.R. is a 48-year-old woman who comes to the clinic reporting hip pain.

Subjective Data

- States that it is "getting hard to get around"
- Reports gradual weight gain of 40 lb over past 20 years
- Lives in a rural community with no sidewalks
- Spends her free time watching television
- Reports a history of type 2 diabetes, shortness of breath, hypertension, osteoarthritis
- Had knee replacement surgery at age 46 for osteoarthritis
- Tried orlistat (Xenical) but hated the side effects

Objective Data

Physical Assessment

- 5 ft, 6 in tall; weighs 230 lb; BMI 37 kg/m^2, waist circumference of 40 in
- Has obese, nontender, soft, round abdomen
- BP 160/100 mm Hg
- Moderate pain with range of motion of both hips

Laboratory Results

- Fasting glucose 250 mg/dL (13.9 mmol/L)
- Total cholesterol 205 mg/dL (5.3 mmol/L)
- Triglyceride 298 mg/dL (3.36 mmol/L)
- HDL cholesterol 31 mg/dL (0.8 mmol/L)
- LDL cholesterol 114 mg/dL

Interprofessional Care

- Referral to a community weight loss program
- Consultation with bariatric surgeon
- Diagnosed with bilateral osteoarthritis of the hips

Discussion Questions

1. ***Recognize:*** What risk factors may have led to S.R.'s obesity?
2. ***Analyze:*** Based on the assessment, what complications of obesity does S.R. have? Why did she develop them?
3. ***Analyze:*** Describe the significance of her laboratory results.
4. ***Plan:*** Is S.R. a candidate for bariatric surgery? Why or why not?
5. ***Plan:*** How could a comprehensive community weight loss program be beneficial to S.R.?
6. ***Prioritize:*** What are her priority clinical problems?
7. ***Act:*** What teaching would you provide as part of an effective weight loss program?
8. ***Evaluate:*** What parameters do you need to continue to monitor?

Answers available at http://evolve.elsevier.com/Lewis/medsurg.

BRIDGE TO NCLEX EXAMINATION

The number of the question corresponds to the same-numbered outcome at the beginning of the chapter.

1. Which statement *best* describes the cause of obesity?
   a. Obesity primarily results from a genetic predisposition.
   b. Psychosocial factors can override the effects of genetics in causing obesity.
   c. Genetic factors are more important than environmental factors in causing obesity.
   d. Obesity is the result of complex interactions between genetic and environmental factors.
2. Health risks associated with obesity include *(select all that apply)*
   a. colorectal cancer.
   b. rheumatoid arthritis.
   c. polycystic ovary syndrome.
   d. nonalcoholic steatohepatitis.
   e. systemic lupus erythematosus.
3. The obesity classification that is *most* often associated with cardiovascular health problems is
   a. primary obesity.
   b. secondary obesity.
   c. gynoid fat distribution.
   d. android fat distribution.
4. The *best* nutrition therapy plan for a person who is obese
   a. is high in animal protein.
   b. is fat-free and low in carbohydrates.
   c. restricts intake to under 800 calories per day.
   d. lowers calories with foods from all the basic groups.
5. This bariatric surgical procedure involves creating a gastric pouch that is reversible, and no malabsorption occurs. Which procedure is this?
   a. Vertical gastric banding
   b. Biliopancreatic diversion
   c. Roux-en-Y gastric bypass
   d. adjustable gastric banding

6. A patient with extreme obesity has undergone Roux-en-Y gastric bypass surgery. In planning postoperative care, the nurse expects that the patient
   a. may have severe diarrhea early in the postoperative period.
   b. will not be allowed to ambulate for 1 to 2 days postoperatively.
   c. will have small amounts of oral liquids within the first 24 hours.
   d. will require nasogastric suction until the drainage is pale yellow.
7. Which criteria must be met for a diagnosis of metabolic syndrome? *(select all that apply)*
   a. Hypertension
   b. High triglycerides
   c. Elevated plasma glucose
   d. Increased waist circumference
   e. Decreased low-density lipoproteins

1. d; 2. a, c, d; 3. d; 4. d; 5. d; 6. c; 7. a, b, c, d.

For rationales to these answers and even more NCLEX review questions, visit http://evolve.elsever.com/Lewis/medsurg.

EVOLVE WEBSITE/RESOURCES LIST

http://evolve.elsevier.com/Lewis/medsurg
Review Questions (Online Only)
Key Points
Answer Keys for Questions
- Rationales for Bridge to NCLEX Examination Questions
- Answer Guidelines for Case Study

Student Case Study
- Patient With Obesity and Osteoarthritis

Conceptual Care Map Creator
Audio Glossary
Content Updates

REFERENCES

1. Centers for Disease Control and Prevention: Overweight and obesity. Retrieved from www.cdc.gov/obesity/data/adult.html.
2. Kumar RB, Aronne LJ: Obesity. In Feldman M, editor: *Sleisenger and Fordtran's gastrointestinal and liver disease*, ed 11, Philadelphia, 2021, Elsevier.
3. Maratos-Flier E: Obesity. In Melmed S, et al.: *Williams textbook of endocrinology*, ed 14, Philadelphia, 2020, Elsevier.
*4. Landecho MF, Tuero C, Valentí V, Bilbao I, de la Higuera M, Frühbeck G: Relevance of leptin and other adipokines in obesity-associated cardiovascular risk, *Nutrients* 11:2664, 2019.
5. Eat Smart, Move More South Carolina: Why low-income and food insecure people are vulnerable to overweight and obesity. Retrieved from http://eatsmartmovemoresc.org/why-low-income-and-food-insecure-people-are-vulnerable-to-overweight-and-obesity/.
6. Cleveland Clinic: Obesity and heart disease. Retrieved from https://my.clevelandclinic.org/health/articles/17308-obesity--heart-disease.
7. American Cancer Society: Does body weight affect cancer risk? Retrieved from https://www.cancer.org/cancer/cancer-causes/diet-physical-activity/body-weight-and-cancer-risk/effects.html#.
*8. Jung FU, Luck-Sikorski C: Overweight and lonely? A representative study on loneliness in obese people and its determinants, *Obesity Facts* 12:440, 2019.
9. National Heart, Blood, and Lung Institute: Assessing your weight and health risk. Retrieved from https://www.nhlbi.nih.gov/health/educational/lose_wt/risk.htm#.
10. Centers for Disease Control and Prevention: Losing weight. Retrieved from https://www.cdc.gov/healthyweight/losing_weight/index.html#.
11. Taylor J: Looking beyond lifestyle: a comprehensive approach to the treatment of obesity in the primary care setting, *J Nurse Pract* 16:74, 2020.
*12. Freire R: Scientific evidence of diets for weight loss: different macronutrient composition, intermittent fasting, and popular diets, *Nutrition* 69:110549, 2020.
*13. Wadden TA, Tronieri JS, Butryn ML: Lifestyle modification approaches for the treatment of obesity in adults, *Am Psychol* 75:235, 2020.
*14. Bays H, McCarthy W, Christensen S: *Obesity algorithm*, Denver, 2020, Obesity Medicine Association.
*15. Andromalos L, Crowley N, Brown J, et al.: Nutrition care in bariatric surgery: an academy evidence analysis center systematic review, *J Acad Nutr Diet* 119:678, 2019.
*16. Ghiassi S, Morton JM: Safety and efficacy of bariatric and metabolic surgery, *Curr Obesity Reports* 9:159, 2020.
*17. Carron M, Safaee Fakhr B, Ieppariello G, Foletto M: Perioperative care of the obese patient, *Brit J Surg* 107:e39, 2020.
*18. Mechanick JI, Apovian C, Brethauer S, et al.: Clinical practice guidelines for the perioperative nutrition, metabolic, and nonsurgical support of patients undergoing bariatric procedures–2019 update, *Endocr Pract* 25:1, 2019.
*19. Hirode G, Wong RJ: Trends in the prevalence of metabolic syndrome in the United States, 2011-2016, *JAMA* 323:2526, 2020.

*Evidence-based information for clinical practice.

46

Upper Gastrointestinal Problems

Kara Ann Ventura

http://evolve.elsevier.com/Lewis/medsurg/

CONCEPTUAL FOCUS

Fluid and Electrolytes
Nutrition
Pain
Sleep
Stress
Tissue Integrity

LEARNING OUTCOMES

1. Describe the etiology, complications, and interprofessional and nursing management of nausea and vomiting.
2. Discuss the etiology, clinical manifestations, and interprofessional and nursing management of common oral inflammations and infections.
3. Describe the etiology, clinical manifestations, complications, and interprofessional and nursing management of oral cancer.
4. Explain the types, pathophysiology, clinical manifestations, complications, and interprofessional and nursing management of gastroesophageal reflux disease and hiatal hernia.
5. Relate the pathophysiology, clinical manifestations, complications, and interprofessional management of esophageal cancer, diverticula, achalasia, and esophageal strictures.
6. Compare acute and chronic gastritis, including the etiology, pathophysiology, and interprofessional and nursing management.
7. Distinguish gastric and duodenal ulcers, including the etiology, pathophysiology, clinical manifestations, complications, and interprofessional and nursing management.
8. Outline the clinical manifestations and interprofessional and nursing management of stomach cancer.
9. Explain the common etiologies, clinical manifestations, and interprofessional and nursing management of upper gastrointestinal bleeding.
10. Identify common types of foodborne illnesses and nursing responsibilities related to food poisoning.

KEY TERMS

achalasia
Barrett esophagus
dysphagia
esophageal cancer
esophagitis
gastritis
gastroesophageal reflux disease (GERD)
hiatal hernia
nausea
peptic ulcer disease (PUD)
stomach (gastric) cancer
stress-related mucosal disease (SRMD)
vomiting

This chapter reviews several upper gastrointestinal (GI) problems and the care of the patient undergoing upper GI surgery. These include nausea and vomiting, oral and gastric cancers, gastroesophageal reflux, ulcerative disease, inflammatory and infectious bowel disorders, GI bleeding, and structural problems. Conceptually, patients with impaired GI function may have malnutrition from decreased intake. Many are at risk for altered fluid, electrolyte, and acid-base balance. Problems with eating, drinking, or talking may cause pain and impair the ability to communicate. Pain can disrupt sleep and cause fatigue. Problems swallowing increase the risk for aspiration.

NAUSEA AND VOMITING

Nausea and vomiting are the most common manifestations of GI disease. Although nausea and vomiting can occur independently, they are closely related and usually treated as one problem. **Nausea** is a feeling of discomfort in the epigastrium with a conscious desire to vomit. **Vomiting** is the forceful ejection of partially digested food and secretions *(emesis)* from the upper GI tract.

Etiology and Pathophysiology

Nausea and vomiting occur in a wide variety of GI problems and in many conditions unrelated to GI disease. These include pregnancy, infection, central nervous system (CNS) problems (e.g., meningitis, tumor), and cardiovascular disease (CVD) (e.g., myocardial infarction, heart failure). They can occur with psychologic states (e.g., stress, fear) or when the GI tract becomes overly irritated, excited, or distended. Patients may have nausea and vomiting after surgery with general anesthesia or as a drug side effect (e.g., chemotherapy, opioids). Women are more likely to have nausea and vomiting associated with anesthesia and motion sickness.[1]

A vomiting center in the medulla coordinates the multiple components involved in vomiting. This center receives input from various stimuli. Neural impulses reach the vomiting center via afferent pathways through branches of the autonomic nervous system. Receptors for these afferent fibers are found in the GI tract, kidneys, heart, and uterus. When stimulated, these receptors relay information to the vomiting center, which then initiates the vomiting reflex (Fig. 46.1).

Vomiting is a complex act. It requires the coordinated activity of several structures: closure of the glottis, deep inspiration with contraction of the diaphragm in the inspiratory position, closure of the pylorus, relaxation of the stomach and lower esophageal sphincter (LES), and contraction of the abdominal muscles with increasing intraabdominal pressure. These simultaneous activities force the stomach contents up through the esophagus, into the pharynx, and out the mouth.

The chemoreceptor trigger zone (CTZ), found in the brainstem, responds to chemical stimuli from drugs, toxins, and labyrinthine stimulation (e.g., motion sickness). Once stimulated, the CTZ transmits impulses directly to the vomiting center. This activates the autonomic nervous system, resulting in both parasympathetic and sympathetic stimulation. Sympathetic activation causes tachycardia, tachypnea, and diaphoresis. Parasympathetic stimulation causes relaxation of the LES, an increase in gastric motility, and increased saliva.

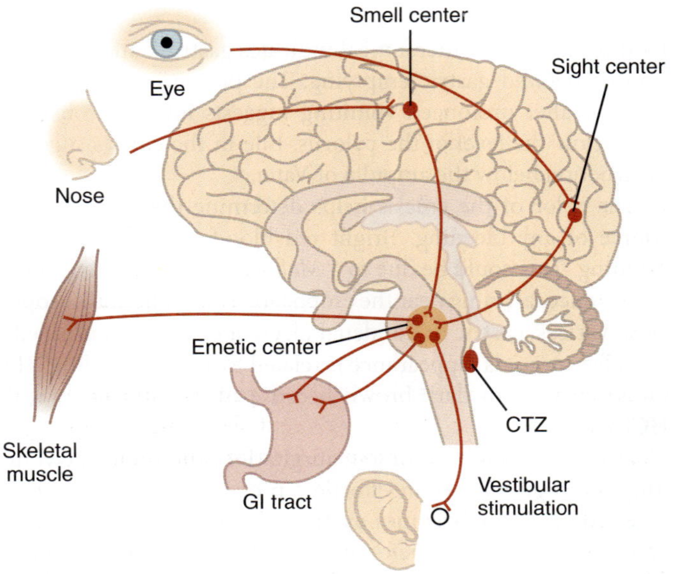

Fig. 46.1 Stimuli involved in the act of vomiting. *CTZ,* Chemoreceptor trigger zone.

Clinical Manifestations

Nausea is subjective. *Anorexia* (lack of appetite) usually accompanies nausea. When nausea and vomiting occur over a long period, dehydration can develop rapidly. Water and essential electrolytes (e.g., potassium, sodium, chloride) are lost. As vomiting persists, the patient may have severe electrolyte imbalances, fluid volume loss, and, eventually, circulatory failure.

Metabolic alkalosis can result from loss of gastric hydrochloric (HCl) acid. Metabolic acidosis can occur with vomiting of small intestine contents. However, metabolic acidosis is less common than metabolic alkalosis. Weight loss resulting from fluid loss can occur in a short time with severe vomiting.

Interprofessional Care

In managing nausea and vomiting, the goals of care are to determine and treat the underlying cause, recognize and correct any complications, and provide symptomatic relief.

Drug Therapy

The use of drugs to treat nausea and vomiting depends on the cause (Table 46.1). Many antiemetic drugs act in the CNS via the CTZ to block the neurochemicals that trigger nausea and vomiting. When the cause has not been determined, use drugs with caution. Using antiemetics before knowing the cause can mask the underlying problem and delay diagnosis and treatment.

DRUG ALERT

Promethazine

- Avoid parenteral routes because of the risk for severe tissue injury.
- Use oral or rectal formulations.

5-HT_3 (Serotonin) receptor antagonists are effective in reducing chemotherapy-induced vomiting (CINV), postoperative nausea and vomiting (PONV), and nausea and vomiting related to migraine headache and anxiety. Dexamethasone is given with other antiemetics to manage acute and delayed CINV.[2] Neurokinin-1 receptor antagonists (NK_1RAs) (e.g., aprepitant [Emend], rolapitant [Varubi]) can treat CINV and PONV.

DRUG ALERT

Metoclopramide (Reglan)

- Chronic use or high doses carry the risk for tardive dyskinesia.
- Tardive dyskinesia is a neurologic condition characterized by involuntary and repetitive movements of the body (e.g., extremity movements, lip smacking).
- It may persist after stopping the drug.

TABLE 46.1 Drug Therapy
Nausea and Vomiting

Drug	Mechanism of Action	Side Effects
Anticholinergics		
scopolamine transdermal	Block cholinergic pathways to vomiting center	Dry mouth, somnolence
Antihistamines		
dimenhydrinate (Dramamine) diphenhydramine hydroxyzine meclizine (Antivert)	Block histamine receptors that trigger nausea and vomiting	Dry mouth, hypotension, sedation, rashes, constipation
Cannabinoids		
dronabinol (Marinol) nabilone (Cesamet)	Inhibit vomiting control mechanism in the medulla oblongata	Dry mouth, amnesia, ataxia, confusion, coordination problems, dizziness, somnolence
Corticosteroids		
dexamethasone	Not well understood how it prevents nausea and vomiting	Hyperglycemia, insomnia, euphoria
Dopamine D2/D3 Receptor Antagonist		
amisulpride (Barhemsys)	Block dopaminergic receptors in the CTZ	Chills, hypokalemia, hypotension, abdominal distention
5-HT$_3$ (Serotonin) Antagonists		
granisetron ondansetron (Zofran) palonosetron (Aloxi)	Block action of serotonin	Constipation, diarrhea, headache, fatigue, malaise, ↑ liver function tests
Phenothiazines		
chlorpromazine prochlorperazine promethazine	Act in the CNS level of the CTZ. Block dopamine receptors that trigger nausea and vomiting	Dry mouth, hypotension, sedation, rashes, constipation
Prokinetic		
metoclopramide (Reglan)	Inhibit action of dopamine. ↑ Gastric motility and emptying	CNS side effects ranging from anxiety to hallucinations, extrapyramidal side effects, including tremor and dyskinesias
Substance P/Neurokinin-1 Receptor Antagonists		
aprepitant (Emend) netupitant and palonosetron (Akynzeo) rolapitant (Varubi)	Block interaction of substance P at NK-1 receptor	Headache, hiccups, fatigue, constipation, diarrhea, anorexia

An oral cannabinoid (e.g., dronabinol) may be part of the plan to manage CINV. Because of the potential for abuse and sedation, this is an option only when other therapies are not effective.

❖ NURSING MANAGEMENT: NAUSEA AND VOMITING

◆ Assessment

Each patient with prolonged or persistent nausea or vomiting needs a thorough assessment. You need to be able to identify the patient who is at high risk. Assess the patient for precipitating factors and describe the contents of the emesis. Table 46.2 presents subjective and objective data to obtain from a patient with nausea and vomiting.

When food is the precipitating cause of nausea and vomiting, help the patient identify the specific food. Determine when it was eaten, prior history with the food, and whether anyone else who ate the food is sick. Emesis containing partially digested food several hours after a meal indicates gastric outlet obstruction or delayed gastric emptying. The presence of fecal odor and bile after prolonged vomiting suggests intestinal obstruction below the level of the pylorus. Bile in the emesis suggests obstruction below the ampulla of Vater.

The color of the emesis helps determine the presence and source of any bleeding. Bright red blood occurs with active bleeding. This could be due to a *Mallory-Weiss tear* (disruption of the mucosal lining near the esophagogastric junction), esophageal varices, gastric or duodenal ulcer, or cancer. Vomitus with a "coffee-grounds" appearance is related to gastric bleeding. The blood changes to dark brown because of its interaction with HCl acid.

Discern among vomiting, regurgitation, and projectile vomiting. *Regurgitation* is an effortless process in which partially digested food slowly comes up from the stomach. Retching or vomiting rarely occurs before it. *Projectile vomiting* is a forceful expulsion of stomach contents without nausea. It often occurs with brain and spinal cord tumors.

TABLE 46.2 NURSING ASSESSMENT

Nausea and Vomiting

Subjective Data

Important Health Information

Health history: GI problems, chronic indigestion, food allergies, pregnancy, infection, CNS problems, recent travel, eating disorders, metabolic problems, cancer, CVD, renal disease

Medications: Antiemetics, digitalis, opioids, ferrous sulfate, aspirin, aminophylline, alcohol, antibiotics, chemotherapy. General anesthesia

Surgery or other treatments: Recent surgery

Functional Health Patterns

Nutritional-metabolic: Amount, frequency, character, and color of vomitus. Dry heaves. Anorexia, weight loss

Activity-exercise: Weakness, fatigue

Cognitive-perceptual: Abdominal tenderness or pain

Coping–stress tolerance: Stress, fear

Objective Data

General

Lethargy, sunken eyeballs

GI

Amount, frequency, character (e.g., projectile), content (undigested food, blood, bile, feces), and color of vomitus (red, coffee-grounds, green-yellow)

Skin

Pallor, dry mucous membranes, poor skin turgor

Urinary

Decreased output, concentrated urine

Possible Diagnostic Findings

Altered serum electrolytes (especially hypokalemia), metabolic alkalosis, abnormal upper GI findings on endoscopy or abdominal x-rays

The timing of nausea and vomiting can help determine its cause. Early morning vomiting is common in pregnancy. Emotional stressors may elicit vomiting during or right after eating. Those with *cyclic vomiting syndrome* have recurring episodes of nausea, vomiting, and fatigue that last from a few hours up to 10 days.

◆ Clinical Problems

Clinical problems for the patient with nausea and vomiting may include:

- Fluid imbalance
- Electrolyte imbalance
- Nutritionally compromised
- Impaired GI function

More information on clinical problems and interventions are in eNursing Care Plan 41.1 (available on the website for this chapter).

◆ Planning

The overall goals are that the patient with nausea and vomiting will (1) have minimal or no nausea and vomiting, (2) have normal electrolyte levels and hydration status, and (3) return to their normal fluid and nutrient intake.

◆ Implementation

◆ Acute Care

Most people with nausea and vomiting are at home. When symptoms persist, the patient may need hospitalized to diagnose the underlying problem. Until we confirm a diagnosis, the patient is NPO and given IV fluids. The patient with persistent vomiting, a possible bowel obstruction, or paralytic ileus may need a nasogastric (NG) tube connected to suction to decompress the stomach. Secure the NG tube to prevent its movement in the nose and back of the throat. This can stimulate nausea and vomiting.

With prolonged vomiting, there is a chance of dehydration and acid-base and electrolyte imbalances. Record intake and output. Monitor vital signs and assess for signs of dehydration. Maintain a quiet, odor-free environment. Provide oral care. Observe for changes in mentation. Pulmonary aspiration is a concern when vomiting occurs in older or unconscious patients or in those with an impaired gag reflex. To prevent aspiration, put the patient who cannot manage self-care in a semi-Fowler's or side-lying position.

◆ Nutrition Therapy

The patient with severe vomiting needs IV fluid therapy with electrolyte and glucose replacement until able to tolerate oral intake. Start oral nutrition beginning with clear liquids once symptoms have subsided. A patient may be reluctant to resume intake because of fear of symptoms recurring. Water is the initial fluid of choice for oral rehydration. Have the patient sip small amounts of room temperature fluids (5 to 15 mL) every 15 to 20 minutes. Other options include carbonated beverages with the carbonation removed at room temperature and warm tea. Very hot or cold liquids are often hard to tolerate. Broth and sports drinks (e.g., Gatorade) are high in sodium, so give them with caution. Dry toast, crackers, and plain gelatin may be helpful.

As the patient's condition improves, provide a diet high in carbohydrates and low in fat. Bland foods, such as a baked potato, rice, cooked chicken, and cereal, are ideal. Many patients do not tolerate coffee, spicy foods, highly acidic foods, and those with strong odors. Tell the patient to eat food slowly and in small amounts to prevent stomach distension. Liquids taken between meals rather than with meals reduce distention. Consult a dietitian about nutritious foods that the patient can tolerate.

CHECK YOUR PRACTICE

You are caring for a newly admitted 76-year-old man who reports vomiting for the past 3 days. He says, "I cannot keep anything down, not even water."

- What assessment do you need to perform?
- What findings would show he is dehydrated?
- What are your priority nursing interventions?

◆ Ambulatory Care

Teach the patient and caregiver (1) how to manage nausea, (2) ways to prevent nausea and vomiting, and (3) how to maintain fluid and nutrition intake. Tell them to keep the immediate environment quiet, free of noxious odors, and well ventilated. Avoiding sudden changes of position and unnecessary activity are helpful. Encourage the use of relaxation techniques, frequent rest periods, and diversion. Provide effective pain management. Cleansing the

TABLE 46.3 Oral Infections and Inflammation

Infection or Inflammation	Cause	Manifestations	Treatment
Aphthous stomatitis (canker sore)	• Recurrent and chronic form of infection • Related to systemic disease, trauma, stress, or unknown causes	• Painful ulcers of mouth and lips • White or gray shallow ulcer surrounded by redness	• Corticosteroids (topical or systemic) • Tetracycline oral suspension
Gingivitis	• Neglected oral hygiene, malocclusion, missing or irregular teeth, faulty dentistry • Eating soft rather than fibrous foods	• Inflamed gingivae and interdental papillae • Bleeding during tooth brushing • Development of pus, abscess formation with loosening of teeth (periodontitis)	• Prevention through health teaching, dental care, gingival massage, professional cleaning of teeth • Eat fibrous foods • Conscientious brushing habits with flossing
Herpes simplex (cold sore, fever blister) (see Table 25.6)	• Herpes simplex virus (type 1 or 2) • Risk factors of upper respiratory tract infections, excessive exposure to sunlight, food allergies, emotional tension, onset of menstruation	• Lip lesions, mouth lesions, vesicle formation (single or clustered) • Shallow, painful ulcers	• Spirits of camphor, corticosteroid cream, mild antiseptic mouthwash, viscous lidocaine • Remove or control risk factors • Antiviral agents (e.g., acyclovir, valacyclovir)
Oral candidiasis (moniliasis or thrush)	• *Candida albicans* (yeastlike fungus) • Debilitation • Prolonged high-dose antibiotic or corticosteroid therapy	• Pearly, bluish white "milk-curd" membranous lesions on mucosa of mouth and larynx • Sore mouth, yeasty halitosis	• Miconazole buccal tablets (Oravig) • Nystatin or amphotericin B as oral suspension or buccal tablets • Good oral hygiene
Parotitis (inflammation of parotid gland, surgical mumps)	• *Staphylococcus* species usually • *Streptococcus* species occasionally • Debilitation and dehydration with poor oral hygiene • Extended NPO status	• Pain in area of gland and ear • Absence of salivation • Purulent exudate from gland, redness, ulcers	• Antibiotics, mouthwashes, warm compresses • Preventive measures, such as chewing gum, sucking on hard candy • Adequate fluid intake
Stomatitis (inflammation of mouth)	• Trauma, pathogens, irritants (tobacco, alcohol) • Renal, liver, hematologic diseases • Side effect of chemotherapy and radiation	• ↑ Saliva • Halitosis • Sore mouth	• Remove or treat cause • Oral hygiene with soothing solutions, topical medications • Soft, bland diet
Vincent's infection (acute necrotizing ulcerative gingivitis, trench mouth)	• Fusiform bacteria, Vincent spirochetes • Risk factors of stress, excessive fatigue, poor oral hygiene • Nutrition deficiencies (B and C vitamins)	• Painful, bleeding gingivae • Eroding necrotic lesions of interdental papillae • Ulcers that bleed • ↑ Saliva with metallic taste, fetid mouth odor • Anorexia, fever, malaise	• Physical and mental rest • Avoid smoking and alcohol • Soft, nutritious diet • Correct oral hygiene habits • Topical applications of antibiotics • Mouth irrigations with chlorhexidine and saline solutions

face and hands with a cool washcloth and providing mouth care between episodes increase the person's comfort level. When symptoms occur, stop all foods and drugs until the acute phase is over.

If you suspect a medication is the cause, notify the HCP at once. The HCP may change the dose or prescribe a new drug. Tell the patient that stopping the drug without consulting the HCP may have adverse effects on their health. The patient should take an antiemetic drug only if prescribed by the HCP. Taking over-the-counter (OTC) drugs to relieve symptoms may make the problem worse.

Some patients find that acupressure or acupuncture at specific points reduces PONV.[3] Others use herbs, such as ginger and peppermint oil. Changes in body position or exercise may help some patients.

◆ Evaluation

Expected outcomes for the patient with nausea and vomiting include:

- Be comfortable, with minimal or no nausea and vomiting
- Have normal electrolyte levels
- Able to maintain adequate intake of fluids and nutrients

Gerontologic Considerations: Nausea and Vomiting

The older adult with nausea and vomiting needs careful assessment and monitoring, especially during periods of fluid loss and rehydration therapy. They are more likely to have heart or renal problems that place them at greater risk for life-threatening fluid and electrolyte imbalances. Excess fluid and electrolyte replacement may have adverse consequences for a person with heart failure or renal disease. The older adult with a decreased level of consciousness has a high risk for aspirating.

Older adults are especially susceptible to the CNS side effects of antiemetic drugs. These drugs may cause confusion and increase fall risk. Doses should be reduced, and efficacy closely evaluated. Use safety precautions.

ORAL INFLAMMATION AND INFECTIONS

Oral inflammations and infections are shown in Table 46.3. They may be due to specific mouth diseases or related to systemic problems, such as leukemia or vitamin deficiency. The patient who is immunosuppressed (e.g., receiving chemotherapy) or using corticosteroid inhalant treatment for asthma is at risk for oral infections (e.g., candidiasis). Oral infections may predispose the patient to infections in other body organs. For example, the oral cavity is a potential reservoir for respiratory pathogens. Oral pathogens are associated with diabetes and heart disease.[4]

Managing oral problems focuses on identifying the cause, eliminating infection, providing comfort measures, and maintaining intake. They can severely impair oral intake. Regular and good oral and dental hygiene reduces oral infections and inflammation.

ORAL CANCER

There are 2 types of oral cancer: *oral cavity cancer,* which starts in the mouth, and *oropharyngeal cancer*. It develops in the part of the throat just behind the mouth (the oropharynx). *Head and neck squamous cell carcinoma* (HNSCC) is a broad term used for cancers of the oral cavity, pharynx, and larynx. Most oral cancer lesions occur on the lower lip. Other common sites are the lateral border and undersurface of the tongue, labial commissure, and buccal mucosa. Each year 51,540 Americans are diagnosed with oral cancer. An estimated 10,030 people die.[5]

Oral cancer is more common after age 35. The average age at diagnosis is 65 years. It is 2 times more common in men than in women (Box 46.1). The 5-year survival rate is 84% for localized cancer and 65% for all stages of oral cavity and pharynx cancer combined.[5] Lip cancer has the most favorable prognosis. The visibility of lip lesions usually leads to an earlier diagnosis.

BOX 46.1 PROMOTING HEALTH EQUITY

Oral, Pharyngeal, and Esophageal Problems

Oral Cancer
- Incidence and mortality rates are highest in Black men
- Death rates are decreasing in whites and increasing in nonwhites

Esophageal Cancer
- Highest incidence is in non-Hispanic white men
- Lowest incidence occurs in Asian Americans, Pacific Islanders, and Hispanics

Stomach Cancer
- Asian Americans and Pacific Islanders, Blacks, and Hispanics have the highest rates
- Asian Americans have the highest survival rates

Etiology and Pathophysiology

We do not know the exact cause of oral cancer. There are several risk factors (Table 46.4). About 75% to 90% report a history of either tobacco or frequent alcohol use. More than 30% of patients with lip cancer have outdoor occupations, showing that prolonged exposure to sunlight is a risk factor. Irritation from the pipe stem resting on the lip is a factor in pipe smokers. Human papillomavirus (HPV) contributes to 25% of oral cancer cases. HPV-associated oropharyngeal cancer is associated with multiple sexual partners, especially multiple oral sex partners.[6]

Clinical Manifestations

Common manifestations are shown in Table 46.4. Patients may report nonspecific symptoms such as chronic sore throat, sore mouth, and voice changes. *Leukoplakia,* called "smoker's patch," is a white patch on the mouth mucosa or tongue. It is a precancerous lesion, with 15% transforming into cancer. The patch becomes *keratinized* (hard and leathery), which is called hyperkeratosis. Leukoplakia results from chronic irritation, especially from smoking. *Erythroplasia* (erythroplakia), a red velvety patch on the mouth or tongue, is another precancerous lesion. More than 50% of cases of erythroplasia progress to squamous cell cancer. About 30% of patients with oral cancer have an asymptomatic neck mass.

Lip cancer usually appears as an indurated, painless ulcer on the lip. The first sign of tongue cancer is an ulcer or area of thickening. The tongue may be sore or painful, especially when eating hot or highly seasoned foods. Lesions are most likely to develop in the proximal half of the tongue. Some patients have limited tongue movement. Later symptoms include increased saliva, slurred speech, **dysphagia** (difficulty swallowing), toothache, and earache.

Diagnostic Studies

Diagnostic tests can identify oral dysplasia, which is a precursor to oral cancer (Table 46.5). Oral exfoliative cytologic study involves scraping the suspicious lesion and spreading the scraping on a slide for microscopic examination. The toluidine blue test is a screening test for oral cancer. When toluidine blue is

TABLE 46.4 Types and Characteristics of Oral Cancer

Location	Risk Factors	Manifestations	Treatment
Lip	Constant overexposure to sun, ruddy and fair complexion, recurrent herpetic lesions, pipe stem irritation, syphilis, immunosuppression	Indurated, painless ulcer	Surgery, radiation
Oral cavity	Poor oral hygiene, tobacco usage (pipe and cigar smoking, snuff, chewing tobacco), chronic alcohol use, chronic irritation (jagged tooth, ill-fitting prosthesis, chemical or mechanical irritants), HPV	Leukoplakia, erythroplakia, ulcers, sore spot, rough area, pain, dysphagia, a lump or thickening in the cheek A sore throat or a feeling that something is stuck Difficulty chewing and speaking (later signs)	Surgery (mandibulectomy, radical neck dissection, resection of buccal mucosa), internal and external radiation
Tongue	Tobacco and alcohol use, chronic irritation, syphilis	Ulcer or area of thickening, soreness, or pain Limited tongue movement ↑ Saliva, slurred speech, dysphagia, toothache, earache (later signs)	Surgery (hemiglossectomy or glossectomy), radiation

applied topically to stain an area, cancer cells take up the dye. A negative cytologic smear or negative toluidine blue test does not necessarily rule out cancer. Once cancer is diagnosed, CT scan, MRI, and positron emission tomography (PET) are used for staging cancer.

Interprofessional Management: Oral Cancer

Management usually consists of surgery, radiation, chemotherapy, or a combination of these. The curative treatments are usually surgery and radiation.

Surgical Therapy

Surgery is the most effective treatment, especially for early-stage disease.[7] The procedure done depends on the location and extent of the tumor. Some patients with small tumors in the mouth and throat are candidates for minimally invasive robotic-assisted surgery. However, many surgeries are radical procedures involving extensive resections. Some examples are partial *mandibulectomy* (removal of the mandible), *hemiglossectomy* (removal of half of the tongue), *glossectomy* (removal of the tongue), resections of the buccal mucosa and floor of the mouth, and radical neck dissection.

Radical neck dissection includes wide excision of the primary lesion with removal of the regional lymph nodes, the deep cervical lymph nodes, and their lymphatic channels. The structures that are removed or transected depend on the extent of the primary lesion. They include the sternocleidomastoid muscle and other closely associated muscles, internal jugular vein, mandible, submaxillary gland, part of the thyroid and parathyroid glands, and spinal accessory nerve. The patient usually has a tracheostomy. Drainage tubes inserted into the surgical area are connected to suction to remove fluid and blood. Head and neck surgery is described in more detail in Chapter 29.

Nonsurgical Therapy

Radiation therapy may be used alone to treat small cancers or when lesions cannot be removed. Patients usually do not have radiation before surgery because it is hard to remove radiated tissue. The tissue becomes fibrotic and heals slower. Most patients begin radiation about 6 weeks after surgery.

TABLE 46.5 Interprofessional Care

Oral Cancer

Diagnostic Assessment
- History and physical assessment
- Biopsy
- Oral exfoliative cytology
- Toluidine blue test
- CT, MRI, PET scans

Management
- Surgical excision
- Radiation therapy
- Chemotherapy
- Nutrition therapy

Chemotherapy can shrink lesions before surgery, decrease metastasis, sensitize cancer cells to radiation, or treat distant metastases. Common chemotherapy drugs include fluorouracil, cisplatin, carboplatin, paclitaxel, docetaxel, and hydroxyurea. A common combination is cisplatin and fluorouracil.[8] This combination is more effective than either drug alone. Chemotherapy is discussed in Chapter 16.

Palliative treatment is the best management when the prognosis is poor, the cancer is inoperable, or the patient decides against surgery. Palliation aims to treat the symptoms and make the patient more comfortable. If it becomes hard for the patient to swallow, placing a gastrostomy tube will allow for adequate nutrition intake. Give analgesic drugs freely. Frequent suctioning of the oral cavity is needed when swallowing becomes difficult. Other palliative and end-of-life nursing measures are discussed in Chapter 10.

Nutrition Therapy

Many patients are malnourished before surgery. They may need placement of a percutaneous endoscopic gastrostomy (PEG) and enteral nutrition (EN) before radiation treatment or surgery. After radical neck surgery, the patient may be unable to ingest nutrients orally because of mucositis, swelling, location of sutures, or problems swallowing. Parenteral nutrition (PN) is given for the first 24 to 48 hours. After that time, EN is given via NG, gastrostomy, or jejunostomy tube. See Chapter 44 for information on EN. Cervical esophagostomy and pharyngostomy are options for some patients.

Assess for feeding tolerance. Adjust the amount, time, and formula if nausea, vomiting, diarrhea, or distention occurs. Give small amounts of water when the patient can swallow. Observe for choking. Suction as needed to prevent aspiration.

NURSING MANAGEMENT: ORAL CANCER

Assessment

Subjective and objective data to obtain from a patient with oral cancer are outlined in Table 46.6.

Clinical Problems

Clinical problems for the patient with oral cancer may include:
- Nutritionally compromised
- Pain
- Difficulty coping

Planning

The overall goals are that the patient with cancer of the oral cavity will (1) have a patent airway, (2) be able to communicate, (3) have adequate intake to maintain nutrition, and (4) have relief of pain and discomfort.

Implementation

You play a key role in the early detection and treatment of oral cancer. Identify patients at risk (Table 46.4) and provide information about risk factors (Box 46.2). Review information about smoking cessation with the patient who smokes or uses snuff or chewing tobacco.

TABLE 46.6 NURSING ASSESSMENT

Oral Cancer

Subjective Data

Important Health Information

Health history: Recurrent oral herpetic lesions, HPV infection or vaccination, syphilis, exposure to sunlight

Medications: Immunosuppressants

Surgery or other treatments: Removal of prior tumors or lesions

Functional Health Patterns

Health perception–health management: Alcohol and tobacco use, pipe smoking. Poor oral hygiene

Nutritional-metabolic: Reduced oral intake, weight loss, difficulty chewing food, increased saliva, intolerance to some foods or temperatures of food

Cognitive-perceptual: Mouth or tongue soreness or pain, toothache, earache, neck stiffness, dysphagia, difficulty speaking

Objective Data

GI

Areas of thickening or roughness, ulcers, leukoplakia, or erythroplakia on the tongue or oral mucosa. Limited tongue movement. Increased saliva, drooling. Slurred speech. Foul breath odor

Skin

Indurated, painless ulcer on lip. Painless neck mass

Possible Diagnostic Findings

Positive exfoliative smear cytology (microscopic examination of cells removed by scraping), positive biopsy

BOX 46.2 PROMOTING POPULATION HEALTH

Health Impact of Good Oral Hygiene

- Improves quality of life
- Lowers risk for teeth loss
- Reduces pain and disability
- Aids in early detection of oral and craniofacial cancers
- Decreases cost of care needed from dental professionals
- Decreases risk for periodontal disease, gingivitis, and dental caries

Early detection of oral cancer is important. Teach the patient to report unexplained pain or soreness of the mouth, unusual bleeding, dysphagia, sore throat, voice changes, or swelling or lump in the neck. Refer any person with an ulcerative lesion that does not heal within 2 to 3 weeks to the HCP.

Preoperative care for the patient who will have a radical neck dissection must consider the patient's physical and psychosocial needs. Physical preparation is the same as that for any major surgery, with special emphasis on oral hygiene. Include information on postoperative communication and feeding. See Chapter 29 for more information about the nursing management of a patient undergoing a radical neck dissection.

◆ Evaluation

Expected outcomes for the patient with oral cancer include:

- Have no respiratory complications
- Be able to communicate

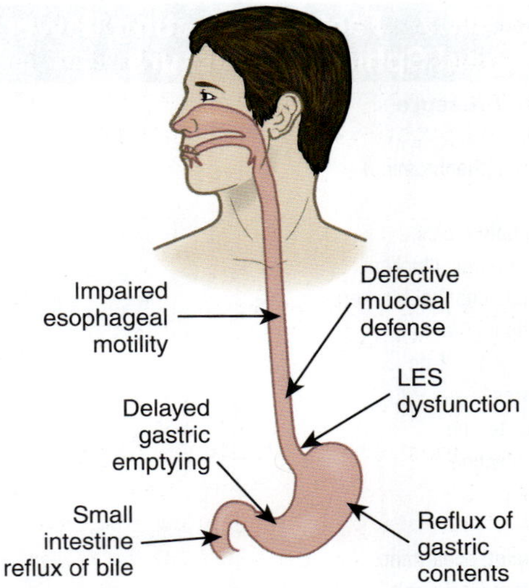

Fig. 46.2 Factors involved in the pathogenesis of GERD.

- Maintain an adequate intake to maintain nutrition
- Have minimal pain and discomfort with eating, drinking, and talking

ESOPHAGEAL PROBLEMS

GASTROESOPHAGEAL REFLUX DISEASE

Gastroesophageal reflux disease (GERD) is a symptom of mucosal damage caused by reflux of stomach acid into the lower esophagus. GERD is not a disease but a syndrome. It is the most common upper GI problem. About 15 million Americans have GERD symptoms each day.[9]

Etiology and Pathophysiology

GERD has no one single cause (Fig. 46.2). GERD results when the reflux of acidic gastric contents into the esophagus overwhelms the esophageal defenses. Gastric HCl acid and pepsin secretions in refluxate cause esophageal irritation and inflammation *(esophagitis)*. If it contains intestinal proteolytic enzymes (e.g., trypsin) and bile, this further irritates the esophageal mucosa. The degree of inflammation depends on the amount and composition of the gastric reflux and on the esophagus's mucosal defense mechanisms.

One of the primary factors causing GERD is an incompetent LES. Normally, the LES acts as an antireflux barrier. An incompetent LES lets gastric contents move from the stomach to the esophagus when the patient is supine or has an increase in intraabdominal pressure.

Decreased LES pressure can be due to certain foods and drugs (Table 46.7). Obesity is a risk factor. In an obese person the intraabdominal pressure increases, which can worsen GERD. Cigarette and cigar smoking can contribute to GERD. Hiatal hernia, discussed in the next section, often causes GERD. Some drugs, such as nonsteroidal antiinflammatory drugs (NSAIDs) and potassium, can irritate the esophageal mucosa, causing *medication-induced esophagitis*.

TABLE 46.7 Factors Affecting Lower Esophageal Sphincter Pressure

Decrease Pressure
- Alcohol
- Chocolate (theobromine)
- Drugs
  - Anticholinergics
  - β-Adrenergic blockers
  - Calcium channel blockers
  - Diazepam (Valium)
  - Morphine sulfate
  - Nitrates
  - Progesterone
  - Theophylline
- Fatty foods
- Nicotine
- Peppermint, spearmint
- Tea, coffee (caffeine)

Increase Pressure
- Bethanechol (Urecholine)
- Metoclopramide (Reglan)

Clinical Manifestations

The symptoms of GERD vary from person to person. We consider persistent mild symptoms (more than twice a week) or moderate to severe symptoms once a week as GERD.

Heartburn *(pyrosis)* is the most common symptom. Heartburn is a burning, tight sensation felt intermittently beneath the lower sternum and spreading upward to the throat or jaw. It may occur after ingesting food or drugs that decrease the LES pressure or directly irritate the esophageal mucosa. An HCP should evaluate heartburn that occurs more than twice a week, is severe, is associated with dysphagia, or occurs at night and wakes a person from sleep. Older adults who report the recent onset of heartburn should receive medical evaluation.

GERD-related chest pain can mimic angina. It is described as burning, squeezing, or radiating to the back, neck, jaw, or arms. Chest pain is more common in older adults with GERD. Unlike angina, antacids relieve GERD-related chest pain.

Patients may have dyspepsia or regurgitation. *Dyspepsia* is pain or discomfort centered in the upper abdomen (mainly in or around the midline). Regurgitation is described as hot, bitter, or sour liquid coming into the throat or mouth.

A person with GERD may report respiratory symptoms, including wheezing, coughing, and dyspnea. Nighttime discomfort and coughing can awaken the person, resulting in disturbed sleep. Otolaryngologic symptoms include hoarseness, sore throat, a *globus sensation* (sense of a lump in the throat), hypersalivation, and choking.

Complications

Complications are due to the direct local effects of gastric acid on the esophageal mucosa. **Esophagitis** (inflammation of the esophagus) is a common complication of GERD. Ulcers with esophagitis may be present (Fig. 46.3). Repeated esophagitis may lead to scar tissue formation, stricture, and dysphagia.

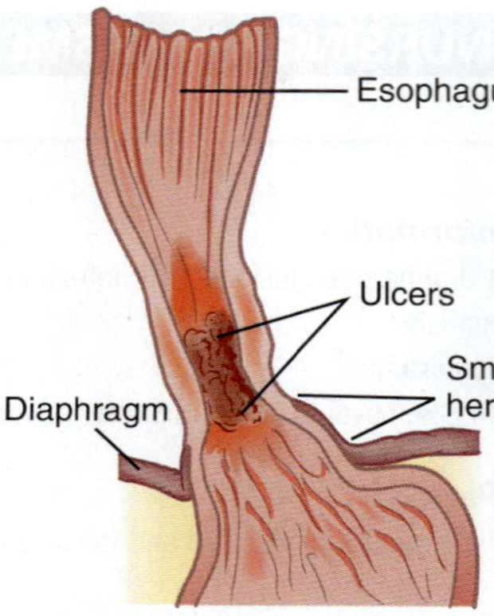

Fig. 46.3 Esophagitis with esophageal ulcers.

A complication of chronic GERD is **Barrett esophagus (BE)** (esophageal metaplasia). *Metaplasia* is the reversible change from one type of cell to another type because of an abnormal stimulus. In BE, the flat epithelial cells in the distal esophagus change into columnar epithelial cells. These cell changes are primarily due to GERD. However, some people with no history of GERD develop BE.

About 5% to 30% of people with chronic GERD have BE.[10] Other risk factors include being over age 60, being male, being white, and having central obesity. BE is a precancerous lesion that increases the patient's risk for esophageal cancer. Because of this risk, those with BE undergo surveillance endoscopy or radiofrequency ablation as needed.

Respiratory complications include cough, bronchospasm, laryngospasm, and cricopharyngeal spasm. These are due to gastric secretions irritating the upper airway. Asthma, chronic bronchitis, and pneumonia may develop from aspiration. Dental erosion, especially in the posterior teeth, may result from acid reflux into the mouth.

Diagnostic Studies

GERD is often diagnosed based on symptoms and the patient's response to behavioral and drug therapies. Diagnostic tests are done when usual therapy is ineffective or when we suspect complications (Table 46.8).

Endoscopy is useful in assessing LES competence and the degree of any inflammation, scarring, and strictures. Biopsy and cytologic specimens can distinguish stomach or esophageal cancer from BE. In addition, the degree of dysplasia (low grade versus high grade) is determined. Manometric studies measure pressure in the esophagus and LES and esophageal motility function. Ambulatory esophageal pH monitoring is an option for those with refractory symptoms and no evidence of mucosal inflammation. Radionuclide tests can detect reflux of gastric contents and the rate of esophageal clearance.

NURSING AND INTERPROFESSIONAL MANAGEMENT: GERD

Most patients with GERD can successfully manage the condition through lifestyle modifications, drug therapy, and nutrition therapy. These approaches require patient teaching and

TABLE 46.8 Interprofessional Care

GERD and Hiatal Hernia

Diagnostic Assessment
- History and physical assessment
- Upper GI endoscopy with biopsy and cytologic analysis
- Esophagram (barium swallow)
- Motility (manometry) studies
- pH monitoring (laboratory or 24 hr ambulatory)
- Radionuclide studies

Management

Conservative
- Elevate head of bed 30 degrees
- Avoid reflux-inducing foods (fatty foods, chocolate, peppermint)
- Avoid alcohol
- Reduce or avoid acidic pH beverages (colas, red wine, orange juice)

Drug Therapy (Table 46.10)
- PPIs
- H_2 receptor blockers
- Antacids
- Prokinetics

Surgical Therapy
- Nissen fundoplication
- Toupet fundoplication

Endoscopic Therapy
- Intraluminal valvuloplasty
- Radiofrequency ablation

TABLE 46.9 PATIENT & CAREGIVER TEACHING

GERD

Include the following instructions when teaching the patient and caregiver about managing GERD:
1. Follow a low-fat diet.
2. Eat small, frequent meals to prevent gastric distention.
3. Avoid alcohol and beverages that contain caffeine.
4. Stopping smoking causes an almost immediate, marked decrease in LES pressure.
5. Do not lie down for 2–3 hr after eating, wear tight clothing around the waist, or bend over, especially after eating.
6. Avoid eating within 3 hr of bedtime.
7. Sleep with head of bed elevated 30 degrees. Use on 4- to 6-in blocks or pillows.
8. Implement measures to reduce weight, if needed.
9. Share concerns about lifestyle changes and living with a chronic illness.

adherence to therapies. When these therapies are ineffective, surgery is an option (Table 46.8).

◆ Lifestyle Modifications

Teach the patient with GERD to avoid factors that trigger symptoms. They should elevate the head of the bed 30 degrees. This can be done using pillows or with 4- to 6-in blocks under the bed. The patient should not be supine for 2 to 3 hours after a meal. A patient and caregiver teaching guide is shown in Table 46.9.

Encourage patients who smoke to stop. If needed, refer the patient to community resources for help in stopping smoking. If stress causes symptoms, teach ways to cope with stress (see Chapter 7). Discuss ways to maintain healthy weight, decrease alcohol use, and increase physical activity.

◆ Drug Therapy

Drug therapy for GERD focuses on decreasing the volume and acidity of reflux, improving LES function, increasing esophageal clearance, and protecting the esophageal mucosa (Table 46.10). Proton pump inhibitors (PPIs) and histamine (H_2) receptor blockers are the most common and effective treatments for symptomatic GERD.[10] The goal of HCl acid suppression treatment is to reduce the acidity of the gastric refluxate. Patients with symptomatic GERD but not esophagitis *(nonerosive GERD)* achieve symptom relief with PPIs and H_2 receptor blockers.

Both PPIs and H_2 receptor blockers are available in prescription or OTC preparations. Teach the patient about side effects. Tell the patient to take medications as prescribed and not to stop without checking with the HCP. Have patients contact the HCP if symptoms persist.

PPIs are more effective in healing esophagitis than H_2 receptor blockers. Therapy should start with once-daily dosing, taken before the first meal of the day. PPIs decrease the incidence of esophageal strictures, a complication of chronic GERD. Long-term PPI use may decrease bone density, kidney disease, and vitamin B_{12} and magnesium deficiency.[11]

DRUG ALERT

PPIs
- Long-term use or high doses may increase the risk for hip, wrist, and spine fractures.
- Patients should take the lowest dose for the shortest duration needed to treat their condition.

H_2 receptor blockers reduce symptoms and promote esophageal healing in 50% of patients. The onset of action of H_2 receptor blockers is 1 hour. Depending on the specific drug, therapeutic effects last up to 12 hours. We can give famotidine and cimetidine orally or IV. Nizatidine is only available orally. Some preparations combine an H_2 receptor blocker with an antacid. For example, Pepcid Complete includes famotidine, calcium carbonate, and magnesium hydroxide.

Adjunctive treatments include antacids and prokinetic drugs. Antacids produce quick, short-lived relief of heartburn. Common antacids consist of magnesium hydroxide or aluminum hydroxide as single preparations or in various combinations (Table 46.10). The neutralizing effects of antacids taken on an empty stomach last only 20 to 30 minutes. They are most effective taken 1 to 3 hours after meals and at bedtime. When taken after meals, their effects may last 3 to 4 hours.

Antacids may be useful in patients with mild, intermittent heartburn. In patients with moderate to severe or frequent symptoms or patients with esophagitis, antacids are not effective in relieving symptoms or healing lesions. After an acute phase of

TABLE 46.10 Drug Therapy

GERD and Peptic Ulcer Disease

Drug	Mechanism of Action	Side Effects
Proton Pump Inhibitors (PPIs)		
dexlansoprazole (Dexilant) esomeprazole (Nexium) lansoprazole (Prevacid) omeprazole (Prilosec) omeprazole and sodium bicarbonate (Zegerid) pantoprazole (Protonix) rabeprazole (Aciphex)	↓ HCl acid secretion by inhibiting the proton pump (H^+-K^+-ATPase) responsible for the secretion of H^+ ↓ Irritation of the esophageal and gastric mucosa	Headache, abdominal pain, nausea, diarrhea, vomiting, flatulence
Histamine (H_2) Receptor Blockers		
cimetidine famotidine (Pepcid) nizatidine	Block the action of histamine on the H_2 receptors to ↓ HCl acid secretion ↓ Conversion of pepsinogen to pepsin ↓ Irritation of the esophageal and gastric mucosa	Headache, abdominal pain, constipation, diarrhea
Antacids, Acid Neutralizers		
Single Substance aluminum hydroxide (Amphojel) calcium carbonate (Tums) sodium bicarbonate (Alka-Seltzer) ***Aluminum and Magnesium*** Maalox, Mylanta aluminum/magnesium trisilicate (Gaviscon)	Neutralize HCl acid Taken 1–3 hr after meals and at bedtime	*Aluminum hydroxide:* Constipation, phosphorus depletion with chronic use *Calcium carbonate:* Constipation or diarrhea, hypercalcemia, milk-alkali syndrome, renal calculi *Magnesium preparations:* Diarrhea, hypermagnesemia. Use with caution in patients with renal problems *Sodium preparations:* Milk-alkali syndrome if used with large amounts of calcium. Use with caution in patients on sodium restrictions
Cholinergic		
bethanechol	↑ LES pressure, ↑ esophageal emptying, ↑ gastric emptying	Lightheadedness, syncope, flushing, diarrhea, stomach cramps, dizziness
Cytoprotective		
sucralfate (Carafate)	Act to form a protective layer and serve as a barrier against acid, bile salts, and enzymes in the stomach	Constipation
Prokinetic		
metoclopramide (Reglan)	Block effect of dopamine ↑ Gastric motility and emptying ↓ Reflux	CNS side effects ranging from anxiety to hallucinations Extrapyramidal side effects (tremor and dyskinesias similar to Parkinson disease)
Prostaglandin (Synthetic)		
misoprostol (Cytotec)	Protect lining of stomach *Cytoprotective:* Increase production of gastric mucus and mucosal secretion of bicarbonate *Antisecretory:* ↓ HCl acid secretion	Abdominal pain, diarrhea, GI bleeding, uterine rupture if pregnant

bleeding, antacids may be given hourly, either orally or through the NG tube. If an NG tube is in place, periodically aspirate the stomach contents and test the pH level. If pH is less than 5, intermittent suction may be used, or the frequency or dosage of the antacid or antisecretory agent increased.

The type and dosage of antacid given depend on side effects and potential drug interactions. Antacids high in sodium are used cautiously in older adults and patients with CVD, liver, and renal disease. Patients with renal failure should not take magnesium preparations because of the risk for magnesium toxicity. An antacid combination of aluminum and magnesium decreases the side effects of both.

Antacids can interact unfavorably with many drugs. They enhance the effects of some drugs, like benzodiazepines and pseudoephedrine. In many instances, antacids decrease the absorption rates of other drugs, such as thyroid hormones, phenytoin, and tetracycline. Adjust the timing of administering medications as needed.

Prokinetics increase LES pressure and improve gastric emptying, which may result in a small improvement in regurgitation and vomiting. Common agents include cisapride, metoclopramide (Reglan), bethanechol, and baclofen. Many have significant side effects, so their use is limited only to those with delayed gastric emptying.

◆ Nutrition Therapy

No specific diet is used to treat GERD. Some patients may need to avoid foods that decrease LES pressure. These include chocolate, peppermint, fatty foods, coffee, and tea (Table 46.7), Some foods (e.g., tomato-based products, orange juice, cola, red wine) and soda may irritate the esophagus.

Tell the patient to avoid late evening meals, nighttime snacking, and milk, especially at bedtime, since these increase gastric acid secretion. Small, frequent meals and drinking fluids between meals help prevent stomach distention. Increased saliva production by chewing gum and oral lozenges may help with mild symptoms. Recommend weight reduction if the patient is overweight.

◆ Surgical Therapy

Antireflux surgery is reserved for patients with complications, such as esophagitis, medication intolerance, stricture, BE, and persistent severe symptoms. The goal of surgery is to reduce reflux by enhancing LES integrity. Most procedures are done laparoscopically. The fundus of the stomach is wrapped around the lower part of the esophagus to reinforce and repair the defective barrier. Nissen and Toupet fundoplications are common laparoscopic antireflux surgeries.

Laparoscopic fundoplication is often an outpatient procedure. Patients at risk for complications, including those with prior upper abdominal surgeries or co-morbidities (e.g., cardiac disease, obesity), may be hospitalized afterwards. Complications include gastric or esophageal injury, splenic injury, pneumothorax, perforation, bleeding, infection, and pneumonia.

After surgery, reflux symptoms should decrease. However, recurrence is possible. In the first month after surgery, the patient may report mild dysphagia. This is caused by edema and should resolve. Teach the patient to report persistent symptoms, such as heartburn and regurgitation.

A LINX Reflux Management System is an option for patients who have symptoms despite maximum medical management. A LINX system is a ring of small, flexible magnets enclosed in titanium beads and connected by titanium wires. Once implanted laparoscopically into the LES, the ring strengthens the weak LES. Under resting (non-swallowing) conditions, the magnetic attraction between the beads helps keep a weak LES closed to prevent reflux. When the person swallows, the force of pressure from the movement of fluids or foods overwhelms the magnetic forces and the fluid or food passes to the stomach. Problems with the system include nausea, swallowing problems, and pain when swallowing food. Patients who have a LINX system cannot have an MRI as it could cause serious harm.

◆ Endoscopic Therapy

Alternatives to surgery include endoscopic mucosal resection (EMR) and radiofrequency ablation. The heat energy delivered through radiofrequencies creates lesions that we think thicken the LES. For patients with high-grade dysplasia, EMR can be used as a diagnostic test to obtain biopsy samples. Biopsy results determine whether cancer is present.

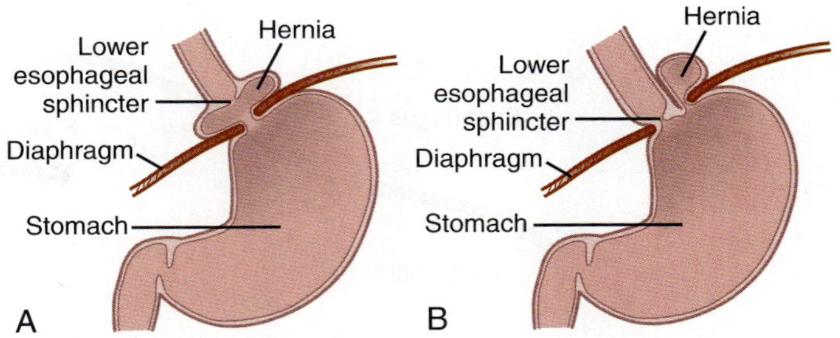

Fig. 46.4 (A) Sliding hiatal hernia. (B) Rolling or paraesophageal hernia.

HIATAL HERNIA

Hiatal hernia is herniation of part of the stomach into the esophagus through an opening, or hiatus, in the diaphragm. We also call it a *diaphragmatic hernia* or *esophageal hernia*. Hiatal hernias are the most common abnormality found on x-ray examination of the upper GI tract. They are common in older adults and occur more often in women.

There are 2 types of hiatal hernias (Fig. 46.4):

1. *Sliding:* The junction of the stomach and esophagus is above the diaphragm. A part of the stomach slides through the hiatal opening in the diaphragm. This occurs when the patient is supine. The hernia usually goes back into the abdominal cavity when the patient is standing upright. This is the most common type.
2. *Paraesophageal* or *rolling:* The fundus and greater curvature of the stomach roll up through the diaphragm, forming a pocket alongside the esophagus. The esophagogastric junction stays in the normal position. Acute paraesophageal hernia is a medical emergency.

Etiology and Pathophysiology

Many factors contribute to the development of a hiatal hernia. Structural changes (weakening of the muscles in the diaphragm around the esophagogastric opening) occur with aging. Factors that increase intraabdominal pressure may predispose patients to developing a hiatal hernia. These include obesity, pregnancy, ascites, tumors, intense physical exertion, and heavy lifting on a continual basis.

Clinical Manifestations and Complications

Some people with hiatal hernia are asymptomatic. When present, manifestations of hiatal hernia are similar to those of GERD.

Complications that may occur include GERD, esophagitis, bleeding from erosion, stenosis (narrowing of the esophagus), ulcerations of the herniated part of the stomach, strangulation of the hernia, and regurgitation with tracheal aspiration.

Diagnostic Studies

An esophagram (barium swallow) may show the protrusion of gastric mucosa through the esophageal hiatus. Endoscopic

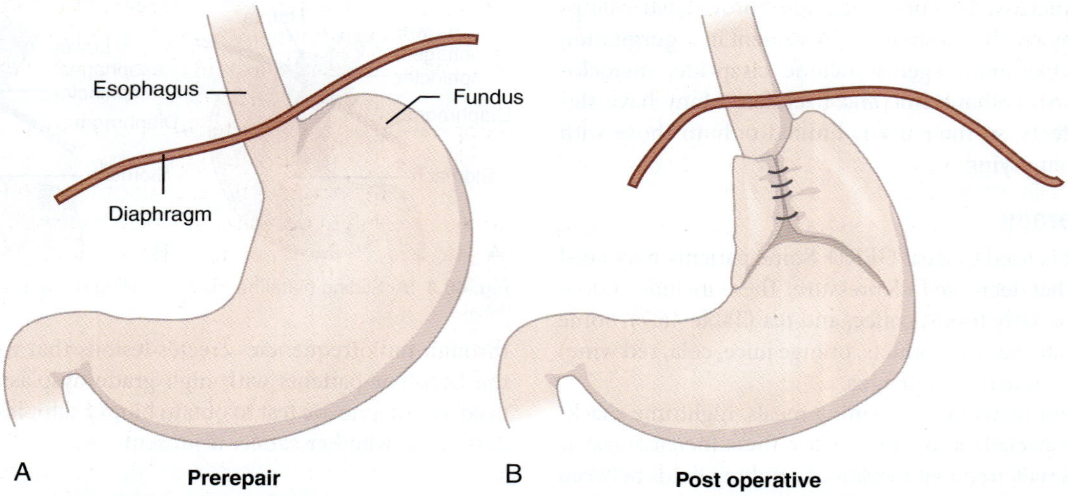

Fig. 46.5 Nissen fundoplication. (A) Fundus of stomach is wrapped around distal esophagus. (B) The fundus is then sutured to itself.

visualization of the lower esophagus gives information on the degree of mucosal inflammation or other abnormalities. Other tests done are the same as those for GERD (Table 46.8).

NURSING AND INTERPROFESSIONAL MANAGEMENT: HIATAL HERNIA

Conservative therapy of hiatal hernia is similar to that described for GERD. Teach the patient to reduce intraabdominal pressure by eliminating constricting garments and avoiding lifting and straining.

Surgical treatment includes reducing the herniated stomach into the abdomen, *herniotomy* (excision of the hernia sac), *herniorrhaphy* (closure of the hiatal defect), fundoplication, and *gastropexy* (attachment of the stomach below the diaphragm to prevent re-herniation). The goals are to reduce the hernia, provide an acceptable LES pressure, and prevent movement of the gastroesophageal junction.

Surgery to repair hiatal hernia is often done laparoscopically by either Nissen or Toupet techniques (Fig. 46.5). The approach used (thoracic or abdominal) depends on the patient.

Gerontologic Considerations: GERD and Hiatal Hernia

The incidence of hiatal hernia and GERD increases with age. Hiatal hernia is associated with weakening of the diaphragm, obesity, kyphosis, or other factors that increase intraabdominal pressure. Older patients may take drugs known to decrease LES pressure (e.g., nitrates, calcium channel blockers, antidepressants). Some older adults are asymptomatic or have less severe symptoms. The first sign may be a serious problem, such as esophageal bleeding from esophagitis or respiratory complications (e.g., aspiration pneumonia) due to aspiration of gastric contents.

The clinical course and management of GERD and hiatal hernia in the older adult are similar to those for the younger adult. Changes in lifestyle, including smoking cessation and elevating the head of the bed on blocks, may be challenging for the older adult. Laparoscopic procedures reduce the risk associated with surgical repair. An older patient with heart and lung problems may not be a good candidate for surgical intervention.

ESOPHAGEAL CANCER

Esophageal cancer is not common. However, the rates are increasing. The United States had 18,400 new cases diagnosed and 16,170 deaths occur from esophageal cancer in 2020. The overall 5-year survival rate is 20%.[12]

Most esophageal cancers are adenocarcinomas. The others are squamous cell tumors. Adenocarcinomas arise from the glands lining the esophagus and resemble cancers of the stomach and small intestine. The incidence of esophageal cancer increases with age. Those between 65 and 75 are at greatest risk. The incidence is higher in men.

Etiology and Pathophysiology

The cause of esophageal cancer is unknown. Key risk factors include BE, smoking, excess alcohol use, and obesity. Current smoking or a history of smoking has a twice greater risk for esophageal cancer. Those with injury to the esophageal mucosa (e.g., from occupational exposure to asbestos and cement dust) are at greater risk. *Achalasia*, a condition marked by delayed emptying of the lower esophagus, is associated with squamous cell cancer.

Most esophageal tumors occur in the middle and lower portions of the esophagus. The tumor usually appears as an ulcerated lesion. It may penetrate the muscular layer and extend outside the wall of the esophagus. Many patients have advanced disease at the time of diagnosis. The cancer spreads via the lymph system. The liver and lung are common sites of metastasis.

Clinical Manifestations and Complications

By the time the patient has symptoms, the tumor is often advanced. Progressive dysphagia is the most common symptom. It may be described as a substernal feeling that food is not passing. At first the dysphagia occurs only with meat, then with soft foods, and eventually with liquids.

Pain develops late. It occurs in the substernal, epigastric, or back areas. Pain usually increases with swallowing. It may radiate to the neck, jaw, ears, and shoulders. If the tumor is in the upper third of the esophagus, symptoms, such as sore throat, choking, and hoarseness, may occur. Most patients lose weight. When esophageal stenosis (narrowing) is severe, regurgitation of blood-flecked esophageal contents is common.

Bleeding occurs if the cancer erodes through the esophagus and into the aorta. Esophageal perforation with fistula formation into the lung or trachea sometimes develops. The tumor may enlarge enough to cause esophageal obstruction, especially in the later stages.

Diagnostic Studies

Endoscopic biopsy is needed to diagnose esophageal cancer. Endoscopic ultrasonography (EUS) is important in staging esophageal cancer. Esophagram (barium swallow) may show narrowing of the esophagus at the tumor site (Table 46.11).

Interprofessional Management

Treatment depends on the tumor's location and whether invasion or metastasis is present. Esophageal cancer usually has a poor prognosis because it is often diagnosed at an advanced stage. The best results occur with a multimodal approach, including surgery, endoscopic ablation, chemotherapy, and radiation therapy. Depending on the location and cancer spread, only chemotherapy and radiation may be used. Palliative therapy consists of restoring swallowing function and maintaining nutrition and hydration.

Surgical Therapy

The types of surgical procedures done are (1) removal of part or all the esophagus *(esophagectomy)* with use of a Dacron graft to replace the resected part, (2) resection of a portion of the esophagus and anastomosis of the remaining portion to the stomach *(esophagogastrostomy)*, and (3) resection of a portion of the esophagus and anastomosis of a segment of colon to the remaining portion *(esophagoenterostomy)*. The surgical approaches may be open (thoracic, abdominal incision) or laparoscopic.

Minimally invasive esophagectomy (e.g., laparoscopic vagal nerve–sparing surgery) is being done more often. The smaller incisions result in decreased intensive care unit (ICU) and hospital stays with fewer pulmonary complications.

TABLE 46.11 Interprofessional Care

Esophageal Cancer

Diagnostic Assessment

- History and physical assessment
- Endoscopy of esophagus with biopsy
- Endoscopic ultrasonography
- Esophagram (barium swallow)
- Bronchoscopy
- CT, MRI, PET scans

Management

- Surgical therapy
  - Esophagectomy
  - Esophagoenterostomy
  - Esophagogastrostomy
- Endoscopic therapy
  - Dilation
  - Endoscopic mucosal resection
  - Laser therapy
  - Photodynamic therapy
  - Radiofrequency ablation
  - Stent or prosthesis placement
- Radiation therapy
- Chemotherapy

Endoscopic Therapy

Endoscopic therapy includes photodynamic therapy, EMR, and radiofrequency ablation. In photodynamic therapy, the patient receives an IV injection of porfimer sodium (Photofrin), a photosensitizer. Although most tissues absorb porfimer, cancer tissue absorbs it to a greater degree. The HCP directs light towards the cancerous area using a fiber passed through an endoscope. The light reacts with porfimer, starting a reaction that destroys the cancer cells. Patients must avoid direct sunlight for up to 6 weeks afterwards.

EMR is an option for some small, very early-stage cancers. It involves removing cancer tissue using an endoscope. Radiofrequency ablation uses electric currents to kill cancer cells by heating them.

Dilation, stent placement, or both can relieve obstruction. Dilation increases the lumen of the esophagus. It often relieves dysphagia and allows for better nutrition. There are various types of dilators. Placement of stents or expandable stents may help when dilation is no longer effective. Stents allow food and liquid to pass through the stenotic area of the esophagus. Self-expandable metal stents are available with features to prevent stent migration and tumor ingrowth. Stents placed before surgery may help improve the patient's nutrition status.

Endoscopic laser therapy may be used in combination with dilation. Laser therapy can be repeated if obstruction recurs as the tumor grows. Sometimes these procedures are combined with radiation therapy.

Radiation Therapy

Depending on the type and stage of esophageal cancer, the patient may receive chemotherapy with or without radiation therapy. Concurrent therapy is given for palliation of symptoms, especially dysphagia, and to increase survival. Some patients receive radiation therapy before surgery.

Chemotherapy

Many different chemotherapy drugs can be used to treat esophageal cancer. Regimens include carboplatin and paclitaxel, cisplatin and irinotecan, and oxaliplatin, paclitaxel, or cisplatin with either fluorouracil or capecitabine. DCF (docetaxel, cisplatin, fluorouracil) is an option for metastatic disease. New therapy focuses on combining chemotherapy with gene therapy. Chemotherapy is discussed in Chapter 16.

Targeted Therapy

Some esophageal cancers have too much HER-2 protein on their cell surfaces, which helps cancer cells to grow. Trastuzumab

(Herceptin) is a drug that targets the HER-2 protein and kills the cancer cells.

Ramucirumab (Cyramza), an angiogenesis inhibitor, binds to the receptor for *vascular endothelial growth factor* (VEGF). It prevents VEGF from binding to the receptor and signaling the body to make more blood vessels. This can help slow or stop the growth and spread of cancer. Ramucirumab treats advanced cancers that start at the gastroesophageal junction. Targeted therapies are discussed in Chapter 16.

Nutrition Therapy

After esophageal surgery, the patient receives IV fluids. A feeding tube may be placed depending on the type of surgery (e.g., esophagogastrectomy). The patient often has a swallowing study before starting oral fluids. When starting fluids, give water (30 to 60 mL) hourly and gradually progress to small, frequent, bland meals. Keep the patient in an upright position for 2 hours after to prevent regurgitation. With EN, observe the patient for signs of intolerance to the feeding or leakage of the feeding into the mediastinum. Symptoms of leakage include pain, fever, and dyspnea (see Chapter 44).

❖ NURSING MANAGEMENT: ESOPHAGEAL CANCER

◆ Assessment

Ask the patient about a history of GERD, hiatal hernia, achalasia, BE, and tobacco and alcohol use. Assess the patient for progressive dysphagia and *odynophagia* (burning, squeezing pain while swallowing). Are there foods or liquids that cause dysphagia? Assess for pain (substernal, epigastric, or back areas), choking, heartburn, hoarseness, cough, anorexia, weight loss, and regurgitation.

◆ Clinical Problems

Clinical problems for the patient with esophageal cancer include:

- Pain
- Nutritionally compromised
- Impaired GI function
- Difficulty coping

◆ Planning

The overall goals are that the patient with esophageal cancer will (1) have relief of symptoms, including pain and dysphagia, (2) achieve optimal nutrition intake, and (3) have a quality of life appropriate to stage of disease and prognosis.

◆ Implementation

◆ Health Promotion

Counsel the patient with GERD, BE, or hiatal hernia about the importance of regular follow-up evaluation. Health counseling should focus on smoking cessation and reducing risk factors for GERD (Table 46.7). Teach the patient to maintain good oral hygiene and diet habits (e.g., intake of fresh fruits and vegetables). Encourage patients to seek medical attention for any esophageal problems, especially dysphagia.

◆ Acute Care

Preoperative care. The patient and caregiver usually react with shock, disbelief, and depression when given the diagnosis of esophageal cancer. Provide emotional and physical support. Clarify test results and provide information. Maintain a positive attitude with respect to the patient's immediate recovery and long-term survival.

Pay attention to the patient's nutrition needs. Many are poorly nourished because of the inability to ingest adequate amounts of food and fluids. A high-calorie, high-protein diet is recommended. Some patients need a liquid form of this diet. Others may need IV fluid replacement or PN. Teach the patient and caregiver how to keep an intake and output record and assess for signs of fluid and electrolyte imbalance. Some treatment protocols include preoperative radiation and chemotherapy.

Meticulous oral care is essential. Cleanse the mouth thoroughly, including the tongue, gingivae, and teeth or dentures. It may be necessary to use swabs or a gauze pad and to scrub the mouth, including the tongue.

Teaching should include information about chest tubes (with a planned open thoracic approach), IV lines, NG tubes, pain management, EN, turning, coughing, and deep breathing. General preoperative care is discussed in Chapter 17.

Postoperative care. During the immediate postoperative period, the patient usually receives care in the ICU for 1 to 2 days. In addition to usual postoperative complications, dysrhythmias may result from the proximity of the pericardium to the surgical site. Other complications include anastomotic leaks, fistula formation, interstitial pulmonary edema, and acute respiratory distress related to the disruption of the mediastinal lymph nodes.

The patient usually has an NG tube in place for 5 to 7 days. The drainage may be bloody for 8 to 12 hours. The drainage gradually changes to greenish yellow. Key nursing actions include assessing the drainage, maintaining the tube, and providing oral and nasal care. Do not irrigate the NG tube, reposition it, or reinsert it without consulting the HCP.

If the chest cavity is entered, postoperative drainage is achieved with chest tube insertion. Assess the amount and type of drainage. Notify the HCP of excess drainage (e.g., over 400 to 600 mL in 8 hours). Chest surgery and drainage tubes are discussed in Chapter 28.

Implement measures to prevent respiratory complications. Have the patient turn, cough and deep breathe, and use an incentive spirometer every 2 hours. Follow VTE prophylaxis measures. Provide effective pain management. Place the patient in a semi-Fowler's or Fowler's position to prevent reflux and aspiration of gastric secretions. When the patient can drink or eat, maintain the upright position for at least 2 hours after eating to assist with gastric emptying.

◆ Ambulatory Care

Many patients need long-term follow-up care after surgery for esophageal cancer. The patient may need chemotherapy and radiation treatment after surgery. Encourage and assist the patient in maintaining adequate nutrition. A permanent feeding gastrostomy may be needed. The patient usually is afraid and anxious about the cancer diagnosis. Know what the HCP has told the patient about the prognosis and provide appropriate counseling.

Referral to a palliative care or home health nurse may be needed. See Chapter 16 for the care of the cancer patient and Chapter 10 for a discussion of palliative and end-of-life care.

◆ Evaluation

Expected outcomes for the patient with esophageal cancer include:

- Maintain a patent airway
- Have relief of pain
- Be able to swallow comfortably and consume adequate intake
- Have a quality of life appropriate to stage of disease and prognosis

OTHER ESOPHAGEAL DISORDERS

Eosinophilic Esophagitis

Eosinophilic esophagitis (EoE) is characterized by swelling of the esophagus from an infiltration of *eosinophils*. People with EoE often have a personal or family history of other allergic diseases. The most common food triggers are milk, egg, wheat, rye, and beef. Environmental allergens, such as pollens, molds, cat, dog, and dust mite allergens, may be involved.

Patients may have severe heartburn, difficulty swallowing, food impaction in the esophagus, nausea, vomiting, and weight loss. The diagnosis is based on symptoms and biopsy findings of eosinophils infiltrating esophageal tissue obtained from endoscopy.

Allergy skin testing helps to determine the person's allergens. Avoiding the foods to which the person has positive allergy tests is the first treatment. Other common treatments include the use of PPIs (Table 46.10) and corticosteroids. Corticosteroids are used to treat EoE when avoiding allergic triggers does not relieve symptoms.

Corticosteroids may be used orally (prednisone) or as a topical therapy with inhaled corticosteroids (e.g., fluticasone). The patient takes a puff of fluticasone, and rather than inhaling it, swallows the medication. This directly delivers the drug to the esophagus. The most common side effect is a yeast infection of the throat (esophageal candidiasis).

Esophageal Diverticula

Esophageal diverticula are saclike outpouchings of 1 or more layers of the esophagus. They occur in 3 main areas: (1) above the upper esophageal sphincter *(Zenker diverticulum)*, which is the most common location, (2) near the esophageal midpoint (traction diverticulum), and (3) above the LES (epiphrenic diverticulum) (Fig. 46.6). Zenker diverticula occur most often in people older than 60 years.

Typical symptoms include dysphagia, regurgitation, chronic cough, aspiration, and weight loss. Food becomes trapped in outpouches. This causes tasting sour food and smelling a foul odor. Complications include malnutrition, aspiration, and perforation. Endoscopy or barium studies can easily establish a diagnosis.

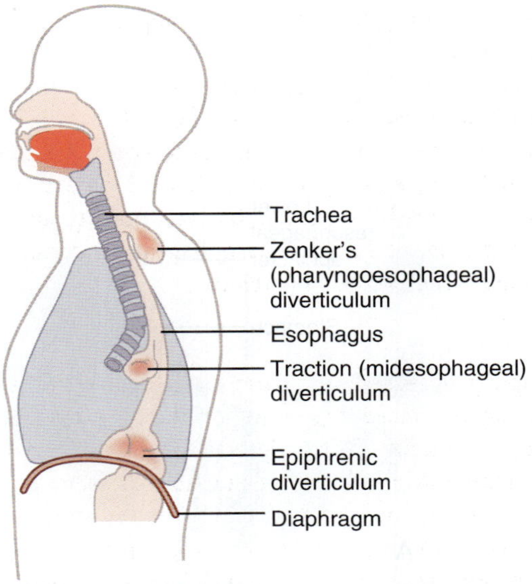

Fig. 46.6 Sites for esophageal diverticula. These hollow outpouchings may occur just above the upper esophageal sphincter (Zenker's), near the midpoint of the esophagus (traction), and just above the LES (epiphrenic).

There is no specific treatment. Some patients find that they can empty the pocket of food that collects by applying pressure at a certain point on the neck. The diet may have to be limited to foods that pass more readily, such as pureed foods. Surgery may be needed if nutrition is disrupted. Endoscopic stapling diverticulotomy or diverticulostomy is associated with decreased complications compared with the open approaches. The most serious surgical complication is esophageal perforation.

Esophageal Strictures

The most common cause of *esophageal strictures* (or narrowing) is chronic GERD. Ingesting strong acids or alkalis, external beam radiation, and surgical anastomosis can also cause strictures. Trauma, such as throat lacerations and gunshot wounds, can lead to strictures from scar formation. Strictures can cause dysphagia and regurgitation, leading to weight loss.

Strictures can be dilated using mechanical *bougies* (dilating instruments) or balloons. Dilation may be done with or without endoscopy, or with fluoroscopy. Surgical excision with anastomosis is sometimes needed. The patient may have a temporary or permanent gastrostomy.

Achalasia

In **achalasia**, peristalsis of the lower two thirds (smooth muscle) of the esophagus is absent. Achalasia is a rare, chronic disorder. The exact cause is unknown. With achalasia, the pressure in the LES increases along with incomplete relaxation. Esophageal obstruction at or near the diaphragm occurs. Food and fluid accumulate in the lower esophagus. The result is dilation of the esophagus above the tapered affected segment of the lower esophagus (Fig. 46.7). There is a selective loss of inhibitory neurons, resulting in unopposed contraction of the LES.

The onset of achalasia is usually slow. Dysphagia is the most common symptom. It occurs with both liquids and solids.

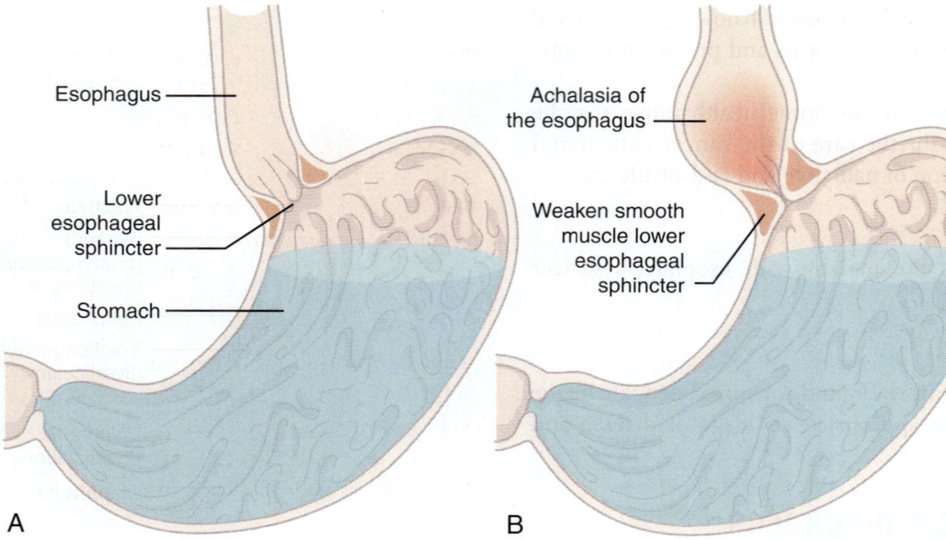

Fig. 46.7 Esophageal achalasia. (A) Healthy esophagus. (B) Achalasia.

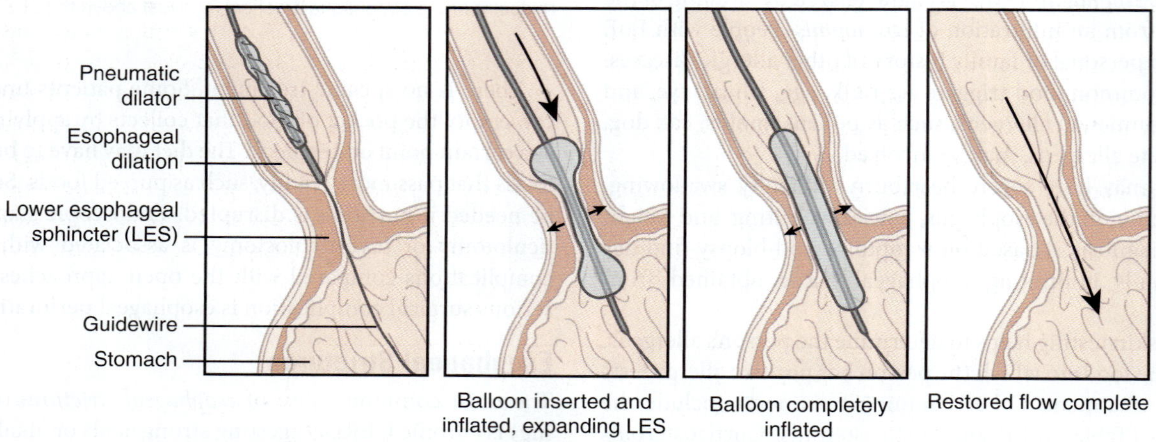

Fig. 46.8 Pneumatic dilation can treat achalasia by maintaining an adequate lumen.

Patients may report a globus sensation and/or substernal chest pain (similar to angina pain) during or right after a meal. About a third have nighttime regurgitation. *Halitosis* (foul-smelling breath) and the inability to eructate (belch) can occur. Patients may report symptoms of GERD and regurgitation of sour-tasting food and liquids, especially when they are lying down. Weight loss is common.

Diagnosis is made with esophagram (barium swallow), manometric evaluation (high-resolution manometry), and/or endoscopic evaluation. Treatment focuses on symptom management. The goals of treatment are to relieve dysphagia and regurgitation, improve esophageal emptying by disrupting the LES, and prevent the development of megaesophagus (enlargement of the lower esophagus).

Endoscopic pneumatic dilation involves dilating the LES muscle using balloons of progressively larger diameter (3.0, 3.5, and 4.0 cm) (Fig. 46.8). It is an outpatient procedure. If this is ineffective, the next option is a Heller myotomy, done laparoscopically. In this procedure, the HCP cuts through the muscles of the LES, allowing food to pass. Because GERD with esophagitis and stricture is a common complication, the patient often has anti-reflux surgery at the same time. The patient typically returns to usual activities 1 to 2 weeks afterward.

Medical therapy is less effective than invasive procedures. The injection of botulinum toxin endoscopically into the LES gives short-term relief of symptoms and improves esophageal emptying. It works by promoting relaxation of the smooth muscle. This treatment is used for older patients for whom surgery and pneumatic dilation may not be appropriate due to other chronic illnesses.

Nitrates (e.g., isosorbide dinitrate) and calcium channel blockers (e.g., nifedipine) relax the LES and may improve dysphagia. They are taken sublingually 10 to 30 minutes before meals. Side effects, drug tolerance, and short duration of action limit their use. Symptomatic treatment consists of eating a semisoft diet, eating slowly, drinking fluid with meals, and sleeping with the head elevated.

Esophageal Varices

Esophageal varices are dilated, tortuous veins occurring in the lower part of the esophagus. They are due to portal hypertension. Esophageal varices are a common complication of liver cirrhosis. They are discussed in Chapter 46. There is a high mortality with variceal bleeding.

STOMACH AND UPPER SMALL INTESTINE PROBLEMS

PEPTIC ULCER DISEASE

Peptic ulcer disease (PUD) is a condition characterized by erosion of the GI mucosa from the digestive action of HCl acid and pepsin. Any part of the GI tract that is in contact with gastric secretions is susceptible to ulcer development. This includes the lower esophagus, stomach, duodenum, and margin of a gastrojejunal anastomosis after surgical procedures. PUD affects about 4.6 million people in the United States each year.[13]

Types

We classify peptic ulcers as acute or chronic (depending on the degree and duration of mucosal involvement) and by location (gastric or duodenal). The *acute ulcer* (Fig. 46.9) causes superficial erosion and minimal inflammation. It is of short duration and resolves quickly when the cause is identified and removed. A chronic ulcer (Fig. 46.10) is of long duration, present continuously for many months or intermittently throughout the person's lifetime. It can erode through the muscular wall with the formation of fibrous tissue. Chronic ulcers are more common than acute ulcers.

Gastric and duodenal ulcers differ in their incidence and presentation (Table 46.12).

Etiology and Pathophysiology

Peptic ulcers develop only in an acid environment. However, an excess of HCl acid is not necessary for ulcer development. Pepsinogen, the precursor of pepsin, changes to pepsin in the presence of HCl acid and a pH of 2 to 3. When food or antacids neutralize the stomach acid level, or drugs block acid secretion, the pH increases to 3.5 or more. At a pH of 3.5 or more, pepsin has little or no proteolytic activity.

The pathophysiology of ulcer development is outlined in Fig. 46.11. The back diffusion of HCl acid into the gastric mucosa results in cellular destruction and inflammation. Histamine is released from the damaged mucosa. This results in vasodilation, increased capillary permeability, and further secretion of acid and pepsin. Fig. 46.12 shows the interrelationship between the mucosal blood flow and disruption of the gastric mucosal barrier. Several factors damage the mucosal barrier.

Helicobacter pylori

The major risk factor for PUD is infection with *Helicobacter pylori.* 80% of gastric and 90% of duodenal ulcers are related to *H. pylori*. In the United States, *H. pylori* affects 20% of persons younger than 30 years and 50% of those older than 60 years. Infection likely occurs during childhood with transmission from family members to the child, possibly through a fecal-oral or oral-oral route. The rate is highest in Hispanics and lowest in East Asians.[14] Most people with *H. pylori* do not develop ulcers. Those infected with *CagA*-positive strains are more likely to have PUD.

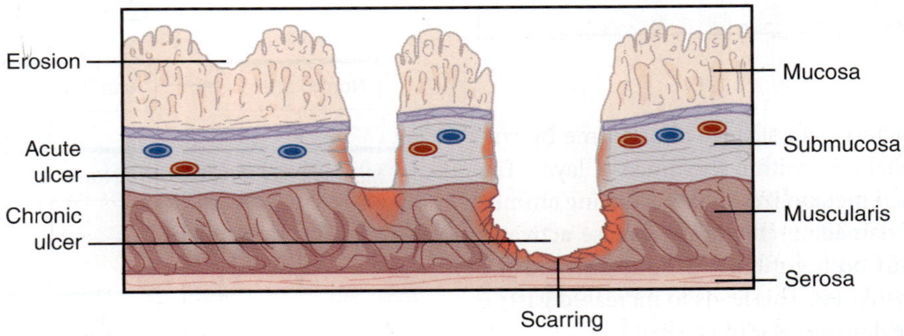

Fig. 46.9 Peptic ulcers, including an erosion, an acute ulcer, and a chronic ulcer. Both the acute ulcer and the chronic ulcer may penetrate the entire wall of the stomach.

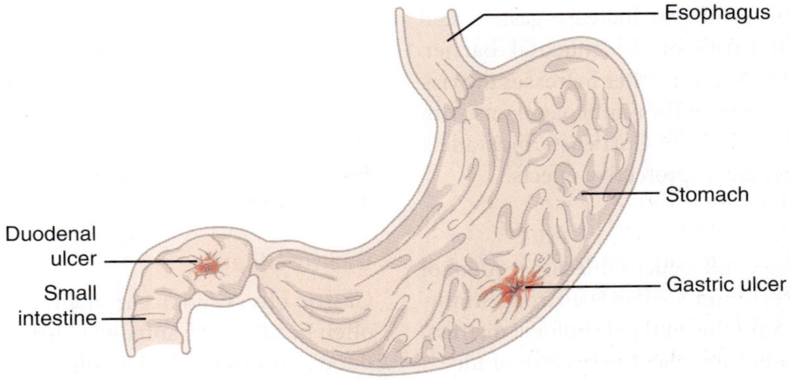

Fig. 46.10 Common sites for gastric and duodenal ulcers.

TABLE 46.12 Comparison of Gastric and Duodenal Ulcers

Gastric Ulcers	Duodenal Ulcers
Lesion	
Superficial, smooth margins. Round, oval, or cone shaped	Penetrating (deformity of duodenal bulb from healing of recurrent ulcers)
Location of Lesion	
Predominantly antrum, also in body and fundus of stomach	First 1–2 cm of duodenum
Gastric Secretion	
Normal to decreased	↑
Incidence	
↑ in women	↑ in men, but increasing in women (especially postmenopausal)
Peak age 50–60 years	Peak age 35–45 years
↑ Cancer risk	No ↑ in cancer risk
H. pylori infection in 80%	*H. pylori* infection in 90%
↑ With incompetent pyloric sphincter and bile reflux	Associated with other diseases (e.g., COPD, pancreatic disease, hyperparathyroidism, ZES, chronic renal failure)
Clinical Manifestations	
Burning or gaseous pressure in epigastrium	Burning, cramping, pressure-like pain across midepigastrium and upper abdomen. Back pain with posterior ulcers
Pain 1–2 hr after meals. If penetrating ulcer, aggravation of discomfort with food	Pain 2–5 hr after meals and midmorning, midafternoon, middle of night. Periodic and episodic. Pain relief with antacids and food
Recurrence Rate	
High	High

In the stomach, the bacteria can survive a long time by colonizing the gastric epithelial cells within the mucosal layer. The bacteria make urease, which metabolizes urea-producing ammonium chloride and other damaging chemicals. Urease activates the immune response with both antibody production and the release of inflammatory cytokines. This leads to increased gastric secretion and causes tissue damage, leading to PUD.

Medication-Induced Injury

NSAID use is responsible for most non–*H. pylori* peptic ulcers. NSAIDs inhibit prostaglandin synthesis, increase gastric acid secretion, and reduce the integrity of the mucosal barrier. NSAID use in the presence of *H. pylori* further increases the risk for PUD. Patients taking corticosteroids or anticoagulants with NSAIDs have a higher risk for PUD.[13] Corticosteroids affect mucosal cell renewal and decrease its protective effects.

Lifestyle Factors

High alcohol intake can cause acute mucosal lesions. Alcohol and smoking stimulate acid secretion. Coffee is a strong stimulant of gastric acid secretion. Smoking and psychologic distress, including stress and depression, can delay the healing of ulcers once they have developed.

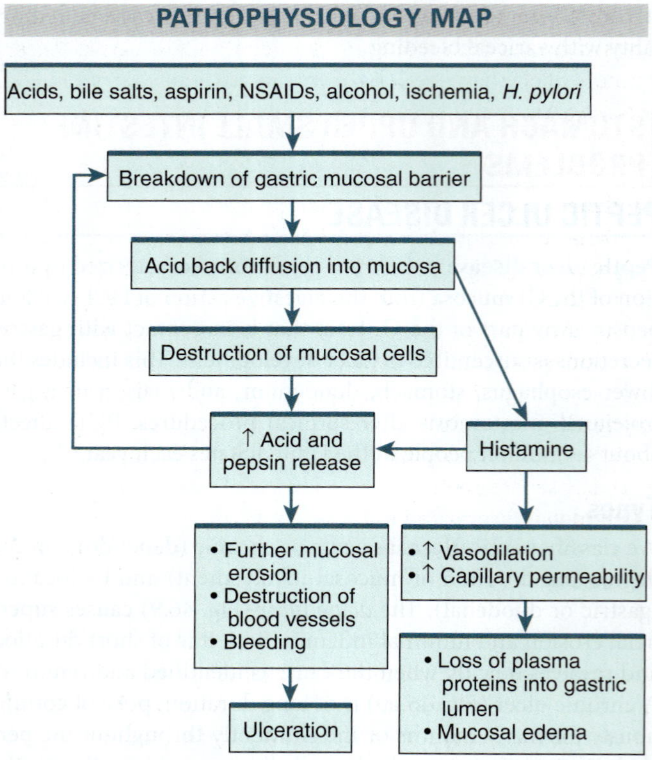

Fig. 46.11 Disruption of gastric mucosa and pathophysiologic consequences of back diffusion of acids.

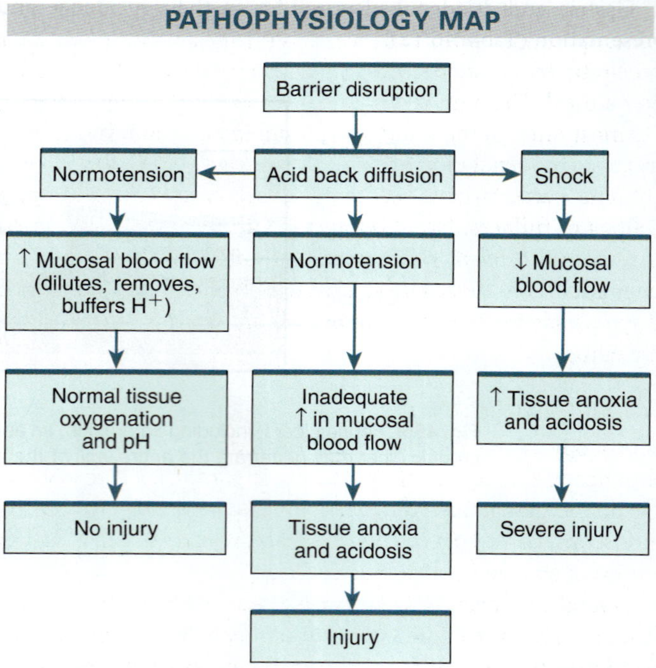

Fig. 46.12 Relationship between mucosal blood flow and disruption of the gastric mucosal barrier.

Gastric Ulcers

Gastric ulcers can occur in any part of the stomach. They most often occur in the antrum. Gastric ulcers are less common than duodenal ulcers. Gastric ulcers are more prevalent in women and those over 50 years of age. Because of the peak incidence of gastric ulcers in older adults, the mortality rate from gastric ulcers is greater than that from duodenal ulcers. Gastric ulcers are more likely than duodenal ulcers to cause an obstruction. *H. pylori,* NSAIDs, and bile reflux are the main risk factors.

Duodenal Ulcers

Duodenal ulcers account for about 80% of all peptic ulcers. Duodenal ulcers occur at any age. The incidence is especially high between 35 and 45 years of age. While there are many factors for duodenal ulcers, *H. pylori* is the most common.

The development of duodenal ulcers is often related to high HCl acid secretion. Those at high risk include people with chronic obstructive pulmonary disease (COPD), cirrhosis, pancreatitis, hyperparathyroidism, chronic kidney disease, and *Zollinger-Ellison syndrome* (ZES). ZES is a rare condition characterized by severe peptic ulceration and HCl acid hypersecretion.

Duodenal ulcers tend to occur continuously for a few weeks or months and then disappear for a time, only to recur some months later.

Clinical Manifestations

In gastric ulcers, the discomfort is generally high in the epigastrium. It occurs about 1 to 2 hours after meals. The pain is described as "burning" or "gaseous." If the ulcer has eroded through the gastric mucosa, food tends to worsen the pain. For some patients, the earliest symptoms are due to a serious complication, such as perforation.

In duodenal ulcers, symptoms occur when gastric acid comes in contact with the ulcers. With meals, food is present to help buffer the acid. Symptoms occur generally 2 to 5 hours after a meal. The pain is described as "burning" or "cramplike." It is most often in the midepigastric region beneath the xiphoid process. Duodenal ulcers can also cause back pain.

Some patients have bloating, nausea, vomiting, and early feelings of fullness. Not all patients with ulcers will have pain or discomfort. *Silent* peptic ulcers are more likely to occur in older adults and those taking NSAIDs. The presence or absence of symptoms is not related to the size of the ulcer or the degree of healing.

Diagnostic Studies

Endoscopy is the most accurate procedure to determine the presence and location of an ulcer.[15] It allows for direct viewing of the gastric and duodenal mucosa (Fig. 46.13). During endoscopy, tissue specimens are taken to determine if *H. pylori* is present and rule out stomach cancer.

Several noninvasive and invasive tests are available to confirm *H. pylori* infection. The gold standard for diagnosing *H. pylori* infection is a biopsy of the antral mucosa with testing for urease (rapid urease testing). Urea is a byproduct of the metabolism of *H. pylori* bacteria. Noninvasive tests include serology, stool, and breath testing. The urea breath and stool antigen tests can identify active infection. Stool tests are not as accurate as the urea breath test. Antibody tests for *H. pylori* can remain positive for years. They are not good for evaluating treatment results.

A barium contrast study may be used to diagnose gastric outlet obstruction or for ulcer detection in those who cannot

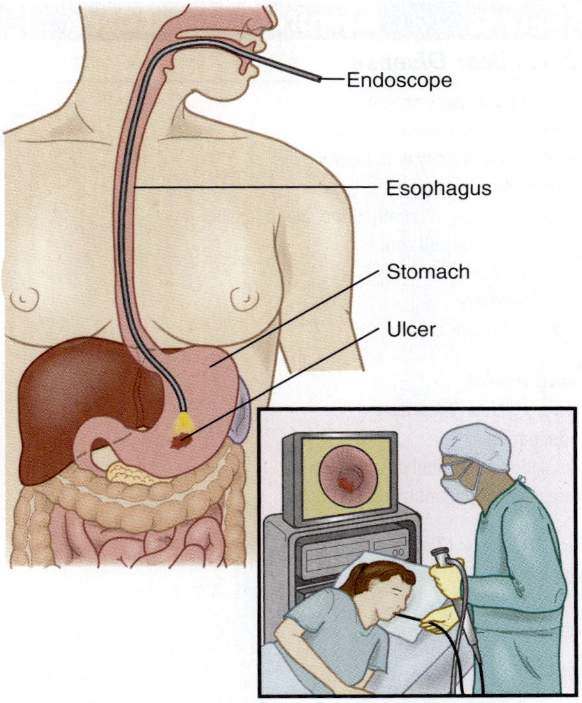

Fig. 46.13 Esophagogastroduodenoscopy (EGD) directly visualizes the mucosal lining of the stomach with a flexible endoscope. Ulcers or tumors can be directly seen, and biopsies obtained.

undergo endoscopy. High fasting serum gastrin levels may show the presence of a possible gastrinoma (ZES). A secretin stimulation test can discern a gastrinoma from other causes of hypergastrinemia.

Laboratory tests, including a CBC, liver enzyme studies, serum amylase, and stool examination, may be done. A CBC may show anemia from ulcer bleeding. Liver enzyme studies help detect any liver problems (e.g., cirrhosis) that may complicate ulcer treatment. Stools are tested for blood. A serum amylase evaluates pancreatic function if we suspect posterior duodenal ulcer penetration of the pancreas.

Interprofessional Management

Conservative Care

Treatment consists of adequate rest, drug therapy, smoking cessation, diet modifications (if needed), and long-term follow-up care (Table 46.13). The aim of treatment is to decrease gastric acidity and enhance mucosal defense mechanisms.

Patients are generally treated in ambulatory care clinics. Pain disappears after 3 to 6 days. Ulcer healing is much slower. Complete healing may take 3 to 9 weeks, depending on ulcer size, treatment, and patient adherence. Endoscopic examination is the most accurate way to monitor ulcer healing. The usual follow-up endoscopic evaluation is done 3 to 6 months after diagnosis and treatment.

Aspirin and nonselective NSAIDs are stopped for 4 to 6 weeks. When aspirin must be continued, co-administration with a PPI, H_2 receptor blocker, or misoprostol may be prescribed. Patients receiving low-dose aspirin (LDA) for CVD and stroke risk who have a history of ulcer disease may need long-term

TABLE 46.13 Interprofessional Care

Peptic Ulcer Disease

Diagnostic Assessment

- History and physical assessment
- Upper GI endoscopy with biopsy
- Endoscopic ultrasound
- *H. pylori* testing of breath, urine, blood, tissue
- Complete blood cell count
- Liver enzymes
- Serum amylase
- Stool testing for blood

Management

Conservative Therapy

- Adequate rest
- Smoking and alcohol cessation
- Stress management (see Chapter 7)

Drug Therapy (Tables 46.10 and 46.14)

- Antibiotics for *H. pylori*
- PPIs
- Adjunctive therapy
  - H_2-receptor blockers
  - Cytoprotective drugs
  - Antacids

Acute Exacerbation Without Complications

- NPO
- NG suction
- Adequate rest
- IV fluid replacement

Drug Therapy (Tables 46.10 and 46.14)

- Antibiotics for *H. pylori*
- PPIs
- Adjunctive therapy
  - H_2 receptor blockers
  - Cytoprotective drugs
  - Antacids
  - Sedatives

Acute Exacerbation With Complications (Bleeding, Perforation, Obstruction)

- NPO
- NG suction
- IV PPI
- Bed rest
- IV fluid replacement
- Blood transfusions
- Stomach lavage (possible)

Surgical Therapy

- Gastric outlet obstruction: Pyloroplasty and vagotomy
- Perforation: Simple closure with omentum graft
- Ulcer removal or reduction
  - Billroth I and II
  - Vagotomy and pyloroplasty

treatment with a PPI. Enteric-coated aspirin decreases localized irritation but does not reduce the overall risk for GI bleeding.

Smoking has an irritating effect on the mucosa and delays mucosal healing. The patient should either stop or severely reduce smoking. Adequate rest, both physical and emotional, is important for ulcer healing and may require some changes in the patient's daily routine. Avoiding or restricting alcohol use will enhance healing.

Drug Therapy

Medications are a key part of therapy (Table 46.10). Drug therapy focuses on reducing gastric acid secretion and, if needed, eliminating *H. pylori* infection. Patients with *H. pylori* infection need treatment with antibiotics and a PPI. After the ulcer has healed, many patients can stop PPI therapy. Some may need to continue low-dose maintenance therapy.

Because ulcers often recur, interrupting or stopping therapy can have harmful results. Strict adherence to the prescribed drug regimen is important. Encourage the patient to adhere to therapy and continue with follow-up care as prescribed. Teach the patient and caregiver about each drug prescribed, why it is ordered, and the expected benefits. Review what to do if pain and discomfort recur or there is blood in vomitus or stools.

Antibiotic therapy. Eradicating *H. pylori* is the most important part of treating PUD in patients positive for *H. pylori.* Antibiotic therapy is prescribed concurrently with a PPI for 14 days (Table 46.14). If the patient has a penicillin allergy, metronidazole is used instead of amoxicillin in the triple-drug regimen. Bismuth can be given alone or as part of a combination capsule containing bismuth, tetracycline, and metronidazole.

Because of the existence of antibiotic-resistant organisms, a growing number of patients do not have *H. pylori* eradicated with a single round of therapy. Talicia is a rifabutin-based treatment for those with resistant H. pylori infection. Each capsule contains omeprazole, amoxicillin, and rifabutin.

Proton pump inhibitors. PPIs are more effective than H_2 receptor blockers in reducing gastric acid secretion and promoting ulcer healing. PPIs are used in combination with antibiotics to treat ulcers caused by *H. pylori*.

Cytoprotective drug therapy. Sucralfate is used for short-term ulcer treatment. It provides mucosal protection for the esophagus, stomach, and duodenum. Sucralfate does not have acid-neutralizing capabilities. Since it is most effective at a low pH, give it at least 60 minutes before or after an antacid. Adverse side effects are minimal. It binds with cimetidine, digoxin, warfarin, phenytoin, and tetracycline, reducing their bioavailability.

Adjunct drugs. H_2 receptor blockers and antacids may be used as adjunct therapy to promote ulcer healing. Antacids increase gastric pH by neutralizing HCl acid. As a result, they reduce the acid content of chyme reaching the duodenum. Some antacids (e.g., aluminum hydroxide) can bind to bile salts, thus decreasing the damaging effects of bile on the gastric mucosa.

Misoprostol is a synthetic prostaglandin analog prescribed to prevent gastric ulcers caused by NSAIDs and LDA. It has protective, and some antisecretory, effects on gastric mucosa. People who need chronic NSAID therapy, such as those with osteoarthritis, may benefit from its use. However, it can cause diarrhea and abdominal pain. It is teratogenic and must be used with caution in women of childbearing age.

Some patients may receive tricyclic antidepressants (e.g., imipramine, doxepin). They may contribute to overall pain

TABLE 46.14 **Drug Therapy**

H. pylori *Infection*

Drug Class	Drug	Triple Therapy	Bismuth Quadruple Therapy	Non-Bismuth Quadruple Therapy
Acid suppression	PPI	20–40 mg, 2 times daily	20–40 mg, 2 times daily	20–40 mg, 2 times daily
Standard antibiotics	Amoxicillin	1 g, 2 times daily		1 g, 2 times daily
	Bismuth compound		2 tablets, 2 times daily	
	Clarithromycin	500 mg, 2 times daily		500 mg, 2 times daily
	Metronidazole		500 mg, 4 times daily	500 mg, 3 times daily
	Tetracycline		500 mg, 4 times daily	

relief through their effects on afferent pain fiber transmission. Their anticholinergic properties result in reduced acid secretion. Anticholinergic drugs are sometimes used for PUD treatment.

Nutrition Therapy

There is no specific diet used to treat PUD. Patients should eat and drink foods and fluids that do not cause any distressing symptoms. Foods that may cause gastric irritation include pepper, carbonated beverages, broth (meat extract), and hot, spicy foods. Caffeine-containing beverages and foods can increase symptoms in some patients. Teach the patient to avoid alcohol use because it can delay healing.

Surgical Therapy

With the use of drug therapy and endoscopic therapy to treat PUD, surgery is less common. Surgery is an option for those with complications that are unresponsive to medical management or concerns about stomach cancer. Gastric surgeries are described later in this chapter.

Complications

The 3 major complications of chronic PUD are GI bleeding, perforation, and gastric outlet obstruction.[15] These complications are emergency situations. The patient may need surgical intervention.

GI Bleeding

GI bleeding is the most common complication of PUD. Duodenal ulcers cause more bleeding episodes than gastric ulcers.

Perforation

Perforation is the most lethal complication of PUD. Perforation risk is highest with large penetrating duodenal ulcers (Fig. 46.14). However, the mortality rate from a perforated gastric ulcer is higher. The patient with gastric ulcers is older and often has concurrent medical problems, which accounts for the higher mortality rate.

With perforation, the ulcer penetrates the serosal surface with spillage of either gastric or duodenal contents into the peritoneal cavity. The contents entering the peritoneal cavity may contain air, saliva, food particles, HCl acid, pepsin, bacteria, bile, and pancreatic fluid and enzymes.

The manifestations of perforation are sudden and dramatic in onset. During the initial phase (up to 2 hours after perforation), the patient has sudden, severe upper abdominal pain that quickly spreads throughout the abdomen. The pain radiates

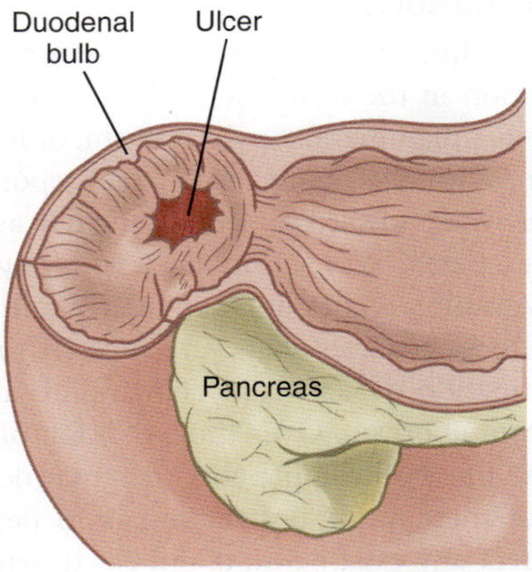

Fig. 46.14 Duodenal ulcer of the posterior wall penetrating the head of the pancreas, resulting in walled-off perforation.

to the back and shoulders. Food or antacids do not relieve the pain. The abdomen appears rigid and board-like. Bowel sounds are usually absent. Nausea and vomiting may occur. Pulse is increased and weak.

Without treatment, bacterial peritonitis may occur within 6 to 12 hours. The intensity of peritonitis is proportional to the amount and duration of the spillage through the perforation. It is hard to determine from symptoms alone whether a gastric or duodenal ulcer has perforated, because the manifestations of peritonitis are the same (see Chapter 47).

The immediate focus of managing a patient with a perforation is to stop the spillage of gastric or duodenal contents into the peritoneal cavity and restore blood volume. An NG tube can provide continuous aspiration and gastric decompression to stop spillage through the perforation. For duodenal aspiration, the tube is placed as near to the perforation site as possible to promote decompression.

Circulating blood volume is replaced with lactated Ringer's and albumin solutions. These solutions substitute for the fluids lost from the vascular and interstitial space as peritonitis develops. Packed RBCs may be needed. A central venous pressure line and an indwelling urinary catheter may be inserted and monitored hourly. The patient with a history of heart disease needs ECG monitoring or a pulmonary artery catheter for assessment of left ventricular function. Broad-spectrum antibiotic therapy is started immediately to treat bacterial peritonitis.

Small perforations may spontaneously seal themselves and symptoms cease. Spontaneous sealing occurs because of fibrin production in response to the perforation. This can lead to fibrinous fusion of the duodenum or gastric curvature to adjacent tissue (mainly the liver) and strictures that can obstruct the flow of intestinal contents and the passage of stool.

Larger perforations need immediate surgical closure. Whether the patient has an open or laparoscopic repair depends on the ulcer's location and HCP preference. The procedure with the least risk to the patient is simple oversewing of the perforation and reinforcement of the area with a graft of omentum. Excess gastric contents are suctioned from the peritoneal cavity during the surgical procedure.

Gastric Outlet Obstruction

Both acute and chronic PUD can cause gastric outlet obstruction. Obstruction in the distal stomach and duodenum is the result of edema, inflammation, pylorospasm, or fibrous scar tissue formation. With obstruction the patient reports discomfort or pain that is worse toward the end of the day as the stomach fills and dilates. Belching or self-induced vomiting may provide some relief. Vomiting is common and often projectile. Vomitus may contain food particles that were ingested hours or days before. Constipation occurs from dehydration and decreased diet intake from anorexia. Over time, dilation of the stomach and visible swelling in the upper abdomen may occur.

The aim of therapy for obstruction is to decompress the stomach, correct any existing fluid and electrolyte imbalances, and improve the patient's general health. An NG tube can provide continuous decompression. This allows the ulcer to begin healing and the inflammation and edema to subside. Pain relief results from decompression.

IV fluids and electrolytes are replaced according to the degree of dehydration, vomiting, and electrolyte imbalance shown by laboratory studies. A PPI or H_2 receptor blocker is used if the obstruction is due to an active ulcer. Balloon dilation can open a pyloric obstruction. Surgery may be needed to remove scar tissue.

TABLE 46.15 NURSING ASSESSMENT

Peptic Ulcer Disease

Subjective Data

Important Health Information

Health history: Chronic kidney disease, pancreatic disease, COPD, serious illness or trauma, hyperparathyroidism, cirrhosis, ZES

Medications: Aspirin, corticosteroids, NSAIDs

Surgery or other treatments: Complicated or prolonged surgery

Functional Health Patterns

Health perception–health management: Chronic alcohol use, smoking, caffeine use. Family history of PUD

Nutritional-metabolic: Weight loss, anorexia, nausea and vomiting, hematemesis, dyspepsia, heartburn, belching

Elimination: Black, tarry stools

Cognitive-perceptual:

- *Duodenal ulcers:* Burning, midepigastric or back pain occurring 2–5 hr after meals and relieved by food; nighttime pain common
- *Gastric ulcers:* High epigastric pain occurring 1–2 hr after meals. Food may precipitate or worsen pain.

Coping–stress tolerance: Acute or chronic stress

Objective Data

General

Anxiety, irritability

Gastrointestinal

Epigastric tenderness

Possible Diagnostic Findings

Anemia. Guaiac-positive stools. Positive blood, urine, breath, or stool tests for *H. pylori*. Abnormal upper GI endoscopic and barium studies

NURSING MANAGEMENT: PEPTIC ULCER DISEASE

Assessment

Subjective and objective data to obtain from a patient with PUD are outlined in Table 46.15.

Clinical Problems

Clinical problems for the patient with PUD may include:

- Pain
- Impaired GI function

Additional information on clinical problems and interventions for the patient with PUD are in eNursing Care Plan 46.2 available on the website for this chapter.

Planning

The overall goals are that the patient with PUD will (1) adhere to the therapeutic regimen, (2) achieve pain relief, (3) be free from complications, (4) have complete healing of the peptic ulcer, and (5) make appropriate lifestyle changes to prevent recurrence.

Nursing Implementation

Health Promotion

You play a key role in identifying those at risk for PUD. Early detection and treatment of ulcers are important in reducing morbidity. Patients who are taking ulcerogenic drugs (e.g., NSAIDs, LDA) are at risk for PUD. Encourage patients to take these drugs with food. Teach patients to report symptoms related to gastric irritation, including epigastric pain, to their HCP.

Acute Care

During an acute exacerbation, the patient often reports increased pain, nausea, and vomiting. Some may have bleeding. Many patients try to cope with the symptoms at home before seeking medical care.

During the acute phase, the patient may be NPO for a few days, have an NG tube connected to intermittent suction, and receive IV fluid replacement. Explain to the patient and caregiver the reasons for these therapies so they understand that the advantages far outweigh any temporary discomfort. Regular mouth care relieves the dry mouth. Cleaning and lubricating the nares decrease soreness. Analysis of gastric contents may include pH testing and analysis for blood, bile, or other substances. When the stomach is empty of gastric secretions, pain decreases, and ulcer healing begins.

The volume of fluid lost, the patient's signs and symptoms, and laboratory test results (hemoglobin, hematocrit, electrolytes) determine the type and amount of IV fluids given. Take vital signs initially and then at least hourly to detect and treat shock. Give IV fluids as ordered. Record intake and output.

Physical and emotional rest is helpful to ulcer healing. The environment should be quiet and restful. Give pain medications as ordered. A mild sedative may help when the patient is anxious and apprehensive. Use good judgment before sedating a person who is becoming increasingly restless because the drug could mask the signs of shock from GI bleeding.

GI bleeding. Changes in vital signs and an increase in the amount and redness of aspirate often signal massive upper GI bleeding. With bleeding, the patient's pain often decreases because the blood helps neutralize the acidic gastric contents. Maintain the patency of the NG tube so that blood clots do not obstruct the tube. If the tube becomes blocked, the patient can develop abdominal distention. Use interventions similar to those described for upper GI bleeding.

Perforation. If the patient with an ulcer develops manifestations of a perforation, notify the HCP immediately. Take vital signs promptly and record them every 15 to 30 minutes. Temporarily stop all oral or NG drugs and feedings. If perforation exists, anything taken orally can add to the spillage into the peritoneal cavity and increase discomfort. Give IV fluid as ordered to replace the depleted plasma volume. Giving pain medications provides comfort.

Those with confirmed perforation will start on antibiotic therapy. If the perforation does not seal spontaneously, surgical closure is needed. Since surgery is done as soon as possible, there may not be time to prepare the patient and family.

Gastric outlet obstruction. Gastric outlet obstruction can happen at any time. It is most likely to occur in the patient whose ulcer is close to the pylorus. The onset of symptoms is usually gradual. Constant NG aspiration of stomach contents can help relieve symptoms. This allows edema and inflammation to subside and permits normal flow of gastric contents through the pylorus.

Regularly irrigate the NG tube with a normal saline solution per agency policy to assist proper functioning. It may be helpful to reposition the patient from side to side so that the tube tip is not constantly lying against the mucosal surface. Maintain accurate intake and output records, especially of the gastric aspirate.

To check for ongoing obstruction, clamp the NG tube intermittently and measure the gastric residual volume. The frequency and amount of time the tube is clamped are related to the amount of aspirate obtained and the patient's comfort level. A common method is to clamp the tube overnight (usually 8 to 12 hours) and measure the gastric residual volume in the morning. When the aspirate falls below 200 mL, it is within a normal range and the patient can begin oral intake of clear liquids. Oral fluids begin at 30 mL/hr and then gradually increase in amount. As the amount of gastric residual decreases, solid foods are added, and the tube removed.

If the patient has resumed oral feedings and you note symptoms of obstruction, promptly inform the HCP. Generally, all that is needed to treat the problem is to resume gastric aspiration until the edema and inflammation resulting from the acute episode resolve. IV fluids with electrolyte replacement keep the patient hydrated during this period. If conservative treatment is not successful, surgery is done after the acute phase has passed.

◆ Ambulatory Care

Patients with PUD have specific needs to prevent recurrence and complications. Teaching should cover aspects of the disease process, drugs, lifestyle changes (alcohol use, smoking), and regular follow-up care. Table 46.16 provides a patient and caregiver teaching guide for PUD. Work with the dietitian to plan ways to incorporate diet modifications.

Teach the patient about prescribed drugs, including their actions, side effects, and dangers if omitted for any reason. Make sure the patient knows not to take OTC drugs (e.g., NSAIDs, LDA) unless approved by the HCP. Some H_2 receptor blockers and PPIs are available without a prescription. Tell the patient to check with the HCP before switching from a prescription to an OTC preparation to avoid side effects and incorrect dosing.

Obtain information about the patient's psychosocial status. The patient may be reluctant to talk about personal stress, their usual ways of coping, smoking habits, or the use of alcohol. Provide information about the negative effects of alcohol and cigarettes on PUD and ulcer healing. Changes such as smoking cessation and alcohol abstinence are hard for many people. The patient may do better in reducing, rather than eliminating, use of these substances. However, the goal is total cessation.

PUD is a chronic, recurring disorder. Teach patients with chronic PUD about potential complications and what to do until they see the HCP. Emphasize the need for long-term follow-up care. Encourage the patient to seek immediate intervention if symptoms return. Some patients have repeated exacerbations. Patients quickly

TABLE 46.16 PATIENT & CAREGIVER TEACHING

Peptic Ulcer Disease

Include the following instructions when teaching the patient and caregiver about management of PUD:

1. Avoid foods that cause epigastric distress, such as acidic foods.
2. Avoid cigarettes. Smoking promoting ulcer development and delays ulcer healing.
3. Reduce or stop alcohol use.
4. Avoid OTC drugs unless approved by the HCP. Many preparations contain ingredients, such as aspirin, which should not be taken unless approved by the HCP. Check with the HCP about the use of NSAIDs.
5. Do not interchange brands of PPIs, antacids, or H_2 receptor blockers that you can buy OTC without checking with the HCP. This can lead to harmful side effects.
6. Follow prescribed drug therapy to prevent a relapse. This includes both antisecretory and antibiotic drugs.
7. Report any of the following:
   - Increased nausea or vomiting
   - Increased epigastric pain
   - Bloody emesis or tarry stools
8. Stress can be related to PUD. Learn and use stress management strategies (see Chapter 7).
9. Share concerns about lifestyle changes and living with a chronic illness.

learn that they often have no discomfort when they omit prescribed drugs, smoke, or drink alcohol. Consequently, they make no or few changes in their lifestyle. After an acute exacerbation, the patient is likely to be more amenable to following the plan of care and open to suggestions for changes in lifestyle.

◆ Evaluation

Expected outcomes for the patient with PUD include:

- Have pain controlled without the use of analgesics
- Commit to self-care and management of the disease
- Be free from complications

Gerontologic Considerations: Peptic Ulcer Disease

Morbidity and mortality rates in older adults with PUD are higher because of concurrent health problems and a decreased ability to withstand hypovolemia. Monitor older adults who use NSAIDs for PUD. In older patients, pain may not be the first symptom of an ulcer. For some patients the first sign is frank gastric bleeding or a decrease in hematocrit. The treatment and management of PUD in older adults are similar to those in younger adults. The emphasis is on preventing gastritis and PUD.

STOMACH CANCER

Stomach (gastric) cancer is an adenocarcinoma of the stomach wall (Fig. 46.15). It accounts for more than 27,600 new cancer cases and 11,010 deaths annually.[16] Asian Americans, Pacific Islanders, Blacks, and Hispanics have the highest rates of stomach cancer. In the United States, the incidence is higher in men by a 2:1 ratio. Stomach cancer mostly affects older people. The average age at the time of diagnosis is 68.[5]

At the time of diagnosis, only 10% to 20% of patients have disease confined to the stomach. The 5-year survival rate in this group is 71%. However, more than 50% have advanced metastatic disease. The overall 5-year survival rate of all people with stomach cancer is about 32%.[17]

Etiology and Pathophysiology

We do not know the exact cause of stomach cancer. It likely begins with a nonspecific mucosal injury because of infection

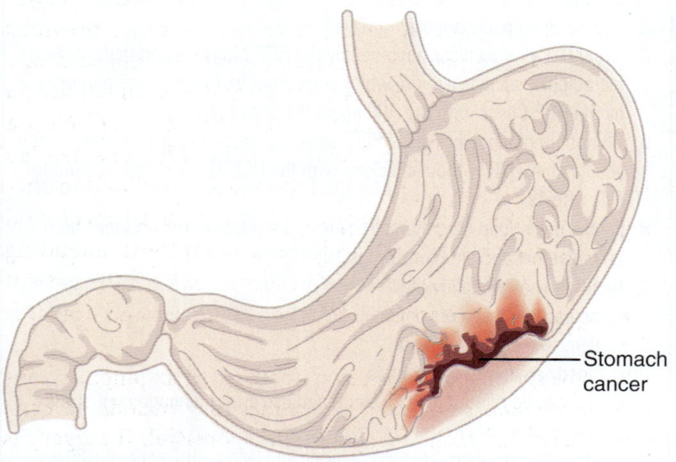

Fig. 46.15 Stomach cancer often begins in cells that line the stomach.

(*H. pylori*), autoimmune-related inflammation, repeated exposure to irritants such as bile or NSAIDs, or tobacco use. It is possible that *H. pylori* and resulting cell changes can induce a sequence of transitions from dysplasia to cancer.

Lifestyle factors influence stomach cancer risk. Increased risk is related to smoking, obesity, and diets high in smoked foods, salted fish and meat, and pickled vegetables. Whole grains and fresh fruits and vegetables reduce stomach cancer risk.

Other risk factors include atrophic gastritis, pernicious anemia, adenomatous polyps, hyperplastic polyps, and *achlorhydria* (absent or low production of gastric HCl). People with lymphoma of the stomach (mucosa-associated lymphoid tissue [MALT]) have a higher risk. Although first-degree relatives of patients with stomach cancer are at increased risk, only about 10% of stomach cancers have an inherited component. 1% stomach cancers are hereditary diffuse gastric cancer (HDGC).[18]

Stomach cancer spreads by direct extension. It typically infiltrates rapidly to the surrounding tissue and liver. Seeding of tumor cells into the peritoneal cavity occurs late in the course of the disease.

Clinical Manifestations

Stomach cancers often spread to adjacent organs before any distressing symptoms occur. Manifestations include unexplained weight loss, indigestion, and abdominal discomfort or pain. Anemia is common. It is caused by chronic blood loss as the lesion erodes through the mucosa or from pernicious anemia (caused by loss of intrinsic factor). The person appears pale and weak. They may report fatigue, weakness, dizziness, and, in extreme cases, shortness of breath. The stool may be positive for occult blood. The patient may report *early satiety*, or a sense of being full sooner than usual. Hard and enlarged supraclavicular lymph nodes suggest metastasis via the thoracic duct. The presence of ascites is a poor prognostic sign.

Diagnostic Studies

The diagnostic studies for stomach cancer are outlined in Table 46.17. Upper GI endoscopy is the best diagnostic tool. The stomach can be distended with air during the procedure, stretching the mucosal folds. Tissue biopsy and histologic examination are important in diagnosing stomach cancer.

Endoscopic ultrasound, CT, MRI, and PET scanning can be used to stage the disease. Laparoscopy is done to determine peritoneal spread.

Blood studies detect anemia and determine its severity. Increased liver enzymes and serum amylase levels may mean liver and pancreas involvement. Stool examination provides evidence of occult or gross bleeding. The presence of tumor markers can help diagnose cancer.

Interprofessional Management

Surgical Therapy

The treatment of choice for stomach cancer is surgical removal of the tumor. The aim is to remove as much of the stomach as needed to remove the tumor and a margin of normal tissue. The location and extent of the lesion, the patient's physical

TABLE 46.17 Interprofessional Care

Stomach Cancer

Diagnostic Assessment	Management

• History and physical assessment
• Endoscopy and biopsy
• CT, MRI, PET scans
• Upper GI barium study
• Exfoliative cytologic study
• Endoscopic ultrasonography
• CBC
• Liver enzymes
• Urinalysis
• Stool examination
• Serum amylase
• Tumor markers
  • α-Fetoprotein
  • Carbohydrate antigen (CA)-19-9, CA-125, CA 72-4
  • Carcinoembryonic antigen (CEA)
	• Surgical therapy
	  • Subtotal gastrectomy (Billroth I or II procedure)
	  • Total gastrectomy with esophagojejunostomy
	• Chemotherapy
	• Radiation therapy
	• Targeted therapy

condition, and the HCP's preference determine the surgery done (e.g., open versus laparoscopic).

Patients with lesions in the antrum or pyloric region generally have either a Billroth I or II procedure (Fig. 46.16). When the lesion is in the fundus, a total gastrectomy with esophagojejunostomy is done (Fig. 46.17). When metastasis has occurred to adjacent organs, such as the spleen, ovaries, or bowel, the surgical procedure is extended as needed. If the tumor extends into the transverse colon, partial colon resection is done.

Preoperative management focuses on correcting nutrition deficits and treating anemia. Packed RBCs transfusions correct the anemia. If gastric outlet obstruction occurs, gastric decompression may be needed before surgery.

Chemotherapy and Radiation Therapy

Many chemotherapy drugs can be used to treat stomach cancer. These include fluorouracil, capecitabine, carboplatin, cisplatin, docetaxel, epirubicin, irinotecan, oxaliplatin, and paclitaxel. Combination therapies offer better outcomes. Examples include ECF (epirubicin, cisplatin, fluorouracil) and docetaxel, irinotecan, oxaliplatin, or cisplatin with fluorouracil or capecitabine.[19] Intraperitoneal chemotherapy may be used to treat metastatic disease. Chemotherapy is discussed in Chapter 16.

Combined radiation therapy and chemotherapy can reduce recurrence or be given as a palliative measure to decrease tumor mass and provide temporary relief of obstruction.

Targeted Therapy

Trastuzumab (Herceptin) and ramucirumab (Cyramza) are targeted therapies used to treat stomach cancer. About 20% of patients have too much HER-2 on the surface of the cancer cells. Trastuzumab targets the HER-2 protein and kills the cancer cells. Ramucirumab binds to the receptor for VEGF and prevents VEGF from binding to the receptor. This prevents the growth and spread of cancer.

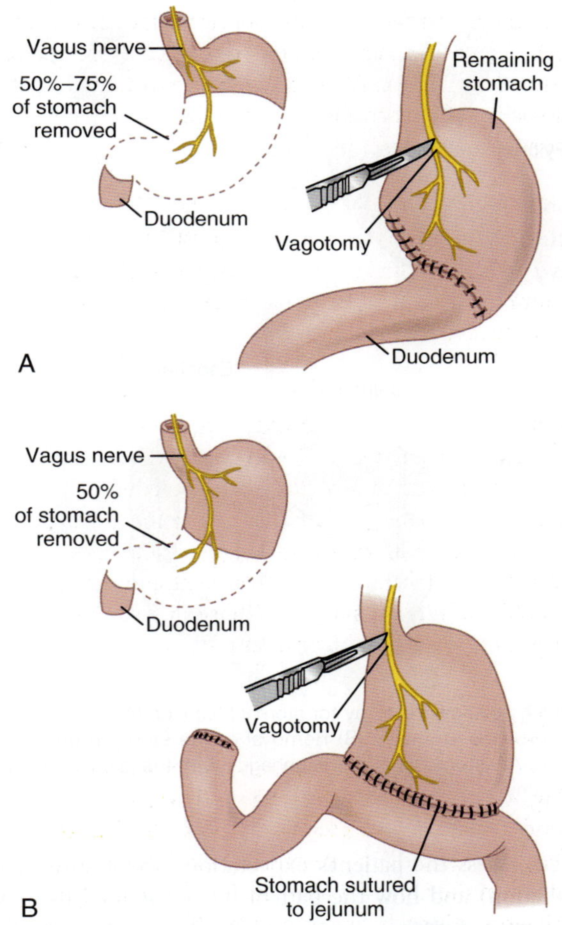

Fig. 46.16 (A) Billroth I procedure (subtotal gastric resection with gastroduodenostomy anastomosis). (B) Billroth II procedure (subtotal gastric resection with gastrojejunostomy anastomosis).

❖ NURSING MANAGEMENT: STOMACH CANCER

◆ Assessment

The assessment of a person with stomach cancer is similar to that for PUD (Table 46.15). Obtain a nutrition assessment, psychosocial history, and physical assessment. Assess how the patient and caregiver are coping with the cancer diagnosis.

The nutrition assessment includes information about appetite and changes in eating patterns over the previous 6 months. Determine the patient's normal weight and any recent weight changes. Unexplained weight loss and anorexia are common. Evaluate the patient's nutrition status. Cachexia may be present if oral intake has been reduced for an extended period. A malnourished patient does not respond well to chemotherapy or radiation therapy and is a poor surgical risk. The patient may have vague abdominal symptoms, including dyspepsia and intestinal gas discomfort or pain. If the patient reports pain, explore where and when it occurs and how it is relieved.

Determine the patient's usual method of coping. A cancer diagnosis and a treatment plan that may include surgery, chemotherapy, or radiation treatment is stressful. If surgery is

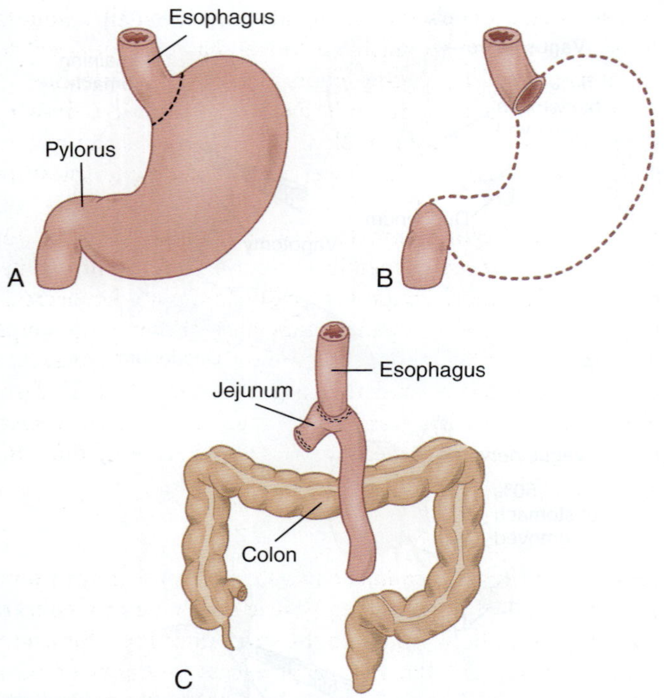

Fig. 46.17 Total gastrectomy for stomach cancer. (A) Normal anatomic structure of the stomach. (B) Removal of the stomach (total gastrectomy). (C) Anastomosis of the esophagus with the jejunum (esophagojejunostomy).

planned, assess the patient's expectations about surgery (cure or palliation) and how the patient has responded to previous surgical procedures.

◆ Clinical Problems

Clinical problems for the patient with stomach cancer include:

- Nutritionally compromised
- Pain
- Impaired GI function
- Difficulty coping

◆ Planning

The overall goals are that the patient with stomach cancer will (1) have minimal discomfort, (2) achieve optimal nutrition status, and (3) maintain a degree of spiritual and psychologic well-being appropriate to the disease stage.

◆ Implementation

◆ Health Promotion

Your role in the early detection of stomach cancer focuses on identifying patients at risk because of problems such as *H. pylori* infection, pernicious anemia, and achlorhydria. Be aware of symptoms of stomach cancer and pertinent findings on physical assessment. Symptoms often occur late and mimic other conditions, such as PUD. Encourage patients with a positive family history of stomach cancer to undergo diagnostic evaluation if anemia, PUD, or vague epigastric distress are present. Recognize the possibility of stomach cancer in a patient who was treated for PUD and did not achieve relief.

◆ Acute Care

When diagnostic tests confirm cancer, the patient and family generally react with shock, disbelief, and depression. Provide emotional and physical support, provide information, and clarify test results. Maintain a positive attitude with respect to the patient's immediate recovery and long-term survival.

Because of changes in appetite and early satiety, the patient may be malnourished. Surgery may be delayed until the patient is more physically able to withstand it. A positive nutrition state enhances wound healing and the ability to deal with infection and other possible postoperative complications. The patient may better tolerate several small meals a day than 3 regular meals. It may be challenging to persuade the patient to eat when they have no appetite and are depressed. Getting the caregiver to help with meals and encourage intake may be helpful. Diet may be supplemented by commercial liquid supplements and vitamins. If the patient is unable to ingest oral feedings, the HCP may prescribe EN or PN (see Chapter 44).

If needed, packed RBCs and fluid volume restoration may be given during the preoperative period. Preoperative teaching and the postoperative care of the patient having stomach cancer surgery is described in the gastric surgery section.

Radiation therapy or chemotherapy is used as an adjuvant to surgery or for palliation. Your role is to provide detailed instructions, reassure the patient, and ensure completion of the designated number of treatments. Assess the patient's knowledge of these therapies. Teach the patient about skin care, need for nutrition and fluid intake, and the use of antiemetic drugs. Specific care of the patient receiving chemotherapy and radiation therapy is discussed in Chapter 16.

◆ Ambulatory Care

When chemotherapy or radiation treatment is continuing after discharge, a referral to home health care may be helpful. The home health nurse can help with recovery and provide support to the patient and caregiver. Provide the patient with a list of available community agencies (e.g., American Cancer Society). Encourage the patient to adhere to the prescribed therapies, keep appointments for chemotherapy or radiation treatments, and keep the HCP informed of changes in physical condition. Recurrence of cancer is common. Patients need regular follow-up examinations and imaging assessments. Long-term management of the cancer patient is discussed in Chapter 16.

◆ Evaluation

Expected outcomes for the patient with stomach cancer include:

- Have minimal discomfort, pain, or nausea
- Achieve optimal nutrition status
- Maintain a degree of psychologic well-being appropriate to the disease stage

GASTROINTESTINAL STROMAL TUMORS

Gastrointestinal stromal tumors (GISTs) are a rare cancer that originates in cells in the wall of the GI tract. These cells, known as *interstitial cells of Cajal,* help control the movement of food and liquid through the stomach and intestines. About 60% of GISTs are in the stomach; 30% are in the small intestine. The rest are in the esophagus, colon, or peritoneum.[20] Most GISTs occur in people between the ages of 50 and 70. While the exact cause is unknown, genetic mutations likely play a role. A few GISTs occur in people with familial mutations in either KIT or platelet-derived growth factor receptor a (PDGFRa) or in those with neurofibromatosis type 1.

The manifestations depend on the part of the GI tract affected. Early manifestations are often subtle. They include early satiety, fatigue, bloating, nausea or vomiting, and a change in bowel habits. Because these are like those of many other GI problems, early detection is difficult. Later manifestations may include GI bleeding and obstruction caused by larger tumors.

GISTs are often found during imaging for other problems. Diagnosis is based on histologic examination of biopsied tissue. Endoscopic ultrasound, CT, or MRI are used to determine the extent of disease.

Surgery offers the only permanent cure. GISTs have usually metastasized by the time of diagnosis or often recur. They are unresponsive to conventional chemotherapy. The discovery of genetic mutations led to the development of tyrosine kinase inhibitor drugs (e.g., imatinib mesylate [Gleevec], sunitinib, regorafenib) that are effective against some GISTs.

GASTRIC SURGERY

Gastric surgeries are done to treat stomach cancer, as well as polyps, perforation, chronic gastritis, and PUD. Surgeries include partial gastrectomy, gastrectomy, vagotomy, and pyloroplasty. Partial gastrectomy with removal of the distal two thirds of the stomach and anastomosis of the gastric stump to the duodenum is a *gastroduodenostomy* or *Billroth I* operation (Fig. 46.16A). If the gastric stump is anastomosed to the jejunum, the surgery is a *gastrojejunostomy* or *Billroth II* operation (Fig. 46.16B). A total gastrectomy involves resecting the lower esophagus, removing the entire stomach, and anastomosis of the esophagus to the jejunum.

Vagotomy, the severing of the vagus nerve, decreases gastric acid secretion. It may be total *(truncal)* or selective *(highly selective vagotomy). Pyloroplasty* is the surgical enlargement of the pyloric sphincter to promote the easy passage of contents from the stomach. It is often done after vagotomy or to enlarge an opening that is constricted from scar tissue.

Postoperative Complications

As with all surgeries, acute postoperative bleeding at the surgical site can occur. Monitoring is similar to that described later under acute upper GI bleeding. The most common long-term postoperative complications from gastric surgery are (1) dumping syndrome, (2) postprandial hypoglycemia, and (3) bile reflux gastritis.

Dumping Syndrome

Dumping syndrome is the direct result of surgical removal of a large part of the stomach and pyloric sphincter. Normally, gastric chyme enters the small intestine in small amounts. After surgery, the stomach no longer has control over the amount of gastric chyme entering the small intestine. A large bolus of hypertonic fluid enters the intestine, drawing fluid into the bowel lumen. This creates a decrease in plasma volume, distention of the bowel lumen, and rapid intestinal transit.

Symptoms begin within 15 to 30 minutes after eating. The patient usually reports generalized weakness, sweating, palpitations, and dizziness. Symptoms are due to the sudden decrease in plasma volume. The patient may have abdominal cramps, *borborygmi* (audible abdominal sounds made by hyperactive intestinal peristalsis), and the urge to defecate. These manifestations usually last less than 1 hour after eating. A short rest period after each meal reduces the chance of dumping syndrome.

Postprandial Hypoglycemia

Postprandial hypoglycemia is a variant of dumping syndrome. It is the result of uncontrolled gastric emptying of a bolus of fluid high in carbohydrate into the small intestine. This causes hyperglycemia and the release of excess amounts of insulin into the circulation. This results in reflex hypoglycemia. Symptoms are like those of any hypoglycemic reaction. They include sweating, weakness, mental confusion, palpitations, tachycardia, and anxiety. Symptoms generally occur 2 hours after eating.

Bile Reflux Gastritis

Gastric surgery that involves either reconstruction or removal of the pylorus can result in reflux of bile into the stomach. Prolonged contact with bile causes damage to the gastric mucosa, chronic gastritis, and PUD.

The main symptom is continuous epigastric distress that increases after meals. Vomiting relieves the distress, but only temporarily. Although only a small number of patients have bile reflux gastritis, caution the patient to notify the HCP of any continuous epigastric distress after meals. Cholestyramine before or with meals has been used to treat this problem. It binds with the bile salts that are the source of gastric irritation.

❖ NURSING MANAGEMENT: GASTRIC SURGERY

◆ Preoperative Care

Surgery can involve either laparoscopic or open surgical techniques. The HCP will provide the necessary information about the procedure and expected outcomes, so the patient can make an informed decision. Help by answering their questions. Teach them what to expect after surgery, including comfort measures, pain relief, coughing and breathing exercises, use of an NG tube, and IV fluid administration. See Chapter 18 for more on preoperative care.

◆ Postoperative Care

Postoperative care focuses on maintaining fluid and electrolyte balance, preventing respiratory complications, maintaining comfort, and preventing infection. Complications include atelectasis, pneumonia, anastomotic leak, deep vein thrombosis, pulmonary embolus, and bleeding. Morbidly obese patients have a higher risk for complications.

After surgery, an NG tube is used for decompression. This decreases pressure on suture lines and allows edema and inflammation resulting from surgical trauma to resolve. Observe the gastric aspirate for color, amount, and odor. Expect small volumes of bloody drainage from the NG for the first 2 to 3 hours because bleeding at the anastomotic site is common. Report bright red bleeding that does not decrease after this period or bleeding that becomes excessive (more than 75 mL/hr) immediately to the HCP. The NG aspirate should gradually darken within the first 24 hours after surgery. Normally the color changes to yellow-green within 36 to 48 hours. After total gastrectomy, the NG tube does not drain a large quantity of secretions because removing the stomach has eliminated the reservoir capacity.

Observe the NG tube closely because blood easily clots and clogs the tube. Notify the HCP immediately if the tube stops draining or appears obstructed with blood. If the tube becomes clogged, the HCP may order periodic gentle irrigations with normal saline solution. It is essential that the NG suction is working and that the tube stays patent so that accumulated gastric secretions do not put a strain on the anastomosis. This can lead to distention of any remaining part of the stomach and result in (1) rupture of the sutures, (2) leakage of gastric contents into the peritoneal cavity, (3) bleeding, and (4) abscess formation. If the tube must be replaced or repositioned, call the HCP to perform this task because of the danger of perforating the gastric mucosa or disrupting the suture line.

While the NG tube is connected to suction, maintain IV therapy. Before the NG tube is removed, the patient begins clear liquids to determine the tolerance level. In a partial gastrectomy, the stomach may be aspirated within 1 or 2 hours to assess the amount remaining and its color and consistency. When the patient tolerates fluids, the NG tube is removed. Solids are added gradually with the goal of resuming a normal diet.

Closely observe the patient for an anastomotic leak and notify the HCP at once if you suspect one. A leak occurs when there is a breakdown of the suture line in an anastomosis that allows gastric or intestinal contents to enter the abdomen or mediastinum. It requires immediate treatment to prevent sepsis and death. Signs and symptoms include tachycardia, dyspnea, fever, abdominal pain, anxiety, and restlessness.

Since most procedures are done laparoscopically, there is less risk for respiratory complications. In an open surgical approach, the incision is in the epigastrium and respiratory complications may occur. Perform a respiratory assessment. Note signs of pneumothorax (e.g., dyspnea, chest pain, cyanosis). Have the patient cough, deep breathe, and use incentive spirometry to expand the lungs. Pain may interfere with deep breathing and coughing. Encourage the patient to splint the area with a pillow. Splinting also protects the abdominal suture line from rupturing during deep breathing and coughing. Encourage early ambulation and frequent position changes.

Give pain medications as needed. Be aware that pain could be from an anastomosis leak rather than typical surgical pain. Abdominal wounds need frequent observation. Note the amount and type of drainage, condition of the incision, and signs of infection. Monitor vital signs to help identify problems such as infection, bleeding, or anastomosis leak. Implement measures to control nausea and vomiting. Measure and record the intake and output. Obtain daily weights.

◆ Nutrition Therapy

You need to understand the patient's surgery and their resulting anatomy. Long-term, many patients have malnutrition, metabolic bone disease, anemia, and weight loss. Nutrition interventions help minimize the occurrence of expected complications and maximize nutrient intake (Table 46.18). Start nutrition teaching as soon as the immediate postoperative period has passed. The dietitian usually provides diet instructions. You must reinforce them. Following diet measures will decrease symptoms and is essential to long-term adherence.

Postoperative wound healing may be impaired because of poor intake. Give potassium and vitamin supplements as ordered. For those who were malnourished preoperatively, a small bowel feeding tube may be placed during surgery. EN may be started on postoperative day 1 and adjusted depending on how oral intake is tolerated. Some may be discharged with nighttime tube feedings. PN is an option if the patient cannot tolerate EN or oral nutrition.

Pernicious anemia is a long-term complication of total gastrectomy and may occur after partial gastrectomy. It is

TABLE 46.18 NUTRITION THERAPY

Postgastrectomy Dumping Syndrome

The amount of time these restrictions should be followed varies. The HCP decides the amount of time to remain on this prescribed diet according to the patient's clinical condition and progress.

Purposes

- Slow the rapid passage of food into the intestine
- Control symptoms of dumping syndrome (dizziness, sense of fullness, diarrhea, tachycardia), which sometimes occurs after a partial or total gastrectomy

Diet Principles

- Divide meals into 6 small feedings to avoid overloading the stomach and intestine at mealtimes.
- Do not take fluids with meals but at least 30–45 min before or after meals. This helps prevent distention or a feeling of fullness.
- Avoid concentrated sweets (e.g., honey, sugar, jelly, jam, candies, pastries, sweetened fruit). They sometimes cause dizziness, diarrhea, and a sense of fullness.
- Protein consumption is unlimited to promote rebuilding of body tissues. Meat and eggs are specific foods to increase in the diet.
- Milk contains lactose, which may be hard to digest. Introduce milk and milk products slowly several weeks after surgery.
- Avoid carbonated beverages and foods that are gas forming to help prevent gastric distention.
- Low-roughage and raw foods are allowed as tolerated a few weeks after surgery.
- Increase complex carbohydrates (e.g., bread, vegetables, rice, potatoes) and fats to meet energy needs.

due to the loss of intrinsic factor, which is made by the parietal cells. *Intrinsic factor* is essential for the absorption of cobalamin in the terminal ileum. Cobalamin is essential for RBC growth and maturation. The patient will require cobalamin replacement therapy (see Chapter 34). Patients should take multivitamins with folate, calcium, vitamin D, and iron for life.

Because partial gastrectomy decreases the stomach's reservoir, patients must reduce their meal size accordingly. For the first few weeks after surgery, the patient should consume soft, bland foods with low fiber and high complex carbohydrates and protein content. Teach the patient to eat in small portions and not to drink fluids with meals. They should avoid simple sugars, lactose, and fried foods. Teach the patient to avoid extreme temperatures in food and to chew food thoroughly.

To avoid hypoglycemic episodes, teach the patient to limit the amount of sugar consumed with each meal and eat small, frequent meals with moderate amounts of protein and fat. The immediate intake of sugared fluids or candy relieves hypoglycemic symptoms.

Ambulatory Care

Patients who have had a total gastrectomy and are frail may need skilled care after discharge. For those going home, assist the patient and caregiver with symptom management. Make plans for pain relief, including comfort measures and the judicious use of analgesics. Teach wound care (if needed) to the primary caregiver. Dressings, special equipment, or special services may be needed. Collaborate with the dietitian to provide teaching about the diet that will optimize nutrition.

GASTRITIS

Gastritis is an inflammation of the gastric mucosa. It is a common problem affecting the stomach. Gastritis may be acute or chronic and diffuse or localized.

Etiology and Pathophysiology

Gastritis occurs as the result of a breakdown in the normal gastric mucosal barrier. This mucosal barrier normally protects the stomach tissue from the corrosive action of HCl acid and pepsin. When the barrier is broken, HCl acid and pepsin can diffuse back into the mucosa. This back diffusion results in tissue edema, disruption of capillary walls with loss of plasma into the gastric lumen, and possible bleeding.

Risk Factors

Table 46.19 lists risk factors and causes of gastritis. Some risk factors are discussed here.

Drug-related gastritis. Drugs contribute to the development of acute and chronic gastritis. NSAIDs and corticosteroids inhibit the synthesis of prostaglandins that protect the gastric mucosa. This makes the mucosa more susceptible to injury. Factors that increase the risk for NSAID-induced gastritis include being female; being over age 60; having a history of ulcer disease; taking anticoagulants, LDA, or corticosteroids; and having a chronic disorder, such as CVD. Some drugs such as digoxin and alendronate have direct irritating effects on the gastric mucosa.

TABLE 46.19 Causes of Gastritis

Drugs
- Aspirin
- Bisphosphonates
- Corticosteroids
- Digitalis
- Iron supplements
- Nonsteroidal antiinflammatory drugs (NSAIDs)

Diet
- Alcohol
- Large amounts of spicy, irritating foods

Microorganisms
- *H. pylori*
- Cytomegalovirus
- *Mycobacterium* species
- *Salmonella* organisms
- *Staphylococcus* organisms
- *Treponema pallidum* (syphilis)

Environmental Factors
- Radiation
- Smoking

Diseases/Disorders
- Burns
- Crohn disease
- Large hiatal hernia
- Physiologic stress
- Reflux of bile and pancreatic secretions
- Renal failure
- Sepsis
- Shock

Other Factors
- Endoscopy procedures
- Nasogastric tube
- Stress

Diet. Diet indiscretions can cause acute gastritis. After binge drinking alcohol, acute damage to the gastric mucosa can range from local injury of superficial epithelial cells to destruction of the mucosa with mucosal congestion, edema, and bleeding. Prolonged damage from repeated alcohol use results in chronic gastritis. Eating large quantities of spicy, irritating foods can cause acute gastritis.

Helicobacter pylori. *H. pylori* infection causes acute gastritis in most infected persons. Chronic gastritis may develop in some. Prolonged inflammation leads to functional changes in the stomach and may cause stomach cancer. *H. pylori* was discussed earlier in this chapter.

Other risk factors. Although not as common as *H. pylori*, other bacterial, viral, and fungal infections can cause chronic gastritis. Gastritis can occur from reflux of bile salts from the duodenum into the stomach because of anatomic changes after surgical procedures (e.g., gastroduodenostomy, gastrojejunostomy). Prolonged vomiting may cause reflux of bile salts. Intense emotional responses and CNS lesions may cause inflammation of the mucosal lining from hypersecretion of HCl acid.

Autoimmune Gastritis

Autoimmune metaplastic atrophic gastritis (also called *autoimmune atrophic gastritis*) is an inherited condition in which there is an immune response directed against parietal cells. It most often affects women of northern European descent. Patients often have other autoimmune disorders. The loss of parietal cells leads to low chloride levels, inadequate production of intrinsic factor, cobalamin (vitamin B_{12}) malabsorption, and pernicious anemia. It increases the risk of stomach cancer.

Clinical Manifestations

The symptoms of *acute gastritis* include anorexia, nausea and vomiting, epigastric tenderness, and a feeling of fullness. GI bleeding is often associated with alcohol use and, at times, is the only symptom. Acute gastritis is self-limiting, lasting from a few hours to a few days. The mucosa should heal completely.

The manifestations of *chronic gastritis* are like those of acute gastritis. Some patients are asymptomatic. However, when parietal cells are lost because of atrophy, the source of intrinsic factor is also lost. *Intrinsic factor* is essential for cobalamin absorption. The lack of cobalamin results in pernicious anemia. Cobalamin deficiency anemia is discussed in Chapter 34.

Diagnostic Studies

Acute gastritis is usually diagnosed based on the patient's symptoms and the presence of risk factors. Occasionally, an endoscopic examination with biopsy is needed to make the diagnosis. Breath, urine, serum, stool, and gastric tissue biopsy tests are done to assess for *H. pylori* infection. A CBC may show anemia from blood loss or lack of intrinsic factor. Stools are tested for occult blood. Serum tests for intrinsic factor and antibodies to parietal cells may be done. A tissue biopsy can rule out gastric cancer.

❖ NURSING AND INTERPROFESSIONAL MANAGEMENT: GASTRITIS

◆ Acute Gastritis

Eliminating the cause and preventing or avoiding it in the future are generally all that is needed to treat acute gastritis. The plan of care is supportive and similar to that described for nausea and vomiting. If vomiting is present, rest, NPO status, and IV fluids may be prescribed. Antiemetics are given (Table 46.1). Monitor for dehydration. It can occur rapidly in acute gastritis with vomiting.

In severe cases of acute gastritis, an NG tube may be used to (1) monitor for bleeding, (2) lavage the precipitating agent from the stomach, or (3) keep the stomach empty and free of noxious stimuli. Clear liquids are resumed when symptoms have subsided. Reintroduce solids gradually.

If the patient is at risk for GI bleeding, frequently check vital signs. Test the vomitus for blood. All the management strategies discussed in the section on upper GI bleeding apply to the patient with severe gastritis.

Drug therapy focuses on reducing irritation of the gastric mucosa and providing symptomatic relief. H_2 receptor blockers (e.g., cimetidine) or PPIs (e.g., omeprazole) reduce gastric HCl acid secretion (Table 46.10). Teach the patient about the therapeutic effects of PPIs and H_2 receptor blockers.

◆ Chronic Gastritis

The treatment of chronic gastritis focuses on evaluating and eliminating the specific cause. Examples include alcohol

TABLE 46.20 Types of Upper GI Bleeding

Type	Manifestations
Obvious bleeding	
• Hematemesis	Bloody vomitus appearing as fresh, bright red blood or "coffee-grounds" appearance (dark, grainy digested blood).
• Melena	Black, tarry stools (often foul smelling) caused by digestion of blood in the GI tract. Black appearance is from the presence of iron.
Occult bleeding	Small amounts of blood in gastric secretions, vomitus, or stools not apparent by appearance. Detectable by guaiac test

cessation or abstaining from drugs. Antibiotic combinations are used to treat *H. pylori* infection (Table 46.14). The patient with pernicious anemia needs lifelong cobalamin therapy (see Chapter 34).

The patient may have to adapt to lifestyle changes and strictly adhere to a drug regimen. Some patients find a nonirritating diet consisting of 6 small feedings a day helpful. Smoking is contraindicated in all forms of gastritis. A team approach in which the HCP, nurse, dietitian, and pharmacist provide consistent information and support will increase the patient's success in making these changes.

UPPER GASTROINTESTINAL BLEEDING

In the United States, the incidence of acute upper GI (UGI) bleeding is 103 cases per 100,000 adults per year.[21] The mortality rate in hospital admitted patients is 14%, with 11% succumbing in the ED.[21] Mortality from an UGI bleed increases with age.

Etiology and Pathophysiology

Table 46.20 describes types of UGI bleeding. The most serious loss of blood from a UGI bleed has a sudden onset. Insidious occult bleeding can also be a major problem. The severity of bleeding depends on whether the origin is venous, capillary, or arterial. Bleeding from an arterial source is profuse. The blood is bright red because it has not been in contact with gastric HCl acid secretion. In contrast, coffee-grounds vomitus means that the blood has been in the stomach for some time. *Melena* (black, tarry stools) occurs with slow bleeding from an upper GI source. The longer the blood passes through the intestines, the darker the stool color because of the breakdown of hemoglobin and release of iron.

Discovering the cause of the bleeding is not always easy. A variety of areas in the GI tract may be involved. Table 46.21 lists common causes of UGI bleeding.

Stomach and Duodenal Origin

Peptic ulcers, due to *H. pylori* infection and NSAID use, are the most common causes of UGI bleeding. About 25% of people on chronic NSAIDs (e.g., ibuprofen) develop ulcer

TABLE 46.21 Causes of Upper GI Bleeding

Stomach and Duodenum	Esophagus

• Drug-induced
  • Corticosteroids
  • NSAIDs
  • Salicylates
• Erosive gastritis
• Polyps
• PUD
• Stress-related mucosal disease
• Stomach cancer
	• Esophageal varices
	• Esophagitis
	• Mallory-Weiss tear
	Systemic Diseases
	• Blood dyscrasias (e.g., leukemia, aplastic anemia)
	• Renal failure

disease. Of these, 2% to 4% will bleed. Even LDA increases risk for GI bleeding. Many OTC preparations contain aspirin. Obtain a careful medication history whenever we suspect UGI bleeding.

Stress-related mucosal disease (SRMD), or *physiologic stress ulcers,* describes mucosal damage in the GI tract associated with serious illness. Damage ranges from small single lesions to multiple gastric ulcers and major bleeding. SRMD most often occurs in critically ill patients who have had severe burns, trauma, or major surgery. Patients with coagulopathy, liver disease, or organ failure and those receiving renal replacement therapy are at highest risk for SRMD.[22]

Esophageal Origin

Bleeding from the esophagus is likely due to chronic esophagitis, Mallory-Weiss tear, or esophageal varices. Chronic esophagitis can be caused by GERD, smoking, alcohol use, and the use of drugs irritating to the mucosa. Esophageal varices most often occur from cirrhosis. Esophageal varices are discussed in Chapter 48.

Diagnostic Studies

Endoscopy is the primary tool for diagnosing the source (e.g., esophageal varices, PUD, gastritis) of UGI bleeding. Angiography is used when endoscopy cannot be done or when bleeding persists after endoscopic therapy. Angiography requires preparation and setup time and may not be appropriate for a high-risk, unstable patient. In this procedure, a catheter is inserted into the femoral artery and advanced to the left gastric or superior mesenteric artery until the site of bleeding is found.

Laboratory studies include CBC, blood urea nitrogen (BUN), serum electrolytes, prothrombin time, partial thromboplastin time, liver enzymes, arterial blood gases (ABGs), and a type and crossmatch for possible blood transfusions. All vomitus and stools are tested for gross and occult blood.

Monitor laboratory results to estimate the effectiveness of therapy. The hemoglobin and hematocrit values are not of immediate help in estimating the degree of blood loss, but they provide a baseline for guiding further treatment. The initial hematocrit may be normal. It may not reflect the loss until 4 to 6 hours after fluid replacement since initially the loss of plasma and RBCs is equal.

Assess the patient's BUN level. With significant bleeding, GI tract bacteria break down proteins, resulting in increased BUN levels. An increased BUN level may also show renal hypoperfusion or renal disease.

Interprofessional Management

A massive UGI hemorrhage is a loss of more than 1500 mL of blood or 25% of intravascular blood volume. Although 80% to 85% of patients with massive hemorrhage spontaneously stop bleeding, the cause must be identified, and treatment started at once.

Emergency Assessment and Management

A complete history of events leading to the bleeding episode is deferred until emergency care has been started. To facilitate early intervention, focus your assessment on identifying signs and symptoms of shock. These include tachycardia, weak pulse, hypotension, cool extremities, prolonged capillary refill, and apprehension. Shock is discussed in Chapter 42.

Urine output is one of the best measures of vital organ perfusion. An indwelling urinary catheter is inserted so that hourly output can be accurately assessed. Hemodynamic monitoring provides an accurate and quick assessment of blood flow and pressure in the cardiovascular system (see Chapter 35). A central venous pressure line may be used for fluid volume status assessment. If the patient has a history of valvular heart disease, coronary artery disease, or heart failure, a pulmonary artery catheter may be needed. Give supplemental O_2 to increase blood O_2 saturation.

The patient is at risk for perforation and peritonitis. Do a thorough abdominal assessment. Note the presence of a tense, rigid, board-like abdomen and the presence or absence of bowel sounds.

The type and amount of fluids infused are based on physical and laboratory findings. Generally, we start an isotonic crystalloid solution (e.g., lactated Ringer's solution). Whole blood, packed RBCs, and fresh frozen plasma may be used for volume replacement in massive hemorrhage. When UGI bleeding is less profuse, isotonic saline solution followed by packed RBCs restores the hematocrit more quickly and does not create complications related to fluid volume overload.

Endoscopic Therapy

The first-line management of UGI bleeding is endoscopy. Endoscopy within the first 24 hours of bleeding is important for diagnosis, determining the need for surgical intervention, and providing treatment.

The goal of endoscopic hemostasis is to coagulate or thrombose the bleeding vessel. Several techniques are used. These include (1) mechanical therapy with clips or bands, (2) thermal ablation, and (3) injection (e.g., epinephrine). Clips and bands directly compress the bleeding vessel. Thermal ablation cauterizes tissue through applying heat to the bleeding site. Common devices include neodymium: yttrium-aluminum-garnet (YAG) laser, monopolar or bipolar electrocoagulation, heater probes, and argon plasma coagulation (APC).[21]

For variceal bleeding, other strategies include variceal ligation, injection sclerotherapy, and balloon tamponade (see Chapter 48).

Surgical Therapy

Surgical intervention is needed when bleeding continues despite therapy and there is an identified site of bleeding. Surgery may be done if the patient continues to bleed after rapid transfusion of up to 2000 mL of whole blood or is still in shock after 24 hours. The site of the bleeding determines the choice of surgery. Mortality rates increase greatly in older patients.

Drug Therapy

During the acute phase of UGI bleeding, drugs are used to decrease bleeding, decrease HCl acid secretion, and neutralize HCl acid. Empiric PPI therapy with high-dose IV bolus and subsequent infusion to decrease acid secretion is often started before endoscopy (Table 46.10).[23] Efforts are made to reduce acid secretion because the acidic environment can alter platelet function and interfere with clot stabilization. This may decrease the amount of bleeding and need for endoscopic therapy.

After an acute phase of bleeding, antacids may be given hourly, either orally or through the NG tube. If an NG tube is in place, aspirate the stomach contents and test periodically for pH level. If pH is less than 5, intermittent suction may be used or the frequency or dosage of the antacid or antisecretory agent increased.

NURSING MANAGEMENT: UPPER GASTROINTESTINAL BLEEDING

Assessment

A thorough assessment is essential when you care for the patient with UGI bleeding. The patient may not be able to give specific information about the cause of the bleeding until immediate physical needs are met. Perform an immediate assessment while getting the patient ready for initial treatment. Assess level of consciousness, vital signs, skin color, and capillary refill. Check the abdomen for distention, guarding, and peristalsis. Vital signs indicate whether the patient is in shock from blood loss and provide a baseline BP and pulse for monitoring the patient's progress. Signs and symptoms of shock include low BP; rapid, weak pulse; increased thirst; cold, clammy skin; and restlessness. Monitor vital signs every 15 to 30 minutes. Inform the HCP of any significant changes.

Once the immediate interventions have begun, the patient or caregiver should answer the following questions: Is there a history of bleeding episodes? Has the patient received blood transfusions? Were there any transfusion reactions? Are there any other illnesses (e.g., liver problems) or medications that may contribute to bleeding or interfere with treatment? Does the patient have a religious preference that prohibits the use of blood or blood products?

Subjective and objective data to obtain from the patient or caregiver are outlined in Table 46.22.

TABLE 46.22 NURSING ASSESSMENT
Upper GI Bleeding

Subjective Data

Important Health Information

Health history: Precipitating events before bleeding episode, prior bleeding episodes and treatment, PUD, esophageal varices, esophagitis, acute and chronic gastritis, stress-related mucosal disease

Medications: Aspirin, NSAIDs, corticosteroids, anticoagulants

Functional Health Patterns

Health perception–health management: Family history of bleeding, smoking, alcohol use

Nutritional-metabolic: Nausea, vomiting, weight loss, thirst

Elimination: Diarrhea. Black, tarry stools. Decreased urine output. Sweating

Activity-exercise: Weakness, dizziness, fainting

Cognitive-perceptual: Epigastric pain, abdominal cramps

Coping–stress tolerance: Acute or chronic stress

Objective Data

General

Fever

Cardiovascular

Tachycardia, weak pulse, orthostatic hypotension, slow capillary refill

GI

Red or coffee-grounds vomitus. Tense, rigid abdomen, ascites. Hypoactive or hyperactive bowel sounds. Black, tarry stools

Neurologic

Agitation, restlessness. Decreasing level of consciousness

Respiratory

Rapid, shallow respirations

Skin

Clammy, cool, pale skin. Pale mucous membranes, nail beds, and conjunctivae. Spider angiomas, jaundice, peripheral edema

Urinary

Decreased urine output, concentrated urine

Possible Diagnostic Findings

↓ Hematocrit and hemoglobin, hematuria. Guaiac-positive stools, emesis, or gastric aspirate. ↓ Levels of clotting factors, ↑ liver enzymes, abnormal endoscopy results

Clinical Problems

Clinical problems for the patient with UGI bleeding include:

- Fluid imbalance
- Inadequate tissue perfusion
- Impaired GI function

Planning

The overall goals are that the patient with UGI bleeding will (1) have no further GI bleeding, (2) have the cause of the bleeding identified and treated, and (3) return to a normal hemodynamic state.

Implementation

Health Promotion

You play a key role in identifying patients at high risk for GI bleeding. Always consider the patient with a history of chronic gastritis, cirrhosis, or PUD at high risk. The patient who has had a UGI bleeding episode is more likely to have another bleed. Patients on LDA and anticoagulants are at risk for UGI bleeding, especially those over 60 years old with a history of PUD.

Teach the patient who takes regular doses of drugs that cause GI toxicity (peptic ulcer formation, bleeding), such as corticosteroids and NSAIDs, about the risk for GI bleeding. They may need to receive long-term treatment with a PPI, H_2 receptor blocker, or misoprostol. Taking these drugs with meals or snacks lessens irritation.

Teach the at-risk patient to avoid known gastric irritants, such as alcohol and smoking, and to take only prescribed medications. OTC drugs can be harmful because they may contain ingredients (e.g., aspirin) that increase the risk for bleeding. Review how to test vomitus or stools for occult blood. Teach them to report positive results promptly to the HCP. Stress the importance of treating an upper respiratory tract infection promptly. Severe coughing or sneezing can increase pressure on the already fragile varices and may result in massive hemorrhage (see Chapter 48).

Patients with blood dyscrasias (e.g., aplastic anemia) or liver problems or those who are taking chemotherapy drugs are at risk due to a decrease in clotting factors and platelets. Teach patients about their disease process, drugs, and increased risk for GI bleeding.

TABLE 46.23 EMERGENCY MANAGEMENT

Acute GI Bleeding

Assessment Findings	Interventions
Abdominal and GI Findings • Abdominal pain • Abdominal rigidity • Hematemesis • Melena • Nausea **Hypovolemic Shock** • ↓ BP • Cool, clammy skin • ↑ HR • ↓ Level of consciousness • Slow capillary refill • ↓ Urine output (<0.5 mL/kg/hr)	**Initial** • If unresponsive, assess circulation, airway, and breathing. • If responsive, monitor airway, breathing, and circulation. • Establish IV access with large-bore catheter and start fluid replacement therapy. Insert a second large-bore catheter if shock present. • Give O_2 via nasal cannula or nonrebreather mask. • Initiate ECG monitoring. • Obtain blood for CBC, clotting studies, and type and crossmatch as needed. • Insert NG tube as needed. • Insert indwelling urinary catheter. • Give IV PPI therapy to decrease acid secretion. **Ongoing Monitoring** • Monitor vital signs, level of consciousness, O_2 saturation, ECG, bowel sounds, and intake/output. • Assess amount and character of emesis. • Keep patient NPO. • Provide reassurance and emotional support to patient and caregiver.

Acute Care

Emergency management of acute GI bleeding is outlined in Table 46.23. Place IV lines, preferably 2, with a 16- or 18-gauge needle for fluid and blood replacement. Give fluid or blood replacement as ordered. An accurate intake and output record is essential so you can assess the patient's hydration status. Measure urine output hourly. If a central venous pressure line or pulmonary artery catheter is in place, record these readings every 1 to 2 hours. Apply ECG monitoring. Monitor vital signs closely, especially in the patient with CVD, because dysrhythmias may occur.

> **CHECK YOUR PRACTICE**
>
> You are admitting a 71-year-old man to the unit from the ED. He has a diagnosis of UGI bleeding. He reports heartburn and pain (6 on a scale of 10) in the upper epigastric region. He just had a 250 mL coffee-grounds emesis.
> - What assessment data do you need to obtain?
> - What are the priority nursing interventions?

Observe the older adult or the patient with CVD closely for signs of fluid overload. However, volume overload and pulmonary edema are concerns in all patients who are receiving large amounts of IV fluids within a short time. Auscultate breath sounds. Closely observe the respiratory effort. Elevate the head of the bed to provide comfort and prevent aspiration.

When an NG tube is present, pay special attention to keeping it in proper position. Check the aspirate for blood. Although gastric lavage (room temperature, cool, iced) is used in some agencies, its effectiveness as a treatment for UGI bleeding is questionable. When lavage is used, around 50 to 100 mL of fluid is instilled at a time into the stomach. The lavage fluid may be aspirated from the stomach or drained by gravity. When aspirating, it is important to stop if you feel resistance. The tip of the NG tube may be up against the gastric mucosal lining. When resistance is a factor, use the gravity method.

Approach the patient in a calm manner to help decrease their anxiety level. Use caution when giving sedatives for restlessness. It is a warning sign of shock and may be masked by the drugs.

Assess the stools for blood (black-tarry, bright red). Black, tarry stools usually indicate prolonged bleeding. Determine if menses is a source of blood in the stool. When vomitus contains blood, but the stool contains no gross or occult blood, the hemorrhage is likely of short duration.

When beginning oral intake, observe the patient for symptoms of nausea and vomiting and a recurrence of bleeding. Start with feedings with clear fluids. Give them hourly until tolerance is determined. Gradually introduce foods if the patient has no signs of problems.

When bleeding is the result of chronic alcohol use, closely observe the patient for delirium tremens as alcohol withdrawal takes place. Symptoms indicating the onset of delirium tremens are agitation, uncontrolled shaking, sweating, and hallucinations. Alcohol withdrawal is discussed in Chapter 11.

Ambulatory Care

Teach the patient and caregiver ways to avoid future bleeding episodes. Encourage the patient and caregiver to adhere to drug therapy. Emphasize not to take any drugs (especially aspirin,

TABLE 46.24 Bacterial Food Poisoning

Type and Cause	Sources	Manifestations	Treatment and Prevention
Botulism Toxin from *Clostridium botulinum;* ingested toxin absorbed from gut and blocks acetylcholine at neuromuscular junction	Improperly canned or preserved food, home-preserved vegetables (most common), preserved fruits and fish, canned commercial products	*Onset:* 12–36 hr *GI:* Nausea, vomiting, abdominal pain, constipation, distention *CNS:* Headache, dizziness, muscular incoordination, weakness, inability to talk or swallow, diplopia, breathing problems, paralysis, delirium, coma	*Treat:* Maintain ventilation, polyvalent antitoxin, guanidine hydrochloric acid (enhances acetylcholine release) *Prevent:* Correct processing of canned foods, boiling of suspected canned foods for 15 min before serving
Clostridial *Clostridium perfringens*	Meat or poultry dishes cooked at lower temperature (stew, pot pie), rewarmed meat dishes, gravies, improperly canned vegetables	*Onset:* 8–24 hr Diarrhea, nausea, abdominal cramps, vomiting (rare), midepigastric pain	*Treat:* Symptomatic, fluid replacement *Prevent:* Correct preparation of meat dishes. Serving food immediately after cooking or rapid cooling of food
Escherichia coli *E. coli* 0157:H7	Contaminated beef, pork, milk, cheese, fish, cookie dough	*Onset:* 8 hr to 1 week (varies by strain) Bloody stools, hemolytic uremic syndrome, abdominal cramping, profuse diarrhea	*Treat:* Symptomatic, fluid and electrolyte replacement *Prevent:* Correct food preparation
Salmonella *Salmonella typhimurium* (grows in gut)	Improperly cooked poultry, pork, beef, lamb, and eggs	*Onset:* 8 hr to several days Nausea and vomiting, diarrhea, abdominal cramps, fever, and chills	*Treat:* Symptomatic, fluid and electrolyte replacement *Prevent:* Correct food preparation
Staphylococcal Toxin from *Staphylococcus aureus*	Meat, bakery products, cream fillings, salad dressings, milk Skin and respiratory tract of food handlers	*Onset:* 30 min to 7 hr Vomiting, nausea, abdominal cramping, diarrhea	*Treat:* Symptomatic, fluid and electrolyte replacement, antiemetics *Prevent:* Immediate food refrigeration, monitoring food handling

NSAIDs) other than those prescribed by the HCP. Support the patient in smoking and alcohol cessation. Long-term follow-up care may be needed because of possible recurrence. Teach the patient and caregiver what to do if acute bleeding occurs in the future.

◆ Evaluation

Expected outcomes for the patient with UGI bleeding include:

- Be free from UGI bleeding
- Maintain normal fluid volume
- Understand potential risk factors and make lifestyle modifications

FOODBORNE ILLNESS

Foodborne illness (food poisoning) is a nonspecific term that describes acute GI symptoms such as nausea, vomiting, diarrhea, and abdominal pain caused by the intake of contaminated food or liquids.[24] Each year 1 in 6 Americans, or 48 million people, gets a foodborne illness. Of these, 128,000 are hospitalized and around 3000 die.[24]

Bacteria account for most foodborne illnesses. The most common source is raw foods that become contaminated during growing, harvesting, processing, storing, shipping, or final preparation. Bacteria multiply quickly when the temperature of food is between 40°F and 140°F. So, bacteria can multiply if hot food is not kept hot enough or cold food is not cold enough. The most common bacterial food poisonings are described in Table 46.24.

Focus interventions on preventing infection. Teaching includes correct food preparation and cleanliness, adequate cooking, and refrigeration (Table 46.25). For the hospitalized patient, emphasize correcting fluid and electrolyte imbalances from diarrhea and vomiting. With botulism, additional assessment and care related to neurologic symptoms are needed (see Chapter 60).

TABLE 46.25 PATIENT & CAREGIVER TEACHING

Preventing Food Poisoning

Include these instructions when teaching the patient and caregiver how to prevent food poisoning:

1. Cook all ground beef and hamburger thoroughly.
   - Use a digital instant-read meat thermometer to ensure thorough cooking. Ground beef can turn brown before disease-causing bacteria are killed.
   - Cook ground beef until a thermometer inserted into several parts of the patty, including the thickest part, reads at least 160°F.
   - People who cook ground beef without using a thermometer can decrease their risk for illness by not eating ground beef patties that are still pink in the middle.
2. If you are served an undercooked hamburger or other ground beef product in a restaurant, send it back for further cooking. Ask for a new bun and a clean plate.
3. Avoid spreading harmful bacteria. Keep raw meat separate from ready-to-eat foods. Wash hands, counters, and utensils with hot soapy water after they touch raw meat. Never place cooked hamburgers or ground beef on the unwashed plate that held raw patties. Wash meat thermometers in between tests of patties that need more cooking.
4. Drink pasteurized milk, juice, or cider. Commercial juice with an extended shelf-life that is sold at room temperature (e.g., juice in cardboard boxes, vacuum-sealed juice in glass containers) is pasteurized. Juice concentrates are heated enough to kill pathogens.
5. Wash fruits and vegetables thoroughly, especially those you are not cooking.
6. Do not eat raw food products that are supposed to be cooked. Follow package directions for cooking at proper temperatures.
7. Avoid eating alfalfa sprouts if you are immunocompromised until you are sure of their safety.

Escherichia coli O157:H7 Poisoning

Most strains of *Escherichia coli* are harmless. They live in the intestines of healthy humans and animals. *E. coli* O157:H7 makes a powerful toxin that can cause severe illness with hemorrhagic colitis and kidney failure. In the very young and older adults, *E. coli* O157:H7 can be life threatening.

E. coli O157:H7 is found primarily in undercooked meats, especially poultry and hamburger. *E. coli* outbreaks have occurred with contaminated leafy vegetables, fruits, and nuts. Infection can occur after drinking raw milk, unpasteurized or contaminated fruit juices, and after swimming in or drinking sewage-contaminated water. Person-to-person contact in families, long-term care, and childcare centers is an important mode of transmission.

Illness starts 1 to 10 days after swallowing the organism and lasts 5 to 10 days. Manifestations include diarrhea (often bloody), vomiting, and abdominal cramping pain. The diarrhea is variable, ranging from mild to bloody. It may start out as watery but may progress to bloody. Systemic complications include hemolytic uremia and thrombocytopenic purpura. Death can occur.

Infection with *E. coli* O157:H7 is diagnosed by detecting the bacteria in the stool. All people who suddenly have diarrhea with blood should have a stool culture for *E. coli* O157:H7.

Treatment involves hydration to maintain blood volume. Patients should avoid antidiarrheal agents. They slow GI motility and can prolong infection. Other therapies may include dialysis and plasmapheresis. We seldom give antibiotics because they increase the risk of complications and do not appear to treat the infection.

A small number of patients, especially young children and older adults develop hemolytic uremic syndrome (HUS). The risk of HUS increases with antibiotic use. With HUS, the RBCs are destroyed, and the kidneys fail. It is a life-threatening condition usually treated in an ICU. Blood transfusions and kidney dialysis are often needed. The mortality rate is around 5%. About one-third of people have abnormal kidney function for years afterward. A few need long-term dialysis. Other long-term complications include hypertension, seizures, blindness, and paralysis.

Case Study

Peptic Ulcer Disease

(iStockphoto/Thinkstock.)

Patient Profile

F.H., a 40-year-old male immigrant from Vietnam, has a 1-year history of epigastric distress. Increasingly, it is not relieved by over-the-counter omeprazole. He is scheduled for an upper endoscopy this morning.

Subjective Data

- Reports increasing substernal pain, especially 2 to 3 hr after eating
- Currently avoids alcohol and is taking an over-the-counter PPI
- Smoking history of 1 pack of cigarettes per day for 20 years
- Has had increasing fatigue with exercise
- Reports occasional black bowel movement

Objective Data

Physical Assessment

- Height 5 ft, 5 in tall and weight 140 lb

Diagnostic Studies

- Endoscopy reveals a duodenal ulcer
- Hgb 10.2 g/dL; Hct 30%
- Histology of biopsied tissue reveals *H. pylori* infection

Interprofessional Care

- Omeprazole 20 mg twice daily × 10 days
- Clarithromycin 500 mg twice daily × 10 days
- Amoxicillin 1 gram twice daily × 10 days

Discussion Questions

1. ***Recognize***: What risk factors does F.H. have for PUD?
2. ***Analyze:*** What assessment findings are consistent with PUD?
3. ***Plan:*** How will you consider F.H.'s cultural preferences in planning care?
4. ***Prioritize:*** Based on the data provided, what are the priority clinical problems?
5. ***Prioritize:*** What are the priority nursing interventions for F.H.?
6. ***Act***: What lifestyle interventions would you recommend for F.H.?
7. ***Evaluation:*** F.H. asks you if the treatment will work and this will be the end of his problems. How will you respond?

Answers available at http://evolve.elsevier.com/Lewis/medsurg.

BRIDGE TO NCLEX EXAMINATION

The number of the question corresponds to the same-numbered outcome at the beginning of the chapter.

1. M.J. calls the clinic and tells the nurse that her 85-year-old mother has been nauseated all day and has vomited twice. Before the nurse hangs up and calls the HCP, she should tell M.J. to
   a. administer antiemetic drugs and assess her mother's skin turgor.
   b. give her mother sips of water and elevate the head of her bed to prevent aspiration.
   c. offer her mother large quantities of Gatorade to decrease the risk for sodium depletion.
   d. give her mother a high-protein liquid supplement to drink to maintain her nutrition needs.
2. The nurse explains to the patient with Vincent's infection that treatment will include
   a. tetanus vaccinations.
   b. viscous lidocaine rinses.
   c. amphotericin B suspension.
   d. topical application of antibiotics.
3. The nurse teaching young adults about behaviors that put them at risk for oral cancer includes
   a. discouraging use of chewing gum.
   b. avoiding use of perfumed lip gloss.
   c. avoiding use of smokeless tobacco.
   d. discouraging drinking of carbonated beverages.

4. Which instructions would the nurse include in a teaching plan for a patient with mild gastroesophageal reflux disease (GERD)?
   a. "The best time to take an as-needed antacid is 1 to 3 hours after meals."
   b. "A glass of warm milk at bedtime will decrease your discomfort at night."
   c. "Do not chew gum; the excess saliva will cause you to secrete more acid."
   d. "Limit your intake of foods high in protein because they take longer to digest."
5. A patient who had an esophagectomy for esophageal cancer develops increasing pain, fever, and dyspnea after starting a full-liquid diet. The nurse recognizes that these symptoms are *most* indicative of
   a. an intolerance to the feedings.
   b. extension of the tumor into the aorta.
   c. leakage of fluids into the mediastinum.
   d. esophageal perforation with fistula formation into the lung.
6. The nurse monitors a patient with gastritis for pernicious anemia due to
   a. chronic autoimmune destruction of cobalamin stores in the body.
   b. progressive gastric atrophy from chronic breakage in the mucosal barrier and blood loss.
   c. a lack of intrinsic factor normally produced by acid-secreting cells of the gastric mucosa.
   d. hyperchlorhydria from an increase in acid-secreting parietal cells and degradation of RBCs.
7. The nurse is teaching the patient and family that peptic ulcers are
   a. caused by a stressful lifestyle and other acid-producing factors, such as *H. pylori*.
   b. inherited within families and reinforced by bacterial spread of *Staphylococcus aureus* in childhood.
   c. promoted by factors that cause oversecretion of acid, such as excess diet fats, smoking, and alcohol use.
   d. promoted by a combination of factors that cause erosion of the gastric mucosa, including certain drugs and *H. pylori*.
8. An optimal teaching plan for an outpatient with stomach cancer receiving radiation therapy should include information about
   a. cancer support groups, alopecia, and stomatitis.
   b. nutrition supplements, ostomy care, and support groups.
   c. prosthetic devices, wound and skin care, and grief counseling.
   d. wound and skin care, nutrition, drugs, and community resources.
9. The discharge teaching plan for the patient after an acute episode of upper GI bleeding includes information about the importance of *(select all that apply)*
   a. limiting alcohol intake to 1 serving per day.
   b. only taking aspirin with milk or bread products.
   c. avoiding taking aspirin and drugs containing aspirin.
   d. only taking drugs prescribed by the health care provider.
   e. taking all drugs 1 hour before mealtime to prevent further bleeding.
10. Several patients come to the urgent care center with nausea, vomiting, and diarrhea that began 2 hours ago while attending a large family reunion potluck dinner. You ask the patients specifically about foods they ingested containing
   a. beef.
   b. meat and milk.
   c. poultry and eggs.
   d. home-preserved vegetables.

1. b; 2. d; 3. c; 4. a; 5. c; 6. c; 7. d; 8. d; 9. c, d; 10. b.

For rationales to these answers and even more NCLEX review questions, visit http://evolve.elsevier.com/Lewis/medsurg.

EVOLVE WEBSITE/RESOURCES LIST

http://evolve.elsevier.com/Lewis/medsurg
Review Questions (Online Only)
Key Points
Answer Keys for Questions
- Rationales for Bridge to NCLEX Examination Questions
- Answer Guidelines for Case Study

Student Case Studies
- Patient With Oral Cancer
- Patient With Peptic Ulcer Disease

Nursing Care Plans
- eNursing Care Plan 46.1: Patient With Nausea and Vomiting
- eNursing Care Plan 46.2: Patient With Peptic Ulcer Disease

Conceptual Care Map Creator
Audio Glossary
Content Updates

REFERENCES

*1. Gan TJ, Belani KG, Bergese S, et al.: Fourth consensus guidelines for the management of postoperative nausea and vomiting, *Anesth Analg* 131:411, 2020.
*2. Vimolchalao V, Sakdejayont S, Wongchanapai P, et al.: The efficacy and safety of the addition of olanzapine to ondansetron and dexamethasone for prevention of chemotherapy-induced nausea and vomiting in patients receiving highly emetogenic chemotherapy, *Int J Clin Oncol* 25:396, 2020.
*3. Shi K, He F, Tang Y, et al.: Acupuncture PC6 for postoperative nausea and vomiting at different times: a protocol for systematic review and meta-analysis, *Medicine* 99:e20452, 2020.
*4. Matsushita K: Analysis of interaction between porphyromonas gingivalis and endothelial cells in vitro, *Methods Mol Biol* 2210:225, 2021.
5. National Cancer Institute: SEER stat fact sheets. Retrieved from http://seer.cancer.gov/statfacts/html.
6. Innerhofer V, Kofler B, Riechelmann H: Sexual behavior and high-risk HPV infection in the head and neck, *Laryngo-Rhino-Otol* 99:647, 2020.

7. The Oral Cancer Foundation: Surgery for oral cancer. Retrieved from https://oralcancerfoundation.org/treatment/surgery/.
8. American Cancer Society: Treating oral cancer. Retrieved from www.cancer.org/cancer/oral-cavity-and-oropharyngeal-cancer/treating.html.
9. American Gastroenterological Association: GERD. Retrieved from www.gastro.org/patient-care/conditions-diseases/gerd.
10. Antunes C, Aleem A, Curtis SA: *Gastroesophageal reflux disease*, StatPearls, 2020.
*11. Koyyada A: Long-term use of proton pump inhibitors as a risk factor for various adverse manifestations, *Therapie* 20:30127, 2020.
12. American Cancer Society: Key statistics for esophageal cancer. Retrieved from https://www.cancer.org/cancer/esophagus-cancer/about/key-statistics.html.
13. OMICS: Peptic ulcer. Retrieved from https://www.omicsonline.org/united-states/peptic-ulcer-peer-reviewed-pdf-ppt-articles/.
14. Sonnenberg A, Turner KO, Genta RM: Interaction between ethnicity and helicobacter pylori infection in the occurrence of reflux disease, *J Clin Gastroenterol* 54:614, 2020.
15. Malik TF, Gnanapandithan K, Singh K: *Peptic ulcer disease*, StatPearls, 2020.
16. American Cancer Society: Key statistics for stomach cancer. Retrieved from https://www.cancer.org/cancer/stomach-cancer/about/key-statistics.html.
17. American Cancer Society: Stomach cancer survival rates. Retrieved from https://www.cancer.org/cancer/stomach-cancer/detection-diagnosis-staging/survival-rates.html.
18. NIH: Stomach cancer. Retrieved from https://rarediseases.info.nih.gov/diseases/7704/stomach-cancer/cases/56850.
19. American Cancer Society: Treating stomach cancer. Retrieved from www.cancer.org/cancer/stomach-cancer/treating.html.
20. Parab TM, DeRogatis MJ, Boaz AM, et al.: Gastrointestinal stromal tumors: a comprehensive review, *J Gastrointest Oncol* 10:144, 2019.
21. Weledji EP: *Acute upper gastrointestinal bleeding: a review*, Surgery in Prac & Sci, 2020.
*22. Schefold JC, Krag M, Marker S, et al.: Outcomes of prophylactic pantoprazole in adult ICU patients receiving dialysis: results of a randomized trial, *Am J Nephrol* 50:312, 2019.
*23. Ye Z, Reintam Blaser A, Lytvyn L, et al.: Gastrointestinal bleeding prophylaxis for critically ill patients: a clinical practice guideline, *BMJ* 368:l6722, 2020.
24. National Digestive Disease Information Clearinghouse: Bacteria and foodborne illness. Retrieved from https;//www.niddk.nih.gov/health-information/digestive-diseases/food-poisoning.

*Evidence-based information for clinical practice.

47

Lower Gastrointestinal Problems

Mariann M. Harding

http://evolve.elsevier.com/Lewis/medsurg/

CONCEPTUAL FOCUS

Cellular Regulation
Elimination
Fluid and Electrolytes
Nutrition
Inflammation
Nutrition
Pain
Stress and Coping

LEARNING OUTCOMES

1. Explain common causes and interprofessional and nursing management of diarrhea, fecal incontinence, and constipation.
2. Describe common causes of acute abdominal pain and nursing management of the patient after a laparotomy.
3. Describe the interprofessional and nursing management of acute appendicitis, peritonitis, and gastroenteritis.
4. Compare and contrast the inflammatory bowel diseases of ulcerative colitis and Crohn's disease, including pathophysiology, clinical manifestations, complications, and interprofessional and nursing management.
5. Distinguish among small and large bowel obstructions, including causes, clinical manifestations, and interprofessional and nursing management.
6. Describe the clinical manifestations and interprofessional and nursing management of colorectal cancer.
7. Select nursing interventions to manage the care of the patient after bowel resection and ostomy surgery.
8. Distinguish between diverticulosis and diverticulitis, including clinical manifestations and interprofessional and nursing management.
9. Compare and contrast the types of hernias, including etiology and surgical and nursing management.
10. Describe the types of malabsorption syndromes and interprofessional care of celiac disease, lactase deficiency, and short bowel syndrome.
11. Describe the types, clinical manifestations, and interprofessional and nursing management of anorectal conditions.

KEY TERMS

anal fistula
appendicitis
bowel obstruction
celiac disease
constipation
Crohn's disease
diarrhea
diverticulitis
fecal incontinence
fistula
gastroenteritis
hemorrhoids
hernia
inflammatory bowel disease (IBD)
irritable bowel syndrome (IBS)
lactase deficiency
ostomy
paralytic ileus
peritonitis
short bowel syndrome (SBS)
steatorrhea
ulcerative colitis (UC)

The wide variety of gastrointestinal (GI) problems discussed in this chapter include diarrhea, constipation, and fecal incontinence; inflammatory and infectious bowel problems; bowel trauma; bowel obstructions; colorectal cancer (CRC); abdominal and bowel surgery (including ostomy formation); and malabsorption problems. Conceptually, patients often have problems with impaired elimination and nutrition. Many have inflammation and pain and are at risk for altered fluid and electrolyte balance. Promoting optimal bowel habits and nutrition are common goals.

DIARRHEA

Diarrhea is the passage of at least 3 loose or liquid stools per day. It may be acute, lasting 14 days or less, or persistent, lasting longer than 14 days. Chronic diarrhea lasts 30 days or longer.

Health care–associated diarrhea is acute diarrhea in a hospitalized patient that was not present on admission and starts after 3 days of being hospitalized. It is fairly common, developing in up to one-third of patients.

Etiology and Pathophysiology

The primary cause of acute diarrhea is ingesting infectious organisms (Table 47.1). Viruses cause most cases of infectious diarrhea in the United States. While some viral infections can

TABLE 47.1 Causes and Manifestations of Acute Infectious Diarrhea

Type of Organism	Manifestations	Source of Infection/Susceptibility
Bacterial		
Campylobacter jejuni	• Diarrhea, abdominal cramps, fever. Sometimes nausea, vomiting • Lasts about 7 days	• Undercooked poultry and unpasteurized milk • Most frequent in summer months
Clostridioides difficile	• Watery diarrhea, fever, anorexia, nausea, abdominal pain	• Prolonged use of antibiotics followed by exposure to feces-contaminated surfaces • Spores on hands and environmental surfaces are extremely hard to kill
Clostridium perfringens	• Diarrhea, abdominal cramps, nausea, vomiting • Occurs 6–24 h after eating contaminated food and lasts about 24 h	• Associated with meats, gravies, stews, dried or precooked foods • Can cause serious illness in anyone, especially older adults
Enterohemorrhagic *Escherichia coli* (e.g., *E. coli* 0157:H7)	• Severe abdominal cramping, bloody diarrhea, vomiting • Low-grade fever • Lasts 5–7 days	• Can cause serious illness, especially in older adults • May progress to life-threatening renal failure • Transmitted in water or food contaminated with infected feces
Enterotoxigenic *E. coli*	• Watery or bloody diarrhea, abdominal cramps • Nausea, vomiting, fever may be present • Lasts 3–4 days	• Most common cause of travelers' diarrhea • Transmitted in water or food contaminated with infected feces
Salmonella	• Diarrhea, fever, abdominal cramps • Lasts 4–7 days	• Reservoir is poultry, reptiles, and other animals (especially turtles, lizards, snakes, chicks, young birds) • Can be transmitted by handling animals • Found in undercooked poultry, meat, foods prepared with raw eggs
Shigella	• Diarrhea (sometimes bloody), fever, stomach cramps • Lasts 5–7 days • Postinfection arthritis may occur	• Transmitted via fecal-oral route or in food or water contaminated with infected feces • Can contaminate recreational water
Staphylococcus	• Nausea, vomiting, abdominal cramps, diarrhea • Usually mild • May cause illness in as little as 30 min • Lasts 1–3 days	• 25%–50% of people are carriers in mucous membranes, skin, or hair • Transmitted in food contaminated by food workers who are carriers or through contaminated milk and cheese
Parasitic		
Cryptosporidium	• Watery diarrhea • Lasts about 2 weeks • May have abdominal cramps, nausea, vomiting, fever, dehydration, weight loss • May be fatal in those who are immunocompromised (e.g., AIDS)	• Lives in human intestines • Transmitted in stool of infected human or animal • Outer shell allows it to live for long periods outside of body and makes it resistant to chlorine • Common cause of waterborne disease (swimming pools, lakes, drinking water, food contaminated with feces)
Entamoeba histolytica	• Diarrhea, abdominal cramping • Only 10%–20% are ill, and symptoms are usually mild • May last 2 weeks	• Fecally contaminated food, water, or hands • Most common in tropical areas • In the United States, high-risk groups include travelers, recent immigrants, and men who have sex with men
Giardia lamblia	• Abdominal cramps, nausea, diarrhea • May interfere with nutrient absorption	• Highly contagious • Transmitted via fecal-oral route • Found in fresh lakes and rivers. Can be transmitted in swimming pools, water parks, and hot tubs
Viral		
Norovirus (Norwalk-like virus)	• Nausea, vomiting, diarrhea, stomach cramping • Rapid onset • Lasts 1–2 days	• Very contagious • Virus is present in stool and emesis
Rotavirus	• Fever, vomiting, profuse watery diarrhea • Lasts 3–8 days	• Highly contagious • Transmitted mainly by fecal-oral route

be deadly, most are mild and last less than 24 hours. So, most patients rarely seek treatment.

Bacterial infection with *Escherichia coli* O157:H7, a type of enterohemorrhagic *E. coli,* is a common cause of bloody diarrhea in the United States. It is transmitted by undercooked beef or chicken contaminated with the bacteria or in fruits and vegetables exposed to contaminated manure. Other pathologic *E. coli* strains are endemic in developing countries and often cause travelers' diarrhea. *Giardia lamblia* is the most common GI parasite that causes diarrhea in the United States.[1]

Infectious organisms attack the intestines in different ways. Some organisms (e.g., Rotavirus A, Norovirus, *G. lamblia*) change the secretion and/or absorption of enterocytes in the small intestine. They do not cause inflammation. Other organisms (e.g., *Clostridioides difficile*) impair absorption by destroying cells, causing inflammation in the colon, and producing toxins that cause damage.

Secretory diarrhea is a common result of bacterial or viral infections. It occurs when ingested pathogens survive in the GI tract long enough to absorb into the enterocytes. The resulting chain reaction changes cell permeability and causes the oversecretion of water, sodium, and chloride into the bowel.

Organisms enter the body in contaminated food (e.g., *Salmonella* in undercooked eggs and chicken) or contaminated drinking water (e.g., *G. lamblia* in contaminated lakes or pools). Travelers often get diarrhea, especially if they travel to countries with poorer sanitation than their own. Infection can spread from person to person via the fecal-oral route. For example, adult day care workers can transmit infection from one resident to another if they do not wash their hands after changing soiled diapers or linens.

A person's age, gastric acidity, intestinal microflora, and immune status influence their susceptibility to pathogens. Older adults are most likely to have life-threatening diarrhea. Since stomach acid kills ingested pathogens, taking drugs to decrease stomach acid (proton pump inhibitors [PPIs]) increases the chance that pathogens will survive.

The healthy human colon normally contains a variety of bacteria, such as *E. coli,* viruses, and fungi we call the normal flora. The normal flora aid in fermentation and provide a microbial barrier against pathogens. Antibiotics kill the normal flora, making the person more susceptible to common viral, parasitic, and bacterial infections. For example, patients receiving broad-spectrum antibiotics (e.g., carbapenems, cephalosporins) are susceptible to pathogenic strains of *C. difficile. C. difficile* infection (CDI) causes the most serious hospital-associated diarrhea and is a common cause of hospital-acquired GI illness.

People who are immunocompromised because of disease (e.g., human immunodeficiency virus [HIV]) or immunosuppressive drugs are susceptible to GI tract infection. Immunocompromised patients receiving jejunal enteral nutrition (EN) are especially prone to CDI and other foodborne infections. Jejunostomy and nasointestinal feedings, which bypass the stomach's acid environment, do not contain the poorly digestible fiber that normal colonic bacteria need for survival.

Diarrhea is not always due to infection. Drugs and food intolerances can cause diarrhea. Large amounts of undigested carbohydrate in the bowel, lactose intolerance, and certain laxatives (e.g., lactulose, sodium phosphate, magnesium citrate) produce osmotic diarrhea. It results from rapid GI transit that prevents fluid and electrolyte absorption. Bile salts and undigested fats lead to excess fluid secretion into the GI tract. Diarrhea from celiac disease and short bowel syndrome (SBS) result from malabsorption in the small intestine.

Clinical Manifestations

Infections that attack the upper GI tract (e.g., Norovirus, *G. lamblia*) usually produce large-volume, watery stools, cramping, and periumbilical pain (Table 47.1). Patients have either a low-grade or no fever and often have nausea and vomiting before diarrhea begins. Infections of the colon and distal small bowel (e.g., *Shigella, Salmonella, C. difficile*) cause fever and frequent bloody diarrhea with a small volume.

Leukocytes, blood, and mucus may be present in the stool, depending on the causative agent. Severe diarrhea may cause life-threatening dehydration, electrolyte problems (e.g., hypokalemia), and acid-base imbalances (metabolic acidosis). CDI can progress to severe colitis and intestinal perforation.

Diagnostic Studies

Stool cultures are usually done only in patients who are very ill; have a fever, bloody diarrhea, or diarrhea lasting longer than 3 days; or were exposed during an outbreak. Those with travelers' diarrhea lasting longer than 14 days should be assessed for parasitic infections. Stools are examined for blood, mucus, white blood cells (WBCs), and parasites.[1] Stool cultures tests can detect common viral, parasitic, and bacterial pathogens from a single stool sample.

Blood cultures should be done in those with signs of sepsis or systemic infection (e.g., high fever) or who are immunocompromised. The WBC count may be high. People with long-standing diarrhea can develop anemia from iron and folate deficiencies. Increased hematocrit, blood urea nitrogen (BUN), and creatinine levels are signs of fluid deficit.

In patients with chronic diarrhea, measuring stool electrolytes, pH, and osmolality helps determine whether the diarrhea is from decreased fluid absorption or increased fluid secretion. Measuring stool fat and undigested muscle fibers may show fat and protein malabsorption conditions. Some patients with secretory diarrhea have high serum levels of GI hormones, such as vasoactive intestinal polypeptide and gastrin.

Interprofessional Care

Treatment of diarrhea depends on the cause. Acute infectious diarrhea is usually self-limiting. The major concerns are preventing transmission, replacing fluid and electrolytes, and protecting the skin. Most patients tolerate oral fluids. Solutions containing glucose and electrolytes may be enough to replace losses from mild diarrhea. If losses are severe, it will be necessary to give IV fluids, electrolytes, vitamins, and nutrition.

Antidiarrheal drugs have limited short-term use. They coat and protect mucous membranes, absorb irritating substances, inhibit intestinal transit, decrease intestinal secretions, or decrease central nervous system stimulation of the GI tract

TABLE 47.2 Drug Therapy

Antidiarrheal Drugs

Drug	Mechanism of Action	Nursing Considerations
bismuth subsalicylate (Pepto-Bismol)	Decreases secretions and has weak antibacterial activity. Used to prevent travelers' diarrhea	May cause tinnitus and confusion. Do not use with GI bleeding
difenoxin with atropine	Decreases peristalsis and intestinal motility	Caution patient to avoid alcohol. May cause drowsiness. Take as directed. Overdose may be life-threatening.
diphenoxylate with atropine (Lomotil)	Opioid and anticholinergic. Decreases peristalsis and intestinal motility	Blurred vision, dry mouth, drowsiness may occur. Take as directed. Overdose may be life-threatening.
loperamide (Imodium, Pepto Diarrhea Control)	Inhibits peristalsis, delays transit, increases absorption of fluid from stools	Caution patient to avoid alcohol. Do not use with GI bleeding. May cause drowsiness. Use caution with hazardous activities.
octreotide acetate (Sandostatin)	Suppresses serotonin secretion, stimulates fluid absorption from GI tract, decreases intestinal motility	Given subcut, IM, IV. May cause gall bladder or liver problems.
paregoric (camphorated tincture of opium)	Opioid. Decreases peristalsis and intestinal motility	Taken after each stool; up to 6 doses per day. May cause drowsiness. Use caution with hazardous activities.

(Table 47.2). Antidiarrheal drugs are not used in treating some infectious diarrheas because they potentially prolong exposure to the organism. They are used cautiously in inflammatory bowel disease (IBD) because of the danger of causing *toxic megacolon* (colon dilation greater than 5 cm).

Antibiotics rarely have a role in treating acute diarrhea. They are given only for certain infections or when the infected person is severely ill or immunosuppressed. The 2 antibiotics recommended for empiric therapy in adults are a fluoroquinolone, such as ciprofloxacin, and azithromycin.

Clostridioides difficile infection

CDI is a particularly hazardous health care–associated infection (HAI). The risk for contracting CDI is highest in patients receiving antimicrobial, chemotherapy, gastric acid–suppressing, or immunosuppressive drugs.[2] *C. difficile* spores can survive for up to 70 days on objects, including commodes, bedside tables, and floors. Health care workers who do not adhere to strict infection control precautions can transmit *C. difficile* from patient to patient. *Lactobacillus* probiotics may be used to prevent CDI or as an adjunct therapy to help prevent the risk for recurrent CDI.

CDI is treated with either oral vancomycin (125 mg 4 times a day) or fidaxomicin (200 mg twice daily) for 10 days.[3] All nonessential antibiotics, stool softeners, laxatives, and antidiarrheal drugs should be stopped. Metronidazole is an option when patients cannot be treated with vancomycin or fidaxomicin. Patients with severe, complicated CDI with shock, hypotension, ileus, or megacolon should receive vancomycin 500 mg 4 times daily orally with IV metronidazole.[2] Patients with an ileus can receive vancomycin via enema.

Recurrent CDI occurs in about 20% of patients. The risk increases with the use of additional antibiotics and CDI recurrences. *Fecal microbiota transplantation* (FMT) is emerging as an effective treatment for recurrent CDI.[2] FMT reestablishes healthy intestinal flora by infusing fecal bacteria obtained from healthy donor stool into the patient's colon. To perform an FMT, feces obtained from the donor is pureed into a liquid slurry consistency using saline, water, or pasteurized cow's milk. The donor stool is then placed in the GI tract via an enema, nasoenteral tube, or during colonoscopy. The major concern with FMT is the potential for transmitting infectious agents in the donor stool. Using feces from donors who have intimate physical contact with the recipient and careful screening minimize this risk. Most patients have diarrhea right after the procedure.

NURSING MANAGEMENT: ACUTE INFECTIOUS DIARRHEA

Assessment

Begin your assessment with a thorough history and physical assessment (Table 47.3). Ask the patient to describe their stool pattern and related symptoms (Fig. 47.1). Focus on the duration, frequency, character, and consistency of stool and the relationship to other symptoms, such as pain and vomiting. Ask about medical conditions that may cause diarrhea and whether the person is taking drugs, such as antibiotics and laxatives, which are known to cause diarrhea, decrease stomach acidity, or cause immunosuppression. Determine whether the patient has traveled to a foreign country or been at a daycare facility recently. Ask if other family members are ill. Assess food preparation practices, food intolerances (e.g., milk), and changes in diet and appetite.

Assess for fever and signs of dehydration (dry skin, low-grade fever, orthostatic changes in pulse and BP, decreased and concentrated urine). Assess the abdomen for distention, pain, and guarding. Inspect the perineal skin for signs of redness and breakdown from diarrhea.

Clinical Problems

Clinical problems for the patient with acute infectious diarrhea include:

- Impaired bowel elimination
- Fluid imbalance
- Electrolyte imbalance

For more information on clinical problems and interventions for diarrhea, see eNursing Care Plan 47.1 on the website for this chapter.

TABLE 47.3 NURSING ASSESSMENT

Diarrhea

Subjective Data

Important Health Information

Health history: Recent travel, hospitalization, infections, stress. Diverticulitis or malabsorption, metabolic disorders, IBD, IBS

Medications: Laxatives or enemas, magnesium-containing antacids, sorbitol-containing suspensions or elixirs, antibiotics, methyldopa, digitalis, colchicine; OTC antidiarrheal drugs

Surgery or other treatments: Stomach or bowel surgery, radiation

Functional Health Patterns

Health perception–health management: Chronic laxative use, malaise

Nutritional-metabolic: Ingestion of fatty and spicy foods, food intolerances. Anorexia, nausea, vomiting, weight loss. Thirst

Elimination: Increased stool frequency, volume, and looseness. Change in color and character of stools. Steatorrhea, abdominal bloating. Decreased urine output

Cognitive-perceptual: Abdominal tenderness, abdominal pain, cramping, tenesmus

Objective Data

General

Lethargy, sunken eyeballs, fever, malnutrition

GI

Frequent soft to liquid stools that may alternate with constipation, altered stool color. Abdominal distention, hyperactive bowel sounds. Pus, blood, mucus, or fat in stools. Fecal impaction

Skin

Pallor, dry mucous membranes, poor skin turgor, perianal irritation

Urinary

Decreased output, concentrated urine

Possible Diagnostic Findings

Abnormal serum electrolyte levels. Anemia, ↑ WBC, eosinophilia, hypoalbuminemia. Positive stool cultures. Ova, parasites, leukocytes, blood, or fat in stool. Abnormal sigmoidoscopy or colonoscopy findings. Abnormal lower GI series

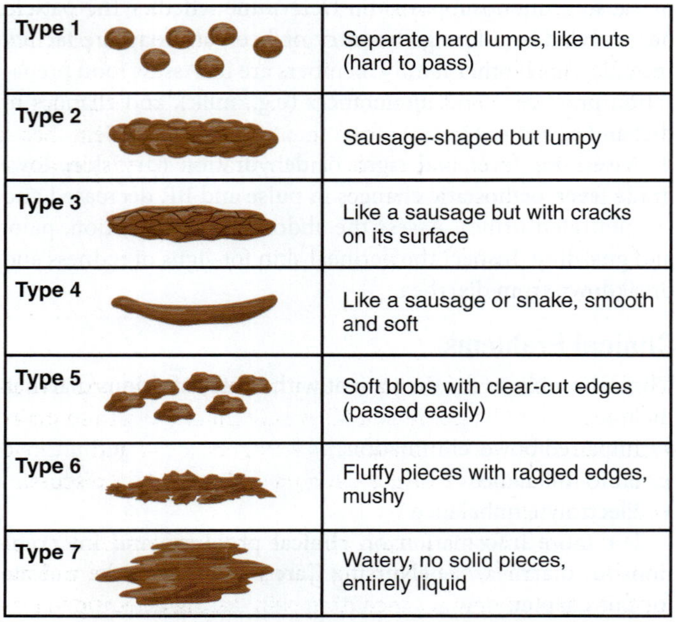

Fig. 47.1 Bristol Stool Scale showing fecal consistency.

TABLE 47.4 NURSING MANAGEMENT

Diarrhea

- Ensure the patient maintains an adequate fluid intake:
  - Encourage oral fluids containing glucose and electrolytes.
  - Administer IV fluids and electrolytes as ordered.
- Administer antidiarrheal and antibiotic drugs as ordered.
- Implement proper isolation and infection control precautions.
- Maintain accurate intake and output records, recording weight daily.
- Assist the patient with keeping the perianal area clean.
- Apply a moisturizing skin barrier cream as needed.
- Have the patient use dibucaine, witch hazel, or sitz baths to reduce perianal irritation and pain.
- Implement measures to make toileting easier for patients, such as:
  - Call light in reach
  - Easy-to-manage clothing
  - Assistive devices available
- Provide privacy for toileting and use a deodorizer.
- Encourage the patient to increase high fiber foods, such as whole-grain breads and cereals, and fresh fruits and vegetables, unless contraindicated.
- Teach the patient to avoid foods and fluids known to worsen diarrhea.

◆ Planning

The overall goals are that the patient with diarrhea will have (1) resumption of normal bowel patterns; (2) normal fluid, electrolyte, and acid-base balance; (3) normal nutrition status; and (4) no perianal/perineal skin breakdown.

◆ Implementation

Nursing management of the patient with diarrhea is outlined in Table 47.4. Consider all cases of acute diarrhea as infectious until the cause is known. Strict infection control precautions are needed to prevent the illness from spreading to others. Wash your hands with soap and water before and after contact with each patient and when handling body fluids of any kind. Teach the patient principles of hygiene, infection control, and the potential dangers of an illness that is infectious to themselves and others. Discuss proper food handling, cooking, and storage with the patient and caregiver (see Tables 46.24 and 46.25).

Viruses and *C. difficile* spores are extremely hard to kill. Meticulous hand washing with soap and water is extremely important in limiting the spread of *C. difficile.* Alcohol-based hand cleaners and ammonia-based disinfectants are ineffective. Immediately put patients with CDI in isolation. Ensure that visitors and all providers wear gloves and gowns. Give infected patients their own disposable stethoscopes and thermometers. Consider all objects in the room contaminated. Ensure surfaces and equipment are disinfected with a 10% bleach solution or a disinfectant labeled as *C. difficile* sporicidal.

FECAL INCONTINENCE

Etiology and Pathophysiology

Fecal incontinence is the involuntary loss of stool. It occurs when the normal structures that maintain continence are damaged or disrupted. Defecation is a voluntary action when the neuromuscular system is intact (see Chapter 43). Problems

TABLE 47.5 Common Causes of Fecal Incontinence

Anal Sphincter Weakness	Neurologic Disease

• Anorectal infection
• Injury
  • Anorectal surgery for hemorrhoids, fistula, fissures
  • Childbirth injury
  • Perineal trauma or pelvic fracture
• Internal sphincter thinning
	• Brain tumor
	• Congenital abnormalities (e.g., spina bifida, myelomeningocele)
	• Dementia
	• Diabetes
	• Multiple sclerosis
	• Neuropathy
	• Spinal cord lesions
	• Stroke

Functional	**Pelvic Floor Dysfunction**
• Physical or mobility problems affecting toileting ability (e.g., frail older person who cannot get to the bathroom in time)	• Fistula • Rectal prolapse
Inflammation	**Other**
• IBD • Radiation	• Chronic constipation • Denervation of pelvic muscles from chronic straining • Diarrhea • Fecal impaction

with motor function (contraction of sphincters and rectal floor muscles) and/or sensory function (ability to perceive the presence of stool or have the urge to defecate) can result in fecal incontinence. Contributing factors include altered bowel habits, weakness or disruption of the internal or external anal sphincter, damage to the pudendal nerve or other nerves that innervate the anorectum, and damage to the anal tissue (Table 47.5).

For women, obstetric trauma is the most common cause of sphincter injury.[4] Aging and menopause are contributing factors. Anorectal surgery can damage the sphincters and pudendal nerves. Radiation for prostate cancer decreases rectal compliance. Neurologic conditions, including stroke and multiple sclerosis, interfere with defecation.

People with normal functioning defecation can have incontinence if mobility problems prevent prompt access to a toilet or stool is accidentally discharged with diarrhea. Chronic constipation can lead to *fecal impaction,* a collection of hardened feces in the rectum or sigmoid colon that a person cannot expel. Incontinence occurs as liquid stool seeps around the hardened feces. Fecal impaction is a common problem in older adults with limited mobility. Straining with constipation contributes to incontinence because it weakens the pelvic floor muscles.

Diagnostic Studies

The diagnosis and effective management of fecal incontinence require a thorough health history and physical assessment. A rectal examination can reveal reduced anal canal muscle tone and contraction strength of the external sphincter and detect internal prolapse, rectocele, hemorrhoids, masses, and fecal impaction. Other tests, such as anorectal manometry, anorectal ultrasonography, and anal electromyography, are done when symptoms persist after treating underlying problems or if certain problems need further evaluation.

Interprofessional Care

Treatment of incontinence depends on the cause. Maintaining normal stool consistency and a bowel management program are important. This includes regular defecation, a high-fiber diet, and increased intake of caffeine-free fluids. Fiber supplements or bulk-forming laxatives, like psyllium (e.g., Metamucil), increase stool bulk, firm the consistency, and promote the sensation of rectal filling. Patients may need to reduce the intake of foods that cause diarrhea and rectal irritation. Common triggers include caffeine, products containing artificial sweeteners, dairy products, high gas-producing vegetables (e.g., broccoli, cabbage, cauliflower), and vegetables containing insoluble fiber (e.g., lettuce, tomatoes, corn).

Fecal incontinence from fecal impaction usually resolves after manual removal of the hard feces and cleansing enemas. Antidiarrheal drugs (e.g., loperamide) are useful in slowing GI transit.

Physical therapy and biofeedback training can improve awareness of rectal sensation, coordinate internal and external anal sphincters, and increase the strength of external sphincter contraction. Biofeedback training requires intact sensory and motor nerves and motivation to learn. It is a safe, painless, and effective treatment.

Mild electrical stimulation of the sacral nerves targets communication problems between the brain and nerves that control the pelvic floor muscles and sphincters. Electrical stimulation can improve quality of life. Some patients may achieve complete continence.

For patients who do not respond to conservative measures, treatment with dextranomer/hyaluronic acid gel (Solesta) may be used. In this treatment, the gel is injected into the deep submucosa of the patient's anal canal. It works by building up tissue in the anal area, narrowing the anal canal and allowing muscles to close better. No anesthesia is given. Postinjection pain and bleeding may occur.

Surgery, such as a sphincter repair procedure, is an option when other conservative treatments fail, the patient has a full-thickness prolapse, or the anal sphincter needs repair. A colostomy is sometimes needed.

❖ NURSING MANAGEMENT: FECAL INCONTINENCE

◆ Assessment

Fecal incontinence is embarrassing, uncomfortable, and irritating to the skin. Its unpredictable nature makes it hard to maintain school or work activities and hampers social and intimate contact. Be sensitive to the patient's feelings when discussing incontinence.

Ask about bowel patterns before the incontinence developed; current bowel habits; stool consistency, volume, and frequency; and symptoms, including pain during defecation and a feeling of incomplete evacuation *(tenesmus)*. The Bristol Stool Scale is helpful to assess stool consistency (see Fig. 47.1). Assess whether the patient has a sensation of urgency to evacuate the bowel or sensation of passing flatus and leaking stool. Ask about daily activities (mealtimes and work), diet, family and social activities, and the degree to which incontinence interferes with these activities.

Check the perineal area for irritation or breakdown. Patients who have fecal incontinence are at risk for *incontinence-associated dermatitis* (IAD). IAD results from chemical irritants in the feces causing skin damage. Symptoms include redness, skin loss, and rash. The location of IAD is usually the perianal or perineal area, buttocks, or upper thighs. Fungal infection is common and seen as a dark red center surrounded by satellite lesions. Your assessment is important in distinguishing IAD from a pressure injury.

◆ Implementation

Regardless of the cause, bowel training is effective for many patients. Knowing the patient's usual bowel pattern can help you plan a bowel program that will achieve optimal stool consistency and establish predictable bowel elimination patterns. For the hospitalized patient, placement on a bedpan, help to a bedside commode, or walks to the bathroom at a regular time daily help to establish regular defecation. The best time to schedule elimination is within 30 minutes after breakfast.

If these techniques are not effective in establishing bowel regularity, administer bisacodyl, a glycerin suppository, or a small phosphate enema 15 to 30 minutes before the usual evacuation time. These preparations stimulate the anorectal reflex. Since stimulation will not occur unless the suppository or enema touches the rectal wall, first check for stool in the rectum and digitally remove it before inserting the laxative. Once a regular pattern is established, stop these drugs. Digital stimulation is another method for stimulating the anorectal reflex. It is often included in bowel programs for people with neurogenic bowels (e.g., from spinal cord injury). Irrigating the rectum and colon (usually with tap water) at regular intervals is another way to achieve continence in patients with neurogenic bowel.

Maintaining perineal skin integrity is a priority, especially in immobile patients. Feces can contaminate wounds, damage skin, cause bladder infections, and spread infections such as *C. difficile*. Fecal containment is essential. One way to contain stool is a stool management system (e.g., Flexi-Seal, DigniCare, Actiflo). These systems funnel liquid stool from the rectum into a containment system. Common features include a retention cuff that sits above the anal sphincter and soft tubing that extends from this cuff to a secure hub that allows a person to change the containment canister when it is full. A system can remain in place for weeks. Their use may decrease the risk for CDI, skin damage from exposure to stool, IAD, and pressure injuries. Do not use a rectal tube or urinary catheter as a stool catheter. They can reduce the responsiveness of the rectal sphincter and ulcerate the rectal mucosa.

Perform frequent skin assessments when using absorbent products. Incontinence pads are an option when the patient is in bed. Briefs should be used only during ambulation or when sitting in a chair. Make sure they are changed promptly after each episode of incontinence.

Use absorbent products in combination with a skin care program. This includes prompt cleansing, moisturizing, and skin protection. Cleanse the skin gently, using a skin cleanser rather than soap and water. Options include a cotton cloth moistened with a hydrating skin cleansing foam, incontinence clean-up cloths, or baby wipes. Avoid products that contain alcohol. They can cause drying of the skin and discomfort if the skin is irritated. Pat the skin dry or use a blow dryer on a cool setting. Do not rub the skin dry. Apply a moisture barrier and, if needed, a skin barrier cream for more protection. For patients unable to care for themselves at home, teach caregivers how to maintain skin integrity.

Fecal incontinence is an overwhelming burden for most patients. Be sensitive to their fears. Teach them ways to reduce incontinence episodes and better cope with them when they do occur. Help patients identify food triggers that may worsen symptoms. Encourage them to avoid those foods and exercise after meals. Tell them to try to use bathrooms when they are available. Patients may be more confident when they use discreet, disposable briefs or pads. Have them wear dark-colored clothing that they can quickly remove for toileting. Ready access to a spare set of clothing and cleansing cloths is important.

CONSTIPATION

People with **constipation** have fewer than 3 stools per week, often accompanied by straining, a feeling of incomplete evacuation, a need for digital assistance to evacuate stool, bloating, and hard or lumpy stools.[5] Constipation is a symptom, not a disease. It can be acute, usually lasting less than 1 week, or chronic, lasting over 3 months.

Etiology and Pathophysiology

Risk factors for chronic constipation include a low-fiber diet, decreased physical activity, or ignoring the defecation urge. Ignoring the urge to defecate for a prolonged period can cause the muscles and mucosa of the rectum to become insensitive to the presence of feces. In addition, the prolonged retention of feces results in drying of stool due to water absorption. The harder and drier the feces, the harder it is to expel. Emotions, including anxiety, depression, and stress, affect the GI tract and can contribute to constipation.

Constipation occurs with diseases that slow GI transit and hamper neurologic function, such as diabetes, Parkinson disease, and multiple sclerosis (Table 47.6).[5] Many drugs, especially opioids, cause constipation (Table 47.7).

Some people think they are constipated if they do not have a daily bowel movement. This can result in chronic laxative use and *cathartic colon syndrome*, a condition in which the colon becomes dilated and atonic (lacking muscle tone). Ultimately, the person cannot defecate without a laxative.

TABLE 47.6 Diseases Associated With Constipation

Colonic Disorders
- Cancer
- Diverticular disease
- IBD
- Intestinal stenosis
- Intussusception
- Luminal or extraluminal obstructing lesions
- Prolapse
- Rectocele

Systemic Disorders
Collagen Vascular Disease
- Amyloidosis
- Systemic lupus erythematosus
- Systemic sclerosis (scleroderma)

Metabolic/Endocrine
- Chronic renal failure
- Diabetes
- Hypercalcemia/hyperparathyroidism
- Hypokalemia
- Hypothyroidism
- Pheochromocytoma
- Pregnancy

Neurologic Disorders
- Autonomic neuropathy (from diabetes)
- Hirschsprung megacolon
- Multiple sclerosis
- Neurofibromatosis
- Parkinson disease
- Spinal cord lesions or injury
- Stroke

TABLE 47.7 Drugs Associated With Constipation

Cardiovascular	• Antihypertensives (β-adrenergic blockers, calcium channel blockers) • Furosemide • Hypolipidemics (cholestyramine, colestipol, statins)
Central nervous system	• Antidepressants (tricyclics, selective serotonin reuptake inhibitors) • Antiepileptics (carbamazepine, phenytoin, clonazepam) • Antipsychotics (butyrophenones, phenothiazines, barbiturates) • Benzodiazepines
GI	• Antacids containing aluminum, calcium • Antidiarrheals • Proton-pump inhibitors • Supplements (bismuth, calcium, iron)
Other	• Analgesics (opiates and derivatives) • Antitussives (codeine, dextromethorphan)

Clinical Manifestations

The clinical presentation varies from mild discomfort to a more severe event mimicking an "acute abdomen." Stools are absent or hard, dry, and difficult to pass. Abdominal distention, bloating, increased flatus, and increased rectal pressure may be present.

Hemorrhoids are a common complication of chronic constipation. They result from venous engorgement caused by repeated *Valsalva maneuvers* (straining) and venous compression from hard, impacted stool. The Valsalva maneuver may have serious outcomes for patients with heart failure, cerebral edema, hypertension, and coronary artery disease. During straining, the patient inspires deeply and holds the breath while contracting abdominal muscles and bearing down. This increases both intraabdominal and intrathoracic pressures and reduces venous return to the heart. The heart rate temporarily decreases along with a decrease in cardiac output. This results in a transient drop in arterial pressure. When the patient relaxes, thoracic pressure falls, resulting in a sudden flow of blood into the heart, increased heart rate, and an immediate rise in arterial pressure. These changes may be fatal for the patient who cannot compensate for the sudden increased blood flow returning to the heart.

Rectal mucosal ulcers and fissures may occur from stool stasis or straining. Diverticulosis is another potential complication of chronic constipation. It is more common in older patients.

In the presence of *obstipation* (absolute constipation with no passage of gas or stool) or fecal impaction from constipation, colonic perforation may occur. Perforation, which is life threatening, causes abdominal pain, nausea, vomiting, fever, and a high WBC count.

Diagnostic Studies

In most patients, the diagnosis of constipation is based on findings from the history and physical assessment. The physical should include an abdominal assessment, inspection of the perianal and rectal region, and digital rectal examination (DRE). Concerning signs include a sudden, persistent change in bowel habits (>6 weeks) in those over 50 years, rectal bleeding or bloody stools, iron deficiency anemia, weight loss, significant abdominal pain, family or personal history of CRC, or IBD and a palpable mass. If any of these are present, tests are needed to rule out serious disease, such as CRC. These may include abdominal x-rays, barium enema, and colonoscopy or sigmoidoscopy. The patient with severe constipation may undergo anorectal manometry, GI tract transit studies, balloon expulsion test, or defecography.

Interprofessional Care

Increasing fiber intake, fluid intake, and exercise can prevent many cases of constipation. Laxatives (Table 47.8) and enemas are an option in treating constipation. All promote bowel movements, but each class works differently. Which one a patient receives depends on the severity and duration of constipation and the patient's health. Daily bulk-forming laxatives (psyllium) can prevent constipation because they work like diet fiber and do not cause dependence. In patients with chronic constipation who do not respond to diet and lifestyle modifications, osmotic laxatives are the next recommended treatment. Stimulant laxatives are given to patients who do not respond to osmotic laxatives. Enemas are fast-acting and offer immediate treatment of constipation but must be used cautiously. Those containing sodium phosphate and magnesium can cause electrolyte imbalances in older adults and patients with heart and kidney problems.

Other therapies target specific patient needs. Peripherally acting opioid receptor antagonists (methylnaltrexone, naldemedine, naloxegol) decrease constipation from opioid use. They do not block the analgesic effects of opioids. Biofeedback therapy

TABLE 47.8 Drug Therapy
Constipation

Mechanism of Action	Indications	Drugs	Nursing Considerations
Bulk Forming			
Absorbs water. Increases bulk, thereby stimulating peristalsis *Action:* Usually within 24 h	Acute and chronic constipation, IBS, diverticulosis	methylcellulose (Citrucel) psyllium (Metamucil, Konsyl, Hydrocil, Fiberall)	Do not use in patients with abdominal pain, nausea, vomiting, those suspected of having appendicitis, biliary tract obstruction, or acute hepatitis. Must be taken with fluids (≥8 oz). Best choice for initial treatment of constipation
Emollients			
Lubricate intestinal tract and soften feces, making hard stools easier to pass. Do not affect peristalsis *Action:* Softeners in 72 h, lubricants in 8 h	Acute and chronic constipation, fecal impaction, anorectal conditions	*Softeners:* docusate (Colace, Surfak) *Lubricants:* mineral oil (Fleet Mineral Oil Enema)	Can block absorption of fat-soluble vitamins, such as vitamin K, which may increase risk for bleeding in patients on anticoagulants
Prosecretory Drugs			
Increases intestinal fluid secretion through direct action on epithelial cells, speeding colonic transit *Action:* Usually within 24 h	Chronic idiopathic constipation, IBS-C (women only)	linaclotide (Linzess) lubiprostone (Amitiza) plecanatide (Trulance)	Do not use in patients with history of mechanical GI obstruction. Can cause nausea and watery diarrhea
Saline and Osmotic Solutions			
Cause retention of fluid in intestinal lumen, reducing stool consistency and increasing volume *Action:* Within 15 min to 3 hr	Chronic constipation, bowel preparation for diagnostic tests and surgery	lactulose magnesium salts (magnesium citrate, Milk of Magnesia) sodium phosphates (Fleet Enema) polyethylene glycol (MiraLAX, GoLYTELY)	May cause abdominal distention, diarrhea. Overuse of magnesium or sodium phosphates in older adults or those with renal failure can lead to fluid and electrolyte imbalances. Least effective agents in this class
Stimulants			
Increases peristalsis and speeds colonic transit by irritating colon wall and stimulating enteric nerves *Action:* Usually within 12 h	Acute constipation, bowel preparation for diagnostic tests and surgery	anthraquinones (cascara sagrada, senna) sennosides (Ex-Lax, Senokot) bisacodyl (Correctol, Dulcolax)	Cause melanosis coli (brown or black pigmentation of colon). Most widely abused laxatives. Should not be used in patients with impaction or obstipation

may help patients who have constipation because of *anismus* (uncoordinated contraction of the anal sphincter during straining).

A patient with severe constipation related to bowel motility or mechanical disorders may need more intense treatment. A patient with unrelenting constipation may need a colostomy, ileostomy, or continent fecal diversion. These procedures are discussed later in this chapter.

Nutrition Therapy

Diet is a key factor in preventing and treating constipation. Many patients have improved symptoms when they increase their fiber intake. Fiber is found in fruits, vegetables, and grains (Table 47.9). Wheat bran and prunes are especially effective for preventing and treating constipation. Whole wheat and bran are high in insoluble fiber.

Fiber adds to the stool bulk directly by attracting water. Adequate fluid intake (2 L/day) is essential. Large, bulky stools move through the colon much more quickly than small stools. However, the recommended fluid intake may be contraindicated in a patient with heart disease or renal failure. Tell the patient that increasing fiber intake may initially increase gas production because of fermentation in the colon, but this effect decreases over several days.

NURSING MANAGEMENT: CONSTIPATION

Assessment

Determine the patient's usual defecation patterns and habits. Ask the patient about the onset and duration of symptoms, the shape and consistency of the stool, and any difficulty with evacuation (see Fig. 47.1). Is the patient straining during defecation? Is there a feeling of incomplete evacuation or the need to use fingering to expel the feces? Ask about diet, exercise, laxative use, and history that could contribute to problems with defecation. Table 47.10 outlines the subjective and objective data to obtain from a patient with constipation.

Implementation

Tailor the nursing management of constipation to your assessment of the patient's symptoms. Teach the patient about the role of diet, adequate fluid intake, and regular exercise in preventing and treating constipation (Table 47.11). Emphasize the importance of a high-fiber diet. Stress using laxatives and enemas as ordered.

TABLE 47.9 NUTRITION THERAPY

High-Fiber Foods

	Fiber/ Serving (g)	Serving Size	Calories/ Serving
Vegetables			
Asparagus	3.5	½ cup	18
Beans			
• Navy	8.4	½ cup	80
• Kidney	9.7	½ cup	94
• Lima	8.3	½ cup	63
• Pinto	8.9	½ cup	78
• String	2.1	½ cup	18
Broccoli	3.5	½ cup	18
Carrots, raw	1.8	½ cup	15
Corn	2.6	½ medium ear	72
Peas, canned	6.7	½ cup	63
Potatoes			
• Baked	1.9	½ medium	72
• Sweet	2.1	½ medium	79
Squash, acorn	7.0	1 cup	82
Tomato, raw	1.5	1 small	18
Fruits			
Apple	2.0	½ large	42
Blackberries	6.7	¾ cup	40
Orange	1.6	1 small	35
Peach	2.3	1 medium	38
Pear	2.0	½ medium	44
Raspberries	9.2	1 cup	42
Strawberries	3.1	1 cup	45
Grain Products			
Bread, whole wheat	1.3	1 slice	59
Cereal			
• All Bran (100%)	8.4	⅓ cup	70
• Corn Flakes	2.6	¾ cup	70
• Shredded Wheat	2.8	1 biscuit	70
Popcorn	3.0	3 cups	62

Teach the patient to establish a regular time to defecate and not to suppress the urge to defecate. Defecation is easiest when the person is sitting on a commode with the knees higher than the hips. The sitting position allows gravity to aid defecation, and flexing the hips straightens the angle between the anal canal and rectum so that stool flows out more easily. Place a footstool in front of the toilet to promote flexion of the hips. It is challenging to defecate while sitting on a bedpan. For a patient in bed, raise the head of the bed as high as the patient can tolerate.

The sights, odors, and sounds of defecation embarrass most people. Provide as much privacy as possible and use an odor eliminator. Encourage patients to maintain abdominal muscle tone. Prompt patients to contract abdominal muscles several times a day. Sit-ups and straight-leg raises can help improve abdominal muscle tone.

For the patient whose perceived constipation is related to rigid beliefs about bowel function, start a discussion about these concerns. Give appropriate information on normal bowel function and discuss the adverse consequences of overuse of laxatives and enemas.

TABLE 47.10 NURSING ASSESSMENT

Constipation

Subjective Data

Important Health Information

Health history: Colorectal disease, neurologic problems, bowel obstruction, environmental changes, cancer, IBD, diabetes

Medications: Table 47.7

Functional Health Patterns

Health perception–health management: Chronic laxative, enema use. Rigid beliefs about bowel function. Malaise

Nutritional-metabolic: Changes in diet or mealtime. Fiber and fluid intake. Anorexia, nausea

Elimination: Change in usual bowel patterns. Hard, difficult-to-pass stool, decrease in stool frequency and amount. Flatus, abdominal distention. Straining, tenesmus, rectal pressure. Fecal incontinence (if impacted)

Activity-exercise: Daily activity routine. Immobility, sedentary lifestyle

Cognitive-perceptual: Dizziness, headache, anorectal pain. Abdominal pain on defecation

Coping–stress tolerance: Acute or chronic stress

Objective Data

General

Lethargy

Skin

Anorectal fissures, hemorrhoids, abscesses

GI

Abdominal distention. Hypoactive or absent bowel sounds. Palpable abdominal mass. Fecal impaction. Small, hard, dry stool. Stool with blood

Skin

Anorectal fissures, hemorrhoids, abscesses

Possible Diagnostic Findings

Guaiac-positive stools. Abdominal x-ray showing stool in lower colon

ACUTE ABDOMINAL PAIN AND LAPAROTOMY

Etiology and Pathophysiology

Acute abdominal pain is pain of recent onset. It may signal a life-threatening problem, so it requires immediate attention. Causes include damage to organs in the abdomen and pelvis, which leads to inflammation, infection, obstruction, bleeding, and perforation (Fig. 47.2). Perforation of the GI tract results in irritation of the *peritoneum* (serous membrane lining the abdominal cavity) and peritonitis. Hypovolemic shock occurs from bleeding or obstruction and peritonitis, causing large amounts of fluid to move from the vascular space into the abdomen.

Clinical Manifestations

Pain is the most common symptom of an acute abdominal problem. The patient may have nausea, vomiting, diarrhea, constipation, flatulence, fatigue, fever, rebound tenderness, and bloating.

Diagnostic Studies

Diagnosis begins with a complete history and physical assessment. Description of the pain (frequency, timing, duration,

TABLE 47.11 PATIENT & CAREGIVER TEACHING

Constipation

Include the following instructions when teaching the patient and caregiver about managing constipation:

1. Eat Fiber

Eat 20 to 30 g of fiber per day. Gradually increase the amount of fiber eaten over 1 to 2 weeks. Fiber softens hard stool and adds bulk to stool, promoting evacuation. Eat prunes or drink prune juice daily. Prunes stimulate defecation.

- Foods high in fiber: raw vegetables and fruits, beans, breakfast cereals (All-Bran, oatmeal)
- Fiber supplements: Metamucil, Citrucel, FiberCon

2. Drink Fluids

Fluid softens hard stools. Drink 2 L/day. Drink water or fruit juices. Avoid caffeinated coffee, tea, and cola. Caffeine stimulates fluid loss through urination.

3. Exercise Regularly

Walk, swim, or bike at least 3 times per week. Contract and relax abdominal muscles when standing or by doing sit-ups to strengthen muscles and prevent straining. Exercise stimulates bowel motility and moves stool through the colon.

4. Establish a Regular Time to Defecate

First thing in the morning or after the first meal of the day is the best time because people often have the urge to defecate at this time.

5. Do Not Delay Defecation

Respond to the urge to have a bowel movement as soon as possible. Delaying defecation results in hard stools and a decreased "urge" to defecate. Water is absorbed from stool by the colon over time. The colon becomes less sensitive to the presence of stool in the rectum.

6. Record Your Bowel Elimination Pattern

Develop a habit of recording on your calendar when you have a bowel movement. Regular monitoring of bowel movement will help you identify a problem early.

7. Use Laxatives and Enemas as Ordered

Do not overuse laxatives and enemas because they cause dependence. People who overuse them become unable to have a bowel movement without them.

location), accompanying symptoms, and sequence of symptoms (e.g., pain before or after vomiting) provide vital clues about the origin of the problem. Note the patient's position. The fetal posture is common with peritoneal irritation (e.g., appendicitis). The patient may be supine with outstretched legs with visceral pain. Restlessness and inability to find a comfortable position occur with obstructions from kidney stones and gallstones.

Physical assessment includes assessment of the abdomen, rectum, and pelvis. A complete blood count (CBC), urinalysis, abdominal x-ray, and ECG are done, along with an ultrasound or CT scan. Women of childbearing age may need a pregnancy test to rule out an ectopic pregnancy.

Interprofessional Care

Emergency management of the patient with acute abdominal pain is shown in Table 47.12. The goal is to identify and treat the cause and monitor and treat complications, especially shock. Carefully use pain medications to provide pain relief without interfering with diagnostic accuracy when patients have nontraumatic acute abdominal pain.

An immediate surgical consult may be needed. The HCP may perform a diagnostic laparoscopy to inspect the surface of abdominal organs, obtain biopsy specimens, perform laparoscopic ultrasounds, and remove organs. A laparotomy is done when laparoscopic techniques are inadequate. If the cause of the acute abdomen can be surgically removed (e.g., inflamed appendix) or surgically repaired (e.g., ruptured abdominal aneurysm), surgery is considered definitive therapy.

❖ NURSING MANAGEMENT: ACUTE ABDOMINAL PAIN

◆ Assessment

For the patient with acute abdominal pain, take vital signs immediately and again at frequent intervals. Increased pulse and decreasing BP indicate impending shock. A fever suggests an inflammatory or infectious process. Intake and output give essential information about the adequacy of vascular volume. Altered mental status occurs with poor cerebral perfusion. Skin color, skin temperature, and peripheral pulse strength give information about perfusion.

Inspect the abdomen for distention, masses, abnormal pulsation, symmetry, hernias, rashes, scars, and pigmentation changes. Auscultate bowel sounds. Decreased or absent bowel sounds in a quadrant may occur with a bowel obstruction, peritonitis, or paralytic ileus. Perform gentle palpation to help determine the location and level of the patient's pain. Assess for involuntary guarding and rigidity, which occur with peritoneal irritation.

Ask the patient about the onset, location, intensity, duration, frequency, and character of pain. Note whether the pain has spread or moved to new sites (quadrants) and what makes the pain worse or better. Ask if the pain is related to other symptoms, such as nausea, vomiting, changes in bowel and bladder habits, or vaginal discharge in women. Assessment of vomiting includes the amount, color, consistency, and odor of the emesis. Ask about usual and changes in bowel patterns and habits.

◆ Clinical Problems

Clinical problems for the patient with acute abdominal pain include:

- Pain
- Fluid imbalance
- Risk for infection

◆ Planning

The overall goals are that the patient with acute abdominal pain will have (1) relief of abdominal pain, (2) resolution of inflammation, (3) freedom from complications (especially hypovolemic shock), and (4) normal nutrition status.

◆ Implementation

General care for patients with acute abdominal pain involves managing fluid and electrolyte imbalances, pain, and anxiety. Assess the quality and intensity of pain at regular intervals.

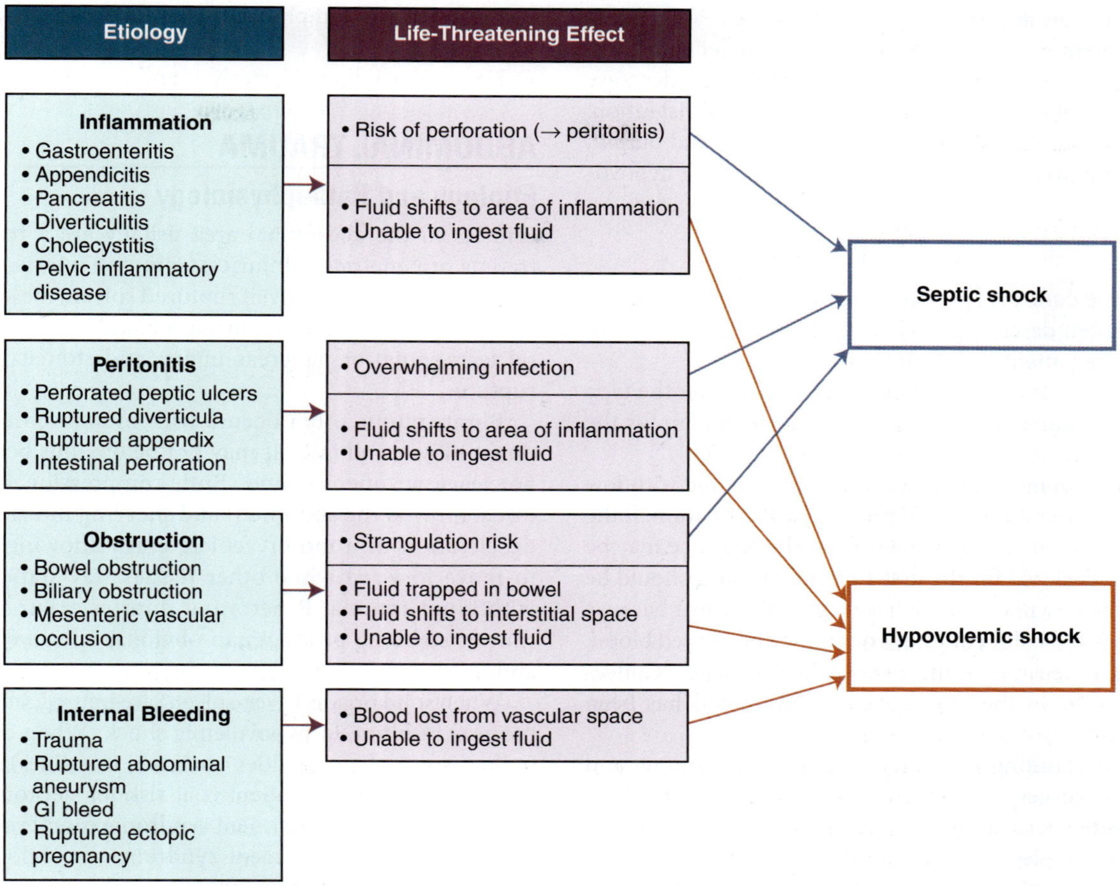

Fig. 47.2 Cause of acute abdominal pain and pathophysiologic sequelae.

TABLE 47.12 EMERGENCY MANAGEMENT

Acute Abdominal Pain

Etiology	Assessment Findings	Interventions
Gynecologic Problems • Pelvic inflammatory disease • Ruptured ectopic pregnancy • Ruptured ovarian cyst **Infectious Disease** • *Escherichia coli* 0157:H7 • *Giardia* • *Salmonella* **Inflammation** • Appendicitis • Cholecystitis • Diverticulitis • Gastritis • IBD • Pancreatitis • Pyelonephritis **Vascular Problems** • Mesenteric vascular occlusion • Ruptured aortic aneurysm **Other** • Obstruction or perforation of abdominal organ • GI bleeding or ischemia • Myocardial infarction • Trauma	**Abdominal and GI Findings** • Diffuse, localized, dull, burning, or sharp abdominal pain or tenderness • Abdominal distention • Abdominal rigidity • Diarrhea • Hematemesis • Melena • Nausea and vomiting • Rebound tenderness **Hypovolemic Shock** • ↓ BP • Cool, clammy skin • ↓ Level of consciousness • ↑ HR • ↓ Urine output (<0.5 mL/kg/h)	**Initial** • Ensure patent airway. • Apply O_2 via nasal cannula or nonrebreather mask. • Establish IV access with large-bore catheter and infuse warm normal saline or lactated Ringer's solution. Insert another large-bore catheter if shock present. • Obtain blood for CBC and electrolyte levels. • Obtain blood for amylase level, pregnancy tests, clotting studies, and type and crossmatch as appropriate. • Insert indwelling urinary catheter. • Obtain urinalysis. • Insert NG tube as needed. **Ongoing Monitoring** • Monitor vital signs, level of consciousness, O_2 saturation, and intake/output. • Obtain pain assessment. • Assess amount and character of emesis. • Anticipate surgical intervention. • Keep patient NPO.

Provide medication and other comfort measures. Maintain a calm environment and give information to help decrease anxiety. A nasogastric (NG) tube with low suction may decrease vomiting and relieve discomfort from gastric distention. Conduct ongoing assessments of vital signs, intake and output, and level of consciousness, which are key indicators of hypovolemic shock.

◆ Acute Care

Preoperative care. Preoperative care includes the emergency care of the patient described in Table 47.12 and general care of the preoperative patient (see Chapter 18).

Postoperative care. Postoperative care depends on the type of surgery. See eNursing Care Plan 20.1, a general plan for the postoperative patient, on the website for Chapter 20.

After surgery, some patients will have an NG tube with low suction to empty the stomach and prevent gastric dilation. If the upper GI tract was entered, drainage from the NG tube may be dark brown to dark red for the first 12 hours. Later it should be light yellowish-brown, or it may have a greenish tinge because of bile. If a dark red color continues or you see bright red blood, notify the HCP because of the risk for hemorrhage. "Coffee-grounds" granules in the drainage mean the blood has been changed by acidic gastric secretions.

Nausea and vomiting are common after a laparotomy and result from the surgery, decreased peristalsis, or pain medications. Antiemetics, such as ondansetron (Zofran), may be given. Monitor fluid and electrolyte status along with BP, heart rate, and respirations. See Chapter 46 for information about managing nausea and vomiting.

Swallowed air and reduced peristalsis from decreased mobility, manipulation of the abdominal organs during surgery, and anesthesia can result in abdominal distention and gas pains. Early ambulation helps restore peristalsis, expel flatus, and reduce gas pain. Gradually, as intestinal activity increases, distention and gas pain disappear.

◆ Ambulatory Care

Preparation for discharge begins soon after surgery. Teach the patient and caregiver about any modifications in activity, care of the incision, diet, and drug therapy. Initially, the patient starts on clear liquids after surgery and then, if tolerated, progresses to a regular diet.

Early ambulation speeds recovery. Normal activities are resumed gradually with planned rest periods. Patients often have restrictions not to lift anything heavier than a few pounds. The patient and caregiver should be aware of possible complications. Teach them to notify the HCP at once if fever is greater than 101°F (38.6°C), vomiting, pain, weight loss, incisional drainage, or changes in bowel function occur.

◆ Evaluation

The expected outcomes are that the patient with acute abdominal pain will:

- Have resolution of the cause of the acute abdominal pain
- Experience relief of abdominal pain and discomfort
- Be free from complications, especially hypovolemic shock and sepsis
- Have normal fluid, electrolyte, and nutrition status

ABDOMINAL TRAUMA

Etiology and Pathophysiology

Injuries to the abdominal area usually are a result of blunt trauma or penetrating injuries. Common injuries of the abdomen include lacerated liver, ruptured spleen, mesenteric artery tears, diaphragm rupture, urinary bladder rupture, great vessel tears, renal or pancreas injury, and stomach or intestine rupture.

Blunt trauma often occurs with motor vehicle accidents, direct blows, and falls. It may not be obvious because it does not leave an open wound. Both compression injuries (e.g., direct blow to the abdomen) and shearing injuries (e.g., rapid deceleration in a motor vehicle crash allowing some tissue to move forward while other tissues stay stationary) occur with blunt trauma. Penetrating injuries occur when a gunshot or stabbing produces an obvious, open wound into the abdomen.

When solid organs (liver, spleen) are injured, bleeding can be profuse, resulting in hypovolemic shock. When contents from hollow organs (e.g., bladder, stomach, intestines) spill into the peritoneal cavity, the patient is at risk for peritonitis. In addition, abdominal compartment syndrome can develop.

Abdominal compartment syndrome, or abdominal hypertension, is excessively high pressure in the abdomen. Anything that increases the volume in the abdominal cavity (e.g., edematous organs, bleeding) increases abdominal pressure. This high pressure restricts ventilation, potentially leading to respiratory failure. The high pressure decreases cardiac output, venous return, and arterial perfusion of organs. Decreased perfusion to the kidneys can lead to renal failure.

Clinical Manifestations

Careful assessment provides important clues to the type and severity of injury. Intraabdominal injuries are often associated with rib fractures, fractured pelvis, spinal injury, and thoracic injury. If the patient was in an automobile accident, a contusion or abrasion across the lower abdomen may indicate internal organ trauma from the seat belt. Seat belts can produce blunt trauma to abdominal organs by pressing the intestine and pancreas into the spinal column.

Classic manifestations of abdominal trauma are (1) guarding and splinting of the abdominal wall (indicating peritonitis); (2) a hard, distended abdomen (occurs with intraabdominal bleeding); (3) decreased or absent bowel sounds; (4) abrasions or bruising over the abdomen; (5) abdominal pain; (6) hematemesis or hematuria; and (7) signs of hypovolemic shock (Table 47.13). Bruising around the umbilicus *(Cullen sign)* or flanks *(Grey Turner sign)* may mean retroperitoneal hemorrhage. Loss of bowel sounds occurs with peritonitis. If the diaphragm ruptures, you may hear bowel sounds (if present) in the chest. Auscultation of bruits indicates arterial damage.

TABLE 47.13 EMERGENCY MANAGEMENT

Abdominal Trauma

Etiology	Assessment Findings	Interventions
Blunt • Assault with a blunt object • Crush injury • Explosions • Falls • Motor vehicle collisions • Pedestrian event **Penetrating** • Gunshot wounds • Impalement • Knife • Other missiles	**Abdominal and GI Findings** • Abdominal distention • Abdominal pain with palpation • Abdominal rigidity • Absent or ↓ bowel sounds • Hematemesis • Hematuria • Nausea and vomiting • Rebound tenderness **Hypovolemic Shock** • ↓ BP • ↑ HR • ↓ Level of consciousness • Tachypnea **Surface Findings** • Abrasions, bruising on abdominal wall, flank, or peritoneum • Impaled object • Open wounds: lacerations, eviscerations, puncture wounds, gunshot wounds	**Initial** • If unresponsive, assess circulation, airway, and breathing. • If responsive, monitor airway, breathing, and circulation. • Apply appropriate O_2 therapy. • Control external bleeding with direct pressure or sterile pressure dressing. • Establish IV access with 2 large-bore catheters and infuse normal saline or lactated Ringer's solution. • Obtain blood for type and crossmatch and CBC. • Remove clothing. • Stabilize impaled objects with bulky dressing—*do not remove.* • Cover protruding organs or tissue with sterile saline dressing. • Insert indwelling urinary catheter if there is no blood at the meatus, pelvic fracture, or boggy prostate. • Obtain urine for urinalysis. • Insert NG tube if no evidence of facial trauma. • Anticipate diagnostic peritoneal lavage. **Ongoing Monitoring** • Monitor vital signs, level of consciousness, O_2 saturation, and urine output. • Maintain patient warmth using blankets, warm IV fluids, or warm humidified O_2.

Diagnostic Studies

Laboratory tests include a baseline CBC and urinalysis. Even when bleeding, the patient will have normal hemoglobin and hematocrit because fluids are lost at the same rate as the red blood cells. Deficiencies are evident after fluid resuscitation begins. Blood in the urine may be a sign of kidney or bladder damage. Other laboratory work includes arterial blood gases, prothrombin time, electrolytes, BUN and creatinine, and type and crossmatch (in anticipation of possible blood transfusions). An abdominal CT scan and focused abdominal ultrasound are the most common diagnostic methods, but the patient must be stable before going for CT. Diagnostic peritoneal lavage can detect blood, bile, intestinal contents, and urine in the peritoneal cavity.

Interprofessional and Nursing Care

Emergency management of abdominal trauma is outlined in Table 47.13. Volume expanders or blood are given if the patient is hypotensive. An NG tube with low suction will decompress the stomach and prevent aspiration. Frequent, ongoing assessment is needed to monitor fluid status, detect deterioration in condition, and determine the need for surgery. The decision about whether to do surgery depends on clinical findings, diagnostic test results, and the patient's response to conservative management. Do not remove an impaled object until skilled care is available. Removal may cause further injury and bleeding.

CHRONIC ABDOMINAL PAIN

Chronic abdominal pain may originate from abdominal structures or be referred from a site with the same or a similar nerve supply. The pain is often described as dull, aching, or diffuse. Common causes include irritable bowel syndrome (IBS), peptic ulcer disease, chronic pancreatitis, hepatitis, pelvic inflammatory disease, adhesions, and vascular insufficiency.

Diagnosing the cause of chronic abdominal pain begins with a thorough history and description of specific pain characteristics, including severity, location, duration, and onset. Assess pain frequency and factors that increase or decrease the pain, such as eating, defecation, and activities. Endoscopy, CT scan, MRI, laparoscopy, and barium studies may be done. Treatment for chronic abdominal pain depends on the underlying cause.

IRRITABLE BOWEL SYNDROME

Irritable bowel syndrome (IBS) is a disorder characterized by chronic abdominal pain and altered bowel patterns. Patients may have diarrhea or constipation, or a mix of both. IBS affects women 2 to 2.5 times more often than men.

IBS has no known cause. Psychologic stressors (e.g., depression, anxiety, panic disorders, posttraumatic stress disorder) are associated with the development and exacerbation of IBS. Many people with IBS have a family member with the disorder. Patients may report a history of GI infections and adverse reactions to food. Diet intolerances that may contribute to symptoms include gluten and fermentable oligo-, di-, and monosaccharides and polyols (FODMAPs). Examples of oligosaccharides are wheat and rye products, some fruits and vegetables, onions, garlic, legumes, and nuts. The disaccharide lactose is found in milk and milk products. Fructose is a monosaccharide found in honey, apples, pears, and high-fructose corn syrup. Polyols are found in apples, pears, stone fruits, cauliflower, mushrooms, and artificial sweeteners, like sorbitol.

IBS is diagnosed solely on symptoms. The Rome IV criteria for diagnosing IBS require the presence of abdominal pain and/or discomfort at least 1 day per week for 3 months that is associated with 2 or more of the following: related to defecation, change in stool frequency, and change in the stool form.[6] Depending on the stool patterns, IBS is categorized as IBS with constipation (IBS-C), IBS with diarrhea (IBS-D), IBS mixed, and IBS unsubtyped. Other common symptoms include abdominal distention, nausea, flatulence, bloating, urgency, mucus in the stool, and sensation of incomplete evacuation. Non-GI symptoms may include fatigue, headache, and sleep problems.

The key to diagnosis is a thorough history and physical assessment. Ask patients to describe symptoms, health history (including psychosocial factors, such as stress and anxiety), family history, and drug and diet history. Determine if and how IBS symptoms interfere with school, work, and social activities. Diagnostic tests are used to rule out other disorders, such as CRC, IBD, endometriosis, and malabsorption disorders (lactose intolerance, celiac disease).

No single therapy is effective for all patients with IBS. Treatment includes psychologic support, diet and lifestyle changes, and drugs to regulate stool output and reduce discomfort. Patients may benefit from keeping a diary of symptoms, diet, and episodes of stress to help identify any factors that trigger the IBS symptoms. Cognitive behavior therapy and stress management techniques may help a patient cope. Participating in regular exercise reduces bloating, constipation, and stress-related symptoms.

Review with the patient foods that are high in FODMAPs. Teach them to follow a low-FODMAP diet.[7] If dairy products tend to cause symptoms, yogurt may be the best option because of the lactobacillus bacteria it contains. Probiotics can improve symptoms. Tell the patient with flatulence to avoid common gas-producing foods, such as broccoli and cabbage. For those with IBS-C, encourage a high-fiber diet to produce soft, painless bowel movements.

Drug therapy focuses on the dominant bowel symptom and pain. All patients with IBS may receive benefit from antidepressants and antispasmodic agents (hyoscyamine, dicyclomine). Antispasmodics decrease GI motility and smooth muscle spasms, reducing pain and diarrhea.

Treatment for IBS-D includes rifaximin, the opioid agonist eluxadoline (Viberzi), and the selective serotonin 5-HT_3 antagonist alosetron.[6] Eluxadoline decreases colonic contractions to reduce diarrhea and pain. Alosetron is only given to women with severe IBS-D that did not respond to other therapy. Because of serious side effects (severe constipation, ischemic colitis), it is available only in a restricted access program. Eluxadoline and alosetron are taken daily. Rifaximin is given as a 2-week course of treatment with repeated courses as needed. Loperamide may help some patients.

DRUG ALERT

Alosetron (Lotronex)

- Taking this drug can cause severe constipation and ischemic colitis (reduced blood flow to the intestines).
- Teach the patient to stop the drug and contact the HCP if constipation, rectal bleeding, bloody diarrhea, or abdominal pain occurs.

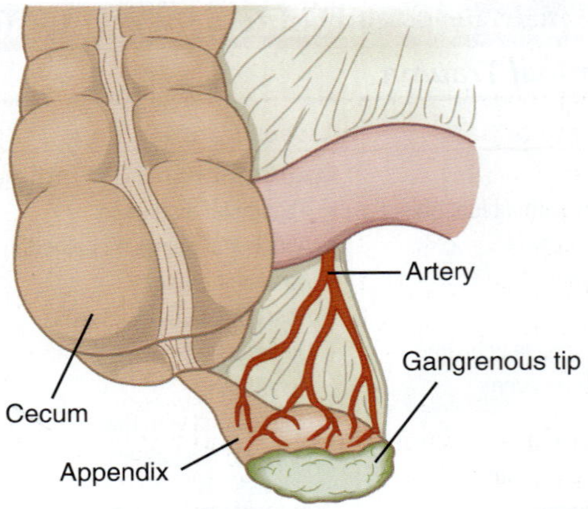

Fig. 47.3 In appendicitis, the blood supply of the appendix is impaired by inflammation and bacterial infection, which may result in gangrene.

Besides laxative therapy, those with IBS-C may take linaclotide (Linzess). It is contraindicated in patients with a history of mechanical obstruction or prior bowel surgery. Women with IBS-C may benefit from lubiprostone (Amitiza).

INFLAMMATORY DISORDERS

APPENDICITIS

Appendicitis is inflammation of the appendix, a narrow blind tube that extends from the inferior part of the cecum (Fig. 47.3). It is the most common reason for emergency abdominal surgery.

Etiology and Pathophysiology

About 7% of people will develop appendicitis sometime during their lifetime.[8] It is most common in those 10 to 30 years of age. Appendicitis is thought to be caused by luminal obstruction. Obstruction results in distention, venous engorgement, and the accumulation of mucus and bacteria. This can lead to gangrene, perforation, and peritonitis.

Clinical Manifestations

Diagnosis can be difficult because many patients do not have classic symptoms. Appendicitis typically begins with dull periumbilical pain, followed by anorexia, nausea, and vomiting. The pain is persistent and continuous, eventually shifting to the right lower quadrant and localizing at *McBurney point* (halfway between the umbilicus and right iliac crest). A low-grade fever may develop. Further assessment reveals rigidity, rebound tenderness, and muscle guarding. Positive psoas (pain with extension of right thigh), obturator (pain with passive internal rotation of the flexed thigh), and Rovsing signs (increased right lower quadrant pain occurring with left lower quadrant palpation) lend to the diagnosis.[8] Coughing or sneezing worsens pain. The patient usually prefers to lie still, often with the right leg flexed.

Diagnostic Studies and Interprofessional Care

The assessment includes a complete history, physical assessment, and a differential WBC count. Most patients have a mildly to moderately high WBC count. A urinalysis is done to rule out genitourinary conditions that mimic appendicitis. CT scan is the preferred diagnostic procedure. However, ultrasound and MRI are options.

If there is a delay in diagnosis and treatment, the appendix can rupture, and the resulting peritonitis can be fatal. The standard treatment is an immediate *appendectomy* (surgical removal of appendix). If the inflammation is localized, surgery should be done as soon as the diagnosis is made. Antibiotics and fluid resuscitation are started before surgery.

If the appendix has ruptured and there is evidence of peritonitis or an abscess, giving IV fluids and antibiotic therapy for 6 to 8 hours before the appendectomy helps prevent dehydration and sepsis.

NURSING MANAGEMENT: APPENDICITIS

Managing the patient who potentially has appendicitis focuses on preventing fluid volume deficit, relieving pain, and preventing complications. To ensure the stomach is empty in case surgery is needed, keep the patient NPO until the HCP evaluates the patient. Monitor vital signs and perform ongoing assessment to detect any deterioration in condition. Give IV fluids, analgesics, and antiemetics as ordered. Provide comfort measures.

Postoperative care for the patient who had an appendectomy is similar to the patient after a laparotomy. Patients are usually discharged within 24 hours after an uncomplicated laparoscopic appendectomy. Ambulation begins a few hours after surgery, and the diet is advanced as tolerated. Those who had a perforation usually have a longer length of stay and need IV antibiotic therapy. Most patients resume normal activities 2 to 3 weeks after surgery.

CHECK YOUR PRACTICE

A 28-year-old female patient comes to the emergency department with acute abdominal pain.

- What manifestations would make you suspect appendicitis is the cause of the abdominal pain?

PERITONITIS

Etiology and Pathophysiology

Peritonitis, inflammation of the peritoneum, may result from contamination of the peritoneal cavity with bacteria, irritating chemicals, or both. Common causes are listed in Table 47.14. Primary peritonitis occurs when blood-borne organisms enter the peritoneal cavity. It is not related to any other intraabdominal problem. For example, ascites from cirrhosis of the liver provides an excellent environment for bacteria to flourish.

Secondary peritonitis is much more common. It occurs when abdominal organs perforate or rupture and release their contents (bile, enzymes, bacteria) into the peritoneal cavity.

TABLE 47.14 Common Causes of Peritonitis

Primary

- Blood-borne organisms
- Cirrhosis with ascites

Secondary

- Appendicitis with rupture
- Blunt or penetrating trauma to abdominal organs
- Diverticulitis with rupture
- Intestinal cancer
- Ischemic bowel disorders
- Pancreatitis
- Perforated intestine, uterus, urinary bladder, stomach
- Perforated peptic ulcer
- Peritoneal dialysis
- Postoperative (breakage of anastomosis)

Common causes include a ruptured appendix, perforated ulcer, diverticulitis, and trauma from gunshot or knife wounds.

Intestinal contents and bacteria irritate the normally sterile peritoneum and produce an initial chemical peritonitis. Bacterial peritonitis develops a few hours later. The resulting inflammatory response leads to massive fluid shifts (peritoneal edema) and adhesions as the body tries to wall off the infection.

Clinical Manifestations

Severe, continuous abdominal pain is the most common symptom of peritonitis. A universal sign is tenderness over the involved area. Rebound tenderness, rigidity, and spasm are other signs of peritoneal irritation. Patients may lie still and take only shallow breaths because movement worsens the pain. Abdominal distention, fever, tachycardia, tachypnea, nausea, vomiting, and altered bowel habits may be present. These manifestations vary, depending on the severity and acuteness of the underlying condition. Complications include hypovolemic shock, sepsis, intraabdominal abscess formation, paralytic ileus, and acute respiratory distress syndrome. Peritonitis can be fatal if treatment is delayed.

Diagnostic Studies and Interprofessional Care

A CBC is done to determine elevations in WBC count and hemoconcentration from fluid shifts (Table 47.15). Peritoneal aspiration may be done with the fluid analyzed for blood, bile, pus, bacteria, fungus, and amylase content. An abdominal x-ray may show dilated loops of bowel consistent with paralytic ileus, free air if perforation has occurred, or air and fluid levels if an obstruction is present. Ultrasound and CT scans may be useful in identifying ascites and abscesses. Peritoneoscopy may be helpful in the patient without ascites. It allows for direct examination of the peritoneum and the ability to obtain biopsy specimens for diagnosis.

Patients with milder cases of peritonitis or those who are poor surgical risks receive conservative care. Treatment consists of antibiotics, NG suction, analgesics, and IV fluid administration. Surgery is indicated to locate the cause of the inflammation, drain purulent fluid, and repair any damage, such as to perforated organs.

TABLE 47.15 Interprofessional Care

Peritonitis

Diagnostic Assessment

- History and physical assessment
- CBC, including WBC differential
- Serum electrolytes
- Abdominal x-ray
- Abdominal paracentesis and culture of fluid
- CT scan or ultrasound
- Peritoneoscopy

Management

Preoperative or Nonoperative

- NPO status
- IV fluid replacement
- NG to low-intermittent suction
- O_2 PRN
- PN as needed

Drug Therapy

- Analgesics (e.g., morphine)
- Antibiotic therapy
- Antiemetics as needed

Postoperative

- NPO status
- NG to low-intermittent suction
- Semi-Fowler's position
- IV fluids with electrolyte replacement
- PN as needed
- Blood transfusions as needed

Drug Therapy

- Antibiotic therapy
- Sedatives and opioids
- Antiemetics as needed

NURSING MANAGEMENT: PERITONITIS

Assessment

Assessing the patient's pain, including the location, is important and may help to determine the cause of peritonitis. Assess for the presence and quality of bowel sounds, increasing abdominal distention, abdominal guarding, nausea, fever, and manifestations of hypovolemic shock.

Clinical Problems

Clinical problems for the patient with peritonitis include:

- Pain
- Fluid imbalance
- Impaired GI function
- Risk for infection

Planning

The overall goals are that the patient with peritonitis will have (1) resolution of inflammation, (2) relief of abdominal pain, (3) freedom from complications (especially sepsis, hypovolemic shock), and (4) normal nutrition status.

Implementation

The patient with peritonitis is extremely ill and needs skilled supportive care. Establish IV access so that you can give replacement fluids lost to the peritoneal cavity and have access for antibiotic therapy. Monitor the patient for pain and response to analgesics. You may position the patient with knees flexed to increase comfort. Sedatives may relieve anxiety and promote rest.

Accurate monitoring of intake and output and electrolyte status is essential to determine replacement therapy. Frequently monitor vital signs. Give antiemetics to decrease nausea and vomiting and prevent further fluid and electrolyte losses. Place the patient on NPO status. The patient may need an NG tube to decrease gastric distention and further leakage of bowel contents into the peritoneum. Give oxygen therapy as needed.

If the patient had an open surgical procedure, drains are inserted to remove purulent drainage and excess fluid. Postoperative care is similar to that for the patient who had a laparotomy.

GASTROENTERITIS

Gastroenteritis is an inflammation of the mucosa of the stomach and small intestine. Features of *acute gastroenteritis* are sudden diarrhea accompanied by nausea, vomiting, fever, and abdominal cramping. Viruses are the most common cause of gastroenteritis (Table 47.1).

Norovirus is a leading cause of foodborne outbreaks of acute gastroenteritis. Laboratory testing to identify norovirus is useful when a number of people simultaneously have gastroenteritis and there is a clear avenue for virus transmission, such as a shared location or food.

Most cases of gastroenteritis are self-limiting. Encourage oral fluids containing glucose and electrolytes to prevent and treat dehydration. Older adults and chronically ill patients may be unable to consume enough fluids to make up for fluid loss. If dehydration occurs, IV fluid replacement may be needed. Nursing management of the patient with gastroenteritis is the same as for the patient with acute diarrhea.

INFLAMMATORY BOWEL DISEASE

Inflammatory bowel disease (IBD) is a chronic inflammation of the GI tract characterized by periods of remission interspersed with periods of exacerbation. We classify IBD as either Crohn's disease or ulcerative colitis (UC) based on clinical manifestations (Table 47.16). As the name suggests, **ulcerative colitis** is usually limited to the colon. **Crohn's disease** can involve any segment of the GI tract from the mouth to the anus. About 1.3 million Americans have IBD. It often begins during the teenage years and early adulthood. IBD has a second peak in the 6th decade.

Etiology and Pathophysiology

We do not know the exact cause of IBD. IBD is an autoimmune disease involving an immune reaction to a person's own intestinal tract. We think that it results from an overactive,

TABLE 47.16 Comparison of Ulcerative Colitis and Crohn's Disease

Characteristic	Ulcerative Colitis	Crohn's Disease
Clinical		
Usual age at onset	Teens to mid-30s; after 60	Teens to mid-30s; after 60
Abdominal pain	Common, severe constant	Common, cramping
Diarrhea	Common	Common
Fever (intermittent)	During acute attacks	Common
Malabsorption and nutrition deficiencies	Minimal incidence	Common
Rectal bleeding	Common	Sometimes
Tenesmus	Common	Rare
Weight loss	Rare	Common, may be severe
Pathologic		
Location	Usually starts in rectum and spreads in a continuous pattern up the colon	Occurs anywhere along GI tract. Most common site is distal ileum
Cobblestoning of mucosa	Rare	Common
Depth of involvement	Mucosa	Entire thickness of bowel wall (transmural)
Distribution	Continuous areas of inflammation	Healthy tissue interspersed with areas of inflammation (skip lesions)
Pseudopolyps	Common	Rare
Small bowel involvement	Minimal	Common
Complications		
Cancer	↑ Incidence of CRC after 10 years of disease	↑ Incidence of small intestinal cancer ↑ Incidence of CRC but less than with ulcerative colitis
C. difficile infection	↑ Incidence and severity	↑ Incidence and severity
Perforation	Common (because of toxic megacolon)	Common (because inflammation involves entire bowel wall)
Perianal abscess and fistulas	Rare	Common
Strictures	Occasional	Common
Toxic megacolon	More common	Rare

inappropriate, or sustained immune response to environmental and bacterial triggers in a genetically susceptible person. The resulting inflammation causes widespread tissue destruction.

The incidence and frequency of IBD varies depending on geographic location and racial or ethnic background. The highest rates are in the Northern Hemisphere and industrialized nations. The risk for having IBD is greater in urban compared with rural areas and those of White and Ashkenazic Jewish origin than in other racial and ethnic groups.[9] The strongest risk factor is family history. Many people with IBD have a family member with the disorder.

Lifestyle factors, such as diet, smoking, and stress, increase susceptibility by changing the environment of the GI microbial flora. We think that diet factors unique to industrialized countries contribute to the development of IBD. A high intake of refined sugar, total fats, polyunsaturated fatty acid (PUFA), and omega-6 fatty acids seems to increase the risk for IBD. Eating more raw fruits, vegetables, omega-3–rich foods, and fiber decreases risk.[9] Use of nonsteroidal antiinflammatory drugs (NSAIDs), antibiotics, and oral contraceptives also increase risk.[9]

Genetic Link

IBD occurs more often in family members of people with IBD, especially monozygotic twins. To date, we have found over 200 genes associated with IBD. Certain genetic mutations are associated with Crohn's disease, others with UC, and many with both.

The number of gene variations suggests that IBD is a group of diseases that produce similar types of mucosal destruction. The path from genetic mutation to abnormal immune responses varies depending on which gene or genes are affected. Several of the genes are involved in protective functions of the intestines. Others have a role in the immune system, especially in the maturation and function of T cells. Genetic variation may explain differences in patient responses to drug therapies for IBD.

Many of the major genes related to Crohn's disease, including *NOD2, ATG16L1, IL23R,* and *IRGM,* are involved in immune system function. The proteins made from these genes help the immune system sense and respond appropriately to bacteria in the lining of the GI tract. *NOD2* gene changes are associated with a form of Crohn's disease that affects the ileum in persons of northern European descent. Changes in the *NOD2* gene prevent normal immune responses, allowing bacteria to grow unchecked and invade intestinal cells. This causes chronic inflammation and digestive problems.[10]

IBD is more likely to occur in those with other genetic syndromes, including cystic fibrosis. An increased prevalence occurs in the presence of other inflammatory disorders with genetic susceptibility, such as psoriasis and multiple sclerosis.

Pattern of Inflammation in Ulcerative Colitis vs. Crohn's Disease

The pattern of inflammation differs between Crohn's disease and UC (Fig. 47.4). Crohn's disease can occur anywhere in the GI tract, from the mouth to the anus. It most often involves the distal ileum and proximal colon. Segments of normal bowel can occur between diseased portions, so-called "skip" lesions. The inflammation in Crohn's disease involves all layers of the bowel wall. Typically, ulcerations are deep, longitudinal, and penetrate between islands of inflamed edematous mucosa, causing the classic cobblestone appearance. Strictures at the areas of inflammation can cause bowel obstruction. Since the inflammation goes through the entire wall, microscopic leaks can allow bowel contents to enter the peritoneal cavity and cause abscesses or peritonitis. In active Crohn's disease, fistulas are common.

UC is a disease of the colon and rectum. It usually starts in the rectum and moves in a continual fashion toward the cecum. Mild inflammation may occur in the terminal ileum. The inflammation and ulcerations occur in the mucosal layer, the innermost layer of the bowel wall. Fistulas and abscesses are rare since inflammation does not extend through all bowel wall

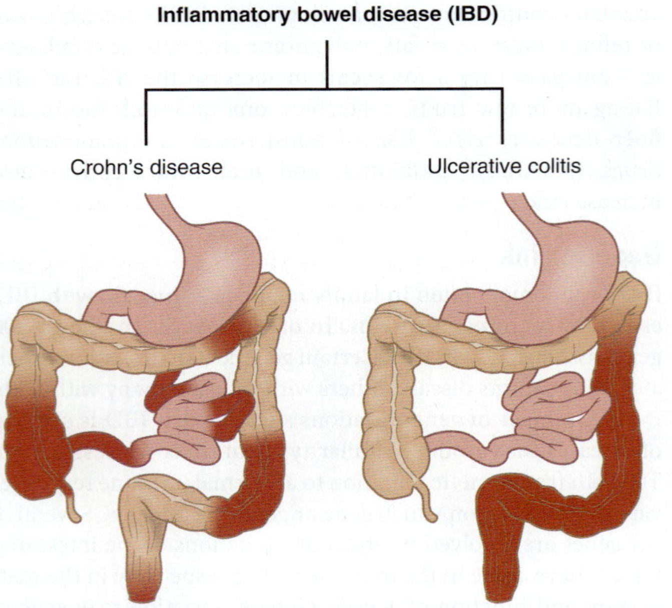

Fig. 47.4 Comparison of distribution patterns of UC and Crohn's disease.

layers. Because water and electrolytes are not absorbed through inflamed mucosa, diarrhea with large fluid and electrolyte losses is common. Breakdown of cells results in protein loss through the stool. Areas of inflamed mucosa form *pseudopolyps,* tongue-like projections into the bowel lumen.

Clinical Manifestations

Both forms of IBD are chronic disorders with mild to severe acute exacerbations that occur at unpredictable intervals. Although the manifestations of Crohn's disease and UC are similar (diarrhea, weight loss, abdominal pain, fever, fatigue), there are differences (Table 47.16).

In Crohn's disease, diarrhea and cramping abdominal pain are common symptoms. If the small intestine is involved, weight loss occurs from inflammation of the small intestine, causing malabsorption. Rectal bleeding sometimes occurs with Crohn's disease, although not as often as with UC.

In UC, the primary problems are bloody diarrhea and abdominal pain. Pain may vary from the mild lower abdominal cramping associated with diarrhea to severe, constant pain from acute perforations. With *mild disease,* diarrhea may consist of no more than 4 semiformed stools daily that contain small amounts of blood. The patient may have no other manifestations. In *moderate disease,* the patient has increased stool output (up to 10 stools/day), increased bleeding, and systemic symptoms (fever, malaise, mild anemia, anorexia). In *severe disease,* diarrhea is bloody, contains mucus, and occurs 10 to 20 times a day. In addition, fever, rapid weight loss (greater than 10% of total body weight), anemia, tachycardia, and dehydration are present.

Complications

Patients with IBD have both local (confined to the GI tract) and systemic (extraintestinal) complications (Fig. 47.5). GI tract complications include hemorrhage, strictures, perforation (with possible peritonitis), abscesses, fistulas, CDI, and toxic megacolon. Toxic megacolon is more common with UC. Patients with toxic megacolon are at risk for perforation and may need an emergency colectomy. Perineal abscesses and fistulas occur in up to a third of patients with Crohn's disease. CDI increases in frequency and severity in patients with IBD.

IBD is related to an increased risk for CRC. Those with Crohn's disease are at increased risk for small intestinal cancer. This makes regular cancer screening important in persons with IBD.[11]

People with IBD may have systemic complications, such as multiple sclerosis and ankylosing spondylitis. Some are related to the inflammatory activity in the bowel. They occur with active inflammation and improve when the IBD improves. Other complications include malabsorption, liver disease (primary sclerosing cholangitis), and osteoporosis. Routine liver function tests are important because primary sclerosing cholangitis can lead to liver failure. Both men and women with IBD are at risk for osteoporosis. They need a bone density scan at baseline and every 2 years.

Diagnostic Studies

The diagnosis of IBD includes ruling out diseases with similar symptoms and figuring out whether the patient has Crohn's disease or UC. The symptoms of early Crohn's disease are like those of IBS. Diagnostic studies provide information about disease severity and complications. A CBC typically shows iron deficiency anemia from blood loss. A high WBC count may be a sign of toxic megacolon or perforation. Decreased serum sodium, potassium, chloride, bicarbonate, and magnesium levels occur due to fluid and electrolyte losses from diarrhea and vomiting. Hypoalbuminemia is present with severe disease because of poor nutrition or protein loss. Increased erythrocyte sedimentation rate, C-reactive protein, and WBCs reflect inflammation. The stool is examined for blood, pus, and mucus. Stool cultures can determine if infection is present.

Imaging studies, such as double-contrast barium enema, small bowel series (small bowel follow-through), transabdominal ultrasound, CT, and MRI, are useful for diagnosing IBD. Colonoscopy allows for examination of the entire large intestine lumen and sometimes the distal ileum. The HCP can determine the extent of inflammation, ulcerations, pseudopolyps, and strictures and obtain biopsy specimens for a definitive diagnosis. Since a colonoscope can enter only as far as the distal ileum, capsule endoscopy (see Chapter 43) may be needed to diagnose Crohn's disease in the small intestine.

Interprofessional Care

The goals of treatment of IBD are to (1) rest the bowel, (2) control inflammation, (3) correct malnutrition, (4) provide symptomatic relief, and (5) improve quality of life. There is no cure for IBD. Treatment relies on drugs to treat the inflammation and maintain remission (Table 47.17). Several drugs are available to treat IBD. Since the recurrence rate is high after surgical treatment of Crohn's disease, drugs are the preferred treatment. Hospitalization is needed if the patient does not respond to drug therapy, the disease is severe, or complications are suspected.

Drug Therapy

The goal of drug treatment in IBD is to induce and maintain remission. Five major classes of drugs are used: aminosalicylates, antimicrobials, corticosteroids, immunomodulators, and biologic therapies (Table 47.18). Drug choice depends on the location and severity of inflammation. Initial treatment for UC includes a corticosteroid for symptom relief with an aminosalicylate or a biologic therapy, depending on the severity of the disease. The management of Crohn's disease also includes biologic therapy, along with a corticosteroid.[12] These therapies can be used alone or as combination therapy.[12]

Drugs containing 5-aminosalicylic acid (5-ASA) treat both UC and Crohn's disease. They are much more effective for UC.[13] Their exact mechanism of action is unclear. We think they suppress the production of proinflammatory cytokines and other inflammatory mediators in the intestine. People can take aminosalicylates orally or rectally. Oral forms are available with different coatings that affect where the medication is released in the GI tract. This allows for more effective treatment of specific symptoms. Rectal use offers the advantage of delivering the 5-ASA directly to the affected tissue. This is useful in treating inflammation in the rectum and/or large intestine. The combination of oral and rectal therapy is better than oral or rectal therapy alone.

Biologics reduce IBD-related inflammation by blocking specific proteins that play a role in inflammation. There are 4 main classes: anti-TNF agents, alpha 4-integrin inhibitors, interleukin (IL)-12/23 antagonists, and Janus kinase (JAK) inhibitors.[12]

The anti-TNF agent infliximab (Remicade) is given IV to induce and maintain remission in patients with UC and Crohn's disease and in patients with draining fistulas. The other anti-TNF agents are given subcutaneously.[13] They all have similar

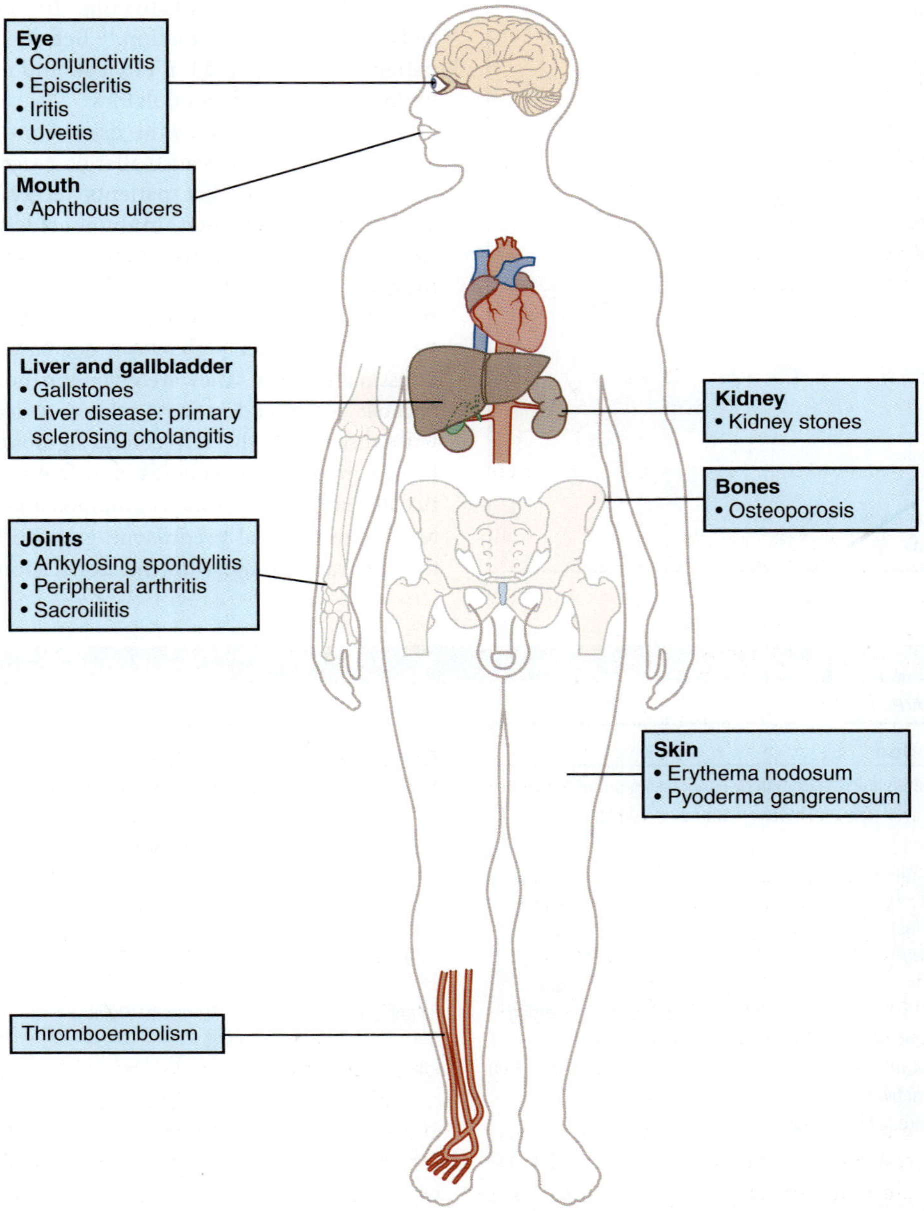

Fig. 47.5 Extraintestinal manifestations of IBD.

side effects. The most common ones are upper respiratory and urinary tract infections, headaches, nausea, joint pain, and abdominal pain. More serious effects include reactivation of hepatitis and tuberculosis (TB); opportunistic infections; and cancers, especially lymphoma. Patients are tested for TB and hepatitis before treatment begins. Therapy must be delayed if an active infection is present. They cannot receive live virus immunizations. Teaching includes how to prevent and recognize early signs and symptoms of infection, including fever, cough, malaise, and dyspnea.

TABLE 47.17 Interprofessional Care

Inflammatory Bowel Disease

Diagnostic Assessment

- History and physical assessment
- CBC, erythrocyte sedimentation rate
- Serum chemistries
- Testing of stool for occult blood and infection
- Capsule endoscopy
- Radiologic studies with barium contrast
- Sigmoidoscopy and/or colonoscopy with biopsy
- Ultrasound studies

Management

- High-calorie, high-vitamin, high-protein diet
- EN during exacerbations
- Drug therapy (Table 47.18)
  - Aminosalicylates
  - Antimicrobials
  - Biologic therapies
  - Corticosteroids
  - Immunomodulators
- Physical and emotional rest
- Referral for counseling or support group
- Surgical therapy (Table 47.19)

Alpha 4-integrin inhibitors include natalizumab (Tysabri) and vedolizumab (Entyvio). They inhibit leukocyte adhesion by blocking α_4-integrin, an adhesion molecule. Use is limited to those who have not had an adequate response with other therapies (corticosteroids, immunomodulators, anti-TNF agents). Both are given by IV infusion. Side effects include increased risk for infection, liver toxicity, and hypersensitivity reactions. Because of the risk for progressive multifocal leukoencephalopathy, natalizumab is available only through a restricted program.[13]

The IL-12/23 antagonists, ustekinumab and risankizumab, are given to patients with severe UC and Crohn's disease. They bind IL-12 and IL-23, preventing the activation of T-helper and natural killer cells.[14] Precautions and side effects are similar to the anti-TNF agents. The first dose of ustekinumab is given IV followed by injections every 8 weeks.

JAK inhibitors are the newest drugs used to treat UC. They suppress the immune system by blocking the JAK enzyme and preventing it from activating the specific immune system cells that cause inflammation.[12] Before starting tofacitinib, the patient must be tested for TB. It should not be given with other biologics or immunomodulators.

Patients need to know the risks before starting biologic therapy. The agents may cause allergic reactions. They are immunogenic, meaning that patients receiving them often make antibodies against them. Immunogenicity leads to acute infusion reactions and delayed hypersensitivity-type reactions. The drugs are most effective when given at regular intervals. Infusion reactions are more likely if a drug is stopped and then restarted.

Corticosteroids prevent or decrease inflammation of the intestinal mucosa. They are given for the shortest possible time because of the side effects related to long-term use. Patients with disease in the left colon, sigmoid, and rectum benefit from suppositories, enemas, and foams. They deliver the corticosteroid directly to the inflamed tissue with minimal systemic effects. Oral prednisone is given to patients with mild to moderate disease who did not respond to either 5-ASA or

TABLE 47.18 Drug Therapy

Inflammatory Bowel Disease

Class	Action	Examples
5-Aminosalicylates (5-ASA)	Decrease inflammation by suppressing proinflammatory cytokines and other inflammatory mediators	*Systemic:* balsalazide (Colazal), mesalamine (Asacol, Apriso, Delzicol, Lialda, Pentasa), olsalazine (Dipentum), sulfasalazine (Azulfidine) *Topical:* 5-ASA enema, foam, suppositories
Antimicrobials	Prevent or treat secondary infection	ciprofloxacin (Cipro), clarithromycin (Biaxin), metronidazole (Flagyl)
Biologic therapies	*Anti-TNF agents:* Inhibit the cytokine tumor necrosis factor (TNF)	adalimumab (Humira), certolizumab pegol (Cimzia), golimumab (Simponi), infliximab (Remicade)
	Integrin receptor antagonists: Prevent migration of leukocytes from bloodstream to inflamed tissue	natalizumab (Tysabri), vedolizumab (Entyvio)
	IL-12/23 antagonists: Bind IL-12 and IL-23, preventing the activation of T-helper and natural killer cells	Risankizumab (Skyrizi), ustekinumab (Stelara)
	JAK inhibitors: Block the JAK enzyme, preventing it from activating immune cells that cause inflammation	tofacitinib (Xeljanz)
Corticosteroids	Decrease inflammation	*Systemic:* corticosteroids (prednisone, budesonide); hydrocortisone, methylprednisolone (IV for severe IBD) *Topical:* hydrocortisone suppository, foam (Cortifoam), enema (Cortenema)
Immunomodulators	Suppress immune response	azathioprine, cyclosporine, methotrexate, 6-mercaptopurine

topical corticosteroids. Those with severe inflammation may need a short course of IV corticosteroids. Corticosteroids must be tapered to very low levels when surgery is planned to prevent postoperative complications (e.g., infection, delayed wound healing, fistula formation).

Immunomodulators are given for several reasons. They can maintain remission after corticosteroid therapy. Patients who do not respond to 5-ASA, corticosteroids, or antibiotics; have side effects from corticosteroids; or have fistulas may benefit. They have a delayed onset of action and are not useful for acute flare-ups.

These drugs require regular CBC monitoring because they can suppress the bone marrow and lead to infections and bleeding. Some develop liver and pancreas problems. Many patients have flu-like symptoms with use. Women of childbearing age must avoid pregnancy when taking methotrexate because use can cause birth defects and fetal death.

Surgical Therapy

Ulcerative colitis. Indications for surgery for UC are outlined in Table 47.19. Surgical procedures used include (1) proctocolectomy with ileal pouch/anal anastomosis (IPAA) and (2) proctocolectomy with permanent ileostomy. Since UC affects only the colon, a total proctocolectomy is curative. For more detail, see the section on bowel resection and ostomy surgery later in this chapter and Table 47.28.

Crohn's disease. Surgery for Crohn's disease is usually done for complications such as obstructions or those who do not respond to therapy (Table 47.19). Most patients with Crohn's disease eventually need surgery. The most common surgery involves resecting the diseased segments with reanastomosis of the remaining intestine. Unfortunately, the disease often recurs at the anastomosis site. Repeated removal of sections of the small intestine can lead to SBS. *Short bowel syndrome* occurs when either surgery or disease leaves too little small intestine surface area to maintain normal nutrition and hydration. Lifetime fluid boluses and parenteral nutrition (PN) may be needed. For more detail, see the section on short bowel syndrome.

The other common surgery for Crohn's disease is a stricture-plasty. This opens narrowed areas obstructing the bowel. Since the intestine stays intact, it reduces the risk of developing short-bowel syndrome and its associated complications. Recurrences at the site are uncommon.

TABLE 47.19 Indications for Surgery for IBD

- Bowel obstruction
- Drain abdominal abscess
- Fistulas
- Inability to decrease corticosteroids
- Lack of response to conservative therapy
- Massive hemorrhage
- Perforation, impending or actual
- Severe anorectal disease
- Strictures
- Suspicion of cancer

Nutrition Therapy

The goals of diet management are to (1) provide adequate nutrition without worsening symptoms, (2) correct and prevent malnutrition, (3) replace fluid and electrolyte losses, and (4) prevent weight loss. Many patients with IBD are malnourished.[15] This makes an individualized diet an important part of treating IBD. Patients need a balanced, healthy diet with enough calories, protein, and nutrients. Consult a dietitian about the ideal diet.

Nutrition problems are due to decreased oral intake, blood loss, and, depending on the location of the inflammation, impaired absorption. Patients may reduce food intake to reduce diarrhea. Inflammatory mediators reduce appetite. Blood loss and malabsorption lead to iron deficiency anemia (see Chapter 34). The patient may need oral iron supplements. IV iron is an option for those who cannot tolerate oral iron or if anemia is severe.[15] Zinc deficiency can result from ostomies or diarrhea. Zinc supplements may be needed.

Disease of the terminal ileum reduces absorption of cobalamin and bile acids. Reduced cobalamin contributes to anemia. Those who develop anemia should receive cobalamin injections. Bile salts are important for fat absorption and contribute to osmotic diarrhea. Cholestyramine, an ion-exchange resin that binds unabsorbed bile salts, helps control diarrhea.

Drug therapy can contribute to nutrition problems. Patients taking sulfasalazine or methotrexate should take folate (folic acid) daily to decrease the chance of folate deficiency.[15] Those receiving corticosteroids are prone to osteoporosis and need calcium supplements. Potassium supplements may be needed with corticosteroids.

During an acute exacerbation, patients with IBD may not be able to tolerate a regular diet. Liquid enteral feedings are preferred over PN because atrophy of the gut and bacterial overgrowth occur when the GI tract is not used. EN is high in calories and nutrients, lactose-free, and easily absorbed. They help achieve remission and improve nutrition status. EN is discussed in Chapter 44.

There are no universal food triggers for IBD, but some may find that certain foods cause diarrhea. A food diary helps to identify problem foods to avoid. Patients are typically taught to then avoid or limit foods that cause GI distress or worsen symptoms.

❖ NURSING MANAGEMENT: INFLAMMATORY BOWEL DISEASE

◆ Assessment

Table 47.20 outlines the subjective and objective data to obtain from a patient with IBD.

◆ Clinical Problems

Clinical problems for the patient with IBD include:

- Impaired bowel elimination
- Nutritionally compromised
- Difficulty coping
- Pain

For more information on clinical problems and interventions for IBD, see eNursing Care Plan 47.2 on the website for this chapter.

TABLE 47.20 NURSING ASSESSMENT

IBD

Subjective Data

Important Health Information

Health history: Infection, autoimmune disorders

Medications: Antidiarrheal drugs

Functional Health Patterns

Health perception–health management: Family history of ulcerative colitis, Crohn's disease. Fatigue, malaise

Nutritional-metabolic: Nausea, vomiting, anorexia. Weight loss

Elimination: Diarrhea. Blood, mucus, pus in stools

Cognitive-perceptual: Lower abdominal pain (worse before defecation), cramping, tenesmus

Objective Data

General

Intermittent fever, emaciated appearance, fatigue

Cardiovascular

↑ HR, ↓ BP

GI

Abdominal distention, hyperactive bowel sounds, abdominal cramps

Skin

Pale skin with poor turgor, dry mucous membranes. Skin lesions, anorectal irritation, skin tags, cutaneous fistulas

Possible Diagnostic Findings

Anemia, ↑ WBC. Electrolyte imbalance, hypoalbuminemia, vitamin, and trace metal deficiencies. Guaiac-positive stool. Abnormal sigmoidoscopy, colonoscopy, and/or barium enema findings

◆ Planning

The overall goals are that the patient with IBD will (1) have fewer and less severe acute exacerbations, (2) maintain normal fluid and electrolyte balance, (3) be free from pain or discomfort, (4) adhere to medical regimens, (5) maintain nutrition balance, and (6) have an improved quality of life.

◆ Implementation

◆ Acute Care

During the acute phase, focus your attention on hemodynamic stability, pain control, fluid and electrolyte balance, and nutrition support. Maintain accurate intake and output records. Monitor the number and appearance of stools. Assess for the presence of blood in stools and emesis. Give IV fluids, electrolytes, analgesics, and antiinflammatory drugs as prescribed. Monitor serum electrolytes, CBC, and vital signs, being alert for changes related to diarrhea and dehydration. If the patient has orthostatic hypotension, teach the patient to change position slowly and use safety precautions.

Help the patient stay clean, dry, and free of odor until the diarrhea is under control. Place a deodorizer in the room. Meticulous perianal skincare using plain water (no harsh soap) with a moisturizing skin barrier cream prevents skin breakdown. Dibucaine, witch hazel, sitz baths, and other soothing compresses or ointments may reduce perianal irritation and pain.

Calculate the adequacy of the daily calorie intake. Obtain a daily weight. Assess the abdomen, including bowel sounds, as needed. Consult with a dietitian about diet modifications and the need for nutrition supplements.

Postoperative care after surgery for IBD is similar to that described in the bowel resection and ostomy surgery section and in the general nursing care of the postoperative patient (see Chapter 20).

◆ Ambulatory Care

IBD is a chronic illness. Assist the patient in accepting the chronicity of IBD and learning ways to cope with its recurrent, unpredictable nature. Teaching includes (1) the importance of rest and diet management, (2) perianal care, (3) drug action and side effects, (4) symptoms of recurrence of disease, (5) when to seek medical care, and (6) ways to reduce stress. Excellent teaching resources, written in easily comprehensible language, are available from the Crohn's and Colitis Foundation of America (www.crohnscolitisfoundation.org).

It is important to establish rapport and encourage the patient to talk about self-care (Box 47.1). Ask patients what you can do to promote their self-care. An explanation of all procedures and treatments helps to build trust, decrease apprehension, and increase self-control. Once you have established a therapeutic relationship, talk with those who smoke who have Crohn's disease about quitting since it can cause more severe disease.

The patient and caregiver may need your help setting realistic short- and long-term goals. Patients may have severe fatigue, which limits their energy for physical activity. Rest is important. Patients may lose sleep because of frequent episodes of diarrhea and abdominal pain. Nutrition deficiencies and anemia worsen fatigue and leave the patient feeling weak. Teach them to schedule activities around rest periods.

Many patients have intermittent exacerbations and remissions of symptoms. Given the chronicity and uncertainty related to the frequency and severity of flares, many patients struggle with depression and anxiety. Behavioral therapy may help patients deal with their feelings about the disease and help to manage their symptoms. Because of the relationship between emotions and the GI tract, teach the patient ways to manage stress (see Chapter 7). Suggest the patient seek support through a local or online support group from the Crohn's and Colitis Foundation of America.

◆ Evaluation

The expected outcomes are that the patient with IBD will:

- Have a decrease in the number of diarrhea stools
- Maintain body weight within a normal range
- Be free from pain and discomfort
- Use effective coping strategies

Gerontologic Considerations: Inflammatory Bowel Disease

A second peak in the occurrence of IBD is in the 6th decade. The cause, natural history, and clinical course of IBD are similar to those seen in younger patients. However, in older patients, proctitis and left-sided UC are more common. Diagnosis is

BOX 47.1 EVIDENCE-BASED PRACTICE

Self-Management Education for Ulcerative Colitis

You are caring for G.K., a 32-year-old patient with ulcerative colitis. G.K. tells you that dealing with disease symptoms has affected his ability to participate in favorite outdoor activities such as hiking, biking, and cross-country skiing. He describes unpredictable symptom fluctuations that have left him afraid to travel. He says the pain has led to frequent job absences. After previously prescribed medications were ineffective in symptom management, he confirms he recently began taking tofacitinib (Xeljanz).

Making Clinical Decisions

Synthesis of Best Available Evidence

Research suggests self-management education can help patients with IBD effectively address their symptoms, maintain independence, and improve function.

Clinician Expertise

The unit's EBP committee recently worked with the clinical nurse specialist (CNS) to develop a standardized education program for patients with IBD. The program includes several options based on patients' interest and willingness to participate. You know the program's goal is to help patients manage their symptoms so they can have improved quality of life through more comfortable participation in desired activities. You believe G.K. could benefit from the information. After watching a video presentation, G.K. has many questions, so you arrange a 1-on-1 session with the CNS to talk more about self-management strategies.

Patient Preferences and Values

"I'm open to anything that may help me," G. K. says. "I think these suggestions can be easily followed to help me management by colitis."

Implications for Nursing Practice

1. How would you informally assess G.K.'s understanding of disease self-management after his meeting with the CNS?
2. If G.K. adopted the self-management strategies identified in the education program, what would you expect about his future ability to take part in outdoor activities?

Reference for Evidence

Magharei M, Jaafari S, Mansouri P, et al.: Effects of self-management education on self-efficacy and quality of life in patients with ulcerative colitis: a randomized controlled clinical trial, *IJCBNM* 7:32, 2019.

sometimes difficult in older adults since IBD can be confused with CDI, diverticulitis, or colitis.

Though interprofessional care is similar, challenges exist. Drug therapy and surgery have an increased risk for adverse events, hospitalization, and mortality. Immunomodulator and biologic therapies have a higher risk for infection and cancer. Anemia and malnutrition are more common. They are more vulnerable to volume depletion from diarrhea. Those with physical limitations may have trouble managing fecal urgency and multiple trips to the bathroom without help.

BOWEL OBSTRUCTION

A **bowel obstruction**, or intestinal obstruction, occurs when intestinal contents cannot pass through the GI tract. The obstruction may occur in the small (SBO) or large (LBO) intestine. It can be partial or complete, simple or strangulated. Partial obstructions do not completely occlude the intestinal lumen, allowing for some fluid and gas to pass through. They usually resolve with conservative treatment. A complete obstruction totally occludes the lumen and usually requires surgery. A simple obstruction has an intact blood supply; a strangulated one does not.

Types of Bowel Obstruction

The causes of bowel obstructions are either mechanical or nonmechanical.

Mechanical

In *mechanical obstruction,* there is a physical obstruction of the intestinal lumen. Most obstructions occur in the small intestine. Surgical adhesions are the most common cause of SBO. They can occur within days of surgery or years later (Fig. 47.6). Other causes of SBO are hernia, cancer, strictures from Crohn's disease, and intussusception after bariatric surgery. The most common cause of LBO is CRC (malignant obstruction), followed by diverticular disease. Other causes include adhesions, ischemia, volvulus, and Crohn's disease.

Nonmechanical

A *nonmechanical obstruction* occurs with reduced or absent peristalsis due to altered neuromuscular transmission of the parasympathetic innervation to the bowel. It may result from a neuromuscular or vascular disorder. **Paralytic ileus** (lack of intestinal peristalsis and bowel sounds) is the most common form of nonmechanical obstruction. It occurs to some degree after any abdominal surgery. Other causes of paralytic ileus include peritonitis, inflammatory responses (e.g., acute pancreatitis, acute appendicitis), electrolyte imbalances (especially hypokalemia), and thoracic or lumbar spinal fractures.

Pseudo-obstruction is a GI motility disorder that mimics a mechanical obstruction. The patient has symptoms of obstruction but without any cause found with imaging. Several conditions are associated with pseudo-obstruction. These include neurologic conditions, drugs, endocrine and metabolic problems, lung disease, trauma, and burns.[16]

Vascular obstructions are rare. They result from an interference with the blood supply to a part of the intestines. The most common causes are emboli and atherosclerosis of the mesenteric arteries. Emboli may originate from thrombi in patients who have chronic atrial fibrillation, diseased heart valves, and prosthetic valves. Venous thrombosis may occur in conditions of low blood flow, such as heart failure and shock.

Etiology and Pathophysiology

About 6 to 8 L of fluid enter the small intestine daily. Most of the fluid is absorbed before it reaches the colon. Around 75% of intestinal gas is swallowed air. When an obstruction occurs, fluid, gas, and intestinal contents accumulate proximal to the obstruction. Distention reduces fluid absorption and initially stimulates intestinal secretions. Distal to the obstruction, the bowel empties and then collapses. As distention increases in the proximal bowel, intraluminal bowel

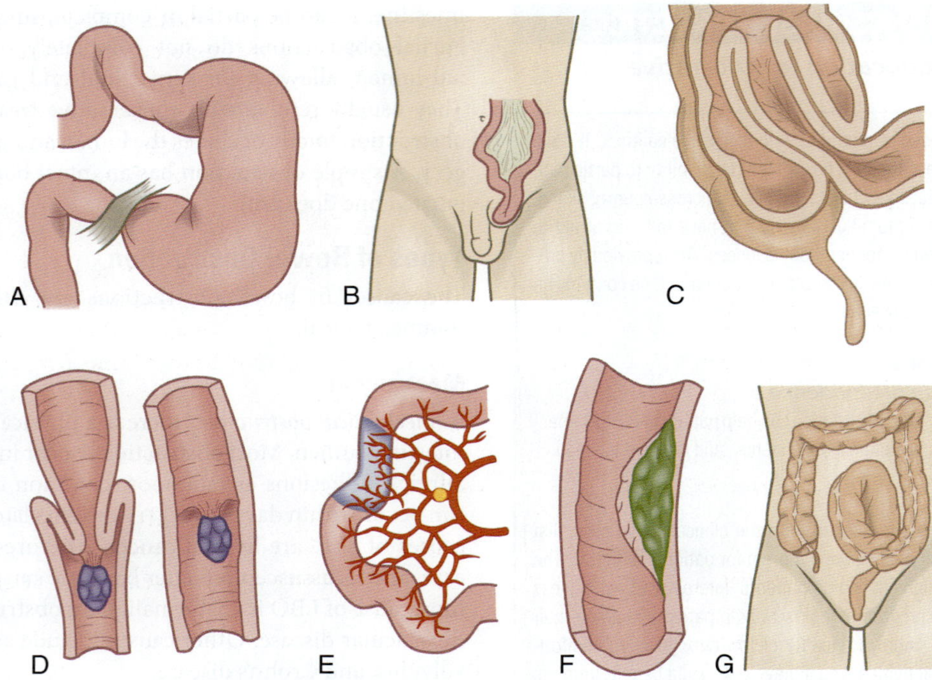

Fig. 47.6 Bowel obstructions. (A) Adhesions. (B) Strangulated inguinal hernia. (C) Ileocecal intussusception. (D) Intussusception from polyps. (E) Mesenteric occlusion. (F) Neoplasm. (G) Volvulus of the sigmoid colon.

pressure rises. The increased pressure leads to an increase in capillary permeability and extravasation of fluids and electrolytes into the peritoneal cavity. Eventually, the intestinal muscle becomes fatigued, and peristalsis stops. Retention of fluids in the intestine and peritoneal cavity leads to a severe decrease in circulating blood volume. This leads to hypotension and hypovolemic shock.

If blood flow is inadequate, bowel tissue becomes ischemic, then necrotic, and the bowel may perforate. In the most dangerous situation, the bowel becomes so distended that the blood flow stops, causing edema, cyanosis, and gangrene of a bowel segment. This is called *intestinal strangulation* or *intestinal infarction.* If not quickly corrected, the bowel will become necrotic and rupture, leading to infection, septic shock, and death.

Clinical Manifestations

The 4 hallmark manifestations of an obstruction are abdominal pain, nausea and vomiting, distention, and constipation. The order and degree these appear vary by the cause, location, and type of obstruction (Table 47.21). Colicky abdominal pain is usually the first symptom. In SBO, the pain is often of sudden onset. It occurs at 4- to 5-minute intervals for proximal obstructions and less often for distal obstructions. The nature of the vomiting gives a clue to the level of obstruction. In a proximal obstruction, patients rapidly develop nausea and vomiting. It may be projectile and contain bile. Vomiting usually gives temporary relief from abdominal pain in higher obstructions. Vomiting from a more distal small bowel obstruction is more gradual in onset and more fecal and foul smelling. Bowel sounds may be high-pitched above the area of obstruction. Bowel sounds are usually absent with paralytic ileus.

TABLE 47.21 Manifestations of Small and Large Bowel Obstructions

	SMALL INTESTINE		
Manifestation	**Proximal**	**Distal**	**Large Intestine**
Onset	Rapid	Rapid	Gradual
Vomiting	Frequent and copious	Less frequent	Late or absent
Pain	Colicky, cramping, occurs at frequent intervals	Colicky, occurs more intermittently	Persistent, cramping
Bowel movement	Feces for a short time	Gradual constipation	Obstipation
Abdominal distention	Minimal	↑	↑

Signs of LBO include abdominal distention, either obstipation or a marked change in bowel function, and lack of flatus. The patient has persistent, cramping abdominal pain. Bowel sounds are usually present and become progressively hypoactive. Vomiting is rare. Strangulation causes severe, constant pain that is rapid in onset.

With both types, abdominal tenderness and rigidity occur. The patient appears acutely ill, with signs of dehydration and sepsis. These include tachycardia, dry mucous membranes, and hypotension. The patient's temperature may rise above 100°F (37.8°C).

The location of the obstruction determines the extent of fluid, electrolyte, and acid-base imbalances. If the obstruction is high (e.g., upper duodenum), metabolic alkalosis may result from the loss of gastric hydrochloric (HCl) acid through vomiting or NG intubation and suction. When the obstruction is in the small intestine, dehydration occurs rapidly. Dehydration and electrolyte imbalances do not occur early in large bowel obstruction.

Diagnostic Studies

Perform a thorough history and physical assessment. Imaging can identify an obstruction and guide decisions about surgery. Abdominal x-rays, CT scan, or contrast enema may be done. Sigmoidoscopy or colonoscopy provides direct visualization of an LBO.

Blood tests include a CBC and blood chemistries. A high WBC count may mean strangulation or perforation. Increased hematocrit values may reflect hemoconcentration. Decreased hemoglobin and hematocrit values may mean bleeding from cancer or strangulation with necrosis. Serum electrolytes, BUN, and creatinine are monitored to assess the degree of dehydration. Metabolic alkalosis can develop from vomiting.

Interprofessional Care

The treatment goal is to regain intestinal patency and resolve the obstruction. Treatment of a bowel obstruction depends on the cause. If a strangulated obstruction or perforation is present, the patient will need emergency surgery to relieve the obstruction and survive. In some, especially those due to surgical adhesions, an obstruction may resolve without surgery. If needed, the patient may have an NG tube for decompression. Some patients need PN to allow bowel rest and improve nutrition status before surgery.

Stents can be placed via endoscopic or fluoroscopic procedures. They are used for palliative purposes or as "a bridge to surgery," allowing a patient to avoid emergency surgery. This gives the health care team time to correct fluid volume and other problems, thus improving surgical outcomes. Corticosteroids with antiemetic properties that decrease edema and inflammation may be used with stent placement.

Surgery may involve simply resecting the obstructed segment of bowel and anastomosing the remaining healthy bowel back together. Partial or total colectomy, colostomy, or ileostomy may be done when extensive obstruction or necrosis is present. Sometimes, an obstruction can be removed nonsurgically. Colonoscopy offers a means to remove polyps, dilate strictures, and remove and destroy tumors with a laser.

NURSING MANAGEMENT: BOWEL OBSTRUCTION

Assessment

An obstruction is a potentially life-threatening condition. Major concerns are preventing fluid and electrolyte imbalances and early recognition of deterioration in the patient's condition (e.g., hypovolemic shock, sepsis, bowel strangulation). Your care begins with a detailed history and physical assessment. Determine the location, duration, intensity, and frequency of abdominal pain. The patient is often restless and constantly changes position to relieve the pain.

Record the onset, frequency, color, odor, and amount of vomitus. Assess bowel function, including the passage of flatus. Auscultate for bowel sounds and document their character and location. Inspect the abdomen for scars, visible masses, and distention. Assess whether abdominal tenderness or rigidity is present. Measure the abdominal girth. Check for signs of peritoneal irritation (e.g., muscle guarding, rebound pain). If the HCP decides to wait to see if the obstruction resolves on its own, assess the patient regularly. Notify the HCP of changes in vital signs, changes in bowel sounds, decreased urine output, increased abdominal distention, and pain.

Maintain a strict intake and output record, including emesis and tube drainage. A urinary catheter allows for hourly monitoring of urine output. Report if the urine output is less than 0.5 mL/kg of body weight per hour. This indicates inadequate vascular volume and the potential for acute kidney injury. Rising serum creatinine and BUN levels are other indicators of acute kidney injury.

Monitor laboratory and arterial blood gas values. A patient with a high obstruction is more likely to have metabolic alkalosis. A patient with a low obstruction is at greater risk for metabolic acidosis.

Clinical Problems

Clinical problems for the patient with an obstruction include:

- Pain
- Impaired GI function
- Fluid imbalance

Planning

The overall goals are that the patient with an obstruction will have (1) relief of the obstruction and return to normal bowel function, (2) minimal to no discomfort, and (3) normal fluid and electrolyte and acid-base status.

Implementation

Care of the patient with an obstruction focuses on measures to promote comfort and fluid and electrolyte balance (Table 47.22). Nursing care of the patient after surgery for an obstruction is similar to care of the patient after a laparotomy.

POLYPS OF LARGE INTESTINE

Colonic polyps arise from the mucosal surface of the colon and project into the lumen. They may be *sessile* (flat, broad-based, and

TABLE 47.22 NURSING MANAGEMENT

Patient With a Bowel Obstruction

- Give IV fluids and electrolyte replacement as ordered
- Monitor for signs of dehydration and electrolyte imbalances
- Place the patient on NPO status
- Implement pain management measures and promote a restful environment
- Maintain a strict intake and output record
- Insert an indwelling urinary catheter, report if the urine output is less than 0.5 mL/kg/h
- Provide frequent oral care and water-soluble lubricant for the lips
- Implement measures to control nausea and vomiting (see Chapter 46)
- Check the NG tube every 4 hours for patency

attached directly to the intestinal wall) or *pedunculated* (attached to the bowel wall by a thin stalk). Polyps tend to be sessile when small and become pedunculated as they enlarge (Fig. 47.7). They may be found anywhere in the large intestine. As patients age, polyps are increasingly present in the proximal colon. Most patients with polyps are asymptomatic. Rectal bleeding and occult blood in the stool are the most common signs.

Types of Polyps

The most common types of polyps are hyperplastic and adenomatous. *Hyperplastic polyps* are noncancerous. They rarely grow larger than 5 mm and never cause clinical symptoms. Other benign polyps include inflammatory polyps, lipomas, and juvenile polyps.

Adenomatous polyps are neoplastic and closely linked to colorectal adenocarcinoma. There are 3 types: tubular, tubulovillous, and villous. Villous or large adenomatous polyps are more likely to have cancers develop in them. Removing adenomatous polyps decreases the occurrence of CRC.

Genetic Link

Familial adenomatous polyposis (FAP) is the most common polyposis syndrome (Box 47.2).[17] FAP is a genetic disorder characterized by hundreds or sometimes thousands of polyps in the colon that appear during adolescence and early adulthood. They eventually become cancerous, usually by age 40. Since CRC is inevitable, the colon and rectum are removed, usually by age 25, by proctocolectomy with an IPAA or an ileostomy. Patients with classic FAP are at risk for cancers of the thyroid, stomach, small intestine, liver, and brain, so lifetime cancer surveillance is essential.

Diagnostic Studies and Interprofessional Care

Colonoscopy, sigmoidoscopy, barium enema, and virtual colonoscopy (CT or MRI colonography) are used to discover polyps. Colonoscopy is preferred because it allows for evaluation of the total colon. All polyps are considered abnormal and should be removed *(polypectomy)*. Polyps can be removed during colonoscopy or sigmoidoscopy. They cannot be removed during barium enema and virtual colonoscopy. After polypectomy, watch the patient for rectal bleeding, fever, severe abdominal pain, and abdominal distention. These may indicate hemorrhage or perforation.

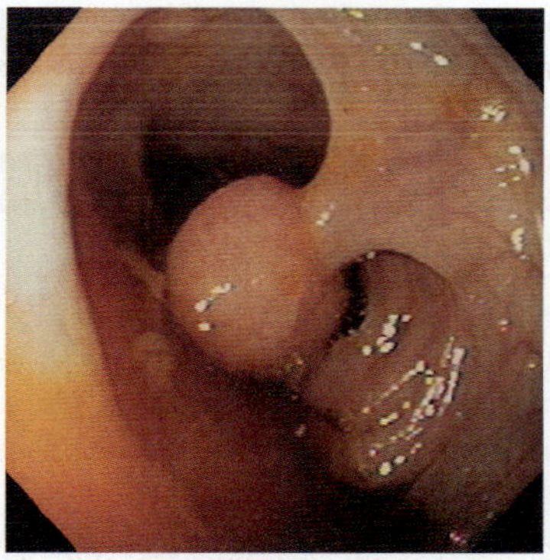

Fig. 47.7 Endoscopic image of pedunculated polyp in descending colon. (Courtesy David Bjorkman, MD, University of Utah School of Medicine, Department of Gastroenterology. In McCance KL, Huether SE: *Pathophysiology: the biologic basis for disease in adults and children,* ed 6, St Louis, 2010, Mosby.)

COLORECTAL CANCER

CRC is the second leading cause of cancer-related deaths. Annually about 148,000 people in the United States are diagnosed with CRC, and 53,000 people die from CRC.[18]

The risk of CRC is higher in men. The risk for CRC increases with age. While about 85% of new CRC cases are detected in people older than 50, this rate has been slowly decreasing. The number of cases in people aged 20 to 49 years is rising and is expected to continue to do so.[19] This is thought to be related to diet, physical inactivity, and increasing rates of obesity (Box 47.3).

Etiology and Pathophysiology

Unlike some other cancers, no single risk factor accounts for most cases of CRC (Table 47.23). The risk is highest in those

BOX 47.2 GENETICS IN CLINICAL PRACTICE

Familial Adenomatous Polyposis (FAP)

Genetic Basis
- Autosomal dominant FAP
  - Classic form of disease
  - Mutations in adenomatous polyposis coli *(APC)* gene
  - Normally this is a tumor suppressor gene involved in DNA repair
  - Normally this gene makes a protein that keeps polyps from developing in the colon
  - 50% of the offspring of a parent with FAP carry the *FAP* gene
- Autosomal recessive FAP
  - Autosomal recessive disorder
  - Mutations in the *mutY* homolog *(MUTYH)* gene
  - Normally this gene is involved in DNA repair
  - Characterized by fewer polyps, typically <100

Incidence
- Affects 1 in 7000–22,000 people
- Causes 1% of all CRC

Genetic Testing
- DNA testing is available

Clinical Implications
- Anyone with a family history of FAP should undergo genetic testing during childhood
- If the FAP gene is present, colorectal screening begins at puberty, and annual colonoscopy begins at age 16
- Persons with a family history of FAP can benefit from genetic counseling

BOX 47.3 PROMOTING HEALTH EQUITY

Colorectal Cancer

- Blacks are most likely to develop and die from CRC.
- CRC may occur at an earlier age in Blacks and Hispanics.
- Hispanics and Asians are the least likely to undergo CRC screening.

TABLE 47.23 Risk Factors for Colorectal Cancer

- Alcohol (≥4 drinks/week)
- Cigarette smoking
- Family history of CRC in first-degree relative
- Family or personal history of familial adenomatous polyposis (FAP)
- Family or personal history of hereditary nonpolyposis colorectal cancer (HNPCC) syndrome
- Obesity (body mass index ≥30 kg/m^2)
- Personal history of CRC, IBD, or diabetes
- Red meat (≥7 servings/week)

BOX 47.4 GENETICS IN CLINICAL PRACTICE

Hereditary Nonpolyposis Colorectal Cancer (HNPCC) or Lynch Syndrome

Genetic Basis

- Autosomal dominant disorder
- Mutations in *MSH2, MLH1, MSH6,* or *PMS2* genes
- These genes are involved with the repair of mistakes in DNA replication

Incidence

- Affects 1 in 500–2000 people

Genetic Testing

- DNA testing is available

Clinical Implications

- Accounts for 3%–5% of all CRC
- Depending on the genetic mutation, the risk for developing CRC is from 50%–80%
- If colon polyps are present, they occur at an earlier age than do polyps in the general population and are more prone to become cancerous
- Have increased risk for stomach, brain, ovary, uterus, skin, urinary tract, small bowel, and bile ducts cancers
- Colonoscopy is recommended every 1–2 years
- Women with HNPCC should undergo ovarian and endometrial cancer screening

with first-degree relatives with CRC and people with IBD. About 20% of cases of CRC occur in patients with a family history of CRC. Hereditary forms of CRC, including FAP (see Box 47.2) and hereditary nonpolyposis colorectal cancer (HNPCC) syndrome (Box 47.4), account for another 5% of cases.[20]

About 30% to 50% of people with CRC have an abnormal *KRAS* gene. The *KRAS* gene, which is primarily involved in regulating cell division, belongs to a class of genes known as *oncogenes.* When mutated, oncogenes have the potential to cause normal cells to become cancerous.

Maintaining a healthy weight, being physically active, limiting alcohol use, not smoking, and eating a diet with large amounts of fruits, vegetables, and grains may decrease the risk for CRC.

CRC usually starts as a polyp on the inner lining of the colon or rectum that grows over a period of 10 to 20 years. Most polyps are adenomas, which arise from the cells that make mucus. As the tumor grows, the cancer invades and penetrates the wall of the colon or rectum (Fig. 47.8). Eventually, cancer cells gain

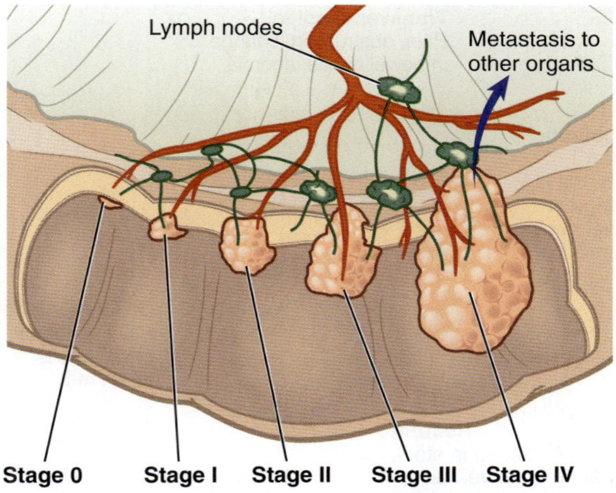

Fig. 47.8 The 5 stages of CRC. Stage 0 cancer has not grown beyond the mucosal layer. Stage I cancer has grown beyond the mucosa into the submucosa, but no lymph nodes are involved. Stage II cancer has grown beyond the submucosa into the muscle, but there is no lymph node involvement or metastasis. Stage III cancer is any tumor with lymph node involvement but no metastasis. Stage IV cancer is any tumor with lymph node involvement and metastasis.

access to the lymph nodes and vascular system and spread to distant sites. Since venous blood leaving the colon and rectum flows through the portal vein and the inferior rectal vein, the liver is a common site of metastasis. The cancer spreads from the liver to other sites, including the lungs, bones, and brain. CRC can also spread directly into adjacent structures.

Clinical Manifestations

CRC develops slowly. Symptoms often do not appear until the disease is advanced. Nonspecific findings in early disease include fatigue and weight loss. As the disease progresses, the patient may have abdominal pain and tenderness with a change in bowel habits. There may be a palpable abdominal mass, hepatomegaly, ascites

Bleeding can occur with both right- and left-sided CRC. Bleeding on the right side is more common than on the left side. It is often unrecognized, and an early manifestation is often anemia. Hematochezia (fresh blood in the stool) is more often caused by left-sided CRC than right-sided CRC.

Right-sided cancers are more likely to cause diarrhea. Left-sided cancers are usually detected later and could present with bowel obstruction (Fig. 47.9). Complications of CRC include obstruction, bleeding, perforation, peritonitis, and fistula formation.

Diagnostic Studies

Obtain a thorough history with close attention to family history (Table 47.24). Since symptoms of CRC often are not evident until the disease is advanced, there is an increased emphasis on screening. Beginning at age 45 and continuing until age 75, those at average risk for developing CRC should have screening tests to detect both polyps and cancer based on 1 of these testing schedules:

- Flexible sigmoidoscopy (every 5 years)
- Colonoscopy (every 10 years)

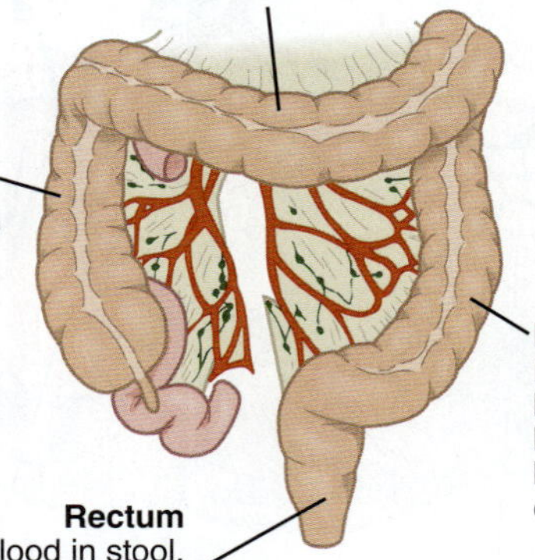

Fig. 47.9 Signs and symptoms of CRC by location of primary tumor. (Modified from McCance KL, Huether SE: *Pathophysiology: the biologic basis for disease in adults and children*, ed 6, St Louis, 2010, Mosby.)

TABLE 47.24 Interprofessional Care

Colorectal Cancer

Diagnostic Assessment

- History and physical assessment
- DRE
- Testing of stool for occult blood
- CBC
- Liver function tests
- Barium enema
- Sigmoidoscopy and/or colonoscopy with biopsy
- Abdominal CT scan, ultrasound, or MRI
- Carcinoembryonic antigen (CEA) test

Management

- Surgery
  - Right hemicolectomy
  - Left hemicolectomy
  - Abdominal-perineal resection
  - Laparoscopic colectomy
  - Low anterior resection
- Chemotherapy
- Targeted therapy
- Radiation therapy

- Double-contrast barium enema (every 5 years)
- CT colonography (virtual colonoscopy) (every 5 years)
- Tests that primarily find cancer include:
  - High-sensitivity fecal occult blood test (FOBT) (every year)
  - Fecal immunochemical test (FIT) (every year)
  - Stool DNA test (every 3 years)

Colonoscopy is the gold standard for CRC screening. It allows the entire colon to be examined, biopsies obtained, and polyps removed and sent to the laboratory for examination. People at average risk for CRC should undergo colonoscopy every 10 years beginning at age 45.

TABLE 47.25 Tumor, Node, Metastasis (TNM) Classification of Colorectal Cancer

T	Primary Tumor
T_x	Cannot assess primary tumor because of incomplete information.
T_{is}	Carcinoma in situ. Cancer is in earliest stage and has not grown beyond mucosa layer.
T_1	Tumor has grown beyond mucosa into the submucosa.
T_2	Tumor has grown through submucosa into muscularis propria.
T_3	Tumor has grown through the muscularis propria into the pericolorectal tissues.
T_4	Tumor invades the visceral peritoneum or invades or adheres to adjacent organ or structure.
N	Lymph Node Involvement
N_x	Cannot assess lymph nodes.
N_0	No regional lymph node involvement is found.
N_1	Cancer is found in 1–3 nearby lymph nodes.
N_2	Cancer is found in 4 or more nearby lymph nodes.
M	Metastasis
M_x	Cannot assess presence of metastasis.
M_0	No distant metastasis seen.
M_1	Distant metastasis is present.

Persons at risk (Table 47.23) should begin screening earlier and have screening done more often. Those who have a first-degree relative who developed CRC before age 60 or have 2 first-degree relatives with CRC should have a colonoscopy every 5 years beginning at age 40 or 10 years earlier than when the youngest relative developed cancer. Those who have 1 first-degree relative who had CRC after age 60 should have a colonoscopy every 10 years beginning at age 40.[20]

Less favorable, but acceptable, screening methods include stool testing for fecal blood. The FOBT and FIT look for blood in the stool. These tests must be done yearly since tumor bleeding occurs at intervals and may easily be missed if a single test is done. Stool DNA tests (PreGen-Plus, Cologuard) can detect cells with DNA mutations that may occur with CRC in the stool.

Once tissue biopsies confirm the diagnosis of CRC, the patient needs a CBC to check for anemia and liver function tests. A CT scan, PET scan, or MRI will be done to detect metastases and determine the depth of penetration of the tumor into the bowel wall.

Carcinoembryonic antigen (CEA) is a complex glycoprotein sometimes made by CRC cells. It may be used to detect CRC and monitor for recurrence after surgery or chemotherapy. It is not the best screening tool because of the large number of false-positive findings. CEA levels also may be increased in non-colon cancers (e.g., gastric, pancreatic, breast, thyroid cancers) as well as some noncancerous conditions, like IBD, pancreatitis, cirrhosis, and chronic obstructive pulmonary disease.

Interprofessional Care

The prognosis and treatment of CRC correlate with the pathologic staging of the disease. The most common staging system is the tumor, node, metastasis (TNM) staging (Table 47.25). As with other cancers, prognosis worsens with greater size and depth of tumor, lymph node involvement, and metastasis (Table 47.26).

TABLE 47.26 Classification System Used to Stage Colorectal Cancer

Stage[a]	TNM[b]	5-Year Survival Rate (%)
0	$T_{is} N_0 M_0$	>96
I	$T_1 N_0 M_0$	92
	$T_2 N_0 M_0$	87
II	$T_3 N_0 M_0$	70–80
III	Any T, $N_{1\text{-}2} M_0$	53–84
IV	Any T, any N, M_1	12

[a]Staging system is shown in Fig. 47.8.
[b]See Table 47.25.

Surgical Therapy

Goals of surgical therapy include (1) complete resection of the tumor, (2) a thorough exploration of the abdomen to determine if the cancer has spread, (3) removing all lymph nodes that drain the area where the cancer is located, and (4) restoring bowel continuity to promote normal bowel function.

Some polyps can be removed during colonoscopy, while others require surgery. Polypectomy during colonoscopy can be used to resect CRC in situ. It is considered successful when the resected margin of the polyp is free of cancer, the cancer is well-differentiated, and there is no apparent lymphatic or blood vessel involvement.

The decision for surgical treatment depends on the staging and location of the cancer and the ability to restore normal bowel function and continence. Surgical therapy for stage I and stage II colon cancers include removing the tumor, surrounding tissues, and nearby lymph nodes. The remaining cancer-free ends are sewn back together (anastomosis) when possible. Laparoscopic surgery is sometimes used, especially for tumors in the left colon. Chemotherapy is used after surgery for high-risk stage II tumors. Stage III tumors are treated with surgery and chemotherapy. Radiation and chemotherapy may be done before surgery to reduce tumor size.

In rectal cancer, the location and size of the tumor determine the course of treatment. Local excision may be an option. If the tumor is in the distal rectum (1 to 2 cm from the anorectal junction) and the sphincters cannot be preserved, the patient will undergo an *abdominal-perineal resection (APR)*. An APR involves removing the entire rectum with the tumor, and the patient will have a permanent colostomy.

If the tumor is in the mid or proximal rectum, it may be possible to preserve the sphincters with a low anterior resection (LAR). A LAR involves removing the rectum and anastomosing the colon to the anal canal. A temporary ostomy may be done to divert stool and allow time for the anastomosis to heal. Another option if the anal sphincters remain is for the HCP to create an alternative reservoir with either a colonic J-pouch or coloplasty (Fig. 47.10). A LAR is increasingly common because of advancements in laparoscopy and stapling techniques.

When the tumor is not resectable or metastasis is present, palliative surgery can control hemorrhage or relieve a bowel obstruction. Chemotherapy and radiation can control the spread and provide pain relief. A few patients with limited lung or liver metastases can achieve a cure after primary and metastatic tumor resection and chemotherapy.

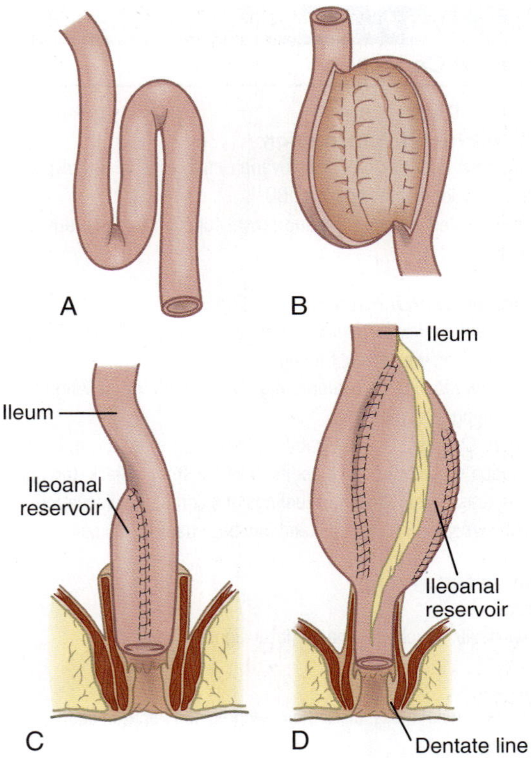

Fig. 47.10 Ileoanal pouch (reservoir). (A) Formation of a pouch. (B) Posterior suture lines completed. (C) J-shaped configuration for ileoanal pouch (J-pouch). (D) S-shaped configuration for ileoanal pouch (S-pouch).

Chemotherapy and Targeted Therapy

Chemotherapy can be used to shrink the tumor before surgery, as an adjuvant therapy after bowel resection, and as palliative treatment for nonresectable cancer. Adjuvant chemotherapy is recommended for patients with stage III tumors. Current protocols include varying doses of oxaliplatin (Eloxatin) with either fluorouracil (FU) and leucovorin (LV) or capecitabine (Xeloda). Irinotecan can be given with FU and LV alone or with oxaliplatin.[21] Capecitabine or FU can be used alone in patients for whom oxaliplatin therapy is not appropriate.

Several targeted therapies have a role in treating metastatic CRC. Angiogenesis inhibitors inhibit the blood supply to tumors. These include aflibercept (Zaltrap), bevacizumab (Avastin), and ramucirumab (Cyramza). Cetuximab (Erbitux) and panitumumab (Vectibix) block the epidermal growth factor receptor. These drugs are often given with a combination chemotherapy regimen.

Regorafenib (Stivarga) is a multikinase inhibitor that blocks several enzymes that promote cancer growth. It, or Lonsurf, a combination of trifluridine and tipiracil, are given to patients with metastatic CRC who are no longer responding to other therapies. Trifluridine impairs DNA function and angiogenesis. Tipiracil prevents the rapid metabolism of trifluridine, thus increasing its bioavailability.

Radiation Therapy

Some patients may receive radiation therapy as an adjuvant to surgery and chemotherapy or as a palliative measure for those

TABLE 47.27 NURSING ASSESSMENT
Colorectal Cancer

Subjective Data
Important Health Information
Health history: Previous breast or ovarian cancer, familial polyposis, villous adenoma, adenomatous polyps, IBD
Medications: Medications affecting bowel function (e.g., laxatives, antidiarrheal drugs)

Functional Health Patterns
Health perception–health management: Family history of colorectal, breast, or ovarian cancer; weakness, fatigue
Nutritional-metabolic: High-calorie, high-fat, low-fiber diet. Anorexia, nausea and vomiting, weight loss
Elimination: Change in bowel habits, alternating diarrhea and constipation, defecation urgency. Rectal bleeding, mucoid stools. Black, tarry stools. Flatus, decrease in stool caliber. Feelings of incomplete evacuation
Cognitive-perceptual: Abdominal and low back pain, tenesmus

Objective Data
General
Pallor, cachexia, lymphadenopathy (later signs)

GI
Palpable abdominal mass, distention, ascites, and hepatomegaly (liver metastasis)

Possible Diagnostic Findings
Anemia. Guaiac-positive stools, palpable mass on DRE. Positive sigmoidoscopy, colonoscopy, barium enema, or CT scan. Positive biopsy

with metastatic cancer. As a palliative measure, the primary goal is to reduce tumor size and provide symptomatic relief. Radiation therapy is described in Chapter 15.

NURSING MANAGEMENT: COLORECTAL CANCER

Assessment

Table 47.27 outlines the subjective and objective data to obtain from a patient with CRC.

Clinical Problems

Clinical problems for the patient with CRC include:

- Altered bowel elimination
- Anxiety
- Difficulty coping

Planning

The overall goals are that the patient with CRC will have (1) normal bowel elimination patterns, (2) quality of life appropriate to the disease progression, (3) relief of pain, and (4) feelings of comfort and well-being.

Implementation

Health Promotion

Encourage all persons over 45 to have regular CRC screening. Help identify those at high risk who need screening at an earlier age. Discuss with patients how taking part in cancer screening helps decrease mortality rates. Realize that barriers exist, including lack of accurate information and fear of diagnosis.

Endoscopic and radiographic procedures can only reveal polyps when the bowel has been properly prepared. Provide teaching about bowel cleansing for outpatient diagnostic procedures and give cleansing preparations to inpatients (see more on diagnostic procedures in Chapter 43).

Acute Care

Nursing care for the patient after a bowel resection is discussed in depth in the next section. If enough healthy bowel remained that the HCP could reconnect the bowel ends, normal bowel function is maintained. Routine postoperative care is appropriate. Patients with more extensive surgery, such as an APR, may have an open wound and drains (e.g., Jackson-Pratt, Hemovac) and a permanent ostomy. Postoperative care includes sterile dressing changes, care of drains, and patient and caregiver teaching about the ostomy.

Ambulatory Care

Psychologic support for the patient and caregiver dealing with the diagnosis of cancer is important. Discuss the patient's feelings about the prognosis and future screening. Patients need much emotional support. The special needs of the cancer patient are discussed in Chapter 16. You may need to address issues surrounding palliative care, end-of-life issues, and hospice (see Chapter 10).

Patients with CRC need to know how to manage changes that result from cancer and cancer treatment. Those who had sphincter-sparing surgery may have diarrhea and incontinence of feces and gas. They may need antidiarrheal drugs or bulking agents to control the diarrhea, but overuse can result in constipation. A consult with a dietitian or wound, ostomy, and continence nurse (WOCN) may help patients and caregivers understand how to manage food and fluid options. Ostomy rehabilitation, including teaching and ongoing support, should be available for all ostomy patients. Patients with skin changes from incontinence and/or radiation therapy will need help with managing these conditions.

Evaluation

The expected outcomes for the patient with CRC are that the patient will:

- Have minimal changes in bowel elimination patterns
- Achieve optimal nutrition intake
- Experience quality of life appropriate to disease progression
- Have feelings of comfort and well-being

BOWEL RESECTION AND OSTOMY SURGERY

Surgical resection of the bowel may be done to (1) remove cancer; (2) repair a perforation, fistula, or traumatic injury; (3) relieve an obstruction or stricture; and (4) treat an abscess, inflammatory disease, or hemorrhage (Table 47.28). For example, if a person has stage III CRC, the HCP will remove the diseased part of the colon along with a margin of healthy tissue. It may be a prophylactic procedure for those with complications

TABLE 47.28 Common Intestinal Surgical Procedures

Procedure	Description
Abdominal-perineal resection (APR)	Removal of the entire rectum with creation of a permanent colostomy
Anterior rectosigmoid resection	Removal of part of descending colon, the sigmoid colon, and upper rectum with the descending colon anastomosed to remaining rectum
Colectomy	Removal of the entire colon with the ileum anastomosed to the rectum
Left hemicolectomy	Removal of splenic flexure, descending colon, and sigmoid colon with the transverse colon anastomosed to rectum
Low anterior resection (LAR)	Removal of the rectum and with anastomosis of the colon to the anal canal. Temporary ileostomy or colostomy may be done to divert stool and allow time for the anastomosis to heal. After 8–12 weeks, the ostomy can be "taken down," and the ends of the colon surgically reconnected
Proctocolectomy with ileostomy	Removal of the colon, rectum, and anus with closure of the anal opening. End of the terminal ileum is brought out through the abdominal wall to form a permanent ileostomy
Proctocolectomy with ileal pouch/anal anastomosis (IPAA)	2 surgeries, 8–12 weeks apart. The first includes colectomy, rectal mucosectomy, ileal pouch (reservoir) construction, ileoanal anastomosis, and temporary ileostomy. Diverting ileostomy is done, and an ileal pouch is created and anastomosed directly to the anus (Fig. 47.10). Second surgery involves closure of the ileostomy to direct stool toward the new pouch
Right hemicolectomy	Removal of ascending colon and hepatic flexure with the ileum anastomosed to transverse colon

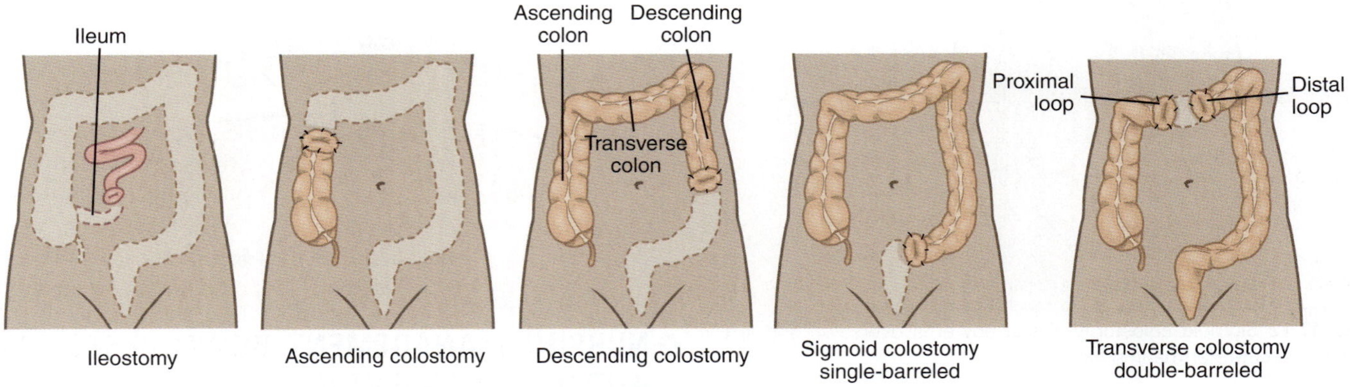

Fig. 47.11 Types of ostomies.

from IBD. Patients at high risk for CRC, such as those with FAP, and patients with UC may have a total colectomy and an ileostomy.

Ostomy

An **ostomy** is a surgically created opening on the abdomen that allows the discharge of body waste when the normal elimination route is no longer possible. The outermost part that is visible is a *stoma*. The stoma is the result of the large or small bowel being brought to the outside of the abdomen and sutured in place. When a stoma is created as a fecal diversion, feces will drain through the stoma instead of the anus.

Ostomies are named according to their location and type (Fig. 47.11). An ostomy in the ileum is an ileostomy. An ostomy in the colon is a colostomy. The ostomy is further characterized by its anatomic site (ascending, transverse, descending, sigmoid). The more distal the ostomy, the more functioning bowel remains, and the more likely that the intestinal contents will resemble the feces that would have been eliminated from an intact colon and rectum. Ileostomy output will be a liquid to thin paste since it did not enter the colon. Patients have no control over ileostomy drainage; it is involuntary. An ileostomy drains frequently, and the patient must wear an ostomy pouch to collect the drainage. In contrast, sigmoid colostomy output resembles normal formed stool. Some patients can regulate emptying time with colostomy irrigation and may not need to wear a pouch. See Table 47.29 for a comparison of colostomies and ileostomies.

Ostomies may be temporary or permanent. For example, the person with a draining fistula may need a temporary ostomy to prevent stool from reaching the diseased area. Cancer involving the rectum requires a permanent ostomy if all bowel distal to the ostomy is removed.

Permanent ostomies may be continent or traditional. *Continent ileostomies* (e.g., Koch pouch, Barnett Continent Ileal Reservoir) use 40 to 45 cm of the terminal ileum to fashion an internal pouch, nipple valve, and abdominal stoma. The pouch replaces the rectum as a reservoir for stool. It can hold around 500 mL of material. Continent ostomies are an option for patients who have had a prior APR with ileostomy for UC or FAP. Patients must be motivated and compliant. They must drain the pouch manually by inserting a catheter through the nipple valve. At first, this is done every 1 to 2 hours. As the pouch enlarges, the frequency decreases to 4 times daily and as needed. They must keep the stool consistency relatively fluid by following a low-residue diet.

The major types of traditional ostomies include end, double-barreled, and loop ostomy.

TABLE 47.29 Comparison of Ileostomy and Colostomy

		COLOSTOMY		
Characteristic	**Ileostomy**	**Ascending**	**Transverse**	**Sigmoid**
Stool consistency	Liquid to semiliquid	Semiliquid	Semiliquid to semiformed	Formed
Fluid requirement	↑	↑	Possibly ↑	No change
Bowel regulation	No	No	No	Yes, if there is a history of a regular bowel pattern
Pouch and skin barriers	Yes	Yes	Yes	Dependent on regulation
Indications for surgery	UC, Crohn's disease, diseased or injured colon, familial polyposis, trauma, cancer	Perforating diverticulum in lower colon, trauma, rectovaginal fistula, inoperable tumors of colon, rectum, or pelvis	Same as for ascending	Cancer of the rectum or rectosigmoid area, perforating diverticulum, trauma

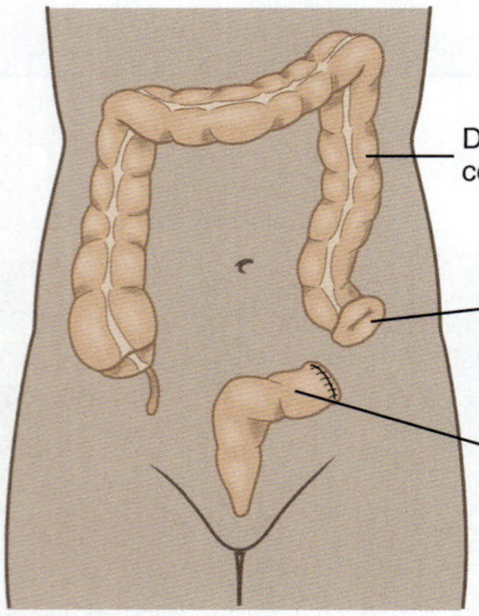

Fig. 47.12 Sigmoid colostomy. Distal bowel is oversewn and left in place to create Hartmann pouch.

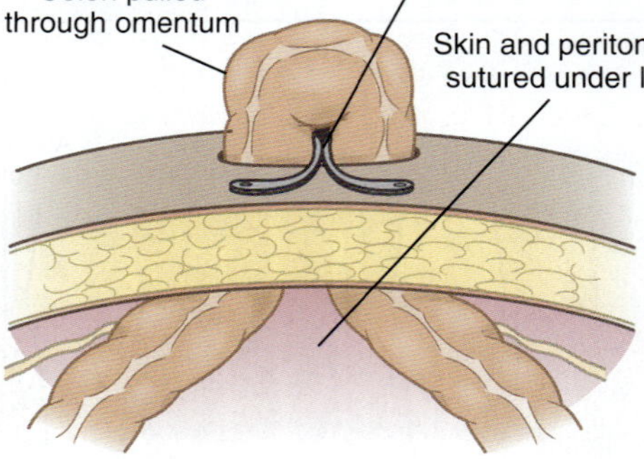

Fig. 47.13 Loop colostomy.

End stoma. An end stoma is made by dividing the bowel and bringing out the proximal end as a single stoma, making a colostomy or ileostomy. The distal part of the GI tract is surgically removed, or the distal segment is oversewn and left in the abdominal cavity with its mesentery intact. If the distal bowel is removed, the stoma is permanent. When the distal bowel is oversewn and not removed, the procedure is called a *Hartmann pouch* (Fig. 47.12). With a Hartmann pouch, the potential exists for the bowel to be reanastomosed and the stoma closed (referred to as a *takedown*).

Loop stoma. A loop stoma is made by bringing a loop of bowel to the abdominal surface and then opening the anterior wall of the bowel to provide fecal diversion. This results in 1 stoma with a proximal opening for feces and a distal opening for mucus drainage from the distal colon. An intact posterior wall separates the 2 openings. A plastic rod holds the loop of bowel in place for 7 to 10 days after surgery to prevent it from slipping back into the abdominal cavity (Fig. 47.13). A loop stoma is usually temporary.

Double-barreled stoma. To create a double-barreled stoma, the HCP divides the bowel, and both the proximal and distal ends are brought through the abdominal wall as 2 separate stomas (Fig. 47.11). The proximal stoma is the functioning stoma. The distal, nonfunctioning stoma is a *mucus fistula*. A double-barreled stoma is usually temporary.

NURSING MANAGEMENT: BOWEL RESECTION AND OSTOMY SURGERY

Preoperative Care

Care that is unique to ostomy surgery includes (1) psychologic preparation for the ostomy, (2) educational preparation, and (3) selecting the best site for the stoma. Ideally, the management of patients facing ostomy surgery begins preoperatively (Box 47.5). If available, a WOCN should visit with the patient and caregiver to determine the patient's ability to perform self-care, identify support systems, and determine any modifications that could promote learning during recovery.

Psychologic preparation and emotional support are particularly important as the person begins to cope with the changes in body image and elimination. The patient and caregiver should understand the extent of the surgery planned. It is normal for them to have questions about the procedures. Provide them with opportunities to share concerns and questions. This will enhance the patient's feelings of control and ability to cope.

A WOCN should choose the site where the ostomy will be and mark the abdomen before surgery. The site should be within the rectus muscle, on a flat surface, and in a place that the patient is able to see. A flat site makes it much easier to create a good seal and avoid bag leakage. Being able to see the stoma makes caring for it easier. Whenever possible, it should be discreetly hidden under clothing and appropriate for normal activities.

BOX 47.5 EVIDENCE-BASED PRACTICE

Preoperative Ostomy Education

F.S., a 68-year-old patient, and his wife meet you in the preoperative clinic. F.S. is scheduled for colostomy surgery for severe diverticular disease. As part of your interview, he tells you he has tried a high-fiber diet, fiber supplements, and probiotics to manage his condition. He was also prescribed oral antibiotics on many occasions. These treatments were not effective. The HCP recommended surgery after he developed rectal bleeding.

Making Clinical Decisions

Synthesis of Best Available Evidence

Research has reinforced the value of preoperative stoma site marking and early education. These measures are critical to achieving a better-situated stoma, with fewer complications related to appliance adherence and leakage. Preoperative education reduces the patient's anxiety. Decreased anxiety allows the patient to more easily learn the skills needed to care for a new ostomy. Routine preoperative education is a critical part of the Enhanced Recovery After Surgery (ERAS) initiative. This leads to shorter hospital stays through evidence-based changes in care delivery.

Clinician Expertise

As part of the preoperative education for F.S., you review what a stoma is and how it is created. Pictures of the sections of the bowel and types of stomas are highlighted in the patient information packet. You show F.S. and his wife several different pouching systems as options for postoperative use. F.S. performs a return demonstration of pouch emptying and changing. You discuss general ostomy care, as well as bathing, diet changes, and travel. The WOCN completes the stoma site marking. You review with F.S. the expectations for stool output the first 6 weeks after surgery.

Patient Preferences and Values

F.S. voices anxiety about the upcoming surgery and his ability to manage the colostomy. However, he and his wife are engaged in the educational session and ask many questions. They express hope that they will be able to travel to see their grandchildren again after he recovers from surgery.

Implications for Nursing Practice

- 1. How would you assess readiness to learn for F.S.?
- 2. How could you determine the anxiety level for F.S. before and after the session?
- 3. What teaching would need to be reinforced after surgery?

Reference for Evidence

Harris MS, Kelly K, Parise C: Does preoperative ostomy education decrease anxiety in the new ostomy patient? *J Wound Ostomy Continence* 47:137, 2020.

◆ Postoperative Care

If the patient's wound is closed or partially closed, assess the integrity of the incision. Monitor for complications, including delayed wound healing, hemorrhage, fistulas, and infections. Assess the wound regularly and record bleeding, excess drainage, and unusual odor. Monitor for edema, redness, and drainage, as well as fever and a high WBC count. Observe the skin and the area around any drains for signs of inflammation. Keep the area around any drains clean and dry.

A patient who has an open wound with packing needs meticulous care. Reinforce dressings and change them often during the first several hours postoperatively when drainage is likely to be profuse. Carefully assess all drainage for amount, color, and consistency. The drainage is usually serosanguineous.

TABLE 47.30 Characteristics of Stoma

Characteristic	Description or Cause
Color	
Rose to brick-red	Viable stoma mucosa
Pale	Anemia
Blanching, dark red to dusky blue or purple	Inadequate blood supply to the stoma or bowel
Brown-black	Necrosis
Edema	
Mild to moderate edema	Normal in initial postoperative period. Trauma to the stoma
Moderate to severe edema	Obstruction of the stoma, allergic reaction to food, gastroenteritis
Bleeding	
Small amount	Oozing from stoma mucosa when touched is normal because of its high vascularity
Moderate to large amount	Lower GI bleeding, coagulation factor deficiency, stomal varices from portal hypertension

If an ostomy is present, assess the stoma and place a clear pouching system. The stoma should be rosy pink to red and mildly swollen (Table 47.30). Assess and document stoma color every 4 hours and ensure that there is no excess bleeding. Report any sustained color changes or bleeding to the HCP. Edema will resolve over the first 6 weeks.

The colostomy starts functioning when peristalsis returns. Record the volume, color, and consistency of the drainage. When a colostomy is done on a colon that was not cleaned out before surgery, stool will drain when peristalsis returns. If the bowel was cleansed preoperatively, it will not begin producing stool until a few days after the patient is eating again. Excessive amounts of gas are common during the first 2 weeks. Because this can be distressing to patients, assure them this is temporary.

In the first 24 to 48 hours after surgery, the amount of drainage from an ileostomy may be negligible. When peristalsis returns, ileostomy output may be as high as 1500 to 1800 mL/24 hr. If the small bowel is shortened by surgery, drainage may be greater. This is because the patient has lost the absorptive functions provided by the colon and the delay provided by the ileocecal valve. Observe the patient for fluid deficits and electrolyte imbalances, particularly potassium and sodium. Over a period of days to weeks, the proximal small bowel adapts and increases fluid absorption. Then, feces will thicken to a paste-like consistency, and the volume will decrease to around 500 mL/day. Patients, especially those with Crohn's disease, are at risk for developing a bowel obstruction during the first 30 days after surgery.

After an IPAA, initially, patients may have 4 to 6 stools or more daily. Adaptation over the next 3 to 6 months will result in fewer bowel movements. The patient can control defecation at the anal sphincter.

After intraoperative manipulation of the anal canal, transient incontinence of mucus may occur. Have the patient start Kegel exercises about 4 weeks after surgery to strengthen the pelvic floor and sphincter muscles (see Table 50.18). Perianal skincare is important to protect the epidermis from mucous drainage and maceration. Teach the patient to gently clean the skin with a mild cleanser, rinse well, and dry thoroughly. A moisture barrier ointment and a perineal pad may be used. Some patients have phantom rectal pain or still feel as if they need to have a bowel movement. This is normal and often subsides over time. Be astute in distinguishing phantom sensations from perineal abscess pain.

◆ Sexual Function

Problems with sexual function depend on the surgery. Pelvic surgery can disrupt nerve and vascular supplies to the genitalia. Unfortunately, any pelvic surgery that removes the rectum has the potential of damaging the parasympathetic nerve plexus. The HCP should discuss the possibility with the patient.

For men, the main concern may be erection and ejaculation. Erection depends on intact parasympathetic and nonadrenergic noncholinergic nerves as well as an adequate blood supply. Sympathetic nerve damage in the presacral area can disrupt the ability to ejaculate. This can occur with the APR procedure. Sexual problems may be temporary and resolve in 3 to 12 months. Nerve-sparing surgical techniques are used when possible to preserve sexual function.

For women, nerve damage can result in vaginal dryness and decreased sensation in the vagina and clitoris, making arousal and achieving orgasm more challenging. Experimenting with positions and using lubrication may help.

Sexual function and sexuality concerns affect most patients with an ostomy. The patient may fear rejection by a partner or that others will not find them desirable. Discuss sexuality and sexual function. Help the patient realize that it takes time to adjust to the pouch and to body changes before feeling secure with sexual functioning.

Teach the patient to empty the pouch before sexual activities. Some may apply a smaller pouch or use a pouch cover during sexual activity. Women may consider wearing open panties, a short slip, or similar lingerie. Men may consider wearing a wrap or cummerbund around the midsection to secure the pouch.

◆ Colostomy Care

Patients with new ostomies have complex needs and require frequent assessment, planning, intervention, and evaluation (Table 47.31). Two major aspects of nursing care are (1) patient and caregiver teaching about ostomy care and (2) emotional support as the patient copes with a change in body image. With shorter hospital stays, patient teaching should focus on the critical aspects that patients need to master. Teaching must include (1) basic skills about managing the ostomy (e.g., changing the pouch), (2) diet, and (3) how to get help for problems. Home care and outpatient follow-up may be helpful, especially if there is access to a WOCN. Patient and caregiver teaching is outlined in Table 47.32. Nursing care for the patient with an ostomy is discussed in eNursing Care Plan 47.3 on the website.

An appropriate pouching system is vital to protect the skin and provide dependable stool collection. Most pouching systems have an adhesive skin barrier and a pouch to collect the feces. If the abdominal stoma site has bends or creases, it is hard to get a good seal, and the skin barrier will pull away faster. Since the excess weight of collected stool pulls the wafer away from the skin, empty ostomy bags when one-third full.

TABLE 47.31 NURSING MANAGEMENT

Ostomy Care

- Assess and document stoma and peristomal skin appearance.
- For patient with a new ostomy, assess patient's preparation for ostomy care.
- Assist the patient with managing the psychologic impact of the stoma and its effect on body image and self-esteem.
- Choose appropriate ostomy pouching system for patient.
- Monitor the volume, color, and odor of the ostomy drainage.
- Develop plan of care for skincare around the ostomy.
- Teach ostomy self-care to patient and caregiver (Table 47.32).
- Irrigate new colostomy, if indicated.
- Teach patient and caregivers about appropriate diet choices (Table 47.33).
- Supervise AP:
  - Empty ostomy bag and measure liquid contents.
  - Place the ostomy pouching system for an established ostomy.
  - Assist stable patient with colostomy irrigation.

TABLE 47.32 PATIENT & CAREGIVER TEACHING

Ostomy Self-Care

Include the following points when teaching the patient and/or caregiver about self-care of an ostomy:

1. Explain what an ostomy is and how it functions.
2. Describe the underlying condition that resulted in the need for an ostomy.
3. Demonstrate and allow the patient and caregiver to practice the following:
   - Remove the old skin barrier, cleanse the skin, and correctly apply new skin barriers.
   - Apply, empty, clean, and remove the pouch.
   - Empty the pouch before it is one-third full to prevent leakage.
4. Irrigate the colostomy to regulate bowel elimination (optional).
5. Explain how to contact the WOCN.
6. Describe how to obtain ostomy supplies.
7. Explain diet and fluid management, including:
   - Well-balanced diet and supplements to prevent nutrition problems
   - Foods to avoid to reduce diarrhea or gas (see Table 47.33)
   - Fluid intake of least 3000 mL/day to prevent dehydration (unless contraindicated)
   - Increase fluid intake during hot weather, excess perspiration, and diarrhea to replace losses and prevent dehydration
   - Describe symptoms of fluid and electrolyte imbalance
   - How to contact the dietitian
   - Chew food very well to reduce the chance of blockage
   - Explain how to recognize problems (fever, diarrhea, skin irritation, stomal problems)
8. Describe community resources to assist with emotional and psychologic adjustment to the ostomy.
9. Explain the importance of follow-up care.
10. Describe the ostomy's potential effects on sexual activity, social life, work, and recreation and ways to manage these changes.

Use a transparent pouch in the initial postoperative period so that you can easily assess stoma viability and pouch application by the patient. Each time the pouch is changed, assess the skin for irritation. If the peristomal skin is irritated and raw, more products may have to be applied. Do not allow feces to remain on the skin, or irritation will quickly develop. Change a pouch that has failed at once.

A colostomy in the ascending and transverse colon has semiliquid stools. Have the patient use a drainable pouch. A drainable pouch may last up to 4 to 7 days. A colostomy in the sigmoid or descending colon has semiformed or formed stools. The patient can use a drainable pouch or a disposable, closed-end pouch changed every day. Charcoal filters can deodorize and automatically release flatus. They are available for both types of pouches.

An option when the stoma is in the distal colon is colostomy irrigation. It may be used to stimulate emptying of the colon. The patient may need to wear only a pad or small pouch over the stoma if spillage should occur between irrigations. Irrigation requires manual dexterity and adequate vision. People who irrigate should have ostomy bags in case they develop diarrhea.

Teach the patient about the importance of fluids and a healthy diet. The effect of food on stoma output is individual. Most patients with colostomies can eat anything they want. However, some choose to avoid certain foods because of possible increased gas, odor, or stoma output (Table 47.33).

The patient can resume activities of daily living within 6 to 8 weeks but should avoid heavy lifting. The patient's physical condition determines when they can resume sports. Swimming with an ostomy pouch intact is not a problem. The patient can bathe and shower with or without the pouching system in place because water does not harm the stoma.

◆ Ileostomy Care

Nursing care for a patient with an ileostomy is similar to that for a patient with a colostomy. Because the stool from an ileostomy is caustic to the skin, a secure pouching system is important. The patient must always wear a pouch since regularity is not possible with an ileostomy. An open-ended, drainable pouch is best, so drainage can be easily emptied.

Patients need to increase fluid intake to at least 2 to 3 L/day or more when there are excess fluid losses from heat and sweating. They may need to ingest more sodium. Patients must learn signs and symptoms of fluid and electrolyte imbalance so that they can take appropriate action.

TABLE 47.33 NUTRITION THERAPY

Effects of Food on Stoma Output

Odor Producing	Gas Forming	Diarrhea Causing
Alcohol	Beans	Alcohol
Asparagus	Beer	Beer
Broccoli	Cabbage family	Cabbage family
Cabbage	Carbonated beverages	Coffee
Eggs	Cheeses (strong)	Fruits (raw)
Fish	Onions	Green beans
Garlic	Sprouts	Spicy foods
Onions		Spinach

An ileostomy is susceptible to obstruction because the lumen is less than 1 inch in diameter. It may narrow further at the point where the bowel passes through the fascia/muscle layer of the abdomen. Foods such as nuts, raisins, popcorn, coconut, mushrooms, olives, stringy vegetables, foods with skins, dried fruits, and meats with casings must be chewed very well before swallowing.

◆ Psychologic Adaptation to an Ostomy

The patient's response to a new ostomy is highly individualized. Some have minimal difficulty and view their ostomy positively. It may be curative if their presenting condition was UC or a step toward remission if the diagnosis was CRC. Other patients may have a grief reaction from the change in body image. They may be angry, depressed, or fearful. Concerns about stool leaking, odor, sounds of flatus, pouch reliability, and changes in lifestyle are all common worries. Information, emotional support, and mastering basic skills will help patients learn to live a full life with an ostomy and accept the changes in body image.

Provide information in an easily understood manner and help patients develop confidence and competence in managing the stoma. The patient's emotional state may limit the ability to take part in teaching and ostomy care. Help the patient identify ways of coping. Support from the caregiver, family, and friends is vital. It reassures the patient of their value despite having the ostomy. Encourage patients to share their concerns and ask questions.

New ostomy patients will have questions on a variety of topics ranging from managing gas to intimacy to travel. Give the names and contact information for support groups. The Wound Ostomy Continence Nurses Society *(www.wocn.org)*, local support groups, and United Ostomy Associations of America *(www.ostomy.org)* provide practical information about living with an ostomy. Online support groups are also available. Some hospitals have a visitor's program. These programs give the patient and caregiver an opportunity to talk with a person who has adjusted well to an ostomy and had some of the same feelings and concerns they have.

DIVERTICULOSIS AND DIVERTICULITIS

Diverticula are saccular dilations or outpouchings of the mucosa that develop in the colon (Fig. 47.14). Diverticulosis is the

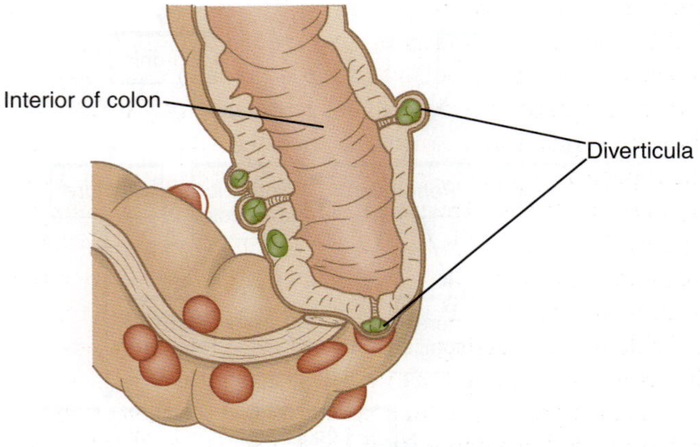

Fig. 47.14 Diverticula are outpouchings of the colon. When they become inflamed, the condition is diverticulitis. The inflammatory process can spread to the surrounding area in the intestine.

presence of multiple noninflamed diverticula. **Diverticulitis** is inflammation of 1 or more diverticula, resulting in perforation into the peritoneum. Clinically, diverticular disease covers a spectrum from asymptomatic, uncomplicated diverticulosis to diverticulitis with complications, such as perforation, abscess, fistula, and bleeding. Diverticula are common, especially in older adults, but most people never develop diverticulitis.

Etiology and Pathophysiology

Diverticula may occur anywhere in the GI tract but are most common in the left (descending, sigmoid) colon. They seem to occur at weak points in the intestinal wall, such as where the blood vessels pass through the muscle layer. The cause is thought to include both genetic and environmental factors. We think the main contributing factors are diet and lifestyle. The disease is more prevalent in Western, industrialized populations, where people tend to consume diets low in fiber and high in red meat and refined carbohydrates.[22] Diverticula are uncommon in vegetarians. Other risk factors are obesity, inactivity, smoking, excess alcohol use, and NSAID use.

Clinical Manifestations and Complications

Most patients with diverticulosis have no symptoms. Those with symptoms typically have abdominal pain, bloating, flatulence, and changes in bowel habits. In more serious situations, the diverticula bleed, or diverticulitis develops. The most common signs and symptoms of diverticulitis are acute pain in the left lower quadrant, distention, decreased or absent bowel sounds, nausea, vomiting, and systemic symptoms of infection. Older adults with diverticulitis may be afebrile, with a normal WBC count and little, if any, abdominal tenderness. Diverticulitis can cause erosion of the bowel wall and perforation into the peritoneum (Fig. 47.15). A localized abscess develops when the body walls off the perforated area. Peritonitis develops if it cannot be contained. Bleeding can be extensive but usually stops spontaneously.

PATHOPHYSIOLOGY MAP

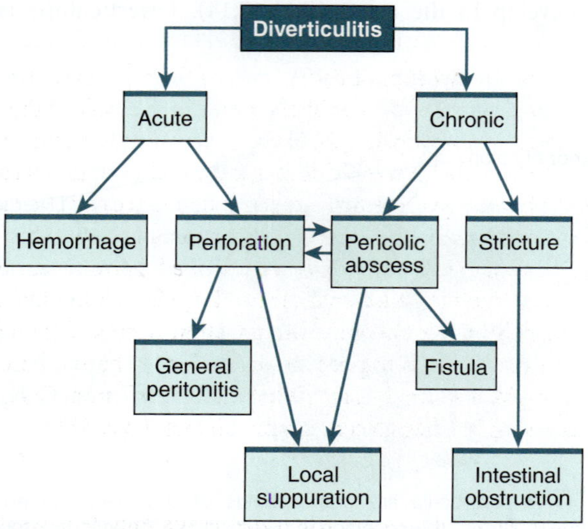

Fig. 47.15 Complications of diverticulitis.

Diagnostic Studies

Diverticular disease can be asymptomatic. It is typically found during routine sigmoidoscopy or colonoscopy. Diagnosis of diverticulitis is based on the physical assessment, CBC, and imaging (Table 47.34).[22] The preferred diagnostic test is a CT scan with oral contrast. Abdominal x-rays, ultrasound, and MRI are other options.

Interprofessional and Nursing Care

In acute diverticulitis, the goal of treatment is to let the colon rest and the inflammation subside (Table 47.35). Some patients can be managed at home with a clear liquid diet, bed rest, and analgesics. Hospitalization is needed if symptoms are severe, the

TABLE 47.34 Interprofessional Care

Diverticulosis and Diverticulitis

Diagnostic Assessment

- History and physical assessment
- Testing of stool for occult blood
- CBC
- Urinalysis
- CT scan with oral contrast
- Abdominal and/or chest x-ray
- MRI
- Ultrasound

Management

Conservative Therapy

- High-fiber diet
- Fiber supplements
- Weight loss (if overweight)
- Smoking cessation

Acute Care: Diverticulitis

- Antibiotic therapy
- NPO status
- IV fluids
- Analgesics
- NG suction
- Surgery
  - Possible resection of involved colon
  - Possible temporary colostomy

TABLE 47.35 NURSING MANAGEMENT

Acute Diverticulitis

- Give IV fluids and electrolyte replacement as ordered.
- Place the patient on NPO status, moving to clear liquids with improvement.
- Administer IV fluids and antibiotics as ordered.
- Observe for signs of abscess, bleeding, and peritonitis.
- Monitor the WBC count.
- Implement pain management measures.
- Keep the patient on bedrest.
- Maintain a strict intake and output record.
- Provide frequent oral care and water-soluble lubricant for the lips.
- Institute NG suctioning and check every 4 hours for patency.

patient is unable to tolerate oral fluids, there are systemic manifestations of infection (fever, significant ↑ WBC), or the patient has co-morbid conditions (e.g., immunosuppression).

Patients with reoccurring diverticulitis or complications, such as an abscess or obstruction, may need surgery. The usual surgical procedure involves resection of the involved colon with a primary anastomosis.[22] If the HCP is not able to anastomose the colon, the patient will have a temporary diverting colostomy. After the colon heals, the temporary colostomy can be taken down and the ends of the colon reconnected.

Provide patients with diverticular disease with a full explanation of the condition. Patients who understand the disease process well and adhere to the prescribed regimen are less likely to have an exacerbation. Teach them the importance of following a high-fiber diet, mainly from fruits and vegetables with a decreased intake of fat and red meat (Table 47.9). Encourage a fluid intake of at least 2 L/day.

A patient with diverticular disease should avoid increased intraabdominal pressure because it may precipitate an attack. Factors that increase intraabdominal pressure are straining at stool, vomiting, bending, heavy lifting, and wearing tight, restrictive clothing. Weight loss (see Chapter 45) is important for the person with obesity. Encourage smoking cessation.

FISTULAS

A **fistula** is an abnormal tract between 2 hollow organs or a hollow organ and the skin. Fistulas are named by the track that they take from one body part to another. For example, an enterocutaneous fistula is an opening between the small intestine and skin. An enterovaginal fistula is between the small intestine and vagina, allowing stool and gas to drain through the vagina.

A GI fistula occurs between the lumen of the GI tract and another organ. GI fistulas are a serious complication associated with increased morbidity and mortality, extended hospital stays, and increased costs. Most fistulas occur after surgery or trauma. Other times fistulas can form with IBD, cancer, perforation, radiation, diverticulitis, or pancreatitis.[23] Fistulas are classified as simple or complex and by the amount of output. A simple fistula has only one short, direct tract. A complex fistula is associated with an abscess, involves multiple organs, and may open into the base of a wound. High-output fistulas drain more than 500 mL/day, moderate-output fistulas drain 200 to 500 mL/day, and low-output fistulas drain less than 200 mL/day.

Fever and abdominal pain are early signs of a fistula. Other manifestations depend on the type. With an enterocutaneous fistula, there may be pus or intestinal contents draining through the skin opening. Patients with a colocutaneous (colon to skin) fistula may have stool or pus draining through the opening. If a colovesical (colon to urinary tract) fistula is present, manifestations include fecaluria (passing stool with urination), recurrent urinary tract infections, dysuria, and hematuria.

Interprofessional and Nursing Care

Treatment of fistula requires (1) identifying the fistula tract, (2) maintaining fluid and electrolyte balance, (3) controlling infection, (4) protecting the surrounding skin, (5) managing output, and (6) providing nutrition support. Managing a fistula is often a difficult and complex process. It can be disheartening for the patient and caregiver. Surgery may be needed if there are complications.

Appropriate fluid and electrolyte replacement can be challenging, especially when the patient has a high-output fistula. Keep an accurate intake and output record. Monitor urine output and the volume of fistula output as these guide fluid replacement. Assess the character of the drainage, noting the color, consistency, and odor. Monitor laboratory values. Low serum levels of potassium, magnesium, and phosphorus from the loss of GI fluids are common. Give IV fluids and electrolyte replacement as ordered. Measure vital signs frequently and be alert for signs of dehydration.

Many patients are NPO as this reduces intestinal output. They may receive acid suppression with a proton-pump inhibitor or histamine H_2-receptor blocker. Antimotility drugs (e.g., loperamide) decrease intestinal fluid loss.[23]

Malnutrition is a significant problem, especially if the patient is NPO or has a small intestinal fistula. Consult a dietitian. High-calorie, high-protein PN or EN is needed to provide enough calories and protein to replace losses and support healing.[23] Many patients need trace elements (e.g., copper, zinc, magnesium) and vitamin supplements.

Maintaining skin integrity and optimizing healing are essential. Consult a WOCN if available. Low-output fistulas may be managed with a simple absorbent dressing. A high-output enterocutaneous fistula often needs advanced techniques, including specialty pouches; barrier creams, powders, and sealants to protect the skin; and negative pressure wound therapy.

CHECK YOUR PRACTICE

A 51-year-old woman is 4 days postop after a proctocolectomy for UC. You note 2.5 cm of redness in the center of her incision with heavy, foul-smelling tan drainage pooling on her skin. Suspecting she is developing an enterocutaneous fistula, you notify the HCP and WOCN.

- What will you do to protect her skin?

HERNIAS

A **hernia** is a protrusion of tissue, such as the intestines, through an abnormal opening or a weakened area in the wall of the cavity in which it is normally contained. A hernia may occur in any part of the body, but it usually occurs within the abdominal cavity. *Reducible* hernias easily return into the abdominal cavity. Reducing can be done manually or may occur spontaneously when the person lies supine. *Irreducible,* or *incarcerated,* hernias cannot be placed back into the abdominal cavity. They have abdominal contents trapped in the opening. Strangulation occurs if the blood supply to the contents trapped in an irreducible hernia becomes compromised. The result is an acute bowel obstruction. Gangrene and necrosis of the hernia contents are possible (Box 47.6).

Types

An *umbilical hernia* occurs when the rectus muscle is weak (as with obesity) or the umbilical opening does not close after birth

(Fig. 47.16A). A *femoral hernia* occurs when there is a protrusion through the femoral ring into the femoral canal. It appears as a bulge below the inguinal ligament. Femoral hernias easily strangulate (Fig. 47.16B).

The *inguinal hernia* is the most common type of hernia and occurs at the point of weakness in the abdominal wall where the spermatic cord (in men) or the round ligament (in women) emerges (Fig. 47.16C).

Ventral or *incisional hernias* are due to weakness of the abdominal wall at the site of a previous incision. They occur most often in those who are obese, have had multiple surgeries in the same area, or have had inadequate wound healing because of poor nutrition or infection. Peristomal hernias are ventral hernias.

Clinical Manifestations

Pain is the classic symptom of a hernia. It may worsen with activities that increase intraabdominal pressure, such as lifting, coughing, and straining. A hernia may be readily visible, especially when the person tenses the abdominal muscles. If the hernia becomes strangulated, the patient will have severe pain and symptoms of bowel obstruction, such as vomiting, cramping, abdominal pain, and distention.

Interprofessional and Nursing Care

Diagnosis of a hernia is usually based on history and physical assessment. Ultrasound, CT, and MRI can help identify a hernia and determine the contents. Laparoscopic surgery is the treatment of choice. The surgical repair of a hernia, known as a *herniorrhaphy,* is usually an outpatient procedure. Reinforcing the weakened area with wire, fascia, or mesh is known as a *hernioplasty.* Emergency surgery is needed for strangulated hernias or inflamed, irreducible hernias. Surgery for strangulated hernias involves resecting the involved area with possible placement of a temporary colostomy.

After a hernia repair, the patient may have problems voiding. Measure intake and output. Observe for a distended bladder. Scrotal edema is a painful complication after an inguinal hernia repair. A scrotal support with application of an ice bag and elevating the scrotum may help relieve pain and edema. Encourage deep breathing but not coughing. Teach patients to splint the incision and keep their mouths open when coughing or sneezing is unavoidable. The patient may be restricted from heavy lifting (>10 lb) for 6 to 8 weeks.

BOX 47.6 BIOLOGIC SEX CONSIDERATIONS

Hernia

Men
- More likely to have inguinal hernias
- Have a 25% lifetime risk for developing an inguinal hernia

Women
- More likely to have femoral hernias, especially older women
- Have less than a 5% lifetime risk for developing an inguinal hernia
- More likely to have umbilical hernias

MALABSORPTION SYNDROME

Malabsorption results from impaired absorption of fats, carbohydrates, proteins, minerals, and vitamins. The stomach, small intestine, liver, and pancreas regulate normal digestion and absorption. Digestive enzymes ordinarily break down nutrients so that absorption can take place. Malabsorption may occur if this process is interrupted at any point. Several problems can cause malabsorption (Table 47.36). Lactose intolerance is the most common malabsorption disorder, followed by IBD, celiac disease, tropical sprue, and cystic fibrosis.

The most common signs of malabsorption are weight loss and diarrhea. Other signs include fatigue, abdominal pain, and **steatorrhea** (bulky, foul-smelling, yellow-gray, greasy stools with putty-like consistency) (Table 47.37).

A complete history and physical along with testing are needed to make a diagnosis. Laboratory studies include a CBC, prothrombin time (to see if vitamin K absorption is adequate), liver function tests, and serum levels of vitamin A, carotene, electrolytes, iron, and calcium. Stool studies include assessing for fat (e.g., Sudan III stain), doing a microbiologic analysis, and assessing secretory function through elastase or chymotrypsin testing to assess pancreatic function.

Imaging studies include a CT scan and endoscopy. Barium studies can identify structural problems. Capsule endoscopy is

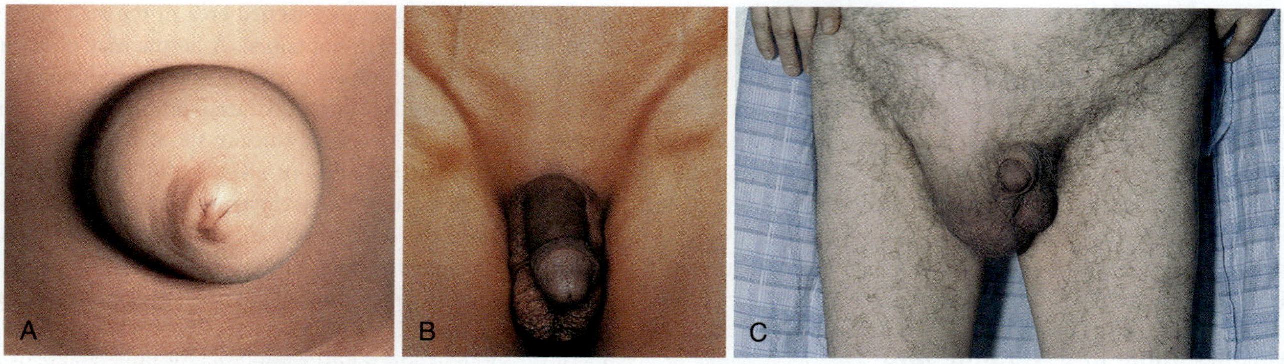

Fig. 47.16 (A) Umbilical hernia. (B) Femoral hernias (note swelling below the inguinal ligaments). (C) Right inguinal hernia. (A and B, From Zitelli BJ, McIntire SC, Nowalk AJ: *Zitelli and Davis' atlas of pediatric physical diagnosis,* ed 6, Philadelphia, 2012, Saunders. C, From Swartz MH: *Textbook of physical diagnosis: history and examination,* ed 6, Philadelphia, 2010, Saunders.)

TABLE 47.36 Causes of Malabsorption

Bacterial Proliferation
- Parasitic infection
- Tropical sprue

Biochemical or Enzyme Deficiencies
- Biliary tract obstruction
- Chronic pancreatitis
- Cystic fibrosis
- Lactase deficiency
- Pancreatic insufficiency
- Zollinger-Ellison syndrome

Disturbed Lymphatic and Vascular Circulation
- Heart failure
- Ischemia
- Lymphangiectasia
- Lymphoma

Small Intestinal Mucosal Disruption
- Celiac disease
- Crohn's disease
- Whipple disease

Surface Area Loss
- Billroth II gastrectomy
- Distal ileal resection, disease, or bypass
- SBS

useful in assessing the small intestine for changes in mucosal integrity and inflammation. Treatment depends on the cause.

CELIAC DISEASE

Celiac disease is an autoimmune disease that causes damage to the small intestinal mucosa. It is triggered by ingesting gluten, a protein in wheat, barley, and rye. It can occur at any age and has a wide variety of symptoms. *Celiac sprue* and *gluten-sensitive enteropathy* are other names for celiac disease.

Celiac disease is not the same disease as *tropical sprue*, a chronic disorder occurring primarily in tropical areas. Tropical sprue causes progressive disruption of jejunal and ileal tissue, resulting in nutrition problems. It is treated with folic acid and tetracycline.

Celiac disease affects about 1 in 100 people worldwide.[24] First-degree relatives of someone with celiac disease have a 10% chance of developing the disorder. It is associated with other autoimmune diseases, particularly rheumatoid arthritis and type 1 diabetes. It is slightly more common in women. Symptoms often begin in childhood.

Etiology and Pathophysiology

Three factors necessary for developing celiac disease are genetic predisposition, gluten ingestion, and an immune-mediated response. About 95% of people with celiac disease have human leukocyte antigen (HLA) allele HLA-DQ2. The other 5% have HLA-DQ8. However, not everyone with these genetic markers develops celiac disease. Some people with celiac disease do not have either of these HLA alleles.

TABLE 47.37 Manifestations of Malabsorption

Manifestations	Pathophysiology
Cardiovascular	
Hypotension	Dehydration
Peripheral edema	Protein malabsorption, protein loss in diarrhea
Tachycardia	Hypovolemia, anemia
GI	
Diarrhea	Impaired absorption of water, sodium, fatty acids, bile salts, carbohydrates
Flatulence	Bacterial fermentation of unabsorbed carbohydrates
Glossitis, cheilosis, stomatitis	Deficiency of iron, riboflavin, cobalamin, folic acid, other vitamins
Steatorrhea	Undigested and unabsorbed fat
Weight loss	Malabsorption of fat, carbohydrates, protein leading to loss of calories. Decrease in caloric intake or ↑ use of calories
Hematologic	
Anemia	Impaired absorption of iron, cobalamin, folic acid
Hemorrhagic tendency	Vitamin C deficiency. Vitamin K deficiency inhibiting production of clotting factors II, VII, IX, and X
Musculoskeletal	
Bone pain	Osteoporosis from impaired calcium absorption. Osteomalacia from hypocalcemia, hypophosphatemia, inadequate vitamin D
Muscle wasting	Protein malabsorption
Tetany	Hypocalcemia, hypomagnesemia
Weakness, muscle cramps	Anemia, electrolyte depletion (especially potassium)
Neurologic	
Altered mental status	Dehydration
Night blindness	Thiamine deficiency, vitamin A deficiency
Paresthesias	Cobalamin deficiency
Peripheral neuropathy	Cobalamin deficiency
Skin	
Brittle nails	Iron deficiency
Bruising	Vitamin K deficiency
Dermatitis	Fatty acid deficiency, zinc deficiency, niacin, other vitamin deficiencies
Hair thinning and loss	Protein deficiency

As with other autoimmune diseases, the tissue destruction that occurs with celiac disease is the result of chronic inflammation. Gluten contains specific peptides called *prolamins*. Partial digestion of gluten releases the prolamin peptides, which are absorbed into the intestinal submucosa. In genetically susceptible persons, the peptides bind to HLA-DQ2 and/or HLA-DQ8 and activate an inflammatory response. Inflammation damages the microvilli and brush border of the small intestine, decreasing the amount of surface area available for nutrient absorption. Damage is most severe in the duodenum, probably because it has more exposure to gluten. The inflammation lasts as long as gluten ingestion continues.

Clinical Manifestations

Classic manifestations of celiac disease include foul-smelling diarrhea, abdominal pain, flatulence, and abdominal distention. Some people have no obvious GI symptoms and may instead have atypical signs and symptoms. These include joint pain, liver problems, fatigue, peripheral neuropathy, and reproductive problems.[24] An intensely pruritic, vesicular skin lesion called *dermatitis herpetiformis*. It is sometimes present and occurs as a rash on the buttocks, scalp, face, elbows, and knees.

Protein, fat, and carbohydrate absorption is affected. Weight loss, muscle wasting, and other signs of malnutrition may be present. Abnormal serum folate, iron, and cobalamin levels can lead to anemia. Patients may have lactose intolerance and need to refrain from lactose-containing products until the disease is under control. Inadequate calcium intake and vitamin D absorption can lead to decreased bone density and osteoporosis.

Diagnostic Studies

Early diagnosis and treatment can prevent complications. Screening is recommended for close relatives of people known to have the disease, young patients with decreased bone density, those with anemia if other causes are ruled out, and certain autoimmune diseases.

Celiac disease is diagnosed by findings from the history and physical assessment and serology testing. Have the patient complete diagnostic testing before starting a gluten-free diet since the diet will change the results. The best serologic test is the tissue transglutaminase IgA antibody, plus an IgA antibody.[24] Though not done as often, histologic evidence is the gold standard for confirming the diagnosis. Biopsies show flattened mucosa and noticeable losses of villi. Genotyping involves testing for HLA-DQ2 and/or HLA-DQ8 antigens.

Interprofessional and Nursing Care

A strict gluten-free diet (Table 47.38) is the only effective treatment for celiac disease. Most patients need to stay on a gluten-free diet for the rest of their lives. Periodic nutrition evaluations and laboratory monitoring are done to monitor for anemia and malnutrition. They often require a daily vitamin and mineral supplement. The patient should undergo bone density screening every 2 to 3 years.

Refer all patients for a diet consultation. You can work with a dietitian to teach the patient how to eat a nutritionally adequate diet while considering food preferences, cultural traditions, and food availability. Teach the patient to read medication and food labels. Some medications and many food additives, preservatives, and stabilizers contain gluten. Although pure oats do not contain gluten, wheat, rye, and barley can contaminate oat products during the milling process. The patient needs to know where to buy gluten-free products. Good sources are health food stores, many grocery stores, and Internet sites.

Maintaining a gluten-free diet can be hard, especially when traveling or eating in restaurants. Many describe feeling embarrassed or like a burden when having to discuss gluten-free menu options with restaurant staff or when dining in others' homes. Mobile phone users will find apps listing gluten-free menu options at popular restaurants helpful. Many restaurants now indicate which food choices are gluten-free. The Celiac Disease Foundation (www.celiac.org) provides suggestions for maintaining a gluten-free diet and living with celiac disease.

TABLE 47.38 NUTRITION THERAPY
Celiac Disease

Foods that contain or often contain gluten:
- Baked goods, including muffins, cookies, cakes, pies, donuts, rolls
- Barley
- Bread, including wheat bread, white bread, and bagels
- Breakfast foods, such as pancakes, French toast
- Crackers
- Dressings, croutons
- Flour
- Flour tortillas
- Gluten stabilizers
- Granola
- Oats
- Pasta, noodles
- Pizza
- Rye
- Wheat

Foods that may contain gluten:
- Candy and candy bars
- Cream-based soups
- Energy bars
- French fries
- Potato chips, tortilla chips
- Processed lunch meat
- Salad dressings, marinades

LACTASE DEFICIENCY

Lactase deficiency is a condition in which the lactase enzyme is deficient or absent. Lactase is the enzyme that breaks down lactose into 2 simple sugars: glucose and galactose. Primary lactase insufficiency is often a result of genetic factors. Certain ethnic or racial groups, especially those with Asian or African ancestry, develop low lactase levels in childhood.[25] Less common causes include premature birth and congenital lactase deficiency, a rare genetic disorder. Lactose malabsorption can occur when conditions leading to bacterial overgrowth promote lactose fermentation in the small bowel or when intestinal mucosal damage interferes with absorption. The latter occurs with IBD and celiac disease.

Many do not have symptoms if they ingest lactose in small amounts.[25] When symptoms are present, they include bloating, flatulence, cramping abdominal pain, and diarrhea. Diarrhea results from the excess, undigested lactose in the small intestine attracting water molecules, which prevents them from being properly absorbed. Symptoms generally occur within 30 minutes to several hours after ingesting lactose. Lactose problems are often diagnosed with lactose tolerance tests, hydrogen breath tests, or genetic testing.[25]

Treatment aims to improve patient symptoms and prevent malnutrition. Limiting lactose in the diet by avoiding milk and milk products generally results in symptom improvement. Many lactose-free milk products are readily available. Lactase tablets are available as an over-the-counter (OTC) product. They break down the lactose present in ingested milk. Some have improved symptoms by taking prebiotics or probiotics that produce lactase in the gut.

Teach the patient which foods to limit. Cheese has less lactose than milk and ice cream. Live culture yogurt has less lactose because the bacteria help digest the lactose. Teach the patient to read labels to detect any hidden sources of lactose. Some people tolerate lactose better if taken with meals. Since limiting milk and milk products can lead to calcium deficiency, supplements may be needed to prevent osteoporosis.

SHORT BOWEL SYNDROME

Short bowel syndrome (SBS) is a condition in which the small intestine does not have enough surface area to absorb enough nutrients. This leaves the person unable to meet energy, fluid, electrolyte, and nutrition needs to stay healthy on a normal diet. Causes of SBS include diseases that damage the intestinal mucosa, surgical removal of too much small intestine (e.g., with Crohn's disease, cancer), and congenital defects.

SBS is likely to develop in patients with a loss of 50% to 75% of the small intestine. The length and area of the small intestine present and the presence of the colon and ileocecal valve affect the patient's outcome. SBS is common in patients with a jejunoileal anastomosis. Parts of the jejunum and ileum are removed. The remaining parts are connected to the colon or an ostomy is formed. If the terminal ileum, ileocecal valve, and colon are intact, the patient will rarely have problems with SBS.

Clinical Manifestations

SBS results in reduced nutrient, fluid, and electrolyte absorption. This leads to dehydration, weight loss, diarrhea, malnutrition, vitamin deficiencies, and electrolyte imbalances. Other manifestations include abdominal pain, flatulence, and steatorrhea. The patient may develop lactase deficiency and bacterial overgrowth. Those who are malnourished may have manifestations from specific deficiencies. For example, patients may have peripheral neuropathy from vitamin B_{12}, vitamin E, copper, or thiamine deficiencies or fatigue due to anemia from decreased folate or iron.

Interprofessional Care

The treatment goals are that the patient will maintain normal nutrition, achieve a good quality of life, and be free from complications. The main treatment is nutrition support involving PN, EN, medications, and a tailored diet. In the immediate period after a major bowel resection, patients receive PN to replace fluid, electrolyte, and nutrient losses and rest the bowel. They may need PN indefinitely. EN and a normal diet are gradually resumed to stimulate the remaining intestine to function better. Some can eventually stop PN.

The patient requires a diet that maximizes nutrient and fluid absorption and decreases stool output. Refer the patient to a dietitian. The ideal diet is high in protein and complex carbohydrates and low in fat and simple sugars. Soluble fiber is encouraged if the colon is present. The patient should eat at least 6 small meals per day to increase the time of contact between food and the intestine. Oral vitamin and mineral supplements may be needed. Patients with severe malabsorption may need PN or EN at night (see Chapter 44).

Patients often take multiple medications. US Food and Drug Administration–approved drugs for the treatment of SBS include somatropin, glutamine, and teduglutide (Gattex). Somatropin enhances intestinal adaption and increases the flow of water, electrolytes, and nutrients into the bowel. Glutamine improves intestinal absorption. Teduglutide increases the surface area of the intestine and improves intestinal absorption of fluids and nutrients.

Antisecretory and antimotility drugs reduce fluid losses and GI motility. These include PPIs or H_2-blockers, α-adrenergic receptor agonists (e.g., clonidine), octreotide, and opioid antidiarrheal drugs (see Table 47.2). For patients who have limited ileal resections, cholestyramine reduces diarrhea resulting from unabsorbed bile acids by increasing their excretion in feces. Bile acids stimulate intestinal fluid secretion and reduce colonic fluid absorption. Antibiotic therapy is used to prevent bacterial overgrowth.

Intestinal transplantation is done at a few specialized transplant centers in the United States. It is considered the only long-term treatment option for patients with intestinal failure who have significant complications from PN or nutrition failure. The leading cause of intestinal failure is SBS. Transplantation may include the intestine alone, liver and intestine, or multivisceral combinations (stomach, duodenum, jejunum, ileum, colon, and/or pancreas).

ANORECTAL PROBLEMS

HEMORRHOIDS

Hemorrhoids are abnormally dilated hemorrhoidal veins. They may be internal (above the internal sphincter) or external (outside the external sphincter) (Figs. 47.17 and 47.18).

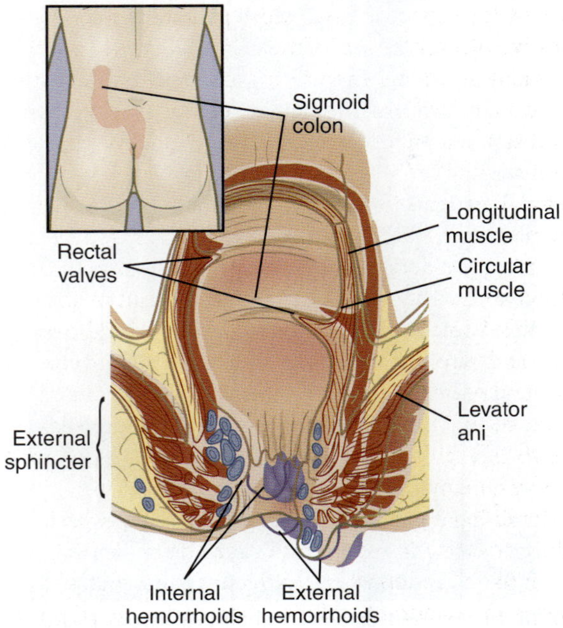

Fig. 47.17 Anatomic structures of the rectum and anus with external and internal hemorrhoids.

Hemorrhoids can appear periodically, depending on the amount of anorectal pressure.

Etiology and Pathophysiology

Hemorrhoids are thought to develop because of increased anal pressure and weakening of the connective tissue that supports the hemorrhoidal veins. Weakened supporting tissue allows for downward displacement of the hemorrhoidal veins, causing them to dilate. Blood flow through the veins of the hemorrhoidal plexus is impaired. An intravascular clot in the venule results in a thrombosed external hemorrhoid. Many factors increase the risk for hemorrhoids. These include pregnancy, constipation, straining to defecate, diarrhea, heavy lifting, prolonged standing and sitting, obesity, and ascites.[26]

Clinical Manifestations

Hemorrhoids are the most common reason for bleeding with defecation. Internal hemorrhoids most often cause painless, bright red bleeding with stools, on the toilet paper, or dripping into the toilet water. If internal hemorrhoids become constricted, the patient will report pain. Internal hemorrhoids can prolapse into the anal canal or externally. Symptoms of prolapse include pressure with defecation and a protruding mass.

External hemorrhoids are reddish-blue and seldom bleed. There may be itching, burning, and edema. They usually do not cause pain unless thrombosis (blood clots) is present. Thrombosed hemorrhoids are a bluish-purple tinge and palpable at the anal orifice. They usually cause pain and inflammation. The clot can erode through the overlying stretched skin, causing bleeding with defecation. Constipation or diarrhea can worsen these symptoms.

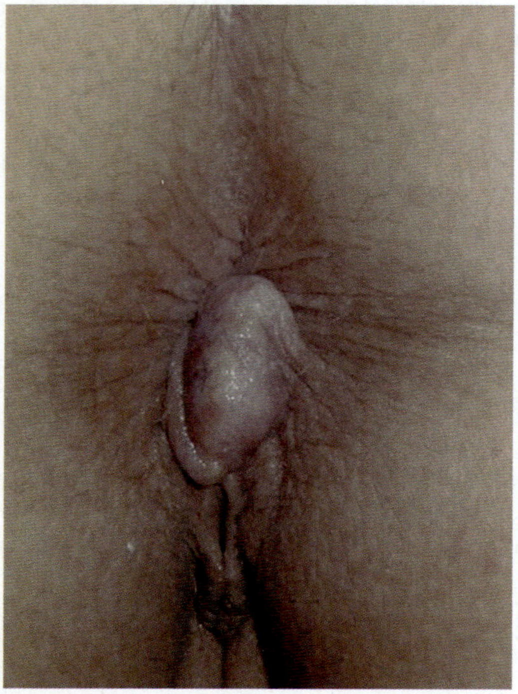

Fig. 47.18 Thrombosed external hemorrhoid. (From Hall J: Modern management of hemorrhoidal disease, *Gastroenterol Clin North Am* 42:759, 2013.)

It is easy to diagnose external hemorrhoids with visual inspection and DRE. DRE, anoscopy, and sigmoidoscopy are used to diagnose internal hemorrhoids.

Interprofessional and Nursing Care

First-line therapy typically involves normalizing stool consistency by treating constipation or diarrhea. Teach the patient measures to prevent constipation (see Table 47.11). A high-fiber diet and increased fluid intake prevent constipation and reduce straining. This allows engorgement of the veins to subside. The resulting stool bulk may decrease stool leakage and itching. Teach the patient to avoid straining and limiting time sitting on the toilet. Warm sitz baths (15 to 20 minutes, 2 or 3 times each day) may help to reduce discomfort and swelling. Teach the patient to seek medical care for severe symptoms of hemorrhoids (e.g., excessive pain or bleeding, prolapsed hemorrhoids).

OTC ointments, creams, and suppositories specifically made for hemorrhoid treatment can be used to shrink the mucous membranes and relieve pain. These drugs often contain anesthetics, corticosteroids, protectants, or antiseptics. Corticosteroid use should be limited to 1 week or less to prevent side effects, such as contact dermatitis and mucosal atrophy. Stool softeners can keep the stools soft. NSAIDs can be taken for pain.

Prolapsed or bleeding internal hemorrhoids or thrombosed external hemorrhoids may need medical treatment. Nonsurgical approaches (rubber band ligation, infrared coagulation, sclerotherapy, laser treatment) are options. Rubber band ligation is the most widely used technique. The HCP inserts an anoscope to identify the hemorrhoid and then ligates it with a rubber band. The rubber band around the hemorrhoid constricts circulation. The tissue becomes necrotic, separates, and sloughs off. There is some local discomfort with this procedure, but no anesthetic is needed.

A *hemorrhoidectomy* is the surgical excision of hemorrhoids. Surgery is needed when there is marked prolapse, excessive pain or bleeding, or large or multiple thrombosed hemorrhoids. After removing the hemorrhoids, the tissue is either sutured, and the wound heals by primary intention, or the area is left open, and healing takes place by secondary intention.

Nursing care after a hemorrhoidectomy focuses on pain control and promoting wound healing (Table 47.39). Be aware that

TABLE 47.39 NURSING MANAGEMENT

Care of the Patient After a Hemorrhoidectomy

- Administer analgesics as ordered, especially before bowel movements.
- Administer stool softeners and bulking agents as ordered.
- Administer warm sitz baths 15 to 20 min, 2 or 3 times each day.
- Encourage the patient to change positions frequently.
- Apply ice to the area several times a day for 10 min at a time.
- Teach the patient to use a pressure relief cushion, not a ring or "doughnut" when sitting.
- Have the patient use baby wipes or medicated pads instead of toilet paper.
- Assess for rectal bleeding, especially in those taking anticoagulants.
- Provide as much privacy as possible when providing wound care and performing assessments.
- Teach the patient care of the anal area, symptoms of complications (especially bleeding), and ways to avoid constipation and straining.

although the procedure is minor, the pain is severe and feared by many. There are several analgesic regimens using a combination of drugs. Most patients receive multimodal analgesia. This may involve an opioid and NSAID in conjunction with topical preparations that provide anesthesia or reduce internal sphincter spasms, such as topical lidocaine, 2% diltiazem, and glyceryl trinitrate.

The patient usually dreads the first bowel movement and often resists the urge to defecate. Give pain medication before the bowel movement to reduce discomfort. Stool softeners (e.g., docusate) and bulking agents are given to help form a soft, bulky stool that is easier to pass. If the patient does not have a bowel movement within 2 or 3 days, an oil-retention enema is given.

A warm sitz bath provides comfort and keeps the anal area clean. A sponge ring in the sitz bath helps relieve pressure on the area. Initially, do not leave the patient alone because of the possibility of weakness or fainting. The patient may have packing in the rectum to absorb drainage, with a T-binder to hold the dressing in place. Packing is usually removed on the first or second postoperative day.

ANAL FISSURE

An *anal fissure* is a linear skin tear in the anal mucosa. Many times, the inciting event is trauma from passing hard stools. Other fissures are related to trauma (anal intercourse, foreign body insertion, childbirth), local infection (syphilis, gonorrhea, *Chlamydia,* herpes simplex virus, HIV), or inflammation. An anal fissure is acute when it is of recent onset (less than 6 weeks) and chronic if it has been present for a longer period. Chronic fissures have a characteristic appearance that includes perianal skin tags and fibrotic edges.

Anal tissue ulcerates because of ischemia caused by a combination of high pressure in the internal anal sphincter and poor blood supply to the area. The ischemic tissue may ulcerate spontaneously or when traumatized by factors such as hard stools, which would not normally cause tissue breakdown. Ischemia must be corrected for a fissure to heal.

The hallmark of an anal fissure is severe anal pain. It is worse with defecation and with direct pressure on the site, such as from sitting. Acute fissures tend to bleed slightly. Patients may report red blood on the toilet paper. Constipation results because of fear of pain when having bowel movements.

Anal fissures are easy to diagnose with a physical assessment. Conservative care with fiber supplements, increased fluid intake, sitz baths, and topical analgesics is successful in most cases, especially if the fissure is acute. Pain is managed by softening stools with a bulk-producing agent (psyllium) or stool softener and warm sitz baths (15 to 20 minutes, 3 times per day). Topical calcium channel blockers decrease rectal pressure and allow the fissure to heal without sphincter damage. Local injections of botulinum toxin can decrease rectal pressure.

If conservative treatment fails, a lateral internal sphincterotomy is the recommended surgical procedure. It carries the risk of postoperative incontinence. Postoperative nursing care is the same as the care for the patient who had a hemorrhoidectomy.

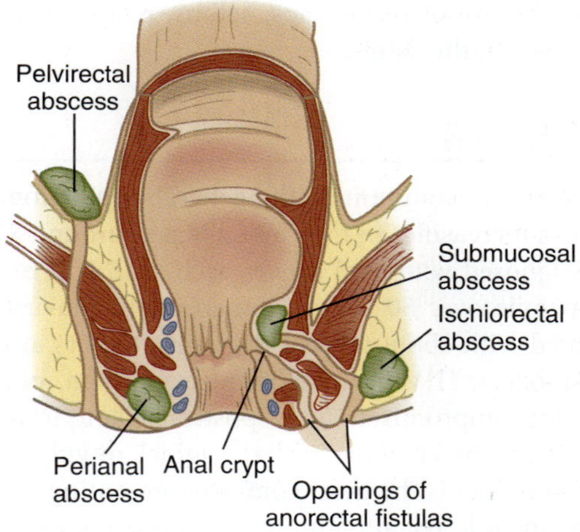

Fig. 47.19 Common sites of anorectal abscesses and fistula formation.

ANORECTAL ABSCESS

An *anorectal abscess* is a collection of perianal pus (Fig. 47.19). The abscess results from obstruction of the anal glands, leading to infection and abscess formation. Abscess formation occurs with anal fissures, trauma, or IBD. The most common causative organisms are *E. coli,* staphylococci, and streptococci. Manifestations include local severe pain and swelling, foul-smelling drainage, tenderness, and fever. Sepsis can occur as a complication. Anorectal abscesses are diagnosed by rectal examination.

Anorectal abscesses require surgical drainage. Larger abscesses need packing afterward with impregnated gauze or placement of drains (e.g., Penrose) to promote drainage. The area then heals by granulation. Patients who have diabetes, cellulitis, or are immunocompromised (e.g., chemotherapy) may need antibiotic therapy. Nursing care includes warm, moist heat applications and changing packing daily. The patient is usually more comfortable lying on the abdomen or side. A low-fiber diet is given. The patient may leave the hospital with the wound still open. Teach the patient about wound care and the importance of sitz baths, thorough cleaning after urinating or bowel movements, and follow-up visits with the HCP.

ANAL FISTULA

An **anal fistula** is an abnormal tunnel from the anus or rectum to the surface of the skin around the anus or the vagina. About 80% of anal fistulas are due to an anorectal abscess or infection. Other causes include Crohn's disease, cancer, chronic diarrhea, trauma, or radiation.[27]

Feces may enter the fistula and cause an infection. There may be persistent, bloody, or purulent discharge or stool leakage from the fistula. The patient may need to wear a pad to avoid staining clothes.

Surgical treatment of an anal fistula depends on the location and nature of the fistula. In a fistulotomy, the HCP opens the fistula, and healthy tissue is allowed to granulate in the wound. Care is the same as after a hemorrhoidectomy. Options for complex fistulas include ligation of the intersphincteric fistula tract

(LIFT) or the use of rectal flaps, setons, plugs, or fibrin glue injections to seal the fistula.

ANAL CANCER

Anal cancer is uncommon in the general population, but the incidence is increasing. In the United States, around 8700 people are diagnosed with anal cancer each year. It is more common in people over 50 years. Human papillomavirus (HPV) is associated with about 90% of the cases. Others at high risk include smokers, HIV-positive homosexual men, people who are immunocompromised (e.g., posttransplant immunosuppression), and women with cervical, vaginal, or vulvar cancer.

Rectal bleeding is the most common presenting sign. Other symptoms include rectal pain, itching, pressure, or a full feeling. Symptoms may be constant and worsen with sex or bowel movements. There may be a change in bowel frequency or size. The patient may report increased straining.[28]

It is especially important to screen high-risk persons using DRE and anal Pap tests. In an anal Pap test, the anal lining is swabbed, and the cells are examined to identify any cell changes (e.g., dysplasia, neoplasia). A high-resolution anoscopy allows the HCP to visualize the mucosa and obtain a biopsy. An endoanal *(endorectal) ultrasound* may be done.

Treatment of anal cancer depends on the size and depth of the lesions. It is primarily treated with a combination of low-dose radiation and chemotherapy. Chemotherapy regimens include combinations of mitomycin, cisplatin, and FU.[28] Options for precancerous lesions are surgical removal or treatment with topical imiquimod (Aldara) and FU. If the tumor involves the rectum and requires removal of the anal sphincters, the anus is sutured shut and a permanent ostomy created.

PILONIDAL SINUS

A *pilonidal sinus* is a small tract under the skin between the buttocks in the sacrococcygeal area. It is thought to be of congenital origin. It may have several openings and is lined with epithelium and hair, hence the name *pilonidal* ("a nest of hair"). The skin is moist, and movement of the buttocks causes the short, wiry hair to penetrate the skin. If the irritated skin becomes infected, it forms a pilonidal cyst or abscess. There are no symptoms with a pilonidal sinus unless there is an infection. Then the patient may have pain and swelling at the base of the spine.

An abscess requires incision and drainage. The wound may be closed or left open to heal by secondary intention. The wound is packed, and sitz baths are ordered. Nursing care includes warm, moist heat applications when an abscess is present. The patient is usually more comfortable lying on the abdomen or side. Teach the patient to avoid contaminating the dressing when urinating or defecating and to avoid straining whenever possible.

Case Study

Colorectal Cancer

(©iStockphoto/ Thinkstock.)

Patient Profile

L.C., a 58-year-old Native American man, is from a Pueblo tribe in northern New Mexico. L.C.'s wife and family drove 50 miles to take him to the Indian Health Service hospital because of his deteriorating health (see the case study in Chapter 43).

Subjective Data

- See the case study in Chapter 43.
- Currently rates pain as a 7 on a scale of 0–10
- States he is not passing flatus

Objective Data

Physical Assessment

- 5 ft 9 in tall, weight 132 lb
- BP 140/72, Heart rate 90, RR 20, temperature 99.4°F (37.4°C), O_2 saturation 97% on room air
- Wound site and staples are intact, dry, without bleeding or signs of infection
- Abdomen slightly distended with hypoactive bowel sounds
- Lungs clear to auscultation, slightly diminished in posterior bases

Laboratory Tests

- CT scan and colonoscopy show 2 medium-sized tumors in the transverse colon
- Hgb of 8.8 g/dL, Hct of 24%.

Interprofessional Care

Surgical Procedure

- Had a transverse hemicolectomy with lymph node biopsies
- Pathology results: Adenocarcinoma, has invaded the muscle wall of colon, 2 of 5 lymph nodes are positive for cancer

Postoperative

- Feels like his life has ended and does not want to leave the hospital
- States that there is "no one" to take care of him at his home, and he is far away from the hospital

Follow-Up Treatment

Scheduled for outpatient chemotherapy

Discussion Questions

1. ***Recognize***: What signs and symptoms of CRC did L.C. have (see the case study in Chapter 43)?
2. ***Analyze***: What stage of CRC does L.C. likely have? What treatment is recommended for this stage of CRC?
3. ***Plan:*** What is a culturally sensitive way for you to support L.C. and his family in making decisions about his health care?
4. ***Plan:*** What referrals may be indicated at this time?
5. ***Prioritize:*** Based on the assessment data, what are the priority clinical problems?
6. ***Prioritize:*** What are the priority nursing interventions for L.C. at this stage of his illness?
7. ***Act:*** How could you provide emotional support to L.C. and his family?
8. ***Act:*** L.C. is worried that other members of his family may have colon cancer. What can you tell him about the recommendations for CRC screening?
9. ***Evaluate:*** What outcomes would indicate nursing interventions were successful?

Answers available at http://evolve.elsevier.com/Lewis/medsurg.

BRIDGE TO NCLEX EXAMINATION

The number of the question corresponds to the same-numbered outcome at the beginning of the chapter.

1. The *most* appropriate therapy for a patient with acute diarrhea caused by a viral infection is to
   - **a.** increase fluid intake.
   - **b.** administer an antibiotic.
   - **c.** administer an antimotility drug.
   - **d.** quarantine the patient to prevent spread of the virus.
2. A 35-year-old female patient is admitted to the emergency department with acute abdominal pain. Which medical diagnoses should you consider as possible causes of her pain? *(select all that apply)*
   - **a.** Gastroenteritis
   - **b.** Ectopic pregnancy
   - **c.** Gastrointestinal bleeding
   - **d.** Irritable bowel syndrome
   - **e.** Inflammatory bowel disease
3. Assessment findings suggestive of peritonitis include *(select all that apply)*
   - **a.** abdominal pain.
   - **b.** rebound tenderness.
   - **c.** a soft, distended abdomen.
   - **d.** shallow respirations with bradypnea.
   - **e.** observing that the patient is lying still.
4. In planning care for the patient with Crohn's disease, the nurse recognizes that a major difference between ulcerative colitis and Crohn's disease is that Crohn's disease
   - **a.** often results in toxic megacolon.
   - **b.** causes fewer nutrition deficiencies than ulcerative colitis.
   - **c.** often recurs after surgery, while ulcerative colitis is curable with a colectomy.
   - **d.** is manifested by rectal bleeding and anemia more often than is ulcerative colitis.
5. The nurse performs an abdominal assessment of a patient with a possible bowel obstruction, knowing that manifestations of an obstruction in the large intestine are *(select all that apply)*
   - **a.** persistent abdominal pain.
   - **b.** marked abdominal distention.
   - **c.** diarrhea that is loose or liquid.
   - **d.** colicky, severe, intermittent pain.
   - **e.** profuse vomiting that relieves abdominal pain.
6. A patient with stage I colorectal cancer is scheduled for surgery. Patient teaching for this patient would include an explanation that
   - **a.** chemotherapy will begin after the patient recovers from the surgery.
   - **b.** both chemotherapy and radiation can be used as palliative treatments.
   - **c.** follow-up colonoscopies will be needed to ensure that the cancer does not recur.
   - **d.** a wound, ostomy, and continence nurse will visit the patient to identify the site for the ostomy.
7. The nurse determines a patient undergoing ileostomy surgery understands the procedure when the patient states
   - **a.** "I should only have to change the pouch every 4 to 7 days."
   - **b.** "The drainage in the pouch will look like my normal stools."
   - **c.** "I may not need to wear a drainage pouch if I irrigate it daily."
   - **d.** "Limiting my fluid intake should decrease the amount of output."
8. In contrast to diverticulitis, the patient with diverticulosis
   - **a.** has rectal bleeding.
   - **b.** often has no symptoms.
   - **c.** usually develops peritonitis.
   - **d.** has localized cramping pain.
9. A nursing intervention that is *most* appropriate to decrease postoperative edema and pain after an inguinal herniorrhaphy is to
   - **a.** maintain the patient on bedrest.
   - **b.** allow the patient to stand to void.
   - **c.** support the incision during coughing.
   - **d.** apply a scrotal support with an ice bag.
10. The nurse determines that the goals of diet teaching have been met when the patient with celiac disease selects from the menu
    - **a.** scrambled eggs and sausage.
    - **b.** buckwheat pancakes with syrup.
    - **c.** oatmeal, skim milk, and orange juice.
    - **d.** yogurt, strawberries, and rye toast with butter.
11. What should a patient be taught after a hemorrhoidectomy?
    - **a.** Take mineral oil before bedtime.
    - **b.** Eat a low-fiber diet to rest the colon.
    - **c.** Use a daily oil-retention enema to empty the colon.
    - **d.** Take prescribed pain medications before a bowel movement.

1. a; 2. a, b, c, d, e; 3. a, b, e; 4. c; 5. a, b; 6. c; 7. a; 8. b; 9. d; 10. a; 11. d.

For rationales to these answers and even more NCLEX review questions, visit http://evolve.elsevier.com/Lewis/medsurg.

EVOLVE WEBSITE/RESOURCES LIST

http://evolve.elsevier.com/Lewis/medsurg

Review Questions (Online Only)

Key Points

Answer Keys for Questions

- Rationales for Bridge to NCLEX Examination Questions
- Answer Guidelines for Case Study

Student Case Study

- Patient With Ulcerative Colitis

Nursing Care Plans

- eNursing Care Plan 47.1: Patient With Acute Infectious Diarrhea

- eNursing Care Plan 47.2: Patient With Inflammatory Bowel Disease
- eNursing Care Plan 47.3: Patient With a Colostomy/Ileostomy

Conceptual Care Map Creator
Audio Glossary
Content Updates

REFERENCES

*1. Carrasco-Labra A, Lytvyn L, Falck-Ytter Y, Surawicz CM, Chey WD: AGA technical review on the evaluation of functional diarrhea and diarrhea-predominant irritable bowel syndrome in adults (IBS-D), *Gastroenterol* 157:859, 2019.

*2. Ng K: *Updates in the management of Clostridium difficile* for adults, *US Pharmacist* 44:HS9, 2019.

*3. Rao K, Malani PN: Diagnosis and treatment of *Clostridioides (Clostridium) difficile* infection in adults in 2020, *JAMA* 323:1403, 2020.

* 4. Kumar N, Kumar D: Fecal incontinence and rectal prolapse, *Ind J Gastroenterol* 38:465, 2019.

*5. Bharucha AE, Lacy BE: Mechanisms, evaluation, and management of chronic constipation, *Gastroenterol* 158:1232, 2020.

*6. Brenner DM, Sayuk GS: Current US Food and Drug Administration-approved pharmacologic therapies for the treatment of irritable bowel syndrome with diarrhea, *Adv Ther* 37:83, 2020.

*7. Selvaraj SM, Wong SH, Ser HL, Lee LH: Role of low FODMAP diet and probiotics on gut microbiome in irritable bowel syndrome, *Progress in Microbes & Molecular Biology* 18:2020.

*8. Krzyzak M, Mulrooney SM: Acute appendicitis review: background, epidemiology, diagnosis, and treatment, *Cureus* 12:e8562, 2020.

*9. Piovani D, Danese S, Peyrin-Biroulet L, Nikolopoulos GK, Lytras T, Bonovas S: Environmental risk factors for inflammatory bowel diseases: an umbrella review of meta-analyses, *Gastroenterol* 157:647, 2019.

10. US National Library of Medicine: NOD2 gene. Retrieved from https://ghr.nlm.nih.gov/gene/NOD2#conditions.

*11. Nebbia M, Yassin NA, Spinelli A: Colorectal cancer in inflammatory bowel disease, *Clin Colon Rectal Surg* 33:305–317, 2020.

12. Dillon DL, Crimaldi JE: Pathway-driven management of inflammatory bowel disease. *JNP* 24, 2020.

13. Gade AK, Douthit NT, Townsley E: Medical management of Crohn's disease, *Cureus* 12, 2020.

14. Hazel K, O'Connor A: Emerging treatments for inflammatory bowel disease, *Ther Adv Chronic Dis* 11, 2020.

*15. Bischoff SC, Escher J, Hébuterne X, et al: ESPEN practical guideline: clinical nutrition in inflammatory bowel disease, *Clin Nutr* 39:632, 2020.

16. Harnsberger CR: Acute colonic pseudo-obstruction, *Semin Colon Rectal Surg* 30:100690, 2019.

17. US National Library of Medicine: Familial adenomatous polyposis. Retrieved from https://ghr.nlm.nih.gov/condition/familial-adenomatous-polyposis#diagnosis.

18. American Cancer Society: Key statistics for colorectal cancer. Retrieved from www.cancer.org/cancer/colon-rectal-cancer/about/key-statistics.html.

19. American Cancer Society: Colorectal cancer rates rise in young adults. Retrieved from https://www.cancer.org/latest-news/colorectal-cancer-rates-rise-in-younger-adults.html.

20. American Cancer Society: Colorectal cancer screening guidelines. Retrieved from www.cancer.org/cancer/colon-rectal-cancer/detection-diagnosis-staging/acs-recommendations.html.

21. National Cancer Institute: Colon cancer treatment. Retrieved from www.cancer.gov/types/colorectal/hp/colon-treatment-pdq#link/_125.

*22. Hall J, Hardiman K, Lee S, et al: The American Society of Colon and Rectal Surgeons clinical practice guidelines for the treatment of left-sided colonic diverticulitis, *Dis Colon Rectum* 63:728, 2020.

23. Nussbaum MS, McFadden DW: Gastric, duodenal, and small intestinal fistulas. In *Shackelford's surgery of the alimentary tract*, ed 8, Philadelphia, 2019, Elsevier.

24. Celiac Disease Foundation: Celiac disease. Retrieved from https://celiac.org/celiac-disease/understanding-celiac-disease-2/what-is-celiac-disease/.

*25. Misselwitz B, Butter M, Verbeke K, Fox MR: Update on lactose malabsorption and intolerance, *Gut* 68:2080, 2019.

*26. Margetis N: Pathophysiology of internal hemorrhoids, *Ann Gastroenterol* 32:264, 2019.

*27. Gardner IH, Siddharthan RV, Tsikitis VL: Benign anorectal disease: hemorrhoids, fissures, and fistulas, *Ann Gastroenterol* 33:9, 2020.

28. The Anal Cancer Foundation: Anal cancer. Retrieved from https://www.analcancerfoundation.org/anal-cancer/.

*Evidence-based information for clinical practice.

48

Liver, Biliary Tract, and Pancreas Problems

Mary C. Olson and Christine M. Cervini

http://evolve.elsevier.com/Lewis/medsurg/

CONCEPTUAL FOCUS

Health Promotion
Infection
Inflammation
Nutrition
Pain

LEARNING OUTCOMES

1. Distinguish among the types of viral hepatitis.
2. Describe the interprofessional and nursing management of the patient with viral hepatitis.
3. Explain the pathophysiology, clinical manifestations, complications, and interprofessional and nursing management of the patient with cirrhosis.
4. Describe the clinical manifestations and management of liver cancer.
5. Distinguish between acute and chronic pancreatitis related to pathophysiology, clinical manifestations, complications, and interprofessional and nursing management.
6. Explain the clinical manifestations and interprofessional and nursing management of the patient with pancreatic cancer.
7. Describe the pathophysiology, clinical manifestations, and interprofessional care of gallbladder disorders.
8. Describe the nursing management of the patient undergoing surgical treatment of cholecystitis and cholelithiasis.

KEY TERMS

acute liver failure
acute pancreatitis
ascites
asterixis
cholecystitis
cholelithiasis
chronic pancreatitis
cirrhosis
esophageal varices
gastric varices
hepatic encephalopathy
hepatitis
hepatorenal syndrome
jaundice
nonalcoholic fatty liver disease (NAFLD)
nonalcoholic steatohepatitis (NASH)
portal hypertension

This chapter focuses on the management of patients with a wide range of liver, pancreatic, and gallbladder problems. These organs are closely positioned together anatomically and highly associated with their digestive functions. Liver and pancreas problems can lead to altered nutrient absorption and use, causing malnutrition and impaired elimination. Inflammation may be present, with the patient having pain, nausea, and vomiting. Nursing care focuses on helping the patient and caregiver manage symptoms and develop ways to cope with the diagnosis and, sometimes, prognosis. Health promotion focuses on reducing risk through immunizations and avoiding substance use.

LIVER PROBLEMS

HEPATITIS

Hepatitis is inflammation of the liver. The most common cause is viral. Other causes include substances (e.g., alcohol, medications, chemicals), autoimmune diseases, and metabolic problems.

TABLE 48.1 Characteristics of Hepatitis Viruses

Incubation Period and Mode of Transmission	Sources of Infection	Infectivity
Hepatitis A Virus (HAV)		
Incubation: 15–50 days (average 28) Fecal-oral (primarily fecal contamination and oral ingestion)	• Contaminated food, milk, water, shellfish • Crowded conditions (e.g., day care, nursing home) • Persons with subclinical infections, infected food handlers, sexual contact, IV drug users • Poor personal hygiene • Poor sanitation	• Most infectious during 2 weeks before onset of symptoms • Infectious until 1–2 weeks after the start of symptoms
Hepatitis B Virus (HBV)		
Incubation: 115–180 days (average 56–96) Percutaneous (parenteral) or mucosal exposure to blood or blood products Sexual contact Perinatal transmission	• Contaminated needles, syringes, and blood products • HBV-infected mother (perinatal transmission) • Sexual activity with infected partners. Asymptomatic carriers • Tattoos or body piercing with contaminated needles	• Before and after symptoms appear • Infectious for months • Carriers continue to be infectious for life
Hepatitis C Virus (HCV)		
Incubation: 14–180 days (average 56) Percutaneous (parenteral) or mucosal exposure to blood or blood products High-risk sexual contact Perinatal contact	• Blood and blood products • Needles and syringes • Sexual activity with infected partners, low risk	• 1–2 weeks before symptoms appear • Continues during clinical course • 75%–85% go on to develop chronic HCV and remain infectious
Hepatitis D Virus (HDV)		
Incubation: 2–26 weeks HBV must precede HDV Chronic carriers of HBV always at risk	• Same as HBV • Can cause infection only when HBV is present	• Blood infectious at all stages of HDV infection
Hepatitis E Virus (HEV)		
Incubation: 15–64 days (average 26–42 days) Fecal-oral route	• Contaminated water, poor sanitation • Found in Asia, Africa, and Mexico • Not common in United States but is increasing in some areas	• Not known • May be similar to HAV

Viral Hepatitis

There are several types of viral hepatitis. We designate each type by a letter (A, B, C, D, E). The different types have similar manifestations. Their modes of transmission and disease course vary (Table 48.1). Some can lead to chronic liver disease. Other less common viruses can also cause liver disease. These include cytomegalovirus (CMV), Epstein-Barr virus (EBV), herpesvirus, coxsackievirus, and rubella virus.

Hepatitis A Virus

Hepatitis A is a self-limiting infection. It can cause a mild flu-like illness and jaundice. In more severe cases, it can cause acute liver failure. Hepatitis A virus (HAV) is a ribonucleic acid (RNA) virus. It is transmitted primarily through the fecal-oral route. It often occurs in small outbreaks caused by fecal contamination of food or drinking water.

Poor hygiene, improper food handling, homelessness, crowded situations, and poor sanitary conditions are risk factors. Transmission occurs between family members, institutionalized persons, and children in daycare centers. Foodborne outbreaks are usually due to food contaminated by an infected food handler. People at increased risk for infection include drug users (both IV and non-injection drugs), men who have sex with men (MSM), and persons traveling to developing countries.[1]

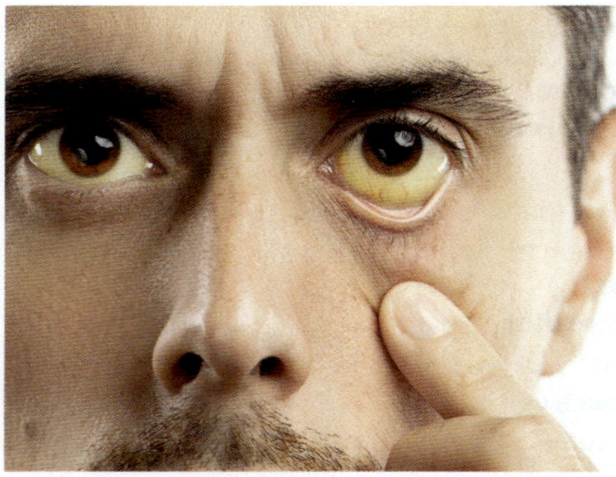

Fig. 48.1 Jaundiced person. (© Jun/iStock.com.)

The greatest risk for transmission occurs before symptoms appear. The virus is in feces 1 to 2 weeks before the onset of symptoms and at least 1 week after the onset of illness (Fig. 48.1). This means it can be carried and transmitted by persons who have undetectable infection. It is present only briefly in blood, usually less than 3 weeks. Fecal excretion can occur in infants for months.

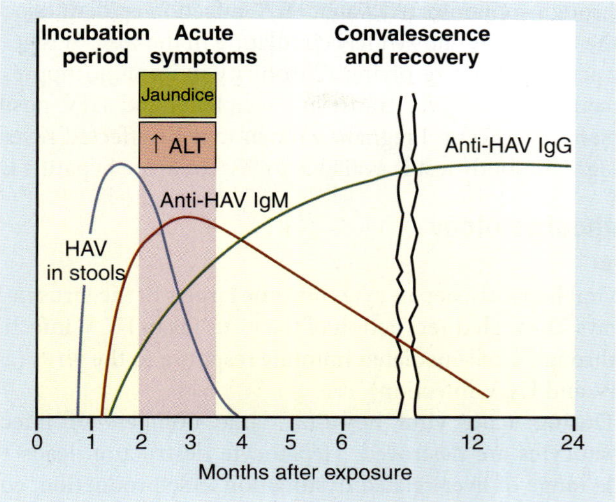

Fig. 48.2 Course of infection with hepatitis A virus *(HAV). ALT,* Alanine aminotransferase. (From McCance KL, Huether SE: *Pathophysiology: the biologic basis for disease in adults and children,* ed 6, St Louis, 2010, Mosby.)

Antibody to HAV immunoglobulin M (IgM) (HAV IgM) appears during the acute phase. The presence of HAV IgM indicates acute hepatitis. Levels stay high for about 8 weeks. HAV IgG without HAV IgM indicates past infection. IgG antibody provides lifelong immunity (Fig. 48.2). HAV vaccination and thorough hand washing are the best ways to prevent outbreaks. In the United States, the incidence of HAV is low among children and adolescents due to vaccination and highest among adults due to low vaccination rates.[2]

Hepatitis B Virus

Hepatitis B virus (HBV) is a blood-borne pathogen that can cause either acute or chronic hepatitis. The global prevalence of HBV is 3.5% to 3.9%. The disease burden is largely in Sub-Saharan Africa, Western Pacific Regions, and Southeast Asia (Box 48.1). The United States has policies to prevent HBV transmission through immunizations of newborns, children, and high-risk populations.[3]

HBV is a deoxyribonucleic acid (DNA) virus. It can be transmitted in several ways: (1) perinatally from mothers infected with HBV to their infants; (2) percutaneously (e.g., IV drug use, accidental needle-stick punctures); or (3) via small cuts on mucosal surfaces and exposure to infectious blood, blood products, or other body fluids (e.g., semen, vaginal secretions, saliva).

Sexual transmission is a common mode of HBV transmission. MSM (especially those practicing unprotected anal intercourse) are at an increased risk for HBV infection. Most believe that casual encounters, like hugging, kissing, and sharing utensils do not transmit the disease.

Other at-risk persons include those who live with chronically HBV-infected persons, patients on hemodialysis, health care personnel, public safety workers, blood product recipients, prisoners, Veterans, and homelessness.

HBV has been detected in almost every body fluid. Infected semen, cervicovaginal secretions, and saliva contain much lower HBV concentrations than blood, but the virus can be transmitted via these secretions. If gastrointestinal (GI) bleeding occurs, virus in the blood can contaminate feces. There is no evidence of fecal-oral transmission. Organ and tissue transplantation is another potential source of infection. In some patients with acute HBV, there is no readily identifiable risk factor.

HBV is a complex structure with 3 distinct antigens: surface antigen (HBsAg), core antigen (HBcAg), and e antigen (HBeAg). Each antigen, along with its corresponding antibody, may appear or disappear in serum depending on the phase of infection and immune response.

In most people who acquire HBV infection as an adult, the infection completely resolves without any long-term complications. In those who develop chronic HBV infections, there is an association with liver cancer and severe liver inflammation and scarring (fibrosis). Those who become chronically infected have an increase in comorbidities. These include cardiovascular disease, hypertension, hyperlipidemia, renal disease, and osteoporosis.[3]

Screening for HBV includes identifying those at high risk for infection and testing the blood for the presence of hepatitis B surface antigen (HBsAg), hepatitis B antibody (anti-HBs), and hepatitis B core antibody (anti-HBc). The presence of anti-HBs in the blood indicates immunity from the HBV vaccine or from past HBV infection (Fig. 48.3). HBsAg in the serum for 6 months or longer after infection indicates chronic HBV infection.

BOX 48.1 PROMOTING HEALTH EQUITY

Liver, Pancreas, and Gallbladder Problems

Hepatitis

- Hepatitis B has a higher incidence among Asian Americans and Pacific Islanders
- Hepatitis C has a higher incidence among Blacks
- Deaths from hepatitis C are more common in Blacks

Liver and Pancreatic Cancer

- Primary liver cancer has the highest incidence in Hispanics
- Pancreatic cancer occurs more often among Blacks

Gallbladder Disease

- Whites and Native Americans have the highest incidence of gallbladder disease

Hepatitis C Virus

Hepatitis C virus (HCV) causes a type of hepatitis that can result in both acute illness and chronic infection. Acute HCV can be hard to detect unless a diagnosis is made with laboratory testing. The most common causes of acute HCV outbreaks are among IV drug users and MSM with HIV infection.

HCV is a blood-borne RNA virus that is primarily transmitted percutaneously. The most common mode of HCV transmission is the sharing of contaminated needles and equipment among IV drug users. High-risk sexual behavior especially among MSM is associated with increased risk.

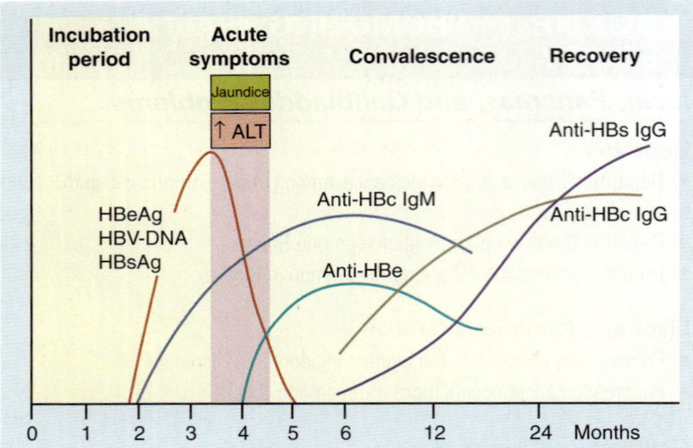

Fig. 48.3 Course of infection with hepatitis B virus *(HBV). ALT,* Alanine aminotransferase; *anti-HBc,* antibody to hepatitis B core antigen; *anti-HBe,* antibody to HBeAg; *anti-HBs,* antibody to HBsAg; *HBeAg,* hepatitis B e antigen; *HBsAg,* hepatitis B surface antigen. (From McCance KL, Huether SE: *Pathophysiology: the biologic basis for disease in adults and children,* ed 6, St Louis, 2010, Mosby.)

Many people infected with HCV develop chronic infection. However, because signs and symptoms of HCV infection are generally mild, most people are unaware of their infection. We think that greater than 50% of people in the United States infected with HCV are undiagnosed. About 20% develop cirrhosis and eventually liver failure and/or liver cancer if left untreated. HCV hepatitis is a common reason for liver transplantation in the United States.[4]

Persons at risk for HCV infection are also at risk for HBV and HIV infections. About 30% to 40% of HIV-infected patients also have HCV. This high rate of co-infection is primarily related to IV drug use. Co-infection with HIV and HCV places the patient at greater risk for progression to cirrhosis if HCV is untreated. A positive antibody test for HCV (anti-HCV) is followed by a positive viral load test to confirm active infection because an anti-HCV can also indicate a past infection.

With the use of direct-acting antiviral (DAA) medications, it is possible to cure HCV in almost all cases. There is no vaccine for HCV. However, with DAA regimens and the ability to cure HCV, the focus in chronic HCV is now on efforts to prevent transmission, screening, and provide needed health care.[5]

Hepatitis D Virus

Hepatitis D virus (HDV), also called *delta virus,* is uncommon in the United States. HDV is a defective single-stranded RNA virus that cannot survive on its own. It requires HBV surface Ag to serve as its outer shell and to infect the hepatocyte. So, only those who with HBV infection can be infected with HDV. It can be acquired at the same time as HBV or a person with HBV can be infected with HDV later. HDV is transmitted like HBV. It causes more rapid progression of liver disease and mortality than HBV infection alone. There is no vaccine for HDV. However, HBV vaccination reduces the risk for HDV co-infection.[6]

Hepatitis E Virus

Like HAV, the hepatitis E virus (HEV) is an RNA virus transmitted by the fecal-oral route. The usual mode of transmission is through contaminated water. HEV infection epidemics occur in the tropics, but it is widely circulating in the west. It is generally acute and self-resolving. Chronicity in immunosuppressed persons, such as liver transplant recipients and HIV positive persons, can occur. Pregnant women may be affected severely. An IgM antibody test is available to test for acute hepatitis E.[7]

Pathophysiology

Liver

In viral hepatitis, hepatocytes become targets of the virus in 1 of 2 ways: through direct action of the virus (as in HCV infection) or through a cell-mediated immune response to the virus (as in HBV and HCV infection).

During acute viral hepatitis, large numbers of infected hepatocytes are destroyed. Hepatocyte destruction leads to a wide range of liver-related dysfunction. Bile production, coagulation, blood glucose, and protein metabolism can be affected. Detoxification and processing of drugs, hormones, and metabolites (e.g., ammonia from protein catabolism) may be disrupted.

After acute infection resolves, liver cells can regenerate. If no complications occur, the liver can resume its normal appearance and function. In some patients, the acute hepatitis can become so severe and irreversible that they develop liver failure or die.

Chronic viral hepatitis can be insidious and silent, causing persistent and continual destruction of infected hepatocytes. Over time scar tissue can develop, which leads to fibrosis, cirrhosis, and compromised liver function. Fibrosis can lead to cirrhosis and liver failure. Cirrhosis is a generally irreversible condition that can increase one's risk for liver dysfunction, portal hypertension, and primary liver cancer.

Systemic Effects

In the early phases of hepatitis infection, antigen-antibody complexes between the virus and its corresponding antibody may form circulating immune complexes. The circulating immune complexes activate the complement system (see Chapter 12). The manifestations of this activation are rash, angioedema, arthritis, fever, and malaise. *Cryoglobulinemia* (abnormal proteins found in the blood), glomerulonephritis, vasculitis, and involvement of other organs can occur from immune complex activation.

Clinical Manifestations and Complications

We classify the manifestations of the different viral hepatitis infections into acute hepatitis and chronic hepatitis (Table 48.2).

Acute Hepatitis

Many patients with acute hepatitis have no symptoms. They may not even know they are infected. Others may have anorexia, lethargy, nausea, vomiting, skin rashes, diarrhea or constipation, malaise, fatigue, muscle pain, joint pain, other flu-like symptoms, and right upper quadrant (RUQ) tenderness (caused by liver inflammation).

Although the acute phase of viral hepatitis varies depending on the type of hepatitis, it usually lasts from 1 to 6 months. During this time, the patient may have a decreased sense of smell and find food repugnant. Smokers may have distaste for cigarettes. Physical assessment often reveals hepatomegaly, lymphadenopathy, abdominal tenderness, and sometimes splenomegaly. The acute phase is the period of maximal infectivity.

A patient in the acute phase of hepatitis may be *icteric* (jaundiced) or anicteric. **Jaundice**, a yellowish discoloration of body tissues, results from a change in normal bilirubin metabolism or disruption of the flow of bile into the hepatic or biliary duct systems. Table 48.3 describes the types of jaundice. The urine may appear darker due to the kidneys excreting excess bilirubin. If conjugated bilirubin cannot pass into the intestines from the liver because of obstruction or inflammation of the bile ducts, the stools will be clay colored.

TABLE 48.2 Manifestations of Hepatitis

Acute Hepatitis	Chronic Hepatitis
• Anorexia	• ↑ ALT, AST (may be normal in some people)
• Clay-colored stools	• Ascites and lower extremity edema
• Dark urine	• Asterixis ("liver flap")
• Diarrhea, constipation	• ↑ Bilirubin
• Fatigue, lethargy, malaise	• Bleeding problems (thrombocytopenia, easy bruising, prolonged clotting time)
• Flu-like symptoms (e.g., headache)	• Fatigue, malaise
• Hepatomegaly	• Hepatic encephalopathy: confusion, problems concentrating, easy agitation
• Jaundice	• Hepatomegaly
• Joint and muscle pain	• Jaundice
• Low-grade fever	• Joint and muscle pain
• Lymphadenopathy	• Palmar erythema
• Nausea, vomiting	• Spider angiomas
• Pruritus	
• RUQ tenderness	
• Splenomegaly	
• ↓ Taste and smell	
• Weight loss	

Pruritus (intense generalized itching) sometimes accompanies jaundice. It occurs from the accumulation of bile salts beneath the skin. Itching can be intolerable to the patient.

As jaundice fades, the convalescent phase begins. The convalescent phase can last for weeks to months, with an average of 2 to 4 months. During this period, patients often have malaise and fatigue. Hepatomegaly remains for several weeks. Splenomegaly (if present) subsides during this period.

Most patients with acute viral hepatitis recover completely. Almost all cases of acute hepatitis A resolve. However, some patients may have a relapse in the first 2 to 3 months after the infection. The disappearance of jaundice does not mean the patient has totally recovered. Some HBV infections and most HCV infections result in chronic hepatitis.

The overall mortality rate for acute hepatitis is less than 1%. The mortality rate is higher in older adults and those with underlying debilitating illnesses (including chronic liver disease).

Complications of acute hepatitis include chronic hepatitis, cirrhosis, portal hypertension, and liver cancer. Sometimes, acute liver failure (fulminant hepatic failure) may occur. It is a serious condition with a poor prognosis. Manifestations include encephalopathy, coagulation problems, and jaundice. Multiple complications can develop. A liver transplant may cure these patients.

Chronic Hepatitis

Table 48.2 shows the manifestations of chronic hepatitis. Chronic HBV is more likely to develop if the person acquired the infection at birth or during childhood. Chronic HBV can remain asymptomatic for years. Complications such as cirrhosis, liver failure, and liver cancer develop in 15% to 40% of people with HBV.[3]

HCV infection is more likely than HBV to become chronic. Many patients with chronic HCV infection develop chronic

TABLE 48.3 Classification of Jaundice

	Hemolytic Jaundice	Hepatocellular Jaundice	Obstructive Jaundice
Causes	• Blood transfusion reactions, hemolytic anemia, sickle cell crisis	• Cirrhosis, hepatitis, liver cancer	• Cirrhosis, hepatitis, liver cancer • Common bile duct obstruction from stone(s), biliary strictures, pancreatic cancer, sclerosing cholangitis
Description	• Caused by increased breakdown of RBCs, which produces an increased amount of unconjugated bilirubin in blood • Liver is unable to handle increased load	• Results from liver's altered ability to take up bilirubin from blood or to conjugate or excrete it • In hepatocellular disease, damaged hepatocytes leak bilirubin	• Results from decreased or obstructed flow of bile through liver or biliary duct system • Obstruction may occur in intrahepatic or extrahepatic bile ducts • Intrahepatic obstructions are due to swelling or fibrosis of the liver's canaliculi and bile ducts
Diagnostic Findings			
Serum Bilirubin			
Unconjugated (indirect)	↑	↑	↑
Conjugated (direct)	Normal	↑ or ↓ (severe disease)	↑
Urine Bilirubin	Negative	↑	↑
Urobilinogen			
Stool	↑	Normal, ↓	↓
Urine	↑	Normal, ↑	↓

TABLE 48.4 Diagnostic Studies
Viral Hepatitis

Virus	Tests	Significance
A (HAV)	HAV immunoglobulin M (IgM)	Acute infection
	HAV immunoglobulin G (IgG)	Previous infection or immunization Not routinely done in clinical practice
B (HBV)	HBsAg (hepatitis B surface antigen)	Marker of infectivity Present in acute or chronic infection Positive in chronic carriers
	Anti-HBs (hepatitis B surface antibody)	Indicates previous infection with HBV or immunization
	HBeAg (hepatitis B e antigen)	Indicates high infectivity Used to determine the clinical management of patients with chronic HBV
	Anti-HBe (hepatitis B e antibody)	Indicates previous infection In chronic HBV, indicates a low viral load and low degree of infectivity
	Anti-HBc (antibody to hepatitis B core antigen) IgM	Indicates acute infection Does not appear after vaccination
	Anti-HBc IgG	Indicates previous infection or ongoing infection with HBV Does not appear after vaccination
	HBV DNA quantitation	Indicates active ongoing viral replication Best indicator of viral replication and effectiveness of therapy in patient with chronic HBV
	HBV genotyping	Indicates the genotype of HBV
C (HCV)	Anti-HCV (antibody to HCV)	Marker for acute or chronic infection with HCV
	HCV RNA quantitation	Indicates active ongoing viral replication
	HCV genotyping	Indicates the genotype of HCV
D (HDV)	Anti-HDV	Present in past or current infection with HDV
	HDV Ag (hepatitis D antigen)	Present within a few days after infection
E (HEV)	Anti-HEV IgM and IgG	Present 1 week to 2 months after illness onset
	HEV RNA quantitation	Indicates active ongoing viral replication

liver disease, cirrhosis, portal hypertension, and liver cancer if untreated. In some patients, co-infection with HIV may cause complications or require treatment modification.

Skin manifestations may include spider angiomas, palmar erythema, and gynecomastia. Some patients with advanced fibrosis have spleen, liver, or cervical lymph node enlargement.

In patients with decompensated cirrhosis, *hepatic encephalopathy*, a potentially life-threatening spectrum of neurologic, psychiatric, and motor disturbances can occur. Hepatic encephalopathy results from the liver's inability to remove toxins (especially ammonia) from the blood.

Ascites is the accumulation of excess fluid in the peritoneal cavity. It is a common manifestation of hepatitis (especially from cirrhosis due to chronic hepatitis). Fluid accumulates due to reduced protein levels in the blood, which reduces the plasma oncotic pressure.

Diagnostic Studies

The only definitive way to distinguish among the types of viral hepatitis is by testing the patient's blood for the specific antigen or antibody (Table 48.4). In some types of viral hepatitis, we can test the blood for the viral load (viral level). Many liver function tests show significant abnormalities, as shown in Table 48.5.

Several tests are available to determine the presence of HCV. The screening test for HCV infection is HCV antibody testing. Antibodies can be detected within 4 weeks of infection. If the antibody test is positive, HCV RNA testing assesses for chronic

TABLE 48.5 Diagnostic Findings in Acute Hepatitis

Test	Abnormal Finding	Cause
Alkaline phosphatase	Moderately ↑	Impaired excretory function of liver
γ-Glutamyl transpeptidase (GGT)	↑	Liver cell injury
Aminotransferases		
• Aspartate aminotransferase (AST)	↑ in acute phase Decreases as jaundice disappears	Liver cell injury
• Alanine aminotransferase (ALT)	↑ in acute phase Decreases as jaundice disappears	Liver cell injury
Prothrombin time	Prolonged	↓ Prothrombin production by liver
Serum proteins		
• Albumin	Normal or ↓	Liver cell injury
• γ-Globulin	Normal or ↓	Impaired clearance from liver
Total bilirubin (serum)	↑ to about 8–15 mg/dL (137–257 μmol/L)	Liver cell injury
Urinary bilirubin	↑	Conjugated hyperbilirubinemia
Urinary urobilinogen	↑ 2–5 days before jaundice	↓ Urobilinogen reabsorption

infection and quantifies viral load. A positive result confirms chronic infection. A few patients may have a false-positive HCV antibody result with a negative HCV RNA test. If we suspect recent HCV infection, HCV RNA testing is usually done because it may take several weeks or longer for HCV antibodies to develop.

HCV RNA testing may be used for immunocompromised patients (e.g., patients with HIV). Because of altered or delayed antibody response to HCV, these patients may not have detectable antibody levels even if they are infected with HCV.

Viral genotype testing is done in patients receiving drug therapy for HBV or HCV infection. HBV has at least 8 different genotypes (A to H). In some centers, we do HBV genotyping before starting treatment. HBV genotype may be useful in predicting disease course and treatment outcomes. HBV core Ab (HBVcAb) IgG shows if the patient has a history of recovered HBV infection. HBV may reactivate in these patients if they become immunosuppressed.

HCV has 6 genotypes and more than 50 subtypes. In the United States, HCV genotype 1 causes 70% of HCV infections. For patients who test positive for HCV, we do genotyping before starting drug therapy. The genotype determines the choice and duration of therapy. It is one of the strongest predictors of a patient's response to drug therapy.

A liver biopsy is done in acute hepatitis if the diagnosis is in doubt. In chronic hepatitis, a liver biopsy allows for histologic examination of liver cells and determination of the degree of inflammation, fibrosis, or cirrhosis that may be present. A patient who has a bleeding disorder may not be able to have a percutaneous liver biopsy because of the risk for bleeding. In these patients, a transjugular biopsy may be done. This type of biopsy consists of obtaining liver tissue through a rigid cannula introduced into a hepatic vein, normally using jugular venous access.

Noninvasive assessment of liver fibrosis is increasingly replacing the need for liver biopsy. One option is the use of ultrasound elastography (e.g., FibroScan), which uses an ultrasound transducer to determine the degree of liver fibrosis. Magnetic resonance elastography (MRE) is another noninvasive imaging technique to measure liver fibrosis. FibroSure (FibroTest) is an example of one of several biomarkers that uses the results of serum tests to assess the extent of hepatic fibrosis.[8]

Interprofessional Care

There is no specific treatment for acute viral hepatitis. Most patients are managed at home. Emphasis is on providing adequate nutrition and measures to rest the body and help the liver to regenerate and repair (Table 48.6). Rest reduces the metabolic demands on the liver and promotes liver cell regeneration. The degree of rest depends on the severity of symptoms. Usually, alternating periods of activity and rest are adequate. Teaching should include the importance of avoiding alcohol and notifying contacts for testing and prophylaxis, if needed.

In patients with chronic viral hepatitis, care may involve liver specialists, infectious disease specialists, pharmacists, dietitians, and mental health or substance use specialists. The role and extent of involvement of team members is based on the patient's specific needs.

TABLE 48.6 Interprofessional Care

Viral Hepatitis

Diagnostic Assessment
- History and physical assessment
- Liver function tests (Table 48.5)
- PT time and INR
- Hepatitis testing (Table 48.4)
  - *Hepatitis A (HAV):* HAV IgM, HAV IgG, HAV total antibody
  - *Hepatitis B (HBV):* HBsAg, anti-HBs, HBeAg, anti-HBe, anti-HBc IgM and IgG, HBV DNA quantitation, HBV genotyping
  - *Hepatitis C (HCV):* Anti-HCV, HCV RNA quantitation, HCV genotyping
  - *Hepatitis D (HDV):* Anti-HDV, HDV Ag, HDV RNA
  - *Hepatitis E (HEV):* Anti-HEV IgM, anti-HEV IgG
- FibroScan
- FibroSure (FibroTest)

Management

Acute and Chronic
- Well-balanced diet
- Vitamin supplements
- Rest (degree of strictness varies)
- Avoiding alcohol and drugs detoxified by liver

Chronic HBV and HCV
- Drug therapy (Table 48.7)

Drug Therapy

Acute hepatitis. There are no drug therapies for treating acute HAV infection. Treatment of acute HBV may be indicated only in patients with severe hepatitis and liver failure.

In acute HCV, some patients may choose to be monitored for spontaneous clearance of the infection. Patients who choose treatment may receive one of the DAAs. DAAs are discussed later in the section on chronic hepatitis.

Supportive drug therapy may include antihistamines for generalized itching and antiemetics for nausea.

Chronic hepatitis B. Drug therapy for chronic HBV focuses on decreasing viral load and liver enzymes, and in turn, slowing the rate of disease progression. Long-term goals are preventing the development of cirrhosis, portal hypertension, liver failure, and liver cancer. Current drug therapies do not eradicate the virus. They suppress viral replication and prevent complications. First-line therapies primarily include nucleoside and nucleotide analogs (Table 48.7) and sometimes interferon therapy.

Nucleoside and nucleotide analogs. Nucleoside and nucleotide analogs inhibit viral DNA replication. HBV reproduces by making copies of its viral DNA nucleosides and nucleotides. The nucleoside and nucleotide analog drugs mimic normal building blocks for DNA but are actually faulty viral DNA building blocks. Once they become included in the viral DNA, they halt DNA synthesis.

Nucleoside and nucleotide analogs do not prevent all viral reproduction. They can substantially lower viral load or the amount of virus in the body. These drugs include lamivudine (Epivir), adefovir (Hepsera), entecavir (Baraclude), telbivudine (Tyzeka), and tenofovir (Viread). They are used to treat chronic

TABLE 48.7 Drug Therapy

Viral HBV and HCV

Drug Class	Examples	Mechanism of Action	Indication
Immune modulator	pegylated interferon (Pegasys, PegIntron)	Has antiviral, antiproliferative, immune-regulating actions	Chronic HBV
Nucleoside and nucleotide analogs	adefovir[a] entecavir (Baraclude) lamivudine (Epivir HBV) telbivudine (Tyzeka)[a] tenofovir (Vemlidy, Viread)	Inhibits HBV DNA polymerase enzyme by competing with natural substrates. Prevents viral replication	Chronic HBV
Direct-acting antivirals for HCV			
NS3/4A protease inhibitors	glecaprevir[b] grazoprevir[c] voxilaprevir[b]	Blocks viral protease enzyme. Prevents viral replication in genotype 1 HCV	Chronic HCV
NS5A inhibitors	elbasvir[b] ledipasvir[c] pibrentasvir[b] velpatasvir[b]	Blocks nonstructural protein 5A (NS5A) at early stage in RNA HCV replication	Chronic HCV
NS5B polymerase inhibitors	sofosbuvir (Sovaldi)	Nucleotide inhibitor and non-nucleoside inhibitor of HCV polymerase. Prevent replication of RNA HCV	Chronic HCV
Combination therapies	elbasvir + grazoprevir (Zepatier) ledipasvir + sofosbuvir (Harvoni) Pibrentasvir + glecaprevir (Mavyret) velpatasvir + sofosbuvir (Epclusa) velpatasvir + sofosbuvir + voxilaprevir (Vosevi)	Drugs are combined in 1 tablet. Drugs may be from the same or different classes.	Chronic HCV

[a]Not preferred
[b]Used only in combination therapy.
[c]CYP3A inhibitor used to enhance the pharmacokinetics of the other agents.

HBV when there is evidence of significant active viral replication and liver inflammation.[9]

These drugs also decrease liver damage and decrease serum liver enzyme levels. Most patients with HBV need long-term treatment. When these drugs are stopped, many patients' (except those who have seroconverted) HBV DNA and liver enzyme levels return to pretreatment levels.

Severe exacerbations can develop after ending treatment. If these drugs are stopped for any reason, we monitor the patient's liver enzymes for several months.

Interferon. Interferon is a naturally occurring immune protein made by the body during an infection to recognize and respond to pathogens. It has antiviral, antiproliferative, and immune-modulating effects (see Chapter 14). Pegylated interferon (PEG-Intron, Pegasys) is given by subcutaneous injection. The many side effects of therapy, including flu-like symptoms (e.g., fever, malaise, fatigue), make adherence hard for some patients. The availability of better tolerated and more effective oral treatments limits interferon use. However, it is still used to treat some patients with HBV because it can have an increased viral response.

Patients receiving interferon should have blood counts and liver function tests every 4 to 6 weeks. Depression is a side effect of therapy. We must screen patients for depression and other mood disorders before starting treatment and monitor them frequently while on therapy.

Chronic hepatitis C. Treatment of chronic HCV is patient specific. It is based on the genotype of the HCV, severity of liver disease, and presence of other health problems (e.g., HIV). The goal of drug therapy is eradicating the virus and preventing HCV-related complications.

Treatment for HCV primarily includes the use of DAAs (Table 48.7), which block proteins needed for HCV replication. Patients normally complete 12 weeks of DAA therapy. Almost all (>95%) of those who complete DAA treatment see a cure of their chronic HCV infection.[4,5]

Many patients with HIV also have HCV. Patients who have stable HIV and intact immune systems ($CD4^+$ counts greater than 200/μL) receive HCV treatment with the goal of eradicating HCV and reducing the risk for progression to cirrhosis. HCV treatment plans are equally effective for HCV/HIV coinfected and HCV mono-infected patients.

Patients with advanced fibrosis or cirrhosis can receive drug therapy if liver decompensation (e.g., ascites, variceal rupture, jaundice, wasting, encephalopathy) is not present.

Nutrition Therapy

No special diet is part of the treatment of viral hepatitis. Emphasize a well-balanced diet that the patient can tolerate. During acute viral hepatitis, adequate calories are important because the patient usually loses weight. If the patient does not tolerate fat content because of decreased bile production, it should be reduced. The patient may receive vitamin supplements, particularly B-complex and vitamin K. If anorexia, nausea, and vomiting are severe, we may give IV glucose solutions or supplemental enteral nutrition (EN). Fluid and electrolyte balance must be maintained.

TABLE 48.8 NURSING ASSESSMENT

Hepatitis

Subjective Data

Important Health Information

Health history: Hemophilia, cancer, exposure to infected persons, ingestion of contaminated food or water. Exposure to benzene, carbon tetrachloride, or other hepatotoxic agents. Crowded, unsanitary living conditions. Exposure to contaminated needles. Recent travel, organ transplant recipient, exposure to new drug regimens, hemodialysis, transfusion of blood or blood products before 1992. HIV status (if known)

Medications: Use and misuse of acetaminophen, new medications or supplements

Functional Health Patterns

Health perception–health management: IV drug and chronic alcohol use. Malaise, distaste for cigarettes (in smokers), high-risk sexual behaviors

Nutritional-metabolic: Weight loss, anorexia, nausea, vomiting. Feeling of RUQ fullness

Elimination: Dark urine, light-colored stools, constipation or diarrhea, skin rashes, hives

Activity-exercise: Fatigue, muscle pain, joint pain

Cognitive-perceptual: RUQ pain, liver tenderness, headache, itching

Role-relationship: Exposure as health care worker, resident in long-term care institution, incarceration, homelessness

Objective Data

General

Low-grade fever, lethargy, lymphadenopathy

GI

Hepatomegaly, splenomegaly

Skin

Rash or other skin changes, jaundice, icteric sclera, injection sites

Possible Diagnostic Findings

↑ Liver enzyme levels. ↑ Serum total bilirubin, hypoalbuminemia, anemia, bilirubin in urine and urobilinogen. Prolonged PT time. Positive tests for hepatitis, including HAV IgM, HBsAg, anti-HBs, HBeAg, anti-HBe, anti-HBc IgM and IgG, HBV DNA quantitation, anti-HCV, HCV RNA quantitation, anti-HDV, HDV Ag. Abnormal liver scan, abnormal results on liver biopsy

HAV, Hepatitis A virus; *HBcAg,* hepatitis B core antigen; *HBeAg,* hepatitis B e antigen; *HBsAg,* hepatitis B surface antigen; *HBV,* hepatitis B virus; *HCV,* hepatitis C virus; *HDV Ag,* hepatitis D antigen; *HDV,* hepatitis D virus.

NURSING MANAGEMENT: VIRAL HEPATITIS

Assessment

Subjective and objective data that you should obtain from a person with hepatitis are outlined in Table 48.8.

Clinical Problems

Clinical problems for the patient with viral hepatitis may include:

- Nutritionally compromised
- Activity intolerance
- Risk for bleeding

Additional information on clinical problems and interventions for the patient with hepatitis is presented in eNursing Care Plan 48.1 available on the website for this chapter.

Planning

The overall goals are that the patient with viral hepatitis will (1) have relief of discomfort, (2) be able to resume normal activities, and (3) return to normal liver function without complications.

Implementation

Health Promotion

Viral hepatitis is a public health problem. Your role is important in the prevention and control of this disease. It is helpful to understand the epidemiology of the different types of viral hepatitis when considering appropriate control measures. Preventive and control measures for hepatitis A, B, and C are outlined in Table 48.9.

A suggested guideline for general practice to prevent you from contracting viral hepatitis from diagnosed and undiagnosed patients and carriers is for you to wear personal protective equipment (PPE) when fecal or blood contamination is likely in handling (1) soiled bedpans, urinals, and catheters and (2) when the patient's bed linens are soiled by body excreta or secretions.

Hepatitis A. Viral hepatitis outbreaks are usually due to HAV. Preventive measures include personal and environmental hygiene and health education to promote good sanitation. Hand washing is the most important precaution. Teach about careful hand washing after bowel movements and before eating.

Isolation is not needed for HAV infection. For a patient with HAV infection, use infection control precautions. Place the patient who is incontinent of stool or has poor personal hygiene in a private room.

Vaccination is the best protection against HAV. All children at 1 year of age should receive the vaccine. Adults at risk should also receive the vaccine. These include travelers to areas with increased rates of hepatitis A, MSM, IV and noninjecting drug users, and homelessness. Others who should receive the vaccine include persons with clotting factor disorders (e.g., hemophilia) and chronic liver disease.

HAV vaccine is inactivated HAV protein. There are 2 forms of HAV vaccine in the United States: Havrix and Vaqta. Primary immunization consists of 1 dose given IM in the deltoid muscle. A booster is recommended 6 to 12 months after the first dose to ensure adequate antibody titers and long-term protection. Primary immunization provides immunity within 30 days after 1 dose in more than 97% to 100% of those vaccinated.[2]

Twinrix, a combined HAV and HBV vaccine, is available for people over 18 years of age. It consists of 3 doses, given on a 0-, 1-, and 6-month schedule (the same schedule as the single HBV vaccine). Twinrix may be given to high-risk persons, including patients with chronic liver disease, IV drug users, patients on hemodialysis, MSM, and people with clotting factor disorders who receive therapeutic blood products. The side effects are mild. They include soreness and redness at the injection site.

Both HAV vaccine and immune globulin (IG) are used to prevent HAV infection after exposure to an infected person *(postexposure prophylaxis).* The vaccine is used for preexposure prophylaxis. We can give IG either before or after exposure. IG gives temporary (1 to 2 months) passive immunity. It is effective

TABLE 48.9 Prevention of Viral Hepatitis

Hepatitis A

General Measures

- Hand washing
- Proper personal hygiene
- Environmental sanitation
- Control and screening (signs, symptoms) of food handlers
- Serologic screening for those carrying virus
- Active immunization: HAV vaccine

Use of Immune Globulin

- Early administration (1–2 weeks after exposure) to those exposed
- Prophylaxis for travelers to areas where hepatitis A is common if not vaccinated with HAV vaccine

Special Considerations for Health Care Personnel

- *HAV,* Hepatitis A virus; *HBcAg,* hepatitis B core antigen; *HBeAg,* hepatitis B e antigen; *HBsAg,* hepatitis B surface antigen; *HBV,* hepatitis B virus; *HCV,* hepatitis C virus; *HDV Ag,* hepatitis D antigen; *HDV,* hepatitis D virus.
- *HAV,* Hepatitis A virus; *HBcAg,* hepatitis B core antigen; *HBeAg,* hepatitis B e antigen; *HBsAg,* hepatitis B surface antigen; *HBV,* hepatitis B virus; *HCV,* hepatitis C virus; *HDV Ag,* hepatitis D antigen; *HDV,* hepatitis D virus.

Hepatitis B and C

Percutaneous Transmission

- Screening of donated blood
- *HBV:* HBsAg
- *HCV:* Anti-HCV
- Use of disposable needles and syringes

Sexual Transmission

- Acute exposure: HBIG administration to sexual partner of HBsAg-positive person
- Give HBV vaccine series uninfected sexual partners
- Use condoms for sexual intercourse

General Measures

- Hand washing
- Avoid sharing toothbrushes and razors
- HBIG administration for one-time exposure (needle stick, contact of mucous membranes with infectious material)
- Active immunization: HBV vaccine

Special Considerations for Health Care Personnel

- Use infection control precautions
- Reduce contact with blood or blood-containing secretions
- Handle the blood of patients as potentially infective
- Dispose of needles properly
- Use needleless IV access devices when available

for preventing HAV if given within 2 weeks after exposure. IG is given to persons who do not have HAV antibodies and were exposed by close (household, daycare center) contact with persons who have HAV or foodborne exposure. Because patients with HAV are most infectious just before the onset of symptoms, those exposed through household contact or foodborne outbreaks should receive the HAV vaccine. They may receive IG based on risk factors. Although IG may not prevent infection, it may lessen the illness to a subclinical infection.

Hepatitis B. The best way to reduce HBV infection is to identify those at risk, screen them for HBV, and vaccinate those who are not infected. Teach those at high risk for contracting HBV to reduce risks by following good hygienic practices, including hand washing and using gloves when expecting contact with blood. Patients should not share razors, toothbrushes, and other personal items. Teach patients to use a condom for sexual intercourse. In addition, the partner should be vaccinated.

The HBV vaccine is the best means of prevention. The HBV vaccines (Recombivax HB, Engerix-B) contain HBsAg. HBsAg promotes the synthesis of specific antibodies directed against HBV. The vaccine is given in a series of 3 IM injections in the deltoid muscle. It is given on a 0-, 1-, and 6-month schedule. The vaccine is 95% effective. Minor reactions include transient fever and soreness at the injection site. The vaccine can be given in pregnancy. A newer formulation of the HBV vaccine (Heplisav-B) is approved for persons 18 years or older. It is given in 2 doses, spaced 4 weeks apart. Use is not approved in pregnancy.

The traditional HBV vaccine of 3 doses is normally given in childhood. The first dose of HBV vaccine should be given at birth. The vaccine series is completed by age 6 to 18 months. Older children and adolescents who did not receive the HBV vaccine should be vaccinated.[9] It is important to vaccinate adults who are in the at-risk groups and are not immune. Household members of the patient with HBV should be tested and vaccinated if they are HBsAg and antibody negative. HBV vaccination is recommended for patients with chronic kidney disease before they start dialysis. Dialysis patients should routinely have their antibody titer levels checked to determine the need for revaccination.

For postexposure prophylaxis, the HBV vaccine series and hepatitis B immune globulin (HBIG) are given. HBIG has antibodies to HBV and confers temporary passive immunity. HBIG is prepared from the plasma of donors with a high titer of anti-HBs. HBIG is recommended for postexposure prophylaxis in cases of needle stick, mucous membrane contact, or sexual exposure and for infants born to mothers who are positive for HBsAg. Ideally, we should give HBIG within 24 hours of exposure. Giving antiviral therapy (e.g., tenofovir) to pregnant women in the third trimester with viral levels over 200,000 IU/mL can prevent the small risk for neonatal infection that may occur even with postnatal immunization and vaccination.

The Centers for Disease Control and Prevention (CDC) recommends following standard precautions for the patient with HBV (see Table 15.9). This includes using disposable needles and syringes and disposing of them in puncture-resistant units without recapping, bending, or breaking.

Hepatitis C. No vaccine is currently available for HCV. So, it is important to identify those at high risk for contracting HCV and teach them how to reduce their risks. Measures to prevent HCV transmission include (1) screening of blood, organ, and tissue donors; (2) using infection control precautions; and (3) modifying high-risk behavior.

BOX 48.2 EVIDENCE-BASED PRACTICE

Screening and Testing of Hepatitis C Virus

You are caring for S.B., a 32-year-old man who often visits the community clinic with health concerns. He arrives today saying he feels "tired." He tells you a friend was recently diagnosed with hepatitis C virus (HCV), and he wants "a shot" to keep from "getting it." You see on the medical record that he injects drugs and has not been tested for HCV.

Making Clinical Decisions

Best Available Evidence

Currently, most HCV-infected persons are undiagnosed and therefore untreated. We recommend testing for patients with known risk factors for HCV. Rapid diagnostic tests (RDTs), including oral HCV antibody (Ab) RDTs, have excellent sensitivity and specificity for HCV Ab detection.

Clinician Expertise

You know a major risk factor for HCV is IV drug use. You understand early diagnosis of HCV is important for best patient outcomes and preventing transmission to others.

Patient Preferences and Values

S.B. tells you he is "busy today," but he can come back tomorrow for HCV testing.

Implications for Nursing Practice

1. What information would you provide to S.B. on HCV testing, symptoms, and transmission?
2. Since S.B. is now willing to be tested for HCV, how would you determine barriers to the informed consent process?
3. Should S.B. test positive for HCV, what other information will you provide him?

Reference for Evidence

Center for Disease Control and Prevention: Viral hepatitis: hepatitis C FAQs for health professionals. Retrieved from www.cdc.gov/hepatitis/hcv/hcvfaq.htm.

In the United States, many people have undiagnosed HCV. The US current screening guidelines recommend one time opt-out HCV testing for everyone 18 years and older. Annual HCV screening is recommended for IV drug users (Box 48.2).

Acute Care

In patients with hepatitis, assess for the presence and degree of jaundice. In light-skinned persons, jaundice is usually seen first in the sclera of the eyes and later in the skin. In dark-skinned persons, jaundice is seen in the hard palate of the mouth and inner canthus of the eyes. The urine may have a dark-brown or brownish-red color from bilirubin excretion from the kidneys. Comfort measures to relieve itching, headache, and joint pain are helpful.

CHECK YOUR PRACTICE

You are caring for a patient with acute hepatitis. He has decreased appetite from severe nausea and vomiting. He is admitted to the hospital for IV hydration and monitoring. The patient says, "I'm so weak, and I feel like I'm going to vomit all the time. Isn't there something you can do to help me?"

- How would you handle this situation?
- What information and teaching will you give him?

Ensuring that the patient receives adequate nutrition is not always easy. The anorexia and distaste for food may cause nutrition problems. Assess the patient's tolerance of specific foods and eating pattern. Small, frequent meals may be preferable to 3 large ones and may help prevent nausea. Often a patient with hepatitis finds that anorexia is not as severe in the morning, so it is easier to eat a good breakfast than a large dinner. Include measures to stimulate the appetite, such as mouth care, antiemetics, and attractively served meals in pleasant surroundings. Drinking carbonated beverages and avoiding very hot or cold foods may help ease anorexia. Adequate fluid intake (2500 to 3000 mL/day) is important.

Rest is a critical factor in promoting hepatocyte regeneration. Assess the patient's response to the rest and activity plan. Modify it as needed based on liver function tests and symptoms.

Psychologic and emotional rest is as essential as physical rest. Limited activity may produce anxiety and restlessness in some patients. Diversion activities, such as reading and hobbies, may help a patient cope with the plan of care and ensure adequate rest.

Ambulatory Care

Most patients with viral hepatitis are cared for at home. Assess the patient's knowledge of nutrition and provide any needed dietary teaching. Caution the patient about overexertion and the need to follow the HCP's advice about when to return to work. For patients who have fatigue, tell them to plan activities after periods of rest when energy levels are highest. Teach the patient and caregiver how to prevent transmission to other family members and symptoms to report to the HCP.

Assess the patient for any complications. These include bleeding tendencies with increasing prothrombin (PT) time values, encephalopathy, bloody or tarry stools, vomiting of blood, or high liver enzymes. Note a sudden increase in weight and abdominal girth, which may indicate fluid retention and/or ascites.

Teach the patient to have regular follow-ups for at least 1 year after the diagnosis of hepatitis. Because relapses occur with HBV and HCV, teach the patient the symptoms of recurrence and the need for follow-up care. All patients with chronic HBV or HCV should avoid alcohol as it can accelerate disease progression. Remind patients who are positive for HBsAg (chronic carrier status) or HCV antibody that they cannot be blood donors.

Evaluation

Expected outcomes are that the patient with hepatitis will

- Maintain food and fluid intake adequate to meet nutrient needs
- Avoid alcohol and other hepatotoxic agents
- Show gradual increase in activity tolerance
- Perform daily activities with scheduled rest periods

DRUG- AND CHEMICAL-INDUCED LIVER DISEASES

Excessive alcohol use can cause injury and necrosis of liver tissue. The manifestations can range from a mild elevation in liver enzymes to acute alcoholic hepatitis. Advanced fibrosis and cirrhosis can occur after decades of excess alcohol use. Patients may have serious liver disease caused by another chronic disease (e.g., chronic viral infection) in combination with alcoholic liver disease, which can compound the problem.

Acute alcoholic hepatitis is a syndrome of hepatomegaly, jaundice, increased liver enzymes (AST, ALT, alkaline phosphate), and low-grade fever. Ascites and prolonged PT time are possible. These manifestations may improve if alcohol intake ceases.

Even at the end-stage of cirrhosis, abstinence can result in significant reversal in some patients. If liver function does not recover after abstaining from alcohol for 6 months or longer, liver transplantation may be an option.[10]

Chemical hepatotoxicity is liver injury caused by exposure to certain compounds (e.g., carbon tetrachloride, gold compounds). Some agents can cause hepatotoxicity, while others may induce cholestasis, necrosis, or liver cancer. Fortunately, because of the decreased use of these agents, the incidence of chemically induced liver toxicity has decreased since the 1980s.

Drug-induced liver injury (DILI) can present similarly to other forms of liver disease. The pattern of injury depends on the drug causing the reaction. Many drugs can cause an increase in liver enzymes and in severe cases jaundice and acute liver failure. The main cause of DILI is antimicrobial agents, especially amoxicillin-clavulanate. The most common cause of acute liver failure is acetaminophen. In patients with chemical hepatotoxicity or DILI, all drugs identified as the cause of liver injury should be stopped.[11]

DRUG ALERT

Acetaminophen

- Safe when taken at recommended levels.
- Its prevalence in a variety of pain relievers, fever reducers, and cough medicines may mean that patients do not know they are taking several drugs that all contain acetaminophen. This can cause an overdose.
- Acute liver failure can occur because of overdosing, either intentionally or unintentionally.
- Combining the drug with alcoholic beverages increases the risk for liver damage.

AUTOIMMUNE, GENETIC, AND METABOLIC LIVER DISEASES

Autoimmune Hepatitis

Autoimmune hepatitis is a chronic inflammatory liver disorder in which the patient's own immune system attacks the liver. The cause is unknown. It is characterized by the presence of autoantibodies and high levels of serum immunoglobulins. It often occurs with other autoimmune diseases.

Most patients with autoimmune hepatitis are women. Laboratory tests useful in the diagnosis include antinuclear antibody (ANA), anti-smooth muscle antibody (ASMA), and antimitochondrial antibody (AMA) testing. A liver biopsy can confirm the diagnosis and guide the treatment decision.

Although autoimmune hepatitis can cause acute liver failure, the spectrum of disease is variable. Most patients develop chronic hepatitis. Untreated autoimmune hepatitis can progress to cirrhosis. Prednisone with or without azathioprine (Imuran) is the recommended treatment for active autoimmune hepatitis. Cyclosporine, tacrolimus (Prograf), budesonide (Entocort), methotrexate, mercaptopurine, and mycophenolate mofetil (CellCept) are options in those who do not respond to prednisone and azathioprine. Mycophenolate is most often used for those who are intolerant to azathioprine.[12]

Wilson Disease

Wilson disease is an autosomal recessive disorder involving cellular copper transport. A defect in biliary excretion leads to copper accumulation in the liver. This causes progressive liver injury and cirrhosis.

Once cirrhosis occurs, copper leaks into the plasma, leading to multiple problems, including neurologic and psychiatric symptoms. The hallmark of Wilson disease is corneal Kayser-Fleischer rings. These are brownish-red rings seen in the cornea near the limbus on eye examination. Low serum ceruloplasmin levels and markedly elevated copper concentrations from liver biopsy samples are present. Diagnosis is based on clinical findings. First-degree relatives of patients with Wilson disease need to be screened for the disease.[13]

The recommended first treatment of symptomatic patients or those with active disease is chelating agents, such as D-penicillamine or trientine (Syprine). They promote the excretion of urinary copper. Zinc acetate (Galzin), another therapy, interferes with copper absorption. Once we have reduced the amount of copper in the body, treatment focuses on preventing copper from building up again. Liver transplantation may be an option with severe liver damage.

Hemochromatosis

Hemochromatosis is a condition in which excess iron accumulates in the body. It is mainly caused by a genetic defect *(hereditary hemochromatosis)*. Iron accumulation in the liver can also be caused by liver disease and chronic blood transfusions used to treat thalassemia and sickle cell disease.[14] Hemochromatosis is discussed in Chapter 34.

Alpha-1 antitrypsin (AAT) deficiency is a genetic disorder that causes an accumulation of AAT in the liver that leads to fibrosis and lung disease. There is no treatment. We recommend patients avoid other causes of liver injury such as alcohol use and fatty liver.[15]

Primary Biliary Cholangitis

Primary biliary cholangitis (PBC), also known as primary biliary cirrhosis, is a chronic disease of the small bile ducts of the liver. In PBC, there is a T cell-mediated attack of the small bile duct cells. This causes a loss of bile ducts and cholestasis (blockage of bile flow). Over time, this leads to liver fibrosis and cirrhosis.

Most patients diagnosed with PBC are middle-aged women. The disease is associated with other autoimmune disorders, such as rheumatoid arthritis, Sjögren syndrome, and scleroderma. High serum alkaline phosphatase, AMA, ANA, and serum lipid levels are present.

The goals of treatment are suppressing ongoing liver damage, preventing complications, and symptom management.

Drugs for PBC include ursodiol, a bile acid, and obeticholic acid (Ocaliva). These drugs decrease bile in the liver. Care focuses on preventing or minimizing malabsorption, hyperlipidemia, vitamin deficiencies, anemia, and fatigue. Care is taken to manage skin disorders, such as itching and xanthomas (cholesterol deposits in the skin). Cholestyramine is used to treat itching. Patients are monitored for progression to cirrhosis. Liver transplantation is an option for end-stage liver disease in patients with PBC.[16]

Primary Sclerosing Cholangitis

Primary sclerosing cholangitis (PSC) is characterized by chronic inflammation, fibrosis, and narrowing of the medium and large bile ducts both inside and outside the liver. We do not know the cause. Most patients with PSC also have ulcerative colitis or, less often, Crohn disease. Complications include cholangitis, cholestasis with jaundice, bile duct cancer, and cirrhosis.

Drug therapy has no proven benefit, although many HCPs use ursodiol. Treatment is directed at reducing the incidence of biliary complications and screening for bile duct and colorectal cancer, which is related to the high incidence of ulcerative colitis. Patients with advanced liver disease may need liver transplantation.

Nonalcoholic Fatty Liver Disease and Nonalcoholic Steatohepatitis

Nonalcoholic fatty liver disease (NAFLD) refers to a wide spectrum of liver diseases ranging from a fatty liver (steatosis) to **nonalcoholic steatohepatitis (NASH)** to cirrhosis.[17] The term *nonalcoholic* is used because NAFLD and NASH occur in people who do not consume excess amounts of alcohol.

The fundamental characteristic of NAFLD is the accumulation of fatty infiltration in the hepatocytes. In NASH, the fat accumulation is associated with varying degrees of inflammation and fibrosis of the liver. If NASH is untreated, it can lead to cirrhosis, liver cancer, and liver failure.

NASH occurs in 3% to 6% of the US population. It is more prevalent in patients with metabolic disease and obesity. About 20% of patients with NASH progress to cirrhosis. NASH should be considered in patients with risk factors, including obesity, diabetes, hyperlipidemia, and hypertension (or *metabolic syndrome*).

Elevated liver function tests (ALT, AST) are often the first sign of NAFLD. Ultrasound and CT scans can be used to diagnose NAFLD. Definitive diagnosis is by a liver biopsy.

There is no currently approved drug for NAFLD. The goal of therapy is weight loss of at least 10% of body weight, if overweight or obese, and exercise. Bariatric surgery for morbidly obese persons reduces the risk of NAFLD. Reducing other risk factors, including hyperlipidemia, hypertension, and diabetes, is important.

CIRRHOSIS

Cirrhosis is the end stage of liver disease.[18] It is characterized by extensive degeneration and destruction of the liver cells. This results in the replacement of liver tissue by fibrosis (scar tissue) and regenerative nodules that occur from the liver's attempt to repair itself (Fig. 48.4). The development of cirrhosis usually happens after decades of chronic liver disease.

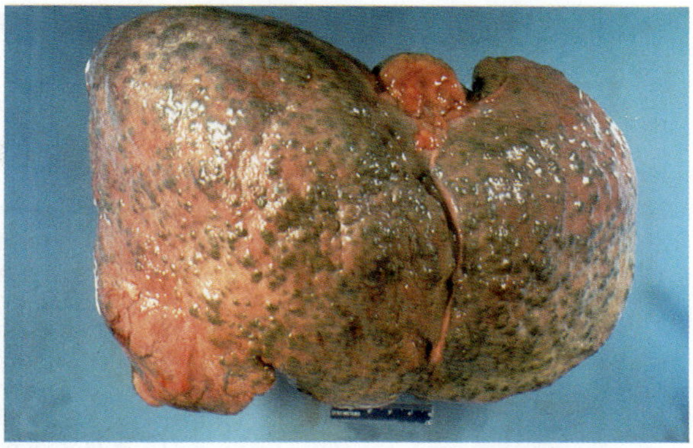

Fig. 48.4 Cirrhosis from alcohol use. The characteristic diffuse nodularity of the surface is due to the combination of regeneration and scarring of the liver. (From Kumar V, Abbas AK, Aster JC, et al.: *Robbins and Cotran pathologic basis of disease,* ed 8, Philadelphia, 2010, Saunders.)

Etiology and Pathophysiology

Any chronic liver disease can cause cirrhosis. The most common causes in the United States are chronic HCV infection, NASH, and alcohol-induced liver disease. In patients with alcohol-induced liver disease, malnutrition adds to the damage caused by the alcohol itself. Some cases of nutrition-related cirrhosis have resulted from extreme dieting, malabsorption, and obesity. Environmental factors and genetic predisposition may lead to the development of cirrhosis.

Chronic inflammation and cell necrosis from viral hepatitis can result in progressive fibrosis and cirrhosis. Chronic hepatitis combined with alcohol use has a synergistic effect in accelerating liver damage. Biliary causes include PBC and PSC.

Cardiac cirrhosis includes a spectrum of liver problems that result from long-standing, severe, right-sided heart failure. It causes hepatic venous congestion, parenchymal damage, necrosis of liver cells, and fibrosis over time. Treatment is aimed at managing the patient's underlying heart failure.

In cirrhosis, the liver cells try to regenerate, but the regenerative process is disorganized. This results in abnormal blood vessel and bile duct architecture. The overgrowth of new and fibrous connective tissue distorts the liver's normal lobular structure, resulting in lobules of irregular size and shape with impeded blood flow. Eventually, irregular and disorganized liver regeneration, poor cell nutrition, and hypoxia (from inadequate blood flow and scar tissue) result in decreased liver function.

Clinical Manifestations

Early Manifestations

Patients may be unaware of their liver condition because there are few symptoms in early-stage disease. If a person does have symptoms, these may include fatigue or an enlarged liver. Blood tests may show normal liver function (compensated cirrhosis). The diagnosis of cirrhosis is often made later when a patient presents with symptoms of more advanced liver disease.

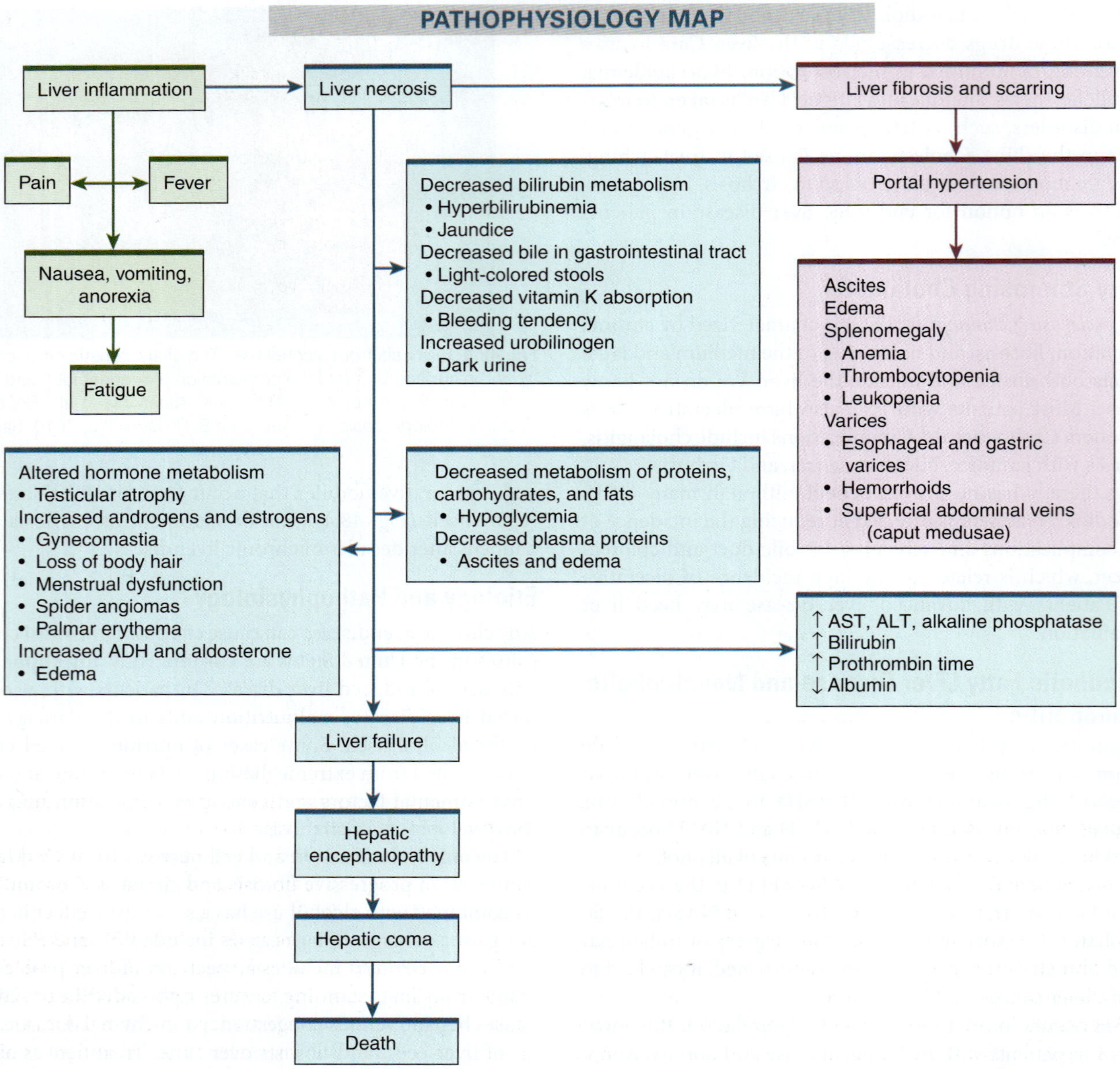

Fig. 48.5 Continuum of liver dysfunction in cirrhosis and resulting manifestations. (Adapted from Huether SE, McCance KL: *Understanding pathophysiology,* ed 5, St Louis, 2012, Mosby.)

Late Manifestations

Late manifestations result from liver failure and portal hypertension (Fig. 48.5). Jaundice, peripheral edema, and ascites develop gradually. Other late manifestations include skin lesions, hematologic problems, endocrine problems, and peripheral neuropathies (Fig. 48.6). In the advanced stages, the liver becomes small and nodular. Liver function is dramatically impaired.

Jaundice. Jaundice results from decreased ability to conjugate and excrete bilirubin into the small intestines (Table 48.3). There is an overgrowth of connective tissue in the liver, which compresses the bile ducts and leads to an obstruction. This results in an increase in the bilirubin in the vascular system, and jaundice occurs. The jaundice may be minimal or severe, depending on the degree of liver damage.

Skin lesions. Various skin manifestations often occur with cirrhosis. *Spider angiomas* (telangiectasia or spider nevi) are small, dilated blood vessels with a bright red center point and spiderlike branches. They occur on the nose, cheeks, upper trunk, neck, and shoulders. *Palmar erythema* (a red area that blanches with pressure) occurs on the palms of the hands. Both lesions are due to an increase in circulating estrogen due to the damaged liver's inability to metabolize steroid hormones.

Hematologic problems. Hematologic problems include thrombocytopenia, leukopenia, anemia, and coagulation problems. We think thrombocytopenia, leukopenia, and anemia are caused by the splenomegaly that results from the backup of blood from the portal vein into the spleen (portal hypertension). Overactivity of the enlarged spleen results in increased removal of blood cells from circulation. Anemia can result from inadequate red blood cell (RBC) production and survival, poor diet, poor folic acid absorption, and bleeding from varices.

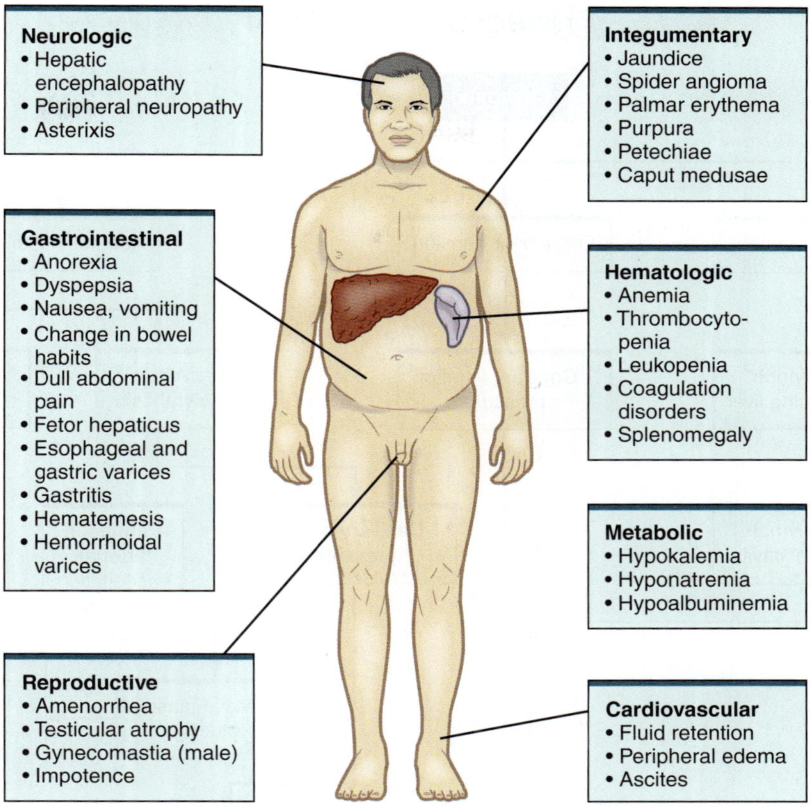

Fig. 48.6 Systemic manifestations of cirrhosis.

Coagulation problems result from the liver's inability to make prothrombin and other factors essential for blood clotting. Manifestations include nosebleeds, purpura, petechiae, easy bruising, gingival bleeding, and heavy menses.

Endocrine problems. The liver plays a vital role in the metabolism of hormones, such as estrogen and testosterone. In men with cirrhosis, gynecomastia, loss of axillary and pubic hair, testicular atrophy, and impotence with loss of libido may occur because of increased estrogen levels. Younger women with cirrhosis may develop amenorrhea. Older women may have vaginal bleeding. If the liver does not metabolize aldosterone properly, it can lead to hyperaldosteronism with sodium and water retention and potassium loss.

Peripheral neuropathy. Peripheral neuropathy is a common finding in alcoholic cirrhosis. It is probably due to a diet deficiency of thiamine, folic acid, and cobalamin. The neuropathy usually results in sensory and motor symptoms, but sensory symptoms may dominate.

Complications

Complications include portal hypertension, esophageal and gastric varices, peripheral edema, abdominal ascites, hepatic encephalopathy, and hepatorenal syndrome. Patients who are cirrhotic but have no obvious complications have *compensated cirrhosis.* Those who have 1 or more complications have *decompensated cirrhosis.*

Portal Hypertension and Esophageal and Gastric Varices

In patients with cirrhosis, the liver undergoes structural changes. These changes lead to obstruction of blood flow in and out of the liver. This results in increased pressure within the liver's circulatory system (portal hypertension). **Portal hypertension** is characterized by increased venous pressure in the portal circulation, splenomegaly, large collateral veins, ascites, and gastric and esophageal varices.[19]

To reduce pressure, the body develops alternate circulatory pathways, referred to as *collateral circulation.* The collateral channels often form in the lower esophagus, anterior abdominal wall, parietal peritoneum, and rectum. Varicosities (distended veins) develop in areas where the collateral and systemic circulations communicate, resulting in esophageal and gastric varices, *caput medusae* (ring of varices around the umbilicus), and hemorrhoids.

Esophageal varices are a complex of tortuous, enlarged veins at the lower end of the esophagus. **Gastric varices** are found in the upper part of the stomach. These varices are fragile and do not tolerate high pressure, so they can bleed easily. Large varices are more likely to bleed. Esophageal varices can cause variceal hemorrhages with a 5-year mortality of 20%. The patient may present with melena or hematemesis. Ruptured esophageal varices are the most life-threatening complication of cirrhosis and considered a medical emergency.

Peripheral Edema and Ascites

Peripheral edema occurs in the lower extremities and presacral area. Peripheral edema can occur before, concurrently with, or after ascites development. Edema results from decreased colloidal oncotic pressure from impaired liver synthesis of albumin and increased portacaval pressure from portal hypertension.

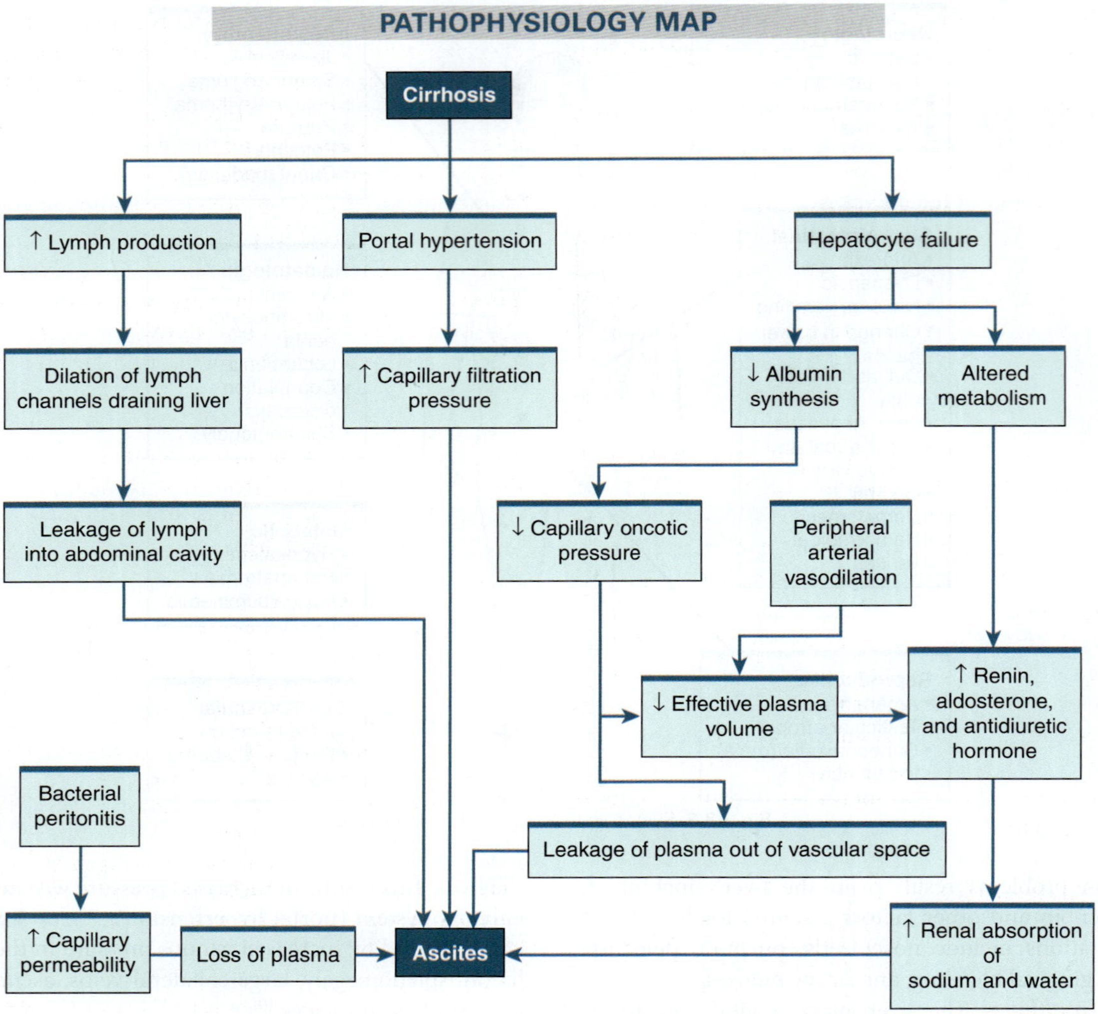

Fig. 48.7 Mechanisms for development of ascites. (Adapted from Huether SE, McCance KL: *Understanding pathophysiology,* ed 5, St Louis, 2012, Mosby.)

Ascites is the accumulation of serous fluid in the peritoneal or abdominal cavity. It is a common manifestation of cirrhosis. Several mechanisms lead to ascites. One mechanism occurs with portal hypertension, which causes proteins to shift from the blood vessels into the lymph space (Fig. 48.7). When the lymphatic system is unable to carry off the excess proteins and water, they leak into the peritoneal cavity. The osmotic pressure of the proteins pulls more fluid into the peritoneal cavity (Table 48.10).

A second mechanism of ascites formation is hypoalbuminemia resulting from the liver's decreased ability to synthesize albumin. Hypoalbuminemia results in decreased colloidal oncotic pressure.

A third mechanism of ascites is hyperaldosteronism, which occurs when the damaged hepatocytes metabolize aldosterone. The increased aldosterone level causes increased sodium reabsorption by the renal tubules. Sodium retention, combined with an increase in antidiuretic hormone in blood, leads to further water retention and edema. Edema decreases intravascular volume with decreased renal blood flow and glomerular filtration.

TABLE 48.10 Factors Involved in Ascites

Factor	Mechanism
↑ Hepatic lymph flow	Leaking of protein-rich lymph from surface of cirrhotic liver
Hyperaldosteronism	↑ Aldosterone secretion stimulated by ↓ renal blood flow ↓ Liver catabolism of circulating aldosterone
Impaired water excretion	↑ Antidiuretic hormone stimulated by ↓ renal blood flow
Portal hypertension	↑ Resistance of blood flow through liver
↓ Serum colloidal oncotic pressure	Impaired liver synthesis of albumin Loss of albumin into peritoneal cavity

Ascites is manifested by abdominal distention with weight gain (Fig. 48.8). If the ascites is severe, the increase in abdominal pressure from the fluid accumulation may cause eversion of the umbilicus. Abdominal striae with distended abdominal wall veins may be present. Patients may have signs of dehydration and a decrease in urine output. Hypokalemia is common. It is due to an excessive loss of potassium caused by hyperaldosteronism.

Low potassium levels can also result from diuretic therapy used to treat the ascites. Those with severe ascites are at risk for pleural effusion.

Because of decreased immune function with cirrhosis, patients with ascites are at risk for *spontaneous bacterial peritonitis* (SBP). SBP is a bacterial infection of the ascitic fluid. In SBP, bacteria normally found in the intestines move into the peritoneal space. The bacteria most often responsible for the infection are a gram-negative enteric pathogen, such as *Escherichia coli*. SBP is a common complication of hospitalized patients with cirrhosis and ascites. Worsening vasodilation contributes to the development of SBP.

Hepatic Encephalopathy

Hepatic encephalopathy is a neuropsychiatric manifestation of liver disease. The pathogenesis is multifactorial.[20] It includes the neurotoxic effects of ammonia, abnormal neurotransmission, astrocyte swelling, and inflammatory cytokines. A major source of ammonia is the bacterial and enzymatic deamination of amino acids in the intestines. The ammonia that results from deamination normally goes to the liver via the portal circulation where it is converted to urea. The kidneys then excrete urea. When blood is shunted past the liver via the collateral vessels or the liver is so damaged that it is unable to convert ammonia to urea, the ammonia levels in the systemic circulation increase. The ammonia crosses the blood-brain barrier and produces neurologic manifestations.

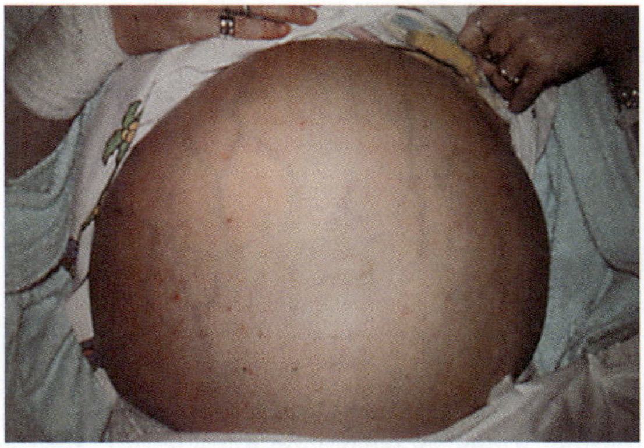

Fig. 48.8 Gross ascites. (From Butcher GP: *Gastroenterology: an illustrated colour text,* London, 2004, Churchill Livingstone.)

Factors that increase ammonia may precipitate hepatic encephalopathy (Table 48.11). Hepatic encephalopathy can occur after placement of a transjugular intrahepatic portosystemic shunt (TIPS). TIPS reduces portal hypertension by diverting blood flow around the liver.

Manifestations include neurologic and mental status changes. These include impaired consciousness and inappropriate behavior, ranging from sleep problems to trouble concentrating to deep coma. Changes may occur suddenly from an increase in ammonia in response to bleeding varices or infection or gradually as blood ammonia levels slowly increase. We often use a grading system to classify the stages of hepatic encephalopathy (Table 48.12).

A characteristic manifestation is **asterixis** (flapping tremors). This may take several forms, with the most common involving the arms and hands. When asked to hold the arms and hands stretched out, the patient is unable to hold this position and performs a series of rapid flexion and extension movements of the hands.

TABLE 48.11 Risk Factors for Hepatic Encephalopathy

Factor	Mechanism
Cerebral depressants (e.g., opioids)	↓ Metabolism by liver, causing ↑ drug levels and cerebral depression
Constipation	↑ Ammonia production from bacterial action on feces
Dehydration	Potentiates ammonia toxicity
GI bleeding	↑ Ammonia in GI tract
Hypokalemia	Potassium needed by brain to metabolize ammonia
Hypovolemia	↑ Ammonia because of hepatic hypoxia Impaired cerebral, liver, and renal function because of ↓ blood flow
Infection	↑ Metabolic rate and cerebral sensitivity to toxins
Metabolic alkalosis	Facilitate transport of ammonia across blood-brain barrier ↑ Renal production of ammonia
↑ Metabolism	↑ Workload of liver
Paracentesis	Loss of sodium and potassium ions ↓ Blood volume
Uremia (renal failure)	Retention of nitrogenous metabolites

TABLE 48.12 Grading Scale for Hepatic Encephalopathy

Grade	Level of Consciousness	Intellectual Function	Neurologic Findings
0	Normal to minimal change	Subtle to no change in personality, behavior, memory, concentration	Asterixis absent May have abnormal psychometric test
1	Lack of awareness, sleep disturbance	Short attention span, impaired computational skills, personality change, impaired short-term memory, mild confusion, depression	Incoordination, asterixis may be absent
2	Lethargy, drowsiness	Disoriented to time, inappropriate behavior, deficits in executive function	Asterixis, abnormal reflexes
3	Somnolent, arousable	Disoriented to time, loss of meaningful conversation, marked confusion, incomprehensible speech	Asterixis, abnormal reflexes
4	Not arousable, comatose	Absent	Decerebrate May be responsive to painful stimuli

Writing impairments include difficulty moving the pen or pencil from left to right and *apraxia* (inability to construct simple figures). Other signs include hyperventilation, hypothermia, twitching of the tongue, and grimacing and grasping reflexes. *Fetor hepaticus* (musty, sweet odor of the patient's breath) occurs in some patients. This odor is from the accumulation of digestive by-products that the liver is unable to degrade.

Hepatorenal Syndrome

Hepatorenal syndrome is a type of renal failure with azotemia, oliguria, and intractable ascites. In this syndrome, the kidneys have no structural problems. The cause is complex. The final common pathway is likely to be portal hypertension along with liver decompensation, resulting in splanchnic and systemic vasodilation and decreased arterial blood volume. As a result, renal vasoconstriction occurs, and renal failure follows. Liver transplantation can reverse renal failure. In the patient with cirrhosis, hepatorenal syndrome can follow diuretic therapy, GI bleeding, or paracentesis.

Diagnostic Studies

Patients with cirrhosis have abnormalities in most of their liver function tests. Enzyme levels, including alkaline phosphatase, AST, ALT, and γ-glutamyl transpeptidase (GGT), are initially high due to their release from inflamed liver cells. However, in end-stage liver disease, AST and ALT levels may be normal due to the death and loss of hepatocytes. Patients will also have low serum total protein and albumin, increased serum bilirubin (Table 48.3) and globulin levels, and prolonged PT time. Low cholesterol levels reflect changes in fat metabolism.

A liver biopsy can identify liver cell changes. It is the gold standard for a definitive diagnosis of cirrhosis. Although a liver ultrasound may be able to detect cirrhosis, it is not a reliable diagnostic test for cirrhosis. Ultrasound elastography (Fibroscan) is a noninvasive test used to quantify the degree of liver fibrosis.

Interprofessional Care

The goal of treatment is to slow the progression of cirrhosis and to prevent and treat any complications. Interprofessional care measures are listed in Table 48.13. Management of specific problems from cirrhosis is described next.

TABLE 48.13 Interprofessional Care

Cirrhosis

Diagnostic Assessment

- History and physical assessment
- Liver function tests
- Serum albumin
- Serum electrolytes
- PT time
- Complete blood count
- Liver biopsy (percutaneous needle)
- Liver ultrasound (e.g., FibroScan)
- Upper endoscopy (esophagogastroduodenoscopy)
- CT scan, MRI

Management

Conservative Therapy

- Rest
- B-complex vitamins
- Avoiding alcohol
- Minimizing or avoiding aspirin, acetaminophen, and NSAIDs

Ascites

- Low-sodium diet
- Diuretics
- Paracentesis (if needed)

Esophageal and Gastric Varices

- Endoscopic band ligation or sclerotherapy
- Balloon tamponade
- TIPS

Drug Therapy

- Nonselective β-blocker (e.g., propranolol)
- octreotide (Sandostatin)
- vasopressin

Hepatic Encephalopathy

Drug Therapy

- Antibiotics (rifaximin [Xifaxan])
- lactulose

Ascites

Management of ascites focuses on sodium restriction, diuretics, and fluid removal. Patients may need to limit sodium intake to 2 g/day. Very low-sodium intake can result in reduced nutrient intake and malnutrition. The patient is usually not on restricted fluids unless severe ascites develops. Monitor fluid and electrolyte balance. An albumin infusion may help maintain intravascular volume and adequate urine output by increasing plasma colloid oncotic pressure.

Diuretic therapy is an important part of management. Often a combination of drugs that work at multiple sites of the nephron is more effective than a single agent. Spironolactone (Aldactone) is an effective diuretic, even in patients with severe ascites. Spironolactone is an aldosterone antagonist and potassium sparing. A high-potency loop diuretic (e.g., furosemide) is often used with a potassium-sparing drug. Hyponatremia is a common problem in patients with cirrhosis on diuretics. It causes an increase in water excretion, resulting in an increase in serum sodium concentration.

A *paracentesis* is a sterile procedure in which a catheter is used to withdraw fluid from the abdominal cavity. This procedure can diagnose a medical condition or relieve pain, pressure, or problems breathing. In the patient with cirrhosis, this procedure is done for the patient with impaired respiration or abdominal discomfort caused by severe ascites who does not respond to diuretic therapy. It is only a temporary measure because the fluid tends to reaccumulate rapidly.

TIPS is used to treat ascites that does not respond to diuretics. A peritoneovenous shunt is a surgical procedure that provides continuous reinfusion of ascitic fluid into the venous system. It is rarely used due to the high rate of complications.

Esophageal and Gastric Varices

The main therapeutic goal for esophageal and gastric varices is to prevent bleeding and variceal rupture by reducing portal pressure.[21] The patient who has esophageal and/or gastric varices should avoid alcohol, aspirin, and nonsteroidal antiinflammatory drugs (NSAIDs).

All patients with cirrhosis should have an upper endoscopy (esophagogastroduodenoscopy [EGD]) to screen for varices. Patients with varices who are at risk for bleeding often receive a nonselective β-blocker (nadolol, propranolol) to reduce bleeding risk. β-Blockers decrease high portal pressure, which decreases the risk for rupture.[22]

When variceal bleeding occurs, the first step is to stabilize the patient and manage the airway. IV therapy is started and may include giving blood products. Care then moves toward stopping the bleeding, identifying the source, and applying interventions to prevent further bleeding. Management that involves a combination of drug therapy, and endoscopic therapy is more successful than either approach alone.

Drug therapy for bleeding varices may include the somatostatin analog octreotide (Sandostatin) or vasopressin. Both produce vasoconstriction of the splanchnic arterial bed, decrease portal blood flow, and decrease portal hypertension. Octreotide is used more often because it has fewer side effects than vasopressin.

At the time of endoscopy, band ligation or sclerotherapy of varices may be used to prevent rebleeding. Endoscopic variceal ligation (EVL, or "banding") is done by placing a small rubber band (elastic O-ring) around the base of the *varix* (enlarged vein). Sclerotherapy involves injecting a sclerosing solution into the swollen veins through a needle placed through the endoscope.

Balloon tamponade is an option when endoscopy does not control acute esophageal or gastric variceal hemorrhage. Balloon tamponade controls the bleeding by mechanical compression of the varices. Several types of tubes are available. The Sengstaken-Blakemore tube has 2 balloons, gastric and esophageal, with 3 lumens: 1 for the gastric balloon, 1 for the esophageal balloon, and 1 for gastric aspiration.

! SAFETY ALERT

Balloon Tamponade

- Label each lumen to avoid confusion.
- Secure the tube to prevent movement of the tube that could result in airway occlusion.
- Deflate balloons for 5 min every 8–12 hr per agency policy to prevent tissue necrosis.

Supportive measures during an acute variceal bleed include giving fresh frozen plasma and packed RBCs, vitamin K, and proton pump inhibitors (PPIs; e.g., pantoprazole). Lactulose and rifaximin (Xifaxan) may be given to prevent hepatic encephalopathy from breakdown of blood and the release of ammonia in the intestine. Antibiotics are given to prevent bacterial infection.

Because of the high incidence of recurrent bleeding with each bleeding episode, continued therapy is necessary. Long-term management of patients who have had an episode of bleeding includes nonselective β-blockers, repeated band ligation of the varices, and portosystemic shunts in patients who develop recurrent bleeding.

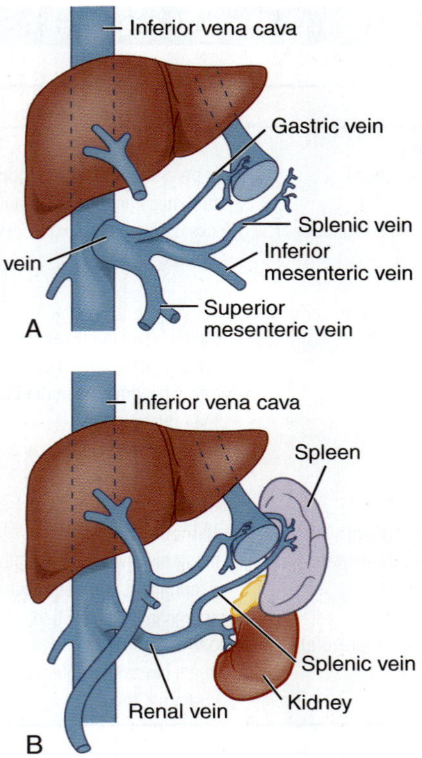

Fig. 48.9 Portosystemic shunts. (A) Portacaval shunt. The portal vein is anastomosed to the inferior vena cava, diverting blood from the portal vein to the systemic circulation. (B) Distal splenorenal shunt. The splenic vein is anastomosed to the renal vein. The portal venous flow stays intact while esophageal varices are selectively decompressed. (The short gastric veins are decompressed.) The spleen conducts blood from the high pressure of the esophageal and gastric varices to the low-pressure renal vein.

Shunting procedure. Nonsurgical and surgical methods of shunting blood away from the varices are available. Shunting procedures tend to be done more after a second major bleeding episode than during an initial bleeding episode. *TIPS* is a nonsurgical procedure in which a tract (shunt) between the systemic and portal venous systems is created to redirect portal blood flow. A catheter is placed in the jugular vein and then threaded through the superior and inferior vena cava to the hepatic vein. The wall of the hepatic vein is punctured, and the catheter is directed to the portal vein. Stents are positioned along the passageway, overlapping in the liver tissue and extending into both veins.

This procedure reduces portal venous pressure and decompresses the varices, thus controlling bleeding. TIPS does not interfere with a future liver transplantation. Limitations of TIPS include the increased risk for hepatic encephalopathy (toxin-containing blood bypasses the liver) and stenosis of the stent. TIPS is contraindicated in patients with severe hepatic encephalopathy, liver cancer, severe hepatorenal syndrome, and portal vein thrombosis.

Various surgical shunting procedures can decrease portal hypertension by diverting some of the portal blood flow while allowing adequate liver perfusion. Currently, the surgical shunts most often used are the portacaval shunt and the distal splenorenal shunt (Fig. 48.9).

TABLE 48.14 Drug Therapy

Cirrhosis

Drug	Mechanism of Action
Diuretics	
furosemide (Lasix)	Acts on distal tubule and loop of Henle to ↓ reabsorption of sodium and water
spironolactone (Aldactone)	Blocks actions of aldosterone, potassium sparing
Other Therapy	
lactulose	Acidifies feces in bowel and traps ammonia, causing its elimination in feces
magnesium sulfate	Corrects hypomagnesemia that may occur with liver dysfunction
nadolol propranolol	↓ Portal venous pressure and esophageal variceal bleeding
neomycin sulfate rifaximin (Xifaxan)	↓ Bacterial flora, thus reducing ammonia formation
octreotide (Sandostatin) vasopressin	Hemostasis and control of bleeding in esophageal and gastric varices, constricts splanchnic arterial bed
PPIs (e.g., pantoprazole)	↓ Gastric acidity
Vitamin K	Corrects clotting problems from decreased vitamin K levels

Hepatic Encephalopathy

The goal of management of hepatic encephalopathy is to reduce ammonia formation. Lactulose, a drug that traps ammonia in the gut, reduces ammonia formation in the intestines. We can give it orally, as an enema, or through a nasogastric (NG) tube. The drug's laxative effect expels the ammonia from the colon. Antibiotics, such as rifaximin, may be given, especially in patients who do not respond to lactulose. Regular and frequent bowel movements are necessary to minimize ammonia buildup, so use measures to prevent constipation.

Control of hepatic encephalopathy also involves treating risk factors (Table 48.10). This includes preventing and controlling GI bleeds and, in the case of a bleed, removing the blood promptly from the GI tract to decrease the protein accumulation in the gut.

Drug Therapy

There is no specific drug therapy for cirrhosis. However, several drugs are used to treat symptoms and complications of advanced liver disease (Table 48.14).

Nutrition Therapy

The diet for the patient who has cirrhosis without complications is high in calories (3000 cal/day). It is high in carbohydrate content with moderate to low levels of fat.

A patient with alcoholic cirrhosis often has protein-calorie malnutrition. Oral supplements containing protein from branched-chain amino acids that are metabolized by the muscles may be needed. These supplements provide protein that the liver can more easily metabolize. Parenteral nutrition (PN) or EN are given for severe malnutrition (see Chapter 44).

The patient with ascites and edema receives a low-sodium diet. The degree of sodium restriction depends on the patient's condition.

TABLE 48.15 NURSING ASSESSMENT

Cirrhosis

Subjective Data

Important Health Information

Health history: Viral, toxic, or idiopathic hepatitis. Alcohol use, metabolic syndrome, chronic biliary obstruction and infection, severe right-sided heart failure

Medications: Adverse reaction to any medication. Use of anticoagulants, aspirin, NSAIDs, acetaminophen

Functional Health Patterns

Health perception–health management: Chronic alcohol use. Weakness, fatigue

Nutritional-metabolic: Anorexia, weight loss, dyspepsia, nausea and vomiting, gingival bleeding. Dry, yellow skin, bruising

Elimination: Dark urine, decreased urine output, light-colored or black stools, flatulence, change in bowel habits.

Cognitive-perceptual: Dull, RUQ or epigastric pain. Numbness, tingling of extremities. Itching

Sexuality-reproductive: Impotence, amenorrhea

Objective Data

General

Fever, cachexia, wasting of extremities

GI

Abdominal distention, ascites, distended abdominal wall veins, palpable liver and spleen, foul breath. Hematemesis. Black, tarry stools. Hemorrhoids

Neurologic

Altered mentation, asterixis

Reproductive

Gynecomastia, testicular atrophy, and impotence (men); loss of libido (men and women); amenorrhea or heavy menses (women)

Respiratory

Shallow, rapid respirations. Nosebleeds

Skin

Icteric sclera, jaundice, petechiae, bruising, spider angiomas, palmar erythema, alopecia, loss of axillary and pubic hair, peripheral edema

Possible Diagnostic Findings

Anemia, thrombocytopenia; leukopenia. ↓ Serum albumin, potassium. Abnormal liver function studies. ↑ INR, ↓ platelets, ↑ ammonia, ↑ bilirubin levels. Abnormal abdominal ultrasound, CT, or MRI

Teach the patient and caregiver about the degree of restriction. Review which foods are high in sodium. Teach the patient to read labels for sodium content (see Fig. 44.5). Offer suggestions about how to make the diet more palatable. Seasonings, like garlic, parsley, onion, lemon juice, and spices may make food more appetizing. Collaborate with a dietitian about dietary strategies.

NURSING MANAGEMENT: CIRRHOSIS

Assessment

Subjective and objective data that you should obtain from a person with cirrhosis are outlined in Table 48.15.

Clinical Problems

Clinical problems for the patient with cirrhosis may include:

- Nutritionally compromised
- Ineffective tissue perfusion
- Activity intolerance
- Fluid imbalance

Additional information on clinical problems and interventions for the patient with cirrhosis is presented in eNursing Care Plan 48.2 available on the website for this chapter.

Planning

The overall goals are that the patient with cirrhosis will (1) have relief of discomfort, (2) have minimal to no complications, and (3) return to as normal a lifestyle as possible.

Implementation

Health Promotion

Common risk factors include alcohol use, malnutrition, viral hepatitis, biliary obstruction, obesity, and right-sided heart failure. Prevention and early treatment of cirrhosis focus on reducing or eliminating these risk factors. Urge patients to abstain from alcohol. Encourage those with chronic alcohol use to enroll in support programs that help patients maintain sobriety. The treatment of alcohol use is discussed in Chapter 11.

Adequate nutrition, especially for the person who uses alcohol and other people at risk for cirrhosis, is essential to promote normal liver regeneration. Identify and treat acute hepatitis early so that it does not progress to chronic hepatitis and cirrhosis.

Acute Care

Care for the patient with cirrhosis focuses on conserving the patient's strength while maintaining muscle strength and tone. When the patient needs complete bed rest, implement measures to prevent pneumonia, thromboembolic problems, and pressure injuries. Modify the activity and rest schedule according to signs of improvement (e.g., decreasing jaundice, improved liver function studies).

Anorexia, nausea and vomiting, pressure from ascites, and poor eating habits interfere with adequate nutrient intake. Oral hygiene before meals may improve the patient's taste sensation. Make between-meal snacks available so that the patient can eat them at times when food is best tolerated. Offer preferred foods whenever possible. Explain the reason for any dietary restrictions to the patient and caregiver.

Assess the patient's physical status. Is jaundice present? Where is it seen—sclera, skin, hard palate? What is the progression of jaundice? If the pruritis accompanies jaundice, use measures to relieve itching. Cholestyramine or hydroxyzine (Atarax) may help. Cholestyramine is a resin that binds bile salts in the intestine, increasing their excretion in the feces. It comes in powder form that you mix with milk or juice. Side effects include nausea, vomiting, diarrhea or constipation, and skin reactions. It may bind with other medications, so check drug-to-drug interactions. Other measures to relieve itching include baking soda or moisturizing bath oils (Alpha Keri), lotions containing calamine, antihistamines, soft or old linens, and control of the temperature (not too hot and not too cold). Keep the patient's nails short and clean. Teach patients to rub with their knuckles rather than scratch with their nails when they cannot resist scratching.

Note the color of urine and stools and assess for improvement or normalization of color. When jaundice is present, the urine is often dark brown, and the stool is gray or tan.

Edema and ascites require your assessment and intervention. Accurate calculation and recording of intake and output, daily weights, and measurements of extremities and abdominal girth help in the ongoing assessment of the location and extent of the edema. Mark the abdomen with a permanent marker so that you measure the girth at the same location each time.

Provide appropriate care for the patient having a paracentesis (Table 48.16).

TABLE 48.16 NURSING MANAGEMENT

Care of the Patient Undergoing Paracentesis

Preprocedure

- Have the patient void or insert an indwelling catheter.
- Obtain baseline vital signs and pulse oximetry. Weigh patient, inspect and palpate abdomen, and assess abdominal girth. Assess bladder for distention and determine last voiding.
- Assess baseline laboratory values (e.g., CBC, electrolytes, coagulation studies).
- Give any sedation or analgesia, if ordered.
- Teach patient to remain immobile during the procedure.
- Help the patient to a high-Fowler (sitting) position with feet on the floor.

Postprocedure

- Perform assessment and compare with baseline: vital signs, pulse oximetry, abdominal girth, abdominal pain. Note any signs of hypovolemia.
- Have the patient sit on the side of the bed or place in high-Fowler's position.
- Label and send the fluid for laboratory analysis.
- Check the dressing for bleeding and/or leakage of ascitic fluid.
- Give IV fluid and/or albumin as ordered.
- Measure any drainage and describe the collected fluid.
- Reweigh the patient and monitor intake and output.
- Maintain bedrest per agency protocol.

CHECK YOUR PRACTICE

You are caring for a patient with advanced cirrhosis and ascites. The patient tells you that he is having increased shortness of breath.

- What is your concern?
- What would you do?

Dyspnea is a frequent problem for the patient with severe ascites. A semi-Fowler's or Fowler's position allows for maximal respiratory efficiency. Use pillows to support the arms and chest to increase the patient's comfort and ability to breathe. Monitor the patient's O_2 level and vital signs.

Meticulous skin care is essential because the edematous tissues are prone to break down. Use an alternating-air pressure mattress or other special mattress. Adhere to a turning schedule (minimum of every 2 hours). Support the abdomen with pillows. If the abdomen is taut, cleanse it gently. The patient will tend to avoid moving because of abdominal discomfort and dyspnea. Range-of-motion exercises are helpful. Implement measures such as coughing and deep breathing to prevent respiratory problems. The lower extremities may be elevated. If scrotal edema is present, a scrotal support gives some comfort.

When the patient is taking diuretics, monitor serum sodium, potassium, chloride, and bicarbonate levels. Monitor renal function (blood urea nitrogen [BUN], serum creatinine) routinely and with any change in the diuretic dosage. Observe for signs of fluid and electrolyte imbalance, especially hypokalemia. Dysrhythmias, hypotension, tachycardia, and generalized muscle weakness may occur with hypokalemia. Muscle cramping, weakness, lethargy, and confusion may be present with hyponatremia from water excess.

Observe for and provide nursing care for any hematologic problems. These include bleeding tendencies, anemia, and increased susceptibility to infection.

Assess the patient's response to altered body image resulting from jaundice, spider angiomas, palmar erythema, ascites, and gynecomastia. The patient may have anxiety and embarrassment about these changes. Explain these phenomena and be a supportive listener. Provide nursing care with concern and encouragement to help the patient maintain their self-esteem.

Bleeding varices. If the patient has esophageal or gastric varices, observe for any signs of bleeding from the varices, such as hematemesis and melena. If hematemesis occurs, assess the patient for bleeding and call the HCP. Be ready to transfer the patient to the endoscopy suite and/or assist with equipment to control the bleeding. Maintain the patient's airway. Patients with bleeding varices are usually admitted to the intensive care unit (ICU).

Balloon tamponade is an option for patients who have bleeding that is unresponsive to band ligation or sclerotherapy. When balloon tamponade is used, explain to the patient and caregiver the use of the tube and how the balloon is inserted. Check the balloons for patency. It is usually the HCP's responsibility to insert the tube by either the nose or mouth. Then, the gastric balloon is inflated with 250 mL of air, and the tube is retracted until resistance (lower esophageal sphincter) is felt. The tube is secured by placing a piece of sponge or foam rubber at the nostrils (nasal cuff). For continued bleeding, the esophageal balloon is then inflated. A sphygmomanometer is used to measure and maintain the desired pressure at 20 to 40 mm Hg. An x-ray confirms the balloon's position.

Monitor for complications of rupture or erosion of the esophagus, regurgitation and aspiration of gastric contents, and occlusion of the airway by the balloon. If the gastric balloon breaks or deflates, the esophageal balloon will slip upward, obstructing the airway and causing asphyxiation. If this happens, cut the tube or deflate the esophageal balloon. Keep scissors at the bedside. Minimize regurgitation by oral and pharyngeal suctioning and keeping the patient in a semi-Fowler's position.

The patient is unable to swallow saliva because the inflated esophageal balloon occludes the esophagus. Encourage the patient to expectorate. Provide an emesis basin and tissues. Frequent oral and nasal care offers relief from the taste of blood and irritation from mouth breathing.

Hepatic encephalopathy. Nursing care focuses on maintaining a safe environment, sustaining life, and assisting with measures to reduce the formation of ammonia. Patients with hepatic encephalopathy may be confused and at risk for falls or other injuries. Assess the patient's level of responsiveness (e.g., reflexes, pupillary reactions, orientation). Note any sensory and motor problems (e.g., hyperreflexia, asterixis, motor coordination). Assess for fluid, electrolyte, and acid-base imbalances. Evaluate the response to treatment measures.

Assess neurologic status at least every 2 hours. Include an exact description of the patient's behavior. Plan your care of the patient based on the severity of the encephalopathy. In patients with altered levels of consciousness or whose airway may become compromised, have emergency equipment readily available. Any GI bleeding may worsen encephalopathy. Institute measures to prevent falls or injuries.

Control factors known to precipitate encephalopathy as much as possible. Measures to minimize constipation are important to reduce ammonia production. Give drugs, laxatives, and enemas as ordered. Encourage fluids, if not contraindicated. Assess the patient taking lactulose for diarrhea and excessive fluid and electrolyte losses.

◆ Ambulatory Care

The patient with cirrhosis may be faced with a prolonged course and the chance of life-threatening problems and complications. The patient and caregiver need to understand the importance of continual health care and medical supervision. Supportive measures include proper diet, rest, avoiding potentially hepatotoxic drugs, such as acetaminophen in high doses, and abstaining from alcohol. Abstinence from alcohol is important and results in improvement in most patients. However, some patients find abstinence difficult and need emotional support. Explore your own attitude toward the patient whose cirrhosis is from chronic alcohol use (Box 48.3). Always provide care without being condescending or judgmental. Treat patients with respect and concern for their well-being (see Chapter 11).

Cirrhosis is a chronic disease. People can live many years with symptoms and complications from cirrhosis. Cirrhosis affects all aspects of the patient's life. They may need to make major lifestyle changes, especially if chronic alcohol use is the primary cause. Provide information about community support programs, such as Alcoholics Anonymous, for help with chronic alcohol use.

Teach the patient and caregiver about complications and when to seek medical attention (Table 48.17). Include instructions about adequate rest periods, how to detect early signs of complications, skin care, drug therapy side effects, observation for bleeding, and protection from infection.

Referral to a community or home health nurse may help ensure patient adherence to prescribed therapy. Home care for the patient with cirrhosis focuses on helping the patient with activities of daily living while maintaining the highest level of wellness possible.

◆ Evaluation

Expected outcomes are that the patient with cirrhosis will:

- Maintain food and fluid intake adequate to meet nutrient needs

BOX 48.3 ETHICAL/LEGAL DILEMMAS

Rationing

Situation

T.H., a 43-year-old female patient with cirrhosis, is frequently admitted to the hospital. She has been told that her continued alcohol use will inevitably lead to her death. She now has GI bleeding and needs blood transfusions. She has a rare blood type that is hard to match. Should you ask for an ethics consult?

Ethical/Legal Points for Consideration

- *Rationing,* or the controlled distribution of scarce resources, is a difficult ethical problem. The needs of an individual patient or group of patients are weighed against the needs of many patients, who may have a greater chance of recovery, and the availability of resources.
- Health interests can supersede the interests or rights of a person. For example, in anticipation of an anthrax attack, the government could confiscate all relevant antibiotics and restrict their use to treat the disease.
- Two individual rights that must be considered are the (1) constitutional right to privacy and (2) right to consent to or refuse medical procedures and therapy.
- The competent adult is the only person who may consent to or refuse treatment for their health care problems.
- If T.H. consents to a blood transfusion, an intervening party may be allowed to refuse that treatment only given substantial intervening circumstances and not as a threat to compel adherent future behavior.
- If involved parties cannot reach an agreement, legal intervention by way of a court order may become necessary.

Discussion Questions

1. Do you think patients with diseases that have a behavioral component, like substance use, deserve aggressive treatment?
2. Would you request an ethics consult in T.H.'s case?

TABLE 48.17 PATIENT & CAREGIVER TEACHING

Cirrhosis

When teaching the patient and caregiver about management of cirrhosis, do the following:

1. Explain that cirrhosis is a chronic illness and requires continual health care.
2. Teach the symptoms of complications and when to seek medical attention to enable prompt treatment.
3. Teach the patient to avoid potentially hepatotoxic over-the-counter drugs, because the diseased liver is unable to metabolize them.
4. Encourage abstinence from alcohol. Continued use increases the rate of liver disease progression and risk for liver complications.
5. Teach the patient with esophageal or gastric varices to avoid aspirin and NSAIDs to prevent bleeding.
6. Teach the patient with portal hypertension and varices that straining at stool, coughing, sneezing, and retching and vomiting may increase the risk for variceal hemorrhage.

- Maintain skin integrity with relief of edema and itching
- Have normal fluid and electrolyte balance
- Acknowledge and get treatment for a substance use problem

ACUTE LIVER FAILURE

Acute liver failure, or *fulminant hepatic failure,* is a potentially life-threatening clinical syndrome.[22] It is characterized by a rapid onset of severe liver dysfunction in someone with no history of liver disease. It is often accompanied by hepatic encephalopathy.

The most common cause is drugs, usually acetaminophen. Other drugs that can cause acute liver failure include isoniazid, sulfa-containing drugs, and anticonvulsants. Herbal and dietary supplements can also cause acute liver failure. Drugs can cause hepatocyte damage by disrupting essential intracellular processes or causing an accumulation of toxic metabolic products. Other causes can include autoimmune hepatitis, viral hepatitis, especially HBV. HAV is a less common cause.

Outcomes depend on the cause. Cerebral edema, cerebellar herniation, and brainstem compression are the most common causes of death. Liver transplantation has a significant survival benefit in patients with a low probability of spontaneous recovery.

Clinical Manifestations and Diagnostic Studies

Manifestations include jaundice, coagulation problems, and encephalopathy. Changes in cognitive function are often the first clinical sign. Patients are susceptible to a wide variety of complications. These include cerebral edema, renal failure, hypoglycemia, metabolic acidosis, sepsis, and multiorgan failure.

Serum bilirubin is high. The PT time is prolonged. Liver enzyme levels (AST, ALT) are often markedly increased. Other laboratory tests include blood chemistries (especially glucose, since hypoglycemia may be present and need correction), complete blood count (CBC), acetaminophen level, screening for other drugs and toxins, viral hepatitis serology (especially HAV and HBV), serum ceruloplasmin (enzyme synthesized in liver) and α_1-antitrypsin levels, iron levels, ammonia levels, and autoantibodies (ANAs and ASMAs).

CT or MRI can provide information about the liver size and contour, presence of ascites or tumors, and patency of the blood vessels.

Interprofessional and Nursing Care

Acute liver failure may progress rapidly, with hour-by-hour changes in consciousness. The patient is usually transferred to the ICU once the diagnosis is made. Planning for transfer to a transplant center should begin in patients with grade 1 or 2 encephalopathy because they may worsen rapidly. Early transfer is important because the risks involved with patient transport may increase or even prevent transfer if stage 3 or 4 encephalopathy develops (Table 48.12).

Renal failure is a frequent complication. It may be due to dehydration, hepatorenal syndrome, or acute tubular necrosis. The frequency of renal failure is greater with acetaminophen overdose or other toxins with which direct renal toxicity occurs. Although few patients die of renal failure alone, it often increases the mortality risk and may worsen the prognosis. Protect renal function by maintaining adequate fluid balance, avoiding nephrotoxic agents (e.g., aminoglycosides, NSAIDs), and promptly identifying and treating infection.

Monitoring and management of hemodynamic and renal function, as well as glucose, electrolytes, and acid-base status, are critical. Conduct frequent neurologic evaluations for signs of increased intracranial pressure. Position the patient with the head elevated at 30 degrees. Avoid excessive patient stimulation. Maneuvers that cause straining or Valsalva-like movements may increase intracranial pressure (ICP). See more about ICP monitoring in Chapter 61.

Assess the patient regularly for baseline level of consciousness and orientation. Report any changes to the HCP. Avoid the use of any sedatives due to their effects on mental status. The effects can be confused with worsening encephalopathy. Use only minimal doses of benzodiazepines due to their delayed metabolism by the failing liver. Closely observe the patient to prevent injuries and pad bedrails to avoid injury from possible seizures. Monitor intake and output for renal function. Provide good skin and oral care to avoid breakdown and infection.

Changes in level of consciousness may compromise oral intake. Many patients receive vitamin supplementation. Other factors, such as coagulation problems, may influence whether we start EN. An NG tube may be irritating to the nasal and esophageal mucosa and cause bleeding.

LIVER CANCER

Primary liver cancer starts in the liver. The most common types of liver cancer are hepatocellular carcinoma (HCC) and intrahepatic cholangiocarcinoma (bile duct cancer). In 2018, there were about 42,220 cases of liver cancer with 30,200 liver cancer deaths in the United States.[23] Worldwide liver cancer is the 5th most common cancer and 2nd most common cause of cancer death.

Liver cancer is the most common cause of death in patients with cirrhosis. Cirrhosis caused by HCV is the most common cause of HCC in the United States, followed by NAFLD. About 2% of patients with cirrhosis develop liver cancer each year.

In primary liver cancer, lesions may be singular or numerous and nodular or diffusely spread over the entire liver. Some tumors infiltrate other organs, such as the gallbladder, or move into the peritoneum or the diaphragm. Primary liver cancer often metastasizes to the lung.

Metastatic cancer in the liver is more common than primary liver cancer (Fig. 48.10). The liver is a common site of metastatic growth because of its high rate of blood flow and extensive capillary network. Cancer cells in other parts of the body are often carried to the liver via the portal circulation.

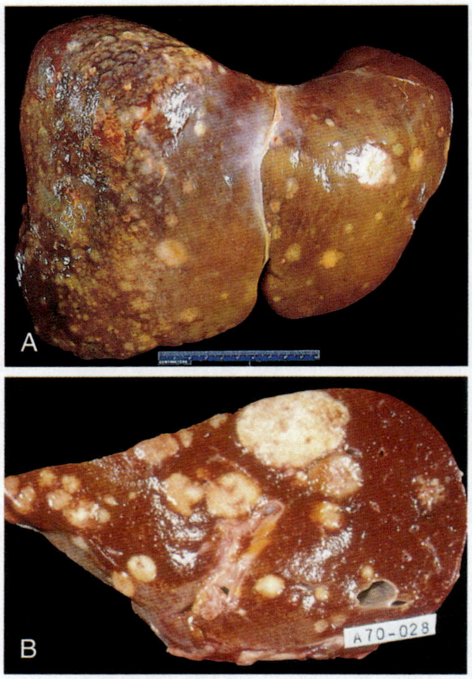

Fig. 48.10 Multiple hepatic metastases from a primary colon cancer. (A) Gross specimen showing outside of liver. (B) Liver section showing metastatic lesions. (*A*, From Kumar V, Abbas AK, Fausto N: *Robbins and Cotran pathologic basis of disease,* ed 7, Philadelphia, 2005, Saunders. *B*, From Kumar V, Abbas AK, Aster JC, et al.: *Robbins and Cotran pathologic basis of disease,* ed 8, Philadelphia, 2010, Saunders.)

Clinical Manifestations and Diagnostic Studies

The manifestations of early liver cancer can be absent or subtle. They are often a result of the underlying cirrhosis rather than from the actual liver tumor(s). The patient may present with hepatomegaly, splenomegaly, fatigue, peripheral edema, ascites, and other complications from portal hypertension. In late stages, patients will often have fever/chills, jaundice, anorexia, weight loss, palpable mass, and RUQ pain.

Diagnostic and screening tests for liver cancer are ultrasound, CT, and MRI. Recent advancements in MRI scanning have allowed for accurate diagnosis and staging of liver cancers without the need for a percutaneous biopsy. Sometimes, a biopsy is only done when diagnostic imaging studies are inconclusive or tissue is needed to guide treatment. Risks of a biopsy include bleeding and potential tumor cell seeding along the needle tract. Serum α-fetoprotein (AFP) levels combined with ultrasound have a high rate of detection of early-stage HCC.

Interprofessional and Nursing Care

Prevention of liver cancer focuses on identifying and treating chronic HBV and HCV infections. Treatment of chronic alcohol use may lower the risk for liver cancer. Screening for at-risk patients (e.g., those with cirrhosis) usually involves a combination of serum AFP and CT, MRI, or ultrasound imaging of the liver.

Treatment depends on the stage of cancer: number, size, and location of tumors; involvement of any blood vessels; patient age and overall health; and extent of underlying liver disease. Liver resection (partial hepatectomy) offers the best chance for a cure. However, only about 15% of people have enough healthy liver tissue for this to be an option. The underlying cirrhosis and portal hypertension often compromise liver function and may cause liver failure after surgery. Many patients are diagnosed at an advanced stage of cancer when surgery is not an option. For those patients who have early-stage liver cancer and impaired liver function, liver transplantation offers a good prognosis.

Nonsurgical therapies include percutaneous ablation, chemoembolization, radioembolization, and systemic therapies. In ablation, a thin needle is inserted into the core of the tumor. Then, various substances can be injected (ethanol, acetic acid) and the temperature of the probe (radiofrequency, microwave, cryotherapy) can be altered to destroy the tumor. This procedure is done percutaneously, laparoscopically, or through an open incision. It is limited by the number, size, and location of liver tumors. It is usually offered to patients with early-stage liver cancer. Complications are uncommon but include infection, bleeding, dysrhythmias, and skin burn.

In patients with multinodular HCC or intermediate-stage liver cancer, embolization of the tumors is another intervention. There are 2 usual options: transarterial chemoembolization (TACE) or transarterial radioembolization (TARE). TACE and TARE are minimally invasive procedures done by interventional radiologists. A catheter is placed via the femoral artery or radial artery and advanced to the arterial blood supply of the tumors. Either a chemotherapy drug (TACE) or radioactive beads (TARE) along with embolizing agents are then injected into the arteries of the tumor(s) region. TACE works by shutting off the blood supply to the tumors and exposing the tumor cells to the chemotherapy drug. TARE destroys the tumor(s) by slowly releasing radioactive material directly to the site of the tumor. It can take up to 3 months for complete results.

Systemic therapy options include chemotherapy and immune-based therapy, such as monoclonal antibodies, tyrosine kinase inhibitors, and immune checkpoint inhibitors (see Table 16.13).[24] These drugs have the potential to slow tumor progression and prolong life. Nursing care focuses on keeping the patient as comfortable as possible. Since these patients have the same problems as any patient with advanced liver disease, the interventions discussed for cirrhosis apply to these patients.

Although the prognosis for patients with liver cancer is poor, it is improving with early screening and surveillance programs for those with chronic hepatitis and/or cirrhosis. The cancer often progresses rapidly, with patients having complications from the advancing cancer and declining liver function. Without treatment, death may occur within 6 to 12 months, most often from hepatic encephalopathy or massive blood loss from GI bleeding.

LIVER TRANSPLANTATION

Liver transplantation has become an option for many people with end-stage liver disease or localized HCC. Liver disease related to errors of metabolism, specifically NAFLD, is the leading reason for liver transplantation followed by chronic viral hepatitis.[25] Other reasons include congenital biliary abnormalities (biliary atresia), inborn errors of metabolism, sclerosing cholangitis, acute liver failure, and chronic end-stage liver disease. In 2018, 11,514 patients were listed for a liver transplant in the United States with 8250 patients receiving a transplant.

Liver transplant candidates must go through a rigorous transplant evaluation prior to being placed on the transplant list. This is done to confirm the diagnosis of end-stage liver disease and to assess for other co-morbid conditions (e.g., cardiovascular disease, chronic kidney disease) that may affect the patient's surgical outcome. The evaluation includes physical assessment, laboratory tests (CBC, liver function tests), cardiac and pulmonary evaluations, endoscopy, CT scan, and psychologic testing. Potential recipients receive counseling about cigarette smoking and alcohol abstinence. Contraindications include severe extrahepatic disease, advanced HCC or other cancer, ongoing drug or chronic alcohol use, and inability to understand or adhere with the rigorous posttransplant care.

Liver transplantation is done using both deceased (cadaver) and live donor livers. The live donor liver transplant was first developed for children whose parents wanted to serve as donors. Today, some liver transplant centers are performing live liver transplant procedures for adults. In this procedure, the living person donates a part of their liver to another. However, live liver donation poses potential risks to the donor, including biliary problems, hepatic artery thrombosis, wound infection, postoperative ileus, and pneumothorax.

Because of the limited number of donor livers, when a liver becomes available for transplant, it may be divided into 2 parts (split liver transplant) and implanted into 2 recipients. The decision to use a split donor liver is based on the donor's size and health. The recipients of the split liver generally are smaller than the donor. The success rate of split liver transplantation is lower than that of whole organ transplantation.

Postoperative complications include bleeding, infection, and rejection. However, the liver is subject to a less aggressive immunologic attack than other organs, like the kidneys. Transplants and immunosuppressive therapy are discussed in Chapter 14.

Immunosuppressive therapy generally involves a combination of corticosteroids, a calcineurin inhibitor (cyclosporine or tacrolimus), and an antiproliferative agent (e.g., azathioprine). Tacrolimus is superior to cyclosporine in liver transplants. Standard immunosuppressive regimens often change over the course of the recipient's life. Corticosteroid withdrawal is relatively safe to do in liver transplant recipients.

About 80% of patients live more than 5 years after liver transplant. Long-term survival depends on the cause of liver failure (e.g., localized HCC, chronic HBV or HCV, biliary disease). Patients who have liver disease from HBV or HCV often have reinfection of the transplanted liver. For patients with HBV, treatment after surgery with IV HBIG and a nucleoside or nucleotide analog (used to treat HBV infection) has reduced the rates of reinfection of the transplanted liver. For patients with HCV, treatment with the new DAAs that can cure HCV infection has provided the opportunity to use HCV-positive liver grafts. The need for liver transplant may decrease in the HCV population. Research is ongoing to decide if DAAs should be started before or after transplant.

The patient who had a liver transplant needs highly skilled nursing care, either in an ICU or other specialized unit. After surgery, we monitor electrolyte levels, neurologic status, and urine output and note signs of bleeding, infection, and rejection. Common respiratory problems are pneumonia, atelectasis, and pleural effusions. To prevent these complications, encourage the patient to cough, deep breathe, use incentive spirometry, and frequently reposition. Measure the drainage from the Jackson–Pratt drain, NG tube, and T tube and note the color and consistency of the drainage at regular intervals.

The first 2 months after surgery are critical for monitoring for infection. Causes of infection can be viral, fungal, or bacterial. Fever may be the only sign of infection. Adhering to

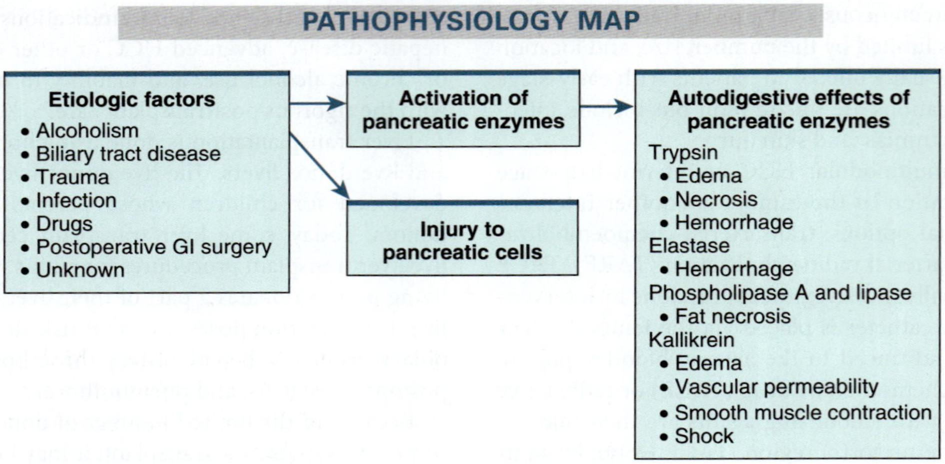

Fig. 48.11 Pathogenic process of acute pancreatitis.

the medication plan can be hard, especially in the beginning. Emotional support and teaching for the patient and caregiver are essential to the success of the patient with a liver transplant.

Gerontologic Considerations: Liver Disease in the Older Adult

The incidence of liver disease increases with age. The liver's size and metabolic breakdown of drugs decrease, and hepatobiliary function changes. The liver has a decreased capacity to respond to injury. This especially applies to regeneration after injury. Transplanted livers take longer to regenerate in the older adult.

Older adults are particularly vulnerable to DILI. This is due to several factors, including the increased use of multiple prescription and OTC drugs, which can lead to drug interactions and potential drug toxicity. Age-related decreases in liver function result in decreased drug metabolism and a decreased ability to recover from drug-induced injury.

A growing number of older adults have chronic HCV and the resulting cirrhosis. We may find antibodies to HCV and high liver enzymes during a routine health assessment in asymptomatic patients.

Lifetime health behaviors may influence the development of chronic liver disease in the older adult. Chronic alcohol use and obesity can contribute to cirrhosis, fatty liver inflammation (NASH), and liver failure. Because of many older adults' concomitant cardiovascular and lung diseases and possible anticoagulant therapy, variceal bleeding can cause significant morbidity and mortality and needs immediate medical intervention. In the older adult with liver disease, we sometimes misdiagnose hepatic encephalopathy as dementia.

Because older adults tend to have more comorbid conditions, transplantation may have more risks for complications. Therefore, older adults may not be good candidates for liver transplants.

PANCREAS PROBLEMS

ACUTE PANCREATITIS

Acute pancreatitis is an acute inflammation of the pancreas.[26] Spillage of pancreatic enzymes into surrounding pancreatic tissue causes autodigestion and severe pain. The degree of inflammation varies from mild edema to severe hemorrhagic necrosis.

Etiology and Pathophysiology

Many factors can cause injury to the pancreas. In the United States, the most common cause is gallbladder disease (gallstones), which is more common in women. The second most common cause is chronic alcohol use. This is more common in men.

Other less common causes include drug reactions, pancreatic cancer, and hypertriglyceridemia (serum levels over 1000 mg/dL). Biliary sludge and microlithiasis, a mix of cholesterol crystals and calcium salts, can be present in patients with acute pancreatitis.

The most common pathogenic mechanism in acute pancreatitis is autodigestion of the pancreas (Fig. 48.11). The causative factors injure pancreatic cells or activate the pancreatic enzymes in the pancreas rather than in the intestine. This may be due to reflux of bile acids into the pancreatic ducts through an open or distended sphincter of Oddi. This reflux may be caused by blockage created by gallstones. Obstruction of pancreatic ducts results in pancreatic ischemia.

The exact mechanism by which chronic alcohol use predisposes a person to pancreatitis is not known. We think that alcohol increases the production of digestive enzymes in the pancreas.

The pathophysiologic involvement of acute pancreatitis is either *mild pancreatitis* (*edematous* or *interstitial pancreatitis*) or *severe pancreatitis* (*necrotizing pancreatitis*) (Fig. 48.12). In severe pancreatitis, about half the patients have permanent decreases in pancreatic endocrine and exocrine function. Patients with severe pancreatitis are at high risk for developing pancreatic necrosis, organ failure, and septic complications. This results in an overall fatality rate of 9%.

Clinical Manifestations

Abdominal pain is the main manifestation. The pain is due to distention of the pancreas, peritoneal irritation, and biliary tract obstruction. It is usually in the left upper quadrant but may be

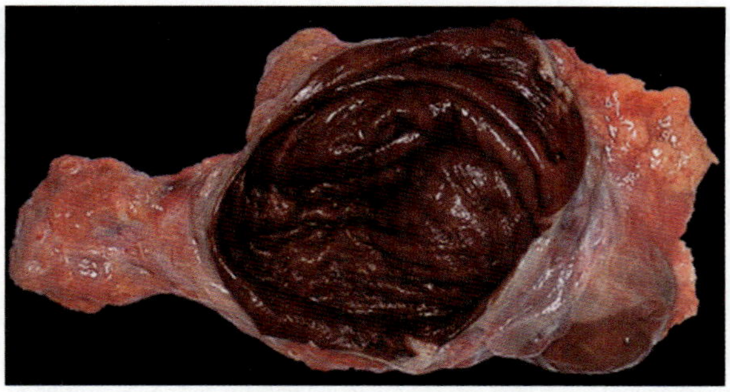

Fig. 48.12 Pancreatitis with large pseudocyst. (From Connolly A, Finkbeiner W, Ursell P, et al.: *Atlas of gross autopsy pathology*, ed 3, Philadelphia, 2016, Elsevier.)

mid-epigastric. It often radiates to the back due to the retroperitoneal location of the pancreas. The pain has a sudden onset. It is described as severe, deep, piercing, and continuous or steady. Eating worsens the pain. Pain is not relieved by vomiting and may be accompanied by flushing, cyanosis, and dyspnea. It often starts when the patient is recumbent. The patient may assume various positions involving flexion of the spine to try to relieve the severe pain.

Other manifestations include nausea and vomiting, low-grade fever, leukocytosis, hypotension, tachycardia, and jaundice. Abdominal tenderness with muscle guarding is common.

Bowel sounds may be decreased or absent. Paralytic ileus may occur and causes marked abdominal distention. The lungs are often involved with crackles present. Intravascular damage from circulating trypsin (a proteolytic enzyme) may cause areas of cyanosis or greenish to yellow-brown discoloration of the abdominal wall. Other areas of bruising are the flanks (*Grey Turner spots* or *sign,* a bluish flank discoloration) and the periumbilical area (*Cullen sign,* a bluish periumbilical discoloration). These result from seepage of bloodstained exudate from the pancreas and may occur in severe cases.

Shock may occur from bleeding into the pancreas, toxemia from the activated pancreatic enzymes, or hypovolemia due to fluid shift into the retroperitoneal space (massive fluid shifts).

Complications

The severity of acute pancreatitis depends on the extent of pancreatic destruction. Acute pancreatitis can be life threatening. Some patients recover completely. Others have recurring attacks, and some develop chronic pancreatitis.

Two significant local complications are pseudocyst and abscess. A *pancreatic pseudocyst* is an accumulation of fluid, pancreatic enzymes, tissue debris, and inflammatory exudates surrounded by a wall next to the pancreas. Manifestations are abdominal pain, palpable epigastric mass, nausea, vomiting, and anorexia. The serum amylase level is often high. CT, MRI, and endoscopic ultrasound (EUS) may detect a pseudocyst. The cysts usually resolve spontaneously within a few weeks but may perforate, causing peritonitis or rupture into the stomach or the duodenum. Treatment options include surgical drainage, percutaneous catheter placement and drainage, and endoscopic drainage.

When a pseudocyst gets infected, a *pancreatic abscess* results from extensive necrosis in the pancreas. It may rupture or perforate into adjacent organs. Manifestations of an abscess include upper abdominal pain, abdominal mass, high fever, and leukocytosis. Pancreatic abscesses need prompt surgical drainage to prevent sepsis.

TABLE 48.18 Diagnostic Findings

Acute Pancreatitis

Laboratory Test	Abnormal Finding
Serum amylase	↑
Serum lipase	↑
Urinary amylase	↑
Blood glucose	↑
Serum calcium	↓
Serum triglycerides	↑

The main systemic complications are cardiovascular and pulmonary (pleural effusion, atelectasis, pneumonia, and acute respiratory distress syndrome [ARDS]). Pulmonary complications are due to the passage of exudate-containing pancreatic enzymes from the peritoneal cavity through transdiaphragmatic lymph channels. Enzyme-induced inflammation of the diaphragm occurs, with the result being atelectasis caused by reduced diaphragm movement. Trypsin can activate prothrombin and plasminogen, increasing the patient's risk for intravascular thrombi, pulmonary emboli, and DIC. Hypotension can occur from fluid shifts and sepsis.

Tetany, which can be caused by hypocalcemia, is a sign of severe disease. It is due in part to the combining of calcium and fatty acids during fat necrosis. We do not understand the exact mechanisms of how or why hypocalcemia occurs. Patients with severe acute pancreatitis are at risk for abdominal compartment syndrome from intraabdominal hypertension and edema.

Diagnostic Studies

The primary diagnostic tests for acute pancreatitis are serum amylase and lipase (Table 48.18). The serum amylase level is usually high early and stays high for 24 to 72 hours. Serum lipase level is high in acute pancreatitis. It is an important test because other disorders (e.g., mumps, cerebral trauma) may increase serum amylase levels. Other serum findings include an increase in liver enzymes, triglycerides, glucose, and bilirubin and a decrease in calcium.

Diagnostic testing is aimed at determining the cause. An abdominal ultrasound, x-ray, or contrast-enhanced CT scan may identify pancreatic problems. CT scan is the best imaging test for pancreatitis and related complications, such as pseudocysts and abscesses. ERCP is an option (although ERCP can cause acute pancreatitis), along with EUS, magnetic resonance cholangiopancreatography (MRCP), and angiography. Chest x-rays may show atelectasis and pleural effusions.

Interprofessional Care

Goals of interprofessional care include (1) pain relief, (2) prevent or alleviate shock, (3) reduce pancreatic secretions, (4) correct fluid and electrolyte imbalances, (5) prevent or treat infection, and (6) remove the precipitating cause, if possible (Table 48.19).

TABLE 48.19 Interprofessional Care

Acute Pancreatitis

Diagnostic Assessment

- History and physical assessment
- Serum amylase and lipase
- Blood glucose
- Serum calcium
- Serum triglycerides
- Flat plate of the abdomen
- Abdominal ultrasound
- Endoscopic ultrasound (EUS)
- MRCP
- ERCP
- Contrast-enhanced CT of pancreas
- Chest x-ray

Management

- NPO with NG tube to suction
- Albumin (if shock present)
- IV calcium gluconate (10%) (if tetany present)
- Lactated Ringer's solution

Drug Therapy

- Pain medication (e.g., morphine)
- PPI (e.g., omeprazole)
- Antibiotics (if necrotizing pancreatitis)

TABLE 48.20 Drug Therapy

Acute and Chronic Pancreatitis

Drug	Mechanism of Action
Acute Pancreatitis	
Antacids	Neutralize gastric hydrochloric (HCl) acid secretion ↓ Production and secretion of pancreatic enzymes and bicarbonate
Antispasmodics (e.g., dicyclomine)	↓ Vagal stimulation, motility, pancreatic outflow (↓ volume and concentration of bicarbonate and enzyme secretion) Contraindicated in paralytic ileus
Carbonic anhydrase inhibitor (acetazolamide)	↓ Volume and bicarbonate concentration of pancreatic secretion
Morphine	Pain relief
PPIs (e.g., omeprazole)	↓ HCl acid secretion (HCl acid stimulates pancreatic activity)
Chronic Pancreatitis	
Insulin	Treat diabetes or hyperglycemia, if needed
Pancreatic enzyme products (pancrelipase [Pancrease, Zenpep, Creon, Viokace])	Replacement therapy for pancreatic enzymes

Conservative Therapy

Treatment focuses on supportive care. This includes aggressive hydration, pain management, managing metabolic complications, and minimizing pancreatic stimulation. Treatment and control of pain are very important. We may give IV opioid analgesics. Pain medications may be given with an antispasmodic agent. Atropine and other anticholinergic drugs are avoided when paralytic ileus is present because they can decrease GI mobility, making the problem worse. Other drugs that relax smooth muscles (spasmolytics), such as nitroglycerin or papaverine, may be used. Supplemental O_2 is used to maintain O_2 saturation greater than 95%. In patients with severe pancreatitis, we monitor serum glucose levels for hyperglycemia.

If shock is present, we give blood volume replacements. The patient may receive plasma or plasma volume expanders, such as dextran or albumin. Lactated Ringer's solution or other electrolyte solutions can correct fluid and electrolyte problems. Central venous pressure readings can help determine fluid replacement requirements. Vasoactive drugs, such as dopamine, may be needed to increase systemic vascular resistance in those with hypotension.

It is important to reduce or suppress pancreatic enzymes to decrease stimulation of the pancreas and allow it to rest. We do this in several ways. First, the patient is NPO. Second, NG suction may be used to reduce vomiting and gastric distention and to prevent gastric acidic contents from entering the duodenum. Certain drugs are given to suppress gastric acid secretion (Table 48.20).

The inflamed and necrotic pancreatic tissue is a good medium for bacterial growth. In patients with acute necrotizing pancreatitis, infection is the leading cause of morbidity and mortality. Therefore, it is important to prevent infections. Because many of the organisms come from the intestine, EN reduces the risk for necrotizing pancreatitis. Monitor the patient closely so that antibiotic therapy can be started early if necrosis and infection occur. Endoscopic- or CT-guided percutaneous aspiration with Gram stain and culture may be done.

Surgical Therapy

When the acute pancreatitis is related to gallstones, an urgent ERCP plus endoscopic *sphincterotomy* (severing of the muscle layers of the sphincter of Oddi) may be done. Laparoscopic cholecystectomy may follow ERCP to reduce the potential for recurrence. Surgery may be done when the diagnosis is uncertain or for the patient does not respond to conservative therapy.

A patient may need drainage of necrotic fluid collections. This is done surgically, under CT guidance, or endoscopically. Percutaneous drainage of a pseudocyst can be done, and a drainage tube left in place.

Drug Therapy

Several different drugs are used to prevent and treat problems associated with pancreatitis (Table 48.20). Currently, there are no drugs that cure pancreatitis.

Nutrition Therapy

Initially, the patient with acute pancreatitis is NPO to reduce pancreatic secretion. Depending on the severity of the pancreatitis, we start EN. Because of infection risk, PN is reserved for patients who cannot tolerate EN (see Chapter 44). If the patient receives IV lipids, monitor blood triglyceride levels.

As pancreatitis resolves, the patient resumes oral intake. When food is allowed, start with small, frequent feedings.

The diet is high in carbohydrate content because that is the least stimulating to the exocrine part of the pancreas. Suspect intolerance to oral foods when the patient reports pain, has increasing abdominal girth, or has increased serum amylase and lipase levels. Supplemental fat-soluble vitamins may be given.

CHECK YOUR PRACTICE

The family member of your patient approaches you and is upset that her mother has not been given any food. The patient is admitted for acute pancreatitis. "My mother has been here for 8 hours and she is starving. Why can't you give her something to eat?"

- How would you respond?
- What information and teaching would you provide?

NURSING MANAGEMENT: ACUTE PANCREATITIS

Assessment

Subjective and objective data that should be obtained from a person with acute pancreatitis are outlined in Table 48.21.

Clinical Problems

Clinical Problems for the patient with acute pancreatitis may include:

- Pain
- Fluid imbalance
- Electrolyte imbalance
- Nutritionally compromised

Additional information on clinical problems and interventions for the patient with acute pancreatitis is presented in eNursing Care Plan 48.3 available on the website for this chapter.

Planning

The overall goals are that the patient with acute pancreatitis will have (1) pain relief, (2) normal fluid and electrolyte balance, (3) minimal to no complications, and (4) no recurrent attacks.

Implementation

Health Promotion

The major factors involved in health promotion are (1) assessing the patient for risk factors and (2) encouraging early treatment of these factors to prevent acute pancreatitis. Encourage the patient to cease alcohol intake, especially if they have had pancreatitis before. Recurrent attacks of pancreatitis may become milder or disappear if they stop alcohol use. Encourage early diagnosis and treatment of biliary tract disease, such as gallstones.

Acute Care

During the acute phase, it is important to monitor vital signs. Hypotension, fever, and tachypnea may compromise hemodynamic stability. Monitor the response to IV fluids. Closely assess fluid and electrolyte balance. Frequent vomiting, along with gastric suction, may result in decreased chloride, sodium, and potassium levels.

TABLE 48.21 NURSING ASSESSMENT

Acute Pancreatitis

Subjective Data

Important Health Information

Health history: Biliary tract disease, alcohol use, abdominal trauma, duodenal ulcers, infection, metabolic disorders

Medications: Thiazides, NSAIDs

Surgery or other treatments: Surgery on the pancreas, stomach, duodenum, or biliary tract. Endoscopic retrograde cholangiopancreatography (ERCP)

Functional Health Patterns

Health perception–health management: Chronic alcohol use, fatigue

Nutritional-metabolic: Nausea and vomiting, anorexia

Activity-exercise: Dyspnea

Cognitive-perceptual: Severe midepigastric or left upper quadrant pain that may radiate to the back, worsened by food and alcohol intake, unrelieved by vomiting

Objective Data

Cardiovascular

Tachycardia, hypotension

GI

Abdominal distention, tenderness, and muscle guarding. Decreased bowel sounds

General

Restlessness, anxiety, low-grade fever

Respiratory

Tachypnea, basilar crackles

Skin

Flushing, diaphoresis, discoloration of abdomen and flanks, cyanosis, jaundice. Decreased skin turgor, dry mucous membranes

Possible Diagnostic Findings

- ↑ Serum amylase and lipase, leukocytosis, hyperglycemia, hypocalcemia. Abnormal ultrasound and CT scans of pancreas, abnormal ERCP or MRCP

Respiratory failure may develop in the patient with severe acute pancreatitis. Assess respiratory function (e.g., lung sounds, O_2 saturation levels). If ARDS develops, the patient may need intubation and mechanical ventilation support.

SAFETY ALERT

Respiratory Distress in Acute Pancreatitis

- Assess for respiratory distress in the patient with severe acute pancreatitis.
- Listen to lung sounds and monitor O_2 saturation on a regular basis.

Because hypocalcemia can occur, observe for symptoms of tetany, including jerking, irritability, and muscular twitching. Numbness or tingling around the lips and in the fingers is an early sign of hypocalcemia. Assess the patient for a positive Chvostek sign or Trousseau sign (see Fig. 17.15). Give calcium gluconate as ordered to treat symptomatic hypocalcemia. Monitor serum magnesium levels since hypomagnesemia may develop.

A major focus of your care is pain relief. Pain and restlessness can increase the metabolic rate and contribute to hemodynamic instability. Opioids may be used for pain relief. Assess and document the duration of pain relief. Comfortable positioning, frequent changes in position, and relief of nausea and vomiting help reduce the restlessness that usually accompanies the pain. Assuming positions that flex the trunk and draw the knees up to the abdomen may decrease pain. A side-lying position with the head elevated 45 degrees decreases tension on the abdomen and may help.

For the patient who is on NPO status or has an NG tube, provide frequent oral and nasal care to relieve the dryness of the mouth and nose. Oral care is essential to prevent parotitis. If the patient is taking anticholinergics to decrease GI secretions, the mouth will be especially dry. If the patient is taking antacids to neutralize gastric acid secretion, they should be sipped slowly or inserted in the NG tube.

Observe for fever and other signs of infection in the patient with acute pancreatitis. Respiratory tract infections are common and cause the patient to take shallow, guarded abdominal breaths. Measures to prevent respiratory tract infections include turning, coughing, deep breathing, and assuming a semi-Fowler's position.

Assess for signs of paralytic ileus, renal failure, and mental changes. Determine the blood glucose level to assess damage to the β cells of the islets of Langerhans in the pancreas.

Patients who had surgery to drain necrotic fluid or treat a cyst may need special wound care for an anastomotic leak or a fistula. To prevent skin irritation, use skin barriers (e.g., Stomahesive, Karaya Paste), pouching, and drains. In addition to protecting the skin, pouching allows a more accurate determination of fluid losses and increases patient comfort. Sterile pouching systems are available. Consult with a clinical specialist or wound, ostomy, and continence nurse (WOCN).

◆ Ambulatory Care

After acute pancreatitis, the patient may need home care follow-up. Because of loss of physical and muscle strength, physical therapy may be needed. Continued care to prevent infection and detect any complications is important. Counseling about abstinence from alcohol is important to prevent the patient from experiencing future attacks of acute pancreatitis and developing chronic pancreatitis. Because nicotine can stimulate the pancreas, they should avoid smoking.

Teach the patient and caregiver about the treatment plan, including the importance of taking the required medications and following the recommended diet. Diet teaching should include fat restriction. Fats stimulate cholecystokinin secretion, which then stimulates the pancreas. Encourage carbohydrates as they are less stimulating to the pancreas. Teach the patient to avoid crash and binge dieting because they can precipitate attacks.

Teach the patient and caregiver to recognize and report symptoms of infection, diabetes, or steatorrhea (foul-smelling, fatty stools). These changes indicate ongoing destruction of pancreatic tissue and pancreatic insufficiency. The patient may need exogenous enzyme supplementation.

◆ Evaluation

The expected outcomes are that the patient with acute pancreatitis will:

- Have adequate pain control
- Maintain adequate fluid and electrolyte balance
- Be knowledgeable about the treatment plan to restore health
- Get help for alcohol use and smoking cessation (if needed)

CHRONIC PANCREATITIS

Chronic pancreatitis is a continuous, prolonged, inflammatory, and fibrosing process of the pancreas. The pancreas is progressively destroyed as it is replaced by fibrotic tissue. Strictures and calcifications may occur in the pancreas.

Etiology and Pathophysiology

The most common cause of nonobstructive pancreatitis (the most common type of chronic pancreatitis) is chronic alcohol use. There is inflammation and sclerosis, mainly in the head of the pancreas and around the pancreatic duct. In some people who drink alcohol, a genetic factor may predispose them to the direct toxic effect of the alcohol on the pancreas.

The most common cause of obstructive pancreatitis is inflammation of the sphincter of Oddi from gallstones. Cancer of the ampulla of Vater, duodenum, or pancreas can also cause this type of chronic pancreatitis.

Chronic pancreatitis may follow acute pancreatitis. It may occur with systemic diseases (e.g., systemic lupus erythematosus), autoimmune pancreatitis, and cystic fibrosis. Some patients may not have an identifiable risk factor (idiopathic pancreatitis).

Clinical Manifestations

As with acute pancreatitis, a major manifestation of chronic pancreatitis is abdominal pain. The patient may have episodes of acute pain, but it usually is chronic (recurrent attacks at intervals of months or years). The attacks may become more frequent until they are almost constant. Sometimes they decrease as pancreatic fibrosis develops. The pain occurs in the same areas as in acute pancreatitis. It is usually described as a heavy, gnawing feeling or sometimes as burning and cramp-like. Food or antacids do not relieve the pain.

Other manifestations include symptoms of pancreatic insufficiency. These include malabsorption with weight loss, constipation, mild jaundice with dark urine, steatorrhea, and diabetes. The steatorrhea may become severe, with voluminous, foul-smelling, fatty stools. Some abdominal tenderness may be present.

Chronic pancreatitis can cause a variety of complications. These include pseudocyst formation, bile duct or duodenal obstruction, pancreatic ascites or pleural effusion, splenic vein thrombosis, pseudoaneurysms, and pancreatic cancer.

Diagnostic Studies

Confirming the diagnosis of chronic pancreatitis can be hard. The diagnosis is based on the patient's signs and symptoms, laboratory studies, and imaging. In chronic pancreatitis, serum amylase and lipase levels may be increased slightly or not at all, depending on the degree of pancreatic fibrosis. Serum bilirubin and alkaline phosphatase levels may be increased. There is usually mild leukocytosis and a high sedimentation rate.

ERCP can visualize the pancreatic and common bile ducts. Imaging studies, such as CT, MRI, MRCP, and abdominal ultrasound, can show a variety of changes, including calcifications, ductal dilation, pseudocysts, and enlargement of the pancreas.

Stool samples are examined for fecal fat content. Deficiencies of fat-soluble vitamins and cobalamin, glucose intolerance, and diabetes may occur. A secretin stimulation test can assess the degree of pancreatic dysfunction.

Interprofessional and Nursing Care

When the patient with chronic pancreatitis has an acute attack, the therapy is identical to that for acute pancreatitis. At other times, the focus is on preventing further attacks, pain relief, and controlling pancreatic exocrine and endocrine insufficiency. It sometimes takes frequent doses of analgesics (morphine, fentanyl patch) to relieve the pain if diet measures and enzyme replacement are not effective.

Diet, pancreatic enzyme replacement, and diabetes control are ways to control pancreatic insufficiency. Small, bland, frequent meals that are low in fat decrease pancreatic stimulation. Smoking can accelerate progression of chronic pancreatitis. Teach the patient not to consume alcohol and caffeinated beverages. If the patient is dependent on alcohol, refer the patient to other resources as needed (see Chapter 11).

Pancreatic enzyme products, such as pancrelipase, contain amylase, lipase, and trypsin. They are used to replace the deficient pancreatic enzymes. The enzymes are usually enteric coated to prevent their breakdown or inactivation by gastric acid. They are usually taken with meals and snacks. Teach the patient and caregiver to monitor stools for steatorrhea to help determine the effectiveness of the enzymes. Bile salts may be given to help with fat-soluble vitamin (A, D, E, and K) absorption and prevent further fat loss.

If diabetes develops, the patient needs insulin (most often) or oral hypoglycemic agents. Teach the patient about testing blood glucose levels and drug therapy (see Chapter 53). While acid-neutralizing drugs (e.g., antacids) and acid-inhibiting drugs (e.g., H_2-receptor blockers, PPIs) may be given to control gastric acidity, they have little overall effect on patient outcomes. Antidepressants can reduce any neuropathic pain.

Treatment sometimes requires endoscopic therapy or surgery. When biliary disease is present or obstruction or pseudocyst develops, surgery may be needed. Surgical procedures can divert bile flow or relieve ductal obstruction. A choledochojejunostomy diverts bile around the ampulla of Vater, where there may be spasm or hypertrophy of the sphincter. In this procedure, the common bile duct is anastomosed into the jejunum. Another surgical diverting procedure is the Roux-en-Y pancreatojejunostomy. The pancreatic duct is opened, and an anastomosis made with the jejunum. Pancreatic drainage procedures can relieve ductal obstruction and are often done with ERCP. Some patients may have an ERCP with sphincterotomy and/or stent placement at the site of obstruction. These patients need follow-up procedures, such as ERCP, to either exchange or remove the stent.

PANCREATIC CANCER

Most pancreatic tumors are adenocarcinomas that begin in the epithelium of the ductal system. More than half of the tumors occur in the head of the pancreas. As the tumor grows, the common bile duct becomes obstructed and obstructive jaundice develops. Tumors starting in the body or tail often remain silent until their growth is advanced. Most cancers have metastasized at the time of diagnosis. Pancreatic cancer has a low incidence rate of around 1.6%. The median age at diagnosis is around 68 years of age.[27] The prognosis of a patient with cancer of the pancreas is poor. Most patients die within 5 to 12 months of diagnosis. The 5-year survival rate is only 9%.

Etiology and Pathophysiology

The cause of pancreatic cancer is unknown. The most established risk factor is cigarette smoking. Smokers are 2 to 3 times more likely to develop pancreatic cancer than nonsmokers. The risk is related to both the duration and number of cigarettes smoked. Other risk factors include chronic pancreatitis, diabetes, age, family history of pancreatic cancer, high-fat diet, and exposure to chemicals, such as benzidine. Blacks have the highest incidence of pancreatic cancer.

Clinical Manifestations

The signs and symptoms of pancreatic cancer are similar to those of chronic pancreatitis.[28] They include abdominal pain (dull, aching), anorexia, rapid and progressive weight loss, nausea, and jaundice. Common manifestations with cancer of the head of the pancreas are pain, jaundice, and weight loss. In general, pain is common and is related to the cancer's location. The pain is often in the upper abdomen or left hypochondrium and often radiates to the back. It is often related to eating and occurs at night. Extreme, unrelenting pain is related to extension of the cancer into the retroperitoneal tissues and nerve plexuses. Pruritus may accompany obstructive jaundice. Weight loss is due to poor digestion and absorption caused by a lack of digestive enzymes from the pancreas.

Diagnostic Studies

Abdominal ultrasound or EUS, spiral CT scan, ERCP, MRI, and MRCP are the most often used diagnostic imaging techniques for pancreatic cancer. EUS involves imaging the pancreas with the use of an endoscope positioned in the stomach and duodenum. EUS also allows for fine-needle aspiration of the tumor for biopsy. CT scan is often the first study and gives information on metastasis and vascular involvement of the tumor. ERCP allows us to see the pancreatic duct and biliary system. With ERCP, pancreatic secretions and tissue can be obtained for biopsy and analysis of tumor markers. MRI, PET, PET/CT scans, and MRCP may be done to confirm a cancer diagnosis and determine staging. They can also monitor progress and response to therapy.

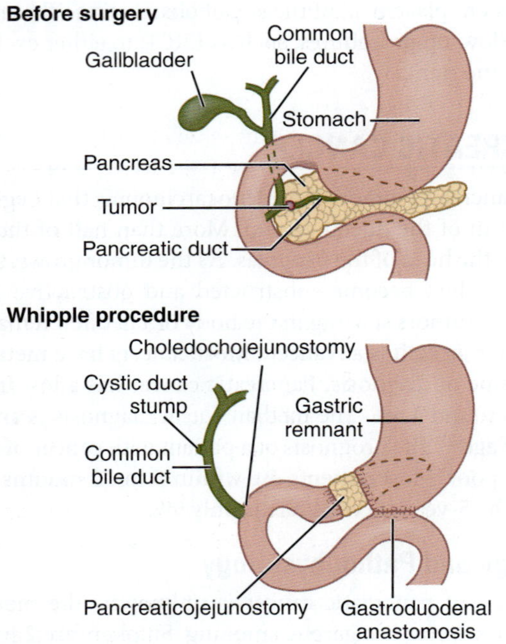

Fig. 48.13 Whipple procedure or radical pancreaticoduodenectomy. This surgery involves resecting the proximal pancreas, adjoining duodenum, distal part of the stomach, and distal part of the common bile duct. An anastomosis of the pancreatic duct, common bile duct, and stomach to the jejunum is done. (From Butcher GP: *Gastroenterology: an illustrated colour text,* London, 2004, Churchill Livingstone.)

Tumor markers are used both for diagnosing pancreatic cancer and monitoring the response to treatment. Cancer-associated antigen 19-9 (CA 19-9) is increased in pancreatic cancer. It is the most commonly used tumor marker. However, CA 19-9 also can be increased in gallbladder cancer and benign conditions, such as acute and chronic pancreatitis, hepatitis, and biliary obstruction.

Interprofessional Care

Surgery is the most effective treatment for pancreatic cancer. Only 15% to 20% of patients have resectable tumors at the time of diagnosis. With the use of neoadjuvant chemotherapy (treatment before surgery), more patients can eventually become surgical candidates. The type of surgery depends on the size and location of the tumor. Pancreatic head tumors require the classic Whipple procedure or pancreaticoduodenectomy (Fig. 48.13). In the Whipple surgery, the proximal pancreas (proximal pancreatectomy), along with duodenum (duodenectomy), distal segment of the common bile duct, and distal part of the stomach (partial gastrectomy) are removed. The pancreatic duct, common bile duct, and stomach are anastomosed to the jejunum. Pancreatic body and/or tail tumors require a distal pancreatectomy procedure. Sometimes, a total pancreatectomy is done. It causes diabetes and the patient must receive insulin therapy and pancreatic enzyme supplements for life. If the pancreatic tumor cannot be removed surgically, palliative measures, such as a cholecystojejunostomy, to relieve biliary obstruction and/or endoscopically placed biliary stents, can be done.

Radiation therapy alone has little effect on survival but may help with pain relief. External radiation is most common, but implanting internal radiation seeds into the tumor has been used. The role of chemotherapy is limited and can have a significant side effect profile. Chemotherapy usually consists of fluorouracil and gemcitabine (Gemzar) either alone or in combination with agents such as capecitabine (Xeloda), paclitaxel (Abraxane), erlotinib (Tarceva), or irinotecan (Onivyde). Erlotinib is a targeted therapy drug (see Chapter 16).

NURSING MANAGEMENT: PANCREATIC CANCER

Because the patient with pancreatic cancer has many of the same problems as the patient with pancreatitis, nursing care includes many of the same measures. Provide symptomatic and supportive nursing care. This includes giving medications and providing comfort measures to relieve pain. Psychologic support is essential, especially during times of distress.

Adequate nutrition is important. Frequent and supplemental feedings may be needed. Include measures to stimulate the appetite as much as possible and to manage anorexia, nausea, and vomiting. If the patient is receiving radiation therapy, observe for adverse reactions, such as anorexia, nausea, vomiting, and skin irritation.

The prognosis for a patient with pancreatic cancer is poor. Help the patient and caregiver cope with the diagnosis and prognosis. Chapter 10 provides information on palliative and end-of-life care.

BILIARY TRACT PROBLEMS

CHOLELITHIASIS AND CHOLECYSTITIS

The most common disorder of the biliary system is **cholelithiasis** (stones in the gallbladder) (Fig. 48.14). The gallstones may lodge in the neck of the gallbladder or in the cystic duct. **Cholecystitis** (inflammation of the gallbladder wall) is usually associated with gallstones. They usually occur together, although a person can have gallstones without cholecystitis. Cholecystitis may be acute or chronic.

Gallbladder disease is a common health problem in the United States. Up to 10% of American adults have cholecystitis caused by gallstones. The actual number is not known because many persons with stones are asymptomatic. *Cholecystectomy* (removal of the gallbladder) is among the most common surgeries done in the United States.

Gallstones are more common in women, especially multiparous women and women over 40 years of age (Box 48.4). Postmenopausal women on estrogen replacement therapy and younger women on oral contraceptives are at an increased risk for gallbladder disease. Oral contraceptives affect cholesterol production and increase gallbladder cholesterol saturation. Other factors are a sedentary lifestyle, a familial tendency, and obesity. Obesity causes increased secretion of cholesterol in bile. The incidence of gallbladder disease is especially high in the Native American population.

Fig. 48.14 Cholesterol gallstones in a gallbladder that was removed. (From Kumar V, Abbas AK, Aster JC, et al.: *Robbins and Cotran pathologic basis of disease,* ed 8, Philadelphia, 2010, Saunders.)

BOX 48.4 BIOLOGIC SEX CONSIDERATIONS

Cholelithiasis

Men

- Incidence is lower in men

Women

- Pregnancy and estrogen replacement therapy increase risk
- Obesity increases the risk, especially for women

Etiology and Pathophysiology

Cholelithiasis

We do not know the cause of gallstones. They develop when the balance that keeps cholesterol, bile salts, and calcium in solution is changed so that these substances precipitate. Other components of bile that precipitate into stones are bilirubin and protein. Mixed cholesterol stones, which are mainly cholesterol, are the most common gallstones.

Conditions that lead to gallstone formation include supersaturation of bile with cholesterol, decreased bile acids that dissolve cholesterol, excess mucus production, and gallbladder dysmotility and stasis. Normally, bile contains enough chemicals to dissolve the cholesterol the liver excretes. If the liver excretes more cholesterol than bile can dissolve, the excess cholesterol may form into crystals and eventually stones. The bile secreted by the liver may be supersaturated with cholesterol (lithogenic bile). The bile in the gallbladder then becomes supersaturated with cholesterol and precipitation of cholesterol occurs in the gallbladder. Bile stasis can promote the progression of supersaturation and changes in the chemical composition of the bile (biliary sludge). Immobility, pregnancy, and inflammatory or obstructive lesions in the biliary system decrease bile flow. Hormonal factors during pregnancy may cause delayed emptying of the gallbladder, resulting in bile stasis.

The stones may stay in the gallbladder or migrate to the cystic duct or the common bile duct. They cause pain as they pass through the ducts. Stones can lodge in the ducts and cause an obstruction. Small stones are more likely to move into a duct and cause obstruction. Table 48.22 describes the changes and manifestations that occur when the stones obstruct the common bile duct. If the blockage occurs in the cystic duct, the bile can continue to flow into the duodenum directly from the liver. However, when the bile in the gallbladder cannot escape, bile stasis may lead to cholecystitis.

Cholecystitis

Cholecystitis is most often associated with obstruction caused by gallstones or biliary sludge. Cholecystitis in the absence of obstruction *(acalculous cholecystitis)* occurs most often in older adults and in patients who are critically ill. Acalculous cholecystitis is also associated with prolonged immobility and fasting, prolonged PN, and diabetes. We think the main cause of this illness is bile stasis. Critically ill patients are more predisposed because of increased bile viscosity due to fever and dehydration and because of prolonged absence of oral feeding resulting in a decrease or absence of cholecystokinin-induced gallbladder contraction. Other risk factors include adhesions, cancer, anesthesia, and opioids.

Once acalculous cholecystitis is present, secondary infection with enteric pathogens, including *E. coli, Enterococcus faecalis, Klebsiella, Pseudomonas,* and *Proteus,* is common. Perforation occurs in severe cases.

Inflammation is the major issue. It may be confined to the mucous lining or involve the entire wall of the gallbladder. During an acute attack of cholecystitis, the gallbladder is edematous and hyperemic. It may be distended with bile or pus. The cystic duct is also involved and may become occluded. The wall of the gallbladder becomes scarred after an acute attack. Decreased functioning will occur if large amounts of tissue become fibrotic.

Clinical Manifestations

Gallstones may cause a range of symptoms. The severity depends on whether the stones are stationary or mobile and whether obstruction is present. When a stone is lodged in the ducts or when stones are moving through the ducts, spasms may result in response to the stone. This sometimes causes severe pain, which is termed *biliary colic,* even though the pain is rarely colicky. The pain is more often steady. The pain can be excruciating and accompanied by tachycardia, diaphoresis, and prostration. The severe pain may last up to an hour, and when it subsides, there is residual RUQ tenderness. Pain often occurs 3 to 6 hours after a high-fat meal or when the patient lies down.

When total obstruction occurs, symptoms related to bile blockage occur (Table 48.22). If the common bile duct is obstructed, no bilirubin will reach the small intestine to be converted to urobilinogen. Thus, the kidneys will excrete bilirubin, causing dark amber to brown urine.

Manifestations of cholecystitis vary from indigestion to moderate to severe pain, fever, chills, and jaundice. Initial symptoms of acute cholecystitis include indigestion and acute pain and RUQ tenderness. Pain may be referred to the right shoulder and scapula. There may be nausea and vomiting, restlessness, and diaphoresis. Inflammation results in leukocytosis and fever. Physical findings include RUQ or epigastrium tenderness and abdominal rigidity. Chronic cholecystitis may present with a history of fat intolerance, dyspepsia, heartburn, and flatulence.

Complications

Complications of gallstones and cholecystitis include gangrenous cholecystitis, subphrenic abscess, pancreatitis, *cholangitis*

TABLE 48.22 Manifestations of Obstructed Bile Flow

Manifestation	Cause
Bleeding tendencies	Lack of or ↓ Vitamin K absorption, resulting in ↓ prothrombin production
Clay-colored stools	No bilirubin reaching small intestine to be converted to urobilinogen
Dark amber to brown urine, which foams when shaken	↑ Water-soluble (conjugated) bilirubin elimination in urine
Fever and chills	Bacterial reflux from biliary tract to systemic circulation
Intolerance for fatty foods	No bile in small intestine for fat digestion
Jaundice	No bile flow into duodenum, bilirubin accumulates in blood
Pruritus	Deposition of bile salts in skin tissues
Steatorrhea	Undigested fatty components of food are eliminated in stool. Occurs because no bile in small intestine, thus preventing emulsion, digestion, and absorption of fat
Urobilinogen absent in urine	No bilirubin reaching small intestine to be converted to urobilinogen

(inflammation of biliary ducts), biliary cirrhosis, fistulas, and rupture of the gallbladder, which can cause bile peritonitis. In older adults and those with diabetes, gangrenous cholecystitis and bile peritonitis are the most common complications of cholecystitis. *Choledocholithiasis* (stone in the common bile duct) may occur, producing symptoms of obstruction.

Diagnostic Studies

Ultrasound is often used to diagnose gallstones (see Table 43.11). It is especially useful for patients with jaundice (because it does not depend on renal function) and those who are allergic to contrast medium. ERCP allows for visualization of the gallbladder, cystic duct, common hepatic duct, and common bile duct. Bile taken during ERCP is sent for culture to identify possible infecting organisms.

Percutaneous transhepatic cholangiography is the insertion of a needle directly into the gallbladder duct followed by injection of contrast materials. It is generally done after ultrasound shows a bile duct blockage.

Laboratory tests may show an increased WBC count because of inflammation. Serum enzymes (e.g., alkaline phosphatase, ALT, and AST), direct and indirect bilirubin levels, and urinary bilirubin levels may be increased if an obstructive process is present (Table 48.3). Serum amylase is increased if the pancreas is involved.

Interprofessional Care

Once gallstones become symptomatic, a cholecystectomy is usually done. However, in some cases, conservative therapy may be considered.

Conservative Therapy

Cholelithiasis. The treatment of gallstones depends on the stage of disease. Bile acids (cholesterol solvents), such as ursodiol and chenodiol, are used to dissolve stones. However,

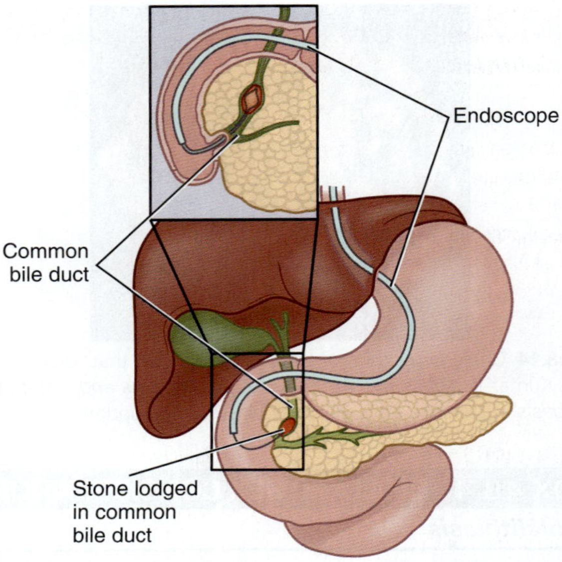

Fig. 48.15 During endoscopic sphincterotomy, an endoscope is advanced through the mouth and stomach until its tip sits in the duodenum opposite the common bile duct. *Inset,* After widening the duct mouth by incising the sphincter muscle, the HCP advances a basket attachment into the duct and snags the stone.

the gallstones may recur. We usually do not treat gallstones with drugs because of the high use and success of laparoscopic cholecystectomy.

ERCP with endoscopic sphincterotomy (papillotomy) may be used to remove stones (Fig. 48.15). ERCP allows for visualization of the biliary system, dilation (balloon sphincteroplasty), and placement of stents and sphincterotomy. Special catheters with wire baskets or inflatable balloon tip may be used for stone removal.[29] When a stent is placed, it is generally removed or changed after a few months.

Extracorporeal shock-wave lithotripsy (ESWL) is an alternative treatment used when endoscopic approaches cannot remove stones. In ESWL, a lithotripter uses high-energy shock waves to disintegrate gallstones. It usually takes 1 to 2 hours to disintegrate the stones. The stone fragments pass through the common bile duct and into the small intestine. Usually, ESWL and oral dissolution therapy are used together.

Cholecystitis. During an acute episode of cholecystitis, treatment focuses on pain control, control of infection with antibiotics, and maintaining fluid and electrolyte balance (Table 48.23). Treatment is supportive and focused on symptom management. If nausea and vomiting are severe, NG tube insertion and gastric decompression may be used to prevent further gallbladder stimulation. A cholecystostomy may be used to drain purulent material from the obstructed gallbladder. Opioids are given for pain management. Anticholinergics can decrease GI secretions and counteract smooth muscle spasms.

Surgical Therapy

Laparoscopic cholecystectomy is the treatment of choice for symptomatic gallstones. About 90% of cholecystectomies are done laparoscopically. In this procedure, the gallbladder is

TABLE 48.23 Interprofessional Care

Cholelithiasis and Acute Cholecystitis

Diagnostic Assessment

- History and physical assessment
- Ultrasound
- ERCP
- Percutaneous transhepatic cholangiography
- Liver function tests
- WBC count
- Serum bilirubin

Management

Conservative Therapy

- IV fluid
- NPO with NG tube, later progressing to low-fat diet
- Antiemetics
- Analgesics
- Fat-soluble vitamins (A, D, E, and K)
- Anticholinergics (antispasmodics)
- Antibiotics (for secondary infection)
- Transhepatic biliary catheter
- ERCP with sphincterotomy (papillotomy)
- Extracorporeal shock-wave lithotripsy

Dissolution Therapy

- Chenodiol
- Ursodiol

Surgical Therapy

- Laparoscopic cholecystectomy
- Incisional (open) cholecystectomy

removed through 1 to 4 small punctures in the abdomen. The HCP makes a small cut below the umbilicus and inserts a needle into the area. CO_2 gas is passed into the abdomen to expand the area. This allows the HCP to see the organs more clearly and gives more room to work. The HCP inserts the laparoscope, which has a camera attached, and grasping forceps into the abdomen through the punctures. Using closed-circuit monitors to view the abdominal cavity, the HCP retracts and dissects the gallbladder and removes it with the forceps. The few contraindications to laparoscopic cholecystectomy include peritonitis, cholangitis, gangrene or perforation of the gallbladder, portal hypertension, and serious bleeding disorders.

This is a safe and routine procedure with minimal morbidity and quick recovery time. Most patients have minimal postoperative pain. They are discharged the day of surgery or the day after. They can usually resume normal activities and return to work within 1 week. The main complication is injury to the common bile duct.

Some patients may need an incisional (open) cholecystectomy. This involves removing the gallbladder through a right subcostal incision. A T tube may be placed in the common bile duct during a common bile duct exploration surgery (Fig. 48.16). It keeps the duct patent until the edema from the trauma of exploring and probing the duct subsides. It allows excess bile to drain while the small intestine is adjusting to receiving a continuous flow of bile.

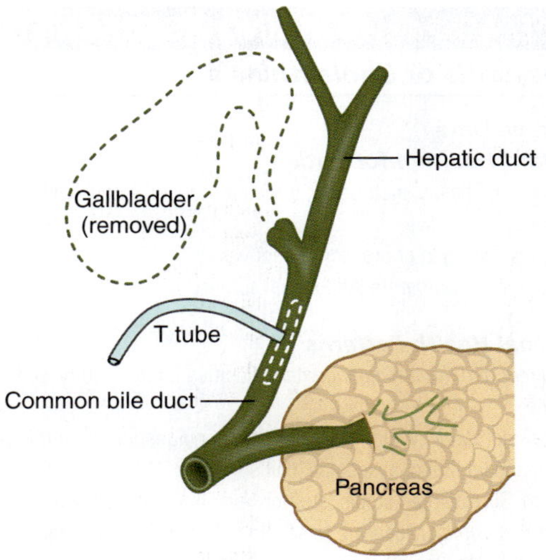

Fig. 48.16 Placement of T tube. *Dotted lines* show parts removed.

Transhepatic Biliary Catheter

The transhepatic biliary catheter can be used preoperatively in biliary obstruction and in liver dysfunction from obstructive jaundice. It also can be part of palliative care when inoperable liver, pancreatic, or bile duct cancer obstructs bile flow. The catheter is used when endoscopic drainage has been unsuccessful. The catheter is inserted percutaneously and allows for decompression of obstructed extrahepatic bile ducts so that bile can flow freely. After placement of the catheter into the obstructed duct internally, the external catheter is connected to a drainage bag. Encourage patients to replace fluids lost in the drainage bag with electrolyte-rich drinks. Cleanse the skin around the catheter insertion site daily with an antiseptic. Observe for bile leakage at the insertion site and any signs or symptoms of an occluded or malfunctioning drain. These include sudden abdominal pain, nausea, fever, or chills.

Drug Therapy

The most common drugs used in the treatment of gallbladder disease are analgesics, anticholinergics (antispasmodics), fat-soluble vitamins, and bile salts. Morphine may be used initially for pain management. Anticholinergics, such as atropine and other antispasmodics, may be used to relax the smooth muscle and decrease ductal tone.

The patient with chronic gallbladder disease or any biliary tract obstruction may need fat-soluble vitamin (A, D, E, and K) replacement. Bile salts can help with digestion and vitamin absorption. Cholestyramine may provide relief from itching.

Nutrition Therapy

People have fewer gallbladder problems if they eat smaller, more frequent meals with some fat at each meal to promote gallbladder emptying. If obesity is a problem, recommend a reduced-calorie diet. The diet should be low in saturated fats (e.g., butter, shortening, lard) and high in fiber and calcium. Avoid rapid weight loss because it can promote gallstone formation.

After a laparoscopic cholecystectomy, teach the patient to have liquids for the rest of the day and eat light meals for a few days.

TABLE 48.24 NURSING ASSESSMENT

Cholecystitis or Cholelithiasis

Subjective Data

Important Health Information

Health history: Obesity, multiparity, infection, cancer, extensive fasting, pregnancy

Medications: Estrogen or oral contraceptives

Surgery or other treatments: Abdominal surgery

Functional Health Patterns

Health perception–health management: Positive family history, sedentary lifestyle

Nutritional-metabolic: Weight loss, anorexia, indigestion, fat intolerance, nausea and vomiting, dyspepsia, chills

Elimination: Clay-colored stools, steatorrhea, flatulence. Dark urine

Cognitive-perceptual: Moderate to severe RUQ pain that may radiate to the back or scapula. Itching

Objective Data

Cardiovascular

Tachycardia

GI

Palpable gallbladder, abdominal guarding, and distention

General

Fever, restlessness

Respiratory

Tachypnea, splinting during respirations

Skin

Jaundice, icteric sclera, diaphoresis

Possible Diagnostic Findings

↑ Serum liver enzymes, alkaline phosphatase, and bilirubin. Absence of urobilinogen in urine, ↑ urinary bilirubin, leukocytosis. Abnormal gallbladder ultrasound

After an incisional cholecystectomy, the patient will progress from liquids to a regular diet once bowel sounds have returned. The amount of fat in the postoperative diet depends on the patient's tolerance of fat. A low-fat diet may be helpful if the flow of bile is reduced (usually only in the early postoperative period) or if the patient is overweight. Sometimes the patient must restrict fats for 4 to 6 weeks. Otherwise, no special diet is needed other than to eat nutritious meals and avoid excess fat intake.

NURSING MANAGEMENT: GALLBLADDER DISEASE

Assessment

Subjective and objective data that should be obtained from a person with gallbladder disease are outlined in Table 48.24.

Clinical Problems

Clinical problems for the patient having gallbladder surgery may include:

- Pain
- Impaired GI function

Planning

The overall goals are that the patient with gallbladder disease will have (1) relief of pain and discomfort, (2) no complications, and (3) no recurrent attacks of cholecystitis or gallstones.

Implementation

Health Promotion

Be aware of predisposing factors for gallbladder disease in health screening. Teach patients at risk the early manifestations and to see their HCP if these manifestations occur. Patients with chronic cholecystitis may not have acute symptoms and may not seek help until jaundice and biliary obstruction occur. Earlier detection in these patients is important so that they can be managed with a low-fat diet and monitored more closely.

Acute Care

Nursing goals for the patient receiving conservative therapy include (1) treat pain, (2) relieve nausea and vomiting, (3) provide comfort and emotional support, (4) maintain fluid and electrolyte balance and nutrition, and (5) observe for complications.

The patient with acute cholecystitis or gallstones often has severe pain. Give the drugs ordered to relieve the pain as needed before pain becomes severe. Observe for side effects of the drugs as part of the continued assessment. Nursing comfort measures, such as comfortable positioning and oral care, are appropriate.

Some patients have more severe nausea and vomiting than others. For these patients, an NG tube and gastric decompression may be needed. Eliminating intake of food and fluids prevents further stimulation of the gallbladder. Maintain accurate intake and output NG suction. For patients with less severe nausea and vomiting, antiemetics are usually adequate. When the patient is vomiting, provide comfort measures, such as frequent mouth rinses. Remove any vomitus at once from the patient's view. Provide oral hygiene and care of nares. If itching occurs with jaundice, use measures to relieve itching. These can include antihistamines or other treatments as previously discussed.

Assess for symptom progression and complications. Observe for signs of obstruction of the ducts by stones. These include jaundice; clay-colored stools; dark, foamy urine; steatorrhea; fever; and increased WBC count.

When manifestations of obstruction are present (Table 48.22), bleeding may result from decreased prothrombin production by the liver. Common sites to observe for bleeding are the mucous membranes of the mouth, nose, gingivae, and injection sites. When giving injections, use a small-gauge needle and apply gentle pressure afterward. Know the patient's PT time and use it to guide your assessment.

Assess for infections. Monitor vital signs. A temperature elevation with chills and jaundice may indicate choledocholithiasis.

Your care of the patient after ERCP with papillotomy includes assessing for complications, such as pancreatitis, perforation, infection, and bleeding. Monitor the patient's vital signs. Abdominal pain, fever, and increasing amylase and lipase may indicate acute pancreatitis. The patient should be on bed rest for several hours and NPO until the gag reflex returns. Teach the patient the need for follow-up if the stent is to be removed or changed.

Postoperative care. Postoperative nursing care after a laparoscopic cholecystectomy includes monitoring for complications, such as bleeding, making the patient comfortable, and preparing the patient for discharge. Patients may report referred pain to the shoulder because of the CO_2 that the HCP uses to inflate the abdominal cavity during surgery. It may not be released or absorbed by the body. The CO_2 can irritate the phrenic nerve and diaphragm, causing some difficulty breathing. Place the patient on their left side with right knee flexed to move the gas pocket away from the diaphragm. Encourage deep breathing along with movement and ambulation. NSAIDs or codeine can usually relieve pain. The patient starts clear liquids and can walk to the bathroom to void. Most patients go home the same day.

Postoperative nursing care for incisional cholecystectomy focuses on promoting ventilation and preventing respiratory complications. Other nursing care is the same as general postoperative nursing care (see Chapter 20).

If the patient has a T tube (Fig. 48.16), maintain the system, and monitor T-tube function and drainage. The T tube is usually connected to a closed gravity drainage system. If the Penrose or Jackson-Pratt drain or the T tube is draining large amounts of bile, it is helpful to use a sterile pouching system to protect the skin. Encourage the patient to replace any lost fluids and electrolytes.

◆ Ambulatory Care

When the patient has conservative therapy, nursing care depends on the patient's symptoms and on whether surgery is planned. Provide any diet teaching. The diet is usually low in fat. The patient may need to take fat-soluble vitamin supplements. If needed, review a weight-reduction diet. Teach the patient signs and symptoms of obstruction (e.g., stool and urine changes, jaundice, itching). Explain the importance of continued health care follow-up.

The patient who had a laparoscopic cholecystectomy is discharged soon after the surgery, so home care and teaching are important (Table 48.25).

After an incisional cholecystectomy, tell the patient to avoid heavy lifting for 4 to 6 weeks. Usual sexual activities, including intercourse, can be resumed as soon as the patient feels ready, unless otherwise instructed by the HCP.

Sometimes, the patient needs to remain on a low-fat diet for 4 to 6 weeks. Provide patient-centered diet teaching. A weight-reduction program may be helpful if the patient is overweight. Most patients tolerate a regular diet with no problems but should avoid excess fats.

TABLE 48.25 PATIENT & CAREGIVER TEACHING

Postoperative Laparoscopic Cholecystectomy

Postoperative teaching should include:

1. Remove the bandages on the puncture sites the day after surgery and you can shower.
2. Notify your HCP if any of the following signs and symptoms occurs:
   - Redness, swelling, bile-colored drainage or pus from any incision
   - Severe abdominal pain, nausea, vomiting, fever, chills
3. You can gradually resume normal activities.
4. Return to work within 1 week of surgery.
5. You can resume your usual diet. Many tolerate a low-fat diet better for several weeks after surgery.

◆ Evaluation

The overall expected outcomes are that the patient with gallbladder disease will:

- Appear comfortable and have pain relief
- Remain free from complications

GALLBLADDER CANCER

Gallbladder cancer has an incidence rate of 1.4 per 100,000 in women and 0.8 per 100,000 in men in the United States.[30] Most gallbladder cancers are adenocarcinomas. Many patients are asymptomatic. The early symptoms are insidious and similar to those of chronic cholecystitis and gallstones. This makes the diagnosis difficult. Most cancers are found incidentally. Many have advanced disease at the time of diagnosis leading to high mortality rates. Later symptoms are usually those of biliary obstruction.

Diagnosis and staging of gallbladder cancer are done using EUS, abdominal ultrasound, CT, MRI, and/or MRCP. When found early, surgery can be curative. Several factors influence successful surgical outcomes. These include the depth of cancer invasion, extent of liver involvement, venous or lymphatic invasion, and lymph node metastasis. Extended cholecystectomy with lymph node dissection has improved outcomes for those with gallbladder cancer.

When surgery is not an option, endoscopic stenting of the biliary tract can reduce obstructive jaundice. Adjuvant therapies, including radiation therapy and chemotherapy, may be used depending on the disease state. Overall, gallbladder cancer has a poor prognosis.

Nursing management involves palliative care with special attention to nutrition, hydration, skin care, and pain relief. Nursing care measures used for patients with cholecystitis and gallstones and for the patient with cancer (see Chapter 16) are appropriate.

Case Study

Cirrhosis

(© sbeagle/iStock/Thinkstock.)

Patient Profile

M.B. has cirrhosis. He has been vomiting for 2 days and noticed blood in the toilet when he vomited. He lives 40 miles from the nearest hospital. He had one of his ranch hands drive him to the hospital. His medical history includes chronic HCV, depression, and stage II chronic kidney disease.

Subjective Data

- Estranged from his 2 children since his divorce 3 years ago
- Has had cirrhosis for 12 years
- States he drank heavily for 20 years but has been sober for the past 2 years
- Reports anorexia, nausea, and abdominal discomfort

Objective Data

Physical Assessment

- Has moderate ascites
- Has jaundice of sclera and skin
- Has 4+ pitting edema of the lower extremities
- Liver and spleen are palpable

Laboratory Values

- Total bilirubin: 15 mg/dL (257 mmol/L)
- AST: 190 U/L (3.2 μkat/L)
- ALT: 210 U/L (3.5 μkat/L)
- Platelets: 45,000/μL
- eGFR: 62 mL/min
- ECG is below

Discussion Questions

1. ***Recognize***: Based on the history, what type of cirrhosis does M.B. likely have?
2. ***Recognize***: Describe the pathophysiologic changes that occur in the liver as cirrhosis develops.
3. ***Analyze***: Explain the significance of the results of his laboratory values and ECG findings.
4. ***Analyze***: What are possible causes of his GI bleeding?
5. ***Plan***: If M.B. begins to show signs and symptoms of hepatic encephalopathy, what would you monitor? What measures would be used to control or decrease the encephalopathy?
6. ***Prioritize:*** Based on the assessment data, what are the priority clinical problems?
7. ***Act:*** What interventions do you need to implement in this situation?
8. ***Act:*** M.B. discusses his prognosis with you. He says, "There is no hope. I might as well keep drinking." How would you respond to his statement?
9. ***Evaluate:*** What would you need to monitor to decide if care was effective?
10. ***Safety:*** Given M.B.'s bleeding history and current laboratory values, identify areas of injury risk and specify actions you will take to ensure patient safety.
11. Develop a conceptual care map for M.B.

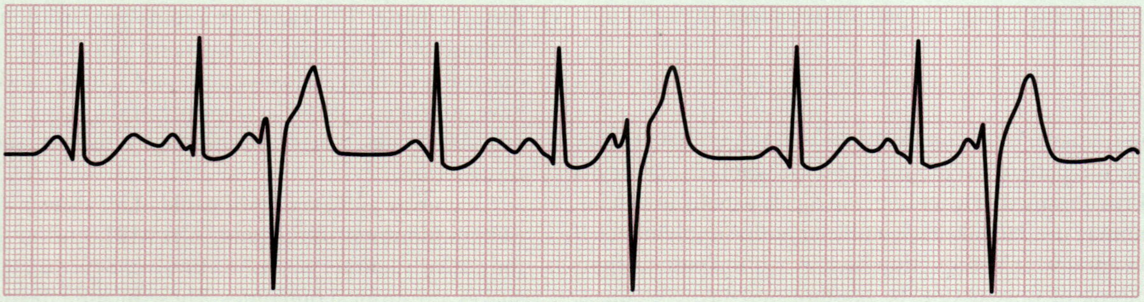

Answers and a corresponding conceptual care map available at evolve.elsevier.com/Lewis/medsurg.

BRIDGE TO NCLEX EXAMINATION

The number of the question corresponds to the same-numbered outcome at the beginning of the chapter

1. The nurse anticipates the preferred treatment for a patient with acute hepatitis A infection will include
   a. interferon.
   b. supportive care.
   c. hepatitis A vaccine.
   d. direct-acting antivirals.

2. A person needs postexposure prophylaxis for hepatitis B with hepatitis B immune globulin (HBIG). When should HBIG be given after exposure?
   a. Within 24 hours
   b. Between 1 and 2 weeks
   c. At 1 month and 6 months
   d. At 1 month, 4 months, and 6 months

3. A patient with late-stage cirrhosis develops portal hypertension. Which complications can develop from this condition? (*select all that apply*)
   a. Ascites
   b. Esophageal varices
   c. Decreased bilirubin
   d. Decreased spleen size
   e. Increased albumin levels

4. A patient with cancer that has metastasized to the liver has symptoms of fluid retention, including edema and ascites. To determine the effectiveness of diuretic therapy on ascites, what should the nurse assess?
   a. Bowel sounds
   b. Abdominal girth
   c. Recent blood work
   d. Mucous membranes

5. Which intervention would the nurse expect for a patient admitted with acute pancreatitis?
   a. Keep the patient NPO
   b. Abdominal paracentesis
   c. Start enteral feedings to prevent malnutrition
   d. Administer acetaminophen every 4 hours for pain relief
6. The patient diagnosed with pancreatic cancer underwent a Whipple procedure 2 days ago. Which clinical problem has the highest priority?
   a. Anticipatory grieving
   b. Fluid volume imbalance
   c. Impaired tissue integrity
   d. Nutritionally compromised
7. Which finding can indicate gallstones and gallbladder obstruction?
   a. Dark colored stools
   b. Pain in the left lower abdomen
   c. Referred pain to the right shoulder
   d. Improved symptoms with high-fat meals
8. Discharge teaching for the patient who underwent laparoscopic cholecystectomy should include the need to
   a. abstain from alcohol.
   b. avoid eating low-fat meals.
   c. obtain hepatitis A vaccine.
   d. call if there are changes in stool or urine color.

1. b; 2. a; 3. a, b; 4. b; 5. a; 6. b; 7. c; 8. d.

For rationales to these answers and even more NCLEX review questions, visit https://evolve.elsevier.com/Lewis/medsurg.

EVOLVE WEBSITE/RESOURCES LIST

https://evolve.elsevier.com/Lewis/medsurg
Review Questions (Online Only)
Key Points
Answer Keys for Questions
- Rationales for Bridge to NCLEX Examination Questions
- Answer Guidelines for Case Study
- Answer Guidelines for Managing Care of Multiple Patients Case Study (Section 9)

Student Case Studies
- Patient With Acute Pancreatitis and Septic Shock
- Patient With Cholelithiasis/Cholecystitis
- Patient With Cirrhosis
- Patient With Hepatitis

Nursing Care Plans
- eNursing Care Plan 48.1: Patient With Acute Viral Hepatitis
- eNursing Care Plan 48.2: Patient With Cirrhosis
- eNursing Care Plan 48.3: Patient With Acute Pancreatitis

Conceptual Care Map Creator
Conceptual Care Map for Case Study
Audio Glossary
Content Updates

REFERENCES

*1. Snyder M, McGinty M, Shearer M: Outbreaks of hepatitis A in US communities, 2017-2018: firsthand experiences and operational lessons from public health responses, *Am J Public Health* 109:S297, 2019.

*2. Nelson N, Weng M, Hofmeister M, et al.: Prevention of hepatitis A virus infection in the US: recommendations of the advisory committee on immunization practices, 2020, *MMWR (Morb Mortal Wkly Rep)* 69:1, 2020.

*3. Likhitsup A, Lok A: Understanding the natural history of hepatitis B virus infection and the new definitions of cure and the endpoints of clinical trials, *Clin Liver Dis* 23:401, 2019.

*4. American Association for the Study of Liver Disease/Infectious Disease Society of America: HCV guidance: recommendations for testing, managing, and treating hepatitis C. Retrieved from www.hcvguidelines.org.

*5. Gardenier D, Olson M, Hepatitis C: In 2019: are we there yet? *J Nurse Pract* 15:415, 2019.

6. Koh C, Da B, Glenn J: HBV/HDV coinfection: a challenge for therapeutics, *Clin Liver Dis* 23:55, 2019.

*7. Horvatits T, Schulze Zur Wiesch J, Polywka S, et al.: Significance of anti-nuclear antibodies and cryoglobulins in patients with acute and chronic HEV infection, *Pathogens* 9:755, 2020.

*8. Agbim U, Asrani S: Non-invasive assessment of liver fibrosis and prognosis: an update on serum and elastography markers, *Expert Rev Gastroenterol Hepatol* 13:361, 2019.

9. Indolfi G, Eaterbrook P, Dusheiko G, et al.: Hepatitis B virus infection in children and adolescents, *Lancet* 4:466, 2019.

10. Hosseini N, Shor J, Szabo G: Alcoholic hepatitis: a review, *Alcohol* 54:408, 2019.

11. Hoofnagle J, Björnsson E: Drug-induced liver injury: types and phenotypes, *N Engl J Med* 381:264, 2019.

*12. Mack C, Adams D, Assis D, et al.: Diagnosis and management of autoimmune hepatitis in adults and children: 2019 practice guidance and guidelines from the American Association for the Study of Liver Diseases, *Hepatology* 72:672, 2020.

13. Sandal T, Laursen T, Munk D, et al.: The prevalence of Wilson's disease: an update, *Hepatology* 71:722, 2020.

*14. Kowdley K, Brown K, Ahn J, et al.: ACG clinical guideline: hereditary hemochromatosis, *Am J Gastroenterol* 114:1202, 2019.

15. Strand P, McElvane N, Lomas D: Alpha (1)-antitrypsin deficiency, *N Engl J Med* 382:1443, 2020.

*16. Younossi Z, Bernstein D, Shiffman ML, et al.: Diagnosis and management of primary biliary cholangitis, *Am J Gastroenterol* 114:48, 2019.

17. Sheka A, Adeyi O, Thompson J, et al.: Nonalcoholic steatohepatitis: a review, *J Am Med Assoc* 323:1175, 2020.

*18. Smith A, Baumgartner K, Bositis C: Cirrhosis: diagnosis and management, *Am Fam Physician* 100:759, 2019.

19. Turbo L, Garcia-Rosa G: Portal hypertension pathogenesis and diagnosis, *Clin Liver Dis* 3:573, 2019.

20. Yanny B, Winters A, Boutros S, et al.: Hepatic encephalopathy: challenges, burden, and diagnostic and therapeutic approach, *Clin Liver Dis* 23:607, 2020.

21. Kovacs TOG, Jensen DM: Varices: esophageal, gastric, and rectal, *Clin Liver Dis* 23:25, 2019.

22. Stravitz R, Lee W: Acute liver failure, *Lancet* 394:10201, 2019.

23. Yang J, Hainaut P, Gores G, et al.: A global view of hepatocellular carcinoma: trends, risk, prevention and management, *Nat Rev Gastroenterol Hepatol* 16:589, 2019.
*24. Bejjani A, Finn R: The place of novel therapies in the American Association for the Study of Liver Diseases guidelines for hepatocellular carcinoma, *Clin Liver Dis* 14:2, 2019.
25. Marrero J: Obesity and liver disease: the new era of liver transplantation, *Hepatology* 70:2, 2019.
26. Lee PJ, Papachristour GI: New insights into acute pancreatitis, *Nat Rev Gastroenterol Hepatol* 16:479, 2019.
27. Khalaf N, El-Serag HB, Abrams HR, et al.: Burden of pancreatic cancer: from epidemiology to practice, *Clin Gastroenterol Hepatol* S1542:30276, 2020.
*28. Lucas A, Kastinos F: Screening for pancreatic cancer, *J Am Med Assoc* 322:5, 2019.
*29. Kedia P, Tarnasky P: Endoscopic management of complex biliary stone disease, *Gastrointest Endosc Clin N Am* 29:257, 2019.
30. Rawla P, Sunkara T, et al.: Epidemiology of gallbladder cancer, *Clin Exp Hepatol* 5:93, 2019.

*Evidence-based information for clinical practice.

Case Study

Applying Clinical Judgment With Multiple Patients

The following 4 patients are among the 7 you are assigned to care for today on the medical unit. You have 1 LPN and 1 AP who are assigned to help you.

 (© iStockphoto/ Thinkstock.)	M.S. is a 70-year-old woman who was admitted with weakness and malnutrition. She is 5 ft, 4 in tall and weighs 100 lb, with a 30-lb weight loss in past 2 months. Her history includes a recent stroke with hemiparesis and dysphagia. She has been NPO for the past 24 hours and started EN via PEG tube placed yesterday afternoon.
 (© Christa Brunt/ iStock/Thinkstock.)	S.R. is a 48-year-old woman admitted with chest pain. She has a history of type 2 diabetes, hypertension, and osteoarthritis. She is 5 ft, 6 in tall and weighs 230 lb. Her last 2 glucose levels were over 250 mg/dL and she received sliding scale insulin. Cardiac enzymes and ECG are all normal. She is scheduled to have a cardiac stress test at 10 AM. Vital signs: 160/110, 102, RR 22, O_2 saturation 94% with O_2 2 L/min via nasal cannula.
 (© iStockphoto/ Thinkstock.)	F.H., a 40-year-old man, was admitted yesterday with upper GI bleeding. He had just finished treatment with omeprazole, clarithromycin, and amoxicillin for a duodenal ulcer and *H. pylori*. He came to the ED yesterday with severe epigastric pain and melena. He is on a pantoprazole IV infusion and scheduled for a repeat EGD today.
 (© sbeagle/iStock/ Thinkstock.)	M.B. is a 58-year-old man admitted early this morning with upper GI bleeding. He has had cirrhosis for 12 years. He reports vomiting for 2 days. He currently has anorexia, nausea, and abdominal discomfort with severe ascites, jaundice, and 4+ pitting edema. His liver enzymes are high and platelet count is 45,000/μL. Vital signs: 102/54, 102, RR 22, O_2 saturation 94% with O_2 2 L/min via nasal cannula.

1. Highlight all the findings above that require your follow-up.
2. After receiving report, which patient should you see first?
3. Which tasks could you delegate to the LPN? *(Select all that apply.)*
   a. Administer a bolus enteral tube feeding to M.S.
   b. Assess M.S.'s PEG tube dressing and bowel sounds.
   c. Administer a scheduled dose of oral lactulose solution to M.B.
   d. Teach F.H.'s wife about his disease because she speaks English.
   e. Perform bedside glucose reading and administer sliding scale insulin to S.R.
4. Which diagnostic finding would you report to the HCP immediately?
   a. Blood glucose level 220 mg/dL for S.R.
   b. Hemoglobin 6.9 g/dL and hematocrit 21% for F.H.
   c. Serum sodium 134 mEq/L and potassium 3.4 mEq/L for M.S.
   d. Total bilirubin 3.2 mg/dL with positive urine bilirubin for M.B.
5. As you are assessing M.B., the LPN tells you that F.H. just vomited a large amount of bright red blood. What initial action would be *most* appropriate?
   a. Have the LPN administer an antiemetic to F.H.
   b. Ask the LPN to notify F.H.'s HCP immediately.
   c. Leave M.B.'s room to perform a focused assessment on F.H.
   d. Ask the AP to obtain a unit of packed RBCs from the blood bank.

Case Study Progression

When you enter F.H.'s room, he tells you that his pain actually feels somewhat relieved since he vomited. However, you note that his skin is cool and clammy, his BP is 90/54 mm Hg, and his heart rate is 116 bpm. You notify his HCP.

6. Which interventions would you expect the HCP to order for F.H.? *(select all that apply)*
   a. Stat hemoglobin and hematocrit
   b. Emergent endoscopy with band ligation
   c. Discontinue the pantoprazole (Protonix) infusion
   d. Start a second IV site and administer a 500 mL normal saline bolus
   e. Contact HCP and notify operating room that patient is unstable and needs surgery
7. You see that you need to complete M.B.'s medication reconciliation for the new HCP orders. Choose the most likely options for the information missing from the table below by selecting from the lists of options provided.

Medication	Dose, Route, Frequency	Drug Class	Indication
Propranolol	1	β-blocker	Decrease portal venous pressure
2	100 mg PO daily	Potassium-sparing diuretic	Excrete fluid with ascites
Lactulose	15 mL PO twice daily	Laxative	3
Vasopressin	10 units subcut 3 times daily	4	Decrease portal blood flow

Case Study—cont'd

Options for 1	Options for 2	Options for 3	Options for 4
20 mg IV every 12 hours 320 mg PO twice daily 640 mg PO daily	acetazolamide chlorothiazide spironolactone	Decrease bacterial flora Decrease gastric acidity Fecal elimination of ammonia	Anticoagulant Antihypertensive Hormone analog

8. Which intervention to treat ascites would you expect the HCP to order for M.B.? *(select all that apply)*
   a. Thoracentesis
   b. 2 g sodium diet
   c. Diuretic therapy
   d. 1800 mL/day fluid restriction
   e. Shunt insertion from peritoneum to heart
9. While you are administering M.S.'s bolus feeding of EN, you perform her assessment. For each assessment finding, use an X to indicate whether the interventions were Effective (helped to meet expected outcomes), Ineffective (did not help to meet expected outcomes), or Unrelated (not related to the expected outcomes).

Assessment Finding	Effective	Ineffective	Unrelated
Swallowing without difficulty			
Weight gain of 2 lb in 1 week			
Periodic diarrheal stools			
Improved activity intolerance			
Increased muscle strength			
Wound around PEG tube not healing properly			

10. After giving M.S. the bolus feeding, it would be *most* important to
    a. assess for gastric residual.
    b. obtain an abdominal x-ray.
    c. keep head of bed elevated 30–45 degrees.
    d. record the total amount of fluid administered.
11. As you enter the nurse's station, you overhear derogatory comments made by the AP to the LPN about S.R.'s weight. Which response would be *most* appropriate?
    a. Report the incident to charge nurse for follow-up.
    b. Talk to the AP to discuss a possible HIPAA violation.
    c. Talk to S.R. about the impact of AP's bias on the patient's self-image.
    d. Set up an in-service to teach staff members to recognize obesity as a disease process.

Answers available at http://evolve.elsevier.com/Lewis/medsurg.

49

Assessment: Urinary System

Teresa Turnbull

http://evolve.elsevier.com/Lewis/medsurg/

CONCEPTUAL FOCUS

Elimination

Fluids and Electrolytes

LEARNING OUTCOMES

1. Identify the anatomic location and functions of the kidneys, ureters, bladder, and urethra.
2. Explain the physiologic events involved in the formation and passage of urine from glomerular filtration to voiding.
3. Obtain significant subjective and objective data related to the urinary system from a patient.
4. Link the age-related changes of the urinary system to the differences in assessment findings.
5. Perform a physical assessment of the urinary system using appropriate techniques.
6. Distinguish normal from abnormal findings of a physical assessment of the urinary system.
7. Describe the purpose, significance of results, and nursing responsibilities related to diagnostic studies of the urinary system.
8. Evaluate findings of a urinalysis.

KEY TERMS

costovertebral angle (CVA)
creatinine
cystoscopy, Table 49.12
glomerular filtration rate (GFR)
glomerulus
nephron
renal biopsy, Table 49.12
urinalysis

Adequate kidney function is essential to health. If a person has complete kidney failure and treatment is not provided, death is inevitable. This chapter discusses the structures and functions, assessment, and diagnostic studies of the urinary system.

STRUCTURES AND FUNCTIONS OF URINARY SYSTEM

The *upper urinary system* consists of 2 kidneys and 2 ureters. The *lower urinary system* consists of a urinary bladder and urethra (Fig. 49.1). Urine is formed in the kidneys, drains through the ureters to be stored in the bladder, and then passes out of the body through the urethra.

Kidneys

The kidneys are the principal organs of the urinary system. The primary functions of the kidneys are to (1) regulate the volume and composition of extracellular fluid (ECF) and (2) excrete waste products from the body. The kidneys also function to control BP, make erythropoietin, activate vitamin D, and regulate acid-base balance.

Macrostructure

The paired kidneys are bean-shaped organs located retroperitoneally (behind the peritoneum) on either side of the vertebral column at about the level of the 12th thoracic (T12) vertebra to the 3rd lumbar (L3) vertebra. Each kidney weighs 4 to 6 oz (113 to 170 g) and is about 5 in (12.5 cm) long. The right kidney, positioned at the level of the twelfth rib, is lower than the left. An adrenal gland lies on top of each kidney.

Each kidney is surrounded by a significant amount of fat and connective tissue that cushion, support, and help the kidney to maintain its position. A thin, smooth layer of fibrous membrane called the *capsule* covers the surface of each kidney. The capsule protects the kidney and serves as a shock absorber if this area is traumatized from a sudden force or strike. The *hilus* on the medial side of the kidney serves as the entry site for the renal artery and nerves and as the exit site for the renal vein and ureter.

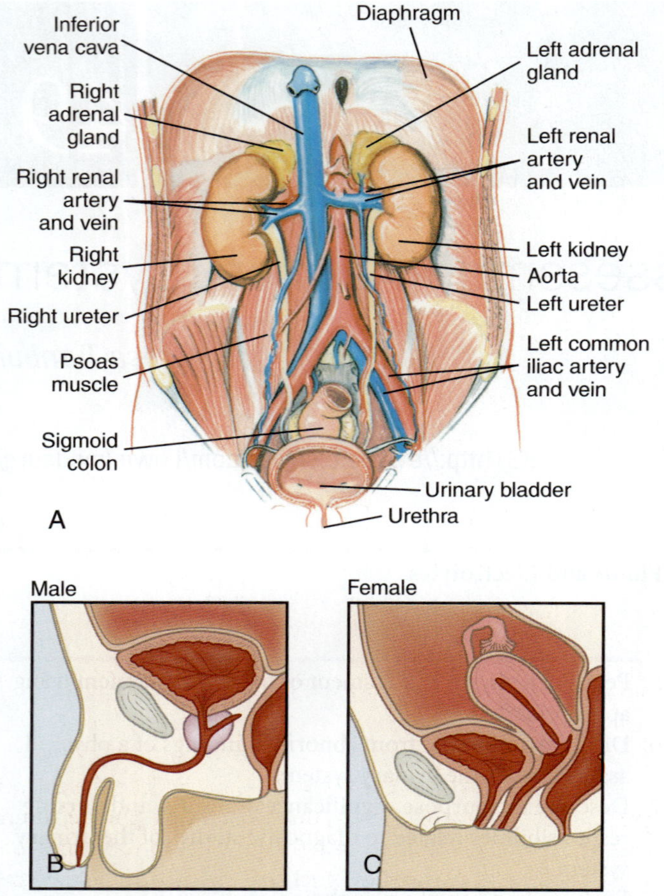

Fig. 49.1 Organs of the urinary system. (A) Upper urinary tract in relation to other anatomic structures. (B) Male urethra in relation to other pelvic structures. (C) Female urethra.

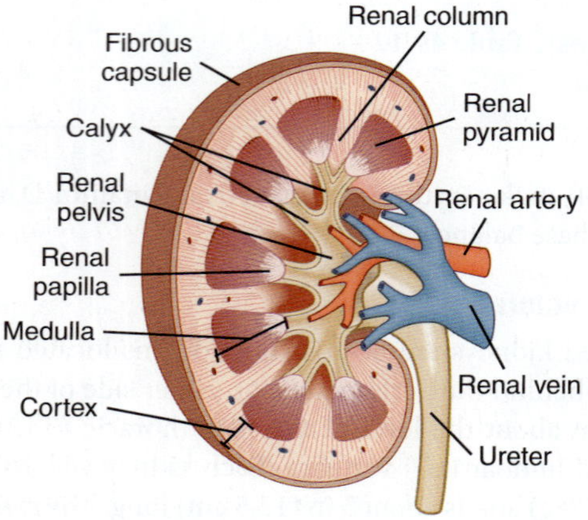

Fig. 49.2 Longitudinal section of the kidney.

The *parenchyma* is the actual tissue of the kidney (Fig. 49.2). The outer layer of the parenchyma is the *cortex*. The inner layer is the *medulla*. The medulla consists of a number of pyramids. The apices (tops) of these pyramids are the *papillae,* through which urine passes to enter the calyces. The minor calyces widen and merge to form major calyces, which form a funnel-shaped sac called the *renal pelvis*. The minor and major calyces transport urine to the renal pelvis, from there it drains through the ureter to the bladder. The renal pelvis can store a small volume of urine (3 to 5 mL).

Microstructure

The **nephron** is the functional unit of the kidney. Each kidney has around 1 million nephrons. Each nephron is composed of the glomerulus, Bowman capsule, and a tubular system. The tubular system consists of the proximal convoluted tubule, loop of Henle, distal convoluted tubule, and collecting tubules (Fig. 49.3). The glomerulus, Bowman capsule, proximal tubule, and distal tubule are in the cortex of the kidney. The loop of Henle and collecting tubules are in the medulla. Several collecting tubules join to form a single collecting duct. The collecting ducts eventually merge into a pyramid that empties via the papilla into a minor calyx.

Blood Supply

Blood flow to the kidneys, around 1200 mL/min, accounts for 20% to 25% of the cardiac output. Blood reaches the kidneys via the renal artery, which arises from the aorta and enters the kidney through the hilus. The renal artery divides into secondary branches and then into still smaller branches, each of which forms an afferent arteriole. The afferent arteriole divides into a capillary network, the **glomerulus**, which is a collection of up to 50 capillaries (Fig. 49.3). The capillaries of the glomerulus unite in the efferent arteriole. This efferent arteriole splits to form a capillary network, the peritubular capillaries, which surround the tubular system. All peritubular capillaries drain into the venous system. The renal vein empties into the inferior vena cava.

Physiology of Urine Formation

Urine formation is the outcome of a complex, multistep process of filtration, reabsorption, secretion, and excretion of water, electrolytes, and metabolic waste products. Although urine formation is the result of this process, the primary functions of the kidneys are to filter the blood and maintain the body's internal homeostasis.

Glomerular function. Urine formation begins at the glomerulus, where blood is filtered. The glomerulus is a semipermeable membrane that allows filtration (Fig. 49.3). The hydrostatic pressure of the blood within the glomerular capillaries causes a portion of blood to be filtered across the semipermeable membrane into Bowman capsule. There, the filtered portion of the blood (glomerular filtrate) begins to pass down to the tubule. Filtration is more rapid in the glomerulus than in ordinary tissue capillaries because the glomerular membrane is porous. The glomerular filtrate is similar in composition to blood except that it lacks blood cells, platelets, and large plasma proteins. Under normal conditions, capillary pores are too small to allow the loss of these large blood components. However, in many kidney diseases, capillary permeability increases, which allows plasma proteins and blood cells to pass into the urine.

The amount of blood filtered each minute by the glomeruli is the **glomerular filtration rate (GFR)**. The normal GFR is about 125 mL/min. The peritubular capillary network reabsorbs most of the glomerular filtrate before it reaches the end

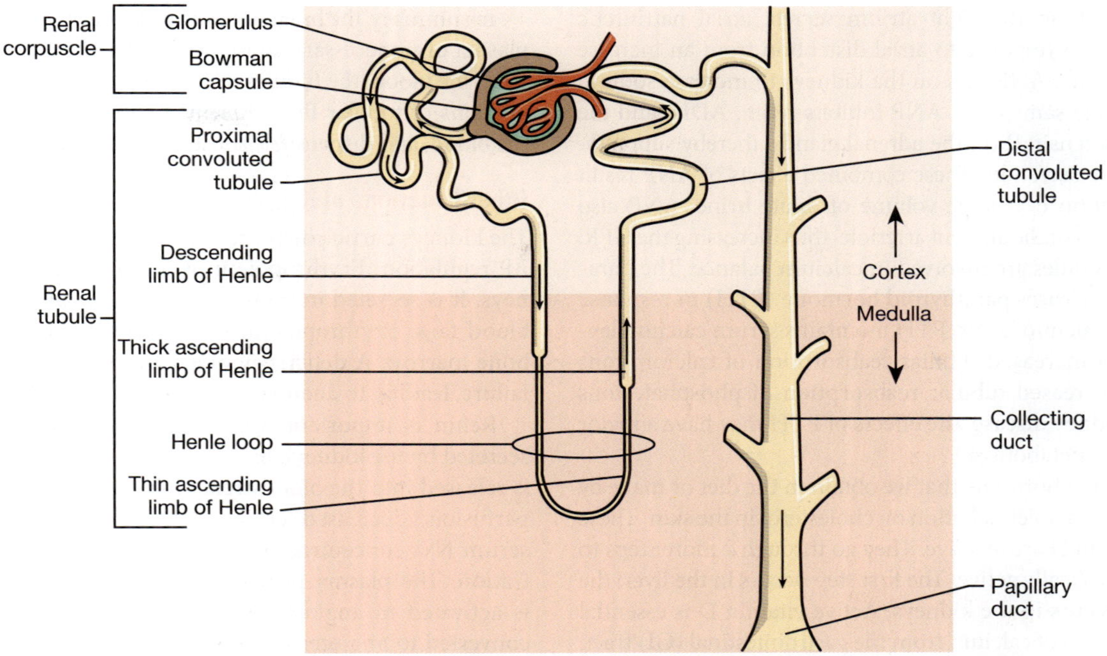

Fig. 49.3 The nephron is the basic functional unit of the kidney. This illustration of a single nephron unit shows the surrounding blood vessels. (Modified from Thibodeau GA, Patton KT: *The human body in health and disease,* ed 4, St Louis, 2005, Mosby.)

TABLE 49.1 Functions of Nephron Segments

Segment	Function
Glomerulus	Selective filtration
Proximal tubule	Reabsorption of 80% of electrolytes and water, glucose, amino acids, HCO_3^- Secretion of H^+ and creatinine
Loop of Henle	Concentration of filtrate Reabsorption of Na^+ and Cl^- in ascending limb and water in descending loop
Distal tubule	Reabsorption of water (regulated by ADH) and HCO_3^- Regulation of Ca^{2+} and PO_4^{2-}—by parathyroid hormone Regulation of Na^+ and K^+ by aldosterone Secretion of K^+, H^+, ammonia
Collecting duct	Reabsorption of water (requires ADH)

of the collecting duct. Therefore only 1 mL/min (on average) is excreted as urine.

Tubular function. The tubules and collecting ducts are responsible for the reabsorption of essential materials and excretion of nonessential ones (Table 49.1). They carry out these functions by reabsorption and secretion. *Reabsorption* is the passage of a substance from the lumen of the tubules through the tubule cells and into the capillaries. This process involves both active and passive transport mechanisms. Tubular *secretion* is the passage of a substance from the capillaries through the tubular cells into the lumen of the tubule. Reabsorption and secretion cause many changes in the composition of the glomerular filtrate as it moves through the entire length of the tubule.

In the proximal convoluted tubule, about 80% of the electrolytes are reabsorbed. Normally, this includes all glucose, amino acids, and small proteins. As reabsorption continues in the loop of Henle, water is conserved, which is important for concentrating the filtrate. The descending loop is permeable to water and moderately permeable to sodium, urea, and other solutes. In the ascending limb, chloride ions (Cl^-) are actively reabsorbed, followed by passive reabsorption of sodium ions (Na^+). About 25% of the filtered sodium is reabsorbed in the ascending limb.

Two key functions of the distal convoluted tubules are final regulation of water balance and acid-base balance. Antidiuretic hormone (ADH) is needed for water reabsorption in the kidney. It is important in water balance. ADH makes the distal convoluted tubules and collecting ducts permeable to water. This allows water to be reabsorbed into the peritubular capillaries and eventually returned to the circulation.

Osmoreceptors in the anterior hypothalamus detect decreases in plasma osmolality. These osmoreceptors send neural input to *superoptic nuclei cells* in the hypothalamus. These superoptic nuclei cells have neuronal axons that end in the posterior pituitary gland and act to inhibit ADH secretion. In the absence of ADH, the tubules are essentially impermeable to water. Thus, any water in the tubules leaves the body as urine.

Aldosterone (released from the adrenal cortex) acts on the distal tubule to cause reabsorption of Na^+ and water. In exchange for Na^+, potassium ions (K^+) are excreted. Circulating blood volume and plasma concentrations of Na^+ and K^+ influence aldosterone secretion.

Acid-base regulation involves reabsorbing and conserving most of the bicarbonate (HCO_3^-) and secreting excess hydrogen ions (H^+). The distal tubule has different ways to keep the pH of ECF within a range of 7.35 to 7.45 (see Chapter 17).

Myocyte cells in the right atrium secrete atrial natriuretic peptide (ANP) in response to atrial distention from an increase in plasma volume. ANP acts on the kidneys to increase sodium excretion. At the same time, ANP inhibits renin, ADH, and the action of angiotensin II on the adrenal glands, thereby suppressing aldosterone secretion. These combined effects of ANP result in the production of a large volume of dilute urine. ANP also causes relaxation of the afferent arteriole, thus increasing the GFR.

The renal tubules are involved in calcium balance. The parathyroid gland releases parathyroid hormone (PTH) in response to low serum calcium levels. PTH maintains serum calcium levels by causing increased tubular reabsorption of calcium ions (Ca^{2+}) and decreased tubular reabsorption of phosphate ions (PO_4^{2-}). In kidney disease, the effects of PTH may have a major effect on bone metabolism.

Vitamin D is a hormone that we obtain in the diet or make by the action of ultraviolet radiation on cholesterol in the skin. These forms of vitamin D are inactive. They go through 2 more steps to become metabolically active. The first step occurs in the liver; the second step occurs in the kidneys. Active vitamin D is essential for the absorption of calcium from the gastrointestinal (GI) tract. The patient with kidney failure (also called *renal failure*) will have a deficiency of the active metabolite of vitamin D and problems with calcium and phosphate balance (see Chapter 52).

In summary, the basic function of nephrons is to cleanse blood plasma of unnecessary substances. After the glomerulus has filtered the blood, the tubules select the unwanted from the wanted portions of tubular fluid. Essential constituents are returned to the blood, and dispensable substances pass into urine.

Other Functions of Kidneys

The kidneys participate in red blood cell (RBC) production and BP regulation. Erythropoietin is a hormone made in the kidneys. It is secreted in response to hypoxia and decreased renal blood flow. Erythropoietin stimulates RBC production in the bone marrow. A deficiency of erythropoietin occurs in kidney failure, leading to anemia.

Renin is important in BP regulation. Renin is made and secreted by the kidney's juxtaglomerular cells (Fig. 49.4). Renin is released into the bloodstream in response to decreased renal perfusion, decreased arterial BP, decreased ECF, decreased serum Na^+ concentration, and increased urinary Na^+ concentration. The plasma protein angiotensinogen (from the liver) is activated to angiotensin I by renin. Angiotensin I is then converted to angiotensin II by angiotensin-converting enzyme (ACE). ACE is found on the inner surface of all blood vessels, with especially high levels in the vessels of the lungs. Angiotensin II stimulates the release of aldosterone from the adrenal cortex.

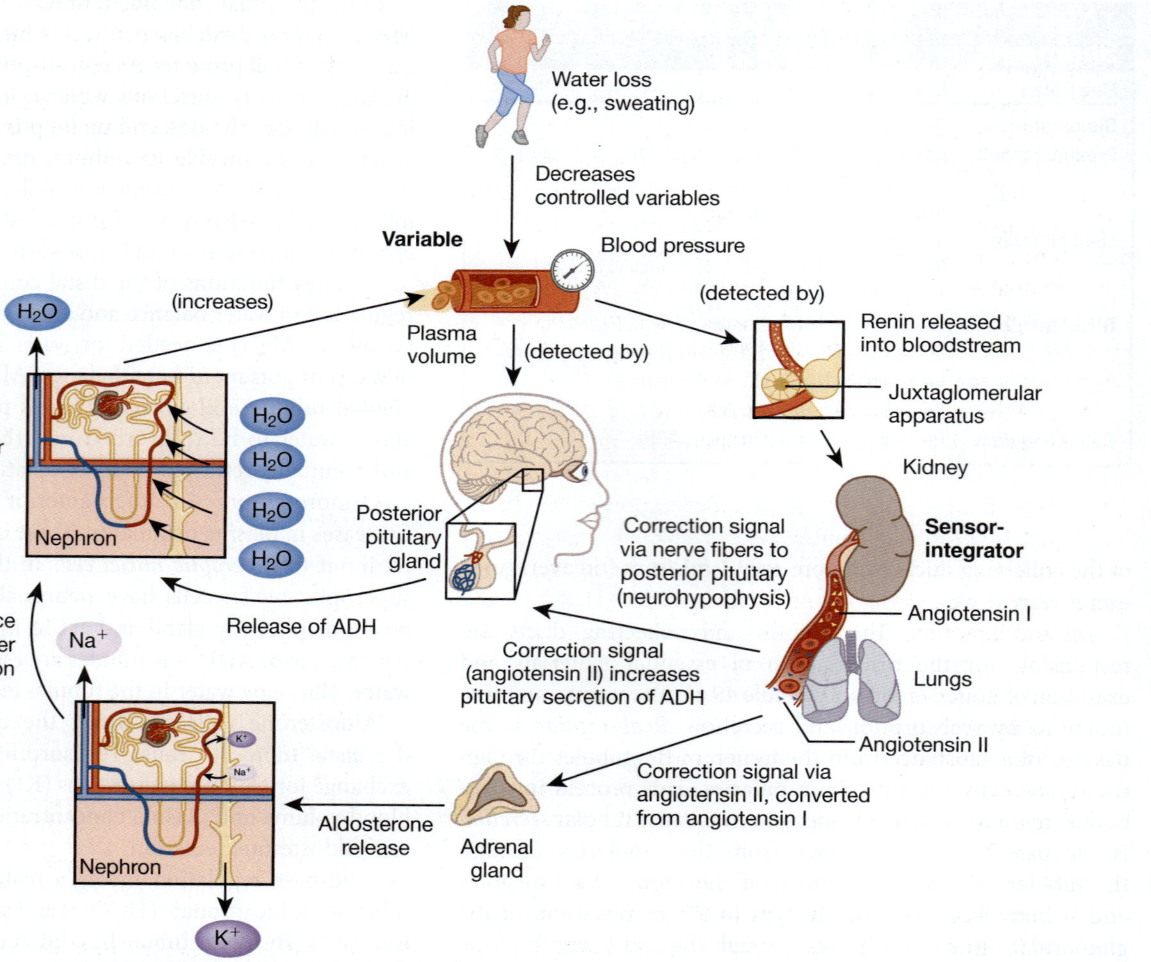

Fig. 49.4 Feedback renin-angiotensin-aldosterone system to fluid loss.

This causes Na^+ and water retention, leading to increased ECF volume. Angiotensin II also causes increased peripheral vasoconstriction. An elevated BP inhibits renin release. Excessive renin production caused by impaired renal perfusion may be a contributing factor in causing hypertension (see Chapter 36).

Most body tissues make prostaglandins (PGs) from the precursor arachidonic acid in response to appropriate stimuli. (See Chapter 12 and Fig. 12.2 for more about PGs.) In the kidney, PG synthesis (mainly PGE_2 and PGI_2) occurs mainly in the medulla. These PGs have a vasodilating action, thus increasing renal blood flow and promoting Na^+ excretion. They counteract the vasoconstrictive effect of substances such as angiotensin and norepinephrine. Renal PGs may have a systemic effect in lowering BP by decreasing systemic vascular resistance. The significance of renal PGs is related to the kidneys' role in causing hypertension. In renal failure with a loss of functioning tissue, these renal vasodilator factors are also lost, which may contribute to hypertension (see Chapter 36).

Ureters

The ureters are tubes that carry urine from the renal pelvis to the bladder (Fig. 49.1). Each ureter is about 10 to 12 inches (25 to 30.5 cm) long and 0.08 to 0.3 inches (0.2 to 0.8 cm) in diameter. Arranged in a mesh-like outer layer, circular and longitudinal smooth muscle fibers contract to promote the peristaltic, 1-way flow of urine through the ureters. Distention, neurologic and endocrine influences, and drugs can affect these muscle contractions.

The narrow area where each ureter joins the renal pelvis is the *ureteropelvic junction* (UPJ). The ureters insert into either side of the bladder base at the *ureterovesical junctions* (UVJs). Because the ureteral lumens are narrowest at these junctions, the UPJ and UVJ are often sites of obstruction. The narrow ureteral lumens can be easily obstructed internally (e.g., urinary stones) or externally (e.g., tumors, adhesions, inflammation). Sympathetic and parasympathetic nerves, along with the vascular supply, surround the mucosal lining of the ureters. Stimulation of these nerves during passage of a stone may cause acute, severe pain, termed *renal colic*.

Because the renal pelvis holds only 3 to 5 mL of urine, kidney damage can result from a backflow of more than that amount of urine. The UVJ relies on the ureter's angle of bladder insertion and muscle fiber attachments with the bladder to prevent the backflow *(reflux)* of urine, which predisposes a person to an ascending infection. The distal ureter enters the bladder laterally at its base. It then courses obliquely through the bladder wall for about 1.5 cm and intermingles with muscle fibers of the bladder base. Circular and longitudinal bladder muscle fibers adjacent to the imbedded ureter help secure it. When bladder pressure rises (e.g., during voiding or coughing), muscle fibers that the ureter shares with the bladder base contract first, promoting ureteral lumen closure. Next, the bladder contracts against its base, ensuring UVJ closure and preventing urine reflux through the junction.

Bladder

The urinary bladder is located behind the symphysis pubis and anterior to the vagina and rectum (Fig. 49.5). Its primary functions are to serve as a reservoir for urine and to eliminate waste products from the body. Like the stomach, the bladder is a stretchable, saclike organ that contracts when it is empty.

The *trigone* is the triangular area formed by the 2 ureteral openings and bladder neck at the base of the bladder. The trigone is attached to the pelvis by many ligaments. It does not change its shape during bladder filling or emptying. The bladder muscle *(detrusor)* is composed of layers of intertwined smooth muscle fibers. These fibers are capable of considerable distention during bladder filling and contraction during emptying. It is attached to the abdominal wall by an umbilical ligament, the *urachus*. Because of this attachment, as the bladder fills, it rises toward the umbilicus. The dome and the anterior and lateral aspects of the bladder expand and contract.

Normal adult urine output is around 1500 mL/day, which varies with food and fluid intake. The volume of urine at night is less than half of that formed during the day because of hormonal influences (e.g., ADH). This diurnal pattern of urination is normal. Typically, a person will urinate 5 or 6 times during the day and sometimes at night.

On average, 200 to 250 mL of urine in the bladder cause moderate distention and the urge to urinate. When the quantity of urine reaches 400 to 600 mL, the person feels uncomfortable. Bladder capacity varies with the person, but generally ranges from 600 to 1000 mL. Evacuation of urine is termed *urination, micturition,* or *voiding*.

The bladder has the same mucosal lining as that of the renal pelvises, ureters, and bladder neck. The bladder is lined by transitional cell epithelium referred to as the *urothelium*. Unique to the urinary tract, the urothelium is resistant to absorption of urine. This means that after waste products (made by the kidneys) have left the kidneys, they cannot be reabsorbed in the

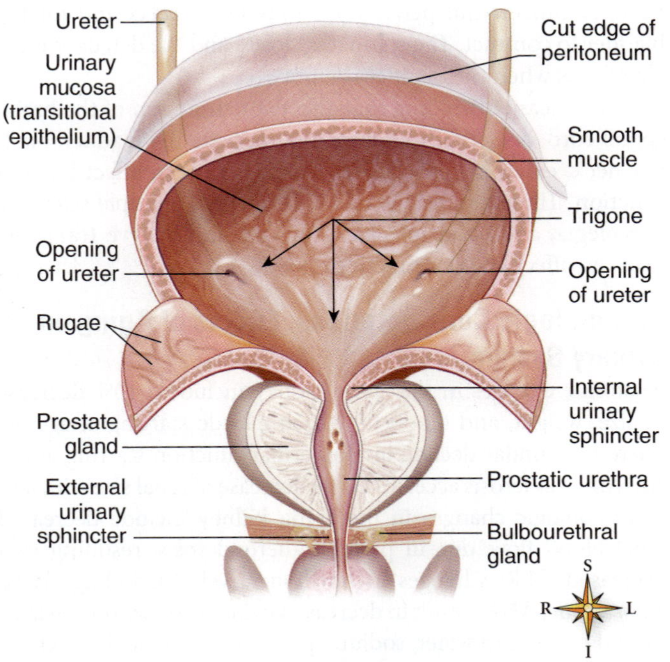

Fig. 49.5 Distended male urinary bladder. (From Patton KT, Thibodeau GA: *The human body in health & disease*, ed 7, St Louis, 2018, Mosby.)

urinary system. Microscopically, urothelium is only several cells deep. However, as urine enters the bladder, these cells can stretch to accommodate filling. As the bladder empties, the urothelium resumes its multicellular layer formation.

Urethra

The urethra is a small tube that incorporates the smooth muscle of the bladder neck and extends to the striated muscle of the external meatus. The urethra's primary functions are to (1) control voiding and (2) serve as a conduit for urine from the bladder to the outside of the body during voiding.

The female urethra is 1 in to 2 in (2.5 cm to 5 cm) long and lies behind the symphysis pubis but anterior to the vagina (Fig. 49.1C). The male urethra, which is about 8 in to 10 in (20 cm to 25 cm) long, starts at the bladder neck and extends the length of the penis (Fig. 49.1B).

Urethrovesical Unit

Together, the bladder, urethra, and pelvic floor muscles form the *urethrovesical unit.* Voluntary control of this unit is defined as *continence.* Stimulating and inhibiting impulses are sent from the brain through the thoracolumbar (T11 to L2) and sacral (S2 to S4) areas of the spinal cord to control voiding. Bladder distention stimulates stretch receptors within the bladder wall. Impulses are transmitted to the sacral spinal cord and then to the brain, causing a desire to urinate.

If you cannot void at a given time, inhibitor impulses in the brain are stimulated and transmitted back through the thoracolumbar and sacral nerves innervating the bladder. In a coordinated fashion, the detrusor muscle accommodates to the pressure (does not contract) while the sphincter and pelvic floor muscles tighten (contract) to resist bladder pressure.

If you can void, cerebral inhibition is voluntarily suppressed. Impulses are transmitted via the spinal cord for the bladder neck, sphincter, and pelvic floor muscles to relax and for the bladder to contract. The sphincter closes, and the detrusor muscle relaxes when the bladder is empty.

Any disease or trauma that affects the function of the brain, spinal cord, or nerves that directly innervate the bladder, bladder neck, external sphincter, or pelvic floor can affect bladder function. These conditions include diabetes, multiple sclerosis, paraplegia, and quadriplegia. Drugs affecting nerve transmission can affect bladder function.

Gerontologic Considerations: Effects of Aging on Urinary System

Anatomic changes in the aging kidney include a 10% decrease in size, weight, and blood flow each decade starting at age 30. There is a similar decline in glomerular function starting at age 40.[1] Atherosclerosis accelerates the decrease of renal size with age.

Physiologic changes in the aging kidney include decreased renal blood flow, due in part to atherosclerosis, resulting in a decreased GFR. Changes in hormone levels (including ADH, aldosterone, ANP) result in decreased urinary concentrating ability and changes in water, sodium, potassium, and acid excretion. Despite these changes, older adults maintain homeostasis unless they have other problems. After abrupt changes in blood volume, acid load, or other insults, the kidney may not be able to function effectively because much of its renal reserve has been lost.[1]

Physiologic changes occur in the aging urethra and bladder. The female urethra, bladder, vagina, and pelvic floor lose elasticity and muscle support. Consequently, older women are more prone to bladder infections and incontinence. The prostate surrounds the proximal urethra. As men age, the prostate enlarges. This can affect urinary patterns, causing hesitancy, retention, slow stream, and bladder infections.

Constipation, often experienced by older adults, can affect urination. Partial urethral obstruction may occur because the rectum is close to the urethra. Age-related changes in the urinary system and differences in assessment findings are outlined in Table 49.2.

ASSESSMENT OF URINARY SYSTEM

Subjective Data

Important Health Information

Health history. Ask the patient about the presence or history of kidney disease or other urologic problems. Note specific urinary problems, such as cancer, infections, benign prostatic hyperplasia (BPH), and stones. Are there other health problems that may affect kidney function? These include hypertension, diabetes, gout, connective tissue disorders (e.g., systemic lupus erythematosus), hepatitis, human immunodeficiency virus (HIV) infection, neurologic problems (e.g., stroke, back injury), and trauma.[2]

TABLE 49.2 GERONTOLOGIC ASSESSMENT DIFFERENCES

Urinary System

Gerontologic Changes	Differences in Assessment Findings
Kidney	
• ↓ Amount of renal tissue	• Less palpable
• ↓ Number of nephrons and renal blood vessels. Thickened basement membrane of Bowman capsule and glomeruli	• ↓ Creatinine clearance, ↑ BUN level, ↑ serum creatinine
• ↓ Function of loop of Henle and tubules	• Changes in drug excretion, nocturia, loss of normal diurnal excretory pattern because of ↓ ability to concentrate urine; less concentrated urine
Ureter, Bladder, and Urethra	
• ↓ Elasticity and muscle tone	• Palpable bladder after urination because of retention
• Weakening of urinary sphincter	• Stress incontinence (especially during Valsalva maneuver), dribbling of urine after urination
• ↓ Bladder capacity and sensory receptors	• Frequency, urgency, nocturia, overflow incontinence
• Estrogen deficiency leading to thin, dry vaginal tissue	• Stress or overactive bladder, dysuria
• ↑ Prevalence of unstable bladder contractions	• Overactive bladder
• Prostate enlargement	• Hesitancy, frequency, urgency, nocturia, straining to urinate, retention, dribbling

Medications. Assess the patient's current and past use of medications. Include over-the-counter drugs, prescription drugs, and herbal therapies. Drugs affect the urinary tract in several ways. Many drugs can be nephrotoxic (Table 49.3). Certain drugs may alter the quantity and character of urine output (e.g., diuretics). Several drugs change the color of urine. Phenazopyridine (Pyridium) turns urine orange. Nitrofurantoin turns urine dark yellow to brown. Anticoagulants may cause hematuria. Many antidepressants, calcium channel blockers, antihistamines, and drugs used for neurologic and musculoskeletal problems affect the ability of the bladder or sphincter to contract or relax normally.

Surgery or other treatments. Ask the patient about hospitalizations related to renal or urologic problems. Were there any urinary problems during past pregnancies? Ask about the duration, severity, and patient's perception of any problem and its treatment. Have they had surgery, especially pelvic surgery, and urinary tract instrumentation (e.g., catheterization)? Ask the patient about any radiation or chemotherapy treatment for cancer.

Case Study

Patient Introduction

(© iStockphoto/ Thinkstock.)

A.K. is a 28-year-old man who comes to the emergency department (ED) in acute distress with severe abdominal pain. The pain began about 6 hours ago after he finished a 10-mile run as part of his training for a marathon. He says that the pain has steadily increased, and he is nauseous. His urine is a dark, smoky color.

Discussion Questions

1. What are the possible causes of A.K.'s abdominal pain, nausea, and urine color?
2. What type of assessment would be most appropriate for A.K.: comprehensive, focused, or emergency? On what basis did you make that decision?
3. What assessment questions will you ask him?

You will learn more about A.K. and his condition as you read through this assessment chapter.

Answers available at http://evolve.elsevier.com/Lewis/medsurg.

TABLE 49.3 Potentially Nephrotoxic Agents

Antimicrobials	Other Drugs	Other Agents
• aminoglycosides	• ACE inhibitors	• Gold
• amphotericin B	• captopril	• Heavy metals
• antivirals	• cimetidine	
• cephalosporins	• cisplatin	
• polymyxin B	• cocaine	
• sulfonamides	• cyclosporine	
• vancomycin	• heroin	
	• lithium	
	• methotrexate	
	• nitrosoureas (e.g., carmustine)	
	• NSAIDs (e.g., ibuprofen, indomethacin)	
	• quinine	
	• rifampin	
	• salicylates (large quantities)	
	• statins	

Functional Health Patterns

Table 49.4 lists key questions to ask a patient with problems related to the renal system.

Health perception–health management pattern. Ask about the patient's general health. Abnormal kidney function may be suspected if the patient reports changes in weight or appetite, excess thirst, fluid retention, headache, pruritus, blurred vision, or "feeling tired all the time." An older adult may report malaise and nonlocalized abdominal discomfort as the only symptoms of a urinary tract infection (UTI). In older adults with a UTI, family members may report the patient is disoriented, has fallen, or has increased confusion.

Obtain a smoking history. Cigarette smoking is a major risk factor for bladder and kidney cancer. Smokers who work with cancer-causing chemicals have an especially high risk for bladder cancer.

Exposure to certain chemicals can affect the urinary system. Aromatic amines and some organic chemicals increase the risk for bladder cancer. Phenol and ethylene glycol are examples of nephrotoxic chemicals. Obtain an occupational history. Machinists, painters, hairdressers, printers, and truck drivers have an increased risk for bladder cancer.[3]

Information about places where a patient has lived is important. Persons living in the U.S. Southeast have the highest incidence of urinary stones (referred to as "stone belt"). This may be caused by differences in temperature, humidity, and sunlight.[4] A person living in Middle Eastern countries or Africa can acquire certain parasites that can cause cystitis or bladder cancer (Box 49.1).

Nutritional-metabolic pattern. The usual quantity and types of fluid a patient drinks are important in relation to urinary tract disease. Dehydration may contribute to UTIs, stone formation, and kidney failure. Large intake of specific foods, such as dairy products or foods high in proteins, may lead to stone formation. Asparagus may cause the urine to smell musty. Red urine caused by beet ingestion may be mistaken for bloody urine. Caffeine, alcohol, carbonated beverages, some artificial sweeteners, or spicy foods often worsen urinary inflammatory diseases. Green tea and some herbal teas cause diuresis. An unexplained weight gain may be the result of fluid retention from a kidney problem. Anorexia, nausea, and vomiting can dramatically affect fluid status and require careful monitoring.

Elimination pattern. Questions about urine elimination patterns are the cornerstone of the health history in the patient with a lower urinary tract disorder. Begin with asking how the patient manages urine elimination. Ask about daytime (diurnal) voiding frequency and the frequency of nocturia. Pelvic organ prolapses, particularly advanced anterior vaginal prolapse, may cause suprapubic pressure, frequency, urgency, and incontinence from urinary retention. Ask about other bothersome lower urinary tract symptoms, including urgency, incontinence, or urinary retention. Table 49.5 lists some common manifestations of urinary tract disorders.

Changes in the color and appearance of urine are often significant and need evaluated. If blood is visible in the urine, determine if it occurs at the beginning of, throughout, or at the end of urination. This is harder for the female patient.

TABLE 49.4 HEALTH HISTORY

Urinary System

Health Perception–Health Management
- How is your energy level compared with 1 year ago?
- Do you have any vision changes?[a]
- Have you ever smoked? If yes, how many packs per day?
- Tell me about the types of jobs you have had.

Nutritional-Metabolic
- How is your appetite?
- Has your weight changed over the past year?[a]
- Do you take vitamins, herbs, or any other supplements?[a]
- How much and what kinds of fluids do you drink daily?
- How many dairy products and how much meat do you eat?
- Do you drink coffee? Colas? Tea?
- Do you spice your food heavily?[a]

Elimination
- Are you able to sit through a 2-hr meeting or ride in a car for 2 hr without urinating?
- Do you awaken at night to urinate? If so, how many times does this occur during an average night?
- Do you ever have blood in your urine?[a] If so, at what point in the urination does it occur?
- Have you noticed any change in the color or smell of your urine?[a]
- Do you ever pass urine when you do not intend to? When?
- Do you use special devices or supplies for urine elimination or control?[a]
- How often do you move your bowels?
- Do you ever have constipation or diarrhea?[a]
- Do you ever have problems controlling your bowels?[a]

Activity-Exercise
- Have you noticed any changes in your ability to perform your usual daily activities?[a]
- Do certain activities worsen your urinary problem?[a]
- Has your urinary problem caused you to alter or stop any activity or exercise?[a]
- Do you need help getting to the bathroom?[a]

Sleep-Rest
- Do you awaken at night from an urge to urinate?[a] How does this disturb your sleep?
- Do you awaken at night from pain or other problems and urinate as a matter of routine before returning to sleep?[a]
- Do you have daytime sleepiness and fatigue because of nighttime urination?[a]

Cognitive-Perceptual
- Do you ever have pain when you urinate?[a] If so, where is the pain?

Self-Perception–Self-Concept
- How does your urinary problem make you feel about yourself?
- Do you perceive your body differently since you have developed a urinary problem?

Role-Relationship
- Does your urinary problem interfere with your relationships with family or friends?[a]
- Has your urinary problem caused a change in your job status or affected your ability to work?[a]

Sexuality-Reproductive
- Has your urinary problem caused any change in your sexual pleasure or performance?
- Do hygiene concerns interfere with sexual activities?

Coping–Stress Tolerance
- Do you feel able to manage your urinary problem? If not, explain.
- What strategies are you using to cope with your urinary problem?

Values-Beliefs
- Has your present illness affected your belief system?[a]
- Are your treatment decisions related to your urinary problem in conflict with your value system?[a]

[a]If yes, describe.

BOX 49.1 GENETIC RISK ALERT

- Polycystic kidney disease and congenital urinary tract abnormalities (e.g., Alport syndrome [congenital nephritis]) are genetic disorders.
- A family history of certain renal or urologic problems increases the chance of similar problems occurring in the patient.
- For any disease reported in the health history, ask if other family members also have/had the same or similar diseases.

Assess bowel function. Problems with fecal incontinence may signal neurologic causes for bladder problems because of shared nerve pathways. Constipation and fecal impaction can partially obstruct the urethra, causing inadequate bladder emptying, overflow incontinence, and infection.

Determine the patient's method of managing a urinary problem. A patient may already be using a catheter or collection device. Sometimes, a patient must assume a specific position to urinate or perform maneuvers, such as pressing on the lower abdomen (Credé's method) or straining (Valsalva maneuver), to empty the bladder.

Activity-exercise pattern. Assess the patient's level of activity. A sedentary person is more likely to have stasis of urine than an active person and, thus, is predisposed to infection and stones. Bone demineralization in a person with limited physical activity can cause increased urine calcium precipitation.

An active person may find that increasing activity worsens the urinary problem. The patient who has had prostate surgery or who has weakened pelvic floor muscles may leak urine when trying certain activities, such as running. Some men develop chronic inflammatory prostatitis or epididymitis after heavy lifting or long-distance driving.

Sleep-rest pattern. Nocturia is a common and a particularly bothersome symptom that often leads to sleep deprivation, daytime sleepiness, and fatigue. It occurs in multiple problems affecting the lower urinary tract. These include urinary incontinence, urinary retention, and interstitial cystitis. Nocturia may be related to polyuria from kidney disease, poorly controlled diabetes, alcohol use, excess fluid intake, liver disease, heart failure, or obstructive sleep apnea.

TABLE 49.5 Manifestations of Urinary System Disorders

	SPECIFIC MANIFESTATIONS RELATED TO URINARY SYSTEM				
General Manifestations	**Edema**	**Pain**	**Patterns of Urination**	**Urine Output**	**Urine Composition**
• Anorexia	• Ankle	• Dysuria	• Change in stream	• Anuria	• Color (red, brown, yellowish green)
• ↑ BP	• Ascites	• Flank or costovertebral angle	• Dribbling	• Oliguria	• Concentrated
• Blurred vision	• Facial (periorbital)	• Groin	• Dysuria	• Polyuria	• Dilute
• Change in weight	• Generalized	• Suprapubic	• Frequency		• Hematuria
• Chills	• Sacral		• Hesitancy of stream		• Pyuria
• Cognitive changes			• Incontinence		
• Fatigue			• Nocturia		
• Headaches			• Retention		
• Nausea and vomiting			• Stress incontinence		
• Thirst			• Urgency		

When assessing nocturia, determine if the need to urinate causes the person to arise from sleep or if pain or other symptoms interrupt sleep. Ask if the person urinates as a matter of habit before returning to bed. Up to 1 episode of nocturia is normal in younger adults, and up to 2 episodes are acceptable in adults ages 65 years or older. If an older adult has more than 2 episodes during the night, assess the amount and timing of fluid intake. This information will help determine if further assessment is needed.

Cognitive-perceptual pattern. Assess the level of mobility, visual acuity, and dexterity. These are important factors to evaluate, especially when urine retention or incontinence is a problem. Determine if the patient is alert, understands instructions, and can recall instructions when needed.

If urinary incontinence is present, ask how the patient is managing the problem. Recognize that incontinence is often distressing and embarrassing. Discuss the problem with the patient with sensitivity.

Pain is a frequent symptom of renal and urologic problems. The patient may report dysuria, groin pain, costovertebral pain, or suprapubic pain. Assess pain and document the location, character, and duration. The absence of pain when other urinary symptoms exist is significant. Many urinary tract cancers are painless in the early stages.

Self-perception–self-concept pattern. Some problems, such as incontinence, urinary diversion procedures, and chronic fatigue (may occur with anemia), can result in loss of self-esteem and a negative body image.

Role-relationship pattern. Urinary problems can affect many aspects of a person's life, including the ability to work and relationships with others. These factors have implications for treatment and management of the patient's condition.

Urinary system problems may be serious enough to cause problems in job-related and social situations. Chronic dialysis therapy often makes regular employment or management of home and family responsibilities difficult. Concurrent poor health and negative body image can seriously affect existing roles.

Sexuality-reproductive pattern. Assess the effect of renal problems on the patient's sexual satisfaction. Problems related to personal hygiene and fatigue can negatively affect sexual relationships. Although urinary incontinence is not directly related to sexual problems, it often has a devastating effect on self-esteem and social and intimate relationships. Counseling both the patient and partner may be needed.

Case Study

Subjective Data

(© iStockphoto/ Thinkstock.)

A focused subjective assessment of A.K. revealed the following:

Medical History: History of 1 isolated incidence of gout 6 years ago. He stopped drinking alcohol with no further occurrence. Appendectomy 12 years ago.

Medications: None.

Health Perception–Health Management: A.K. states that he is usually healthy. He does not smoke or drink alcohol. He has never had this type of pain before. Describes the pain as being sharp and colicky (coming in waves). Rates the pain as 9 on a scale of 0 to 10.

Nutritional-Metabolic: A.K. is currently on a high-protein diet as he trains for the marathon. He eats a lot of chicken, beef, and seafood. He drinks milk-based protein shakes and water after exercising but admits that he does not think he drinks enough to replace fluid loss from perspiration. He drinks coffee for energy but denies eating chocolate or other sweets. He avoids sodas.

Elimination: Denies any history of problems with urination, constipation, or diarrhea. This is the first time he has ever noticed a change of color in his urine.

Activity-Exercise: Prides himself on his ability to exercise and run without difficulty.

Sleep-Rest: Does not awaken at night to urinate.

Cognitive-Perceptual: Denies pain on urination.

Self-Perception–Self-Concept: Believes he can monitor himself and maintain a healthy lifestyle.

Coping–Stress Tolerance: Worried that this pain may interfere with his marathon training.

Discussion Questions

1. Which subjective assessment findings concern you most?
2. What would be your priority assessment of A.K.?
3. What should be included in the physical assessment? What would you be looking for?

You will learn more about the physical assessment of the urinary system in the next section.

Answers available at http://evolve.elsevier.com/Lewis/medsurg.

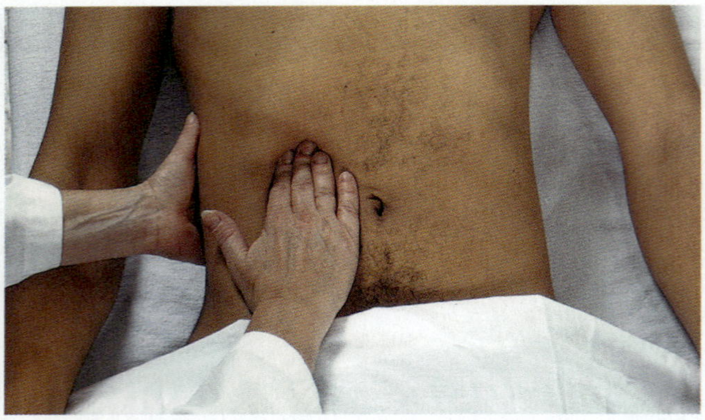

Fig. 49.6 Palpating the right kidney. (From Jarvis C: *Physical examination and health assessment,* ed 8, St Louis, 2020, Elsevier.)

Objective Data

Physical Assessment

Inspection. Assess for changes in the following:

- *Skin:* Pallor, yellow-gray cast, excoriations, changes in turgor, bruises, texture (e.g., rough, dry skin)
- *Mouth:* Stomatitis, ammonia breath odor
- *Face and extremities:* Generalized edema, peripheral edema
- *Abdomen:* Abdominal contour for midline mass in lower abdomen (may indicate bladder distention and urinary retention) or unilateral mass (sometimes seen in adults, indicating kidney enlargement from large tumor or polycystic kidney)
- *Weight:* Weight gain from edema. Weight loss and muscle wasting in kidney failure
- *General health:* Fatigue, lethargy, and decreased alertness

Palpation. The kidneys are posterior organs protected by the abdominal organs, ribs, and heavy back muscles. A landmark useful in locating the kidneys is the **costovertebral angle (CVA)** formed by the rib cage and the vertebral column. The normal-sized left kidney is rarely palpable because the spleen lies directly on top of it. Occasionally, the lower pole of the right kidney is palpable.

To palpate the right kidney, place your left (anterior) hand behind and support the patient's right side between the rib cage and the iliac crest (Fig. 49.6). Elevate the right flank with the left hand. Use your right hand to palpate deeply for the right kidney. The lower pole of the right kidney may be felt as a smooth, rounded mass that descends on inspiration. If the kidney is palpable, note its size, contour, and tenderness. Kidney enlargement is suggestive of cancer or other serious renal problems.

The urinary bladder is normally not palpable unless it is distended with urine. If the bladder is full, it may be felt as a smooth, round, firm organ and is sensitive to palpation.

Percussion. Tenderness in the flank area may be detected by fist percussion *(kidney punch).* Perform fist percussion by striking the fist of one hand against the dorsal surface of the other hand, which is placed flat along the posterior CVA margin (Fig. 49.7). Normally, this action should not elicit pain. If CVA tenderness and pain are present, it may indicate a kidney infection or polycystic kidney disease.[5]

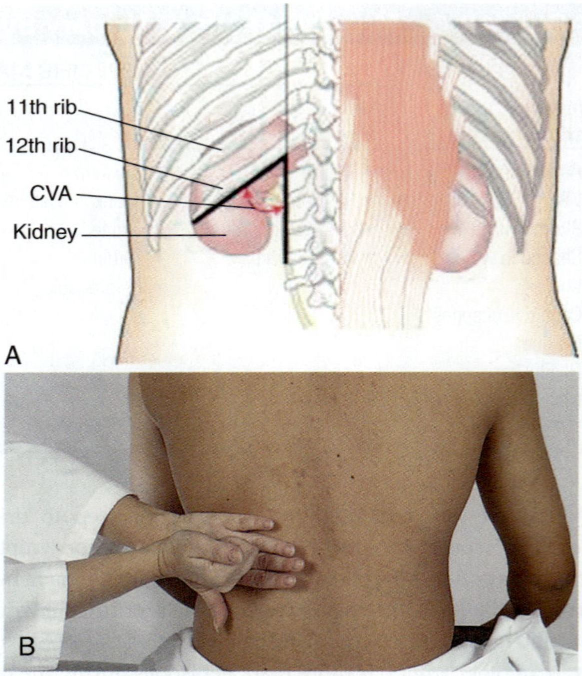

Fig. 49.7 (A) Costovertebral angle. (B) Indirect fist percussion of the costovertebral angle *(CVA).* To assess the kidney, place one hand over the twelfth rib at the CVA on the back. Thump that hand with the ulnar edge of the other fist. (From Jarvis C: *Physical examination and health assessment,* ed 8, St Louis, 2020, Elsevier.)

TABLE 49.6 Normal Physical Assessment of Urinary System

- No costovertebral angle tenderness
- Nonpalpable kidney and bladder
- No palpable masses

A bladder does not percuss until it contains at least 150 mL of urine. If the bladder is full, dullness is heard above the symphysis pubis. A distended bladder may be percussed as high as the umbilicus.

Auscultation. Use the diaphragm of the stethoscope to auscultate bowel sounds, since the bowels can affect the urinary system.

Table 49.6 shows how to record the normal physical assessment findings of the urinary system. Table 49.7 describes assessment abnormalities of the urinary system. Assessment findings may vary in the older adult. Table 49.2 presents the age-related changes in the urinary system and differences in assessment findings. Use a *focused assessment* to evaluate the status of previously identified urinary system problems and monitor for signs of new problems (Table 49.8).

TABLE 49.7 ASSESSMENT ABNORMALITIES

Urinary System

Finding	Description	Possible Etiology and Significance
Anuria	Technically no urination (24-h urine output <100 mL)	Acute kidney injury, end-stage renal disease (ESRD), bilateral ureteral obstruction
Burning on urination	Stinging pain in urethral area	Urethral irritation, UTI, urethral stones
Dysuria	Painful or difficult urination	UTI, interstitial cystitis, urethral stones, and wide variety of pathologic conditions
Enuresis	Involuntary nocturnal urination	Lower urinary tract disorder
Frequency	↑ Incidence of urination	Acutely inflamed bladder, retention with overflow, excess fluid intake, intake of bladder irritants, urethral stones
Hematuria	Blood in the urine	Cancer of genitourinary tract, blood dyscrasias, kidney disease, UTI, stones in kidney or ureter, anticoagulants
Hesitancy	Delay or difficulty in initiating urination	Partial urethral obstruction, BPH
Incontinence	Inability to voluntarily control discharge of urine	Neurogenic bladder, bladder infection, injury to external sphincter
Nocturia	Frequent urination at night	Kidney disease with impaired concentrating ability, bladder obstruction, heart failure, diabetes, post renal transplant, excess evening and nighttime fluid intake
Oliguria	↓ Amount of urine in a time period (24-hr urine output of 100–400 mL)	Severe dehydration, shock, transfusion reaction, kidney disease, ESRD
Pain	Suprapubic pain (related to bladder), urethral pain (irritation of bladder neck), flank pain, CVA tenderness	Infection, urinary retention, foreign body in urinary tract, urethritis, pyelonephritis, renal colic, stones
Pneumaturia	Passage of urine containing gas	Fistula connections between bowel and bladder, gas-forming UTI
Polyuria	Large volume of urine in a time period	Diabetes, diabetes insipidus, chronic kidney disease, diuretics, excess fluid intake, obstructive sleep apnea
Retention	Inability to urinate even though bladder contains excess amount of urine	Finding after pelvic surgery, childbirth, catheter removal, anesthesia; urethral stricture or obstruction; neurogenic bladder
Stress incontinence	Involuntary urination with ↑ pressure (sneezing or coughing)	Weakness of sphincter control, lack of estrogen, urinary retention

TABLE 49.8 FOCUSED ASSESSMENT

Urinary System

Use this checklist to ensure that you complete key assessment steps.

Subjective

Ask the patient about any of the following and note responses.

Painful urination	Y	N
Changes in color of urine (blood, cloudy)	Y	N
Change in characteristics of urination (decreased, excessive)	Y	N
Problems with frequent nighttime urination (nocturia)	Y	N

Objective: Diagnostic

Check the following laboratory results for critical values.

Blood urea nitrogen	✓
Serum creatinine	✓
Urinalysis	✓
Urine culture and sensitivity	✓

Objective: Physical Assessment

Inspect

Abdomen	✓
Urinary meatus for inflammation or discharge	✓

Palpate

Abdomen for bladder distention, masses, or tenderness	✓

Percuss

Costovertebral angle for tenderness	✓

Case Study

Objective Data: Physical Assessment

(© iStockphoto/ Thinkstock.)

A focused assessment of A.K. reveals the following:

A.K. is lying with his knees bent and drawn to his abdominal area. He appears restless and keeps moving from back to side to reduce his discomfort. Vital signs are as follows: BP 156/70, apical pulse 108, respiratory rate 24, temperature 37.4°C, O_2 saturation 96% on room air. Awake, alert, and oriented × 3. Lungs are clear to auscultation. Apical pulse is regular. Abdomen nondistended with + bowel sounds in all 4 quadrants. No rebound tenderness. Positive left costovertebral tenderness. Voiding small amounts of dark, smoky urine.

Discussion Questions

1. Which physical assessment findings concern you most?
2. Based on the results of the subjective and physical assessment findings, what diagnostic studies do you think may be ordered for A.K.?

You will learn more about diagnostic studies related to the urinary system in the next section.

Answers available at http://evolve.elsevier.com/Lewis/medsurg.

DIAGNOSTIC STUDIES OF URINARY SYSTEM

Many diagnostic studies are used to assess urinary system problems. Tables 49.9, 49.10, 49.11, and 49.12 describe the most common studies. Select studies are described in more detail here.

Urine Studies

Urinalysis

Urinalysis is one of the first studies done to evaluate disorders of the urinary tract (Table 49.9). Results from the urinalysis

TABLE 49.9 Urinalysis

General examination of urine to establish baseline information or provide data to establish a tentative diagnosis and determine if further studies are needed.
Before: Wash perineal area before collecting specimen.
During: Try to obtain first urinated morning specimen.
After: Ensure specimen is examined within 1 hr of urinating.

Test	Normal	Abnormal Finding	Possible Cause and Significance
Bilirubin	None	Present	Liver problems. May appear before jaundice is visible (see Chapter 48).
Casts	None Occasional hyaline	Present	Molds of the renal tubules that may contain protein, WBCs, RBCs, or bacteria. Noncellular casts (hyaline in appearance) occasionally found in normal urine.
Color	Amber yellow	Dark, smoky color Yellow-brown to olive green Orange-red or orange-brown Cloudiness of freshly voided urine Colorless urine	Hematuria. Excess bilirubin. phenazopyridine (Pyridium), rifampin. UTI Excess fluid intake, kidney disease, or diabetes insipidus.
Culture for organisms	No organisms in bladder $<10^4$ organisms/mL result of normal urethral flora	Bacteria counts $>10^5$/mL	UTI; most common organisms are *E. coli,* enterococci, *Klebsiella, Proteus,* streptococci.
Glucose	None	Glycosuria	Diabetes, low renal threshold for glucose reabsorption (if blood glucose level is normal). Pituitary problems.
Ketones	None	Present	Altered carbohydrate and fat metabolism in diabetes and starvation; dehydration, vomiting, severe diarrhea.
Odor	Aromatic	Ammonia-like odor Unpleasant odor	Urine allowed to stand. UTI.
Osmolality	50–1200 mOsm/kg (50–1200 mmol/kg)	<50 mOsm/kg >1200 mOsm/kg	Tubular dysfunction. Kidney lost ability to concentrate or dilute urine.
pH	4.6–8.0 (average, 6.0)	>8.0	UTI. Urine allowed to stand at room temperature (bacteria decompose urea to ammonia).
Protein	Random protein (dipstick): 0–trace	Persistent proteinuria	Characteristic of acute and chronic kidney disease, especially involving glomeruli. Heart failure.
	24-h protein (quantitative): 50–80 mg/day		In absence of disease: high-protein diet, strenuous exercise, dehydration, fever, stress, contamination by vaginal secretions.
RBCs	0–4/hpf	<4.0 >4/hpf	Respiratory or metabolic acidosis. Stones, cystitis, cancer, glomerulonephritis, tuberculosis, kidney biopsy, UTI, trauma.
Specific gravity	1.005–1.030 Maximum concentrating ability of kidney in morning urine (1.025–1.030)	Low High Fixed at about 1.010	Dilute urine, excess diuresis, diabetes insipidus. Dehydration, albuminuria, glycosuria. Renal inability to concentrate urine; end-stage renal disease.
WBCs	0–5/hpf	5/hpf	UTI, inflammation.

hpf, High-powered field.

TABLE 49.10 Diagnostic Studies

Urine

Study	Description and Purpose	Nursing Responsibility
Composite urine collection	Measures specific components, such as electrolytes, glucose, protein, 17-ketosteroids, catecholamines, creatinine, and minerals. Composite urine specimens collected over a period ranging from 2 to 24 hr.	*During:* Have patient urinate and discard this 1st urine specimen. Note this time as the start of the test. Save all urine from subsequent urinations in a container for designated period. At end of period, ask patient to urinate, and add this urine to container. Remind patient to save all urine during study period. Specimens may need refrigerated or preservatives added to container used for collecting urine.
Concentration test	Evaluates renal concentration ability. Measured by specific gravity readings. *Reference interval:* 1.005–1.030.	*Before:* Have patient fast after given time in evening (in usual procedure). *During:* Collect 3 urine specimens at hourly intervals in morning.

TABLE 49.10 Diagnostic Studies—cont'd

Urine

Study	Description and Purpose	Nursing Responsibility
Creatinine clearance	Creatinine is a waste product of protein breakdown (primarily body muscle mass). Clearance of creatinine by kidney approximates the GFR. Calculated as follows: $\text{Creatinine clearance} = \frac{\text{Urine creatinine (mg/dL)} \times \text{Urine volume (mL/min)}}{\text{Serum creatinine (mg/dL)}}$ Reference interval: *Male*: 107–139 mL/min/1.73 m^2 *Female:* 87–107 mL/min/1.73 m^2 (corrected for body surface area).	*During:* Collect 24-hr urine specimen. Discard 1st urination when test is started. Save urine from all subsequent urinations for 24 hr. Have patient urinate at end of 24 hr and add specimen to collection. Measure serum creatinine during 24-hr period.
Protein determination		
• Dipstick (Albustix, Combistix)	Detects protein (primarily albumin) in urine. *Reference interval:* 0 to trace.	*During:* Dip end of stick in urine and read result by comparison with color chart on label as directed. Grading is from 0 to 4+. Interpret with caution. Positive result may not indicate significant proteinuria. Some drugs may give false-positive readings.
• Quantitative protein test	24-hr collection gives a more accurate indication of amount of protein in urine. Persistent proteinuria usually indicates glomerular kidney disease. *Reference interval:* 50–80 mg/day (mainly albumin).	*During:* Perform 24-hr urine collection as above.
Residual urine	Determines amount of urine left in bladder after urinating. Finding may be abnormal in problems with bladder innervation, sphincter impairment, BPH, urethral strictures. *Reference interval:* ≤50 mL urine (↑ with age).	*During:* Immediately after patient urinates, catheterize patient or use bladder ultrasound equipment. If a large amount of residual urine is obtained, HCP may want catheter left in bladder.
Urine culture ("clean catch," "midstream")	Confirms suspected UTI and identifies causative organisms. Normally, bladder is sterile, but urethra contains bacteria and a few WBCs. *Reference interval:* If properly collected, stored, and handled: $<10^3$ organisms/mL usually indicates no infection. 10^3–10^5/mL is usually not diagnostic. Test may need repeated. $>10^5$/mL indicates infection.	*During:* Use sterile container for collection of urine. Touch only outside of container. *For women:* Wipe the periurethral area from front to back, dry the area thoroughly with sterile swab, separate labia with one hand. *For men:* Retract foreskin (if present), cleanse glans around urethra, replace foreskin after cleaning. After cleaning, have patient start voiding, and collect the specimen 1–2 sec after voiding starts. The initial voided urine flushes out most contaminants in the urethra and perineal area. Catheterization may be needed if patient is unable to cooperate with procedure.
Urine cytologic study	Identifies abnormal cellular structures that occur with bladder cancer. Used to follow the progress of bladder cancer after treatment.	*During:* Obtain specimens by voiding, catheterization, or bladder irrigation. Do not use morning's 1st voided specimen because epithelial cells may change in appearance in urine held in bladder overnight. *After:* Specimen should be fresh or brought to laboratory within the hour. An alcohol-based fixative is then added to preserve the cellular structure.

TABLE 49.11 Blood Studies

Urinary System

Test	Reference Interval	Significance
Bicarbonate	22–26 mEq/L (22–26 mmol/L).	Most patients in renal failure have metabolic acidosis and low serum HCO_3^- levels.
Blood urea nitrogen (BUN)	10–20 mg/dL (3.6–7.1 mmol/L)	Used to detect renal problems. Concentration of urea in blood is regulated by rate at which kidney excretes urea. Nonrenal factors may ↑ BUN (e.g., cell destruction from infections, fever, GI bleeding, trauma, athletic activity, excessive muscle breakdown).
BUN/creatinine ratio	12:1–20:1	Increased ratio may be due to conditions that ↓ blood flow to kidneys (e.g., heart failure, dehydration, GI bleeding) or increased protein intake. Decreased ratio may occur with liver disease (from ↓ urea formation) and malnutrition.
Calcium (total)	9.0–10.5 mg/dL (2.25–2.62 mmol/L)	Main mineral in bone and aids in muscle contraction, neurotransmission, and clotting. In kidney disease, ↓ Ca^{2+} reabsorption leads to renal osteodystrophy.
Creatinine	*Male*: 0.6–1.2 mg/dL (53–106 μmol/L) *Female:* 0.5–1.1 mg/dL (49.97 μmol/L)	More reliable than BUN as a determinant of renal function. Creatinine is a product of muscle and protein metabolism. It is released at a constant rate.
Phosphorus	3.0–4.5 mg/dL (0.97–1.45 mmol/L)	Phosphorus balance is inversely related to Ca^{2+} balance. In kidney disease, phosphorus levels are high because the kidney is the primary excretory organ.
Potassium	3.5–5.0 mEq/L (3.5–5.0 mmol/L)	Kidneys excrete majority of body's potassium. In kidney disease, K^+ determinations are critical because K^+ is one of the first electrolytes to become abnormal. High K^+ levels >6 mEq/L can lead to muscle weakness and dysrhythmias.
Sodium	136–145 mEq/L (136–145 mmol/L)	Main extracellular electrolyte determining blood volume. Values usually stay within normal range until late stages of renal failure.
Uric acid	*Male:* 4.0–8.5 mg/dL (0.24–0.51 mmol/L) *Female:* 2.7–7.3 mg/dL (0.16–0.43 mmol/L)	Used as screening test for disorders of purine metabolism. Can indicate kidney disease. Values depend on renal function, rate of purine metabolism, and diet intake of food rich in purines.

TABLE 49.12 Diagnostic Studies

Urinary System

Study	Description and Purpose	Nursing Responsibility
Endoscopy		
Cystoscopy	Inspects interior of bladder with a tubular lighted scope (cystoscope) (Fig. 49.8). Can be used to insert ureteral catheters, remove stones, obtain biopsy specimens of bladder lesions, treat bleeding lesions. Lithotomy position is used. Done under local or general anesthesia, depending on patient's needs and condition. Complications include urinary retention, urinary tract hemorrhage, bladder infection, and bladder perforation.	*Before:* Give IV fluids if general anesthesia is to be used. Ensure consent form is signed. Explain procedure to patient. Give preoperative medication. *After:* Explain that burning on urination, pink-tinged urine, and urinary frequency are expected effects. Observe for bright red bleeding, which is not normal. Help with ambulation because orthostatic hypotension may occur. Offer warm sitz baths, heat, mild analgesics to relieve discomfort.
Radiologic Procedures		
Computed tomography (CT) scan (CT urogram)	Visualizes kidneys, ureters, and bladder. Can detect tumors, abscesses, suprarenal masses (e.g., adrenal tumors), and obstructions. Done with or without contrast media. Contrast is iodine based.	*Before:* Before contrast medium used, evaluate renal function. Assess if patient is allergic to shellfish, since the contrast is iodine based. Patient may need to be NPO 4 hr prior to study. *During:* Warn patient that contrast injection may cause a feeling of being warm and flushed. Patient must lie completely still during scan. *After:* Encourage patient to drink fluids to avoid renal problems with any contrast.
Cystogram	Visualizes bladder and evaluates vesicoureteral reflux. Evaluates patients with neurogenic bladder and recurrent UTIs. Can delineate abnormalities of bladder (e.g., diverticula, stones, tumors). Contrast media instilled into bladder via cystoscope or catheter.	*Before:* Explain procedure to patient. *During:* If done via cystoscope, follow nursing care related to cystoscopy.
Intravenous pyelogram (IVP)	Visualizes urinary tract after IV injection of contrast media. Evaluates size and shape of kidneys, ureters, and bladder. Cysts, tumors, and ureteral obstructions distort normal appearance of these structures. Patient with decreased renal function should not have IVP because contrast media can be nephrotoxic.	*Before:* Cathartic or enema given night before. Assess patient for iodine sensitivity to avoid anaphylactic reaction. *During:* Warn patient that contrast injection may cause a feeling of being warm and flushed. *After:* Force fluids to avoid renal problems with contrast.
Kidneys, ureters, bladder (KUB)	X-ray examination of abdomen and pelvis. Delineates size, shape, and position of kidneys, ureter, and bladder. Can see radiopaque stones and foreign bodies.	*Before:* No special preparation needed.
Loopogram	Detects obstructions, anastomotic leaks, stones, and reflux when patient has a urinary pouch or ileal conduit. Because urinary diversions are created with bowel, there is risk for absorption of contrast media.	*Before:* Explain procedure to patient. *During:* Monitor patient for reactions to the contrast media.
Magnetic resonance angiography	Visualizes renal vasculature. Gadolinium-enhanced studies allow visualization of renal artery.	Same as renal arteriogram. Does not require femoral artery puncture.
Magnetic resonance imaging (MRI)	Visualizes kidneys. Not proven useful for detecting urinary stones or calcified tumors.	*Before:* Oral and/or IV contrast injection may be used. Check for pregnancy, allergies, and renal function before test. Have patient remove all metal objects. Remove metallic foil patches. Contraindicated for persons with implanted metallic devices or other metal fragments unless noted to be MRI safe. Ask about any staples, plates, dental bridges, or other metal appliances. Patient may need to be fasting. Assess for claustrophobia and the need for antianxiety medication. *During:* Patient must lie completely still during scan.
Nephrostogram (antegrade pyelogram)	Evaluates upper urinary tract when patient has allergy to contrast media, decreased renal function, or abnormalities that prevent passage of a ureteral catheter. Contrast media may be injected percutaneously into renal pelvis or via a nephrostomy tube that is already in place when determining tube function or ureteral integrity after trauma or surgery.	*Before:* Explain procedure and prepare patient as for IVP. *During and after:* Watch for signs of complications (e.g., hematuria, infection, hematoma).
Renal arteriogram (angiogram)	Visualizes renal blood vessels. Can aid in diagnosing renal artery stenosis (Fig. 49.9), extra or missing renal blood vessels, and renovascular hypertension. Can aid in distinguishing between a renal cyst and renal tumor. Included in workup of a potential renal transplant donor. A catheter is inserted into the femoral artery and passed up the aorta to the level of renal arteries (Fig. 49.10). Contrast media is injected to outline renal blood supply.	*Before:* Cathartic or enema may be used the night before. Before injection of contrast material, assess for iodine sensitivity. Tell patient they may feel a transient warm feeling along the course of blood vessel when contrast media is injected. *After:* Place a pressure dressing over femoral artery injection site. Observe site for bleeding and inflammation. Have patient maintain bed rest with affected leg straight. Take peripheral pulses in the involved leg every 30–60 min to detect occlusion of blood flow (from thrombus or emboli).

TABLE 49.12 Diagnostic Studies—cont'd

Urinary System

Study	Description and Purpose	Nursing Responsibility
Renal biopsy	Obtains renal tissue for examination to determine type of kidney disease or to follow progress of kidney disease. Usually done as a skin (percutaneous) biopsy through needle insertion into lower lobe of kidney under CT or ultrasound guidance. Absolute contraindications are bleeding disorders, single kidney, and uncontrolled hypertension. Relative contraindications include suspected renal infection, hydronephrosis, and possible vascular lesions.	*Before:* Type and crossmatch patient for blood. Ensure consent form is signed. Assess coagulation status through patient history, medication history, CBC, hematocrit, prothrombin time, and bleeding and clotting time. Patient should not be taking aspirin or warfarin. *After:* Apply pressure dressing and keep patient on affected side for 30–60 min. Bed rest for 24 hr. Vital signs every 5–10 min, first hour. Assess for flank pain, hypotension, decreasing hematocrit, fever, chills, urinary frequency, dysuria, and gross or microscopic hematuria. Inspect biopsy site for bleeding. Teach patient to avoid lifting heavy objects for 5–7 days and to not take anticoagulant drugs until allowed by HCP.
Renal scan	Evaluates anatomic structures, perfusion, and function of kidneys. IV radioactive isotopes are injected. Radiation detector probes are placed over kidney and scintillation counter monitors radioactive material in kidney. Radioisotope distribution in kidney is scanned and mapped. Shows location, size, and shape of kidney and assesses blood flow, glomerular filtration, tubular function, and urinary excretion. Abscesses, cysts, and tumors may appear as cold spots because of nonfunctioning tissue. Monitors function of a transplanted kidney.	*Before:* No diet or activity restriction. Tell patient that there should not be any pain or discomfort during test.
Renal ultrasound	Detects renal or perirenal masses (tumors, cysts) and obstructions. Small external ultrasound probe is placed on patient's skin. Conductive gel applied to skin. Noninvasive procedure involves passing sound waves into body structures and recording images as they are reflected. Computer interprets tissue density based on sound waves and displays it in picture form. Safe for patients with renal failure.	*Before:* Explain procedure to patient. No bowel preparation needed. *During:* Because radiation exposure is avoided, can obtain repeated images over a brief period.
Retrograde pyelogram	X-ray of urinary tract taken after injection of contrast material into kidneys. May be done if an IVP does not visualize the urinary tract or has decreased renal function. A cystoscope is inserted, and ureteral catheters are inserted through it into renal pelvis. Contrast media is injected through catheters.	*Before:* Prepare patient as for IVP. Tell patient that there may be pain from distention of pelvis and discomfort from cystoscope. Anesthesia may be given for procedure. *After:* Complications similar to those for cystoscopy.
Urethrogram	Similar to a cystogram. Contrast media is injected retrograde into urethra to identify strictures, diverticula, or other urethral pathologic conditions. When urethral trauma is suspected, a urethrogram is done before catheterization.	*Before:* Explain procedure to patient.
Voiding cystourethrogram (VCUG)	Voiding study of bladder opening (bladder neck) and urethra. Bladder is filled with contrast media. Fluoroscopic films are taken to visualize bladder and urethra. After urination, another film is taken to assess for residual urine. Can detect abnormalities of lower urinary tract, urethral stenosis, bladder neck obstruction, vesicoureteral reflux, and prostatic enlargement.	*Before:* Explain procedure to patient.
Urodynamic Studies		
Cystometrogram	Evaluates bladder's capacity to contract and expel urine. Involves insertion of catheter and instillation of water or saline solution into bladder. Measurements of pressure exerted against bladder wall are recorded. If measuring abdominal pressure, a 2nd tube is inserted into rectum or vagina. This tube is attached to a small fluid-filled balloon to allow pressure recording.	*Before:* Explain procedure to patient. *During:* Ask patient about sensations of bladder filling, usually including the first desire (urge) to urinate, a strong desire to urinate, and perception of bladder fullness. *After:* Observe patient for manifestations of UTI after procedure.
Radionuclide cystography (RNC)	Detects and grades vesicoureteral reflux. Like VCUG with a small dose of radioisotope tracer instilled into the bladder via urethral catheter. More sensitive than VCUG, and radiation dose is 1/1000 that of the VCUG.	*Before:* Explain procedure to patient as in VCUG.

Continued

TABLE 49.12 Diagnostic Studies—cont'd

Urinary System

Study	Description and Purpose	Nursing Responsibility
Sphincter electromyography (EMG)	Recording of electrical activity created when nervous system stimulates muscle tissue. By placing needles, percutaneous wires, or patches near the urethra, pelvic floor muscle activity can be assessed. During the cystometrogram, sphincter EMG is used to identify voluntary pelvic floor muscle contractions and response of these muscles to bladder filling, coughing, and other provocative maneuvers.	*Before:* Explain procedure to patient.
Urine flow study (uroflow)	Measures urine volume in a single voiding expelled in a period. Used to (1) assess the degree of outflow obstruction caused by such conditions as BPH, (2) assess bladder or sphincter dysfunction effects on voiding, and (3) evaluate effects of treatment for lower urinary tract problems. Graphic displays can illustrate straining and intermittent flow patterns or other abnormal voiding disorders. *Normal maximum flow rate:* Men: 20–25 mL/sec; women: 25–30 mL/sec. Volume voided and patient's age can affect the flow rate.	*Before:* Explain procedure to patient. *During:* Ask the patient to start the test with a comfortably full bladder, urinate into a designated container, and try to empty completely. *After:* Measure residual urine volume immediately after a urinary flow study because this will help identify degree of chronic urinary retention that often occurs with abnormal flow patterns.
Videourodynamics	Combination of cystometrogram, sphincter EMG, and/or urinary flow study with anatomic imaging of the lower urinary tract, typically via fluoroscopy. Used in selected cases to identify an obstructive lesion and characterize anatomic changes in bladder and lower urinary tract.	*Before:* Explain procedure to patient.
Voiding pressure flow study	Combines a urinary flow rate, cystometric pressures (intravesical, abdominal, and detrusor pressures), and sphincter EMG for detailed evaluation of micturition. Completed by assisting the patient to a specialized toilet to urinate while the various pressure tubes and EMG apparatus remain in place.	*Before:* Explain procedure to patient.
Whitaker study	Measures the pressure differential between renal pelvis and bladder. Ureteral obstruction can be assessed. Percutaneous access to renal pelvis obtained by placing a catheter in renal pelvis. A catheter is placed in bladder. Fluid is perfused through the percutaneous tube or needle at a rate of 10 mL/min. Pressure data are then collected. Pressure measurements are combined with fluoroscopic imaging to find the level of obstruction.	*Before:* Explain procedure to patient.

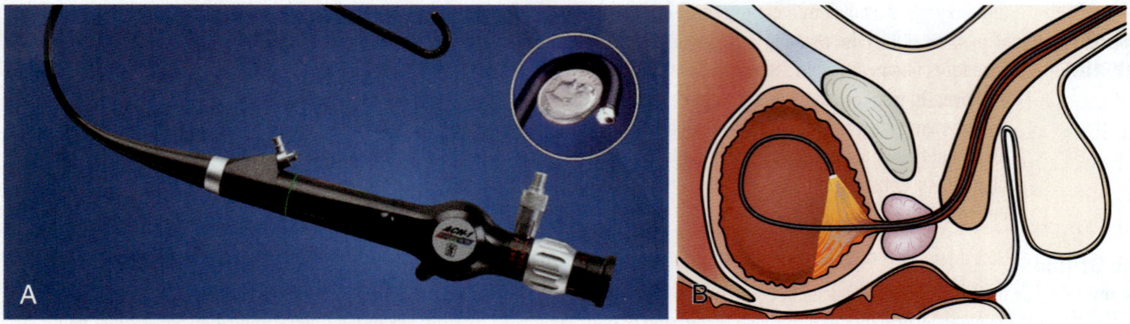

Fig. 49.8 Cystoscopic examination of the bladder in a man. (A) Flexible cystonephroscope. (B) Scope inserted into bladder. (A, Courtesy Circon Corporation, Santa Barbara, CA.)

may show abnormalities, suggest the need for further studies, or show progression in a previously diagnosed disorder.

Although a specimen may be collected at any time of the day for a routine urinalysis, it is best to obtain the first specimen urinated in the morning. This concentrated specimen is more likely to contain abnormal constituents if they are present in the urine. The specimen should be examined within 1 hour of urinating. Otherwise, bacteria multiply rapidly, RBCs hemolyze, *casts* (molds of renal tubules) disintegrate, and the urine becomes alkaline because of urea-splitting bacteria. If it is not

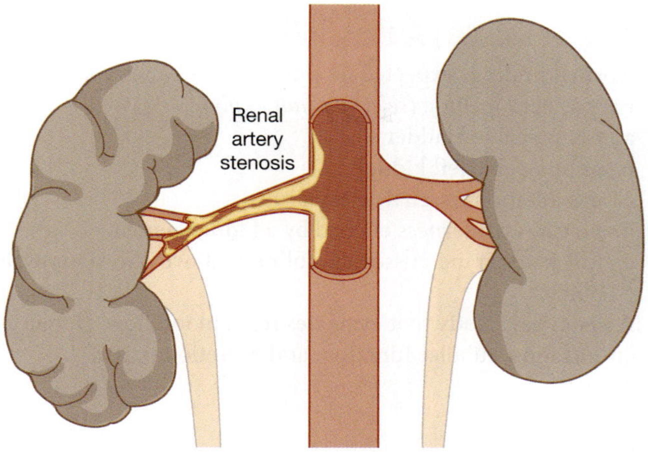

Fig. 49.9 Left renal artery stenosis *(arrow)*.

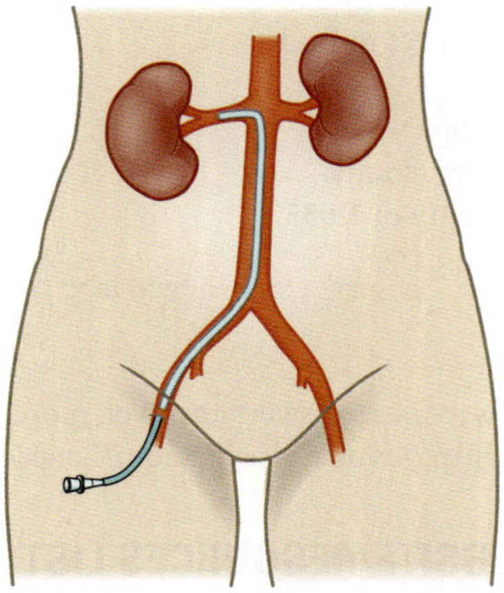

Fig. 49.10 Catheter insertion for a renal arteriogram.

possible to send the specimen to the laboratory immediately, refrigerate it. However, for the best results, coordinate specimen collection with routine laboratory hours.

Creatinine Clearance

A common test used to analyze urinary system disorders is creatinine clearance. **Creatinine** is a waste product made by muscle breakdown. Urinary excretion of creatinine is a measure of the amount of active muscle tissue in the body, not of body weight. Therefore, people with larger muscle mass have higher values. Creatinine levels stay remarkably constant for each person because they are not significantly affected by protein ingestion, exercise, water intake, or rate of urine production.

Since almost all creatinine is excreted by the kidneys, creatinine clearance is the most accurate indicator of renal function. The result of a creatinine clearance test closely approximates that of the GFR. Normal creatinine clearance values range from 87 to 139 mL/min (Table 49.11). After age 40, the creatinine clearance rate decreases at a rate of about 1 mL/min/year. We should obtain a blood specimen to measure serum creatinine during the period of urine collection.

Urodynamic Studies

Urodynamic studies measure urinary tract function. Urodynamic tests study the storage of urine within the bladder and the flow of urine through the urinary tract to the outside of the body. A combination of techniques may be used for a detailed assessment of urinary function (Table 49.12).

Radiologic Studies

Many radiologic studies require a bowel preparation the evening before the study to clear the lower GI tract of feces and flatus. Because the kidneys lie in a retroperitoneal location, colon contents can obstruct visualization of the urinary tract. If the bowel preparation does not adequately clear the lower GI tract, the study may be unsuccessful and need rescheduled. Common bowel preparations include enemas, magnesium citrate, and bisacodyl (Dulcolax) tablets or suppositories. Patients with kidney failure should not receive some bowel preparations, such as magnesium citrate and saline laxative enema, because the kidneys cannot excrete the magnesium (see Chapter 51).

Iodine-based contrast media used in some diagnostic studies may cause contrast-induced kidney injury (CIN) and allergic reactions. Keeping the patient hydrated is important. Some patients may need IV fluids started hours before the procedure. N-acetylcysteine—a renal vasodilator and antioxidant—is sometimes given to reduce the incidence of CIN. It can be given by oral or IV route.

When a patient has multiple diagnostic studies, it is important to maintain hydration. The patient is at risk for dehydration when they have had nothing by mouth for consecutive days, extended time in the radiology department, and bowel preparations. Severe dehydration, especially in debilitated or older patients and patients with diabetes, may lead to acute kidney injury. Ensure that the patient is hydrated and given adequate nourishment between studies. Check with the HCP about insulin dosage for patients with diabetes who are NPO.

Case Study

Objective Data: Diagnostic Studies

(© iStockphoto/ Thinkstock.)

The HCP orders the following initial diagnostic studies for A.K.:

- CBC, basic metabolic panel (electrolytes, BUN, creatinine)
- Urinalysis, culture if indicated
- Renal ultrasound

A.K.'s CBC and metabolic panel results are within normal limits. His urinalysis shows moderate hematuria. A renal ultrasound shows several stones in the left ureter. There is no hydronephrosis at present. The HCP prescribes IV opioids for pain management and admits A.K. to a medical unit.

Discussion Questions

1. Which diagnostic study results are abnormal?
2. Which diagnostic study results are of most concern to you?

Answers available at http://evolve.elsevier.com/Lewis/medsurg.

BRIDGE TO NCLEX EXAMINATION

The number of the question corresponds to the same-numbered outcome at the beginning of the chapter.

1. A renal stone in the pelvis of the kidney will change the patient's kidney function by interfering with the
   a. structural support of the kidney.
   b. regulation of the concentration of urine.
   c. entry and exit of blood vessels at the kidney.
   d. collection and drainage of urine from the kidney.
2. A patient with kidney disease has oliguria and a creatinine clearance of 40 mL/min. These findings most directly reflect abnormal function of
   a. tubular secretion.
   b. glomerular filtration.
   c. capillary permeability.
   d. concentration of filtrate.
3. The nurse identifies a risk for urinary stones in a patient who relates a health history that includes
   a. dehydration.
   b. hyperaldosteronism.
   c. serotonin deficiency.
   d. adrenal insufficiency.
4. Diminished ability to concentrate urine, associated with aging of the urinary system, is due to
   a. a decrease in bladder sensory receptors.
   b. a decrease in the number of functioning nephrons.
   c. decreased function of the loop of Henle and tubules.
   d. thickening of the basement membrane of Bowman capsule.
5. During physical assessment of the urinary system, the nurse
   a. performs fist percussion to detect tenderness in the flank area.
   b. expects a dull percussion sound when 100 mL of urine is present in the bladder.
   c. percusses above the symphysis pubis to determine the level of urine in the bladder.
   d. palpates the lower pole of the right kidney as a smooth mass that descends on expiration.
6. Normal findings expected on physical assessment of the urinary system include *(select all that apply)*
   a. nonpalpable bladder.
   b. nonpalpable left kidney.
   c. auscultation of renal artery bruit.
   d. no CVA tenderness elicited by a kidney punch.
   e. full bladder percusses as dullness above the symphysis pubis.
7. A diagnostic study that evaluates renal blood flow, glomerular filtration, tubular function, and excretion is a(n)
   a. IVP.
   b. VCUG.
   c. renal scan.
   d. loopogram.
8. On reading the urinalysis results of a dehydrated patient, the nurse would expect to find
   a. a pH of 8.4.
   b. RBCs of 4/hpf.
   c. color: yellow, cloudy.
   d. specific gravity of 1.035.

1. d; 2. b; 3. a; 4. c; 5. a; 6. a, b, d, e; 7. c; 8. d.

For rationales to these answers and even more NCLEX review questions, visit http://evolve.elsevier.com/Lewis/medsurg.

EVOLVE WEBSITE/RESOURCES LIST

http://evolve.elsevier.com/Lewis/medsurg
Review Questions (Online Only)
Key Points
Answer Keys for Questions
- Rationales for Bridge to NCLEX Examination Questions
- Answer Guidelines for Case Study

Conceptual Care Map Creator
Audio Glossary
Content Updates

REFERENCES

1. Chou Y, Chen Y: Aging and renal disease: old questions for new challenges, *Aging Dis* 12:515, 2020.
2. National Institute of Diabetes and Digestive and Kidney Disease: Chronic kidney disease. Retrieved from https://www.niddk.nih.gov/health-information/kidney-disease/chronic-kidney-disease-ckd.
3. American Cancer Society: Bladder cancer risk factors. Retrieved from https://www.cancer.org/cancer/bladder-cancer/causes-risks-prevention/risk-factors.html.
4. Song L, Maalouf NM: Nephrolithiasis. Retrieved from https://www.ncbi.nlm.nih.gov/books/NBK279069/.
5. Jarvis C: *Physical examination and health assessment*, ed 8, St Louis, 2020, Elsevier.

50

Renal and Urologic Problems

Cynthia Ann Smith

http://evolve.elsevier.com/Lewis/medsurg/

CONCEPTUAL FOCUS

Elimination
Fluids and Electrolytes
Infection
Pain

LEARNING OUTCOMES

1. Discuss the pathophysiology, clinical manifestations, and interprofessional and nursing management of urinary tract infections, cystitis, urethritis, and pyelonephritis.
2. Distinguish the etiology, clinical manifestations, and nursing and interprofessional management of acute poststreptococcal glomerulonephritis, Goodpasture syndrome, and chronic glomerulonephritis.
3. Describe the common causes, clinical manifestations, and interprofessional and nursing management of nephrotic syndrome.
4. Compare and contrast the etiology, clinical manifestations, and interprofessional and nursing management of various types of urinary calculi.
5. Distinguish the common causes and management of renal trauma, renal vascular problems, and hereditary kidney diseases.
6. Describe the clinical manifestations and nursing and interprofessional management of kidney and bladder cancers.
7. Describe the common causes and management of urinary incontinence and urinary retention.
8. Distinguish among urethral, ureteral, suprapubic, and nephrostomy catheters regarding indications for use and nursing responsibilities.
9. Explain the nursing management of the patient undergoing nephrectomy or urinary diversion surgery.

KEY TERMS

calculus
cystitis
glomerulonephritis
hydronephrosis
ileal conduit
interstitial cystitis (IC)
lithotripsy
nephrolithiasis
nephrosclerosis
nephrotic syndrome
polycystic kidney disease (PKD)
pyelonephritis
renal artery stenosis
stricture
urethritis
urinary incontinence (UI)
urinary retention
urinary tract infection (UTI)
urosepsis

A wide range of renal and urologic problems contribute to impaired elimination. This chapter discusses problems of the upper urinary tract (kidneys and ureter) and lower urinary tract (bladder and urethra). Many patients are at risk for fluid, electrolyte, and acid-base imbalances because of the kidneys' vital role in homeostasis. The person may have discomfort, incontinence, disrupted sleep, and impaired skin integrity.

INFECTIOUS AND INFLAMMATORY URINARY PROBLEMS

URINARY TRACT INFECTION

Urinary tract infections (UTIs) are infections of the urinary tract. They are the most common outpatient infection. *Escherichia coli* is the most common pathogen causing a UTI. It causes 75% of cases without urinary tract structural

TABLE 50.1 Common Causes of UTIs

- *Candida* species
- *Enterobacter*
- *Enterococcus*
- *Escherichia coli*
- *Klebsiella pneumoniae*
- *Proteus mirabilis*
- *Pseudomonas aeruginosa*
- *Serratia*
- *Staphylococcus aureus*
- *Streptococci*, Group B

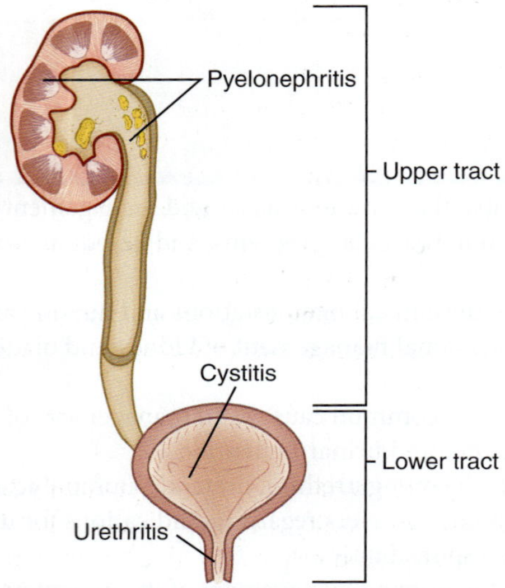

Fig. 50.1 Sites of infections in the upper and lower urinary tracts.

abnormalities or stones and 65% of complicated UTIs (Table 50.1).[1]

Fungal and parasitic infections sometimes cause UTIs. These are more common in patients who are immunosuppressed, have diabetes or kidney problems, or received multiple courses of antibiotic therapy. They may also occur in persons who live in or have traveled to certain developing countries.

Rec'd Multiple rounds of ABT.

Classification of Urinary Tract Infection

UTIs can be broadly described as an upper or lower UTI according to its location within the urinary system (Fig. 50.1). We use specific terms to describe the location of a UTI. For example, **pyelonephritis** implies inflammation (usually caused by infection) of the renal parenchyma and collecting system. **Cystitis** is an inflammation of the bladder. **Urethritis** is an inflammation of the urethra. **Urosepsis** is a UTI that has spread systemically. It is a life-threatening condition requiring emergency treatment.

We also classify a UTI as complicated or uncomplicated. *Uncomplicated UTIs* occur in an otherwise normal urinary tract. They usually only involve the bladder. *Complicated UTIs* occur in a person with an underlying disease or with a structural or functional problem in the urinary tract. Examples include obstruction, stones, catheters, abnormal genitourinary (GU) tract, acute kidney injury (AKI), chronic kidney disease (CKD), kidney transplant, diabetes, or neurologic disease. They can

TABLE 50.2 Risk Factors for UTIs

Anatomic Factors
- Congenital defects leading to obstruction or urinary stasis
- Fistula exposing urinary stream to skin, vagina, or fecal stream
- Obesity
- Shorter female urethra and colonization from normal vaginal flora

Factors Compromising Immune Response
- Aging
- Diabetes
- HIV infection

Factors Increasing Urinary Stasis
- Extrinsic obstruction (tumor, fibrosis compressing urinary tract)
- Intrinsic obstruction (stone, tumor of urinary tract, urethral stricture, BPH)
- Renal impairment
- Urinary retention (e.g., neurogenic bladder)

Foreign Bodies
- Catheters (indwelling, external condom catheter, ureteral stent, nephrostomy tube, intermittent catheterization)
- Urinary tract instrumentation (cystoscopy)
- Urinary tract stones

Functional Disorders
- Constipation
- Voiding dysfunction with detrusor sphincter muscle incoordination

Other Factors
- Habitual delay of urination ("nurse's bladder," "teacher's bladder")
- Pregnancy
- Menopause
- Sexual activity (women)
- Poor personal hygiene
- Use of spermicidal agents, contraceptive diaphragm (women), bubble baths, feminine sprays

also occur when a person has developed antibiotic resistance, is immunocompromised, has pregnancy-induced changes, or has recurrent infection. The person with a complicated infection is at risk for pyelonephritis, urosepsis, and renal damage.

Etiology and Pathophysiology

The urinary tract above the urethra is normally sterile. Several mechanical and physiologic defense mechanisms aid in maintaining sterility and preventing UTIs. These defenses include normal voiding with complete bladder emptying, ureterovesical junction (UVJ) competence, and ureteral peristaltic activity that propels urine toward the bladder. The antibacterial properties of urine are maintained by a slightly acidic pH (6.0 to 7.5) and abundant antimicrobial proteins and peptides that interfere with the bacterial growth. A change in any of these defense mechanisms increases the risk for a UTI (Table 50.2).

The organisms that usually cause UTIs originate in the perineum. They are introduced via the ascending route from the urethra. Most infections are caused by gram-negative bacilli normally found in the gastrointestinal (GI) tract. However, gram-positive organisms, such as streptococci, enterococci, and *Staphylococcus saprophyticus,* can also cause UTIs.

TABLE 50.3 Lower Urinary Tract Symptoms (LUTS)

Symptoms	Description
Emptying Symptoms	
Dysuria	• Painful or difficult urination
Hesitancy	• Difficulty starting urine stream • Delay between initiation of urination (because of urethral sphincter relaxation) and beginning of flow of urine • Diminished urinary stream
Intermittency	• Interruption of urinary stream while voiding
Postvoid dribbling	• Urine loss after completing voiding
Urinary retention or incomplete emptying	• Inability to empty urine from bladder • Caused by atonic bladder or obstruction of urethra • Can be acute or chronic
Storage Symptoms	
Incontinence	• Involuntary or accidental urine loss or leakage
Nocturia	• Awakened by urge to void 2 or more times during sleep • May be diurnal or nocturnal depending on sleep schedule
Nocturnal enuresis	• Adults: loss of urine during sleep
Urgency	• Sudden, strong, or intense desire to void immediately • Often accompanied by frequency
Urinary frequency	• More than 8 times in 24-h period • Often <200 mL each voiding

A common factor contributing to ascending infection is urologic instrumentation (e.g., catheterization, cystoscopic examinations). Instrumentation allows bacteria that are normally present at the opening of the urethra to enter the urethra or bladder. Sexual intercourse promotes "milking" of bacteria from the vagina and perineum. It may cause minor urethral trauma that predisposes women to UTIs.

UTIs can result from hematogenous transmission, in which blood-borne bacteria invade the kidneys, ureters, or bladder from elsewhere in the body. For a kidney infection to occur this way, there must be prior injury to the urinary tract, such as obstruction of the ureter, damage caused by stones, or renal scars.

UTIs are the most common health care–associated infection (HAI). They are mainly due to the use of an indwelling catheter. *Catheter-associated urinary tract infections (CAUTIs)* are often caused by *E. coli* and, less often, *Pseudomonas* organisms. CAUTIs lead to extended hospital stays, increased health care costs, and increased mortality.[2]

Clinical Manifestations

Manifestations of UTIs range from painful urination in uncomplicated urethritis or cystitis to severe systemic illness with abdominal or back pain, fever, and sepsis.

Lower urinary tract symptoms (LUTS) occur in patients who have UTIs of the upper urinary tract, as well as those confined to the lower tract. Symptoms are related to either bladder storage or bladder emptying (Table 50.3). These include dysuria, frequency (voiding more than every 2 hours), urgency, and suprapubic discomfort or pressure. The urine may have grossly visible blood (hematuria) or sediment, giving it a cloudy appearance. Upper UTIs (involving the renal parenchyma, pelvis, and ureters) typically causes fever, chills, and flank pain. A UTI confined to the lower urinary tract does not usually have systemic manifestations. People with significant bacteriuria may have no symptoms or may have nonspecific symptoms, such as fatigue or anorexia.

Remember that the common manifestations of a UTI are often absent in older adults. Older adults tend to have general abdominal discomfort rather than dysuria and suprapubic pain. They may have impaired cognition or overall clinical deterioration. Because older adults are less likely to have a fever with a UTI, temperature is an unreliable sign of a UTI.[3]

Multiple problems may produce LUTS similar to the symptoms of a UTI. For example, patients with bladder tumors or those receiving intravesical chemotherapy or pelvic radiation usually have urinary frequency, urgency, and dysuria. Interstitial cystitis/painful bladder syndrome produces urinary symptoms that are similar to and sometimes confused with a UTI.

A small number of healthy persons have some bacteria colonizing the bladder. We call this asymptomatic bacteriuria. It does not justify screening or treatment except in pregnant women, those with a recent kidney transplant, or those having a urologic procedure.

Diagnostic Studies

In a patient suspected of having a UTI, first obtain a dipstick urinalysis. This test can identify the presence of nitrites (indicating bacteriuria), white blood cells (WBCs), and leukocyte esterase (an enzyme present in WBCs, indicating pyuria). Microscopic urinalysis can confirm these findings. Bacterial counts of 10^5 colony-forming units per milliliter (CFU/mL) or higher typically indicate a clinically significant UTI. However, counts as low as 10^2 to 10^3 CFU/mL in a person with signs and symptoms are indicative of UTI.

After confirmation of bacteriuria and pyuria, we may do a urine culture. A urine culture is needed in persistent bacteriuria, recurring UTIs (more than 2 or 3 per year), or complicated, CAUTI, or HAI UTIs. We may culture urine when the infection is not responsive to empiric therapy or the diagnosis is questionable.

A voided midstream technique *(clean-catch urine sample)* is best for obtaining a urine culture in most circumstances (see Table 49.8). When we cannot obtain an adequate clean-catch specimen, we may do catheterization. A specimen from catheterization gives more accurate results than a clean-catch specimen.

A urine culture with *sensitivity testing* can determine the bacteria's susceptibility to a variety of antibiotic drugs. The results allow the HCP to choose an antibiotic known to be capable of destroying the bacteria causing a UTI in a specific patient.

Some patients need imaging studies of the urinary tract. An ultrasound or CT scan may be done if we suspect an obstruction or UTIs recur.

Interprofessional Care

The interprofessional care and drug therapy of UTIs are outlined in Table 50.4. Once a UTI has been diagnosed, appropriate antimicrobial therapy is started. An antibiotic may be chosen

TABLE 50.4 Interprofessional Care

UTI

Diagnostic Assessment
- History and physical assessment
- Urinalysis (midstream, "clean-catch" voided specimen)
- Urine for culture and sensitivity (if indicated)
- Imaging studies of urinary tract (if indicated): CT scan, ultrasound, cystoscopy

Management

Uncomplicated UTI
- Patient teaching
- Adequate fluid intake (8 to 9 8-oz glasses/day)

Drug Therapy
- Antibiotics
  - fluconazole (in patients with fungal UTI)
  - fosfomycin (Monurol)
  - nitrofurantoin (Macrodantin, Macrobid)
  - TMP/SMX (Bactrim, Bactrim DS)
  - trimethoprim alone (in patients with sulfa allergy)
  - cephalexin

Recurrent UTI
- Repeat urinalysis
- Urine culture and sensitivity testing
- Adequate fluid intake (8 to 9 8-oz glasses/day)
- Repeat patient teaching
- Imaging studies of urinary tract (if indicated): see above

Drug Therapy
- Antibiotic: nitrofurantoin, TMP/SMX
- Sensitivity-guided antibiotic therapy: ampicillin, amoxicillin, 1st- or 2nd-generation cephalosporin, fluoroquinolones
- 3- to 6-month trial of suppressive or prophylactic antibiotic therapy
- Postcoital antibiotic prophylaxis: cephalexin, nitrofurantoin, TMP/SMX, fosfomycin, trimethoprim

based on the HCP's best judgment *(empiric therapy)* or the results of sensitivity testing.

Uncomplicated UTIs are treated with a short-term course of antibiotics, typically for 3 days. In contrast, complicated UTIs need a longer period of treatment, lasting 7 to 14 days or more.[4] Many residents of long-term care facilities, especially women, have chronic asymptomatic bacteriuria. However, we usually only treat symptomatic UTIs.

First-choice drugs to treat uncomplicated or initial UTIs are trimethoprim/sulfamethoxazole (TMP/SMX), nitrofurantoin, cephalexin, and fosfomycin.[4] TMP/SMX has the advantages of being inexpensive and taken twice daily. Nitrofurantoin is taken 3 or 4 times daily, but a twice-daily formulation is available.

DRUG ALERT

Nitrofurantoin (Macrodantin)
- Avoid use if the creatinine clearance <30 mL/min.
- Notify HCP at once if fever, chills, cough, chest pain, dyspnea, rash, or numbness or tingling of fingers or toes develops.

Other antibiotics used in the treatment of uncomplicated UTI include ampicillin, amoxicillin, and cephalosporins. Fluoroquinolones (e.g., levofloxacin, ciprofloxacin) are given to treat complicated UTIs. *E. coli* resistance to TMP/SMX, β-lactams, and ciprofloxacin is an increasing problem in the United States. In patients with UTIs from fungi, fluconazole (Diflucan) is the preferred therapy.

A urinary analgesic, such as oral phenazopyridine, may relieve discomfort caused by severe dysuria. Phenazopyridine is an azo dye excreted in urine. There it exerts a topical analgesic effect on the urinary tract mucosa. It is taken up to 2 concurrent days. Teach patients that this drug causes the urine to turn orange or red.

Patients who have repeated UTIs may receive prophylactic or suppressive antibiotics. A low dose of TMP/SMX, nitrofurantoin, or another antibiotic taken daily may prevent recurring UTIs. A single dose may be taken after an event likely to provoke a UTI, such as sexual intercourse. While suppressive therapy is often effective short term, use is limited because of the risk for antibiotic resistance, which leads to breakthrough infections with increasingly virulent pathogens.

NURSING MANAGEMENT: URINARY TRACT INFECTION

Assessment

Subjective and objective data that you should obtain from a patient with a UTI are shown in Table 50.5.

Clinical Problems

Clinical problems for the patient with a UTI may include:
- Impaired urinary elimination
- Infection
- Pain
- Deficient knowledge

More information on clinical problems and interventions for the patient with a UTI is presented in eNursing Care Plan 50.1 (available on the website for this chapter).

Planning

The overall goals are that the patient with a UTI will have (1) relief from bothersome symptoms, (2) no upper urinary tract involvement, and (3) no recurrence.

Implementation

Health Promotion

It is important to recognize people who are at risk for a UTI. These include debilitated persons, older adults, patients who are immunocompromised (e.g., cancer, diabetes), and patients treated with immunosuppressive drugs or corticosteroids. Health promotion measures can help decrease the frequency of UTIs and support early detection of infection. These activities include teaching preventive measures, including (1) emptying the bladder regularly and completely, (2) evacuating the bowel regularly, (3) wiping the perineal area from front to back after voiding and defecation, and (4) drinking an adequate amount of liquid each day.

TABLE 50.5 NURSING ASSESSMENT
UTI

Subjective Data

Important Health Information

Health history: Previous UTI. Urinary stones, reflux, strictures, or retention. Neurogenic bladder, pregnancy, BPH, bladder cancer, sexually transmitted infection.

Medications: Antibiotics, anticholinergics, antispasmodics

Surgery or other treatments: Recent urologic instrumentation (catheterization, cystoscopy)

Functional Health Patterns

Cognitive-perceptual: Suprapubic or low back pain, bladder spasms, dysuria, burning on urination

Elimination: Urinary frequency, urgency, hesitancy, dysuria, nocturia

Health perception–health management: Urinary hygiene practices. Lassitude, malaise

Nutritional-metabolic: Nausea, vomiting, anorexia. Chills and fever

Sexuality-reproductive: Sexual activity, use of spermicidal agents or contraceptive diaphragm (women)

Objective Data

General

Fever, chills, dysuria

Atypical presentation in older adults: afebrile, absence of dysuria, loss of appetite, altered mental status

Urinary

Hematuria. Cloudy, foul-smelling urine

Possible Diagnostic Findings

Leukocytosis. Urinalysis positive for bacteria, pyuria, RBCs, WBCs, and nitrites. Positive urine culture. Ultrasound, CT scan, MRI, voiding cystourethrogram (VCUG), cystoscopy showing urinary tract abnormalities

BOX 50.1 EVIDENCE-BASED PRACTICE
Nurse-Driven Protocol for Catheter Removal

You are caring for M.B., a 42-year-old patient who had a total vaginal hysterectomy for dysfunctional uterine bleeding. She had an indwelling urinary catheter placed before surgery. On the 1st postoperative day, M.B. asks you when the catheter will be removed.

Making Clinical Decisions

Synthesis of Best Available Evidence

CAUTI still represents a notable source of infection in hospitalized patients. A single CAUTI can increase cost of care by $600 to $20,000. Because the Centers for Medicare and Medicaid Services requires public reporting of CAUTI as an indicator for hospital reimbursement, hospital leaders have led efforts to develop CAUTI prevention bundles. Traditionally, physicians have been responsible for ordering urinary catheter removal. However, research has shown physicians tend to leave catheters in place without appropriate indications and may be unaware the patient continues to have an indwelling urinary catheter. Nurse-driven protocols for directed assessment of catheter need and decision for removal may be a way to decrease catheter days and CAUTI occurrence.

Clinician Expertise

As part of the unit's efforts to decrease occurrence of CAUTI, you have received education on daily assessment of specific indications for continued catheterization. In your agency, use of an indwelling catheter typically does not exceed 24 hours after a hysterectomy. You have assessed M.B. based on identified criteria and found the time appropriate for urinary catheter removal. You explain the process to M.B. and prepare to remove the indwelling urinary catheter.

Patient Preferences and Values

M.B. expresses concern about getting a UTI related to catheterization.

Implications for Nursing Practice

1. How would you explain the catheter removal protocol and its rationale to M.B.?
2. How can you demonstrate engagement with and ownership of this unit practice?

Reference for Evidence

Tyson AF, Campbell EF, Spangler LR, et al.: Implementation of a nurse-driven protocol for catheter removal to decrease catheter-associated urinary tract infection rate in a surgical trauma ICU, *J Intensiv Care Med* 35:738, 2020.

Routine and thorough perineal hygiene is important for all hospitalized patients, especially after using a bedpan, after a bowel movement, or if fecal incontinence is present. Answer call lights quickly. Offer the bedpan or urinal to bedridden patients at frequent intervals. These measures can prevent incontinence and decrease the number of incontinence episodes.

Prevention of CAUTI. All patients undergoing catheterization of the urinary tract are at risk for developing CAUTI. You play a key role in preventing CAUTI. Avoiding unnecessary catheterization and early removal of indwelling catheters are the most effective means for reducing CAUTI (Box 50.1). Always follow aseptic technique during these procedures. Wash your hands before and after contact with each patient. Wear gloves for care of urinary catheters. The American Nurses Association offers an evidence-based clinical tool for decreasing CAUTI.[5]

◆ Acute Care

Acute care for a patient with a UTI includes ensuring adequate fluid intake unless contraindicated. Maintaining adequate fluid intake may be hard because of the patient feeling that fluid intake will make the pain and urinary frequency worse. Tell patients that fluids will increase frequency of urination but will also dilute the urine, making the bladder less irritable. Fluids will help flush out bacteria before they have a chance to colonize in the bladder. Teach them to avoid caffeine, alcohol, citrus juices, chocolate, and highly spiced foods or beverages because they are bladder irritants.

Applying heat to the suprapubic area or lower back may relieve the discomfort. Have the patient apply a heating pad (turned to its lowest setting) against the back or suprapubic area. A warm shower or sitting in a tub of warm water filled above the waist can give temporary relief.

Teach the patient about the prescribed drug therapy, including side effects. Emphasize the importance of taking the full course of antibiotics. Often patients stop antibiotic therapy once symptoms disappear. This can lead to inadequate treatment, recurrent infection, or bacterial resistance to antibiotics.

Sometimes a second drug or a reduced dosage of drug is given after the first course to suppress bacterial growth in patients

[TA]BLE 50.6 PATIENT & CAREGIVER [TE]ACHING

UTI

When teaching a patient and caregiver measures to prevent a recurrence of a UTI, include:

1. Take all antibiotics as prescribed. Symptoms may improve after 1–2 days of therapy, but organisms may still be present.
2. Practice appropriate hygiene, including:
   - Carefully clean the perineal region by separating the labia in females, or in males pulling back the foreskin if present when cleansing.
   - Wipe from front to back after urinating.
   - Cleanse with warm soapy water after each bowel movement.
3. Empty the bladder before and after sexual intercourse.
4. Void regularly, about every 3–4 hours during the day.
5. Maintain adequate fluid intake.
6. Avoid vaginal douches and harsh soaps, bubble baths, powders, and sprays in the perineal area.
7. Report to the HCP symptoms or signs of recurrent UTI (e.g., fever, cloudy urine, pain on urination, urgency, frequency).

susceptible to recurrent UTI. Teach the patient to monitor for signs of improvement (e.g., cloudy urine becomes clear) as well as a decrease in or cessation of symptoms. Tell patients to report to their HCP any (1) persistence of bothersome LUTS beyond the antibiotic treatment course, (2) onset of flank pain, or (3) fever.

◆ Ambulatory Care

Teach the patient and caregiver about the need for ongoing care (Table 50.6). This includes (1) taking antimicrobial drugs as ordered, (2) maintaining adequate daily fluid intake, (3) voiding regularly (every 3 to 4 hours), and (4) voiding before and after intercourse. Have the patient temporarily stopping using a diaphragm.

If treatment is complete and the symptoms are still present, teach the patient to get follow-up care. Recurrent symptoms typically occur within 1 to 2 weeks after completing therapy. If the patient has followed the treatment plan, a relapse indicates the need for further evaluation.

◆ Evaluation

The expected outcomes are that the patient with a UTI will

- Have normal urinary elimination patterns
- Report relief of bothersome urinary tract symptoms
- State knowledge of the treatment plan

ACUTE PYELONEPHRITIS

Etiology and Pathophysiology

Pyelonephritis is an inflammation of the renal parenchyma and collecting system, including the renal pelvis (Fig. 50.2). The most common cause is bacterial infection. Fungi, protozoa, or viruses can also infect the kidney.[6]

Urosepsis is a systemic infection arising from a urologic source. Its prompt diagnosis and effective treatment are critical because it can lead to septic shock and death unless promptly treated. Septic shock is discussed in Chapter 42.

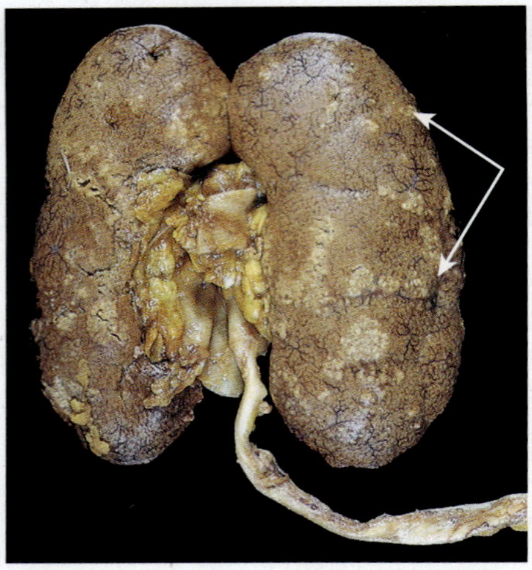

Fig. 50.2 Acute pyelonephritis. Cortical surface shows grayish-white areas of inflammation and abscess formation *(arrows)*. (From Kumar V, Abbas AK, Aster JC, et al.: *Robbins and Cotran pathologic basis of disease,* ed 8, Philadelphia, 2010, Saunders.)

Pyelonephritis usually begins with colonization and infection of the lower urinary tract via the ascending urethral route. Bacteria normally found in the GI tract, including *E. coli* or *Proteus, Klebsiella,* or *Enterobacter* species, often cause pyelonephritis. A preexisting factor can be present, like *vesicoureteral reflux* (retrograde [backward] movement of urine from lower to upper urinary tract) or dysfunction of the lower urinary tract (e.g., obstruction from benign prostatic hyperplasia [BPH], stricture, stones).

Acute pyelonephritis often starts in the renal medulla and spreads to the adjacent cortex. Pregnancy-induced physiologic changes in the urinary system are an important risk factor for acute pyelonephritis. Recurring episodes of pyelonephritis, especially in the presence of obstructive abnormalities, can lead to chronic pyelonephritis (discussed later).

Clinical Manifestations and Diagnostic Studies

The classic manifestations include (1) fever/chills, (2) nausea/vomiting, (3) malaise, and (4) flank pain. There may be LUTS, such as dysuria, urgency, and frequency. *Costovertebral angle tenderness* to percussion (costovertebral angle [CVA] pain) is typically present on the affected side. In some cases of pyelonephritis, renal scarring and decreased kidney function can occur. Potentially life-threatening urosepsis can occur.

Urinalysis results may show pyuria, bacteriuria, and varying degrees of hematuria. WBC casts in the urine may indicate renal parenchyma involvement. Urine cultures with sensitivities are done when pyelonephritis is suspected. Blood cultures may be done on hospitalized patients with more severe illness.

Ultrasound can identify anatomic abnormalities, hydronephrosis, renal abscesses, or an obstructing stone. CT scans are the preferred imaging studies. They can assess for signs of infection in the kidney and complications of pyelonephritis, such as impaired renal function, scarring, chronic pyelonephritis, or abscesses.

Interprofessional Care

The diagnostic tests and interprofessional care of acute pyelonephritis are outlined in Table 50.7. Patients with severe infections

TABLE 50.7 Interprofessional Care
Acute Pyelonephritis

Diagnostic Assessment

- History and physical assessment
- Urinalysis
- Urine for culture and sensitivity
- Imaging studies: ultrasound (initially), CT scan, MRI, cystoscopy, voiding cystourethrogram (VCUG)
- CBC count with WBC differential
- Blood culture (if bacteremia is suspected)
- Percussion for flank (CVA) pain

Management

Mild Symptoms

- Outpatient management or short hospitalization
- Adequate fluid intake
- NSAIDs or antipyretic drugs
- Follow-up urine culture and imaging studies

Drug Therapy

- Empirically selected broad-spectrum antibiotics: fluoroquinolones (ciprofloxacin, levofloxacin), cephalosporins preferred. TMP/SMX or an oral B-lactam can be used if infection expected to be susceptible
- Short course of IV antibiotics, such as an extended spectrum cephalosporin or penicillin, fluroquinolone (e.g., ciprofloxacin, levofloxacin), or an aminoglycoside without or with amoxicillin
- Switch to sensitivity-guided therapy when urine and blood culture results available

Severe Symptoms

- Hospitalization
- Adequate fluid intake (IV initially; switch to oral fluids as nausea, vomiting, and dehydration subside)
- NSAIDs or antipyretic drugs to reverse fever and relieve discomfort
- Follow-up urine culture and imaging studies

Drug Therapy

- IV antibiotics
  - Empirically selected broad-spectrum antibiotics: carbapenem (e.g., imipenem, meropenem), vancomycin, daptomycin, linezolid
  - Switch to sensitivity-guided antibiotic therapy when results of urine and blood culture are available
- Oral antibiotics when patient tolerates oral intake

or complicating factors, such as nausea and vomiting with dehydration, need hospitalized.

The patient with mild symptoms may be treated as an outpatient with antibiotics for 5 to 14 days (Table 50.7). IV antibiotics are often given initially in the hospital to rapidly establish high serum and urinary drug levels.[6] When initial treatment resolves acute symptoms and the patient can tolerate oral fluids and drugs, they can be discharged on oral antibiotics for 14 more days. Symptoms and signs typically improve or resolve within 48 to 72 hours after starting therapy.

Relapses may be treated with a different course of antibiotics. Antibiotic prophylaxis also may be used for recurrent infections. The effectiveness of therapy is based on bacterial growth on urine culture.

Urosepsis is characterized by bacteriuria and bacteremia (bacteria in blood). Close observation and vital sign monitoring are essential. Prompt recognition and treatment of septic shock may prevent irreversible damage or death.

NURSING MANAGEMENT: ACUTE PYELONEPHRITIS

Assessment

Subjective and objective data that you should obtain from a patient with pyelonephritis are similar to those for the patient with a UTI (Table 50.5).

Clinical Problems

Clinical problems for the patient with pyelonephritis include those for the patient with a UTI.

Planning

The overall goals are that the patient with pyelonephritis will have (1) normal renal function, (2) no complications, (3) relief of pain, and (4) no recurrence of symptoms.

Implementation

Health promotion and maintenance measures are similar to those for cystitis. Early treatment for cystitis can prevent ascending infections. Because patients with structural abnormalities of the urinary tract are at high risk for infection, stress the need for regular medical care.

Interventions vary depending on the severity of symptoms. Teach the patient about the disease process. Emphasize (1) taking antibiotic therapy as prescribed, (2) having a follow-up urine culture, and (3) recognizing signs of recurrence or relapse (Table 50.6). Encourage the patient to drink at least 8 glasses of fluid every day, even after the infection has been treated. Rest will increase patient comfort.

The patient who has frequent relapses or reinfections may receive long-term, low-dose antibiotics. Making certain the patient understands the reason for therapy is important to increase adherence.

Evaluation

The expected outcomes for the patient with pyelonephritis are the same as for UTI.

CHRONIC PYELONEPHRITIS

In *chronic pyelonephritis,* the kidneys are continually infected. This leads to inflammation and fibrosis (scarring). There may be a loss of renal function and renal atrophy (shrinkage). Chronic pyelonephritis is usually the result of significant anatomic abnormalities, such as vesicoureteral reflux or recurring infections involving the upper urinary tract. It can rarely occur due to a substantial inflammatory response from an infection.

Radiologic imaging studies can confirm the diagnosis of chronic pyelonephritis and possible contributing factors. A renal biopsy can show the loss of functioning nephrons, infiltration of the parenchyma with inflammatory cells, and fibrosis.

The level of renal function in chronic pyelonephritis depends on whether 1 or both kidneys are affected, the extent of scarring, and the presence of coexisting infection. Chronic pyelonephritis can progress to end-stage renal disease (ESRD). Monitoring and treating infection and correcting any underlying contributing factors are important. Care of the patient with CKD is discussed in Chapter 51.

URETHRITIS

Urethritis is inflammation of the urethra. Causes include a bacterial or viral infection (e.g., herpes simplex virus), *Trichomonas*, monilial infection (especially in women), chlamydial infection, *Mycoplasma*, and gonorrhea.

In men, the causes of urethritis are usually sexually transmitted. Purulent discharge can indicate a gonococcal urethritis. A clear or mucoid discharge typically signifies a nongonococcal urethritis. Sexually transmitted infections are discussed in Chapter 57. Urethritis can cause bothersome LUTS, including dysuria, urgency, and frequency, similar to those seen with cystitis. Men may have penile burning.

In women, urethritis can be hard to diagnose. It should be considered when WBCs are present on urinalysis but there are no bacteria. It often produces bothersome LUTS, but urethral discharge may not be present.

Treatment of urethritis is based on identifying and treating the cause and providing symptomatic relief. Drugs used for bacterial infections include TMP/SMX, doxycycline (Vibramycin), ceftriaxone, and nitrofurantoin. Metronidazole (Flagyl) and tinidazole (Tindamax) are options for treating *Trichomonas* infection. Drugs used to treat monilial infections include nystatin, clotrimazole, or fluconazole. In chlamydial infections, doxycycline or azithromycin are options. Women with negative urine cultures and no pyuria usually do not respond to antibiotics.

Warm sitz baths may temporarily relieve bothersome symptoms. Teach the patient to (1) avoid using vaginal deodorant sprays and contraceptive gels, (2) cleanse the perineal area after bowel movements and voiding, and (3) avoid sexual intercourse for at least 7 days. Tell patients with sexually transmitted urethritis to refer their sex partners for evaluation and testing if they had sexual contact in the 60 days before the onset of the patient's symptoms or diagnosis.

URETHRAL DIVERTICULA

Urethral diverticula are localized outpouchings of the urethra. Women have a much higher incidence than men. The rare cases in males usually are associated with congenital lower urinary tract anomalies or surgical trauma.

Risk factors include obstructed periurethral glands or infection. The periurethral glands are found along the distal two-thirds of the urethra. Other risk factors include urethral trauma, vaginal delivery, urethral instrumentation, and urethral dilation.

Classic symptoms include dysuria, postvoid dribbling, and dyspareunia (painful intercourse). Other symptoms include frequency (voiding more often than every 2 hours), urgency, suprapubic discomfort or pressure, pelvis or urethral pain, and a feeling of incomplete bladder emptying. Urinary incontinence (UI) is often present. However, women can also be asymptomatic.

The urine may have gross blood (hematuria) or sediment, which gives it a cloudy appearance. The diverticula can protrude into the anterior vaginal wall, causing an anterior wall mass. The mass may be felt on assessment. When palpated, the mass is often quite tender and can express urine and/or purulent discharge through the urethra.

Radiographic studies, such as ultrasound and MRI, are helpful in determining the size of the diverticulum in relation to the urethral lumen. A urethroscopy may be of benefit. It is done as an adjunct to radiologic studies.

Surgical options include transvaginal diverticulectomy, marsupialization (creation of a permanent opening) of the diverticular sac into the vagina *(Spence procedure)*, and urethroscopic surgical excision. Stress UI, infection, bleeding, and urethral-vaginal fistula are potential complications of the surgery.

INTERSTITIAL CYSTITIS/PAINFUL BLADDER SYNDROME

Interstitial cystitis (IC) is a chronic, painful disease of the bladder characterized by urgency, frequency, and pain in the bladder and/or pelvis. IC is also called bladder pain syndrome or painful bladder syndrome (PBS). The term *IC/PBS* refers to cases of urinary pain that we cannot attribute to other causes, such as UTI or urinary stones. IC/PBS is more common in women. It affects about 3 to 8 million women and 1 to 4 million men each year.[7]

The cause of IC/PBS is unknown. It is likely multifactorial. Possible causes include neurogenic hypersensitivity of the lower urinary tract, changes in mast cells in the muscle and/or mucosal layers of the bladder, bladder attacked by the immune system, or production of a toxic substance in the urine.

Clinical Manifestations and Diagnostic Studies

The 2 primary manifestations of IC/PBS are pain and bothersome LUTS (e.g., frequency, urgency). People with severe cases may void as often as 60 times in a day, including nighttime urination. The pain is usually in the suprapubic area, but may involve the vagina, labia, or entire perineal region, including the rectum and anus. The pain varies from mild to severe. The pain may get worse with bladder filling, postponed urination, physical exertion, pressure against the suprapubic area, certain foods, exercise, or prolonged sitting. Voiding temporarily relieves pain. Bothersome LUTS are similar to a UTI. The condition may be misdiagnosed as a recurring or chronic UTI or, in men, chronic prostatitis.

The patient may have periods of remission and exacerbation. Women often report pain that occurs before menstruation. Sexual intercourse or emotional stress can worsen pain. Some patients have symptoms that disappear altogether after a period of weeks to months. Others have persistent symptoms over months to years.

IC/PBS is a diagnosis of exclusion. A history and physical assessment can rule out other problems that have similar symptoms, such as cancer, infection, or pelvic abnormalities. Urine cultures do not find any bacteria or other organisms in the urine. Cystoscopic examination may reveal a small bladder capacity, Hunner lesions (distinct inflammatory areas on the bladder wall), and glomerulations (superficial ulcerations with pinpoint bleeding). These findings, though, are not always present.

Interprofessional Care

No single treatment consistently reverses or relieves symptoms. Various therapies have been effective, including nutrition and drug therapy. People with IC/PBS do not respond to antibiotic therapy. They rarely need surgery.

Eliminating foods and beverages that are likely to irritate the bladder may give some symptom relief. Common bladder irritants include coffee and tea (caffeinated and decaffeinated); alcohol; citrus products; carbonated drinks; chocolate; foods containing vinegar, curries, or hot peppers; and foods or beverages likely to lower urinary pH, including fruits such as cranberries. An over-the-counter (OTC) supplement called *calcium glycerophosphate* (Prelief) or 1 tablespoon of baking soda mixed with water alkalinizes the urine. It may provide relief from the irritating effects of some foods. Recipes and menus for a well-balanced diet that avoids bladder-irritating foods and beverages are available at the website for the Interstitial Cystitis Association (www.ichelp.org).

The tricyclic antidepressants, amitriptyline (preferred) and nortriptyline, may reduce burning and urinary frequency. Pentosan polysulfate sodium (Elmiron) is the only oral agent approved for treating IC symptoms. It enhances the protective effects of the glycosaminoglycan layer of the bladder and relieves pain by reducing the irritative effects of urine on the bladder wall. This drug provides relief over time (weeks to months). It does not give immediate relief for acute symptoms. Due to reports of macular eye changes, this medication has an FDA approved warning label regarding eye toxicity.

Pelvic physical therapy and bladder hydrodistention therapy may be useful. Dimethyl sulfoxide (DMSO) can be directly instilled into the bladder through a small catheter. DMSO improves inflammation and desensitizes pain receptors in the bladder wall. Heparin, lidocaine, or sodium bicarbonate can also be instilled into the bladder to relieve acute symptoms. Intradetrusor botulinum toxin and cyclosporine A may be of some help.

Surgery is an option to improve severe, debilitating pain. Sacral neuromodulation or fulguration (using high-frequency energy to destroy a lesion) and resection of Hunner lesions are options. Urinary diversion, such as an ileal conduit, without or with removal of the bladder, is an option when other measures fail. Unfortunately, some patients have pain within the urinary diversion, which means that some factor in the urine may contribute to IC/PBS in some cases.

◆ NURSING MANAGEMENT: IC/PBS

Assess the characteristics of the pain with IC/PBS. Ask the patient about specific diet or lifestyle factors that relieve pain or make it worse. Teach the patient to keep a bladder log or voiding diary over a period of at least 3 days to determine voiding frequency and patterns of nocturia. Keeping a pain record at the same time may be useful.

A UTI may occur during IC/PBS management because of diagnostic instrumentation and frequent bladder instillations. A UTI is likely to cause an acute exacerbation of bothersome LUTS and urinary frequency, as well as dysuria (not typically present with IC/PBS), odorous urine, and hematuria.

Because stress can worsen symptoms or cause flare-ups, stress management techniques such as relaxation breathing and imagery (see Chapter 7) may be helpful. Using lubrication or changing positions may decrease pain from sexual intercourse.

Discuss proper nutrition, especially considering the broad diet restrictions often needed to control IC-related pain. Tell the patient to take a multivitamin containing no more than the recommended daily allowance for essential vitamins. They should avoid high-potency vitamins because they may irritate the bladder. The patient should avoid clothing that creates suprapubic pressure, such as pants with tight belts or waistlines. Information about diet, coping with the need for frequent urination, and coping with the emotional burden of IC/PBS are available from the Interstitial Cystitis Association (www.ichelp.org). Reassurance that IC/PBS is a real condition experienced by others and that it can be treated may relieve the anxiety, anger, guilt, and frustration related to having chronic pain and voiding dysfunction in the absence of a clear-cut diagnosis and treatment strategy.

GENITOURINARY TUBERCULOSIS

Genitourinary tuberculosis (GUTB) is the 3rd most common type of extrapulmonary tuberculosis. Between 2% and 20% of patients with pulmonary TB develop GUTB. Onset can occur 1 to 33 years after the primary lung infection.[8,9] When the kidney is first infected with bacilli, the patient is often asymptomatic and may have incidental microscopic hematuria and/or pyuria. With progression of the infection to involve the bladder, symptoms of urgency, frequency, dysuria, and/or nocturia develop in about 50% of patients. A third of patients have back pain and gross hematuria.

A diagnosis of GUTB is based on finding *Mycobacterium tuberculosis* bacilli in the urine. A CT scan with contrast and ultrasound can help determine the extent and severity of the disease. A TB skin test should be done.

Long-term complications of GUTB depend on the duration of the disease. Scarring of the renal parenchyma, calcifications, hydronephrosis, and ureteral strictures can occur. The earlier treatment is started, the less likely renal failure will develop. The patient may need long-term urologic follow-up. Care of the patient with TB is discussed in Chapter 30.

IMMUNOLOGIC KIDNEY PROBLEMS

GLOMERULONEPHRITIS

Glomerulonephritis (inflammation of the glomeruli) affects both kidneys equally. It is the 3rd leading cause of ESRD in the

TABLE 50.8 Causes and Risk Factors for Glomerulonephritis (GN)

Cause or Risk Factor	Description
Conditions Causing Scarring of Glomeruli	
Diabetic nephropathy	• Primary cause of end-stage renal disease in the United States (see Chapter 51) • Microvascular changes of diffuse glomerulosclerosis involving thickening of the glomerular basement membrane
Focal segmental glomerulosclerosis	• Characterized by scattered scarring of glomeruli • May result from another disease or occur for unknown reasons
Hypertension	• Nephrosclerosis is a complication of hypertension • GN can cause hypertension
Immune Diseases	
Anti-GBM disease	• Autoimmune disorder that causes lung and kidney disease • Causes bleeding into lungs and GN
Immunoglobulin A (IgA) nephropathy	• Results from deposits of IgA in the glomeruli • Characterized by recurrent episodes of hematuria
Scleroderma	• Disease of unknown cause characterized by widespread changes in connective tissue and vascular lesions in many organs (see Chapter 69) • In the kidney, vascular lesions are associated with fibrosis • Severity of renal involvement varies
Systemic lupus erythematosus (SLE)	• Autoimmune disorder characterized by the involvement of several tissues and organs, especially joints, skin, and kidneys (see Chapter 69) • GN often occurs in SLE and has a poor prognosis
Infections	
Infective endocarditis	• Bacteria can cause an infection of 1 or more of the heart valves (see Chapter 40) • People at risk include those with a heart defect, such as a damaged or artificial heart valve • GN may be due to glomerular membrane deposits of complement and immunoglobulin
Poststreptococcal glomerulonephritis	• GN may develop 1–3 weeks after a streptococcal throat infection or 3–6 weeks after a skin infection • Antibodies (Ab) to strep antigen (Ag) develop and the Ag-Ab deposit in the glomeruli, causing inflammation
Viral infections	• Viral infections can trigger GN • Common viruses include HIV, hepatitis B, and hepatitis C viruses
Vasculitis	
Granulomatosis with Polyangiitis	• Form of vasculitis affecting small and medium blood vessels • Most often affects kidneys, lungs, and upper respiratory tract
Polyarteritis nodosa	• Rare disease, possibly autoimmune, that affects small and medium blood vessels • Can affect any organ but common in heart, kidneys, and intestines
Other Causes	
Amyloidosis	• Caused by infiltration of tissues with amyloid (hyaline substance) • Hyaline bodies consist largely of protein • Kidney involvement is common • Proteinuria is often the first clinical manifestation
Illegal drug use	• People who use these drugs are at increased risk for GN

United States. Although the glomerulus is the primary site of inflammation, tubular and interstitial changes with vascular scarring and hardening *(glomerulosclerosis)* in the kidney can occur.[10]

A variety of conditions are associated with glomerulonephritis. These range from kidney infections, drugs toxic to the kidneys, problems with the immune system, and systemic diseases (Table 50.8). Glomerulonephritis can be acute or chronic. With *acute glomerulonephritis,* symptoms come on suddenly. They may be temporary or reversible. An example of this is acute poststreptococcal glomerulonephritis (APSGN). *Chronic glomerulonephritis* typically progresses slowly and can lead to irreversible renal failure.

Diagnostic studies and the history, including any recent infection, such as a sore throat or upper respiratory tract infection, or a diagnosis of diabetes, aid in identifying the type of glomerulonephritis present.

Acute Poststreptococcal Glomerulonephritis

Acute poststreptococcal glomerulonephritis is the most common type of acute glomerulonephritis worldwide. It is most common in children aged 5 to 7 years old and adults older than 60 years. APSGN develops about 1 to 6 weeks after an infection of the tonsils, pharynx, or skin (e.g., streptococcal sore throat, impetigo) by nephrotoxic strains of group A β-hemolytic streptococci.[11] The person makes antibodies to the streptococcal antigen. Although the exact mechanism is not known, tissue injury occurs as the antigen-antibody complexes are deposited in the glomeruli, complement is activated (see Chapter 12), and inflammation results.

Manifestations vary. They include generalized edema, hypertension, oliguria, hematuria, and proteinuria. Fluid retention occurs because of decreased glomerular filtration. At first, edema appears in low-pressure tissues, such as those around the eyes *(periorbital edema)*. Later it progresses to involve the whole body. Red to brown urine occurs with bleeding in the upper urinary tract. The degree of proteinuria varies with the severity of the glomerulonephritis. Hypertension results from increased extracellular fluid volume. The patient may have abdominal or flank pain. Sometimes the patient may be asymptomatic. The problem is found on routine urinalysis.

The diagnosis of APSGN is based on a complete history and physical assessment. An immune response to the streptococci is often shown by the streptozyme test. It measures 5 different streptococcal antibodies, including antistreptolysin-O (ASO). The finding of decreased complement components (especially C3 and CH50) indicates an immune-mediated response. A renal biopsy can confirm the disease.

Dipstick urinalysis and urine sediment microscopy can show significant numbers of red blood cells (RBCs) with or without casts. Proteinuria may range from mild to severe. Blood tests include blood urea nitrogen (BUN) and serum creatinine to assess the extent of renal impairment.

NURSING AND INTERPROFESSIONAL MANAGEMENT: ACUTE POSTSTREPTOCOCCAL GLOMERULONEPHRITIS

More than 90% of patients with APSGN recover completely or improve rapidly with supportive management. Accurate recognition and assessment are critical. Chronic glomerulonephritis can develop if the patient is not treated appropriately.

Management focuses on symptomatic relief. Rest is recommended until the signs of glomerular inflammation (proteinuria, hematuria) and hypertension subside. Restricting sodium and fluid intake and giving diuretics can reduce edema. Severe hypertension is treated with antihypertensive drugs. We may restrict protein intake if there is evidence of an increase in nitrogenous wastes (e.g., increased BUN). The protein restriction varies with the degree of proteinuria. Low-protein, low-sodium, fluid-restricted diets are discussed in Chapter 51. Antibiotics are given if the streptococcal infection is still present.

One of the most important ways to prevent APSGN is to encourage early diagnosis and treatment of sore throats and skin lesions. If a culture is positive for streptococci, treatment with the appropriate antibiotic therapy is essential. Encourage the patient to take the full course of antibiotics to ensure that the bacteria are completely gone. Good personal hygiene is a key factor in preventing the spread of cutaneous streptococcal infections.

In most cases, recovery from the acute glomerulonephritis is complete. However, in rare cases, hypertension, proteinuria, and/or renal insufficiency can occur.

Chronic Glomerulonephritis

Chronic glomerulonephritis is a syndrome of permanent and progressive renal fibrosis involving the glomeruli. It can progress to ESRD. Most types of glomerulonephritis and nephrotic syndrome can eventually lead to chronic glomerulonephritis. Some people who develop chronic glomerulonephritis have no history of kidney disease. We may not find the cause of chronic glomerulonephritis. An inherited disorder (e.g., Alport syndrome) or an autoimmune disorder may be the cause.

With chronic glomerulonephritis, symptoms develop slowly over time. Patients are often unaware that progressive kidney impairment is occurring, even if it is severe, until they have a diagnostic evaluation. Chronic glomerulonephritis is often discovered by finding an abnormality on a urinalysis, high BP, or increased serum creatinine.

The syndrome is characterized by proteinuria, hematuria, and the slow development of uremia (see Chapter 51) because of decreasing renal function. Chronic glomerulonephritis progresses insidiously toward ESRD over a course of several years.

Manifestations include varying degrees of hematuria (ranging from microscopic to gross), proteinuria, and urinary excretion of various formed elements, including RBCs, WBCs, and casts. Increased BUN and serum creatinine levels are common. Ultrasound and CT scans are the preferred radiologic studies. A renal biopsy may be done to determine the cause of the glomerulonephritis.

The history provides vital information. Assess exposure to drugs (e.g., nonsteroidal antiinflammatory drugs [NSAIDs]) and infections (e.g., hepatitis). Evaluate the patient for other immune disorders, such as systemic lupus erythematosus (SLE). The patient may not recall any history of renal problems.

Treatment depends on the cause of the chronic glomerulonephritis. It includes supportive and symptomatic care. Management of CKD is discussed in Chapter 51.

Anti-Glomerular Basement Membrane Disease

Anti-glomerular basement membrane (GBM) disease (formerly called Goodpasture syndrome) is an autoimmune disease characterized by antibodies that attack the glomerular and alveolar basement membranes. Damage to the kidneys and lungs results when binding of the antibody causes an inflammatory reaction mediated by complement activation (see Chapter 12).

GBM is a rare disease that occurs mainly in older children and adults, especially those in their 30s and 60s to 70s. The manifestations can include weakness, pallor, and pulmonary symptoms, such as cough, mild shortness of breath, hemoptysis, crackles, and pulmonary insufficiency. Renal involvement includes hematuria, proteinuria, and anemia. It can proceed quickly to renal failure. Pulmonary involvement can occur before or at the same time as glomerular abnormalities.

Current management includes glucocorticoids, immunosuppressive drugs (e.g., cyclophosphamide, rituximab), plasmapheresis (see Chapter 14), and, if needed, dialysis. Plasmapheresis removes the circulating anti–GBM antibodies. Immunosuppressive therapy inhibits further antibody production. Those with ESRD due to the disease may be a candidate for a kidney transplant. GBM disease rarely occurs in the transplanted kidney.

Encourage smoking cessation. The patient receives care appropriate for a critically ill patient who has AKI (see Chapter 51) and respiratory distress (see Chapter 32). Death is often from bleeding in the lungs and respiratory failure.

Rapidly Progressive Glomerulonephritis

Rapidly progressive glomerulonephritis (RPGN) is a type of glomerular disease with glomerular crescent formations. In contrast to chronic glomerulonephritis, which develops slowly and progresses over many years, RPGN is characterized by more rapid, progressive loss of renal function over days to months.

There are 3 types of RPGN: (1) anti-GBM disease, (2) due to immune complex disease (e.g., SLE, postinfectious), (3) or due to pauci-immune disease where no or few immune deposits are seen on electron or immunofluorescence microscopy.

Manifestations almost always include renal insufficiency. They include hypertension, edema, hematuria, and reduced urine output. Treatment aims include correcting fluid overload, hypertension, and uremia and reducing inflammatory injury to the kidney. Treatment often includes corticosteroids and cyclophosphamide. Plasmapheresis may be an option. Dialysis or a kidney transplant may be considered for the patient with RPGN who has progressed to ESRD. After a kidney transplant, RPGN may recur.

NEPHROTIC SYNDROME

Nephrotic syndrome results when the glomerulus is excessively permeable to plasma protein, causing proteinuria that leads to low plasma albumin and edema.

Etiology and Clinical Manifestations

Common causes of nephrotic syndrome are listed in Table 50.9. Minimal change disease is the most common cause in children. For adults, 30% of nephrotic syndrome cases are due to systemic disease such as diabetes, SLE, or amyloidosis.[12]

The common manifestations are peripheral edema, massive proteinuria, hyperlipidemia, hypoalbuminemia, and foamy urine. The increased glomerular membrane permeability is responsible for the massive excretion of protein in the urine. This results in decreased total serum protein and subsequent edema formation. Ascites and *anasarca* (massive, generalized edema) develop if there is severe hypoalbuminemia.

The diminished plasma oncotic pressure from the decreased serum proteins stimulates hepatic lipoprotein synthesis, which results in hyperlipidemia. Significant increases in the lipid profile (e.g., cholesterol, LDL triglycerides) can occur. Fat bodies (fatty casts) often appear in the urine, causing foamy urine.

Immune responses are impaired. As a result, there is an increased risk of infection. Calcium and skeletal abnormalities may occur, including hypocalcemia, blunted calcium response to parathyroid hormone, hyperparathyroidism, and osteomalacia.

TABLE 50.9 Causes of Nephrotic Syndrome

Primary Glomerular Disease
- Focal-segmental glomerulosclerosis
- Membranous glomerulopathy
- Minimal-change disease

Secondary Causes

Cancers
- Hodgkin lymphoma
- Leukemias
- Solid tumors of lungs, colon, stomach, breast, renal, prostate

Drugs
- Captopril
- Heroin
- Lithium
- NSAIDs
- Penicillamine

Infections
- Bacterial (streptococcal, syphilis)
- Protozoal (malaria)
- Viral (hepatitis, HIV, mononucleosis)

Multisystem Disease
- Amyloidosis
- Diabetes
- SLE

Hypercoagulability is a serious issue for those with nephrotic syndrome. Hypercoagulability increases the risk for arterial and venous thromboembolism, including pulmonary embolism and deep vein or renal thrombus.

Interprofessional and Nursing Care

Specific treatment of nephrotic syndrome depends on the cause. The goals are to cure or control the primary disease and relieve the symptoms. Corticosteroids and cyclophosphamide may be used. Prednisone has been effective to varying degrees for some causes of nephrotic syndrome (e.g., membranous glomerulonephritis, lupus nephritis). Managing diabetes is important when nephrotic syndrome is related to diabetes.

Angiotensin-converting enzyme inhibitor or angiotensin receptor blocker drugs may reduce urine protein losses. Diuretics (typically loop diuretics) can improve edema.

The treatment of hyperlipidemia includes lipid-lowering agents (see Table 37.6). Anticoagulant therapy may be given if thrombosis is present.

The patient is placed on a low-sodium (less than 2 g/day), low-moderate protein (1 g/kg/day) diet. If urine protein losses are high (more than 10 g/day), more protein may be needed. Patients are usually anorexic. They can become malnourished from the excess loss of protein in the urine. Serve small, frequent meals in a pleasant setting to encourage intake.

A major nursing focus is on managing edema. Assess edema by (1) weighing the patient daily, (2) recording intake and output, and (3) measuring abdominal girth or extremity size. Compare this information daily to assess the effectiveness of treatment. Clean edematous skin carefully. Avoid trauma to the skin.

Because the patient is susceptible to infection, teach the patient to avoid exposure to persons with known infections. Support for the patient, especially in helping cope with an altered body image, is essential. They may feel embarrassment and shame because of their edematous appearance.

OBSTRUCTIVE UROPATHIES

Urinary obstruction refers to any anatomic or functional condition that blocks or impedes the flow of urine (Fig. 50.3). It may be congenital or acquired. Damaging effects from an obstruction affect the urinary system above the level of the obstruction. The severity of these effects depends on the location, duration of obstruction, amount of pressure or dilation, and presence of urinary stasis or infection. Infection increases the risk for irreversible damage.[13]

When obstruction occurs at the level of the bladder neck or prostate, significant bladder changes can occur. Detrusor muscle fibers *hypertrophy* (increase in size) to contract harder to push urine out a narrower pathway. Over a long period, the detrusor loses its ability to compensate for this resistance, eventually leading to a large residual urine volume in the bladder.

When *bladder outlet obstruction* is present, pressure increases during bladder filling or storage. This pressure can be transmitted to the ureters. Pressure can lead to *reflux* (backflow, or backward movement, of urine), *hydroureter* (ureteral dilation and distention), vesicoureteral reflux (backflow of urine from

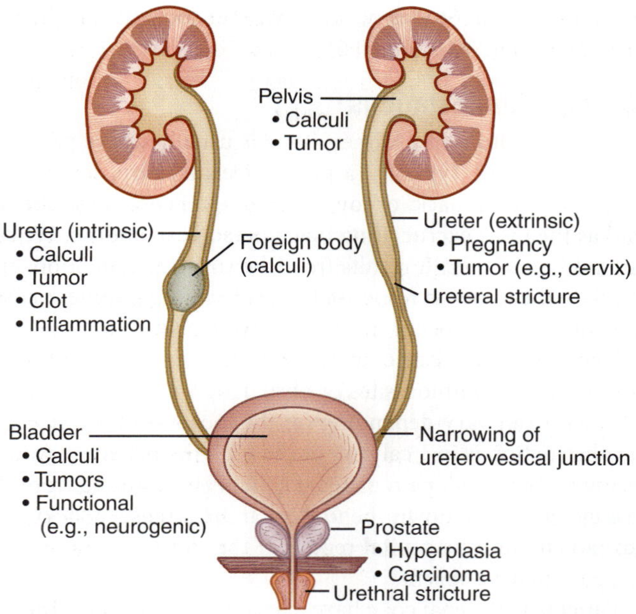

Fig. 50.3 Sites and causes of upper and lower urinary tract obstruction.

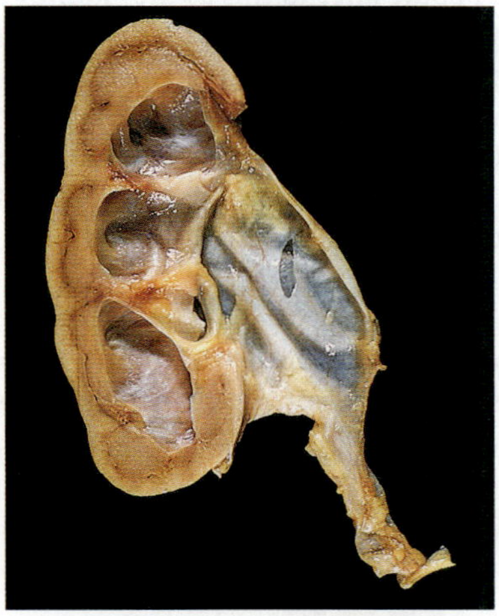

Fig. 50.4 Hydronephrosis of the kidney. Note the marked dilation of the pelvis and calyces and thinning of the renal parenchyma. (From Kumar V, Abbas AK, Aster JC, et al.: *Robbins and Cotran pathologic basis of disease,* ed 8, Philadelphia, 2010, Saunders.)

the lower to upper urinary tract), and **hydronephrosis** (dilation or enlargement of the renal pelvises and calyces) (Fig. 50.4). Chronic pyelonephritis and renal atrophy may develop. If only 1 kidney is obstructed, the other kidney may try to compensate by enlarging.

Partial obstruction may occur in the ureter or at the ureteropelvic junction (UPJ) (where the renal pelvis narrows into the ureter). If the pressure stays low or moderate, the kidney may continue to dilate with no noticeable loss of function. Urinary stasis and reflux increase the risk for pyelonephritis. If only 1 kidney is involved, and the other kidney is functioning, the patient may be asymptomatic.

If both kidneys or only 1 functioning kidney is involved (e.g., if the patient has only 1 kidney), changes in renal function (e.g., increased BUN and serum creatinine levels) occur. Progressive obstruction can lead to renal failure. Treatment involves finding and relieving the blockage. This can include insertion of a tube (e.g., urethral, ureteral), surgical correction of the primary problem, or diversion of the urinary stream above the level of blockage.

BOX 50.2 BIOLOGIC SEX CONSIDERATIONS

Urinary Tract Stones

Men

- More likely to have urinary stones, except for struvite stones

Women

- More likely to have struvite stones associated with UTI

URINARY TRACT CALCULI

In their lifetime, 11% of men and 7% of women in the United States will have **nephrolithiasis** (kidney stone disease, renal calculi) (Box 50.2). The term **calculus** refers to the stone, and *lithiasis* refers to stone formation.

Most patients are middle-aged adults. The risk for developing kidney stones increases with age.[14] Stone formation occurs more often in Whites and Asians. The incidence is higher in persons with a family history of stone formation. Stones recur in up to 50% of patients. In the United States, the incidence of stone disease is highest in the South and Southwest. Stone formation occurs more often in the summer months, supporting the possible contributing factors of a hot climate and dehydration.

Etiology and Pathophysiology

Many factors are involved in the incidence and type of stones. These factors include climate, diet, genetic, metabolic, and lifestyle (Table 50.10). No single theory accounts for stone formation in all cases. Crystals, when in a supersaturated concentration, can precipitate and unite to form a stone. Keeping urine dilute and free flowing reduces the risk for recurrent stone formation in many people.

We think kidney stones form when certain crystal-forming substances are not diluted by the kidney and/or the kidney's ability to keep crystals from sticking together is reduced. Urinary pH, solute load, and inhibitors in the urine affect stone formation. The higher the pH (alkaline), the less soluble are calcium and phosphate. The lower the pH (acidic), the less soluble are uric acid and cystine. When a substance is not very soluble in fluid, it is more likely to precipitate out of solution.

Other key factors in stone formation include obstruction with associated urinary stasis and UTI with urea-splitting bacteria (e.g., *Proteus, Klebsiella, Pseudomonas,* and some species of staphylococci). These bacteria cause the urine to become alkaline and contribute to the formation of struvite stones. Infected stones, trapped in the kidney (Fig. 50.5), may assume a staghorn configuration as the stone branches to occupy a larger part of the collecting system. These stones can lead to a renal infection, hydronephrosis, and loss of kidney function.

TABLE 50.10 Risk Factors for Urinary Tract Stones

Climate
- Warm climates that cause increased fluid loss, low urine volume, and increased urine solute concentration

Diet
- Excess amounts of tea or fruit juices that increase urinary oxalate level
- Large intake of diet proteins that increases uric acid excretion
- Large intake of salt, low calcium intake
- Low fluid intake that increases urine concentration

Genetic Factors
- Family history of stone formation, cystinuria, gout, or renal acidosis

Lifestyle
- Immobility
- Obesity
- Sedentary occupation

Metabolic
- Abnormalities that result in increased urine pH, calcium, oxalate, or uric acid levels, or low citrate

Genetic factors may contribute to stone formation. Cystinuria, an autosomal recessive disorder, causes a large increase in the urinary excretion of cystine.

Types of Urinary Stones

The 5 main types of stones are (1) calcium oxalate, (2) calcium phosphate, (3) cystine, (4) struvite (magnesium ammonium phosphate), and (5) uric acid (Table 50.11). Calcium stones are the most common. Stone composition may be mixed. For example, calcium stones can be calcium oxalate, calcium phosphate, or a mix of both. Stones occur in various locations in the urinary tract (Figs. 50.3 and 50.5).

Clinical Manifestations

The first symptom of a kidney stone is usually severe pain that begins suddenly. Typically, a person feels a sharp, severe pain in the flank area, back, or lower abdomen. People describe the pain as the most excruciating that a person can endure. We call this pain *renal colic*. It results from the stretching, dilation, and spasm of the ureter in response to the obstructing stone. Nausea and vomiting may occur due to the severe pain.

Urinary stones cause manifestations when they obstruct urinary flow. Common sites of obstruction are at the UPJ and UVJ. Pain can vary depending on the location of the stone. If the obstruction is in a calyx or at the UPJ, the patient may have costovertebral flank pain or renal colic. Pain resulting from the passage of a stone down the ureter can be intense, colicky, and can radiate into the genital region. If the stone is nonobstructing, pain may be absent.

Patients with renal colic have a hard time being still. They go from walking to sitting to lying down, and then they repeat the process. Some people refer to this as the "kidney stone dance."

The patient may be in mild shock with cool, moist skin. As a stone nears the UVJ, pain moves around toward the abdomen and down toward the lower quadrant. Men may have testicular pain, while women may have labial pain. Both men and women can have groin pain. The patient may have manifestations of a UTI with dysuria, fever, and chills.

Diagnostic Studies

We can easily diagnose stones with either a noncontrast CT scan or ultrasound. A complete urinalysis helps confirm the diagnosis of a urinary stone by assessing for hematuria and

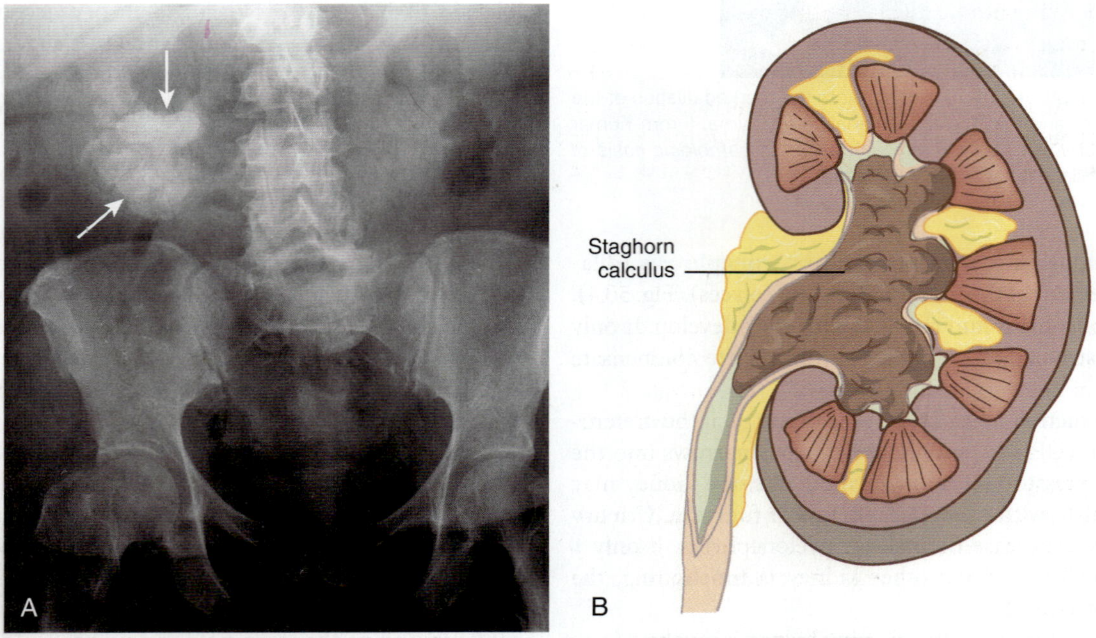

Fig. 50.5 (A) Bilateral staghorn stones *(arrows)* shown on x-ray. (B) Staghorn stone. The renal pelvis is filled with a large stone that is shaped to its contours, resembling the horns of a stag. (A, From Torigian DA, Ramchandani P: *Radiology secrets plus*, ed 4, Philadelphia, 2017, Elsevier.)

TABLE 50.11 **Types of Urinary Tract Stones**

Characteristics	Predisposing Factors	Treatment
Calcium Oxalate		
Most common type of stone. More frequent in men. *Incidence:* 70%–80%	Idiopathic hypercalciuria, hyperoxaluria, independent of urinary pH, family history	Increase hydration. Reduce oxalate intake, animal protein, and sodium. Increase intake of calcium, fruits, and vegetables. Give thiazide diuretics. Give potassium citrate to maintain alkaline urine. Avoid vitamin C and calcium supplements.
Calcium Phosphate		
Mixed stones (typically), with struvite or oxalate stones. *Incidence:* 15%	Alkaline urine, primary hyperparathyroidism	Increase hydration. Treat underlying causes and other stones. Reduce sodium and animal protein intake. Increase calcium intake.
Cystine		
Genetic autosomal recessive defect. Defective absorption of cystine in GI tract and kidney, excess concentrations causing stone formation. *Incidence:* 1%–2%	Acidic urine	Increase hydration. Give α-penicillamine, captopril, or tiopronin to prevent cystine crystallization. Give potassium citrate to keep urine alkaline.
Struvite (Magnesium Ammonium Phosphate)		
More common in women. Always associated with UTIs. Large staghorn type (usually) (Fig. 50.5). *Incidence:* 1%	UTIs (Urease-producing bacteria, usually *Proteus*)	Give antimicrobial agents, acetohydroxamic acid. Typically need surgery to remove stone. Take measures to acidify urine.
Uric Acid		
Predominant in men. *Incidence:* 5%–8%	Gout, acidic urine, high uric acid	Increase hydration. Reduce urinary concentration of uric acid. Alkalinize urine with potassium citrate. Consider allopurinol. Reduce purine intake (Table 50.12).

crystalluria. Measuring urine pH is useful in the diagnosis of struvite stones (tendency to alkaline or high pH) and uric acid or cystine stones (tendency to acidic or low pH).

Retrieval and analysis of the stone(s) is important in diagnosing an underlying problem contributing to stone formation. We measure serum calcium, phosphorus, sodium, potassium, bicarbonate, uric acid, BUN, and creatinine levels. Patients who have recurrent stone formation have a 24-hour urinary measurement of calcium, phosphorus, magnesium, sodium, oxalate, citrate, cysteine, sulfate, potassium, uric acid, and total urine volume.

Interprofessional Care

Care of a patient with stones consists of 2 concurrent approaches. The first approach is aimed toward managing the acute attack by treating the pain, infection, and/or obstruction. Opioids and/or NSAIDS can relieve renal colic pain. Before using NSAIDs, make sure there is no contraindication because of renal function. Most stones are 4 mm or less in size and pass spontaneously. However, it may take weeks for a stone to pass.

α-Adrenergic blockers, such as tamsulosin (Flomax) or terazosin, which relax the smooth muscle in the ureter, can help stone passage. These drugs also relax the muscle tissue in the prostate in men with BPH.

The second approach is aimed toward determining the cause of the stone formation and preventing further stone development. Is there a history of prolonged illness with immobilization, dehydration, or disease or surgery involving the GI or GU tract? Is there a personal or family history of stone formation? What is their geographic residence? Obtain a nutrition assessment, including fluid intake and the intake of vitamins C and D. Review their activity pattern (active or sedentary). Obtain a complete medication history.

Therapy for active stone formers requires a comprehensive management approach, with an emphasis on teaching. Adequate hydration, sodium restrictions, diet changes, and drugs are used to minimize urinary stone formation (Table 50.11). Depending on the specific problem underlying the stone formation, various drugs are prescribed. These drugs prevent stone formation in several ways. These include altering urine pH, preventing excessive urinary excretion of a substance, or correcting a primary disease (e.g., hyperparathyroidism).

Treatment of struvite stones typically requires surgical intervention (e.g., percutaneous nephrolithotomy). Medical therapy alone is generally not effective in controlling infection of the urea-splitting bacterium. Chronic antibiotic therapy may be given to patients unable to tolerate surgery. It may also be given after surgically removing a stone. Acetohydroxamic acid may be used in those with a retained stone or with recurrent struvite stones. Acetohydroxamic acid inhibits urease produced by bacteria.

Endourology, lithotripsy, or open surgical stone removal may be used if (1) stones are too large for spontaneous passage (usually greater than 5 mm); (2) stones with bacteriuria

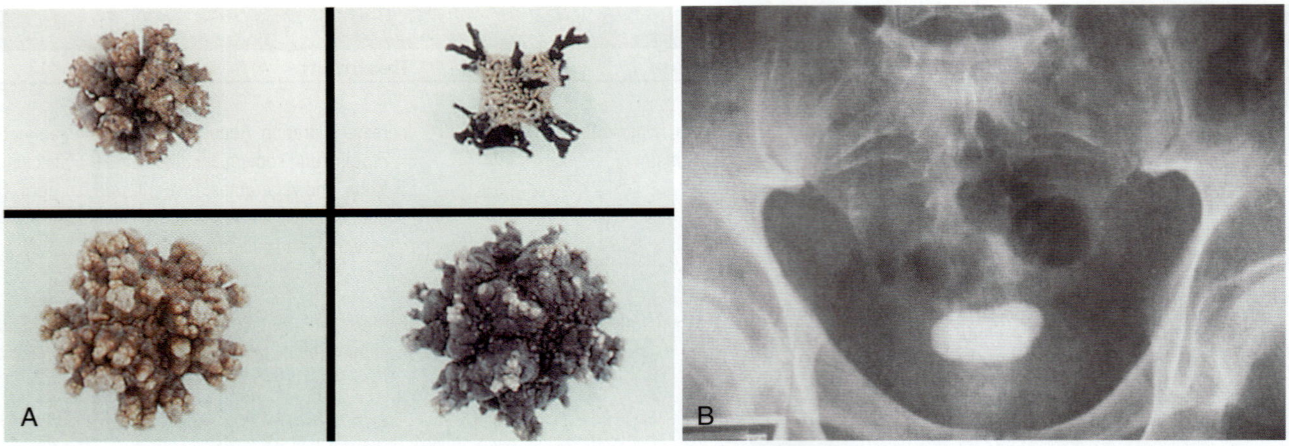

Fig. 50.6 (A) Calcium oxalate stones. (B) Abdominal x-ray showing large bladder stone. (From Bullock N, Doble A, Turner W, et al.: *Urology: an illustrated colour text,* London, 2008, Churchill Livingstone.)

or symptomatic infection are present; (3) stones are causing impaired renal function; (4) stones are causing persistent pain, nausea, or paralytic ileus; (5) patient is unable to be treated medically; and (6) patient has only 1 kidney.[15]

Endourologic Procedures

If the stone is in the bladder, a cystoscopy is done to remove small stones. For larger stones (Fig. 50.6), a *transurethral or percutaneous suprapubic cystolitholapaxy* is done. In this procedure, ultrasonic or laser energy or an instrument called a *lithotrite* (stone crusher) is used to break up the stone. The bladder is then irrigated, and the crushed stones washed out. A *cystoscopic lithotripsy* uses ultrasonic waves to break up stones. Sometimes, we may need to remove the stone with an open suprapubic cystotomy. Complications of these procedures include hemorrhage, retained stone fragments, and infection.

Flexible or rigid *ureteroscopes* can remove stones from the renal pelvis and upper urinary tract. Ultrasonic, laser, or electrohydraulic lithotripsy may be used in conjunction with ureteroscopy to break up the stone.

In *percutaneous nephrolithotomy,* a nephroscope is inserted into the kidney pelvis through a track (using a sheath) in the skin. The track is created in the patient's back. The kidney stones can be fragmented using ultrasound, electrohydraulic, or laser lithotripsy. The stone fragments are removed, and the pelvis is then irrigated. A percutaneous nephrostomy tube can be left in place to make sure that the ureter stays unobstructed. Complications include bleeding, injury to adjacent structures, and infection.

Lithotripsy

Lithotripsy is a procedure used to break up stones, thus allowing them to pass from the urinary tract. Lithotripsy techniques include (1) laser lithotripsy, (2) extracorporeal shock-wave lithotripsy (ESWL), (3) ultrasonic lithotripsy, and (4) electrohydraulic lithotripsy. *Laser lithotripsy* is used to shatter ureteral and large bladder stones. To access ureteral stones, a ureteroscope is used to get close to the stone. A small fiber is inserted up the scope so that the tip (which emits the laser energy) can come in contact with the stone. A holmium laser in direct contact with the stone is often used. The intense energy breaks the stone into small pieces. The pieces are then extracted or flushed out. This minimally invasive treatment usually requires general anesthesia.

In *extracorporeal shock-wave lithotripsy (ESWL),* the patient is anesthetized (spinal or general) to ensure they stay in the same position during the procedure. The HCP uses fluoroscopy or ultrasound to focus the lithotripter over the stone. Then, a high-voltage spark generator produces high-energy acoustic shock waves that shatters the stone. The small pieces of stone are then excreted in the urine. Complications of ESWL include incomplete breakup of the stone, which can lead to possible obstruction, kidney damage, decreased renal function, and elevated BP.

In *ultrasonic lithotripsy,* high-frequency sound waves are used to break the stone into sand-like particles. The patient receives general or spinal anesthesia. In *electrohydraulic lithotripsy,* electrical shock waves are used to break the stone into small fragments. The patient needs general anesthesia.

Complications of lithotripsy are rare. They include hemorrhage, infection, and obstruction. Hematuria is common and can last a few days to a few weeks. The first few times that the patient voids, the urine is often bright red. As the bleeding subsides, the urine can become dark red or a smoky color. Antibiotics are given afterward to reduce the risk for infection.

Afterward, the patient usually has mild to moderate pain. Severe colicky pain can occur as the pieces of stone pass. Most patients can return to their normal activities in a day or 2. For those with a large stone, a self-retaining ureteral stent may be placed to aid in passing the shattered stone. This helps prevent obstruction. The stent is typically removed within 2 weeks after lithotripsy. Encourage fluids to help dilute the urine and reduce the pain from passing stone fragments.

Surgical Therapy

A small group of patients need open surgical procedures. The primary indications for surgery include pain, infection, and obstruction. The type of surgery depends on the location of

TABLE 50.12 NUTRITION THERAPY

Urinary Tract Stones

Depending on the type of stone, modifying the diet can be helpful in preventing reoccurrence.

Calcium

High: Milk, cheese, ice cream, yogurt, sauces containing milk; all beans (except green beans), lentils; fish with fine bones (e.g., sardines, kippers, herring, salmon); dried fruits, nuts; Ovaltine, chocolate, cocoa

Oxalate

High: Dark roughage, spinach, rhubarb, asparagus, cabbage, tomatoes, beets, nuts, celery, parsley, runner beans; grapefruit, orange, raspberries; chocolate, cocoa, instant coffee, Ovaltine, tea; Worcestershire sauce

Purine

High: Sardines, anchovies, herring, mussels, scallops, organ meats, kidney, goose

Moderate: Chicken, salmon, crab, veal, mutton, bacon, pork, beef, ham

the stone. A *nephrolithotomy* is an incision into the kidney to remove a stone. A *pyelolithotomy* is an incision into the renal pelvis for stone removal. If the stone is in the ureter, a *ureterolithotomy* is done. A *cystotomy* may be indicated for bladder stones. For open surgery on the kidney or ureter, the patient often has a flank incision directly below the diaphragm and across their side. The most common complications after surgery for stone removal are bleeding and infection.

Nutrition Therapy

To manage an obstructing stone, the patient should drink adequate fluids to avoid dehydration. Do not force excess fluids because it does not promote the passage of stones in the urine. Forcing fluids may increase the pain or precipitate renal colic.

After an episode of urolithiasis, encourage a high fluid intake (around 3 L/day) to produce a urine output of at least 2.5 L/day unless contraindicated. High urine output prevents supersaturation of minerals (i.e., dilutes the concentration of urine) and promotes excretion of minerals within the urine, thus preventing stone formation. Increasing fluid intake is important for patients at risk for dehydration, including those who (1) are active in sports, (2) live in a dry climate, (3) perform physical exercise, (4) have a family history of stone formation, or (5) work outside or in an occupation that requires a great deal of physical activity. Water is the preferred fluid. Limit colas, coffee, and tea intake because they increase the risk for recurring urinary stones.

A low-sodium diet is best. High-sodium intake increases calcium excretion in the urine. Table 50.12 shows foods high in calcium, oxalate, and purines.

❖ NURSING MANAGEMENT: URINARY TRACT STONES

◆ Assessment

Subjective and objective data you should obtain from a patient with urinary tract stones are outlined in Table 50.13.

TABLE 50.13 NURSING ASSESSMENT

Urinary Tract Stones

Subjective Data

Important Health Information

Health history: Recent or chronic UTI. Immobilization. Previous urinary tract stones, obstruction, or kidney disease with urinary stasis. Gout, BPH, hyperparathyroidism, chronic diarrhea

Medications: Prior use of medication for prevention of stones or treatment of UTI, allopurinol, analgesics, loop diuretics, thiazide diuretics

Surgery or other treatments: External urinary diversion, long-term indwelling urinary catheter

Functional Health Patterns

Health perception–health management: Family history of urinary tract stones, sedentary lifestyle

Nutritional-metabolic: Nausea, vomiting. Intake of purines, calcium, salt, oxalates, phosphates, and OTC supplements. Low fluid intake. Chills

Elimination: Decreased urine output, urinary urgency, frequency, feeling of bladder fullness

Cognitive-perceptual: Acute, severe, colicky pain in flank, back, abdomen, groin, or genitalia. Burning on urination, dysuria. Anxiety

Objective Data

General

Guarding, back pain, fever, dehydration

GI

Abdominal distention, absence of bowel sounds

Skin

Warm, flushed skin or pallor with cool, moist skin (mild shock)

Urinary

Oliguria, hematuria, tenderness on palpation of renal areas, passage of stone or stones

Possible Diagnostic Findings

↑ BUN and serum creatinine levels. Urinalysis showing RBCs, WBCs, pyuria, crystals, casts, minerals, bacteria. ↑ Uric acid, calcium, phosphorus, oxalate, or cystine values on 24-h urine sample. Stones or anatomic changes on x-ray, CT scan, or renal/bladder US. Direct visualization of obstruction on cystourethroscopy

◆ Clinical Problems

Clinical problems for the patient with urinary tract stones include:

- Impaired urinary elimination
- Pain
- Deficient knowledge

More information on clinical problems and interventions for the patient with urinary tract stones is presented in eNursing Care Plan 50.2 (on the website for this chapter).

◆ Planning

The overall goals are that the patient with urinary tract stones will have (1) pain relief, (2) no urinary tract obstruction, and (3) knowledge of ways to prevent stone recurrence.

◆ Implementation

Most people who have had urinary stones can lower their risk for recurrence by changing their lifestyle and diet habits.

Adequate fluid intake is important to produce a urine output of around 2.5 L/day. Consult with the HCP about the patient's specific recommendations for fluid intake. The moderately active, ambulatory person should drink about 3 to 4 L/day. Fluid intake must be higher in the active person who works outdoors or who regularly engages in athletic activities.

Preventive measures for a person who is on bed rest or is immobile for a prolonged time include maintaining an adequate fluid intake, turning the patient every few hours, and helping the patient sit or stand, if possible, to maximize urinary flow.

Other preventive measures focus on reducing metabolic or secondary risk factors. For example, diet restriction of purines may be helpful for the patient at risk for developing uric acid stones. Teach the patient the dosage, scheduling, and potential side effects of drugs used to reduce the risk for stone formation (Table 50.11). You may teach some patients to monitor urinary pH or urine output.

Pain management is a key nursing responsibility when a patient has an obstructing stone and renal colic. To retrieve any spontaneously passed stones, strain all urine with a gauze or a urine strainer. Encourage ambulation to promote movement of the stone from the upper to the lower urinary tract. To ensure safety, tell the patient who has acute renal colic to ask for help when ambulating, especially if they are receiving opioid analgesics.

◆ Evaluation

The expected outcomes are that the patient with urinary tract stones will:

- Maintain free flow of urine with minimal hematuria
- Report satisfactory pain relief
- State understanding of disease process and ways to prevent recurrence

STRICTURES

A ureteral or urethral **stricture** is a narrowing of the lumen of the ureter or urethra.

Ureteral Strictures

Ureteral strictures can affect the entire length of the ureter, from the UPJ to UVJ. While these can be congenital, they are usually from adhesions or scar formation after surgery or radiation. They may be due to extrinsic factors, such as large tumors in the peritoneal cavity. Depending on its severity, ureteral obstruction can threaten kidney function.

Manifestations include mild to moderate colic, flank pain, and CVA tenderness. This pain may be moderate to severe in intensity, especially if the patient drinks a large volume of fluids, such as alcohol, over a brief period. Infection is unusual unless a stone or foreign object, such as a stent or nephrostomy tube, is present.

The obstruction of a ureteral stricture may be temporarily bypassed by placing a stent using endoscopy or by diverting urine flow through a nephrostomy tube placed in the renal pelvis of the affected kidney. Definitive correction requires surgery. Ureteral strictures under 1 cm can be treated using an endoscopic procedure *(endoureterotomy)*. In some patients, open surgery may be done to excise the stenotic area and reanastomose the ureter to the contralateral ureter *(ureteroureterostomy)* or to the renal pelvis. Alternatively, distal ureteral strictures may be treated by a *ureteroneocystostomy* (reimplantation of the ureter into the bladder wall).

Urethral Strictures

A *urethral stricture* is the result of fibrosis or inflammation of the urethral lumen. Causes of urethral strictures include trauma, urethritis (especially after gonococcal infection), surgical intervention or repeated catheterizations (iatrogenic), or a congenital defect of the urethra. Once the process of inflammation and fibrosis begins, the lumen of the urethra narrows and its compliance (ability to close or open in response to bladder filling or voiding) is compromised. Meatal stenosis, a narrowing of the urethral opening at the tip of the penis, develops due to irritation in this region. It is more common in circumcised patients.

Manifestations include a diminished force of the urinary stream, straining to void, sprayed stream, postvoid dribbling, or a split urine stream. The patient may report feelings of incomplete bladder emptying with urinary frequency and nocturia. Moderate to severe obstruction of the bladder outlet may lead to acute urinary retention. The patient may have a history of urethritis, difficulty with insertion of a urinary catheter, or trauma involving the penis or the perineum. However, many patients are unable to recall any such events, thus leading to a diagnosis of an idiopathic stricture. A history of UTI is common, especially if the stricture involves the distal urethra. Retrograde urethrography (RUG), ultrasound urethrography, voiding cystourethrogram, and cystourethroscopy are used to identify stricture length, location, and caliber.

Initial management can include dilation. With dilation, we place a metal instrument (urethral sound) or a series of progressively larger stents (followers) into the urethra to expand the lumen. Alternatively, the patient may have an endoscopic urethrotomy, a closed procedure involving an incision of the urethra. An open surgical procedure *(urethroplasty)* may be done for an obstructive urethral stricture. Shorter strictures may be treated by resecting the fibrotic area followed by reanastomosis of the urethra. Longer strictures may require the use of a skin flap as a substitute urethral segment.

RENAL TRAUMA

Renal trauma can be blunt or penetrating. *Blunt trauma* is the most common cause. Injury to the kidney can occur with sports injuries, motor vehicle accidents, and falls. Renal trauma is especially likely when the patient injures the abdomen, flank, or back. Around 10% of patients with abdominal trauma also have renal trauma. *Penetrating injuries* may result from violent encounters (e.g., gunshot, stabbing incidents).

The severity of renal trauma depends on the extent of the injury. Obtain a history of trauma to the area of the kidneys. Gross or microscopic hematuria may be present. Diagnostic studies include contrast-enhanced CT and CT pyelography. Both the injured kidney and the uninvolved kidney need evaluated. Patients with renal trauma are often admitted for observation. Up to 60% to 70% need surgery.[16]

Nursing care depends on the type of trauma and the extent of any associated injuries. Interventions related to renal trauma include (1) assess cardiovascular status and monitor for shock, especially in a penetrating injury; (2) ensure adequate fluid intake and monitor intake and output; (3) provide for pain relief; (4) assess for hematuria and myoglobinuria; and (5) evaluate the patient and vital signs frequently.

RENAL VASCULAR PROBLEMS

Vascular problems involving the kidney include (1) nephrosclerosis, (2) renal artery stenosis, and (3) renal vein thrombosis.

NEPHROSCLEROSIS

Nephrosclerosis is sclerosis of the small arteries and arterioles of the kidney. The decreased blood flow results in ischemia, interstitial fibrosis, and necrosis of parts of the kidney. *Benign nephrosclerosis* usually occurs in adults over 60 years old. It is caused by vascular changes from hypertension and narrowing of blood vessels. Vascular changes account for most of the loss of renal function from aging. The degree of nephrosclerosis is related to the severity of hypertension. The patient with benign nephrosclerosis generally does not progress to significant loss of renal function or ESRD.

With accelerated nephrosclerosis (acute hypertensive or malignant nephrosclerosis), we see a significantly high BP (systolic BP ≥180 and/or diastolic BP ≥120 mm/Hg) with concurrent acute impairment of 1 of more organ systems. It can begin suddenly and is a medical emergency. With renal involvement, damage to the kidney can progress rapidly.

The availability and use of antihypertensive drugs have improved the prognosis for patients with nephrosclerosis. Treatment for benign nephrosclerosis is the same as that for essential hypertension (see Chapter 36). Malignant nephrosclerosis is treated with antihypertensive therapy. We generally lower the BP over a 24-hour period. The prognosis for a patient with untreated or refractive malignant hypertension is poor. These conditions can lead to death.

RENAL ARTERY STENOSIS

Renal artery stenosis is a partial occlusion of 1 or both renal arteries and their major branches. It can be due to atherosclerotic narrowing or fibromuscular hyperplasia. Renal artery stenosis can be a cause of secondary hypertension. When hypertension develops suddenly or is difficult to treat, renal artery stenosis should be considered.

Diagnostic tests used to assess for renal artery stenosis include a renal duplex Doppler ultrasonography, CT or MRI angiography, and renal arteriography.

The goals of therapy are to control BP and restore perfusion to the kidney. Percutaneous transluminal renal angioplasty, with or without stenting, for unilateral renal artery stenosis can be done but only if there is a high chance of success.

Surgical revascularization of the kidney is an option in complex cases. Revascularization may result in the patient's BP becoming normotensive. Surgery usually involves anastomosis between the kidney and another major artery, usually the splenic artery or aorta. In some cases of unilateral renal involvement, unilateral nephrectomy may be done.

RENAL VEIN THROMBOSIS

Renal vein thrombosis may occur unilaterally or bilaterally. It can develop acutely or chronically. Causes include trauma, extrinsic compression (e.g., tumor, aortic aneurysm), kidney cancer, pregnancy, contraceptive use, and nephrotic syndrome.

The patient can be asymptomatic, or have acute flank pain/tenderness, hematuria, fever, worsening renal function, and/or worsening proteinuria. Anticoagulation is used to prevent progression and the development of an embolus. The patient may undergo percutaneous thrombectomy. Other options include thrombolysis and placement of suprarenal IVC filters. Surgical thrombectomy is rarely needed.

HEREDITARY KIDNEY DISEASES

Hereditary kidney diseases involve developmental abnormalities of the renal parenchyma. Renal cysts occur with both inherited and non-inherited disorders. They can be simple or complex. In evaluating renal cysts, it is important to tell simple cyst(s) from those due to diseases such as PKD, kidney cancer, or a kidney abscess.

POLYCYSTIC KIDNEY DISEASE

Polycystic kidney disease (PKD) is a common genetic disorder. In PKD, cysts form in the kidneys that can cause the kidneys to change shape and enlarge over time. PKD affects 500,000 people in the United States. The disease usually progresses from loss of kidney function to ESRD by age 65 in 85% of patients.[17] It is the 4th leading cause of ESRD, affecting 5% of those with ESRD. A nongenetic PKD (acquired cystic kidney disease [ACKD]) can occur in those with severe kidney scarring and damage who typically receive dialysis. After 8 years on dialysis, 90% of patients will have ACKD.[17]

Genetic Link

PKD has 2 hereditary forms: one usually diagnosed in early childhood and one in adulthood. The childhood form of PKD is a rare autosomal recessive disorder that is often rapidly progressive (Box 50.3). The adult form of PKD is an autosomal dominant disorder (ADPKD) and accounts for 90% of all PKD cases. If 1 parent has the disease, there is a 50% chance that the disease will pass to the child.

ADPKD involves both kidneys. It occurs in both men and women. Large, thin-walled cysts that are several millimeters to several centimeters in diameter fill the cortex and medulla (Fig. 50.7). The cysts enlarge and destroy surrounding tissue by compression. They are filled with fluid and may contain blood or pus. ADPKD kidneys can become enlarged and look like they are filled with golf balls.

BOX 50.3 GENETICS IN CLINICAL PRACTICE

Polycystic Kidney Disease (PKD)

	Adult	Child
Genetic basis	Autosomal dominant	Autosomal recessive
Incidence	1 in 400–1000	1 in 20,000–40,000
Gene location	• *PKD1* gene on chromosome 16 or *PKD2* gene on chromosome 4 • Genes code for polycystins (proteins that promote normal kidney development and function) • Mutations in genes lead to formation of thousands of cysts that disrupt the normal function of kidneys and other organs	• Polycystic kidney and hepatic disease *(PKHD1)* gene on chromosome 6p21, DZIP1L gene may be affected • PKHD1 gene codes for fibrocystin • Mutations in gene leads to cyst formation
Genetic testing	DNA testing available	DNA testing available
Age of onset	Kidney function usually starts worsening in the 40s, but symptoms can start earlier	Infancy or childhood
Clinical implications	• Multisystem involvement • Systemic hypertension is common, occurs in 60% of patients before kidney function worsens • Increased risk for cerebral aneurysms • Those at risk should be screened	• Up to 30% of affected newborns die within one week after birth • If infant survives the newborn period, chances of survival are good • Often need dialysis or transplant by adulthood

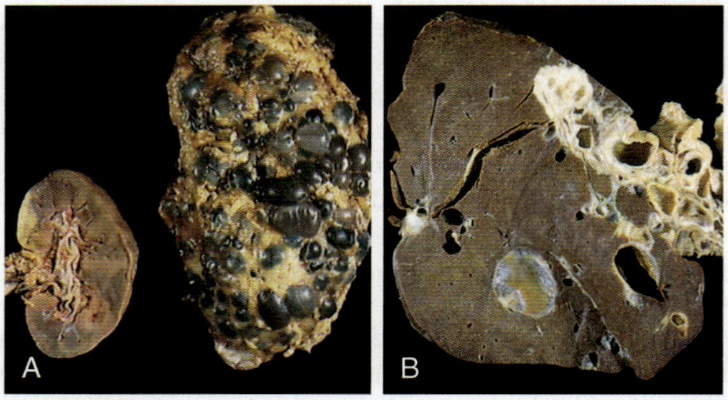

Fig. 50.7 (A) Comparison of polycystic kidney with normal kidney. (B) Cysts in the liver. (A, From Brundage DJ: *Renal disorders,* St Louis, 1992, Mosby. B, From Kumar V, Abbas AK, Fausto N: *Robbins and Cotran pathologic basis of disease,* ed 7, Philadelphia, 2005, Saunders.)

ADPKD can be symptomless for many years. Signs and symptoms usually develop between 30 and 50 years of age.[17] Symptoms can appear when the renal cysts begin to enlarge. Often the first manifestations are hypertension, hematuria, proteinuria, loss of kidney function, and/or a feeling of pain or heaviness in the back, side, or abdomen.

Both acute and chronic pain is a common problem. Acute pain can develop from kidney stone formation, UTIs, or cyst hemorrhage. The pain can be constant and severe in those with enlarged kidneys. Bilateral, enlarged kidneys are often palpable. Those with ADPKD can have no symptoms, which can delay diagnosis.

ADPKD can affect the liver (liver cysts [Fig. 50.7]), pancreas, heart (abnormal heart valves), blood vessels (aneurysms), and intestines (diverticulosis). The most serious complication is a cerebral aneurysm, which can rupture.

Diagnosis is based on manifestations, family history, ultrasound (best screening measure), or CT scan (provides more precise images).

❖ Interprofessional and Nursing Care

There is no cure for PKD. Tolvaptan is an approved treatment for treating rapidly progressive ADPKD. It works to slow growth of renal cysts, helping to preserve kidney function. Other treatment aims include preventing or treating UTIs. Nephrectomy may be done if pain, bleeding, or infection becomes a chronic, serious problem. Dialysis and kidney transplant may be needed to treat ESRD (see Chapter 51).

When the patient begins to have progressive renal failure, the interventions depend on the remaining renal function. Measures we use are the same as those for managing ESRD. They include diet changes, fluid restriction, drugs (e.g., antihypertensives), and help for the patient and family in coping with having a chronic disease.

The patient with ADPKD often has children by the time the disease is diagnosed. Those children should receive genetic counseling. The patient needs counseling about plans for having more children. You can find more resources at the PKD Foundation website (www.pkdcure.org).

CHECK YOUR PRACTICE

You are doing a rotation in the dialysis unit. You have been doing vital sign checks on a 45-year-old man who receives dialysis 3 times/week. When you ask him why he is on dialysis, he tells you that he has ADPKD. After further discussion, he tells you that he has 1 son who is now 23 years old, but they do not speak. He does not want to tell him about his medical problems or why he is on dialysis.

- How would you respond to this patient?

MEDULLARY CYSTIC KIDNEY DISEASE

In *medullary cystic kidney disease,* cysts form in the medulla, or center, of the kidneys. It is a rare, autosomal dominant disorder. The patient has loss of renal function often starting in their teens. Most progress to ESRD by the time they are age 65. The kidneys are typically normal or small in size with significant tubular-interstitial fibrosis. Defects in the kidneys' concentrating ability result in polyuria, which is a hallmark of the disease. Hyperuricemia is common. Genetic counseling may be helpful in family planning. Treatment measures are those related to ESRD (see Chapter 51). A similar disease, familial juvenile nephronophthisis, is found in young children. It is autosomal recessive and leads to 15% of pediatric ESRD cases.

ALPORT SYNDROME

Alport syndrome, or *chronic hereditary nephritis,* is an inherited disease that affects the glomeruli. The basic defect is a mutation in a gene for collagen that results in altered synthesis of the glomerular basement membrane.[18]

There are 3 genetic types of Alport syndrome: X-linked, autosomal recessive type, and autosomal dominant type. In X-linked, the most common type, the earliest manifestation is chronic asymptomatic microscopic hematuria. These patients can have progressive hearing loss and deformities of the lens of the eye. Ocular changes and sensorineural hearing loss occur with the autosomal recessive type but are rare in the autosomal dominant type.

Alport syndrome can cause progressive kidney damage, leading to ESRD. Those with X-linked and autosomal recessive type generally progress to ESRD between ages 16 and 35. People with autosomal dominant Alport syndrome usually develop ESRD around ages 45 to 60.

There is no specific treatment. Care is supportive. Corticosteroids and cytotoxic drugs are not effective. A kidney transplant is usually successful. The disease itself does not recur after a kidney transplant, but there is small risk of developing anti-GBM antibody disease.

URINARY TRACT TUMORS

KIDNEY CANCER

Tumors that arise from the cortex, pelvis, or calyces may be benign or cancerous. Eighty percent of *kidney cancers* develop in the renal cortex with 8% in the renal pelvis. Nephroblastoma is a common type of pediatric kidney cancer. The lifetime risk of developing kidney cancer is 1 in 80 for females and 1 in 46 for males.[19]

Most cases of kidney cancer are renal cell carcinomas (renal adenocarcinoma) (Fig. 50.8). It occurs twice as often in men as in women. The average age at diagnosis is 64 years. It is rare in those under 45 years old. Smoking and obesity are significant risk factors. An increased incidence occurs in first-degree relatives of people who have or had renal cell cancer. Other risk factors include hypertension and exposure to certain chemicals such as trichloroethylene and cadmium. Blacks have slightly higher rates of renal cell cancer.

Clinical Manifestations and Diagnostic Studies

Early-stage kidney cancer usually has no symptoms, so many patients go undiagnosed until the disease has significantly progressed. Many are diagnosed as incidental findings on imaging studies used to evaluate symptoms for unrelated conditions.

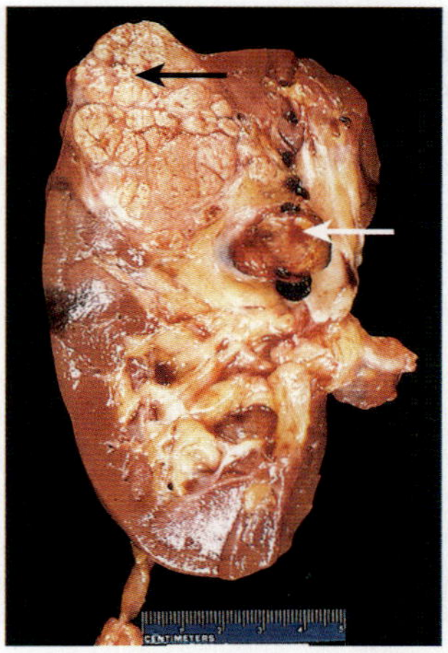

Fig. 50.8 Cross section of kidney with renal cell cancer. The cancer *(black arrow)* is on the pole of the kidney. Note that the renal vein is involved and thrombosed *(white arrow)*. (From Kumar V, Abbas AK, Fausto N: *Robbins and Cotran pathologic basis of disease,* ed 7, Philadelphia, 2005, Saunders.)

Kidney tumors cause symptoms by compressing, stretching, or invading structures near or within the kidney. The most common presenting symptoms are hematuria and flank pain. Other manifestations include weight loss, fever, anemia, fatigue, hypercalcemia, and/or a palpable mass in the flank or abdomen.

About 33% of patients have metastasis at the time of diagnosis. Local extension of kidney cancer into the renal vein and vena cava is common (Fig. 50.8). The most common sites of metastases include lungs, lymph nodes, bone, and liver.

CT scan is often used in the diagnosis and can detect small kidney tumors. Ultrasound has improved the ability to determine between a solid mass tumor and a cyst. This is significant because most masses detected on imaging are cysts. Partial nephrectomy or nephrectomy are typically done at the time of biopsy.

Interprofessional and Nursing Care

Preventive measures, including quitting smoking, maintaining a healthy weight, controlling BP, and reducing exposure to toxins, help reduce the incidence of kidney cancer. Patients in high-risk groups should be aware of their increased risk. Teach them about early manifestations (e.g., hematuria, flank pain). A cure for kidney cancer may be possible if it is found and treated early.

Table 50.14 outlines the interprofessional care of the patient with kidney cancer. Staging provides a basis for determining treatment options. The following is a simple description of staging of kidney cancer based on the primary tumor:

Stage I: The tumor can be up to 7 cm in diameter and is confined to the kidney.

Stage II: The tumor is larger than a stage I tumor but still confined to the kidney.

Stage III: The tumor extends beyond the kidney to the surrounding tissue. Has not spread to the adrenal gland or to Gerota fascia.

Stage IV: Cancer spreads outside the kidney beyond Gerota fascia. Can involve multiple lymph nodes or spread to distant parts of the body, such as bones, brain, liver, or lung.

The treatment of choice for some kidney cancers is a partial nephrectomy (for smaller tumors), simple total nephrectomy,

TABLE 50.14 Interprofessional Care

Kidney Cancer

Diagnostic Assessment	Management

• History and physical assessment
• Urinalysis
• Ultrasound
• Abdominal CT scan
• MRI
• Renal biopsy
• Renal scan
	• Surgical therapy
	  • Partial nephrectomy
	  • Radical nephrectomy
	• Ablation
	  • Cryoablation
	  • Radiofrequency ablation
	• Radiation therapy
	• Chemotherapy
	• Immunotherapy
	• Targeted therapy

or a radical nephrectomy (for larger tumors). Radical nephrectomy involves removal of the kidney, adrenal gland, surrounding fascia, and draining lymph nodes. Nephrectomy can be done by a conventional (open) approach or laparoscopically. Other treatment options include cryoablation (freezing technique) and radiofrequency ablation (destroying tumor by using radiofrequency heat). These procedures can be used when surgery is not an option (e.g., patient has comorbid conditions) and for small renal tumors.

Kidney cancer is relatively resistant to most chemotherapy drugs. While kidney cancer can be resistant to radiation therapy, it may be useful in certain situations, such as metastasis to bone, brain, or lungs.

Immunotherapy, including α-interferon and interleukin-2 (IL-2), is a treatment option in metastatic disease (see Chapter 16.) Another drug used as immunotherapy is nivolumab (Opdivo) without or with ipilimumab (anti-CTLA-4 antibody). Nivolumab targets PD-1, a protein on T cells that normally helps keep these cells from attacking other cells in the body. By blocking PD-1, this drug boosts the immune response against cancer cells. This can shrink some tumors or slow their growth.

Targeted therapy is another treatment option for metastatic kidney cancer. Kinase inhibitors, a class of targeted therapies, block certain proteins (kinases) that play a role in tumor growth and cancer progression. Kinase inhibitors include sunitinib (Sutent), sorafenib (Nexavar), cabozantinib (Cabometyx), and axitinib (Inlyta). Bevacizumab (Avastin) inhibits the formation of new blood vessel growth to the tumor. Temsirolimus (Torisel) and everolimus (Afinitor) inhibit a specific protein known as the mechanistic target of rapamycin (mTOR).[20] These drugs are discussed in Table 16.13. The mechanisms of action are shown in Fig. 16.16.

The diagnosis of kidney cancer is devastating. Often the cancer has already metastasized by the time a person is diagnosed. See more about the care of the patient with cancer in Chapter 16.

BLADDER CANCER

Bladder cancer is the most common cancer of the urinary system.[21] About 83,730 new cases are diagnosed each year. About 17,240 deaths occur every year. Bladder cancer is most common in older adults. 90% of cases occur in those over the age of 55.

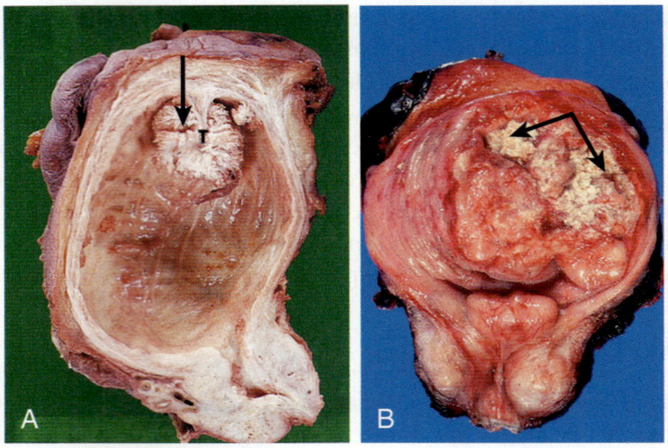

Fig. 50.9 (A) Papillary transitional cell cancer *(T)* seen arising from the dome of the bladder as a cauliflower-like lesion *(arrow)*. (B) Opened bladder showing advanced stage bladder cancer. Yellow areas are ulcerations and necrosis *(arrows)*. (A, From Stevens A, Lowe J: *Pathology: Illustrated review in colour,* ed 2, London, 2000, Mosby. B, From Kumar V, Abbas AK, Fausto N: *Robbins and Cotran pathologic basis of disease,* ed 7, Philadelphia, 2005, Saunders.)

It is far more common in men and in Whites.[22] Some bladder tumors are benign papillomatous growths (Fig. 50.9).

Urothelial cancer, or transitional cell cancer (TCC), is by far the most common type of bladder cancer. TCC can easily spread to other urinary tract areas given that the mucosal lining throughout the urinary tract is the same. Cancer recurrence within the bladder is common.

About half of bladder cancers are related to cigarette smoking.[21] Other risk factors include workplace exposure to certain chemicals. Others at risk include those treated with pelvic radiation for cancer; patients who received cyclophosphamide or aristolochic acid; and those who have indwelling catheters for long periods. People with chronic, recurrent urinary tract stones, often in the bladder, and chronic lower UTIs have an increased risk for non-urethral bladder cancer such as squamous cell carcinoma.

Clinical Manifestations and Diagnostic Studies

Microscopic or gross, painless hematuria (chronic or intermittent) is the most common manifestation of bladder cancer. Bladder irritability with dysuria, frequency, and urgency may also be the first signs and symptoms.

When cancer is suspected, the patient has a complete urologic work-up. This includes obtaining urine specimens to identify any cancer cells. Exfoliated cells from the bladder's epithelial surface are often found in voided specimens. Urine cytology and testing for bladder tumor antigens can be done. CT without and with contrast is the recommended study of choice. Alternatively, IV pyelogram or MRI are options. Cancer is confirmed by cystoscopy and biopsy.[23]

❖ NURSING AND INTERPROFESSIONAL MANAGEMENT: BLADDER CANCER

Most bladder cancers are diagnosed at an early stage when the cancer is treatable. Before starting treatment, bladder cancers

TABLE 50.15 Interprofessional Care

Bladder Cancer

Diagnostic Assessment

- History and physical assessment
- Urinalysis
- Urine cytology studies
- Cystoscopy with biopsy
- CT scan

Management

- Surgical therapy
  - Transurethral resection of bladder tumor
  - Partial cystectomy
  - Radical cystectomy
- Radiation therapy
- Immunotherapy
- Targeted drug therapy
- Intravesical immunotherapy
  - Bacille Calmette-Guérin (BCG)
  - α-interferon (Intron A)
- Intravesical chemotherapy
  - epirubicin
  - gemcitabine
  - mitomycin
  - valrubicin (Valstar)
- Systemic chemotherapy and immunotherapy

are graded based on the cell type and staged based on the extent and invasiveness of the cancer. We use a grading system to classify the cancerous potential of tumor cells, using a scale from well differentiated (closely resembling the normal tissue) to undifferentiated (poorly differentiated).

Clinical staging of bladder cancer is determined by the depth of invasion of the bladder wall and surrounding tissue. The following is a simple description of staging of bladder cancer:

Stage I: Cancer is in the inner lining of the bladder but has not invaded the bladder muscle wall.

Stage II: Cancer has invaded the bladder wall but is still confined to the bladder.

Stage III: Cancer has spread through the bladder wall to surrounding tissue.

Stage IV: Cancer has spread to the bowels, prostate, vagina, and/or uterus.

Interprofessional care of bladder cancer includes surgery, radiation, chemotherapy, targeted therapy, immunotherapy, and intravesical therapy (Table 50.15).

Surgical Therapy

Surgical therapy includes a variety of procedures. *Transurethral resection of the bladder tumor* (TURBT) is used for superficial lesions of the bladder's inner lining. The HCP uses a wire loop inserted through the cystoscope or a resectoscope with an attached loop to remove the tumor and tissue, which are sent for pathologic evaluation. After the tumor is removed, the tissue in the area where the tumor was may be burned. This is called fulguration. Cells can also be destroyed with a high-energy laser. Those with a low- or intermediate-risk tumor may get a one-time dose of intravesical chemotherapy in the immediate postoperative period. Repeat TURBT is often done 6 weeks later for those with higher-grade tumors. The primary disadvantages of TURBT include the chance of incomplete removal of the tumor, bleeding, and bladder perforation.[24]

A *segmental cystectomy (partial cystectomy)* is used to treat larger tumors or those that involve only 1 area of the bladder. The part of the bladder wall containing the tumor is removed along with a margin of normal tissue.

When the tumor is invasive and involves muscle, a radical cystectomy with urinary diversion is the treatment of choice. A *radical cystectomy* involves removal of the bladder, prostate, and seminal vesicles in men and the bladder, uterus, cervix, anterior vagina, and ovaries in women. After a radical cystectomy, a new way for urine to leave the body, or urinary diversion, must be created.[24]

Postoperative instructions for any of these procedures include drinking a large volume of fluid for the first week afterward. Teach the patient to monitor the color and consistency of the urine. Hematuria is common, but the blood in the urine should not contain clots and/or appear thick.

Give analgesics and stool softeners for a brief period after the procedure. Help the patient and family cope with fears about cancer, surgery, and sexuality. Emphasize the importance of regular follow-up care. Follow-up cystoscopies are done on a regular basis after surgery for bladder cancer.

Radiation Therapy, Chemotherapy, Targeted Therapy, and Immunotherapy

Radiation therapy can be used in combination with cystectomy or as the primary therapy when the cancer is inoperable or the patient refuses surgery. Chemotherapy is often used in combination with radiation. Targeted therapy includes FGFR inhibitors (e.g., erdafitinib) that affect proteins that help the cancer cells grow. Immunotherapy can be used to treat bladder cancer. Options include immune checkpoint inhibitors, PD-1 and PD-L1 inhibitors, and intravesical BCG.

Intravesical Therapy

In intravesical therapy, chemotherapy or immunotherapy is placed directly into the bladder by a urethral catheter.[23] The drug is then retained for 1 to 2 hours. During that time, the patient may have to change position every 15 minutes so the solution washes over the entire bladder. The patient's bladder must be empty before instillation. Intravesical therapy is usually given once per week for 6 to 12 weeks. Maintenance therapy after the initial induction regimen may be given.

Bacillus Calmette-Guérin (BCG), a weakened strain of *Mycobacterium bovis,* is the treatment of choice for high-risk bladder tumors. It can also treat intermediate risk tumors. BCG stimulates the immune system to attack the cancer cells. Interferon-alpha therapy may be given with BCG. Other intravesical chemotherapy options include mitomycin, epirubicin, gemcitabine, and valrubicin.[23]

Most patients have irritative voiding symptoms and hematuria after intravesical therapy. BCG may cause flu-like symptoms, increased urinary frequency, hematuria, and, rarely, systemic infection. Other side effects of chemotherapy (e.g., nausea, vomiting, hair loss) do not occur with intravesical chemotherapy.

Encourage patients to increase their daily fluid intake and quit smoking. Assess the patient for secondary UTI. Stress the need for routine urologic follow-up. The patient may have fears or concerns about sexual activity or bladder function that we must address. Because of the high rate of disease recurrence and progression in bladder cancer, follow-up studies are important.

BLADDER DYSFUNCTION

URINARY INCONTINENCE

Urinary incontinence (UI) is an involuntary leakage of urine. Although UI is more prevalent among older adults, it is not a natural consequence of aging. UI has a major effect on quality of life and contributes to emotional, social, and potential serious health problems, especially in older adults.

Etiology and Pathophysiology

UI occurs when bladder pressure exceeds urethral closure pressure. Anything that interferes with internal and/or external urethral sphincter control can result in UI. There are many risk factors for UI. These include obesity, BPH, smoking, recurrent UTIs, GU surgeries, vaginal delivery, impaired functional status, certain drugs, certain neurologic problems, and a family history of UI (Box 50.4). Patients may have more than 1 type of UI (Table 50.16). The combination of stress and urge incontinence is called mixed incontinence.

Diagnostic Studies

The basic evaluation for UI includes a focused history, physical assessment, and a urinalysis. Obtain information about the onset of UI, factors that provoke urinary leakage, any associated systemic symptoms, use of caffeine and alcohol, medications taken, and associated conditions. Pay special attention to factors known to produce transient UI, especially when the onset of urine loss is sudden. It may be useful to have the patient keep a bladder log or voiding diary. Have them record the timing of urinations, episodes of urinary leakage, and frequency of nocturia for a period of 1 to 7 days (minimum of 3 days if possible). Nursing staff can keep this record if the person is in an inpatient or long-term care facility.

Begin the assessment with looking at general health and functional issues related to urination, including mobility, dexterity, and cognitive function. A pelvic examination may be done. Carefully inspect the perineal skin for signs of erosion or rashes related to UI. Is there any pelvic organ prolapse? Assess local innervation and pelvic floor muscle strength. Perform a digital examination of the pelvic floor muscle to assess for weakness or tension.

A urinalysis can identify factors contributing to transient UI (e.g., UTI, diabetes). A bladder stress test can be useful when we suspect stress incontinence. Measuring postvoid residual (PVR) urine may be of use. PVR volume is obtained by asking the patient to void, followed by catheterization or use of a bladder ultrasound (preferably within 10 to 20 minutes).

Some patients have urodynamic testing. Imaging studies of the upper and lower urinary tract (e.g., ultrasound) and cystoscopy may also be done.

> **BOX 50.4 BIOLOGIC SEX CONSIDERATIONS**
>
> ***Urinary Incontinence***
>
> **Men**
> - A common manifestation of BPH and prostate cancer
> - More likely to have overflow incontinence caused by urinary retention
>
> **Women**
> - Have a higher prevalence of UI
> - More likely to have stress and urge incontinence

Interprofessional Care

Many cases of UI can be cured or significantly improved. Transient, reversible factors are first corrected, followed by management of the type of UI (Table 50.16). In general, we try less invasive treatments before more invasive ones (e.g., surgery). The choice of the initial treatment is patient specific, based on patient preference, the type and severity of UI, and associated anatomic defects.

Several behavioral therapies may improve UI (Table 50.17). Pelvic floor muscle training (Kegel exercises) is used to treat UI, especially stress UI (Table 50.18).[25] Biofeedback can help the patient identify, isolate, contract, and relax the pelvic muscles. Bladder training may help.

Drug Therapy

Drug therapy varies according to the UI type (Table 50.19). There are no drugs approved to treat stress UI. In urge and reflex UI, drugs play a key role.

Anticholinergic drugs (muscarinic receptor blockers) block the action of acetylcholine at muscarinic receptors. They relax the bladder muscle and inhibit overactive detrusor contractions (Table 50.19). Side effects include dry mouth and eyes, constipation, blurred vision, and sleepiness.

Botox (onabotulinumtoxin A) can be used to treat UI from detrusor overactivity. Botox is injected into the bladder. It results in bladder relaxation, an increase in its storage capacity, and a decrease in UI.

> **DRUG ALERT**
>
> ***Antimuscarinic Agents***
>
> - Overdosage can result in severe anticholinergic effects.
> - These effects include constipation, decreased sweating, eye pain, blurred vision, and difficulty starting urination and/or completely emptying the bladder.

Surgical Therapy

Surgical techniques vary depending on the type of UI. Surgical correction of stress UI is aimed at making the urinary structures more receptive to intraabdominal pressure and augmenting the urethral resistance of the internal sphincter. It may involve

TABLE 50.16 Types of Urinary Incontinence

Description	Causes	Treatment
Functional Incontinence		
• Loss of urine resulting from cognitive, functional, environmental factors	• Neurologic and/or muscular limitations (e.g., severe arthritis) • Cognitive problems (e.g., dementia) • Psychologic issues • Environment barriers	• Modifying the environment or care plan to facilitate regular, easy access to toilet and promote patient safety • Includes better lighting, ambulatory assistance equipment, clothing alterations, timed voiding, different toileting equipment
Incontinence After Trauma or Surgery		
• In women, vesicovaginal or urethrovaginal fistula may occur • In men, inadequate urethral sphincter function, can lead to stress, urge, overflow, or mixed UI	• Fistulas may occur as a complication of pregnancy and delivery of baby, after hysterectomy or invasive cancer of cervix, or after radiation therapy • Incontinence is a postoperative complication of radical prostatectomy, and rarely transurethral resection of the prostate	• External condom catheter • Penile clamp • Sling surgery (male) • Surgery to correct fistula • Periurethral balloons
Overflow Incontinence		
• Occurs when pressure of urine in overfull bladder overcomes sphincter control and/or detrusor underactivity • Leakage of small amounts of urine is frequent or continual throughout day and night • Concurrent incomplete bladder emptying • Bladder can stay distended and is usually palpable	• Caused by bladder or urethral outlet obstruction (bladder neck obstruction, urethral stricture, pelvic organ prolapse) or by underactive detrusor muscle caused by myogenic or neurogenic factors (e.g., herniated disc, diabetic neuropathy) • May occur after pelvic floor surgery • Neurogenic bladder (flaccid type)	• Urinary catheterization to decompress bladder • α-Adrenergic blockers (Table 50.20) • 5α-Reductase inhibitors (Table 50.20) to decrease outlet resistance • Bethanechol to enhance bladder contractions • Intermittent catheterization • Intravaginal device, such as a pessary, to support prolapse • Surgery to correct underlying problem
Reflex Incontinence		
• Condition occurs with no warning, periodic involuntary urination • Urination can be frequent, large in volume, and occurs equally during day and night	• CNS problems, including, multiple sclerosis, brain tumors, CVA, Parkinson disease, spinal cord injuries	• Treat underlying cause • Intermittent self-catheterization • Behavioral therapy including bladder training, pelvic floor muscle exercises • Certain medications may be useful: anticholinergics, B3-adrenergic agonist, tricyclic antidepressants, topical estrogen (women)
Stress Incontinence		
• Sudden increase in intraabdominal pressure causes involuntary passage of urine • Can occur during coughing, laughing, sneezing, or physical activities, such as heavy lifting, exercising • Leakage usually is in small amounts and may not be daily	• Most common in women with relaxed pelvic floor musculature (from delivery, use of instrumentation during vaginal delivery, or multiple pregnancies) • Structures of female urethra atrophy when estrogen decreases • Prostate surgery for BPH or prostate cancer	• Pelvic floor muscle exercises (e.g., Kegel exercises), weight loss if obese, topical estrogen products, transurethral bulking agents, surgery • Continence pessary. Use of duloxetine may be of aid
Urge Incontinence		
• Often referred to as overactive bladder • Occurs randomly when urgency precedes involuntary urination • Leakage is periodic but can be frequent and varies in amount • Nocturnal frequency and incontinence are common	• Caused by uncontrolled contraction or overactive detrusor muscle • Bladder escapes central inhibition and contracts reflexively • Conditions include: • CNS problems (e.g., stroke, Alzheimer disease, brain tumor, Parkinson disease) • Bladder disorders (e.g., cancer, radiation effects, interstitial cystitis) • Interference with spinal inhibitory pathways (e.g., cancer in spinal cord, spondylosis) • Bladder outlet obstruction or conditions of unknown cause	• Treat underlying cause • Biobehavioral interventions (bladder retraining with urge suppression, decrease in diet irritants, bowel regularity, pelvic floor muscle exercises) • Anticholinergic drugs (Table 50.20) • mirabegron (Myrbetriq) • Vaginal estrogen creams • Containment devices (e.g., external condom catheters) • Absorbent products

TABLE 50.17 Interventions for Urinary Incontinence

Intervention	Description
Lifestyle changes	Self-management to reduce or eliminate risk factors, including: • Smoking cessation • Weight reduction • Bowel regimen • Reduction of bladder irritants (e.g., caffeine, aspartame artificial sweetener, citrus juices) • Fluid modifications for those with urge incontinence
Scheduled Voiding Regimens	
Bladder retraining and urge-suppression strategies	Scheduled toileting with progressive voiding intervals. Includes teaching of urge control using relaxation and distraction techniques, self-monitoring, reinforcement techniques, and other strategies, such as conscious contraction of pelvic floor muscles.
Habit retraining	Scheduled toileting with adjustments of voiding intervals (longer or shorter) based on the person's voiding pattern.
Prompted voiding	Scheduled toileting that requires prompts to void from a caregiver (typically every 3 hr). Used in conjunction with operant conditioning techniques to reward people for maintaining continence and appropriate toileting.
Timed voiding	Toileting on a fixed schedule (typically every 2–3 hr during waking hours).
Pelvic Floor Muscle Rehabilitation	
Biofeedback	Feedback from vaginal pressure sensor about pelvic floor contractions.
Electrical stimulation	Application of low-voltage electric current to sacral and pudendal afferent fibers through vaginal, anal, or surface electrodes. Used to inhibit bladder overactivity and improve awareness, contractility, and efficiency of pelvic muscle contraction.
Pelvic floor muscle (Kegel) exercises or training	Table 50.18.
Vaginal weight training	Active retention of vaginal weights (devices designed and shaped to exercise and strengthen pelvic floor muscles) at least twice a day. Typically used in combination with pelvic floor muscle exercises.
Anti-Incontinence Devices	
Incontinence clamps (penile compression devices)	Mechanical fixed compression applied to the penis to prevent any flow or leakage via the urethra. Must be released to void.
Intraurethral occlusive device (urethral plug)	Device worn in the urethra to provide mechanical obstruction to prevent urine leakage. Removed for voiding and after several hours of wearing.
Intraurethral valve pump	Replaceable urinary prosthesis for use in women who have impaired detrusor contractility (cannot contract muscles to push urine out of the bladder). Draws urine out to empty bladder and blocks urine flow when continence is desired.
Intravaginal support devices (pessaries)	Devices support bladder neck, relieve minor pelvic organ prolapse, and change pressure transmission to the urethra.
Containment Devices	
Absorbent products	Variety of reusable and disposable pads and undergarment systems.
External collection devices	External catheter (condom) systems (e.g., penile sheaths) direct urine into a drainage bag. Most often used by men.

repositioning the urethra and/or creating a backboard of support to stabilize the urethra and bladder neck and make them more receptive to changes in intraabdominal pressure. Another technique for stress UI augments the urethral resistance of the intrinsic sphincter with a sling or periurethral injectable.

Placement of a suburethral sling, typically midurethral, using the person's own fascia or a synthetic material, can correct stress UI in women. Complications include vascular and bowel injury, urinary retention, mesh or sling erosion, infection, urgency, and bladder perforation. Suburethral slings have better success rates compared to conservative therapy.

A bulking agent can be injected underneath the mucosa of the urethra to correct stress UI in women or men. Bulking agents include glutaraldehyde cross-linked bovine collagen (GAX collagen), autologous fat, carbon beads, carbon hydroxylapatite, and polydimethylsiloxane injections. Although treatment with bulking agents avoids the risk from open surgery, reinjection is typically needed after several years.

In artificial urethral sphincter surgery, the bladder sphincter that no longer works is replaced with an artificial one. An inflatable cuff is placed around the urethra internally. The patient inflates it to stop the flow and deflates it when the need to empty occurs. The patient must be able to work the internal pump. It is usually done in men. This procedure is done only as a last resort.[26]

❖ NURSING MANAGEMENT: URINARY INCONTINENCE

It is important to recognize both the physical and emotional problems from UI. Maintain and enhance the patient's dignity, privacy, and feelings of self-worth. This involves a 2-step

TABLE 50.18 PATIENT & CAREGIVER TEACHING

Pelvic Floor Muscle (Kegel) Exercises

Include the following instructions when teaching the patient to perform Kegel exercises:

What Are the Pelvic Floor Muscles?

- Your pelvic floor muscles provide support for your bladder and rectum and, in women, the vagina and uterus.
- If the muscles weaken or are damaged, they cannot support these organs and their position can change.
- This causes problems with the normal bladder and rectal function.
- If you have weak pelvic floor muscles, you may want to do special exercises to make the muscles stronger, prevent unwanted urine leakage, and lessen urinary urgency.

Finding the Pelvic Floor Muscles

- Without tensing the muscles of your leg, buttocks, or abdomen, imagine that you are trying to control the passing of gas or pinching off a stool.
- Imagine you are in an elevator full of people and feel the urge to pass gas. What do you do?
- You tighten or pull in the ring of muscle around your rectum.
- You should feel a lifting sensation in the area around the vagina or a pulling in of your rectum.

How to Do the Exercises

1. Squeeze the pelvic floor muscles.
2. Hold the muscle contraction for 3–5 seconds building up over time to longer and harder contractions.
3. Relax the pelvic floor muscles for 3–5 seconds.

Do these exercises 10 times at 3 different times of the day each day.

When to Do These Exercises

- You can do these exercises anytime and anywhere.
- You can do these exercises in any position but sitting or lying down may be the easiest.

How Long Does It Take Before I Notice a Change?

After a few weeks or months of doing these exercises, you should start to see less urine leakage and urinary urgency.

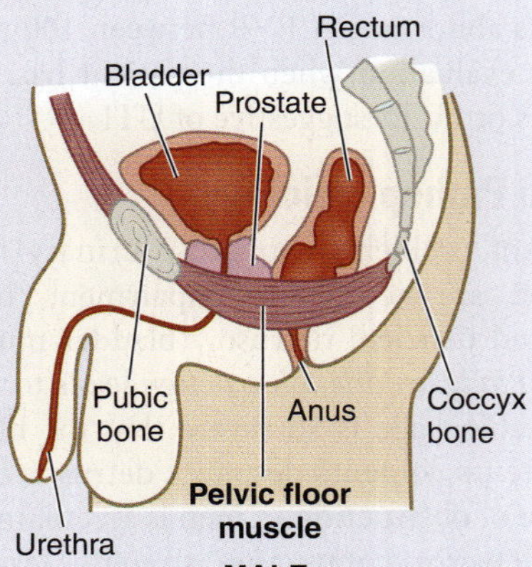

MALE

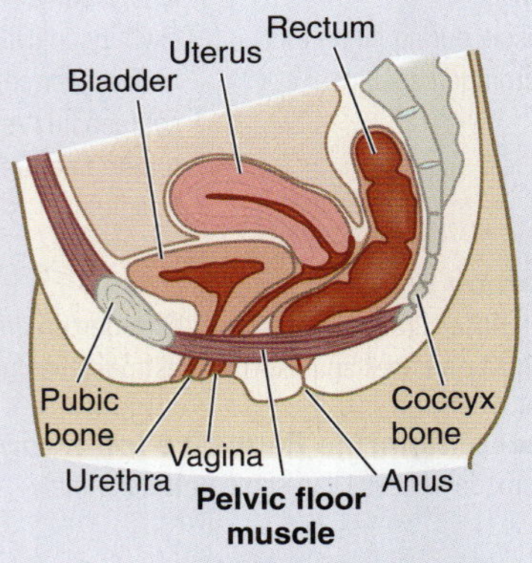

FEMALE

(Courtesy Diane Newman.)

approach with (1) containment devices to manage existing urinary leakage and (2) a plan to reduce or resolve the factors leading to UI.

CHECK YOUR PRACTICE

You are doing BP and glucose screening at the community senior center. While you are checking the BP on a 78-year-old woman, she starts to sob quietly. You tell her that her BP is 134/84 and gently place your hand on her arm. You ask her what is wrong. She tells you, "I have to pee all the time. I soak the bed, and my husband won't sleep with me anymore. I am washing sheets and my clothes all the time. Our whole house smells like urine."

- How would you respond to her?

Management options are shown in Tables 50.17 and 50.18. They include lifestyle interventions such as teaching the patient about consuming an adequate volume of fluids and reducing or eliminating bladder irritants, especially caffeine and alcohol, from the diet. Have the patient maintain a regular, flexible schedule of urination, usually every 3 to 4 hours while awake. Advise patients to quit smoking because it increases the risk for stress UI. Teach patients about the relationships among constipation, UI, and urinary retention. Aggressive management of constipation is recommended. Begin with ensuring adequate fluid intake, increasing fiber, lightly exercising, and judiciously using stool softeners. The management of constipation is discussed in Chapter 47.

Behavioral treatments include scheduled voiding regimens (timed voiding, habit training, prompted voiding), bladder retraining, and pelvic floor muscle training. Assess how the patient contains urine and offer alternatives if needed (Table 50.20). Many women use feminine hygiene pads. Many people use household products, such as rags, paper towels, or folded toilet tissue. Unfortunately, none of these products is designed to wick urine away from the skin, prevent soiling of clothing, and eliminate odor.

Provide information on products specifically designed to contain urine. For example, patients with mild to moderate UI often benefit from incontinent pads containing superabsorbent

TABLE 50.19 Drug Therapy

Voiding Dysfunction

Class and Mechanism of Action	Drug
α-Adrenergic Blockers	
Reduce urethral sphincter resistance to urinary outflow	alfuzosin (Uroxatral) doxazosin (Cardura) phenoxybenzamine (Dibenzyline) prazosin (Minipress) silodosin (Rapaflo) tamsulosin (Flomax) terazosin
5α-Reductase Inhibitors	
Suppress androgen resulting in epithelial atrophy and decrease in prostate size	dutasteride (Avodart) finasteride (Proscar)
β_3-Adrenergic Agonist	
Improves bladder's storage capacity by relaxing bladder muscle during filling	mirabegron (Myrbetriq)
Anticholinergics (Muscarinic Receptor Blockers)	
Reduce overactive bladder contractions in urge incontinence Relax bladder muscle during filling and improves the storage capacity of bladder	darifenacin (Enablex) fesoterodine (Toviaz) oxybutynin (Ditropan, Oxytrol Transdermal System) solifenacin (Vesicare) tolterodine (Detrol, Detrol LA) trospium
Hormone Therapy	
Local application reduces urethral irritation and increases host defenses against UTI	estrogen cream (Premarin) estrogen vaginal ring (Estring)
Serotonin-Norepinephrine Reuptake Inhibitor	
Unclear mechanism, decreases UI in some patients	Duloxetine
Tricyclic Antidepressants	
Reduce sensory urgency and burning pain of interstitial cystitis Reduce overactive bladder contractions	Amitriptyline imipramine (Tofranil)

TABLE 50.20 NURSING MANAGEMENT

Caring for the Patient With Incontinence

- Assess for risk factors for UI or urinary retention.
- Determine type of UI that patient has.
- Develop plan of care to decrease UI.
- Teach patient ways to decrease UI, such as pelvic floor muscle (Kegel) exercises.
- Assist patient in choosing appropriate products to contain urine.
- Delegate to the LPN/VN:
  - Use bladder scanner to estimate the postvoid residual volume (PVR).
  - Catheterize patient and measure PVR.
  - Give medications to decrease UI or urinary retention.
- Supervise AP:
  - Help patient to commode or bedpan at regular intervals.
  - Clean patient and provide skin care.
  - Notify RN about new-onset UI in a previously continent patient.

material, designed to absorb many times its weight in water. Patients with higher-volume urine loss or those with both urinary and fecal incontinence may need disposable or reusable incontinence protective underwear, briefs, or pad/pant systems.

In inpatient or long-term care facilities, nursing management of UI includes maximizing toilet access. This may take the form of offering the urinal or bedpan or helping the patient to the bathroom every 3 to 4 hours or at scheduled times. Ensure that toilets are accessible to patients and provide privacy to allow effective urine elimination. See Table 50.20.

URINARY RETENTION

Urinary retention is the inability to empty the bladder when a person voids or the accumulation of urine in the bladder because of an inability to void. In some cases, there is urinary leakage or postvoid dribbling, called *overflow UI*. *Acute urinary retention* is the total inability to pass urine via micturition. It is a medical emergency. *Chronic urinary retention* is an incomplete bladder emptying despite urination. The PVR volumes in patients with chronic urinary retention vary widely. Normal PVR is under 50 mL and for the elderly, 50 to 100 mL. A PVR over 200 mL is abnormal. A PVR between 100 to 200 mL can justify further evaluation when the patient has issues such as recurring UTIs or LUTS suggestive of UTI.

Etiology and Pathophysiology

Several different problems can cause urinary retention. The most common are neurologic impairment, bladder outlet obstruction, and deficient detrusor (bladder muscle) contraction strength. *Bladder outlet obstruction* leads to urinary retention when the blockage is so severe that the bladder can no longer evacuate its contents despite a detrusor contraction. A common cause of obstruction in men is an enlarged prostate.

Deficient detrusor contraction strength leads to urinary retention when the muscle is no longer able to contract with enough force or for enough time to completely empty the bladder. Common causes include neurologic impairment, diabetic neuropathy, overdistention, chronic alcohol use, and drugs (e.g., anticholinergic drugs).

Diagnostic Studies

The diagnostic studies for urinary retention are similar to the ones used for UI. Other studies include PVR measurement, ultrasound, urodynamic evaluation, video urodynamic evaluation, cystourethroscopy, and electromyography.

Interprofessional Care

Behavioral therapies for UI may be used in the management of urinary retention. Scheduled toileting and double voiding may be effective in chronic urinary retention with moderate PVR volumes. *Double voiding* is an attempt to maximize bladder evacuation. The patient is asked to void, sit on the toilet for 3 to 4 minutes, and void again before exiting the bathroom.

Catheterization may be needed. Intermittent catheterization allows the patient to remain free of an indwelling catheter with its associated risk of CAUTI and urethral irritation. In some situations, an indwelling catheter is preferred (e.g., if the patient is unwilling or unable to perform intermittent catheterization). An indwelling catheter is also used when urethral obstruction makes intermittent catheterization uncomfortable or infeasible.

Drug Therapy

Several drugs may be given to promote bladder evacuation. For the patient with dysfunctional voiding, an α-adrenergic blocker may be prescribed. These drugs relax the smooth muscle of the bladder neck and prostatic urethra and may decrease urethral resistance. Examples of α-adrenergic blockers are listed in Table 50.20. They are given to patients with BPH and may help with bladder neck or detrusor sphincter dyssynergia (muscle incoordination).

Surgical Therapy

Surgical interventions are used to manage retention from an obstruction. Transurethral or open surgical techniques are used to treat benign or cancerous prostatic enlargement, bladder neck contracture, urethral strictures, or dyssynergia of the bladder neck. Pelvic reconstruction using an abdominal or transvaginal approach can correct bladder outlet obstruction in women with severe pelvic organ prolapse.

While surgery has had a minimal role in the management of urinary retention caused by deficient detrusor contraction strength, there are procedures that may be helpful. Sacral neuromodulation involves a stimulator device and placement of a lead wire into the S3 foramen. Placement of an intraurethral valve pump, which empties the patient's bladder on command, may be an option.

NURSING MANAGEMENT: URINARY RETENTION

Acute urinary retention is a medical emergency that requires prompt recognition and bladder drainage. Insert a catheter as ordered. Use a catheter with a retention balloon in anticipation of the need for an indwelling catheter.

Teach the patient with acute urinary retention and the patient predisposed to these episodes ways to minimize risk. Have them pay attention to when they need to urinate and to void when they feel the need to do so. Take medications as prescribed. Pelvic floor muscle exercises may be helpful. Teach the patient to drink small amounts throughout the day and avoid the intake of large volumes of fluid over a brief period. Tell the patient (if chilled) to warm up before trying to void. They should avoid excess alcohol use because it leads to polyuria and a diminished awareness of the need to void until the bladder is distended. Tell patients that sitting in a tub of warm water or taking a warm shower may help them void. If these measures do not lead to successful urination, have the patient seek immediate care.

Patients with chronic urinary retention may be managed by behavioral methods, indwelling or intermittent catheterization, surgery, or drugs. Scheduled toileting and double voiding are the primary behavioral interventions used for chronic retention. Scheduled toileting can reduce, rather than expand, bladder capacity. In this case, have the patient void every 3 to 4 hours regardless of the desire to void. This is especially useful in the patient with chronic overdistention, diabetes, or chronic alcohol use with a large bladder capacity and diminished or delayed sensations of bladder filling and urgency.

CATHETERIZATION

INDICATIONS FOR AND COMPLICATIONS OF CATHETERIZATION

Urinary catheterization is often used in the management of the hospitalized patient. Indications for short-term urinary catheterization are listed in Table 50.21. Catheterization for sterile urine specimens may be needed if the patient has a history of complicated UTI. The risk for CAUTI is too high to perform catheterization for (1) routine acquisition of a urine specimen for laboratory analysis or (2) the convenience of the health care team or caregivers. A catheter should be the last resort to provide the patient with a dry environment to prevent skin breakdown and protect dressings or skin lesions.

Having a catheter is not without serious complications. Complications that are seen with long-term use (more than 28 days) of indwelling catheters include CAUTI, bladder spasms, periurethral abscess, chronic pyelonephritis, urosepsis, urethral trauma or erosion, fistula or stricture formation, and stones. CAUTIs are the most common HAI.

Aseptic technique is mandatory when inserting a urinary catheter (Table 50.22). After insertion, maintaining the closed drainage system and preventing infection are major nursing responsibilities. Do not routinely irrigate the catheter. Only irrigate if ordered. While the catheter is in place, manage fluid intake and provide for the patient's comfort. Address the psychologic

TABLE 50.21 Indications for Urinary Catheterization

Indwelling Catheter
- Relieve urinary retention caused by lower urinary tract obstruction, paralysis, or inability to void
- Bladder decompression preoperatively and operatively for lower abdominal or pelvic surgery
- Facilitate surgical repair of urethra and surrounding structures
- Splinting of ureters or urethra to promote healing after surgery or other trauma in area
- Accurate measurement of urine output
- Contamination of stage III or IV pressure injuries with urine that has impeded healing, despite appropriate personal care for the incontinence
- Terminal illness or severe impairment, which makes positioning or clothing changes uncomfortable, or which is associated with intractable pain

Intermittent (Straight, In-and-Out) Catheter
- Relieve urinary retention caused by lower urinary tract obstruction, paralysis, or inability to void
- Study of anatomic structures of urinary system
- Urodynamic testing
- Collect sterile urine sample in certain situations
- Instill medications into bladder
- Measure residual urine after voiding (postvoid residual [PVR]) if portable ultrasound not available

TABLE 50.22 NURSING MANAGEMENT

Care of the Patient With a Urethral Catheter

The following measures can be used to manage patients with a urethral catheter and prevent a CAUTI.

- Determine need for catheterization, but HCP must order.
- Choose appropriate type and size of catheter.
- Insert catheter using sterile technique.
- Develop plan of care to decrease risk for CAUTI.
- Teach catheter care to the patient, especially one who is ambulatory.
- Maintain a sterile, closed drainage system.
- Do not disconnect the distal urinary catheter and proximal drainage tube except for catheter irrigation (if ordered).
- Use sterile technique whenever the collecting system is open. If frequent irrigations are needed in short-term catheterization to maintain catheter patency, a triple-lumen catheter may be preferable, permitting continuous irrigations within a closed system.
- A routine catheter change is not needed if the patient is catheterized for less than 2 weeks. For long-term use of an indwelling catheter, replace the catheter based on patient assessment and not on a routine changing schedule.
- If ordered, aspirate small volumes of urine for culture from the catheter sampling port using a sterile syringe and needle. Prepare the puncture site with an antiseptic solution.
- With long-term use of a catheter, a leg bag may be used. If the collection bag is reused, wash it in soap and water and rinse thoroughly. When it is not reused immediately, fill it with 1/2 cup of vinegar and drain. Vinegar is effective against *Pseudomonas* and other organisms and eliminates odors.
- Remove the catheter as early as possible. Intermittent catheterization and external catheters are alternatives that have less risk of CAUTI.
- Ensure that AP:
  - Maintain unobstructed downhill flow of urine.
  - Empty the collecting bag regularly and accurately record the urine output.
  - Provide perineal care (once or twice a day and when needed), cleaning the meatus-catheter junction with soap and water.
  - Do not use lotion or powder near the catheter.
  - Anchor catheter using a securement device. Anchor catheter to upper thigh in women and lower abdomen in men to prevent catheter movement and urethral tension.

implications of urinary drainage. Patient concerns can include embarrassment, an altered body image, and fear that care of the catheter will result in increased dependency.

CATHETER CONSTRUCTION

Catheters vary in construction materials, size of the lumen, and tip shape (Fig. 50.10). Catheter materials include polyvinyl chloride, red rubber, silicone, and latex. Some are DEHP-free. Catheters coated with antimicrobial agents may prevent CAUTIs.

A coudé tip catheter is often used in men. We size catheters using the French scale. Each French unit (Fr) equals 0.33 mm of diameter. The diameter listed is the external diameter of the catheter. The size used varies with the patient's size and the purpose of catheterization. In women, urethral catheter sizes 10Fr to 12Fr are the most common. In men, the most common sizes are 14Fr to 16Fr. Balloon sizes are either 5 or 30 mL. The primary problem resulting from too large a catheter is tissue erosion from excessive pressure on the meatus or urethra.

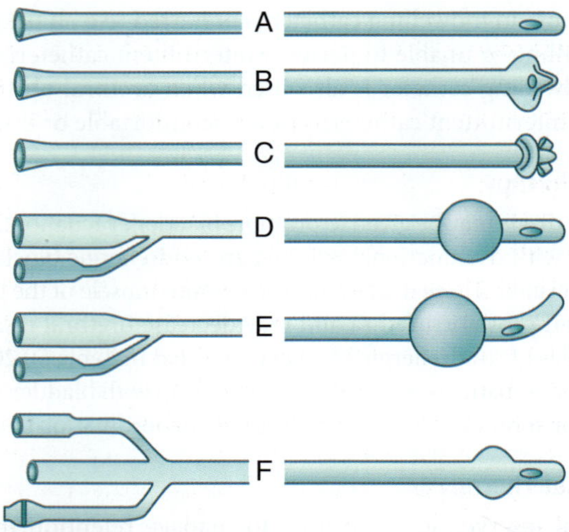

Fig. 50.10 Types of urinary catheters. (A) Simple urethral catheter. (B) Mushroom-tip de Pezzer catheter (can be for suprapubic catheterization). (C) Wing-tip Malecot catheter (wings hold catheter in place for temporary drainage). (D) Indwelling urethral catheter with inflated balloon. (E) Indwelling Tiemann catheter with coudé tip (slightly curved tip allows for passage past obstruction). (F) 3-Way indwelling catheter (third lumen can be used for irrigation).

TYPES OF CATHETERS

Four routes are used for urinary tract catheterization: urethral, ureteral, suprapubic, and via a nephrostomy tube.

Urethral Catheterization

Urethral catheterization is the most common route of catheterization. It involves the insertion of a catheter through the external meatus into the urethra, past the internal sphincter, and into the bladder.

Ureteral Catheters

A *ureteral catheter* is often called a ureteral stent. It is placed through the ureters into the renal pelvis. The catheter is inserted either (1) by being threaded up the urethra and bladder to the ureters under cystoscopic observation or (2) by surgical insertion through the abdominal wall into the ureters. The ureteral catheter is used either during surgery with removal immediately afterward or after surgery to splint the ureters and prevent them from being obstructed by edema.

A self-retaining ureteral catheter is often inserted after a lithotripsy procedure or when ureteral obstruction from adjacent tumors or fibrosis threatens renal function. They can be placed short or long term. When used long term, we replace the catheter every 3 to 6 months. A double-J ureteral catheter is often used. It allows the patient to ambulate. One end coils up in the kidney pelvis, while the other coils in the bladder.

Care of these catheters is similar to that of urethral catheters. Avoid situations that could cause dislodgement or displacement of the catheter. If the output is decreased, notify the HCP immediately.

Suprapubic Catheters

Suprapubic catheterization requires surgical placement. It is the oldest method of urinary diversion. The 2 ways to insert a suprapubic catheter are (1) through an open approach with a small incision made in the abdominal wall or (2) through a percutaneous approach. The catheter is placed while the patient is under general anesthesia for another procedure or at the bedside with a local anesthetic. The catheter may be sutured into place. Tape the catheter to prevent dislodgment. Teaching includes the need to stay well hydrated and how to monitor for infection, catheter obstruction or kinking, and urinary leakage around the catheter.

Suprapubic catheters can be used either short or long term. Common situations where a suprapubic catheter may be placed include acute urinary retention, urethra trauma, need for long-term urinary diversion, and to aid in treating a complicated UTI. The catheter should be changed at least each month.

A suprapubic catheter is prone to poor drainage because of mechanical obstruction of the catheter tip by the bladder wall, sediment, and clots. To ensure patency of the tube (1) prevent tube kinking by coiling the excess tubing and maintaining gravity drainage, (2) have the patient turn from side to side, and (3) milk the tube. If these measures are not effective, obtain an order from the HCP to irrigate the catheter using sterile technique.

If the patient has bladder spasms that are hard to control, urinary leakage may result. Oxybutynin or solifenacin can decrease bladder spasms.

Nephrostomy Tubes

The *nephrostomy tube* (catheter) is typically inserted on a temporary basis but can be placed long term to preserve renal function. Nephrostomy tubes are placed most often for urinary obstruction. The tube is inserted through a small flank incision directly into the pelvis of the kidney and attached to connecting tubing for closed drainage. The principle is the same as with other catheters—that is, the catheter should never be kinked, twisted, or tugged on. If the patient has excessive pain in the area or if there is excess drainage around the tube, check the catheter for patency. Use aseptic technique when performing irrigation. Gently instill no more than 5 mL of sterile saline solution at one time to prevent overdistention of the kidney pelvis and renal damage. Good wound care is critical. Infection, including pyelonephritis, is a common complication.

Intermittent Catheterization

An alternative approach to a long-term indwelling catheter is *intermittent catheterization,* often referred to as "straight" or "in-and-out" catheterization. The main goal of intermittent catheterization is to prevent urinary retention, stasis, and compromised blood supply to the bladder caused by prolonged pressure.[27]

It can be used short or long term and for conditions such as neurogenic bladder dysfunction (e.g., spinal cord injuries, chronic neurologic diseases). Barriers to intermittent catheterization include obesity, patient unwillingness, discomfort due to the catheterization, urinary obstruction, and limited upper extremity strength and/or movement.

The technique consists of inserting a urethral catheter into the bladder every 4 to 6 hours, including first thing upon awakening and before going to bed. Some patients perform intermittent catheterization only once or twice a day to measure residual urine and ensure an empty bladder.

The techniques for intermittent catheterization vary. Catheters can be sterile (single use) or clean (multiple use). Research shows no evidence that any technique (sterile or clean), catheter type (coated or uncoated), method (single-use or multiple-use), person (self or other), or strategy is better than any other.

We often use sterile technique in the hospital or long-term care facility. Depending on agency policy, you will see clean technique used.[27] Clean intermittent catheterization done correctly at home does not seem to increase the risk for UTIs and is more cost-effective. For home care, clean technique includes good hand washing with soap and water. Teach patients to wash and rinse the catheter before and after catheterization.

Using a lubricant makes catheterization more comfortable and minimizes trauma. Catheters come coated (pre-lubricated) or uncoated. Patients may prefer one type of catheter for use at home and another type while at work or during travel. The patient, caregiver, or HCP may insert the catheter.

Teach the patient to observe for signs of UTI so it can be treated early. Some patients receive prophylactic antibiotics. Complications include urethritis, urethral sphincter damage (especially if there is a forceful catheterization against a closed sphincter), urethral stricture, and creation of a false passage. Urethral damage from intermittent catheterization in men is similar to problems seen with indwelling catheterization.

URINARY TRACT SURGERY

RENAL AND URETERAL SURGERY

The most common indications for nephrectomy are a renal tumor, polycystic kidneys that are bleeding or severely infected, massive traumatic injury to the kidney, and the elective removal of a kidney for transplant into a person with ESRD. Surgery involving the ureters and kidneys can be done to remove stones that become obstructive, correct congenital anomalies, and divert urine when necessary. It is important that the patient having a nephrectomy has 1 working kidney to maintain normal renal function.

Surgical Procedure

Nephrectomy can be done by a conventional (open) approach or laparoscopically. In the open approach, an incision of about 8 to 12 inches is made through several layers of muscle. The incision can be made in the flank or abdominal area.

Laparoscopic Nephrectomy

With a laparoscopic nephrectomy, there are 3 to 5 puncture sites. When removing a kidney for donation, 1 incision is enlarged to 6 to 9 cm so the kidney can be removed in 1 piece. The kidney can also be removed through morcellation. Once dissected, the kidney is placed in a special sac then broken into smaller pieces before being removed from the patient. Compared with conventional nephrectomy, the laparoscopic approach is less painful, involves a shorter hospital stay, and has a much faster recovery.

Preoperative Management

The basic needs of the patient having renal and ureteral surgery are similar to those of any patient who has surgery (see Chapters 18 through 20). Before surgery ensure adequate fluid intake and a normal electrolyte balance. Tell the patient that if there is a flank incision, surgery will require a hyperextended, side-lying position. This position often causes the patient to have muscle aches after surgery.

Postoperative Management

Specific postoperative needs of a patient are related to urine output, respiratory status, and abdominal distention.

Urine Output

In the immediate postoperative period, measure and record the urine output at least every 1 or 2 hours. Measure drainage from the various catheters and record it separately. Do not clamp or irrigate the catheter or tube without a specific order. The total urine output should be at least 0.5 mL/kg/hr. It is important to assess for urine drainage on the dressing and to estimate this amount. Observe and monitor the color and consistency of urine. Urine with increased amounts of mucus, blood, or sediment may occlude the drainage tubing or catheter.

Weigh the patient daily using the same scale. Have the patient wear similar clothing and dressings each time. A significant change in daily weight can indicate retention of fluids, which places the patient at risk for heart failure. Fluid retention can increase the work required of the remaining kidney to perform its functions.

Respiratory Status

A nephrectomy can be done through a flank incision just below the diaphragm. It is important to ensure adequate ventilation. The patient is often reluctant to turn, cough, and breathe deeply because of the incisional pain. Give adequate pain medication to ensure the patient's comfort and ability to perform coughing and deep-breathing exercises. Have the patient use an incentive spirometer every 2 hours while awake. Early and frequent ambulation helps maintain respiratory function.

Abdominal Distention

Abdominal distention is present to some degree in most patients who have had surgery on their kidneys or ureters. It is often due to paralytic ileus caused by manipulation and compression of the bowel during surgery. We restrict oral intake until bowel sounds are present (usually 24 to 48 hours after surgery). Give IV fluids as ordered until oral intake resumes. Progression to a regular diet follows.

URINARY DIVERSION

Urinary diversion procedures are done when urine needs to be redirected from the bladder. Common reasons include bladder cancer, neurogenic bladder, congenital anomalies, strictures, trauma to the bladder, and chronic bladder inflammation. Numerous urinary diversion techniques and bladder substitutes are possible. These include an incontinent urinary diversion, a continent urinary diversion catheterized by the patient, or an orthotopic neobladder bladder so that the patient voids urethrally.[28] Surgical procedures for urinary diversion are described in Table 50.23 and Fig. 50.11. Urinary diversion may be done with or without cystectomy.

Incontinent Urinary Diversion

Incontinent urinary diversion is diversion to the skin, requiring a pouch. The simplest form is the cutaneous ureterostomy. However, complications (e.g., scarring, ureteral strictures) have led to the more frequent use of ileal or colonic conduits. The most common incontinent urinary diversion procedure is the **ileal conduit** (ileal loop). In this procedure a 4- to 6-in (10- to 15-cm) segment of the ileum is converted into a conduit for urinary drainage. The colon (colon conduit) can also be used. The ureters are anastomosed into one end of the conduit, and the other end of the bowel is brought out through the abdominal wall to form a stoma (Fig. 50.12). Although the mesentery still supports the bowel segment, it is completely isolated from the GI tract. The bowel is anastomosed and continues to function normally.

TABLE 50.23 Urinary Diversion Surgery

Description	Advantages	Disadvantages	Special Considerations
Cutaneous Ureterostomy			
Ureters excised from bladder and brought through abdominal wall, and stoma is created. Ureteral stomas may be created from both ureters, or ureters may be brought together, and 1 stoma created.	No need for major surgery.	External pouch needed because of continuous urine drainage. Possible stricture or stenosis of small stoma.	Periodic catheterizations may be needed to dilate stomas to maintain patency.
Ileal Conduit			
Ureters implanted into part of ileum or colon that has been resected from GI tract. Abdominal stoma is created.	Relatively good urine flow with few physiologic alterations.	External pouch needed to continually collect urine.	Surgery is complex. Increased risk for complications. Metabolic complications include electrolyte imbalances. Meticulous attention is necessary to care for stoma and collecting device.
Nephrostomy			
Catheter inserted into pelvis of kidney. Procedure may be done to 1 or both kidneys. May be temporary or permanent. Most often done in advanced disease as palliative procedure.	No need for major surgery.	High risk for renal infection.	May have to change nephrostomy tube every 10–12 weeks. Never clamp the catheter.

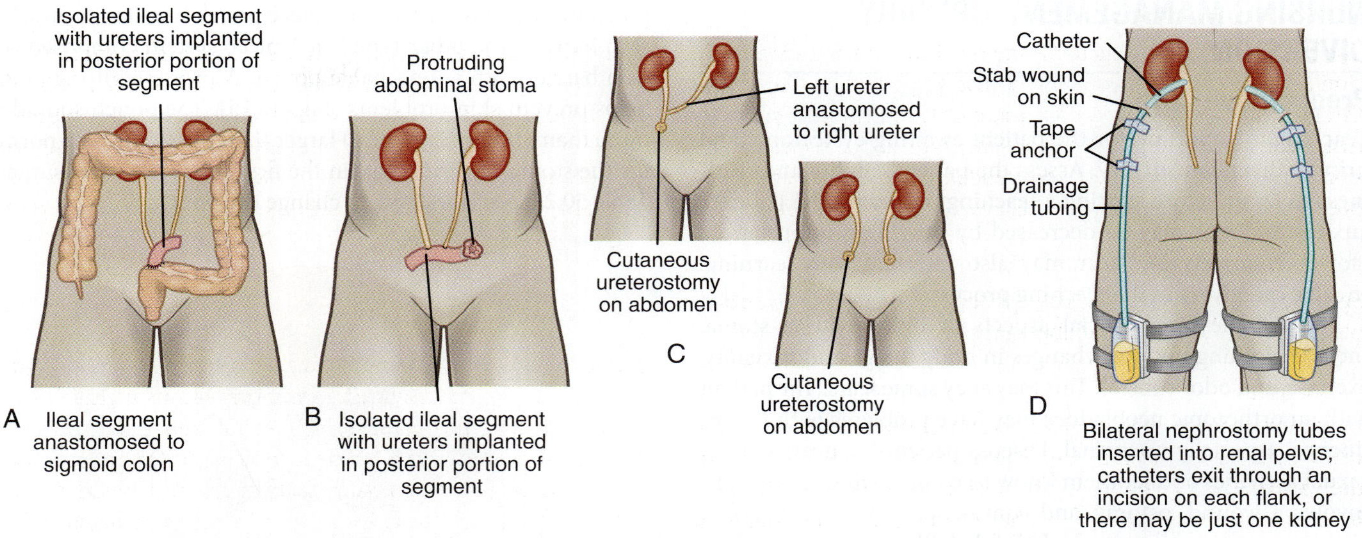

Fig. 50.11 Methods of urinary diversion. (A) Ureteroileosigmoidostomy. (B) Ileal loop (ileal conduit). (C) Ureterostomy (transcutaneous ureterostomy and bilateral cutaneous ureterostomies). (D) Nephrostomy.

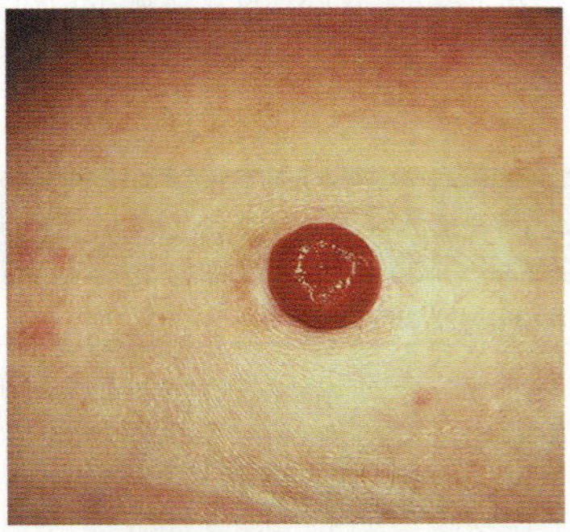

Fig. 50.12 Urinary stoma. Symmetric, no skin breakdown, protrudes about 1.5 cm. Mucosa is healthy red. This configuration is flat when the patient is upright or supine. (Courtesy Lynda Brubacher, Virginia Mason Hospital, Seattle, WA.)

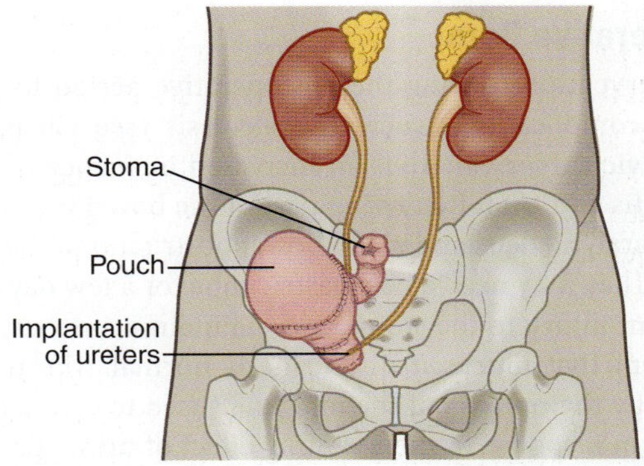

Fig. 50.13 Creation of a Kock pouch with implantation of ureters into one intussuscepted part of the pouch and creation of a stoma with the other intussuscepted part.

Because there is no valve and no voluntary control over the stoma, drops of urine flow from the stoma every few seconds, requiring a permanent external collecting device. The visible stoma and need for external collection devices are disadvantages. The lifelong need to care for and deal with the stoma and collection devices may be difficult. These problems have led to the increasing use of continent diversions and neobladder bladder substitutes.

Continent Urinary Diversions

A *continent urinary diversion* is an intraabdominal urinary reservoir that can be catheterized. Continent diversions are internal pouches created similarly to the ileal conduit. Reservoirs are constructed from the ileum, ileocecal segment, or ascending colon. Large segments of bowel are altered to prevent peristaltic action. A surgically created valve and the large, low-pressure reservoir helps prevent involuntarily leakage. The patient with a continent reservoir needs to self-catheterize every 4 to 6 hours but does not need to wear external attachments. Patients may wear a small bandage on the stoma to collect any mucous drainage or excess drainage. Examples of continent diversions are the Kock (Fig. 50.13), Indiana (most often used), and Miami pouches. The main difference among the diversions is the bowel segment used. For example, the Indiana pouch uses part of the ilium, cecum, and ascending colon as the reservoir.

Orthotopic Bladder Reconstruction

Orthotopic bladder reconstruction, or orthotopic neobladder, is the construction of a new bladder in the bladder's normal anatomic position, with discharge of urine through the urethra. The neobladder is surgically shaped from intestinal segments to make a low-pressure reservoir. An isolated segment of the terminal ileum is often used. The ureters and urethra are sutured into the neobladder. There are multiple procedure types based on the type of intestine and the construction technique used.

Orthotopic bladder reconstruction has become a more viable option if cancer does not involve the bladder neck or prostate apex. Ideal patients have normal renal and liver function, longer than 1- to 2-year life expectancy, adequate motor skills, and no history of inflammatory bowel disease or colon cancer. The advantage of an orthotopic bladder is that it allows for natural micturition. Incontinence is a possible problem. Intermittent catheterization may be needed.

❖ NURSING MANAGEMENT: URINARY DIVERSION

Preoperative Care

Teaching is important for the patient awaiting cystectomy and urinary diversion surgery. Assess the patient's ability and readiness to learn before starting a teaching program. The patient's anxiety and fear may be decreased by providing information. However, anxiety and fear may also interfere with learning. Involve caregivers in the teaching process.

Discuss the psychosocial aspects of living with a stoma. Include clothing options, changes in body image and sexuality, exercise, and odor control. This may allay some fears. The patient with an orthotopic neobladder may have problems with incontinence, especially nocturnal. Discuss patients' concerns about sexual activities and let them know that counseling is available. Involve a wound, ostomy, and continence nurse (WOCN). A visit from an ostomate can be helpful. Additional interventions are discussed in eNursing Care Plan 50.3 for the patient with an ileal conduit (on the website for this chapter).

Postoperative Care

Plan interventions during the postoperative period to prevent surgical complications, such as atelectasis (see Chapter 20). After pelvic surgery, there is an increased incidence of thrombophlebitis and UTI. Removing part of the bowel increases the risk of paralytic ileus and small bowel obstruction. The patient is NPO. They may need a nasogastric tube for a few days.

Prevent injury to the stoma and maintain urine output. Tell the patient that mucus in the urine is normal. The mucus is secreted by the mucosa of the intestine (used to create the ileal conduit) in response to the irritating effect of urine. Encourage a high fluid intake to "flush" the ileal conduit or continent diversion and prevent obstruction.

Provide meticulous care for the skin around the stoma. Alkaline encrustations with dermatitis may occur when alkaline urine comes in contact with exposed skin (Fig. 50.14). The urine is often kept slightly acidic to prevent alkaline encrustations. Other common peristomal skin problems include yeast infections, product allergies, and shearing-effect excoriations.

The patient is fitted for a pouching system to collect urine passed out of the stoma. It may need refitted later, depending on the degree of stoma healing and shrinkage. There are 2 types of pouching systems. There is a 1-piece pouch that has an attached skin barrier. The other type is a 2-piece system composed of a skin barrier with a detachable pouch. A properly fitting pouch helps prevent skin problems (Fig. 50.15). The pouch should be more than 1/8th inch (3 mm) larger than the stoma. It is normal for the stoma to shrink within the first few weeks after surgery. Table 50.24 describes how to change the pouch.

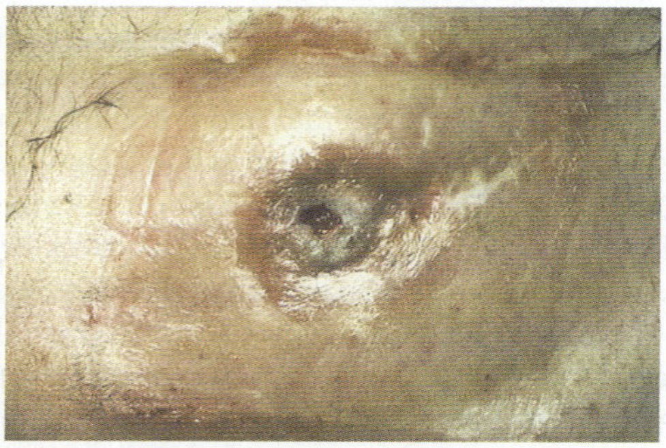

Fig. 50.14 Ammonia salt encrustation from alkaline urine. (Courtesy Lynda Brubacher, Virginia Mason Hospital, Seattle, WA.)

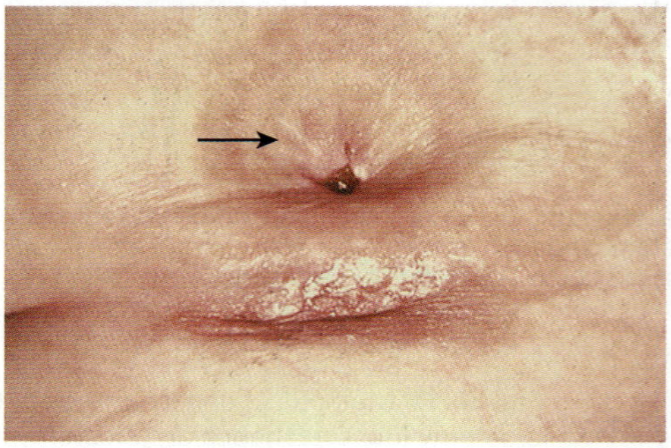

Fig. 50.15 Retracted urinary stoma with pressure injury from faceplate above stoma *(arrow)*. (Courtesy Lynda Brubacher, Virginia Mason Hospital, Seattle, WA.)

TABLE 50.24 PATIENT & CAREGIVER TEACHING

Ileal Conduit Appliances

Include the following instructions when teaching a patient or a caregiver how to change an ileal conduit appliance:

Temporary

1. Cut hole in pouch to fit over stoma (pouch 0.1 in [0.2 cm] larger than stoma).
2. Remove old pouch.
3. Clean area gently and remove old adhesive.
4. Wash area with warm water.
5. Place wick (rolled-up 4 × 4–in pad) over stoma to keep area dry during rest of procedure.
6. Dry skin around stoma.
7. Unless recommended by WOCN or HCP, avoid using creams or powders on the skin around the stoma.
8. Apply pouch by first smoothing its edges toward side and lower part of body.
9. Remove wick and complete application of pouch.
10. If patient is usually in bed, apply pouch so that it lies toward side of body.
11. If patient is ambulatory, apply pouch so that it lies vertically.
12. Connect drainage tubing to pouch.
13. Keep drainage pouch on same side of bed as stoma.

Permanent

1. Keep pouch in place for 3–4 days. May need changed more or less often as needed.
2. Change pouch when fluid intake has been restricted for several hours.
3. Sit or stand in front of mirror.
4. Can moisten edge of faceplate with warm water or adhesive solvent and gently remove.
5. Use warm water and a washcloth to clear the skin around the stoma. Use soap to remove any adhesive solvent.
6. Dry skin and inspect.
7. Place wick (rolled-up 4 × 4–inch pad) over stoma to keep skin free of urine.
8. Place pouch over stoma.

Teach the patient with a continent diversion (e.g., Indiana pouch) to catheterize at first every few hours. Over time this can be extended to every 4 to 6 hours. Irrigation of the pouch with normal saline or sterile water is often needed.

Patients with a neobladder may have postoperative urinary retention and need catheterization. It may take up to 6 months for them to regain bladder control. Patients empty their neobladders by relaxing their outlet sphincter muscles and bearing down with their abdominal muscles. Since there is no longer neurologic feedback between the reservoir and the brain, the patient should not expect a normal desire to void. To avoid bladder overdistention, patients should void at least every 2 to 3 hours, sit during voiding, and practice pelvic floor muscle relaxation to aid voiding.

Discharge teaching includes teaching the patient about symptoms of obstruction and infection and care of the ostomy. Acceptance of the surgery and changes in body image ensures the patient's best adjustment to a urinary diversion. Concerns include fear that the stoma will be offensive to others and will interfere with sexual, personal, professional, and recreational activities. Teach the patient that few activities will be restricted because of the urinary diversion. Meeting and sharing feelings with similar patients can help.

Tell the patient and caregiver about where to buy supplies, emergency telephone numbers, location of ostomy clubs, and follow-up visits with a WOCN. Follow-up with an HCP is important to monitor the patient's recovery, detect complications, and assess renal function.

Case Study

Painful Bladder and Frequent Urination

(© marilook/iStock/Thinkstock.)

Patient Profile

L.T., a 38-year-old woman, comes to the HCP's office today for the 8th time in the past year for a history of pelvic pain with urinary frequency during the day, nocturia, and urgency to void. All previous urine cultures have been negative for bacteria. A recent evaluation by her gynecologist was negative for endometriosis.

Subjective Data

- Has a history of suprapubic and vaginal pain, urinary frequency, and urgency
- Reports bladder pain that increases with bladder filling
- States this is her 3rd attack of suprapubic pain and painful urination in 2 months
- Constant pain and discomfort that is physically and emotionally exhausting
- Worried that she has cancer, and no one cares
- Had 4 pregnancies with uneventful vaginal deliveries
- Normal menstrual cycles
- Her husband and she rarely have sexual intercourse because she has pain with intercourse
- Has a bowel movement every day. Denies constipation and/or diarrhea
- Recalls having many UTIs as a child

Objective Data

Physical Assessment

- Lungs clear. BP 132/86. Heart rate 86/min. Respiratory rate 18/min. Abdomen soft, tender in suprapubic region.

Diagnostic Studies

- Urinalysis today: normal
- Previous urine cytology ordered to rule out cancer: normal
- Recent referral to urologist for cystoscopy, which was done 2 weeks ago

Interprofessional Care

- Cystoscopy results show glomerulations and Hunner lesions
- Urologist diagnosed interstitial cystitis
- Urologist prescribed pentosan (Elmiron), which she has not started yet
- Follow-up in 4 weeks with the urologist

Discussion Questions

1. ***Recognize***: After taking L.T.'s history, would you consider a UTI as a cause of her symptoms? Why or why not?
2. ***Analyze***: What additional testing and assessment would be helpful?
3. ***Analyze***: What is the significance of the cystoscopy findings?
4. ***Analyze***: What is the reason for the use of pentosan?
5. ***Prioritize:*** What are the priority clinical problems?
6. ***Act:*** How can you help L.T. deal with her diagnosis and treatment plan?
7. ***Act***: Why is it important to involve the dietitian in L.T.'s care?
8. ***Act:*** L.T. asks you how she can control her interstitial cystitis. How would you respond?

Answers available at http://evolve.elsevier.com/Lewis/medsurg.

BRIDGE TO NCLEX EXAMINATION

The number of the question corresponds to the same-numbered outcome at the beginning of the chapter.

1. The nurse teaches the female patient who has frequent UTIs to
   a. take tub baths with bubble bath.
   b. void before and after sexual intercourse.
   c. take prophylactic sulfonamides for the rest of her life.
   d. restrict fluid intake to prevent the need for frequent voiding.
2. One of the *most* important nursing roles in relation to acute poststreptococcal glomerulonephritis (APSGN) is to
   a. promote early diagnosis and treatment of sore throats and skin lesions.
   b. encourage patients to obtain antibiotic therapy for upper respiratory tract infections.
   c. teach patients that long-term prophylactic antibiotic therapy is needed to prevent recurrence.

d. monitor for respiratory symptoms that indicate the disease is affecting the alveolar basement membrane.

3. The edema that occurs in nephrotic syndrome is due to
   a. increased hydrostatic pressure caused by sodium retention.
   b. decreased aldosterone secretion from adrenal insufficiency.
   c. increased fluid retention caused by decreased glomerular filtration.
   d. decreased colloidal osmotic pressure caused by loss of serum albumin.
4. The nurse's *first priority* in managing the care of the patient with severe renal colic is to
   a. administer opioids as prescribed.
   b. obtain supplies for straining all urine.
   c. encourage fluid intake of 3 to 4 L/day.
   d. keep the patient NPO in preparation for surgery.
5. The nurse recommends genetic counseling for the children of a patient with
   a. nephrotic syndrome.
   b. chronic pyelonephritis.
   c. malignant nephrosclerosis.
   d. adult-onset polycystic kidney disease.
6. Which factor from the patient's history does the nurse identify as a risk factor for kidney and bladder cancer?
   a. Aspirin use
   b. Tobacco use
   c. Chronic alcohol use
   d. Use of artificial sweeteners
7. In planning nursing interventions to increase bladder control in the patient with urinary incontinence, the nurse includes *(select all that apply)*
   a. teaching the patient to use Kegel exercises.
   b. clamping and releasing a catheter to increase bladder tone.
   c. teaching the patient biofeedback mechanisms to train pelvic floor muscles.
   d. counseling the patient concerning choice of incontinence containment device.
   e. developing a fluid modification plan, focusing on decreasing intake before bedtime.
8. A patient with a ureterolithotomy returns from surgery with a nephrostomy tube in place. Postoperative nursing care includes
   a. clamping the tube for 10 minutes every hour to decrease spasms.
   b. encouraging fluids of at least 2 to 3 L/day after nausea has subsided.
   c. notifying the provider if nephrostomy tube drainage is more than 30 mL/hr.
   d. irrigating the nephrostomy tube with 10 mL of normal saline solution as needed.
9. A patient has had a cystectomy and ileal conduit diversion. Four days after surgery, the nurse notes mucous shreds in the pouch. The nurse would
   a. notify the provider.
   b. notify the charge nurse.
   c. irrigate the drainage tube.
   d. document it as a normal observation.

1. b; 2. a; 3. d; 4. a; 5. d; 6. b; 7. a, c; 8. b; 9. d.

For rationales to these answers and even more NCLEX review questions, visit http://evolve.elsevier.com/Lewis/medsurg.

EVOLVE WEBSITE/RESOURCES LIST

http://evolve.elsevier.com/Lewis/medsurg
Review Questions (Online Only)
Key Points
Answer Keys for Questions
- Rationales for Bridge to NCLEX Examination Questions
- Answer Guidelines for Case Study

Student Case Studies
- Patient With Bladder Cancer and Urinary Diversion
- Patient With Glomerulonephritis and Acute Kidney Injury

Nursing Care Plans
- eNursing Care Plan 50.1: Patient With a Urinary Tract Infection
- eNursing Care Plan 50.2: Patient With Urinary Tract Calculi
- eNursing Care Plan 50.3: Patient With an Ileal Conduit

Conceptual Care Map Creator
Audio Glossary
Content Updates

REFERENCES

1. Medina J, Castillo-Pino E: An introduction to the epidemiology and burden of urinary tract infections, *Ther Adv Urol* 11, 2019.
*2. Gould CV, Umscheid CA, Agarwal RK, et al.: Healthcare Infection Control Practices Advisory Committee: guideline for prevention of catheter-associated urinary tract infections. Retrieved from https://www.cdc.gov/infectioncontrol/pdf/guidelines/cauti-guidelines-H.pdf.
3. Zeng G, Zhu W, Lam W, Bayramgil A: Treatment of urinary tract infections in the old and fragile, *World J Urol* 38:2709, 2020.
*4. University of Rochester: Guidelines for the diagnosis and management of urinary tract infections. Retrieved from www.rochesterpatientsafety.com/Images_Content/Site1/Files/Pages/UTI_Treatment_Guidelines.pdf.
5. American Nurses Association: ANA CAUTI prevention tool. Retrieved from www.nursingworld.org/practice-policy/work-environment/health-safety/infection-prevention/ana-cauti-prevention-tool/.
*6. European Association of Urology: Urological infections guidelines. Retrieved from http://uroweb.org/guideline/urological-infections/#3.
7. National Institute for Diabetes and Digestive and Kidney Diseases (NIDDKD): Interstitial cystitis/painful bladder syndrome. Retrieved from www.niddk.nih.gov/health-information/health-topics/urologic-disease/interstitial-cystitis-painful-bladder-syndrome.
8. Lessnau K, Bylud JR, Deters LA, et al.: Tuberculosis of the genitourinary system. Retrieved from http://emedicine.medscape.com/article/450651-overview.

9. Mert A, Guzelburc V, Guven S: Urinary tuberculosis: still a challenge, *World J Urol* 38:2693, 2020.
10. NIDDKD: Glomerular diseases. Retrieved from www.niddk.nih.gov/health-information/kidney-disease/glomerular-diseases.
11. Bhimma R: Acute poststreptococcal glomerulonephritis. Retrieved from https://emedicine.medscape.com/article/980685-overview.
12. Sinnakirouchenan R: Nephrotic syndrome. Retrieved from http://emedicine.medscape.com/article/244631-overview.
13. US National Library of Medicine: Obstructive uropathy. Retrieved from https://medlineplus.gov/ency/article/000507.htm.
*14. American Urological Association (AUA): Medical management of kidney stones. Retrieved from https://www.auanet.org/guidelines/kidney-stones-medical-mangement-guideline.
*15. AUA/Endourology Society: Surgical management of stones: AUA/Endourology Society guideline. Retrieved from www.auanet.org/guidelines/surgical-management-of-stones-(aua/endourological-society-guideline-2016.
*16. AUA: Urotrauma guideline. Retrieved from https://www.auanet.org/guidelines/urotrauma-guideline.
*17. Kidney Disease: Improving global outcomes: Autosomal dominant polycystic kidney disease (ADPKD). Retrieved from https://kdigo.org/wp-content/uploads/2017/02/KDIGO-ADPKD-Supplemental-Full-Report-FINAL.pdf.
18. Genetics Home Reference: Alport syndrome. Retrieved from https://ghr.nlm.nih.gov/condition/alport-syndrome#diagnosis.
19. American Cancer Society (ACS): Key statistics about kidney cancer 2021. Retrieved from www.cancer.org/cancer/kidney-cancer/about/key-statistics.html.
*20. AUA: Renal mass and localized renal cancer: AUA guideline. Retrieved from www.auanet.org/guidelines/renal-mass-and-localized-renal-cancer-new-(2017).
*21. Kwan ML, Garren B, Nielsen ME, Tang L: Lifestyle and nutritional modifiable factors in the prevention and treatment of bladder cancer, *Urol Oncol: Semin Ori* 37:380, 2019.
22. ACS: Key statistics about bladder cancer 2021. Retrieved from www.cancer.org/cancer/bladder-cancer/about/key-statistics.html.
*23. AUA, SUO: Diagnosis and treatment of non-muscle invasive bladder cancer: AUA/SUO joint guideline. Retrieved from https://www.auanet.org//guidelines/bladder-cancer-non-muscle-invasive-guideline.
*24. AUA, ASCO, ASTRO, SUO: Treatment of non-metastatic muscle-invasive bladder cancer: AUA/ASCO/ASTRO/SUO guideline. Retrieved from https://www.auanet.org/guidelines/bladder-cancer-non-metastatic-muscle-invasive-guideline.
25. US National Library of Medicine: Kegel exercises-self-care. Retrieved from https://medlineplus.gov/ency/patientinstructions/000141.htm.
*26. AUA, SUFU: Female pelvic medicine and urogenital reconstruction: surgical treatment of female stress urinary incontinence: AUA/SUFU guidelines. Retrieved from www.auanet.org/guidelines/stress-urinary-incontinence-(sui)-new-(aua/sufu-guideline-2017).
*27. Southern Health National Health Services Foundation Trust: Urinary catheter care guidelines. Retrieved from www.southernhealth.nhs.uk/_resources/assets/inline/full/0/70589.pdf.
28. NIDDKD: Urinary diversion. Retrieved from https://www.niddk.nih.gov/health-information/urologic-diseases/urinary-diversion.

*Evidence-based information for clinical practice.

51

Acute Kidney Injury and Chronic Kidney Disease

Hazel A. Dennison

http://evolve.elsevier.com/Lewis/medsurg/

CONCEPTUAL FOCUS

Acid-Base Balance
Adherence
Coping
Elimination
Fluids and Electrolytes
Nutrition

LEARNING OUTCOMES

1. Outline criteria used to classify acute kidney injury using the acronym RIFLE (*R*isk, *I*njury, *F*ailure, *L*oss, *E*nd-stage renal disease).
2. Relate the clinical course of acute kidney injury.
3. Explain the interprofessional and nursing management of a patient with acute kidney injury.
4. Define chronic kidney disease and delineate its 5 stages based on the glomerular filtration rate.
5. Identify risk factors for chronic kidney disease.
6. Explain the conservative interprofessional care and related nursing management of the patient with chronic kidney disease.
7. Distinguish among renal replacement therapy options for persons with end-stage renal disease.
8. Compare and contrast nursing interventions for patients on peritoneal dialysis and hemodialysis.
9. Discuss the role of nurses in managing patients who receive a kidney transplant.

KEY TERMS

acute kidney injury (AKI)
acute tubular necrosis (ATN)
anuria
arteriovenous fistula (AVF)
arteriovenous grafts (AVGs)
automated peritoneal dialysis (APD)
azotemia
chronic kidney disease (CKD)
CKD mineral and bone disorder (CKD-MBD)
continuous ambulatory peritoneal dialysis (CAPD)
continuous renal replacement therapy (CRRT)
dialysis
end-stage renal disease (ESRD)
hemodialysis (HD)
peritoneal dialysis (PD)
uremia

Kidney failure, also called *renal failure,* is the partial or complete impairment of kidney function. It results in the inability to excrete metabolic waste products and water. Kidney failure contributes to problems with all body systems. Patients have problems with fluid, electrolyte, and acid-base imbalance. Adhering to diet therapy and the treatment plan can be challenging. The patient must deal with changes in lifestyle, occupation, family relationships, and self-image that can lead to withdrawal and depression. The patient grieves the loss of kidney function and independence.

We classify kidney failure as acute or chronic (Table 51.1). Acute kidney injury (AKI) has a rapid onset. Chronic kidney disease (CKD) is gradual with a progressive decline in kidney function.

ACUTE KIDNEY INJURY

Acute kidney injury (AKI) is the term used to encompass the entire scope of the syndrome, ranging from a slight deterioration in kidney function to severe impairment. AKI is characterized by a rapid loss of kidney function with or without decreased urine output. This loss is accompanied by progressive increases in blood urea nitrogen (BUN), creatinine, and potassium. The severity of dysfunction can range from a small increase in serum creatinine or reduction in urine output to the development of **azotemia**, an accumulation of nitrogenous waste products (urea nitrogen, creatinine) in the blood.

AKI can develop over hours or days. Although AKI is potentially reversible, it has a high mortality rate.[1] AKI usually affects people with other life-threatening problems (Table 51.2).[2] It often follows severe, prolonged hypotension, hypovolemia, or exposure to a nephrotoxic agent. Hospitalized patients develop AKI at a high rate (1 in 5) and have a high mortality rate. When AKI develops in an intensive care unit (ICU) patient, the mortality rate can be as high as 80%.[2]

Etiology and Pathophysiology

The causes of AKI are multiple and complex. We categorize them as prerenal, intrarenal (or intrinsic), and postrenal causes (Table 51.2 and Fig. 51.1).

Prerenal

Prerenal causes are factors that reduce systemic circulation, causing decreased renal blood flow. The decrease in blood flow leads to decreased glomerular perfusion and filtration of the kidneys.

It is important to distinguish prerenal oliguria from the oliguria of intrarenal AKI. In prerenal oliguria there is no damage to the kidney tissue (parenchyma). The oliguria is caused by a decrease in circulating blood volume (e.g., severe dehydration, heart failure [HF], decreased cardiac output). Prerenal oliguria

TABLE 51.1 Comparison of AKI and CKD

	AKI	CKD
Onset	Sudden	Gradual, often over many years
Most common cause	Acute tubular necrosis	Diabetic nephropathy
Diagnostic criteria	Acute reduction in urine output *AND/OR* ↑ Serum creatinine	GFR <60 mL/min/1.73 m² for >3 months *AND/OR* Kidney damage >3 months
Reversibility	Potentially	Progressive and irreversible
Main cause of death	Infection	CVD

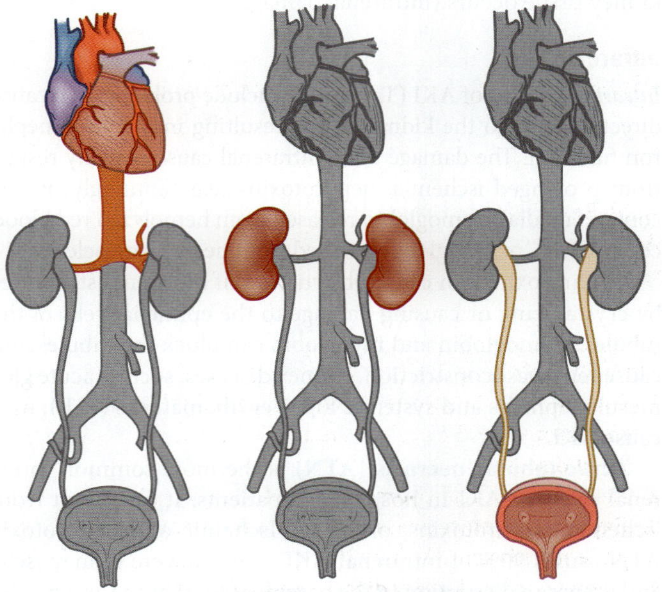

Fig. 51.1 Prerenal, intrarenal, and postrenal causes of AKI.

TABLE 51.2 Common Causes of AKI

Prerenal	Intrarenal	Postrenal
Decreased Cardiac Output • Cardiogenic shock • Dysrhythmias • HF • MI **Decreased Peripheral Vascular Resistance** • Anaphylaxis • Neurologic injury • Septic shock **Decreased Renovascular Blood Flow** • Bilateral renal vein thrombosis • Embolism • Hepatorenal syndrome • Renal artery thrombosis **Hypovolemia** • Burns • Dehydration • Excessive diuresis • GI losses (diarrhea, vomiting) • Hemorrhage • Hypoalbuminemia	**Interstitial Nephritis** • Allergies: antibiotics (sulfonamides, rifampin), NSAIDs, ACE inhibitors • Infections: bacterial (acute pyelonephritis), viral (Epstein-Barr), fungal (candidiasis) **Nephrotoxic Injury** • Chemical exposure: ethylene glycol, lead, arsenic, carbon tetrachloride • Contrast media • Drugs: aminoglycosides (gentamicin, amikacin), amphotericin B • Hemolytic blood transfusion reaction • Severe crush injury **Other** • Acute glomerulonephritis • Malignant hypertension • Prolonged prerenal ischemia • Systemic lupus erythematosus • Thrombotic disorders • Toxemia of pregnancy	• BPH • Bladder cancer • Calculi formation • Neuromuscular disorders • Prostate cancer • Spinal cord disease • Strictures • Trauma (back, pelvis, perineum)

is readily reversible with proper treatment.[3] With a decrease in circulating blood volume, autoregulatory mechanisms that increase angiotensin II, aldosterone, norepinephrine, and antidiuretic hormone try to preserve blood flow to essential organs. Prerenal azotemia results in decreased sodium excretion (less than 20 mEq/L), increased sodium and water retention, and decreased urine output. Prerenal problems can contribute to intrarenal AKI. If decreased perfusion persists for an extended time, the kidneys lose their ability to compensate and damage to kidney tissue occurs (intrarenal damage).

Intrarenal

Intrarenal causes of AKI (Table 51.2) include problems that cause direct damage to the kidney tissue, resulting in impaired nephron function. The damage from intrarenal causes usually results from prolonged ischemia, nephrotoxins (e.g., aminoglycosides, contrast media), hemoglobin released from hemolyzed red blood cells (RBCs), or myoglobin released from necrotic muscle cells.

Nephrotoxins can cause obstruction of intrarenal structures by crystallizing or causing damage to the epithelial cells of the tubules. Hemoglobin and myoglobin can block the tubules and cause renal vasoconstriction. Kidney diseases, such as acute glomerulonephritis and systemic lupus erythematosus (SLE), may cause AKI.

Acute tubular necrosis (ATN) is the most common intrarenal cause of AKI in hospitalized patients. It can result from ischemia, nephrotoxins, or sepsis. Ischemic and nephrotoxic ATN causes 90% of intrarenal AKI cases.[3] Severe kidney ischemia causes a disruption in the basement membrane and patchy destruction of the tubular epithelium. Nephrotoxic agents cause necrosis of tubular epithelial cells, which slough off and plug the tubules. Other risk factors for ATN while in the hospital include major surgery, shock, blood transfusion reaction, muscle injury from trauma, and prolonged hypotension. ATN is potentially reversible if the basement membrane is not destroyed and the tubular epithelium regenerates.

Postrenal

Postrenal causes of AKI involve mechanical obstruction in the outflow of urine. With the flow of urine obstructed, urine refluxes into the renal pelvis, impairing kidney function. The most common postrenal causes are benign prostatic hyperplasia (BPH), prostate cancer, stones, trauma, and extrarenal tumors. Bilateral ureteral obstruction leads to *hydronephrosis* (kidney dilation), increase in hydrostatic pressure, and tubular blockage, resulting in a progressive decline in kidney function. If bilateral obstruction is relieved within 48 hours of onset, complete recovery is likely. Prolonged obstruction can lead to tubular atrophy and irreversible kidney fibrosis. Postrenal causes of AKI account for less than 10% of AKI cases.[3]

Clinical Manifestations

Prerenal and postrenal AKI that has not caused intrarenal damage usually resolves quickly with treatment. When tissue damage occurs from either prerenal or postrenal causes, or when damage occurs directly as with intrarenal causes, AKI has a prolonged course. Clinically, AKI may progress through phases: oliguric, diuretic, and recovery. When a patient does not recover from AKI, CKD may develop.

The RIFLE classification describes the stages of AKI (Table 51.3). *R*isk, the first stage of AKI, is followed by *I*njury, which is the second stage. Then AKI increases in severity to the last, or third, stage, *F*ailure. The 2 outcome variables are *L*oss and *E*nd-stage renal disease.[3]

TABLE 51.3 Diagnostic Criteria

RIFLE Classification for Acute Kidney Injury

Stage	GFR Criteria	Urine Output Criteria	Clinical Example
Risk	Serum creatinine increased × 1.5 *OR* GFR decreased by 25%	Urine output <0.5 mL/kg/hr for 6 hr	• 68-year-old patient with type 2 diabetes, hypertension, CAD, CKD • Scheduled for emergency coronary artery bypass graft • Serum creatinine is 1.8 mg/dL (increased), weight 60 kg • Calculated GFR is 35 mL/min/1.73 m^2 • Has stage 3b CKD
Injury	Serum creatinine increased × 2 *OR* GFR decreased by 50%	Urine output <0.5 mL/kg/hr for 12 hr	• During surgery, hypotensive for a sustained period • Diagnosed with acute tubular necrosis • After surgery: serum creatinine is 3.6 mg/dL, urine output reduced to 28 mL/hr
Failure	Serum creatinine increased × 3 *OR* GFR decreased by 75% *OR* Serum creatinine >4 mg/dL with acute rise ≥0.5 mg/dL	Urine output <0.3 mL/kg/hr for 24 hr (oliguria) *OR* Anuria for 12 hr	• 72 hr after surgery, develops ventilator-associated pneumonia and sepsis while in ICU • Serum creatinine rises to 5.2 mg/dL, urine output drops to 10 mL/hr • BP remains low despite dopamine therapy
Loss	Persistent acute kidney failure. Complete loss of kidney function >4 weeks	—	• Starts on continuous venovenous hemodialysis • After 3 weeks of therapy has a cardiopulmonary arrest and does not survive
End-stage renal disease	Complete loss of kidney function >3 months	—	—

Oliguric Phase

Next, we will discuss the most common manifestations of AKI.

Urinary changes. The most common initial manifestation of AKI is *oliguria*, a reduction in urine output to less than 400 mL/day. It usually occurs within 1 to 7 days of the injury to the kidneys. If the cause is ischemia, oliguria often occurs within 24 hours. When nephrotoxic drugs are involved, the onset may be delayed for as long as 1 week. This phase lasts on average 10 to 14 days. It can last months in some cases. The longer the oliguric phase lasts, the poorer the prognosis for complete recovery of kidney function.[1]

Nonoliguric AKI has a urine output greater than 400 mL/day. About 50% of patients will be nonoliguric. This makes their initial diagnosis more difficult.[2]

While changes in urine output often do not correspond to changes in glomerular filtration rate (GFR), they can help us determine the cause of AKI. For example, **anuria** (no urine output) is usually seen with urinary tract obstruction. Oliguria often occurs with prerenal causes. Nonoliguric AKI occurs with acute interstitial nephritis and ATN.[2]

A urinalysis may show casts, RBCs, and white blood cells (WBCs). Casts form from mucoprotein impressions of the necrotic renal tubular epithelial cells, which slough into the tubules. The specific gravity may be fixed at around 1.010, with urine osmolality at about 300 mOsm/kg (300 mmol/kg). This is the same specific gravity and osmolality of plasma, thus reflecting tubular damage and the loss of concentrating ability by the kidney. Proteinuria may be present if AKI is related to glomerular membrane dysfunction.

Fluid volume. Hypovolemia (volume depletion) has the potential to worsen all forms of AKI. Fluid replacement is often enough to treat many forms of AKI, especially prerenal causes. When urine output decreases, fluid retention occurs. The severity of the manifestations depends on the extent of the fluid overload. In the case of reduced urine output (anuria, oliguria), the neck veins may become distended with a bounding pulse. Edema and hypertension may develop. Fluid overload can eventually lead to HF, pulmonary edema, and pericardial and pleural effusions.

Metabolic acidosis. In the normal kidney, excess hydrogen ions are excreted to keep a physiologic balance of the blood pH. Impaired kidneys cannot excrete hydrogen ions or the acid products of metabolism. Serum bicarbonate (HCO_3^-) production decreases from defective reabsorption and regeneration of HCO_3^- ions. Serum HCO_3^- is depleted through buffering of acidic hydrogen ions and metabolic end products. The patient with severe acidosis may develop rapid, deep respirations to try to compensate by increasing CO_2 exhalation.

Sodium balance. Damaged tubules cannot conserve sodium. Urinary sodium excretion may increase, resulting in normal or below-normal levels of serum sodium. Excess sodium intake is avoided because it can lead to volume expansion, hypertension, and HF. Uncontrolled hyponatremia or water excess can lead to cerebral edema.

Potassium excess. The kidneys normally excrete 80% to 90% of the body's potassium. In AKI the serum potassium level increases because the kidney's normal ability to excrete potassium is impaired. The risk for hyperkalemia increases if AKI is caused by massive tissue trauma because the damaged cells release potassium into the extracellular fluid (ECF). Bleeding and blood transfusions may cause cellular destruction, releasing more potassium into the ECF. Metabolic acidosis worsens hyperkalemia as hydrogen ions enter the cells, and potassium is driven out of the cells into the ECF.

While patients with hyperkalemia are often asymptomatic, some may have weakness with severe hyperkalemia. Acute or rapid development of hyperkalemia may result in electrocardiogram (ECG) changes (see Fig. 17.14). These changes include peaked T waves, widening of the QRS complex, and ST segment depression.[4] Because cardiac muscle is intolerant of acute increases in potassium, emergency treatment of hyperkalemia is needed.

Hematologic problems. Several hematologic problems occur in patients with AKI. Hospital-acquired AKI often occurs in patients who have multiorgan failure. Leukocytosis is often present. The most common cause of death in AKI is infection. The most common sites of infection are the urinary and respiratory systems.

Waste product accumulation. The kidneys are the main excretory organs for urea (an end product of protein metabolism) and creatinine (an end product of endogenous muscle metabolism). BUN and serum creatinine levels are increased in kidney disease. An increased BUN level also can be caused by dehydration, corticosteroids, or catabolism resulting from infections, fever, severe injury, or GI bleeding. The best serum indicator of AKI is creatinine because it is not affected by other factors.

Neurologic problems. Neurologic changes can occur as the nitrogenous waste products accumulate in the brain and other nervous tissue. The manifestations can be as mild as fatigue and difficulty concentrating and escalate to seizures, stupor, and coma.

Diuretic Phase

During the diuretic phase of AKI, daily urine output is usually around 1 to 3 L. It may reach 5 L or more. The nephrons are still not fully functional even as urine output increases. The high urine volume is caused by osmotic diuresis from the high urea concentration in the glomerular filtrate and the inability of the tubules to concentrate the urine. In this phase, the kidneys have recovered their ability to excrete wastes but not to concentrate the urine. Hypovolemia and hypotension can occur from massive fluid losses.

Patients who had an oliguric phase will have greater diuresis as kidney function returns. Large losses of fluid and electrolytes require us to monitor for hyponatremia, hypokalemia, and dehydration. The diuretic phase may last 1 to 3 weeks. Near the end of this phase, the patient's acid-base, electrolyte, and waste product (BUN, creatinine) values stabilize.

Recovery Phase

The recovery phase begins when the GFR increases, allowing the BUN and serum creatinine levels to decrease. Major improvements occur in the first 1 to 2 weeks of this phase. It may take

12 months for kidney function to stabilize. The patient's overall health, severity of kidney injury, and number and type of complications influence their outcome. Some patients do not recover and progress to end-stage renal disease (ESRD). The older adult is less likely to have a complete recovery of kidney function. Patients who recover may achieve clinically normal kidney function but remain in an early stage of CKD.

Diagnostic Studies

The history is essential for diagnosing the cause of AKI. Consider prerenal causes when there is a history of dehydration, hypotension, or blood loss. Suspect intrarenal causes if the patient was exposed to nephrotoxic drugs or contrast media. A history of changes in the urinary stream, stones, BPH, or bladder or prostate cancer suggests postrenal causes.

Although changes in urine output and serum creatinine occur late in the course of AKI, they are known diagnostic indicators. An increase in serum creatinine may not be present until there is a loss of more than 50% of kidney function. The rate of increase in serum creatinine is important as a diagnostic indicator in determining the severity of injury.

Urinalysis is an important diagnostic test. Urine sediment containing abundant cells, casts, or proteins suggests intrarenal disorders. The urine osmolality, sodium content, and specific gravity help in distinguishing the causes of AKI. Urine sediment may be normal in both prerenal and postrenal AKI. In intrarenal problems, hematuria, pyuria, and crystals may be seen. Other testing may be done (Table 51.4). A kidney ultrasound is often the first test done. It provides imaging without exposure to nephrotoxic contrast agents. It can evaluate kidney disease and urinary tract obstruction. A renal scan can assess abnormalities in kidney blood flow, tubular function, and the collecting system. A CT scan can show lesions, masses, obstructions, and vascular anomalies. A renal biopsy is the best way to confirm intrarenal causes of AKI.

Having an MRI or magnetic resonance angiography (MRA) study with the contrast media gadolinium is not advised in patients with kidney failure. Giving gadolinium can be potentially fatal.

TABLE 51.4 Interprofessional Care

Acute Kidney Injury

Diagnostic Assessment

- History and physical assessment
- Identify cause
- Serum creatinine and BUN levels
- Serum electrolytes
- Urinalysis
- Renal ultrasound
- Renal scan
- CT scan

Management

- Treat cause
- Fluid restriction (600 mL plus previous 24-hr fluid loss)
- Nutrition therapy
  - Adequate protein intake (0.8–1.0 g/kg/day) depending on degree of catabolism
  - Enteral nutrition
  - PN
  - Diet restrictions (potassium, phosphate, sodium)
- Measures to lower potassium (if high) (Table 51.5)
- Calcium supplements or phosphate-binding agents
- Dialysis (if necessary)
- Continuous RRT (if necessary)

Interprofessional Care

Because AKI is potentially reversible, the main goals of treatment are to eliminate the cause, manage the signs and symptoms, and prevent complications while the kidneys recover (Table 51.4). The first step is to determine if there is adequate intravascular volume and cardiac output to ensure adequate kidney perfusion.[4] Diuretic therapy may be given. It usually includes loop diuretics (e.g., furosemide [Lasix], bumetanide) or an osmotic diuretic (e.g., mannitol). If AKI is established, forcing fluids and diuretics will not be effective and may be harmful. Closely monitor fluid intake during the oliguric phase of AKI.

The general rule for calculating the fluid restriction is to add all losses for the previous 24 hours (e.g., urine, diarrhea, emesis, blood) plus 600 mL for insensible losses (e.g., respiration, diaphoresis). For example, if a patient excreted 300 mL of urine on Tuesday with no other losses, the fluid allocation on Wednesday would be 900 mL.

Hyperkalemia is one of the most serious complications in AKI because it can cause life-threatening dysrhythmias. Therapies used to treat high potassium levels are listed in Table 51.5. Both insulin and sodium bicarbonate are temporary measures for treating hyperkalemia by promoting a transient shift of potassium into the cells. Potassium will eventually diffuse back into the bloodstream. Calcium gluconate raises the threshold at which dysrhythmias occur, temporarily stabilizing the myocardium. Sodium polystyrene sulfonate (Kayexalate) and dialysis remove potassium rapidly from the body.

Conservative therapy may be all that is necessary until kidney function improves. If conservative therapy is not effective in treating AKI, then *renal replacement therapy* (RRT) is used. Controversy exists about the timing of RRT in AKI.[5] The most common indications for RRT in AKI are (1) volume overload, resulting in compromised cardiac and/or pulmonary status; (2) high serum potassium level; (3) metabolic acidosis (serum HCO_3^- level less than 15 mEq/L [15 mmol/L]); (4) BUN level greater than 120 mg/dL (43 mmol/L); (5) significant change in mental status; and (6) pericarditis, pericardial effusion, or cardiac tamponade.[6] Although laboratory values provide rough parameters, the best guideline is the clinical status of the patient.

Of the several RRT therapy options available, there is no consensus about the best approach.[6] Even though peritoneal dialysis (PD) is a viable option for RRT, it is not often used. Intermittent hemodialysis (HD) and continuous renal replacement therapy (CRRT) have both been used effectively.

CRRT is provided continuously over 24 hours through cannulation of a vein or catheter placement. CRRT has much slower blood flow rates compared with intermittent HD. HD is the method of choice when changes are needed emergently. It

TABLE 51.5 Therapies for High Potassium Levels

Regular Insulin IV
- Potassium moves into cells when insulin is given
- IV glucose given concurrently to prevent hypoglycemia
- IV Calcium Gluconate often given concurrently to improve cardiac contractility
- When effects of insulin decrease, potassium shifts back out of cells

Sodium Bicarbonate
- May be considered to correct acidosis and cause a shift of potassium into cells

Calcium Gluconate IV
- Generally used in advanced cardiac toxicity (evidence of hyperkalemic ECG changes)
- Raises the threshold for excitation, resulting in dysrhythmias

Sodium Polystyrene Sulfonate (Kayexalate)
- Given by mouth or retention enema
- When resin is in the bowel, potassium is exchanged for sodium
- Produces osmotic diarrhea, allowing for evacuation of potassium-rich stool
- Removes 1 mEq of potassium per 1 g of drug
- Do not give to a patient with a paralytic ileus as bowel necrosis can occur

Patiromer (Veltassa) and Sodium Zirconium Cyclosilicate (SZC)
- Oral suspension that binds potassium in GI tract
- Used to treat patients with CKD
- Do not use as an emergency drug for life-threatening hyperkalemia
- Has a delayed onset of action
- Do not give to a patient with a paralytic ileus as bowel necrosis can occur

Hemodialysis
- Most effective therapy to remove potassium
- Works within a short time

Diet Restriction
- Potassium intake is limited to 40 mEq/day
- Used to prevent recurrent elevation, not for acute elevation

is technically more complicated because it requires special staff and equipment and vascular access. The patient needs anticoagulation therapy to prevent blood clotting when the blood makes contact with the dialysis circuit. Rapid fluid shifts during HD may cause hypotension.

Nutrition Therapy

The goal of nutrition therapy in AKI is to provide adequate calories to prevent catabolism despite restrictions that prevent electrolyte and fluid problems and azotemia. Intake must provide adequate calories (30 to 35 kcal/kg and 0.8 to 1.0 g of protein/kg of desired body weight) to prevent the breakdown of body protein.

Adequate energy should mainly come from carbohydrate and fat sources to prevent ketosis from endogenous fat breakdown and gluconeogenesis from muscle protein breakdown. Essential amino acids may be supplemented. Potassium and sodium are regulated per plasma levels. Sodium is restricted as needed to prevent edema, hypertension, and HF.[7] Fat intake is increased so that the patient receives at least 30% to 40% of total calories from fat. IV fat emulsion infusions provide a good source of nonprotein calories. If a patient cannot maintain adequate oral intake, enteral nutrition is the preferred route for nutrition support (see Chapter 44). When the GI tract is not functional, parenteral nutrition (PN) can provide adequate nutrition. The patient treated with PN may need daily HD or CRRT to remove the excess fluid. Concentrated PN formulas are available to minimize fluid volume.

NURSING MANAGEMENT: ACUTE KIDNEY INJURY

Assessment

Several assessments are essential for developing the plan of care. Daily weights, strict intake and output, and vital signs are key. Daily monitoring of urine output has prognostic value. It is crucial for determining therapy and daily fluid volume replacement. Assess the urine for color, specific gravity, glucose, protein, blood, and sediment. Note the patient's general appearance, including skin color. Is there any edema, neck vein distention, or bruises? If a patient is receiving dialysis, check the access site for inflammation and exudate. Assess mental status and level of consciousness. Check the oral mucosa for dryness and inflammation. Auscultate the lungs for crackles, wheezes, or decreased breath sounds. Monitor the heart for an S_3 gallop, murmurs, or a pericardial friction rub. Assess ECG readings for dysrhythmias. Review all laboratory values and diagnostic test results.

Clinical Problems

Clinical problems for the patient with AKI include:
- Electrolyte imbalance
- Fluid imbalance
- Risk for infection
- Anxiety

Planning

The overall goals are that the patient with AKI will (1) completely recover without any loss of kidney function, (2) maintain normal fluid and electrolyte balance, (3) have decreased anxiety, and (4) adhere to and understand the need for careful follow-up care.

Implementation

Health Promotion

Prevention and early recognition of AKI are the most important aspects of care. Prevention is directed toward identifying and monitoring high-risk populations, controlling exposure to nephrotoxic drugs and industrial chemicals, and preventing prolonged episodes of hypotension and hypovolemia. In the hospital, factors that increase the risk for developing AKI are preexisting CKD, older age, massive trauma, major surgery, extensive burns, HF, sepsis, and obstetric complications.[8]

Contrast-induced nephropathy (CIN) can occur when contrast media for diagnostic studies causes nephrotoxic injury. In patients with diabetes receiving metformin, the drug should be held for 48 hours prior to and after the use of contrast media to decrease the risk for lactic acidosis. The best way to avoid CIN is to avoid exposure to contrast media by using other diagnostic tests, such as ultrasound. If contrast media is given to a high-risk patient, ensure adequate fluid intake. They should receive the lowest possible dose or a lower osmolality contrast agent.[9]

Monitor the patient's weight, intake and output, and fluid and electrolyte balance. Assess and record extrarenal losses of fluid from vomiting, diarrhea, hemorrhage, and increased insensible losses. Prompt replacement of significant fluid losses helps prevent ischemic tubular damage from trauma, burns, and extensive surgery. Intake and output and weight are valuable indicators of fluid volume status. Aggressive diuretic therapy for the patient with fluid overload from any cause can lead to decreased renal blood flow.

Monitor kidney function in persons who are taking drugs that are potentially nephrotoxic (see Table 49.3). These drugs should be used sparingly in the high-risk patient. When they must be used, they should be given in the smallest effective doses for the shortest possible periods. Caution the patient about over-the-counter (OTC) analgesics (especially nonsteroidal antiinflammatory drugs [NSAIDs]). They may worsen kidney function in the patient with mild CKD.

Angiotensin-converting enzyme (ACE) inhibitors can decrease perfusion pressure and cause hyperkalemia. If other measures, such as diet changes and diuretics, cannot control hyperkalemia, ACE inhibitors may have to be reduced or stopped. However, ACE inhibitors are often used to prevent proteinuria and progression of kidney disease, especially in patients with diabetes.

◆ Acute Care

The patient with AKI is critically ill and may have comorbid problems (e.g., diabetes, cardiovascular disease [CVD]) in addition to kidney injury. Focus on the patient holistically since they will have many physical and emotional needs. Usually, the changes caused by AKI arise suddenly. The patient needs help in understanding that kidney disease may affect the entire body's functions.

You have a key role in managing fluid and electrolyte balance during the oliguric and diuretic phases. Observe and record intake and output. Take daily weights with the same scale at the same time each day to detect excessive gains or losses of body fluid (1 kg is equivalent to 1000 mL of fluid). Assess for signs and symptoms of hypervolemia (in the oliguric phase) or hypovolemia (in the diuretic phase), potassium and sodium problems, and other electrolyte imbalances that may occur in AKI (see Chapter 17).

Because infection is the leading cause of death in AKI, meticulous aseptic technique is critical. Protect the patient from those with infectious diseases. Be alert for local manifestations of infection (e.g., swelling, redness, pain) as well as systemic manifestations (e.g., fever, malaise, leukocytosis).

If a patient with renal failure has an infection, be aware that they may not have a fever. Patients with AKI have a blunted febrile response to infection (e.g., pneumonia). If antibiotics are given to treat infection, we carefully consider the type, frequency, and dosage because the kidneys are the main route of excretion for many antibiotics. Dosages may be decreased depending on the patient's level of kidney function if the drug is eliminated by the kidneys. Nephrotoxic drugs (see Table 49.3) should be used with caution.

Perform good skin care. Take measures to prevent pressure injuries as mobility may be impaired. Mouth care is important to prevent stomatitis, which develops when ammonia (made by bacterial breakdown of urea) in saliva irritates the mucous membranes.

◆ Ambulatory Care

Recovery from AKI is highly variable. It depends on whether other body systems fail, the patient's general health and age, the length of the oliguric phase, and the severity of nephron damage. Protein and potassium intake are dictated by kidney function. Regular evaluation of kidney function is necessary. Teach the patient the signs and symptoms of recurrent kidney disease. Emphasize measures to prevent the recurrence of AKI.

The long-term convalescence of 3 to 12 months may cause psychosocial and financial hardships for the patient, caregiver, and family. Make appropriate referrals for counseling. If the kidneys do not recover, the patient will need to transition to life on chronic dialysis or a possible transplant.

◆ Evaluation

The expected outcomes are that the patient with AKI will

- Regain and maintain normal fluid and electrolyte balance
- Adhere to the treatment regimen
- Have no complications
- Have a complete recovery

Gerontologic Considerations: Acute Kidney Injury

Older adults are at an increased risk for AKI. The GFR declines with age. In older adults, impaired function of other organ systems from CVD or diabetes can increase the risk for AKI. The aging kidney is less able to compensate for changes in fluid volume, solute load, and cardiac output. Dehydration is a predisposing factor. It can occur from polypharmacy (diuretics, laxatives, drugs that suppress appetite or consciousness), acute febrile illness, and immobility.

Other common causes of AKI in the older adult include hypotension, diuretic therapy, aminoglycoside therapy, obstructive disorders (e.g., BPH), surgery, infection, and contrast media. Mortality rates are similar for older and younger patients. Patients over 65 years of age are less likely to recover from AKI. Despite this, age is not a barrier to offering RRT.

CHRONIC KIDNEY DISEASE

Chronic kidney disease (CKD) involves progressive, irreversible loss of kidney function. More than 26 million American adults, or 1 out of every 9, have CKD. CKD is much more

TABLE 51.6 Risk Factors for CKD

Risk Factors	Prevention and Management
Age >60 years	Prevent insult or injury to kidneys
Cardiovascular disease	Institute risk factor reduction measures
Diabetes	Achieve optimal glycemic control
Ethnic minority (e.g., Black, Native American)	Teach about ↑ risk and assist with appropriate screening (BP measurement, urinalysis)
Exposure to nephrotoxic drugs	Limit exposure and give sodium bicarbonate as treatment
Family history of CKD	Teach about ↑ risk and assist with appropriate screening
Hypertension	Maintain BP in normal range with ACE inhibitors or ARBs

common than AKI (Table 51.1). We partially attribute the increasing prevalence of CKD to increased risk factors, including an aging population, and increased rates of obesity, diabetes, and hypertension.

Because the kidneys are highly adaptive, CKD is often not recognized until there has been considerable loss of nephrons. Patients with CKD are often asymptomatic. This often results in CKD being underdiagnosed and untreated. We think about 70% of people with CKD are unaware that they have the disease.[10]

CKD has many different causes. The leading ones are diabetes (about 50%) and hypertension (about 25%) (Table 51.6).[11,12] Less common causes include glomerulonephritis, cystic diseases, and urologic diseases. Kidney diseases are discussed in Chapter 50.

Kidney Disease Improving Global Outcomes (KDIGO) Clinical Practice Guidelines defines CKD as either the presence of kidney damage or a decreased GFR less than 60 mL/min/1.73 m^2 for longer than 3 months.[11] Table 51.7 shows the stages of CKD. The last stage of kidney disease, **end-stage renal disease (ESRD)**, occurs when the GFR is less than 15 mL/min. At this point, RRT (dialysis, transplant) is needed to maintain life.[11]

Over half a million Americans are receiving treatment for ESRD. Despite all the technologic advances in life-sustaining treatment with dialysis, patients with ESRD have a high mortality rate. As the stage of kidney disease progresses, the mortality rate increases. Mortality rates are as high as 19% to 24% for patients with ESRD on dialysis.[12,13]

The prognosis and course of CKD are highly variable. They depend on the cause, patient's health and age, and adequacy of health care follow-up (Box 51.1). Some people live normal, active lives with kidney disease, while others may rapidly progress to ESRD (stage 5).

Since 1972, the United States has covered most of the costs of dialysis through Medicare benefits. Under Title XVIII of the Social Security Act, ESRD was recognized as a disability. Medicare pays for 80% of eligible charges. The state, private insurance, or patient covers the rest.[14]

Clinical Manifestations

As kidney function deteriorates, all body systems become affected. The manifestations result from retained urea,

TABLE 51.7 Diagnostic Criteria

Stages of CKD

Description	GFR (mL/min/1.73 m^2)	Clinical Action Plan
Stage 1 Kidney damage with normal or ↑ GFR	≥90	Diagnosis and treatment CVD risk reduction Slow progression
Stage 2 Kidney damage with mild ↓ GFR	60–89	Estimation of progression
Stage 3a Moderate ↓ GFR	45–59	Evaluation and treatment of complications
Stage 3b Moderate ↓ GFR	30–44	More aggressive treatment of complications
Stage 4 Severe ↓ GFR	15–29	Preparation for RRT (dialysis, kidney transplant)
Stage 5 Kidney failure	<15 (or dialysis)	RRT (if uremia present and patient desires treatment)

BOX 51.1 PROMOTING HEALTH EQUITY

Chronic Kidney Disease

Blacks
- Have a high risk for CKD as a complication of hypertension
- Have the highest rate of CKD, nearly 4 times that of Whites

Native Americans
- Have a rate of CKD twice that of Whites
- Rate of CKD is 6 times higher among Native Americans with diabetes than among other ethnic groups with diabetes

Hispanics
- Rate of CKD in Hispanics is 1.5 times higher than in non-Hispanic Whites

creatinine, phenols, hormones, electrolytes, and water. **Uremia** is a syndrome in which kidney function declines to the point that symptoms may develop in multiple body systems (Fig. 51.2). It often occurs when the GFR is 15 mL/min or less. The manifestations of uremia vary depending on the cause, comorbid problems, age, and degree of adherence to the treatment plan. Many patients are tolerant of the changes caused by declining kidney function because they occur gradually.[10]

Urinary System

In the early stages of CKD, patients usually do not report any change in urine output. Since diabetes is the main cause of CKD, polyuria may be present, but not necessarily from kidney disease. As CKD progresses, patients have increasing difficulty

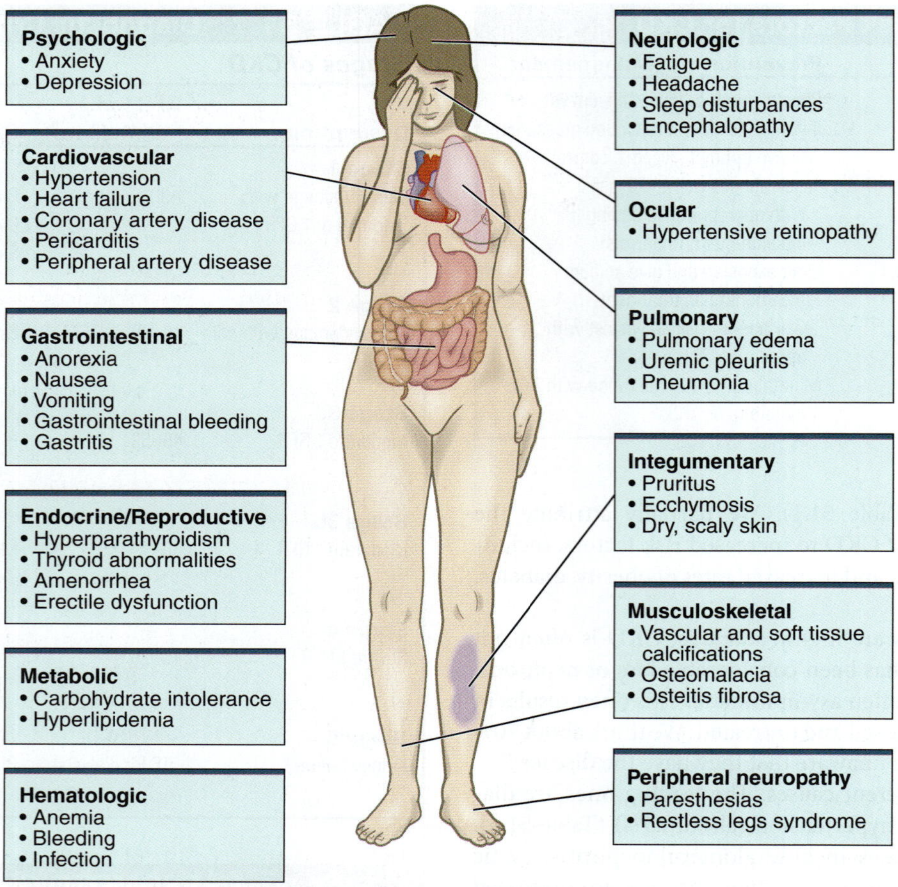

Fig. 51.2 Possible manifestations of CKD.

with fluid retention and need diuretic therapy. After a period on dialysis, patients may develop anuria.

Metabolic Disturbances

Waste product accumulation. As the GFR decreases, the BUN and serum creatinine levels increase. The BUN increase is not only from kidney disease but also protein intake, fever, corticosteroids, and catabolism. For this reason, serum creatinine clearance determinations (calculated GFR) are more accurate indicators of kidney function than BUN or creatinine (Table 51.8). Significant increases in BUN contribute to nausea, vomiting, lethargy, fatigue, impaired cognition, and headaches.

Altered carbohydrate metabolism. Impaired glucose metabolism, from cellular insensitivity to the normal action of insulin, causes defective carbohydrate metabolism. Mild to moderate hyperglycemia and hyperinsulinemia may occur.

Insulin and glucose metabolism may improve (but not to normal values) after starting dialysis. Patients with diabetes who use insulin before starting dialysis may need less insulin therapy when they start dialysis, and their kidney disease progresses. Patients with diabetes who develop uremia may need less insulin than before the onset of CKD. Insulin, which depends on the kidneys for excretion, stays in the circulation longer. Insulin dosing is patient specific. We monitor glucose levels carefully.

> **CHECK YOUR PRACTICE**
>
> You are working in a community-based HD unit. One of your patients is a 56-year-old woman who has been on HD for 3 weeks. You are reviewing her medications with her. She is surprised that her dose of glargine insulin has been decreased. She tells you, "I have been a diabetic for 10 years. This is the first time ever that my dose of insulin has been decreased."
>
> • How would you respond?

Elevated triglycerides. Hyperinsulinemia stimulates hepatic triglyceride production. Many patients develop dyslipidemia, with increased very-low-density lipoproteins (VLDLs), increased low-density lipoproteins (LDLs), and decreased high-density lipoproteins (HDLs). The altered lipid metabolism is related to decreased levels of the enzyme lipoprotein lipase, which is important in the breakdown of lipoproteins. Most patients with CKD die from CVD.[12]

Electrolyte and Acid-Base Imbalances

Potassium. Hyperkalemia is a serious electrolyte disorder associated with CKD. Fatal dysrhythmias can occur when the serum potassium level reaches 7 to 8 mEq/L (7 to 8 mmol/L). Hyperkalemia results from the kidneys excreting less potassium, the breakdown of cellular protein, bleeding, and metabolic acidosis. Potassium may come from foods, diet supplements, drugs, and IV infusions.

TABLE 51.8 Indicators of Kidney Function

This example shows why serum creatinine alone is a poor indicator of kidney function. Calculation of GFR is considered the best index to estimate kidney function as shown by the following example.

	PATIENT EXAMPLE	
Estimation of GFR	**76-Year-Old Woman (Weight 56 kg)**	**28-Year-Old Man (Weight 74 kg)**
Serum creatinine	1.4 mg/dL	1.4 mg/dL
GFR, estimated by the Cockcroft-Gault formula: (140–Age) × (Weight in kg) × (0.85 if female)/(72 × Cr)	30.2 mL/min	82.2 mL/min
GFR, estimated by MDRD equation: 186 × $(Creatinine/88.4)^{-1.154}$ × $(Age)^{-0.203}$ × (0.742 if female) × (1.21 if Black)	47 mL/min/1.73 m^2	64 mL/min/1.73 m^2

Sodium. Sodium may be high, normal, or low in kidney disease. Because of impaired sodium excretion, sodium is retained with water. If large quantities of water are retained, dilutional hyponatremia occurs. Sodium retention can contribute to edema, hypertension, and HF. Sodium intake is patient specific but is often restricted to 2 g/day.

Calcium and phosphate. Calcium and phosphate changes are discussed in the section on the musculoskeletal system.

Magnesium. Magnesium is mainly excreted by the kidneys. Hypermagnesemia is often not a problem unless the patient is ingesting magnesium (e.g., magnesium citrate, antacids containing magnesium). Manifestations can include absent reflexes, decreased mental status, dysrhythmias, and hypotension.

Metabolic acidosis. Metabolic acidosis results from the kidneys' impaired ability to excrete excess acid and from defective reabsorption and regeneration of HCO_3^-. The average adult makes 80 to 90 mEq of acid per day. This acid is normally buffered by HCO_3^-. In kidney disease, plasma HCO_3^-, which is an indirect measure of acidosis, usually falls to a new steady state at around 16 to 20 mEq/L (16 to 20 mmol/L). The decreased plasma HCO_3^- reflects its use in buffering metabolic acids. The HCO_3^- level often does not progress below this level because H^+ production is balanced by buffering from bone demineralization.

Hematologic System

Anemia. Normocytic, normochromic anemia is associated with CKD. Anemia in CKD is due to decreased erythropoietin production. Erythropoietin normally stimulates precursor cells in the bone marrow to make RBCs (erythropoiesis). Other factors contributing to anemia are nutrition deficiencies, decreased RBC life span, increased RBC hemolysis, frequent blood samplings, and GI bleeding. For patients receiving maintenance HD, blood loss in the dialyzer can contribute to the anemic state. Increased parathyroid hormone (PTH) (made to compensate for low serum calcium levels) can inhibit erythropoiesis, shorten RBC survival, and cause bone marrow fibrosis, which can result in decreased numbers of hematopoietic cells.

Sufficient iron stores are needed for erythropoiesis. Many patients with kidney disease are iron deficient and need iron supplementation. Oral iron supplements may not be effective for the person with CKD. GI side effects can cause adherence problems. Medications, such as proton pump inhibitors or phosphate binders, decrease absorption. Patients on dialysis may need IV iron to restore iron levels. Folic acid, needed for RBC maturation, is dialyzable because it is water soluble. Many patients receive folic acid supplements (1 mg/day).[15]

Bleeding tendencies. The most common cause of bleeding in uremia is a defect in platelet function. This problem is caused by impaired platelet aggregation and impaired release of platelet factor III. Changes in the coagulation system occur due to increased concentrations of both factor VIII and fibrinogen. The altered platelet function, hemorrhagic tendencies, and GI bleeding susceptibility can usually be corrected with regular HD or PD.

Infection. Patients with advanced CKD have an increased risk of infection. This is due to changes in WBC function and altered immune response and function. Both cellular and humoral immune responses are suppressed. Other factors contributing to the increased risk for infection include hyperglycemia and external trauma (e.g., catheters, needle insertions into vascular access sites).

Cardiovascular System

The most common cause of death in patients with CKD is CVD. Leading causes of death are myocardial infarction (MI), ischemic heart disease, peripheral arterial disease, HF, cardiomyopathy, and stroke.[16] CVD and CKD are so closely linked that if patients develop cardiac events (e.g., MI, HF), kidney function is evaluated. Traditional CVD risk factors, such as hypertension and increased lipids, are common in CKD patients.

CVD may be related to vascular calcification and arterial stiffness. Calcium deposits in the vascular medial layer can cause stiffening of the blood vessels. The mechanisms involved are multifactorial. They include (1) vascular smooth muscle cells changing into chondrocytes or osteoblast-like cells, (2) high total body amount of calcium and phosphate resulting from abnormal bone metabolism, (3) impaired renal excretion, and (4) drug therapies to treat the bone disease (e.g., calcium-phosphate binders).[17]

Hypertension, which is prevalent in patients with CKD, is both a cause and a consequence of CKD. Hypertension is worsened by sodium retention and increased ECF volume.[16] In some people, increased renin production contributes to hypertension. Hypertension and diabetes are contributing risk factors for vascular complications.[11,12] Long-standing hypertension, ECF volume overload, and anemia contribute to development of left ventricular hypertrophy that may eventually lead to cardiomyopathy and HF. Hypertension can cause retinopathy, encephalopathy, and nephropathy. Because of the many effects of hypertension, BP control is one of the most important therapeutic goals in CKD management.[12,16]

Patients with CKD are susceptible to dysrhythmias from hyperkalemia and decreased coronary artery perfusion. Uremic pericarditis can develop and sometimes progresses to pericardial effusion and cardiac tamponade. Pericarditis typically presents with a friction rub, chest pain, and low-grade fever.

Respiratory System

With severe acidosis, the respiratory system may try to compensate with Kussmaul breathing, which increases CO_2 removal by exhalation (see Chapter 17). Dyspnea may occur because of fluid overload, pulmonary edema, uremic pleuritis (pleurisy), pleural effusions, and respiratory infections (e.g., pneumonia).

GI System

Stomatitis with exudates and ulcerations, a metallic taste in the mouth, periodontal disease, and *uremic fetor* (a urinous odor of the breath) often occur in CKD. Anorexia, nausea, and vomiting may develop if CKD progresses to ESRD and is not treated with dialysis. Weight loss and malnutrition may occur. Diabetic *gastroparesis* (delayed gastric emptying) can compound the effects of malnutrition for patients with diabetes. GI bleeding is a risk because of mucosal irritation and the platelet defect.

Constipation may be due to ingesting iron salts or calcium-containing phosphate binders. Limits on fluid intake and physical inactivity increase the risk for constipation.

Neurologic System

Neurologic changes are expected as kidney disease progresses. They are the result of increased nitrogenous waste products, electrolyte imbalances, metabolic acidosis, and atrophy and demyelination of nerve fibers.

The central nervous system (CNS) becomes depressed, resulting in lethargy, apathy, decreased ability to concentrate, fatigue, irritability, and altered mental ability. Seizures and coma may result from a rapidly increasing BUN and hypertensive encephalopathy.

Peripheral neuropathy initially manifests as a slowing of nerve conduction to the extremities. The patient may have paresthesias in the feet and legs as a burning sensation. Eventually, motor involvement may lead to bilateral foot drop, muscular weakness and atrophy, and loss of deep tendon reflexes. Muscle twitching, jerking, *asterixis* (hand-flapping tremor), and nighttime leg cramps may occur. In patients with diabetic neuropathy, uremic neuropathy can compound symptoms. Those with advanced stage 5 CKD may develop restless legs syndrome.

Dialysis should improve general CNS problems and may slow or halt the progression of neuropathies. Motor neuropathy may not be reversible. The treatment for neurologic problems is dialysis or a transplant. Altered mental status, a late manifestation of CKD stage 5, rarely occurs unless the patient has chosen not to have RRT.

Musculoskeletal System

CKD mineral and bone disorder (CKD-MBD) develops as a systemic disorder of mineral and bone metabolism caused by progressive deterioration in kidney function (Fig. 51.3). Activated vitamin D is necessary to optimize absorption of calcium from the GI tract. As kidney function declines, less vitamin D is converted to its active form, resulting in decreased serum levels. Low levels of active vitamin D result in decreased serum calcium levels.[17]

PATHOPHYSIOLOGY MAP

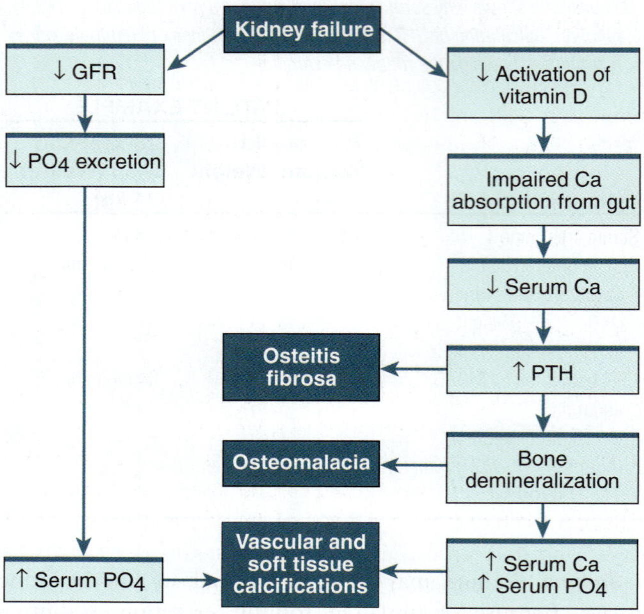

Fig. 51.3 Mechanisms of CKD-MBD. *GFR,* Glomerular filtration rate; *PTH,* parathyroid hormone.

Serum calcium levels are regulated primarily by PTH. When hypocalcemia occurs, the parathyroid gland secretes PTH, which stimulates bone demineralization, releasing calcium from the bones. Phosphate is also released, leading to high serum phosphate levels. Hyperphosphatemia also results from decreased phosphate excretion by the kidneys. It decreases serum calcium levels and further reduces the kidneys' ability to activate vitamin D.

Low serum calcium, increased phosphate, and decreased vitamin D contribute to stimulation of the parathyroid gland and excretion of PTH. PTH acts on the bone to increase remodeling. The accelerated rate of bone remodeling causes a weakened bone matrix and places the patient at a higher risk for fractures. Low ionized calcium levels can lead to tetany (see Chapter 17). However, in CKD, it is unusual for hypocalcemia to be symptomatic. In the acidotic state associated with CKD, more calcium is in the ionized form than is bound to protein.

CKD-MBD is a common complication of CKD. It results in skeletal, vascular, and soft tissue (extraskeletal) complications. Skeletal complications include (1) *osteomalacia* (results from demineralization from slow bone turnover and defective mineralization of newly formed bone) and (2) *osteitis fibrosa* (decalcification of the bone and replacement of bone tissue with fibrous tissue).

Soft tissue complications result from vascular calcifications. Vascular calcifications are a significant contributing factor to CVD. Irritation from calcium deposits in the eye can cause "uremic red eye." Cardiac calcifications can disrupt the conduction system and cause cardiac arrest. The gold standard for diagnosing CKD-MBD is a bone biopsy.

Skin

A small number of patients develop refractory itching that can have a devastating impact on their well-being and quality of life. Itching has multiple causes, including dry skin, calcium-phosphate deposition in the skin, and sensory neuropathy. It is more common in patients receiving dialysis than in the earlier stages of CKD. The itching may be so intense that it can lead to bleeding or infection from scratching. Uremic frost is a rare condition in which urea crystallizes on the skin. It is usually seen only when BUN levels are very high (e.g., over 200 mg/dL).

Reproductive System

Both men and women can have infertility and a decreased libido. Women usually have low levels of estrogen, progesterone, and luteinizing hormone, causing anovulation and menstrual changes (usually amenorrhea). Menses and ovulation may return after starting dialysis. Men have loss of testicular consistency, decreased testosterone levels, and low sperm counts.

Sexual problems may be caused by anemia, which causes fatigue and decreased libido. Peripheral neuropathy can cause impotence in men and anorgasmia in women. Other factors that may cause changes in sexual function are psychologic problems (e.g., anxiety, depression), physical stress, and drug side effects. Sexual function may improve with maintenance dialysis and become normal after a successful transplant.

Patients who become pregnant while receiving dialysis have been able to carry a fetus to term, but there is significant risk to the mother and infant. Pregnancy in patients with a kidney transplant is more common, but there is still considerable risk to the mother and fetus.

Psychologic Changes

Personality and behavioral changes, emotional lability, withdrawal, and depression often occur in patients with CKD. Fatigue and lethargy contribute to the feeling of illness. The changes in body image caused by edema, skin changes, and access devices (e.g., fistulas, catheters) may lead to anxiety and depression. Decreased ability to concentrate and slowed mental activity can give the appearance of dullness and disinterest in the environment. The patient must deal with significant changes in lifestyle, occupation, family responsibilities, and financial status. Long-term survival depends on medications, diet restrictions, dialysis, and possibly a transplant. The patient grieves the loss of kidney function and independence.

Diagnostic Studies

Persistent proteinuria is usually the first sign of kidney damage.[18] Screening for CKD involves a dipstick evaluation of protein in the urine or evaluation for albuminuria, which is not detected with routine urinalysis. The urine of patients with diabetes must be checked for albuminuria if no protein is present on routine urinalysis. A person with persistent proteinuria (1+ protein on standard dipstick testing 2 or more times over a 3-month period) should have further assessment of risk factors and a diagnostic workup with blood and urine tests to evaluate for CKD.

A urinalysis can detect RBCs, WBCs, protein, casts, and glucose. A renal ultrasound can detect any obstructions and determine the size of the kidneys. Other diagnostic studies (Table 51.9) help establish the diagnosis and cause of CKD. A kidney biopsy may be needed to provide a definitive diagnosis.

TABLE 51.9 Interprofessional Care

CKD

Diagnostic Assessment
- History and physical assessment
- Identify reversible kidney disease
- Renal ultrasound, renal scan, CT scan
- Renal biopsy
- BUN, serum creatinine, and creatinine clearance levels
- Serum electrolytes
- Lipid profile
- Urinalysis
- Protein-to-creatinine ratio in 1st morning voided specimen
- Hematocrit and hemoglobin levels

Management
- Correct fluid volume overload or deficit
- RRT (dialysis, kidney transplant)
- Nutrition therapy (Tables 51.10 and 17.7)
- Measures to lower potassium (Table 51.5)

Drug Therapy
- Calcium supplementation, phosphate binders, or both
- Antihypertensive therapy
- ACE inhibitors or ARBs
- Erythropoietin therapy
- Lipid-lowering drugs
- Adjust drug dosages to degree of renal function

Serum creatinine alone poorly reflects kidney function. GFR is the preferred way to determine kidney function. There are several GFR calculators. The equations used most often are the Cockcroft-Gault formula and Modification of Diet in Renal Disease (MDRD) Study equation (Table 51.8). MDRD is the preferred method of calculation.[19]

Interprofessional Care

The overall goals of CKD therapy are to preserve existing kidney function, reduce the risks for CVD, prevent complications, and provide for the patient's comfort. Early recognition, diagnosis, and treatment can prevent the progression of kidney disease. Patients with CKD need a referral to a nephrologist early in the course of the disease. Every effort is made to detect and treat potentially reversible causes of kidney failure (e.g., HF, dehydration, infections, nephrotoxins, urinary tract obstruction, glomerulonephritis, renal artery stenosis).

Patients with CKD have a high incidence of CVD. More patients die from CVD than live to need dialysis. When a patient has CKD, therapy is aimed at treating CVD plus slowing the progression of kidney disease (Table 51.9).

A focus during stages 1 through 4 (Table 51.7) before the need for dialysis (stage 5) includes controlling blood pressure, hyperparathyroidism, CKD-MBD, anemia, and dyslipidemia. The next section focuses on the drug and nutrition aspects of care.

Drug Therapy

Hyperkalemia. We use several strategies to manage hyperkalemia (Table 51.5). These include restricting high-potassium foods and drugs. Acute hyperkalemia may need treatment with IV glucose and insulin or IV 10% calcium gluconate.

Sodium polystyrene sulfonate, a cation-exchange resin, is often given to lower potassium levels in stage 4 CKD. Sodium polystyrene sulfonate has an osmotic laxative action and ensures potassium evacuation from the bowel. Tell the patient to expect some diarrhea. Since sodium polystyrene sulfonate exchanges sodium ions for potassium ions, observe the patient for sodium and water retention. If changes appear in the ECG, such as peaked T waves and widened QRS complexes, HD may be done to remove excess potassium.

Patiromer (Veltassa) is an oral suspension that binds potassium in the GI tract. It can treat hyperkalemia in persons with CKD. It should not be used in emergency situations to treat hyperkalemia because of its delayed onset of action. Because patiromer binds other oral medications, it must be taken at least 6 hours before or after other oral medications. Sodium zirconium cyclosilicate (SZC) is another long-term drug for hyperkalemia. It is an oral solution that should be given at least 2 hours apart from other medications.[20]

Hypertension. For some, the progression of CKD can be delayed by controlling hypertension.[16] Treatment of hypertension includes (1) weight loss (if needed), (2) lifestyle changes (e.g., exercise, avoid alcohol use, smoking cessation), (3) diet recommendations (DASH Diet), and (4) antihypertensive drugs. Most patients need 2 or more drugs to reach target BP. The treatment of hypertension is discussed in Chapter 36.

Drug therapy depends on whether the patient has diabetes. ACE inhibitors and ARBs are given to patients with diabetes and those with nondiabetic proteinuria.[11] They decrease proteinuria and may delay the progression of CKD. They must be used with caution as they can further decrease the GFR and increase serum potassium levels.

Measure the BP with the patient in the supine, sitting, and standing positions to assess the effect of antihypertensive drugs. Teach the patient and caregiver how to monitor the BP at home and what readings require immediate intervention.

CKD-MBD. Interventions for CKD-MBD include limiting phosphorus intake, giving phosphate binders, supplementing vitamin D, and controlling hyperparathyroidism.[17] Phosphate intake is not usually restricted until the patient needs RRT. At that time, phosphate is usually limited to about 1 g/day, but diet control alone is usually not enough.

Phosphate binders include calcium-based binders, such as calcium acetate, and calcium carbonate. They bind phosphate in the bowel and then excrete it in the stool. Giving calcium increases the calcium load which increased the risk for vascular calcifications. When calcium levels are increased or there is evidence of existing vascular or soft tissue calcifications, non–calcium-based phosphate binders are used. These include lanthanum carbonate (Fosrenol), sevelamer carbonate (Renvela), and iron-based, calcium-free phosphate binders, such as sucroferric oxyhydroxide (Velphoro) and ferric citrate (Auryxia).

To be most effective, give phosphate binders with each meal. Constipation is a frequent side effect. Stool softeners may be needed.

Because bone disease (osteomalacia) is associated with excess aluminum, aluminum preparations should be used with caution in patients with kidney disease. Do not use magnesium-containing antacids (e.g., Maalox, Mylanta) because magnesium depends on the kidneys for excretion.

Hypocalcemia is a problem in the later stages of CKD due to the inability of the GI tract to absorb calcium in the absence of active vitamin D. If hypocalcemia persists even if the serum phosphate levels are normal, supplemental calcium and vitamin D may be given. Assess vitamin D levels to determine the need for a supplement. If the levels are low, vitamin D is given in the form of cholecalciferol.

Treatment of secondary hyperparathyroidism in ESRD patients requires the activated form of vitamin D because the kidneys cannot activate vitamin D. Active vitamin D is available as oral or IV calcitriol (Rocaltrol), IV paricalcitol (Zemplar), or oral or IV doxercalciferol (Hectorol). Their use can reduce high PTH levels. Cinacalcet (Sensipar), a calcimimetic agent, can control secondary hyperparathyroidism. Calcimimetics mimic calcium and increase the sensitivity of the calcium receptors in the parathyroid glands. As a result, the parathyroid glands detect calcium at lower serum levels and decrease PTH secretion.

If parathyroid disease becomes severe, a subtotal or total parathyroidectomy may be done to decrease the synthesis and secretion of PTH. In most cases, a total parathyroidectomy is done and parathyroid tissue transplanted into the forearm. The transplanted cells make PTH as needed. If PTH production becomes excessive, some cells can be removed from the forearm.

Hypercalcemia may occur with calcium and vitamin D supplementation. If hypercalcemia occurs, vitamin D may be withheld, and calcium-based phosphate binders replaced with non–calcium-based phosphate binders.

Anemia. Anemia is caused by the kidneys making less erythropoietin. We give exogenous erythropoietin (EPO) to treat anemia. One option is epoetin alfa (Epogen, Procrit). It can be given IV or subcutaneously, usually 2 or 3 times per week. Darbepoetin alfa (Aranesp) is longer acting and can be given weekly or biweekly.

Hemoglobin and hematocrit levels may take 2 to 3 weeks to increase. Higher doses of EPO increase the risk of thromboembolic events and death from serious CV events (MI, HF, stroke). The recommendation is to use the lowest possible dose of EPO. EPO can increase BP. It is contraindicated in uncontrolled hypertension. The increased BP is due to hemodynamic changes (e.g., increased whole blood viscosity) that occur as the anemia is corrected.

Treatment of CKD-related anemia is patient specific with the goal being to reduce the need for blood transfusions. There is no target hemoglobin or widely accepted EPO dosing strategy. Teach people who are prescribed EPO about the risks and benefits and allow them to decide about their treatment plan.

EPO therapy may lead to iron deficiency from the increased demand for iron to support erythropoiesis. Iron supplements are

TABLE 51.10 NUTRITION THERAPY

CKD

	Pre-ESRD	Hemodialysis	Peritoneal Dialysis
Calcium	About 1000–1500 mg/day	Patient specific	Patient specific
Calories	30–35 kcal/kg/day	30–35 kcal/kg/day	25–35 kcal/kg/day (includes calories from dialysate glucose absorption)
Fluid allowance	As desired or depends on urine output	Urine output plus 600–1000 mL	Unrestricted if weight and BP controlled and residual renal function
Iron	Supplement recommended if receiving erythropoietin	Supplement recommended if receiving erythropoietin	Supplement recommended if receiving erythropoietin
Phosphate	Patient specific or 1.0–1.8 g/day	Patient specific or about 0.6–1.2 g/day	Patient specific or about 0.6–1.2 g/day
Potassium	Based on laboratory values	Patient specific or about 2–4 g/day	Usually not restricted
Protein	Patient specific or 0.6–1.0 g/kg/day (low protein)	1.2 g/kg/day	1.2–1.3 g/kg/day
Sodium	Patient specific or 1–3 g/day	Patient specific or 2–3 g/day	Patient specific or 2–4 g/day

recommended if the plasma ferritin concentrations fall below 100 ng/mL. Most CKD patients receive an iron supplement.

Iron can be given by mouth or IV. Oral use is limited due to GI side effects, which decrease adherence. Oral iron should not be taken at the same time as phosphate binders because calcium binds the iron, preventing its absorption. Tell the patient that iron may make the stool dark in color. Most patients receiving HD are prescribed IV iron sucrose (Venofer) or sodium ferric gluconate complex (Ferrlecit). Supplemental folic acid (1 mg/day) is usually given because it is needed for RBC formation and removed by dialysis.

Blood transfusions are avoided unless the patient has an acute blood loss or symptomatic anemia (i.e., dyspnea, excess fatigue, tachycardia, palpitations, chest pain). Transfusions increase the development of antibodies. This makes it harder to find a compatible donor for a kidney transplant. Multiple blood transfusions may lead to iron overload since each unit of blood has about 250 mg of iron.

Dyslipidemia. Dyslipidemia, a risk factor for CVD, is a common problem in CKD. Statins (HMG-CoA reductase inhibitors), such as atorvastatin (Lipitor), can lower LDL cholesterol levels (see Table 37.6). Statins should be used in patients with CKD, especially those with diabetes, not yet on dialysis.[13,16]

Fibrates (fibric acid derivatives), such as gemfibrozil (Lopid), are used to lower triglyceride levels (see Table 37.6) and can increase HDLs. Specific drugs used in these classes depend on the patient response and HCP recommendation.

Complications of drug therapy. The kidneys partially or totally excrete many drugs. CKD causes decreased elimination that leads to an accumulation of drugs and the potential for drug toxicity. Drug doses and frequency are adjusted based on the severity of the kidney disease. Increased sensitivity may result as drug levels increase in the blood and tissues. Drugs of particular concern include digoxin, diabetic agents (metformin, glyburide), antibiotics (e.g., vancomycin, gentamicin), and opioid drugs.

Nutrition Therapy

Protein restriction. The current diet for the person with CKD is designed to maintain good nutrition (Table 51.10). Calorie-protein malnutrition is a potential, serious problem that results from altered metabolism, anemia, dental problems, anorexia, and nausea (Box 51.2). Other factors leading to malnutrition include depression and complex diets that restrict protein, phosphorus, potassium, and sodium.

BOX 51.2 EVIDENCE-BASED PRACTICE

Oral Health and CKD

You work in an outpatient HD clinic. A new patient, K.D., is a 56-year-old woman with CKD who is scheduled for HD 3 times a week. During her first visit, you note several discolored teeth and swollen gums and suspect periodontal disease. When you ask K.D. about her oral care, she tells you she has not seen a dentist "in years." "Now that you mention it," she says, "my mouth always feels dry. Even when I try to drink a lot of water, it doesn't seem to help. Nothing tastes right." K.D. agrees when you tell her you would like to discuss her oral care options with her nephrology provider. K.D. comments, "My mother paid an arm and a leg for dental work. I don't even have enough money for a co-pay."

Making Clinical Decisions

Synthesis of Best Available Evidence

Research has identified a strong relationship between CKD and periodontitis. For patients who are undergoing dialysis, periodontal disease can increase the risk of CVD and mortality. Poor oral health can affect the ability to eat, taste, and swallow, and lead to dry mouth, gingivitis, dental caries, and pain.

Clinician Expertise

You contact the nurse practitioner (NP) at the nephrologist's office to discuss K.D.'s oral health. The NP tells you the patient has seemed defensive in past discussions about oral care. The NP says he is encouraged by her conversation with you. He confirms K.D. is insured and tells you he will make a referral to a local free clinic for dental care to minimize the cost.

Patient Preferences and Values

When you report to K.D. about the plan, she agrees to explore the options the NP and you are exploring.

Implications for Nursing Practice

1. What would you suggest as part of the oral care plan for K.D.?
2. How would you prepare K.D. for the dental work she is likely to need?

Reference for Evidence

Wallace K, Shafique S, Piamjariyakul U: The relationship between oral health and hemodialysis treatment among adults with CKD: a systematic review, *Nephrol Nurs J* 46(375), 2019.

Frequent monitoring of laboratory tests and anthropometric measurements are needed to evaluate nutrition status. All patients with CKD should be referred to a dietitian for nutrition teaching.

For CKD stages 1 through 4, many HCPs encourage a diet with normal protein intake. For the patient on HD, protein is not routinely restricted. The patient should avoid high-protein diets and supplements because they may overburden the diseased kidneys.[21]

Protein guidelines for PD differ from those for HD because of protein loss through the peritoneal membrane. During PD, protein intake must be high enough to compensate for the losses so that the nitrogen balance is maintained. The recommended protein intake is at least 1.2 g/kg of ideal body weight (IBW) per day. This can be increased depending on the patient's needs.

For patients with malnutrition or inadequate caloric or protein intake, commercially prepared products that are high in protein but low in sodium and potassium are available (e.g., Nepro, Amin-Aid). As an alternative, the patient may use liquid or powder breakfast drinks.

Fluid restriction. Water and any other fluids are not routinely restricted in patients with CKD stages 1 to 5 who are not receiving HD. To reduce fluid retention, diuretics are often used. Patients on HD have a more restricted fluid intake than patients on PD. For those on HD, as their urine output decreases, fluids are restricted. Recommended fluid intake depends on the daily urine output. Generally, 600 mL (from insensible loss) plus an amount equal to the previous day's urine output is allowed for a patient on HD.

Foods that are liquid at room temperature (e.g., gelatin, ice) are counted as fluid intake. Space fluid allotment throughout the day so that the patient does not become thirsty. Teach patients to limit fluid intake so that weight gains are no more than 1 to 3 kg between dialyses (interdialytic weight gain).

Sodium and potassium restriction. Teach patients with CKD to restrict sodium. Sodium-restricted diets may vary from 2 to 4 g/day. Teach the patient to avoid high-sodium foods, such as processed meats, canned soups and stews, cold cuts, and many dressings (see Table 38.8). Salt substitutes should be avoided in potassium-restricted diets because they contain potassium chloride.

Potassium restriction depends on the kidneys' ability to excrete potassium. Restrictions range from 2000 to 3000 mg (39 mg = 1 mEq). Teach patients receiving HD to avoid foods that are high in potassium (see Table 17.7). Patients using PD do not usually need potassium restrictions. They may need oral potassium supplementation because of the loss of potassium with dialysis exchanges.

Phosphate restriction. As kidney function declines, phosphate elimination by the kidneys is decreased. The patient develops high phosphorus levels. By the time a patient reaches ESRD, they need to limit phosphate to around 1 g/day. Foods that are high in phosphate include meat and dairy products (e.g., milk, ice cream, cheese, yogurt, pudding). Many foods that are high in phosphate are also high in protein. When patients eat a diet containing protein, phosphate binders are given to control the phosphate level.

NURSING MANAGEMENT: CHRONIC KIDNEY DISEASE

Assessment

Obtain a complete history of any existing kidney disease or family history of kidney disease. Some kidney disorders, including Alport syndrome and polycystic kidney disease, have a genetic component. Other problems that can lead to CKD are diabetes, hypertension, and SLE.

Because many drugs are potentially nephrotoxic, obtain a medication history. Decongestants and antihistamines that contain pseudoephedrine and phenylephrine cause vasoconstriction and lead to an increase in BP. Magnesium and aluminum from antacids can accumulate in the body because they cannot be excreted. Some antacids have high levels of salt. This contributes to hypertension.

NSAIDs (aspirin, ibuprofen, naproxen) can contribute to the development of AKI and progression of CKD, especially when taken in higher doses than recommended. If taken as prescribed, these analgesics are usually considered safe.[22]

Assess the patient's diet habits and discuss any problems with intake. Measure height and weight. Evaluate any recent weight changes.

CKD and its long-term treatment affect virtually every area of a person's life, including family relationships, social and work activities, self-image, and emotional state. Assess the patient's support systems. The choice of treatment may be related to support systems available.

Clinical Problems

Clinical problems for patients with CKD include:

- Fluid imbalance
- Electrolyte imbalance
- Impaired cardiac function
- Difficulty coping

More information on clinical problems and interventions for the patient with CKD is presented in eNursing Care Plan 51.1, available on the website for this chapter.

Planning

The overall goals are that a patient with CKD will (1) adhere to the treatment plan, (2) have effective coping strategies, and (3) continue with activities of daily living within their limitations.

Implementation

Health Promotion

Identify those at risk for CKD. At-risk persons include those diagnosed with diabetes or hypertension and people with a personal or family history of kidney disease or repeated urinary tract infections (UTIs). They should have regular checkups that include a routine urinalysis and calculation of the estimated GFR.

People with diabetes need to have their urine checked for albuminuria if routine urinalysis is negative for protein. Teach patients with diabetes to report any changes in urine appearance (color, odor), frequency, or volume to the HCP. If a patient needs a potentially nephrotoxic drug, it is important

BOX 51.3 PROMOTING POPULATION HEALTH

Prevention and Detection of CKD

- Early detection and treatment are the ways to reduce CKD.
- Ensure diagnosis and treatment of diabetes as it is the leading cause of CKD.
- Monitor BP to detect elevations so that treatment can be started early.
- Treat hypertension appropriately as it is the 2nd leading cause of CKD.

TABLE 51.11 PATIENT & CAREGIVER TEACHING

CKD

Include the following information in the teaching plan for the patient and caregiver:

1. Diet (sodium, potassium, phosphate) and fluid restrictions.
2. Common problems patient will encounter in modifying diet and fluid intake.
3. Signs and symptoms of electrolyte imbalance, especially high potassium.
4. Alternative ways of reducing thirst, such as sucking on ice cubes, lemon, or hard candy.
5. Reasons for prescribed drugs and common side effects. *Examples:*
   - Phosphate binders (including calcium supplements used as phosphate barriers) should be taken with meals.
   - Take calcium supplements prescribed to treat hypocalcemia on an empty stomach, but not at the same time as iron supplements.
   - Iron supplements should be taken between meals.
6. The importance of reporting any weight gain >4 lb (2 kg), increasing BP, shortness of breath, edema, increasing fatigue or weakness, or confusion or lethargy
7. Need for support and encouragement. Share concerns about lifestyle changes, living with a chronic illness, and decisions about type of dialysis or transplantation.

to monitor kidney function with serum creatinine, BUN, and GFR. Those at risk must take measures to prevent or delay the progression of CKD. Most important are measures to reduce the risk or progression of CVD (Box 51.3). These include glycemic control for patients with diabetes (see Chapter 53), BP control (see Chapter 36), and lifestyle modifications, including smoking cessation.

◆ Acute Care

Most of the care of the patient with CKD occurs on an outpatient basis. In-hospital care is needed for management of complications and kidney transplant.

◆ Ambulatory Care

Encourage patients to take part in their care. Teach the patient and caregiver about the diet, drugs, and follow-up care (Table 51.11). The patient needs to understand the drugs and common side effects. Because patients with CKD take many medications, a pillbox organizer or a list of the drugs and the times of administration may be helpful. Tell the patient to avoid OTC drugs such as NSAIDs and aluminum- and magnesium-based laxatives and antacids. Teach the patient to take daily BP readings. They need to watch for signs and symptoms of fluid overload, hyperkalemia, and other electrolyte imbalances.

The dietitian should meet with the patient and caregiver on a regular basis for diet planning. A diet history and consideration of cultural variations help with diet planning and adherence. The rate of progression of CKD is dependent on the type of kidney disease and presence of other comorbid problems.

The patient can complete an evaluation for a kidney transplant prior to the need to start dialysis. Patients may receive a transplant before ever having to start dialysis. Even though a transplant offers the best outcome for many ESRD patients, the critical shortage of donor organs limits this option for many patients.

Most patients need either PD or HD. Most patients use HD. Explain to the patient and caregiver what is involved in PD or HD. Offer information about all treatment options so that the patient can be involved in the decision-making process, giving a sense of control over life-altering decisions. Tell the patient that even while on dialysis, transplant is still an option. Let the patient know that if a transplanted organ fails, the patient can return to dialysis.

Discuss palliative care as needed. Patients themselves often start the conversation about palliative care. Focus the discussion on moving from the curative approach to promotion of comfort care and consideration of hospice care. Listen to the patient and caregiver, allowing them to do most of the talking and pay special attention to their hopes and fears. Palliative and end-of-life care is discussed in Chapter 10.

◆ Evaluation

The expected outcomes are that the patient with CKD will maintain

- Fluid and electrolyte levels within normal ranges
- An acceptable weight with no more than a 10% weight loss

DIALYSIS

Dialysis is the movement of fluid and molecules across a semipermeable membrane from one compartment to another. Clinically, dialysis is a technique in which substances move from the blood through a semipermeable membrane and into a dialysis solution *(dialysate)*. It corrects fluid and electrolyte imbalances and removes waste products in kidney failure. It also can be used to treat drug overdoses.

The 2 methods of dialysis available are **peritoneal dialysis (PD)** and **hemodialysis (HD)** (Table 51.12).[23,24] In PD the peritoneal membrane acts as the semipermeable membrane.[23] In HD an artificial membrane (usually made of cellulose-based or synthetic materials) is used as the semipermeable membrane and is in contact with the patient's blood.[24]

Dialysis is started when the patient's uremia can no longer be adequately treated with conservative medical management. Generally, this is when the GFR is less than 15 mL/min/1.73 m^2.[24] This criterion can vary widely in different clinical situations. The nephrologist decides when to start dialysis based on the patient's clinical status. Certain uremic complications, such as encephalopathy, neuropathies, hyperkalemia, pericarditis,

TABLE 51.12 Comparison of Peritoneal Dialysis and Hemodialysis

Advantages	Disadvantages
Peritoneal Dialysis (PD)	
• Immediate initiation in almost any hospital • Less complicated than hemodialysis • Portable system with CAPD • Fewer diet restrictions • Short training time • Usable in patient with vascular access problems • Less cardiovascular stress • Home dialysis possible • Preferable for patient with diabetes	• Bacterial or chemical peritonitis • Protein loss into dialysate • Exit site and tunnel infections • Self-image problems with catheter placement • Hyperglycemia • Surgery for catheter placement • Contraindicated in patient with multiple abdominal surgeries, trauma, unrepaired hernia • Requires completion of education program • Catheter can migrate • Best instituted with willing partner
Hemodialysis (HD)	
• Rapid fluid removal • Rapid removal of urea and creatinine • Effective potassium removal • Less protein loss • Lowering of serum triglycerides • Home dialysis possible • Can place temporary access at bedside	• Vascular access problems • Diet and fluid restrictions • Heparinization may be necessary • Extensive equipment necessary • Hypotension during dialysis • Added blood loss that contributes to anemia • Specially trained personnel necessary • Surgery for permanent access placement • Self-image problems with permanent access

and accelerated hypertension, indicate a need for immediate dialysis.

Most patients with ESRD are treated with dialysis because (1) there is a lack of donated organs, (2) some patients are physically or mentally unsuitable for a transplant, or (3) some patients do not want transplants. An increasing number of people, including older adults and those with complex medical problems, are receiving maintenance dialysis. A patient's age is not a factor in determining candidacy for dialysis.[22]

General Principles of Dialysis

Solutes and water move across the semipermeable membrane from the blood to the dialysate or from the dialysate to the blood per concentration gradients. Diffusion, osmosis, and ultrafiltration are involved in dialysis (Fig. 51.4). *Diffusion* is the movement of solutes from an area of greater concentration to an area of lesser concentration. In kidney failure, urea, creatinine, uric acid, and electrolytes (potassium, phosphate) move from the blood to the dialysate with the net effect of lowering their concentration in the blood. RBCs, WBCs, and plasma proteins are too large to diffuse through the pores of the membrane. Small-molecular-weight substances can pass from the dialysate into a patient's blood, so we must monitor and control the water purity used for dialysis.

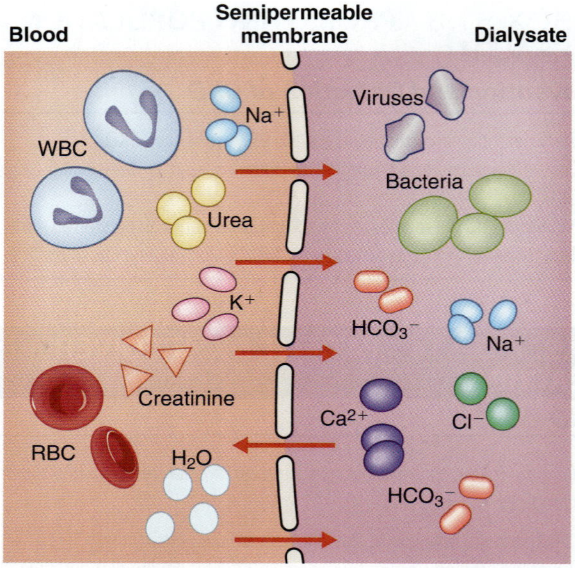

Fig. 51.4 Osmosis and diffusion across a semipermeable membrane.

Osmosis is the movement of fluid from an area of lesser concentration to an area of greater concentration of solutes. Glucose in the dialysate creates an osmotic gradient across the membrane, pulling excess fluid from the blood.

Ultrafiltration (water and fluid removal) results when there is an osmotic gradient or pressure gradient across the membrane. In PD, excess fluid is removed by increasing the osmolality of the dialysate (osmotic gradient) by adding glucose. In HD, the gradient is created by increasing pressure in the blood compartment (positive pressure) or decreasing pressure in the dialysate compartment (negative pressure). ECF moves into the dialysate because of the pressure gradient. The excess fluid is removed by creating a pressure differential between the blood and the dialysate solution with a combination of positive pressure in the blood compartment and negative pressure in the dialysate compartment.

PERITONEAL DIALYSIS

PD started to come into widespread use in the 1970s. That was when we developed soft, pliable peritoneal solution bags and continuous PD. The passage of the Executive Order on Advancing American Kidney Health in 2019 supported transplants and home dialysis. This led to more patients in the United States receiving PD.[23]

Catheter Placement

Peritoneal access is obtained by inserting a catheter through the anterior abdominal wall (Fig. 51.5). The catheter is about 24 in (60 cm) long and has 1 or 2 Dacron cuffs. The cuffs act as anchors and prevent the migration of microorganisms into the peritoneum. Within a few weeks, fibrous tissue grows into the Dacron cuff, holding the catheter in place and preventing bacterial penetration into the peritoneal cavity. The tip of the catheter rests in the peritoneal cavity. It has many perforations spaced along the distal end of the tubing, allowing fluid movement through the catheter.

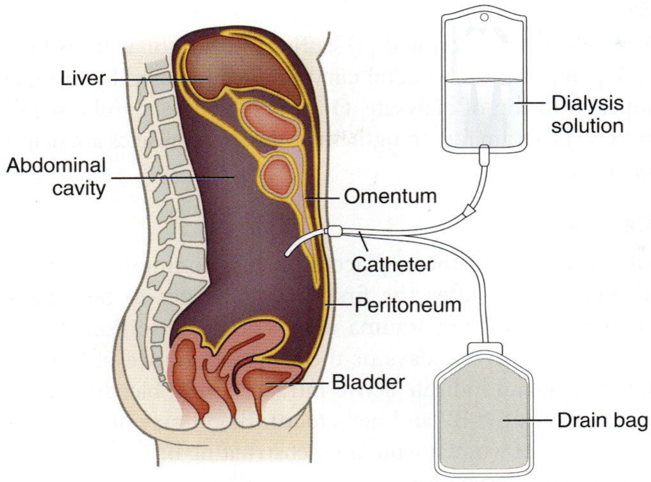

Fig. 51.5 PD showing peritoneal catheter inserted into peritoneal cavity.

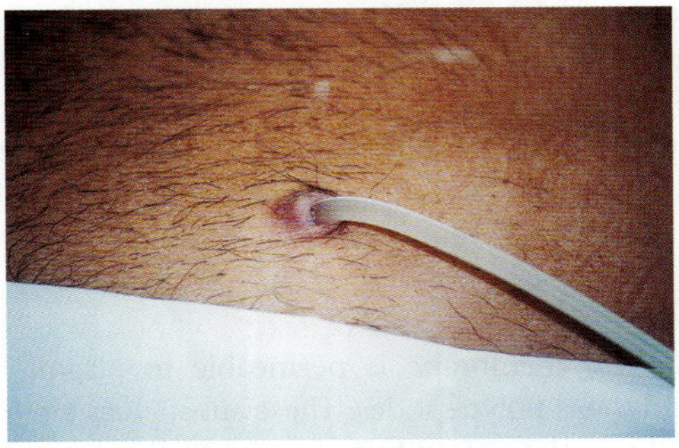

Fig. 51.6 Peritoneal catheter exit site. (Courtesy Mary Jo Holechek, Baltimore, MD.)

The technique for catheter placement varies. It is usually placed surgically so that the catheter can be seen directly, minimizing potential complications. Patient preparation for catheter insertion includes emptying the bladder and bowel, weighing the patient, and obtaining a signed consent form. After placement, PD may be started at once with low-volume exchanges or delayed for 2 weeks pending healing and sealing of the exit site. Once the catheter incision site is healed, the patient may shower and then pat the catheter and exit site dry.[23] Daily catheter care varies. Some patients just wash with soap and water and go without a dressing (Fig. 51.6). Others need daily dressing changes. Showering is preferred to bathing.

In PD it is critical to maintain aseptic technique to avoid peritonitis. Several tubing connections and devices are available to help maintain an aseptic system. Teach all patients to check their catheter site for signs of infection.

Dialysis Solutions and Cycles

PD is done by putting dialysis solution into the peritoneal space. The 3 phases of the PD cycle are inflow (fill), dwell (equilibration), and drain. Together, the 3 phases are an *exchange*. For manual PD, it takes about 30 to 50 minutes to complete an exchange. During *inflow*, a prescribed amount of solution, usually 2 L, is infused through an established catheter over about 10 minutes. The flow rate may be decreased if the patient has pain. After infusing the solution, the inflow clamp is closed.

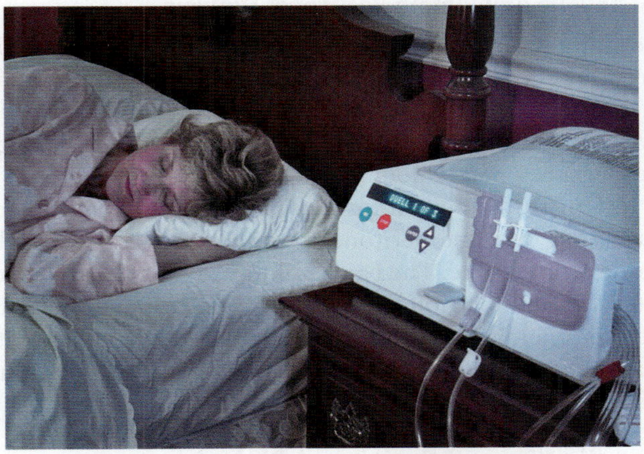

Fig. 51.7 Automated PD can be used while the patient is sleeping.

The next part of the cycle is the *dwell* phase, or equilibration. This is when diffusion and osmosis occur between the patient's blood and peritoneal cavity. The duration of the dwell time is usually between 4 and 6 hours. *Drain* time takes 15 to 30 minutes. It may be facilitated by gently massaging the abdomen or changing position. The cycle starts again with the infusion of another 2 L of solution.

PD solutions vary. The exchange volume is mainly determined by the size of the peritoneal cavity. An average-size person typically uses a 2-L exchange. A larger person may need a 3-L exchange volume. Smaller exchange volumes are used for patients with a smaller body, pulmonary compromise (the added pressure of the large volume may cause respiratory problems), or inguinal hernias.

Ultrafiltration (fluid removal) during PD depends on osmotic forces. Dextrose is the most often used osmotic agent in PD solutions. It is safe and inexpensive. It is associated with high rates of peritoneal glucose absorption. This can lead to problems with hypertriglyceridemia, hyperglycemia, and long-term peritoneal membrane dysfunction.

Alternatives to dextrose PD solution include icodextrin and amino acid solutions. Icodextrin is a commercially available iso-osmolar preparation. It induces ultrafiltration by its oncotic effect. Amino acid PD solutions are an option for patients who need nutrition supplementation.

Peritoneal Dialysis Systems

Automated Peritoneal Dialysis

Automated peritoneal dialysis (APD) is the most popular form of PD because it allows patients to do dialysis while they sleep. An automated device called a *cycler* delivers the dialysate for APD (Fig. 51.7). The automated cycler times and controls the fill, dwell, and drain phases. The machine cycles 4 or more exchanges per night with 1 to 2 hours per exchange. Alarms and monitors built into the system make it safe for the patient to sleep while dialyzing. The patient disconnects from the machine in the morning. They usually leave fluid in the abdomen during the day.

It is hard to achieve the required solute and fluid clearance solely with nighttime APD. One or 2 daytime manual exchanges may be needed to ensure adequate dialysis.

Continuous Ambulatory Peritoneal Dialysis

Continuous ambulatory peritoneal dialysis (CAPD) is done every few hours during the day. The patient may perform an exchange of 2 L of peritoneal dialysate 4 times daily, with dwell times averaging 4 hours. A common schedule includes exchanges at 7 AM, 12 noon, 5 PM, and 10 PM.

In CAPD, the person instills 2 to 3 L of dialysate from a plastic bag into the peritoneal cavity through a disposable administration line. The bag and line are then disconnected. After the equilibration period, the line is reconnected to the catheter, the dialysate (effluent) is drained from the peritoneal cavity, and a new 2- to 3-L bag of dialysate solution is infused.

Complications of Peritoneal Dialysis

Exit Site Infection

Infection of the peritoneal catheter exit site is most often caused by *Staphylococcus aureus* or *Staphylococcus epidermidis* (from skin flora). Manifestations include redness at the site, tenderness, and drainage. Superficial exit site infections caused by these organisms generally resolve with antibiotic therapy. If not treated quickly, subcutaneous tunnel infections may progress and cause peritonitis, requiring catheter removal.

Peritonitis

Peritonitis results from contact contamination or an exit site or tunnel infection. Most often it occurs because of improper technique when connections for exchanges are contaminated. Peritonitis is usually caused by *S. aureus* or *S. epidermidis*. It rarely results from bacteria in the intestine crossing into the peritoneal cavity.

The main manifestations are abdominal pain, rebound tenderness, and cloudy peritoneal effluent with a WBC count greater than 100 cells/μL (more than 50% neutrophils) or bacteria in the peritoneal effluent shown by Gram stain or culture. GI manifestations may include diarrhea, vomiting, abdominal distention, and hyperactive bowel sounds. Fever may be present. To determine if the peritoneal effluent is cloudy, drain the effluent and place the drained bag on reading material, such as a newspaper. If you cannot read the print through the effluent, it is cloudy.

Cultures, Gram stain, and a WBC differential of the peritoneal effluent are used to confirm the diagnosis of peritonitis. Antibiotics can be given orally, IV, or intraperitoneally. In most cases, the patient is treated on an outpatient basis.

The formation of adhesions in the peritoneum can result from repeated infections and interferes with the peritoneal membrane's ability to act as a dialyzing surface. Repeated infections may require the removal of the peritoneal catheter and a temporary or permanent change of modality to HD.

Hernias

Increased intraabdominal pressure from the dialysate volume can cause hernias to develop in predisposed persons, such as multiparous women and older men. After hernia repair, PD often can be resumed after several days using small dialysate volumes and keeping the patient supine.

Lower Back Problems

Increased intraabdominal pressure can cause or worsen lower back pain. The lumbosacral curvature is increased by intraperitoneal infusion of dialysate. Orthopedic binders and a regular exercise program for strengthening the back muscles are helpful for some patients.

Bleeding

After peritoneal catheter placement, it is common for the PD effluent drained after the first few exchanges to be pink or slightly bloody from trauma after catheter insertion. Bloody effluent over several days or the new appearance of blood in the effluent can indicate active intraperitoneal bleeding. If this occurs, check the BP and hematocrit. Blood may be present in the effluent of women who are menstruating or ovulating. This requires no intervention.

Pulmonary Complications

Atelectasis, pneumonia, and bronchitis may occur from repeated upward displacement of the diaphragm, resulting in decreased lung expansion. Longer dwell times increase the risk for pulmonary problems. Frequent repositioning and deep-breathing exercises can help. When the patient is lying in bed, elevate the head of the bed to prevent these problems.

Protein Loss

The peritoneal membrane is permeable to plasma proteins, amino acids, and polypeptides. These substances are lost in the dialysate fluid. The amount of loss is usually about 0.5 g/L of dialysate drainage, but it can be as high as 10 to 20 g/day. This loss may increase to as much as 40 g/day during episodes of peritonitis as the peritoneal membrane becomes more permeable. Unresolved peritonitis can cause excessive protein loss that can result in malnutrition. PD may need to stop temporarily or sometimes permanently.

Effectiveness of Chronic Peritoneal Dialysis

Mortality rates are similar between in-center HD patients and PD patients for the first few years. After about 2 years, mortality rates for patients receiving PD increase, especially for the older person with diabetes and patients with a prior history of CVD.[23]

The main advantage of PD is its simplicity. It is a home-based program, increasing patient participation in their care. Learning the skills needed to do PD usually involves a 3- to 7-day training program. There is no need for special water systems. Equipment setup is fairly simple.

HEMODIALYSIS

Vascular Access Sites

HD requires a very rapid blood flow and access to a large blood vessel. Obtaining vascular access is one of the biggest problems associated with HD. Enough time is needed to determine the best arteriovenous (AV) access for HD. The types of vascular access include AV fistulas (AVFs), AV grafts (AVGs), and temporary vascular access.[25]

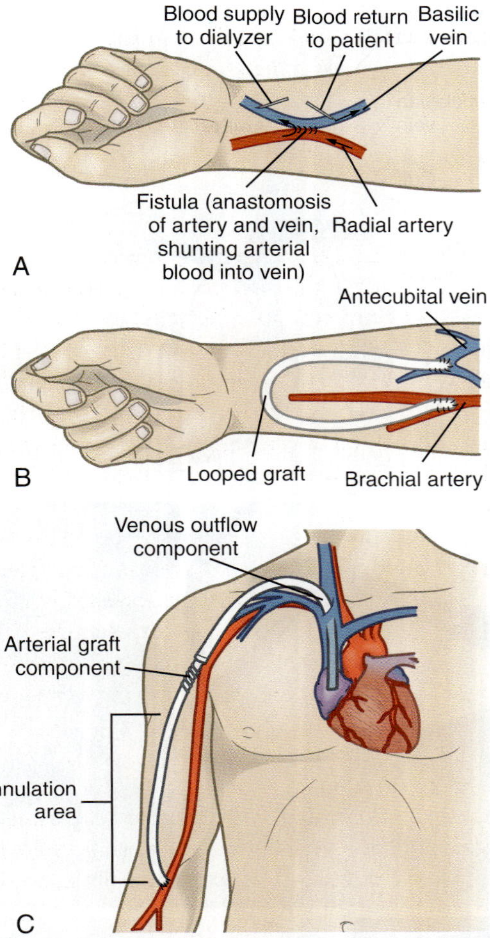

Fig. 51.8 Vascular access for hemodialysis. (A) AVF. (B) AVG. (C) HeRO Graft.

Arteriovenous Fistulas and Grafts

A subcutaneous **arteriovenous fistula (AVF)** is usually created in the forearm or upper arm with an anastomosis between an artery and a vein (usually cephalic or basilic) (Figs. 51.8A and 51.9). The fistula allows arterial blood to flow through the vein.

The vein becomes "arterialized," increasing in size and developing thicker walls. The arterial blood flow is essential to supply the rapid blood flow needed for HD. As the fistula matures, it is more amenable to repeated venipunctures. Maturation may take 6 weeks to months. AVF should be placed at least 3 months before starting HD. A fistula is the preferred access for HD.

Normally, a *thrill* (buzzing sensation) can be felt by palpating the fistula, and a *bruit* (rushing sound) can be heard with a stethoscope. The thrill and bruit are created by arterial blood moving at a high velocity through the vein.

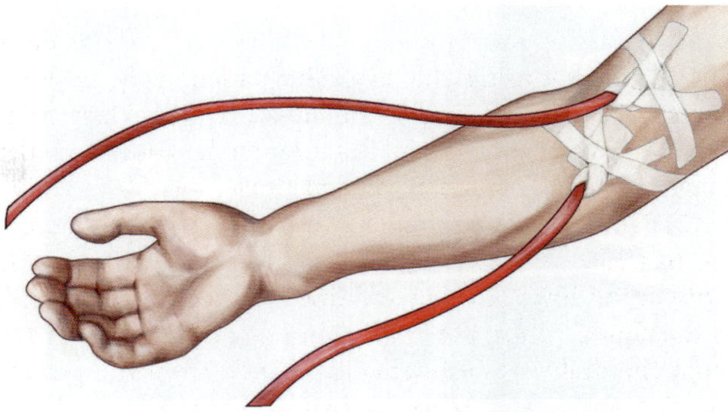

Fig. 51.9 AVF with cannulation needles for HD access.

AVFs are harder to create in patients with a history of severe peripheral vascular disease (e.g., people with diabetes), those with prolonged IV drug use, and obese women. These persons may need a synthetic graft.

Arteriovenous grafts (AVGs) are made of synthetic materials (polytetrafluoroethylene [PTFE, Teflon]). They form a "bridge" between the arterial and venous blood supplies. Grafts are placed under the skin and surgically anastomosed between an artery (usually brachial) and a vein (usually antecubital) (Fig. 51.8B). An interval of 2 to 4 weeks is usually needed to allow the graft to heal, but it may be used earlier. Because grafts are made of artificial materials, they are more likely than AVFs to become infected and tend to form clots. When AVG infections occur, they may need surgically removed, since it is hard to resolve infection from the synthetic material.

A common problem is central venous stenosis (CVS) or occlusion. CVS is serious because the central veins are the final pathway for blood flow to the heart. As CVS progresses, vascular access for HD is often lost.

A special bridge graft can be used in patients when other access options are exhausted. The Hemodialysis Reliable Outflow (HeRO) consists of 2 pieces: a reinforced tube to bypass blockages in veins and a graft anastomosed to an artery for HD access (Fig. 51.8C). It is placed under the skin, like both a fistula and standard graft. It bypasses the venous system and provides blood flow directly from a target artery to the heart. You may find it harder to auscultate the bruit or feel the thrill because of the absence of a venous anastomosis.

Surgical creation of AV access for HD has several risks. These include distal ischemia *(steal syndrome)* and pain because too much arterial blood is being shunted or "stolen" from the distal

CHECK YOUR PRACTICE

It is your first time working with a HD patient on your unit. You are helping a HD tech "hook up" a 56-year-old man to HD. He has been on HD for 5 years due to polycystic kidney disease. You take his vital signs, palpate his AV fistula, and then use your stethoscope to auscultate the AV fistula. You are concerned because you feel a super-strong pulse and hear a very loud "whoosh" sound. The patient turns to you and just smirks, "I bet you have never had a thrill like that."

- You are very flustered and not sure how to respond. What should you say to him?

SAFETY ALERT

AV Fistulas and Grafts

- Never perform BP measurements, IV line insertion, or venipuncture in an extremity with AV access.
- These precautions are taken to prevent infection and clotting of the vascular access.
- Place signs in patient's room and label the arm with a band that says, "No BP, blood draws, or IV in this arm."

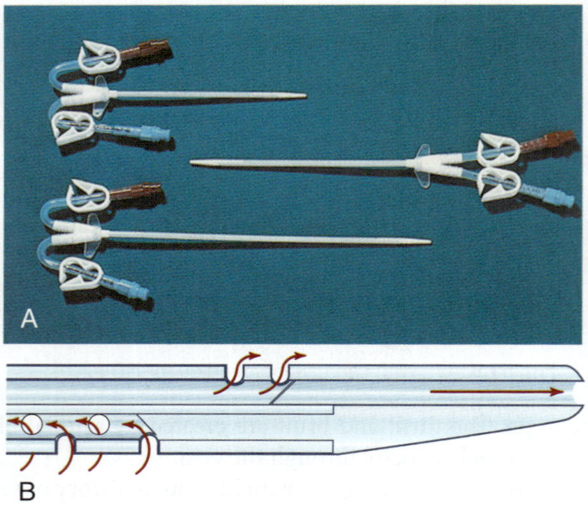

Fig. 51.10 Temporary double-lumen vascular access catheter for acute hemodialysis. (A) Soft, flexible double-lumen tube is attached to a Y hub. (B) The distance between the arterial intake lumen and the venous return lumen typically provides recirculation rates of 5% or less. (A, Courtesy Quinton Instrument Co., Seattle, WA.)

extremity. Manifestations of steal syndrome are pain distal to the access site, numbness or tingling of fingers that may worsen during HD, and poor capillary refill. Aneurysms can develop in the AV access and can rupture if left untreated.

Temporary Vascular Access

When immediate vascular access is needed, catheterization of the internal jugular or femoral vein is done. A flexible catheter inserted at the bedside into 1 of these large veins gives access to the circulation without surgery (Fig. 51.10). The catheters usually have a double external lumen with an internal septum separating the 2 internal segments. One lumen is used for blood removal and the other for blood return (Fig. 51.11A and B). Temporary catheters have high rates of infection, dislodgment, and malfunction. A patient should not be discharged from the hospital with a temporary catheter in place.

Long-term cuffed HD catheters are often used for temporary vascular access. These catheters give temporary access while the patient is waiting for fistula placement or as long-term access when other forms of access have failed. They exit on the upper chest wall and are tunneled subcutaneously to the internal or external jugular vein (Fig. 51.11C). The catheter tip rests in the right atrium. It has 1 or 2 subcutaneous Dacron cuffs that prevent infection from tracking along the catheter and anchor the catheter, eliminating the need for sutures.

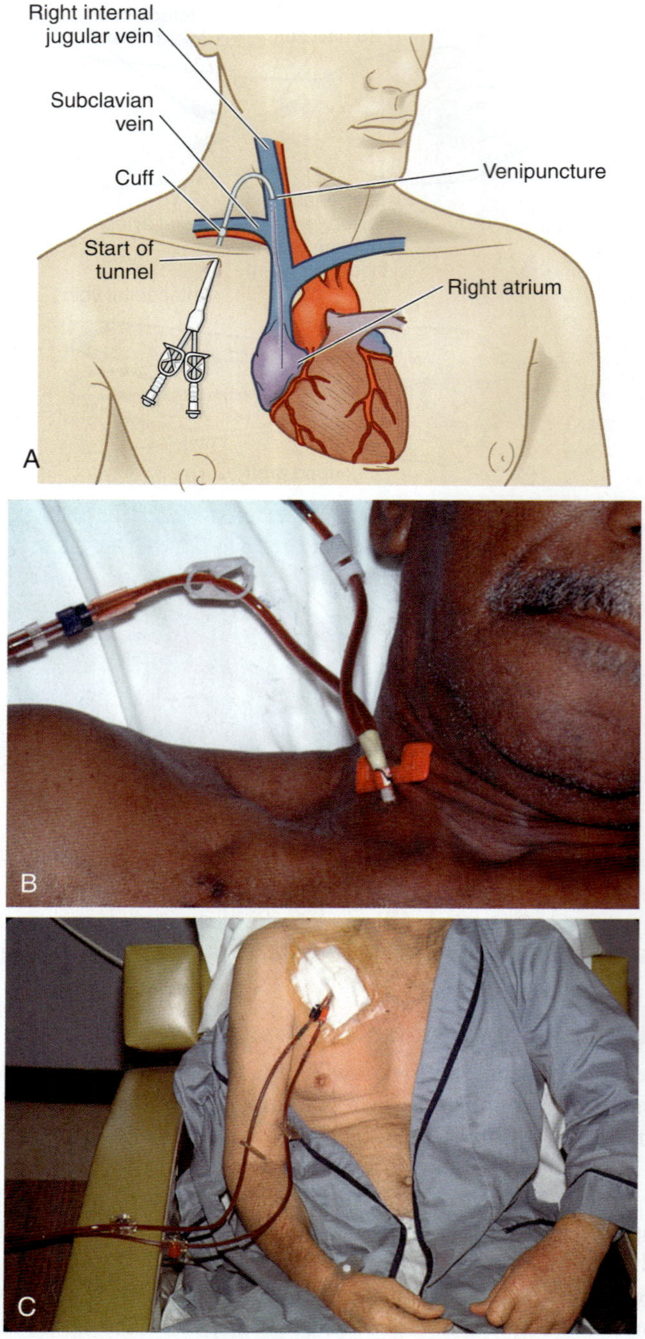

Fig. 51.11 (A) Right internal jugular placement for a tunneled, cuffed semipermanent catheter. (B) Temporary hemodialysis catheter in place. (C) Long-term cuffed hemodialysis catheter. (B and C, Courtesy Dr. Stephen Van Voorst, MD.)

Dialyzers

The HD dialyzer is a plastic cartridge that has thousands of parallel hollow tubes or fibers. The fibers are semipermeable membranes made of cellulose-based or other synthetic materials. The blood is pumped into the top of the cartridge and dispersed into all the fibers. Dialysis fluid *(dialysate)* is pumped into the bottom of the cartridge and bathes the outside of the fibers. Ultrafiltration, diffusion, and osmosis occur across the pores of this semipermeable membrane. When the dialyzed blood reaches the end of the thousands of semipermeable fibers, it converges into a single tube that returns it to the patient. Dialyzers differ in surface area, membrane composition and thickness, clearance of waste products, and removal of fluid.

Procedure for Hemodialysis

The needles used for HD are large bore, usually 14 to 16 gauge. They are inserted into the fistula or graft to obtain vascular access. One needle pulls blood from the circulation to the HD

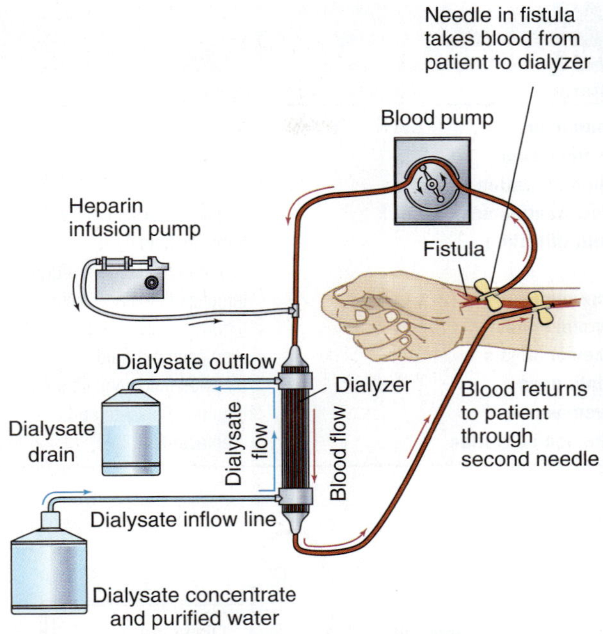

Fig. 51.12 Parts of a hemodialysis system. Blood is removed via a needle inserted in a fistula or via catheter lumen. A pump moves the blood to the dialyzer. Heparin is infused either as a predialysis bolus or through a heparin pump to prevent clotting. Dialysate flows in the opposite direction of the blood. The dialyzed blood is returned to the patient through a second needle or catheter lumen. Dialysate with waste products and ultrafiltrate are drained and discarded.

machine. The other needle returns the dialyzed blood to the patient. The needles are attached via tubing to dialysis lines. If a patient has a catheter, the 2 blood lines are attached to the 2 catheter lumens. The needle closer to the fistula (red catheter lumen) pulls blood from the patient to the dialyzer using a blood pump. Blood is returned from the dialyzer to the patient through the second needle (blue catheter lumen).[24]

When blood comes in contact with a foreign material, such as the dialyzer, it tends to clot. We add heparin to the blood to prevent clotting.

In addition to the dialyzer, we use a dialysate delivery and monitoring system (Fig. 51.12). This system pumps the dialysate through the dialyzer, countercurrent to the blood flow. To end the treatment, saline solution returns the blood in the extracorporeal circuit back to the patient through the vascular access. The needles are removed from the patient. Firm pressure is applied to the venipuncture sites until the bleeding stops.

Before beginning treatment, assess fluid status (weight, BP, peripheral edema, lung and heart sounds), condition of vascular access, and temperature. The difference between the last post-dialysis weight and the present predialysis weight determines the ultrafiltration or the amount of weight (from fluid) to be removed. While the patient is on HD, take vital signs at least every 30 to 60 minutes because rapid BP changes may occur.

Settings and Schedules for Hemodialysis

Most HD patients are treated in a community-based center and dialyze for 3 to 4 hours 3 days/week. Other schedule options are short daily HD and long nighttime HD. The patient receiving long nighttime HD has the advantage of sleeping while dialyzing. Each nighttime treatment lasts 6 to 8 hours. The patient dialyzes up to 6 times per week.

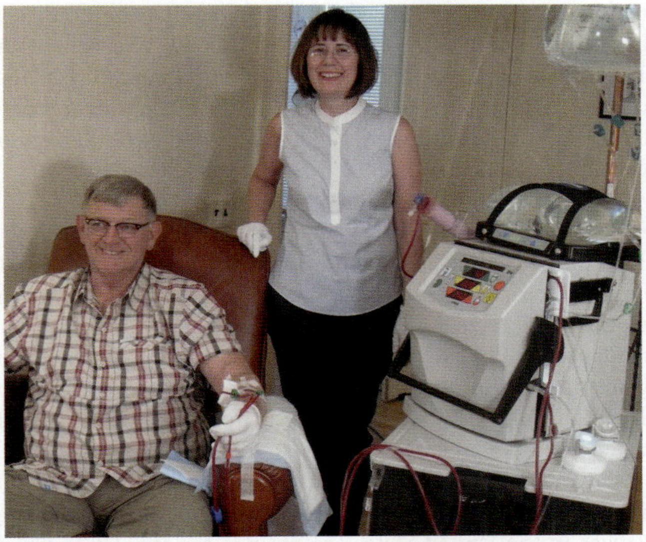

Fig. 51.13 Home hemodialysis is growing in popularity, and machines are more compact. (From NxStage Medical, Inc, Lawrence, MA.)

Home HD may be an option (Fig. 51.13). The use of home HD often depends on a patient's family support. One of the main advantages of home HD is that it allows greater freedom in choosing dialysis times. In short daily HD, the patient dialyzes for 2½ to 3 hours per session 5 to 6 days/week. Short daily HD is usually done at home.

Patients who choose daily or nighttime dialysis may have fewer uremic symptoms, tend to need fewer medications, and have fewer HD-related side effects (e.g., hypotension, cramps). In addition, they have more autonomy. Although daily home HD offers the potential of significant health benefits, only about 2% of HD patients dialyze at home.

Complications of Hemodialysis

Hypotension

Hypotension that occurs during HD often results from rapid removal of vascular volume (hypovolemia), decreased cardiac output, and decreased systemic vascular resistance. The drop in BP may cause lightheadedness, nausea, vomiting, seizures, vision changes, and chest pain from cardiac ischemia. The usual treatment for hypotension includes decreasing the volume of fluid removed and infusing 0.9% saline solution.

Muscle Cramps

We do not completely understand the cause of muscle cramps in HD. Risk factors for developing muscle cramps include hypotension, hypovolemia, high ultrafiltration rate (UFR), and low-sodium dialysis solution. Treatment includes reducing the UFR and giving fluids (saline, glucose, mannitol). Hypertonic saline is not recommended since the sodium load can be problematic. Hypertonic glucose is preferred.

Loss of Blood

Blood loss may result from blood not being completely rinsed from the dialyzer, accidental separation of blood tubing, dialysis membrane rupture, or bleeding after removing the needles at the end of HD. If a patient has received too much heparin or has clotting problems, postdialysis bleeding can occur. It is essential to rinse back all blood, avoid excess anticoagulation, and hold firm but nonocclusive pressure on access sites until the risk for bleeding has passed.

Hepatitis

Hepatitis B used to have an unusually high prevalence in HD patients, but the incidence today is low. Lower transfusion requirements, screening, and vaccinations have lowered the incidence. Outbreaks of hepatitis B still occur, likely from breaks in infection control practices. To prevent transmission, all patients and personnel in dialysis units receive hepatitis B vaccine.

Hepatitis C virus (HCV) causes most cases of hepatitis in HD patients (see Chapter 48). About 10% of patients receiving dialysis in the United States are positive for anti-HCV, which indicates a previous infection. Infection control precautions are mandated in caring for the patient with hepatitis C to protect the patient and staff (see Chapter 15). Currently no vaccine is available for hepatitis C.

Effectiveness of Hemodialysis

HD is still an imperfect therapy for management of ESRD. It cannot fully replace the normal biologic functions of the kidneys.[24] It can ease many of the symptoms of CKD and, if started early, can prevent certain complications. It does not alter the accelerated rate of CVD and the related high mortality rate. The yearly death rate of patients receiving maintenance HD is around 19% to 24%. CVD (stroke, MI) causes most deaths. Infectious complications are the second leading cause of death.[13,21]

Adaptation to maintenance HD varies considerably. At first, many patients feel positive about the dialysis because it makes them feel better and keeps them alive, but there is often great ambivalence about whether it is worthwhile. Dependence on a machine is a reality. In response to their illness, patients may be nonadherent, depressed, and show suicidal tendencies. Key nursing goals are to (1) help the patient to maintain a healthy self-image and (2) return the patient to the highest level of function possible, including returning to work.

CONTINUOUS RENAL REPLACEMENT THERAPY

Continuous renal replacement therapy (CRRT) is a method for treating AKI. It provides a means by which uremic toxins and fluids are removed while acid-base status and electrolytes are adjusted slowly and continuously in a hemodynamically unstable patient. The principle of CRRT is to dialyze patients in a more physiologic way (over 24 hours), just like the kidneys. CRRT is contraindicated if a patient has life-threatening manifestations of uremia (hyperkalemia, pericarditis) that need rapid treatment. CRRT can be used in conjunction with HD.

Several types of CRRT are available (Table 51.13). CRRT often uses a venovenous approach. Examples include continuous venovenous hemofiltration (CVVH), continuous venovenous hemodialysis (CVVHD), and continuous venovenous hemodiafiltration (CVVHDF).

TABLE 51.13 Continuous Renal Replacement Therapies

Therapy	Abbreviation	Purpose
Continuous venovenous hemofiltration	CVVH	Removes fluid and solutes Requires replacement fluid
Slow continuous ultrafiltration	SCUF	Simplified version of CVVH Removes fluid No fluid replacement required
Continuous venovenous hemodialysis	CVVHD	Removes fluids and solutes Requires dialysate and replacement fluid
Continuous venovenous hemodiafiltration	CVVHDF	Removes fluids and solutes Requires dialysate and replacement fluid

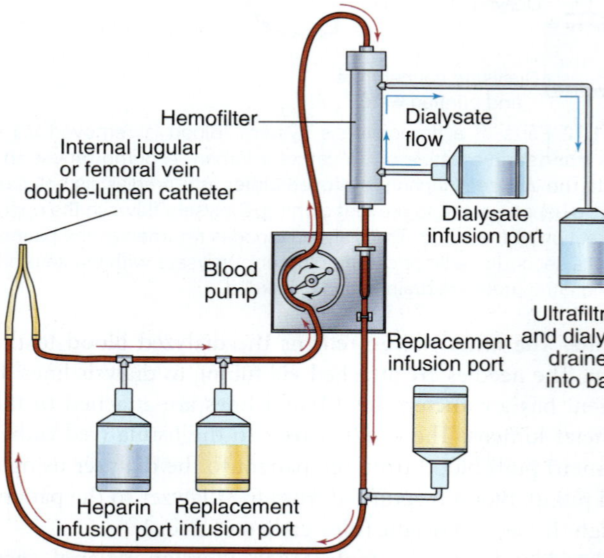

Fig. 51.14 Basic schematic of continuous venovenous therapies. A blood pump is needed to pump blood through the circuit. Replacement ports are used for instilling replacement fluids and can be given prefilter or postfilter. Dialysate port is used for infusing dialysis solution. Regardless of modality, ultrafiltrate is drained via the ultrafiltration drain port.

Vascular access for CRRT is achieved with a double-lumen catheter as used in HD (Figs. 51.10 and 51.11) placed in the jugular or femoral vein. A blood pump propels the blood through the circuit. A highly permeable, hollow-fiber hemofilter removes plasma water and nonprotein solutes, which are collectively termed *ultrafiltrate.* The UFR may range from 0 to 500 mL/h. Under the influence of hydrostatic pressure and osmotic pressure, water and nonprotein solutes pass out of the filter into the extracapillary space and drain through the ultrafiltrate port into a collection device (drainage bag) (Fig. 51.14). The remaining fluid continues through the filter and returns to the patient via the return port of the double-lumen catheter.

As ultrafiltrate drains out of the hemofilter, fluid and electrolyte replacements can be infused through a port found before or after the filter as the blood returns to the patient. Replacement fluid is designed to replace volume and solutes, such as sodium, chloride, HCO_3^-, and glucose. The infusion rate of replacement fluid is determined by the degree of fluid and electrolyte imbalance. Replacement fluid infused into the infusion port before the hemofilter allows for greater clearance of urea and can decrease filter clotting. An infusion port after the filter dilutes intravascular fluid and decreases the concentration of unwanted solutes, such as BUN, creatinine, and potassium. Anticoagulants are given to prevent blood clotting. They may be infused as a bolus at the start of CRRT or through an infusion port before the hemofilter.

The type of CRRT is determined by the patient's needs. Some types involve giving replacement fluids. CVVHD and CVVHDF use dialysate. Dialysis fluid is attached to the distal end of the hemofilter, and the fluid is pumped countercurrent to the blood flow (Fig. 51.14). As in HD, diffusion of solutes and ultrafiltration via hydrostatic pressure and osmosis occur. This is an ideal treatment for a patient who needs both fluid and solute control but cannot tolerate the rapid fluid shifts associated with HD.

Several features of CRRT differ from HD:

- The blood pump in CRRT runs at a slower (150 mL/min average) rate. This may improve hemodynamic stability.
- Continuous rather than intermittent. Fluid volume can be removed over days (24 hours to more than 2 weeks) versus hours (3 to 4 hours).
- Solute removal can occur by *convection* (no dialysate needed) in addition to osmosis and diffusion.
- Causes less hemodynamic instability (e.g., hypotension)
- Does not need constant monitoring by a specialized HD nurse but does require a trained ICU nurse
- Does not require complicated HD equipment

CRRT can be continued as long as 30 to 40 days. Change the hemofilter every 24 to 48 hours because of loss of filtration efficiency or potential for clotting. The ultrafiltrate should be clear yellow. Specimens may be obtained for serum chemistries. If the ultrafiltrate becomes bloody or blood tinged, suspect a rupture in the filter membrane. Stop treatment to prevent blood loss.

Specific nursing care includes obtaining weights and monitoring and documenting laboratory values daily to ensure adequate fluid and electrolyte balance. Assess hourly intake and output, vital signs, and hemodynamic status. Although we expect central venous pressure and pulmonary artery pressure to decrease, there should be little change in mean arterial pressure or cardiac output. Assess and maintain the patency of the CRRT system. Care for the patient's vascular access site to prevent infection. Once the patient's AKI is resolved or there is a decision to withdraw treatment, CRRT is stopped, and the needle(s) removed.

WEARABLE ARTIFICIAL KIDNEY

The wearable artificial kidney is a miniaturized dialysis machine that can be worn on the body. The carrier resembles a tool belt. The device connects to a patient via a catheter. Like conventional dialysis machines, it filters the blood of ESRD patients. Unlike current portable or stationary dialysis machines, it can run continuously on batteries. The present version weighs about 10 lb. Future modifications could make it lighter and more streamlined.[26] The WAK has greatly improved the quality of life for some ESRD patients.

KIDNEY TRANSPLANTATION

Major advances have been made in kidney transplants since the first live donor kidney transplant was done in 1954 between identical twins. These advances include organ procurement and preservation, surgical techniques, tissue typing and matching, immunosuppressant therapy, and preventing and treating graft rejection. General information about organ transplants is in Chapter 14.

Even though a kidney transplant is the best treatment option for patients with ESRD, fewer than 4% have a transplant. This is due to the large disparity between the supply and demand for kidneys. Every year thousands are waiting for kidney transplants (more than 120,000 are currently on the list), yet only about 24,000 transplants take place every year. Most die while waiting. Transplants from a deceased (cadaveric) donor usually require a prolonged waiting period, with differences in waiting time depending on age, gender, and race. Average wait times in the United States for a deceased kidney usually range from 2 to 5 years.[27]

Kidney transplants are very successful. 1-year graft survival rates are over 90% for deceased donor transplants and 95% for live donor transplants.[27] An advantage of a kidney transplant compared with dialysis is that it reverses many of the pathophysiologic changes associated with renal disease. It eliminates the dependence on dialysis and the accompanying diet and lifestyle restrictions. A transplant is less expensive than dialysis after the first year.

Recipient Selection

Appropriate recipient selection is important for a successful outcome. Candidacy is determined by a variety of medical and psychosocial factors (Box 51.4). These factors vary among transplant centers. Some programs exclude patients who are morbidly obese or continue to smoke despite smoking cessation interventions. A careful evaluation is done to identify and minimize potential complications after the transplant. Certain patients, particularly those with CVD and diabetes, are considered high risk. They must be carefully evaluated and then monitored closely after the transplant.[28]

For a small number of patients who are approaching ESRD, a *preemptive transplant* (before dialysis is needed) is possible if they have a living donor. This approach is best for patients with diabetes because they have a much higher mortality rate on dialysis.

Contraindications to a transplant include advanced cancer, refractory or untreated heart disease, chronic respiratory failure, extensive vascular disease, chronic infection, and unresolved psychosocial disorders (e.g., nonadherence to treatment plan, alcohol use, drug use). Being HIV-positive or having hepatitis B or C infection is not a contraindication.

The patient may need other surgeries before having a transplant. Coronary artery bypass or coronary angioplasty may be needed for advanced coronary artery disease. Cholecystectomy may be necessary for patients with a history of gallstones,

BOX 51.4 ETHICAL/LEGAL DILEMMAS

Allocation of Resources

Situation

T.H., a transplant nurse coordinator, is considering her feelings about 2 patients who are being evaluated for placement on the deceased kidney transplant waiting list. One patient is a 40-year-old schoolteacher. She is married and has 2 children. The other patient is a 22-year-old unemployed man. He misses 3 or 4 dialysis treatments per month and does not take his antihypertensive drugs consistently.

Ethical/Legal Points for Consideration

- Ethical principles that are important in the allocation of human organs include utility and justice.
- Allocation policies based on utility require we use standardized outcome measures to give a rough estimate about which allocation would produce the greatest good. Factors considered include patient survival, quality of life, availability of alternative treatments, and age.
- We must give equal respect and concern to each patient. Allocation based on social characteristics (e.g., race, socioeconomic class, gender) conflict with the principle of justice and violate constitutional law.
- Constitutional laws prohibit discrimination based on race, gender, religion, and ethnic background. It is highly unlikely that these standard prohibitions will change. It is possible that definitions of unhealthy behavior, such as substance use, alcohol use, smoking, and obesity, may be used to screen out candidates.
- Nurses are concerned about social justice because of their health advocacy role. Today the situation is immensely more complex because of the cost and availability of care.

Discussion Questions

1. What does the American Nurses Association Code of Ethics say about how you as a nurse should view patients?
2. What are your thoughts about which patient should receive the next available kidney transplant?
3. Can you assign value to the lives of various patients? Who is worth more?

biliary obstruction, or cholecystitis. On rare occasions, bilateral nephrectomies are done for patients with refractory hypertension, recurrent UTIs, or grossly enlarged kidneys from polycystic kidney disease. In general, the recipient's own kidneys are not removed before receiving a kidney transplant.

Histocompatibility Studies

Histocompatibility studies, including human leukocyte antigen (HLA) testing and crossmatching, are discussed in Chapter 14.

Donor Sources

Kidneys for transplants are obtained from compatible blood-type deceased donors, blood relatives, emotionally related (close and distant) living donors (e.g., spouses, distant cousins), and altruistic living donors who are known (friends) or unknown to the recipient. Living donation accounts for around 27% of all kidney transplants in the United States. Most transplant centers regard them as the preferred donation modality.[27]

Live Donors

Live donors undergo an extensive evaluation to ensure that they are in good health and have no history of disease that would place them at risk for developing kidney disease or operative complications. Crossmatches are done at the time of the evaluation and about a week before the transplant to ensure that no antibodies to the donor are present or that the antibody titer is below the allowed level. Advantages of a live donor kidney include (1) better patient and graft survival rates regardless of histocompatibility match, (2) immediate organ availability, (3) immediate function due to minimal *cold time* (kidney out of body and not getting blood supply), and (4) the opportunity to have the recipient in the best possible health since the surgery is elective.

The potential donor sees a nephrologist for a complete history and physical assessment and laboratory and diagnostic studies. Laboratory studies include a 24-hour urine study for creatinine clearance and total protein, complete blood count, and chemistry and electrolyte profiles. Hepatitis B and C, HIV, and cytomegalovirus (CMV) testing is done to assess for transmitted diseases. An ECG and chest x-ray are done. A renal ultrasound and renal arteriogram or 3-dimensional CT scan is done to ensure that the blood vessels supplying each kidney are adequate and that no anomalies exist and to see which kidney will be used in the transplant.

A transplant psychologist or social worker determines if the person is emotionally stable and able to deal with the issues related to organ donation. All donors must be informed about the risks and benefits of donation, the potential short- and long-term complications, and what to expect during the hospitalization and recovery phases. Kidney donation is considered safe without any long-term health consequences. Although the recipient's insurance covers the costs of the evaluation and surgery, no compensation is available for lost wages during the posthospitalization recovery period. This period can last 6 weeks or longer.

When there is ABO incompatibility between a donor and recipient, paired donor exchange is a viable alternative. *Paired organ donation* occurs when one donor/recipient pair who are incompatible or poorly matched with each other find another donor/recipient pair with whom they can exchange kidneys. Thus, a spouse (person A) who wants to donate a kidney to his wife (person B) but is incompatible is paired with another donor/recipient pair involving a son with ESRD (person C) and his mother (person D). In this example, person A would donate his kidney to person C, and person D would donate her kidney to person B. Paired organ donation is the practice of matching biologically incompatible donor/recipient pairs to permit transplantation of both candidates with a well-matched organ.

Another option for ABO incompatibility or a positive crossmatch between the donor and recipient is to use plasmapheresis to remove antibodies from the recipient. This allows transplant candidates to receive kidneys from live donors with blood types that we have traditionally considered incompatible. After the transplant, the patient has more plasmapheresis treatments.

Deceased Donors

Deceased (cadaver) kidney donors are fairly healthy persons who have an irreversible brain injury and are declared brain dead. The most common causes of injury are cerebral trauma from motor vehicle accidents or gunshot wounds, intracerebral or subarachnoid hemorrhage, and anoxic brain damage caused by cardiac arrest. The brain-dead donor must have effective CV function and be supported on a ventilator to preserve the organs.

Even if the donor carried a signed donor card, permission from the donor's legal next of kin is still requested after brain death has been declared. That is why it is important for you to talk with your family about your wishes before losing the capacity to convey your desires.

In deceased kidney donation, the kidneys are removed and preserved. They can be preserved for up to 72 hours. Most transplant surgeons prefer to transplant kidneys before the cold time (time outside of the body when being transported from the deceased donor to the recipient) reaches 24 hours. Prolonged cold time increases the chance that the kidney will not function immediately. ATN may develop.

The United Network for Organ Sharing (UNOS) distributes deceased donor kidneys using an objective computerized point system. The kidney allocation system (KAS) provides all donor kidneys a kidney donor profile index (KDPI). The KDPI includes 10 donor factors that evaluate the risk for a kidney transplant failure. The KDPI can help predict how long a kidney may function. Each kidney transplant candidate gets an Estimated Post-Transplant Survival (EPTS) score. This score ranges from 0% to 100%. The score is related to how long a candidate will need a functioning kidney transplant when compared with other candidates. For example, a person with an EPTS score of 20% is likely to need a kidney longer than 80% of other candidates. The EPTS score is based on age, length of time on dialysis, previous transplants, and having diabetes.[29]

When a donor becomes available, the donor's key information is compared with the data of all patients awaiting a transplant locally and nationwide. When a kidney arrives at the recipient's transplant center, a final crossmatch is done. It must be negative for the deceased donor transplant to proceed.

The only exception is if a patient needs an emergency transplant or if a donor and recipient match on all 6 HLA antigens (zero antigen mismatch). The patient meeting either of these criteria goes to the top of the list. Emergency transplants receive priority because the patient is facing imminent death if not transplanted. If a zero-antigen mismatch patient is found nationally, since statistically these grafts have better survival rates, one of the donor kidneys must be sent to that recipient's transplant center regardless of location.

Surgical Procedure

Live Donor

A transplant surgeon performs the live donor nephrectomy. The donor's surgery begins 1 to 2 hours before the recipient's surgery. The recipient is surgically prepared for the kidney transplant in a nearby operating room.

Laparoscopic donor nephrectomy is the most common technique for removing a kidney in a living donor. Laparoscopic nephrectomy is discussed in Chapter 50. After the kidney is removed, it is flushed with a chilled, sterile electrolyte solution and prepared for immediate transplant into the recipient. The use of this procedure is minimally invasive, with fewer risks and shorter recovery time than an open procedure. The laparoscopic approach significantly decreases hospital stay, pain, operative blood loss, debilitation, and length of time off work. For these reasons, the number of people willing to donate a kidney has increased significantly.

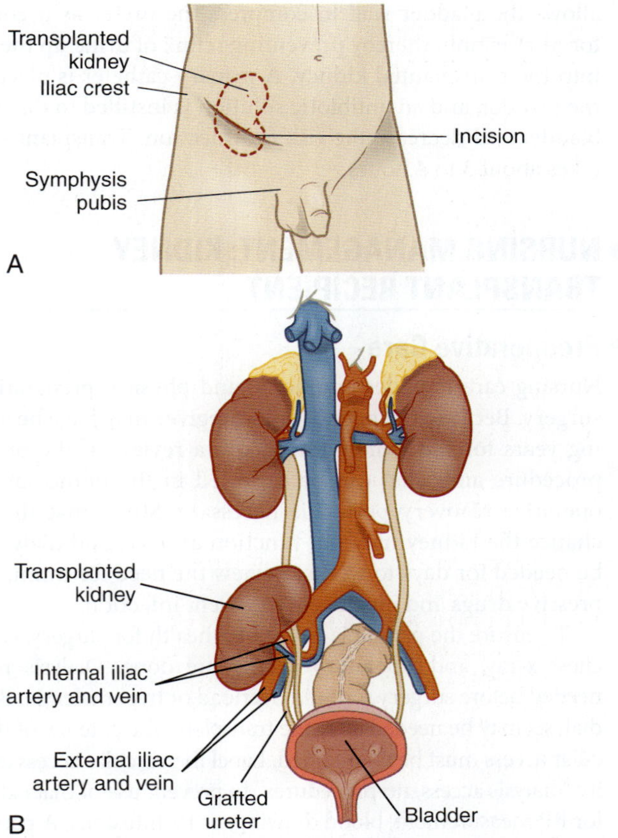

Fig. 51.15 (A) Surgical incision for a renal transplant. (B) Surgical placement of transplanted kidney.

For an open (conventional) nephrectomy, the donor is placed in the lateral decubitus position on the operating table so that the flank is exposed laterally. An incision is made at the level of the eleventh rib. The rib may have to be removed to see the kidney.

Kidney Transplant Recipient

The transplanted kidney is usually placed extraperitoneally in the iliac fossa (Fig. 51.15). The right iliac fossa is preferred to facilitate anastomoses of the blood vessels and ureter and minimize the occurrence of paralytic ileus.

Rapid revascularization is critical to prevent ischemic injury to the kidney. The donor artery is anastomosed to the recipient's internal iliac (hypogastric) or external iliac artery. The donor vein is anastomosed to the recipient's external iliac vein. When the anastomoses are complete, the clamps are released, and blood flow to the kidney is reestablished. The kidney should become firm and pink. Urine may begin to flow from the ureter at once. The donor ureter is then tunneled through the bladder submucosa before entering the bladder cavity and being sutured in place. This approach is called *ureteroneocystostomy*. This allows the bladder wall to compress the ureter as it contracts for micturition, thereby preventing reflux of urine up the ureter into the transplanted kidney. A urinary catheter is placed into the bladder, and an antibiotic solution is instilled to distend the bladder and decrease the risk for infection. Transplant surgery takes about 3 to 4 hours.

NURSING MANAGEMENT: KIDNEY TRANSPLANT RECIPIENT

Preoperative Care

Nursing care includes emotional and physical preparation for surgery. Because the patient and caregiver may have been waiting years for the kidney transplant, a review of the operative procedure and what can be expected in the immediate postoperative recovery period is necessary. Stress that there is a chance the kidney may not function at once, and dialysis may be needed for days to weeks. Review the need for immunosuppressive drugs and measures to prevent infection.

To ensure the patient is in the best health for surgery, an ECG, chest x-ray, and laboratory studies are done. Dialysis may be needed before surgery for fluid overload or hyperkalemia. Because dialysis may be needed after the transplant, the patency of the vascular access must be maintained. Label the vascular access extremity "dialysis access, no procedures" to prevent use of that extremity for BP measurement, blood drawing, or IV infusions. A patient on PD must empty the peritoneal cavity of all dialysate solution before going to surgery and have the PD catheter capped.

Postoperative Care

Live Donor

Postoperative care for the donor is similar to that after open (conventional) or laparoscopic nephrectomy (Chapter 50). Monitor renal function to assess for impairment and the hematocrit to assess for bleeding. Donors usually have more pain than the recipient. Donors who had an open surgical approach may have more pain than those after a laparoscopic approach.

Donors who had an open approach are usually discharged from the hospital in 4 or 5 days and return to work in 6 to 8 weeks. With a laparoscopic approach, donors are discharged from the hospital in 2 to 4 days and return to work in 4 to 6 weeks. The surgeon sees the donor 1 to 2 weeks after discharge.

Nurses caring for the living donor must acknowledge the precious gift that this person has given. The donor has taken physical, emotional, and financial risks to help the recipient. It is vital that the donor is not forgotten after surgery. The donor will need support if the donated organ does not work at once or for some reason fails.

Kidney Transplant Recipient

The priority during the postoperative period is maintaining fluid and electrolyte balance. Kidney transplant recipients require close monitoring and spend the first 12 to 24 hours in the ICU. Large volumes of urine may be made soon after the blood supply to the transplanted kidney is reestablished. This diuresis is due to the (1) new kidney's ability to filter BUN, which acts as an osmotic diuretic; (2) abundance of fluids given during the surgery; and (3) initial renal tubular dysfunction, which inhibits the kidney from concentrating urine normally. Urine output during this phase may be as high as 1 L/hr and gradually decreases as the BUN and serum creatinine levels return toward normal. Urine output is replaced with fluids milliliter for milliliter hourly for the first 12 to 24 hours.

Central venous pressure readings are essential for monitoring fluid status. Dehydration must be avoided to prevent renal hypoperfusion and renal tubular damage. Assess for hyponatremia and hypokalemia. They can occur with rapid diuresis. Treatment with potassium supplements or infusion of 0.9% normal saline may be needed. IV sodium bicarbonate may be given if the patient develops metabolic acidosis from a delay in the return of kidney function.

ATN in the transplanted kidney can occur because of prolonged cold times causing ischemic damage or the use of marginal cadaveric donors (those who are medically suboptimal). While the patient is in ATN, dialysis is needed to maintain fluid and electrolyte balance. Some patients have high-output ATN with the ability to excrete fluid but not metabolic wastes or electrolytes. Other patients have oliguric or anuric ATN. These patients are at risk for fluid overload in the immediate postoperative period. Assess closely for the need for dialysis. ATN can last from days to weeks, with gradually improving kidney function. Most patients with ATN are discharged from the hospital on dialysis. This is discouraging for the patient, who needs reassurance that renal function usually improves. Dialysis is stopped when urine output increases and serum creatinine and BUN begin to normalize.

A sudden decrease in urine output in the early postoperative period is a cause for concern. It may be due to dehydration, rejection, a urine leak, or obstruction. A common cause of early obstruction is a blood clot in the urinary catheter. Maintain catheter patency since the catheter stays in the bladder for 3 to 5 days to allow the ureter-bladder anastomosis to heal. If you suspect blood clots, gentle catheter irrigation (if ordered) can reestablish patency.

Identify and address discharge planning and teaching needs early. Patient teaching ensures a smooth transition from the hospital to home. Include how to recognize signs of rejection, infection, and any complications of surgery. Frequent blood tests and clinic visits help to detect rejection early.

Immunosuppressive Therapy

The goal of immunosuppression is to adequately suppress the immune response to prevent rejection of the transplanted kidney while maintaining sufficient immunity to prevent overwhelming infection. Immunosuppressive therapy is discussed in Chapter 14.

Complications of Transplantation

Complications of PD, HD, and kidney transplants are compared in Table 51.14.

Rejection

Rejection is a major problem after a kidney transplant. Rejection can be hyperacute, acute, or chronic. The types of rejection are

TABLE 51.14 Complications of Dialysis and Transplantation

Peritoneal Dialysis (PD)	Hemodialysis (HD)	Transplantation

• Abdominal pain
• Carbohydrate abnormalities
• Catheter outflow
• CVD
• Encapsulating sclerosing peritonitis
• Exit site infection
• Hernias
• Lipid abnormalities
• Lower back pain
• Peritonitis
• Protein loss
• Pulmonary problems
  • Atelectasis
  • Pneumonia
  • Bronchitis
	• CVD
	• Disequilibrium syndrome
	• Exsanguination
	• Hepatitis
	• Hypotension
	• Infection, including sepsis
	• Muscle cramp
		• Cancers
		• Corticosteroid-related complications
		• CVD
		• Recurrent kidney disease
		• Susceptible to infection
		• Transplant rejection
		  • Hyperacute
		  • Acute
		  • Chronic

discussed in Chapter 14. Patients with chronic rejection may be placed on the transplant list to be retransplanted before they need dialysis.

Infection

Infection is a significant cause of mortality after a transplant. The transplant recipient is at risk for infection because of suppression of the body's normal defense mechanisms by surgery, immunosuppressive drugs, and the effects of ESRD. Underlying systemic illness, such as diabetes or SLE, malnutrition, and older age, can further compound the negative effects on the immune response. The signs and symptoms of infection can be subtle. You must be astute in your assessment of the recipient because prompt diagnosis and treatment of infection improves patient outcomes.

The common infections seen in the first month after a transplant are like those of any postoperative patient. These include pneumonia, wound infections, UTIs, and IV line and drain infections. Fungal and viral infections are common due to the patient's immunosuppressed state. Fungal infections include *Candida, Cryptococcus,* and *Aspergillus* organisms and *Pneumocystis jirovecii.* Fungal infections are hard to treat, require prolonged treatment periods, and often involve the administration of nephrotoxic drugs. Transplant recipients usually receive prophylactic antifungal drugs to prevent these infections, such as clotrimazole, fluconazole, and trimethoprim/sulfamethoxazole.

Viral infections, including CMV, Epstein-Barr virus, herpes simplex virus (HSV), and varicella-zoster virus, can be primary infections or reactivations of existing disease. Primary infections occur as new infections from an exogenous source such as the donated organ or a blood transfusion. Reactivation occurs when a virus exists in a patient and becomes reactivated because of immunosuppression.

CMV is one of the most common viral infections. If a recipient has never had CMV and receives an organ from a donor with a history of CMV, antiviral prophylaxis will be needed (e.g., ganciclovir, valganciclovir). To prevent HSV infections, the patient receives oral acyclovir for several months after the transplant.

Cardiovascular Disease

CVD is the leading cause of death after a kidney transplant.[28] Transplant recipients have an increased incidence of atherosclerotic vascular disease. Hypertension, dyslipidemia, diabetes, smoking, rejection, infections, and increased homocysteine levels (many of which existed prior to the transplant) can all contribute to CVD. Immunosuppressants can worsen hypertension and dyslipidemia.

Teach the patient to control risk factors, such as high cholesterol, triglycerides, and blood glucose and weight gain. Adherence to the prescribed antihypertensive regimen is essential to prevent CV events and damage to the new kidney.

Cancers

The overall incidence of cancer in kidney transplant recipients is greater than in the general population, mainly because of immunosuppressive therapy. Not only do immunosuppressants suppress the immune system to prevent rejection, but they suppress the ability to fight infection and the production of abnormal cells, including cancer cells.

The most common types of cancer after transplant are (1) skin cancers—basal and squamous cell cancers and melanoma—and (2) posttransplant lymphoproliferative disorder (PTLD). Most PTLDs are of B-cell origin, related to Epstein-Barr virus (EBV). They cause aggressive lymphomas (Hodgkin and non-Hodgkin lymphoma). Most cases of PTLD occur within the first year of transplant.

Patients are also at risk for cancers of the colorectum, breast, cervix, liver, stomach, oropharynx, anus, vulva, and penis. Regular screening for cancer is an important part of the transplant recipient's preventive care. Teach the patient to avoid sun exposure by using protective clothing and sunscreens to minimize the incidence of skin cancers.

Recurrence of Original Kidney Disease

Recurrence of the original disease that destroyed the native kidneys occurs in some kidney transplant recipients. It is most common with certain types of glomerulonephritis, immunoglobulin A (IgA) nephropathy, diabetic nephropathy, and focal segmental sclerosis. Disease recurrence can result in the loss of a functioning kidney transplant. We must advise patients before the transplant if they have a disease known to recur.

Corticosteroid-Related Complications

Aseptic necrosis of the hips, knees, and other joints can result from chronic corticosteroid therapy and renal osteodystrophy. Other problems related to corticosteroids include peptic ulcer disease, diabetes, cataracts, dyslipidemia, infections, and cancers. The use of tacrolimus and other immunosuppressants has allowed corticosteroid doses to be much lower than they were in the past.

Many transplant programs have started corticosteroid-free drug regimens because of the problems of long-term corticosteroid use. Other centers withdraw patients from corticosteroids after the transplant. For patients who stay on corticosteroids, vigilant monitoring for side effects and prompt treatment is essential. Corticosteroid therapy as immunosuppression is discussed in Chapter 14.

Gerontologic Considerations: Chronic Kidney Disease

The incidence of CKD in the United States is increasing most rapidly in older adults. The most common diseases leading to CKD in older adults are hypertension and diabetes.[30]

The care of older patients is particularly challenging because of the normal physiologic changes of aging and the increased presence of disabilities, chronic diseases, and comorbid problems. Physiologic changes include decreased cardiopulmonary function, bone loss, immunodeficiency, altered protein synthesis, impaired cognition, and altered drug metabolism. Malnutrition is common in these patients for a variety of reasons. These include lack of mobility, social isolation, physical disability, and impaired cognitive function.

When conservative therapy for CKD is no longer effective, the older patient needs to consider the best treatment modality based on physical and emotional health, personal preferences, and availability of support. Quality-of-life measures show no justification for excluding the older adult from dialysis programs. Rationing dialysis based on age alone is not a reasonable decision for health care professionals to make. Older adults have successfully used dialysis, especially PD. Many choose treatment with in-center HD due to a lack of help in the home and reluctance to manage the technology of home HD or PD. Establishing vascular access for HD may be difficult because of atherosclerotic changes.

Although a transplant is an option, older adults are carefully screened to ensure that the benefits outweigh the risks.[31] Although a living donor is preferable, this may not be an option for many older patients.

The most common cause of death in older ESRD patients is CVD (MI, stroke), followed by withdrawal from dialysis. If a competent patient decides to withdraw from dialysis, it is essential to support the patient and family. Ethical issues (Box 51.5) include patient competency, benefit versus burden of treatment, and futility of treatment. Withdrawal from treatment is not a failure if the patient is well informed and comfortable with the decision.

BOX 51.5 ETHICAL/LEGAL DILEMMAS

Withdrawing Treatment

Situation

L.R., a 70-year-old patient with diabetes and ESRD, has been on dialysis for 10 years. He tells you that he wants to stop his dialysis. His quality of life has declined during the past 2 years since his wife died. He is not a transplant candidate.

Ethical/Legal Points for Consideration

- Informed consent includes the legal right to refuse treatment. However, the right to refuse may be difficult if (1) it is contrary to the wishes of family and friends, (2) the treatment is still effective, and (3) the treatment has been in place for some time.
- Quality-of-life decisions often outweigh the benefit against the burden of treatment. When a treatment becomes too burdensome, the patient, if competent, may request to withdraw the treatment.
- It must be determined whether some other treatable problem, such as depression, may be clouding the patient's judgment.
- Although there is no ethical or legal difference between withdrawing treatment and withholding treatment, withdrawing treatment feels different because it requires an action.
- Some health care professionals become conflicted when asked to withdraw treatment, since they may think they are contributing to the patient's premature death.
- If a decision is made to withdraw treatment, the interprofessional care team, patient, and family should develop a follow-up plan that includes palliative care and hospice support.

Discussion Questions

1. How should you respond to L.R.'s request?
2. What is the American Nurses Association's position on withdrawing or withholding treatment that no longer benefits the patient or causes suffering?

Case Study

Chronic Kidney Disease

(© iStockphoto/ Thinkstock.)

Patient Profile

M.B. is a 56-year-old college professor. He is having a well visit with his primary HCP. He has not seen an HCP in a little over a year. M.B. reports malaise, frequent urination, and "increasing thirst." His history includes borderline hypertension and dyslipidemia. He smokes 1 pack of cigarettes per day. His efforts to quit have been unsuccessful.

Subjective Data

- Family history: father died of an MI at age 62, brother had coronary artery bypass graft (CABG) at age 50, mother died from complications of diabetes
- Becomes "winded" when walking from his car to his office at the university
- Wakes up at night to urinate and has more frequent urination
- Increasing thirst

Objective Data

Laboratory Data

- Calculated creatinine clearance using the MDRD equation: 42 mL/min/1.73 m^2
- Serum creatinine 6.5 mg/dL
- BUN 85 mg/dL
- Serum glucose 264 mg/dL
- Hgb 13 g/dL
- Serum cholesterol 236 mg/dL

Physical Assessment

- Weight 220 lb, height 5 ft, 11 in
- BP 168/104 mm Hg

Case Study—cont'd

Chronic Kidney Disease

Discussion Questions

1. ***Recognize:*** What may have caused M.B.'s kidney disease?
2. ***Analyze:*** What stage of chronic kidney disease does he have?
3. ***Analyze:*** Identify the abnormal diagnostic study results and why each would occur.
4. ***Plan:*** How can the interprofessional team work together with M.B. to plan the best form of renal replacement therapy?
5. ***Prioritize:*** Based on the assessment data provided, what are the priority clinical problems?
6. ***Prioritize:*** What are the most important treatment measures that the interprofessional team can provide for M.B.?
7. ***Act:*** What interventions would help promote M.B.'s self-management of his disease?
8. ***Act:*** M.B. tells you that he has not been taking his BP medications regularly. When he asks you how important they are, what will you tell him?

Answers available at http://evolve.elsevier.com/Lewis/medsurg.

BRIDGE TO NCLEX EXAMINATION

The number of the question corresponds to the same-numbered outcome at the beginning of the chapter.

1. The nurse using RIFLE to determine the early stage of AKI evaluates the patient's
- **a.** blood pressure and urine osmolality.
- **b.** fractional excretion of urinary sodium.
- **c.** estimation of GFR with the MDRD equation.
- **d.** serum creatinine or urine output from baseline.

2. During the oliguric phase of AKI, the nurse monitors the patient for *(select all that apply)*
- **a.** hypotension.
- **b.** ECG changes.
- **c.** hypernatremia.
- **d.** pulmonary edema.
- **e.** urine with high specific gravity.

3. When a patient is in the diuretic phase of AKI, the nurse must monitor for which serum electrolyte imbalances?
- **a.** Hyperkalemia and hyponatremia
- **b.** Hyperkalemia and hypernatremia
- **c.** Hypokalemia and hyponatremia
- **d.** Hypokalemia and hypernatremia

4. The nurse assesses the patient with chronic kidney disease with the understanding that this condition is characterized by
- **a.** progressive irreversible destruction of the kidneys.
- **b.** a rapid decrease in urine output with an elevated BUN.
- **c.** an increasing creatinine clearance with a decrease in urine output.
- **d.** prostration, somnolence, and confusion with coma and imminent death.

5. Nurses can screen patients at risk for developing chronic kidney disease. Those considered to be at increased risk include *(select all that apply)*
- **a.** older Black patients.
- **b.** patients more than 60 years old.
- **c.** those with a history of pancreatitis.
- **d.** those with a history of hypertension.
- **e.** those with a history of type 2 diabetes.

6. Which points must the nurse consider when planning nutrition support for patients with chronic kidney disease? *(select all that apply)*
- **a.** Sodium may be restricted in someone with advanced CKD.
- **b.** Fluid is not usually restricted for patients on peritoneal dialysis.
- **c.** Decreased fluid intake and a low-potassium diet are needed for a patient on hemodialysis.
- **d.** Decreased fluid intake and a low-potassium diet are needed for a patient on peritoneal dialysis.
- **e.** Decreased fluid intake and a diet in protein-rich foods are part of a diet for a patient on hemodialysis.

7. An ESRD patient receiving hemodialysis is considering asking a relative to donate a kidney for a transplant. In helping the patient decide about treatment, the nurse informs the patient that
- **a.** successful transplant usually provides better quality of life than that offered by dialysis.
- **b.** if rejection of the transplanted kidney occurs, no further treatment for the renal failure is available.
- **c.** hemodialysis replaces normal kidney functions, and they do not have to live with the continual fear of rejection.
- **d.** immunosuppressive therapy after a transplant makes the person ineligible to receive other treatments if the kidney fails.

8. To assess the patency of a newly placed arteriovenous graft, the nurse should *(select all that apply)*
- **a.** monitor the BP in the affected arm.
- **b.** irrigate the graft daily with low-dose heparin.
- **c.** palpate the area of the graft to feel a normal thrill.
- **d.** listen with a stethoscope over the graft to detect a bruit.
- **e.** assess the pulses and neurovascular status distal to the graft.

9. A kidney transplant recipient has had fever, chills, and dysuria over the past 2 days. What is the *first* action that the nurse should take?
- **a.** Assess temperature and start workup to rule out infection.
- **b.** Reassure the patient that this is common after a transplant.
- **c.** Provide warm covers to the patient and give 1 gram oral acetaminophen.
- **d.** Notify the nephrologist that the patient has manifestations of acute rejection.

1. d; 2. b, d; 3. c; 4. a; 5. a, b, d, e; 6. a, b, c; 7. a; 8. c, d; 9. a.

For rationales to these answers and even more NCLEX review questions, visit http://evolve.elsevier.com/Lewis/medsurg.

EVOLVE WEBSITE/RESOURCES LIST

http://evolve.elsevier.com/Lewis/medsurg
Review Questions (Online Only)
Key Points
Answer Keys for Questions
- Rationales for Bridge to NCLEX Examination Questions
- Answer Guidelines for Case Study
- Answer Guidelines for Managing Care of Multiple Patients Case Study (Section 10)

Student Case Studies
- Patient With Glomerulonephritis and Acute Kidney Injury
- Patient With Kidney Transplant

Nursing Care Plan
- eNursing Care Plan 51.1: Patient With Chronic Kidney Disease

Conceptual Care Map Creator
Audio Glossary
Content Updates

REFERENCES

*1. Banda J: Predictors of acute kidney injury and mortality in intensive care unit at a teaching tertiary hospital ID, *Indian J Crit Care Med* 24:116, 2020.
*2. Igiraneza GD, Finklestein V, et al.: Challenges in the recognition and management of acute kidney injury by hospitals in resource-limited settings, *Kidney Int Rep* 5:991, 2020.
3. Thongprayoon C, Hansrivijit P, Kovvuru K, et al.: Diagnostics, risk factors, treatment and outcomes of acute kidney injury in a new paradigm, *J Clin Med* 9:1104, 2020.
*4. Bell S, Siddiqui M, De Souza N, et al.: Major adverse cardiovascular outcomes following acute kidney injury: an observational cohort study, *Nephrol Dial Transplant* 35:3, 2020.
*5. Matsuura R, Doi K, Hamasaki Y, et al.: RRT Selection for AKI patients with critical illness, *Semin Nephrol* 40:498, 2020.
*6. Zhao Y, Chen Y: Effect of renal replacement therapy modalities on renal recovery and mortality for acute kidney injury: a PRISMA–compliant systematic review and meta–analysis, *Semin Dial* 33:127, 2020.
7. Siew ED, Liu KD, Bonn J, et al.: Improving care for patients after hospitalization with AKI, *Clin J Am Soc Nephrol* 31:2237, 2020.
*8. Desai AP, Knapp SM, Orman ES, et al.: Changing epidemiology and outcomes of acute kidney injury in hospitalized patients with cirrhosis: a US population-based study, *J Hepatol* 73:1092, 2020.
*9. Hong WY, Kabach M, Feldman G, et al.: IV fluids for the prevention of contrast-induced nephropathy in patients undergoing coronary angiography and cardiac catheterization, *Expert Rev Cardiovasc Ther* 18:33, 2020.
*10. Molnar AO, Akbari A, Brimble S: Perceived and objective kidney disease knowledge in patients with advanced CKD followed in a multidisciplinary CKD clinic. *Can J Kidney Health Dis* 7, 2020.
*11. De Boer IH, Caramori ML, Chan JC, et al.: Executive summary of the 2020 KDIGO diabetes management in CKD Guideline: evidence-based advances in monitoring and treatment, *Kidney Int* 98:4, 2020.
*12. Flack JM, Adekola B: Blood pressure and the new ACC/AHA hypertension guidelines, *Trends Cardiovasc Med* 30:160, 2020.
*13. Fu R, Sekercioglu N, Mathur MB, et al.: Dialysis initiation and all-cause mortality among incident adult patients with advanced CKD: a meta-analysis with bias analysis, *Kidney Med* 3:1, 2021.
14. US Department of Health and Human Services: ESRD: General information. Retrieved from https://www.cms.gov/Medicare/End-Stage-Renal-Disease/ESRDGeneralInformation.
15. Sanjeev N, Mayuri T: Anemia management in dialysis patients: a PIVOT and a new path? *Curr Opin Nephrol Hypertens* 29:351, 2020.
16. Bonekamp NE, Spiering W, Nathoe HM, et al.: Applicability of blood pressure lowering drug trials to real-world patients with cardiovascular disease, *Hypertension* 77:356, 2020.
17. Cannata-Andía JB, Martín-Carro B, Martín-Vírgala J, et al.: Chronic kidney disease—mineral and bone disorders: pathogenesis and management, *Calcif Tissue Int* 108:410, 2020.
18. Panagiotis IG, Agarwal R: Hypertension in chronic kidney disease: diagnosis, classification, and therapeutic targets, *Am J Hypertens*, 2020.
19. Sehgal AW: Race and the false precision of glomerular filtration rate estimates, *Ann Inter Med* 173:1008, 2020.
*20. Roger SD, Lavin PT, Lerma EV, et al.: Long-term safety and efficacy of sodium zirconium cyclosilicate for hyperkalemia in patients with mild/moderate versus severe/end-stage chronic kidney disease: comparative results from an open-label, Phase 3 study, *Nephrol Dial Transplant* 36:137, 2021.
*21. Hu EA, Coresh J, Anderson CA, et al.: Adherence to healthy dietary patterns and risk of CKD progression and all-cause mortality: findings from the CRIC (Chronic Renal Insufficiency Cohort) Study, *AKJD* 77:235, 2021.
22. National Kidney Foundation: Treatment and support. Retrieved from https://www.kidney.org/treatment-support.
23. National Kidney and Urologic Diseases Information Clearinghouse (NKUDIC): Treatment methods for kidney disease: peritoneal dialysis. Retrieved from http://kidney.niddk.nih.gov/health-information/kidney-failure/peritoneal-dialysis.
24. NKUDIC: Treatment methods for kidney disease: hemodialysis. Retrieved from http://kidney.niddk.nih.gov/health-information/kidney-disease/kidney-failure/hemodialysis.
*25. Lok CE, Huber TS, Lee T, et al.: KDOQI clinical practice guideline for vascular access: 2019 update, *AJKD* 75:S1, 2020.
26. Himmelfarb J, Ratner B: Wearable artificial kidney: problems, progress and prospects, *Nat Rev Nephrol* 16:558, 2020.
27. Hart A, Smith JM, Skeans MA, et al.: OPTN/SRTR 2018 annual data report: kidney, *Amer J Transplant* 20:1, 2020.
28. De Lima JJ, Gowdak L, David-Neto E, et al.: Early cardiovascular events and cardiovascular death after renal transplantation: role of pretransplant risk factors, *Clin Exp Nephrol* 25:545, 2021.
29. Organ procurement and transplant network kidney allocation system. Retrieved from https://optn.transplant.hrsa.gov/learn/professional-education/kidney-allocation-system/.
*30. Lai S, Amabile MI, Mazzaferro S, et al.: Association between multidimensional prognostic index and hospitalization and mortality among older adults with CKD on conservative or on replacement therapy, *J Clin Med* 9:3965, 2020.
*31. Oskoui T, Pandya R, Weiner DE, et al.: Advance care planning among older adults with advanced non–dialysis-dependent CKD and their care partners: perceptions versus reality, *Kidney Med* 2:116, 2020.

*Evidence-based information for clinical practice.

Case Study

Applying Clinical Judgment With Multiple Patients

You are working on the medical-surgical unit and have been assigned to care for the following 4 patients. You are also assigned to receive the next admission. You have 1 AP on your team to help you.

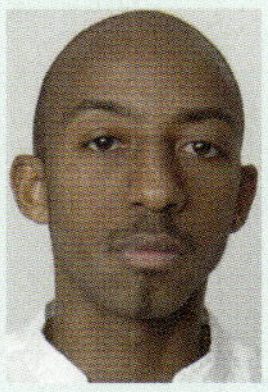 (© iStockphoto/ Thinkstock)	A.K., a 28-year-old man, was admitted with several kidney stones in the left ureter. He is receiving IV morphine sulfate for pain. His current pain level is 4 (1 to 10 scale). He is voiding dark, smoky-colored urine. He has positive costovertebral tenderness. Vital signs: 156/70, 94, RR 24.
 (© iStockphoto/ Thinkstock.)	S.U., a 29-year-old woman with type 1 diabetes, was admitted with acute pyelonephritis from a recent UTI. She has bilateral flank pain and abdominal tenderness. UA shows pyuria and hematuria. Blood culture results are pending. The next dose of IV antibiotics is due at 0900. Laboratory results: WBC 14,800/μL, glucose 215 mg/dL. Vital signs: 126/74, 94, RR 20, temp 101.5°F (38.6°C).
 (© iStockphoto/ Thinkstock.)	M.B., a 56-year-old man, was admitted with uncontrolled hypertension and CKD. He smokes 1 pack of cigarettes per day and is having some nicotine withdrawal symptoms. BP on admission was 224/102. He is receiving IV metoprolol (Lopressor) 5 mg q4h prn for SBP >180 mm Hg. Laboratory results: BUN 85 mg/dL, creatinine 6.5 mg/dL, glucose 264 mg/dL. Vital signs: 178/86, 88, RR 18.
 (© iStockphoto/ Thinkstock.)	D.M., an 82-year-old woman, was admitted with dehydration, heart failure, and acute kidney injury. She is confused. Her potassium is 6.3 mEq/L. Her urine output for the past 8 hours was 90 mL. Vital signs: 142/86, 98, RR 22.

1. Highlight all the findings above that require your follow-up.
2. After receiving report, which patient should you see first? Second?
3. Which tasks could you delegate to the AP? (*select all that apply*)
   a. Obtain vital signs on M.B.
   b. Strain A.K.'s voided urine.
   c. Report D.M.'s potassium level to the HCP.
   d. Measure D.M.'s urine output and report the results to the RN.
   e. Assess S.U. for manifestations of sepsis and diabetic ketoacidosis.
4. As you are assessing D.M., the AP tells you that M.B.'s BP is 190/96. He is asymptomatic. Then the charge nurse calls and tells you that you will receive a patient with heart failure from the ED in the next 20 min. Which action would be *most* appropriate?
   a. Ask the charge nurse to assign the new admission to someone else.
   b. Have the AP admit the new patient while you administer M.B.'s IV metoprolol.
   c. Call the ED and have them hold the new admission until after you have assessed all your patients.
   d. Ask the charge nurse to give M.B.'s IV metoprolol while you complete your assessment of D.M. and S.U.

Case Study Progression

As you complete your assessment of D.M., you note she has 1+ pitting edema in her lower extremities. Her BP is 160/90 mm Hg, heart rate 108 beats/min, and respiratory rate 32/min. Auscultation reveals crackles in the lung bases and O_2 saturation is 88% on room air. The skin is cool, and she is reporting dyspnea.

5. Based on these assessment findings, you suspect D.M. is experiencing ____1____. You notify the HCP, expecting orders for ____2____, ____2____, and ____2____.

Options for 1	Options for 2
Pulmonary edema	12-lead ECG and continuous ECG monitoring
Pulmonary embolism	furosemide
Unstable angina	heparin
	nitroglycerin
	O_2 therapy

6. A.K. is reporting pain rated as 8 (1 to 10 scale) and requests IV morphine. What would you do first?
   a. Assess the patency of A.K.'s IV site.
   b. Prepare the dose using sterile technique.
   c. Determine the last time A.K. received IV morphine.
   d. Scan A.K.'s ID band and the medication according to agency policy.
7. You begin S.U.'s scheduled infusion of IV ceftriaxone and perform her assessment. Use an X for the nursing actions listed below that are Indicated (appropriate or necessary), Contraindicated (could be harmful), or Nonessential (makes no difference or not necessary) for S.U. at this time.

Nursing Action	Indicated	Contraindicated	Nonessential
Monitor BUN and creatinine levels.			
Maintain intake and output.			
Medicate with ibuprofen every 6 hr as needed for pain.			
Initiate a fluid restriction.			
Encourage her to void every 3–4 hr while awake.			
Assess for the presence of bowel sounds every 4 hr.			

8. Which statement would be *most* appropriate when teaching S.U. about her kidney infection?
   a. "The damage to your kidneys will likely require dialysis."
   b. "You will need to be in the hospital for a 2-week course of IV antibiotics."
   c. "It is very important that you maintain adequate hydration to flush your kidneys."
   d. "You will not need further antibiotics once you are discharged from the hospital."

Continued

Case Study—cont'd

9. As the AP prepares the room for the patient being admitted from the ED, you overhear her telling a coworker that she does all your work for you. What is your *best* initial action?
   a. Report the incident to the charge nurse for follow-up.
   b. Ask the AP to discuss her concerns with you in private.
   c. Tell the AP how much you appreciate and value her input on your team.
   d. Immediately clarify the situation by telling the AP all the tasks you are completing.
10. You are reviewing S.U.s latest assessment findings. For each assessment finding, use an X to indicate whether the interventions were Effective (helped to meet expected outcomes), Ineffective (did not help to meet expected outcomes), or Unrelated (not related to the expected outcomes).

Assessment Finding	Effective	Ineffective	Unrelated
BUN 55 mg/dL, creatinine 3.5 mg/dL			
Reports wiping front to back after voiding			
No flank pain or dysuria			
Voiding clear, yellow urine 5–6 times per day			
Lungs clear to auscultation			
UA shows hematuria			

52

Assessment: Endocrine System

Julia A. Hitch

http://evolve.elsevier.com/Lewis/medsurg/

CONCEPTUAL FOCUS

Homeostasis
Hormonal Regulation
Reproduction
Stress

LEARNING OUTCOMES

1. Describe the common characteristics and functions of hormones.
2. Identify the locations of the endocrine glands.
3. Describe the functions of hormones secreted by the pituitary, thyroid, parathyroid, and adrenal glands and the pancreas.
4. Obtain significant subjective and objective assessment data related to the endocrine system from a patient.
5. Perform a physical assessment of the endocrine system using the appropriate techniques.
6. Link age-related changes in the endocrine system to differences in assessment findings.
7. Distinguish normal from common abnormal findings of a physical assessment of the endocrine system.
8. Describe the purpose, significance of results, and nursing responsibilities related to diagnostic studies of the endocrine system.

KEY TERMS

aldosterone
antidiuretic hormone (ADH)
catecholamines
circadian rhythm
corticosteroid
cortisol
hormones
insulin
negative feedback
positive feedback
thyroxine (T_4)
triiodothyronine (T_3)
tropic hormones

STRUCTURES AND FUNCTIONS OF ENDOCRINE SYSTEM

Glands

Endocrine glands include the hypothalamus, pituitary, thyroid, parathyroids, adrenals, pancreas, ovaries, testes, and pineal gland (Fig. 52.1). These glands make and release special chemical messengers called *hormones.* The endocrine system has 5 general functions: (1) a role in reproductive and central nervous system (CNS) development in the fetus, (2) stimulating growth and development during childhood and adolescence, (3) sexual reproduction, (4) maintaining homeostasis, and (5) responding to emergency demands.

Hormones

Hormones are chemical substances made by endocrine glands that control and regulate the activity of certain target cells or organs. Many are made in one part of the body and control and regulate the activity of certain cells or organs in another part of the body. The thyroid gland makes the hormone thyroxine, which affects many body tissues when released directly into the circulation. Other hormones act locally on cells where they are released and never enter

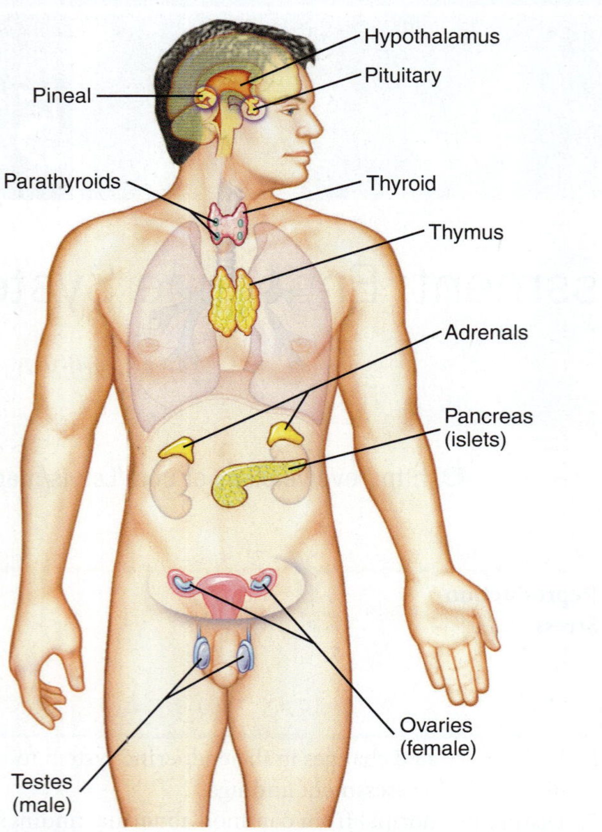

Fig. 52.1 Location of the major endocrine glands. The parathyroid glands lie on the posterior surface of the thyroid gland. (Modified from Patton KT, Thibodeau GA: *Anatomy and physiology,* ed 8, St Louis, 2013, Mosby.)

the bloodstream. We call this local effect *paracrine action.* The action of sex steroids on the ovary is an example of paracrine action.

Most hormones have common characteristics. They are (1) secreted in small amounts at variable but predictable rates, (2) regulated by feedback systems, and (3) able to bind to specific target cell receptors. Table 52.1 reviews the main hormones, the glands or tissues that make the hormones, their target organs or tissues, and their functions.

The endocrine system and nervous system have a strong connection. *Catecholamines* (e.g., epinephrine), secreted by the adrenal gland, travel through the bloodstream and affect multiple organ systems. When secreted by nerve cells in the brain and peripheral nervous system, these same substances act as neurotransmitters, sending important impulses across nerve synapses.

Organs can act as endocrine glands by secreting hormones. For example, the kidneys secrete erythropoietin. It stimulates red blood cell production. The heart secretes atrial natriuretic peptide (ANP). The gastrointestinal (GI) tract secretes many peptide hormones (e.g., gastrin) that aid in digestion. These hormones are discussed in their respective assessment chapters.

Hormone Receptors

Hormones exert their effects by recognizing their target tissues and attaching to receptor sites in a "lock-and-key" type of mechanism. This means a hormone will act only on cells with a receptor specific to that hormone (Fig. 52.2).

Lipid-Soluble and Water-Soluble Hormones

We classify hormones by their chemical structure as lipid soluble or water soluble. The difference in solubility is important in understanding how the hormone interacts with the target cell (Fig. 52.3). Lipid-soluble hormones (steroids, thyroid) are bound to plasma proteins as they travel to target cells. They cross the cell membrane by simple diffusion. Water-soluble hormones (insulin, growth hormone [GH], prolactin) circulate freely in the blood and act directly on target tissues.

Regulation of Hormonal Secretion

Specific mechanisms control endocrine activity by either stimulating or inhibiting hormone synthesis and secretion. These include positive and negative feedback, nervous system control, and physiologic rhythms.

Simple feedback. **Negative feedback** relies on the blood level of a hormone or other chemical compound regulated by the hormone (e.g., glucose). It is the most common type of endocrine feedback system. It results in the gland increasing or decreasing the release of a hormone. An example of negative feedback is calcium and parathyroid hormone (PTH) regulation. Low blood levels of calcium stimulate the parathyroid gland to release PTH. PTH acts on the bone, intestine, and kidneys to increase blood calcium levels. The increased blood calcium level then inhibits further PTH release (Fig. 52.4).

With **positive feedback**, increasing hormone levels cause another gland to release a hormone that stimulates further release of the first hormone. Something must stop the release of the first hormone (e.g., follicle death), or its release will continue. The ovarian hormone estradiol works by this type of feedback. Increased estradiol levels made by the follicle during the menstrual cycle result in the production and release of follicle-stimulating hormone (FSH) by the anterior pituitary. FSH causes further increases in estradiol until the death of the follicle. This results in a drop in FSH serum levels.

Nervous system control. Nervous system activity directly affects some endocrine glands. Pain, fear, sexual excitement, and other stressors can stimulate the nervous system to control hormone secretion. For example, when the CNS senses or perceives stress, the sympathetic nervous system (SNS) secretes catecholamines (e.g., epinephrine), which maximize heart and lung function and vision to deal with the stress more effectively. Chronic exposure to some stressors can cause persistent increases in heart rate and BP and changes in the endocrine system. This puts patients at risk for chronic disease, such as hypertension and heart disease. Stress-related effects are discussed in Chapter 7.

Rhythms. A common physiologic rhythm is the **circadian rhythm**. It is a 24-hour rhythm that is driven by sleep-wake or dark-light 24-hour (diurnal) cycles. Hormone levels and the responsiveness of target tissues fluctuate predictably during these cycles. Cortisol, made by the adrenal cortex, rises early in the day, declines toward evening, and rises again toward

TABLE 52.1 Endocrine Glands and Hormones

Hormones	Target Tissue	Functions
Anterior Pituitary (Adenohypophysis)		
Adrenocorticotropic hormone (ACTH)	Adrenal cortex	Fosters growth of adrenal cortex Stimulates corticosteroid secretion
Gonadotropic hormones • Follicle-stimulating hormone (FSH) • Luteinizing hormone (LH)	Reproductive organs	Stimulates sex hormone secretion, reproductive organ growth, reproductive processes
Growth hormone (GH), or somatotropin	All body cells	Promotes protein anabolism (growth, tissue repair) and lipid mobilization and catabolism
Melanocyte-stimulating hormone (MSH)	Melanocytes in skin	↑ Melanin production in melanocytes
Prolactin	Ovary and mammary glands in women	Stimulates milk production in lactating women. ↑ Response of follicles to LH and FSH
	Testes in men	Stimulates testicular function in men
Thyroid-stimulating hormone (TSH), or thyrotropin	Thyroid gland	Stimulates synthesis and release of thyroid hormones, growth and function of thyroid gland
Posterior Pituitary (Neurohypophysis)		
Antidiuretic hormone (ADH)	Renal tubules, vascular smooth muscle	Promotes reabsorption of water from the renal tubules, vasoconstriction
Oxytocin	Uterus, mammary glands	Stimulates milk secretion, uterine contractility
Thyroid		
Calcitonin	Bone tissue	Regulates calcium and phosphorus serum levels. ↓ Serum Ca^{2+} levels
Thyroxine (T_4)	All body tissues	Precursor to T_3
Triiodothyronine (T_3)	All body tissues	Regulates metabolic rate of all cells and processes of cell growth and tissue differentiation
Parathyroids		
Parathyroid hormone (PTH) or parathormone	Bone, intestine, kidneys	Regulates calcium and phosphorus serum levels. Promotes bone demineralization and ↑ intestinal absorption of Ca^{2+}. ↑ Serum Ca^{2+} levels
Adrenal Medulla		
Epinephrine (adrenaline)	Catecholamine	↑ In response to stress. Enhances and prolongs effects of sympathetic nervous system
Norepinephrine (noradrenaline)	Catecholamine	↑ In response to stress. Enhances and prolongs effects of sympathetic nervous system
Adrenal Cortex		
Androgens (e.g., dehydroepiandrosterone [DHEA], androsterone) and estradiol	Reproductive organs	Promotes growth spurt in adolescence, secondary sex characteristics, and libido in both sexes
Corticosteroids (e.g., cortisol, hydrocortisone)	All body tissues	Promotes metabolism. ↑ In response to stress. Antiinflammatory
Mineralocorticoids (e.g., aldosterone)	Kidney	Regulates sodium and potassium balance and thus water balance
Pancreas (Islets of Langerhans)		
Amylin (from β cells)	Liver, stomach	↓ Gastric motility, glucagon secretion, and endogenous glucose release from liver. ↑ Satiety
Glucagon (from α cells)	General	Stimulates glycogenolysis and gluconeogenesis
Insulin (from β cells)	General	Promotes glucose transport from the blood into the cell
Pancreatic polypeptide	General	Influences regulation of pancreatic exocrine function and metabolism of absorbed nutrients
Somatostatin	Pancreas	Inhibits insulin and glucagon secretion
Gonads		
Women: Ovaries		
Estrogen	Reproductive system, breasts	Stimulates development of secondary sex characteristics, preparation of uterus for fertilization, and fetal development. Stimulates bone growth
Progesterone	Reproductive system	Maintains lining of uterus needed for successful pregnancy
Men: Testes		
Testosterone	Reproductive system	Stimulates development of secondary sex characteristics, spermatogenesis

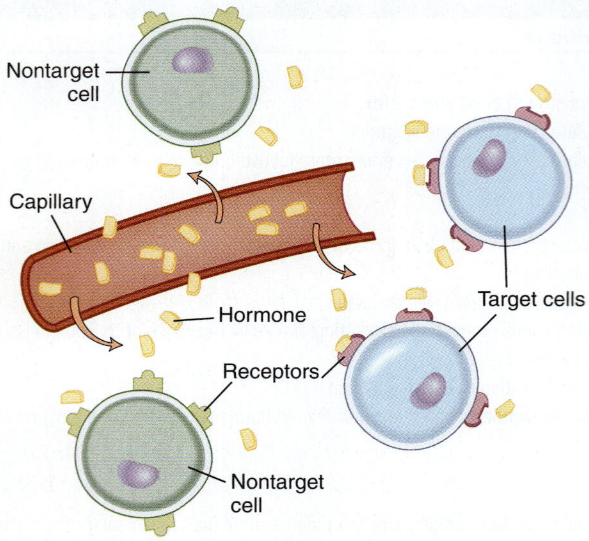

Fig. 52.2 The target cell concept. Hormones act only on cells with receptors specific to that hormone since the receptor's shape determines which hormone can react with it. This is an example of the lock-and-key model of biochemical reactions.

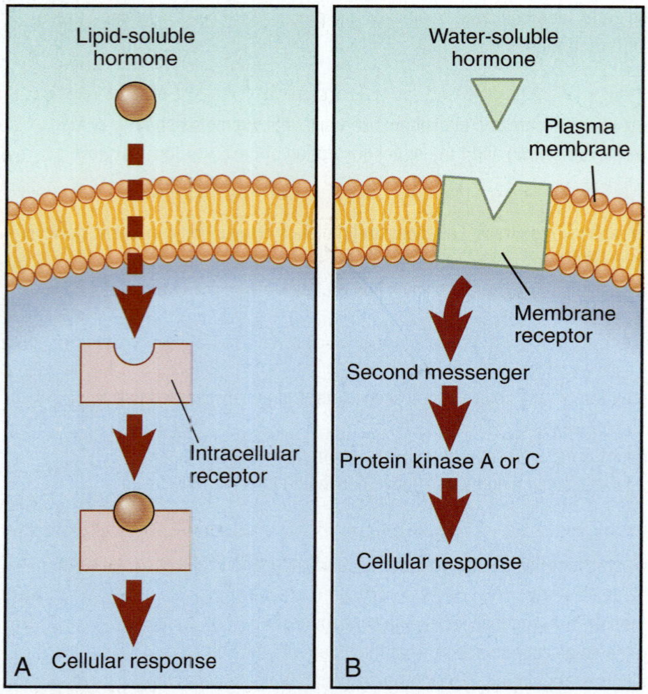

Fig. 52.3 (A) Lipid-soluble hormones (e.g., steroid hormones) penetrate the cell membrane and interact with intracellular receptors. (B) Water-soluble hormones (e.g., protein hormones) bind to receptors in the cell membrane. The hormone-receptor interaction stimulates various cell responses. (Modified from McCance KL, Huether SE: *Pathophysiology: the biologic basis for disease in adults and children*, ed 6, St Louis, 2010, Mosby.)

the end of sleep to peak by morning (Fig. 52.5). GH, thyroid-stimulating hormone (TSH), and prolactin levels peak during sleep. Reproductive cycles are often longer than 24 hours *(ultradian)*. An example is the menstrual cycle. We must consider these rhythms when interpreting laboratory results for hormone levels.

Hypothalamus

Although many call the pituitary gland the "master gland" of the endocrine system, most of its functions rely on its interrelationship with the hypothalamus. The hypothalamus releases substances that either stimulate or inhibit the production and release of hormones from the pituitary gland (Table 52.2). Examples of these hormones include corticotropin-releasing hormone (CRH) and thyrotropin-releasing hormone (TRH). Somatostatin inhibits GH release.

Neurons in the hypothalamus receive input from the CNS, including the brainstem, limbic system, and cerebral cortex. These neurons create a circuit that helps coordinate the endocrine system and autonomic nervous system (ANS). The hypothalamus also coordinates the expression of complex behavioral responses, such as anger, fear, and pleasure.

Pituitary

The pituitary gland *(hypophysis)* is in the sella turcica under the hypothalamus at the base of the brain above the sphenoid bone (Fig. 52.1). The infundibular *(hypophyseal)* stalk connects the pituitary and hypothalamus. The stalk relays information between the hypothalamus and pituitary, creating a strong neuroendocrine connection. The pituitary consists of 2 main parts, the anterior lobe *(adenohypophysis)* and posterior lobe *(neurohypophysis)*. A smaller intermediate lobe makes melanocyte-stimulating hormone (MSH).

Anterior Pituitary

The anterior lobe of the pituitary accounts for 80% of the gland by weight. The hypothalamus regulates the anterior lobe through releasing and inhibiting hormones. These hypothalamic hormones reach the anterior pituitary through a network of capillaries known as the *hypothalamus-hypophyseal portal system.* These releasing and inhibiting hormones, in turn, affect the secretion of 6 hormones from the anterior pituitary (Fig. 52.6).

We refer to several hormones secreted by the anterior pituitary as **tropic hormones**. Tropic hormones control the secretion of hormones by other glands. TSH stimulates the thyroid gland to secrete thyroid hormones. Adrenocorticotropic hormone (ACTH) stimulates the adrenal cortex to secrete corticosteroids. FSH stimulates secretion of estrogen and the development of ova in women and sperm in men. Luteinizing hormone (LH) stimulates ovulation in women and secretion of sex hormones in both men and women.

Growth hormone affects the growth and development of all body tissues. It has many biologic actions, including a role in protein, fat, and carbohydrate metabolism. *Prolactin,* or lactogenic hormone, stimulates the breast development needed for lactation after childbirth.

Posterior Pituitary

The posterior pituitary is composed of nerve tissue and is essentially an extension of the hypothalamus. Communication

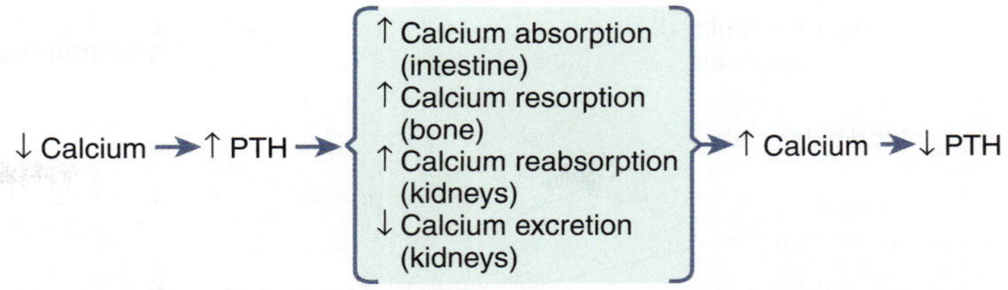

Fig. 52.4 Feedback mechanism between PTH and calcium.

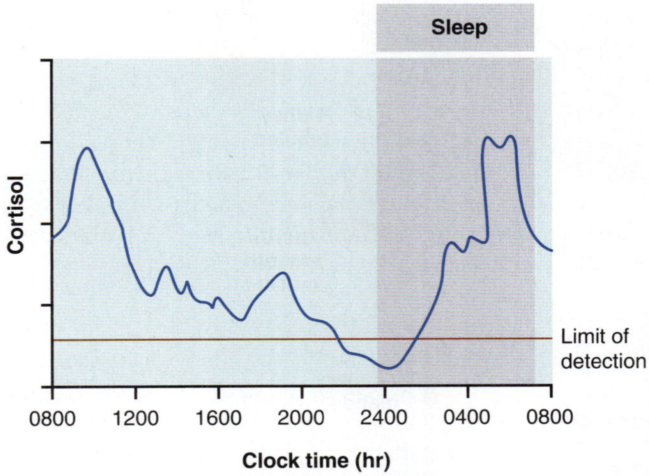

Fig. 52.5 Circadian rhythm of cortisol secretion.

TABLE 52.2 Hormones of the Hypothalamus

The following hormones from the hypothalamus target the anterior pituitary:

Releasing Hormones
- Corticotropin-releasing hormone (CRH)
- Thyrotropin-releasing hormone (TRH)
- Growth hormone–releasing hormone (GHRH)
- Gonadotropin-releasing hormone (GnRH)
- Prolactin-releasing factor (PRF)

Inhibiting Hormones
- Somatostatin (inhibits growth hormone release)
- Prolactin-inhibiting factor (PIF)

between the hypothalamus and posterior pituitary occurs through nerve tracts. The hormones secreted by the posterior pituitary, **antidiuretic hormone (ADH)** and oxytocin, are made in the hypothalamus. These hormones travel down the nerve tracts from the hypothalamus to the posterior pituitary and are stored there until stimuli trigger their release (Fig. 52.6).

The main physiologic role of ADH *(arginine vasopressin)* is to regulate fluid volume. It causes the renal tubules to reabsorb water, making the urine more concentrated. A rise in plasma osmolality or hypovolemia causes specialized neurons in the hypothalamus, called *osmoreceptors,* to stimulate ADH release from the posterior pituitary (Fig. 52.7). When ADH release is inhibited, renal tubules do not reabsorb water, resulting in more dilute urine. Volume receptors in large veins, heart atria, and carotid arteries that sense pressure changes (from hypovolemia) also contribute to ADH control. ADH is also a potent vasoconstrictor.

Pineal Gland

The pineal gland is in the brain. It is composed of photoreceptive cells. Its primary function is the secretion of the hormone *melatonin.* Melatonin secretion increases in response to exposure to the dark and decreases in response to light exposure. The gland helps to regulate circadian rhythms and the reproductive system at the onset of puberty.

Thyroid Gland

The thyroid gland is in the anterior part of the neck in front of the trachea. It consists of 2 encapsulated lateral lobes connected by a narrow isthmus (Fig. 52.8). The thyroid gland is highly vascular. Its size is related to TSH secretion by the anterior pituitary. The 3 hormones made and secreted by the thyroid gland are thyroxine (T_4), triiodothyronine (T_3), and calcitonin.

Thyroxine and Triiodothyronine

Thyroxine (T_4) accounts for 90% of thyroid hormone made by the thyroid gland. **Triiodothyronine (T_3)** is much more potent and has greater metabolic effects. The thyroid gland directly secretes about 20% of circulating T_3. The rest comes from the conversion of T_4 after its release into the bloodstream. Iodine is needed to synthesize T_3 and T_4. Both hormones affect metabolic rate, caloric requirements, O_2 consumption, carbohydrate and lipid metabolism, growth and development, brain function, and other nervous system activities. More than 99% of thyroid hormones are bound to plasma proteins, especially thyroxine-binding globulin made by the liver. Only the unbound "free" hormones are biologically active.

TSH from the anterior pituitary gland stimulates thyroid hormone production and release. When circulating levels of thyroid hormone are low, the hypothalamus releases TRH. TRH causes the anterior pituitary to release TSH. High circulating thyroid hormone levels inhibit the secretion of both TRH from the hypothalamus and TSH from the anterior pituitary gland.

Calcitonin

Calcitonin is made by C cells (parafollicular cells) of the thyroid gland in response to high circulating calcium levels.

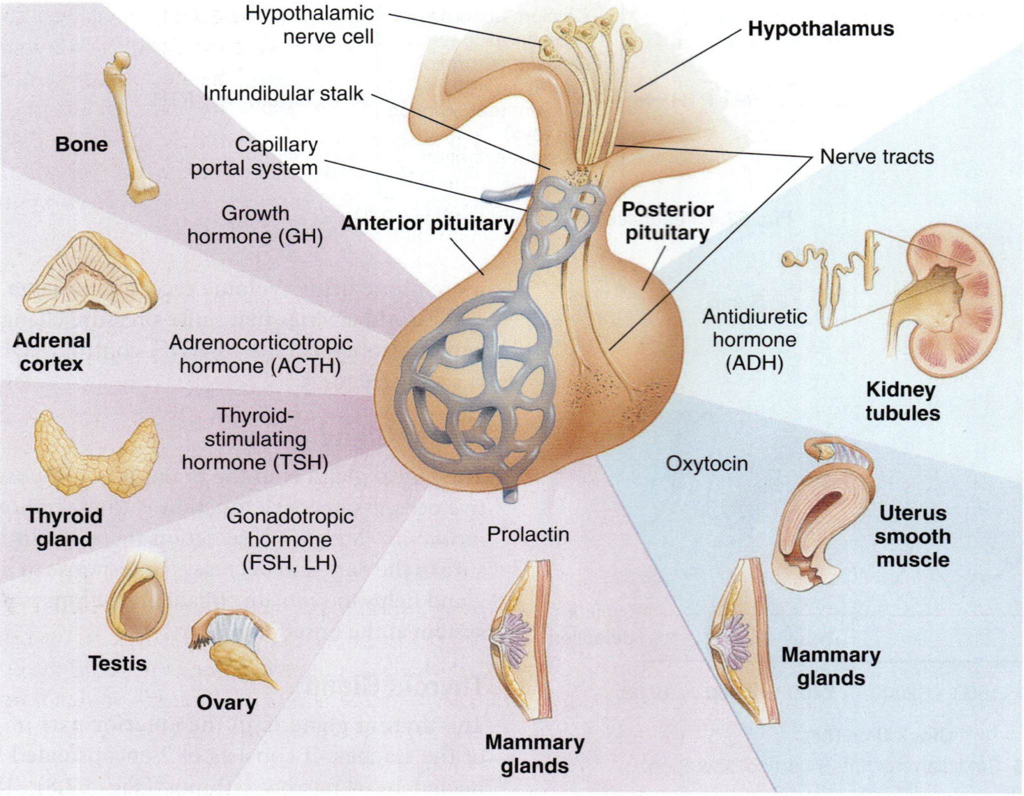

Fig. 52.6 Relationship between the hypothalamus, pituitary, and target organs. The hypothalamus communicates with the anterior pituitary via a capillary system and with the posterior pituitary via nerve tracts. The anterior and posterior pituitary hormones are shown with their target tissues. (Modified from Patton KT, Thibodeau GA: *Anatomy and physiology,* ed 8, St Louis, 2013, Mosby.)

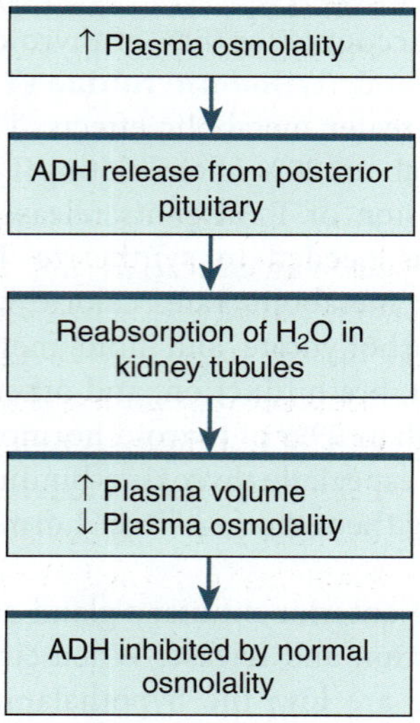

Fig. 52.7 Relationship of plasma osmolality to ADH release and action.

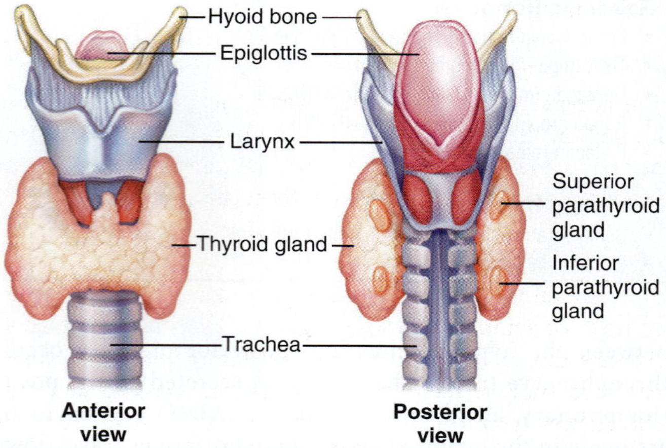

Fig. 52.8 Thyroid and parathyroid glands. Note the surrounding structures. (From Thibodeau GA, Patton KT: *The human body in health and disease,* ed 4, St Louis, 2005, Mosby.)

Calcitonin lowers serum calcium levels by (1) inhibiting the transfer of calcium from the bone to blood, (2) increasing calcium storage in bone, and (3) increasing renal excretion of calcium and phosphorus. Calcitonin and PTH regulate calcium balance.

Parathyroid Glands

There are usually 2 pairs of parathyroid glands lying behind each thyroid lobe (Fig. 52.8). Although there are usually 4 glands, their number may range from 2 to 6.

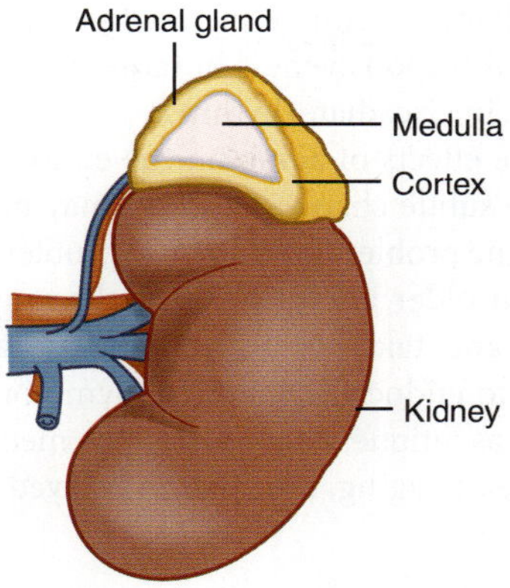

Fig. 52.9 The adrenal gland is composed of the adrenal cortex and the adrenal medulla.

Parathyroid Hormone

The parathyroid glands secrete PTH, or *parathormone.* Its major role is to regulate serum calcium levels. PTH increases serum calcium levels by acting on bone, the kidneys, and indirectly on the GI tract. PTH stimulates the transfer of calcium from the bone into the blood. In the kidney, PTH promotes calcium reabsorption (moving calcium from the renal tubules back into the bloodstream) and phosphate excretion. PTH stimulates the renal conversion of vitamin D to its most active form (1,25-dihydroxyvitamin D_3). This form of vitamin D promotes calcium and phosphorus absorption in the GI tract. PTH secretion is regulated by a negative feedback system. When serum calcium or magnesium levels are low, PTH secretion increases. When serum calcium or active vitamin D levels are high, PTH secretion falls.

Adrenal Glands

The adrenal glands are small, paired, highly vascular glands located on the upper part of each kidney. Each gland consists of 2 parts: medulla and cortex (Fig. 52.9). Each part has distinct functions and acts independently from the other.

Adrenal Medulla

The adrenal medulla is the inner part of the adrenal gland. It consists of sympathetic postganglionic neurons. The medulla secretes the **catecholamines** *epinephrine* (adrenaline), *norepinephrine* (noradrenaline), and *dopamine.* We consider catecholamines neurotransmitters when secreted by neurons and hormones when secreted by the adrenal medulla. They are an essential part of the SNS's "fight or flight" response.

Adrenal Cortex

The adrenal cortex is the outer part of the adrenal gland. It secretes several steroid hormones, including *glucocorticoids, mineralocorticoids,* and *androgens.* Cholesterol is the precursor for steroid hormone synthesis. Glucocorticoids (e.g., cortisol) are named for their effects on glucose metabolism. They inhibit the inflammatory response and are considered antiinflammatory. Mineralocorticoids (e.g., aldosterone) are essential for maintaining fluid and electrolyte balance. The term **corticosteroid** refers to both glucocorticoids and mineralocorticoids.

Cortisol. **Cortisol**, the most abundant and potent glucocorticoid, is necessary to maintain life and protect the body from stress. It is secreted in a diurnal pattern (Fig. 52.5). A negative feedback mechanism controls cortisol secretion. The release of CRH from the hypothalamus stimulates the anterior pituitary to secrete ACTH.

A key function of cortisol is regulating blood glucose concentration by stimulating hepatic glucose formation *(gluconeogenesis).* Cortisol inhibits peripheral glucose use in the fasting state, inhibits protein synthesis, and stimulates the mobilization of glycerol and free fatty acids. It helps maintain vascular integrity and fluid volume through its action on mineralocorticoid receptors. Cortisol decreases the inflammatory response by stabilizing the membranes of cellular lysosomes and preventing increased capillary permeability. Stress, burns, infection, fever, acute anxiety, and hypoglycemia increase cortisol levels.

Aldosterone. **Aldosterone** is a potent mineralocorticoid that maintains extracellular fluid volume. It acts on the renal tubule to promote renal reabsorption of sodium and excretion of potassium and hydrogen ions. Hyponatremia, hyperkalemia, and angiotensin II stimulate aldosterone synthesis and secretion. ANP and hypokalemia inhibit aldosterone synthesis and release.

Adrenal androgens. The adrenal cortex secretes small amounts of androgens. They are converted to sex steroids in peripheral tissues: testosterone in men and estrogen in women. The most common adrenal androgens are dehydroepiandrosterone (DHEA) and androstenedione. Because they are precursors to other sex steroids, their actions are like those of testosterone and estrogen. In postmenopausal women, the main source of estrogen is the peripheral conversion of adrenal androgens to estrogen.

Pancreas

The pancreas is a long, tapered, lobular, soft gland located behind the stomach and anterior to the first and second lumbar vertebrae. The pancreas has both exocrine and endocrine functions. The hormone-secreting part of the pancreas is the *islets of Langerhans.* The islets account for less than 2% of the gland. They consist of 4 types of hormone-secreting cells: α, β, delta, and F cells. The α cells make and secrete the hormone glucagon. The β cells make and secrete insulin and amylin. Delta cells make and secrete somatostatin. F (or PP) cells secrete pancreatic polypeptide.

Glucagon

Pancreatic α cells release *glucagon* in response to low blood glucose levels, protein ingestion, and exercise. Glucagon increases blood glucose, providing fuel for energy by stimulating glycogenolysis (breakdown of glycogen into glucose), gluconeogenesis (formation of glucose from noncarbohydrate molecules), and ketogenesis. Glucagon and insulin function in a reciprocal manner to maintain normal blood glucose levels.

Insulin

Insulin is the main regulator of metabolism and storage of ingested carbohydrates, fats, and proteins. Insulin facilitates glucose transport into cells, transport of amino acids across muscle membranes, and the synthesis of amino acids into protein in the peripheral tissues. However, the brain, nerves, lens of the eye, hepatocytes, erythrocytes, and cells in the intestinal mucosa and kidney tubules are not dependent on insulin for glucose uptake. After a meal, insulin is responsible for how we use and store nutrients *(anabolism)*. An increased blood glucose level is the major stimulus for insulin synthesis and secretion. Low blood glucose levels, glucagon, somatostatin, hypokalemia, and catecholamines usually inhibit insulin secretion.

Gerontologic Considerations: Effects of Aging on Endocrine System

Normal aging has many effects on the endocrine system (Table 52.3). These include (1) decreased hormone production and secretion, (2) altered hormone metabolism and biologic activity, (3) decreased responsiveness of target tissues to hormones, and (4) changes in circadian rhythms.

Assessing the effects of aging on the endocrine system may be difficult. The subtle changes of aging may mimic manifestations of endocrine problems. Endocrine problems may manifest differently in an older adult. Older adults may have multiple co-morbidities and take medications that change the body's usual response to endocrine function. Symptoms of endocrine problems, such as fatigue, constipation, or mental impairment, may be attributed to aging, resulting in delayed treatment.

TABLE 52.3 GERONTOLOGIC ASSESSMENT DIFFERENCES

Endocrine System

Changes	Clinical Significance
Thyroid	
Atrophy of thyroid gland ↓ T_3, T_4, TSH secretion ↑ Nodules	↑ Incidence of hypothyroidism Most older adults maintain adequate thyroid function Thyroid hormone replacement dose lower in older adults
Parathyroid	
↑ PTH secretion ↑ Basal level of PTH	↑ Calcium resorption from bone Hypercalcemia, hypercalciuria (may reflect defective renal mechanism)
Adrenal Cortex	
Adrenal cortex becomes more fibrotic and slightly smaller ↓ Cortisol metabolism ↓ Plasma levels of adrenal androgens and aldosterone	↓ Metabolic clearance rate for glucocorticoids
Adrenal Medulla	
↑ Secretion and basal level of norepinephrine ↓ β-Adrenergic receptor response to norepinephrine	↓ Responsiveness to β-adrenergic agonists and receptor blockers May partly explain ↑ incidence of hypertension with aging
Pancreas	
↑ Fibrosis and fatty deposits in pancreas ↑ Glucose intolerance with ↓ sensitivity to insulin	May partly contribute to ↑ incidence of diabetes with advanced aging
Gonads	
Women: ↓ Estrogen secretion	Have menopausal symptoms ↑ Risk for arteriosclerosis and osteoporosis
Men: ↓ Testosterone secretion	Men may or may not have symptoms

Case Study

Patient Introduction

(© iStockphoto/Thinkstock.)

L.M. is a 35-year-old woman who comes to the clinic saying she is "just not feeling well." Her husband, H.M., is with her. L.M. states that she has gained a lot of weight despite trying to watch her diet and just seems to be getting more and more tired. H.M. voices concerns about the changes in his wife's energy level.

Discussion Questions

1. What are the possible causes of L.M.'s weight gain, fatigue, and irritability?
2. What would be your priority assessment of L.M.?
3. What questions would you ask L.M.?

You will learn more about L.M. and her condition as you read this assessment chapter.

Answers available at http://evolve.elsevier.com/Lewis/medsurg.

ASSESSMENT OF ENDOCRINE SYSTEM

Endocrine problems generally result from too much or too little of a specific hormone. The onset of symptoms is often gradual. Subtle or vague symptoms are often attributed to other physiologic or psychologic causes. Patients may present with fluid and electrolyte imbalances, altered tissue perfusion, changes in heart rhythm, or changes in skin integrity that can be interpreted as other problems. Some patients may present with acute symptoms that are life threatening and need immediate intervention.

Subjective Data

Information obtained from the patient can provide important clues about endocrine system function. Obtain a thorough history from the patient and/or a caregiver if the patient's mental acuity is compromised.

Important Health Information

Health history. Patients with endocrine problems often present with nonspecific complaints. They may report not just one but a group of symptoms. The most common presenting problems include fatigue, weakness, menstrual problems, and weight changes. It is important to determine if the onset of symptoms has been gradual or sudden and what the patient has done about them.

Because some of the more general signs of problems are the easiest to overlook, evaluate any reported or observed changes in weight, appetite, skin, libido, mental acuity, emotional stability, or energy levels.

Medications. Ask about the use of all medications, herbs, and diet supplements. Ask about the reason for taking the drug, the dosage, and the length of time the drug has been taken. Are they using hormone replacements, such as insulin, thyroid hormone, or corticosteroids (e.g., prednisone)? This will alert you to potential adverse drug events. For example, corticosteroids may increase blood glucose levels and cause bone loss with long-term use. Thyroid agents may cause tachycardia or dysrhythmias. Drug-to-drug interactions and adverse effects of nonhormonal medications can contribute to endocrine problems.

Surgery or other treatments. Ask about medical, surgical, and obstetric history. Include the number of pregnancies and live births. Assess growth patterns and stages of physical and emotional development. For example, knowing about radiation therapy to the head and neck is important when you suspect thyroid or pituitary problems.

Functional Health Patterns

Key questions to ask the patient with an endocrine problem are outlined in Table 52.4.

TABLE 52.4 HEALTH HISTORY

Endocrine System

Health Perception–Health Management
- What is your usual day like?
- Have you noticed any changes in your ability to perform your usual activities compared with last year? 5 years ago?[a]

Nutritional-Metabolic
- What are your weight and height?
- How much do you want to weigh?
- Have there been any changes in your appetite or weight?[a]
- Have you noticed any changes in the distribution of the hair anywhere on your body?[a]
- Have you noticed any changes in the color of your skin, especially on your face, neck, hands, or body creases?[a]
- Has the texture of your skin changed? For example, does it seem thicker and drier than it used to?[a]
- Have you noticed any problems swallowing, throat pain, or hoarseness? Is the top button on your shirt or blouse hard to button?[a]
- Do you feel more nervous than you used to? Do you notice your heart pounding or that you sweat when you do not think you should be sweating?
- Is it hard to hold things because of shakiness of your hands?[a]
- Do you feel that most rooms are too hot or too cold? Do you often have to put on a sweater, or feel as though you need to open windows when others in the room seem comfortable?[a]
- Do you have, or have you had any wounds that were slow to heal?[a]

Elimination
- Do you have to get up at night to urinate? If so, how many times? Do you keep water by your bed at night?
- Have you ever had a kidney stone?[a]
- Describe your usual bowel pattern. Have you noted any bowel changes?[a]
- Do you use anything, such as laxatives, to help you move your bowels?[a]

Activity-Exercise
- What is your usual activity pattern during a typical day?
- Do you have a planned exercise program? If yes, what is it and have you had to make any changes in this routine lately? If so, why, and what kinds of changes?
- Do you have fatigue with or without activity?[a]
- Have you had any trouble breathing?[a]

Sleep-Rest
- How many hours do you sleep at night? Do you feel rested on awakening?
- Are you ever awakened by sweating during the night?[a]
- Do you have nightmares?[a]

Cognitive-Perceptual
- How is your memory? Have you noticed any changes?[a]
- Have you had any blurring or double vision?[a]
- When was your last eye examination?

Self-Perception–Self-Concept
- Have you noticed any changes in your physical appearance or size?[a]
- Are you concerned about your weight?[a]
- Do you feel you are able to do what you think you can do? If not, why not?
- Does your health problem affect how you feel about yourself?[a]

Role-Relationship
- Do you have a support system or partner? Are you married? Do you have any children? Do you think you are able to take care of your family and home? If not, why not?
- Where do you work? What kind of work do you do? Are you able to do what is expected of you and what you expect of yourself?
- Are you retired? What type of work did you do before you retired? How do you spend your time now that you have retired?

Sexuality-Reproductive

Women
- When did you start to menstruate? Was this earlier or later than other women in your family?
- When was your last menstrual period? Do you have scant, heavy, or irregular menstrual flows?
- How many children have you had? How much did they weigh at birth? Were you told you had diabetes during any pregnancy?[a]
- Are you menopausal? If so, for how long?
- Are you trying to get pregnant but cannot?[a]
- Are you postmenopausal? If so, do you have any bleeding from your uterus?

Men
- Have you noticed any changes in your ability to get and maintain an erection?[a]
- Are you trying to have children but cannot?[a]

Coping–Stress Tolerance
- What kind of stressors do you have?
- How do you deal with stress or problems?
- What is your support system? To whom do you turn when you have a problem?

Value-Belief
- Do you think medicine should still be taken even though you feel okay?
- Do any of your prescribed therapies cause any conflict in your value-belief system?[a]

[a]If yes, describe.

BOX 52.1 GENETIC RISK ALERT

Pituitary

- Nephrogenic diabetes insipidus can be inherited as a sex-linked or autosomal disorder.

Thyroid

- Genetics has a role in many cases of hypothyroid and hyperthyroid problems.
- Hashimoto thyroiditis, the most common cause of hypothyroidism, and Graves' disease, a cause of hyperthyroidism, are autoimmune disorders. Both likely result from a combination of genetic and environmental factors.

Multiple Endocrine Neoplasia (MEN)

- MEN involves tumors in 2 or more different endocrine glands.
- The features of MEN are relatively consistent within a family.
- Medullary thyroid cancer is common in MEN type 2.[2]

Diabetes

- Genetics has a strong role in the development of type 1 and type 2 diabetes.

Health perception–health management pattern. Heredity plays a key role in the development of endocrine problems (Box 52.1). Ask about first-degree relatives with diabetes, thyroid disease, or endocrine gland cancers since these conditions have a familial tendency. A genetic assessment of family members may be needed.

Nutritional-metabolic pattern. Changes in appetite and weight can indicate an endocrine problem. Ask about a history of weight distribution and changes. Weight loss with increased appetite may occur with hyperthyroidism or diabetes. Weight gain may occur with hypothyroidism or hypocortisolism. Obese persons are more likely to develop type 2 diabetes.

Ask if there have been problems with nausea, vomiting, or diarrhea. An enlarged thyroid gland can cause problems swallowing or a change in neck size. Increased SNS activity, including nervousness, palpitations, sweating, and tremors, may occur with thyroid problems or a rare tumor of the adrenal medulla *(pheochromocytoma)*. Heat or cold intolerance occurs with hyperthyroidism or hypothyroidism, respectively.

Ask about changes in the patient's skin, especially on the face, neck, hands, or body creases. Changes in skin texture and skin that seems thicker or drier may suggest an endocrine problem. A patient with hypothyroidism or excess GH may have skin that feels coarse or leathery. Ask if the patient has noticed any change in the distribution of hair anywhere on the body.

Elimination pattern. Because maintaining fluid balance is a key role of the endocrine system, questions related to fluid intake and elimination patterns may uncover endocrine problems. For example, increased thirst and urination can indicate diabetes (pancreas problem) or diabetes insipidus (pituitary problem). Ask about the frequency and consistency of bowel movements. Diarrhea can occur with hyperthyroidism or thyroid cancer. Constipation occurs with hypothyroidism, hypoparathyroidism, and hypopituitarism.

Activity-exercise pattern. Determine if there are any acute or gradual changes in energy level or persistent fatigue. A patient with chronic fatigue from hypothyroidism, hypocortisolism, or diabetes may report changes in activity level.

Sleep-rest pattern. Ask the patient how many hours they typically sleep and if they feel rested on awakening. Sleep problems can result from nocturia, nightmares, anxiety, depression, or insomnia that occur with diabetes or thyroid problems.

Cognitive-perceptual pattern. Memory deficits may occur with hypothyroidism and changes in sodium levels. Inappropriate secretion of antidiuretic hormone (SIADH) or pituitary tumors can cause hyponatremia. These issues can occur gradually. Gathering information from the patient and family about memory, cognitive abilities, and balance can increase the chances of an earlier diagnosis.

Self-perception–self-concept pattern. Many endocrine problems may affect a patient's self-esteem because of associated changes in physical appearance. For example, weight gain from hypothyroidism or exophthalmos and goiter from hyperthyroidism can cause body image concerns.

Role-relationship pattern. Questions related to roles and relationships can highlight depression, chronic fatigue, and sleep problems. With chronic fatigue, depression, and anxiety, patients and their families will have stressed relationships. Questions related to home life and the patients' ability to fulfill their role in the family will aid in identifying problems.

Sexuality-reproductive pattern. The endocrine system regulates GH, prolactin, LH, FSH, testosterone, and estrogen. Therefore, menstrual problems, hirsutism, infertility, decreased libido, and growth problems can result from endocrine problems. Some women develop hypothyroidism during or after menopause. Other patients begin to develop type 2 diabetes during middle age when sex hormones are changing. Assess for abnormal secondary sex characteristics, such as facial hair *(hirsutism)* in women. Obtain a detailed history of menstruation and pregnancy. Menstrual problems can occur with disorders of the ovaries and pituitary, thyroid, and adrenal glands. A history of large-birth-weight babies or gestational diabetes increases the risk of developing type 2 diabetes. Male sexual problems may include impotence, infertility, or the lack of development of secondary sexual characteristics. Retrograde ejaculation can occur in diabetes.

Coping–stress tolerance pattern. Because stress worsens some endocrine conditions, ask patients about their stress level and usual coping patterns. Patients with adrenal insufficiency have difficulty dealing with stress. These patients are at risk for developing hypotension and fluid and electrolyte imbalance.

Value-belief pattern. Determining a patient's ability to make lifestyle changes is an important nursing function. Identify the patient's value-belief patterns so that you can help to determine appropriate treatment plans. This is especially important in a condition such as diabetes, which may require major lifestyle changes. Other disorders, such as hypothyroidism, may be managed with medications but need lifelong monitoring.

Case Study

Subjective Data

(© iStockphoto/ Thinkstock.)

A focused subjective assessment of L.M. revealed the following information:

- ***Medical History:*** Denies any medical or surgical history. Has not seen an HCP for 8 years.
- ***Medications:*** None.
- ***Health Perception–Health Management:*** L.M. works as a receptionist for a local law firm and says it is all she can do to make it through the workday. She often wakes up with a headache and goes to bed with the same headache, describing it as a dull, throbbing ache between her eyes. She rates the pain as a 4 on a scale of 0 to 10 and states that ibuprofen does not ease the pain. The pain is typically worse on arising in the morning. It slowly decreases during the day. She does not have the energy she had 6 months ago. She used to enjoy gardening and going out with friends but now can barely manage work and coming home.
- ***Nutritional-Metabolic:*** L.M. reports a steady weight gain over the past 6 months, mainly in her abdominal area. She feels as if she looks pregnant but knows that is not possible. Her appetite has decreased, but she is not able to lose any weight. She says she feels "bloated." She reports growth of facial hair and notices she is bruising easily. L.M. denies problems with swallowing, hoarseness, palpitations, or tremors.
- ***Elimination:*** Denies any changes or problems with urination or bowel movements.
- ***Activity-Exercise:*** L.M. states that she has no ambition to exercise. She is just too tired at the end of the workday and has no energy on the weekends either. She reports leg cramps with walking.
- ***Sleep-Rest:*** Sleeps 10+ h at night but does not feel rested on awakening.
- ***Cognitive-Perceptual:*** L.M. finds herself easily angered and irritable, often snapping at coworkers and her husband. She says this is not her usual self. At first, she thought it was because she was dealing with a constant, dull headache. Lately, she has noticed that her vision is blurry, making work and life more stressful.
- ***Self-Perception–Self-Concept:*** L.M. says that she cannot believe what she sees when she looks in the mirror. She feels as if she has aged 10 years over the past 6 months. She has gained weight in her face, neck, and trunk. Her scalp hair is thinning, and she is growing a beard. She tells you she feels "old and ugly"!
- ***Coping–Stress Tolerance:*** L.M. states that she is finding it harder to cope with the stresses of her job, her relationship with her husband, and life in general. She believes her emotions are very "raw and labile," so different from the easy-going, smiling person she had once prided herself in being.

Discussion Questions

1. Which subjective assessment findings concern you most?
2. Based on the subjective assessment findings, what should you include in the physical assessment? What would you be looking for?

You will learn more about the physical assessment of the endocrine system in the next section.

Answers available at http://evolve.elsevier.com/Lewis/medsurg.

Objective Data

Assessment is performed using objective data from the physical assessment and diagnostic tests. Except for the thyroid and testes, most endocrine glands are inaccessible to direct assessment. It is essential to understand the actions of hormones to assess the function of a gland by monitoring the target tissue.

Physical Assessment

Use the following general assessment when evaluating endocrine function. Specific clinical findings for the various endocrine problems are discussed in Chapters 53 and 54. Endocrine problems may cause changes in mental and emotional status. Throughout the assessment, note the patient's orientation, alertness, memory, cognitive abilities, affect, personality, and appropriateness of their behavior.

Take a full set of vital signs. Variations in temperature, heart rate, and BP can occur with a variety of endocrine problems. Obtain height and weight. Calculate body mass index (BMI) to assess nutrition status.

Integument. Assess the color and texture of the skin, hair, and nails. Note the overall skin color and pigment. Decreased skin pigment can occur in hypopituitarism, hypothyroidism, and hypoparathyroidism. Hyperpigmentation, or "bronzing" of the skin, especially on knuckles, elbows, knees, genitalia, and palmar creases, is a classic finding with Addison disease. Palpate the skin for texture and moisture. Examine hair distribution on the head, face, trunk, genitalia, and extremities. Assess the hair's appearance and texture. Hair loss, excess hair growth, or dull, brittle hair may suggest endocrine problems. Changes in genital hair distribution can occur with hormone problems. Assess for bruising and delayed wound healing.

Head. Inspect the size and contour of the head. Facial features should be symmetric. Hyperreflexia and facial muscle contraction upon percussion of the facial nerve *(Chvostek sign)* may occur in hypoparathyroidism. Inspect the eyes for position, symmetry, and shape. Large and protruding eyes (exophthalmos) can occur with hyperthyroidism. Assess visual acuity. Visual field loss may occur with a pituitary tumor. In the mouth, inspect the buccal mucosa, condition of teeth, and tongue size. Note hair distribution on the scalp and face. Vision and hearing loss are common in acromegaly from excess GH.[3]

Neck. The thyroid gland is not usually visible during inspection. A feature that distinguishes the thyroid from other masses in the neck is its upward movement on swallowing. Inspect the neck while the patient swallows a sip of water. The neck should appear symmetric without lumps or bulging.

Palpate the thyroid for size, shape, symmetry, tenderness, and any nodules. *Goiter,* an enlarged thyroid gland, can occur with hyperthyroidism or hypothyroidism. Do not press too hard or massage an enlarged thyroid gland. This can cause a sudden release of thyroid hormone into an already overloaded system. An experienced clinician should perform palpation in patients with a known diagnosis of hyperthyroidism.

Perform palpation using a posterior or anterior approach. For *anterior palpation,* stand in front of the patient with the patient's neck flexed. Place your thumb horizontally with the upper edge along the lower border of the cricoid cartilage. Then move your thumb over the isthmus as the patient swallows water. Place your fingers laterally to the anterior border of the sternocleidomastoid muscle and palpate each lateral lobe before and while the patient swallows water.[4]

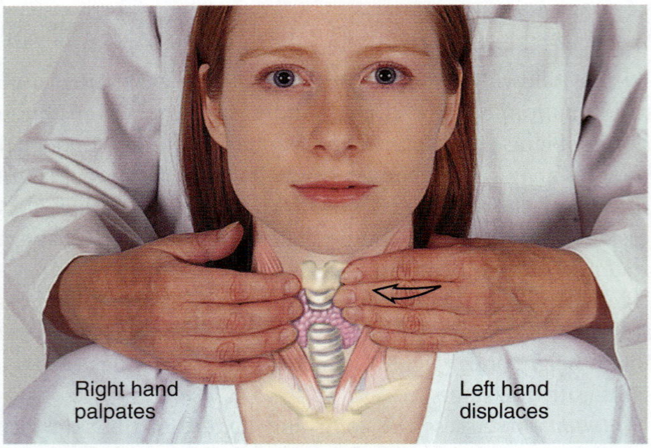

Fig. 52.10 Posterior palpation of the thyroid gland. (From Jarvis C: *Physical examination and health assessment,* ed 6, St Louis, 2012, Saunders.)

For *posterior palpation,* stand behind the patient (Fig. 52.10). With the thumbs of both hands resting on the nape of the patient's neck, use your index and middle fingers of both hands to feel for the thyroid isthmus and the anterior surfaces of the lateral lobes. Ask the patient to flex the neck slightly forward and to the right to relax the neck muscles. Displace the thyroid cartilage to the right with your left hand and fingers. Palpate with your right hand after placing the thumb deep and behind the sternocleidomastoid muscle with the index and middle fingers in front of it. Ask the patient to swallow water and feel for the thyroid to move up. In a normal person, the thyroid is often not palpable. If palpable, it usually feels smooth with a firm consistency. It is not tender with gentle pressure.[4]

If nodules, enlargement, asymmetry, or hardness (abnormal findings) are present, refer the patient for further evaluation. Auscultate the lateral lobes of an enlarged thyroid gland with the stethoscope bell to hear a *bruit,* a soft swishing sound that can occur with a goiter or hyperthyroidism.

Thorax. Inspect the thorax for shape and characteristics of the skin. Note the presence of breast gynecomastia in men. Auscultate lung sounds and heart sounds. Note any adventitious lung sounds (wheezing, decreased sounds) or extra heart sounds. Signs of fluid overload or heart failure may be present in patients with SIADH or hypothyroidism.

Abdomen. Inspect the contour of the abdomen. Note the symmetry and color. Cushing syndrome (hypercortisolism) causes the skin to be fragile, resulting in purple-blue striae across the abdomen. Note general obesity or truncal obesity. Auscultate bowel sounds.

Extremities. Assess the size, shape, symmetry, and general proportion of hands and feet. Patients with acromegaly from pituitary tumors may have large hands and feet. Inspect the skin for pigment changes, lesions, and edema. Assess muscle strength and deep tendon reflexes. Are there any tremors? Muscle spasms of the hand elicited on application of an occlusive BP cuff for 3 minutes *(Trousseau sign)* may occur in hypoparathyroidism.

Genitalia. Assessment abnormalities related to the endocrine system are outlined in Table 52.5. A focused assessment of the endocrine system is shown in Box 52.2.

Case Study

Objective Data: Physical Assessment

(© iStockphoto/ Thinkstock.)

A focused assessment of L.M. reveals the following:

L.M. appears somewhat anxious. Her BP is 190/80, heart rate 84, respiratory rate 20, temp 98.6°F (37°C). Her weight is 160 lb. She is 5 ft, 4 in tall. L.M.'s face is reddened and puffy. She appears to have a lump on the back of her neck and shoulders. There is some acne on her face and some hair growth on her upper lip and chin area. Her abdomen is protruding, but her arms and legs are thin. She has +1 edema in her ankles bilaterally. There are several bruises on her upper and lower extremities, as well as purple stretch marks on her abdomen.

Discussion Questions

1. Which physical assessment findings concern you most?
2. Based upon the subjective and objective assessment data presented so far, what are 3 priority clinical problems?
3. What diagnostic studies would you expect to be ordered?

You will learn more about diagnostic studies related to the endocrine system in the next section.

Answers available at http://evolve.elsevier.com/Lewis/medsurg.

DIAGNOSTIC STUDIES OF ENDOCRINE SYSTEM

Diagnostic studies of the endocrine system are shown in Tables 52.6 and 52.7. Pertinent findings from the history and physical assessment guide the selection of diagnostic studies. Imaging studies can identify pituitary tumors, thyroid nodules, or adrenal tumors. Laboratory studies may include direct measurement of the hormone level or an indirect measure of gland function by evaluating blood or urine components affected by the hormone, such as glucose or electrolytes. We can measure releasing and stimulating hormones. For example, we can evaluate thyroid function by measuring TSH.

We can assess hormones with constant basal levels, such as T_4, with a single measurement. Note the time of the sample collection on the laboratory slip. Information about night shift work is important for hormones with circadian or sleep-related secretion (e.g., cortisol). Evaluating other hormones may require multiple blood samplings. Examples include suppression tests (e.g., dexamethasone) and stimulation tests (e.g., glucose tolerance). In these situations, it is often necessary to obtain IV access to give the testing medication and fluids and draw multiple blood samples.

Pituitary gland problems can manifest in a wide variety of ways because of the number of hormones produced. Many diagnostic studies evaluate these hormones either directly or indirectly.

Several tests are available to evaluate thyroid function. The most sensitive and accurate laboratory test is the measurement of TSH. It is often the first test performed to evaluate thyroid function.[5]

TABLE 52.5 ASSESSMENT ABNORMALITIES

Endocrine System

Finding	Description	Possible Etiology and Significance
Cardiovascular		
Chest pain	Angina caused by increased metabolic demands, effusions	Hyperthyroidism, hypothyroidism
Dysrhythmias	Tachycardia, atrial fibrillation	Hypothyroidism, hyperthyroidism, hypoparathyroidism, hyperparathyroidism, pheochromocytoma
Fluid overload or signs of heart failure	Crackles in the lungs, peripheral edema, shortness of breath	SIADH, hypothyroidism, myxedema
Hypertension	High BP caused by ↑ metabolic demands and catecholamines	Hyperthyroidism, pheochromocytoma, Cushing syndrome
GI		
Constipation	Passage of infrequent hard stools	Hypothyroidism, hyperparathyroidism
Head and Neck		
Exophthalmos	Eyeball protrusion from orbits	Hyperthyroidism because of fluid accumulation in eye and retroorbital tissue
Goiter	Generalized enlargement of thyroid gland	Hyperthyroidism, hypothyroidism, iodine deficiency
Moon face	Periorbital edema and facial fullness	Cushing syndrome because of ↑ cortisol secretion
Myxedema	Puffiness, periorbital edema, masklike affect	Hydrophilic mucopolysaccharides infiltrating dermis in patients with hypothyroidism
Thyroid nodule(s)	Localized enlargement of thyroid gland	May be benign or malignant
Vision changes	↓ Visual acuity and/or ↓ peripheral vision	Pituitary gland enlargement or tumor leading to pressure on optic nerve
Integument		
Bruises easily	Multiple bruises over various parts of body	Cushing syndrome
Changes in hair distribution	Hair loss	Hypothyroidism, hyperthyroidism, ↓ pituitary secretion
	↓ Axillary and pubic hair	Cortisol deficiency
	Hirsutism (excess facial hair on women)	Cushing syndrome, prolactinoma (a pituitary tumor)
Changes in skin texture	Thick, cold, dry skin	Hypothyroidism
	Thick, leathery, oily skin	GH excess (acromegaly)
	Warm, smooth, moist skin	Hyperthyroidism
Depigmentation (vitiligo)	Patchy areas of light skin	May be a marker of autoimmune endocrine problems
Edema	Generalized edema	Mucopolysaccharide accumulation in tissue in hypothyroidism
Hyperpigmentation	Darkening of the skin, especially in skinfolds and creases	↑ Secretion of MSH from Addison disease, acanthosis nigricans
Skin ulcers	Areas of ulcerated skin, most often found on legs and feet	Peripheral neuropathy and peripheral vascular disease, which are contributory factors in the development of diabetic foot ulcers
Striae	Purplish red marks below the skin surface. Usually seen on abdomen, breasts, and buttocks	Cushing syndrome
Musculoskeletal		
Changes in muscular strength or muscle mass	Generalized weakness and/or fatigue	Common with many endocrine problems, including pituitary, thyroid, parathyroid, and adrenal problems
		Diabetes, diabetes insipidus
	↓ Muscle mass	GH deficiency and Cushing syndrome from protein wasting
Enlargement of bones and cartilage	Coarsening of facial features. ↑ In size of hands and feet over several years	GH excess in adults. Seen in acromegaly due to pituitary dysfunction
Neurologic		
↑ Deep tendon reflexes	Hyperreflexia	Hyperthyroidism, hypoparathyroidism
Lethargy	State of mental sluggishness or somnolence	Hypothyroidism
Seizure	Sudden involuntary contraction of muscles	Pituitary tumor
		Hypervolemia and hyponatremia with SIADH
		Complication of diabetes, severe hypothyroidism
Tetany	Intermittent involuntary muscle spasms usually involving the extremities	Severe hypocalcemia that can occur with hypoparathyroidism
Nutrition		
Changes in weight	Weight loss	Hyperthyroidism caused by ↑ in metabolism, type 1 diabetes
	Weight gain	Hypothyroidism, Cushing syndrome, type 2 diabetes

Continued

TABLE 52.5 ASSESSMENT ABNORMALITIES—cont'd

Endocrine System

Finding	Description	Possible Etiology and Significance
Glucose levels altered	↑ Serum glucose	Diabetes, Cushing syndrome, GH excess
Reproductive		
Changes in reproductive function	Menstrual irregularities, ↓ libido, ↓ fertility, impotence	Pituitary hypofunction, GH excess, thyroid problems, adrenocortical problems
Other		
↓ Urine output	↓ Water reabsorption from kidney tubules	SIADH
Polydipsia	Excessive thirst	Extreme water losses in diabetes (with severe hyperglycemia), diabetes insipidus, dehydration
Polyuria	Excess urine output	Diabetes (from hyperglycemia) or diabetes insipidus (due to ↓ ADH)
Thermoregulation	Cold insensitivity	Hypothyroidism caused by a slowing of metabolic processes
	Heat intolerance	Hyperthyroidism caused by excessive metabolism

BOX 52.2 FOCUSED ASSESSMENT

Endocrine System

Use this checklist to ensure you complete key assessment steps.

Subjective

Ask the patient about any of the following and note responses.

Excessive or increased thirst	Y	N
Excess or decreased urination	Y	N
Excessive hunger	Y	N
Heat or cold intolerance	Y	N
Excessive sweating	Y	N
Recent weight gain or loss	Y	N

Objective: Diagnostic

Check the following laboratory results for critical values.

Potassium	✓
Glucose	✓
Sodium	✓
Glycosylated hemoglobin (A1C)	✓
Thyroid studies: TSH, T_3, T_4	✓
Serum osmolality	✓

Objective: Physical Assessment

Inspect/Measure

Body temperature	✓
Height and weight	✓
Alertness and emotional state	✓
Skin for changes in color and texture	✓
Hair for changes in color, texture, and distribution	✓

Auscultate

Heart rate, BP	✓

Palpate

Extremities for edema	✓
Skin for texture and temperature	✓
Neck for thyroid size, shape	✓

Follow-up tests ordered when the TSH level is abnormal include total T_4, free T_4, and total T_3. Free T_4 is the unbound thyroxine. It more accurately reflects thyroid function than total T_4.

The only hormone secreted by the parathyroid glands is PTH. Because PTH regulates serum calcium and phosphate levels, these levels reflect problems with PTH secretion. For this reason, parathyroid gland testing typically includes PTH, serum calcium, and serum phosphate levels.

Tests assessing adrenal cortex function focus on measuring blood plasma and urine levels of the 3 types of hormones secreted: glucocorticoids, mineralocorticoids, and androgens. Urine studies often require a 24-hour urine collection to eliminate the impact of short-term fluctuations in plasma hormone levels.

The tests used to evaluate glucose metabolism are important in the diagnosis and management of diabetes. See Chapter 53 for information about diagnostic studies for diabetes.

Case Study

Objective Data: Diagnostic Studies

(© iStockphoto/ Thinkstock.)

The HCP orders the following initial diagnostic studies to be drawn in the morning after an 8-h fast:

- CBC, basic metabolic panel (electrolytes, BUN, creatinine)
- Fasting blood glucose (FBG)
- TSH, free T_4
- Plasma cortisol levels
- Plasma ACTH levels

CBC results reveal a WBC of 12,200/μL and a decreased lymphocyte count at 800 cells/μL. The rest of the CBC is within normal limits (WNL). The FBG is 130 mg/dL. The plasma cortisol and ACTH levels are high. Thyroid studies are WNL.

Discussion Questions

1. Which diagnostic study results are of most concern to you?
2. Do you expect the HCP to order any other diagnostic studies for L.M.?
3. What are our care priorities for L.M. at this time?

Answers available at http://evolve.elsevier.com/Lewis/medsurg.

TABLE 52.6 Serology and Urine Studies

Endocrine System

Study	Reference Interval	Purpose and Description	Nursing Responsibility
Adrenal Studies			
Blood Studies			
Adrenal steroid precursors • Androstenediones (AD) • Dehydroepiandrosterone (DHEA) • Dehydroepiandrosterone sulfate (DHEA S) • 11-Deoxycortisol	AD • *Female:* 0.05–2.05 ng/mL • *Male:* 0.04–1.06 ng/mL DHEA • *Female:* 0.14–7.88 ng/mL • *Male:* 0.11–6.73 ng/mL DHEA S • *Female:* 7–488 mcg/dL • *Male:* 7–371 mcg/dL 11-Deoxycortisol • *Adults:* 10–79 ng/dL	Assesses for congenital adrenal hyperplasia, sex hormones abnormalities, adrenal or gonadal tumors.	*Before*: Tanner stage I–V of physical development needed for accurate assessment. Determine date of last menstrual period (LMP) for females. Test should be done 1 week before or after menstrual cycle. *After*: Note date of LMP on laboratory slip.
Adrenocorticotropic hormone (ACTH, corticotropin)	• *Female:* 6–58 pg/mL • *Male:* 7–69 pg/mL	Measures amount of ACTH made by the anterior pituitary gland. Levels determine if there is an overproduction or underproduction of cortisol and whether cause is an adrenal gland or pituitary gland abnormality.	*Before:* Patient should be NPO after midnight. Do morning blood draw between 6 and 8 AM. *During:* Use prechilled blood tube and place on ice.
ACTH stimulation test with cosyntropin (Cortisol stimulation test)	*Rapid test:* Cortisol levels increase more than 7 mcg/dL higher than baseline *24-Hr test:* Cortisol levels >40 mcg/dL *3-Day test:* Cortisol levels greater than 40 mcg/dL	Used to evaluate cause of adrenal insufficiency. If cortisol levels increase after cosyntropin injection, the cause of adrenal insufficiency is the pituitary gland. If there is no or little rise in cortisol levels, the cause of adrenal insufficiency is the adrenal gland.	*Before*: Obtain baseline cortisol level at beginning of cosyntropin infusion. *During*: Inject bolus of IV cosyntropin with a plastic syringe. Draw cortisol samples 30 and 60 min after bolus. Monitor site and rate of IV infusion. Ensure sample collection at appropriate times.
Aldosterone	*Supine:* 3–10 ng/dL (0.08–0.30 nmol/L) *Upright:* • *Female:* 5–30 ng/dL (0.14–0.08 nmol/L) • *Male:* 6–22 ng/dL (0.17–0.61 nmol/L)	Used to identify hyperaldosteronism. Helps distinguish primary aldosteronism from adrenal disease versus secondary aldosteronism from extraadrenal disease.	*Before:* Morning blood sample is preferred. Tell patient that the required position (supine/sitting/standing) must be maintained for 2 h before specimen is drawn.
Cortisol (hydrocortisone, serum cortisol)	• *8 AM:* 5–23 mcg/dL (138–635 nmol/L) • *4 PM:* 3–13 mcg/dL (83–359 nmol/L)	Measures serum cortisol level to evaluate adrenal activity. Cortisol levels are normally highest in the morning, slowly drop during the day, and are lowest around midnight.	*Before:* Sample should be drawn in morning. Note if patient works night shift. Mark time of blood draw on laboratory slip. Stress and excess physical activity produce elevated results.
Dexamethasone suppression (DST, prolonged/rapid DST, cortisol suppression test, ACTH suppression test)	Prolonged method: • *Low dose:* >50% reduction of plasma cortisol and 17-hydroxycorticosteroid (17-OCHS) • *High dose:* >50% reduction of plasma cortisol and 17-OCHS Rapid (overnight) method: • Plasma cortisol levels suppressed to <2 mcg/dL	Helps to identify and determine cause of adrenal hyperactivity (e.g., Cushing syndrome).	*Before*: Patient should fast for 8–10 hr prior. Do not test acutely ill patients or those under stress. Stress-stimulated ACTH may override suppression. Screen patient for drugs, such as estrogen and corticosteroids, which may give false-positive results. *Overnight method:* Dexamethasone 1 mg (low dose) or 4 mg (high dose) is given at 2300 to suppress secretion of corticotropin-releasing hormone. Plasma cortisol sample is drawn at 0800.
Metanephrine, plasma free (fractionated metanephrine)	*Normetanephrine:* <0.5 nmol/L or 18–111 pg/mL by HPLC *Metanephrine:* <0.9 nmol/L or 12–60 pg/mL by HPLC	Used to identify pheochromocytoma of the adrenal or extraadrenal glands.	*Before:* Ask about recent history of vigorous exercise, high stress levels, or starvation (may artificially ↑ levels). Assess for drugs (e.g., caffeine, alcohol, levodopa, nitroglycerin, acetaminophen, and those containing epinephrine or norepinephrine) that can alter results.

Continued

TABLE 52.6 Serology and Urine Studies—cont'd

Endocrine System

Study	Reference Interval	Purpose and Description	Nursing Responsibility
Urine Studies			
Cortisol (hydrocortisone, urine cortisol, free cortisol)	24-Hr specimen: <100 mcg/24 hr (<276 nmol/day)	Measures urine cortisol level to evaluate adrenal activity.	*Before*: Explain 24-hr urine collection and need to avoid stressful situations and excessive physical exercise. Assess for drug use (e.g., reserpine, diuretics, phenothiazines, insulin, amphetamines) that may alter results.
17-Hydroxycorticosteroids (17-OCHS)	24-Hr specimen: *Adults:* • *Male:* 3–10 mg/24 hr (8.3–27.6 μmol/day) • *Female:* 2–8 mg/24 hr (5.2–22.1 μmol/day)	Measures 17-OCHS, a cortisol metabolite, to evaluate adrenocortical function. Older adults may have slightly lower values.	*Before*: Explain 24-hr urine collection and need to avoid stressful situations and excess physical exercise. Assess for drug use (e.g., erythromycin, spironolactone) that may alter results.
17-Ketosteroids (17-KS)	24-Hr specimen: • *Male:* 6–20 mg/24 hr (20–70 μmol/day) • *Female:* 6–17 mg/24 hr (20–60 μmol/day)	Evaluates adrenocortical and gonadal functions by measuring urinary androgen metabolites. Older adults may have slightly lower values.	*Before:* Explain 24-hr urine collection.
Vanillylmandelic acid (VMA)	24-Hr specimen: <6.8 mg/24 hr (<35 μmol/24 hr)	Measures the excretion of catecholamine metabolite. Used to identify catecholamine-producing tumors, such as pheochromocytoma.	*Before*: Explain 24-hr urine collection. Must follow VMA-restricted diet 2–3 days before and during the urine collection. *During*: Keep 24-hr urine collection at pH <3.0 with HCl acid as preservative. Keep on ice.
Pancreatic Studies			
Blood Studies			
C-Peptide (connecting peptide insulin, insulin C-peptide, proinsulin C-peptide)	*Fasting:* 0.78–1.89 ng/mL (0.26–0.62 nmol/L) *1 hr after glucose load:* 5–12 ng/mL	Measures amount of C-peptide, which is released with insulin. Distinguishes between type 1 (low levels) and type 2 diabetes (normal or high levels).	*Before:* Patient should fast 8–12 hr prior. Water intake is allowed.
Glucagon	50–100 pg/mL (50–100 ng/L)	Assesses for glucagonoma (α islet cell tumor). Evaluates pancreatic function, especially in people with diabetes who have low blood glucose (hypoglycemia).	*Before:* Patient should fast 8–12 hr prior. Water intake is allowed.
Glucose (blood sugar, fasting blood glucose [FBG])	*Fasting* (defined as no caloric intake for at least 8 hr): 74–106 mg/dL (4.1–5.9 mmol/L) *Casual* (defined as any time of day): ≤200 mg/dL (<11.1 mmol/L)	Aids in the diagnosis of diabetes.	*Before:* Patient should fast 8–12 hr prior. Water intake is allowed. Assess for the many drugs that may influence results.
Glucose, postprandial (2-hour postprandial glucose [2-h PPG])	*0–50 years:* <140 mg/dL (<7.8 mmol/L) *50–60 years:* <150 md/dL *60 years and older:* <160 mg/dL	Aids in the diagnosis of diabetes.	*Before:* Patient should fast 8–12 hr, then eat a meal of at least 75 g of carbohydrate. Patient must fast after eating this meal until blood is drawn. No exercise during test.
Glucose tolerance test (GTT, oral glucose tolerance [OGTT])	*Nonpregnancy:* *Fasting:* <110 mg/dL (<6.1 mmol/L *1 hr:* <180 mg/dL (<11.1 mmol/L) 2 *hr:* <140 mg/dL (<7.8 mmol/L)	Assesses glucose levels in people with symptoms of (hypoglycemia). Aids in the diagnosis of diabetes.	*Before:* Patient should fast 8–12 hr prior. Many drugs may influence results, including caffeine and smoking. Ensure that patient's diet 3 days before test includes 150–300 g of carbohydrate with intake of at least 1500 cal/day.
Glycosylated hemoglobin (GHb, GHB, glycohemoglobin, hemoglobin A1C [Hb A1C], diabetic control index, glycated protein)	*Nondiabetic adult/child:* 4%–5.6%	Measures the average blood glucose for the past 90 days. Used to diagnose and screen diabetes treatment plans.	*Before:* Tell patient that fasting is not necessary and that blood sample will be drawn.

TABLE 52.6 Serology and Urine Studies—cont'd

Endocrine System

Study	Reference Interval	Purpose and Description	Nursing Responsibility
Insulin assay	6–26 μU/mL (43–186 pmol/L)	Assesses insulin levels in people with symptoms of hypoglycemia. Assesses for insulinomas and carbohydrate and lipid absorption abnormalities.	*Before:* Patient should fast 8–12 hr prior. Water intake is allowed.
Urine Studies			
Glucose (urine sugar)	*Random specimen:* negative *24-hr specimen:* 50–300 mg/day (0.3–1.7 mmol/day)	Measures amount of glucose in the urine. Assesses diabetes management.	*Before:* Use freshly voided urine. Many drugs alter glucose readings. Follow directions exactly to avoid errors.
Ketones	None or negative	Measures amount of ketones in the urine. Assesses for diabetic ketoacidosis, a life-threatening condition seen most often in people with type 1 diabetes.	*Before:* Use freshly voided urine specimen. Test is often done with glucose test. Follow directions exactly. Certain drugs can produce false-positive or false-negative results.
Parathyroid Studies			
Blood Studies			
Calcium (total)	9.0–10.5 mg/dL (2.25–2.62 mmol/L)	Assesses the function of the parathyroid gland and calcium absorption.	*Before:* Patient must fast 8–12 hr prior. Assess for drug use (e.g., albuterol, heparin, diuretics) that may alter results. *After:* Keep sample on ice.
Calcium (ionized)	4.5–5.6 mg/dL (1.05–1.3 mmol/L)	Free form of total calcium. Unchanged by inconsistent serum albumin levels that occur in certain populations, such as critically ill patients.	As above.
Parathyroid hormone (PTH, parathormone)	*Intact (whole):* 10–65 pg/mL (10–65 ng/L) *N terminal:* 8–24 pg/mL *C terminal:* 50–330 pg/mL	Used to determine the cause of changes in calcium levels caused by parathyroid or nonparathyroid problems. Monitored in patients with chronic kidney disease, especially those on dialysis.	*Before:* Patient should fast 8–12 hr prior. Obtain sample in the morning. *During:* Obtain serum calcium level at same time. *After:* Mark time of blood draw on laboratory slip.
Phosphate (PO4), phosphorus (P)	3.0–4.5 mg/dL (0.97–1.45 mmol/L)	Measures amount of inorganic phosphate in the blood. Assesses for problems related to calcium and phosphorus disorders.	*Before:* Patient must fast 8–12 hr prior. If possible, hold IV fluids containing glucose for 8 hr prior.
Pituitary Studies			
Blood Studies			
Antidiuretic hormone (ADH, vasopressin, Arginine vasopressin [AVP])	1–5 pg/mL	Assesses for diabetes insipidus (DI) or SIADH.	*Before:* Patient must fast 8–12 hr prior.
Gonadotropins • Follicle-stimulating hormone (FSH) assay • Luteinizing hormone (LH assay, Lutropin)	*FSH (Adult)* • *Male:* 1.42–15.4 IU/L • *Female:* *Follicular phase:* 1.37–9.9 IU/L *Ovulatory phase:* 6.17–17.2 IU/L *Luteal phase:* 1.09–9.2 IU/L *Postmenopause:* 19.3–100.6 IU/L *LH (Adult)* • *Male:* 1.24–7.8 IU/L • *Female:* *Follicular phase:* 1.68–15 IU/L *Ovulatory phase:* 21.9–56.6 IU/L *Luteal phase:* 0.61–16.3 IU/L *Postmenopause:* 14.2–52.3 IU/L	Assesses for pituitary, puberty or infertility conditions, and menopause.	*Before:* Tell patient that fasting is not necessary and that blood sample will be drawn. *During:* Note on the laboratory slip time of LMP or whether woman is menopausal.

Continued

TABLE 52.6 Serology and Urine Studies—cont'd

Endocrine System

Study	Reference Interval	Purpose and Description	Nursing Responsibility
Growth hormone (GH, human growth hormone [HGH], somatotropin hormone [SH])	• *Men:* <5 ng/mL • *Women:* <10 ng/mL	Evaluates GH secretion and pituitary gland function.	*Before:* Patient must fast 8–12 hr prior. Emotional and physical stress may alter results. Indicate patient fasting status and recent activity level on the laboratory slip.
GH stimulation (GH provocation, insulin tolerance test [ITT], arginine test)	GH levels >10 mg/mL	Aids in identifying GH deficiency and conditions caused by decreased pituitary hormone production.	*Before*: Patient must fast 10–12 hr prior. Water is allowed on morning of test. Establish IV access for medication administration and blood sampling. *During*: Continually assess for hypoglycemia and hypotension. Keep 50% dextrose and 5% dextrose IV solution at the bedside in case severe hypoglycemia occurs.
Insulin-like growth factor (IGF-1, somatomedin C, insulin-like growth factor binding proteins [IGF BP])	42–110 ng/mL	Evaluates GH and pituitary gland function. Provides a more accurate reflection of mean plasma concentration of GH because it is not subject to circadian rhythm and fluctuations.	*Before:* Patient must fast 8–12 hr prior.
Urine Studies			
Water deprivation (ADH stimulation)	*Neurogenic DI:* >9% rise in urine osmolality *Nephrogenic DI:* <9% rise in urine osmolality *Psychogenic polydipsia:* <9% rise in urine osmolality	Distinguishes among neurogenic, nephrogenic, or psychogenic DI.	*Before*: Obtain baseline weight and urine and plasma osmolality. Should be done only if serum sodium is normal and urine osmolality is <300 mOsm/kg. *During*: Patient may need to fast. Severe dehydration may occur. Assess urine hourly for volume and specific gravity. Send hourly urine samples to laboratory for osmolality determination. Send blood samples for sodium and osmolality every 2 hr. Stop test and rehydrate if patient's weight drops >2 kg at any time. *After*: Rehydrate with oral fluids. Check orthostatic BP and pulse to ensure adequate fluid volume.
Thyroid Studies			
Blood Studies			
Antithyroglobulin antibody (thyroid autoantibody, thyroid antithyroglobulin antibody, thyroglobulin antibody, thyroid peroxidase antibody [TPO])	<116 IU/mL	Measures thyroid antibody levels. Aids in diagnosing autoimmune thyroid disease and separates it from other forms of thyroiditis. One or more antibody tests may be ordered depending on symptoms.	*Before:* Explain blood draw procedure to the patient.
Thyroglobulin (Tg, thyrogen-stimulated thyroglobulin)	• *Male:* 0.5–53 ng/mL • *Female:* 0.5–43.0 ng/mL	Identifies functioning thyroid tissue and thyroid cancer cells. Used primarily as a tumor marker for patients being treated for thyroid cancer.	As above.
Thyroid-stimulating hormone (TSH, thyrotropin)	2–10 μU/mL	Most sensitive diagnostic test for evaluating thyroid function. Helps in distinguishing primary (thyroid), secondary (pituitary), and tertiary (hypothalamus) hypothyroidism.	As above.
Thyroxine-binding globulin (TBG, thyroid-binding globulin)	*10–19 years:* • *Male:* 1.4–2.6 mg/dL • *Female:* 1.4–3.0 mg/dL *20 years:* 1.7–3.6 mg/dL *Oral contraceptives:* 1.5–5.5 mg/dL	Measures TBG, the main thyroid hormone protein carrier. Used to assess thyroid function when T_4 and T_3 levels are abnormal.	As above.

TABLE 52.6 Serology and Urine Studies—cont'd

Endocrine System

Study	Reference Interval	Purpose and Description	Nursing Responsibility
Thyroxine, total and Free (T_4, thyroxine screen, FT_4)	*Free T_4:* 0.8–2.8 ng/dL (10–36 pmol/L) *Total T_4:* • *Male:* 4–12 mcg/dL (51–154 nmol/L) • *Female:* 5–12 mcg/dL (64–154 nmol/L) • >60 years: 5–11 mcg/dL (64–142 nmol/L)	Used to evaluate thyroid function and monitor thyroid replacement or suppressive therapy. Free T_4 levels not affected by protein levels like total T_4 is, so it is thought to be more precise marker of thyroid function.	As above.
Triiodothyronine (total T_3 radioimmunoassay [T_3 by RIA], free T_3)	*16–20 years:* 80–210 ng/dL *20–50 years:* 70–205 ng/dL (1.2–3.4 nmol/L) *>50 years:* 40–180 ng/dL (0.6–2.8 nmol/L)	Evaluates thyroid function. Free T_3 measures the active component of total T_3. Used to diagnose hyperthyroidism if TSH is abnormal and T_4 levels are normal. May be used to monitor drug therapy.	As above.
T_3 uptake (thyroid hormone–binding ratio [THBR], T_3 resin uptake)	24%–39%	Used with T_4 to assess thyroid function. Indirectly measures binding capacity of thyroid-binding globulin	As above.

TABLE 52.7 Radiologic Studies

Endocrine System

Study	Description and Purpose	Nursing Responsibility
Adrenal arteriography (angiography; adrenal)	Assesses for arterial obstructive conditions and/or tumors of the adrenal glands.	*Before*: Assess for allergies, especially to contrast dye. Have patient fast 6–12 hr prior. Give sedative and other drugs, as ordered. *During*: Patient will feel flushed when dye is injected. *After:* Check pressure dressing site after procedure. Monitor BP, pulse, and circulation distal to injection site. Place compression device over site. Maintain IV and/or oral fluid intake.
Computed tomography (CT)	*Abdominal:* Used to detect adrenal hyperplasia and tumors or pancreatic abnormalities, such as pancreatitis, tumors, or cysts. *Brain:* Used to detect a pituitary tumor and its size. *Neck:* Can locate thyroid nodules and assess for thyroid cancer.	*Before:* Before contrast medium used, evaluate renal function. Assess if patient is allergic to shellfish since the contrast is iodine based. Patient may need to be NPO 4 hr prior to study. If the patient is taking metformin, hold it the day of the test to prevent hypoglycemia or acidosis. *During:* Warn patient that contrast injection may cause a feeling of being warm and flushed. Patient must lie completely still during scan. *After:* Encourage patient to drink fluids to avoid renal problems with any contrast.
Magnetic resonance cholangiopancreatography (MRCP)	Assesses for the source of pancreatitis and can detect pancreatobiliary tumors.	*Before*: Patient may need to be fasting. Oral and/or IV contrast injection may be used. Check for pregnancy, allergies, and renal function. *During*: Patient must lie completely still during scan.
Magnetic resonance imaging (MRI)	*Abdominal:* Can distinguish benign tumors from adrenal cancers. *Brain:* Study of choice for radiologic evaluation of the pituitary gland and hypothalamus. Used to identify tumors in these glands.	*Before:* Oral and/or IV contrast injection may be used. Check for pregnancy, allergies, and renal function before test. Have patient remove all metal objects. Ask about any history of surgical insertion of staples, plates, dental bridges, or other metal appliances. Remove metallic foil patches. Patient may need to be fasting. Assess for claustrophobia and the need for antianxiety medication. *During:* Patient must lie completely still during scan.
Parathyroid scan (parathyroid scintigraphy)	Used to find the parathyroid glands. Radioactive isotopes are taken up by cells in parathyroid glands. Obtains image of the glands and any abnormally active areas.	*Before:* Check for iodine allergy. Some foods and medications are restricted a few weeks before the scan.
Radioactive iodine (RAIU) uptake	Direct measure of thyroid activity and evaluates function of thyroid nodules. *For 2–4 hr:* 3%–19%. *For 24 hr:* 11%–30%.	*Before:* Radioactive iodine given orally or IV. Check for allergies. *During:* Uptake by the thyroid gland is measured with a scanner at several time intervals, such as 2–4 hr and at 24 hr. *After:* Encourage patient to increase fluid intake as radionuclide takes 6–24 hr to be eliminated from body.
Thyroid scan	Used to evaluate nodules of thyroid. Benign nodules appear as warm spots because they take up radionuclide. Cancer tumors appear as cold spots because they tend not to take up radionuclide.	*Before:* Radioactive isotopes are given orally or IV. Check for allergies. *After*: Encourage patient to increase fluid intake as radionuclide takes 6–24 hr to be eliminated from body.
Thyroid ultrasound	Evaluates thyroid nodules to determine size and characteristics (cystic or solid tumors). Used to observe management and surveillance of nodules and unaffected portions of the gland.	*Before:* Explain that gel and a transducer will be used over the neck. The test lasts 15 min. No fasting or sedation required.

BRIDGE TO NCLEX EXAMINATION

The number of the question corresponds to the same-numbered outcome at the beginning of the chapter.

1. A characteristic common to all hormones is that they
a. circulate in the blood bound to plasma proteins.
b. influence cellular activity of specific target tissues.
c. accelerate the metabolic processes of all body cells.
d. enter a cell and change the cell's metabolism or gene expression.

2. A patient is receiving radiation therapy for renal cancer. The nurse monitors the patient for signs and symptoms of damage to the
a. pancreas.
b. thyroid gland.
c. adrenal glands.
d. posterior pituitary gland.

3. A patient has a serum sodium level of 152 mEq/L (152 mmol/L). The normal hormonal response to this situation is
a. release of ADH.
b. release of ACTH.
c. secretion of aldosterone.
d. secretion of corticotropin-releasing hormone.

4. When obtaining subjective data from a patient during assessment of the endocrine system, the nurse asks specifically about
a. energy level.
b. intake of vitamin C.
c. employment history.
d. frequency of sexual intercourse.

5. An appropriate technique to use during physical assessment of the thyroid gland is
a. asking the patient to hyperextend the neck during palpation.
b. percussing the neck for dullness to define the size of the thyroid.
c. having the patient swallow water during inspection and palpation of the gland.
d. using deep palpation to determine the extent of a visibly enlarged thyroid gland.

6. Endocrine problems often go unrecognized in the older adult because
a. symptoms are often attributed to aging.
b. older adults rarely have identifiable symptoms.
c. endocrine problems are uncommon in an older adult.
d. older adults usually have endocrine problems with lesser symptoms.

7. Abnormal findings during an endocrine assessment include *(select all that apply)*
a. excess facial hair on a woman.
b. blood pressure of 100/70 mm Hg.
c. soft, formed stool every other day.
d. 3-lb weight gain over last 6 months.
e. hyperpigmented coloration in lower legs.

8. A patient has a total serum calcium level of 3 mg/dL (1.5 mEq/L). If this finding reflects hypoparathyroidism, the nurse expects further diagnostic testing to reveal
a. decreased serum PTH.
b. increased serum ACTH.
c. increased serum glucose.
d. decreased serum cortisol levels.

1. b; 2. c; 3. a; 4. a; 5. c; 6. a; 7. a, e; 8. a.

For rationales to these answers and even more NCLEX review questions, visit http://evolve.elsevier.com/Lewis/medsurg.

EVOLVE WEBSITE/RESOURCES LIST

http://evolve.elsevier.com/Lewis/medsurg
Review Questions (Online Only)
Key Points
Answer Keys for Questions
- Rationales for Bridge to NCLEX Examination Questions
- Answer Guidelines for the Case Study

Conceptual Care Map Creator
Audio Glossary

REFERENCES

1. American Institute of Stress: Effects of stress. Retrieved from https://www.stress.org.
*2. Prete A, de Souza PB, Censi S, et al.: Update on fundamental mechanisms of thyroid cancer, *Front Endocrinol* 11:102, 2020.
3. National Organization for Rare Disorders: Acromegaly. Retrieved from https://rarediseases.org/rare-diseases/acromegaly/.
4. Swartz MH: *Textbook of physical diagnosis: history and examination*, ed 8, Philadelphia, 2020, Elsevier Health Sciences.
5. Pagana K, Pagana T, Pagana TN: *Mosby's manual of diagnostic and laboratory tests*, ed 15, St Louis, 2020, Mosby.

*Evidence-based information for clinical practice.

53

Diabetes

Jane K. Dickinson

http://evolve.elsevier.com/Lewis/medsurg/

CONCEPTUAL FOCUS

Glucose Regulation
Infection
Nutrition
Self-Management
Sensory Perception

LEARNING OUTCOMES

1. Describe the pathophysiology and clinical manifestations of diabetes.
2. Distinguish between type 1 and type 2 diabetes.
3. Describe the interprofessional care of a patient with diabetes.
4. Describe the role of nutrition and exercise in managing diabetes.
5. Discuss the nursing management of a patient with newly diagnosed diabetes.
6. Describe the nursing management of a patient with diabetes in the ambulatory and home care settings.
7. Relate the pathophysiology of acute and chronic complications of diabetes to the clinical manifestations.
8. Explain the interprofessional care and nursing management of a patient with acute and chronic complications of diabetes.

KEY TERMS

basal-bolus plan
blood glucose monitoring (BGM)
dawn phenomenon
diabetes mellitus (DM)
diabetes-related ketoacidosis (DKA)
diabetes-related nephropathy
diabetes-related neuropathy
diabetes-related retinopathy
hyperosmolar hyperglycemia syndrome (HHS)
impaired fasting glucose (IFG)
impaired glucose tolerance (IGT)
insulin resistance
prediabetes
Somogyi effect

This chapter presents the pathophysiology, manifestations, complications, and management of diabetes (DM). The potential for long-term complications from DM makes it a challenging disease. DM is associated with adult blindness, end-stage renal disease (ESRD), and nontraumatic lower-limb amputations. People with DM have a higher risk of heart disease and stroke. Managing DM requires making daily decisions about food intake, blood glucose monitoring (BGM), medication, and exercise. You play a vital role in promoting the patient's self-management of DM through providing comprehensive patient and caregiver education.

DIABETES

Diabetes mellitus (DM), or diabetes, is a chronic multisystem disease characterized by hyperglycemia from abnormal insulin production, impaired insulin use, or both. DM is a prevalent and growing health problem throughout the world. In the United States, an estimated 34.2 million people, or 10.5% of the population, have DM. Prediabetes affects 88 million adults.[1] About 7.3 million people with DM have not been diagnosed and are unaware that they have the disease. DM is the 7th leading cause of death in the United States.[2]

Etiology and Pathophysiology

Current theories link the causes of DM, singly or in combination, to genetic, autoimmune, and environmental factors (e.g., virus, higher weight). Regardless of its cause, DM is mainly a disorder of glucose metabolism related to absent or insufficient insulin supply and/or ineffective use of the available insulin.

The American Diabetes Association (ADA) recognizes 4 different classes of DM. The 2 most common are type 1 and type

TABLE 53.1 Comparison of Type 1 and Type 2 DM

Factor	Type 1 DM	Type 2 DM
Age at onset	More common in young people but can occur at any age	More common in adults but can occur at any age Incidence increasing in children
Type of onset	Signs and symptoms usually abrupt, although disease process may be present for several years	Gradual, may go undiagnosed for years
Prevalence	Accounts for 5%–10% of all types of DM	Accounts for 90%–95% of all types of DM
Endogenous insulin	Absent	Initially increased in response to insulin resistance. Secretion decreases over time
Environmental factors	Virus, toxins	Higher weight, lack of exercise
Islet cell antibodies	Often present at onset	Absent
Primary defect	Absent or minimal insulin production	Insulin resistance, decreased insulin production over time, and changes in adipokines production
Symptoms	Polydipsia, polyuria, polyphagia, fatigue, weight loss without trying	Often none. Fatigue, recurrent infections. May also have polyuria, polydipsia, and polyphagia, blurred vision
Ketosis	Present at onset or during insulin deficiency	Usually not present; can occur during infection or high stress
Insulin therapy	Required for all	Required for some. Progressive disease. Insulin may need to be added to treatment plan
Body type	Thin, normal, or obese	Often overweight or obese with visceral adiposity ("apple shape"). May be normal
Nutrition therapy	Essential	Essential
Vascular and neurologic complications	Frequent	Frequent

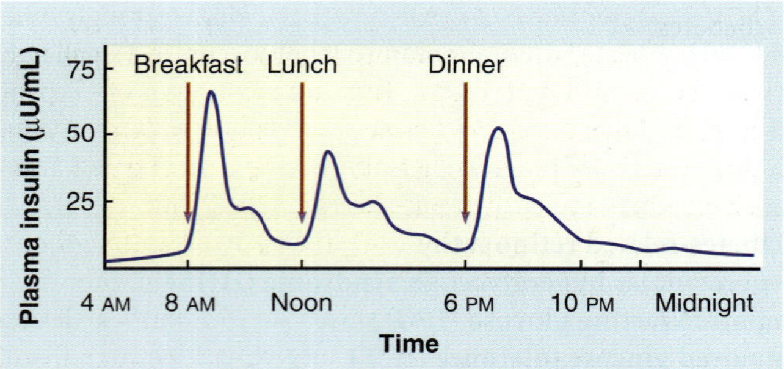

Fig. 53.1 Normal endogenous insulin secretion. After meals, insulin concentrations rise rapidly in blood and peak at about 1 hour. Then insulin concentrations promptly decline toward preprandial values as carbohydrate absorption from the GI tract declines. After carbohydrate absorption from the GI tract is complete and during the night, insulin concentrations are low and fairly constant, with a slight increase at dawn.

2 DM (Table 53.1). Another type is maturity onset diabetes of the young (MODY). The 2 other classes are gestational DM and other specific types of DM with various causes.

Normal Glucose and Insulin Metabolism

Insulin is a hormone made by the β cells in the islets of Langerhans of the pancreas. Under normal conditions, the pancreas continuously releases insulin into the bloodstream in small amounts. Release increases when we ingest food (Fig. 53.1). Insulin lowers glucose and facilitates a stable, normal glucose range of about 74 to 106 mg/dL (4.1 to 5.9 mmol/L). The amount of insulin secreted daily by an adult is about 40 to 50 U or 0.6 U/kg of body weight.

Insulin promotes glucose transport from the bloodstream across the cell membrane to the cytoplasm of the cell (Fig. 53.2).

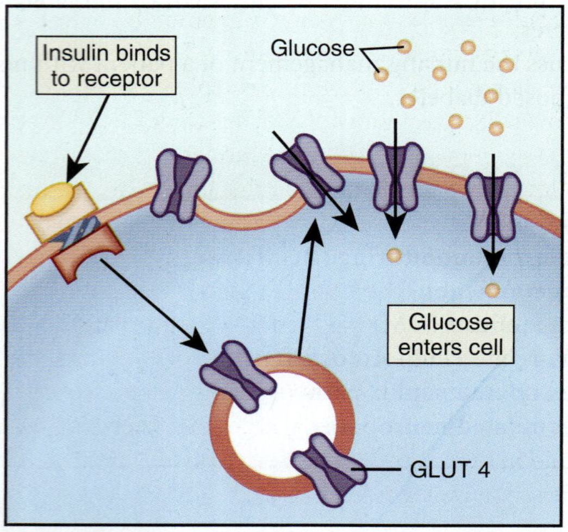

Fig. 53.2 Normal glucose metabolism. Insulin binds to receptors along the cell walls of muscle, adipose, and liver cells. Glucose transport proteins *(GLUT 4s)* then attach to the cell wall and allow glucose to enter the cell. There it is either stored or used to make energy.

Cells break down glucose to make energy. Liver and muscle cells store excess glucose as glycogen. The rise in plasma insulin after a meal inhibits gluconeogenesis, enhances fat deposition of adipose tissue, and increases protein synthesis. For this reason, insulin is an *anabolic,* or storage, hormone. The fall in insulin level during normal overnight fasting promotes the release of stored glucose from the liver, protein from muscle, and fat from adipose tissue.

Skeletal muscle and adipose tissue have specific receptors for insulin and are considered insulin-dependent tissues. Insulin is required to "unlock" these receptor sites, allowing the transport of glucose into the cells to be used for energy. Other tissues (e.g., brain, liver, blood cells) do not directly depend on insulin for

BOX 53.1 GENETICS IN CLINICAL PRACTICE

Diabetes

Type 1 DM	Type 2 DM	MODY
Genetic Basis		
• Increased susceptibility (40%–50%) when a person has specific human leukocyte antigens (HLA-DR3 and HLA-DR4) • Polygenic (>40 genes influence susceptibility)	• Polygenic (>25 genes influence susceptibility)	• Autosomal dominant • Monogenic (single gene) • Caused by mutations in any of 6 MODY genes (types 1–6) • Gene mutations lead to β-cell dysfunction
Risk to Offspring		
• Risk to offspring of mothers with DM is 1%–4% • Risk to offspring of fathers with DM is 5%–6% • When 1 identical twin has type 1 DM, the other gets DM about 30%–40% of the time	• Risk to offspring is 8%–14% • When 1 identical twin has type 2 DM, the other gets DM about 60%–75% of the time	• If 1 parent has MODY, a child has a 50% chance of developing DM • If 1 parent has MODY, a child has a 50% chance of being a carrier
Clinical Implications		
• Result of complex interaction of genetic, autoimmune, and environmental factors	• Result of complex genetic interactions and other metabolic factors • Environmental factors, such as body weight and exercise, can sometimes modify metabolic factors	• Accounts for 1%–5% of people with DM • Young age of onset (often before age 25) • Not related to obesity or hypertension • Treatment depends on the genetic mutation that caused MODY

glucose transport but require an adequate glucose supply for normal function. Although liver cells are not insulin-dependent tissue, insulin receptor sites on the liver facilitate uptake of glucose and its conversion to glycogen.

Other hormones (glucagon, epinephrine, growth hormone [GH], cortisol) work against the effects of insulin. They are *counterregulatory hormones.* These hormones increase glucose levels by (1) stimulating glucose production and release by the liver and (2) decreasing the movement of glucose into the cells. The counterregulatory hormones and insulin work together to maintain glucose levels within the normal range by regulating the release of glucose for energy during food intake and periods of fasting.

Insulin is synthesized from its precursor, proinsulin. Enzymes split proinsulin to form insulin and C-peptide. The 2 substances are released in equal amounts. Therefore, measuring C-peptide in serum and urine is a useful indicator of pancreatic β-cell function and insulin levels.

Type 1 Diabetes

Type 1 diabetes accounts for about 5% to 10% of all people with DM. Type 1 DM generally affects people under 40 years of age, although it can occur at any age.[3]

Etiology and pathophysiology. Type 1 DM is an autoimmune disorder in which the body develops antibodies against insulin and/or the pancreatic β cells that make insulin. This eventually results in not enough insulin for a person to survive. A genetic predisposition and exposure to a virus are factors that may contribute to developing immune-related type 1 DM (Box 53.1).

Genetic Link

Predisposition to type 1 DM is related to human leukocyte antigens (HLAs) (see Chapter 14). In theory, when a person with certain HLA types is exposed to a viral infection, the β cells of the pancreas are destroyed, either directly or through an autoimmune process. The HLA types with an increased risk for type 1 DM include HLA-DR3 and HLA-DR4.

Idiopathic diabetes is a form of type 1 DM that is strongly inherited and not related to autoimmunity. It only occurs in a small number of people with type 1 DM. They are most often of Hispanic, African, or Asian ancestry.[4] *Latent autoimmune diabetes in adults* (LADA) is a slowly progressing autoimmune form of type 1 DM. It occurs in adults and is often mistaken for type 2 DM.

Onset of disease. In type 1 DM, the islet cell autoantibodies responsible for β-cell destruction are present for months to years before the onset of symptoms. Manifestations develop when the person's pancreas can no longer make enough insulin to maintain normal glucose. Once this occurs, the onset of symptoms is usually rapid. Patients often present with impending or actual ketoacidosis. The patient usually has a history of recent and sudden weight loss and the classic symptoms of *polydipsia* (excessive thirst), *polyuria* (frequent urination), and *polyphagia* (excessive hunger).

The person with type 1 DM requires insulin from an outside source *(exogenous insulin)* to sustain life. Without insulin, the patient will develop diabetes-related ketoacidosis (DKA), a life-threatening condition causing metabolic acidosis. Newly diagnosed patients may have a remission, or "honeymoon period," for 3 to 12 months after starting treatment. During this time, the patient needs little injected insulin because β-cell insulin production is still sufficient for healthy glucose levels. Eventually, as more β cells are destroyed, and glucose levels increase, the honeymoon period ends. The patient then requires insulin on a permanent basis.

Type 2 Diabetes

Type 2 diabetes accounts for about 90% to 95% of people with DM.[5] Many risk factors contribute to developing type 2 DM. These include having a family history of type 2 DM, being

BOX 53.2 PROMOTING HEALTH EQUITY

DM

- Native Americans and Alaska Natives have the highest prevalence of DM (23.5%)[6]
- Rates of DM are higher among Blacks (20.4%), Hispanics (22.1%), than among Whites (12.1%), and Asians (14.0%)[6]

overweight or obese, and being older. Although it occurs less often in children, the incidence is increasing due to the increasing prevalence of childhood obesity. Type 2 DM is more prevalent in some ethnic populations (Box 53.2). This increase is related to genetic predisposition, environmental factors, and diet choices.

Etiology and pathophysiology. Type 2 DM is characterized by a combination of inadequate insulin secretion and insulin resistance. The pancreas usually makes some *endogenous* (self-made) insulin. However, the body either does not make enough insulin, does not use it effectively, or both. The presence of endogenous insulin is a major distinction between type 1 and type 2 DM. In type 1 DM, there is an absence of endogenous insulin.

Genetic Link

Although we do not fully understand the genetics of type 2 DM, it is likely that multiple genes are involved (Box 53.1). We have found genetic mutations that lead to insulin resistance and a higher risk for obesity in many people with type 2 DM. Persons with a first-degree relative with the disease are 10 times more likely to develop type 2 DM.

Metabolic abnormalities have a role in developing type 2 DM (Fig. 53.3). The first factor is **insulin resistance**. This is a condition in which body tissues do not respond to the action of insulin because insulin receptors are unresponsive, insufficient in number, or both. Most insulin receptors are located on skeletal muscle, fat, and liver cells. When insulin is not properly used, the entry of glucose into the cell is impeded, causing hyperglycemia. In the early stages of insulin resistance, the pancreas responds to high glucose levels by producing more insulin (if β cell function is normal). This creates a temporary state of hyperinsulinemia that coexists with hyperglycemia.

A second factor in developing type 2 DM is a marked decrease in the ability of the pancreas to make insulin. The β cells become fatigued from the compensatory overproduction of insulin or when β-cell mass is lost. We do not know the reason the β cells fail to adapt. It may be due to the adverse effects of chronic hyperglycemia or high circulating free fatty acids. In addition, the α cells of the pancreas increase production of glucagon.

This leads to a third factor, which is inappropriate glucose production by the liver. Instead of properly regulating the release of glucose in response to blood levels, the liver does so in a haphazard way that does not correspond to the body's needs at the time.

A fourth factor is the production of hormones and cytokines by adipose tissue *(adipokines)*. Adipokines secreted by adipose

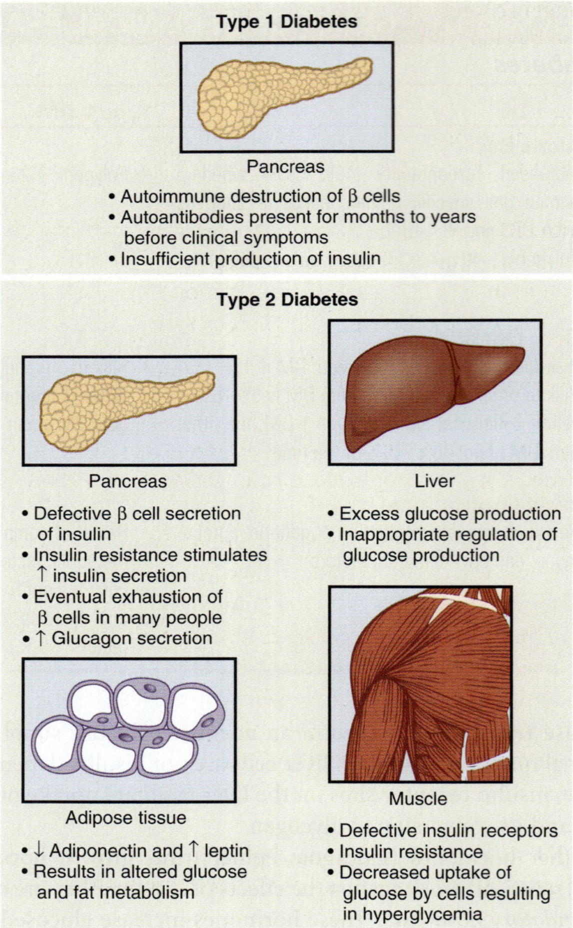

Fig. 53.3 Altered mechanisms in type 1 and type 2 DM.

tissue appear to play a role in glucose and fat metabolism. They are likely to contribute to developing type 2 DM.[7] We think adipokines cause chronic inflammation, a factor involved in insulin resistance, type 2 DM, and cardiovascular disease (CVD). The 2 main adipokines thought to affect insulin sensitivity are adiponectin and leptin. Finally, the brain, kidneys, and gut have roles in developing type 2 DM. We are continuously learning more about metabolic factors and developing type 2 DM.

People with *metabolic syndrome* have an increased risk of developing type 2 DM. Metabolic syndrome has 5 components: increased glucose levels, abdominal obesity, high BP, high triglyceride levels, and decreased high-density lipoprotein (HDL) levels (see Table 45.11). A person with 3 of the 5 components is considered to have metabolic syndrome.[8] Overweight persons with metabolic syndrome can reduce their risk for DM through food choices and regular physical activity. See Chapter 45 for more about metabolic syndrome.

Onset of disease. The disease onset in type 2 DM is usually gradual. The person may go for many years with undetected hyperglycemia and few, if any, symptoms. Many people are diagnosed on routine laboratory testing or when they undergo treatment for other conditions, and they have high glucose or glycosylated hemoglobin (A1C) levels. The signs and symptoms of hyperglycemia develop when about 50% to 80% of β cells are no longer secreting insulin. At the time of diagnosis, the average person has had type 2 DM for 6½ years.

Prediabetes

Persons diagnosed with prediabetes are at increased risk for developing type 2 DM. **Prediabetes** is defined as **impaired glucose tolerance (IGT), impaired fasting glucose (IFG)**, or both. It is an intermediate stage between normal glucose homeostasis and DM. Glucose levels are high but not high enough to meet the diagnostic criteria for DM.[4] A diagnosis of IGT is made if the 2-hour oral glucose tolerance test (OGTT) values are 140 to 199 mg/dL (7.8 to 11.0 mmol/L). IFG is diagnosed when fasting glucose levels are 100 to 125 mg/dL (5.56 to 6.9 mmol/L).

Persons with prediabetes usually do not have symptoms. However, long-term damage to the body, especially the heart and blood vessels, may already be occurring. It is important for people to undergo screening and understand risk factors for DM. People with prediabetes can take action to prevent or delay their developing type 2 DM. Encourage those with prediabetes to have their glucose level and A1C checked regularly and monitor for symptoms of DM, such as fatigue or frequent infections. Maintaining a healthy weight, exercising regularly, and making healthy food choices reduce the risk for developing type 2 DM in those with prediabetes.

Gestational Diabetes

Gestational diabetes develops during pregnancy and occurs in about 2% to 10% of pregnancies in the United States.[9] Women with gestational DM have a higher risk for cesarean delivery. Their babies are at increased risk for perinatal death, birth injury, and neonatal complications. Women who are at high risk for gestational DM are screened at the first prenatal visit. Those at high risk include women who are obese, are of advanced maternal age, or have a family history of DM. We screen women with an average risk for gestational DM using an OGTT at 24 to 28 weeks of gestation. Most women with gestational DM have normal glucose levels within 6 weeks postpartum. Women with a history of gestational DM have up to a 63% chance of developing type 2 DM within 16 years. Gestational DM and managing the pregnant patient with DM are specialized areas not covered in detail here. Consult an obstetric text for more information.

Other Specific Types of Diabetes

DM occurs in some people because of another medical condition or treatment of a medical condition that causes abnormal glucose levels. Conditions that may cause DM can result from injury to, interference with, or destruction of the β-cell function in the pancreas. These include Cushing syndrome, hyperthyroidism, pancreatitis, cystic fibrosis, hemochromatosis, and parenteral nutrition. Common drugs that can induce DM include corticosteroids (prednisone), thiazides, phenytoin (Dilantin), and atypical antipsychotics (e.g., clozapine [Clozaril]). DM caused by medical conditions or drugs can resolve when the underlying condition is treated or the drug is discontinued.

Clinical Manifestations

Type 1 Diabetes

Because the onset of type 1 DM is rapid, the first manifestations are usually acute. The classic symptoms are *polyuria, polydipsia,* and *polyphagia.* The osmotic effect of excess glucose in the bloodstream causes polydipsia and polyuria. Polyphagia is a result of cell malnourishment when insulin deficiency prevents cells from using glucose for energy. Weight loss may occur because the body cannot get glucose and instead breaks down fat and protein to try to make energy. Weakness and fatigue may result because cells lack needed energy from glucose. DKA, a complication most common in those with untreated type 1 DM, has additional manifestations.

Type 2 Diabetes

The manifestations of type 2 DM are often nonspecific. Although not common, it is possible for a person with type 2 DM to have classic symptoms associated with type 1 DM, including polyuria, polydipsia, and polyphagia. Some of the common manifestations of type 2 DM are fatigue, recurrent infections, recurrent vaginal yeast or candida infections, prolonged wound healing, and vision problems.

Diagnostic Studies

The diagnosis of DM is made using 1 of 4 methods (Table 53.2). If a patient has a hyperglycemic crisis or clear symptoms of hyperglycemia (polyuria, polydipsia, polyphagia) with a random plasma glucose level of 200 mg/dL or greater, repeat testing is not needed. Otherwise, criteria 1 through 3 require confirmation by repeat testing to rule out laboratory error. The repeat test should be the same test used initially. For example, if a random high glucose was the initial measurement, that same measure should be used to confirm a diagnosis.

The accuracy of laboratory results depends on patient preparation and attention to the many factors that influence the results. Factors that can falsely increase values include recent severe restrictions of carbohydrate intake, acute illness, drugs (e.g., contraceptives, corticosteroids), and restricted activity, such as bed rest. A patient with impaired gastrointestinal (GI) absorption or who has recently taken acetaminophen may have false-negative results.

A1C measures the amount of glycosylated hemoglobin (Hgb) as a percentage of total Hgb. For example, an A1C of 6.5% means that 6.5% of the total Hgb has glucose attached

TABLE 53.2 Diagnostic Criteria

DM

The diagnosis of DM is made using 1 of 4 methods:

1. A1C of 6.5% or higher
2. Fasting plasma glucose (FPG) level of 126 mg/dL (7.0 mmol/L) or greater. *Fasting* is defined as no caloric intake for at least 8 hours
3. A 2-hour plasma glucose level of 200 mg/dL (11.1 mmol/L) or greater during an OGTT, using a glucose load of 75 g
4. In a person with classic symptoms of hyperglycemia (polyuria, polydipsia, unexplained weight loss) or hyperglycemic crisis, a random plasma glucose level of 200 mg/dL (11.1 mmol/L) or greater

to it. The amount of glycosylated Hgb depends on the glucose level. When glucose levels are high over time, the amount of glucose attached to Hgb increases. This glucose stays attached to the red blood cell (RBC) for the life of the cell (about 120 days). Therefore, A1C provides an average measure of glucose levels over the previous 2 to 3 months. Increases in the A1C reflect higher average glucose levels. A1C does not, however, consider fluctuations in glucose. It does not give a good indicator of how often someone has high or low glucose levels. An advantage of the A1C includes greater convenience since fasting is not needed. Diseases affecting RBCs (e.g., iron deficiency anemia, sickle cell anemia) can influence the A1C and should be considered when interpreting results.

Teach patients with DM and prediabetes to have their A1C regularly monitored to determine how well they are meeting their glycemic goals. The ADA identifies an A1C goal for patients with DM of less than 7.0%. The American College of Endocrinology recommends an A1C of less than 6.5%. When the A1C is maintained at near-normal levels, the risk for developing microvascular and macrovascular complications is greatly reduced. For people with prediabetes, monitoring the A1C can detect overt DM and provide feedback on efforts to prevent DM.

More people with DM are using continuous glucose monitoring (CGM). CGM reports include "time in range." It is a more accurate way to look at daily glucose levels and fluctuations than A1C. Until CGM is more widely used, A1C remains a good tool for monitoring glucose over time.

Fructosamine is another way to assess glucose levels. It is formed by a chemical reaction of glucose with plasma protein. It reflects glycemia in the previous 1 to 3 weeks. Fructosamine levels may show a change in glucose levels before A1C does. It is used for people with hemoglobinopathies or short-term measurement of glucose levels, for instance, after a change in medication or during pregnancy.

Islet cell autoantibody testing can help distinguish between autoimmune type 1 DM and DM from other causes. Autoantibodies can develop into 1 or several autoantigens, including GAD65, IA-2, or insulin.

Interprofessional Care

The goals of DM management are to reduce symptoms, promote well-being, prevent acute complications related to hyperglycemia and hypoglycemia, and prevent or delay the onset and progression of long-term complications. These goals are most likely to be met when the patient maintains glucose levels as near to normal as possible. Meeting goals for what we refer to as the "ABCs of Diabetes" can help patients manage DM and lower their risk for heart attack and stroke. The ABCs refer to (1) A1C, (2) blood pressure, and (3) cholesterol. Only 19.2% of adults meet the target goals for all 3 steps.[10] Patient teaching, which enables the patient to self-manage their own care, is essential to achieve glycemic goals. Nutrition therapy, drug therapy, exercise, and BGM are the tools used in managing DM (Table 53.3).

The 3 major types of glucose-lowering agents (GLAs) used in DM treatment are insulin, oral agents (OAs), and noninsulin injectable agents.[11] All persons with type 1 DM require insulin. For some people with type 2 DM, a healthy eating plan, regular physical activity, and maintaining a healthy body weight are enough to attain safe glucose levels. Eventually, most people will need medication because type 2 DM is a progressive disease.

TABLE 53.3 Interprofessional Care

DM

Diagnostic Assessment
- History and physical assessment
- Blood tests, including glucose levels (Table 53.2), A1C, fructosamine, lipid profile, BUN and creatinine, electrolytes, islet cell autoantibodies
- Urine for complete urinalysis, albuminuria, and acetone (if indicated)
- BP
- ECG (if indicated)
- Funduscopic examination (dilated eye examination)
- Dental examination
- Neurologic examination, including monofilament test for sensation to lower extremities
- Ankle-brachial index (ABI) (if indicated)
- Foot (podiatric) examination
- Monitoring of weight

Management
- Patient and caregiver teaching and follow-up programs
- Nutrition therapy (Table 53.9)
- Exercise therapy (Tables 53.10 and 53.11)
- Blood glucose monitoring (BGM) (Table 53.12)

Drug Therapy
- Insulin (Fig. 53.3 and Tables 53.4 and 53.5)
- Oral agents (OAs) and noninsulin injectable agents (Table 53.8)
- Enteric-coated aspirin (81–162 mg/day)
- ACE inhibitors (see Table 36.6)
- Angiotensin II receptor blockers (ARBs) (see Table 36.6)
- BP medications (see Table 36.6)

Drug Therapy: Insulin

Exogenous (injected) insulin is needed when someone has inadequate insulin to meet specific metabolic needs. People with type 1 DM require exogenous insulin to survive. They often use multiple daily injections of insulin (often 4 or more) or continuous insulin infusion via an insulin pump to adequately manage glucose levels. People with type 2 DM may need exogenous insulin during periods of severe stress, such as illness or surgery. Since type 2 DM is progressive, over time, the combination of nutrition, exercise, OAs, and noninsulin injectable agents may no longer adequately manage glucose levels. At that point, we add exogenous insulin to their management plan. People with type 2 DM may also need up to 4 injections per day to adequately maintain their glucose levels. Insulin pumps may be an option for patients with type 2 DM.

Types of Insulin

Today, people use genetically engineered human insulin made in laboratories. The insulin is derived from common bacteria (e.g., *Escherichia coli*) or yeast cells using recombinant DNA technology. Types of insulin differ by their onset, peak action, and duration (Fig. 53.4). They are categorized as rapid-acting, short-acting, intermediate-acting, and long-acting insulin (Table 53.4).

INSULIN PREPARATION	ONSET, PEAK, DURATION	EXAMPLE
Rapid acting lispro (Humalog) aspart (NovoLog, Fiasp) glulisine (Apidra)	*Onset:* 10–30 min *Peak:* 30 min–3 hr *Duration:* 3–5 hr	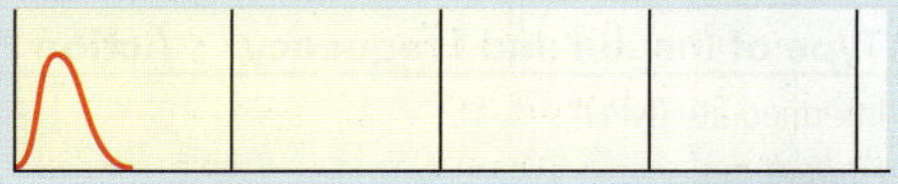
Short acting Regular (Humulin R, Novolin R)	*Onset:* 30 min–1 hr *Peak:* 2–5 hr *Duration:* 5–8 hr	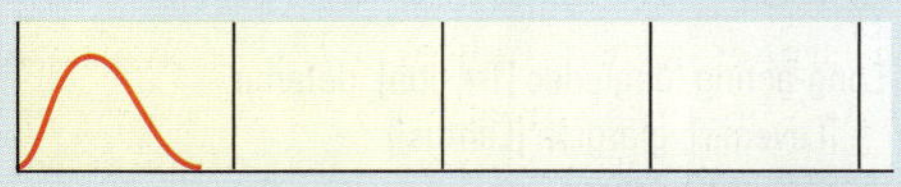
Intermediate acting NPH (Humulin N, Novolin N)	*Onset:* 1.5–4 hr *Peak:* 4–12 hr *Duration:* 12–18 hr	
Long acting glargine (Lantus, Toujeo, Basaglar) detemir (Levemir) degludec (Tresiba)	*Onset:* 0.8–4 hr *Peak:* Less defined or no pronounced peak *Duration:* 16–24 hr	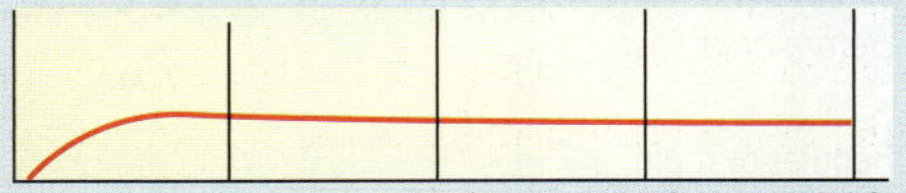
Inhaled insulin Afrezza	*Onset:* 12–15 min *Peak:* 60 min *Duration:* 2.5–3 hr	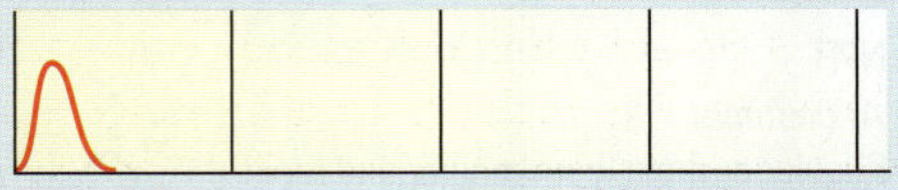

Fig. 53.4 Commercially available insulin preparations showing onset, peak, and duration of action. Patient responses to each type of insulin are different and affected by many factors.

TABLE 53.4 Drug Therapy

Types of Insulin

Classification	Examples
Rapid-acting insulin	aspart (NovoLog, Fiasp) glulisine (Apidra) lispro (Humalog)
Short-acting insulin	regular (Humulin R, Novolin R)
Intermediate-acting insulin	NPH (Humulin N, Novolin N)
Long-acting insulin	degludec (Tresiba) detemir (Levemir) glargine (Basaglar, Lantus, Toujeo) insulin glargine (Basaglar)
Combination therapy (premixed)	aspart protamine/aspart 70/30[a] (NovoLog Mix 70/30) degludec/aspart 70/30 (Ryzodeg) lispro protamine/lispro 75/25[a] (Humalog Mix 75/25) lispro protamine/lispro 50/50[a] (Humalog Mix 50/50) NPH/regular 70/30[a] (Humulin 70/30, Novolin 70/30) NPH/regular 50/50[a] (Humulin 50/50)
More concentrated insulin	Humulin R U-500 Toujeo U-300 (insulin glargine) Humalog U-200 (insulin lispro)
Inhaled insulin	Afrezza

[a]These numbers refer to percentages of each type of insulin.

Insulin Plans

Table 53.5 shows examples of insulin plans. The insulin approach that most closely mimics endogenous insulin production is the **basal-bolus plan** (often called *intensive or physiologic insulin therapy*). It consists of multiple daily insulin injections or an insulin pump together with frequent BGM or CGM. Injections include rapid- or short-acting (bolus) insulin before meals and intermediate- or long-acting (basal) background insulin once or twice a day. The goal is to achieve a glucose level as close to normal as possible, as much of the time as possible. We refer to this as "time in range."

Other, less intense plans can promote healthy glucose levels for some people. Ideally, the patient and the HCP work together to choose a plan. Selection criteria are based on the desired and feasible glucose levels and the patient's lifestyle, food choices, and activity. If a less intense plan is not giving the person optimal results, the HCP may encourage a more intense approach.

Mealtime Insulin (Bolus)

To manage postprandial glucose levels, the timing of rapid- and short-acting insulin in relation to meals is crucial. Rapid-acting synthetic insulin analogs, which include aspart (NovoLog, Fiasp), glulisine (Apidra), and lispro (Humalog), have an onset of action of about 15 minutes. They should be injected within 15 minutes of eating. The rapid-acting analogs most closely mimic natural insulin secretion in response to a meal.

TABLE 53.5 Drug Therapy

Insulin Plans

Plan	Type of Insulin and Frequency	Action Profile	Comments
Once a day Single dose	Intermediate (NPH) *At bedtime*	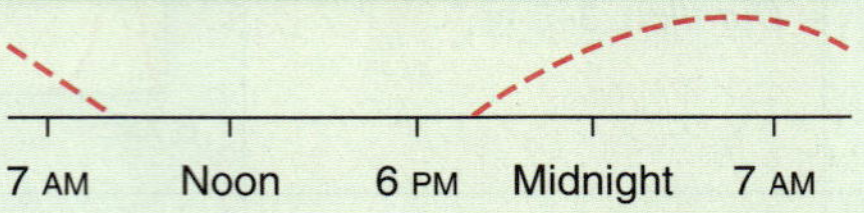	1 injection should provide nighttime coverage.
	OR Long-acting (degludec [Tresiba], detemir [Levemir], glargine [Lantus]) *In am or at bedtime*	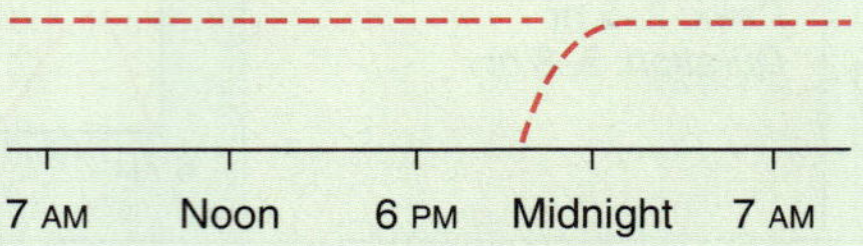	1 injection may last up to 24 hr with fewer defined peaks and less chance for hypoglycemia. Does not cover postprandial glucose levels.
Twice a day Split-mixed dose	NPH and regular or rapid (both regular and rapid are shown on the diagram) *Before breakfast and at dinner*	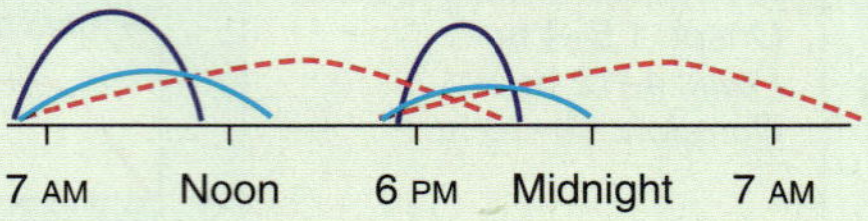	2 injections provide coverage for 24 hr. Person must eat at certain times to avoid hypoglycemia.
Three times a day Combination of mixed and single dose	NPH and regular or rapid (both regular and rapid are shown on the diagram) *Before breakfast* + Regular or rapid *Before dinner* + NPH *At bedtime*	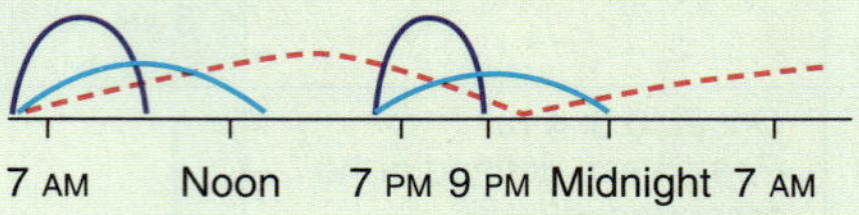	3 injections provide coverage for 24 h, especially during early AM hours. Decreased potential for 2–3 AM hypoglycemia.
Basal-bolus Multiple dose	Regular or rapid (both regular and rapid are shown on the diagram) *Before breakfast, lunch, and dinner* + Long-acting (degludec, detemir, or glargine) *Once or twice a day* *OR*	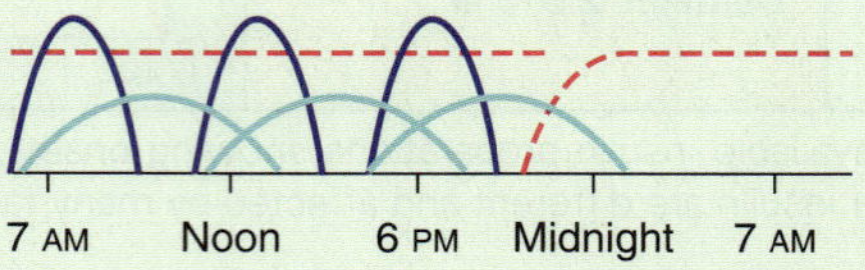	More flexibility at mealtimes and for amount of food intake. Good postprandial coverage. Preprandial glucose checks and following a patient-centered plan are beneficial. People with type 1 DM require basal insulin to cover 24 hr. Most physiologic approach, other than pump.
	Regular or rapid (both regular and rapid are shown on the diagram) *Before breakfast, lunch, and dinner* + NPH *Twice a day*	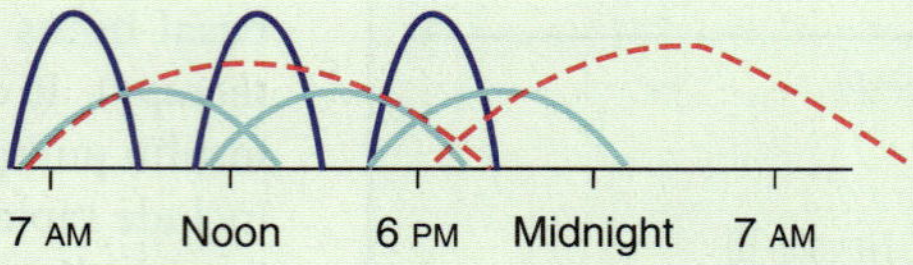	

——— Rapid-acting (lispro, aspart, glulisine) insulin.
——— Short-acting (regular) insulin.
- - - - Intermediate-acting (NPH) or long-acting (glargine, detemir, degludec) insulin.

Short-acting regular insulin has an onset of action of 30 to 60 minutes. It is injected 30 to 45 minutes before a meal to ensure that the insulin is working at the same time as meal absorption. Because timing an injection 30 to 45 minutes before a meal is hard for some people to do with their lifestyles, those taking insulin with their meals often prefer the flexibility of rapid-acting insulins. Short-acting insulin is more likely to cause hypoglycemia because of a longer duration of action.

Long- or Intermediate-Acting (Basal) Background Insulin

In addition to mealtime insulin, people with type 1 DM use a long- or intermediate-acting basal (background) insulin to maintain glucose levels in between meals and overnight. Without 24-hour background insulin, people with type 1 DM are more prone to developing DKA. Many people with type 2 DM who use OAs will need basal insulin to adequately manage glucose levels.

The long-acting insulins include degludec (Tresiba), detemir (Levemir), and glargine (Lantus, Toujeo, Basaglar). Long-acting insulin is released steadily and continuously. For most people, it does not have a peak of action. The action time for long-acting insulin varies (Fig. 53.4). Although they can be given once daily, detemir is often given twice daily. Because they lack peak action time, the risk for hypoglycemia with this type of insulin is greatly reduced. Glargine and detemir must not be diluted or mixed with any other insulin or solution in the same syringe. If

OAs and long-acting insulin are not adequate to achieve glycemic goals, people with type 2 DM may need to add mealtime insulin.

Intermediate-acting insulin (NPH) can be used as basal insulin. It has a duration of 12 to 18 hours. The disadvantage of NPH is that its action peaks 4 to 12 hours after injection, which can result in hypoglycemia. NPH can be mixed with short- and rapid-acting insulins. It is never given IV.

CHECK YOUR PRACTICE

You are preparing your patient's order for NPH insulin. When you look at the vial, you notice that it is cloudy. You think that you should throw away the vial because it has become contaminated.

- Before you take this action, what should you do?

All insulins are clear solutions except NPH, lispro protamine, and aspart protamine. They are cloudy because they contain a protein called protamine, which makes them work longer. These insulins must be gently agitated before administration.

Combination Insulin Therapy

For those who want to use only 1 or 2 injections per day, a short- or rapid-acting insulin is mixed with intermediate-acting insulin in the same syringe. This allows the person to have both mealtime and basal coverage without having to give 2 separate injections. Although this may be more appealing, most people achieve target glucose levels with basal-bolus therapy. Patients may mix the 2 types of insulin themselves or use a commercially premixed formula or pen (Table 53.4). Premixed formulas offer convenience as people do not have to draw up and mix insulin from 2 different vials. This is helpful to those who lack the visual, manual, or cognitive skills to mix insulin themselves. However, it is harder to achieve target glucose levels because there is less opportunity for flexible dosing based on need.

Insulin Storage

As a protein, insulin has special storage considerations. Extreme temperatures alter insulin and can make it less effective. Insulin vials and pens in use may be left at room temperature for up to 4 weeks. The room temperature cannot be higher than 86°F (30°C) or below freezing (<32°F [0°C]). Teach patients to avoid exposing their insulin to direct sunlight. A person who is traveling in hot climates may store insulin in a thermos or cooler to keep it cool (not frozen). Store unopened insulin vials and pens in the refrigerator.

People who are traveling or caregivers of patients with impaired vision or who cannot fill their own syringes may prefill insulin syringes. Prefilled syringes with 2 different insulins are stable for up to 1 week when stored in the refrigerator. Syringes with only 1 type of insulin are stable for up to 30 days.

Teach patients to store syringes in a vertical position with the needle pointed up to avoid clumping of suspended insulin in the needle. Before injection, gently roll prefilled syringes between the palms 10 to 20 times to warm the insulin and resuspend the particles. Some insulin combinations cannot be prefilled and stored because the mixture can alter the onset, action, and/or peak times of either insulin. Consult a reference as needed when mixing and prefilling different types of insulin.

Insulin Administration

Routine doses of insulin are given by subcutaneous injection. Regular insulin can be given IV when immediate onset of action is desired. Insulin is not taken orally because it is inactivated by gastric fluids. Teach patients to avoid injecting insulin IM because rapid and unpredictable absorption could result in hypoglycemia.

Insulin injection. The steps in giving a subcutaneous insulin injection are outlined in Table 53.6. Teach this technique to new insulin users and review it periodically with long-term users. Never assume that because the patient already uses insulin, they know and practice the correct insulin injection technique. The patient may not have understood prior instructions, or changes in eyesight may result in incorrect preparation.[12] The patient may not see air bubbles in the syringe or may improperly read the scale on the syringe. The patient receiving mixed insulins in the same syringe needs to learn the right technique for combining them if they are not using commercially prepared premixed insulin.

The speed with which peak serum concentrations are reached varies with the injection site. The fastest subcutaneous absorption is from the abdomen, followed by the arm, thigh, and buttock. Although the abdomen is often the preferred injection site, other sites work well (Fig. 53.5). Caution the patient about injecting into a site that will be exercised. For example, injecting into the thigh and then going jogging could increase body heat and circulation. This could increase the rate of insulin absorption and speed the onset of action, causing hypoglycemia.

Teach patients to rotate the injection within and between sites. This allows for better insulin absorption. It may be helpful

TABLE 53.6 PATIENT & CAREGIVER TEACHING

Preparing an Insulin Injection

Include the following instructions when teaching the patient and caregiver about insulin therapy:

1. Wash hands thoroughly.
2. Always inspect insulin bottle before using it. Make sure that it is the right type and concentration, expiration date has not passed, and top of bottle is in perfect condition. Insulin solutions (except for NPH, lispro protamine, aspart protamine) should look clear and colorless. Discard if it appears discolored or you see particles in the solution.
3. For intermediate-acting insulins (which are normally cloudy), gently roll the insulin bottle between the palms of hands to mix the insulin. Do not agitate clear insulins. Do not shake insulin to minimize introduction of air bubbles.
4. Choose right injection site (Fig. 53.5).
5. Ensure that the site is clean and dry.
6. Push the needle straight into the skin (90-degree angle). If you are very thin, muscular, or using an 8- or 12-mm needle, you may need to pinch the skin and/or use a 45-degree angle.
7. Push the plunger all the way down, leave needle in place for 5 sec to ensure that all insulin is injected, and then remove needle.
8. Destroy and dispose of single-use syringe safely.

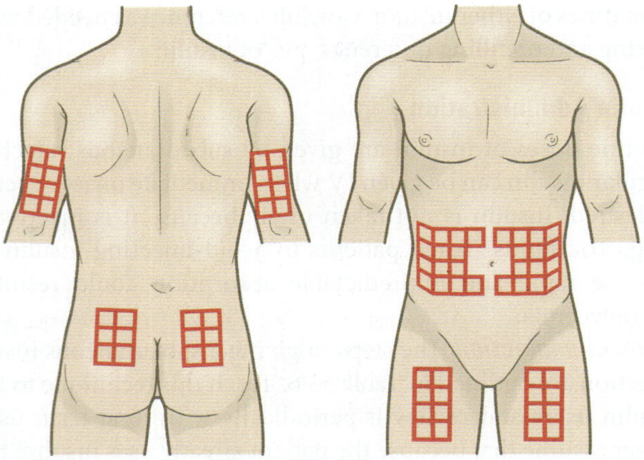

Fig. 53.5 Insulin injection sites.

to think of the abdomen as a checkerboard, with each ½-in square representing an injection site. Injections are rotated systematically across the board, with each injection site at least ½ to 1 inch away from the previous injection site. It can be helpful to inject fast-acting insulin into faster-absorbing sites and slow-acting insulin into slower absorbing sites.

Most commercial insulin is available as U100. This means that 1 mL contains 100 U of insulin. U100 insulin must be used with a U100-marked syringe. Disposable plastic insulin syringes are available in a variety of sizes, including 1.0, 0.5, and 0.3 mL. The 0.5-mL size is for doses of 50 U or less. The 0.3-mL syringe is for doses of 30 U or less. The 0.5- and 0.3-mL syringes are in 1-unit increments. This provides more accurate delivery when the dose is an odd number. The 1.0-mL syringe is necessary for patients who inject more than 50 U of insulin. The 1.0-mL syringe is in 2-unit increments. When patients change from a 0.3- or a 0.5-mL to a 1.0-mL syringe, tell them of the dose increment difference.

Insulin syringe needles come in 3 lengths: 5 mm (3/16 in), 8 mm (5/16 in), and 12.7 mm (½ in).[13] Needle gauges vary among syringes. The needle gauges available are 28, 29, 30, and 31. The higher the gauge number, the smaller the diameter. This results in a more comfortable injection. Only the person using the syringe should recap the needle. Patients performing self-injection can prepare the site with routine hygiene, such as washing with soap and rinsing with water.

! SAFETY ALERT

- Never recap a needle used for a patient.
- When injecting a patient, prepare the site with alcohol to prevent health care–associated infection.

Insulin is typically injected at a 90-degree angle. For very thin or muscular patients in the hospital, perform injections at a 45-degree angle. At home, patients inject at a 90-degree angle using the shortest needle desired. We no longer pinch up the skin to avoid IM injection because of the use of short needles.

An insulin pen is a compact device loaded with an insulin cartridge that serves the same function as a needle and syringe (Fig. 53.6). Pen needles are available in lengths of 4 mm (5/32 in),

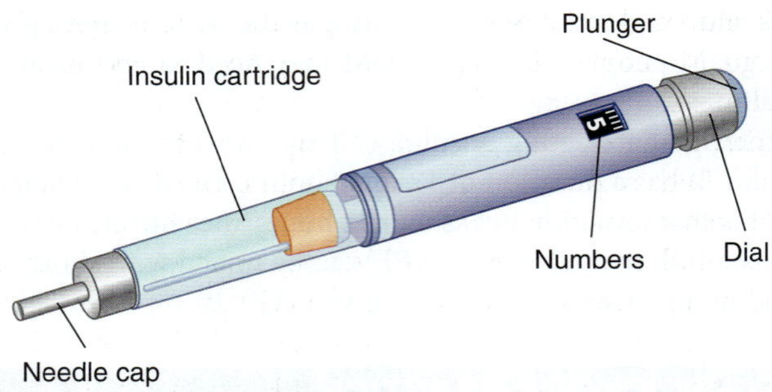

Fig. 53.6 Parts of insulin pen.

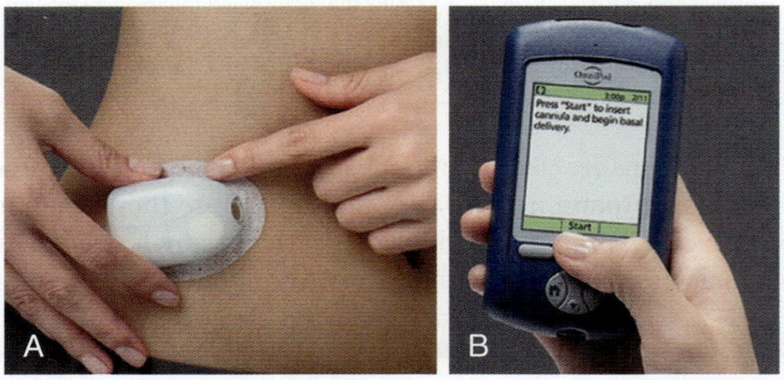

Fig. 53.7 (A) OmniPod Insulin Management System. The Pod holds and delivers insulin. (B) The Personal Diabetes Manager (PDM) wirelessly programs insulin delivery via the Pod. The PDM has a built-in glucose meter. (Courtesy of Insulet Corporation.)

5 mm (3/16 in), 8 mm (5/16 in), and 12.7 mm (½ in) and in 3 gauges: 29, 31, and 32. Insulin pens offer convenience and flexibility. They are portable, are more discreet than using a vial and syringe, and provide consistent and accurate dosing. For patients with poor vision, the pen is a better option. They can hear the pen click as they dial the dose. Insulin pens come packaged with printed instructions, including pictures of the steps to take when using the pen. These instructions are helpful when teaching new pen users and reviewing technique with current users. Smart pens connect with a phone app that provides many reminders and helps people calculate doses.

Insulin pump. An *insulin pump* delivers a continuous subcutaneous insulin infusion through a small device worn on the belt, in a pocket, or under clothing.[14] Insulin pumps use rapid-acting insulin. It is loaded into a reservoir or cartridge and connected via plastic tubing to a catheter inserted into the subcutaneous tissue. Insulet Corporation has an insulin pump that is a tubing-free system (Fig. 53.7). All insulin pumps are programmed to deliver a continuous infusion of rapid-acting insulin 24 hours a day, known as the *basal rate.* Basal insulin can be temporarily increased or decreased based on carbohydrate intake, activity, or illness. Pump users need different basal rates at different times of the day.

At mealtime, the user programs the pump to deliver a bolus infusion of insulin appropriate to the amount of carbohydrate ingested and an additional amount, if needed, to bring down or "correct" high preprandial glucose. The infusion set is changed every 2 to 3 days and placed in a new site to avoid infection and promote good insulin absorption. Insulin pump users check their glucose level at least 4 times per day and/or use a CGM system. Monitoring 8 times or more per day is common.

A major advantage of the insulin pump is the potential for keeping glucose levels in a tighter range with the goal of eliminating both high and low glucose. With careful programming and constant monitoring, this is possible because insulin delivery is similar to the normal physiologic pattern. Pumps offer users more flexibility with meals and activities. Potential challenges of pump therapy include infection at the insertion site, an increased risk for DKA if the infusion is disrupted, the cost of the pump and supplies, and being attached to a device.

Hybrid closed-loop insulin pumps deliver insulin automatically by adjusting basal doses constantly throughout the day. The person must program bolus doses, which is why they are called "hybrid."

Problems With Insulin Therapy

Problems associated with insulin therapy include hypoglycemia, allergic reactions, lipodystrophy, and the Somogyi effect. Hypoglycemia is discussed later in this chapter. Table 53.7 outlines guidelines for assessing patients treated with insulin and other GLAs.

Allergic reactions. Local inflammatory reactions to insulin may occur. These include itching, redness, and burning around the injection site. Local reactions may be self-limiting within 1 to 3 months or may improve with a low dose of antihistamine. A true insulin allergy is rare. It is manifested by a systemic response with urticaria and possibly anaphylactic shock. Preservatives in the insulin and the latex or rubber stoppers on the vials have caused allergic reactions.

Lipodystrophy. *Lipodystrophy* (changes in subcutaneous fatty tissue) may occur if the same injection sites are used frequently. *Atrophy*, which is uncommon, is the wasting of subcutaneous tissue. It presents as indentations in injection sites. *Hypertrophy* happens more often and is a thickening of the subcutaneous tissue. It eventually regresses if the person does not use the site for at least 6 months. Injecting into a hypertrophied site may cause erratic insulin absorption.

Somogyi effect and dawn phenomenon. Hyperglycemia in the morning may be due to the **Somogyi effect**. A high dose of insulin causes a decline in glucose levels during the night. As a result, counterregulatory hormones (e.g., glucagon, epinephrine, GH, cortisol) are released. They stimulate lipolysis, gluconeogenesis, and glycogenolysis, which in turn cause rebound hyperglycemia. The danger of this effect is that when glucose levels are measured in the morning, hyperglycemia is present, and the patient (or the HCP) may increase the insulin dose.

If a patient has morning hyperglycemia, checking glucose levels between 2:00 and 4:00 AM for hypoglycemia will help determine if the cause is the Somogyi effect. The patient may report headaches on awakening and recall having night sweats or nightmares.

The **dawn phenomenon** is also characterized by hyperglycemia that is present on awakening. Two counterregulatory hormones (GH and cortisol), which are excreted in increased amounts in the early morning hours, may be the cause of this phenomenon. The dawn phenomenon affects many people with DM. It tends to be most severe when GH is at its peak in adolescence and young adulthood.

Careful assessment is needed to diagnose the Somogyi effect or dawn phenomenon because the treatment for each differs. The treatment for Somogyi effect is a bedtime snack, reducing the dose of insulin, or both. The treatment for dawn phenomenon is an increase in insulin or an adjustment in administration time. Your assessment must include insulin dose, injection sites, and variability in the time of meals or insulin administration. Ask the patient to measure and document bedtime, nighttime

TABLE 53.7 Assessing the Patient Treated With Glucose-Lowering Agents

Category	Assessment
For Patient With Newly Diagnosed DM or for Reevaluation of Drug Plan	
Affective	• What emotions and attitudes are patient and caregiver displaying concerning DM diagnosis and insulin or other treatment?
Cognitive	• Is patient or caregiver able to understand why insulin or other drugs are part of DM management? • Is patient or caregiver able to understand concepts of asepsis, combining insulins, and drug side effects? • Is patient able to remember to take >1 dose/day? • Does patient take medications at right times in relation to meals?
Psychomotor	• Is patient or caregiver physically able to prepare and give accurate drug doses?
For Patient Follow-up	
Effectiveness of therapy	• Is patient having symptoms of hyperglycemia? • Does glucose record show glucose levels in or out of the target range? • Is A1C in a safe range and consistent with glucose records?
Self-management behaviors	• If patient is having hyperglycemia or hypoglycemia, how do they manage the episodes? • Has patient determined reason for hyperglycemia or hypoglycemia? • How much insulin or other drug is patient taking and at what time of day? Is patient adjusting insulin dose? Under what circumstances and by how much? • Has the exercise pattern changed? • Is patient making healthy food choices? Are meals taken at times corresponding to peak insulin action?
Side effects of therapy	• Is atrophy or hypertrophy present at injection sites? • Has patient had hypoglycemia? If so, how often? What time of day? What were the symptoms of hypoglycemia? • Are there reports of nightmares, night sweats, or early morning headaches? • Has patient had a skin rash or GI upset since taking DM drugs? • Has patient gained or lost weight?

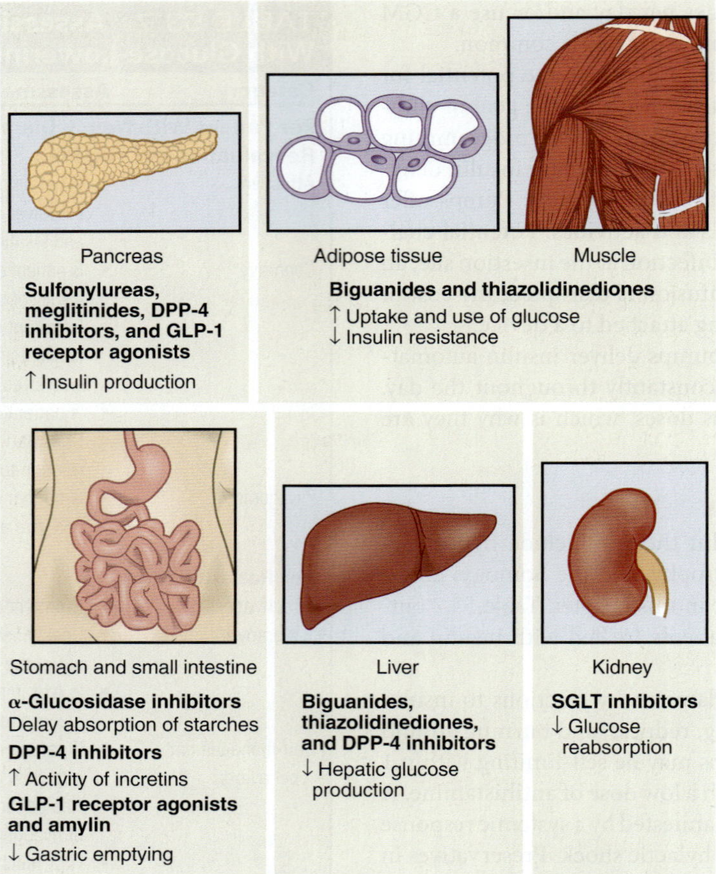

Fig. 53.8 Sites and mechanisms of action of type 2 DM drugs. *DDP-4,* Dipeptidyl peptidase; *GLP-1,* glucagon-like peptide-1; *SGLT,* sodium-glucose co-transporter.

(between 2:00 and 4:00 AM), and morning fasting glucose levels on several occasions. If the predawn levels are less than 60 mg/dL (3.3 mmol/L) and signs and symptoms of hypoglycemia are present, the insulin dosage should be reduced. If the 2:00 to 4:00 AM glucose is high, the insulin dosage should be increased. Counsel the patient on appropriate bedtime snacks.

Inhaled Insulin

Afrezza is a rapid-acting inhaled insulin. It is given at the beginning of each meal or within 20 minutes after starting a meal. Afrezza must be used in combination with long-acting insulin in those with type 1 DM. It should not be used to treat DKA. People with chronic lung disease, such as asthma or COPD, or who smoke should not use Afrezza because bronchospasm can occur. Other side effects include hypoglycemia, cough, and throat pain or irritation.

Drug Therapy: Oral and Noninsulin Injectable Agents

OAs and noninsulin injectable agents work to improve the mechanisms by which the body makes and uses insulin and glucose. These drugs primarily work on 3 defects of type 2 DM: (1) insulin resistance, (2) decreased insulin production, and (3) increased liver glucose production (Fig. 53.8). They may be used in combination with drugs from other classes or with insulin to achieve glucose goals. Table 53.8 lists OAs and noninsulin injectable agents.

Biguanides

The most widely used OA is metformin. It is the only drug in the biguanide class available in the United States. Metformin is the most effective first-line treatment for type 2 DM. Forms of metformin include Glucophage (immediate-release), Glucophage XR (extended-release), Fortamet (extended-release), and Riomet (liquid). The primary action of metformin is to reduce glucose production by the liver. It enhances insulin sensitivity at the tissue level and improves glucose transport into the cells. It has beneficial effects on lipid levels.

Because it may cause moderate weight loss, metformin may be useful for people with type 2 DM and prediabetes who are overweight or obese. It may prevent type 2 DM in those with prediabetes who are younger than age 60 and have risk factors, such as hypertension or a history of gestational DM.

Patients who are having surgery or radiologic procedures that involve the use of a contrast medium need to temporarily discontinue metformin before surgery or the procedure. This reduces the risk of contrast-induced kidney injury (CIN) (see Chapter 49). They should not resume the metformin until 48 hours afterward once their serum creatinine has been checked and is normal.

TABLE 53.8 Drug Therapy

Oral Agents and Noninsulin Injectable Agents

Type	Mechanism of Action	Side Effects	Considerations
Oral Agents			
α-Glucosidase Inhibitors			
acarbose (Precose) miglitol (Glyset)	Delays absorption of complex carbohydrates (starches) from GI tract	Gas, abdominal pain, diarrhea	Take with the first bite of each main meal.
Biguanides			
metformin (Fortamet Glucophage, Glucophage XR, Glumetza, Riomet)	↓ Liver glucose production. ↑ Insulin sensitivity. Improves glucose uptake by tissues, especially muscles	Diarrhea, lactic acidosis	Must be held 1–2 days before IV contrast media given and for 48 hr after. Take with food to minimize GI side effects.
Dipeptidyl Peptidase-4 (DPP-4) Inhibitors			
alogliptin (Nesina) linagliptin (Tradjenta) saxagliptin (Onglyza) sitagliptin (Januvia)	↑ Activity of incretins. ↑ Insulin release from pancreatic β-cells. ↓ Liver glucose production	Pancreatitis, allergic reactions	Take with or without food.
Dopamine Receptor Agonists			
bromocriptine (Cycloset)	Activates dopamine receptors in central nervous system. Unknown how it improves glucose levels	Orthostatic hypotension, nausea, headache, fatigue	Take with food at the same time each day. Teach the patient to change positions slowly.
Meglitinides			
nateglinide repaglinide	Stimulates a rapid and short-lived release of insulin from the pancreas	Weight gain, hypoglycemia	Take any time from 30 min before each meal right up to the time of the meal. They should not be taken if a meal is skipped.
Sodium-Glucose Co-Transporter 2 (SGLT2) Inhibitors			
canagliflozin (Invokana) dapagliflozin (Farxiga) empagliflozin (Jardiance) ertugliflozin (Steglatro)	↓ Renal glucose reabsorption. ↑ Urinary glucose excretion	Increased risk of genital and urinary tract infections. Hypoglycemia	Take in the morning before the first meal of the day. Teach the patient to drink 1–2 glasses of water each day above their normal intake.
Sulfonylureas			
glimepiride (Amaryl) glipizide (Glucotrol, Glucotrol XL) glyburide (DiaBeta, Glynase)	↑ Insulin release from pancreatic islets. ↓ Glycogenolysis and gluconeogenesis. Enhances cellular sensitivity to insulin	Weight gain, hypoglycemia	Take 30 min before meals. Avoid alcohol use.
Thiazolidinediones			
pioglitazone (Actos) rosiglitazone (Avandia)	↑ Glucose uptake in muscle. ↓ Endogenous glucose production	Weight gain, edema. *Pioglitazone:* ↑ Risk for bladder cancer and worsen heart failure. *rosiglitazone:* ↑ Risk for cardiovascular events (e.g., myocardial infarction, stroke)	Taken with or without food.
Combination Oral Therapy			
Actoplus Met, Actoplus Met XR	Same as for metformin and pioglitazone	See side effects for individual drugs	
Duetact	Same as for pioglitazone and glimepiride	Same as above	
Glucovance	Same as for metformin and glyburide	Same as above	
Glyxambi	Same as for empagliflozin and linagliptin	Same as above	
Invokamet, Invokamet XR	Same as for canagliflozin and metformin	Same as above	
Janumet, Janumet XR	Same as for metformin and sitagliptin	Same as above	
Jentadueto, Jentadueto XR	Same as for linagliptin and metformin	Same as above	
Kazano	Same as for alogliptin and metformin	Same as above	
Kombiglyze	Same as for saxagliptin and metformin	Same as above	
Oseni	Same as for alogliptin and pioglitazone	Same as above	
PrandiMet	Same as for metformin and repaglinide	Same as above	

Continued

TABLE 53.8 Drug Therapy—cont'd

Oral Agents and Noninsulin Injectable Agents

Type	Mechanism of Action	Side Effects	Considerations
Qtern	Same as for dapagliflozin and saxagliptin	Same as above	
Qternmet XR	Same as for dapagliflozin, saxagliptin, and metformin XR	Same as above	
Segluromet	Same as for metformin and ertugliflozin	Same as above	
Steglujan	Same as for sitagliptin and ertugliflozin	Same as above	
Synjardy, Synjardy XR	Same as metformin and empagliflozin	Same as above	
Trijardy	Same as for empagliflozin, linagliptin, and metformin XR	Same as above	
Xigduo	Same as for dapagliflozin and metformin	Same as above	
Noninsulin Injectable Agents			
Amylin Analogs			
pramlintide (Symlin)	Slows gastric emptying. ↓ Glucagon secretion and endogenous glucose output from liver. ↑ Satiety	Hypoglycemia, nausea, vomiting, decreased appetite, headache	Inject subcutaneously into the thigh or abdomen before meals. Do not inject into the arm because absorption from the arm is too variable.
Glucagon-Like Peptide-1 (GLP-1) Receptor Agonists			
albiglutide (Tanzeum) dulaglutide (Trulicity) exenatide (Byetta) exenatide extended-release (Bydureon) liraglutide (Victoza) lixisenatide (Adlyxin) semaglutide (Ozempic)	↑ Insulin release. ↓ Glucagon secretion and slow gastric emptying. ↑ Satiety	Nausea, vomiting, hypoglycemia, diarrhea, headache	The delayed gastric emptying may affect the absorption of other oral drugs. Tell patients to take fast-acting oral agents at least 1 hr before injecting a GLP-1 agonist drug.

DRUG ALERT

Metformin

- Do not use in patients with kidney disease, liver disease, or heart failure. Lactic acidosis is a rare complication of metformin accumulation.
- IV contrast media that contain iodine pose a risk for CIN, which could worsen metformin-induced lactic acidosis.
- To reduce risk for CIN, discontinue metformin 2 days before the procedure.
- May be resumed 48 hours after the procedure, assuming kidney function is normal.
- Do not use in people who drink excess amounts of alcohol.

Sulfonylureas

Sulfonylureas include glimepiride (Amaryl), glipizide (Glucotrol, Glucotrol XL), and glyburide (DiaBeta, Glynase). Their primary action is to increase insulin production by the pancreas. This makes hypoglycemia the major side effect.

Meglitinides

Like sulfonylureas, nateglinide and repaglinide increase insulin production by the pancreas. However, because they are more rapidly absorbed and eliminated than sulfonylureas, they are less likely to cause hypoglycemia. When taken just before meals, pancreatic insulin production increases during and after the meal, mimicking the normal response to eating.

α-Glucosidase Inhibitors

These drugs, also known as "starch blockers," work by slowing down carbohydrate absorption in the small intestine. Acarbose and miglitol (Glyset) are the available drugs in this class. They are most effective in lowering postprandial glucose. Their effectiveness is measured by checking 2-hour postprandial glucose levels.

Thiazolidinediones

Thiazolidinediones, sometimes called "insulin sensitizers," include pioglitazone (Actos) and rosiglitazone (Avandia). They are most effective for people who have insulin resistance. These drugs improve insulin sensitivity, transport, and use at target tissues. Because they do not increase insulin production, they do not cause hypoglycemia when used alone. These drugs are rarely used because of their adverse effects. Rosiglitazone can cause cardiovascular events (e.g., myocardial infarction [MI]). It can be obtained only through restricted access programs. Pioglitazone can worsen heart failure (HF). Use is associated with an increased risk for bladder cancer.

Dipeptidyl Peptidase-4 Inhibitors

Normally, the intestines release incretin hormones throughout the day. When glucose levels are normal or high, incretins increase insulin synthesis and release from the pancreas and decrease liver glucose production. Incretin levels increase after a meal. The 2 main incretin hormones are gastric inhibitory peptide [GIP] and glucagon-like peptide-1 [GLP-1]). They are quickly inactivated by the enzyme dipeptidyl peptidase-4 (DPP-4).

DPP-4 inhibitors (also called *gliptins*) come in pill form. They include alogliptin (Nesina), linagliptin (Tradjenta), saxagliptin (Onglyza), and sitagliptin (Januvia). DPP-4 inhibitors block the action of DPP-4, which inactivates incretin hormones. The result is an increase in insulin release, a decrease in glucagon secretion, and a decrease in liver glucose production. Since the DPP-4 inhibitors are glucose-dependent, they have a lower potential for hypoglycemia. Their main benefit over other drugs with similar effects is the absence of weight gain as a side effect.

Sodium-Glucose Co-Transporter 2 (SGLT2) Inhibitors

Normally, sodium-glucose transporters reabsorb glucose from the kidneys back into the bloodstream. SGLT2 inhibitors work by blocking glucose reabsorption by the kidney, increasing urinary glucose excretion. Drugs in this class include canagliflozin (Invokana), dapagliflozin (Farxiga), and empagliflozin (Jardiance).

Dopamine Receptor Agonist

Bromocriptine (Cycloset) is a dopamine receptor agonist that improves glucose levels. The mechanism of action is unknown. We think people with type 2 DM have low dopamine levels in the morning. These low dopamine levels may interfere with the body's ability to control glucose. Bromocriptine increases dopamine receptor activity. It can be used alone or with another type 2 DM treatment.

Combination Oral Therapy

Many combination drugs are currently available (Table 53.8). These drugs combine different classes of DM medications in 1 pill. An advantage of combination therapy is that the patient takes fewer pills, thus making it easier to take medication.

Glucagon-Like Peptide-1 Receptor Agonists

GLP-1 receptor agonists stimulate GLP-1 (an incretin hormone). It is decreased in people with type 2 DM. These drugs increase insulin synthesis and release from the pancreas, inhibit glucagon secretion, slow gastric emptying, and reduce food intake by increasing satiety. They may be used alone or with another type 2 DM treatment when OAs have not achieved optimal glucose levels.

Except for semaglutide (Rybelsus), which is given orally, they are all given using a subcutaneous injection in a prefilled pen. Exenatide (Byetta) is given twice daily. Liraglutide (Victoza) is given once daily. Albiglutide (Tanzeum), dulaglutide (Trulicity), and exenatide extended-release (Bydureon) are given once every 7 days.

DRUG ALERT

Exenatide (Byetta)

- Acute pancreatitis and kidney problems may occur.

DRUG ALERT

Liraglutide (Victoza) and Dulaglutide (Trulicity)

- Do not use in patients with a personal or family history of medullary thyroid cancer.
- Acute pancreatitis may occur.

Amylin Analogs

Pramlintide (Symlin) is the only available amylin analog. Amylin is a hormone secreted by the β cells of the pancreas in response to food intake. It slows gastric emptying, reduces glucagon secretion, and increases satiety. People with type 1 or type 2 DM with high glucose levels on insulin therapy take pramlintide with their mealtime insulin. It is only used concurrently with insulin and is not a replacement for insulin. The drug cannot be mixed in the same syringe with insulin.

The concurrent use of pramlintide and insulin increases the risk for severe hypoglycemia during the 3 hours after injection, especially in those with type 1 DM. Teach patients to eat a meal with at least 250 calories and fast-acting glucose on hand in case hypoglycemia develops. When using pramlintide, the bolus insulin dose should be reduced.

DRUG ALERT

Pramlintide (Symlin)

- Can cause severe hypoglycemia when used with insulin.

Other Drugs Affecting Glucose Levels

Both the patient and the HCP must be aware of drug interactions that can potentiate hypoglycemia and hyperglycemia effects. For example, β-adrenergic blockers can mask symptoms of hypoglycemia and prolong the hypoglycemic effects of insulin. Loop diuretics can worsen hyperglycemia by inducing potassium loss.

Nutrition Therapy

Patient-centered nutrition therapy, consisting of counseling, education, and ongoing monitoring, is a cornerstone of care for people with DM and prediabetes. Changing eating habits can be challenging for many people.[15] Achieving nutrition goals requires a coordinated team effort that considers the person's behavioral, cognitive, socioeconomic, cultural, and religious backgrounds and preferences. Because of these complexities, a dietitian with expertise in DM management should work with the person with DM. The dietitian starts with a nutrition assessment and develops a patient-centered food plan. Other team members may include nurses, certified diabetes care and education specialists (CDCESs), clinical nurse specialists, social workers, and other HCPs.

ADA guidelines state that, within the context of an overall healthy eating plan, a person with DM can eat the same foods as a person without DM. This means that the same principles of healthy nutrition that apply to the general population apply to the person with DM. Table 53.9 describes nutrition guidelines

TABLE 53.9 NUTRITION THERAPY

DM

Component	Recommendations
Total carbohydrate	• Include carbohydrate from fruits, vegetables, grains, legumes, and low-fat milk • Monitor by carbohydrate counting, exchange lists, or use of appropriate proportions • Fiber intake at 14 g/1000 kcal/day • Nonnutritive sweeteners are safe when consumed within FDA daily intake levels
Protein	Individualize goals
Fat	• Individualize goals • ≥2 servings of fish per week to provide polyunsaturated fatty acids • Consume fats from plant products
Alcohol	• Limit to moderate amount (maximum 1 drink per day for women, 2 drinks per day for men) • Consume alcohol with food to reduce risk for nocturnal hypoglycemia in those using insulin or drugs that promote insulin secretion • Moderate alcohol consumption has no acute effect on glucose and insulin concentrations • Carbohydrate taken with alcohol (mixed drink) may raise glucose

Source: ADA: Lifestyle management: standards of medical care in diabetes, *Diabetes Care* 43:S50, 2020.

for people with DM. According to the ADA, the overall goal of nutrition therapy is to help people with DM make healthy food choices that will lead to achieving and/or maintaining safe and healthy glucose levels.[16] Additional goals include:

- Maintain glucose levels as close to normal as safely possible to prevent or reduce the risk for DM-related complications.
- Achieve lipid profiles and BP levels that reduce the risk for CVD.
- Prevent or slow the rate of development of chronic complications by modifying nutrient intake and lifestyle.
- Address nutrition needs while considering personal and cultural preferences and respecting the person's willingness or ability to change eating and dietary habits.
- Maintain the pleasure of eating by encouraging a variety of healthy food choices.

Type 1 Diabetes

People with type 1 DM base their meal planning on usual food intake and preferences balanced with insulin and exercise patterns. The patient coordinates insulin dosing with eating habits and activity in mind. Day-to-day consistency in timing and amount of food eaten makes it much easier to manage glucose levels, especially for those using conventional, fixed insulin plans. Those using rapid-acting insulin can adjust the dose before each meal based on the current glucose level and the carbohydrate content of the meal. Intensified insulin therapy, such as multiple daily injections or the use of an insulin pump, allows considerable flexibility in food selection and can be adjusted for changes from usual eating and exercise habits. This does not diminish or replace the need for healthy food choices and a well-balanced diet.

Type 2 Diabetes

Nutrition therapy in type 2 DM emphasizes achieving glucose, lipid, and BP goals.[17] Modest weight loss may improve insulin sensitivity. Therefore, weight loss is recommended for all persons with DM who are overweight or obese.

There is no one proven strategy or method. A nutritionally adequate meal plan with appropriate serving sizes, a reduction of saturated and *trans* fats, and lower carbohydrates can decrease calorie consumption. Spacing meals is another strategy that spreads nutrient intake throughout the day. A weight loss of 5% to 7% of body weight often improves glucose levels, even if desirable weight is not achieved. Weight loss is best achieved by a moderate decrease in calories and regular exercise. Adopting new behaviors and attitudes can promote long-term health behavior changes. Monitoring glucose levels, A1C, lipids, and BP gives feedback on how well the goals of nutrition management are being met.

Food Composition

A healthy balance of nutrients is essential to maintain glucose levels and overall health. Energy from food intake can be balanced with the patient's energy output. Teach patients to outline their meal plan with their lifestyle and health goals in mind. There is no special eating plan for people with DM. The person can work with their HCP to determine which plan works best for them, keeping in mind portions and effects on glucose, lipids, and BP. The following are general recommendations for nutrient balance.

Carbohydrate. Carbohydrates are an important source of energy, fiber, vitamins, and minerals. They are needed by all people, including those with DM. Foods containing carbohydrate from whole grains, fruits, vegetables, and low-fat dairy are part of a healthy meal plan. The ADA recommends individualizing carbohydrate intake as there is no ideal amount for all people with DM.

All persons benefit from including dietary fiber as part of a healthy meal plan. The current recommendation for people with DM is to consume a minimum of 14 grams of fiber per 1000 kcal. At least half of any grain intake should come from whole intact grains.

Nutritive and nonnutritive sweeteners may be included in a healthy meal plan in moderation. Nonnutritive sweeteners include the sugar substitutes saccharine, aspartame, sucralose, stevia, neotame, and acesulfame-K.

Fat. Fat provides energy, transports fat-soluble vitamins, and provides essential fatty acids. The ADA recommends 20% to 35% of total calorie intake from fat. People with DM benefit from eating fewer carbohydrate foods that are higher in total fat. Healthy fats are those that come from plants, such as olives, nuts, and avocados.

Protein. The amount of daily protein in the diet for people with DM and normal kidney function is the same as the general population. The ADA recommends individualizing protein intake. Teach patients to choose lean protein whenever possible.

Alcohol. Alcohol inhibits gluconeogenesis by the liver. This can cause severe hypoglycemia in people who take insulin or OAs that increase insulin secretion. Alcohol use can make DM harder to manage. Create a trusting environment in which patients feel comfortable talking openly about their alcohol use.

Moderate alcohol use can be safely included in the meal plan if the person monitors glucose levels and is not at risk for other alcohol-related problems. Moderate use is defined as 1 drink per day for women and 2 drinks per day for men. A person can reduce the risk for alcohol-induced hypoglycemia by eating carbohydrates when drinking alcohol. Mixed drinks often contain sweetened mixers and can increase glucose levels. To decrease the carbohydrate content, recommend using sugar-free mixes and drinking dry, light wines.

Patient Teaching Related to Nutrition Therapy

Most often, the dietitian initially teaches the principles of nutrition management. Whenever possible, work with dietitians as part of the DM care team. Some patients who have limited insurance coverage or live in remote areas do not have access to a dietitian. In these cases, you may need to assume responsibility for teaching basic nutrition principles to patients with DM.

Carbohydrate counting is a meal planning technique used to keep track of the amount of carbohydrate eaten at each meal and per day. Teach patients to keep carbohydrate intake within a healthy range. The amount of total carbohydrate per day depends on glucose levels, age, weight, activity level, patient preference, and drug plan. A serving size of carbohydrate is 15 g. A typical adult might start with 45 to 60 g of carbohydrate per meal. Some patients tailor insulin doses to the amount of carbohydrate foods that they will consume at the meal, with a set number of units of insulin given per gram of carbohydrate (e.g., 1 U/15 g carbohydrate, 2 U/25 g carbohydrate). Teach the patient about the foods that contain carbohydrate, how to read food labels, and appropriate serving sizes.

Diabetes exchange lists are another method for meal planning. Instead of counting carbohydrates, the person uses a meal plan with specific numbers of helpings from a list of exchanges for each meal and snack. The exchanges are starches, fruits, milk, meats, vegetables, fats, and free foods. The person chooses foods from the various exchanges based on the prescribed meal plan. This method may be easier for some people than carbohydrate counting. It also encourages a well-balanced meal plan. Another advantage is that this approach helps the person limit portion sizes and overall food intake, an important part of weight management.

The MyPlate method can help the person see how much vegetables, starch, and meat should fill a 9-in plate.[18] The recommendation is that each meal has half of the plate filled with nonstarchy vegetables, one-fourth filled with a starch, and one-fourth filled with a protein. An 8-oz glass of nonfat milk and a small piece of fresh fruit complete the meal.

Whenever possible, include family members and caregivers in nutrition education and counseling, especially the person who cooks for the household. However, the responsibility for maintaining a healthy eating plan still belongs to the person with DM. Reliance on another person to make health decisions interferes with the patient's ability to develop self-care skills, which are essential in managing DM. Foster independence, even in patients with visual or cognitive problems.

TABLE 53.10 Activities That Affect Caloric Expenditure

Light Activity (100–200 kcal/hr)	Moderate Activity (200–350 kcal/hr)	Vigorous Activity (400–900 kcal/hr)
• Fishing	• Active housework	• Aerobic exercise
• Light housework	• Bicycling (light)	• Bicycling (vigorous)
• Secretarial work	• Bowling	• Hard labor
• Teaching	• Dancing	• Ice skating
• Walking casually	• Gardening	• Outdoor sports
	• Golf	• Running
	• Roller skating	• Soccer
	• Walking briskly	• Tennis
		• Wood chopping

Discuss traditional and favorite foods with the patient. Explore the influences of culture on food choices and meal planning with the patient. Individualize food choices considering the patient's preferences and culturally appropriate foods. Nutrition resources designed for members of different cultural groups are available from the ADA.

Exercise

Regular, consistent exercise is an essential part of DM and prediabetes management. The ADA recommends that people with DM engage in at least 150 minutes/week (30 minutes, 5 days/week) of a moderate-intensity aerobic activity (Table 53.10). The ADA encourages people with DM to perform resistance training 2 to 3 times a week unless contraindicated.

Exercise decreases insulin resistance and can have a direct effect on lowering glucose levels. It contributes to weight loss, which further decreases insulin resistance. The therapeutic benefits of regular activity may result in a decreased need for DM drugs to reach target glucose goals in people with type 2 DM. Regular exercise may help reduce triglyceride and low-density lipoprotein (LDL) cholesterol levels, increase HDL, reduce BP, and improve circulation.

Encourage patients to be active every day and decrease the amount of time sitting. Medical clearance may be needed for new, intensive exercise programs. Teach patients to start slowly and gradually progress toward the desired goal. Patients who use insulin, sulfonylureas, or meglitinides are at increased risk for hypoglycemia when they increase physical activity, especially if they exercise at the time of peak drug action or eat too little to maintain adequate glucose levels. This can also occur if a normally sedentary patient with DM has an unusually active day.

The glucose-lowering effects of exercise can last up to 48 hours after the activity, so it is possible for hypoglycemia to occur long after the activity. People who use drugs that can cause hypoglycemia should exercise about 1 hour after a meal or have a 10- to 15-g carbohydrate snack and check their glucose before exercising. It is preferable not to increase caloric intake for exercise. If needed, they can eat small carbohydrate snacks every 30 minutes during exercise to prevent hypoglycemia. Patients using drugs that place them at risk for hypoglycemia should always carry a fast-acting source of carbohydrate, such

TABLE 53.11 PATIENT & CAREGIVER TEACHING

Exercise for Patients With DM

Include the following information in the exercise teaching plan for the patient and caregiver:

1. Exercise does not have to be vigorous to be effective. The glucose-reducing effects of exercise can be reached with activity such as brisk walking.
2. Choose activities that are enjoyable to foster regularity.
3. Use properly fitting footwear to avoid rubbing or injury.
4. The exercise session includes a warm-up period and a cool-down period. Start the exercise program gradually and increase slowly.
5. Exercise is best done after meals when the glucose level is rising.
6. Exercise plans are patient-specific and monitored by the HCP.
7. Monitor glucose levels before, during, and after exercise to determine the effect exercise has on glucose levels at specific times of the day.
8. Before exercise, if glucose ≤100 mg/dL, eat a 15-g carbohydrate snack. After 15–30 min, recheck glucose levels. Delay exercise if <100 mg/dL. Talk to HCP about lowering drug dose(s) if hypoglycemia occurs consistently.
9. Before exercise, if glucose ≥250 mg/dL in a person with type 1 DM and ketones are present, delay vigorous activity until ketones are gone. Drink fluids.
10. Exercise-induced hypoglycemia may occur several hours after completing exercise.
11. Planned or spontaneous exercise is still important when taking a glucose-lowering medication.
12. Compensate for extensive planned and spontaneous activity by monitoring glucose levels and adjusting the insulin dose (if taken) and food intake.

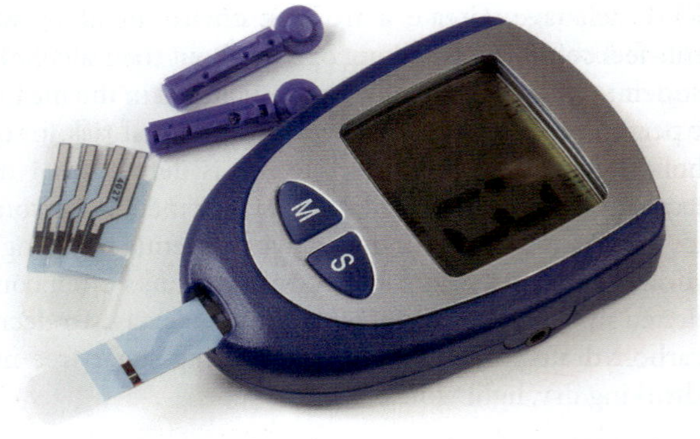

Fig. 53.9 Blood glucose meters are used to measure glucose levels. (© iStock.com/kolesnikovserg.)

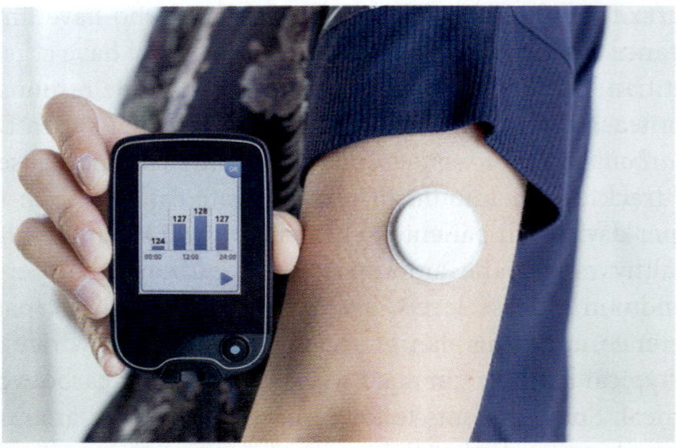

Fig. 53.10 Continuous blood glucose meter showing a reading after scanning the sensor of the glucose monitoring system placed on the arm. (Click_and_Photo/iStock.com.)

as glucose tablets or hard candies, when exercising. If they have frequent lows from exercise, the dose may need to be lowered. Table 53.11 describes exercise guidelines for people with DM.

The body can perceive strenuous activity as stress, causing a release of counterregulatory hormones and a temporary increase in glucose. In a person with type 1 DM who has hyperglycemia and ketones, exercise can worsen these conditions. Teach these patients to delay activity if the glucose level is over 250 mg/dL and ketones are present in the urine. If hyperglycemia is present without ketosis, it is not necessary to postpone exercise.

Blood Glucose Monitoring

Blood glucose monitoring (BGM) is a critical part of DM management. By providing a current glucose reading, BGM lets the patient make decisions about food intake, activity patterns, and drug dosages. It produces accurate records of daily glucose fluctuations and trends and alerts the patient to acute episodes of hyperglycemia and hypoglycemia. BGM provides patients with a tool for achieving and maintaining specific glycemic goals. It is recommended for all people who use insulin to manage their DM. Other patients with DM use BGM to help achieve and maintain glycemic goals and monitor for acute fluctuations in glucose related to drugs, food, and exercise.

The frequency of BGM depends on several factors. These include the patient's glycemic goals, type of DM, drug plan, patient's ability to check glucose independently, access to supplies and equipment, and patient's willingness and ability to do so. The recommendation for patients who use multiple insulin injections or insulin pumps is to monitor their glucose 4 to 8 times each day. Patients using less frequent insulin injections, noninsulin therapy, or nutrition management may use BGM as often as needed to achieve their glycemic goals.

People who perform BGM use portable blood glucose meters. A wide variety of blood glucose meters are available (Fig. 53.9). Disposable lancets are used to get a small drop of capillary blood (usually from a finger stick) that is placed in a reagent strip. After a specified time, the meter displays a reading of the capillary glucose value. Technology is rapidly changing. More convenient systems are introduced on an ongoing basis.

CGM systems are another route for monitoring glucose (Fig. 53.10).[19] More people with type 1 DM are using CGMs. These systems are slowly being used by more people with type 2 DM. Insurance coverage and cost are the most common limiting factors. Some insulin pumps have CGM integrated as part of the system.

Using a sensor inserted subcutaneously, the CGM systems display new glucose values every 1 to 5 minutes. CGM assesses interstitial glucose, which lags behind blood glucose by 5 to 10 minutes. The person inserts the sensor using an automatic insertion device. Data are sent from the sensor to a transmitter, which displays the glucose value on either an insulin pump or a pager-like receiver. The CGM can be used with or without an insulin pump. Newer CGMs can "share" data with a smartphone.

CGMs help the patient and HCP identify trends and patterns in glucose levels. The goal is to increase "time in range" (70 to 180 mg/dL) and have fewer highs and lows. They are useful for managing insulin therapy or when continuous glucose readings are important. They alert the person to episodes of hypoglycemia and hyperglycemia. This allows them to take corrective action quickly.

Blood glucose meters are reliable when used consistently and correctly. It is not necessary to compare their readings to laboratory readings. If the A1C result does not correspond to the glucose readings on the home meter, troubleshoot any problems with the meter, technique, strips, and hand washing.

Because errors in BGM technique can cause errors in management strategies, patient teaching is essential. Follow the initial instruction with regular reassessment. Review the instructions that come with each product. If a product has a control solution, teach patients to use and interpret control solutions. A control should be done when first using a blood glucose meter or when there is a reason to believe that the readings are not correct. Table 53.12 lists the steps to include when teaching the patient how to perform BGM.

People with type 1 DM often check their glucose before meals. This is because many people use insulin pumps or multiple daily injections and base the insulin dose on the amount of carbohydrate in a meal or the preprandial glucose value. Checking glucose 2 hours after the first bite of food helps a person determine if the bolus insulin dose was adequate for that meal.

Teach patients to check glucose whenever they suspect hypoglycemia and then take immediate action. During times of illness, check glucose levels at 4-hour intervals (or more) to determine the effects of the illness on glucose levels. Teach the patient to check glucose before and after exercise to determine the effects of exercise on glucose levels. This is especially important for the patient with type 1 DM.

A patient with impaired vision, cognitive impairment, or limited dexterity needs careful assessment to see if BGM can be done independently. Nurses preparing patients for discharge from the hospital and nurses working in home health and outpatient settings may need to identify caregivers who can assume this responsibility. Adaptive devices are available to help patients with certain limitations. These include talking monitors and other equipment for the visually impaired.

TABLE 53.12 PATIENT & CAREGIVER TEACHING

Blood Glucose Monitoring (BGM)

Include the following instructions when teaching the patient and caregiver about BGM:

1. Wash and dry hands completely. It is not necessary to clean the site with alcohol, and it may interfere with results.
2. If it is hard to get an adequate drop of blood for monitoring, warm the hands in warm water or let the arms hang dependently for a few minutes before making the finger puncture.
3. A lancing device is often used. Place the lancet in the device, following the instructions that come with it. If the puncture is made on the finger, use the side of the finger pad rather than near the center. There are fewer nerve endings along the side of the finger pad.
4. Set lancing device to make a puncture just deep enough to get a sufficiently large drop of blood. Unnecessarily deep punctures may cause pain and bruising. Current meters need very small amounts of blood.
5. Follow instructions on meter for checking the glucose level.
6. Record results. Compare with personal glucose goals.

Pancreas Transplantation

Pancreas transplantation is an option for select persons with type 1 DM. Candidates include patients who have ESRD and have had or plan to have a kidney transplant. Kidney and pancreas transplants are often done together, or a pancreas may be transplanted after a kidney transplant. If renal failure is not present, the ADA recommends that pancreas transplantation be considered only for people who meet 3 criteria: (1) a history of frequent, acute, and severe metabolic complications (e.g., hypoglycemia, hyperglycemia, DKA) requiring medical attention; (2) clinical and emotional problems with the use of insulin therapy that are so severe as to be incapacitating; and (3) consistent failure of insulin-based management to prevent acute complications.

Successful pancreas transplantation can improve quality of life, primarily by eliminating the need for insulin therapy and frequent BGM. Transplantation can eliminate acute complications experienced by people with type 1 DM (e.g., hypoglycemia, hyperglycemia). However, transplantation is only partially successful in reversing the renal and neurologic complications of DM. The patient will need lifelong immunosuppression to prevent rejection of the organ. Complications can result from immunosuppressive therapy. Immunosuppressive therapy is discussed in Chapter 14.

Pancreatic islet cell transplantation is another potential treatment measure. During this procedure, the islets are harvested from the pancreas of a deceased organ donor. Most recipients need islets from 2 or more pancreases. The islets are infused via a catheter through the upper abdomen into the portal vein of the liver. With only the islets transplanted, pain and recovery time are less than with whole pancreas transplants. Currently, this procedure is experimental in the United States. Research is continuing to explore the best ways to implant the islet cells and prevent their rejection.

NURSING MANAGEMENT: DIABETES

Assessment

Table 53.13 provides initial subjective and objective data you should obtain from a person with DM. After the initial assessment, perform periodic patient assessments on a regular basis.

Clinical Problems

Clinical problems for the patient with DM may include:

- Altered blood glucose level
- Deficient knowledge
- Risk for injury
- Impaired endocrine function
- Neurologic problem

TABLE 53.13 NURSING ASSESSMENT

DM

Subjective Data

Important Health Information

Health history: Mumps, rubella, coxsackievirus, or other viral infections. Recent trauma, infection, or stress. Pregnancy, gave birth to infant >9 lb. Pancreatitis, Cushing syndrome, acromegaly, family history of type 1 or type 2 DM

Medications: Use of insulin, OAs, noninsulin injectables, corticosteroids, diuretics, phenytoin

Surgery or other treatments: Any recent surgery

Functional Health Patterns

Health perception–health management: Positive family history, malaise

Nutrition-metabolic: Obesity, weight loss (type 1), weight gain (type 2). Thirst, hunger, nausea, and vomiting. Poor healing (especially involving the feet), eating habits

Elimination: Constipation or diarrhea, frequent urination, frequent bladder infections, nocturia, urinary incontinence

Activity-exercise: Muscle weakness, fatigue

Cognitive-perceptual: Abdominal pain, headache, blurred vision, numbness or tingling of extremities, pruritus

Sexuality-reproductive: ED, frequent vaginal infections, vaginal dryness, or pain, ↓ libido

Adaptation: Depression, irritability, apathy

Value-belief: Health beliefs, commitment to lifestyle changes involving food, medication, and activity patterns

Objective Data

Cardiovascular

Hypotension.[a] Weak, rapid pulse[a]

Eyes

Soft, sunken eyeballs.[a] History of vitreal hemorrhages, cataracts

GI

Dry mouth, vomiting.[a] Fruity breath[a]

Musculoskeletal

Muscle wasting[a]

Neurologic

Altered reflexes, restlessness, confusion, stupor, coma[a]

Respiratory

Rapid, deep respirations (Kussmaul respirations)[a]

Skin

Dry, warm, inelastic skin. Pigmented lesions (on legs), ulcers (especially on feet), loss of hair on toes, acanthosis nigricans

Possible Findings

Serum electrolyte abnormalities. Fasting glucose level ≥126 mg/dL. OGTT >200 mg/dL, random glucose ≥200 mg/dL. Leukocytosis. ↑ BUN, creatinine, triglycerides, cholesterol, LDL, VLDL. ↓ HDL. A1C >6.0% (A1C >7.0% in those with diagnosed DM), glycosuria, ketonuria, albuminuria. Acidosis

[a]Indicates manifestations of DKA.

Additional information on clinical problems and interventions for the patient with DM is presented in eNursing Care Plan 53.1, available on the website.

◆ Planning

The overall goals are for the patient with DM to (1) engage in self-care behaviors to actively manage DM, (2) have few or no hyperglycemia or hypoglycemia emergencies, (3) maintain safe and healthy glucose levels, (4) reduce the risk for chronic complications, and (5) adjust lifestyle to accommodate the DM plan with minimal stress. The goal is for the patient with DM to safely and effectively fit DM into life rather than living life around DM.

◆ Implementation

◆ Health Promotion

Your role in health promotion is to identify, monitor, and teach the patient at risk for DM. Obesity is a key risk factor for type 2 DM. The ADA recommends routine screening for type 2 DM for all adults who are overweight or obese (BMI 25 kg/m^2 or greater) or have 1 or more risk factors. A DM risk test is available at www.diabetes.org/risk-test. The DM risk test determines if the person is at risk for prediabetes or DM based on the number of risk factors present. For people who do not have risk factors for DM, begin screening at age 45. Table 53.14 provides criteria to screen for prediabetes and DM. If results are normal, repeat screening at 3-year intervals.

Primary prevention is a cost-effective approach (Box 53.3). Current recommendations for primary prevention include lifestyle modifications for at-risk people. A modest weight loss of 5% to 7% of body weight and 150 minutes of physical activity a week lowers the risk for developing type 2 DM by 34% to 58%.

TABLE 53.14 Screening for DM in Asymptomatic, Undiagnosed Persons

Who to Screen

1. Consider screening all adults who are overweight (BMI >25 kg/m^2) and have risk factors for DM:
   - First-degree relative with DM
   - Physically inactive
   - Members of a high-risk ethnic population (e.g., Black, Hispanic, Native American, Asian American,[a] Pacific Islander)
   - Women who delivered a baby weighing >9 lb or were diagnosed with gestational DM
   - Hypertensive (≥140/90 mm Hg) or on therapy for hypertension
   - HDL cholesterol level ≤35 mg/dL (0.90 mmol/L) and/or a triglyceride level ≥250 mg/dL (2.82 mmol/L)
   - Women with polycystic ovary syndrome
   - A1C ≥5.7%, IGT, or IFG on previous screening
   - Other conditions associated with insulin resistance (e.g., acanthosis nigricans)
2. In the absence of the above criteria, screening for DM should begin at age 45 years.
3. If results are normal, repeat screening at least every 3 years, with more frequent screening depending on initial results and risk status.

What Measurements to Use

To screen for DM or to assess risk of future DM, A1C, FPG, or 2-hr OGTT is appropriate (Table 53.2).

[a]Consider screening Asian Americans with a BMI of 23 kg/m^2 or higher.

BOX 53.3 PROMOTING POPULATION HEALTH

Preventing DM

- Aim for 150 min of moderate activity each week.
- Maintain a healthy weight through a nutritionally balanced diet.
- Follow a diet low in saturated and *trans* fat, total calories, and processed foods and high in whole grains, fruits, and vegetables.
- If overweight and over age 45, have yearly screening for DM.
- Avoid cigarette smoking or tobacco products.
- Limit alcohol use to moderate levels.
- Follow the prescribed treatment plan for hypertension.

Acute Care

Acute situations involving the patient with DM include hypoglycemia, DKA, and hyperosmolar hyperglycemic syndrome (HHS). Management for these situations is discussed in more detail later in this chapter. Other areas of acute care relate to management during acute illness and surgery (Table 53.15).

Acute illness and surgery. Emotional and physical stress can increase the glucose level and cause hyperglycemia. Because stress is unavoidable, certain situations may require more intense treatment, such as extra insulin and more frequent BGM, to maintain glycemic goals and avoid hyperglycemia.

Acute illness, injury, and surgery may evoke a counterregulatory hormone response, causing hyperglycemia. Even common illnesses, such as an upper respiratory tract infection or the flu, can cause this response. Encourage patients to check glucose at least every 4 hours when they are ill. Teach acutely ill patients with type 1 DM and glucose greater than 240 mg/dL (13.3 mmol/L) to check urine for ketones every 3 to 4 hours.

Teach patients to contact the HCP when glucose levels are over 300 mg/dL twice in a row, or urine ketone levels are moderate to high. A patient with type 1 DM may need an increase in insulin to prevent DKA. High glucose levels can lead to poor healing and infection. A patient with type 2 DM may need insulin therapy to prevent or treat hyperglycemia symptoms and avoid an acute hyperglycemia emergency. In critically ill patients, insulin therapy may be started if the glucose is persistently greater than 180 mg/dL. These patients have a higher targeted glucose goal, which is usually 140 to 180 mg/dL. Food intake is important during times of stress and illness when the body needs extra energy. If patients can eat normally, they can continue with their regular meal plan while increasing the intake of noncaloric fluids, such as water, sugar-free gelatin, and other decaffeinated beverages, and continue taking OAs, noninsulin injectable agents, and insulin as prescribed. When illness causes patients to eat less than normal, they can continue to take OAs, noninsulin injectable agents, and/or insulin as prescribed while supplementing food intake with carbohydrate-containing fluids. Examples include low-sodium soups, juices, and regular, sugar-sweetened decaffeinated soft drinks. It is important to tell the patient to contact an HCP if they are unable to keep down food or fluid.

During the intraoperative period, we often adjust the DM plan to ensure safe and healthy glucose levels. The patient receives IV fluids and insulin (if needed) just before, during, and after surgery when there is no oral intake. Explain to the patient with type 2 DM who has been taking OAs that this is a temporary measure, not a sign of worsening DM.

When caring for an unconscious surgical patient receiving insulin, be alert for signs of hypoglycemia, such as sweating, tachycardia, and tremors. Frequent glucose monitoring can prevent episodes of hypoglycemia.

TABLE 53.15 NURSING MANAGEMENT

Caring for the Patient With DM

- Assess for risk factors for prediabetes and type 1 and type 2 DM.
- Teach the patient and caregiver about DM management, including BGM, drug therapy, nutrition, activity, and managing hypoglycemia.
- Develop a plan to avoid hypoglycemia or hyperglycemia in a patient with DM who is acutely ill or having surgery.
- Assess for acute complications and implement appropriate actions for hypoglycemia, DKA, and HHS.
- In patients with acute complications, perform or directly supervise actions, including IV fluid and insulin administration.
- Assess for chronic complications, including CVD, retinopathy, nephropathy, neuropathy, and foot complications.
- Teach the patient and caregiver about prevention and management of chronic complications.
- Supervise LPN/VNs, and in some states and settings APs, administer insulin, noninsulin injectable agents, and OAs to stable patients.

Collaborate With Other Team Members

Dietitian
- Obtain a diet history from the patient.
- Work with patient and caregiver to create a patient-centered meal plan.
- Provide instructions for meal plan as needed.

Physical Therapist
- Assess patient's current level of fitness.
- Develop an exercise plan with the patient.

Occupational Therapist
- Teach patients with impaired vision how to use devices to draw up and measure insulin.
- Provide teaching on how to use a talking glucose meter or any glucose meter one-handed.
- Develop protective techniques for activities that involve exposure to heat, cold, and sharp objects.

Social Worker
- Aid the patient in finding resources to meet medical and financial needs.
- Help with coping with DM, including managing problems within the family or workplace.

Ambulatory Care

Successful DM management involves ongoing interaction among the patient, caregiver, and health care team. Because DM is a complex chronic condition, a great deal of patient contact takes place in outpatient and home settings. The major goal of patient care in these settings is to enable the patient (with the help of a caregiver as needed) to reach an optimal level of independence in self-management.

Many patients face challenges in reaching these goals. DM increases the risk for other chronic conditions that can affect self-management. These include impaired vision, lower extremity problems that affect mobility, and other functional limitations related to a stroke. Other barriers may include feelings of inadequacy about their abilities, unwillingness to make behavior changes, ineffective coping strategies, and cognitive problems. If the patient is not able to manage DM, a family member may be able to assume part of this role. If the patient or caregiver cannot make decisions related to DM management, consider a referral to a CDCES, social worker, or other resources within the community. These resources can help the patient and family in outlining a feasible treatment program that meets their capabilities.

Assess the ability of patients and caregivers in performing activities such as BGM and insulin injection. Assistive devices for self-administration of insulin include syringe magnifiers, vial stabilizers, and dosing aids for the visually impaired. In some cases, referrals can help the patient achieve their self-care goal. These may include an occupational therapist, a social worker, a home care nurse, a home health aide, or a dietitian.

A diagnosis of DM affects each person in many profound ways. Self-management of DM is demanding. People with DM continually face lifestyle choices that affect the foods they eat, their activities, and demands on their time and energy. The requirements of scheduled meals, BGM, medication, and insulin management may interfere with the patient's other responsibilities. Any change in the daily routine can be hard. In addition, they face the challenge of preventing or dealing with the complications of DM.

Assess the patient's knowledge of DM and lifestyle preferences when planning a teaching program (Box 53.4). What does it mean to the person to have DM? Assess the patient's knowledge frequently so that you can help with gaps in knowledge or correct misinformation.

Identify the patient's support system. Include them in planning, teaching, and counseling. When we include family members and other persons close to the patient, they can support the patient's self-management. They can also provide care if self-care is not possible. Encourage the family and caregivers to provide emotional support and encouragement as the patient deals with the reality of living with a chronic disease.

The goals of DM education are to match the level of self-management to the patient's ability so that they can become the most active participant possible. Patients who actively manage their DM care have better outcomes than those who do not. For this reason, advocate for an educational approach that facilitates informed decision-making by the patient. We call this the *empowerment approach* to education. People with DM trust their HCPs more if they make them feel like a partner in their care.[20]

Tables 53.16 and 53.17 present guidelines to use for patient and caregiver teaching. The ADA offers resources for patients in the form of pamphlets, booklets, books, and their website. The ADA publishes materials and sponsors conferences for health care professionals concerned with DM care, education, and research. The ADA website (www.diabetes.org) has extensive information for the public and health care professionals. Most drug companies that make DM-related products have free education materials for patients and HCPs. You need to stay current in your DM knowledge so that you can effectively teach and support patients with DM.

BOX 53.4 EVIDENCE-BASED PRACTICE

Interactive Self-Management and DM

You are a member of a nurse-led diabetes care team that interacts with adult patients throughout the hospital. You have a referral to meet with A.Y., a 62-year-old woman with type 2 DM. Quarterly A1C results over the past year ranged from 6.9% to 9.4%. She knows that keeping glucose levels close to normal can help prevent long-term complications. A.Y. tells you she wants to be more involved in her care and make changes to her eating habits. You see that she is motivated and wants to learn how to better manage her DM.

Making Clinical Decisions

Best Available Evidence

The delivery of education and skills related to DM self-management is person-centered. These include guiding patients to make food choices that lead to stabilizing glucose levels as measured by A1C levels or TIR, increased knowledge and self-efficacy, and reduced DM-related distress.

Clinician Expertise

You know interactive self-management strategies are effective in helping patients stabilize glucose levels. There are several options for eating approaches in patients with DM who manage their own care. You discuss the multiple influences on success in glucose management and tell her that team members will help her identify any barriers to self-care.

Patient Preferences and Values

A.Y. shows a strong interest in taking more control of her DM and wishes to receive information on exercise, BGM, and diet.

Implications for Nursing Practice

1. What options for interactive self-management will you offer A.Y.?
2. As you empower A.Y. to manage her care, why is it important to assess her knowledge and skills?
3. What parameters will you use to assess if she is able to manage her own care?

Reference for Evidence

Kloss KA, Funnell MM, Piatt GA, Nwankwo R: One size does not fit all: nutrition strategies for people with diabetes, *Nursing* 50:32–38, 2020.

Insulin therapy. Nursing responsibilities for the patient receiving insulin include proper administration, assessing the patient's response to insulin therapy, and teaching the patient about administration, storage, and side effects of insulin (Table 53.6). Table 53.7 lists guidelines for assessing a patient using GLAs, including insulin and OAs.

Assess the new user of insulin for their ability to safely manage therapy. This includes the ability to understand the interaction of insulin, food, and activity and to recognize and treat the symptoms of hypoglycemia appropriately. If the patient does not have the cognitive skills to do these things, identify and teach another responsible person. The patient or caregiver must have the cognitive and manual skills needed to prepare and inject insulin. Otherwise, additional resources will be needed to assist the patient. For patients with cognitive, physical, and other barriers, consider referral to a CDCES. A CDCES has the

TABLE 53.16 PATIENT & CAREGIVER TEACHING

DM Management

Include the following instructions when teaching the patient and caregiver how to manage DM:

Component	What to Teach
Disease process	• Introduce the pancreas and the islets of Langerhans. • Describe how insulin is made and what affects its production. • Discuss the relationship between insulin and glucose. • Explain the difference between type 1 and type 2 DM.
Drug therapy	• Ensure that the patient understands the drug plan • Account for a patient's physical or other limitations or inabilities for self-medication. If necessary, involve the family or caregiver in proper use of medication. • Discuss all side effects and safety issues.
Exercise	• Discuss the effect of regular exercise on managing glucose and improving cardiovascular function and general health.
Meal planning	• Stress the importance of a well-balanced diet as part of a DM management plan. • Explain the impact of carbohydrates on glucose levels.
Monitoring glucose	• Teach correct BGM. • Include when to check glucose levels, how to record them, and how to adjust insulin levels, if necessary.
Risk reduction	• Ensure that the patient understands and appropriately responds to the signs and symptoms of hypoglycemia and hyperglycemia (Table 53.18). • Stress the importance of proper foot care (Table 53.23), regular eye examinations, and consistent BGM. • Teach the patient about the effect that stress can have on glucose.
Psychosocial	• Help the patient identify resources that are available to help with the adjustment and answer questions about living with a chronic condition such as DM.

specialized knowledge and skills to promote self-care behaviors for these patients.

Many people are fearful when they first begin using insulin. Some find it hard to self-inject because they are afraid of needles or the pain associated with an injection. Others may think that they do not need insulin or that they will have hypoglycemia after an injection. Explore the patient's underlying fears before beginning the teaching. Assessing the patient's beliefs and concerns about starting insulin will guide the teaching, counseling, and plan of care. Having open discussion with patients, providing educational materials and programs, and working with a CDCES are all beneficial for patients starting insulin.

TABLE 53.17 PATIENT & CAREGIVER TEACHING

Instructions for the Patient With DM

Include the following essential instructions for DM management for the patient and caregiver:

Glucose Levels

- Monitor your glucose at home and record results in a log.
- Take your insulin, OA, and/or noninsulin injectable agent as prescribed.
- Take insulin consistently, especially when you are sick.
- Keep an adequate supply of insulin on hand at all times.
- Obtain A1C blood test every 3–6 months as an indicator of your long-term glucose levels.
- Be aware of symptoms of hypoglycemia and hyperglycemia.
- Always carry a form of rapid-acting glucose so that you can treat hypoglycemia quickly.
- Teach family members how and when to use glucagon if you are unresponsive because of hypoglycemia.

Exercise

- Learn how exercise and food affect your glucose levels.
- Remember that exercise will usually lower your glucose level.
- Begin an exercise program after approval from HCP.

Food

- Work with a dietitian to create a patient-specific meal plan.
- Make healthy food choices and eat regular meals at regular times.
- Choose foods low in saturated and *trans* fat. Know your cholesterol level.
- Limit the amount of alcohol you drink.
- Be aware that excess alcohol use may lead to unpredictable low glucose events.
- Avoid fad diets.
- Limit regular soda and fruit juice.

Other Guidelines

- Have an annual eye examination by an ophthalmologist.
- Obtain annual urine monitoring for protein.
- Examine your feet at home.
- Wear comfortable, well-fitting shoes to help prevent foot injury. Break-in new shoes gradually.
- Always carry identification that says you have DM.
- Have other medical problems treated, especially high BP and high cholesterol.
- Have a yearly influenza vaccination.
- Quit or never start smoking cigarettes or using nicotine products.
- Avoid applying heat or cold directly to your feet.
- Do not go barefoot.
- Keep skin moisturized by applying cream to surfaces of feet, but not between toes.

Follow-up assessment of the patient who has been using insulin therapy includes inspecting injection sites for signs of lipodystrophy and other reactions, reviewing insulin preparation and injection technique, taking a history of the occurrence of hypoglycemia, and assessing how they managed hypoglycemia. Reviewing the recorded glucose readings is vital in assessing how the patient is doing and making any needed adjustments.

Oral and noninsulin injectable agents. Your responsibilities for the patient taking OAs and noninsulin injectable agents are similar to those for the patient taking insulin. Proper storage and administration, assessing the patient's use of and response to these drugs, and teaching the patient and family are all essential nursing actions.

Your assessment is valuable in determining the most appropriate drug for a patient. Factors such as the patient's mental status, eating habits, home environment, learning ability, resources, attitude toward DM, and medication history all play a significant role in determining the most appropriate drug. For example, frail older adults who live alone are at high risk for severe hypoglycemia because low glucose is often undetected or untreated. This is especially true for patients with cognitive impairment. In these cases, an OA that does not cause hypoglycemia, or a shorter-acting OA, would be most appropriate.

Patient teaching is essential. Some patients may assume that their DM is not a serious condition if they are only taking a pill to treat it. Teach the patient that OAs help manage glucose and prevent serious long- and short-term complications. Discuss how OAs and noninsulin injectable agents are part of the DM plan with food choices and activity. Stress the importance of following their meal and activity plans. Teach patients not to take extra pills if they have overeaten. If the patient uses sulfonylureas and metformin, teach the patient how to prevent, recognize, and manage hypoglycemia.

Personal hygiene. The potential for infection requires diligent skin and dental hygiene practices. Because of the susceptibility to periodontal disease, encourage daily brushing and flossing and regular dental visits. When having dental work done, teach the patient to tell the dentist they have DM.

Routine care includes regular bathing, with an emphasis on foot care.[21] Teach patients to inspect their feet daily, avoid going barefoot, and wear shoes that are supportive and comfortable. If cuts, scrapes, or burns occur, treat them promptly and monitor them carefully. Wash the area and apply a nonabrasive or nonirritating antiseptic ointment. Cover the area with a dry, sterile pad. Teach patients to notify the HCP at once if the injury does not begin to heal within 24 hours or if signs of infection develop.

Medical identification and travel. Teach the patient to always carry medical identification indicating that they have DM. Police, paramedics, and many private citizens know to look for this identification when working with sick or unconscious persons. An identification card (Fig. 53.11) can supply valuable information, such as the name of the HCP; the type of DM; and the type and dosage of insulin, noninsulin injectable agents, or OAs.

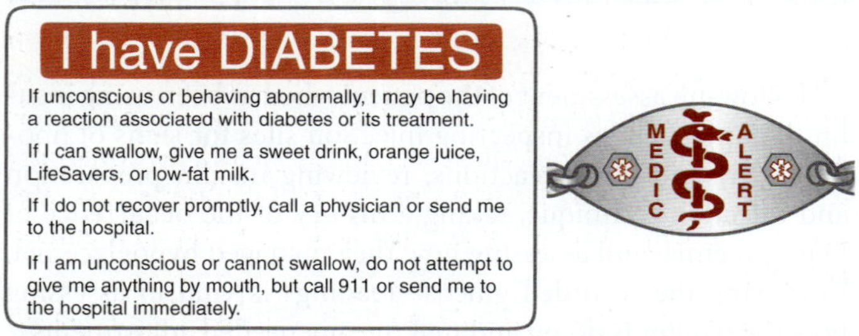

Fig. 53.11 Medical alerts. A patient with DM should carry a card and wear a bracelet or necklace that indicates DM. If the patient with DM is unconscious, these measures will ensure prompt and appropriate attention.

Travel for a person with DM requires planning. Being sedentary for long periods may raise the person's glucose level. Encourage the patient to get up and walk at least every 2 hours to lower the risk for deep vein thrombosis and prevent high glucose levels. Teach the patient to have a full set of DM care supplies in their carry-on luggage when traveling by plane, train, or bus. This includes BGM equipment, insulin, noninsulin injectable agents, OAs, syringes, insulin pens, and pen needles.

Best practices for traveling with DM supplies change frequently. Encourage patients to check TSA guidelines before traveling at https://www.diabetes.org/resources/know-your-rights/what-can-i-bring-with-me. Notify screeners if an insulin pump is used so that they can inspect it while it is on the body, rather than removing it.

For patients who use insulin or OAs that can cause hypoglycemia, keep snack items and a quick-acting carbohydrate source for treating hypoglycemia in the carry-on luggage. Keep extra insulin available in case a bottle breaks or is lost. For longer trips, carry a full day's supply of food in case of canceled flights, delayed meals, or closed restaurants. If the patient is planning a trip out of the country, it is wise to have a letter from the HCP explaining that the patient has DM and requires all the materials, especially syringes, for ongoing health care.

When travel involves time zone changes, the patient can contact the HCP to plan an appropriate insulin schedule. During travel, most patients find it helpful to keep watches set to the time of the city of origin until they reach their destination. The key to travel when taking insulin is to know the type of insulin being taken, its onset of action, the anticipated peak time, and mealtimes.

◆ Evaluation

The expected outcomes are that the patient with DM will

- State key elements of the treatment plan
- Describe measures that may prevent or slow progression of chronic complications
- Maintain a balance of nutrition, activity, and insulin availability that results in stable, safe, and healthy glucose levels
- Have no injury from decreased sensation in the feet

ACUTE COMPLICATIONS OF DIABETES

The acute complications of DM arise from events associated with hyperglycemia and hypoglycemia. Hyperglycemia (high glucose) occurs when there is not enough insulin working. Hypoglycemia (low glucose) occurs when there is too much insulin working. Many signs and symptoms of hyperglycemia and hypoglycemia overlap. It is important to distinguish between them because hypoglycemia worsens rapidly and is a serious threat if action is not immediately taken. Table 53.18 compares the manifestations, causes, management, and prevention of hyperglycemia and hypoglycemia.

DIABETES-RELATED KETOACIDOSIS (DKA)

Etiology and Pathophysiology

DKA is caused by a profound deficiency of insulin. It is characterized by hyperglycemia, ketosis, acidosis, and dehydration.

TABLE 53.18 Comparison of Hyperglycemia and Hypoglycemia

Hyperglycemia	Hypoglycemia
Manifestations	
• High glucose • ↑ Urination • ↑ Appetite followed by anorexia • Weakness, fatigue • Blurred vision • Headache • Glycosuria • Nausea and vomiting • Abdominal cramps • Progression to DKA or HHS • Mood swings	• Glucose <70 mg/dL (3.9 mmol/L) • Cold, clammy skin • Numbness of fingers, toes, mouth • Tachycardia • Emotional changes • Headache • Nervousness, tremors • Faintness, dizziness • Unsteady gait, slurred speech • Hunger • Changes in vision • Seizures, coma
Causes	
• Illness, infection • Corticosteroids • Too much food • Too little or no DM medication • Inactivity • Emotional, physical stress • Poor absorption of insulin	• Alcohol intake without food • Too little food—delayed, omitted, inadequate intake • Too much DM medication • Too much exercise without adequate food intake • DM medication or food taken at wrong time • Loss of weight without change in medication • Use of β-adrenergic blockers interfering with recognition of symptoms
Clinical Course	
• More gradual onset • Definition of high glucose varies by person, based on personal glucose targets	• More rapid onset • Pattern of manifestations changes over time
Treatment	
• Get medical care • Continue DM medication as prescribed • Check glucose frequently and check urine for ketones. Record results • Drink fluids at least on an hourly basis • Contact HCP about ketonuria	• Follow the Rule of 15. • See Table 53.19 for emergency treatment of hypoglycemia.
Preventive Measures	
• Take prescribed dose of medication at proper time • Accurately give insulin, noninsulin injectables, OA • Make healthy food choices • Follow sick-day rules when ill • Check glucose routinely • Wear or carry DM identification	• Take prescribed dose of medication at proper time • Accurately give insulin, noninsulin injectables, OA • Coordinate eating with medications • Eat adequate food intake needed for calories for exercise • Be able to recognize symptoms and treat them immediately • Carry simple carbohydrates • Teach family and caregiver about symptoms and treatment • Check glucose routinely • Wear or carry DM identification

PATHOPHYSIOLOGY MAP

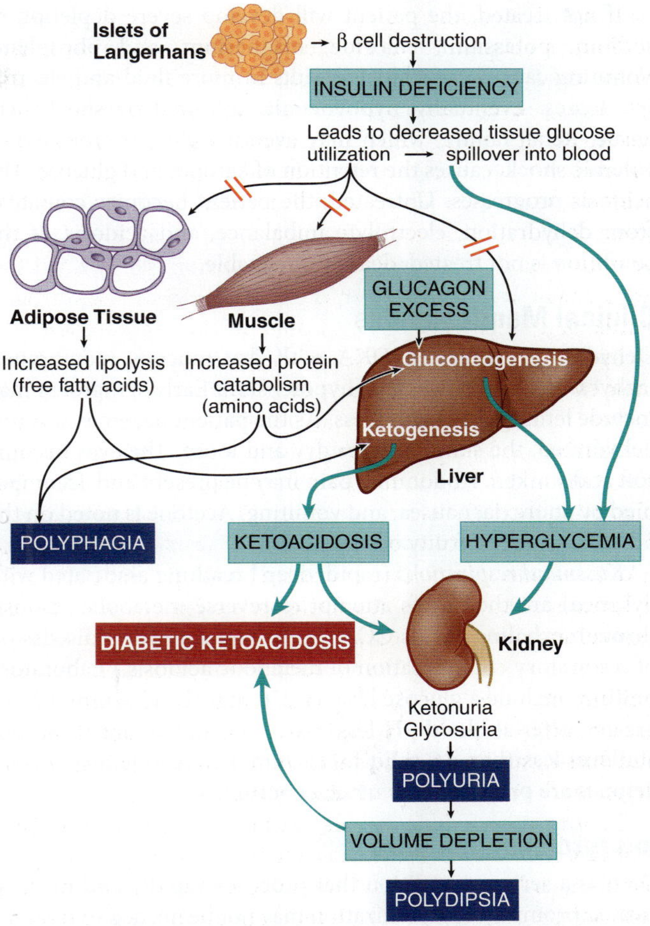

Fig. 53.12 Metabolic events leading to DKA. (Modified from Kumar V, Abbas AK, Aster JC, et al.: *Robbins and Cotran pathologic basis of disease*, ed 8, Philadelphia, 2010, Saunders.)

It is most likely to occur in people with type 1 DM. DKA may occur in people with type 2 DM in conditions of severe illness or stress in which the pancreas cannot meet the extra demand for insulin. Precipitating factors include illness; infection; inadequate insulin dosage; undiagnosed type 1 DM; lack of education, understanding, or resources; and neglect.

When the circulating supply of insulin is insufficient, glucose cannot be properly used for energy. The body compensates by breaking down fat stores as a secondary source of fuel (Fig. 53.12). Ketones are acidic by-products of fat metabolism that can cause serious problems when they become excessive in the blood. Ketosis alters the pH balance, causing metabolic acidosis to develop. Ketonuria occurs when ketone bodies are excreted in the urine. During this process, the kidney excretes cation electrolytes with the anionic ketones to try to maintain balance.

Insulin deficiency impairs protein synthesis and causes excessive protein degradation. This results in nitrogen losses from the tissues. Insulin deficiency stimulates glucose production from amino acids (from proteins) in the liver and leads to further hyperglycemia. Because of insulin deficiency, the body cannot use the additional glucose, and the glucose level rises further. This adds to the osmotic diuresis.

If not treated, the patient will develop severe depletion of sodium, potassium, chloride, magnesium, and phosphate. Vomiting caused by acidosis results in more fluid and electrolyte losses. Eventually, hypovolemia, followed by shock, will ensue. Renal failure, which may eventually occur from hypovolemic shock, causes the retention of ketones and glucose. The acidosis progresses. Untreated, the patient becomes comatose from dehydration, electrolyte imbalance, and acidosis. If the condition is not treated, death is inevitable.

Clinical Manifestations

Dehydration occurs in DKA with dry mucous membranes, tachycardia, and orthostatic hypotension. Early symptoms may include lethargy and weakness. As the patient becomes severely dehydrated, the skin becomes dry and loose. The eyes become soft and sunken. Abdominal pain may be present and accompanied by anorexia, nausea, and vomiting. Acetone is noted on the breath as a sweet, fruity odor.

Kussmaul respirations (rapid, deep breathing associated with dyspnea) are the body's attempt to reverse metabolic acidosis through exhaling excess CO_2. (See Chapter 17 for a discussion of respiratory compensation of metabolic acidosis.) Laboratory findings include a glucose level of 250 mg/dL (13.9 mmol/L) or greater, arterial blood pH less than 7.30, and serum bicarbonate level less than 16 mEq/L (16 mmol/L). Moderate to large ketones are present in the urine or serum.

Interprofessional Care

DKA is a serious condition that proceeds rapidly and must be treated promptly. Hospitalization may not be needed to treat the patient with DKA. If fluid and electrolyte imbalances are not severe and glucose levels can be safely monitored at home, DKA can be managed on an outpatient basis (Table 53.19). Other factors to consider when deciding where we manage the patient include the presence of fever, nausea, vomiting, and diarrhea; altered mental status; the cause of the DKA; and availability of communication with the HCP (every few hours). Patients with DKA who have an illness such as pneumonia or a urinary tract infection (UTI) usually need admitted to the hospital.

Refer to Table 53.20 for the emergency management of a patient with DKA. Because fluid imbalance is potentially life-threatening, the first goal of therapy is to establish IV access and begin fluid and electrolyte replacement. Typically, the initial fluid therapy involves an IV infusion of 0.45% or 0.9% NaCl at a rate to raise BP and restore urine output to 30 to 60 mL/h. When glucose levels approach 250 mg/dL (13.9 mmol/L), 5% to 10% dextrose is added to prevent hypoglycemia and a sudden drop in glucose that can cause cerebral edema. Rapid rehydration, especially with hypotonic IV solutions, can cause cerebral edema.

The aim of fluid and electrolyte therapy is to replace extracellular and intracellular water and to correct deficits of sodium, chloride, bicarbonate, potassium, phosphate, and magnesium. Monitor patients with kidney or heart problems for fluid overload. Obtain a serum potassium level before starting insulin. If the patient is hypokalemic, giving insulin will further decrease potassium levels, making early potassium replacement essential. Although initial serum potassium may be normal or high, levels can rapidly decrease once therapy starts as insulin drives potassium into the cells, leading to life-threatening hypokalemia.

IV insulin therapy is given to correct hyperglycemia and hyperketonemia. It is important to prevent rapid drops in serum glucose to avoid cerebral edema. A glucose reduction of 36 to 54 mg/dL/hr (2 to 3 mmol/L/hr) will avoid complications. Insulin allows water and potassium to enter the cell along with glucose and can lead to a depletion of vascular volume and hypokalemia. Monitor the patient's fluid balance and potassium levels.

TABLE 53.19 Interprofessional Care

DKA and HHS

Diagnostic Assessment
- History and physical assessment
- Blood studies, including glucose, CBC, pH, ketones, electrolytes, BUN, arterial or venous blood gases
- Urinalysis, including specific gravity, glucose, acetone

Management
- IV fluid administration
- IV administration of short-acting insulin
- Electrolyte replacement
- Assess mental status
- Record of intake and output
- Central venous pressure monitoring (if indicated)
- Monitoring glucose levels
- Assess blood and urine for ketones
- ECG monitoring
- Assess cardiovascular and respiratory status

CHECK YOUR PRACTICE

A 22-year-old female with DKA has a glucose level of 554 mg/dL. You are trying to regulate her IV rate. You know that giving IV fluids too rapidly and quickly, lowering the serum glucose, can lead to cerebral edema. You also know that incorrect fluid replacement, especially with hypotonic fluids, can cause a sudden fall in serum sodium that can cause cerebral edema.
- What are the best clinical indicators of successful treatment of DKA?
- What is your role as a nurse in caring for this patient?

HYPEROSMOLAR HYPERGLYCEMIA SYNDROME

Hyperosmolar hyperglycemia syndrome (HHS) is a life-threatening syndrome that can occur in patients with DM who are able to make enough insulin to prevent DKA but not enough to prevent severe hyperglycemia, osmotic diuresis, and extracellular fluid depletion (Fig. 53.13). HHS is less common than DKA (Table 53.19). It often occurs in patients over 60 years of age with type 2 DM.

Common causes include UTIs, pneumonia, sepsis, an acute illness, and newly diagnosed type 2 DM. HHS is often related to impaired thirst sensation and/or a functional inability to replace fluids. There is usually a history of inadequate fluid intake, increasing mental depression or impaired cognition, and polyuria.

TABLE 53.20 EMERGENCY MANAGEMENT

DKA

Etiology	Assessment Findings	Interventions
• Undiagnosed DM • Inadequate treatment of existing DM • Insulin not taken as prescribed • Illness, infection • Change in eating, insulin, or exercise plan • Malfunction of insulin pump/non-delivery of insulin	• Abdominal pain • Breath odor of ketones (fruity) • Dry mouth • Eyes appearing sunken • Fever • Flushed, dry skin • Glucosuria and ketonuria • Increasing restlessness, confusion, lethargy • Labored breathing (Kussmaul respirations) • Nausea and vomiting • Rapid, weak pulse • Serum glucose >250 mg/dL (13.9 mmol/L) • Thirst • Urinary frequency	**Initial** • Ensure patent airway. • Give O_2 via nasal cannula or nonrebreather mask. • Establish IV access with large-bore catheter. • Begin fluid resuscitation with 0.9% NaCl solution 1 L/h until BP stabilized and urine output 30–60 mL/h. • Begin continuous regular insulin drip 0.1 U/kg/h. • Identify history of DM, time of last food, and time and amount of last insulin injection. **Ongoing Monitoring** • Monitor vital signs, level of consciousness, ECG, O_2 saturation, and urine output. • Assess breath sounds for fluid overload. • Monitor serum glucose and serum potassium. • Give potassium to correct hypokalemia. • Give sodium bicarbonate if severe acidosis (pH <7.0). • Add dextrose to IV fluid for glucose <250 mg/dL.

The main difference between HHS and DKA is that the patient with HHS usually has enough circulating insulin so that ketoacidosis does not occur. Because HHS has fewer symptoms in the earlier stages, glucose levels can climb quite high before the problem is recognized. The higher glucose levels increase serum osmolality and cause more severe neurologic manifestations, such as somnolence, coma, seizures, hemiparesis, and aphasia. Since these manifestations resemble a stroke, immediate determination of the glucose level is critical for correct diagnosis and treatment.

Laboratory values in HHS include a glucose level greater than 600 mg/dL (33.33 mmol/L) and a marked increase in serum osmolality. Ketone bodies are absent or minimal in both blood and urine.

Interprofessional Care

HHS is a medical emergency. It has a high mortality rate. The management of HHS is similar to DKA. It includes immediate IV administration of insulin and either 0.9% or 0.45% NaCl. HHS usually requires large volumes of fluid replacement. This should be done slowly and carefully. Patients with HHS are often older and may have heart or kidney problems, requiring hemodynamic monitoring to avoid fluid overload during fluid replacement. When glucose levels fall to about 250 mg/dL (13.9 mmol/L), IV fluids containing dextrose are given to prevent hypoglycemia.

Electrolytes are monitored and replaced as needed. Hypokalemia is not as significant in HHS as it is in DKA, although fluid losses may result in milder potassium deficits that require replacement. Assess vital signs, intake and output, laboratory values, and cardiac monitoring to check the efficacy of fluid and electrolyte replacement. This includes monitoring serum osmolality and frequently assessing cardiac, renal, and mental status. Once the patient is stable, begin attempts to detect and correct the underlying cause.

❖ NURSING MANAGEMENT: DIABETES-RELATED KETOACIDOSIS AND HYPEROSMOLAR HYPERGLYCEMIA SYNDROME

Closely monitor the hospitalized patient with appropriate blood and urine tests. You must monitor glucose and urine for output and ketones and use laboratory data to determine appropriate patient care.

Monitor the administration of (1) IV fluids to correct dehydration, (2) insulin therapy to reduce glucose and serum ketone levels, and (3) electrolytes given to correct electrolyte imbalance. Assess renal status and cardiopulmonary status related to hydration and electrolyte levels. Monitor level of consciousness.

Assess for signs of potassium imbalance resulting from low levels of insulin and osmotic diuresis (see Chapter 17). When insulin treatment is started, potassium levels may rapidly decrease as potassium moves into the cells once insulin is available. This movement of potassium into and out of extracellular fluid influences cardiac function. ECG monitoring is useful in detecting changes in potassium levels (see Fig. 17.14). Assess vital signs often to identify fever, hypovolemic shock, tachycardia, and Kussmaul respirations.

HYPOGLYCEMIA

Hypoglycemia, or low glucose, occurs when there is too much insulin in proportion to available glucose in the blood. This causes the glucose level to drop to less than 70 mg/dL (3.9 mmol/L). When glucose drops below 70 mg/dL, the body

PATHOPHYSIOLOGY MAP

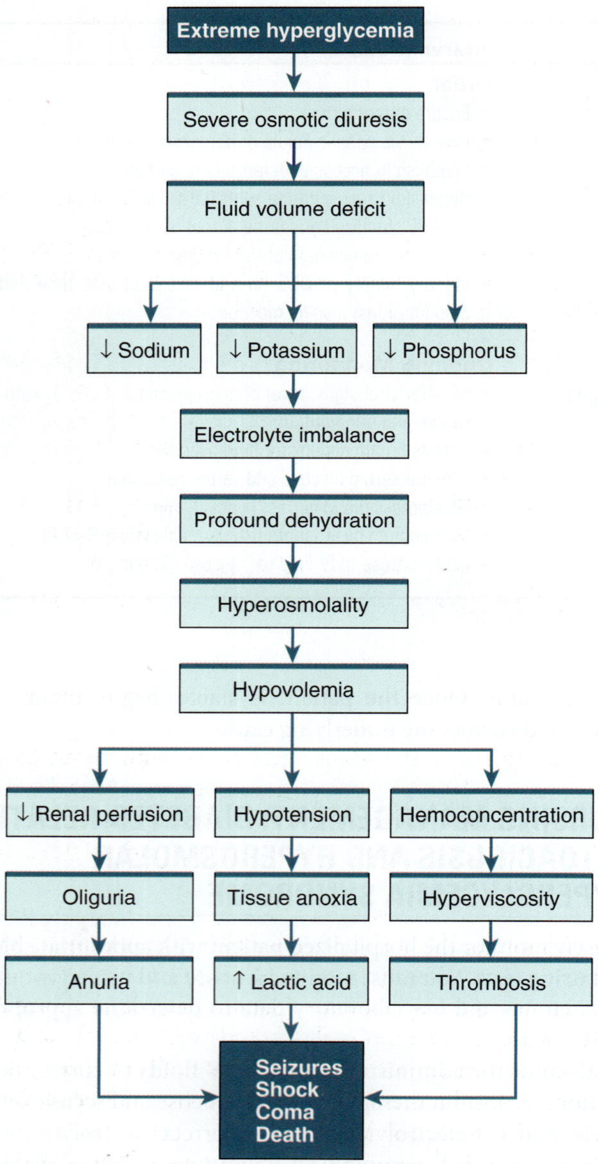

Fig. 53.13 Pathophysiology of hyperosmolar hyperglycemic syndrome. (Modified from Urden LD, Stacy KM, Lough ME: *Critical care nursing: diagnosis and management*, ed 6, St Louis, 2010, Mosby.)

releases counterregulatory hormones and activates the autonomic nervous system. Suppressing insulin secretion and producing glucagon and epinephrine provide a defense against hypoglycemia. Epinephrine release causes manifestations that include shakiness, palpitations, nervousness, diaphoresis, anxiety, hunger, and pallor. Because the brain needs a constant supply of glucose in sufficient quantities to function properly, hypoglycemia can affect mental functioning. These "neuroglycopenia" manifestations are difficulty speaking, visual changes, stupor, confusion, and coma. Manifestations of hypoglycemia can mimic alcohol intoxication. Untreated hypoglycemia can progress to loss of consciousness, seizures, coma, and death.

Hypoglycemia unawareness is a condition in which a person does not have the warning signs and symptoms of hypoglycemia until the glucose level reaches a critical point. Then the person may become incoherent and combative or lose consciousness. This is often a result of DM-related autonomic neuropathy that interferes with the secretion of counterregulatory hormones that cause these symptoms. Patients at risk for hypoglycemia unawareness include those who have had repeated episodes of hypoglycemia, older adults, and patients who use β-adrenergic blockers. Using intensive treatment to lower glucose levels in patients who have or are at risk for hypoglycemia unawareness may not be an appropriate goal. These patients usually keep glucose levels somewhat higher than those who can detect and manage the onset of hypoglycemia.

Causes of hypoglycemia are often related to a mismatch in the timing of food intake and the peak action of insulin or OAs that increase insulin secretion. Common causes include receiving too much insulin or medication, ingesting too little food, delaying the time of eating, and performing unusual or unexpected exercise. Hypoglycemia can occur at any time. It most often occurs when the OA or insulin is at its peak of action or when the patient's daily routine is disrupted without adequate adjustments in diet, drugs, and activity. Hypoglycemia is most common with insulin therapy. It can occur with noninsulin injectable agents and OAs and may persist for an extended time because of the longer duration of action of these drugs.

Symptoms of hypoglycemia may occur when a very high glucose level falls too rapidly (e.g., a glucose level of 300 mg/dL [16.7 mmol/L] falling quickly to 150 mg/dL [10 mmol/L]). Although the glucose level is above normal by definition and measurement, the sudden metabolic shift can cause hypoglycemia symptoms. Aggressively managing glucose levels, lowering high glucose levels for the first time, or lowering glucose with insulin after a long period of hyperglycemia can cause this situation.

❖ NURSING AND INTERPROFESSIONAL MANAGEMENT: HYPOGLYCEMIA

Hypoglycemia can usually be quickly reversed with effective treatment. At the first sign of hypoglycemia, check the glucose, if possible. If it is less than 70 mg/dL (3.9 mmol/L), immediately begin treatment for hypoglycemia. If the glucose is greater than 70 mg/dL, look for other possible causes of the signs and symptoms. If the patient has manifestations of hypoglycemia and monitoring equipment is not available, or the patient has a history of fluctuating glucose levels, assume hypoglycemia, and start treatment.

Follow the "Rule of 15" to treat hypoglycemia (Table 53.21). A glucose value less than 70 mg/dL is treated by ingesting 15 to 20 g of a simple (fast-acting) carbohydrate, such as 4 to 6 oz of fruit juice or a regular soft drink. Encourage the patient to carry or have available glucose tablets, gels, and powders for use in such situations. Recheck the glucose 15 minutes later. If the value is still less than 70 mg/dL, ingest 15 to 20 g more of carbohydrate and recheck the glucose in 15 minutes. If no significant improvement occurs after 2 or 3 doses, contact the HCP. After an acute episode of hypoglycemia, the patient may need a snack with carbohydrate and protein if the next meal is more than an hour away or if they are being active.

TABLE 53.21 EMERGENCY MANAGEMENT

Hypoglycemia

Etiology	Assessment Findings	Interventions
• Too little food—delayed, omitted, inadequate intake • Too much DM medication • Too much exercise without adequate food intake • DM medication or food taken at wrong time • Alcohol use without food intake	• Glucose <70 mg/dL (3.9 mmol/L) • Cold, clammy skin • Numbness of fingers, toes, mouth • Tachycardia • Emotional changes • Headache • Nervousness, tremors • Faintness, dizziness • Unsteady gait, slurred speech • Hunger • Changes in vision • Seizures, coma	**Initial** • Check glucose. • Determine cause of hypoglycemia (after correcting condition). **Management** ***Conscious Patient*** • Have patient eat or drink 15–20 g of quick-acting carbohydrate (4–6 oz of regular soda, 5–8 LifeSavers, 1 Tbsp syrup or honey, 4 tsp jelly, 4–6 oz orange juice, commercial dextrose products [per label instructions]). • Wait 15 min. Check glucose level. • If glucose is still <70 mg/dL, have patient eat or drink another 15–20 g of carbohydrate. • Once the glucose level is stable, give patient additional food of carbohydrate plus protein or fat (e.g., crackers with peanut butter or cheese) if the next meal is more than 1 h away or patient is engaged in physical activity. • Immediately notify HCP or emergency service (if patient outside hospital) if symptoms do not subside after 2 or 3 doses of quick-acting carbohydrate. ***Worsening Symptoms or Unconscious Patient*** • 1 mg glucagon subcutaneous or IM or IV administration of 20–50 mL of 50% glucose. • Turn the patient on the side to prevent aspiration.

Avoid treatment with carbohydrates that contain fat, such as candy bars, cookies, whole milk, and ice cream. The fat in those foods will slow glucose absorption and delay the response to treatment. Do not overtreat with large quantities of quick-acting carbohydrates because a rapid fluctuation to hyperglycemia can occur.

In an acute care setting, patients with hypoglycemia may receive 20 to 50 mL of 50% dextrose IV. If the patient is not alert enough to swallow and no IV access is available, another option is to give 1 mg of glucagon by IM or subcutaneous injection. An IM injection in a site such as the deltoid muscle will result in a quicker response. Glucagon stimulates the liver to convert glycogen to glucose and makes glucose rapidly available. Nausea is a common reaction after glucagon injection. To prevent aspiration if vomiting occurs, turn the patient on the side until they are alert. Patients with minimal glycogen stores will not respond to glucagon. This includes patients with alcohol-related liver disease, starvation, and adrenal insufficiency. Teach family members and others likely to be present if severe hypoglycemia occurs when and how to inject glucagon.

Once the episode is resolved, explore with the patient the reasons why the situation developed. This assessment may indicate the need for further patient teaching to avoid future episodes of hypoglycemia.

CHRONIC COMPLICATIONS ASSOCIATED WITH DIABETES

ANGIOPATHY

Chronic complications associated with DM are primarily those of end-organ disease from damage to blood vessels *(angiopathy)* from chronic hyperglycemia (Fig. 53.14). Angiopathy is a leading cause of DM-related deaths, with about 68% of deaths caused by CVD and 16% caused by strokes for those ages 65 or older.[22] These chronic blood vessel dysfunctions are divided into 2 categories: macrovascular and microvascular complications.

Several theories exist as to how and why chronic hyperglycemia damages cells and tissues. Possible causes include (1) the accumulation of damaging by-products of glucose metabolism, such as sorbitol, which damage nerve cells; (2) the formation of abnormal glucose molecules in the basement membrane of small blood vessels, such as those that circulate to the eyes and kidneys; and (3) a problem with RBC function that leads to a decrease in tissue oxygenation.

The Diabetes Control and Complications Trial (DCCT), a landmark study in DM management, showed the risk for microvascular complications is reduced in people with type 1 DM by keeping glucose levels as near to normal as possible for as much of the time as possible *(tight or intensive therapy)*.[23] Those who maintained tight glucose levels reduced their risk for developing eye and kidney problems, common microvascular complications. Intensive treatment of type 2 DM greatly lowers the risk of developing DM-related eye and kidney problems.[24] Based on these findings, the ADA issued treatment goals to maintain glucose levels as near to normal as possible. Specific targets for each patient must consider their risk for severe or undetected hypoglycemia as a side effect of intensive management.

Because of the devastating effects of long-term complications, people with DM need scheduled and ongoing monitoring for the detection and prevention of chronic complications. The ADA recommendations for ongoing evaluation are shown in Table 53.22. It is essential that patients understand the importance of regular follow-up visits.

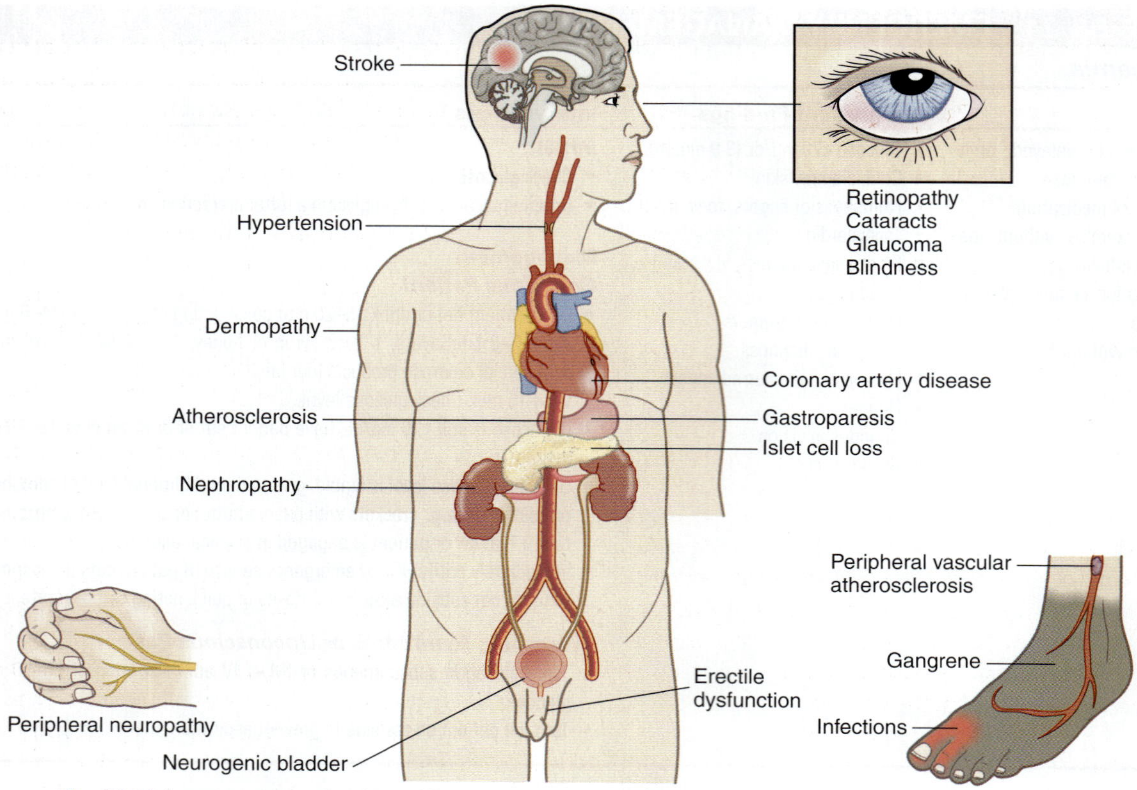

Fig. 53.14 Long-term complications of DM. (From Kumar V, Abbas AK, Aster JC, et al.: *Robbins and Cotran pathologic basis of disease*, ed 8, Philadelphia, 2010, Saunders.)

TABLE 53.22 Monitoring for Long-Term Complications Related to DM

Complication	Type of Examination	Frequency
Retinopathy	• Funduscopic: dilated eye examination • Fundus photography	• Annually
Nephropathy	• Urine for albuminuria • Serum creatinine	• Annually
Neuropathy (foot and lower extremities)	Visual examination of foot • Comprehensive foot • Vision examination • Sensory testing with monofilament and tuning fork • Palpation (pulses, temperature, callus formation)	• Daily by patient • Every visit to HCP • Annually[a]
CVD	• Risk factor assessment: hypertension, dyslipidemia, smoking, family history of premature coronary artery disease, and presence of albuminuria • Exercise stress testing (may include stress ECG, stress echocardiogram, stress nuclear imaging)	• Every visit • At least annually • As needed, based on risk factors

[a]If patients have a history of foot ulcers, loss of sensation in their feet, or other foot abnormalities, the recommendation is to have a foot examination at every visit.

Source: ADA: Standards of medical care in diabetes, *Diabetes Care* 43:S135, 2020.

Macrovascular Complications

Macrovascular complications are diseases of the large- and medium-size blood vessels that occur with greater frequency and with an earlier onset in people with DM. Macrovascular diseases include cerebrovascular, cardiovascular, and peripheral vascular disease. Women with DM have a 4 to 6 times increased risk for CVD. Men with DM have a 2 to 3 times increased risk for CVD compared with those without DM.

There are several modifiable risk factors associated with macrovascular complications. These include obesity, smoking, hypertension, high fat intake, and sedentary lifestyle. The ADA recognizes that DM alone is a CVD risk factor. The ADA recommends yearly screening for CVD risk factors in people with DM.[25]

Insulin resistance is important in developing CVD and implicated in the pathogenesis of essential hypertension and dyslipidemia. We do not completely understand the role of insulin resistance in the pathogenesis of CVD. It seems to combine with dyslipidemia in contributing to greater risk for CVD in people with DM.

Optimizing BP in patients with DM is significant in preventing CVD and kidney disease. Treating hypertension in those with DM results in a decrease in macrovascular and microvascular complications. Hypertension in people with DM causes an increase in mortality greater than for those with hypertension without DM. The ADA recommends BP screening at every visit for people with DM. They recommend lifestyle counseling for BP greater than 130/80 mm Hg and treatment to achieve a target BP of less than 140/90 mm Hg for most patients with DM. Hypertension is discussed in Chapter 36, and coronary artery disease is discussed in Chapter 37.

People with DM have an increase in lipid abnormalities that contribute to their increased risk for CVD. The ADA recommends screening all adults for dyslipidemia when they are diagnosed with DM and starting statin therapy as needed. Dosing is based on the presence of age and other CVD risk factors. The ADA advocates treating hyperlipidemia with lifestyle interventions, including nutrition therapy, exercise, weight loss, and smoking cessation.

Smoking is especially dangerous for people with DM. It significantly increases the risk for blood vessel and CVD, stroke, and lower extremity amputation.

Microvascular Complications

Microvascular complications result from thickening of the vessel membranes in the capillaries and arterioles (small vessels) in response to chronic hyperglycemia. Although microangiopathy can be found throughout the body, the areas most noticeably affected are the eyes (retinopathy), kidneys (nephropathy), and nerves (neuropathy). Microvascular changes are present in some people with type 2 DM at the time of diagnosis.

RETINOPATHY

Etiology and Pathophysiology

Diabetes-related retinopathy refers to the microvascular damage to the retina because of chronic hyperglycemia, nephropathy, and hypertension in people with DM. DM-related retinopathy is the leading cause of new cases of adult blindness.

We classify retinopathy as nonproliferative or proliferative. In *nonproliferative retinopathy,* the most common form, partial occlusion of the small blood vessels in the retina, causes microaneurysms to develop in the capillary walls. The walls of these microaneurysms are so weak that capillary fluid leaks out, causing retinal edema and eventually hard exudates or intraretinal hemorrhages. This may cause mild to severe vision loss, depending on which parts of the retina are affected. If the center of the retina (macula) is affected, vision loss can be severe.

Proliferative retinopathy, the most severe form, involves the retina and vitreous. When retinal capillaries become occluded, the body compensates by forming new blood vessels to supply the retina with blood, a process called *neovascularization.* These new vessels are very fragile and bleed easily, causing vitreous contraction. Eventually, light cannot reach the retina as the vessels break and bleed into the vitreous cavity. The patient sees black or red spots or lines. If these new blood vessels pull the retina while the vitreous contracts, causing a tear, partial or complete retinal detachment will occur. If the macula is involved, vision is lost. Without treatment, more than half of people with proliferative diabetic retinopathy will be blind.

Persons with DM are prone to other visual problems. Glaucoma occurs because of the occlusion of the outflow channels from neovascularization. This type of glaucoma is hard to treat and often results in blindness. Cataracts develop at an earlier age and progress more rapidly in people with DM.

Interprofessional Care

The earliest and most treatable stages of DM-related retinopathy often cause no changes in the vision. Teach patients with type 2 DM to have a dilated eye examination by an ophthalmologist or a specially trained optometrist at the time of diagnosis and annually thereafter for early detection and treatment. Those with type 1 DM need to have a dilated eye examination within 5 years after the onset of DM and then annually.

The best approach to managing DM-related eye disease is to prevent it by maintaining healthy glucose levels and managing hypertension. Laser photocoagulation therapy can reduce the risk for vision loss in patients with proliferative retinopathy or macular edema and, sometimes, nonproliferative retinopathy. Laser photocoagulation destroys the ischemic areas of the retina that make growth factors that encourage neovascularization. A patient who develops vitreous hemorrhage and retinal detachment may need to undergo vitrectomy. *Vitrectomy* is the aspiration of blood, membrane, and fibers from the inside of the eye through a small incision just behind the cornea. (Photocoagulation and vitrectomy are discussed in Chapter 22.)

A fluocinolone acetonide intravitreal implant (Iluvien) is used to treat retinopathy. It is an injectable microinsert that provides sustained treatment through continuous delivery of corticosteroid fluocinolone acetonide for 36 months. Iluvien is injected in the back of the eye with an applicator that uses a 25-gauge needle, which allows for a self-sealing wound.

Vascular endothelial growth factor (VEGF) plays a key role in developing DM-related retinopathy. We are currently studying drugs injected into the eye that block the action of VEGF and reduce inflammation for their effectiveness in treating retinopathy.[26]

NEPHROPATHY

Diabetes-related nephropathy is associated with damage to the small blood vessels that supply the glomeruli of the kidney. It is the leading cause of ESRD in the United States and is seen in 20% to 40% of people with DM. Risk factors include hypertension, genetic predisposition, smoking, and chronic hyperglycemia. Keeping glucose levels in a healthy range is critical in preventing DM-related nephropathy.

Patients are screened for nephropathy annually with a random spot urine collection to assess for albuminuria and measure the albumin-to-creatinine ratio. Serum creatinine is measured to give an estimate of the glomerular filtration rate and the degree of kidney function.

Patients with albuminuria receive either ACE inhibitor drugs (e.g., lisinopril) or angiotensin II receptor blockers (e.g., losartan). Both these drug classes are used to treat hypertension and delay the progression of nephropathy in patients with DM. Hypertension significantly accelerates the progression of nephropathy. Aggressive BP management is indicated for Patients with DM and hypertension. Patients with DM and hypertension need aggressive BP management (see Chapter 36). See Chapter 51 for a discussion of renal failure.

NEUROPATHY

Diabetes-related neuropathy is nerve damage that occurs from the metabolic imbalances associated with DM. About 60% to 70% of patients with DM have some degree of neuropathy. The most common type affecting persons with DM is sensory neuropathy. This can lead to the loss of sensation in the lower extremities. Coupled with other factors, it significantly increases the risk for complications that result in lower limb amputation. More than 60% of nontraumatic amputations in the United States occur in people with DM. Neuropathy can precede, accompany, or follow the diagnosis of DM. Screening for neuropathy begins at the time of diagnosis in patients with type 2 DM and 5 years after diagnosis in patients with type 1 DM.[27]

Etiology and Pathophysiology

We do not completely understand the pathophysiology of DM-related neuropathy. Theories include metabolic, vascular, and autoimmune factors. The prevailing theory is that persistent hyperglycemia leads to an accumulation of sorbitol and fructose in the nerves that causes damage. How they cause damage is unknown. The result is reduced nerve conduction and demyelination. Ischemic damage by chronic hyperglycemia in blood vessels that supply the peripheral nerves is implicated in developing DM-related neuropathy.

Classification

The 2 major categories of DM-related neuropathy are *sensory neuropathy,* which affects the peripheral nervous system, and *autonomic neuropathy.* Each type has several forms.

Sensory Neuropathy

The most common form of sensory neuropathy is distal symmetric polyneuropathy. It affects the hands and/or feet bilaterally. We sometimes call this *stocking-glove neuropathy.* Characteristics include loss of sensation, abnormal sensations, pain, and paresthesias. Patients describe the pain as burning, cramping, crushing, or tearing. It is usually worse at night and may occur only at that time. The paresthesias may be associated with tingling, burning, and itching sensations. The patient may report a feeling of walking on pillows or numb feet. The skin can become so sensitive (hyperesthesia) that the patient cannot tolerate even light pressure from bed sheets. Complete or partial loss of sensitivity to touch and temperature is common. Foot injury and ulcerations can occur without the patient ever having pain (Fig. 53.15). Neuropathy can cause atrophy of the small muscles of the hands and feet, causing deformity and limiting fine movement.

Managing glucose is the only treatment for DM-related neuropathy. It is effective in many, but not all, cases. Drug therapy may be used to treat neuropathic symptoms, especially pain. At the start of therapy, symptoms usually increase, followed by relief of pain in 2 to 3 weeks.

Common drugs used include topical creams (e.g., capsaicin), tricyclic antidepressants (e.g., amitriptyline), selective serotonin and norepinephrine reuptake inhibitors (e.g., duloxetine), and antiseizure drugs (e.g., gabapentin). Capsaicin is a moderately effective topical cream made from chili peppers. It depletes the accumulation of pain-mediating chemicals in the peripheral sensory neurons. The cream is applied 3 or 4 times a day.

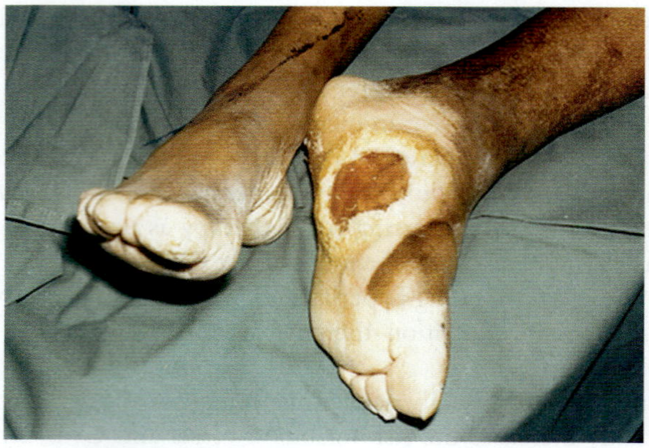

Fig. 53.15 Neuropathy: neurotrophic ulceration.

Tricyclic antidepressants are moderately effective in treating DM-related neuropathy. They inhibit the reuptake of norepinephrine and serotonin, which are neurotransmitters thought to play a role in pain transmission. We think duloxetine relieves pain by increasing the levels of serotonin and norepinephrine, which improves the body's ability to regulate pain. Antiseizure drugs decrease the release of neurotransmitters that transmit pain.

Autonomic Neuropathy

Autonomic neuropathy can affect nearly all body systems and lead to hypoglycemia unawareness, bowel incontinence and diarrhea, and urinary retention. *Gastroparesis* (delayed gastric emptying) is a complication of autonomic neuropathy that can cause anorexia, nausea, vomiting, gastroesophageal reflux, and persistent feelings of fullness. Gastroparesis can trigger hypoglycemia by delaying food absorption. Cardiovascular problems from autonomic neuropathy include postural hypotension, resting tachycardia, and painless MI. Assess for postural hypotension to determine if the patient is at risk for falls. Teach the patient with postural hypotension to change from a lying or sitting position slowly.

DM can affect sexual function. Erectile dysfunction (ED) in men with DM is common. It is often the first manifestation of autonomic neuropathy. ED is associated with other factors, including vascular disease, high glucose levels, endocrine problems, psychogenic factors, and other drugs. Decreased libido is a problem for some women with DM. Candida and nonspecific vaginitis are common. ED and sexual problems require sensitive counseling for both the patient and the patient's partner. See Chapter 59 for more about ED.

A neurogenic bladder may develop as the sensation in the inner bladder wall decreases, causing urinary retention. A patient with retention has infrequent voiding, difficulty voiding, and a weak stream of urine. Emptying the bladder every 3 hours in a sitting position helps prevent stasis and infection. Tightening the abdominal muscles during voiding and using the Credé maneuver (mild massage downward over the lower abdomen and bladder) may help with complete bladder emptying.

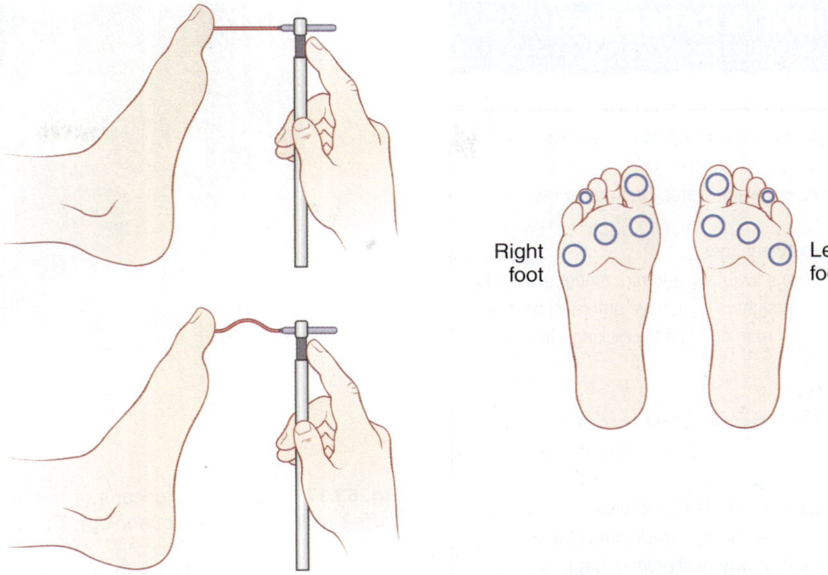

Fig. 53.16 Monofilament testing. Press the monofilament lightly until it bows in each area of the foot that should be tested. Record the presence of sensation in that area. (From Dehn R: *Essential clinical procedures*, St. Louis, 2021, Elsevier.)

Cholinergic agonist drugs, such as bethanechol (Urecholine), may be used. The patient may need to learn self-catheterization (see Chapter 50).

COMPLICATIONS OF FEET AND LOWER EXTREMITIES

People with DM are at high risk for foot ulcerations and lower extremity amputations. The development of DM-related foot complications can be the result of a combination of microvascular and macrovascular diseases that place the patient at risk for injury and serious infection. Sensory neuropathy and peripheral artery disease (PAD) are risk factors for foot complications. Clotting abnormalities, impaired immune function, and autonomic neuropathy have a role. Smoking has a negative effect on lower extremity blood vessels and increases the risk for amputation.

Sensory neuropathy is a major risk factor for lower-extremity amputation in people with DM. *Loss of protective sensation* (LOPS) often prevents the patient from being aware that a foot injury has occurred. Improper footwear and injury from stepping on foreign objects while barefoot are common causes of undetected foot injury in the person with LOPS. Because the primary risk factor for lower extremity amputation is LOPS, annual screening with monofilament testing is important (Fig. 53.16).

PAD increases the risk for amputation by reducing blood flow to the lower extremities. With decreased blood flow, oxygen, white blood cells (WBCs), and vital nutrients are not available to the tissues. Wounds take longer to heal, and the risk for infection increases. Signs of PAD include intermittent claudication, pain at rest, cold feet, loss of hair, delayed capillary refill, and dependent rubor. PAD is diagnosed by history, ankle-brachial index (ABI), and angiography. Management includes reducing risk factors, especially smoking, and managing cholesterol and hypertension. Bypass or graft surgery is needed in some patients. PAD is discussed in Chapter 41.

If the patient has LOPS or PAD, aggressive measures must be taken to teach the patient how to prevent foot ulcers. These measures include choosing proper footwear, including protective shoes. Teach the patient to carefully avoid injury to the foot, practice diligent skin and nail care, inspect the foot thoroughly each day, and treat small problems promptly. Guidelines for patient teaching are listed in Table 53.23.

Proper care of a foot ulcer is critical for wound healing. Several forms of treatment can be used. Casting can redistribute the weight on the plantar surface of the foot. Wound care for the ulcer can include debridement, dressings, advanced wound healing products, vacuum-assisted closure, ultrasound, hyperbaric O_2, and skin grafting.

Neuropathic arthropathy, or *Charcot's foot,* results in ankle and foot changes that lead to joint problems and footdrop. These changes occur gradually. They promote an abnormal distribution of weight over the foot. This increases the chances of developing a foot ulcer as new pressure points appear. Foot deformity should be recognized early, and proper footwear fitted before ulceration occurs.

SKIN COMPLICATIONS

Up to two-thirds of persons with DM develop skin problems. DM-related dermopathy, the most common skin lesion, is characterized by reddish-brown, round or oval patches. They initially are scaly, then they flatten out and become indented. The lesions appear most often on the shins but can occur on the front of the thighs, forearm, side of the foot, scalp, and trunk.

Acanthosis nigricans is a manifestation of insulin resistance. It can appear as a velvety light brown to black skin thickening,

TABLE 53.23 PATIENT & CAREGIVER TEACHING

Foot Care

Include the following instructions when teaching the patient and caregiver about foot care:

1. Wash feet daily with mild soap and warm water. First, test water temperature with elbow.
2. Pat feet dry gently, especially between toes.
3. Examine feet daily for cuts, blisters, swelling, and red, tender areas. Do not depend on feeling sores. If eyesight is poor, have others inspect feet.
4. Use lanolin on feet to prevent skin from drying and cracking. Do not apply between toes.
5. Use mild foot powder on sweaty feet.
6. Do not use commercial remedies to remove calluses or corns.
7. Cleanse cuts with warm water and mild soap, covering with clean dressing. Do not use iodine, rubbing alcohol, or strong adhesives.
8. Report skin infections or nonhealing sores to HCP at once.
9. Cut toenails evenly with rounded contour of toes. Do not cut down corners. The best time to trim nails is after a shower or bath.
10. Separate overlapping toes with cotton or lamb's wool.
11. Avoid open-toe, open-heel, and high-heel shoes. Leather shoes are preferred to plastic ones. Wear slippers with soles. Do not go barefoot. Inspect feet, socks, and shoes for foreign objects before putting on.
12. Wear clean, absorbent (cotton or wool) socks or stockings that have not been mended. Colored socks must be colorfast.
13. Do not wear clothing that leaves impressions, hindering circulation.
14. Do not use hot water bottles or heating pads to warm feet. Wear socks for warmth.
15. Guard against frostbite.
16. Exercise feet daily either by walking or by flexing and extending feet in suspended position. Avoid prolonged sitting, standing, and crossing of legs.

mainly on flexures, axillae, and the neck (Fig. 53.17). *Necrobiosis lipoidica diabeticorum* usually appears as red-yellow lesions, with atrophic skin that becomes shiny and transparent, revealing tiny blood vessels under the surface. This condition is uncommon. It occurs more often in young women. It may appear before other signs and symptoms of DM. Because the thin skin is prone to injury, special care must be taken to protect affected areas from injury and ulceration.

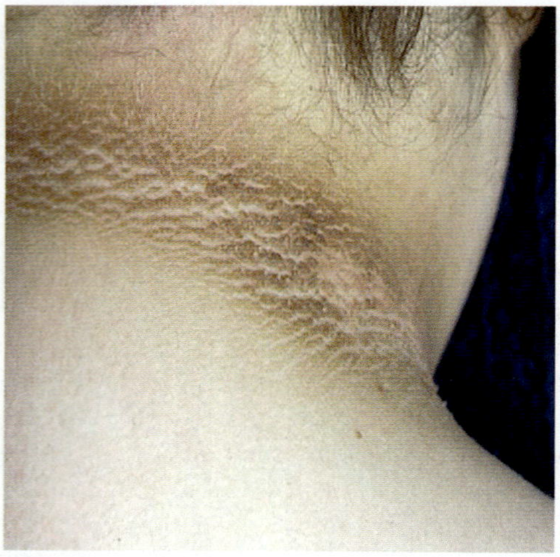

Fig. 53.17 Acanthosis nigricans of the neck. (From Strauss J: *Yen and Jaffe's reproductive endocrinology*, St Louis, 2019, Elsevier.)

INFECTION

A person with DM is more susceptible to infections because of a defect in the mobilization of WBCs and impaired phagocytosis by neutrophils and monocytes. Recurring or persistent infections, such as *Candida albicans,* boils, and furuncles in the undiagnosed patient often lead the HCP to suspect DM. Loss of sensation (neuropathy) may delay the detection of an infection.

Persistent glycosuria may predispose people to bladder infections, especially those with a neurogenic bladder. Decreased circulation resulting from angiopathy can prevent or delay the immune response. Antibiotic therapy has prevented infection from being a major cause of death in patients with DM. The treatment of infections must be prompt and vigorous. Teach patients to prevent infection by practicing good hand hygiene, avoiding exposure to persons who have a communicable illness, and getting an annual influenza vaccine and pneumococcal vaccine.

PSYCHOLOGIC CONSIDERATIONS

People with DM have high rates of distress, anxiety, and eating disorders. Depression and distress contribute to diminished DM self-care, feelings of helplessness related to chronic illness, and poor outcomes. DM distress encompasses the stress, fear, and burden of living with and managing a demanding chronic disease. Assess patients for manifestations of depression and/or DM distress.

Disordered eating behaviors (DEBs) can occur in people with both type 1 and type 2 DM. DEBs include anorexia, bulimia, binge eating, excessive calorie restriction, and intense exercise. Adolescent girls with DM are more than twice as likely to develop DEB than those who do not have DM.[28] Patients may intentionally decrease their dose of insulin or omit the dose. This is called "diabulimia." It leads to weight loss, hyperglycemia, and glycosuria because the food ingested cannot be used for energy without adequate insulin. Insulin omission and DEBs can have serious consequences, including retinopathy, neuropathy, lipid abnormalities, DKA, and death.

Open communication is critical to identify these behaviors early. Refer patients with DEB to a mental health professional with expertise in DEB and an understanding of DM management.

Gerontologic Considerations: DM

DM is present in more than 25% of persons over 65 years of age. This age group is the fastest-growing segment of the population developing DM. Older people with DM have higher rates of premature death, functional disability, and coexisting illnesses, such as hypertension and stroke, than those without DM. The prevalence of DM increases with age. A major reason for this is that the aging process is associated with a reduction in β-cell function, decreased insulin sensitivity, and altered carbohydrate metabolism. Aging is associated with conditions that are more likely to be treated with drugs that impair insulin action (e.g., corticosteroids, antihypertensives, phenothiazines). Undiagnosed and untreated DM is more common in older adults. This in part occurs because manifestations of DM, such as low energy levels, dizziness, confusion, and chronic UTIs, are wrongly attributed to normal age-related changes.

Several factors affect setting glycemic goals for an older adult. One is that hypoglycemia unawareness is more common in older adults, making them more likely to have adverse consequences from glucose-lowering therapy. They may have problems that could interfere with the ability to treat hypoglycemia. Other factors include the patient's desire for treatment and coexisting medical problems, such as cognitive impairment. Compounding the challenge, DM increases the rate of cognitive decline. Although treatment is needed to prevent complications, intensive DM management may be hard and dangerous to achieve, especially in older adults.

Meal planning and exercise are recommended therapy for older adults with DM. Consider functional limitations that may interfere with physical activity and the ability to prepare meals. Because of the physiologic changes that occur with aging, the therapeutic outcome for the older adult who receives OAs may be altered. Assess renal function and creatinine clearance in those over 80 years of age taking metformin. Monitor those taking sulfonylurea drugs (e.g., glipizide) for hypoglycemia and kidney and liver problems. Insulin therapy may be started if OAs are not effective. However, older adults are more likely to have limitations in the dexterity and visual acuity needed for accurate insulin administration. Insulin pens may be a safer alternative.

Patient education issues include those related to altered vision, mobility, cognitive status, and functional ability. Plan patient teaching based on individual needs. Use a slower pace with simple printed or audio materials in patients with cognitive and functional limitations. Include the family or caregivers in the teaching. Consider the patient's financial and social situation and the effect of multiple drugs, eating habits, and quality-of-life issues.

Case Study

DKA

(© katrinaelena/iStock/Thinkstock.)

Patient Profile

N.B., a 48-year-old farmer, is in the emergency department after his wife found him unconscious in the barn. They live 40 miles from the nearest hospital. He has a medical history of type 1 DM, hypertension, and DM-related neuropathy.

Subjective Data (Provided by Wife)

- Diagnosed with type 1 DM 15 years ago
- Takes 40 U/day of insulin via insulin pump: 5 U of lispro insulin bolus with breakfast, 5 U bolus with lunch, and 10 U bolus with dinner plus 20 U of basal insulin
- Has history of gastroenteritis for 1 week with vomiting and anorexia
- Stopped taking mealtime boluses 2 days ago when he was unable to eat
- Has not changed his infusion set in 5 days

Objective Data

Physical Assessment

- Respirations deep with rate 36 breaths/min
- Fruity acetone smell on breath
- Skin flushed and dry
- Heart rate 118 beats/min; BP 98/60 mm Hg

Diagnostic Studies

- Glucose level 730 mg/dL (40.5 mmol/L)
- Blood pH 7.26

Discussion Questions

1. ***Recognize***: Briefly explain the pathophysiology behind N.B.'s DKA.
2. ***Recognize***: What factors precipitated his developing DKA?
3. ***Analyze***: What clinical manifestations of DKA does this patient exhibit?
4. ***Analyze***: What distinguishes this case history from one of HHS or hypoglycemia?
5. ***Prioritize:*** Based on the assessment data presented, what are the priority clinical problems?
6. ***Prioritize:*** What is the priority nursing intervention for N.B.?
7. ***Act:*** What teaching do you need to provide for N.B. and his family?
8. ***Act:*** N.B.'s wife asks you if she should have given her husband insulin when he got sick. How would you respond?
9. ***Act:*** How can the health care team be most effective in caring for N.B.?
10. ***Evaluate:*** What outcomes would indicate that the health care team was effective in caring for N.B.?
11. Develop a conceptual care map for N.B.

Answers and a corresponding concept map available at http://evolve.elsevier.com/Lewis/medsurg.

BRIDGE TO NCLEX EXAMINATION

The number of the question corresponds to the same-numbered outcome at the beginning of the chapter.

1. The nurse is assessing a patient newly diagnosed with type 1 diabetes. Which symptom reported by the patient correlates with the diagnosis?
   a. Excessive thirst
   b. Gradual weight gain
   c. Overwhelming fatigue
   d. Recurrent blurred vision
2. When distinguishing between persons with type 1 diabetes from type 2 diabetes, the nurse is aware that
   a. persons with type 1 diabetes require insulin therapy.
   b. autoantibodies to pancreatic β-cells are found in type 2 diabetes.
   c. persons with type 1 diabetes may be managed with metformin alone.
   d. hyperosmolar hyperglycemia syndrome is more common in type 1 diabetes.

BRIDGE TO NCLEX EXAMINATION—cont'd

3. Goals of managing the patient with diabetes include *(select all that apply)*
   a. keeping the target A1C greater than 9%.
   b. teaching self-monitoring of glucose levels.
   c. preventing complications of hypoglycemia.
   d. monitoring for ophthalmologic complications.
   e. maintaining the LDL cholesterol greater than 100 mg/dL (2.6 mmol/L).
4. Which patient statement demonstrates an understanding of the role of exercise in managing diabetes?
   a. "I cannot exercise if I am taking insulin and metformin."
   b. "Exercise increases insulin resistance, so I will need a higher dose of insulin."
   c. "It is better to exercise before a meal if I take medication that causes hypoglycemia."
   d. "My insulin dose may need to be changed if I have low glucose levels after exercising."
5. You are caring for a patient with newly diagnosed type 2 diabetes who was started on metformin. What information should you include in discharge teaching? (*Select all that apply.*)
   a. Need to reduce physical activity
   b. Eliminate all forms of sugar from diet
   c. Use of a portable blood glucose meter
   d. Hypoglycemia prevention, symptoms, and treatment
   e. Procedures that require IV contrast media are contraindicated
6. What is the *priority* action for the nurse to take if the patient with type 2 diabetes reports headache, nervousness, and dizziness?
   a. Administer glucagon.
   b. Give insulin as ordered.
   c. Check the patient's glucose level.
   d. Assess for other signs of neurologic stroke.
7. A patient with diabetes has a serum glucose level of 824 mg/dL (45.7 mmol/L) and is unresponsive. After assessing the patient, the nurse suspects diabetes-related ketoacidosis rather than hyperosmolar hyperglycemia syndrome based on the finding of
   a. polyuria.
   b. severe dehydration.
   c. rapid, deep respirations.
   d. decreased serum potassium.
8. Which are appropriate therapies for patients with diabetes? *(Select all that apply.)*
   a. Use of statins to reduce CVD risk
   b. Use of diuretics to treat nephropathy
   c. Use of β-blockers to treat retinopathy
   d. Use of serotonin agonists to decrease appetite
   e. Use of ACE or ARB inhibitors to treat nephropathy

1. a; 2. a; 3. b, c, d; 4. d; 5. c, d; 6. c; 7. c; 8. a, e.

For rationales to these answers and even more NCLEX review questions, visit http://evolve.elsevier.com/Lewis/medsurg.

EVOLVE WEBSITE/RESOURCES LIST

http://evolve.elsevier.com/Lewis/medsurg
Review Questions (Online Only)
Key Points
Answer Keys for Questions
- Rationales for Bridge to NCLEX Examination Questions
- Answer Guidelines for Case Study

Student Case Studies
- Patient With Type 1 Diabetes and Diabetes-Related Ketoacidosis
- Patient With Type 2 Diabetes and Hyperosmolar Hyperglycemia Syndrome

Nursing Care Plans
- eNursing Care Plan 53.1: Patient With Diabetes

Conceptual Care Map Creator
- Conceptual Care Map for Case Study

Audio Glossary
Content Updates

REFERENCES

1. Centers for Disease Control and Prevention (CDC): National diabetes statistics report. Retrieved from https://www.cdc.gov/diabetes/pdfs/data/statistics/national-diabetes-statistics-report. Pdf, 2020.
2. CDC: National vital statistics report: Final data from 2017. Retrieved from https://www.cdc.gov/nchs/data/nvsr/nvsr68/nvsr68_09-508.pdf.
3. CDC: Type 1 diabetes. Retrieved from https://www.cdc.gov/diabetes/basics/type1.html.

*4. American Diabetes Association (ADA): Classification and diagnosis of diabetes: standards of care in diabetes—2021, *Diabetes Care* 44:S15, 2021.

5. ADA: Statistics about diabetes. Retrieved from https://www.diabetes.org/resources/statistics/statistics-about-diabetes.

*6. Cheng YJ, Kanaya AM, Araneta MR, et al.: Prevalence of diabetes by race and ethnicity in the United States, 2011-2016, *J Am Med Assoc* 322:2389, 2019.

*7. Jausmann J, Waechtershaeuser A, Behnken I, et al.: The role of adipokines in the improvement of diabetic and cardiovascular risk factors within a 52-week weight-loss programme for obesity, *Obes Res Clin Pract* 13:440, 2019.

*8. Ter Horst R, Van den Muckhof ICL, Schraa K, et al.: Sex-specific regulations of inflammation and metabolic syndrome in obesity, *Arterioscler Thromb Vasc Biol* 40:1787, 2020.

9. CDC: Gestational diabetes. Retrieved from https://www.cdc.gov/diabetes/basics/gestational.html.
10. National Institute of Diabetes and Digestive and Kidney Diseases: Diabetes, heart disease, and stroke. Retrieved from https://www.niddk.nih.gov/health-information/diabetes/overview/preventing-problems/heart-disease-stroke.

*11. Doyle-Delgado K, Chamberlain JJ, Shubrook JK, et al.: Pharmacologic approaches to glycemic treatment of type 2 diabetes: synopsis of the 2020 ADA's standards of medical care in diabetes clinical guideline, *Ann Intern Med* 173:813, 2020.
12. Chin G, Robins M: Teaching patients with type 2 diabetes to self-administer insulin, *Aust J Gen Pract* 48:251, 2019.
13. BD: Insulin syringes. Retrieved from https://www.bd.com/en-us/offerings/capabilities/diabetes-care/insulin-syringes.
14. Joslin Diabetes Center: Insulin pump. Retrieved from https://www.joslin.org/patient-care/diabetes-education/diabetes-learning-center/insulin-pumps.
*15. ADA: Facilitating behavior change and well-being to improve health outcomes: standards of medical care in diabetes—2021, *Diabetes Care* 44:S53, 2021.
16. ADA: Nutrition. Retrieved from https://www.diabetes.org/healthy-living/recipes-nutrition.
17. Evert AB, Dennison M, Gardner CD, et al.: Nutrition therapy for adults with diabetes or prediabetes: a consensus report, *Diabetes Care* 42:731, 2019.
18. U.S. Department of Agriculture: MyPlate. Retrieved from https://www.myplate.gov/.
19. Funtanilla VD, Caliendo T, Hillas O: Continuous glucose monitoring: a review of available systems, *P T* 44:550, 2019.
20. Dickinson JK, Guzman SJ, Maryniuk MD, et al.: The use of language in diabetes care and education, *Diabetes Care* 40:1790, 2017. (Classic).
*21. ADA: Microvascular complications and foot care: standards of medical care in diabetes—2021, *Diabetes Care* 44:S151, 2021.
*22. ADA: Cardiovascular disease and risk management: standards of medical care in diabetes—2021, *Diabetes Care* 44:S125, 2021.
*23. Diabetes Control and Complications Trial Research Group: The effect of intensive treatment of diabetes on the development and progression of long-term complications in insulin-dependent diabetes mellitus, *N Engl J Med* 329:977, 1993. (Classic).
*24. Zoungas S, Arima H, Gerstein HC, et al.: Effects of intensive glucose control on microvascular outcomes in patients with type 2 diabetes: a meta-analysis of individual participant data from randomised controlled trials, *Lancet Diabetes Endocrinol* 5:431, 2017.
*25. ADA: Comprehensive medical evaluation and assessment of comorbidities: standards of medical care in diabetes—2021, *Diabetes Care* 44:S40, 2021.
26. Zhao M, Sun Y, Jiang Y: Anti-VEGF therapy is not a magic bullet for diabetic retinopathy, *Eye* 34:609, 2020.
*27. Khdour MR: Treatment of diabetic peripheral neuropathy: a review, *J Pharm Pharmacol* 72:863, 2020.
*28. Rancourt D, Foster N, Bollepalli S, et al.: Test of the modified dual pathway model of eating disorders in individuals with type 1 diabetes, *Int J Eat Disord* 52:630, 2019.

*Evidence-based information for clinical practice.

54

Endocrine Problems

Ann H. Crawford

http://evolve.elsevier.com/Lewis/medsurg/

CONCEPTUAL FOCUS

Coping
Fluids and Electrolytes
Hormonal Regulation
Nutrition
Perfusion
Reproduction
Thermoregulation
Tissue Integrity

LEARNING OUTCOMES

1. Explain the pathophysiology, clinical manifestations, and interprofessional and nursing management of the patient with an anterior pituitary gland problem.
2. Describe the pathophysiology, clinical manifestations, and interprofessional and nursing management of the patient with a posterior pituitary gland problem.
3. Explain the pathophysiology, clinical manifestations, and interprofessional and nursing management of the patient with a thyroid problem.
4. Describe the pathophysiology, clinical manifestations, and interprofessional and nursing management of the patient with a parathyroid problem.
5. Identify the pathophysiology, clinical manifestations, and interprofessional and nursing management of the patient with an adrenal cortex problem.
6. Describe the pathophysiology, clinical manifestations, and interprofessional and nursing management of the patient with an adrenal medulla problem.
7. Outline the side effects of corticosteroid therapy.

KEY TERMS

acromegaly
Addison disease
Cushing syndrome
diabetes insipidus (DI)
goiter
Graves disease
hyperaldosteronism
hyperparathyroidism
hyperthyroidism
hypoparathyroidism
hypopituitarism
hypothyroidism
myxedema
pheochromocytoma
syndrome of inappropriate antidiuretic hormone (SIADH)
thyroid cancer
thyroiditis
thyrotoxicosis

The endocrine system is made up of several organs and glands involved in the synthesis and secretion of hormones which affect every body system. Because hormones have a wide range of action, problems with their regulation may cause homeostatic changes that can affect many aspects of a person's life. The severity varies widely. There may be adverse effects on perfusion, metabolism, skin integrity, and nutrition. Regulating fluid and electrolyte balance and temperature may be difficult. The patient may have problems with growth and fertility and reproductive processes because these are hormone dependent. There may be a wide range of psychologic responses, including anxiety and depression.

ANTERIOR PITUITARY GLAND PROBLEMS

The pituitary gland is considered the master gland of the endocrine system. The anterior pituitary gland secretes growth hormone (GH), prolactin, and 4 tropic hormones—adrenocorticotropic hormone (ACTH), thyroid-stimulating hormone (TSH), follicle-stimulating hormone (FSH), and luteinizing hormone (LH).

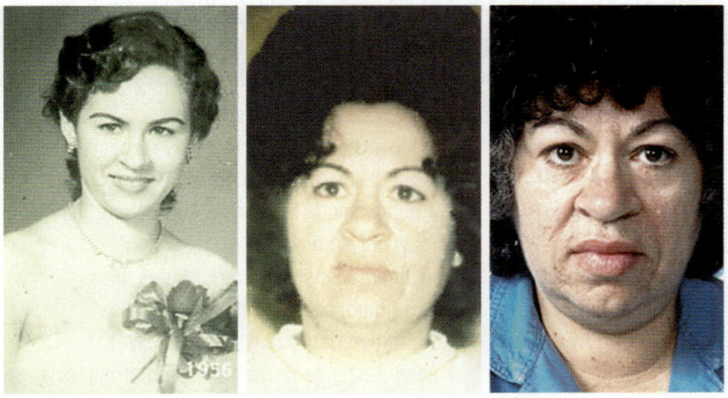

Fig. 54.1 Progressive development of facial changes from acromegaly. (Courtesy Linda Haas, Seattle, WA.)

These hormones affect growth, sexual maturation, reproduction, metabolism, stress response, and fluid balance. As a result, pituitary gland disorders manifest in a variety of ways.

Pituitary gland tumors account for 5% to 20% of primary intracranial tumors.[1] The most common, a pituitary adenoma, is a slow-growing, benign tumor. It often occurs in adults between 40 and 60 years of age. Hypersecretory pituitary adenomas secrete an excess of a specific hormone causing manifestations related to the action of that hormone. The most common are prolactinomas and GH- and ACTH-secreting adenomas.[1]

ACROMEGALY

Acromegaly is a rare condition characterized by an overproduction of GH. Around 3 cases per 1 million people in the United States are diagnosed annually.[2] It affects both genders equally. The mean age at the time of diagnosis is 40 to 45 years old.

Etiology and Pathophysiology

Acromegaly most often occurs because of a benign GH-secreting pituitary adenoma. The excess GH results in an overgrowth of soft tissues and bones in the hands, feet, and face. Because the problem develops after epiphyseal closure, the bones of the arms and legs do not grow longer.

Clinical Manifestations

The changes resulting from excess GH in adults can occur slowly, over many years. They may go unnoticed by the person, family, and friends. Thickening and enlargement of the bony and soft tissues on the face, feet, and head occur (Fig. 54.1). Patients may have proximal muscle weakness and joint pain that can range from mild to crippling. Carpal tunnel syndrome and peripheral neuropathy may be present.

Tongue enlargement causes dental and speech problems. The voice deepens because of hypertrophy of the vocal cords. Sleep apnea may occur because of upper airway narrowing and obstruction from increased amounts of pharyngeal soft tissues. The skin becomes thick, leathery, and oily with acne outbreaks.

Vision changes may occur from pressure on the optic nerve from a pituitary adenoma. Headaches are common. Since GH antagonizes the action of insulin, glucose intolerance and manifestations of diabetes may occur, including increased thirst and *polyuria* (increased urination).

The life expectancy of those with acromegaly is reduced by 5 to 10 years. They are prone to cardiovascular disease (CVD), diabetes, and colorectal cancer.[3] Even if patients are cured or the disease is well controlled, manifestations such as joint pain and deformities often remain.

Diagnostic Studies

In addition to the history and physical assessment, a diagnosis requires evaluating plasma insulin-like growth factor-1 (IGF-1) levels and GH response to an oral glucose tolerance test (OGTT). IGF-1 mediates the peripheral actions of GH. As GH levels rise, so do IGF-1 levels. Since GH is released in a pulsatile fashion, we need several samples to obtain an accurate assessment. Serum IGF-1 levels are more constant, giving a reliable diagnostic measure of acromegaly. During an OGTT, GH concentration normally falls because glucose inhibits GH secretion. In acromegaly, GH levels do not fall and in some cases GH levels rise.

MRI or high-resolution CT scan with contrast can detect pituitary adenomas. A complete eye examination, including visual fields, is done because a tumor may cause pressure on the optic chiasm or optic nerves.

Interprofessional and Nursing Care

The patient's prognosis depends on the age at onset, age when treatment started, and tumor size. The overall goal is to return the patient's GH levels to normal. Treatment consists of surgery, radiation therapy, drug therapy, or a combination of these. Treatment can stop bone growth and reverse tissue hypertrophy. However, sleep apnea, diabetes, and cardiac problems may persist.

Surgery (hypophysectomy) is the treatment of choice. It offers the best chance for a cure and optimal symptom management, especially for smaller pituitary tumors.[4] Surgery results in an immediate reduction in GH levels. IGF-1 levels fall within a few weeks. Patients with larger tumors or those with GH levels greater than 45 ng/mL may need adjuvant radiation or drug therapy. Surgery and radiation therapy for pituitary tumors are discussed later in this chapter.

Drug therapy is an option for patients whose surgery did not result in a cure and/or in combination with radiation therapy. The main drug used is octreotide (Sandostatin), a somatostatin analog. It reduces GH levels to normal in many patients. Octreotide is given by subcutaneous injection 3 times a week. Long-acting somatostatin analogs, octreotide (Sandostatin LAR), pasireotide (Signifor), and lanreotide SR (Somatuline Depot), are available as IM injections given every 4 weeks. GH levels are measured every 2 weeks to guide drug dosing and then every 6 months until the desired response is achieved.

Dopamine agonists (e.g., bromocriptine, cabergoline) may be given alone or with somatostatin analogs if surgery does not result in a complete remission. These drugs reduce GH secretion from the tumor.

GH antagonists (e.g., pegvisomant [Somavert]) reduce the effect of GH in the body by blocking liver production of IGF-1. Most patients taking this drug achieve normal IGF-1 levels with symptom improvement.[3]

Serial photographs showing improvement in appearance may be helpful to the patient's recovery. Psychosocial effects of acromegaly include body image problems, sexual problems, and depression. Fatigue and sleep problems may persist after surgery. Patients will need strategies for dealing with these symptoms. Referral to a support group may be helpful.

EXCESSES OF OTHER TROPIC HORMONES

Excess prolactin or tropic hormone (e.g., ACTH, TSH) secretion by the anterior pituitary gland will cause other endocrine glands to overproduce certain hormones. An excess of these hormones (discussed later in the chapter) can cause significant problems in metabolism and general health.

A prolactin-secreting adenoma is known as a *prolactinoma.* They account for about 40% of pituitary tumors.[5] Women with prolactinomas may have galactorrhea, anovulation, infertility, infrequent or absent menses, decreased libido, and hirsutism. In men, impotence, decreased sperm density, and libido may result. Compression of the optic chiasm can cause vision changes and signs of increased intracranial pressure, including headache, nausea, and vomiting.

Because prolactinomas do not typically grow, drug therapy is usually the first-line treatment. The dopamine agonists cabergoline and bromocriptine are given to block prolactin release. Surgery may be an option, depending on the extent and size of the tumor. Radiation therapy can reduce the risk for tumor recurrence for patients with large tumors.

PITUITARY GLAND HYPOFUNCTION

Hypopituitarism is a rare disorder that involves a decrease in 1 or more of the pituitary hormones. A deficiency of only 1 pituitary hormone is called *selective hypopituitarism.* Total failure of the pituitary gland results in deficiency of all pituitary hormones—a condition called *panhypopituitarism.* The most common hormone deficiencies from hypopituitarism involve GH and gonadotropins (e.g., LH, FSH).

Etiology and Pathophysiology

The usual cause of pituitary hypofunction is a pituitary tumor. Autoimmune disorders, infections, pituitary infarction (Sheehan syndrome), or destruction of the pituitary gland (from trauma, radiation, surgery) can also cause hypopituitarism. The incidence varies among populations, with a higher mortality in women.

Anterior pituitary hormone deficiencies can lead to end-organ failure. TSH and ACTH deficiencies are life threatening. ACTH deficiency can lead to acute adrenal insufficiency and hypovolemic shock from sodium and water depletion.

Clinical Manifestations and Diagnostic Studies

The manifestations vary with the type and degree of dysfunction. Early manifestations of a space-occupying lesion include headaches, vision changes (decreased visual acuity, decreased peripheral vision), loss of smell, nausea and vomiting, and seizures. Manifestations associated with hyposecretion of the target glands vary widely (Table 54.1).

TABLE 54.1 Manifestations of Hypopituitarism

Hormone Deficiency	Manifestations
Adrenocorticotropic hormone (ACTH)	Involves cortisol deficiency: weakness, fatigue, headache, dry and pale skin, ↓axillary and pubic hair, ↓ resistance to infection, fasting hypoglycemia
Follicle-stimulating hormone (FSH) and luteinizing hormone (LH)	*Women:* Menstrual irregularities, loss of libido, changes in secondary sex characteristics (e.g., ↓ breast size) *Men:* Testicular atrophy, ↓ spermatogenesis, loss of libido, impotence, ↓ facial hair and muscle mass
Growth hormone (GH)	Subtle, nonspecific findings: truncal obesity, osteoporosis, ↓ muscle mass and strength, weakness, fatigue, depression, or flat affect
Thyroid-stimulating hormone (TSH)	Mild form of primary hypothyroidism: fatigue, cold intolerance, constipation, lethargy, weight gain

In addition to a history and physical assessment, diagnostic studies such as MRI and CT can identify a pituitary tumor. Laboratory tests generally involve the direct measurement of pituitary hormones (e.g., TSH) or an indirect determination of the target organ hormones (e.g., triiodothyronine [T_3], thyroxine [T_4]). See Chapter 52 for more information about diagnostic studies.

Interprofessional and Nursing Care

The treatment for hypopituitarism often consists of surgery or radiation therapy followed by lifelong hormone therapy. Surgery and radiation therapy for pituitary tumors are discussed in the next section. Appropriate hormone therapy is used (e.g., corticosteroids, thyroid hormone). Hormone therapies for thyroid hormone and corticosteroids are discussed later in this chapter.

Somatropin (Genotropin, Humatrope, Omnitrope) is recombinant human GH. It is used for long-term hormone therapy in adults with GH deficiency. These patients respond well to GH replacement. They have increased energy, increased lean body mass, a feeling of well-being, and improved body image. Side effects include fluid retention with swelling in the feet and hands, muscle and joint pain, and headache. GH is given daily as a subcutaneous injection, preferably in the evening. The dosing is variable and adjusted based on symptoms, IGF-1 levels, and side effects.

Although gonadal deficiency is not life threatening, hormone therapy will improve sexual function and general well-being. It is contraindicated in those with certain medical conditions, such as phlebitis, pulmonary embolism, breast cancer, and prostate cancer. Estrogen and progesterone replacement therapy may be given to hypogonadal women to treat hot flashes, vaginal dryness, and decreased libido (see Chapter 58). Testosterone is used to treat men with gonadotropin deficiency. The benefits of testosterone therapy include a return of male secondary sex characteristics, improved libido, and increased muscle mass, bone mass, and bone density. Hormone therapy for men is discussed in Chapter 59.

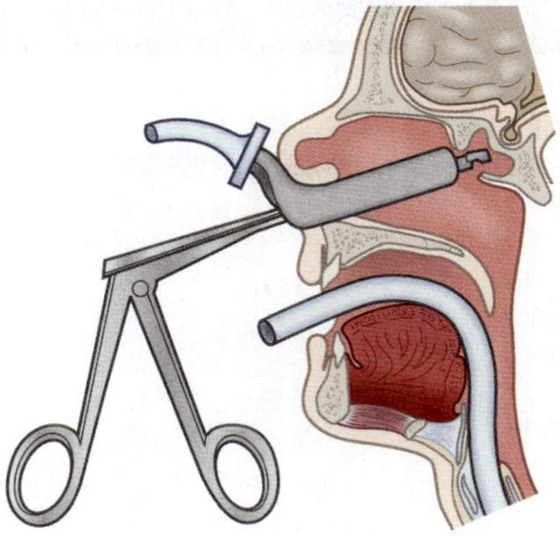

Fig. 54.2 Surgery on the pituitary gland is most often done by a transsphenoidal approach. An incision is made in the inner aspect of the upper lip and gingiva. The sella turcica is entered through the floor of the nose and sphenoid sinuses.

PITUITARY SURGERY

A *hypophysectomy* is the surgical removal of the pituitary gland. It is the treatment of choice for tumors in the pituitary area, especially smaller pituitary adenomas. Most surgeries are done by an endoscopic *transsphenoidal* approach (Fig. 54.2). When the entire pituitary gland is removed, there is permanent loss of all pituitary hormones. The patient will need lifelong replacement therapy of thyroid hormone, sex hormones, and glucocorticoids.[6]

Radiation therapy can reduce the size of a tumor before surgery. It is also used when surgery does not produce a cure or when patients are not candidates for surgery. The full effects may take months to years. Radiation therapy may lead to hypopituitarism, which then requires lifelong hormone replacement therapy. Stereotactic radiosurgery (Gamma Knife surgery, proton beam, linear accelerator) is an option for small, surgically inaccessible pituitary tumors or in place of conventional radiation.

NURSING MANAGEMENT: PITUITARY SURGERY

After surgery, assess the patient for the presence of a hematoma compressing the optic nerve or optic chiasma. Monitor peripheral vision, visual acuity, extraocular movements, and pupillary response. Report changes at once. Prompt intervention may prevent vision changes from becoming permanent (Table 54.2).

Cerebrospinal fluid (CSF) leaks and nosebleeds are other common complications after surgery. The HCP may place a petroleum jelly–coated ribbon of gauze or a balloon-tipped catheter (like an indwelling urinary catheter) in the sphenoid sinus. It is usually removed after 24 hours. It can be left in for 2 to 3 days if there is concern for bleeding or CSF leak. The patient must not blow the nose for at least 48 hours after surgery. They need to avoid vigorous coughing, sneezing, and straining at stool.

Monitor the "moustache" dressing regularly for any drainage. Check any clear drainage with a urine dipstick for glucose and protein. If present, notify the HCP of a possible CSF leak. A sample can be sent to the laboratory. A glucose level greater than 30 mg/dL (1.67 mmol/L) indicates CSF leakage from an open connection with the brain. If this happens, the patient is at increased risk for meningitis.

A persistent and severe generalized or supraorbital headache may indicate CSF leakage into the sinuses. A CSF leak usually resolves within 72 hours when treated with head elevation and bed rest. If the leak persists, daily spinal taps can reduce pressure to below-normal levels.

Keep the head of the bed elevated at a 30-degree angle. This avoids pressure on the sella turcica and decreases headaches. Monitor pupillary response, speech patterns, and extremity strength to detect neurologic complications. Gentle mouth care every 4 hours keeps the surgical site clean and free of debris. Have the patient avoid brushing their teeth for at least 10 days to protect the suture line.

Fluid and electrolyte problems can occur if diabetes insipidus (DI) develops.[7] Transient DI may occur because of the loss of antidiuretic hormone (ADH), which is stored in the posterior lobe of the pituitary gland, or cerebral edema from manipulation of the pituitary during surgery. DI may be permanent after surgery. To assess for DI, monitor urine output and measure specific gravity. Report a urine output of more than 200 mL/hr for more than 3 consecutive hours or a specific gravity level of less than 1.005. Patients with DI will have a high serum sodium and extreme thirst. We treat DI by giving desmopressin acetate (DDAVP). Fluid replacement may be needed to avoid hypovolemia from high urine output.

Syndrome of inappropriate antidiuretic hormone secretion (SIADH) can occur after any intracranial surgery. SIADH typically occurs later than DI, usually around the 4th postoperative day. It may occur due to manipulation of the pituitary and other structures causing release of ADH. The fluid retention caused

TABLE 54.2 NURSING MANAGEMENT

Care of the Patient After Pituitary Surgery

- Monitor vital signs. Assess peripheral pulses and watch for orthostatic hypotension.
- Monitor neurologic and cognitive status (e.g., level of consciousness, orientation, speech) hourly for the first 24 h and then every 4 h.
- Assess extremity strength and reflexes.
- Monitor field of vision, visual acuity, extraocular movements, and pupillary response. Notify HCP of any changes.
- Assess dressing for type and amount of drainage. Notify HCP for excessive bleeding or CSF drainage.
- Maintain strict intake and output and monitor fluid balance. Assess for DI or SIADH.
- Keep head of bed elevated at least 30 degrees.
- Encourage deep-breathing exercises and incentive spirometer use.
- Monitor for pain and give analgesic medications as prescribed.
- Encourage high-fiber diet to decrease risk for constipation.
- Perform oral care every 4 hr.
- Teach the patient to:
  - Avoid vigorous coughing, sneezing, and blowing the nose
  - Avoid bending over at the waist or straining at stool (Valsalva maneuver) due to risk for increased intracranial pressure
  - Avoid use of toothbrushes until incision heals
  - Follow replacement hormone therapy plan

PATHOPHYSIOLOGY MAP

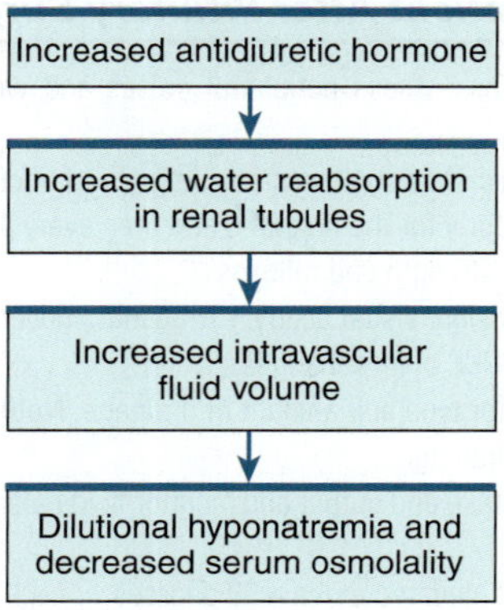

Fig. 54.3 Pathophysiology of SIADH. (Modified from Urden LD, Stacy KM, Lough ME: *Critical care nursing: diagnosis and management,* ed 6, St Louis, 2010, Mosby.)

by circulating ADH leads to dilutional hyponatremia. Sodium levels of less than 125 mEq/L will present as headache, vomiting, and decreased level of consciousness. DI and SIADH are discussed in the next section.

The patient needs lifelong ADH, cortisol, and thyroid hormone replacement after a hypophysectomy. Surgery may result in permanent loss or deficiencies in FSH and LH. This can lead to decreased fertility. Assist the patient in working through the grieving process associated with these losses.

POSTERIOR PITUITARY GLAND PROBLEMS

The hormones secreted by the posterior pituitary are ADH and oxytocin. ADH, also called *arginine vasopressin* (AVP) or vasopressin, has a key role in regulating water balance and serum osmolarity (see Chapter 52). The main problems result from either overproduction or underproduction of ADH.

SYNDROME OF INAPPROPRIATE ANTIDIURETIC HORMONE

Etiology and Pathophysiology

Syndrome of inappropriate antidiuretic hormone (SIADH) results from an overproduction of ADH or the release of ADH despite normal or low plasma osmolarity (Fig. 54.3). ADH increases the permeability of the renal distal tubule and collecting duct, which leads to the reabsorption of water into the circulation. Extracellular fluid volume expands, plasma osmolality declines, glomerular filtration rate increases, and sodium levels decline (dilutional hyponatremia). Thus features of SIADH are fluid retention, serum hypoosmolality, dilutional hyponatremia, hypochloremia, and concentrated urine in the presence of normal or increased intravascular volume.

SIADH occurs more often in older adults. The most common cause is cancer, especially small cell lung cancer (Table 54.3). SIADH tends to be self-limiting when caused by head trauma or drugs. It can be chronic when caused by tumors or metabolic diseases.

TABLE 54.3 Causes of SIADH

Cancer
- Colorectal cancer
- Lymphoid cancers (Hodgkin lymphoma, non-Hodgkin lymphoma, lymphocytic leukemia)
- Pancreatic cancer
- Prostate cancer
- Small cell lung cancer
- Thymus cancer

CNS Disorders
- Brain tumors
- Cerebral atrophy
- Guillain-Barré syndrome
- Head injury (skull fracture, subdural hematoma, subarachnoid hemorrhage)
- Infection (encephalitis, meningitis)
- Stroke
- Systemic lupus erythematosus

Drug Therapy
- Carbamazepine (Tegretol)
- Chemotherapy agents (vincristine, vinblastine, cyclophosphamide)
- General anesthesia agents
- Opioids
- Oxytocin
- Thiazide diuretics
- Selective serotonin reuptake inhibitor (SSRI) antidepressants
- Tricyclic antidepressants

Miscellaneous Conditions
- Adrenal insufficiency
- COPD
- HIV
- Hypothyroidism
- Lung infection (pneumonia, tuberculosis, lung abscess)
- Positive pressure mechanical ventilation

Clinical Manifestations and Diagnostic Studies

The patient with SIADH has low urine output and increased body weight. At first, the patient has thirst, dyspnea on exertion, and fatigue. Mild hyponatremia causes muscle cramping, irritability, and headache. As the serum sodium level falls (usually below 120 mEq/L [120 mmol/L]), manifestations become more severe and include vomiting, abdominal cramps, and muscle twitching. As plasma osmolality and serum sodium levels continue to decline, cerebral edema may occur, leading to lethargy, confusion, seizures, and coma.

The diagnosis is made by simultaneous measurements of urine and serum osmolality. Dilutional hyponatremia is indicated by a serum sodium less than 135 mEq/L, serum osmolality less than 280 mOsm/kg (280 mmol/kg), and urine specific gravity greater than 1.030. A serum osmolality much lower than the urine osmolality shows the body is inappropriately excreting concentrated urine in the presence of dilute serum.

Interprofessional and Nursing Care

When assessing patients at risk and those who have confirmed SIADH, be alert for low urine output with a high specific gravity, a sudden weight gain without edema, or a decreased serum sodium level. Monitor intake and output, vital signs, and heart and lung sounds. Obtain daily weights. Observe for signs of hyponatremia, including seizures, headache, vomiting, and decreased neurologic function.

Treatment is directed at the underlying cause.[8] Medications that stimulate ADH release should be avoided or discontinued (Table 54.3). If symptoms are mild and serum sodium is greater than 125 mEq/L (125 mmol/L), the only treatment may be a fluid restriction of 800 to 1000 mL/day. This restriction should result in weight loss and a gradual rise in serum sodium concentration and osmolality. An improvement in symptoms should accompany normalization of serum sodium and osmolality. Provide the patient with frequent oral care and distractions to decrease discomfort related to thirst from the fluid restriction.

A loop diuretic, such as furosemide (Lasix), may be used to promote diuresis. Since loop diuretics cause sodium loss, the serum sodium must be at least 125 mEq/L (125 mmol/L). Because furosemide increases potassium, calcium, and magnesium loss, the patient may need supplements. Demeclocycline also may be given. It blocks the effect of ADH on the renal tubules, resulting in more dilute urine.

Initiate seizure and fall precautions if the patient has an altered sensorium or is having seizures. Keep the head of the bed flat or elevated no more than 10 degrees. This promotes venous return to the heart and increases left atrial filling pressure, thus reducing ADH release. Frequent turning, positioning, and range-of-motion exercises are important to maintain skin integrity and joint mobility.

In cases of severe hyponatremia (less than 120 mEq/L), especially in the presence of neurologic manifestations, such as seizures, small amounts of IV hypertonic saline solution (3% sodium chloride) may be given. We must correct hyponatremia slowly. The level should not increase by more than 8 to 12 mEq/L in the first 24 hours. Quickly increasing levels can cause osmotic demyelination syndrome with permanent damage to nerve cells in the brain. A fluid restriction of 500 mL/day may be needed for those with severe hyponatremia.

Vasopressor receptor antagonists block the activity of ADH. They are used to treat euvolemic hyponatremia in hospitalized patients. Two drugs are approved for use in the United States: conivaptan (Vaprisol) and tolvaptan (Samsca). Conivaptan is given IV; tolvaptan is given orally. Neither should be given to patients with liver disease because they worsen liver function.

Help the patient with chronic SIADH to self-manage their treatment. In chronic SIADH, a fluid restriction of 800 to 1000 mL/day is recommended. Ice chips or sugarless chewing gum help decrease thirst. Teach them to supplement the diet with sodium and potassium, especially if taking loop diuretics. Have the patient obtain a daily weight to monitor changes in fluid balance. Teach the patient the symptoms of fluid and electrolyte imbalances, especially those involving sodium and potassium (see Chapter 17).

DIABETES INSIPIDUS

Etiology and Pathophysiology

Diabetes insipidus (DI) is caused by deficient production or secretion of ADH or a decreased renal response to ADH.[9] The decrease in ADH results in fluid and electrolyte imbalances caused by increased urine output and increased plasma osmolality (Fig. 54.4). Depending on the cause, DI may be transient or a chronic, lifelong condition. There are several types of DI (Table 54.4). Central DI is the most common form.

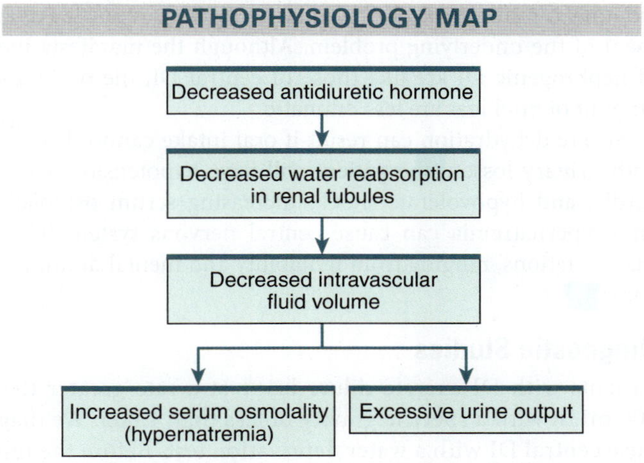

Fig. 54.4 Pathophysiology of diabetes insipidus.

TABLE 54.4 Types of Diabetes Insipidus

Type	Cause
Central (neurogenic) DI	Interference with ADH synthesis, transport, or release *Examples:* Brain tumor, head injury, brain surgery, CNS infections
Nephrogenic DI	Inadequate renal response to ADH despite presence of adequate ADH *Examples:* Drug therapy (especially lithium), renal damage, hereditary renal disease
Primary DI	Excess water intake *Examples:* Structural lesion in thirst center, psychologic disorder

Clinical Manifestations

Key features of DI are polydipsia and polyuria. The patient excretes large quantities of urine (2 to 20 L/day) with a very low specific gravity (less than 1.005) and urine osmolality of less than 100 mOsm/kg (100 mmol/kg). Serum osmolality is increased (usually greater than 295 mOsm/kg [295 mmol/kg]) because of hypernatremia (serum sodium greater than 145 mg/dL) from pure water loss in the kidneys. Most patients compensate for fluid loss by drinking large amounts of water so that serum osmolality stays normal or is somewhat increased. The patient may be tired from nocturia and have generalized weakness. Uncorrected hypernatremia can cause brain shrinkage and intracranial bleeding.

The onset of central DI is usually acute and accompanied by excess fluid loss. After intracranial surgery, central DI has a triphasic pattern: (1) an acute phase with an abrupt onset of polyuria, (2) an interphase in which urine volume normalizes, and (3) a third phase in which central DI may become permanent. The third phase occurs 10 to 14 days after surgery. Central DI from head trauma is often self-limiting. It improves with treatment of the underlying problem. Although the manifestations of nephrogenic DI are like those of central DI, the onset and amount of fluid loss are less dramatic.

Severe dehydration can result if oral intake cannot keep up with urinary losses. The patient will have hypotension, tachycardia, and hypovolemic shock. Increasing serum osmolality and hypernatremia can cause central nervous system (CNS) manifestations, ranging from irritability and mental dullness to coma.

Diagnostic Studies

Patients with DI excrete dilute urine at a rate greater than 200 mL/h with a specific gravity of less than 1.005. We diagnose central DI with a water deprivation test. Before the test, we measure body weight, and urine osmolality, volume, and specific gravity. The patient is deprived of water for 8 to 12 hours and then given DDAVP subcutaneously or nasally. Patients with central DI have a dramatic increase in urine osmolality (from 100 to 600 mOsm/kg) and a significant decrease in urine volume. The patient with nephrogenic DI will not be able to increase urine osmolality to greater than 300 mOsm/kg.

Another test to distinguish central DI from nephrogenic DI is to measure the ADH level after giving an analog of ADH (e.g., desmopressin). If the cause is central DI, the kidneys will respond to the hormone by concentrating urine. If the kidneys do not respond in this way, the cause is nephrogenic.

Interprofessional and Nursing Care

Management of DI includes early detection, maintaining adequate hydration, and patient teaching for self-management. A clinical goal is maintaining fluid and electrolyte balance.

For central DI, fluid and hormone therapy are the cornerstone of treatment. We replace fluids orally or IV, depending on the patient's condition and ability to drink copious amounts. In acute DI, IV hypotonic saline or dextrose 5% in water (D_5W) is given and titrated to replace urine output. If IV glucose solutions are used, monitor serum glucose levels. Hyperglycemia and glycosuria can lead to osmotic diuresis, which increases the fluid volume deficit. Monitor BP, heart rate, urine output, level of consciousness, and specific gravity. They may be done hourly in the acutely ill patient. Assess for signs of acute dehydration. Maintain an accurate record of intake and output and daily weights to determine fluid volume status. Adjustments in fluid replacement should be made accordingly.

DDAVP, an analog of ADH, is the hormone replacement of choice for central DI. Another ADH replacement drug is aqueous vasopressin. DDAVP can be given orally, IV, subcutaneously, or as a nasal spray. Assess the response to DDAVP by monitoring pulse, BP, level of consciousness, intake and output, and specific gravity. Medications such as carbamazepine (Tegretol) can help decrease thirst associated with central DI.

Because the kidney is unable to respond to ADH in nephrogenic DI, hormone therapy has little effect. Instead, the treatment includes a low-sodium diet and thiazide diuretics (e.g., chlorothiazide), which may reduce flow to the ADH-sensitive distal nephrons. Limiting sodium intake to no more than 3 g/day often helps decrease urine output. If a low-sodium diet and thiazide drugs are not effective, indomethacin may be prescribed. It is a nonsteroidal antiinflammatory drug (NSAID) that helps increase renal responsiveness to ADH.

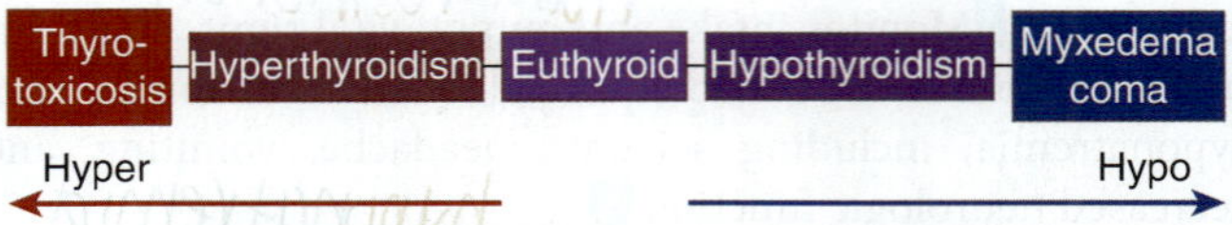

Fig. 54.5 Continuum of thyroid dysfunction.

TABLE 54.5 Goitrogens

Thyroid Inhibitors	Select Foods
• Iodine in large doses	• Broccoli
• Methimazole (Tapazole)	• Brussels sprouts
• Propylthiouracil (PTU)	• Cabbage
	• Cauliflower
Other Drugs	• Kale
• Amiodarone	• Mustard
• Lithium	• Peanuts
• p-Aminosalicylic acid	• Strawberries
• Salicylates	• Turnips
• Sulfonamides	

THYROID GLAND PROBLEMS

Thyroid gland problems are among the most common endocrine disorders. The thyroid hormones T_4 and T_3 regulate energy metabolism and growth and development. Thyroid gland problems include goiter, benign and malignant nodules, inflammatory conditions leading to hyperthyroidism, and hypothyroidism (Fig. 54.5).

GOITER

A **goiter** is an enlarged thyroid gland. The person may have an overactive thyroid (hyperthyroidism) or an underactive thyroid (hypothyroidism). The most common cause of goiter worldwide is a lack of diet iodine. In the United States, where most people use iodized salt, goiter is more often due to the overproduction or underproduction of thyroid hormones or to nodules that develop in the thyroid gland. *Goitrogens* (foods or drugs that contain thyroid-inhibiting substances) can cause a goiter (Table 54.5).

A nontoxic goiter is a diffuse enlargement of the thyroid gland that does not result from cancer or inflammation. The thyroid hormone levels are normal. *Nodular goiters* are thyroid hormone–secreting nodules. They function independently of TSH stimulation. There may be multiple nodules (multinodular goiter) or a single nodule (solitary autonomous nodule). The nodules are usually benign follicular adenomas. If these nodules cause hyperthyroidism, they are called *toxic nodular goiters*.[10] This type of goiter is often found in patients with Graves disease

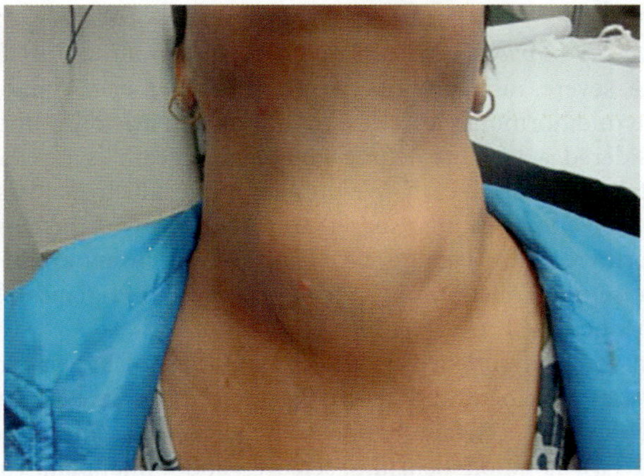

Fig. 54.6 Goiter. (From Iyomasa RM, Tagliarini JV, Rodrigues SA, et al.: Laryngeal and vocal alterations after thyroidectomy, *Braz J Otorhinolaryngol* 85:3, 2019.)

(Fig. 54.6). Toxic nodular goiters occur equally in men and women. Although they can appear at any age, they most often occur in people over 40 years of age.

We measure TSH and T_4 levels to determine whether a goiter is associated with normal thyroid function, hyperthyroidism, or hypothyroidism. Thyroid antibodies (e.g., thyroid peroxidase [TPO] antibody) show the presence of *thyroiditis* (inflammation of the thyroid). Treatment with thyroid hormone may prevent further thyroid enlargement. Surgery can remove large goiters. Goiter as a manifestation of thyroid disorders is discussed in the next sections.

THYROIDITIS

Thyroiditis, an inflammation of the thyroid gland, encompasses several clinical disorders. It is a frequent cause of goiter. We think that *subacute granulomatous thyroiditis* is caused by a viral infection. *Acute thyroiditis* is due to bacterial or fungal infection. Subacute and acute forms of thyroiditis have an abrupt onset. The patient reports pain in the thyroid area or radiating to the throat, ears, or jaw. Systemic manifestations include fever, chills, sweats, and fatigue.

Hashimoto thyroiditis (chronic autoimmune thyroiditis) is caused by the destruction of thyroid tissue by antibodies.[11] It is the most common cause of hypothyroid goiters in the United States. Risk factors include female gender, a family history, older age, and White ethnicity. The goiter, which is the hallmark of Hashimoto thyroiditis, may develop gradually or rapidly. If it enlarges rapidly, it may compress structures in the neck (e.g., trachea, laryngeal nerves), changing the voice and affecting breathing. As antibodies destroy thyroid tissue, there may be a transient phase of hyperthyroidism due to leaking thyroid hormone from the damaged tissues.

Silent, painless thyroiditis, which may be early Hashimoto thyroiditis, can occur in postpartum women. This condition is usually seen in the first 6 months after delivery. It may be due to an autoimmune reaction to fetal cells in the mother's thyroid gland.

At first, T_4 and T_3 levels increase in subacute, acute, and silent thyroiditis. They decrease with time. Suppressed radioactive iodine uptake (RAIU) occurs in subacute and silent thyroiditis. In Hashimoto thyroiditis, T_4 and T_3 levels are usually low and the TSH level is high. Antithyroid antibodies are present in Hashimoto thyroiditis.

Recovery from acute or subacute thyroiditis may be complete in weeks or months without any treatment. If the cause is bacterial, treatment may include antibiotics or surgical drainage. In the subacute and acute forms, NSAIDs (e.g., aspirin, naproxen) can relieve symptoms. With more severe pain, corticosteroids (e.g., prednisone up to 40 mg/day) can relieve discomfort. Propranolol (Inderal) or atenolol (Tenormin) may relieve cardiovascular symptoms related to a hyperthyroid state. The patient who is hypothyroid needs thyroid hormone therapy.

Nursing care includes patient teaching about the disease process and treatment. Teach the patient not to stop medications abruptly. Tell the patient to remain under close health care supervision so that progress can be monitored. Teach the patient to report to the HCP any change in symptoms, such as trouble breathing or swallowing, swelling to face and extremities, or rapid weight gain or loss. Those receiving thyroid hormone need to know the expected side effects and ways to manage them.

The patient with Hashimoto thyroiditis is at risk for other autoimmune diseases, such as Addison disease, pernicious anemia, or Graves disease. Teach the patient the signs and symptoms of these disorders, especially Addison disease.

HYPERTHYROIDISM

Hyperthyroidism is hyperactivity of the thyroid gland with sustained increase in synthesis and release of thyroid hormones.[12] It occurs in women more than men, with the highest frequency in persons 20 to 40 years old (Box 54.1). The most common form is Graves disease. Other causes include toxic nodular goiter, thyroiditis, excess iodine intake, pituitary tumors, and thyroid cancer. Since hyperthyroidism may be caused by iodinated contrast media used in CT scans and other radiologic studies, monitor those who are at risk closely after iodinated contrast media exposure. TSH↓ - Secondary cause.

Thyrotoxicosis refers to the physiologic effects or clinical syndrome of hypermetabolism resulting from excess circulating levels of T_4, T_3, or both. Hyperthyroidism and thyrotoxicosis usually occur together. Subclinical hyperthyroidism occurs when the patient has a serum TSH level below 0.4 mU/L but normal T_4 and T_3 levels. Overt hyperthyroidism is defined by low or undetectable TSH and increased T_4 and T_3 levels. The patient may or may not have symptoms of hyperthyroidism. T3↓ T4↑

Etiology and Pathophysiology

Graves disease is an autoimmune disease characterized by thyroid enlargement and excess thyroid hormone secretion. It accounts for 75% of the cases of hyperthyroidism. We do not

BOX 54.1 BIOLOGIC SEX CONSIDERATIONS
Endocrine Problems

Men
- Ectopic ACTH production is more common.

Women
- Thyroid disorders are more common.
- Graves disease affects 5 times more women.
- Thyroid nodules and thyroid cancer affect up to 4 times as many women.
- Hyperparathyroidism affects twice as many women.
- Cushing disease and primary hyperaldosteronism are more common.

know the exact cause. Risk factors, such as a lack of iodine, smoking, infection, and stress, may interact with genetic factors to cause Graves disease.

In Graves disease, the patient develops antibodies to TSH receptors. These antibodies attach to the receptors and stimulate the thyroid gland to release T_3, T_4, or both. Excess thyroid hormones lead to the manifestations of thyrotoxicosis. Remissions and exacerbations occur, with or without treatment. It may progress to destruction of the thyroid tissue, causing hypothyroidism. Graves disease is associated with the presence of other autoimmune disorders, including rheumatoid arthritis, pernicious anemia, systemic lupus erythematosus, Addison disease, celiac disease, and vitiligo.

Clinical Manifestations

The manifestations are related to the effect of excess circulating thyroid hormones. They directly increase metabolism and tissue sensitivity to sympathetic nervous system stimulation.

Palpation of the thyroid gland may reveal a goiter. When the thyroid gland is excessively large, you may be able to see a goiter (Fig. 54.6). Auscultating the thyroid gland may reveal bruits from the increased blood supply. Another common finding is *ophthalmopathy,* a term used to describe abnormal eye appearance or function. A classic finding in Graves disease is *exophthalmos,* a protrusion of the eyeballs from the orbits (see Fig. 22.9). Exophthalmos results from increased fat deposits and fluid (edema) in the orbital tissues and ocular muscles. The increased pressure forces the eyeballs outward. The upper lids are usually retracted and elevated, with the sclera visible above the iris. When the eyelids do not close completely, the exposed corneal surfaces become dry and irritated. Corneal ulcers and loss of vision can occur. Changes in the ocular muscles result in muscle weakness, causing diplopia.

Other manifestations are outlined in Table 54.6. Abnormal laboratory findings are shown in Table 54.7. A patient in the early stages of hyperthyroidism may only have weight loss and increased nervousness. *Acropachy* (clubbing of the digits) may occur with advanced disease (Fig. 54.7). Manifestations (e.g., palpitations, tremors, weight loss) in older adults do not differ significantly from those of younger adults (Table 54.8). In older patients who are confused and agitated, we may suspect dementia and delay the diagnosis.

Complications

Acute thyrotoxicosis (thyrotoxic crisis or *thyroid storm)* is an acute, severe, rare condition that occurs when excess amounts of thyroid hormones are released into the circulation. Although considered a life-threatening emergency, death is rare when treatment is started early. We think that it results from stressors (e.g., infection, trauma, surgery) in a patient with preexisting hyperthyroidism. Patients having a thyroidectomy are at risk because manipulation of the hyperactive thyroid gland results in the increased release of hormones.

In acute thyrotoxicosis, all the symptoms of hyperthyroidism are prominent and severe. Manifestations include severe tachycardia, heart failure, shock, hyperthermia (up to 106°F [41.1°C]), agitation, delirium, seizures, abdominal pain, vomiting, diarrhea, and coma.

Diagnostic Studies

The primary laboratory findings used to confirm the diagnosis of hyperthyroidism are low or undetectable TSH levels (<0.4 mU/L) and increased free T_4 levels. Total T_3 and T_4 levels may be assessed, but they are not as definitive. Total T_3 and T_4 determine both free and bound (to protein) hormone levels. The free hormone is the only biologically active form of these hormones.

The RAIU test can distinguish Graves disease from other forms of thyroiditis. The patient with Graves disease shows a diffuse, homogeneous uptake of 35% to 95%, while the patient with thyroiditis shows an uptake of less than 2%. The person with a nodular goiter has an uptake in the high normal range.

Interprofessional Care

The goals of care are to block the adverse effects of excess thyroid hormone, suppress oversecretion of thyroid hormone, and prevent complications.[13] There are several treatment options. They include antithyroid medications, radioactive iodine (RAI) therapy, and surgery (Table 54.9). Supportive therapy is aimed at managing respiratory distress, reducing fever, replacing fluid, and eliminating or managing the initiating stressor(s).

The choice of treatment is influenced by the patient's age and preferences, coexistence of other diseases, and pregnancy status.

Drug Therapy

Drugs used to treat hyperthyroidism include antithyroid drugs, iodine, and β-adrenergic blockers. These drugs are useful in treating thyrotoxic states but are not curative. Radiation therapy or surgery may be needed.

Antithyroid drugs. The first-line antithyroid drugs are propylthiouracil and methimazole (Tapazole). These drugs inhibit thyroid hormone synthesis. Reasons for use include Graves disease in the young patient, hyperthyroidism during pregnancy, and the need to achieve a euthyroid state before surgery or radiation therapy. Propylthiouracil is generally used for patients who are in the first trimester of pregnancy, had an adverse reaction to methimazole, or need a rapid reduction in symptoms. It is the first line therapy in thyrotoxicosis since it blocks the peripheral conversion of T_4 to T_3. An advantage of propylthiouracil is that it achieves the therapeutic goal of being euthyroid more quickly.

TABLE 54.6 Manifestations of Thyroid Problems

	Hyperfunction	Hypofunction
Cardiovascular System	• ↑ BP • ↑ Rate and force of cardiac contractions • Bounding, rapid pulse • ↑ Cardiac output • Systolic murmurs • Dysrhythmias • Palpitations • Angina	• ↑ Capillary fragility • ↓ Rate and force of contractions • Varied changes in BP • Cardiac hypertrophy • Distant heart sounds • Anemia • Heart failure • Angina
GI System	• ↑ Appetite, thirst • Weight loss • ↑ Peristalsis • Diarrhea, frequent defecation • ↑ Bowel sounds • Splenomegaly • Hepatomegaly	• ↓ Appetite • Weight gain • Nausea and vomiting • Constipation • Distended abdomen • Enlarged, scaly tongue • Celiac disease
Musculoskeletal System	• Fatigue • Weakness • Proximal muscle wasting • Dependent edema • Osteoporosis	• Fatigue • Weakness • Muscular aches and pains • Slow movements • Arthralgia
Nervous System	• Hyperactive deep-tendon reflexes • Depression • Lack of ability to concentrate • Rapid speech • Insomnia • Difficulty focusing eyes • Nervousness • Fine tremor of fingers and tongue • Lability of mood, delirium • Restlessness • Personality changes of irritability, agitation • Stupor, coma	• Prolonged relaxation of deep tendon reflexes • Anxiety, depression • Slowed mental processes • Slow, slurred speech • Sleepiness • Apathy • Lethargy • Forgetfulness • Hoarseness • Stupor, coma • Paresthesias
Reproductive System	• Menstrual irregularities • Amenorrhea • ↓ Libido • ↓ Fertility • Impotence and gynecomastia in men	• Prolonged menstrual periods or amenorrhea • ↓ Libido • Infertility
Respiratory	• Dyspnea on mild exertion • ↑ Respiratory rate	• Dyspnea • ↓ Breathing capacity
Skin	• Warm, smooth, moist skin • Thin, brittle nails detached from nail bed (onycholysis) • Hair loss (may be patchy) • Clubbing of fingers (thyroid acropachy) (Fig. 54.7) • Palmar erythema • Fine, silky hair • Premature graying (in men) • Diaphoresis • Vitiligo • Pretibial myxedema (infiltrative dermopathy)	• Dry, thick, inelastic, cold skin • Thick, brittle nails • Dry, sparse, coarse hair • Poor turgor of mucosa • Generalized interstitial edema • Puffy face • ↓ Sweating • Pallor
Other	• Goiter (Fig. 54.6) • Intolerance to heat • Lid lag, stare • Eyelid retraction • Exophthalmos • ↑ Temperature	• Goiter • Hearing problems • Intolerance to cold • ↑ Risk for infection • ↑ Sensitivity to opioids, barbiturates, anesthesia

However, it must be taken 3 times per day. Methimazole is given in a single daily dose.

Improvement usually begins 1 to 2 weeks after the start of drug therapy. We usually see results within 4 to 8 weeks. Therapy is usually continued for 6 to 15 months to allow for spontaneous remission, which occurs in 20% to 40% of patients. Teach the patient the importance of adhering to the drug plan. Abruptly stopping drug therapy can result in a return of hyperthyroidism.

Iodine. Iodine is available as saturated solution of potassium iodine (SSKI) and Lugol solution. Iodine is used with other antithyroid drugs to prepare the patient for thyroidectomy or for treatment of thyrotoxicosis. Quickly giving large doses of iodine inhibits T_3 and T_4 synthesis and blocks the release of these hormones into circulation. It decreases the vascularity of the thyroid gland, making surgery safer and easier. The maximal effect usually occurs within 1 to 2 weeks. Because of a reduction in the therapeutic effect, long-term iodine therapy is not effective in controlling hyperthyroidism.

Iodine is mixed with water or juice and given after meals. Sipping it through a straw decreases the chance of it staining the teeth. Assess the patient for signs of iodine toxicity, such as swelling of the buccal mucosa and other mucous membranes, excess salivation, nausea and vomiting, and skin reactions. If toxicity occurs, stop administering iodine and notify the HCP.

β-Adrenergic blockers. β-Adrenergic blockers are used for symptomatic relief of thyrotoxicosis. They block the effects of sympathetic nervous stimulation, thereby decreasing tachycardia, nervousness, irritability, and tremors. Propranolol is usually given with antithyroid agents. Atenolol is the preferred

TABLE 54.7 Laboratory Results for Hyperthyroid and Hypothyroid Patients

		HYPOTHYROID	
Test	**Hyperthyroid**	**Primary**	**Secondary**
Thyroid-stimulating hormone (TSH)	↓	↑	↓
T_4 (thyroxine)	↑	↓	↓
Total cholesterol	N	↑	↑
Low-density lipoproteins (LDLs)	↓	↑	↑
Triglycerides	N	↑	↑
Creatine kinase (CK)	N	↑	↑
Basal metabolic rate (BMR)	↑	↓	↓
Thyroid peroxidase (TPO) antibody	N	+ (in autoimmune hypothyroidism)	N

N, Normal; +, positive.

TABLE 54.8 Comparison of Hyperthyroidism in Younger and Older Adults

	Younger Adult	**Older Adult**
Common causes	Graves disease in >90% of cases	Graves disease or toxic nodular goiter
Common symptoms	Nervousness, irritability, weight loss, heat intolerance, warm moist skin	Anorexia, weight loss, apathy, lassitude, depression, confusion
Goiter	Present in >90% of cases	Present in ~50% of cases
Ophthalmopathy	Exophthalmos (Fig. 54.6) present in 20%–40% of cases	Exophthalmos less common
Cardiac features	↑ HR and palpitations common but without heart failure	Angina, dysrhythmia (especially atrial fibrillation with rapid ventricular response), heart failure may occur

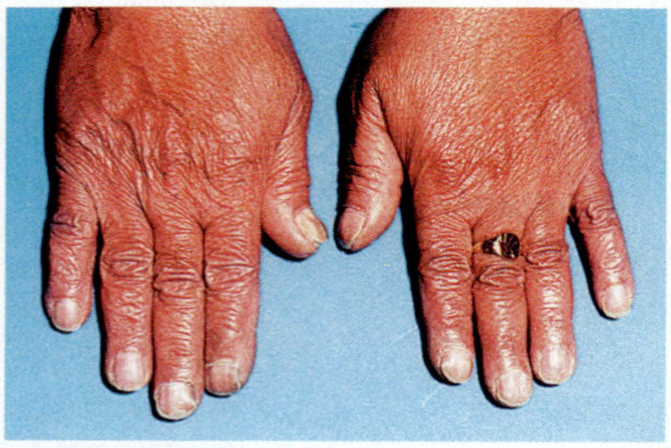

Fig. 54.7 Thyroid acropachy. Digital clubbing and swelling of fingers. (From Chew SL, Leslie D: *Clinical endocrinology and diabetes: an illustrated colour text,* Edinburgh, 2006, Churchill Livingstone.)

TABLE 54.9 Interprofessional Care

Hyperthyroidism

Diagnostic Assessment
- History and physical assessment
- Ophthalmologic examination
- ECG
- Laboratory tests
  - TSH levels, serum free T_4
  - Thyroid antibodies (e.g., thyroid peroxidase [TPO] antibody)
  - Total serum T_3 and T_4
- Radioactive iodine uptake (RAIU)

Management

Drug Therapy
- Antithyroid drugs
  - Methimazole (Tapazole)
  - Propylthiouracil
- Iodine (SSKI)

Radiation Therapy
- Radioactive iodine

Surgical Therapy
- Subtotal thyroidectomy

Nutrition Therapy
- High-calorie, high-protein diet
- Frequent meals

β-adrenergic blocker for use in the hyperthyroid patient with asthma or heart disease.

Radioactive Iodine Therapy

RAI therapy is the treatment of choice for most nonpregnant adults. RAI damages or destroys thyroid tissue, thus limiting thyroid hormone secretion. RAI has a delayed response. The maximum effect may not be seen for up to 3 months. For this reason, the patient is usually treated with antithyroid drugs and propranolol before and for 3 months after starting RAI until the effects of radiation become apparent. Although RAI is usually effective, 80% of patients have posttreatment hypothyroidism, resulting in the need for lifelong thyroid hormone therapy. Teach the patient the symptoms of hypothyroidism and to seek medical help if these symptoms occur.

RAI therapy is usually given on an outpatient basis. A pregnancy test is done before starting therapy for all women who have menstrual cycles. Tell the patient that radiation thyroiditis and parotitis are possible and may cause dryness and irritation of the mouth and throat. Relief may be obtained with frequent sips of water, ice chips, or a salt and soda gargle 3 or 4 times per day. Make this gargle by dissolving 1 tsp of salt and 1 tsp of baking soda in 2 cups of warm water. The discomfort should subside in 3 to 4 days. A mixture of antacid (Mylanta or Maalox), diphenhydramine, and viscous lidocaine can be used to swish and spit, increasing patient comfort when eating.

parathyroid - reg CA.

To limit radiation exposure to others, teach the patient receiving RAI home precautions. These include (1) using private toilet facilities, if possible; (2) flushing 2 or 3 times after each use; (3) separately laundering towels, bed linens, and clothes daily at home; and (4) not preparing food for others that needs prolonged handling with bare hands. They should avoid being close to pregnant women and children for 7 days after therapy. ↓ CA - laryngospasm

Surgical Therapy

A thyroidectomy is done for those who have (1) a large goiter causing tracheal compression, (2) a lack of response to antithyroid therapy, or (3) thyroid cancer (Fig. 54.8). Surgery may be done when a person is not a candidate for RAI. One advantage that thyroidectomy has over RAI is a more rapid reduction in

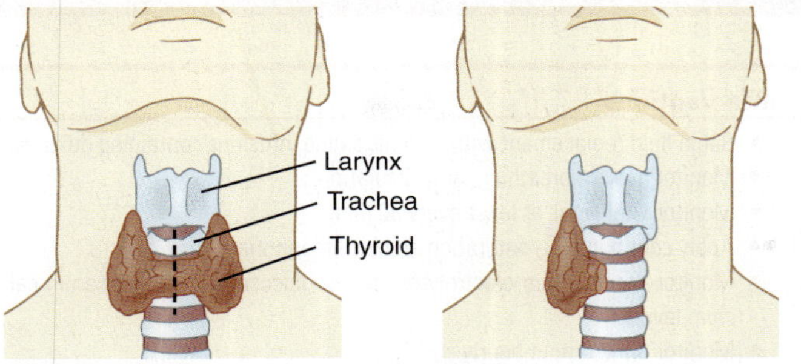

Fig. 54.8 Subtotal thyroidectomy. Part of the thyroid gland is removed.

T_3 and T_4 levels. A *subtotal thyroidectomy* is the preferred surgical procedure. It involves removing a large portion (90%) of the thyroid gland.

Some patients may have minimally invasive endoscopic or robotic thyroidectomy. Endoscopic thyroidectomy is appropriate for patients with small nodules (less than 3 cm) and no evidence of cancer. Robotic surgery is best for those who are not overweight and have small nodules on only 1 side of the gland. Advantages of these procedures include less scarring, less pain, and a faster return to normal activity.

Nutrition Therapy

With the increased metabolic rate in hyperthyroid patients, there is a high risk for nutrition problems. A high-calorie diet (4000 to 5000 cal/day) may be needed to satisfy hunger, prevent tissue breakdown, and decrease weight loss. The patient may need 6 full meals a day and snacks high in protein, carbohydrates, minerals, and vitamins. The protein content should be 1 to 2 g/kg of ideal body weight. Increase carbohydrate intake to compensate for increased metabolism. Carbohydrates provide energy and decrease the use of body-stored protein. Teach the patient to avoid highly seasoned and high-fiber foods because they can further stimulate the already hyperactive GI tract. Have the patient avoid caffeine-containing liquids, such as coffee, tea, and cola, to decrease the restlessness and sleep problems. Refer the patient to a dietitian for help in meeting their nutrient needs.

NURSING MANAGEMENT: HYPERTHYROIDISM

Assessment

Subjective and objective data you should obtain from a person with hyperthyroidism are outlined in Table 54.10.

Clinical Problems

Clinical problems for the patient with hyperthyroidism include:

- Activity intolerance
- Nutritionally compromised

Additional information on clinical problems and interventions is presented in eNursing Care Plan 54.1 for the patient with hyperthyroidism (available on the website for this chapter).

TABLE 54.10 NURSING ASSESSMENT

Hyperthyroidism

Subjective Data

Important Health Information

Health history: Preexisting goiter. Recent infection or trauma, immigration from iodine-deficient area, autoimmune disease

Medications: Thyroid hormones, herbal therapies that may contain thyroid hormone

Functional Health Patterns

Health perception–health management: Positive family history of thyroid or autoimmune disorders

Nutritional-metabolic: Iodine intake, weight loss, ↑ appetite, thirst, nausea, vomiting

Elimination: Diarrhea, polyuria, sweating

Activity-exercise: Dyspnea on exertion, palpitations, muscle weakness, fatigue

Sleep-rest: Insomnia

Cognitive-perceptual: Chest pain, nervousness, heat intolerance, pruritus

Sexuality-reproductive: ↓ Libido, impotence, gynecomastia (in men), amenorrhea (in women)

Coping–stress tolerance: Emotional lability, irritability, restlessness, personality changes, delirium

Objective Data

Cardiovascular

↑ HR, bounding pulse, systolic murmurs, dysrhythmias, ↑ BP, bruit over the thyroid gland

Eyes

Exophthalmos, eyelid retraction, infrequent blinking

General

Agitation, rapid speech and body movements, anxiety, restlessness, fever, enlarged or nodular thyroid gland

GI

↑ Bowel sounds. ↑ Appetite, diarrhea, weight loss, liver and/or spleen enlargement

Neurologic

Hyperreflexia; diplopia. Fine tremors of hands, tongue, eyelids

Musculoskeletal

Muscle wasting

Reproductive

Menstrual irregularities, infertility, impotence, gynecomastia in men

Respiratory

Tachypnea, dyspnea on exertion

Skin

Warm, diaphoretic, velvety skin. Thin, loose nails. Fine, silky hair and hair loss. Palmar erythema, clubbing, white pigmentation of skin (vitiligo), diffuse edema of legs and feet

Possible Diagnostic Findings

↑ T_3, ↑ T_4, ↑ T_3 *resin* uptake, ↓ or undetectable TSH. Chest x-ray showing enlarged heart. ECG findings of tachycardia, atrial fibrillation

Planning

The overall goals are that the patient with hyperthyroidism will (1) have relief of symptoms, (2) have no serious complications

TABLE 54.11 **EMERGENCY MANAGEMENT**

Acute Thyrotoxicosis

Cause	Assessment Findings	Interventions

• Infection, surgery, trauma in a patient with hyperthyroidism
• Thyroidectomy
	• Abdominal pain
	• Agitation
	• Delirium
	• Diarrhea
	• Fever (up to 106°F [41.1°C])
	• Heart failure
	• Seizures
	• Severe tachycardia
	• Shock
	• Vomiting
		• Begin fluid replacement with isotonic saline infusions containing dextrose.
		• Monitor airway, breathing, and circulation.
		• Monitor vital signs at least every 30 min.
		• Apply continuous O_2 saturation and ECG monitoring.
		• Monitor serial serum electrolytes, serum glucose, ABGs, and serum calcium levels.
		• Monitor urine output hourly.
		• Apply ice packs and cooling blankets to reduce fever. Acetaminophen as needed.
		• Provide pulmonary hygiene.
		• Assess for manifestations of heart failure or pulmonary edema (e.g., extra heart sounds, adventitious lung sounds).
		• Decrease O_2 demands by decreasing anxiety and pain.
		• Restrict visitors, if needed.
		• Give prescribed drugs and monitor effects:
		  • β-Adrenergic blockers
		  • Antithyroid agents
		  • Iodine compounds
		  • Glucocorticoids

related to the disease or treatment, (3) maintain balanced nutrition, and (4) cooperate with the therapeutic plan.

Implementation

Acute Care

Patients with hyperthyroidism are usually treated in an outpatient setting. However, those who develop acute thyrotoxicosis or undergo thyroidectomy need hospitalization and acute care.

Acute thyrotoxicosis. Acute thyrotoxicosis requires aggressive treatment, often in an intensive care unit (ICU).[14] Give medications that block thyroid hormone production and sympathetic nervous system effects. Provide supportive therapy, including monitoring for dysrhythmias and decompensation, ensuring adequate oxygenation, and giving IV fluids to replace fluid and electrolyte losses. This is important in the patient who has fluid losses from vomiting and diarrhea (Table 54.11).

Ensuring adequate rest may be a challenge because of the patient's irritability and restlessness. Provide a calm, cool, quiet room. Use light bed coverings and change the linen often if the patient is diaphoretic. Encourage and assist with exercise involving large muscle groups (tremors can interfere with small-muscle coordination) to allow the release of nervous tension and restlessness. Establish a supportive, trusting relationship to promote coping by a patient who is irritable, restless, and anxious.

If exophthalmos is present, there is a risk for corneal injury related to irritation and dryness. The patient may have orbital pain. To relieve eye discomfort and prevent corneal ulceration, apply artificial tears to soothe and moisten conjunctival membranes. Restricting salt may help reduce periorbital edema. The patient should sit upright as much as possible to promote fluid drainage from the periorbital area.

Dark glasses reduce glare and prevent irritation from smoke, air currents, dust, and dirt. If the eyelids cannot be closed, lightly tape them shut for sleep. To maintain flexibility, teach the patient to exercise the intraocular muscles several times a day by turning the eyes in the complete range of motion. Good grooming can help promote self-esteem from an altered body image. If the exophthalmos is severe, treatment options include corticosteroids, radiation of retroorbital tissues, orbital decompression, or corrective lid or muscle surgery.

Thyroid surgery. When a subtotal thyroidectomy is planned, the patient must be adequately prepared to avoid complications. Before surgery, antithyroid drugs, iodine, and β-adrenergic blockers may be given to achieve a euthyroid state. Iodine also decreases the vascularization of the thyroid gland, reducing the risk for hemorrhage.

Teach the patient about routine postoperative care and comfort and safety measures. Show the patient how to support the head manually while turning in bed, since this minimizes stress on the suture line after surgery. The patient should practice neck range-of-motion exercises. Tell the patient that talking is likely to be difficult for a short time after surgery. Review the importance of performing leg exercises.

Postoperative care. Postoperative complications include hypothyroidism, damage to or inadvertent removal of parathyroid glands (causing hypoparathyroidism and hypocalcemia), hemorrhage, injury to the recurrent or superior laryngeal nerve, thyrotoxicosis, and infection. Recurrent laryngeal nerve damage leads to vocal cord paralysis. If both cords are paralyzed, spastic airway obstruction will occur, requiring an immediate tracheostomy.

! SAFETY ALERT

Airway Obstruction

- Airway obstruction after thyroid surgery is an emergency.
- Keep O_2, suction equipment, and a tracheostomy tray available in the patient's room.

TABLE 54.12 NURSING MANAGEMENT

Care of the Patient After Thyroid Surgery

- Assess vital signs every 15 min until stable and then every 30 min for the first 24 hr after surgery.
- Monitor airway and respiratory status (patency, rate, rhythm, depth, and effort).
- Assess the patient every 2 hr for 24 hr for signs of hemorrhage or tracheal compression (e.g., irregular breathing, neck swelling, frequent swallowing, choking, blood on the dressings, and sensations of fullness at the incision site).
- Assist the patient with coughing and deep breathing.
- Apply supplemental O_2 with humidification as ordered.
- Have suction equipment and a tracheostomy kit available for immediate use.
- Assess the ability to speak aloud, noting voice quality, tone, and any problems speaking. Notify the HCP of any permanent hoarseness or loss of vocal volume.
- Monitor calcium levels. Assess for signs of tetany and hypocalcemia (e.g., tingling in toes, fingers, around the mouth; muscular twitching; apprehension) and any trouble with speaking or hoarseness. Check Trousseau sign and Chvostek sign (see Fig. 17.15).
- Keep IV calcium (calcium gluconate, calcium chloride) available for immediate use.
- Assess condition of operative site and dressing. Monitor the area under the patient's neck and shoulders for drainage.
- Keep the patient in a semi-Fowler position. Support the head and neck with pillows. Avoid neck flexion to prevent tension on the suture line.
- Provide comfort measures and give analgesic medications as prescribed.

Respiration may become difficult because of excess swelling of the neck tissues, hemorrhage, and hematoma formation. *Laryngeal stridor* (harsh, vibratory sound) may occur because of edema of the laryngeal nerve. It may be related to tetany from hypocalcemia, which occurs if the parathyroid glands were removed or damaged during surgery. To treat tetany, have IV calcium salts (e.g., calcium gluconate) available.

Assess the patient frequently for signs of bleeding or tracheal compression (Table 54.12). The patient should expect some hoarseness for 3 or 4 days after surgery because of edema. Monitor vital signs. Assess for any signs of hypocalcemia from hypoparathyroidism. If recovery is uneventful, the patient ambulates within hours after surgery. Give fluids as soon as tolerated. A soft diet starts the day after surgery.

The appearance of the incision may be distressing to the patient. Reassure the patient that the scar will fade in color and eventually look like a normal neck wrinkle. A scarf, jewelry, a high collar, or other covering can effectively camouflage the scar.

Ambulatory care. Teach the patient and caregiver that thyroid hormone balance will be monitored periodically. Most patients have a period of relative hypothyroidism soon after surgery because of the substantial reduction in the size of the thyroid. The remaining tissue usually hypertrophies over time and recovers the ability to make hormones. We usually do not give thyroid hormone because the exogenous hormone inhibits pituitary production of TSH and delays or prevents the restoration of normal gland function and tissue regeneration.

To prevent weight gain, caloric intake must be greatly reduced to less than the amount that was needed before surgery. Adequate iodine is needed to promote thyroid function, but excesses can inhibit the thyroid gland. Seafood once or twice a week or normal use of iodized salt should provide enough iodine intake. Encourage regular exercise to stimulate the thyroid gland. Teach the patient to avoid high environmental temperatures because they inhibit thyroid regeneration.

Regular follow-up care is needed. The patient should see the HCP biweekly for a month and then at least semiannually to assess thyroid function. Tell the patient who had a complete thyroidectomy about the need for lifelong thyroid hormone replacement. Teach the patient the signs and symptoms of thyroid failure and to seek medical care promptly if these develop.

◆ Evaluation

The expected outcomes are that the patient with hyperthyroidism will:

- Have relief of symptoms
- Have no serious complications related to the disease or treatment
- Cooperate with the therapeutic plan
- Maintain balanced nutrition

HYPOTHYROIDISM

Hypothyroidism is a deficiency of thyroid hormone that causes a general slowing of the metabolic rate.[15] About 4% of the U.S. population has mild hypothyroidism, with about 0.3% having more severe disease. Hypothyroidism is more common in women (Box 54.1). Subclinical hypothyroidism occurs when the TSH is greater than 4.5 mU/L, but the T_4 levels are normal. Up to 10% of women older than 60 years have subclinical hypothyroidism. Patients with overt hypothyroidism have increased TSH and decreased T_4 levels. Critically ill patients may present with nonthyroidal illness syndrome (NTIS).[15] Those with NTIS have low T_3, T_4, and TSH levels.

hair loss BP-↓ HR-↓ RR-↓ temp ↓ wt-↑

Etiology and Pathophysiology

We classify hypothyroidism as primary or secondary. *Primary hypothyroidism* is caused by destruction of thyroid tissue or defective hormone synthesis. *Secondary hypothyroidism* is caused by pituitary disease with decreased TSH secretion or hypothalamic dysfunction with decreased thyrotropin-releasing hormone (TRH) secretion. Hypothyroidism can be brief and related to thyroiditis or stopping thyroid hormone therapy.

Iodine deficiency is the most common cause of hypothyroidism worldwide. In the United States, the most common cause of primary hypothyroidism is atrophy of the thyroid gland. This atrophy is the result of Hashimoto thyroiditis or Graves disease. These autoimmune diseases destroy the thyroid gland. Hypothyroidism can develop after treatment for hyperthyroidism, specifically thyroidectomy or RAI therapy. Drugs such as amiodarone, which contains iodine,

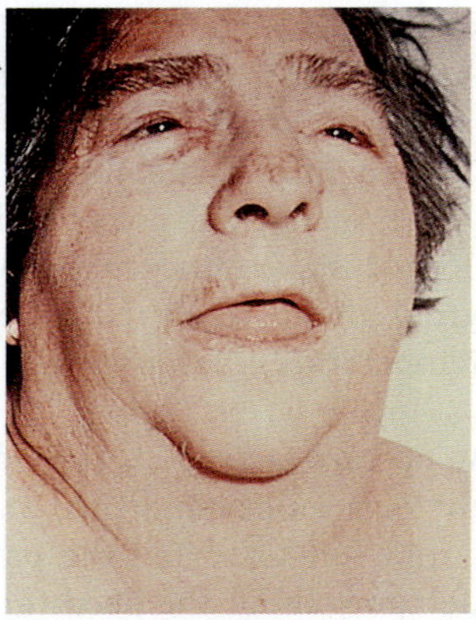

Fig. 54.9 Common features of myxedema. Dull, puffy skin; coarse, sparse hair; periorbital edema; and prominent tongue. (Courtesy Paul W. Ladenson, MD, The Johns Hopkins University and Hospital, Baltimore, MD. From Seidel HM, Ball JW, Dains JE, et al, editors: *Mosby's guide to physical examination,* ed 6, St Louis, 2006, Mosby.)

and lithium, which blocks hormone production, can cause hypothyroidism.

Hypothyroidism that develops in infancy *(cretinism)* results from thyroid hormone deficiencies during fetal or early neonatal life. In the United States, we screen all infants for decreased thyroid function at birth.

Clinical Manifestations

With hypothyroidism we see a slowing of body processes (Table 54.6). Manifestations vary depending on the severity and the duration of thyroid deficiency and the patient's age at the onset of the deficiency. Symptoms may develop over months to years, unless hypothyroidism occurs after a thyroidectomy, after thyroid ablation, or during treatment with antithyroid drugs.

The patient is often tired and lethargic. There may be personality and mental changes, including impaired memory, slowed speech, decreased initiative, and somnolence. Many appear depressed. Weight gain is a result of a decreased metabolic rate.

Hypothyroidism may cause significant cardiovascular problems, especially in a person with a history of CVD. It can cause decreased cardiac contractility and decreased cardiac output. The patient may have low exercise tolerance and shortness of breath on exertion. High serum cholesterol and triglyceride levels and the accumulation of mucopolysaccharides in the intima of small blood vessels can result in coronary atherosclerosis. Anemia is common.

Patients with severe, long-standing hypothyroidism may have **myxedema**. Myxedema results from the accumulation of hydrophilic mucopolysaccharides in the dermis and other tissues (Fig. 54.9). It alters the physical appearance of the skin and subcutaneous tissues with puffiness, facial and periorbital edema, and a mask-like affect. Patients may have an altered self-image related to their altered appearance.

In the older adult, we may attribute manifestations of hypothyroidism (fatigue, cold and dry skin, hair loss, constipation, cold intolerance) to normal aging. For this reason, the patient's

TABLE 54.13 Interprofessional Care

Hypothyroidism

Diagnostic Assessment	Management
• History and physical assessment	• Thyroid hormone replacement (e.g., levothyroxine)
• Serum TSH and free T_4	• Monitor thyroid hormone levels and adjust dosage (if needed)
• Total serum T_3 and T_4	• Nutrition therapy to promote weight loss
• Thyroid peroxidase (TPO) antibodies	• Patient and caregiver teaching (Table 54.14)

symptoms may not raise suspicion of an underlying condition. Older adults who have confusion, lethargy, and depression should be screened for thyroid disease.

Complications

The mental sluggishness, drowsiness, and lethargy of hypothyroidism may progress gradually or suddenly to a notable impairment of consciousness or coma. This situation, termed *myxedema coma,* is a medical emergency. Cause of myxedema coma include infection, drugs (especially opioids, tranquilizers, and barbiturates), exposure to cold, and trauma. Manifestations include low temperature, hypotension, and hypoventilation. Cardiovascular collapse can result from hypoventilation, hyponatremia, hypoglycemia, and lactic acidosis. For the patient to survive myxedema coma, we must support vital functions and give IV thyroid hormone replacement.

Diagnostic Studies

The most reliable laboratory tests for thyroid function are TSH and free T_4. These values, correlated with findings from the history and physical assessment, confirm the diagnosis of hypothyroidism. Serum TSH levels help determine the cause. Serum TSH is high when the defect is in the thyroid and low when it is in the pituitary or the hypothalamus. The presence of thyroid antibodies suggests an autoimmune origin. Other abnormal laboratory findings are high cholesterol and triglycerides, anemia, and increased creatine kinase (Table 54.7).

Interprofessional Care

The treatment goal for a patient with hypothyroidism is to restore a euthyroid state as safely and quickly as possible with hormone therapy (Table 54.13). A low-calorie diet can promote weight loss or prevent weight gain.

Levothyroxine (Synthroid) is the drug of choice to treat hypothyroidism. In the young and otherwise healthy patient, the maintenance replacement dosage is based on the patient's response and laboratory findings. When beginning thyroid hormone therapy, the first dosages are low to avoid increases in resting heart rate and BP. In the patient with compromised cardiac status, careful monitoring is needed when starting and adjusting the dosage because the usual dose may increase myocardial O_2 demand. This may cause angina and dysrhythmias.

DRUG ALERT

Levothyroxine (Synthroid)

- Carefully monitor patients with CVD who take this drug.
- Monitor heart rate and report pulse greater than 100 beats/min or an irregular heartbeat.
- Promptly report chest pain, weight loss, nervousness, tremors, or insomnia.

In a patient without side effects, the dose is increased at 4- to 6-week intervals as needed based on the TSH levels. It may take up to 8 weeks before the full effect of hormone therapy is seen. Levothyroxine has a peak of action of 1 to 3 weeks. The patient must regularly take replacement medication. Lifelong thyroid therapy is usually needed.

NURSING MANAGEMENT: HYPOTHYROIDISM

Assessment

Careful assessment may reveal early and subtle changes in a patient suspected of having hypothyroidism. Note any history of hyperthyroidism and treatment with antithyroid medications, RAI, or surgery. Ask the patient about using iodine-containing medications (Table 54.5). Note any changes in appetite, weight, activity level, speech, memory, and skin (e.g., increased dryness or thickening). Assess for cold intolerance, constipation, and signs of depression. Further assessment should focus on heart rate, tenderness over the thyroid gland, and edema in the extremities and face.

Clinical Problems

Clinical problems for the patient with hypothyroidism may include:

- Activity intolerance
- Constipation
- Nutritionally compromised

Additional information on clinical problems and interventions is presented in the eNursing Care Plan 54.2 for the patient with hypothyroidism (available on the website for this chapter).

Planning

The overall goals are that the patient with hypothyroidism will (1) have relief of symptoms, (2) maintain a euthyroid state, (3) maintain a positive self-image, and (4) adhere with lifelong thyroid therapy.

Implementation

Health Promotion

Routine screening of thyroid function is not recommended. High-risk persons should be screened for subclinical thyroid disease. Risk factors include being female, White ethnicity, advancing age or having type 1 diabetes, Down syndrome, family history of thyroid disease, goiter, previous hyperthyroidism, and external beam radiation in the head and neck area.[17]

Acute Care

Most people with hypothyroidism are treated on an outpatient basis. The person who develops myxedema coma needs acute nursing care, often in the ICU. They often need mechanical respiratory support and cardiac monitoring.

Give thyroid hormone therapy and all other medications IV because severe gastric hypomotility may prevent the absorption of oral agents. Monitor the core temperature for hypothermia that often occurs in myxedema and myxedema coma. Use gentle soap and moisturize often to prevent skin breakdown. Frequent position changes and a low-pressure mattress help maintain skin integrity.

Monitor the patient's progress by assessing vital signs, body weight, intake and output, and edema. Cardiac assessment is especially important because the cardiovascular response to hormone therapy determines the medication regimen. Note energy level and mental alertness. They should improve within 2 to 14 days and continue a steady progression to normal levels. Neurologic status and TSH levels are used to determine continuing treatment.

Ambulatory care. Provide patient teaching about medication management and complications (Table 54.14). At first the hypothyroid patient may have a hard time processing complex instruction. Give written instructions, repeat the information often, and assess the patient's comprehension level.

Stress the need for lifelong drug therapy and avoiding abruptly stopping drugs. Caution patients against doubling up on doses for any reason. Some patients notice weight loss and are tempted to increase dosing to achieve a desired weight. Teach the patient the expected and unexpected side effects, including the signs and symptoms of hypothyroidism and hyperthyroidism (Table 54.6). The manifestations of overdose are the same as hyperthyroidism. Tell the patient to contact the HCP at once

TABLE 54.14 PATIENT & CAREGIVER TEACHING

Hypothyroidism

Include the following instructions when teaching the patient and caregiver about management of hypothyroidism:

1. Discuss the importance of thyroid hormone therapy:
   - Need for lifelong therapy
   - Taking thyroid hormone in the morning before food
   - Need for regular follow-up care and monitoring of thyroid hormone levels
2. Caution the patient not to switch brands of the hormone since the bioavailability of thyroid hormones may differ.
3. Emphasize the need for a comfortable, warm environment because of cold intolerance.
4. Teach ways to prevent skin breakdown. Use soap sparingly, and apply lotion to skin.
5. Caution the patient, especially if an older adult, to avoid sedatives. If they must be used, suggest that the lowest dose be used. Caregiver should closely monitor mental status, level of consciousness, and respirations.
6. Discuss ways to minimize constipation, including:
   - Gradual increase in activity and exercise
   - Increased fiber in diet
   - Use of stool softeners
   - Regular bowel elimination time
   - Tell patient to avoid using enemas. They cause vagal stimulation, which can be hazardous if heart disease is present.

if symptoms, such as orthopnea, dyspnea, rapid pulse, palpitations, chest pain, nervousness, or insomnia, are present.

The patient with diabetes should check glucose levels at least daily because the return to the euthyroid state often increases insulin requirements. Thyroid drugs increase the effects of anticoagulants. Stress the need to remain under close medical observation until stable. Drug interactions are an important reason for patients to consult the HCP before switching brands of thyroid replacement medication. Switching brands may change bioavailability of the drug and physiologic response.

With treatment, striking transformations occur in both appearance and mental function. Most adults return to a normal state. Cardiovascular conditions may persist after correcting the hormone imbalance. Relapses occur if treatment is interrupted.

◆ Evaluation

The expected outcomes are that the patient with hypothyroidism will:

- Have relief from symptoms
- Maintain a euthyroid state with normal thyroid hormone and TSH levels
- Avoid complications of therapy
- Adhere to lifelong therapy

THYROID NODULES AND CANCER

A *thyroid nodule* (growth in the thyroid gland) may be benign or malignant (thyroid cancer). More than 95% of thyroid gland nodules are benign. The risk of developing a thyroid nodule increases with age. Benign nodules are usually not dangerous, but they can cause tracheal compression if they become too large. The risk of developing a thyroid nodule increases with age.

Thyroid cancer is the most common type of endocrine cancer. Around 62,450 new cases of thyroid cancer are diagnosed each year. The incidence of thyroid cancer has increased significantly in the past 25 years. It is the most rapidly increasing cancer in the United States. Thyroid cancer affects more women. The incidence is higher in Whites and Asian Americans.[18] Adults at risk include those who had head and neck radiation therapy during childhood, were exposed to radioactive fallout, or have a personal or family history of goiter.

Types of Thyroid Cancer

The 4 main types of thyroid cancer are papillary, follicular, medullary, and anaplastic. *Papillary* thyroid cancer is the most common type. It accounts for about 70% to 80% of thyroid cancers. Papillary cancer tends to grow slowly. It initially spreads to lymph nodes in the neck.

Follicular thyroid cancer makes up about 15% of thyroid cancers. It tends to occur in older patients. Follicular cancer first metastasizes into the cervical lymph nodes and then spreads to the neck, lungs, and bones.

Medullary thyroid cancer, accounts for only 10% of thyroid cancers. It is more likely to occur in families and be associated with other endocrine problems. It is diagnosed by genetic testing for a proto-oncogene called *RET*. Medullary thyroid cancer is a type of multiple endocrine neoplasia (MEN). It is often poorly differentiated and associated with early metastasis.

Anaplastic thyroid cancer occurs in less than 2% of patients with thyroid cancer. It is the most advanced and aggressive thyroid cancer. The patient is least likely to respond to treatment and has a poor prognosis.

Clinical Manifestations and Diagnostic Studies

The primary manifestation of thyroid cancer is a painless, palpable nodule or nodules in an enlarged thyroid gland. Most nodules are found during routine palpation of the neck. Firm, palpable, cervical masses suggest lymph node metastasis. Some patients may have trouble swallowing or breathing if tumor growth invades the trachea or esophagus. Hemoptysis and airway obstruction may occur if the trachea is involved. Patients generally are euthyroid.

Nodular enlargement of the thyroid gland or palpation of a mass requires further evaluation. Ultrasound is often the first test used. Follow-up testing may involve CT, MRI, and ultrasound-guided fine-needle aspiration (FNA). An FNA is done when a tissue sample for pathologic examination is needed. A thyroid scan may be done. The scan shows whether nodules on the thyroid are "hot" or "cold." "Hot" tumors take up RAI. They are almost always benign. If the nodule does not take up the RAI, it appears "cold." There is a higher risk for being cancer.

Increased serum calcitonin is associated with medullary thyroid cancer. In papillary and follicular cancers, thyroglobulin is high. In families with a history of medullary thyroid cancer, we encourage family members to have genetic testing and thyroid screening on a regular basis.

Interprofessional and Nursing Care

Surgical removal of the tumor is the main treatment for thyroid cancer. Procedures range from unilateral total lobectomy to near-total thyroidectomy with bilateral lobectomy. Lymph nodes in the neck may be removed to determine if the cancer has spread. Some patients may receive RAI after surgery to destroy any remaining cancer cells. RAI therapy improves survival rates in patients with papillary and follicular thyroid cancer. External beam radiation may be given as palliative treatment for patients with metastatic thyroid cancer.

Many thyroid cancers are TSH dependent. Thyroid hormone therapy in high doses is often prescribed to inhibit TSH secretion. Chemotherapy, including doxorubicin, may be used for advanced disease. Targeted therapies for metastatic cancer include Vandetanib (Caprelsa), lenvatinib (Lenvima), sorafenib tosylate (Nexavar), and cabozantinib (Cometriq). These drugs inhibit tyrosine kinases, enzymes that promote the growth of cancer cells. Nursing care for the patient with thyroid cancer is similar to that of a patient undergoing thyroidectomy. Because of the surgical site location and the risk for hypocalcemia, the patient needs frequent postoperative assessment. Assess the patient for airway obstruction, bleeding, and tetany since the parathyroid gland may have been disturbed or removed during surgery.

MULTIPLE ENDOCRINE NEOPLASIA

Multiple endocrine neoplasia (MEN) is an inherited condition characterized by hormone-secreting tumors.[19] It is caused by the mutation of 1 of 2 genes, *MEN1* or *RET,* that normally control cell growth. Tumors may develop in childhood or later in life.

The 2 major types of MEN are type 1 and type 2. Both types are often inherited as autosomal dominant disorders. Persons with type 1 often have parathyroid gland hyperactivity (hyperparathyroidism). Other signs may include hyperactivity of the pituitary gland (prolactinoma) and pancreas (gastrinoma). In most cases, the tumors are initially benign. Some tumors later become malignant. Persons with type 2 neoplasia often have medullary thyroid carcinoma. They may develop pheochromocytoma (tumor of the adrenal glands).

Treatment includes conservative management (watchful waiting), drugs to block the effects of excess hormone, and surgical removal of the gland and/or tumor. Patients must have regular screening visits with the HCP so that new tumors may be detected early and existing tumors carefully monitored.

PARATHYROID GLAND PROBLEMS

HYPERPARATHYROIDISM

Etiology and Pathophysiology

Hyperparathyroidism is a condition involving an increased parathyroid hormone (PTH) secretion. PTH helps regulate serum calcium and phosphate levels by stimulating bone resorption of calcium, renal tubular reabsorption of calcium, and activation of vitamin D. Thus PTH oversecretion causes increased serum calcium levels.

Hyperparathyroidism is either primary, secondary, or tertiary. *Primary hyperparathyroidism* is due to an increased PTH secretion that leads to problems with calcium, phosphate, and bone metabolism.[20] It affects 25 of 100,000 persons per year. The peak incidence is in the 40s and 50s. It affects twice as many women as men. The most common cause is a benign tumor (adenoma) in the parathyroid gland. Patients who have had head and neck radiation have an increased risk for developing a parathyroid adenoma. Long-term lithium therapy is also associated with primary hyperparathyroidism.

Secondary hyperparathyroidism is a compensatory response to conditions that induce or cause hypocalcemia, the main stimulus of PTH secretion. These include vitamin D deficiencies, malabsorption, chronic kidney disease, and hyperphosphatemia.

Tertiary hyperparathyroidism occurs when there is hyperplasia of the parathyroid glands and a loss of negative feedback from circulating calcium levels. Thus there is autonomous PTH secretion even with normal calcium levels. This may happen in patients who have a kidney transplant after a long period of dialysis treatment for chronic kidney disease (see Chapter 51).

High PTH levels usually lead to hypercalcemia and hypophosphatemia. Multiple body systems are affected (Table 54.15). Decreased bone density can occur because of the effect of PTH on osteoclastic (bone resorption) and osteoblastic (bone formation) activity. The kidneys cannot reabsorb the excess calcium. This leads to high urinary calcium levels (hypercalciuria). This urinary calcium, along with a large amount of urinary phosphate, can lead to stone formation.

Clinical Manifestations and Complications

Manifestations range from an asymptomatic person (diagnosed through testing for unrelated problems) to a patient with overt symptoms. The manifestations are due to hypercalcemia (Table 54.15). Loss of appetite, constipation, fatigue, emotional disorders, shortened attention span, and muscle weakness, especially in the proximal muscles of the lower extremities, often occur. Complications include osteoporosis, renal failure, kidney stones, pancreatitis, cardiac changes, and long bone, rib, and vertebral fractures.

Diagnostic Studies

Patients with hyperparathyroidism have increased PTH levels. Serum calcium levels usually exceed 10 mg/dL (2.50 mmol/L). Because of its inverse relation with calcium, the serum phosphorus level is usually less than 3 mg/dL (0.1 mmol/L). Asymptomatic hypercalcemia is often found through a routine chemistry panel.

Other increased values include urine calcium, serum chloride, uric acid, creatinine, amylase (if pancreatitis is present), and alkaline phosphatase (in the presence of bone disease). Bone density measurements may be used to detect bone loss. Conversely, those with bone loss on a screening dual energy x-ray absorptiometry (DEXA) scan should be screened for hypercalcemia. MRI, CT, and/or ultrasound can detect an adenoma.

Interprofessional Care

The goal of treatment is to relieve symptoms and prevent complications caused by excess PTH. The choice of therapy depends on the urgency of the situation, degree of hypercalcemia, and underlying cause of the disorder.

Surgical Therapy

The most effective treatment of primary and secondary hyperparathyroidism is surgery. Surgery involves partial or complete removal of the parathyroid glands. The most common procedure involves endoscopy. It is done on an outpatient basis. Criteria for surgery include increased serum calcium levels (more than 1 mg/dL above the upper limit of normal), hypercalciuria (greater than 400 mg/day), markedly reduced bone mineral density, overt symptoms (e.g., neuromuscular effects, kidney stones), or age under 50 years. Parathyroidectomy leads to a rapid reduction of high calcium levels.

Patients who have multiple parathyroid glands removed may undergo autotransplantation of normal parathyroid tissue in the forearm or near the sternocleidomastoid muscle. This allows PTH secretion to continue with normal calcium levels. If autotransplantation is not possible or if it fails, the patient will need to take calcium supplements for life.

Nonsurgical Therapy

A conservative approach is often used in patients who are asymptomatic or have mild symptoms. Ongoing care includes regular measurement of serum PTH, calcium, phosphorus, alkaline phosphatase, creatinine and blood urea nitrogen (BUN) (to assess renal function), and urinary calcium excretion. Annual x-rays and DEXA scans assess for metabolic bone loss. Continued ambulation and avoiding immobility are important. Diet measures include high fluid and moderate calcium intake.

TABLE 54.15 Manifestations of Parathyroid Problems

Hyperfunction	Hypofunction
Cardiovascular System	
• ↑ BP	• ↓ BP
• Angina	• Edema
• Dysrhythmias	• Dysrhythmias
• Shortened ST segment	• Elongation of ST segment
• Shortened QT interval	• Prolonged QT interval
• ↑ Digitalis effect	• ↓ Cardiac output
Gastrointestinal System	
• Vague abdominal pain	• Abdominal cramps
• Anorexia	• Fecal incontinence (in older adult)
• Nausea and vomiting	• Malabsorption
• Constipation	
• Pancreatitis	
• Peptic ulcer disease	
• Cholelithiasis	
• Weight loss	
Laboratory Findings	
• ↑ Calcium	• ↓ Calcium
• ↓ Phosphorus	• ↑ Phosphorus
Musculoskeletal System	
• Weakness, fatigue	• Weakness, fatigue
• Skeletal pain	• Painful muscle cramps
• Backache	• Skeletal x-ray changes, osteosclerosis
• Pain on weight bearing	• Soft tissue calcification
• Osteoporosis	• Problems walking
• Pathologic fractures of long bones	
• Compression fractures of spine; kyphosis	
• ↓ Muscle tone, muscle atrophy	
Neurologic System	
• Lethargy, weakness, fatigue	• Weakness, fatigue
• Psychosis, depression	• Depression
• Depressed reflexes	• Hyperreflexia, muscle cramps
• Personality changes	• Personality changes
• Irritability	• Irritability
• Impaired memory	• Impaired memory
• Delirium, confusion, coma	• Disorientation, confusion (in older adult)
• Headache	• Headache, ↑ intracranial pressure
• Poor coordination	• Tetany, seizures
• Gait abnormalities	• Positive Chvostek and Trousseau signs
• Psychomotor retardation	• Tremor
• Paresthesias	• Paresthesias of lips, hands, feet
Renal/Urinary System	
• Hypercalciuria	• Urinary frequency
• Kidney stones	• Urinary incontinence
• Urinary tract infections	
• Polyuria	
Skin	
• Skin necrosis	• Dry, scaly skin
• Moist skin	• Hair loss on scalp and body
	• Brittle nails, transverse ridging
	• Lack of tooth enamel
Visual System	
• Impaired vision	• Eye changes, including lenticular opacities, cataracts, papilledema
• Corneal calcification	

Severe hypercalcemia is managed with IV sodium chloride and loop diuretics, such as furosemide, to increase urinary calcium excretion. Several drugs help to lower calcium levels, but they do not treat the underlying problem. Bisphosphonates (e.g., alendronate) inhibit osteoclastic bone resorption, normalizing serum calcium levels and improving bone mineral density. IV bisphosphonates (e.g., pamidronate) can quickly lower serum calcium in patients with dangerously high levels. Phosphates are given if the patient has normal renal function and low serum phosphate levels.

Calcimimetic agents (e.g., cinacalcet [Sensipar]) increase the sensitivity of calcium receptors on the parathyroid gland, resulting in decreased PTH secretion and calcium blood levels. They are useful in treating secondary hyperparathyroidism in those with chronic kidney disease on dialysis or in patients with parathyroid cancer.

❖ NURSING MANAGEMENT: HYPERPARATHYROIDISM

Nursing care for the patient after a parathyroidectomy is similar to that for a patient after thyroidectomy. The major complications are bleeding and fluid and electrolyte problems. *Tetany,* a condition of neuromuscular hyperexcitability from a sudden decrease in calcium levels, is another concern. It is usually apparent early in the postoperative period but may develop over several days. Mild tetany, characterized by unpleasant tingling of the hands and around the mouth, may be present but should decrease over time. If tetany becomes more severe (e.g., muscular spasms, laryngospasms), IV calcium may be given. IV calcium gluconate should be readily available for patients after parathyroidectomy in case acute tetany occurs.

Monitor intake and output to evaluate fluid status. Assess calcium, potassium, phosphate, and magnesium levels frequently. Monitor Chvostek and Trousseau signs (see Fig. 17.15). Encourage mobility to promote bone calcification.

If surgery is not done, treatment to relieve symptoms and prevent complications is started. Help the patient to adapt the meal plan to their lifestyle. A referral to a dietitian may be helpful. Because immobility can worsen bone loss, stress the importance of an exercise program. Encourage the patient to keep the regular follow-up appointments. Teach the patient the symptoms of hypocalcemia and hypercalcemia and to report them if they occur. Hypocalcemia and hypercalcemia are discussed in Chapter 17.

HYPOPARATHYROIDISM

Hypoparathyroidism is an uncommon condition associated with inadequate circulating PTH. It is characterized by hypocalcemia due to a lack of PTH to maintain serum calcium levels. PTH resistance at the cellular level may occur *(pseudohypoparathyroidism)*. This is caused by a genetic defect resulting in hypocalcemia despite normal or high PTH levels. It is often associated with hypothyroidism and hypogonadism.

The most common cause is iatrogenic. This may include accidental removal of the parathyroid glands or damage to the vascular supply of the glands during neck surgery (e.g., thyroidectomy). Idiopathic hypoparathyroidism resulting from the absence, fatty replacement, or atrophy of the glands is rare. It usually occurs early in life and may be associated with other endocrine disorders. Affected patients may have antiparathyroid antibodies. Severe hypomagnesemia (e.g., malnutrition, alcohol use, renal failure) can suppress PTH secretion. Other causes include tumors and heavy metal poisoning.

The features of acute hypoparathyroidism are due to hypocalcemia (Table 54.15). Sudden decreases in calcium levels cause tetany, characterized by tingling of the lips and stiffness in the extremities. Painful tonic spasms of smooth and skeletal muscles can cause dysphagia and laryngospasms, which compromise breathing. Lethargy, anxiety, and personality changes may occur. Abnormal laboratory findings include decreased serum calcium and PTH and increased phosphate levels.

Interprofessional and Nursing Care

Treatment goals are to treat acute complications, such as tetany, maintain normal serum calcium levels, and prevent long-term complications. Emergency treatment of tetany after surgery requires IV calcium administration.

Give IV calcium slowly. Use ECG monitoring when giving calcium, because high serum calcium levels can cause hypotension, serious dysrhythmias, or cardiac arrest. The patient who takes digoxin is especially vulnerable. Assess IV patency. Calcium chloride can cause venous irritation and inflammation. Extravasation may cause cellulitis, necrosis, and tissue sloughing.

Rebreathing may partially relieve the acute neuromuscular symptoms from hypocalcemia, including muscle cramps and mild tetany. Have the patient breathe in and out of a paper bag or breathing mask. This reduces CO_2 excretion from the lungs, increases carbonic acid levels in the blood, and lowers the pH. A lower pH (acidic environment) enhances calcium ionization. This causes more total body calcium to be available in the active form.

> **CHECK YOUR PRACTICE**
>
> You are caring for a 62-year-old patient admitted to your unit from the PACU. The patient had a total thyroidectomy for papillary thyroid cancer. As you are preparing to give oral pain medication, the patient says his mouth feels "numb" like it does after he goes to the dentist. The patient asks if this is normal.
>
> - How do you respond?
> - What complication do you suspect could be occurring?
> - What assessments do you need to make?
> - Describe the actions needed if this complication is occurring.

Teach the patient how to manage long-term drug and nutrition therapy. Most patients receive oral calcium supplements, magnesium supplements, and vitamin D. We usually do not recommend PTH replacement because of the expense and need for parenteral administration. Vitamin D (e.g., 1,25-dihydroxycholecalciferol, calcitriol) is used to enhance intestinal calcium absorption. It increases calcium levels rapidly and is quickly metabolized.

A high-calcium meal plan includes foods, such as dark green vegetables, soybeans, and tofu. Tell the patient to avoid foods containing oxalic acid (e.g., spinach, rhubarb) because they inhibit calcium absorption. Teach the patient about the need for follow-up care, including monitoring of calcium levels 3 or 4 times a year.

ADRENAL CORTEX PROBLEMS

Adrenal cortex steroid hormones have 3 main classifications: glucocorticoids, mineralocorticoids, and androgens. Glucocorticoids regulate metabolism, increase glucose levels, and are critical in the physiologic stress response. The primary glucocorticoid is cortisol. Mineralocorticoids regulate sodium and potassium balance. The primary mineralocorticoid is aldosterone. Androgens contribute to growth and development in both genders and to sexual development in men. The term *corticosteroid* refers to any of these 3 types of hormones made by the adrenal cortex.

CUSHING SYNDROME

Etiology and Pathophysiology

Cushing syndrome is a clinical condition that results from chronic exposure to excess corticosteroids, especially glucocorticoids.[21] Several conditions can cause Cushing syndrome. The most common is iatrogenic administration of exogenous corticosteroids (e.g., prednisone). About 85% of the cases of endogenous Cushing syndrome are due to an ACTH-secreting pituitary adenoma (Cushing disease). Less common causes include adrenal tumors and ectopic ACTH production by tumors (usually of the lung or pancreas) outside of the hypothalamic-pituitary-adrenal axis. Cushing disease and primary adrenal tumors are more common in women in the 20- to 40-year-old age-group. Ectopic ACTH production is more common in men (Box 54.1).

Clinical Manifestations

Manifestations occur in most body systems. They are related to excess corticosteroid levels (Table 54.16). Although signs of glucocorticoid excess usually predominate, symptoms of mineralocorticoid and androgen excess can occur.

Corticosteroid excess causes pronounced changes in physical appearance (Fig. 54.10). Weight gain is the most common. It results from the accumulation of adipose tissue in the trunk (centripetal obesity), face ("moon face"), and cervical areas ("buffalo hump") (Fig. 54.11). Hyperglycemia occurs because of glucose intolerance from cortisol-induced insulin resistance and increased gluconeogenesis by

TABLE 54.16 Manifestations of Adrenocortical Problems

System	Cushing Syndrome	Addison Disease
Glucocorticoids		
General appearance	Truncal obesity, thin extremities, rounding of face (moon face), fat deposits on back of neck and shoulders (buffalo hump) (Fig. 54.11)	Weight loss, emaciation
Cardiovascular	↑ BP, hypervolemia, edema of lower extremities	↓ BP, tendency to develop refractory shock, vasodilation
GI	↑ Secretion of pepsin and HCl acid, risk for peptic ulcer disease, anorexia	Anorexia, nausea and vomiting, cramping abdominal pain, diarrhea
Immune	Inhibition of immune response, suppression of allergic response	Tendency for coexisting autoimmune diseases
Metabolic	Hyperglycemia, negative nitrogen balance, dyslipidemia	↓ Sodium, insulin sensitivity, fever
Musculoskeletal	Muscle wasting in extremities, fatigue, osteoporosis, awkward gait, back pain, weakness, compression fractures	Fatigue
Psychologic	Euphoria, irritability, depression, insomnia, anxiety	Depression, exhaustion or irritability, confusion, delusions
Renal/urinary	Glycosuria, hypercalciuria, risk for kidney stones	
Skin	Thin, fragile skin, purplish red striae (Fig. 54.12). Petechial hemorrhages, bruises. Florid cheeks (plethora), acne, poor wound healing	Bronzed or smoky hyperpigmentation of face, neck, hands (especially creases) (Fig. 54.13), buccal membranes, nipples, genitalia, and scars (if pituitary function normal). Vitiligo, alopecia
Mineralocorticoids		
Cardiovascular	↑ BP, hypervolemia	Hypovolemia, tendency toward shock, decreased cardiac output
Fluid and electrolytes	Marked sodium and water retention, edema, marked ↓ potassium, alkalosis	Sodium loss, ↓ volume of extracellular fluid, ↑ potassium, salt craving
Androgens		
Musculoskeletal	Muscle wasting and weakness	↓ Muscle size and tone
Reproductive	*Women:* Menstrual irregularities and enlargement of clitoris *Men:* Gynecomastia and testicular atrophy	*Women:* ↓ Libido in women *Men:* No effect in men
Skin	Hirsutism, acne, hyperpigmentation	↓ Axillary and pubic hair (in women)

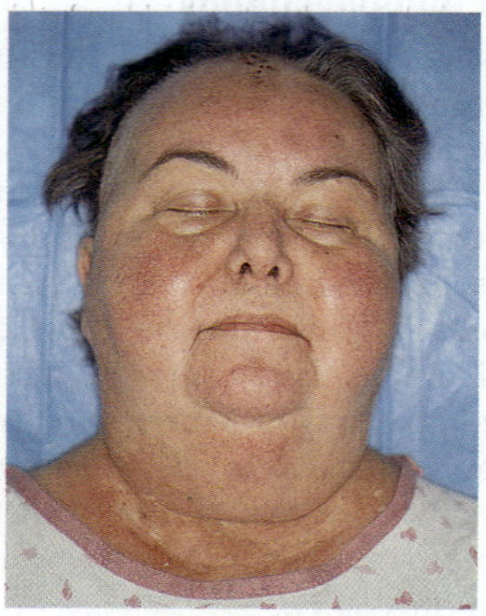

Fig. 54.10 Cushing syndrome. Facies include a rounded face ("moon face") with thin, reddened skin. Hirsutism may be present. (From Seidel HM, Ball JW, Dains JE, et al.: *Mosby's guide to physical examination*, ed 6, St Louis, 2006, Mosby.)

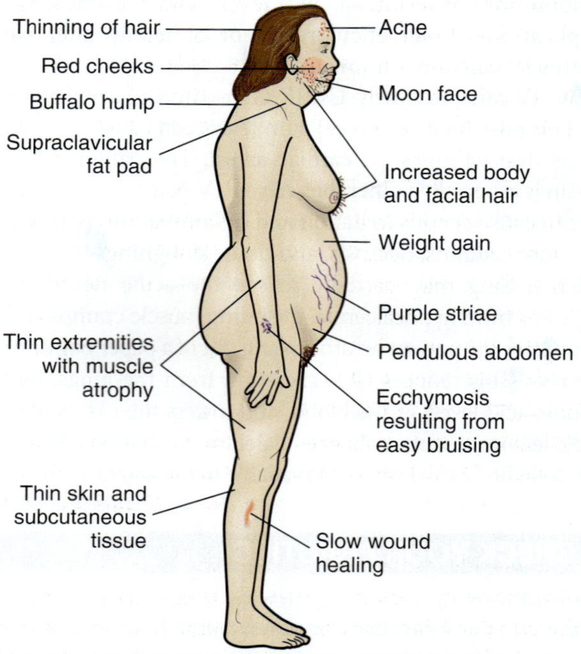

Fig. 54.11 Common characteristics of Cushing syndrome.

the liver. Muscle wasting causes weakness, especially in the extremities. A loss of bone matrix leads to osteoporosis and back pain. The loss of collagen makes the skin weaker, thinner, and more easily bruised. Purplish red striae (usually depressed below the skin surface) appear on the abdomen, breast, or buttocks (Fig. 54.12). Catabolic processes lead to a delay in wound healing.

Mineralocorticoid excess may cause hypokalemia from potassium excretion and hypertension from fluid retention. Adrenal androgen excess may cause severe acne, the development of male characteristics in women, and feminization in men. Menstrual problems and hirsutism in women and gynecomastia and impotence in men occur more often with adrenal cancer.

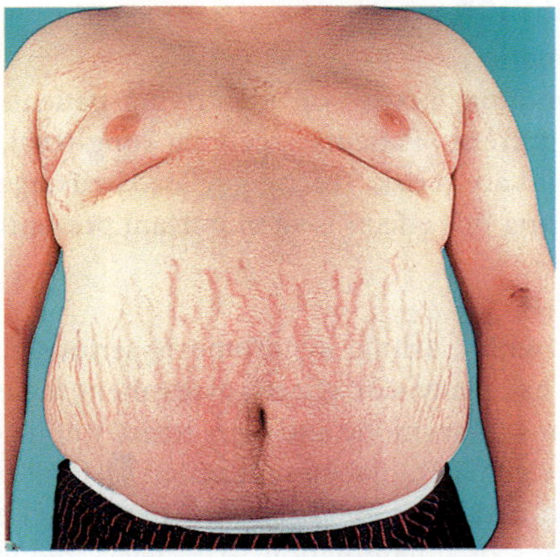

Fig. 54.12 Cushing syndrome. Truncal obesity; broad, purple striae; and easy bruising (left antecubital fossa). (From Chew SL, Leslie D: *Clinical endocrinology and diabetes: an illustrated colour text,* Edinburgh, 2006, Churchill Livingstone.)

Diagnostic Studies

Diagnosing Cushing syndrome begins with confirming increased plasma cortisol levels. We use 3 tests: (1) midnight or late-night salivary cortisol, (2) low-dose dexamethasone suppression test, and (3) 24-hour urine cortisol. Urine cortisol levels higher than 100 mcg/24 hr indicate Cushing syndrome. Urine levels of 17-ketosteroids may be high. A CT scan or MRI of the pituitary and adrenal glands can detect a tumor.

Plasma ACTH levels may be low, normal, or high, depending on the underlying cause. High or normal ACTH levels indicate Cushing disease. Low or undetectable levels indicate an adrenal or medication cause. Other findings that may be present but are not diagnostic of Cushing syndrome include leukocytosis, lymphopenia, eosinopenia, hyperglycemia, glycosuria, hypercalciuria, and osteoporosis. Hypokalemia and alkalosis occur with ectopic ACTH syndrome and adrenal cancer.

Interprofessional Care

The primary goal of treatment is to normalize hormone secretion. The treatment depends on the underlying cause (Table 54.17). If the cause is a pituitary adenoma, the standard treatment is surgical removal of the pituitary tumor using the transsphenoidal approach. Radiation therapy is an option for patients who are not surgical candidates.

An adrenalectomy is done if Cushing syndrome is caused by adrenal tumors or hyperplasia. Sometimes, bilateral adrenalectomy is needed. A laparoscopic approach is used unless adrenal cancer is suspected. Then an open surgical adrenalectomy is usually done.

Patients with ectopic ACTH-secreting tumors are best managed by removing the tumor (usually lung or pancreas). This is usually possible when the tumor is benign. If a cancerous tumor has already metastasized, surgical removal may not be possible or successful.

When the patient is a poor candidate for surgery or prior surgery has failed, we can try drug therapy. The goal of drug therapy is to suppress the synthesis and secretion of cortisol from the adrenal gland *(medical adrenalectomy).* Drugs used include ketoconazole and mitotane. These are used cautiously because they are often toxic at the dosages needed to reduce cortisol secretion. Hydrocortisone or prednisone may be needed to avoid adrenal insufficiency. Mifepristone (Korlym) can help control hyperglycemia in patients with endogenous Cushing syndrome who have type 2 diabetes.

If Cushing syndrome developed because of prolonged use of corticosteroids (e.g., prednisone), we may try several options. We can gradually discontinue corticosteroid therapy, reduce the corticosteroid dose, or convert to alternate-day dosing. Gradual tapering of the corticosteroids is necessary to avoid potentially life-threatening adrenal insufficiency. In alternate-day dosing, twice the daily dosage of a shorter-acting corticosteroid is given every other morning to minimize hypothalamic-pituitary-adrenal suppression, growth suppression, and altered appearance. This plan is not an option if the corticosteroids are given as hormone therapy.

TABLE 54.17 Interprofessional Care

Cushing Syndrome

Diagnostic Assessment

- History and physical assessment
- Dexamethasone suppression test
- 24-Hr urine for free cortisol and 17-ketosteroids
- Plasma and salivary cortisol levels
- Plasma ACTH levels
- CBC with WBC differential
- Blood chemistries for sodium, potassium, glucose
- CT scan, MRI

Management

Pituitary Adenoma

- Transsphenoidal resection
- Radiation therapy

Adrenocortical Adenoma, Cancer, or Hyperplasia

- Adrenalectomy (open or laparoscopic)
- Drug therapy (e.g., ketoconazole, mitotane, mifepristone [Korlym])

Ectopic ACTH-Secreting Tumor

- Treatment of the tumor (surgical removal or radiation)

Exogenous Corticosteroid Therapy

- Discontinue or change the dose of exogenous corticosteroids

NURSING MANAGEMENT: CUSHING SYNDROME

Assessment

Subjective and objective data that should be obtained from a patient with Cushing syndrome are outlined in Table 54.18.

Clinical Problems

Clinical problems for the patient with Cushing syndrome may include:

- Risk for infection
- Nutritionally compromised

TABLE 54.18 NURSING ASSESSMENT

Cushing Syndrome

Subjective Data

Important Health Information

Health history: Pituitary tumor (Cushing disease). Adrenal, pancreatic, or pulmonary cancer. GI bleeding, frequent infections

Medications: Corticosteroids

Functional Health Patterns

Health perception–health management: Malaise

Nutritional-metabolic: Weight gain, anorexia. Prolonged wound healing, easy bruising

Elimination: Polyuria

Activity-exercise: Weakness, fatigue

Sleep: Insomnia, poor sleep quality

Cognitive-perceptual: Headache. Back, joint, bone, and rib pain. Poor concentration and memory

Self-perception–self-concept: Negative feelings about changes in personal appearance

Sexuality-reproductive: Amenorrhea, impotence, ↓ libido

Coping–stress tolerance: Anxiety, mood changes, emotional lability, psychosis

Objective Data

Cardiovascular

↑ BP

General

Truncal obesity, supraclavicular fat pads, buffalo hump, moon face

Musculoskeletal

Muscle wasting, thin extremities, awkward gait

Reproductive

Gynecomastia, testicular atrophy (in men), enlarged clitoris (in women)

Skin

Hirsutism of body and face, thinning of head hair. Thin, friable skin. Acne, petechiae, purpura, hyperpigmentation. Purplish red striae on breasts, buttocks, and abdomen. Edema of lower extremities

Possible Diagnostic Findings

Hyperglycemia, ↓ potassium, dyslipidemia, polycythemia, lymphocytopenia, eosinopenia. ↑ Plasma cortisol, ↑ salivary cortisol. High, low, or normal ACTH levels. Abnormal dexamethasone suppression test. ↑ Urine free cortisol, 17-ketosteroids. Glycosuria, hypercalciuria. Osteoporosis on x-ray

- Disturbed body image
- Impaired tissue integrity

Additional information on clinical problems and interventions is presented in eNursing Care Plan 54.3 for the patient with Cushing syndrome (available on the website for this chapter).

◆ Planning

The overall goals are that the patient with Cushing syndrome will (1) have relief of symptoms, (2) avoid serious complications, (3) maintain a positive self-image, and (4) actively take part in the therapeutic plan.

◆ Implementation

◆ Health Promotion

Health promotion focuses on identifying patients at risk for Cushing syndrome. Patients receiving long-term, exogenous corticosteroids are at risk. Teaching related to using medications and monitoring side effects is an important preventive measure.

◆ Acute Care

The patient with Cushing syndrome is seriously ill. Because the therapy has many side effects, assessment focuses on signs and symptoms of hormone and drug toxicity and complicating conditions (e.g., CVD, diabetes, infection). Monitor vital signs, daily weight, and glucose. Assess for infection. Because signs and symptoms of inflammation (e.g., fever, redness) may be minimal or absent, assess for pain, loss of function, and purulent drainage. Monitor for signs and symptoms of thromboembolic events, such as pulmonary emboli (e.g., sudden chest pain, dyspnea, tachypnea).

Another important focus of care is emotional support. Changes in appearance, such as truncal obesity, multiple bruises, hirsutism in women, and gynecomastia in men, can be distressing. The patient may feel unattractive, repulsive, or unwanted. You can help by being sensitive to the patient's feelings and offering respect and unconditional acceptance (Box 54.2). Reassure the patient that the physical changes and much of the emotional lability will resolve when hormone levels return to normal.

If treatment involves surgical removal of a pituitary adenoma, an adrenal tumor, or 1 or both adrenal glands, nursing care will include preoperative and postoperative care.

Preoperative care. Before surgery, the patient should be in optimal physical condition. Hypertension and hyperglycemia must be under control. Hypokalemia must be corrected with diet and potassium supplements. A high-protein diet helps correct protein depletion. Preoperative teaching depends on the type of surgery planned (hypophysectomy or adrenalectomy). Include information about the expected care after surgery.

Postoperative care. Surgery on the adrenal glands poses great risks. Because the adrenal glands are vascular, there is an increased risk for bleeding. After both laparoscopic and open adrenalectomy, the patient may have a nasogastric tube, a urinary catheter, IV therapy, and central venous pressure monitoring. Initiate VTE prophylaxis.

Manipulating glandular tissue during surgery may release large amounts of hormones into the circulation. This can produce marked fluctuations in the metabolic processes affected by these hormones. After surgery, BP, fluid balance, and electrolyte levels may be unstable due to these hormone fluctuations.

High doses of corticosteroids (e.g., hydrocortisone) are given IV during surgery and for several days afterward to ensure adequate responses to the stress of the procedure. If large amounts of endogenous hormone were released into the systemic circulation during surgery, the patient is likely to have hypertension, increasing the risk for bleeding. High corticosteroid levels cause problems with glycemic control, increase risk for infection, and delay wound healing.

The critical period for circulatory instability is 24 to 48 hours after surgery. During this time, you must be alert for signs of

BOX 54.2 EVIDENCE-BASED PRACTICE

Health-Related Quality of Life in Patients With Cushing Syndrome

You are working in the endocrinology clinic when B.F., a 47-year-old patient, checks in for an appointment. B.F. was diagnosed with Cushing syndrome after long-term use of glucocorticoid inhalers for treatment of asthma but is now in biochemical remission. His wife is with him today. When B.F. is having blood drawn for laboratory testing, his wife tells you he seems depressed and rarely sleeps through the night. She adds, "He battled so hard to get that disease in remission…did everything he was supposed to do…but he doesn't seem to enjoy life now."

Making Clinical Decisions

Synthesis of Best Available Evidence

Long-term exposure to excessive cortisol affects a patient's health. This can affect health-related quality of life. While cortisol secretion can normalize (biochemical remission), clinical features of Cushing syndrome may be slower to resolve (e.g., obesity, muscle weakness, skin changes). Research suggests patients may have difficulty achieving recovery of all social, professional, and personal aspects of daily functioning.

Sleep problems have been found through self-report of patients in remission of Cushing syndrome. Impaired sleep can affect quality of life, including psychologic aspects of well-being. Research suggests physical activity may affect sleep quality.

Clinician Expertise

When B.F. returns to the examination room after laboratory testing, you take his vital signs and begin usual intake questions. You also ask, "How have you been sleeping? Do you have enough energy for regular activity?" The patient looks at his wife but initially says nothing. You continue, "We know from research that people like you, who are in biochemical remission from Cushing syndrome, may have poor sleep quality and may even become depressed during their clinical recovery. Physical activity can not only improve sleep but can help with some of the other symptoms that may be bothering you."

Patient Preferences and Values

B.F. responds, "Some days I don't really feel like doing much, but I know I need to get active again to try to lose weight. Are there any limits to what I can do?" You encourage B.F. responding, "Let's talk about the things you like to do that will help you become more active again."

Implications for Nursing Practice

1. What aspects of health-related quality of life may be affected by Cushing syndrome?
2. How can we best address these issues with our patients?

Reference for Evidence

Moyers SA, Tiemensma J: The association between physical activity, sleep, and quality of life in in patients in bio-chemical remission from Cushing's syndrome, *Qual Life Res* 29:2089, 2020.

corticosteroid imbalance. Report any rapid or significant changes in BP, respirations, or heart rate. Monitor intake and output carefully and assess for imbalances. Give IV corticosteroids as ordered. The dosage is adjusted depending on the patient's manifestations and fluid and electrolyte balance. Oral doses are given as tolerated. After IV corticosteroids are withdrawn, keep the IV line open for quick administration of corticosteroids or vasopressors. Obtain morning urine samples at the same time each morning for cortisol measurement to evaluate the surgery's effectiveness.

If corticosteroid dosage is tapered too quickly after surgery, acute adrenal insufficiency may develop. Vomiting, weakness, dehydration, and hypotension are signs of hypocortisolism. The patient may have painful joints, itching, or peeling skin and severe emotional problems. Report these signs and symptoms so that drug doses can be adjusted as needed.

The patient is usually kept on bed rest until the BP stabilizes. Be alert for subtle signs of infection because the usual inflammatory responses are suppressed. To prevent infection, provide meticulous care when changing the dressing and during any other procedures that involve access to body cavities, circulation, or areas under the skin.

◆ Ambulatory Care

Discharge teaching is based on the patient's lack of endogenous corticosteroids and resulting inability to react physiologically to stressors. Consider a home health nurse referral, especially for older adults, because of the need for ongoing evaluation and teaching. Teach the patient to always wear a Medic Alert bracelet and carry medical identification and instructions in a wallet or purse. Teach the patient to avoid exposure to extreme temperatures, infections, and emotional situations. Stress may cause acute adrenal insufficiency because the remaining adrenal tissue cannot meet an increased hormone demand. Many patients need lifetime replacement therapy. They should be prepared for it to take several months to adjust the hormone dose satisfactorily. Teach patients to adjust their corticosteroid replacement therapy by their stress levels. Consult with the patient's HCP to determine the parameters for dosage changes if this plan is feasible. If the patient cannot adjust their own medication or if weakness, fainting, fever, or nausea and vomiting occur, the patient should contact the HCP for a possible adjustment in corticosteroid dosage.

◆ Evaluation

The expected outcomes are that the patient with Cushing syndrome will:

- Have no signs or symptoms of infection
- Maintain weight appropriate for height
- State acceptance of appearance and treatment plan
- Show healing of skin and maintaining intact skin

ADRENOCORTICAL INSUFFICIENCY

Etiology and Pathophysiology

Adrenocortical insufficiency (hypofunction of the adrenal cortex) may be from a primary cause (**Addison disease**) or a secondary cause (lack of pituitary ACTH secretion). In Addison disease, all 3 classes of adrenal corticosteroids (glucocorticoids, mineralocorticoids, and androgens) are reduced. In secondary adrenocortical insufficiency, corticosteroids and androgens are deficient but mineralocorticoids rarely are. ACTH deficiency may be caused by pituitary disease or suppression of the hypothalamic-pituitary axis because of the use of exogenous corticosteroids.

Up to 80% of Addison disease cases in the United States are caused by an autoimmune response.[22] Autoimmune adrenalitis causes the adrenal cortex to be destroyed by antibodies. This

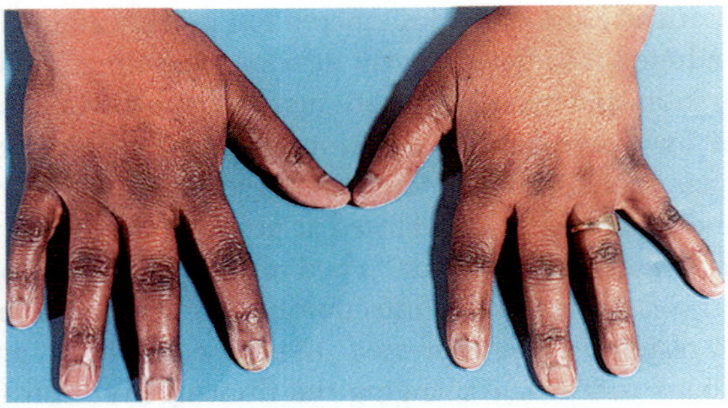

Fig. 54.13 Hyperpigmentation typically seen in Addison disease. (From Chew SL, Leslie D: *Clinical endocrinology and diabetes: an illustrated colour text,* Edinburgh, 2006, Churchill Livingstone.)

results in loss of glucocorticoid, mineralocorticoid, and adrenal androgen hormones. Addison disease can be present along with other endocrine problems. This is known as *autoimmune polyglandular syndrome*. It is most common in white females. Those with autoimmune adrenalitis often have other autoimmune disorders, such as type 1 diabetes, autoimmune thyroid disease, pernicious anemia, and celiac disease.

Although tuberculosis causes Addison disease worldwide, it is now an uncommon cause in the United States. Other causes include amyloidosis, fungal infections (e.g., histoplasmosis), acquired immunodeficiency syndrome (AIDS), and metastatic cancer. Iatrogenic Addison disease may be due to adrenal hemorrhage, often related to anticoagulant therapy, chemotherapy, or bilateral adrenalectomy. Adrenal insufficiency most often occurs in adults younger than 60 years of age. It affects both genders equally.

Clinical Manifestations

Because manifestations do not tend to become evident until 90% of the adrenal cortex is destroyed, the disease is often advanced before it is diagnosed. The manifestations have a slow onset and include anorexia, nausea, progressive weakness, fatigue, and weight loss. Increased ACTH causes the striking bronze-colored skin hyperpigmentation. It is seen mainly in sun-exposed areas of the body, at pressure points, over joints, and in the creases, especially palmar creases (Fig. 54.13). Skin changes are likely due to increased secretion of β-lipotropin (which contains melanocyte-stimulating hormone [MSH]). MSH is increased because of decreased negative feedback and subsequent low corticosteroid levels. Other manifestations include abdominal pain, diarrhea, headache, orthostatic hypotension, salt craving, and joint pain. Irritability and depression may occur in primary adrenal hypofunction.

Patients with secondary adrenocortical hypofunction may have many signs and symptoms similar to those of patients with Addison disease. However, they usually do not have hyperpigmented skin because ACTH levels are low.

Complications

Patients with adrenocortical insufficiency are at risk for acute adrenal insufficiency *(addisonian crisis)*.[23] It is a life-threatening emergency caused by insufficient adrenocortical hormones or a sudden sharp decrease in these hormones. Triggers of addisonian crisis is include (1) stress (e.g., infection, surgery), (2) sudden withdrawal of corticosteroid hormone therapy, (3) adrenal surgery, or (4) sudden pituitary gland destruction.

During acute adrenal insufficiency, the patient has severe manifestations of glucocorticoid and mineralocorticoid deficiencies. These include hypotension, tachycardia, dehydration, hyponatremia, hyperkalemia, hypoglycemia, fever, weakness, and confusion. Hypotension may lead to shock. Circulatory collapse from adrenal insufficiency is often unresponsive to the usual treatment (vasopressors and fluid replacement). GI manifestations include severe vomiting, diarrhea, and pain in the abdomen. Pain may occur in the lower back and legs.

Diagnostic Studies

The ACTH stimulation test is a common test to diagnose adrenal insufficiency. Baseline cortisol and ACTH levels are measured, and the patient is given an IV injection of synthetic ACTH (cosyntropin). Cortisol and ACTH levels are rechecked after 30 and 60 minutes. The normal response is a rise in blood cortisol levels. People with Addison disease have little or no increase in cortisol levels. Those with primary adrenal insufficiency have a high ACTH level.

When the response to the ACTH test is abnormal, a corticotropin-releasing hormone (CRH) stimulation test may be done. The patient is given an IV injection of synthetic CRH, and blood is taken after 30 and 60 minutes. Those with Addison disease have high ACTH levels but no cortisol. People with secondary adrenal insufficiency from pituitary or hypothalamus problems do not make ACTH or have a delayed response.

Other abnormal laboratory findings may include hyperkalemia, hypochloremia, hyponatremia, hypoglycemia, anemia, and increased BUN levels. An ECG may show low voltage and peaked T waves caused by hyperkalemia. CT scans and MRI can identify other causes, including tumors, fungal infections, tuberculosis, or adrenal calcification.

Interprofessional and Nursing Care

Treatment focuses on managing the underlying cause when possible. The mainstay is often lifelong hormone therapy with glucocorticoids and mineralocorticoids (Table 54.19). Overall, patients who take their medications consistently can expect a normal life expectancy. Hydrocortisone, the most common form of hormone therapy, has both glucocorticoid and mineralocorticoid properties. Mineralocorticoids are replaced with fludrocortisone. Women need androgen replacement with dehydroepiandrosterone (DHEA) as their only source of androgen production is the adrenal glands. Increased salt is added to the diet.

As a nurse, you have a key role in the long-term management of Addison disease. The serious nature of the disease and the need for lifelong hormone therapy necessitate a comprehensive teaching plan. Table 54.20 outlines the major areas to include in a teaching plan.

Glucocorticoids are usually given in divided doses, two-thirds in the morning and one-third in the afternoon. Mineralocorticoids are given once daily, preferably in the morning. This schedule reflects normal circadian rhythm in

TABLE 54.19 Interprofessional Care

Addison Disease

Diagnostic Assessment
- History and physical assessment
- ACTH stimulation test
- Serum cortisol and ACTH
- Urine cortisol and aldosterone
- CRH suppression test
- Serum electrolytes
- CT scan, MRI

Management
- Daily glucocorticoid (e.g., prednisone, hydrocortisone) replacement (two-thirds on awakening in morning, one-third in late afternoon)
- Daily mineralocorticoid (fludrocortisone) in morning
- ↑ Salt in the diet
- Androgen replacement with dehydroepiandrosterone (DHEA) for women
- Salt additives for excess heat or humidity
- ↑ Doses of glucocorticoid for stress situations (e.g., surgery, hospitalization)

TABLE 54.20 PATIENT & CAREGIVER TEACHING

Addison Disease

Include the following information in the teaching plan for the patient with Addison disease and the caregiver:

1. Names, dosages, and actions of drugs
2. Symptoms of overdosage and underdosage
3. Conditions requiring increased dosage (e.g., trauma, infection, surgery, emotional crisis)
4. Action to take related to changes in medication
   - Increased dose of corticosteroid
   - Self-administration of large dose of corticosteroid IM
   - Consult with HCP
5. Preventing infection and need for prompt and vigorous treatment of existing infections
6. Need for lifelong replacement therapy
7. Need for lifelong medical supervision
8. Need to carry medical identification
9. Fall prevention
10. Adverse effects of corticosteroid therapy and prevention techniques
11. Special instruction for patients with diabetes and management of glucose when taking corticosteroids

endogenous hormone secretion and decreases the side effects of corticosteroid therapy. Teach patients using mineralocorticoid therapy how to take their BP, increase salt intake, and report any significant changes to the HCP.

The patient with Addison disease needs an increased dosage of corticosteroids in stressful situations to prevent addisonian crisis. Examples of situations requiring corticosteroid adjustment are fever, influenza, tooth extraction, and rigorous physical activity, such as playing sports on a hot day or distance running. Provide written and verbal instructions on when to change the dose. Review stress management techniques. If vomiting or diarrhea occurs, as may happen with gastroenteritis, the patient should notify the HCP at once. They may need electrolyte replacement and IV cortisol administration.

Teach patients the signs and symptoms of corticosteroid deficiency and excess (Cushing syndrome) and to report these signs to the HCP so that the drug dose can be adjusted. The patient should wear an identification bracelet (Medic Alert) and carry a wallet card saying they have Addison disease so that appropriate therapy can be started in an emergency. The patient should carry an emergency kit with 100 mg of IM hydrocortisone and syringes. Teach the patient and caregiver how to give an IM injection.

When the patient with Addison disease is hospitalized, nursing care focuses on monitoring the patient while correcting fluid and electrolyte balance. Assess vital signs and neurologic status. Monitor for signs of fluid volume deficit and electrolyte imbalance. Obtain a daily weight, and keep an accurate intake and output record. Take a medication history to see if there are drugs that can interact with corticosteroids. These drugs include oral hypoglycemics, cardiac glycosides, oral contraceptives, anticoagulants, and NSAIDs.

Note changes in BP, weight gain, weakness, and other manifestations of Cushing syndrome. Guard the patient against exposure to infection and help with daily hygiene. Protect the patient from noise, light, and environmental temperature extremes. The patient cannot cope with these stresses because of the inability to make corticosteroids.

Addisonian crisis is a life-threatening emergency requiring aggressive management. Treatment is directed toward shock management and high-dose hydrocortisone replacement. Large volumes of IV fluid are given to reverse hypotension and electrolyte imbalances until BP returns to normal.

CORTICOSTEROID THERAPY

Corticosteroids are effective in treating many problems (Table 54.21). However, long-term corticosteroid therapy at therapeutic doses often leads to serious complications and side effects (Table 54.22). For this reason, corticosteroid therapy is not recommended for minor chronic conditions. Therapy should be reserved for problems that have a risk for death, permanent loss of function, or for which short-term therapy is likely to produce remission or recovery. We must weigh the potential benefits of treatment against the risks.

CHECK YOUR PRACTICE

You are working in the outpatient clinic. Your 30-year-old female patient has Cushing syndrome from high doses of prednisone use for autoimmune hepatitis. At her office visit today, she tells you, "I haven't been taking my prednisone because I'm gaining weight and I'm not happy with the way I look."
- How would you respond to her?

A beneficial effect of corticosteroids in one situation may be a harmful one in another. For example, decreasing inflammation in arthritis is an important therapeutic effect, but increasing the risk for infection is a harmful effect. Suppressing inflammation and the immune response may help save lives in persons with

TABLE 54.21 Drug Therapy

Diseases/Disorders Treated With Corticosteroids

Hormone Therapy
- Adrenal insufficiency
- Congenital adrenal hyperplasia

Therapeutic Effect

Allergic Reactions
- Anaphylaxis
- Bee stings
- Contact dermatitis
- Drug reactions
- Serum sickness
- Urticaria

Connective Tissue Problems
- Mixed connective tissue disorders
- Polymyositis
- Polyarteritis nodosa
- Rheumatoid arthritis
- Systemic lupus erythematosus

Endocrine Problems
- Hypercalcemia
- Hashimoto thyroiditis
- Thyrotoxicosis

GI Problems
- Inflammatory bowel disease
- Celiac disease

Liver Problems
- Alcoholic hepatitis
- Autoimmune hepatitis

Neurologic Problems
- Cerebral edema and increased intracranial pressure
- Head trauma

Pulmonary Diseases
- Aspiration pneumonia
- Asthma
- Chronic obstructive pulmonary disease

Other Problems
- Skin diseases
- Cancer, leukemia, lymphoma
- Immunosuppression
- Inflammation
- Nephrotic syndrome

anaphylaxis and in those receiving an organ transplant, but it can activate latent tuberculosis and increase the risk for infection and cancer. The vasopressive effect of corticosteroids is critical in allowing a person to function in stressful situations but can cause hypertension when used for drug therapy.

Detailed teaching is needed to ensure patient adherence. Corticosteroids given as nonreplacement therapy are taken once daily or once every other day. They should be taken early in the morning with food to decrease GI irritation. Because exogenous corticosteroid use may suppress endogenous ACTH and cortisol (suppression is time and dose dependent), emphasize the danger of abruptly stopping corticosteroid therapy to patients and caregivers. Corticosteroids taken for longer than 1 week will suppress adrenal production, and oral corticosteroids must be tapered. Ensure that higher doses of corticosteroids are prescribed in situations of physical or emotional stress.

Corticosteroid-induced osteoporosis is an important concern for patients who receive corticosteroid treatment for long periods (longer than 3 months).[24] Therapies to reduce bone resorption include increased calcium intake, vitamin D supplements, bisphosphonates (e.g., alendronate), and a low-impact exercise program. Measures to minimize the side effects and complications of corticosteroid therapy are outlined in Table 54.23.

HYPERALDOSTERONISM

Hyperaldosteronism (Conn syndrome) is characterized by excess aldosterone secretion. The main effects of aldosterone are (1) sodium retention and (2) potassium and hydrogen ion excretion. Thus the hallmark of this disease is hypertension with hypokalemic alkalosis. *Primary hyperaldosteronism* (PA) is most often caused by a small solitary adrenocortical adenoma. Sometimes, multiple lesions are involved and are associated with bilateral adrenal hyperplasia.

PA affects women more than men and usually occurs between 30 and 50 years of age. A genetic link has been found in some patients. PA causes up to 2% of all cases of hypertension. *Secondary hyperaldosteronism* occurs in response to a nonadrenal cause of increased aldosterone levels, such as renal artery stenosis, renin-secreting tumors, and chronic kidney disease.

Increased aldosterone levels cause sodium retention and potassium excretion. Sodium retention leads to hypernatremia, hypertension, and headache. Edema does not usually occur because the rate of sodium excretion increases, preventing more severe sodium retention. Potassium wasting leads to hypokalemia, which causes generalized muscle weakness, fatigue, dysrhythmias, glucose intolerance, and metabolic alkalosis that may lead to tetany.

Hyperaldosteronism should be suspected in hypertensive patients with hypokalemia who are not being treated with diuretics. PA causes increased sodium and aldosterone levels, decreased potassium levels, and decreased renin activity. A CT scan or MRI can detect an adenoma. If a tumor is not found, plasma 18-hydroxycorticosterone is measured after overnight bed rest. A level greater than 50 ng/dL indicates an adenoma.

DRUG ALERT

Corticosteroids
- Teach the patient not to abruptly stop these drugs.
- Monitor the patient for signs of infection.
- Have patients with diabetes closely monitor glucose.

TABLE 54.22 Drug Therapy

Effects and Side Effects of Corticosteroids
- Delayed wound healing with ↑ risk for wound dehiscence
- Fat from extremities redistributed to trunk and face
- Glucose intolerance
- Hypertension with ↑ risk for heart failure
- Hypocalcemia related to anti–vitamin D effect
- Hypokalemia
- ↑ Risk for infection
- Infection develops more rapidly and spreads more widely
- Mood and behavior changes
- Pathologic fractures, especially compression fractures of the vertebrae (osteoporosis)
- Peptic ulcer disease
- Pituitary ACTH synthesis suppressed
- Skeletal muscle atrophy and weakness
- Suppressed inflammatory response

Interprofessional and Nursing Care

The preferred treatment for PA is surgical removal of the adenoma (adrenalectomy).[25] A laparoscopic approach is most often used. Before surgery, patients should receive potassium-sparing diuretics (e.g., spironolactone) and antihypertensive agents to

TABLE 54.23 PATIENT & CAREGIVER TEACHING

Corticosteroid Therapy

Include the following instructions when teaching the patient and caregiver to manage corticosteroid therapy:

1. Follow a diet high in protein, calcium (at least 1500 mg/day), and potassium and low in fat and concentrated simple carbohydrates, such as sugar, syrups, and candy.
2. Ensure adequate rest and sleep, such as daily naps and avoiding caffeine late in the day.
3. Take part in an exercise program to help maintain bone integrity.
4. Recognize edema and ways to restrict sodium intake to <2000 mg/day if edema occurs.
5. Monitor glucose levels and recognize symptoms of hyperglycemia (e.g., polydipsia, polyuria, blurred vision). Report hyperglycemic symptoms or capillary glucose levels >120 mg/dL (10 mmol/L).
6. Notify HCP if heartburn after meals or epigastric pain that is not relieved by antacids occurs.
7. See an eye specialist yearly to assess for cataracts.
8. Use safety measures, such as getting up slowly from bed or a chair and good lighting, to avoid accidental injury.
9. Maintain appropriate hygiene practices.
10. Avoid contact with persons with colds or other contagious illnesses to prevent infection.
11. Inform all HCPs about long-term corticosteroid use.
12. Recognize need for higher doses of corticosteroids in times of physical and emotional stress.
13. Never abruptly stop the corticosteroids because this could lead to addisonian crisis and death.

normalize potassium levels and BP. Spironolactone and eplerenone block the binding of aldosterone to the mineralocorticoid receptor in the terminal distal tubules and collecting ducts of the kidney, thus increasing sodium and water excretion and potassium retention. Oral potassium supplements and sodium restrictions may be needed. However, potassium supplementation and a potassium-sparing diuretic should not be started simultaneously because of the risk for hyperkalemia.

Patients with bilateral adrenal hyperplasia are treated with a potassium-sparing diuretic. Calcium channel blockers may be used to control BP. Dexamethasone may be used to decrease adrenal hyperplasia.

Nursing care includes careful assessment of fluid and electrolyte balance (especially potassium) and cardiovascular status. Monitor BP frequently before and after surgery because unilateral adrenalectomy is successful in controlling hypertension in only 80% of patients with an adenoma. Teach patients receiving spironolactone about the possible side effects of gynecomastia, impotence, and menstrual disorders, as well as the signs and symptoms of hypokalemia and hyperkalemia. Review how to monitor their BP and the need for frequent monitoring. Stress the need for continued health care.

ADRENAL MEDULLA PROBLEMS

PHEOCHROMOCYTOMA

Pheochromocytoma is a rare condition caused by a tumor in the adrenal medulla. It affects the chromaffin cells, resulting in excess production of catecholamines (epinephrine, norepinephrine). The most dangerous immediate effect is severe hypertension. If left untreated, it may lead to encephalopathy, diabetes, cardiomyopathy, multiple organ failure, and death. It most often occurs in young to middle-aged adults. Pheochromocytoma may be inherited in persons with MEN.

The most striking findings are severe, episodic hypertension accompanied by severe, pounding headache; tachycardia with palpitations; profuse sweating; and unexplained abdominal or chest pain. Attacks can be induced by direct trauma, mechanical pressure to the tumor, stress (e.g., surgery, exercise, defecation, sexual intercourse, alcohol use, smoking), or many drugs, including antihypertensives, opioids, radiologic contrast media, and tricyclic antidepressants. Attacks can last from a few minutes to several hours.

The simplest and most reliable diagnostic test is measurement of urinary fractionated metanephrines (catecholamine metabolites) and fractionated catecholamines and creatinine, usually done as a 24-hour urine collection.[26] Values are increased in at least 95% of persons with pheochromocytoma. Serum catecholamines may be increased during an "attack." CT scans and MRI can detect tumors. Do not palpate the abdomen of a patient with suspected pheochromocytoma. It may cause the sudden release of catecholamines and severe hypertension.

Interprofessional and Nursing Care

The main treatment is surgical removal of the tumor. Treatment with α- and β-adrenergic receptor blockers is needed before surgery to control BP and prevent an intraoperative hypertensive crisis. Therapy begins with an α-adrenergic receptor blocker (e.g., doxazosin, prazosin, phenoxybenzamine) 10 to 14 days before surgery to reduce BP. After adequate α-adrenergic blockade, β-adrenergic receptor blockers (e.g., propranolol) are used to decrease tachycardia and dysrhythmias. If β-blockers are started too early, unopposed α-adrenergic stimulation can cause a hypertensive crisis. Therapy can cause orthostatic hypotension. Teach the patient to change positions slowly.

Surgery is usually done using a laparoscopic approach. Removing the adrenal tumor often cures the hypertension, but it does persist in about 10% to 30% of patients. If surgery is not an option, metyrosine (Demser) can decrease catecholamine production by the tumor.

Case finding is an important nursing role. The diagnosis of pheochromocytoma is often missed. Any patient with hypertension and symptoms of sympathoadrenal stimulation should be referred to an HCP. Assess for the classic triad of symptoms of pheochromocytoma: severe pounding headache, tachycardia, and profuse sweating. Monitor the BP often if the patient is having an "attack."

Make the patient as comfortable as possible. Monitor glucose levels to assess for diabetes. Patients need rest, proper nutrition, and emotional support during this period. Surgical care is similar to that for any patient undergoing adrenalectomy. Note that BP fluctuations from catecholamine excesses tend to be severe and must be carefully monitored. Emphasize the importance of follow-up and routine BP monitoring because hypertension may persist even when the tumor is removed.

Case Study

Graves Disease

(© Hemera Technologies/AbleStock.com/Thinkstock.)

Patient Profile

R.D., a 52-year-old woman, was admitted to the hospital with a high fever. No infection is found. Based upon her history, assessment, and laboratory findings, the HCP diagnosed R.D. with Graves disease.

Subjective Data

- Reports recent job loss because she is no longer able to tolerate work-related stress
- Symptoms include fatigue, unintentional weight loss, insomnia, palpitations, vision problems, sweating, heat intolerance

Objective Data

Physical Assessment

- Fever of 104°F (40°C)
- BP of 150/80 mm Hg, pulse of 132 beats/min, and respiratory rate of 26 breaths/min
- Hot, moist skin
- Fine tremors of the hands
- 4+ deep tendon reflexes and muscle strength of 1 to 2 out of 5
- Swelling to the anterior neck
- Excessive tearing of the eyes

Interprofessional Care

- Subtotal thyroidectomy planned for 2 months later
- Started on methimazole (Tapazole) and propranolol (Inderal LA)

Discussion Questions

1. ***Recognize***: Explain the cause of R.D.'s symptoms.
2. ***Analyze***: What diagnostic studies were probably ordered? What would the results have been to establish the diagnosis of Graves disease?
3. ***Analyze***: Why was surgery delayed?
4. ***Prioritize:*** What is the interprofessional team's top priority at this time for R.D.?
5. ***Prioritize:*** Based on the assessment data presented, what are the priority clinical problems?
6. ***Plan:*** What are her teaching needs at this time?
7. ***Act:*** What teaching will you provide after surgery so that R.D. can successfully self-manage her care?
8. ***Evaluate:*** What is the expected outcome of drug therapy?
9. ***Safety:*** Why is R.D. counseled to give up her long-standing cigarette smoking habit?

Answers available at http://evolve.elsevier.com/Lewis/medsurg.

BRIDGE TO NCLEX EXAMINATION

The number of the question corresponds to the same-numbered outcome at the beginning of the chapter.

1. Which interventions would the nurse include in the care for a patient who underwent transsphenoidal excision of the pituitary gland? (*select all that apply*)
   - **a.** Frequent monitoring of serum and urine osmolarity
   - **b.** Assessment of visual acuity and extraocular movement
   - **c.** Keeping the patient in a recumbent position at all times
   - **d.** Teaching the patient about the need for lifelong hormone therapy
   - **e.** Instructing the patient to blow their nose frequently to relieve cerebral pressure
2. A patient with lung cancer develops SIADH. Which are anticipated findings?
   - **a.** Hypernatremia and hyperkalemia
   - **b.** Thirst, muscle cramping, and headache
   - **c.** High urine output, weight gain, and vomiting
   - **d.** Weight gain and decreased glomerular filtration rate
3. The nurse reviews the laboratory results of a patient with primary hypothyroidism. The nurse would expect to find
   - **a.** a low TSH.
   - **b.** an elevated TSH.
   - **c.** an elevated free T_4.
   - **d.** decreased low-density lipoproteins (LDLs).
4. After thyroid surgery, the nurse suspects damage of the parathyroid glands when the patient develops
   - **a.** hyperthermia and severe tachycardia.
   - **b.** hypercalcemia and shortness of breath.
   - **c.** laryngospasms and tingling in the hands and feet
   - **d.** hypophosphatemia, hypertension, vomiting, and chest pain.
5. The nurse teaching the patient with Addison disease determines additional teaching is needed when the patient states
   - **a.** "I should take my prednisone twice a day."
   - **b.** "I should call my HCP if I develop vomiting or diarrhea."
   - **c.** "If I get influenza, I should decrease my prednisone dose."
   - **d.** "I will pick up my emergency hydrocortisone from the pharmacy."
6. A nursing priority for a patient who underwent removal of a pheochromocytoma includes
   - **a.** assessing for weight gain.
   - **b.** administering IV calcium.
   - **c.** close monitoring of blood pressure.
   - **d.** restricting fluid and sodium intake.
7. To control the side effects of corticosteroid therapy, the nurse teaches the patient who is taking corticosteroids to
   - **a.** limit calcium intake.
   - **b.** perform glucose monitoring for hyperglycemia.
   - **c.** avoid immunizations due to high risk for infections.
   - **d.** stop steroids immediately if the patient gains weight.

1. a, b, d; 2. b; 3. b; 4. c; 5. c; 6. c; 7. b.

For rationales to these answers and even more NCLEX review questions, visit http://evolve.elsevier.com/Lewis/medsurg.

EVOLVE WEBSITE/RESOURCES LIST

http://evolve.elsevier.com/Lewis/medsurg

Review Questions (Online Only)
Key Points
Answer Keys for Questions
- Rationales for Bridge to NCLEX Examination Questions
- Answer Guidelines for Case Study

Student Case Studies
- Patient With Addison Disease
- Patient With Cushing Syndrome
- Patient With Hyperthyroidism

Nursing Care Plans
- eNursing Care Plan 54.1: Patient With Hyperthyroidism
- eNursing Care Plan 54.2: Patient With Hypothyroidism
- eNursing Care Plan 54.3: Patient With Cushing Syndrome

Conceptual Care Map Creator
Audio Glossary
Content Updates

REFERENCES

1. American Cancer Society: About pituitary tumors. Retrieved from https://www.cancer.org/cancer/pituitary-tumors/about/what-is-pituitary-tumor.html.
2. National Institute of Diabetes and Digestive, and Kidney Diseases: Acromegaly. Retrieved from https://www.niddk.nih.gov/health-information/endocrine-diseases/acromegaly
3. Pituitary Network Association: Acromegaly. Retrieved from https://pituitary.org/knowledge-base/disorders/acromegaly
*4. Sarkar S, Chacko AG: Surgery for acromegaly, *Neurol India* 68:44, 2020.
*5. Chanson P, Maiter D: The epidemiology, diagnosis and treatment of prolactinomas, *Best Pract Res Clin Endocrinol Metab* 33:2, 2019.
*6. Araujo-Castro M, Pascual-Corrales E, Martínez San Millan JS, et al.: Postoperative management of patients with pituitary tumors submitted to pituitary surgery, *Endocrine* 69:1, 2020.
*7. Nadel J, Couldwell WT: Management of water and sodium disturbances after transsphenoidal resection of pituitary tumors, *Neurol India* 68:101, 2020.
8. Mentrasti G, Scortichini L, Torniai M, et al.: SIADH: optimal management, *Ther Clin Risk Manag* 16:663, 2020.
9. Refardt J, Winzeler B, Christ-Crain M: Diabetes insipidus, *Endocrin Metab Clin North Am* 49:517, 2020.
10. Simsir Y, Cetinkalp S, Kabalak T: Review of factors contributing to nodular goiter and thyroid carcinoma, *Med Princ Pract* 29:1, 2020.
*11. Ralli M, Angeletti D, Fiore M, et al.: Hashimoto's thyroiditis: an update on pathogenic mechanisms, diagnostic protocols, therapeutic strategies, and potential malignant transformation, *Autoimmun Rev* 19:10, 2020.
12. McDermott MT: Hyperthyroidism, *Ann Intern Med* 172:7, 2020.
*13. Brito JP, Payne S, Ospina NS, et al: Patterns of use, efficacy, and safety of treatment options for patients with Graves' disease: a nationwide population-based study. *Thyroid* 30, 2020.
*14. Modarresi M, Amro A, Amro M, et al: Management of cardiogenic shock due to thyrotoxicosis: a systematic literature review. *Curr Cardiol Rev* 16, 2020.
15. Chiovato L, Magri F, Carlé A: Hypothyroidism in context: where we've been and where we're going, *Adv Ther* 36:47, 2019.
*16. Bragg S, Ramsetty A, Bunt C: Refining your approach to hypothyroidism treatment, *J Fam Pract* 69:2, 2020.
*17. Reyes Domingo F, Avey MT, Doull M: Screening for thyroid dysfunction and treatment of screen-detected thyroid dysfunction in asymptomatic, community-dwelling adults: a systematic review, *Syst Rev* 8, 2019.
*18. Seib CD, Sosa JA: Evolving understanding of the epidemiology of thyroid cancer, *Endocrinol Metab Clin North Am* 48:23, 2019.
19. McDonnell JE, Gild ML, Clifton-Bligh RJ, et al.: Multiple endocrine neoplasia, *Intern Med J* 49:954, 2019.
20. Machado NN, Wilhelm SM: Diagnosis and evaluation of primary hyperparathyroidism, *Surg Clin North Am* 99:659, 2019.
*21. Chabre O, Cristante J: Treatment of Cushing's syndrome: what place for medical treatment? *Acta Endocrinol* 15:2, 2019.
*22. Saverino S, Falorni A: Autoimmune Addison's disease, *Best Pract Res Clin Endocrinol Metab* 34:1, 2020.
23. Rathbun KM, Nguyen M, Singhal M: Addisonian crisis. Retrieved from https://pubmed.ncbi.nlm.nih.gov/28722962/
*24. Adami G, Saag KG: Glucocorticoid-induced osteoporosis: 2019 concise clinical review, *Osteoporos Int* 30:6, 2019.
*25. Funder J: Primary aldosteronism: treatment of the disease, and new therapeutic approaches, *Best Pract Res Clin Endocrinol Metab* 34:2, 2020.
26. Sbardella E, Grossman AB: Pheochromocytoma: an approach to diagnosis, *Best Pract Res Clin Endocrinol Metab* 34:2, 2020.

*Evidence-based information for clinical practice.

55

Assessment: Reproductive System

Ashton T. Strachan

http://evolve.elsevier.com/Lewis/medsurg/

CONCEPTUAL FOCUS

Hormonal Regulation
Reproduction
Sexuality

LEARNING OUTCOMES

1. Describe the structures and functions of the male and female reproductive systems.
2. Outline the functions of the major hormones essential for the functioning of the male and female reproductive systems.
3. Explain the physiologic changes during the stages of a sexual response.
4. Link the age-related changes of the reproductive system to the differences in assessment findings.
5. Obtain significant subjective and objective data related to the reproductive system and information about sexual function.
6. Perform a physical assessment of the reproductive system using the appropriate techniques.
7. Distinguish normal from common abnormal findings of a physical assessment of the reproductive system.
8. Describe the purpose, significance of results, and nursing responsibilities related to diagnostic studies of the reproductive system.

KEY TERMS

amenorrhea
epididymis
estrogen
gonads
menarche
menopause
menstrual cycle
progesterone
spermatogenesis
testosterone
uterus
vulva

STRUCTURES AND FUNCTIONS OF MALE AND FEMALE REPRODUCTIVE SYSTEMS

The male and female reproductive systems consist of primary (essential) organs and secondary (accessory) organs. The primary reproductive organs are the **gonads**. The female gonads are the ovaries. The male gonads are the testes. The main purpose of the gonads is secretion of hormones and production of gametes (ova and sperm, sex cells that unite during fertilization to form a new cell called a *zygote*). Secondary organs begin their maturity at puberty under the influence of sex hormones. They are responsible for (1) transporting and nourishing the ova (eggs) and sperm, and (2) preserving and protecting the fertilized ova.

Male Reproductive System

The 3 main roles of the male reproductive system are (1) sperm production and transportation, (2) deposition of sperm in the female reproductive tract, and (3) hormone secretion. The primary male organs are the testes. Secondary organs include ducts (epididymis, ductus deferens, ejaculatory duct, urethra), sex glands (prostate gland, Cowper glands, seminal vesicles), and the external genitalia (scrotum, penis) (Fig. 55.1).

Testes

The paired testes are ovoid, smooth, firm organs. They measure 1.4 to 2.2 in (3.5 to 5.6 cm) long and 0.8 to 1.2 in (2 to 3 cm) wide. They lie within the scrotum. It is a loose protective sac composed of a thin outer layer of skin over a tough connective tissue layer. Within the testes, coiled structures, called the seminiferous tubules, form *spermatozoa* (immature sperm). The process of sperm production is called **spermatogenesis**. Males make sperm throughout their reproductive life cycle. Interstitial cells lie between the seminiferous tubules. These cells make the male sex hormone, testosterone.

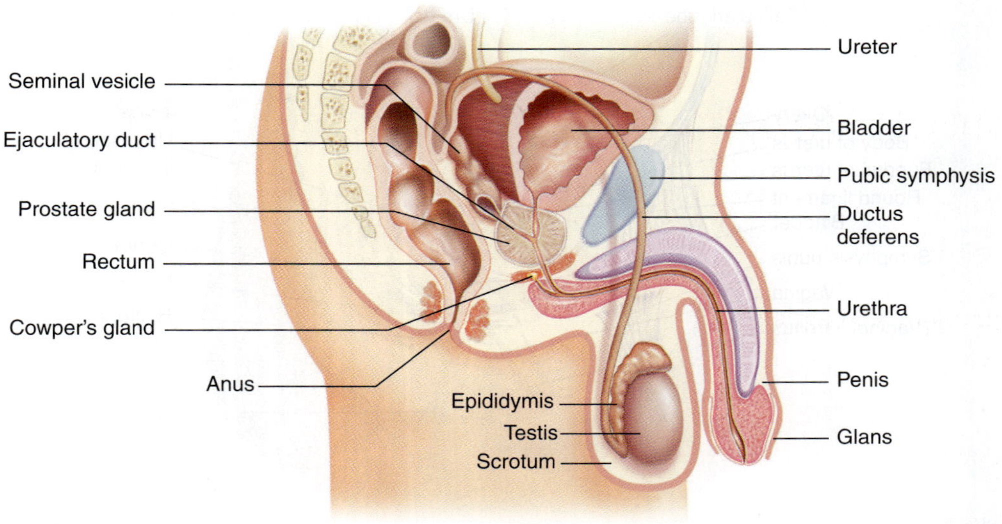

Fig. 55.1 Male reproductive tract. (Modified from Patton KT, Thibodeau GA: *Anatomy and physiology*, ed 8, St Louis, 2013, Mosby.)

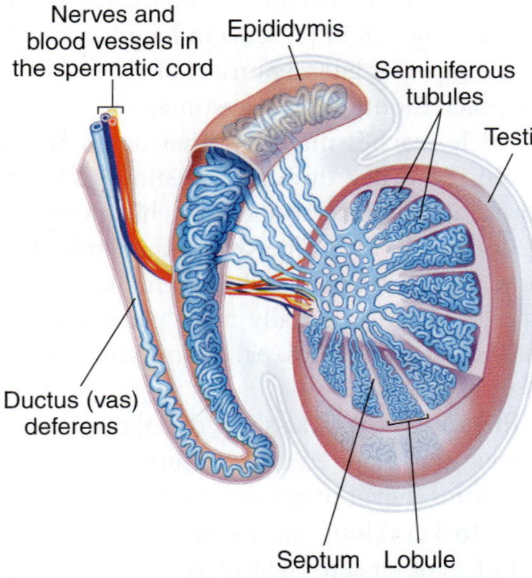

Fig. 55.2 Seminiferous tubules, testis, epididymis, and ductus (vas) deferens in the male. (Modified from Patton KT, Thibodeau GA: *Anatomy and physiology*, ed 8, St Louis, 2013, Mosby.)

Ducts

Sperm formed in the seminiferous tubules move through a series of ducts. These ducts transport sperm from the testes to the outside of the body. As sperm exit the testes, they enter and pass through the epididymis, ductus deferens, ejaculatory duct, and urethra.

The **epididymis** is a comma-shaped structure found behind and on top of each testis within the scrotum (Figs. 55.1 and 55.2). It is a long, tightly coiled structure that, uncoiled, measures about 20 ft in length.[1] The epididymis transports sperm as they mature. Sperm exit the epididymis through a long, thick tube called the *ductus deferens*.

The ductus deferens (also called the *vas deferens*) is continuous with the epididymis within the scrotal sac. It travels upward through the scrotum and continues through the inguinal ring into the abdominal cavity. The spermatic cord is composed of a connective tissue sheath that encloses the ductus deferens, arteries, veins, nerves, and lymph vessels as it ascends through the inguinal canal (Fig. 55.2). In the abdominal cavity, the ductus deferens travels up, over, and behind the bladder. Behind the bladder, the ductus deferens joins the seminal vesicle to form the ejaculatory duct (Fig. 55.1).

The ejaculatory duct passes downward through the prostate gland, connecting with the urethra. The urethra extends from the bladder, through the prostate, and ends in a slit-like opening (the meatus) on the ventral side of the *glans,* the tip of the penis. During ejaculation, sperm travel through the urethra and out of the penis.

Glands

The seminal vesicles, prostate gland, and Cowper (bulbourethral) glands are the accessory glands. These glands make and secrete seminal fluid *(semen),* which surrounds the sperm and forms the *ejaculate.* The ejaculate fluid serves as a medium for the transport of sperm. It creates an alkaline, nutritious environment that promotes sperm motility and survival.

The seminal vesicles lie behind the bladder, between the bladder and rectum. The ducts of the seminal vesicles fuse with the ductus deferens to form the ejaculatory ducts. They enter the prostate gland, which lies beneath the bladder. Its posterior surface is in contact with the rectal wall. The prostate normally measures 0.8 in (2 cm) wide and 1.2 in (3 cm) long. It is divided into right and left lateral lobes and an anteroposterior median lobe. Cowper glands lie on each side of the urethra and slightly behind it, just below the prostate. The ducts of these glands enter directly into the urethra.

External Genitalia

The external male genitalia consist of the penis and scrotum. The penis consists of a shaft and tip, called the *glans.* The glans is covered by a fold of skin, the prepuce (or foreskin), that forms at the junction of the glans and shaft of the penis. In circumcised males, the prepuce has been removed. The shaft consists

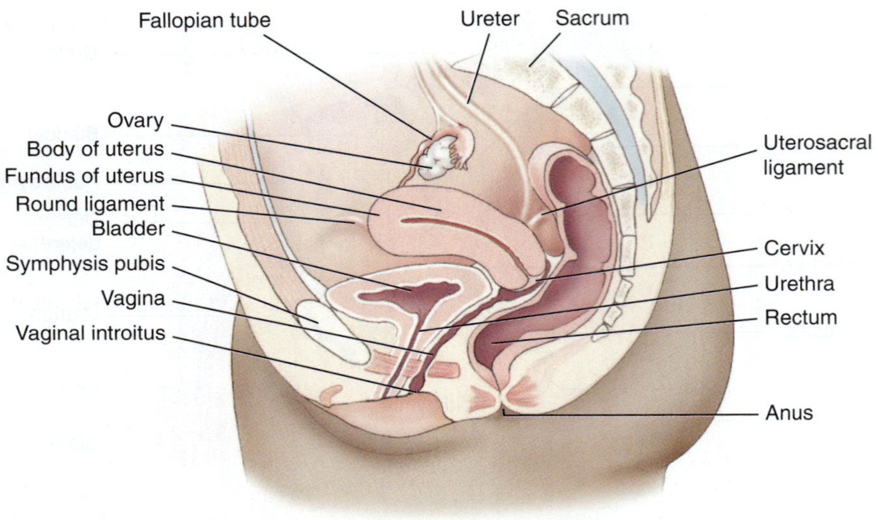

Fig. 55.3 Female reproductive tract. (Modified from McKenry L, Tessier E, Hogan M: *Mosby's pharmacology in nursing,* St Louis, 2006, Mosby.)

of erectile tissue composed of the corpus cavernosum, corpus spongiosum (fibrous sheath that encases the erectile tissue), and urethra. The skin covering the penis is thin, loose, and hairless.

Female Reproductive System

The 3 main roles of the female reproductive system are (1) ova production, (2) hormone secretion, and (3) protect and facilitate the development of the fetus in a pregnant female. The primary female organs are the paired ovaries. Secondary organs include the ducts (fallopian tubes), uterus, vagina, sex glands (Bartholin glands, breasts), and external genitalia (vulva).

Pelvic Organs

Ovaries. The ovaries are found on either side of the uterus, just behind and below the fallopian tubes (Fig. 55.3). The almond-shaped ovaries are firm and solid. They are around 0.6 in (1.5 cm) wide and 1.2 in (3 cm) long. Their functions include ovulation and secretion of the 2 major reproductive hormones: estrogen and progesterone.

The outer zone of the ovary has follicles with germ cells, or *oocytes.* Each follicle contains a primordial (immature) oocyte surrounded by granulosa and theca cells. These 2 layers protect and nourish the oocyte until the follicle reaches maturity and ovulation occurs. However, not all follicles reach maturity. In a process termed *atresia,* most of the immature follicles become smaller and are reabsorbed by the body. Thus, the number of follicles declines from 700,000 at birth to around 300,000 at *menarche* (first menstruation).[2] This is the female's lifetime supply of sex cells. As a woman ages, the number and quality of oocytes decline. A normal healthy woman releases around 300 to 500 oocytes by ovulation during the reproductive years.[3]

Fallopian tubes. The fallopian tubes transport the ovum toward the uterus, facilitating fertilization or implantation. The tubes are uterine appendages that end by curling around the ovary. The distal ends of the fallopian tubes consist of fingerlike projections called *fimbriae.* They sweep the ovum from the ruptured ovarian follicle (ovulation) into the fallopian tube. The tubes, which average 4.8 in (12 cm) in length, extend from the fimbriae to the superior lateral borders of the uterus.

Normally, each month during a woman's reproductive years, 1 ovarian follicle reaches maturity. That ovum is ovulated, or expelled, from the ovary through the stimulus of the gonadotropic hormones: follicle-stimulating hormone (FSH) and luteinizing hormone (LH). The ovum then travels through a fallopian tube, where fertilization by sperm may occur (if sperm are present). Fertilization usually takes place within the outer one third of the fallopian tubes. An ovum can be fertilized up to 72 hours after its release.

Uterus. The **uterus** is a pear-shaped, hollow, muscular organ found between the bladder and rectum (Fig. 55.3). In the mature *nulliparous* (never pregnant) woman, the uterus is about 2.4 to 3.2 in (6 to 8 cm) long and 1.6 in (4 cm) wide. The uterine walls consist of an outer serosal layer, the *perimetrium;* a middle muscular layer, the *myometrium;* and an inner mucosal layer, the *endometrium.*

The uterus consists of the fundus, body (or corpus), and cervix (Fig. 55.3). The body makes up about 80% of the uterus. It connects with the cervix at the isthmus, or neck. The cervix is the lower part of the uterus. It projects into the anterior wall of the vaginal canal. It makes up about 15% to 20% of the uterus in the nulliparous female. The cervix consists of the *ectocervix,* the outer part that protrudes into the vagina, and the *endocervix,* the canal in the opening of the cervix. The cervical canal is 0.8 to 1.6 in (2 to 4 cm) long. The opening of the cervix is the *cervical os* (Fig. 55.4).

The ectocervix is covered with squamous epithelial cells. This gives it a smooth, pinkish appearance. The endocervix is lined with columnar epithelial cells, which give it a rough, reddened appearance. The junction at which the 2 types of epithelial cells (squamous and columnar) meet is the *squamocolumnar junction* (Fig. 55.4). Cells sampled from the squamocolumnar junction are examined as part of a Papanicolaou (Pap) test, which is part of cervical cancer screening.

The cervical os is relatively tightly closed. It does allow for menses to be expelled and sperm to enter the uterus. Mucus made by the cervix (under the influence of estrogen) facilitates the entrance of sperm into the uterus. Under normal conditions, the cervical mucus becomes watery, stretchy, and more abundant at ovulation. The postovulatory cervical mucus, under the influence of progesterone, is thick and inhibits sperm passage. The cervix can stretch to allow passage of a fetus during the birth process. The columnar epithelium, under hormonal influence, provides elasticity during labor.

Vagina. The vagina is a tubular structure 3 to 4 in (7.6 to 10 cm) long. The anterior vaginal wall lies along the urethra and bladder. The posterior vaginal wall is next to the rectum. It is lined with squamous epithelium. In reproductive-age women, the vagina has multiple transverse folds called *rugae.* Vaginal secretions consist of cervical mucus, desquamated epithelium, and, during sexual stimulation, a watery secretion. These fluids help protect against vaginal infection. The muscular and erectile tissue of the vaginal walls allows enough dilation and contraction to accommodate the passage of the fetus during labor and penetration of the penis during intercourse.

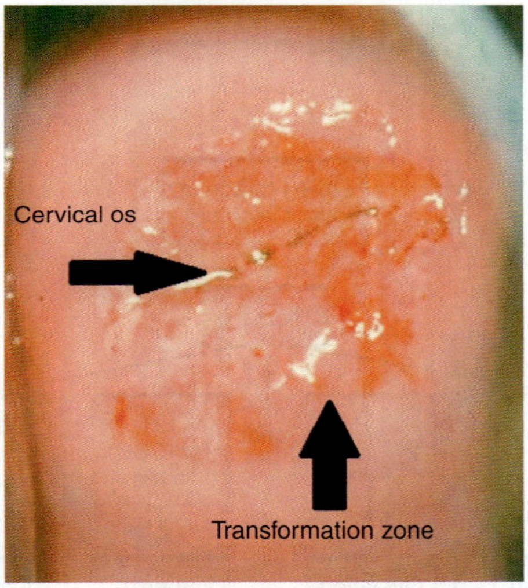

Fig. 55.4 Cervical os and squamocolumnar junction (transformation zone). (Courtesy Candy Tedschi, NP, Great Neck, NY.)

External Genitalia

The external part of the female reproductive system (Fig. 55.5) is often called the **vulva.** It consists of the mons pubis, labia majora, labia minora, vestibule, clitoris, urethral meatus, Skene glands, vaginal introitus (opening), and Bartholin glands.

The *mons pubis* is a fatty layer lying over the pubic bone. It is covered with coarse hair that lies in a triangular pattern. The labia majora are folds of adipose tissue that form the outer borders of the vulva. The hairless labia minora form the borders of the vaginal orifice and extend anteriorly to enclose the clitoris.

The *vestibule* is the space between the labia minora that is seen when they are held apart. It extends from the clitoris to the *posterior fourchette* (a mucous membrane band that forms the posterior ends of the labia minora). The perineum is the area between the vagina and anus. The vaginal introitus (vaginal opening) is surrounded by thin membranous tissue called the *hymen.* It is usually perforated and has many variations in shape. In the adult woman, the hymen usually appears as folds or hymenal tags *(caruncula e myrtiformes).* It separates the external genitalia from the vagina.

The *clitoris* is erectile tissue that becomes engorged during sexual excitation. It lies anterior to the urethral meatus and the vaginal orifice. It is usually covered by the prepuce. Clitoral stimulation is an important part of sexual activity for many women.

Ducts of the Skene glands lie alongside the urinary meatus and correspond to the prostate gland in males. We think they help lubricate the urinary meatus. Bartholin glands are found at the posterior and lateral aspects of the vaginal orifice. They secrete a thin, mucoid material we think contributes slightly to lubrication during sexual intercourse. These glands are not usually palpable unless sebaceous-like cysts form or they are swollen from an infection, such as a sexually transmitted infection (STI). Bartholin glands correspond to Cowper glands in males.

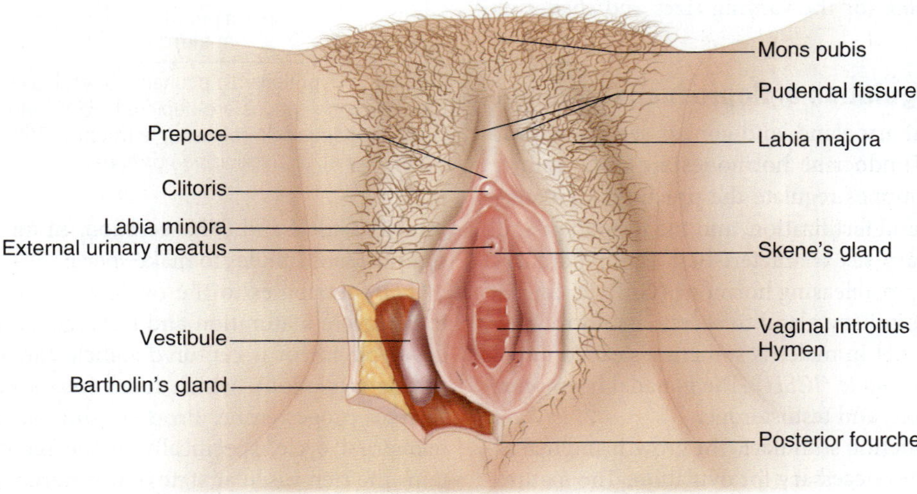

Fig. 55.5 External female genitalia. (Modified from Patton KT, Thibodeau GA: *Anatomy and physiology,* ed 8, St Louis, 2013, Mosby.)

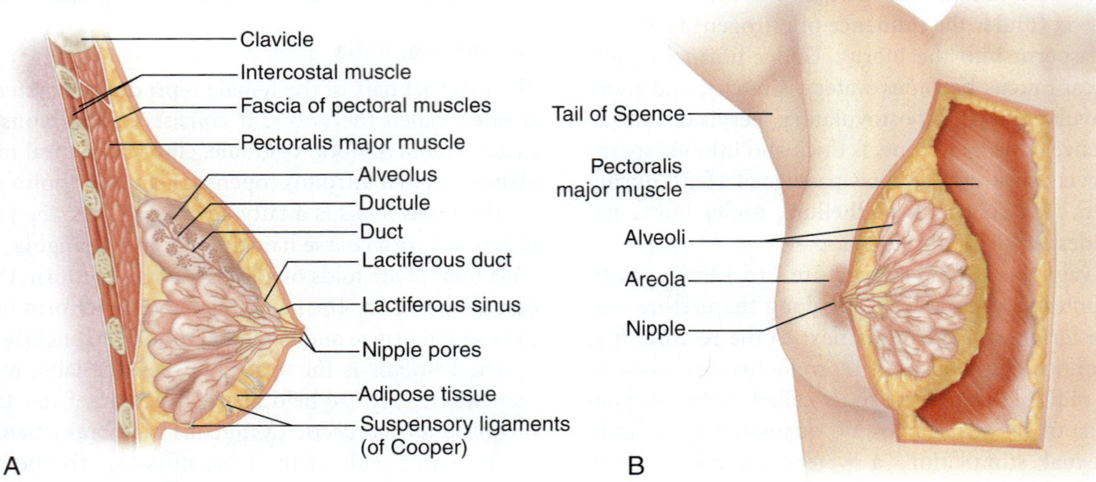

Fig. 55.6 The lactating female breast. (A) Glandular structures are anchored to the overlying skin and the pectoralis muscle by suspensory ligaments of Cooper. Each lobule of glandular tissue is drained by a lactiferous duct that eventually opens through the nipple. (B) Anterior view of a lactating breast. In nonlactating breasts, glandular tissue is less evident, with adipose tissue making up most of the breast. (Modified from Patton KT, Thibodeau GA: *Anatomy and physiology*, ed 8, St Louis, 2013, Mosby.)

Breasts

The breasts are a secondary sex characteristic that develops during puberty in response to estrogen and progesterone. Cyclic hormonal changes lead to regular changes in breast tissue to prepare it for lactation when fertilization and pregnancy occur.

The breasts extend from the 2nd to the 6th ribs. The extension of breast tissue into the upper-outer quadrant into the axilla is an area referred to as the *tail of Spence* (Fig. 55.6). The fully mature breast is dome shaped and has a pigmented center called the *areola*. The areolar region contains Montgomery tubercles, which are similar to sebaceous glands. They help lubricate the nipple. During lactation, the alveoli secrete milk. The milk then flows into a ductal system and is transported to the lactiferous sinuses. The nipple has 15 to 20 tiny openings through which the milk flows during breastfeeding. The fibrous and fatty tissue that supports and separates the channels of the mammary duct system is responsible for the varying sizes and shapes of the breasts.

Neuroendocrine Regulation of Reproductive System

The hypothalamus, pituitary gland, and gonads secrete several hormones (Fig. 55.7). (Endocrine hormones are discussed in Chapter 52.) These hormones regulate the processes of ovulation, sperm formation, and fertilization, and the formation and function of the secondary sex characteristics. The hypothalamus secretes gonadotropin-releasing hormone (GnRH). GnRH stimulates the anterior pituitary gland to secrete its hormones, including FSH and LH. LH in males is sometimes called *interstitial cell–stimulating hormone (ICSH)*. The gonadal hormones are estrogen, progesterone, and testosterone.

In women, FSH production stimulates the growth and maturity of the ovarian follicles necessary for ovulation. The mature follicle makes estrogen, which suppresses the release of FSH. Inhibin is another hormone secreted by the ovarian follicle. It

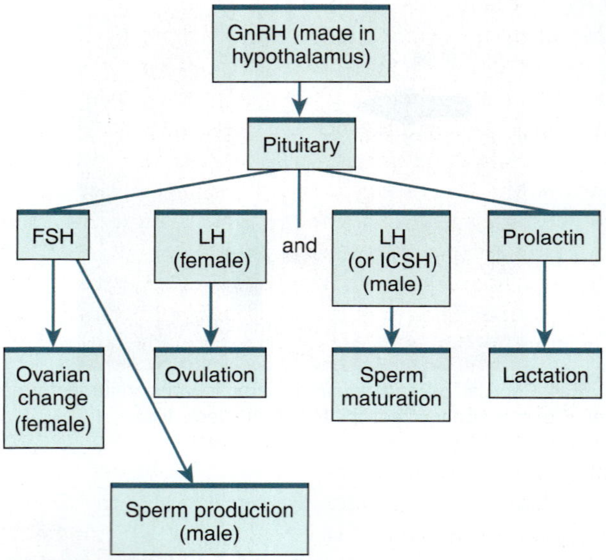

Fig. 55.7 Hypothalamic-pituitary-gonadal axis. Only the major pituitary hormone actions are depicted. *FSH,* Follicle-stimulating hormone; *GnRH,* gonadotropin-releasing hormone; *ICSH,* interstitial cell–stimulating hormone; *LH,* luteinizing hormone.

inhibits GnRH and FSH secretion. In men, FSH stimulates the seminiferous tubules to make sperm.

LH contributes to the ovulatory process. It causes follicles to complete maturation and undergo ovulation. LH affects the development of a ruptured follicle (area where ovum exited during ovulation), which turns into a corpus luteum, which secretes progesterone. **Progesterone** plays a major role in the menstrual cycle, specifically in the secretory phase. It maintains the rich vascular state of the uterus in preparation for fertilization and implantation. Adequate progesterone is needed to maintain an implanted ovum. Like estrogen, progesterone

TABLE 55.1 Gonadal Feedback Mechanisms

Negative Feedback

Female

↓Estrogen → ↑GnRH (hypothalamus) → ↑FSH (pituitary) → ↑Estrogen (ovaries)

Male

↓Testosterone → ↑GnRH (hypothalamus) → ↑FSH and LH (or ICSH) (pituitary) → ↑Testosterone (testes)

Positive Feedback

↑Estrogen → ↑GnRH (hypothalamus) → ↑LH (pituitary)

FSH, Follicle-stimulating hormone; *GnRH,* gonadotropin-releasing hormone; *ICSH,* interstitial cell–stimulating hormone; *LH,* luteinizing hormone.

is involved in the body changes associated with pregnancy. In men, LH triggers testosterone production by the interstitial cells of the testes and is essential for the full maturation of sperm.

In women, prolactin stimulates the development and growth of the mammary glands. During lactation, it initiates and maintains milk production. In men, prolactin has no known function.

In women the ovaries make the gonadal hormones, estrogen and progesterone. Small amounts of an estrogen precursor are also made in the adrenal cortices. **Estrogen** is essential to the development and maintenance of the secondary sex characteristics, proliferative phase of the menstrual cycle immediately after menstruation, and uterine changes essential to pregnancy. In men, most estrogen is made in the adrenal cortices. We do not understand the role of estrogen in men.

In men, the major gonadal hormone is testosterone, which is made by the testes. **Testosterone** is responsible for the development and maintenance of secondary sex characteristics and adequate spermatogenesis. In women, the adrenal glands and ovaries make small amounts of androgens.

The circulating levels of gonadal hormones are controlled mainly by a *negative feedback process.* Receptors within the hypothalamus and pituitary are sensitive to the circulating blood levels of the hormones (Table 55.1). Increased hormone levels stimulate a hypothalamic response to decrease the high circulating levels. Likewise, low circulating levels provoke a hypothalamic response that increases the low circulating levels. For example, low circulating testosterone levels stimulate the hypothalamus to secrete GnRH. This triggers the anterior pituitary to secrete greater amounts of FSH and LH, which in turn cause an increase in the testosterone production. The high level of testosterone signals a decrease in GnRH production, and thus FSH and LH.

In women, however, there is a slight variation in the control of gonadal hormones. The circulating levels are controlled through a combination of both a negative and positive feedback system. A *negative feedback control* mechanism exists similar to that described for men. Low circulating estrogen levels stimulate the hypothalamus to increase its production of GnRH. GnRH stimulates the pituitary to secrete greater amounts of FSH and LH, resulting in increased estrogen production by the ovaries. Higher levels of circulating estrogen result in a decreasing secretion of GnRH and thus a decrease in the secretion of FSH by the pituitary.

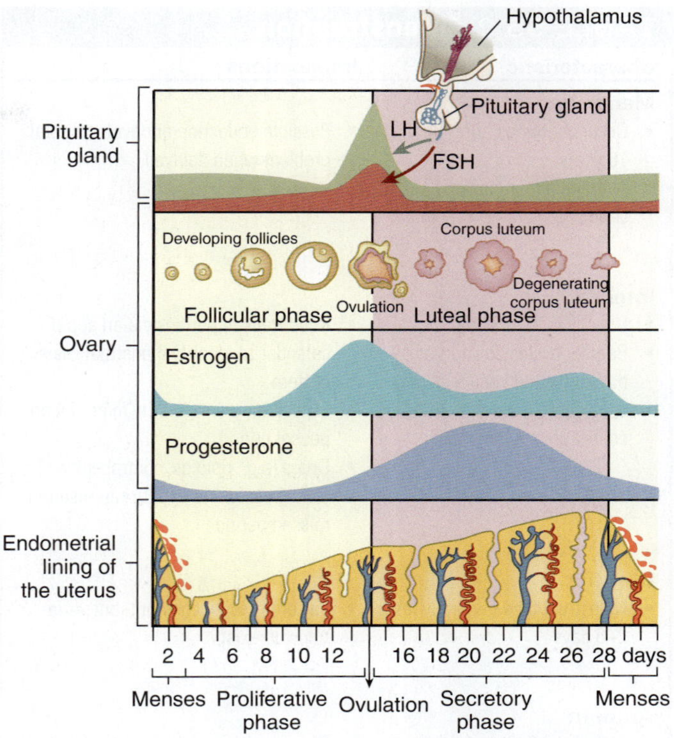

Fig. 55.8 Events of the menstrual cycle. The *lines* depict the changes in blood hormone levels, the development of the follicles, and the changes in the endometrium during the cycle. (Modified from Patton KT, Thibodeau GA: *Anatomy and physiology,* ed 8, St Louis, 2013, Mosby.)

Women also have a *positive feedback control* mechanism. Here, with increased levels of circulating estrogen, more GnRH is made, resulting in an increased level of LH from the pituitary. Likewise, low estrogen levels result in a lower level of LH.

Menarche

Menarche is the first episode of menstrual bleeding, indicating that a girl has reached puberty. Menarche usually occurs at around 12 to 13 years of age but can occur as early as 10 years of age in some girls. Menstrual cycles are often irregular for the first 1 to 2 years after menarche because of *anovulatory cycles* (cycles without ovulation).

Menstrual Cycle

The major functions of the ovaries are ovulation and the secretion of hormones. These functions are accomplished during the normal **menstrual cycle,** a monthly process mediated by the hormonal activity of the hypothalamus, pituitary gland, and ovaries. Menstruation occurs during each month in which an ovum is not fertilized (Fig. 55.8). The length of the menstrual cycle ranges from 21 to 35 days, with an average of 28 days. Most women have regular cycles. Irregular cycles may occur and can be due to a variety of factors, such as hormonal fluctuations, medications, or conditions, such as uterine fibroids. Table 55.2 describes characteristics of the menstrual cycle.

TABLE 55.2 Menstruation

Characteristic	Implications
Menarche	
• Occurs between ages 10 and 16 years • Average age at onset is 12–13 years	• Possible endocrine or developmental problem when delayed.
Interval	
• Usually is 21–35 days • Regular cycles as short as 17 days or as long as 45 days are considered normal if pattern is consistent for the person	• Keep track of periods via an app or calendar to identify menstrual cycle pattern • Expect some irregularity in perimenopausal period • Drugs (e.g., opioids, contraceptives) and stressful life events can result in missed periods
Duration	
• Menstrual flow generally lasts 2–8 days	• Pattern is fairly constant, but variations do exist
Amount	
• Menstrual flow varies from 20–80 mL per menses. Average is 30 mL • Amount varies among women and in same woman at different times • It is usually heaviest first 2 days	• Count pads or tampons used per day • Average tampon or pad (when completely saturated) absorbs 20–30 mL • Very heavy flow is indicated by complete soaking of 2 pads in 1–2 hr • Flow increases and then gradually decreases in perimenopausal period • IUD or drugs, such as anticoagulants and thiazides, can cause heavy menses • Women with uterine fibroids may have increased or heavy menses
Composition	
• Menstrual discharge is mixture of endometrium, blood, mucus, and vaginal cells • Dark red, less viscous than blood, and usually does not clot	• Clots indicate heavy flow or vaginal pooling

We divide the menstrual cycle into 3 phases. They are labeled in relation to uterine and ovarian changes: (1) the *proliferative*, or *follicular, phase*; (2) the *secretory*, or *luteal, phase*; and (3) the *menstrual*, or *ischemic, phase*. The menstrual cycle begins on the 1st day of menstruation. It usually lasts 4 to 6 days. The 1st day of the menstrual cycle is known as the last menstrual period (LMP). During menstruation, estrogen and progesterone levels are low, but FSH levels begin to increase. During the follicular phase, a single follicle matures fully under FSH stimulation. The mechanism that ensures that usually only 1 follicle reaches maturity is not known. The mature follicle stimulates estrogen production, causing a negative feedback with resulting decreased FSH secretion.

Although FSH stimulates the 1st stage of follicular maturation, complete maturation and ovulation occur only in the presence of LH. When estrogen levels peak on about the 12th day of the cycle, there is a surge of LH. This triggers ovulation 1 or 2 days later. After ovulation, LH promotes the development of the corpus luteum, a temporary functional cyst that forms with the ruptured follicle.

The fully developed corpus luteum continues to secrete estrogen and initiates progesterone secretion. If fertilization occurs, estrogen and progesterone continue to be secreted because of the continued activity of the corpus luteum from stimulation by human chorionic gonadotropin (hCG). If fertilization does not take place, menstruation occurs because of a decrease in estrogen production and progesterone withdrawal.

During the *follicular phase*, the endometrial lining of the uterus undergoes change. As more estrogen is made, the endometrial lining goes through proliferative changes, including an increase in the length of blood vessels and glandular tissue.

With ovulation and the resulting increased levels of progesterone, the *luteal* (or *secretory*) *phase* begins. If the corpus luteum regresses (when fertilization does not occur) and estrogen and progesterone levels fall, the endometrial lining can no longer be supported. As a result, the blood vessels contract, and tissue begins to slough (fall away). This sloughing results in menses and the start of the menstrual phase.

Menopause

Menopause is the physiologic cessation of menses from declining ovarian function. It is considered complete after 1 year of **amenorrhea** (absence of menstruation). Menopause is discussed in Chapter 58.

Phases of Sexual Response

The sexual response is a complex interplay of psychologic and physiologic phenomena. It is influenced by several variables (e.g., stress, illness). The changes that occur during sexual excitement are similar for men and women. Masters and Johnson described the sexual response in terms of the excitement, plateau, orgasmic, and resolution phases.[4]

Male Sexual Response

The penis and urethra are essential to the transport of sperm during intercourse. This transport is facilitated by penile erection in response to sexual stimulation during the *excitement phase*. Erection results from the filling of the large venous sinuses within the erectile tissue of the penis. In the flaccid state the sinuses hold only a small amount of blood. During an erection, they are congested with blood. Because the penis is richly endowed with sympathetic, parasympathetic, and pudendal nerve endings, it is readily stimulated to erection. The loose skin of the penis becomes taut from venous congestion. This tautness allows for easy insertion during penetrative sex.

As the man reaches the *plateau phase*, the erection is maintained. The penis increases in diameter from a slight increase in vasocongestion. Testicle size also increases. Sometimes the glans penis becomes reddish purple.

The contractions of the penile and urethral musculature during the *orgasmic phase* propel the sperm outward through the meatus. In this process, termed *ejaculation,* sperm are released into the ductus deferens. Sperm advance through the urethra, where fluids from the prostate and seminal vesicles are added to the ejaculate. The sperm continue their path through the urethra, receiving a small amount of fluid from the Cowper glands. They are finally ejaculated through the urinary meatus. *Orgasm* is characterized by the rapid release of vasocongestion and muscular tension through rhythmic contractions. This occurs primarily in the penis, prostate gland, and seminal vesicles. After ejaculation, a man enters the *resolution phase.* The penis undergoes involution, gradually returning to its unstimulated, flaccid state.

Female Sexual Response

The changes that occur in a woman during sexual excitation are similar to those in a man. In response to stimulation, the clitoris becomes congested and vaginal lubrication increases from secretions from the cervix, Bartholin glands, and vaginal walls. This initial response is the excitation phase.

As excitation is maintained in the plateau phase, the vagina expands, and the uterus is elevated. In the orgasmic phase, contractions occur in the uterus from the fundus to the lower uterine segment. There is a slight relaxation of the cervical os, which helps the entrance of the sperm, and rhythmic contractions of the vagina. Muscular tension is rapidly released through rhythmic contractions in the clitoris, vagina, and uterus. A resolution phase follows, in which these organs return to their preexcitation state. However, women do not have to go through the resolution (refractory) recovery state before they can be orgasmic again. They can be multiorgasmic without resolution between orgasms.

Gerontologic Considerations: Effects of Aging on Reproductive Systems

With advancing age, changes occur in the reproductive systems (Table 55.3). In women, many of these changes are related to decreased estrogen production due to menopause.[5] Decreased estrogen and other sex steroids in postmenopausal women causes breast and genital atrophy, reduced bone mass, and increased rate of atherosclerosis. Vaginal dryness may occur, which can lead to urogenital atrophy and changes in the composition of the vaginal *microbiome* (the aggregate of microorganisms and their genetic material).[6]

Testosterone levels decline in men as they age. Manifestations of this decline are more gradual in men. They can be physical, psychologic, or sexual. Changes include an increase in prostate size and a decrease in testosterone level, sperm production, muscle tone of the scrotum, and size and firmness of the testicles. Erectile dysfunction (ED) and sexual problems occur in some men because of these changes (Box 55.1).

Many factors affect sexuality in later life. Gradual changes occur in the sexual response. The cumulative effects of these changes, as well as the negative social attitude toward sexuality in older adults, can affect the sexual practices of older adults. Illness, disability, medicines, and surgeries can affect a person's ability to take part in sexual activities.

Nurses play a vital role in providing accurate and unbiased information about sexuality and age. Emphasize the normalcy of sexual activity in older adults and refer them to resources that address such issues.

TABLE 55.3 GERONTOLOGIC ASSESSMENT DIFFERENCES

Reproductive Systems

Structure	Changes	Assessment Findings Abnormalities
Male		
Breasts	Enlargement	Gynecomastia (abnormal enlargement)
Penis	↓ Subcutaneous fat	Easily retractable foreskin (if uncircumcised) ↓ Size Fewer sustained erections
Prostate	Benign hyperplasia	Enlargement, urinary obstruction, incontinence
Testes	↓ Testosterone production	↓ Size, firmness
Female		
Breasts	↓ Subcutaneous fat, increased fibrous tissue, ↓ skin turgor	Less resilient, looser, more pendulous tissue ↓ Size Duct around nipple may feel like stringy strand
Ovaries	↓ Ovarian function	Nonpalpable ovaries are normal postmenopause
Urethra	↓ Muscle tone, mucosal thinning	Possible UTIs, painful urination (dysuria), urgency, frequency, incontinence
Uterus	↓ Thickness of myometrium	Uterine prolapse
Vagina	Tissue atrophy, ↓ muscle tone, alkaline pH	Mucosa becomes pale, dry, smooth and thins Vagina narrows and shortens
Vulva	↓ Skin turgor	Atrophy ↓ Amount of pubic hair ↓ Size of clitoris and labia

BOX 55.1 BIOLOGIC SEX CONSIDERATIONS

Effects of Aging on Sexual Function

Men

- ↑ Stimulation necessary for erection
- ↓ Force of ejaculation
- ↓ Ability to attain or sustain erection
- ↓ Size and rigidity of the penis at full erection
- ↓ Libido and interest in sex

Women

- ↓ Vaginal lubrication
- ↓ Sensitivity with labia shrinking and more clitoris exposed
- Difficulty maintaining arousal
- Difficulty achieving orgasm
- ↓ Libido and interest in sex

Case Study

Patient Introduction

(© Benjamin A. Peterson/Mother Image/mother image/Fuse/Thinkstock.)

C.W. is a 23-year-old woman who is being seen for pelvic pain and irregular menstrual bleeding for the past several months. She takes oral contraceptive pills (OCPs) but occasionally forgets to take them. C.W. takes naproxen as needed for pain.

Discussion Questions

1. What are the possible causes for C.W.'s irregular menstrual bleeding?
2. What assessment questions would you ask C.W.?
3. How would you individualize the assessment based on her age, ethnic/cultural background, and condition?

You will learn more about C.W. and her condition as you read through this assessment chapter.

Answers available at http://evolve.elsevier.com/Lewis/medsurg.

ASSESSMENT OF MALE AND FEMALE REPRODUCTIVE SYSTEMS

Subjective Data

Important Health Information

In addition to general health information, obtain information specifically related to the reproductive system. Many people consider reproduction and sexual issues personal and private. The extent and depth of the interview about a patient's sexuality and reproductive health depend on your expertise and the patient's needs and willingness to discuss the topic. Assess your comfort with your own sexuality because any discomfort in questioning becomes obvious to the patient.

A professional demeanor is important when taking a reproductive or sexual history. Develop trust with the patient. Conduct interviews in an environment that provides reassurance, confidentiality, and a nonjudgmental attitude. Be sensitive, use gender-neutral terms when asking about partners, and maintain an awareness of a patient's culture and beliefs. Begin with the least sensitive information (e.g., menstrual history) before asking questions about more sensitive issues, such as sexual practices or STIs.

Health history. The health history should include information about major illnesses, hospitalizations, immunizations, and surgeries. Ask about any infections involving the reproductive system, including STIs. Take a complete obstetric and gynecologic history from patients assigned female at birth.

Mumps and rubella affect reproductive function. Mumps in young men increases the risk for sterility. Bilateral testicular atrophy may occur from mumps-related orchitis. Ask male patients if they have had mumps, were immunized with the mumps vaccine, or have any signs of sterility.

Rubella is a concern to women of childbearing age. Having rubella during the first 3 months of pregnancy increases the risk for congenital anomalies. So, encourage rubella immunization for all women of childbearing age who are not immunized or have not had the disease. Antibody titers can determine rubella immunity. Do not immunize a woman if they are already pregnant.[7] Advise patients to avoid becoming pregnant for 1 month after vaccination, or ideally, after immunity has been confirmed by antibody titers.

Ask the patient about current health status and any acute or chronic health problems. Chronic illnesses, such as cardiovascular disease, respiratory problems, anemia, cancer, and kidney and urinary tract problems, may affect the reproductive system and sexual functioning.

Ask questions relating to possible endocrine problems, including diabetes, hypothyroidism, and hyperthyroidism. These disorders directly interfere with women's menstrual cycles and sexual performance. Men with diabetes may have ED and retrograde ejaculation. In women with uncontrolled diabetes, pregnancy may pose significant health risks to both the woman and fetus.

Determine if the patient had a stroke. In men, strokes may cause physiologic or psychologic ED. Men who had a myocardial infarction (MI) may have ED because of fear that sexual activity could precipitate another MI. Post-MI medication, such as β-blockers, may affect a man's ability to achieve an erection.[8] Although most patients have concerns about sexual activity after an MI, many are not comfortable expressing these fears to the nurse. Be sensitive to this concern.

Note any allergies. Is the patient allergic to latex or drugs, including sulfonamides, macrolides, cephalosporins, tetracyclines, or penicillin? These drugs are often used to treat reproductive and genitourinary (GU) problems, such as STIs and urinary tract infections (UTIs). Silicone and latex are often used in diaphragms and condoms. An allergy to these substances precludes their use as contraception.

Medications. Obtain a complete medication history. Include the reason for use, dosage, and length of time that the drug has been taken. Ask about the use of herbal products and diet and nutrition supplements. Psychotropic agents may interfere with sexual performance. Antihypertensives, such as amlodipine (Norvasc), lisinopril, propranolol (Inderal), and clonidine, may cause ED. Drugs such as alcohol, marijuana, barbiturates, amphetamines, or cocaine can affect the reproductive system.

In women, note the use of hormonal contraceptives and hormone therapy (HT). The long-term use of combined HT (specifically a combination of oral conjugated equine estrogen and a progestin, *medroxyprogesterone acetate*) increases the risk for stroke, breast cancer, deep vein thrombosis, and gallbladder disease.[9] These risks are higher in women who also use tobacco products. Women may seek treatment based on the degree of symptoms and associated morbidities to help balance their quality of life with menopausal symptoms.[10]

A history of cholecystitis and hepatitis is important because these conditions may be contraindications for the use of OCPs. OCPs often aggravate cholecystitis. Chronic liver inflammation generally precludes the use of estrogen products because they are metabolized by the liver. Chronic obstructive pulmonary disease may be a contraindication to OCP use because progesterone thickens respiratory secretions.

Surgery or other treatments. Note any surgical procedures. Common surgeries involving the female reproductive system are listed in Table 58.7. Record any therapeutic or spontaneous abortions and type of intervention (medical versus surgical abortion).

TABLE 55.4 HEALTH HISTORY

Reproductive System

Health Perception–Health Management
- How would you describe your overall health?
- Describe the health of your family members. Any history of breast, uterine, ovarian, or prostate cancer?[a]

Women
- Do you perform breast self-examination? Any concerns?
- When was your last Pap test and the results?[a]
- Any prior abnormalities with your Pap tests?
- When was your last mammogram and the results?[a]
- Any prior abnormalities with your mammograms?

Men
- Do you perform testicular self-examination? Any concerns?

Nutritional-Metabolic
- Describe what you usually eat and drink.
- Have you had any changes in weight?[a]
- How do you feel about your current weight?
- Do you take any nutrition supplements, such as calcium or vitamins?[a]
- Do you have any diet restrictions?[a]

Elimination
- Do you have problems with urination (e.g., pain, burning, dribbling, incontinence, frequency)?[a]
- Have you had bladder infections? If so, when? How often?
- Do you have problems with bowel movements?[a]
- Do you have any constipation, loose stools, or blood with stools?[a]
- Do you use laxatives?[a]

Activity-Exercise
- What activities do you typically do each day?
- Do you have enough energy for your desired activities?

Sleep-Rest
- How many hours do you typically sleep each night?
- Do you feel rested after sleep?
- Do you have any problems sleeping?[a]

Cognitive-Perceptual
- Do you have pain? If yes, where?
- Do you have pain during sexual activity?[a]

Self-Perception–Self-Concept
- How would you describe yourself?
- Have there been any recent changes that have made you feel differently about yourself?[a]
- Are you having any problems that are affecting your sexuality?[a]

Role-Relationship
- Describe your living arrangements. With whom do you live?
- Do you have a significant other? If yes, is this relationship satisfying?
- Are you having any role-related problems in your family?[a] At work?[a]
- What are the relationships among your family members?

Sexuality-Reproductive
- Are you sexually active? If so, how many partners do you have?
- What kind of sex do you engage in (oral, vaginal, anal)?
- How do you protect yourself against sexually transmitted infections and unwanted pregnancy?
- Are you satisfied with your present means of sexual expression? If not, explain.
- Have you had any recent changes in your sexual practices?[a]

Women
- How old were you when you had your first menstrual period? (Menarche)
- What was the first day of your last menstrual period?
- Describe your period. How many days does it last? How often does it come (e.g., every 28 days)?
- Do you have pain with your period? Do you pass clots?
- Do you feel your flow is heavy or excessive?
- How old were you when you went through menopause?
- Have you had any postmenopausal bleeding or spotting?[a]
- Pregnancy history: How many times have you been pregnant? How many living children do you have? Have you ever had any miscarriages or abortions? Did they need medical intervention?

Men
- Do you have any problem obtaining or sustaining an erection?
- Do you have any problems with ejaculation?

Coping–Stress Tolerance
- Have there been any major changes in your life within the past couple of years?[a]
- What is stressful in your life right now?
- How do you handle health problems when they occur?
- Do you feel safe in your home? Work? Has anyone ever tried to hurt or harm you?

Value-Belief
- What beliefs do you have about your health and illnesses?
- Do you use home remedies?[a]
- Is religion an important part of your life?[a]
- Do you think that any of your personal beliefs or values may be compromised because of your treatment?[a]

[a] If yes, describe.

Functional Health Patterns

The key questions to ask a patient with a reproductive problem are outlined in Table 55.4.

Health perception–health management pattern. Discuss the patient's perception of their own health and measures that they take to maintain health. Ask about self-examination practices and screenings. Mammography and periodic cervical Pap tests are key to a woman's health. Men are at risk for testicular and prostate cancer. However, controversy exists about the benefits of routine screening for these cancers.[11] All patients should discuss the benefits and risks of screening with their HCP.

BOX 55.2 GENETIC RISK ALERT

- Breast, ovarian, uterine, and prostate cancer have known genetic risk factors.
- Having a 1st-degree relative with any of these cancers significantly increases the risk for cancer for the patient.
- The risk increases if several family members have had these cancers over succeeding generations.
- Persons with a known hereditary predisposition to breast or ovarian cancer can use this information to make informed decisions about how to minimize their risks.

An accurate family history is vital. Ask about a history of cancer, especially cancer of the reproductive organs (Box 55.2). Note a family history of diabetes, hypothyroidism, hyperthyroidism, hypertension, stroke, angina, MI, endocrine problems, or anemia.

Assess the patient's lifestyle choices. Determine whether a patient has smoked or currently smokes, the amount (if any) of alcohol use, or if they use illicit drugs. Risks associated with smoking include ectopic pregnancy, miscarriage, an increased risk for perinatal mortality and morbidity, placental abnormalities, preterm delivery, and congenital facial defects of the fetus.[12] Smoking increases the risk for mortality in women who use OCPs. Smoking in women is also related to early menopause. Decreased sperm counts and ED are seen in male smokers. Smoking is a known cofactor for persistence of *human papillomavirus* (HPV) infection for oral and anogenital cancers among men and women.[13]

Nutritional-metabolic pattern. Anemia is a common problem in women in their reproductive years, especially during pregnancy and the postpartum period. Evaluate the adequacy of the diet with this in mind. Iron deficiency anemia is the most common cause of anemia in menstruating females.

Take a thorough nutrition and psychologic history to assess for the presence of an eating disorder. Anorexia nervosa can cause amenorrhea and other problems, such as osteoporosis. Obesity can be related to polycystic ovarian syndrome and may be a precursor to type 2 diabetes.

From early adolescence, teach women about adequate calcium and vitamin D intake to prevent osteoporosis. Estimate the patient's daily calcium intake to determine whether supplementation is needed. Evaluate folic acid intake for women in their reproductive years because a deficiency can result in spina bifida and other fetal neural tube defects.[14]

Elimination pattern. Many gynecologic problems can result in GU problems. Urinary incontinence is common in older women. Factors associated with incontinence include relaxation of the pelvic musculature caused by multiple births, advancing age, fibroid tumors, diabetes, obesity, and weight gain. Condom, diaphragm, and spermicide use increases the risk for UTIs. Men may have urethritis, an inflammation of the urethra, which may be caused by an STI. Urethritis can cause painful urination. Benign prostatic hyperplasia (BPH) is common in older men. It can cause urinary retention or difficulty in starting the urinary stream.

Activity-exercise pattern. Record the amount, type, and intensity of activity and exercise. Lack of weight-bearing exercise is an important factor in the development of osteoporosis, especially in postmenopausal women. Anemia can result in fatigue and activity intolerance and interfere with performing activities of daily living. Adolescent females who engage in excessive leanness sports may have *female athlete triad.* It is characterized by secondary amenorrhea, low energy availability, and osteoporosis.[15]

Sleep-rest pattern. Sleep patterns may be affected during the postpartum period and while raising young children. Hot flashes and sweating during perimenopause can cause serious sleep interruption when the woman awakens in a drenching sweat. The need to change her clothing and bedding further disrupts sleep. Insomnia is common among perimenopausal women. Daytime fatigue can result from sleep problems. In men, frequent urination at night related to prostate enlargement or HT for prostate cancer can disturb sleep.

Cognitive-perceptual pattern. Pelvic pain can occur with various gynecologic disorders, such as pelvic inflammatory disease, ovarian cysts, and endometriosis. *Dyspareunia* (painful intercourse) can be problematic for women in the postmenopausal period. The pain with intercourse can create a reluctance to take part in sexual activity and strain relationships with sexual partners. Refer women with dyspareunia to their HCP.

Self-perception–self-concept pattern. Changes that occur with aging, such as pendulous breasts and vaginal dryness in women and decreased penis size in men, may lead to distress. The subtle changes associated with sexuality and advancing age may affect self-concept.

Role-relationship pattern. Obtain information about the family structure and occupation. Ask about recent changes in work-related relationships or family conflict. Assess the patient's role in the family as a starting point to determine family dynamics. Changes within the family, such as marriage, divorce, or birth of a child, affect roles and relationships.

Sexuality-reproductive pattern. For women, obtain a menstrual and a chronologic obstetric history. The menstrual history includes the first day of the LMP, description of menstrual flow, age of menarche, and, if applicable, age at menopause. Menstrual history data are used in the detection of pregnancy, infertility, and many gynecologic problems. Have the patient describe any changes in her usual menstrual pattern to determine whether the change is transient and unimportant or connected with a more serious problem. Terminology that describes abnormal uterine bleeding patterns is discussed in Chapter 58.

Identify changes in menstrual patterns from the use of OCPs, intrauterine devices (IUDs), birth control patches, vaginal rings, progestin-only implants, or medroxyprogesterone injections. OCPs usually decrease the amount and duration of flow. Some IUDs are used for both contraception and as a nonsurgical treatment for heavy menstrual bleeding. However, some IUDs increase menstrual flow.

The obstetric history includes the number of pregnancies, full-term births, preterm births, stillbirths, living children, and abortions (including spontaneous [miscarriage], ectopic, induced). Document the course of each pregnancy. Include the duration of each pregnancy, date of delivery, problems that occurred, and any medical or surgical treatment that was needed.

Table 55.5 outlines *The 5 Ps of Sexual Health* approach for taking a sexual history. Never assume a patient's sexual orientation. Ask patients about their general satisfaction with their sexuality. Ask them about sexual beliefs and practices and whether they achieve orgasm. Explore any unexplained change in sexual practices or performance. Reproductive problems can cause physiologic or psychologic problems that can lead to painful intercourse, ED, sexual problems, or infertility.

Coping–stress tolerance pattern. The stress related to situations such as pregnancy or menopause increases dependence on support systems. Determine whom the support people are in the patient's life. The diagnosis of an STI can cause stress for the patient and partner. Explore ways to manage this stress with patients by encouraging them to share their concerns.

Value-belief pattern. Sexual and reproductive functioning is closely related to cultural, religious, moral, and ethical values. Be aware of your own beliefs in these areas. Recognize and

TABLE 55.5 Sexual History Format

The Five Ps of Taking a Sexual History[a]

The 5 *Ps*	Questions
1. **Partners**	• Are you currently sexually active? (yes or no) • Do you have sex with men, women, or both? • In the past 2 months, with how many partners have you had sex? • In the past 12 months, with how many partners have you had sex?
2. **Practices**	• To understand your risk for STIs, I need to understand the kind of sex you have had recently. • Genital (penis in the vagina) • Anal (penis in the anus) • Oral (mouth on penis, vagina, or anus)
3. **Protection from STIs**	• Do you and your partner(s) use any protection against STIs? • What kind? • How often?
4. **Past history of STIs**	• Have you ever had an STI? • What type? • When? • How were you treated?
5. **Pregnancy prevention**	• Are you or your partner trying to get pregnant? • If not, what are you doing to prevent pregnancy?

[a]Modify this guide as needed to be culturally appropriate, based on culture or gender dynamics.
Adapted from https://www.cdc.gov/std/treatment/sexualhistory.pdf.

Case Study

Subjective Data

(© Benjamin A. Peterson/Mother Image/mother image/Fuse/Thinkstock.)

A focused assessment of C.W. revealed the following information:

Health Perception–Health Management: In good health. Pap smear 2 years ago was normal. Has not had any surgeries

Nutritional-Metabolic: 5 ft 2 in, 130 lb (BMI 23.7 kg/m^2)

Elimination: Denies any changes with urination or bowel movements

Activity-Exercise: Exercises at gym 2 times a week

Cognitive-Perceptual: Denies dyspareunia

Self-Perception–Self Concept: In graduate school and hopes to graduate next year.

Role-Relationship: Single, lives with 2 other young women in off-campus housing

Sexuality-Reproductive: Menarche at age 12. Last menstrual period 2 weeks ago. Menses is usually every 28 days, lasting 2 days, but has noted irregular bleeding with increased pelvic pain over past few months. Sexually active with men and women, with 6 lifetime partners. In a mutually monogamous relationship of 2 years duration with a male partner. Practices vaginal and oral sex.

Coping–Stress Tolerance: Denies stressors

Value-Belief: Raised Catholic, but does not attend mass

Discussion Questions

1. Which subjective assessment findings concern you most?
2. What should be included in the physical assessment?

You will learn more about physical assessment of the reproductive system in the next section.

Answers available at http://evolve.elsevier.com/Lewis/medsurg.

sensitively react to the patient's personal beliefs associated with reproductive and sexuality issues.

Objective Data

Physical Assessment: Male

The assessment of the external male genitalia includes inspection and palpation of the pubis, penis, and scrotum. The patient may be lying or standing. The standing position is preferred. Sit in front of the standing patient. Use gloves when assessing the male genitalia.

If breast cancer is suspected or there is a strong family history of breast cancer in a male patient, a clinical breast examination is conducted in the same pattern for a male patient as a female breast examination (see Fig. 56.1).

Pubis. Assess for hair distribution and presence of body lice. Normally, the hair is in a diamond-shaped pattern and coarser than scalp hair. The absence of hair is not normal unless the man is shaving or waxing the pubic hair. Carefully assess the skin for irritation and inflammation.

Penis and scrotum. Inspect the penis for any lesions, bleeding, or swelling. Note the location of the urethral meatus and the presence of a foreskin. If present, retract the foreskin and note any redness, discharge, irritation, lesions, or swelling from the meatus. Replace the foreskin over the glans after observation. Inspect the scrotum by lifting each testis to inspect all sides of the scrotal sac. Palpate the testes for tenderness or masses. The left testis usually hangs lower than the right. An undescended testis *(cryptorchidism)* is a major risk factor for testicular cancer and a potential cause of male infertility.

Anus. Note if the buttocks have any lesions, swelling, or inflammation. Spread the buttocks apart with both hands to expose the anus. Inspect the anal sphincter and perineal regions for fissures, lesions, masses, and hemorrhoids. The anus should be free from inflammation or skin changes.

Physical Assessment: Female

Physical assessment often begins with inspection and palpation of the breasts and axillae, then proceeds to the abdomen and genitalia. Examining the abdomen provides an opportunity to detect pain or any masses that may involve the GU system. Abdominal assessment is discussed in Chapter 43.

Breasts. To perform a breast examination, first examine the breasts by visual inspection. With the patient seated, inspect the breasts for symmetry, size, shape, skin color, vascular patterns, dimpling, and unusual lesions. Ask the patient to put the arms at the sides, arms overhead, lean forward, and press hands on hips. Observe for any abnormalities during these maneuvers. Palpate the axillae and clavicular areas for enlarged lymph nodes.

After the patient assumes the supine position, place a pillow under the back on the side to be examined. Ask the patient to put the arm above and behind the head. This flattens breast tissue and make palpation easier. Then palpate the breast in a systematic fashion, preferably using a vertical line (see Fig. 56.1). Use the distal finger pads of the index, middle, and ring fingers for palpation. Include the axillary tail of Spence. This area of the breast lies adjacent to the upper outer quadrant. It is where most breast cancer develops. Palpate the area around the areolae for masses. Document the color, consistency, and odor of any discharge. For patients at average risk who have no breast symptoms, the benefit of routine clinical breast examinations to detect early breast cancer is unclear. Teach patients to be familiar with how their breasts feel and report any changes or concerns to the HCP.[16]

External genitalia. The assessment of the external female genitalia includes inspection and palpation of the mons pubis, vulva, and anus. Use gloves for the assessment. Assess for hair distribution, presence of body lice, lesions, redness, edema, or discharge. Many women remove hair from the genital region via shaving, waxing, or laser hair removal. They may develop folliculitis (infection of the hair follicle). Separate the labia to fully inspect the clitoris, urethral meatus, and vaginal orifice. Spread the buttocks apart to inspect the anus for fissures, lesions, and hemorrhoids.

Internal pelvic examination. HCPs with advanced or specialized training usually do this part of the examination. During the speculum examination, the HCP inspects the walls of the vagina and cervix for inflammation, discharge, polyps, and suspicious growths. A Pap test and specimens for nucleic acid amplification tests (NAATs) for STI sampling and microscopic examination may be obtained. After the speculum examination, a bimanual examination may be done to assess the size, shape, and consistency of the uterus and ovaries. The ovaries and tubes are not normally palpable.

Table 55.6 gives an example of a recording format for the physical assessment findings. Tables 55.7 through 55.9 summarize assessment abnormalities of the breasts, female reproductive system, and male reproductive system, respectively.

A *focused assessment* is used to evaluate the status of previously identified reproductive problems and to monitor for signs of new problems. A focused assessment of the reproductive system is presented in Box 55.3.

Case Study

Objective Data: Physical Assessment

(© Benjamin A. Peterson/Mother Image/mother image/Fuse/Thinkstock.)

Focused assessment of C.W. reveals the following:

BP is 108/72 mm Hg; her pulse is 78 beats/min and regular. Temp 97.8°F. Skin warm and dry without lesions. No cyanosis of lips, mucous membranes, or nail beds. Thyroid is slightly enlarged. Abdomen soft and nontender. External genitalia examination is normal. Bimanual examination by the HCP is negative for cervical motion tenderness, uterine anomalies. She has pain on left side with palpation of a soft mass consistent with an ovarian cyst.

Discussion Questions

1. Based on the subjective and objective assessment findings, what diagnostic tests would you anticipate being ordered for C.W.?

You will learn more about diagnostic studies related to the reproductive system in the next section.

Answers available at http://evolve.elsevier.com/Lewis/medsurg.

TABLE 55.6 Normal Physical Assessment of the Reproductive System

Male	Female
Breasts	
Nipples soft. No lumps, nodules, swelling, or enlarged tissue noted.	Symmetric without dimpling. Nipples soft. No drainage, retraction, or lesions noted. No masses or tenderness. No lymphadenopathy.
External Genitalia	
Diamond-shaped hair distribution. No penile lesions or discharge noted. Scrotum symmetric, no masses, descended testes. No inguinal hernia.	Triangular hair distribution. Genitalia dark pink, no lesions, redness, swelling, or inflammation in perineal region. No vaginal discharge noted. No tenderness with palpation of Skene ducts and Bartholin glands.
Anus	
No hemorrhoids, fissures, or lesions noted.	No hemorrhoids, fissures, or lesions noted.

DIAGNOSTIC STUDIES OF REPRODUCTIVE SYSTEMS

The most common diagnostic studies used to assess the reproductive systems are described in Tables 55.10 through 55.14. Diagnostic studies of the endocrine system may also be done in a person with a reproductive system problem (see Tables 52.6 and 52.7).

Case Study

Objective Data: Diagnostic Studies

(© Benjamin A. Peterson/Mother Image/mother image/Fuse/Thinkstock.)

The following laboratory and diagnostic tests are ordered for C.W.:

C.W. has a urine pregnancy test, urinalysis, pelvic and transvaginal ultrasound, complete blood count (CBC), thyroid stimulating hormone (TSH), and testing for STIs (HIV, syphilis, gonorrhea, chlamydia). Her results are:

Urine pregnancy test: Negative
Urinalysis: Normal
CBC: hemoglobin, 14.1 g/dL, hematocrit, 36.5%, WBC 11.5
TSH: 0.3 IU/L
HIV Antigen/Antibody: Nonreactive (Negative)
Syphilis: Nonreactive (Negative)
Gonorrhea and chlamydia tests: Negative

The pelvic and transvaginal ultrasound revealed a normal uterus and ovaries with good blood flow and a 4-cm ovarian cyst.

Discussion Questions

1. Which diagnostic and laboratory test results are of concern to you?
2. What patient teaching can you provide C.W. based on her diagnostic test results?

Answers available at http://evolve.elsevier.com/Lewis/medsurg.

TABLE 55.7 ASSESSMENT ABNORMALITIES

Breast

Finding	Description	Possible Cause and Significance
Dimpling	Unilateral, recent onset, no pain	Cancer
Nipple inversion or retraction	Recent onset, redness, pain, unilateral	Abscess, inflammation, cancer
	Recent onset (usually within past year), unilateral, nontender	Cancer
Nipple scaling or irritation	Unilateral or bilateral, crusting, possible ulceration	Paget disease, eczema, infection
Nipple secretions		
• Galactorrhea (female)	Milky, no relationship to lactation, unilateral or bilateral, intermittent or consistent	Drug therapy, especially phenothiazines, tricyclic antidepressants, methyldopa. Hypofunction or hyperfunction of thyroid or adrenal glands. Hypothalamus or pituitary tumor. Excess estrogen. Prolonged suckling or breast foreplay
• Galactorrhea (male)	Milky, bilateral	Chorioepithelioma of testes, pituitary tumor
• Multicolored or dark green discharge	Thick, sticky, often bilateral	Ductal ectasia
• Purulent	Gray-green or yellow color. Often unilateral. May have pain, redness, induration, nipple inversion	Puerperal (after birth) mastitis or abscess
	Same as above but usually without nipple inversion	Infected sebaceous cyst
• Serosanguineous or bloody drainage	Unilateral	Papillomatosis (widespread development of nipple-like growths), intraductal papilloma, cancer (male and female)
• Serous discharge	Clear appearance, unilateral or bilateral, intermittent or consistent	Intraductal papilloma
Nodules, lumps, or masses	Multiple, bilateral, well-delineated, soft or firm, mobile cysts. Pain. Premenstrual occurrence	Fibrocystic changes
	Rubbery consistency, fluid-filled interior, pain	Ductal ectasia
	Soft, mobile, well-delineated cyst, painless	Lipoma, fibroadenoma
	Redness, tenderness, induration	Infected sebaceous cysts, abscesses
	Usually singular, hard, irregularly shaped, poorly delineated, nonmobile	Cancer

TABLE 55.8 ASSESSMENT ABNORMALITIES

Female Reproductive System

Finding and Description	Possible Cause and Significance
Vulvar Discharge	
Thin gray or white, copious flow, malodorous or fishy, vulvar irritation	Bacterial vaginosis infection
White, thick, curdy, itching, redness, no odor or yeast-like smell	Candidiasis (*Candida* or yeast infection), vaginitis
Mucopurulent discharge; bloody discharge	*Chlamydia trachomatis* or *Neisseria gonorrhoeae* infection, menstruation, trauma, cancer
Frothy green or yellow color; malodorous	*Trichomonas vaginalis*
Vulvar Growths	
Soft, fleshy growth, nontender	Condyloma acuminatum (genital warts)
Flat and warty appearance, nontender	Condyloma latum
Same as either of above, possible pain	Cancer
Reddened base, vesicles, and small erosions; pain	Lymphogranuloma venereum, genital herpes, chancroid
Indurated, firm ulcers, no pain	Chancre (syphilis), granuloma inguinale
Vulvar Redness	
Bright or beefy red color, itching	*Candida albicans*, allergy, chemical vaginitis
Reddened base, painful vesicles or ulcerations	Genital herpes
Macules or papules, itching	Chancroid, contact dermatitis, scabies, pediculosis
Abdominal Pain, Tenderness, or Pelvic Masses	
Intermittent or consistent tenderness in right or left lower quadrant	Salpingitis, ectopic pregnancy, ruptured ovarian cyst, pelvic inflammatory disease, tubal or ovarian abscess
Periumbilical location, consistent occurrence	Cystitis, endometritis, ectopic pregnancy
Abdominal or pelvic pain, especially with menses, radiates to back, rectum or vagina.	Endometriosis
Pelvic masses	Fibroids, ovarian cysts, cancer

TABLE 55.9 ASSESSMENT ABNORMALITIES

Male Reproductive System

Finding and Description	Possible Cause and Significance
Inguinal Masses	
Bulging unilateral mass during straining	Inguinal hernia
1– 3 cm nodules	Lymphadenopathy
Penile Discharge	
Clear to purulent color, minimal to copious flow	Urethritis or gonorrhea, *Chlamydia trachomatis* infection, trauma
Penile Growths or Masses	
Indurated, smooth, disk-like appearance. Painless, single lesion	Chancre (syphilis)
Papular to irregularly shaped ulceration with pus, no induration	Chancroid
Ulceration with induration and nodularity	Cancer
Flat, wartlike nodule	Condyloma latum
Raised, fleshy, moist, elongated projections with single or multiple projections	Condyloma acuminatum (genital warts)
Localized swelling with retracted, tight foreskin	Paraphimosis (inability to replace foreskin to its normal position after retraction), trauma
Scrotal Masses	
Localized swelling with tenderness, unilateral or bilateral	Epididymitis, testicular torsion, orchitis (mumps)
Swelling, tenderness	Incarcerated hernia
Swelling without pain. Unilateral or bilateral. Translucent, cordlike, or wormlike appearance	Hydrocele, spermatocele, varicocele, hematocele
Firm, nodular testes or epididymis. Often unilateral	Tuberculosis, cancer
Scrotal or Penile Redness	
Macules and papules	Scabies, pediculosis
Vesicles, Erosions, or Ulcers	
Painful, reddened base. Vesicular or small erosions	Genital herpes, balanitis, chancroid
Painless, singular, small erosion with eventual lymphadenopathy	Lymphogranuloma venereum, cancer

BOX 55.3 FOCUSED ASSESSMENT

Reproductive System

Use this checklist to ensure the key assessment steps have been done.

Subjective

Ask the patient about any of the following and note responses.

Vaginal or vulvar: discharge, lesions, itching, unusual bleeding, odor	Y	N
Penile pain, lesions, discharge	Y	N
Drugs: OCPs, antihypertensives, psychotropics, hormones	Y	N
Clinical assessment of reproductive systems (breast, pelvis, testicular, prostate) and results	Y	N
Pain: abdomen, pelvis, or genitalia	Y	N

Objective: Diagnostic

Check the following for results and critical values.

Serum/urine hCG	✓
Serum PSA	✓
CBC	✓
Hormone studies (testosterone, progesterone, estrogen, FSH, LH, TSH)	✓
NAAT STI results (e.g., *Chlamydia*, gonorrhea, *Trichomonas*)	✓
Testing for other STIs (HIV, syphilis)	
In office testing (e.g., wet mounts, pH assessment)	✓
Mammography and/or breast ultrasound	✓
Ultrasound: abdominal, pelvic, transvaginal, prostate	✓

Objective: Physical Assessment

Inspect

External genitalia for redness, swelling, discharge, lesions	✓
Breasts for swelling, dimpling, retraction, drainage, redness, skin changes, masses	✓

Palpate

Breast tissue for masses or tenderness	✓
External genitalia: tenderness, pain	✓

CBC, Complete blood count; *FSH,* follicle-stimulating hormone; *hCG,* human chorionic gonadotropin; *LH,* luteinizing hormone; *NAAT,* Nucleic acid amplification test; *PSA,* Prostate-specific antigen; *STI,* sexually transmitted infection; *TSH,* thyroid stimulating hormone.

TABLE 55.10 Serology Studies

Male and Female Reproductive Systems

Study	Reference Interval	Description and Purpose
Anti-müllerian hormone (AMH)	*Female:* 13–45 years: 0.9–9.5 ng/mL >45 years: <1.0 ng/mL	Measures ovarian function. Level reflects size of the remaining egg supply ("ovarian reserve"). May be done when a woman has manifestations of polycystic ovarian syndrome (PCOS). Used to monitor AMH-producing ovarian tumor. Females with ↑ AMH levels have a better response to ovarian stimulation during fertility treatments.

TABLE 55.10 Serology Studies—cont'd

Male and Female Reproductive Systems

Study	Reference Interval	Description and Purpose
Estradiol	*Female:* Follicular phase: 20–350 pg/mL (73–1285 pmol/L) Luteal phase: 30–450 pg/mL (110–1652 pmol/L) Postmenopause: ≤20 pg/mL (≤73 pmol/L) *Male:* 10–50 pg/mL (37–184 pmol/L)	Measures ovarian function. Useful in assessing estrogen-secreting tumors and precocious female puberty. Can confirm perimenopausal status. ↑ Levels in men may indicate testicular tumor.
Follicle-stimulating hormone (FSH)	In 24-hr urine samples: *Female:* Follicular phase: 2–15 U/24 hr Midcycle: 8–60 U/24 hr Luteal phase: 2–10 U/24 hr Postmenopause: 35–100 U/24 hr *Male:* 3–11 U/24 hr In blood: *Female:* Follicular phase: 1.37–9.9 mU/mL Ovulatory phase: 6.17–17.2 mU/mL Luteal phase: 1.09–9.2 mU/mL Postmenopause: 19.3–100.6 mU/mL *Male:* 1.42–15.4 mU/mL	Assesses gonadal function. Abnormal levels may indicate pituitary problem. ↑ in menopause. Can confirm menopausal status.
Human chorionic gonadotropin (hCG)	Qualitative: Negative Quantitative: <5 mIU/mL (<5 IU/L) (males and nonpregnant females)	Detects pregnancy. Detects hydatidiform mole and chorioepithelioma (in men and women). Done with urine or blood.
Luteinizing hormone (LH)	*Female:* Premenopause: 5–25 IU/L, with higher peaks at ovulation Postmenopause: 14–52.3 IU/L *Male:* 1.8–8.6 IU/L	Associated with ovulation in women and testosterone production in men. Used in women in the workup of infertility and menstrual irregularities.
Progesterone	*Female:* Follicular phase: 15–70 ng/dL (0.5–2.2 nmol/L) Luteal phase: 200–2500 ng/dL (6.4–79.5 nmol/L) Postmenopause: <40 ng/dL (1.28 nmol/L) *Male:* 13–97 ng/dL (0.4–3.1 nmol/L)	Assesses infertility, monitors success of drugs for infertility or the effect of progesterone treatment. Determines whether ovulation is occurring. Diagnoses problems with adrenal glands and some cancers.
Prolactin	*Female:* 3.8–23.2 ng/mL (3.8–23.2 mg/L) *Male:* 3.0–14.7 ng/mL (3.0–14.7 mg/L)	Detects pituitary problems that can cause amenorrhea, decreased libido, and impotence.
Prostate-specific antigen (PSA)	*Male:* <2.5 ng/mL (<2.5 mcg/L)	Detects prostate problems.
Testosterone	In 24-hr urine samples: *Female:* 2–12 mcg/24 hr (6.9–41.6 nmol/24 hr) *Male:* 40–135 mcg/24 hr (139–469 nmol/24 hr) In blood: *Female:*15–70 ng/dL (0.52–2.43 nmol/L) *Male:* 280–1100 ng/dL (10.4–38.17 nmol/L)	Detects tumors and developmental anomalies of the testicles. Used to assess male infertility.

TABLE 55.11 Radiologic Studies

Male and Female Reproductive Systems

Study	Description and Purpose
CT scan of pelvis	Detects tumors in the pelvis.
Mammography	X-ray image used to assess breast tissue. Detects benign and malignant masses. See Chapter 56 for mammography screening guidelines.
MRI	Radio waves and magnetic field used to assess soft tissue. Useful after an abnormal mammogram or in women with dense breast tissue. Breast MRI may be with mammography to detect breast cancer in women at high risk for breast cancer. Used to diagnose abnormalities in female and male reproductive systems.
Ultrasound (US) (breast, pelvic, testicular, transvaginal [TV], rectal [TRUS])	Measures and records high-frequency sound waves as they pass through tissues of variable density. Breast US: Used to detect fluid-filled masses and for follow-up screening after mammography in women with dense breast tissue. Pelvic and TV US: In women, used to detect pelvic masses, such as ectopic pregnancy, ovarian cysts, fibroids, and cancer. Testicular US: Detects testicular masses and testicular torsion. TRUS: Used to diagnose prostate tumors.

TABLE 55.12 Interventional Studies

Study	Description and Purpose	Nursing Responsibility
Colposcopy	Direct visualization of cervix with binocular microscope. Allows magnification of cervix and study of cellular abnormalities. Used as follow-up for abnormal Pap test. Cervical biopsy(ies) may be taken. Assesses for vaginal or vulvar dysplasia.	*Before:* Teach patient about the procedure. Tell patient this test is similar to a speculum examination. *After.* If a biopsy was done, tell patient there may be some vaginal bleeding and to avoid sexual intercourse until healed.
Conization	Cone-shaped sample of squamocolumnar tissue of cervix removed for direct study.	*Before:* Teach patient about the procedure. Requires anesthesia. *After:* Tell patient to avoid sexual intercourse and tampons for 3–4 weeks. May have some discharge or spotting for 1 week. 3 weeks follow-up necessary.
Dilation and curettage (D&C)	Surgery procedure that dilates cervix and allows curetting of endometrial lining. Used in assessment of abnormal bleeding and cytologic evaluation of lining.	*Before:* Teach patient about procedure and sedation. *After:* Assess degree of bleeding with frequent pad check during first 24 hr.
Hysterosalpingogram (HSG)	Involves instillation of contrast media through cervix into uterine cavity and through fallopian tubes. X-ray images taken to detect abnormalities of uterus and its adnexa (ovaries and tubes) as contrast progresses through them. Often part of infertility assessment (e.g., to detect adhesions, abnormal uterine shape, blockage of tubal pathways).	*Before:* Teach patient about procedure and that it may be uncomfortable. Contrast medium given. *After:* Tell patient she may have slight vaginal bleeding and cramping. Monitor for foul-smelling vaginal discharge, severe pain, fever, or chills.
Hysteroscopy	Allows visualization of uterine lining through insertion of scope through cervix. Used to diagnose and treat abnormal bleeding, such as polyps and fibroids. Biopsy may be done during procedure. May be part of infertility assessment.	*Before:* Should be NPO for at least 6 hr prior. May be done in the HCP's office or an outpatient setting. *After:* Tell patient that mild cramping and slight bloody discharge is normal.
Laparoscopy	Allows visualization of pelvic structures via fiberoptic scopes inserted through small abdominal incisions. Instillation of CO_2 into the abdominal cavity improves visualization. Used in diagnostic assessment of uterus, tubes, and ovaries (Fig. 55.9). Often used for tubal sterilization or part of infertility assessment.	*Before:* Prepare patient for surgery with preoperative teaching and sedation. *After:* Tell patient referred shoulder pain is likely from residual gas in the abdomen. A heating pad may help. A slight discharge or spotting for 2–5 days is normal.
Loop electrosurgical excision procedure (LEEP)	Excision of cervical tissue via an electrosurgical instrument. Diagnoses and treats cervical dysplasia. Minimal amount of tissue removed and preserves childbearing ability.	*Before:* Teach about procedure. May be done in the HCP's office. Patient may feel slight tingling or abdominal cramping during procedure. *After:* Tell patient that discharge, bleeding, and cramping may occur for 1–3 days.
Ultrasound-guided biopsy	Use of ultrasound guidance while performing a biopsy. Ultrasound used to direct the biopsy needle into the region of interest and obtain a sample of tissue. Can diagnose infection, inflammation, or mass.	*Before:* Teach about procedure. Usually done as an outpatient. *After:* Tell patient to monitor for signs and symptoms of infection at biopsy site.

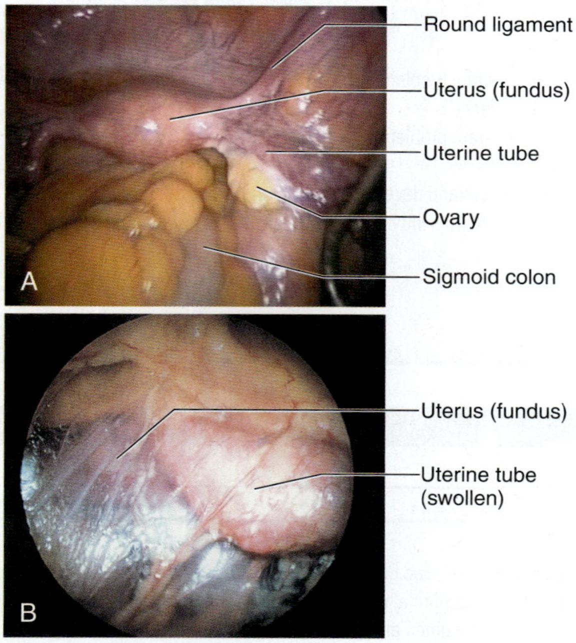

Fig. 55.9 Laparoscopic views of the female pelvis. (A) Normal image. (B) Pelvic inflammatory disease. Note reddish inflammatory membrane covering and fixing the ovary and uterus to the surrounding structures. (A, From Abrahams P, Marks S, Hutching R: *McMinn's color atlas of human anatomy,* ed 5, Philadelphia, 2003, Saunders. B, From Symonds EM, MacPherson MB: *Color atlas of obstetrics and gynecology,* London, 1994, Mosby Wolfe.)

TABLE 55.13 Cytology and Microbiologic Studies

Study	Description and Purpose
Cultures	Specimens from urine to assess for gonorrhea, chlamydia, or UTIs. Rectal and throat cultures may be taken depending on data from sexual history.
Gram stain	Used for rapid detection of gonorrhea. Presence of gram-negative intracellular diplococci generally needs treatment. Not highly accurate for women. Alternative chlamydia test.
Nucleic acid amplification test (NAAT)	Nonculture test used to identify small amounts of DNA or RNA in test samples. Sensitivity similar to culture tests. Uses ligase or polymerase chain reaction that amplifies the signal of the nucleic acids in the test sample so that they are easier to identify. Preferred method to test for gonorrhea, chlamydia, and trichomoniasis. Can be done on a wide variety of samples, including vaginal, endocervical, urethral, urine, rectal, and pharyngeal.
Papanicolaou (Pap) test	Microscopic study of exfoliated cervical cells to detect abnormal cells. *Conventional cytology* entails fixing cells directly to a slide at the time of collection and sending the slide to the laboratory for interpretation. In *liquid-based cytology* the specimen is sent to the laboratory in a liquid solution that preserves it and is processed for microscopic evaluation at the laboratory. Testing for HPV may be done on specimen obtained for liquid-based Pap test.
Wet mounts	Direct microscopic examination of vaginal discharge specimen is done immediately after collection. Determines presence or absence and number of *Trichomonas* organisms, bacteria, white and red blood cells, and candidal buds or hyphae.

TABLE 55.14 Fertility Studies

Study	Description and Purpose
Basal body temperature assessment	Indirectly indicates whether ovulation has occurred. Temperature rises at ovulation and stays high during secretory phase of normal menstrual cycle.
Semen analysis	Assesses semen for volume (2–5 mL), viscosity, sperm count (>20 million/mL), sperm motility (60% motile), and percent of abnormal sperm (60% with normal structure).
Serum anti-müllerian hormone, estradiol, FSH, progesterone	Same as serology studies. See Table 55.10.
Urinary LH	Over-the-counter "ovulation predictor kits." Identifies midcycle LH surge that precedes ovulation by 1–2 days.

BRIDGE TO NCLEX EXAMINATION

The number of the question corresponds to the same-numbered outcome at the beginning of the chapter.

1. A normal male reproductive function that may be altered in a patient who had an orchiectomy (removal of testes) is the production of
   a. PSA.
   b. GnRH.
   c. testosterone.
   d. seminal fluid.
2. Follicle stimulating hormone (FSH) *(select all that apply)*
   a. results in ovulation.
   b. initiates lactation in women.
   c. affects development of ruptured follicles in women.
   d. stimulates seminiferous tubules to make sperm in men.
   e. stimulates growth and maturity of ovarian follicles in women.
3. Male orgasm is characterized by
   a. engorgement of testicles.
   b. resolution and involution of the penis.
   c. filling of the venous sinuses within erectile tissue of the penis.
   d. rapid release of vasocongestion and muscular tension through rhythmic contractions.
4. An age-related finding when assessing an older man's reproductive system is
   a. increased libido.
   b. increased skin turgor.
   c. increase in prostate size.
   d. increase in muscle tone.
5. The 5Ps of sexual history taking includes asking questions about *(select all that apply)*
   a. sexual practices.
   b. gender of partners.
   c. erectile dysfunction.
   d. use of alcohol or drugs while having sex.
   e. past treatment of sexually transmitted infections
6. When performing a breast exam on a patient, which positions are recommended? *(select all that apply)*
   a. Sitting, leaning forward
   b. While sitting and arms raised
   c. Sitting with hands placed on hips
   d. Laying supine with hands by their side
   e. On their side, with one hand on the hip
7. Which condition would the nurse suspect in a patient with a red, tender vulvar lesion?
   a. Genital herpes
   b. Endometriosis
   c. *Neisseria gonorrhoeae*
   d. Condyloma acuminatum
8. The nurse is caring for a patient scheduled for a transvaginal ultrasound. The nurse explains to the woman that
   a. the procedure treats cervical dysplasia.
   b. bleeding and discharge are common after the procedure.
   c. the procedure involves curettage of the endometrial lining.
   d. the uterus, ovaries, and potential abnormal findings can be visualized.

1. c; 2. d, e; 3. d; 4. c; 5. a, b, e; 6. a, b, c; 7. a; 8. d.

For rationales to these answers and even more NCLEX review questions, visit http://evolve.elsevier.com/Lewis/medsurg.

EVOLVE WEBSITE/RESOURCES LIST

http://evolve.elsevier.com/Lewis/medsurg
Review Questions (Online Only)
Key Points
Answer Keys for Questions
- Rationales for Bridge to NCLEX Examination Questions
- Answer Guidelines for Case Study

Conceptual Care Map Creator
Audio Glossary
Content Updates

REFERENCES

1. National Cancer Institute (NCI): Male reproductive system. Retrieved from https://training.seer.cancer.gov/anatomy/reproductive/male/.
2. NCI: Female reproductive system. Retrieved from https://training.seer.cancer.gov/anatomy/reproductive/female/response.html.
3. Rogel Cancer Center Michigan Medicine: Normal ovarian function. Retrieved from https://www.rogelcancercenter.org/fertility-preservation/for-female-patients/normal-ovarian-function.

4. Masters WH, Johnson E: *Human sexual response*, Boston, 1966, Little Brown. (Classic).
5. Knudtson J, McLaughlin JE: Effects of aging on the female reproductive system. Retrieved from https://www.merckmanuals.com/home/women-s-health-issues/biology-of-the-female-reproductive-system/effects-of-aging-on-the-female-reproductive-system.
6. Santoro N, Roeca C, Peters BA, et al.: The menopause transition: signs, symptoms, and management options, *J Clin Endocrinol Metab* 106:1, 2021.
7. Centers for Disease Control and Prevention (CDC): Pregnancy and rubella. Retrieved from https://www.cdc.gov/rubella/pregnancy.html.
8. Medline Plus: Aging changes in the male reproductive system. Retrieved from https://medlineplus.gov/ency/article/004017.htm.
*9. The American College of Obstetricians and Gynecologists: Combined hormonal birth control: pill, patch, and ring. Retrieved from https://www.acog.org/womens-health/faqs/combined-hormonal-birth-control-pill-patch-ring.
10. Mayo Clinic: Menopause diagnosis and treatment. Retrieved from https://www.mayoclinic.org/diseases-conditions/menopause/diagnosis-treatment/drc-20353401.
11. American Cancer Society (ACS): Can prostate cancer be found early? Retrieved from https://www.cancer.org/cancer/prostatecancer/detailedguide/prostate-cancer-detection.
12. CDC: Health effects of cigarette smoking. Retrieved from https://www.cdc.gov/tobacco/data_statistics/fact_sheets/health_effects/effects_cig_smoking/.
13. Medscape: Human papilloma virus. Retrieved from https://emedicine.medscape.com/article/219110-overview#a4.
14. CDC: Recommendations: Women and folic acid. Retrieved from https://www.cdc.gov/ncbddd/folicacid/recommendations.html.
*15. American Academy of Family Physicians: Female athlete triad. Retrieved from https://familydoctor.org/condition/female-athlete-triad/.
*16. ACS: ACS recommendations for the early detection of cancer. Retrieved from https://www.cancer.org/healthy/find-cancer-.

*Evidence-based information for clinical practice.

Breast Problems

Deena D. Dell

http://evolve.elsevier.com/Lewis/medsurg/

CONCEPTUAL FOCUS

Coping
Cellular Regulation
Infection
Pain
Sexuality

LEARNING OUTCOMES

1. State screening guidelines for the early detection of breast cancer.
2. Explain the types, causes, clinical manifestations, and interprofessional and nursing management of common benign breast problems.
3. State the risk factors for breast cancer.
4. Describe the pathophysiology and clinical manifestations of breast cancer.
5. Describe the interprofessional and nursing management of breast cancer.
6. Specify the physical and psychologic aspects of nursing management for the patient undergoing breast cancer surgery.
7. Explain the indications for, types and complications of, and nursing management after reconstructive breast surgery.

KEY TERMS

ductal ectasia
fibroadenoma
fibrocystic changes
galactorrhea
gynecomastia
intraductal papilloma
lumpectomy
lymphedema
mammoplasty
mastalgia
mastitis
Paget disease

Breast problems are a significant health concern for women. Whether the actual diagnosis is a benign condition or cancer, the initial discovery of a lump or change in the breast often triggers intense feelings of anxiety and fear. The potential loss of a breast, or part of a breast, may be devastating for many women because of the significant psychologic, social, sexual, and body image implications associated with it.

The most common breast problems are fibrocystic changes, fibroadenoma, intraductal papilloma, ductal ectasia, and breast cancer. In a woman's lifetime, there is a 1 in 8 (12%) chance that she will be diagnosed with breast cancer.[1] Although rare, breast cancer does occur in men. Being aware of personal risk, including genetic factors, and taking part in recommended screening are important health promotion activities.

ASSESSMENT OF BREAST PROBLEMS

Breast Cancer Screening Guidelines

Screening guidelines for the early detection of breast cancer vary depending on a woman's age and risk (Table 56.1).[2] Average risk women include those with no personal history of breast cancer, a strong family of breast cancer, a genetic mutation known to increase breast cancer, and has not had chest radiation therapy before the age of 30.

Women at increased risk for breast cancer (family history, genetic link, prior breast cancer, history of thoracic radiation therapy, or certain atypical findings on a prior breast biopsy) should talk with their HCP about the benefits and limitations of starting screening earlier with 3D mammography and breast magnetic resonance imaging (MRI) and having more frequent clinical breast encounters. A clinical encounter includes an assessment of risk factors, instruction in ways to reduce the risk factors, and a clinical breast examination (CBE).[3]

Consistent breast self-examination (BSE) may be a useful way to increase self-awareness of how one's breasts normally look and feel. However, research has shown that BSE has no effect on reducing deaths from breast cancer. However, you still need to teach women the importance of knowing how their breasts look and feel and to report breast changes (e.g., nipple discharge, a lump) to their HCP.[3]

If a woman wants to learn about BSE, include information about the potential benefits and limitations. Allow time for questions and a return demonstration. For women who choose to perform BSE, teach the method described at www.breastcancer.org/symptoms/testing/types/self_exam/.

TABLE 56.1 Breast Cancer Screening Guidelines

The American Cancer Society (ACS) recommends the following guidelines for screening women at average risk for breast cancer:

- Women should undergo regular screening mammography starting at age 45 years
- Women should be offered the chance to begin annual screening between the ages of 40 and 44
- Women aged 45–54 years should be screened annually
- Women 55 years and older can switch to every other year screening or can continue screening annually
- Women should continue screening if their overall health is good, and they have a life expectancy of 10 years or longer
- The ACS does not recommend CBE as screening for breast cancer

Diagnostic Studies

Radiologic Studies

We use several techniques to screen for breast problems or help diagnose a suspicious physical finding. *Mammography* is used to view the breast's internal structure using x-rays (Fig. 56.1). It can detect suspicious lumps that cannot be felt. Mammography has significantly improved the early and accurate detection of breast cancer. Improved imaging technology has reduced the radiation dose from mammography.

A comparison of current and prior mammograms may show early tissue changes. Because some tumors metastasize late, early detection by mammography allows for earlier treatment and the prevention of metastasis. In younger women, mammography is less sensitive because of the greater density of breast tissue, resulting in more false-negative results. Having dense breasts makes mammographic detection of cancer more difficult.

With *digital mammography* x-ray images are digitally coded and stored in a computer (Fig. 56.1). It is more accurate than traditional film mammography in younger women with dense breasts. The availability and associated costs of digital mammography are issues with this technology.

3D mammography, or tomosynthesis mammography, produces a 3D image of the breast. It gives a clearer view of overlapping breast tissue structures. It can increase the number of cancers detected and decrease the number of false-positive results (a result stating a cancer is present when it is not).

Calcifications are the most easily recognized mammogram abnormality (Fig. 56.1). They are deposits of calcium crystals that form in the breast. Causes include inflammation, trauma, and aging. Although most calcifications are benign, they may occur with breast cancer.

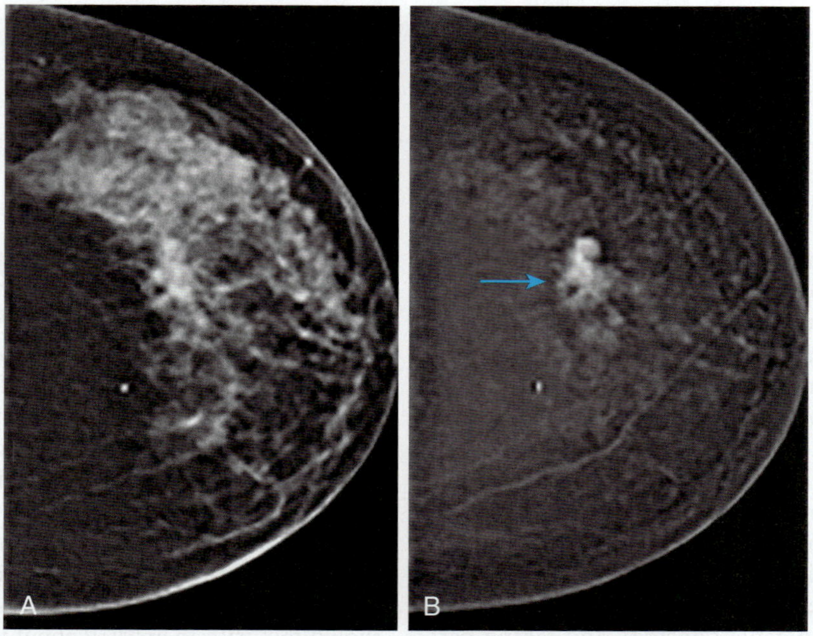

Fig. 56.1 Screening mammogram showing dense breast tissue and benign, scattered microcalcifications. (A) Using conventional x-rays. (B) Using digital x-rays. (From Patel B, Lobbes M, Lewin J: Contrast enhanced spectral mammography: a review, *Semin Ultrasound CT MR* 39:70, 2018e.)

About 10% to 15% of all breast cancers cannot be seen on mammography. They may be detected by palpation or other breast imaging studies, such as ultrasound and MRI. If the clinical findings are suspicious and the mammogram is normal, an ultrasound or MRI may be done. Based on these findings, a biopsy may be done.

Ultrasound is used in conjunction with mammography to discern a solid mass from a cystic mass, to evaluate a mass in a pregnant or lactating woman, and to locate and biopsy a suspicious lesion. MRI is recommended as a screening tool in addition to mammography for women who are at high risk for breast cancer (e.g., first-degree relative with a *BRCA* mutation).

Biopsies

A definitive diagnosis of a suspicious area is made by analyzing biopsied tissue. Biopsy techniques include *fine-needle aspiration* (FNA), core (core needle), vacuum-assisted, and excisional biopsies.

FNA biopsy is done by inserting a needle into a lesion to sample fluid from a breast cyst, remove cells from intercellular spaces, or sample cells from a solid mass. Before the procedure, the breast area is first locally anesthetized. Then, the needle is placed into the breast, and fluid and cells are aspirated into a syringe. Usually, 3 or 4 passes are made. If the results are negative with a suspicious lesion, another biopsy may be necessary.

A *core (core needle) biopsy* involves removing small samples of breast tissue using a hollow "core" needle. For palpable lesions, this is done by fixing the lesion with one hand and performing a needle biopsy with the other. In the case of nonpalpable lesions, *stereotactic mammography,* ultrasound, or MRI image guidance is used. Stereotactic mammography uses computers to pinpoint the exact location of a breast mass based on mammograms. With ultrasound, the HCP watches the needle on the ultrasound monitor to help guide it to the area of concern. A core biopsy is more accurate because it removes more tissue than an FNA.

Vacuum-assisted biopsy is a version of core biopsy that uses a vacuum technique to help collect the tissue sample. In core biopsy, several separate needle insertions are used to obtain multiple samples. During vacuum-assisted biopsy, the needle is inserted only once into the breast, and the needle can be rotated, allowing for multiple samples through a single needle insertion.

Minimally invasive breast biopsies have become the standard of care for diagnosing abnormalities found either on imaging studies or through CBE. However, in some cases, an *excisional biopsy* is recommended. An excisional biopsy is done in an operating room.

BENIGN BREAST PROBLEMS

MASTALGIA

Mastalgia, or breast pain, is the most common breast-related symptom reported in women. The most common form is *cyclic mastalgia,* which coincides with the menstrual cycle.[4] Women describe it as diffuse bilateral breast tenderness or heaviness. Breast pain may last 2 or 3 days or most of the month. It is related to hormonal sensitivity. Symptoms often decrease with menopause.

Noncyclic mastalgia has no relationship to the menstrual cycle. It can continue into menopause. Pain may be constant or intermittent throughout the month and last for several years. Symptoms include a burning, aching, or soreness in the breast. It usually affects only 1 breast. The pain may be from trauma, fat necrosis, ductal ectasia, costochondritis, or arthritic pain in the chest or neck radiating to the breast.

For patients with breast pain, mammography and targeted ultrasound are often done to exclude cancer and provide information on the cause of the pain. Reassure women that mastalgia is not a usual sign of breast cancer.[4]

There is no specific treatment for breast pain. Some relief for cyclic pain may occur by reducing intake of caffeine and fat; taking vitamin E or gamma-linolenic acid (evening primrose oil); and continually wearing a supportive bra. Compresses, ice, analgesics, and antiinflammatory drugs may help. Tamoxifen may provide relief in up to 70% of women with few side effects. Bromocriptine, a prolactin inhibitor, may provide some with relief. It causes GI upset and lightheadedness. Danazol is an FDA-approved treatment. The androgenic side effects (acne, edema, hirsutism) make this therapy unacceptable for many women.

BREAST INFECTIONS

Mastitis

Mastitis is an inflammatory breast condition. It occurs most often in lactating women (Table 56.2). *Lactational mastitis* presents as a localized area that is red, painful, and tender to palpation. Fever is often present. The infection develops when pathogens (usually staphylococci) gain access to the breast through a cracked nipple. In its early stages, mastitis can be cured with antibiotics. Breastfeeding should continue unless an abscess is forming, or there is purulent drainage. The mother may wish to use a nipple shield or to hand-express milk from the involved breast until the pain subsides. The woman should see her HCP promptly to begin antibiotic therapy. Any breast that stays red, tender, and not responsive to antibiotics requires follow-up care and evaluation for inflammatory breast cancer.[4,5]

Mastitis sometimes develops in women who are not lactating. This is called *periductal mastitis.* It occurs most often in regular smokers aged late 20s to early 30s. Treatment is the same as for lactating mastitis.

Lactational Breast Abscess

If lactational mastitis persists after several days of antibiotic therapy, a lactational breast abscess may be present. In this condition, the skin may become red and edematous over the involved breast, often with a corresponding palpable mass. The patient may have a fever. Antibiotics alone are insufficient treatment for a breast abscess. Ultrasound-guided drainage of the abscess or surgical incision and drainage are done. The drainage is cultured, and sensitivities are obtained. Antibiotic therapy is started. Breastfeeding can continue in most cases with ongoing treatment.

TABLE 56.2 Common Benign Breast Problems

Disorder	Risk Factors	Clinical Manifestations
Lactational mastitis	Occurs in up to 33% of postpartum lactating mothers (both primipara and multipara). Usually within first 3 months after birth	• Warm to touch, indurated, painful, often unilateral • Most often caused by *Staphylococcus aureus*
Fibrocystic changes	Most common between ages 30 and 50	• Not usually discrete masses—nodularity instead • Usually accompanied by cyclic pain and tenderness • Mass(es) often cyclic in occurrence (movable, soft)
Cysts	Most common over age 35. Incidence decreases after menopause. Develop in over half of women in North America	• Palpable fluid-filled mass (movable, soft, tender) • Multiple cysts can occur and recur • Rarely associated with breast cancer
Fibroadenoma	Often occurs in teens and those in their 20s	• Palpable mass (firm, movable), usually 1–3 cm in size • Rarely associated with breast cancer
Fat necrosis	Many women report a history of trauma to breast	• Usually a hard, tender, mobile, indurated mass with irregular borders
Ductal ectasia	Most common in women over 60 years old. Considered a normal part of aging. May be due to duct obstruction or mastitis	• Nipple fixation, usually accompanied by nipple discharge of thick gray material • Breast pain often present

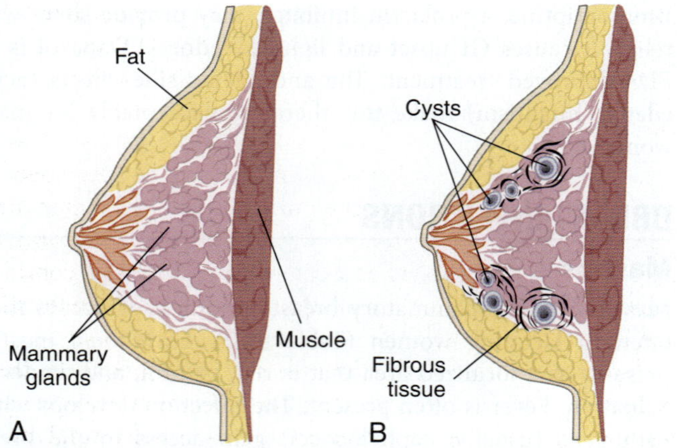

Fig. 56.2 (A) Normal breast tissue. (B) Fibrocystic breast tissue.

FIBROCYSTIC CHANGES

Fibrocystic changes are benign conditions characterized by changes in breast tissue (Fig. 56.2).[6,7] Fibrocystic changes are the most common breast disorder. They occur in more than 30% to 60% of women of reproductive age. Fibrocystic changes occur most often between ages 30 and 50 but may begin under 21 years of age in as many as 10% of women. Many women report premenstrual abnormalities, early menarche or late menopause, or a history of spontaneous abortion. Others at risk include nulliparous women and nonusers of oral contraceptives.

Fibrocystic changes include excess fibrous tissue, hyperplasia of the epithelial lining of the mammary ducts, proliferation of mammary ducts, and cysts. We think these changes are due to a heightened responsiveness of breast tissue to circulating estrogen and progesterone. They may cause pain from chronic inflammation, edema, nerve irritation, and fibrosis. Pain and nodularity often increase over time. They tend to subside after menopause unless the woman is taking high doses of estrogen replacement. Symptoms often worsen in the premenstrual phase and subside after menstruation.

Manifestations of fibrocystic breast changes include 1 or more palpable lumps that are often round, well delineated, and freely movable within the breast (Table 56.2). Discomfort ranging from tenderness to pain may occur. The lump usually increases in size and sometimes tenderness before menstruation. Cysts may enlarge or shrink rapidly. Nipple discharge from fibrocystic breasts is often green or dark brown, not bloody.

Alone, fibrocystic changes do not increase breast cancer risk. Masses or nodules can appear in both breasts. They often occur in the upper, outer quadrants and usually bilaterally.

Mammography may be helpful in distinguishing fibrocystic changes from breast cancer. In some women, the breast tissue is so dense that it is hard to obtain a mammogram. In these situations, ultrasound can better distinguish a fluid-filled cyst from a solid mass.

Interprofessional and Nursing Care

With the discovery of a discrete mass in the breast by a woman or the HCP, aspiration or biopsy may be done. If the nodularity is recurrent, we may wait 7 to 10 days to see if any changes are related to the menstrual cycle. With large or frequent cysts, an excisional biopsy may be preferred over repeated aspiration. An excisional biopsy may be done if (1) no fluid is found on aspiration, (2) the fluid is hemorrhagic, or (3) a residual mass remains after fluid aspiration.

Severe fibrocystic changes may make palpating the breast more difficult. Teach the woman with cystic changes to maintain regular follow-up care with the HCP. Encourage breast self-awareness and to report any changes found so they can be evaluated.

Treatment for a fibrocystic condition is similar to that described earlier for mastalgia. Teach the woman with fibrocystic breasts that she may expect cysts to reoccur in 1 or both breasts until menopause and that the cysts may enlarge or become painful just before menstruation. Reassure her that the cysts do not "turn into" cancer. Tell her that the HCP should examine any new lump that does not respond in a cyclic manner over 1 to 2 weeks.

FIBROADENOMA

Fibroadenoma is the most common cause of discrete benign breast lumps in young women. It generally occurs in women in their teens and 20s. They occur more often in Black than White women.

The possible cause may be increased estrogen sensitivity in a localized area of the breast. Fibroadenomas are usually small (but can be large [2 to 3 cm]), painless, round, well delineated, and very mobile. They are usually solid, firm, and rubbery in consistency. There is no accompanying retraction or nipple discharge. The fibroadenoma may appear as a single unilateral mass, although multiple bilateral fibroadenomas may occur. Growth is slow and often ceases when the size reaches 2 to 3 cm. Menstruation does not affect size. However, pregnancy can stimulate dramatic growth.

Fibroadenomas are easily detected by physical assessment. They may be visible on mammography and ultrasound. However, definitive diagnosis requires FNA, core, or excisional biopsy and tissue examination to exclude a cancer. Treatment can include observation with regular monitoring if cancer is not present, there are no symptoms, and the mass stays less than 3 cm. A fibroadenoma that increases in size and/or is symptomatic should be removed by surgical resection or, in some cases, cryotherapy. All new lesions should be evaluated by breast ultrasound and possible biopsy.

NIPPLE DISCHARGE

Nipple discharge may occur spontaneously or because of nipple manipulation. Secretions can be clear, serous, bloody, or brown to green. A milky secretion is due to inappropriate lactation, or **galactorrhea**.

Disorders associated with nipple discharge include benign breast conditions, such as fibrocystic changes, intraductal papilloma, or ductal ectasia. It may be a result of certain medicines or endocrine or neurologic problems. Sometimes there is no known cause. In most cases, nipple discharge is not caused by cancer. However, spontaneous, unilateral discharge that can be reproduced on exam warrants further evaluation. A cytology slide of the secretion can help determine the specific cause and recommended treatment.

ATYPICAL HYPERPLASIA

Atypical hyperplasia is usually found after a biopsy is done to evaluate a suspicious area found on a mammogram or during a CBE. It can be in either the ducts (atypical ductal hyperplasia) or in the lobules (atypical lobular hyperplasia). Both increase the risk for breast cancer. To follow up on a diagnosis of atypical hyperplasia, an excisional biopsy or lumpectomy may be done to remove all the affected tissue.[6]

INTRADUCTAL PAPILLOMA

An **intraductal papilloma** is a benign, soft or hard, wart-like growth found in the mammary ducts. It is usually unilateral. Typically, the nipple has a bloody discharge that can be intermittent or spontaneous. Most intraductal papillomas are beneath the areola. They may be hard to palpate. They usually occur in women 35 to 55 years of age. A single duct or several ducts may be involved. Papillomas have a slightly increased risk for developing breast cancer, so a core biopsy is recommended. If there are any abnormal cells, surgical excision of the papilloma and the involved duct or duct system is done.[8]

DUCTAL ECTASIA

Ductal ectasia (duct dilation) is a benign breast disease of perimenopausal and postmenopausal women involving the ducts in the subareolar area. It usually involves several bilateral ducts. Nipple discharge is the main symptom. Ductal ectasia is initially painless but may progress to burning, itching, pain around the nipple, and swelling in the areolar area. Inflammatory signs are often present. The nipple may retract. The discharge may become bloody in more advanced disease. It is not associated with cancer. If an abscess develops, warm compresses and antibiotics are usually effective treatments. Therapy consists of close follow-up examinations or surgical excision of the involved ducts.

MALE GYNECOMASTIA

Gynecomastia is a transient, noninflammatory enlargement of 1 or both breasts. It is the most common breast problem in men. The condition is usually temporary and benign. Gynecomastia itself is not a risk factor for breast cancer. The most common cause is a change in the normal ratio of active androgen to estrogen in plasma or within the breast itself.[9]

Gynecomastia can occur in puberty. During puberty, there is often a transient relative imbalance between estrogen and testosterone, leading to gynecomastia. It usually resolves by age 20 years when the person reaches adult androgen-to-estrogen ratios. Reassure the parent and teenager about the benign nature of the condition.

Gynecomastia can also be a sign of other problems. It may occur with testicular tumors, adrenal cancer, pituitary adenomas, hyperthyroidism, and liver disease. It can be a side effect of drug therapy, particularly with estrogen and androgen, digitalis, isoniazid, ranitidine, and spironolactone. Marijuana use can also cause gynecomastia.

Senescent Gynecomastia

Senescent gynecomastia occurs in many older men. The likely cause is high plasma estrogen levels with the increased conversion of androgens to estrogens in peripheral circulation. Although initially unilateral, the tender, firm, centrally located enlargement may become bilateral. A discrete, circumscribed mass with gynecomastia must be biopsied to determine if it is the rare breast cancer in males. Senescent hyperplasia needs no treatment. It usually regresses within 6 to 12 months.

Gerontologic Considerations: Age-Related Breast Changes

The loss of subcutaneous fat and structural support and the atrophy of mammary glands often result in pendulous breasts in the postmenopausal woman. Encourage older women to wear a well-fitting bra. Adequate support can improve physical appearance and reduce pain in the back, shoulders, and neck. It can also prevent *intertrigo,* dermatitis caused by friction between opposing surfaces of skin.

The decrease in glandular tissue makes a breast mass easier to palpate. This decreased density likely results from age-related decreases in estrogen. Rib margins may be palpable in a thin woman and can be confused with a mass. That is why it is so important that women become familiar with their own breasts and what is normal for them. Because the incidence of breast cancer increases with age, encourage breast awareness in older women. Encourage them to have an annual mammogram and CBE and have any breast-related concern evaluated by their HCP.

BREAST CANCER

Breast cancer is the most common cancer in American women except for skin cancer. It is second only to lung cancer as the leading cause of death from cancer in women. In the United States, more than 276,480 new cases of invasive breast cancer and more than 48,530 cases of in situ breast cancer are diagnosed each year. Another 2620 cases of breast cancer happen in men. About 42,690 deaths occur each year from breast cancer.[10]

The incidence of breast cancer is slowly decreasing, with a slight drop in the number of deaths from breast cancer. This decline may be due to the decreased use of hormone therapy after menopause as well as earlier detection and treatment advances. Breast cancer survivors are the largest group of any cancer survivors.

Etiology and Risk Factors

We do not completely understand the cause of breast cancer. We know there are several risk factors (Table 56.3). Risk factors appear to be cumulative and interacting. So, the presence of multiple risk factors may greatly increase the overall risk, especially for women with a positive family history.

Risk Factors for Women

The strongest risk factors include female gender and advancing age.[10] Women are at far greater risk than men. 99% of breast cancers occur in women. Increasing age increases the risk for developing breast cancer. The incidence of breast cancer in women under 25 years of age is very low. Risk increases gradually until age 55. After age 55, the incidence increases dramatically.

Hormonal regulation of the breast is related to cancer development, but we do not understand exactly how. The hormones estrogen and progesterone may act as tumor promoters to stimulate breast cancer growth if cancer changes in the cells have already occurred. The Women's Health Initiative study showed that combined hormone therapy (estrogen plus progesterone) (1) increases the risk for breast cancer after as little as 2 years use and (2) increased the risk for having a larger, more advanced breast cancer at diagnosis. However, this risk decreases within 5 years of stopping hormone therapy. Some studies show that using estrogen therapy alone for longer than 15 years (for women with a prior hysterectomy) increases long-term risk. A link also exists between oral contraceptive use and increased risk for breast cancer. This risk decreases when use stops and is gone after 10 years.

Modifiable risk factors include excess weight gain during adulthood, sedentary lifestyle, smoking, fat intake, obesity, nightshift work, and alcohol use. Environmental factors, such as radiation exposure and using hair dyes and straighteners, may play a role.

Genetic Link

Family history of breast cancer is an important risk factor, especially if the family member also had ovarian cancer, was

TABLE 56.3 Risk Factors for Breast Cancer

Risk Factor	Comments
Age ≥55 years	Majority found in postmenopausal women After age 60, ↑ in incidence
Alcohol use	Drinking ≥1 alcoholic beverage per day may have an ↑ risk
Benign breast disease with atypical epithelial hyperplasia, lobular carcinoma in situ	Atypical changes in breast biopsy ↑ risk
Chemicals in environment, cosmetics (parabens, phthalates), food	Emerging risk: may be hormone disruptors
Early menarche (before age 12), late menopause (after age 55)	A long menstrual history ↑ risk
Exposure to ionizing radiation	Radiation damages DNA (e.g., prior treatment for Hodgkin lymphoma)
Family history	Breast cancer, ovarian, pancreatic and high-grade prostate cancer in a first-degree relative, particularly when premenopausal or bilateral
Female	Women account for 99% of breast cancer cases
First full-term pregnancy after age 30, nulliparity, no breastfeeding	Prolonged exposure to unopposed estrogen ↑ risk
Genetic factors *(BRCA1, BRCA2, P53, PTEN, PALB2, ATM, CHEK2, NBM)*	Gene mutations play a role in up to 10% of breast cancer cases
Hair chemicals in permanent dyes and hair straightening products	Emerging risk: especially in Black women
Height, being taller	May be due to factors related to early growth
Hormone use	Use of estrogen and/or progesterone as hormone therapy, especially in postmenopausal women
Light exposure at night	Emerging risk: seen in night shift workers
Long-term heavy smoking	May ↑ risk, especially in women who begin smoking before first pregnancy
Obesity, weight gain after menopause	Fat cells store estrogen, which ↑ the risk for developing breast cancer
Personal history of breast, colon, endometrial, or ovarian cancer	Personal history significantly ↑ risk for breast cancer, risk for cancer in other breast, and recurrence
Physical inactivity	Risk ↑s most after menopause
Race and ethnicity	See Box 56.2

premenopausal, or had bilateral breast cancer. Having any first-degree relative (mother, father, sister, brother, daughter) with breast cancer doubles a woman's risk for breast cancer, especially if the relative was diagnosed at a young age.[11] A breast cancer risk assessment tool for HCPs is available *(www.cancer.gov/bcrisktool)*. Genetic counseling must be considered for a person at high risk for breast cancer.

Up to 10% of all breast cancers are hereditary. This means that the person inherited specific genetic abnormalities that contribute to breast cancer development (Box 56.1). Most inherited cases of breast cancer are related to mutations in 2 genes: *BRCA1* and *BRCA2*. *BRCA* stands for *BR*east *CA*ncer. Everyone has *BRCA* genes. The *BRCA1* gene, found on chromosome 17, is a tumor suppressor gene that inhibits tumor development when functioning normally. The *BRCA2* gene, found on chromosome 11, is another tumor suppressor gene. Women with a mutation of this gene have a similar risk for breast cancer.[11]

BOX 56.1 GENETICS IN CLINICAL PRACTICE

Breast Cancer

Genetic Basis
- Mutations occur in *BRCA1* and/or *BRCA2* genes.
- Normally, these genes are tumor suppressor genes involved in DNA repair.
- Transmission is autosomal dominant.
- Other genes (e.g., *ATM, CHEK2, TP53, PTEN, PALB2, NBM, NF1, STK11, CHD1, READ 56C, BRIP1, BARD1, STK11, MSI, NTRK*) may increase the risk for breast cancer.

Incidence
- Up to 10% of breast cancers are related to *BRCA1* and *BRCA2* gene mutations.
- As many as 1 in 300–800 women in the United States have *BRCA1* and *BRCA2* gene mutations.[12]
- Women with *BRCA1* and *BRCA2* gene mutations have a 41%–90% lifetime risk for developing breast cancer along with an increased risk for developing cancer in the other breast.
- Mutations in *BRCA* genes may cause as many as 90% of all inherited breast cancers.
- *BRCA1* and *BRCA2* gene mutations are associated with early-onset breast cancer that is more likely to involve both breasts.
- Men with mutations in *BRCA1* and *BRCA2* have an increased risk for breast cancer and prostate cancer.
- Family history of both breast and ovarian cancer increases the risk for having a *BRCA* mutation.

Genetic Testing
- DNA testing is available for *BRCA1* and *BRCA2* gene mutations.
- Genetic tests can analyze an entire panel of genes.

Clinical Implications
- Bilateral oophorectomy and/or bilateral mastectomy reduces the risk for breast cancer and ovarian cancer in women with *BRCA1* and *BRCA2* mutations.
- Women with *BRCA* mutations have a higher risk for developing ovarian, colon, pancreatic, and uterine cancers.[12]
- Genetic counseling and testing for *BRCA* mutations should be offered to patients whose personal or family history puts them at high risk for a genetic predisposition to breast cancer.

In addition to *BRCA* gene mutations, we have identified many other abnormal genes that increase a person's risk of developing breast cancer. These include the genes that normally suppress tumor growth, including *PALB2* (which partners with *BRCA* to suppress tumor growth), *TP53, CHEK2, PTEN*. Other genes that may be abnormal include *ATM* and *NBM* (help repair damaged DNA), *CDH1* (makes a protein to bind cells together), and *STK11* (provides instructions to make a tumor suppressor enzyme).[12]

Most people (90%) who develop breast cancer do not have an abnormal breast cancer gene or a family history of breast cancer. Their cancer is associated with genetic changes that occurred after they were born (somatic mutations). There is no risk for passing on the mutated gene to children.

Risk Factors for Men

Risk factors for breast cancer in men include estrogen use, hyperestrogenism, a family history of breast cancer, and radiation exposure. Examining the male breast should be a routine part of a physical assessment. Men in *BRCA*-positive families should consider genetic testing. Teach men who test positive for a *BRCA* gene mutation to be aware of how their breasts look and feel and to report any changes to their HCP. They should have a CBE every year starting at age of 35.[13] We do not recommend screening mammography as research shows this to be of no benefit. Men with a history of breast cancer treated with lumpectomy should have an ipsilateral annual mammogram. Men with a history of breast cancer and a genetic mutation with an increased risk of breast cancer should have a contralateral mammogram.[14] These men should begin prostate screening at age 35 as they have an increased risk for prostate cancer.

Prophylactic Oophorectomy and Mastectomy

In women with *BRCA1* or *BRCA2* mutations, prophylactic bilateral oophorectomy can decrease the risk for breast and ovarian cancers. Removing the ovaries lowers the risk for breast cancer because the ovaries are the main source of estrogen in a premenopausal woman.

CHECK YOUR PRACTICE

You are doing a preoperative assessment on a woman who having an elective mastectomy because she has a high risk for breast cancer based on her BRCA testing. You note that she appears nervous. She asks you, "Do you think I'm being too aggressive by having this surgery?"
- How would you respond to her?

Removing the ovaries does not reduce the risk for breast cancer in postmenopausal women because the ovaries are not the main producers of estrogen in these women. Women with *BRCA* mutations also have a higher risk for developing breast cancer in the unaffected (contralateral) breast. They may, as might any woman who has a high risk for developing breast cancer choose, in consultation with her HCP and genetic counselor, to undergo prophylactic bilateral mastectomy.

TABLE 56.4 Classification of Breast Cancer

Based on Tissue Type
- Ductal carcinoma (affects milk ducts)
  - Medullary
  - Tubular
  - Colloid (mucinous)
- Lobular carcinoma (affects milk-producing glands)
- Other
  - Inflammatory
  - Paget disease
  - Phyllodes tumor

Based on Invasiveness
Noninvasive (In situ)
- Ductal carcinoma in situ (DCIS)
- Pure Paget disease

Invasive (Spreading to Other Locations)
- Invasive ductal carcinoma
- Invasive lobular carcinoma

Based on Hormone Receptor and Genetic Status
Estrogen and Progesterone Receptor Status
- Estrogen receptor positive
- Estrogen receptor negative
- Progesterone receptor positive
- Progesterone receptor negative

HER-2 Genetic Status
- HER-2 positive
- HER-2 negative

Pathophysiology

The main components of the breast are lobules (milk-producing glands) and ducts (milk passages that connect the lobules and the nipple). In general, breast cancer arises from the epithelial lining of the ducts *(ductal carcinoma)* or from the epithelium of the lobules *(lobular carcinoma).* Breast cancers may be in situ (within the duct) or invasive (invading through the duct wall).

Metastatic breast cancer is breast cancer that has spread to other organs. The most common sites are the bone, liver, lung, and brain. Cancer growth rates can range from slow to rapid. Factors that affect cancer prognosis are tumor size, axillary node involvement (the more nodes involved, the worse the prognosis), tumor differentiation, estrogen and progesterone receptor (PR) status, and *human epidermal growth factor receptor 2* (HER-2) status. HER-2 is a protein that helps regulate cell growth.[15]

Types of Breast Cancer

Breast cancer is not just one disease, but a group of diseases characterized by different pathologic findings and clinical behaviors. Breast cancer can be classified as (1) ductal, lobular, or other or (2) noninvasive or invasive (Table 56.4). We can also classify it based on hormonal status and genetic subtypes.

Noninvasive Breast Cancer

Around 20% of breast cancers are noninvasive. Noninvasive cancer stays within the milk ducts or lobules. They do not grow into or invade normal tissues within or beyond the breast. They are sometimes called carcinoma in situ ("in the same place") or pre-cancers. These cancers include *ductal carcinoma in situ* (DCIS) and pure Paget disease.

DCIS tends to be unilateral. It may progress to invasive breast cancer if left untreated. Treatment options include breast-conserving treatment (lumpectomy) with or without radiation therapy, total mastectomy with or without sentinel lymph node biopsy (SLNB), and/or hormone therapy (e.g., tamoxifen) to prevent recurrences.[16]

In the past, *lobular carcinoma in situ* (LCIS) was considered a noninvasive breast cancer. It is now classified as a benign condition that is a risk factor for developing breast cancer. No surgical or radiation treatment is indicated for LCIS. Hormone therapy may be used as a preventive measure to reduce breast cancer risk for some patients.

Invasive Ductal Carcinoma

Invasive (infiltrating) ductal carcinoma is the most common type of breast cancer. It accounts for about 80% of all invasive breast cancers. It starts in the milk ducts and then breaks through the walls of the duct, invading the surrounding tissue. From there, it may metastasize to other parts of the body. Subtypes of invasive ductal carcinoma include medullary, tubular, colloid (mucinous), papillary, and metaplastic.

Invasive Lobular Carcinoma

Invasive (infiltrating) lobular carcinoma begins in the lobules (milk-producing glands) of the breast. It accounts for about 10% to 15% of invasive breast cancers. The cancer cells can break out of the lobule and metastasize to other areas of the body. Invasive lobular carcinoma usually presents as a subtle thickening in the upper outer quadrant of the breast. It is often not detected by mammography.

Other Types of Breast Cancer

Inflammatory breast cancer. *Inflammatory breast cancer* is an aggressive and fast-growing breast cancer with a high risk for metastasis. It accounts for about 1% to 3% of all breast cancers. In the early stages, it is often mistaken for mastitis. However, the inflammatory changes do not improve with antibiotics. Cancer cells block the lymph channels in the skin of the breast. Because of skin involvement, the breast looks red, feels warm, and has a thickened appearance that is often described as looking like an orange peel *(peau d'orange).* Sometimes, the breast develops ridges and small bumps that look like hives. A breast mass may not be present. Changes may not show up on mammograms, making diagnosis difficult. Inflammatory breast cancer has a worse prognosis as compared to invasive ductal and lobular breast cancers.[17]

Paget disease. Paget disease is a rare breast cancer that starts in the breast ducts and spreads to the nipple and areola. It causes about 1% of all breast cancers. It is different from Paget disease of the bone (see Chapter 68). Most women with Paget disease have underlying ductal carcinoma. Only in rare cases is the cancer confined to the nipple (in situ) and not invasive.

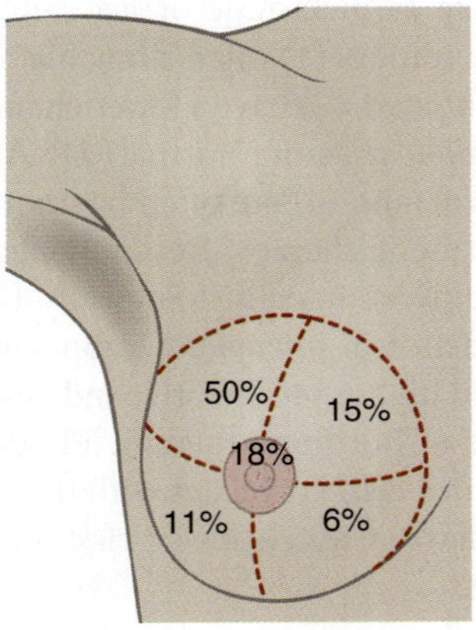

Fig. 56.3 Distribution of where breast cancer occurs.

Itching, burning, bloody nipple discharge with superficial skin erosion and ulceration may be present. A pathologic examination of the lesion confirms the diagnosis. Nipple changes are often diagnosed as an infection or dermatitis, which can lead to treatment delays.

The treatment of Paget disease is surgical removal of the involved tissue by either central lumpectomy or mastectomy with or without sentinel node (SLN) biopsy. Radiation therapy may be used after surgery. The prognosis is good when the cancer is confined to the nipple.

Phyllodes tumor. A phyllodes tumor is a very rare tumor that develops in the connective tissue (stroma) of the breast. The tumors tend to grow quickly, within a period of weeks or months, to a size of 2 to 3 cm or sometimes larger. Although most are benign, some are cancerous. Treatment is usually excision with a wide margin. Axillary surgery is not necessary.

Triple-Negative Breast Cancer

A patient whose breast cancer tests negative for all 3 receptors (estrogen, progesterone, HER-2) has *triple-negative breast cancer.*[18] The incidence of triple-negative breast cancer is higher in Blacks, Hispanics, premenopausal women, and those with a *BRCA1* mutation. These patients tend to have more aggressive tumors with a poorer prognosis. These cancers do not respond to hormone therapy or therapy for HER-2. Chemotherapy is more successful for treating triple-negative breast cancer.

Clinical Manifestations

Breast cancer is usually detected as a lump or thickening in the breast or mammography abnormality. It occurs most often in the upper, outer quadrant of the breast, which is the location of most of the glandular tissue (Fig. 56.3). Breast cancers vary in their growth rate. If palpable, breast cancer is characteristically hard and may be irregularly shaped, poorly delineated, nonmobile, and nontender.

A small number of breast cancers cause nipple discharge. The discharge is usually unilateral. It may be clear or bloody. Nipple retraction may be present. Peau d'orange may occur due to plugging of the dermal lymphatics. In large cancers, infiltration, induration, and dimpling (pulling in) of the overlying skin may occur.

TABLE 56.5 Sites of Breast Cancer Recurrence and Metastasis

Site	Manifestations
Local Recurrence	
Skin, chest wall	Firm, discrete nodules. Sometimes pruritic, usually painless, often in or near a scar
Regional Recurrence	
Lymph nodes	Enlarged nodes in axilla or supraclavicular area, usually nontender
Distant Metastasis	
Bone marrow	Anemia, infection, ↑ bleeding, bruising, petechiae. Weakness, fatigue, mild confusion, lightheadedness, dyspnea
Brain	Headache, unilateral sensory loss, focal muscular weakness, hemiparesis, incoordination (ataxia), nausea and vomiting not related to medication, cognitive changes
Liver	Abdominal distention. Right lower quadrant abdominal pain sometimes radiating to scapular area. Nausea and vomiting, anorexia, weight loss. Weakness and fatigue. Hepatomegaly, ascites, jaundice. Peripheral edema. High liver enzymes
Lung (including lung nodules and pleural effusions)	Shortness of breath, tachypnea, nonproductive cough
Skeletal	Localized pain of gradually increasing intensity, percussion tenderness at involved sites, pathologic fracture caused by involvement of bone cortex
Spinal cord	Progressive back pain, localized and radiating. Change in bladder or bowel function. Loss of sensation in lower extremities

Complications

The main complication of breast cancer is recurrence (Table 56.5). Recurrence may be *local* or *regional* (skin or soft tissue near the mastectomy site, axillary or internal mammary lymph nodes) or distant. Widely disseminated or metastatic disease involves the growth of cancerous breast cells in parts of the body distant from the breast. Most often involved are the bone, lung, brain, and liver. Metastases primarily occur through the lymphatics, usually those of the axilla (Fig. 56.4). However, metastatic disease can occur anywhere.

Diagnostic Studies

In addition to radiologic and biopsy studies used to diagnose breast cancer, we use other tests to predict the risk for local or systemic recurrence. These tests include axillary lymph node analysis, tumor size, estrogen and PR status, cell-proliferative indices (number of cells that are dividing), and genomic assays.

Axillary Lymph Node Analysis

Axillary lymph node involvement is an important prognostic factor in breast cancer. *Axillary lymph nodes* are often examined

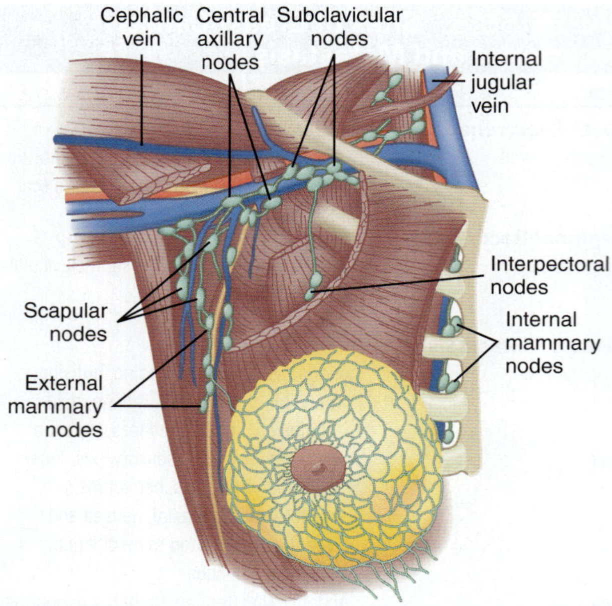

Fig. 56.4 Lymph nodes and drainage in the axilla. The sentinel lymph node is usually found in the external mammary nodes. A complete axillary dissection would remove all nodes. (From Donegan WL, Spratt JS: *Cancer of the breast*, ed 3, Philadelphia, 1988, Saunders.)

to see if cancer has spread to the axilla on the same side of the breast as the cancer (Fig. 56.4). The more nodes involved, the greater the risk for recurrence.

A *sentinel lymph node biopsy* helps to identify the lymph node(s) that drain first from the tumor site. Those nodes are *sentinel node(s)*. In SLNB, a radioisotope and/or blue dye, which will travel the same route as the cancer, is injected into the affected breast. Then, in surgery, the HCP determines if the radioisotope (using radioactive detector) or dye (visually see blue nodes) is found in any SLNs. A local incision is made in the axilla, and the HCP dissects the blue-stained and/or radioactive SLNs. Generally, with SLNB, 1 to 4 axillary lymph nodes are removed. The nodes are sent for pathologic analysis. If the SLNs are negative, no further axillary surgery is needed.

If the SLNs are positive or the SLN cannot be identified, the patient may have a complete *axillary lymph node dissection* (ALND). In an ALND, the HCP will typically remove 12 to 20 lymph nodes. SLNB is less invasive and has a lower mortality rate than ALND.

Tumor Size

Tumor size is a prognostic variable. In general, the larger the tumor, the poorer the prognosis. The wide variety of biologic types of breast cancer explains the variability of disease behavior. In general, the more well differentiated (like the original cell type) the tumor, the less aggressive it is. The cells of poorly differentiated (unlike the original cell type) tumors appear morphologically disorganized, and they are more aggressive.

Estrogen and Progesterone Receptor Status

Estrogen receptor (ER) and progesterone receptor (PR) status is another diagnostic test useful for decisions about treatment and prognosis. Hormone receptor testing is done with any newly diagnosed primary or metastatic breast cancer and on DCIS. Receptor-positive tumors (1) often show histologic evidence of being well differentiated, (2) have a lower chance for recurrence, (3) often have a *diploid* (more normal) DNA content and low proliferative indices, and (4) are often hormone dependent and responsive to hormone therapy. Receptor-negative tumors (1) are often poorly differentiated histologically, (2) often recur, (3) have a high incidence of *aneuploidy* (abnormally high or low DNA content) and higher proliferative indices, and (4) are usually unresponsive to hormone therapy. Ploidy status (number of chromosomes in a cell) correlates with tumor aggressiveness. Diploid tumors have a much lower risk for recurrence than aneuploid tumors.

Genomic Assay

An important *genomic assay* is to determine HER-2, which is a prognostic indicator. Overexpression of HER-2 is associated with unusually aggressive tumor growth, a greater risk for recurrence, and a poorer prognosis. It is overexpressed in 10% to 20% of patients with breast cancer. The presence of HER-2 helps in the selection and sequence of drug therapy and predicts the patient's response to treatment. HER-2 testing is done with any newly diagnosed primary or metastatic breast cancer.

A *gene expression assay* test uses a sample of the breast cancer tissue to analyze the activity of a group of genes that can affect how a cancer is likely to behave and respond to treatment. Knowing whether certain genes are present or absent, or overly active or not active enough, can provide information about the risk for recurrence and the expected benefit of chemotherapy or hormone therapy. The 21-gene recurrence (OncotypeDX) test is the most often used genomic test.[19] Other genomic tests are MammaPrint, PAM50 (Prosigna), EndoPredict, and the Breast Cancer Index.

Cell-Proliferative Indices

Cell-proliferative indices indirectly measure the rate of tumor cell proliferation. The number of tumor cells in the synthesis (S) phase of the cell cycle (see Fig. 16.1) is another important prognostic indicator. Although cell-proliferative indices are not a routine part of the cancer pathology evaluation, patients with cells that have high S-phase fractions have a higher risk for recurrence and earlier cancer death.

Interprofessional Care

A wide range of treatment options is available (Table 56.6). The treatment plan is often determined by prognostic factors, the clinical stage, and biology of the cancer.

Breast Cancer Staging

The most widely accepted staging method for breast cancer is the TNM system. This system uses anatomic factors of tumor size (T), nodal involvement (N), and presence of metastasis (M) to determine the stage of disease (Table 56.7). The stages range from 0 to IV, with stage 0 being in situ cancer with no lymph node involvement and no metastasis. Stage IV indicates metastatic spread, regardless of tumor size or lymph node involvement. This system is used worldwide to communicate

TABLE 56.6 Interprofessional Care

Breast Cancer

Diagnostic Assessment

Prediagnosis

- Health history, including risk factors
- Physical assessment, including breast and lymph nodes
- Mammography
- Ultrasound (if indicated)
- Breast MRI (if indicated)
- Biopsy

Postdiagnosis

- Lymph node analysis
- Estrogen and progesterone receptor status
- Cell-proliferative indices
- HER-2 marker
- Genetic assays (e.g., MammaPrint, Oncotype DX)

Staging

- Complete blood count
- Liver function tests
- Chest x-ray (if indicated)
- CT scan of chest, abdomen, pelvis (if indicated)
- PET/CT, MRI, bone scans (if indicated)

Management

Surgical Therapy

- Breast-conserving surgery (lumpectomy) with SLNB and/or axillary lymph node dissection
- Simple (total) mastectomy with SLNB and/or axillary lymph node dissection
- Modified radical mastectomy
- Reconstructive surgery

Radiation Therapy

- External radiation
- Brachytherapy
- Palliative radiation therapy

Drug Therapy (Table 56.9)

- Chemotherapy
- Hormone therapy
- Immunotherapy
- Targeted therapy

TABLE 56.7 Staging of Breast Cancer

Stage	Tumor Size	Lymph Node Involvement	Metastasis
0	TIS (tumor in situ)	No	No
I			
A	<2 cm	No	No
B	<2 cm	<2 mm	No
II			
A	No evidence of tumor ranging to 5 cm	No, or 1–3 axillary nodes and/or internal mammary nodes	No
B	Ranging from ≤2 to >5 cm	No, or 1–3 axillary nodes and/or internal mammary nodes	No
III			
A	Ranging ≤2 to >5 cm	Yes, 1–9 axillary nodes and/or internal mammary nodes	No
B	Any size with extension to chest wall or skin	No, or 1–9 axillary nodes and/or internal mammary nodes	No
C	Any size	Yes, ≥10 axillary nodes, internal mammary nodes, or infraclavicular nodes	No
IV	Any size	Any type of nodal involvement	Yes

the size of a breast cancer and the extent to which it has spread. It provides an accurate prediction of the outcome of a group of patients.

The latest cancer staging guidelines add biologic factors in making the final determination of the stage. These enable more accurate determination of prognosis and appropriate systemic therapy. These factors include tumor grade, hormone receptor expression, HER-2 overexpression and/or amplification, and genomic panels.

For example, some larger tumors are considered stage I instead of stage II based on their biology. For patients with hormone receptor–positive, HER2-negative, lymph node–negative tumors, and a low-risk gene recurrence score, regardless of T size, place into the same prognostic category as T1a-T1b N0 M0. Patients with triple-negative tumors have survival equal to that of patients with disease 1 TNM stage higher who have ER, PR, or HER2-positive expressing tumors.

Surgical Therapy

Surgery is the main treatment for breast cancer. Table 56.8 describes the most common procedures used to treat breast cancer. The most common options for operable breast cancer are (1) breast conservation surgery (lumpectomy [segmental mastectomy]) and (2) mastectomy with or without reconstruction. Most women diagnosed with early-stage breast cancer (tumors smaller than 5 cm) are candidates for either surgery. The overall survival rate with lumpectomy and radiation is the same as with mastectomy.[15]

Breast reconstruction is an option for any woman having surgery for breast cancer. Women having a mastectomy can have breast reconstruction at the time of the surgery or months or even years later. Some women choose to not have reconstruction and use a breast prosthesis instead.

Breast-conserving surgery. Breast-conserving surgery, or **lumpectomy**, involves removing the entire tumor along with a margin of normal surrounding tissue (Fig. 56.5A). In some cases, it may take 2 or 3 more surgeries to remove all the cancer from the margins. After surgery, radiation therapy is usually delivered to the entire breast, ending with a boost to the tumor bed. If the risk for recurrence is high, the patient may receive chemotherapy before starting radiation.

TABLE 56.8 Surgical Procedures for Breast Cancer

Procedure	Side Effects	Complications	Patient Issues
Breast-Conserving Surgery (Lumpectomy) With Radiation Therapy			
Excision of tumor with no tumor at margins, sentinel lymph node biopsy (SLNB) and/or axillary lymph node dissection (ALND) Radiation therapy	Arm swelling Breast edema Breast soreness Sensory changes in breast and arm Skin reactions	*Short-term:* moist desquamation[a] hematoma, seroma, infection *Long-term:* fibrosis,[a] lymphedema,[b] myositis, pneumonitis,[a] rib fractures[a]	Impaired arm mobility[b] Prolonged treatment[a] Texture and sensitivity changes in breast
Mastectomy			
Simple Mastectomy Removal of breast, preservation of pectoralis muscle, SLNB may be done at same time ***Modified Radical Mastectomy*** Removal of breast with ALND, pectoralis muscle is spared	Chest wall tightness, scar Impaired range of motion Lymphedema Phantom breast sensations Sensory changes	*Short-term:* skin flap necrosis, seroma, hematoma, infection *Long-term:* sensory loss, muscle weakness, lymphedema	Body image Impaired arm mobility Incision Loss of breast Need for prosthesis
Breast Implants and Tissue Expansion			
Expander used to slowly stretch tissue. Saline gradually injected into reservoir over weeks to months Insertion of implant under musculofascial layer of chest wall Fat grafting can sometimes replace implant	Chest wall tightness Pain	*Short-term:* skin flap necrosis, wound separation, seroma, hematoma, infection *Long-term:* capsular contractions, displacement of implant	Body image HCP visits to expand implants Potential added surgeries for nipple construction, symmetry
Breast Reconstruction Tissue Flap Procedures[c]			
Transverse Rectus Abdominis Musculocutaneous (TRAM) Flap			
Musculocutaneous flap (muscle, skin, fat, blood supply) is transposed from abdomen to the mastectomy site May be done concurrently with mastectomy	Pain related to 2 surgical sites and extensive surgery	*Short-term:* delayed wound healing, infection, skin flap necrosis, abdominal hernia, hematoma	Longer postoperative recovery
Deep Inferior Epigastric Artery Perforator (DIEP) Flap			
Free flap that transfers skin and fat from the abdomen to the chest. Differs from TRAM flap because no muscle is moved	More time in surgery than pedicle TRAM flap Pain related to 2 surgical sites	Needs close monitoring first 24–48 hr after surgery. If flap fails, patient needs surgery	Less pain and impaired movement than with a pedicle TRAM flap

[a]Specific to radiation therapy.
[b]If ALND (less likely with SLNB).
[c]This list is not inclusive; other breast reconstruction options are available.

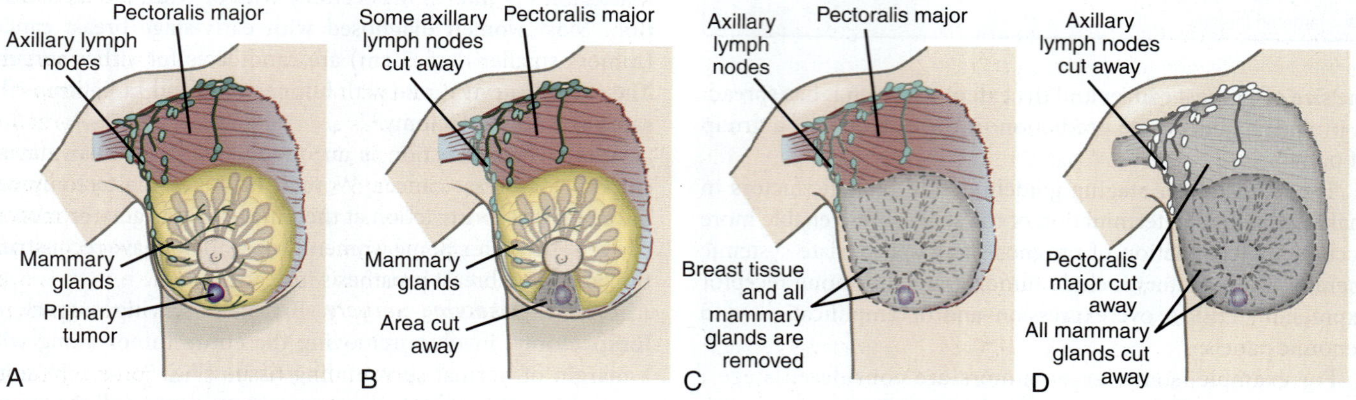

Fig. 56.5 Breast cancer surgery. (A) Preoperative. (B) Lumpectomy. (C) Simple mastectomy. (D) Modified radical mastectomy.

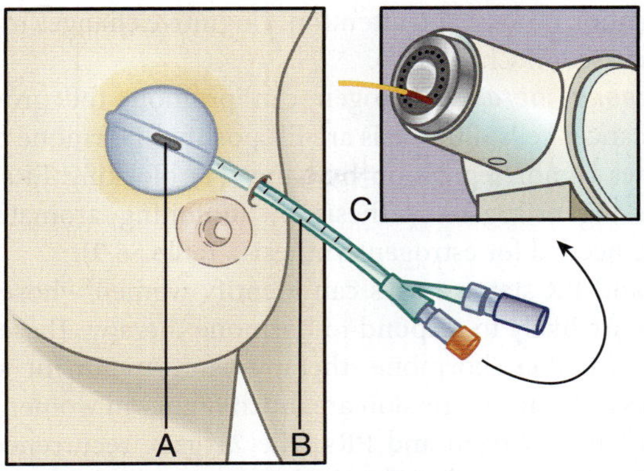

Fig. 56.6 High-dose brachytherapy for breast cancer. The MammoSite system involves the insertion of a single small balloon catheter *(B)* at the time of the lumpectomy or shortly thereafter into the tumor resection cavity (the space that is left after the HCP removes the tumor). A tiny radioactive seed *(A)* is inserted into the balloon, connected to an afterloader *(C)*, and delivers the radiation therapy.

Not everyone is a candidate for breast conservation surgery. Contraindications include breast size too small in relation to the tumor size to yield an acceptable cosmetic result, multifocal masses and calcifications, multicentric masses (in more than 1 quadrant), diffuse calcifications in more than 1 quadrant, or prior radiation therapy. Because of the time commitment (5 to 7 weeks of daily radiation therapy treatments) and travel distances to access radiation therapy treatment centers, some patients may choose mastectomy over breast conservation surgery.

Mastectomy. A *total* or *simple mastectomy* removes the entire breast. A *modified radical mastectomy* includes removal of the breast and axillary lymph nodes. It preserves the pectoralis major muscle (Fig. 56.5B). For women desiring breast reconstruction, a skin-sparing mastectomy provides the best cosmetic result and does not increase the chance of the cancer recurring. In a *nipple-sparing mastectomy,* the nipple and/or areola are left in place and the breast tissue under them is removed. Women who have a small, low-grade cancer near the outer part of the breast, with no signs of cancer in the skin or near the nipple, may be able to have nipple-sparing surgery.

For women who have a mastectomy, breast reconstruction can be done with the mastectomy or it can be delayed. Some women choose not to have reconstruction. There are 2 main types of breast reconstruction procedures: implant reconstruction or procedures that use autologous tissue transplantation (pedicled or microsurgical flaps from the abdomen, back, buttocks or thigh, and/or fat grafting) (Table 56.8).

Radiation Therapy

Radiation therapy is one *adjuvant (additional)* therapy that can be used after surgery. It is used for breast cancer to (1) prevent local breast cancer recurrences after breast-conserving surgery; (2) prevent local and lymph node recurrences after mastectomy; or (3) relieve pain caused by local, regional, or distant cancer spread.

External radiation therapy. When radiation therapy is a primary treatment, it is usually done after surgery. The decision to use radiation after mastectomy is based on the chance that local, residual cancer cells are present. Radiation of the axilla and/or supraclavicular nodes may be done when lymph nodes are involved to decrease the risk for axillary recurrence. Radiating a localized area does not prevent distant metastasis.

With traditional whole breast, and in some cases regional lymph node, treatment, the area is radiated 5 days per week over the course of about 5 to 7 weeks. An external beam of radiation delivers daily fractions to a total dose of 46 to 50 Gy (4500 to 5000 cGy). Patients who have had breast-conserving surgery may receive a "boost" dose of radiation to the area where the original tumor was located. It is given by external beam and adds 4 to 8 more treatments to the total number given.[15]

Newer and preferred regimens use a type of accelerated external beam radiation called hypofractionation. This type of radiation has a shortened schedule, daily for 3 to 4 weeks, with a total dose of 40 to 42.5 Gy.[15]

Fatigue, skin changes, and breast edema are temporary side effects of external radiation therapy. Nursing care of the patient receiving radiation therapy is discussed in Chapter 16.

Brachytherapy. *Brachytherapy* (internal radiation) is used for partial-breast radiation. It is an alternative to traditional external radiation treatment for some patients with early-stage breast cancer.[15] This method has the same chance for local recurrence as whole breast radiation. However, the cosmetic results may not be as good.

Brachytherapy is minimally invasive. The radiation is delivered directly into the cavity left after a tumor is surgically removed by a lumpectomy. Because the radiation is concentrated and focused on the area with the highest risk for tumor recurrence, it only requires 5 treatments. Therapy is delivered using a multicatheter method or balloon-catheter system.

In the *multicatheter method* (e.g., SAVI) many small catheters are placed in the breast at the site of the tumor. The SAVI is inserted through a small incision, and the catheter bundle expands uniformly. The ends of the catheters stick out through little holes in the skin. Small radioactive seeds are placed in the catheters. The seeds are left in place just long enough to deliver the radiation dose (e.g., 5 to 10 minutes) and then removed. The radiation does not stay in the body between treatments or after the last treatment is over.

In the *balloon-catheter system,* a balloon is placed where the tumor was located. The balloon is filled with fluid, to keep it in place, then radioactive seeds are inserted (Fig. 56.6). Radiation is emitted by a tiny radioactive seed attached by a wire to an afterloader, a computer-controlled machine. The seed travels through the MammoSite applicator into the inflated balloon. As with the multicatheter system, the radiation does not stay in the body between treatments or after the last treatment is over. After the last session, the balloon is deflated, and the system is removed.

Palliative radiation therapy. Reducing the primary tumor mass with radiation often results in a decrease in pain. Radiation is a treatment option for symptomatic metastatic lesions in such sites as bone, soft tissue organs, brain, and chest. It often relieves pain and is successful in controlling recurrent or metastatic disease.

Drug Therapy

Drug therapy includes chemotherapy, hormone therapy, immunotherapy, and targeted therapy. When drug therapy is given before surgery, we call it *neoadjuvant therapy.* Neoadjuvant therapy is given to shrink the size of the tumor enough to make surgical removal possible or allow for breast-conserving surgery in women who would have been recommended to have a mastectomy. It also allows time for genetic testing to occur (if appropriate) so a patient can make more informed treatment decisions. It provides evidence whether the tumor is responsive to the selected agent(s).

Drug therapy after surgery is called *adjuvant therapy*. Drug therapy can decrease the rate of recurrence and increase the length of survival. Because of the risk for recurrent disease, nearly all patients with evidence of node involvement, particularly those who are hormone receptor negative, will have some type of drug therapy. Some patients, especially those with a more aggressive tumor, have a higher risk for recurrent or metastatic disease. They may receive drug therapy even when there is no evidence of node involvement. Weighing the risks and benefits of drug therapy is a complex process.

Chemotherapy. Chemotherapy is the use of cytotoxic drugs to destroy cancer cells. A combination of drugs is usually better than using a single drug. Combination treatment is best because the drugs have different mechanisms of action and work at different parts of the cell cycle. When used in the neoadjuvant and adjuvant setting, chemotherapy is usually given for 3 to 6 months. However, a patient with metastasis may receive chemotherapy for the rest of their life.

Common combination-therapy protocols in the adjuvant and neoadjuvant setting are (1) CMF: cyclophosphamide, methotrexate, and fluorouracil; (2) AC: doxorubicin and cyclophosphamide, with or without the addition of a taxane, such as paclitaxel (Taxol) or docetaxel (Taxotere); or (3) CEF or CAF: cyclophosphamide, epirubicin (Ellence) or doxorubicin, and fluorouracil.

DRUG ALERT

Doxorubicin

- Monitor for signs of cardiotoxicity and heart failure (e.g., shortness of breath, pedal edema, decreased activity tolerance, dysrhythmias, ECG changes).
- Tell the patient not to have immunizations without the HCP's approval.

Teach patients to avoid contact with those who recently received live virus vaccines and those with infections. Because chemotherapy affects healthy cells, many side effects accompany chemotherapy. The incidence and severity of common side effects are related to specific drug combinations, drug schedule, and dosage. The most common side effects involve rapidly dividing cells in the gastrointestinal tract (nausea, anorexia, weight loss), bone marrow (anemia), and hair follicles (hair loss).

Cognitive changes during and after treatment can occur. We often call this *"chemo brain."* These changes include problems with memory, focus, and attention. Cognitive changes in cancer are discussed in Chapter 16.

Hormone therapy. Estrogen can promote the growth of breast cancer cells if the cells are ER positive. Hormone therapy promotes tumor regression by either (1) blocking ERs or (2) suppressing estrogen synthesis by inhibiting aromatase, an enzyme needed for estrogen synthesis (Table 56.9).

ER and PR status assays can identify women whose breast cancers are likely to respond to hormone therapy. These assays predict whether hormone therapy is a treatment option. Chances of tumor regression are much higher in women whose tumors have estrogen and PRs. The 21-gene recurrence score (OncotypeDX) can identify which women with hormone-positive breast cancer can be treated with hormone therapy alone and do not need chemotherapy.

Premenopausal women with ER-positive breast cancers may benefit from the removal or suppression of their ovaries. Ovarian ablation can be done surgically or by using luteinizing hormone-releasing hormone (LHRH) analogs, such as goserelin (Zoladex) or leuprolide (Lupron).

Estrogen receptor blockers. ER blockers include tamoxifen, toremifene (Fareston), and fulvestrant (Faslodex). Tamoxifen has been the hormone therapy of choice in ER-positive women at all stages of breast cancer for the past 30 years. It also may be used in high-risk women to prevent breast cancer. Common side effects include hot flashes, mood swings, vaginal discharge and dryness, and other effects associated with decreased estrogen. It increases the risk for blood clots, cataracts, stroke, and endometrial cancer in postmenopausal women.

DRUG ALERT

Tamoxifen

- Irregular vaginal bleeding or spotting may occur.
- Decreased visual acuity, corneal opacity, and retinopathy can occur in women receiving high doses (240–320 mg/day for >17 months). These problems may not be reversible.
- Teach the patient to immediately report any vision changes.
- Monitor for signs of VTE and stroke, including shortness of breath, leg cramps, and weakness.

Aromatase inhibitors. Aromatase inhibitors lower estrogen levels by stopping aromatase, an enzyme in fat tissue, from changing other hormones into estrogen. These drugs include anastrozole (Arimedex), letrozole (Femara), and exemestane (Aromasin). They do not stop the ovaries from making estrogen. Thus, they are of little benefit and may be harmful in premenopausal women. They are used to treat breast cancer in postmenopausal women.

Because they block estrogen production in postmenopausal women, osteoporosis and bone fractures may occur. Side effects include night sweats, nausea, and joint and muscle pain.

Estrogen receptor modulators. Raloxifene (Evista) is a selective ER modulator that has both estrogen-agonistic effects on bone and estrogen-antagonistic effects on breast tissue (see Chapter 68).

TABLE 56.9 Drug Therapy

Breast Cancer

Drug Class	Mechanism of Action	Indications
Hormone Therapy		
Aromatase Inhibitors		
anastrozole (Arimidex) exemestane (Aromasin) letrozole (Femara)	Prevents estrogen production by inhibiting aromatase	ER-positive breast cancer in postmenopausal women only
Estrogen Receptor (ER) Blockers		
fulvestrant (Faslodex)	Blocks ERs and increases their degradation	ER-positive breast cancer in postmenopausal women only
tamoxifen	Selectively blocks ERs	ER-positive breast cancer in premenopausal and postmenopausal women Used as a preventive measure in high-risk premenopausal and postmenopausal women
toremifene (Fareston)	Blocks ERs	ER-positive breast cancer in postmenopausal women only
Estrogen Receptor Modulator		
raloxifene (Evista)	In breast, blocks the effect of estrogen. In bone, promotes effect of estrogen and prevents bone loss	Postmenopausal women
Targeted Therapy		
HER-2 Inhibitors		
lapatinib (Tykerb)	Blocks the function of HER-2 related kinases inside the cell	HER-2-positive breast cancer
margetuximab-cmkb (Margenza) pertuzumab (Perjeta) trastuzumab (Herceptin) trastuzumab-pkrb (Herzuma) trastuzumab-qyyp (Trazimera)	Blocks HER-2 receptor	HER-2-positive breast cancer
ado-trastuzumab emtansine (Kadcyla)	Trastuzumab with a chemotherapy drug called DM1	HER-2-positive breast cancer
fam-trastuzumab deruxtecan-nxki (Enhertu)	HER-2 directed antibody and a topoisomerase inhibitor	Advance or metastatic HER-2 positive breast cancer after 2 other HER-2 therapies
Kinase Inhibitors		
abemaciclib (Verzenio) palbociclib (Ibrance) ribociclib (Kisqali)	CDK4/6 Kinase inhibitors	ER-positive, HER-2-negative breast cancer in postmenopausal women
neratinib (Nerlynx) tucatinib (Tukysa)	Tyrosine kinase inhibitor	Advance or metastatic HER-2 positive breast cancer after 1 other HER-2 therapy, includes patients with brain metastasis
alpelisib (Piqray)	P13 kinase inhibitor	PIK3CA mutated, HER-2 negative advanced breast cancer
everolimus (Afinitor)	mTOR inhibitor suppressing T cell activation and proliferation	ER-positive, HER-2-negative breast cancer in postmenopausal women
olaparib (Lynparza) talazoparib (Talzenna)	PARP inhibitors	Patients with metastatic breast cancer positive for BRCA mutations
entrectinib (Rozlytrek) larotrectinib (Vitrakvi)	NTRK inhibitors	In NTRK + breast cancers (very rare) when no other options exist
Immunomodulators		
atezolizumab (Tecentriq)	PD-1 inhibitor	PD-L1 positive triple negative advanced or metastatic breast cancer
pembrolizumab (Keytruda)	PD-'1 inhibitor	Any MSI-H breast cancer when no other options exist
sacituzumab govitecan-hziy (Trodelvy)	Monoclonal antibody that targets Trop-2 protein and a topoisomerase 1 inhibitor	Metastatic triple negative disease after 2 other therapies

Targeted Therapy

As we learn more about genetic changes in breast cancer, we have developed drugs that specifically target cells that have altered gene expression. One of these genetic changes is the overexpression of HER-2. Tumors that overexpress the HER-2 protein tend to be more aggressive and are more likely to recur.

HER-2 inhibitors work by attaching to the HER-2 receptors on the surface of the breast cancer cells and blocking them from receiving signals that tell them to proliferate. Trastuzumab

(Herceptin) is one HER-2 inhibitor. It can be used alone or in combination with chemotherapy agents. The most common side effects are flu-like symptoms (fever, chills, myalgia), nausea and vomiting, diarrhea, and infusion reactions. A possible, but more serious, side effect is heart damage. Trastuzumab-qyyp (Trazimera) and trastuzumab-pkrb (Herzuma) are biosimilars of trastuzumab.

DRUG ALERT

Trastuzumab (Herceptin)

- Use with caution in women with preexisting heart disease.
- Monitor for signs of heart failure.

Other drugs that target HER-2 include pertuzumab (Perjeta), ado-trastuzumab emtansine (Kadcyla), and lapatinib (Tykerb). Neratinib (Nerlynx) is an option for extended adjuvant therapy for some high-risk women. Using 2 of these agents together for neoadjuvant therapy can increase the number of tumors that become undetectable. Survival improves when used for adjuvant therapy.

Kinase inhibitors prevent cells from dividing, thus slowing cancer growth. Drugs in this class include palbociclib (Ibrance), ribociclib (Kisqali), and abemaciclib (Verzenio). They are used for ER-positive, HER-2-negative cancer in postmenopausal women

Other targeted drugs include everolimus (Afinitor). It works by blocking mTOR, a protein that normally promotes cell growth and division. The PARP inhibitors olaparib (Lynparza) and talazoparib (Talzenna) are used in patients with metastatic breast cancer positive for BRCA mutations. Alpelisib (Piqray) a PI3K inhibitor, is used for patients with advanced or metastatic disease with a PIK3CA-mutation. For the rare breast cancers that test positive for NTRK fusion genes, the NTRK inhibitors larotrectinib (Vitrakvi) and entrectinib (Rozlytrek) may be tried after other treatments are exhausted. Immunotherapy and targeted therapy are discussed in Chapter 16.

Immunotherapy

Atezolizumab (Tecentriq), an immune checkpoint inhibitor, is the first FDA-approved immunotherapy agent. It is used with chemotherapy to treat locally advanced triple-negative breast cancer in patients with a PD-L1 (programmed death ligand 1) positive biomarker. Adding pembrolizumab (Keytruda) to chemotherapy as part of neoadjuvant therapy for triple-negative breast cancer increased the chance of a complete response (disappearance of the tumor) regardless of PD-L1 status. Pembrolizumab is an option with advanced breast cancer that tests MSI-H (microsatellite instability-high) when no other therapies are available.

Culturally Competent Care: Breast Cancer

Differences exist among racial and ethnic groups in the incidence, mortality rate, and care related to breast cancer (Box 56.2). In addition, cultural differences may involve gender roles, health beliefs, religion, family structure, socioeconomic factors

BOX 56.2 PROMOTING HEALTH EQUITY

Breast Cancer

- White and Black women have the highest incidence of breast cancer.
- Black women have lower survival rates from breast cancer than White women, even when diagnosed at an early stage.
- Hispanic and Black women are more likely to be diagnosed at a later stage of breast cancer than white women.
- Triple-negative breast cancer has a higher incidence in Black and Hispanic women.
- Mortality rates are lower among Hispanic and Asian/Pacific Islander women.
- Breast cancer is the most commonly diagnosed cancer among Hispanic women.
- Indian/Alaskan native women have the lowest rate of breast cancer screening of any ethnic group.

(e.g., poverty), and lack of health insurance. Lack of education may influence disparities related to access to health care and having recommended surveillance examinations.[20]

Cultural values strongly influence how a person responds to and copes with breast cancer and treatment. Diverse cultural norms influence health beliefs and behaviors. Cultural values and meanings (body image, sexuality, modesty, motherhood) associated with the breasts affect breast cancer screening, diagnosis, and treatment. Women may delay screening or treatment for varying reasons, including an acceptance of disease as inevitable fate or "God's will," a mistrust of Western medicine, lack of health care benefits, fear, or the stigma of a cancer diagnosis.

NURSING MANAGEMENT: BREAST CANCER

Assessment

You must consider many factors when assessing a patient with a breast problem. The history helps establish a diagnosis. Investigate the presence of nipple discharge, pain, rate of growth of the lump, breast asymmetry, and correlation with the menstrual cycle.

Carefully record the size and location of the lump(s). Assess the lesion, including consistency, mobility, and shape. If nipple discharge is present, note the color and consistency. Does it occur from 1 or both breasts?

Subjective and objective data to obtain from a person suspected of having or diagnosed with breast cancer are outlined in Table 56.10.

Clinical Problems

Clinical problems for the care of a patient diagnosed with breast cancer vary. After diagnosis and before a treatment plan has been selected, the following would apply:

- Difficulty coping
- Deficient knowledge
- Negative self-image

If surgery is planned, the nursing diagnoses and interventions may include those in eNursing Care Plan 56.1 (available on the website for this chapter).

TABLE 56.10 NURSING ASSESSMENT

Breast Cancer

Subjective Data

Important Health Information

Health history: Benign breast disease with atypical changes. Previous unilateral breast cancer. Menstrual history (early menarche with late menopause), pregnancy history (nulliparity or first full-term pregnancy after age 30). Endometrial, ovarian, or colon cancer. Hyperestrogenism and testicular atrophy (in men)

Medicines: Hormones, especially as postmenopausal hormone therapy and in oral contraceptives. Infertility treatments

Surgery or other treatments: Exposure to therapeutic radiation (e.g., Hodgkin lymphoma or thyroid radiation)

Functional Health Patterns

Health perception–health management: Family history of breast cancer (young age at diagnosis). History of abnormal mammogram or atypical prior biopsy. Palpable change found on BSE. Known *BRCA* mutation carrier, first-degree relative of *BRCA* carrier (but untested)

Nutritional-metabolic: Obesity; unexplained severe weight loss (may indicate metastasis)

Activity-exercise: Level of usual activity

Cognitive-perceptual: Changes in cognition, headache, bone pain (may indicate metastasis)

Sexuality-reproductive: Unilateral nipple discharge (clear, milky, bloody). Change in breast contour, size, or symmetry

Coping–stress tolerance: Psychologic stress

Self-perception–self-concept: Anxiety about threat to self-esteem

Objective Data

General

Axillary and supraclavicular lymphadenopathy

GI

Hepatomegaly, jaundice, ascites (may indicate liver metastasis)

Respiratory

Pleural effusions (may indicate metastasis)

Skin

Hard, irregular, nonmobile breast lump most often in upper, outer sector, possibly fixated to fascia or chest wall. Thickening of breast. Nipple inversion or retraction, erosion. Edema ("peau d'orange"), redness, induration, infiltration, or dimpling (in later stages). Firm, discrete nodules at mastectomy site (may indicate local recurrence). Peripheral edema (may indicate metastasis)

Possible Diagnostic Findings

Finding of mass or change in tissue on breast examination. Abnormal mammogram, ultrasound, or breast MRI. Positive results of FNA or surgical biopsy; similar results with a needle biopsy

◆ Planning

The overall goals are that the patient with breast cancer will (1) take part in decision-making related to treatment, (2) adhere to the therapeutic plan, (3) communicate about and manage the side effects of therapy, (4) be supported by significant others and the health care team, and (5) adhere to recommended follow-up and surveillance after treatment.

◆ Implementation

◆ Health Promotion

Review the risk factors in Table 56.3. Maintaining a healthy weight, exercising regularly, limiting alcohol, eating nutritious food, and never smoking (or quitting if currently smoking) are ways to reduce risk.

Encourage women to adhere to the breast cancer screening guidelines shown in Table 56.1. Those at high risk need a personalized plan with the HCP. Early detection can decrease mortality from breast cancer.

Along with these lifestyle choices, there are other risk-reduction options for those at high risk. Genetic testing for *BRCA* and other gene mutations is available. People with a personal history of breast cancer, especially those diagnosed at age 45 or earlier; those older with unknown family history; those with a second breast cancer at any age; those of Ashkenazi Jewish ancestry; males of any age: and anyone with 1 or more close relatives with breast, ovarian, pancreatic, or high-grade prostate cancers should be tested. If testing was done in the past and was negative, a conversation about repeat testing with a genetic counselor is worthwhile as newer tests examine a much wider range of genes.

Prophylactic surgery decisions require a great deal of thought, patience, and discussion with the HCP, genetic counselor, and family. In women with an abnormal *BRCA1* or *BRCA2* gene, prophylactic oophorectomy may reduce their risk of developing breast and ovarian cancer. In deciding whether and when to undergo this surgery, women should receive counseling about the risks and benefits of prophylactic oophorectomy, including fertility issues.

Patients need to consider the options and make decisions with which they feel comfortable. Removing both breasts and ovaries does not eliminate the risk for breast cancer. A small risk exists that cancer can develop in the areas where the breasts used to be. Close follow-up is necessary even after prophylactic surgery.

◆ Acute Care

The times of waiting for the initial biopsy results and waiting for the HCP to make treatment recommendations are difficult for patients and their families. Even after the HCP has discussed treatment options, the patient often relies on you to clarify and expand on these options. During this stressful time, the patient may not be coping effectively. Explore the patient's usual decision-making processes, help them evaluate the advantages and disadvantages of the options, and provide information relevant to the decision. Clarify any unresolved issues with the HCP. Provide support to the patient and family after they make decisions (Box 56.3).

Provide the patient with enough information to ensure informed consent. Some patients seek extensive, detailed information to maintain a sense of control. Others avoid information to decrease anxiety and fear. Be sensitive to the person's need for and preferred type of information. These include (1) instructions on pain control and what to expect after surgery (e.g., dressing and drain care, turning, coughing, deep breathing), (2) a review of mobility restrictions and postoperative exercises, and (3) an explanation of the recovery period.

BOX 56.3 EVIDENCE-BASED PRACTICE

Breast Cancer Treatment

C.P. is a 56-year-old woman who was diagnosed with stage IIIA breast cancer. Her treatment plan is to receive neoadjuvant chemotherapy and then have surgery and radiation. C.P. tells you that she will have surgery and radiation but does not want chemotherapy because she is afraid of the side effects.

Making Clinical Decisions

Best Available Evidence

The use of chemotherapy before surgery reduces the size and extent of the tumor, thus making the surgery more likely to succeed. It reduces the chance more extensive treatment will be needed.

Clinician Expertise

Neoadjuvant chemotherapy is usually recommended for stage IIIA breast cancer. The common side effects (e.g., nausea, vomiting, fatigue) can be managed with appropriate treatment.

Patient Preferences and Values

C.P. does not want chemotherapy and prefers to take her chances. If the cancer comes back, she will have chemotherapy.

Implications for Nursing Practice

1. Why is it important to discuss with C.P. the reason chemotherapy is recommended?
2. What information would you share with her about treatment side effects and how they can be managed?
3. You note her spouse appears attentive and supportive. How will you involve him in C.P.'s care?

Reference for Evidence

National Comprehensive Cancer Network: NCCN guidelines for patients: invasive breast cancer: 2020. Retrieved from https://www.nccn.org/patients/guidelines/content/PDF/breast-invasive-patient.pdf.

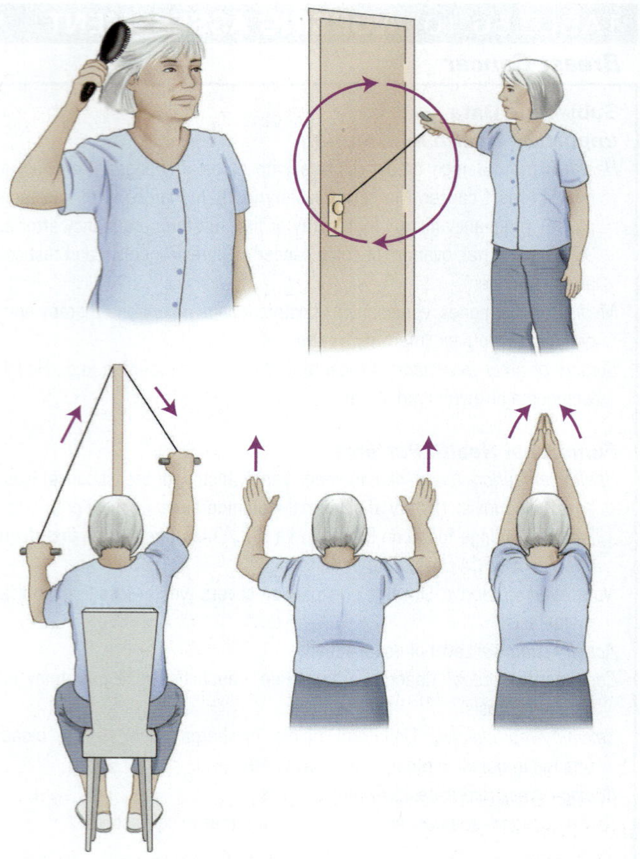

Fig. 56.7 Postoperative exercises for the patient with a mastectomy or lumpectomy with axillary lymph node sampling and/or dissection.

The woman who has breast-conserving surgery usually has an uncomplicated postoperative course with variable pain intensity. Pain depends primarily on the extent of the lymph node sampling procedure. If an ALND has been done or if the patient had a mastectomy, drains are generally left in place and patients are discharged home with them. Teach the patient and family how to manage the drains at home.

Most patients are discharged from the hospital 24 to 48 hours after a mastectomy, depending on if reconstructive surgery was done. Restoring arm function on the affected side after breast cancer surgery is a key nursing goal. Arm and shoulder exercises, which are started gradually, may begin prior to discharge (Fig. 56.7). These exercises aim to prevent contractures and muscle shortening, maintain muscle tone, and improve lymph and blood circulation. The difficulty and pain encountered in performing what used to be simple tasks may cause frustration and depression. The goal of all exercise is a gradual return to full range of motion.

Minimize discomfort by giving analgesics regularly when the patient is in pain and about 30 minutes before starting exercises. When the patient can shower, the warm water on the involved shoulder often relaxes the muscle and reduces joint stiffness.

Explain the specific follow-up plan to the patient and emphasize the importance of ongoing monitoring and self-care. After surgery, teach the patient to report symptoms, such as fever, inflammation at the surgical site, redness, and unusual swelling. Other changes to report are new back pain, weakness, shortness of breath, and change in mental status, including confusion.

For women who have had a mastectomy without breast reconstruction, a variety of products are available. Your role is to present the choices and resources. Options include garments such as camisoles with soft breast prosthetic inserts or a fitted prosthesis with a bra. Should the woman choose a breast prosthesis, a certified fitter can help her choose a comfortable, more permanent weighted prosthesis and bra. This is generally done 4 to 8 weeks after surgery.

Lymphedema. **Lymphedema** is an accumulation of lymph in soft tissue. It can occur because of the lymph node sampling procedure or radiation therapy (Fig. 56.8). When the axillary nodes cannot return lymph fluid to the central circulation, the fluid accumulates in the arm, hand, or breast, causing obstructive pressure on the veins and venous return. The patient may have heaviness, impaired motor function in the arm, and numbness and paresthesia of the fingers. Cellulitis and progressive fibrosis of the skin can result from untreated lymphedema.

Upper extremity lymphedema can occur at any point after treatment for breast cancer. Teach the patient ways to prevent and reduce lymphedema. These include no BP readings, venipunctures, or injections on the affected arm, if possible. The affected arm should not be dependent for long periods. Caution

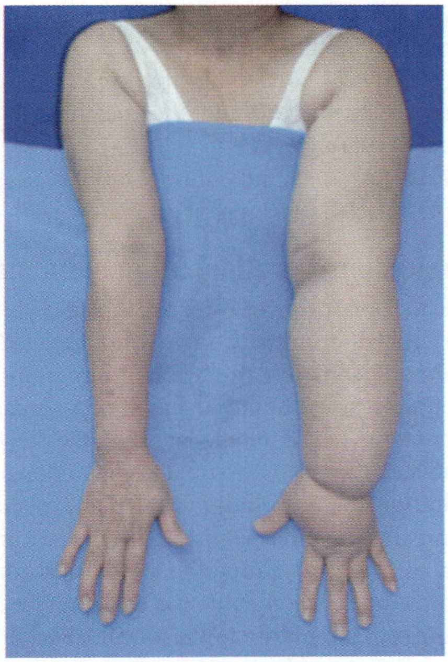

Fig. 56.8 Lymphedema. Accumulation of fluid in the tissue after excision of lymph nodes. (From Pappalardo M, Cheng M: *Principles and practice of lymphedema surgery*, 6:39, St Louis, 2022, Elsevier.)

should be used to prevent infection, burns, or compromised circulation on the affected side. Encourage exercise and maintaining a normal weight.

If trauma to the arm occurs, teach the patient to thoroughly wash the area with soap and water and observe. A topical antibiotic ointment and a bandage or other sterile dressing may be needed.

With acute lymphedema, we usually start complete decongestive therapy. Specially trained professionals perform this therapy. It consists of a massage-like technique to mobilize the subcutaneous accumulation of fluid. This may be followed by the use of compression bandaging and an intermittent pneumatic compression sleeve. The sleeve applies mechanical massage to the arm and helps move lymph drainage up toward the heart. Elevating the arm so that it is level with the heart and performing isometric exercises reduce the fluid in the arm. To maintain maximum volume reduction, the patient may need to wear a fitted compression sleeve during waking hours and preventively during air travel.

Post–breast therapy pain syndrome. *Post–breast therapy pain syndrome* (PBTPS) occurs in some people who have had procedures for breast cancer. It is often caused by injury to nerves during surgery. However, it also can be due to chemotherapy and radiation therapy. The most common theory is that PBTPS results from injury to intercostobrachial nerves. These are sensory nerves that exit the chest wall muscles and provide sensation to the shoulder and upper arm.

Because of its multiple causes, PBTPS symptoms can range from mild to debilitating. Common symptoms include chest and upper arm pain, tingling down the arm, continuous aching and burning, numbness, shooting or pricking pain, and unbearable itching that persists beyond the normal 3-month healing time. Edema may be present.

Treatment includes nonsteroidal antiinflammatory drugs (NSAIDs), low-dose antidepressants, topical anesthetics (e.g., EMLA [lidocaine and prilocaine]), and antiseizure drugs (e.g., gabapentin). Other treatments include biofeedback, physical therapy to prevent "frozen shoulder" syndrome from inadequate movement, guided imagery, and psychologic counseling with a therapist trained in the management of chronic pain syndromes.

Phantom breast pain. *Phantom breast pain* is feeling pain in the breast after the breast was removed with mastectomy. It occurs for the same reasons phantom limb sensation occurs after limb amputations. The brain continues to send signals to nerves in the breast area that were cut during surgery, even though the breast is no longer physically there.

CHECK YOUR PRACTICE

You are working in the breast clinic and doing a postoperative assessment on a 56-year-old woman who had a right radical mastectomy 6 weeks ago. She is reporting sharp, prickly feelings in her right arm. She tells you, "I feel pain in the breast that was removed. Am I going crazy? That breast is not even attached to my body anymore!"

- How would you respond and what follow-up would you provide?

Psychosocial support. Throughout history, the female breast has been a symbol of beauty, femininity, sexuality, and motherhood. The potential loss of a breast, or part of a breast, may be devastating for many women because of the significant psychologic, social, sexual, and body image implications associated with it. In some cases, psychosocial concerns may increase the physical effects of cancer, such as pain, fatigue, sleep problems, fear of recurrence, and cognitive changes. Men diagnosed with breast cancer may feel isolation and embarrassment related to the diagnosis. You must be aware of resources for men (https://malebreastcancercoalition.org).

Screening all cancer patients for psychosocial distress is a Commission on Cancer accreditation requirement.[21] From the time of diagnosis through treatment, survivorship, or metastatic disease, the patient may have signs of distress or tension (e.g., tachycardia, muscle tension, sleep problems, restlessness, changes in appetite or mood). Assess the patient's body language and affect during periods of high stress and indecision so that you can begin appropriate interventions.

Be sensitive to the psychologic impact that a cancer diagnosis and breast surgery can have on patients and their families. With an accepting attitude and the offer of resources, you can help the patient cope with feelings of fear, anger, anxiety, and depression (Table 56.11).

Refer patients to support resources, such as Breastcancer.org (www.Breastcancer.org), American Cancer Society (www.cancer.org), Living Beyond Breast Cancer (www.lbbc.org), Susan G. Komen for the Cure (ww5.komen.org), the Cancer Support Community, or local breast cancer organizations. The National Cancer Institute provides materials to help you meet the special needs of patients with breast cancer. In addition to in-person and online support programs, free smart phone applications are available through national cancer

TABLE 56.11 NURSING MANAGEMENT

Managing Distress in Breast Cancer

- Screen all patients for distress.
- Provide a safe environment for expressing feelings.
- Identify sources of support and strength, such as the partner, family, and spiritual or religious practices.
- Encourage the patient to identify and learn personal coping strengths.
- Promote communication among the patient, family, and friends.
- Assess the willingness, availability, and resilience of family and friends to serve as supportive caregivers.
- Provide teaching and answer questions about the disease, treatment options, and reproductive, fertility, or lactation issues (if appropriate).
- Make resources available for mental health counseling.
- Offer information about local and national community resources.

organizations that provide reliable and current information for the patient and family.

Many HCPs do not adequately address sexual concerns. If you are comfortable, begin a discussion of sexuality by inviting questions about relationships or intimacy concerns. Often, the patient's partner and/or family members need help dealing with their emotional reactions to the diagnosis and surgery before they can provide effective support for the patient. There are no physical reasons why a mastectomy would prevent sexual satisfaction. A woman taking hormone therapy may have a decreased sexual drive or vaginal dryness. She may need to use lubrication to prevent pain during intercourse. If difficulty adjusting or other problems develop, single or couples counseling may be useful to deal with the emotional side of a cancer diagnosis.

Depression and anxiety may occur with the continued stress and uncertainty of a cancer diagnosis. A patient's self-esteem and identity may be threatened. The support of family and friends and taking part in a cancer support group and/or counseling are important aspects of care that may improve the patient's quality of life.

Survivorship. Almost 3 million breast cancer survivors are alive in the United States, making this population the largest group of cancer survivors. We expect this number to grow due to an aging population and improved methods for early detection and treatment. After treatment for breast cancer, the patient will have ongoing survivorship care.[22]

A history and physical assessment is recommended 1 to 4 times per year as clinically appropriate for 5 years, then annually thereafter. Teach breast cancer survivors to perform monthly BSE and chest wall self-examination and report any changes to their HCP. Local recurrence of breast cancer is usually at the surgical site. Breast cancer survivors should have an annual mammogram. Other breast imaging studies, such as a breast ultrasound or breast MRI, should be done only as an adjunct to mammography and not for annual routine surveillance. Cancer survivorship is discussed in Chapter 16.

◆ Evaluation

Expected outcomes are that the patient after breast cancer surgery will:

- Identify activities that can reduce postoperative edema and improve mobility
- Show effective use of coping strategies
- Discuss feelings about and the meaning of changes in physical appearance
- Identify community and online resources, personal counseling resources, and support groups

Gerontologic Considerations: Breast Cancer

A major risk for breast cancer is increasing age. More than half of all breast cancers occur in women who are age 55 or older. Older women are less likely to have mammograms. Screening and treatment decisions should be based on a woman's general health status rather than biologic age since health status has a greater influence on tolerance to treatment and long-term prognosis. In addition to comorbidities and life expectancy, treatment decisions for the older woman with breast cancer should be based on nutrition and functional status; vision, gait, and balance; and the presence of dementia or depression.

Breast cancer treatment is similar for older patients, including the use of surgery, radiation therapy, and drug therapy. For healthy older women, breast cancer survival rates are similar to those of younger women when matched by cancer stage.

MAMMOPLASTY

Mammoplasty is the surgical change in the size or shape of the breast. It may be done electively for cosmetic purposes to either enlarge or reduce the size of the breasts. It also may be done to reconstruct the breast after a mastectomy.

A professional, nonjudgmental attitude and clear information about surgical breast options are most useful for women engaged in decision making about mammoplasty. The desire to change the appearance of the breasts has special significance for each woman as she attempts to change or recreate her body image. Be aware of the cultural value that the woman places on the breast. Help the patient set realistic expectations about what mammoplasty can achieve and possible complications (e.g., hematoma formation, hemorrhage, infection). If an implant is involved, capsular contracture and loss of the implant are possible.

Breast Reconstruction

Breast reconstructive surgery is a type of surgery for women who have had all or part of a breast removed. It can achieve symmetry and restore or preserve body image. It may be done simultaneously with a mastectomy or some time afterward. The timing of reconstructive surgery is based on the patient's physical and psychologic needs.[23]

Indications

The main indications for breast reconstruction are to improve self-image, regain a sense of normalcy, and assist in coping with the loss of the breast. It restores the contour of the breast without the use of an external prosthesis. Reconstruction techniques cannot restore lactation, nipple sensation, or erectility. Although the breast will not fully resemble its premastectomy appearance,

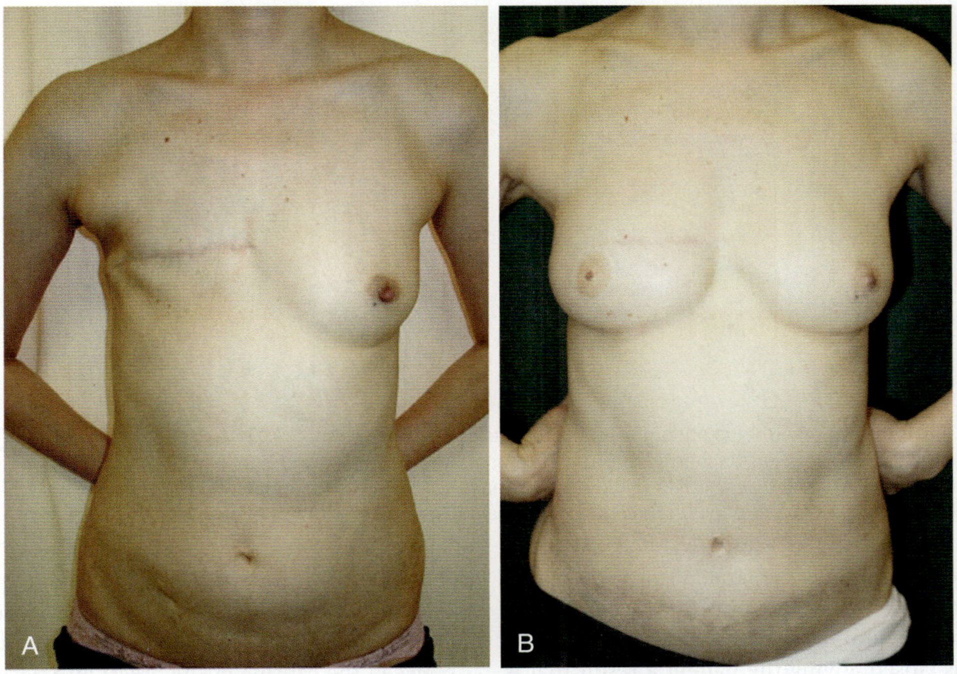

Fig. 56.9 (A) Appearance of chest after right modified mastectomy. (B) Breast reconstruction after nipple-areolar reconstruction. (From Satake T, Muto M, Kou S, et al.: Contralateral unaffected breast augmentation using zone IV as a SIEA flap during unilateral DIEP flap breast reconstruction, *J Plast Reconstr Aesthet Surg* 72:1537, 2019.)

the reconstructed appearance usually is an improvement over the mastectomy scar (Fig. 56.9).

Types of Reconstruction

Breast implants and tissue expansion. Implants have a silicone shell filled with either silicone gel or saline.[24] Some newer types use a cohesive gel, which is a thicker silicone gel. Implant surgery can be done in 1 or 2 stages. In the 1-stage procedure, the implant is placed at the same time as the mastectomy. The implant is usually placed under the pectoralis muscle.

In the 2-stage procedure, a tissue expander is inserted after the mastectomy. The expander stretches the skin and muscle at the mastectomy site before inserting permanent implants (Fig. 56.10). It is placed in a pocket under the pectoralis muscle, which protects the implant and provides soft tissue coverage. The expander is minimally inflated, then gradually filled by weekly injections of sterile saline solution. This procedure stretches the skin and muscle and can be painful. A small magnet embedded in most expanders helps locate the port where the fluid is injected. A woman should not have an MRI with a magnet in place.

The expander can be (1) surgically removed and a permanent implant is inserted or (2) remain in place to become the implant, thus eliminating the need for a second surgery. Tissue expansion does not work well in those with extensive scar tissue from surgery or radiation therapy.

The body's natural response to the presence of a foreign substance is the formation of a fibrous capsule around the implant. If excessive capsular formation occurs because of infection, hematoma, trauma, or reaction to a foreign body, a contracture can develop, resulting in deformity. Although HCPs differ in their approaches to the prevention of contracture formation, gentle manual massage around the implant is routine. Other adverse outcomes include wrinkling, scarring, asymmetry, pain, and infection at the incision site. There is a small chance of anaplastic large cell lymphoma. This has mostly occurred with textured implants.

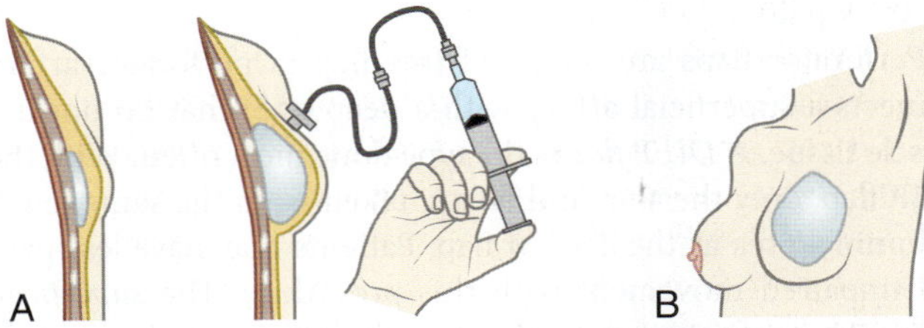

Fig. 56.10 (A) Tissue expander with gradual expansion. (B) Tissue expander in place after mastectomy.

Tissue flap procedures. We can use autologous (person's own) tissue to recreate a breast mound. In autologous reconstruction, tissue from the abdomen, back, thighs, or buttocks is used to create a reconstructed breast. The most common types of tissue flap procedures are *transverse rectus abdominis musculocutaneous (TRAM) flap, deep inferior epigastric artery perforator (DIEP) flap,* and *latissimus dorsi flap.*

The TRAM flap is a common flap surgery. The rectus abdominis muscles are paired flat muscles running from the rib cage down to the pubic bone. Arteries running inside the muscles provide branches at many levels, and these branches supply the fat and skin across a large expanse of the abdomen.

There are 2 different types of TRAM flaps: pedicle and free. In a pedicle flap, the tissue stays attached to the rectus muscle and is tunneled under the skin to the patient's chest (Fig. 56.11).

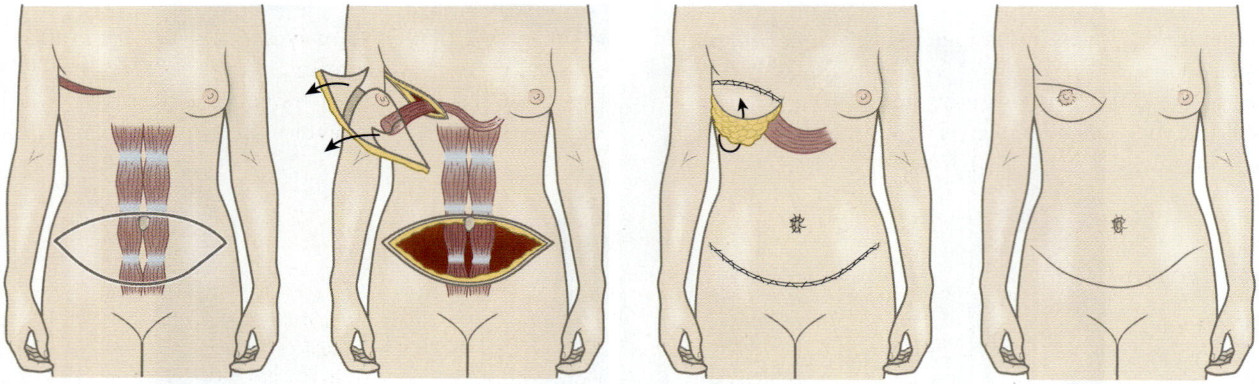

A B C D

Fig. 56.11 Transverse rectus abdominis musculocutaneous (TRAM) flap. (A) TRAM flap is planned. (B) The abdominal tissue, while attached to the rectus muscle, nerve, and blood supply, is tunneled through the abdomen to the chest. (C) The flap is trimmed to shape the breast. The lower abdominal incision is closed. (D) Nipple and areola are reconstructed after the breast is healed.

In a free flap, the tissue is completely separated from the muscle and its blood supply and moved to the new place on the patient's chest. The tissue is molded and fashioned to form a breast. The abdominal incision is closed, giving the patient a result that is similar to having an abdominoplasty ("tummy tuck"). The procedure can last 6 to 8 hours with recovery taking 6 to 8 weeks. Some patients have report pain and fatigue for up to 3 months. Complications include bleeding, seroma, hernia, infection, and low back pain.

Perforator flaps are a type of free flap (a perforator artery connects a superficial artery with a deep one) that do not use muscle tissue. A *DIEP flap* is the type done most often. With the DIEP flap, only the skin and fat are taken from the same lower abdominal area as the TRAM flap. Patients may have less pain and impaired movement with this procedure. The *superficial inferior epigastric artery perforator (SIEAP)* is another option using the abdominal area.

The *latissimus dorsi flap* is a pedicle flap. In this type of flap, a block of skin and muscle from the patient's back replaces tissue removed during mastectomy. A small implant may be needed under the flap to gain reasonable breast shape and size. A disadvantage of this technique is a scar on the back.

Less often, flaps are taken from the buttocks, hips, or thighs. The transverse upper gracilis flap, or inner thigh flap, is one type of free flap. Tissue, including the gracilis muscle, is taken from the bottom fold of the buttock extending into the inner thigh. The inferior or superior gluteal artery perforators are used for flaps taken from the buttocks.

Nipple-areolar reconstruction. Many patients undergoing breast reconstruction also have nipple-areolar reconstruction. Nipple reconstruction gives the reconstructed breast a much more natural appearance (Fig. 56.9C). Nipple-areolar reconstruction is usually done a few months after breast reconstruction. Tissue to construct a nipple may be taken from the opposite breast or from a small flap of tissue on the reconstructed breast mound. Most often, the areola is tattooed with a permanent pigmented dye. Improved techniques allow skilled tattoo artists to create a complete 3D nipple-areola complex. Polyurethane removable nipples are also available.

Breast Augmentation

In *augmentation mammoplasty* (procedure to enlarge the breasts), an implant is placed in a surgically created pocket between the capsule of the breast and pectoral fascia or ideally under the pectoralis muscle.

Breast Reduction

For some women, large breasts can be a source of physical and psychologic discomfort. They can interfere with normal daily activities, such as walking, using a computer, and driving a car. The weight of large breasts can lead to back, shoulder, and neck problems, including degenerative nerve changes. Overly large breasts can interfere with self-esteem, self-image, and comfort in wearing some clothing. Reducing breast size can have positive effects on the patient's psychologic and physical health.

Reduction mammoplasty is done by resecting wedges of tissue from the upper and lower quadrants of the breast. The excess skin is removed. The areola and nipple are relocated on the breast. Lactation usually can still occur if massive amounts of tissue are not removed, and the nipples are left connected during surgery.

Breast Lift

A breast lift, or mastopexy, is a surgical procedure that changes the shape of the breasts. During a breast lift, excess skin is removed, and the tissue reshaped to raise the breast. Most women who have this procedure do so to lift sagging breasts. A breast lift does not change the size of the breast. It is often done with breast augmentation or reduction.

❖ NURSING MANAGEMENT: BREAST AUGMENTATION AND REDUCTION

Breast augmentation and breast reduction may be done in the outpatient surgical area or involve overnight hospitalization. General anesthesia is used. Drains are generally placed in the surgical site to prevent hematoma formation and then removed when drainage is under 20 to 30 mL/day. Assess drainage for color and odor to detect infection or hemorrhage. Monitor the temperature. Change dressings as needed using sterile technique.

After surgery, assure the woman that the breast's appearance will improve when healing is complete. Depending on HCP preference, the patient may wear a bra that provides good support continuously for 2 or 3 days after breast reduction or augmentation. Depending on the extent of the surgery, most women resume normal activities within 2 to 3 weeks. They must avoid strenuous exercise for several weeks.

Case Study

Breast Cancer

(© XiXinXing/iStock/Thinkstock.)

Patient Profile

A.K., a 62-year-old married Asian American woman, was diagnosed with a 1.3 cm estrogen- and progesterone-positive, HER-2–negative breast cancer. She had a lumpectomy and sentinel lymph node biopsy (SLNB) with possible axillary node dissection.

Interprofessional Care

Preoperative

- When she is seen in the clinic 1 week before surgery, she was crying uncontrollably and said, "My husband does not want to look at me anymore. He is afraid of what I am going to look like with a flat chest."
- "I cannot sleep, and I just pace the floor at night."
- "My mother died of breast cancer when she was 60, and my sister got it when she was 40."
- Expresses concern that her 2 daughters (34 and 32) and their daughters are going to get "this horrible disease."
- Appointment made with genetic counselor

Operative Procedure

- Lumpectomy and SLNB; 4 lymph nodes removed
- Tumor was removed with clear margins
- No cancer cells in the sentinel lymph nodes
- Tissue specimen sent for a 21-gene recurrence score genomic test

Postoperative

- Does not want to leave hospital and refuses to get out of bed
- Swelling and restricted range of motion in right arm
- Pain not controlled well with pain medication
- Oncology social worker and physical therapy to see patient

Follow-Up Findings and Treatment

- Scheduled for external radiation and a consult with medical oncologist to discuss hormone therapy
- 21-Gene recurrence score is 11, low risk; genetic panel negative
- A.K. joined support group for cancer patient and husband joined support group for caregivers

Discussion Questions

1. ***Recognize***: What in A.K.'s breast cancer experience with her family members may influence her coping response?
2. ***Analyze***: What complication did she develop after surgery?
3. ***Plan:*** How will you include cultural preferences in A.K.'s plan of care?
4. ***Plan:*** Which exercises will A.K. need to perform after surgery?
5. ***Prioritize:*** What is the most important information you would provide A.K. about radiation treatment and hormone therapy?
6. ***Act:*** What information would you provide A.K. about her surgery and why the 21-gene recurrence test was done?
7. ***Act:*** What information would you provide A.K. and her daughters? What early detection measures are important for them to know?
8. ***Act:*** What types of referrals may be indicated for A.K.?
9. ***Evaluate:*** What outcomes would indicate nursing interventions were successful for A.K.?

Answers and a corresponding conceptual care map available at http://evolve.elsevier.com/Lewis/medsurg.

BRIDGE TO NCLEX EXAMINATION

The number of the question corresponds to the same-numbered outcome at the beginning of the chapter.

1. A nurse planning a community program on breast cancer screening guideline would include which recommendation about screening in average risk women?
   a. Women over age 55 should discontinue screening.
   b. Women 40 to 45 should receive a clinical breast exam.
   c. Women aged 45 to 54 years should get annual mammograms.
   d. Women should have the option of beginning annual screening at age 35.
2. Which intervention would the nurse include in the plan of care for a young woman with preductal mastitis?
   a. Administer antibiotics as ordered.
   b. Teach the woman about a breast biopsy.
   c. Counsel her on the need for genetic breast cancer screening.
   d. Explain the role of radiation therapy as a treatment alternative.
3. Which are considered risk factors for breast cancer in women? (*select all that apply*)
   a. Having menarche at age 17
   b. Being a woman over age 60
   c. Previous history of ovarian cancer
   d. Having a brother with breast cancer
   e. Stopping oral contraceptives 15 years ago
4. A patient with breast cancer has a lumpectomy with sentinel lymph node biopsy that is positive for cancer. You explain that, of the other tests done to determine the risk for cancer recurrence or spread, the results that support the more favorable prognosis are (*select all that apply*)
   a. well-differentiated tumor.
   b. estrogen receptor-positive tumor.
   c. overexpression of HER-2 cell marker.
   d. involvement of 2 to 4 axillary nodes.
   e. aneuploidy status from cell proliferation studies.

5. The nurse teaches a patient starting immune based therapy for breast cancer that this treatment works by
   a. blocking HER-2 receptors.
   b. increasing estrogen production.
   c. increasing the number of macrophages.
   d. preventing the production of aromatase.
6. A priority in providing care for a patient who underwent mastectomy includes
   a. teaching the patient to shower with cool water.
   b. measuring blood pressures in both upper extremities.
   c. instructing the patient to limit movement to promote healing.
   d. encouraging exercises to restore arm function on the affected side.
7. A patient with breast cancer who underwent mastectomy is asking about reconstructive surgery. Which information would the nurse provide?
   a. It can restore lactation.
   b. Nipple sensation may not return.
   c. The triceps muscle is used as a tissue flap for breast reconstruction.
   d. Patients must wait 3 months after mastectomy before reconstruction can begin.

1. c; 2. a; 3. b, c, d; 4. a, b; 5. a; 6. d; 7. b

For the rationales to these answers and even more NCLEX review questions, visit http://evolve.elsevier.com/Lewis/medsurg.

EVOLVE WEBSITE/RESOURCES LIST

http://evolve.elsevier.com/Lewis/medsurg
Review Questions (Online Only)
Key Points
Answer Keys for Questions
- Rationales for Bridge to NCLEX Examination Questions
- Answer Guidelines for Case Study

Student Case Study
- Patient With Breast Cancer

Nursing Care Plan
- eNursing Care Plan 56.1: Patient After Breast Surgery

Conceptual Care Map Creator
- Conceptual Care Map for Case Study

Audio Glossary
Content Updates

REFERENCES

1. American Cancer Society (ACS): Cancer facts and figures 2020. Retrieved from https://www.cancer.org/content/dam/cancer-org/research/cancer-facts-and-statistics/annual-cancer-facts-and-figures/2020/cancer-facts-and-figures-2020.pdf.
2. ACS: Breast cancer early detection and diagnosis. Retrieved from https://www.cancer.org/cancer/breast-cancer/screening-tests-and-early-detection.html.
*3. National Comprehensive Cancer Network (NCCN): NCCN guidelines: breast cancer screening and diagnosis. Retrieved from https://www.nccn.org/professionals/physician_gls/pdf/breast-screening.pdf.
4. Gilmore R, Lange J: Benign breast disease. In Cameron J, editor: *Current surgical therapy*, ed 13, Atlanta, 2020, Elsevier.
5. Elsevier Point of Care: Mastitis. Retrieved from https://www.clinicalkey.com.
6. Nye L: Breast diseases. In *Conn's current therapy 2021*, Philadelphia, 2021, Elsevier.
7. Whitney E, Sciscone A: Fibrocystic breast disease. In *Ferri's clinical advisor*, Philadelphia, 2020, Elsevier.
8. Li A, Kirk L: Intraductal papilloma. Retrieved from https://www.ncbi.nlm.nih.gov/books/NBK519539/.
9. Satpathy H: Gynecomastia. In *Ferri's clinical advisor*, Philadelphia, 2020, Elsevier.
10. ACS: Breast cancer: Risk factors and prevention. Retrieved from https://www.cancer.org/cancer/breast-cancer/risk-and-prevention.html.
11. National Cancer Institute: Genetics and breast and gynecologic cancers PDQ®—health professional version. Retrieved from https://www.cancer.gov/types/breast/hp/breast-ovarian-genetics-pdq.
12. Breastcancer.org: Genetic testing. Retrieved from https://www.breastcancer.org/symptoms/testing/genetic.
*13. Hasset M, Somerfield M, Baker E, et al.: Management of male breast cancer: ASCO guideline, *J Clin Oncol* 38:1849, 2020.
14. Koh J, Kim M: Introduction of a new staging system of breast cancer for radiologists: an emphasis on the prognostic stage, *Korean J Radiol* 20:69, 2019.
*15. NCCN: NCCN guidelines, version 5, 2020: breast cancer. Retrieved from https://www.nccn.org/professionals/physician_gls/pdf/breast.pdf.
16. James TA, Palis B, McCabe R, et al.: Evaluating the role of sentinel lymph node biopsy in patients with DCIS treated with breast conserving surgery, *Am J Surg* 220:654, 2020.
17. Chippa V, Barazi H: Inflammatory breast cancer. Retrieved from https://www.ncbi.nlm.nih.gov/books/NBK564324/.
18. Green H, Schwartzberg L: Expert insights on triple-negative breast cancer: preparing for the next wave of treatments, *J Adv Prac Oncol* 11:266, 2020.
19. About OncotypeDX breast DCIS score. Retrieved from https://www.oncotypeiq.com/en-US/breast-cancer/patients-and-caregivers/stage-0-dcis/about-the-test.
20. Yedjou C, Sims J, Miele L, et al.: Health and racial disparity in breast cancer, *Adv Exp Med Biol* 1152:31, 2020.
*21. American College of Surgeons Commission on Cancer: Optimal resources for cancer care 2020 standards. Survivorship care. Retrieved from https://www.facs.org/-/media/files/quality-programs/cancer/coc/optimal_resources_for_cancer_care_2020_standards.ashx.
*22. ACS: ACS/American Society of Clinical Oncology breast cancer survivorship care guideline. Retrieved from https://www.cancer.org/health-care-professionals/american-cancer-society-survivorship-guidelines/breast-cancer-survivorship-care-guidelines.html.
23. ACS: Breast reconstructive surgery. Retrieved from https://www.cancer.org/cancer/breast-cancer/reconstruction-surgery.html.
24. Food and Drug Administration: Breast implants. Retrieved from https://www.fda.gov/medical-devices/implants-and-prosthetics/breast-implants.

*Evidence-based information for clinical practice.

57

Sexually Transmitted Infections

Daniel P. Worrall

http://evolve.elsevier.com/Lewis/medsurg/

CONCEPTUAL FOCUS

Infection
Pain
Reproduction
Sexuality

LEARNING OUTCOMES

1. Identify factors contributing to sexually transmitted infections (STIs) in the United States.
2. Describe the etiology, clinical manifestations, complications, and diagnostic studies for chlamydia, gonorrhea, trichomoniasis, genital herpes, genital warts, and syphilis.
3. Compare and contrast primary genital herpes with recurrent genital herpes.
4. Explain the interprofessional care and treatment of chlamydia, gonorrhea, trichomoniasis, genital herpes, genital warts, and syphilis.
5. Discuss the assessment for patients who have an STI.
6. Describe the nursing management of patients with STIs.
7. Summarize the nursing role in the prevention and control of STIs.

KEY TERMS

chlamydial infections
genital herpes
genital warts
gonorrhea
sexually transmitted infections (STIs)
syphilis
trichomoniasis

Sexually transmitted infections (STIs) are infectious diseases that spread through sexual contact with the penis, vagina, anus, mouth, or sexual fluids of an infected person. Many do not view STIs as a serious health threat because most are easily treated. However, complications of STIs are serious. They can include infertility and cancer. Having an STI can affect a person's well-being, their relationships, and their sexual lives. Patient education, counseling, and referrals are essential nursing roles for promoting health and optimal sexual well-being.

Mucosal tissues in the genitals (urethra in men, vagina in women), rectum, and mouth are especially susceptible to the bacteria and viruses that cause STIs. A list of common STIs is shown in Table 57.1. Some STIs, such as human papillomavirus (HPV), can spread from direct skin-to-skin contact with an infected person. Other STIs, such as human immunodeficiency virus (HIV), may be contracted via blood products, semen, or vaginal secretions or be transmitted from mother to baby during pregnancy or labor and delivery. Some STIs can spread through *autoinoculation* (spread of infection by touching or scratching an infected area and transferring it to another part of the body). STIs cannot typically be transmitted from casual contact or inanimate objects.

FACTORS AFFECTING INCIDENCE OF STIs

Rates of STIs in the United States are at an all-time high. According to recent data, 26 million new infections are diagnosed in the United States each year. STIs affect 1 in 5 adults and result in $16 billion in health care costs.[1] Although all sexually active persons are at risk, some populations have a greater burden of infection. Socioeconomic factors, decreased condom use, and cuts to STD programs across the country are contributors.[2] Having one STI can increase the risk for getting another. It is also possible for a person to have more than one STI at a time.

All STIs have an *incubation period*. It is the time from initial infection to the time when symptoms first appear or screening tests for the infection are positive. This can lead to the transmission of disease from an asymptomatic (but infected)

TABLE 57.1 Causes of STIs

STI	Cause
Bacterial Infections	
Chlamydial	*Chlamydia trachomatis*
Gonorrhea	*Neisseria gonorrhoeae*
Syphilis	*Treponema pallidum*
Viral Infections	
Genital herpes	Herpes simplex virus (HSV 1 or 2)
Genital warts (condylomata acuminata)	Human papillomavirus (HPV)
Human immunodeficiency virus infection (HIV)	Human immunodeficiency virus (HIV) (see Chapter 15)
Hepatitis B and C	Hepatitis B and C viruses (see Chapter 48)
Molluscum	*Molluscum contagiosum*
Parasitic/Protozoan Infection	
Trichomoniasis	*Trichomonas vaginalis*

person to another person, even before any signs or symptoms begin.

In the United States, all cases of gonorrhea, chlamydia, and syphilis must be reported to public health authorities for surveillance purposes for federally funded control programs and partner notification. Surveillance and partner notification are a major part of the effort to prevent and control the spread of STIs. Nurses and other HCPs play a vital role. They are mandated to report STIs to public health authorities. Despite this requirement, only a small number of infections are reported. This means that the cases of gonorrhea, chlamydia, and syphilis reported in the United States annually do not represent the actual number of infections.

Many factors contribute to the high rate of STIs.[2] Earlier reproductive maturity and increased longevity make for a longer sexual life span. Other factors include greater sexual freedom, individual sexual behaviors, the media's increasing emphasis on sexuality without mentioning safer sex, and sexual network characteristics. Alcohol and substance use can further contribute to unsafe sexual practices by impairing judgment. Risk factors for STIs are outlined in Table 57.2.

STIs affect certain groups of people disproportionately (Box 57.1). This includes youth and young adults under age 25, men having sex with men (MSM), transgender women, and those who are socially and economically disadvantaged.[3] Many minority groups have rates of STIs greater than that of Whites, including Asians, Native American Indian/Alaskan Native, and Native Hawaiian/Other Pacific Islanders.[4]

Trends in methods of contraceptive use affect the rate of STIs. The male condom is the best form of protection (other than abstinence) against STIs. While condom use has increased in the United States, many people do not use condoms. Most women use hormonal (e.g., oral contraceptive pills, patch, injectables) or long-acting reversible contraceptives (e.g., intrauterine devices). These do not provide barrier protection against STIs.

This chapter covers the most common STIs. HIV infection is covered in Chapter 15. Anyone who contracts an STI may also be at risk for HIV infection. HIV pre-exposure prophylaxis

TABLE 57.2 Risk Factors for STIs

High-Risk Behaviors
- Alcohol or substance use (inhibits judgment)
- Having new sexual partners
- Having more than 1 sexual partner
- Having sexual partners who have/have had multiple partners
- Inconsistent or incorrect use of condoms or other barrier methods
- Exchanging sex for money, shelter, or other needs

High-Risk Medical History
- Having 1 STI is a risk factor for getting another
- Not being vaccinated for STIs or other infections that may be transmitted through some forms of sexual activity (HPV, hepatitis A and B)
- Receiving multiple courses of non-occupational postexposure prophylaxis to prevent HIV infection

High-Risk Populations
- Adolescents and young adults (under age 25)
- Ethnicity/race (e.g., Black, American Indian/Alaskan Native, Native Hawaiian/Other Pacific Islander, Hispanic)
- MSM
- Persons in correctional facilities
- Transgender women
- Victims of sexual assault
- Women

BOX 57.1 PROMOTING HEALTH EQUITY

STIs

Incidence of STIs
- Depending on their age and gender, Black persons have
  - The highest number of chlamydial infections
  - More than 50% of cases of gonorrhea
  - Nearly 35% of cases of syphilis
  - More than 40.4% of congenital syphilis cases
  - A higher seroprevalence of herpes simplex type 2
- Hispanic persons
  - Infected with chlamydia and gonorrhea at a higher rate than Whites
  - 23% of all syphilis cases
  - 32.6% of all congenital syphilis cases
- Men who have sex with men (MSM)
  - Have the largest proportion of gonorrhea infections
  - Are more likely to test positive for antimicrobial resistant strains of gonorrhea
  - 64% of all syphilis cases
  - Are at increased risk for HIV, hepatitisC, and HSV-2

Factors Influencing Disparities
- Social and economic disadvantages can make it hard for people to care for their overall health, including their sexual health.
- People who cannot afford basic necessities may have trouble accessing and affording quality sexual health services.
- Fear and distrust of HCPs and institutions can negatively affect racial and ethnic minorities from seeking health care.
- In communities where is a higher prevalence of STIs, it may be hard to reduce the risk for infection because a person faces a higher chance of having an infected partner than in those communities with a lower prevalence.

(PrEP) or non-occupational postexposure prophylaxis (nPEP) may be appropriate for these persons. See Chapter 15 for more about PrEP and nPEP.

STIs CHARACTERIZED BY DISCHARGE, CERVICITIS, OR URETHRITIS

CHLAMYDIAL INFECTIONS

Chlamydia is the most common reportable STI in the United States. Nearly 2 million cases are reported annually. Incidence is on the rise.[2] As many infections are asymptomatic, we believe the actual number of cases is significantly higher, around 4 million.[1]

Etiology and Pathophysiology

Chlamydial infections are caused by *Chlamydia trachomatis,* a gram-negative bacterium and intracellular pathogen. *Chlamydia* is transmitted through vaginal, anal, or oral sex. Ejaculation does not have to occur for transmission. The incubation period for chlamydia is 1 to 3 weeks. Prior infection with *Chlamydia* does not provide protection from reinfection. This means that people who were treated for chlamydia can always be reinfected.

The most common site for infection in men is the urethra. Infection in the male urethra is called *urethritis.* The most common site for infection for women is the cervix. Infection of the female cervix is called *cervicitis.* Men and women can get chlamydia of the rectum from receptive anal sex or the oropharynx from giving oral sex. Because the vagina acts as a natural reservoir for infectious secretions, STI transmission is more efficient from men to women than it is from women to men.

There are many serotypes of *C. trachomatis.* The more common are the cause of nongonococcal urethritis (NGU) in men or cervicitis in women. There is a small subset of serotypes that can cause another STI, lymphogranuloma venereum (LGV), when spread to the rectum. Although rare, this is more common in MSM.

Clinical Manifestations

Patients with chlamydia often have no symptoms. If symptoms develop in men, they may have pain with urination (dysuria) or urethral discharge. Rarely, men have testicular pain or swelling caused by infection of the epididymis (Fig. 57.1). In women, symptoms include mucopurulent vaginal discharge (mucus with pus), abnormal vaginal bleeding, dysuria, and pain with intercourse. Symptoms of rectal chlamydia include anorectal pain, discharge or bleeding, anal pruritus, tenesmus, mucus-coated stools, or painful bowel movements. Most patients with chlamydia in the throat will have no symptoms. A few may have a sore throat.

Complications

Complications often develop from poorly managed, inaccurately diagnosed, or undiagnosed chlamydia. Although men rarely have long-term complications from infection, epididymitis can result in male infertility. More often, chlamydia can affect a woman's reproductive tract, resulting in *pelvic inflammatory disease* (PID).[5] PID can damage fallopian tubes and increase a woman's risk for an ectopic pregnancy, infertility, and chronic pelvic pain. The risk for developing PID increases with repeated infection. The more episodes of PID, the more likely a woman will experience infertility. Although rare, patients can develop reactive arthritis, an autoimmune response to infection with *C. trachomatis.*

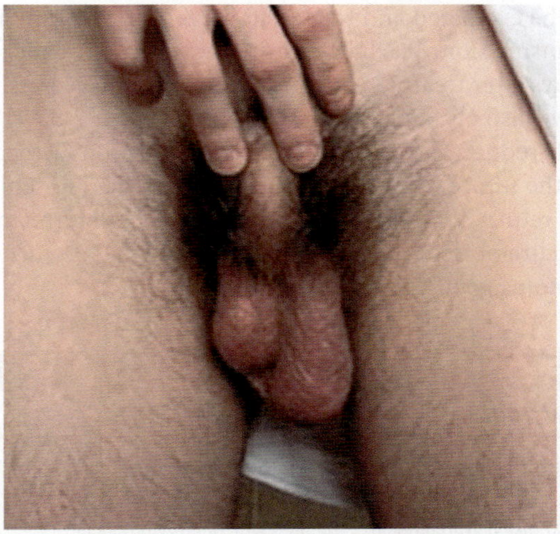

Fig. 57.1 Unilateral testicular swelling from chlamydial epididymitis. (From Jordan S, Geisler W: *Infectious diseases,* St. Louis, 2017, Elsevier.)

TABLE 57.3 Interprofessional Care

Chlamydial Infections

Diagnostic Assessment
- History and physical assessment
- Nucleic acid amplification test (NAAT)
- Testing for other STIs (gonorrhea, HIV, syphilis)

Management
- Doxycycline
- Alternative regimen: azithromycin or levofloxacin
- Teach to abstain from sexual contact for 7 days after completing treatment
- Treat all sexual partners, who must also wait 7 days before resuming sexual contact

Diagnostic Studies

Diagnosis of an STI requires an accurate sexual history, a physical assessment, and laboratory tests specific to each infection. The preferred method for diagnosing chlamydia is a nucleic acid amplification test (NAAT) (Table 57.3). NAAT is used to identify small amounts of DNA or RNA in test samples. NAAT can be done on urine, rectal, and oropharyngeal swabs; endocervical or vaginal swabs from women; and urethral swabs from men.

Interprofessional Care

The preferred treatment is doxycycline (Vibramycin) twice a day for 7 days (Table 57.3).[6] All sexual contacts within 60 days should be evaluated and treated to prevent reinfection and further transmission. Teach patients to abstain from sexual contact for 7 days after treatment or until all partners have been treated and have also abstained from sexual contact for 7 days. Review ways to reduce risk of reinfection or infection with another STI in the future. Anyone diagnosed and treated for chlamydia should return for repeat testing 3 months after treatment to ensure cure or detect reinfection. Tell patients to return sooner if symptoms persist or recur.

DRUG ALERT

Doxycycline (Vibramycin)

- Take doses on an empty stomach either 1 h before eating or 2 h after eating.
- Avoid taking with antacids, iron products, or dairy products.
- Remain upright for at least 30 min after taking a dose.
- Patients should avoid prolonged or excessive exposure to sunlight.
- Pregnant women should not take doxycycline.

Unfortunately, there is a high rate of recurrence. This often occurs when the sexual partners of infected people are not treated. This "ping-pong" effect (treatment, reexposure, reinfection) can end only when both partners are treated appropriately. Because of this issue, we recommend *expedited partner therapy* (EPT).[7] With EPT, HCPs give drugs or prescriptions to patients with STIs to give to partners without their examining the partner. EPT varies from state to state, but few states prohibit EPT. EPT is often not recommended for partners of MSM because of a higher risk for coexisting infections, especially undiagnosed syphilis or HIV. It is not recommended for female partners who are symptomatic because of the risk for PID.

CHECK YOUR PRACTICE

You are caring for a 28-year-old woman who is being treated for pelvic inflammatory disease (PID). This is the second time in 2 months that she has been diagnosed with an STI. The patient says she has not been with anyone else except her regular partner. She says, "I don't know why I have this again. The doctor gave me the pills, and I took them."

- How would you respond?
- What do you think is causing her symptoms?

GONOCOCCAL INFECTIONS

Gonorrhea is the second most common reportable STI in the United States. Like chlamydia, incidence is on the rise. There are nearly 600,000 cases reported each year. We think the actual number of cases is around 1.6 million.[2]

Etiology and Pathophysiology

Gonorrhea is caused by *Neisseria gonorrhoeae,* a gram-negative, diplococcus bacterium. Gonorrhea can be transmitted by exposure to sexual fluids during vaginal, anal, or oral sex. Ejaculation does not have to occur for it to be transmitted. The incubation period ranges from 1 to 14 days. Prior infection does not provide protection from reinfection. The most common site for infection for men is the urethra and for women, the cervix.

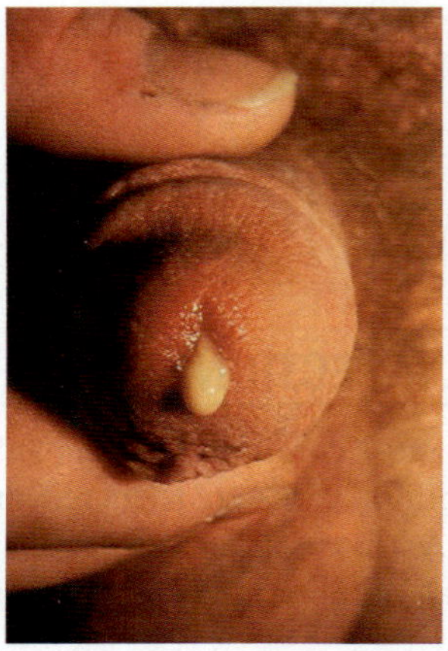

Fig. 57.2 Profuse, purulent drainage in a patient with gonorrhea. (From Marx J, Walls R, Hockberger R: *Rosen's emergency medicine: concepts and clinical practice,* ed 7, St Louis, 2010, Mosby.)

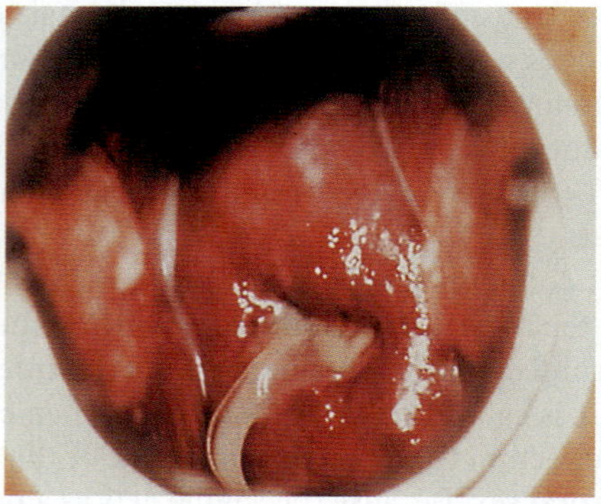

Fig. 57.3 Endocervical gonorrhea. Cervical redness and edema with discharge. (From Morse S, Moreland A, Holmes K: *Atlas of sexually transmitted diseases and AIDS,* London, 1996, Mosby-Wolfe.)

Clinical Manifestations

The initial site of infection in men is usually the urethra. Most men will be symptomatic within a few days of infection. The most common symptoms of gonococcal urethritis are dysuria, purulent urethral discharge (Fig. 57.2), or epididymitis. Most women are asymptomatic or have minor symptoms that they often overlook. In women, common symptoms are increased vaginal discharge, dysuria, frequency, or bleeding after sex. Often, redness and swelling occur at the cervix or urethra along with a purulent exudate (Fig. 57.3).

Anyone can contract rectal gonorrhea during anal intercourse or oropharyngeal gonorrhea during oral sex. Symptoms of rectal infection include mucopurulent rectal discharge or bleeding, anorectal pain, anal pruritus, tenesmus, mucus-coated stools, or painful bowel movements. Most patients with gonorrhea in the throat have no symptoms. A few may have a sore throat (Box 57.2).

Complications

Because men are more often symptomatic and seek treatment earlier, they are less likely to develop serious complications.

BOX 57.2 BIOLOGIC SEX CONSIDERATIONS

STIs

Men

- Syphilis and gonorrhea more common, especially in MSM
- More likely to have symptoms of genital infection
- Genital infection results in fewer complications
- Easier to diagnose because of less complex anatomy
- Less likely to seek medical care unless symptomatic

Women

- Anatomy increases risk for STIs
- Less likely to show early signs of genital infection
- Trichomoniasis and herpes simplex type 2 more common
- Are screened for and therefore more likely to be diagnosed with HPV
- Have more frequent and serious complications related to STIs (e.g., PID, infertility)

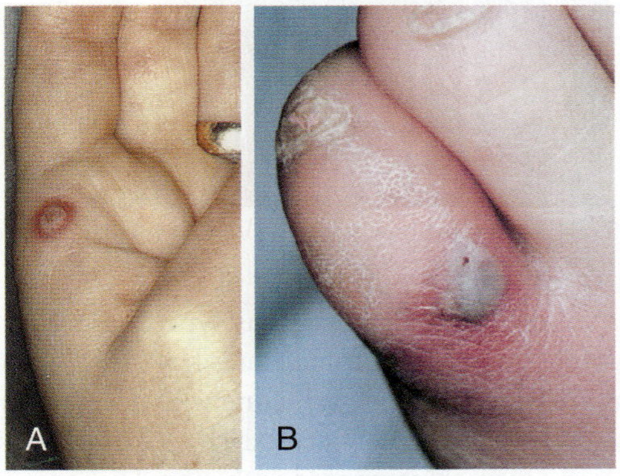

Fig. 57.4 Skin lesions with disseminated gonococcal infection. (A) On the hand. (B) On the fifth toe. (A, From Cohen J, Powderly WG: *Infectious diseases,* ed 2, St Louis, 2004, Mosby. B, From Mandell GL, Bennett JE, Dolin R: *Mandell, Douglas, and Bennett's principles and practice of infectious diseases,* ed 7, Philadelphia, 2010, Churchill Livingstone.)

Those who do can develop epididymitis, a progression of the infection to the testes. It can cause infertility.

Because women are more likely to be asymptomatic and therefore seldom seek early treatment, serious complications are more common. Untreated gonorrhea can cause an infection in the Bartholin glands or Skene glands or result in PID. PID increases risk for ectopic pregnancy, infertility, and chronic pelvic pain.

Although rare, patients can develop disseminated gonococcal infection (DGI). DGI can cause skin lesions, fever, arthralgia, arthritis, and/or endocarditis (Fig. 57.4).

Neonates can develop gonococcal conjunctivitis *(ophthalmia neonatorum)* from exposure to an infected mother during delivery that can result in permanent blindness. Almost all states have laws or health department regulations requiring the use of prophylactic eye treatment of all newborns to prevent such infections. Because of improved prenatal screening for gonorrhea and prophylactic treatment plans, *ophthalmia neonatorum* caused by gonorrhea is rare.

Diagnostic Studies

For men, a presumptive diagnosis of gonorrhea is made if there is a history of sexual contact with a new or infected partner followed within a few days by the development of urethral discharge. For women, making a diagnosis based on symptoms is difficult. Most women are asymptomatic or have symptoms that may be confused with other conditions, such as a urinary tract infection.

The preferred method for diagnosing gonorrhea is through an NAAT (Table 57.4). This can be done on endocervical or vaginal swabs from women, urethral swabs from men, and urine, rectal, and oropharyngeal swabs. A culture may be used to diagnose infection. Gram stains of urethral secretions can be used, but the sensitivity is not as good as other methods.

TABLE 57.4 Interprofessional Care

Gonococcal Infections

Diagnostic Assessment

- History and physical assessment
- Gram-stained smears of urethral or endocervical exudate
- Culture for *N. gonorrhoeae* with antibiotic sensitivity testing if available
- Nucleic acid amplification test (NAAT) to detect *N. gonorrhoeae*
- Testing for other STIs (syphilis, HIV, chlamydial infection)

Management

- Uncomplicated gonorrhea: high-dose ceftriaxone IM
- Gonorrhea with chlamydia coinfection: high-dose ceftriaxone IM plus doxycycline
- Treatment of sexual contacts
- Teach to abstain from sexual contact for 7 days after treatment
- Treat all sexual partners, who must also wait 7 days before resuming sexual contact
- Reexamination if symptoms persist or recur after treatment

Interprofessional Care

Because of a short incubation period and high infectivity, we often start treatment without waiting for positive test results. Over the years, *N. gonorrhoeae* has developed resistance to many classes of antibiotics, including fluoroquinolones (e.g., ciprofloxacin, levofloxacin), tetracyclines (e.g., doxycycline), and macrolides (e.g., azithromycin). First-line treatment is now high-dose IM ceftriaxone (Table 57.4).[8] Patients who persistently test positive after treatment should have culture of the infected site with antibiotic sensitivity testing to check for resistance.

As with chlamydia, all sexual contacts within 60 days should be evaluated and treated to prevent reinfection and further transmission. Teach patients to abstain from sexual contact for 7 days after treatment, or until all partners have been treated and have also abstained from sexual contact for 7 days. Anyone diagnosed and treated for gonorrhea should return for repeat testing 3 months after treatment to ensure cure or detect reinfection.

TRICHOMONIASIS

Trichomoniasis ("trich") is an STI caused by the protozoan parasite *Trichomonas vaginalis*. It is another common STI in the United

States, affecting around 3.7 million people.[6] It is much more common among women than men, especially among women with HIV. This infection is often overlooked compared with other STIs. However, better testing methods have improved detection.

Etiology and Pathophysiology

Trichomonas can be transmitted by exposure to sexual fluids during vaginal, anal, or oral sex, even if ejaculation does not occur. The incubation period is usually 1 week to 1 month but can be much longer. Prior infection does not provide protection from reinfection.

The most common site for infection in men is the urethra and in women is the cervix. It is uncommon for *Trichomonas* to infect the rectum. It is not known to infect the oropharynx. Routine screening should be considered for women in high-risk populations, those receiving care in high-risk settings, and women seeking care for vaginal discharge.[5,6]

Clinical Manifestations

Most people do not have symptoms. Men may have burning with urination, ejaculation, or urethral discharge. Women may have painful urination, vaginal itching, painful intercourse, bleeding after sex, or a yellow-green discharge with a foul odor. The cervix can have a "strawberry" appearance.

Complications

The main complications of untreated infection are related to the inflammation and irritation that it causes in the genital tract. Inflammation makes an infected person more likely to contract or transmit another STI, particularly HIV. Trichomoniasis is associated with PID in women with HIV.

Diagnostic Studies

The preferred method of diagnosing trichomoniasis is by NAAT testing of vaginal or endocervical secretions or urine. Other methods include culture, point-of-care testing, or direct visualization of trichomonads under the microscope. Identifying motile trichomonads in vaginal secretions confirms infection. Tests can be done on liquid-based cervical Pap samples. In men, NAAT testing is recommended.[6]

Interprofessional Care

Patients and their partners should be treated with either metronidazole (Flagyl) or tinidazole (Tindamax). Teach patients to abstain from sexual contact for 7 days after treatment or until all sexual partners have completed a full course of treatment and abstained from sexual contact for 7 days. Tell patients to return if symptoms persist or recur. Any sexual partner within the preceding 60 days should be treated. Teach patients to use condoms or other barrier methods with every sexual contact. Because of a high rate of recurrence, recommend repeat testing 3 months after treatment.

STIs CHARACTERIZED BY GENITAL LESIONS OR ULCERS

GENITAL HERPES INFECTIONS

Genital herpes is a common, lifelong, incurable but treatable infection. There are 2 strains of herpes: herpes simplex virus type 1 (HSV-1) and herpes simplex virus type 2 (HSV-2). Around 18.6 million people in the United States have HSV-2.[1] Most new infections are transmitted by someone who does not know they are infected. The rate of new genital HSV-2 infections is twice as high among women compared with men. Hispanic and Black persons are more likely to be infected.[3,4]

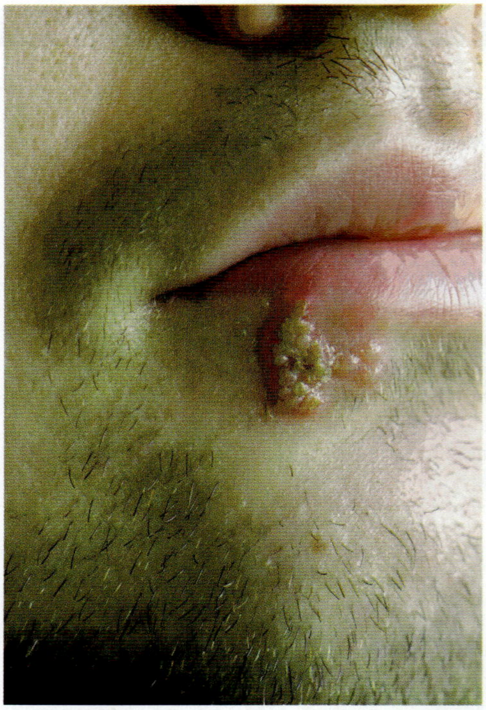

Fig. 57.5 Herpes simplex virus (HSV). (© iStock.com/zeleno.)

Etiology and Pathophysiology

The virus enters through the mucous membranes or breaks in the skin during contact with an infected person. The virus reproduces inside the cell and spreads to the surrounding cells. Then the virus enters the peripheral or autonomic nerve endings and ascends to the sensory or autonomic nerve ganglion near the infection site. There, it often becomes dormant. Viral reactivation (recurrence or "outbreak") occurs when the virus descends to that initial site of infection, either the mucous membranes or skin.

When a person is infected with HSV-1 or HSV-2, the virus persists within the person for life. Transmission of either strain of HSV to others occurs easiest through direct contact with skin or mucous membranes when an infected person is symptomatic. However, both can be transmitted without any apparent symptoms, called *asymptomatic viral shedding*. It is impossible to predict when asymptomatic shedding will occur or for how long. HSV-2 is more likely to shed than HSV-1.

HSV-1 was mainly associated with oral lesions, known as "cold sores" or "fever blisters" (Fig. 57.5), and HSV-2 with anogenital disease.[9] We now know that HSV-1 or HSV-2 can cause genital, anal, or orolabial infections, though it is rare to have HSV-2 infection of the mouth. In most cases, HSV-1 infections are more common "above the waist," involving the gingivae, dermis, upper respiratory tract, and rarely the central nervous system (CNS). HSV-2 almost always infects sites "below the

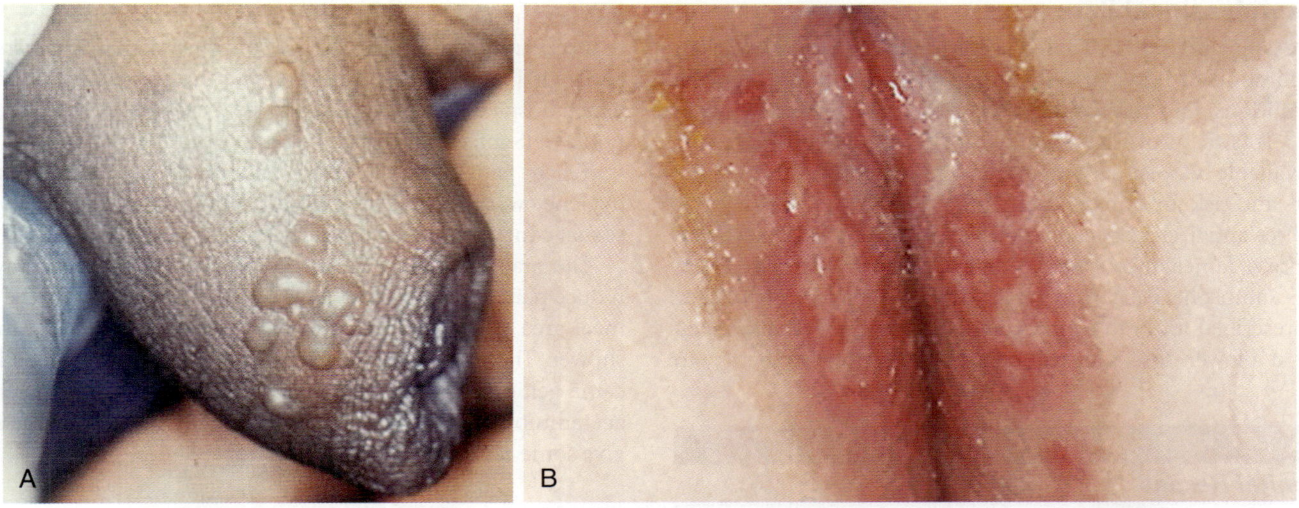

Fig. 57.6 Herpes simplex virus type 2. (A) Vesicular stage. Clear, grouped vesicles on the penis. (B) Ulcerative stage. Vesicles and ulceration of vulvar area. (From Elsevier Point of Care, St. Louis, 2020, Elsevier Health Sciences.)

waist," or the genital tract, perineum, or anus. Having 1 type does not protect against getting the other.

Clinical Manifestations

Primary Episode

A *primary (initial) episode* of genital herpes has an incubation of 2 to 12 days. Most people do not have any recognizable symptoms of primary HSV genital infection. If symptoms do occur, they follow a series of stages. During the *prodromal stage*, the period before lesions appear, the patient may have burning, itching, or tingling at the site of inoculation. In the *vesicular stage*, few to multiple small, often painful vesicles (blisters) may appear on the buttock, inner thigh, penis, scrotum, vulva, perineum, perianal region, vagina, or cervix. The vesicles have large quantities of infectious viral particles (Fig. 57.6). Next, in the *ulcerative stage,* the lesions rupture and form shallow, moist ulcerations. In the *final stage,* spontaneous crusting and epithelialization of the erosions occur.

Regional (inguinal node) lymphadenopathy and systemic flu-like symptoms, including fever, headache, malaise, and myalgia, may occur with the primary episode. Urination may be painful from the urine touching active lesions. The whole process from prodrome to healing varies. It may take up to 3 weeks. Autoinoculation can occur if active lesions are touched or scratched, causing additional and potentially recurrent infection at extragenital sites.

Recurrent Episodes

Recurrent genital herpes occurs in many people during the year after the primary episode. The symptoms of recurrent episodes are less severe. The lesions usually heal more quickly. HSV-1 genital infections recur less often than HSV-2 genital infections. Over time, both decrease in frequency.

Common triggers of recurrence include stress, fatigue, sunburn, general illness, immunosuppression, menses, or local trauma at the site of infection. Many patients can predict a recurrence by noticing the prodromal symptoms of tingling, burning, and itching at the site where the lesions will recur. The greatest risk for transmitting infection exists when active lesions are present. However, it is possible to transmit the virus when no visible lesions or symptoms are present. Most HSV transmission occurs during these asymptomatic periods.[9]

Complications

Both HSV-1 and HSV-2 can cause rare but serious complications, including blindness, encephalitis, and aseptic meningitis. Autoinoculation can result in extragenital lesions in the buttocks, groin, thighs, fingers, and eyes. Genital ulcers increase the risk for contracting HIV. HSV lesions can be more severe and more persistent in HIV-infected patients.

Pregnant women with HSV can transmit the virus to the baby, especially if the virus is shed while the infant passes through the birth canal. Women with a primary episode of HSV near the time of delivery have the highest risk for transmitting genital herpes to the neonate. The virus can infect the neonate's skin, eyes, mouth, or the CNS or become widespread and cause significant mortality. An active genital lesion at the time of delivery is an indication for cesarean delivery.

One of the most profound consequences for people with genital herpes is the overall impact it can have on their psychologic well-being, relationships, and sexual lives. Help teach patients to understand how to talk to sexual partners about HSV. Refer patients who need counseling. Teach patients with herpes that it is a common, manageable, non–life-threatening condition. Help them to understand their treatment options.

Diagnostic Studies

Diagnosis is often based on the patient's reported symptoms, then confirmed by visual examination. Viral culture or PCR from open skin eruptions can be used to diagnose HSV and distinguish between HSV-1 and HSV-2. Highly accurate blood tests for antibodies are available for HSV-1 and HSV-2. Antibodies usually appear by 12 weeks after exposure. These tests do not show the location of the infection.

Interprofessional Care

There is no cure for HSV infection. Antiviral drugs can shorten the duration of HSV viral shedding, shorten the healing time of eruptions, and reduce the frequency of outbreaks by up to 80%.[9] Treatment of HSV should start before diagnostic results are available because early treatment reduces the duration of the ulcers and risk for transmission (Table 57.5).

Three antiviral agents are available for treating HSV: acyclovir (Zovirax), famciclovir (Famvir), and valaciclovir (Valtrex). These drugs inhibit herpetic viral replication (see Table 15.10). They are prescribed for both primary and recurrent infections. Taken daily at a lower dose, they can be used as suppressive therapy to decrease frequency and severity of anogenital recurrences. They reduce, but not eliminate, the risk of transmission to others. IV acyclovir is reserved for severe or life-threatening infections in which hospitalization is needed to treat eye or widespread infections, CNS infections (e.g., meningitis), or pneumonitis.

Teach patients with active outbreaks to maintain good hygiene, wear loose-fitting cotton undergarments, and avoid sexual contact until the outbreak has completely healed.

The main goal is to keep eruptions clean and dry. Ways to reduce pain with urination include pouring water onto the perineal area while voiding to dilute the urine or voiding in the shower. The patient may need a local anesthetic, such as lidocaine gel, or analgesics, such as ibuprofen, acetaminophen, or acetaminophen with codeine. Ice packs to the affected area can give some relief.

TABLE 57.5 Interprofessional Care

Genital Herpes

Diagnostic Assessment
- History and physical assessment
- Antibody assay for HSV type
- Viral isolation by culture, PCR testing

Management
- Identify triggering factors
- Abstain from sexual contact while lesions are present and until fully healed
- Symptomatic care
- Confidential counseling and testing for HIV

Primary (Initial) Infection (see Table 15.10)
- Acyclovir, valacyclovir, or famciclovir

Recurrent Episodic Infection
- Acyclovir, valacyclovir, or famciclovir for shorter duration

Suppressive Therapy
- Acyclovir, valacyclovir, or famciclovir daily at a lower dose

Severe Infection
- IV acyclovir until clinical improvement, followed by oral antiviral therapy

GENITAL WARTS

Genital warts *(condylomata acuminata)* are caused by HPV. There are around 150 types of HPV. At least 40 strains are sexually transmitted.[6,9] "Low-risk" strains of the virus can cause warts on the skin. "High-risk" strains can lead to cancers of the genital tract, anus, or oropharynx. HPV types 6 and 11 cause about 90% of genital and anal warts. HPV types 16 and 18 cause about 70% of cervical cancer, as well as most anal and some throat cancers. Around 16 million people in the United States have HPV.[1] Many sexually active people will be infected with some type of HPV at some point in their lives. In most states, HPV is not a reportable infection. Cervical HPV infection is discussed in Chapter 58.

Etiology and Pathophysiology

HPV is transmitted by skin-to-skin contact, most often during vaginal or anal sex. It can also be transmitted during nonpenetrating sexual activity. The basal epithelial cells infected with HPV undergo transformation and proliferation to form a warty growth (Fig. 57.7). The incubation period can range from weeks

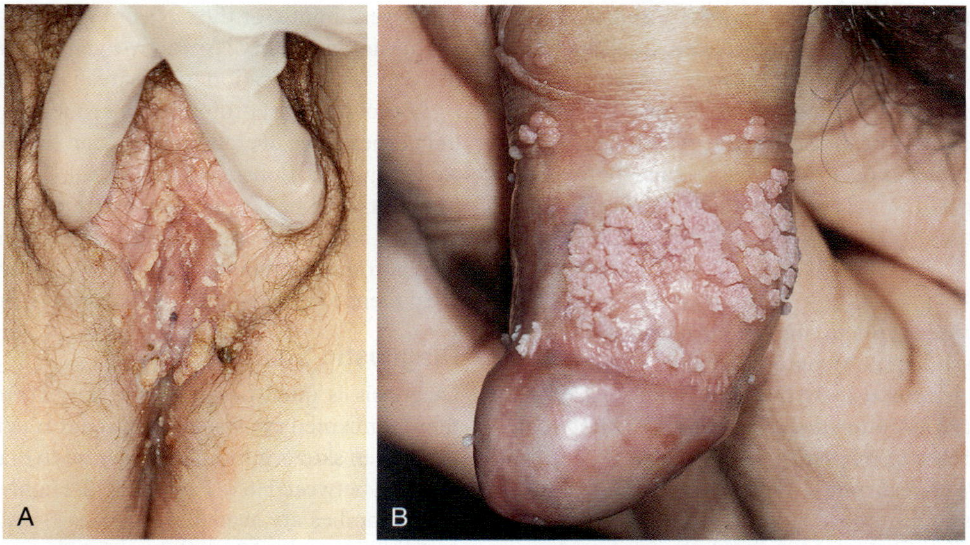

Fig. 57.7 Genital warts. (A) Vulvar warts. (B) Multiple warts on the penis. (From Habif TP: *Clinical dermatology,* ed 6, St Louis, 2015, Mosby.)

to months to years. Infection with 1 type of HPV does not prevent infection with another type.

In most people, HPV is transient (virus is "cleared" or resolves spontaneously after 1 to 2 years). However, it can persist even when the warts themselves are not visible after treatment. We do not know whether removing visible warts helps a person to clear the virus, cures the virus, or reduces their ability to transmit the virus.[10]

Clinical Manifestations

Most people with HPV do not know that they are infected because they have no symptoms. Genital or anal warts are discrete single or multiple papillary growths. They may grow and coalesce to form large, cauliflower-like masses, although most patients will have few lesions. Growths may be pink, pink-flesh colored, or hyperpigmented depending on the skin type.

In men, warts occur on the penis and scrotum, in or around the anus, or in the urethra. In women, warts occur on the inner thighs, vulva, vagina, or cervix, perineum, or internal or external anus (Fig. 57.7). There are usually no other signs or symptoms. Itching may occur with anogenital warts. Bleeding on defecation may occur with anal warts.

Diagnostic Studies

Most early lesions caused by HPV are undetectable by visual examination. A diagnosis of genital warts can be made based on the characteristic appearance of the lesions (Fig. 57.7). Warts may be confused with *condylomata lata* of secondary syphilis, cancer, or benign growths. Testing should be done to rule out other conditions. At present, the only definitive diagnostic procedure is biopsy of any questionable growth. Testing for cervical HPV is discussed in Chapter 58.

Complications

Genital and anal warts have few long-term complications. The HPV strains that cause warts do not cause cancer. For some people, HPV lesions can cause psychosocial burden due to the cosmetic appearance of lesions or the need for long courses of HPV-related treatment. During pregnancy, warts tend to grow rapidly and increase in size. Infection with "high-risk" strains of HPV (especially types 16 and 18) can lead to cancers of the cervix, vagina, vulva, penis, anus, and oropharynx.

Interprofessional Care

HPV Vaccine

It may be possible to eradicate some HPV types over the next few decades, especially if all youth are vaccinated. A 9-valent vaccine (Gardasil 9) is the only vaccine available in the United States. It protects against HPV types 6, 11, 16, 18, and 5 other high-risk HPV types.[11] The vaccine is given in 2 or 3 IM doses over a 6-month period. There are few side effects. The CDC recommends that all children, male and female, be vaccinated at age 11 to 12. Vaccination can be started as early as age 9. Routine vaccination is recommended up to age 26 (Box 57.3). Gardasil 9 is also approved for use in those ages 27 through 45 who may be at risk.[12]

BOX 57.3 EVIDENCE-BASED PRACTICE

HPV Vaccine and Young Males

T.N. is a 19-year-old man who is being seen in the health care center for a urinary tract infection. After reviewing his health history, you learn he has not yet received the HPV vaccine. When asked, he tells you "I am not at risk because HPV really only affects girls."

Making Clinical Decisions

Best Available Evidence

Males ages 9 to 26 can be vaccinated with 9-valent/9vHPV (Gardasil 9) to reduce the incidence of HPV infections and HPV-related cancers (e.g., penile, anal, throat). The vaccine protects against the 2 HPV types (6 and 11) that cause 90% of anogenital warts. Vaccination rates for HPV lag all other vaccinations for young people.

Clinician Expertise

You know younger men may not be aware of the recommendations for the HPV vaccine. The vaccine was first approved to prevent cervical, vulvar, and vaginal cancer in females ages 9 through 26. Since there is no routine screening for HPV-related cancers except cervical cancer, a vaccine that prevents most of these cancers is critical. You know that T.N. will need the 3-dose series (0, 1 to 2, 6 months) to complete his immunization.

Patient Preferences and Values

T.N. states he never has unprotected sex and does not like injections.

Implications for Nursing Practice

1. Why is it important to discuss the risks and benefits of the vaccine to T.N.?
2. How would you respond to T.N., who has heard that only females need the vaccine?
3. How can you address T.N.'s concerns about his dislike of injections?

Reference for Evidence

CDC: Human papillomavirus vaccination and cancer prevention. Retrieved from https://www.cdc.gov/vaccines/vpd/hpv/index.html.

HPV vaccine offers protection against strains causing 90% of anogenital warts and cervical cancers. This protection extends to other HPV-related cancers, including penile, anal, and throat cancers. Remember that the vaccine does not treat active HPV infection. Ideally persons should receive the vaccine before the start of sexual activity or before the potential for infection.

Drug Therapy

Treatment of genital or anal warts is hampered by the high proportion of asymptomatic and undiagnosed infections and lack of curative treatment. The primary goal of treatment is the removal of symptomatic warts.

In-office treatment consists of chemical or ablative (removal with laser or electrocautery) methods. A common treatment is the use of trichloroacetic acid (TCA) or bichloroacetic acid (BCA) applied directly to the wart surface. Petroleum jelly applied with a cotton swab to the surrounding normal skin can minimize irritation. A sharp, stinging pain is often felt with initial acid contact, but this quickly subsides.

Patient-applied treatments are also available. Podofilox liquid and gel are available by prescription (Condylox, Condylox Gel). The patient applies the solution or gel for 3 successive days. Treatment can be repeated for up to 4 weeks or until

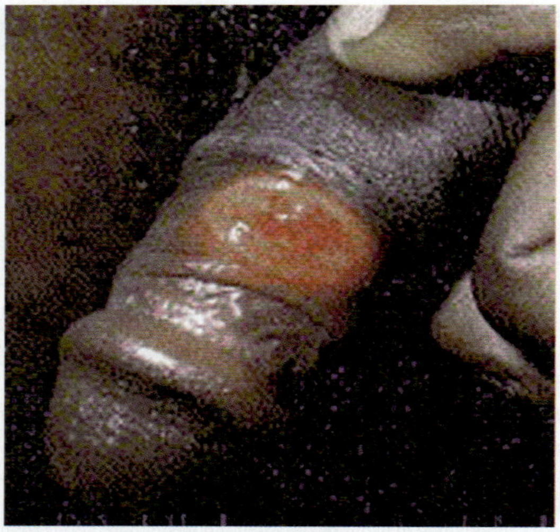

Fig. 57.8 Primary syphilis chancre. (From Morse S, Holmes K, Ballard R: *Atlas of sexually transmitted diseases and AIDS*, ed 4, London, 2010, Saunders.)

resolution of the lesions. Imiquimod cream (Aldara, Zyclara) is an immune response modifier applied at bedtime, either 3 times per week (Aldara) or nightly for up to 16 weeks (Zyclara). Sinecatechin ointment (Veregen) is a green tea derivative that has antioxidant properties. It is applied 3 times daily for up to 16 weeks.

Treatment of warts may not decrease infectivity because the HPV-causing warts may still be present. Anogenital warts are hard to treat and often need more than 1 treatment or modality. Therapy should be modified if a patient has not improved or cannot tolerate the side effects of certain treatments.

If the warts do not resolve with topical therapies, treatments such as cryotherapy with liquid nitrogen, electrocautery, laser therapy, local α-interferon injections, or surgical excision may be done. Teach patients that, because treatment does not destroy the virus (merely the infected tissue), recurrence and reinfection are possible. Long-term follow-up is needed.

SYPHILIS

Syphilis is a sexually transmitted bacterial infection that can cause serious long-term complications if not identified and treated appropriately. Over 130,000 cases of syphilis are reported each year in the United States. As with other infections, we think this number is much higher.[1] Incidence is sharply on the rise. The population most affected by syphilis is MSM, with the highest rates among MSM of color.[3,4]

Etiology and Pathophysiology

Syphilis is caused by *Treponema pallidum,* a bacterial spirochete. It is transmitted by direct contact with a syphilitic ulcer called a *chancre* or through the mucosal membranes of an infected person. A chancre can occur externally on the genitals, anus, or lips or internally in the vagina, rectum, or mouth or tongue (Fig. 57.8). Transmission can occur during vaginal, anal, or oral sex. The incubation period can range from 10 to 90 days (average 21 days). Having the infection does not provide protection from reinfection, even after successful treatment. An infected pregnant woman can transmit syphilis to her fetus during her pregnancy. There is a high risk for stillbirth or having babies who develop complications after birth, including seizures and death. Unfortunately, the incidence of congenital syphilis in the United States has risen 185% since 2014.[1]

TABLE 57.6 Stages of Syphilis

Primary
- *Infectivity:* Highly infectious
- *Duration of stage:* 3–6 weeks
- Single or multiple chancres (painless indurated lesions) of penis, vulva, lips, mouth, vagina, and rectum) (Fig. 57.8). Occurs 10–90 days after inoculation
- Regional lymphadenopathy (microorganisms drain into the lymph nodes)
- Exudate and blood from chancre are highly infectious

Secondary
- *Infectivity:* Highly infectious
- *Duration of stage:* Occurs a few weeks after primary chancre heals, lasts 1–2 years
- Flu-like symptoms: malaise, fever, sore throat, headaches, fatigue, arthralgia, generalized adenopathy
- Mucous patches in mouth (Fig. 57.9), tongue, or cervix
- Symmetric, nonpruritic rash bilaterally that appears on trunk, palms, and/or soles (Fig. 57.10)
- *Condylomata lata* (moist, weeping warts) in the anogenital area
- Weight loss, alopecia

Latent
- *Infectivity:* Early (<1 year)—infectious; late (≥1 year)—noninfectious
- *Duration of stage:* Throughout life or progression to late stage
- No signs or symptoms
- Diagnosis based on positive specific treponemal antibody test together with normal CSF and absence of clinical manifestations

Late
- *Infectivity:* Noninfectious
- *Duration of stage:* Chronic (without treatment), occurs 1–20 years after initial infection
- Gummas (chronic, destructive lesions affecting any organ of body, especially skin, bone, liver, mucous membranes) (Fig. 57.11)
- Cardiovascular: Aneurysms, heart valve insufficiency, heart failure, aortitis
- Neurosyphilis: Can occur at any stage of syphilis
- General paresis: Personality changes from minor to psychotic, tremors, physical and mental deterioration
- Tabes dorsalis (ataxia, areflexia, paresthesias, lightning pains, damaged joints)

Clinical Manifestations

Syphilis is called "*The Great Imitator*" because it can present with a variety of signs and symptoms that mimic other diseases. Compared with other STIs, syphilis is harder to recognize, which can delay treatment. If it is not diagnosed and treated, specific clinical stages occur with the progression of the disease (Table 57.6).

The primary stage is the development of a chancre at the site of transmission. This can appear days to months following infection. In most patients, it occurs by 3 weeks. Chancres can

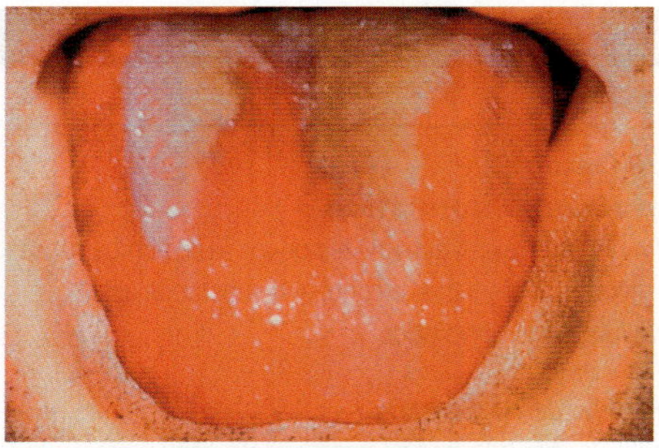

Fig. 57.9 Secondary syphilis. Mucous patch in the mouth. (From Mandell GL, Bennett JE, Dolin R: *Mandell, Douglas, and Bennett's principles and practice of infectious diseases,* ed 7, Philadelphia, 2010, Churchill Livingstone.)

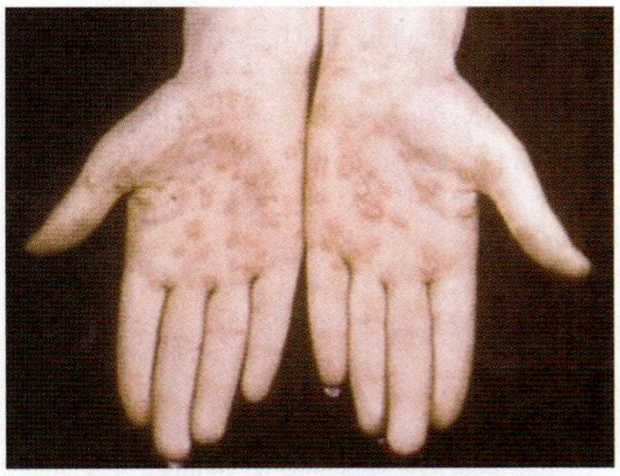

Fig. 57.10 Secondary syphilis. Palmar rash. (From Centers for Disease Control and Prevention Public Health Image Library. Courtesy Robert Sumpter.)

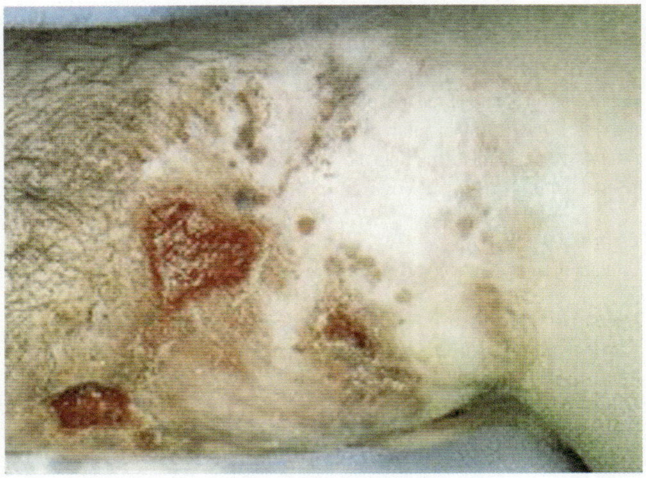

Fig. 57.11 Destructive skin gummas from tertiary syphilis. (From Gawkrodger D, Ardern-Jones M: *Dermatology,* ed 6, St Louis, 2016, Mosby.)

be found on the genitals but often go unnoticed when inside the mouth, vagina, or anus. As the chancre begins to heal or shortly after, patients will progress to the secondary stage of infection if untreated. This stage is usually characterized by a maculopapular rash. The classic rash appears as round, reddish "spots" on the palms of the hands or soles of the feet. It may involve the trunk or extremities. Without treatment, the rash will resolve, but the patient still has syphilis and is infectious for some time. There may be other systemic symptoms at this stage.

Tertiary, or late syphilis, is the final stage. Patients will not have obvious symptoms. During this stage, the organism is silently causing organ damage over many years. The formation of *gummas*, an inflammatory tumor-like response to syphilis, can lead to serious complications.

Complications

Gummas may cause irreparable damage to skin, bone, or liver. In cardiovascular syphilis, the resulting aneurysm may press on structures such as the intercostal nerves, causing pain. The risk for rupture exists as the aneurysm increases in size. Scarring of the aortic valve can cause aortic valve insufficiency and heart failure.

Neurosyphilis occurs when *T. pallidum* invades the CNS. It can occur at any stage of syphilis. Visual impairment, *tabes dorsalis* (progressive locomotor ataxia), and dementia are rare, extreme manifestations.

Chancres on or inside the genitalia or anus enhance HIV transmission. Patients with HIV and syphilis are at greatest risk for significant CNS involvement. They may need more intensive treatment than other patients with syphilis.

Diagnostic Studies

Blood tests can diagnose syphilis. We classify tests for syphilis as those done for screening and those done that help to stage the infection and ensure an infected person was effectively treated. The fluorescent treponemal antibody absorption (FTA-Abs) test, *T. pallidum* particle agglutination (TP-PA) test, and syphilis qualitative enzyme-linked immunoassay (EIA) treponemal tests detect antibodies to *T. pallidum.* They are positive if a patient has ever been infected with syphilis. They remain positive even after treatment, so another test is used to ensure cure and determine when someone has been reinfected.

Nontreponemal tests detect antibodies that are not specific for syphilis. These include the Venereal Disease Research Laboratory (VDRL) test and the rapid plasma reagin (RPR) test. These tests usually become positive 10 to 14 days after the appearance of a chancre. When positive or "reactive," the test will read as a titer and will increase exponentially (e.g., 1:1, 1:2, 1:4, 1:8). This titer will continue to climb, reaching levels of up to 1:2048 during the primary and secondary stages of infection. Following treatment, this titer will fall back to "nonreactive" or negative. It will take time for this to happen, usually several months. If the titer does not return to nonreactive or continues to elevate, this could indicate treatment failure or reinfection.

False-negative and false-positive test results can occur with the nontreponemal tests (VDRL, RPR). A false-negative result may occur with primary syphilis if the test is done before the person has had time to make these nonspecific antibodies. A false-positive may occur in patients who have other diseases or inflammatory conditions that produce these nonspecific antibodies. In addition, if treatment with antibiotics is started early in suspected cases of syphilis, the serologic nontreponemal test may not react or elevate.

Interprofessional Care

Because of the serious complications of untreated syphilis, screening programs for high-risk groups are important for

TABLE 57.7 Interprofessional Care

Syphilis

Diagnostic Assessment
- History and physical assessment
- Treponemal and/or nontreponemal serologic testing
- Testing for other STIs (HIV, gonorrhea, chlamydial infection)

Management
- Antibiotic therapy:
  - Penicillin G benzathine
  - Doxycycline or tetracycline (if penicillin contraindicated)
- Confidential counseling and testing for HIV infection
- Surveillance
- Repeat of nontreponemal tests at 6 and 12 months
- Cerebrospinal fluid examination at 1 year if treatment involves alternative antibiotics or treatment failure has occurred

reducing morbidity and mortality. The evaluation of all patients with syphilis should include HIV testing. The CDC recommends annual syphilis testing for HIV patients (Table 57.7).[6]

Drug Therapy

Management is aimed at starting treatment early. Penicillin G benzathine is the recommended treatment for all stages (Table 57.7). When penicillin is contraindicated, doxycycline or tetracycline may be used with close follow-up. Aqueous procaine penicillin G is the treatment of choice for neurosyphilis. Treatment cannot reverse damage that is already present in the later stages of the disease. All sexual contacts from the preceding 90 days should be treated. Reexamination and follow-up testing are recommended every 6 months for up to 2 years to ensure cure. Repeat HIV testing should be done on all HIV-negative patients diagnosed with primary or secondary syphilis given the higher risk for HIV transmission during these stages.

NURSING MANAGEMENT: STIs

Assessment

Subjective and objective data that you should obtain from a person with an STI are outlined in Table 57.8. Screen patients based on risk history and sexual behaviors. Assess the patient's risk for contracting an STI. Questions to ask include the number of sexual partners (in the last month, year), gender of partners ("Do you have sex with men, women, or both? Transgender, nonbinary?"), type of birth control used (if applicable), use of condoms or other barrier methods, and history of an STI. Do they use social media or other networking apps to meet partners? Do they use drugs and alcohol or exchange sex for drugs or money? Are there violence and personal safety concerns?[13] Plan teaching based on the patient's responses.

Interpersonal skills needed for this interview include respect, compassion, and a nonjudgmental attitude. Tailor counseling to the patient and protect their privacy. Sexual practices are deeply personal. Interview patients alone, without parents or partners present whom they may not want to disclose all activities in front of. Provide a safe space to encourage honest discussion.

TABLE 57.8 NURSING ASSESSMENT

STIs

Subjective Data

Important Health Information

Sexual health history: Sexual activity, history of STIs, number of sexual partners, unsafe sexual practices, alcohol and substance use, social media apps

Medications: Allergy to antibiotics

Functional Health Patterns

Health perception–health management: Unsafe sexual practices, drug and/or alcohol use

Nutritional-metabolic: Nausea, vomiting, anorexia. Pharyngitis, oral lesions, chills. Alopecia

Elimination: Dysuria, urinary frequency, urethral discharge, pain with bowel movements

Cognitive-perceptual: Arthralgia, headache, painful, burning lesions, itching or irritation at infected site

Sexuality-reproductive: Dyspareunia, vaginal or penile discharge, bleeding with sex, genital or perianal lesions

Objective Data

General

Fever, lymphadenopathy (generalized or inguinal)

GI

Rectal discharge, rectal lesions

Reproductive

Cervical mucopurulent discharge, cervical erythema, cervical bleeding; penile purulent discharge, epididymitis, proctitis, genital lesions

Skin

Syphilis: Primary: Painless, indurated genital, oral, or perianal lesions

Secondary: Bilateral, symmetric rash on palms, soles, or entire body. Mucous patches on mouth or tongue; alopecia; condylomata lata

Genital herpes: Painful genital or anal vesicular lesions

Genital warts: Single or multiple, flesh-colored, hyperpigmented, genital or anal warts

Urinary

Urethral discharge, erythema

Possible Diagnostic Findings

Chlamydia: Positive NAAT cervical, urethral, anal, oropharyngeal, or urine samples

Gonorrhea: Positive cultures or NAAT from cervical, urethral, anal, oropharyngeal, or urine samples

Genital herpes: Positive HSV-1 or HSV-2 serum antibody test. Positive viral culture or PCR from an active lesion indicating HSV-1 or HSV-2

Syphilis: Positive findings on fluorescent treponemal antibody absorption (FTA-Abs) test, *T. pallidum* particle agglutination (TP-PA) test, or syphilis qualitative enzyme-linked immunoassay (EIA) test and/or a reactive VDRL or RPR test with elevated titer

Trichomoniasis: ↑ pH and positive motile protozoa on wet preparation of discharge. Positive FDA-approved rapid test or liquid-based Pap positive for trichomoniasis

Start by asking patients how they define themselves, including their gender identity and sexual preferences. Finally, do not assume that older people are not at risk. Sex and sexuality are dynamic across the life cycle. Sexually active older adults can be at risk for STIs.[13]

BOX 57.4 PROMOTING POPULATION HEALTH

Preventing STIs

- Follow "safer" sex practices every time you have sexual contact and be responsible for your own protection.
- Have sexual activity only in an established, monogamous relationship, and limit the number of sexual partners otherwise.
- Obtain vaccinations to help prevent some types of HPV.
- Know your sex partners. Be comfortable saying "no" to sexual activity.
- Limit alcohol use to moderate levels, and avoid substance use.
- If you are sexually active and at risk, obtain testing regularly and encourage partners to do the same.

CHECK YOUR PRACTICE

You are working on the medicine unit caring for a 68-year-old man admitted for IV penicillin for neurosyphilis. The nurse whom you are working with says, "I can't believe a man that old got syphilis."

- How would you respond?
- What should you discuss with your colleague?

◆ Clinical Problems

Clinical problems for the patient with an STI include:

- Impaired sexual functioning
- Infection
- Deficient knowledge

◆ Planning

The overall goals are that the patient with an STI will (1) understand the mode of transmission of STIs and the risks related to STIs, (2) complete treatment and return for appropriate follow-up, (3) notify or assist in notifying sexual contacts about their need for testing and treatment, (4) abstain from sexual contact until the infection is resolved and all partners have been treated, and (5) show knowledge of safer sex practices.

◆ Implementation

◆ Health Promotion

Many approaches to stopping the spread of STIs have had varying degrees of success (Box 57.4). Be prepared to discuss "safer" sex practices and harm reduction with all patients, not only those you perceive to be at risk. These practices include abstinence, monogamy, avoiding high-risk sexual behaviors, and correctly using condoms and other barriers with every sexual act. Sexual abstinence is the only certain method of avoiding all STIs, but few people consider this option. Limiting sexual contacts to an established, monogamous relationship in which both partners have been tested for STIs can reduce the risk. Addressing issues related to drug and alcohol use is important for promoting healthy sexual behavior.

Be prepared to teach special populations about their risks, including people of different racial and ethnic backgrounds, men having sex with men (MSM), and transgender persons (Table 57.9). Encourage routine testing in people who are at higher risk so STIs can be identified early. This will help to decrease the potential for complications and reduce transmission to others.

TABLE 57.9 Working With Special Populations

When working with the following populations at risk for STIs, consider cultural, behavioral, social networking, and other factors that may place them at increased risk.

Racial and Ethnic Minorities

- When approaching patients of different backgrounds, be sensitive to their culture, religion, and social norms.
- Remember that there may be limited access to care, varying education levels, and lower health literacy among certain populations.
- Use an interpreter when communicating with non–English-speaking patients.
- Acknowledge that some communities may not be open to talking about sex or sexual practices for religious or cultural reasons.
- Be aware that some men in the Black, Hispanic, or Middle Eastern communities may not be comfortable disclosing that they are having sex with other men. They may be in a relationship with a female partner due to cultural or community pressures.

Men Who Have Sex With Men

- Assess risk for STIs. Be comfortable asking questions about sexual identity and practices, including insertive and receptive anal sex. Do not assume all MSM engage in the same sexual activities.
- Ask about social media and networking apps used to connect with other men for casual dating and sex. These have been traced to outbreaks of STIs.
- Counsel HIV-uninfected MSM with an STI about options for HIV prevention, including pre-exposure prophylaxis (PrEP) and non-occupational postexposure prophylaxis (nPEP) (see Chapter 15).

Transgender Persons

- *Transgender man* is a term used to describe a person assigned as female at birth but who identifies as male. *Transgender woman* is a term used to describe a person assigned as male at birth but who identifies as female.
- Not all transgender persons have had gender reassignment surgery and may still have the anatomy present at birth. Screen these persons for STIs based on both risk history and site of exposure. For example, a transgender man may still have a vagina and cervix, requiring a vaginal exam and testing for trichomoniasis.

A teaching guide for the patient with an STI is shown in Table 57.10.

Measures to prevent infection. Help patients to be aware of specific signs and symptoms of infection. Encourage patients to take notice of a sexual partner's genitalia before sex. They should note any discharge, sores, blisters, lesions, or rashes. This can help them to make good decisions about whether to continue sexual activity with safer-sex modifications or to choose not to have sexual contact at all. Remind patients that most STIs may have no symptoms but can still be transmitted. Emphasize that when they have sex, they are exposed to the infections of everyone with whom their partner has ever had sex.

Proper condom use is a highly effective mechanical barrier to infections that may be transmitted by or to a penis. Partners should openly discuss any objections to condom use, such as interference with spontaneity and the presence of a barrier. Information about the mechanics of sexual arousal and incorporating a condom into sex can help to overcome resistance to

TABLE 57.10 PATIENT & CAREGIVER TEACHING

STIs

When teaching a patient with an STI:

1. Explain precautions to take, such as
   - Using condoms and other barrier methods with every sexual encounter
   - When being monogamous, defining what monogamy means with your partner
   - Limiting the number of sexual partners
   - Asking potential partners about their sexual history
   - Asking potential partners if they have been tested for STIs
   - Avoiding sex with partners who have visible oral, inguinal, genital, perineal, or anal lesions or those who use IV drugs
   - Voiding and washing genitalia and surrounding area after sex to flush out/wash away organisms to reduce potential for transmitting infection
2. Explain the importance of taking all antibiotics or antiviral agents as prescribed. Symptoms will improve after 1–2 days of treatment, but organisms may still be present.
3. Teach patients diagnosed with gonorrhea, chlamydia, syphilis, or trichomoniasis that all sexual partners need treatment to prevent transmission and reinfection.
4. Teach patients to abstain from sexual contact during and for 7 days after treatment. Review the use of condoms or other barrier methods when sexual activity is resumed to prevent spread of infection and reinfection.
5. Explain the importance of follow-up examination and retesting at least once after treatment (if appropriate) to confirm complete cure.
6. Allow patients and partners to voice their concerns and clarify areas that need explanation.
7. Teach patients about the signs and symptoms of complications and need to report problems to their HCP to ensure proper follow-up and early treatment of reinfection.
8. Tell patients of the infectious nature of these infections to avoid a false sense of security, which may result in careless sexual practices or poor personal hygiene.
9. Tell patients about health department requirements for anonymously reporting certain STIs.

its use. Refusing sexual activity with any partner who will not use a condom is a safe and legitimate option.

The *female condom,* a lubricated polyurethane sheath designed for vaginal use, is an option for some women. Teach patients to avoid the spermicide nonoxynol 9 (N-9), which can be used alone to prevent pregnancy or as a condom lubricant. N-9 is one of the least effective methods of birth control when used alone. It can be irritating to the vagina and rectum, increasing the risk for acquiring an STI.

Screening programs. Screening programs are a way to identify, treat, prevent, and control the spread of STIs. At present, there are CDC-recommended screening programs for certain populations, including young people, MSM, pregnant women, and anyone at increased risk for exposure to an STI (e.g., new partners, multiple relationships, not using condoms).[6]

Case finding. Interviewing and case finding are other methods used to control the spread of STIs. These activities are directed toward finding and examining all sexual contacts of patients with reportable STIs so that they receive treatment. Public health professionals, often nurses, are aware of the social implications of STIs and the need for discretion in finding partners. Sexual contacts are not told about the origin of the information naming them as a contact or the timing of exposure to ensure patient privacy mandates.

Partner notification and treatment impose a heavy burden on public health departments. As a result, notification often becomes the responsibility of the infected partner. The infected partner may choose not to tell sexual partners, and the partners may choose not to seek treatment. Unfortunately, this perpetuates the disease.

Educational programs. Actively encourage your community to provide better education about STIs for its citizens. High-risk populations (e.g., young people under age 25) should be a prime target for such programs. STI rates are rising in older adults.[2] Older adults are less likely to use condoms and often have a hard time starting discussions about sexual health issues.

Knowledge and understanding can decrease the incidence of STIs. Encourage the HPV vaccine before the start of sexual activity. Accurate and current information may help reduce parental fears related to the vaccine. Consider stressing the prevention of cancer as a reason for the vaccine. This may be more productive and less controversial, thus making the parent and adolescent more receptive.

◆ Acute Care

Psychologic support. The diagnosis of an STI may be met with a variety of emotions, such as embarrassment, shame, guilt, anger, or even a desire for vengeance. Encourage the patient to voice feelings. Couples in marital or committed relationships have an added problem when an STI is diagnosed if they must face the implication of sexual activity outside the relationship. The STI raises other concerns about their relationship and may serve as an incentive for further problem solving. A referral for professional counseling to explore the impact of the STI on their relationship may be needed.

A patient with genital herpes is faced with the fact that future outbreaks will occur and that no cure is available. This can be frustrating and disruptive to the patient's physical, emotional, social, and sexual life. Help the patient identify and avoid any factors that may precipitate outbreaks, such as stress, local trauma, or sun exposure. Tell the patient that the frequency and severity of recurrences will decrease over time. Stress that herpes is a common, manageable condition and does not pose a risk to their overall health.

Genital or anal warts involve a prolonged course of treatment. Clearing the virus takes time and is not always possible. Patients can become frustrated and distressed due to frequent office visits, associated costs, potential for unpleasant treatment side effects, and effects of the infection on future health and sexual relationships. Support and a willingness to listen to the patient's concerns are needed. Local or online support groups are available for almost all STIs. Help patients to connect with support groups.

Follow-up. If you work in public health facilities, clinics, or other outpatient settings, you are more likely to care for a patient with an STI than if you work in a hospital setting. Whatever the setting, as a nurse, you can teach about treatment measures, such as the purpose and side effects of prescribed drugs, and the need for follow-up care (Table 57.10).

BOX 57.5 ETHICAL/LEGAL DILEMMAS

Confidentiality and HIPAA

Situation

D.G. is a 25-year-old male who recently tested positive for chlamydia. You tell him to tell his sexual partners of the infection so they may be treated. He refuses to tell her girlfriend because she will then know that he had sex with someone else. You later learn that a nursing student who was in the clinic that day is a friend of his girlfriend and told her that the girlfriend is likely infected and should have STI testing.

Ethical/Legal Points for Consideration

- Each state has requirements for reporting communicable diseases and other health-related data. Inform the patient of the reporting requirements for communicable diseases.
- Nurses and other HCPs have both a legal and an ethical obligation to maintain confidentiality of patient information. The Health Insurance Portability and Accountability Act (HIPAA) ensures the privacy of personal health information.
- The duty to maintain confidentiality is not absolute and may be limited, as needed, to protect the patient or other parties, or by law or regulation, such as mandated reporting for safety or public health reasons.
- Your main obligation is to the patient seeking care. Teaching is one way to establish a partnership with this patient. Share information about the effects of the disease, the consequences of reinfection, and the effect of the disease on others who may not know that they are infected. Then encourage the patient to tell his partners of the diagnosis and discuss the option of EPT where applicable.

Discussion Questions

1. What are your state's requirements for reportable conditions?
2. In your opinion, what is the best way to balance the needs of an individual patient with those of the public?
3. What are the risks to agencies for the breach of confidentiality and HIPAA?

Reference

Code of Ethics for Nurses. Retrieved from https://www.nursingworld.org/practice-policy/nursing-excellence/ethics/code-of-ethics-for-nurses/.

Single-dose treatment for gonorrhea, chlamydia, and syphilis helps prevent problems from nonadherence with drug therapy. Stress to the patient receiving multiple-dose therapy the need to complete the prescribed treatment. Teach the patient about problems resulting from nonadherence. All patients should return to the treatment center for repeat testing of the infected sites or for serologic testing at designated times to determine the effectiveness of the treatment. Explaining to the patient that they may not be cured with the first treatment can reinforce the need for a follow-up visit. Tell the patient to inform sexual partners of the need for testing and treatment as a contact, regardless of whether they are free of or have symptoms (Box 57.5).

Hygiene measures. Emphasize the importance of certain hygiene measures, such as frequent hand washing. Tell the patient not to scratch infection sites, to avoid autoinoculation of STIs that can be spread to other parts of the body. Washing with soap and water and voiding after sex may have some benefit in decreasing the exposure to STIs but does not give adequate protection against transmission. Teach patients not to douche after sex. It can push bacteria higher into the reproductive tract or undermine local immune responses.

Sexual activity. Sexual abstinence is needed during the communicable phase of any STI. Long-term precautions must be taken with those STIs that are chronic or recurrent. Emphasize that even single-dose treatments can take up to 1 week to clear the infection. Thus the patient is infectious during this period and should avoid all sexual contact. Remind patients that all partners must be treated as contacts to prevent reinfection. Emphasize the importance of using condoms or other barrier methods to help prevent the spread of infection and reinfection after all have been treated. Remind patients that complications can follow if sexual activity occurs before treatment completion or if all partners are not treated appropriately. Patients need to discuss re-treatment or continued treatment with an HCP. During treatment, the patient can choose to relate to a partner in an intimate way that avoids penetrative, oral-genital contact, or skin-to-skin contact.

◆ Ambulatory Care

Because many STIs are cured with a single dose or short course of antibiotic therapy, many patients are casual about the outcome. The consequences of this attitude can include delays in treatment, nonadherence with instructions, treatment failure, reinfection, and complications. Complications are serious and costly and can include future infertility.

Patients with infection-related complications may need prolonged treatment and surgery. Major surgery, such as resection of an aneurysm or aortic valve replacement, may be needed to treat cardiovascular problems caused by syphilis. Pelvic surgery and procedures to correct fertility problems from an STI may be needed. If not successful, patients may need assisted reproductive technologies to achieve future pregnancy. Because young people ages 15 to 24 represent about 50% of new STIs annually, almost every state and the District of Columbia have laws that allow minors to consent to STI services without parental involvement. However, the minimum age does vary by state.

◆ Evaluation

Expected outcomes for the patient with an STI are that the patient will:

- Understand the course, modes of transmission, and treatment options for the STI
- Relate the potential long-term complications of untreated infection
- Adhere to treatment plan and the follow-up protocol
- Understand the importance of partner notification and treatment
- Practice STI risk-reducing behaviors

Case Study

Gonococcal Infection

(© ajr_images/ iStock.com.)

Patient Profile

B.D. is a 24-year-old MSM seen in the outpatient clinic with dysuria and yellow penile discharge for the past 2 days. He is sexually active with a new partner. B.D. reports having had oral and unprotected anal sex as the insertive partner 1 week ago. He was treated in the past for chlamydia.

Subjective Data

- He and his partner used condoms at the beginning of their relationship but stopped recently
- His partner has no symptoms
- Appears worried

Objective Data

- Penis: Meatus is red
- Moderate amount of yellowish penile discharge
- Testicles are nontender, no local lymph adenopathy
- Urine NAAT is positive for *N. gonorrhoeae*

Interprofessional Care

- ceftriaxone 500 mg IM × 1 dose

Discussion Questions

1. ***Recognize:*** What are B.D.'s risk factors for acquiring gonorrhea?
2. ***Analyze:*** What complications could occur if B.D.'s infection is not treated?
3. ***Plan:*** What impact is the diagnosis likely to have on B.D.'s self-image? On his relationship with his sexual partner?
4. ***Prioritize:*** What is the priority of care for B.D.?
5. ***Act:*** B.D. mentions he and his partner are on pre-exposure prophylaxis (PrEP) for protection against HIV. How would you advise him on STI prevention?
6. ***Act:*** What instructions should B.D. receive to ensure successful treatment? To prevent reinfection? To prevent further transmission?
7. ***Safety:*** B.D. tells you he is worried about how his partner will react when he discloses this information. What assistance in notifying his partner should you consider?

Answers available at http://evolve.elsevier.com/Lewis/medsurg.

BRIDGE TO NCLEX EXAMINATION

The number of the question corresponds to the same-numbered outcome at the beginning of the chapter.

1. The nurse planning a prevention program for sexually transmitted infections (STIs) notes which factors are associated with the increased incidence of STIs? *(select all that apply)*
   - **a.** Alcohol and drug use
   - **b.** Asymptomatic infections
   - **c.** Being upper middle class
   - **d.** Use of long-acting contraceptives
   - **e.** Being placed in a correctional facility
2. The nurse is reviewing treatment orders for a pregnant woman diagnosed with chlamydia. What is *most* important to consider?
   - **a.** Infection may involve the throat or anus.
   - **b.** Doxycycline should not be used as treatment.
   - **c.** Symptoms of chlamydia are often absent in women.
   - **d.** Repeat testing is needed 3 months after treatment to ensure cure.
3. The nurse plans to include in the teaching plan for a patient with herpes who is prescribed an antiviral agent that daily use of the medication
   - **a.** cures the infection over time.
   - **b.** masks the symptoms of other STIs.
   - **c.** eliminates the risk of transmission to others.
   - **d.** reduces the frequency and severity of recurrent episodes.
4. Which laboratory tests would the nurse evaluate to confirm suspected syphilis in a patient who denies a prior history of syphilis?
   - **a.** Antibiotic resistance testing to select an appropriate treatment
   - **b.** Treponemal-specific test with an antinuclear antibody (ANA)
   - **c.** Complete blood count (CBC) to assess for a shift in white blood cells
   - **d.** Treponemal-specific test, and a follow-up rapid plasma reagin (RPR) if positive
5. Which STIs can be asymptomatic? *(Select all that apply.)*
   - **a.** Syphilis
   - **b.** Chlamydia
   - **c.** Genital warts
   - **d.** Genital herpes
   - **e.** Gonorrhea of the throat
6. When educating patients about preventing STIs, the nurse should highlight *(select all that apply)*
   - **a.** the appropriate use of oral contraceptives.
   - **b.** how alcohol and substance use may increase risk.
   - **c.** sexual positions that can be used to avoid infection.
   - **d.** the need for annual Pap tests for women with HPV.
   - **e.** sexual practices that are considered high-risk behaviors.
7. A student nurse is assisting the staff nurse with an admission history for a patient with pelvic inflammatory disease from gonorrhea. Which action by the student nurse requires the nurse to intervene?
   - **a.** Obtains a history of alcohol and substance use
   - **b.** Asks questions considering the patient's ethnic background and education
   - **c.** Reviews sexual activities in a respectful, compassionate, nonjudgmental manner
   - **d.** Interviews the patient with the partner present to determine if the partner is at risk

1. a, b, d, e; 2. b; 3. d; 4. d; 5. a, b, c, d, e; 6. b, e; 7. d.

For rationales to these answers and even more NCLEX review questions, visit http://evolve.elsevier.com/Lewis/medsurg.

EVOLVE WEBSITE/RESOURCES LIST

http://evolve.elsevier.com/Lewis/medsurg
Review Questions (Online Only)
Key Points
Answer Keys for Questions
- Rationales for Bridge to NCLEX Examination Questions
- Answer Guidelines for Case Study

Conceptual Care Map Creator
Audio Glossary
Content Updates

REFERENCES

1. Centers for Disease Control and Prevention (CDC): Sexually transmitted infections prevalence, incidence, and cost estimates in the United States. Retrieved from https://www.cdc.gov/std/statistics/prevalence-2020-at-a-glance.htm.
2. CDC: New CDC report: STDs continue to rise in the U.S. Retrieved from https://www.cdc.gov/nchhstp/newsroom/2019/2018-STD-surveillance-report-press-release.html.
3. CDC: STDs in racial and ethnic minorities. Retrieved from https://www.cdc.gov/std/stats18/minorities.htm.
4. CDC: Sexually transmitted disease surveillance 2018. Retrieved from https://www.cdc.gov/std/stats18/STDSurveillance2018-full-report.pdf.
5. CDC: STDs in women and infants. Retrieved from https://www.cdc.gov/std/stats18/womenandinf.htm.

*6. CDC: Sexually transmitted infections treatment guidelines. Retrieved from https://www.cdc.gov/std/treatment-guidelines/default.htm.

*7. CDC: Expedited partner therapy. Retrieved from https://www.cdc.gov/std/ept/.

*8. St Cyr S, Barbee L, Workowski KA, et al.: Update to CDC's treatment guidelines for gonococcal infection, *MMWR Morb Mortal Wkly Rep* 69:1911, 2020.

9. CDC: Genital HSV infections. Retrieved from https://www.cdc.gov/std/tg2015/herpes.htm.

10. CDC: Human papillomavirus (HPV) infection. Retrieved from https://www.cdc.gov/std/tg2015/hpv.htm.

*11. Zhang S, Batur P: Human papillomavirus in 2019: an update on cervical cancer prevention and screening guidelines, *Cleve Clin J Med* 86:173, 2019.

*12. Meites E, Szilagyi PG, Chesson HW, et al.: Human papillomavirus vaccination for adults: updated recommendations of the advisory committee on immunization practices, *MMWR Morb Mortal Wkly Rep* 68:698, 2019.

13. CDC: A guide to taking a sexual history. Retrieved from https://www.cdc.gov/std/treatment/sexualhistory.pdf.

*Evidence-based information for clinical practice.

58

Female Reproductive Problems

Robyn Schafer

http://evolve.elsevier.com/Lewis/medsurg/

CONCEPTUAL FOCUS

Cellular Regulation
Hormonal Regulation
Infection
Inflammation
Pain
Reproduction
Sexuality

LEARNING OUTCOMES

1. Outline strategies for the diagnosis and treatment of female infertility.
2. Identify risk factors and nursing and interprofessional management of early pregnancy loss and ectopic pregnancy.
3. Describe the etiology and clinical manifestations of menstrual problems, abnormal uterine bleeding, and polycystic ovary syndrome.
4. Describe physiologic changes related to menopause and management of perimenopausal symptoms.
5. Outline the etiology and clinical manifestations of lower genital tract infections and pelvic inflammatory disease.
6. Identify the pathophysiology and appropriate interprofessional and nursing care for benign gynecologic problems.
7. Explain the clinical manifestations, diagnostic studies, and treatment of gynecologic cancers.
8. Discuss the interprofessional and nursing care for victims of sexual assault.

KEY TERMS

abnormal uterine bleeding (AUB)
dilation and curettage (D&C)
dysmenorrhea
early pregnancy loss
ectopic pregnancy
endometriosis
fibroids (leiomyomas)
infertility
menopause
pelvic inflammatory disease (PID)
pelvic organ prolapse
perimenopause
polycystic ovary syndrome (PCOS)
premenstrual syndrome (PMS)
sexual assault
sexual dysfunction
spontaneous abortion

Sexual functioning and satisfaction are important aspects of well-being across the lifespan. Problems with gynecologic and female sexual health profoundly affect health and well-being. This chapter discusses common female reproductive system problems. Care often includes screening and prevention, health teaching and promotion, and assessment and treatment of complications.

While these are referred to as female reproductive system problems, the terms "female" and "woman" may not reflect the gender identity of patients with these problems. These problems may be relevant in transgender, gender-nonconforming, and gender-diverse persons assigned female sex at birth. Use of gendered terms here is not meant to exclude any person who has these problems.

INFERTILITY

Infertility is defined as the inability to conceive after at least 1 year of regular intercourse without contraception.[1] Around 15% of heterosexual couples experience infertility. It is more common with advancing age. The process of assessing and managing infertility is often stressful and emotionally difficult for patients and their partners.

TABLE 58.1 Diagnostic Criteria

Infertility

Infertility is diagnosed after a person has not been able to conceive after:

- 12 months of regular (frequent) intercourse without contraception in those less than 35 years of age; OR
- 6 months of regular (frequent) intercourse without contraception in those 35 years of age and older.

TABLE 58.2 Interprofessional Care

Infertility

Diagnostic Assessment

- History and physical assessment of both partners
  - Detailed menstrual, sexual, reproductive, and gynecologic history
  - Height, weight, and body mass index
  - Pelvic examination
- Laboratory tests (as indicated)
  - CBC
  - Thyroid-stimulating hormone (TSH)
  - STI screening
  - Hormone levels (FSH, LH, antimüllerian hormone, progesterone, prolactin)
- Imaging
  - Transvaginal ultrasound
  - Hysterosalpingogram

Management

- Lifestyle changes
- Drug therapy (Table 58.3)
- Surgery
- Assisted reproductive technologies (ARTs)

TABLE 58.3 Drug Therapy

Infertility

Class	Drugs	Mechanism of Action
Aromatase inhibitor	letrozole (Femara)	↓ Estrogen by preventing the conversion of androgens to estrogens in the ovaries
Biguanide	glucophage (Metformin)	↓ Hyperinsulinemia. May lead to enhanced spontaneous ovulation with PCOS
Gonadotropin	follicle-stimulating hormone (Gonal-f) human chorionic gonadotropin (hCG) human menopausal gonadotropin (Menopur)	Stimulates follicle growth and maturation by mimicking the body's natural hormones
Selective estrogen receptor modulator (SERM)	clomiphene citrate (Clomid)	Stimulates ovulation by binding estrogen receptors in the hypothalamus. Leads to ↑ gonadotropin-releasing hormone (GnRH) production and ↑ LH and FSH secretion in the pituitary

Etiology and Pathophysiology

Infertility affects men and women equally. We describe it as being caused by male or female factors. There may also be a combination of factors. In as many as 30% of cases, no specific cause is identified. Factors that cause male infertility are discussed in Chapter 59. The most common causes of female infertility are hormone imbalances, anatomic or structural problems of the reproductive tract, and other unexplained causes.

Diagnostic Studies

Formal evaluation of infertility is usually done after 12 months of regular, unprotected intercourse (Table 58.1). Earlier evaluation is appropriate in women over the age of 35 or in the presence of known medical or physical problems. Evaluation starts with a history and physical assessment (Table 58.2). Based on the findings, laboratory tests and diagnostic imaging may be done. These explore common causes of infertility, including diminished ovarian reserve, ovulatory dysfunction, and structural problems of the fallopian tubes and uterus.[2] A semen analysis of the male partner is often part of the infertility workup.

❖ Interprofessional and Nursing Management

There are multiple treatment options for infertility. These include lifestyle changes, drug therapy, and surgery. The approach is tailored to the underlying cause. A patient-centered approach to care is essential in treating infertility. Patients and, when appropriate, their partners should be involved in determining the plan of care and weighing the efficacy, safety, and advantages and disadvantages of various treatment options. These procedures may be expensive and stressful. Provide an overview of infertility evaluation, treatments, and alternatives to help reduce stress. Teaching about fertility, ovulation, and intercourse is important. This information often improves conception rates.

Lifestyle changes include weight loss, smoking cessation, and reduced alcohol and caffeine intake. Intercourse is timed around ovulation. Medical treatment for female infertility focuses on stimulating the ovaries (known as *ovulation induction*). Table 58.3 reviews common drugs used in fertility treatment. Surgery may address blockages in the ovarian tubes or uterine problems. Finally, *assisted reproductive technology* (ART) procedures include insemination through intracervical insemination (ICI), intrauterine insemination (IUI), or in vitro fertilization (IVF). The National Infertility Association (RESOLVE) is a useful resource to support patients in exploring treatment options.[3]

PREGNANCY LOSS

Pregnancy loss is the term used to describe the loss of a nonviable pregnancy up to 20 weeks gestation. **Early pregnancy loss** occurs in the first trimester (the first 13 weeks of pregnancy). It is the most common type of pregnancy loss. *Abortion* is another term used to describe the loss of a previable pregnancy or the elective termination of pregnancy at any stage. We classify

TABLE 58.4 Types of Spontaneous Abortion

Type	Description
Complete abortion	All products of conception (POC) are expelled
Incomplete abortion	Passage of some but not all POC through the cervix
Inevitable abortion	Pregnancy loss cannot be prevented due to opening of the cervix or rupture of amniotic membranes
Infected (septic) abortion	Serious maternal infection occurring with any type of abortion
Missed abortion	Nonviable POC remain in the uterus
Threatened abortion	Vaginal bleeding in a pregnancy prior to 20 weeks' gestation in the absence of cervical dilation

abortions as spontaneous or induced. Pregnancy loss can lead to grief and psychological distress.

Spontaneous Abortion

Spontaneous abortion is the natural loss of pregnancy before 20 weeks of gestation. Many refer to this as a "miscarriage." Types of spontaneous abortions are listed in Table 58.4. Around 20% of pregnancies result in spontaneous abortion. Most occur in the first trimester. They are often related to embryonic chromosomal abnormalities. Other common causes include endocrine problems, maternal infection, uterine abnormalities (e.g., uterine fibroids, endometriosis), immune factors, and environment factors. Risk factors for spontaneous abortion include age greater than 35 years, history of prior pregnancy loss, and chronic medical problems such as diabetes, obesity, or thyroid disease. Stress and substance use are also related to an increased risk.

Patients experiencing a spontaneous abortion often present with vaginal bleeding and cramping. Following a history and physical assessment, transvaginal ultrasound imaging is recommended for diagnosis. Bloodwork is done to assess serum human chorionic gonadotropin levels (hCG, also called β-hCG or "beta"). We have few interventions to prevent pregnancy loss. We used to place patients with threatened abortions on bed rest. Research shows this practice has more potential to be harmful than helpful. So, we no longer recommend bed rest.

There are 3 approaches to treatment of spontaneous abortion: (1) expectant management, (2) drug therapy, and (3) surgery.[4] A patient-centered approach should be used to determine the plan of care based on the patient's preferences and values. Provide patients with information about treatment options. Discuss the risks and benefits of each. Involving patients in decision making leads to the best mental health outcomes. Any patients with signs of acute complications such as hemorrhage or infection need emergency care.

Expectant management involves waiting for the pregnancy tissue (also called *products of conception [POC]*) to pass on its own. When appropriate criteria are met, this approach is about 75% effective in the 1st trimester. This option is the least invasive. However, it is not as predictable or effective as other approaches. Patient teaching about warning signs is needed. We need to monitor for complications and have a clear plan for follow-up.

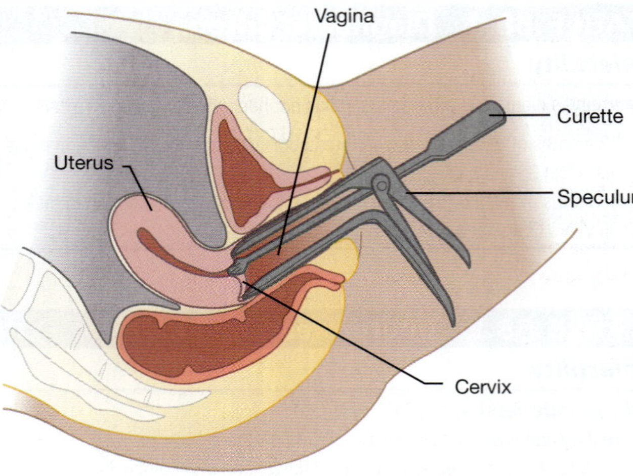

Fig. 58.1 D&C.

Drug therapy involves drugs such as misoprostol (Cytotec) and mifepristone (Mifeprex) to open the cervix and induce passage of the POC from the uterus. This approach offers more predictable timing of the POC than expectant management. It is less invasive than surgery. The ability to prescribe and dispense mifepristone is restricted in the United States.[5] This limits its accessibility in some settings. Teaching about side effects and anticipatory guidance is essential to safety in this approach.

Surgery of an abortion involves **dilation and curettage (D&C)** (Fig. 58.1). With a D&C, the cervix is dilated and the uterine contents removed using either manual vacuum aspiration (MVA) or electric vacuum aspiration (EVA). This approach is the most invasive of spontaneous abortion treatment options. But it is highly effective and offers rapid resolution of pregnancy loss.

Teach patients to call the HCP for heavy vaginal bleeding, fever, foul-smelling vaginal discharge, or severe pain. Discuss the use of pain medications, such as ibuprofen. Give resources or referrals for psychologic support and grief counseling to reduce mental health complications such as depression and anxiety. Review contraceptive options or planning for a subsequent pregnancy. Ovulation can resume within days or weeks after a pregnancy loss. Historically, we told patients to abstain from vaginal intercourse and wait several weeks or months before trying to become pregnant again. However, these practices do not reduce complications like infection or recurrent pregnancy loss and are no longer recommended.

Induced Abortion

Induced abortion is the elective termination of a pregnancy. There are several ways to induce an abortion. In the United States, the most common ways are medical abortion and aspiration (sometimes called surgical) abortion (Table 58.5). The approach used depends on the gestational length of the pregnancy, patient preference, and availability of care. State laws and agency regulations affect abortion care. Cost can be a significant factor since most patients pay out-of-pocket for abortion services. Engage patients in decision making about the risks, benefits, and alternatives to help them make the most appropriate decision. Provide patients information about all available options and referral to a setting that provides safe abortion care.[6]

TABLE 58.5 Comparison of Common Ways to Induce Abortions

Method	Aspiration Abortion	Medication Abortion
Description	Products of conception are removed through medical instruments that are introduced through the cervix and attached to manual or electric vacuum aspirator	Use of a combination of oral or buccal drugs (most often mifepristone and misoprostol) to soften and dilate the cervix and expel the pregnancy tissue
Timing	Up to 14 weeks gestation	Up to 10 weeks gestation
Success rate	High (99%)	High (98%–99%)
Common side effects	Abdominal cramping, vaginal bleeding	GI distress, abdominal cramping, vaginal bleeding
Health care visits	Requires 1 visit (often to an abortion care center)	May require multiple visits. Drugs must be taken in 2 doses 2 days apart. Follow-up care advised to ensure complete passage of tissue

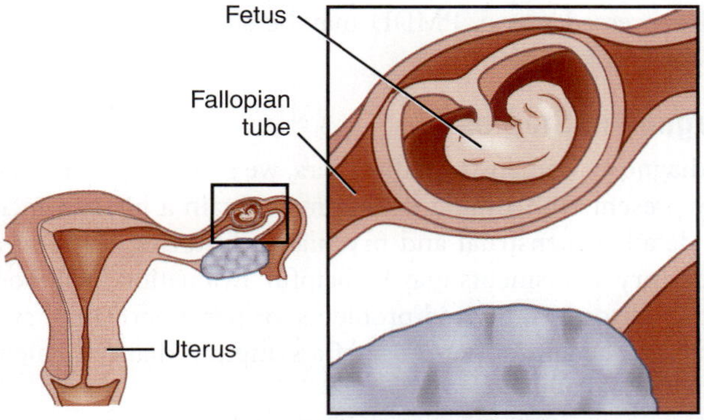

Fig. 58.2 Ectopic pregnancy in the fallopian tube.

Nursing care for induced abortion includes assessment, psychosocial support, and teaching. Patients who are RhD-negative blood type should receive Rho(D) immune globulin (Rhogam) for alloimmunization prevention. While rare, potential complications include infection, hemorrhage, uterine perforation, or incomplete abortion. Teach patients about the warning signs of complications, such as heavy vaginal bleeding, severe abdominal cramping or pain, fever, or foul-smelling vaginal discharge. Induced abortions do not negatively affect future pregnancies. Ovulation can occur within 2 weeks following an induced abortion. Menses often returns within 2 months. Therefore, when pregnancy is not desired, explore contraceptive options.

ECTOPIC PREGNANCY

An ectopic pregnancy is the implantation of a fertilized ovum outside the uterus. Almost all ectopic pregnancies occur within the fallopian tube (Fig. 58.2). When this happens, there is a risk that the pregnancy will rupture the fallopian tube. This can lead to excessive intrabdominal blood loss. It is a life-threatening emergency. Early detection of ectopic pregnancy is essential to reduce mortality.

Etiology and Pathophysiology

Tubal complications or blockages from infection, surgery, or deformity increase the chance that implantation will occur in the fallopian tube. While rare, ectopic pregnancies can occur in other sites such as the cervix, ovaries, surgical scar tissue, or abdominal wall. Embryos that implant outside of the uterine lining are unable to develop normally. As the embryo grows, it can cause organ rupture leading to severe internal bleeding and, if untreated, death.

Risk factors include a history of ectopic pregnancy, tubal surgery or deformity, or pelvic infection. Assisted reproduction and previous induced abortion also increase risk. Intrauterine conception greatly reduces the likelihood of intrauterine pregnancy. Therefore, when pregnancy does occur in a person with an intrauterine device (IUD), there is a higher risk of it being an ectopic pregnancy.

Clinical Manifestations

In an ectopic pregnancy, symptoms often occur 6 to 8 weeks after the last (normal) menstrual period (LMP). The main symptoms are abdominal or pelvic pain and unexplained vaginal bleeding. Secondary symptoms include those of early pregnancy, such as absent or late menses, nausea, frequent urination, and breast tenderness. Pain is typically caused by distention of the fallopian tube. This pain is often described as vague, sharp, or unilateral. Some patients do not have any pain. When present, vaginal bleeding can vary in quantity and color from scant brown spotting to bright red, heavy bleeding. In severe cases, patients have severe, sharp, unilateral pelvic or abdominal pain and sudden onset of vaginal bleeding. Any patients who present with severe hemorrhage or symptoms of shock such as hypotension or feeling dizzy or faint should be treated as a medical emergency.

Diagnostic Studies

Physical assessment, diagnostic imaging, and laboratory studies are used to diagnose an ectopic pregnancy. The presence of cervical motion or adnexal tenderness or an adnexal mass on pelvic examination are common findings. Serial transvaginal ultrasound and measurement of serum hCG are useful in confirming or ruling out ectopic pregnancy.

CHECK YOUR PRACTICE

You are working in the ED. Your patient is a 29-year-old woman who presents with acute abdominal pain, scant vaginal bleeding, and a positive home pregnancy test. The HCP suspects an ectopic pregnancy. The patient is crying, "I am going to lose this baby, and we have been trying so hard to have one."

- As her nurse, what are your priorities?
- How would you respond to her?

Interprofessional and Nursing Management

There are 3 ways to treat an ectopic pregnancy: drug therapy, surgery, or expectant management. Drug therapy with methotrexate may be an option if an ectopic pregnancy is diagnosed early and the patient is stable. Methotrexate stops the growth of rapidly dividing cells, including fetal and early placenta cells, by inhibiting DNA synthesis and disrupting cell multiplication. It is given as a single- or multiple-dose IM injection. The most common side effect is cramping or abdominal pain, which usually occurs during the first 2 to 3 days after treatment. When therapy is ineffective, or a patient has severe symptoms or high risk of rupture, surgery is needed. Surgical options include a *salpingectomy* (removal of the fallopian tube) or *salpingostomy* (surgically opening the tube and removing the pregnancy tissue). Surgery may be done laparoscopically. For a small number of low-risk patients, expectant management with close monitoring may be an option.

Nursing care includes closely monitoring symptoms and vital signs. Assess for signs of shock. Teach patients about ectopic pregnancy and treatment options. Provide emotional support. Prepare patients for diagnostic procedures, drug therapy, or surgery. Follow up with additional laboratory tests or imaging as appropriate based on the treatment approach and symptoms.

PROBLEMS RELATED TO MENSTRUATION

Wide variation exists among normal menstrual cycle length and bleeding duration, quantity, and character (see Table 55.2). The menstrual cycle may be irregular the first few years after *menarche* (first menstruation) and in *perimenopause* (the years preceding menopause). Common perimenstrual problems include premenstrual syndromes (PMS) and painful menses. Patients may have bleeding that is absent or irregular in amount, frequency, duration, or timing. Hyperandrogenic disorders like polycystic ovary syndrome (**PCOS**) can cause menstrual problems. We discuss each of these in the following sections.

PREMENSTRUAL DISORDERS

Most women have physical and emotional symptoms during specific menstrual cycle phases. For example, many have mild bloating, breast tenderness, or mood swings in the premenstrual phase. While often referred to as PMS, these mild symptoms do not meet the criteria for PMS. Clinically, the term **premenstrual syndrome (PMS)** is used in situations in which 1 or more recurrent physical and behavior symptoms cause severe distress or interfere with daily functioning. PMS can affect health, relationships, work performance, or academic performance. *Premenstrual dysphoric disorder* (PMDD) is a severe form of PMS that often includes behavior and affective symptoms.

Etiology and Pathophysiology

We do not know the exact cause of premenstrual disorders. Most likely, they are the result of a combination of hormone and psychosocial factors. Genetics, nutrition, drug therapy, and underlying medical or mental health problems may be contributing factors.

Clinical Manifestations

PMS presents with a wide variety of recurrent, cyclical symptoms. Symptoms may be physical, emotional, behavioral, or cognitive. Onset of symptoms occurs in the luteal phase of the menstrual cycle. Resolution of symptoms occurs within days of onset of menses. Common physical symptoms are breast discomfort, bloating and swelling, headache, and cramping. Emotional symptoms include mood swings, irritability, and feeling anxious or depressed. Changes in behavior such as food cravings or increased appetite are common. Some patients have cognitive symptoms like difficulty concentrating. With PMDD, patients often have irritability, anger, fatigue, anxiety, and depressed mood. PMDD may be superimposed on other psychiatric conditions.

Diagnostic Studies

To diagnose premenstrual disorders, we rule out problems that may present with similar symptoms. Obtain a history, including detailed menstrual and psychiatric histories. Physical and laboratory assessments may be helpful. Evaluation for mood or anxiety disorders, thyroid problems, or perimenopausal symptoms may be appropriate. Use of a symptom diary or calendar can aid the diagnosis.

Interprofessional Care and Nursing Management

Care focuses on symptom management. A holistic approach including lifestyle and behavior interventions, complementary and alternative therapies, and consideration of drug options may best meet the patient's needs.

Health promotion should include guidance and support for improved nutrition, exercise, sleep, and stress management. Behavior interventions such as relaxation techniques may be helpful. Cognitive behavioral therapy may be used to manage moderate to severe symptoms. Drug treatment options include selective serotonin reuptake inhibitors (SSRIs) and/or combined hormonal contraceptives such as an oral contraceptive pill (OCP). Some herbal remedies such as *vitex agnus castus* (chasteberry) and nutrition supplements may help reduce symptoms in some persons.[7]

Nursing care includes teaching about the condition and ways to manage symptoms (Table 58.6). Acknowledging the diagnosis can be therapeutic and validating. Helping patients monitor their symptoms and set realistic goals can improve functioning and quality of life. Patients with PMDD are at increased for suicide. Provide counseling and resources for suicide prevention.

DYSMENORRHEA

Dysmenorrhea is painful menstruation. It is one of the most common gynecologic problems. Although most women have some discomfort during menses, dysmenorrhea is cyclic pain that interferes with activities of daily living. It can be primary or secondary. In *primary dysmenorrhea*, no underlying problem or disease process is causing the symptoms. In *secondary dysmenorrhea*, the symptoms are due to an underlying pathology such as endometriosis or uterine fibroids.

TABLE 58.6 Interprofessional Care

Premenstrual Disorders

Diagnostic Assessment

- Health history including medication, menstrual, psychiatric history
- Symptom diary
- Physical assessment
- Laboratory studies as indicated

Management

- Health promotion (diet, sleep, exercise)
- Stress reduction
- Cognitive behavioral therapy
- Nutrition therapy
- Drug therapy
  - SSRIs
  - Combined hormonal contraceptives

Etiology and Pathophysiology

Primary dysmenorrhea is thought to be caused by excess production of prostaglandin, a hormone secreted by the *endometrium* (uterine lining) during menstruation. Prostaglandin stimulates the uterus to contract. Uterine contractions and constriction of small endometrial blood vessels lead to tissue ischemia and increased sensitization of pain receptors. This results in painful menstrual cramps. As menstruation continues, prostaglandin levels decrease, and menstrual cramping improves. Primary dysmenorrhea is most common in adolescents around the time of menarche.

Secondary dysmenorrhea has similar symptoms of pain during menses but is caused by a uterine pathology. The most common causes of secondary dysmenorrhea are endometriosis, adenomyosis, or uterine fibroids. There may also be an association between dysmenorrhea and chronic pain conditions.

Clinical Manifestations

Both forms of dysmenorrhea present with the same symptoms. Patients have painful uterine cramping with the start of menses. Symptoms often resolve spontaneously within 2 or 3 days after onset. Patients may also have back pain, nausea and vomiting, and symptoms of premenstrual disorders. Dysmenorrhea can impair patients' functioning and quality of life. Severe dysmenorrhea can lead to absenteeism and decreased productivity at work or school. Depending on the cause, secondary dysmenorrhea may be associated with *dyspareunia* (painful intercourse), heavy or irregular vaginal bleeding, or infertility.

Diagnostic Studies

Evaluation begins with the history. Obtain detailed menstrual and sexual histories. Because dysmenorrhea has a genetic component, take a focused family history. Use of a symptom diary may help aid diagnosis. A diagnosis of primary dysmenorrhea can be made based on the presentation of symptoms in the absence of other suspected causes of pain. Pelvic examination may not be necessary for adolescents who are not at risk for sexually transmitted infections (STIs) and present with classic symptoms of primary dysmenorrhea. If we suspect secondary dysmenorrhea, assessment will include a pelvic examination and transvaginal or pelvic ultrasound imaging.

CHECK YOUR PRACTICE

In an outpatient clinic, your 28-year-old patient is reporting symptoms of PMS. She tells you, "Lately, before my period comes, I spend the entire day in bed. I'm in pain. I'm anxious and overwhelmed. I just can't function like this anymore."

- How would you respond?
- What can she do to improve her symptoms?

Interprofessional Care

Treatment for primary dysmenorrhea includes drug and nonpharmacologic therapies. Nonpharmacologic options include use of heat, exercise, and complementary and alternative therapy such as transcutaneous electrical nerve stimulation (TENS) or acupuncture. First-line drug therapy includes nonsteroidal antiinflammatory drugs (NSAIDs). NSAIDs inhibit prostaglandins and decrease pain. If NSAIDs are ineffective or patients want contraception, hormone therapies such as oral conceptive pills may be appropriate.

Treatment of secondary dysmenorrhea depends on the cause. Some patients' symptoms are improved by the same approaches used to treat primary dysmenorrhea. However, management of the underlying problem may be needed to relieve symptoms. Some patients may need surgical treatment. Common surgical treatments for dysmenorrhea include *endometrial ablation* (surgical destruction of the uterine lining) and *hysterectomy* (removal of the uterus) (Table 58.7).

Nursing care includes teaching about the cause, symptoms, and treatment options for dysmenorrhea. Validate the patient's pain and experience. Provide psychosocial support. Teach patients about lifestyle changes and nonpharmacologic options. Regular exercise and good nutrition to improve symptoms. Provide teaching about drug therapy. Follow-up on test results as appropriate. Develop a plan to evaluate the effectiveness of treatment and provide follow-up care.

ABNORMAL UTERINE BLEEDING

Abnormal uterine bleeding (AUB) is any uterine bleeding that is abnormal in quantity, duration, or timing. It is one of the most common gynecologic concerns. AUB can have significant negative effects on quality of life. AUB is defined as either acute or chronic. *Acute AUB* is an episode of uterine bleeding (in a non-pregnant woman of reproductive age) that requires immediate treatment. *Chronic AUB* is abnormal uterine bleeding that has been present for most of the past 6 months. The most common forms of AUB are heavy menstrual bleeding (menses that are heavy or prolonged), intermenstrual bleeding (bleeding between menses), and irregular bleeding (ovulatory dysfunction). Historically, several terms were used to describe AUB. These include dysfunctional uterine bleeding (DUB), menorrhagia, and metrorrhagia. Though their use is no longer recommended, you may still hear them used in some settings.

TABLE 58.7 Common Gynecologic Surgeries

Type of Surgical Procedure	Description
Dilation and Curettage (D&C)	Opening (dilation) of cervix and removal (scraping) of endometrial tissue
Endometrial Ablation	Destroys endometrial lining using heat, cold, or electrical energy
Hysterectomy	Removal of the uterus Several different types: • Vaginal: uterus is removed through an incision in the vagina • Abdominal: uterus is removed through an incision in the abdomen • Laparoscopic: uses a laparoscope and instrument inserted through abdominal incisions • Robotic-assisted laparoscopy: uses a surgical robot to manipulate surgical instruments
Hysteroscopy	Examination of uterine cavity using a hysteroscope (lighted, flexible viewing instrument), inserted through the cervix
Myomectomy	Removal of fibroids from the uterus, leaving the uterus in place
Oophorectomy	Removal of the ovary, can be unilateral or bilateral
Salpingectomy	Removal of the fallopian tube, can be unilateral or bilateral
Uterine artery embolization	Minimally invasive surgery to inject embolic agents into uterine arteries to block blood supply to uterine fibroids
Vaginectomy	Removal of vagina, may be partial or total
Vulvectomy	Removal of part or all the vulva

The absence of menses (*amenorrhea*) is also a common menstrual abnormality. We describe amenorrhea as primary or secondary. *Primary amenorrhea* refers to the failure of menstrual cycles to begin by 16 years of age. *Secondary amenorrhea* occurs when menstrual cycles stop for more than 3 months in women with previously regular menstrual cycles or more than 6 months in those with irregular menses.

Etiology and Pathophysiology

There are many different problems that cause AUB. The most common causes are outlined in the PALM-COEIN classification system for AUB (Fig. 58.3). PALM stands for common structural causes of bleeding: polyps, adenomyosis, leiomyoma, and malignancy or hyperplasia. The COEIN acronym represents common nonstructural causes: coagulopathy, ovulatory dysfunction, endometrial dysfunction, iatrogenic, and not otherwise classified. AUB may also be related to drug therapy such as hormonal contraception. Common causes of amenorrhea are listed in Table 58.8.

Clinical Manifestations

AUB is defined in contrast to normal menstruation. Bleeding that is outside the norms of frequency, duration, volume, and timing is classified as abnormal. For example, normal menstruation occurs every 24 to 38 days, lasts no more than 8 days, and has a blood loss that does not interfere with quality of life. Normal menstruation is discussed in Chapter 55.

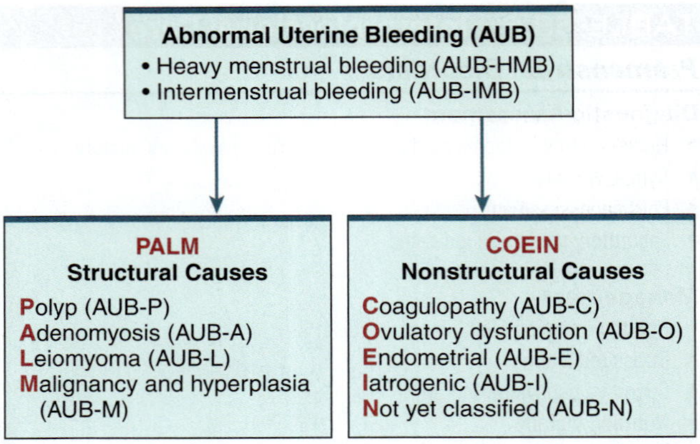

Fig. 58.3 PALM-COIEN classification system for abnormal uterine bleeding. (Used with permission from Munro MG, Critchley HO, Broder MS, et al.: FIGO classification system [PALM–OEIN] for causes of AUB in nongravid women of reproductive age, *Int J Gynecol Obstet* 11:3, 2011.)

TABLE 58.8 Common Causes of Amenorrhea

Anatomic
- Abnormality in müllerian development (e.g., absence of uterus)
- Imperforate hymen
- Intrauterine adhesions (e.g., Asherman syndrome)

Hormone
- Hypothalamic dysfunction
- Ovarian dysfunction (e.g., Turner syndrome)
- PCOS
- Pituitary problems (e.g., pituitary tumors)
- Thyroid problems

Other
- Drug therapy (e.g., hormonal contraceptives)
- Lifestyle (e.g., low body weight, stress, excessive exercise)
- Pregnancy, breastfeeding, menopause

Diagnostic Studies

Evaluation of AUB begins with the history, including detailed menstrual, sexual, gynecologic, and obstetric histories. Physical assessment should determine rule out other (non-uterine) potential sources of bleeding. For example, bleeding could be coming from another site in the urinary, GI, or genital tracts. Pelvic examination is useful to assess for any masses or structural problems. A pregnancy test is appropriate in sexually active patients to rule out pregnancy-related causes of bleeding. Depending on the suspected cause of AUB, laboratory tests to assess for hormone imbalances, coagulation problems, or thyroid problems may be done. HCPs may assess for STIs and anemia. A progesterone challenge test may be done. Other possible diagnostic studies include cervical cancer screening (Pap test), pelvic or transvaginal ultrasound, endometrial biopsy, and hysteroscopy or saline infusion sonohysterography (SIS).

Interprofessional Care

Treatment for AUB depends on the cause (Table 58.9).[8] Treatment goals may be to improve quality of life or prevent

TABLE 58.9 Interprofessional Care

Abnormal Uterine Bleeding

Diagnostic Assessment

- History
  - Detailed menstrual history
  - Bleeding patterns, perceived severity of bleeding (clots, soaking through clothing)
- Physical assessment
  - Inspection of the source of bleeding
  - Pelvic examination
  - Evaluation for obesity/hirsutism (suggestive of PCOS)
- Laboratory tests (as indicated)
  - Pregnancy test
  - CBC
  - Thyroid-stimulating hormone (TSH)
  - STI screening
  - Screening for bleeding disorders
  - Hormone levels (e.g., FSH, LH, prolactin, testosterone)
  - Liver and renal function tests
- Imaging studies and tissue sampling
  - Transvaginal/pelvic ultrasound
  - Saline infusion sonohysterography
  - Endometrial biopsy
  - Hysteroscopy

Management

Based on the cause, may include:

- Hormone therapy
- NSAIDS
- Tranexamic acid (Lysteda)
- Antibiotics
- Surgery
  - D&C
  - Endometrial ablation
  - Uterine artery embolization
  - Hysterectomy

further complications such as cancer and severe anemia. Future fertility goals are important in guiding the treatment plan. Care for *heavy menstrual bleeding (HMB)* focuses on medical or surgical treatments. Drug therapy for HMB includes hormone therapy such as OCPs, NSAIDs, and tranexamic acid (Lysteda). IUDs are another option for HMB. Another approach for HMB is surgical therapy such as D&C, endometrial ablation, uterine artery embolization, or hysterectomy (Table 58.7). There are also medical and surgical treatment options for intermenstrual or irregular bleeding. These options include hormone therapy, antibiotics for suspected infections, and polyp removal (polypectomy).

Nursing care focuses on patient teaching. Teach about the menstrual cycle and characteristics of normal bleeding to help patients identify variations (see Table 55.2). Encourage patients to report excessively heavy bleeding, passing of clots, or bleeding of extended duration. Nutrition teaching is appropriate, especially for adolescents and those at risk for anemia. Ensure that patients understand the cause of their bleeding and the various treatment options. Follow up to assess treatment effectiveness and improvement in symptoms and quality of life.

TABLE 58.10 Diagnostic Criteria

PCOS

A diagnosis of PCOS is made based on the presence of 2 of the 3 following:

1. Menstrual irregularity (infrequent menstruation or anovulation)
2. Signs of hyperandrogenism or elevated serum androgen levels
3. Polycystic ovaries on ultrasound

Polycystic Ovary Syndrome

Polycystic ovary syndrome (PCOS) is an endocrine disorder that affects menstruation and fertility. This syndrome is characterized by menstrual irregularity, ovulatory dysfunction, and hyperandrogenism. It is the most common cause of infertility. The cause of PCOS is not known. We think there are multiple etiologies, including complex genetic and environmental factors. The underlying pathophysiology includes excessive androgen production in the ovaries, often accompanied by insulin resistance. There are numerous long-term health consequences associated with PCOS. Patients with PCOS are at increased risk for diabetes, cardiovascular disease, mood disorders, and endometrial cancer.

Clinical Manifestations

Manifestations include signs of hyperandrogenism such as hirsutism and acne, irregular menstrual cycles, and obesity. Amenorrhea or oligomenorrhea and anovulation are common. Hyperandrogenism may present with acne, hirsutism, or male-pattern hair loss. Signs of insulin resistance, such as metabolic syndrome, may be present.

Diagnostic Studies

Table 58.10 outlines the diagnostic criteria for PCOS. A diagnosis of PCOS should be considered in a female of reproductive age based on the presence of classical manifestations of irregular menstrual cycles with signs of hyperandrogenism, as described above. Laboratory tests and pelvic imaging are not needed to make a diagnosis. However, testing may be useful to identify high androgen levels in the absence of symptoms. These diagnostic studies can also rule out other potential causes of symptoms such as pregnancy or non-classic congenital adrenal hyperplasia. Polycystic ovaries may be visible on ultrasound, although this is not required for diagnosis (Fig. 58.4).

Interprofessional Care

The approach to treating PCOS depends on the symptoms and desire for pregnancy. For overweight patients, weight loss is recommended. Weight loss results in improved ovulatory dysfunction. Hormonal contraceptives are often used to reduce symptoms of hyperandrogenism. Spironolactone (Aldactone), a diuretic, may be prescribed for its antiandrogenic effects. For patients with undesired infertility, an aromatase inhibitor, letrozole (Femara), can induce ovulation. Approaches to reducing hirsutism include cosmetic measures (e.g., waxing, electrolysis, laser hair removal) and topical therapies like depilatory agents or eflornithine hydrochloride (Vaniqa) cream. In some patients, insulin-lowering drugs such as metformin are given to treat PCOS. Resources such as the National PCOS Association's PCOS Challenge may be helpful to provide support and resources to patients with PCOS.[9]

DRUG ALERT

Spironolactone (Aldactone)

- Check for drug interactions.
- Monitor for hypotension and electrolyte imbalances.
- Discuss the importance of a low-potassium diet.

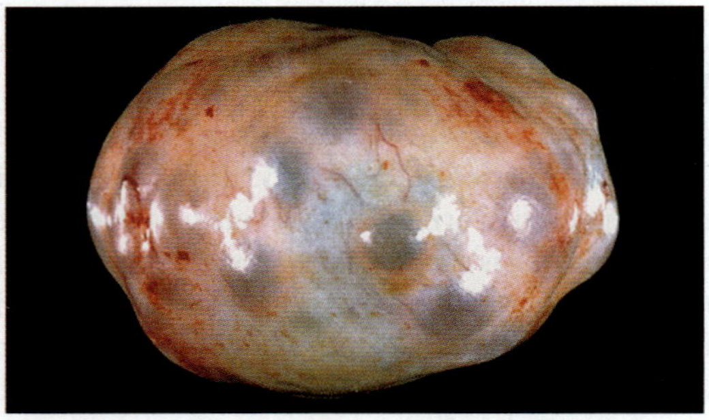

Fig. 58.4 PCOS. (From Kumar V, et al.: *Robbins and Cotran pathologic basis of disease*, ed 7, Philadelphia, 2005, Saunders.)

MENOPAUSE

Menopause is the cessation of menstruation. *Natural menopause* is the permanent cessation of menstrual periods. It is diagnosed retrospectively after 12 months of amenorrhea without any other suspected cause. The age of natural menopause ranges from 40 to 58 years, with a median age of 52 years. The menopausal transition is known as **perimenopause**. Perimenopause often begins about 4 years before the *final menstrual period (FMP)* but can be much earlier or later. Menopause and perimenopausal symptoms are a major health focus for women during midlife. The Stages of Reproductive Aging Workshop (STRAW) +10 System describes reproductive aging in women (Fig. 58.5). Common menopause terminology is defined in Table 58.11.

Etiology and Pathophysiology

Natural menopause occurs in response to normal physiologic changes of aging in the hypothalamic-pituitary-ovarian axis. Fluctuations in hormone levels cause perimenopausal

Menarche (at start of stage −5) — FMP (0) (between stages −1 and +1a)

Stage	−5	−4	−3b	−3a	−2	−1	+1a	+1b	+1c	+2
Terminology	Reproductive				Menopausal transition		Postmenopause			
	Early	Peak	Late		Early	Late	Early			Late
					Perimenopause					
Duration	*Variable*				*Variable*	1-3 years	2 years (1+1)		3-6 years	*Remaining lifespan*
Principal criteria										
Menstrual cycle	Variable to regular	Regular	Regular	Subtle changes in flow/ length	*Variable length* persistent ≥7-day difference in length of consecutive cycles	Interval of amenorrhea of ≥60 days				
Supportive criteria										
Endocrine										
FSH			Low	Variable*	↑ Variable*	↑ >25 iU/L**	↑ Variable		Stabilizes	
AMH			Low	Low	Low	Low	Low		Very low	
Inhibin B				Low	Low	Low	Low		Very low	
Antral follicle count			Low	Low	Low	Low	Very low		Very low	
Descriptive characteristics										
Symptoms						Vasomotor symptoms *likely*	Vasomotor symptoms *most likely*			*Increasing* symptoms of urogenital atrophy

* Blood draw on cycle days 2–5. ↑ = elevated.

** Approximate expected level based on assays using current international pituitary standard.

Fig. 58.5 Stages of Reproductive Aging Workshop + 10 staging system for reproductive aging in women. (Source: Harlow SD, Gass M, Hall JE, et al.: Executive summary of the Stages of Reproductive Aging Workshop + 10: addressing the unfinished agenda of staging reproductive aging, *J Clin Endocrinol Metab* 2012. © 2012, The Endocrine Society.)

TABLE 58.11 Menopause Terminology

Term	Definition
Final menstrual period (FMP)	Last menstrual period; the point of menopause
Induced menopause	Menopause resulting from medical or surgical intervention
Menopause	A point in time 12 consecutive months after the FMP
Natural menopause	Menopause resulting from normal, spontaneous, physiologic changes
Perimenopause	Period of transition before menopause. Often lasts around 4 years. Associated with fluctuations in hormone levels
Postmenopause	Period of time after menopause. Characterized by symptoms associated with decreased estrogen and progesterone
Primary ovarian insufficiency	Temporary or permanent menopause at <40 years of age. May be called premature menopause

TABLE 58.12 Symptoms Associated With Perimenopause

- Changes in menstrual bleeding patterns
- Depression
- Headache
- Joint pain
- ↓ Libido
- Memory loss
- Poor concentration
- Sexual dysfunction
- Sleep problems
- Urinary frequency/urgency
- Vaginal dryness
- Vasomotor symptoms (e.g., hot flashes)

symptoms. Menopause can also be induced. *Induced menopause* occurs after surgical intervention to remove the ovaries or due to side effects of chemotherapy, radiation therapy, or other drugs. *Primary ovarian insufficiency* is permanent or temporary menopause that occurs at less than 40 years of age. Causes include drugs, chromosomal abnormalities, or health problems such as endocrine or autoimmune disorders.

Clinical Manifestations

Perimenopause is characterized by erratic hormone fluctuations and irregular menstrual cycles. Common symptoms of perimenopause are outlined in Table 58.12. The experience of perimenopause varies widely. Many women have vasomotor changes such as hot flashes or hot flushes. These are often experienced as an intense heat sensation. They may be accompanied by profuse sweating. Sleep disruptions, mood changes, and decreased sexual function are common. Some find perimenopausal systems greatly disrupt their quality of life and well-being, while others may report no bothersome symptoms. In postmenopause, estrogen and progesterone deficiency increases the risk for cardiovascular disease, urogenital atrophy, bone mineral density loss, dementia, and various types of cancer.

Diagnostic Studies

Menopause is a retrospective diagnosis. It can only be made after 12 consecutive months of amenorrhea in the absence of other causes. A diagnosis of perimenopause is based on manifestations. We begin with the history, including menstrual and sexual histories and physical assessment. A symptom diary may be useful to aid diagnosis. Laboratory tests are not needed in women over age 45 with typical perimenopausal symptoms. Some HCP measure serum follicle-stimulating hormone (FSH). However, FSH varies widely throughout the menstrual cycle and is therefore not a reliable indicator of perimenopause. HCPs should assess for other potential causes of clinical manifestations such as pregnancy or thyroid disease. Further assessment is needed in women under 40 years of age or those with atypical symptoms. This may include laboratory assessment of hormone levels or diagnostic imaging such as pelvic ultrasound.

Interprofessional Care

Treatment options for menopausal symptoms include options to target specific symptoms and systemic effects. The North American Menopause Society (NAMS) has patient information, tools, and a mobile app to help patients and HCPs engage in patient-centered care around treatment decisions.[10]

Drug therapy centers on hormone therapy. Hormone therapy typically starts with estrogen. There are many different forms of estrogen, including oral pills, transdermal patches, intramuscular injection, transvaginal ring, and topical creams, lotions, and sprays. Patient preference and symptoms often inform which preparation they use. For patients with an intact uterus (e.g., have not had a hysterectomy), progesterone must be given with estrogen to prevent endometrial cancer from estrogen-related endometrial hyperplasia. Progesterone also comes in several different forms and combinations. These include various pills, patches, vaginal administrations (capsule, ring, cream, gel), and an IUD.

A patient-centered approach to treatment is important. We need to address the patient's needs and preferences against the potential risks from hormone therapy. Assess for contraindications to hormone therapy such as a history of breast cancer, coronary heart disease, stroke, thromboembolic disorders, or liver disease. Hormone therapy can greatly reduce bothersome symptoms and improve quality of life. However, this must be balanced against the potential for increased risk of breast and endometrial cancer and cardiovascular disease. For patients who are not candidates for hormone therapy or want alternatives, there are some nonhormone drug treatment options. These include antidepressants (SSRIs or SNRIs), gabapentin, and antihypertensives. Despite their widespread use, there is not a strong body of evidence to support the safety and efficacy of herbal or other complementary and alternative therapies for symptoms.

❖ NURSING MANAGEMENT: MENOPAUSE

Menopause is a time of great physical and psychologic transition. Many women have symptoms for years during the perimenopausal period, while others transition without any difficulty. Menopause may be occurring simultaneously with role

TABLE 58.13 **Vaginal Infections Associated With Vaginitis**

Infection	Manifestations	Treatment Options
Bacterial vaginosis (bacterial infection)	"Fishy" odor Gray or white vaginal discharge	Oral or vaginal antibiotics • clindamycin (Cleocin) • metronidazole (Flagyl) • tinidazole (Tindamax)
Trichomonas vaginalis (protozoan infection)	Genital itching and inflammation Dysuria Frothy, thin, yellowish-greenish vaginal discharge Deep red or pink cervix and vagina ("strawberry cervix")	Antifungal agents • metronidazole (Flagyl) • tinidazole (Tindamax) Treatment of partner(s)
Vulvovaginal candidiasis (yeast infection)	Vaginal itching Red, swollen vulva Thick, white, curdy vaginal discharge	Oral or vaginal antifungals • butoconazole (Gynazole) • clotrimazole (Gyne-Lotrimin) • fluconazole (Diflucan) • miconazole (Monistat)

changes in personal and professional life. Many patients will not seek treatment for common menopausal symptoms such as hot flashes, sleep disturbances, and mood changes. Asking patients about midlife health issues, including menopausal symptoms during routine health encounters, can help identify concerns.

Teach patients about menopause and common symptoms. Provide support for physical, psychological, and emotional effects of menopause. Discuss lifestyle changes that can improve symptoms and quality of life. These include diet changes, exercise, clothing selection, and sleep hygiene. Support stress reduction and management strategies. Encourage smoking cessation. Recommend increased water intake to reduce dryness and hot flashes. Suggest wearing breathable or moisture-wicking fabrics and layered clothing to improve comfort during hot flashes. Suggest environmental changes such as room temperature, use of fans, or special cooling bedding.

Review the risks, benefits, and alternatives of various treatment options. Other therapies include vaginal lubricants and moisturizers and the intake of soy isoflavones through diet or supplements. Ensure patients are getting adequate intake or supplementation of calcium and vitamin D to reduce risk of bone fractures (see Table 68.16). Encourage health promotion measures such as depression screening, bone density screening, mammography, and ways to reduce risk of cardiovascular disease.

LOWER GENITAL TRACT INFECTIONS

Lower genital tract infections include infections resulting from a disruption in the vaginal microbiome and STIs. The *vaginal microbiome* contains microorganisms like yeast and healthy bacteria that protect against infection by maintaining an acidic environment. Inflammation of the vagina, known as *vaginitis*, can occur from a disruption of the vaginal flora. Vaginal infections associated with vaginitis are shown in Table 58.13. STIs are discussed in Chapter 57. If not treated, lower genital tract infections can lead to long-term health problems.

Etiology and Pathophysiology

Many problems can cause vaginitis. Common problems associated with vaginitis are bacterial vaginosis, vulvovaginal candidiasis, and STIs such as trichomoniasis. Exposure to irritating substances and foreign bodies (such as tampons or condoms) left in the vagina can disrupt the vaginal microbiome and cause lower genital infections.

Bacterial vaginosis is characterized by a disruption in the microbiota shifting away from healthy *Lactobacillus* species towards other organisms such as anaerobic bacteria leading to a rise in vaginal pH. Bacterial vaginosis can be transmitted by sexual activity, especially receptive oral sex. Having other STIs, vaginal douching, and smoking are also risk factors for bacterial vaginosis.

The second most common cause of vaginitis symptoms is vulvovaginal candidiasis. *Vulvovaginal candidiasis* is caused by an overgrowth of *Candida*, a naturally occurring part of the vaginal flora. The cause of the disruption of normal vaginal flora is not always known. Certain drugs (e.g., broad-spectrum antibiotics), behaviors (e.g., vaginal douching), and chronic problems (e.g., diabetes) increase the risk of vulvovaginal candidiasis.

STIs such as *trichomoniasis*, a protozoan infection, can also cause vaginitis. STIs are passed from person to person through sexual contact. They are caused by bacteria, viruses, or parasites. They are transmitted through bodily fluids such as blood, semen, and vaginal fluids. High-risk sexual behaviors such as having multiple sex partners increase the risk for STIs. The most common STIs are chlamydia, trichomoniasis, genital herpes, and human papillomavirus (HPV). Common STIs are listed in Table 58.14 and discussed in Chapter 57.

Clinical Manifestations

The manifestations depend on the type of infection. Many persons are asymptomatic. Others will have specific symptoms such as skin or mucosal lesions, cervical inflammation or tenderness, or enlarged lymph nodes. Vaginal discharge that is abnormal in color, quantity, odor, or consistency is a common symptom. For example, a "fishy" odor is a common symptom of bacterial vaginosis. Discharge that is thick, white, and curdy is characteristic of vulvovaginal candidiasis. Many patients have itching, burning, or irritation. Pain during intercourse or urination is common.

TABLE 58.14 Common STIs

Bacterial vaginosis
Chancroid
Chlamydia
Gonorrhea
Hepatitis
Herpes simplex virus
Human immunodeficiency virus (HIV)
Human papillomavirus (HPV)
Pelvic inflammatory disease (PID)
Pubic lice or crabs
Scabies
Syphilis
Trichomoniasis
Zika virus

❖ Interprofessional and Nursing Management

Assessment for lower genital infections starts with the history, including a sexual history. Routine screening for vaginitis infections is not recommended in asymptomatic persons. For patients with lower genital tract infection symptoms, the physical assessment should include pelvic and speculum examination. Evaluating vaginal secretions by pH testing, microscopic examination, culture, and/or other laboratory tests aid in diagnosis. Treatment options depend on the type of infection (Table 58.13). Options include topical and oral therapies. Screening and treatment for STIs are discussed in Chapter 57. A follow-up visit is often recommended to evaluate treatment effectiveness and teach sexual health and contraception.

Teach patients about behavior and lifestyle measures to reduce the risk for infection. This includes keeping the vulvar area dry and avoiding products like harsh laundry detergents, scented menstrual products, or spermicides that can cause irritation. Discuss how to clean the vulva and vagina to reduce infections by using only gentle and unscented soaps to clean externally and avoiding douching. Review sexual practices to prevent infections, such as inserting only clean objects (like washed hands or sex toys) into the vagina and using water or silicone-based lubricants. Smoking cessation and nutrition teaching may help minimize the risk of infection.

Review symptoms that indicate a problem and help women seek care promptly. Discussing problems that concern the patient's genitalia or sexual intercourse is often hard. Use a nonjudgmental attitude to make women feel more comfortable while empowering them to ask questions.

When a woman is diagnosed with a genital infection, ensure that she fully understands the treatment. Provide information about comfort measures to improve symptoms. If she is using a vaginal medication for the first time, show her the applicator and how to fill it. Teach where and how the applicator should be inserted using visual aids or models. Vaginal creams should be inserted before going to bed so the drug will remain in the vagina for a long period.

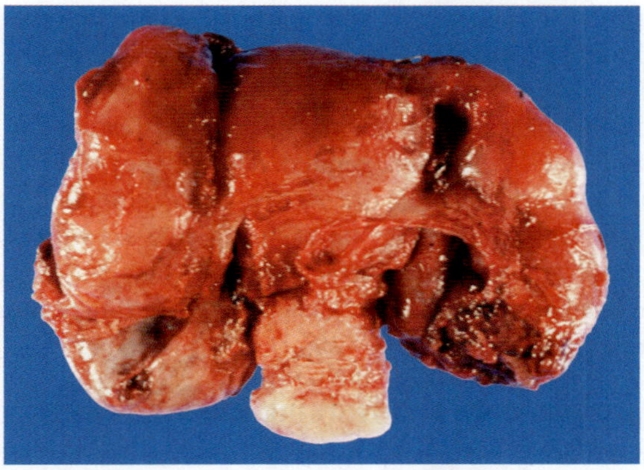

Fig. 58.6 Pelvic inflammatory disease (PID). (From Kumar V, et al.: *Robbins and Cotran pathologic basis of disease*, ed 8, Philadelphia, 2010, Saunders.)

PELVIC INFLAMMATORY DISEASE

Pelvic inflammatory disease (PID) is a clinical syndrome that includes a spectrum of infectious and inflammatory diseases of the upper genital tract. Ascending organisms cause inflammation in the endometrium, fallopian tubes, ovaries, and pelvic peritoneum (Fig. 58.6). There are about 1 million cases of PID each year in the United States. PID is most common among sexually active young women.

Etiology and Pathophysiology

PID is caused by an infectious organism ascending from the vagina or upper urogenital tract. Untreated sexually transmitted *Neisseria gonorrhoeae* and *Chlamydia trachomatis* are common causes of PID, as are microbes associated with bacterial vaginosis. Organisms can ascend past the endocervical barrier through normal processes like menstruation or gynecologic procedures (e.g., IUD insertion). Other risk factors include high-risk sexual behaviors, young age, vaginal douching, recent cervical manipulation, and history of PID.

Clinical Manifestations

The classic presentation of acute PID is pelvic or lower abdominal pain with tenderness in the cervix, uterus, or adnexa. Pain varies from mild to severe. The pain often occurs with intercourse and urination. Movement, such as walking, can increase the pain. Spotting after intercourse and purulent cervical or vaginal discharge may occur. Fever and chills may be present.

Complications

If not diagnosed and treated promptly, PID can cause serious complications. These include infertility, ectopic pregnancy, chronic pelvic pain, or tubo-ovarian abscess (TOA). These complications result from scarring, adhesions, or obstruction of the fallopian tubes. TOA or perihepatitis (Fitz-Hugh Curtis Syndrome) are potential immediate and serious risks of untreated PID.

Interprofessional Care

A health and sexual history and physical assessment are important to explore the presenting symptoms and rule out other causes of abdominal or pelvic pain. Physical assessment will include abdominal, pelvic, and speculum examinations. While no laboratory tests are needed to begin treatment, microscopic examination of vaginal discharge and testing for gonorrhea and chlamydia can support the diagnosis. Testing for other STIs such as HIV is recommended. A pregnancy test is done to rule out a possible ectopic pregnancy. Ultrasound, endometrial biopsy, or laparoscopy may be useful to rule out other potential complications. Some HCPs may order blood tests, such as a complete blood count (CBC), erythrocyte sedimentation rate, or C-reactive protein.

Interprofessional and Nursing Management

Treatment is started promptly, often based on the presentation, without waiting for laboratory results. PID is usually treated on an outpatient basis with a combination of broad-spectrum antibiotics (see Table 15.8). Antibiotic regimens recommended by the Centers for Disease Control and Prevention (CDC) are outlined in Chapter 57. Symptoms should improve within 72 hours of starting treatment. Hospitalization may be needed for patients with suspected PID who do not respond within 48 to 72 hours. Patients who are pregnant or present with severe symptoms such as high fever or nausea and vomiting may be hospitalized. In those instances, IV antibiotics, further tests, or surgery may be needed. Recent sexual partners should be treated presumptively for gonorrhea and chlamydia.

Prevention, early recognition, and prompt treatment can prevent PID and associated complications. Subjective and objective data that you should obtain from the patient with PID are outlined in Table 58.15. For hospitalized patients, you have a key role in implementing drug therapy and monitoring the patient's health status. Record vital signs. Note the character, amount, color, and odor of any vaginal discharge. Assess patient's pain and provide analgesics and supportive measures to decrease pain.

Teaching about PID is important. Provide anticipatory guidance about symptom improvement. Teach patients the importance of completing the prescribed therapy. Advise them to abstain from sexual intercourse until treatment is completed and sexual partners have been treated. Provide teaching about sexual practices and health screening to reduce transmission of STIs in the future.

TABLE 58.15 NURSING ASSESSMENT

PID

Subjective Data

Important Health Information

Health history: Previous STIs or PID. Recent IUD insertion, termination of pregnancy, or gynecologic procedure.

Sexual history: Age of first sexual encounter. Number and sex of sexual partners. Exposure to partner with STIs. Types of sexual activities. Use of condoms and other preventative measures for STIs.

Medications: Hormone agents, including contraception.

Allergies: Allergies to antibiotics or other drugs.

Functional Health Patterns

Health perception–health management: Malaise

Nutritional-metabolic: Nausea, vomiting; chills, fever

Elimination: Urinary frequency, urgency

Cognitive-perceptual: Lower abdominal pain, pelvic pain, low back pain, onset of pain just after a menstrual cycle; dyspareunia, dysuria, vulvar pruritus

Sexuality-reproductive: Abnormal vaginal discharge, unscheduled vaginal bleeding

Objective Data

Reproductive

Mucopurulent cervicitis, vulvar maceration, vaginal discharge (heavy and purulent to thin and mucoid), cervical motion tenderness, uterine or adnexal tenderness. Inflammatory masses on palpation

Possible Diagnostic Findings

White blood cells on wet mount (saline microscopy of vaginal fluid), ↑ erythrocyte sedimentation rate, laboratory confirmation of gonorrheal or chlamydial infection, abscess or inflammation on ultrasonography

BENIGN GYNECOLOGIC PROBLEMS

Many different benign problems affect the female reproductive organs. While they are benign in that they are not life-threatening or cancerous, they can still significantly impact quality of life. Problems that affect the skin, such as vulvar dermatoses, are discussed in Chapter 55. This section focuses on those benign conditions affecting the cervix, uterus, or adnexa.

Some patients with these conditions present with symptoms such as bleeding or pain. Others have no symptoms. They are diagnosed based on findings from a physical assessment or other procedure. Assessment includes a detailed health and sexual history and physical assessment with pelvic and speculum examinations. Diagnostic imaging is often helpful. For many of these conditions, no treatment is necessary. In those instances, care centers on confirming the diagnosis of the benign condition, providing teaching and reassurance, and recommending supportive measures to reduce any bothersome symptoms. In other cases, medical or surgical treatments may improve patients' quality of life.

Cervical Problems

The cervix may have benign growth or lesions such as cervical ectropion, cysts, or polyps. These may be seen with a speculum examination (Fig. 58.7). *Cervical ectropion* occurs when the cervix becomes slightly everted, exposing underlying cells which may be more sensitive or prone to bleeding. This condition is not due to underlying pathology. It is common in adolescents and pregnancy.

Nabothian cysts (mucus or epithelial inclusion cysts) are another common finding on speculum examination. They are caused by mucus-producing cells being covered by epithelial cellular growth. Nabothian cysts do not usually cause symptoms or require treatment. They may resolve spontaneously.

Cervical polyps are another benign growth that may be found during routine speculum examination. Polyps are usually red or purple and small, measuring less than 3 cm in length. Their cause is not known. We believe hormone factors play a role. Polyps may be removed if they are large or cause complications, such as bleeding after intercourse.

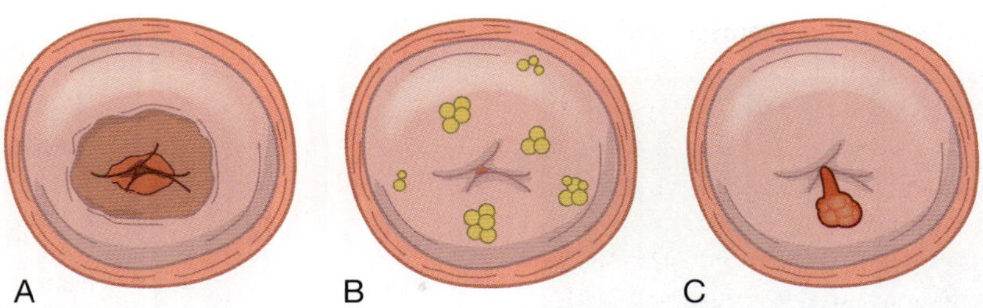

Fig. 58.7 Benign cervical lesions: (A) cervical ectropion. (B) Nabothian cyst. (C) Cervical polyp.

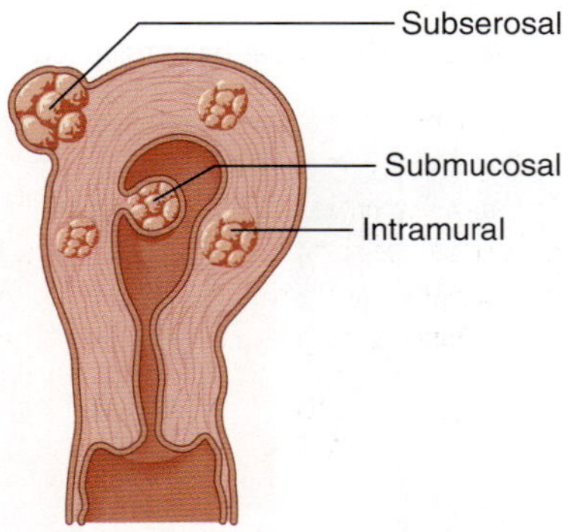

Fig. 58.8 Uterine fibroids. (From McCance KL, Huether SE: *Pathophysiology: the biologic basis for disease in adults and children*, ed 6, St. Louis, 2010, Mosby.)

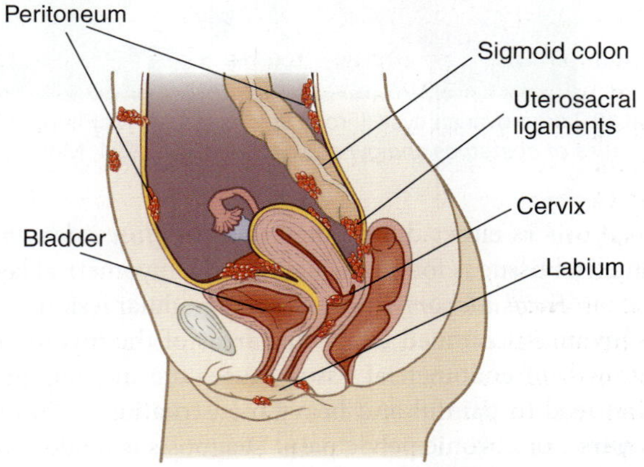

Fig. 58.9 Common sites of endometriosis.

Uterine Problems

The most common benign uterine problems are uterine fibroids, endometriosis, and adenomyosis. Uterine **fibroids** (or leiomyomas, myomas) are non-cancerous smooth-muscle tumors. They appear most often in women of reproductive age. We think they are caused by hormone and genetic factors. We classify fibroids based on their location in the uterus. The most common types are subserosal, intermural, or submucosal (Fig. 58.8).

Many patients with fibroids have no symptoms. Others will have pelvic pain, AUB, or infertility. On physical assessment, the uterus may be enlarged or irregularly shaped. Pelvic ultrasound is used to confirm the diagnosis. The approach to treatment depends on the patient's age, severity of symptoms, and desire for pregnancy. Expectant management may be appropriate since most fibroids reduce in size after menopause. Drug therapy, such as hormonal contraception or gonadotropin-releasing hormone (GnRH) agonists, can reduce HMB and pain. Surgical interventions such as removal of uterine fibroids (myomectomy), hysterectomy, or uterine artery embolization may be used for severe symptoms impacting quality of life or fertility.

Endometriosis is a benign inflammatory condition in which endometrial tissue accumulates outside the endometrium of the uterus.[11] The most frequent sites for endometriosis are in or near the ovaries, uterosacral ligaments, and uterovesical peritoneum (Fig. 58.9). We think endometriosis is caused by a combination of hormone, genetic, and immune factors. Retrograde menstruation (menstrual blood and endometrial tissue flow backward into the pelvis during menses) may be a factor.

Endometriosis may be suspected based on manifestations of infertility, HMB, and pain. Pain may be chronic or occur during menses, intercourse, urination, or defecation. Tenderness or nodules in the pelvic region may be noted on physical assessment. Some patients may not have any symptoms but are diagnosed with endometriosis during fertility treatment or gynecologic surgery. Laparoscopy with biopsy is needed for a definitive diagnosis. Imaging such as ultrasound and MRI may be used to aid in the diagnosis.

Management includes both medical and surgical approaches. The treatment depends on the patient's age, desire for pregnancy, severity of symptoms, and extent and location of the disease. Drug therapy is used to relieve pain, reduce inflammation, and suppress endometrial tissue growth. Common agents include NSAIDs, hormonal contraceptives, aromatase inhibitors, and GnRH analogs (such as leuprolide [Lupron]).

The only cure for endometriosis is surgical removal of all endometrial tissue and adhesions. For women with infertility or who desire pregnancy, efforts are made to restore pelvic anatomy to allow the ovaries and fallopian tubes to work better. Therapy may involve removing implants blocking the fallopian tube. Adhesions are removed from the tubes, ovaries, and pelvic structures.

DRUG ALERT

Leuprolide (Lupron)

- Assess for pregnancy before starting therapy.
- Monitor for dysrhythmias, palpitations.
- Teach patient to use nonhormonal contraceptive measures during therapy.

Adenomyosis is the benign growth of endometrial tissue in the myometrium of the uterus. It is most common in middle-aged women. We do not know the cause. We describe

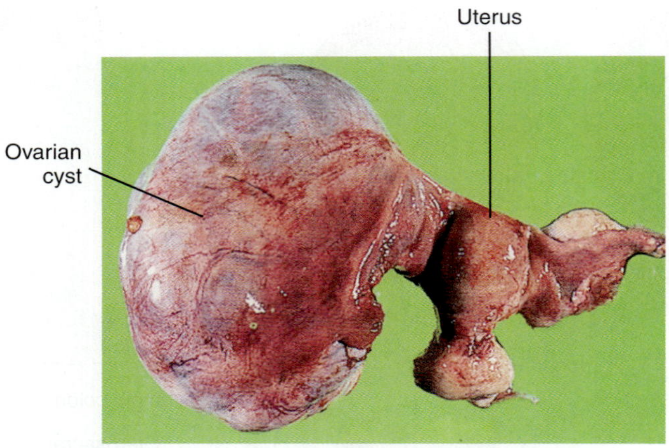

Fig. 58.10 Large ovarian cyst. (From Symonds EM, McPherson MBA: *Colour atlas of obstetrics and gynecology*, London, 1994, Mosby.)

adenomyosis as either diffuse or focal. In *diffuse adenomyosis*, endometrial tissue is found throughout the myometrial layer of the uterus. *Focal adenomyosis* consists of nodular lesions (called adenomyomas) confined to specific areas of the myometrium. The growth of endometrial tissue causes uterine enlargement and can lead to painful and heavy menstruation, pain during intercourse, or chronic pelvic pain. Diagnosis is made through pelvic ultrasound or MRI. Adenomyosis is often treated with hysterectomy. Uterine artery embolization or ablation can improve symptoms in some patients. Hormonal contraceptives and GnRH agonists are options for patients who prefer nonsurgical approaches.

Adnexal Masses

Adnexal masses are those found in the ovary, fallopian tube, or connective tissue. There are many different causes of adnexal masses. HCPs need to consider and assess for serious conditions such as ectopic pregnancy, TOA, or cancer. The most common benign adnexal masses are ovarian cysts and benign tumors.

Follicular or *corpus luteal cysts* are associated with normal, physiologic ovarian function (see Chapter 55). Occasionally, these cysts may become enlarged or painful (Fig. 58.10). Diagnosis is made by ultrasound or MRI. Cysts usually resolve spontaneously. In rare instances, complications such as rupture or torsion (being severely twisted) may cause pain and bleeding requiring surgical treatment.

Adnexal masses can also be caused by benign tumors, such as dermoid cysts or endometriomas. A dermoid cyst (teratoma) is an ovarian germ cell tumor. Patients with teratomas are often asymptomatic. The cysts may be identified incidentally on pelvic examination or imaging. Surgical removal of the cyst (cystectomy) is recommended since they may become cancerous. Endometriomas are a type of benign mass resulting from growth of endometrial tissue in the adnexal region. They are considered a form of endometriosis.

Pelvic Organ Prolapse

Pelvic organ prolapse is a common, benign condition in which the pelvic organs herniate to or beyond the vaginal walls. Types of prolapse include *cystocele* or urethrocele (prolapse of the bladder) (Fig. 58.11), *rectocele* or enterocele (bulging of the rectum in the vagina) (Fig. 58.12), and *uterine prolapse* (descent of the uterus into the vaginal canal). We describe uterine prolapse by degrees (Fig. 58.13). In first-degree prolapse, the cervix rests in the lower part of the vagina. Second-degree prolapse means the cervix is at the vaginal opening. Third-degree prolapse means the uterus protrudes through the introitus.

The cause of pelvic organ prolapse is pelvic floor dysfunction from weak pelvic floor muscles or connective tissue. Patients may have physiologic pelvic organ prolapse as they age. Other

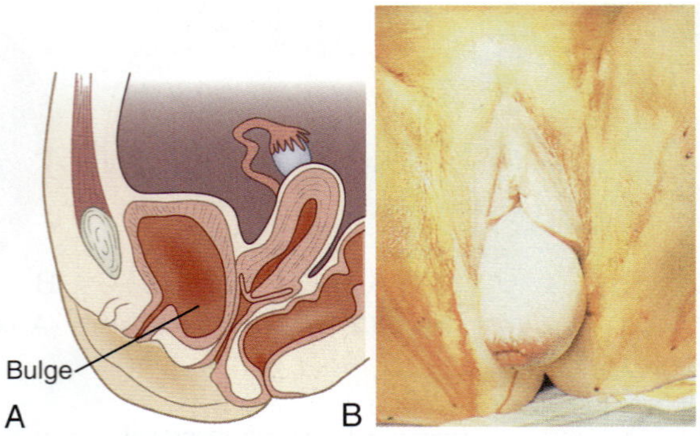

Fig. 58.11 (A) Cystocele. (B) Bladder has prolapsed into the vagina.

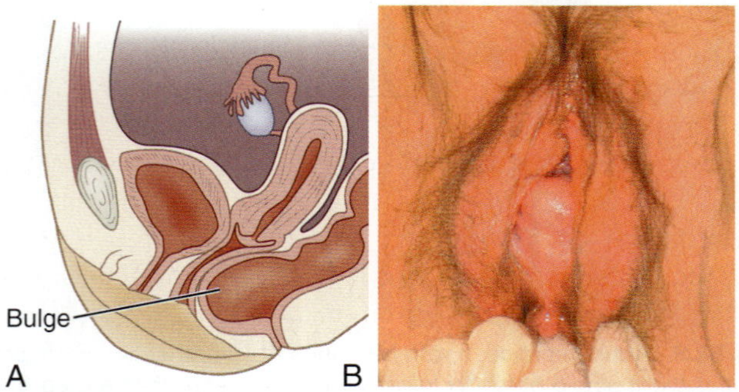

Fig. 58.12 (A) Rectocele. (B) Rectum has prolapsed into the vagina. (B, From Townsend CM: *Sabiston textbook of surgery*, ed 18, St. Louis, 2009, Mosby.)

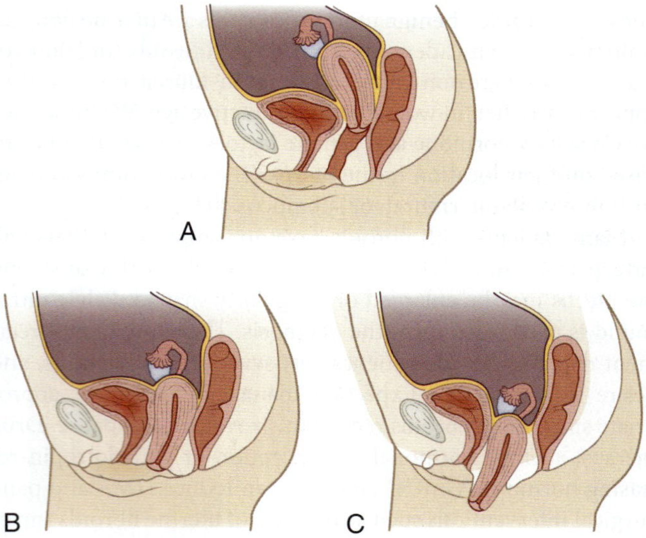

Fig. 58.13 Uterine prolapse. (A) First-degree. (B) Second-degree. (C) Third-degree.

TABLE 58.16 Symptoms of Gynecologic Cancers

Symptom	Cervical Cancer	Ovarian Cancer	Uterine Cancer	Vaginal Cancer	Vulvar Cancer
Abdominal or back pain		X			
Abnormal vaginal bleeding or discharge	X	X	X	X	
Bloating		X			
Changes in vulva color or skin, such as a rash, sores, or warts					X
Feeling full too quickly or difficulty eating		X			
Pelvic pain or pressure		X	X		
Urgent or frequent need to urinate and/or constipation		X		X	
Vulvar pain, itching, burning, tenderness of the vulva					X

Adapted from *CDC gynecological cancer symptoms*, CDC publication #22-0099, August 2016.

risk factors include having multiple pregnancies, history of vaginal births, obesity, connective tissue disorders, and chronic constipation.[12]

Some patients with pelvic organ prolapse have no symptoms. For others, this condition can be very uncomfortable and limit their quality of life and daily functioning. Pelvic pressure or bulging is a common concern. Other manifestations are difficulty with urination and defecation, decreased sexual function, and backache.

Evaluation starts with the history and physical assessment, including abdominal and pelvic examination. The assessment includes evaluation of pelvic floor function. The Pelvic Organ Prolapse Quantification (POP-Q) tool from the American Urogynecologic Society is used to assess and grade the stage of prolapse.[13]

A patient-centered approach is important to identify the severity and impact of symptoms and goals for treatment. Treatment is often unnecessary in the absence of bothersome symptoms such as pelvic pain/pressure, sexual dysfunction, or bowel or bladder dysfunction. In those cases, patient teaching and reassurance are appropriate. Lifestyle changes such as weight loss, managing constipation, and eliminating heavy lifting can improve minor symptoms. Nonsurgical interventions include pelvic floor physical therapy (see Table 50.18) or vaginal pessaries (a silicone supportive device inserted into the vagina, similar to a diaphragm). When these interventions are ineffective or symptoms are severe, surgery may be needed. Surgical options include hysterectomy, suspension of prolapsed organs, and repair of vaginal walls.

FISTULA

A *fistula* is an abnormal opening between internal organs or between an organ and the exterior of the body. Gynecologic procedures cause most urinary tract fistulas. Other causes include injury during childbirth and disease processes such as cancer. Fistulas may develop between the vagina and bladder, urethra, ureter, or rectum. When *vesicovaginal* fistulas (between the bladder and vagina) develop, some urine leaks into the vagina. With *rectovaginal* fistulas (between the rectum and vagina), flatus and feces escape into the vagina. In both instances, excoriation and irritation of the vaginal and vulvar tissues occur and may lead to severe infections. In addition to wetness, offensive odors may develop, causing embarrassment and limiting socialization.

Interprofessional and Nursing Management

Because small fistulas may heal spontaneously within a matter of months, treatment may not be needed. If the fistula does not heal, surgical repair is needed. The fistulectomy may result in the patient having an ileal conduit or temporary colostomy. Surgical repair is not always effective, even in the best conditions.

After surgery, emphasize ways to avoid stress on the repaired areas and prevent infection. Ensure the indwelling catheter, usually in place for 7 to 10 days, is patent. Encourage the patient to maintain an adequate fluid intake to provide for internal catheter irrigation. Change perineal pads often. Give stool softeners or mild laxatives as ordered. Our encouragement and reassurance help the patient cope.

FEMALE REPRODUCTIVE SYSTEM CANCERS

There are 5 main types of gynecologic cancer: cervical, ovarian, uterine, vaginal, and vulvar.[14] Combined, these cancers affect around 100,000 patients each year in the United States. While they are relatively rare compared to other forms of cancer, it is important to understand screening and diagnosis of gynecologic cancers. Signs and symptoms of gynecologic cancers are shown in Table 58.16. When cancer is present, patients are referred to gynecologic oncologists. Depending on the extent of the cancer, treatment options include surgery, chemotherapy, or radiation (see Chapter 16).

CERVICAL CANCER

Historically, cervical cancer was a common cause of cancer-related death. However, as cervical cancer screening and prevention measures have become widespread, the mortality rate from cervical cancer has significantly declined. One of the key measures in preventing cervical cancer is vaccination for high-risk strains of HPV, the leading cause of cervical cancer (see Chapter 57).

Cervical cancer is the only gynecologic cancer with a reliable screening approach. There is a 2-fold approach to screening for cervical cancer: (1) testing for the virus that causes most cervical cancer (HPV) and (2) screening for cellular changes to the

TABLE 58.17 Cervical Cancer Screening

Age	Recommendation
<21 years	No screening
21–29 years	Cervical cytology (Pap test) every 3 years
25-29 years	Human papillomavirus (HPV) testing alone may be an option, but Pap tests are preferred
30–65 years	3 options for screening: • Pap test every 3 years • HPV testing every 5 years • Co-testing (Pap test and HPV) every 5 years
>65 years	No screening after adequate negative prior screening results

Adapted from PDQ® Screening and Prevention Editorial Board: *PDQ cervical cancer screening*, Bethesda, MD, National Cancer Institute. Available at https://www.cancer.gov/types/cervical/patient/cervical-screening-pdq.

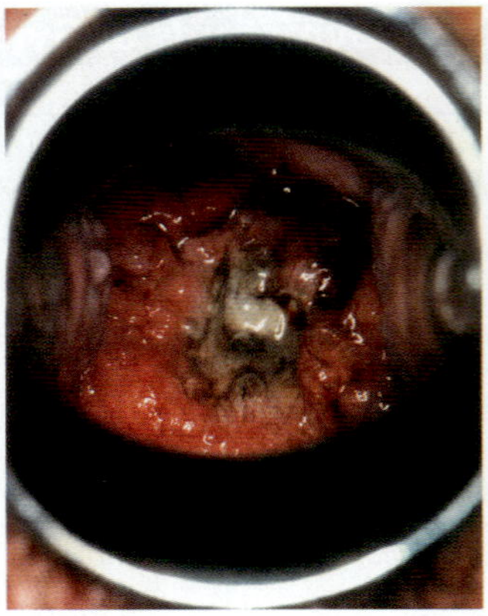

Fig. 58.14 Cervical cancer. (From Drake RL, et al.: *Gray's anatomy for students*, ed 2, Edinburgh, 2010, Churchill Livingstone.)

cervix (Pap test). The *Pap test* (also called Papanicolaou test or Pap smear) is a method of screening for precancerous or cancerous cervical lesions. The specimen is obtained through speculum examination and an endocervical sampler (e.g., spatula, brush). Testing for high-risk HPV infections (that cause these cervical cellular changes) can be done using the same technique. Cervical cancer screening options include either cytology (Pap test alone), primary HPV testing (HPV alone), or co-testing (both cytology and HPV testing).

There are different screening recommendations (Table 58.17). The US Preventive Services Task Force (USPSTF) supports screening all women between the ages of 21 to 29 years who have a cervix with cytology every 3 years. Between the ages 30 and 65, they recommend either screening every 3 years with cytology or every 5 years with either primary HPV testing or cotesting.[15] The American Cancer Society takes a slightly different approach.[16] These guidelines support screening in low-risk women with a cervix starting at 25 years of age. From ages 25 to 65, they recommend primary HPV testing every 5 years. If this option is not available, then cotesting every 5 years or cytology every 3 years are acceptable options. This approach maximizes outcomes and reduces unnecessary procedures in younger patients, in whom HPV often resolves spontaneously. Those at increased risk for cervical cancer due to immunosuppression, HIV infection, or in utero exposure to diethylstilbestrol (DES) may be screened more often.

Early cervical cancer often has no symptoms. An unusual discharge, AUB, or postcoital bleeding eventually occurs. The discharge is usually thin and watery but becomes dark and foul smelling as the disease advances. Vaginal bleeding first presents as spotting. As the tumor enlarges, bleeding becomes heavier and more frequent. Pain is a late symptom. It is followed by weight loss, anemia, and cachexia.

Management of abnormal findings should follow the American Society of Colposcopy and Cervical Pathology (ASCCP) guidelines.[17] The ASCCP has both an online and mobile app to guide HCPs in screening and management recommendations. The primary diagnostic method is colposcopy. *Colposcopy* is an outpatient procedure where the HCP examines the cervix using a magnification device (colposcope) after applying an acetic acid solution (Fig. 58.14). When abnormalities are seen on colposcopy, a biopsy may be done. Cryotherapy, loop electrosurgical excision procedure (LEEP), laser therapy, or cone biopsy can remove abnormal cells and prevent progression to cervical cancer. Treatment depends on the stage of the cancer and if fertility is a concern. The main treatment for early cancer is surgery or radiation therapy (Table 58.7). Care for more advanced cancer can include a combination of surgery, chemotherapy, and radiation.

OVARIAN CANCER

Ovarian cancer is the 5th leading cause of cancer death in women. Each year in the United States, around 21,000 women are diagnosed with ovarian cancer, and about 14,000 die. Ovarian cancer often affects pstmenopausal women. Risk factors include a personal or family history of cancer, genetic predisposition (Box 58.1), family history of Lynch syndrome (hereditary nonpolyposis colorectal cancer [HNPCC]), endometriosis, nulliparity (never having given birth), and infertility. Women who have given birth, breastfed, or used hormonal contraceptive pills for 5 or more years have a reduced risk of ovarian cancer. These factors may have a protective effect because they reduce the number of ovulatory cycles over the lifetime.

There are 3 major types of ovarian cancer. About 90% of ovarian cancers are epithelial cancers that arise from surface epithelial cells. Germ cell tumors account for another 3%, and sex cord stromal, 2%. Histologic grading is important to determine the prognosis. Intraperitoneal dissemination is common in ovarian cancer. It metastasizes to the uterus, bladder, bowel, and omentum. In advanced disease, it can spread to the stomach, colon, liver, and other parts of the body.

Early ovarian cancer usually has no obvious symptoms. There may be nonspecific symptoms such as pelvic or abdominal pain, bloating, urinary urgency or frequency, and difficulty eating or feeling full quickly. In later stages, abdominal enlargement with ascites (fluid in the abdominal cavity), unexplained weight loss or gain, nausea, and abnormal vaginal discharge or bleeding may occur. Adnexal mass or lymphadenopathy may be present on physical exam. A mass may also be identified on pelvic imaging such as ultrasound or MRI. No accurate screening test exists for early detection of ovarian cancer. For those

BOX 58.1 GENETICS IN CLINICAL PRACTICE

Ovarian Cancer and BRCA Genetic Mutations

Genetic Basis

- Normally these genes are tumor suppressor genes involved in DNA repair
- Transmission is autosomal dominant
- Mutations are passed down from either mother or father

Incidence

- About 15% of cases of ovarian cancer are related to *BRCA1* and *BRCA2* mutations.
- Women with *BRCA1* mutations have a 40% lifetime risk for developing ovarian cancer.
- Women with *BRCA2* mutations have a 15% lifetime risk for developing ovarian cancer.
- Family history of both breast and ovarian cancer increases the risk of having a BRCA mutation.

Genetic Testing

- DNA testing is available for *BRCA1/2* genetic mutations.
- All patients with ovarian cancer should be offered testing for *BRCA1/2* mutations.

Clinical Implications

- Genetic counseling and testing for *BRCA* mutations should be offered to those with a personal or family history that puts them at increased risk for ovarian cancer.
- Bilateral salpingectomy-oophorectomy reduces the risk for ovarian cancer in women with *BRCA1/2* mutations.

at increased risk, screening may include serum tumor marker CA-125 and pelvic ultrasound.

The CA-125 test is positive in 80% of women with advanced ovarian cancer. CA-125 is also used to monitor the course of the disease and response to treatment. The problem is that CA-125 levels can be high with other cancers (e.g., pancreatic cancer) or with benign gynecologic problems, including fibroids and endometriosis.

Options for high-risk women based on family and health history include prophylactic removal of the ovaries and fallopian tubes and the use of OCPs. While salpingo-oophorectomy significantly reduces the risk for ovarian cancer, it does not completely eliminate the risk for cancer in the peritoneum.

The initial treatment for all stages of ovarian cancer is a total abdominal hysterectomy and bilateral salpingo-oophorectomy (TAH-BSO) with removal of as much of the tumor as possible (e.g., tumor debulking). Depending on the grade and stage of cancer, treatment options include intraperitoneal and systemic chemotherapy, intraperitoneal instillation of radioisotopes, and external abdominal and pelvic radiation therapy. Combination chemotherapy and radiation therapy should be considered before a single-modality treatment.

The most used chemotherapy agents are taxanes (paclitaxel, docetaxel) and platinums (carboplatin, cisplatin). Among the targeted therapies used to treat advanced ovarian cancer are bevacizumab (Avastin), rucaparib (Rubraca), and olaparib (Lynparza). Rucaparib and olaparib are PARP inhibitors. They block enzymes involved in repairing damaged DNA. They are used for women with cancer associated with defective *BRCA* genes.

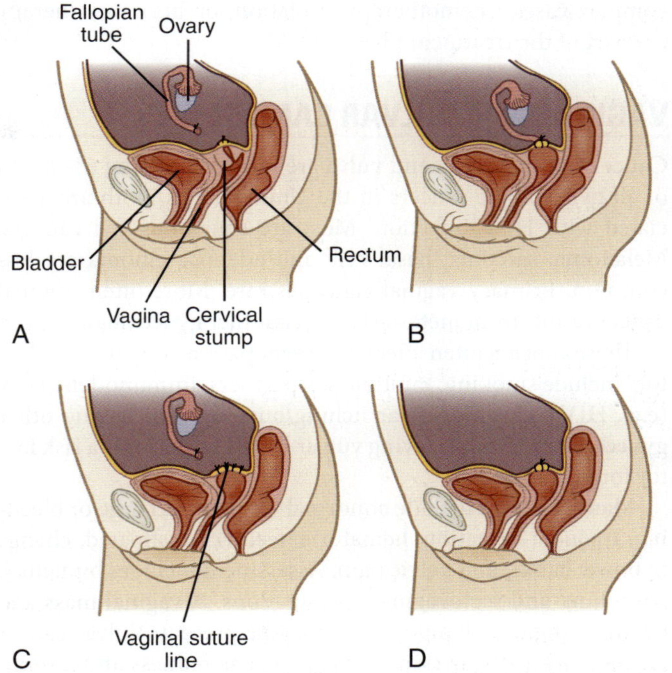

Fig. 58.15 Hysterectomies. (A) Subtotal hysterectomy. Cervical stump, fallopian tubes, and ovaries remain. (B) Total hysterectomy. Fallopian tubes and ovaries remain. (C) Vaginal hysterectomy. Fallopian tubes and ovaries remain. (D) Total hysterectomy, salpingectomy, and oophorectomy. Uterus, fallopian tubes, and ovaries are removed.

UTERINE CANCER

Uterine cancer is the most common gynecologic cancer in high-income countries. It is 2nd globally after cervical cancer. Cancer of the endometrium (lining of the uterus) is the most common site and type of uterine cancer. Other types of uterine cancer are rare, such as gestational trophoblastic tumors (hydatidiform mole) and uterine sarcoma. Endometrial cancer affects 1% to 2% of women in the United States, mainly those over 50.

The major risk factor for endometrial cancer is exposure to estrogen, especially unopposed estrogen therapy (without progesterone). Obesity is a risk factor because of increased estrogen in adipose tissue. Other risk factors include family history of cancer or Lynch syndrome, infertility, and use of tamoxifen. Protective factors include taking OCPs, breastfeeding, increased number of pregnancies, and physical activity.

AUB (especially postmenopause) is the classic sign of endometrial cancer. Other exam findings are often normal. Late symptoms can include dysuria, dyspareunia, unintentional weight loss, and pelvic pain. A thickened endometrium may be seen on ultrasound.

There is no routine screening test for uterine cancer. Diagnosis of endometrial cancer is based on tissue sampling, usually obtained by endometrial biopsy. Alternatively, HCPs may obtain a specimen using curettage or following hysterectomy. Most patients with endometrial cancer have a good prognosis due to early diagnosis. Surgery (total hysterectomy and bilateral salpingo-oophorectomy) is the main treatment for uterine cancer (Table 58.7). It is often curative (Fig. 58.15). For complex cases, chemotherapy, radiation, or hormone therapy are part of the treatment plan.

VAGINAL AND VULVAR CANCER

Cancers of the vagina and vulva are rare, comprising 6% to 7% of all gynecologic cancers in the United States. Both are associated with HPV infection. Most are squamous cell cancers. Melanoma, sarcoma, basal cell, and adenocarcinoma are less common. Primary vaginal cancer is rare. More often, vaginal cancer results from metastasis from another gynecologic cancer.

These cancers often affect postmenopausal women. Risk factors include smoking, multiple sex partners, immunodeficiency (e.g., HIV), chronic vulvar itching/burning, and having other gynecologic cancers. Having vulvar lichen sclerosus is a risk factor for vulvar cancer.

Manifestations include abnormal vaginal discharge or bleeding, frequent urination, hematuria, feeling constipated, change in bowel habits, and pelvic pain. Assessment includes bimanual, speculum, and rectovaginal examinations. A vaginal mass and enlarged inguinal lymph nodes may be present. Vulvar cancer presents with vulvar skin changes such as redness and lesions. Vulvar itching or burning, dysuria, dyspareunia, and pelvic pain may be present. Diagnostic evaluation often includes cytology, colposcopy, and biopsy. Treatment depends on the location, size, and stage of the cancer. Options include surgery, radiation, and/or chemotherapy.

NURSING MANAGEMENT: FEMALE REPRODUCTIVE SYSTEM CANCERS

The overall goals of nursing care are that the patient will (1) take part in treatment decisions, (2) achieve satisfactory pain and symptom management, (3) recognize and report complications, (4) maintain quality of life, and (5) practice cancer detection. Key concerns for the patient with gynecologic cancer include pain, disturbed body image, and impaired sexual functioning.

Health promotion is an important aspect of nursing care. Teach patients about the importance of HPV vaccination and cervical cancer screening. HPV vaccination can reduce the risk of vaginal and vulvar cancers. Teach about risk factors for cancers of the reproductive system. When high-risk behaviors are identified, help patients change their lifestyles to decrease risk.

Acute Intervention Related to Surgery

Types of surgery of the female reproductive tract are described in Table 58.7. All patients have a degree of anxiety while waiting for cancer surgery. The prospect of major gynecologic surgery increases these concerns. Some women may focus on the effect the surgery will have on their appearance and sexual functions. Discuss the woman's feelings and concerns about her surgery. Be willing to listen since this can provide considerable support.

Standard preoperative care includes perineal or abdominal preparation and urinary catheter insertion (see Chapter 18). After surgery, pain management, bowel and bladder care, and encouraging ambulation and exercise are important. Initiate venous thromboembolism (VTE) prophylaxis. Teach the patient about postoperative care and expectations for recovery. Radiation therapy is discussed in Chapter 16.

> **CHECK YOUR PRACTICE**
>
> You are working in the preoperative surgery holding unit. Your patient is a 60-year-old who is scheduled for a TAH-BSO for endometrial cancer. When you ask her how she is doing, she tells you that she is worried because "life will never be the same."
>
> - How would you approach this situation?
> - What information would you provide?

Sexual Dysfunction

Female sexual response is a complex process affected by multiple biologic, psychological, cultural, and environmental factors. **Sexual dysfunction** is a complication of sexual desire, arousal, orgasm, or pain that causes personal distress. Out of every 8 women, 1 reports sexual dysfunction. It can strongly affect quality of life. Common types of sexual dysfunction include sexual interest/arousal disorder, orgasmic disorder, genitopelvic pain/penetration disorder, and medication-induced sexual dysfunction.

There are many potential causes of sexual dysfunction. They include psychological issues (e.g., anxiety, relationship stress), medication or substance use (e.g., SSRIs, hormone agents), medical problems (e.g., diabetes, hypertension), structural problems (e.g., female genital mutilation, gynecologic surgery), gynecologic problems (e.g., endometriosis, uterine fibroids), and physiologic changes (e.g., breastfeeding, menopause).[18] Sexual dysfunction may also be caused by a combination of personal or relationship factors.

Women with sexual dysfunction may present with concerns of low libido or sexual arousal, difficulty in achieving orgasm, genital or pelvic pain, pain with penetration, medication- or substance-induced changes in sexual response, or other distress with sexual activities.

Given the complexity and sensitivity of sexual dysfunction, it may be appropriate to provide a referral to an HCP with experience in female sexual medicine for assessment, diagnosis, and treatment. Assessment begins with the history, including gynecologic, obstetric, sexual, menstrual, and psychiatric histories. Symptom diaries and symptom checklists can help to define the extent and type of dysfunction. Physical assessment may include speculum and pelvic examination. In the absence of underlying medical conditions, laboratory tests are not part of diagnosing sexual dysfunction.

The management is patient-centered and specific to the condition. A team approach may be needed. This may include counseling, sex education and sexual skills training, physical therapy, and gynecologic care. Stress reduction, cognitive–behavioral therapy, and relationship counseling are often important aspects of treatment. Teaching anatomy, sexual response, and methods to achieve sexual health goals can improve sexual functioning. Pelvic floor physical therapy can reduce pain.

Management includes both drugs and nonpharmacologic treatment options. If the patient takes drugs associated with sexual dysfunction, such as certain antidepressants or antipsychotics, they may be discontinued. Hormone therapy or use of ospemifene (Osphena), a selective estrogen receptor modulator [SERM]), may help with sexual dysfunction due to menopause or estrogen deficiency. Transdermal testosterone, flibanserin (Addyi), a serotonin receptor agonist/antagonist, or bremelanotide (Vyleesi), a melanocortin receptor agonist, may be used to treat sexual interest and arousal disorders. Bupropion, an antidepressant, may be appropriate for dysfunction associated with psychological conditions. Vaginal lubricants and moisturizers, topical anesthesia, and vaginal dilators can improve pain symptoms.

Nursing care starts with an understanding of normal female sexual response. Approach patients with a non-judgmental, sex-positive attitude to support patients in discussing their concerns. Provide teaching about sexual health and functioning. Suggest books or other appropriate resources for additional information. Review safe sex practices and measures to prevent unintended pregnancy. Teach patients about lifestyle changes to support sexual health and well-being. Encourage patients to follow treatment plans. Provide sexual medicine specialists, sex or couples therapists, or pelvic floor physical therapy referrals. Follow up to assess the effectiveness of treatment and next steps to promote sexual health.

SEXUAL ASSAULT

Sexual violence is any sexual activity in which consent was not freely given. It is a serious public health problem that affects millions of people each year. Nearly 1 in 3 women will experience some form of sexual violence in their lifetime. Sexual violence may take many forms, such as unwanted sexual contact, sexual coercion, or rape. Persons of all ages, races, genders, sexual orientations, and socioeconomic statuses experience sexual violence. It has long-lasting consequences on physical and mental health. Nurses play an important role in caring for survivors of sexual violence in both the short and long term. This section focuses on gynecologic nursing care for women who have been recent victims of sexual assault.

Sexual assault is nonconsensual sexual contact, such as penetration of the victim's body. The terms sexual assault and rape are often used interchangeably. Rape is completed or attempted nonconsensual vaginal, anal, or oral penetration, no matter how slight, with any object or part of the body (such as a finger or penis). There are many complex factors associated with an increased risk of sexual assault. Most often, sexual assault is committed by someone known to the victim. The perpetrator is a stranger in only about 20% of cases.

Many victims will not seek medical attention. Others may wait days or even weeks after the assault to seek care. Victims may present with physical trauma or injury on any area of the body, in addition to psychological trauma. A medical forensic exam may be needed to collect evidence. You should be familiar with the legal definition of sexual crimes and rape in your state.[19] A forensic examination is not mandatory. It requires informed consent. HCPs may be asked to testify if sexual assault charges are filed.

Nursing care for a sexual assault victim is complex. Due to the unique needs of caring for sexual assault victims, involve a specially trained provider such as a sexual assault nurse examiner (SANE). Assessment of victims of sexual assault includes (1) treatment of acute traumatic injuries including anogenital injuries, (2) evaluation for STIs, (3) pregnancy screening and prevention, (4) assessment and support for psychological health, and (5) forensic examination (Table 58.18).

First, we must establish consent for care and ensure the patient's physical and psychological safety. Caring for any acute traumatic injuries or urgent medical problems is the priority. Once the patient is stable, contact appropriate services such as a social worker, psychiatric HCP, rape advocate, medical forensic examiner, or SANE. Explain that you are not offering to clean

TABLE 58.18 Assessment of Victims of Sexual Assault

1. Medicolegal
   - Informed consent for assessment and care
   - Informed consent for forensic examination and collection of evidence
   - Appropriate "chain of evidence" documentation
2. History
   - Details of the assault (who, what, when, where)
   - Activities since assault that may affect evidence collection (e.g., changed clothes, showered, douched)
   - Review of symptoms, including any loss of consciousness or memory loss
   - Alcohol or drug intake
   - Health history including menstrual, gynecologic, contraceptive, sexual, and immunization history
3. Physical assessment
   - Vital signs and general appearance
   - Psychological assessment
   - Extragenital and/or anogenital trauma (e.g., bruising, lacerations, abrasions, edema, redness)
   - Pelvic and speculum examination
4. Laboratory tests and diagnostic imaging
   - STI testing (e.g., HIV, hepatitis B, syphilis, chlamydia, gonorrhea, trichomonas)
   - Microscopic analysis of vaginal fluids
   - Pregnancy test
   - Toxicology, as appropriate for victims who may have been drugged
   - Radiology for trauma assessment
5. Forensic samples
   - Clothing
   - Anogenital and/or oral swabs
   - Combed specimens from scalp or pubic hair
   - Fingernail scrapings or clippings
   - Blood, urine, saliva, and hair samples
6. Treatment considerations
   - Care of any traumatic injuries and pain management
   - Empiric treatment for STIs (e.g., gonorrhea, chlamydia)
   - PEP treatment for HIV
   - Tetanus and hepatitis B boosters
   - Emergency contraception
   - HPV vaccination
   - Psychological support and referrals for mental health services
   - Protection of legal rights and compliance with mandatory reporting based on local requirements
   - Recommendation of continued follow-up and services of rape crisis center

the patient until evidence has been collected. Collaborate with the health care team to obtain a history, perform a physical assessment, and collect forensic evidence. Monitor vital signs and emotional status. Provide emotional support. Perform baseline screening for HIV and STIs. Teach patients that it is often not possible to assess for STIs after a recent sexual assault and stress the importance of seeking follow-up care for this screening. Discuss pregnancy prevention measures such as emergency contraception. Provide referrals for counseling services and follow-up care.

Case Study

PCOS

(© Juanmonino/iStock.com.)

Patient Profile

B.C., a 26-year-old female, presents with difficulty getting pregnant. She states she and her male partner have been trying to conceive for almost a year. She has never been pregnant and has no history of STIs. She reports menarche at age 14, irregular menses, and no periods in the past 3 months. She states she hoped she might be pregnant but has had multiple negative urine pregnancy tests. She has been feeling somewhat depressed and has not been sleeping well for the past year. She is not currently taking any drugs and reports no allergies.

Subjective Data

- History of chronic hypertension
- No reports of pelvic or urinary pain, vaginal discharge, or bleeding
- Denies nausea, breast tenderness, fatigue
- Recent weight gain (20 pounds in the past 6 months)

Objective Data

- BP 140/92 mm Hg, pulse 82 beats/min, respirations 14 breaths/min
- Height 5 ft, 6 in; weight 187 lb; BMI 30 kg/m^2
- Acne, facial hair present on upper lip and chin
- Normal pelvic and speculum examination

Diagnostic Studies

- Pregnancy test negative
- Depression screen negative
- Total testosterone and 17-hydroxyprogesterone within normal limits

Plan of Care

- Weight loss, diet, and exercise
- Referral for counseling and infertility treatment

Discussion Questions

1. ***Recognize:*** What criteria are needed to make a diagnosis of PCOS?
2. ***Analyze:*** What is the relationship between PCOS and infertility?
3. ***Plan:*** B.C. asks you about her chances of conceiving without fertility treatments. How would you respond, and what type of teaching would you provide?
4. ***Prioritize:*** Based on the assessment data, what are the priority clinical problems?
5. ***Act:*** B.C. doesn't understand how her weight gain, facial hair, and sleeping problems are related to her irregular periods and difficulty getting pregnant. How would you help her understand her condition and the recommended treatment?
6. ***Safety:*** What measures can B.C. take to avoid long-term health complications associated with PCOS?

Answers available at http://evolve.elsevier.com/Lewis/medsurg.

BRIDGE TO NCLEX EXAMINATION

The number of the question corresponds to the same-numbered outcome at the beginning of the chapter.

1. A 33-year-old patient expresses difficulty in achieving pregnancy and asks when a fertility evaluation is appropriate. The nurse advises a formal evaluation is appropriate after
   a. 35 years of age.
   b. 1 or more spontaneous pregnancy losses.
   c. 12 months of regular, unprotected intercourse.
   d. 6 months of lifestyle and behavioral modifications.
2. The nurse reviews the ultrasound report for a woman with a suspected ectopic pregnancy, knowing that it is most often located in the
   a. cervix.
   b. ovaries.
   c. endometrium.
   d. fallopian tube.
3. An appropriate question to ask a patient with painful menstruation to distinguish primary from secondary dysmenorrhea is
   a. "When did you start experiencing painful menstruation?"
   b. "Does your pain become worse with activity or overexertion?"
   c. "Have you had a recent personal crisis or change in your lifestyle?"
   d. "Do non-steroidal antiinflammatory drugs (NSAIDs) like ibuprofen help your pain?"
4. The nurse teaching a woman with an intact uterus about hormone therapy states that it is essential to
   a. start vitamin E and B-complex supplements.
   b. use vaginal lubricants in penetrative sexual activities.
   c. avoid selective serotonin reuptake inhibitor antidepressant agents.
   d. take progesterone with estrogen to reduce the risk of endometrial cancer.
5. The nurse suspects that the patient with vaginal itching and thick, curdy, white discharge most likely has
   a. chlamydia.
   b. bacterial vaginosis.
   c. human papilloma virus.
   d. vulvovaginal candidiasis.
6. In caring for a patient with endometriosis, the nurse teaches that common interventions to treat this condition include *(select all that apply)*
   a. NSAIDs.
   b. antibiotics.
   c. oral contraceptives.
   d. intrauterine device.
   e. surgical removal of tissue.

7. Teaching about cancer prevention includes information that the only gynecologic cancer with reliable routine screening is cancer of the
   a. cervix.
   b. uterus.
   c. vagina.
   d. ovaries.
8. The *first* nursing intervention for a patient who has been sexually assaulted is to
   a. contact a support person.
   b. treat acute traumatic injuries.
   c. examine and document anogenital trauma.
   d. collect specimens for forensic examination.

1. c; 2. d; 3. a; 4. d; 5. d; 6. a, c, e; 7. a; 8. b.

For rationales to these answers and even more NCLEX review questions, visit http://evolve.elsevier.com/Lewis/medsurg.

EVOLVE WEBSITE/RESOURCES LIST

http://evolve.elsevier.com/Lewis/medsurg
Review Questions (Online Only)
Key Points
Answer Keys for Questions
- Rationales for Bridge to NCLEX Examination Questions
- Answer Guidelines for Case Study

Student Case Study
- Patient With PCOS

Nursing Care Plan(s)
- eNursing Care Plan 58.1: Patient Having Abdominal Hysterectomy

Conceptual Care Map Creator
Audio Glossary
Content Updates

REFERENCES

*1. Practice Committee of the American Society for Reproductive Medicine: Definitions of infertility and recurrent pregnancy loss: a committee opinion, *Fertil Steril* 113:583, 2020.
*2. American College of Obstetricians and Gynecologists: Infertility workup for the women's health specialist: ACOG Committee opinion, number 781, *Obstet Gynecol* 133:e377, 2019.
3. RESOLVE: The National Infertility Association. Retrieved from https://resolve.org/.
*4. Innovative Education in Reproductive Health: Early pregnancy loss: managing, counseling, and diagnosis. Retrieved from https://www.innovating-education.org/course/early-pregnancy-loss/.
5. US Food and Drug Administration: Post market drug safety information for patients and providers: Mifeprex (mifepristone) information. Retrieved from https://www.fda.gov/drugs/postmarket-drug-safety-information-patients-and-providers/mifeprex-mifepristone-information.
6. Abortion Care Network: Find a clinic. Retrieved from https://abortioncarenetwork.org/find-a-clinic/.
*7. National Center for Complementary and Integrative Health: Chasteberry. Retrieved from https://www.nccih.nih.gov/health/chasteberry.
*8. Kaunitz AM: Abnormal uterine bleeding in reproductive-age women, *JAMA* 321:2126, 2019.
9. National PCOS Association: PCOS challenge. Retrieved from https://pcoschallenge.com/.
*10. North American Menopause Society. Retrieved from https://www.menopause.org.
11. American Society for Reproductive Medicine: Endometriosis examples. Retrieved from https://www.reproductivefacts.org/resources/educational-videos/videos/full-length-videos/videos/endometriosis/.
*12. American College of Obstetricians and Gynecologists and the American Urogynecologic Society: Pelvic organ prolapse, *FPMRS* 25:397, 2019.
13. American Urogynecologic Society: POP-Q interactive assessment tool. Retrieved from https://www.augs.org/patient-services/pop-q-tool/.
*14. Centers for Disease Control and Prevention: Gynecologic cancers. Retrieved from https://www.cdc.gov/cancer/gynecologic/index.htm.
*15. Curry SJ, Krist AH, Owens DK, et al.: Screening for cervical cancer: US preventive services task force recommendation statement, *JAMA* 320:674, 2018.
*16. Fontham ETH, Wolf AMD, Church TR, et al.: Cervical cancer screening for individuals at average risk: 2020 guideline update from the American Cancer Society, *CA Cancer J Clin* 70:321, 2020.
*17. Perkins RB, Guido RS, Castle PR, et al.: 2019 ASCCP risk-based management consensus guidelines for abnormal cervical cancer screening tests and cancer precursors, *J Low Genit Tract Dis* 24:102, 2020.
*18. American College of Obstetricians and Gynecologists' Committee on Practice Bulletins—Gynecology: ACOG practice bulletin no. 213: female sexual dysfunction, *Obstet Gynecol* 134:203, 2019.
19. RAINN (Rape, Abuse, & Incest National Network): State law database. Retrieved from https://apps.rainn.org/policy/.

*Evidence-based information for clinical practice.

59

Male Reproductive Problems

Anthony Lutz

http://evolve.elsevier.com/Lewis/medsurg/

CONCEPTUAL FOCUS

Cellular Regulation
Infection
Pain
Reproduction
Sexuality

LEARNING OUTCOMES

1. Describe the pathophysiology, clinical manifestations, and interprofessional and nursing management of benign prostatic hyperplasia.
2. Describe the pathophysiology, clinical manifestations, and interprofessional care of prostate cancer.
3. Explain the nursing management of prostate cancer.
4. Specify the pathophysiology, clinical manifestations, and interprofessional and nursing management of prostatitis and problems of the penis and scrotum.
5. Explain the clinical manifestations and interprofessional care of testicular cancer.
6. Describe the pathophysiology, clinical manifestations, and interprofessional and nursing management of problems related to male sexual function.
7. Discuss the psychologic and emotional implications related to male reproductive problems.

KEY TERMS

benign prostatic hyperplasia (BPH)
epididymitis
erectile dysfunction (ED)
orchitis
paraphimosis
phimosis
prostate cancer
prostatitis
radical prostatectomy
testicular cancer
testicular torsion
transurethral resection of the prostate (TURP)
vasectomy

This chapter discusses male reproductive system problems. These involve a variety of structures, including the prostate, penis, urethra, testes, epididymis, and rectum (Fig. 59.1). Many of these problems can profoundly affect sexuality and reproduction. Sexual dysfunction from prostate problems or erectile dysfunction (ED) can cause psychologic and body image problems. The patient may have anxiety because of a perceived loss of his sex role, self-esteem, or quality of sexual interaction with his partner. Patient teaching and counseling are essential for promoting health and optimal sexual well-being.

PROBLEMS OF THE PROSTATE GLAND

BENIGN PROSTATIC HYPERPLASIA

Benign prostatic hyperplasia (BPH) is a condition in which the prostate gland increases in size, disrupting the outflow of urine from the bladder through the urethra. Half of men will have some signs of BPH by the age of 50. That number increases to more than 70% for men 60 to 69 years old.[1]

Etiology and Pathophysiology

There are several factors that may play a role in the development and progression of BPH. We think that hormonal changes associated with aging are a contributing factor. Dihydroxytestosterone (DHT), one of several sex hormones, stimulates prostate cell growth. Excess DHT can cause overgrowth of prostate tissue. As men age, they continue to make and accumulate high levels of DHT, resulting in prostate enlargement.

Another possible cause of BPH is an increased proportion of estrogen as compared with testosterone. Throughout their lives, men make testosterone and small amounts of estrogen. As men age, the amount of testosterone they make decreases, leaving a higher proportion of estrogen. A higher amount of estrogen

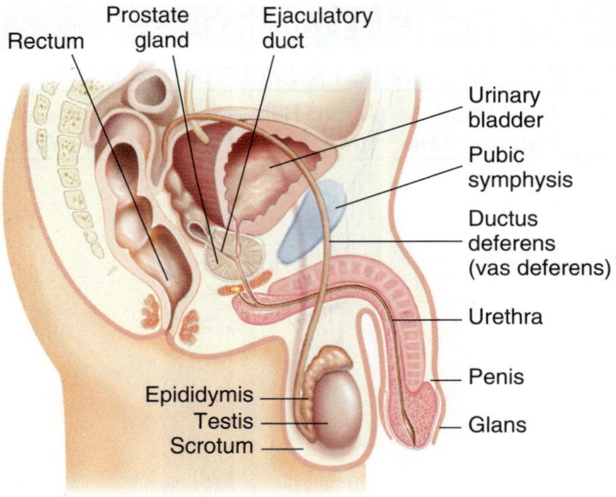

Fig. 59.1 Areas of the male reproductive system in which problems are likely to develop.

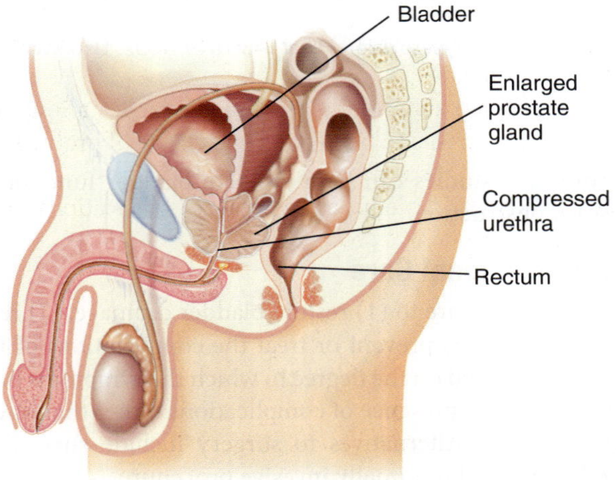

Fig. 59.2 BPH. The enlarged prostate compresses the urethra.

within the prostate gland increases the activity of substances (including DHT) that promote prostate cell growth.

BPH usually develops in the inner part of the prostate, called the transition zone. As the transition zone of the prostate enlarges, it gradually compresses the urethra, leading to partial or complete obstruction (Fig. 59.2). This compression of the urethra leads to the development of clinical manifestations. There is no direct relationship between overall prostate size and the severity of manifestations or degree of obstruction.[2] The location of the enlargement is most significant in the development of obstructive symptoms (Fig. 59.3). For example, it is possible for mild prostate enlargement to cause severe obstructive symptoms or for extreme prostate enlargement to cause few obstructive symptoms.

Risk factors for BPH include aging, obesity (especially increased waist circumference), lack of physical activity, a high intake of red meat and animal fat, alcohol use, ED, smoking, and diabetes.[3] A family history of BPH in a first-degree relative also may be a risk factor.

Clinical Manifestations

Manifestations occur gradually. They may go unnoticed until prostate enlargement has been present for some time. Early symptoms may not cause many problems because the bladder can compensate for a small amount of resistance to urine flow. As the severity of urethral obstruction increases, symptoms gradually worsen.

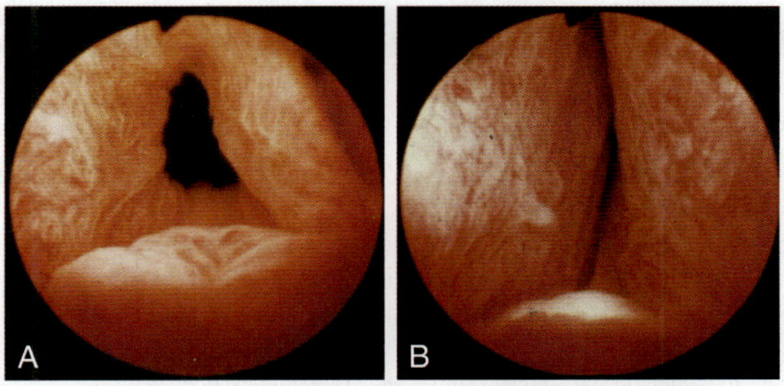

Fig. 59.3 Views of the prostate by cystoscopy. (A) Normal appearance. (B) Moderate BPH with urethral obstruction. (From Townsend CM, Beauchamp RD, Evers BM, et al.: *Sabiston textbook of surgery,* ed 19, Philadelphia, 2012, Saunders.)

We place symptoms into 2 groups: irritative and obstructive. *Irritative symptoms* include nocturia, urinary frequency, urgency, dysuria, bladder pain, and incontinence. These symptoms are related to inflammation or infection. Nocturia is often the first symptom that the patient notices. *Obstructive symptoms,* caused by prostate enlargement, include a decrease in the caliber and force of the urinary stream, difficulty in starting a stream, intermittency (stopping and starting stream several times while voiding), and dribbling at the end of urination. These symptoms are due to the increased effort of the bladder as it tries to empty through the decreased diameter of the urethra. As a group, both irritative and obstructive symptoms are considered lower urinary tract symptoms (LUTS).

The American Urological Association (AUA) symptom index (AUA-SI) for BPH (Table 59.1) is a widely used tool to assess voiding symptoms from obstruction.[4] This tool is not diagnostic. It helps determine the extent of symptoms and guide treatment. Higher scores on this tool mean greater symptom severity.

Complications

Some men may have acute urinary retention. They will have the sudden and painful inability to urinate. Treatment involves the inserting a catheter to drain the bladder. Surgery may be needed in severe situations. Bladder damage can occur if treatment is delayed.

Urinary tract infection (UTI) can be a complication of BPH. Since the bladder is unable to empty completely, bacteria can grow in the residual urine that remains in the bladder and cause infection. In more severe cases, infection can progress into the kidney and cause pyelonephritis. In severe cases, infection can spread into the bloodstream and sepsis can develop. Bladder calculi (stones) may develop because of the alkalinization of the residual urine. So, the finding of bladder stones often indicates obstruction related to BPH.

Renal failure can occur due to *hydronephrosis* (distention of the renal pelvis and calyces by urine that cannot flow through the ureter to the bladder).

TABLE 59.1 AUA Symptom Index to Determine Severity of Prostatic Problems

	AUA SYMPTOM SCORE[a] (CIRCLE 1 NUMBER ON EACH LINE)					
Questions	**Not At All**	**Less Than 1 Time in 5**	**Less Than Half the Time**	**About Half the Time**	**More Than Half the Time**	**Almost Always**
Over the Past Month						
1. How often do you have the sensation that your bladder is not completely empty after you finish urinating?	0	1	2	3	4	5
2. How often do you have to urinate again, less than 2 hr after you finish urinating?	0	1	2	3	4	5
3. How often do you stop and start again several times when you urinate?	0	1	2	3	4	5
4. How often do you find it difficult to postpone urination?	0	1	2	3	4	5
5. How often do you have a weak urinary stream?	0	1	2	3	4	5
6. How often do you have to push or strain to begin urination?	0	1	2	3	4	5
7. How many times do you usually get up to urinate from the time you go to bed at night until the time you get up in the morning?	0 (None)	1 (1 time)	2 (2 times)	3 (3 times)	4 (4 times)	5 (5 times or more)
Sum of circled numbers (AUA Symptom Score): _____						

[a]Score is interpreted as follows: 0–7, mild; 8–19, moderate; 20–35, severe.
Source: Barry MJ, Fowler FJ, O'Leary MP, et al.: The AUA symptom index for benign prostatic hyperplasia, *J Urol* 148:1549, 1992. Used with permission.

Diagnostic Studies

A detailed history and physical assessment are important. Diagnostic studies are outlined in Table 59.2. A digital rectal examination (DRE) is done to estimate the prostate size, symmetry, and consistency. In BPH, the prostate is symmetrically enlarged, firm, and smooth.

A urinalysis (UA) and urine culture with sensitivities can detect bacteria, nitrites, leukocyte esterase, white blood cells (WBCs), or microscopic hematuria (RBCs), which could indicate infection or inflammation.

A prostate-specific antigen (PSA) blood test can screen for prostate cancer. Patients with BPH may have slightly increased PSA levels. PSA is released into the bloodstream by both benign and malignant prostate cells. Serum creatinine levels can assess for renal insufficiency. If creatinine levels are high, a renal ultrasound may show hydronephrosis. Because symptoms of BPH and neurogenic bladder are similar, a neurologic examination may be done.

In patients with an abnormal DRE and high PSA, a transrectal ultrasound (TRUS) can be ordered as a stand-alone imaging test. We more often do a TRUS-guided prostate biopsy. An alternative option is a pelvic MRI with attention to the prostate. If abnormal areas are seen on MRI, these areas can be targeted on a TRUS prostate biopsy (MRI-fusion targeted biopsy). Insurance coverage of pelvic MRI is sometimes an issue. Studies have shown that assessment with MRI prior to biopsy and MRI-targeted biopsy are better than standard TRUS biopsy in men at risk for prostate cancer.[5]

Uroflowmetry (measures the volume of urine expelled from the bladder) is helpful to determine the extent of urethral blockage and the treatment needed. Postvoid residual urine volume can determine the degree of urine flow obstruction. Cystoscopy is done if the diagnosis is unclear or to see the degree of prostatic enlargement. If the diagnostic picture is unclear, urodynamic/pressure flow studies can help evaluate bladder function and assess for obstruction.

Interprofessional Care

The goals of care are to (1) restore bladder drainage, (2) relieve symptoms, and (3) prevent or treat the complications of BPH. Treatment is based on the degree to which the symptoms bother the patient or the presence of complications rather than the size of the prostate. Alternatives to surgery include surveillance, drug therapy, and minimally invasive procedures.

The most conservative treatment is called *active surveillance*, or watchful waiting. When the patient has mild symptoms (AUA symptom scores of 0 to 7), we usually take a wait-and-see approach. Teaching patients to make lifestyle changes can help relieve early or mild symptoms. Making diet changes (decreasing intake of bladder irritants, like caffeine, alcohol, carbonated drinks, artificial sweeteners, and spicy or acidic foods), avoiding certain drugs (e.g., decongestants, anticholinergics), and restricting evening fluid intake may improve symptoms. A timed voiding schedule (also called "bladder retraining") may reduce symptoms and eliminate the need for further treatment. If the patient begins to have signs or symptoms that indicate an increase in obstruction, further treatment is needed.

Drug Therapy

The 2 main classes of drugs to treat BPH include 5α-reductase inhibitors and α-adrenergic receptor blockers. Combination therapy using both types of drugs may be more effective in reducing symptoms than using 1 drug alone. An erectogenic drug can also be used to help treat BPH.

5α-reductase inhibitors. 5α-Reductase inhibitors work by reducing the size of the prostate gland. They block the 5α-reductase type 1 and 2 isoenzymes, which are necessary for the conversion of testosterone to DHT (main intraprostatic

TABLE 59.2 Interprofessional Care

BPH

Diagnostic Assessment

- History and physical assessment with DRE
- UA and urine culture and sensitivities
- PSA
- Serum creatinine
- Postvoid residual (by ultrasound)
- Renal ultrasound (if increased serum creatinine, evaluate for hydronephrosis)
- TRUS
- Uroflowmetry
- Cystoscopy
- Urodynamic/pressure flow studies

Management

Active Surveillance

- Annual PSA and DRE
- Repeat AUA symptom score and postvoid residual if any symptoms change

Drug Therapy

- 5α-Reductase inhibitors (e.g., dutasteride, finasteride)
- α-Adrenergic receptor blockers (e.g., alfuzosin, doxazosin, tamsulosin)
- Combination 5α-reductase inhibitor and α-adrenergic receptor blocker (e.g., dutasteride plus tamsulosin [Jalyn])
- Erectogenic drugs (e.g., tadalafil)

Minimally Invasive Therapy (Table 59.3)

- Laser enucleation of the prostate (HoLEP or ThuLEP)
- Photoselective vaporization of the prostate (PVP)
- Prostatic urethral lift (PUL)
- Transurethral microwave thermotherapy (TUMT)
- Transurethral needle ablation (TUNA)
- Water vapor thermal therapy

Surgical Therapy (Table 59.3)

- Transurethral incision of the prostate (TUIP)
- Transurethral resection of the prostate (TURP)
- Simple prostatectomy (open, laparoscopic, robotic assisted)

androgen). Prostate size is directly related to the amount of DHT. By blocking DHT, overly enlarged prostates can decrease in size. These agents are more effective for men with larger prostates who have bothersome symptoms.

Finasteride (Proscar) inhibits only the type 2 isoenzyme. It is an appropriate treatment for men who have a moderate to severe symptom score on the AUA-SI (Table 59.1). Although most men who are treated with the drug have symptom improvement, it can take 6 months to be effective. It must be taken on a regular basis to have an effect. Because it blocks the enzyme needed for conversion of testosterone to DHT, decreased libido is a common side effect.

Serum PSA levels may appear decreased by 50% when taking finasteride. Therefore, to "correct" for the apparent decrease caused by finasteride, the HCP should double the PSA value for a patient who has been on a 5α-reductase inhibitor for at least 6 months. This allows for a more accurate comparison to premedication PSA levels. Dutasteride (Avodart) has the same effect on prostatic tissue as finasteride. It is a dual inhibitor of 5α-reductase types 1 and 2 isoenzymes.

These drugs may lower the risk for some prostate cancers. However, using them to prevent prostate cancer is not recommended, and research is ongoing. Patients who develop a high PSA level while taking these drugs should have further evaluation. Encourage the patient to discuss the need for prostate cancer screening with the HCP.

DRUG ALERT

Finasteride (Proscar)

- Women who may be or are pregnant should not touch tablets due to potential risk to male fetus (anomaly).

α-Adrenergic receptor blockers. α-Adrenergic receptor blockers are another drug treatment option for BPH. These drugs selectively block α_1-adrenergic receptors, which are abundant in the prostate and increased in hyperplastic prostate tissue. They offer symptom relief by relaxing the smooth muscle of the prostate that surrounds the urethra, thus facilitating urinary flow through the urethra. These agents do not decrease the size of the prostate.

α-Adrenergic blockers include alfuzosin (Uroxatral), doxazosin (Cardura), prazosin (Minipress), tamsulosin (Flomax), and silodosin (Rapaflo). Symptom improvement can often be seen within days to weeks of starting therapy. Because they relax the smooth muscle of the prostatic urethra, a common side effect is retrograde ejaculation. The combination of a 5α-reductase inhibitor (dutasteride) and an α-adrenergic receptor blocker (tamsulosin) is available in a single oral medication (Jalyn).

Erectogenic drugs. Tadalafil (Cialis) can be used in men who have symptoms of BPH alone or in combination with ED. It can be effective in reducing symptoms for both conditions.

Herbal therapy. Some patients take plant extracts, such as saw palmetto *(Serenoa repens)*. However, research shows that saw palmetto has no benefit over a placebo.[6] Advise patients to discuss herbal therapies with their HCP.

Minimally Invasive Therapy

Minimally invasive therapies are becoming more common as an alternative to watchful waiting and surgery (Table 59.3). A benefit of these procedures is a decreased length of stay in the hospital. They are associated with fewer adverse events. Many minimally invasive therapies have outcomes comparable to surgery.

Photoselective vaporization of the prostate. *Photoselective vaporization of the prostate* (PVP) uses a high-power green laser light to vaporize prostate tissue. Laser therapy through visual or ultrasound guidance is an effective alternative to transurethral resection of the prostate (TURP). The laser beam is delivered through a fiber instrument inserted into the meatus and through the urethra. It can cut, coagulate, and vaporize prostatic tissue. Improvements in urine flow and symptoms are almost immediate. PVP works well for larger prostate glands. Irritative voiding symptoms may persist for several weeks.

Laser enucleation of the prostate. Laser enucleation also involves delivering a laser beam transurethrally through a fiber instrument. It is used for rapid coagulation and vaporization of prostatic tissue, with better coagulative properties in the tissue

TABLE 59.3 Treatment for BPH

Description	Advantages	Disadvantages
Minimally Invasive		
Laser Enucleation of the Prostate		
Laser beams used to rapidly vaporize and coagulate prostate tissue. Laser does not penetrate deep tissue. 2 types of lasers in this class: holmium laser enucleation of the prostate (HoLEP), thulium laser enucleation of the prostate (ThuLEP).	• Outpatient procedure • Better coagulative properties in tissue compared with TURP • Comparable results to TURP and PVP • Minimal bleeding • Fast recovery time	• Catheter needed after for 24–48 hr • Irritative voiding symptoms, urinary incontinence • Hematuria • Retrograde ejaculation • May be more difficult to perform compared with PVP
Photoselective Vaporization of the Prostate (PVP)		
Uses a laser beam to cut or destroy part of the prostate. May be more effective for small to moderate-sized prostates.	• Short procedure • Comparable results to TURP • Minimal bleeding • Fast recovery time • Rapid symptom improvement • Very effective	• Catheter needed up to 7 days after due to edema and urinary retention • Delayed sloughing of tissue • Takes several weeks to reach optimal effect • Retrograde ejaculation
Prostatic Urethral Lift (PUL)		
Permanent transprostatic implants/tension sutures placed transurethrally via cystoscope. Mechanically open the prostatic urethra by compressing the prostate tissue/parenchyma.	• Outpatient procedure • ED, urinary incontinence, and retrograde ejaculation are minimal • No change in PSA since no prostate tissue ablated	• Lack of long-term durability/results • Treatment response rates slightly lower when compared with TURP • If unsuccessful, may need repeat PUL or TURP in the future
Transurethral Microwave Thermotherapy (TUMT)		
Use of microwave radiating heat to produce coagulative necrosis of the prostate.	• Outpatient procedure • ED, urinary incontinence, and retrograde ejaculation are rare • Mild effects: bladder spasm, hematuria, dysuria	• Potential for damage to surrounding tissue • Urinary catheter needed after for 2–7 days • Not appropriate for men with rectal problems
Transurethral Needle Ablation (TUNA)		
Low-wave radiofrequency used to heat the prostate, causing necrosis.	• Outpatient procedure • ED, urinary incontinence, and retrograde ejaculation are rare • Precise delivery of heat to desired area • Very little pain • Early return to activities	• Urinary retention common • Irritative voiding symptoms • Hematuria for up to a week • May need a catheter for a short time after
Transurethral Vaporization of Prostate (TUVP)		
Electrosurgical modification of the standard TURP. Vaporization and desiccation used together to destroy prostatic tissue. Can use a variety of energy delivery mediums (e.g., button, rollerball, vaportrode).	• Minimal risks • Minimal bleeding and sloughing	• Retrograde ejaculation • Intermittent hematuria
Water Vapor Thermal Therapy		
Heated water vapor/steam used to destroy obstructive prostate tissue. Delivered transurethrally via hand-held device with a retractable needle that releases the water vapor in 9-second doses.	• Outpatient procedure • Can be done in an outpatient office setting • ED, urinary incontinence, and retrograde ejaculation are rare • Precise delivery of steam to desired area • Very little pain	• Relatively new, so lack of long-term results • Irritative voiding symptoms and UTI • Hematuria
Surgical Therapy		
Transurethral Incision of Prostate (TUIP)		
Involves transurethral incisions into prostatic tissue to relieve obstruction. Effective for small to moderate prostates.	• Outpatient procedure • Minimal complications • Low occurrence of ED or retrograde ejaculation • Outcomes similar to TURP	• Urinary catheter needed after

TABLE 59.3 **Treatment for BPH—cont'd**

Description	Advantages	Disadvantages
Transurethral Resection of Prostate (TURP)		
Use of excision and cauterization to remove prostate tissue via cystoscope. Standard for treatment of BPH.	• ED unlikely	• Bleeding, clot retention • Retrograde ejaculation • Catheter needed after
Simple Prostatectomy (Open, Laparoscopic, or Robotic Assisted)		
Surgery of choice for men with large prostates (often >100 g), bladder damage, or other complicating factors. If open, involves an external incision with retropubic or perineal approach (Fig. 59.6). If laparoscopic and/or robotic assisted, involves several small abdominal incisions and 1 slightly larger incision near the umbilicus.	• Complete visualization of the prostate and surrounding tissue	• ED • Bleeding • Pain • Risk for infection

compared with TURP. There are 2 types of lasers in this class: holmium laser enucleation of the prostate (HoLEP) and thulium laser enucleation of the prostate (ThuLEP). Neither penetrate deep tissue, which decreases side effects.

Prostatic urethral lift. *Prostatic urethral lift* (PUL) is a relatively new minimally invasive treatment. PUL involves permanent transprostatic implants or tension sutures delivered transurethrally via cystoscope. They mechanically open the prostatic urethra by compressing the prostate tissue. This alters prostate anatomy without ablating any tissue. So far, PUL has been done only in prostates less than 80 g in size and without an obstructive median lobe.[2] There is a lack of long-term data on the durability of PUL over time and the rates of needing either repeat treatment or progression to TURP.

Transurethral microwave thermotherapy. *Transurethral microwave thermotherapy* (TUMT) involves the delivery of microwaves directly to the prostate through a transurethral probe. The microwaves increase the temperature of the prostate tissue to about 113°F (45°C). The heat causes death of tissue, relieving the obstruction. A rectal temperature probe is used during the procedure to ensure that the temperature in the rectum stays less than 110°F (43.5°C) to prevent rectal tissue damage. The procedure takes about 90 minutes. It is an outpatient procedure.

Urinary retention is a common complication. Patients often go home with an indwelling catheter for 2 to 7 days to maintain urinary flow and facilitate the passing of small clots or necrotic tissue. Antibiotics, pain medication, and bladder antispasmodics are used to treat and prevent postprocedure problems. Anticoagulant therapy should be stopped 10 days before treatment.

Transurethral needle ablation. *Transurethral needle ablation* (TUNA) is another procedure that increases the temperature of prostate tissue, thus causing localized necrosis. TUNA differs from TUMT in that low-wave radiofrequency is used to heat the prostate. Only prostate tissue in direct contact with the needle is affected. This allows for more precise removal of the target tissue. Most patients have an improvement in symptoms. It is done in an outpatient unit or HCP's office using local anesthesia and IV or oral sedation. TUNA takes about 30 minutes.

CHECK YOUR PRACTICE

You are caring for a patient who is scheduled for a transurethral needle ablation for BPH. He appears anxious. He tells you he is worried about not being able to urinate normally after the procedure.

- What type of information and teaching would you provide?

Transurethral vaporization of the prostate. *Transurethral vaporization of the prostate* (TUVP) is an electrosurgical modification of the standard TURP. Vaporization and desiccation are used together to destroy obstructive prostatic tissue. There are a variety of energy delivery mediums that can be used to deliver the energy (e.g., button, rollerball, vaportrode). This is why many call it a "button TURP." The results, side effects, and long-term outcomes are equal to TURP. Because TUVP uses a bipolar energy delivery surface, an energy current is not passed through the patient's body to a grounding pad. This allows the HCP to use saline irrigation during the procedure, which decreases the risk for TUR syndrome.

Water vapor thermal therapy. *Water vapor thermal therapy* uses heated water vapor/steam to destroy obstructive prostate tissue. The steam is delivered transurethrally directly into the prostate by a hand-held device with a retractable needle. It releases the heated water vapor in 9-second doses. It is potentially a good option for a patient who is looking to minimize the risk for postprocedure ED. This treatment has been done only on prostates less than 80 g in size. It lacks long-term durability data.

Surgical Therapy

Invasive treatment of symptomatic BPH involves surgery. The approach used depends on the size and location of the prostatic enlargement and patient factors, such as age and surgical risk. Table 59.3 describes common surgeries.

Surgery is indicated when a decrease in urine flow causes pain, persistent residual urine, acute urinary retention because

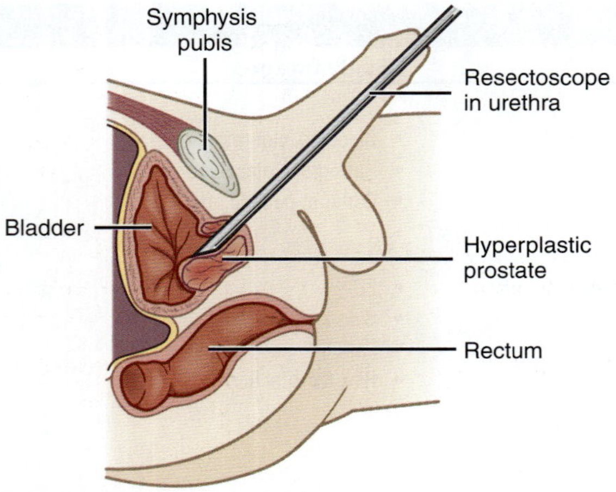

Fig. 59.4 Transurethral resection of the prostate.

of obstruction with no reversible precipitating cause, or hydronephrosis. Intermittent catheterization or insertion of an indwelling catheter can temporarily reduce symptoms and bypass the obstruction. However, avoid long-term catheter use because of the increased risk for infection.

Transurethral incision of the prostate. Transurethral incision of the prostate (TUIP) is a surgical procedure done under local anesthesia for men with moderate to severe symptoms. Several small incisions are made into the prostate gland to expand the urethra, which relieves pressure on the urethra and improves urine flow. TUIP is an option for patients with a small or moderately enlarged prostate gland.

Transurethral resection of the prostate. **Transurethral resection of the prostate (TURP)** involves the removal of prostate tissue using a resectoscope inserted through the urethra. TURP is the gold standard for surgical treatment of obstructing BPH. Most patients have marked improvements in symptoms and urinary flow rates.

In TURP there is no external incision. A resectoscope is inserted through the urethra to excise and cauterize obstructing prostatic tissue (Fig. 59.4). A large 3-way indwelling catheter with a 30-mL balloon is inserted into the bladder after the procedure to provide hemostasis and to facilitate urinary drainage. If there is a large amount of hematuria with clots after surgery, then the bladder can be irrigated, either continuously or intermittently, for the first 24 hours to prevent obstruction from blood clots.

TURP has a relatively low risk. We do have to assess for transurethral resection syndrome (TUR or TURP syndrome). Signs and symptoms include nausea, vomiting, confusion, bradycardia, and hypertension. TUR syndrome is due to hyponatremia from long operative times and prolonged intraoperative bladder irrigation with iso-osmolar fluid. If the HCP uses saline irrigation during the procedure, the risk for TUR syndrome dramatically decreases.

Other complications include bleeding and clot retention. Because bleeding is a common complication, patients taking aspirin, warfarin, or other anticoagulants must stop taking these several days before surgery. BPH medications are stopped after the procedure.

TABLE 59.4 NURSING ASSESSMENT

BPH

Subjective Data

Important Health Information

Medications: Testosterone supplementation
Surgery or other treatments: Previous BPH treatment

Functional Health Patterns

Health perception–health management: Knowledge of the condition
Nutritional-metabolic: Voluntary fluid restriction
Elimination: Urinary urgency, diminution in caliber and force of urinary stream. Hesitancy in starting voiding. Postvoid dribbling, urinary retention, urinary incontinence
Sleep-rest: Nocturia
Cognitive-perceptual: Dysuria, sensation of incomplete voiding, bladder discomfort
Sexuality-reproductive: Anxiety about sexual dysfunction

Objective Data

General

Older adult male

Urinary

Distended bladder on palpation. Smooth, firm, elastic enlargement of prostate on rectal examination

Possible Diagnostic Findings

Enlarged prostate on ultrasonography, bladder neck obstruction on cystoscopy, residual urine with postvoiding ultrasound or catheterization. WBCs, bacteria, or microscopic hematuria with bladder infection. ↑ Serum creatinine levels with renal involvement

NURSING MANAGEMENT: BENIGN PROSTATIC HYPERPLASIA

Because you will be most directly involved in care of patients with BPH having surgery, the focus of nursing management in this section is on preoperative and postoperative care.

Assessment

Subjective and objective data that you should obtain from a patient with BPH are outlined in Table 59.4.

Clinical Problems

Clinical problems for the patient with BPH before surgery may include:

- Pain
- Risk for infection
- Impaired urinary elimination

Clinical problems and interventions for the patient with BPH who has surgery are presented in eNursing Care Plan 59.1 (available on the website for this chapter).

Planning

The overall preoperative goals for the patient having surgery are to (1) restore urinary drainage; (2) resolve any UTI; and (3) understand the upcoming procedure, implications for sexual function, and urinary control. The overall postoperative goals are to have (1) no complications, (2) restoration of urinary control, (3) complete bladder emptying, and (4) satisfying sexual expression.

◆ Implementation

◆ Health Promotion

Health promotion focuses on early detection and treatment of BPH. When symptoms of BPH are present, further diagnostic screening may be needed (Table 59.2).

Some men find that consuming alcohol, caffeine, or other bladder irritants tends to increase prostatic voiding symptoms because the diuretic effect increases bladder distention and overactivity. Compounds found in common cough and cold remedies, such as pseudoephedrine (e.g., Sudafed) and phenylephrine, often worsen the symptoms of BPH. These drugs are α-adrenergic agonists that cause smooth muscle contraction. If this occurs, the patient should avoid these drugs.

Teach patients with obstructive symptoms to urinate every 2 to 3 hours and when they first feel the urge. This will minimize urinary stasis and acute urinary retention. Teach patients to maintain a normal level of fluid so that they do not become dehydrated. The patient may think that if he restricts fluid intake, symptoms will be less severe. This actually increases the risk of infection while concentrating his urine.

◆ Acute Care

The following discussion focuses on perioperative care for the patient undergoing a TURP.

Preoperative care. Antibiotics are usually given before any invasive genitourinary (GU) procedure. UTI must be treated before surgery. Restoring urinary drainage and encouraging a high fluid intake (2 to 3 L/day unless contraindicated) are helpful in managing infection. Prostatic obstruction may result in acute retention or inability to void. Urinary drainage must be restored before surgery.

A urethral foley catheter may be needed to restore bladder drainage. In many health care settings, 2% lidocaine gel is inserted into the urethra before catheter placement. The lidocaine gel acts as a lubricant, provides local anesthesia, and helps open the urethral lumen. If a sizable obstruction of the urethra exists, the HCP may need to use a special catheter or dilation tools to pass through the obstruction. Aseptic technique is important to avoid introducing bacteria into the bladder.

Patients may be concerned about the impact of the impending surgery on sexual function. Provide an opportunity for the patient and partner to express their concerns. Tell the patient that ejaculate volume may be decreased or absent after the procedure. Most types of prostatic surgery result in some degree of *retrograde ejaculation*. This is a condition in which some semen travels back into the bladder during orgasm instead of traveling out of the penis. This may decrease orgasmic sensations felt during ejaculation. Retrograde ejaculation is not harmful. The semen is voided with the next urination.

Postoperative care. The main complications after surgery are bleeding, bladder spasms, urinary incontinence, and infection. Adjust the plan of care to the type of surgery, reasons for surgery, and patient's response to surgery.

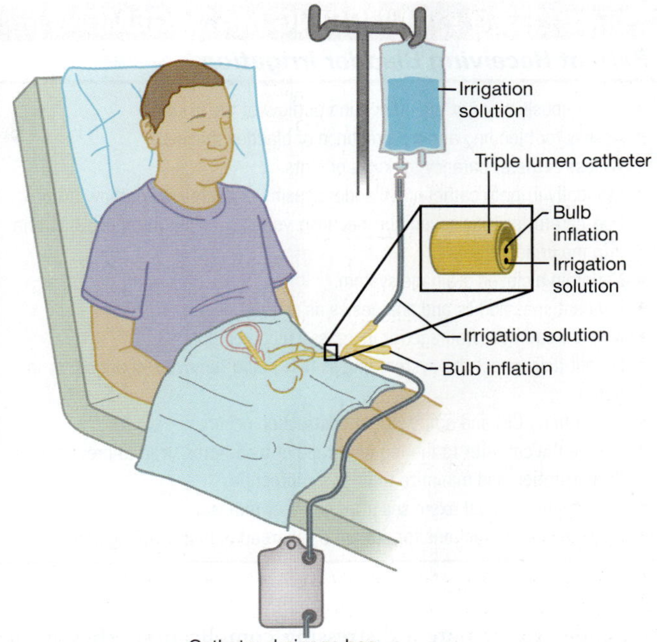

Fig. 59.5 Bladder irrigation with a triple lumen urinary catheter.

After surgery, the patient will have a standard 2-way foley catheter or a 3-way urethral catheter. Bladder irrigation is typically done to remove clotted blood from the bladder and ensure drainage of urine (Fig. 59.5). The bladder is irrigated either manually on an intermittent basis or more often, as continuous bladder irrigation (CBI) with sterile normal saline solution or another prescribed solution. If the bladder is manually irrigated, instill 50 mL of irrigating solution. Then withdraw with a syringe to remove clots that may be in the bladder and catheter. Painful bladder spasms often occur with manual irrigation.

With CBI, irrigating solution is continuously infused and drained from the bladder. The rate of infusion is based on the color of drainage. The urine drainage should be light pink without clots. Continuously monitor the inflow and outflow of the irrigant (Table 59.5). If outflow is less than inflow, assess the catheter patency for kinks or clots. If the outflow is blocked and patency cannot be reestablished by manual irrigation, stop the CBI and notify the HCP.

Blood clots are expected after prostate surgery for the first 24 to 36 hours. However, large amounts of bright red blood in the urine can indicate bleeding. Bleeding may occur from catheter displacement, dislodgment of a large clot, or increased abdominal pressure.

Release or displacement of the catheter dislodges the balloon that provides counterpressure on the operative site. Traction on the catheter may be applied to provide counterpressure (tamponade) on the bleeding site in the prostate, thereby decreasing bleeding. Such traction can result in local necrosis if pressure is applied for too long. Pressure should be relieved on a scheduled basis by qualified personnel.

The patient should avoid activities that increase abdominal pressure in the recovery period. These include sitting or walking for prolonged periods and straining to have a bowel movement (Valsalva maneuver).

TABLE 59.5 NURSING MANAGEMENT

Patient Receiving Bladder Irrigation

- Continuously monitor the inflow and outflow of the irrigant.
- Assess for bleeding and the presence of bladder spasms.
- Assess catheter patency for kinks or clots.
- Manually irrigate catheter if bladder spasms or decreased outflow occurs.
- Use careful aseptic technique because you can easily introduce bacteria into the urinary tract.
- Maintain a closed drainage system.
- Give antispasmodics and analgesics as needed.
- Monitor catheter drainage for increased blood or clots.
- Do not disconnect the system unless it is being removed, changed, or irrigated.
- Discontinue CBI and notify HCP if obstruction occurs.
- Secure the catheter to the leg with tape or a catheter strap to prevent urethral irritation and minimize the risk for infection.
- Teach patient Kegel exercises after catheter removal.
- Provide care instructions for patient discharged with indwelling catheter.

Bladder spasms are a distressing complication. They occur because of irritation of the bladder mucosa from the insertion of the resectoscope, presence of a catheter, or clots leading to catheter obstruction. If bladder spasms develop, check the catheter for clots. If present, remove the clots by irrigation so that urine can flow freely. Tell the patient not to urinate around the catheter because this increases the chance of spasm. Belladonna and opium suppositories or other antispasmodics (e.g., oxybutynin), along with relaxation techniques, can relieve pain and decrease spasm.

We often remove the catheter 2 to 4 days after surgery. The patient should have a voiding trial after catheter removal. If he cannot urinate, he will have a catheter reinserted for a day or so or perform clean intermittent self-catheterization (see Chapter 50).

Sphincter tone may be poor right after catheter removal, resulting in urinary incontinence or dribbling. This is a common but distressing situation for the patient. Performing Kegel exercises (pelvic floor muscle technique) 10 to 20 times per hour while awake (see Table 50.18) can strengthen sphincter tone. Encourage the patient to practice starting and stopping the stream several times during urination. This helps the patient to target the correct pelvic floor muscles when doing Kegel exercises.

It can take several weeks to achieve urinary continence. In some instances, control of urine may never be fully regained. Continence can improve for up to 12 months. If continence has not been achieved by that time, the patient may be referred to a continence clinic. A variety of methods, including biofeedback, have been used to achieve positive results.

Teach the patient how to use a penile clamp, a condom catheter, or incontinence pads or briefs to avoid embarrassment from dribbling. In severe cases, an occlusive cuff that serves as an artificial sphincter can be surgically implanted to restore continence. Help the patient find ways to manage the problem that allow him to continue socializing and interacting with others. Urinary incontinence is discussed in Chapter 50.

Observe the patient for signs of infection. If an external wound is present (e.g., from an open, laparoscopic, or robotic-assisted prostatectomy), assess the area for redness, heat, swelling, and purulent drainage. Take special care if a perineal incision is present because of the proximity of the anus. Avoid rectal procedures, such as rectal temperatures and enemas. The insertion of well-lubricated belladonna and opium suppositories is acceptable.

Diet intervention and stool softeners are important to prevent the patient from straining while having bowel movements. Straining increases the intraabdominal pressure, which can lead to bleeding at the operative site. A diet high in fiber promotes the passage of stool.

◆ Ambulatory Care

Discharge planning and home care issues are important after prostate surgery. Teaching, especially about the procedure and the possible complications, directly impacts quality of life. Teaching includes (1) caring for an indwelling catheter (if present), (2) managing urinary incontinence, (3) maintaining fluid intake, (4) observing for signs and symptoms of urinary tract and wound infection, (5) preventing constipation, (6) avoiding heavy lifting (more than 10 lb [4.5 kg]), and (7) refraining from driving or intercourse after surgery as directed by the HCP.

The patient may have a change in sexual function after surgery (Box 59.1). Recovery depends on the type of surgery done and the interval of time between when symptoms first appeared and the date of surgery. For example, it may 2 years for complete sexual function to return after nerve-sparing prostatectomy. Many men have retrograde ejaculation because of trauma to the internal urethral sphincter. ED may occur if the nerves are cut or damaged during surgery. The patient may have anxiety over the change because of a perceived loss of his sex role, self-esteem, or quality of sexual interaction with his partner. Discuss these changes with the patient and his partner and allow them to ask questions and express their concerns. Sexual counseling and treatment options may be needed if ED becomes a chronic issue.

The bladder may take 2 months to return to its normal capacity. Teach the patient to drink at least 2 to 3 L of fluid per day and urinate every 2 to 3 hours to flush the urinary tract. Teach the patient to avoid or limit the amounts of bladder irritants, such as caffeine products, citrus juices, and alcohol. Because the patient may have incontinence or dribbling, he may incorrectly believe that decreasing fluid intake will relieve this problem.

Urethral strictures may result from instrumentation or catheterization. Treatment may include teaching the patient intermittent clean self-catheterization or having a urethral dilation.

Tell the patient to discuss the need for a yearly DRE with his HCP if he has had any procedure other than complete removal of the prostate. Hyperplasia or cancer can occur in the remaining prostatic tissue.

◆ Evaluation

The expected outcomes are that the patient with BPH who has surgery will report:

- Acceptable pain control
- Improved urinary function with no pain or incontinence

BOX 59.1 EVIDENCE-BASED PRACTICE

Effect of a Sexual Health Discharge Program

You are caring for D.P., a 62-year-old patient who had a TURP. D.P. has been on your surgical unit for 2 days and is ready for discharge. As you are reviewing postoperative self-care, you discuss D.P.'s understanding of the possible effects of surgery on sexual function.

Making Clinical Decisions

Synthesis of Best Available Evidence

A TURP often is associated with stress incontinence, stricture, and erectile and ejaculatory dysfunction. Patients may have distress about their sexual function and sexuality. Managing sexual problems is an important part of holistic care for a patient recovering after TURP.

Clinician Expertise

Standardized discharge instructions after TURP include information about the hospital's nurse-led sexual health program available to patients who had a TURP. You explain to D.P. that the program is based on a thorough review of the literature and consults with urology experts. The program involves 3 weekly 1-hr group sessions with the urology nurse practitioner.

Patient Preferences and Values

D.P. responds, "I wasn't excited about having this surgery. However, I was up to the bathroom many times during the night…I can't remember the last time I had a full night's sleep…and I know that was disruptive for my wife. Now that the surgery is behind me, I need to find my way to a complete recovery."

Implications for Nursing Practice

1. What topics on sexual function after TURP should we address before discharge?
2. Should we include patients' partners in the discharge program?

Reference for Evidence

Bayat R, Shahsavari H, Faghihzadeh H, et al.: Effect of the nurse-led sexual health discharge program on the sexual function of older patients undergoing transurethral resection of prostate: a randomized controlled trial, *Geriatrics* 5, 2020.

PROSTATE CANCER

Prostate cancer is a tumor of the prostate gland. Prostate cancer is the most common cancer among men, excluding skin cancer. It is the second leading cause of cancer death in men, exceeded only by lung cancer. The American Cancer Society (ACS) estimates that in 2021 there will be 248,530 men diagnosed with prostate cancer, and 34,130 men will die from prostate cancer. A man has a 1 in 8 risk for developing prostate cancer in his lifetime. More than 3.1 million men in the United States are prostate cancer survivors.[7]

Etiology and Pathophysiology

Prostate cancer is a slow-growing, androgen-dependent cancer. It is most likely to develop in the outer part of the prostate, called the peripheral zone. It can spread by 3 routes: by direct extension, through the lymph system, or through the bloodstream. Spread by direct extension involves the seminal vesicles, urethral mucosa, bladder wall, and external sphincter. The cancer later spreads through the lymphatic system to the regional lymph nodes. The bloodstream is the mode of spread to the axial skeleton (e.g., pelvic bones, head of the femur, lower lumbar spine), liver, and lungs.

BOX 59.2 PROMOTING HEALTH EQUITY

Cancers of the Male Reproductive System

Prostate Cancer

- Black men have the highest rate of prostate cancer.
- Black men are diagnosed with prostate cancer at an earlier age, have more advanced disease at the time of diagnosis, and have a higher mortality rate than do White men.
- Although the mortality rate for prostate cancer among Black men is high, the mortality rate is declining.
- Asian American men have a lower incidence and lower mortality rates from prostate cancer than White men.

Testicular Cancer

- Testicular cancer occurs most often among White men.

Age, ethnicity, and family history are known risk factors for prostate cancer (Box 59.2). The incidence of prostate cancer rises markedly after age 50. The median age at diagnosis is 66 years old. However, many cases occur in younger men. They sometimes have a more aggressive type of cancer.

Diet factors and obesity may be related to prostate cancer. A diet high in red and processed meat and high-fat dairy products along with a low intake of vegetables and fruits may increase the risk for prostate cancer. Environment may play a role. There is an increased prevalence of prostate cancer in farmers and commercial pesticide applicators. This might be due to chemicals found in pesticides. It is not clear if smoking is a risk factor.

Genetic Link

Currently no known single gene causes prostate cancer. Some genes or gene mutations are more common in men with prostate cancer. From a genetics viewpoint, we classify prostate cancer into 3 categories.

Most prostate cancers (about 75%) are *sporadic,* which means that damage to the genes occurs by chance after a person is born. Prostate cancer that runs in a family, called *familial prostate cancer,* is less common (about 20%). It occurs because of a combination of genes and environment or lifestyle factors. Familial prostate cancer is when 2 or more first-degree relatives (father, brother, son) have prostate cancer.

Hereditary (inherited) prostate cancer is rare (5% to 10%). It occurs when gene mutations are passed down in a family from 1 generation to the next. In hereditary prostate cancer, a family has any of the following characteristics: (1) 3 or more first-degree relatives with prostate cancer, (2) prostate cancer in 3 generations on the same side of the family, and (3) 2 or more close relatives (father, brother, son, grandfather, uncle, nephew) on the same side of the family diagnosed with prostate cancer before age 55.

Having a family history does not mean that a man will develop prostate cancer. It means that he has an increased risk. Men with a family history of prostate cancer should talk with their HCP about their concerns. It is important for the HCP to obtain a detailed family history. Depending on the findings, a referral to a genetic counselor may be appropriate.

Hereditary breast and ovarian cancer (HBOC) syndrome is associated with mutations in the *BRCA1* and/or *BRCA2* genes (BRCA stands for *BR*east *CA*ncer). Women with HBOC have an increased risk for breast and ovarian cancer. Men with HBOC have an increased risk for breast cancer and prostate cancer. Mutations in *BRCA1* and *BRCA2* cause only a small number of familial prostate cancers. Genetic testing may be appropriate for families with prostate cancer that have HBOC.

Clinical Manifestations and Complications

Prostate cancer typically has no symptoms in the early stages. Eventually, the patient may have LUTS similar to those of BPH. Pain in the lumbosacral area that radiates down to the hips or the legs, when combined with urinary symptoms, may indicate metastasis.

The tumor can spread to pelvic lymph nodes, bones, bladder, lungs, and liver. Once the tumor has spread to distant sites, the major problem becomes pain. As the cancer spreads to the bones (common site of metastasis), pain can become severe, especially in the back and legs because of spinal cord compression and bone destruction.

Diagnostic Studies

Most men in the United States with prostate cancer are diagnosed by PSA screening. As prostate cancer screening has become more widespread, smaller cancers are being found in older men. In most cases, slow-growing cancers probably do not need to be treated. Many men live and die *with* prostate cancer, but most will not die *from* it.

Men can make an informed decision with their HCP about whether to be screened for prostate cancer. Men should be told about the potential risks (e.g., subsequent evaluation and treatment that may not be needed) and benefits (early detection of prostate cancer) of PSA screening before being tested. After this discussion, men who want to be screened may have an annual PSA test and DRE. On DRE, an abnormal prostate may feel hard, nodular, and asymmetric.

The AUA states that men ages 55 to 69 have the greatest potential benefit from PSA screening. They recommend shared decision making and potential screening every 2 years. Men at higher risk (Black men, men with a first-degree relative with prostate cancer) should have a more personalized screening schedule.

The ACS recommends men decide about screening after they discuss information about the risks and benefits with their HCP.[8] This discussion should take place at:

- Age 50 for men who are at average risk for prostate cancer and expected to live at least 10 more years.
- Age 45 for men at high risk for developing prostate cancer. This includes Blacks and men who have a first-degree relative (father, brother, son) diagnosed with prostate cancer at an early age (younger than age 65).
- Age 40 for men at even higher risk (those with more than 1 first-degree relative who had prostate cancer at an early age).

High PSA levels do not always indicate prostate cancer. Mild PSA increases may occur with aging, BPH, recent ejaculation, constipation, prostatitis, or after long bike rides. Cystoscopy, indwelling urethral catheters, and prostate biopsies may cause transient increases in PSA levels.

Neither PSA nor DRE is a definitive diagnostic test for prostate cancer. If PSA levels are continually high or if the DRE is abnormal, a biopsy of the prostate tissue is usually done. Biopsy can confirm the diagnosis of prostate cancer. The biopsy is typically done using a transrectal approach. In a TRUS procedure, an ultrasound probe allows the HCP to see abnormalities in the prostate. When a suspicious area is found, biopsy needles are inserted through the wall of the rectum into the prostate to obtain tissue samples. A pathologic examination of the specimen is done to assess for cancer. For patients at a high risk for infection with a transrectal biopsy, or with a history of prior post-biopsy sepsis, a transperineal approach is another option if it is available. There can be a lower risk for infection with the transperineal approach as the biopsy needles do not pierce the rectal wall. It is typically done in the operating room.

Another approach for biopsies is to use an MRI/ultrasound fusion biopsy. In this approach, pelvic MRI 3-dimensional images are fused with real-time, TRUS images. This technique is more accurate than the traditional approach. Typically, men who undergo this procedure have a history of a previous negative ultrasound-guided biopsy and increasing PSA. This approach may also be used for men who are on active surveillance. Recent studies show risk assessment with MRI before biopsy and MRI-targeted biopsy are better than standard TRUS biopsy in men at risk for prostate cancer who have not had a prostate biopsy before.[5]

PSA is used to monitor the success of treatment. When treatment has been successful, with either prostatectomy or hormone therapy, PSA levels should decrease to undetectable levels. With successful radiation therapy, the PSA level should decrease to a very low number (the nadir) and remain stable near that number. The regular measurement of PSA levels after treatment is important to evaluate the effectiveness of treatment and possible recurrence of prostate cancer.[8]

With advanced prostate cancer, serum alkaline phosphatase can be increased because of bone metastases. Other tests used to determine the location and extent of the spread of the cancer may include a nuclear medicine whole body bone scan, a CT scan of the abdomen and pelvis, and an MRI of the pelvis with special attention to the prostate.

Interprofessional Care

Chemoprevention of prostate cancer is an active area of research. Finasteride and dutasteride, used to treat BPH, may reduce the chance for getting prostate cancer. Men who are concerned about prostate cancer should discuss with their HCP the risks and benefits of taking finasteride or dutasteride.

Early recognition and treatment are important to control tumor growth, prevent metastasis, and preserve quality of life. Most patients with prostate cancer are diagnosed when the cancer is at a local or regional stage.[8] The 5-year survival rate with a diagnosis at this stage is almost 100%.

The most common classification system for determining the extent of prostate cancer is the tumor, node, and metastasis (TNM) system (Table 59.6). The tumor is graded based on tumor histology using 2 different grading systems: the Gleason

TABLE 59.6 Staging of Prostate Cancer

Stage	Tumor Size	Lymph Node Involvement	Metastasis	PSA Level	Gleason Score
I	Not felt on DRE. Not seen by visual imaging.	No	No	<10	≤6
II	Felt on DRE. Seen by imaging. Tumor confined to prostate.	No	No	10–20	6–7
III	Cancer outside prostate. Possible spread to seminal vesicles.	No	No	Any level	Any score
IV	Any size.	Any nodal involvement.	Yes	Any level	Any score

Adapted from ACS: How is prostate cancer staged? Retrieved from https://www.cancer.org/Cancer/ProstateCancer/DetailedGuide/prostate-cancer-staging.

score and the Grade Group. The Gleason score grades the tumor from 3 to 5 based on the degree of glandular differentiation. Grade 3 represents the most well-differentiated or lowest grade (most like the original cells), and grade 5 represents the most poorly differentiated (unlike the original cells) or highest grade. The 2 most commonly occurring patterns of cells are graded, and the 2 scores are added together to create a Gleason score. Gleason score ranges from 6 to 10. Currently the lowest risk Gleason score is Gleason 6 (3+3).

The Grade Group system grades the cells based on their differentiation. The Grade Group assigns the tumor a number on a scale from 1 to 5. Grade Group 1 is the lowest risk, and Grade Group 5 the highest risk. Currently, the Gleason score and the Grade Group system are used together. A low-risk, well-differentiated prostate cancer specimen may be graded a Grade Group 1, Gleason 6 (3+3) prostate cancer. The trend is moving toward Grade Group scoring only.

The PSA level at diagnosis and the Gleason score and Grade Group are used with the TNM system to determine the stage of the tumor, which is vital to determine treatment options.

The care of the patient with prostate cancer depends on the stage of the cancer and the patient's overall health (Table 59.7). None of the diagnostic options can predict the progression of prostate cancer. At all stages, there is more than one treatment option depending on the stage, Gleason score, and PSA. The decision of which treatment to pursue should be made jointly by patients, their partners, and the health care team.[8]

TABLE 59.7 Interprofessional Care

Prostate Cancer

Diagnostic Assessment

- History and physical assessment with DRE
- PSA
- TRUS or pelvic MRI
- Prostate biopsy
- Whole body bone scan (to assess for bone metastases)
- CT abdomen and pelvis with contrast (to assess for metastatic disease)

Management

Active Surveillance

- Closely monitor PSA and DRE (annually, at minimum)
- Repeat/surveillance prostate biopsies
- Repeat imaging
- Consider genomic testing on biopsy tissue, if appropriate

Surgery

- Radical prostatectomy
- Cryotherapy
- Orchiectomy (for metastatic disease)

Radiation Therapy

- External beam for primary, adjuvant, and recurrent disease
- Brachytherapy

Drug Therapy

- Androgen deprivation therapy (Table 59.7)
- Chemotherapy for metastatic disease

Active Surveillance

Low-grade prostate cancer is slow growing. Therefore a conservative approach is active surveillance, or "watchful waiting." This strategy is appropriate when the patient has (1) a life expectancy of less than 10 years (low risk for dying of the disease); (2) a low-grade, low-stage tumor; and (3) serious coexisting medical conditions. With active surveillance, patients are typically followed with frequent PSA measurements and DRE to monitor the progress of the disease. Significant changes in PSA level, DRE, or the development of symptoms warrant a reevaluation of treatment options.

Surgical Therapy

Radical prostatectomy. With radical prostatectomy, the entire prostate gland, seminal vesicles, and part of the bladder neck (ampulla) are removed. The entire prostate is removed because the cancer tends to be in many different places within the gland. A pelvic lymph node dissection is typically done at the same time as prostatectomy to assess for nodal metastases in the local pelvic area. Typically, a higher number of lymph nodes are removed if the prostate cancer is higher grade/higher risk on biopsy. Surgery is usually not an option for advanced-stage disease except to relieve symptoms from obstruction.

Traditional surgical approaches for an open radical prostatectomy include retropubic and perineal approaches (Fig. 59.6). With the *retropubic* approach, a low midline abdominal incision is made to access the prostate gland and the pelvic lymph nodes can be dissected. With the *perineal* resection, an incision is made between the scrotum and anus.

With a robotic assisted (e.g., da Vinci system) prostatectomy, the HCP sits at a computer console while controlling

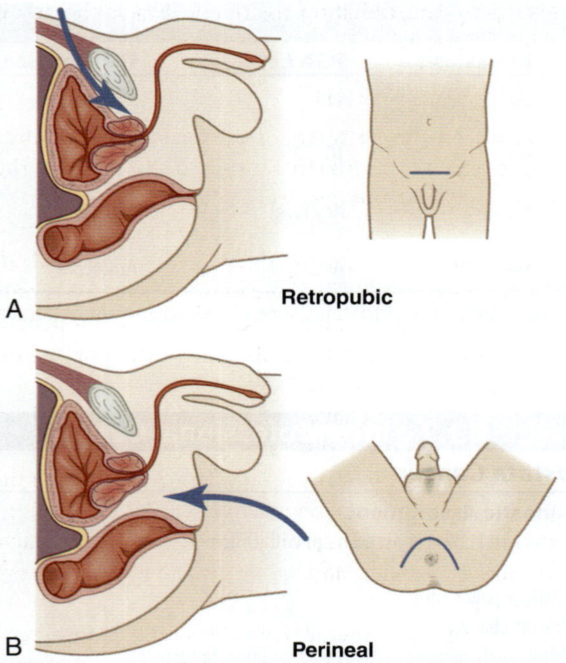

Fig. 59.6 Common approaches used to perform a prostatectomy. (A) Retropubic approach involves a midline abdominal incision. (B) Perineal approach involves an incision between the scrotum and the anus.

high-resolution cameras and microsurgical instruments. Robotics is being used more often since it allows for increased precision, visualization, and dexterity by the HCP when removing the prostate gland. It results in less bleeding, less pain, and a faster recovery compared with other approaches.[9]

After surgery, the patient has a large indwelling catheter with a 10- or 30-mL balloon placed in the bladder via the urethra. A drain is left in the surgical site to aid in removing drainage from the area. This drain is typically removed after a few days. Because the perineal approach has a higher risk for infection (location of the incision related to the anus), careful dressing changes and perineal care after each bowel movement are important for comfort and to prevent infection. Depending on the type of surgery, the length of hospital stay ranges from 1 to 3 days.

Two major adverse outcomes after a radical prostatectomy are ED and urinary incontinence. The incidence of ED depends on the patient's age, preoperative sexual function, whether nerve-sparing surgery was done, and the HCP's expertise. Sexual function tends to return gradually over at least 24 months or more. Phosphodiesterase type 5 (PDE5) inhibitor drugs may help improve sexual function.

Problems with urinary control may occur for the first few months after surgery because the bladder must be reattached to the urethra after the prostate is removed. Over time, the bladder adjusts, and most men regain urinary continence. Kegel exercises strengthen the pelvic floor muscles and the urinary sphincter. They may help improve continence (see Table 50.18). Other complications of surgery include bleeding, lymphocele, urinary retention, infection, wound dehiscence, and VTE.

Nerve-sparing procedure. Near the prostate gland are neurovascular bundles that maintain erectile function. The preservation of these bundles during a prostatectomy is possible while still removing all the cancer. Nerve-sparing prostatectomy is not indicated for patients with cancer outside of the prostate gland. Although the risk for ED is reduced with this procedure, there is no guarantee that potency will be maintained.

Cryotherapy. *Cryotherapy* (cryoablation) is a surgical technique that destroys cancer cells by freezing the tissue. It has been used both as an initial treatment and as a second-line treatment after radiation therapy has failed. A TRUS probe is inserted to see the prostate gland. Probes containing liquid nitrogen are then inserted into the prostate. Liquid nitrogen delivers freezing temperatures, thus destroying the tissue. The treatment takes about 2 hours under general or spinal anesthesia. It does not involve an abdominal incision.

Complications include damage to the urethra and, in rare cases, an urethrorectal fistula (an opening between the urethra and rectum) or a urethrocutaneous fistula (an opening between the urethra and skin). Tissue sloughing, ED, urinary incontinence, prostatitis, and bleeding can occur.

Radiation Therapy

Radiation therapy is another common treatment option. Radiation therapy may be the only treatment, or it may be used in combination with surgery or with hormone therapy. Salvage radiation therapy given for prostate cancer recurrence after a radical prostatectomy may improve survival in some men.

External beam radiation. External beam radiation is the most widely used method of delivering radiation treatments for prostate cancer. This therapy can be used to treat cancer confined to the prostate and/or surrounding tissue. Patients are usually treated on an outpatient basis 5 days a week for 4 to 8 weeks. Each treatment lasts less than 1 hour.

Side effects from radiation can be acute (occurring during treatment or within 90 days that follow) or delayed (occurring months or years after treatment). The most common side effects involve changes to the skin (dryness, redness, irritation, pain), gastrointestinal tract (diarrhea, abdominal cramping, bleeding, radiation proctitis), urinary tract (dysuria, hematuria, frequency, hesitancy, urgency, nocturia, radiation cystitis), and sexual function.[10] Fatigue may occur. There is a rare risk for secondary cancers after radiation to the pelvic area (e.g., bladder cancer, rectal cancer). In patients with localized prostate cancer, cure rates with external beam radiation are comparable with those with radical prostatectomy.

Brachytherapy. *Brachytherapy* involves placing radioactive seed implants into the prostate gland. This delivers high doses of radiation directly to the tissue while sparing the surrounding tissue (rectum and bladder). The radioactive seeds are placed in the prostate gland with a needle through a grid template guided by TRUS (Fig. 59.7) to ensure correct placement of the seeds.

Because brachytherapy is a 1-time outpatient procedure, many patients find this more convenient than external beam radiation treatment. Brachytherapy is best suited for patients with early-stage disease. The most common side effect is the development of urinary irritative or obstructive problems.

Some men may have ED. The AUA-SI (Table 59.1) can measure urinary function for patients undergoing brachytherapy and can be part of nursing management. For those with more advanced tumors, brachytherapy may be used in combination with external beam radiation treatment. Brachytherapy is discussed in Chapter 16.

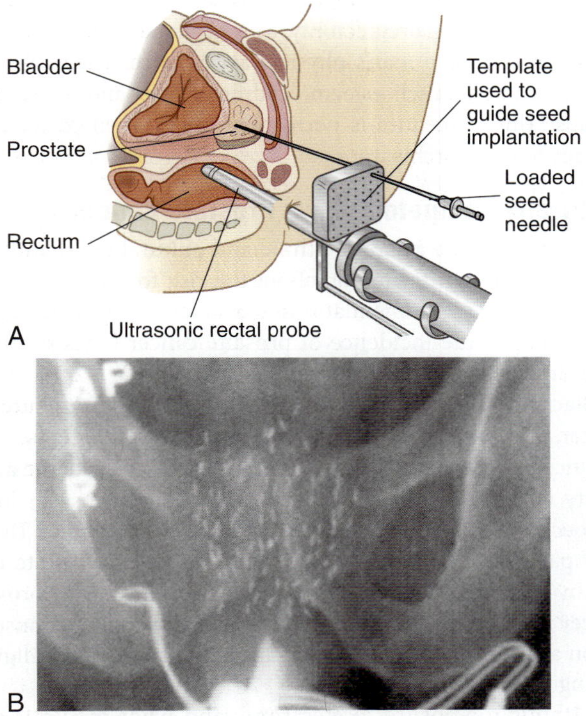

Fig. 59.7 (A) Prostate brachytherapy. Implantation of radioactive seeds with a needle guided by ultrasound and a template grid. (B) Radioactive seeds. (B, From Abeloff MD, Armitage JO, Niederhuber JE, et al., editors: *Abeloff's clinical oncology,* ed 4, Philadelphia, 2008, Churchill Livingstone.)

Drug Therapy

Drug therapy for the treatment of advanced or metastatic prostate cancer includes androgen deprivation (hormone) therapy, chemotherapy, or a combination of both.

Androgen deprivation therapy. Prostate cancer growth is largely dependent on the presence of androgens. *Androgen deprivation therapy* (ADT) reduces the levels of circulating androgens to reduce the tumor growth. Androgen deprivation can be produced by inhibiting androgen production or blocking androgen receptors (Table 59.8).

One of the biggest challenges with ADT is that almost all tumors treated become resistant to this therapy *(hormone refractory)* within a few years. A high PSA level is often the first sign that this therapy is no longer effective. Patients taking ADT have an increased risk for cardiovascular side effects, including high serum cholesterol and triglyceride levels and coronary artery disease.[11]

Osteoporosis and fractures may occur in those receiving ADT. Drugs recommended to reduce bone mineral loss include zoledronic acid (Reclast) and raloxifene (Evista). Zoledronic acid is a bisphosphonate therapy given IV. A rare complication of therapy is osteonecrosis of the jaw. Denosumab (Prolia, Xgeva), a drug that slows the breakdown of bone, may be used to increase bone mass in men with nonmetastatic prostate cancer.

Androgen synthesis inhibitors. The hypothalamus produces luteinizing hormone–releasing hormone (LHRH), which stimulates the anterior pituitary to produce luteinizing hormone (LH) and follicle-stimulating hormone (FSH). LH

TABLE 59.8 Drug Therapy

Androgen Deprivation Therapy for Prostate Cancer

Therapy	Mechanism of Action	Side Effects
Androgen Receptor Blockers		
apalutamide (Erleada) bicalutamide (Casodex) darolutamide (Nubeqa) enzalutamide (Xtandi) nilutamide (Nilandron)	• Block action of testosterone by competing with receptor sites	• Loss of libido, ED • Hot flashes • Breast pain, gynecomastia
Androgen Synthesis Inhibitors		
CYP17 Enzyme Inhibitor		
abiraterone (Zytiga)	• Inhibits CYP17, an enzyme needed to produce testosterone • Inhibits testosterone synthesis from testes, adrenal glands, and prostate cancer cells	• Joint swelling, fluid retention • Muscle aches • Hot flashes • Diarrhea
LHRH Agonists		
goserelin (Zoladex) leuprolide (Eligard, Lupron Depot) triptorelin (Trelstar)	• ↓ Secretion of LH and FSH • ↓ Testosterone production	• Hot flashes, gynecomastia, ↓ libido, ED • Depression, mood changes
LHRH Antagonist		
degarelix (Firmagon)	• Blocks LH receptors • Immediate testosterone suppression	• Pain, redness, swelling at injection site • ↑ Liver enzymes

stimulates the testicular Leydig cells to make testosterone. *LHRH agonists* super stimulate the pituitary, downregulating the LHRH receptors and leading to a refractory condition in which the anterior pituitary is unresponsive to LHRH. These drugs cause an initial transient increase in LH and FSH; testosterone abruptly rises resulting in a *flare*. Symptoms may worsen during this time. However, with continued administration, LH and testosterone levels decrease.

LHRH agonists include goserelin (Zoladex), leuprolide (Lupron Depot, Eligard), and triptorelin (Trelstar) (Table 59.8). These drugs produce a chemical castration similar to the effects of an orchiectomy. They are given by subcutaneous or IM injections on a regular basis.

Degarelix (Firmagon) is an LHRH antagonist. It lowers testosterone levels to castration levels. Unlike the LHRH agonists, degarelix does not cause a testosterone flare because it acts directly to block LH and FSH receptors. It is given as a subcutaneous injection. Results are seen in 3 days.

Abiraterone (Zytiga) works by inhibiting an enzyme, CYP17, which is needed to produce testosterone. This drug is given orally to men with castration-resistant prostate cancer, usually in combination with prednisone. It improves overall survival by 4 to 5 months.

Androgen receptor blockers. Androgen receptor blockers are another classification of antiandrogen drugs that compete with circulating androgens at the receptor sites. These drugs include bicalutamide (Casodex), enzalutamide (Xtandi), apalutamide (Erleada), darolutamide (Nubeqa), and nilutamide (Nilandron). They are taken orally each day. They be used in combination with an LHRH agonist (e.g., goserelin). Combining an androgen receptor blocker with an LHRH agonist results in combined androgen blockade.

Chemotherapy. Chemotherapy is limited to treatment for those with hormone-refractory prostate cancer (HRPC) in late-stage disease. In HRPC the cancer is progressing despite treatment. This occurs in patients who have taken an antiandrogen for a certain period. The goal of chemotherapy is mainly palliative. Common chemotherapy drugs include cabazitaxel (Jevtana), cyclophosphamide, docetaxel (Taxotere), estramustine (Emcyt), mitoxantrone, paclitaxel (Abraxane), and vinblastine.

Men with advanced prostate cancer who have HRPC may receive a vaccine (sipuleucel-T [Provenge]). We do not know exactly how, but the vaccine stimulates the patient's immune system against the cancer. Use prolongs survival by about 4 months. It is individually prepared for each man by a process that combines his own WBCs with granulocyte-macrophage colony-stimulating factor (GM-CSF), which then attacks the prostate tumor cells.

Radiotherapy. Radium-223 dichloride (Xofigo) can be used in the treatment of patients with castration-resistant prostate cancer, symptomatic bone metastases, and no known visceral metastatic disease. It is an alpha particle–emitting radiotherapy drug that mimics calcium and forms complexes with hydroxyapatite at areas of increased bone turnover, such as bone metastases.

Orchiectomy. A bilateral orchiectomy is the surgical removal of the testes. It may be done alone or after prostatectomy. It is the gold standard for androgen deprivation. For advanced stages of prostate cancer, an orchiectomy is an option for cancer control, with rapid relief of bone pain associated with advanced tumors. Orchiectomy may shrink the prostate, thus relieving urinary obstruction in the later stages of disease when surgery is not an option. After an orchiectomy, weight gain and loss of muscle mass can change a man's physical appearance. These physical changes can affect self-esteem, leading to grief and depression. Because this procedure is permanent, many men prefer drug therapy over an orchiectomy.

Culturally Competent Care: Prostate Cancer

Nurses need to be aware of ethnic and cultural considerations when providing information about the risk for prostate cancer and screening recommendations. Consider not only the ethnic differences in the incidence of prostate cancer but also differences in health promotion practices.

Black men have the highest mortality rates from prostate cancer, in part because their prostate cancer often is more advanced at the time of diagnosis (Box 59.2). Despite the availability of screening measures, Black men and those in lower socioeconomic groups may not access these services. This is only partially related to knowledge levels about prostate cancer. In comparison with White men, Black men with prostate cancer report more problems with financial access to transportation and health care costs. They describe using more religious coping strategies.[12]

Although exposure to electronic and print media is successful in informing some men about prostate cancer, the effectiveness differs significantly based on demographic variables, such as ethnicity, age, education level, and socioeconomic level. Ideally, all men should be aware of the risks of prostate cancer and the screening methods available. Consider the best method to communicate this information to men of all cultures and ethnicities to promote understanding and participation in prostate cancer screening for men in at-risk groups.

NURSING MANAGEMENT: PROSTATE CANCER

Assessment

Subjective and objective data that you should obtain from a patient with prostate cancer are outlined in Table 59.9.

Clinical Problems

Clinical problems for the patient with prostate cancer depend on the stage of the cancer. These may include:

- Deficient knowledge
- Pain
- Impaired urinary elimination
- Impaired sexual function
- Difficulty coping

Planning

The overall goals are that the patient with prostate cancer will (1) be an active participant in the treatment plan, (2) have acceptable pain control, (3) follow the treatment plan, (4) understand

TABLE 59.9 NURSING ASSESSMENT
Prostate Cancer

Subjective Data
Important Health Information
Medications: Testosterone supplements. Use of any drugs affecting urinary tract such as morphine, anticholinergics, monoamine oxidase inhibitors, tricyclic antidepressants

Functional Health Patterns
Health perception–health management: Positive family history. ↑ Fatigue and malaise
Nutritional-metabolic: High-fat diet. Anorexia, weight loss (may indicate metastasis)
Elimination: Hesitancy or straining to start stream, urinary urgency, frequency, retention with dribbling, weak stream, hematuria
Sleep-rest: Nocturia
Cognitive-perceptual: Dysuria. Low back pain radiating to legs or pelvis, bone pain (may indicate metastasis). Pain level
Self-perception–self-concept: Anxiety about self-concept

Objective Data
General
Older adult male. Pelvic lymphadenopathy (late sign)

Urinary
Distended bladder on palpation. Unilaterally hard, enlarged, fixed prostate on rectal examination

Possible Diagnostic Findings
Serum PSA. Serum alkaline phosphatase. Nodular and irregular prostate on ultrasonography, positive biopsy results. Anemia

the effect of the treatment plan on sexual function, and (5) find an acceptable way to manage bladder and bowel function.

◆ Implementation

◆ Health Promotion

One of the most important roles in relation to prostate cancer is to encourage patients, in consultation with their HCPs, to have annual prostate screening (PSA and DRE). Because of their increased risk for prostate cancer, Black men and other men at high risk, such as those with a family history of prostate cancer, should discuss the need for annual PSA and DRE beginning at age 45.[7]

◆ Acute Care

Care of the patient having a radical prostatectomy is similar to surgical procedures for BPH. Care of the patient receiving radiation therapy and chemotherapy are discussed in Chapter 16. Another consideration is the patient's psychologic response to the cancer diagnosis. Provide sensitive, caring support for the patient and his family to help them cope with the diagnosis. Prostate cancer support groups are available for men and their families to encourage them to be active, informed participants in their own care.

◆ Ambulatory Care

Teach catheter care if the patient is discharged with an indwelling catheter in place. Teach the patient to clean the urethral meatus with soap and water once a day; always keep the collection bag lower than the bladder; and keep the catheter securely anchored to the inner thigh or abdomen. Tell them to report any signs of bladder infection, such as bladder spasms, fever, or hematuria. They should maintain a high fluid intake.

If urinary incontinence is a problem, encourage the patient to practice pelvic floor muscle exercises (Kegel exercises) at every urination and throughout the day. Continuous practice during the 4- to 6-week healing process improves the success rate. Products used for incontinence specifically designed for men are available through home care product catalogs and retail stores. Urinary incontinence is discussed in Chapter 50.

Palliative and end-of-life care are often appropriate and beneficial to the patient with advanced disease and his family (see Chapter 10). Common problems with advanced prostate cancer include fatigue, bladder outlet obstruction and ureteral obstruction (caused by compression of the urethra and/or ureters from tumor mass or lymph node metastasis), severe bone pain and fractures (from bone metastasis), spinal cord compression (from spinal metastasis), and leg edema (from lymphedema, VTE). Nursing care must focus on managing these problems.

Pain management is important. Pain control involves ongoing pain assessment, giving prescribed medications (both opioid and nonopioid agents), and nonpharmacologic methods of pain relief (e.g., relaxation breathing). Pain management is discussed in Chapter 9.

◆ Evaluation

The outcomes are that the patient with prostate cancer will:

- Be an active participant in the treatment plan
- Have acceptable pain control
- Follow the treatment plan
- Understand the effect of the treatment on sexual function
- Find an acceptable way to manage bladder or bowel function

PROSTATITIS

Etiology and Pathophysiology

Prostatitis is a broad term that describes a group of inflammatory and noninflammatory conditions affecting the prostate gland. Prostatitis is one of the most common urologic disorders. We believe that 10% of all men in the United States will have prostatitis in their lifetime.[13] Almost 2 million men are treated for prostatitis every year.

The 4 categories of prostatitis syndromes are (1) acute bacterial prostatitis, (2) chronic bacterial prostatitis, (3) chronic prostatitis/chronic pelvic pain syndrome, and (4) asymptomatic inflammatory prostatitis. The most common type is nonbacterial.

Both acute and chronic bacterial prostatitis generally result from organisms reaching the prostate gland by ascending from the urethra, descending from the bladder, or invading via the bloodstream or the lymphatic channels. Common causative organisms are *Escherichia coli* (most common), *Klebsiella, Pseudomonas, Enterobacter, Proteus, Chlamydia trachomatis, Neisseria gonorrhoeae,* and group D streptococci.

Chronic bacterial prostatitis differs from acute prostatitis in that it involves recurrent episodes of infection. It is the most common reason for recurrent UTIs in adult men.

Chronic prostatitis/chronic pelvic pain syndrome describes a syndrome of prostate and urinary pain in the absence of an obvious infectious process. The cause of this syndrome is not known. It may occur after a viral illness, or with a sexually transmitted infection (STI), especially in younger adults. A culture reveals no causative organisms. WBCs may be found in prostatic secretions.

Asymptomatic inflammatory prostatitis is usually diagnosed in those who have no symptoms but are found to have an inflammatory process in the prostate. These patients are usually diagnosed during the evaluation of other GU tract problems. WBCs are present in the seminal fluid from the prostate. We do not know the cause.

Clinical Manifestations and Complications

Common manifestations of acute prostatitis include fever, chills, back pain, and perineal pain. Acute urinary symptoms such as dysuria, urinary frequency, urgency, and cloudy urine may occur. The patient may progress to acute urinary retention caused by prostatic swelling if he remains untreated. With DRE, the prostate is extremely swollen, extremely tender, and boggy. The clinical features of prostatitis can mimic those of a UTI. However, remember that acute cystitis is not common in men.

Manifestations of chronic prostatitis are similar but generally milder than those of acute bacterial prostatitis. They include irritative voiding symptoms (frequency, urgency, dysuria), backache, perineal and pelvic pain, and ejaculatory pain. Obstructive symptoms are rare unless there is coexisting BPH. With DRE, the prostate feels enlarged and soft or boggy. It may be slightly tender with palpation. Chronic prostatitis can predispose the patient to recurrent UTIs.

Complications include epididymitis and cystitis. Sexual function may be affected. Manifestations include postejaculation pain, libido problems, and ED. Prostatic abscess is a potential but rare complication.

Diagnostic Studies

Because patients with prostatitis have urinary symptoms, a UA and urine culture and sensitivities are needed. Often WBCs and bacteria are present. The patient with a fever needs blood cultures and a complete blood count (CBC) to check the WBC count. The PSA test may be done to rule out prostate cancer. However, PSA levels are often increased with prostatic inflammation or infection. Thus, when inflammation or infection is present, the PSA may not be diagnostic.

Microscopic evaluation and culture of expressed prostate secretion can potentially be useful in the diagnosis of prostatitis. Expressed prostate secretion is obtained using a premassage and postmassage test. The patient is asked to void into a specimen cup just before and just after a vigorous prostate massage. Prostatic massage (for expressed prostate secretion) is becoming less common unless all other diagnostic options are exhausted. It should not be done if acute bacterial prostatitis is suspected. Compression is extremely painful and can increase the risk for bacterial spread. TRUS is not useful in the diagnosis of prostatitis. However, TRUS or MRI can rule out an abscess in the prostate.

Interprofessional and Nursing Care

Common antibiotics used for acute and chronic bacterial prostatitis include fluoroquinolones (e.g., ciprofloxacin, levofloxacin, ofloxacin), clindamycin, cephalexin, doxycycline, trimethoprim/sulfamethoxazole (Bactrim), or tetracycline. Antibiotics are usually given orally for up to 4 weeks for acute bacterial prostatitis. However, if the patient has high fever or other signs of impending sepsis, they need hospitalized and IV antibiotics.

Chronic bacterial prostatitis may be treated with oral antibiotic therapy for 8 to 12 weeks. Antibiotics may be given for a lifetime if the patient is immunocompromised. A short course of oral antibiotics is usually prescribed for those with chronic prostatitis in case of bacterial infection. However, antibiotic therapy is often ineffective for patients whose prostatitis is not due to bacteria.

Patients with bacterial prostatitis tend to have a great amount of pain. The pain resolves as the infection resolves. However, they may have residual pain for several weeks after a course of antibiotics because it takes time for the prostate to return to normal. Managing pain for patients with chronic prostatitis is more difficult because the pain persists for weeks to months. No single approach provides relief for everyone. Antiinflammatory agents (e.g., ibuprofen, naproxen) may be used for pain control, but these drugs provide only some pain relief.

Warm sitz baths may help to relieve pain. α-Adrenergic blockers (e.g., tamsulosin, alfuzosin) relax muscle tissue in the prostate. They are effective in reducing pain for some men.

Acute urinary retention can develop in acute prostatitis, requiring insertion of a urinary catheter. However, passage of a catheter through an inflamed urethra is contraindicated in acute prostatitis. The patient may need a suprapubic catheter. Repetitive prostatic massage may be recommended as an adjunct therapy. It can relieve congestion within the prostate by squeezing out excess prostatic secretions, providing pain relief. Like massage, measures to stimulate ejaculation (masturbation, intercourse) may help to drain the prostate and provide some relief.

Encourage the patient to drink plenty of fluids. Men with acute bacterial prostatitis have increased fluid needs from fever and infection. Managing fever is important (see Table 12.5).

PROBLEMS OF THE PENIS

We describe problems of the penis as congenital, problems of the prepuce, problems with the erectile mechanism, and cancer. Penis problems are rare once we exclude STIs (see Chapter 57).

CONGENITAL PROBLEMS

Hypospadias is a urologic problem in which the urethral meatus is on the ventral surface of the penis. This can be anywhere from the corona to the perineum. Causes include hormonal influences in utero, environmental factors, and genetic factors.

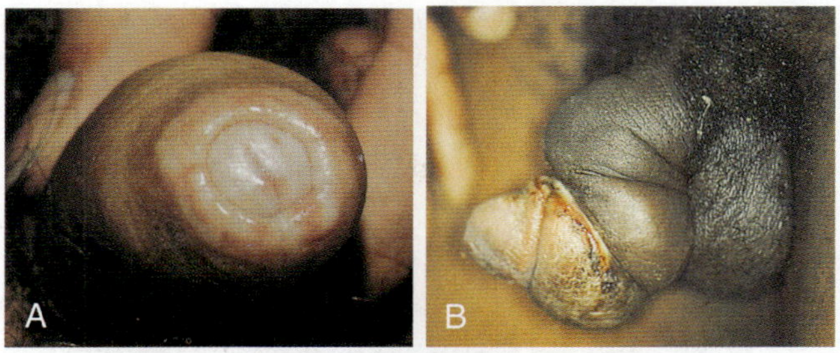

Fig. 59.8 (A) Phimosis: inability to retract the foreskin due to secondary lesions on the prepuce (foreskin). (B) Paraphimosis: ulcer with edema from foreskin remaining contracted over the prepuce (foreskin).

Surgical repair of hypospadias, especially those that are close to the scrotum or perineum, is usually done while the boy is young. Surgery may be done if it is associated with *chordee* (a painful downward curvature of the penis during erection) or if it prevents intercourse or normal urination. Surgery may be considered for cosmetic reasons or emotional well-being in older boys and adult men.

PROBLEMS OF PREPUCE

Problems of the prepuce (foreskin) are not as common in the United States as in most other countries because circumcision (surgical removal of the foreskin of the penis) is a routine procedure for many male infants. When these conditions do occur, they can be very painful and potentially an emergency. It is important to be familiar with these problems so proper treatment and pain relief can be promptly provided.

Phimosis is a tightness or constriction of the foreskin around the head of the penis, making retraction difficult (Fig. 59.8A). It is caused by chronic inflammation of the foreskin. It is usually related to poor hygiene techniques that allow bacterial and yeast organisms to become trapped under the foreskin. Topical corticosteroid cream, with or without an antifungal, applied 2 or 3 times daily to the exterior and interior of the tip of the foreskin may be effective in the initial treatment of inflammation. Definitive treatment is either circumcision or a dorsal slit surgery.

Paraphimosis is tightness of the foreskin resulting in the inability to pull it forward from a retracted position, thus preventing normal return over the glans. It is a urologic emergency. A tightly retracted phimotic ring can compromise arterial flow to the glans. An ulcer can develop if the foreskin stays contracted (Fig. 59.8B). Paraphimosis can occur when the foreskin is pulled back during bathing, use of urinary catheters, or intercourse and is not placed back in the forward position. Replacement of the foreskin after careful cleaning helps prevent this condition. The goal of treatment is to return the foreskin to its natural position over the glans penis through manual reduction. One strategy involves pushing the glans back through the prepuce by applying constant thumb pressure while the index fingers pull the prepuce over the glans. Ice and/or hand compression on the foreskin, glans, and penis may be applied before to reduce edema. Treatment may include antibiotics or warm soaks. Definitive treatment is either circumcision or a dorsal slit.

PROBLEMS OF ERECTILE MECHANISM

Priapism is a painful erection lasting longer than 4 hours. It is caused by complex vascular and neurologic factors that result in an obstruction of venous outflow in the penis. Conditions that may be associated with priapism include sickle cell disease, diabetes, trauma to the spinal cord, degenerative lesions of the spine, and drugs (e.g., cocaine, trazodone). Vasoactive drugs (e.g., alprostadil) injected into the corpora cavernosa for ED can cause priapism. Complications include penile tissue necrosis caused by lack of blood flow or hydronephrosis from bladder distention. Without immediate medical treatment, the risk for permanent ED is high.

Treatment varies depending on the cause. Patients with sickle cell disease may need a blood exchange transfusion. Other patients may be treated with sedatives, an injection of a smooth muscle relaxant directly into the penis, or aspiration and irrigation of the corpora cavernosa with a large-bore needle.

Peyronie disease is caused by plaque formation in the corpora cavernosa of the penis that results in inelasticity during erection. The palpable, nontender, hard plaque formation may occur spontaneously or result from trauma to the penile shaft. The plaque prevents adequate blood flow into the spongy tissue, which results in a curvature during erection. The condition is not dangerous but can result in painful erections, ED, or embarrassment. Patients may improve slightly over time, stabilize, or need surgery. Collagenase clostridium histolyticum (Xiaflex) and intralesional verapamil (ILV) are other options. Each is given as a series of injections into the plaque. The goal of therapy is to reduce the curvature and avoid surgery.

CANCER OF PENIS

Cancer of the penis is rare in the United States. More than 95% are squamous cell carcinoma. It occurs more often in men who have human papillomavirus (HPV) infection and phimosis or uncircumcised men.[14] The tumor may appear as a superficial ulceration or a pimple-like nodule. Pain is rare. This contributes to a delay in seeking treatment. The nontender warty lesion may be mistaken for a genital wart. Treatment in the early stages is laser removal of the growth. A radical resection of the penis may be done if the cancer has spread. Surgery, radiation, or chemotherapy are options, depending on the extent of the disease, lymph node involvement, or metastasis.

PROBLEMS OF SCROTUM AND TESTES

It is important for the patient to see the HCP if he feels any scrotal lumps or painful areas in the scrotum or testes. He would not be able to tell normal variations from cancer when performing self-examination. An incidental finding of a "scrotal lump" may result in high anxiety.

INFLAMMATORY AND INFECTIOUS PROBLEMS

Skin Problems

The skin of the scrotum is susceptible to several common skin problems. The most common are fungal infections, dermatitis

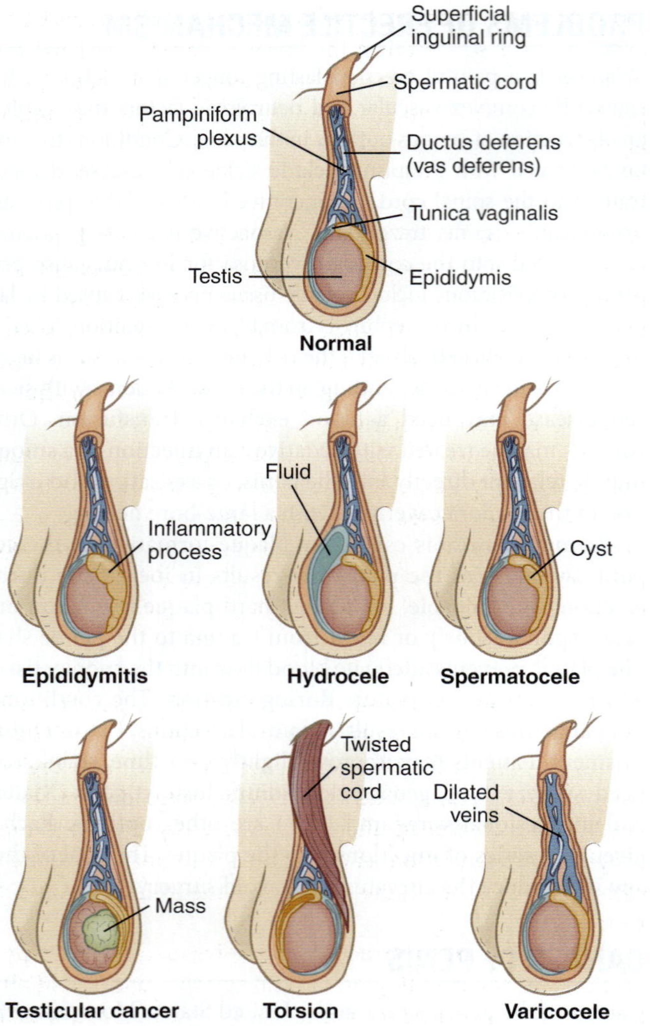

Fig. 59.9 Scrotal masses.

(neurodermatitis, contact dermatitis, seborrheic dermatitis), and parasitic infections (scabies, lice). These conditions involve discomfort but cause few severe complications (see Chapter 25).

Epididymitis

Epididymitis is an acute, painful inflammatory process of the epididymis (Fig. 59.9). It is often due to an infectious process, trauma, or urinary reflux down the ductus (vas) deferens. It is usually unilateral. Swelling may progress to the point that the epididymis and testis are indistinguishable. In men younger than 35 years of age, the most common cause is gonorrhea or chlamydial infection. In men older than 35, the most common cause is *E. coli* infection. BPH and prostatitis are common contributors in older men.

The use of antibiotics is important. We treat both partners if the transmission is through sexual contact. Encourage patients to refrain from sexual intercourse until treatment is complete. They should use a condom if they do engage in intercourse. Conservative treatment consists of elevating the scrotum, ice packs, and analgesics. Ambulation places the scrotum in a dependent position and increases pain. Acute tenderness

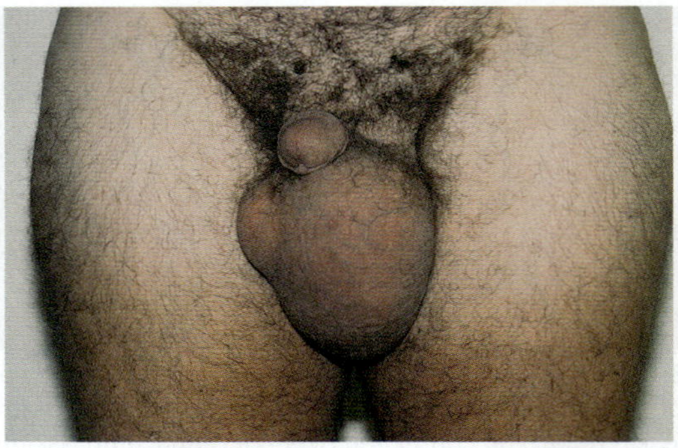

Fig. 59.10 Hydrocele. (From Swartz MH: *Textbook of physical diagnosis*, ed 6, Philadelphia, 2010, Saunders.)

subsides within 1 week, although some pain and swelling may last for weeks or months.

Orchitis

Orchitis is an acute inflammation of the testis. In orchitis, the testis is painful, tender, and swollen. It generally occurs after an episode of bacterial or viral infection, such as mumps, pneumonia, tuberculosis, or syphilis. It can be a side effect of epididymitis, trauma, infectious mononucleosis, influenza, catheterization, or complicated UTI. Mumps orchitis contributes to infertility. It can be avoided by childhood vaccination against mumps. Treatment is similar to that for epididymitis.

CONGENITAL PROBLEMS

Cryptorchidism (undescended testes) is failure of the testes to descend into the scrotal sac before birth. It is the most common congenital testicular condition. The condition may occur bilaterally or unilaterally. It is more common on the right. We believe it is a contributing factor to male infertility if corrective surgery is not done by age 2. The incidence of testicular cancer is higher if the condition is not corrected before puberty. Surgery is done to locate and suture the testis or testes to the scrotum.

ACQUIRED PROBLEMS

Hydrocele

A *hydrocele* is a nontender, fluid-filled mass that results from interference with lymphatic drainage of the scrotum and swelling of the tunica vaginalis that surrounds the testis (Figs. 59.9 and 59.10). Diagnosis is aided by shining a flashlight through the scrotum (transillumination). No treatment is needed unless the swelling becomes large and uncomfortable, then surgical repair is needed. Hydrocele repair is avoided in men who have not started their family or seek to add to their family as repair can contribute to subfertility or infertility.

Spermatocele

A *spermatocele* is a firm, sperm-containing cyst of the epididymis. It may be visible with transillumination (Fig. 59.9). The cause is unknown. They can become large, tense, and painful. Their size can wax and wane with time. Spermatocele repair is avoided in men who have not started their family or seek to add to their family as repair can contribute to subfertility or infertility.

Varicocele

A *varicocele* is a dilation of the veins that drain the testes (Fig. 59.9). The scrotum can feel worm-like when palpated if the venous dilation is significant. We do not know the cause of the problem. A varicocele is usually on the left side of the scrotum because of retrograde blood flow from the left renal vein.

Varicoceles are associated with 40% to 50% of cases of infertility. We think that the varicocele damages the sperm. Surgery is considered if fertility is a concern. Repair options include injecting a sclerosing agent or surgical ligation of the spermatic vein.

Testicular Torsion

Testicular torsion involves a twisting of the spermatic cord that supplies blood to the testes and epididymis (Fig. 59.9). It is considered a surgical emergency. It most often occurs in males younger than age 20. It can occur spontaneously or because of trauma or an anatomic abnormality.

The patient has severe, sudden onset of scrotal pain, tenderness, swelling, nausea, and vomiting. The pain does not usually subside with rest or elevating the scrotum. The cremasteric reflex is absent on the side of the swelling. Normal anatomic landmarks are lost due to tissue edema.

A Doppler ultrasound is done to assess blood flow within the testicle. Decreased or absent blood flow confirms the diagnosis. Torsion is an emergency! If the blood supply to the affected testicle is not restored within 4 to 6 hours, ischemia to the testis will occur, leading to necrosis. Unless the torsion resolves spontaneously, surgery to untwist the cord and restore the blood supply must be done emergently.

TESTICULAR CANCER

Etiology and Pathophysiology

Testicular cancer is relatively rare. It accounts for less than 1% of all cancers found in males. However, it is the most common cancer in young men between 15 and 34 years of age. In the United States, about 9560 new cases occur annually.[15]

Testicular tumors are more common in males who have had undescended testes (cryptorchidism) or a family history of testicular cancer or anomalies. Other predisposing factors include orchitis, human immunodeficiency virus (HIV) infection, maternal exposure to exogenous estrogen, and testicular cancer in the other testis.

Most testicular cancers develop from 2 types of embryonic germ cells: seminomas and nonseminomas. Seminoma germ cell cancers are the most common but are the least aggressive. Nonseminoma testicular germ cell tumors are rare but very aggressive. Non–germ cell tumors arise from other testicular tissue. These include Leydig cell and Sertoli cell tumors. They cause less than 10% of testicular cancers.

Clinical Manifestations

Testicular cancer may have a slow or rapid onset depending on the type of tumor (Fig. 59.9). There may be a painless, firm lump in the scrotum and scrotal swelling. Some patients report a dull ache or heavy sensation in the lower abdomen, perianal area, or scrotum. Acute pain is the first symptom in about 10% of patients. Manifestations of advanced disease vary. They include lower back or chest pain, cough, and dyspnea.

Diagnostic Studies

Palpation of the scrotal contents is the first step in diagnosing testicular cancer. A cancerous mass is firm and does not transilluminate. Ultrasound is done if testicular cancer is suspected (e.g., palpable mass) or when persistent or painful testicular swelling is present. Serum tumor markers are done to assess α-fetoprotein (AFP), lactate dehydrogenase (LDH), and human chorionic gonadotropin (hCG) levels.

A chest x-ray, CBC, basic metabolic panel, and liver function tests may be done. Anemia may be present. Liver function levels may be increased in metastatic disease. If cancer is confirmed by pathology, then a CT scan of the abdomen and pelvis (and possibly the chest) is done to further stage and assess for metastases.

Interprofessional and Nursing Care

Testicular cancer is one of the most curable types of cancer. Treatment generally involves a radical inguinal orchiectomy (removal of the affected testis, spermatic cord, and regional lymph nodes). Some patients with early-stage disease do not need further treatment after an orchiectomy. Retroperitoneal lymph node dissection and removal also may be done in early-stage disease. These nodes are the primary route for metastasis.

Postorchiectomy treatment may involve radiation therapy or chemotherapy depending on the stage of the cancer. Radiation therapy is mainly used for patients with a seminoma, which is very sensitive to radiation. Radiation does not work well for nonseminomas.

Testicular germ cell tumors are more sensitive to systemic chemotherapy than any other adult solid tumor. Chemotherapy protocols use a combination of agents, including bleomycin, cisplatin, etoposide, and ifosfamide (Ifex). Retroperitoneal lymph node dissection may be done after chemotherapy as adjunct therapy in patients with advanced testicular cancer.

> **CHECK YOUR PRACTICE**
>
> You are working on the urologic oncology unit caring for a 24-year-old man who recently had an orchiectomy for testicular cancer. He appears quiet and nonengaged when you assess him. He says, "I'm never going to have a normal sex life."
>
> - How would you respond? What kind of support and information would you provide?

The prognosis for men with testicular cancer has greatly improved; 95% obtain complete remission if the disease is found in the early stages. Because of treatment successes, many men with testicular cancer are long-term survivors.

However, some drugs used to treat testicular cancer can cause serious long-term side effects. These include lung problems,

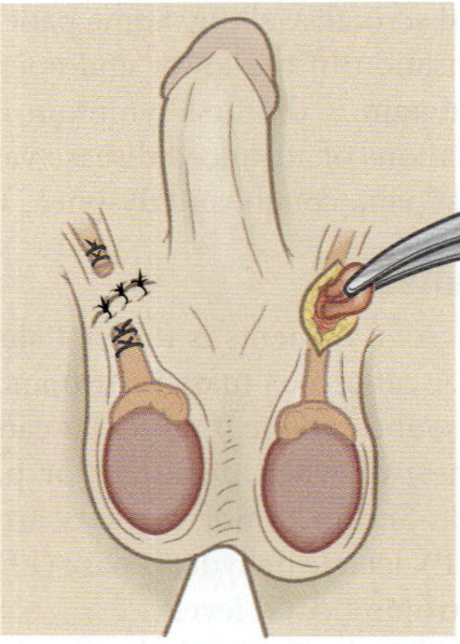

Fig. 59.11 Vasectomy procedure. The ductus deferens is ligated or resected for sterilization.

kidney damage, nerve damage (which can cause numbness and tingling), and hearing loss (from nerve damage). Secondary cancers can occur after chemotherapy (see Chapter 16).

All patients with testicular cancer need surveillance and regular physical assessments, chest x-rays, CT scans, and serum tumor markers (hCG, AFP, LDH). The goal is to detect relapse when the tumor burden is minimal.

Pretreatment subfertility or impaired fertility is identified at diagnosis. Chemotherapy with cisplatin and/or pelvic radiation often damages the testicular germ cells. However, spermatogenesis can return in some patients. Because of the high risk for infertility, the cryopreservation of sperm in a sperm bank before treatment begins should be discussed and recommended. Ejaculatory dysfunction may result from retroperitoneal lymph node dissection. These issues may be hard to discuss with the newly diagnosed patient. Men may feel the disease is a threat to their masculinity and self-worth.

SEXUAL FUNCTION

VASECTOMY

Vasectomy is the bilateral surgical ligation or resection of the ductus deferens done for the purpose of sterilization (Fig. 59.11). The procedure takes only 15 to 30 minutes. It is usually done with the patient under local anesthesia on an outpatient basis. Although vasectomy is considered a permanent form of sterilization, successful vasectomy reversals *(vasovasostomy, vasoepididymostomy)* are common.

After vasectomy, the patient should not notice any difference in the look or feel of the ejaculate because its major components are seminal and prostatic fluid. The patient must use a different form of contraception until semen examination reveals no sperm. Sperm cells continue to be made by the testes but are stored in the epididymis and reabsorbed by the body rather than being passed through the ductus deferens. Vasectomy does not affect the hormone production, ability to ejaculate, or physiologic mechanisms related to erection or orgasm. Psychologic adjustment may be a problem after surgery. It may be hard for the patient to separate vasectomy from castration at a subconscious level. Some men develop psychogenic ED or feel the need to be more sexually active than they were to prove their masculinity.

TABLE 59.10 Common Risk Factors for ED

Drug Induced • Alcohol • Antiandrogens • Antihypertensives • Antilipidemic agents • Major tranquilizers (diazepam [Valium], alprazolam [Xanax]) • Marijuana, cocaine • Nicotine • Tricyclic antidepressants (e.g., amitriptyline [Elavil])	**Neurologic** • Cerebrovascular disease • Parkinson disease • Trauma to the spinal cord • Tumors or transection of spinal cord **Psychologic** • Anxiety • Depression • Stress
Endocrine • Diabetes • Hypogonadism • Obesity	**Vascular** • Atherosclerosis • Hypertension • Peripheral vascular disease
Genitourinary • Radical prostatectomy • Renal failure	**Other** • Aging

ERECTILE DYSFUNCTION

Erectile dysfunction (ED) is the inability to attain or maintain an erection that allows satisfactory sexual activity. Although sexual function is a topic that many persons are uncomfortable discussing, health care professionals must be able and willing to address ED.

ED is a condition that is significant because of its prevalence. More than 10 million men in the United States have ED. It can occur at any age, although the incidence increases with age. We estimate that 50% of men between ages 40 and 70 have at least some degree of ED. ED is increasing in all sexually active males. In younger men, the increase is attributed to substance use (e.g., recreational drugs, alcohol), stress, and anxiety. Middle-aged men are more likely to have ED due to chronic medical conditions (e.g., diabetes, hypertension) or treatment for these conditions (e.g., antihypertensive drugs) that may cause ED.

Etiology and Pathophysiology

ED can be due to many factors (Table 59.10). Common causes include diabetes, vascular disease, drug side effects, result of surgery (e.g., prostatectomy), trauma, chronic illness, stress, difficulty in a relationship, or depression. Since ED results from reduced blood flow to the penis, there is a potential association with cardiovascular disease because the risk factors for both disorders are the same.

Normal physiologic age-related changes are associated with changes in erectile function. They may be an underlying cause of ED for some men. Table 55.3 lists age-related changes in sexual function. Review age-related changes (if necessary) to reassure an anxious older man about normal changes in his sexual abilities.

Clinical Manifestations and Complications

The typical symptom is a patient's self-report of problems with erectile activity, describing an inability to attain or maintain an erection. The symptoms may occur only occasionally, may be continual with a gradual onset, or may have a sudden onset. A gradual onset of symptoms is usually due to physiologic factors. A sudden or rapid onset of symptoms may be related to psychologic issues. It is common for younger men who seek care for ED to be diagnosed with diabetes, hypertension, depression, or cholesterol abnormalities during their evaluation for ED.

A man's inability to perform sexually can cause great distress in his interpersonal relationships and interfere with his concept of himself as a man. It can affect the relationship between the man and his partner. ED can lead to personal issues, including anger, anxiety, and depression.

Diagnostic Studies

The first step in the diagnosis of ED is a thorough sexual, health, and psychosocial history. Self-administered assessment and treatment-related questionnaires may be used as primary screening tools. For example, the International Index of Erectile Function (IIEF) assesses a man's response to 5 key areas of male sexual function: erectile function, orgasmic function, sexual desire, intercourse satisfaction, and overall satisfaction.

The physical assessment should focus on secondary sexual characteristics. Note if secondary sexual characteristics reflect the person's chronologic age (Tanner stage). A DRE is done to assess prostate size, consistency, and presence of nodules. Assess BP and peripheral pulses. Auscultate the femoral arteries.

Further testing is typically based on findings from the history and physical assessment. A serum glucose, hemoglobin A1C (Hb A1C), and lipid profile are recommended to rule out diabetes. Hormonal levels for testosterone, prolactin, LH, and thyroid hormones may identify endocrine-related problems. PSA level and a CBC may help to identify other diseases.

Other diagnostic tests may be done to diagnose ED. Nocturnal penile tumescence and rigidity testing is a noninvasive method that involves the continuous measurement of penile circumference and axial rigidity during sleep. These tests distinguish between physiologic or psychogenic causes of ED. Vascular studies, including penile arteriography, penile blood flow study, and duplex Doppler ultrasound studies, can assess penile blood inflow and outflow. These tests help to identify vascular problems interfering with erection.

Interprofessional and Nursing Care

The goal of ED therapy is for the patient and his partner to achieve a satisfactory sexual relationship. The treatment for ED can be based on the underlying cause. In general, men are moved directly into treatment without a costly workup. A variety of treatment options are available (Table 59.11). Advise patients that no option will restore ejaculation or tactile sensations if they were absent before treatment.

It is important to determine if ED is reversible before treatment is started. For example, if ED is a side effect of prescribed drugs, other treatments can be explored. With an established diagnosis of testicular failure (hypogonadism), androgen replacement therapy may be part of the prescribed treatment.

For men with ED that is psychologic in nature, counseling (with or without his partner) is recommended. This counseling should be carried out by a qualified sex therapist.

The man with ED needs a great deal of emotional support for both himself and his partner. Men often do not feel comfortable discussing their problems because of their perceptions of society's expectations of a man's sexual abilities. Many men delay seeking medical care or expect immediate solutions to ED. The health care team should provide a support system and accurate information.

TABLE 59.11 Interprofessional Care

ED

Diagnostic Assessment
- History and physical assessment
- Sexual history
- Serum glucose and lipid profile
- Testosterone, prolactin, and thyroid hormone levels
- Nocturnal penile tumescence and rigidity testing
- Vascular studies

Management
- Modify reversible causes
- Sexual counseling

Drug Therapy
- avanafil (Stendra)
- sildenafil (Viagra)
- tadalafil (Cialis)
- vardenafil (Levitra, Staxyn)

Devices and Implants
- Intraurethral medication pellet
- Intracavernosal self-injection
- Penile implants
- Vacuum erection device (VED)

Erectogenic Drugs

PDE5 inhibitors cause smooth muscle relaxation and increased blood flow into the corpus cavernosum, promoting penile erection. These drugs include avanafil (Stendra), sildenafil (Viagra), tadalafil (Cialis), and vardenafil (Levitra, Staxyn). Most are taken orally before sexual activity. These drugs are generally safe and effective for the treatment of most types of ED. They are ineffective in the absence of arousal.

Side effects include headaches, leg/back pain, dyspepsia, flushing, and nasal congestion. Rare side effects are blurred or blue-green vision problems, sudden hearing loss, and an erection lasting more than 4 hours (priapism). Teach the patient to seek immediate medical attention if any of these reactions occur. Because these drugs may potentiate the hypotensive effect of nitrates, they are contraindicated for those taking nitrates (e.g., nitroglycerin).

Some men seek other ways to obtain ED medications. This includes compounding pharmacies and online pharmacies. This may be due to both the cost of ED medications and the lack of insurance coverage for them.

DRUG ALERT

Phosphodiesterase Type 5 (PDE5) Inhibitors

- Should not be used with nitrates (nitroglycerin) in any form.
- Can potentiate hypotensive effects of nitrates.

Vacuum Erection Devices

Vacuum erection devices (VEDs) are suction devices that are applied to a flaccid penis then produce an erection by pulling blood up into the corporeal bodies. A penile ring or constrictive band is placed around the base of the penis to retain venous blood, preventing the erection from subsiding.

Intraurethral Devices and Intracavernosal Injections

Intraurethral devices include the use of vasoactive drugs applied as a topical gel or a medication pellet inserted into the urethra using a medicated urethral system for erection (MUSE) device. Intracavernosal self-injections may be combined with medication injected directly into the corpus cavernosum.

Alprostadil (Caverject, Edex) is a vasoactive drug that enhances blood flow into the penile arteries. It can be given either by injection or as a transurethral pellet (suppository). When given as a suppository, the drug is placed into the opening at the tip of the penis. When injected, a needle and syringe is used to inject the drug directly into the corpus cavernosum. Trimix (a combination product) includes alprostadil, papaverine, and phentolamine.

Penile Implants

Penile implants are placed into the corporeal bodies to provide an erection firm enough for penetration. The inflatable implant consists of cylinders in the penis, a small pump in the scrotum, and a reservoir in the lower abdomen. The main complications of penile prostheses are infection, erosions, and, rarely, mechanical failure. Implantation requires surgery. It can sometimes be done in an outpatient setting.

Sexual Counseling

Sexual counseling can be recommended at any point during treatment for ED. It may be most valuable in cases with a component of psychogenic ED. Counseling should address psychologic or interpersonal factors that may enhance sexual expression, as well as other factors that are of concern. Counseling can be effective for the patient. It can include his partner, especially if he is involved in a long-term relationship.

HYPOGONADISM

Hypogonadism is a gradual decline in androgen secretion that occurs in most men as they age. Thus we also call it *late onset-hypogonadism* or *hypogonadism of old age*. It can begin as early as age 40. The primary male androgen that is reduced is testosterone (Fig. 59.12). It is unclear what causes the decline in testosterone. Obesity is a contributing factor.

Manifestations of low testosterone include decreased libido, fatigue, ED, depression and mood swings, and sleep problems. Since many of these manifestations can be associated with aging, some patients may not mention this to their HCP, or the HCP may not recognize these manifestations as signs of low testosterone. Long-term effects of low testosterone include loss of muscle mass and strength, which may contribute to an increased risk for falls and fractures.

Hypogonadism is diagnosed with a blood test and physical assessment. Replacement testosterone therapy is considered if

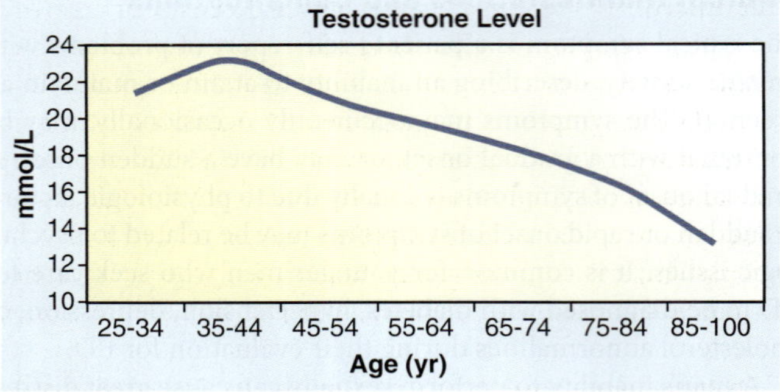

Fig. 59.12 Changes in testosterone plasma level in men as they age.

total serum testosterone levels are less than 300 ng/dL on 2 separate early morning measurements/occasions and the patient has manifestations of low testosterone.[16] Therapy may be started earlier depending on severity of symptoms. Testosterone replacement therapy (TRT) should not be started until the patient, in consultation with his HCP, considers the risks and benefits of therapy. Potential risks of TRT include lowered levels of high-density lipoprotein (HDL) cholesterol, increased hematocrit, and worsening sleep apnea, although these are rare. Since TRT may cause increased growth of prostate tissue, TRT is contraindicated in patients with unmanaged BPH or prostate cancer. Before treatment is started, a DRE and PSA test should be done. Once TRT begins, the HCP should closely monitor the patient.

Replacement therapy is available in different forms, including injection, transdermal, topical, buccal, or intranasal preparations. IM injections, such as testosterone cypionate (Depo-Testosterone) and testosterone enanthate, are available in varying doses. These drugs create a cyclic rise and fall in serum testosterone levels. The highest levels occur 2 to 3 days after the injection. Testosterone levels slowly decrease until the next injection. One side effect of IM TRT is that men may report mood swings with the hormone fluctuations.

Transdermal preparations, including patches and gels (e.g., Androderm, Testim), are often prescribed. They are applied to the skin at product-specific sites, including the back, arm, and abdomen. Skin irritation is a common side effect.

Emphasize to the patient the importance of hand washing with soap and water after applying testosterone preparations to the skin. Have the patient cover the area with clothing until the preparation has dried. Women of childbearing age and children should not touch testosterone products. Testosterone may cause early signs of puberty in young children and changes (virilization) in the external genitalia of a female fetus.

INFERTILITY

Infertility in a couple is the inability to conceive after 1 year of frequent unprotected intercourse. Infertility is a problem with the couple, not of a person. For this reason, both partners must be involved in evaluating infertility. Some estimate up to 40% of infertility cases are related to male factors.[17]

Problems of the hypothalamic-pituitary system, testicular disorders, and problems of the ejaculatory system can cause male infertility. We consider the physical causes of infertility in 3 categories: pretesticular, testicular, and posttesticular. The *pretesticular* or endocrine causes occur in only about 3% of the cases. They can generally be treated with medication or surgery.

Testicular problems make up 50% of the cases. The most common cause of male infertility is a varicocele. Other factors that influence the testes include infection (e.g., mumps virus, STIs, bacterial infections), congenital anomalies, drugs, radiation, substance use (alcohol, nicotine, drugs), and environmental hazards.

Posttesticular causes account for 5% to 7% of the cases. Obstruction, infection, and the result of a surgical procedure are the primary causes. The remaining 40% are *idiopathic,* or of unknown causes.

A careful health history and assessment may reveal the cause of infertility. The history is a starting point for determining cause and treatment. The history should include age; occupation; past injury, surgery, or infections of the genital tract; lifestyle issues (e.g., hot tubs, weight training, wearing tight undergarments); sexual practices; frequency of intercourse; and emotional factors, such as stress level. Have they fathered a child? Record the use of drugs, such as chemotherapeutic agents, anabolic steroids or testosterone, sulfasalazine, cimetidine, and recreational drugs. These drugs can reduce the sperm count. The assessment may identify a varicocele, Peyronie disease, or other physical findings.

The first test in the male infertility evaluation is a semen analysis to evaluate sperm concentration, motility, and morphology. Hormone studies, including plasma testosterone and serum LH and FSH measurements, are helpful. Be tactful in dealing with the male patient undergoing infertility studies. Many cultures equate fertility and masculinity. Both male and female partners should undergo evaluation simultaneously to avoid potential treatment delays.

Treatment options for the man include drugs, conservative lifestyle changes (e.g., avoiding scrotal heat, substance use, high stress), in vitro fertilization techniques, and corrective surgery. Infertility can seriously strain a relationship. The couple may need counseling and discussion of alternatives if they do not achieve conception. Female infertility is discussed in Chapter 58.

Case Study

Benign Prostatic Hyperplasia With Acute Urinary Retention

(© IPGGutenbergUKLtd/iStock/Thinkstock.)

Patient Profile

B.G., a 60-year-old Black man with hypertension, COPD, and coronary artery disease, presents to the emergency department because of an inability to void for the past 13 h.

Subjective Data

- Reports the urge to void, and pain in the lower abdomen
- Reports gradually worsening dysuria for 2 days prior to presentation
- Appears restless, anxious, and agitated

Objective Data

- Has prostate enlargement on digital rectal examination
- Has a tender and palpable bladder above the umbilicus
- Urinalysis (from catheter): >100 WBC, 30 RBC, positive bacteria and nitrites
- PSA test: 8 ng/mL

Interprofessional Care

- Indwelling urinary catheter inserted by emergency department nurse, with 900-mL cloudy urine drained from the bladder with relief of symptoms
- Admitted for observation

Discussion Questions

1. ***Recognize:*** What risk factors do you identify for prostate problems?
2. ***Analyze:*** Interpret the high PSA level.
3. ***Analyze:*** Based on the assessment, what problem does B.G. have?
4. ***Plan:*** What treatment options are possible?
5. ***Prioritize*** What is the most important problem to manage right now?
6. ***Act*** What teaching will you provide so B.G. can successfully self-manage care?
7. ***Evaluate:*** What do you need to continually monitor?
8. ***Safety:*** What risk factors does B.G. have for DVT? Infection?

Answers available at http://evolve.elsevier.com/Lewis/medsurg.

BRIDGE TO NCLEX EXAMINATION

The number of the question corresponds to the same-numbered outcome at the beginning of the chapter.

1. Postoperatively, a patient who had a green light laser photoselective vaporization of the prostate (PVP) has continuous bladder irrigation (CBI) with a 3-way urinary catheter with a 30-mL balloon. On assessment, CBI outflow is light pink. The patient reports bladder spasms with the catheter in place. The nurse would
   - **a.** inflate the balloon to 35 mL to decrease bulk in the bladder.
   - **b.** stop the irrigation and notify the HCP of possible obstruction.
   - **c.** deflate the balloon and then reinflate to ensure that the catheter is patent.
   - **d.** tell him spasms are expected and he should not try to urinate around the catheter.
2. Which factors would place a patient at a higher risk for prostate cancer? *(select all that apply)*
   - **a.** Older than 65 years
   - **b.** Asian or Native American
   - **c.** Long-term use of an indwelling urethral catheter
   - **d.** Father diagnosed with early-stage prostate cancer
   - **e.** History of undescended testicle and testicular cancer
3. A patient who is recovering from a radical prostatectomy for prostate cancer expresses concern that he will have erectile dysfunction. In responding to this patient, the nurse would keep in mind that
   - **a.** testosterone therapy will improve his libido.
   - **b.** PDE5 inhibitors are contraindicated in prostatectomy patients.

   c. erectile dysfunction can occur even with a nerve-sparing procedure.
   d. he will not be able to ejaculate which will decrease his desire for sex.
4. The nurse explains to the patient with chronic bacterial prostatitis who is undergoing antibiotic therapy that *(select all that apply)*
   a. all patients require hospitalization.
   b. treatment is generally 8 to 12 weeks.
   c. α-adrenergic blockers can help with pain.
   d. long-term therapy may be needed in immunocompromised patient.
   e. if the condition is not treated appropriately, he is at risk for prostate cancer.
5. Assessment findings that may be present in a patient with testicular cancer include
   a. painful ejaculation.
   b. urinary incontinence.
   c. painless mass in the scrotal area.
   d. rapid onset of dysuria with scrotal swelling and fever.
6. Which points would the nurse include in a teaching plan for a patient with erectile dysfunction? *(select all that apply)*
   a. The most common cause is benign prostatic hypertrophy.
   b. Only men who are 65 years or older benefit from PDE5 inhibitors.
   c. There are medications and devices that can be used to help with erections.
   d. This condition can be caused by psychologic problems like anxiety or depression.
   e. If they take a PDE5 inhibitor, they may experience a headache and nasal congestion.
7. When discussing a male patient's reproductive organs, the nurse should
   a. arrange to have male nurses care for the patient.
   b. look away and avoid eye contact with the patient.
   c. maintain a nonjudgmental attitude toward his sexual practices.
   d. use medical terms and anatomic names for his genitalia and sexual organs.

1. d; 2. a; 3. c; 4. b, d; 5. c; 6. c, d, e; 7. c.

For rationales to these answers and even more NCLEX review questions, visit http://evolve.elsevier.com/Lewis/medsurg.

EVOLVE WEBSITE/RESOURCES LIST

http://evolve.elsevier.com/Lewis/medsurg
Review Questions (Online Only)
Key Points
Answer Keys for Questions
- Rationales for Bridge to NCLEX Examination Questions
- Answer Guidelines for Case Study
- Answer Guidelines for Managing Care of Multiple Patients Case Study (Section 11)

Student Case Study
- Patient With Benign Prostatic Hyperplasia

Nursing Care Plan
- eNursing Care Plan 59.1: Patient Having Prostate Surgery

Conceptual Care Map Creator
Audio Glossary
Content Updates

REFERENCES

1. Powley G, Briolat G: Benign prostatic hyperplasia. In Lajiness M, Quallich S, editors: *The nurse practitioner in urology*, ed 2, Switzerland, 2020, Springer Nature.
*2. Parsons JK, Dahm P, Kohler TS, et al.: Surgical management of lower urinary tract symptoms attributed to benign prostatic hyperplasia: AUA Guideline amendment 2020, *J Urol* 204:799, 2020.
*3. ElJalby M, Thomas D, Elterman D, et al.: The effect of diet on BPH, LUTS and ED, *World J Urol* 37:1001, 2019.
4. Barry M, Fowler F, O'Leary M, et al.: The AUA symptom index for benign prostatic hyperplasia, *J Urol* 148:1549, 1992. (Classic).
*5. Kasivisvanathan V, Stabile A, Neves J, et al.: Magnetic resonance imaging-targeted biopsy versus systematic biopsy in the detection of prostate cancer: a systematic review and meta-analysis, *Eur Urol* 76:284, 2019.
*6. Abreu-Mendes P, Silva J, Cruz F: Pharmacology of the lower urinary tract: update on LUTS treatment, *Ther Adv Urol* 12:1, 2020.
7. American Cancer Society (ACS): Key statistics for prostate cancer. Retrieved from https://www.cancer.org/cancer/prostate-cancer/about/key-statistics.html.
8. ACS: Early detection, diagnosis, and staging. Retrieved from https://www.cancer.org/cancer/prostate-cancer/detection-diagnosis-staging.html.
*9. Desai A, Hudnall M, Weiner A, et al.: Contemporary comparison of open to robotic prostatectomy at a Veteran's Affairs hospital, *Mil Med* 184:e330, 2019.
10. Oncolink: Possible side effects of radiation treatment for prostate cancer. Retrieved from https://www.oncolink.org/cancers/prostate/treatments/possible-side-effects-of-radiation-treatment-for-prostate-cancer.
*11. Cardwell C, O'Sullivan J, Jain S, et al.: The risk of cardiovascular disease in prostate cancer patients receiving androgen deprivation therapies, *Epidemiology* 31:432, 2020.
*12. Dess R, Hartman H, Mahal B, et al.: Association of black race with prostate cancer-specific and other-cause mortality, *JAMA Oncol* 5:975, 2019.
*13. Farmer T, Johnston M, Milica A, et al.: Chronic prostatitis/chronic pelvic pain syndrome: a literature review of NIH III prostatitis, *Curr Bladder Dysfunct Rep* 14:83, 2019.
*14. Douglawi A, Masterson T: Penile cancer epidemiology and risk factors, *Curr Opin Urol* 29:145, 2019.
*15. Gilligan T, Lin D, Aggarwal R, et al.: Testicular cancer. NCCN clinical practice guidelines in oncology, version 2.2020. Retrieved from https://www.nccn.org.
*16. Julien D, Sessanna L, Campbell N: A comparative analysis of testosterone therapy and phosphodiesterase 5 inhibitor monotherapy and combined therapy in men with erectile dysfunction and low testosterone levels, *Urol Nurs* 40:11, 2020.
*17. Flyckt R, Falcone T: Infertility: a practical framework, *Cleve Clin J Med* 86:473, 2019.

*Evidence-based information for clinical practice.

Case Study

Applying Clinical Judgment With Multiple Patients

You are working on the medical-surgical unit. The following are 4 of the 6 patients you have been assigned to care for this shift. An LPN and AP assist another RN and you.

 (© iStockphoto/ Thinkstock.)	L.M. is a 35-year-old woman admitted for hypertension caused by newly diagnosed Cushing syndrome. She has been depressed and crying because of her appearance. Vital signs: 164/94, 84, RR 18.
 (© iStockphoto/ Thinkstock.)	N.B. is a 48-year-old man admitted to the ICU 2 days ago in diabetic ketoacidosis (DKA). He was transferred to the clinical unit yesterday evening. Laboratory results: glucose 296 mg/dL.
 (© XiXinXing/ iStock/Thinkstock.)	A.K. is a 68-year-old woman with cancer of her right breast. She had a partial mastectomy and axillary node dissection yesterday. She has a Jackson-Pratt drain in her right chest. Her last pain medication was given 1 hour ago, at which time she rated her pain as a 7 (0–10 scale).
 (© Jupiterimages/ Photos.com/ Thinkstock.)	R.D., a 52-year-old woman with Graves disease, had a subtotal thyroidectomy yesterday. Is to start a soft diet and ambulate in the hall this morning. In report it was noted that her voice has become slightly "hoarse" in the last hour.

1. Highlight all the findings above that require your follow-up.
2. After receiving report, which patient should you see first? Second?
3. Which tasks could you delegate to AP? (*Select all that apply*)
   a. Assist N.B. to ambulate in the hallway.
   b. Obtain daily weights for L.M. and N.B.
   c. Take R.D.'s vital signs and report the results to you.
   d. Assess A.K.'s mastectomy incision for signs of infection.
   e. Listen to L.M. talk about her feelings while helping her with AM care.
4. While you are assessing R.D., the LPN tells you that A.K.'s chest dressing is totally saturated with bloody drainage. Which *initial* action would be most appropriate?
   a. Ask the LPN to call the laboratory for a stat hemoglobin (Hgb) and hematocrit (Hct) on A.K.
   b. Tell the LPN to reinforce the dressing with sterile 4 × 4 gauze pads.
   c. Have the LPN stay with R.D. while you assess A.K.'s Jackson-Pratt drain.
   d. Ask the LPN to stay with A.K., have the AP monitor R.D. while you call A.K.'s HCP.

Case Study Progression

A.K.'s Jackson-Pratt drain was not functioning properly. You get it working and change the chest dressing. The incision is well approximated without signs of infection. When you leave the room, the Jackson-Pratt has a small amount of serosanguineous drainage in it. As you enter R.D.'s room, you notice she is having a carpal spasm on the same arm on which the LPN is taking her BP. You obtain a focused assessment and notify the health care provider.

4. Which assessment findings would be *most* important to include in a discussion with the health care provider about R.D.? *(select all that apply)*
   a. Patient is anxious
   b. Hoarseness of voice
   c. Most recent Hgb and Hct
   d. Carpal spasm upon inflation of BP cuff
   e. BP of 138/76 and heart rate of 78
5. Based on R.D.'s assessment findings, the priority need will be prevention of ____1____. To reduce this risk, the most important intervention is to ____2____.

Options for 1	Options for 2
bleeding	administer IV calcium gluconate
respiratory distress	increase IV fluids and apply a pressure dressing
thyrotoxicosis	start O_2 therapy

6. Which intervention would be of *highest* priority in caring for L.M.?
   a. Assess her for fall risk.
   b. Assess her for signs and symptoms of hypoglycemia.
   c. Teach her the need for a high-carbohydrate, low-protein diet.
   d. Reassure her that her physical appearance will improve with treatment.
7. You are concerned N.B. may redevelop DKA. For each of assessment finding, use an X to indicate whether it is Expected (no follow-up is required) or Requires Follow-up (could be harmful to the patient) at this time.

Assessment Finding	Expected	Requires Follow-up
Potassium 2.7 mEq/L		
Lungs sounds clear bilaterally		
Restlessness		
Slightly labored respirations		
Reports of dizziness when ambulating		
Skin pink, warm, and dry		

8. You see that you need to review N.B.'s medication record for new HCP orders. Choose the most likely options for the information missing from the table by selecting from the lists of options provided.

Continued

Case Study—cont'd

Medication	Dose, Route, Frequency	Drug Class	Indication
Insulin glargine	1	Long-acting insulin	Decrease glucose levels
2	20 mEq IV in 250 mL 0.9% over 2 hr	Electrolyte replacement	Reverse low potassium levels
enoxaparin sodium	40 units subcut daily	Anticoagulant	3
Ondansetron	4 mg IV q8hr as needed	4	Reduce feelings of nausea and vomiting

Options for 1	Options for 2	Options for 3	Options for 4
20 units IV daily 22 units subcut daily 100 units subcut daily	Magnesium, potassium, sodium sulfates Penicillin G potassium Potassium chloride	Decrease insulin resistance Reduce risk of atrial fibrillation VTE prophylaxis	Antiemetic Antihypergly-cemic Hormone analog

9. The LPN is assigned to give medications to N.B., including his sliding scale Novolog insulin with lunch. The AP, who is also a senior nursing student, tells you that the LPN gave N.B.'s insulin at least 30 minutes after the patient ate his lunch. What is your *best* initial action?
   a. Report the incident to the charge nurse for follow up.
   b. Talk to the LPN about the importance of timely medication administration.
   c. Ask the LPN what time the insulin was given and when the patient ate breakfast.
   d. Ask the AP to first discuss the concern with the LPN to follow lines of communication.

60

Assessment: Nervous System

Kristen J. Costello

http://evolve.elsevier.com/Lewis/medsurg/

CONCEPTUAL FOCUS

Cognition
Functional Ability
Intracranial Regulation
Sensory Perception

LEARNING OUTCOMES

1. Compare the functions of neurons and glial cells.
2. Explain the anatomic location and functions of the cerebrum, brainstem, cerebellum, spinal cord, peripheral nerves, and cerebrospinal fluid.
3. Identify the major arteries supplying the brain.
4. Describe the functions of the 12 cranial nerves.
5. Compare the functions of the 2 divisions of the autonomic nervous system.
6. Link the age-related changes in the neurologic system to the differences in assessment findings.
7. Obtain significant subjective and objective data related to the nervous system from a patient.
8. Perform a physical assessment of the nervous system using the appropriate techniques.
9. Discern normal from abnormal findings of a physical assessment of the nervous system.
10. Describe the purpose, significance of results, and nursing responsibilities related to diagnostic studies of the nervous system.

KEY TERMS

autonomic nervous system (ANS)
blood-brain barrier
central nervous system (CNS)
cerebrospinal fluid (CSF)
cranial nerves (CNs)
dermatome
glial cells
lower motor neurons (LMNs)
meninges
neurons
neurotransmitters
peripheral nervous system (PNS)
reflex
synapse
upper motor neurons (UMNs)

The nervous system is one of the most complex systems. It controls all the body's activities. Having a good understanding of the nervous system is critical to be able to analyze and interpret clinical findings. This chapter reviews the structures and functions, assessment, and diagnostic studies of the nervous system.

STRUCTURES AND FUNCTIONS OF NERVOUS SYSTEM

The nervous system is responsible for the control and integration of the body's many activities. It is divided into the central nervous system and peripheral nervous system. The **central**

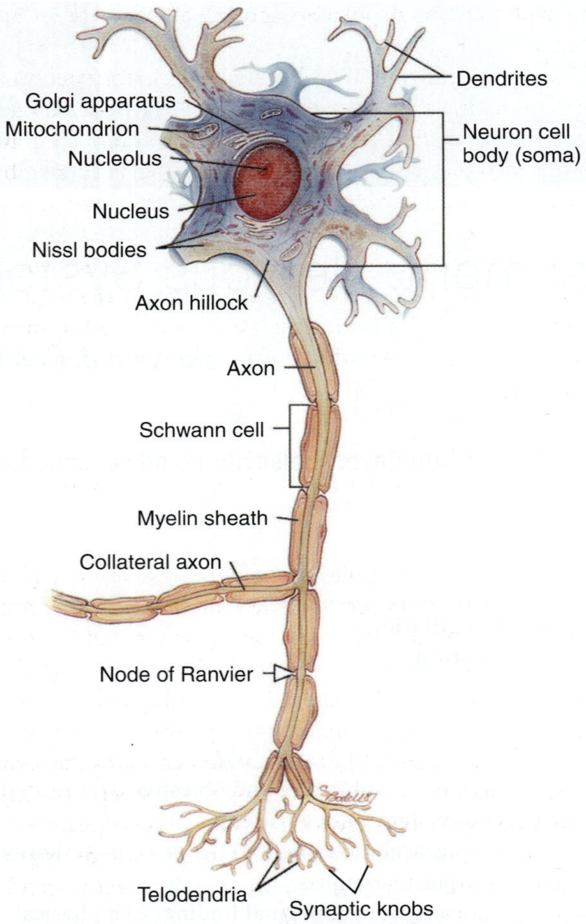

Fig. 60.1 Structural features of neurons: dendrites, cell body, and axons. (Modified from Thibodeau GA, Patton KT: *Anatomy and physiology,* ed 8, St Louis, 2013, Mosby.)

nervous system (CNS) consists of the brain, spinal cord, and cranial nerves I and II. The peripheral nervous system (PNS) consists of cranial nerves III to XII, spinal nerves, and peripheral components of the autonomic nervous system (ANS).

Cells of Nervous System

The nervous system is made up of 2 types of cells: neurons and supportive glial cells.

Neurons

Neurons are the main functional unit of the nervous system. Neurons come in many shapes and sizes. They share 3 characteristics: (1) *excitability,* or the ability to generate a nerve impulse; (2) *conductivity,* or the ability to transmit an impulse; and (3) the ability to influence other neurons, muscle cells, or glandular cells.

A typical neuron consists of a cell body, multiple dendrites, and an axon (Fig. 60.1). The *cell body* contains the nucleus and cytoplasm. It is the metabolic center of the neuron. *Dendrites* are short processes extending from the cell body. They receive impulses or signals from other neurons and conduct them toward the cell body. The *axon* projects varying distances from the cell body. The axon carries nerve impulses to other neurons or to end organs, such as smooth and striated muscles and glands.

Many axons in the CNS and PNS are covered by a *myelin sheath*. It is a white, lipid protein substance that acts as an insulator for impulse conduction. Axons may be myelinated or unmyelinated, as in the case of smaller nerve fibers.

Glial Cells

Glial cells (glia, neuroglia) provide support, nourishment, and protection to neurons. Glial cells make up about half of the brain and spinal cord mass. Glial cells are divided into microglia and macroglia. *Microglia* are specialized macrophages capable of phagocytosis. They protect the neurons. These cells are mobile within the brain. They multiply when the brain is damaged.

Macroglial cells include astrocytes, oligodendrocytes, and ependymal cells. *Astrocytes* are found mainly in gray matter. They provide structural support to neurons. Their delicate processes form the *blood-brain barrier* with the endothelium of the blood vessels. They play a role in *synaptic transmission* (impulse conduction between neurons). When the brain is injured, astrocytes act as phagocytes for cleaning up neuronal debris. They help restore the neurochemical milieu and provide support for repair. Proliferation of astrocytes contributes to the formation of scar tissue *(gliosis)* in the CNS.

Oligodendrocytes produce the myelin sheath of nerve fibers in the CNS. They are found mainly in the white matter of the CNS. *Ependymal cells* line the brain ventricles. They aid in cerebrospinal fluid (CSF) secretion.

Nerve Regeneration

If the axon of the nerve cell is damaged, the cell tries to repair itself. Damaged nerve cells try to grow back to their original destinations by sprouting many branches from the damaged ends of their axons. Axons in the CNS are generally less successful than peripheral axons in regeneration.[1]

Schwann cells myelinate the nerve fibers in the PNS. Injured nerve fibers in the PNS can regenerate by growing within the protective myelin sheath of the Schwann cells if the cell body is intact and the environment is optimal.[2] The final result of nerve regeneration depends on the number of axon sprouts that join with the appropriate Schwann cell columns and reinnervate appropriate end organs.

Neurons have long been thought to be nonmitotic. That is, after being damaged, neurons could not be replaced. Recent research shows a subset of astrocytes proliferate after some CNS injuries, and neurogenesis may occur from stem cells.[3] These findings support the fact that the patient will have a certain amount of recovery after injury involving the neurons.

Nerve Impulse

The purpose of a neuron is to initiate, receive, and process messages about events both within and outside the body. The initiation of a neuronal message *(nerve impulse)* involves the generation of an action potential. A series of action potentials travel along the axon. When the impulse reaches the end of the nerve fiber, a chemical interaction involving neurotransmitters transfers the impulse across the junction *(synapse)* between

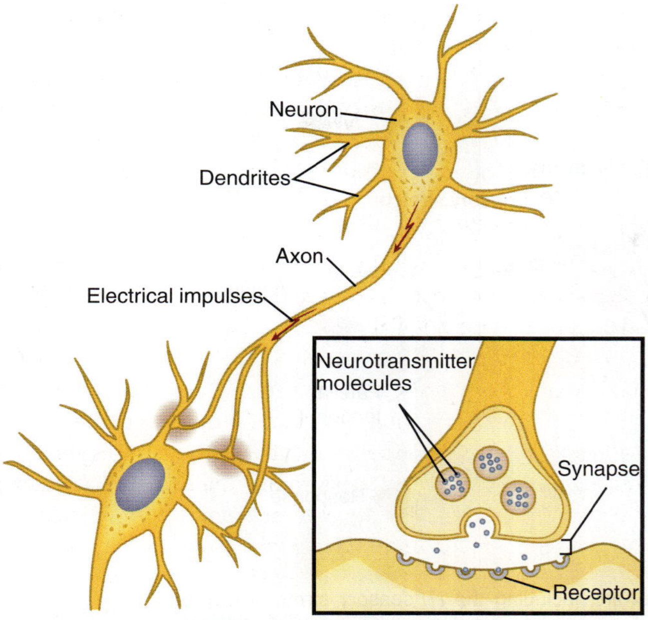

Fig. 60.2 Impulse generation between neurons. Synapse shown with neurotransmitters and receptors.

nerve cells. This chemical interaction generates another set of action potentials in the next neuron. These events are repeated until the nerve impulse reaches its destination.

Because of its insulating capacity, myelination of axons speeds the conduction of an action potential. Many peripheral nerve axons have *nodes of Ranvier* (gaps in the myelin sheath) that allow an action potential to travel much faster by jumping from node to node. We call this *saltatory* (hopping) *conduction.* In an unmyelinated fiber, conduction is slower. The wave of depolarization travels the entire length of the axon, with each part of the membrane becoming depolarized in turn.

Synapse

A **synapse** is the structural and functional junction between 2 neurons. It is where the nerve impulse is transmitted from one neuron to another. The nerve impulse also can be transmitted from neurons to glands or muscles. The essential structures of synaptic transmission are a presynaptic terminal, synaptic cleft, and receptor site on the postsynaptic cell (Fig. 60.2).

Neurotransmitters

Neurotransmitters are chemicals that affect the transmission of impulses across the synaptic cleft. *Excitatory neurotransmitters* (e.g., epinephrine, norepinephrine, glutamate) activate postsynaptic receptors that increase the chance that an action potential will be generated. *Inhibitory neurotransmitters* (e.g., serotonin, γ-aminobutyric acid [GABA], dopamine) activate postsynaptic receptors to decrease the chance that an action potential will be generated. For example, endorphins block pain transmission while substance P makes nerves more sensitive to pain.

In general, the net effect (excitatory or inhibitory) depends on the number of presynaptic neurons releasing neurotransmitters on the postsynaptic cell. A presynaptic cell that releases an excitatory neurotransmitter does not always cause the postsynaptic cell to depolarize enough to generate an action potential.

When many presynaptic cells release excitatory neurotransmitters on a single neuron, the sum of their input is enough to generate an action potential. Neurotransmitters continue to combine with the receptor sites at the postsynaptic membrane until they are inactivated by enzymes, taken up by the presynaptic endings, or diffuse away from the synaptic region. Drugs and toxins can affect neurotransmitters by changing their function or blocking their attachment to receptor sites on the postsynaptic membrane. Cerebral microdialysis can be used to measure neurotransmitter levels in the cerebral cortex (see Chapter 61).

Central Nervous System

The components of the CNS include the cerebrum (cerebral hemispheres), brainstem, cerebellum, and spinal cord.

Spinal Cord

The *spinal cord* is continuous with the brainstem and exits from the cranial cavity through the foramen magnum. A cross section of the spinal cord reveals gray matter that is centrally located in an H shape and surrounded by white matter. The gray matter contains the cell bodies of voluntary motor neurons, preganglionic autonomic motor neurons, and association neurons (interneurons). The white matter contains the axons of the ascending sensory and descending motor fibers. The myelin surrounding these fibers gives them their white appearance. The spinal pathways or tracts are named for the point of origin and the point of destination (e.g., spinocerebellar tract [ascending], corticospinal tract [descending]).

Ascending tracts. In general, the ascending tracts carry specific sensory information to higher levels of the CNS. This information comes from special sensory receptors in the skin, muscles and joints, viscera, and blood vessels. It enters the spinal cord by way of the dorsal roots of the spinal nerves. The ascending tracts are organized by sensory modality and anatomy. The fasciculus gracilis and the fasciculus cuneatus (*dorsal* or *posterior columns*) carry information about touch, deep pressure, vibration, position sense, and kinesthesia (appreciation of movement, weight, and body parts). The *spinocerebellar tracts* carry information about muscle tension and body position to the cerebellum for coordination of movement. The *spinothalamic tracts* carry pain and temperature sensations.

Other ascending tracts may also carry sensory information. The signs and symptoms of various neurologic problems suggest there are other pathways for touch, position sense, and vibration.

Descending tracts. Descending tracts carry impulses that are responsible for muscle movement. Important descending tracts are the corticobulbar and corticospinal tracts, collectively termed the *pyramidal tract.* These tracts carry voluntary impulses from the cerebral cortex to the cranial and peripheral nerves. Another group of descending motor tracts carries impulses from the extrapyramidal system (all motor systems except the pyramidal) concerned with voluntary movement. It includes pathways originating in the brainstem, basal ganglia,

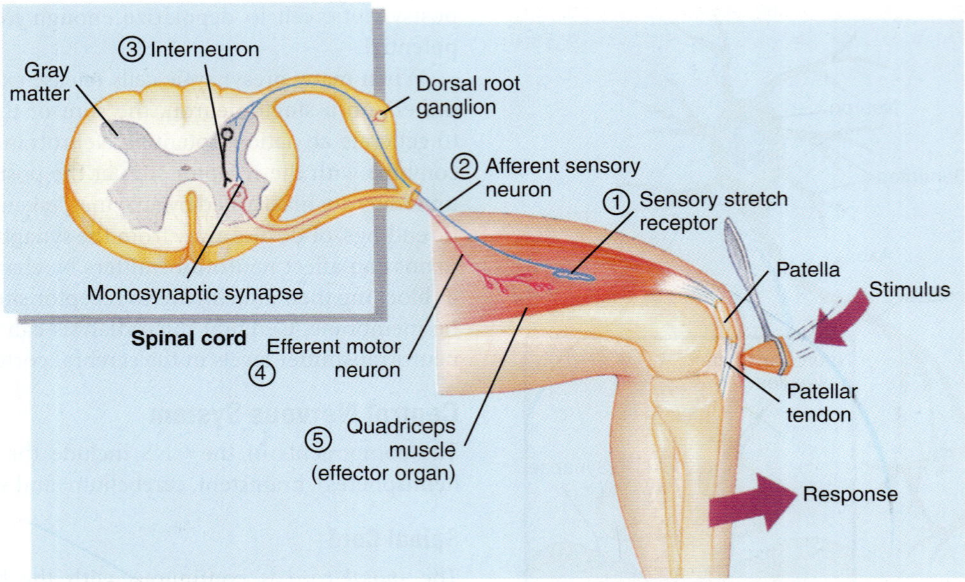

Fig. 60.3 Basic diagram of the patellar "knee jerk" reflex arc, including the *(1)* sensory stretch receptor, *(2)* afferent sensory neuron, *(3)* interneuron, *(4)* efferent motor neuron, and *(5)* quadriceps muscle (effector organ). (Modified from Thibodeau GA, Patton KT: *Anatomy and physiology,* ed 6, St Louis, 2007, Mosby.)

and cerebellum. The motor output exits the spinal cord through the ventral roots of the spinal nerves.

Reflex arc. A reflex is an involuntary response to stimuli. In the spinal cord, reflex arcs play an important role in maintaining muscle tone, which is essential for body posture. The components of a monosynaptic reflex arc (Fig. 60.3) are a receptor organ, afferent neuron, effector neuron, and effector organ (e.g., skeletal muscle). The afferent neuron synapses with the efferent neurons in the gray matter of the spinal cord, producing an involuntary response. More complex reflex arcs involve interneurons in addition to the afferent neuron influencing the effector neuron.

Lower and upper motor neurons. Upper motor neurons (UMNs) originate in the cerebral cortex and project downward. The corticobulbar tract ends in the brainstem, and the corticospinal tract descends into the spinal cord. These neurons influence skeletal muscle movement. UMN lesions generally cause weakness or paralysis, disuse atrophy, hyperreflexia, and increased muscle tone (spasticity).

Lower motor neurons (LMNs) are the final common pathway through which descending motor tracts influence skeletal muscle. The cell bodies of LMNs, which send axons to innervate the skeletal muscles of the arms, trunk, and legs, are found in the anterior horn of the corresponding segments of the spinal cord (e.g., cervical segments contain LMNs for the arms). LMNs for skeletal muscles of the eyes, face, mouth, and throat are found in the corresponding segments of the brainstem. These cell bodies and their axons make up the somatic motor components of the cranial nerves (CNs). LMN lesions generally cause weakness or paralysis, denervation atrophy, hyporeflexia or areflexia, and decreased muscle tone (flaccidity).

Brain

The brain has 3 major intracranial components: cerebrum, brainstem, and cerebellum.

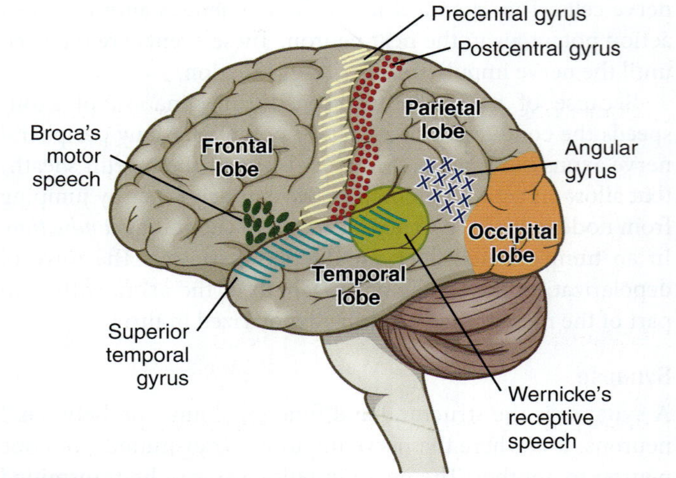

Fig. 60.4 Left hemisphere of cerebrum, lateral surface, showing major lobes and areas of the brain.

Cerebrum. The *cerebrum* is composed of the right and left cerebral hemispheres. It is divided into 4 lobes: frontal, temporal, parietal, and occipital (Fig. 60.4). The functions of the cerebrum are multiple and complex (Table 60.1). The *frontal lobe* controls higher cognitive function, memory retention, voluntary eye movements, voluntary motor movement, and motor functions involved in speech production *(Broca area)*. The *temporal lobe* integrates somatic, visual, and auditory data. It contains *Wernicke receptive speech area*. The *parietal lobe* interprets spatial information. It contains the sensory cortex. Processing of sight takes place in the *occipital lobe*.

The division of the cerebrum into lobes is useful to delineate portions of the neocortex (gray matter), which makes up the outer layer of the cerebral hemispheres. Neurons in specific parts of the neocortex are essential for various complex and

TABLE 60.1 Function of Cerebrum

Part	Location	Function
Cortical Areas		
Motor		
Primary	Precentral gyrus	Motor control and movement on opposite side of body
Supplemental	Anterior to precentral gyrus	Facilitates proximal muscle activity, including activity for stance and gait, and spontaneous movement and coordination
Sensory		
Association areas	Parietal lobe	Integrates somatic and sensory input
	Posterior temporal lobe	Integrates visual and auditory input for language comprehension
	Anterior temporal lobe	Integrates past experiences
	Anterior frontal lobe	Controls higher order processes (e.g., judgment, reasoning)
Auditory	Superior temporal gyrus	Registers auditory input
Somatic	Postcentral gyrus	Sensory response from opposite side of body
Visual	Occipital lobe	Registers visual images
Language		
Comprehension	Wernicke area in dominant posterior temporal lobe	Integrates auditory language (understanding of spoken words)
Expression	Broca area in dominant frontal lobe	Regulates motor speech
Basal Ganglia	Near lateral ventricles of both cerebral hemispheres	Controls and refines learned and automatic movements
Thalamus	Below and slightly posterior to basal ganglia	Relays sensory and motor input to and from cerebrum
Hypothalamus	Below and anterior to thalamus	Regulates endocrine and autonomic functions
Limbic System	Lateral to hypothalamus	Influences emotional behavior and basic drives, such as feeding and sexual behavior

sophisticated functions. These include language, memory, and interpreting visual-spatial relationships.

The basal ganglia, thalamus, hypothalamus, and limbic system are specific groups of neuron clusters in the cerebrum. The *basal ganglia* are found centrally in the cerebrum and midbrain. Most of them are on both sides of the thalamus. The function of the basal ganglia includes the initiation, execution, and completion of voluntary movements, learning, emotional response, and automatic movements associated with skeletal muscle activity (e.g., swallowing saliva, blinking, swinging the arms while walking).

The *thalamus* lies directly above the brainstem (Fig. 60.5). It is the major relay center for sensory input from the body, face, retina, and cochlear and taste receptors. Motor relay nuclei in the thalamus connect the cerebellum and basal ganglia to the frontal cortex.

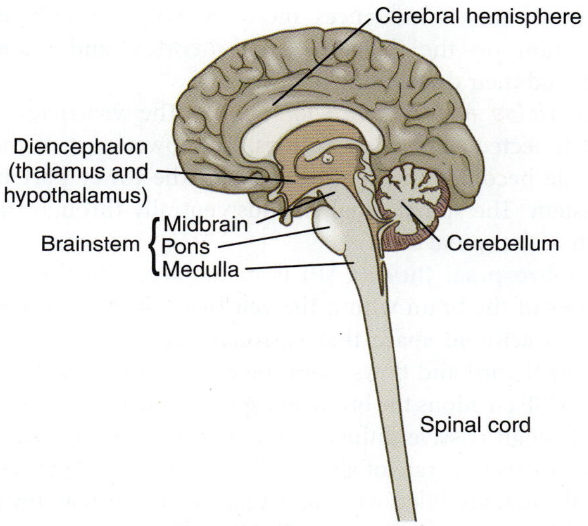

Fig. 60.5 Major divisions of the CNS.

The *hypothalamus* is just below the thalamus and slightly in front of the midbrain. It exerts a direct influence on release of hormones from the anterior pituitary gland. It has a rich capillary connection to the pituitary gland to aid in the transport of hormones. These hormones include thyroid-stimulating hormone, growth hormone, luteinizing hormone, and prolactin-releasing hormone (see Chapter 52). In contrast, the supraoptic and paraventricular neurons travel directly through the pituitary stalk to the posterior pituitary. There, they release vasopressin and oxytocin. The hypothalamus contains the satiety center that regulates appetite. With input from the limbic system, it regulates body temperature, water balance (through influence on vasopressin secretion), circadian rhythm, and expression of emotion. The *limbic system* is found near the inner surfaces of the cerebral hemispheres. It is concerned with emotion, aggression, feeding behavior, and sexual response.

Brainstem. The *brainstem* includes the midbrain, pons, and medulla (Fig. 60.5). Ascending and descending fibers to and from the cerebrum and cerebellum pass through the brainstem. The nuclei of CNs III through XII are in the brainstem. The vital centers concerned with respiratory, vasomotor, and heart function are in the medulla. The brainstem contains the centers for sneezing, coughing, hiccupping, vomiting, sucking, and swallowing.

We find the *reticular formation* in the brainstem. It is a diffusely arranged group of neurons and their axons that extends from the medulla to the thalamus and hypothalamus. The reticular formation relays sensory information, influences excitatory and inhibitory control of spinal motor neurons, and controls vasomotor and respiratory activity. The *reticular activating system* (RAS) is a complex system that requires communication among the brainstem, reticular formation, and cerebral cortex. The RAS regulates arousal and sleep-wake transitions.

Cerebellum. The *cerebellum* is in the posterior cranial fossa below the occipital lobe. It coordinates voluntary movement and maintains trunk stability and equilibrium. The cerebellum receives information from the cerebral cortex, muscles, joints, and inner ear. It influences motor activity through axonal connections to the thalamus, motor cortex, and brainstem nuclei and their descending pathways.

Ventricles and cerebrospinal fluid. The ventricles are 4 interconnected fluid-filled cavities. The lower part of the 4th ventricle becomes the central canal in the lower part of the brainstem. The spinal canal extends centrally through the full length of the spinal cord.

Cerebrospinal fluid (CSF) is made largely in the choroid plexuses of the brain within the ventricles. It circulates within the subarachnoid space that surrounds the brain, brainstem, and spinal cord and flows from the cranial cavity to the spinal cavity. CSF cushions the brain and spinal cord and carries nutrients through passive diffusion and active transport. We make CSF at an average rate of about 500 mL/day. The ventricles and central canal are filled with an average of 150 mL at any given time. Changes in the rate of CSF production or absorption can occur. This leads to a change in the volume within the ventricles and central canal. Too much CSF results in *hydrocephalus*.

CSF circulates throughout the ventricles and seeps into the subarachnoid space surrounding the brain and spinal cord. It is absorbed mainly through the *arachnoid villi* (tiny projections into the subarachnoid space) into the intradural venous sinuses and eventually into the venous system.

Analyzing CSF composition provides useful diagnostic information related to certain nervous system diseases. We often measure CSF pressure in patients with actual or suspected intracranial injury. Increased intracranial pressure, indicated by increased CSF pressure, can force downward (central) herniation of the brain and brainstem. The signs marking this event are part of the herniation syndrome (see Chapter 61).

Peripheral Nervous System

The PNS includes all the neuronal structures that lie outside the CNS. It consists of the spinal and CNs, their associated ganglia (groupings of cell bodies), and parts of the ANS.

Spinal Nerves

The spinal cord can be seen as a series of spinal segments, each on top of another with no visible boundaries. In addition to the cell bodies, each segment has a pair of dorsal (afferent) sensory nerve fibers or roots and ventral (efferent) motor fibers or roots. They innervate a specific region of the body. This combined motor-sensory nerve is called a *spinal nerve* (Fig. 60.6). The cell bodies of the voluntary motor system are in the anterior horn of the spinal cord gray matter. The cell bodies of the autonomic (involuntary) motor system are in the anterolateral part of the spinal cord gray matter. The cell bodies of sensory fibers are in the dorsal root ganglia just outside the spinal cord. On exiting the spinal column, each spinal nerve divides into ventral and dorsal rami, a collection of motor and sensory fibers that eventually goes to peripheral structures (e.g., skin, muscles, viscera).

A **dermatome** is the area of skin innervated by the sensory fibers of a single dorsal root of a spinal nerve (Fig. 60.7). The dermatomes give a general picture of somatic sensory innervation by spinal segments. A *myotome* is a muscle group innervated by the primary motor neurons of a single ventral root. The

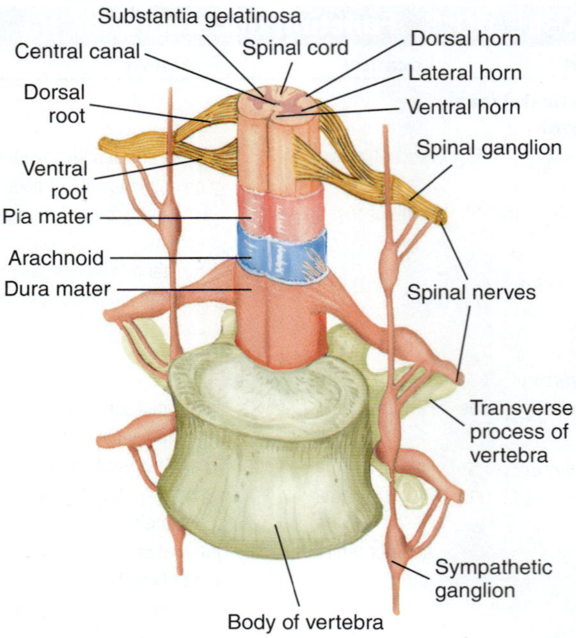

Fig. 60.6 Cross section of spinal cord showing attachments of spinal nerves and coverings of the spinal cord.

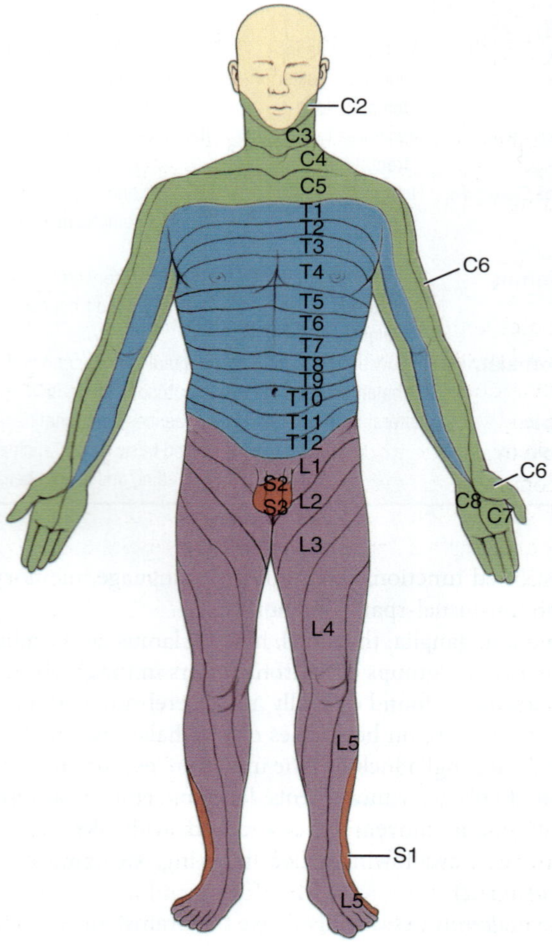

Fig. 60.7 Dermatomes of the body. (From Herlihy B: *The human body in health and illness,* ed 4, St Louis, 2011, Saunders.)

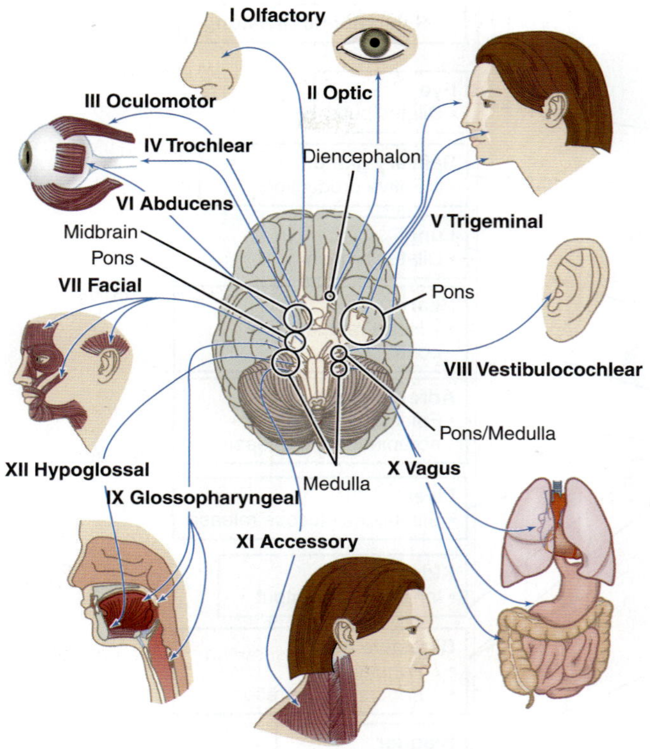

Fig. 60.8 The cranial nerves are numbered by the order in which they leave the brain. (Redrawn from McCance KL, Huether SE: *Pathophysiology: the biologic basis for disease in adults and children*, ed 6, St Louis, 2010, Mosby.)

dermatomes and myotomes of a given spinal segment overlap with those of adjacent segments because of the development of ascending and descending collateral branches of nerve fibers.

Cranial Nerves

The **cranial nerves (CNs)** are the 12 paired nerves composed of cell bodies with fibers that exit from the cranial cavity. Unlike the spinal nerves, which always have both afferent sensory and efferent motor fibers, some CNs are only sensory, some only motor, and some both.

Table 60.4 (later in this chapter) outlines the motor and sensory components of the CNs. Fig. 60.8 shows the position of the CNs in relation to the brain and spinal cord. Just as the cell bodies of the spinal nerves are in specific segments of the spinal cord, cell bodies (nuclei) of the CNs are in specific segments of the brainstem. Exceptions are the nuclei of the olfactory and optic nerves. The primary cell bodies of the olfactory nerve are in the nasal epithelium. The cell bodies of the optic nerve are in the retina.

Autonomic Nervous System

The **autonomic nervous system (ANS)** is divided into the sympathetic and parasympathetic systems. The ANS governs involuntary functions of heart muscle, smooth muscle, and glands through both efferent and afferent pathways. The 2 systems function together to maintain a relatively balanced internal environment. The preganglionic cell bodies of the *sympathetic nervous system* (SNS) are found in spinal segments T1 through L2. The major neurotransmitter released by the postganglionic fibers of the SNS is norepinephrine. The neurotransmitter released by the preganglionic fibers is acetylcholine.

The preganglionic cell bodies of the *parasympathetic nervous system* (PSNS) are found in the brainstem and sacral spinal segments (S2 through S4). Acetylcholine is the neurotransmitter released at both preganglionic and postganglionic nerve endings.

SNS stimulation activates the mechanisms required for the "fight-or-flight" response that occurs throughout the body (Fig. 60.9). In contrast, the PSNS is geared to act in localized and discrete regions. It conserves and restores the body's energy stores. The ANS provides dual and often reciprocal innervation to many structures. For example, the SNS increases the rate and force of heart contraction and the PSNS decreases the rate and force.

Cerebral Circulation

Knowing the distribution of the brain's major arteries is essential for evaluating the signs and symptoms of cerebrovascular disease and trauma. The brain's blood supply arises from the internal carotid arteries (anterior circulation) and the vertebral arteries (posterior circulation) (Fig. 60.10).

The internal carotid arteries provide blood flow to the anterior and middle portions of the cerebrum. The vertebral arteries join to form the basilar artery. It branches to supply the middle and lower parts of the temporal lobes, occipital lobes, cerebellum, brainstem, and part of the diencephalon. The main branch of the basilar artery is the posterior cerebral artery. The *circle of Willis* is formed by communicating arteries that join the basilar and internal carotid arteries (Fig. 60.11). It plays a key role in cerebral blood flow. Interestingly, research shows the formation of the circle of Willis varies greatly. Imaging shows that many people have an incomplete formation.[4]

Superior to the circle of Willis, 3 pairs of arteries supply blood to the left and right hemispheres. The anterior cerebral artery feeds the medial and anterior portions of the frontal lobes. The middle cerebral artery feeds the outer portions of the frontal, parietal, and superior temporal lobes. The posterior cerebral artery feeds the medial portions of the occipital and inferior temporal lobes. Venous blood drains from the brain through the dural sinuses, which form channels that drain into the 2 jugular veins.

Blood-Brain Barrier

The **blood-brain barrier** is a physiologic barrier between blood capillaries and brain tissue. This barrier protects the brain from harmful agents, while allowing nutrients and gases to enter. The structure of brain capillaries differs from that of other capillaries. Substances that normally pass into most tissues are prevented from entering brain tissue. Lipid-soluble compounds enter the brain easily. Water-soluble and ionized drugs enter the brain and the spinal cord slowly. Thus, the blood-brain barrier affects drug penetration. Only some drugs can enter the CNS from the bloodstream.

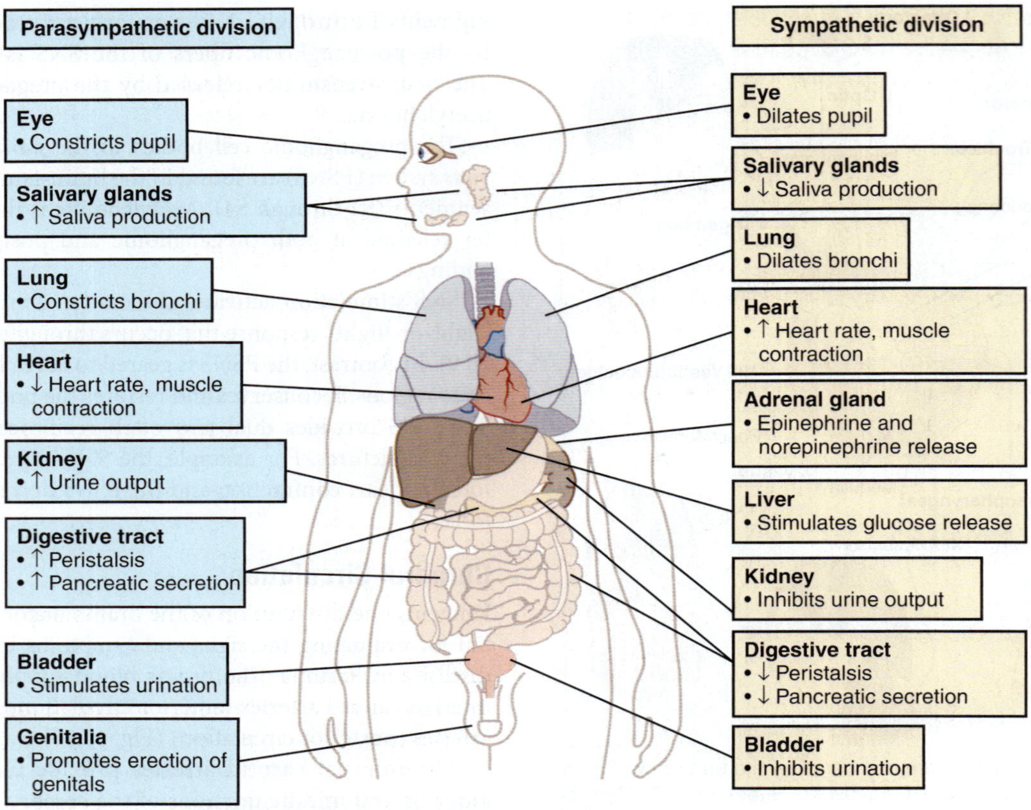

Fig. 60.9 Effects of the sympathetic and parasympathetic systems.

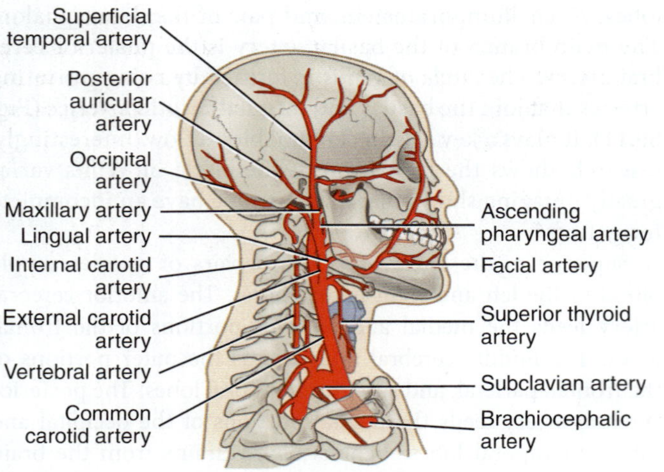

Fig. 60.10 Arteries of the head and neck. Brachiocephalic artery, right common carotid artery, right subclavian artery, and their branches. The major arteries to the head are the common carotid and vertebral arteries. (Modified from Thibodeau GA, Patton KT: *Anatomy and physiology,* ed 8, St Louis, 2013, Mosby.)

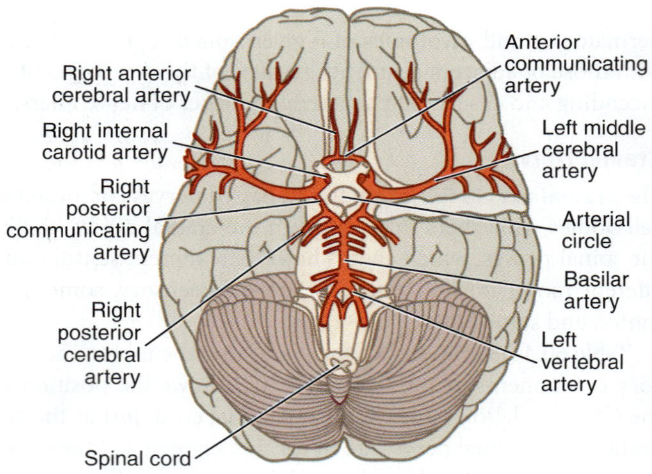

Fig. 60.11 Arteries at the base of the brain. The arteries that compose the circle of Willis are the 2 anterior cerebral arteries joined to each other by the anterior communicating cerebral artery and to the posterior cerebral arteries by the posterior communicating arteries. (Modified from Thibodeau GA, Patton KT: *Anatomy and physiology,* ed 8, St Louis, 2013, Mosby.)

Protective Structures

Meninges

The **meninges** consist of 3 protective membranes that surround the brain and spinal cord: the dura mater, arachnoid, and pia mater (Fig. 60.12). The thick *dura mater* forms the outermost layer. The *falx cerebri* is a fold of the dura that separates the 2 cerebral hemispheres. It slows expansion of brain tissue in conditions such as a rapidly growing tumor or acute hemorrhage. The *tentorium cerebelli* is a fold of dura that separates the cerebral hemispheres from the posterior fossa (which contains the brainstem and cerebellum).

The *arachnoid* layer is a fragile, web-like membrane that lies between the dura mater and *pia mater* (the vascular innermost layer of the meninges). The area between the arachnoid layer and pia mater *(subarachnoid space)* is filled with CSF. Structures such as arteries, veins, and CNs passing to and from the brain and skull must pass through the subarachnoid space. A larger subarachnoid space in the region of the 3rd and 4th lumbar vertebrae is the area used to obtain CSF during a lumbar puncture (LP).

Skull

The *skull* protects the brain from external trauma. It is composed of 8 cranial bones and 14 facial bones. Although the top and sides of the inside of the skull are fairly smooth, the bottom surface is uneven. It has many ridges, prominences, and foramina (holes through which blood vessels and nerves enter the intracranial vault). The largest hole is the *foramen magnum,* through which the brainstem extends to the spinal cord. The foramen magnum is the only major space for the expansion of brain contents when increased intracranial pressure occurs.

Vertebral Column

The *vertebral column* protects the spinal cord, supports the head, and provides flexibility. The vertebral column is made up of 33 individual vertebrae: 7 cervical, 12 thoracic, 5 lumbar, 5 sacral (fused into 1), and 4 coccygeal (fused into 1). Each vertebra has a central opening through which the spinal cord passes. A series of ligaments holds the vertebrae together. Intervertebral discs occupy the spaces between vertebrae, allowing cushion and movement of the column. Fig. 60.13 shows the natural curvature of the spinal column and its relation to the trunk.

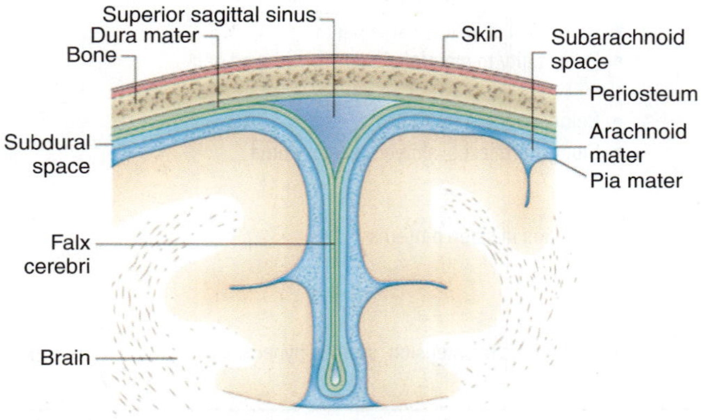

Fig. 60.12 Meninges.

Gerontologic Considerations: Effects of Aging on Nervous System

Aging affects several parts of the nervous system. In the CNS, the gradual loss of neurons in certain areas of the brainstem, cerebellum, and cerebral cortex begins in early adulthood. With loss of neurons, the ventricles widen or enlarge, brain weight decreases, and cerebral blood flow decreases. CSF production declines.

In the PNS, degenerative changes in myelin cause a decrease in nerve conduction. Coordinated neuromuscular activity, such as maintaining BP in response to changing from a lying to a standing position, is altered with aging. As a result, older adults are more likely to have orthostatic hypotension. Similarly, coordination of neuromuscular activity to maintain body temperature becomes less efficient with aging. Older adults are less able to adapt to extremes in environmental temperature. They are more vulnerable to hypothermia and hyperthermia.

Other changes include decreases in memory, vision, hearing, taste, smell, vibration, position sense, muscle strength, and reaction time. Decreases in taste and smell may result in decreased intake in the older adult. Reduced hearing and vision can result in perceptual confusion.[5] Problems with balance and coordination can put the older adult at risk for falls.[6] Changes in assessment findings result from age-related changes in the nervous system (Table 60.2). Consider other underlying causes before attributing changes to aging.

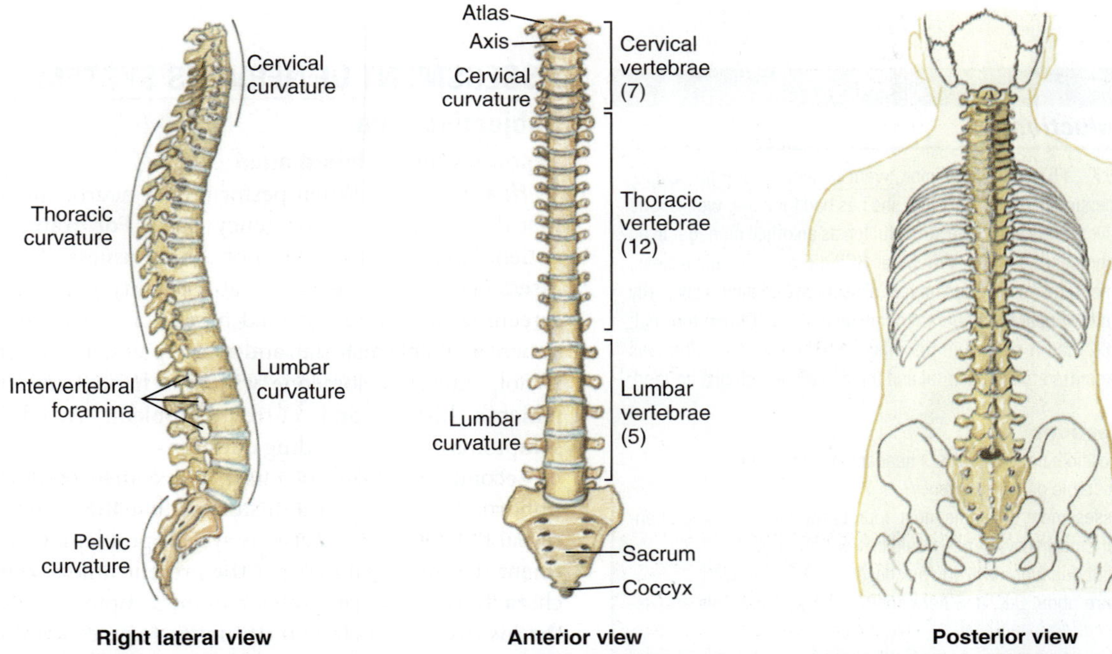

Fig. 60.13 The vertebral column (3 views). (Modified from Thibodeau GA, Patton KT: *Anatomy and physiology,* ed 8, St Louis, 2013, Mosby.)

TABLE 60.2 GERONTOLOGIC ASSESSMENT DIFFERENCES

Nervous System

Component	Changes	Differences in Assessment Findings
Central Nervous System		
Brain	↓ Cerebral blood flow and metabolism Cerebral tissue atrophy and ↑ size of ventricles ↓ Efficiency of temperature-regulating mechanism ↓ Neurotransmitters, loss of neurons ↓ O_2 supply	• Altered balance, vertigo, syncope, ↑ postural hypotension • Changes in gait and ambulation • Changes in mental functioning • ↓ Kinesthetic sense • ↓ Ability to adapt to environmental temperature • ↓ Proprioception, ↓ sensory input • Slowed conduction of nerve impulses, with slowed response time
Peripheral Nervous System		
Cranial and Spinal Nerves	Cell degeneration, death of neurons Loss of myelin and ↓ conduction time	• ↓ Reaction time in specific nerves • ↓ Speed and intensity of neuronal reflexes
Functional Divisions		
Motor	↓ Muscle bulk	• ↓ Strength, tone, agility
Sensory[a]	Atrophy of taste buds Degeneration and loss of fibers in olfactory bulb Degenerative changes in nerve cells in inner ear, cerebellum, and proprioceptive pathways ↓ Electrical activity ↓ Sensory receptors	• ↓ Sense of touch, pain, and temperature • Slowing of or change in sensory reception • Malnutrition, weight loss • ↓ Sense of smell • Poor ability to maintain balance, widened gait
Reflexes	↓ Deep tendon reflexes ↓ Sensory conduction velocity	• Below-average reflex score • Sluggish reflexes, slowed reaction time
Reticular Formation		
Reticular activating system	Modification of hypothalamic function ↓ Stage IV sleep	• Changes in sleep patterns
Autonomic Nervous System		
Sympathetic nervous system and parasympathetic nervous system	Morphologic features of ganglia Slowed autonomic nervous system responses	• Orthostatic hypotension, systolic hypertension

[a]Specific changes related to the eye are listed in Table 22.1. Specific changes related to the ear are listed in Table 23.1.

Case Study

Patient Introduction

(© TatyanaGI/iStock/Thinkstock.)

J.K., a 57-year-old woman, went to see her HCP for severe, persistent headaches that she has had for a few weeks. She lives alone and has a stressful job as an office manager in an engineering office. When her HCP did a neurologic assessment, he noted that she had a visual field deficit, especially in the upper left quadrant of her visual field. During the visit, J.K. had a seizure in his office. Staff called 911. She was admitted to the hospital and the on-call neurologist notified.

Discussion Questions

1. What are the possible causes of J.K.'s headaches and seizure?
2. Is her condition stable or an emergency?
3. What type of assessment would be most appropriate for J.K.: comprehensive, focused, or emergency? What would be your priority?
4. What assessment questions will you ask her?

You will learn more about J.K. and her condition as you read this assessment chapter.

Answers available at http://evolve.elsevier.com/Lewis/medsurg.

ASSESSMENT OF NERVOUS SYSTEM

Subjective Data

Important Health Information

Health history. When performing a neurologic assessment, first determine if an emergency exists. For example, does the patient have decreasing level of consciousness? The neurologic assessment is done when an abnormality is identified during screening or can be expected based on patient history. Is the patient a reliable historian and able to give detailed information? If not, interview someone with first-hand knowledge of the patient's history and current problem. Avoid suggesting symptoms or asking leading questions.

Second, the mode of onset and course of the illness are important aspects of the history. Often these facts alone can reveal the nature of a nervous system problem. Obtain all pertinent data in the history of the present illness, especially the characteristics and progression of the symptoms. In some cases, the history may include birth injury (e.g., cerebral palsy from hypoxia) and/or other neurologic insults, such as a traumatic brain injury, stroke, or degenerative disease.

Growth and developmental history can be important in determining if a nervous system problem was present at an early age. Ask about major developmental tasks, such as walking and talking. Obtain a family history (Box 60.1).

Medications. Obtain a medication history. Include the use of sedatives, opioids, tranquilizers, and mood-elevating drugs. Many drugs have neurologic side effects. Ask the patient to describe their treatment plan to determine adherence to prescribed therapies.

Surgery or other treatments. Ask about any surgery involving any part of the nervous system, such as head, spine, or sensory organs. If a patient had surgery, determine the date, procedure, recovery, and current status. Note any history of eye surgery to determine the relevance of abnormal pupil assessment.

BOX 60.1 GENETIC RISK ALERT

- Huntington disease is a genetically transmitted, autosomal dominant disorder.
- Major neurologic disorders that may have a genetic basis include multiple sclerosis (MS), headaches, Parkinson disease, and Alzheimer disease. The presence of these problems in a family history increases the chance of similar problems occurring in the patient.
- A family history may show if a neurologic problem has a genetic basis.

Functional Health Patterns

Key questions to ask a patient with a neurologic problem are outlined in Table 60.3.

Health perception–health management pattern. Ask about the patient's health practices that affect the nervous system. Include substance use, smoking, adequate nutrition, BP management, safe participation in physical and recreational activities, and use of seat belts or helmets. Ask about hospitalizations for neurologic problems.

If the patient has an existing neurologic problem, assess how it affects daily living and the ability to perform self-care. Ask someone who knows the patient well whether they have noticed any mental or physical changes in the patient. The patient with a neurologic problem may not be aware of it or may be a poor historian.

Nutritional-metabolic pattern. Neurologic problems can result in poor nutrition. Problems related to chewing, swallowing, facial nerve paralysis, and muscle coordination could make it difficult for the patient to ingest adequate nutrients. Certain vitamins, such as thiamine (B_1), niacin, and pyridoxine (B_6), are essential for the health of the CNS. Deficiencies in any of these can result in nonspecific problems, such as depression, apathy, neuritis, weakness, confusion, and irritability. Cobalamin (vitamin B_{12}) deficiency can occur in

TABLE 60.3 HEALTH HISTORY

Nervous System

Health Perception–Health Management
- What are your usual daily activities?
- Do you use alcohol, tobacco, or recreational drugs?[a]
- What safety practices do you follow in a car? On a motorcycle? On a bicycle?
- Do you have hypertension? If so, how is it managed?
- Have you ever been hospitalized for a neurologic problem?[a]
- Do you take any medication to manage neurologic problems? If so, what?

Nutritional-Metabolic
- Are you able to feed yourself?
- Do you have any problems getting adequate nutrition because of chewing or swallowing problems, facial nerve paralysis, or poor muscle coordination?[a]
- Give a 24-hr diet recall.

Elimination
- Do you have bowel or bladder incontinence?[a]
- Do you ever have problems with urinary hesitancy, urgency, retention?[a]
- Do you postpone your bowel movements?[a]

Activity-Exercise
- Describe any problems you have with usual activities and exercise because of a neurologic problem.
- Do you have weakness or lack of coordination?[a]
- Are you able to perform your personal hygiene needs alone?[a]

Sleep-Rest
- Describe your sleep pattern.
- When you have trouble sleeping, what do you do?

Cognitive-Perceptual
- Have you noticed any changes in your memory?[a]
- Do you have dizziness, heat or cold sensitivity, numbness, or tingling?[a]
- Do you have chronic pain?[a]
- Do you have any problem with verbal or written communication?[a]
- Have you noticed any changes in vision or hearing?[a]

Self-Perception–Self-Concept
- How do you feel about yourself, about who you are?
- Describe your general emotional pattern.

Role-Relationship
- Have you had changes in roles such as spouse, parent, or primary wage earner?[a]

Sexuality-Reproductive
- Are you satisfied with your sexual function?[a]
- Are problems related to your sexual function causing tension in an important relationship?[a]
- Do you feel the need for professional counseling related to your sexual function?[a]

Coping–Stress Tolerance
- Describe your usual coping pattern.
- Do you think your present coping pattern is adequate to meet the stressors of your life?[a]
- What needs are unmet by your current support system?

Value-Belief
- Describe any culturally specific beliefs and attitudes that may influence your care.

[a]If yes, describe.

older adults. They may have problems with vitamin absorption from supplements as well as natural food sources, such as meat, fish, and poultry. Untreated, cobalamin deficiency can cause mental function decline. In the patient with brain injury, early nutrition support can markedly improve outcomes.[7]

Elimination pattern. Bowel and bladder problems often occur with neurologic problems, such as stroke, head injury, spinal cord injury, MS, and dementia. To plan appropriate interventions, determine if the bowel or bladder problem was present before or after the current neurologic event. Retention and incontinence of urine and feces are common problems. For example, nerve root compression (as occurs in cauda equina conditions) leads to a sudden onset of incontinence. Note key details, such as number of episodes, accompanying sensations or lack of sensations, and measures to control the problem.

Activity-exercise pattern. Many neurologic disorders can cause problems with mobility, strength, and coordination. These problems can affect the patient's usual activity and exercise patterns and increase the risk for falls.[6] Assess the person's activities of daily living. Neurologic problems can affect the ability to perform motor tasks, which increases the risk for injury.

Sleep-rest pattern. Sleep pattern changes can be both a cause and a response to neurologic problems. Pain and reduced ability to change position because of muscle weakness and paralysis could interfere with sleep quality. Hallucinations from dementia or drugs can interrupt sleep. Assess sleep pattern and bedtime routines.

Cognitive-perceptual pattern. Because the nervous system controls cognition and sensory integration, many neurologic problems affect these functions. Consider culture, age, and education when assessing communication because they play a role in our interaction with others. Assess memory, language, calculation ability, problem-solving ability, insight, and judgment. Ask the patient hypothetical questions, such as "What is a reasonable price for a cup of coffee?" or "What would you do if you saw a car crash outside your house?" Do the patient's plans and goals match the physical and mental capabilities? Note the presence of factors affecting intellectual capacity, such as impaired cognition, hallucinations, delusions, and dementia.

Assess a person's ability to use and understand language. Appropriateness of responses is a useful indicator of cognitive and perceptual ability. Determine the patient's understanding and ability to carry out needed treatments. Neurologic-related cognitive changes can interfere with the patient's understanding of the disease and adherence to treatment.

Pain is common with many neurologic problems. It is often the reason a patient seeks care. Carefully assess the patient's pain. Pain assessment is discussed in Chapter 9.

Self-perception–self-concept pattern. Neurologic problems can drastically change a patient's control over life and create dependency on others for meeting daily needs. Physical appearance and emotional control can be affected. Sensitively ask about the patient's evaluation of self-worth, perception of abilities, body image, and general emotional pattern.

Role-relationship pattern. Physical impairments, such as weakness and paralysis, can alter or limit participation in usual roles and activities. Cognitive changes can permanently alter a person's ability to maintain previous roles. These changes can dramatically affect the patient and caregiver. Ask the patient if a role change has occurred (e.g., spouse or breadwinner) because of neurologic problems and determine how long it has lasted. Caregivers should take part in decision making when neurologic problems affect the patient's ability to make decisions.

Sexuality-reproductive pattern. Assess the person's ability to take part in sexual activity. Many neurologic problems can affect sexual response. Cerebral lesions may inhibit the desire phase or the reflex responses of the excitement phase. The hypothalamus stimulates the pituitary gland to release hormones that influence sexual desire. Brainstem and spinal cord lesions may partially or completely interrupt the desire or ability to have intercourse. Neuropathies and spinal cord lesions may prevent reflex activities of the sexual response or affect sensation and decrease desire. Despite neurologic changes in sexual function, many persons can achieve satisfying expression of intimacy and affection.

Coping–stress tolerance pattern. The physical sequelae of a neurologic problem can strain a patient's coping ability. Often the problem is chronic, and the patient must learn new coping skills. Assess if the patient's coping skills are adequate to deal with the stress of this problem. Evaluate the patient's support system.

Value-belief pattern. Many neurologic problems have serious, long-term, life-changing effects. Determine what these effects are because they can strain the patient's belief system. Assess if any religious or cultural beliefs could affect the treatment plan.

Case Study

Subjective Data

(© TatyanaGl/ iStock/ Thinkstock.)

After her admission to the hospital, a subjective assessment of J.K. revealed the following information:

Medical History: No history of seizures, migraine, or other headache prior to the current headaches and seizure.

Medications: lisinopril 10 mg PO daily.

Health Perception–Health Management: Never smoked. Occasional social alcohol use. Reports good health other than mild hypertension.

Nutritional-Metabolic: J.K. is 5 ft, 5 in tall; weight 145 lb.

Activity-Exercise: Moderate activity. No formal exercise or participation in sports.

Cognitive-Perceptual: Says her headaches led her to get her eyes tested. Has had only minor decrease in visual acuity.

Coping–Stress Tolerance: Is depressed and fearful. She is worried that something serious is wrong. Denies dizziness, change in hearing, or memory deficits.

Discussion Questions

1. Which subjective assessment findings concern you the most?
2. Based on these subjective assessment findings, what should be included in the physical assessment?

You will learn more about the physical assessment of the neurologic system in the next section.

Answers available at http://evolve.elsevier.com/Lewis/medsurg.

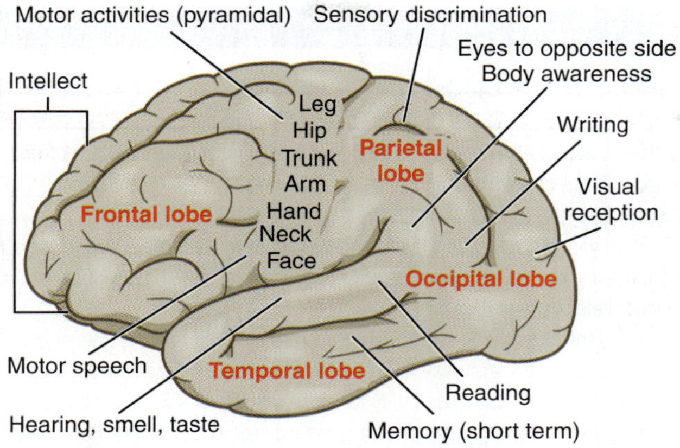

Fig. 60.14 Each area of the brain controls a particular activity.

Objective Data

Physical Assessment

The standard neurologic assessment helps determine the presence, location, and nature of nervous system disease (Fig. 60.14). The assessment looks at 6 categories of function: mental status, CN function, motor function, sensory function, cerebellar function, and reflexes.[8] Develop a consistent pattern of completing the neurologic assessment to remember to include each element for every patient encounter.

Mental status. Assessing mental status (cerebral function) gives a general impression of how the patient is functioning. It involves determining complex and high-level cerebral functions governed by many areas of the cerebral cortex. The mental status assessment begins during the start of the interview. It is ongoing throughout your interaction with the patient. For example, assess language and memory when asking the patient for details of the illness and past events. Consider the patient's age, cultural background, and level of education when evaluating mental status.

The components of the mental status assessment include:

- *General appearance and behavior:* Assess level of consciousness (awake, asleep, comatose), motor activity, body posture, dress and hygiene, facial expression, and speech pattern. Begin your assessment when you first see the patient. A patient who has deficits in self-care as shown by poor grooming is more likely to have other cognitive problems.
- *Cognition:* Note orientation to time, place, person, and situation. Note memory, general knowledge, insight, judgment, problem solving, and calculation. Common questions are "Who were the last 3 presidents?" "What do people use to cut paper?" "Can you count backward from 100 by 7s?" We often use a structured mental status questionnaire to assess these functions and provide baseline data for evaluating changes over time. Common tools include the Mini-Mental State Examination (MMSE)[8] (see Table 64.10) and Montreal Cognitive Assessment (MoCA). Delirium is an acute and transient disorder of cognition that can occur at any time during a patient's illness. As discussed in Chapter 64, delirium is often an early indicator of various illnesses (see Table 64.17). The Confusion Assessment Method tool is used to assess for delirium (see Table 64.19).
- *Mood and affect:* Note any agitation, anger, depression, or euphoria, and the appropriateness of these states. Use suitable questions to reveal the patient's feelings.

Cranial nerves. Testing each CN is an essential part of the neurologic assessment (Table 60.4).

Olfactory nerve. Chronic rhinitis, sinusitis, and heavy smoking may decrease the sense of smell. Problems with smell may occur with a tumor involving the olfactory bulb or a basilar skull fracture that has damaged the olfactory fibers. *Anosmia* (loss of sense of smell) and *hyposmia* (reduced sense of smell) is an early sign in Parkinson disease and Alzheimer disease.[9]

Optic nerve. Visual field defects may arise from lesions of the optic nerve, optic chiasm, or tracts that extend through the temporal, parietal, or occipital lobes. Visual field changes resulting from brain lesions include *hemianopsia* (half of the visual field is affected), *quadrantanopia* (1/4 of the visual field is affected), *bitemporal hemianopsia* (bilateral peripheral vision is affected), or monocular vision. It may be hard to test acuity if the patient does not read English or is aphasic.

Oculomotor, trochlear, and abducens nerves. Because the oculomotor (CN III), trochlear (CN IV), and abducens (CN VI) nerves help move the eye, we test them together (Table 60.4). With weakness or paralysis of an eye muscle, the eyes do not move together, and the patient has a *disconjugate gaze.* Note the presence and direction of *nystagmus* (fine, rapid jerking movements of the eyes), even though this condition most often indicates vestibulocerebellar problems (Fig. 60.15).

Because the oculomotor nerve exits at the top of the brainstem at the tentorial notch, it can be compressed easily by expanding mass lesions. When this occurs, sympathetic input to the pupil is unopposed; the pupil changes shape and becomes dilated. The lack of pupillary constriction is an early sign of central herniation (see Chapter 61).

Two abbreviations we often use to record the reaction of the pupils are *PERRL* (*P*upils are *E*qual [in size], *R*ound, and *R*eactive to *L*ight) and *PERRLA* (*P*upils are *E*qual, *R*ound, and *R*eactive to *L*ight and *A*ccommodation). The *PERRL* abbreviation is appropriate when accommodation cannot be assessed, as in an unconscious patient. Test convergence and accommodation by having the patient focus on your finger as it moves toward the patient's nose.

Another function of the oculomotor nerve is to keep the eyelid open. Damage to the nerve can cause *ptosis* (drooping eyelid), pupillary abnormalities, and eye muscle weakness.

Motor system. The motor system assessment includes strength, tone, coordination, and symmetry of the major muscle groups. Test muscle strength by asking the patient to push and pull against the resistance of your arm as it opposes flexion and extension of the patient's muscle. Test all 4 extremities and note any asymmetry in strength or movement. Ask the patient to offer resistance at the shoulders, elbows, wrists, hips, knees, and ankles. Mild arm weakness is demonstrated by downward drifting of the arm or pronation of the palm *(pronator drift).*

The pronator drift test is an excellent measure of strength in the upper extremities. It is especially sensitive when the patient has a potential for vasospasm or increasing edema in 1 cerebral hemisphere. Ask the patient to close the eyes and hold the arms

TABLE 60.4 Cranial Nerves

Function and Assessment

Nerve	Function	Assessment
I Olfactory	*Sensory:* from olfactory (smell)	Ask patient to close 1 nostril at a time and identify easily recognized odors (e.g., coffee). Any asymmetry in sense of smell is important.
II Optic	*Sensory:* from retina of eyes (vision)	Examine each eye separately. *Visual fields:* Position yourself opposite the patient. Ask them to look at the bridge of your nose and indicate when an object (finger, pencil tip) presented from the periphery of each of the visual fields is seen (Fig. 60.15). *Visual acuity:* Ask patient to read a Snellen chart. Record the number on the lowest line the patient can read with 50% accuracy. The patient who wears glasses should wear them during testing unless they are used only for close reading. If a Snellen chart is not available, ask the patient to read newsprint for gross assessment of acuity. Record the distance from patient to newsprint needed for accurate reading.
III Oculomotor	*Motor:* to 4 eye movement muscles and levator palpebrae muscle *Parasympathetic:* smooth muscle in eyeball	Ask the person to hold the head steady and to follow the movement of your finger, pen, or penlight only with the eyes. Hold the target back about 12 inches so that the person can focus on it comfortably. Move the target to each of the 6 positions (right and up, right, right and down, left and up, left, left and down), hold it momentarily, and then move back to center. Progress clockwise. A normal response is parallel tracking of the object with both eyes. Check for pupillary constriction and *accommodation* (pupils constricting with near vision). To test pupillary constriction, shine a light into the pupil of 1 eye; look for ipsilateral constriction of the same pupil and contralateral (consensual) constriction of the opposite eye. Note the size and shape of the pupils. The optic nerve must be intact for this reflex to occur.
IV Trochlear	*Motor:* to 1 eye movement muscle, the superior oblique muscle	See testing for CN III. Because the oculomotor (CN III), trochlear (CN IV), and abducens (CN VI) nerves help move the eye, they are tested together.
V Trigeminal		
• Ophthalmic branch	*Sensory:* from forehead, eye, superior nasal cavity	*Sensory:* Have patient close eyes and identify light touch (cotton wisp) and pinprick in each of the 3 divisions (ophthalmic, maxillary, and mandibular) of nerve on both sides of face.
• Maxillary branch	*Sensory:* from inferior nasal cavity, face, upper teeth, mucosa of superior mouth	*Motor:* Ask patient to clench teeth and then palpate masseter muscles just above the mandibular angle. Muscles should feel equally strong on both sides.
• Mandibular branch	*Sensory:* from surfaces of jaw, lower teeth, mucosa of lower mouth, and anterior tongue *Motor:* to muscles of mastication	*Corneal (blink) reflex:* Assesses CN V and CN VII simultaneously. Sensory component (corneal sensation) is innervated by the ophthalmic division of CN V. The motor component (eye blink) is innervated by the facial nerve (CN VII). Have patient look up and away. Then from the other side, lightly touch the cornea with cotton wisp. Look for normal blink reaction of both eyes. Repeat on other side.
VI Abducens	*Motor:* to the lateral rectus muscle of the eye (1 eye movement)	See testing for CN III. Because CN III, CN IV, and CN VI nerves help move the eye, they are tested together.
VII Facial	*Motor:* to facial muscles of expression and cheek muscle *Sensory:* taste from anterior 2/3 of tongue	Ask patient to raise eyebrows, close eyes tightly, purse lips, draw back the corners of mouth in an exaggerated smile, and frown. Note any asymmetry in the facial movements because this can indicate damage to nerve.
VIII Vestibulocochlear		
• Vestibular branch	*Sensory:* from equilibrium sensory organ (vestibular apparatus)	Not routinely tested unless the patient has dizziness, vertigo, unsteadiness, or auditory problems.
• Cochlear branch	*Sensory:* from auditory sensory organ (cochlea), hearing	Have patient close eyes and indicate when they hear the rustling of your fingertips. For more precise assessment of hearing, perform the Weber and Rinne tests or use an audiometer (see Table 23.6).
IX Glossopharyngeal	*Sensory:* from pharynx and posterior tongue, including taste *Motor:* to superior pharyngeal muscles	Glossopharyngeal and vagus nerves (CN IX and CN X) are tested together because both innervate the pharynx. To test the gag reflex, touch the sides of the posterior pharynx or soft palate with a tongue blade. If the reflex is weak or absent, the patient is in danger of aspirating food or secretions. For the awake, cooperative patient, ask the patient to say "ah." Note the bilateral symmetry of elevation of the soft palate. If a patient has an endotracheal tube, the cough reflex (elicited when the suction catheter contacts the *carina* of the respiratory tree) is a method of assessing the vagus nerve.

TABLE 60.4 Cranial Nerves—cont'd

Function and Assessment

Nerve	Function	Assessment
X Vagus	*Sensory:* from much of viscera of thorax and abdomen *Motor:* to larynx and middle and inferior pharyngeal muscles *Parasympathetic:* to heart, lungs, most of digestive system	See testing for CN IX. Glossopharyngeal and vagus nerves (CN IX and CN X) are tested together because both innervate the pharynx.
XI Accessory	*Motor:* to sternocleidomastoid and trapezius muscles	Ask patient to shrug the shoulders and to turn head to either side against resistance. Sternocleidomastoid and trapezius muscles should contract smoothly. Note symmetry, atrophy, or fasciculation of muscle.
XII Hypoglossal	*Motor:* to muscles of tongue	Ask to protrude tongue. It should protrude in midline. Next ask the patient to move the tongue up and down and side to side. Finally, the patient should be able to push the tongue to either side against the resistance of a tongue blade. Note any asymmetry, atrophy, or fasciculation.

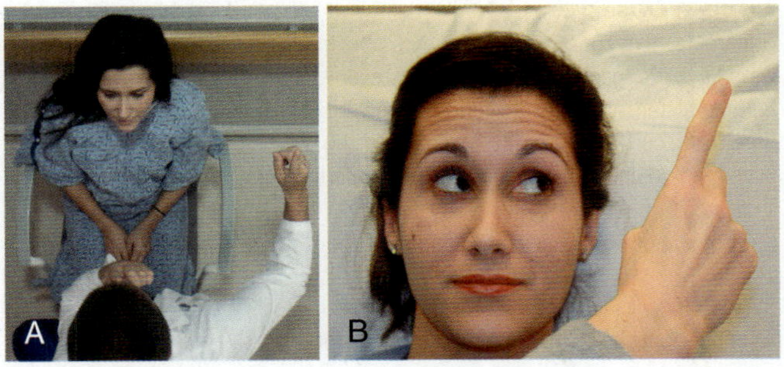

Fig. 60.15 (A) Nurse checking visual fields. (B) Nurse checking extraocular movement (EOM). (Courtesy DaiWai Olson, RN, PhD, CCRN, Dallas, TX.)

out with palms facing up (like they are holding a large pizza). The patient should hold this position for 30 seconds. Downward drift with palm pronation indicates a problem in the opposite motor cortex. Asking the patient to raise the foot from the bed or to bend the knees up in bed is a good assessment of lower extremity strength.

Test muscle tone by passively moving the limbs through their range of motion. You should identify a slight resistance to these movements. Abnormal tone is described as *hypotonia* (flaccidity) or *hypertonia* (spasticity). Note any involuntary movements, such as tics, tremor, *myoclonus* (spasm of muscles), *athetosis* (slow, writhing, involuntary movements of extremities), *chorea* (involuntary, purposeless, rapid motions), and *dystonia* (impaired muscle tone).

Test cerebellar function by assessing balance and coordination. A good screening test for both balance and muscle strength is to observe stature (posture while standing) and gait. Note the pace and rhythm of the gait. Observe for normal symmetric and oppositional arm swing. The patient's ability to ambulate helps to determine the level of nursing care needed and the risk for falling.

The finger-to-nose test (having the patient alternately touch the nose, then touch the examiner's finger) and the heel-to-shin test (having the patient stroke the heel of 1 foot up and down the shin of the opposite leg) assess coordination and cerebellar function. Reposition your finger while the patient is touching the nose so that the patient must adjust to a new distance each time your finger is touched. These movements should be performed smoothly and accurately. Other tests include asking the patient to pronate and supinate both hands rapidly and to do a shallow knee bend, first on 1 leg and then on the other. Note dysarthria or slurred speech because it is a sign of incoordination of the speech muscles.

Sensory system. We evaluate several modalities in the somatic sensory assessment. Each modality is carried by a specific ascending pathway in the spinal cord before it reaches the sensory cortex. As a rule, perform the assessment with the patient's eyes closed and avoid providing the patient with clues. Ask "How does this feel?" rather than "Is this sharp?" In the routine assessment, sensory testing of the anterior torso, posterior torso, and all extremities is sufficient. However, if you identify a problem in sensory function, delineate the boundaries of that dysfunction carefully along the dermatome.

Touch, pain, and temperature. Light touch is usually tested first using a cotton wisp or light pinprick. Gently touch each extremity. Ask the patient to indicate when they feel the stimulus. Test pain by alternately touching the skin with the sharp and dull end of a pin. Tell the patient to respond "sharp" or "dull." Assess each limb separately.

Extinction is assessed by simultaneously touching both sides of the body symmetrically. Normally, the simultaneous stimuli are both perceived (sensed). An abnormal response occurs when the patient perceives the stimulus on only 1 side. The other stimulus is *extinguished.*

Test the sensation of temperature by applying tubes of warm and cold water to the skin and asking the patient to identify the stimuli with the eyes closed. If pain sensation is intact, you do not have to assess temperature sensation because the same ascending pathways carry both sensations.

Vibration sense. Assess vibration sense by applying a vibrating tuning fork to the fingernails and bony prominences of the hands, legs, and feet. Ask the patient if the vibration or "buzz" is felt. Then ask the patient to indicate when the vibration ceases.

Position sense. Assess position sense *(proprioception)* by placing your thumb and forefinger on either side of the patient's

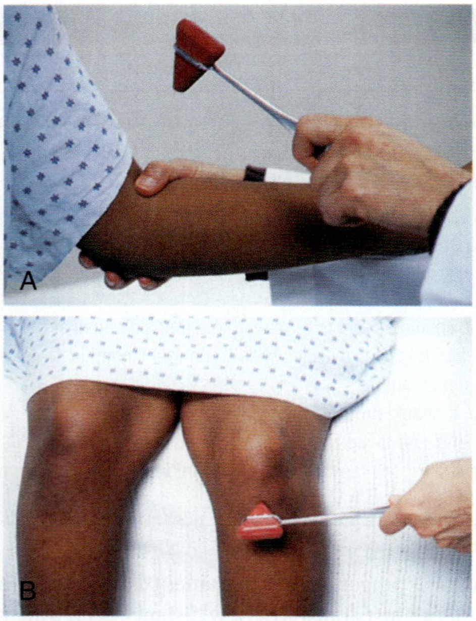

Fig. 60.16 The examiner strikes a swift blow over a stretched tendon to elicit a stretch reflex. (A) Biceps reflex. (B) Patellar reflex.

forefinger or great toe and gently moving their digit up or down. Ask the patient to close the eyes and state the direction in which the digit is moved.

Another test of proprioception is the Romberg test. Ask the patient to stand with feet together and then close their eyes. If the patient can maintain balance with the eyes open but sways or falls with the eyes closed (i.e., a positive Romberg test), vestibulocochlear problems in the posterior columns of the spinal cord may be present. Be aware of patient safety during this test.

Cortical sensory functions. Several tests assess cortical integration of sensory perceptions (which occurs in the parietal lobes). Explain these tests to the patient beforehand, while their eyes are still open. Assess *2-point discrimination* by placing the 2 points of a calibrated compass on the tips of the fingers and toes. The minimum recognizable separation is 4 to 5 mm in the fingertips and a greater degree of separation elsewhere. This test is important in diagnosing diseases of the sensory cortex and PNS.

Test *graphesthesia* (ability to feel writing on skin) by having the patient identify numbers traced on the palm of the hands. Test *stereognosis* (ability to perceive the form and nature of objects) by having the patient close the eyes and identify the size and shape of easily recognized objects (e.g., coins, keys, safety pin) placed in the hands.

Reflexes. Tendons have receptors that are sensitive to stretch. A reflex contraction of the skeletal muscle occurs when the tendon is stretched. In general, we test the biceps, triceps, brachioradialis, patellar, and Achilles tendon reflexes. Initiate a simple muscle stretch reflex by briskly tapping the tendon of a stretched muscle, usually with a reflex hammer (Fig. 60.16). Measure the response (muscle contraction of the corresponding muscle) on a 0 to 5 scale as follows: 0 = absent reflex; 1 = weak response, seen only with reinforcement; 2 = normal response; 3 = brisk response; 4 = hyperreflexia with nonsustained clonus; and 5 = hyperreflexia with sustained clonus. *Clonus,* an abnormal response, is a continued rhythmic contraction of the muscle with continuous application of the stimulus.

Elicit the *biceps reflex,* with the patient's arm partially flexed and palm up, by placing your thumb over the biceps tendon in the antecubital space and striking the thumb with a hammer. The normal response is flexion of the arm at the elbow or contraction of the biceps muscle that you can feel with your thumb.

Elicit the *triceps reflex* by striking the triceps tendon above the elbow while the patient's arm is flexed. The normal response is extension of the arm or visible contraction of the triceps.

Elicit the *brachioradialis reflex* by striking the radius 3 to 5 cm above the wrist while the patient's arm is relaxed. The normal response is flexion and supination at the elbow or visible contraction of the brachioradialis muscle.

Elicit the *patellar reflex* by striking the patellar tendon just below the patella. The patient can be sitting or lying, as long as the leg being tested hangs freely. The normal response is extension of the leg with contraction of the quadriceps.

Gently dorsiflex the patient's foot at the ankle. Elicit the *Achilles tendon reflex* by striking the Achilles tendon while the patient's leg is flexed at the knee. The normal response is plantar flexion at the ankle.

A *focused assessment* is used to assess the status of previously identified neurologic problems and to monitor for signs of new problems. A focused assessment of the neurologic system is shown in Box 60.2.

BOX 60.2 FOCUSED ASSESSMENT

Nervous System

Use this checklist to make sure the key assessment steps have been done.

Subjective

Ask the patient about any of the following and note responses.

Blackouts/loss of memory	Y	N
Weakness, numbness, tingling in arms or legs	Y	N
Headaches, especially new onset	Y	N
Loss of balance/coordination	Y	N
Orientation to person, place, time, and situation	Y	N

Objective: Diagnostic

Check the following diagnostic results for critical values.

Lumbar puncture	✓
CT or MRI of brain	✓
EEG	✓

Objective: Physical Assessment

Inspect/Observe

General level of consciousness/orientation	✓
Oropharynx for gag reflex and soft palate movement	✓
Peripheral sensation of light touch and pinprick (face, hands, feet)	✓
Smell with coffee or soap	✓
Eyes for extraocular movements, PERRLA, peripheral vision, nystagmus	✓
Gait for smoothness and coordination	✓

Palpate

Strength of neck, shoulders, arms, and legs for fullness and symmetry	✓

Percuss

Reflexes	✓

TABLE 60.5 Normal Physical Assessment of the Nervous System

Parameter	Findings
Mental status	• Alert and oriented, orderly thought processes • Appropriate mood and affect
Cranial nerves May be recorded as "CN I to XII intact"	• Smell intact to soap or coffee • Visual fields full to confrontation • Intact extraocular movements • No nystagmus. PERRLA • Intact facial sensation to light touch and pinprick • Full facial movements • Hearing intact bilaterally • Intact gag and swallow reflexes. Symmetric smile. Midline protrusion of tongue • Full strength with head turning and shoulder shrugging
Motor system	• Normal gait and station. Normal tandem walk. Negative Romberg test • Normal and symmetric muscle bulk, tone, strength • Smooth performance of finger-nose, heel-shin movements
Sensory system	• Intact sensation to light touch, position sense, pinprick, heat, and cold
Reflexes	• Biceps, triceps, brachioradialis, patellar, and Achilles tendon reflexes 2/5 bilaterally • Toes pointed down with plantar stimulation

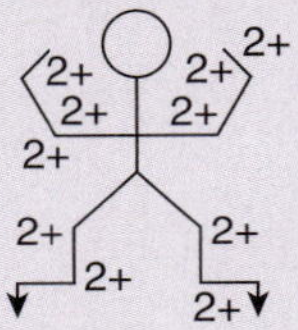

Table 60.5 is an example of a normal neurologic physical assessment. Abnormal assessment findings of the neurologic system are shown in Table 60.6.

Case Study

Objective Data: Physical Assessment

(© TatyanaGl/iStock/Thinkstock.)

A physical assessment of J.K. reveals the following:

- BP 145/80, HR 78, RR 20, T 98.6°F (37°C)
- Alert, oriented, and appropriate, but anxious
- Strength 5/5 on all extremities
- Visual field deficits in upper left quadrant of visual field

Discussion Questions

1. Which physical assessment findings concern you most?
2. Based on the results of the subjective and physical assessment, what diagnostic studies do you think may be ordered for J.K.?

You will learn more about diagnostic studies related to the neurologic system in the next section.

Answers available at http://evolve.elsevier.com/Lewis/medsurg.

DIAGNOSTIC STUDIES OF NERVOUS SYSTEM

Many diagnostic studies are available to assess the nervous system. CSF analysis provides information about a variety of CNS diseases. Normal CSF is clear, colorless, odorless, and free of red blood cells. It contains little protein. Normal CSF values are listed in Table 60.7. CSF may be obtained through LP or, on occasion, ventriculostomy.

TABLE 60.6 ASSESSMENT ABNORMALITIES

Nervous System

Finding	Description	Possible Cause and Significance
Cranial Nerves		
Dysphagia	Difficulty swallowing	Lesions involving motor pathways of CN IX and CN X (including lower brainstem)
Ophthalmoplegia	Paralysis of eye muscles	Lesions in brainstem
Eyes		
Anisocoria	Inequality of pupil size	Oculomotor nerve injury Sympathetic pathway injury
Diplopia	Double vision	Lesions affecting nerves of extraocular muscles, cerebellar damage
Homonymous hemianopsia	Loss of vision in 1 side of visual field	Lesions in the contralateral occipital lobe
Papilledema	"Choked disc," swelling of optic nerve head	Increased intracranial pressure
Mental Status		
Altered consciousness	Stuporous, mute, ↓ response to verbal cues or pain	Intracranial lesions, metabolic problem, psychiatric disorders
Anosognosia	Inability to recognize bodily defect or disease	Lesions in right parietal cortex
Motor System		
Apraxia	Inability to perform learned movements despite having desire and physical ability to perform them	Cerebral cortex lesion
Ataxia	Lack of coordination of movement	Lesions of sensory or motor pathways, cerebellum Antiseizure drugs, sedatives, hypnotic drug toxicity (including alcohol)
Dyskinesia	Impaired voluntary movement, resulting in fragmentary or incomplete movements	Disorders of basal ganglia, idiosyncratic reaction to psychotropic drugs
Hemiplegia	Paralysis on 1 side	Stroke and other lesions involving contralateral motor cortex

Continued

TABLE 60.6 ASSESSMENT ABNORMALITIES—cont'd

Nervous System

Finding	Description	Possible Cause and Significance
Nystagmus	Jerking or bobbing of eyes as they track moving object	Lesions in cerebellum, brainstem, vestibular system Antiseizure drugs, sedatives, hypnotic toxicity (including alcohol)
Reflexes		
Deep tendon reflexes	↓ or absent motor response	Lower motor neuron lesions
Extensor plantar response	Toes pointing up with plantar stimulation	Suprasegmental or upper motor neuron lesion
Sensory System		
Analgesia	Loss of pain sensation	Lesion in spinothalamic tract or thalamus. Analgesic drugs
Anesthesia	Absence of sensation	Lesions in spinal cord, thalamus, sensory cortex, or peripheral sensory nerve. Anesthesia drugs
Astereognosis	Inability to recognize form of object by touch	Lesions in parietal cortex
Paresthesia	Abnormal sensation, such as numbness or tingling	Lesions in the posterior column or sensory cortex
Speech		
Aphasia, dysphasia	Loss of or impaired language faculty (comprehension, expression, or both)	Left cerebral cortex lesion
Dysarthria	Lack of coordination in articulating speech	Cerebellar or CN lesion Antiseizure drugs, sedatives, hypnotic drug toxicity (including alcohol)
Spinal Cord		
Bladder dysfunction		
• Atonic (autonomous)	Absence of muscle tone and contractility, enlargement of capacity, no sensation of discomfort, overflow with large residual, inability to voluntarily empty	Early stage of spinal cord injury
• Hypertonic	↑ Muscle tone, ↓ capacity, reflex emptying, dribbling, incontinence	Lesions in pyramidal tracts (efferent pathways)
• Hypotonic	More ability than atonic bladder but less than normal	Interruption of afferent pathways from bladder
Paraplegia	Paralysis of lower extremities	Spinal cord transection or mass lesion (thoracolumbar region)
Tetraplegia (quadriplegia)	Paralysis of all extremities	Spinal cord transection or mass lesion (cervical region)

TABLE 60.7 Cerebrospinal Fluid Analysis

Parameter	Normal Value
Specific gravity	1.007
pH	7.35
Appearance	Clear, colorless
RBCs	None
WBCs	0–5 cells/μL (0–5 × 10^6 cells/L)
Protein	
• Lumbar	15–45 mg/dL (0.15–0.45 g/L)
• Cisternal	15–25 mg/dL (0.15–0.25 g/L)
• Ventricular	5–15 mg/dL (0.05–0.15 g/L)
Glucose	40–70 mg/dL (2.2–3.9 mmol/L)
Microorganisms	None
Pressure	60–150 mm H_2O

During LP, the HCP aspirates CSF through a needle inserted into the L3-4 or L4-5 interspace. A manometer attached to the needle is used to obtain CSF pressure. CSF is withdrawn in a series of tubes and sent for analysis. LP is contraindicated in the presence of increased intracranial pressure because of the risk for downward herniation from CSF removal or if there is infection at the intended puncture site. Nursing care of the patient undergoing LP is outlined in Table 60.8.

Tables 60.9 and 60.10 describe a number of other studies. Nerve, muscle, brain, and arterial tissues biopsies are useful in diagnosing several disorders (e.g., tumors, infectious disease, degenerative diseases). A brain biopsy is usually done using a stereotactic procedure.

TABLE 60.8 NURSING MANAGEMENT

Care of the Patient Undergoing Lumbar Puncture

Preprocedure

- Obtain vital signs and a baseline neurologic assessment. Notify HCP of signs of increased intracranial pressure (see Chapter 61).
- Assess coagulation studies to reduce the risk for epidural hematoma.
- Teach patient and caregiver about procedure. Tell the patient they may feel temporary, sharp pain or tingling radiating down the leg as a sterile needle is passed between 2 lumbar vertebrae.
- Give sedative and analgesia, as ordered.
- Have patient void.
- Place patient in a side-lying or sitting position. (Fig. 60.17)

Postprocedure

- Monitor neurologic signs and vital signs.
- Monitor for headache intensity and drainage from the puncture site.
- Apply pressure and a pressure dressing to the puncture site.
- Keep the patient in a reclining position for 1 hour or up to several hours to decrease the risk for spinal headache. The patient may to turn from side to side as long as the head is not raised.
- Properly label CSF specimens and send to laboratory.
- Teach the patient to report numbness, tingling, and movement of the extremities; pain at the injection site; and the inability to void.
- Encourage fluids with a straw to replace the CSF that was removed.
- Give ordered analgesia, as needed.

TABLE 60.9 Radiologic Studies

Nervous System

Study	Description and Purpose	Nursing Responsibility
Cerebral angiography	Serial x-ray visualization of intracranial and extracranial blood vessels done to detect vascular lesions (aneurysms, hematomas, arteriovenous malformations) and brain tumors. Catheter is inserted into the femoral (sometimes brachial) artery and passed through the aortic arch into the base of a carotid or a vertebral artery for injection of contrast medium. Timed-sequence radiographic images obtained as contrast flows through arteries, smaller vessels, and veins.	*Before:* Assess patient for stroke risk because thrombi may be dislodged during procedure. May need to be NPO. *During:* Warn patient that contrast injection may cause a feeling of being warm and flushed. Patient must lie completely still during scan. *After:* Monitor neurologic signs and VS every 15–30 min for first 2 hr, every hour for next 6 hr, then every 2 hr for 24 hr. Maintain bed rest for 6 hr (1 hr if a closure device is used). Assess for bleeding. Report any neurologic status changes.
CT scan	Provides a rapid means of obtaining radiographic images of the brain (Fig. 60.18A). Computer-assisted x-ray of multiple cross sections of body parts to detect problems such as hemorrhage, tumor, cyst, edema, infarction, brain atrophy, and other abnormalities. Contrast medium may be used to enhance visualization of brain structures.	*Before:* Note renal function before contrast medium used. Assess if patient is allergic to shellfish since the contrast is iodine based. Patient may need to be NPO 4 hr prior. If the patient is taking metformin, hold it the day of the test to prevent kidney damage. *During:* Warn patient that contrast injection may cause a feeling of being warm and flushed. Patient must lie completely still during scan. *After:* Encourage patient to drink fluids to avoid renal problems with any contrast.
• CT angiography (CTA)	Noninvasive imaging of vascular system (e.g., aneurysms). Evaluates blood volume, flow, and mean transit time as a measure of perfusion. Has fewer complications than cerebral angiography and is less expensive.	Similar to CT (see above).
MRI	Imaging of brain, spinal cord, and spinal canal by means of magnetic energy (Fig. 60.18B). Used to detect strokes, MS, tumors, trauma, herniation, and seizures. Provides greater detail than CT and improved resolution (detail) of intracranial structures. Takes a longer time to complete and may not be appropriate in life-threatening emergencies. Contrast medium may be used to enhance visualization. The contrast agent *gadolinium* has a lower incidence of allergy than iodine used in CT.	*Before:* Oral and/or IV contrast injection may be used. Check for pregnancy, allergies, and renal function. Have patient remove all metal objects. Ask about any history of surgical insertion of staples, plates, dental bridges, or other metal appliances. Remove metallic foil patches. Patient may need to be fasting. Assess for claustrophobia and the need for antianxiety medication. *During:* Patient must lie completely still.
• Magnetic resonance angiography (MRA)	Uses differential signal characteristics of flowing blood to evaluate extracranial and intracranial blood vessels. Provides both anatomic and hemodynamic information. Can be done with contrast medium.	Similar to MRI (see above).
• Functional MRI (fMRI)	MRI technique that provides time-related images that evaluate how the brain responds to various stimuli. Makes it possible to detect the brain areas that are involved in a task, process, or an emotion.	Similar to MRI (see above).

Continued

TABLE 60.9 Radiologic Studies—cont'd

Nervous System

Study	Description and Purpose	Nursing Responsibility
• MR spectroscopy (MRS)	Noninvasive test. Measures biochemical changes in the brain, especially the presence of tumors. Compares chemical composition of normal brain tissue with abnormal tumor tissue. Can detect tissue changes in stroke and epilepsy.	Similar to MRI (see above).
Myelogram	X-ray of spinal cord and vertebral column after injection of contrast medium into subarachnoid space. Used to detect spinal lesions (e.g., herniated or ruptured disc, spinal tumor).	*Before:* Give sedative as ordered. Have patient empty bladder. Tell patient that test is done with patient on tilting table that is moved during test. *After:* Patient should lie flat for 1–2 hr to prevent spinal headache. Encourage fluids. Monitor neurologic signs and VS. Headache, nausea, and vomiting may occur.
Positron emission tomography (PET)	Measures metabolic activity of brain to assess cell death or damage. Uses radioactive material that shows up as a bright spot on the image. Used to diagnose stroke, Alzheimer disease, seizure disorders, Parkinson disease, tumors.	*Before:* Explain procedure to patient. Tell patient not to take sedatives or tranquilizers. Have patient empty bladder. Insert 2 IV lines. *During:* Patient may be asked to perform different activities during test.
Single-photon emission computed tomography (SPECT)	Method of scanning similar to PET but uses more stable substances and different detectors. Radiolabeled compounds are injected, and their photon emissions can be detected. Resulting images are accumulation of labeled compound. Assesses blood flow and O_2 and glucose metabolism in the brain. Used to diagnose strokes, brain tumors, and seizure disorders.	Similar to PET (see above).
Skull and spine x-rays	Simple x-ray of skull and spinal column. Done to detect fractures, bone erosion, calcifications, abnormal vascularity.	*Before:* Remove any radiopaque objects that can interfere with results. Explain procedure to patient. *During:* Avoid excessive exposure of patient and self.
Ultrasound		
Carotid artery duplex scan	Noninvasive study. Assesses the degree of stenosis of carotid and vertebral arteries. Combines ultrasound and Doppler technology. Probe is placed over the carotid artery and slowly moved along the course of common carotid artery. Frequency of reflected ultrasound signal corresponds to blood velocity. Increased blood flow velocity can indicate stenosis of a vessel.	*Before:* Explain procedure to patient.
Transcranial Doppler	Same technology as carotid duplex but evaluates blood flow velocities of intracranial blood vessels. Probe placed on skin at various "windows" in the skull (areas in the skull that have only a thin bony covering) to record velocities of the blood vessels.	*Before:* Explain procedure to patient.

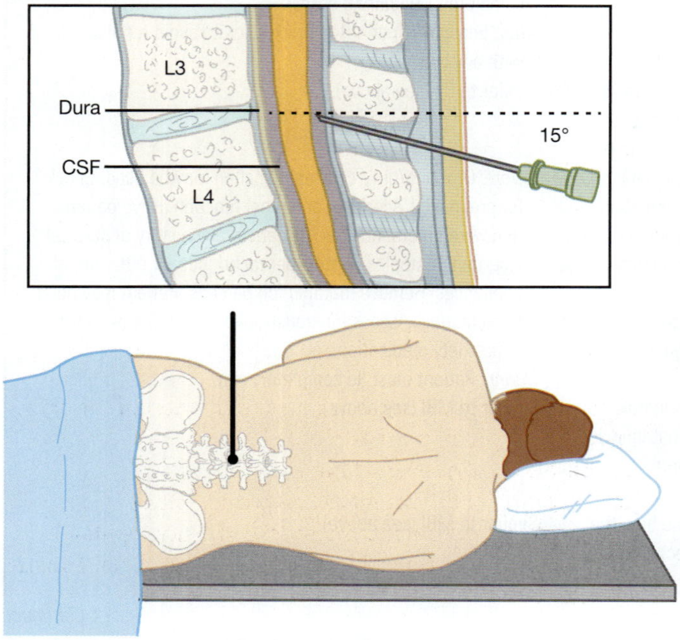

Fig. 60.17 The lateral position for a LP. The hips, knees, and neck are flexed with the knees bent up towards the chest.

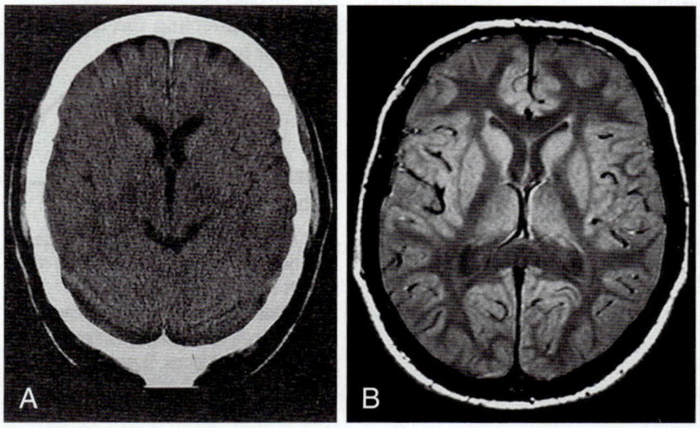

Fig. 60.18 Normal images of the brain. (A) CT scan. (B) MRI. (From Fuller G, Manford M: *Neurology: an illustrated colour text,* ed 3, New York, 2010, Churchill Livingstone.)

TABLE 60.10 Electrographic Studies

Nervous System

Study	Description and Purpose	Nursing Responsibility
Electroencephalography (EEG)	Electrical activity of brain recorded using scalp electrodes. Evaluates seizure disorders, cerebral disease, CNS effects of systemic diseases, brain injury, brain death. Specific tests may be done to evaluate brain's electrical response to lights and loud noises.	*Before:* Tell patient procedure is noninvasive and without danger of electric shock. Determine if any medications (e.g., tranquilizers, antiseizure drugs) should be withheld. *After:* Resume medications. Have patient wash electrode paste out of hair.
Electromyography (EMG)	Recording of electrical activity associated with innervation of skeletal muscle. Needle electrodes are inserted into the muscle to record specific motor units. Normal muscle at rest shows no electrical activity. Electrical activity occurs only when the muscle contracts. Activity may be altered in muscle diseases (e.g., myopathic conditions), disorders of muscle innervation (e.g., segmental or LMN lesions, peripheral neuropathic conditions).	*Before:* Explain procedure. Tell patient that pain and discomfort are common with insertion of needles. HCPs may restrict stimulants (e.g., caffeine) 2–3 hr prior. *After:* Assess needle sites for hematoma or inflammation. Give as-needed analgesics.
Electroneurography (nerve conduction studies)	Measures nerve conduction velocity of peripheral nerves. Involves applying a brief electrical stimulus to a distal portion of a sensory nerve and recording the resulting wave of depolarization at a point proximal to the stimulation. The time between the stimulus onset and the first wave of depolarization at the recording electrode is measured. Damaged nerves have slower conduction velocities.	*Before:* Explain procedure to patient. For example, a stimulus can be applied to the forefinger and a recording electrode placed over the median nerve at the wrist will detect the speed of the conduction.
Evoked potentials	Electrical activity associated with nerve conduction along sensory pathways is recorded by electrodes placed on skin and scalp. A stimulus generates the impulse. Increases in the normal time from stimulus onset to a given peak (latency) indicate slowed nerve conduction or nerve damage. Used to diagnose disease (e.g., MS), locate nerve damage, and monitor function during surgery. Can diagnose disorders of the visual or auditory systems because it shows if a sensory impulse is reaching the right part of brain.	*Before:* Explain procedure to patient. Have patient shampoo hair before test.
Magnetoencephalography (MEG)	Uses a biomagnetometer to detect magnetic fields generated by neural activity. Can accurately pinpoint the part of the brain involved in a stroke, seizure, or other disorder or injury. Measures extracranial magnetic fields and scalp electric field (EEG).	*Before:* Explain procedure to patient. MEG, a passive sensor, does not make physical contact with patient.

Case Study

Objective Data: Diagnostic Studies

(© TatyanaGl/ iStock/ Thinkstock.)

MRI/MRA results show a temporal-parietal glioblastoma that has extended into margins of the occipital lobes.

Discussion Questions

1. Are these the diagnostic studies that you expected to be ordered?
2. Why are these diagnostic study results of concern to you?

This case study is continued in Chapter 62.

Answers available at http://evolve.elsevier.com/Lewis/medsurg.

BRIDGE TO NCLEX EXAMINATION

The number of the question corresponds to the same-numbered outcome at the beginning of the chapter.

1. In a patient with a disease that affects the myelin sheath of nerves, such as multiple sclerosis, the glial cells affected are the
   a. microglia.
   b. astrocytes.
   c. ependymal cells.
   d. oligodendrocytes.
2. A patient taking a drug that impairs function of the extrapyramidal system may have loss of
   a. sensations of pain and temperature.
   b. regulation of the autonomic nervous system.
   c. integration of somatic and special sensory inputs.
   d. automatic movements associated with skeletal muscle activity.

3. During the neurologic assessment, the nurse finds the patient has speech problems with weakness of the right arm and lower face. The nurse would expect a CT scan to show pathology in the distribution of the
   a. basilar artery.
   b. left middle cerebral artery.
   c. right anterior cerebral artery.
   d. left posterior communicating artery.
4. A patient is seen in the emergency department after diving into the pool and hitting the bottom with a blow to the face that hyperextended the neck and scraped the skin off the nose. The patient reports double vision when looking down. During the neurologic assessment, the nurse finds the patient is unable to abduct either eye. The nurse recognizes this finding is related to
   a. a basal skull fracture.
   b. an injury to CN VI on both sides.
   c. a stiff neck from the hyperextension injury.
   d. facial swelling from the scrape on the bottom of the pool.
5. Stimulation of the parasympathetic nervous system results in *(select all that apply)*
   a. constriction of the bronchi.
   b. dilation of skin blood vessels.
   c. increased secretion of insulin.
   d. increased blood glucose levels.
   e. relaxation of the urinary sphincters.
6. When assessing the muscle strength of an older adult, the nurse cannot compare the findings with those of a younger adult because
   a. nutrition status is better in young adults.
   b. muscle tone and strength decrease in older adults.
   c. muscle strength should be the same for all adults.
   d. most young adults exercise more than older adults.
7. A patient is admitted with a headache, fever, and general malaise. The HCP has asked that the patient be prepared for a lumbar puncture. What is a *priority* nursing action to avoid complications?
   a. Review laboratory results for changes in the white cell count.
   b. Give acetaminophen for the headache and fever before the procedure.
   c. Notify the provider if signs of increased intracranial pressure are present.
   d. Administer antibiotics before the procedure to treat the potential meningitis.
8. During neurologic testing, the patient can perceive pain elicited by pinprick. Based on this finding, the nurse may omit testing for
   a. position sense.
   b. patellar reflexes.
   c. temperature perception.
   d. heel-to-shin movements.
9. A patient's eyes jerk while the patient looks to the left. The nurse records this finding as
   a. nystagmus.
   b. CN VI palsy.
   c. ophthalmic dyskinesia.
   d. oculocephalic response.
10. The nurse is caring for a patient with peripheral neuropathy who is scheduled for EMG studies tomorrow morning. The nurse should
    a. ensure the patient has an empty bladder.
    b. instruct the patient about the risk for electric shock.
    c. ensure the patient has no metallic jewelry or metal fragments.
    d. teach the patient that pain may be experienced during the study.

1. d; 2. d; 3. b; 4. b; 5. a, b, c, e; 6. b; 7. c; 8. c; 9. a; 10. d.

For rationales to these answers and even more NCLEX review questions, visit http://evolve.elsevier.com/Lewis/medsurg.

EVOLVE WEBSITE/RESOURCES LIST

http://evolve.elsevier.com/Lewis/medsurg
Review Questions (Online Only)
Key Points
Answer Keys for Questions
- Rationales for Bridge to NCLEX Examination Questions
- Answer Guidelines for Case Study

Conceptual Care Map Creator
Audio Glossary
Content Updates

REFERENCES

1. Wahane S, Halawani D, Zhou X, et al.: Epigenetic regulation of axon regeneration and glial activation in injury responses, *Front Genet*, 2019.
2. Nocera G, Jacob C: Mechanisms of Schwann cell plasticity involved in peripheral nerve repair after injury, *Cell Mol Life Sci* 77:3977, 2020.
3. Boghadadi A, Teo L, Bourne J: The neuroprotective role of reactive astrocytes after central nervous system injury, *J Neurotrauma* 37:681, 2020.
*4. Ravikanth R, Philip B: Magnetic resonance angiography determined variations in the circle of Willis: analysis of a large series from a single center, *TCMJ* 31:52, 2019.
5. NIH MedlinePlus: Aging changes in the senses. Retrieved from https://www.nlm.nih.gov/medlineplus/ency/article/004013.htm.
*6. Papalia G, Papalia R, Balzani LA, et al.: The effects of physical exercise on balance and prevention of falls in older people: a systematic review and meta-analysis, *J Clin Med* 9:2595, 2020.
*7. Kurtz P, Rocha E: Nutrition therapy, glucose control, and brain metabolism in traumatic brain injury: a multimodal monitoring approach, *Front Neurosci* 14:190, 2020.
8. Shahrokhi M, Asuncion R: Neurologic exam. Retrieved from https://www.ncbi.nlm.nih.gov/books/NBK557589/.
*9. Ubeda-Banon I, Saiz-Sanchez D, Flores-Cuadrado A, et al.: The human olfactory system in two proteinopathies: Alzheimer's and Parkinson's diseases, *Transl Neurodegener* 9:22, 2020.

*Evidence-based information for clinical practice.

61

Acute Intracranial Problems

Kristen J. Costello

http://evolve.elsevier.com/Lewis/medsurg/

CONCEPTUAL FOCUS

Cognition
Functional Ability
Intracranial Regulation
Mobility
Safety
Sensory Perception

LEARNING OUTCOMES

1. Explain the mechanisms that maintain normal intracranial pressure.
2. Describe the common etiologies, clinical manifestations, and interprofessional care of the patient with increased intracranial pressure.
3. Describe the nursing management of the patient with increased intracranial pressure.
4. Compare types of head injury by mechanism of injury and clinical manifestations.
5. Describe the interprofessional and nursing management of the patient with a head injury.
6. Compare the types, clinical manifestations, and interprofessional care of patients with brain tumors.
7. Discuss the nursing management of the patient with a brain tumor.
8. Describe the nursing management of the patient undergoing cranial surgery.
9. Distinguish among the primary causes and interprofessional and nursing management of brain abscess, meningitis, and encephalitis.

KEY TERMS

cerebral edema
coma
concussion
contusion
diffuse axonal injury (DAI)
encephalitis
epidural hematoma
Glasgow Coma Scale (GCS)
head injury
intracerebral hematoma
intracranial pressure (ICP)
meningitis
nuchal rigidity
subdural hematoma
unconsciousness

The body has various mechanisms by which it regulates the intracranial space to promote optimal brain function. Acute intracranial problems can disrupt these processes, leading to increased intracranial pressure (ICP), reduced blood flow to the brain, and brain tissue damage. This chapter discusses the mechanisms that maintain normal ICP and problems that lead to increased ICP.

INTRACRANIAL REGULATION

Understanding the dynamics of ICP is important in caring for patients with neurologic problems. The skull is an enclosed space with 3 essential volume components: brain tissue, blood, and cerebrospinal fluid (CSF) (Fig. 61.1). Brain tissue makes up about 78% of this volume. Blood in the arterial, venous, and capillary network makes up 12% of the volume. The remaining 10% is the volume of CSF.

We categorize brain injury in 2 phases, primary and secondary injury. *Primary injury* occurs at the initial time of an injury (e.g., impact of car accident, blunt-force trauma). It results in displacement, bruising, or damage to any cranial component (brain tissue, blood, CSF).

Secondary injury is the resulting hypoxia, ischemia, hypotension, edema, or increased ICP that follows the primary injury. Secondary injury can occur several hours to days after the initial injury. It is the modifiable concern when managing brain

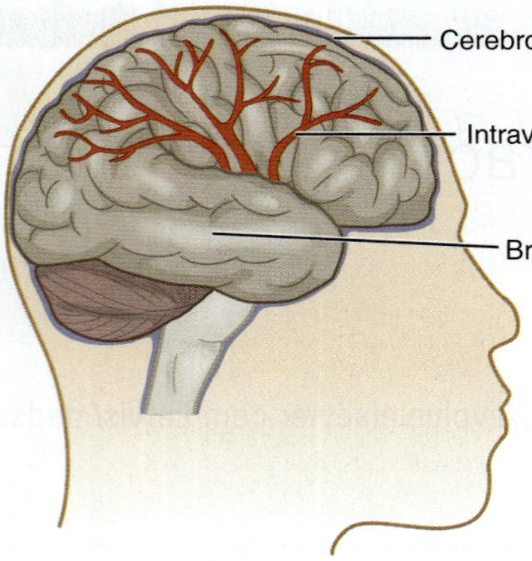

Fig. 61.1 Components of the brain.

injury. Management of the patient with an acute intracranial problem must include managing secondary injury and preventing increased ICP.

Normal Intracranial Pressure

Intracranial pressure (ICP) is the hydrostatic force measured in the brain CSF compartment. Under normal conditions in which intracranial volume stays relatively constant, the balance among the 3 components (brain tissue, blood, CSF) maintains ICP. Factors that influence ICP under normal conditions are changes in (1) arterial pressure, (2) venous pressure, (3) intraabdominal and intrathoracic pressure, (4) posture, (5) temperature, and (6) blood gases, especially CO_2 levels. The degree to which these factors increase or decrease the ICP depends on the brain's ability to adapt to changes.

The Monro-Kellie doctrine states that the 3 components must stay at a relatively constant volume within the closed skull. If the volume of any 1 of the 3 components increases within the skull and the volume from another component is displaced, the total intracranial volume will not change.[1] This hypothesis is applicable only in situations in which the skull is closed. The hypothesis does not apply in persons with displaced skull fractures or craniectomy (removal of part of the skull).

We can measure ICP in the ventricles, subarachnoid space, subdural space, epidural space, or brain tissue with a pressure transducer.[2] Normal ICP ranges from 5 to 15 mm Hg. A sustained pressure greater than 20 mm Hg is abnormal.

Normal Compensatory Adaptations

In applying the Monro-Kellie doctrine, the body can adapt to volume changes within the skull in 3 different ways to maintain a normal ICP. The first compensatory mechanisms can include changes in CSF volume. CSF volume can be changed by altering CSF absorption or production, and by displacing CSF into the spinal subarachnoid space. Second, changes in intracranial blood volume can occur through the collapse of cerebral veins and dural sinuses, regional cerebral vasoconstriction or dilation, and changes in venous outflow. Third, brain tissue volume compensates through distention of the dura or compression of brain tissue.

Initially an increase in volume does not increase ICP because of these compensatory mechanisms. However, there is a limited ability to compensate for changes in volume. As the volume increase continues, ICP rises. Decompensation occurs. This results in compression and ischemia.

Cerebral Blood Flow

Cerebral blood flow (CBF) is the amount of blood in milliliters passing through 100 g of brain tissue in 1 minute. The global CBF is about 50 mL/min/100 g of brain tissue. Maintaining blood flow to the brain is critical because the brain requires a constant supply of O_2 and glucose. The brain uses 20% of the body's O_2 and 25% of its glucose.[3]

Autoregulation of Cerebral Blood Flow

The brain regulates its own blood flow in response to its metabolic needs despite wide fluctuations in systemic arterial pressure. *Cerebral autoregulation* is the automatic adjustment in the diameter of the cerebral blood vessels by the brain to maintain a constant blood flow with changes in arterial BP. The purpose of autoregulation is to ensure a consistent CBF to provide for the metabolic needs of brain tissue and maintain cerebral perfusion pressure (CPP) within normal limits.

The lower limit of systemic arterial pressure at which autoregulation is effective is a mean arterial pressure (MAP) of 70 mm Hg. Below this, CBF decreases, and symptoms of cerebral ischemia, such as syncope and blurred vision, occur. The upper limit of systemic arterial pressure at which autoregulation is effective is a MAP of 150 mm Hg. When this pressure is exceeded, the vessels are maximally constricted and further vasoconstrictor response is lost.

The *cerebral perfusion pressure* is the pressure needed to ensure blood flow to the brain. CPP is equal to the MAP minus the ICP (CPP = MAP − ICP). See the example in Table 61.1. Normal CPP is 60 to 100 mm Hg. As CPP decreases, autoregulation fails and CBF decreases. A CPP of less than 50 mm Hg is associated with ischemia and neuron death. A CPP of less than 30 mm Hg results in ischemia. It is incompatible with life. This is why it is important to maintain MAP when ICP is increased.

Although CPP is clinically useful, it does not consider the effect of cerebrovascular resistance. Cerebrovascular resistance is generated by the arterioles within the cranium. It links CPP and blood flow as follows:

$$\text{CPP} = \text{Flow} \times \text{Resistance}$$

When cerebrovascular resistance is high, blood flow to brain tissue is impaired. Normally, autoregulation maintains an adequate CBF and CPP by adjusting the diameter of cerebral blood vessels and metabolic factors that affect ICP.

CPP may not reflect perfusion pressure in all parts of the brain. There may be local areas of swelling and compression that limit perfusion pressure. Thus these patients may need a higher CPP to prevent localized tissue damage. For example, a patient with an acute stroke may need a higher BP, increasing MAP and CPP, to increase perfusion to the brain and prevent further tissue damage.

TABLE 61.1 Calculating Cerebral Perfusion Pressure (CPP)

$CPP = MAP - ICP$

$MAP = DBP + 1/3\,(SBP - DBP)$

OR

$$MAP = \frac{SBP + 2\,(DBP)}{3}$$

Example: Systemic BP = 122/84 mm Hg
MAP = 97 mm Hg
ICP = 12 mm Hg
CPP = 85 mm Hg

Factors Affecting Cerebral Blood Flow

CO_2, O_2, and hydrogen ion concentration affect cerebral blood vessel tone. An increase in the partial pressure of CO_2 in arterial blood ($PaCO_2$) relaxes smooth muscle, dilates cerebral vessels, decreases cerebrovascular resistance, and increases CBF. A decrease in $PaCO_2$ constricts cerebral vessels, increases cerebrovascular resistance, and decreases CBF.

Cerebral O_2 tension of less than 50 mm Hg results in cerebrovascular dilation. Dilation decreases cerebrovascular resistance, increases CBF, and increases O_2 tension. However, if O_2 tension is not increased, anaerobic metabolism begins, resulting in a buildup of lactic acid. As lactic acid increases and hydrogen ions accumulate, the environment becomes more acidic. Within this acidic environment, further vasodilation occurs in a continued attempt to increase blood flow. The combination of a severely low partial pressure of O_2 in arterial blood (PaO_2) and increased hydrogen ion concentration (acidosis), which are both potent cerebral vasodilators, may produce a state in which autoregulation is lost and compensatory mechanisms do not meet tissue metabolic demands.

CBF can be affected by cardiac or respiratory arrest, systemic bleeding, and other pathophysiologic states (e.g., diabetic coma, infections, toxicities). Regional CBF can be affected by trauma, tumors, cerebral bleeding, or stroke. When regional or global autoregulation is lost, CBF is no longer maintained at a constant level but is directly influenced by changes in systemic BP, hypoxia, or catecholamines.

INCREASED INTRACRANIAL PRESSURE

Mechanisms of Increased Intracranial Pressure

Increased ICP is a potentially life-threatening situation that results from an increase in any or all the 3 components (brain tissue, blood, CSF) within the skull. Increased ICP is clinically significant because it decreases CPP and increases risks for brain ischemia and infarction. It has a poor prognosis.[4] Common causes of increased ICP include a mass (e.g., hematoma, contusion, abscess, tumor) and cerebral edema (from brain tumors, hydrocephalus, head injury, brain inflammation).

These cerebral insults increase the formation and spread of cerebral edema. This may result in hypercapnia, cerebral acidosis, impaired autoregulation, and systemic hypertension. Edema distorts brain tissue, further increasing the ICP, and leads to even more tissue hypoxia and acidosis. Fig. 61.2 shows the progression of increased ICP.

PATHOPHYSIOLOGY MAP

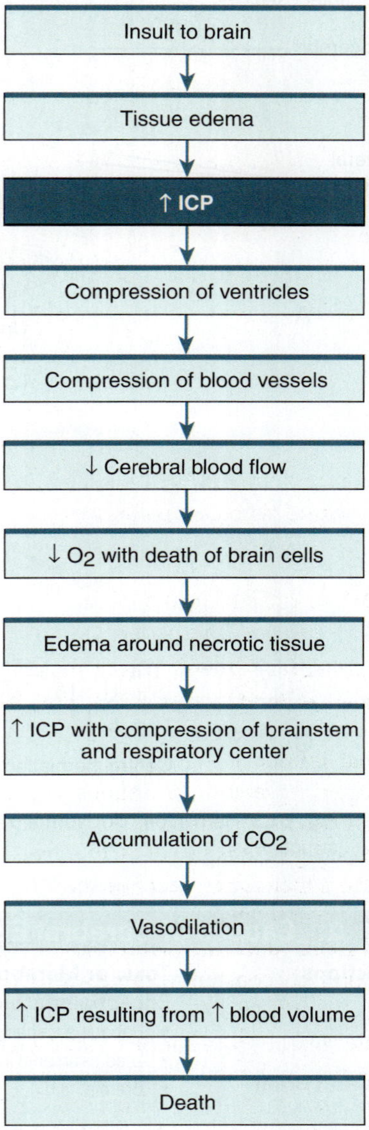

Fig. 61.2 Progression of increased ICP.

It is critical to maintain CBF to preserve tissue and thus minimize secondary injury. Sustained increases in ICP result in brainstem compression and brain herniation. *Herniation* occurs as the brain tissue is forcibly shifted from a compartment of greater pressure to a compartment of less pressure.

Displacement and herniation of brain tissue can cause a potentially reversible process to become irreversible. Ischemia and edema are further increased, compounding the preexisting problem. Compression of the brainstem and cranial nerves (CNs) may be fatal. Fig. 61.3 shows types of herniation. Herniation forces the cerebellum and brainstem downward through the foramen magnum. If compression of the brainstem is unrelieved, respiratory arrest will occur due to compression of the respiratory control center in the medulla. In this situation, intense pressure is placed on the brainstem. If herniation continues, brainstem death is imminent.

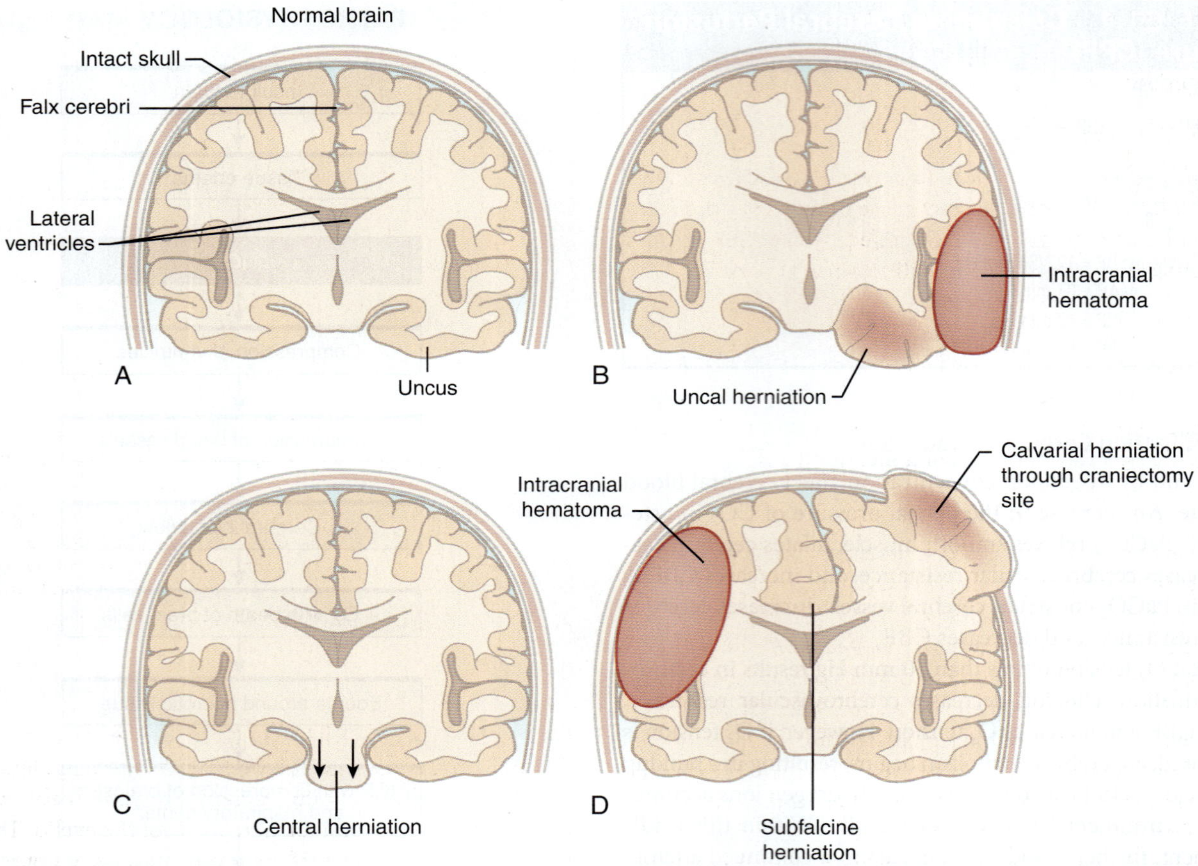

Fig. 61.3 Herniation. (A) Normal relationship of intracranial structures. (B, C, and D) Shifts of intracranial structures.

TABLE 61.2 Causes of Cerebral Edema

Cerebral Infections
- Encephalitis
- Meningitis

Head Injuries and Brain Surgery
- Contusion
- Hemorrhage
- Posttraumatic brain swelling

Mass Lesions
- Brain abscess
- Brain tumor (primary, metastatic)
- Hematoma (intracerebral, subdural, epidural)
- Hemorrhage (intracerebral, cerebellar, brainstem)

Toxic or Metabolic Encephalopathies
- Hepatic encephalopathy
- Lead or arsenic intoxication
- Uremia

Vascular Insult
- Anoxic and ischemic episodes
- Cerebral infarction (thrombotic or embolic)
- Venous sinus thrombosis

Cerebral Edema

There are a variety of causes of **cerebral edema** (increased accumulation of fluid in the extravascular spaces of brain tissue) (Table 61.2). Cerebral edema results in an increase in tissue volume that can increase ICP. The extent and severity of the original insult are factors that determine the degree of cerebral edema.

There are 3 types of cerebral edema: vasogenic, cytotoxic, and interstitial. A patient may have more than 1 type.

Vasogenic Cerebral Edema

Vasogenic cerebral edema is the most common type of cerebral edema. It occurs mainly in the white matter. It results from disruption of the blood-brain barrier. This allows large molecules (protein, blood products) to enter brain tissue. This exposes brain cells to toxic products from the blood and results in an osmotic gradient that causes fluid to flow from the intravascular to extravascular space. The result is an increase in the extracellular fluid volume. Systemic BP, site of the brain injury, and extent of the blood-brain barrier defect influence the extent of the spread of edema.

Edema may produce a continuum of symptoms. These range from headache to a decrease in consciousness, including **coma** (profound state of unconsciousness) and focal (specific to a certain area of the brain) neurologic deficits. In cases of cerebral edema, a headache can quickly progress to coma and death. So, you must be vigilant in your assessment.

Cytotoxic Cerebral Edema

Cytotoxic cerebral edema results from disruption of the integrity of the cell membranes. It develops from destructive lesions or trauma to brain tissue, resulting in cerebral hypoxia or anoxia and syndrome of inappropriate antidiuretic hormone (SIADH) secretion. In this type of edema, the blood-brain barrier stays intact. Cerebral edema occurs from fluid and protein shifts from the extracellular space directly into the cells, with subsequent swelling and loss of cellular function.

Interstitial Cerebral Edema

Interstitial cerebral edema is usually a result of hydrocephalus. *Hydrocephalus* is a buildup of fluid in the brain. It is manifested by ventricular enlargement. It can be due to excess CSF production, obstruction of flow, or an inability to reabsorb the CSF.

Clinical Manifestations

The manifestations of increased ICP can take many forms, depending on the cause, location, and rate of increases in ICP. Any patient who becomes unconscious acutely, regardless of the cause, should be suspected of having increased ICP.

Change in Level of Consciousness

Level of consciousness (LOC) is the most sensitive and reliable indicator of neurologic status. Changes in LOC are a result of impaired CBF, which causes O_2 deprivation to the cells of the cerebral cortex and reticular activating system (RAS). The RAS is found in the brainstem, with neural connections to many parts of the nervous system. An intact RAS can maintain a state of wakefulness even in the absence of a functioning cerebral cortex. Interruptions of impulses from the RAS or changes in functioning of the cerebral hemispheres can cause **unconsciousness,** an abnormal state of complete or partial unawareness of self or environment.

The patient's state of consciousness is defined by their clinical responses and pattern of brain activity (recorded by an electroencephalogram [EEG]). A change in consciousness may be dramatic (as in coma) or subtle (e.g., flattening of affect, change in orientation, decrease in level of attention). In the deepest state of unconsciousness (e.g., coma), the patient does not respond to painful stimuli. Corneal and pupillary reflexes are absent. The patient cannot swallow or cough and is incontinent of urine and feces. The EEG pattern shows suppressed or absent neuronal activity.

Changes in Vital Signs

Increasing pressure on the thalamus, hypothalamus, pons, and medulla causes changes in vital signs.

Manifestations such as *Cushing triad* (systolic hypertension with a widening pulse pressure, bradycardia with a full and bounding pulse, irregular respirations) may be present. They often do not appear until ICP has been increased for some time or is suddenly and markedly increased (e.g., head trauma). Cushing triad as a medical emergency. It is a sign of brainstem compression and impending death. A change in body temperature may occur because increased ICP affects the hypothalamus.

> **CHECK YOUR PRACTICE**
>
> You are monitoring vital signs of an 82-year-old woman who has a head injury. She fell while walking on the sidewalk, hitting her head on a fire hydrant. She was confused on admission with stable vital signs: BP 150/86, pulse 84, respirations 14/min; 2 hr after admission, her vital signs are BP 166/74, pulse 54, respirations 10 to 16/min.
>
> - What is your interpretation of her vital signs?

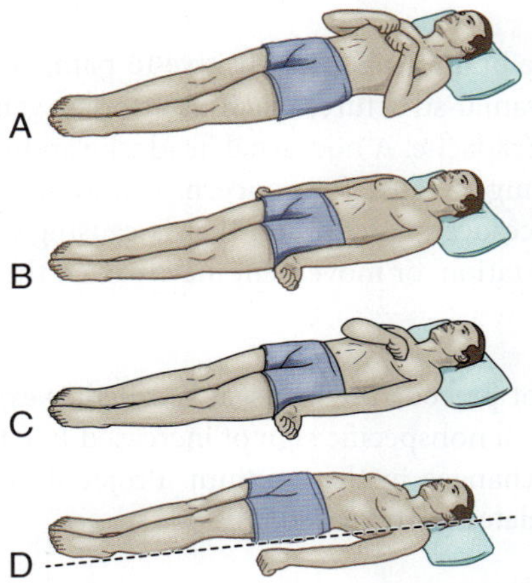

Fig. 61.4 Decorticate and decerebrate posturing. (A) Decorticate response. Flexion of arms, wrists, and fingers with adduction in upper extremities. Extension, internal rotation, and plantar flexion in lower extremities. (B) Decerebrate response. All 4 extremities in rigid extension, with hyperpronation of forearms and plantar flexion of feet. (C) Decorticate response on right side of body and decerebrate response on left side of body. (D) Opisthotonic posturing.

Ocular Signs

Compression of CN III, the oculomotor nerve, results in pupil dilation on the same side *(ipsilateral)* as the mass lesion. There may be sluggish or no pupil response to light, inability to move the eye upward and adduct, and ptosis of the eyelid. These signs result from the brain shifting from midline, compressing the trunk of CN III, and paralyzing the muscles controlling pupillary size and shape. In this situation, a fixed, unilateral, dilated pupil is a neurologic emergency that indicates brain herniation.

Other CNs may be affected, including the optic (CN II), trochlear (CN IV), and abducens (CN VI) nerves. Signs of problems with these CNs include blurred vision, diplopia, and changes in extraocular eye movements. *Central herniation* may initially manifest as sluggish but equal pupil response. *Uncal herniation* may cause a dilated unilateral pupil. *Papilledema* (an edematous optic disc seen on retinal examination) is a nonspecific sign of persistent increases in ICP.

Decrease in Motor Function

As the ICP continues to rise, the patient has changes in motor ability. A *contralateral* (opposite side of the mass lesion) hemiparesis or hemiplegia may develop depending on the location of the source of the increased ICP. If painful stimuli are used to elicit a motor response, the patient may localize to the stimuli or withdraw from it.

Noxious stimuli may elicit *decorticate* (flexor) or *decerebrate* (extensor) posturing (Fig. 61.4). Decorticate posture consists of internal rotation and adduction of the arms with flexion of the elbows, wrists, and fingers. It is a result of interruption of voluntary motor tracts in the cerebral cortex. Extension of the legs may be seen. A decerebrate posture may indicate more serious damage. It results from disruption of motor fibers in the midbrain and brainstem. In this position, the arms are stiffly extended, adducted, and hyperpronated. There is hyperextension of the legs with plantar flexion of the feet.

Headache

Although the brain itself is insensitive to pain, compression of other intracranial structures, such as arteries, veins, and CNs, can cause a headache. A nocturnal headache and/or a headache in the morning is cause for concern. It may indicate a tumor or other space-occupying lesion that is causing increased ICP. Straining, agitation, or movement may worsen the pain.

Vomiting

Vomiting, not preceded by nausea, is called *unexpected vomiting*. It is often a nonspecific sign of increased ICP that is related to pressure changes in the cranium. Projectile vomiting may occur. It is related to increased ICP.

Complications

The major complications of uncontrolled increased ICP are inadequate cerebral perfusion and cerebral herniation (Fig. 61.3). To help you understand cerebral herniation, we are going to describe 2 important structures in the brain. The *falx cerebri* is a thin wall of dura that folds down between the cortex, separating the 2 cerebral hemispheres. The *tentorium cerebelli* is a rigid fold of dura that separates the cerebral hemispheres from the cerebellum (Fig. 61.3). It is called the *tentorium* (meaning tent) because it forms a tent-like cover over the cerebellum.

Tentorial herniation (central herniation) occurs when a mass lesion in the cerebrum forces the brain to herniate downward through the opening created by the brainstem (the foramen magnum). Uncal herniation occurs when there is lateral and downward herniation. Cingulate herniation occurs when there is lateral displacement of brain tissue beneath the falx cerebri.

Diagnostic Studies

Diagnostic studies can be used to identify the cause of increased ICP (Table 61.3). CT and MRI can discover many conditions that can cause increased ICP and assess the effect of treatment.

Other tests include EEG, cerebral angiography, ICP measurement, brain tissue oxygenation measurement via the LICOX catheter (described later), positron emission tomography (PET), transcranial Doppler studies, and evoked potential studies. In general, a lumbar puncture (LP) is contraindicated when we suspect increased ICP. The reason is that cerebral herniation could occur from the sudden release of the pressure in the skull from the area above the LP.

In some agencies, a hand-held near-infrared scanner (Infrascanner) is used to detect life-threatening intracranial bleeding. The scanner directs a wavelength of light that can penetrate tissue and bone. Blood from intracranial hematomas absorbs the light differently from other areas of the brain. Transcranial doppler can monitor changes in cerebrovascular resistance.

TABLE 61.3 Interprofessional Care

Increased Intracranial Pressure

Diagnostic Assessment

- History and physical assessment
- Vital signs, neurologic assessments, ICP measurements
- Skull, chest, and spinal x-ray studies
- CT scan, MRI, cerebral angiography, EEG, PET
- Transcranial Doppler studies
- Infrascanner
- ECG
- Evoked potential studies
- Lumbar puncture (not done if there is a risk for herniation)
- Laboratory studies, including CBC, coagulation profile, electrolytes, serum creatinine, ABGs, ammonia level, drug and toxicology screen
- CSF analysis (protein, WBC, glucose)

Management

- Elevate head of bed to 30 degrees with head in a neutral position
- Mechanical ventilation
- ICP monitoring
- Cerebral oxygenation monitoring ($PbtO_2$, $SjvO_2$)
- Maintain $PaO_2 \geq 100$ mm Hg
- Maintain fluid balance and assess osmolality
- Maintain systolic arterial pressure between 100 and 160 mm Hg
- Maintain CPP >60 mm Hg
- Reduction of cerebral metabolism (e.g., high-dose barbiturates)

Drug Therapy

- Osmotic diuretic (mannitol)
- Hypertonic saline
- Antiseizure drugs (e.g., phenytoin)
- Corticosteroids for brain tumors, bacterial meningitis
- Histamine (H_2)-receptor antagonist (e.g., cimetidine) or proton pump inhibitor (e.g., pantoprazole to prevent GI ulcers and bleeding)

Monitoring ICP and Cerebral Oxygenation

Indications for Intracranial Pressure Monitoring

ICP monitoring is used to guide care when the patient is at risk for or has increased ICP.[4] It may be used in patients with a variety of neurologic problems, including stroke, hemorrhage, tumor, infection, or traumatic brain injury (TBI). ICP should be monitored in patients admitted with a *Glasgow Coma Scale* (GCS) score of 8 or less and an abnormal CT scan or MRI. These results indicate that the patient may have bleeding, contusion, edema, or other problems.

Methods of Measuring ICP

Patients with conditions known to increase ICP, except those with irreversible problems or advanced neurologic disease, usually undergo ICP monitoring in an ICU. Multiple methods and devices are available to monitor ICP (Fig. 61.5).

The gold standard for monitoring ICP is the *ventriculostomy*, in which a specialized catheter is inserted into the lateral ventricle and coupled to an external transducer (Figs. 61.6 and 61.7). This technique directly measures the pressure within the ventricles, facilitates removal and/or sampling of CSF, and allows for intraventricular drug administration. The transducer is external. We must ensure that the transducer is level with the foramen of Monro (interventricular foramen). The system must also be at the ideal height (Fig. 61.8A). A reference point for this foramen is the tragus of the ear. Every time the patient is repositioned, assess the system to ensure it is level.

The *fiberoptic catheter*, an alternative technology, uses a sensor transducer found within the catheter tip. The sensor tip is

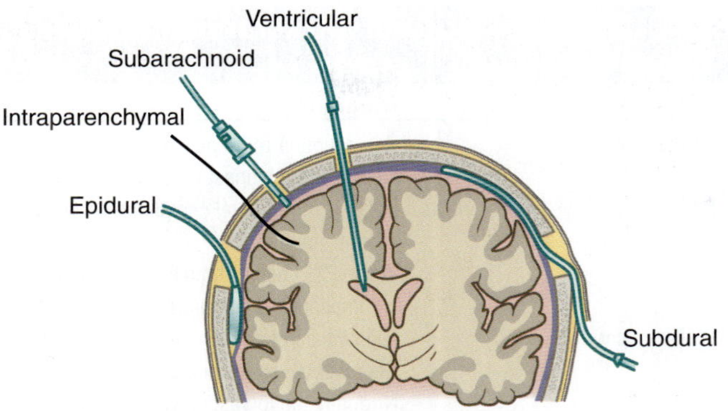

Fig. 61.5 Coronal section of brain showing potential sites for placement of ICP monitoring devices.

placed within the ventricle or the brain tissue and gives a direct measurement of brain pressure.

The *air pouch/pneumatic technology* uses an air-filled pouch to measure ICP. The pouch is at the of a catheter that maintains a constant volume. The pressure changes within the cranium are transmitted through the changes exerted on this pouch to the monitor.

ICP is represented on the monitor as a mean pressure in millimeters of mercury (mm Hg). If a CSF drainage device is in place, the drain must be closed for at least 6 minutes to ensure an accurate reading. Record the waveform strip along with other pressure monitoring waveforms. The normal ICP waveform has 3 phases (Fig. 61.6 and Table 61.4). It is important to monitor the ICP waveform and the mean CPP. When ICP is normal, P1, P2, and P3 resemble a staircase. As ICP increases, P2 rises above P1. This indicates poor ventricular compliance (Fig. 61.6). Consider the rate at which changes occur and the patient's condition. Neurologic deterioration may not occur until the ICP increase is pronounced and sustained. Immediately report to the HCP any increase in ICP, either as a mean increase in pressure or as an abnormal waveform configuration.

Causes of inaccurate ICP readings include CSF leaks around the monitoring device, obstruction of the intraventricular catheter (from tissue or blood clot), a difference between the height of the catheter and the transducer, kinks in the tubing, and incorrect height of the drainage system relative to the patient's reference point. Bubbles or air in the tubing can dampen the waveform.

Infection is a serious complication with ICP monitoring. Factors that contribute to infection include ICP monitoring more than 5 days, use of a ventriculostomy, a CSF leak, and a concurrent systemic infection. Routinely assess the insertion site and use aseptic technique. Monitor the CSF for a change in drainage color or clarity.

Cerebrospinal Fluid Drainage

With a ventricular catheter, it is possible to control ICP by removing CSF (Fig. 61.7). The HCP typically orders a specific level at which to start drainage (e.g., if ICP is greater than 20 mm Hg) and the frequency of drainage (intermittent or continuous). Draining CSF relieves pressure inside the skull (Fig. 61.8B).

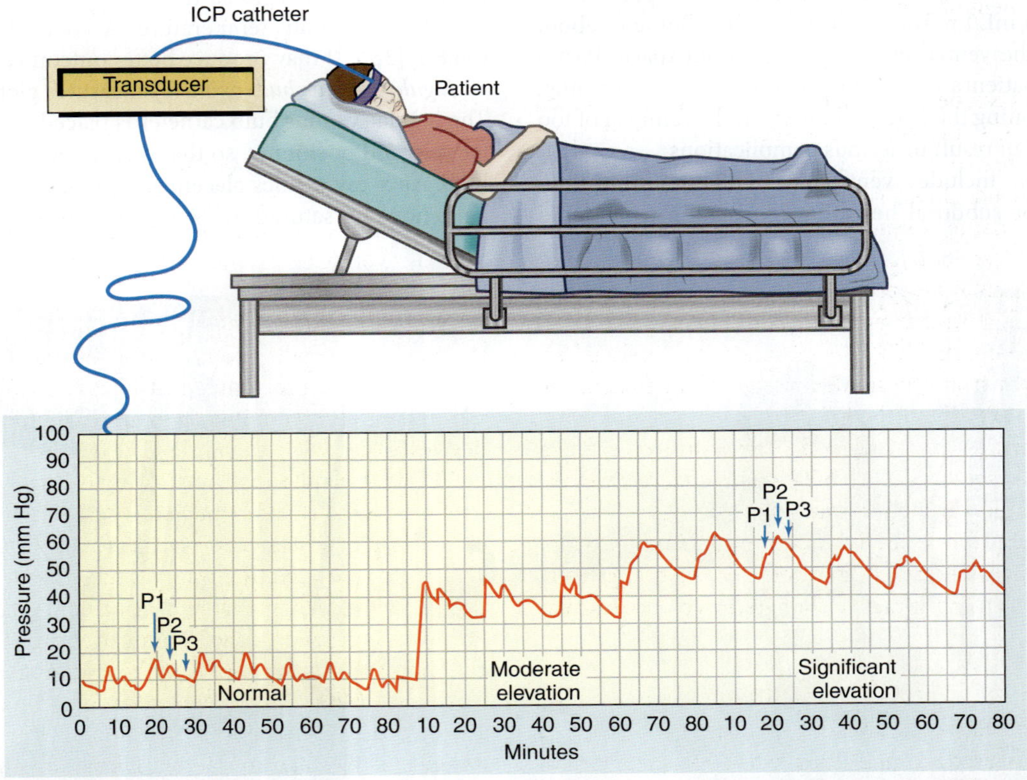

Fig. 61.6 ICP monitoring can continuously measure ICP. The ICP tracing shows normal, elevated, and plateau waves. At high ICP, the P2 peak is higher than the P1 peak, and the peaks become less distinct and plateau. (Modified from Copstead-Kirkhorn LC, Banasik JL: *Pathophysiology,* ed 5, St Louis, 2013, Mosby.)

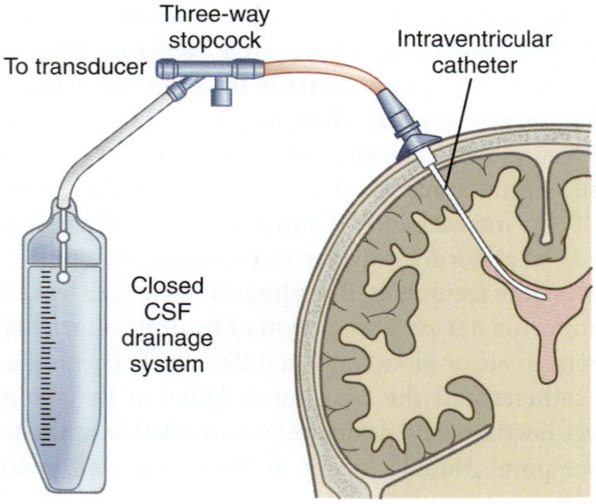

Fig. 61.7 Ventriculostomy in place. Cerebrospinal fluid *(CSF)* can be drained via a ventriculostomy when ICP exceeds the upper pressure parameter set by the HCP. Intermittent drainage involves opening the 3-way stopcock to allow CSF to flow into the drainage bag for brief periods (30 to 120 seconds) until the pressure is less than the upper pressure parameters.

Although CSF removal decreases ICP and improves CPP, there are no universal guidelines for CSF removal. Guidelines are typically based on agency or HCP preference.[5]

The 2 options for CSF drainage are intermittent or continuous. With intermittent drainage, you open the system at the indicated ICP and allow CSF to drain for 2 to 3 minutes. Then close the stopcock to return the ventriculostomy to a closed system. With continuous ICP drainage, carefully monitor the volume of CSF drained. Keep in mind that normal CSF production is about 20 to 30 mL/hr. There is a total CSF volume of about 150 mL within the ventricles and subarachnoid space. Post a sign above the patient's bed to notify anyone before turning, moving, or suctioning the patient, to prevent the removal of too much CSF. This can result in serious complications.

Complications include ventricular collapse, infection, and herniation or subdural hematoma formation from rapid decompression. Use strict aseptic technique during dressing changes or sampling of CSF to prevent infection. Keep the system intact to ensure that the ICP readings are accurate because treatment is based on the pressures.

TABLE 61.4 Normal Intracranial Pressure Waveforms

Waveform (Fig. 61.6)	Meaning
P1 Percussion wave	Represents arterial pulsations. Normally the highest of the 3 waveforms.
P2 Rebound wave or tidal wave	Reflects intracranial compliance or relative brain volume. When P2 is higher than P1, intracranial compliance is compromised.
P3 Dicrotic wave	Follows dicrotic notch. Represents venous pulsations. Normally the lowest waveform.

Cerebral Oxygenation Monitoring

Technology is available to measure cerebral oxygenation and assess perfusion. Three intracranial devices used in ICU settings are the LICOX catheter, Neurovent catheter, and jugular venous bulb catheter.

The LICOX and Neurovent catheters are placed in healthy white matter of the brain (Fig. 61.9). These catheters measure brain oxygenation and temperature. They provide continuous monitoring of the O_2 pressure in brain tissue ($PbtO_2$). The normal range for $PbtO_2$ is 20 to 40 mm Hg. A low $PbtO_2$ level indicates ischemia or regional tissue hypoxia.[4] These catheters can also measure brain temperature. A cooler brain temperature (96.8°F [36°C]) may produce better outcomes.

Jugular venous bulb oximetry measures global O_2 extraction. The jugular venous bulb catheter is placed in the internal jugular vein and positioned so that the catheter tip is in the jugular bulb. An x-ray verifies placement. This catheter measures jugular venous O_2 saturation ($SjvO_2$), which indicates total venous

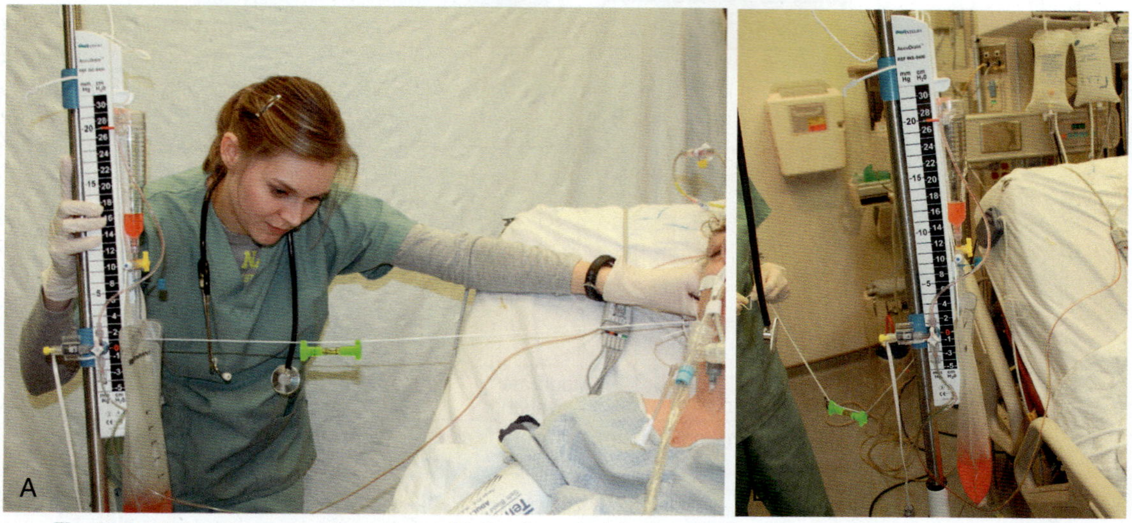

Fig. 61.8 (A) Leveling a ventriculostomy. (B) Cerebrospinal fluid is drained into a drainage system. (Courtesy Meg Zomorodi, RN, PhD, CNL, Raleigh, NC.)

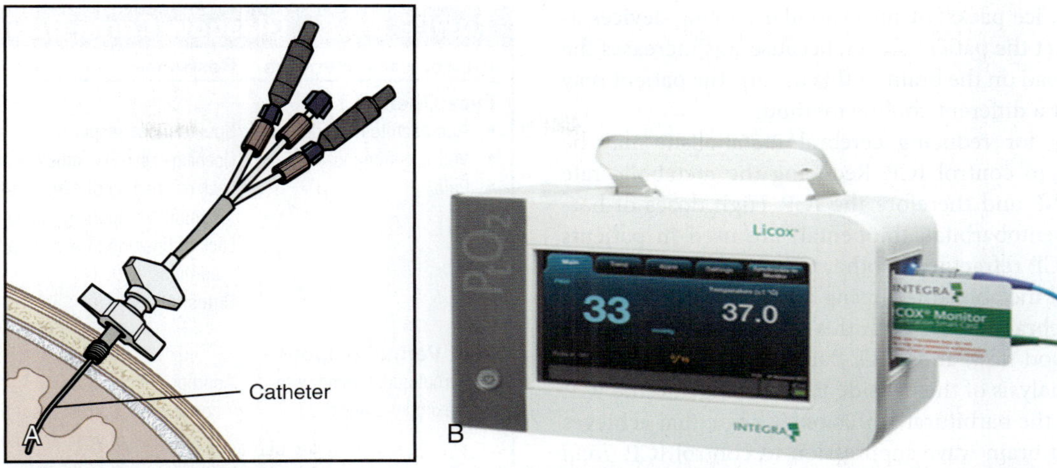

Fig. 61.9 (A) The LICOX brain tissue O_2 system involves insertion of a catheter. (B) The system measures O_2 in the brain ($PbtO_2$), brain tissue temperature, and ICP. (B, Courtesy of Integra LifeSciences Corporation, Plainsboro, NJ.)

brain tissue extraction of O_2. This is a measure of cerebral O_2 supply and demand. The normal $SjvO_2$ range is 60% to 75%. Values less than 50% indicate impaired cerebral oxygenation.[4]

In addition to measuring ICP and brain oxygenation, many HCPs are now looking at multimodality monitoring in TBI and intracranial hypertension. This technology includes brain microdialysis (measurement of small molecules), continuous EEG, and blood flow monitoring.

Interprofessional Care

The goals of interprofessional care (Table 61.3) are to (1) identify and treat the underlying cause of increased ICP and (2) support brain function. The earlier the condition is recognized and treated, the better the patient outcome. A careful history is important in the search for the underlying cause. The underlying cause of increased ICP is usually an increase in blood (bleeding), brain tissue (tumor or edema), or CSF (hydrocephalus) in the brain.

For any patient with increased ICP, it is important to maintain adequate oxygenation to support brain function and prevent secondary injury. An endotracheal tube or tracheostomy may be needed to maintain adequate ventilation. Arterial blood gas (ABG) analysis guides the O_2 therapy. The goal is to maintain the PaO_2 at 100 mm Hg or greater and to keep $PaCO_2$ in normal range at 35 to 45 mm Hg. The patient may need mechanical ventilation to ensure adequate oxygenation.

If increased ICP is caused by a mass (e.g., tumor, hematoma), surgical removal of the mass is the best treatment. In aggressive situations, a craniectomy (removal of part of skull) may be done to reduce ICP and prevent herniation.

Drug Therapy

Drug therapy plays an important part in managing increased ICP. Mannitol (Osmitrol) (25%) is an osmotic diuretic given IV. It decreases ICP through plasma expansion and an osmotic effect. The immediate plasma-expanding effect reduces the hematocrit and blood viscosity. This increases CBF and cerebral O_2 delivery. Mannitol creates a vascular osmotic gradient. The decrease in the total brain fluid content causes fluid to move from the tissues into the blood vessels, reducing the ICP. Monitor fluid and electrolyte status when osmotic diuretics are used. Mannitol may be contraindicated with renal disease and increased serum osmolality.

Hypertonic saline solution is another option. It produces massive movement of water out of edematous swollen brain cells and into blood vessels. This movement can reduce swelling and improve CBF. During an infusion, monitor BP and serum sodium levels because intravascular fluid volume excess can occur. Hypertonic saline infusion is just as effective as mannitol when treating increased ICP. They are often used concurrently when caring for a patient with a severe brain injury.[4]

Corticosteroids (e.g., dexamethasone) are used to treat vasogenic edema around tumors and abscesses. These drugs are not recommended for TBI. Corticosteroids stabilize the cell membrane and inhibit prostaglandin synthesis (see Fig. 12.2), preventing the formation of proinflammatory mediators. Corticosteroids also improve neuronal function by improving CBF and restoring autoregulation.

Complications of corticosteroids include hyperglycemia, infections, and gastrointestinal (GI) bleeding. Monitor fluid intake, electrolyte, and glucose levels. Perform blood glucose monitoring at least every 6 hours. Patients receiving corticosteroids should receive a histamine (H_2)-receptor blocker (e.g., cimetidine, ranitidine) or proton pump inhibitor (e.g., pantoprazole) to prevent GI ulcers and bleeding.

IV 0.9% sodium chloride is the preferred solution for giving secondary medications. If 5% dextrose in water or 0.45% sodium chloride is used, serum osmolality decreases and an increase in cerebral edema may occur.

Metabolic demands, such as fever (greater than 100.4°F [38°C]), agitation, shivering, pain, and seizures, can increase ICP. Implement measures to reduce these metabolic demands to lower the ICP in the at-risk patient. Monitor patients for seizure activity. They may need prophylactic antiseizure medication. Maintain the temperature at 96.8°F to 98.6°F (36°C to 37°C) by using antipyretics (e.g., acetaminophen), cool baths, cooling blankets, ice packs, or intravascular cooling devices as needed. Do not let the patient shiver, because this increases the metabolic workload on the brain. If this occurs, the patient may need sedatives or a different cooling method.

Drug therapy for reducing cerebral metabolism may be an effective way to control ICP. Reducing the metabolic rate decreases the CBF and therefore the ICP. High doses of barbiturates (e.g., pentobarbital, thiopental) are used in patients with increased ICP refractory to other treatments. Barbiturates decrease cerebral metabolism, causing a decrease in ICP and a reduction in cerebral edema. With this treatment, monitor the patient's ICP, blood flow, and EEG. Barbiturate dosing is typically based on analysis of the bedside EEG tracing and the ICP. The HCP orders the barbiturate infusion at a rate that achieves a desired level of brain wave suppression to control ICP. *Total burst suppression,* recognized by the absence of spikes showing brain activity on the EEG monitor, shows that maximal therapeutic effect has been achieved.

Nutrition Therapy

Because malnutrition promotes continued cerebral edema, maintaining optimal nutrition is important. The patient with increased ICP is in a hypermetabolic and hypercatabolic state that increases the need for glucose as fuel for metabolism of the injured brain. If the patient cannot maintain an adequate oral intake, we should start other means of meeting nutrition needs, such as enteral feedings or parenteral nutrition.

Early feeding after brain injury may improve patient outcome.[5] Nutrition replacement should meet caloric needs by at least day 5 after injury.[5] Fluid and electrolyte status and metabolic needs should guide feedings or supplements. The patient should be kept in a euvolemic fluid state. Continuously evaluate the patient based on clinical factors such as urine output, insensible fluid loss, serum and urine osmolality, and serum electrolytes.

NURSING MANAGEMENT: INCREASED INTRACRANIAL PRESSURE

Assessment

You can obtain subjective data about the patient with increased ICP from the patient, caregiver, or family member who is familiar with the patient. Describe LOC by noting the specific behaviors seen. Assess LOC, body functions, and vital signs.

Glasgow Coma Scale

The **Glasgow Coma Scale (GCS)** is a quick, practical, and standard system for assessing the LOC. The 3 areas assessed in the GCS are the patient's ability to (1) open the eyes when a verbal or painful stimulus is applied, (2) speak, and (3) obey commands. Specific assessments evaluate the patient's response to varying degrees of stimulus. Three indicators of response are evaluated: (1) opening of the eyes, (2) best verbal response, and (3) best motor response (Table 61.5).

Specific behaviors observed as responses to the testing stimulus are given a numeric value. Your responsibility is to elicit the best response on each of the scales. The subscale scores are especially important if a patient is untestable in an area. For example, severe periorbital edema may make eye opening impossible.

TABLE 61.5 Glasgow Coma Scale

Appropriate Stimulus	Response	Score
Eyes Open		
• Approach to bedside	Spontaneous response.	4
• Verbal command	Opening of eyes to name or command.	3
• Pain	Lack of opening of eyes to previous stimuli but opening to pain.	2
	Lack of opening of eyes to any stimulus.	1
	Untestable.[a]	U
Best Verbal Response		
• Verbal questioning with maximum arousal	Appropriate orientation, conversant. Correct identification of self, place, year, and month.	5
	Confusion. Conversant, but disorientation in 1 or more spheres.	4
	Inappropriate or disorganized use of words (e.g., cursing), lack of sustained conversation.	3
	Incomprehensible words, sounds (e.g., moaning).	2
	Lack of sound, even with painful stimuli.	1
	Untestable.[a]	U
Best Motor Response		
• Verbal command (e.g., "raise your arm, hold up 2 fingers")	Obedience of command.	6
• Pain (pressure on proximal nail bed)	Localizes pain, lack of obedience but presence of attempts to remove offending stimulus.	5
	Flexion withdrawal,[a] flexion of arm in response to pain without abnormal flexion posture.	4
	Abnormal flexion, flexing of arm at elbow and pronation, making a fist.	3
	Abnormal extension, extension of arm at elbow usually with adduction and internal rotation of arm at shoulder.	2
	Lack of response.	1
	Untestable.[a]	U

[a]Added to the original scale by some centers.

The total GCS score is the sum of the numeric values assigned to each of the 3 areas. The higher the scores, the higher the level of brain functioning. The highest GCS score is 15 for a fully alert person. The lowest possible score is 3. A GCS score of 8 or less generally indicates coma. Plot the results of the GCS scores on a graph. Use the data to determine if the patient is stable, improving, or deteriorating.

The GCS offers several advantages in the assessment of the unconscious patient. It allows different health care professionals to arrive at the same conclusion about the patient's status. It can be used to determine between different or changing states.

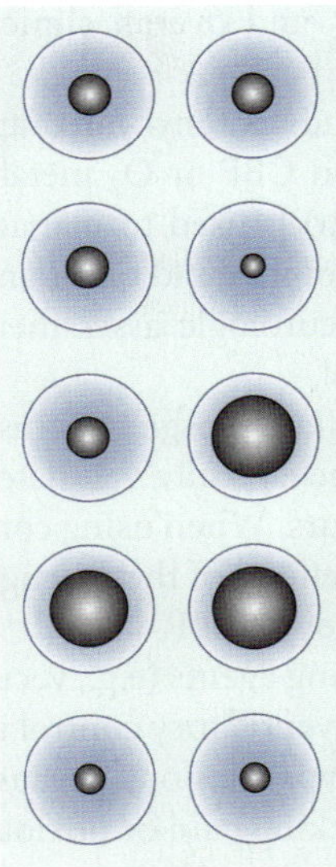

Fig. 61.10 Pupillary check for size and response.

Pattern	Location of Lesion	Description
1. Cheyne-Stokes 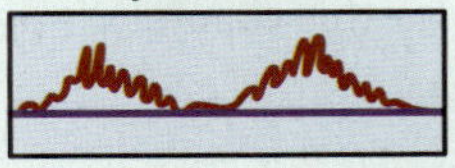	Bilateral hemispheric disease or metabolic brain dysfunction	Cycles of hyperventilation and apnea
2. Central neurogenic hyperventilation 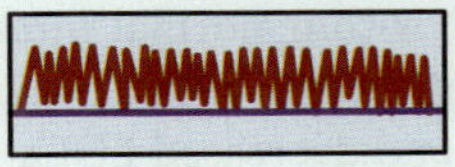	Brainstem between lower midbrain and upper pons	Sustained, regular rapid and deep breathing
3. Apneustic breathing 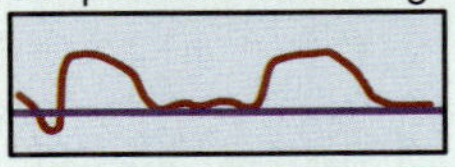	Mid or lower pons	Prolonged inspiratory phase or pauses alternating with expiratory pauses
4. Cluster breathing 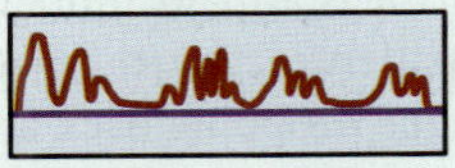	Medulla or lower pons	Clusters of breaths follow each other with irregular pauses between
5. Ataxic breathing 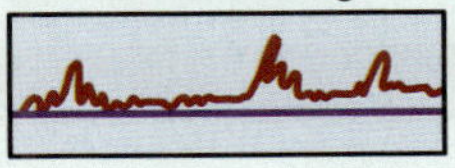	Reticular formation of the medulla	Completely irregular with some breaths deep and some shallow. Random, irregular pauses, slow rate

Fig. 61.11 Common abnormal respiratory patterns associated with coma.

Although the GCS is the standard assessment tool for LOC, we sometimes use other scales, such as the *Full Outline of Unresponsiveness (FOUR) scale*.[6] In cases of stroke or hemorrhage with increased ICP, use the NIH Stroke Scale (see Table 62.12). Other key neurologic assessments include CN assessment and motor and sensory testing. CN assessment is outlined in Table 60.4.

◆ Neurologic Assessment

Compare the pupils for size, shape, movement, and reactivity (Fig. 61.10). If the oculomotor nerve (CN III) is compressed, the pupil on the affected side *(ipsilateral)* becomes larger until it fully dilates. If ICP continues to increase, both pupils dilate.

Test pupillary reaction with a penlight. The normal reaction is brisk constriction when the light is shone directly into the eye. Note a consensual response (slight constriction in the opposite pupil) at the same time. A sluggish reaction can indicate early pressure on CN III. A fixed pupil unresponsive to light stimulus usually indicates increased ICP. However, there are other causes of a fixed pupil. These include direct injury to CN III, previous eye surgery, atropine administration, and mydriatic eye drops.

In some agencies, HCPs are using a hand-held device *(pupillometer)* to measure the pupil reactivity and size. The device removes any subjectivity from the pupil evaluation.

Assess eye movements controlled by CN III, CN IV, and CN VI in the patient who is awake and able to follow commands. They can be used to assess brainstem function. Testing the corneal reflex gives information about CN V and CN VII. If this reflex is absent, start routine eye care to prevent corneal abrasion (see Chapter 22).

We can test the eye movements of the uncooperative or unconscious patient with the use of head movements (oculocephalic) and caloric stimulation (oculovestibular). To test the oculocephalic reflex (doll's eye reflex), turn the patient's head briskly to the left or right while holding the eyelids open. A normal response is movement of the eyes across the midline in the direction opposite that of the turning. Next, quickly flex and then extend the neck. Eye movement should be opposite to the direction of head movement—up when the neck is flexed and down when it is extended. Abnormal responses can help locate an intracranial lesion. We usually only do this test as part of the evaluation of brain death.

To test the oculovestibular reflex (cold caloric), position the patient with the head of bed elevated. Instill a syringe of ice-cold water into the external auditory ear canal. Then, assess the patient's eyes for a total of 1 minute. The absence of eye movement or response indicates severe neurologic demise. This test requires patent external auditory ear canals and tympanic membranes.

Test all 4 extremities for strength. Note any asymmetry in strength or movement. Assess the motor response of the unconscious or uncooperative patient by observation of spontaneous movement. If no spontaneous movement is possible, apply a pain stimulus to the patient and note the response. Resistance to movement during passive range of motion exercises is another measure of strength. Do not include hand squeezing as part of the assessment of motor movement in the unconscious or uncooperative patient. This is a reflex action and can misrepresent the patient's status.

Record vital signs, including BP, pulse, respiratory rate, and temperature. Be aware of Cushing triad, which indicates severely increased ICP. Note the respiratory pattern. Specific respiratory patterns are associated with severely increased ICP (Fig. 61.11).

◆ Clinical Problems

Clinical problems for the patient with increased ICP include:

- Increased intracranial pressure
- Inadequate tissue perfusion
- Risk for injury

Additional information on clinical problems and interventions for patients with increased ICP is presented in eNursing Care Plan 61.1 (available on the website for this chapter).

◆ Planning

The overall goals for the patient with increased ICP are to (1) maintain a patent airway, (2) have ICP within normal limits, (3) have normal fluid, electrolyte, and nutrition balance, and (4) prevent complications from immobility and decreased LOC.

◆ Implementation

◆ Acute Care

Respiratory function. Maintaining a patent airway is critical in the patient with increased ICP. It is a major nursing responsibility. As the LOC decreases, the patient is at an increased risk for airway obstruction from the tongue dropping back and occluding the airway or from accumulation of secretions.

! SAFETY ALERT

Altered Breathing

- Be alert to altered breathing in a patient with increased ICP.
- Snoring sounds indicate obstruction and require immediate intervention.

Remove secretions by suctioning as needed. An oral airway facilitates breathing and provides an easier suctioning route in the comatose patient. In general, any patient with a GCS of 8 or less or an altered LOC who is unable to maintain a patent airway or effective ventilation needs intubation and mechanical ventilation.

Frequently monitor and evaluate the ABG values. Take measures to maintain the levels within prescribed or acceptable parameters. Appropriate ventilatory support can be ordered based on PaO_2 and $PaCO_2$ values.

Prevent hypoxia and hypercapnia to minimize secondary injury. Suctioning and coughing cause transient decreases in PaO_2 and increase ICP. Keep suctioning to a minimum and less than 10 seconds in duration. Give 100% O_2 before and after to prevent decreases in the PaO_2. To avoid cumulative increases in the ICP with suctioning, limit suctioning to 2 passes per suction procedure, if possible. Patients with increased ICP are at risk for lower CPP during suctioning.

Try to prevent abdominal distention, since it can interfere with respiratory function. Inserting a nasogastric (NG) tube to aspirate the stomach contents can prevent distention, vomiting, and aspiration. However, in patients with facial and skull fractures, an NG tube is contraindicated due to risk for inadvertent intracranial placement. Oral insertion of a gastric tube is preferred.

Sedation. Pain, anxiety, and fear related to the primary injury, therapeutic procedures, or noxious stimuli can increase ICP and BP, thus complicating the patient's management and recovery. The appropriate choice or combination of sedatives, paralytics, and analgesics for symptom management is a challenge. Giving these agents may alter the neurologic state, thus masking true neurologic changes. We may need to temporarily stop drug therapy to appropriately assess neurologic status. The choice, dose, and combination of agents may vary depending on the patient's history, neurologic state, and overall clinical presentation.

Opioids, such as morphine sulfate and fentanyl, are rapid-onset analgesics with minimal effect on CBF or O_2 metabolism. The IV sedative propofol (Diprivan) is used to manage anxiety and agitation in the ICU because of its rapid onset and short half-life. We can do an accurate neurologic assessment soon after stopping an infusion of propofol.

Dexmedetomidine (Precedex), an α_2-adrenergic agonist, is used for continuous IV sedation of mechanically ventilated patients in the ICU setting for up to 24 hours. When using continuous IV sedatives, be aware of the side effects of these drugs, especially hypotension. Hypotension can lower CPP.

Nondepolarizing neuromuscular blocking agents (e.g., vecuronium) are useful for achieving complete ventilatory control in the treatment of refractory intracranial hypertension. Because these agents paralyze muscles without blocking pain or noxious stimuli, they must be used in combination with sedatives, analgesics, or benzodiazepines.

Benzodiazepines, although useful for sedation, are usually avoided when managing the patient with increased ICP because of the hypotensive effect and long half-life. They are usually given as an adjunct to neuromuscular blocking agents.

The patient should be in a quiet, calm environment with minimal noise and interruptions. Observe the patient for signs of agitation, irritation, or frustration. Teach the caregiver and family about decreasing stimulation. Coordinate with team members to minimize procedures that may cause agitation.

Fluid and electrolyte balance. Fluid and electrolyte problems can have an adverse effect on ICP. Closely monitor IV fluids with the use of an accurate IV infusion control device or pump. Intake and output, accounting for insensible losses, and daily weights are important parameters in assessing fluid balance.

Monitor serum electrolytes, especially glucose, sodium, potassium, magnesium, and osmolality. Discuss abnormal values with the HCP.

Monitor urine output to detect problems related to diabetes insipidus and inappropriate secretion of antidiuretic hormone (SIADH). Diabetes insipidus is caused by a decrease in antidiuretic hormone (ADH). It results in increased urine output and hypernatremia. The usual treatment of diabetes insipidus is fluid replacement, vasopressin, or desmopressin acetate (DDAVP) (see Chapter 54). If it is not quickly identified and treated, severe dehydration will occur.

SIADH is caused by excess secretion of ADH. SIADH results in decreased urine output and dilutional hyponatremia. It may result in cerebral edema, changes in LOC, seizures, and coma. SIADH is described in Chapter 54.

Monitoring ICP. ICP monitoring is used with other parameters to guide the care of the patient and assess their response to treatment. Suctioning, hypoxemia, and arousal from sleep are factors that can increase ICP. Be alert to these factors and try to minimize them. Increased intrathoracic pressure can increase ICP by impeding the venous return. So, the patient should avoid coughing, straining, sneezing, and the Valsalva maneuver.

Body position. Proper head positioning is important. Maintain the patient in the head-up position. Keep the head in a midline position, avoiding extreme neck flexion. Flexion can cause venous obstruction and contribute to increased ICP. Adjust the body position to decrease the ICP and improve the CPP. Elevating the head of the bed promotes drainage from the head and decreases the vascular congestion that can produce cerebral edema. However, raising the head of the bed more than 30 degrees can decrease the CPP by lowering systemic BP. Carefully evaluate the effects of elevating the head of the bed on both ICP and CPP. Position the bed so that it lowers the ICP while optimizing the CPP and other indices of cerebral oxygenation.

Turn the patient with slow, gentle movements. Rapid changes in position may increase ICP. Prevent discomfort when turning and positioning the patient because pain or agitation increases pressure. Avoid extreme hip flexion to decrease the risk for raising the intraabdominal pressure, which increases ICP. Decorticate or decerebrate posturing is a reflex response in some patients with increased ICP. Turning, skin care, and even passive range of motion can elicit these posturing reflexes.

Provide the physical care to minimize complications of immobility, such as atelectasis and contractures. Turn the patient at least every 2 hours.

Protection from injury. The patient with increased ICP and decreased LOC needs protection from self-injury. Confusion, agitation, and the possibility of seizures increase the risk for injury. Use restraints carefully in the agitated patient. If restraints are necessary to keep the patient from removing tubes or falling out of bed, they should be secure enough to be effective. Observe the skin area under the restraints regularly for irritation. Agitation may increase with the use of restraints, which indicates the need for other measures to protect the patient from injury. Light sedation with sedative agents may be needed. Having a family member stay with the patient may have a calming effect.

Place the patient with or at risk for seizures on seizure precautions. These include padded side rails, an Ambu bag at the bedside, readily available suction, accurate and timely administration of antiseizure drugs, and close observation. Antiseizure prophylaxis against early seizures (within the first 7 to 10 days) is recommended in severe brain injury. This practice is controversial for mild to moderate brain injury.[7]

The patient can benefit from a quiet, nonstimulating environment. Use a calm, reassuring approach. Touch and talk to the patient, even one who is in a coma.

Psychologic considerations. Be aware of the psychologic well-being of patients and their families. There is a need for support, information, and teaching of both patients and families. Anxiety over the diagnosis and prognosis can be distressing to the patient, caregiver, family, and nursing staff. Your competent and assured manner in performing care is reassuring to everyone involved. Short, simple explanations are appropriate. Allow the patient and caregiver to acquire the amount of information they desire. Assess the family members' desires to help with providing care for the patient and allow for their participation as appropriate. Encourage interprofessional management (e.g., social work, chaplain) involving the patient and family in decision making as much as possible.

◆ Evaluation

The expected outcomes are that the patient with increased ICP will:

- Maintain ICP and cerebral perfusion within normal parameters
- Have no serious increases in ICP during or after care activities
- Have no complications of immobility

HEAD INJURY

Head injury includes any injury or trauma to the scalp, skull, or brain. A serious form of head injury is *traumatic brain injury* (TBI). Statistics about head injuries are incomplete because many victims die at the injury scene, or the condition is minor so the patient does not seek health care. Around 2.8 million persons are treated each year in US emergency departments (EDs) for TBI. Of those, 57,000 die and 282,000 are hospitalized. Of those hospitalized, 20% will die.[8] At least 5.3 million Americans (2% of the US population) currently live with disabilities resulting from TBI.

The most common causes of head injury are falls and motor vehicle accidents. Other causes include firearms, assaults, sports-related trauma, recreational injuries, and war-related injuries.[8] Men are twice as likely to sustain a TBI.

Head trauma has a high potential for a poor outcome (Box 61.1). Deaths from head trauma occur at 3 points after injury: immediately after the injury, within 2 hours after injury, and about 3 weeks after injury.[9] Most deaths occur immediately after the injury, either from the direct head trauma or from massive bleeding and shock. Deaths occurring within a few hours of the trauma are caused by progressive worsening of the brain injury or bleeding.[10]

Deaths occurring 3 weeks or more after the injury result from multisystem failure. Expert nursing care in the weeks after the injury is crucial in decreasing mortality and optimizing outcomes.[11]

Types of Head Injuries

Scalp Lacerations

Scalp lacerations are an easily recognized type of external head trauma. Because the scalp contains many blood vessels with poor constrictive abilities, profuse bleeding occurs with most scalp lacerations. Even relatively small wounds can bleed significantly. The major complications with scalp laceration are blood loss and infection.

Skull Fractures

Skull fractures often occur with head trauma. Skull fractures are described in several ways: (1) linear or depressed, (2) simple, comminuted, or compound, and (3) closed or open (Table 61.6). Fractures may be closed or open, depending on the presence of a scalp laceration or extension of the fracture into the air sinuses or dura. The type and severity of a skull fracture depend on the velocity, momentum, direction, and shape (blunt or sharp) of the injuring agent and site of impact.

The location of the fracture determines the manifestations (Table 61.7). For example, a basilar skull fracture is a special type

BOX 61.1 ETHICAL/LEGAL DILEMMAS

Brain Death

Situation

The emergency nurse receives a call from emergency response system (ERS) personnel, who are in route with R.G., a young man involved in a motorcycle crash. He was not wearing a helmet and has a large open skull fracture. Transport from the accident scene was delayed by 45 min because of a severe thunderstorm and the location. R.G. has fixed, dilated pupils and is in cardiac arrest. Estimated arrival at the hospital is still another 30 min because of the weather. ERS personnel request permission to stop resuscitation efforts.

Ethical/Legal Points for Consideration

- Criteria for brain death include coma or unresponsiveness, absence of brainstem reflexes, and apnea (see Chapter 10).
- In a situation in which the professional responsible for determining a state of death is in remote contact with the patient but the monitoring devices available provide virtual contact with the patient, a remote diagnosis of death may be legally acceptable.
- CPR is not appropriate when survival is not expected or the patient is expected to survive without the ability to communicate. Quantitative futility implies that survival is not expected after CPR under given circumstances. In the absence of mitigating factors, prolonged resuscitative efforts are unlikely to be successful and can be stopped if there is no return of spontaneous circulation at any time during 30 minutes of cumulative advanced life support.
- It is ethical for ED personnel to stop treatment started by ERS personnel in the prehospital setting if there is valid, after-the-fact evidence that these interventions are now inappropriate.

Discussion Questions

1. What are your feelings about cessation of brain function versus cessation of heart and lung function as the criteria for death?
2. What are your state's laws or practices about stopping CPR efforts by ERS personnel in the field?

TABLE 61.6 Types of Skull Fractures

Type	Description	Cause
Comminuted	Multiple linear fractures with fragmentation of bone into many pieces	Direct, high-momentum impact
Compound	Depressed skull fracture and scalp laceration with communicating pathway to intracranial cavity	Severe head injury
Depressed	Inward indentation of skull	Powerful blow
Linear	Break in continuity of bone without change of relationship of parts	Low-velocity injuries
Simple	Linear or depressed skull fracture without fragmentation or communicating lacerations	Low to moderate impact

of linear fracture involving the base of the skull. Manifestations can evolve over the course of several hours. They vary with the location and severity of fracture. These may include CN deficits, Battle sign (postauricular bruising), and periorbital bruising (raccoon eyes) (Fig. 61.12). This fracture is often due to a tear in the dura and subsequent leakage of CSF.

TABLE 61.7 Manifestations of Skull Fractures

Fracture Location	Manifestations
Basilar	CSF or brain otorrhea, bulging of tympanic membrane caused by blood or CSF, Battle sign, tinnitus or hearing difficulty, rhinorrhea, facial paralysis, conjugate deviation of gaze, vertigo
Frontal	Exposure of brain to contaminants through frontal air sinus, possible association with air in forehead tissue, CSF rhinorrhea, pneumocranium (air between cranium and dura mater)
Orbital	Periorbital bruising (raccoon eyes), optic nerve injury
Parietal	Deafness, CSF or brain otorrhea, bulging of tympanic membrane caused by blood or CSF, facial paralysis, loss of taste, Battle sign
Posterior fossa	Occipital bruising resulting in cortical blindness, visual field defects, rare appearance of ataxia or other cerebellar signs
Temporal	Boggy temporal muscle because of extravasation of blood, oval-shaped bruise behind ear in mastoid region (Battle sign), CSF otorrhea, middle meningeal artery disruption, epidural hematoma

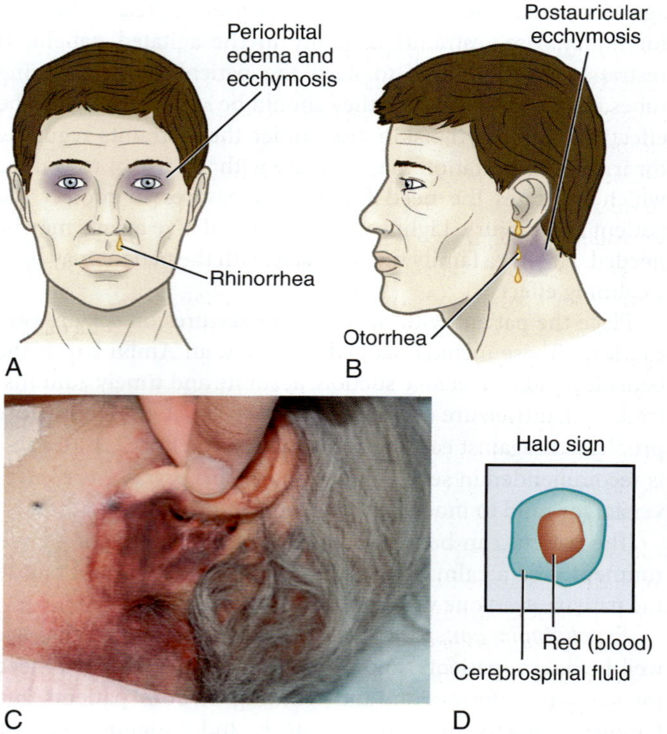

Fig. 61.12 (A) Raccoon eyes and rhinorrhea. (B) Battle sign (postauricular bruising) with otorrhea. (C) Battle sign. (D) Halo or ring sign (see text). (C, From Takahashi C, Okudera H, Kobayashi K, et al.: An extensive retropharyngeal haematoma associated with pyramidal fracture, *Injury Extra* 40:162, 2009.)

Rhinorrhea (CSF leakage from the nose) or *otorrhea* (CSF leakage from the ear) can confirm that a fracture has traversed the dura (Fig. 61.12). Rhinorrhea may also manifest as postnasal sinus drainage. Rhinorrhea may be overlooked unless we assess the patient for this finding. The risk for meningitis is high with a CSF leak. Antibiotics should be given as a preventive measure.

We use 2 ways to test whether fluid leaking from the nose or ear is CSF. One method is to test the leaking fluid with a Dextrostix or Tes-Tape strip to see if glucose is present. CSF gives a positive reading for glucose. If blood is present in the fluid, testing for glucose is unreliable because blood also contains glucose. In this event, look for the *halo* or *ring* sign (Fig. 61.12D). Allow the leaking fluid to drip onto a white gauze pad (4 × 4) or towel, and then observe the drainage. Within a few minutes, the blood coalesces into the center, and a yellowish ring encircles the blood if CSF is present. Note the color, appearance, and amount of leaking fluid because both tests can give false-positive results.

The major complications of skull fractures are intracranial infections, hematoma, and meningeal and brain tissue damage.

Head Trauma

We categorize brain injuries as diffuse (generalized) or focal (localized). In a *diffuse* injury (e.g., concussion, diffuse axonal injury), damage to the brain is not localized to 1 area. In a *focal injury* (e.g., contusion, hematoma), damage is localized to a specific area of the brain. We also classify brain injury as *minor* (GCS 13 to 15), *moderate* (GCS 9 to 12), or *severe* (GCS 3 to 8).

Diffuse injury. A **concussion** is a sudden transient mechanical head injury with disruption of neural activity and a change in the LOC. It is a minor diffuse head injury. Typical signs include a brief disruption in LOC, amnesia about the event (retrograde amnesia), and headache. The patient may or may not lose total consciousness. The manifestations are often of short duration. It usually resolves spontaneously. A concussion is usually considered benign.

For some, the signs and symptoms may be the beginning of a more serious, progressive problem, especially in a patient with a history of a concussion or head injury. If the patient has not lost consciousness or if the loss of consciousness lasts less than 5 minutes, the patient is usually discharged with instructions to notify the HCP if symptoms persist or if behavior changes occur. Give the patient and caregiver instructions for observation and accurate reporting of symptoms or changes in neurologic status.

Postconcussion syndrome may develop in some patients, usually from 2 weeks to 2 months after the injury. Manifestations include persistent headache, lethargy, personality and behavior changes, shortened attention span, decreased short-term memory, and changes in intellectual ability. This syndrome can significantly affect the patient's abilities to perform activities of daily living.

Diffuse axonal injury. **Diffuse axonal injury (DAI)** is widespread axonal damage occurring after a mild, moderate, or severe TBI. The damage occurs primarily around axons in the subcortical white matter of the cerebral hemispheres, basal ganglia, thalamus, and brainstem.[12] Initially, we thought DAI occurred because the tensile forces of trauma sheared axons, resulting in axonal disconnection. There is increasing evidence that axonal damage is not preceded by an immediate tearing of the axon from the traumatic impact. Instead, the trauma changes the function of the axon, resulting in axon swelling and disconnection. This process takes 12 to 24 hours to develop. It may persist longer.

The clinical signs of DAI vary. They may include a decreased LOC, increased ICP, decortication or decerebration, and global cerebral edema. Patients with DAI who survive the initial event are admitted to ICU. There, they will be vigilantly watched for signs of increased ICP and treated accordingly. Patients with severe injury have a poor functional prognosis.[13]

Focal injury. Focal injury can be minor to severe and localized to an area of injury. Focal injury consists of lacerations, contusions, hematomas, and CN injuries.

Lacerations involve actual tearing of the brain tissue. They often occur in depressed and open fractures and penetrating injuries. Tissue damage is severe. Surgical repair of the laceration is impossible because of the nature of brain tissue. Management consists of antibiotics (until meningitis is ruled out) and preventing secondary injury from increased ICP. If bleeding is deep into the brain tissue, focal and generalized signs develop.

With major head trauma, many delayed responses can occur. These include bleeding, hematoma formation, seizures, and cerebral edema. Intracerebral hemorrhage is generally due to a cerebral laceration. This bleeding manifests as a space-occupying lesion accompanied by unconsciousness, hemiplegia on the contralateral side, and a dilated pupil on the ipsilateral side. As the hematoma expands, signs of increased ICP become more severe. Subarachnoid hemorrhage and intraventricular hemorrhage can occur from head trauma.

A **contusion** is bruising of the brain tissue within a focal area. It is usually associated with a closed head injury. A contusion often occurs at a fracture site. There may be areas of bleeding, infarction, necrosis, and edema.

With contusion, the phenomenon of *coup-contrecoup injury* may occur (Fig. 61.13). Injuries can range from minor to severe. Damage from coup-contrecoup injury occurs when the brain moves inside the skull due to high-energy or high-impact injury mechanisms. Contusions or lacerations occur both at the site of the direct impact of the brain on the skull *(coup)* and at a second area of damage on the opposite side away from injury *(contrecoup)*, leading to multiple contused areas. *Contrecoup* injuries tend to be more severe. The overall prognosis depends on the amount of bleeding around the contusion site.

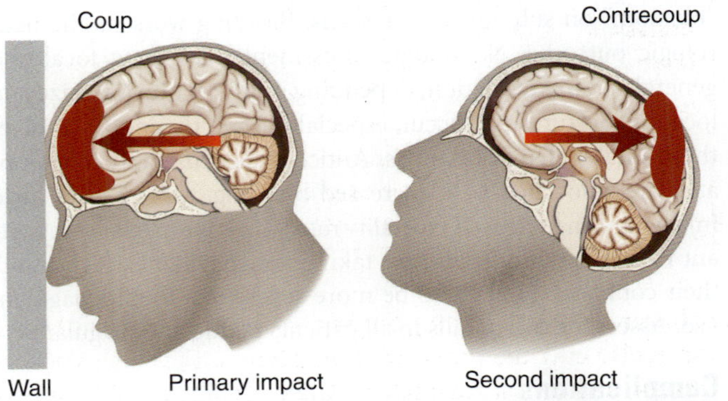

Fig. 61.13 Coup-contrecoup injury. After the head strikes the wall, a coup injury occurs as the brain strikes the skull (primary impact). The contrecoup injury (the second impact) occurs when the brain strikes the skull surface opposite the site of the original impact.

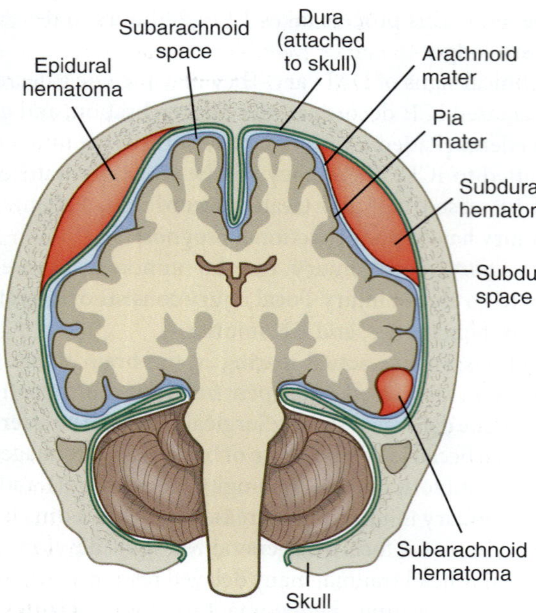

Fig. 61.14 Locations of epidural, subdural, and subarachnoid hematomas. (From Copstead-Kirkhorn LC, Banasik JL: *Pathophysiology,* ed 4, St Louis, 2010, Mosby.)

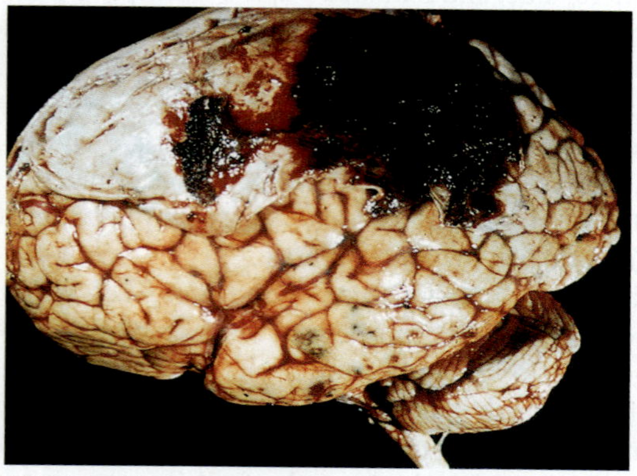

Fig. 61.15 Epidural hematoma covering a portion of the dura. Multiple small contusions are seen in the temporal lobe. (From Kumar V, Abbas AK, Aster JC, et al.: *Robbins and Cotran pathologic basis of disease,* ed 8, Philadelphia, 2010, Saunders.)

Contusions may continue to bleed or rebleed and appear to "blossom" on subsequent CT scans. Bleeding worsens the neurologic outcome. Neurologic assessment may show focal and generalized manifestation, depending on the contusion's size and location. Seizures can occur, especially when the injury involves the frontal or temporal lobes. Anticoagulant use and coagulopathy are associated with increased bleeding, more severe head injury, and an increased mortality rate.[14] This is especially important with older adults who are taking anticoagulants. If they fall, their contusion is likely to be more severe due to anticoagulant use. Assess for risk of falls in all patients taking anticoagulants.

Complications

Epidural Hematoma

An **epidural hematoma** results from bleeding between the dura and inner surface of the skull (Figs. 61.14 and 61.15). An epidural hematoma is a neurologic emergency. It is usually due to a linear fracture crossing a major artery in the dura, causing a tear. It can have a venous or arterial origin. Venous epidural hematomas are due to a tear of the dural venous sinus and develop slowly. With arterial hematomas, the middle meningeal artery lying under the temporal bone is often torn. Bleeding occurs into the epidural space, which lies between the dura and inner surface of the skull (Fig. 61.14). Because this is arterial bleeding, the hematoma develops rapidly.

Classic signs include an initial period of unconsciousness at the scene, with a brief lucid interval followed by a decrease in LOC. Other manifestations may be a headache, nausea and vomiting, or focal findings. Rapid surgical treatment to evacuate the hematoma and prevent cerebral herniation, along with medical management for increasing ICP, dramatically improves outcomes.

TABLE 61.8 Types of Subdural Hematomas

Occurrence After Injury	Progression of Symptoms	Treatment
Acute		
24–48 hr after severe trauma	Immediate deterioration	Craniotomy, evacuation, and decompression
Subacute		
48 hr–2 weeks after severe trauma	Decline in mental status as hematoma develops. Progression dependent on size and location of hematoma	Evacuation and decompression
Chronic		
Weeks or months, usually >20 days after injury. Often injury seemed trivial or was forgotten by patient	Nonspecific, nonlocalizing progression. Progressive change in LOC	Evacuation and decompression, membranectomy

Subdural Hematoma

A **subdural hematoma** occurs from bleeding between the dura mater and arachnoid layer of the meninges (Fig. 61.14). A subdural hematoma usually results from injury to the brain tissue and its blood vessels. The veins that drain from the surface of the brain into the sagittal sinus are the source of most subdural hematomas. Because it is usually venous in origin, a subdural hematoma may be slower to develop. However, an arterial bleed can cause a subdural hematoma. In this case it develops more rapidly.

Subdural hematomas may be acute, subacute, or chronic (Table 61.8). An *acute subdural hematoma* manifests within hours of the injury.[14] The signs and symptoms are similar to those of brain tissue compression in increased ICP. They include decreasing LOC and headache. The size of the hematoma determines the presentation and prognosis. The patient's appearance may range from drowsy and confused to unconscious. The ipsilateral pupil dilates and becomes fixed if ICP is significantly increased. Blunt-force injuries that produce acute subdural hematomas may cause significant underlying brain injury, resulting in cerebral edema. The resulting increase in ICP from the cerebral edema can increase morbidity and mortality despite surgery to evacuate the hematoma.

A *subacute subdural hematoma* usually occurs within 2 to 14 days of the injury. After the initial bleeding, this hematoma may appear to enlarge over time as the breakdown products of the blood draw fluid into the subdural space.

A *chronic subdural hematoma* develops over weeks or months after a seemingly minor head injury.[14] They are more common in older adults because of a potentially larger subdural space from brain atrophy. With atrophy, the brain stays attached to the supportive structures and tension is increased. This makes it subject to tearing. Because the subdural space is larger, the presenting problem is focal symptoms rather than signs of increased ICP.[14] Patients with a history of alcohol use are prone to subdural hematomas because of an increased incidence of falls.

There may be a delay in diagnosing a subdural hematoma in the older adult because symptoms mimic other health problems in this age-group, such as confusion, lethargy, and memory loss. Manifestations of a subdural hematoma are often attributed to vascular disease (stroke, transient ischemic attack [TIA]) or dementia.

CHECK YOUR PRACTICE

You are doing BP screenings in the senior center when you meet a 76-year-old man and his wife. As you perform their BP screening, the wife tells you that her husband has been getting severe headaches, is dizzy, and sometimes has difficulty talking. Based on your advice, they go to an urgent care center, where a CT scan is done. The results show he has a chronic subdural hematoma. When you find out the diagnosis, you are puzzled because you thought he was having a stroke and cannot understand how he got a subdural hematoma.

- If you had been the nurse, what would you have done differently when screening this man?

Intracerebral Hematoma

Intracerebral hematoma occurs from bleeding within the brain tissue. It occurs in about 16% of head injuries. It usually happens in the frontal and temporal lobes, possibly from rupture of intracerebral vessels at the time of injury. The size and location of the hematoma are key in determining the patient's outcome.

Diagnostic Studies

In general, the diagnostic studies are similar to those used for a patient with increased ICP (Table 61.3). CT scan is the best test to evaluate for head trauma. It allows for rapid diagnosis and intervention in the acute care setting. MRI, PET, and evoked potential studies may be used to diagnose head injuries. An MRI scan is more sensitive than the CT scan in detecting small lesions. Transcranial Doppler studies can measure CBF velocity. A cervical spine x-ray series, CT scan, or MRI of the spine may be done since cervical spine trauma often occurs at the same time as a head injury.

Interprofessional Care

Emergency management of the patient with a head injury is outlined in Table 61.9. The key treatment of head injuries is prompt diagnosis and surgery (if needed). We also institute measures to prevent secondary injury by treating cerebral edema and managing increased ICP. For the patient with concussion and contusion, observation and management of increased ICP are the main management strategies.

The treatment of skull fractures is usually conservative. For depressed fractures and fractures with loose fragments, a craniotomy is done to elevate the depressed bone and remove the free fragments. If large amounts of bone are destroyed, the bone may be removed (craniectomy). A cranioplasty will be needed later.

In cases of large acute subdural and epidural hematomas or those that have significant neurologic impairment, the blood must be removed through surgical evacuation. A craniotomy is usually done to see and allow control of the bleeding vessels. Burr-hole openings may be used in an extreme emergency for a more rapid decompression, followed by a craniotomy. A drain may be placed after surgery for several days to prevent blood from reaccumulating. When extreme swelling is expected (e.g., DAI, bleeding), a craniectomy may be done. This involves removing a piece of skull to reduce the pressure inside the skull. It reduces the risk for herniation.

NURSING MANAGEMENT: HEAD INJURY

Assessment

A patient with a head injury always has the potential to develop increased ICP, which has higher mortality rates and poorer functional outcomes. Objective data are obtained by applying the GCS (Table 61.5), assessing and monitoring neurologic status, and determining whether a CSF leak has occurred. Nursing assessment related to increased ICP is discussed later in this chapter. Assessment of the patient with a head injury is outlined in Table 61.10.

Clinical Problems

Clinical problems for the patient who has a head injury may include:

- Increased intracranial pressure
- Inadequate tissue perfusion
- Altered temperature

Planning

The overall goals are that the patient with an acute head injury will (1) maintain adequate cerebral oxygenation and perfusion, (2) stay afebrile, (3) be free of discomfort, (4) be free from infection, (5) have adequate nutrition, and (6) attain maximal cognitive, motor, and sensory function.

Implementation

Health Promotion

One of the best ways to prevent head injuries is to prevent car and motorcycle accidents. Be active in campaigns that promote driving safety (Box 61.2). Speak to driver education classes about the dangers of distracted driving and driving after drinking alcohol or using drugs. Helmets for motorcycle riders is the most effective way to increase survival after crashes.

TABLE 61.9 EMERGENCY MANAGEMENT

Head Injury

Etiology	Assessment Findings	Interventions
Blunt • Assault • Fall • Motor vehicle collision • Sports injury **Penetrating** • Arrow • Gunshot • Knife	**Central Nervous System** • Asymmetric facial movements • Combativeness • Confusion • CSF leaking from ears or nose • Decerebrate or decorticate posturing • Depressed or hyperactive reflexes • Dilated or unequal pupils, photophobia • Flaccidity • Garbled speech, abusive speech • GCS score <12 • Incontinence • Involuntary movements • ↓ LOC • Seizures **Respiratory** • Central neurogenic hyperventilation • Cheyne-Stokes respirations • ↓ O_2 saturation • Pulmonary edema **Surface Findings** • Bruises or contusions on face, Battle sign (bruising behind ears) • Fracture or depressions in skull • Raccoon eyes (dependent bruising around eyes) • Scalp lacerations	**Initial** • If unresponsive, assess circulation, airway, and breathing. • If responsive, monitor airway, breathing, and circulation. • Assume neck injury with head injury. • Stabilize cervical spine. • Apply O_2 via nonrebreather mask. • Establish IV access with 2 large-bore catheters to infuse normal saline or lactated Ringer solution. • Intubate if GCS score <8. • Control external bleeding with sterile pressure dressing. • Remove patient's clothing. **Ongoing Monitoring** • Maintain normothermia using blankets, warm IV fluids, as needed. • Monitor vital signs, LOC, O_2 saturation, cardiac rhythm, GCS score, pupil size and reactivity. • Expect intubation if gag reflex is impaired or absent. • Assess for rhinorrhea, otorrhea, scalp wounds. • Give fluids cautiously to prevent fluid overload and increasing ICP.

◆ Acute Care

Management at the scene can have a significant impact on the outcome of a head injury. Emergency management of head injury is outlined in Table 61.9. The general goal of nursing management of the patient with head injury is to maintain cerebral oxygenation and perfusion and prevent secondary cerebral ischemia.

Surveillance or monitoring for changes in neurologic status is critically important because the patient's condition may deteriorate rapidly, requiring emergency surgery. Appropriate nursing interventions are started if surgery is anticipated. Because of the close association between hemodynamic status and cerebral perfusion, be aware of any coexisting injuries or conditions.

Explain the need for frequent neurologic assessments to the patient and caregiver. Behavior manifestations can result in a frightened, disoriented patient who is combative and resists help. Your approach should be calm and gentle. A family member may be available to stay with the patient to decrease their anxiety and fear. An important need of the caregiver and family members in the acute injury phase is information about the patient's diagnosis, treatment plan, and reason for the interventions. Other teaching points are described in Table 61.11.

Perform neurologic assessments at intervals based on the patient's condition. The GCS is useful in assessing the LOC (Table 61.5). Report any signs of a deteriorating neurologic state, no matter how subtle, such as a decreasing LOC or motor strength, to the HCP. Monitor the patient's condition closely.

The major focus of nursing care for the patient with a brain injury relates to increased ICP (see eNursing Care Plan 61.1). However, some problems need specific nursing intervention.

Eye problems may include loss of the corneal reflex, periorbital bruising and edema, and diplopia. Loss of the corneal reflex may require lubricating eye drops or taping the eyes shut to prevent abrasion. Periorbital bruising and edema decrease with time. Cold and, later, warm compresses provide comfort and hasten healing. Wearing an eye patch can relieve diplopia. Consider a consult with an ophthalmologist.

Fever may occur from injury to or inflammation of the hypothalamus. Fever can increase CBF, cerebral blood volume, and ICP. Increased metabolism from fever increases metabolic waste. This causes further cerebral vasodilation. Avoid fever with a goal of a temperature of 96.8°F to 98.6°F (36°C to 37°C) as the standard of care. Use interventions to reduce fever and prevent shivering (see Table 12.5).

If CSF rhinorrhea or otorrhea occurs, inform the HCP at once. The head of the bed may be raised to decrease the CSF pressure so that a tear can seal. A loose collection pad may be placed under the nose or over the ear. Do not place a dressing in the nasal or ear cavities. Record the amount of drainage each shift. Teach the patient not to sneeze or blow the nose. Do not use NG tubes. Do not perform nasotracheal suctioning because of the high risk for meningitis.

Implement measures specific to the care of the immobilized patient, such as those related to bladder and bowel function,

TABLE 61.10 NURSING ASSESSMENT

Head Injury

Subjective Data

Important Health Information

Health history: Mechanism of injury: motor vehicle collision, sports injury, industrial incident, assault, falls

Medications: Anticoagulant drugs

Functional Health Patterns

Health perception–health management: Alcohol or recreational drugs. Risk-taking behaviors

Cognitive-perceptual: Headache, mood or behavior change, mentation changes, aphasia, dysphasia, impaired judgment

Coping–stress tolerance: Fear, denial, anger, aggression, depression

Objective Data

Cardiovascular

Impending herniation: Cushing triad (systolic hypertension with widening pulse pressure, bradycardia with full and bounding pulse, irregular respirations)

GI

Vomiting, projectile vomiting, bowel incontinence

Musculoskeletal

Motor deficit/impairment, weakness, palmar drift, paralysis, spasticity, decorticate or decerebrate posturing, muscular rigidity or increased tone, flaccidity, ataxia

Neurologic

Altered LOC, altered mental status, seizure activity, pupil dysfunction, cranial nerve deficit(s)

Respiratory

Rhinorrhea, impaired gag reflex, inability to maintain a patent airway. Impending herniation: altered/irregular respiratory rate and pattern

Skin

Lacerations, contusions, abrasions, hematoma, Battle sign, periorbital edema and bruising, otorrhea, exposed brain matter

Urinary

Bladder incontinence

Possible Diagnostic Findings

Location and type of hematoma, edema, skull fracture, and/or foreign body on CT scan and/or MRI; abnormal EEG; positive toxicology screen or alcohol level, ↓ or ↑ blood glucose level; ↑ ICP

skin care, and infection. Nausea and vomiting may be a problem. Administer antiemetics drugs as ordered. Acetaminophen or small doses of codeine can help to control headache.

If the patient's condition deteriorates, they may need intracranial surgery. The patient may need a burr-hole opening or craniotomy, depending on the underlying injury. The emergency nature of the surgery may hasten the usual preoperative preparation. Consult with the HCP to determine specific preoperative nursing measures.

The patient is often unconscious before surgery, making it necessary for a family member to sign the consent form for surgery. This is a difficult and frightening time for the patient's caregiver and family and requires sensitive nursing management. The suddenness of the situation makes it especially hard for the family to cope. Use a team approach, including social workers, to help the patient and family throughout the hospitalization and recovery time.

BOX 61.2 PROMOTING POPULATION HEALTH

Reducing the Risk for Head Injuries

- Always wear car seat belts in motor vehicles.
- Do not drive after using drugs or alcohol.
- Do not text and drive or drive distracted.
- Wear helmets while bicycling, skating, skateboarding, skiing, and playing contact sports.
- Athletes should follow safe playing techniques and the rules of the game.
- Assess home safety and implement any corrective measures needed.
- Older adults should continue to exercise regularly to improve strength and balance.
- Follow workplace safety precautions, including wearing helmets and protective gear.

TABLE 61.11 PATIENT & CAREGIVER TEACHING

Head Injury

Include the following instructions when teaching the patient and caregiver about care during the first 2 or 3 days after a head injury:

1. Notify your HCP immediately if you have signs and symptoms that may indicate complications. These include:
   - Increased drowsiness (e.g., difficulty arousing, confusion)
   - Nausea or vomiting
   - Worsening headache or stiff neck
   - Seizures
   - Vision changes (e.g., blurring) or sensitivity to light (photophobia)
   - Behavior changes (e.g., irritability, anger)
   - Motor problems (e.g., clumsiness, difficulty walking, slurred speech, weakness in arms or legs)
   - Sensory problems (e.g., numbness)
   - Heart rate <60 beats/min
2. Have someone stay with you.
3. Abstain from alcohol.
4. Check with your HCP before taking drugs that may increase drowsiness, including muscle relaxants, tranquilizers, and opioid analgesia.
5. Avoid driving, using heavy machinery, playing contact sports, and taking hot baths.

◆ Ambulatory Care

Once their condition has stabilized, the patient is usually transferred for acute rehabilitation management. There may be chronic problems related to motor and sensory deficits, communication, memory, and intellectual functioning. Conditions we may need to manage include nutrition problems, bowel and bladder problems, spasticity, dysphagia, and hydrocephalus. Many of the principles for managing the patient with a stroke are appropriate for these patients (see Chapter 62).

Seizure disorders may occur in patients with nonpenetrating head injury. Seizures may develop during the first week after the head injury or not until years later. Antiseizure drugs may be used prophylactically to manage posttraumatic seizure activity. However, this practice is controversial.

The mental and emotional sequelae are often the most incapacitating problems. One of the consequences of TBI is that the person may not realize that a brain injury has occurred. Many patients with head injuries who were comatose for more than 6 hours may have some personality change. They may have loss of concentration and memory and defective memory processing. Personal drive may decrease. Apathy may increase. Euphoria and mood swings, along with a seeming lack of awareness of the seriousness of the injury, may occur. The patient's behavior may indicate a loss of social restraint, judgment, tact, and emotional control.

Progressive recovery may continue for years. Specific nursing management in the posttraumatic phase depends on specific residual deficits. Being able to return to work and maintaining employment are challenges during the recovery period.[15] The patient's outward physical appearance does not necessarily reflect what has happened in the brain. It is not a good indicator of how well the patient will ultimately function in the home or work environment.

Give the family special consideration. They need to understand what is happening. The family often has unrealistic expectations of the patient as the coma begins to recede. They may expect full return to pretrauma status. In reality, the patient usually has a reduced awareness and ability to interpret environmental stimuli. Prepare the family for the patient's emergence from coma. Explain that the process of awakening often takes several weeks. Help the patient and family to remain hopeful. Arrange for social work and chaplain consults for the family.

When it is time for discharge planning, the patient, caregiver, and family may benefit from specific instructions to avoid family-patient friction. Special "no" policies may include no alcohol use, no driving, no use of firearms, no working with hazardous implements and machinery, and no unsupervised smoking. Help the family in involving the patient in family activities whenever possible. Family members, especially spouses, go through role transition as the role changes from that of spouse to that of caregiver. Provide guidance and referrals for financial aid, childcare, and other personal needs.

◆ Evaluation

The expected outcomes are that the patient with a head injury will:

- Maintain normal CPP
- Achieve maximal cognitive, motor, and sensory function
- Have no infection or fever

BRAIN TUMORS

There are an estimated 23,400 people diagnosed each year with brain tumors in the United States. The brain is also a frequent site for metastasis from other sites.[16] Males have a slightly higher incidence of brain tumors (Box 61.3). Brain tumors most often occur in middle-aged persons, but they may be seen at any age.

BOX 61.3 PROMOTING HEALTH EQUITY

Brain Tumors

- Whites have a higher incidence of malignant brain tumors than do Blacks.
- White males have the highest incidence of malignant brain tumors.
- Blacks have the highest incidence of benign brain tumors.

Types

Brain tumors can occur in any part of the brain or spinal cord. They may be *primary,* arising from tissues within the brain, or *secondary,* resulting from a metastasis of cancer from elsewhere in the body.[16] Metastatic brain tumors are the most common brain tumor. The cancers that most often metastasize to the brain are lung and breast.

We usually classify primary brain tumors according to the tissue from which they arise (Table 61.12). Meningiomas are the most common primary brain tumor. Other common brain tumors are gliomas (e.g., astrocytoma, glioblastoma [most common form of glioma]).

More than half of brain tumors are malignant. They infiltrate the brain tissue and are not amenable to complete surgical removal. Other tumors may be histologically benign but are located such that complete removal is not possible.

Brain tumors rarely metastasize outside the central nervous system (CNS) because they are contained by structural (meninges) and physiologic (blood-brain) barriers. Table 61.12 compares the most common brain tumors. Sites of common tumors are shown in Fig. 61.16.

Clinical Manifestations and Complications

The manifestations of brain tumors depend mainly on their location and size (Table 61.13). A wide range of manifestations are possible. Headache is common. Tumor-related headaches tend to be worse at night and may awaken the patient. The headaches are usually dull and constant but sometimes throbbing. Seizures are common in gliomas and brain metastases. Brain tumors can cause nausea and vomiting from increased ICP. Cognitive dysfunction, including memory problems and mood or personality changes, is common, especially in patients with brain metastases. Muscle weakness, sensory losses, aphasia, and visual-spatial dysfunction may occur.

If the tumor mass obstructs the ventricles or occludes the outlet, ventricular enlargement (hydrocephalus) can occur. As the brain tumor expands, it may produce manifestations of increased ICP, cerebral edema, or obstruction of the CSF pathways. Unless treated, all brain tumors eventually cause death from increasing tumor volume leading to increased ICP.

Diagnostic Studies

An extensive history and a comprehensive neurologic examination are done in the workup of a patient with a suspected brain tumor. The history and physical assessment may provide data with respect to location. New onset of seizures or adult-onset migraines may indicate a brain tumor and should be assessed. Diagnostic studies are similar to those used for a patient with increased ICP (Table 61.3).

TABLE 61.12 Types of Brain Tumors

Type	Tissue of Origin	Characteristics
Acoustic neuroma (schwannoma)	Cells that form myelin sheath around nerves. Often affects cranial nerve VIII	Many grow on both sides of the brain. Usually benign or low grade.
Gliomas		
• Astrocytoma	Supportive tissue, glial cells, and astrocytes	Can range from low grade to moderate grade.
• Ependymoma	Ependymal epithelium	Range from benign to highly malignant. Most are benign and encapsulated.
• Glioblastoma	Primitive stem cell (glioblast)	Highly malignant and invasive. Among the most devastating of primary brain tumors.
• Medulloblastoma	Primitive neuroectodermal cell	Highly malignant and invasive. Metastatic to spinal cord and remote areas of brain.
• Oligodendroglioma	Oligodendrocytes	Benign (encapsulation and calcification).
Hemangioblastoma	Blood vessels of brain	Rare and benign. Surgery is curative.
Meningioma	Meninges	Can be benign or malignant. Most are benign.
Metastatic tumors	Lungs and breast (most common)	Malignant.
Pituitary adenoma	Pituitary gland	Usually benign.
Primary central nervous system lymphoma	Lymphocytes	↑ Incidence in transplant recipients and AIDS patients.

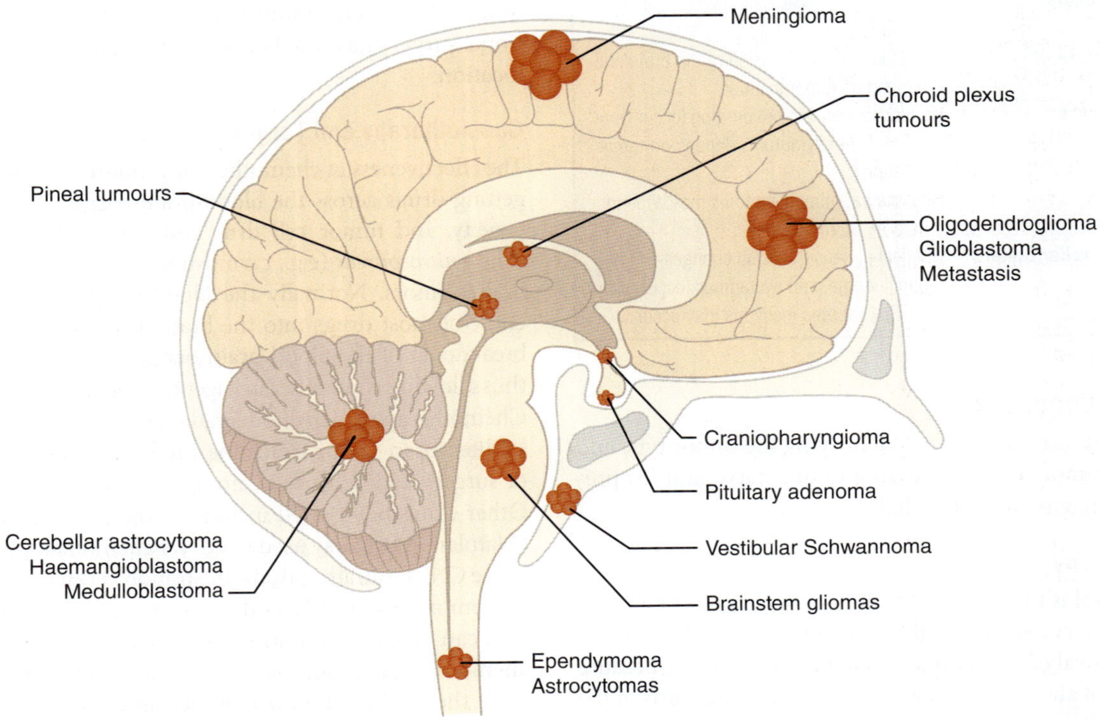

Fig. 61.16 Common sites of occurrence for CNS tumors.

CT with contrast and MRI are used to identify the lesion's location. The sensitivity of MRI and PET scans allows for detection of small tumors and may provide better diagnostic information than a CT scan. Other tests include magnetic resonance spectroscopy, functional MRI (fMRI), and single-photon emission computed tomography (SPECT). An EEG can rule out seizures but is of less importance. Cerebral angiography can assess blood flow to the tumor and further localize the tumor. Other studies are done to rule out a primary lesion elsewhere in the body. Endocrine studies are helpful when a pituitary adenoma is suspected (see Chapter 54).

The correct diagnosis of a brain tumor can be made by obtaining tissue for histologic study. In most patients, tissue is obtained at the time of surgery. Computer-guided stereotactic biopsy is also an option. A smear or frozen section can be done in the operating room for a preliminary interpretation of the histologic type. With this information, the HCP can make a better decision about the extent of surgery.

TABLE 61.13 Manifestations of Brain Tumors

Tumor Location	Manifestations
Brainstem tumors	Headache on awakening, drowsiness, vomiting, ataxic gait, facial muscle weakness, hearing loss, dysphagia, dysarthria, "crossed eyes" or other visual changes, hemiparesis
Cerebellopontine tumors	Tinnitus and vertigo, deafness
Cerebral hemisphere	
• Frontal lobe (unilateral)	Unilateral hemiplegia, seizures, memory deficit, personality and judgment changes, visual changes
• Frontal lobe (bilateral)	Symptoms of unilateral frontal lobe tumors. Ataxic gait
• Parietal lobe	Speech problems (if tumor is in the dominant hemisphere), inability to write, spatial disorders, unilateral neglect
• Occipital lobe	Vision changes and seizures
• Temporal lobe	Few symptoms. Seizures, dysphagia, hallucinations, auras
Fourth ventricle and cerebellar tumors	Headache, nausea, and papilledema (occur from ↑ ICP). Ataxic gait and changes in coordination
Meningeal tumors	Symptoms of compression of the brain and depend on tumor location
Metastatic tumors	Headache, nausea, or vomiting (occur from ↑ ICP). Other symptoms depend on tumor location
Subcortical	Hemiplegia; other symptoms may depend on area of infiltration
Thalamus and sellar tumors	Headache, nausea, vision changes, papilledema, and nystagmus (occur from ↑ ICP). Diabetes insipidus may occur

Interprofessional Care

Treatment goals are aimed at (1) identifying the tumor type and location, (2) removing or decreasing tumor mass, and (3) preventing or managing increased ICP.

Surgical Therapy

Surgical removal is the preferred treatment for brain tumors. The outcome of surgery depends on the tumor's type, size, and location. Complete removal of brain tumors is not always possible because the tumor is not always accessible or may involve vital parts of the brain. Surgery can reduce tumor mass, which decreases ICP, provides relief of symptoms, and extends survival time.

Meningiomas and oligodendrogliomas can usually be completely removed. The more invasive gliomas and medulloblastomas may be only partially removed. Stereotactic surgery is used to perform a biopsy and remove small brain tumors. Computer-guided stereotactic biopsy, ultrasound, fMRI, and cortical mapping can localize brain tumors during surgery.

Ventricular Shunts

Hydrocephalus due to a tumor obstructing the CSF flow can be treated by placing a ventricular shunt. A catheter with 1-way valves is placed in the lateral ventricle and then tunneled under the skin to drain CSF into the peritoneal cavity. Rapid decompression of ICP can cause total body collapse and weakness. Headache may be prevented by gradually introducing the patient to the upright position.

Manifestations of shunt malfunction, which are related to increased ICP, include decreasing LOC, restlessness, headache, blurred vision, or vomiting. This may require shunt revision or replacement. Infection may occur, with high fever, headache, and stiff neck. Antibiotics are used to treat the infection. In some situations, the shunt is replaced. CSF drainage is managed with an extraventricular drainage system while the infection is treated.

Radiation Therapy and Stereotactic Radiosurgery

Radiation therapy may be used as a follow-up measure after surgery. Radiation seeds can be implanted into the brain. Cerebral edema and rapidly increasing ICP may be a complication of radiation therapy. These problems can usually be managed with high doses of corticosteroids (e.g., dexamethasone, methylprednisolone). Radiation therapy is discussed in Chapter 16.

Stereotactic radiosurgery is a method of delivering a highly concentrated dose of radiation to a precise location within the brain. Stereotactic radiosurgery may be used when conventional surgery has failed or is not an option because of the tumor location.

Chemotherapy and Targeted Therapy

The effectiveness of chemotherapy is limited by the difficulty with getting drugs across the blood-brain barrier, tumor cell heterogeneity, and tumor cell drug resistance. Chemotherapy drugs called *nitrosoureas* (e.g., carmustine, lomustine) are used to treat brain tumors. Normally the blood-brain barrier prohibits the entry of most drugs into the brain. Cancer tumors can cause a breakdown of the blood-brain barrier in the area of the tumor, thus allowing chemotherapy agents to be used to treat the cancer. Chemotherapy-laden biodegradable wafers (e.g., Gliadel wafer [polifeprosan with carmustine implant]) implanted at the time of surgery can deliver chemotherapy directly to the tumor site. Other drugs being used include methotrexate and procarbazine (Matulane). One way used to deliver chemotherapy drugs directly to the CNS is intrathecal administration via an Ommaya reservoir.

Temozolomide (Temodar) is an oral chemotherapy agent that can cross the blood-brain barrier. In contrast with many chemotherapy drugs, which require metabolic activation to exert their effects, temozolomide can convert spontaneously to a reactive agent that directly interferes with tumor growth. It does not interact with other common drugs taken by patients with brain tumors, such as antiseizure drugs, corticosteroids, and antiemetics.

DRUG ALERT

Temozolomide (Temodar)

- Causes myelosuppression. Before using, the absolute neutrophil count should be ≥1500/µL and platelet count should be ≥100,000/µL.
- To reduce nausea and vomiting, take on empty stomach or at bedtime.

Bevacizumab (Avastin) is used to treat patients with glioblastoma that continues to progress after standard therapy. Bevacizumab is a targeted therapy that inhibits the action of vascular endothelial growth factor, which helps form new blood vessels. These vessels can feed a tumor, helping it to grow, and provide a pathway for cancer cells to circulate in the body.

Other Therapies

The Optune System is used to treat glioblastoma that recurs or progresses after receiving chemotherapy and radiation therapy. With this system, electrodes are placed on the surface of the patient's scalp to deliver low intensity, changing electrical fields called *tumor treatment fields* (TTFs) to the tumor site.

NURSING MANAGEMENT: BRAIN TUMORS

Assessment

Ask about the medical history, intellectual abilities and educational level, and history of nervous system infections and trauma. Is there a history of dementia? Loss of emotional control, confusion, disorientation, memory loss, impulsivity, and depression may be signs of a frontal lobe lesion. The patient often does not perceive these changes. Having the patient or caregiver explain the problem can be helpful to determine the patient's limitations and obtain information about the patient's insight into the problems. Structure the initial assessment to provide baseline data of the patient's neurologic status. Use this information to design a realistic patient-specific care plan.

Assess the patient's LOC, motor abilities, sensory perception, integrated function (including bowel and bladder function), and balance and proprioception. Determine the presence of seizures, syncope, nausea and vomiting, and headaches or other pain. Assess the coping abilities of the patient, caregiver, and family. Watching a patient perform activities of daily living and listening to the patient's conversation can be part of the neurologic assessment. Record all initial data to provide a baseline for comparison to determine whether the patient's condition is improving or deteriorating.

Clinical Problems

Clinical problems for the patient with a brain tumor may include:

- Inadequate tissue perfusion
- Pain
- Anxiety
- Neurologic problem

Planning

The overall goals are that the patient with a brain tumor will (1) maintain normal ICP, (2) maximize neurologic functioning, (3) achieve control of pain and discomfort, and (4) be aware of the long-term implications with respect to prognosis and cognitive and physical functioning.

Implementation

Help the caregiver and family understand what is happening to the patient and support the family. A tumor of the frontal lobe can cause behavior and personality changes. These changes can be disturbing and frightening to the caregiver and family. They can also cause a distancing to occur between the family and patient.

The confused patient with behavior instability can be a challenge. Protecting the patient from self-harm is an important part of nursing care. Essential interventions include close supervision of activity, use of side rails, judicious use of restraints, appropriate sedatives, padding of the rails and the area around the bed, and a calm, reassuring approach.

Tumors in the temporal lobe can cause hallucinations. Perceptual problems from frontal and parietal lobe tumors contribute to disorientation and confusion. Minimize environmental stimuli, create a routine, and use reality orientation for the confused patient.

Seizures, which often occur with brain tumors, are managed with antiseizure drugs. Use seizure precautions for the patient's protection. Some behavior changes seen in the patient are a result of seizure disorders and can improve with adequate seizure control. Patients at risk for seizures may be unable to drive. Be aware of the extra resources needed and collaborate with the social worker and family. Seizure disorders are discussed in Chapter 63.

Motor and sensory problems interfere with activities of daily living. Encourage the patient to provide as much self-care as physically possible. Self-image often depends on the patient's ability to take part in care within the limitations of the physical deficits.

Language deficits may be present. Motor (expressive) or sensory (receptive) dysphasia may occur. The problem with communication can be frustrating for the patient and may interfere with your ability to meet the patient's needs. Try to establish a communication system that both the patient and staff can use.

Nutrition intake may be decreased because of the patient's inability to eat, loss of appetite, or loss of desire to eat. Assess nutrition status and ensure adequate nutrition intake. Encourage the patient to eat. Some patients may need enteral or parenteral nutrition (see Chapter 44).

Provide help and support during the adjustment phase and in long-range planning. Social work and home health nurses may help the caregiver with discharge planning. They can help the family adjust to role changes and psychosocial and socioeconomic factors. Issues related to palliative and end-of-life care must be discussed with both the patient and family (see Chapter 10).

Evaluation

The expected outcomes are that the patient with a brain tumor will:

- Achieve control of pain, vomiting, and other discomforts
- Maintain ICP within normal limits
- Have maximal neurologic function given the location and extent of the tumor
- Maintain optimal nutrition status
- Accept the long-term consequences of the tumor and its treatment

TABLE 61.14 Indications for Cranial Surgery

Indication	Cause	Surgical Procedure
Aneurysm repair	Dilation of weak area in arterial wall (usually near anterior portion of circle of Willis)	Dissection and clipping or coiling of aneurysm
Arteriovenous (AV) malformation	Congenital tangle of arteries and veins (often in middle cerebral artery)	Excision of malformation
Brain abscess	Bacteria that caused intracranial infection	Excision or drainage of abscess
Brain tumors	Benign or malignant cell growth	Excision or partial resection of tumor
Hydrocephalus	Overproduction of cerebrospinal fluid, obstruction to flow, defective reabsorption	Placement of ventriculoperitoneal or (rarely) ventriculoatrial shunt
Intracranial bleeding	Rupture of cerebral vessels because of trauma or stroke	Surgical evacuation through burr holes or craniotomy
Skull fractures	Trauma to skull	Debridement of fragments and necrotic tissue, elevation and realignment of bone fragments

TABLE 61.15 Types of Cranial Surgery

Type	Description
Burr hole	Opening into the cranium with a drill. Used to remove localized fluid and blood beneath the dura.
Craniectomy	Excision into the cranium to cut away bone flap.
Cranioplasty	Repair of cranial defect resulting from trauma, malformation, or previous surgery. Artificial material used to replace damaged or lost bone.
Craniotomy	Opening into cranium with removal of bone flap and opening the dura to remove a lesion, repair a damaged area, drain blood, or relieve ↑ ICP.
Shunt procedures	Alternative pathway to redirect cerebrospinal fluid from one area to another using a tube or implanted device. Examples include ventricular shunt and Ommaya reservoir.
Stereotactic procedure	Precise localization of a specific area of the brain using a frame or frameless system based on 3-dimensional coordinates. Used for biopsy, radiosurgery, or dissection.

CRANIAL SURGERY

Indications for cranial surgery are related to brain tumors, CNS infection (e.g., abscess), vascular abnormalities, craniocerebral trauma, seizure disorder, or intractable pain (Table 61.14).

Types

Various cranial surgeries are outlined in Table 61.15.

Craniotomy

Depending on the location of the pathologic condition, a *craniotomy* may be frontal, parietal, occipital, temporal, suboccipital, or a combination of any of these. The HCP drills a set of burr holes and uses a saw to connect the holes to remove the bone flap (Fig. 61.17). Sometimes operating microscopes are used to magnify the site. After surgery, the bone flap is secured with small plates or wired shut. Sometimes drains are placed to remove fluid and blood. Patients usually receive care in the ICU until stable.

Stereotactic Radiosurgery

Stereotactic procedures use a precision apparatus (often computer guided) to help the HCP precisely target an area of the brain. Stereotactic biopsy can be done to obtain tissue samples for histologic examination. CT scanning and MRI image the targeted tissue. With the patient under general or local anesthesia, the HCP drills a burr hole or creates a bone flap for an entry site and then introduces a probe and biopsy needle. Stereotactic procedures are used for removal of small brain tumors and abscesses, drainage of hematomas, ablative procedures for extrapyramidal diseases (e.g., Parkinson disease), and repair of arteriovenous malformations. A major advantage of the stereotactic approach is a reduction in damage to surrounding tissue.

Stereotactic radiosurgery is not a form of surgery in the traditional sense. Instead, radiosurgery uses high-dose radiation to destroy precisely targeted tumor cells and other abnormal growths. Computers create 3-dimensional images of the brain. These images are used to guide the focused radiation while the patient's head is held still in a stereotactic frame (Fig. 61.18). The ionizing radiation can be generated by a linear accelerator, Gamma Knife, or CyberKnife. The dose of radiation is delivered in a single treatment lasting a few hours or in multiple sessions. Side effects include fatigue, headache, and nausea.

In combination with stereotactic procedures to identify and localize tumor sites, lasers can be used to destroy tumors. Lasers work by creating thermal energy, which destroys the tissue on which it is focused. Laser therapy provides the benefit of reducing damage to surrounding tissue.

❖ NURSING MANAGEMENT: CRANIAL SURGERY

◆ Implementation

◆ Acute Care

The general nursing care for the patient undergoing cranial surgery is similar regardless of the cause. It is similar to that for the patient with increased ICP. The patient (if conscious and coherent), caregiver, and family will be concerned about the potential physical and emotional problems that can result from surgery. The uncertainty about the prognosis and outcome requires compassionate nursing care in the preoperative period.

Preoperative teaching is important in allaying the fears of the patient, caregiver, and family and in preparing them for the postoperative period. Provide general information about the type of surgery and what they can expect afterwards. Explain that some hair may be shaved to allow for better exposure and to prevent contamination. The hair is usually removed in the

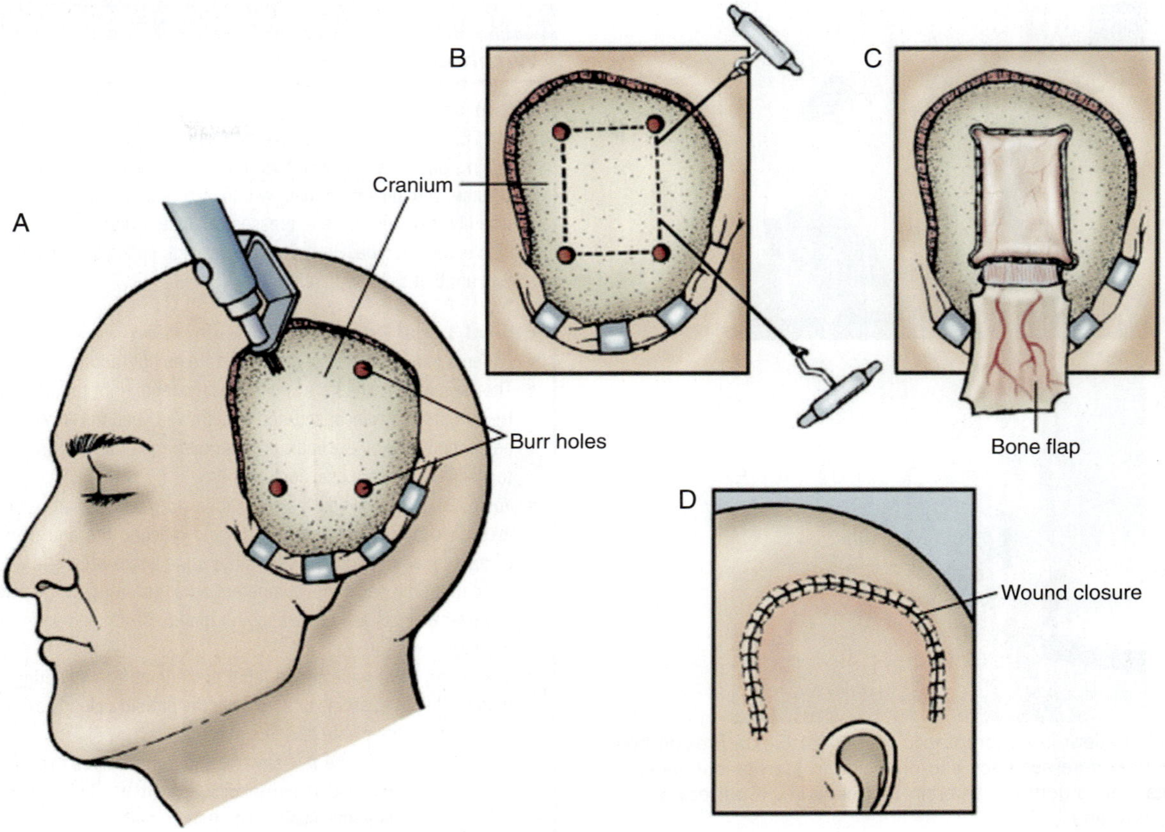

Fig. 61.17 Craniotomy. (A) Burr holes are drill into skull. (B) Skull is cut between burr holes with a surgical saw. (C) Bone flap is turned back to expose cranial contents. (D) Bone flap is replaced and wound closed. (From Monahan F, Sands J, Neighbors M, et al.: *Phipps' medical-surgical nursing: health and illness perspectives,* ed 9, St Louis, 2007, Mosby.)

operating room after induction of anesthesia. Tell them that the patient will be in an ICU or special care unit after surgery.

The main goal of care after cranial surgery is preventing increased ICP. Frequent assessment of the patient's neurologic status is essential during the first 48 hours. Closely monitor fluid and electrolyte levels and serum osmolality to detect changes in sodium regulation, the onset of diabetes insipidus, or severe hypovolemia. Manage problems associated with increased ICP.

Monitor the patient for pain and nausea. Nausea and vomiting are common after surgery. Administer antiemetic drugs as ordered. Do not give promethazine. It can increase somnolence and change the accuracy of a neurologic assessment.

Although the brain itself does not have pain receptors, patients often report headache caused by edema or pain at the incision site. Control pain with short-acting opioids and monitor neurologic status.

The dressing is usually in place for a few days. When the incision over the skull is in the anterior or middle fossa, elevate the head of the bed at least 30 degrees. If the surgical approach is in the posterior fossa or they have a burr hole, keep the patient flat or at a slight elevation (10 to 15 degrees).

Turning and positioning the patient will depend on the site of the operation. If a bone flap was removed (craniectomy), do not position the patient on the operative side. Place a sign at the head of the bed, alerting everyone of the craniectomy site and position of the surgical site. Observe the dressing for color, odor, and amount of drainage. Notify the HCP immediately of any excess bleeding or clear drainage. Check drains for placement. Assess the area around the dressing. Scalp care should include meticulous care of the incision to prevent wound infection. Cleanse the area and treat it following agency protocol or the HCP's orders. Once the dressing is removed, use an antiseptic soap for washing the scalp. The psychologic impact of hair removal can be lessened by using a wig, turban, scarves, or cap. For the patient who is receiving radiation, teach the patient to use a sunblock and head covering if any sun exposure is expected.

◆ Ambulatory Care

The patient's rehabilitative potential depends on the reason for the surgery, postoperative course, and their general state of health. Base your care on a realistic appraisal of these factors. Specific rehabilitation potential cannot be determined until cerebral edema and increased ICP subside postoperatively (Box 61.4). An overall goal is to foster independence for as long as possible and to the highest degree possible.

Take care to maintain as much function as possible through measures such as careful positioning, meticulous skin and mouth care, regular range of motion exercises, bowel and bladder care, and adequate nutrition. Address the needs and problems of each patient individually because many variables affect the plan.

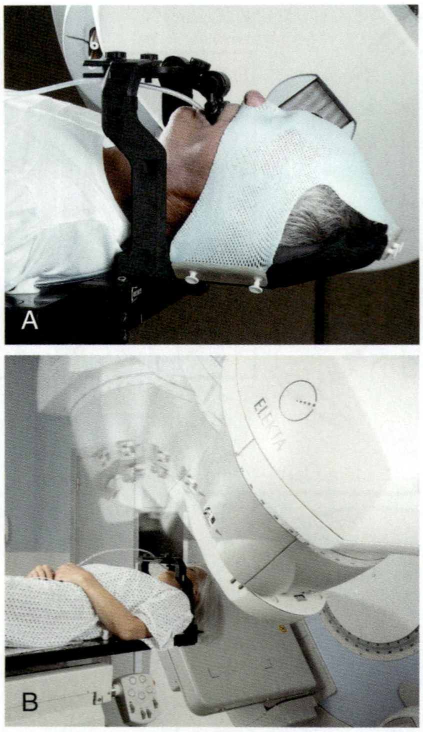

Fig. 61.18 (A) Patient in a stereotactic frame. (B) Elekta Fraxion head frame helps to ensure accuracy and precision in stereotactic radiation therapy of cancer targets in the brain and cranium. (Courtesy Elekta, Stockholm, Sweden.)

Collaborate with other specialists. The physical therapist may provide an exercise plan to regain functional deficits. A speech therapist will help the patient with communication and swallowing skills. The patient's mental and physical deterioration, including seizures, personality disorganization, apathy, and wasting, is difficult for both family and health care professionals. Cognitive and emotional residual deficits are often harder to accept than are motor and sensory losses. Social workers can help the patient and family adapt to changes in their home life, work, and financial circumstances.

BOX 61.4 ETHICAL/LEGAL DILEMMAS

Withholding Treatment

Situation

C.J., a 26-year-old patient in a permanent vegetative state after a craniotomy for brain trauma, is diagnosed with her 15th bladder infection. As the home care nurse, you must determine whether to seek antibiotics for this infection. The family members have expressed a concern that no heroic measures be used to extend her life. However, they are not willing to stop enteral nutrition. Should antibiotics be withheld?

Ethical/Legal Points for Consideration

- Patients in a persistent vegetative state do not recover.
- The main legal issue here is who has the legal right to refuse or consent to treatment for this incapacitated patient. You need to know if a guardian has been appointed by the court or if her parents retain a form of guardianship to make health care decisions for her.
- You need to know when the vegetative state began; that is, did the patient ever have the right to consent having reached the age of majority as a competent adult or did the vegetative state begin while she was a minor? If the patient did become a competent adult before the vegetative state, did she ever express any preference for quality-of-life and end-of-life decision making?
- The courts have widespread legal precedents for accepting the decision of the patient's guardian or parents or the patient's clearly expressed preferences for quality-of-life decision making.
- Life-sustaining treatment is any treatment that serves to prolong life without reversing the underlying medical condition. Common life-sustaining treatments include mechanical ventilation, dialysis, chemotherapy, antibiotics, and artificial nutrition and hydration.
- There is no ethical distinction between withdrawing and withholding life-sustaining treatment. If there is not adequate evidence of the incompetent patient's preferences and values, the decision should be based on the best interests of the patient (i.e., what outcome will promote the patient's well-being).

Discussion Questions

1. How would you approach C.J.'s family?
2. What are your feelings about providing nutrition, hydration, and treatments that will prolong life in a patient for whom there is no hope of recovery?
3. What options are available to the family for the care of their daughter once a decision is made about withholding antibiotics?

INFLAMMATORY CONDITIONS OF THE BRAIN

Brain abscesses, meningitis, and encephalitis are the most common inflammatory conditions of the brain and spinal cord (Table 61.16). Inflammation can be caused by bacteria, viruses, fungi, and chemicals (e.g., contrast media used in diagnostic tests, blood in the subarachnoid space). CNS infections may occur via the bloodstream, by extension from a primary site, or along cranial and spinal nerves.

The mortality rate for inflammatory conditions of the brain is about 10% to 15% in the general population. Rates are higher rates in older and immunosuppressed patients. Some who recover have long-term neurologic deficits, including hearing loss.[17]

BACTERIAL MENINGITIS

Meningitis is an acute inflammation of the meningeal tissues surrounding the brain and spinal cord. Meningitis usually occurs in fall, winter, or early spring. It is often related to a viral respiratory disease. Older adults and persons who are debilitated are affected more often. College students living in dormitories and people living in institutions (e.g., prisoners) have a high risk for meningitis. Untreated bacterial meningitis has a high mortality rate.[17]

Etiology and Pathophysiology

Streptococcus pneumoniae and *Neisseria meningitidis* are the leading causes of bacterial meningitis. *N. meningitides* has at least 13 different subtypes (serogroups), with 5 of them (A, B, C, Y, W) causing most cases. *Haemophilus influenzae* was once the most common cause of bacterial meningitis. *H. influenzae* vaccine has significantly decreased meningitis from this organism.

The organisms usually gain entry to the CNS through the upper respiratory tract or bloodstream. However, they may

TABLE 61.16 Comparison of Cerebral Inflammatory Conditions

	Meningitis	Encephalitis	Brain Abscess
Cause	Bacteria (*Streptococcus pneumoniae, Neisseria meningitidis*, group B streptococci, viruses, fungi)	Bacteria, fungi, parasites, herpes simplex virus (HSV), other viruses (e.g., West Nile virus)	Streptococci, staphylococci through bloodstream
Cerebrospinal Fluid (Reference Interval)			
• Pressure (<20 mm H_2O)	↑ Bacterial: 200–500 Viral: ≤250	Normal to slight ↑	↑
• WBC count (0–5 cells/μL)	Bacterial: >1000/μL (mainly neutrophils) Viral: 25–500/μL (mainly lymphocytes)	500/μL, neutrophils (early), lymphocytes (later)	25–300/μL (neutrophils)
• Protein (15–45 mg/dL [0.15–0.45 g/L])	Bacterial: >500 mg/dL Viral: 50–500 mg/dL	Slight ↑	Normal
• Glucose (50–77 mg/dL [2.2–3.9 mmol/L])	Bacterial: ↓ 5–40 Viral: Normal or low >40	Normal	↓ or absent
• Appearance	Bacterial: Turbid, cloudy Viral: Clear or cloudy	Clear	Clear
Diagnostic Studies	CT scan, Gram stain, smear, culture, PCR	CT scan, EEG, MRI, PET, PCR, IgM antibodies to virus in serum or CSF	CT scan
Treatment	Antibiotics, dexamethasone, supportive care, prevent ↑ ICP	Supportive care, prevent ↑ ICP, acyclovir (Zovirax) for HSV	Antibiotics, incision and drainage Supportive care

enter by direct extension from penetrating skull wounds or through fractured sinuses in basilar skull fractures.

The inflammatory response to the infection tends to increase CSF production with a moderate increase in ICP. In bacterial meningitis the purulent secretions quickly spread to other areas of the brain through the CSF and cover the CNs and other intracranial structures. If this process extends into the brain parenchyma or if concurrent encephalitis is present, cerebral edema and increased ICP become more of a problem. Closely observe all patients for manifestations of increased ICP. ICP can increase from swelling around the dura and increased CSF volume.

Clinical Manifestations

Fever, severe headache, nausea, vomiting, and **nuchal rigidity** (neck stiffness) are key signs of meningitis. Photophobia, a decreased LOC, and signs of increased ICP may be present. Coma is associated with a poor prognosis. It occurs in 5% to 10% of patients with bacterial meningitis. Seizures occur in one third of all cases. The headache becomes progressively worse. It may be accompanied by vomiting and irritability.

If the infecting organism is a meningococcus, a skin rash is common. Petechiae may be seen on the trunk, lower extremities, and mucous membranes. Perform a *tumbler test* by pressing the base of a drinking glass against the rash. The rash does not blanch or fade under pressure.

Complications

The most common acute complication of bacterial meningitis is increased ICP. Most patients have increased ICP. It is the major cause of an altered mental status.

Another complication is residual neurologic dysfunction. It often involves many CNs. CN irritation can have serious sequelae. The optic nerve (CN II) is compressed by increased ICP. Papilledema is often present. Blindness may occur. When CN III, CN IV, and CN VI are irritated, ocular movements are affected. Ptosis, unequal pupils, and diplopia are common. Irritation of CN V results in sensory losses and loss of the corneal reflex. Irritation of CN VII results in facial paresis. Irritation of CN VIII causes tinnitus, vertigo, and deafness. The dysfunction usually disappears within a few weeks. However, hearing loss may be permanent.

Hemiparesis, dysphasia, and hemianopsia may occur. These signs usually resolve over time. If they do not, suspect a cerebral abscess, subdural empyema, subdural effusion, or persistent meningitis. Acute cerebral edema may cause seizures, CN III palsy, bradycardia, hypertensive coma, and death.

Headaches may occur for months after the diagnosis of meningitis until the irritation and inflammation have completely resolved. It is important to implement pain management for chronic headaches.

A noncommunicating hydrocephalus may occur if the exudate causes adhesions that prevent the normal flow of CSF from the ventricles. CSF reabsorption by the arachnoid villi may be obstructed by the exudate. In this situation, surgical implantation of a shunt is the only treatment.

Waterhouse-Friderichsen syndrome is a complication of meningococcal meningitis. The syndrome is manifested by petechiae, disseminated intravascular coagulation (DIC), adrenal hemorrhage, and circulatory collapse. DIC and shock, which are some of the most serious complications of meningitis, are associated with meningococcemia. DIC is discussed in detail in Chapter 34.

Diagnostic Studies

When a patient has manifestations suggestive of bacterial meningitis, a blood culture and CT scan should be done. Diagnosis is usually verified by doing an LP with CSF analysis (Table 61.16). An LP should be done only after the CT scan has ruled out an obstruction in the foramen magnum to prevent a fluid shift resulting in herniation.

TABLE 61.17 Interprofessional Care

Bacterial Meningitis

Diagnostic Assessment
- History and physical assessment
- Analysis of CSF (for protein, WBC, glucose), Gram stain, and culture
- CBC, coagulation profile, electrolyte levels, glucose, platelet count
- Blood culture
- CT scan, MRI, PET scan
- Skull x-ray studies

Management
- Rest
- IV fluid
- Hypothermia

Drug Therapy
- IV antibiotics
  - ampicillin, penicillin
  - cephalosporin (e.g., ceftriaxone)
- codeine for headache
- dexamethasone
- acetaminophen or aspirin for temperature >100.4°F (38°C)
- IV phenytoin
- IV mannitol (Osmitrol) for diuresis

Specimens of the CSF, sputum, and nasopharyngeal secretions are taken for culture before the start of antibiotic therapy to identify the causative organism. A Gram stain is done to detect bacteria. The predominant white blood cell type in the CSF with bacterial meningitis is neutrophils.

X-rays of the skull may show infected sinuses. CT scans and MRI may be normal in uncomplicated meningitis. In other cases, CT scans may show signs of increased ICP or hydrocephalus.

Interprofessional Care

Bacterial meningitis is a medical emergency. Rapid diagnosis based on history and physical assessment is crucial because the patient is usually in a critical state when health care is sought. When meningitis is suspected, antibiotic therapy is begun after the collection of specimens for cultures, even before the diagnosis is confirmed (Table 61.17).

Ampicillin, penicillin, vancomycin, cefuroxime, ceftriaxone, and ceftazidime are the main drugs given to treat bacterial meningitis. Dexamethasone may be given before or with the first dose of antibiotics. Collaborate with the HCP to manage the headache, fever, and nuchal rigidity from meningitis.

NURSING MANAGEMENT: BACTERIAL MENINGITIS

Assessment

Initial assessment should include vital signs, neurologic assessment, fluid intake and output, and evaluation of the lungs and skin.

Clinical Problems

Clinical problems for the patient with bacterial meningitis may include:

- Increased ICP
- Inadequate tissue perfusion
- Altered body temperature
- Pain

Additional information on clinical problems and interventions for the patient with bacterial meningitis is presented in eNursing Care Plan 61.2 (available on the website for this chapter).

Planning

The overall goals for the patient with bacterial meningitis are to (1) return to maximal neurologic functioning, (2) resolve the infection, and (3) control pain and discomfort.

Implementation

Health Promotion

Prevention of respiratory tract infections through vaccination programs for pneumococcal pneumonia and influenza is important. Meningococcal vaccines are available that protect against the serogroups that occur most often in the United States. They will not prevent all cases. Two types of meningococcal vaccines are available in the United States:

- Meningococcal conjugate vaccines (MCV4) (Menactra, Menveo)
- Serogroup B meningococcal vaccines (Bexsero, Trumenba)

Early treatment of respiratory tract and ear infections is important. Persons who have close contact with anyone who has bacterial meningitis should receive prophylactic antibiotics.

Acute Care

The patient with bacterial meningitis is usually acutely ill. The fever is high, and head pain is severe. Irritation of the cerebral cortex may cause seizures. Changes in mental status and LOC depend on the degree of increased ICP. Assess vital signs, neurologic status, intake and output, skin, and lung sounds at regular intervals based on the patient's condition. Administer antibiotics as scheduled to maintain therapeutic blood levels.

Head and neck pain with movement requires attention. Codeine provides some pain relief without undue sedation for most patients. Assist the patient to a position of comfort, often curled up with the head slightly extended. Elevate the head of the bed slightly. A darkened room and a cool cloth over the eyes relieve photophobia.

All patients have some degree of mental distortion and hypersensitivity. They may be frightened and misinterpret the environment. Make every attempt to minimize environmental stimuli and prevent injury. For the patient with delirium, low lighting may decrease hallucinations. A familiar person at the bedside may have a calming effect. Be efficient with care while conveying an attitude of caring and unhurried gentleness. The use of touch and a soothing voice to give simple explanations of activities is helpful. If seizures occur, assess the patient and take protective measures. Give antiseizure drugs, such as phenytoin or levetiracetam (Keppra), as ordered. Manage problems associated with increased ICP.

Fever is vigorously treated because it increases cerebral edema and the risk for seizures. In addition, neurologic damage may result from a high fever over a prolonged time. Acetaminophen or aspirin may be used to reduce fever. If the fever is resistant to aspirin or acetaminophen, more vigorous means are needed (e.g., cooling blanket). Do not to reduce the temperature too rapidly because shivering may result, causing a rebound effect and increasing the temperature and ICP. Wrap the extremities in soft towels or a blanket covered with a sheet to reduce shivering. If a cooling blanket is not available or desirable, tepid sponge baths with water may be effective in lowering the temperature. Protect the skin from excessive drying and injury and prevent breaks in the skin.

Because high fever increases the metabolic rate and insensible fluid loss, assess the patient for dehydration and adequacy of fluid intake. Diaphoresis further increases fluid losses and should be noted on the output record. Calculate replacement fluids as 800 mL/day for respiratory losses and 100 mL for each degree of temperature greater than 100.4°F (38°C). Supplemental feeding (e.g., enteral nutrition) may be needed to maintain adequate nutrition.

Meningococcal meningitis is highly contagious. Maintain respiratory isolation until the cultures are negative. Other causes of meningitis may pose minimal to no infection risk with patient contact. They do not need isolation.

◆ Ambulatory Care

After the acute period has passed, the patient needs several weeks of recovery before resuming normal activities. In this period, stress the importance of adequate nutrition. Encourage a high-protein, high-calorie diet in small, frequent feedings.

Muscle rigidity may persist in the neck and backs of the legs. Progressive range of motion exercises and warm baths are useful. Have the patient gradually increase activity as tolerated, but encourage adequate rest and sleep.

Residual effects can result in sequelae such as dementia, seizures, deafness, hemiplegia, and hydrocephalus. Assess vision, hearing, cognitive skills, and motor and sensory abilities after recovery. Provide the patient with appropriate referrals as needed. Throughout the acute and recovery periods, be aware of the anxiety and stress felt by the caregiver and other family members.

◆ Evaluation

The expected outcomes are that the patient with bacterial meningitis will:

- Have appropriate cognitive function
- Maintain body temperature within normal range
- Report satisfaction with pain control

VIRAL MENINGITIS

The most common causes of viral meningitis are enteroviruses, arboviruses, human immunodeficiency virus, and herpes simplex virus (HSV). Enteroviruses most often spread through direct contact with respiratory secretions. Viral meningitis usually presents as a headache, fever, photophobia, and stiff neck.[17] The fever may be moderate or high.

The Xpert EV test can rapidly diagnose viral meningitis. A sample of CSF is used to determine if enterovirus is present. Results are available within hours of symptom onset.[17]

The CSF can be clear or cloudy, and the typical finding is lymphocytosis. Organisms are not seen on Gram stain or acid-fast smears. Polymerase chain reaction (PCR) used to detect viral-specific deoxyribonucleic acid (DNA) or ribonucleic acid (RNA) is a sensitive method for diagnosing CNS viral infections.

Antibiotics should be given after the LP while awaiting the results of the CSF analysis. Antibiotics are the best defense for bacterial meningitis. We can easily discontinue them if the meningitis is found to be viral.

Viral meningitis is managed symptomatically because the disease is self-limiting. Full recovery is expected. Rare sequelae include persistent headaches, mild mental impairment, and incoordination.

BRAIN ABSCESS

Brain abscess is an accumulation of pus within the brain tissue from a local or systemic infection. Direct extension from an ear, tooth, mastoid, or sinus infection is the main cause. Other causes include spread from a distant site (e.g., pulmonary infection, bacterial endocarditis), skull fracture, and prior brain trauma or surgery. Streptococci and *Staphylococcus aureus* are the most common infective organisms.

Manifestations are similar to those of meningitis and encephalitis. They include headache, fever, and nausea and vomiting. Signs of increased ICP may include drowsiness, confusion, and seizures. Focal symptoms may reflect the local area of the abscess. For example, visual field defects and seizures are common with a temporal lobe abscess. Vision problems and hallucinations may accompany an occipital abscess. CT and MRI are used to diagnose a brain abscess.

Antimicrobial therapy is the main treatment. Other manifestations are treated symptomatically. If drug therapy is not effective, the abscess may have to be drained or removed if it is encapsulated.

Nursing care is similar to those for a patient with meningitis or increased ICP. If the patient had surgical drainage or removal, the nursing care is similar to that of a patient having cranial surgery.

ENCEPHALITIS

Encephalitis is an acute inflammation of the brain. It is a serious and sometimes fatal disease. Several thousand cases occur in the United States each year. It is usually caused by a virus. Many different viruses can cause encephalitis. Some are associated with certain seasons of the year or endemic to certain geographic areas.

Ticks and mosquitoes transmit epidemic encephalitis. Examples include eastern equine, La Crosse, St. Louis, West Nile, and western equine.[17] Nonepidemic encephalitis may occur as a complication of measles, chickenpox, or mumps. HSV encephalitis is the most common cause of acute nonepidemic viral encephalitis. Cytomegalovirus encephalitis occurs in patients with acquired immunodeficiency syndrome (AIDS).

Clinical Manifestations and Diagnostic Studies

Encephalitis can be acute or subacute. The onset is typically nonspecific, with fever, headache, nausea, and vomiting. CNS signs appear on day 2 or 3. They vary from minimal changes in mental status to coma. Virtually any CNS problem can occur, including hemiparesis, tremors, seizures, CN palsies, personality changes, impaired memory, amnesia, and dysphasia.

Early diagnosis and treatment of viral encephalitis are essential for favorable outcomes. Diagnostic findings are shown in Table 61.16. Brain imaging techniques include CT, MRI, and PET. PCR tests allow for early detection of HSV and West Nile encephalitis. West Nile virus should be strongly considered in adults over 50 years old who develop encephalitis or meningitis in summer or early fall. The best diagnostic test for West Nile virus is a blood test that detects viral RNA. This test is also used to screen donated blood, organs, cells, and tissues.

Interprofessional and Nursing Care

Encephalitis prevention focuses on mosquito control. Measures include cleaning rain gutters, removing old tires, draining bird baths, and removing water where mosquitoes can breed. Insect repellent should be used during mosquito season.

The management of encephalitis, including West Nile virus infection, is symptomatic and supportive. In the initial stages of encephalitis, many patients need intensive care. We treat seizure disorders with antiseizure drugs. Prophylactic treatment with antiseizure drugs may be used in severe cases of encephalitis.

Acyclovir (Zovirax) is used to treat encephalitis caused by HSV infection. Its use reduces mortality rates, although neurologic complications may still occur. For maximal benefit, it should start before the onset of coma. Treatment of cytomegalovirus encephalitis in AIDS patients is discussed in Chapter 15.

Case Study

Traumatic Brain Injury

(© Comstock/Thinkstock.)

Patient Profile

C.G. is a 30-year-old Army veteran who comes to the outpatient clinic reporting chronic headaches (rating of 8 [0 to 10 scale]) and trouble sleeping. During his service, he was deployed for 15 months to Afghanistan. His wife has noticed some personality changes since his discharge from military service. She is concerned that he has posttraumatic stress disorder (PTSD).

Subjective Data

- Reports that he has been depressed lately but attributes it to headache and difficulty returning to civilian life
- Headache is worse in the morning or when he lies down
- Uses tobacco and drinks coffee throughout the day
- Has trouble sleeping
- Reports "incidents" of heavy combat and blasts with a loss of consciousness. Cannot remember how many times
- Unable to obtain a more through history as he becomes quite agitated

Objective Data

- During your assessment, you note that C.G. is looking around the room and jumps when the phone rings next door
- Loss of short-term memory (remembers 1 of 3 items)
- Heart rate ranges from 100 to 130 beats/min
- ECG strip is shown below:

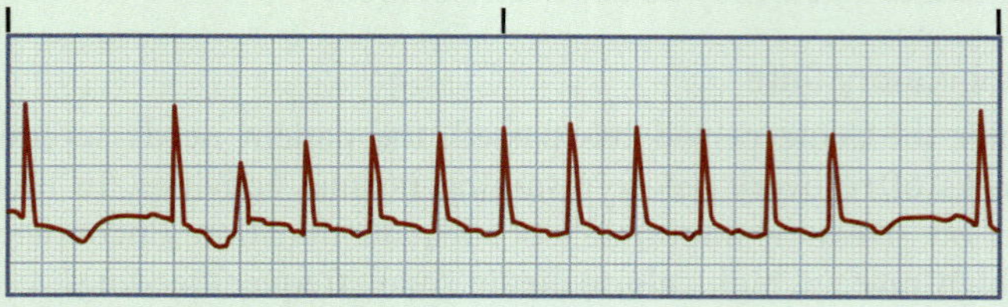

- Systolic BP ranges from 120 to 160 mm Hg
- Right pupil, 3 mm sluggishly reactive; left pupil, 3 mm briskly reactive

Diagnostic Studies

- CT of the head: negative for skull fracture, hematoma, or bleeding. Cerebral edema present, with cingulate herniation on the right side
- MRI of the head: Mild diffuse axonal injury

Discussion Questions

1. ***Recognize:*** What could be the cause of C.G.'s hypertension, tachycardia, and ECG rhythm?
2. ***Analyze:*** In addition to PTSD, what do his manifestations suggest?
3. ***Prioritize:*** Based on the assessment data presented, what are the priority clinical problems?
4. ***Prioritize:*** What priority interventions should be implemented?
5. ***Plan:*** How can the interprofessional team work together to meet his needs?
6. ***Safety:*** Are there any safety concerns for this patient or his wife?
7. ***Act:*** What interventions and support can help his wife?

Answers available at http://evolve.elsevier.com/Lewis/medsurg.

BRIDGE TO NCLEX EXAMINATION

The number of the question corresponds to the same-numbered outcome at the beginning of the chapter.

1. Vasogenic cerebral edema increases intracranial pressure by
   a. shifting fluid in the gray matter.
   b. disrupting the blood-brain barrier.
   c. leaking molecules from the intracellular fluid to the capillaries.
   d. altering the osmotic gradient flow into the intravascular component.

2. A patient with intracranial pressure monitoring has a pressure of 12 mm Hg. The nurse understands that this pressure reflects
   a. a severe decrease in cerebral perfusion pressure.
   b. an alteration in the production of cerebrospinal fluid.
   c. the loss of autoregulatory control of intracranial pressure.
   d. a normal balance among brain tissue, blood, and cerebrospinal fluid.

3. A nurse plans care for the patient with increased intracranial pressure with the knowledge that the *best* way to position the patient is to
   a. keep the head of the bed flat.
   b. elevate the head of the bed to 30 degrees.
   c. maintain patient on the left side with the head supported on a pillow.
   d. use a continuous-rotation bed to continuously change patient position.
4. The nurse is alert to a possible acute subdural hematoma in the patient who
   a. has a linear skull fracture crossing a major artery.
   b. has focal symptoms of brain damage with no recollection of a head injury.
   c. develops decreased level of consciousness and a headache within 48 hours of a head injury.
   d. has an immediate loss of consciousness with a brief lucid interval followed by decreasing level of consciousness.
5. During admission of a patient with a severe head injury to the emergency department, the nurse places the *highest* priority on assessment of
   a. airway patency.
   b. presence of a neck injury.
   c. neurologic status with the Glasgow Coma Scale.
   d. cerebrospinal fluid leakage from the ears or nose.
6. A patient suspected of having a brain tumor has memory deficits, visual changes, weakness of right upper and lower extremities, and personality changes. The nurse determines that the tumor is likely located in the
   a. frontal lobe.
   b. parietal lobe.
   c. occipital lobe.
   d. temporal lobe.
7. Management of a patient with a brain tumor includes *(select all that apply)*
   a. discussing with the patient methods to control inappropriate behavior.
   b. using diversion techniques to keep the patient stimulated and motivated.
   c. assisting and supporting the family in understanding any changes in behavior.
   d. limiting self-care activities until the patient has regained maximum physical functioning.
   e. planning for seizure precautions and teaching the patient and the caregiver about antiseizure drugs.
8. The nurse on the clinical unit is assigned to 4 patients. Which patient should she assess *first*?
   a. Patient with a skull fracture whose nose is bleeding
   b. A patient with an acute stroke who is confused and whose daughter is present
   c. Patient with meningitis who is suddenly agitated and reporting a headache of 10 on a 0 to 10 scale
   d. Patient 2 days postoperative after a craniotomy for a brain tumor who has had continued vomiting
9. A nursing measure that can reduce the potential for seizures and increased intracranial pressure in the patient with bacterial meningitis is
   a. administering codeine for relief of head and neck pain.
   b. controlling fever with prescribed drugs and cooling techniques.
   c. maintaining strict bed rest with the head of the bed slightly elevated.
   d. keeping the room dark and quiet to minimize environmental stimulation.

1. b; 2. d; 3. b; 4. c; 5. a; 6. a; 7. c, e; 8. c; 9. b.

For rationales to these answers and even more NCLEX review questions, visit http://evolve.elsevier.com/Lewis/medsurg.

EVOLVE WEBSITE/RESOURCES LIST

http://evolve.elsevier.com/Lewis/medsurg
Review Questions (Online Only)
Key Points
Answer Keys for Questions
- Rationales for Bridge to NCLEX Examination Questions
- Answer Guidelines for Case Study

Student Case Studies
- Patient With Head Injury
- Patient With Meningitis

Nursing Care Plans
- eNursing Care Plan 61.1: Patient With Increased Intracranial Pressure
- eNursing Care Plan 61.2: Patient With Meningitis

Conceptual Care Map Creator
Audio Glossary
Content Updates

REFERENCES

1. Cushing H: *Studies in intracranial physiology and surgery*, London, 1925, Oxford University Press. (Classic).
2. M. Plus. Intracranial pressure monitoring. Retrieved from https://medlineplus.gov/ency/article/003411.htm.
3. Seidman R: Cerebrovascular disease. Retrieved from https://medicine.stonybrookmedicine.edu/pathology/neuropathology/chapter2. (Classic).
*4. Shizodimos T, Soulountsi V, Iasonidou C, et al.: An overview of management of intracranial hypertension in the intensive care unit, *J Anesth* 34:741, 2020.
5. Brain Trauma Foundation: Guidelines for the management of severe traumatic brain injury. Retrieved from https://braintrauma.org/uploads/03/12/Guidelines_for_Management_of_Severe_TBI_4th_Edition.pdf. (Classic).
6. Foo C, Loan J, Brennan P: The relationship of the FOUR Score to patient outcome: a systematic review, *J Neurotrauma* 36, 2019.
*7. Harris L, Hateley S, Tsang K, et al.: Impact of anti-epileptic drug choice on discharge in acute traumatic brain injury patients, *J Neurol* 267:1774, 2020.
8. Taylor CA, Bell JM, Breiding MJ, et al.: Traumatic brain injury–related emergency department visits, hospitalizations, and deaths—United States, 2007 and 2013, *MMWR* 66:1, 2017. (Classic).

9. Sobrino J, Shafi S: Timing and causes of death after injuries, *Proc - Bayl Univ Med Cent* 26(2), 2013. (Classic).

*10. Eastridge B, Holcom J, Shakelford S: Outcomes of traumatic hemorrhagic shock and the epidemiology of preventable death from injury, *Transfusion* 59:1423, 2019.

*11. Othman S, et al.: Effect of integrative nursing practices on cognitive recovery among severe traumatic brain injury patients, *JNEP* 10, 2020.

12. Mesfin F, et al: Diffuse axonal injury. Retrieved from https://www.ncbi.nlm.nih.gov/books/NBK448102/.

*13. Svedung Wettervik T, Lenell S, Enblad P, et al.: Pre-injury antithrombotic agents predict intracranial hemorrhagic progression, but not worse clinical outcome in severe traumatic brain injury, *Acta Neurochir* 163:1403, 2021.

14. Harvard Health: Subdural hematoma Retrieved from https://www.health.harvard.edu/a_to_z/subdural-hematoma-a-to-z.

*15. Hart T, Ketchum JM, O'Neil-Pirozzi TM, et al.: Neurocognitive status and return to work after moderate to severe traumatic brain injury, *Rehabil Psychol* 64:435, 2019.

16. National Cancer Institute: Cancer of the brain. Retrieved from https://seer.cancer.gov/statfacts/html/brain.html.

17. National Institute of Neurological Disorders and Stroke: Meningitis and encephalitis fact sheet. Retrieved from https://www.ninds.nih.gov/Disorders/Patient-Caregiver-Education/Fact-Sheets/Meningitis-and-Encephalitis-Fact-Sheet.

*Evidence-based information for clinical practice.

62

Stroke

Michelle Bussard

http://evolve.elsevier.com/Lewis/medsurg/

CONCEPTUAL FOCUS

Family Dynamics
Functional Ability
Intracranial Regulation
Mobility
Safety
Sensory Perception

LEARNING OUTCOMES

1. Describe the incidence of and risk factors for stroke.
2. Explain mechanisms that affect cerebral blood flow.
3. Compare and contrast the etiology and pathophysiology of ischemic and hemorrhagic strokes.
4. Correlate the clinical manifestations of stroke with the underlying pathophysiology.
5. Identify diagnostic studies done for patients with strokes.
6. Distinguish the interprofessional care for patients with ischemic strokes and hemorrhagic strokes.
7. Describe the acute nursing management of a patient with a stroke.
8. Describe the rehabilitative nursing management of a patient with a stroke.
9. Explain the psychosocial impact of a stroke on the patient, caregiver, and family.

KEY TERMS

aneurysm
aphasia
cerebrovascular accident (CVA)
dysarthria
dysphasia
embolic stroke
hemorrhagic strokes
intracerebral hemorrhage
ischemic stroke
stroke
subarachnoid hemorrhage (SAH)
thrombotic stroke
transient ischemic attack (TIA)

Stroke occurs when there is (1) *ischemia* (inadequate blood flow) to a part of the brain or (2) *hemorrhage* (bleeding) into the brain that results in the death of brain cells. In a stroke, functions such as movement, sensation, thinking, talking, or emotions that were controlled by the affected area of the brain are lost or impaired. The severity of the loss of function varies based on the location and extent of the brain damage.

The terms *brain attack* and **cerebrovascular accident (CVA)** are also used to describe stroke. The term *brain attack* communicates the urgency of recognizing the warning signs of a stroke and treating it as a medical emergency, as we do with a heart attack (Table 62.1). After the onset of a stroke, immediate medical attention is crucial to decrease disability and the risk of death.

Stroke is a major public health concern. About 800,000 people have a stroke each year.[1] An estimated 7 million adults in the United States have had a stroke.[1] With an aging population, we can expect these numbers to increase. However, stroke can occur at any age. 34% of strokes occur in people younger than 65 years old.[2]

Stroke is currently the fifth most common cause of death in the United States.[1] More than 150,000 deaths occur each year from stroke.[3] While deaths due to stroke have declined, stroke is the leading cause of serious long-term disability. 15% to 30% have a permanent disability.[4]

Common long-term disabilities include *hemiparesis* (partial paralysis on 1 side), inability to walk, complete or partial dependence for activities of daily living (ADLs), *aphasia* (dysfunction in communication), and depression. In addition to the physical, cognitive, and emotional impact of the stroke on the survivor, the stroke affects the lives of the stroke patient's caregiver and family. A stroke is a lifelong change for both the stroke survivor

TABLE 62.1 PATIENT & CAREGIVER TEACHING

FAST Warning Signs of Stroke

FAST is an easy way to remember the signs of stroke. Include the following information in the teaching plan for a patient at risk for stroke and the patient's caregiver:

F	Face drooping	Does one side of the face droop, or is it numb? Ask the person to smile. Is the smile uneven?
A	Arm weakness	Is one arm weak or numb? Ask the person to raise both arms. Does one arm drift downward?
S	Speech difficulties	Is speech slurred? Is the person unable to speak or hard to understand? Ask the person to repeat a simple sentence like "The sky is blue." Is the sentence repeated correctly?
T	Time	Time is CRITICAL! If someone shows any of these signs (even if they go away), call 911 and get the person to the hospital. Note the time when the signs first appeared.

In addition, report the sudden onset of the following:

- Confusion
- Numbness or weakness, especially in 1 side of the body
- Severe headache with no known cause
- Trouble seeing in one or both eyes
- Trouble walking, dizziness, loss of balance or coordination

Source: ASA: FAST. Retrieved from www.strokeassociation.org/STROKEORG/WarningSigns/Stroke-Warning-Signs-and-Symptoms_UCM_308528_SubHomePage.jsp.

and family. Be mindful of this impact when caring for patients who survive stroke.

PATHOPHYSIOLOGY OF STROKE

Anatomy of Cerebral Circulation

Blood is supplied to the brain by 2 major pairs of arteries: internal carotid arteries (anterior circulation) and vertebral arteries (posterior circulation). The carotid arteries branch to supply most of the (1) frontal, parietal, and temporal lobes; (2) basal ganglia; and (3) part of the diencephalon (thalamus and hypothalamus). The major branches of the carotid arteries are the middle cerebral and anterior cerebral arteries. The vertebral arteries join to form the basilar artery, which branches to supply the middle and lower parts of the temporal lobes, occipital lobes, cerebellum, brainstem, and part of the diencephalon. The main branch of the basilar artery is the posterior cerebral artery. The anterior and posterior communicating arteries connect the anterior and posterior cerebral circulation at the *circle of Willis* by (Fig. 62.1). Fig. 60.10 shows the arteries at the base of the brain. Genetic variations in this area are common. All connecting vessels may not be present.

Regulation of Cerebral Blood Flow

The brain needs a continuous supply of blood to provide the O_2 and glucose that neurons need to function. Blood flow must be maintained at 750 to 1000 mL/min (55 mL/100 g of brain tissue), or 20% of the cardiac output, for optimal brain function. If blood flow to the brain is totally interrupted (e.g., cardiac arrest), neurologic metabolism is altered in 30 seconds, metabolism stops in 2 minutes, and cell death occurs in 5 minutes.

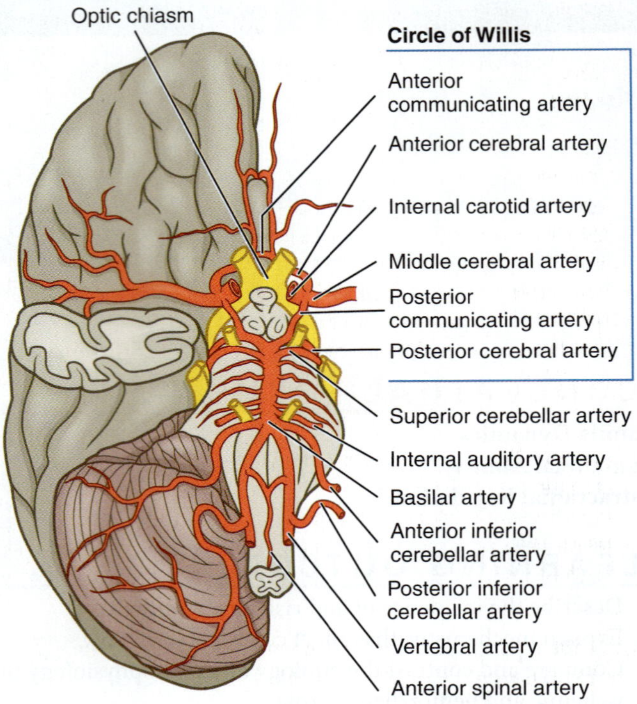

Fig. 62.1 Cerebral arteries and the circle of Willis. The top of the temporal lobe has been removed to show the course of the middle cerebral artery.

The brain is normally protected from changes in mean systemic arterial BP over a range from 50 to 150 mm Hg by a mechanism known as *cerebral autoregulation.* This involves changes in the diameter of cerebral blood vessels in response to changes in pressure so that the blood flow to the brain stays constant. When cerebral ischemia occurs, autoregulation may be impaired, making the brain dependent on systemic BP. CO_2 is a potent cerebral vasodilator. Changes in arterial CO_2 levels have a huge effect on cerebral blood flow (CBF). Increased CO_2 levels increase CBF. Decreased CO_2 levels decrease CBF. Very low arterial oxygen (O_2) levels (partial pressure of arterial O_2 less than 50 mm Hg) or increases in hydrogen ion concentration also increase CBF.

Factors that affect blood flow to the brain include systemic BP, cardiac output, and blood viscosity. During normal activity, O_2 requirements vary. Changes in cardiac output, vasomotor tone, and distribution of blood flow normally maintain adequate blood flow to the brain. Cardiac output must be reduced by one-third before CBF is reduced. Changes in blood viscosity affect CBF, with decreased viscosity increasing blood flow.

Collateral circulation may develop over time to compensate for a decrease in CBF. An area of the brain can potentially receive blood supply from another blood vessel even if blood supply from the original vessel has been cut off (e.g., because of thrombosis). In other words, the vessels in the brain make an "alternative route" for blood flow to reach damaged areas, thus preventing a stroke.

Intracranial pressure (ICP) influences CBF. Increased ICP causes brain compression and reduced CBF. A major goal when

BOX 62.1 PROMOTING HEALTH EQUITY

Stroke

Blacks

- Have the highest incidence of strokes
- Have a rate of first strokes that is twice that of any other ethnic group
- Are 3 times more likely than Whites to have an ischemic stroke and 4 times more likely to have a hemorrhagic stroke
- Have increased rates of hypertension, diabetes, and sickle cell anemia, which may be related to the high incidence of strokes
- Have high rates of smoking and obesity, 2 risk factors for stroke
- Are twice as likely to die from a stroke as Whites

Other Ethnicities

- Hispanics, Native Americans, and Asian Americans have a higher incidence of strokes than Whites
- Hispanics have a high incidence of diabetes, an important risk factor
- Native Americans are more likely than Whites to have at least 2 risk factors for stroke

caring for a patient after a stroke is to reduce secondary injury from increased ICP (see Chapter 61).

RISK FACTORS FOR STROKE

The most effective way to decrease the burden of stroke is prevention and teaching, especially about risk factors. We divide risk factors into nonmodifiable and modifiable. Stroke risk increases with multiple risk factors. Thus, primary prevention focuses on reducing modifiable risk factors. This can dramatically reduce the chance of stroke.[5]

Nonmodifiable Risk Factors

Nonmodifiable risk factors include age, gender, ethnicity or race, and family history or heredity. Stroke risk increases with age, doubling each decade after 55 years of age. Two-thirds of all strokes occur in persons older than 65 years. Strokes are more common in men, but more women die from stroke than men. Because women tend to live longer than men, they have more opportunity to have a stroke.[2]

Blacks have twice the incidence of stroke and a higher death rate from stroke compared to any other ethnic group (Box 62.1). This may be related in part to higher rates of hypertension, obesity, and diabetes.[2]

Genetic risk factors are important in the development of vascular disease, including stroke. A person with a family history of stroke has an increased risk of having a stroke. We think that genes encoding products involved in lipid metabolism, thrombosis, and inflammation are genetic factors for stroke. People who have at least 2 first-degree relatives with a history of subarachnoid hemorrhage (SAH) or aneurysm should be screened to rule out anomalies in their cerebral vasculature.[5]

Modifiable Risk Factors

Modifiable risk factors are those that can potentially be altered through lifestyle changes and medical treatment, thus reducing the risk for stroke. They include hypertension, heart disease, diabetes, smoking, obesity, sleep apnea, metabolic syndrome, lack of physical exercise, poor diet, and drug and alcohol use. We think modifiable risk factors cause 90% of strokes.[6]

Hypertension is the single most important modifiable risk factor. It is often undetected and inadequately treated. Increases in systolic BP (SBP) and diastolic BP (DBP) independently increase stroke risk. Treating hypertension reduces stroke risk up to 50%. New recommendations by the American Heart Association (AHA) include home BP monitoring with a goal of SBP less than 140 mm Hg.[4]

Heart disease, including atrial fibrillation, myocardial infarction (MI), cardiomyopathy, cardiac valve abnormalities, and congenital heart defects, is a risk factor for stroke. Atrial fibrillation causes about 25% of strokes.[6] People with atrial fibrillation are 5 times more likely to have a stroke than people with a regular heart rhythm. The incidence of atrial fibrillation increases with age. Oral anticoagulants (e.g., warfarin, dabigatran) and adherence to their therapy play a key role in stroke prevention.

Diabetes is a significant risk factor for stroke. Stroke risk in people with diabetes is 5 times higher than in those without diabetes.[6]

Smoking nearly doubles the risk for ischemic stroke. Smokers are 4 times as likely to have a hemorrhagic stroke than nonsmokers.[5] The risk from smoking decreases substantially over time after the smoker quits. After 5 to 10 years of no tobacco use, former smokers have the same risk for stroke as nonsmokers.

The effect of alcohol on stroke risk depends on the amount consumed. Women who drink more than 1 alcoholic drink per day and men who drink more than 2 alcoholic drinks per day are at higher risk for hypertension, which increases their chance of stroke. Illicit drug use, especially cocaine use, increases stroke risk.[6]

A waist circumference to hip circumference ratio equal to or above the mid-value for the population increases the risk for ischemic stroke 3-fold. Obesity is associated with hypertension, high blood glucose, and increased blood lipid levels, all of which increase stroke risk.[6] Physical inactivity increases stroke risk. Benefits of physical activity can occur with even light to moderate regular activity. The AHA recommends 150 minutes of moderate-intensity exercise or 75 minutes of vigorous-intensity exercise per week to reduce stroke risk.[4] Nutrition teaching is important. A diet high in fat and low in fruits and vegetables may increase stroke risk.

The early forms of birth control pills that had high levels of progestin and estrogen increased a woman's chance of having a stroke, especially if the woman smoked. Newer, low-dose oral contraceptives have lower risks for stroke except in those who have hypertension and smoke. The AHA recommends smoking cessation and alternatives to estrogen oral contraceptives for those women to reduce their risk of stroke.[4]

Women who have migraines with aura have an increased risk for stroke. Other conditions that may increase stroke risk include inflammatory conditions (e.g., rheumatoid arthritis), sickle cell disease, and blood clotting disorders, such as factor V Leiden mutation.[5]

Transient Ischemic Attack

Another risk factor associated with stroke is a history of a **transient ischemic attack (TIA)**. A TIA is a transient episode of neurologic dysfunction caused by focal brain, spinal cord, or retinal ischemia, but without acute infarction of the brain. Symptoms typically last less than 1 hour.

Teach the patient to seek treatment for any stroke symptoms since there is no way to predict if a TIA will resolve or if it will progress to a stroke. In general, one-third of those who had a TIA do not have another, one-third have more TIAs, and one-third progress to stroke.[7] TIAs may be due to microemboli that temporarily block the blood flow. TIAs are a warning sign of progressive cerebrovascular disease. The signs and symptoms of a TIA depend on the blood vessel that is involved and the area of the brain that is ischemic. If the carotid system is involved, patients may have a temporary loss of vision in 1 eye *(amaurosis fugax)*, transient hemiparesis, numbness or loss of sensation, or a sudden inability to speak. Signs of a TIA involving the vertebrobasilar system may include tinnitus, vertigo, darkened or blurred vision, diplopia, ptosis, dysarthria, dysphagia, ataxia, and unilateral or bilateral numbness or weakness.

CHECK YOUR PRACTICE

You are talking with your uncle at your family reunion. He knows that you are a nurse and seems very eager to talk with you. He tells you that earlier this morning, he was having problems talking, got dizzy, and then "blanked" out for a while. He found himself just lying on the floor in his room. He says, "I think it is just all the excitement of the reunion."

- How would you respond?

A TIA is considered a medical emergency since it can lead to an ischemic stroke. Teach people at risk for TIAs to seek medical attention at once with any stroke-like symptoms and to identify the time of onset of symptoms. The ABCD² score is a tool used to predict stroke risk after a TIA (Table 62.2).[8]

TABLE 62.2 ABCD² Score

The ABCD² score is a risk assessment tool. It is designed to predict the risk for stroke 2 days after a transient ischemic attack (TIA). Calculate the score by adding up points for 5 factors.

Risk Factor	Points
Age ≥60 year	1
Systolic BP ≥140 mm Hg *OR* diastolic BP ≥90 mm Hg	1
Clinical features of TIA (choose 1)	
Unilateral weakness with or without impaired speech *OR*	2
Impaired speech without unilateral weakness	1
Duration	
TIA duration ≥60 min *OR*	2
TIA duration 10–59 min	1
Diabetes	1
Total ABCD² Score	0–7

ABCD² Score	2-Day Stroke Risk (%)	Care Needed
0–3	1.0	Hospitalization not needed unless there is another indication (e.g., new atrial fibrillation)
4–5	4.1	Hospitalization in most situations
6–7	8.1	Hospitalization

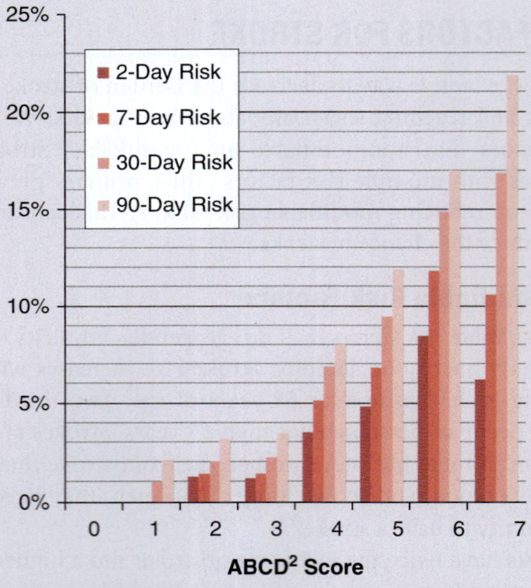

Permission obtained from National Stroke Association. Retrieved from https://www.stroke.org.

TYPES OF STROKE

Unlike a TIA, in which ischemia occurs without infarction, a stroke results in infarction (cell death). We classify strokes as ischemic or hemorrhagic based on the cause and underlying pathophysiologic findings (Fig. 62.2 and Table 62.3).

Ischemic Stroke

An **ischemic stroke** results from inadequate blood flow to the brain from partial or complete occlusion of an artery.[9] We classify ischemic strokes as thrombotic or embolic strokes.

Thrombotic Stroke

A **thrombotic stroke** occurs from injury to a blood vessel wall and formation of a blood clot (Fig. 62.2A). The lumen of the blood vessel becomes narrowed, and, if it becomes occluded, infarction occurs. Thrombosis develops readily where atherosclerotic plaques have already narrowed blood vessels. Thrombotic stroke is the most common cause of stroke. It accounts for about 60% of strokes.[2] They are more common in older adults, especially those with high cholesterol, atherosclerosis, or diabetes. Most thrombotic strokes are associated with hypertension or diabetes, both of which accelerate atherosclerosis. Many times, a TIA precedes thrombotic strokes.

The extent of the stroke depends on rapidity of onset, size of the damaged area, and presence of collateral circulation. Most patients with ischemic stroke do not have a decreased level of consciousness (LOC) in the first 24 hours, unless it is due to a brainstem stroke or other condition, such as seizure, increased ICP, or hemorrhage. Manifestations of ischemic stroke may progress in the first 72 hours as infarction and cerebral edema increase.

Embolic Stroke

Embolic stroke occurs when an embolus lodges in and occludes a cerebral artery, resulting in infarction and edema of the area

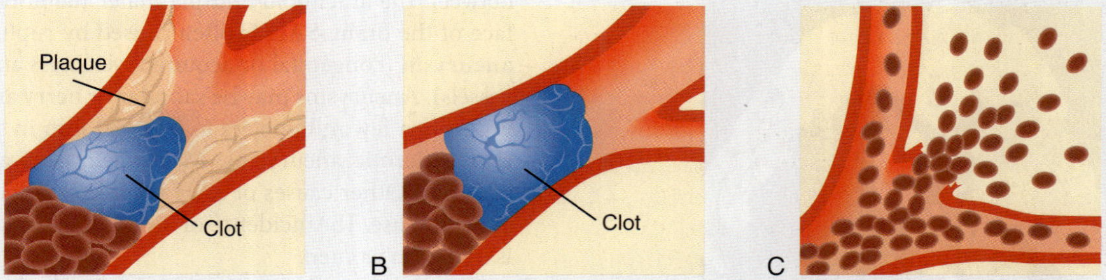

A **Thrombotic stroke.** The process of clot formation (thrombosis) results in a narrowing of the lumen, which blocks the passage of the blood through the artery.

B **Embolic stroke.** An embolus is a blood clot or other debris circulating in the blood. When it reaches an artery in the brain that is too narrow to pass through, it lodges there and blocks the flow of blood.

C **Hemorrhagic stroke.** A burst blood vessel may allow blood to seep into and damage brain tissues until clotting shuts off the leak.

Fig. 62.2 Major types of stroke.

TABLE 62.3 **Types of Stroke**

Gender and Age	Warning and Onset	Prognosis
Ischemic		
Incidence: 87% of strokes		
Embolic		
Men more than women	*Warning:* TIA (uncommon) *Onset:* Sudden onset, most likely to occur during activity	Single event, signs, and symptoms develop quickly, usually some improvement, recurrence common without aggressive treatment of underlying disease.
Thrombotic		
Men more than women Oldest median age	*Warning:* TIA (30%–50% of cases) *Onset:* Often during or after sleep	Stepwise progression, signs, and symptoms develop slowly, usually some improvement, recurrence in 20%–25% of survivors.
Hemorrhagic		
Incidence: 13% of strokes		
Intracerebral		
Slightly higher in women	*Warning:* Headache (25% of cases) *Onset:* Activity (often)	Progression over 24 h. Poor prognosis, fatality more likely with presence of coma.
Subarachnoid		
Slightly higher in women Youngest median age	*Warning:* Headache (common) *Onset:* Activity (often), sudden onset, most often related to head trauma	Usually single sudden event, fatality more likely with presence of coma.

TIA, Transient ischemic attack.

supplied by the involved vessel (Fig. 62.2B). Embolism is the second most common cause of stroke.[2] Most emboli originate in the endocardial (inside) layer of the heart when a plaque breaks off from the endocardium and enters the circulation. The embolus travels upward to the cerebral circulation and lodges where a vessel narrows or bifurcates (splits). Heart conditions, including atrial fibrillation, MI, infective endocarditis, valvular heart prostheses, patent foramen ovale, and atrial septal defects, cause most embolic ischemic strokes.[2] Less common causes of emboli include air and fat from long bone (e.g., femur) fractures. Embolic strokes can affect any age group. Rheumatic heart disease is a cause of embolic stroke in young to middle-aged adults. An embolus from an atherosclerotic plaque is more common in older adults.

The patient with an embolic stroke often has severe manifestations that occur suddenly. Warning signs are less common than with thrombotic stroke. The embolic stroke often occurs rapidly, giving little time to accommodate an obstructed blood vessel by developing collateral circulation. The patient is usually conscious. They may have a headache. The effects of the emboli are initially characterized by severe neurologic deficits, which can be temporary if the clot breaks up and allows blood to flow. Smaller emboli then continue to obstruct smaller vessels, which in turn involve smaller portions of the brain with fewer deficits noted.

The prognosis is related to the amount of brain tissue deprived of its blood supply. Recurrence of embolic stroke is common unless the underlying cause is aggressively treated.

Hemorrhagic Stroke

Hemorrhagic strokes result from bleeding into the brain tissue itself (intracerebral or intraparenchymal hemorrhage) or into the subarachnoid space or ventricles (SAH or intraventricular hemorrhage).

Intracerebral Hemorrhage

Intracerebral hemorrhage is bleeding within the brain caused by a rupture of a vessel (usually in the basal ganglia) (Fig. 62.2C). The prognosis of patients with intracerebral hemorrhage is poor. The 30-day mortality rate is 40% to 80%. Half of the deaths occur within the first 48 hours.[2]

Hypertension is the most common cause of intracerebral hemorrhage (Fig. 62.3). Other causes include vascular

Fig. 62.3 Massive hypertensive hemorrhage rupturing into a lateral ventricle of the brain. (From Kumar V, Abbas AK, Aster JC, et al.: *Robbins and Cotran pathologic basis of disease,* ed 8, Philadelphia, 2010, Saunders.)

malformations, coagulation disorders, anticoagulant and thrombolytic drugs, trauma, brain tumors, and ruptured aneurysms. Hemorrhage often occurs during periods of activity. Most often, there is a sudden onset of symptoms, with progression over minutes to hours because of ongoing bleeding.

Manifestations include neurologic deficits, headache, nausea, vomiting, decreased LOC, and hypertension. The extent of the symptoms varies depending on the amount, location, and duration of the bleeding. A blood clot within the closed skull can result in a mass that causes pressure on brain tissue, displaces brain tissue, and decreases CBF, leading to ischemia and infarction.

Most intracerebral hemorrhages occur in the cerebral lobes, cerebellum, pons, thalamus, subcortical white matter, internal capsule, or a part of the basal ganglia called the putamen. At first, patients have a severe headache with nausea and vomiting. Manifestations of putaminal and internal capsule bleeding include weakness of 1 side (including the face, arm, and leg), slurred speech, and deviation of the eyes. Progression of symptoms related to a severe hemorrhage includes hemiplegia, fixed and dilated pupils, abnormal body posturing, and coma. Thalamic hemorrhage results in hemiplegia with more sensory than motor loss. Bleeding into the subthalamic areas of the brain leads to problems with vision and eye movement. Cerebellar hemorrhages are characterized by severe headache, vomiting, loss of ability to walk, dysphagia, dysarthria, and eye movement changes.

Hemorrhage in the pons is the most serious because basic life functions (e.g., respiration) are rapidly affected. Hemorrhage in the pons can be characterized by hemiplegia leading to complete paralysis, coma, abnormal body posturing, fixed pupils, hyperthermia, and death.

Subarachnoid Hemorrhage

Subarachnoid hemorrhage (SAH) occurs when there is intracranial bleeding into the cerebrospinal fluid (CSF)–filled space between the arachnoid and pia mater membranes on the surface of the brain. SAH is often caused by rupture of a cerebral **aneurysm** (congenital or acquired weakness and ballooning of vessels). Aneurysms may be saccular or berry aneurysms, ranging from a few millimeters to 20 to 30 mm in size, or fusiform atherosclerotic aneurysms. Most aneurysms are in the circle of Willis. Other causes of SAH include trauma and illicit drug (cocaine) use. The incidence of SAH increases with age. The rate is higher in women.

The patient may have warning signs and symptoms if the ballooning artery applies pressure to brain tissue. Minor warning symptoms may result from leaking of an aneurysm before major rupture. In general, cerebral aneurysms are viewed as a "silent killer" since people do not have warning signs or symptoms of an aneurysm until rupture has occurred.

> **CHECK YOUR PRACTICE**
>
> You are watching your husband's "for fun" soccer game. He leaves the game and is kneeling on the ground. When you try to assess what is going on, he says, "I've got a terrible headache. It just started." Knowing that he sometimes gets headaches when he is stressed, you ask him if he is feeling stressed. He almost screams back at you, "NO! This is the worst headache of my life!"
>
> - What are 3 priority interventions?

Loss of consciousness may or may not occur. The patient's LOC may range from alert to comatose, depending on the severity of the bleed. Other manifestations include focal neurologic deficits (including cranial nerve deficits), nausea, vomiting, seizures, and stiff neck.

Complications of aneurysmal SAH include rebleeding before surgery or other therapy is started and cerebral vasospasm (narrowing of the blood vessels), which can result in cerebral infarction. Cerebral vasospasm is likely due to an interaction between the metabolites of blood and the vascular smooth muscle. This occurs when the subarachnoid blood clots break down or dissolve, releasing metabolites that can cause endothelial damage and vasoconstriction. The release of endothelin (a potent vasoconstrictor) may play a key role in inducing cerebral vasospasm after SAH. Patients with SAH who are at risk for vasospasm are often in the intensive care unit (ICU) (up to 14 days) until the threat of vasospasm is reduced. Peak time for vasospasm is 6 to 10 days after the initial bleed.

Despite improvements in surgical techniques and management, many patients with SAH die. Some die almost immediately when a rupture occurs. Others die from subsequent bleeding. Survivors can have significant deficits, including cognitive problems.

CLINICAL MANIFESTATIONS

Neurologic manifestations do not significantly differ between ischemic and hemorrhagic stroke. The reason for this is that neural tissue destruction is the basis for neurologic dysfunction caused by both types of stroke. The manifestations are related to the location of the stroke. Specific manifestations related to

TABLE 62.4 Stroke Manifestations Related to the Artery Involved

Artery	Manifestations
Anterior cerebral	Motor and/or sensory deficit (contralateral), sucking or rooting reflex, rigidity, gait problems, loss of proprioception and fine touch
Middle cerebral	*Dominant side:* Aphasia, motor and sensory deficit, hemianopsia
	Nondominant side: Neglect, motor and sensory deficit, hemianopsia
Posterior cerebral	Hemianopsia, visual hallucination, spontaneous pain, motor deficit
Vertebral	Cranial nerve deficits, diplopia, dizziness, nausea, vomiting, dysarthria, dysphagia, and/or coma

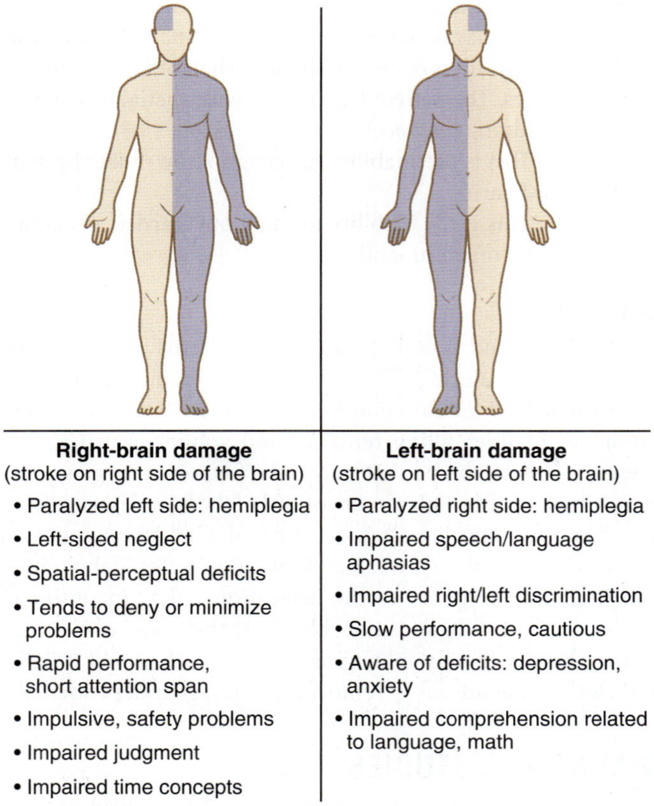

Fig. 62.4 Manifestations of right-brain and left-brain stroke.

the type of stroke were discussed in the previous section. The general manifestations of ischemic and hemorrhagic stroke are discussed together here.

A stroke can affect many body functions, including motor activity, bladder and bowel function, intellect, spatial perception, personality, affect, sensation, swallowing, and communication. The functions affected are directly related to the artery involved and area of the brain that it supplies (Table 62.4). Manifestations related to right- and left-brain damage differ somewhat. These are shown in Fig. 62.4.

Motor Function

Motor deficits are the most obvious effect of stroke. Motor deficits include impaired (1) mobility, (2) respiratory function, (3) swallowing and speech, (4) gag reflex, and (5) self-care abilities. Symptoms are caused by the destruction of motor neurons in the pyramidal pathway (nerve fibers from the brain that pass through the spinal cord to the motor cells). The characteristic motor deficits include loss of skilled voluntary movement *(akinesia),* impaired integration of movements, changes in muscle tone, and altered reflexes. The initial *hyporeflexia* (depressed reflexes) progresses to *hyperreflexia* (hyperactive reflexes) for most patients.

Motor deficits after a stroke follow certain specific patterns. Because the pyramidal pathway crosses at the level of the medulla, a lesion on 1 side of the brain affects motor function on the opposite side of the body (contralateral). The arms and legs of the affected side may be weakened or paralyzed to different degrees depending on which part of and to what extent the cerebral circulation was compromised. A stroke affecting the middle cerebral artery leads to greater weakness in the upper extremity than the lower extremity. The affected shoulder tends to rotate internally, and the hip rotates externally. The affected foot is plantar flexed and inverted. An initial period of flaccidity may last from days to several weeks. It is related to nerve damage. Muscle spasticity follows the flaccid stage. It is related to interruption of upper motor neuron influence.

Communication

The left hemisphere is dominant for language skills in right-handed persons and in most left-handed persons.[9] Language disorders involve expression and comprehension of written and spoken words. The patient may have **aphasia**. Types of aphasia include *receptive aphasia* (loss of comprehension), *expressive aphasia* (inability to produce language), or *global aphasia* (total inability to communicate). Aphasia occurs when a stroke damages the dominant hemisphere of the brain.

Dysphasia refers to impaired ability to communicate. However, in most settings, the terms *aphasia* and *dysphasia* are used interchangeably. Aphasia is the more common term used. Patterns of aphasia may differ since a stroke affects different portions of the brain. We describe aphasia as *nonfluent* (minimal speech activity with slow speech that requires obvious effort) or *fluent* (speech is present but has little meaningful communication) (Table 62.5). Most types of aphasia are mixed, with both impaired expression and understanding. A massive stroke may result in global aphasia.

Many stroke patients have **dysarthria**, a problem with the muscular control of speech. Impairment may involve pronunciation, articulation, and phonation. Dysarthria does not affect the meaning of communication or language comprehension. It does affect the mechanics of speech. Some patients have a combination of aphasia and dysarthria.

Affect

Patients who had a stroke may have a hard time controlling their emotions. Emotional responses may be exaggerated or unpredictable. Depression and feelings due to changes in body image and loss of function can make this worse.[10] Mobility and communication problems increase frustration.

CHECK YOUR PRACTICE

You are working in the outpatient stroke clinic, counseling the family of one of your favorite patients. He is a well-respected 65-year-old businessman who has returned home after a stroke. His family tells you that during meals, he becomes frustrated and begins to cry because of the difficulty getting food into his mouth and chewing. His family cannot understand why a previously very competent man is so emotional.

- What teaching will you provide the family?
- What measures can you take to support the family?

TABLE 62.5 Types of Aphasia

Type	Characteristics
Broca's	• Type of nonfluent aphasia • Damage to frontal lobe of brain • Often speak in short phrases that make sense but take great effort • Often omit small words (e.g., is, and, the) • May say, "Walk dog," meaning, "I will take the dog for a walk," or "Book 2 table," for "There are 2 books on the table" • Typically understands others' speech • Often aware of their difficulties and can become easily frustrated
Global	• Type of nonfluent aphasia • Results from damage to extensive portions of language areas of brain • Have severe communication difficulties • May be limited in ability to speak or understand language
Wernicke's	• Type of fluent aphasia • Damage occurs in left temporal lobe, although it can result from damage to right lobe • May speak in long sentences that have no meaning, add unnecessary words, and even create made-up words • May say, "You know that smoodle pinkered and that I want to get him round and take care of him like you want before" • Usually have great difficulty understanding speech • Often unaware of their mistakes • Often difficult to follow what person is trying to say
Other	• Results from damage to different language areas in brain • Some may have trouble repeating words and sentences, even though they can speak and understand the meaning of the word or sentence • May have trouble naming objects, even though they know what the object is and what its use is

Intellectual Function

A stroke may impair both memory and judgment. These impairments can occur with strokes affecting either side of the brain. A left-brain stroke is more likely to result in memory problems related to language. Patients with a left-brain stroke often are cautious in making judgments.

The patient with a right-brain stroke tends to be impulsive and move quickly. An example is that they try to rise quickly from a wheelchair without locking the wheels or raising the footrests. On the other hand, people with a left-brain stroke would move slowly and cautiously from the wheelchair. Patients with either type of stroke may find it hard to make generalizations, interfering with their ability to learn.

Spatial-Perceptual Problems

Those who had a stroke on the right side of the brain are more likely to have problems with spatial-perceptual orientation. However, this can also occur in people with left-brain stroke. Patients may or may not be aware of their spatial-perceptual problems. You need to assess for these problems as they will affect rehabilitation and recovery.

Spatial-perceptual problems fall within 4 categories:

- An incorrect perception of self and illness. In this situation, patients may deny their illnesses or not recognize their own body parts. This results from parietal lobe damage.
- Spatial neglect. This occurs when the patient neglects all input from the affected side (erroneous perception of self in space). This may be worsened by *homonymous hemianopsia,* in which blindness occurs in the same half of the visual fields of both eyes. The patient has trouble with spatial orientation, such as judging distances.
- *Agnosia.* This is the inability to recognize an object by sight, touch, or hearing.
- *Apraxia.* This is the inability to carry out learned, sequential movements on command.

Elimination

Most urinary and bowel elimination problems are temporary. When a stroke affects 1 hemisphere of the brain, the prognosis for normal bladder function is excellent. At least partial sensation for bladder filling remains, and voluntary urination is present. At first, the patient may have frequency, urgency, and incontinence. Although motor control of the bowel is usually not a problem, patients are often constipated. Constipation is associated with immobility, weak abdominal muscles, dehydration, and decreased response to the defecation reflex. Incontinence may occur if the patient is not able to say they need to eliminate or they have difficulty managing clothing. Scheduled toileting and clothes that are easily removed encourage independence.

DIAGNOSTIC STUDIES

When manifestations of a stroke occur, diagnostic studies (Tables 62.6 and 62.7) are done to (1) confirm that it is a stroke and not another type of brain lesion and (2) identify the likely cause of the stroke. Diagnostic study results also guide decisions about therapy. A key assessment is to determine the time of the onset of symptoms. This is important for all types of stroke, especially ischemic strokes, since time can affect treatment decisions.

When a person suspected of TIA or stroke arrives in the emergency department or mobile stroke unit, it is important for them to rapidly undergo either a noncontrast head CT or MRI. These tests can rapidly distinguish between ischemic and hemorrhagic stroke. They help determine the size and location of the stroke and treatment options. MRI is more effective in identifying ischemic stroke than CT scans. However, a CT scan is a rapid diagnostic tool to rule out hemorrhage. Serial scans

TABLE 62.6 Diagnostic Studies
Stroke

Diagnosis of Stroke (Including Extent of Involvement)
- CT scan
- CT angiography (CTA)
- CT/MRI perfusion and diffusion imaging
- MRI
- Magnetic resonance angiography (MRA)

Cerebral Blood Flow
- Carotid angiography
- Carotid duplex scanning
- Cerebral angiography
- Digital subtraction angiography
- Transcranial doppler ultrasonography

Cardiac Assessment
- Cardiac markers (troponin, creatine kinase-MB)
- Chest x-ray
- Echocardiography (transthoracic, transesophageal)
- ECG

Additional Studies
- Coagulation studies: prothrombin time, activated partial thromboplastin time
- CBC (including platelets)
- Electrolyte panel with blood glucose
- Lipid profile
- Renal and hepatic studies

may be used to assess the effectiveness of treatment and to evaluate recovery.

CT angiography (CTA) provides visualization of cerebral blood vessels. It can be done after or at the same time as the noncontrast CT scan. CTA can give an estimate of perfusion and detect filling defects in the cerebral arteries. Magnetic resonance angiography (MRA) can detect vascular lesions and blockages, similar to CTA. CT/MRI perfusion and diffusion imaging may be done.

If the suspected cause of the stroke includes emboli from the heart, diagnostic cardiac tests should be done. Cardiac imaging is recommended because many strokes are caused by blood clots from the heart. Blood tests can help identify conditions contributing to stroke and guide treatment (Table 62.6).

Angiography can identify cervical and cerebrovascular occlusion, atherosclerotic plaques, and malformation of vessels. Cerebral angiography can find the source of SAH. Risks of angiography include dislodging an embolus, causing vasospasm, inducing further hemorrhage, and provoking an allergic reaction to contrast media.

Intraarterial digital subtraction angiography (DSA) involves injecting a contrast agent to visualize blood vessels in the neck and the large vessels of the circle of Willis. It reduces the dose of contrast material, uses smaller catheters, and shortens the length of the procedure compared with conventional angiography. It is considered safer than cerebral angiography because there is less vascular manipulation.

TABLE 62.7 Interprofessional Care
Acute Stroke

Diagnostic Assessment
- History and physical assessment
- Diagnostic studies (Table 62.6)

Management
Drug Therapy
- Platelet inhibitors (e.g., aspirin)
- Anticoagulation therapy for patients with atrial fibrillation

Surgical Therapy
- Carotid endarterectomy
- Stenting of carotid artery
- Transluminal angioplasty
- Surgical interventions for aneurysms at risk for bleeding

Acute Care
- Maintain airway
- Fluid therapy
- Treat cerebral edema
- Prevent secondary injury

Ischemic Stroke
- Tissue plasminogen activator (tPA) IV or intraarterial
- Endovascular therapy

Hemorrhagic Stroke
- Surgical decompression if indicated
- Clipping or coiling of aneurysm

Role of Interprofessional Team Members
Speech Therapy
- Assess swallowing reflex
- Evaluate patient for communication defects (e.g., aphasia)

Occupational Therapy
- Evaluate ability to perform self-care
- Teach to perform activities of daily living and adapting tasks

Physical Therapy
- Recommend functional position
- Assess function and, together with patient, plan a rehabilitation program

Transcranial doppler (TCD) ultrasonography is a noninvasive study that measures the velocity of blood flow in the major cerebral arteries. TCD is effective in detecting microemboli and vasospasm. It is ideal for the patient suspected of having an SAH. Carotid duplex scanning is used to detect the cause of the stroke and stratify patients for either medical management or carotid intervention if they have carotid stenosis.

An LP can determine if red blood cells are present in the CSF if we suspect SAH and the CT does not show hemorrhage. An LP is avoided if the patient is suspected of having an obstruction in the foramen magnum or other signs of increased ICP because of the danger of herniation of the brain downward. This could lead to pressure on cardiac and respiratory centers in the brainstem and potentially death.

BOX 62.2 PROMOTING POPULATION HEALTH

Stroke Prevention

- Reduce salt and sodium intake.
- Maintain a normal body weight.
- Follow a diet low in saturated fat and high in fruits and vegetables.
- Limit alcohol use to moderate levels.
- Maintain a systolic BP less than 140 mm Hg.
- Avoid cigarette smoking and tobacco products.
- Maintain a normal blood glucose level and control diabetes.
- Follow the prescribed treatment plan for diagnosed heart problems.
- Moderate exercise for 150 min/week or vigorous exercise for 75 min/week.

The LICOX system may be used as a diagnostic tool to evaluate the progression of stroke. LICOX measures brain oxygenation and temperature.

INTERPROFESSIONAL CARE

Preventive Therapy

Primary prevention is a priority for decreasing morbidity and mortality from stroke. The goals of stroke prevention include adopting a healthy lifestyle and managing modifiable risk factors (Box 62.2). Health promotion focuses on (1) healthy diet, (2) weight control, (3) regular exercise, (4) no smoking, (5) limiting alcohol use, and (6) BP management. Patients with known risk factors (e.g., diabetes, hypertension, obesity, high serum lipids, cardiac disease) need close management.

Preventive Drug Therapy

We use measures to prevent the development of a thrombus or embolus in patients with TIAs since they are at high risk for stroke. Antiplatelet drugs are a first-line treatment to prevent stroke in patients who had a TIA. Aspirin, at a dose of 81 mg/day, is the most often used antiplatelet agent. Other agents include ticlopidine, clopidogrel (Plavix), dipyridamole (Persantine), and combined dipyridamole and aspirin (Aggrenox).

DRUG ALERT

Ticlopidine and Clopidogrel (Plavix)

- Inform all HCPs and dentists that the drug is being taken before scheduling surgery or major dental procedures.
- Therapy may be stopped 10–14 days before surgery if the antiplatelet effect is not desired.

For patients with atrial fibrillation, oral anticoagulation can include warfarin (Coumadin) and the direct factor Xa inhibitors: rivaroxaban (Xarelto), dabigatran (Pradaxa), and apixaban (Eliquis). The primary advantage of direct factor Xa inhibitors compared to warfarin is that they do not need close monitoring or dosage adjustments. Statins (e.g., simvastatin, lovastatin) are effective in stroke prevention for those with high cholesterol levels who had a TIA.

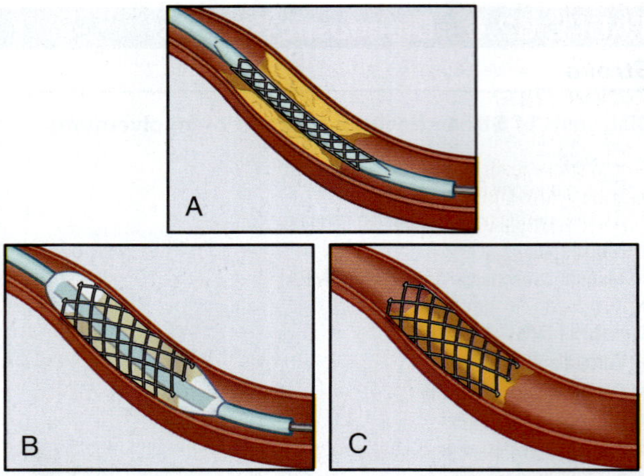

Fig. 62.5 Brain stent used to treat blockages in cerebral blood flow. (A) A balloon catheter is used to implant the stent into an artery of the brain. (B) The balloon catheter is moved to the blocked area of the artery and then inflated. The stent expands due to inflation of the balloon. (C) The balloon is deflated and withdrawn, leaving the stent permanently in place, holding the artery open, and improving the flow of blood.

Left Atrial Appendage Occlusion

The left atrial appendage (LAA) is a pouch that extends off the left atrium. We think the LAA is the source of many stroke-causing emboli in patients with atrial fibrillation. Removing or occluding the LAA decreases the risk of strokes. LAA occlusion can help prevent blood clot formation in patients with atrial fibrillation. It is an alternative for patients who cannot use oral anticoagulants, such as warfarin. After LAA occlusion, patients may be able to stop taking anticoagulants.

A special stapler can be used to remove the LAA. Or, the HCP can place sutures that manually occlude the LAA. There are also special LAA occlusion devices (e.g., AtriClip, Watchman). These devices are positioned around the LAA and then closed, like a clamp, shutting off the blood supply. This prevents blood from flowing into and out of the LAA.

Patent Foramen Ovale

Patients with a patent foramen ovale have a hole between the left and right atriums. Blood clots can pass through this opening and go to the brain, leading to ischemia. An occlusion device implanted in the opening can prevent clot dislodgment.[11]

Surgical/Endovascular Therapy for TIA and Stroke Prevention

Surgical interventions for patients with TIAs due to carotid disease include carotid endarterectomy (CEA), transluminal angioplasty, and stenting. In a *carotid endarterectomy*, the atheromatous lesion is removed from the carotid artery to improve blood flow.

Transluminal angioplasty involves inserting a balloon to open a stenosed artery in the brain and improve blood flow. The balloon is threaded up to the carotid artery through a catheter inserted in the femoral artery.

Stenting involves the intravascular placement of a stent to try to maintain patency of the artery (Fig. 62.5). The stent can be inserted during an angioplasty. Once in place, the system can be used with a tiny filter that opens like an umbrella. The

TABLE 62.8 60 Minute Door-to-Needle Time Interval Goals

Action	*Time*
Door to physician	≤10 min
Door to stroke team	≤15 min
Door to CT/MRI initiation	≤25 min
Door to CT/MRI interpretation	≤45 min
Door to needle time	≤60 min

Adapted from American Heart Association: Target: stroke. Retrieved from https://www.heart.org/-/media/files/professional/quality-improvement/target-stroke/target-stroke-phase-iii/9-17-update/ds14860-time-interval-one-pager_v2.pdf?la=en.

TABLE 62.9 Stroke (STK) Core Measure Set

Measure	Topic
STK-1	Venous thromboembolism (VTE) prophylaxis
STK-2	Discharged on antithrombotic therapy
STK-3	Anticoagulation therapy for atrial fibrillation/flutter
STK-4	Thrombolytic therapy
STK-5	Antithrombotic therapy by end of hospital day 2
STK-6	Discharged on statin medication
STK-8	Stroke education
STK-10	Assessed for rehabilitation

Source: The Joint Commission: Stroke core measures. Retrieved from https://www.jointcommission.org/stroke.

filter catches and removes the debris that is stirred up during the stenting procedure before it floats to the brain, where it can trigger a stroke. Stenting is a less invasive strategy for revascularization in patients unable to withstand the CEA because of coexisting medical conditions.

Care after stenting or angioplasty includes neurovascular assessment and BP management. Monitor vital signs. Assess for complications, including stent occlusion and bleeding. Minimize the risk for bleeding at the insertion site by keeping the patient's leg straight for the prescribed time.

Acute Care for Ischemic Stroke

During initial evaluation, the single most important point in the patient's history is the time of onset of symptoms. Care goals during the acute phase are preserving life, preventing further brain damage, and reducing disability (Table 62.7).

For emergency care, patients should be transported to the closest certified stroke center. If one is not available, the patient should be sent to the closest place offering emergency stroke care.[12] Some communities have a mobile stroke unit that offers onsite emergency CT and point of care testing.[13] Meeting the AHA's Door-to-Needle or Door-to-Device time initiative promotes better patient outcomes (Table 62.8). [14] The stroke (STK) core measures (Table 62.9) are proven standards of care that reduce complications, also leading to better outcomes (Table 62.9).

Table 62.10 outlines the emergency management of the patient with a stroke. In the unresponsive person, acute care begins with assessing circulation, airway, and breathing. Patients may have difficulty keeping an open and clear airway because of a decreased LOC or decreased or absent gag and swallowing reflexes. Maintaining adequate oxygenation is important. O_2 administration, artificial airway insertion, intubation, and mechanical ventilation may be needed. Perform a baseline neurologic assessment. Monitor closely for signs of increasing neurologic deficit. Many patients worsen in the first 24 to 48 hours.

Elevated BP is common right after a stroke. It may be a protective response to maintain cerebral perfusion. However, it can be detrimental. In patients with an ischemic stroke who do not receive fibrinolytic therapy, the use of drugs to lower BP is recommended only if BP is markedly increased (SBP greater than 220 mm Hg or DBP greater than 120 mm Hg). In a patient who is going to have fibrinolytic therapy, the BP must be less than 185/110 mm Hg and then maintained at or below 180/105 mm Hg for at least 24 hours after fibrinolytic therapy. In an acute stroke, IV antihypertensives, such as labetalol and nicardipine, are preferred. Although low BP right after a stroke is uncommon, we correct hypotension and hypovolemia if present.

Fluid and electrolyte balance must be controlled carefully. The goal is to keep the patient adequately hydrated to promote perfusion and decrease further brain injury. Overhydration may compromise perfusion by increasing ICP and cerebral edema. Adequate fluid intake during acute care is a priority. Monitor urine output to make sure the patient does not become dehydrated.

If secretion of antidiuretic hormone (ADH) increases in response to the stroke, urine output decreases, and fluid is retained. Low serum sodium (hyponatremia) may occur. IV solutions with glucose and water are avoided because they are hypotonic and may further increase cerebral edema and ICP. Glycemic control should be maintained. In general, decisions about fluid and electrolyte replacement therapy are based on the extent of intracranial edema, manifestations of increased ICP, central venous pressure levels, electrolyte levels, and intake and output.

Increased ICP is more likely to occur with hemorrhagic strokes but can occur with ischemic strokes. Increased ICP from cerebral edema usually peaks in 72 hours and may cause brain herniation. Management of increased ICP includes practices that improve venous drainage. These include elevating the head of the bed, keeping the head and neck in alignment, and avoiding hip flexion. Other measures for reducing ICP include managing fever (goal temperature of 96.8°F to 98.6°F [36°C to 37°C]), drug therapy to prevent seizures, pain management, and preventing constipation. CSF drainage may be used in some patients to reduce ICP. The specific management of increased ICP is discussed in Chapter 61.

Drug Therapy for Ischemic Stroke

Fibrinolytic therapy should not be delayed. Recombinant tissue plasminogen activator (tPA) is used to produce localized fibrinolysis by binding to the fibrin in the thrombi. The fibrinolytic action of tPA occurs as the plasminogen is converted to plasmin, whose enzymatic action then digests fibrin and fibrinogen, thus breaking down the clot. Other fibrinolytic agents cannot be substituted for tPA. Fibrinolytic therapy is discussed in Chapter 37.

IV tPA can reestablish blood flow through a blocked artery and prevent cell death in patients with the acute onset of ischemic stroke. tPA must be given within 3 to 4½ hours of the onset of signs of ischemic stroke.[15] We must screen patients carefully

TABLE 62.10 EMERGENCY MANAGEMENT

Stroke

Etiology	Assessment Findings	Interventions
• Aneurysm • Arteriovenous malformation • Embolism • Hemorrhage • Sudden vascular compromise causing disruption of blood flow to brain • Thrombosis • Trauma	• Altered level of consciousness • Bladder or bowel incontinence • ↑ BP • Difficulty swallowing • Facial drooping on affected side • Heart rate ↑ or ↓ • Numbness, weakness, or paralysis of part of body • Respiratory distress • Seizures • Severe headache • Speech or visual changes • Unequal pupils • Vertigo	**Initial** • If unresponsive, assess circulation, airway, and breathing. • If responsive, monitor airway, breathing, and circulation. • Call stroke code or stroke team. • Remove dentures. • Perform pulse oximetry. • Maintain adequate oxygenation (SaO_2 >95%) with supplemental O_2, if needed. • Establish IV access with normal saline. • Maintain BP according to guidelines. • Remove clothing. • Obtain CT scan or MRI. • Perform baseline laboratory tests (including blood glucose) immediately and treat if hypoglycemic. • Position head in midline. • Elevate head of bed 30 degrees if no symptoms of shock or injury. • Institute seizure precautions. • Anticipate thrombolytic therapy for ischemic stroke. • Keep patient NPO until swallow reflex evaluated. **Ongoing Monitoring** • Monitor vital signs and neurologic status, including level of consciousness (NIH Stroke Scale), motor and sensory function, pupil size and reactivity, SaO_2, and cardiac rhythm. • Reassure patient and family.

before they receive tPA. Screening includes a noncontrast CT scan or MRI to rule out hemorrhagic stroke; blood tests for coagulation disorders; screening for recent history of gastrointestinal (GI) bleeding, stroke, or head trauma within the past 3 months; major surgery within 14 days; or recent active internal bleeding within 22 days.[15]

During tPA infusion, closely monitor the patient's vital signs and neurologic status to assess for improvement or for potential deterioration related to intracerebral hemorrhage. Control of BP (SBP less than 185 mm Hg) is critical during treatment and for 24 hours following.

Patients with an ischemic stroke may receive an intraarterial tPA infusion if mechanical thrombectomy is not an option. To be effective, intraarterial tPA must be given within 6 hours of the onset of stroke symptoms. With intraarterial tPA, the HCP inserts a thin, flexible catheter into an artery (usually the femoral artery) and guides the catheter (using angiogram) to the area of the clot. The tPA is given through the catheter and immediately targets the clot. Less tPA is needed when it is delivered directly to the clot, reducing the risk for intracranial hemorrhage.

Anticoagulant (e.g., heparin) use in the emergency phase after an ischemic stroke is not recommended because of the risk for intracranial hemorrhage. Aspirin at a higher dose may be started within 24 to 48 hours after the onset of an ischemic stroke. Complications of high dose aspirin include GI bleeding. Aspirin should be given cautiously if the patient has a history of peptic ulcer disease.

After the patient has stabilized and to prevent further clot formation, patients with strokes caused by thrombi and emboli may be treated with anticoagulants and platelet inhibitors. For patients with atrial fibrillation, oral anticoagulant options include warfarin and direct factor Xa inhibitors (e.g., rivaroxaban [Xarelto], dabigatran [Pradaxa], apixaban [Eliquis]). Platelet inhibitors include aspirin, ticlopidine, clopidogrel, and dipyridamole. The use of statins is effective for the patient after an ischemic stroke.

Endovascular Therapy for Ischemic Stroke

Stent retrievers are a way of opening blocked arteries in the brain by using a removable stent system.[16] During the procedure, a catheter is used to guide the small stent from the femoral or radial artery into the part of the artery where a blood clot has formed. The stent expands the interior walls of the artery and allows blood to get to the patient's brain immediately to prevent as much brain damage as possible. The clot seeps into the mesh of the stent. Then, after a few minutes, the stent and clot are removed together. Stent retrievers are becoming the most effective way of managing ischemic stroke.[16]

Acute Care for Hemorrhagic Stroke

Drug Therapy for Hemorrhagic Stroke

Anticoagulants and platelet inhibitors are contraindicated in patients with hemorrhagic strokes. Drug therapy for patients with hemorrhagic stroke involves managing hypertension. Oral and IV agents may be used to maintain BP within a normal to high-normal range (SBP less than 160 mm Hg). Seizure prophylaxis is patient-specific.[17]

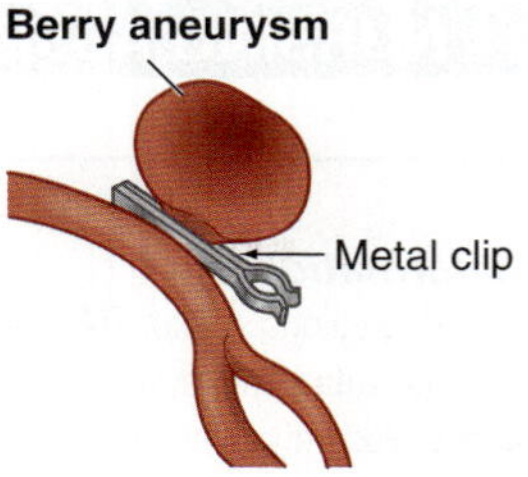

Fig. 62.6 Clipping of aneurysms.

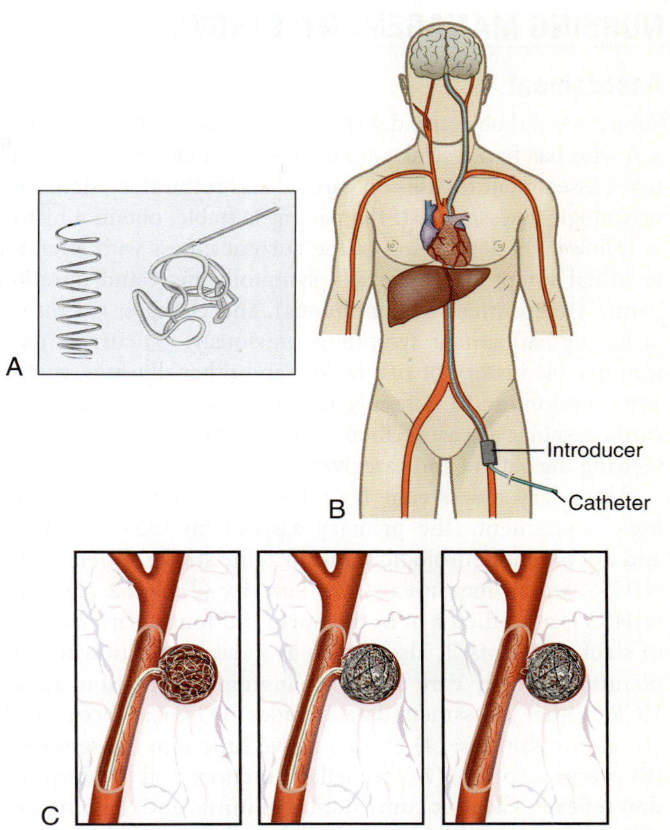

Fig. 62.7 Guglielmi detachable coil (GDC). (A) A coil is used to occlude an aneurysm. Coils are made of soft, spring-like platinum. The softness of the platinum allows the coil to assume the shape of irregularly shaped aneurysms while posing little threat of rupture of the aneurysm. (B) A catheter is inserted through an introducer (small tube) in an artery in the leg. The catheter is threaded up to the cerebral blood vessels. (C) Platinum coils attached to a thin wire are inserted into the catheter and then placed in the aneurysm until the aneurysm is filled with coils. Packing the aneurysm with coils prevents the blood from circulating through the aneurysm, reducing the risk for rupture.

Surgical Therapy for Hemorrhagic Stroke

Surgical interventions for hemorrhagic stroke include immediate evacuation of aneurysm-induced hematomas or cerebellar hematomas larger than 3 cm. Those who have an arteriovenous malformation (AVM) may have a hemorrhagic stroke if the AVM ruptures. The treatment of AVM is surgical resection and/or radiosurgery. Catheter embolization of affected vessels can block the blood supply to the AVM.

SAH is usually caused by a ruptured aneurysm. Patients may have multiple aneurysms. Treatment of an aneurysm often involves clipping or coiling the aneurysm to prevent rebleeding (Figs. 62.6 and 62.7). In clipping the aneurysm, the HCP places a metallic clip on the neck of the aneurysm to block blood flow and prevent rupture. The clip stays in place for life.

Interventional radiology procedures include coiling and flow diversion. With coiling, a hydrogel-coated platinum coil is inserted into the lumen of the aneurysm (Fig. 62.7). Guglielmi detachable coils (GDCs) give immediate protection against hemorrhage by reducing the blood pulsations within the aneurysm. Eventually, a thrombus forms within the aneurysm. Then the aneurysm becomes sealed off from the parent vessel by the formation of an endothelialized layer of connective tissue. Flow diverters placed in the parent blood vessel divert blood flow away from an aneurysm.

After clipping or coiling, hyperdynamic therapy (hemodilution-induced hypertension using vasoconstricting agents, such as phenylephrine or dopamine, and hypervolemia) may be started to increase the mean arterial pressure and cerebral perfusion. Volume expansion is achieved with crystalloid or colloid solutions.

With SAH, bleeding from a damaged vessel causes blood to accumulate between the brain and skull. The leaked blood can irritate, damage, or destroy the surrounding brain cells. When blood enters the subarachnoid space, it mixes with the CSF. This can block CSF circulation, thus increasing pressure on the brain. The open spaces in the brain (ventricles) may enlarge, causing hydrocephalus. This further increases ICP (due to the large accumulation of blood) and can result in further brain injury. Inserting a ventriculostomy for CSF drainage can dramatically improve these situations by reducing ICP.[18] Goals for managing ICP are the same for patients with SAH as they are for patients dealing with acute stroke. The management of ICP is discussed in Chapter 61.

Patients with SAH may receive the calcium channel blocker nimodipine to treat cerebral vasospasms and minimize cerebral damage. We think it dilates narrowed blood vessels around the area of the bleeding, so blood flows more easily. This minimizes cerebral damage

DRUG ALERT

Nimodipine

- Assess BP and apical pulses before administration.
- If pulse is ≤60 beats/min or systolic BP is <90 mm Hg, hold the medication and contact the HCP.

Rehabilitation Care

After the stroke patient has stabilized for 12 to 24 hours, care goals shift from preserving life to lessening disability and reaching optimal function. Many of the interventions started in the acute phase are continued during this phase. The patient may be evaluated by a physiatrist (a physician who specializes in physical medicine and rehabilitation). Some aspects of rehabilitation begin in the acute care phase as soon as the patient is stable. Specific rehabilitation measures are discussed in the section on Ambulatory Care.

❖ NURSING MANAGEMENT: STROKE

◆ Assessment

Subjective and objective data that you should obtain from a person who has had a stroke are detailed in Table 62.11. The primary assessment focuses on cardiac and respiratory status and neurologic assessment. If the patient is stable, obtain a history as follows: (1) description of the current illness with attention to initial symptoms, especially symptom onset and duration, nature (intermittent or continuous), and changes; (2) history of having had similar symptoms previously; (3) current medications; (4) history of risk factors and other illnesses, such as hypertension; and (5) family history of stroke, aneurysm, or cardiovascular diseases. Obtain this information through interviewing the patient and caregivers.

Secondary assessment includes a comprehensive neurologic assessment. The primary assessment tool to evaluate and document neurologic status in acute stroke patients is the NIHSS, which measures stroke severity (Table 62.12).[19] The NIHSS is a predictor of both short- and long-term outcomes of stroke patients. It also serves as a data collection tool for planning patient care and exchanging information among HCPs. Other assessment data includes (1) LOC; (2) cognition; (3) motor abilities; (4) cranial nerve function; (5) sensation; (6) proprioception; (7) cerebellar function; and (8) deep tendon reflexes. Clear documentation of initial and ongoing neurologic assessment is essential to note changes in the patient's status.

◆ Clinical Problems

Clinical problems for the person with a stroke may include:

- Neurologic problems
- Increased intracranial pressure
- Impaired communication
- Difficulty coping
- Risk for aspiration
- Musculoskeletal problems
- Risk for injury

More information on clinical problems and interventions are presented in eNursing Care Plan 62.1 (available on the website for this chapter).

◆ Planning

Establish the goals of nursing care together with the patient, caregiver, and family. Typical goals are that the patient will (1) maintain a stable or improved LOC, (2) attain maximum physical functioning, (3) attain maximum self-care abilities and skills, (4) maintain stable body functions (e.g., bladder control), (5) maximize communication abilities, (6) maintain adequate nutrition, (7) avoid complications, and (8) maintain effective personal and family coping.

◆ Implementation

◆ Health Promotion

You have a key role in promoting a healthy lifestyle. Teaching should focus on stroke prevention, especially for persons with known risk factors. Most strokes are caused by modifiable risk factors. Measures to reduce risk factors for stroke are similar to those for coronary artery disease (see Chapter 37).

Uncontrolled or undiagnosed hypertension is the primary cause of stroke. Therefore, you need to be involved in BP screening and ensuring that patients adhere to their antihypertensive

TABLE 62.11 NURSING ASSESSMENT

Stroke

Subjective Data

Important Health Information

Health history: Hypertension, previous stroke, TIA, aneurysm, cardiac disease (including recent myocardial infarction, dysrhythmias, heart failure, valvular heart disease, infective endocarditis), hyperlipidemia, polycythemia, blood clotting disorders, diabetes, gout

Family history: Neurologic disorders, aneurysms, stroke, TIA, diabetes, hypertension, coronary artery disease

Medications: Oral contraceptives; use of and adherence with antihypertensive and anticoagulant therapy; illicit substance use

Functional Health Patterns

Health perception–health management: Alcohol use, smoking, drug use

Nutritional-metabolic: Anorexia, nausea, vomiting. Dysphagia, altered sense of taste and smell

Elimination: Change in bowel and bladder patterns

Activity-exercise: Loss of movement and sensation. Syncope, weakness on one side, generalized weakness, easy fatigability

Cognitive-perceptual: Numbness, tingling of one side of the body, loss of memory. Change in speech, language, problem-solving ability. Pain, headache (possibly sudden and severe) (hemorrhage). Visual changes. Denial of illness

Objective Data

Cardiovascular

↑ BP, ↑ HR, carotid bruit

General

Emotional lability, lethargy, apathy or combativeness, fever

Gastrointestinal

Loss of gag reflex, bowel incontinence, decreased or absent bowel sounds, constipation

Neurologic

Contralateral motor and sensory deficits, including weakness, paresis, paralysis, anesthesia. Unequal pupils, hand grasps. Akinesia, aphasia (expressive, receptive, global), dysarthria (slurred speech), agnosia, apraxia, visual deficits, perceptual or spatial problems, altered level of consciousness (drowsiness to deep coma), and Babinski sign, ↓ followed by ↑ deep tendon reflexes, flaccidity followed by spasticity, amnesia, ataxia, personality change, nuchal rigidity, seizures

Respiratory

Loss of cough reflex, labored or irregular respirations, tachypnea, wheezes (aspiration), airway occlusion (tongue), apnea, coughing when eating, or delayed coughing

Urinary

Frequency, urgency, incontinence

Possible Diagnostic Findings

Positive CT, CT angiography, MRI, magnetic resonance angiography, or other neuroimaging scans showing size, location, and type of lesion. Positive Doppler ultrasonography and angiography showing stenosis

TABLE 62.12 National Institutes of Health Stroke Scale

Description

The NIH Stroke Scale (NIHSS) is a 15-item neurologic examination used to evaluate the effect of an acute stroke. Total scores on the NIHSS range from 0 to 42, with higher values reflecting more severity.

Procedure for Use

A trained observer rates the patient's ability to answer questions and perform activities. Ratings for each item are scored, and there is an allowance for untestable (UN) items. If an item is left untested, a detailed explanation must be clearly written on the form. Training can be completed free at www.nihstrokescale.org.

Item	Scale Definition
Level of consciousness	0 = Alert 1 = Not alert, but arousable by minor stimulation 2 = Not alert, requires repeated stimulation to get attention 3 = Responds only with reflex motor or autonomic effects or unresponsive, flaccid, areflexic
Level of consciousness questions	0 = Answers both questions correctly 1 = Answers 1 question correctly 2 = Answers neither question correctly
Level of consciousness commands	0 = Performs both tasks correctly 1 = Performs 1 task correctly 2 = Performs neither task correctly
Best gaze	0 = Normal 1 = Partial gaze palsy 2 = Forced deviation, or total gaze paresis
Visual	0 = No visual loss 1 = Partial hemianopsia 2 = Complete hemianopsia 3 = Bilateral hemianopsia or blind
Facial palsy	0 = Normal symmetric movement 1 = Minor paralysis 2 = Partial paralysis 3 = Complete paralysis of 1 or both sides
Motor and drift (for each extremity)	0 = No drift 1 = Drift 2 = Some effort against gravity 3 = No effort against gravity, limb falls 4 = No movement UN = Amputation
Limb ataxia	0 = Absent 1 = Present in 1 limb 2 = Present in 2 limbs
Sensory	0 = Normal 1 = Mild to moderate sensory loss 2 = Severe to total sensory loss
Best language	0 = No aphasia, normal 1 = Mild to moderate aphasia 2 = Severe aphasia 3 = Mute, no usable speech or auditory comprehension
Dysarthria	0 = Normal 1 = Mild to moderate 2 = Severe UN = Intubated or other physical barrier
Extinction or inattention	0 = No abnormality 1 = Inattention or extinction to bilateral stimulation 2 = Does not recognize own hand
Distal motor function	0 = Normal (no flexion after 5 sec) 1 = At least some extension but not fully extended 2 = No voluntary extension after 5 sec

Source: National Institutes of Health: NIH Stroke Scale. Retrieved from https://www.stroke.nih.gov/resources/scale.htm.

therapy. If a person has diabetes, it is important that it is well controlled. If a person has atrial fibrillation, anticoagulant therapy may reduce the risk for stroke. Because smoking is a major risk factor for stroke, help patients to stop smoking (see Chapter 11).

Another important aspect of health promotion is teaching patients and families about early symptoms of stroke or TIA. Table 62.1 presents information on when to seek health care for these symptoms.

◆ Acute Care

Respiratory system. During the acute phase after a stroke, management of the respiratory system is a nursing priority. Stroke patients are vulnerable to respiratory problems. Advancing age and immobility increase the risk for atelectasis and pneumonia.

Interventions to support adequate respiratory function are tailored to meet the patient's specific needs (Table 62.13). Some stroke patients, especially those with brainstem or hemorrhagic stroke, may need endotracheal intubation and mechanical ventilation. An oropharyngeal airway in a comatose patient may prevent the tongue from falling back and obstructing the airway and provide access for suctioning. Alternatively, a nasopharyngeal airway may be used to provide airway protection and access. When an artificial airway is needed for a prolonged time, a tracheostomy may be done.

Frequently assess airway patency and function. Provide O_2 therapy as ordered. Suction the patient as needed and encourage deep breathing. In patients who are on mechanical ventilation, oral care at least every 2 hours reduces the risk of ventilator-assisted pneumonia.

Position the patient to prevent aspiration. Risk for aspiration pneumonia is high because of impaired consciousness or dysphagia. Dysphagia after stroke is common. Airway obstruction can occur because of problems with chewing and swallowing, food pocketing (food remaining in the buccal cavity of the

TABLE 62.13 NURSING MANAGEMENT

Caring for the Patient With an Acute Stroke

- Assess manifestations of stroke and determine when they started.
- Screen patient for contraindications for tissue plasminogen activator (tPA) therapy.
- Infuse tPA for patients with ischemic stroke who meet the criteria for tPA administration.
- Assess respiratory status and start needed actions, such as O_2, oropharyngeal or nasopharyngeal airways, suctioning.
- Position patient to prevent aspiration and atelectasis.
- Assess neurologic status, including intracranial pressure (ICP), if needed.
- Monitor cardiovascular status, including hemodynamic monitoring, if needed.
- Calculate intake and output, noting imbalances.
- Regulate IV infusions and adjust fluid intake to patient needs.
- Assess patient's ability to swallow in conjunction with the speech therapist.
- Give scheduled anticoagulant and antiplatelet drugs.
- Implement measures to prevent venous thromboembolism and skin breakdown.
- Delegate to AP:
  - Obtain vital signs and report these to RN.
  - Measure and record urine output.
  - Help with positioning and turning patient at least every 2 h.
  - Perform passive and active range-of-motion exercises.

mouth), and the tongue falling back. Enteral nutrition (EN) places the patient at risk for aspiration pneumonia. Screen all patients for their ability to swallow. Keep them NPO until dysphagia is ruled out.

Patients who have an unclipped or uncoiled aneurysm may have rebleeding and further increased ICP with coughing or suctioning. Care is aimed at reducing these interventions while maintaining a patent airway.

Neurologic system. Perform ongoing neurologic assessments, including the NIHSS, mental status, pupillary response, and extremity movement and strength. A decreasing LOC may indicate increasing ICP. Monitor ICP and cerebral perfusion pressure if the patient is in ICU. Record your assessment promptly to communicate the patient's neurologic status to the stroke team.

Cardiovascular system. Nursing goals for the cardiovascular system are aimed at maintaining homeostasis. Many patients with stroke have decreased cardiac reserves from cardiac disease. Fluid retention, overhydration, dehydration, or BP changes may further compromise cardiac efficiency. Central venous pressure, pulmonary artery pressure, or hemodynamic monitoring may be used to assess fluid balance and cardiac function in the ICU.

Monitor vital signs and maintain ECG monitoring. Hypertension sometimes occurs after a stroke as the body tries to increase CBF. It is important to assess for orthostatic hypotension before ambulating the patient for the first time. Neurologic changes can occur with a sudden decrease in BP.

Calculate intake and output, noting imbalances. Regulate IV infusions and adjust fluid intake to meet the patient's needs. Monitor lung sounds for crackles and wheezes, which may indicate pulmonary congestion.

The patient is at risk for venous thromboembolism (VTE), especially in the weak or paralyzed lower extremity. VTE is related to immobility, loss of venous tone, and decreased muscle pumping activity in the leg. The most effective prevention is to keep the patient moving. Teach the patient active range-of-motion (ROM) exercises if the patient has voluntary movement in the affected extremity. For the patient with hemiplegia, perform passive ROM exercises several times a day. Other measures to prevent VTE include positioning to minimize the effects of dependent edema and using intermittent pneumatic compression devices. VTE prophylaxis may include low-molecular-weight heparin (e.g., enoxaparin [Lovenox]). Your assessment includes observing for swelling of the lower extremities, noting unusual warmth of the leg, and asking the patient about pain in the calf.

Musculoskeletal system. The nursing goal for the musculoskeletal system is to maintain optimal function by preventing joint contractures and muscular atrophy. In the acute phase, ROM exercises and positioning are important nursing interventions. Passive ROM exercise is begun on the first day of hospitalization. Muscle atrophy from lack of innervation and activity can develop after a stroke, so exercise is an important intervention for rehabilitation and recovery.

The paralyzed or weak side needs special attention when the patient is positioned. Position each joint higher than the joint proximal to it to prevent dependent edema. Specific deformities on the weak or paralyzed side that may be present include internal rotation of the shoulder; flexion contractures of the hand, wrist, and elbow; external rotation of the hip; and plantar flexion of the foot. Subluxation of the shoulder on the affected side is common. Careful positioning and moving of the affected arm may prevent the development of a painful shoulder condition. Immobilization of the affected upper extremity may precipitate a painful shoulder-hand syndrome.

Interventions to promote musculoskeletal function include (1) trochanter roll at the hip to prevent external rotation; (2) hand cones (not rolled washcloths) to prevent hand contractures; (3) arm supports with slings and lap boards to prevent shoulder displacement; and (4) avoidance of pulling the patient by the arm to avoid shoulder displacement; and (5) posterior leg splints or high-top tennis shoes to prevent footdrop.

Using a footboard for patients with spasticity is controversial. Rather than preventing plantar flexion (footdrop), the sensory stimulation of a footboard against the bottom of the foot increases plantar flexion. Likewise, experts disagree on whether hand splints decrease spasticity. The decision about using footboards or hand splints is made on an individual patient basis.

Integumentary system. The skin of the patient with stroke is susceptible to breakdown related to loss of sensation, decreased circulation, and immobility. Advanced age, poor nutrition, dehydration, edema, and incontinence compound the risk.

Measures to prevent skin breakdown include (1) pressure relief by position changes, special mattresses, or wheelchair cushions; (2) good skin hygiene; (3) emollients applied to dry skin; and (4) early mobility. An example of a position change schedule is side-back-side, with a maximum duration of 2 hours for any position. Position the patient on the weak or paralyzed side for only 30 minutes. Controlling pressure is key in both preventing and treating skin breakdown. Use pillows under lower extremities to reduce pressure on the heels. See more information on preventing pressure injuries in Chapter 12.

Gastrointestinal system. The most common bowel problem after stroke is constipation. Fluid and fiber intake goals are determined with the stroke team based on the patient's nutrition and fluid status. Patients may be prophylactically placed on stool softeners and/or fiber (psyllium [Metamucil]). Laxatives, suppositories, or additional stool softeners may be ordered if the patient does not respond to increased fluid and fiber. Enemas are used only if suppositories and digital stimulation are ineffective because they cause vagal stimulation and increase ICP. Physical activity promotes bowel function. If a patient has liquid stools, check for stool impaction.

Bowel retraining may be needed and continued into the rehabilitation phase. A bowel management program consists of placing the patient on the bedpan or bedside commode or taking the patient to the bathroom at a regular time daily to reestablish bowel regularity. A good time for a bowel movement is 30 minutes after breakfast because eating stimulates the gastrocolic reflex and peristalsis. The timing may need adjusted as bowel habits vary.

Urinary system. In the acute stage of stroke, the primary urinary problem is poor bladder control, resulting in incontinence. Take steps to promote normal bladder function and avoid the use of indwelling catheters. If an indwelling catheter is used initially, remove it as soon as the patient is medically and neurologically stable. Long-term use of an indwelling catheter is associated with urinary tract infections and delayed bladder retraining.

Avoid bladder overdistention. An intermittent catheterization program may be used for patients with urinary retention to lower the risk of urinary infections. An alternative to intermittent catheterizations for a male patient is an external catheter. External catheters do not address problems with urine retention.

Often the patient has functional incontinence, which is associated with communication, mobility, and dressing problems. A bladder retraining program consists of (1) adequate fluid intake, with most of it given between 7:00 AM and 7:00 PM; (2) scheduled toileting every 2 hours using bedpan, commode, or bathroom while encouraging the usual position for urinating (standing for men, sitting for women); (3) observing for signs of restlessness, which may indicate the need for urination; and (4) assessing for bladder distention by palpation. Encourage patients to wear pants without drawstrings, buttons, or zippers. These can be hard to manage if motor or sensory deficits exist.

Assessing postvoid residual volume is often done using bladder ultrasound. The ultrasound measures how much urine is in the bladder after voiding. If urine stays in the bladder, incomplete emptying is a problem and may cause urinary tract infections. A coordinated program by the entire nursing staff is needed to achieve urinary continence.

Nutrition. The patient's nutrition needs require quick assessment and treatment. The patient may initially receive IV infusions to maintain fluid and electrolyte balance. Patients with severe impairment may need EN or parenteral nutrition. Patients should have their nutrition needs addressed in the first 24 hours of admission because nutrition is important for recovery and healing.[20]

Many patients have dysphagia after a stroke. Keep patients NPO until a speech therapist performs a swallowing evaluation. This should be done in the first 24 hours after the stroke.[20] You or another health care team member may perform the screen if a speech therapist cannot perform the formal evaluation.

Before starting feeding, assess the gag reflex. If the gag reflex is absent, defer the feeding and begin exercises to stimulate swallowing. The speech therapist or occupational therapist is usually responsible for designing this program. However, you may be involved in helping to develop the program in some clinical settings.

> **! SAFETY ALERT**
>
> ***Oral Feeding After Stroke***
>
> - Dysphagia is common after stroke.
> - Keep the patient on NPO status until a speech therapist does a swallowing evaluation.

To assess swallowing ability, elevate the head of the bed to an upright position (unless contraindicated). Give the patient a small amount of crushed ice or ice water to swallow. If the gag reflex is present and the patient can swallow safely, you may proceed with feeding.

The speech therapist may recommend various foods. Foods should be easy to swallow and provide enough texture, temperature (warm or cold), and flavor to stimulate a swallow reflex. Crushed ice can be used as a stimulant. Pureed foods are not usually the best choice because they are often bland or too smooth. Thin liquids are often hard to swallow and may promote coughing. We can thicken thin liquids with a commercially available thickening agent. Avoid milk products because they tend to increase the viscosity of mucus and increase salivation.

Mouth care before feeding helps stimulate sensory awareness and salivation and can help swallowing. Keep the patient in the high-Fowler's position, preferably in a chair, for the feeding and 30 minutes afterward. While feeding, keep the head flexed forward. Place food in the unaffected side of the mouth. Teach the patient to swallow and then swallow again. Follow feedings with good oral hygiene because food may collect in the affected side of the mouth.

A dietitian can help determine the daily caloric intake based on the patient's size, weight, and activity level. If the patient is unable to take in an adequate oral diet and dysphagia persists, a percutaneous endoscopic gastrostomy (PEG) tube may be used for EN (Box 62.3). EN is described in Chapter 44.

The inability to feed one's self can be frustrating and may result in malnutrition and dehydration. Interventions to promote self-feeding include using the unaffected upper extremity to eat; employing assistive devices, such as rocker knives, plate guards, and nonslip pads for dishes; and removing unnecessary items from the tray or table, which can reduce spills. Provide a

BOX 62.3 EVIDENCE-BASED PRACTICE

Enteral Nutrition and Stroke Rehabilitation

In your role as a clinical nurse on a stroke rehabilitation unit, you often care for patients who need enteral nutrition (EN) to meet their nutrient needs. In caring for 87-year-old E.R., a female who had a stroke, you realize you often interrupt scheduled feedings to accommodate physical therapy or off-unit testing.

Making Clinical Decisions

Synthesis of Best Available Evidence

EN is critical for patients with impaired swallowing. Without EN, the patient, after a stroke, is at risk of decline. Because of interruptions, however, most patients receive only about 60% of their nutrient requirements through EN.

Clinician Expertise

As a member of the EBP Committee, you identify interrupted enteral feedings as a clinical problem. You express concern at the committee meeting that patients may not be meeting their nutrient needs based on current EN ordering practices. You suggest that this could affect their length of stay and potential for achieving optimal health. Committee members agree. After reviewing the literature, the group decides to recommend volume-based tube feeding (VBTF) as a way to adjust feedings throughout the day to meet each patient's nutrition goals. Committee members note VBTF has been mainly used in acute care settings but suggest this is an opportunity to optimize nutrition support for patients after stroke.

Patient Preferences and Values

You reconnect E.R.'s enteral feeding after her return from physical therapy. She says, "I thought I was finished with that. It seems like I'm always connected to some tube, yet I never have any energy."

Implications for Nursing Practice

1. How could VTBF better address patients' caloric needs?
2. What outcomes may be affected if patients have adequate caloric intake?

Reference for Evidence

Bonomo A, Blume DL, Davis K, Kim HJ: Implementing volume-based feeding to optimize delivery of enteral nutrition, *Crit Care Nurse* 41:16, 2021.

calm environment (e.g., turn off the television) to decrease sensory overload and distraction. Introduce these interventions in the acute care setting so that maximum rehabilitation can occur once the patient is discharged. We evaluate the effectiveness of the diet program in terms of weight, adequate hydration, and patient satisfaction.

Communication. During the acute stage of stroke, your role in meeting the patient's psychologic needs is primarily supportive. Speech, comprehension, and language deficits are the most difficult problems for the patient and caregiver. Assess the patient for the ability to speak and understand. The patient's response to simple questions can guide you in structuring explanations and instructions. If the patient cannot understand words, use gestures to support verbal cues. Collaborate with the speech therapist to assess and develop a plan of care to enhance communication.

Interventions that support communication include (1) communicating often and meaningfully; (2) allowing time for the patient to comprehend and answer; (3) using simple, short sentences; (4) using visual cues; (5) structuring conversation so that it allows simple answers by the patient; and (6) praising the patient honestly for improvements with speech.

TABLE 62.14 Communicating With a Patient With Aphasia

The following are guidelines for communicating with a patient with aphasia:

1. Decrease environmental stimuli that may be distracting and disrupting to communication efforts.
2. Treat the patient as an adult.
3. Speak with normal volume and tone.
4. Present a single thought or idea at a time.
5. Keep questions simple or ask questions that can be answered with "yes" or "no."
6. Let the person speak. Do not interrupt. Allow time for the person to complete thoughts.
7. Make use of gestures as an alternative form of communication. Encourage this by saying, "Show me . . . ." or "Point to what you want."
8. Do not pretend to understand the person if you do not. Calmly say you do not understand. Encourage the use of nonverbal communication or ask the person to write out what they want.
9. Give the patient time to process information and generate a response before repeating a question or statement.
10. Allow body contact (e.g., clasp of a hand, touching) as much as possible. Realize that touching may be the only way the patient can express feelings.
11. Organize the patient's day by preparing and following a schedule (the more familiar the routine, the easier it will be).
12. Do not push communication if the person is tired or upset. Aphasia worsens with fatigue and anxiety.
13. Teach communication techniques to caregivers and family members.

An alert patient is usually anxious because of what has happened and problems with communication or the inability to communicate. Verbal stimuli can easily overwhelm the patient with aphasia. Give the patient extra time to understand and respond to communication. Guidelines for communicating with a patient who has aphasia are outlined in Table 62.14. A picture board may be helpful for communicating with the stroke patient. The speech therapist often does further evaluation and treatment of language and communication deficits once the patient has stabilized. It is important to teach the caregiver and family these communication strategies.

Sensory-perceptual problems. Patients who had a stroke often have perceptual deficits. Patients with a stroke on the right side of the brain usually have difficulty judging position, distance, and rate of movement. These patients are often impulsive and impatient. They tend to deny problems related to strokes. They may not correlate spatial-perceptual problems with the inability to perform activities, such as guiding a wheelchair through the doorway. They best understand directions given verbally. Break down the task into simple steps for ease of understanding. The patient with a right-brain stroke and left hemiplegia is at higher risk for injury because of mobility problems. Environmental control (e.g., removing clutter, using good lighting) aids in concentration and safer mobility. Provide nonslip socks at all times. One-sided neglect is common for people with right-brain stroke. You may need to help or remind the patient to dress the weak or paralyzed side or shave the forgotten side of the face.

Patients with a left-brain stroke (right hemiplegia) often are slower in organizing and performing tasks. They tend to have impaired spatial discrimination. These patients usually admit to

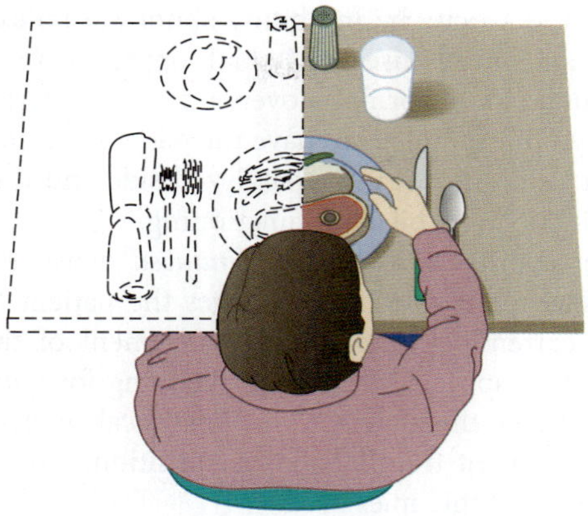

Fig. 62.8 Spatial and perceptual deficits in stroke. Perception of a patient with homonymous hemianopsia shows that food on the left side is not seen and thus is ignored. (Modified from Hoeman SP: *Rehabilitation nursing,* ed 2, St Louis, 1995, Mosby.)

deficits and have a fearful, anxious response to a stroke. Their behaviors are slow and cautious. Nonverbal cues and instructions are helpful for patients who had a left-brain stroke.

Homonymous hemianopsia (blindness in the same half of each visual field) is common after a stroke. Persistent disregard of objects in part of the visual field should alert you to this possibility. At first, help the patient to compensate by arranging the environment within the patient's perceptual field, such as arranging the food tray so that all foods are on one side to accommodate for the field of vision (Fig. 62.8). Later, the patient learns to compensate for the visual defect by consciously attending to or by scanning the neglected side. Weak or paralyzed extremities are carefully checked for adequacy of dressing, hygiene, and trauma.

It is often hard to distinguish between a visual field cut and a neglect syndrome. Both problems may occur with strokes affecting either the right or the left side of the brain. A person may have both homonymous hemianopsia and a neglect syndrome, which increases the inattention to the weak or paralyzed side. Neglect syndrome results in decreased safety awareness and places the patient at high risk for injury. Immediately after the stroke, anticipate safety hazards and provide protection from injury. Safety measures include closely observing the patient, elevating side rails, lowering the height of the bed, and using video monitors. Avoid using restraints and soft vests because these may agitate the patient.

Other visual problems may include *diplopia* (double vision), loss of the corneal reflex, and *ptosis* (drooping eyelid), especially if the stroke is in the vertebrobasilar distribution. Diplopia is often treated with an eye patch. If the corneal reflex is absent, the patient is at risk for corneal abrasion. Prevent corneal abrasions with artificial tears or gel to keep the eyes moist and an eye shield (especially at night). We usually do not treat ptosis unless it inhibits vision.

Coping. A stroke is usually a sudden, very stressful event. Stroke is often a family disease, affecting the family emotionally, socially, and financially and changing roles and responsibilities within the family. The stroke patient and family may perceive the stroke as a threat to life and their accustomed lifestyle. Reactions to this threat vary considerably. They may involve fear, apprehension, denial of the severity of the stroke, depression, anger, and sorrow. During the acute phase of caring for the stroke patient and caregiver, interventions that promote coping involve teaching and providing emotional support.

Give clear, understandable explanations about what has happened and diagnostic and therapeutic procedures. Reinforce as needed. Decision making and upholding the patient's wishes during this challenging time are important. Advance directives should be honored. Update the family daily and hold family meetings about feeding tube placement or tracheostomy.

Give the caregiver and family a careful, detailed explanation of what has happened to the patient. However, if the family is anxious and upset during the acute phase, you may have to repeat explanations later. Because family members usually have not had time to prepare for the illness, they may need help in arranging care for family members or pets and for transportation and finances. A social services referral is often helpful.

It is challenging to keep the patient with aphasia adequately informed. Use demeanor and touch to convey support. When communicating with a patient who has a communication deficit, speak in a normal volume and tone. Keep questions simple. Present one thought or idea at a time. To decrease frustration, let the patient speak without interruption and make use of gestures. Use writing and communication boards.

◆ Ambulatory Care

Care transitions. The patient is usually discharged from the acute care setting to home, an intermediate- or long-term care facility, or a rehabilitation facility. Ideally, discharge planning with the patient and caregiver starts early in the hospitalization and promotes a smooth transition between care settings. The stroke team provides guidance for the appropriate care needed after discharge. Factors that are considered include the patient's medical needs and independence in performing ADLs, caregiver's ability to provide care, and community setting. If the patient needs a short- or long-term health care facility, the team can make appropriate referrals that allow time to select and arrange for care.

If the patient is returning home, the team can make referrals for needed equipment and services. You can prepare the patient and caregiver through teaching. Evaluate the transition plan for any barriers. Follow-up care is carefully planned to allow continued nursing care; physical, occupational, and speech therapy; and medical care. Identify community resources to provide recreational activities, group support, spiritual assistance, respite care, adult day care, and home assistance based on the patient's needs.

Rehabilitation. *Rehabilitation* is the process of maximizing the patient's capabilities and resources to promote optimal functioning related to physical, mental, and social well-being. Many interventions started in the acute phase of care continue throughout rehabilitation. The goals of rehabilitation are to prevent deformity and maintain and improve function. Ongoing rehabilitation is essential to maximize the patient's abilities. Most patients recover in the first 6 months after a stroke, with a maximum benefit 1 year after a stroke.[1]

Rehabilitation requires an interprofessional team approach so that the patient and caregiver can benefit from the team's combined, expert care. The team must communicate and coordinate care to achieve the patient's goals. As a nurse, you can facilitate this process and are often the key to successful rehabilitation efforts. The rehabilitation team is composed of many other members. These include physicians; psychiatrists or psychologists; physical, occupational, speech, vocational, recreational, and respiratory therapists; registered dietitians; social workers; pharmacists; and chaplains.

Physical therapy focuses on mobility, progressive ambulation, transfer techniques, and equipment needed for mobility. Occupational therapy emphasizes retraining for skills of daily living, including eating, dressing, hygiene, and cooking. Occupational therapists are skilled in cognitive and perceptual evaluation and training. Speech therapy focuses on speech, communication, cognition, and eating abilities.

The rehabilitation nurse assesses the patient, caregiver, and family with attention to the patient's (1) rehabilitation potential, (2) physical status, (3) complications caused by the stroke or other chronic conditions, (4) cognitive status, (5) family resources and support, and (6) expectations related to the rehabilitation program.

Musculoskeletal function. The initial assessment consists of determining the stage of recovery of muscle function. If the muscles are still flaccid several weeks after the stroke, the prognosis for regaining function is poor, and care focuses on preventing further loss.

Most patients begin to show signs of spasticity with exaggerated reflexes within 48 hours after the stroke. Spasticity at this phase denotes progress toward recovery. As improvement continues, small voluntary movements of the hip or shoulder may be accompanied by involuntary movements in the rest of the extremity. The last stage of recovery occurs when the patient has voluntary control of isolated muscle groups.

Interventions advance in a manner of progressive activity. Balance training is the first step. It begins with the patient sitting up in bed or dangling the legs over the edge of the bed. Assess tolerance by noting dizziness or syncope caused by vasomotor instability. Loss of postural stability is common after stroke. When the non-dominant hemisphere is involved, walking apraxia and loss of postural control are usually apparent. The patient may be unable to sit upright and tends to fall sideways. Provide support with pillows or cushions.

Assess whether patients autocorrect their posture when sitting on the edge of the bed. If the patient can straighten their posture instead of leaning to the weaker side, the patient may be ready for the next step of transferring from bed to chair. Place the chair beside the bed so that the patient can lead with the stronger arm and leg. The patient sits on the side of the bed, stands, places the strong hand on the far wheelchair arm, and sits down. You may either supervise the transfer or provide minimal aid by guiding the patient's strong hand to the wheelchair arm, standing in front of the patient while blocking the patient's knees with your knees to prevent knee buckling, and guiding the patient into a sitting position.

In some rehabilitation units, the Bobath method is used as an approach to mobility. The Bobath method helps the patient gain control over spasticity by inhibiting abnormal reflex patterns. Therapists and nurses use the Bobath approach to encourage normal muscle tone, normal movement, and bilateral function of the body. An example is to have the patient transfer into the wheelchair using the weak or paralyzed side and the stronger side to facilitate more bilateral functioning.

Another approach is *constraint-induced movement therapy* (CIMT) (Fig. 62.9). CIMT encourages the patient to use the weakened extremity by restricting movement of the normal extremity. This approach can be challenging for patients. It is used only under the supervision of physical or occupational therapy. Movement training, skill acquisition, stretching, and exercise are other therapies used.[21]

Supportive or assistive equipment, such as canes, walkers, and leg braces, may be needed on a short- or long-term basis for mobility. The physical therapist usually selects the right supportive device(s) to meet individual needs and instructs the patient about use. Include physical therapy activities into the patient's daily routine for added practice and repetition of rehabilitation efforts (Fig. 62.10).

Stroke survivorship and coping. The patient may have many losses, including sensory, intellectual, communicative, functional, role behavior, emotional, social, and vocational losses. The patient, caregiver, and family often go through the process of grief and mourning associated with the losses. Some patients develop long-term depression, with symptoms including anxiety, weight loss, fatigue, poor appetite, and sleep problems. The time and energy needed to perform previously simple tasks can result in anger and frustration.

The magnitude of disability and changes in total function can leave patients wondering if they can ever return to their "old self." Loss of independence may be a major concern. The ability to perform ADLs may require many adaptive changes because of physical, emotional, perceptual, and cognitive deficits. There may be limited family members, including adult children, living nearby to provide help. Patients may become fearful and depressed because they think they may have another stroke or die. The fear can become immobilizing and interfere with effective rehabilitation.

The patient, caregiver, and family need help coping with the losses from the stroke. Provide assistance by (1) supporting communication between the patient and family; (2) discussing lifestyle changes resulting from stroke deficits; (3) discussing changing roles and responsibilities within the family; (4) being an active listener to allow the expression of fear, frustration, and anxiety; (5) including the family and patient in short- and long-term goal planning and patient care; (6) supporting family conferences; and (7) identifying support groups and referrals as needed. Stroke support groups in rehabilitation facilities and the community are helpful in terms of mutual sharing, education, coping skills, and understanding.

Changes may occur in the patient-partner relationship. The dependency resulting from a stroke may threaten the relationship. The partner may be older or have chronic health problems that affect their ability to care for the stroke survivor. The patient may not want anyone other than the partner to provide care, thus putting a significant burden on the partner. There may be

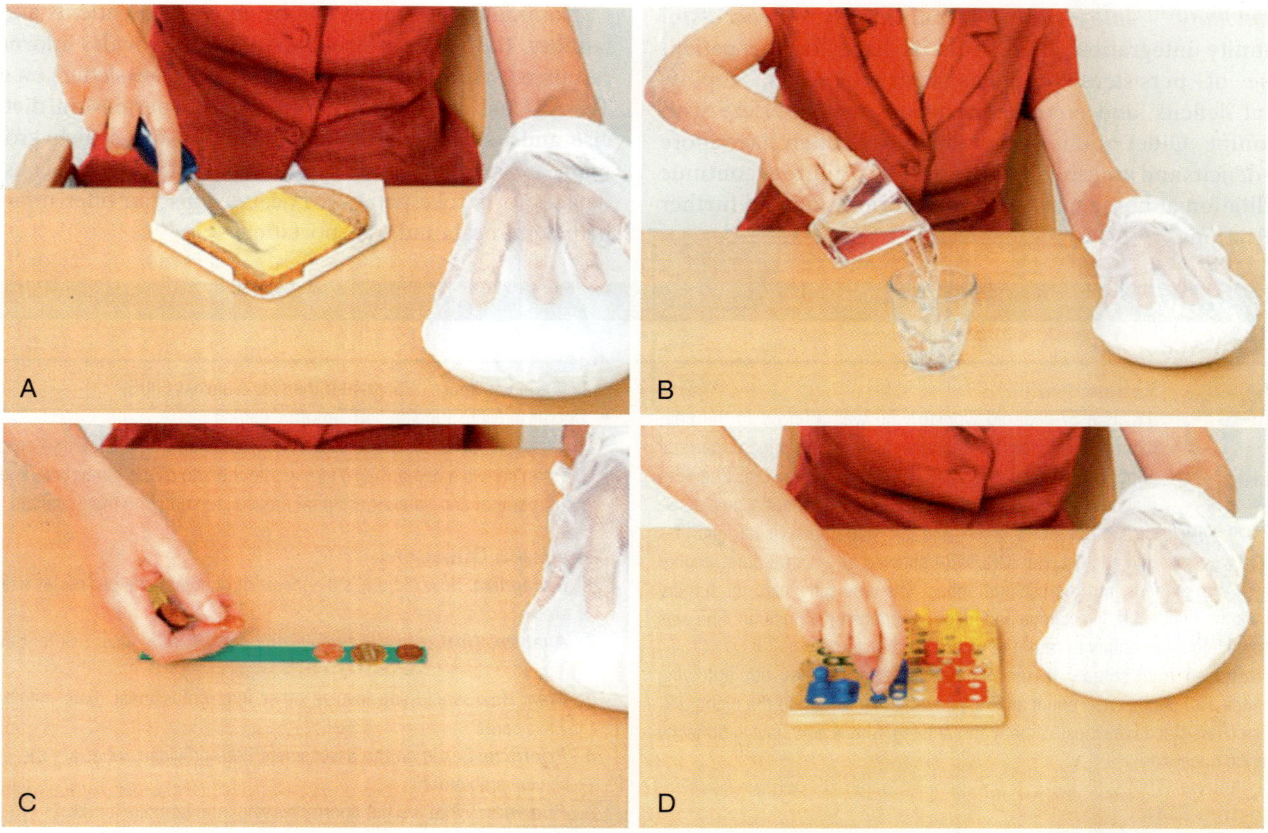

Fig. 62.9 Constraint-induced movement therapy after stroke. (From Kwakkel G, Veerbeek JM, van Wegen EE, et al.: Constraint-induced movement therapy after stroke, *Lancet Neurol* 14:224, 2015. Reprinted with permission from Elsevier.)

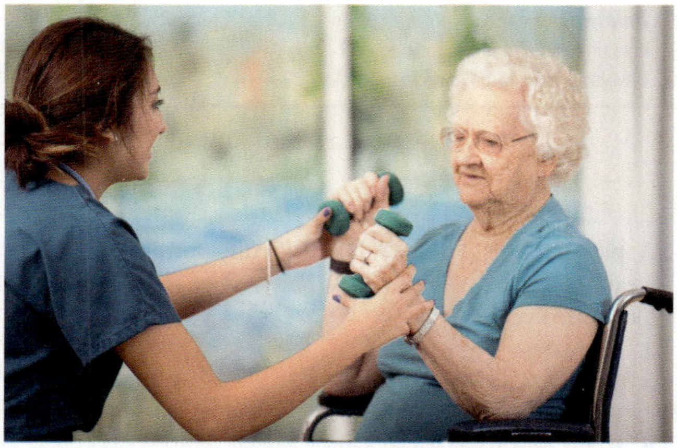

Fig. 62.10 A patient who had a stroke works with a physical therapist to improve arm strength. (© Thinkstock 78783452.)

limited family members, including adult children, living nearby to provide help.

Patients who had a stroke often have emotional responses that are not appropriate or typical for the situation. They may appear apathetic, depressed, fearful, anxious, weepy, frustrated, and angry. Some patients, especially those with a stroke on the left side of the brain (right hemiplegia), have exaggerated mood swings. The patient may be unable to control emotions and suddenly burst into tears or laughter. This behavior is out of context and often unrelated to the patient's underlying emotional state. Interventions for atypical emotional response are to (1) distract the patient who suddenly becomes emotional, (2) explain to the patient and family that emotional outbursts may occur after a stroke, (3) maintain a calm environment, and (4) avoid shaming or scolding the patient during emotional outbursts.

Maladjusted dependence with inadequate coping occurs when the patient does not maintain optimal functioning for self-care, family responsibilities, decision making, or socialization. This situation can cause resentment from both the patient and family with a negative cycle of interpersonal dependency and control. Family therapy is often helpful. Caregivers and family members must cope with 3 aspects of the patient's behavior: (1) recognition of behavioral changes resulting from neurologic deficits that are not changeable, (2) responses to multiple losses by both the patient and family, and (3) behaviors that may have been reinforced during the early stages of stroke as a continued dependency.

Sexual function. A patient who had a stroke may be concerned about the loss of sexual function. Many patients are comfortable talking about their anxieties and fears about sexual function if you are comfortable and open to the topic. You can start a discussion about the topic with the patient and spouse or significant other. Common concerns include impotence and the chance of another stroke occurring during sex. Interventions include teaching about (1) optional positioning of partners, (2) timing for peak energy periods, and (3) patient and partner counseling.

Community integration. Traditionally, successful community integration after stroke is hard for the patient because of persistent problems with cognition, coping, physical deficits, and emotional changes that interfere with functioning. Older adults who had a stroke often have more severe deficits and multiple health problems. Failure to continue rehabilitation at home may result in deterioration and further complications.

Community resources can be an asset to patients and their families. The National Stroke Association provides information, resources, referral services, and quarterly newsletters on stroke. The ASA has information about stroke, hypertension, diet, exercise, and assistive devices. They also sponsor self-help groups in many areas. Easter Seals supplies wheelchairs and other assistive devices for stroke patients. Local groups can offer more daily help with meals and transportation.

Case Study

Stroke

(© iStockphoto/ Thinkstock.)

Patient Profile

J.K. is a 57-year-old woman who was referred to the neurosurgery service for management of a temporal-parietal glioblastoma (see the Case Study in Chapter 60). She was diagnosed after presenting with persistent headaches, a seizure in her HCP's office, and left-side upper visual field loss and neglect. Her MRI/MRA showed a temporal-parietal glioblastoma that extends into the occipital lobes. She was scheduled for surgery to debulk the tumor. J.K. lives alone and holds a management position. She was concerned about her ability to return to work after her surgery.

J.K. returned from surgery to the neurosurgery unit drowsy but following commands. Her pupils were equal and responded to light. During the night, J.K. developed left-sided weakness of both arm and leg. She is now having difficulty answering questions.

Subjective Data

- Left arm and leg are weak and feel numb
- Trying to answer questions but looks confused and cannot follow commands

Objective Data

- BP 150/90 mm Hg
- Right gaze preference
- Left homonymous hemianopsia
- Left arm weakness (3/5) greater than leg weakness (4/5)
- Decreased sensation on both left arm and leg
- Has speech but not clear. Difficulty with word finding and following commands
- CT scan shows a hemorrhagic stroke into the site of the tumor bed, and temporal-parietal and anterior occipital areas extending into the thalamus

Discussion Questions

1. ***Recognize***: How did J.K.'s diagnosis of glioblastoma put her at risk for a stroke?
2. ***Analyze:*** What potential complications is J.K. at highest risk for developing?
3. ***Plan:*** How would you involve other interprofessional team members in J.K.'s care?
4. ***Prioritize:*** Based on the assessment data provided, what are the priority clinical problems?
5. ***Prioritize:*** What are the priority nursing interventions for J.K.?
6. ***Act***: What nursing interventions can you delegate to AP?
7. ***Act:*** What strategies can you implement to improve communication for J.K.?
8. ***Act:*** How can you address J.K.'s concerns about her finances and self-care?
9. ***Safety:*** How can you ensure safety for J.K. in light of her homonymous hemianopsia and left-sided neglect?
10. Develop a conceptual care map for J.K.

Answers available at http://evolve.elsevier.com/Lewis/medsurg.

BRIDGE TO NCLEX EXAMINATION

The number of the question corresponds to the same-numbered outcome at the beginning of the chapter.

1. Which patient has the *highest* risk for having a stroke?
   a. A 45-year-old Native American with obesity
   b. A 65-year-old Black man with hypertension
   c. A 35-year-old Asian American woman who smokes
   d. A 32-year-old White woman taking oral contraceptives
2. The factor related to cerebral blood flow that *most* often determines the extent of cerebral damage from a stroke is the
   a. O_2 content of the blood.
   b. amount of cardiac output.
   c. level of CO_2 in the blood.
   d. degree of collateral circulation.
3. Information provided by the patient that would help distinguish a hemorrhagic stroke from a thrombotic stroke includes
   a. sensory changes.
   b. a history of hypertension.
   c. presence of motor weakness.
   d. sudden onset of severe headache.
4. A patient after a stroke has difficulty finding words and weakness in his right arm. What area of the brain is *most* likely involved?
   a. Brainstem
   b. Vertebral artery
   c. Left middle cerebral artery
   d. Right middle cerebral artery
5. Which test would provide the best initial diagnostic information for a patient who presents to the emergency department with a potential stroke?
   a. Noncontrast head CT
   b. Cerebral angiography
   c. Transcranial doppler ultrasonography
   d. Intraarterial digital subtraction angiography
6. A patient having TIAs is scheduled for a carotid endarterectomy. The nurse explains that the purpose of this procedure is to
   a. decrease cerebral edema.
   b. reduce the brain damage that occurs during a stroke in evolution.

   c. prevent a stroke by removing atherosclerotic plaques blocking cerebral blood flow.
   d. provide a circulatory bypass around thrombotic plaques obstructing cranial circulation.

7. For a patient who is suspected of having a stroke, the *most* important piece of information that the nurse would obtain is
   a. time of the patient's last meal.
   b. time at which stroke symptoms first appeared.
   c. patient's hypertension history and management.
   d. family history of stroke and other cardiovascular diseases.

8. Bladder training in a male patient who has urinary incontinence after a stroke includes
   a. limiting fluid intake.
   b. helping the patient to stand to void.
   c. keeping a urinal in place at all times.
   d. catheterizing the patient every 4 hours.

9. A patient who recently had a stroke is home after one month of rehabilitation. The home care nurse is concerned when the patient says *(select all that apply)*
   a. "I just don't want to do anything anymore."
   b. "My daughter visits twice a day and helps me."
   c. "I just can't sleep at night. I wake up every hour."
   d. "I understand that my atrial fibrillation caused my stroke."
   e. "I have no problem going up the stairs. Why is everyone so worried?"

1. b; 2. d; 3. d; 4. c; 5. a; 6. c; 7. b; 8. b; 9. a, c, e.

For rationales to these answers and even more NCLEX review questions, visit http://evolve.elsevier.com/Lewis/medsurg.

EVOLVE WEBSITE/RESOURCES LIST

http://evolve.elsevier.com/Lewis/medsurg
Review Questions (Online Only)
Key Points
Answer Keys for Questions
- Rationales for Bridge to NCLEX Examination Questions
- Answer Guidelines for Case Study

Student Case Studies
- Patient With Hypertension and Stroke
- Patient With Stroke

eNursing Care Plans
- eNursing Care Plan 62.1: Patient With Stroke

Conceptual Care Map Creator
- Conceptual Care Map for Case Study

Audio Glossary
Content Updates

REFERENCES

1. National Stroke Association (NSA): Stroke survivors. Retrieved from https://www.stroke.org/we-can-help/survivors.
2. Center for Disease Control and Prevention (CDC): Stroke facts. Retrieved from https://www.cdc.gov/stroke/facts.htm.
3. CDC: Causes of death. Retrieved from https://www.cdc.gov/nchs/fastats/leading-causes-of-death.htm.
*4. Arnett DK, Blumenthal RS, Albert MA, et al.: 2019 ACC/AHA Guideline on the primary prevention of cardiovascular disease: a report of the ACC/AHA Task Force on Clinical Practice Guidelines, *J Am Coll Cardiol* 140:e596, 2019.
*5. Abraham G, Malik R, Yonova-Doing E, et al.: Genomic risk score offers predictive performance comparable to clinical risk factors for ischemic stroke, *Nat Commun* 11:1036, 2020.
6. National Institute of Neurological Disorders and Stroke: Brain basics: preventing stroke. Retrieved from https://www.ninds.nih.gov/Disorders/Patient-Caregiver-Education/Preventing-Stroke.
7. AHA/ASA: Transient ischemic attacks. Retrieved from https://www.strokeassociation.org/STROKEORG/AboutStroke/TypesofStroke/TIA/TIA-Transient-Ischemic-Attack_UCM_310942_Article.jsp.
8. NSA: ABCD^2 score. Retrieved from https://www.stroke.org/tia-abcd2-tool/.
9. AHA/ASA: Ischemic strokes. Retrieved from https://www.strokeassociation.org/STROKEORG/AboutStroke/TypesofStroke/IschemicClots/Ischemic-Strokes-Clots_UCM_310939_Article.jsp.
*10. van Rijsbergen MWA, Mark RE, Kop WJ, et al.: Psychological factors and subjective cognitive complaints after stroke: beyond depression and anxiety, *Neuropsychol Rehabil* 29:1671, 2019.
11. Abbott: Amplatzer PFO occluder. Retrieved from https://www.structuralheartsolutions.com/us/index.php?id=104&L=0.
*12. Powers WJ, Rabinstein AA, Ackerson T, et al.: Guidelines for the early management of patients with acute ischemic stroke, *Stroke* 50:e344, 2019.
13. Cleveland Clinic: Mobile stroke unit. Retrieved from https://consultqd.clevelandclinic.org/treatment-on-mobile-stroke-unit-improves-functional-outcomes-in-acute-ischemic-stroke/.
14. AHA: Target: stroke phase III. Retrieved from https://www.heart.org/-/media/files/professional/quality-improvement/target-stroke/target-stroke-phase-iii/9-17-update/ds14860-time-interval-one-pager_v2.pdf?la=en.
*15. Berekashvili K, Zha AM, Abdel-Al M, et al.: Emergency medicine physicians accurately select acute stroke patients for tissue-type plasminogen activator treatment using a checklist, *Stroke* 51:663, 2020.
*16. Khanna O, Sweid A, Mouchtouris N, et al.: Radial artery catheterization for neuroendovascular procedures, *Stroke* 50:2587, 2019.
17. Keigher KM: Large vessel occlusion in the acute stroke patient: identification, treatment, and management, *Crit Care Nurs Clin North Am* 32:21, 2020.
18. Watson J: Subarachnoid hemorrhage surgery. Retrieved from https://emedicine.medscape.com/article/247090-overview.
19. ASA: NIH Stroke Scale International. Retrieved from https://www.nihstrokescale.org.
*20. Park KD, Kim TH, Lee SH: The Gugging Swallowing Screen in dysphagia screening for patients with stroke: a systematic review, *Int J Nurs Stud* 107:103588, 2020.
21. Stinear CM, Lang CE, Zeiler S, et al.: Advances and challenges in stroke rehabilitation, *Lancet Neurol* 19:348, 2020.

*Evidence-based information for clinical practice.

63

Chronic Neurologic Problems

Cynthia Amerson

http://evolve.elsevier.com/Lewis/medsurg/

CONCEPTUAL FOCUS

Cognition
Coping
Functional Ability
Inflammation
Intracranial Regulation
Mobility
Safety

LEARNING OUTCOMES

1. Compare the etiology, clinical manifestations, and interprofessional and nursing management for types of primary headaches.
2. Describe the clinical manifestations, diagnostic studies, and interprofessional and nursing management of seizure disorder and restless legs syndrome.
3. Discern the clinical manifestations and nursing and interprofessional management of multiple sclerosis, Parkinson disease, myasthenia gravis, amyotrophic lateral sclerosis, and Huntington disease.
4. Explain the potential impact of chronic neurologic disease on well-being.
5. Outline the major goals of nursing care for the patient with a chronic, progressive neurologic disease.

KEY TERMS

absence seizure
amyotrophic lateral sclerosis (ALS)
aura
cluster headache
focal-onset seizures
generalized-onset seizures
Huntington disease (HD)
migraine headache
multiple sclerosis (MS)
myasthenia gravis (MG)
myasthenic crisis
Parkinson disease (PD)
restless legs syndrome (RLS)
seizure
seizure disorder
status epilepticus
tension-type headache (TTH)
tonic-clonic seizure

This chapter discusses headaches, chronic neurologic disorders, and degenerative neurologic disorders. Chronic neurologic disorders include seizure disorder and restless legs syndrome (RLS). *Degenerative nerve diseases* lead to nerve damage that worsens as the diseases progress. These neurologic problems have no cure. Treatment aims to reduce symptoms and help the patient maintain optimal function. Many have a genetic basis.

Degenerative nerve diseases include multiple sclerosis (MS), Parkinson disease (PD), myasthenia gravis (MG), amyotrophic lateral sclerosis (ALS), and Huntington disease (HD). They affect many activities, including vision, balance, movement, speech, swallowing, and heart and lung function. Patients with these diseases have similar concerns and problems. They must deal with the disease and its impact on quality of life. Many patients have concerns about safety, mobility, self-care, and coping. Patients and their caregivers often need psychosocial support, especially as the disease progresses and disability worsens.

HEADACHES

Headache is one of the most common types of pain. Most people have functional headaches, such as migraine or tension-type headaches. Others have organic headaches caused by intracranial or extracranial disease.

Pain-sensitive structures in the head include venous sinuses, dura, cranial blood vessels, and some nerves. There are 3 divisions of the trigeminal nerve (cranial nerve [CN] V), facial nerve (CN VII), glossopharyngeal nerve (CN IX), vagus nerve (CN X), and the first 3 cervical nerves. Pain occurs when these structures experience pull, displacement, inflammation, or swelling. Because these nerves have both motor and sensory functions, increased pain intensity and symptoms can occur when a person moves.

We classify headaches as primary or secondary. This is based on the International Headache Society (IHS) guidelines outlining characteristics of headaches.[1] *Primary headaches* include tension-type, migraine, and cluster headaches (Table 63.1). They are not caused by a disease or another medical problem. *Secondary headaches* are caused by another disease or problem, such as sinus infection, neck injury, or brain tumor.

A patient may have more than 1 type of headache. The history and neurologic assessment are key to deciding the type of headache. The assessment is often normal. Unexplained abnormal findings require further diagnostic studies.

TENSION-TYPE HEADACHE

Tension-type headache (TTH), or *stress headache*, is the most common type of headache. It is characterized by its bilateral location and pressing or tightening quality. TTH is usually of

TABLE 63.1 Interprofessional Care

Comparison of Headaches

Tension-Type Headaches	Migraine Headache	Cluster Headache
Location		
Bilateral, bandlike pressure at base of skull	Unilateral in 60%, may switch sides; often anterior location	Unilateral, radiating up or down from 1 eye
Quality		
Constant, squeezing, tightness	Throbbing, synchronous with pulse	Severe, bone crushing
Frequency		
Cycles for many years	Periodic, cycles of several months and years	May have months or years between attacks. Attacks occur in clusters over a period of 2–12 weeks
Duration		
30 min–7 days	4–72 hr	5 min–3 hr
Time and Mode of Onset		
Not related to time	May be preceded by prodromal symptoms or aura Onset after awakening Improves with sleep	Nocturnal, often awakens person from sleep
Associated Symptoms		
Palpable neck and shoulder muscle tension Stiff neck Tenderness	Aura: visual, sensory, aphasic Irritability, sweating Nausea, vomiting Photophobia Phonophobia Prodromal symptoms: sensory, motor, or psychic phenomena	Facial flushing or pallor Unilateral lacrimation, ptosis, rhinitis
Treatment: Abortive and Symptomatic Drugs		
Nonopioid analgesics: aspirin, acetaminophen, NSAIDs Analgesic combinations • butalbital/acetaminophen/caffeine • butalbital/aspirin/caffeine (Fiorinal) Muscle relaxants	α-Adrenergic blockers • ergotamine • dihydroergotamine NSAIDs Serotonin receptor agonists • almotriptan • eletriptan (Relpax) • frovatriptan (Frova) • naratriptan (Amerge) • rizatriptan (Maxalt) • sumatriptan (Imitrex) • zolmitriptan (Zomig) Combination • acetaminophen/caffeine/aspirin • sumatriptan/naproxen (Treximet) CGRP antagonists • Lasmiditan (Reyvow)	α-Adrenergic blockers Serotonin receptor agonists • almotriptan • eletriptan • frovatriptan • naratriptan • rizatriptan • sumatriptan • zolmitriptan High-flow 100% O_2

Continued

TABLE 63.1 Interprofessional Care—cont'd

Comparison of Headaches

Tension-Type Headaches	Migraine Headache	Cluster Headache
Treatment: Preventive		
Antiseizure drugs • topiramate (Topamax) • divalproex (Depakote) β-Adrenergic blockers Botulinum toxin A mirtazapine (Remeron) Muscle relaxation training Selective serotonin reuptake inhibitors • fluoxetine (Prozac) • paroxetine (Paxil) Tricyclic antidepressants • amitriptyline • doxepin • nortriptyline	Antiseizure drugs β-Adrenergic blockers Botulinum toxin A CGRP antagonists Tricyclic antidepressants	α-Adrenergic blockers • ergotamine tartrate Antiseizure drugs • gabapentin • topiramate Corticosteroids CGRP antagonists Lithium verapamil

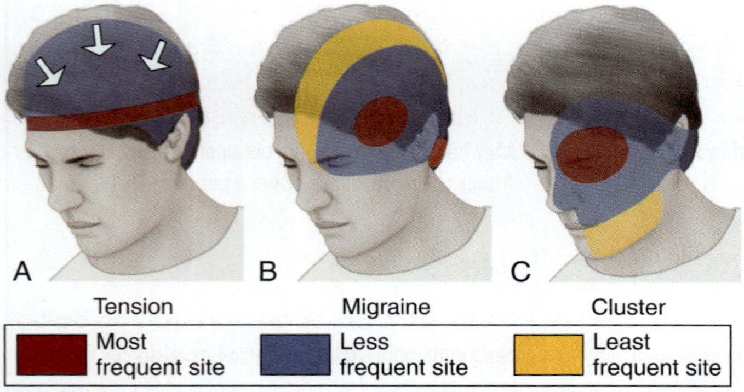

Fig. 63.1 Location of pain for common headache syndromes. (A) Tension headache is often described as feeling of a weight in or on the head or a band squeezing the head. (B) Migraine headache is usually unilateral, in the temple on 1 side of the head. The pain can be bilateral. (C) Cluster headache pain is focused in and around 1 eye.

mild or moderate intensity. It can last from minutes to days. TTHs are divided by frequency into episodic or chronic. Chronic TTH occurs more than 15 days per month. It can lead to decreased quality of life and severe disability.[1]

Etiology and Pathophysiology

We do not know the cause of TTH. It may have a neurobiologic basis similar to migraine headaches. Triggers may include stress, anxiety, or depression. They may develop after exposure to caffeine or smoking. Many patients have tight cervical muscles and general pain in the back, hip, and knees. For some, episodic headaches evolve into chronic headaches. Headaches may occur intermittently for weeks, months, or even years.

Clinical Manifestations

Patients often have a bilateral frontal-occipital headache (Fig. 63.1). They describe the pain as a constant, dull pressure or bandlike. There may be increased cervical and neck muscle tone with neck pain. The patient may have sensitivity to light *(photophobia)* or sound *(phonophobia)*. There is no nausea or vomiting. Activity does not make the pain worse. There are no *prodromal symptoms* (warning symptoms of impending headache). Many patients have a combination of migraine headache and TTH, with features of both occurring together.

TABLE 63.2 Interprofessional Care

Headaches

Diagnostic Assessment

- History and physical assessment
  - Neurologic assessment
  - Inspect for local infection
  - Palpate head for tenderness, bony swellings
  - Auscultate for bruits over major arteries, especially neck
- Laboratory studies
  - CBC
  - Electrolytes
  - Urinalysis
- Diagnostic studies
  - Angiography
  - CT scan, MRA, MRI
  - EEG
  - LP

Management

- Drug therapy (Table 63.1)
- Biofeedback
- Cognitive-behavioral therapy
- Relaxation therapy
- Sleep modification therapy

Diagnostic Studies

The history may be the most useful tool for diagnosing TTH (Table 63.2). If TTH is present during physical assessment, we may see increased resistance to passive movement of the head and head and neck tenderness. Electromyography (EMG) may show sustained contraction of neck, scalp, or facial muscles. However, the patient may not have increased muscle tension

BOX 63.1 BIOLOGIC SEX CONSIDERATIONS

Headaches

Men
- Cluster headaches are 3 to 7 times more common.
- Have more exercise-induced headaches.

Women
- Migraine headaches are 3 times more common.
- Have more tension-type headache.

with an EMG, even during a headache. Imaging is done when symptoms raise concern about a possible pathologic cause.

MIGRAINE HEADACHE

Migraine headache is a recurring headache characterized by unilateral throbbing pain. Migraines are most common between the ages of 25 and 55. One in 4 US households have someone with migraines. Migraines account for up to 5 million emergency room visits a year.[2] The IHS divides migraines into 2 categories: migraine without aura and migraine with aura. Migraine without aura is more common.[1]

Etiology and Pathophysiology

We do not know the exact cause of migraines. They likely result from complex interactions between trigeminal neuron, vascular, genetic, hormonal, and environment factors causing vasodilation and inflammation in the brain.[3] Current theory suggests a complex series of neurovascular events starts the headache. People who have migraines have a state of neuron hyperexcitability in the cerebral cortex, especially in the occipital cortex. Genetics may play a role. 50% of people with migraine have first-degree relatives with the disorder.[3]

Migraines are related to many disorders. These include seizure disorder, ischemic stroke, asthma, depression, anxiety, hypertension, and irritable bowel syndrome.[4] In many cases, migraines have no known precipitating events.[5] Other risk factors include age, female gender, obesity, low education level, and stressful life events (Box 63.1).

For some patients, specific factors may trigger a headache. Triggers include hormone fluctuations, environment factors like bright lights or loud noises, barometric pressure changes, skipping meals, odors, alcohol, depression, lack of sleep, and stress. Common food triggers include caffeine, monosodium glutamate, and high tyramine foods (red wine, aged cheese).[5]

Clinical Manifestations

Prodromal symptoms and an aura may precede the headache phase by several hours or days. Prodromal symptoms occur before the onset of aura or headache. Common prodromal symptoms include a change in activity level, depression, fatigue, pallor, yawning, or difficulty concentrating.[6] Aura occurs in about 25% of patients. An **aura** is a group of neurologic symptoms that occur before a headache begins but may continue into the headache. The symptoms of an aura are completely reversible. There are 3 main types of auras: visual, sensory, and aphasic. Visual symptoms, such as flashes of bright lights, blind spots, distortions, or zigzag lines, are the most common type of aura. Sensory auras may start as tingling or numbness in the fingers or in the mouth, voices that do not exist, or unusual odors. Aphasic aura presents as speech problems.[7]

A migraine may last 4 to 72 hours. Patients often describe the pain as steady, pounding, or throbbing. It is synchronous with the pulse and worsens with movement. The pain is usually unilateral (Fig. 63.1). During the headache, patients may try to avoid noise, light, odors, people, and stress.

! SAFETY ALERT
- A severe headache accompanied by a stiff neck, vomiting, confusion, weakness, double vision, a rash, or difficulty arousing requires emergent evaluation.
- These signs may indicate life-threatening illness.

Diagnostic Studies

The diagnosis is usually based on the history. Neurologic and other diagnostic examinations are often normal (Table 63.2). No specific laboratory or radiologic test can diagnose migraine headache. Neuroimaging techniques (e.g., head CT scan, MRI) are not part of the routine evaluation unless the neurologic assessment is abnormal. If atypical features are present, further testing is done.

CLUSTER HEADACHE

Cluster headache is the most severe form of primary headache. It is classified as a *trigeminal autonomic cephalalgia* (TAC). Cluster headache effects the trigeminal nerve (CN V) and has associated autonomic symptoms (e.g., tears, stuffy nose). Age at onset is often 20 to 50 years, but they can start at any age. They more often affect persons who smoke and men (Box 63.1).[8]

Etiology and Pathophysiology

We do not know the cause nor how cluster headache occurs. Imaging studies show activation of the hypothalamus and trigeminal vascular complex at the onset.[8] There may be a genetic influence. Many attacks occur at night, waking the person 1 to hours after falling asleep. Alcohol, caffeine, and tyramine foods can be diet triggers. Pain often starts within 1 hour of a drink. Strong odors (e.g., gasoline, paint fumes) or getting overheated are other triggers.[9] Cluster headaches may occur at high altitudes when less O_2 is available in the atmosphere.

Clinical Manifestations

Patients have severe, intense pain lasting from 15 minutes to 3 hours. The pain is sharp and stabbing, described as excruciating. It is usually around the eye, radiating to the temple, forehead, cheek, nose, teeth, or jaw along the CN V pathway (Fig. 63.1). Patients have characteristic autonomic features include swelling around the eye, lacrimation (tearing), facial flushing or pallor, nasal congestion or running, and miosis (pupil constriction). During the headache, the patient may be agitated and restless, unable to sit still or relax.[9]

Repeated headaches occur in clusters, recurring regularly. A cluster typically lasts 4 to 12 weeks. Then, the patient goes into remission for months to years. Headaches usually occur at the same time in the day and as often as 8 times a day. Because cluster periods often occur seasonally, headaches may be mistaken for allergy symptoms. About 20% of patients have chronic headaches without pain-free intervals.[9]

Diagnostic Studies

The diagnosis is based on the history.[9] Asking patients to keep a headache diary can be useful. CT scan, MRI, or magnetic resonance angiography (MRA) may rule out an aneurysm, tumor, or infection. A lumbar puncture (LP) may rule out other disorders with similar symptoms (Table 63.2).

OTHER TYPES OF HEADACHES

Other types of headaches can occur. They may be related to external and internal changes (cold, cough, hormone disruption, seasonal). A headache may be from external head trauma or the first symptom of a more serious illness. Headache can occur with subarachnoid hemorrhage, brain tumors, intracranial masses, vascular abnormalities, trigeminal neuralgia, systemic illness (e.g., infection), and eye, nose, or teeth problems. Because of the varied causes of headache, assessment is important. Assess personality, life adjustment, environment, and living situation with the physical assessment.

INTERPROFESSIONAL CARE: HEADACHES

If no systemic disease is the cause, the type of headache guides the therapy. Tables 63.1 and 63.3 show therapies for preventing and managing headaches.

Cognitive-behavioral therapy, sleep modification therapy, and relaxation therapy used alone, or in conjunction with drug therapy, may help some patients (see Chapter 7). Biofeedback involves using physiologic monitoring equipment that gives the patient information about muscle tension and peripheral blood flow. The patient is trained to relax the muscles and raise the finger temperature. Positive reinforcement occurs when the patient makes these changes. Acupuncture, acupressure, and hypnosis are options for some patients.

Drug Therapy

Tension-Type Headache

Drug therapy for TTH usually involves aspirin, acetaminophen, or nonsteroidal antiinflammatory drugs (NSAIDs) used alone or in combination with caffeine, a sedative, or a muscle relaxant. These analgesics may be only partly effective, even with use of the maximum dose. Stronger analgesics provide no added benefit. Tricyclic antidepressants, some antiseizure medications, or muscle relaxants may be used as preventative therapy.

Many of these drugs have serious side effects. Caution the patient about the long-term use of aspirin or aspirin-containing drugs because they can cause gastrointestinal (GI) bleeding and bleeding problems in some patients. Drugs containing acetaminophen can cause kidney damage with chronic use and liver damage when taken in large doses or with alcohol. Psychoactive medications and antiseizure medications may be sedating and interfere with daily activities.

Migraine Headache

The aim of drug treatment in an acute migraine is stopping or decreasing the symptoms. Many people with mild or moderate migraine headache can get relief with NSAIDs, aspirin, or caffeine-containing analgesics. For moderate to severe headache pain, triptans are the first line of therapy (Table 63.1).[2]

Triptans (e.g., sumatriptan) affect selected serotonin receptors. They reduce neurogenic inflammation of cerebral blood vessels and cause vasoconstriction. Some patients respond better to certain triptans than to others. Triptans are most effective when taken at the start of a migraine headache or during the aura. Sumatriptan is available in several dosage forms and delivery systems (oral, subcutaneous, nasal spray, transdermal). It is also the only ultrafast-acting triptan. A combination of oral sumatriptan and naproxen sodium (Treximet) is more effective for symptom relief than either drug alone. Because triptans cause vasoconstriction, they are contraindicated for people with heart disease (e.g., angina, myocardial infarction, hypertension) or stroke.[2]

When triptans are contraindicated or ineffective, we can give other drugs (Table 63.1). Vasoconstrictors used to treat acute migraine include dihydroergotamine (Dhe 45) and other ergot-based agents. Patients with cardiovascular disease or those taking other vasoconstrictors should use these drugs cautiously.[2] The serotonin (5-HT) receptor agonist lasmiditan (Reyvow) increases serotonin and reduces inflammation and pain during a migraine.[8]

DRUG ALERT

Sumatriptan (Imitrex)

- Should not be used by patients with a history of:
  - Ischemic cardiac, cerebrovascular, or peripheral vascular problems.
  - Uncontrolled hypertension (may increase BP).
- Excess dosage may cause tremor and decrease respirations.

Preventive treatment is important in managing migraine headache. The decision to start preventive treatment is made based on frequency, severity, and disability related to headaches. Patients with migraine may take preventative drugs if they must take triptans more than 3 days a week for migraine symptoms. Several different classes of drugs are used.

Antiseizure drugs (e.g., topiramate, divalproex, valproate) may be taken daily for migraine prevention. Common side effects include hypoglycemia and cognitive changes. They take 2 to 3 months to reach full effectiveness. Antiseizure drugs should never be abruptly stopped because seizures may develop. We must provide thorough teaching to promote safe use. Extended-release forms promote adherence, with fewer cognitive effects.[3]

Commonly prescribed β-adrenergic blockers include propranolol (Inderal), metoprolol (Lopressor), and atenolol (Tenormin). They should be used cautiously in patients with asthma and diabetes. Tricyclic antidepressants like amitriptyline are another option.

Botulinum toxin A (Botox) may be an effective prophylactic treatment for adults who have chronic migraines at least 15 days each month or migraines that do not respond to other medications. Botox is given by multiple injections around the head and neck into the pain fibers involved in headaches. Maximum benefit may not be seen for up to 6 months. During this time, the patient should continue their regular medications. Injections are usually given every 3 months. The most common reactions are neck pain and headache. A slight risk exists for the toxin to migrate to other areas of the face and neck, causing swallowing and breathing difficulties. Teach the patient to seek immediate medical attention if this occurs.

CGRP antagonists block the effect of CGRP. CGRP is a small protein involved with pain transmission. It is highly prevalent in the sensory nerves that supply the head and neck. Levels increase during a migraine attack. Injectable agents include erenumab (Aimovig), fremanezumab (Ajovy), and galcanezumab (Emgality).[8] Ubrogepant (Ubrelvy) is given orally.

Other prophylactic treatments for migraine include supraorbital transcutaneous electrical stimulation, vagal nerve stimulation (VNS), and single pulse transcranial magnetic stimulation. These treatments use energy stimulation to prevent headache.[10] Herbal treatments that may be helpful in migraine prophylaxis include riboflavin, coenzyme Q10, magnesium, melatonin, and feverfew.[11]

Cluster Headache

Triptans (e.g., sumatriptan, zolmitriptan) are the standard of treatment for occasional cluster headache. Nasal administration or subcutaneous injection is appropriate. As discussed earlier, they are contraindicated for some patients. Options for patients with refractory cluster headaches include invasive nerve blocks, deep brain stimulation (DBS), vagal or trigeminal stimulators, and ablative neurosurgical procedures (e.g., percutaneous radiofrequency).[3]

High-flow 100% O_2 by non-rebreather mask is well-tolerated, safe, and effective as an alternative treatment. O_2 delivered at a rate of 7 to 12 L/min for 20 minutes may relieve headache by causing vasoconstriction and reducing inflammation in the brain. Treatment can be repeated after a 5-minute rest.

Those with chronic cluster headache often seek preventive treatment. High-dose verapamil is the first-choice drug to prevent cluster headache. The patient needs careful monitoring during treatment. An electrocardiogram (ECG) should be done with every dose increase and every 6 months.

Other Headaches

Patients with frequent headaches may overuse drugs used for headache treatment. *Medication overuse headache* (MOH) is the term used to describe a new type of headache or marked worsening of a preexisting headache condition. Drugs known to cause this problem are acetaminophen, aspirin, NSAIDs (e.g., ibuprofen), triptans, barbiturates, and ergotamine.[1,2,8] MOH often occurs daily and is present on wakening. Patients may have nausea, restlessness, weakness, lack of energy, decreased memory, difficulty concentrating, depression, and irritability. Treatment involves stopping the offending drug and using alternative agents, such as amitriptyline.

TABLE 63.3 NURSING ASSESSMENT
Headaches

Subjective Data

Important Health Information

Health history: Seizures, cancer, recent fall or other trauma, cranial infection, stroke. Asthma or allergies. Relationship of headache to overwork, stress, menstruation, exercise, food, sexual activity, travel, bright lights, or noxious environmental stimuli

Medications: Hydralazine, bromides, nitroglycerin, ergotamine (withdrawal), NSAIDs (in high daily doses), estrogen preparations, oral contraceptives, OTC medications

Surgical interventions or other treatments: Craniotomy, sinus surgery, facial surgery

Functional Health Pattern

Health perception–health management: Positive family history. Malaise

Nutritional-metabolic: Ingesting alcohol, caffeine, cheese, chocolate, monosodium glutamate, aspartame, lunch meats (nitrites in cured meats), sausage, hot dogs, onions, avocados. Anorexia, nausea, vomiting (migraine premonitory symptom); unilateral lacrimation (cluster)

Activity-exercise: Vertigo, fatigue, weakness, paralysis, fainting

Sleep-rest: Insomnia

Cognitive-perceptual

- *Tension type:* Bilateral, bandlike, dull and persistent, base-of-skull headache, neck tenderness
- *Migraine:* Aura. Unilateral, severe, throbbing headache (possible switching of side). Vision changes, photophobia, phonophobia, dizziness, tingling or burning sensations
- *Cluster:* Unilateral and severe, nocturnal headache. Nasal stuffiness

Self-perception–self-concept: Depression

Coping–stress tolerance: Stress, anxiety, irritability, withdrawal

Objective Data

General

Anxiety, apprehension

Musculoskeletal

Resistance of head and neck movement, nuchal rigidity (meningeal, tension type), palpable neck and shoulder muscle tension (tension type)

Neurologic

Restlessness (cluster), hemiparesis (migraine)

Skin

Migraine: Generalized edema (premonitory symptom) pallor, diaphoresis

Cluster: Forehead diaphoresis, pallor, unilateral facial flushing with cheek/eye edema, conjunctivitis

Possible Diagnostic Findings

Evidence of disease, deformity, or infection on brain imaging (CT, MRI, MRA), cerebral angiogram, LP, EEG, EMG

❖ NURSING MANAGEMENT: HEADACHES

◆ Assessment

Table 63.3 outlines subjective and objective data to obtain from a patient with headaches. The history is key and focused on specific details of the headaches. Include location and type of pain, onset, frequency, duration, relation to events (emotional, psychologic, physical), and time of day of the occurrence. A thorough history may suggest headache is due to other problems or drug therapies.

Ask the patient to keep a diary of headaches with specific details. This can help identify the type of headache and precipitating events. Avoiding diet triggers is helpful for most patients with cluster and migraine headache. If there is a history of primary headache, ask if the character, intensity, or location of the headache has changed. The answer may be an important clue about the cause of the headache.

◆ Clinical Problems

Clinical Problems for the patient with headaches may include:

- Pain
- Deficient knowledge

Additional information on clinical problems and interventions is presented in eNursing Care Plan 63.1 for the patient with headaches (available on the website for this chapter).

◆ Planning

The overall goals are that the patient with headaches will (1) have reduced or no pain, (2) understand triggering events and treatments, (3) use positive coping strategies to deal with pain, and (4) have increased quality of life and decreased disability.

◆ Implementation

Patients benefit from engaging in stress reduction techniques.[9] An inability to cope with daily stresses can cause headaches. Effective treatment may involve helping the patient examine the daily routine, recognize stressful situations, and develop effective coping strategies. Help the patient identify precipitating factors and develop ways to avoid or minimize them. Encourage daily exercise, relaxation periods, and socialization as ways to decrease headaches. Suggest meditation, yoga, biofeedback, and other ways to reduce stress and address headache pain. Encourage a consistent daily routine with adequate sleep and regular well-balanced meals.[12]

Table 63.4 shows a teaching guide for the patient with headaches. Teach the patient about drugs prescribed for preventive and symptomatic treatment. Encourage the patient with migraines to seek a quiet, dimly lit environment. Massage and cool or hot packs or cool packs to the neck and head can help.

Provide diet teaching if headaches are triggered by food. Encourage the patient to eliminate foods that may provoke headaches. Active challenge testing (designed specifically to provoke symptoms) with suspect foods may help determine specific causative agents.

◆ Evaluation

Expected outcomes are that the patient with headaches will:

- Report satisfaction with pain management
- Use measures appropriately to manage pain
- Report an increase in quality of life

TABLE 63.4 PATIENT & CAREGIVER TEACHING

Headaches

Include the following instructions when teaching the patient with headaches and the patient's caregiver:

1. Keep a diary or calendar of headaches and possible precipitating events.
2. Avoid possible headache triggers:
   - Drugs, such as ergot-containing preparations (ergotamine tartrate) and monoamine oxidase inhibitors
   - Fatigue
   - Foods
     - Alcohol (especially red wine)
     - Amines (cheese, chocolate)
     - Aspartame
     - Caffeine
     - Fermented or marinated foods, vinegar
     - Ice cream
     - Monosodium glutamate
     - Nitrites (meats, such as hot dogs)
     - Onions
     - Oranges
     - Tomatoes
   - Nicotine
3. Learn the purpose, action, dosage, and side effects of drugs taken.
4. Self-administer sumatriptan nasally or subcutaneously, if prescribed.
5. Use stress management techniques (see Chapter 7).
6. Take part in regular exercise.
7. Avoid smoking and exposure to environmental triggers, such as strong perfumes.
8. Contact HCP if any of the following occur:
   - Symptoms become more severe, last longer than usual, or are resistant to medication
   - Nausea and vomiting (if severe or not typical), change in vision, or fever occurs with the headache
   - Problems occur with any drugs

CHRONIC NEUROLOGIC DISORDERS

Seizure Disorder

A **seizure** is a sudden abnormal, excessive, electrical discharge of neurons in the brain. During a seizure, multiple neurons fire at a rate much faster than normal, causing involuntary movements, sensory phenomena, emotional expression, and unusual behaviors.[13] Seizures may accompany a variety of disorders or occur without any apparent cause.

Seizure disorder, or *epilepsy,* is a group of neurologic diseases marked by recurring seizures. If a person has 2 or more seizures more than 24 hours apart without an underlying problem that caused the seizure, they may have seizure disorder. Seizures from systemic and metabolic problems are not seizure disorder if they stop when the underlying problem is corrected.

It is the 4th most common neurologic disorder. About 3.4 million or 1.2% of Americans have seizure disorder. 1 in 26 people will develop seizure disorder during their lifetime.[14] It effects men and women of all ages, races, and ethnic backgrounds.[15]

Etiology and Pathophysiology

For most persons, the cause of seizure disorder is unknown. These cases are known as *idiopathic generalized epilepsy*

(IGE). Known causes include stroke, brain tumors, cerebral infection, traumatic brain injury, hypoxic birth injury, neurodevelopmental disorders (e.g., autism spectrum disorders), or neurodegenerative disease (e.g., Alzheimer).[15] Other common causes include low or very high glucose levels, abnormal serum electrolytes (sodium, magnesium, calcium), eclampsia with pregnancy, lack of sleep, and alcohol withdrawal. Children may have seizures with high fever. Medical problems that may cause seizures include hypertension, sepsis, and heart, lung, liver, or kidney diseases. Immune factors may influence seizure disorder. Patients with autoimmune disease, like systemic lupus erythematosus (SLE) and MS, have inflammatory changes in the brain increasing seizure risk. Research into the role of neural antibodies and seizures is ongoing.

Seizure disorder is characterized by a group of abnormal neurons that seem to fire without a clear cause. This may happen due to the release of excitatory neurotransmitters or by an absence of neuroinhibitory activity. Both allow abnormal excitement of neurons, leading to excessive discharge of electrical activity. Any stimulus that causes the neuron's cell membrane to depolarize can cause this firing which spreads by physiologic pathways. Localizing the *seizure focus* (the place where the seizure originates) is critical to the success of any surgical treatment.

Genetic Link

One or more genetic abnormalities affect up to 70% of people with seizure disorder.[13] Seizure disorder can develop from the interaction between genetics and the environment. Some genetic diseases cause brain malformations that lead to a seizure disorder. Gene mutations that cause a low seizure threshold, a change in nutrient metabolism, or neural migration in brain development can lead to seizure disorder. Patients with chromosomal disorders (e.g., Down syndrome) often have seizure disorder.[13]

Clinical Manifestations

Specific manifestations of seizure are determined by the site of the electrical disturbance. The International League Against Epilepsy has developed a classification system for seizures. This system divides seizures into 3 major classes based on where the seizure activity begins: *generalized onset, focal onset*, and unknown onset.[16] 60% of patients have focal seizures (Table 63.5). Seizures within each classification as *motor* or *nonmotor* and by level of awareness. These descriptors address what occurs during the seizure. It may not be easy to figure out what type of seizure a patient is having. Seizures may begin with a single focus but may spread and become generalized throughout the brain.

Depending on the type, a seizure may occur in 4 phases: (1) *prodromal phase,* with sensations or behavior changes that precede a seizure by hours or days; (2) *aural phase,* with a sensory warning that is similar each time a seizure occurs and is part of the seizure; (3) *ictal phase,* from 1st symptoms to the end of seizure activity; and (4) *postictal phase,* the recovery period after the seizure. Not all patients have every phase.

TABLE 63.5 Classification of Seizures

Generalized Onset Seizure
(Involves both hemispheres of brain)
- Motor seizure
  - Atonic
  - Clonic
  - Epileptic spasms
  - Myoclonic
  - Myoclonic-atonic
  - Myoclonic-tonic-clonic
  - Tonic
  - Tonic-clonic
- Nonmotor (Absence) seizure
  - Typical
  - Atypical
  - Myoclonic
  - Eyelid myoclonia

Focal-Onset Seizure
(Limited to 1 hemisphere of brain)
- Aware (no impairment of awareness/consciousness)
- Impaired awareness (impairment of awareness/consciousness)
- Motor onset
  - Automatisms
  - Atonic
  - Clonic
  - Epileptic spasms
  - Hyperkinetic
  - Myoclonic
  - Tonic
- Nonmotor onset
  - Autonomic
  - Behavior arrest
  - Cognitive
  - Emotional
  - Sensory

Unknown Onset Seizure
(Due to inadequate information or inability to assign to other categories above)

Adapted from Fisher RS, Cross JH, D'Souza C, et al.: Instruction manual for the ILAE 2017 operational classification of seizure types, *Epilepsia* 58:4, 2017.

Generalized-Onset Seizures

Generalized-onset seizures start over wide areas of both sides of the brain. They are characterized by bilateral, synchronous neural discharges. In most cases, the patient has impaired consciousness for a few seconds to several minutes. Generalized seizures are either motor or nonmotor. Motor movements are bilateral.

Tonic-clonic seizure. **Tonic-clonic seizure** (formerly called grand mal) is the most common generalized-onset motor seizure. During a tonic-clonic seizure, the patient loses consciousness and, if upright, falls to the ground. The body stiffens (tonic phase) for 10 to 20 seconds and then the extremities jerk (clonic phase). This may last 30 to 40 seconds up to several minutes. Cyanosis, excessive salivation, tongue or cheek biting, and incontinence may occur during the seizure.

In the postictal phase, the patient usually has muscle soreness, feels tired, and may sleep for several hours. Some patients do not feel normal for several hours or days after a seizure. The patient has no memory of the seizure.

Other generalized-onset motor seizures. Other types of generalized-onset motor seizures include tonic and clonic. A tonic seizure involves a sudden onset of increased tone in the extensor muscles, contributing to sudden stiff movements. Tonic seizures most often occur in sleep and affect both sides of the body. Patients will fall if they are standing when the seizure occurs. Tonic seizures usually last less than 20 seconds. The patient usually stays aware. Clonic seizures begin with loss of awareness and sudden loss of muscle tone, followed by rhythmic limb jerking that may or may not be symmetric.

A generalized *atonic seizure* (or *drop attack*) involves a brief, sudden loss of tone. It may affect just the head and neck or result in the person falling to the ground. Seizures typically last a few seconds. There is a brief loss of consciousness and a brief post ictal confusion. Patients with atonic seizure are at great risk for head injury. They often need protective helmets.

Generalized-onset nonmotor (absence) seizures. Absence seizure most often occurs in children. They rarely occur beyond adolescence. This type of seizure occurs more often in girls. It usually begins between ages 4 and 8. They may stop altogether as the child matures or evolve into another type of seizure. A *typical absence seizure* is marked by a sudden onset brief staring spell that resembles daydreaming and sudden recovery. It often goes unnoticed because it lasts less than 10 to 20 seconds. Usually, the patient is unresponsive when spoken to during the seizure.[3]

In *atypical absence seizure,* the staring spell is accompanied by other signs and symptoms, such as eye blinking or jerking movements of the lips and repetitive finger movements (automatisms). This type of seizure often lasts as much as 30 seconds, with a gradual beginning and end. If the patient has existing cognitive problems, it may be hard to tell seizure activity from usual behavior. Atypical absence seizures usually continue into adulthood.

Focal-Onset Seizures

Focal-onset seizures (formerly called *partial* or *partial focal seizures*) are the other major class of seizures (Table 63.5). Focal seizures begin in 1 hemisphere of the brain in a localized region of the cortex. They cause sensory, motor, cognitive, or emotional manifestations based on the function of the involved area of the brain. For example, if the discharging focus is in the medial aspect of the postcentral gyrus, the patient may have paresthesia in the leg on the side opposite the focus. This can help discern the type of seizure.

Focal seizures are motor or nonmotor. Motor activities include atonic (loss of tone, relaxed muscles), tonic (sustained stiffening), clonic (rhythmic jerking), or myoclonic (very rapid, irregular, brief jerking).[8] Some people show strange behavior, such as lip smacking, picking at clothes, or other repetitive, purposeless actions (automatisms). With a focal nonmotor seizure, the patient can have emotional manifestations or autonomic symptoms.[13]

A patient with focal-onset seizure may be described as aware or impaired awareness. In *focal awareness seizures*, patients are conscious and alert, but have unusual feelings or sensations. They may have sudden and unexplainable feelings of joy, anger, sadness, or nausea. They may hear, smell, taste, see, or feel things that are not real. Some have localized twitching.

In a *focal impaired awareness seizure*, patients have a loss of consciousness or a change in awareness producing a dreamlike state. Their eyes are open. They make movements that may seem purposeful, but they cannot interact with others. During a seizure, some people may do things that can be dangerous or embarrassing, such as walking into traffic or removing their clothes. They may continue an activity started before the seizure, such as counting coins or choosing items from a grocery shelf. After the seizure they do not remember the activity performed during the seizure. Seizures usually last 1 to 2 minutes. Patients may be tired or confused after the seizure and not return to normal activity for hours. The degree of awareness can be unspecified.

Psychogenic Nonepileptic Seizures

Psychogenic nonepileptic seizures (PNES) imitate seizures but are triggered by emotional events not neuronal activity. Because of the close resemblance, we may misdiagnose PNES as seizure disorder. Proper diagnosis usually requires video-EEG monitoring during the attack.[13] A history of emotional or physical abuse or a specific traumatic event often emerges. Treatment includes cognitive behavioral therapy and serotonin reuptake inhibitors.[13]

Complications

Physical

People with seizure disorder have a higher mortality rate than the general population. Severe injury, or death, can result from trauma suffered during a seizure. Patients who lose consciousness during a seizure are at greatest risk. Other deaths are due to accidents during seizures, death from an underlying disease, sudden unexpected death in epilepsy (SUDEP), or status epilepticus.

Status epilepticus (SE) is a state of continuous seizure activity. We define SE as any seizure lasting longer than 5 minutes or occurring so close together the patient cannot recover between them.[17] The patient does not return to consciousness between seizures. The longer a seizure lasts, the less likely it is to stop without drug therapy.

SE is a neurologic emergency. It can occur with any type of seizure. The highest incidence occurs in children and older adults. In adults it is most common with stroke, metabolic problems, or low therapeutic levels of seizure medications. Most patients who have SE do not have a history of seizure disorder.[13]

During repeated seizures, the brain uses more energy than the body can supply. As neurons become exhausted and cease to function, permanent brain damage may result. *Convulsive status epilepticus* (CSE) is the most common form. It occurs with prolonged or repeated tonic-clonic or other motor seizures. The goal of therapy is to rapidly end clinical and electrical seizure activity before neuronal damage occurs. Without effective, prompt treatment, CSE can lead to respiratory insufficiency, hypoxemia, dysrhythmias, hyperthermia, and systemic acidosis. The prognosis is related to the cause, length of the seizures, patient's age, and time to treatment.[13]

We use the term *nonconvulsive status epilepticus* to describe long or repeated focal impaired awareness seizures. Symptoms may be subtle, making it hard to tell recovery from seizure symptoms.

Refractory status epilepticus (RSE) is continuous seizure activity despite administration of first- and second-line therapy. RSE has a high risk for mortality and neurologic damage. This highlights the need for rapid escalation of treatment for CSE to avoid progression. *Super refractory SE* is a refractory condition that continues or recurs 24 hours or more after starting anesthesia treatment. It also includes cases in which seizure activity returns after withdrawal of anesthesia drugs or persists after 7 days of continuous general anesthesia.

Subclinical seizures are a form of SE in which a sedated patient seizes but there are no external signs because of sedative use. For example, a patient under sedation for ventilatory support in the intensive care unit (ICU) could have a seizure without physical movements and we miss the seizure occurrence.

SUDEP affects about 1.6 in 1000 persons with uncontrolled seizures each year.[18] Most cases occur during or right after a seizure. It is most often from tonic-clonic seizures. SUDEP is more common at night, in those taking multiple antiseizure drugs, and in patients with poorly managed seizure activity. We think that people who acquire seizure disorder at a young age or who drink alcohol are higher at risk. We do not know the exact cause. Ictal and postictal apnea and hypoxia are believed to play a role.[18] Specific teaching about medication adherence and disease awareness is critical for at-risk people.

Psychosocial

Perhaps the most common complication of seizure disorder is the effect on a patient's lifestyle. Patients may have psychosocial problems related to having chronic seizures. An increased incidence of depression occurs in people who have seizures that are difficult to control.

A diagnosis of seizure disorder carries a social stigma. Patients may be victims of discrimination in employment and educational opportunities. Transportation may be difficult if state law does not allow the person to drive. Screen patients often for depression. Encourage them to pursue available treatment options.

Diagnostic Studies

The most useful diagnostic tool is an accurate, comprehensive description of seizures and the patient's health history (Table 63.6). If a patient is diagnosed with seizure disorder, the seizure type must be correctly identified to determine the correct treatment.

The EEG is useful if it shows abnormalities. Abnormal findings help determine the type of seizure and pinpoint the seizure focus. An EEG should be done within 24 hours of a suspected seizure. Only a small number of patients with seizure disorder have abnormal EEG findings the first time they have an EEG.

TABLE 63.6 Interprofessional Care

Seizure Disorder

Diagnostic Assessment

History and Physical Assessment
- Health history
  - Birth and developmental
  - Significant illnesses and injuries
  - Family history
- Febrile seizures
- Comprehensive neurologic assessment
- Seizure history
- Precipitating factors
- Antecedent events
- Seizure description (aura, onset, duration, frequency, postictal state)

Diagnostic Studies
- CBC, metabolic panel
- Urinalysis
- LP for CSF analysis
- CT, MRI, MRA, MRS, PET scan
- EEG

Management
- Antiseizure drugs (Table 63.8)
- Surgery
- Vagal nerve stimulation
- Deep brain stimulation
- Responsive neurostimulation
- Counseling
- Physical therapy

Repeated EEGs, continuous EEG monitoring, or video-EEG may be needed to detect abnormalities. Many patients with seizure disorder have normal EEG results between seizures. Magnetoencephalography (MEG) may be done with the EEG. MEG has greater sensitivity in detecting small magnetic fields of neuron activity.

A complete blood count (CBC), serum chemistries, liver and kidney function tests, and urinalysis assess for metabolic problems. A CT scan or MRI should be done in any new-onset seizure to rule out a structural lesion. If an MRI shows a spot or lesion but EEG results differ, MEG can see if the brain waves are coming from the lesion. Other imaging tests (e.g., PET, SPECT) or angiography may be done in some situations.

Interprofessional Care

Most seizures do not require emergency medical care because they are self-limiting and rarely cause injury (Table 63.6). However, if SE or injury occurs, or if the event is a first-time seizure, medical care should be sought immediately. Table 63.7 outlines emergency care of the patient with a tonic-clonic seizure.

Drug Therapy

The main treatment for seizure disorder is antiseizure drugs (Table 63.8). Because a cure is not possible, the goal of therapy is to prevent seizures with minimal drug side effects. Most drugs

TABLE 63.7 EMERGENCY MANAGEMENT

Tonic-Clonic Seizures

Etiology

Drug-Related
- Ingestion, inhalation
- Overdose
- Withdrawal of alcohol, opioids, antiseizure drugs

Head Trauma
- Cerebral contusion
- Epidural hematoma
- Intracranial hematoma
- Subdural hematoma
- Traumatic birth injury

Idiopathic

Infection
- Encephalitis
- Meningitis
- Sepsis

Intracranial Events
- Brain tumor
- Hypertensive crisis
- Increased ICP due to clogged shunt
- Stroke
- Subarachnoid hemorrhage

Medical Problems
- Heart, liver, lung, or kidney disease
- SLE

Metabolic Problems
- Fluid and electrolyte imbalance
- Hypoglycemia

Other
- Cardiac arrest
- High fever
- Psychiatric problems

Assessment Findings

Aural Phase
- Bowel and bladder incontinence
- Diaphoresis
- Loss of consciousness
- Pallor, flushing, or cyanosis
- Peculiar sensations that precede seizure
- Tachycardia
- Warm skin

Tonic Phase
- Continuous muscle contractions

Hypertonic Phase
- Extreme muscular rigidity lasting 5–15 sec

Clonic Phase
- Rigidity and relaxation alternating in rapid succession

Postictal Phase
- Altered level of consciousness, lethargy
- Confusion and headache
- Repeated tonic-clonic seizures for several min

Interventions

Initial
- Ensure patent airway.
- Protect patient from injury during seizure. Do not restrain. Pad side rails.
- Remove sharp objects and glasses.
- Never force anything between patient's clenched teeth.
- Remove or loosen tight clothing.
- Establish IV access.
- Stay with patient until seizure has passed.
- Anticipate giving phenytoin, benzodiazepines (e.g., diazepam, midazolam, lorazepam) to try to stop seizures.
- Suction as needed.
- Assist ventilations if patient does not breathe spontaneously after seizure.
- Anticipate need for intubation.

Ongoing Monitoring
- Monitor vital signs, level of consciousness, O_2 saturation, Glasgow Coma Scale results, pupil size and reactivity.
- Reassure and orient patient after seizure.
- Give IV dextrose for hypoglycemia.
- Maintain NPO till awake with gag reflex.

stabilize nerve cell membranes and prevent spread of the epileptic discharge. Therapy should begin with a single drug based on the patient's age, weight, and type, frequency, and cause of seizure. Dosage should be increased until seizures are under control or toxic side effects occur. Antiseizure drugs successfully control seizures for about 70% of patients. The other 30% do not respond to antiseizure drugs. They have *medically refractory epilepsy* (drug resistant epilepsy).

If seizure control is not achieved with a single drug, we can change the dose or timing of administration or add a second drug. About one-third of patients need combination therapy for control. Patients should discuss their treatment with the HCP. Our goal is to provide the best control with the least amount of medication. Each drug has a therapeutic range. Above that range, most patients have toxic side effects, and below that range, most continue to have seizures. Therapeutic drug ranges are guides for therapy. If seizures are well controlled with a subtherapeutic level, the dose does not have to be increased. Likewise, if a drug level is above the therapeutic range and the patient has good seizure control without toxic side effects, the dose does not have to be decreased. Drug levels are monitored if seizures continue to occur, frequency increases, or drug adherence is questioned. Because they have a large therapeutic range, many newer drugs do not require drug-level monitoring.

The main drugs to treat tonic-clonic and focal-onset seizures are phenytoin, carbamazepine (Tegretol), and divalproex (Depakote). The drugs used most often to treat generalized onset nonmotor and myoclonic seizures include ethosuximide (Zarontin), divalproex, and clonazepam (Klonopin). Treatments for focal seizures are carbamazepine, lamotrigine (Lamictal), or levetiracetam (Keppra). Pregabalin (Lyrica) is an added treatment for focal aware or impaired awareness seizures not successfully controlled with 1 medication. Table 63.8 lists other drugs used for seizure treatment. Some drugs are effective for multiple seizure types.

TABLE 63.8 **Drug Therapy**

Select Antiseizure Agents

Drug	Route	Side Effects	Considerations
GABA Analogs			
gabapentin (Neurontin)	PO	Ataxia Dizziness Drowsiness Vision changes Weight gain	Monitor weight. Avoid pregnancy. Use safety measures if CNS effects occur. Avoid alcohol.
pregabalin (Lyrica)	PO	Dizziness Drowsiness Edema Vision problems Weight gain	Avoid pregnancy. Use safety measures if CNS effects occur. Avoid alcohol. Monitor weight.
vigabatrin (Sabril)	PO	Dizziness Drowsiness Impaired memory Vision changes	Stop if vision changes occur. Avoid pregnancy. Use safety measures if CNS effects occur. Avoid alcohol.
Hydantoins			
phenytoin (Dilantin) fosphenytoin (Cerebyx, Sesquient)	IV, PO IM, IV	Ataxia Drowsiness GI distress Gingival hyperplasia Liver toxicity Nystagmus Rash	Avoid alcohol, direct sunlight. Monitor drug levels. Monitor site when giving IV. Monitor CBC and liver function tests. May change urine color to pink or red-brown. Maintain good oral hygiene.
Iminostilbenes			
carbamazepine (Tegretol) oxcarbazepine (Trileptal)	PO PO	Bleeding Dizziness Gait changes GI distress Headache Rash Vision problems	Take with meals; avoid grapefruit juice. Avoid direct sunlight. Monitor drug levels, CBC, and liver function tests. Avoid pregnancy. Use safety measures if CNS effects occur. Avoid alcohol.
Miscellaneous			
brivaracetam (Briviact)	IV, PO	Dizziness GI distress Suicidal thoughts	Avoid alcohol. Monitor for depression.
cenobamate (Xcopri)	PO	Dizziness Drowsiness Suicidal thoughts Vision problems	Use safety measures if CNS effects occur. Monitor for depression. Avoid alcohol.
clonazepam (Klonopin)	PO	Confusion Dizziness Drowsiness	Do not stop suddenly. Use safety measures if CNS effects occur. Can develop tolerance. Monitor liver function tests.
divalproex (Depakote)	PO	Bleeding Drowsiness GI distress Liver toxicity Suicidal thoughts Vision changes Weight gain	Use safety measures if CNS effects occur. Monitor for depression. Monitor CBC, liver function tests. Monitor weight.
eslicarbazepine (Aptiom)	PO	Depression Drowsiness GI distress Rash Speech problems Vision changes	Monitor for depression. Avoid alcohol. Use safety measures if CNS effects occur. Avoid pregnancy. Monitor liver function tests.

Continued

TABLE 63.8 Drug Therapy—cont'd

Select Antiseizure Agents

Drug	Route	Side Effects	Considerations
ethosuximide (Zarontin)	PO	Drowsiness GI distress Liver toxicity Rash	Monitor liver function tests. Use safety measures if CNS effects occur. Avoid alcohol. Avoid pregnancy. Stop if rash occurs.
felbamate (Felbatol)	PO	Decreased appetite with weight loss Liver toxicity Vision changes	Monitor CBC, liver function tests. Monitor weight.
lacosamide (Vimpat)	IV, PO	Dizziness Drowsiness Dysrhythmias GI distress	Use safety measures if CNS effects occur. Avoid alcohol. Avoid pregnancy.
lamotrigine (Lamictal)	PO	Dizziness Drowsiness GI distress Rash Vision changes	Use safety measures if CNS effects occur. Monitor liver function tests. Stop if rash occurs.
levetiracetam (Keppra)	PO	Dizziness GI distress Suicidal thoughts	Avoid alcohol. Monitor for depression.
perampanel (Fycompa)	PO	Anxiety Dizziness GI distress Suicidal thoughts	Give at bedtime. Monitor for depression. Avoid alcohol. Use safety measures if CNS effects occur. Avoid pregnancy.
tiagabine (Gabitril)	PO	Agitation Dizziness GI distress Rash Suicidal thoughts	Monitor for depression. Avoid in pregnancy. Avoid alcohol. Use safety measures if CNS effects occur.
topiramate (Topamax)	PO	Ataxia Drowsiness GI distress Vision changes	Stop if vision changes occur. Use safety measures if CNS effects occur. Avoid alcohol. Avoid pregnancy.
valproic acid (Depakene)	PO	Bleeding Drowsiness GI distress Weight gain	Avoid use in pregnancy. Take with food; avoid carbonated beverages. Monitor bleeding times, CBC, drug levels, liver function tests. Use safety measures if CNS effects occur.
zonisamide (Zonegran)	PO	Confusion Drowsiness Gait changes GI distress Kidney stones	Use safety measures if CNS effects occur. Encourage fluids.

Treatment of SE requires a rapid-acting antiseizure drug. The drugs most often used are benzodiazepines. Options include midazolam IM autoinjector (Seizalam) and buccal or intranasal midazolam (Nayzilam).[17] If a patient has an IV, then IV lorazepam is preferred. Because these are short-acting drugs, we follow their administration with long-acting drugs, such as fosphenytoin. Ongoing administration of IV antiseizure and anesthetic drugs is needed if the seizures are not stopping.[13]

Because many antiseizure drugs (e.g., phenytoin, phenobarbital, ethosuximide, lamotrigine, topiramate) have a long half-life, they can be given once or twice a day. This increases the patient's adherence because the drug does not have to be taken at work or school.

DRUG ALERT

Antiseizure Drugs

- Abrupt withdrawal after long-term use may cause seizures.
- If weaning is to occur, the patient must be seizure free for a prolonged period (e.g., 2–5 years) and have a normal neurologic assessment and EEG.

Side effects of antiseizure drugs involve the CNS. They include vision changes, drowsiness, ataxia, and mental slowness. Neurologic assessment for dose-related toxicity involves testing for nystagmus and evaluating hand and gait coordination, cognitive function, and general alertness.

Gerontologic Considerations: Drug Therapy for Seizure Disorder

Many older adults have a first single seizure, then do not have another seizure. To be considered for antiseizure drug therapy, older adults should have recurrent seizures, an obvious structural predisposition for seizures, or onset of seizure disorder presenting as SE. Older adults are more responsive to antiseizure drugs than younger adults, but they also are more likely to have side effects at lower serum drug levels.

Because the liver metabolizes phenytoin, it should not be used in older patients with liver problems. The potential effects on cognitive function and bone demineralization make carbamazepine less desirable for older adults. Many newer antiseizure drugs offer greater treatment benefit to older adults. Compared with older drugs, gabapentin, lamotrigine, oxcarbazepine (Trileptal), and levetiracetam may be safer, with fewer effects on cognitive function and fewer drug interactions.

Surgical Therapy

People with a defined site of seizure origin (epileptogenic zone) can benefit from surgical resection of that focal area, laser ablation, or radiosurgery over continued use of antiseizure drugs. For severe cases, hemispherectomy can be done. Most HCPs recommend staying on seizure control medication for 2 years after surgery.[13] About 65% of patients are seizure free after surgery, depending on surgery type.[8]

Not all patients benefit from surgery. Extensive preoperative evaluation is important. This includes continuous EEG monitoring and other tests to ensure precise localization of the focal point. Surgical treatment destroys or removes brain tissue, so it is best for seizures that do not arise from critical areas.

Other Therapies

VNS, a form of neuromodulation, is used as an adjunct to drugs when an accessible focal point cannot be identified for surgical removal. The exact mechanism of action is unknown. It may increase blood flow to specific brain areas or raise levels of neurotransmitters. In VNS, a surgically implanted electrode in the neck is programmed to deliver electrical impulses to the CN X at specific intervals or when the pulse elevates. Elevated pulse often occurs with seizures. The patient can also activate the electrode with a magnet if they sense a seizure is imminent. Adverse effects include coughing, hoarseness, dyspnea, and tingling in the neck. Batteries need replaced every 3 to 10 years. Benefits of VNS increase with time.[13] Contraindications include a history of dysrhythmias or sleep apnea.

Responsive neurostimulation (NeuroPace RNS System) is like a pacemaker. It continually monitors the EEG to detect abnormalities, then responds to seizure activity by delivering electrical stimulation to a precise location. The device is placed under the skin, outside the skull, with connections to electrodes over the area of seizure focus. The HCP uses a programmable wand to collect information about seizure activity. This can be used to assess treatment efficacy. This modality is an option for persons who are not surgical candidates or have multiple areas of seizure focus.

DBS consists of electrodes placed by a neurosurgeon in the brain at defined areas. They are connected to a neurostimulator (like a pacemaker) that delivers electrical stimulation at preset cycles, not in response to seizure activity. The device can collect information from the brain that can be used in treatment decisions. Effectiveness improves over time. Other neurostimulators include repetitive transcranial magnetic stimulation.[13]

A ketogenic diet is a special high-fat, low-carbohydrate diet that helps control seizures in some people. A person on this diet makes ketones that pass into the brain, where they replace glucose as an energy source. Meals are carefully planned to restrict the amount of protein and carbohydrate. Patients who take anticoagulants need close monitoring for bleeding. Most people must continue their use of antiseizure medication but may take smaller doses or fewer medications. Seizures may worsen if the diet is stopped abruptly. Long-term effects of the diet are not clear.

NURSING MANAGEMENT: SEIZURE DISORDER

Assessment

Subjective and objective data to obtain from a patient with seizure disorder are outlined in Table 63.9. Obtain data related to a specific seizure episode from a witness.

Clinical Problems

Clinical Problems for the patient with seizure disorder may include:

- Impaired respiratory function
- Difficulty coping
- Risk for injury

Additional information on clinical problems and interventions for the patient with seizure disorder is presented in eNursing Care Plan 63.2 (available on the website for this chapter).

Planning

The overall goals are that the patient with seizure disorder will (1) be free from injury during a seizure, (2) have optimal function while taking antiseizure drugs, and (3) have satisfactory psychosocial function.

Implementation

Health Promotion

Following general safety measures (e.g., wearing helmets to reduce risk for head injury) can prevent some seizure disorders. Improved perinatal care has reduced fetal trauma and hypoxia and thus brain damage leading to seizure disorder.

Help the patient identify events or situations that cause seizures. Provide suggestions for handling them better. The patient should practice good general health habits. Teach them to avoid excess alcohol use, fatigue, and loss of sleep. Help the patient

TABLE 63.9 NURSING ASSESSMENT
Seizure Disorder

Subjective Data

Important Health Information

Health history: Seizures, birth defects or injuries, anoxic episodes. CNS trauma, tumors, or infections. Stroke, metabolic disorders, alcohol use, exposure to metals or carbon monoxide, hepatic or renal failure, fever, pregnancy, SLE

Medications: Adherence to antiseizure medication plan. Barbiturate or alcohol withdrawal. Use or overdose of cocaine, amphetamines, lidocaine, theophylline, penicillin, lithium, phenothiazines, tricyclic antidepressants, benzodiazepines

Functional Health Patterns

Health perception–health management: Family history

Cognitive-perceptual: Headaches, aura, mood, or behavioral changes before seizure. Mentation changes, abdominal pain, muscle pain (postictal).

Self-perception–self-concept: Anxiety, depression. Loss of self-esteem, social isolation

Sexuality-reproductive: Decreased sexual drive, erectile dysfunction. Increased sexual drive (postictal)

Objective Data

Cardiovascular

Hypertension, tachycardia or bradycardia (ictal)

General

Precipitating factors, including severe metabolic acidosis or alkalosis, hyperkalemia, hypoglycemia, dehydration, water intoxication

GI

Bowel incontinence, excessive salivation

Musculoskeletal

Weakness, paralysis, ataxia (postictal)

Neurologic

Generalized Onset

Tonic-clonic: Loss of consciousness, muscle tightening, then jerking. Dilated pupils. Hyperventilation, then apnea. Postictal somnolence

Absence: Altered consciousness (5–30 s), minor facial motor activity

Focal Onset

Aware: Aura. Focal sensory, motor, cognitive, or emotional phenomena (focal motor)

Impaired awareness: Altered consciousness with inappropriate behaviors, automatisms, amnesia of event

Respiratory

Abnormal respiratory rate, rhythm, or depth. Apnea (ictal). Absent or abnormal breath sounds, possible airway occlusion

Skin

Bitten tongue, soft tissue damage, cyanosis, diaphoresis (postictal)

Urinary

Incontinence

Possible Diagnostic Findings

Positive toxicology screen or blood alcohol level. Altered serum electrolytes, acidosis or alkalosis, very low blood glucose, ↑ blood urea nitrogen or serum creatinine, abnormal liver function tests, ammonia; abnormal CT scan or MRI of head, abnormal findings from LP. Abnormal discharges on EEG

handle stress constructively. Maintaining healthy weight and engaging in regular exercise can help manage seizures and other health problems.

◆ Acute Care

Nursing care for a hospitalized patient with seizure disorder or a patient who has had seizures due to other factors involves observation and treatment of the seizure, patient and caregiver teaching, and psychosocial intervention. Provide acute care for the seizure and maintain patient safety (Table 63.10).

CHECK YOUR PRACTICE

You are making your morning rounds and go to check a patient who was admitted the night before with increased seizure activity. When you go to the room, the roommate is yelling, "Help, help!" You find the patient is on the floor jerking and stiffening and not responding to you.

- What should you do?

When a seizure occurs, carefully observe and record details of the event. The diagnosis and subsequent treatment often rest on the seizure description. What events preceded the seizure? When did the seizure occur? How long did each phase (aural [if any], ictal, postictal) last? What occurred during each phase?

Note patient description of aura (if any); the exact onset of the seizure; the course and nature of the seizure activity (awareness, motor movements, automatisms); body parts involved, their sequence of involvement, and autonomic signs, such as dilated pupils, excessive salivation, altered breathing, cyanosis, flushing, diaphoresis, or incontinence. Assessment of the postictal period should include a detailed description of the level of consciousness, vital signs, pupil size and position of the eyes, memory loss, muscle soreness, speech disorders (aphasia, dysarthria), weakness or paralysis, sleep period, and the duration of each sign or symptom.

! SAFETY ALERT
Seizure

During a seizure, you should:

- Maintain a patent airway for the patient.
- Protect the patient's head, turn the patient to the side, loosen constrictive clothing, ease patient to the floor (if seated).
- Do not restrain the patient.
- Do not place any objects in the patient's mouth.

After the seizure, the patient may need repositioning to open and maintain the airway, suctioning, and O_2. A seizure can be frightening for the patient and others who witnessed it. Assess

TABLE 63.10 NURSING MANAGEMENT

Care of the Patient With Seizure Disorder

- Initiate safety precautions for the patient at risk for seizures.
- Assess and record details of seizure events, including events preceding the seizure; length of each phase of the seizure; course and nature of seizure activity; and level of consciousness, vital signs, and activity during the postictal period.
- Assess airway patency, and position patient to maintain airway during and after seizures.
- Give IV antiseizure medications to the patient with SE.
- Give oral antiseizure medications as scheduled.
- Make appropriate referrals to community agencies to help the patient with the financial impact of seizure disorder, work training, employment, and living arrangements.
- Provide patient and caregiver teaching (Table 63.11).
- In the ambulatory and home care setting, evaluate patient self-management of medications and lifestyle.
- Supervise AP:
  - Place suction equipment, bag-valve-mask, and O_2 at the patient's bedside.
  - Remove potentially harmful objects from the bedside and pad side rails.
  - Immediately report any seizure activity to the RN.
  - Provide no food or fluid until awake
  - Obtain vital signs during the postictal period.

Collaborate With Other Team Members

Respiratory Therapist

- Assess airway patency and suction as needed.
- Assist ventilations if patient does not breathe spontaneously after seizure.
- Assist with intubation if needed.

Social Worker

- Help patient identify and obtain needed resources.
- Offer counseling to develop positive coping skills.

their level of understanding and provide information about how and why the event occurred. This is an excellent chance for you to discuss any misconceptions about seizures.

◆ Ambulatory Care

Preventing recurring seizures is the major treatment goal. You have a vital role in teaching the patient and caregiver (Table 63.11). Maintaining a seizure diary can be helpful in ongoing management. Encourage the patient to keep regular appointments with the HCP.

Medication nonadherence can be a problem. Take measures to increase adherence to the prescribed drug plan. Help the patient understand that for treatment to be effective, drugs must be taken regularly and consistently. Review details of the drug plan and what to do if a dose is missed. Usually, the dose is made up if the omission is remembered within 24 hours. Caution the patient not to adjust drug dosages without HCP guidance because this can increase seizure frequency and cause SE.

You need to know about drug side effects so you can teach patients and start proper treatment. Review side effects the patient needs to report. For example, common side effects of phenytoin are gingival hyperplasia (excess growth of gingival tissue) and hirsutism, especially in young adults. Good dental hygiene, including regular tooth brushing and flossing, can decrease gingival hyperplasia. If gingival hyperplasia is extensive, gingivectomy may be done and phenytoin replaced with another drug.

Teach caregivers the emergency management of tonic-clonic seizures (Table 63.7). Remind them they do not need to call an ambulance or send a person to the hospital after a single seizure unless the seizure is prolonged (longer than 5 minutes), another seizure immediately follows, injury has occurred, or it is unknown if this was a first-time seizure.

Patients may have concerns or fears related to recurrent seizures, incontinence, or loss of self-control. Support patients

TABLE 63.11 PATIENT & CAREGIVER TEACHING

Seizure Disorder

Include the following information in the teaching plan for the patient with seizure disorder:

1. Take antiseizure medications as prescribed. Report all drug side effects to the HCP.
2. When needed, blood is drawn to ensure therapeutic drug levels. Schedule regular visits with the HCP to discuss treatment options.
3. Do not add any supplements without HCP approval.
4. Use nondrug techniques, such as relaxation therapy and diet modification, to try to reduce the number of seizures.
5. Be aware of community and online resources for education and help with tracking and explaining seizure activity.
6. Wear a medical alert bracelet or necklace and carry an identification card.
7. Avoid excess alcohol use, fatigue, and loss of sleep.
8. Eat regular meals and snacks in between if feeling shaky, faint, or hungry.
9. Be knowledgeable as a woman of childbearing age about antiseizure medications and contraceptive use.

Caregivers should receive the following information:

Focal-Onset Seizures

1. Stay calm. Guide patient to safety to prevent injury but do not restrain.
2. Observe for asymmetry of activity and focus on specific actions, such as lip smacking and abnormal movements.
3. Assess patient's level of consciousness and ability to converse and respond appropriately.
4. Note the time the seizure started and stopped. Take note of the time of return to baseline.
5. Provide respect and explanation of occurrence.

Generalized-Onset Tonic-Clonic Seizures

1. When seizure occurs outside the hospital setting, activate EMS if (1) the duration is greater than 5 min; (2) events recur without the patient recovering to baseline; (3) the patient is unable to establish a normal breathing pattern, is injured or pregnant; or (4) you do not know if this is a first-time seizure event.
2. Maintain patient safety. Lower the patient to the floor or bed, remove glasses if worn, and loosen restrictive clothing.
3. Do not place anything in the patient's mouth. Patient's teeth/dentures may be damaged. Caregiver may be bitten.
4. Position patient on side (if possible) to improve the patient's ability to drain oral secretions.
5. Note the time the seizure started and stopped. Take note of the time of return to baseline.
6. Assess for any injury and lingering motor weakness.

through teaching and by helping them use effective coping mechanisms. Perhaps the greatest challenge is adjusting to any limitations imposed by the illness. Discrimination in employment is a serious problem facing the person with seizure disorder. For issues relating to job discrimination, refer patients to the state department of vocational rehabilitation or the U.S. Equal Employment Opportunity Commission (EEOC).

Help the patient find community resources. Local support groups may be identified through the Epilepsy Foundation (EF). This volunteer agency offers varied services to patients with a seizure disorder (www.epilepsy.com). Refer the patient who is an eligible veteran to a Department of Veterans Affairs medical center that provides comprehensive care. Refer the patient who needs counseling to a community mental health center.

Social workers and government programs can help with financial implications and living arrangements. State agencies specializing in vocational rehabilitation services can provide vocational assessment, counseling, and funding for training. They can help with job placement for patients whose seizures are not well controlled. Financial assistance for transportation and medical costs may be available.

Driving laws for patients who have had a seizure vary from state to state. They may require up to a year seizure free before reissuing a driver's license. The EF provides current information on driving laws for each state.

Medical alert bracelets, necklaces, and identification cards are available through the EF, local pharmacies, or companies specializing in identification devices (e.g., Medic Alert). Using medical identification is optional.

Encourage the patient to learn more about seizures through self-education. Many organizations and agencies that offer services to patients with seizure disorder offer teaching aids and support.

◆ Evaluation

Expected outcomes are that the patient with seizure disorder will:

- Have a breathing pattern adequate to meet O_2 needs
- Have no seizure-related injury
- Perform optimal-self management

RESTLESS LEGS SYNDROME

Etiology and Pathophysiology

Restless legs syndrome (RLS) *(Willis-Ekbom disease)* is a movement disorder with unpleasant sensory (paresthesia) and motor abnormalities of 1 or both legs. It is a relatively common sleep problem. Around 3% to 8% of the U.S. population has RLS.[19] RLS is more common in older adults and in women. RLS is lifelong and has no cure. Symptoms may disappear for a while, but they eventually reappear.[20]

There are 2 types of RLS: primary (idiopathic) and secondary. Most people have primary RLS. Secondary RLS can occur with metabolic problems from iron deficiency, renal disease and hemodialysis, or neuropathy as in MS. Many pregnant women develop RLS. Symptoms may be worsened by sleep deprivation, sleep apnea, stress, sedentary lifestyle, obesity, alcohol, nicotine, caffeine use, diabetes, peripheral neuropathy, and some medications (antihistamines, antiemetics, lithium, and some antipsychotics).[19,20] RLS has a genetic link. Those with primary RLS, especially those with an onset before 40 report family links.[21]

We do not know the exact cause of primary RLS. It may be a problem in the brain's basal ganglia circuits that use the neurotransmitter dopamine (DA). DA helps with smooth and purposeful movements. Disruption in these pathways can cause involuntary movement. We think DA levels fall throughout the day, and this causes muscle spasm and involuntary movement.[21]

Clinical Manifestations

The severity of RLS sensory symptoms ranges from infrequent minor discomfort (numbness, tingling, "pins and needles") to severe pain. A small number have severe symptoms that affect their quality of life and need drug therapy. Sensory symptoms often appear first. Patients describe a tingling, itching, "creepy-crawling," or throbbing feeling in their calf muscle, accompanied by an irresistible urge to move.[20] Symptoms most often begin when the patient is inactive or lying still. It is most common at night. Some patients have pain after sitting long periods. Patients can have pain in the arms too.[19]

Pain at night can disrupt sleep. Physical activity, such as walking, stretching, rocking, or kicking, often relieves the pain. In severe cases, patients sleep only a few hours at night. This causes daytime fatigue and disrupts the daily routine. Motor problems include voluntary restlessness and periodic, involuntary movements. Fatigue worsens symptoms. RLS worsens over time. Symptoms become more frequent and last longer.

Diagnostic Studies

RLS is diagnosed largely based on the history or the report of the bed partner about nighttime activities. The HCP may ask the patient to keep a sleep diary to aid in diagnosis and treatment. Diagnosis of RLS can be made when the patient meets 5 specific criteria: (1) overwhelming urge to move the legs, often accompanied by uncomfortable or unpleasant sensations in the legs; (2) urge to move the legs worsens during rest or inactivity; (3) urge to move the legs is partially or totally relieved by movement, as long as the activity continues; (4) urge to move the legs becomes worse in the evening or night; and (5) these features are not due to another problem.[22]

The patient may have polysomnography studies during sleep to discern RLS from other problems that can disturb sleep. Periodic leg movements are not exclusive to RLS. Blood tests, such as a CBC, serum ferritin, and renal function tests, may help exclude secondary causes of RLS. A patient with diabetes may have paresthesia caused by peripheral neuropathy.

Interprofessional Care

The goal of care is to reduce patient discomfort and distress and improve sleep quality. When RLS is due to renal failure or iron deficiency, treating these problems may decrease symptoms. Lifestyle changes may help persons with mild to moderate RLS. For example, decreasing the use of caffeine, alcohol, or tobacco; maintaining regular sleep habits; exercising; relaxation techniques; and massaging and stretching the legs may be helpful. The patient should avoid antihistamine-containing medications (e.g., diphenhydramine).

If nondrug measures fail, drug therapy is an option. No specific medication effectively manages RLS for all patients. The main drugs used to treat RLS increase the amount of DA in the brain. DA agonists (e.g., ropinirole [Requip], pramipexole [Mirapex], rotigotine [Neupro]) can treat pain and provide more restful sleep. These drugs can cause impulse disorders (gambling, shopping).[20]

The antiseizure drugs gabapentin, enacarbil (Horizant), or pregabalin are first-line drugs for RLS. They may decrease the sensory sensations and nerve pain. The patient with iron deficiency anemia may need to start iron supplements. Other supplements that may help RLS include magnesium, zinc, and vitamin D.[20]

Other drugs may relieve some symptoms of RLS. Very low doses of opioids (e.g., oxycodone) may help patients with severe symptoms who do not respond to other drug therapies. Since the main side effect of opioids is constipation, the patient may need a stool softener or laxative. Clonidine and propranolol help some patients. Short-acting benzodiazepines (e.g., clonazepam, lorazepam) may help patients obtain more restful sleep. They should only be used if no other treatments work.[20]

Medical devices approved for use with RLS include a foot wrap that applies pressure to the foot and lower leg and a vibration and counter stimulation device (Relaxis) that competes with and decreases RLS sensations. Some HCPs recommend pneumatic compression devices.[20]

DEGENERATIVE NEUROLOGIC DISORDERS

MULTIPLE SCLEROSIS

Multiple sclerosis (MS) is a chronic, unpredictable, progressive, degenerative disorder of the CNS. It is characterized by disseminated demyelination of nerve fibers of the brain and spinal cord. MS can affect people of any age. The onset of MS is usually between ages 20 and 40 years. MS affects every patient differently. Some will have little permanent effect while others have progressive illness leading to severe disability.[23] People diagnosed at 50 years of age or older often have more progressive disease. MS affects women 2 to 3 times more often.

Almost a million people are living with MS in the United States. MS becomes more prevalent further away from the equator. MS effects people of all ethnic groups but is most prevalent in people of Northern European ancestry.[24] There is some evidence that maintaining adequate levels of vitamin D reduces the risk of MS.

Etiology and Pathophysiology

We do not know the cause of MS. It is unlikely due to a single cause, but a combination of genetic and environment factors. The primary problem is an autoimmune process driven by activated T cells. 15% of MS patients have a blood relative with the disease. We have found over 230 genetic variables that play a small part in MS risk.[13]

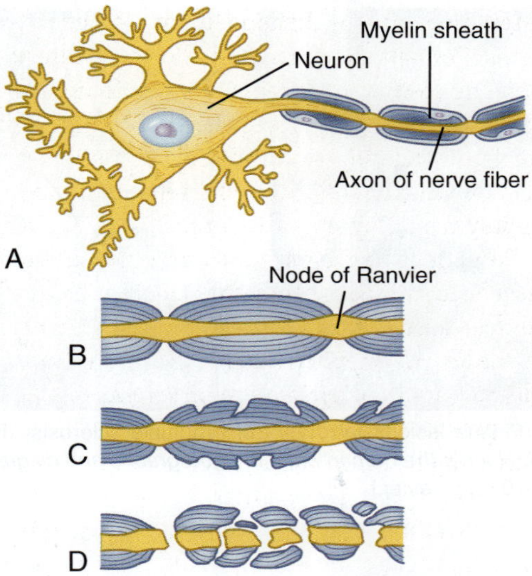

Fig. 63.2 Pathogenesis of multiple sclerosis. (A) Normal nerve cell with myelin sheath. (B) Normal axon. (C) Myelin breakdown. (D) Myelin totally disrupted; axon not functioning.

MS may develop in a genetically susceptible person after an environmental exposure, such as a viral infection. Some viral proteins are structurally similar to myelin. We believe viruses or other antigens activate T Cells, although we have not found a causative virus. The T cells cross the blood-brain barrier and begin the inflammatory process. T cells mistake the myelin protein for the viral antigen. Successive antigen-antibody reactions within the CNS activates the inflammatory response and lead to further demyelination and destruction.

MS is marked by 3 processes: chronic inflammation, demyelination, and gliosis in the CNS. The immune system attack on the myelin proteins causes damage to the myelin sheath (Fig. 63.2A–C). Transmission of nerve impulses still occurs, but it is slowed. The patient may have impaired function (e.g., weakness, numbness). Inflammation ceases and full recovery or partial recovery can occur. Symptoms all or partially disappear. At that point, the patient has a remission.

As inflammation continues or recurs, nearby oligodendrocytes are affected. Myelin loses the ability to regenerate. Eventually damage occurs to the underlying axon. This disrupts nerve impulse transmission. Nerve function is lost permanently (Fig. 63.2D). White, grey, and axonal matter are all eventually effected. As inflammation subsides, glial scar tissue replaces damaged tissue. This leads to the formation of hard, rigid plaques (Fig. 63.3). These plaques are found throughout the white matter of the CNS.[8] In late disease cerebral cortex atrophy occurs.

MS reduces life expectancy by about 7 years.[13] Often, death does not come from MS exacerbations. It is usually caused by infection or complications of immobility (e.g., pneumonia).

Clinical Manifestations

The onset of MS is often slow and gradual. Vague symptoms occur periodically over months or years. Because they do not prompt the patient to seek medical attention, MS may not be diagnosed until long after the first symptom. For some patients,

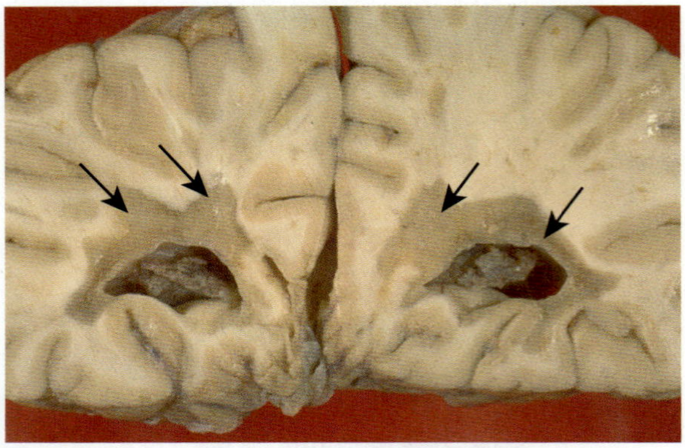

Fig. 63.3 Plaque lesions *(arrows)* from multiple sclerosis. (From Vanderah TW: *Nolte's the human brain in photographs and diagrams*, ed 5, St. Louis, 2020, Elsevier.)

MS is marked by rapid, progressive deterioration. Others have remissions and exacerbations. With repeated exacerbations, the overall trend is progressive deterioration in neurologic function.

Because changes from MS have a spotty distribution in the CNS, symptoms vary based on the area of CNS involvement. Some patients have severe symptoms early in the disease. Some may have minimal symptoms for several years. The classification scheme of MS, with 4 primary patterns, is based on the clinical course (Table 63.12).

Vision changes like blurred or double vision, red-green color distortion, or blindness in 1 eye may be the first sign (Fig. 63.4). Many patients describe extremity muscle weakness and problems with coordination and balance. Those symptoms may affect walking or standing. MS can cause partial or complete paralysis in the worst cases. Most have numbness and tingling.

TABLE 63.12 Patterns of Multiple Sclerosis

Category	Characteristics
Relapsing-remitting	• Clearly defined attacks of worsening neurologic function *(relapses)* with partial or complete recovery *(remission)*. • 85% of people first diagnosed with this type.
Primary-progressive	• Steadily worsening neurologic function from the beginning with minor improvements but no distinct relapses or remissions. • 10% of people first diagnosed with this type.
Secondary-progressive	• A relapsing-remitting initial course, followed by progression with or without occasional relapses, minor remissions, and plateaus. • New treatments may slow progression. • Most people initially diagnosed with relapsing-remitting MS eventually transition to this type.
Progressive-relapsing	• Progressive disease from onset, with clear acute relapses, with or without full recovery. Periods between relapses are characterized by continuing progression. • 5% of people with MS.

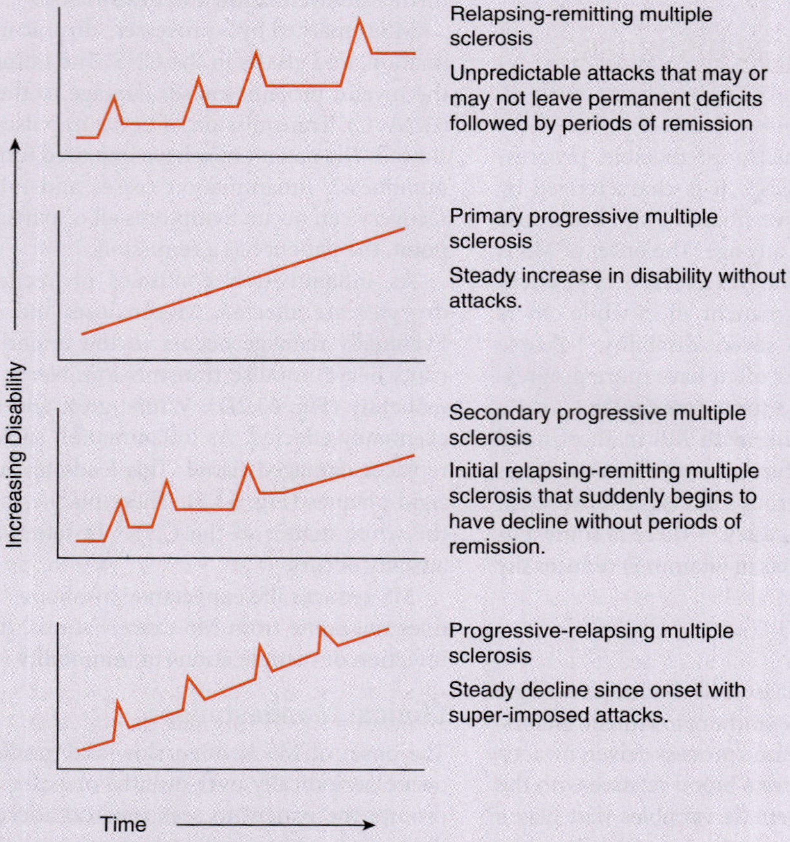

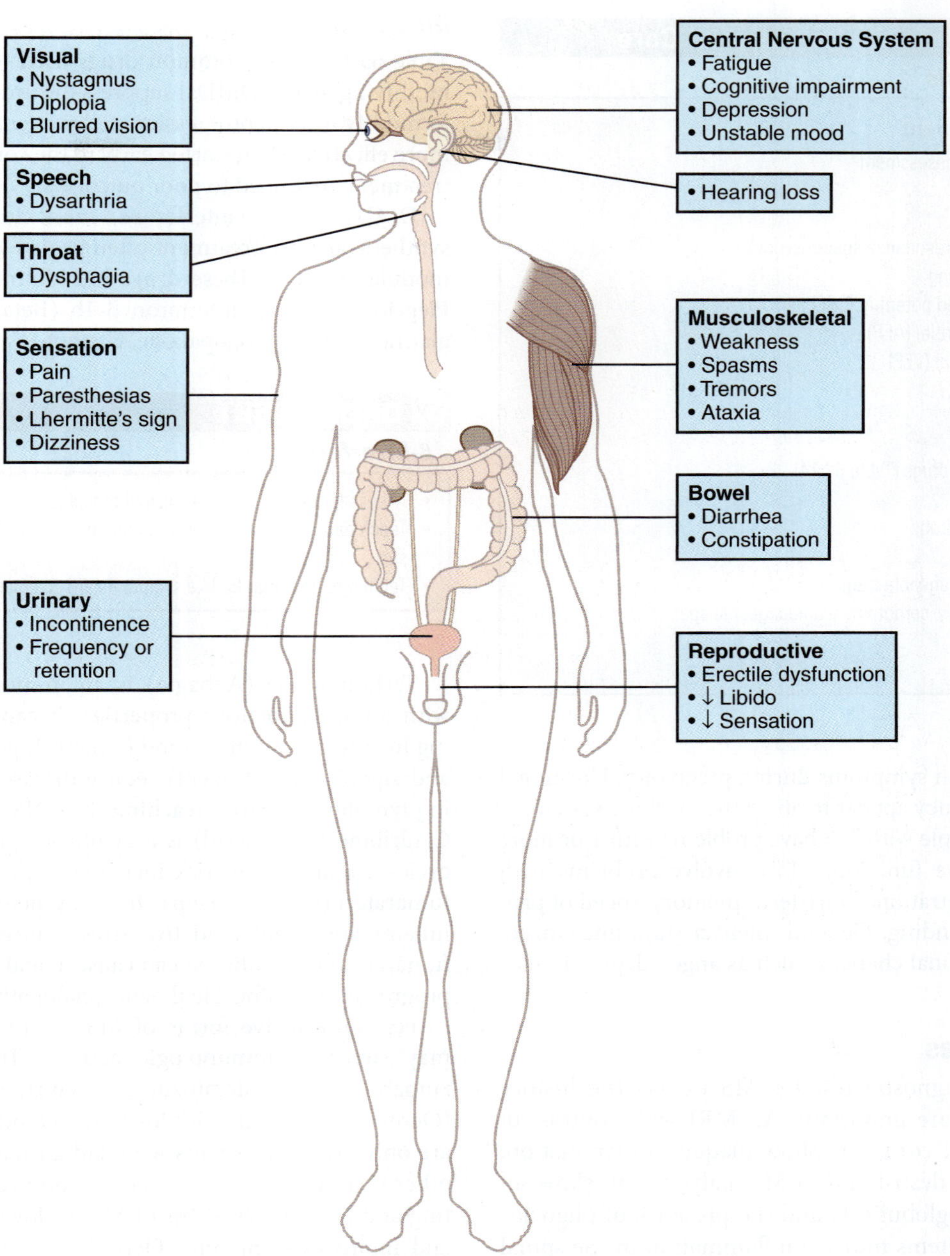

Fig. 63.4 Manifestations of multiple sclerosis.

Lhermitte's sign is a temporary sensory symptom described as an electric shock going down the spine or into the limbs with neck flexion. Some patients report pain, especially around the low thoracic and abdominal regions. Labeled the "MS hug," this is from muscle spasm in intercostal and abdominal muscles. Other frequent problems include speech problems, hearing loss, tremors, and dizziness. Possible cerebellar signs include nystagmus, ataxia, dysarthria, and dysphagia. Many patients have severe, even disabling fatigue. Heat, humidity, deconditioning, and medication side effects worsen fatigue.

A rigid plaque in areas of the CNS that control elimination can alter bowel and bladder function. Bowel problems usually involve constipation. Urinary problems vary. A common problem is *spastic* (uninhibited) bladder. The bladder has a small capacity for urine, and its contractions are unchecked. The result is urinary urgency and frequency, often with dribbling or incontinence.

A *flaccid* (hypotonic) bladder occurs with a lesion in the reflex arc controlling bladder function. The patient often has urinary retention because there is no sensation or desire to void, no pressure, and no pain. A combination of spastic and flaccid bladder can occur. Urinary problems can be diagnosed with urodynamic studies.

Sexual problems occur in many people. Physiologic erectile dysfunction may result from spinal cord involvement in men. Women may have decreased libido, difficulty with orgasm, painful intercourse, and decreased vaginal lubrication. Decreased sensation can prevent a normal sexual response. The emotional effects of chronic illness and the loss of self-esteem contribute to loss of sexual response. Some women with MS have remission

TABLE 63.13 **Interprofessional Care**

Multiple Sclerosis

Diagnostic Assessment

- History and physical assessment
- CSF analysis
- CT scan
- MRI, MRS (magnetic resonance spectroscopy)
- Evoked potential testing
- Somatosensory evoked potential (SSEP)
- Auditory evoked potential (AEP)
- Visual evoked potential (VEP)

Management

- Drug therapy
  - Disease modifying drugs (Table 63.14)
  - Corticosteroids
  - Symptom specific drugs
- Surgical therapy
- Thalamotomy (unmanageable tremor)
- Neurectomy, rhizotomy, cordotomy (unmanageable spasticity)
- Physical therapy
- Occupational therapy

or an improvement in symptoms during pregnancy. Hormonal changes with pregnancy appear to affect the immune system.

About half of people with MS have problems with 1 or more domains of cognitive function. Most involve problems with multitasking, concentration, short-term memory, speed of processing, and word finding. General intellect stays unchanged. There may be emotional changes, such as anger, depression, or euphoria.

Diagnostic Studies

No one specific diagnostic test for MS exists. The history and manifestations are important. An MRI with contrast of the brain and spinal cord may show plaques, inflammation, atrophy, and tissue destruction. CSF analysis may show an increase in immunoglobulin G and the presence of oligoclonal banding. These items indicate inflammation in the spinal fluid. Evoked potential responses are often delayed because of decreased nerve conduction from the eye and ear to the brain.[13]

Diagnostic criteria for MS specify that the patient must have (1) evidence of at least 2 inflammatory demyelinating lesions in at least 2 different locations within the CNS, (2) 2 or more attacks occurring at different times (usually 1 month or more apart), and (3) all other diagnoses ruled out. If evidence exists for only 1 lesion or only 1 clinical attack has occurred, the HCP will monitor the patient for another attack or confirm the presence of oligoclonal banding in the CSF.[13]

Interprofessional Care

No cure currently exists for MS. Care is aimed at treating the disease process and providing symptomatic relief (Table 63.13). No cases of MS are alike. We tailor therapy to the disease pattern and symptoms of each patient.

Drug Therapy

Table 63.14 shows common drugs used to treat MS. Disease-modifying drugs (DMDs) suppress the immune system in order to modify disease progression and prevent relapses. DMDs are more effective when started early in the course of MS. Delays in treatment are linked to poor outcomes.

DMDs include interferons, monoclonal antibodies, and synthetic agents. Treatment often begins with use of immunomodulator drugs. These drugs include interferon β-1a (Rebif, Plegridy, Avonex), interferon β-1b (Betaseron, Extavia), and glatiramer acetate (Copaxone, Glatopa).

DRUG ALERT

β-Interferon

- Assess for depression and suicidal thoughts.
- Teach patient to wear sunscreen and protective clothing when exposed to sun.
- Tell the patient that flu-like symptoms are common after starting therapy.

Teriflunomide (Aubagio) is an immunomodulatory agent with antiinflammatory properties. It can cause life-threatening liver toxicity. Fingolimod (Gilenya), ponesimod (Ponvory), and siponimod (Mayzent) reduce disease activity by preventing lymphocytes from reaching the CNS and causing damage. Cladribine (Mavenclad) is a cytotoxic agent taken orally in 2 cycles a year. Cancer risk increases with cladribine. Dimethyl fumarate (Tecfidera) helps the body defend itself against the inflammation and oxidative stress caused by MS. Dimethyl fumarate and fingolimod can cause a fatal viral brain infection, progressive multifocal leukoencephalopathy (PML).[25]

For more active forms of MS, IV monoclonal antibodies may suppress immunologic activity. These include natalizumab (Tysabri), alemtuzumab (Lemtrada), and ocrelizumab (Ocrevus). Due to the risk for PML and other side effects, these are only given to patients who had an inadequate response to other treatments. Ocrelizumab is approved for relapsing remitting and progressive forms of MS. It slows disease progression and improves symptoms. Ocrelizumab increases the risk for infection and breast cancer.[25]

IV corticosteroids (e.g., prednisone) can be used to treat acute MS exacerbations. They reduce edema and acute inflammation at the site of demyelination. They speed recovery, but do not affect the residual neurologic impairment from the exacerbation.[23] Therapeutic plasma exchange (plasmapheresis) and IV immunoglobulin G may be considered for a short time when treatment with corticosteroids alone does not achieve symptom improvement.

Many other drugs are used to treat the various MS symptoms. These may include drugs for spasticity, fatigue, tremor, vertigo or dizziness, depression, pain, bowel and bladder problems, sexual problems, and cognitive changes. For example, amantadine, modafinil (Provigil), and fluoxetine (Prozac) are used to treat fatigue. Anticholinergics (oxybutynin, propantheline) can treat bladder spasms. Tricyclic antidepressants and antiseizure drugs help with chronic pain. Dalfampridine

TABLE 63.14 Drug Therapy

Disease-Modifying Drugs for Multiple Sclerosis

Drug	Considerations
Injectable	
β-1a interferon (Rebif, Plegridy, Avonex) β-1b interferon (Betaseron, Extavia)	• Teach self-injection techniques. • Rotate injection sites. • Report side effects. • Treat flu-like symptoms with an NSAID or acetaminophen. • Monitor for depression.
glatiramer acetate (Copaxone, Glatopa)	• Teach self-injection techniques. • Monitor liver function tests.
ofatumumab (Kesimpta)	• Teach self-injection techniques. • Avoid pregnancy • Monitor liver function tests.
Oral Agents	
cladribine (Mavenclad)	• Avoid pregnancy. • No contact with large crowds and people who have an infection. • Follow cancer screening guidelines. • Monitor liver tests.
dimethyl fumarate (Tecfidera)	• Report side effects
fingolimod (Gilenya)	• Report side effects. • Monitor BP and heart rate regularly. • Avoid pregnancy.
monomethyl fumarate (Bafiertam)	• Report side effects. • Avoid pregnancy.
ponesimod (Ponvory)	• Report side effects. • Avoid pregnancy.
siponimod (Mayzent)	• Report side effects. • Monitor blood pressure and heart rate regularly. • Avoid pregnancy.
teriflunomide (Aubagio)	• Report side effects. • Avoid pregnancy. • No contact with large crowds and people who have an infection. • Monitor liver function tests.
IV infusions	
alemtuzumab (Lemtrada) natalizumab (Tysabri) ocrelizumab (Ocrevus)	• Report side effects. • Avoid pregnancy. • Monitor for infusion-related reactions. • Follow cancer screening guidelines.

(Ampyra) may improve walking speed.[23] It is a selective potassium channel blocker that improves nerve conduction in damaged nerve segments. Use may cause seizures, especially at higher doses. Bethanechol is a common treatment for urinary retention.

Other Therapies

Spasticity is a major problem for patients with MS. Severe muscle spasticity can be treated with stretching, physical therapy, baclofen, intrathecal pumps, or onabotulinumtoxin A (Botox).[23] Other options include surgery (e.g., neurectomy, rhizotomy, cordotomy) or dorsal-column electrical stimulation. Tremors that become unmanageable with drugs can be treated with thalamotomy or DBS.

Fig. 63.5 Water therapy provides exercise and recreation for the patient with a chronic neurologic disease. (© Photos.com/AbleStock.com/Thinkstock.)

Neurologic problems sometimes improve with physical therapy. Exercise improves daily function for patients not having an exacerbation. Exercise decreases spasticity, increases coordination, and retrains unaffected muscles to act for impaired ones. Water exercise is especially beneficial (Fig. 63.5). Water, which gives buoyancy to the body, allows the patient to have more control and perform activities that would otherwise be impossible.

❖ NURSING MANAGEMENT: MULTIPLE SCLEROSIS

◆ Assessment

Subjective and objective data that you should obtain from a patient with MS are outlined in Table 63.15.

◆ Clinical Problems

Clinical problems for the patient with MS may include:

- Musculoskeletal problems
- Fatigue
- Difficulty coping
- Impaired urinary elimination

Additional information on clinical problems and interventions for the patient with MS is presented in the eNursing Care Plan 63.3 (available on the website for this chapter).

TABLE 63.15 NURSING ASSESSMENT

Multiple Sclerosis

Subjective Data

Important Health Information

Health history: Recent or past viral infections or vaccinations, other recent infections, residence in cold or temperate climates, physical or emotional stress, pregnancy, exposure to extremes of heat and cold

Medications: Adherence to treatment plan (corticosteroids, immunomodulators, immunosuppressants, cholinergics, anticholinergics, antispasmodics)

Functional Health Patterns

Health perception–health management: Positive family history; malaise

Nutritional-metabolic: Weight loss; difficulty in chewing, dysphagia

Elimination: Urinary frequency, urgency, dribbling or incontinence, retention; constipation

Activity-exercise: Generalized muscle weakness, muscle fatigue; tingling and numbness; ataxia (clumsiness)

Cognitive-perceptual: Eye, back, leg, joint pain; painful muscle spasms; vertigo; blurred or lost vision; diplopia; tinnitus

Sexuality-reproductive: Impotence, decreased libido

Coping–stress tolerance: Anger, depression, euphoria, social isolation

Objective Data

General

Apathy, inattentiveness

Musculoskeletal

Muscle weakness, paresis, paralysis, spasms, foot dragging, dysarthria

Neurologic

Nystagmus, ataxia, tremor, spasticity, hyperreflexia, decreased hearing

Skin

Pressure injury

Possible Diagnostic Findings

↓ T suppressor cells, demyelinating lesions on MRI or MRS scans, ↑ IgG or oligoclonal banding in CSF, delayed evoked potential responses

◆ Planning

The overall goals are that the patient with MS will (1) maximize neuromuscular function, (2) maintain independence in activities of daily living (ADL) for as long as possible, (3) manage fatigue, (4) optimize psychosocial well-being, (5) adjust to the illness, and (6) reduce factors that trigger exacerbations.

◆ Implementation

The patient with MS should be aware of triggers that may cause worsening of the disease. These include infection, trauma, live virus immunizations, childbirth, stress, and change in climate. Each person responds differently to triggers. Help the patient identify triggers and develop ways to avoid them or decrease their effects. Becoming overheated worsens symptoms of MS. If the patient lives in a warm climate, cooling vests may help maintain function. Avoiding the midday heat will help manage symptoms in the summer.

During the diagnostic phase, reassure the patient that tests are done to rule out other neurologic disorders, even if a tentative diagnosis of MS has been made. Help the patient to deal with anxiety caused by the diagnosis of a disabling illness. The patient with newly diagnosed MS may need support with the grieving process.

During an acute exacerbation, the patient may be immobile and confined to bed. The focus of nursing care at this phase is to prevent complications of immobility. These include respiratory complications, UTIs, and pressure injuries. Visual symptoms may make driving, reading, performing self-care, and even watching television difficult. Preparation for unexpected exacerbations can make coping with the physical changes easier.

Bladder control is a concerning and potentially embarrassing problem. Drug therapy may help some patients. You may need to teach self-catheterization. Constipation is common. Stress a diet high in fiber and maintaining activity.

Discuss ways to reduce illness. This includes avoiding fatigue, extremes of heat and cold, and exposure to infection. Encourage early treatment of infection when it occurs. Teach the patient to seek a good balance of exercise and rest. They should minimize caffeine intake and eat a healthy diet. The patient should know the treatment plan, drug side effects, how to identify and manage side effects, and drug interactions. Teach the patient to notify the HCP at the first signs of exacerbation.

The patient and caregivers must make many emotional adjustments because of disease unpredictability, the need for lifestyle changes, and the challenge of avoiding or decreasing precipitating factors. The uncertainty of disease progression, along with fatigue and decreased mobility, can cause anxiety and depression. The National Multiple Sclerosis Society and its local chapters offer a variety of services to meet the needs of patients with MS.

◆ Evaluation

The expected outcomes are that the patient with MS will:

- Maintain or improve muscle strength and mobility
- Maintain urinary continence
- Make decisions about health and lifestyle modifications to manage MS
- Maintain independence in ADL

PARKINSON DISEASE

Parkinson disease (PD) is a chronic, progressive neurodegenerative disorder characterized by slowness in the initiation and execution of movement *(bradykinesia),* increased muscle tone *(rigidity),* tremor at rest, and gait changes. It is the most common form of *parkinsonism,* a syndrome of several disorders characterized by similar symptoms.

Almost 1 million Americans are living with PD in the United States. Around 60,000 persons are diagnosed each year. Occurrence of PD increases with age, with average age of onset around 70 years. Around 4% of people with PD are diagnosed before age 50 years. Men are 1.5 times more likely to have PD.[26]

Etiology and Pathophysiology

We do not know the exact cause of PD. We think it is an interplay of genetic and environment risk factors. Traumatic brain injury has been shown to increase the risk of PD. Exposure to industrial manganese, pesticides, herbicides (paraquat), industrial solvents, and chemicals (polychlorinated biphenyl) may increase risk.[27]

Parkinsonism is a syndrome made up of disorders that mimic PD. Many forms of secondary *(atypical)* parkinsonism exist. Because of the similarity, PD and parkinsonism can be confused. Symptoms of parkinsonism have occurred after exposure to a variety of chemicals and metals. Drug-induced parkinsonism can follow therapy with metoclopramide, methyldopa, lithium, haloperidol, or chlorpromazine. It can be seen after the use of illicit drugs like methamphetamine. After removing the cause, symptoms of parkinsonism often disappear. Other causes include hydrocephalus, neurodegenerative disorders, hypoparathyroidism, infections, stroke, tumor, and trauma.

The changes in PD occur in many areas of the brain. There is degeneration of the DA-producing neurons in the substantia nigra of the midbrain (Figs. 63.6 to 63.8). This disrupts the normal balance between DA and acetylcholine (ACh) in the basal ganglia. DA is essential for normal function of the extrapyramidal motor system, including control of posture, support, and voluntary motion. Initial symptoms of PD do not occur until 60% to 80% of DA-producing neurons are lost.[28] Signals to the corpus striatum, which causes smooth and purposeful movement, are impaired. The loss of nerve endings that make norepinephrine also influence symptoms of PD.

Unusual clumps of protein called *Lewy bodies* are found in the brains of patients with PD.

We do not know what causes Lewy bodies to form. Their presence indicates abnormal brain function. Lewy body dementia is discussed in Chapter 64.

Genetic Link

We do not fully understand how genetic changes cause PD or influence the risk for developing PD. Around 20% to 25% of patients with PD have a family history of PD.[13] Several gene mutations have been linked to various forms of PD. These genes include SNCA, LRRK2, DJ1, PRKN, PINK1, and GBA. Despite these discoveries, causative genes have only been found in 10% of PD patients. Genetics plays a larger role in early onset PD. Up to 50% of those with disease onset before 50 have PARK2 mutations.[13]

Clinical Manifestations

The onset of PD is gradual, with ongoing progression. Only 1 limb or 1 side of the body may be involved at first. Common

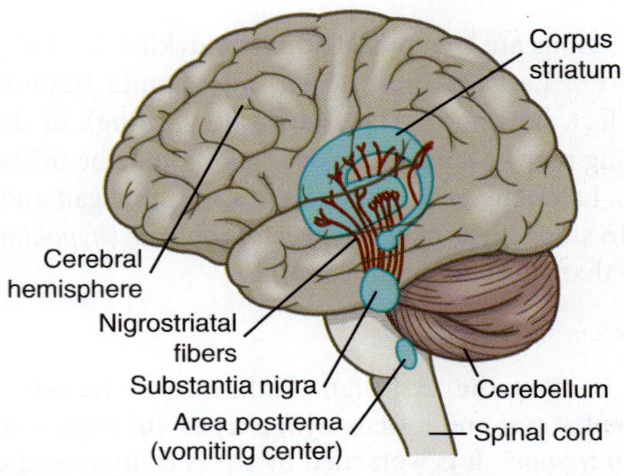

Fig. 63.6 Nigrostriatal disorders produce parkinsonism. Left-sided view of the human brain showing the substantia nigra and the corpus striatum *(shaded area)* lying deep within the cerebral hemisphere. Nerve fibers extend upward from the substantia nigra, divide into many branches, and carry dopamine to all regions of the corpus striatum.

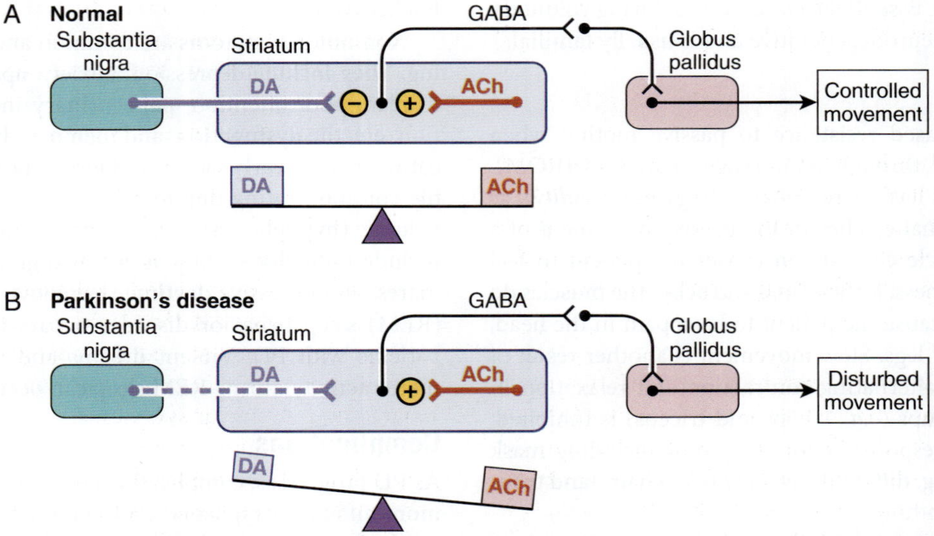

Fig. 63.7 A deficit in dopamine *(DA)* exists in PD. This deficit creates an imbalance between DA and the excitatory neurotransmitter acetylcholine *(ACh)*. (A) In a healthy person, DA released from neurons in the substantia nigra inhibits the firing of neurons in the striatum that release γ-aminobutyric acid *(GABA)*. Conversely, neurons in the striatum, which release ACh, excite the GABAergic neurons. Under normal conditions, inhibitory actions of DA are balanced by excitatory actions of ACh, and controlled movement results. (B) In PD, neurons in the substantia nigra that supply DA to the striatum degenerate. When a deficit of DA occurs, excitatory effects of ACh go unopposed and disturbed movements (tremor, rigidity) result. (From Lehne RA: *Pharmacology for nursing care,* ed 8, St Louis, 2013, Saunders.)

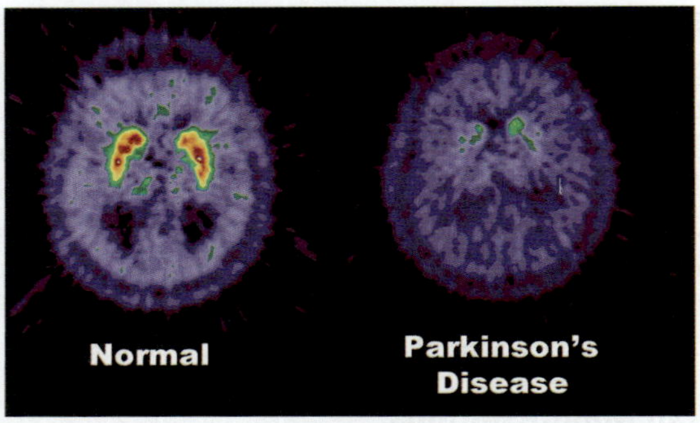

Fig. 63.8 In PD, PET scan showing reduced fluorodopa uptake in the basal ganglia *(right)* compared with a normal control *(left)*. (From Aminoff MJ, Daroff RB: *Encyclopedia of the neurological sciences,* Waltham, MA, 2003, Academic Press.)

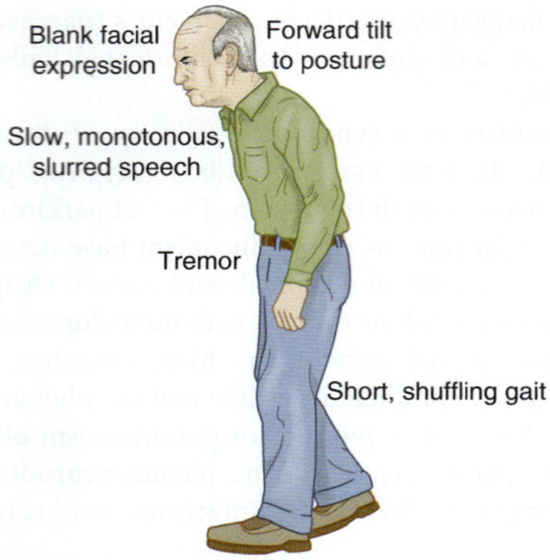

Fig. 63.9 Characteristic appearance of a patient with PD.

manifestations are tremors, rigidity, bradykinesia, and postural instability.[28] Early in the disease, only a mild tremor, a flattened affect, slowing of ADLs (dressing, feeding), or decreased arm swing may be seen. Shoulder rigidity may be mistaken for arthritis. Later, the patient may have a shuffling gait and appear unable to stop. There may be speech problems *(hypokinetic dysarthria)* that affect communication.

Tremor

Tremor is often the first sign. Parkinsonian tremor is more prominent at rest and lessens with purposeful movement (*nonintention tremor*). It is worsened by stress or increased concentration. The hand tremor is described as "pill rolling" because the thumb and forefinger appear to move in a rotary fashion as if rolling a pill or coin. This tremor can affect handwriting, causing it to trail off toward the ends of words. Tremor can involve the diaphragm, tongue, lips, and jaw.

Some people have a benign *essential tremor* that is mistakenly diagnosed as PD. Essential tremor occurs during voluntary movement. It is not neurodegenerative and is usually familial.

Rigidity

Rigidity is the increased resistance to passive motion when the limbs are moved through their range of motion (ROM). Parkinsonian rigidity has a jerky quality *(cogwheel rigidity),* as if there were occasional catches in the passive movement of a joint. Sustained muscle contraction causes the patient to feel stiff with muscle soreness, feeling tired and achy. The muscles do not relax. They may cause the patient to have pain in the head, upper body, spine, or legs. Slow movement is another result of rigidity because the alternating contraction and relaxation in opposing muscle groups (e.g., biceps and triceps) is inhibited. Rigidity is partially responsible for symptoms including mask face, lack of arm swing, difficulty getting out of chairs, and trouble with buttoning clothing.

Bradykinesia

In PD, bradykinesia (slowness of movement) is present in both spontaneous and automatic movements. All movement is slower. Tasks that were once easy are now frustratingly slow. Bradykinesia is due to the decreased impulses from the basal ganglia. In the unaffected person, automatic movements are involuntary and occur subconsciously. They include blinking of the eyelids, swinging of the arms while walking, swallowing saliva, using facial and hand movements, and making minor movements to adjust posture. The patient with PD lacks this natural activity. This accounts for the stooped, bent forward posture, masked face (deadpan expression), drooling of saliva, and shuffling gait (festination) that are typical of a person with PD (Fig. 63.9).

Postural Instability

Postural instability is common. Patients may describe being unable to stop themselves from going forward *(propulsion)* or backward *(retropulsion)*. This increases their risk of falling. Assessment of postural instability includes the "pull test." The examiner stands behind the patient and gives a tug backward on the shoulder, causing the patient to lose their balance and fall backward.

Nonmotor symptoms are common and can be very disturbing. They include depression, anxiety, apathy, fatigue, inability to plan, poor attention, pain, urinary incontinence, constipation, erectile dysfunction, and memory changes. Problems with eating include early satiety and loss of taste. Patients have trouble communicating due to a lack of expressive voice and low volume (hypophonia).[28] Sleep problems are common. They include difficulty staying asleep at night, restless sleep, nightmares, and excessive daytime sleepiness. Rapid eye movement (REM) sleep behavior disorder occurs in about one-third of patients with PD. Violent dreams and potentially dangerous motor activity during REM sleep can occur.[32]

Complications

As PD progresses, complications increase. Swallowing becomes more difficult (dysphagia) and malnutrition or aspiration may result. Increasing weakness may lead to immobility problems. Orthostatic hypotension is common. Along with loss of postural reflexes, it can cause falls or other injury. The increased fall risk means caregivers must be aware of environment conditions that may contribute to falls.

Other complications include dyskinesias (spontaneous, involuntary movements), weakness, and neuropsychiatric

TABLE 63.16 Interprofessional Care

Parkinson Disease

Diagnostic Assessment
- History and physical assessment
- Positive response to antiparkinsonian drugs
- MRI

Management
- Antiparkinsonian drugs (Table 63.17)
- Surgical therapy
- Deep brain stimulation
- Ablation
- Physical therapy
- Occupational therapy
- Speech therapy
- Dietitian consult for nutrition therapy

problems (e.g., depression, hallucinations). Dementia often results. It is associated with increased mortality.

Diagnostic Studies

No specific diagnostic test exists for PD. The diagnosis is based on the history and clinical features. Clinical diagnosis requires the presence of 2 of the 4 main manifestations (tremor, rigidity, bradykinesia, and postural instability) and asymmetric onset. Disease is confirmed with a positive response to antiparkinsonian drugs (levodopa or DA agonist). MRI and CT are usually normal in PD. They will be done to rule out other diagnosis. DaTscan, a special CT scan, may be done to detect DA function in the brain and distinguish PD from similar diseases.[29]

Interprofessional Care

Because PD has no cure, care focuses on symptom management (Table 63.16).

Drug Therapy

Table 63.17 outlines the drugs commonly used in PD. Drug therapy for PD is aimed at correcting the imbalance of neurotransmitters within the CNS. Antiparkinsonian drugs either enhance the release or supply of DA (dopaminergic) or block the effects of the overactive cholinergic neurons in the striatum (anticholinergic) (Fig. 63.7).

Drug doses are carefully adjusted. Excess amounts of dopaminergic drugs can worsen rather than relieve symptoms *(paradoxical intoxication)*. The use of only 1 drug is best. Fewer side effects occur. The dose is easier to adjust than when several drugs are used. However, as PD progresses, the patient often needs combination therapy.

Levodopa with carbidopa (Sinemet) is the primary treatment for symptomatic patients. Levodopa is a chemical precursor of DA. It can cross the blood-brain barrier. There, it is converted to DA in the basal ganglia. Carbidopa inhibits the enzyme dopa-decarboxylase, which breaks down levodopa before it reaches the brain. The net result of using this combination is that more levodopa reaches the brain. Levodopa has many side effects and drug interactions. Prolonged use often results in dyskinesias and "off/on" periods when the drug will unpredictably stop or start working.

DRUG ALERT

Carbidopa/Levodopa (Sinemet)

- Monitor for signs of dyskinesia.
- Stress that effects may be delayed for several weeks to months.
- Teach patient or caregiver to report any uncontrolled movement of face, eyelids, mouth, tongue, arms, hands, or legs; mental changes; palpitations; and problems urinating.

Many patients receive carbidopa/levodopa early in the disease course for the management of motor symptoms. While it will reduce symptoms, use does not stop the progression of PD.[28] HCPs may prefer to start therapy with a DA receptor agonist, a drug that directly stimulates DA receptors. Ropinirole (Requip) and pramipexole (Mirapex) may be used alone or in combination with carbidopa/levodopa. Many of these drugs are available in extended-release forms that improve the patient's ability to adhere to treatment plans. Rotigotine (Neupro), another DA receptor agonist, is a transdermal patch applied once daily. The DA receptor agonist apomorphine (Apokyn, Kynmobi) can improve movement in hypomobility ("off") episodes. Patients must take it with an antiemetic drug because it causes severe nausea and vomiting when taken alone. It cannot be taken with antiemetics in the serotonin (5-HT3) receptor antagonist class (e.g., ondansetron). This combination can lead to very low BP and loss of consciousness.

DRUG ALERT

Apomorphine

- May be taken up to 5 times per day.
- Take BP and pulse before and after administration.
- May cause falls, dizziness, and spontaneous sleepiness.
- Take with an antiemetic (not $5HT_3$ antagonist).

Anticholinergic drugs, such as trihexyphenidyl and benztropine (Cogentin), decrease the activity of Ach. Providing balance between cholinergic and dopaminergic actions can help with tremors and rigidity.

Monoamine oxidase type B (MAO-B) inhibitors like selegiline, rasagiline (Azilect), and safinamide (Xadago) may be used in combination with carbidopa/levodopa.[28] Inhibiting MAO-B, the enzyme that degrades DA, increases DA levels. However, MAO-B inhibitors are less effective at treating motor symptoms than DA receptor agonists.

Entacapone (Comtan) and opicapone (Ongentys) block the enzyme catechol *O*-methyltransferase (COMT), which breaks down levodopa in the peripheral circulation. This prolongs the effect of carbidopa/levodopa. They are used as adjuncts to therapy when the patient's response to levodopa is wearing off at the end of the dosing interval.

After 3 to 5 years of standard PD treatments, many patients have episodes of hypomobility (e.g., inability to

TABLE 63.17 Drug Therapy

Parkinson Disease

Drug	Mechanism of Action	Side Effects	Considerations
Dopaminergics			
Dopamine Precursors			
levodopa (L-dopa) levodopa/carbidopa (Sinemet)	Converted to dopamine (DA) in basal ganglia	Dry mouth GI distress	Do not take with meals. Limit Vitamin B6 intake. Teach about ways to decrease dry mouth.
Dopamine Receptor Agonists			
pramipexole (Mirapex) ropinirole (Requip, Requip XL) rotigotine (Neupro [transdermal patch])	Stimulate DA receptors	Dizziness GI distress Hallucinations Insomnia Orthostatic BP	Monitor orthostatic BP. Change positions slowly. Use safety measures if CNS effects occur. Rotate patch sites.
Dopamine Agonists			
amantadine apomorphine (Apokyn)	Blocks NMDA-type glutamate receptors, increases DA release, and blocks DA reuptake Stimulates postsynaptic DA receptors	Dizziness Insomnia Chest pain Drowsiness GI distress Liver toxicity Sweating	Do not stop abruptly. Use safety measures if CNS effects occur. Monitor liver function tests. Rotate injection sites. Give in abdomen, thigh, upper arm.
Anticholinergics			
benztropine (Cogentin) trihexyphenidyl	Block cholinergic receptors, thus helping to balance cholinergic and dopaminergic activity	Dizziness Dry mouth Urinary retention Vision changes	Stop if swallowing problems occur. Avoid alcohol, hot weather. Use safety measures if CNS effects occur.
Antihistamine			
diphenhydramine	Has anticholinergic effect	Drowsiness Dry mouth Urinary retention Vision changes	Avoid alcohol. Use safety measures if CNS effects occur. Do not take with MAO inhibitors.
Monoamine Oxidase Type B Inhibitors			
rasagiline (Azilect) safinamide (Xadago) selegiline	Block breakdown of DA	Dizziness Dry mouth Headache Orthostatic BP	Use safety measures if CNS effects occur. Avoid tyramine-containing foods. Many drug interactions. Avoid direct sunlight. Change positions slowly.
Catechol O-Methyltransferase (COMT) Inhibitors			
entacapone (Comtan) opicapone (Ongentys)	Block COMT and slow the breakdown of levodopa, thus prolonging the action of levodopa	Confusion Dizziness GI distress Hypotension	Only give with levodopa. Avoid pregnancy. Use safety measures if CNS effects occur.

rise from chair, speak, or walk; "off "episodes). Off episodes can occur toward the end of a dosing interval with standard medications (end-of-dose wearing off) or at unpredictable times (spontaneous "on/off"). A combination of carbidopa, levodopa, and entacapone (Stalevo) is available for patients with end-of-dose wearing off. This combination is typically prescribed for patients with advanced PD and intense motor fluctuations.[28] Rivastigmine (Exelon) or donepezil (Aricept) is used to treat dementia. Amitriptyline may be used to treat depression.

Surgical Therapy

Surgical procedures to relieve PD symptoms are used in patients who do not respond to drug therapy or have developed severe motor complications. Surgical procedures include DBS and ablation. The most common surgical treatment is DBS. This involves placing an electrode in the thalamus, globus pallidus, or subthalamic nucleus and connecting it to a generator placed in the upper chest (like a pacemaker) (Fig. 63.10). The device is programmed to deliver a specific current to the targeted brain location. DBS is preferred to ablation procedures

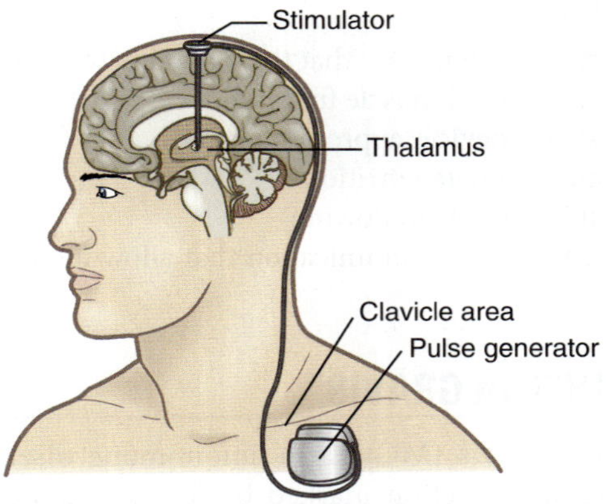

Fig. 63.10 DBS can be used to treat tremors and uncontrolled movements of PD. Electrodes are surgically placed in the brain and connected to a neurostimulator (pacemaker device) in the chest.

because it is reversible and programmable. DBS reduces the increased neuronal activity produced by DA depletion. It can improve motor function and reduce dyskinesia. DBS is indicated for patients who have had PD over 5 years, with dyskinesias, and are unable to tolerate or not controlled with drug therapy.[13]

Ablation surgery involves finding, targeting, and destroying an area of the brain affected by PD. The goal is to destroy tissue that produces abnormal chemical or electrical impulses leading to tremors or other symptoms. Typical targets of ablation are the thalamus *(thalamotomy)* and globus pallidus *(pallidotomy)*. Gamma knife surgery uses multiple radiation beams to target and destroy the target tissue. Unilateral focused ultrasound uses MRI-guided high-intensity ultrasound to destroy target tissue that is causing tremors and other symptoms.

NURSING MANAGEMENT: PARKINSON DISEASE

Assessment

Subjective and objective data that you should obtain from a patient with PD are outlined in Table 63.18.

Clinical Problems

Clinical problems for the patient with PD may include:

- Neurologic problem
- Nutritionally compromised
- Risk for injury
- Impaired communication
- Difficulty coping

Additional information on clinical problems and interventions for the patient with PD is presented in eNursing Care Plan 63.4 (available on the website for this chapter).

Planning

The overall goals are that the patient with PD will (1) maximize neurologic function, (2) maintain independence in ADLs for as long as possible, (3) prevent injury, and (4) optimize well-being.

TABLE 63.18 NURSING ASSESSMENT

Parkinson Disease

Subjective Data

Important Health Information

Health history: CNS trauma, cerebrovascular disorders, exposure to metals and carbon monoxide, encephalitis or other infections

Medications: Major tranquilizers, especially haloperidol (Haldol), and phenothiazines, reserpine, methyldopa, amphetamines

Functional Health Patterns

Health perception–health management: Fatigue

Nutritional-metabolic: Excessive salivation, dysphagia, weight loss

Elimination: Constipation, incontinence, excessive sweating

Activity-exercise: Difficulty in initiating movements, frequent falls, loss of dexterity, slowing of movements, micrographia (handwriting deterioration)

Sleep-rest: Insomnia, nightmares, daytime sleepiness

Cognitive-perceptual: Diffuse pain in head, shoulders, neck, back, legs, and hips. Muscle soreness and cramping

Self-perception–self-concept: Depression, mood swings, hallucinations

Objective Data

Cardiovascular

Postural hypotension

General

Blank (masked) facial expression, slow and monotonous speech, infrequent blinking

GI

Drooling

Musculoskeletal

Cogwheel rigidity, dysarthria, bradykinesia, contractures, stooped posture, shuffling gait

Neurologic

Tremor at rest, first in hands (pill rolling), later in legs, arms, face, and tongue. Aggravation of tremor with anxiety, absence in sleep. Poor coordination, cognitive impairment and dementia, impaired postural reflexes

Skin

Seborrhea, dandruff; ankle edema

Possible Diagnostic Findings

No specific tests. Diagnosis based on history and physical findings and ruling out of other diseases. Improvement with levodopa confirms diagnosis.

Nursing Implementation

Because PD is a chronic degenerative disorder with no acute exacerbations, teaching and nursing care are directed toward maintaining good health, encouraging independence, and avoiding complications, such as contractures, aspiration, and falls. Problems due to bradykinesia can be addressed by relatively simple measures.

CHECK YOUR PRACTICE

You are working in a rehabilitation facility with a new patient, a 78-year-old man with PD. He was at your facility briefly 6 months ago with a fractured hip after falling in his yard. The family has asked to talk with you about their fear of taking him for a walk in the hallways because he is so unstable.

- What advice would you give them?

Promoting physical exercise is a major nursing concern. Exercise can limit the effects of decreased mobility, such as muscle atrophy, contractures, and constipation. Although exercise will not stop disease progress, it will enhance the patient's functional ability. The American Parkinson Disease Association (www.apdaparkinson.org) can connect patients and families with support groups, and they publish booklets and fact sheets with helpful exercises that can be used by caregivers and health care professionals.

A physical therapist can design a personal exercise program to strengthen and stretch specific muscles. Speech therapists can design a plan to help with speaking and swallowing. An occupational therapist can help the patient with ways to increase self-care measures, including eating and dressing.

Work with caregivers to find ways to promote independence and self-care. The patient can get out of a chair better by using an upright chair with arms and placing the back legs of the chair on small (2-inch) blocks. Encourage environmental changes to improve safety. These include removing rugs and excess furniture to avoid stumbling and using an elevated toilet seat to help the patient get on and off the toilet. Elevating the legs can decrease dependent ankle edema. Clothing can be simplified by using slip-on shoes and Velcro hook-and-loop fasteners or zippers on clothing, instead of buttons. Allow extra time for all ADL.

A well-balanced diet is important. Malnutrition and constipation can result from poor nutrition. Patients who have dysphagia and bradykinesia need appetizing foods that are easy to chew and swallow. The diet should have adequate fiber to reduce constipation.

Eating 6 small meals a day may be less tiring than eating 3 large meals a day. Plan ample time for eating to avoid frustration. Cut food into bite-sized pieces. Protein ingestion can impair the absorption of levodopa. Limiting protein intake to the evening meal can decrease this problem. Discuss with the HCP about including vitamin B_6 in a multivitamin and fortified cereals. Vitamin B_6 intake can inhibit levodopa, but this does not occur when taking carbidopa with levodopa.

Effective management of sleep problems can improve quality of life. Some patients find satin nightwear or satin sheets helpful. Teaching about sleep hygiene practices is discussed in Chapter 8.

In the early stages of PD, patients often have depression and anxiety. Patients need to adjust their lifestyle, including work and home responsibilities. As PD progresses, the impact on psychologic well-being increases. Help the patient by listening, providing teaching, gently correcting distorted thoughts, and encouraging social interactions. Psychologic therapy and counseling can be helpful.

The patient begins with subtle changes in cognitive function that can progress to dementia. This causes increased caregiver burden and may lead to long-term care placement. Information on care of the patient with dementia is discussed in Chapter 64.

Family members (e.g., spouse, children) care for most patients with PD. Their burden increases as the disease progresses. The caregiver's physical and mental health may also decline. Help them find appropriate resources.

◆ Evaluation

The expected outcomes are that the patient with PD will:

- Maintain optimal muscle function
- Use assistive devices appropriately
- Maintain adequate nutrition
- Have unimpaired swallowing
- Use methods of communication that allow interaction with others

MYASTHENIA GRAVIS

Myasthenia gravis (MG) is an autoimmune disease of the neuromuscular junction marked by fluctuating weakness of certain skeletal muscles that worsens with activity. MG can occur in anyone. Around 40 per 100,000 people have MG in the United States. It affects people of all ages and races. In women, MG often starts between ages 20 to 30. Men usually develop MG in their 50s.[30]

Etiology and Pathophysiology

MG is caused by an autoimmune process in which antibodies attack and destroy ACh receptors. This results in fewer ACh receptor (AChR) sites at the neuromuscular junction. This prevents ACh molecules from attaching to receptors and stimulating muscle contraction. We think the thymus gives incorrect instructions to developing immune cells causing them to make AChR antibodies. Anti-AChR antibodies are found in the serum of most patients with MG. MuSK and LRP4 antibodies, which also reduce AChR, are present in some patients as well. Some patients have no autoantibodies.

Clinical Manifestations and Complications

The key feature of MG is fluctuating weakness of skeletal muscles. MG affects multiple muscle groups. Muscles engaged in repetitive movements are affected the most. This includes muscles used to move the eyes and eyelids, chew, swallow, speak, and breathe. Muscles are often strongest in the morning. They become exhausted with continued activity. Muscle weakness is prominent by the end of the day. A period of rest usually restores strength.

In more than half of patients, the first muscles involved are the ocular muscles, causing ptosis (drooping of the eyelids) in 1 or both eyes and double vision (Fig. 63.11).[8] MG does not progress beyond the ocular muscles in most patients. When facial muscles are affected, facial mobility and expression can be impaired. Patients may have difficulty chewing and swallowing food. Speech is affected. The voice often is hoarse or fades after long conversations. The muscles of the trunk and limbs easily fatigue. Of these, the proximal muscles of the neck, shoulder, and hip are more often affected than the distal muscles. No other neural problems occur. No sensory loss occurs, and reflexes are normal. Muscle atrophy is rare.

The course of MG is highly variable. Patients may have short-term remissions, stabilize, or have severe progressive disease. Fatigue, pregnancy, illness, trauma, temperature extremes, stress, and hypokalemia can exacerbate MG. Some drugs can worsen MG symptoms, including β-adrenergic blockers,

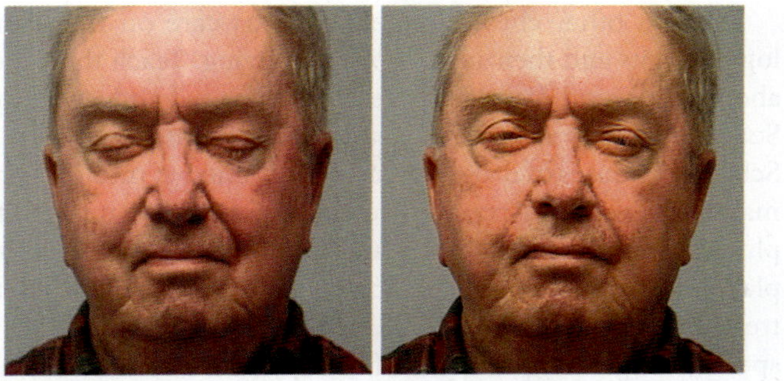

Fig. 63.11 "Peek" sign in myasthenia gravis. During sustained forced eyelid closure, he is unable to bury his eyelashes *(left)*. After 30 seconds, he cannot keep the lids fully closed *(right)*. (From Sanders DB, Massey JM: Clinical features of myasthenia gravis. In AG Engel, editor: *Neuromuscular junction disorders: handbook of clinical neurology,* New York, 2008, Elsevier.)

calcium channel blockers, lithium, quinidine, and aminoglycoside antibiotics.[30]

Myasthenic crisis is an acute worsening of muscle weakness triggered by respiratory infection, surgery, stress, pregnancy, exposure to certain drugs, or starting corticosteroid treatment. The major complications of a myasthenic crisis results from muscle weakness in areas that affect swallowing and breathing. This can result in aspiration or respiratory insufficiency. The patient may need a ventilator or noninvasive respiratory support (BiPAP).

Diagnostic Studies

The diagnosis can be based on the history and physical assessment. Other tests may be used for confirmation. Single-fiber EMG is highly sensitive in confirming MG.[30] EMG may show a decreased response to repeated stimulation of the hand muscles that shows muscle fatigue.

The response to an edrophonium test can indicate MG. Edrophonium, an anticholinesterase agent, is given IV. It blocks the enzyme acetylcholinesterase, the enzyme that breaks down ACh. A patient with MG has rapid improvement in muscle strength for a short time after receiving edrophonium.[30] Atropine, a cholinergic antagonist, should be readily available to counteract the effects of edrophonium when it is used diagnostically. In patients with a confirmed diagnosis of MG, a chest CT scan may be done to evaluate the thymus.

Interprofessional Care

Drug Therapy

Drug therapy for MG includes anticholinesterase drugs, alternate-day corticosteroids, and immunosuppressants (Table 63.19). Anticholinesterase drugs enhance transmission at the neuromuscular junction. Inhibiting acetylcholinesterase with an anticholinesterase inhibitor prolongs the action of ACh and improves impulse transmission at the neuromuscular junction. Pyridostigmine (Mestinon) is the best drug of this group for the long-term treatment of MG.

Tailoring the dose to avoid a myasthenic or cholinergic crisis often presents a challenge. Inadequate dosing can cause myasthenic crisis. Excessive dosing will cause a cholinergic crisis, which occurs due to too much cholinesterase inhibition. Cholinergic crisis symptoms are very similar to myasthenic crisis. Features of a cholinergic crisis include involuntary muscle contraction, extreme weakness, flaccid muscle paralysis, sweating, excessive salivation, diarrhea, and constricted pupils. In a cholinergic crisis, giving edrophonium increases muscle weakness. The use of corticosteroids in addition to edrophonium have reduced the incidence of cholinergic crisis.

Corticosteroids (specifically prednisone) are used to suppress the immune response. Other drugs used for immunosuppression include azathioprine (Imuran), mycophenolate (CellCept), and cyclosporine (Sandimmune). Up to 80% of patients who receive corticosteroids have marked improvement. These benefits must be weighed with concerns about their chronic use. Eculizumab (Soliris), an IV monoclonal antibody, stops the autoimmune response. Over time, it improves symptoms.[31] Vyvgart (efgartigimod), another IV infusion, is the first drug in a class of drugs called FcRn Inhibitors. It is used to treat adults who are anti-AChR antibody positive.

Surgical Therapy

Because the thymus gland in the patient with MG appears to enhance the production of AChR antibodies, removing the thymus gland causes improvement in most patients. A few patients achieve cure after thymectomy.

Other Therapies

Plasmapheresis and IV immunoglobulin G can yield short-term improvement in symptoms. They are indicated for patients in myasthenic crisis or before surgery when corticosteroids must be avoided. Plasmapheresis directly removes circulating AChR antibodies from the plasma, leading to a decrease in symptoms. IV immunoglobulin binds antibodies thus preventing their action.

TABLE 63.19 Interprofessional Care

Myasthenia Gravis

Diagnostic Assessment

- History and physical assessment
  - Fatigability with prolonged upward gaze (2–3 min)
  - Muscle weakness
- EMG
- Edrophonium test
- Acetylcholine receptor antibodies
- Chest x-ray

Management

- Drug therapy
  - Anticholinesterase agents
  - Corticosteroids
  - Immunosuppressive agents
  - FcRn inhibitors
- Surgery (thymectomy)
- Plasmapheresis
- IV immunoglobulin G

TABLE 63.20 Comparison of Myasthenic and Cholinergic Crises

Myasthenic Crisis	Cholinergic Crisis
Causes	
Exacerbation of myasthenia after precipitating factors, failure to take drug as prescribed, or drug dose too low	Overdose of anticholinesterase drugs resulting in ↑ ACh at the receptor sites, remission (spontaneous or after thymectomy)
Differential Diagnosis	
Improved strength after IV administration of anticholinesterase drugs	Weakness within 1 h after ingestion of anticholinesterase drugs
↑ Weakness of skeletal muscles manifesting as ptosis, bulbar signs (e.g., difficulty swallowing, difficulty articulating words), dyspnea	↑ Weakness of skeletal muscles manifesting as ptosis, bulbar signs, dyspnea Effects on smooth muscle include pupillary miosis, salivation, diarrhea, nausea or vomiting, abdominal cramps, ↑ bronchial secretions, sweating, lacrimation

NURSING MANAGEMENT: MYASTHENIA GRAVIS

Assessment

Assess the severity of MG by asking the patient about fatigue, what body parts are affected, and how severely they are affected. Some patients become so fatigued they cannot work or even walk. Assess the patient's coping abilities and understanding of MG. Obtain a thorough medication history. Many drugs are contraindicated or must be used with caution in patients with MG.

Objective data should include respiratory rate and depth, O_2 saturation, arterial blood gas analyses, and pulmonary function tests. Assess for respiratory distress in patients with acute myasthenic crisis. Assess muscle strength of all face and limb muscles, swallowing, speech (volume and clarity), and cough and gag reflexes.

Clinical Problems

Clinical problems for the patient with MG may include:

- Impaired respiratory function
- Activity intolerance
- Risk for injury
- Neurologic Problem

Planning

The overall goals are that the patient with MG will (1) have a return of normal muscle strength, (2) manage fatigue, (3) avoid complications, and (4) maintain quality of life.

Implementation

The patient with MG who is admitted to the hospital usually has a respiratory tract infection or is in acute myasthenic crisis. Nursing care is aimed at maintaining adequate ventilation, continuing drug therapy, and watching for side effects of therapy. Be able to tell a cholinergic from myasthenic crisis (Table 63.20) because their causes and treatment differ greatly.

As with other chronic illnesses, focus care on the neurologic deficits and their impact on daily living. Teach the patient about a balanced diet that can easily be chewed and swallowed. Semisolid foods may be easier to eat than solids or liquids. Scheduling doses of drugs to reach peak action at mealtime may make eating easier. Arrange diversional activities that need little physical effort and match the patient's interests. Help the patient plan ADLs to avoid fatigue. Focus teaching on adherence to the treatment plan, complications, potential adverse reactions to specific drugs, complications of therapy (crisis conditions), and what to do about them. Explore community resources, such as the Myasthenia Gravis Foundation of America and MG support groups.

Evaluation

The expected outcomes are that the patient with MG will:

- Maintain optimal muscle function
- Be free from side effects of drugs
- Have no complications
- Maintain a quality of life appropriate to the disease course

AMYOTROPHIC LATERAL SCLEROSIS

Amyotrophic lateral sclerosis (ALS) is a rare progressive neuromuscular disorder marked by loss of motor neurons. ALS usually leads to death 3 to 5 years after diagnosis. A few patients may survive for more than 10 years. Many call ALS *Lou Gehrig's disease* after the famous baseball player who was stricken with it in 1939. The best-known patient with ALS is physicist Stephen Hawking. He was diagnosed at age 21 years and lived with ALS for over 50 years. The median age of onset is 55 years. ALS is more common in Whites, men, and military veterans. About 30,000 Americans have ALS.[32]

In ALS, upper and lower motor neurons in the brainstem and spinal cord gradually degenerate. We do not know the cause. Early in the disease mitochondrial changes occur and excess glutamate (an excitatory neurotransmitter) damages the neurons.[33] Destroyed motor neurons cannot produce or transport signals to muscles. Consequently, electrical and chemical messages originating in the brain do not reach the muscles to activate them. Factors that we suspect affect ALS include smoking, athleticism, metals, solvents, radiation, electromagnetic fields, pesticides, and viruses.[32]

About 10% of ALS cases are genetic. We have found mutations in more than a dozen genes that cause familial ALS (FALS). The most common genes are *C9ORF72* and SOD1.[8]

Progressive muscle weakness and atrophy are the classic sign of ALS. Early symptoms of weakness vary. Some have "limb-onset ALS," initially affecting the arms or legs. The person may have trouble with tasks requiring fine motor skills (e.g., writing, typing) or notice they are tripping, dropping things, or stumbling more often. Those who first have problems with slurred speech or swallowing have "bulbar onset" ALS.

Muscle wasting and involuntary contractions and twitching result from the denervation of the muscles and lack of stimulation and use. Other symptoms include pain, sleep disorders, spasticity and hyperreflexia, drooling, emotional lability, constipation, and esophageal reflux. Eventually the patient may not be able to communicate. As the ability to move decreases, swallowing is impaired leading to aspiration. ALS does not affect intelligence but affected people may have problems with decision making and memory. Death often results from compromised respiratory function due to muscle weakness and paralysis.

No cure exists for ALS. Two drugs may slow the decline. Riluzole (Rilutek) reduces damage to motor neurons by decreasing the release of glutamate. Edaravone (Radicava) is a free radical scavenger that we think relieves effects of oxidative stress, a likely factor in progression of ALS.[32] It is given IV in 14-day cycles.

The course of ALS is devastating because the patient is cognitively intact while wasting away. Common problems are grief and impaired role performance. Care focuses on (1) facilitating communication, (2) reducing aspiration risk, (3) early identification of respiratory problems, (4) decreasing pain from muscle weakness, (5) decreasing risk for fall-related injury, (6) providing diversional activities, such as reading and companionship, and (7) providing compassionate end-of-life care. Moderate-intensity, endurance-type exercises for the trunk and limbs may help to reduce spasticity.

Support the patient and caregivers emotionally. This includes grieving related to the loss of motor function and impending death. Discuss advance directives and artificial ventilation with the patient and caregiver. Provide the caregiver with support and resources to combat the fatigue and stressors they experience.

HUNTINGTON DISEASE

Huntington disease (HD) is a progressive, degenerative brain disorder causing deterioration of physical, emotional, and cognitive abilities. It is a genetically transmitted, autosomal dominant disorder (Box 63.2). The offspring of a person with HD have a 50% risk for inheriting it. Diagnosis is often made after the affected person has had children. The United States has about 30,000 affected people. The onset of HD is usually between ages 30 and 55 years.[34] Patients live 15 to 20 years after diagnosis.[34]

The diagnostic process begins with a review of the family history and clinical symptoms. Genetic testing confirms excessive CAG protein repeats in the *HTT* gene.[35] People who are asymptomatic but who have a positive family history of HD must decide if they want genetic testing. If the test is positive, the person will develop HD. However, we do not know when the disease will develop. If a person has HD in the family, genetic testing is recommended to aid in family planning. Refer those wishing to have a child who does not carry the gene to a fertility specialist.

The pathologic process of HD involves the basal ganglia and extrapyramidal motor system. HD involves a deficiency of the neurotransmitters ACh and γ-aminobutyric acid (GABA). The net effect is an excess of DA, which leads to symptoms that are the opposite of those of parkinsonism.

Manifestations include movement disorder and cognitive and psychiatric problems. The movement disorder is marked by abnormal and excessive involuntary movements *(chorea)*. These are writhing, twisting movements of the face, limbs, and body. The movements get worse as the disease progresses. Movements are uncoordinated. Patients have difficulty with movement sequences (getting out of bed, getting out of a chair). Inability to sustain movement occurs. Because facial movements involving speech, chewing, and swallowing are affected, aspiration and malnutrition are likely. The gait deteriorates. Ambulation eventually becomes impossible. Eventually all psychomotor processes, including the ability to eat and talk, are impaired.

BOX 63.2 GENETICS IN CLINICAL PRACTICE

Huntington Disease (HD)

Genetic Basis

- Autosomal dominant disorder
- Caused by mutation in *HTT* gene found on chromosome 4
- A single copy of altered gene (heterozygous) is enough to cause HD
- Offspring of a person with HD have a 50% chance of inheriting the disease-causing allele

Incidence

- Occurs in 3 to 7 in 100,000 people of European ancestry
- Less common in other populations

Genetic Testing

- DNA testing is available
- DNA testing can be done on fetal cells obtained by amniocentesis or chorionic villus sampling
- Preimplantation genetic diagnosis can be done on embryos before implantation and pregnancy
- No test is available to predict when symptoms will develop

Clinical Implications

- Consider genetic counseling if there is a family history of HD
- A positive result means the patient will eventually develop HD
- A negative test means the person does not carry the mutated gene and will not develop HD

Psychiatric symptoms are often present in the early stage of HD, even before the onset of motor symptoms. Depression is common. Other psychiatric symptoms include anxiety, agitation, impulsivity, apathy, social withdrawal, moodiness, and stubbornness.[35] Cognitive deterioration is more variable. Many have slowed mental processing. They have difficulty thinking through a problem and will have trouble putting tasks in order. HD involves perception, memory, attention, and learning problems. Cognitive problems will progress to dementia. At the end of the disease, the patient will be nonverbal, bedridden, and require help with all ADLs.

The most common cause of death is pneumonia, followed by suicide. Other causes of death include injuries related to falls and other complications.

Because HD has no cure, treatment is palliative. Drugs are available to control movements and behavioral problems. Tetrabenazine (Xenazine) and Deutetrabenazine (Austedo) are used to treat chorea. They decrease the amount of DA available at synapses of the nerves and thus reducing the involuntary movements. Other medications to lessen the chorea disorder include neuroleptics and benzodiazepines.

Cognitive disorders are treated as needed with nondrug therapies (e.g., counseling, memory books). Selective serotonin reuptake inhibitors, such as sertraline (Zoloft), are an option for depression. Antipsychotic medication, such as haloperidol or risperidone, may be needed.

The goal of nursing management is to provide the most comfortable environment possible for the patient and caregiver by maintaining physical safety, treating symptoms, and providing emotional and psychologic support.

Because of the chorea, caloric requirements are high. The patient may need as many as 4000 to 5000 cal/day to maintain body weight. As HD progresses, meeting caloric needs becomes a greater challenge when the patient has difficulty swallowing and holding the head still. Depression and mental deterioration can compromise nutrition intake. Enteral or parenteral nutrition may be needed as the disease progresses.

End-of-life issues need to be discussed with the patient and caregiver. These include care in the home or long-term care facility, artificial methods of feeding, advance directives, use of antibiotics to treat infections, and guardianship. Address these topics throughout the course of the disease as the patient and caregiver adapt to increasing disability.

Case Study

Seizure Disorder With Headache

(© Purestock/Thinkstock.)

Patient Profile

C.A. is a 28-year-old woman diagnosed with seizure disorder at age 17. At that time, she had a heat-related injury and electrolyte imbalance causing a tonic-clonic seizure. She had a second seizure 2 months later and was placed on divalproex. She has had no further seizures until 6 months ago. In the past 6 months, she has had 2 generalized onset seizures and developed throbbing headaches after both episodes. She now has frequent headaches. C.A. says she is planning a wedding and taken on more responsibilities at work. She is afraid the headaches and seizures will cause her to lose her job and interfere with her wedding.

Subjective Data

- Describes throbbing headache pain on the right side of her forehead
- Has vomited during headaches
- Describes vision changes, including blurring and flashing zig zag lights before the start of a headache
- Headache occurs several times a week and last several hours
- Headaches have not improved with ibuprofen or acetaminophen

Objective Data

- Neurologic assessment shows no abnormal findings
- Serum divalproex levels are within therapeutic range
- EEG and CT of head normal
- CBC and metabolic panel are within normal limits

Discussion Questions

1. ***Recognize:*** What assessment findings are important?
2. ***Analyze:*** What type of headache is C.A. describing?
3. ***Plan:*** What therapy do you expect for her headaches and seizures?
4. ***Prioritize:*** Based on the assessment data, what are the priority clinical problems?
5. ***Act:*** What teaching will you provide so C.A. can manage her care?
6. ***Act:*** What lifestyle changes would you recommend?
7. ***Evaluate:*** What outcomes would indicate C.A.'s care has been successful?
8. ***Safety:*** To ensure C.A.'s safety, what nursing interventions are needed?

Answers available at http://evolve.elsevier.com/Lewis/medsurg.

BRIDGE TO NCLEX EXAMINATION

The number of the question corresponds to the same-numbered outcome at the beginning of the chapter.

1. A patient in urgent care reports a stabbing headache around his left eye and nasal stuffiness. He says, "This pain is horrible; it is worse than my heart attack last year." The provider orders sumatriptan nasal spray now for headache relief. The nurse would take what action?
   a. Administer a puff to each nostril now.
   b. Take vital signs prior to administration.
   c. Contact the provider about administering the medication to this patient.
   d. Teach the patient to self-administer the medication at the start of the migraine.
2. The rapid response team is called to the cafeteria. They find a 22-year-old with a known seizure disorder having a tonic-clonic seizure. What actions will be taken during the seizure? *(select all that apply)*
   a. Establish IV access.
   b. Insert an oral airway.
   c. Gently hold the arms to prevent injury.
   d. Administer the patient's intranasal midazolam.
   e. Turn the person to their side and pad their head.
3. A 28-year-old patient whose mother has Huntington disease is discussing family planning with the nurse. The patient says they want to have a child but are concerned. What statement will the nurse make?
   a. "Both parents must have the gene for your child to inherit this disease."
   b. "If you have the Huntington mutation, you will not be able to have children."
   c. "Only about 1 in 10 people who have the gene pass it to their children."
   d. "Genetic testing can be done to determine if you can pass this trait to a child."
4. The nurse conducts a home visit for a patient with Parkinson disease taking levodopa/carbidopa daily. The patient has stopped eating meals with his family and has lost 3 pounds since the last visit a week ago. What action will the nurse take?
   a. Plan 6 small high-protein meals a day.
   b. Provide information on a high-fat ketogenic diet.

c. Evaluate their ability with eating, swallowing, and use of assistive devices.
d. Collaborate with the HCP about every other day levodopa/carbidopa dosing.

5. A patient with multiple sclerosis receives natalizumab every 6 months and modafinil and dalfampridine daily. What assessment findings would indicate that the treatment plan was successful? *(select all that apply)*
   a. Blurred vision
   b. Improved walking
   c. Decreased fatigue
   d. No change in spasticity
   e. Reduced exacerbation frequency

1. c; 2. a, d, e; 3. d; 4. c; 5. b, c, e.

For rationales to these answers and even more NCLEX review questions, visit http://evolve.elsevier.com/Lewis/medsurg.

EVOLVE WEBSITE/RESOURCES LIST

http://evolve.elsevier.com/Lewis/medsurg
Review Questions (Online Only)
Key Points
Answer Keys for Questions
- Rationales for Bridge to NCLEX Examination Questions
- Answer Guidelines for Case Study

Student Case Studies
- Patient With Parkinson's Disease and Hip Fracture
- Patient With Seizures

Nursing Care Plans
- eNursing Care Plan 63.1: Patient With Headaches
- eNursing Care Plan 63.2: Patient With Seizure Disorder
- eNursing Care Plan 63.3: Patient With Multiple Sclerosis
- eNursing Care Plan 63.4: Patient With Parkinson's Disease

Conceptual Care Map Creator
- Conceptual Care Map for Case Study

Audio Glossary
Content Updates

REFERENCES

1. International Headache Society: Guidelines. Retrieved from https://ichd-3.org/.
2. Oliver N: Migraine management in the emergency department, *J Emerg Nurs* 46:518, 2020.
3. Ferri F: *Ferri's Clinical Advisor 2022*, Philadelphia, 2022, Elsevier.
4. American Migraine Foundation: Comorbidities of migraine. Retrieved from https://americanmigrainefoundation.org/resource-library/comorbidities-of-migraine.
5. Healthline: Migraine triggers. Retrieved from https://www.healthline.com/health/migraine/triggers.
6. International Headache Society (AHS): Migraine. Retrieved from https://ichd-3.org/1-migraine.
7. AHS: Types of aura. Retrieved from https://americanheadachesociety.org/news/types-of-aura/.
8. Goldman L, Schafer A: *Goldman-Cecil Medicine*, ed 26, Philadelphia, 2020, Elsevier.
9. The Migraine Trust: Cluster headache. Retrieved from https://www.migrainetrust.org/about-migraine/types-of-migraine/other-headache-disorders/cluster-headache.
10. AHS: Noninvasive migraine treatment options. https://americanheadachesociety.org/news/non-invasive-migraine-treatment-options-qa-dr-stewart-tepper/.
11. AHS: Incorporating nutraceuticals for migraine prevention. Retrieved from https://americanheadachesociety.org/news/incorporating-nutraceuticals-for-migraine-prevention.
12. AHS: How do I discuss lifestyle modifications with my migraine patient? Retrieved from https://americanheadachesociety.org/wp-content/uploads/2021/01/AHS-First-Contact-Lifestyle-Recommendations.pdf.
13. Jankovic J, Mazziotta JC, Pomeroy SL, Newman NJ: *Bradley and Daroff's neurology in clinical practice*, ed 8, Philadelphia, 2022, Elsevier.
14. Center for Disease Control (CDC): Epilepsy fast facts. Retrieved from https://www.cdc.gov/epilepsy/about/fast-facts.htm.
15. National Institute of Neurologic Disorders and Stroke (NINDS): The epilepsies and seizures: hope through research. Retrieved from https://www.ninds.nih.gov/Disorders/Patient-Caregiver-Education/Hope-Through-Research/Epilepsies-and-Seizures-Hope-Through#3109_8.

*16. International League Against Epilepsy: Operational classification of seizure types. Retrieved from https://www.ilae.org/guidelines/definition-and-classification/operational-classification-2017.

17. Wieruszewski ED, Brown CS, Leung JG, et al.: Pharmacologic management of status epilepticus, *AACN Adv Crit Care* 31:349, 2020.
18. CDC: SUDEP. Retrieved from https://www.cdc.gov/epilepsy/about/sudep/.
19. Drugs.com: Restless leg syndrome. Retrieved from https://www.drugs.com/health-guide/restless-legs-syndrome.html.
20. The Sleep Foundation: Restless Leg Syndrome (RLS) treatment. Retrieved from https://www.sleepfoundation.org/restless-legs-syndrome/treatment.
21. NHS Inform: Restless leg syndrome. Retrieved from https://www.nhsinform.scot/illnesses-and-conditions/brain-nerves-and-spinal-cord/restless-legs-syndrome#causes-of-restless-legs-syndrome.
22. Restless Leg Syndrome Foundation: Symptoms & diagnosis. Retrieved from https://www.rls.org/understanding-rls/symptoms-diagnosis.
23. NINDS: Multiple sclerosis: hope through research. Retrieved from https://www.ninds.nih.gov/Disorders/Patient-Caregiver-Education/Hope-Through-Research/Multiple-Sclerosis-Hope-Through-Research#myelin.
24. National Multiple Sclerosis Society: Who gets MS? Retrieved from https://www.nationalmssociety.org/What-is-MS/Who-Gets-MS.
25. Multiple Sclerosis Association of America: Long term treatments for multiple sclerosis. Retrieved from https://mymsaa.org/ms-information/treatments/long-term/.

*26. Parkinson's Foundation: Statistics. Retrieved from https://www.parkinson.org/Understanding-Parkinsons/Statistics.

27. Parkinson's Foundation: Environmental factors. Retrieved from https://www.parkinson.org/Understanding-Parkinsons/Causes/Environmental-Factors.

28. NINDS: Parkinson's disease: hope through research. Retrieved from https://www.ninds.nih.gov/disorders/patient-caregiver-education/hope-through-research/parkinsons-disease-hope-through-research#causes.
29. American Parkinson's Disease Association: Diagnosing Parkinson's. Retrieved from https://www.apdaparkinson.org/what-is-parkinsons/diagnosing/.
30. National Organization for Rare Disorders: Myasthenia gravis. Retrieved from https://rarediseases.org/rare-diseases/myasthenia-gravis/.
31. Conquer Myasthenia Gravis: What makes MG worse. Retrieved from https://www.myastheniagravis.org/about-mg/what-makes-mg-worse/.
32. NINDS: Amyotrophic lateral sclerosis fact sheet. Retrieved from http://www.ninds.nih.gov/Disorders/Patient-Caregiver-Education/Fact-Sheets/Amyotrophic-Lateral-Sclerosis-ALS-Fact-Sheet#who.
33. ALS Association: Disease mechanisms. Retrieved from https://www.als.org/research/research-we-fund/scientific-focus-areas/disease-mechanisms.
34. NIH National Center for Advancing Translational Sciences: Huntington's disease. Retrieved from https://rarediseases.info.nih.gov/diseases/6677/huntington-disease.
35. NINDS: Huntington's disease. Retrieved from https://www.ninds.nih.gov/Disorders/Patient-Caregiver-Education/Hope-Through-Research/Huntingtons-Disease-Hope-Through#4.

*Evidence-based information for clinical practice.

64

Dementia and Delirium

Janice Smolowitz

http://evolve.elsevier.com/Lewis/medsurg/

CONCEPTUAL FOCUS

Caregiving
Cognition
Family Dynamics
Functional Ability
Safety

LEARNING OUTCOMES

1. Define dementia and delirium.
2. Classify the different etiologies of dementia.
3. Explain the pathophysiology for different types of dementia.
4. Discuss the clinical manifestations of mild cognitive impairment.
5. Describe the clinical manifestations, diagnostic studies, and nursing and interprofessional care for a patient with dementia.
6. Discuss the clinical manifestations, diagnostic studies, and nursing and interprofessional care for a patient with Alzheimer disease.
7. Explain the etiology, pathophysiology, clinical manifestations, diagnostic studies, and nursing and interprofessional care for a patient with delirium.

KEY TERMS

Alzheimer disease (AD)
delirium
dementia
dementia with Lewy bodies (DLB), Table 64.3
frontotemporal lobar degeneration (FTLD), Table 64.3
mild cognitive impairment (MCI)
mixed dementia
retrogenesis
sundowning

This chapter discusses dementia and delirium, with a focus on the nursing management of patients with Alzheimer disease (AD). Cognitive impairment refers to any deficit in intellectual functioning, including problems with memory, orientation, attention, and concentration. The consequences of cognitive impairment can be devastating for the person and caregivers. Dementia adversely affects functional ability and the person's ability to work, fulfill responsibilities, and perform activities of daily living (ADL). There is a high risk for many problems, including injury, impaired nutrition, and social isolation.

Persons with dementia and delirium may have symptoms of depression. Depression and dementia are often mistaken for one another, especially among older adults. Manifestations of depression, especially among older adults, may include sadness, difficulty concentrating, fatigue, apathy, feelings of despair, and inactivity. When depression is severe, poor concentration and inattention may result, causing memory and functional impairment. When dementia and depression occur together, there can be marked intellectual decline. Table 64.1 compares key features of dementia, delirium, and depression. Your ability to interview the patient and family members about presenting symptoms and signs can help with early diagnosis and treatment.

DEMENTIA

Dementia is a disorder characterized by a decline from the previous level of function in 1 or more cognitive domains: complex attention, executive function, language, learning and memory, perceptual-motor, and social cognition.[1,2] The cognitive decline interferes with the ability to function and perform daily activities. This decline does not occur with the onset of acute confusion, such as delirium, or the onset of another major mental problem, such as depression.

The number of patients diagnosed with dementia is increasing. AD is the most common form of dementia.[3] It accounts for 60% to 80% of all cases of dementia (Fig. 64.1).

TABLE 64.1 Comparison of Dementia, Delirium, and Depression

Feature	Dementia	Delirium	Depression
Onset	Subtle, gradual	Abrupt, although initially can be subtle	Often coincides with life changes. Often abrupt
Progression	Slow	Abrupt. Can fluctuate from day to day	Variable, rapid to slow but may be uneven
Duration	Years (average of 8, can be longer)	Hours to days to weeks. Can be prolonged	Can be several months to years, especially if not treated
Thinking	Difficulty with abstract thinking, impaired judgment, words difficult to find	Disorganized, distorted. Slow or accelerated incoherent speech	Intact but with apathy, fatigue. May be indecisive. Feels a sense of hopelessness. May not want to live
Perception	Misperceptions often present. Delusions and hallucinations	Distorted. Delusions and hallucinations	May deny or be unaware of depression. May have feelings of guilt
Psychomotor behavior	May pace or be hyperactive. As disease progresses, may not be able to perform tasks or movements when asked	Variable. Can be hyperactive or hypoactive, or mixed	Often withdrawn and hypoactive
Sleep-wake cycle	Sleeps during the day. Frequent awakenings at night. Fragmented sleep	Disturbed sleep. Reversed sleep-wake cycle	Disturbed, often with early morning awakening

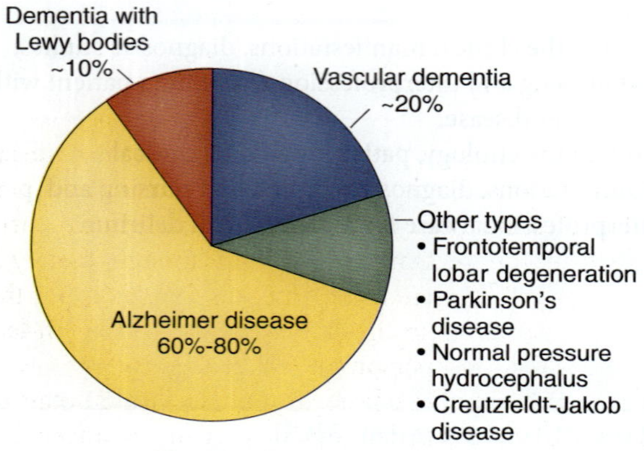

Fig. 64.1 Causes of dementia.

Etiology and Pathophysiology

Dementia is caused by treatable and untreatable conditions. Table 64.2 describes types of dementia and their underlying causes. Treatable causes may initially be reversible. However, irreversible changes can occur with prolonged exposure or disease.

The most common causes are neurodegenerative conditions that cannot be reversed (Table 64.3). Most of these are due to AD.[4] Other causes include dementia with Lewy bodies (DLB), frontotemporal dementia (FTD), and Parkinson disease with dementia (PDD). Vascular or multi-infarct dementia (VaD) is a loss of cognitive function caused by vascular disease. VaD may be caused by a single infarct (stroke) or multiple strokes.[5] It is more common in men. Subcortical dementia is the most common type of VaD. It occurs when small vessels deep in the brain develop thick walls and become stiff. This reduces blood flow, which damages the nerve fibers that carry signals to white matter. This process can cause infarcts near the base of the brain.[6]

Mixed dementia occurs when 2 or more types of dementia are present at the same time. It is characterized by the hallmark abnormalities of AD and another type of dementia. Usually, the other type of dementia is VaD, but it can be other types.

Normal pressure hydrocephalus is a rare disorder characterized by an obstruction in the flow of cerebrospinal fluid (CSF). This causes a buildup of CSF in the brain. Manifestations include dementia, urinary incontinence, and difficulty walking. Meningitis, encephalitis, or head injury may cause the condition. If diagnosed early, it is treatable by surgery in which a shunt is inserted to divert the fluid away from the brain.

Clinical Manifestations

The onset of manifestations varies depending on the cause. Manifestations of neurologic degeneration usually occur gradually and progress over time. Symptoms of VaD may appear abruptly or progress in a stepwise pattern. While the cause of dementia cannot be determined based only on the history of symptom progression, patterns can guide your thinking about the cause. An acute change that occurs over days to weeks or subacute change that occurs over weeks to months may indicate an infectious or metabolic cause of dementia, such as encephalitis, meningitis, hypothyroidism, or drug-related dementia. Other manifestations of dementia are discussed in the section on clinical manifestations of AD.

Diagnostic Studies

The diagnosis is focused on determining the cause (e.g., reversible versus irreversible). An important first step is a thorough medical, neurologic, and psychologic history. During the history, give special attention to the cognitive and behavior changes that have occurred. Family members and significant others can give important information. Obtain information about (1) problems with judgment; (2) reduced interest in hobbies/activities; (3) repeating questions, stories, or statements; (4) trouble learning how to use a tool or appliance; (5) forgetting the month or year; (6) problems handling financial affairs; (7) difficulty remembering appointments; and (8) consistent problems with thinking and/or memory.

Obtain information about diet and nutrition, alcohol use, and medications. Include herbal supplements and recreational substances in the medication history. Ask about drugs that can

TABLE 64.2 Causes of Dementia

Type of Dementia	Cause
Neurodegenerative disorders	• AD • Amyotrophic lateral sclerosis (ALS) • Dementia with Lewy bodies (DLB) • Down syndrome • Frontotemporal lobar degeneration (FTLD) • Huntington disease • Parkinson disease
Vascular diseases	• Chronic subdural hematoma[a] • Subarachnoid hemorrhage[a] • Vascular (multi-infarct) dementia
Immunologic diseases or infections	• AIDS • Encephalitis[a] • Infections (e.g., Creutzfeldt-Jakob disease) • Meningitis[a] • Multiple sclerosis • Neurosyphilis[a] • Systemic exertion intolerance disease • Systemic lupus erythematosus[a]
Medications[b]	• Anticholinergics • Antiparkinsonian drugs • Cardiac drugs: digoxin, methyldopa • Cocaine • Heroin • Hypnotics • Opioids • phenytoin (Dilantin) • Tranquilizers
Metabolic or nutrition diseases	• Alcohol use disorder • Cobalamin (vitamin B12) deficiency[a] • Folate deficiency[a] • Hyperthyroidism[a] • Hypothyroidism[a] • Thiamine (vitamin B1) deficiency[a]
Systemic diseases	• Dialysis dementia[a] • Hepatic encephalopathy[a] • Uremic encephalopathy[a] • Wilson disease
Trauma	• Head injury[a]
Tumors	• Brain tumors (primary)[a] • Metastatic tumors[a]
Ventricular disorders	• Hydrocephalus[a]

[a]Potentially reversible.
[b]These are examples of drugs that may cause cognitive impairment that is potentially reversible.

impair cognition, such as analgesics, anticholinergics, psychotropics, and sedative-hypnotics.

The physical assessment is done to assess for other potential medical conditions. For example, slow movement, rigidity, asymmetric tremor of an extremity, and shuffling gait suggest Parkinsonism. Dementia, urinary incontinence, and ataxic gait suggest normal pressure hydrocephalus. The neurologic assessment includes a mental status examination or screening test. Agreement among findings from the assessment, screening tests, and history help confirm the presence of dementia.

Based on the history and physical assessment, diagnostic studies are ordered to confirm the most likely cause and exclude other possible conditions. Routine screening tests include electrolyte panel, liver function tests, serum vitamin B_{12} level, complete blood count (CBC), and thyroid function tests.[3–5] Specialized laboratory tests, such as red blood cell folate in a patient with alcohol use disorder or ionized serum calcium in a patient with multiple myeloma, are ordered based on history. Head CT or MRI may show strokes, tumors, and other changes. Positron emission tomography (PET) can examine brain activity. In some instances, genetic testing may be considered based on family history.

Interprofessional and Nursing Care

If there is an identifiable cause, treatment is aimed at treating that cause. Other management measures are similar to the care of patients with AD (described later in this chapter). Preventive measures for VaD include treating risk factors, such as hypertension, diabetes, smoking, hypercholesterolemia, and dysrhythmias. Stroke is discussed in Chapter 62. Drugs given to patients with AD are also useful for patients with VaD.

ALZHEIMER DISEASE

Alzheimer disease (AD) is a chronic, progressive, irreversible neurodegenerative brain disease. It most often affects persons age 65 and older. More than 6.2 million people are currently living with AD in the United States.[3] It is thought that by 2050, this number will increase to 12.7 million people.[3] AD is the 6th leading cause of death in the United States. It is the 5th-leading cause of death among persons age 65 and older.

Only a small number of people younger than 60 years of age develop AD. When AD develops in someone younger than 60 years, it is called *early-onset AD.* AD that occurs in people over 60 years old is called *late-onset AD.*

AD progresses slowly. It has a long preclinical phase, which may last up to 20 years. The average clinical duration is 4 to 8 years. Some patients have lived for 20 years after diagnosis.

The burden of caring for a patient with AD is well documented. In 2020, family members and friends provided $257 billion of informal (unpaid) care for persons with AD.[3] This estimate includes 15.3 billion hours of assistance. Reasons for providing informal care include wanting the person to remain at home (65%), being able to stay close to the person (48%), and feeling obligated to provide care (38%). Many informal caregivers are women. More than 60% of caregivers are married and living with a partner or are in a long-term relationship. 30% of caregivers are age 65 or older. 64% of informal caregivers report that caregiving is stressful (Box 64.1). Nearly 92% say it is also rewarding.[4,5]

Etiology

We do not know the exact cause of AD.[7,8] It is likely a combination of multiple factors (Box 64.2).

Aging

The greatest risk factor for AD is age. Most people with AD are diagnosed at age 65 or older. While age is the greatest risk factor,

TABLE 64.3 Neurodegenerative Causes of Dementia

Neurodegenerative Disorder	Characteristics	Management
Dementia With Lewy Bodies (DLB)		
• Characterized by presence of Lewy bodies (abnormal deposits of protein α-synuclein) in brainstem and cortex • Has features of both AD and Parkinson disease	• Diagnosis based on manifestations • Typically have manifestations of parkinsonism (extrapyramidal signs [bradykinesia, rigidity, postural instability, but not always a tremor]), hallucinations, short-term memory loss, unpredictable cognitive shifts, sleep problems • Pneumonia is a common complication	• Drugs may include levodopa/carbidopa and acetylcholinesterase inhibitors • Manage dementia and problems related to dysphagia and immobility • Swallowing problems can lead to impaired nutrition • At risk for falls from impaired mobility and balance
Frontotemporal Lobar Degeneration (FTLD)		
• Due to atrophy of frontal and temporal lobes of brain • In Pick disease, a type of FTLD, brain may have abnormal microscopic deposits called Pick bodies • Often misdiagnosed as a psychiatric problem because of strange behaviors	• Changes in behavior, sleep, eventually memory • Progresses relentlessly • May lead to language impairment, erratic behavior, dementia • Tends to occur at a younger age than does AD, typically about age 60	• No specific treatment • Antidepressants and antipsychotics to treat behavior manifestations
Vascular (Multi-Infarct) Dementia		
• Due to a single infarct (stroke) or multiple strokes • Prognosis is poor • Symptoms may begin suddenly, with decline after each small stroke	• More common in men • Typically begins between the ages 60 and 75 • Symptoms are similar to AD • Often occurs with AD	• See Chapter 62 • No treatment • Focus is on preventing future strokes by controlling problems that put people at high risk for stroke

BOX 64.1 PROMOTING HEALTH EQUITY

AD

- 36% of Blacks, 18% of Hispanics, and 19% of Asian Americans believe discrimination is a barrier to care for persons with AD.
- More than 50% of non-White caregivers report discrimination when navigating health care services, feeling that providers do not listen because of their race, color, or ethnicity.
- 41% of persons who provide unpaid care for a Black person and 32% of persons who provide unpaid care for a Hispanic persons say race makes it harder for them to obtain health care.

Source: Alzheimer's Association: 2021 Alzheimer's disease facts and figures.

BOX 64.2 BIOLOGIC SEX CONSIDERATIONS

AD

Women

- Nearly two-thirds of people with AD are women.
- Women are more likely to develop AD than men, mainly because they live longer.
- About twice as many women as men die each year from AD.

AD is not a normal part of aging and age alone does not cause the disease.

Family History

Family history of AD is an important risk factor. Persons with a first-degree relative (parent or sibling) with dementia are more likely to develop AD. Those who have more than 1 first-degree relative with dementia are at even higher risk for developing AD.

Genetic Link

Persons with a clear pattern of inheritance within a family have familial AD (FAD). FAD is associated with onset before age 60 and a more rapid disease course. We refer to cases as sporadic when there is no familial connection.

The first gene associated with late-onset and sporadic forms of AD was the epsilon (E)-4 allele of the apolipoprotein E *(ApoE)* gene on chromosome 19. *ApoE* contains the instructions to make a protein that helps to carry cholesterol and other types of fat in the bloodstream. *ApoE* may have a role in clearing amyloid plaques. *ApoE* mutations result in more amyloid deposits.

ApoE comes in several different alleles or forms. Three alleles occur most often. People inherit 1 allele (e.g., *ApoE-2, ApoE-3, ApoE-4*), from each parent. The presence of *ApoE-4* increases the risk of developing late-onset AD (Box 64.3).

In patients with early-onset AD, we have identified 3 key genes: presenilin-1 *(PSEN1)*, presenilin-2 *(PSEN2)*, and amyloid precursor protein *(APP)*. When these genes mutate, they cause brain cells to overproduce β-amyloid. *PSEN1* mutations cause AD before age 60 and often before age 50. *PSEN2* causes early-onset FAD.

Cardiovascular Factors

Brain health is closely linked to the health of the heart and blood vessels. Brain functioning depends on a good blood supply and nutrients delivered to it by that blood supply.

Many factors increase the risk for CVD. These include diabetes, hypertension, obesity, hypercholesterolemia, and smoking. Diabetes dramatically increases the risk of developing AD and other types of dementia. Diabetes can contribute to dementia in several ways. Chronic high levels of insulin and glucose may be directly toxic to brain cells. Insulin resistance, which causes high

BOX 64.3 GENETICS IN CLINICAL PRACTICE

AD

Genetic Basis

Early Onset (Familial) (<60 Years Old at Onset)

- Autosomal dominant disorder
- Various mutations in the following genes:
  - Amyloid precursor protein *(APP)* gene on chromosome 21
  - Presenilin-1 *(PSEN1)* gene on chromosome 14
  - Presenilin-2 *(PSEN2)* gene on chromosome 1

Late Onset (Sporadic) (>60 Years Old at Onset)

- Genetically more complex than early-onset AD
- Apolipoprotein E-4 *(ApoE-4)* allele on chromosome 19 increases risk for developing AD
- Presence of the *ApoE-2* allele is associated with a lower risk for AD

Incidence

Early Onset

- Rare form of AD, accounts for <5% of cases
- 50% risk for disease for children of affected parents
- May occur in people as young as 30 years

Late Onset

- *ApoE-4* is present in 40%–65% of people with late-onset AD
- Many *ApoE-4*–positive people do not develop AD

Genetic Testing

Early Onset

- Genetic screening is available for mutations on chromosomes 1, 14, and 21

Late Onset

- Blood test can identify which *ApoE* allele a patient has but cannot predict who will develop disease
- In a patient who meets the clinical criteria for AD, finding *ApoE-4* increases the reliability of the diagnosis

Clinical Implications

- Genetic testing for family members of patients with early-onset AD may be appropriate.
- Testing should be done only with formal genetic counseling, especially when asymptomatic family members are involved.
- If a person tests positive for *ApoE-4*, it does not mean they will develop AD.

blood glucose and can lead to type 2 diabetes, may interfere with the body's ability to break down amyloid, a protein that forms brain plaques in AD. High blood glucose and high cholesterol have a role in atherosclerosis, which contributes to VaD.[8]

Diabetes may contribute to poor memory and decreased mental function in other ways. Diabetes causes microangiopathy, which damages small blood vessels throughout the body. Ongoing damage to blood vessels in the brain may be one reason people with diabetes are at a higher risk for cognitive problems as they age. People with diabetes may lose brain volume, especially gray matter, as the disease progresses.

Head Trauma

Head trauma is a risk factor for dementia. Professional football players and military veterans who had a traumatic brain injury or posttraumatic stress disorder have an increased risk for AD and other types of dementia.[4,6]

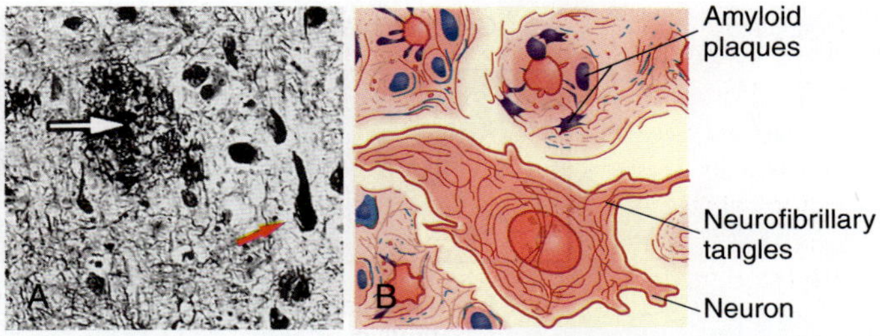

Fig. 64.2 Pathologic changes in AD. (A) Plaque with central amyloid core *(white arrow)* next to a neurofibrillary tangle *(red arrow)* on the histologic specimen from a brain autopsy. (B) Schematic representation of amyloid plaque and neurofibrillary tangle.

Pathophysiology

Changes in the brain's structure and function with AD include (1) amyloid plaques, (2) neurofibrillary tangles, (3) loss of connections between neurons, and (4) neuron death.[7,8] Fig. 64.2 shows the pathologic changes in AD.

As a part of aging, people develop some plaques in their brain tissue. In AD, more plaques appear in certain parts of the brain affecting memory. In AD, plaques develop first in areas of the brain used for memory and cognitive function, including the hippocampus. The hippocampus is important in forming and storing short-term memories. Eventually, AD attacks the cerebral cortex, especially the areas responsible for language and reasoning.

Plaques consist of clusters of insoluble deposits of a protein called β-amyloid, other proteins, remnants of neurons, non-nerve cells such as microglia (cells that surround and digest damaged cells or foreign substances), and other cells, such as astrocytes. β-Amyloid is cleaved from APP, which is associated with the cell membrane (Fig. 64.3). We do not know the normal function of APP. Genetic factors may play a critical role in how the brain processes the β-amyloid protein. Overproduction of β-amyloid is an important risk factor for AD. Abnormally high levels of β-amyloid cause cell damage either directly or by eliciting an inflammatory response and ultimately neuron death.

Neurofibrillary tangles are abnormal collections of twisted protein threads inside nerve cells. The main component of these structures is a protein called tau. Tau proteins in the central nervous system (CNS) provide support for intracellular structure through their support of microtubules. Tau proteins hold the microtubules together like railroad ties. In AD, tau protein is altered. As a result, the microtubules twist together in a helical fashion (Fig. 64.3). This forms the neurofibrillary tangles found in the neurons of people with AD.

Plaques and neurofibrillary tangles are not unique to patients with AD or dementia. They are also found in the brains of people without cognitive impairment. However, they are more abundant in the brains of those with AD.

The other feature of AD is the loss of connections between neurons and neuron death. These processes result in structural damage. Affected parts of the brain begin to shrink in a process

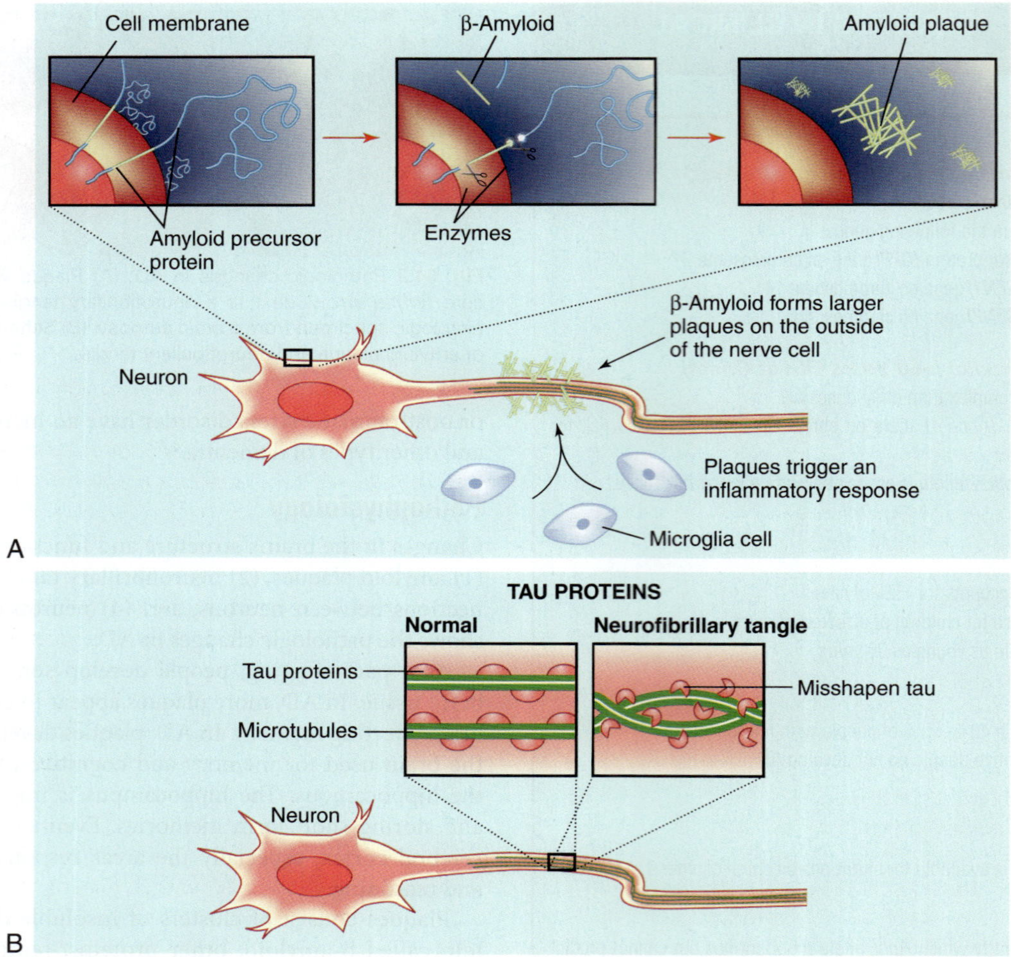

Fig. 64.3 Current theories about the development of AD. (A) Abnormal amounts of β-amyloid are cleaved from the amyloid precursor protein (APP) and released into the circulation. The β-amyloid fragments come together in clumps to form plaques that attach to the neuron. Microglia react to the plaque. This results in an inflammatory response. (B) Tau proteins provide structural support for the neuron microtubules. Chemical changes in the neuron cause structural changes in tau proteins. This results in twisting and tangling (neurofibrillary tangles).

called brain atrophy. By the final stage of AD, brain tissue has shrunk significantly (Fig. 64.4).

Clinical Manifestations

Research suggests AD causes pathologic changes in the brain at least 15 years before manifestations appear.[9] The Alzheimer's Association has developed a list of 10 warning signs that are common manifestations of AD (Table 64.4).

Symptoms do not always directly relate to abnormal changes in the brain caused by AD. We describe the stages of AD as mild, moderate, and severe (Table 64.5). The rate of progression from mild to severe is highly variable and ranges from 3 to 20 years.

The initial manifestations are usually related to changes in cognitive functioning. The person may have memory loss, mild disorientation, or trouble with words and numbers. Often, a family member reports the patient's declining memory to the HCP.

Normal age-related memory decline is characterized by mild changes that do not interfere with ADLs (Table 64.6). In AD, the memory loss initially relates to recent events, with remote memories still intact. With time and progression of AD, memory loss includes both recent and remote memory. It affects the ability to perform self-care.

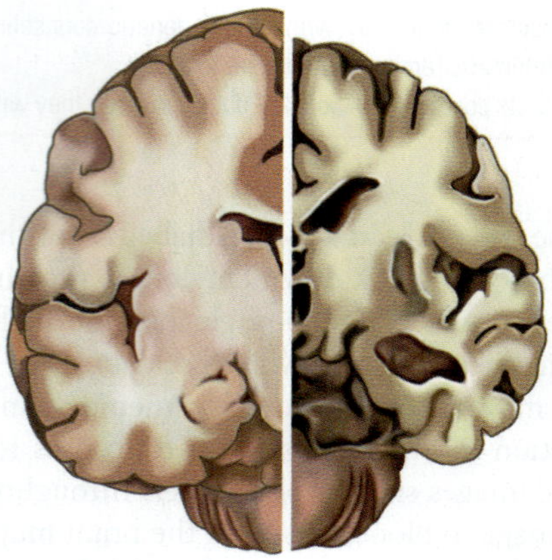

Fig. 64.4 Effects of AD on the brain. This figure compares a normal brain *(left)* with a brain affected by AD *(right)*.

As AD progresses, personal hygiene deteriorates, as does the ability to concentrate and maintain attention.[10,11] Ongoing loss

TABLE 64.4 PATIENT & CAREGIVER TEACHING

Early Warning Signs of AD

Include the following information in the teaching plan for the patient with AD:

1. Memory loss that affects job skills
   - Frequent forgetfulness or unexplainable confusion at home or in the workplace may signal that something is wrong.
   - This type of memory loss goes beyond forgetting an assignment, colleague's name, deadline, or phone number.
2. Problems with abstract thinking
   - For the patient with AD, this goes beyond challenges, such as balancing a checkbook.
   - The patient with AD may not be able to recognize numbers or do basic calculations.
3. Difficulty doing familiar tasks
   - It is normal for most people to become distracted and to forget something (e.g., leave something on the stove too long).
   - People with AD may cook a meal, then forget not only to serve it but also that they made it.
4. Poor or decreased judgment
   - Many people from time to time may choose not to dress appropriately for the weather (e.g., not bringing a coat or sweater on a cold evening).
   - The patient with AD may dress inappropriately in more noticeable ways, such as wearing a bathrobe to the store or a sweater on a hot day.
5. Problems with language
   - Most people have trouble finding the "right" word from time to time.
   - People with AD may forget simple words or substitute inappropriate words, making their speech difficult to understand.
6. Misplacing things
   - For many people, temporarily misplacing keys, purses, or wallets is a normal, albeit frustrating, event.
   - The patient with AD may put items in inappropriate places (e.g., eating utensils in clothing drawers) but have no memory of how they got there.
7. Changes in mood
   - Most people have mood changes.
   - The patient with AD tends to have more rapid mood swings for no apparent reason.
8. Changes in personality
   - As most people age, they may have some change in personality (e.g., become less tolerant).
   - The patient with AD can change dramatically, either suddenly or over time. For example, someone who is easygoing may become angry, suspicious, or fearful.
9. Loss of initiative
   - The patient with AD may become and remain uninterested and uninvolved in many or all their usual pursuits.

Adapted from Alzheimer's Association: 10 Early signs and symptoms of Alzheimer's. Retrieved from https://www.alz.org/alzheimers_disease_know_the_10_signs.asp.

of neurons can cause the person to act in unpredictable ways. Behavior manifestations, such as agitation or aggression, result from changes that take place within the brain. These behaviors are neither intentional nor controllable by the person. Some people have delusions and hallucinations.

As AD progresses, more cognitive impairments occur. These include aphasia (difficulty comprehending language and oral communication), apraxia (inability to manipulate objects or perform purposeful acts), visual agnosia (inability to recognize objects by sight), and dysgraphia (difficulty communicating by writing). Eventually, they cannot recall long-term memories. The person may not recognize family members and friends. Later in the disease, the ability to communicate and perform ADLs is lost. Some tend to wander. In the late stages of AD, the person is unresponsive, incontinent, and needs total care.[12]

Retrogenesis

Retrogenesis is the process in which the decline in AD mirrors, in reverse order, brain development that occurs from birth.[13] Thus, it compares the developmental stages of childhood with the deterioration of patients with AD. As seen in Fig. 64.5, a relationship exists between developmental stage and deterioration of function. For example, it is appropriate for a patient in the moderate stage to feel good about putting together puzzles that belong to his 3-year-old grandson. In fact, they may play well together on the same task or project.

Diagnostic Criteria

The National Institute on Aging and the Alzheimer's Association have criteria and guidelines for diagnosing AD. Guidelines address the use of imaging and biomarkers that may help determine whether changes are due to AD.

AD is considered on a spectrum (Table 64.7). The stages are preclinical AD, mild cognitive impairment, and dementia due to AD. Dementia is the last stage.

Preclinical Stage

A long lag exists between pathologic changes in the brain and manifestations of AD. The future goal would be to modify the disease process of AD before it becomes symptomatic. Once plaques and tangles have formed in sufficient quantity, it may be too late to intervene to prevent the disease or its progression. Although current attempts at modifying the disease process have not been successful, research is ongoing.

Mild Cognitive Impairment

Mild cognitive impairment (MCI) is the second stage in the AD spectrum. It is a state of cognitive function in which persons have problems with memory, language, or other essential cognitive functions. The problems are severe enough to be noticed by the person having them and by others and can be found on screening tests. Family members may see changes in the person's abilities (Table 64.6). To the casual observer, the person with MCI may seem normal. Because the problems do not interfere with daily activities, the patient does not meet the criteria for being diagnosed with dementia.

We classify MCI based on the cognitive skills affected. MCI that primarily affects memory is called amnestic MCI. With amnestic MCI, a person may forget important information that they would have recalled easily, such as appointments. The person is often aware of the change in memory. MCI that affects other cognitive skills is non-amnestic MCI. Skills that may be affected include the ability to make sound decisions or complete a complex task.[11]

Between 15% and 20% of people 65 years and older have MCI. They are at high risk for developing AD. Some people with

TABLE 64.5 Stages of AD

Mild	Moderate	Severe
• Forgetfulness beyond what is seen in a normal person • Short-term memory impairment, especially for new learning • Loss of initiative and interests • May forget recent events or the names of people or things • Impatient • May no longer be able to solve simple math problems • Slowly loses the ability to plan and organize	• Memory loss and confusion become more obvious • Has more trouble organizing, planning, and following directions • May need help getting dressed • May start having incontinence • Trouble recognizing family members and friends • Agitation, restlessness • May lack judgment and begin to wander, gets lost • May have trouble sleeping • Delusions, hallucinations, paranoia • Behavior problems	• Severe impairment of all cognitive functions • Little memory, unable to process new information • Unable to perform self-care activities • Often needs help with daily needs • May not be able to talk • Cannot understand words • May have problems eating, swallowing • May not be able to walk or sit up without help • Immobility • Incontinence

TABLE 64.6 Comparison of Normal Forgetfulness and Memory Loss

Normal Forgetfulness	Memory Loss in Mild Cognitive Impairment	Memory Loss in AD
• Sometimes misplaces keys, eyeglasses, or other items	• Often misplaces items	• Forgets what an item is used for or puts it in an inappropriate place
• Momentarily forgets an acquaintance's name	• Often forgets people's names and is slow to recall them	• May not remember knowing a person
• Sometimes has to search for a word	• Has increasing difficulty finding desired words	• Begins to lose language skills and may withdraw from social interaction
• Sometimes forgets to run an errand	• Begins to forget important events and appointments	• Loses sense of time, does not know what day it is
• May forget an event from the distant past	• May forget recent events or newly learned information	• Seriously impaired recent memory and problems learning and remembering new information
• When driving, may momentarily forget where to turn, but quickly orients self	• Becomes temporarily lost more often, may have trouble understanding and following a map	• Becomes easily disoriented or lost in familiar places, sometimes for hours
• Jokes about memory loss	• Worries about memory loss, family and friends notice lapses	• May have little or no awareness of cognitive problems

Adapted from Rabins P: Memory. In *The Johns Hopkins white papers,* Baltimore, 2007, Johns Hopkins University.

MCI show no progression and do not go on to develop AD. An estimated 15% of people with MCI will eventually develop AD.

Treatment consists of ongoing monitoring. Assessing for changes in memory and thinking skills that indicate a worsening of symptoms or a progression to AD or another dementia is critical (Table 64.4).

Diagnostic Studies

No definitive diagnostic test exists for AD. The diagnosis is primarily a diagnosis of exclusion. In patients with cognitive impairment, there is increased emphasis on early and careful evaluation. Many conditions can cause manifestations of dementia. Some are treatable or reversible (Table 64.2).

When all other conditions that can cause cognitive impairment have been excluded, a clinical diagnosis of AD can be made. A comprehensive evaluation includes a health history, physical assessment, neurologic and mental status assessments, and laboratory tests (Table 64.8). A definitive diagnosis of AD requires an examination of brain tissue at autopsy and findings of neurofibrillary tangles and plaques.

Neuroimaging allows us to detect changes early in the disease and monitor treatment response. In AD, multiple brain structures atrophy and the volume of the brain correlates with neurodegeneration. CT or MRI may show brain atrophy in the later stages of the disease. This finding occurs in other diseases and can be seen in people without cognitive impairment. PET scanning can help discern AD from other forms of dementia (Fig. 64.6). PET determines brain metabolism using glucose tracers. PET can detect amyloid.

Guidelines identify 2 biomarker categories: (1) those that show the level of β-amyloid accumulation in the brain and (2) those that show if nerve cells in the brain are injured or degenerating. Biomarkers include (1) CSF neurochemical markers: β-amyloid and tau proteins, and (2) imaging biomarkers: volumetric MRI and PET. The level of tau in the CSF is an indication of neurodegeneration. Plasma levels of tau or β-amyloid are not of any value in diagnosing AD. There are some other imaging biomarkers we use in special clinical settings. They may help in some cases to increase the level of certainty about a diagnosis of AD.

Neuropsychologic testing is important for diagnostic purposes and to establish a baseline for evaluating changes over time. They are repeated at regular intervals during the course of care to assess changes in cognitive status. Common tools include the Mini-Cog (Table 64.9), Mini-Mental State Examination (MMSE) (Table 64.10), and Montreal Cognitive Assessment (MoCA). Brief screenings, such as the Mini-Cog, are useful for ongoing screening, especially when time is limited. The clock drawing test can be used as part of the Mini-Cog or by itself to assess cognitive function (Fig. 64.7). The MMSE takes about

Stage	Alzheimer's Disease	Reisberg Stage*	Developmental Age	Diversion/Distraction Activities
Mild	No difficulty at all	1		
	Some memory trouble begins to affect job/home. Forgets familiar names.	2		
	Much difficulty maintaining job performance. Withdrawal from difficult situations.	3	12+ yr	Can function with understanding. Enjoy things previously enjoyed—watch TV, play and listen to music, play games.
	Can no longer hold a job, plan and prepare meals, handle personal finances, etc. Driving becomes difficult, although can drive to familiar places.	4	8–12 yr	Can still enjoy simple games, watch TV and videos. Enjoys family photos and memories.
Moderate	Can no longer select proper clothing for occasion or season. Needs help to remain safe in home. Forgets to bathe.	5	5–7 yr	Needs age-appropriate toys and games.
	Requires assistance with dressing.	6a	4–5 yr	Enjoy many of the same activities as preschoolers.
	Requires assistance with bathing.	6b	4–5 yr	
	Can no longer use toilet without assistance.	6c	4 yr	
	Urinary incontinence	6d	3–4.5 yr	
	Fecal incontinence	6e	2–3 yr	
Severe	Speech now limited to about words per day.	7a	15 mo	Enjoys infant toys, mobiles, dangling ribbons.
	Speech now limited to 1 word per day.	7b	1 yr	
	Can no longer walk without assistance.	7c	1 yr	
	Can no longer sit up without assistance.	7d	6–10 mo	
	Can no longer smile.	7e	2–4 mo	
	Can no longer hold up head.	7f	1–3 mo	

Fig. 64.5 Retrogenesis (back to birth) in AD. *Based on Functional Assessment Staging. (From Reisberg B: Functional Assessment Staging [FAST], *Psychopharmacol Bull* 24:653, 1988.)

TABLE 64.7 Diagnostic Criteria *AD*

Stage	Description	Recommendations for Biomarkers
Preclinical AD	• Brain changes, including amyloid buildup and other early neuron changes, may already be in process • At this point, significant symptoms are not yet evident • In some people, PET scans and CSF analysis can detect amyloid buildup	• Use of imaging and biomarker tests at this stage are only for research • Biomarkers are still being developed, not used by clinicians in general practice
Mild cognitive impairment (MCI) due to AD	• MCI stage is marked by symptoms of memory problems, enough to be noticed and measured, but not compromising a patient's independence • May or may not progress to AD	• Used primarily by researchers • May be used in specialized clinical settings to supplement standard tests to help determine possible causes of MCI • May help confirm that the patient's impairment is related to AD
Dementia due to AD	• Characterized by memory, thinking, and behavior symptoms that impair a patient's ability to function in daily life • Dementia marks the terminal stage of AD • Encompasses all stages shown in Table 64.5	• Can increase the level of certainty about a diagnosis of AD • May be used to discern AD from other dementias

Source: National Institute on Aging: Diagnostic criteria for Alzheimer's disease. Retrieved from https://www.nia.nih.gov/health/alzheimers-disease-diagnostic-guidelines.

TABLE 64.8 Interprofessional Care

AD

Diagnostic Assessment

- History and physical assessment,
  - Psychologic evaluation, including depression screening
  - Neuropsychologic testing, including Mini-Cog (Table 64.9) and Mini-Mental State Examination (Table 64.10)
- Brain imaging tests: CT, MRI, PET
- CBC
- ECG
- Glucose, creatinine, BUN
- Vitamin B1, B6, B12 levels
- Thyroid function tests
- Liver function tests

Management

- Drug therapy for cognitive problems (Table 64.11)
- Behavior modification
- Moderate exercise
- Assistance with functional independence
- Assistance and support for caregivers

7 minutes to complete. It gives information about orientation, recall, attention, calculation, language manipulation, and constructional praxis. The MoCA takes about 10 minutes to do. It assesses memory, language, attention, visuospatial, and executive functions.

Interprofessional Care

There is no cure for AD. Treatment does not stop the deterioration of brain cells. Care is aimed at controlling undesirable behavior manifestations and providing support for family caregivers.

Drug Therapy

Although medication for AD is available, these drugs do not cure or reverse the progression of AD (Table 64.11). They help many people for a period of time by leading to a modest decrease in the rate of decline of cognitive function. There is no effect on overall disease progression.[3,7]

Cholinesterase inhibitors block cholinesterase, the enzyme that breaks down acetylcholine in the synaptic cleft (Fig. 64.8). These drugs include donepezil (Aricept), rivastigmine (Exelon), and galantamine (Razadyne). Rivastigmine is available as a patch.

Memantine (Namenda) protects the brain's nerve cells against excess amounts of glutamate, which is released in large amounts by cells damaged by AD. The attachment of glutamate to *N*-methyl-D-aspartate (NMDA) receptors permits calcium to flow freely into the cell, which in turn may lead to cell degeneration. Memantine may prevent this destructive sequence by blocking the action of glutamate.

Treating the depression that is often associated with AD may improve cognitive function. Depression is often treated with selective serotonin reuptake inhibitors. These include fluoxetine (Prozac), sertraline (Zoloft), and citalopram (Celexa). The antidepressant trazodone may help with sleep problems.

Antipsychotic drugs can be used for managing agitation and aggressive behavior, which occurs in some patients. These drugs increase the risk for death and cognitive decline in patients with AD. They should be used only when agitation and psychosis symptoms are severe, are dangerous, and/or cause significant distress to the patient.

❖ NURSING MANAGEMENT: ALZHEIMER DISEASE

◆ Assessment

Subjective and objective data that you should obtain from a patient with AD are outlined in Table 64.12. Useful questions for the patient and caregiver are, "When did you first notice the memory loss?" and "How has the memory loss progressed since then?"

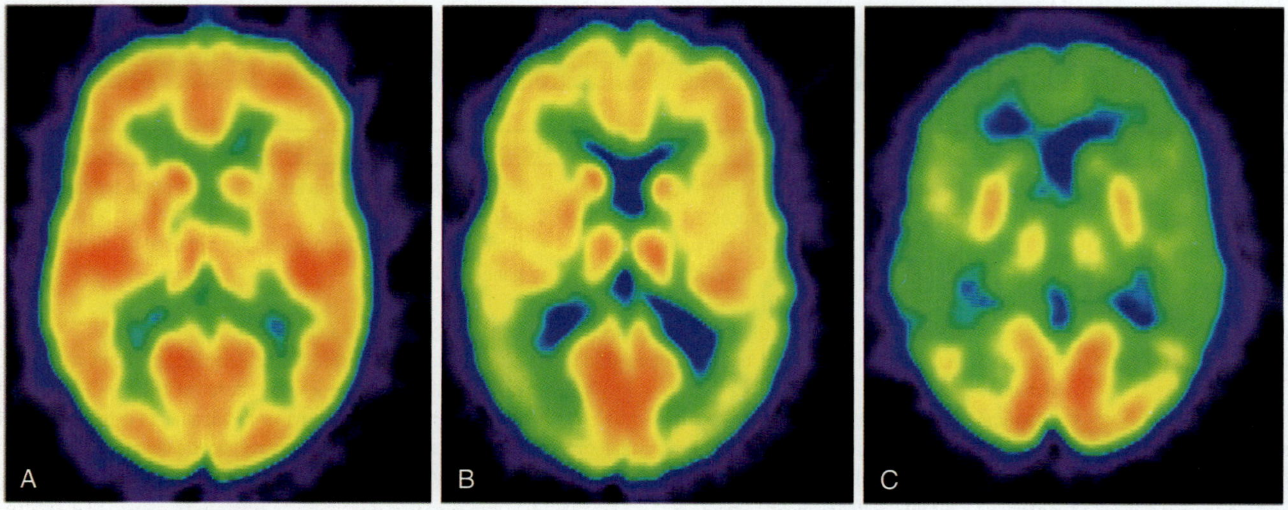

Fig. 64.6 PET scan assist in diagnosing AD. Radioactive fluorine is applied to glucose (fluorodeoxyglucose), and the yellow areas show metabolically active cells. (A) A normal brain. (B) Early AD. (C) Advanced AD, with hypometabolism in many areas of the brain. (From Rice L, Bisdas S: The diagnostic value of FDG and amyloid PET in Alzheimer's disease, *Eur J Radiol* 94:16, 2017.)

TABLE 64.9 The Mini-Cog

The Mini-Cog is used as a brief assessment tool for cognitive impairment. It can be quickly administered and can guide the need for further evaluation.

Administration

- Tell the patient to listen carefully to and remember 3 unrelated words and then to repeat the words. *Example:* apple, table, penny. (This initial step is not scored.) The same 3 words may be repeated to the patient up to 3 times to register all 3 words.
- Tell the patient to draw the face of a clock, either on a blank sheet of paper or on a sheet with the clock circle already drawn on the page. After the patient puts the numbers on the clock face, ask them to draw the hands of the clock to read a specific time (11:10). The test is considered normal if all numbers are present in the correct sequence and position and the hands readably display the requested time.
- Ask the patient to repeat the 3 previously stated words.

Scoring (out of 5 Total Points)

Give 1 point for each recalled word after the clock drawing test.

- Patients recalling none of the 3 words are classified as cognitively impaired (score = 0).
- Patients recalling all 3 words are classified as not cognitively impaired (score = 3).
- Patients with intermediate word recall of 1 or 2 words are classified on the clock drawing test:

The clock drawing test is scored 2 if normal and 0 if abnormal.
Interpretation of results
0–2: Positive screen for dementia
3–5: Negative screen for dementia

Source: Borson S, Scanlan J, Brush M, et al.: The Mini-Cog: a cognitive "vital signs" measure for dementia screening in multi-lingual elderly, *Intern J Geriatr Psychiatry* 15:1021, 2000.

◆ Clinical Problems

Clinical problems for AD may include:

- Impaired cognition
- Risk for injury
- Impaired role performance

Additional information on clinical problems and interventions for the patient with AD is presented in eNursing Care Plan 64.1 (available on the website for this chapter).

◆ Planning

The overall goals are for the patient with AD to (1) maintain functional ability for as long as possible, (2) be in a safe environment, (3) have personal care needs met, and (4) have dignity maintained. The overall goals for the caregiver of a patient with AD are to (1) reduce caregiver stress, (2) maintain personal, emotional, and physical health, and (3) cope with the long-term effects of caregiving.

◆ Implementation

◆ Health Promotion

Can AD be prevented? Although there is no known definitive way to prevent AD, there are several things that we can do to keep our brain healthy and lower the risk of developing dementia (Table 64.13).

Early recognition and treatment of AD are important. Review early signs of AD with patients and families (Table 64.4). In the early stages of AD, patients are often aware that their memory is faulty and do things to mask the problem.

TABLE 64.10 Mini-Mental State Examination (MMSE)

Sample Items

Orientation to Time
"What is the date?"

Registration
"Listen carefully. I am going to say 3 words. You say them back after I stop. Ready? Here they are HOUSE (pause), CAR (pause), LAKE (pause). Now repeat those words back to me." (Repeat up to 5 times but score only the first trial.)

Naming
"What is this?" (Point to a pencil or pen.)

Reading
"Please read this and do what it says." (Show examinee the words CLOSE YOUR EYES on the stimulus form.)

◆ Acute Care

Nursing management of the patient with AD is outlined in Table 64.14. The diagnosis of AD is traumatic for both the patient and family. It is not unusual for the patient to have depression, denial, worry, fear, and feelings of loss and dread. You are in an important position to assess for depression. Antidepressant drugs and counseling may be needed. Family caregivers may be in denial and may not seek medical attention early in the disease. Assess their ability to accept and cope with the diagnosis.

Ongoing monitoring of both the patient and caregiver is important. Patients with AD move through the stages at variable rates. The health care team works with caregivers and patients to manage manifestations, which change over time.

The care the patient needs changes as the disease progresses, which emphasizes the need for regular assessment and support. The severity of the problems and amount of care needed increase over time. The specific manifestations depend on the area of the brain involved. Nursing care focuses on decreasing manifestations, preventing harm, and supporting the patient and caregiver throughout the disease process.

Patients with AD may have other acute and chronic illnesses that require hospitalization or surgery. Hospitalization can be traumatic for the patient with AD and the caregiver. It can precipitate a worsening of dementia or the development of delirium. Caregivers and health care professionals need to help patients who have difficulty explaining their symptoms or recalling their health and medical histories. In the acute care setting, we must observe patients with AD more closely because of safety concerns. They should be frequently reassured and oriented to place and time. Anxiety or disruptive behavior may be reduced by using consistent nursing staff.

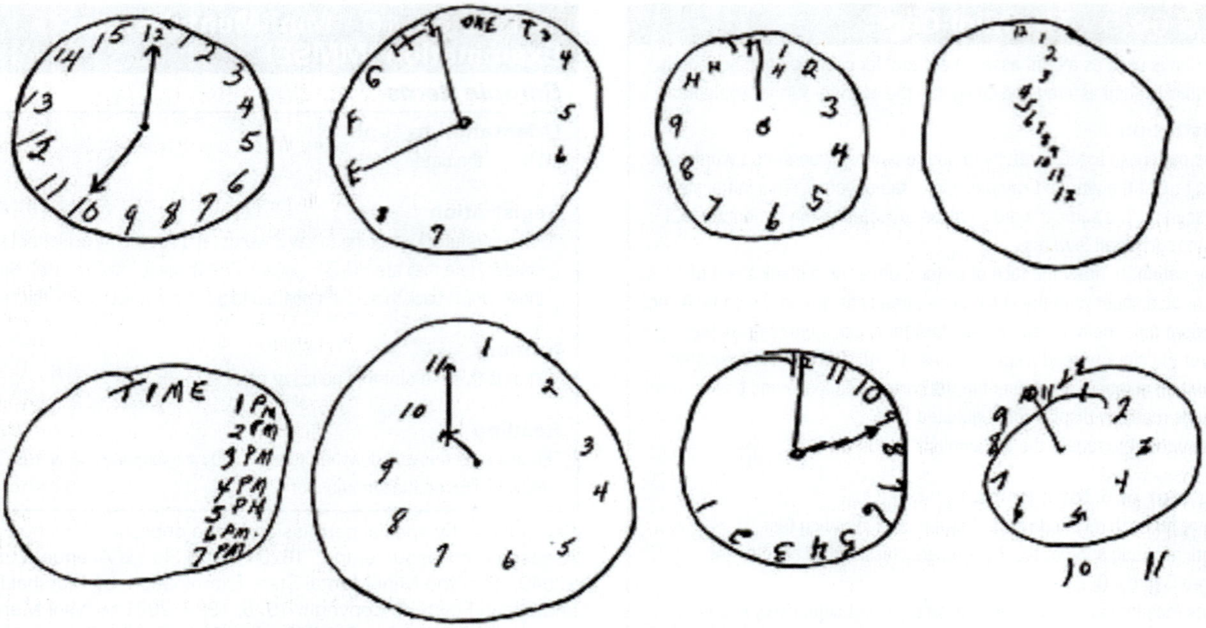

Fig. 64.7 Clock drawing is a simple test that can be used to assess for dementia. The patient is asked to draw a clock, put in all the numbers, and set the hands at 11:10. Clocks drawn by people with AD. (From Mendez M: *Mental status examination handbook*, St. Louis, 2022, Elsevier.)

TABLE 64.11 Drug Therapy

AD

Problem	Drugs
Decreased memory and cognition	Cholinesterase inhibitors
	• donepezil (Aricept)
	• galantamine (Razadyne)
	• rivastigmine (Exelon)
	N-methyl-d-aspartate (NMDA) receptor antagonist
	• memantine (Namenda)
Depression	Selective serotonin reuptake inhibitors (SSRIs)
	• citalopram (Celexa)
	• fluoxetine (Prozac)
	• sertraline (Zoloft)
	• fluvoxamine (Luvox)
	Atypical antidepressants
	• mirtazapine (Remeron)
	• trazodone
Behavior problems (e.g., agitation, physical aggression, disinhibition)	Antipsychotics
	• aripiprazole (Abilify)
	• haloperidol (Haldol)
	• olanzapine (Zyprexa)
	• quetiapine (Seroquel)
	• risperidone (Risperdal)
	Benzodiazepines
	• clonazepam (Klonopin)
	• lorazepam (Ativan)
Sleep problems	• zolpidem (Ambien)

◆ Ambulatory Care

Currently, family members and friends care for many people with AD in their homes. Other patients with AD live in various types of facilities, including long-term care and assisted living. A facility that is good for one patient may not be good for another. What is helpful for a patient at one point in the disease process may be completely different from what is best when the disease progresses.

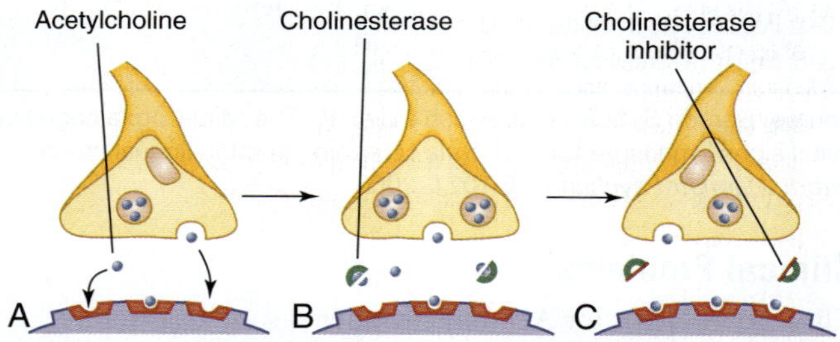

Fig. 64.8 Mechanism of action of cholinesterase inhibitors. (A) Acetylcholine is released from the nerve synapses and carries a message across the synapse. (B) Cholinesterase breaks down acetylcholine. (C) Cholinesterase inhibitors block cholinesterase, thus giving acetylcholine more time to transmit the message.

After the initial diagnosis, patients need to be aware that the progression of the disease is variable. Effective management may slow symptom progression and decrease the burden on the patient, caregiver, and family. Decisions related to care should be made with the patient, family members, and health care team early in the disease. You have a role in advising the patient and caregiver to initiate health care decisions, including advance directives, while the patient has the capacity to do so. This can ease the burden for the caregiver as the disease progresses.

In the early stages of AD, memory aids, such as calendars, may be helpful. Patients often become depressed during this phase. Depression may be related to the diagnosis of an incurable disorder and the impact of the disease on ADL, including

TABLE 64.12 NURSING ASSESSMENT

AD

Subjective Data

Important Health Information

Health history: Repeated head trauma, stroke, CNS infection, family history of dementia

Medications: Use of any drug to decrease symptoms (e.g., tranquilizers, hypnotics, antidepressants, antipsychotics)

Functional Health Patterns

Health perception–health management: Positive family history. Emotional lability

Nutritional-metabolic: Anorexia, malnutrition, weight loss

Elimination: Incontinence

Activity-exercise: Poor personal hygiene, gait instability, weakness, inability to perform activities of daily living

Sleep-rest: Frequent nighttime awakening, daytime napping

Cognitive-perceptual: Forgetfulness, inability to cope with complex situations, difficulty with problem solving (early signs), depression, withdrawal, suicidal ideation (early)

Objective Data

General

Disheveled appearance, agitation

Neurologic

Mild: Loss of recent memory, disorientation to date and time, flat affect, lack of spontaneity. Impaired abstraction, cognition, and judgment

Moderate: Agitation, impaired ability to recognize close family and friends, loss of remote memory, confusion, apraxia, agnosia, alexia (inability to understand written language); aphasia, inability to do simple tasks

Severe: Inability to do self-care, incontinence, immobility, limb rigidity, flexor posturing

Possible Diagnostic Findings

Diagnosis by exclusion, cerebral cortical atrophy on CT scan, poor scores on mental status tests, hippocampal atrophy on MRI scan, abnormal changes on PET

driving, socializing, and taking part in recreational activities. Teach caregivers to perform tasks needed to maximize quality of life and safety of the patient.

Adult day care is one of the options available. They can provide respite for the family and a protective environment. Programs vary in size, structure, physical environment, and staff experience. During the early and moderate stages of AD, the patient can still benefit from stimulating activities that encourage independence and decision making in a protective environment. The patient returns home tired, content, less frustrated, and ready to be with the family. The respite from the demands of care allows the caregiver to be more responsive to the patient's needs.

As the disease progresses, the demands on the caregiver eventually exceed the resources, and the patient may need to be placed in a long-term care facility. Special dementia units are increasingly common. The dementia unit is designed with an emphasis on safety. Many have designated areas that allow the patient to walk freely within the unit. The unit is secured so that the patient cannot wander outside.

TABLE 64.13 PROMOTING POPULATION HEALTH

Decreasing Risk for Cognitive Decline

The following are tips to reduce the risk for cognitive decline and dementia:

1. Avoid harmful substances.
   Excessive drinking and drug use can damage brain cells. Stop smoking because it increases the risk for cognitive decline.
2. Challenge your mind.
   Read often, do crossword puzzles. Play games Keep mentally active. Learn new skills. Go back to school. This strengthens the brain connections and promotes new ones.
3. Exercise regularly.
   Even low to moderate level activity, such as walking or gardening 3 to 5 times per week, can make you feel better. Daily physical activity, even in older adults, can decrease the risk for cognitive decline.
4. Stay socially active.
   Pursue social activities that have meaning to you. Family, friends, church, and a sense of community may all contribute to better brain health.
5. Avoid trauma to the brain.
   Because traumatic brain injury may be a risk factor for developing AD, promote safety in physical activities and driving. Use the car seat belt. Wear a helmet when playing contact sports or riding a bike. Fall proof your home.
6. Take care of mental health.
   Recognize and treat depression early. Depression may cause or worsen memory loss and other cognitive problems.
7. Treat diabetes.
   Better blood glucose control can help prevent the cognitive decline from diabetes.
8. Take care of your heart.
   Risk factors for cardiovascular disease and stroke (hypertension, obesity) negatively affect your cognitive health. Heart health is linked to brain health.
9. Get enough sleep.
   Not getting enough sleep may result in problems with memory and thinking.
10. Get the right fuel.
    A healthy and balanced diet low in fats and sugary foods and high in vegetables and fruits helps to reduce the risk for cognitive decline.

Adapted from Alzheimer's Association: 10 Ways to love your brain. Retrieved from https://www.alz.org/help-support/brain_health/10_ways_to_love_your_brain.

As the disease progresses to the late stage, the patient is severely impaired. They have difficulty with basic functions, including walking and talking. Total care is needed. Specific problems relate to the care of the patient in all phases of AD. These problems are described next.

Behavior problems. Behavior problems occur in about 90% of patients with AD. These problems include repetitiveness or asking the same question repeatedly, delusions, hallucinations, agitation, aggression, altered sleeping patterns, wandering, hoarding, and resisting care. Many times, these behaviors are unpredictable and may challenge caregivers. Caregivers must be aware that these behaviors are not intentional and are often difficult to control. Behavior problems are often the reason that patients are placed in a facility.[10]

These behaviors are often the patient's way of responding to pain, frustration, temperature extremes, or anxiety. When

TABLE 64.14 NURSING MANAGEMENT

Caring for the Patient With AD

Assess the patient on an ongoing basis, including:

- Memory and level of function
- Presence of any co-existing problems
- Ability to perform basic and instrumental activities of daily living
- Diet and fluid intake and develop a plan to ensure adequate intake
- Ability to meet self-care needs related to elimination and hygiene
- Safety concerns

Determine possible precipitating factors for behavior changes and develop strategies to address difficult behavior.

Assess family caregivers' stress level and coping strategies.

Implement a plan to meet areas of identified need in terms of elimination, nutrition, hydration, and hygiene.

Provide for patient needs:

- Communicate with the patient in a therapeutic manner (Table 64.15)
- Use memory aids and reorient to time, place, and person often
- Use distraction to manage agitated behavior
- Institute measures to manage pain, fever, nausea, and other symptoms
- Maintain a consistent daily routine
- Encourage continued mobility if appropriate
- Present changes in the patient's routine gradually, if possible
- If the patient uses eyeglasses or a hearing aid, have them available

Provide a safe, optimal environment by:

- Implement measures to decrease fall risk and address wandering
- Reducing noise and providing adequate nonglare lighting
- Providing a soothing atmosphere
- Assigning consistent nursing staff

Implement measures to promote sleep (see Chapter 8).

Provide caregiver support:

- Make referrals for community services, such as adult day care and respite care
- In long-term care, encourage visitation by significant others as appropriate and include them in planning, providing, and evaluating care to the extent desired
- Teach the patient and caregiver about measures to manage AD (Table 64.16)

Delegate to LPN/VN:

- Monitor for behavior changes that may indicate physiologic problems.
- Check the environment for potential safety hazards.
- Give enteral feedings to patients who are unable to swallow, if ordered.
- Give ordered medications.

Supervise AP:

- Help patients to use the toilet, commode, or bedpan at frequent intervals.
- Provide personal hygiene, skin care, and oral care.
- Help patients with eating.
- Aid patients with daily activities.
- Use bed alarms and surveillance to decrease risk for falls.

Collaborate With Other Team Members

Dietitian

- Assess nutrition status and provide prescribed nutrition support.
- Offer practical suggestions to enhance dietary intake.

Occupational Therapist

- Suggest ways to help patients retain self-care ability as long as possible.

Social Worker

- Help caregivers identify and obtain needed resources.
- Provide support and counseling to caregivers.

these behaviors become problematic, you must plan interventions carefully. Assess the patient's physical status. Check for changes in vital signs, urinary and bowel patterns, and pain that could account for behavior problems. Are there factors in the environment triggering the behavior? Extremes in temperature or excessive noise may lead to behavior changes. When environmental conditions are agitating the patient, either move the patient or remove the stimulus.

When a patient resists or pulls tubes or dressings, cover these items with stretch tube gauze or remove them from the visual field. Reassure the patient that you are present to keep them safe. If the patient cannot state distress, validate their mood. Rephrase the patient's statement to validate its meaning. Closely observe the patient's emotional state.

Nursing strategies that address difficult behavior include redirection, distraction, and reassurance. Table 64.15 lists tips for promoting communication. When a patient is restless or agitated, use redirecting. Change the patient's focus by having them perform activities, such as sweeping, raking, or dusting. Providing snacks, taking a car ride, sitting on a porch swing or rocker, listening to favorite music, watching videotapes, looking at family photographs, or walking may distract an agitated patient. Reassure patients by telling them that they will be protected from danger, harm, or embarrassment. Repetitive activities, including songs, poems, music, massage, aromas, or a favorite object can be soothing. Animal-assisted therapy helps some persons.[14]

Do not threaten to restrain an agitated patient. Ask a calming family member to stay with them. Monitor the patient frequently and record all interventions. As verbal skills decline, you and the caregiver must rely more on the patient's body language to communicate care needs. Positive nursing actions can reduce the use of chemical (drug therapy) restraints.

Antipsychotic drugs may be used to treat disruptive behaviors (Table 64.11). However, they have adverse effects. We should exhaust all other ways of treating behavior issues before starting drug treatment.

CHECK YOUR PRACTICE

You are working in a secure Alzheimer's unit. While making rounds at 1600, you see Dan, one of the APs, screaming at an 84-year-old male resident. When you approach Dan and the resident, you ask what is going on. Dan responds, "Every day about this time he gets so agitated and starts yelling at me, so I yell back."

- How would you handle the situation? What teaching does Dan need?

A specific type of agitation, **sundowning**, is when the patient becomes more confused and agitated in the late afternoon or evening. Behaviors related to sundowning include agitation, aggressiveness, wandering, resistance to redirection, and increased verbal activity, such as yelling. The cause of sundowning is unclear. It may be due to a disruption of circadian rhythms. Other causes include pain, hunger, unfamiliar environment and noise, medications, reduced lighting, and fragmented sleep.[15]

TABLE 64.15 NURSING MANAGEMENT

Promoting Communication With the Patient With AD

Do

- Treat the adult with respect and dignity, even when behavior is childlike.
- Use gentle touch and direct eye contact.
- Remain patient, flexible, calm, and understanding.
- Expect challenging behaviors since AD affects the patient's ability to think logically.
- Give directions using gestures or pictures.
- Simplify tasks. Focus on one thing at a time.
- Avoid questions or topics that require extensive thought, memory, or words.
- Be flexible. If one approach does not work, try another.
- Use distraction, changing the subject, redirecting to another activity.
- Provide reassurance. Praise sincerely for success.

Do Not

- Criticize, correct, or argue.
- Rush or hurry the patient.
- Force participation in activities or events.
- Talk about the patient as if they are not there.
- Blame the patient with AD. Instead, blame the disease.
- Take challenging behaviors personally. These behaviors are due to the disease.
- Use condescending terms, such as "honey" or "sweetie."
- Use threatening gestures.
- Overreact to the patient with AD.
- Try to explain "why" or rationalize.

Managing sundowning can be challenging for you, the patient, and the family. When a patient has sundowning, remain calm and avoid confrontation. Assess the situation for possible causes of the agitation. Helpful interventions include (1) creating a quiet, calm environment; (2) maximizing exposure to daylight by opening blinds and turning on lights during the day; (3) evaluating medications to determine if any could cause sleep problems; (4) limiting naps and caffeine; and (5) consulting with the HCP about drug therapy.

Safety. The patient is at risk for problems related to personal safety. Hazards include falling, ingesting dangerous substances, wandering, injuring others and self with sharp objects, being burned, and being unable to respond to crisis situations. These concerns require careful attention in the home environment to minimize risk. Supervision is needed. As the patient's cognitive function declines over time, they may have problems navigating physical spaces and interpreting environmental cues. Help the caregiver assess the home environment for safety risks.

! SAFETY ALERT

Preventing Falls

Teach the caregiver to take the following steps:

- Have stairwells well lit.
- Make sure the patient can grasp the handrails.
- Tack down carpet edges.
- Remove throw rugs and extension cords.
- Use nonskid mats in the tub or shower.
- Install handrails in the bath and by the commode.

Wandering is a major concern for caregivers. Wandering may be related to loss of memory or to side effects of medications. It may be an expression of a physical or emotional need, restlessness, curiosity, or stimuli that trigger memories of earlier routines. As with other behaviors, observe for factors or events that may precipitate wandering. For example, the patient may be sensitive to stress and tension in the environment. In such cases, wandering may reflect an attempt to leave.

When someone with AD is discovered missing, every second counts. To assist caregivers with finding them, the Alzheimer's Association and the MedicAlert Foundation have created an alliance called MedicAlert + Alzheimer's Association Safe Return.[16] This program includes identification products (e.g., bracelet, necklace, wallet cards), a national photo and information database, a 24-hour toll-free emergency crisis line, local chapter support, and wandering behavior education and training for caregivers and families.

Tracking devices (e.g., global positioning system [GPS]) can be used to find people who wander. These devices can be placed in shoes, sewn into pockets, worn as a bracelet or pendant, or clipped to a belt.

Pain management. Because of difficulties with oral and written language, patients may have a hard time expressing physical problems, including pain. You need to rely on other clues, such as their behavior. Pain can result in changes in behavior, including increased vocalization, agitation, withdrawal, and changes in function. Pain should be recognized and treated promptly and the patient's response monitored.

Eating and swallowing difficulties. Undernutrition is a problem in the moderate and severe stages of AD. Loss of interest in food and decreased ability to self-feed *(feeding apraxia)*, as well as co-morbid conditions, can result in significant nutrition problems. In long-term care facilities, inadequate aid with feeding may add to the problem.

Use pureed foods, thickened liquids, and nutrition supplements when chewing and swallowing become problematic. The patient may need reminders to chew their food and to swallow. A quiet and unhurried environment without distractions (e.g., television) at mealtimes can help. Low lighting, music, and simulated nature sounds may improve eating behaviors. Easy-grip eating utensils and finger foods may allow the patient to self-feed. Offer liquids frequently.

When oral feeding is not possible, explore alternative routes. Nasogastric (NG) feeding may be used for short periods. However, for the long term, the NG tube is uncomfortable and may add to the patient's agitation. A percutaneous endoscopic gastrostomy (PEG) tube is another option. PEG tubes can be problematic since patients with AD are vulnerable to aspiration of feeding formula and tube dislodgment. The potential positive outcomes from nutrition therapies must be considered in light of overall goals and potential adverse effects of the specific therapy. Nutrition therapy is described in Chapter 44.

Oral care. In the late stages, the patient is unable to perform oral self-care. With decreased tooth brushing and flossing, dental problems are likely to occur. Because of swallowing difficulties, patients may retain food in the mouth, adding to the risk for tooth decay. Dental caries and tooth abscess can cause discomfort and increase agitation. Inspect the mouth regularly. Provide mouth care to those who cannot perform self-care.

Infection prevention. Urinary tract infection and pneumonia are the most common infections in patients with AD. Such infections are the cause of death in many patients with AD. Because of feeding and swallowing problems, the patient is at risk for aspiration pneumonia. Immobility can predispose the patient to pneumonia.

Reduced fluid intake, prostate enlargement in men, poor hygiene, and urinary drainage devices can predispose patients to bladder infection. Any manifestations of infection, such as a change in behavior, fever, cough, or pain on urination, require prompt evaluation and treatment.

Skin care. It is important to monitor the patient's skin over time. Note and treat rashes, areas of redness, and skin breakdown. In the late stages, incontinence along with immobility and undernutrition can place the patient at risk for skin breakdown. Keep the skin clean and dry. Change the patient's position regularly to avoid areas of pressure over bony prominences.

Elimination problems. During the moderate and severe stages of AD, urinary and fecal incontinence lead to an increased need for nursing care. Scheduled toileting may help decrease incontinence.

Constipation is a common problem. Causes include immobility, reduced fiber intake, and decreased fluid intake. Treatment includes increased dietary fiber, fiber supplements, and stool softeners. Ways to manage constipation are discussed in Chapter 47.

Caregiver support. More than 16 million Americans provide unpaid care for people with AD or other dementias.[3] Most of these are family members providing care in the home (Fig. 64.9). AD disrupts all aspects of patient and family life. Caregivers for people with AD describe it as very stressful. They often have adverse consequences to their own health.

The chronic and often severe stress of dementia caregiving increases the risk for dementia in spouse caregivers. It could be that the effects from the chronic stress of caregiving affect the hippocampus, a region of the brain responsible for memory.

Fig. 64.9 Caregivers of patients with dementia face incredible challenges. (© KatarzynaBialasiewicz/iStock.com.)

As the disease progresses, the relationship between the caregiver and patient changes. Family roles may be altered or reversed. A child may care for a parent. Decisions must be made, including when to have the patient stop driving or doing activities that may have become dangerous, ask for assistance, and place the patient in adult day care or a long-term care facility. With early-onset AD, the patient is affected during their most productive years in terms of career and family. The consequences can be devastating to the patient and family.

AD seriously affects sexual relationships. As the disease progresses, sexual interest may decline for both the patient and partner. Several reasons account for this, including fatigue, memory impairment, and incontinence. Some patients become sexually driven and uninhibited as the disease progresses.

Work with the caregiver to assess stressors and identify coping strategies to reduce the burden of caregiving. For example, ask which behaviors are most disruptive to family life at a given time. This is likely to change as the disease progresses. Determining what is most disruptive or distressful to the caregiver can help establish priorities.

Patient safety is a high priority. Assess what the caregiver's expectations are about the patient's behavior. Are the expectations reasonable given the progression of the disease? A family and caregiver teaching guide based on the disease stages is shown in Table 64.16. A nursing care plan for the family caregiver (eNursing Care Plan 64.2) is available on the website for this chapter.

Support groups for caregivers and family members (Fig. 64.10) can provide an atmosphere of understanding and give current information about the disease itself and related topics, such as safety, legal, ethical, and financial issues. The Alzheimer's Association has many educational and support systems available to help family caregivers (*www.alz.org*).

◆ Evaluation

Expected outcomes are that the patient with AD will:

- Function at the highest level of cognitive ability
- Perform basic personal care ADLs, by self or with assistance, as needed
- Be injury free

DELIRIUM

Delirium is a state of confusion that develops over days to hours.[1] The patient has decreased ability to direct, focus, sustain, and shift attention and awareness. Deficits in memory, orientation, language, visuospatial ability, or perception may be present. The patient may be hypoactive or hyperactive. Emotional problems include fear, depression, euphoria, or perplexity. Sleep may be disturbed.

These symptoms represent a change from the patient's baseline. They tend to fluctuate throughout the day. They do not occur in the context of a severely reduced level of arousal, such as coma, and cannot be explained by another preexisting, evolving, or established neurocognitive disorder.

Etiology and Pathophysiology

We do not know the exact cause of delirium. A main contributing factor is impaired cerebral oxidative metabolism, in which

TABLE 64.16 PATIENT & CAREGIVER TEACHING

AD

Include the following instructions when teaching families and caregivers the management of the patient with AD:

Mild Stage

- Many treatable (and potentially reversible) conditions can mimic dementia (Table 64.2). Try to establish a diagnosis.
- Get the patient to stop driving. Confusion and poor judgment can impair driving skills and potentially put others at risk.
- Encourage activities such as visiting with friends and family, listening to music, enjoying hobbies, and exercising.
- Provide cues in the home, establish a routine, and determine a specific location where essential items (e.g., glasses) must be kept.
- Do not correct misstatements or faulty memory.
- Register with MedicAlert + Alzheimer's Association Safe Return, a program established by the MedicAlert Foundation and the Alzheimer's Association to locate those who wander from their homes.
- Make plans in terms of advance directives, care options, financial concerns, and personal preference for care.

Moderate Stage

- Install door locks for patient safety.
- Provide protective wear for incontinence.
- Ensure that the home has good lighting, install handrails in stairways and bathrooms, and remove area rugs.
- Label drawers and faucets (hot and cold) to ensure safety.
- Develop ways, such as distraction and diversion, to cope with behavior problems. Identify and reduce potential triggers (e.g., reduce stress, extremes in temperature) for disruptive behavior.
- Provide memory triggers, such as pictures of family and friends.

Severe Stage

- Follow a regular schedule for toileting to reduce incontinence.
- Provide care to meet needs, including oral care and skin care.
- Monitor diet and fluid intake to ensure their adequacy.
- Continue communication through talking and touching.
- Consider placement in a long-term care facility when providing total care becomes too difficult.

Fig. 64.10 Support groups are an effective way to help caregivers cope. (© SDI Productions/iStock.com.)

the brain gets less oxygen and has problems using it. Multiple neurotransmitter abnormalities may be involved. Cholinergic deficiency, excess release of dopamine, and both increased

TABLE 64.17 Risk Factors for Delirium

Demographic Characteristics

- Age 65 years or older
- Male gender

Cognitive Status

- Cognitive impairment
- Dementia
- Depression
- History of delirium

Decreased Oral Intake

- Dehydration
- Malnutrition

Drugs

- Alcohol or drug use or withdrawal
- Aminoglycosides
- Anticholinergics
- Opioids
- Sedative-hypnotics
- Treatment with multiple drugs
- Vasopressors

Environmental

- Admission to ICU
- Pain (especially untreated)
- Restraints use
- Sleep deprivation
- Stress

Functional Status

- Functional dependence
- History of falls
- Immobility

Medical Problems

- Acute infection, sepsis, fever
- Chronic kidney or liver disease
- Electrolyte imbalances
- Fracture or trauma
- Hemodynamic instability
- History of stroke
- Hypertension
- Hypoxia
- Neurologic disease
- Severe acute illness
- Terminal illness

Sensory

- Sensory deprivation
- Sensory overload
- Vision or hearing impairment

Surgery

- Cardiac surgery
- Noncardiac surgery
- Orthopedic surgery
- Prolonged cardiopulmonary bypass

TABLE 64.18 Mnemonic for Causes of Delirium

Dementia, dehydration
Electrolyte imbalances, emotional stress
Lung, liver, heart, kidney, brain
Infection, intensive care unit
Rx drugs
Injury, immobility
Untreated pain, unfamiliar environment
Metabolic disorders

and decreased serotonin activity may contribute to delirium. Proinflammatory cytokines, including interleukin-1 (IL-1), IL-2, IL-6, tumor necrosis factor-α (TNF-α), cytokines, and interferon, appear to play a role.

Delirium is rarely caused by a single factor. Common factors that can lead to delirium are listed in Tables 64.17 and 64.18. Major risk factors include increased age, preexisting dementia, hypertension, alcohol use, and severe illness on admission. Dementia is the leading risk factor for delirium. Likewise, delirium is a risk factor for developing dementia. Delirium may cause permanent neuronal damage and lead to dementia.

Environmental factors that can contribute to delirium include sleep deprivation, stress, sensory overload, and immobilization. Physical conditions such as electrolyte imbalances and severe infections can lead to delirium. Last, certain drugs (e.g., sedatives [benzodiazepines], opioids) are linked with delirium, especially in older or vulnerable patients.[17]

Delirium most often occurs among hospitalized older adults.[18] Up to 60% of older adults hospitalized for medical conditions have delirium at some time during their hospitalization. It is the most common surgical complication among older adults. Older adults have limited compensatory mechanisms to deal with physiologic insults, such as hypoxia, hypoglycemia, and dehydration.

The prevalence of delirium in ICU patients is as high as 87%. It is related to longer hospital stays and higher mortality rates.

Delirium may be the first symptom of life-threatening problems such as pneumonia, urosepsis, or meningitis. It can occur after a relatively minor insult in a vulnerable patient. For example, a patient with underlying health problems, such as heart failure (HF), cancer, cognitive impairment, or sensory limitations, may develop delirium in response to a minor change, such as using a sleeping medication. In other less vulnerable patients, it may take a combination of factors, such as anesthesia, major surgery, mechanical ventilation, infection, and prolonged sleep deprivation, to precipitate delirium. Pain and depression contribute to delirium, especially among older adults.

Clinical Manifestations

Delirium can have a variety of manifestations, ranging from hypoactivity and lethargy to hyperactivity, agitation, and hallucinations. Patients can have mixed delirium, with both hypoactive and hyperactive symptoms. Delirium can develop over the course of hours to days. It usually develops over a 2- to 3-day period. Delirium can last from 1 to 7 days. However, delirium may persist for months or years. Some patients do not fully recover.

During a delirious state, the patient often has a reduced ability to focus, sustain, and shift attention. Memory, judgment, and orientation are impaired. Speech is rapid, rambling, and/or incoherent. Other manifestations often include disorganized thinking, irritability, insomnia, loss of appetite, and restlessness. Later manifestations may include agitation, misperception, misinterpretation, and hallucinations.

Manifestations of delirium are sometimes confused with those of dementia. A key distinction between them is that the patient who has sudden cognitive impairment, disorientation, or clouded sensorium is more likely to have delirium rather than dementia. Table 64.1 compares delirium and dementia.

Diagnostic Studies

Diagnosing delirium is complicated because many critically ill patients cannot communicate their needs. A careful medical, psychologic history, and physical assessment are the first steps in diagnosing delirium and its underlying cause. This includes careful attention to medications, both prescription and OTC. The Confusion Assessment Method (CAM) is a reliable tool for assessing delirium (Table 64.19). The version of the CAM may vary depending on the clinical setting. Determine if delirium is related to underlying dementia.

TABLE 64.19 Confusion Assessment Method (CAM)

Delirium is diagnosed with the presence of features 1 and 2 and either 3 or 4.

Feature 1

Acute Onset and Fluctuating Course

Data usually obtained from a family member or nurse.

Shown by positive responses to the following questions:

- Is there evidence of an acute change in mental status from the patient's baseline?
- Did the (abnormal) behavior fluctuate during the day (i.e., tend to come and go, or increase and decrease in severity)?

Feature 2

Inattention

Shown by positive response to the following question:

- Did the patient have problem focusing attention (e.g., being easily distractible, or having problem keeping track of what was being said)?

Feature 3

Disorganized Thinking

Shown by a positive response to the following question:

- Was the patient's thinking disorganized or incoherent, such as rambling or irrelevant conversation, unclear or illogical flow of ideas, or unpredictable switching from subject to subject?

Feature 4

Altered Level of Consciousness

Shown by any answer other than "alert" to the following question:

- Overall, how would you rate this patient's level of consciousness (alert [normal], vigilant [hyper alert], lethargic [drowsy, easily aroused], stupor [difficult to arouse], or coma [unarousable])?

Adapted from Inouye S, van Dyck C, Alessi C, et al: Clarifying confusion: the confusion assessment method, *Ann Intern Med* 113:941, 1990.

Once delirium has been diagnosed, explore potential causes. Review the health history and medication record. Laboratory tests include CBC, serum electrolytes, blood urea nitrogen (BUN), and creatinine levels; ECG; urinalysis; liver and thyroid function tests; and O_2 saturation. Drug and alcohol levels may be obtained. If unexplained fever or nuchal rigidity is present and meningitis or encephalitis is suspected, a lumbar puncture may be done. CSF is examined for glucose, protein, and bacteria. If the patient's history includes head injury, appropriate x-rays or scans may be ordered. In general, brain imaging studies, such as CT and MRI, are used only when head injury is known or suspected.

❖ NURSING AND INTERPROFESSIONAL MANAGEMENT: DELIRIUM

Treatment is important as many cases of delirium are potentially reversible. In caring for a patient with delirium, you are responsible for prevention, early recognition, and treatment (Table 64.20). Prevention involves recognition of patients at high risk, including those with neurologic disorders, such as dementia or stroke. Table 64.17 lists common risk factors. (Box 64.4)

Care focuses on eliminating precipitating factors. If it is drug induced, medications are discontinued. Keep in mind

TABLE 64.20 NURSING MANAGEMENT

Caring for the Patient With Delirium

Determine the potential cause for delirium and initiate measures to address the cause if appropriate

Regularly assess for manifestations of delirium

- Administer screening tools, such as the CAM (Table 64.19)
- Screen for the presence of any co-existing problems
- Review the results of diagnostic tests

Determine their ability to meet self-care needs related to nutrition, elimination, hydration, and hygiene and implement a plan to meet any areas of identified need

Provide for patient needs:

- Provide the patient with reassurance
- Talk to the patient and reorient to time, place, and person often
- Use distraction to manage agitated behavior
- Institute measures to manage pain, fever, nausea, and other symptoms
- Encourage early mobility if appropriate
- If the patient uses eyeglasses or a hearing aid, have them available

Provide a safe, optimal environment by:

- Reducing noise and providing adequate nonglare lighting
- Providing a soothing atmosphere
- Plan for consistent nursing staff

Implement measures to promote sleep (see Chapter 8)

Teach the patient and caregivers about causes and manifestations of delirium

that delirium can accompany drug and alcohol withdrawal. Depending on the history, drug screening may be done. Fluid and electrolyte imbalances and nutrition deficiencies (e.g., thiamine) are corrected if appropriate. If delirium is from infection, appropriate antibiotic therapy is started. Similarly, if delirium is due to chronic illness, such as chronic kidney disease or HF, treatment focuses on these conditions.

If the problem is related to an overstimulating or an understimulating environment, then changes should be made. Reduce environmental stimuli, including noise and light levels. Limit noise levels by muting phones, setting alarms based on the patient's condition, and reducing unnecessary alarms. Limit overhead paging and all unnecessary noise in patient care areas.

Conversation is an especially stressful noise, especially when it concerns the patient and is held in the presence of, but without participation from, the patient. Reduce this source of stress by finding suitable places for patient-related discussions. Whenever possible, include the patient and caregiver in the discussion.

CHECK YOUR PRACTICE

You are working in the medical ICU. Your patient is an 82-year-old man who had a hip replacement 3 days ago. He was doing well after surgery and then developed bilateral pneumonia. He was transferred to the ICU yesterday. When you walk into his room, you notice his daughter is staring out the window and does not respond to your greeting. When you approach her, you notice she is very upset. When you ask her what is wrong, she bursts out crying, "How can this be? My dad is a brilliant man. Now look at him. He talks to himself. He screams at me. He thinks I am his wife. Mom died 5 years ago. What happened to him?"

- How would you assess the situation?
- What can you do to help the daughter?

BOX 64.4 EVIDENCE-BASED PRACTICE

Postoperative Delirium

You are caring for S.L., an 82-year-old patient who fell and sustained a femoral neck fracture. Fracture repair is scheduled this morning. The patient's daughter is with S.L. During your assessment, S.L. is unable to identify a pain intensity score but tells you, "It doesn't hurt much when I lay very still." S.L. is alert and oriented to person and place but does recall falling. S.L. tells you, "I couldn't find my glasses!" The history includes hypertension and type 2 diabetes, with a recent glycosylated hemoglobin result of 8.2. BP at 0800 was 148/82 mm Hg. You administer the scheduled atenolol 100 mg with a sip of water.

Making Clinical Decisions

Synthesis of Best Available Evidence

Cognitive changes often occur in older adults after surgery, ranging from a transient problem to a persistent decline. The 2 main conditions have been identified as postoperative delirium and postoperative cognitive dysfunction.

Clinician Expertise

S.L.'s risk factors for postoperative delirium, include age, history of diabetes and hypertension, impaired vision, lack of sleep, and current cognitive state. You are prepared to use an assessment tool for delirium as part of your assessment when S.L. returns from surgery. Your interventions would include managing stressors that could precipitate delirium.

Patient Preferences and Values

S.L.'s daughter tells you during her preoperative visit, "My mother seems much calmer and more comfortable. I was really concerned to see her so restless and unsettled. I don't believe she's slept much since the fall."

Implications for Nursing Practice

1. What would you do if your assessment findings suggest delirium?
2. What stressors should be managed to decrease the risk of postoperative delirium?

Reference for Evidence

Hasan TF, Kelley RE, Cornett EM, et al.: Cognitive impairment assessment and interventions to optimize surgical patient outcomes, *Best Practice & Research Clinical Anaesthesiology* 34:225, 2020.

Implement measures to protect the patient from harm. Give priority to creating a calm and safe environment. The presence of a caregiver may help. Provide familiar objects and family photos, transfer the patient to a private room or one closer to the nurses' station, and plan for consistent nursing staff if possible. Use reorientation and behavior interventions. Provide the patient with reassurance and reorienting information as to place, time, and procedures. Clocks, calendars, and lists of scheduled activities are helpful. Removing lines no longer needed and early mobility are effective.

Reorient patients who are confused during assessments to provide comfort and direction. Personal contact through touch and verbal communication can be an important reorienting strategy. If the patient uses eyeglasses or a hearing aid, they should be available because sensory deprivation can precipitate delirium. Avoid the use of restraints. Other interventions, including relaxation techniques, music therapy, and massage, may be appropriate for some patients with delirium.

You may need to address polypharmacy, pain, nutrition status, and potential for incontinence. The patient with delirium is at risk for the adverse consequences of immobility, including skin breakdown. Give attention to increasing physical activity or providing range-of-motion exercises, when appropriate, and maintaining skin integrity.

Focus on supporting the family and caregivers during episodes of delirium. Family members need to understand factors that may have precipitated the delirium, as well as the potential outcomes. Patient education materials are available at www.ICUdelirium.org.

◆ Drug Therapy

Drug therapy is reserved for patients with severe agitation, especially when it interferes with needed medical treatments. Agitation can put the patient at risk for falls and injury. Drug therapy is used cautiously because many of the drugs used to manage agitation have psychoactive properties. Drugs should be used only when nonpharmacologic interventions have failed.

Dexmedetomidine (Precedex), an α-adrenergic receptor agonist, has been used in ICU settings for sedation. The use of low-dose antipsychotics (e.g., haloperidol, risperidone [Risperdal]), though common practice, is controversial. Their use does not change the duration of delirium or the length of hospitalization.

Haloperidol can be given IV, IM, or orally. It will produce sedation. Other side effects include hypotension; extrapyramidal side effects, including *tardive dyskinesia* (involuntary muscle movements of face, trunk, and arms) and *athetosis* (involuntary writhing movements of the limbs); muscle tone changes; and anticholinergic effects. Monitor older patients receiving antipsychotic agents.

Short-acting benzodiazepines (e.g., lorazepam [Ativan]) can be used to treat delirium from sedative and alcohol withdrawal or in conjunction with antipsychotics to reduce extrapyramidal side effects. However, these drugs may worsen delirium caused by other factors and must be used cautiously.

Case Study

Alzheimer Disease

(© iStock/Thinkstock.)

Patient Profile

M.Y., a 78-year-old man, was diagnosed with AD 3 years ago, shortly after his wife died. Today, his 45-year-old son brings him to the emergency department because he wandered from his son's home, fell, and injured his left hip.

Subjective Data

- Can say his name, confused as to place and time
- Denies memory of wandering or falling
- Agitated, trying to get up
- Denies pain

Objective Data

Physical Assessment

- Left leg shorter than the right leg
- Tense and anxious

Diagnostic Studies

- X-ray of left hip indicates a fracture
- Mini-Cog testing indicates cognitive impairment

Discussion Questions

1. ***Recognize*:** What is the pathogenesis of AD?
2. ***Analyze*:** What precipitating factors may have resulted in M.Y.'s fall?
3. ***Plan:*** Surgery is planned to repair his fractured hip. Why is he at risk for delirium?
4. ***Prioritize:*** Based on the assessment data, what are the priority clinical problems?
5. ***Prioritize:*** What is the priority nursing intervention for M.Y.?
6. ***Act:*** What nursing activities can you delegate to assistive personnel (AP)?
7. ***Act:*** What teaching plan should you develop for M.Y. and his son?
8. ***Safety:*** What safety precautions need to be taken when caring for M.Y.?

Answers available at http://evolve.elsevier.com/Lewis/medsurg.

BRIDGE TO NCLEX EXAMINATION

The number of the question corresponds to the same-numbered outcome at the beginning of the chapter.

1. Dementia is defined as a
   - **a.** syndrome that results only in memory loss.
   - **b.** disease associated with abrupt changes in behavior.
   - **c.** disease that is always due to reduced blood flow to the brain.
   - **d.** syndrome characterized by cognitive dysfunction and loss of memory.
2. Vascular dementia is associated with
   - **a.** transient ischemic attacks.
   - **b.** viral infection of nerve tissue.
   - **c.** cognitive changes from cerebral ischemia.
   - **d.** abrupt changes in cognitive function that are irreversible.
3. Assessment findings in a patient with dementia with Lewy bodies (DLB) include
   - **a.** remissions and exacerbations over many years.
   - **b.** memory impairment, muscle jerks, and blindness.
   - **c.** parkinsonian symptoms, including muscle rigidity.
   - **d.** increased intracranial pressure from decreased CSF drainage.
4. Which statement(s) accurately describe(s) mild cognitive impairment? *(select all that apply)*
   - **a.** Cannot be detected by screening tests
   - **b.** The person may appear normal to the casual observer
   - **c.** Family members may see changes in the patient's abilities
   - **d.** Problems the person is experiencing interfere with daily activities
   - **e.** The person is usually aware that there is a problem with their memory
5. A patient with cognitive impairment would receive a clinical diagnosis of dementia based on
   - **a.** CT or MRI.
   - **b.** brain biopsy.
   - **c.** electroencephalogram.
   - **d.** history and cognitive assessment.
6. A priority goal of treatment for the patient with Alzheimer disease is to
   - **a.** maintain patient safety.
   - **b.** maintain or increase body weight.
   - **c.** return to a higher level of self-care.
   - **d.** enhance functional ability over time.

7. Which patient is at the highest risk for developing delirium?
   a. A 50-year-old woman with cholecystitis
   b. A 19-year-old man with a fractured femur
   c. A 42-year-old woman having an elective total hysterectomy
   d. A 78-year-old man admitted to the medical unit with complications of heart failure

1. d; 2. c; 3. c; 4. b, c, e; 5. d; 6. a; 7. d.

For rationales to these answers and even more NCLEX review questions, visit http://evolve.elsevier.com/Lewis/medsurg.

EVOLVE WEBSITE/RESOURCES LIST

http://evolve.elsevier.com/Lewis/medsurg

Review Questions (Online Only)
Key Points
Answer Keys for Questions
- Rationales for Bridge to NCLEX Examination Questions
- Answer Guidelines for Case Study

Student Case Study
- Patient With Alzheimer's Disease

eNursing Care Plans
- eNursing Care Plan 64.1: Patient With Alzheimer's Disease
- eNursing Care Plan 64.2: Family Caregivers

Conceptual Care Map Creator
Audio Glossary
Content Updates

REFERENCES

1. American Psychiatric Association: *Diagnostic and statistical manual of mental disorders*, ed 5, Arlington, VA, 2013, APA. (Classic).
2. U.S. Department of Health and Human Services National Institute on Aging: What is dementia? Symptoms, types, and diagnosis. Retrieved from https://www.nia.nih.gov/health/what-dementia-symptoms-types-and-diagnosis.
*3. Alzheimer's Association: Alzheimer's disease facts and figures. Retrieved from https://www.alz.org/media/documents/alzheimers-facts-and-figures.pdf, 2021.
4. Alzheimer's Association: What is Alzheimer's disease? Retrieved from https://www.alz.org/alzheimers-dementia/what-is-alzheimers.
5. Alzheimer's Society: Types of vascular dementia. Retrieved from https://www.alzheimers.org.uk/.
6. Jankovic J, Mazziotta JC, Pomeroy SL, Newman NJ: *Bradley and Daroff's neurology in clinical practice*, ed 8, Philadelphia, 2022, Elsevier.
7. Jameson JL, Fauci A, Kasper D, et al.: *Harrison's principles of internal medicine*, ed 20, McGraw Hill, 2020.
8. Heuther S, McCance KL: *Understanding pathophysiology*, ed 7, St Louis, 2019, Elsevier.
9. Alzheimer's Association: 10 Early signs and symptoms of Alzheimer's. Retrieved from https://www.alz.org/alzheimers-dementia/10_signs.
10. Denung H, Aldridge Zena K: Understanding behaviors in dementia, *J Comm Nurs* 35:50, 2021.
*11. Yeon L, Kyung Hee L, McConnell E: Mealtime caregiving approaches and behavioral symptoms in persons living with dementia: a longitudinal observational study, *BMC Nursing* 20:104, 2021.
*12. Trinh E, Lee A, Kim KY: End-of-life care of persons with Alzheimer disease: an update for clinicians, *Am J of Hosp Pall Care* 1(1), 2019.
*13. Meguro M, Meguro K, Takahashi K, et al.: Alzheimer's deterioration in intellectual and neurobiological staging supports the retrogenesis model: a double dissociation between verbal/non-verbal judgments and the left/right parieto-temporal glucose metabolism, *Psychogeriatrics* 20:149, 2020.
*14. Yakimicki M, Edwards N, Richards E, et al.: Animal-assisted intervention and dementia: a systematic review, *Clin Nurs Res* 28(9), 2019.
15. Alzheimer's Association: Sleep issues and sundowning. Retrieved from https://www.alz.org/help-support/caregiving/stages-behaviors/sleep-issues-sundowning.
16. Alzheimer's Association: 24/7 Wandering support for a safe return. Retrieved from https://www.alz.org/help-support/caregiving/safety/medicalert-with-24-7-wandering-support.
17. Bennett C: Caring for patients with delirium, *Nursing* 40(17):2019, 2019.
18. Volland J, Fisher A, Drexler D: Preventing and identifying hospital acquired delirium, *Nursing* 50:32, 2020.

*Evidence-based information for clinical practice.

65

Spinal Cord and Peripheral Nerve Problems

Kristen J. Costello

http://evolve.elsevier.com/Lewis/medsurg/

CONCEPTUAL FOCUS

Family Dynamics
Functional Ability
Mobility
Pain
Sensory Perception

LEARNING OUTCOMES

1. Outline the classification of spinal cord injuries and associated clinical manifestations.
2. Describe the clinical manifestations and interprofessional and nursing management of neurogenic and spinal shock.
3. Relate the clinical manifestations of spinal cord injury to the level of disruption and rehabilitation potential.
4. Describe the nursing management of the patient with a spinal cord injury.
5. Explain the types, clinical manifestations, and interprofessional and nursing management of spinal cord tumors.
6. Explain the etiology, clinical manifestations, and interprofessional and nursing management of trigeminal neuralgia and Bell's palsy.
7. Describe the etiology, clinical manifestations, and interprofessional and nursing management of Guillain-Barré syndrome and inflammatory demyelinating polyneuropathy.

KEY TERMS

autonomic dysreflexia
Bell's palsy
Guillain-Barré syndrome (GBS)
neurogenic bladder
neurogenic bowel
neurogenic (vasogenic) shock
paraplegia
spinal cord injury (SCI)
spinal shock
tetanus
tetraplegia
trigeminal neuralgia (TN)

This chapter discusses spinal cord and peripheral nerve problems, including spinal cord injuries, spinal cord tumors, cranial nerve disorders, and polyneuropathies. We focus on the nursing management of the problems encountered by the patient with spinal cord injury (SCI). The potential for disruption of individual growth and development, altered family dynamics, economic loss from unemployment, and the high cost of rehabilitation and long-term health care make SCI a major problem. While many people with SCI can care for themselves independently, those with the highest level of injury need around-the-clock care at home or in a long-term care facility. The nurse's role in providing holistic care can significantly impact the patient's general health and well-being.

SPINAL CORD PROBLEMS

SPINAL CORD INJURY

Spinal cord injury (SCI) is caused by trauma or damage to the spinal cord. It can result in temporary or permanent alteration in spinal cord function. About 17,000 Americans have SCIs each year. Some 282,000 persons in the United States are living with SCI. The average life expectancy for persons with SCI is shortened and has not improved since the 1980s. In the first year after injury, mortality rates are high. There is a 30% chance of rehospitalzation.[1]

Etiology and Pathophysiology

SCI is usually a result of trauma. The 4 most common causes are motor vehicle collisions (38%), falls (30.5%), violence (13.5%), and sports injuries (9%).[1]

Types of Injury

Neurologic damage caused by SCI occurs in 2 phases: *primary injury* (initial physical disruption of the spinal cord) and *secondary injury* (from processes such as ischemia, hypoxia, hemorrhage, edema).

Primary injury. *Primary injury* results from direct physical trauma to the spinal cord due to blunt or penetrating trauma. Trauma can cause spinal cord compression by bone displacement, interruption of blood supply, or distraction from pulling. Penetrating trauma, such as gunshot and stab wounds, can cause tearing and transection.

Secondary injury. *Secondary injury* refers to the ongoing, progressive damage that occurs after the primary injury. Secondary injury causes further permanent damage. It begins a few minutes after injury and lasts for months. The cascade of events results in edema, ischemia, and inflammation. This causes cell death, disruption of the blood-brain barrier, and demyelination. This can extend the level of deficit and worsen long-term outcomes.

The edema from the inflammatory response is especially harmful because of limited space for tissue expansion. Thus, compression of the spinal cord occurs. Edema extends above and below the injury, increasing ischemic damage. Within 24 hours, permanent damage may occur from edema.

Apoptosis (programmed cell death) continues for weeks. It contributes to post-injury demyelination. The inflammatory response at the site of the initial injury focuses on clearing up the initial cellular debris without damaging normal tissue. This results in a central non-neural core of connective tissue that we refer to as a glial scar (Fig. 65.1). The glial scar creates a physical barrier. It restricts the cells in the spinal cord from migration and regeneration. This leads to irreversible nerve damage and permanent neurologic deficit.

Spinal and Neurogenic Shock

Spinal shock may occur shortly after acute SCI. It is characterized by loss of deep tendon and sphincter reflexes, loss of sensation, and flaccid paralysis below the level of injury. This syndrome lasts days to weeks. It often masks post-injury neurologic function.[2]

In contrast to spinal shock, **neurogenic (vasogenic) shock** can occur in cervical or high thoracic injury (T6 or higher). It occurs from unopposed parasympathetic response due to loss of sympathetic nervous system (SNS) innervation. It causes peripheral vasodilation, venous pooling, and decreased cardiac output. Manifestations include significant hypotension (<90 mm Hg), bradycardia, and temperature dysregulation. Neurogenic shock may persist for as long as 5 weeks after injury.[3] Hypotension can result in poor perfusion and oxygenation to the spinal cord and worsen spinal cord ischemia.[3]

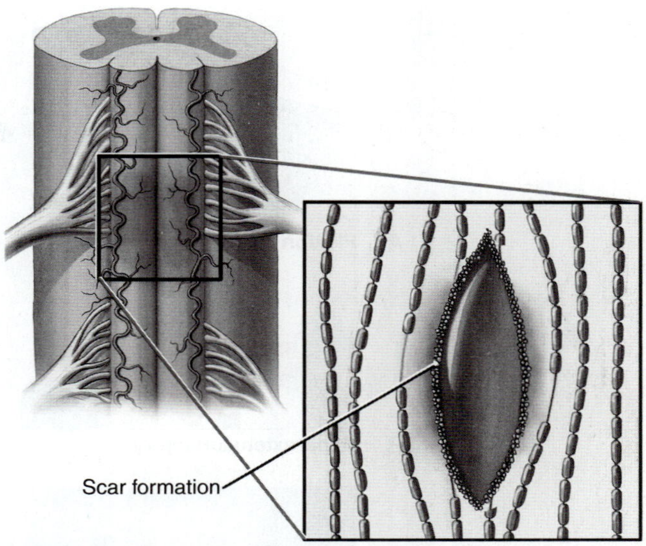

Fig. 65.1 1 to 2 days after the injury, astrocytes proliferate and surround the edges of the fibrotic scar. This confines inflammation to the area of injury protects and neighboring neural tissue from further damage. This process may take 7 to 10 days. (Used with permission from Barrow Neurological Institute, Phoenix, AZ.)

Classification of SCI

SCI is classified by the (1) mechanism of injury, (2) level of injury, and (3) degree of injury.

Mechanisms of injury. The major mechanisms of injury include flexion, flexion-rotation, hyperextension, vertical compression, extension-rotation, and lateral flexion (Fig. 65.2). Flexion-rotation injury is often the most unstable because ligaments that stabilize the spine are torn. This injury most often contributes to severe neurologic deficits.

Level of injury. *Skeletal level* of injury is the vertebral level with the most damage to vertebra and related ligaments. *Neurologic level* is the lowest segment of the spinal cord with normal sensory and motor function on both sides of the body. The level of injury may be cervical, thoracic, lumbar, or sacral. Cervical and lumbar injuries are most common because those areas of the spine are associated with the greatest flexibility and movement.

Injury from C1 to T1 can cause paralysis of all 4 extremities, resulting in **tetraplegia** (formerly called *quadriplegia*). The degree of impairment in the arms after cervical injury depends on the level of injury. The lower the level, the more function is retained in the arms.

Paraplegia (paralysis and loss of sensation in the legs) can occur in SCI below the level of T2.[4] Fig. 65.3 shows affected structures and functions at different levels of cord injury.

Degree of injury. The degree of spinal cord involvement may be complete or incomplete (partial). *Complete cord involvement* results in total loss of sensory and motor function below the level of injury. *Incomplete cord involvement* results in a mixed loss of voluntary motor activity and sensation and leaves some tracts intact. The degree of sensory and motor loss depends on the level of injury and reflects specific damaged nerve tracts.

Five major syndromes are associated with incomplete injuries: central cord syndrome, anterior cord syndrome,

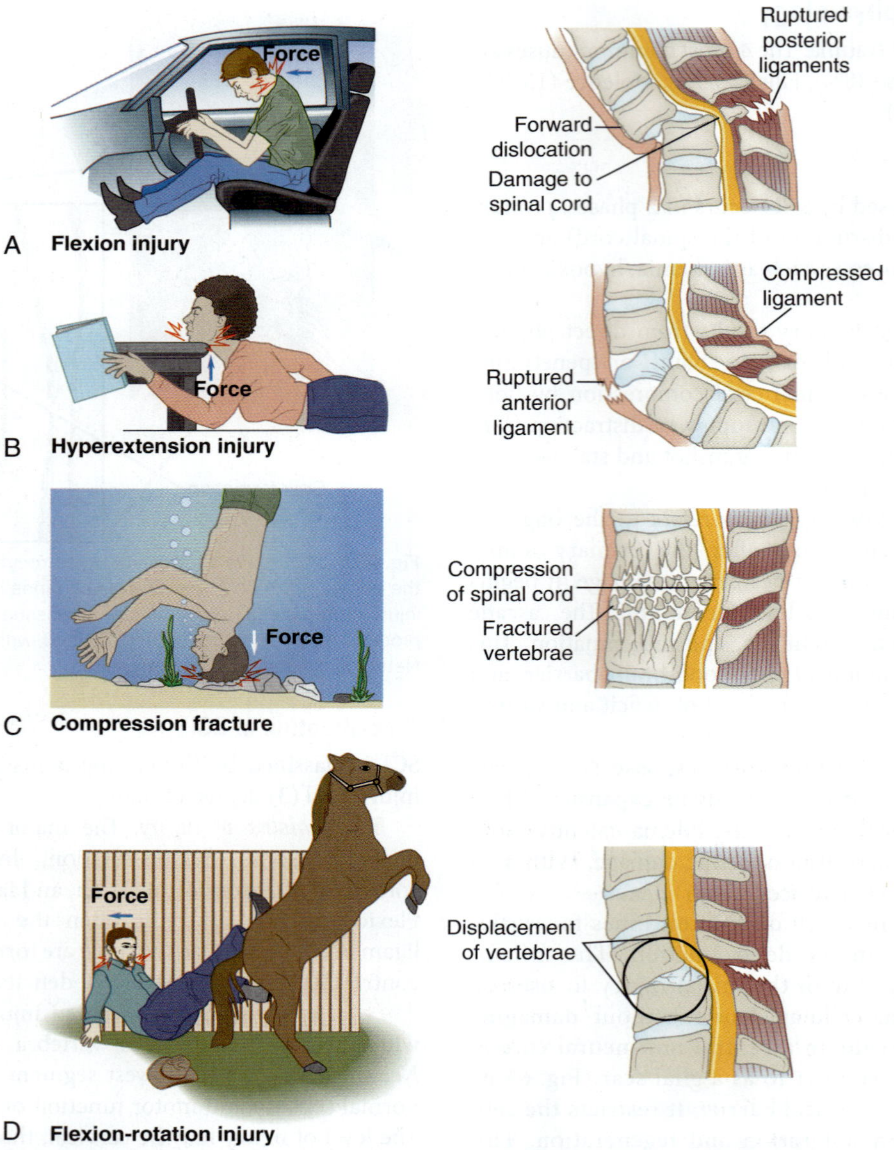

Fig. 65.2 Examples of mechanisms of spinal cord injury. (A) Flexion injury of the cervical spine ruptures the posterior ligaments. (B) Hyperextension injury of the cervical spine ruptures the anterior ligaments. (C) Compression fractures crush the vertebrae and force bony fragments into the spinal canal. (D) Flexion-rotation injury of the cervical spine often results in tearing of ligamentous structures that normally stabilize the spine. (A–C, From Copstead-Kirkhorn LC, Banasik JL: *Pathophysiology,* ed 5, St Louis, 2014, Mosby.)

Brown-Séquard syndrome, cauda equina syndrome, and conus medullaris syndrome (Table 65.1).

Clinical Manifestations

Manifestations of SCI are the result of trauma that causes cord compression, ischemia, edema, and possible cord transection. They are related to the level and degree of injury. The patient with an incomplete injury may have a mix of manifestations.

Motor and Sensory Effects

The American Spinal Injury Association (ASIA) Impairment Scale is used to classify the severity of impairment from SCI. It combines motor and sensory function assessments to determine neurologic level and completeness of injury (Fig. 65.4).[5]

We call the sensory regions *dermatomes*. Each segment of the spinal cord innervates a specific area of skin. A dermatome map is shown in Fig. 60.7. Each dermatome has a recommended point for testing.

The ASIA Impairment Scale is useful for recording changes in neurologic status. It helps us identify rehabilitation goals. Movement and rehabilitation potential related to specific locations of SCI are described in Table 65.2. In general, sensory function closely matches motor function at all levels.

Respiratory System

Respiratory complications closely correspond to the level of injury. Cervical injuries above C3 present special problems because of the total loss of respiratory muscle function.

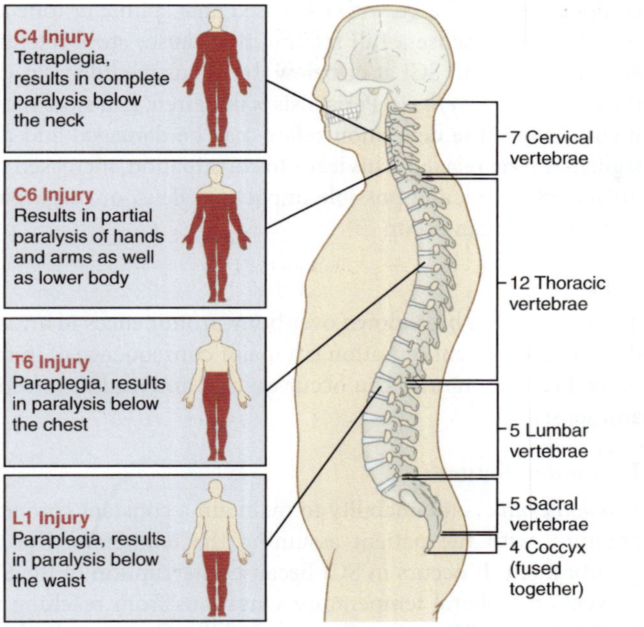

Fig. 65.3 Symptoms, degree of paralysis, and potential for rehabilitation depend on level of spinal injury.

TABLE 65.1 Incomplete Spinal Cord Injury Syndromes

Description	Manifestations
Anterior Cord Syndrome	
• Damage to anterior spinal artery • Results in compromised blood flow to anterior spinal cord • Typically results from acute compression of anterior part of the spinal cord • Common with flexion injury	• Motor paralysis and loss of pain and temperature sensation below level of injury • Since posterior cord tracts are not injured, sensations of touch, position, vibration, and motion remain intact
Brown-Séquard Syndrome	
• Damage to half of the spinal cord • Typically results from penetrating injury to spinal cord	• *Contralateral* (opposite side of injury): Loss of pain and temperature sensation below level of injury • *Ipsilateral* (same side as injury): Loss of motor function, light touch, pressure, position, and vibratory sense
Cauda Equina Syndrome	
• Damage to cauda equina (lumbar and sacral nerve roots)	• Asymmetric distal weakness, patchy sensation in lower extremities • May cause flaccid paralysis of lower extremities • Complete loss of sensation between legs and over buttocks, inner thighs, and backs of legs (*saddle area*) • Areflexic (flaccid) bladder and bowel • Severe, radicular, asymmetric pain
Central Cord Syndrome	
• Damage to central spinal cord • Occurs most often in cervical cord region • More common in older adults • Caused by hyperextension injury in people with degenerative disease	• Motor weakness and altered sensation present in upper extremities • Lower extremities not usually affected • Burning pain in upper extremities
Conus Medullaris Syndrome	
• Damage to conus medullaris (lowest part of spinal cord)	• Motor function in legs may be preserved, weak, or flaccid • Decrease in or loss of sensation in perianal area • Areflexic bowel and bladder • Impotence

These patients have respiratory arrest within minutes of injury if not intubated. Patients with high cervical injury (C3–5) have respiratory insufficiency due to loss of phrenic nerve innervation to the diaphragm and decreased chest and abdominal wall strength.[6] Patients with complete SCI above C5 should be intubated at once. Patients with incomplete SCI injury will have a high degree of variability in their respiratory function.

Cervical and thoracic injuries cause paralysis of abdominal muscles and often the intercostal muscles. The patient cannot cough effectively enough to remove secretions. This increases the risk for aspiration, atelectasis, and pneumonia. Hypoventilation and impairment of the intercostal muscles lead to decreased vital capacity and tidal volume.

Associated traumatic injuries, such as lung contusions, can further compromise lung function. Fluid overload can cause pulmonary edema. Neurogenic pulmonary edema may occur due to a dramatic increase in SNS activity at the time of injury.

Maintaining an arterial saturation above 92% reduces hypoxemia, which can lead to bradycardia and worsen secondary injury. Patients are assessed for respiratory distress, including dyspnea, decreased vital capacity, and pCO_2 greater than 20 mm Hg above baseline, and their ability to manage their secretions. Patients in distress may need mechanical ventilation.

Cardiovascular System

Any cord injury above T6 leads to SNS dysfunction. The result may be bradycardia, peripheral vasodilation, and hypotension (neurogenic shock). Peripheral vasodilation causes relative hypovolemia because of the increase in the capacity of the dilated veins. It reduces venous return of blood to the heart. Cardiac output then decreases, leading to hypotension. Other injuries can cause hemorrhagic shock and further reduce BP. It is essential to identify all causes of hypotension in the person with SCI. Those on β-blockers, young, healthy patients, and older adults may not be tachycardic with bleeding.[6]

Urinary System

Urinary dysfunction occurs in most patients after SCI. **Neurogenic bladder** describes any type of bladder dysfunction related to abnormal or absent bladder innervation. After SCI, the ability of the bladder muscles and the micturition center in the brain to transmit information is impaired. Both the detrusor muscle (bladder wall) and sphincter muscle (a valve around the

American Spinal Injury Association (ASIA) Impairment Scale

☐ **A = Complete.** No sensory or motor function is preserved in the sacral segments S4-5.

☐ **B = Sensory Incomplete.** Sensory but not motor function is preserved below the neurologic level and includes the sacral segments S4-5 (light touch or pin prick at S4-5 or deep anal pressure) AND no motor function is preserved more than three levels below the motor level on either side of the body.

☐ **C = Motor Incomplete.** Motor function is preserved at the most caudal sacral segments for voluntary anal contraction (VAC) OR the patient meets the criteria for sensory incomplete status (sensory function preserved at the most caudal sacral segments [S4-S5]), and has some sparing of motor function more than three levels below the ipsilateral motor level on either side of the body.

☐ **D = Motor Incomplete.** Motor incomplete status as defined above, with at least half (half or more) of key muscle functions below the single neurologic level of injury (NLI) having a muscle grade ≥ 3.

☐ **E = Normal.** If sensation and motor function as tested with the ISNCSCI are graded as normal in all segments, and the patient had prior deficits, then the AIS grade is E. Someone without an initial SCI does not receive an AIS grade.

☐ **ND = Not Determined.** To document the sensory, motor, and NLI levels, the ASIA Impairment Scale grade, and/or the zone of partial preservation (ZPP) when they are unable to be determined based on the examination results.

Fig. 65.4 The ASIA Impairment Scale. (From American Spinal Injury Association.)

top of the urethra) may be overactive due to the lack of brain control. This may cause high bladder pressures and urinary retention. Incontinence results from reflex emptying and failure to store urine.

Depending on the injury, a neurogenic bladder may (1) have no reflex detrusor contractions *(flaccid, hypotonic),* which can result in bladder stretching from overdistention; (2) have hyperactive reflex detrusor contractions *(spastic),* seen in SCI above T12, leading to incontinence; or (3) lack coordination between detrusor contraction and urethral relaxation *(dyssynergia),* resulting in reflux of urine into the kidneys. Reflux into the kidneys can lead to stone formation, hydronephrosis, pyelonephritis, and renal failure.[7]

Gastrointestinal System

Decreased gastrointestinal (GI) motor activity contributes to gastric distention and paralytic ileus. Gastric emptying may be delayed, especially in patients with higher-level SCI. Excessive release of hydrochloric acid (HCl) in the stomach may cause stress ulcers. Dysphagia may be present in patients who need mechanical ventilation, tracheostomy, or anterior spine surgery.

Intraabdominal bleeding may be hard to diagnose because the person with SCI may not have pain or tenderness. Continued hypotension and decreases in hemoglobin and hematocrit may be the only signs of bleeding.

Loss of voluntary control of the bowel results in **neurogenic bowel**. SCI above the level of the conus medullaris results in a *hyperreflexic* bowel with increased rectal and sigmoid compliance. Combined with increased anal sphincter tone and the inability to sense a full rectum, this causes stool retention and constipation.[8] SCI at or below the conus medullaris causes the bowel to be *areflexic*. Peristalsis is impaired, and stool movement is slow. The defecation reflex may be damaged and anal sphincter tone relaxed. This leads to constipation, increased risk for incontinence, and possible impaction, ileus, or megacolon. Hemorrhoids can occur.

Skin

The risk for skin breakdown over bony prominences in areas of decreased or absent sensation is a major consequence of immobility. Pressure injuries can occur quickly and lead to infection and sepsis.

Thermoregulation

Poikilothermia is the inability to maintain a constant core temperature, with the patient assuming the temperature of the environment. It occurs in SCI because interruption of the SNS prevents peripheral temperature sensations from reaching the hypothalamus. There is a decreased ability to sweat or shiver below the level of injury, which affects the ability to regulate body temperature. The degree of poikilothermia depends on the level of injury. Cervical injuries are associated with a greater loss of ability to regulate temperature than are thoracic or lumbar injuries.

Metabolic Needs

The person with SCI has increased nutrition needs due to increased metabolism and more protein breakdown. Lean body mass decreases and muscles atrophy, leading to weight loss. In the acute injury phase, stress on the body from hemodynamic instability and medical interventions, such as surgery, can worsen stress. We should start nutrition support within 72 hours after injury.[6] Adequate nutrition helps prevent skin breakdown, reduce infection, and decrease muscle atrophy. We may give enteral nutrition (EN) or parenteral nutrition (PN) to meet nutrient needs.

Peripheral Vascular Problems

Venous thromboembolism (VTE) is a common problem due to hypercoagulability, venous stasis, and venous endothelial injury.[9] Immobilization promotes venous stasis and thrombi of the lower extremities. It may be hard to detect a deep venous thrombosis (DVT) because usual signs and symptoms, such as pain and tenderness, are not present.

Pain

Pain after SCI differs in type and severity. The patient's physical functioning and emotions influence pain. Pain can be nociceptive or neuropathic.

Nociceptive pain can result from musculoskeletal, visceral, and/or other types of injury (e.g., skin ulceration, headache). Patients often describe musculoskeletal pain as dull or aching. It starts or worsens with movement. Visceral pain is in the thorax, abdomen, and/or pelvis. It may be dull, tender, or cramping.

TABLE 65.2 Level of SCI and Rehabilitation Potential

Movement Remaining	Rehabilitation Potential
Tetraplegia	
C1-3	
• Often fatal • Movement in neck and above, loss of innervation to diaphragm, absence of independent respiratory function	• Able to drive electric wheelchair equipped with portable ventilator by using chin control or mouth stick, headrest to stabilize head • Computer use with mouth stick, head wand, or noise control • Attendant care 24 h/day, able to instruct others
C4	
• Sensation and movement in neck and above • May be able to breathe without ventilator	• Same as C1–3
C5	
• Full neck, partial shoulder, back, biceps • Gross elbow, inability to roll over or use hands • ↓ Respiratory reserve	• Able to drive electric wheelchair with mobile hand supports • Indoor mobility in manual wheelchair • Able to feed self with setup and adaptive equipment • Attendant care 10 h/day
C6	
• Shoulder and upper back abduction and rotation at shoulder • Full biceps to elbow flexion, wrist extension, weak grasp of thumb • ↓ Respiratory reserve	• Able to help with transfer and perform some self-care • Feed self with hand devices • Push wheelchair on smooth, flat surface • Drive adapted van from wheelchair • Independent computer use with adaptive equipment • Attendant care 6 h/day
C7-8	
• All triceps to elbow extension, finger extensors, and flexors • Good grasp with some decreased strength • ↓ Respiratory reserve	• Able to transfer self to wheelchair • Roll over and sit up in bed • Push self on most surfaces • Perform most self-care • Independent use of wheelchair • Able to drive car with powered hand controls (in some patients) • Attendant care 0–6 hr/day
Paraplegia	
T1–6	
• Full innervation of upper extremities • Back, essential intrinsic muscles of hand • Full strength and dexterity of grasp • ↓ Trunk stability, decreased respiratory reserve	• Full independence in self-care and in wheelchair • Able to drive car with hand controls (in most patients) • Independent standing in standing frame
T6–12	
• Full, stable thoracic muscles and upper back • Functional intercostal muscles, resulting in ↑ respiratory reserve	• Full independent use of wheelchair • Able to stand erect with full leg brace, ambulate on crutches with swing (although gait difficult) • Unable to climb stairs
L1–2	
• Varying control of legs and pelvis • Instability of lower back	• Good sitting balance • Full use of wheelchair • Ambulation with long leg braces
L3–4	
• Quadriceps and hip flexors • Absence of hamstring function, flail ankles	• Completely independent ambulation with short leg braces and canes • Unable to stand for long periods

Neuropathic pain occurs from damage to the spinal cord or nerve roots. The pain can be at or below the level of injury. Patients often describe the pain as hot, burning, tingling, pins and needles, cold, and/or shooting. They may be very sensitive to stimuli. Even light touch can cause significant pain. Pain is discussed in Chapter 9.

Diagnostic Studies

CT scan is the preferred imaging study to diagnose the location and degree of injury and the degree of spinal canal compromise. Cervical x-rays are done when a CT scan is not readily available. However, it is hard to see C7 and T1 on a cervical x-ray, decreasing the ability to fully evaluate a cervical spine injury. MRI can assess soft tissue injury, neurologic changes, unexplained neurologic deficits, or worsening neurologic conditions.

We perform a comprehensive neurologic examination and assess the head, chest, and abdomen for other injuries or trauma. Patients with cervical injuries who have altered mental status may need a CT angiogram to rule out vertebral artery damage. Table 41.9 describes studies used to assess the site and extent of a VTE.

Interprofessional Care

Prehospital

Goals immediately after injury include maintaining a patent *airway,* adequate ventilation/*breathing,* and adequate *circulating* blood volume (ABCs) and preventing extension of spinal cord damage (secondary injury). Table 65.3 outlines emergency management of the patient with SCI. Spinal motion should be restricted with a combination of a rigid cervical collar and a supportive backboard with straps. Most patients are kept supine. Some may be placed in reverse Trendelenburg position. Sedation may be given to keep combative patients safe from further injury.

Intubation to secure the airway is done as soon as possible for patients with respiratory distress. End-tidal CO_2 monitoring can help determine the need for rapid sequence intubation (RSI). Patients with stable airways in the field may need intubation at the medical facility. After cervical injury, all body systems must be maintained until we evaluate the full extent of the damage. After stabilization at the injury scene, the person should be transferred to the nearest medical facility. The

TABLE 65.3 EMERGENCY MANAGEMENT

SCI

Etiology	Assessment Findings	Interventions
Blunt Trauma • Compression, flexion, extension, or rotation injuries to spinal column • Diving • Falls • Motor vehicle crash • Pedestrian accidents • Sports injuries **Penetrating Trauma** • Gunshot wounds • Stab wounds • Stretched, torn, crushed, or lacerated spinal cord	• Bowel and bladder incontinence • Changes in sensation • ↓ Rectal sphincter tone • Muscle weakness, paralysis, or flaccidity • Neurogenic shock: hypotension, bradycardia, cool or warm dry skin • Numbness, paresthesia • Pain, tenderness, deformities, or muscle spasms adjacent to vertebral column • Priapism • Spinal shock • Respiratory distress/difficulty breathing • Urinary retention • Wounds, cuts; bruises; on head, face, neck, or back	**Initial** • Ensure patent airway and adequate breathing. • Maintain SaO_2 >90%. Apply O_2 via nasal cannula, nonrebreather mask, or endotracheal tube. • Maintain SBP >90 mm Hg. • Establish IV access with 2 large-bore catheters to infuse normal saline or lactated Ringer's solution. • Immobilize and stabilize cervical spine. • Assess for other injuries. • Control external bleeding. • Obtain appropriate imaging. **Ongoing Monitoring** • Monitor vital signs, level of consciousness, motor and sensory function, O_2 saturation, cardiac rhythm, urine output. • Anticipate need for intubation if in respiratory distress or gag reflex absent. • Maintain normal temperature.

preferred facility is one that specializes in acute SCI care. A thorough assessment determines the degree of deficit and the level and degree of injury.

Acute Care

Interprofessional care during the acute phase for a patient with a cervical injury is described in Table 65.4. Compared to cervical injury, patients with SCI of the thoracic and lumbar vertebrae need less intense support. Respiratory compromise is not as severe at this level of injury. Bradycardia is usually not a problem. Other problems are treated symptomatically.

Obtain a history. How did the incident occur? Assess the extent of injury perceived by the patient or the emergency response system (ERS) personnel right after the event. Initial assessment occurs in the emergency department (ED). It includes managing the person's ABCs and vital signs. Ensure a secure airway. Maintain oxygenation saturation (SaO_2) greater than 92% and mean arterial pressure (MAP) greater than 85 mm Hg. Avoid systolic BP (SBP) less than 90 mm Hg. Neurogenic shock is treated with IV fluids and vasopressors to maintain SBP greater than 90 mm Hg after other causes of hypotension, including bleeding, are ruled out. Appropriate medical interventions and diagnostics are implemented to ensure the patient is hemodynamically stable.

Perform a complete neurologic assessment using the ASIA tool (Fig. 65.5). Muscle groups are tested with and against gravity, alone and against resistance, on both sides of the body. Record strength, symmetry, and spontaneous movement. Complete a sensory assessment, including touch and pain, as tested by pinprick. Start at the toes and work upward toward the head. Assess rectal tone. Note the presence of *priapism.* Voluntary anal contractions indicate incomplete SCI. If time and conditions permit, assess position sense and vibration.

Mechanisms of injury that cause spinal cord trauma, especially involving the cervical cord, may result in brain injury and/or vertebral artery injury. Is there a history of unconsciousness? Note signs of concussion and increased intracranial pressure (see Chapter 61). Assess for musculoskeletal injuries and trauma to internal organs. Because the patient may have altered or no muscle, bone, or visceral sensations below the level of injury, the only clue to internal trauma with bleeding may be a rapidly decreasing BP and increasing pulse. Imaging and diagnostic tests are done to evaluate injuries.

Move the patient in alignment as a unit *(logroll)* during transfers and when repositioning to prevent further injury. Monitor respiratory, cardiac, urinary, and GI functions. The patient may go directly to surgery after the initial evaluation or to the intensive care unit (ICU) for monitoring and management.

Nonoperative stabilization. Nonoperative treatments involve stabilization of the injured spinal segment and decompression, either through traction or realignment. Stabilization eliminates damaging motion at the injury site. It is meant to prevent secondary spinal cord damage caused by narrowing of the spinal canal or continued contusion or compression of the spinal cord at the level of the injury. Early realignment of an unstable fracture-dislocation injury by closed reduction through craniocervical traction is effective and safe.

Surgical therapy. Surgical treatment after acute SCI is used to manage instability and decompress the spinal cord. It may reduce secondary injury and improve the patient's outcome. Early surgery (within 24 hours after the injury) is recommended for persons with central cord syndrome and for adults with acute SCI at any level.[10] The type of surgery depends on the severity and level of the injury, mechanism of injury, and location and degree of compression.

Surgery to stabilize the spine can be done from the back of the spine *(posterior approach)* or from the front of the spine *(anterior approach).* In some cases, both approaches are needed. Fixation involves attaching metal screws, plates, or other devices to the bones of the spine to help keep them aligned. This procedure is

TABLE 65.4 Interprofessional Care

Cervical Cord Injury

Diagnostic Assessment

- History and physical assessment, including complete neurologic examination
- ABGs
- Electrolytes, serum glucose, coagulation profile, hemoglobin, hematocrit
- Urinalysis
- CT scan, MRI, EMG (measure evoked potentials)
- Spinal x-rays
- Serial bedside pulmonary function tests (PFTs)

Management

Acute Care

- Immobilization and stabilization of vertebral column
- ABCs (airway, breathing, circulation)
  - O_2 by high-humidity mask ($PaO_2 > 60$ mm Hg)
  - Intubation (if indicated by ABGs and PFTs)
  - Maintain heart rate (e.g., atropine) and BP (e.g., dopamine) (SBP > 90 mm Hg, MAP > 85)
  - Administer IV fluids
- Insert NG tube and attach to suction.
- Assessment and management of nutrition
- Maintain normal body temperature
- Indwelling urinary catheter
- Pain management
- VTE prophylaxis
- Pressure injury prevention
- Stress ulcer prophylaxis
- Bowel and bladder care and training
- Mobilization once spine stabilized
- Physical, occupational, speech therapy and physiatrist consults

Rehabilitation and Home Care

- Physical therapy (ROM, mobility, strength, equipment)
- Occupational therapy (splints, ADLs training)
- Speech therapy (swallow and cognition)
- Pain management
- Spasticity management
- Bowel and bladder training
- Autonomic dysreflexia prevention
- Pressure injury prevention
- Recreational therapy
- Patient and caregiver teaching

usually done when 2 or more vertebrae are injured. Small pieces of bone may be attached to the injured bones to help them fuse into 1 solid piece. The bone used is obtained from the patient's spinal bone harvested during surgery, from another bone in the patient's body, or from donor bone.

Drug Therapy

Evidence for using methylprednisolone is mixed. Guidelines for managing spinal cord injuries issued by both the American Association of Neurological Surgeons and Congress of Neurological Surgeons do not recommend its use for treating acute SCI.[11] However, the AOSPine 2017 Guidelines suggest a 24-hour infusion of high-dose methylprednisolone within 8 hours of acute SCI.[12] So, some HCPs may give an infusion.

VTE prophylaxis with low-molecular-weight heparin (LMWH) (e.g., enoxaparin) or fixed, low-dose heparin should start within 72 hours after injury unless contraindicated. Contraindications include internal or external bleeding and recent surgery. For those with abnormal kidney function, heparin is best as LMWH is mainly excreted via the kidneys.

Vasopressor agents (e.g., phenylephrine, norepinephrine) are used in the acute phase of injury as adjuvant treatment. They maintain the MAP to improve perfusion to the spinal cord. Use of vasopressors has significant risk for complications. These include ventricular tachycardia, troponin elevation, metabolic acidosis, and atrial fibrillation. Dopamine has more complications than phenylephrine in SCI. Considerations for vasopressor selection include level of injury, patient age, and comorbidities (e.g., heart problems).

❖ NURSING MANAGEMENT: SPINAL CORD INJURY

◆ Assessment

Subjective and objective data you should obtain from a patient with recent SCI are outlined in Table 65.5.

◆ Clinical Problems

Clinical problems for the patient with SCI depend on the severity of the injury and level of dysfunction. Clinical problems for a patient with SCI may include:

- Impaired respiratory function
- Neurologic problem
- Nutritionally compromised
- Inadequate tissue perfusion
- Impaired tissue integrity
- Impaired urinary elimination
- Difficulty coping

Additional information on clinical problems and interventions for the patient with complete cervical SCI is presented in eNursing Care Plan 65.1 (available on the website for this chapter).

◆ Planning

Overall goals are that the patient with an SCI will (1) maintain an optimal level of neurologic functioning; (2) have minimal or no complications of immobility; (3) be able to care for self or direct others to do so; and (4) return home at an optimal level of functioning.

◆ Implementation

◆ Health Promotion

Nursing interventions for the prevention of SCI include identifying high-risk persons and providing teaching. Support measures to combat distracted and impaired driving. Teach people to use child safety seats and helmets for motorcyclists and bicyclists. Promote programs for older adults (e.g., STEADI) aimed at preventing accidental death and injury.[13]

Emphasize the importance of health promotion and screening behaviors after SCI. Health-promoting behaviors after SCI

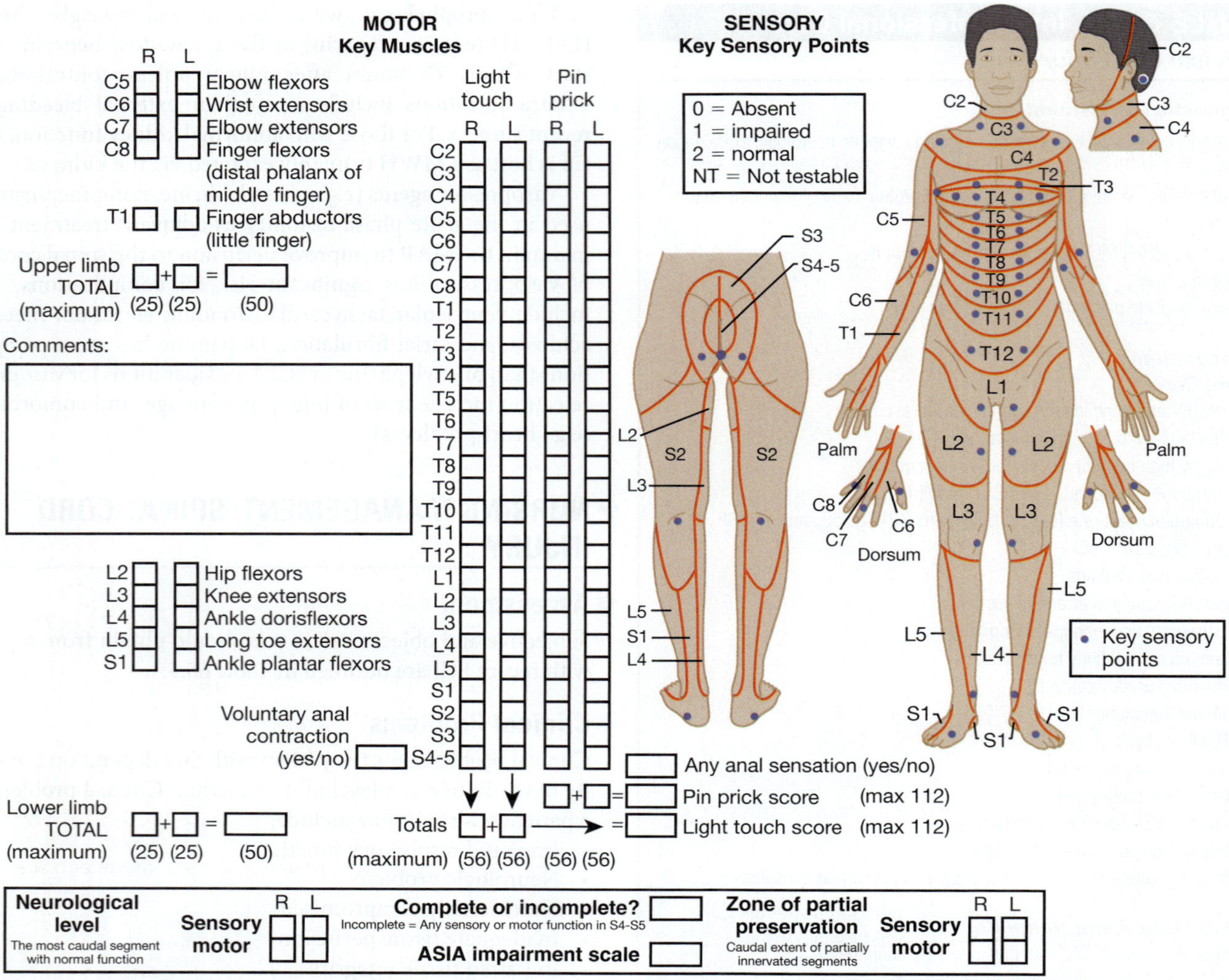

Fig. 65.5 The ASIA Standard Neurological Classification of Spinal Cord Injury is an assessment used to score the motor and sensory impairment and severity of a SCI.

can have a significant impact on the patient's overall health and well-being. Provide teaching and counseling. Refer the patient as needed to smoking cessation or alcohol treatment programs. Explore available recreation programs. They should continue to receive routine care for non-neurologic problems. Make sure facilities are accessible to and accommodate people with SCI. Schedule wheelchair-accessible examination rooms and allow extra time, if needed, for appointments.

◆ Acute Care

High cervical cord injury caused by flexion-rotation is the most complex SCI. It is the focus of this section. Interventions for this type of injury can be modified for patients with less severe injuries.

Immobilization. To restrict spinal motion, maintain the neck in a neutral position. For cervical injuries, closed reduction with skeletal traction is used for early realignment *(reduction)*. Crutchfield (Fig. 65.6) or Gardner-Wells tongs or halo (halo ring) can provide this type of traction. A rope extends from the center of the device over a pulley to weights attached at the end. Traction must be maintained at all times. Possible displacement of the skull pins is a disadvantage of tongs. If pin displacement occurs, hold the patient's head in a neutral position and get help. Immobilize the head while the HCP reinserts the tongs.

> **! SAFETY ALERT**
>
> ***Cervical Spine Injuries***
>
> - Always keep the patient's body in correct alignment.
> - Turn the patient as a unit (e.g., logrolling) to prevent movement of the spine.

No specific guidelines address the maximum weight for traction. The HCP may start with 10 lb and add 5 lb for each level to the injury. The goal is spinal reduction. Awake patients are monitored with x-ray and neurologic and pain assessment. Comatose patients need serial x-rays to evaluate the effects of traction. The need for surgery is determined after the spine is reduced. After cervical fusion or other stabilization surgery, the patient may have a hard cervical collar or sternal-occipital-mandibular immobilizer brace (Fig. 65.7).

TABLE 65.5 NURSING ASSESSMENT
SCI

Subjective Data

Important Health Information

Health history: Motor vehicle crash, sports injury, industrial incident, gunshot or stabbing injury, falls

Functional Health Patterns

Health perception–health management: Use of alcohol or recreational drugs. Risk-taking behaviors

Activity-exercise: Loss of strength, movement, and sensation below level of injury. Dyspnea, inability to breathe adequately ("air hunger")

Cognitive-perceptual: Tenderness, pain at or above level of injury. Numbness, tingling, burning, twitching of extremities

Coping–stress tolerance: Fear, denial, anger, depression

Objective Data

Cardiovascular

Injury above T6: Bradycardia, hypotension, postural hypotension, absence of vasomotor tone

General

Poikilothermia (unable to regulate body heat)

GI

↓ Or absent bowel sounds (paralytic ileus in injuries above T5), abdominal distention, constipation, fecal incontinence, fecal impaction

Musculoskeletal

Muscle atony (in flaccid state), contractures (in spastic state)

Neurologic

Complete: Areflexic, flaccid paralysis and anesthesia below level of injury resulting in tetraplegia (injuries above C8) or paraplegia (injuries below C8), hyperactive deep tendon reflexes and bilaterally positive Babinski test (after resolution of spinal shock)

Incomplete: Mixed loss of voluntary motor activity and sensation

Pain

Neuropathic, musculoskeletal, and/or visceral

Reproductive

Priapism, altered sexual function

Respiratory

Injury at C1–3: Apnea, inability to cough

Injury at C4: Poor cough, diaphragmatic breathing, hypoventilation

Injury at C5–T6: ↓ Respiratory reserve

Skin

Warm, dry skin below level of injury (neurogenic shock)

Urinary

Retention (for injuries at T1–L2), flaccid bladder (acute stages), spasticity with reflex bladder emptying (later stages)

Possible Diagnostic Findings

Location of level and type of bony involvement on spinal x-ray. Injury, edema, compression on CT scan and MRI; positive finding on myelogram

Some patients with spinal fractures with or without acute SCI may not be able to have surgery but still need immobilization for their cervical fracture. In these patients, the halo frame can be attached to a special vest (Halo vest) (Fig. 65.8). This allows the patient to move and ambulate while cervical bones fuse. Surgery is used instead of the halo if the patient has ligament instability from the injury; has severe cervical deformity; or is morbidly obese, older, cachectic, or noncompliant.

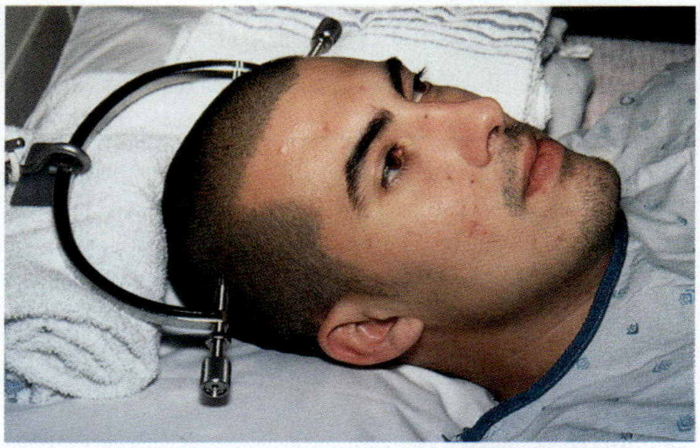

Fig. 65.6 Cervical traction is attached to tongs inserted in the skull. (Courtesy Michael S. Clement, MD, Mesa, AZ.)

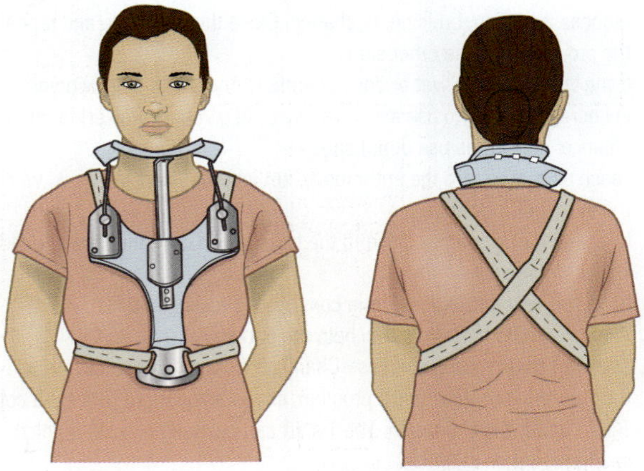

Fig. 65.7 Sternal-occipital-mandibular immobilizer brace.

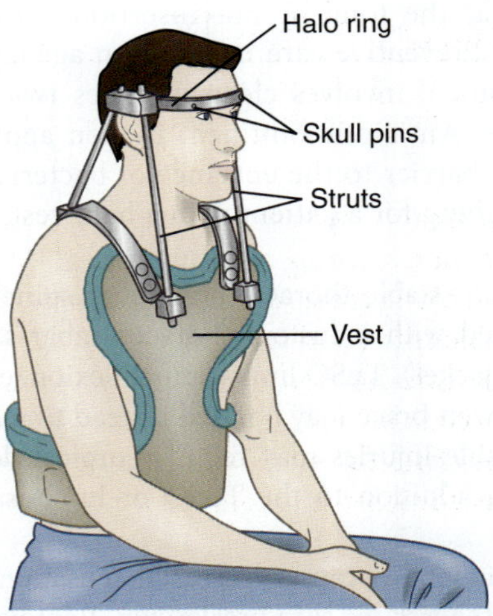

Fig. 65.8 Halo vest. The halo traction brace immobilizes the cervical spine, which allows the patient to ambulate and take part in self-care. (Modified from Urden LD, Stacy KM, Lough ME: *Priorities in critical care nursing*, ed 6, St Louis, 2012, Mosby.)

TABLE 65.6 PATIENT & CAREGIVER TEACHING

Halo Vest Care

Include the following instructions when teaching the patient and caregiver management of a halo vest:

1. Inspect the pins on the halo traction ring. Report to HCP if pins are loose or signs of infection are present, including redness, tenderness, swelling, or drainage at insertion sites.
2. Clean around pin sites carefully with chlorhexidine, water, or half-strength peroxide on a cotton swab as directed.
3. Apply antibiotic ointment as prescribed.
4. For skin care, have patient lie down with the head resting on a pillow to reduce pressure on the brace. Loosen 1 side of the vest. Gently wash the skin under the vest with soap and water, rinse area, and then dry it thoroughly. At the same time, check the skin for pressure points, redness, swelling, bruising, or chafing. Close the open side and repeat the procedure on the other side.
5. If the vest becomes wet or damp, carefully dry it with a blow dryer.
6. Encourage patient to use assistive device (e.g., cane, walker) to improve balance; encourage use of flat shoes.
7. Teach patient to turn the entire body, not just the head and neck, when trying to look sideways.
8. Keep a set of wrenches close to the halo vest in case they are needed for an emergency.
9. Mark the vest strap to maintain consistent buckling and fit.
10. Avoid grabbing bars or vest to help the patient.
11. Keep sheepskin pad under vest. Change and wash pad at least weekly.
12. If perspiration or itching is a problem, encourage patient to wear a cotton T-shirt under the sheepskin. The T-shirt can be modified with a Velcro seam closure on one side.

Infection at the tong or pin insertion sites is a potential problem. Preventive care is based on agency protocol. A common protocol involves cleansing sites twice a day with chlorhexidine. Antibiotic ointment is then applied to act as a mechanical barrier to the entrance of bacteria. Patient and caregiver teaching for a patient with a halo vest is outlined in Table 65.6.

Patients with stable thoracic or lumbar spine injuries may be immobilized with a custom thoracolumbar sacral orthosis (TLSO, body jacket). TLSO limits spinal flexion, extension, and rotation. A Jewett brace may be used instead to restrict forward flexion. Unstable injuries may require surgical decompression and fusion in addition to the TLSO or lumbosacral orthotic (LSO).

Skin care is vital because decreased sensation and circulation increase the risk for skin breakdown. Remove the patient's backboard as soon as possible. Replace it with other forms of immobilization to prevent skin breakdown in the coccygeal and occipital areas. Fit cervical collars properly. Carefully assess areas under any device used for immobilization.

Respiratory problems. Respiratory complications are the leading cause of morbidity and mortality in SCI.[6] Respiratory dysfunction is present in up to 65% of patients with cervical SCI. During the first 48 hours after injury, spinal cord edema may increase the level of dysfunction, and respiratory distress may occur. Injury at or above C4 affects the phrenic nerve. This leads to the diaphragm, and breathing can stop.

Monitor the patient for respiratory compromise. Be prepared for quick action if arrest occurs. Regularly assess (1) breath sounds, (2) arterial blood gases (ABGs), (3) tidal volume, (4) vital capacity, (5) skin color, (6) breathing patterns (especially use of accessory muscles), (7) subjective comments about the ability to breathe, and (8) amount and color of sputum. A PaO_2 greater than 60 mm Hg and a $PaCO_2$ less than 45 mm Hg are acceptable values in a patient with uncomplicated tetraplegia. A patient who is unable to count to 20 aloud without taking a breath needs immediate attention.

Provide measures to maintain ventilation. Apply O_2 and provide appropriate ventilatory support until ABGs stabilize. If the patient is exhausted from labored breathing or ABGs show inadequate oxygenation or ventilation, endotracheal intubation or tracheostomy, and mechanical ventilation is needed. Patients who have chest trauma or difficulty weaning from the ventilator may need a tracheostomy for airway management.

Clearing secretions is vital in reducing the risk for lung complications and possible respiratory failure.[6] Perform tracheal suctioning if crackles or coarse breath sounds are present. Chest physiotherapy and assisted (augmented) coughing can help. Perform assisted coughing either manually or mechanically with an insufflation-exsufflation device. Encourage the use of incentive spirometry.

The older adult has more difficulty responding to hypoxia and hypercapnia. Chest physiotherapy, adequate oxygenation, and proper pain management are needed to maximize respiratory function and gas exchange.

Cardiovascular instability. Heart rate is slowed, often to less than 60 beats/min, because of unopposed vagal response. Any increase in vagal stimulation, as occurs with turning or suctioning, can cause cardiac arrest. Loss of SNS tone in peripheral vessels results in chronic low BP with potential orthostatic hypotension. The lack of muscle tone to aid venous return can cause sluggish blood flow and predispose the patient to VTE. Dysrhythmias may occur.

Frequently assess vital signs. If bradycardia is symptomatic, give an anticholinergic drug, such as atropine. Some patients need a temporary or permanent pacemaker. Maintain SBP greater than 90 mm Hg and keep MAP between 85 and 90 mm Hg for the first 7 days after SCI.[6] Manage hypotension with fluid replacement and a vasopressor agent, such as phenylephrine or norepinephrine.

Maintain a normal blood volume. If blood loss has occurred from other injuries, monitor hemoglobin and hematocrit and give blood according to protocol. Assess the patient for signs of hypovolemic shock from hemorrhage.

Orthostatic hypotension is likely to occur in the patient with injury at T6 and above. The patient may have lightheadedness, dizziness, and nausea. Assess orthostatic BP when mobilizing the patient. Some lose consciousness when moved from the bed to a chair. For symptomatic patients, use an abdominal binder and graduated compression stockings to promote venous return. Drugs used to increase intravascular volume include salt tablets and fludrocortisone. Midodrine may be given to promote blood vessel contraction and increase venous return.

Use LMWH or low-dose heparin in combination with intermittent pneumatic compression devices or graduated compression stockings to promote venous return and reduce the risk for VTE. Remove stockings every 8 hours for skin care. Assess thighs and calves every shift for signs of VTE. Regularly perform range-of-motion (ROM) exercises and stretching. Continue VTE prophylaxis for 3 months after injury.

Fluid and nutrition management. During the first 48 to 72 hours after the injury, the GI tract may stop functioning *(paralytic ileus)*. We may insert a nasogastric (NG) tube if severe ileus occurs. Because the patient cannot have oral intake, monitor fluid, and electrolyte status.

Nutrition should be started within the first 72 hours after injury. Specific solutions and additives are determined by individual requirements. Due to severe catabolism, a high-protein, high-calorie diet is needed for energy and tissue repair. If the patient cannot be fed through the GI system, either orally or through EN, PN should be started to reduce nitrogen losses that occur during the hypermetabolic state.

Once bowel sounds are present, or flatus is passed, and the patient is off mechanical ventilation, they have a formal swallow evaluation. If no risk for aspiration is identified, gradually introduce oral food and fluids. If the patient fails the swallow evaluation or is unable to eat due to an endotracheal tube or tracheostomy, a feeding tube may be placed in the stomach or jejunum (see Chapter 44).

CHECK YOUR PRACTICE

You are working in the spinal cord unit. Your 28-year-old male patient with SCI at T6 weighs 168 lb. When he was admitted 3 weeks ago, he weighed 196 lb. He asks you, "Well, what is my weight? Are you going to make me eat now? You know you can't do that."

- What assessment data do you need to obtain?
- What interventions would help him avoid further weight loss and regain lean body mass?

Patients may have anorexia due to depression, boredom with agency food, or discomfort at being fed (often by a hurried person). Some patients have a normally small appetite. Sometimes refusal to eat is a way of asserting control. If the patient is not eating adequately, assess the cause.

Based on assessment findings, make a contract with the patient with mutual goal setting for the diet. This contract gives the patient increased control and often results in improved intake. General measures also may be effective. For example, provide a pleasant eating environment and allow adequate time to eat (including any self-feeding the patient can achieve). Encourage the family to bring in special foods. Plan social rewards for eating.

Consult a dietitian to ensure evaluation of laboratory markers and develop the treatment plan. Keep a calorie count. Record daily weight to evaluate progress. If possible, have the patient take part in recording calorie intake. Diet supplements may be needed to meet nutrition goals. Increase dietary fiber to promote bowel function.

Bladder and bowel management. Immediately after the injury, urine retention occurs because of the loss of autonomic and reflex control of the bladder and sphincter *(neurogenic bladder)*. Because there is no sensation of fullness, overdistention of the bladder can result in reflux into the kidney and cause renal failure. Bladder overdistention may even result in rupture of the bladder. An indwelling catheter may be inserted soon after injury. Maintain patency of the catheter. Check the catheter to prevent kinking and ensure free flow of urine. Use strict aseptic technique for catheter care to prevent infection. While the catheter is in place, encourage a large fluid intake.

Catheter-acquired urinary tract infection (CAUTI) is a common problem. The best way to prevent CAUTI is regular and complete bladder drainage. Once the patient is stabilized, assess the best means of managing long-term urinary function. Clean intermittent catheterization (CIC) is the preferred method for emptying the bladder. CAUTI and CIC are discussed in Chapter 50.

CIC should be done 4 to 6 times daily to prevent bacterial overgrowth from urinary stasis. Keep urine residuals under 500 mL to prevent bladder distention. If the urine is cloudy or has a strong odor or if the patient develops symptoms of a urinary tract infection (UTI) (e.g., chills, fever, malaise), send a specimen for culture.

Consider age-related changes in renal function. The older adult is more likely to develop renal stones. Older men may have benign prostatic hyperplasia, which may interfere with urinary flow and complicate management of urinary problems. It can affect the ability to complete CIC.

Start a bowel program to combat constipation from neurogenic bowel. This involves inserting a rectal stimulant (suppository or small-volume enema) daily at a regular time, followed by gentle digital stimulation or manual evacuation until evacuation is complete. At first, the program may be done in bed with the patient in the side-lying position. However, as soon as the patient has resumed sitting, the patient should be in the upright position on a padded bedside commode chair. These programs typically take 30 to 60 minutes to complete. Measures to reduce constipation include adequate fluid intake, a diet high in fiber and vegetables, and increased activity and exercise as able.

Temperature control. Monitor the environment closely to maintain an appropriate temperature. Regularly assess the patient's temperature. Do not use excess covers or unduly expose the patient (e.g., during bathing). If an infection with fever develops, implement measures to control temperature (see Table 12.5).

Stress ulcers. Stress ulcers can occur because of the physiologic response to severe trauma and psychologic stress. Peak incidence of stress ulcers is 6 to 14 days after injury. Monitor the hematocrit for a slow drop. Histamine (H_2)-receptor blockers or proton pump inhibitors (e.g., pantoprazole, omeprazole) given prophylactically decrease the secretion of HCl acid and prevents ulcers.

Sensory deprivation. To prevent sensory deprivation, compensate for absent sensations by stimulating the patient above the level of injury. Conversation, music, and interesting foods can be a part of the care plan. If the head of the bed must stay flat, provide prism glasses to help the patient read and watch television.

Help the patient avoid withdrawing from the environment. Promote adequate rest and sleep. Assess for changes in mood. Depression is common.

Pain management. Musculoskeletal nociceptive pain can develop from injuries to bones, muscles, and ligaments. The pain is worse with movement or palpation. Antiinflammatory drugs, such as ibuprofen, may help with pain. Opioids may be used to manage nociceptive pain.

Visceral nociceptive pain is a dull, tender, or cramping pain in the thorax, abdomen, or pelvis. It may originate in the bladder or bowel. Assess bowel and bladder function to avoid bladder distention or constipation. Other causes of nociceptive pain include UTI and renal stones. Notify the HCP if the patient has persistent pain despite treatment. Diagnostic testing may be needed to determine the cause.

Neuropathic pain in the initial phase is usually at the level of SCI. It may occur on one or both sides of the body within the affected dermatome and up to 3 levels below. The patient will describe hot, burning, tingling, shooting, electric pain. Pregabalin (Lyrica) and Gabapentin (Neurontin) may be used to reduce symptoms.

Neuropathic pain can occur months or years after SCI, become chronic, and negatively affect sleep. Mood, sudden noise, constipation, and infection can affect the pain. Teach the patient and caregiver about possible pain triggers and offer relaxation therapy. Other treatments may include tricyclic antidepressants, intrathecal drugs, epidural stimulation, and destructive surgical intervention.

Skin care. The most common long-term complication in SCI is a pressure injury (PI). Healthy skin requires adequate blood circulation. Constant pressure in 1 position can compress blood vessels and limit blood supply, causing cell death and PI. Factors that increase risk for PI include duration of SCI, higher level of injury, smoking, being underweight, and comorbid medical conditions.[14]

Preventing PI requires diligent nursing care. Perform a risk assessment with a daily skin assessment. Areas most vulnerable to breakdown include the sacrum, ischia, trochanters, and heels. Assess surgical incisions for healing and skin integrity under collars and braces. Regularly assess nutrition status. Both weight loss and gain can contribute to skin breakdown. Teach the patient and caregiver about the causes and risk factors for PI development.[15]

A consult with the wound, ostomy, continence nurse (WOCN) can assist with prevention and management strategies (e.g., surface overlays).[15] Monitor incontinence. Implement appropriate neurogenic bowel and bladder management interventions. Apply skin barrier creams.

Carefully position and reposition the patient at least every 2 hours. Gradually increase the times between turns if no redness over bony prominences is seen when turning. While the patient is supine in bed, float the heels to reduce pressure. Consider prophylactic dressings to prevent sacral and heel injury. Move the patient carefully during turns and transfers to avoid stretching and folding of soft tissues *(shear)* or abrasion.

We often place patients on special beds (Fig. 65.9). Kinetic therapy involves continuous side-to-side rotation of a patient to 40 degrees or more to help prevent lung complications. This lateral rotation also redistributes pressure, helping prevent pressure injuries. We may use specialty mattresses.[15] When the patient is moved to a chair or wheelchair, use pressure-relieving cushions. Schedule pressure relief every 15 to 20 minutes when the patient is in a chair. It should last 30 to 60 seconds each time.

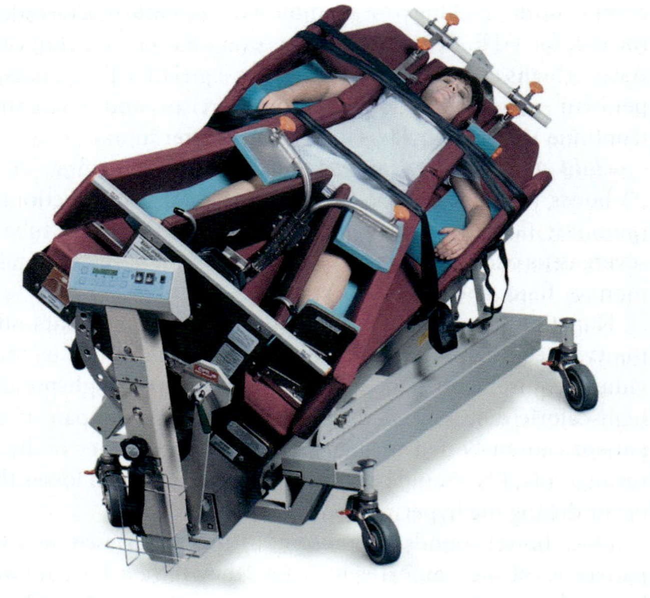

Fig. 65.9 The RotoRest Therapy System helps prevent and treat lung complications for immobile patients, including those with unstable cervical, thoracic, and lumbar fractures. Kinetic therapy, the continual side-to-side bilateral rotation of the patient, redistributes pulmonary blood flow and mobilizes secretions to improve ventilation and perfusion matching. The therapy system helps to prevent pressure injuries. (Courtesy Arjo Huntleigh, Addison, IL.)

Reflexes. Once spinal cord shock is resolved, return of reflexes may complicate rehabilitation. Lacking control from the higher brain centers, reflexes are often hyperactive and have exaggerated responses. Penile erection can occur from a variety of stimuli, causing embarrassment and discomfort. Spasms ranging from mild twitches to convulsive movements below the level of injury may occur. The patient or caregiver may interpret this reflex activity as a return of function. Tactfully explain the reason for the activity. Tell the patient the positive use of these reflexes in sexual, bowel, and bladder retraining. Antispasmodic drugs, such as baclofen (Lioresal), dantrolene (Dantrium), and tizanidine (Zanaflex), may help control spasms. Botulism toxin injections may be given to treat severe spasticity.

Autonomic dysreflexia. The return of reflexes after the resolution of spinal shock means patients with injury at T6 or higher may develop autonomic dysreflexia (AD). **Autonomic dysreflexia (AD)** is a massive, uncompensated cardiovascular reaction mediated by the SNS. It involves stimulation of sensory receptors below the level of the SCI. The intact SNS below the level of injury responds to the stimulation with a reflex arteriolar vasoconstriction that increases BP. The parasympathetic nervous system cannot directly counteract these responses via the injured spinal cord. Baroreceptors in the carotid sinus and aorta sense the hypertension and stimulate the parasympathetic system. This causes a decrease in heart rate. Visceral and peripheral vessels do not dilate because efferent impulses cannot pass through the injured spinal cord. It most often presents in the chronic phase after SCI.[16]

The most common precipitating cause is a distended bladder or rectum. However, any sensory stimulation, including contraction of the bladder or rectum, skin stimulation, or stimulation of pain receptors, can cause AD. AD is a life-threatening condition that requires immediate resolution. Proper identification and elimination of the inciting stimulus for AD can resolve the event. If uncorrected, it can lead to status epilepticus, stroke, myocardial infarction, and even death.

Manifestations include hypertension, throbbing headache, marked diaphoresis above the level of injury, bradycardia (30 to 40 beats/min), piloerection from pilomotor spasm, flushing of the skin above the level of injury, blurred vision or spots, nasal congestion, anxiety, and nausea. Measure BP when a patient with SCI reports a headache. Suspect AD in adults with SBP elevation of 20 to 40 mm Hg above baseline.[16]

Immediate interventions include elevating the head of the bed 45 degrees or sitting the patient upright (to lower the BP) and determining the cause (bowel impaction, urinary retention, UTI, PI, tight clothing). Notify the HCP. The most common cause is bladder irritation. Immediate catheterization to relieve bladder distention may be done. Instill lidocaine jelly in the urethra before catheterization. If a catheter is already in place, check it for kinks or folds. If it is plugged, perform small-volume irrigation slowly and gently to open the catheter or insert a new catheter.

Stool impaction can cause AD. Apply an anesthetic ointment to avoid increasing symptoms, and then perform a digital rectal examination (if trained). Remove all skin stimuli, such as constrictive clothing and tight shoes. Monitor BP often during the episode. If symptoms persist after the source has been relieved, give a rapid-onset and short-duration agent, such as nitroglycerin, nitroprusside, or hydralazine. Continue careful monitoring until vital signs stabilize.

Teach the patient and caregiver to recognize causes and symptoms of AD (Table 65.7). They must understand the life-threatening nature of AD, know how to relieve the cause, and activate the ERS, if needed.

Rehabilitation and Home Care

Rehabilitation of the person with SCI is complex. With physical and psychologic care and intensive and specialized rehabilitation, the patient with SCI can learn to function at the highest level of wellness. All patients with a new SCI should receive comprehensive inpatient rehabilitation in a rehabilitation unit or center that specializes in SCI rehabilitation.[17] Rehabilitation is an interprofessional team effort. Team members include rehabilitation nurses, HCPs, physical therapists, occupational therapists, speech therapists, vocational counselors, psychologists, therapeutic recreation specialists, prosthetists, orthotists, case managers, social workers, and dietitians.

Many problems that begin in the acute period become chronic and continue throughout life. Rehabilitation focuses on retraining physiologic processes and extensive patient and caregiver teaching about how to manage the physiologic and life changes resulting from the injury (Fig. 65.10).

Rehabilitation care depends on the patient's goals and needs. The patient is expected to be involved in therapies and learn self-care for several hours each day. Such intensive work at a time when the patient is dealing with the sudden change in health and function can be stressful. Progress may be slow. The rehabilitation nurse has a key role in providing encouragement, specialized nursing care, and patient and caregiver teaching, and in helping to coordinate efforts of the rehabilitation team.

TABLE 65.7 PATIENT & CAREGIVER TEACHING

Autonomic Dysreflexia

For a patient at risk for autonomic dysreflexia, include the following information in the teaching plan for the patient and caregiver:

1. Signs and symptoms
   - Sudden onset of acute headache.
   - Elevation in BP and/or reduction in pulse rate.
   - Flushed face and upper chest (above level of injury) and pale extremities (below level of injury).
   - Sweating above level of injury.
   - Nasal congestion.
   - Feeling of apprehension.
2. Immediate interventions.
   - Raise the person to a sitting position.
   - Remove the noxious stimulus (fecal impaction, kinked urinary catheter, tight clothing).
   - Call the HCP if above actions do not relieve the signs and symptoms.
3. Measures to decrease the incidence of autonomic dysreflexia
   - Maintain regular bowel function.
   - If manual rectal stimulation is used to promote bowel function, use a local anesthetic to prevent autonomic dysreflexia.
   - Monitor urine output.
   - Teach the patient to wear a Medic Alert bracelet indicating a history of risk for autonomic dysreflexia.

Fig. 65.10 SCI has a major effect on a person's physical, emotional, and psychologic health.

Respiratory rehabilitation. The patient with mechanical ventilation will need around-the-clock caregivers to provide respiratory hygiene and tracheostomy care. The rehabilitation nurse and respiratory therapist should teach patients and caregivers about home ventilator and tracheostomy care. The patient may need chest percussion or postural drainage to manage secretions to lower the risk for atelectasis and

TABLE 65.8 Types of Neurogenic Bladder

Type	Characteristics	Causes	Manifestations
Uninhibited bladder (spastic, overactive)	• No inhibitions influence time and place of voiding • Bladder empties in response to stretching of bladder wall	• Lesions above the pons • Seen in stroke, brain tumor, brain trauma	• Incontinence, frequency, urgency • Voiding is unpredictable and incomplete

Upper motor neuron bladder (flaccid, spastic/overactive)	• Mixed A type (most common):
	  • Bladder is flaccid and external sphincter is spastic, leading to urinary retention.
	• Mixed B type:
	  • Bladder is spastic with flaccid external sphincter leading to urinary incontinence.
		• Lesions between pons and sacral spinal cord
		• Seen in SCI or MS involving the cervicothoracic spinal cord
			• Detrusor-sphincter dyssynergia
			• Can lead to high bladder pressures and kidney damage from urinary reflex
			• Sensory function impaired

Lower motor neuron bladder (flaccid, underactive, areflexic)	• Bladder acts as if all motor functions were paralyzed • Bladder fills without emptying	• Lower motor neuron injury caused by trauma involving S2–4 or below • Lesions of cauda equina, pelvic nerves	• If sensory function intact, patient feels bladder distention and hesitancy • No control of micturition, resulting in urinary retention, over distention of bladder, overflow incontinence, and UTI

pneumonia. Refer to appropriate community agencies as needed.

Some patients with high cervical SCI have improved respiratory function with phrenic nerve stimulators or electronic diaphragmatic pacemakers.[18] These devices are not appropriate for all ventilator-dependent patients. They are safe and effective for those with an intact phrenic nerve. Some ventilators are portable, allowing ventilator-dependent patients with tetraplegia to be mobile and less dependent.

If the patient was weaned from the ventilator during hospitalization, downsizing (gradual decrease in size) and removal of the tracheostomy would be done during rehabilitation. Teach assisted coughing, regular use of incentive spirometry, and breathing exercises to the patient who is not ventilator dependent. They should limit exposure to persons with fever, cold, and cough. Adhering to swallowing precautions (e.g., proper positioning of head and neck) and diet recommendations can prevent aspiration.

Neurogenic bladder. Types of neurogenic bladder are described in Table 65.8. The type of bladder dysfunction determines management options. After the patient's overall condition is stable and assessment shows return of neurologic reflexes, urodynamic testing (see Table 49.11) and a urine culture may be done. Diagnostic and interprofessional care of neurogenic bladder is described in Table 65.9.

The patient with a neurogenic bladder needs a comprehensive program to manage bladder function. The goal is to improve quality of life and safety through preserving renal function, minimizing UTI and bladder stones, and developing a plan for urinary continence. Many factors are considered when selecting a bladder management strategy. These include patient preference, upper extremity function, and caregiver availability. For the selected strategy, teach the patient and caregiver successful self-management. Teach them about the various management techniques, how to obtain supplies, care of supplies and equipment, and when to seek health care.

TABLE 65.9 Interprofessional Care

Neurogenic Bladder

Diagnostic Assessment
- History and physical assessment, including neurologic and pelvic examinations
- Laboratory: Urinalysis, urine culture and sensitivity, blood urea nitrogen, serum creatinine, creatinine clearance
- Urodynamic testing (postvoid residual, cystometric testing, EMG, urethral pressure profile)

Management
- Patient teaching
- Voiding diary
- Bladder retraining: time voiding, manual expression, intermittent catheterization
- Fluid schedule: intake of 1800–2000 mL/day
- Indwelling urinary catheter

Drug Therapy
- Tricyclic antidepressants
- Anticholinergic drugs
- α-Adrenergic blockers
- Antispasmodics
- Botulinum toxin injection into bladder wall

Bladder and/or Urethral Surgical Therapy
- Bladder augmentation
- Sphincter resection or removal *(sphincterotomy)*
- Electrode placement for electrical stimulation
- Urinary diversion
- Urethral stents and balloon dilation
- Artificial urinary sphincter

Various drugs can be used to treat patients with a neurogenic bladder. Anticholinergic drugs (e.g., oxybutynin, tolterodine [Detrol]) may be used to suppress bladder contraction. α-Adrenergic blockers (e.g., terazosin, doxazosin [Cardura]) can relax the urethral sphincter. Antispasmodic drugs (e.g., baclofen) may decrease spasticity of pelvic floor muscles. *Botulinum toxin* is an effective alternative in patients with neurogenic detrusor overactivity who cannot tolerate or have an inadequate response to anticholinergic drugs.[19]

Numerous drainage methods are possible. These include bladder reflex retraining (if partial voiding control remains), indwelling catheter, CIC, and external catheter (condom catheter). Evaluate long-term use of an indwelling catheter because of the associated high incidence of CAUTI, fistula formation, and diverticula. However, this is the best option for some patients. Patients with indwelling catheters need to have adequate fluid intake (at least 3 to 4 L/day). Regularly check the patency of the indwelling catheter. Frequency of routine catheter changes ranges widely depending on the type of catheter used and agency policy.

CIC is the first-line option for bladder management (see Chapter 50). Assessment is essential in selecting the time interval between catheterizations. At first, catheterization is done every 4 hours. Measure bladder volume before catheterization using bladder ultrasound. If less than 200 mL of urine is present, the time interval until catheterization may be extended. If more than 500 mL of urine is present, the time interval is shortened. CIC is usually done 4 to 6 times daily.

Suprapubic catheters are a safe option in select patients. Because of personal preference or the inability to catheterize due to neurologic dysfunction, 30% of patients with SCI use indwelling urethral or suprapubic catheters. The incidence of bacteriuria after catheter introduction is 5% to 10% per day.

Traditional bladder management options include *urinary diversion surgery* for the recurrent UTI patient with renal involvement or repeated stones. Surgical treatment of neurogenic bladder includes bladder neck revision (sphincterotomy), bladder augmentation (augmentation cystoplasty), perineal ureterostomy, cystotomy, vesicostomy, and anterior urethral transplantation. Placement of a sacral cord stimulator, penile prosthesis, or artificial sphincter is possible. Urinary diversion procedures are discussed in Chapter 50.

Neurogenic bowel. Management of bowel evacuation is necessary for the patient with SCI because voluntary control may be lost. Usual measures for preventing constipation include a high-fiber diet and adequate fluid intake (see Table 42.9). Patient and caregiver teaching is needed to promote successful independent bowel management. Guidelines related to bowel management are outlined in Table 65.10.

These measures may not be adequate to stimulate evacuation. Suppositories (e.g., bisacodyl) or small-volume enemas and digital stimulation (done 20 to 30 minutes after suppository insertion) by the nurse or patient may be needed. In the patient with an upper motor neuron injury, digital stimulation can relax the external sphincter to promote defecation. A stool softener can help regulate stool consistency. Oral stimulant laxatives should be used only if absolutely necessary and not on a regular basis.

Valsalva maneuver and manual stimulation are useful in patients with lower motor neuron injuries. Because the Valsalva maneuver requires intact abdominal muscles, it is used in patients with injuries below T12. In general, a bowel movement every other day is adequate. However, consider pre-injury bowel patterns. Fecal incontinence can result from too much stool softener or a fecal impaction.

Timing of defecation is important. Planning bowel evacuation for 30 to 60 minutes after the first meal of the day may enhance success by taking advantage of the gastrocolic reflex induced by eating. This reflex may also be stimulated by drinking a warm beverage right after the meal. Discuss timing of the bowel program so there are no interruptions when the patient is doing therapy (e.g., swimming pool therapy). Record all bowel movements, including amount, time, and consistency.

Spasticity. Spasticity can be both beneficial and undesirable. It aids with mobility, especially for the patient with incomplete SCI. Spasticity improves circulation by promoting venous return, decreasing orthostatic hypotension and the risk for VTE. Unfortunately, the patient with marked spasticity and tone may have difficulty with positioning and mobility from spasms. Spasms can cause significant pain and make activities of daily living (ADLs) difficult.

You can use the Ashworth and Modified Ashworth Scales to evaluate spasticity. Treatment includes ROM exercises to prevent muscle and joint tightness and reduce the risk for contracture. Antispasmodic drugs, such as baclofen or tizanidine, may be given. Botulinum toxin injection is useful for specific muscle involvement.

TABLE 65.10 PATIENT & CAREGIVER TEACHING

Bowel Management After SCI

For the patient with a SCI, include the following information about bowel management in the teaching plan for the patient and caregiver:

1. Optimal nutrition intake includes the following:
   - 3 well-balanced meals each day
   - 2 servings from the milk group
   - 2 or more servings from the meat group, including beef, pork, poultry, eggs, fish
   - 4 or more servings from the vegetable and fruit groups
   - 4 or more servings from the bread and cereal group
2. Fiber intake should be about 20–30 g/day. Increase the amount of fiber eaten gradually over 1–2 weeks.
3. Consume at least 2–3 L of fluid per day unless contraindicated. Drink water or fruit juices (fluid softens hard stools). Limit caffeinated beverages, such as coffee, tea, and cola (caffeine stimulates fluid loss through urination).
4. Avoid foods that produce gas (e.g., beans) or upper GI upset (e.g., spicy foods).
5. Timing: Follow a regular schedule for bowel elimination. A good time is 30 min after the first meal of the day.
6. Position: If possible, an upright position with feet flat on the floor or on a step stool enhances bowel evacuation. Staying on the toilet, commode, or bedpan for longer than 20–30 min may cause skin breakdown. Based on stability, someone may need to stay with the patient.
7. Activity: Exercise is important for bowel function. In addition to improving muscle tone, it increases appetite and GI transit time. Exercise muscles, including stretching, ROM, position changing, and functional movement.
8. Drug treatment: Suppositories may be needed to stimulate a bowel movement. Manual stimulation of the rectum may be helpful in starting defecation. Use stool softeners as needed to regulate stool consistency. Use oral laxatives only if necessary.

TABLE 65.11 PATIENT & CAREGIVER TEACHING

Skin Care After SCI

To prevent skin breakdown in a patient with SCI, include the following instructions when teaching the patient and caregiver:

Change Position Frequently
- If in a wheelchair, lift self and shift weight every 15–30 min.
- If in bed, change position with a regular turning schedule (at least every 2 h) that includes sides, back, and abdomen.
- Use pressure-reducing mattresses and wheelchair cushions (not eggcrate).
- Use pillows to protect bony prominences when in bed.

Monitor Skin Condition
- Inspect skin often for areas of redness, swelling, and breakdown.
- If a wound develops, follow standard wound care procedures.

Protect Skin
- Do not sit too close to fires, space heaters, or other sources of heat.
- Use sunscreen liberally when outdoors.
- Keep fingernails trimmed to avoid scratches and abrasions.
- Do not wear clothes that are too tight or too loose.
- Dress warmly in cold weather to prevent frostbite.
- Do not put hot food in your lap without protection.

Skin care. Prevention of PI is part of the lifelong treatment plan after SCI. Nurses in rehabilitation are responsible for teaching the patient and caregiver about daily skin care. PI may not be noticed until severe damage has occurred. Include information on the importance of adequate nutrition to skin condition. Provide anticipatory guidance about potential risks. Patient and caregiver teaching about skin care is outlined in Table 65.11.

Pain management. The acute pain of the initial injury may persist during the first few weeks of rehabilitation. Chronic pain can result from overuse of muscles in the shoulders and arms for movement and repositioning. Pain often disrupts sleep. Assess, evaluate, and treat pain routinely. Use analgesics and interventions, such as massage and repositioning, to help the patient during therapy. Patients may benefit from referral to a pain management specialist.

Sexuality. Sexuality is an important issue regardless of the patient's age or gender. Open discussion with the patient about sexual rehabilitation is essential. A nurse or other rehabilitation professional trained in sexual counseling should provide support for the patient and the partner. Alternative methods of obtaining sexual satisfaction, such as oral-genital sex, may be options. Explicit films may help, such as a film showing sexual activities of a patient with paraplegia and a nondisabled partner. Use graphics cautiously because they may focus too much on the mechanics of sex rather than on the relationship.

We need to know the level and completeness of injury to understand the male patient's potential for orgasm, erection, fertility, and capacity for sexual satisfaction. Men normally have 2 types of erections: psychogenic and reflex. The process of *psychogenic erection* begins in the brain with sexual thoughts. Signals from the brain are sent through the nerves of the spinal cord to the T10–L2 levels. The signals are then relayed to the penis and trigger an erection. Men with low-level incomplete injuries are more likely to have psychogenic erection than men with higher level incomplete injuries. Men with complete injuries are less likely to have psychogenic erection.[20]

A *reflex erection* occurs with direct physical contact to the penis or other erotic areas. This short-lived, uncontrolled erection is involuntary. It does not require sexually stimulating thoughts. Most men with SCI can have a reflex erection with physical stimulation if the S2–S4 nerve pathways are not damaged.

Treatment for erectile dysfunction includes drugs, vacuum devices, and surgery. Phosphodiesterase inhibitors (e.g., sildenafil [Viagra]) are the first-line treatment in men with SCI between T6 and L5. Sexual stimulation is needed to get an erection after taking the medication. Penile injection of vasoactive substances (papaverine, alprostadil, or a combination) is another treatment. Risks include scarring, bruising, and infection. Use may lead to priapism. Vacuum suction devices use negative pressure to encourage blood flow into the penis. A constriction band placed at the base of the penis maintains the erection. The main surgical option is implantation of a penile prosthesis.[24] Erectile dysfunction is discussed in Chapter 59.

SCI affects male fertility, causing poor sperm motility and ejaculatory dysfunction. Sperm retrieval methods include penile vibratory stimulation and rectal probe electroejaculation. Surgical removal of sperm is a last resort for sperm retrieval. Once retrieved, sperm can be directly injected into an egg via intracytoplasmic sperm injection (ICSI). These techniques have changed the prognosis for men with SCI to father children from unlikely to a reasonable chance of successful outcomes.[20]

The effect of SCI on female sexual response is less clear. A woman of childbearing age with SCI usually stays fertile. The injury does not affect the ability to become pregnant or deliver normally through the birth canal. Menses may cease for as long as 6 months after injury. If sexual activity is resumed, discuss protection against unplanned pregnancy. Pregnancy increases the risk for diabetes and UTI and higher rates of AD, PI, increased spasticity, and catheter-related issues. Labor and delivery have high rates of complications.[21]

Care must be taken not to dislodge an indwelling catheter during sexual activity. A patient with an external catheter should refrain from fluids and remove the catheter before sexual activity. Teach patients about the risk for AD. The bowel program should include evacuation on the morning of sexual activity. Encourage the patient to tell the partner that incontinence is always possible. The woman may need a water-soluble lubricant to supplement decreased vaginal secretions and ease vaginal penetration. Women with some residual pelvic innervation can achieve normal orgasm. Use of the Eros device may help with orgasmic dysfunction.[21]

Grief and depression. Depression after SCI is common and disabling. Patients with SCI may feel an overwhelming sense of loss. They may temporarily lose control over everyday activities as they depend on others for ADLs and for life-sustaining measures. Patients may feel they are useless and burdens to their families. At a life stage when independence is of great importance, they may be totally dependent on others.

TABLE 65.12 Grief Response in SCI

Patient Behavior	Nursing Intervention
Shock and Denial	
Struggle for survival, complete dependence, excessive sleep, withdrawal, fantasies, unrealistic expectations	• Provide honest information. • Use simple diagrams to explain injury. • Encourage patient to begin road to recovery. • Establish agreement to use and improve all current abilities while not denying the possibility of future improvement.
Anger	
Refusal to discuss paralysis, ↓ self-esteem, manipulation, hostile and abusive language	• Coordinate care with patient and encourage self-care. • Support family members. • Use humor appropriately. • Allow patient outbursts of emotions. • Do not allow fixation on injury.
Depression	
Sadness, pessimism, anorexia, nightmares, insomnia, agitation, "blues," suicidal preoccupation, refusal to take part in any self-care activities	• Encourage family involvement and use of community resources. • Plan graded steps in rehabilitation to give success with minimal opportunity for frustration. • Give cheerful and willing assistance with ADLs. • Avoid sympathy. • Use firm kindness.
Adjustment and Acceptance	
Planning for future, actively taking part in therapy, finding personal meaning in experience and continuation of growth, returning to premorbid personality	• Remember patients have unique personalities. • Balance support systems to encourage independence. • Set goals with patient input. • Emphasize potential.

BOX 65.1 ETHICAL/LEGAL DILEMMAS

Right to Refuse Treatment

Situation

R.D., a 25-year-old man, had a SCI to C7-8 after a motorcycle accident. He was diagnosed with anterior cord syndrome and has motor paralysis. He has become very depressed and no longer wishes to live. Because of his emotional state, R.D. is now refusing to eat. Can we force him to receive EN?

Ethical/Legal Points for Consideration

- Withholding treatment in a newly injured but otherwise healthy young adult may present an ethical dilemma for some nurses. They may consider it assisted suicide and believe that it violates the ethical principles of beneficence and nonmaleficence.
- A competent adult has the right to consent to or refuse medical treatment under the right to privacy, the Fourteenth Amendment of the Constitution, and case law (*Cruzan v. Director, Missouri Department of Health,* 497 U.S. 261, 1990. Retrieved from www.supreme.justia.com/cases/federal/us/497/261). Case law has supported the concept that forced treatment is battery (unlawful use of force on somebody). A mentally competent, physically incapacitated adult can refuse EN. The health agency must follow the patient's wishes (*Bouvia v. Superior Court,* 1986. Retrieved from http://law.justia.com/cases/california/calapp3d/179/1127.html).
- To be competent to take part in informed consent or refusal, an adult must be able to understand the information provided about the procedure or treatment, consider choices among available alternatives, and make a choice based on his values and preferences. Depression may not be a factor in determining competency to make informed treatment choices.
- If, after adequate evaluation and treatment for pain, depression, or other medical conditions, the patient persists in his refusal, his wishes must be respected.
- Refusal to eat or drink has never been upheld as illegal, and the alternative—forced eating and drinking—is clearly a violation of patient rights and the criminal act of battery.

Discussion Questions

1. What are your feelings about requests to withhold treatment in a young person with a newly acquired disability?
2. What resources are available to help R.D., his family, and nursing staff deal with this emotionally charged and ethically complex situation?

Working through grief is a hard, lifelong process for which the patient needs support and encouragement. Table 65.12 outlines the grief response to SCI and appropriate nursing interventions. Your role in grief work is to support the patient and family and to allow mourning as part of the rehabilitation process. Maintaining hope is important during the grieving process. It should not be viewed as denial. With recent advances in rehabilitation, the patient is often independent physically and discharged from the rehabilitation center before completing the grief process.

The goal of recovery is related more to adjustment than to acceptance. *Adjustment* implies the ability to go on with living with certain limitations. Problem-based strategies are effective in supporting positive adjustment. When the patient accepts the current new normal, levels of coping and adjustment are improved. Nonacceptance is more predictive of psychologic distress, disengagement, denial, fantasy, and drug, and alcohol use.

Include and encourage the patient to participate in care planning. A primary nurse relationship is helpful. To adjust, the patient needs continual support throughout the rehabilitation process in the form of acceptance, affection, and caring. Be attentive when the patient needs to talk and sensitive to needs at various stages of the grief process.

Although depression during the grief process usually lasts days to weeks, some patients become clinically depressed and need treatment for depression. Evaluation by a psychiatric nurse or psychiatrist is recommended. Treatment may include drugs and therapy. Treatment is maximized when the patient's personal preferences are identified, and care is tailored to patient needs (Box 65.1).

Caregivers need counseling to avoid promoting dependency in the patient through guilt or misplaced sympathy. A support group of family members and friends of patients with SCI can help them increase their participation and knowledge of the grieving process, physical problems, rehabilitation plan, and meaning of the disability.

Fig. 65.11 An increasing number of older adults are living with chronic SCI. (© WavebreakmediaLtd/WavebreakMedia/Thinkstock.)

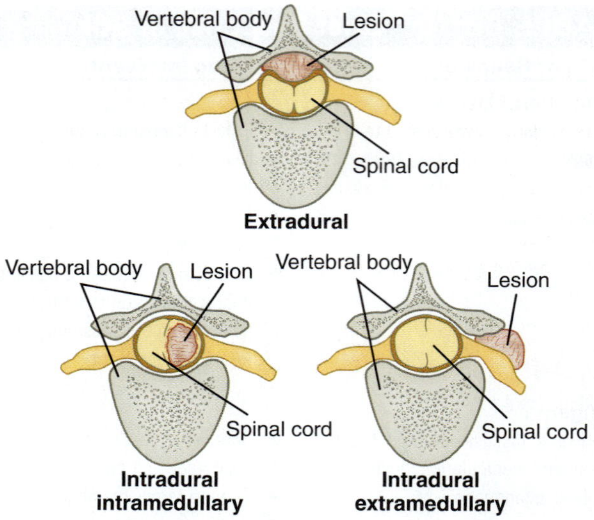

Fig. 65.12 Types of spinal cord tumors.

◆ Evaluation

Expected outcomes are that the patient with SCI will:

- Maintain adequate ventilation and have no signs of respiratory distress
- Maintain adequate circulation and BP
- Maintain intact skin over bony prominences
- Maintain adequate nutrition
- Establish a bowel and bladder management program
- Have no episodes of AD

Gerontologic Considerations: SCI

Because of increased work and recreational activities among older adults, more of them have SCI (Fig. 65.11). Falls are the leading cause of SCI for people age 65 and older. Older adults with traumatic injuries have more complications, are hospitalized longer, and have higher mortality rates.

Chronic illnesses can have a serious impact on older adults living with SCI. As patients with SCI age, both aging changes and length of time since injury can affect functional ability. For example, bowel and bladder dysfunction can increase with the duration and severity of SCI.

Health promotion and screening are important for the older patient with SCI. Daily skin inspections and UTI prevention measures are critical. Regular breast examinations for women and prostate cancer screening for men are recommended. Heart disease is the most common cause of morbidity and mortality among older adults with SCI. The lack of sensation, including chest pain, in persons with high-level injuries may mask acute myocardial ischemia. Altered autonomic nervous system function and decreases in physical activity can place patients at risk for heart problems, including hypertension.

Rehabilitation may take longer because of preexisting conditions and poorer health status at the time of initial injury. An interprofessional approach to rehabilitation is needed to prevent secondary complications.

SPINAL CORD TUMORS

Spinal cord tumors can have a devastating impact due to spinal compression and neurologic dysfunction. We classify tumors as *primary* (arising from some part of spinal cord, dura, nerves, or vessels) or *secondary* (from primary growths in other places in the body that have metastasized to the spinal cord).

Etiology and Pathophysiology

Spinal cord tumors are either *extradural* (outside the dura), *intradural-extramedullary* (between the spinal cord and dura), and *intramedullary* (within the substance of spinal cord itself) (Fig. 65.12 and Table 65.13).

Extradural tumors include metastatic cancer and benign schwannomas. Many patients with cancer will have metastasis to the spine. Metastatic lesions can invade intradurally and compress the spinal cord. Tumors that often metastasize to the spinal epidural space are those that spread to bone, such as prostate, breast, lung, and kidney cancer. Intradural-extramedullary lesions include meningiomas that develop in the arachnoid membrane, schwannomas and neurofibromas that extend from the nerve root, and ependymomas found at the end of the spinal cord. Intramedullary tumors arise from glial or ependymal cells found throughout the entire spinal cord. The most common lesions are astrocytes and ependymomas.[22]

Many spinal cord tumors are slow growing. Their symptoms are due to the mechanical effects of slow compression and irritation of nerve roots, spinal cord displacement, or gradual obstruction of the blood supply. The slowness of growth does not cause secondary injury as in traumatic SCI. Thus, complete functional restoration may be possible when the tumor is removed.

Clinical Manifestations

Both sensory and motor problems may result. The location and extent of the tumor determine the severity and extent of the problem. The most common early symptom of a spinal cord tumor is back pain or pain radiating along the compressed nerve route.[23] Location of the pain depends on the level of compression. Pain may worsen with activity, coughing, straining, and/or lying down. There may be slowly increasing clumsiness, weakness, and spasticity. Paralysis can develop. Sensory disruption occurs

TABLE 65.13 Classification of Spinal Cord Tumors

Type	Incidence	Treatment	Prognosis
Extradural			
Outside spinal cord in extradural space	Metastatic lesions. Benign schwannomas	Relief of cord pressure by surgical laminectomy, radiation, chemotherapy, or combination approach	*Benign:* Excellent with resection *Metastatic:* Poor, treatment usually palliative
Intradural Extramedullary			
Within dura mater but outside spinal cord	Mostly benign. Meningiomas, neurofibromas, schwannomas	Complete surgical removal of tumor (if possible) Partial removal followed by radiation	Usually very good if no damage to cord from compression
Intramedullary			
Within spinal cord	Mostly benign. Astrocytomas, ependymomas	Complete surgical removal of tumor (if possible) Partial removal followed by radiation	Usually very good if no damage to cord from compression Complete surgical resection of astrocytomas difficult

as coldness, numbness, and tingling in 1 or more extremities. Neurogenic bowel and bladder are marked by incontinence, constipation, and urgency with difficulty in starting the flow, progressing to retention with overflow incontinence.

Interprofessional and Nursing Care

Extradural tumors can be seen on routine spinal x-rays. Intradural extramedullary and intramedullary tumors require MRI, CT scan, or CT myelogram for detection. Cerebrospinal fluid (CSF) analysis may reveal tumor cells. Patients with tumors suspicious for metastatic disease need an oncology referral and further diagnostic testing to identify the primary cancer.[22]

Spinal cord compression is an emergency. Relief of ischemia related to the compression is the goal of therapy. Indications for surgery depend on the type of tumor and neurologic deficit. Emergency surgery may be needed to decompress the spinal cord, obtain tissue for biopsy, and help to determine treatment.[22] Primary spinal tumors may be removed with the goal of cure. In patients with metastatic tumors, treatment is mainly palliative. The goal is to restore or preserve neurologic function, stabilize the spine, and alleviate pain.

Radiation and/or chemotherapy are other treatment options. Surgery and radiation therapy may cause more inflammation. Corticosteroids (e.g., dexamethasone) may be used to relieve tumor-related edema.[24]

Relieving pain and maximizing neurologic function are the goals of treatment. Assess neurologic status before and after treatment. Giving analgesia as needed is an important nursing responsibility. Depending on the amount of neurologic dysfunction, care of the patient may be similar to that of a patient recovering from SCI.

CRANIAL NERVE DISORDERS

Cranial nerve disorders are often classified as peripheral neuropathies. The 12 pairs of cranial nerves are considered the peripheral nerves of the brain. The disorders usually involve the motor and/or sensory branches of a single nerve *(mononeuropathies).* Causes of cranial nerve problems include tumors, trauma, infection, inflammatory processes, and idiopathic (unknown) causes. The 2 cranial nerve disorders discussed here are trigeminal neuralgia (TN) and Bell's palsy.

TRIGEMINAL NEURALGIA

Trigeminal neuralgia (TN) *(tic douloureux)* is characterized by sudden, usually unilateral, severe, brief, stabbing, recurrent episodes of pain in the distribution of the trigeminal nerve. It occurs in about 12 per 100,000 Americans each year. TN affects more women. It occurs most often in people over age 50.

We classify TN as *classic* (TN 1) or *atypical* (TN 2). Patients may have both types. The pain intensity and lifestyle disruption that accompany TN can cause marked physical and psychologic dysfunction.

Etiology and Pathophysiology

The trigeminal nerve, the 5th cranial nerve (CN V), has both motor and sensory branches. TN most often affects the sensory (afferent) branches of the second and third divisions (maxillary and mandibular branches) of CN V (Fig. 65.13).

Most cases result from vascular compression of the trigeminal nerve root by an abnormal loop of the superior cerebellar artery. This artery compresses the nerve as it exits the brainstem. Constant compression appears to lead to chronic injury, causing flattening and atrophy of the nerve and damage to the myelin sheath.[25] In some cases, TN may be related to underlying pathology, such as multiple sclerosis (MS), shingles, or masses in the cerebellum or brainstem.

Clinical Manifestations

The first episode of TN is sudden, with a memorable onset. In TN 1, the patient has an abrupt onset of waves of excruciating pain. It is described as a burning, knifelike, or lightning-like shock in the lips, upper or lower gums, cheek, forehead, or side of the nose.[25] Facial twitching, grimacing, and frequent blinking and tearing of the eye can occur during the acute attack (giving rise to the term *tic douloureux*). Some patients may have facial sensory loss. Attacks are usually brief, lasting only seconds to 2 or 3 minutes. Frequency ranges from 1 to over 50 times a day.[26]

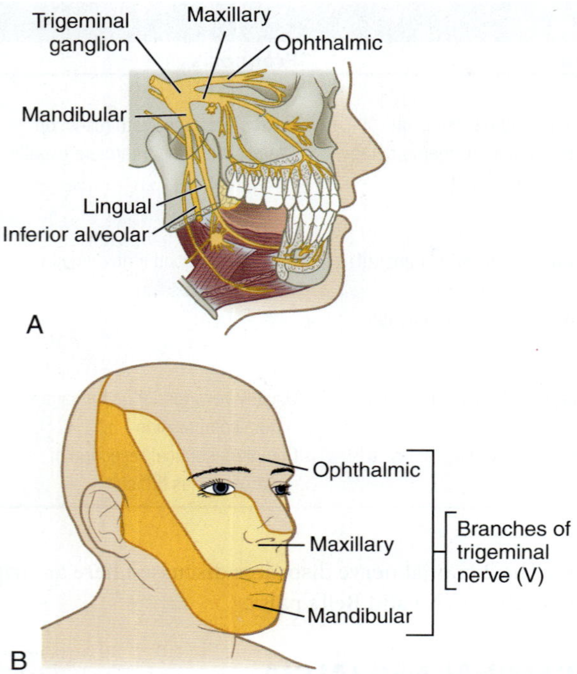

Fig. 65.13 (A) Trigeminal (fifth cranial) nerve and its 3 main divisions: ophthalmic, maxillary, and mandibular nerves. (B) Cutaneous innervation of the head. (Modified from Patton KT, Thibodeau GA: *Anatomy and physiology,* ed 8, St Louis, 2013, Mosby.)

Pain episodes are usually started by a triggering mechanism of light touch at a specific point *(trigger zone)* along the distribution of the nerve branches. Precipitating stimuli include chewing, brushing the teeth, feeling a hot or cold blast of air on the face, washing the face, yawning, or even talking. As a result, the patient may eat improperly, neglect hygienic practices, wear a cloth over the face, and withdraw from interaction with others. The patient may sleep to cope with pain.

TN 2 manifests as constant aching, burning, crushing, or stabbing pain. The pain has a lower intensity and does not subside completely.[25] The distinct attacks of TN 1 do not occur in TN 2.

Diagnostic Studies

Diagnosis is based almost entirely on history and results from physical and neurologic assessments. Other disorders that cause facial pain are ruled out before TN is diagnosed. MRI can rule out sinusitis, cancer, MS, or masses in the cerebellopontine angle. 3D reconstruction and angiography MRI are helpful with seeing the specific brain anatomy, nerve roots, and vasculature involved. Other specialists, such as neuroradiology, neurosurgery, dentistry, maxillofacial surgery, and pain management, may be involved.

Interprofessional Care

Once a diagnosis is made, the goal is to relieve pain with either medical or surgical treatment (Tables 65.14 and 65.15). Electrical nerve stimulation and nerve blocks with local anesthetics or botulinum toxin are options.

Antiseizure drug therapy may reduce pain by stabilizing the neuronal membrane and blocking nerve firing. These drugs are usually effective in treating TN 1 but less effective in TN 2. First-line drugs include carbamazepine (Tegretol) and oxcarbazepine (Trileptal). Topiramate (Topamax), clonazepam (Klonopin), phenytoin, lamotrigine (Lamictal), gabapentin, and valproic acid are other options.[25]

Tricyclic antidepressants, such as amitriptyline or nortriptyline, can help treat the constant burning or aching pain. Analgesics or opioids are usually not effective in controlling pain in TN 1. They may help with pain in TN 2.[25]

If a conservative approach is ineffective or the patient cannot tolerate drug therapy, surgical therapy is available (Table 65.15 and Fig. 65.14). In percutaneous procedures, affected nerve fibers are damaged to eliminate pain. Although most patients are pain-free after any procedures, pain relief lasts the longest with microvascular decompression. About half of treated patients develop recurrent pain within 12 to 15 years.[25]

TABLE 65.14 Interprofessional Care

Trigeminal Neuralgia

Diagnostic Assessment
- History and physical assessment, including neurologic examination
- MRI

Management
- Drug therapy
  - Antiseizure drugs (e.g., carbamazepine, oxcarbazepine, gabapentin [Neurontin])
  - Tricyclic antidepressants (e.g., amitriptyline)
- Local nerve block
- Surgical therapy (Table 65.15)

❖ NURSING MANAGEMENT: TRIGEMINAL NEURALGIA

Patients usually receive outpatient treatment. Assess the attacks in detail, including triggering factors, characteristics, frequency, and pain management techniques. This information helps you to plan care. Evaluate the degree of pain and its effects on the patient's lifestyle, drug use, emotional state, and suicidal tendencies. Note behavior, including withdrawal.

Monitor the patient's response to drug therapy. Note any side effects. Discuss complementary pain management measures, such as acupuncture, biofeedback, and yoga. Environmental assessment is essential during an acute period to decrease triggering stimuli. The room should be kept at an even, moderate temperature and free of drafts. The patient may prefer to complete all self-care activities, fearing someone else will inadvertently cause injury.

Assess nutrition status and hygiene, especially oral. Teach the patient the importance of nutrition, hygiene, and oral care. Convey understanding if oral neglect is apparent. A small, soft-bristled toothbrush or a warm mouthwash helps promote oral care. Hygiene activities are best done when analgesia is at its peak.

Encourage food that is high in protein and calories and easy to chew. Serve food lukewarm. Encourage small, frequent meals.

TABLE 65.15 Therapies for Trigeminal Neuralgia

Procedure	Description
Percutaneous Procedures	
Balloon compression	• Cannula is inserted through cheek and guided to a natural opening in the base of skull. • Soft catheter with a balloon tip is threaded through cannula. • Balloon is inflated and mechanical compression damages trigeminal nerve.
Glycerol rhizotomy (injection into 1 or more branches of trigeminal nerve) (Fig. 65.14)	• Thin needle inserted through puncture in cheek and guided through natural opening in base of skull. • Glycerol is injected into trigeminal ganglion. • Procedure can be repeated multiple times.
Radiofrequency thermal lesioning	• Needle is passed through cheek thorough a natural opening in base of skull. • Patient is awakened, and then a small electric current is passed through the needle, causing tingling. • When the needle is positioned so the tingling occurs in the same area of pain, patient is sedated again, then radiofrequency current is used to destroy part of the nerve. • Can result in facial numbness (although some degree of sensation may be retained), corneal anesthesia, and trigeminal motor weakness
Surgical Procedures	
Microvascular decompression, with or without neurectomy	• Small craniotomy done behind the ear (suboccipital craniotomy). • Blood vessels that appear to be compressing the nerve at the root entry zone where it exits the pons are then displaced and repositioned. • If there is no compression, cutting of the nerve (neurectomy) may be done.
Stereotactic radiosurgery (gamma knife, cyber knife)	• Uses stereotactic localization to focus high doses of radiation to area where trigeminal nerve exits the brainstem. • Radiation causes slow formation of a lesion on nerve and disrupts transmission of pain signals to brain. • Pain relief may take several months.

If oral intake is sharply reduced and the patient is nutritionally compromised, an NG tube can be inserted on the unaffected side for EN.

Appropriate teaching related to surgery depends on the type of procedure planned (e.g., percutaneous). The patient needs to know they will be awake during local procedures to cooperate when corneal and ciliary reflexes and facial sensations are checked. After the procedure, compare the patient's pain with the preoperative intensity. Evaluate the corneal reflex, extraocular muscles, hearing, sensation, and facial nerve function often (see Chapter 60). If the corneal reflex is impaired, take special care to protect the eyes. This includes using artificial tears or eye shields.

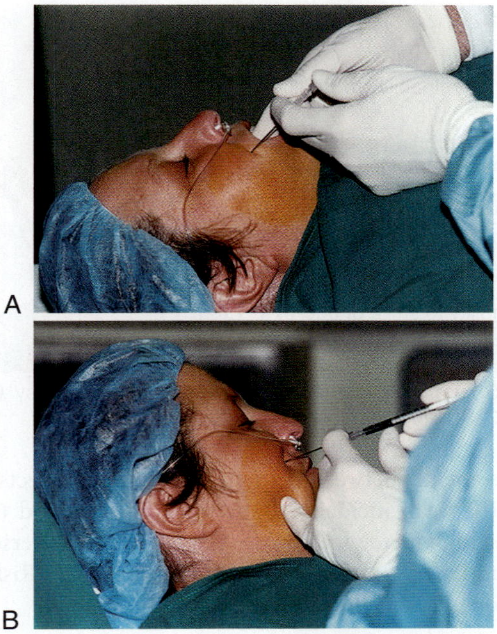

Fig. 65.14 Glycerol rhizotomy for the treatment of trigeminal neuralgia. (A) Patient with trigeminal neuralgia having needle placed. (B) HCP injecting glycerol. (Courtesy Joe Rothrock, Media, PA.)

After a percutaneous radiofrequency procedure, apply an ice pack to the jaw on the operative side for 3 to 5 hours. To avoid injuring the mouth, the patient should not chew on the operative side until sensation has returned. If intracranial surgery was done, general postoperative nursing care after a craniotomy is appropriate. Nursing care related to craniotomy is discussed in Chapter 61.

Plan for regular follow-up care. Teach the patient about drug therapy. Encourage the patient to keep environmental stimuli to a moderate level and use stress management techniques. Long-term management after surgery depends on residual effects of the procedure. If anesthesia is present or the corneal reflex is altered, teach the patient to (1) chew on the unaffected side; (2) avoid hot foods or beverages, which can burn the mucous membranes; (3) check the oral cavity after meals to remove food particles; (4) practice meticulous oral hygiene and continue with semiannual dental visits; (5) protect the face against temperature extremes; (6) use an electric razor; (7) wear a protective eye shield and avoid rubbing eyes; and (8) examine eye regularly for symptoms of infection or irritation.

BELL'S PALSY

Bell's palsy is an acute, usually temporary, facial paresis (or palsy) resulting from damage or trauma of the facial nerve (CN VII). It usually affects only 1 side of the face, but both sides can be affected.

Bell's palsy is the most common facial nerve disorder.[27] Each year, about 40,000 Americans are diagnosed with Bell's palsy.

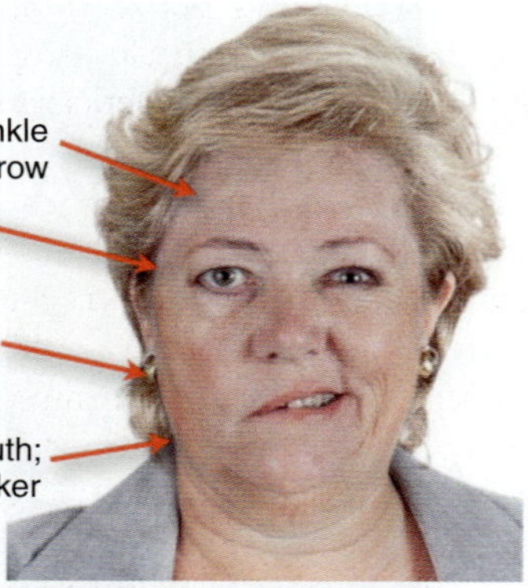

Fig. 65.15 Facial characteristics of a person with Bell's palsy. (© Jo Ann Snover/123RF Stock Photo/123rf.com.)

It occurs equally between men and women and affects any age group. The peak incidence is between ages 15 and 60 years. There is a high incidence during pregnancy and in persons with upper respiratory tract conditions (e.g., flu, colds). Risk factors include obesity, diabetes, and hypertension.[27]

Etiology and Pathophysiology

We do not know the exact cause. Several theories exist. Some think it is a reactivation of herpes simplex virus isoform (HSV-1) and/or herpes zoster virus (HZV). The viral infection causes inflammation, leading to nerve compression and the subsequent clinical features (Fig. 65.15). Another cause may be acute demyelination, similar to what happens in Guillain-Barré syndrome (GBS).

The prognosis is often very good. The extent of nerve damage determines the extent of recovery. Most begin to get better within 2 weeks after the onset and recover some or all facial function within 6 months. There may be residual effects in some cases, including facial asymmetry or abnormal facial movements.

Clinical Manifestations

CN VII is a mixed cranial nerve with motor, sensory, and autonomic function, which accounts for the manifestations. The key feature is the acute onset of unilateral lower motor facial weakness. 50% to 60% have pain around and behind the ear and neck. Other manifestations include drooping of the eyelid and corner of the mouth, drooling, facial twitching, dryness of the eye or mouth, facial numbness, altered taste, hearing loss, and excessive tearing in 1 eye.[27] Most often, these symptoms begin suddenly. They reach their peak within 48 to 72 hours.

Quality of life is often decreased due to eating, swallowing, speech, and taste problems. Patients may have psychologic withdrawal because of changes in appearance, muscle stretching, and facial spasms and contractures. They may have malnutrition, dehydration, mucous membrane trauma, or corneal abrasions.

Diagnostic Studies

Bell's palsy is a clinical diagnosis. No definitive diagnostic test exists. The assessment and typical pattern of onset guide the diagnosis and prognosis. Patients should be referred to a neurologist or otolaryngologist as soon as possible to exclude other neurologic conditions. If indicated, MRI and CT can eliminate other causes for facial paralysis. Blood tests can diagnose infections or other diseases. Electromyography (EMG) can confirm the presence of nerve damage.

Interprofessional Care

Care focuses on relieving symptoms, preventing complications, and protecting the eye on the affected side. Early treatment improves the chance of a complete recovery. Oral corticosteroid therapy to reduce inflammation and swelling should be started within 72 hours of onset.[28] Some patients should also receive an antiviral agent, such as acyclovir (Zovirax). Surgical decompression of the facial nerve is controversial but an option in refractory cases.

❖ NURSING MANAGEMENT: BELL'S PALSY

Mild analgesics can relieve pain. Moist heat can reduce discomfort and aid circulation. Electrical stimulation of the nerve, facial massage, and physical therapy help maintain muscle tone and ease pain. A facial sling may be helpful to support affected muscles, improve lip alignment, and facilitate eating. The facial sling is usually made and fitted by a physical or occupational therapist. When function begins to return, active facial muscle exercises are done several times a day. Tell the patient to protect the face from cold and drafts because trigeminal *hyperesthesia* (extreme sensitivity to pain or touch) may occur.

CHECK YOUR PRACTICE

You are working in the outpatient neurology clinic. Your patient is a 68-year-old woman with Bell's palsy. Her main problem today is dry eyes. When you are doing an assessment, she tells you, "I hate the way I look. I cannot go anywhere, and I am afraid to leave the house. I am so ugly."

- How can you help her cope?
- What can you suggest to increase moisture in the affected eye?

Eye protection is important. The patient may wear dark glasses for protective and cosmetic reasons. Frequent use of artificial tears (methylcellulose) during the day can prevent drying of the cornea. Ointment and an impermeable eye shield can be used at night to retain moisture. Some patients may need to tape the lids closed at night. Teach the patient to report eye pain, drainage, or discharge.

Maintaining good nutrition is important. Teach the patient to chew on the unaffected side of the mouth to avoid trapping food and enjoy the taste of food. After each meal, thorough oral hygiene helps prevent parotitis, caries, and periodontal disease from accumulated residual food.

The change in physical appearance from Bell's palsy can be devastating. Reassure the patient that chances for a full recovery are good. Enlisting support from family and friends is important. Tell the patient most people recover within 3 to 6 months after onset of symptoms.

POLYNEUROPATHIES

GUILLAIN-BARRÉ SYNDROME

Guillain-Barré syndrome (GBS) is an autoimmune process that occurs a few days or weeks after a viral or bacterial infection. GBS is rare, affecting about 1 person in every 100,000.[29] It can occur at any age, but those over age 50 are at greatest risk.[30] The most common type of GBS is *acute inflammatory demyelinating polyneuropathy (AIDP)*. Other types include acute motor axonal neuropathy (AMAN) and acute motor-sensory axonal neuropathy (AMSAN). AMAN is more common in children.

Etiology and Pathophysiology

The cause of GBS is unknown. Both cellular and humoral immune responses likely play a role in AIDP. Humoral responses appear to cause AMAN.[30] After an infection, immune responses cause injury to either the myelin sheath (AIDP) or the nerve axon itself (AMAN). There is edema and inflammation of affected nerves. The result is segmental loss of the myelin sheath with exposed nerve membranes in nerve terminals and the nodes of Ranvier. Transmission of nerve impulses is stopped or slowed. This leads to flaccid paralysis with muscle denervation and atrophy. In the recovery phase, remyelination occurs slowly. Neurologic function returns in a proximal-to-distal pattern.

Most GBS cases follow a viral or bacterial infection of the GI or upper respiratory tract. Cytomegalovirus is the most common viral cause. *Campylobacter jejuni* gastroenteritis is the most common bacterial cause, especially for AMAN. Other related infections include Epstein-Barr virus, *Mycoplasma pneumoniae, Haemophilus influenza,* hepatitis (A, B, E), and Zika virus.[29] Surgery and trauma may trigger GBS.

Clinical Manifestations and Complications

The main features of GBS include acute, ascending, rapidly progressive, symmetric weakness of the limbs. The first symptoms are weakness, *paresthesia* (numbness and tingling), and *hypotonia* (reduced muscle tone) of the limbs. Reflexes in the affected limbs are weak or absent. Maximal weakness is reached in 4 weeks.

Autonomic nervous system dysfunction occurs with AIDP and AMSAN, causing orthostatic hypotension, hypertension, and abnormal vagal responses (bradycardia, heart block, asystole). Other autonomic dysfunction effects include bowel and bladder dysfunction, facial flushing, and diaphoresis. Cranial nerve involvement manifests as facial weakness and paresthesia, extraocular eye movement problems, and dysphagia.

Pain is common. It can include paresthesia, muscular aches and cramps, and hyperesthesia. It is often worse at night. Pain may contribute to decreased appetite and interfere with sleep.

The most serious complication is respiratory failure. It occurs if the paralysis progresses to nerves that innervate the thoracic area. Assess the respiratory system by checking respiratory rate and depth to determine the need for immediate intervention, including intubation and mechanical ventilation. Respiratory infection or UTI may occur. Immobility from paralysis can cause paralytic ileus, muscle atrophy, VTE, PIs, orthostatic hypotension, and nutrition deficiencies.[31]

Diagnostic Studies

Diagnosis is based mainly on history and assessment. Clinical features required for diagnosis include progressive weakness of more than 1 limb and decreased or absent reflexes. Electrolyte levels, liver function tests, creatinine phosphokinase, and erythrocyte sedimentation rates are evaluated. CSF analysis helps exclude other causes. In GBS, the CSF has more protein than normal.[31] Results of EMG and nerve conduction studies (NCS) are used after 2 weeks to confirm the diagnosis. NCS allows the HCP to diagnose the subtype. NCS in AIDP show demyelination. These studies aid in diagnosis and selecting treatment.

Interprofessional and Nursing Care

The management of GBS is supportive. Ventilatory support is critical during the acute phase. Patients may be in ICU for hemodynamic monitoring. Immunomodulating treatments, such as plasma exchange (PE) *(plasmapheresis)* or high-dose IV immunoglobulin (IVIG), are most effective if used within the first 2 weeks of symptom onset. They are equally effective. PE removes antibodies and other immune factors. It is used 5 times, either daily or every other day in the first 2 weeks (see Chapter 14). IVIG interferes with antigen presentation. It is given over 5 days. It is readily available and is the preferred treatment in many centers.[31] After 4 weeks past disease onset, PE and IVIG therapies have little value.

Assessment is important during the acute phase. During the neurologic assessment, evaluate motor and sensory function. Report changes in motor function (e.g., ascending paralysis), reflexes, cranial nerve function (gag, cornea, swallow), and level of consciousness.

Assess respiratory and cardiac function. Monitor ABGs and vital capacity. Closely monitor BP and cardiac rate and rhythm during the acute phase because dysrhythmias, orthostatic hypotension, and increased or decreased BP and heart rate may occur. Vasopressor agents and volume expanders may be needed to treat the low BP. If fever develops, obtain sputum and blood cultures to identify the pathogen. Appropriate antibiotic therapy is then started.

Nutrition needs must be met despite possible delayed gastric emptying, paralytic ileus, and potential for aspiration if the gag reflex is lost. In addition to testing for the gag reflex, note drooling and other problems with secretions that may indicate an inadequate gag reflex. EN or PN may be used to ensure adequate caloric intake.

Throughout the course of the illness, provide support and encouragement to the patient and caregivers. Coordinate early referrals for physical, occupational, and speech therapy. Counseling may help the patient adjust to the sudden disabling syndrome and dependence on others.

Most patients with GBS will start to recover spontaneously at about 28 days. 80% of patients walk independently at 6 months, with 60% making a full recovery in 1 year. GBS patients who have a GI infection, are older in age, have poor upper extremity motor strength, or need mechanical ventilation have a poorer prognosis.[31]

CHRONIC INFLAMMATORY DEMYELINATING POLYNEUROPATHY

Chronic inflammatory demyelinating polyneuropathy (CIDP) is a motor and sensory neuropathy. CIDP is a rare autoimmune disorder affecting 1 to 2 persons per 100,000. CIDP is more common in men and those in their 50s and 60s.

Like GBS, there are different types of CIDP. CIDP differs from GBS in that symptoms gradually occur over 8 weeks, and there is no acute onset. CIDP is not self-limiting (with an end to the acute phase). Early recognition and treatment can help the patient avoid significant disability.

Etiology and Pathophysiology

We do not know the exact cause of CIDP. Evidence supports an autoimmune basis. CIDP seems to be associated with infection, HIV, hepatitis C, Sjögren syndrome, inflammatory bowel disease, melanoma, lymphoma, and diabetes.

Clinical Manifestations and Diagnostic Studies

It is important to recognize the differences between CIPD and GBS to prevent incorrect or delayed treatment. The classic presentation of patients with CIPD includes progressive symptoms lasting over 2 months, more weakness than sensory deficits, symmetric weakness in the arms and legs, impaired sensation (from distal to proximal), paresthesia and dysesthesia, and absent or decreased reflexes in all extremities. Tremors, facial weakness, and papilledema may be present. Sensory ataxia and impaired vibration and pinprick sensation occur more often in CIDP.

CIDP diagnostic tests are similar to those for GBS. CSF shows high protein levels. MRI may show changes. Key identifying features of CIDP include nerve conduction block and slowed conduction velocity, possibly due to demyelination. Nerve biopsy is done when other studies do not confirm a diagnosis.

Interprofessional and Nursing Care

Early recognition and diagnosis of CIDP are key to reducing permanent disability. The goal of treatment is to halt the immune response and stop nerve inflammation and demyelination. Use of IVIG, high-dose corticosteroids, or PE are all effective treatments.

Patients continue therapy until maximum clinical improvement is achieved or until they reach a plateau. Patients need maintenance therapy to prevent relapse or progression. Coordinate appropriate referrals to rehabilitation to promote maximum recovery. Therapy may improve muscle strength, function, and mobility while minimizing muscle atrophy and joint distortion.

TETANUS

Tetanus (lockjaw) is a severe nervous system infection affecting spinal and cranial nerves. In the United States, because of widespread immunization and careful wound care, there are only about 40 to 50 cases per year.[32] The annual worldwide incidence is between 500,000 and 1 million cases.[33]

Tetanus results from the effects of a potent neurotoxin (tetanospasmin) released by the anaerobic bacillus *Clostridium tetani*. The spores of the bacillus are present in soil, garden mold, and manure. Tetanospasmin binds to motor nerves and enters the axons. From there, it can travel to the brain and spinal cord and stop the release of inhibitory neurotransmitters. This causes sustained muscle contraction. Many different muscles can be affected if the toxin reaches the blood or lymph system.[32]

C. tetani enters the body through a wound that provides an appropriate low-O_2 environment for the organisms to mature and make toxin. Examples of such wounds include IV drug use injection sites, human and animal bites, puncture wounds from stepping on a nail, gardening injuries, burns, frostbite, open fractures, and gunshot wounds. The incubation period is typically 4 to 14 days. The shorter the period, the more severe the symptoms.

The hallmark feature of generalized tetanus is muscle rigidity and spasms. Patients may have muscle soreness, cramping, or difficulty swallowing. Facial muscles are affected first with stiffness in the jaw *(trismus)*. They may have a sardonic smile *(risus sardonicus)* from facial muscle contractions. The neck muscles, back, abdomen, and extremities become increasingly rigid as the disease progresses. In severe forms, continuous tonic seizures may occur with *opisthotonos* (extreme arching of the back and retraction of the head). Laryngeal and respiratory spasms cause apnea and anoxia. The slightest noise, jarring motion, or bright light can set off a painful seizure.

Tetanus prevention and immunizations are the most important factors influencing incidence. Adults should receive a tetanus and diphtheria toxoid booster every 10 years.[32] Teach the patient that immediate, thorough cleansing of all wounds with soap and water is important to prevent tetanus. If an open wound occurs and the patient has not been immunized within 5 years, contact the HCP so they can get a tetanus booster.

Tetanus is a medical emergency that requires hospitalization. Patients receive tetanus immune globulin (TIG). It provides temporary immunity by directly providing antitoxin.[32] Drugs to control spasms are essential. Diazepam or barbiturates are given to promote sedation and skeletal muscle relaxation. In severe cases, neuromuscular blocking agents (e.g., vecuronium) are given to paralyze skeletal muscles. Opioid analgesics are used for pain management. A 10- to 14-day course of penicillin, metronidazole, tetracycline, or doxycycline inhibits further growth of *C. tetani*.

Because of laryngospasm and the potential need for neuromuscular blocking drugs, the patient is placed on mechanical ventilation. Sedative agents and opioid analgesics are given to all patients who are pharmacologically paralyzed. IV fluids are needed for proper hydration due to sustained muscle contraction. Any wound should be debrided or abscess drained. Antibiotics may be given to prevent secondary infections.

Case Study

SCI

(© Com-stockImages/Stockbyte/Thinkstock.)

Patient Profile

Acute Phase

S.W., an 18-year-old woman, is admitted to the ED with a cervical SCI. S.W. was swimming at a neighbor's backyard pool. She dove into the shallow end, striking her head on the bottom of the pool. Her friends noticed she did not resurface. They rescued her and brought her to the side of the pool. They maintained neck immobilization until emergency personnel arrived.

Subjective Data

- Awake and alert
- Reporting neck pain
- Anxious and asking why she cannot move her legs
- Asking to see her family

Objective Data

- Weak elbow flexion (biceps) movement bilaterally
- No triceps movement bilaterally
- Gross shoulder movement present bilaterally
- No movement in bilateral lower extremities
- Decreased sensation from the shoulders down
- No bladder or bowel control
- BP 85/50 mm Hg; pulse 56 beats/min; respirations 32 breaths/min and labored

Diagnostic Studies

- CT C-spine shows C5 subluxation and compression fracture
- MRI C-spine shows severe spinal cord compression at C5-6

Interprofessional Care

- Intubated started on mechanical ventilation
- Placed in tongs and traction on arrival to ICU

Discussion Questions

1. ***Recognize:*** What signs and symptoms would indicate respiratory distress? What physiologic problem would cause respiratory distress in S.W.'s injury state?
2. ***Analyze:*** What physiologic problems are causing S.W. to have hypotension and bradycardia?
3. ***Plan:*** What would be the initial treatment for S.W.'s hypotension and bradycardia?
4. ***Prioritize:*** What nursing activities would be a priority on S.W.'s arrival in the ICU?
5. ***Act:*** What interventions can decrease S.W.'s anxiety?

Patient Profile

Rehabilitation Phase

S.W. is now 1-month post injury and has been transferred to a local inpatient SCI rehabilitation center. She is extubated and using a wheelchair to mobilize. She eats 3 meals a day with help and is on a strict bowel and bladder program.

Subjective Data

- Awake and alert but anxious
- Reporting a severe headache, blurred vision, and nausea

Objective Data

- Flushed and diaphoretic above the level of injury
- No bowel movement for 2 days
- BP 235/106 mm Hg, pulse 32 beats/min, respirations 30 breaths/min, and labored

Discussion Questions

1. ***Analyze:*** What physiologic problem is causing S.W.'s hypertension and bradycardia?
2. ***Prioritize:*** What initial priority nursing interventions would be appropriate?
3. ***Plan:*** Once you notify the HCP, what other interventions would be appropriate?
4. ***Act:*** Patient and caregiver involvement in rehabilitation is vital. What teaching will you provide about bowel management?
5. ***Act:*** S.W. and her family are concerned about the risk for autonomic dysreflexia. What effective strategies to prevent autonomic dysreflexia would you discuss with them?
6. ***Evaluation:*** What outcomes would indicate that nursing interventions were successful?

Answers available at http://evolve.elsevier.com/Lewis/medsurg.

BRIDGE TO NCLEX EXAMINATION

The number of the question corresponds to the same-numbered outcome at the beginning of the chapter.

1. During rehabilitation, a patient with spinal cord injury begins to ambulate with long leg braces. Which level of injury does the nurse associate with this degree of recovery?
   a. L1-2
   b. T6-7
   c. T1-2
   d. C7-8
2. A patient with a T4 spinal cord injury has neurogenic shock due to sympathetic nervous system dysfunction. What would the nurse recognize as characteristic of this condition?
   a. Tachycardia
   b. Hypotension
   c. Increased cardiac output
   d. Peripheral vasoconstriction
3. A patient with spinal cord injury has severe neurologic deficits. What is the *most* likely mechanism of injury for this patient?
   a. Compression
   b. Hyperextension
   c. Flexion-rotation
   d. Extension-rotation
4. A patient undergoing rehabilitation for a C7 spinal cord injury tells the nurse he must have the flu because he has a bad headache and nausea. The nurse's *first priority* is to
   a. call the health care provider.
   b. check the patient's temperature.

c. measure the patient's blood pressure.
d. elevate the head of the bed to 90 degrees.

5. The most common early symptom of a spinal cord tumor is
   a. urinary incontinence.
   b. back pain that worsens with activity.
   c. paralysis below the level of involvement.
   d. impaired sensation of pain, temperature, and light touch.
6. During assessment of the patient with trigeminal neuralgia, the nurse should *(select all that apply)*
   a. inspect all aspects of the mouth and teeth.
   b. assess the gag reflex and respiratory rate and depth.
   c. lightly palpate the affected side of the face for edema.
   d. test for temperature and sensation perception on the face.
   e. ask the patient to describe factors that initiate an episode.
7. During routine assessment of a patient with Guillain-Barré syndrome, the nurse finds the patient is short of breath. The patient's respiratory distress is caused by
   a. elevated protein levels in the CSF.
   b. immobility resulting from ascending paralysis.
   c. degeneration of motor neurons in the brainstem and spinal cord.
   d. paralysis ascending to the nerves that stimulate the thoracic area.

1. a; 2. b; 3. c; 4. c; 5. b; 6. a, d, e; 7. d.

For rationales to these answers and even more NCLEX review questions, visit http://evolve.elsevier.com/Lewis/medsurg.

EVOLVE WEBSITE/RESOURCES LIST

http://evolve.elsevier.com/Lewis/medsurg
Review Questions (Online Only)
Key Points
Answer Keys for Questions
- Rationales for Bridge to NCLEX Examination Questions
- Answer Guidelines for Case Study

Student Case Study
- Patient With Spinal Cord Injury

Nursing Care Plan
- eNursing Care Plan 60.1: Patient With a Spinal Cord Injury

Conceptual Care Map Creator
Audio Glossary
Content Updates

REFERENCES

1. National SCI Statistical Center: Spinal cord injury facts and figures at a glance. Retrieved from www.nscisc.uab.edu/Public/Facts%2020.pdf.
2. Ziu E, Mesfin F: Spinal shock. Retrieved from https://www.https://ncbi.nlm.nih.gov/books/NBK448163/.
3. Dave S, Cho JJ: Neurogenic shock. Retrieved from www.ncbi.nlm.nih.gov/books/NBK459361/.
4. National Institute of Health and Human Development: Spinal cord injury. Retrieved from https://www.nichd.nih.gov/health/topics/spinalinjury/conditioninfo/default.
5. Christensen B: ASIA Impairment Scale. Retrieved from https://www.emedicine.medscape.com/article/2172437-overview.

*6. Azzez M, Moscote-Salazar L, Alcala-Cerra G, et al.: Emergency management of traumatic spinal cord injuries, *Int J Number Theory* 17:57, 2020.

*7. Kavanagh A, Baverstock R, et al.: Canadian Urological Association guideline: diagnosis, management, and surveillance of neurogenic lower urinary tract dysfunction, *Can J Urol* 13:e157, 2019.

8. Cedar Sinai: Neurogenic bowel. Retrieved from https://www.cedars-sinai.org/health-library/diseases-and-conditions/n/neurogenic-bowel.html.

*9. Piran S, Schulman S: Thromboprophylaxis in patients with spinal cord injury: a narrative review, *Semin Thromb Hemost* 45:150, 2019.

10. Fehlings M: Spine surgery after spinal cord injury: why timing matters. Retrieved from https://www.spineuniverse.com/conditions/spinal-cord-injury/spine-surgery-after-spinal-cord-injury-why-timing-matters.
11. Della Volpe K: Declining rates of high-dose steroid use for acute spinal cord injury. Retrieved from https://www.spineuniverse.com/professional/news/declining-rates-high-dose-steroid-use-acute-spinal-cord-injury-0.
12. Della Volpe, K. Methylprednisolone use in acute spinal cord injury. Retrieved from https://www.spineuniverse.com/professional/guidelines/methylprednisolone-use-acute-spinal-cord-injury.
13. STEADI: Stopping elderly accidents, deaths and injuries. Retrieved from https://www.cdc.gov/steadi/index.html.

*14. Shiferaw W, Akalu T, Mulugeta H, et al.: The global burden of pressure ulcers among patients with spinal cord injury: a systematic review and meta- analysis, *BMC Muscoskel Disord* 21:1, 2020.

15. Kirman C, Geibel J: What are WOCN guidelines for the prevention of pressure injuries? Retrieved from https://www.medscape.com/answers/190115-82589/what-are-wocn-guidelines-for-the-prevention-of-pressure-injuries-pressure-ulcers.
16. Stephenson R, Klein M: Autonomic dysreflexia in spinal cord injury. Retrieved from https://emedicine.medscape.com/article/322809-overview.
17. Christopher & Dana Reeve Foundation: How do I find a rehabilitation facility? Retrieved from https://www.Christopherreeve.org/living-with-paralysis/newly-paralyzed/how-do-i-find-a-rehabilitation-facility.

*18. Gu Y, Ren S, Shi Y, et al.: Restoration methods of respiratory function for spinal cord injury, *Math Probl Eng*, 2020.

*19. Spin A, Bratu O, et al.: Botulinum toxin in low urinary tract disorders-over 30 years of practice, *Exp Ther Med*, 2020.

20. Christopher & Dana Reeve Foundation Paralysis Resource Center: Sexual health for men. Retrieved from https://www.christopherreeve.org/living-with-paralysis/health/sexual-health/sexual-health-for-men.
21. Christopher & Dana Reeve Foundation Paralysis Resource Center: Sexual health for women. Retrieved from https://www.christopherreeve.org/living-with-paralysis/health/sexual-health/sexual-health-for-women.
22. Ogden A, Kopell B: Intramedullary spinal cord tumors. Retrieved from https://emedicine.medscape.com/article/251133-overview.

23. American Association of Neurological Surgeons: Spinal tumors. Retrieved from https://www.aans.org/Patients/Neurosurgical-Conditions-and-Treatments/Spinal-Tumors.
24. Mayo Clinic: Spinal cord tumor. Retrieved from https://www.mayoclinic.org/diseases-conditions/spinal-cord-tumor/diagnosis-treatment/drc-20350108.
25. National Institute of Health: Trigeminal neuralgia fact sheet. Retrieved from https://www.ninds.nih.gov/Disorders/Patient-Caregiver-Education/Fact-Sheets/Trigeminal-Neuralgia-Fact-Sheet.
26. Khatri M: Tic douloureux. Retrieved from https://www.webmd.com/a-to-z-guides/tic-douloureux#2.
27. National Institute of Neurologic Disorders and Stroke: Bell's palsy. Retrieved from https://www.ninds.nih.gov/Disorders/All-Disorders/Bells-Palsy-Information-Page.
28. Lo B, Herchline T: Bell palsy empiric therapy. Retrieved from https://emedicine.medscape.com/article/2018337-overview.
29. National Institute of Neurologic Disorders and Stroke: Guillain-Barré fact sheet. Retrieved from https://www.ninds.nih.gov/Disorders/Patient-Caregiver-Education/Fact-Sheets/Guillain-Barr%C3%A9-Syndrome-Fact-Sheet.
30. Centers for Disease Control and Prevention: Guillain-Barré syndrome. Retrieved from https://www.cdc.gov/campylobacter/guillain-barre.html.
31. Andary MT, Klein MJ: Guillain-Barré syndrome. Retrieved from https://emedicine.medscape.com/article/315632-overview.
32. Davis DP, Stoppler MC: Tetanus. Retrieved from https://www.emedicinehealth.com/tetanus/article_em.htm#facts_on_tetanus.

*Evidence-based information for clinical practice.

66

Assessment: Musculoskeletal System

Colleen Walsh

http://evolve.elsevier.com/Lewis/medsurg/

CONCEPTUAL FOCUS

Functional Ability
Mobility
Safety

LEARNING OUTCOMES

1. Describe the gross and microscopic anatomy of bone.
2. Explain the classification system for joints and movements at synovial joints.
3. Describe the functions of cartilage, muscles, ligaments, tendons, fascia, and bursae.
4. Link age-related changes in the musculoskeletal system to the differences in assessment findings.
5. Obtain significant subjective and objective assessment data related to the musculoskeletal system from a patient.
6. Perform a physical assessment of the musculoskeletal system using appropriate techniques.
7. Distinguish normal from abnormal findings of a physical assessment of the musculoskeletal system.
8. Describe the purpose, significance of results, and nursing responsibilities related to diagnostic studies of the musculoskeletal system.

KEY TERMS

ankylosis, Table 66.6
arthrocentesis, Table 66.9
arthroscopy, Table 66.9
atrophy, Table 66.6
bone remodeling
contracture, Table 66.6
crepitation, Table 66.6
isometric contractions
isotonic contractions
kyphosis, Table 66.6
lordosis, Table 66.6
range of motion (ROM)
scoliosis
x-ray

The musculoskeletal system is composed of voluntary muscle and 6 types of connective tissue: bone, cartilage, ligaments, tendons, fascia, and bursae. The purpose of the musculoskeletal system is to protect body organs, provide support and stability for the body, store minerals, and allow coordinated movement. This chapter reviews the structure and function of the musculoskeletal system to enable nursing assessment and evaluation of assessment findings.

STRUCTURES AND FUNCTIONS OF MUSCULOSKELETAL SYSTEM

Bone

Function

The main functions of bone are support, protection of internal organs, voluntary movement, blood cell production, and mineral storage. Bones provide the supporting framework that keeps the body from collapsing. It allows the body to bear weight. Bones protect underlying vital organs and tissues. For example, the skull encloses the brain and vertebrae surround the spinal cord. The rib cage protects the lungs and heart.

Bones serve as a point of attachment for muscles and ligaments. Muscles are connected to bones by tendons. Bones act as a lever for muscles. Movement occurs because of muscle contractions applied to these levers. Ligaments provide stability to joints. Bone marrow contains the tissues responsible for making red and white blood cells. Bones serve as a storage site for inorganic minerals, including calcium and phosphorus.[1]

Bone is a dynamic tissue that continuously changes form and composition. It contains both organic material (collagen) and inorganic material (calcium, phosphate). The internal and

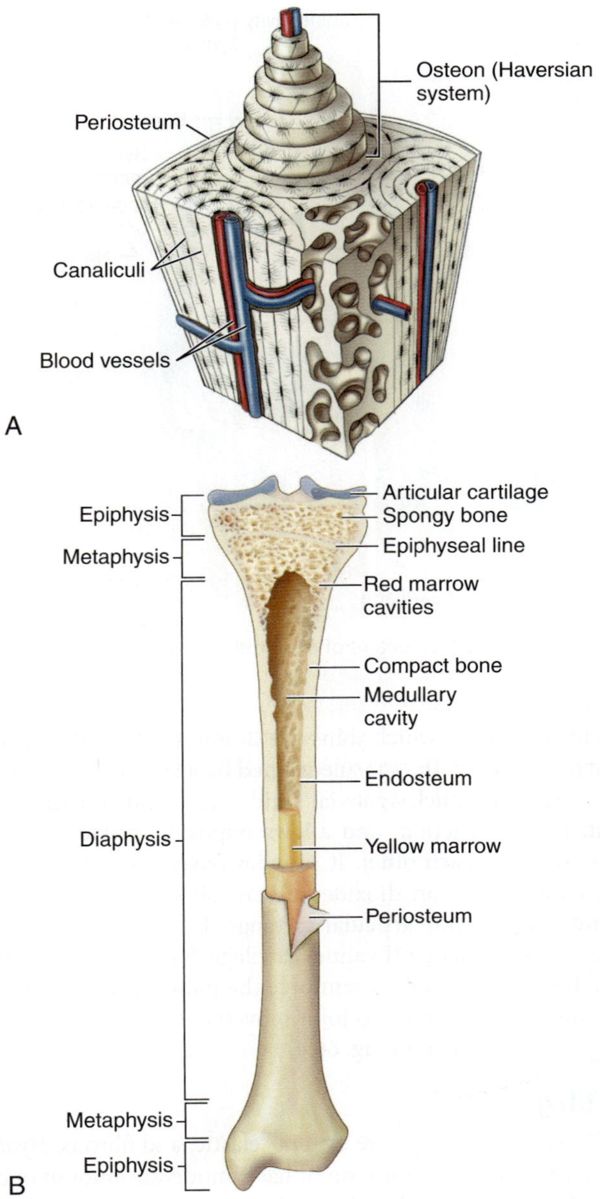

Fig. 66.1 Bone structure. (A) Cortical bone showing numerous structural units called osteons. (B) Anatomy of a long bone (tibia) showing cancellous and compact bone. (A, From Patton KT, Thibodeau GA: *Anatomy and physiology*, ed 9, St Louis, 2016, Mosby. B, From Patton KT, Thibodeau GA: *The human body in health and disease*, ed 7, St Louis, 2018, Mosby.)

external growth and remodeling of bone are ongoing processes that vary throughout the life span.

Microscopic Structure

We classify bone according to structure as *cortical* (compact and dense) or *cancellous* (spongy). In *cortical bone,* cylindrical structural units called *osteons (Haversian systems)* fit closely together to create a dense bone structure (Fig. 66.1A). Within the systems, the Haversian canals run parallel to the bone's long axis. They contain the blood vessels that travel to the bone's interior from the periosteum. Surrounding each osteon are concentric rings called *lamellae,* which indicate mature bone. Smaller canals *(canaliculi)* extend from the Haversian canals to the *lacunae*, where mature bone cells are embedded.

Cancellous bone has a different structure. The lamellae occur along the lines of maximum stress placed on the bone. Cancellous bone is filled with red or yellow marrow. Blood reaches the bone cells by passing through spaces in the marrow.

The 3 types of bone cells are osteoblasts, osteocytes, and osteoclasts.[2] Osteoblasts make organic bone matrix (collagen). They are the basic bone-forming cells. Osteocytes are mature bone cells. Osteoclasts take part in bone remodeling by helping breakdown bone tissue. **Bone remodeling** is the removal of old bone by osteoclasts (resorption) and the deposit of new bone by osteoblasts (ossification). The inner layer of bone is made mostly of osteoblasts with a few osteoclasts.

Gross Structure

The anatomic structure of bone is best represented by a typical long bone, such as the tibia (Fig. 66.1B). Each long bone consists of the epiphysis, diaphysis, and metaphysis. The *epiphysis*, the widened area at each end of a long bone, is made mostly of cancellous bone. The wide epiphysis allows greater weight distribution and provides stability for the joint. The epiphysis is a main location for muscle attachment. Articular cartilage covers the ends of the epiphysis. It provides a smooth, low-friction surface for joint movement.

The *diaphysis* is the main shaft of the long bone. It provides structural support and is composed of cortical bone. The tubular structure of the diaphysis allows it to withstand bending and twisting forces more easily. The *metaphysis* is the flared area between the epiphysis and diaphysis. It is composed of cancellous bone.

The *epiphyseal plate* (physis or growth plate) is the cartilaginous area between the epiphysis and metaphysis. In skeletally immature children who still have open growth plates, the epiphyseal plate actively makes chondrocytes that become mature bone. Chondrocyte division causes longitudinal bone growth in children. Injury to the epiphyseal plate in a growing child can cause the formation of new bone to stop at the growth plate. This leads to a shorter extremity and may contribute to major functional problems. In the adult, the metaphysis and epiphysis become joined when chondrocyte formation at the growth plate stops and bone formation is complete.

The *periosteum* is composed of fibrous connective tissue that covers the bone. Tiny blood vessels penetrate the periosteum to bring nutrition to underlying bone. Musculotendinous fibers attach to the outer layer of the periosteum. Collagen bundles attach the inner layer of the periosteum to the bone. There is no periosteum on the articular surfaces of long bones. These bone ends are covered by articular cartilage.[3]

The medullary *(marrow)* cavity in the center of the diaphysis contains either red or yellow bone marrow.[2] In adults, red marrow is found mainly in the flat bones, such as the pelvis, sternum, and scapula, and cancellous bone at the epiphyseal ends of long bones, such as the femur and humerus. Red bone marrow is involved in blood cell production (hematopoiesis). In the adult, the medullary cavity of long bones contains yellow

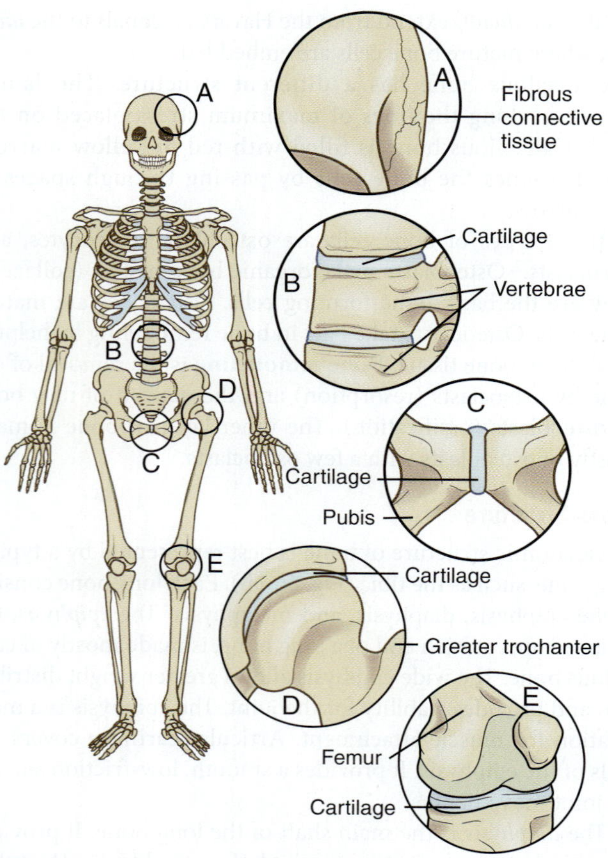

Fig. 66.2 Classification of joints. (A–C) Synarthrotic (immovable) and amphiarthrotic (slightly movable) joints. (D and E) Diarthrodial (freely movable) joints.

bone marrow (mainly adipose tissue). It serves as a storage site for triglycerides.[4] Yellow marrow is involved in hematopoiesis in times of great blood cell need.

Types

The skeleton consists of 206 bones. We classify bones by shape as long, short, flat, irregular, or seismoid.

Long bones have a central shaft (diaphysis) and 2 widened ends (epiphyses) (Fig. 66.1B). Examples include the femur, humerus, and tibia. Short bones are composed of cancellous bone covered by a thin layer of compact bone. Examples include the carpals in the hand and tarsals in the foot.

Flat bones have 2 layers of compact bone separated by a layer of cancellous bone. Flat bones include the pelvis, skull, sternum, ribs, vertebrae, and scapula. The spaces in the cancellous bone contain bone marrow. Irregular bones appear in a variety of shapes and sizes. Examples include the sacrum, mandible, and ear ossicles. *Sesamoid bones* are round or oval bones (such as the patella), which develop in tendons.[3]

Joints

A *joint* (articulation) is a place where the ends of 2 bones are close and move in relation to each other. Joints are classified by the degree of movement that they allow (Fig. 66.2).

The most common joint is the freely movable *diarthrodial* (synovial) type. Each joint is enclosed in a capsule of fibrous

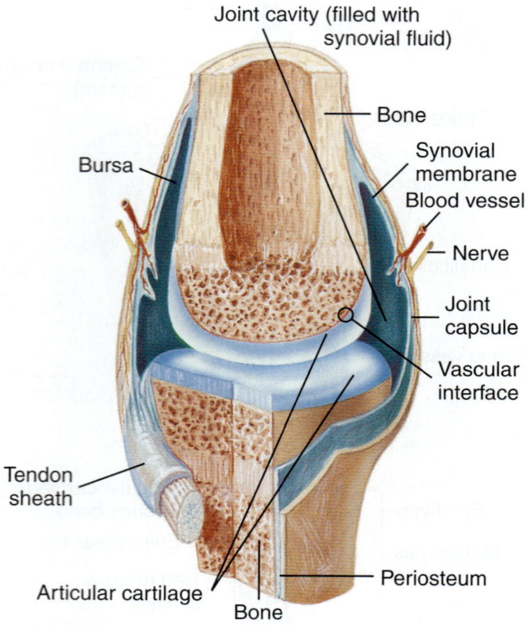

Fig. 66.3 Structure of diarthrodial (synovial) joint.

connective tissue, which joins the 2 bones together to form a cavity (Fig. 66.3). The capsule is lined by a synovial membrane, which secretes thick synovial fluid. This fluid lubricates the joint, reduces friction, and allows opposing surfaces to slide smoothly over each other. It supplies oxygen and nutrients to and removes carbon dioxide and metabolic wastes from the chondrocytes within articular cartilage. The end of each bone is covered with articular (hyaline) cartilage. Supporting structures (e.g., ligaments, tendons) reinforce the joint capsule. They provide limits and stability to joint movement. Types of diarthrodial joints are shown in Fig. 66.4.

Cartilage

The 3 types of *cartilage* are hyaline, elastic, and fibrous. *Hyaline cartilage* is the most common. It has a moderate amount of collagen fibers. It is found in the trachea, bronchi, nose, epiphyseal plate, and articular surfaces of bones.

Elastic cartilage, which has both collagen and elastic fibers, is more flexible than hyaline cartilage. It is found in the ear, epiglottis, and larynx.

Fibrous cartilage (fibrocartilage) consists mostly of collagen fibers. It is a tough tissue that often functions as a shock absorber. Fibrous cartilage is found between the vertebral discs. It forms a protective cushion between the bones of the pelvic girdle, knee, and shoulder.

Cartilage in synovial joints serves as a support for soft tissue and provides the articular surface for joint movement. It protects underlying tissues. Because articular cartilage is avascular, it must receive nourishment by the diffusion of material from the synovial fluid. The lack of a direct blood supply contributes to the slow metabolism of cartilage cells and explains why healing and repair of cartilage tissue occur slowly. The cartilage in the epiphyseal plate is involved in the growth of long bones before reaching physical maturity.[5]

Joint	Movement	Examples	Illustration
Hinge joint	Flexion, extension	Elbow joint (shown), interphalangeal joints, knee joint	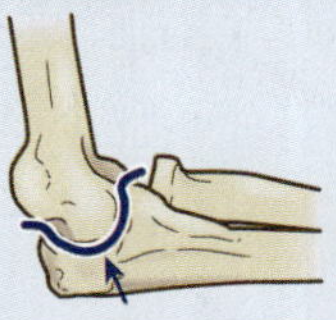
Ball and socket (spheroidal)	Flexion, extension; adduction, abduction; circumduction	Shoulder (shown), hip	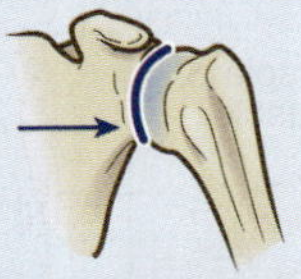
Pivot (rotary)	Rotation	Atlas-axis, proximal radioulnar joint (shown)	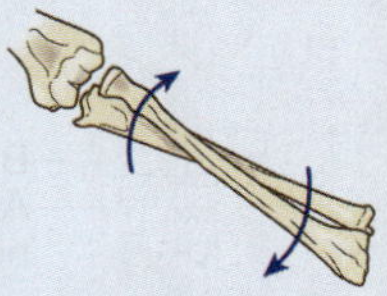
Condyloid	Flexion, extension; abduction, adduction; circumduction	Wrist joint (between radial and carpals) (shown)	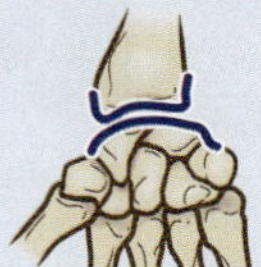
Saddle	Flexion, extension; abduction, adduction; circumduction, thumb-finger opposition	Carpometacarpal joint of thumb (shown)	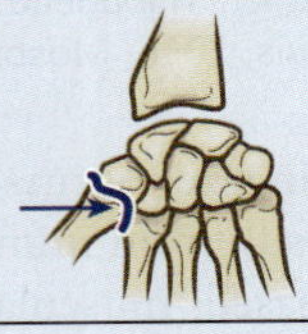
Gliding	One surface moves over another surface	Between tarsal bones, sacroiliac joint, between articular processes of vertebrae, between carpal bones (shown)	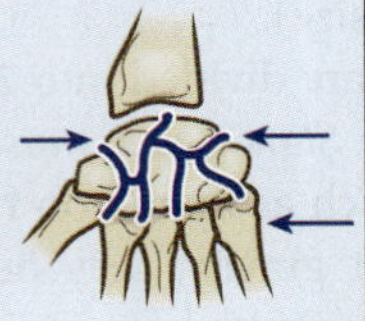

Fig. 66.4 Types of diarthrodial (synovial) joints.

Muscle

Types

The 3 types of muscle tissue are cardiac (striated, involuntary), smooth (nonstriated, involuntary), and skeletal (striated, voluntary) muscle. *Cardiac muscle* is found only in the heart. Its contractions are spontaneous. *Smooth muscle* is found in the walls of hollow structures, such as airways, arteries, gastrointestinal (GI) tract, urinary bladder, and uterus. Smooth muscle contraction is controlled by neuronal and hormonal influences. *Skeletal muscle* requires neuronal stimulation for contraction. It accounts for about half of a human's body weight. We focus on skeletal muscle in the following discussion.

Structure

The skeletal muscle is enclosed by the *epimysium*, a continuous layer of deep fascia. The epimysium helps muscles slide over nearby structures. Connective tissue surrounding and extending into the muscle can be subdivided into fiber bundles *(fasciculi)*. These bundles are covered by *perimysium* and an innermost connective tissue layer called the *endomysium* that surrounds each fiber (Fig. 66.5).[6]

The structural unit of skeletal muscle is the muscle cell or muscle fiber. It is highly specialized for contraction. Skeletal muscle fibers are long, multinucleated cylinders that contain many mitochondria to support their high metabolic activity. Muscle fibers are composed of myofibrils, which in turn are made up of protein contractile filaments. The *sarcomere* is the contractile unit of a myofibril. Each sarcomere consists of *myosin* (thick) filaments and *actin* (thin) filaments. The arrangement of the thin and thick filaments causes the characteristic banding of muscle seen under a microscope. Muscle contraction occurs as thick and thin filaments slide past each other, causing the sarcomeres to shorten.[6]

Contractions

Skeletal muscle contractions allow posture maintenance, body movement, and facial expressions. **Isometric contractions** increase the tension within a muscle but do not produce movement. **Isotonic contractions** shorten a muscle to produce movement. Most contractions are a combination of tension *(isometric)* and shortening *(isotonic)*. Repeated isometric and/or isotonic contractions provide stress to stimulate muscle growth.

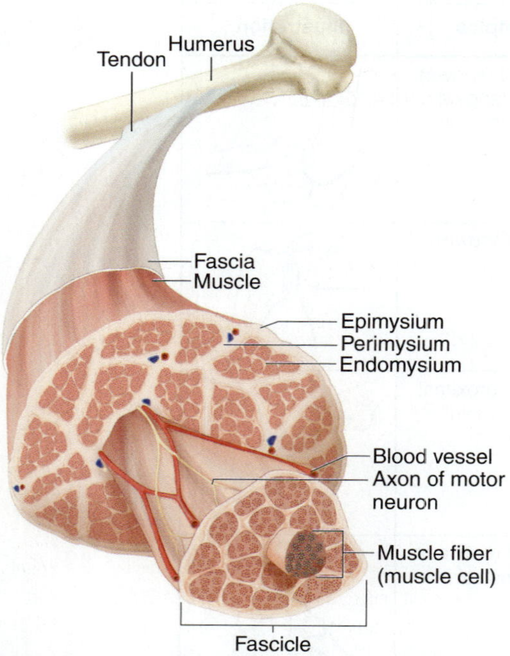

Fig. 66.5 Myofibrils of a skeletal muscle fiber and overall organization of skeletal muscle. (From Patton KT, Thibodeau GA, Douglas M: *Anatomy and physiology*, ed 9, St Louis, 2016, Mosby.)

Muscular *atrophy* (decrease in size) occurs with the absence of contractions. Atrophy can result from immobility or decreased neuronal stimulation. Increased muscular activity leads to *hypertrophy* (increase in size).

Skeletal muscle fibers are divided into 2 groups based on the type of activity they show. *Slow-twitch muscle fibers* support prolonged muscle activity, such as marathon running. Because they support the body against gravity, they help maintain posture. *Fast-twitch muscle fibers* are used for rapid muscle contraction needed for activities, such as blinking the eye, jumping, or sprinting. Fast-twitch fibers tire more quickly than slow-twitch fibers.

Neuromuscular Junction

Skeletal muscle fibers require a nerve impulse to contract. A nerve fiber and the skeletal muscle fibers it stimulates are called a *motor endplate*. The junction between the axon of the nerve cell and the adjacent muscle cell is called the *myoneural* or *neuromuscular junction* (Fig. 66.6).[7]

Presynaptic neurons release acetylcholine. It diffuses across the neuromuscular junction to bind with receptors on the motor endplate of the muscle. In response to this stimulation, the sarcoplasmic reticulum releases calcium into the cytoplasm. The presence of calcium triggers contraction in the myofibrils. When calcium is low, *tetany* (involuntary skeletal muscle contractions) can occur.

Energy Source

The direct energy source for muscle contractions is adenosine triphosphate (ATP). ATP is synthesized through cellular oxidative metabolism in the numerous mitochondria found close to the myofibrils. It is rapidly depleted through conversion to adenosine diphosphate (ADP) and must be rephosphorylated. Phosphocreatine provides a rapid source for the resynthesis

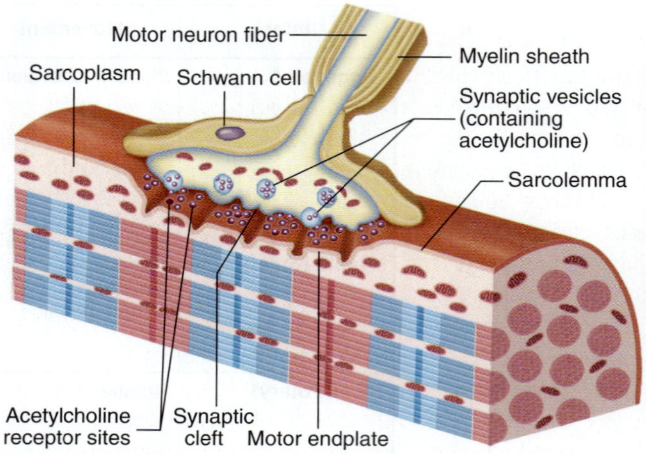

Fig. 66.6 Motor units of a muscle. (From McCance KL, Huether SE: *Pathophysiology: the biological basis for disease in adults and children*, ed 8, St. Louis, 2019, Elsevier.)

of ATP, but it is, in turn, converted to creatine. Glycolysis can serve as a source of ATP when the O_2 supply is inadequate for metabolic needs of the muscle tissue. In this process, 1 glucose molecule is broken down to 2 ATP molecules.

Ligaments and Tendons

Ligaments and tendons are composed of dense, fibrous connective tissue with bundles of closely packed collagen fibers arranged in the same plane for additional strength. *Tendons* attach muscles to bones as an extension of the muscle sheath that adheres to the periosteum. *Ligaments* connect bones to bones (e.g., tibia to femur at knee joint). They have a higher elastic content than tendons.[8] Ligaments provide stability while allowing controlled movement at joints.

Ligaments and tendons have a poor blood supply. This can make their repair after injury a slow process. For example, the stretching or tearing of ligaments that occurs with a sprain may require a long time to mend.

Fascia

Fascia refers to layers of connective tissue with intermeshed fibers that can withstand limited stretching. Superficial fascia lies right under the skin. Deep fascia is a dense, fibrous tissue that surrounds muscle bundles, nerves, and blood vessels. It encloses individual muscles, allowing them to act independently and glide over each other during contraction. Fascia provides strength to muscle tissues.

Bursae

Bursae are small sacs of connective tissue lined with synovial membrane and containing viscous synovial fluid. They are found at bony prominences or joints to relieve pressure and decrease friction between moving parts.[9] Bursae are found between the (1) patella and skin (prepatellar bursae), (2) olecranon process of the elbow and skin (olecranon bursae), (3) head of the humerus and acromion process of the scapula (subacromial bursae), and (4) greater trochanter of the proximal femur and skin (trochanteric bursae). *Bursitis* is an inflammation of a bursa sac. The inflammation may be acute or chronic.

Gerontologic Considerations: Effects of Aging on Musculoskeletal System

Many functional problems experienced by the older adult are related to changes in the musculoskeletal system. Although some changes begin in early adulthood, obvious signs of musculoskeletal impairment may not appear until later adult years. Changes may affect the older adult's ability to complete self-care tasks and pursue usual activities. Effects of musculoskeletal changes may range from mild discomfort and decreased ability to perform ADLs to severe, chronic pain and immobility.

The bone remodeling process changes in the aging adult. Increased bone resorption and decreased bone formation cause a loss of bone density. This contributes to osteopenia and osteoporosis (see Chapter 68). Muscle mass and strength decrease. Almost 30% of muscle mass is lost by age 70. A loss of motor neurons can cause problems with skeletal muscle movement. Tendons and ligaments become less flexible, making movement more rigid.

Osteoarthritis is more likely to affect joints in the aging adult (see Chapter 69). Metabolic bone diseases involve bone tissue deterioration (osteoporosis) and cartilage destruction (osteoarthritis). Carefully distinguish between expected changes and the effects of disease in the aging adult. Symptoms of disease can be treated in many cases, helping the older adult to return to a higher functional level. Table 66.1 outlines age-related changes in the musculoskeletal system and differences in assessment findings.

Assess the impact of age-related changes on functional status. Ask about changes in self-care habits and ability to be independent in the home environment. Functional limitations that are accepted by the older adult as a normal part of aging can often be addressed with preventive strategies.

The risk for falls increases due in part to loss of strength. Aging can also bring changes in the patient's balance, making the person unsteady. *Proprioception* (awareness of self in relation to the environment) may be altered. Identify any musculoskeletal changes that increase the patient's risk for falls. Discuss fall prevention strategies.

TABLE 66.1 GERONTOLOGIC ASSESSMENT DIFFERENCES

Musculoskeletal System

Changes	Differences in Assessment Findings
Bone	
• ↓ Bone density and strength • Slowed remodeling process	• Loss of height and deformity, such as dowager's hump (kyphosis), from vertebral compression and degeneration • Back pain, stiffness • Bony prominences more pronounced • ↑ Risk for osteopenia and osteoporosis
Joints	
• ↑ Risk for cartilage erosion that leads to direct contact between bone ends and overgrowth of bone around joint margins • Loss of water from discs between vertebrae, ↓ height of intervertebral spaces	• Joint stiffness, ↓ mobility, limited ROM, possible crepitation on movement • Pain with motion and/or weight bearing • Loss of height and shortening of trunk from disc compression. Posture change
Muscles	
• ↓ Number and diameter of muscle cells. Replacement of muscle cells by fibrous connective tissue • Loss of elasticity and deterioration of cartilage • ↓ Ability to store glycogen. ↓ Ability to release glycogen as quick energy during stress • ↓ Basal metabolic rate	• ↓ Muscle strength and mass • Abdominal protrusion • ↑ Rigidity in neck, shoulders, back, hips, and knees • ↓ Fine motor dexterity, ↓ agility • Slowed reaction times and reflexes from slowed conduction of nerve impulses along motor units • Earlier fatigue with activity

ASSESSMENT OF MUSCULOSKELETAL SYSTEM

Subjective Data

Important Health Information

Health history. The most common manifestations of musculoskeletal impairment include pain, weakness, deformity, limitation of movement, stiffness, and joint crepitation (crackling sound). Ask the patient about changes in sensation or in the size of a muscle.

Focus questions on symptoms of arthritic and connective tissue diseases (e.g., gout, psoriatic arthritis, systemic lupus erythematosus [SLE]), osteomalacia, osteomyelitis, and fungal infection of bones or joints. Ask the patient about sources of a secondary bacterial infection, such as ears, tonsils, teeth, sinuses, lungs, or genitourinary tract. These infections can enter the bones via the blood, resulting in osteomyelitis or joint destruction. Get a detailed account of the course and treatment of any of these problems.

Certain illnesses are known to affect the musculoskeletal system directly or indirectly. Ask the patient about problems such as tuberculosis, polio, diabetes, parathyroid problems,

Case Study

Patient Introduction

(© pixelhead-photo/iStock/Thinkstock.)

G.A. is a 58-year-old woman whose husband brought her to the emergency department (ED) this morning after she awoke with a sudden onset of excruciating pain in her left great toe. She denies any injury to her foot. She says she has never had this type of pain before.

Discussion Questions

1. What are the possible causes for G.A.'s acute pain in her great toe?
2. Is this condition stable or an emergency?
3. What type of assessment would be most appropriate for G.A.: comprehensive, focused, or emergency? What is the basis for your decision?
4. What assessment questions will you ask G.A.?

You will learn more about how to assess G.A.'s condition as you read this chapter.

Answers available at http://evolve.elsevier.com/Lewis/medsurg.

hemophilia, rickets, soft tissue infection, and neuromuscular disability.

Trauma to the musculoskeletal system is a common reason for seeking medical care. The patient who is a good historian can recount minor and major injuries of the musculoskeletal system. Record information chronologically and include:

- Mechanism and circumstances of the injury (e.g., twist, crush, stretch)
- Methods and duration of treatment
- Current status of the injury
- Need for assistive devices
- Interference with ADLs

Medications. Obtain a complete medication history. Ask about the use of skeletal muscle relaxants, opioids, nonsteroidal antiinflammatory drugs, corticosteroids, and calcium and vitamin D supplements. Review the use of drugs that can have detrimental effects on the musculoskeletal system. Some of these and their potential side effects include antiseizure drugs (osteomalacia), phenothiazines (gait changes), corticosteroids (avascular necrosis, decreased bone and muscle mass), and potassium-depleting diuretics (muscle cramps and weakness). Ask postmenopausal women about the use of hormone therapy.

Surgery or other treatments. Ask about any hospitalizations due to a musculoskeletal problem. Document the reason for hospitalization; the date and duration; and the treatment, including ongoing rehabilitation. Record details of emergency treatment for musculoskeletal injuries. Get specific information about any surgeries, postoperative course, and complications. Ask the patient about total knee or total hip replacements. If the patient had a period of prolonged immobilization, consider the possibility of disuse osteoporosis and muscle atrophy.

Functional Health Patterns

Past or developing musculoskeletal problems can affect the patient's overall health. Use functional health patterns to organize assessment data. Table 66.2 outlines specific questions to ask in relation to functional health patterns.

Health perception–health management pattern. Ask about health practices related to the musculoskeletal system. This includes maintaining normal body weight, avoiding excessive stress on muscles and joints, and using proper body mechanics when lifting objects. Ask the patient about tetanus, pertussis, and polio immunizations.

Safety practices can affect the predisposition for certain injuries and illnesses. Ask about safety practices related to the work environment, home life, recreation, and exercise. For example, if the patient works with computers, do they use ergonomic adaptations that decrease the risk for carpal tunnel syndrome or low back pain? Identifying problems in this area will direct your patient teaching.

Is there a family history of rheumatoid arthritis, SLE, ankylosing spondylitis, osteoarthritis, gout, osteoporosis, and scoliosis (Box 66.1)? A patient may have a genetic predisposition to these or other musculoskeletal problems.

Nutritional-metabolic pattern. The patient's description of a typical day's diet gives clues to areas of nutrition concern that can affect the musculoskeletal system. Adequate intake of vitamins C and D, calcium, and protein is essential for a healthy musculoskeletal system. Nutrition problems can contribute to osteomalacia and osteoporosis. Maintaining normal weight is an important goal. Obesity places added stress on weight-bearing joints, such as the knees, hips, and spine. This increases the risk for cartilage deterioration and ligament instability.

Elimination pattern. Questions about the patient's mobility may reveal problems with ambulating to the toilet. Ask the patient if an assistive device, such as an elevated toilet seat or a grab bar, is needed to manage toileting. Decreased mobility can lead to constipation. Musculoskeletal problems can contribute to bowel or bladder incontinence when ambulation is a problem.

Activity-exercise pattern. Many musculoskeletal problems can affect the patient's activity-exercise pattern. Get a detailed account of the type, duration, and frequency of exercise and recreational activities. What are their warm-up activities? Compare daily, weekend, and seasonal patterns because occasional exercise can be more of a problem than regular exercise. Ask the patient about clumsiness or limitations in movement, pain, weakness, crepitus, or any change in bones or joints that interferes with daily activities.

Occupational activity can affect the musculoskeletal system. For example, a desk job can negatively affect muscle flexibility and strength. Jobs that require heavy lifting or pushing can lead to damage of joints and supporting structures. Ask the patient about work-related musculoskeletal injuries, including treatment and time lost from work.

Sleep-rest pattern. Discomfort from a musculoskeletal problem can interfere with sleep and lead to fatigue. Ask the patient about any changes in sleep patterns. If the patient describes poor sleep because of a musculoskeletal problem, ask about the type of bedding and pillows used, bedtime routine, sleeping partner, and sleeping positions.

Cognitive-perceptual pattern. Fully discuss any reports of pain reported from a musculoskeletal problem. To give a baseline for later reassessment, ask the patient to describe the intensity of the pain on a numeric scale from 0 to 10 (0 = no pain, 10 = most severe pain imaginable). Reassessments over time help to determine the effectiveness of any treatment plan. Ask the patient about measures used to manage pain. Are there any other problems, such as joint swelling or muscle weakness? If so, are there any adjustments that help with the problem?

Self-perception–self-concept pattern. Many chronic musculoskeletal problems lead to deformities and a reduction in activities. This can have a serious negative impact on the patient's body image and sense of personal worth. Assess the patient's feelings about these changes and any effect on interactions with family and friends.

Role-relationship pattern. Impaired mobility and chronic pain from musculoskeletal problems can negatively affect the patient's ability to perform in roles of spouse, parent, and/or employee. The ability to pursue and maintain meaningful social and personal relationships can be affected by musculoskeletal

TABLE 66.2 HEALTH HISTORY

Musculoskeletal System

Health Perception–Health Management Pattern

- Describe your usual daily activities.
- Do you have any problems performing these activities?[a] Describe what you do if you have trouble dressing, preparing meals and feeding yourself, performing basic hygiene, writing, using the phone, or maintaining your home.
- Do you have to lift heavy objects? Does your work or exercise involve repetitive motion or joint stress? Describe any special equipment you use or wear when you work or exercise that helps protect you from injury.
- Do you take any drugs or herbal products to manage your musculoskeletal problem? If so, what are their names and what are the expected effects?

Nutritional-Metabolic Pattern

- What is your usual daily intake of food and snacks?
- Do you have problems preparing your food?
- What diet supplements do you take? Do you take calcium or vitamin D supplements?
- What is your weight? Describe any recent weight loss or gain.

Elimination Pattern

- Does your musculoskeletal problem make it hard for you to reach the toilet in time?[a]
- Do you need any assistive devices or equipment to manage toileting?[a]
- Do you have constipation related to decreased mobility or drugs taken for your musculoskeletal problem?[a]

Activity-Exercise Pattern

- Do you need help in completing your usual daily activities because of a musculoskeletal problem?[a]
- Describe your usual exercise pattern. Do you have musculoskeletal symptoms before, during, or after exercising?[a]
- Are you able to move all your joints comfortably through full range of motion?
- Do you use any prosthetic or orthotic devices?[a]

Sleep-Rest Pattern

- Do you have any problems sleeping because of a musculoskeletal problem?[a]
- Do you need frequent position changes at night?[a]
- Do you wake up at night because of musculoskeletal pain?[a]
- Describe any practices you use to help you sleep at night.[a]

Cognitive-Perceptual Pattern

- Describe any musculoskeletal pain you have. How do you manage your pain? Ask about adjunctive therapies, such as heat and cold, or complementary and alternative therapies, such as acupuncture.

Self-Perception–Self-Concept Pattern

- Have changes in your musculoskeletal system (posture, walking, muscle strength) and decreased ability to do certain things affected how you feel about yourself?[a]
- Have these changes affected your lifestyle?[a]

Role-Relationship Pattern

- Do you live alone?
- Describe how family, friends, or others help you with your musculoskeletal problem.
- Describe the effect of your musculoskeletal problem on your work and your social relationships.

Sexuality-Reproductive Pattern

- Describe any sexual concerns related to your musculoskeletal problem.

Coping–Stress Tolerance Pattern

- Describe how you deal with problems such as pain, weakness, or immobility that have resulted from your musculoskeletal problem.

Value-Belief Pattern

- Describe any cultural practices or religious beliefs that may influence the treatment of your musculoskeletal problem.

[a]If yes, describe.

BOX 66.1 GENETIC RISK ALERT

Autoimmune Diseases

- Many autoimmune diseases of the musculoskeletal system have a genetic basis involving human leukocyte antigens (HLAs).
- These diseases include ankylosing spondylitis, rheumatoid arthritis, and SLE.

Osteoporosis

- Genetic factors contribute to osteoporosis by influencing bone mineral density and bone size, quality, and turnover.

Osteoarthritis, Gout, and Scoliosis

- A genetic predisposition is a contributing risk factor in all these diseases.

Muscular Dystrophy

- The most common types of muscular dystrophy are X-linked recessive disorders.

problems. Carefully ask the patient about role performance and relationships.

If the patient lives alone, any musculoskeletal problem and rehabilitation may make it hard or impossible to continue to do so. Assess how much help is available from family, friends, and other caregivers. Find out if other resources are needed, such as physical therapy and home health care.

Sexuality-reproductive pattern. Ask women about their menstrual history. Premenopausal amenorrhea can contribute to osteoporosis. Pain from musculoskeletal problems can affect the ability to obtain sexual satisfaction. Explore this area in a sensitive way. Help the patient feel comfortable discussing any sexual problems related to pain, movement, and positioning. More information on obtaining data in this area is discussed in Chapter 55.

Coping–stress tolerance pattern. Mobility limitations and pain are serious potential stressors that challenge the patient's coping resources. Recognize the potential for difficulty coping in the patient and family or significant other. Explore if a musculoskeletal problem is causing difficulties in coping and adjusting.

Value-belief pattern. Ask about cultural or religious beliefs that may influence acceptance of treatment for the musculoskeletal problem. These may include recommendations for diet, exercise, medication, and lifestyle changes.

Case Study

Subjective Data

(© pixelhead-photo/iStock/Thinkstock.)

A focused subjective assessment of G.A. revealed the following:

Medical History: Hypertension for 6 years. Type 2 diabetes for 11 years, 40-pack-year smoking history.

Medications: Metformin 500 mg PO bid; hydrochlorothiazide 50 mg PO bid.

Health Perception–Health Management: Currently smokes 1 pack of cigarettes per day. Is trying to quit but finding it difficult. Drinks alcohol at night.

Nutritional-Metabolic: G.A. is 5 ft, 2 in tall and weighs 160 lb (BMI 29.3 kg/m^2). Does not take any nutrition supplements. Avoids milk and other dairy products because they make her "gassy."

Activity-Exercise: Minimally active; does not exercise. Able to perform ADLs without assistance. Denies any history of musculoskeletal problems.

Cognitive-Perceptual: Rates toe pain at 8 on a scale of 0–10. Describes sharp, burning pain that increases in intensity with any movement.

Coping–Stress Tolerance: Is asking for pain medicine "as strong as you can give me."

Discussion Questions

1. What subjective assessment findings concern you most?
2. Is this an appropriate time to talk with G.A. about her weight?
3. Based on these subjective findings, what should be included in the physical assessment?

You will learn more about the physical assessment of the musculoskeletal system in the next section.

Answers available at http://evolve.elsevier.com/Lewis/medsurg

TABLE 66.3 Synovial Joint Movements

Movement	Description
Abduction	Movement of part away from midline of body
Adduction	Movement of part toward midline of body
Circumduction	Circular motion of a body part from a combination of flexion, abduction, extension, and adduction
Dorsiflexion	Flexion of the ankle and toes toward the shin
Eversion	Turning of sole outward away from midline of body
Extension	Straightening of joint that ↑ angle between 2 bones
External rotation	Movement along longitudinal axis away from midline of body
Flexion	Bending of joint from muscle contraction that causes ↓ angle between 2 bones
Hyperextension	Extension in which angle exceeds 180 degrees
Internal rotation	Movement along longitudinal axis toward midline of body
Inversion	Turning of sole inward toward midline of body
Opposition	Moving the first and fifth metacarpals anteriorly from a flattened palm ("cupping position"); makes it possible to hold objects between the thumb and fingers
Plantar flexion	Flexion of the ankle and toes toward the plantar surface of the foot ("toes pointed")
Pronation	Turning of palm downward
Supination	Turning of palm upward

Objective Data

Physical Assessment

The basic musculoskeletal physical assessment involves inspection, palpation, neurovascular assessment, and range of motion, strength, and reflex testing. Other special tests can be used to assess for specific conditions. Conduct a general overview. While obtaining a careful health history, choose areas to concentrate on during the local assessment. Take specific measurements as indicated by the local assessment.

Inspection. Perform a systematic inspection. Start at the head and neck then moving to the upper extremities, lower extremities, and trunk. The regular use of a systematic approach is important to avoid missing any important aspects. Inspect the skin for general color, scars, or other overt signs of previous injury or surgery. Certain skin lesions require further assessment because they can indicate another problem. For example, butterfly rash over the cheeks and nose is a sign of SLE.

Note the patient's general posture and body build, muscle size and symmetry, and symmetry and contour of joints. Observe for any swelling, deformity, nodules or masses, and discrepancies in limb length or muscle size. Use the patient's opposite body part for comparison when you suspect an abnormality.

If the patient can move independently, assess posture and gait by watching the patient walk, stand, and sit. Musculoskeletal and neurologic problems can result in abnormal gait patterns.

Palpation. Palpation usually proceeds head to toe. Examine the neck, shoulders, elbows, wrists, hands, back, hips, knees, ankles, and feet. Warm your hands to prevent muscle spasm, which can interfere with identifying essential landmarks or soft tissue structures. Carefully palpate any specific areas of concern because of a subjective report or abnormal appearance on inspection.

Both superficial and deep palpation are usually done consecutively. Consider the underlying anatomy structures and landmarks you are palpating. Palpate muscles and joints to assess temperature, tenderness, swelling, and crepitation. Establish the relationship of adjacent structures. Note the general contour, local landmarks, and any abnormal prominences. Note the specific anatomic location of any abnormal findings.

Motion. When assessing the patient's joint mobility, evaluate active and passive **range of motion (ROM)**. ROM is the full movement potential of a joint. Common movements that occur at the synovial joints, including *abduction, adduction, flexion,* and *extension,* are described in Table 66.3.

Measurements should be similar for active and passive maneuvers. *Active ROM* means the patient takes their own joints through all movements without assistance. *Passive ROM* occurs when someone else moves the patient's joints without their assistance through the full ROM. Be careful in performing passive ROM because of the risk for injury to underlying structures. If pain or resistance occurs, stop at once.

If you note deficits in active or passive ROM, assess functional ROM to see if joint changes are affecting the ability to perform ADLs. Ask the patient if activities, such as eating, grooming, dressing, and bathing, require help or cannot be done at all.

We use a goniometer to accurately assess ROM. It measures the angle of the joint (Fig. 66.7). We do not usually measure specific degrees of ROM of all joints. If a specific musculoskeletal

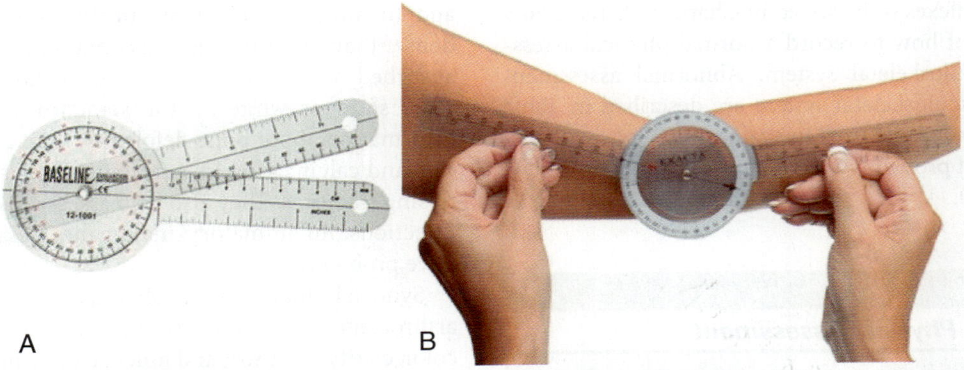

Fig. 66.7 (A) Goniometer. (B) Measurement of joint ROM using a goniometer. (From LaSala TT, Run-Kowzun T, Figueroa M: The effect of a Hatha yoga practice on hamstring flexibility, *J Bodywork Move Therap* 28:439-449, 2021.)

TABLE 66.4 Muscle Strength Scale

0/5	No detection of muscular contraction
1/5	Barely detectable flicker or trace of contraction with observation or palpation
2/5	Active movement of body part with elimination of gravity
3/5	Active movement against gravity only and not against resistance
4/5	Active movement against gravity and some resistance
5/5	Active movement against full resistance without evident fatigue (normal muscle strength)

problem has been identified, measure ROM of the affected joint. A less exact but valuable assessment method is simply to compare the ROM of 1 extremity with that on the opposite side.

Muscle-strength testing. Grade the strength of individual muscles or groups of muscles during contraction on a 5-point scale (Table 66.4). Grade normal muscle strength with full resistance to opposition as a 5/5 bilaterally. To test resistance to opposition, have the patient apply resistance as you exert a force. For example, have the patient try to extend the elbow while you try to flex it. Compare muscle strength with the strength of the opposite extremity. Note any subtle variations in muscle strength when comparing the patient's dominant and nondominant sides. Variations in strength also exist when comparing people.

Measurement. When you note limb length discrepancies or subjective problems, measure limb length and circumferential muscle mass. For example, if you observe an altered gait, measure leg length between the anterosuperior iliac crest and the bottom of the medial malleolus. Then compare it with the similar measurement of the opposite extremity. Measure muscle mass circumferentially at the largest area of the muscle. When recording measurements, record the exact location at which the measurements were obtained (e.g., left quadriceps muscle measured 15 cm above the patella). This tells the next examiner the exact area to measure and ensures consistency with reassessment.

Other. Note the use of an assistive device such as a walker or cane. Assess the patient for proper fit while reviewing the safe and correct technique for using a device. Regularly review with the patient the use of the assistive device to be sure it is still appropriate and safe. Ask the patient if they use the device regularly. If not, assess for reasons for inconsistent use.

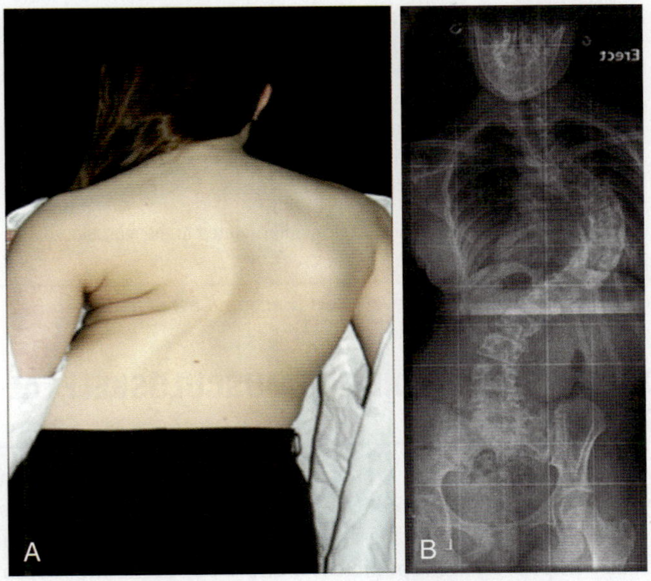

Fig. 66.8 (A) Thoracic scoliosis. (B) X-ray of same patient showing scoliosis greater than 90 degrees. (From Hawary R, Chukwunyerenwa C: Update on evaluation and treatment of scoliosis, *Pediatr Clin North Am* 61:1223, 2014.)

Scoliosis is a lateral S-shaped curvature of the thoracic and lumbar spine. Unequal shoulder and scapula height is usually noted when the patient is observed from the back (Fig. 66.8). Ask the patient to place the hands together above the head as if diving into a swimming pool and slowly bend forward at the waist, allowing assessment of thoracic rib prominence or paravertebral muscle prominence in the lumbar spine. Advanced scoliosis can impair lung and heart function.

The *straight-leg-raising test* is done on the patient with sciatica or leg pain. With the patient supine, passively raise the leg 60 degrees or less. The test is positive if the patient reports pain along the distribution of the sciatic nerve. A positive test shows nerve root irritation from intervertebral disc prolapse and herniation, especially at level L4–5 or L5–S1.

Assessment of reflexes is discussed in Chapter 60. Table 66.5 shows an example of how to record a normal physical assessment of the musculoskeletal system. Abnormal assessment findings of the musculoskeletal system are described in Table 66.6. A *focused assessment* is used to evaluate previously identified musculoskeletal problems and to monitor for signs of new problems (Box 66.2).

Case Study

Objective Data: Physical Assessment

(© pixelhead-photo/iStock/Thinkstock.)

A focused assessment of G.A. reveals the following:

BP 128/94, heart rate 88, respiratory rate 26, temp 96.8°F, O_2 saturation 98%. Alert and oriented × 3. Lungs are clear bilaterally. Left great toe is red and swollen. No open wounds. Tremendous pain on palpation and with any movement of the left great toe. +1 Pedal pulses bilaterally.

Discussion Questions

1. What physical assessment findings concern you most?
2. Based on results of the subjective and physical assessment, what diagnostic studies might you expect to be ordered for G.A.?

You will learn more about diagnostic studies related to the musculoskeletal system in the next section.

Answers available at http://evolve.elsevier.com/Lewis/medsurg.

DIAGNOSTIC STUDIES OF MUSCULOSKELETAL SYSTEM

Many diagnostic studies are used to assess the musculoskeletal system. Tables 66.7 and 66.8 present the most common studies.

Imaging, including x-rays, MRI, and bone scans, has greatly improved orthopedic care. The **x-ray** is the most common diagnostic study used to assess musculoskeletal problems and to monitor treatment effectiveness. Because bones are denser than other tissues and contain calcium, most x-rays are absorbed by the bone tissue and do not penetrate it. Dense areas show as white on the standard x-ray. X-rays provide information about bone deformity, joint congruity, bone density, and calcification in soft tissue. X-rays are useful for diagnosing fractures. They also help assess genetic, developmental, infectious, inflammatory, malignant, metabolic, and degenerative problems.

Synovial fluid can be obtained for analysis through an arthrocentesis (Table 66.9). The fluid is assessed for volume, color, clarity, viscosity, and mucin clot formation. Normal synovial fluid is transparent and colorless or straw colored. It should be scant in amount and of low viscosity. Fluid from an infected joint may be purulent and thick or gray and thin. In gout, the fluid may be whitish yellow. Blood may be aspirated if there is hemarthrosis due to injury or a bleeding disorder.

The mucin clot test indicates the character of the protein portion of the synovial fluid. Normally a white, ropelike mucin clot is formed. In the presence of inflammation, the clot fragments easily. The fluid is examined grossly for floating fat globules, which indicate bone injury. In septic arthritis, protein content is increased, and glucose is considerably decreased. Presence of uric acid crystals suggests a diagnosis of gout. A Gram stain and culture also may be done to assess for the presence and type of infection.

TABLE 66.5 Normal Physical Assessment of the Musculoskeletal System

- Ordinary spinal curvatures
- No muscle atrophy or asymmetry
- No joint swelling, deformity, or crepitation
- No tenderness on palpation of spine, joints, or muscles
- Full ROM of all joints without pain or laxity
- Muscle strength of 5/5

TABLE 66.6 ASSESSMENT ABNORMALITIES
Musculoskeletal System

Finding	Description	Possible Cause and Significance
Achilles' tendonitis	Pain in ankle and posterior calf, initially when running or walking. Can progress to pain at rest.	Stress on Achilles tendon over time causing inflammation.
Ankylosis	Stiffness and fixation of a joint.	Chronic joint inflammation and destruction (e.g., rheumatoid arthritis).
Antalgic gait	Shortened stride with minimal weight bearing on the affected side, resulting in a limp.	Pain or discomfort in the lower extremity on weight bearing. Can be due to trauma or other problems.
Ataxic gait	Staggering, uncoordinated gait often with sway.	Neurogenic problems (e.g., spinal cord lesion).
Atrophy	↓ Size and strength of muscle leading to ↓ function and tone.	Muscle denervation, contracture, prolonged disuse from immobilization.
Boutonnière deformity	Finger abnormality, flexion of proximal interphalangeal (PIP) joint and hyperextension of the distal interphalangeal (DIP) joint of the fingers (see Fig. 69.4B).	Typical deformity of rheumatoid and psoriatic arthritis. Caused by disruption of extensor tendons over the fingers.
Contracture	Resistance of movement of muscle or joint due to fibrosis of supporting soft tissues.	Shortening of muscle or ligaments, tightness of soft tissue, incorrect positioning of immobilized extremity.

TABLE 66.6 ASSESSMENT ABNORMALITIES—cont'd

Musculoskeletal System

Finding	Description	Possible Cause and Significance
Crepitation (crepitus)	Frequent, audible crackling sound with palpable grating that accompanies movement.	Fracture, dislocation, temporomandibular joint dysfunction, osteoarthritis.
Dislocation	Separation of 2 bones from their normal position within a joint.	Trauma, surrounding soft tissue problem.
Festinating gait	While walking, neck, trunk, and knees flex and the body is rigid. Delayed start with short, quick, shuffling steps. Speed may ↑ as if patient is unable to stop (festination).	Neurogenic problems (e.g., Parkinson disease).
Ganglion cyst	Small fluid-filled mass over a tendon sheath or joint, usually on dorsal surface of wrist or foot.	Inflammation of tissues around a joint, which can increase in size or disappear.
Kyphosis (dowager's hump)	Exaggerated thoracic curvature.	Poor posture, tuberculosis, arthritis, osteoporosis, growth disturbance of vertebral epiphyses, vertebral fractures.
Lateral epicondylitis (tennis elbow)	Dull ache along outer aspect of elbow, worsens with twisting and grasping motions.	Injury, inflammation, and/or partial tearing of tendon at its insertion on epicondyle.
Limited range of motion (ROM)	Joint does not achieve expected degrees of motion.	Injury, inflammation, contracture.
Lordosis (swayback)	Exaggerated lumbar curvature.	Other spinal deformities, muscular dystrophy, obesity, flexion contracture of hip, congenital dislocation of hip.
Muscle spasticity	↑ Muscle tone (rigidity) with sustained muscle contractions (spasms); stiffness or tightness may interfere with gait, movement, speech.	Neuromuscular problems, such as multiple sclerosis, cerebral palsy.
Myalgia	General muscle tenderness and pain.	Chronic pain syndromes (e.g., fibromyalgia). Overuse, injury, or strain. May result from statin therapy.
Paresthesia	Numbness and tingling, often described as a "pins and needles" sensation.	Compromised sensory nerves, often due to edema in a closed space (e.g., cast, bulky dressing). Spinal stenosis.
Pes planus (flatfoot)	Abnormal flatness of the sole and arch of the foot.	Hereditary, muscle paralysis, mild cerebral palsy, early muscular dystrophy, injury to posterior tibial tendon.
Plantar fasciitis	Burning, sharp pain on heel and sole of foot. Worse in the morning with first step out of bed.	Chronic degenerative/reparative cycle resulting in inflammation.
Scoliosis	Asymmetric elevation of shoulders, scapulae, and iliac crests with lateral spine curvature (Fig. 66.8).	Idiopathic, congenital or neuromuscular condition, fracture or dislocation, osteomalacia.
Short-leg gait	A limp, unless corrective footwear used.	Leg length discrepancy of 1 in or more, often structural origin (e.g., arthritis, fracture).
Spastic gait	Short steps with dragging of foot. Jerky, uncoordinated, cross-knee (scissor) movement.	Neurogenic problems (e.g., cerebral palsy, hemiplegia).
Steppage gait	↑ Hip and knee flexion to clear the foot from the floor. Foot drop is evident, foot slaps down and along walking surface.	Neurogenic problems (e.g., peroneal nerve injury, paralyzed dorsiflexor muscles).
Subluxation	Partial dislocation of joint.	Instability of joint capsule and supporting ligaments (e.g., trauma, arthritis).
Swan neck deformity	Hyperextension of the PIP joint with flexion of the metacarpophalangeal (MCP) and DIP joints of the fingers (see Fig. 69.4D).	Typical deformity of rheumatoid and psoriatic arthritis. Caused by contracture of muscles and tendons.
Swelling	Enlargement, often of a joint due to fluid collection. Usually leads to pain, stiffness.	Trauma, inflammation.
Tenosynovitis	Superficial swelling, pain, and tenderness along a tendon sheath.	Inflammation that often occurs with infection, injury, or overuse.
Torticollis (wryneck)	Neck is rotated and laterally bent in unusual position to one side.	Prolonged contraction of neck muscles (congenital or acquired).
Ulnar deviation (ulnar drift)	Fingers drift to ulnar side of forearm (see Fig. 69.4A).	Typical deformity of rheumatoid arthritis due to tendon contracture.
Valgum deformity (knock-knees)	When knees are together and there is <1 in (2.5 cm) between the medial malleoli.	Poliomyelitis, congenital deformity, arthritis.
Varum deformity (bowlegs)	When knees are apart and the medial malleoli are together, a space of >1 in (2.5 cm) exists.	Arthritis, congenital deformity.

BOX 66.2 FOCUSED ASSESSMENT

Musculoskeletal System

Use this checklist to be sure key assessment steps have been done.

Subjective

Ask the patient about any of the following and note responses.

Joint pain or stiffness	Y	N
Muscle weakness	Y	N
Bone pain	Y	N

Objective: Diagnostic

Check the results of the following diagnostic studies.

X-ray	✓
MRI or CT scan	✓
Bone scan	✓
Ultrasound	✓

Objective: Physical Assessment

Inspect and Palpate

Spine and extremities (compare sides) for alignment, contour, symmetry, size, gross deformities	✓
Joints for ROM, tenderness or pain, heat, crepitus, swelling	✓
Muscles (compare sides) for size, symmetry, tone, tenderness, or pain	✓
Bones for tenderness or pain	✓

TABLE 66.7 Serology Studies

Musculoskeletal System

Test	Reference Intervals	Description and Purpose
Aldolase	22–59 mU/L	Monitoring of muscular dystrophy, dermatomyositis.
Alkaline phosphatase	30–120 U/L (0.5–2.0 μkat/L)	Enzyme made by osteoblasts, needed for mineralization of organic bone matrix. ↑ in healing fractures, bone cancers, osteoporosis, osteomalacia, Paget disease.
Anticyclic citrullinated (anti-CCP)	Negative or <20.0 U	Assesses presence of CCP antibodies. More specific for rheumatoid arthritis than rheumatoid factor. Positive result indicates high likelihood of RA.
Anti-DNA antibody	<5 IU/mL	Detects serum antibodies that react with DNA. Most specific test for SLE.
Antinuclear antibody (ANA)	Negative at 1:40 dilution	Assesses presence of antibodies capable of destroying nucleus of tissue cells. Positive in 95% of patients with SLE. May be positive with scleroderma, rheumatoid arthritis, small number of normal persons.
Calcium	9.0–10.5 mg/dL (2.25–2.62 mmol/L)	Bone is primary organ for calcium storage. Calcium provides bone with rigid structure. ↓ in osteomalacia, kidney disease, hypoparathyroidism. ↑ in hyperparathyroidism, some bone tumors.
C-reactive protein (CRP)	<1.0 mg/dL	Used to diagnose inflammatory diseases, infections, active widespread cancer. Synthesized by liver. Present in large amounts in serum 18–24 h after onset of tissue damage.
Creatine kinase (CK)	20–200 U/L	Highest concentration found in skeletal muscle. ↑ in muscular dystrophy, polymyositis, traumatic injuries.
Human leukocyte antigen (HLA)–B27	Negative	Antigen often present in autoimmune disorders, such as ankylosing spondylitis, rheumatoid arthritis.
Potassium	3.5–5.0 mEq/L (3.5–5.0 mmol/L)	Released into serum with cell destruction. ↑ with muscle trauma.
Phosphorus	3.0–4.5 mg/dL (0.97–1.45 mmol/L)	Amount present is indirectly related to calcium metabolism. ↓ Level found in osteomalacia. ↑ in chronic kidney disease, healing fractures, osteolytic metastatic tumor.
Rheumatoid factor (RF)	Negative or titer <1:17	Presence of autoantibody (rheumatoid factor) in serum. Not specific for rheumatoid arthritis. Seen in other connective tissue diseases and small number of normal persons.

TABLE 66.8 Diagnostic Studies

Musculoskeletal System

Study	Description and Purpose	Nursing Responsibilities
Basic x-ray	Evaluates structural or functional changes of bones and joints. Can give a general impression of bone density. In anteroposterior view, x-ray beam passes from front to back, allowing 1-dimensional view. Lateral position provides 2-dimensional view.	*Before:* Remove any radiopaque objects that can interfere with results. Explain procedure to patient. *During:* Avoid excess exposure of patient and self.
Bone scan	Injection of radioisotope (usually technetium [Tc]-99 m) that is taken up by bone. Uniform uptake of isotope is normal. ↑ Uptake seen in osteomyelitis, primary and metastatic cancer of bone, certain fractures. ↓ Uptake seen in areas of avascular necrosis.	*Before:* Explain that radioisotope is given 2 hr before procedure. Have patient void before scan. Tell patient that no harm will result from isotopes. *During:* Patient must lie completely still during scan. *After:* Increase fluids after scan.

TABLE 66.8 Diagnostic Studies—cont'd

Musculoskeletal System

Study	Description and Purpose	Nursing Responsibilities
Computed tomography (CT) scan	X-ray beam used with a computer to provide a 3D picture. Used to identify soft tissue abnormalities, bony abnormalities, and various types of musculoskeletal trauma.	*Before:* Evaluate renal function before contrast medium used. Assess if patient is allergic to shellfish since the contrast is iodine based. Patient may need to be NPO 4 h prior to study. If the patient is taking metformin, hold it the day of the test to prevent hypoglycemia or lactic acidosis. *During:* Warn patient that contrast injection may cause a feeling of being warm and flushed. Patient must lie completely still during scan. *After:* Encourage patient to drink fluids to avoid renal problems with any contrast.
Discogram	X-ray of cervical or lumbar intervertebral disc done after injecting contrast media into nucleus pulposus. Permits visualization of intervertebral disc abnormalities.	*Before:* Assess patient for allergy to contrast medium. Explain procedure. *After:* May have mild back pain for 1–2 days. Use as-needed analgesics.
Dual energy x-ray absorptiometry (DEXA)	Measures bone mineral density of spine, femur, forearm, total body. Assesses bone density with minimal radiation exposure. Used to diagnose metabolic bone disease (e.g., osteoporosis), monitor changes in bone density with treatment.	*Before:* Remove any radiopaque objects that can interfere with results. Explain procedure to patient.
Electromyogram (EMG)	Evaluates electrical potential of skeletal muscle contraction. Small-gauge needles are inserted into certain muscles. Needle probes are attached to leads that send information to EMG machine. Recordings of muscle electrical activity are traced on audio transmitter, oscilloscope, and recording paper. Provides information about lower motor neuron dysfunction and primary muscle disease.	*Before:* Explain procedure. Tell patient needle insertion will cause discomfort. Some HCPs restrict stimulants (e.g., caffeine) 2–3 hr prior. *After:* Assess needle sites for hematoma or inflammation. Use as-needed analgesics.
MRI	Radio waves and magnetic field used to view soft tissue. Used to diagnose avascular necrosis, disc disease, tumors, osteomyelitis, ligament tears, cartilage tears. Patient placed inside scanning chamber. Gadolinium may be injected IV to enhance visualization of structures.	*Before:* Oral and/or IV contrast injection may be used. Check for pregnancy, allergies, and renal function before test. Have patient remove all metal objects. Ask about any history of surgical insertion of staples, plates, dental bridges, or other metal appliances. Remove metallic foil patches. Patient may need to be fasting. Assess for claustrophobia and the need for antianxiety medication. *During:* Patient must lie completely still during test.
Myelogram with or without CT	Injection of a radiographic contrast medium into sac around nerve roots. CT scan may follow to show how bone is affecting the nerve roots. Sensitive test for nerve impingement, can detect subtle lesions and injuries.	*Before:* Give sedative as ordered. Have patient empty bladder. Tell patient that test is done with patient on tilting table that is moved during test. *After:* Keep patient flat for 1–2 hr after to prevent spinal headache. Encourage fluids. Monitor neurologic signs and VS. Headache, nausea, and vomiting may occur after.
Somatosensory evoked potential (SSEP)	Evaluates evoked potential of muscle contractions. Electrodes are placed on skin and provide recordings of electrical activity of muscle. Used to identify subtle dysfunction of lower motor neuron and primary muscle disease. Measures nerve conduction along pathways not accessible by EMG. Transcutaneous or percutaneous electrodes applied to the skin help identify neuropathy and myopathy. Used during spinal surgery for scoliosis to detect neurologic compromise when patient is under anesthesia.	*Before:* Tell patient that procedure is like an EMG but does not involve needles. Electrodes are applied to the skin.
Thermography	Uses infrared detector to measure degree of heat radiating from skin surface. Assess cause of inflamed joint and determine response to antiinflammatory drug therapy. Can evaluate skin temperature with complex regional pain syndrome (CRPS).	*Before:* Tell patient that procedure is painless and noninvasive.
Quantitative ultrasound (QUS)	Evaluates bone mineral density, elasticity, and strength of bone using ultrasound rather than radiation. Used to assess heel. Used in infants to help diagnosis congenital dysplasia of the hip (CDH).	*Before:* Tell patient that procedure is painless and noninvasive.

TABLE 66.9 Interventional Studies

Musculoskeletal System

Study	Description and Purpose	Nursing Responsibilities
Arthrocentesis	Incision or puncture of joint capsule to obtain samples of synovial fluid or to remove excess fluid. Local anesthesia and aseptic preparation are used before needle is inserted into joint and fluid aspirated. Used to diagnose joint inflammation, infection, meniscal tears, and subtle fractures.	*Before:* Explain procedure to patient. HCP may have patient be NPO prior. Usually done at bedside or in examination room. *After:* Send samples of synovial fluid to laboratory for examination (if indicated). Apply compression dressing and ice to decrease pain and swelling. Observe for leakage of blood or fluid on dressing. Assess the joint for any pain, fever, or swelling. Review activity restrictions.
Arthroscopy	Insertion of arthroscope into joint to see interior of joint cavity. Can be used for surgery (removal of loose bodies, biopsy); repair of joint structures; diagnosis of problems with meniscus, articular cartilage, ligaments, joint capsule. Structures that can be seen through an arthroscope include knee, shoulder, elbow, wrist, jaw, hip, ankle (Fig. 66.9).	*Before:* Explain procedure to the patient. Can be done in outpatient setting. Local or general anesthesia may be used. HCP may have patient be NPO prior. *After:* Cover wound with sterile dressing. Apply ice to decrease pain and swelling. Observe for bleeding. Assess the joint for any pain, weakness, or swelling. Review activity restrictions.

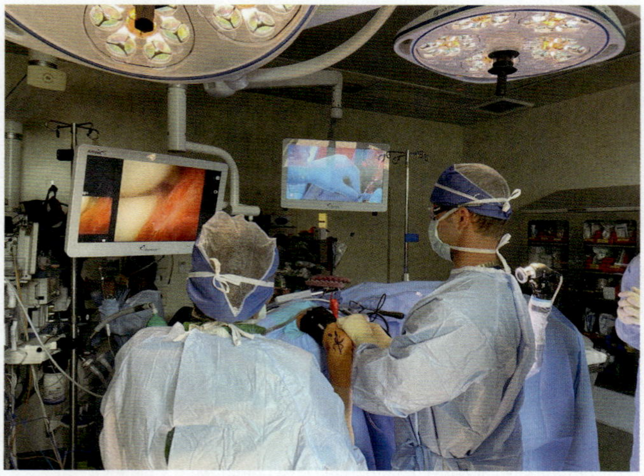

Fig. 66.9 Elbow arthroscopy in progress. Patient is positioned so monitor is clearly visible. (From Fournier M, Corning E, Witt A, et al.: Arthroscopically assisted fixation of terrible triad variant injuries of the elbow with small-bore needle arthroscopy, *Arthrosc Tech* 10:e1469–e1474, 2021.)

Case Study

Objective Data: Diagnostic Studies

(© pixhead-photo/iStock/Thinkstock.)

The HCP in the ED orders the following diagnostic studies:

- X-ray of left foot
- CBC, electrolytes
- Aspiration of the great toe

The x-ray of the foot shows minor soft tissue swelling but no evidence of fracture. Very mild arthritis is noted at the interphalangeal joint of the great toe. CBC and electrolytes are within normal limits. Aspiration of the interphalangeal joint shows clear synovial fluid. Protein and glucose are within normal limits. Microscopic analysis of the synovial fluid shows urate crystals.

Discussion Questions

1. Which diagnostic results are abnormal?
2. What diagnostic study results concern you most?

Answers available at http://evolve.elsevier.com/Lewis/medsurg.

BRIDGE TO NCLEX EXAMINATION

The number of the question corresponds to the same-numbered outcome at the beginning of the chapter.

1. The bone cells that function in the formation of new bone tissue after a patient sustains a fracture are called
   a. osteoids.
   b. osteocytes.
   c. osteoclasts.
   d. osteoblasts.
2. When performing passive range of motion for a patient, the nurse puts the elbow joint through the movements of *(select all that apply)*
   a. flexion and extension.
   b. inversion and eversion.
   c. pronation and supination.
   d. flexion, extension, abduction, and adduction.
   e. pronation, supination, rotation, and circumduction.
3. A patient with a torn ligament in the knee asks what the ligament does. The nurse would respond that ligaments
   a. connect bone to bone.
   b. provide strength to muscle.
   c. lubricate joints with synovial fluid.
   d. relieve friction between moving parts.
4. The increased risk for falls in the older adult is likely due to *(select all that apply)*
   a. changes in balance.
   b. decrease in bone mass.
   c. loss of ligament elasticity.
   d. erosion of articular cartilage.
   e. decrease in muscle mass and strength.
5. The nurse obtained a health history of a patient with a fracture. Which problem, if reported by the patient, would most concern the nurse?

   a. Diabetes
   b. Hypertension
   c. Chronic bronchitis
   d. Nephrotic syndrome

6. When grading muscle strength, the nurse records a score of 3/5, which indicates
   a. no detection of muscular contraction.
   b. a barely detectable flicker of contraction.
   c. active movement against full resistance without fatigue.
   d. active movement against gravity but not against resistance.

7. An abnormal assessment finding of the musculoskeletal system is
   a. equal leg length bilaterally.
   b. ulnar deviation and subluxation.
   c. full range of motion in all joints.
   d. muscle strength of 5/5 in all muscles.

8. A patient is scheduled for a bone scan. The nurse explains that this diagnostic test involves
   a. incision or puncture of the joint capsule.
   b. insertion of small needles into certain muscles.
   c. administration of a radioisotope before the procedure.
   d. placement of skin electrodes to record muscle activity.

1. d; 2. a, c; 3. a; 4. a, b, c, e; 5. a; 6. d; 7. b; 8. c.

For rationales to these answers and even more NCLEX review questions, visit http://evolve.elsevier.com/Lewis/medsurg.

EVOLVE WEBSITE/RESOURCES LIST

http://evolve.elsevier.com/Lewis/medsurg
Review Questions (Online Only)
Key Points
Answer Keys for Questions
- Rationales for Bridge to NCLEX Examination Questions
- Answer Guidelines for Case Study

Conceptual Care Map Creator
Audio Glossary
Content Updates

REFERENCES

1. El Sayed SA, Nezwek TA, Varacallo M: Physiology, bone. Retrieved from https://www.ncbi.nlm.nih.gov/books/NBK441968/.
2. Walker J: Skeletal system 1: the anatomy and physiology of bones, *Nursing Times* 116:38, 2020.
3. Dave HD, Shook M, Varacallo M: Anatomy, skeletal muscle. Retrieved from https://www.ncbi.nlm.nih.gov/books/NBK537236/.
4. Omar A, Marwaha K, Bollu PC: Physiology, neuromuscular junction. Retrieved from https://www.ncbi.nlm.nih.gov/books/NBK470413/.
5. Mercadante JR, Marappa-Ganeshan R. Anatomy: skin bursa. Retrieved from https://www.ncbi.nlm.nih.gov/books/NBK554438/.
*6. Létocart AJ, Mabesoone F, Charleux F, et al.: Muscles adaptation to aging and training: architectural changes: a randomized trial, *BMC Geriatr* 21:48, 2021.
7. Rolvien T, Amling M: Disuse osteoporosis: clinical and mechanistic insights, *Calcif Tissue Int March* 18, 2021.
*8. Rossi F, Martinoli C, Murialdo G, et al.: The primary role of radiological imaging in the diagnosis of rare musculoskeletal diseases. Emphasis on ultrasound, *J Ultrason* 19:187, 2019.

*Evidence-based information for clinical practice.

67

Musculoskeletal Trauma and Orthopedic Surgery

Rebekah Filson

http://evolve.elsevier.com/Lewis/medsurg/

CONCEPTUAL FOCUS

Functional Ability
Infection
Mobility
Pain
Perfusion
Safety

LEARNING OUTCOMES

1. Discuss the etiology, pathophysiology, manifestations, and interprofessional and nursing management of soft tissue injuries.
2. Relate the sequence of events involved in fracture healing.
3. Compare closed reduction, casting, open reduction, and traction in terms of purpose, complications, and nursing management.
4. Assess the neurovascular condition of an injured extremity.
5. Explain common complications of a fracture and fracture healing.
6. Describe the interprofessional and nursing management of patients with various kinds of fractures.
7. Describe indications for and interprofessional and nursing management of the patient with an amputation.
8. Describe types of joint replacement surgery.
9. Prioritize management of the patient having joint replacement surgery.

KEY TERMS

amputation
arthrodesis
arthroplasty
bursitis
carpal tunnel syndrome (CTS)
compartment syndrome
debridement
dislocation
fat embolism syndrome (FES)
fracture
osteotomy
phantom limb sensation
repetitive strain injury (RSI)
sprain
strain
traction

The most common cause of musculoskeletal injury is a traumatic event resulting in fracture, dislocation, subluxation, and/or soft tissue injury. Most of these injuries are not fatal. However, accidents are 1 of the top 3 causes of death for persons ages 1 to 64 years.[1] The costs in terms of pain, disability, and expense are enormous. Nurses play a key role in teaching the public about basic principles of safety and accident prevention.

This chapter discusses musculoskeletal problems resulting from trauma and common orthopedic surgeries. After trauma or surgery, the injured area is often immobilized while healing occurs. We discuss the important role of the nurse in preventing complications (e.g., pressure injuries, constipation, infection, venous thromboembolism [VTE]) and promoting functional ability in patients with fractures and orthopedic surgery.

HEALTH PROMOTION

Teach people to take proper safety precautions to prevent injuries while at home or work, driving, or taking part in sports (Box 67.1). The morbidity from accidents can be reduced if people are aware of environmental hazards, use proper safety equipment, and apply safety and traffic rules. In the work setting, teach employees and employers to use proper safety equipment and decrease workplace hazards. Falls cause many musculoskeletal injuries in the home.

BOX 67.1 PROMOTING POPULATION HEALTH

Reducing the Risk for Musculoskeletal Injuries

- Wear seatbelts.
- Drive within posted speed limits.
- Avoid distracted driving (e.g., no texting, eating, talking on a cell phone).
- Do not drive under the influence of alcohol or drugs (prescribed or illicit).
- Warm up muscles before exercise.
- Use protective athletic equipment (helmets and knee, wrist, and elbow pads).
- Use proper safety equipment at work.

BOX 67.2 PROMOTING POPULATION HEALTH

Reducing Fall Risk

- Assess the living environment for safety risks.
- Wear functional, nonskid, hard-soled shoes.
- Avoid wet or slippery surfaces.
- Remove throw rugs and ensure adequate lighting in the home.
- Maintain clear paths to the bathroom for nighttime use.

Provide preventive teaching to high-risk persons (e.g., people with gait instability, vision impairment) (Box 67.2).

Encourage people, especially older adults, to take part in moderate exercise to help maintain muscle strength and balance. Table 67.1 describes ways to prevent common musculoskeletal problems in the older adult. Stress the importance of adequate calcium and vitamin D intake for bone health.

TABLE 67.1 PATIENT & CAREGIVER TEACHING

Preventing Musculoskeletal Problems in Older Adults

To prevent musculoskeletal problems, include the following instructions when teaching older adults and their caregivers:

1. Use ramps in buildings and at street corners instead of steps to prevent falls.
2. Remove throw rugs from the home.
3. Treat pain and discomfort from osteoarthritis.
   - Rest in positions that decrease discomfort.
   - Use medication as prescribed for pain.
4. Use a walker or cane to help prevent falls.
5. Eat the amount and kind of foods needed to prevent weight gain. Obesity adds stress to joints, which may predispose to osteoarthritis.
6. Get regular and frequent exercise.
   - ADLs provide range-of-motion exercises. Tai Chi may be helpful.
   - Hobbies (e.g., jigsaw puzzles, needlework, model building) exercise finger joints and prevent stiffness.
   - Do daily weight-bearing exercise (e.g., walking) to improve bone health.
7. Use shoes with good support for safety and comfort.
8. Avoid sudden change in position. Rise slowly to a standing position to prevent dizziness, falls, and fractures.
9. Do not walk on uneven surfaces and wet floors.

SOFT TISSUE INJURIES

Soft tissue injuries include sprains, strains, dislocations, and subluxations. They usually result from trauma. As more people have become involved in fitness programs or sports, the incidence of soft tissue injuries has increased. Table 67.2 describes common sports-related injuries. Sports injuries that often result in a visit to the emergency department (ED) for younger patients include sprains and strains, growth plate injuries, and repetitive motion injuries.[2]

SPRAINS AND STRAINS

Sprains and strains often result from abnormal stretching or twisting forces during vigorous activities. These injuries tend to occur around joints and in the spinal muscles.

A **sprain** is an injury to the ligaments surrounding a joint. Sprains are usually caused by a wrenching or twisting motion. Most occur in the ankle, wrist, and knee joints.[3] We classify sprains according to the degree of ligament damage. A *first-degree (mild) sprain* involves tears in only a few fibers, with mild tenderness and minimal swelling. A *second-degree (moderate) sprain* results in partial disruption of the involved tissue with more swelling and tenderness. A *third-degree (severe) sprain* is a complete tear of the ligament with moderate to severe swelling.

A **strain** is an excessive stretching of a muscle and its fascial sheath, often involving the tendon. Most strains occur in the large muscle groups, including the lower back, calf, and hamstrings. We classify strains as first degree (mild or slightly pulled muscle), second degree (moderate or moderately torn muscle), and third degree (severely torn or ruptured muscle). A defect in the muscle may be apparent or palpated through the skin if the muscle is torn. Because areas around joints are rich in nerve endings, the injury can be very painful.

Manifestations of sprains and strains are similar. They include pain, edema, decreased function, and bruising. Continued use of the joint, tendon, or ligament makes pain worse. Edema develops in the injured area because of the local inflammatory response.

Mild sprains and strains are usually self-limiting. Full function generally returns within 3 to 6 weeks. X-rays may be done to rule out a fracture. A severe sprain can cause an *avulsion fracture,* in which the ligament pulls loose a fragment of bone. The joint structure may become unstable, causing subluxation or dislocation. At the time of injury, *hemarthrosis* (bleeding into a joint space or cavity) or disruption of the synovial lining may occur. Severe strains may need surgical repair of the muscle, tendon, or surrounding fascia.

NURSING MANAGEMENT: SPRAINS AND STRAINS

Implementation

Health Promotion

Warming up muscles before exercising and vigorous activity, followed by stretching, may significantly reduce the risk for sprains and strains. Strength, balance, and endurance

TABLE 67.2 Soft Tissue Injuries

Injury	Description	Treatment
Anterior cruciate ligament tear	Tearing of ligament by deceleration forces with pivoting or odd positions of the knee or leg.	PT with rehabilitation, knee brace. If knee instability or further injury, reconstructive surgery may be done.
Impingement syndrome	Entrapment of soft tissues and nerves under coracoacromial arch of shoulder	NSAIDs. Rest until symptoms ↓, then begin gradual ROM and strength exercises.
Ligament injury	Tearing or stretching of ligament. Usually occurs from inversion, eversion, shearing, or torque applied to a joint. Characterized by sudden pain, swelling, and instability	Rest, ice, elevation of extremity if possible, NSAIDs. Protect affected extremity by use of brace. If symptoms persist, surgical repair may be needed.
Meniscus injury	Injury to fibrocartilage discs in knee. Characterized by popping, clicking, tearing sensation, effusion, and/or swelling	Rest, ice, elevation of extremity if possible, NSAIDs. Gradual return to regular activities. If symptoms persist, MRI to assess meniscus injury. Possible arthroscopic surgery.
Rotator cuff tear	Tear within muscle, tendons, or ligaments around shoulder	*If minor tear:* rest, NSAIDs, and gradual mobilization with ROM and strength exercises. *If major tear:* surgical repair.
Shin splints	Inflammation of periosteal bone *(periostitis)* along anterior calf. Caused by improper shoes, overuse, or running on hard pavement	Rest, ice, NSAIDs, proper shoes. Gradual ↑ in activity. If pain persists, x-ray to rule out tibial stress fracture
Tendonitis	Inflammation of tendon due to overuse or incorrect use	Rest, ice, NSAIDs. Gradual return to sport activity. Protective brace *(orthosis)* may be needed if symptoms recur.

BOX 67.3 PROMOTING POPULATION HEALTH

Health Impact of Physical Activity

- Helps with weight management
- Increases lean muscle and decreases body fat
- Helps maintain and improve bone mass
- Increases muscle strength, flexibility, and endurance
- Helps prevent high BP
- Reduces the risk for heart disease, diabetes, and colon cancer
- Enhances sense of well-being and reduces risk for depression

exercises are important (Box 67.3). Strength exercises that involve working against resistance build muscle strength and bone density. Balance exercises, which may overlap with some strength exercises, help prevent falls. Endurance exercises should start at a low level of effort and progress gradually to a moderate level.

◆ Acute Care

If an injury occurs, immediate care focuses on (1) stopping the activity and limiting movement to the injured part, (2) applying ice packs to the injured area, (3) compressing the involved area, (4) elevating the extremity, and (5) providing analgesia as needed (Table 67.3). Most sprains and strains are treated in the outpatient setting.

RICE (*R*est, *I*ce, *C*ompression, *E*levation) may decrease local inflammation and pain for most musculoskeletal injuries. Movement should be restricted with the extremity rested as soon as pain is felt. Unless the injury is severe, prolonged rest is usually not needed.

There are several forms of cold therapy *(cryotherapy)*. Cold causes vasoconstriction in the soft tissue and reduces the transmission and perception of nerve pain impulses. These changes also reduce muscle spasms, inflammation, and edema. Cold is most useful when applied immediately after an injury has occurred and used for 24 to 28 hours. Apply ice no more than 20 to 30 minutes at a time. Do not apply ice directly to the skin.

Compression helps decrease edema and pain. We often use an elastic compression bandage. It can be wrapped around the injured part. To prevent edema and encourage fluid return, wrap the bandage starting distally (at the point farthest from the trunk of the body) and progress proximally (toward the trunk of the body). The bandage is too tight if there is numbness or tingling below the area of compression or pain or more swelling occurs beyond the edge of the bandage. Leave the bandage in place for 30 minutes, then remove it for 15 minutes. Use of an elastic wrap may provide extra support during training, athletic, and work activities.

Elevate the injured part above heart level, even during sleep, for 24 to 48 hours to help mobilize excess fluid from the area and prevent further edema. Mild analgesics and nonsteroidal antiinflammatory drugs (NSAIDs) may be used to manage patient discomfort.

After the acute phase (usually 24 to 48 hours), apply warm, moist heat to the affected part to reduce swelling and provide comfort. Heat applications should not exceed 20 to 30 minutes. Allow a "cool-down" time between applications. Encourage the patient to use the limb if the joint is protected by a cast, brace, splint, or taping. Joint movement maintains nutrition to the cartilage. Movement helps prevent *contracture* (stiffening) of tendons and ligaments. Muscle contraction improves circulation and helps resolve bruising and swelling.

Emphasize the importance of strength and conditioning exercises to prevent reinjury. The physical therapist may help with pain relief by using ultrasound or other interventions. They can teach the patient exercises to improve flexibility and strength.

TABLE 67.3 EMERGENCY MANAGEMENT

Acute Soft Tissue Injury

Cause	Assessment Findings	Interventions
• Crush injury • Direct blows • Falls • Motor vehicle crashes • Sports injuries	• Bruising • ↓ Movement with limited function or inability to bear weight (lower extremity) • ↓ Pulse, coolness, capillary refill >2 sec • ↓ Sensation • Edema • Muscle spasms • Pain, tenderness • Pallor • Shortening or rotation of extremity	**Initial** • Ensure airway, breathing, and circulation. • Perform neurovascular assessment of involved limb. • Elevate involved limb. • Apply compression bandage unless dislocation present. • Apply ice packs to affected area. • Immobilize affected extremity in the position found. Do *not* try to realign or reinsert protruding bones. • Anticipate x-rays of injured extremity. • Give analgesia as needed. • Give tetanus prophylaxis if there is an open fracture. • Give antibiotic prophylaxis for open fracture, large tissue defects, or mangled extremity injury. **Ongoing Monitoring** • Monitor for changes in neurovascular condition. • Implement weight-bearing restrictions as ordered for lower extremity involvement. • Anticipate compartment pressure monitoring if neurovascular assessment changes and compartment syndrome suspected.

DISLOCATIONS

Dislocation is the complete displacement or separation of the articular surfaces of the joint. *Subluxation* is a partial or incomplete displacement of the joint surface. Symptoms of subluxation are similar to a dislocation but are less severe. Many structures contribute to joint stability. Injury to, or excessive laxity of, ligaments is a major factor in dislocations or subluxations. Weak or atrophied muscles can cause chronic joint instability. Fibrocartilage structures, such as the labrum around hip and shoulder sockets and the meniscus at the knee, play an important role in joint stability. Even small tears to these structures can result in recurrent, chronic dislocations or subluxations.

Dislocations typically result from forces on the joint that disrupt the surrounding soft tissue support structures. The joints most often dislocated in the upper extremity include the thumb, elbow, and shoulder. The shoulder most often dislocates anteriorly. Posterior shoulder dislocations are rare. They typically only happen after electrocution or seizure. In the lower extremity, the hip is vulnerable to dislocation from severe trauma, often from motor vehicle crashes (Fig. 67.1). The kneecap *(patella)* may dislocate because of a sharp, direct blow or after a sudden twisting inward motion while the planted foot is pointed outward.

The most obvious sign of a dislocation is deformity. For example, if the hip dislocates in a posterior (or backward) direction, the affected limb may be shorter and internally rotated. Other manifestations include local pain, tenderness, loss of function of the injured part, and swelling of soft tissues near the joint. Major complications include open joint injuries, *intraarticular* fractures (within the joint), *avascular necrosis* (bone cell death from blood supply), and damage to adjacent nerves and blood vessels.

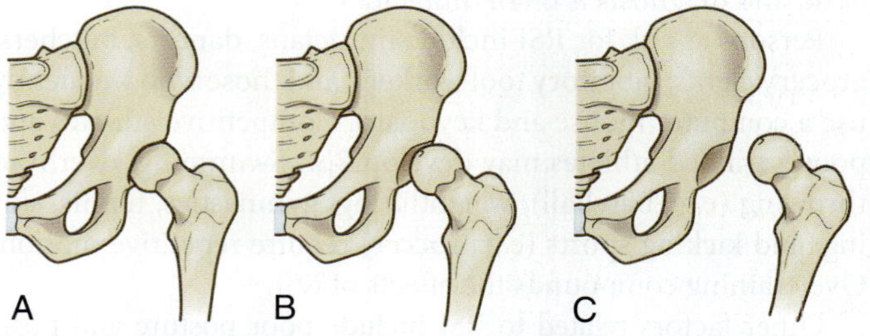

Fig. 67.1 Soft tissue injury of the hip. (A) Normal. (B) Subluxation (partial dislocation). (C) Dislocation.

X-rays can determine the extent of displacement. The joint may be aspirated to assess for hemarthrosis or fat cells. Fat cells in the aspirate indicate a probable intraarticular fracture.

Interprofessional and Nursing Care

A dislocation requires prompt attention. It is often considered an orthopedic emergency because it may be cause significant vascular injury. The longer the joint is dislocated, the greater the risk for avascular necrosis. The femoral head of the hip joint is especially susceptible to avascular necrosis. Compartment syndrome may occur after dislocation due to vascular injury and resulting ischemia. Neurovascular assessment is critical.

The first goal of care of a dislocation is to realign the dislocated part of the joint to its original anatomic position. Closed reduction (no incision) may be done under local or general anesthesia or IV moderate to deep sedation. Anesthesia is often needed to relax the muscle so that the bones can be manipulated. Sometimes, open reduction (joint visualized through surgery) may be needed. After reduction, the extremity is immobilized by a brace, splint, or sling, or by taping, to allow torn ligaments and surrounding tissue to heal.

Nursing care includes pain management and support and protection of the injured joint. After the joint has been reduced and immobilized, motion is usually restricted. A monitored rehabilitation program can prevent further instability and joint problems. Gentle range-of-motion (ROM) exercises may be done if the joint is stable and well supported. An exercise program slowly restores the joint to its original ROM without causing another dislocation. The patient should gradually return to normal activities.

A patient who has dislocated a joint may be at greater risk for repeated dislocations because of damage or laxity to the supporting structures. Activity restrictions may be imposed on the affected joint to decrease the risk for repeated dislocations.

REPETITIVE STRAIN INJURY

Repetitive strain injury (RSI) and *cumulative trauma disorder* are terms used to describe injuries resulting from prolonged force or repetitive movements and awkward postures. RSI is also called *repetitive trauma disorder, nontraumatic musculoskeletal injury, overuse syndrome* (sports medicine), *regional musculoskeletal disorder,* and *work-related musculoskeletal disorder.* Repeated movements strain the tendons, ligaments, and muscles, causing tiny tears that become inflamed. We do not know the exact cause of these disorders. No specific diagnostic tests exist, and diagnosis is often difficult.

Persons at risk for RSI include musicians, dancers, butchers, grocery clerks, vibratory tool workers, and those who frequently use a computer mouse and keyboard. Competitive athletes and poorly trained athletes may develop RSI. Swimming, overhead throwing (e.g., baseball), weightlifting, gymnastics, tennis, skiing, and kicking sports (e.g., soccer) require repetitive motion. Overtraining compounds the effects of RSI.

Other factors related to RSI include poor posture and positioning, poor workspace ergonomics, badly designed workplace equipment (e.g., computer keyboard), and repetitive lifting of heavy objects without sufficient muscle rest. Inflammation, swelling, and pain in the muscles, tendons, and nerves of the neck, spine, shoulder, forearm, and hand may result. Symptoms of RSI include pain, weakness, numbness, or impaired motor function.

RSI can be prevented through education and *ergonomics* (the science that promotes efficiency and safety in the interaction of humans and their work environment). For example, ergonomic considerations for those who work at a desk and use a computer include keeping the hips and knees flexed to 90 degrees with the feet flat, keeping the wrist straight to type, having the top of the computer monitor even with the forehead, and taking at least hourly stretch breaks.

Treatment is supportive. Pain management includes heat or cold therapy, NSAIDs, and rest. Physical therapy (PT) focuses on strength and conditioning exercises. Teach the patient about lifestyle changes and ways to modify equipment and/or activity.

CARPAL TUNNEL SYNDROME

Carpal tunnel syndrome (CTS) is caused by compression of the median nerve. It enters the hand at the wrist through the narrow carpal tunnel (Fig. 67.2). The carpal tunnel is formed by ligaments and bones. CTS is the most common compression neuropathy in the upper extremity. It is associated with hobbies or work that require continuous wrist movement (e.g., musicians, carpenters, computer operators).

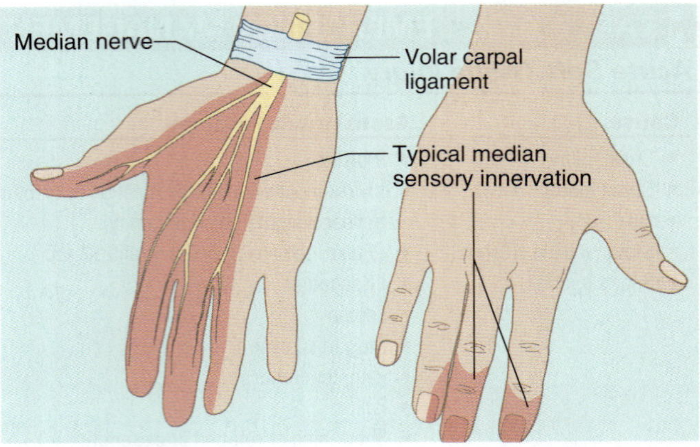

Fig. 67.2 Wrist structures involved in carpal tunnel syndrome. Median nerve distribution. *Shaded areas* show the locations of pain in carpal tunnel syndrome. (From Buttaravoli P: *Minor emergencies,* ed 3, Philadelphia, 2012, Saunders.)

CTS is often caused by pressure from trauma or edema (from inflammation of a tendon *[tenosynovitis]*), cancer, rheumatoid arthritis (RA), or soft tissue masses, such as ganglia. Hormones may be involved because CTS often occurs during the premenstrual period, pregnancy, and menopause. Persons with diabetes, peripheral vascular disease (PVD), and RA have a higher incidence of CTS because of swelling that changes blood flow to the nerve and narrows the carpal tunnel.[4] Women are more likely than men to develop CTS, possibly because of a smaller carpal tunnel.

Manifestations of CTS are impaired sensation, pain, numbness, or weakness in the distribution of the median nerve (Fig. 67.2). Numbness and tingling may awaken the patient at night. Shaking the hands often relieves these symptoms. Clumsiness in performing fine hand movements is common.

The patient may have a positive Tinel sign and Phalen sign. Elicit *Tinel sign* by tapping over the median nerve as it passes through the carpal tunnel in the wrist. A positive response is a sensation of tingling in the distribution of the median nerve over the hand. Test for *Phalen sign* by allowing the wrists to fall freely into maximum flexion and maintain the position for longer than 60 seconds. A positive response is a sensation of tingling in the distribution of the median nerve over the hand. In late stages, atrophy of the muscles around the base of the thumb results in recurrent pain and eventual dysfunction of the hand.

Interprofessional and Nursing Care

To prevent CTS, teach employees and employers to identify risk factors. Adaptive devices, such as wrist splints, may be worn to hold the wrist in a slight extension and relieve pressure on the median nerve. Special keyboard pads and computer mice that help prevent repetitive pressure on the median nerve are available for computer users. Other ergonomic changes include workstation changes, change in body positions, and frequent breaks from work activities.

Care is directed toward relieving the underlying cause of the nerve compression. Early symptoms can usually be relieved by stopping the aggravating movement and by resting the hand and wrist by immobilization in a hand splint. Splints worn at night help keep the wrist in a neutral position. This may reduce night pain and numbness. PT with hand and wrist exercises may lessen symptom severity. A corticosteroid injection directly into the carpal tunnel may give short-term relief. The patient may need to consider a change in occupation because of discomfort and sensory changes.

Carpal tunnel release is generally done if symptoms last more than 6 months or if there is significant impairment to conduction on electromyography (EMG). Surgery involves severing the band of tissue around the wrist to reduce pressure on the median nerve (Fig. 67.2). Surgery is done in the outpatient setting using local anesthesia. The types of carpal tunnel release surgery include open release and endoscopic surgery. In *open release surgery*, an incision is made in the wrist and then the carpal ligament is cut to enlarge the carpal tunnel. *Endoscopic carpal tunnel release* is done through 1 or more small puncture incisions in the wrist and palm. A camera is attached to a tube, and the carpal ligament is cut. The endoscopic approach may allow a faster recovery and cause less discomfort than traditional open release surgery.

Although symptoms may be relieved right after surgery, full recovery may take months. After surgery, assess the hand's neurovascular status. Teach the patient about wound care and assessments to perform at home.

ROTATOR CUFF INJURY

The rotator cuff is made up of 4 muscles in the shoulder: the supraspinatus, infraspinatus, teres minor, and subscapularis muscles. These muscles stabilize the humeral head in the glenoid fossa and assist with ROM of the shoulder and rotation of the humerus.

A tear in the rotator cuff may occur as a gradual, degenerative process due to aging, repetitive stress (especially overhead arm motions), or injury to the shoulder. In sports, repetitive overhead motions, such as in swimming, weightlifting, and swinging a racquet (tennis, racquetball), often cause injury. The rotator cuff can tear because of sudden adduction forces applied to the cuff while the arm is held in abduction. Other causes include (1) falling onto an outstretched arm and hand, (2) a blow to the upper arm, (3) heavy lifting, or (4) repetitive work motions.

Manifestations include shoulder weakness, pain, and decreased ROM. The patient usually has severe pain when the arm is abducted between 60 and 120 degrees (the painful arc). A positive *drop arm test* is a sign of rotator cuff injury. In this test, the arm is abducted 90 degrees, and the patient is asked to slowly lower the arm to the side. If the arm falls suddenly, rotator cuff injury is suspected. An x-ray is not helpful in the diagnosis. MRI can usually confirm a tear.

The patient with a partial tear or cuff inflammation may be treated with rest, ice, and heat, NSAIDs, corticosteroid injections into the subacromial space, ultrasound, and PT. If the patient does not respond to conservative treatment or if a complete tear is present, surgical repair may be done. Most repairs are arthroscopic procedures done as an outpatient (Fig. 67.3). If the tear is extensive, part of the acromion may be surgically removed *(acromioplasty)* to relieve compression of the rotator cuff during movement. A shoulder immobilizer with an abduction pillow is typically used for 6 weeks after surgery to limit shoulder movement. However, the shoulder should not be immobilized for too long because "frozen" shoulder *(arthrofibrosis)* may occur. Pendulum exercises and other passive exercises typically begin the first postoperative day. Active PT starts after 6 weeks of immobilization. Weight restrictions for lifting are usually given. Full recovery may take 6 to 12 months.

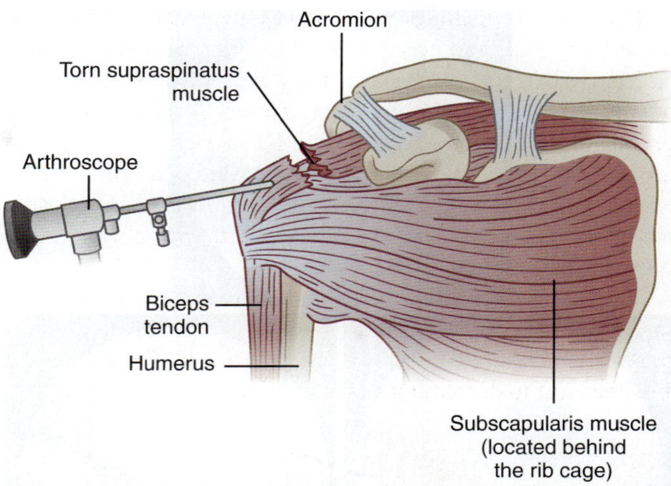

Fig. 67.3 A torn rotator cuff is repaired using arthroscopic surgery.

MENISCUS INJURY

The menisci are crescent-shaped pieces of fibrocartilage in the knee. Menisci are also found in other joints, including the acromioclavicular (AC), sternoclavicular, and temporomandibular joints. Meniscus injuries are associated with ligament sprains common among athletes in sports such as basketball, football, soccer, and hockey.[5] These activities produce rotational stress when the knee is in varying degrees of flexion and the foot is planted or fixed. A blow to the knee can cause shearing of the meniscus between the femoral condyles and tibial plateau, causing a torn meniscus. Older adults and people who have jobs that require squatting or kneeling are at risk for degenerative tears.[5]

Meniscus injuries alone do not usually cause significant edema because most cartilage is avascular. However, an acutely torn meniscus may present with local tenderness, pain, and effusion (Fig. 67.4). Pain occurs with flexion, internal rotation, and then extension of the knee *(McMurray's test)*. The patient may feel that the knee is unstable. They often report that the knee "clicks," "pops," "locks," or "gives way." Quadriceps atrophy is usually present if the injury has been present for some time. Traumatic arthritis may occur from repeated meniscus injury and chronic inflammation.

MRI can confirm the diagnosis before arthroscopy. The patient's age, occupation, sport activities, degree of pain, and dysfunction may affect the decision whether to have surgery.

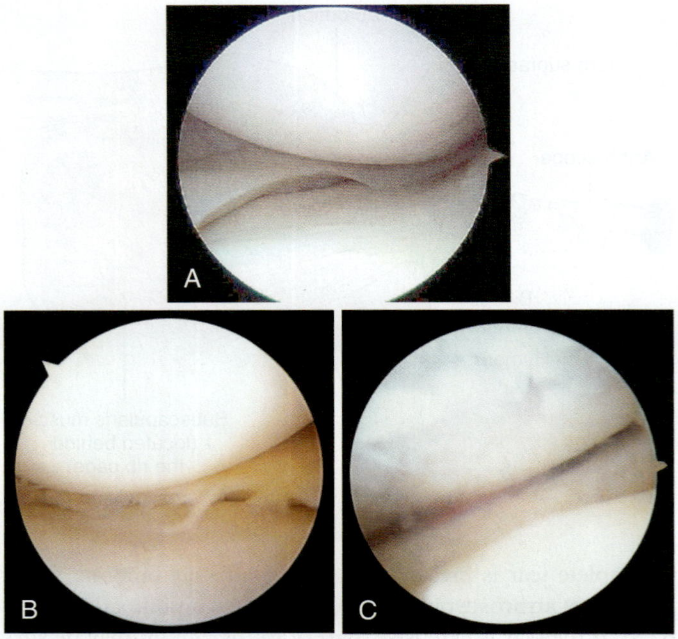

Fig. 67.4 Arthroscopic views of the meniscus. (A) Normal meniscus. (B) Torn meniscus. (C) Surgically repaired meniscus. (A, From David Lintner, MD, Houston, TX, www.drlintner.com. B and C, Courtesy Peter Bonner, Placitas, NM.)

Interprofessional and Nursing Care

Most meniscus injuries are treated in an outpatient setting. The acutely injured knee should be examined within 24 hours of injury. Initial care involves ice, immobilization, and use of crutches with weight bearing as tolerated. Using a knee brace or immobilizer during the first few days after the injury protects the knee and offers some pain relief.

After acute pain has decreased, PT can help the patient regain knee flexion and muscle strength to aid in returning to full function. Teach athletes to do warm-up exercises to reduce the risk for sports-related injuries. In older adults with degenerative meniscus tears, progressive exercise therapy may improve neuromuscular function and muscle strength.

Surgical repair or excision of part of the meniscus *(meniscectomy)* may be needed (see Fig. 67.4). Meniscal surgery is done by arthroscopy. Pain relief may include NSAIDs or other analgesics. Rehabilitation starts soon after surgery. PT includes quadriceps and hamstring strength exercises and ROM. When the patient's strength is back to its preinjury level, they can resume normal activities.

ANTERIOR CRUCIATE LIGAMENT INJURY

Knee injuries account for more than 50% of all sports injuries. The most commonly injured knee ligament is the anterior cruciate ligament (ACL). ACL injuries are usually noncontact injuries that occur when a person pivots, lands from a jump, or stops abruptly when running. Patients often report coming down on the knee, twisting, and hearing a pop, followed by acute knee pain and swelling. The knee may feel unstable. Athletes usually cannot continue playing. ACL injury can result in a partial tear, a complete tear, or an *avulsion* (tearing away) from the bones that form the knee (Fig. 67.5).

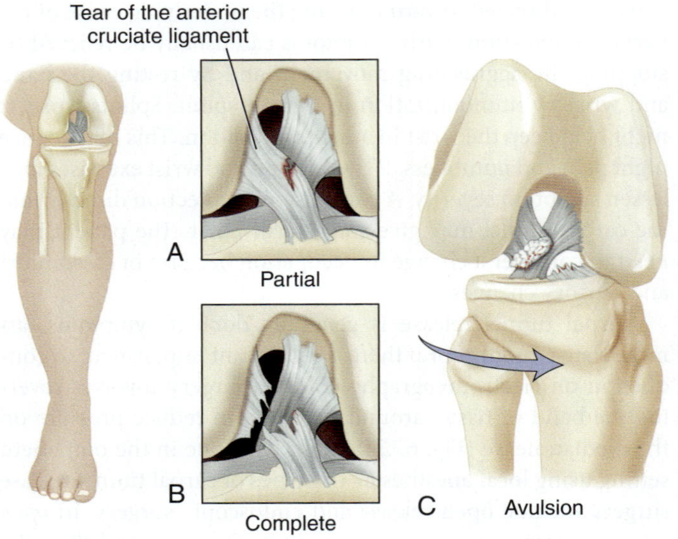

Fig. 67.5 ACL injury. (A) Partial tear. (B) Complete tear. (C) Avulsion.

A positive *Lachman's test* suggests an ACL tear. This test is done by flexing the knee 15 to 30 degrees and pulling the tibia forward while stabilizing the femur. The test is positive for an ACL tear if forward motion of the tibia occurs with the feeling of a soft or indistinct endpoint. MRI can diagnose an ACL tear and coexisting conditions, including a fracture, meniscus tear, and ligament injuries.

Interprofessional and Nursing Care

Prevention programs can significantly reduce ACL injuries in athletes. Conservative treatment for an intact ACL injury includes rest, ice, NSAIDs, elevation, and ambulation as tolerated with crutches. If present, a tight, painful effusion may be aspirated. A knee immobilizer or hinged knee brace may provide support. PT often helps the patient maintain knee joint motion and muscle tone.

Reconstructive surgery is usually recommended for physically active patients who have sustained severe injury to the ACL and meniscus. In reconstruction, the torn ACL tissue is removed and replaced with graft tissue. ROM is encouraged soon after surgery. The knee is placed in a brace or immobilizer. Rehabilitation with PT is critical. Progressive weight bearing is determined by the type of surgery. A safe return to the prior level of function may take 6 to 8 months.

BURSITIS

Bursae are closed sacs that are lined with synovial membrane and contain a small amount of synovial fluid. They are found at sites of friction, such as between tendons and bones and near the joints. **Bursitis** (inflammation of the bursa) results from repeated or excessive trauma or friction, gout, RA, or infection.

Symptoms include warmth, pain, swelling, and limited ROM in the affected part. Common sites are the hands, elbows, shoulders, knees, and greater trochanters of the hip. Improper body

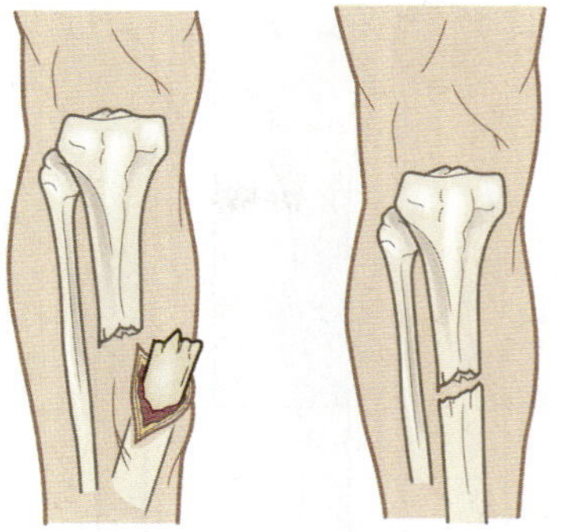

Fig. 67.6 Fracture classification by communication with the external environment.

mechanics, repetitive kneeling (e.g., carpet layers, coal miners, gardeners), jogging in worn-out shoes, and prolonged sitting with crossed legs are common precipitating activities.

Try to determine and correct the cause of the bursitis. Rest is often the only treatment needed. The affected part may be immobilized in a compression dressing or splint. Ice and NSAIDs can reduce pain and inflammation. Aspiration of the bursal fluid and intraarticular corticosteroid injection may be needed. If the bursal wall has become thickened and continues to interfere with normal joint function, surgical excision *(bursectomy)* may be done. Septic bursae may be treated with oral antibiotics but usually need surgical incision and drainage.

FRACTURES

Classification

A **fracture** is a disruption or break in the continuity of bone. Traumatic injuries cause most fractures. Other fractures are due to a disease process, such as cancer or osteoporosis *(pathologic fracture).*

We classify fractures in several ways. Fractures are described as *open* or *closed* based on communication with the external environment (Fig. 67.6). In an *open fracture*, the skin is broken, and bone exposed, causing soft tissue injury. An open fracture usually results from severe external forces. In a *closed fracture*, the skin is intact over the site.

We also describe fractures as complete or incomplete. A fracture is *complete* if the break goes completely through the bone. An *incomplete* fracture occurs partly across a bone shaft, but the bone is still intact. An incomplete fracture is often the result of bending or crushing forces applied to a bone.

Fractures are identified by the direction of the fracture line. Types include linear, oblique, transverse, longitudinal, and spiral fractures (Fig. 67.7).

Finally, we describe fractures as displaced or nondisplaced. In a *displaced* fracture, the 2 ends of the broken bone are separated from each other and out of their normal positions. Displaced fractures are often *comminuted* (more than 2fragments) or *oblique* (Fig. 67.7). In a *nondisplaced* fracture, the bone fragments stay in alignment. Nondisplaced fractures are usually transverse, spiral, or greenstick (Fig. 67.7).

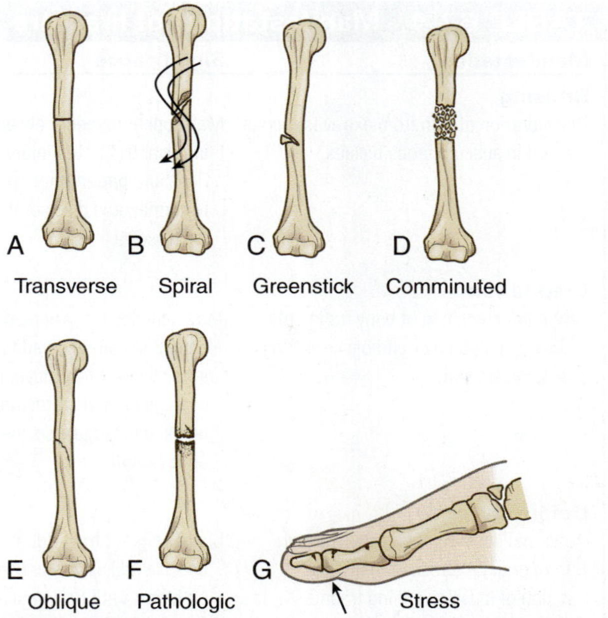

Fig. 67.7 Types of fractures. (A) Transverse fracture: the line of the fracture extends across the bone shaft at a right angle to the longitudinal axis. (B) Spiral fracture: the line of the fracture extends in a spiral direction along the bone shaft. (C) Greenstick fracture: an incomplete fracture with 1 side splintered and the other side bent. (D) Comminuted fracture: a fracture with more than 2 fragments. The smaller fragments appear to be floating. (E) Oblique fracture: the line of the fracture extends across and down the bone. (F) Pathologic fracture: a spontaneous fracture at the site of a diseased bone. (G) Stress fracture: occurs in bone that is subject to repeated stress, such as from jogging or running.

Manifestations

Manifestations include immediate pain, decreased function, and inability to bear weight or use the affected part (Table 67.4). The patient guards and protects the extremity against movement. Obvious deformity may be present.

Fracture Healing

Bone goes through a complex multistage healing process, or union (Fig. 67.8). Healing occurs in 6 stages:

1. *Fracture hematoma:* When a fracture occurs, bleeding creates a hematoma that surrounds the ends of the bone fragments. The hematoma is composed of extravasated blood that changes from a liquid to a semisolid clot in the first 72 hours after injury.
2. *Granulation tissue:* During this stage, active phagocytosis absorbs the products of local necrosis. The hematoma converts to granulation tissue. Granulation tissue (consisting of new blood vessels, fibroblasts, and osteoblasts) forms the basis for new bone substance *(osteoid)* during days 3 to 14 after injury.
3. *Callus formation:* As minerals (calcium, phosphorus, and magnesium) and new bone matrix are deposited in the osteoid, an unorganized network of bone is formed and woven about the fracture parts. *Callus* is mainly composed of cartilage, osteoblasts, calcium, and phosphorus. It usually appears by the end of the second week after injury. An x-ray can show evidence of callus formation.

TABLE 67.4 Manifestations of Fracture

Manifestation	Significance
Bruising	
Discoloration of skin from extravasation of blood in subcutaneous tissues.	May appear immediately after injury and distal to injury. Reassure patient that process is normal, and discoloration will resolve.
Crepitation	
Grating or crunching of bony fragments, causing palpable or audible crunching or popping sensation.	May ↑ chance for nonunion if bone ends are allowed to move excessively. Micromovement of fragments (postfracture) helps in osteogenesis (new bone growth).
Deformity	
Abnormal position of extremity or part from original forces of injury and action of muscles pulling fragment into abnormal position. Seen as a loss of normal bony contours.	Classic sign of fracture. If uncorrected, it may cause problems with bony union and restoration of function of injured part.
Edema and Swelling	
Disruption or penetration of skin or soft tissues by bone fragments, or bleeding into surrounding tissues.	Unchecked bleeding and swelling in closed space can occlude blood vessels and damage nerves (e.g., ↑ risk for compartment syndrome).
Loss of Function	
Disruption of bone or joint, preventing functional use of limb or part.	Fracture must be managed properly to ensure restoration of function to limb or part.
Muscle Spasm	
Irritation of tissues and protective response to injury and fracture.	May displace nondisplaced fracture or prevent it from reducing spontaneously.
Pain and Tenderness	
Muscle spasm due to involuntary reflex action of muscle, direct tissue trauma, ↑ pressure on nerves, movement of fracture fragments.	Prompt the patient to splint muscle around fracture and reduce motion of injured area.

4. *Ossification:* Ossification of the callus occurs from 3 weeks to 6 months after the fracture and continues until the fracture has healed. Callus ossification is sufficient to prevent movement at the fracture site when the bones are gently stressed. However, the fracture is still evident on x-ray. During this stage of *clinical union,* the patient may be allowed limited mobility, or we may remove the cast.
5. *Consolidation:* As callus continues to develop, the distance between bone fragments decreases and eventually closes. Ossification continues and can be equated with *radiologic union,* which occurs when an x-ray shows complete bony union. This phase can occur up to 1 year after injury.

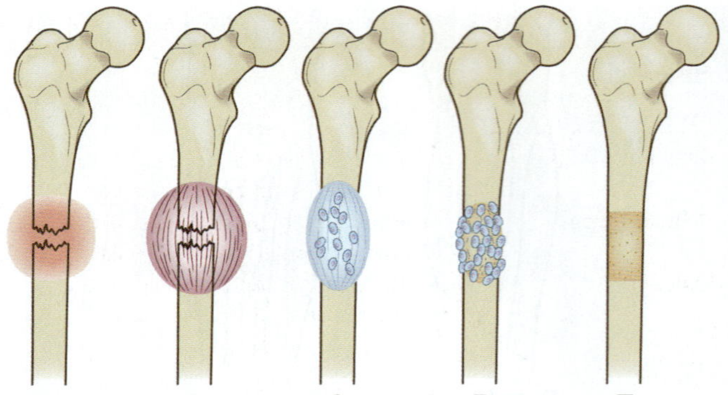

Fig. 67.8 Bone healing (schematic representation). (A) Bleeding at fractured ends of the bone with hematoma formation. (B) Organization of hematoma into fibrous network. (C) Invasion of osteoblasts, lengthening of collagen strands, and deposition of calcium. (D) Callus formation: new bone is built up as osteoclasts destroy dead bone. (E) Remodeling is accomplished as excess callus is resorbed and trabecular bone is laid down.

6. *Remodeling:* Excess bone tissue is resorbed in the last stage of bone healing, and union is complete. Gradual return of the injured bone to its preinjury structural strength and shape occurs. Bone remodels in response to physical loading stress. Initially, stress is provided through exercise. Weight bearing is gradually introduced. New bone is deposited in sites subjected to stress and resorbed at areas of little stress.

Many factors influence the time needed for complete fracture healing. They include displacement and site of the fracture, blood supply, other local tissue injury, immobilization, and use of internal fixation devices (e.g., screws, pins). Ossification may be slowed or even stopped by inadequate immobilization, excessive movement of fracture fragments, infection, poor nutrition, and systemic disease (e.g., diabetes).[6] Healing time for fractures increases with age. For example, an uncomplicated midshaft femur fracture heals in 3 weeks in an infant and in 20 weeks in an adult. Smoking increases fracture healing time. Fracture healing may not occur in the expected time *(delayed union)* or may not occur at all *(nonunion).* Table 67.5 describes complications of fracture healing.

Interprofessional Care

The overall goals of fracture treatment are (1) anatomic realignment of bone fragments through reduction, (2) immobilization to maintain realignment, and (3) restoration of normal or near-normal function of the injured part. Table 67.6 outlines the management of fractures.

Fracture Reduction

Closed reduction. *Closed reduction* is the nonsurgical, manual realignment of bone fragments to their anatomic position. Traction and countertraction are manually applied to the bone fragments to restore position, length, and alignment. Closed reduction is usually done while the patient is under local or general anesthesia. Traction, casting, splints, or orthoses (braces) may be used after reduction to maintain alignment and immobilize the injured part until healing occurs.

TABLE 67.5 Complications of Fracture

Healing

Complication	Description
Angulation	Fracture heals in abnormal position in relation to midline of structure (type of malunion).
Delayed union	Fracture healing progresses more slowly than expected. Healing eventually occurs.
Malunion	Fracture heals in expected time but in unsatisfactory position. May cause deformity or dysfunction.
Myositis ossificans	Deposition of calcium in muscle tissue at site of significant blunt muscle trauma or repeated muscle injury.
Nonunion	Fracture does not heal despite treatment. No x-ray evidence of callus formation.
Pseudoarthrosis	Type of nonunion occurring at fracture site in which a false joint is formed with abnormal movement at site.
Refracture	New fracture occurs at original fracture site.

TABLE 67.6 Interprofessional Care

Fractures

Diagnostic Assessment
- History and physical assessment
- X-ray
- CT scan, MRI

Management

Fracture Reduction
- Manual traction
- Closed reduction
- Skeletal traction
- Open reduction

Fracture Immobilization
- Casting or splinting
- Skeletal traction
- External fixation
- Internal fixation

Open Fractures
- Surgical debridement and irrigation
- Tetanus and diphtheria immunization
- Prophylactic antibiotic therapy

Open reduction. *Open reduction* is the correction of bone alignment through surgery. It usually includes internal fixation of the fracture with wires, screws, pins, plates, intramedullary rods, or nails. The type and location of the fracture, patient age, and concurrent disease influence the decision to use open reduction. The main risks of open reduction are infection, complications of anesthesia, and effects of preexisting medical conditions (e.g., diabetes). However, open reduction internal fixation (ORIF) facilitates early ambulation, decreasing the risk for complications related to prolonged immobility.

Traction. Traction is the application of a pulling force to an injured or diseased body part or extremity. Traction is used to (1) prevent or reduce pain and muscle spasm (e.g., whiplash, unrepaired hip fracture), (2) immobilize a joint or part of the body, (3) reduce a fracture or dislocation, and (4) treat a pathologic joint condition (e.g., tumor, infection). Traction can also (1) provide immobilization to prevent soft tissue damage, (2) promote active and passive exercise, (3) expand a joint space during arthroscopic procedures, and (4) expand a joint space before major joint reconstruction.

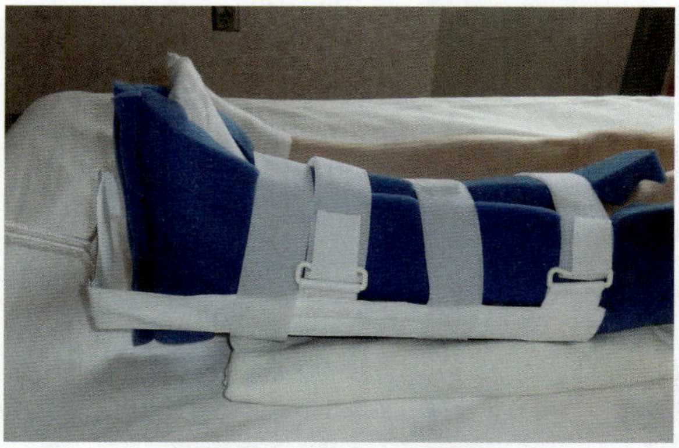

Fig. 67.9 Buck's traction is most often used for fractures of the hip and femur. (Courtesy Mary Wollan, RN, BAN, ONC, Spring Park, MN.)

Traction devices apply a pulling force on a fractured extremity to attain realignment, while *countertraction* pulls in the opposite direction. The most common types of traction are skin traction and skeletal traction. *Skin traction* is generally used for short-term treatment (48 to 72 hours) until skeletal traction or surgery is possible. Tape, boots, or splints are applied directly to the skin. They help decrease muscle spasms in the injured extremity. Traction weights are usually 5 to 10 lb (2.3 to 4.5 kg). *Buck's traction* is a type of skin traction sometimes used for the patient with a hip, knee, or femur fracture (Fig. 67.9). Pelvic or cervical skin traction may require heavier weights applied intermittently. In skin traction, regular skin assessment is a priority because pressure points and skin breakdown may develop quickly. Assess key pressure points every 2 to 4 hours.

Skeletal traction is used to align injured bones and joints or to treat joint contractures and congenital hip dysplasia. It provides a long-term pull that keeps the injured bones and joints aligned. To apply skeletal traction, the HCP inserts a pin or wire into the bone, and weights are attached to align and immobilize the injured body part. Weight for skeletal traction ranges from 5 to 45 lb (2.3 to 20.4 kg). Too much weight can result in delayed union or nonunion. The major complications of skeletal traction are infection at the pin insertion site and the effects of prolonged immobility.

A common type of skeletal traction is balanced suspension traction (Fig. 67.10). Fracture alignment depends on the correct positioning and alignment of the patient while the traction forces stay constant. For extremity traction to be effective, forces must be pulling in the opposite direction *(countertraction)*. Countertraction is supplied by the patient's body weight or by weights pulling in the opposite direction. Elevating the end of the bed can help. Traction must be maintained continuously. Keep the weights off the floor and moving freely through the pulleys.

Fracture Immobilization

Fracture immobilization is achieved with casts, braces, splints, immobilizers, and external and internal fixation devices.

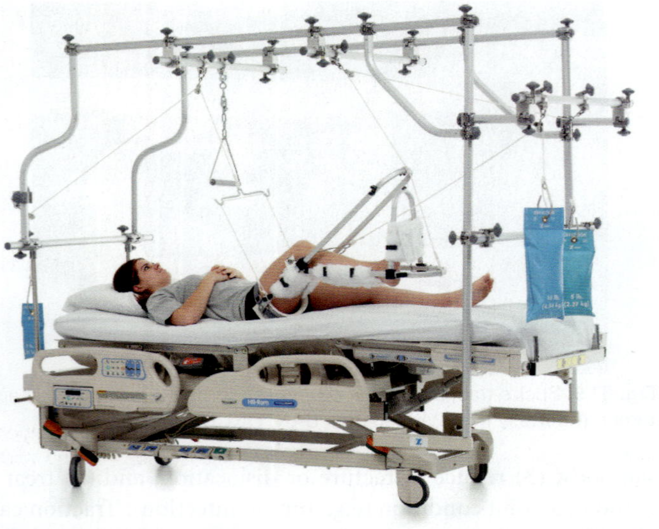

Fig. 67.10 Balanced suspension skeletal traction. Most often used for fractures of the femur, hip, and lower leg. (Courtesy Zimmer, Inc.)

Casts. A *cast* is a temporary immobilization device often applied after closed reduction. A cast usually immobilizes the joints above and below a fracture. This restricts tendon and ligament movement, thus assisting with joint stabilization while the fracture heals. A cast often allows the patient to perform many normal ADLs while providing stability. The 2 most common cast materials are natural (plaster of Paris) and fiberglass. We use fiberglass casts most often because they are lighter, relatively waterproof, and longer wearing than plaster of Paris.[7] They also allow early weight bearing. Plaster of Paris is used mainly for contact casting for treating diabetic foot ulcers.[8]

To apply a cast on an extremity, first cover the affected part with stockinette that is cut longer than the extremity. Then place cotton padding over the stockinette, with extra padding for bony prominences. If using plaster of Paris, immerse it in warm water and then wrap and mold it around the affected part. The number of layers of plaster bandage and the technique of application determine the strength of the cast. The plaster sets within 15 minutes. It is not strong enough for weight bearing until about 36 to 72 hours after application. The decision about weight bearing is made by the HCP. Casts made of fiberglass or other synthetic materials (thermolabile plastic, thermoplastic resins, polyurethane) are activated by submersion in cool or tepid water. Then they are molded to fit the torso or extremity.

Leave a fresh plaster cast uncovered to allow air circulation. Covering the cast allows heat to build up in the cast. This may cause a burn and delay drying. Avoid direct pressure on the cast during the drying period. Handle the cast gently with an open palm to avoid denting the cast. Once the cast is thoroughly dry, the rough edges may be *petaled* to minimize skin irritation. Petaling also prevents plaster of Paris debris from falling into the cast and causing irritation or pressure necrosis. Place several strips (petals) of tape over the rough areas to ensure a smooth cast edge.

Upper extremity injuries. An acute fracture or soft tissue injury of the upper extremity can be immobilized by using a (1) sugar-tong splint, (2) posterior splint, (3) short arm cast, or (4) long arm cast (Fig. 67.11). The *sugar-tong splint* is applied for acute wrist injuries or injuries that may result in significant swelling. Splints are placed over a well-padded forearm, beginning at the phalangeal joints of the hand, extending up the dorsal aspect of the forearm around the distal humerus, and then down the volar aspect of the forearm to the distal palmar crease. The splinting material is wrapped with either elastic bandage or bias stockinette. The sugar-tong posterior splint adjusts for early swelling in the fractured extremity.

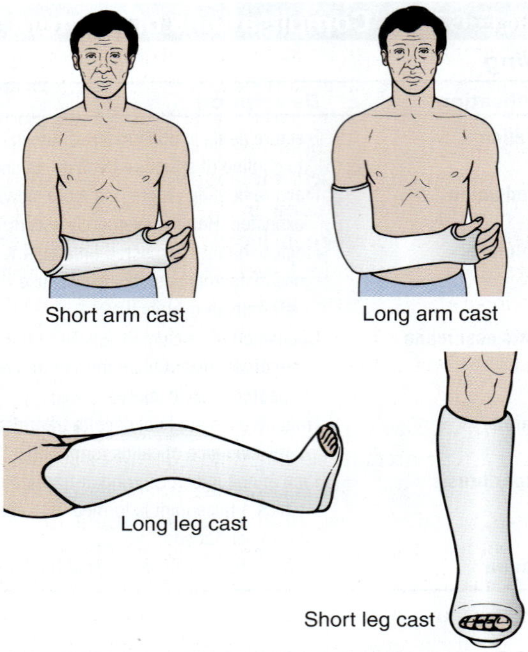

Fig. 67.11 Common types of casts.

The *short arm cast* is often used to treat stable wrist or metacarpal fractures. An aluminum finger splint can be placed in a short arm cast to treat finger injuries. The short arm cast is a circular cast extending from the distal palmar crease to the proximal forearm. This cast immobilizes the wrist and allows unrestricted elbow motion.

The *long arm cast* is often used for stable forearm, elbow, or unstable wrist fractures. It is similar to the short arm cast but extends to the proximal humerus, restricting motion at the wrist and elbow. Support the extremity and reduce edema by elevating the extremity with a sling. When a hanging arm cast is used for a proximal humerus fracture, avoid elevation or use of a supportive sling. The hanging provides traction and maintains fracture alignment.

When a sling is used, ensure the axillary area is well padded to prevent skin breakdown from direct skin-to-skin contact. Apply the sling carefully to avoid putting excess pressure on the neck. Encourage movement of the fingers (unless contraindicated). This decreases edema by enhancing the pumping action of blood vessels. Teach the patient to actively move joints of the upper extremity if not immobilized to prevent stiffness and contractures.

Vertebral injuries. The *body jacket brace* is used for immobilization and support for stable spine injuries of the thoracic or lumbar spine. The brace goes around the chest and abdomen, extending from above the nipple line to the pubis. After applying a brace, assess the patient for superior mesenteric artery syndrome *(cast syndrome).* This condition occurs if the brace is too tight, compressing the superior mesenteric artery against the duodenum. The patient may have abdominal pain, abdominal pressure, nausea, and vomiting. Assess the abdomen for decreased bowel sounds (there may be a window in the brace over the umbilicus). Treatment of cast syndrome includes gastric decompression with a nasogastric (NG) tube and suction. Assess respiratory status, bowel and bladder function, and areas of pressure over the bony prominences, especially the iliac crest. The brace may have to be adjusted or removed if any complications occur.

Lower extremity injuries. Injuries to the lower extremity can be immobilized with a long leg cast, short leg cast, cylinder cast, or prefabricated splint or immobilizer. The usual indications for a long leg cast are an unstable ankle fracture, soft tissue injuries, a fractured tibia, and knee injuries. The cast usually extends from the base of the toes to the groin and gluteal crease. The short leg cast is used for stable ankle and foot injuries. A cylinder cast is used for knee injuries or fractures. It extends from the groin to the malleoli of the ankle. A Robert Jones dressing may be used temporarily to limit mobility of a joint. It is composed of soft padding materials (absorption dressing and cotton sheet wadding), splints, and an elastic wrap or bias-cut stockinette.

With a lower extremity cast or dressing, elevate the extremity above the heart on pillows for the first 24 hours. After that, a casted extremity should not be placed in a dependent position, as this may increase edema. After cast application, observe for signs of compartment syndrome. Note increased pressure, especially in the heel, anterior tibia, head of the fibula, and malleoli. Increased pressure presents as pain or a burning feeling in these areas.

Prefabricated knee and ankle splints and immobilizers are used in many settings. This type of immobilization is easy to apply and remove. This allows us to observe the affected joint for swelling and skin breakdown (Fig. 67.12). Depending on the injury, removing the splint or immobilizer promotes ROM of the affected joint and faster return to function.

The *hip spica cast* is mainly used for femur fractures in children to immobilize the affected extremity and trunk. It extends from above the nipple line to the base of the foot (single spica) and may include the opposite extremity up to an area above the knee (spica and a half) or both extremities (double spica). Assess the patient with a hip spica cast for the same problems associated with the body jacket brace.

External fixation. An *external fixator* is composed of metal pins and wires that are inserted into the bone and attached to external rods to stabilize the fracture while it heals (Fig. 67.13). It can be used to apply traction or to compress fracture fragments and immobilize reduced fragments when the use of a cast or traction is not appropriate. The external device holds fracture fragments in place similar to a surgically implanted internal device. External fixation is mainly used for complex fractures with extensive soft tissue damage, correcting congenital bony defects, nonunion or malunion, and limb lengthening.

External fixation is often used to try to salvage extremities that otherwise may need amputation. Perform ongoing assessment for pin loosening and infection. Infection may require removing the device. Teach the patient and caregiver about meticulous pin care. Although each HCP has a protocol for pin care cleaning, chlorhexidine is often used.[9]

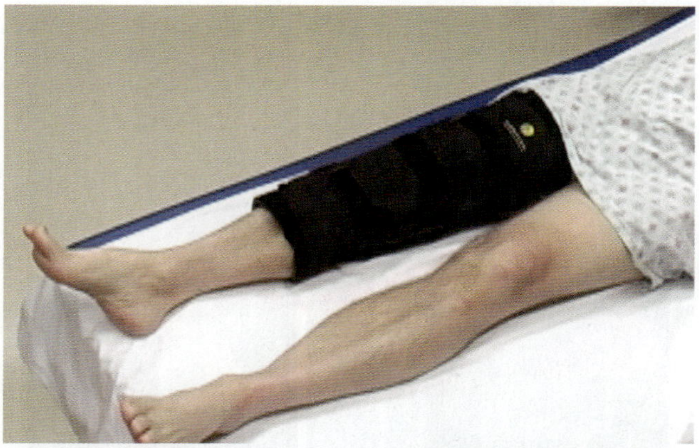

Fig. 67.12 Knee immobilizer. (From Naples RM, Ufberg JW: *Roberts and Hedges' Clinical procedures in emergency medicine and acute care*, Philadelphia, 2020, Elsevier.)

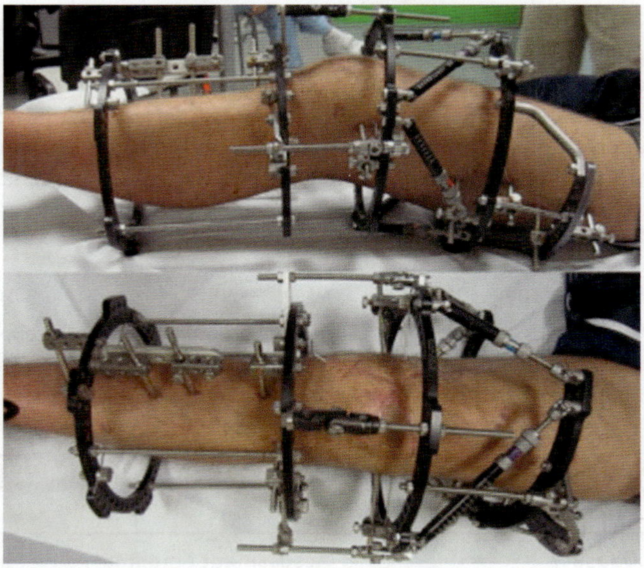

Fig. 67.13 External fixation of tibial fracture. (From Krettke C, Hawi N: *Skeletal trauma: basic science, management, and reconstruction*, ed 6, Philadelphia, 2020, Elsevier.)

Internal fixation. Internal fixation devices (pins, plates, intramedullary rods, metal and bioabsorbable screws) are surgically inserted to realign and maintain position of bony fragments (Fig. 67.14). These metal devices are biologically inert and made from stainless steel, vitallium, or titanium. Proper alignment and bone healing are evaluated regularly by x-rays.

Electrical Bone Growth Stimulation

Electrical bone growth stimulation can promote healing, especially with fracture nonunion or delayed union. It stimulates new bone, cartilage, and blood vessel formation.[10] There are noninvasive, semi-invasive, and invasive methods of electrical bone growth stimulation. Noninvasive stimulators use direct

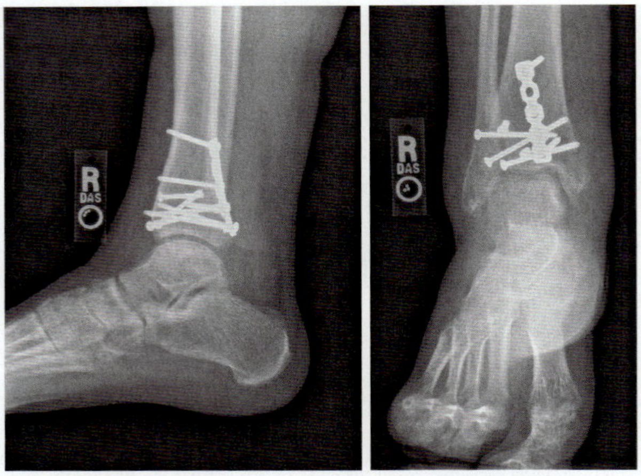

Fig. 67.14 Views of internal fixation devices to stabilize a fractured tibia and fibula. (From Jeremy Lewis, MD, Albuquerque, NM.)

current or pulsed electromagnetic fields (PEMFs) to generate a weak electrical current. Electrodes are typically in a band applied over the patient's skin or cast and worn 10 to 12 hours each day, usually while the patient is sleeping. Semi-invasive or percutaneous bone growth stimulators use an external power supply and electrodes that are inserted through the skin and into the bone. Invasive stimulators require surgical implantation of a current generator in an IM or subcutaneous space. An electrode is implanted in the bone fragments.

Drug Therapy

Patients with fractures have varying degrees of pain. Muscle relaxants, such as carisoprodol (Soma), cyclobenzaprine, or methocarbamol, may be given to manage pain from muscle spasms.

We give tetanus and diphtheria toxoid or tetanus immunoglobulin to the patient with an open fracture when their immunization status cannot be confirmed. Bone-penetrating antibiotics, such as a cephalosporin (e.g., cefazolin), are given prophylactically before surgery.

Nutrition Therapy

Proper nutrition helps ensure optimal soft tissue and bone healing. An adequate energy source promotes muscle strength and tone, builds endurance, and provides energy for ambulation and gait-training skills. The diet must include adequate protein (e.g., 1 g/kg of body weight), vitamins (especially B, C, and D), calcium, potassium, phosphorus, and magnesium. Low serum protein and vitamin C deficiencies interfere with tissue healing. Immobility and bone healing increase calcium needs.

A fluid intake of 2000 to 3000 mL/day promotes optimal bladder and bowel function. Adequate fluid and a high-fiber diet with fruits and vegetables prevent constipation. If immobilized in bed with skeletal traction or in a body jacket brace, the patient should eat 6 small meals. This helps avoid overeating that can cause abdominal pressure and cramping.

❖ NURSING MANAGEMENT: FRACTURES

◆ Assessment

Obtain a brief history of the traumatic episode, mechanism of injury, and position in which the patient was found from the patient or witnesses. As soon as possible, the patient should be transported to an ED. There we do a thorough assessment and start treatment (Table 67.7). Subjective and objective data that

TABLE 67.7 EMERGENCY MANAGEMENT

Fractured Extremity

Cause	Assessment Findings	Interventions
Blunt Trauma • Direct blow • Fall • Forced flexion or hyperextension • Motor vehicle crash • Pedestrian event • Twisting force **Penetrating Trauma** • Blast • Gunshot **Other** • Pathologic condition • Violent muscle contraction (seizures) • Crush injury	• Bruising • ↓ Distal pulses • Deformity or unnatural position of affected limb • Edema • Grating (crepitus) • Loss of function • Muscle spasm • Numbness, tingling • Tenderness, pain • Warmth at site • Wound over injured site, exposure of bone	**Initial** • Treat life-threatening injuries first. • If unresponsive, assess circulation, airway, and breathing. • If responsive, monitor airway, breathing, and circulation. • Control external bleeding with direct pressure or sterile pressure dressing and elevation of the extremity. • Assess neurovascular condition distal to injury before and after splinting. • Elevate injured limb if possible. • Do not try to straighten fractured or dislocated joints. • Do not manipulate protruding bone ends. • Apply ice packs to affected area. • Obtain x-rays of affected limb. • Give tetanus prophylaxis if there is a break in skin integrity. • Mark location of pulses to aid repeat assessment. • Splint fracture site, including joints above and below fracture site. **Ongoing Monitoring** • Assess vital signs, level of consciousness, O_2 saturation, neurovascular condition, pain. • Assess for compartment syndrome (excessive pain, pain with passive stretch of the affected extremity muscles, pallor, paresthesia, with late signs of paralysis and pulselessness). • Assess for FES (dyspnea, chest pain, temperature elevation).

TABLE 67.8 NURSING ASSESSMENT

Fracture

Subjective Data	Objective Data (continued)
Subjective Data **Important Health Information** *Health history:* Traumatic injury, long-term repetitive forces (stress fracture), bone or systemic diseases, prolonged immobility, osteopenia, osteoporosis *Medications:* Corticosteroids (osteoporotic fractures); analgesics *Surgery or other treatments:* First aid treatment of fracture, musculoskeletal surgeries	***General*** Apprehension, guarding of injured site ***Musculoskeletal*** Restricted or lost function of affected part; local bony deformities, abnormal angulation; shortening, rotation, or crepitation of affected part; muscle weakness
Functional Health Patterns *Health perception–health management:* Calcium and vitamin D supplementation *Activity-exercise:* Loss of motion or weakness of affected part, muscle spasms *Cognitive-perceptual:* Sudden and severe pain in affected area; numbness, tingling, loss of sensation distal to injury; ongoing pain that increases with activity (stress fracture)	***Neurovascular*** Paresthesia, absent or ↓ sensation, hypersensation ***Skin*** Lacerations, pallor and cool skin or bluish and warm skin distal to injury; bruising, edema at fracture site
Objective Data ***Cardiovascular*** Reduced or absent pulse distal to injury, ↓ skin temperature, delayed capillary refill	***Possible Diagnostic Findings*** Identification and extent of fracture on x-ray, bone scan, CT scan, or MRI

you should obtain from a person with a fracture are outlined in Table 67.8.

If a fracture is suspected, immobilize the extremity in the position in which it is found. Unnecessary movement increases risk for damage to adjacent nerves and blood vessels. It may also convert a closed fracture to an open fracture.

Neurovascular Assessment

Perform a thorough neurovascular assessment of the affected extremity, distal to the fracture site. Musculoskeletal injuries may cause changes in the neurovascular status of an injured extremity. Poor positioning, physiologic responses to the traumatic injury, and application of a cast or constrictive dressing can cause nerve or vascular damage, usually distal to the injury. Record clinical findings before fracture treatment. This way, if a problem occurs later, it will help determine if it was missed during the original assessment or a result of treatment.

The neurovascular assessment consists of *peripheral vascular assessment* (color, temperature, capillary refill, peripheral pulses, edema) and *peripheral neurologic assessment* (sensation, motor function, pain). Throughout the neurovascular assessment, compare both extremities to obtain an accurate assessment.

Assess an extremity's color (pink, pale, cyanotic) and temperature (hot, warm, cool, cold) around the injury. Pallor or a cool-to-cold extremity below the injury could indicate arterial insufficiency. A warm, cyanotic extremity could indicate poor venous return. Next, assess capillary refill. A delay in returning to its original color (greater than 3 seconds) can occur with arterial insufficiency.

Compare pulses on the unaffected and injured extremities to identify differences in rate or quality. This contralateral evaluation is critical. A decreased or absent pulse distal to the injury can indicate vascular problems and insufficiency. Assess peripheral edema. Pitting edema may be present with severe injury.

Assess ulnar, median, and radial nerve function to evaluate sensation and motor innervation in the upper extremity. Assess motor function by asking the patient to (1) abduct the fingers (ulnar nerve), (2) oppose the thumb and small finger (median nerve), and (3) flex and extend the wrist (or the fingers, if in a cast) (radial nerve). In the lower extremity, assess the patient's ability to perform dorsiflexion (peroneal nerve) and plantar flexion (tibial nerve). Evaluate sensory function of the peroneal nerve by touching the web space between the big and second toes. Stroke the plantar surface (sole) of the foot to assess sensory function of the tibial nerve.

The patient may report *paresthesia* (abnormal sensation [e.g., numbness, tingling]) and hypersensation or hyperesthesia. Partial or full loss of sensation (paresis or paralysis) may be a late sign of neurovascular damage. Teach the patient to immediately report any changes in sensation or the ability to move the digits in the affected extremity.

Clinical Problems

Clinical problems for the patient with a fracture may include:

- Musculoskeletal problem
- Risk for infection
- Pain

Additional information on clinical problems and interventions for the patient with a fracture is presented in eNursing Care Plan 67.1 (on the website for this chapter).

Planning

The overall goals are that the patient with a fracture will (1) have healing with no associated complications, (2) have acceptable pain relief, and (3) achieve maximal rehabilitation potential.

◆ Implementation

◆ Acute Care

Patients with fractures may be treated in an ED or an HCP's office and released to home care. They may need hospitalization for varying amounts of time. Specific nursing measures depend on the setting and type of treatment.

Preoperative care. If surgery is needed to treat a fracture, patients must be prepared. In addition to the usual preoperative nursing care (see Chapter 18), teach the patient about the type of immobilization and assistive devices that will be used. Discuss expected activity limitations after surgery. Assure them that nursing staff will help meet their personal needs until they can resume self-care. Review pain management strategies.

Postoperative care. In general, nursing care after surgery involves monitoring vital signs and applying general principles of postoperative nursing care (see Chapter 20). Perform frequent neurovascular assessment of the affected extremity to detect early and subtle changes. Follow any limitations related to turning, positioning, and extremity support. Minimize pain and discomfort through proper alignment and positioning. Frequently observe dressings or casts for any signs of bleeding or drainage. Report an increase in size of the drainage area to the HCP. If a wound drainage system is in place, regularly measure the volume of drainage and assess its character (e.g., bloody, purulent). Report increased or purulent drainage at once to the HCP. Maintain the patency of any drainage systems, using aseptic technique to avoid contamination.

Other nursing actions depend on the type of immobilization used. A blood salvage and reinfusion system may be used to allow recovery and reinfusion of the patient's own blood. The blood is retrieved from a joint space or cavity; then the patient receives this blood in the form of an autotransfusion. Autotransfusion is discussed in Chapter 31.

Other measures. Patients often have reduced mobility because of a fracture. Plan care to decrease risk for the many possible complications of immobility. Prevent constipation by increasing patient activity. Maintain high fluid intake (more than 2500 mL/day unless contraindicated) and a diet high in bulk and roughage (fresh fruits and vegetables). If these measures are not effective in continuing the patient's normal bowel elimination pattern, give stool softeners, laxatives, or suppositories. Maintain a regular time for elimination to promote bowel regularity (Table 67.9).

Renal stones can develop from bone demineralization due to reduced mobility. Hypercalcemia from demineralization causes a rise in urine pH and stone formation from calcium precipitation. Unless contraindicated, maintain a fluid intake of 2500 mL/day to decrease the risk for stone formation. Renal stones are discussed in Chapter 50.

Rapid deconditioning of the cardiopulmonary system can occur from prolonged bed rest, resulting in orthostatic hypotension and decreased lung capacity. Unless contraindicated, decrease these effects by having the patient sit on the side of the bed, allowing their lower limbs to dangle over the bedside. Have the patient perform standing transfers. When the patient is allowed to increase activity, assess for orthostatic hypotension. Assess patients for signs of VTE. VTE is discussed in Chapter 41.

TABLE 67.9 NURSING MANAGEMENT

Caring for the Patient With a Cast or Traction

- Perform neurovascular assessment on the affected extremity.
- Monitor pain intensity and give prescribed analgesics.
- Determine correct body alignment to enhance traction.
- Monitor skin integrity around cast and at traction pin sites.
- Monitor cast during drying for denting or flattening.
- Teach patient and caregiver about cast care or traction and measures to prevent complications (e.g., ROM exercises).
- Assess for complications of immobility (e.g., constipation, VTE, kidney stones, atelectasis) and develop a plan to minimize those complications.
- Supervise assistive personnel (AP):
  - Position casted extremity above heart level as directed by RN.
  - Apply ice to cast as directed by RN.
  - Maintain body position and integrity of traction (if trained in this procedure).
  - Help with passive and active ROM exercises.
  - Notify RN about reports of pain, tingling, or decreased sensation in the affected extremity.

Collaborate With Physical Therapist

- Assess current mobility and need for assistance.
- Teach safe ambulation with assistive device based on weight-bearing restrictions.
- Establish exercise plan and teach patient to perform exercises safely.
- Coordinate PT with RN so that patient can receive timely analgesia.
- Discuss home environment with patient and identify modifications to promote safety (e.g., stair training).

Collaborate With Occupational Therapist

- Assess impact of patient's condition on ability to perform ADLs.
- Teach use of assistive devices (e.g., long-handled reacher, shoe donner) to promote self-care while maintaining activity restrictions.

Traction. When slings are used with traction, regularly inspect exposed skin areas. Pressure over a bony prominence created by wrinkled sheets or blankets may cause pressure necrosis. Persistent skin pressure may impair blood flow and cause injury to peripheral nerves and blood vessels. Assess skeletal traction or external fixation pin sites for signs of infection. Pin site care may vary. It often includes regularly cleansing with chlorhexidine, rinsing with sterile saline, and drying the area with sterile gauze.

External rotation of the affected extremity is a classic assessment finding for a patient with unrepaired hip fracture. If skin traction is ordered before surgery, apply traction without trying to reposition or realign the extremity. Movement of fracture fragments can occur during repositioning, causing increased pain and possible nerve impingement. Keep the patient in the center of the bed in a supine position to provide adequate countertraction.

If exercise is allowed, encourage patient participation in a simple exercise program based on activity restrictions. Have the patient perform frequent position changes, ROM exercises of unaffected joints, deep-breathing exercises, and isometric exercises. These activities should be done several times each day. Teach the patient to use the trapeze bar (if permitted) to raise the body off the bed for linen changes and placement of the bedpan. Encourage and help the hospitalized patient to stay connected with friends and family by telephone or through social media resources.

TABLE 67.10 PATIENT & CAREGIVER TEACHING

Cast Care

After a cast is applied, include the following instructions when teaching the patient and the caregiver:

Do

1. Apply ice directly over fracture site for first 24 hr (avoid getting cast wet by keeping ice in plastic bag and protecting cast with cloth).
2. Check with HCP before getting fiberglass cast wet.
3. Dry cast thoroughly if inadvertently exposed to water.
   - Blot dry with towel.
   - Use hair dryer on low setting until cast is thoroughly dry.
4. Elevate extremity above heart level for first 48 hr.
5. Regularly move joints above and below cast.
6. Use hair dryer on cool setting for itching inside the cast.
7. Report signs of possible problems to HCP:
   - Increasing pain despite elevation, ice, analgesia.
   - Swelling with pain and discoloration of toes or fingers.
   - Pain during movement.
   - Burning or tingling under cast.
   - Sores or foul odor under cast.
8. Keep appointment to have fracture and cast checked.

Do Not

1. Get cast wet.
2. Remove any padding.
3. Insert any objects inside cast.
4. Bear weight on new cast for 48 hr (not all casts are made for weight bearing; check with HCP when unsure).
5. Cover cast with plastic for prolonged periods.

◆ Ambulatory Care

Cast care. Most uncomplicated fractures are treated in an outpatient setting. Whatever the type of cast material, a cast can interfere with circulation and nerve function if it is applied too tightly or excess edema occurs after application. Frequent neurovascular assessment of the immobilized extremity is critical. Teach the patient to recognize and promptly report tightness of the cast and areas of pressure or discomfort. Explain the importance of elevating the extremity above heart level to promote venous return and applying ice to control or prevent edema during the initial phase. However, if you suspect compartment syndrome, do not elevate the extremity above the heart.

Patient and caregiver teaching is important to prevent complications. Table 67.10 describes patient and caregiver instructions for cast care. Teach the patient to exercise joints above and below the cast. Tell the patient not to scratch or place anything inside the cast because this may cause skin injury and infection. For itching, direct a hair dryer on a cool setting under the cast. Confirm the patient's and caregiver's understanding of these instructions before discharge. A follow-up phone call is appropriate. Home care nursing visits may be needed, especially for the patient with a body jacket brace.

The cast is typically removed in the outpatient setting. Patients often fear being cut by the oscillating blade of the cast saw. Reassure the patient that damage to the skin is unlikely. Teach the patient about possible changes in the appearance of the extremity beneath the cast (e.g., dry, wrinkled skin; atrophied muscle; foul odor). The patient may be scared to use the injured extremity after cast removal.

Ambulation. Know the overall goals of PT in relation to the patient's abilities, needs, and tolerance. The physical therapist is responsible for mobility training and teaching about the use of assistive aids (cane, crutches, walker). Reinforce these instructions. The patient with lower extremity fractures usually starts mobility training when able to sit in bed and dangle the feet over the side. Work with the physical therapist to give analgesia before a PT session.

When the patient begins to ambulate, know their weight-bearing status and the correct technique if the patient is using an assistive device. Ambulation occurs in different degrees of weight-bearing: (1) non–weight-bearing (no weight on the involved extremity), (2) touch-down/toe-touch weight bearing (contact with floor for balance but no weight borne), (3) partial–weight-bearing ambulation (25% to 50% of weight borne), (4) weight bearing as tolerated (based on pain and tolerance), and (5) full–weight-bearing ambulation (no limitations).

Assistive devices. Devices for ambulation range from a cane (can relieve up to 40% of the weight normally borne by a lower limb) to a walker or crutches (may allow for complete non–weight-bearing ambulation). The HCP decides which device is best, balancing the need for maximum stability and safety with the need for maneuverability in small spaces, such as bathrooms. Discuss with the patient lifestyle requirements and help select a device that allows the patient to feel most secure and independent. The technique for using assistive ambulation devices varies. The involved limb is usually advanced at the same time or immediately after advance of the device. The uninvolved limb is advanced last. Canes are held in the hand opposite the involved extremity.

Place a transfer belt (gait belt) around the patient's waist to provide stability while teaching the patient how to use an assistive device. Discourage the patient from reaching for furniture or relying on another person for support. A patient with inadequate upper limb strength or poorly fitted crutches bears weight at the axilla rather than at the hands. This can damage the neurovascular bundle that passes across the axilla. If verbal coaching does not correct the problem, teach the patient another form of ambulation (e.g., walker) until strength is adequate.

Patients who must ambulate without weight bearing need enough upper limb strength to lift their own weight at each step. Because the muscles of the shoulder girdle and upper arm may not be accustomed to this work, patients require focused training for this task. Push-ups, pull-ups using the overhead trapeze bar, and weightlifting develop the triceps and biceps muscles. Straight-leg raises and quadriceps-setting exercises strengthen the quadriceps muscles.

Psychosocial concerns. Short-term rehabilitative goals address the transition from dependence to independence in performing simple ADLs. They are directed at preserving or increasing strength and endurance. Long-term rehabilitative goals are aimed at preventing problems from musculoskeletal

TABLE 67.11 Problems Associated With Musculoskeletal Injuries

Problem	Description	Nursing Considerations
Atrophy	• ↓ Muscle mass occurs from disuse after prolonged immobilization. • Loss of nerve function can cause muscle atrophy.	• Isometric strength exercises as able with immobilization device helps reduce amount of atrophy. • Muscle atrophy interferes with and prolongs rehabilitation process.
Contracture	• Abnormal condition of joint characterized by flexion and fixation. • Caused by atrophy and shortening of muscle fibers and ligaments or by loss of normal elasticity of skin over joint.	• Can be prevented by frequent position change, correct body alignment, active-passive ROM exercises several times a day. • Intervention requires gradual progressive stretching of muscles or ligaments in region of joint.
Footdrop	• Plantar-flexed position of the foot occurs when Achilles's tendon in ankle shortens because it has been allowed to assume an unsupported position. • Peroneal nerve palsy (a compression neuropathy) can cause footdrop and spinal nerve compression.	• For patient with long-term injuries, support foot in neutral position to ↓ risk for footdrop. • Once footdrop has developed, can significantly hinder ambulation and gait training. • May need splint to keep feet in neutral position. • High-top athletic shoes may help. Apply at scheduled times to keep feet in neutral position.
Muscle spasms	• Caused by involuntary muscle contraction after fracture, muscle strain, or nerve injury. • May last several weeks. • Pain from muscle spasms is often intense and can last from several seconds to several minutes.	• Measures to ↓ intensity of muscle spasms are similar to actions for pain management. • Do not massage muscle spasms. Massage may stimulate muscle tissue contraction that ↑ spasm and pain. • Thermotherapy, especially heat, may reduce muscle spasm.
Pain	• Common with fractures, edema, muscle spasm. • May be mild to severe and described as aching, dull, burning, throbbing, sharp, or deep.	• Causes include incorrect positioning and alignment of extremity, incorrect support of extremity, sudden movement of extremity, immobilization device that is applied too tightly or incorrectly, constrictive dressings, motion at fracture site. • Determine causes of pain so that corrective action can be taken.

injury (Table 67.11). During the rehabilitative phase, help the patient adjust to any problems caused by the injury (e.g., separation from family, financial impact, loss of income from inability to work, potential for disability). Assess patients for posttraumatic stress disorder. This is especially important if significant injury to others or fatalities occurred with the incident.

The caregiver may have a key role in providing long-term care. Teach the caregiver how to help with strength and endurance exercises, mobility, and promoting activities that enhance the quality of daily living. Offer support and encouragement while actively listening to the patient's and caregiver's concerns.

◆ Evaluation

The expected outcomes are that the patient with a fracture will:

- Report satisfactory pain management
- Show proper care of cast or immobilizer
- Have uncomplicated bone healing

COMPLICATIONS OF FRACTURES

Most fractures heal without complications. Complications may be direct or indirect. *Direct complications* include infection, problems with bone union, and avascular necrosis. *Indirect complications* include compartment syndrome, VTE, fat embolism syndrome (FES), breakdown of skeletal muscle *(rhabdomyolysis)*, and hypovolemic shock. Most musculoskeletal injuries are not life threatening. Death after a fracture is usually due to damage to underlying organs and vascular structures or complications of the fracture or immobility. Open fractures, fractures with severe blood loss, and fractures that damage vital organs (e.g., lung, heart) are medical emergencies requiring immediate attention.

Infection

Open fractures and soft tissue injuries have a high rate of infection. Communication of the fracture site with the outside environment can contaminate the site with microorganisms or foreign bodies. Damage to the surrounding soft tissue and blood vessels impairs the ability of defense mechanisms to respond to microorganisms. Dying or contaminated tissue is an ideal medium for many common pathogens, including anaerobic bacilli, such as *Clostridium tetani*. Measures to prevent infection and osteomyelitis are important.

Open fractures require surgical debridement. The wound is cleaned by saline lavage in the operating room. Gross contaminants are irrigated and mechanically removed. Contused, contaminated, and devitalized tissue (muscle, subcutaneous fat, skin, and bone fragments) is surgically excised *(debridement)*. The wound may be irrigated with antibiotic solution. Antibiotic-impregnated beads can be placed in the surgical site. Patients usually receive IV antibiotics for at least 3 days.[11] Surgical management and antibiotics have reduced the occurrence of infection. The amount of soft tissue damage determines if the wound is closed at the time of surgery or if it needs repeat debridement, closed suction drainage, and/or skin grafting.

Compartment Syndrome

Compartment syndrome is a condition in which swelling causes increased pressure within a limited space (muscle compartment). Because the fascia surrounding the muscle has limited ability to stretch, continued swelling can cause pressure that compromises the function of blood vessels and nerves in the compartment. Capillary perfusion is reduced below a level needed for tissue life. Compartment syndrome often involves the leg but can occur in any muscle group.

There are 38 compartments in the upper and lower extremities. Two basic causes of compartment syndrome are (1) decreased compartment size resulting from restrictive dressings, splints, casts, excessive traction, or premature closure of fascia; and (2) increased compartment contents due to bleeding, inflammation, edema, or IV infiltration.

Edema can create enough pressure to obstruct circulation and cause venous occlusion, which further increases edema. Arterial flow is eventually compromised, causing ischemia in the extremity. As ischemia continues, muscle and nerve cells are destroyed. Fibrotic tissue eventually replaces healthy tissue. Contracture, disability, and loss of function can occur. Delays in diagnosis and treatment may lead to irreversible muscle and nerve ischemia. The extremity may become functionally useless or severely impaired.

Compartment syndrome is usually due to fractures (especially of long bones), extensive soft tissue damage, and crush injury. Distal humerus and proximal tibial fractures are the most common ones associated with compartment syndrome. Compartment injury can also occur after knee or leg surgery. Prolonged pressure on a muscle compartment may result when someone is trapped under a heavy object or a person's limb is trapped beneath the body because of response to drugs or alcohol.

Clinical Manifestations

Compartment syndrome may occur initially from the body's physiologic response to the injury, or it may be delayed for several days after the original insult or injury. Ischemia can occur within 4 to 8 hours after the onset of compartment syndrome.

One or more of the "6 *Ps*" are specific to compartment syndrome: (1) *pain* out of proportion to the injury that is not managed by opioid analgesics, and *pain* on passive stretch of muscle in the compartment; (2) increasing *pressure* in the compartment; (3) *paresthesia* (numbness and tingling); (4) *pallor*, coolness, and loss of normal color of the extremity; (5) *paralysis* or loss of function; and (6) *pulselessness* (decreased or absent peripheral pulses).

Interprofessional Care

Prompt diagnosis of compartment syndrome is critical. Perform regular neurovascular assessment on all patients with fractures, especially those with injury of the extremities or soft tissue in these areas. Early recognition and effective treatment of compartment syndrome are essential to avoid permanent damage to muscles and nerves.

Carefully assess the location, quality, and intensity pain (see Chapter 9). Pain unrelieved by drugs and out of proportion to the level of injury is one of the *first* signs of compartment syndrome. Paresthesia is also an early sign. Notify the HCP immediately of these changes. Relieving the source of pressure (e.g., cast is cut [bivalved] or dressing loosened by order of the HCP)

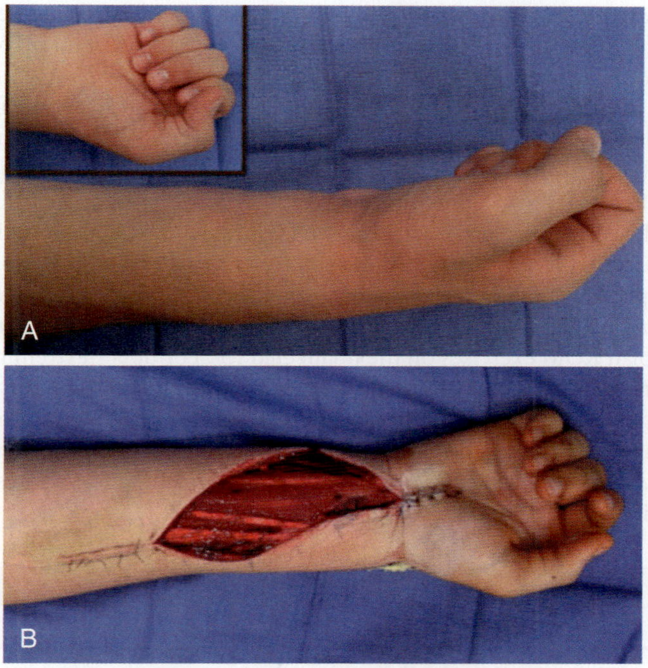

Fig. 67.15 (A) Fracture of the distal radius with distal forearm compartment syndrome. (B) Fasciotomy used to treat compartment syndrome. (From Stevanovic MV, Sharpe F: *Green's operative hand surgery*, ed 7, Philadelphia, 2017, Elsevier.)

typically decreases pain and paresthesia and can avoid compartment syndrome. Reducing traction weight may decrease external pressures on the extremity. Pulselessness and paralysis are late signs of compartment syndrome. Do not wait until these late signs occur to contact the HCP. Amputation may be needed due to prolonged ischemia.

With suspected compartment syndrome, do not elevate the extremity above the heart. Similarly, do not apply cold compresses. They may cause vasoconstriction and worsen compartment syndrome.

Surgical decompression (e.g., fasciotomy) of the involved compartment may be needed (Fig. 67.15). The fasciotomy site is left open for several days to allow adequate soft tissue decompression. Infection resulting from delayed wound closure is a potential problem after fasciotomy. In severe cases of compartment syndrome, amputation is done.

CHECK YOUR PRACTICE

Your 22-year-old male patient had a fall while rock climbing. He returned from surgery 8 hours ago with a long leg cast placed for open fractures of the femur and tibia. He continually reports pain that IV morphine does not seem to help.

- How will you assess his neurovascular condition?
- What signs and symptoms would suggest the development of compartment syndrome?
- What is the most likely intervention if compartment syndrome is developing?

Venous Thromboembolism

Veins of the lower extremities and pelvis are at great risk for clot (thrombus) formation after a fracture, especially a hip fracture. VTE may occur after total hip or total knee replacement surgery. In patients with limited mobility, inactivity of muscles that normally help pump venous blood from the extremities to the heart worsens venous stasis.

Because of the high risk for VTE in the orthopedic surgical patient, prophylactic anticoagulant drugs should be given for at least 10 to 14 days.[12] The most common agents used include (1) warfarin (Coumadin), (2) low-molecular-weight heparin (LMWH) (e.g., enoxaparin [Lovenox], fondaparinux), (3) aspirin, or (4) a factor Xa inhibitor (e.g., rivaroxaban [Xarelto], apixaban).[12] Have the patient dorsiflex and plantar flex the ankle of an affected lower extremity against resistance and perform ROM exercises on the unaffected leg. For upper extremity injuries, have the patient flex and extend the wrist if not immobilized by a cast or splint and perform ROM exercises on the unaffected arm. They may wear compression gradient stockings (antiembolism hose) or using intermittent pneumatic compression devices.[12] VTE is discussed in Chapter 41.

! SAFETY ALERT

Anticoagulant Therapy

- Monitor for signs of bleeding (e.g., nosebleeds, hematuria).
- Teach patient signs of bleeding and what to do if bleeding occurs.
- Teach patient safe self-injection if taking an injectable anticoagulant after discharge.
- Encourage patient to keep appointments for laboratory testing to monitor effects of warfarin (if prescribed).

Fat Embolism Syndrome

Fat embolism syndrome (FES) is characterized by fat globules entering the circulatory system from fractures. They collect in areas with abundant blood vessels, especially the lungs and brain. FES contributes to mortality from fractures. The fractures most often associated with FES are those of the long bones, ribs, tibia, and pelvis. FES can occur after joint replacement, burns, pancreatitis, liposuction, crush injuries, and bone marrow transplantation.[13]

Two theories about FES exist. According to the mechanical theory, fat emboli originate from fat released from the marrow of injured bone. The fat enters systemic circulation, where it travels to other organs. As fat droplets become stuck in small blood vessels, local ischemia and inflammation occur. The biochemical theory suggests hormonal changes caused by trauma or sepsis stimulate systemic release of free fatty acids (e.g., chylomicrons) that form the fat emboli.

Clinical Manifestations

Early recognition of FES is crucial to prevent patient death. Most patients have symptoms within 24 to 48 hours after injury.[13] Severe forms have occurred within hours of injury. Fat emboli in the lungs cause hemorrhagic interstitial pneumonitis with signs and symptoms of acute respiratory distress syndrome (ARDS). These include chest pain, tachypnea, cyanosis, dyspnea, apprehension, tachycardia, and hypoxemia. These symptoms are caused by poor O_2 exchange. Changes in mental status due to hypoxemia are common. Petechiae on the neck, anterior chest wall, axilla, and head may help discern FES from other problems.[13] They may appear due to intravascular thromboses caused by decreased oxygenation. However, not all patients have petechiae. They may fade before they are noticed.

The clinical course of FES may be rapid and acute. In a short time, skin color can change from pallor to cyanosis. The patient may become comatose. No specific laboratory tests aid in the diagnosis. However, certain abnormalities may be present. These include fat cells in blood, urine, or sputum; a decrease of PaO_2 to less than 60 mm Hg; decreased platelet count and hematocrit; and high erythrocyte sedimentation rate (ESR). The ECG may show ST segment and T-wave changes. A chest x-ray may show bilateral pulmonary infiltrates.

Interprofessional care. Management of FES is supportive and related to managing symptoms. The patient needs appropriate respiratory support (see Chapter 28). Administer O_2 to treat hypoxia. ECMO or mechanical ventilation may be an option if a satisfactory PaO_2 cannot be obtained. Some patients develop pulmonary edema and/or ARDS, leading to increased mortality. Most persons survive FES with few complications.

Cardiovascular problems are often managed with IV fluids, pulmonary vasodilators, peripheral vasoconstrictors, and inotropic drugs. There is currently no research supporting the use of steroids, heparin, or dextran in the treatment of FES.[13]

Preventing FES is important. Careful immobilization and handling of a long bone fracture are the most important factors in preventing FES. Reposition the patient as little as possible before fracture immobilization or stabilization to decrease the risk of dislodging fat droplets into the general circulation.

CHECK YOUR PRACTICE

You are caring for a 24-year-old male patient who had a femur fracture in a motorcycle accident last night. He is scheduled for ORIF later today. While doing your assessment, you notice that he seems very restless. You note some axillary petechiae.

- What complication would you suspect is occurring?
- Why is this patient at risk for this complication?
- What is the most important intervention for a patient with this complication?

Rhabdomyolysis

Rhabdomyolysis is a syndrome caused by the breakdown of damaged skeletal muscle cells. This breakdown causes the release of myoglobin into the bloodstream. Myoglobin precipitates and causes obstruction in renal tubules. This results in acute tubular necrosis and acute kidney injury (AKI). Because of possible muscle damage, assess urine output. Common signs are dark reddish-brown urine and symptoms of AKI (see Chapter 51).

TYPES OF FRACTURES

COLLES FRACTURE

A *Colles fracture* is a fracture of the distal radius. The styloid process of the ulna may be involved as well. The injury usually occurs when the patient falls on an outstretched arm and hand.

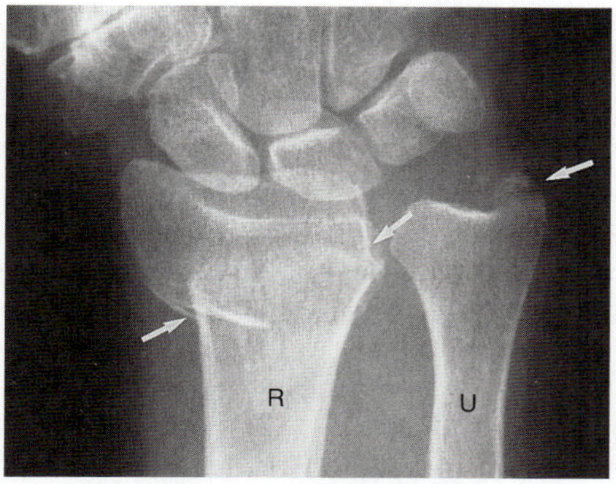

Fig. 67.16 Colles' fracture. Fracture of the distal radius *(R)* and ulnar *(U)* styloid from patient falling on the outstretched hand. (From Mettler FA: *Essentials of radiology*, ed 2, Philadelphia, 2005, Saunders.)

It is one of the most common types of fractures in adults. It most often occurs in patients over 50 years old whose bones are osteoporotic *(fragility fracture)* (Fig. 67.16). A younger person with a Colles' fracture caused by a low-energy force should be referred for an osteoporosis evaluation.

Symptoms include pain in the immediate area of injury, pronounced swelling, and dorsal displacement of the distal fragment (silver-fork deformity). This displacement appears as an obvious deformity of the wrist. The major complication is vascular insufficiency from edema. CTS can be a later complication.

A Colles' fracture is usually managed with closed reduction of the fracture and applying a splint or cast. If displaced, the fracture is typically managed with open reduction and internal or external fixation. Nursing care includes frequent neurovascular assessment and measures to reduce edema. Provide support and protect the extremity. Encourage active movement of the thumb and fingers to reduce edema and increase venous return. Teach the patient to perform active movements of the shoulder to prevent stiffness or contracture.

HUMERAL SHAFT FRACTURE

Fractures involving the shaft of the humerus are common among young and middle-aged adults. The most common symptoms are obvious displacement of the humeral shaft, shortened extremity, abnormal mobility, and pain. Complications include radial nerve injury and injury to the brachial artery due to laceration, transection, or muscle spasm.

Treatment depends on the specific fracture location and displacement. Nonoperative treatment may include a hanging arm cast, shoulder immobilizer, sling and swathe (a type of immobilizer that prevents shoulder movement), or humeral cuff brace (Fig. 67.17).

The humeral cuff brace is typically used to stabilize mid-shaft humerus fractures. Two pieces of molded plastic are fitted together in a clam-shell configuration and held together with Velcro straps. The humeral cuff brace is a good option for nonoperative fracture management if the patient is at increased risk for complications.

When these devices are used, elevate the head of the bed to assist gravity in reducing the fracture. Allow the arm to hang freely when the patient is sitting or standing. Provide measures to protect the axilla and prevent skin breakdown. Carefully place absorbable composite dressing pads (e.g., ABD pads) in the axilla. Change them twice daily or as needed. Skin or skeletal traction may be used for reduction and immobilization.

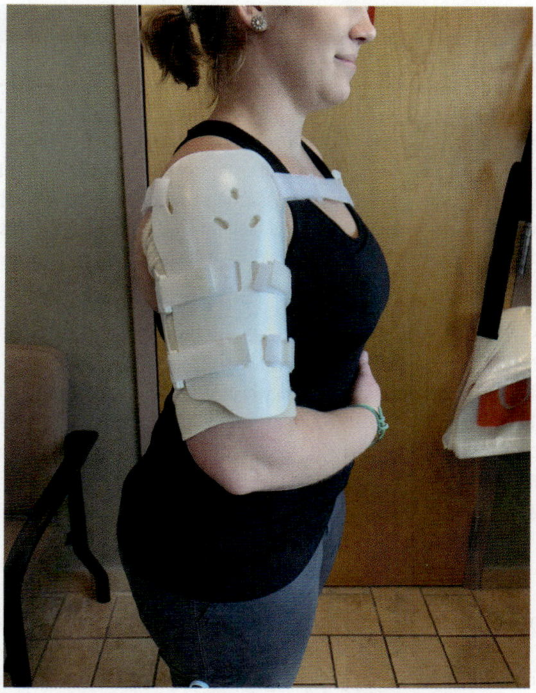

Fig. 67.17 Humeral cuff brace. (Courtesy Matthew C. Price, MS, RN, CNP, ONP-C, RNFA, Columbus, OH.)

During the rehabilitative phase, an exercise program to improve strength and motion of the injured extremity is important. Exercises should include assisted motion of the hand and fingers. The shoulder can be exercised if the fracture is stable. This helps prevent stiffness from frozen shoulder or fibrosis of the shoulder capsule.

CLAVICULAR FRACTURE

The clavicle is a frequently broken bone in children and young adults. Midshaft fractures account for 85% of all clavicle fractures. Injury is usually the result of a fall. Less often it happens from direct trauma to the bone. Common manifestations include pain at the fracture site, with or without obvious deformity, and limited shoulder range of motion. The patient often supports the affected side with the other hand and tilts the head toward the side of the fracture.

Most patients do not need surgery. Surgery is usually done only if the fracture is open. Treatment is aimed at maintaining comfort with splinting, ice, and analgesics. PT includes early ROM and strength exercises. Most clavicle fractures heal without complications. Contact sports should be avoided for 8 to 10 weeks.

PELVIC FRACTURE

Pelvic fractures range from relatively minor to life threatening, depending on the mechanism of injury and associated vascular

BOX 67.4 ETHICAL/LEGAL DILEMMAS

Entitlement to Treatment

Situation

D.C., a 35-year-old English tourist, was in a hang-gliding accident while touring the United States. She was taken to the regional trauma center for treatment of internal injuries, blood loss, and severe pelvic fractures. She has become septic, is now in renal failure, and has ARDS. She has no health insurance. Despite a poor chance of survival, her husband and parents want all possible measures to be taken.

Ethical/Legal Points for Consideration

- Federal law requires hospitals receiving federal funds through Medicare and Medicaid to provide emergency evaluation and treatment to stabilize patients (Emergency Medical Treatment and Active Labor Act [EMTALA]). Once the patient is stabilized, they are under no obligation to continue treatment and may transfer the patient to another facility.
- Discuss with the family treatment goals (e.g., recovery, survival, continued biologic existence, nonabandonment of the patient) and what they mean by wanting "everything done." There is no legal or ethical obligation to continue medical treatment when treatment goals cannot be met.
- Contact with the English consulate may result in collaboration to stabilize the patient and transport her to England.
- Neither HCPs nor hospitals are required to provide medically futile care (care that provides no benefit to the patient).
- Although her home country offers universal health care, D.C. assumed the risk when engaging in a potentially dangerous activity and did not obtain international health insurance coverage for her visit to a foreign country.

Discussion Questions

1. How can the nurse promote discussions with the family about treatment goals for D.C.?
2. Are family members able to state D.C.'s wishes for her own care in such a situation?

damage. They account for only 3% of adult fractures. Pelvic fractures have a high mortality rate. They may cause serious intraabdominal injury, including laceration and hemorrhage of the urethra, bladder, or colon. They can cause acute pelvic compartment syndrome. Paralytic ileus may occur after pelvic fracture. Patients may survive the pelvic injury, only to die from sepsis, FES, or VTE.

Abdominal assessment may show local swelling, tenderness, deformity, unusual pelvic movement, and bruising. Assess the neurovascular condition of the lower extremities and determine associated injuries. Pelvic fractures are diagnosed by x-ray and CT scan.

Treatment depends on the severity of the injury. Stable, nondisplaced fractures require little intervention. Ambulation with weight bearing as tolerated is typically encouraged. Complex or displaced fractures (e.g., open book fracture) need external fixation alone or combined with ORIF (e.g., screws), often done emergently. Use extreme care in handling or moving the patient, to prevent further injury. Because a pelvic fracture can damage other organs, assess bowel and urinary elimination. Regularly perform distal neurovascular assessment. Provide back care with adequate help or while the patient is raised from the bed by independent use of a trapeze (Box 67.4).

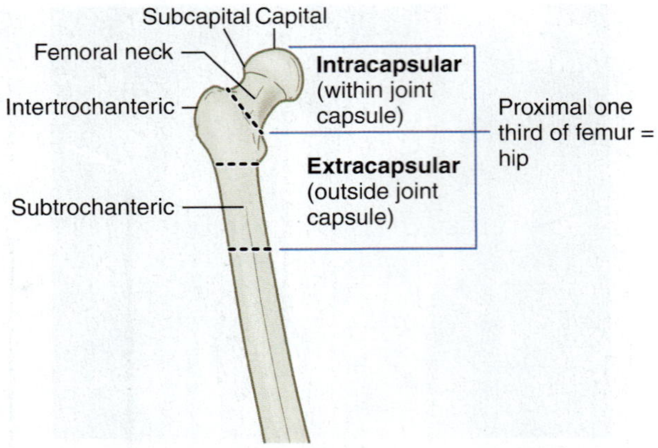

Fig. 67.18 Femur with location of various types of fracture.

HIP FRACTURE

Hip fractures are common in older adults. 95% of hip fractures result from a fall.[14] Many falls occur when getting in or out of a chair or bed. Falls to the side are the most common type seen in frail older adults. More than 300,000 patients are admitted to hospitals each year because of a hip fracture. Up to 37% of those patients die within 1 year of injury. Many older adults develop disabilities that require long-term care. Women suffer 75% of all hip fractures. In adults over 65 years old, hip fracture occurs more often in women because of osteoporosis.

Older adults may have low bone density *(osteopenia)* or osteoporosis, which increases their risk for fragility fractures. Other factors that increase the risk for a hip fracture in older adults include (1) increased risk for falling due to an altered center of gravity and inability to correct a postural imbalance, (2) decreased fat and muscle to act as local tissue shock absorbers, and (3) reduced skeletal strength. Other factors that increase the older adult's risk for falling include (1) gait and balance problems, (2) altered vision and hearing, (3) slowed reflexes, (4) orthostatic hypotension, and (5) medication use.

Hip fracture refers to a fracture of the proximal (upper) third of the femur, which extends 5 cm below the lesser trochanter (Fig. 67.18). Fractures within the hip joint capsule are *intracapsular fractures.* Intracapsular fractures are further identified by their specific locations: (1) *capital* (fracture of the head of the femur), (2) *subcapital* (fracture just below the head of the femur), and (3) *transcervical* (fracture of the femoral neck). These fractures, which are often associated with osteoporosis and minor trauma, are *fragility fractures.*

Extracapsular fractures occur outside the joint capsule. They are either (1) *intertrochanteric* (in a region between the greater and lesser trochanter) or (2) *subtrochanteric* (below the lesser trochanter). Most are caused by severe direct trauma or a fall.

Clinical Manifestations

Manifestations include external rotation, muscle spasm, shortening of the affected extremity, and severe pain and tenderness around the fracture site. Displaced femoral neck fractures may disrupt blood supply to the femoral head, resulting in avascular necrosis of the femoral head.

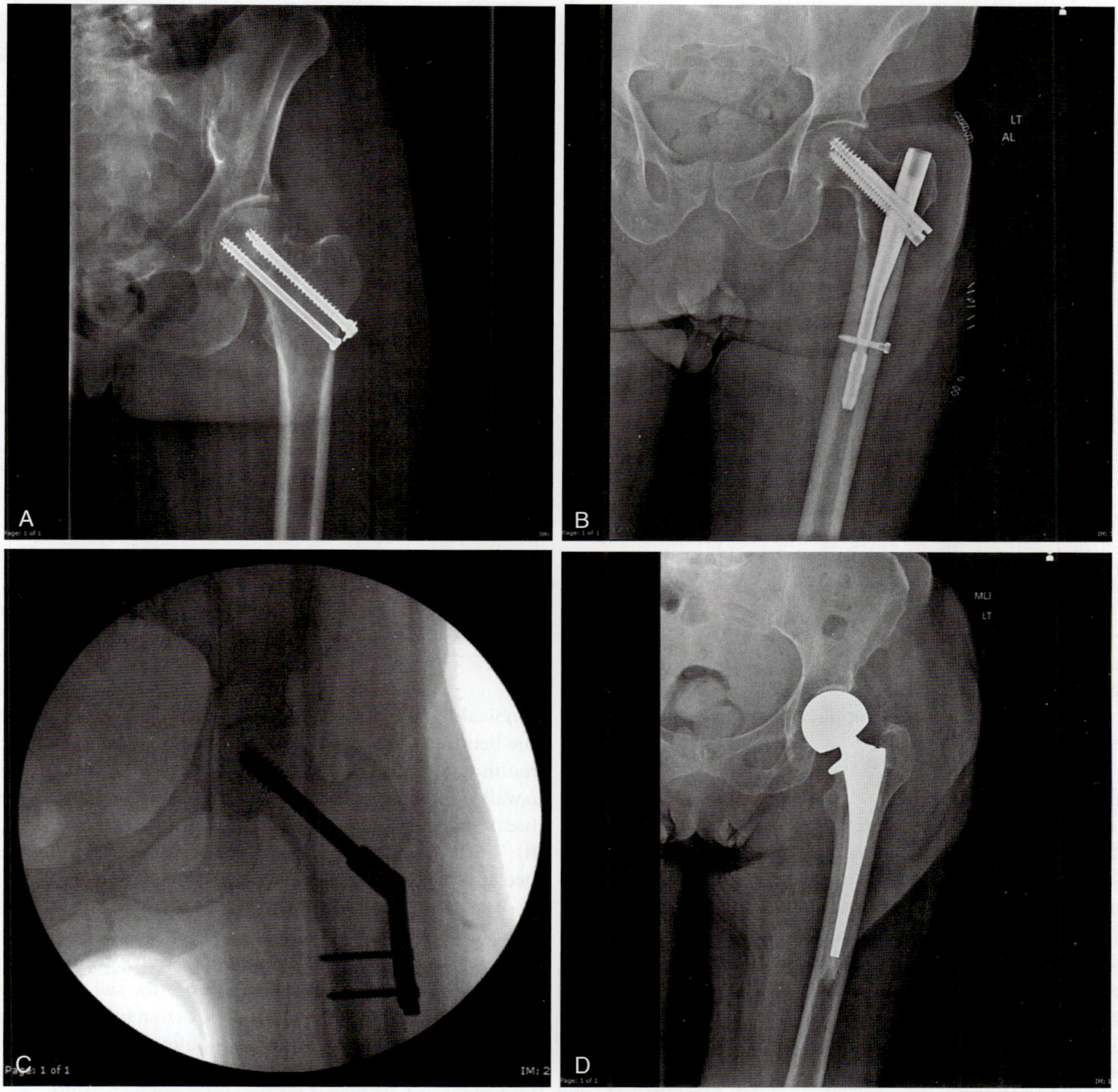

Fig. 67.19 Types of surgical repair for a hip fracture: (A) Closed reduction with percutaneous pinning. (B) Intramedullary nail. (C) Sliding hip screw. (D) Hemiarthroplasty. (Courtesy Matthew C. Price, MS, RN, CNP, ONP-C, RNFA, Columbus, OH.)

Interprofessional Care

Immediate surgery is the standard of care. Initially we may immobilize the affected extremity with Buck's traction (Fig. 67.9) if the patient's physical condition needs stabilized before they can have surgery. Buck's traction may be used for 24 to 48 hours to relieve painful muscle spasms.

Surgical treatment allows for early mobilization and decreases the risk for complications. The type of surgery depends on the location and severity of the fracture and the person's age. Options include (1) closed reduction with percutaneous pinning (CRPP) (minimally invasive surgery to stabilize the femoral neck and head with screws), (2) repair with internal fixation devices (e.g., hip compression screw, intramedullary devices), (3) replacement of the femoral head with a prosthesis (partial hip replacement or *hemiarthroplasty*, often used for fracture of the femoral neck) (Fig. 67.19), and (4) total hip replacement (involves both the femur and acetabulum) (Fig. 67.20).

❖ NURSING MANAGEMENT: HIP FRACTURE

◆ Implementation

◆ Preoperative Care

In addition to the usual preoperative nursing care (see Chapter 18), we may do teaching in the ED. Most patients do not have an extended preoperative period in which to receive instructions. Many are older adults. When planning treatment of the hip

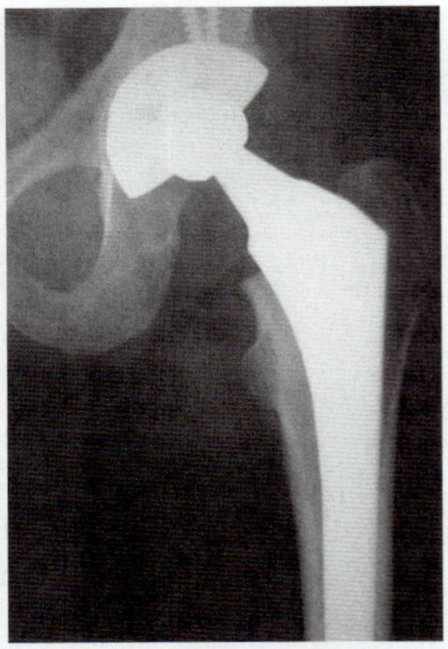

Fig. 67.20 Total hip replacement (arthroplasty) with cementless femoral prosthesis of metal alloy with plastic acetabular socket.

fracture, consider the presence of any chronic health problems (e.g., diabetes, heart disease). We may have to delay surgery briefly until the patient's general health is stabilized. Begin to consider discharge plans because the length of stay after surgery will be no more than a few days.

Before surgery, severe muscle spasms can increase pain. Analgesics or muscle relaxants, comfortable positioning (unless contraindicated), and properly applied traction (if used) can help to manage the spasms.

◆ Postoperative Care

Similar principles of patient care apply to any surgical procedure for hip fractures. In the initial postoperative period, assess vital signs, intake, and output. Monitor respiratory function and encourage deep breathing and coughing. Assess pain and give pain medication. Observe the dressing and incision for signs of bleeding. See eNursing Care Plan 67.2 for the orthopedic surgical patient (available on the website for this chapter).

Neurovascular impairment is possible. Assess the extremity for (1) color, (2) temperature, (3) capillary refill, (4) distal pulses, (5) edema, (6) sensation, (7) motor function, and (8) pain. Decrease edema by elevating the leg when the patient is in bed or in a chair. Pain in the affected extremity can be reduced by maintaining limb alignment with pillows between the patient's knees when turning the patient to the nonoperative side.

Encourage the patient to use the overhead trapeze bar and the opposite side rail to help in position changes. Avoid turning the patient to the affected side unless approved by the HCP. Have the patient exercise the unaffected leg and both arms.

Weight bearing on the involved extremity varies. Limited weight bearing is typically the only restriction for the patient who had ORIF of the hip fracture. The restriction continues until x-rays show adequate healing, usually 6 to 12 weeks. Teach the patient and caregiver about weight-bearing status after surgery.

The physical therapist usually supervises exercises for the affected extremity and ambulation when the HCP allows it. The patient is usually out of bed the first postoperative day. A

TABLE 67.12 PATIENT & CAREGIVER TEACHING

Posterior Hip Replacement

After a hip replacement by posterior surgical approach, include the following instructions when teaching a patient and caregiver:

Do

- Use an elevated toilet seat.
- Place chair inside shower or tub and remain seated while washing.
- Use pillow between legs for first 6 weeks when lying on nonoperative side or when supine.
- Keep hip in neutral, straight position when sitting, walking, or lying.
- Notify HCP at once if severe pain, deformity, or loss of function occurs.
- Discuss personal risk factors for prosthetic joint infection with HCP and dentist before dental work.

Do Not

- Flex hip greater than 90 degrees (e.g., sitting in low chairs or toilet seats).
- Adduct hip (e.g., bring legs together at knees).
- Internally rotate hip (e.g., turn toward planted foot on affected side).
- Cross legs at knees or ankles.
- Put on own shoes or stockings without adaptive device (e.g., long-handled shoehorn or stocking-helper) for 4–6 weeks.
- Sit on chairs without arms. The arms of chairs will help the patient rise to a standing position.

physical therapist can teach the patient how to transfer out of the bed to a chair. In collaboration with the physical therapist, monitor the patient's ambulation for proper use of crutches or a walker. To be discharged home, the patient must show proper use of crutches or a walker over a functional distance (about 150 ft). The patient must be able to transfer to and from a chair and bed and to go up and down stairs.

If hemiarthroplasty or total joint replacement was done by a *posterior approach* (incision posterior to the midline of the greater trochanter down the femoral shaft), measures to prevent dislocation must be used (Table 67.12). Tell the patient and caregiver about positions and activities that increase the risk for dislocation (more than 90 degrees of flexion, adduction across the midline [crossing of legs and ankles], internal rotation of hip). Many daily activities reproduce these positions. These include (1) putting on shoes and socks, (2) crossing the legs or feet while seated, (3) assuming the side-lying position incorrectly, (4) standing up or sitting down while the hip is flexed more than 90 degrees relative to the chair, and (5) sitting on low seats, especially low toilet seats. Teach the patient to avoid these activities until the soft tissue capsule around the hip has healed enough to stabilize the prosthesis (usually at least 6 weeks).

Elevated toilet seats and chair alterations (e.g., raising the seat with a folded blanket, keeping a straight back) are needed. Avoid placing a soft pillow in a seat because sitting on it can cause internal rotation. If a foam abduction wedge is ordered to prevent joint dislocation, place it between the patient's legs (Fig. 67.21). Apply the top straps above the knee to avoid putting pressure on the peroneal nerve at the lateral tibial tubercle. Some HCPs want the patient to keep the abductor wedge in place except when bathing or walking.

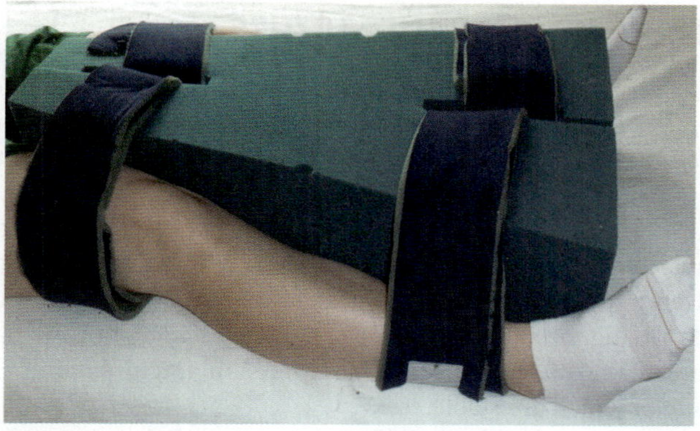

Fig. 67.21 Maintaining abduction after total hip replacement. (Courtesy Mary Wollan, RN, BAN, ONC, Spring Park, MN.)

If hemiarthroplasty or total joint replacement was done by an *anterior approach* (incision is made in the front of the hip with patient lying on the back), the hip muscles are left intact. This approach provides a more stable hip in the postoperative period with a lower rate of complications. Precautions related to motion and weight bearing are few. They typically include instructions to avoid hyperextension.

The patient may not take a tub bath or drive for 4 to 6 weeks. An occupational therapist (OT) may teach the patient to use assistive devices, such as long-handled shoehorns, sock assists, and reachers or grabbers, to avoid bending over to pick up something on the floor. The knees must be kept apart. Teach the patient to never cross the legs or twist to reach behind.

Complications of femoral neck fracture include nonunion, avascular necrosis, dislocation, and osteoarthritis (OA). The affected leg may be shorter if the patient had an intertrochanteric fracture. A cane or shoe lift may be needed for safe ambulation.

Sudden severe pain, a lump in the buttock, limb shortening, and external rotation indicate prosthesis dislocation. This requires closed reduction with moderate to deep sedation or open reduction under general anesthesia to realign the femoral head in the acetabulum. If any of these signs occur (regardless of the setting), keep the patient NPO in anticipation of surgical intervention.

Help the patient and caregiver to adjust to restrictions and dependence because of the hip fracture. Anxiety and depression can easily occur. Creative nursing care and awareness of potential problems can help to prevent them. Tell the patient and caregiver about community services that can help with rehabilitation after hospital discharge.

CHECK YOUR PRACTICE

You are taking care of an 83-year-old patient who fell down the steps outside her house while getting her mail. She was diagnosed with a femoral neck fracture and Colles' fracture. She is returning to the clinical unit after surgery. She had a hemiarthroplasty for the femoral neck fracture and closed reduction of the Colles' fracture.

- Based on these injuries, what are some possible complications?
- How will you mobilize a patient with these injuries?
- What are your discharge concerns?

◆ Ambulatory Care

Hospitalization averages 3 or 4 days. Older adults or patients who live alone may require care in a subacute rehabilitation unit, at a skilled nursing facility, or in an acute rehabilitation facility for a few weeks before returning home. If the patient has skilled nursing needs or is homebound for PT after discharge from postacute care, the HCP may order follow-up home health care.

Home care considerations include ongoing assessment of pain management, monitoring for infection, and VTE prevention. If incision is closed with metal staples, they will be removed at the HCP's office. Teach the patient who is receiving an anticoagulant to report signs of bleeding to the HCP (see Chapter 41). Review how to administer an injectable anticoagulant (if needed). Teach the patient receiving warfarin about required laboratory testing.

Exercises to restore strength and tone in the quadriceps and muscles around the hip are essential to improve function and ROM. These include quadriceps setting (e.g., pressing the kneecap down), gluteal muscle setting (e.g., tightening the buttocks), leg raises in supine and prone positions, and abduction exercises from the supine and standing positions (e.g., swinging the leg out but never crossing midline). The patient continues these exercises for many months after discharge. Teach the exercise program to the caregiver who will be encouraging the patient at home.

A physical therapist assesses ROM, ambulation, and adherence to the exercise program. The patient gradually increases the number of exercise repetitions and may add ankle weights. Swimming and stationary cycling may tone quadriceps and improve cardiovascular fitness. Teach the patient to avoid high-impact exercises and sports, such as jogging and tennis, because they may loosen the implant.

A physical therapist or home care nurse may perform a home assessment to identify hazards that may cause the patient to fall again. Homes can be made safer by (1) eliminating tripping hazards (e.g., throw rugs, uneven surfaces), (2) adding grab bars inside and outside the tub or shower, and beside the toilet, (3) adding railings on both sides of the stairs, and (4) installing better lighting.[14]

Calcium and vitamin D supplementation are given to patients with osteopenia or osteoporosis. A bisphosphonate drug (e.g., alendronate) may be prescribed to decrease bone loss or increase bone density. This reduces the chance of fracture. Osteoporosis is discussed in Chapter 68.

◆ Evaluation

The expected outcomes are that the patient with a hip fracture will:
- Report satisfactory pain management
- Have uncomplicated bone healing
- Take part in exercise therapy

FEMORAL SHAFT FRACTURE

Because the femur can bend slightly to absorb stress, femoral shaft fracture occurs from a severe direct force. The force exerted to cause the fracture (e.g., from a motor vehicle crash or gunshot wound) often also damages the adjacent soft tissue. These injuries may be more serious than the bone injury. Young adults have a high incidence of this type of fracture.

Displacement of fracture fragments often causes increased soft tissue damage. Considerable blood loss (1 to 1.5 L) can occur. The most common types of femoral shaft fracture include transverse, spiral, comminuted, oblique, and open (Figs. 67.6 and 67.7).

A femoral shaft fracture is marked by pain, notable deformity and angulation, shortening of the extremity, and inability to move the hip or knee. Complications include FES; nerve and vascular injury; and problems with bone union, open fracture, and soft tissue damage.

Initial management involves patient stabilization and fracture immobilization. Traction may be used as a temporary measure before surgery or in the patient unable to have surgery. Placement of an *intramedullary rod* is the most common surgical treatment for femoral shaft fracture. The metal rod is placed into the marrow canal of the femur. The rod passes across the fracture to keep fragments in position. Plates and screws also may be used. Internal fixation is preferred. It reduces the hospital stay and complications of prolonged bed rest. External fixation may be used for an open fracture.

After surgery, gluteal and quadriceps isometric exercises promote and maintain strength in the affected extremity. Encourage the patient to perform ROM and strength exercises for all uninvolved extremities to prepare for ambulation. The patient may be allowed to start non–weight-bearing activities with an assistive device (e.g., walker, crutches). Full weight bearing is usually restricted until x-rays show union of fracture fragments. Teach the patient to follow the HCP's instructions for weight bearing.

TIBIAL FRACTURE

Although the tibia is vulnerable to injury because it lacks a covering of anterior muscle, strong force is needed to cause a fracture. As a result, soft tissue damage, devascularization, and open fracture are common. The tibia is a common site for stress fracture. Complications include compartment syndrome, FES, delayed union or nonunion, and possible infection with an open fracture.

Treatment for closed tibial fractures is closed reduction followed by immobilization in a long leg cast. ORIF with intramedullary rods, plate fixation, or external fixation is needed for complex fractures and those with extensive soft tissue damage. An emphasis of care is maintaining quadriceps strength.

Assess the neurovascular condition of the affected extremity at least every 2 hours during the first 48 hours. Have the patient perform active ROM exercises with the uninvolved leg and the upper extremities to build the strength needed for crutch walking. When the HCP has determined the patient is ready for gait training, review principles of crutch walking introduced by the physical therapist. The patient may be non–weight bearing for 6 to 12 weeks, depending on healing. Home nursing visits may be needed to monitor the patient's progress if the patient is homebound.

STABLE VERTEBRAL FRACTURE

In a stable vertebral fracture, the fracture fragments are unlikely to move or cause spinal cord damage. This injury is often confined to the vertebral body (anterior part of the spinal column) in the lumbar region. Sometimes it involves the cervical and thoracic regions. Vertebral bodies are usually protected from displacement by intact spinal ligaments. Stable fractures of the vertebral column are usually caused by motor vehicle crashes, falls, diving, or sports injuries. Patients with osteoporosis have more than 700,000 vertebral compression fractures annually, many of which are stable.

Most patients with stable fractures have only brief periods of disability. If spinal ligaments are significantly disrupted, dislocation of the vertebrae may occur. Instability and injury to the spinal cord may result (unstable fracture). These injuries often require surgery. The most serious complication of vertebral fractures is fracture displacement, which can cause damage to the spinal cord (see Chapter 65). Although stable vertebral fractures are not associated with abnormal spinal cord pathology, all spinal injuries should be considered unstable and potentially serious until diagnostic tests determine the fracture to be stable.

The patient usually has pain and tenderness in the affected region of the spine. There may be a kyphotic deformity (flexion angulation of thoracic vertebrae) known as a *dowager's hump*. We can easily identify this deformity during the physical assessment (see Fig. 68.9). *Lordosis* and cervical spine involvement are possible. Sudden loss of function below the fracture indicates spinal cord impingement and paraplegia. Bowel and bladder problems may occur if there is interruption of the autonomic nervous system nerves or injury to the spinal cord.

The overall goal is to keep the spine in good alignment until union is achieved. Many nursing interventions are aimed at assessing for spinal cord trauma (see Chapter 65). Regularly evaluate vital signs and bowel and bladder function. Monitor the motor and sensory function of peripheral nerves distal to the injured region. Report any decline in neurovascular condition.

Treatment includes pain medication followed by early mobilization and bracing. The mattress should be firm to support the spinal column, relax muscles, decrease edema, and prevent potential compression on nerve roots. Teach the patient to keep the spine straight when turning by moving the shoulders and pelvis together. The patient will need to learn to logroll. Several days after the initial injury, the HCP may apply a specially constructed orthotic device (e.g., thoracolumbar sacral orthosis [TLSO]), a jacket cast, or a removable corset if there is no neurologic deficit. The device gives extra support during healing. It is used for a short period of time.

Lightweight bracing (e.g., Jewett or Bähler-Vogt brace) may be used for patients with stable vertebral compression fractures due to osteoporosis. Patients with osteoporosis may undergo vertebroplasty or balloon kyphoplasty. *Vertebroplasty* uses radioimaging to guide the injection of bone cement into a fractured vertebral body. When hardened, the cement stabilizes the vertebra and prevents further compression. *Balloon kyphoplasty* involves inserting a balloon into the vertebral body and then inflating it. This creates a cavity that is filled with bone cement under low pressure to restore the height of the vertebral body. Kyphoplasty is now the surgery of choice for compression fractures. This is due to the decreased incidence of bone cement leakage into nearby structures (e.g., colon, lung) compared to vertebroplasty. Patients have decreased pain almost at once with these procedures. However, later compression fractures of adjacent vertebrae are a risk.

If the fracture is in the cervical spine, the patient may wear a hard cervical collar. Some cervical fractures are immobilized with a halo vest (see Fig. 65.8). This consists of a plastic jacket or cast fitted about the chest and attached to a halo held in place by skeletal pins inserted into the cranium. These devices immobilize the spine in the fracture area while allowing the patient to ambulate.

The patient with a stable vertebral fracture is discharged after (1) showing safe ambulation, (2) learning care of the cast or orthotic device, and (3) stating ways to address safety and security concerns related to the injury and treatment. Unstable vertebral fractures and spinal cord injuries are the subject of Chapter 65.

FACIAL FRACTURE

A person can fracture any bone of the face. Trauma, such as a motor vehicle crash, assault, or fall, is a common cause. After facial injury it is important to establish and maintain a patent airway and provide adequate ventilation. Suctioning may be needed to remove foreign material and blood. A surgically created airway *(tracheostomy)* may be needed if a patent airway cannot be maintained.

Facial fractures and cervical spine injuries often occur together. All patients with facial injuries should be treated as if they have a cervical injury until proven otherwise by assessment and CT scan or x-ray. Table 67.13 describes clinical manifestations of common facial fractures.

Related soft tissue injury often makes assessment of facial injury difficult. Perform oral and facial assessments after we have treated any life-threatening situations. Carefully assess eye muscles and cranial nerves III, IV, and VI. X-rays help determine the extent of the injury. CT scanning helps discern between bone and soft tissue injury.

TABLE 67.13 Manifestations of Facial Fractures

Fracture	Manifestation
Frontal bone	Rapid edema that may mask underlying fractures
Mandible	Tooth fractures, bleeding, limited motion of mandible
Maxilla	Segmental motion (instability) of maxilla and tooth fracture at socket
Nasal bone	Displacement of nasal bones, nosebleed *(epistaxis)*
Periorbital bone	Possible frontal sinus involvement, entrapment of ocular muscles
Zygomatic arch	Depression of cheek bone *(zygomatic arch)* and entrapment of ocular muscles

Suspect injury to the eye when facial injury occurs, especially if the injury is near the orbit. If an eye-globe rupture is suspected, stop and place a protective shield over the eye. Signs of rupture include vitreous humor forced out of the eye. Brown tissue (iris or ciliary body) may be seen on the surface of the globe or penetrating through a laceration, with an off-center or teardrop-shaped pupil.

Specific treatment depends on the site and extent of the facial fracture and associated soft tissue injury. Immobilization or surgical stabilization may be needed. Maintain a patent airway and adequate nutrition throughout the recovery period.

Be sensitive about changes in appearance that may occur after facial fracture. Changes in appearance may be drastic. Edema and discoloration subside with time, but soft tissue injuries can cause permanent scarring.

MANDIBULAR FRACTURE

Mandibular fracture may result from trauma to the face or jaw. The fracture may be simple, with no bone displacement, or may involve loss of tissue and bone. Mandibular fracture may need immediate treatment to ensure the patient's survival. Long-term treatment is sometimes needed to restore satisfactory appearance and function.

Mandibular fractures may be done therapeutically to correct an underlying alignment problem *(malocclusion)* that cannot be adjusted by orthodontics alone. The mandible is resected during surgery and manipulated forward or backward to correct the occlusion problem.

Surgery includes immobilization, usually by wiring the jaws *(intermaxillary fixation)*. Internal fixation may be done with screws and plates. In a simple fracture with no loss of teeth, the lower jaw is wired to the upper jaw. Wires are placed around the teeth, and then cross-wires or rubber bands are used to hold the lower jaw tight against the upper jaw (Fig. 67.22). Arch bars may be placed on the maxillary and mandibular arches of the teeth. Vertical wires placed between the arch bars hold the jaws together. If teeth are missing or bone is displaced, other forms of fixation may be needed (e.g., metal arch bars in the mouth or insertion of a pin in the bone). Bone grafting may be needed. Immobilization is usually needed for only 4 to 6 weeks because the fractures often heal rapidly.

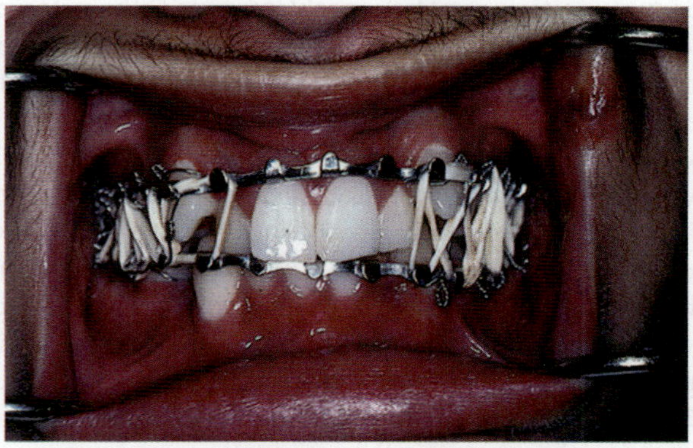

Fig. 67.22 Intermaxillary fixation. (Courtesy R.A. Weinstein, Denver, CO.)

❖ NURSING MANAGEMENT: MANDIBULAR FRACTURE

Teach the patient before surgery about what is involved in the surgery, how their face will look afterward, and changes caused by the surgery. Reassure the patient about the ability to breathe normally, speak, and swallow liquids. Hospitalization for respiratory monitoring is brief unless there are other injuries or problems.

Postoperative care focuses on a patent airway, oral hygiene, communication, pain management, and adequate nutrition. Two potential problems in the immediate postoperative period are airway obstruction and aspiration of vomitus. Because the patient cannot open the jaws, an airway must be maintained. Observe for signs of respiratory distress (e.g., dyspnea; changes in rate, quality, and depth of respirations). After surgery place the patient on the side with the head slightly elevated.

Tape a wire cutter or scissors (for rubber bands) to the head of the bed. Send it with the patient when they are away from the bedside. The wire cutter or scissors may be used to cut the wires or elastic bands in case of an emergency requiring access to the pharynx or lungs (e.g., cardiac arrest or respiratory distress). Keep a picture nearby showing the appropriate wires to cut in an emergency. In some cases, cutting the wires may cause the entire facial and upper jaw structure to shift or collapse and worsen the problem. Keep a tracheostomy or endotracheal tray available.

If the patient begins to vomit or choke, try to clear the mouth and airway. Suction via the nasopharyngeal or oral route, depending on the extent of injury and type of repair. An NG tube can remove fluids and gas from the stomach to help prevent vomiting and aspiration. The NG tube can later be used as a feeding tube. Antiemetics may be given. Teach the patient to clear secretions and vomitus.

Oral hygiene is important. Teach the patient to remove food debris by rinsing the mouth often, especially after meals and snacks. Warm normal saline solution, water, or alkaline mouthwashes may be used. A syringe and soft irrigation catheter or a Water Pik may be effective for thorough oral cleansing. Inspect the mouth several times a day to see that it is clean. Use a tongue depressor to retract the cheeks. Keep the lips, corners of the mouth, and buccal mucosa moist. Cover any sharp edges of the wires with dental wax to prevent irritation of the buccal mucosa.

Communication may be a problem, especially in the early postoperative period. Establish an effective way of communicating before surgery (e.g., dry erase board, texting). The patient can usually speak well enough to be understood within a few days after surgery.

Adequate nutrition may be a challenge because the diet must be liquid. The patient easily tires of sucking through a straw or laboriously using a spoon. Work with the dietitian and patient to plan a diet with adequate calories, protein, and fluids. Liquid protein supplements may improve nutrition. The low-bulk, high-carbohydrate diet and intake of air through the straw contribute to constipation and gas. Ambulation, prune juice, and bulk-forming laxatives may help relieve these problems.

The patient is usually discharged with the wires in place. Encourage the patient to share feelings about the changes in appearance. Discharge teaching should include oral care, diet, how to handle secretions, how and when to use wire cutters or scissors, and when to notify the HCP.

AMPUTATION

An **amputation** is the removal of a body extremity by trauma or surgery. About 2 million Americans live with limb loss.[15] About 185,000 amputations occur each year in the United States. Just over half are due to PVD and diabetes. These patients often have peripheral neuropathy that progresses to deep ulcers and gangrene. Trauma is the other major cause. Injuries have affected over 1700 military veterans since 2003, with several losing more than 1 limb.[16] Other reasons for amputation include thermal injuries, tumors, osteomyelitis, and congenital limb disorders.

Diagnostic Studies

Diagnostic studies depend on the underlying reason for the amputation (Table 67.14). An increased white blood cell (WBC) count with abnormal differential may show infection. Vascular tests such as arteriography, Doppler studies, and venography give information about circulation in the extremity.

Interprofessional Care

Chronic illnesses and infection must be managed before an amputation is done. The goal of surgery is to preserve the greatest extremity length and function while removing all infected, pathologic, or ischemic tissue. Fig. 67.23 shows levels of amputation of upper and lower extremities. The type of amputation

TABLE 67.14 Interprofessional Care

Amputation

Diagnostic Assessment
- History and physical assessment
  - Physical appearance of soft tissues
  - Skin temperature
  - Sensory function
  - Quality of peripheral pulses
- Arteriography
- Venography
- Plethysmography (measures blood flow in the arms or legs)
- Transcutaneous ultrasonic Doppler recordings

Management

Medical
- Appropriate management of underlying disease
- Stabilize trauma victim

Surgical
- Residual limb management
- Immediate or delayed prosthesis fitting

Rehabilitation
- Coordination of prosthesis-fitting and gait-training activities
- Coordination of muscle-strength and PT programs

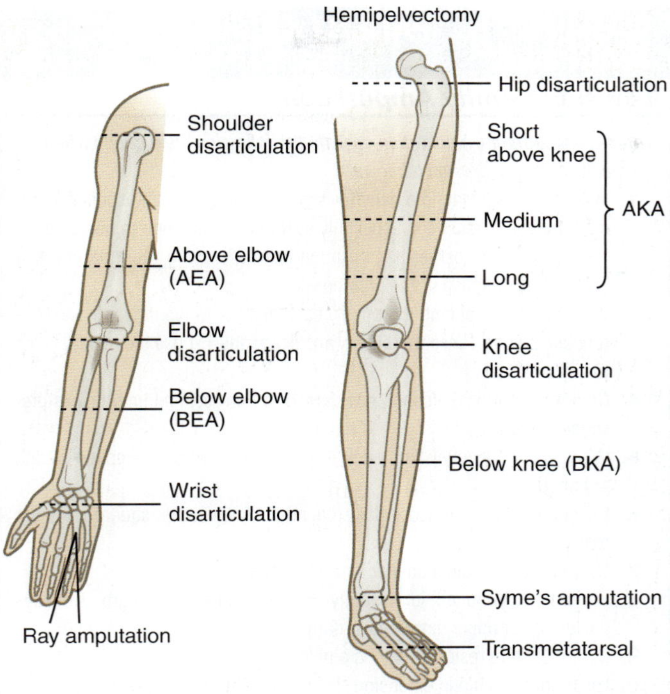

Fig. 67.23 Location and description of amputation sites of the upper and lower extremities. *AKA,* Above-the-knee amputation.

depends on the reason for the surgery. A closed amputation creates a weight-bearing *residual limb* (or stump). An anterior skin flap with dissected soft tissue padding covers the bony part of the residual limb. The skin flap is sutured posteriorly so that the suture line will not be in a weight-bearing area. Take special care to prevent accumulation of drainage, which can cause pressure and harbor bacteria that may cause infection.

Disarticulation is an amputation done through a joint. A *Syme's amputation* is a form of disarticulation at the ankle. After an open amputation *(guillotine amputation),* the surface of the residual limb is left uncovered with skin. This type of surgery is generally done to control actual or potential infection. The wound is usually closed later by a second surgery or closed by skin traction surrounding the residual limb.

NURSING MANAGEMENT: AMPUTATION

Assessment

Assess for any preexisting illnesses. If amputation is planned or elective, as for the patient with PVD, assess the patient's general health. Because most amputations are done for vascular problems, vascular and neurologic assessments are important (see Chapters 35 and 60).

Clinical Problems

Clinical problems for the patient with an amputation may include:

- Impaired tissue integrity
- Pain
- Musculoskeletal problem
- Impaired role performance
- Negative self-esteem

Planning

The overall goals are that the patient with an amputation will (1) have satisfactory pain management, (2) reach maximum rehabilitation potential (with the use of a prosthesis, if indicated), (3) cope with the body image changes, and (4) make satisfying lifestyle adjustments.

Implementation

Health Promotion

Control of illnesses, such as PVD, diabetes, chronic osteomyelitis, and pressure injuries, can eliminate or delay the need for amputation. Teach patients with these problems to carefully examine their lower extremities daily for signs of infection or skin breakdown. If the patient cannot do this, the caregiver should help. Teach the patient and caregiver to report changes in the feet or toes to the HCP. These include decreased or absent sensation, tingling, burning pain, cuts, or abrasions, and changes in skin color or temperature.

Review safety precautions for people taking part in recreational activities and potentially hazardous work. This role is important for the occupational health nurse.

Acute Care

Reasons for amputation and the rehabilitation potential depend on a person's age, diagnosis, occupation, personality, resources, and support system. Be aware of the psychologic and social implications of amputation. Body image problems related to amputation often cause a patient to go through a grieving process. Use therapeutic communication to help the patient and caregiver through this process and develop a realistic attitude about the future.

Preoperative care. Reinforce information that the patient and caregiver have received about reasons for the amputation, proposed prosthesis, and mobility-training program. Help the patient and caregiver understand the need for the amputation. Assure them that rehabilitation can help with quality of life. If the amputation is done emergently after trauma, patient management is physically and emotionally more complicated.

To meet the patient's educational needs, know the level of amputation, type of dressings to be applied, and type of prosthesis to be used. Teach the patient to perform upper extremity exercises, such as push-ups in bed or the wheelchair, to promote arm strength for crutch walking and gait training. Discuss general postoperative nursing care. Review positioning, support, and residual limb care. If a compression bandage will be used after surgery, teach the patient about its purpose and how it will be applied. If immediate prosthesis use is planned, discuss general ambulation expectations. Tell the patient that the amputated limb may feel like it is still present after surgery. This phenomenon, termed **phantom limb sensation**, occurs in many amputees.

Postoperative care. General care for the patient who had an amputation depends largely on the patient's age, general state of health, and reason for the amputation. Monitor patients who had an amputation due to a traumatic injury for posttraumatic stress disorder because they may have had no time to prepare or even take part in the decision to have a limb amputated.

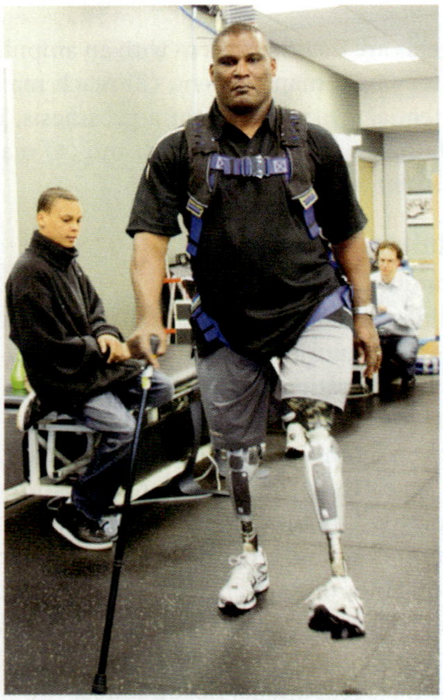

Fig. 67.24 A double amputee fitted with prostheses. (Photo courtesy US Army.)

Prevention and detection of complications are important after surgery. Monitor vital signs. Assess dressings for hemorrhage. Use sterile technique during dressing changes to reduce the risk for wound infection. If an *immediate* postoperative prosthesis has been applied, carefully observe the surgical site. If excess bleeding occurs, notify the HCP at once. Keep a tourniquet available for emergency use.

Proper bandaging ensures the residual limb is shaped and molded for eventual prosthesis fitting (Fig. 67.24). The HCP usually orders a compression bandage to be applied right after surgery to support soft tissues, reduce edema, hasten healing, and minimize pain. Compression also promotes residual limb shrinkage and maturation. This bandage may be an elastic roll applied to the residual limb or a residual limb shrinker, which is an elastic stocking that fits tightly over the residual limb.

At first, the patient always wears the compression bandage except during PT and bathing. Remove and reapply the bandage several times daily. Take care to apply it snugly but not so tight as to interfere with circulation. Wash and change shrinker bandages daily. After the residual limb is healed, bandage it only when the patient is not wearing the prosthesis. Teach the patient to avoid dangling the residual limb over the bedside to decrease edema.

As the patient's condition improves, the HCP and physical therapist start and supervise an exercise program. We start active ROM exercises for all joints as soon as possible after surgery. To prepare for mobility, the patient should increase triceps and shoulder strength for lower limb support. The patient will need to learn to balance the altered body. The lost weight of an amputated limb requires adaptation of proprioception and coordination to prevent falls and injury.

Flexion contractures may delay rehabilitation. The most common and debilitating contracture is hip flexion. Hip adduction contracture is rare. To prevent flexion contractures, have patients avoid sitting in a chair for more than 1 hour with hips flexed or having pillows under the surgical extremity. Unless contraindicated, patients should lie on their abdomen for 30 minutes 3 or 4 times each day and position the hip in extension while prone.

Crutch walking starts as soon as the patient is physically able. Follow orders for weight bearing carefully to avoid injury to the skin flap and delay of tissue healing. Before discharge, teach the patient and caregiver about residual limb care, ambulation, contracture prevention, recognition of complications, exercise, and follow-up care (Table 67.15).

TABLE 67.15 PATIENT & CAREGIVER TEACHING

Lower Extremity Amputation

After lower extremity amputation, include the following instructions when teaching the patient and caregiver:

1. Inspect the residual limb daily for signs of skin irritation, especially redness, abrasion, and odor. Especially evaluate areas prone to pressure.
2. Stop using the prosthesis if irritation develops. Have the area checked before resuming use of the prosthesis.
3. Wash the residual limb thoroughly each night with warm water and bacteriostatic soap. Rinse thoroughly and dry gently. Expose the residual limb to air for 20 min.
4. Do not use lotions, alcohol, powders, or oil on residual limb unless prescribed by the HCP.
5. Wear only a residual limb sock in good condition and supplied by the prosthetist.
6. Change residual limb sock daily. Launder in mild soap, squeeze, lay flat to dry.
7. Use prescribed pain management techniques.
8. Perform ROM to all joints daily. Perform general strength exercises (including for upper extremities) daily.
9. Do not elevate residual limb on a pillow.
10. Lay prone with hip in extension for 30 min, 3 or 4 times daily.

Ambulatory Care

Success of rehabilitation depends on the patient's physical and emotional health. Chronic illness and deconditioning can complicate rehabilitation. The patient's previous ability to ambulate may affect the extent of recovery. Physical and occupational therapy must be a central part of the overall plan of care.

Prostheses

Appropriate timing for the use of a prosthesis depends on satisfactory healing of the residual limb and the patient's general condition. The *delayed* prosthetic fitting may be the best choice for older adults, patients with infection, or patients who had amputations above the knee or below the elbow (Fig. 67.25). A temporary prosthesis may be used for partial weight bearing after sutures are removed. If there are no problems, the patient can bear full weight on a permanent prosthesis about 3 months after amputation.

Not all patients are candidates for prostheses. Using a prosthesis requires significant strength and energy for ambulation. For example, walking with a below-the-knee prosthesis requires 40% more energy than walking on 2 legs. An above-the-knee prosthesis requires 60% more. The seriously ill or debilitated

Fig. 67.25 Mirror therapy, a type of treatment that may reduce phantom limb sensation and pain. (US Navy photo courtesy Mass Communication Specialist Seaman Joseph A. Boomhower.)

patient may not have the upper body strength and energy needed to use a lower extremity prosthesis. Mobility with a wheelchair may be the most realistic goal for this patient.

When healing has occurred satisfactorily, and the residual limb is well molded, the patient is ready for prosthesis fitting. A prosthetist makes a mold of the residual limb and measures landmarks for creation of the prosthesis. The molded limb socket allows the residual limb to fit snugly into the prosthesis. The residual limb is covered with a stocking to ensure good fit and prevent skin breakdown. If the limb continues to shrink, causing a loose fit, a new socket must be made. The patient may need to have the prosthesis adjusted to prevent rubbing and friction between the residual limb and socket. Excessive movement of a loose prosthesis can cause severe skin irritation, breakdown, and gait problems.

Artificial limbs become an integral part of the patient's changed body image. Teach the patient to clean the prosthesis socket daily with mild soap and rinse thoroughly to remove irritants. Leather and metal parts of the prosthesis should not get wet. Encourage the patient to have regular maintenance on the prosthesis. Consider the condition of the patient's shoe. A badly worn shoe alters the gait and can damage the prosthesis.

Phantom Limb Sensations

Patients are often worried about phantom limb sensation because they still perceive pain in the missing part of the limb. As recovery and ambulation progress, phantom limb sensation and pain usually subside. However, the pain may become chronic. The patient may have shooting, burning, or crushing pain as well as feelings of coldness, heaviness, and cramping,

There is no one therapy for phantom limb sensation. Mirror therapy and virtual reality treatment reduce symptoms in some patients (Fig. 67.26). We think these therapies give visual information to the brain, replacing sensory feedback expected from the missing limb.[17]

Upper Limb Amputation

An upper limb amputation is often more devastating than for lower limb amputation. Despite technologic advances, we

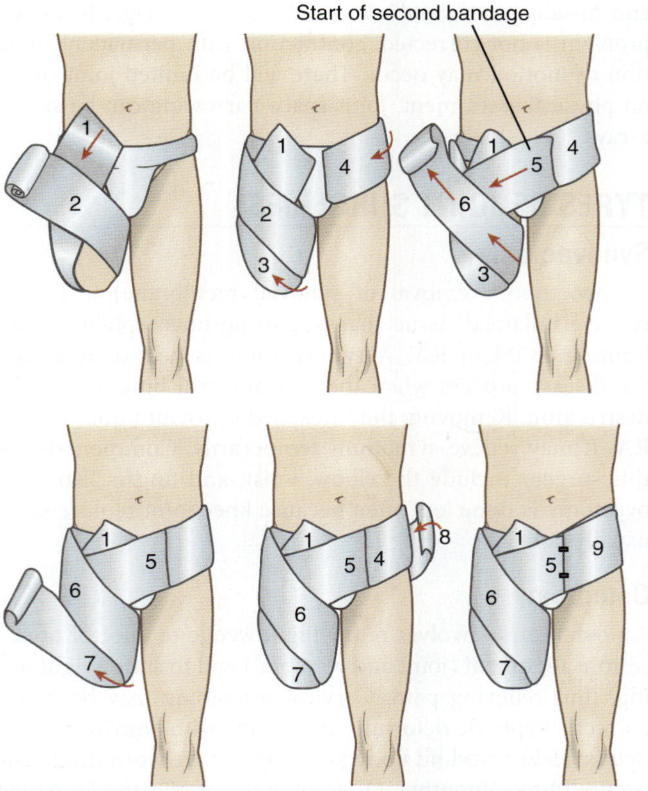

Fig. 67.26 Bandaging for the above-the-knee amputation residual limb. Figure-8 style covers progressive areas of the residual limb; 2 elastic wraps used.

cannot replicate the movements and functional capacity of our hands with upper extremity prostheses. The enforced dependency due to being 1-handed may be depressing and frustrating to the patient. Because most upper extremity amputations result from trauma, the patient likely had little time to adjust or be a part of the decision-making process.

Both immediate and delayed prosthetic fittings are possible for the below-the-elbow amputee. Prosthetic fitting is delayed for the above-the-elbow amputee. The usual functional prosthesis is the arm and hook. A cosmetic hand is available but has limited functional value. As with the lower limb prosthesis, patient motivation and perseverance are major factors contributing to a satisfactory outcome.

Evaluation

The expected outcomes are that the patient with an amputation will:

- Accept changed body image and integrate changes into lifestyle
- Have no evidence of skin breakdown
- Have reduction or absence of pain
- Become mobile within limitations imposed by amputation

COMMON JOINT SURGERIES

Surgery plays a vital role in the treatment and rehabilitation of patients with various joint problems. The goals of surgery are to relieve chronic pain, improve joint motion, correct deformity and misalignment, and remove diseased cartilage. If the joint problem is not corrected, contraction with permanent limitation of motion may occur. There will be limited joint motion on physical assessment. Joint-space narrowing can be seen on x-rays.

TYPES OF JOINT SURGERIES

Synovectomy

Synovectomy (removal of synovial membrane) is done to remove inflamed tissue that is causing unacceptable pain or limiting ROM in RA. A synovectomy is best done early in the disease process when there is minimal bone or cartilage destruction. Removing the thickened synovium does not cure RA. It may relieve symptoms temporarily. Common sites for this surgery include the elbow, wrist, and fingers. Knee synovectomy is done less often because knee joint replacement is usually done.

Osteotomy

An **osteotomy** involves removing a wedge or slice of bone to restore alignment (joint and vertebral) and to shift weight bearing, thus relieving pain. Cervical osteotomy may be used to correct a kyphotic deformity in patients with ankylosing spondylitis. Halo vests and body jacket braces are worn until fusion occurs (3 to 4 months). Osteotomy is not effective in patients with inflammatory joint disease. Femoral osteotomy may provide some pain relief and improve motion in select patients with hip OA. Tibial osteotomy provides pain relief in some patients with knee instability or OA.

Care of a patient who had an osteotomy is similar to that of a patient with ORIF of a fracture at a comparable site. Internal wires, screws and plates, bone grafts, or an external fixator usually fixes the bone in place.

Debridement

Debridement is the removal of debris, such as pieces of bone or cartilage *(loose bodies)* or osteophytes, from a joint using a fiberoptic arthroscope. This procedure is usually done on an outpatient basis on the knee or shoulder. A compression dressing is applied after surgery. Weight bearing is permitted after knee arthroscopy. Patient teaching includes monitoring for signs of infection, managing pain, and restricting activity for 24 to 48 hours.

Arthroplasty

Arthroplasty is the reconstruction or replacement of a joint to relieve pain, improve or maintain ROM, and correct deformity. Arthroplasty is most often done on patients with OA, RA, avascular necrosis, congenital deformities or dislocations, and other systemic problems. Types of arthroplasty include surgical reshaping of the bones of the joints, replacement of part of a joint (hemiarthroplasty), and total joint replacement. Around 1 million Americans have knee and hip replacement surgery annually.[18] Arthroplasty is also available for elbows, shoulders, fingers, wrists, ankles, and feet.

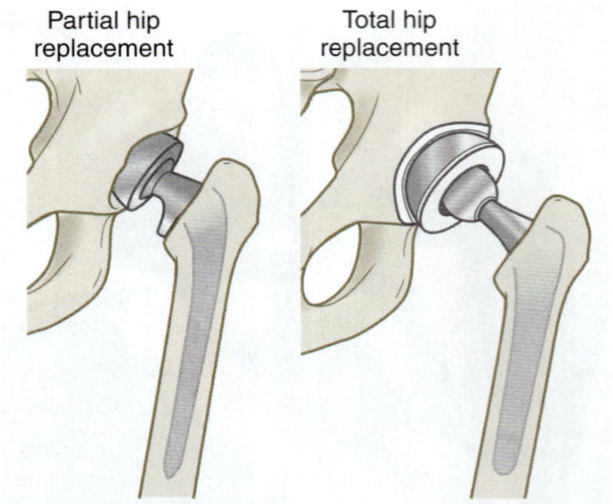

Fig. 67.27 Types of hip replacements.

Total Hip Arthroplasty

Total hip arthroplasty (THA), or a total hip replacement, provides significant relief of pain and improved function for patients with joint deterioration from OA, RA, and other conditions. THA is also used to treat hip fractures.

In THA, the prosthesis (implant) replaces the ball-and-socket joint formed by the upper shaft of the femur and pelvis (Fig. 67.27). Both the ball-and-socket components can be cemented in place with polymethyl methacrylate, which bonds to the bone. They may be inserted without cement (cementless). Cementless THA may provide longer stability by enabling growth of new bone tissue into the porous surface coating of the prosthesis. Cementless devices are better for younger, more active patients and patients with good bone quality as there is better bone growth into the components. The nursing care for a patient who had a THA is discussed in the section on nursing management of a patient with a hip fracture.

Hip Resurfacing Arthroplasty

An alternative to THA is hip resurfacing arthroplasty. It preserves and reshapes the femoral head (ball) rather than replacing it as in THA. The resurfaced femoral head is then capped by a metal prosthesis. Hip resurfacing may be an option for patients younger than age 60 with larger frames. A small number of patients have a femoral neck fracture after hip resurfacing. This is not possible with THA. Metal ions may be released into the bloodstream from the prosthesis. Patients may develop sensitivity or allergy to these ions.[19] Patients receiving a smaller femoral head (including many women) have a higher failure rate with a resurfaced implant when compared with patients receiving THA.

Knee Arthroplasty

Unrelieved pain and instability due to severe deterioration of the knee joint are the main reasons for total knee arthroplasty (TKA) or a total knee replacement (Fig. 67.28). Partial arthroplasty can be done on a patient with OA limited to 1 part (compartment) of the knee.

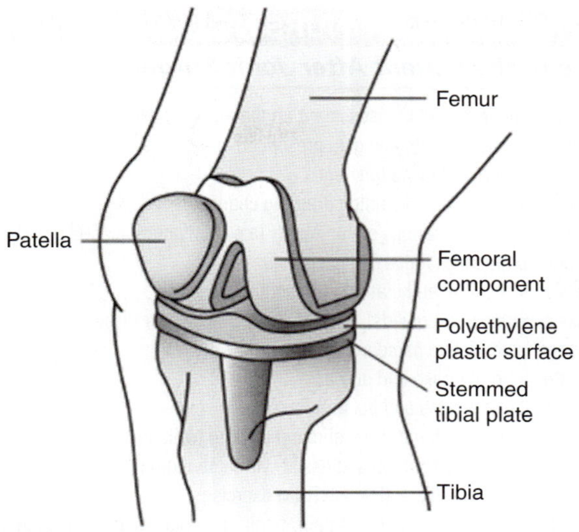

Fig. 67.28 Knee arthroplasty components. Up to 3 bone surfaces can be replaced in a total knee replacement. (Modified from Odom-Forren J: *Drain's perianesthesia nursing,* ed 7, St Louis, 2018, Elsevier.)

Right after surgery a compression dressing may be used to immobilize the knee in extension. This dressing is removed before discharge. If the patient is unable to perform a straight-leg raise, a knee immobilizer or posterior plastic shell to maintain extension may be used during ambulation and at rest for about 4 weeks.

After surgery, emphasis is on pain management and PT. Managing pain is a primary nursing goal. Doing so decreases the risk for complications and speeds the return to function. Adequate analgesia should be ordered at discharge to allow the patient to continue with the exercise program. Effective pain management is key to achieving positive rehabilitation outcomes.

PT begins early with isometric quadriceps setting. Therapy progresses to straight-leg raises and gentle ROM to increase muscle strength and obtain 90-degree knee flexion. Ambulation starts early with walking short distances, progressing to full weight bearing. An active home exercise program involves progressive ROM with muscle strength and flexibility exercises. After TKA, many patients with OA show significant improvement in mobility, motor function tests, and ability to complete daily tasks.

Finger Joint Arthroplasty

A silicone rubber arthroplastic device is used to restore function in the fingers of the patient with RA. Ulnar deviation often causes severe functional limitations of the hand. The main goal of hand surgery is to restore function related to grasp, pinch, stability, and strength rather than to correct cosmetic deformity. Before surgery, the patient should learn hand exercises, including flexion, extension, abduction, and adduction of the fingers.

After surgery, the patient will have a bulk dressing. Keep the hand elevated. Perform regular neurovascular assessment. Monitor for signs of infection. Success of the surgery depends largely on the postoperative treatment plan. An OT plays a key role. After the dressing is removed, a guided splinting program is started. Patients wear splints while sleeping and do hand exercises at least 3 or 4 times a day for 10 to 12 weeks. Teach the patient to avoid lifting heavy objects.

Elbow and Shoulder Arthroplasty

Elbow and shoulder replacements is not as common as other arthroplasties. Shoulder replacements are done in patients with severe pain because of RA, OA, avascular necrosis, or trauma. A special type of shoulder replacement, called a reverse total shoulder arthroplasty, may be done for pain and dysfunction caused by massive, irreparable rotator cuff tears. Shoulder replacement is usually considered if the patient has adequate surrounding muscle strength and bone density.

Rehabilitation is longer and more difficult than with other joint surgeries. If the patient needs elbow and shoulder joint replacements, the elbow is usually done first because elbow pain interferes with shoulder rehabilitation. Most patients have no pain at rest or minimal pain with activity after elbow and shoulder arthroplasty. Functional improvements contribute to better hygiene and increased ability to perform ADLs.

Ankle Arthroplasty

Total ankle arthroplasty (TAA) is indicated for RA, OA, trauma, and avascular necrosis. Although TAA is not widespread, it is a good alternative to fusion for treatment of severe ankle arthritis in certain patients. Available devices include several fixed-bearing devices and a mobile-bearing cementless prosthesis. This device more closely imitates natural ankle function.

Ankle fusion is preferred over arthroplasty because the result is more durable. However, fusion leaves the patient with a stiff foot and the inability to change heel height. TAA achieves a more normal gait pattern. After surgery, the patient may not bear weight for 6 weeks. They need to elevate the extremity to reduce edema and maintain immobilization as directed by the HCP.

Arthrodesis

Arthrodesis is the surgical fusion of a joint. This procedure is done only if articular surfaces are too severely damaged or infected to allow joint replacement or if reconstructive surgery fails. Arthrodesis relieves pain and provides a stable but immobile joint. The fusion is usually done by removing the articular hyaline cartilage and adding bone grafts across the joint surface. The affected joint must be immobilized until bone healing has occurred. Common areas fused are wrist, ankle, cervical spine, lumbar spine, and metatarsophalangeal (MTP) joint of the big toe.

Complications of Joint Surgery

Infection is a serious complication of joint surgery, especially joint replacement surgery. The most common causative organisms are streptococci and staphylococci. Infection may lead to pain and loosening of the prosthesis, often requiring further surgery. Measures to reduce infection include the use of specially designed self-contained operating suites, operating rooms with laminar airflow, and prophylactic antibiotic administration.

VTE is a serious complication after joint surgeries, especially those involving the lower extremities. Provide prophylactic measures, such as anticoagulant drugs, use of intermittent pneumatic compression devices, and early ambulation. Assess patients for signs of VTE. VTE is discussed in Chapter 41.

NURSING AND INTERPROFESSIONAL MANAGEMENT: JOINT SURGERY

Preoperative Care

The primary goal of preoperative assessment is to identify risk factors for postoperative complications so we can implement measures to promote optimal outcomes. A careful history includes (1) medical diagnoses and complications, such as diabetes; (2) pain tolerance and management preferences; (3) current functional level and expectations after surgery; (4) current social support; and (5) home care needs after discharge. The patient should be free from infection, breaks in skin integrity, and acute joint inflammation.

Preoperative teaching about the expected hospital course and postoperative management at home is important for the patient and caregiver. Explain postoperative care, including early mobility, the need to maintain hydration, and VTE prophylaxis. Assure the patient that analgesia will be available. A preoperative PT visit allows practice of postoperative exercises and measurement for crutches or other assistive devices. Provide opportunities for practice with assistive devices.

If lower extremity surgery is planned, assess upper extremity muscle strength and joint function to determine the type of assistive devices needed for ambulation and ADL performance. Discuss ways to maximize the usefulness and longevity of the prosthesis. Patients need to realize that recovery does not occur rapidly. Talking with other people who have had joint arthroplasty may help the patient better understand the reality of rehabilitation.

Begin discharge planning. Review the duration of the hospital stay and expected postoperative events so that the patient and caregiver can prepare. Advanced planning helps to allow for a discharge home. Assess the patient's support. Identify their care partner. Who is going to help the patient at home? Will the patient need homemaker or meal services? It is preferable that the patient goes home after a total joint arthroplasty. Discuss the safety and accessibility of the home environment (e.g., throw rugs, cords). Are the bathroom and bedroom on the first floor? Are door frames wide enough to accommodate a walker? Discharge to a subacute or extended care facility should be planned beforehand. The older patient may need to go to a facility for a few weeks to regain independent living skills, if there is no social support available.

Postoperative Management

Nursing care of the patient having orthopedic surgery is outlined in Table 67.16. Other nursing interventions are presented in eNursing Care Plan 67.2 (available on the website for this chapter). The hospital stay after arthroplasty can be a few hours after surgery to 2 days depending on preoperative planning, postoperative course, and need for PT after surgery. Many hip and knee replacement surgeries are done at ambulatory surgical centers. Same day surgery is a trend expected to increase.

TABLE 67.16 NURSING MANAGEMENT

Care of the Patient After Joint Surgery

- Perform neurovascular assessment on the affected extremity.
- Monitor pain intensity and give prescribed analgesics.
- Maintain correct body alignment.
- Provide wound care, including dressing changes.
- Assess for complications of immobility (e.g., constipation, VTE) and develop a plan to minimize those complications.
- Assist with initial ambulation then help as needed.
- Assist patient, caregiver(s), and family in planning for discharge care.
- Supervise assistive personnel (AP):
  - Record oral intake and output.
  - Obtain vital signs and pulse oximetry.
  - Aid patient with nutrition, elimination, and hygiene needs.
  - Maintain body position and assist with ambulation.
  - Help with passive and active ROM exercises.
  - Notify RN about reports of pain, tingling, or decreased sensation in the affected extremity.

Collaborate With Physical Therapist

- Assess current mobility and need for assistance.
- Teach safe ambulation with assistive device based on weight-bearing restrictions.
- Establish exercise plan and teach patient to perform exercises safely.
- Coordinate PT with RN so that patient can receive timely analgesia.
- Discuss home environment with patient and identify modifications to promote safety.

Regularly perform neurovascular assessment. Give ordered analgesics. Assess patient comfort often during the postoperative period. Monitor for postoperative complications. Teach the patient to report complications. Review signs of infection (e.g., fever, increased pain, drainage) and dislocation of the prosthesis (e.g., pain, loss of function, shortening or malalignment of an extremity).

Assess ROM at regular intervals to promote functional performance. In general, the affected joint is exercised, and we encourage ambulation as early as possible. PT and ambulation enhance mobility, build muscle strength, and reduce the risk for VTE. Specific protocols vary according to the patient, type of prosthesis, and HCP preference.

VTE risk reduction includes hydration, shorter surgery time, early mobility, and use of anticoagulant medications. Most prophylactic anticoagulant drugs are given for at least 10 to 14 days.[12] Some patients need therapy for up to 35 days. If the patient is taking warfarin, therapy starts on the day of surgery, and the INR and prothrombin times are measured daily. Therapy with LMWH (e.g., enoxaparin), apixaban, or rivaroxaban usually starts the morning after surgery.

Case Study

Hip Fracture and Revision Arthroplasty

(© aronaze/ iStock.com.)

Patient Profile

M.C. is a 64-year-old man who had both hips replaced (left 6 years ago, right 2 years ago). He has a history of hypothyroidism. He was admitted to the ED after tripping over a short retaining wall in his backyard while gardening. He landed on his right side.

Subjective Data

- Acute, severe pain in right hip, unable to bear weight on right leg.
- Takes cholecalciferol (vitamin D_3) 1000 IU every day without calcium supplement. States calcium upsets his stomach.
- Reports loss of about 30 lb in the last year through diet and exercise. Exercises 3 times a week.
- Lives in multilevel house with his wife. Bedrooms are on the second level.
- Has smoked ½ pack of cigarettes a day for the 30 years.
- Describes himself as "a very light social drinker."

Objective Data

- 5 ft, 9 in tall, 175 lb

Diagnostic Studies

- X-rays show periprosthetic right proximal femur fracture at the greater trochanter with loss of fixation in the femoral part of the THA
- Normal CBC, chest x-ray
- Serum calcium 8.1 mg/dL

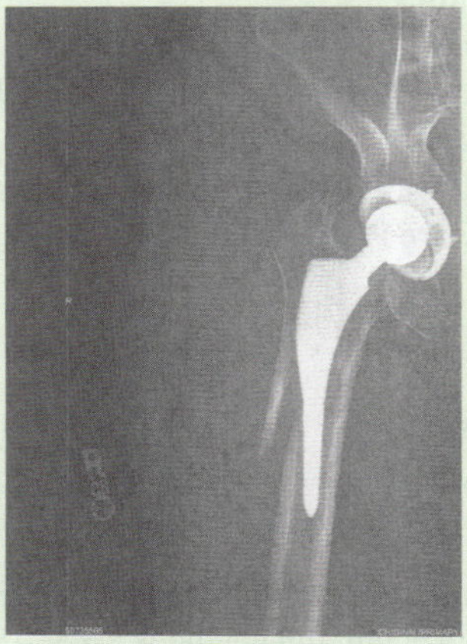

Interprofessional Care

- Revision of femoral part of his right total hip replacement with open reduction of the femoral fracture and fixation with 3 wires
- Medications:
  - IV morphine sulfate 2 mg IV every 3 hr as needed
  - Cefazolin 1 gram IV every 8 hr for 24 hr
  - Enoxaparin 40 mg subcutaneous daily for 4 weeks
  - Calcium citrate 600 mg plus 800 IU vitamin D orally daily
  - Levothyroxine (Synthroid) 125 mcg orally daily
- PT for transfers, gait, and stair training
- Occupational therapy for ADLs training
- Discharge planning based on mobility limitations and need for continued PT and OT

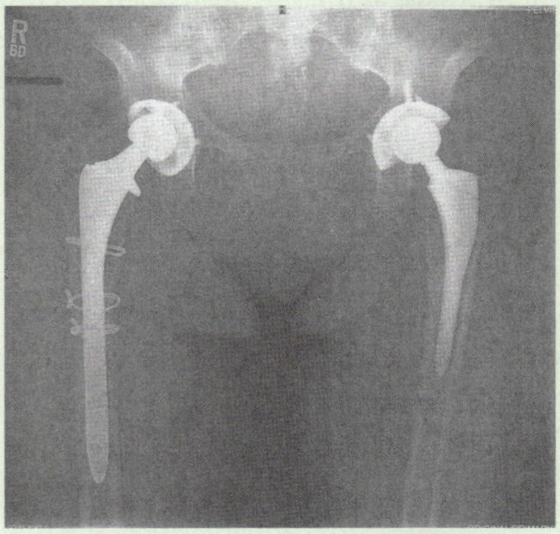

Discussion Questions

1. ***Recognize:*** How do M.C.'s previous total joint surgeries affect his recovery after this surgery?
2. ***Analyze:*** What are the most likely postoperative complications M.C. could develop?
3. ***Analyze:*** In considering his patient profile, what issues can you identify that may affect his bone healing?
4. ***Plan:*** As you plan care for M.C., what are the priority nursing interventions?
5. ***Prioritize:*** What is the interprofessional team's top priority at this time?
6. ***Act:*** What do you need to assess to determine his readiness for discharge?
7. ***Safety:*** What safety precautions should we implement for M.C.?
8. ***Evaluate:*** Why is satisfactory pain management an important postoperative nursing goal for M.C.?
9. ***Evaluate:*** What outcomes would indicate nursing care was effective?

Answers available at http://evolve.elsevier.com/Lewis/medsurg.

BRIDGE TO NCLEX EXAMINATION

The number of the question corresponds to the same-numbered outcome at the beginning of the chapter.

1. The nurse in urgent care suspects an ankle sprain when a patient describes
   a. being hit by another soccer player during a game.
   b. having ankle pain after sprinting around the track.
   c. dropping a 10-lb weight on his lower leg at the health club.
   d. twisting his ankle while running bases during a baseball game.
2. A patient with a humeral fracture is returning for a 4-week checkup. The nurse explains that initial evidence of healing on x-ray is indicated by
   a. formation of callus.
   b. complete bony union.
   c. hematoma at the fracture site.
   d. presence of granulation tissue.

3. A patient with a comminuted fracture of the tibia is to have an open reduction with internal fixation (ORIF) of the fracture. The nurse explains that ORIF is indicated when
   a. the patient cannot tolerate prolonged immobilization.
   b. the patient cannot tolerate the surgery for a closed reduction.
   c. other nonsurgical methods cannot achieve adequate alignment.
   d. a temporary cast would be too unstable to provide normal mobility.
4. The nurse suspects a neurovascular problem based on assessment of
   a. exaggerated strength with movement.
   b. increased redness and heat below the injury.
   c. decreased sensation distal to the fracture site.
   d. purulent drainage at the site of an open fracture.
5. A patient with a stable, closed humeral fracture has a temporary splint with bulky padding applied with an elastic bandage. The nurse suspects early compartment syndrome when the patient has
   a. increasing edema of the limb.
   b. muscle spasms of the lower arm.
   c. bounding pulse at the fracture site.
   d. pain when passively extending the fingers.
6. The nurse would monitor a patient with a pelvic fracture for
   a. changes in urine output.
   b. petechiae on the abdomen.
   c. a palpable lump in the buttock.
   d. sudden increase in blood pressure.
7. The nurse teaches the patient with an above-the-knee amputation that the residual limb should not be routinely elevated because this position promotes
   a. hip flexion contracture.
   b. clot formation at the incision.
   c. skin irritation and breakdown.
   d. increased risk for wound dehiscence.
8. A patient with osteoarthritis is scheduled for total hip arthroplasty. The nurse explains the purpose of this procedure is to *(select all that apply)*
   a. fuse the joint.
   b. replace the joint.
   c. prevent further damage.
   d. improve or maintain ROM.
   e. decrease the amount of destruction in the joint.
9. A patient is scheduled for total ankle replacement. The nurse should tell the patient that after surgery he should avoid
   a. lifting heavy objects.
   b. sleeping on the back.
   c. abduction exercises of the affected ankle.
   d. bearing weight on the affected leg for 6 weeks.

1. d; 2. a; 3. c; 4. c; 5. d; 6. a; 7. a; 8. b, d; 9. d.

For rationales to these answers and even more NCLEX review questions, visit http://evolve.elsevier.com/Lewis/medsurg.

EVOLVE WEBSITE/RESOURCES LIST

http://evolve.elsevier.com/Lewis/medsurg
Review Questions (Online Only)
Key Points
Answer Keys for Questions
- Rationales for Bridge to NCLEX Examination Questions
- Answer Guidelines for Case Study

Student Case Studies
- Patient With Musculoskeletal Trauma
- Patient With Parkinson's Disease and Hip Fracture

Nursing Care Plans
- eNursing Care Plan 67.1: Patient With a Fracture
- eNursing Care Plan 67.2: Patient Having Orthopedic Surgery

Concept Map Creator
Audio Glossary
Content Updates

REFERENCES

1. Centers for Disease Control and Prevention (CDC): Leading causes of death. Retrieved from https://www.cdc.gov/injury/wisqars/facts.html.
2. National Institute of Arthritis and Musculoskeletal and Skin Diseases: Preventing sports injuries in youth: a guide for parents. Retrieved from https://www.niams.nih.gov/Health_Info/Sports_Injuries/child_sports_injuries.asp.
3. American Academy of Orthopaedic Surgeons (AAOS): Sprains, strains, and other soft-tissue injuries. Retrieved from https://www.orthoinfo.org/topic.cfm?topic=A00111.
4. Mayo Clinic: Carpal tunnel syndrome. Retrieved from https://www.mayoclinic.org/diseases-conditions/carpal-tunnel-syndrome/basics/definition/con-20030332.
5. Mayo Clinic: Rotator cuff injury: diagnosis and treatment. Retrieved from https://www.mayoclinic.org/diseases-conditions/rotator-cuff-injury/symptoms-causes/syc-20350225.
6. Sheen JR, Garla VV: Fracture healing overview. Retrieved from: https://www.ncbi.nlm.nih.gov/books/NBK551678/.
7. Swiontkowski MF: Cast and bandaging techniques. In *Manual of Orthopaedics*, 8 ed, Wolters Kluwer, 2020.
8. American Orthopedic Foot and Ankle Society: Foot ulcers and the total contact cast. Retrieved from https://www.aofas.org/footcaremd/conditions/diabetic-foot/Pages/Foot-Ulcers-and-the-Total-Contact-Cast.aspx.

*9. Sáenz-Jalón M, Sarabia-Cobo CM, Bartolome ER, et al.: A randomized clinical trial on the use of antiseptic solutions for the pin-site care of external fixators, *J Trauma Nurs* 27:146, 2020.

*10. Bhavsar MB, Han Z, DeCoster T, et al.: Electrical stimulation-based bone fracture treatment, if it works so well why do not more surgeons use it? *Eur J Trauma Emerg Surg* 46:245, 2020.

11. Rupp M, Popp D, Alt V: Prevention of infection in open fractures: where are the pendulums now? *Injury* 51:S57, 2020.

12. Bartlett MA, Mauck KF, Stephenson CR, et al.: Perioperative venous thromboembolism prophylaxis, *Mayo Clin Proc* 95:277, 2020.
13. Luff D, Hewson DW: Fat embolism syndrome, *BJA Education* 21:322, 2021.
14. CDC: Hip fractures among older adults. Retrieved from https://www.cdc.gov/HomeandRecreationalSafety/Falls/adulthipfx.html.
15. Amputee Coalition: Limb loss statistics. Retrieved from https://www.amputee-coalition.org/limb-loss-resource-center/resources-by-topic/limb-loss-statistics/limb-loss-statistics.
*16. Armstrong AJ, Hawley CE, Darter B, et al.: Operation Enduring Freedom and Operation Iraqi Freedom veterans with amputation: an exploration of resilience, employment, and individual characteristics, *J Vocat Rehabil* 48:167, 2018.
17. Erlenwein J, Diers M, Ernst J, et al.: Clinical updates on phantom limb pain, *Pain Rep* 6:e888, 2021.
*18. Singh JA, Yu S, Chen L, et al.: Rates of total joint replacement in the United States: future projections to 2020–2040 using the national inpatient sample, *J Rheumatol* 46:1134, 2019.
19. AAOS: Hip resurfacing. Retrieved from http://orthoinfo.aaos.org/topic.cfm?topic=A00586.

*Evidence-based information for clinical practice.

68

Musculoskeletal Problems

Diane Ryzner

http://evolve.elsevier.com/Lewis/medsurg/

CONCEPTUAL FOCUS

Functional Ability
Mobility
Pain
Safety

LEARNING OUTCOMES

1. Describe the pathophysiology, clinical manifestations, and interprofessional and nursing management of osteomyelitis.
2. Discern among the types, clinical manifestations, and interprofessional management of bone cancer.
3. Discuss the genetic basis and clinical course of muscular dystrophy.
4. Discern between the causes and characteristics of acute and chronic low back pain.
5. Describe the postoperative nursing management of a patient who had spine surgery.
6. Discuss the etiology and nursing management of common foot problems.
7. Describe the etiology, pathophysiology, clinical manifestations, and nursing and interprofessional management of osteomalacia, osteoporosis, and Paget disease.

KEY TERMS

degenerative disc disease (DDD)
hallux valgus
herniated disc
low back pain
muscular dystrophy (MD)
osteochondroma
osteomalacia
osteomyelitis
osteopenia (Table 68.14)
osteoporosis
osteosarcoma
Paget disease
sarcoma

We were made to move! This chapter reviews a variety of acute and chronic musculoskeletal problems unrelated to trauma that affect the musculoskeletal system. These include osteomyelitis, bone cancer, foot problems, back pain, and metabolic bone diseases. These problems can lead to changes in mobility that affect almost every system in the body. They are a common source of pain and physical limitations that restrict the ability to fully take part in activities of daily living (ADLs), leading to disability. The nurse plays a key role in assessing pain and functional ability and initiating interventions to prevent injury and maintain mobility.

OSTEOMYELITIS

Etiology and Pathophysiology

Osteomyelitis is a severe infection of the bone, bone marrow, and surrounding soft tissue. A number of pathogens can cause osteomyelitis (Table 68.1).[1] *Staphylococcus aureus* is the most common cause.

Infecting microorganisms can invade by indirect or direct entry. *Indirect entry* (hematogenous) is usually from an infection with 1 microorganism. Indirect injury accounts for only 20% of cases. It most often affects children younger than 17 years. Risk factors in adults are older age, debilitation, hemodialysis, sickle cell disease, and IV drug use. The vertebrae are the most common site of infection in adults.[2]

Direct entry (contiguous) osteomyelitis accounts for 80% of case. It most often affects adults.[2] It can occur when an open wound (e.g., penetrating wounds, fractures, surgery) allows microorganisms to enter the body. Osteomyelitis can be related to a foreign body, such as an implant or an orthopedic prosthetic device (e.g., plate, total joint prosthesis). It may occur in the feet of patients with diabetes or vascular disease–related ulcers or in the hips or sacrum near a pressure injury. More than 1 microorganism is usually involved.

TABLE 68.1 **Organisms Causing Osteomyelitis**

Organism	Predisposing Problem
Escherichia coli	Urinary tract infection
Fungi, mycobacteria	Immunocompromised host
Mycobacterium tuberculosis	Tuberculosis
Neisseria gonorrhoeae	Gonorrhea
Pseudomonas	Puncture wounds, IV drug use
Salmonella	Sickle cell disease
Staphylococcus aureus	Pressure injury, penetrating wound, open fracture, orthopedic surgery, vascular insufficiency (e.g., diabetes, atherosclerosis)
Staphylococcus epidermidis	Indwelling prosthetic devices (e.g., joint replacements, fracture fixation devices)
Streptococcus viridans	Abscessed tooth, gingival disease

After entering the blood, microorganisms grow, and pressure increases because of the nonexpanding nature of most bone. This increased pressure eventually leads to ischemia and vascular compromise of the periosteum. The infection spreads through the bone cortex and marrow cavity, obstructing blood flow and causing and necrosis.

Bone death occurs due to ischemia. The area of dead bone eventually separates from the surrounding living bone, forming *sequestra*. The part of the periosteum that continues to have a blood supply forms new bone called *involucrum* (Fig. 68.1). Antibiotics or white blood cells (WBCs) have difficulty reaching the sequestrum through the blood. Thus sequestrum may become a reservoir for microorganisms that spread to other sites, including the lungs and brain. If the sequestrum does not resolve or is not debrided surgically, a sinus tract may develop. Chronic, purulent drainage from the tract results.

Clinical Manifestations and Complications

Acute osteomyelitis refers to the initial infection or an infection of less than 1 month in duration. Local manifestations include constant bone pain that worsens with activity and is unrelieved by rest; swelling, tenderness, and warmth at the site; and restricted movement of the affected part. Systemic manifestations include fever, night sweats, chills, restlessness, nausea, and malaise. Later signs include drainage from skin sinus tracts or the fracture site.

Chronic osteomyelitis is a bone infection that lasts longer than 1 month or an infection that did not respond to initial antibiotic treatment. Chronic osteomyelitis may be a continuous, persistent problem or recurrent, with exacerbations and remissions (Fig. 68.2). Systemic manifestations are lessened. Local signs of infection become more common, including constant bone pain and swelling and warmth at the infection site. Over time, granulation tissue turns to scar tissue. The avascular scar tissue is an ideal site for continued microorganism growth because it cannot be penetrated by antibiotics.

Long-term, and mostly rare, complications of osteomyelitis include septicemia, septic arthritis, pathologic fractures, and amyloidosis.

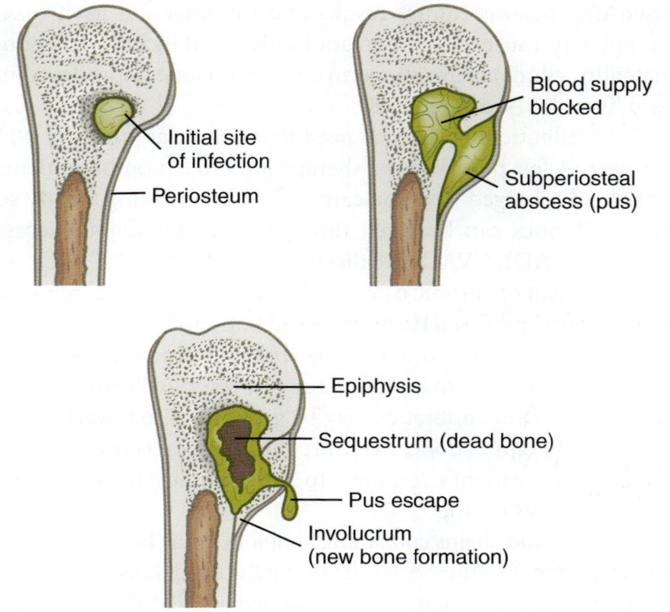

Fig. 68.1 Development of osteomyelitis infection with involucrum and sequestrum.

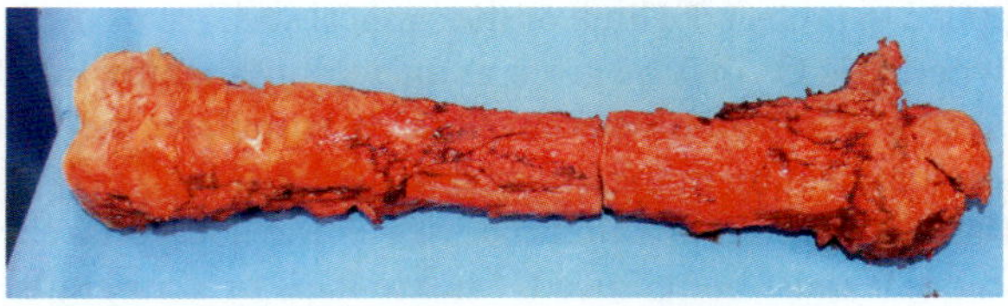

Fig. 68.2 Left femur with severe bone damage due to osteomyelitis. (From Trung DT, Dinh HN, Le NT, et al.: Total femur replacement in a patient with chronic persistence osteomyelitis, *Int J Surg Case Rep* 84:106067, 2021.)

Diagnostic Studies

Bone or soft tissue biopsy is the definitive way to identify the causative agent. Blood and wound cultures are often positive. Increased WBC count and erythrocyte sedimentation rate (ESR) may occur. High C-reactive protein (CRP) may occur with acute infection. Signs of osteomyelitis usually do not appear on x-rays until 2 to 4 weeks after the initial clinical symptoms. By this time, the disease will have progressed. Compared with x-rays, CT scan may be better in assessing the extent of infection. In the acute phase, MRI may be better than CT in detecting bone marrow edema, an early sign of osteomyelitis. Radionuclide bone scans (technetium-99m) also show abnormalities earlier than x-rays. A WBC scan (indium-111–labeled cells) may help pinpoint the area of infection.[2]

Interprofessional Care

Prolonged antibiotic therapy is the treatment of choice for acute osteomyelitis if bone ischemia has not yet occurred. Cultures or a bone biopsy should be done, if possible, before starting drug therapy. Any related soft tissue abscess or ulceration often needs surgical debridement or drainage.

Most patients start on IV antibiotics then switch to oral therapy. However, some may only receive oral agents.[3] The antibiotic used depends on culture results and the infection itself (e.g., complexity, cause). Common antibiotics used include oxacillin, nafcillin, clindamycin, vancomycin, ceftriaxone, ciprofloxacin, and linezolid (see Table 15.8).

IV antibiotic therapy may need to continue at home for 4 to 6 weeks. A few persons need therapy for 3 to 6 months. Patients may be discharged to home care or a skilled nursing facility so the antibiotics can be given through a central venous access device (CVAD). CVADs are discussed in Chapter 17.

Treatment of chronic osteomyelitis includes surgical removal of the poorly perfused tissue and dead bone and extended use of antibiotics. In adults, oral therapy with a fluoroquinolone (e.g., ciprofloxacin) for 6 to 8 weeks may be prescribed instead of IV antibiotics. Oral antibiotics may be given for 4 to 8 weeks after acute IV therapy is done, to ensure the infection is resolved. We monitor the patient's response to drug therapy through bone scans and ESR testing.

Acrylic bead chains containing antibiotics may be implanted to help treat the infection. After debriding the dead, infected tissue, a suction irrigation system may be inserted and the wound closed. Intermittent or constant irrigation of the area with antibiotics may be used. Another option for wound management is negative-pressure wound therapy (discussed in Chapter 12). Casts or braces may be applied to protect the limb or the surgical site.

Hyperbaric O_2 may be given as an adjunct therapy in refractory cases of chronic osteomyelitis. It stimulates new blood growth and healing in the infected tissue.

If an orthopedic prosthetic device is the source of chronic infection, it must be removed. Muscle flaps or skin grafts provide wound coverage over the dead space in the bone. Bone grafts may help to restore blood flow. However, flaps or grafts should never be placed when there is an active or suspected infection.

Amputation may be needed if bone destruction is extensive. Amputation should improve quality of life and may save the patient's life if systemic complications are developing.

NURSING MANAGEMENT: OSTEOMYELITIS

Assessment

Subjective and objective data that you should obtain from a person with osteomyelitis are outlined in Table 68.2.

Clinical Problems

Clinical problems for the patient with osteomyelitis may include:

- Pain
- Musculoskeletal problems
- Infection

Additional information on nursing diagnoses and interventions for the patient with osteomyelitis can be found in eNursing Care Plan 68.1 (available on the website for this chapter).

Planning

The overall goals are that the patient with osteomyelitis will (1) have satisfactory pain and fever management, (2) be free from complications, (3) and adhere to the treatment plan.

TABLE 68.2 NURSING ASSESSMENT

Osteomyelitis

Subjective Data

Important Health Information

Health history: Bone trauma, open fracture, open or puncture wounds, other infections (e.g., streptococcal sore throat, bacterial pneumonia, sinusitis, skin or tooth infection, chronic urinary tract infection)

Medications: Analgesics or antibiotics

Surgery or other treatments: Bone surgery

Functional Health Patterns

Health perception–health management: IV drug and alcohol use. Malaise

Nutritional-metabolic: Anorexia, weight loss. Chills

Activity-exercise: Weakness, paralysis, muscle spasms around affected area

Cognitive-perceptual: Local tenderness over affected area, ↑ pain with movement of affected area

Coping–stress tolerance: Irritability, withdrawal, dependency, anger

Objective Data

General

Restlessness. High, spiking temperature. Night sweats

Musculoskeletal

Restricted movement; wound drainage. Spontaneous fracture

Skin

Diaphoresis. Redness, warmth, edema at site of infection

Possible Diagnostic Findings

Positive blood and/or wound cultures, ↑ ESR, ↑ WBC. Presence of sequestrum and involucrum on x-rays, radionuclide bone scans, CT, and MRI

Implementation

Health Promotion

Control of other current infections (e.g., urinary or respiratory tract, pressure injuries) is important in preventing osteomyelitis. Persons at risk for osteomyelitis are those who are immunocompromised or have diabetes, orthopedic prosthetic implants, or vascular insufficiency. Teach the at-risk patient about the signs of osteomyelitis. Encourage the patient to contact the HCP about bone pain, fever, swelling, and restricted limb movement so that they can start treatment. Teach caregivers about their role in monitoring the patient's health.

Acute Care

Nursing care of the patient with osteomyelitis is outlined in Table 68.3. Some immobilization of the affected limb (e.g., splint, traction) is usually needed to decrease pain and reduce risk for further injury. Carefully handle the limb. Avoid undue manipulation. This may increase pain and cause a pathologic fracture. Assess for pain. Muscle spasms may cause minor to severe pain. Nonsteroidal antiinflammatory drugs (NSAIDs), opioid analgesics, and muscle relaxants may be given.

Dressings are used to absorb drainage from wounds and debride dead tissue from the wound bed. These include dry, sterile dressings; dressings saturated in saline or antibiotic solution; wet-to-dry dressings; and dressings applied with negative-pressure wound therapy. Handle soiled dressings carefully

TABLE 68.3 NURSING MANAGEMENT

Caring for the Patient With Osteomyelitis

- Give IV antibiotics as ordered.
- Assess wound for signs of worsening infection.
- Teach patient and caregiver about antibiotic side effects and length of treatment, signs and symptoms of worsening infection, and use of hyperbaric O_2 if ordered.
- Assess for muscle spasms, and give muscle relaxants as ordered. Assess response.
- Assess pain, and give analgesics as ordered. Assess response.
- Handle affected limb carefully and avoid undue manipulation.
- Assess neurovascular condition of affected limb, and immediately inform HCP of significant changes.
- Encourage nondrug approaches to managing pain (e.g., guided imagery, relaxation breathing) (see Chapter 7).
- Change dressing as ordered using sterile technique.
- Implement contact precautions as needed.
- Supervise AP:
  - Handle affected limb carefully based on RN instruction.
  - Help patient with passive ROM of adjacent joints and active ROM exercises of unaffected limb.
  - Notify RN about reports of pain, tingling, or decreased sensation in the affected extremity.

Collaborate With Physical Therapist

- Assess current mobility and need for aid.
- Teach safe ambulation with assistive device based on weight-bearing restrictions.
- Establish exercise plan and teach patient to perform exercises safely.
- Coordinate PT so that patient can receive timely analgesia.
- Discuss home environment with patient and identify modifications needed (e.g., stair training, bed placement on first level).

Collaborate With Occupational Therapist

- Assess impact of condition on ability to perform ADLs.
- Teach use of assistive devices (e.g., long-handled reacher, shoe donner) to promote self-care while maintaining activity restrictions.

to prevent transfer of bacteria to other areas of the wound. Discard dressings appropriately to prevent spread of infection.

The patient is often placed on bed rest in the early stages of acute infection. Good body alignment and frequent position changes promote comfort and prevent complications related to immobility. Flexion contracture of the affected lower extremity is common. The patient often positions the leg in a flexed position to promote comfort. Footdrop can develop quickly due to Achilles tendon contracture if the foot is not supported in a neutral position by a splint or boot.

Teach the patient the possible adverse reactions from prolonged high-dose antibiotic therapy (see Table 15.8). These include hearing problems, impaired renal function, and neurotoxicity (e.g., limb weakness or numbness, cognitive changes, vision changes, headache, behavior problems). Monitor peak and trough blood levels of most antibiotics. Assess for the overgrowth of *Candida albicans* and *Clostridioides difficile* in the genitourinary (GU) and gastrointestinal (GI) tracts, especially in immunosuppressed and older adult patients. Teach the patient to report any changes in the oral cavity (e.g., whitish yellow, curd-like lesions) or the GU tract (e.g., perianal itching, discharge).

CHECK YOUR PRACTICE

Your patient on the orthopedic unit is a 22-year-old man who was in an all-terrain vehicle accident in a remote area 4 days ago. He is slowly recovering from his head injury and surgical repair of an open fracture of the femur. Yesterday, he was diagnosed with acute osteomyelitis. He is very angry and at times disoriented. When you try to assess his leg, he yells at you, "It hurts. Leave it alone!"

- What are your priorities of care?
- What signs and symptoms would suggest the patient's condition is worsening?

The patient and caregivers may be anxious and discouraged because of the serious nature of osteomyelitis, the uncertainty of the outcome, and the long, costly treatment. Continued emotional support is a key part of nursing management.

◆ Ambulatory Care

Teach the patient and caregiver how to manage the CVAD if receiving IV antibiotics at home. Review how to administer the antibiotic. Reinforce the need for follow-up laboratory testing. Stress the importance of continuing to take the full course of antibiotics prescribed, even after symptoms have improved.

Dressing changes are often needed if the patient has an open wound. The patient and caregiver may need supplies and instruction for completing the dressing change. If the osteomyelitis becomes chronic, the patient needs continued physical and psychologic support.

◆ Evaluation

The expected outcomes are that the patient with osteomyelitis will:

- Have satisfactory pain management
- Adhere to the recommended treatment plan
- Show a consistent increase in mobility and range of motion (ROM)

BONE TUMORS

Primary bone tumors, both benign and malignant, are rare in adults. They account for only around 3% of all tumors. Benign bone tumors are more common than primary malignant tumors. Metastatic bone cancer, in which cancer has spread from another site, is more common.

BENIGN BONE TUMORS

The main types of benign bone tumors are osteochondroma, osteoclastoma, and enchondroma (Table 68.4).

Osteochondroma

Osteochondroma is the most common benign bone tumor. It is characterized by an overgrowth of cartilage and bone near the

TABLE 68.4 Types of Primary Bone Tumors

Types	Description
Benign	
Enchondroma	• Intramedullary cartilage tumor usually found in cavity of a single hand or foot bone • Rarely transforms to cancer • If tumor becomes painful, surgical resection is done • Peak incidence in people ages 10–20 years
Osteochondroma	• Most common benign bone tumor • Often found in pelvis, scapula, or metaphyseal part of long bones • Occurs most often in people ages 10–25 years • May transform to cancer (chondrosarcoma)
Osteoclastoma (giant cell tumor)	• Arises in cancellous ends of arm and leg bones • Around 10% are locally aggressive and may spread to lungs • High rate of local recurrence after surgery and chemotherapy
Malignant	
Chondrosarcoma	• Most often occurs in cartilage in arm, leg, and pelvic bones of adults ages 50–70 years • Can arise from benign bone tumors (osteochondromas) • Wide surgical resection is typically done as tumor rarely responds to radiation and chemotherapy • Survival rate depends on stage, size, and grade of tumor
Ewing sarcoma	• Develops in medullary cavity of pelvis and long bones, especially femur, humerus, and tibia • Usually occurs in children and teenagers • Use of wide surgical resection, radiation, and chemotherapy has improved 5-year survival rate to 60%
Osteosarcoma	• Most common primary bone cancer • Occurs mostly in males ages 10–25 • Most often in pelvis or bones of arms, legs (Fig. 68.3)

end of the bone at the growth plate. They most often occur in the pelvis, scapula, or long bones of the leg.

Manifestations include a painless, hard, immobile mass; shorter-than-normal height for age; soreness of muscles close to the tumor; 1 leg or arm longer than the other; and pressure or irritation with exercise. Some may be asymptomatic. Diagnosis is confirmed using x-ray, CT scan, and MRI.

No treatment is needed for asymptomatic osteochondroma. Patients should have regular screenings to detect progression to cancer. If the tumor is causing pain or neurologic manifestations because of compression, surgical removal is usually done.

MALIGNANT BONE TUMORS

A **sarcoma** is a malignant tumor that develops in bone, muscle, fat, nerve, or cartilage. The most common types of sarcomas are osteosarcoma, chondrosarcoma, and Ewing sarcoma (Table 68.4). In 2020, 3600 new cases of bone and joint cancer are expected in the United States, with an estimated 1720 deaths.[4] Primary tumors occur most often during childhood and young adulthood. They cause bone destruction and have rapid metastasis.

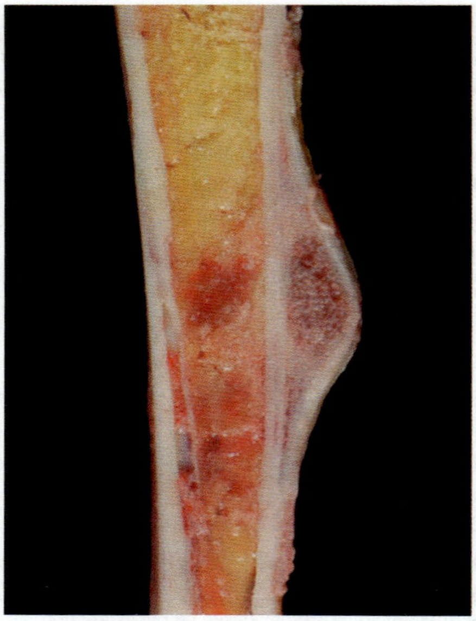

Fig. 68.3 Osteosarcoma. (From Czerniak B: *Dorfman and Czerniak's bone tumors*, ed 2, Philadelphia, 2016, Elsevier.)

Osteosarcoma

Osteosarcoma is a very aggressive bone cancer. It rapidly spreads to distant sites. It often starts in the pelvis or metaphyseal region of the long bones of extremities, especially in the distal femur, proximal tibia, and proximal humerus (Fig. 68.3). Osteosarcoma is the most common bone cancer affecting children and young adults. It can occur in older adults, but not as often. It is most often associated with Paget disease and prior radiation.

The gradual onset of pain and swelling in the affected bone are the most common manifestations. The pain may be worse at night and increase with activity. A minor injury does not cause the cancer but may be how it is found. Metastasis is present in 10% to 20% of people at the time of diagnosis. Diagnosis is confirmed from tissue biopsy, increased serum alkaline phosphatase and calcium, x-ray, CT or PET scans, and MRI.

Chemotherapy (neoadjuvant) may be used before surgery to decrease tumor size. Limb salvage procedures are usually considered if a clear (no cancer present) 6- to 7-cm margin surrounds the lesion. Limb salvage is usually not possible if the patient has major nerve or blood vessel involvement, pathologic fracture, infection, or extensive muscle involvement.

Chemotherapy after amputation or limb salvage (adjuvant) has increased the 5-year survival rate to 70% in people without metastasis. Chemotherapy includes combinations of methotrexate, doxorubicin, cisplatin, ifosfamide, cyclophosphamide, and etoposide.[5]

Metastatic Bone Cancer

The most common type of cancerous bone tumor occurs because of spread *(metastasis)* from a primary tumor at another site. Common primary sites include breast, colon, prostate, lungs, kidney, and thyroid.[6] Metastatic cancer cells travel from the primary tumor to the bone via the lymph and blood supply. Metastatic bone lesions often occur in the spine, ribs, or pelvis.[6] Pathologic fractures at the site of metastasis are common because the bone is weak. High serum calcium occurs as damaged bones release calcium.

Once a primary lesion has been found, bone scans are often done to detect metastatic lesions before they are visible on x-ray. Metastatic bone lesions may occur at any time (even years later) after diagnosis and treatment of the primary tumor. Bone metastasis should be suspected in any patient who has local bone pain and a history of cancer. Surgical stabilization of the bone may be indicated for fracture or to prevent fracture in a high-risk patient. Prognosis depends on the primary type of cancer and any other sites of metastasis. Possible palliative treatment consists of radiation and pain management (see Chapter 16).

❖ NURSING MANAGEMENT: BONE CANCER

Nursing care of the patient with bone cancer does not differ significantly from the general care of the patient with cancer (see Chapter 16). Monitor the tumor site for swelling, changes in circulation, and decreased movement, sensation, or joint function.

Use special care to prevent pathologic fractures and reduce the complications from them. Prevent fractures by careful handling and support of the affected extremity and logrolling the patient. Note weakness caused by anemia and decreased mobility.

Treatment for hypercalcemia may be started if bone decalcification occurs. The patient may be unwilling to exercise or take part in activities because of weakness from the disease and treatment, fear of falling and fracturing a bone, and fear of pain. Provide regular rest periods between activities.

Assess the patient for the location and severity of pain. The pain from bone cancer can be severe. It is often caused by the tumor pressing against nerves and other organs near the bone. New onset or changes in pain severity may indicate pathologic fracture. Ensure adequate pain medication is provided. Sometimes radiation therapy is used as a palliative treatment to shrink the tumor and decrease pain.

Assist the patient and caregiver in managing the diagnosis of bone cancer. Give special attention to managing pain and disability, side effects of chemotherapy, and postoperative care (e.g., after spinal cord decompression or amputation). As with all types of cancer, stress the importance of follow-up care.

MUSCULAR DYSTROPHY

Muscular dystrophy (MD) is a group of genetic diseases characterized by progressive symmetric wasting of skeletal muscles without neurologic involvement. A gradual loss of strength with increasing disability and deformity occurs with all forms of MD. Life expectancy is increasing due to advances in cardiac and respiratory care.

The types of MD differ in the groups of muscles affected, age of onset, rate of progression, and mode of genetic inheritance (Table 68.5). Duchenne MD is the most common type. Duchenne and Becker MDs are X-linked recessive disorders usually seen only in males (Box 68.1).[7]

TABLE 68.5 Select Types of MD

	Genetic Basis	Manifestations
Becker	• X-linked • Mutation of dystrophin gene	• Very similar but less severe than Duchenne MD • Onset ages 5–15 • Slower course of pelvic and shoulder muscle wasting than Duchenne • Cardiomyopathy • Respiratory failure • May survive into 50s
Duchenne	• X-linked • Mutation of dystrophin gene	• Most common form of MD • Primarily affects boys • Onset before age 5 • Progressive weakness of pelvic and shoulder muscles • Unable to walk by age 12 • Cardiomyopathy • Respiratory failure in 20s • Mental impairment
Facioscapulohumeral	• Autosomal dominant • Deletion of chromosome *4q35*	• Onset before age 20 • Slowly progressive weakness of face, shoulder muscles, and upper arms and lower legs • Can affect vision and hearing
Limb-girdle	• Autosomal recessive or autosomal dominant • Mutation in any of at least 15 genes affecting proteins needed for muscle function	• Group of disorders affecting voluntary muscles, especially those of hips and shoulders • Onset ranges from early childhood to early adulthood or later • Slow progressive weakness of hip and shoulder muscles

Other diagnostic studies include muscle serum enzymes (especially creatine kinase), electromyogram (EMG) testing, and muscle fiber biopsy. Classic findings on muscle biopsy include fat and connective tissue deposits, muscle fiber degeneration and necrosis, and a deficiency of dystrophin. An ECG may show abnormalities that suggest cardiomyopathy.

There is no cure for MD. Corticosteroids may slow disease progression for up to 2 years and improve survival.[8] Deflazacort (Emflaza) is the first corticosteroid approved to treat Duchenne MD. Eteplirsen (Exondys 51) is the first disease-modifying drug to treat patients with Duchenne MD who have a certain dystrophin gene mutation.[9]

The main treatment goals are to preserve mobility and independence through exercise, physical therapy, and use of assistive devices. Progressive muscle weakening around the trunk can cause spinal collapse. The patient may be fitted early with an orthotic jacket to give stability and prevent further deformity or injury.

Cardiomyopathy often occurs and causes heart failure.[8] Gradual decreases in pulmonary function often lead to the use of continuous positive airway pressure (CPAP). Eventually

BOX 68.1 GENETICS IN CLINICAL PRACTICE

Duchenne and Becker Muscular Dystrophy (MD)

Genetic Basis

- Caused by various mutations in the dystrophin *(DMD)* gene
- Gene provides instructions for making dystrophin, a protein that helps keep muscle fibers intact
- Dystrophin is found mainly in skeletal and cardiac muscle
- Abnormal dystrophin can cause defects in the muscle fiber and muscle fiber degeneration
- Inherited in an X-linked recessive pattern
- Females in affected families have a 50% chance of inheriting and passing the defective gene to their children

Incidence

- Between 400 and 600 boys are born with MD each year in the United States
- Together they affect 1 in 3500 to 5000 newborn males worldwide

Genetic Testing

- DNA testing can detect mutations in dystrophin gene
- Genetic testing and counseling should be considered for those with a family history of MD

Clinical Implications

- Because there are many types of MD with different genetic bases, knowing the type of MD is important to direct treatment and genetic counseling recommendations.

tracheostomy and mechanical ventilation are needed to support respiratory function.

Encourage communication between the patient and family to cope with the emotional and physical demands of MD. Teach the patient and caregiver range-of-motion (ROM) exercises, principles of good nutrition, and signs of disease progression.

Focus care on keeping the patient active as long as possible. Prolonged bed rest should be avoided because immobility can cause more muscle wasting. As the disease progresses, teach the patient to limit sedentary periods to prevent skin breakdown and respiratory complications. Ongoing medical and nursing care is needed throughout the patient's life.

The Muscular Dystrophy Association (www.mda.org) is an important resource with information about support services for the patient and caregivers. The website gives updates about the latest clinical trials and treatment advances.

LOW BACK PAIN

Low back pain is most often due to a musculoskeletal problem. It may be localized or diffuse. In *localized pain,* patients feel soreness or discomfort when a specific area of the lower back is palpated or pressed. *Diffuse pain* occurs over a larger area and comes from deep tissue.

Low back pain may be radicular or referred. *Radicular pain* is caused by irritation of a nerve root. Radicular pain is not isolated to a single location. Instead, it radiates or moves along a nerve distribution. Sciatica is an example of radicular pain. *Referred pain* is felt in the lower back, but the source of the pain is another location (e.g., kidneys, lower abdomen).

Low back pain affects about 80% of adults in the United States at least once during their lives. Backache is second to headache as the most common pain problem. It is the leading cause of job-related disability and a major contributor to missed work.[10]

Low back pain is common because the lumbar region (1) bears most of the weight of the body, (2) is the most flexible region of the spinal column, (3) has nerve roots that are at risk for injury or disease, and (4) has a naturally poor biomechanical structure. Risk factors include lack of muscle tone, obesity, trauma, poor posture, older age, smoking, pregnancy, prior compression fracture of the spine, spinal problems since birth, and a family history of back pain. Jobs that require repetitive heavy lifting, vibration (e.g., a jackhammer operator), and extended periods of sitting are associated with low back pain.

The causes of low back pain of musculoskeletal origin include (1) acute lumbosacral strain, (2) instability of the lumbosacral bony mechanism, (3) osteoarthritis (OA) of the lumbosacral vertebrae, (4) degenerative disc disease (DDD), and (5) herniation of an intervertebral disc.

ACUTE LOW BACK PAIN

Acute low back pain lasts 4 weeks or less. Most acute low back pain is caused by trauma or an activity that cause undue stress (often hyperflexion) on the lower back. Examples of trauma or activities that cause acute back pain are heavy lifting; overuse of back muscles during yard work; a sports injury; or a sudden jolt, as in a motor vehicle crash.

Often symptoms do not appear at the time of injury. They develop later (usually within 24 hours) because of a gradual increase in pressure on the nerve from an intervertebral disc and/or associated edema. Symptoms may range from muscle ache to shooting or stabbing pain, limited flexibility or ROM, or an inability to stand upright.

Few definitive diagnostic abnormalities are present with nerve irritation and muscle strain. One test is the straight-leg-raising test (see Chapter 66). MRI and CT scans are not done unless trauma or systemic disease (e.g., cancer, spinal infection) is suspected. MRI findings may be limited in the acute phase of an injury due to increased edema near the injury.

NURSING AND INTERPROFESSIONAL MANAGEMENT: ACUTE LOW BACK PAIN

Assessment

Subjective and objective data that you should obtain from the patient with low back pain are outlined in Table 68.6.

Implementation

Acute Care

If acute muscle spasms and accompanying pain are not severe and unbearable, the patient is treated as an outpatient with NSAIDs and muscle relaxants (e.g., cyclobenzaprine). Massage, back manipulation, acupuncture, and cold and hot compresses

TABLE 68.6 NURSING ASSESSMENT

Low Back Pain

Subjective Data

Important Health Information

Health history: Acute or chronic lumbosacral strain/trauma, osteoarthritis, degenerative disc disease, obesity

Medications: Opioid analgesics and NSAIDs, muscle relaxants, corticosteroids, over-the-counter remedies (e.g., topical ointments, patches)

Surgery or other treatments: Back surgery, epidural corticosteroid injections

Functional Health Patterns

Health perception–health management: Smoking, lack of exercise

Nutritional-metabolic: Obesity

Activity-exercise: Poor posture, muscle spasms, activity intolerance

Elimination: Constipation

Sleep-rest: Interrupted sleep

Cognitive-perceptual: Pain in back, buttocks, or leg associated with walking, turning, straining, coughing, leg raising. Numbness or tingling of legs, feet, toes

Role-relationship: Occupations requiring heavy lifting, vibrations, or extended driving. Change in role within family structure due to inability to work and provide income

Objective Data

General

Guarded movement

Musculoskeletal

Tense, tight paravertebral muscles on palpation, ↓ range of motion in spine

Neurologic

Depressed or absent Achilles tendon reflex or patellar tendon reflex. Positive straight-leg-raising test, positive crossover straight-leg-raising test, positive Trendelenburg test

Possible Diagnostic Findings

Localization of site of lesion or disorder on myelogram, CT scan, or MRI. Determination of nerve root impingement on EMG

may help some patients. Severe pain may need a brief course of corticosteroids or opioid analgesics.

Some people may need a brief period (1 to 2 days) of rest at home. They should avoid prolonged bed rest. Most patients do better if they continue their regular activities. Patients should refrain from activities that increase the pain, including lifting, bending, twisting, and prolonged sitting. Symptoms of acute low back pain usually improve within 2 weeks. They often resolve without treatment.

Other nursing interventions for the patient with low back pain are detailed in eNursing Care Plan 68.2 (available on the website for this chapter).

◆ Ambulatory Care

The goal of care is to make an episode of acute low back pain an isolated incident. If the lumbosacral area is unstable, repeated episodes are likely. Teach the patient about the cause of the pain and ways to prevent further episodes. Exercise is aimed at strengthening the supporting muscles. Muscle stretching may be part of the management plan. Referral to a physical therapist or personal trainer to address posture and core and abdomen strength may be appropriate. Reinforce the type and frequency of prescribed exercise and the reason for the program.

TABLE 68.7 PATIENT & CAREGIVER TEACHING

Low Back Problems

Include the following instructions when teaching the patient and caregiver how to manage low back problems:

Do

- Maintain healthy body weight.
- Maintain a neutral pelvic position if standing. Place 1 foot on a low stool if standing for long periods.
- Choose a seat with good lower back support, armrests, and a swivel base. Place a pillow at the lumbar spine to maintain normal curvature. Keep knees and hips level.
- Sleep in a side-lying position with knees and hips bent, and a pillow between the knees for support.
- Sleep on back with a lift under knees and legs or on back with 10-in-high pillow under knees to flex hips and knees.
- Use proper body mechanics when lifting heavy objects. Bend at the knees, not at the waist, and stand up slowly while holding object close to your body.
- Take part in regular strength and flexibility training and low-impact aerobic exercise.
- Use local heat and cold application to relieve muscle tension.

Do Not

- Lean forward without bending knees.
- Lift anything above level of elbows.
- Stand unmoving for prolonged time.
- Sleep on abdomen or on back or side with legs out straight.
- Exercise without consulting HCP if having severe pain.
- Exceed prescribed amount and type of exercises without consulting HCP.
- Smoke or use tobacco products.

Persistent use of poor body mechanics may result in repeated episodes of low back pain. Offer advice when the person does activities that could cause back strain. Some HCPs refer patients with back pain to a formal program called "Back School." Back School is usually taught by an HCP, nurse, or physical therapist. It is designed to teach the patient ways minimize back pain and avoid repeat episodes of pain.

Tips for prevention of back injury are listed in Table 68.7. Recommend flat shoes or shoes with low heels and shock-absorbing shoe inserts for women. Stress the importance of smoking cessation. Tobacco use impairs circulation to the intervertebral discs and contributes to low back pain.

Advise patients to maintain a healthy body weight. Excess body weight places more stress on the lower back. It weakens abdominal muscles that support the lower back. Sleeping position is important. Teach patients to avoid sleeping in a prone position. It causes excessive lumbar lordosis, placing stress on the lower back. Sleeping in a supine or side-lying position with knees and hips flexed prevents pressure on support muscles, ligaments, and lumbosacral joints. Recommend use of a firm mattress.

If the strain is work related, occupational counseling may be needed. Low back pain can cause frustration, pain, and disability. Provide emotional support and understanding care of the patient.

Health care personnel who perform direct patient care activities are at high risk for developing low back pain.[11] Lifting and moving patients, excessive bending or leaning forward, and frequent twisting can result in low back pain. This causes lost productivity and disability. Safe patient handling devices to lift, transfer, and reposition patients are recommended for nurse and patient safety. Serve as a role model by always using proper body mechanics. This includes raising the patient's bed height, bending at the knees, and asking for help in lifting and moving patients.

CHRONIC LOW BACK PAIN

Chronic low back pain lasts more than 3 months or involves a repeated incapacitating episode. It is often progressive. The cause can be hard to determine. Causes include (1) degenerative conditions, such as arthritis or disc disease; (2) osteoporosis or other metabolic bone diseases; (3) weakness from the scar tissue of prior injury; (4) chronic strain on lower back muscles from obesity, pregnancy, or stressful postures on the job; and (5) congenital spine problems.

Spinal Stenosis

Spinal stenosis is a narrowing of the spinal canal, which holds the spinal cord. Stenosis in the lumbar spine is a common cause of chronic low back pain. Spinal stenosis can be acquired or inherited. A common acquired cause is OA. Arthritic changes (bone spurs, calcification of spinal ligaments, disc degeneration) narrow the space around the spinal canal and nerve roots, eventually leading to compression. Inflammation caused by the compression results in pain, weakness, and numbness.

Other acquired conditions that may cause spinal stenosis include rheumatoid arthritis, spinal tumors, Paget disease, and traumatic damage to the vertebral column. Inherited conditions that lead to spinal stenosis include congenital spinal stenosis and scoliosis.

The pain from lumbar spinal stenosis often starts in the lower back and then radiates to the buttock and leg. It is worse with walking or prolonged standing. Numbness, tingling, weakness, and heaviness in the legs and buttocks may be present. History of decreased pain when the patient bends forward or sits is often a sign of spinal stenosis. Cold, damp weather may worsen the pain. In most cases, stenosis slowly progresses.

Interprofessional and Nursing Care

The management and treatment of chronic low back pain are similar to those for acute low back pain. Manage the patient's pain and stiffness with mild analgesics, such as NSAIDs, for daily comfort. Antidepressants (e.g., duloxetine) may help with pain and sleep problems. The antiseizure drug gabapentin may improve walking and relieve leg symptoms.

Weight reduction, rest periods, and exercise and activity throughout the day help keep the muscles and joints mobilized. Physical therapy can significantly reduce pain and improve body posture. Rest and local heat application can decrease pain. Complementary and alternative therapies, such as biofeedback, acupuncture, and yoga, may help reduce pain.

Minimally invasive treatments, such as epidural corticosteroid injections and implanted devices that deliver pain medication, are options for those who do not respond to the usual therapies. Surgery may be done in patients with severe pain who received no benefit from conservative care and/or have continued neurologic deficits.

INTERVERTEBRAL DISC DISEASE

Intervertebral discs separate the vertebrae and help absorb shock for the spine. *Intervertebral disc disease* involves the deterioration, herniation, or other problem with the intervertebral discs. Disc problems can affect the cervical, thoracic, and lumbar spine.

Etiology and Pathophysiology

Degenerative disc disease (DDD) results from loss of fluid in the intervertebral discs with aging. The discs lose their elasticity, flexibility, and shock-absorbing abilities. Unless it is accompanied by pain, DDD is a normal process. The discs become thinner as the *nucleus pulposus* (gelatinous center of the disc) starts to dry out and shrink. This change limits the disc's ability to distribute pressure between vertebrae. The pressure is then transferred to the *annulus fibrosus* (strong outside part of the disc), causing progressive destruction. When the disc is damaged, the nucleus pulposus may seep through a torn or stretched annulus. This is called a **herniated disc** *(slipped disc),* a condition in which a spinal disc bulges outward between the vertebrae (Fig. 68.4).

A herniated disc can result from degeneration with age or repeated stress and trauma to the spine. The most common sites of herniation are the lumbosacral discs, specifically L4-5 and L5-S1. Disc herniation may also occur at C5-6 and C6-7. It may be the result of spinal stenosis. There is a narrowing of the spinal canal that forces the intervertebral disc to bulge.

The spinal nerves emerge from the spinal column through an opening *(intervertebral foramen)* between adjacent vertebrae. Herniated discs can press against these nerves ("pinched nerve"), causing *radiculopathy* (radiating pain, numbness, tingling, decreased strength and/or ROM).

OA of the spine is associated with DDD and the stresses placed on the vertebrae. As the poorly lubricated joints rub against each other, the protective cartilage is damaged and painful bone spurs occur.

Clinical Manifestations

In *lumbar disc disease,* the most common manifestation is low back pain. Radicular pain that radiates down the buttock and below the knee, along the distribution of the sciatic nerve, generally indicates disc herniation. Manifestations of lumbar disc herniation are outlined in Table 68.8. A positive straight-leg-raising test may indicate nerve root irritation (see Chapter 66). Back or leg pain may be reproduced by raising the leg.

Low back pain from other causes may not be accompanied by leg pain. Reflexes may be depressed or absent, depending on the spinal nerve root involved. Numbness and tingling *(paresthesia)* or muscle weakness in the legs, feet, or toes may occur.

Multiple lumbar nerve root compressions *(cauda equina syndrome)* may occur from a herniated disc, tumor, or epidural abscess. Manifestations include severe low back pain, progressive weakness, increased pain, and bowel and bladder incontinence or retention. Saddle anesthesia (loss of or altered sensation of the perineum, buttocks, inner thighs and back of the legs [saddle area]) may be present. Symptoms of cauda equina syndrome may develop suddenly or evolve slowly over time. They may vary in intensity. Cauda equina is a medical emergency. It requires surgical decompression to reduce pressure on the nerves and prevent permanent paralysis.[12]

In *cervical disc disease,* pain radiates into the arms and hands, following the pattern of the involved nerve. Like lumbar disc disease, reflexes may or may not be present. The handgrip is often weak. Because manifestations of cervical disc disease may include shoulder pain and problems, the HCP must rule out shoulder problems as part of the diagnosis.

Diagnostic Studies

X-rays are done to detect any structural defects. A myelogram, MRI, or CT scan is helpful in localizing the damaged site. An epidural venogram or diskogram may be needed if other diagnostic studies are inconclusive. An EMG of the extremities can be done to determine the severity of nerve irritation or to rule out other conditions, such as peripheral neuropathy.

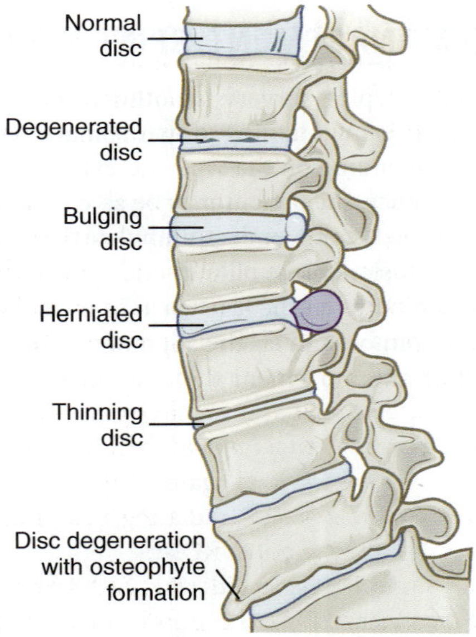

Fig. 68.4 Common causes of degenerative disc damage.

Interprofessional Care

The patient with suspected disc damage is usually managed with conservative therapy (Table 68.9). This includes limiting extremes of spinal movement (e.g., brace, corset, belt), local heat or ice, ultrasound and massage, traction, and transcutaneous electrical nerve stimulation (TENS). Drug therapy to manage pain includes NSAIDs, short-term oral corticosteroids, opioid analgesics, muscle relaxants, antiseizure drugs, and antidepressants.[13] Epidural corticosteroid injections may reduce inflammation and relieve acute pain. However, pain tends to recur if the underlying cause remains.

When symptoms subside, the patient should begin back-strengthening exercises twice a day and continue for life. Teach the patient the principles of good body mechanics. Discourage extremes of flexion and torsion. Most patients heal after 6 months with a conservative treatment plan.[13]

Surgical Therapy

If conservative treatment is unsuccessful, radiculopathy becomes worse, or loss of bowel or bladder control occurs, surgery may be considered. Surgery for a damaged disc is generally done if the patient is in constant pain and/or has a persistent neurologic deficit.

Intradiscal electrothermoplasty (IDET) is a minimally invasive outpatient procedure for treating back and sciatic pain. A needle is inserted into the affected disc with x-ray guidance. A wire is then threaded through the needle and into the disc. As the wire is heated, small nerve fibers that have invaded the degenerating disc are destroyed. The heat also partially melts the annulus fibrosus. This causes the body to make new reinforcing proteins in the fibers of the annulus.

Another outpatient technique is *radiofrequency discal nucleoplasty* (coablation nucleoplasty). Like IDET, a needle is inserted into the disc. Instead of a heated wire, a special radiofrequency probe is used. The probe generates energy that breaks the molecular bonds of the gel in the nucleus pulposus. Up to 20% of the nucleus is removed. This decompresses the disc, reducing pressure on the disc and surrounding nerve roots. Pain relief after varies.

A third minimally invasive procedure involves implanting a device made from titanium, elastomeric compounds, or other materials to decompress and/or stabilize the affected spinal

TABLE 68.8 Manifestations of Lumbar Disc Herniation

Intervertebral Level	Pain	Affected Reflex	Motor Function	Sensation
L3-4	Back to buttocks to posterior thigh to inner calf	Patellar	Quadriceps, anterior tibialis	Inner aspect of lower leg, anterior part of thigh
L4-5	Back to buttocks to dorsum of foot and big toe	None	Anterior tibialis, extensor hallucis longus, gluteus medius	Dorsum of foot and big toe
L5-S1	Back to buttocks to sole of foot and heel	Achilles	Gastrocnemius, hamstring, gluteus maximus	Heel and lateral foot

A disc herniation can involve pressure on more than 1 nerve root.

segment. *Interspinous devices* (ISDs) are implanted between the spinous processes to lift vertebrae off the pinched nerve. Newer ISDs include *interspinous dynamic stabilizers* (ISDSs) and *interspinous stabilizers* (ISSs). *ISSs* reduce the degree of extension of the vertebrae with no effect on spinal stability. *ISDSs* stabilize the spinal segment and provide some spacer properties.[14] Examples of devices include the Wallis, DIAM, X-Stop, and Coflex.

Laminotomy with discectomy (or lumbar discectomy) is the most common surgery. The HCP makes a small incision on the back over the involved disc. A small portion of the lamina is removed to expose the nerve root. Next, the herniated portion of the disc that is causing nerve root compression is removed. The goal is to relieve leg pain. It may or may not relieve back pain. A short hospital stay may be needed.[15]

Two minimally invasive procedures to decompress the nerve root are *microdiscectomy* and *endoscopic microdiscectomy.* In the first procedure, the HCP uses a microscope to see the disc and disc space in order to remove the herniated portion. *Percutaneous discectomy* uses instruments with a tiny camera with fluoroscopy guidance, then uses a laser on the damaged part of the disc.[15]

The goals of artificial disc replacement surgery are to restore movement and eliminate pain. The Charité disc is used in patients with lumbar disc damage from DDD. This disc has a high-density core between 2 cobalt-chromium end plates (Fig. 68.5). After removing the damaged disc, the device is surgically placed in the spine (usually through a small incision below the umbilicus). The disc restores movement at the level of the implant. The ProDisc-L and activL are 2 other types of artificial lumbar discs available.[16]

Options for treating DDD of the cervical spine include the Prestige cervical disc, Mobi-C disc, Secure-C, Simplify, and M6-C artificial cervical disc.

A *spinal fusion* may be needed if the spine is unstable. The spine is stabilized by creating *ankylosis* (fusion) of adjacent vertebrae with a bone graft from the patient's fibula or iliac crest *(autograft)* or from donated cadaver bone *(allograft).* Metal fixation with rods, plates, or screws may be placed to give more stability and decrease vertebral motion. Surgical procedures include posterior lumbar interbody fusion (PLIF), anterior lumbar interbody fusion (ALIF), transforaminal lumbar interbody fusion (TLIF), and extreme lateral interbody fusion (XLIF).[15]

Bone morphogenetic protein (BMP), a genetically engineered protein, may be used to stimulate bone growth of the graft in spinal fusions. A dissolvable sponge soaked with BMP is implanted into the spine. BMP on the sponge stimulates the body's cells to become active and produce bone, promoting fusion. The body absorbs the sponge, leaving living bone behind.

TABLE 68.9 Interprofessional Care

Intervertebral Disc Disease

Diagnostic Assessment
- History and physical assessment
- X-ray
- CT scan
- MRI
- Myelogram
- Diskogram
- EMG

Management

Conservative Therapy
- Restricted activity for several days, limited total bed rest
- Local ice or heat
- Physical therapy
- Analgesics (e.g., tramadol [Ultram])
- NSAIDs
- Muscle relaxants (e.g., cyclobenzaprine)
- Antiseizure drugs (e.g., gabapentin)
- Antidepressants
- Epidural corticosteroid injections

Surgical Therapy
- Intradiscal electrothermoplasty (IDET)
- Radiofrequency discal nucleoplasty
- Interspinous process decompression system (X-Stop)
- Laminectomy with or without spinal fusion
- Discectomy
- Percutaneous laser discectomy
- Artificial disc replacement (e.g., Charité disc)
- Spinal fusion with instrumentation (e.g., plates, screws) or without instrumentation

❖ NURSING MANAGEMENT: SPINE SURGERY

Nursing care after spine surgery is outlined in Table 68.10. A key nursing focus is maintaining proper spinal alignment until it has healed. Depending on the type and extent of surgery and the HCP's preference, the patient may be able to dangle the legs at the side of the bed, stand, or even ambulate the day of surgery.

After lumbar fusion, place pillows under the patient's thighs when supine and between the legs when in the side-lying position to provide comfort and ensure alignment. The patient often fears turning or any movement that may increase pain. Have

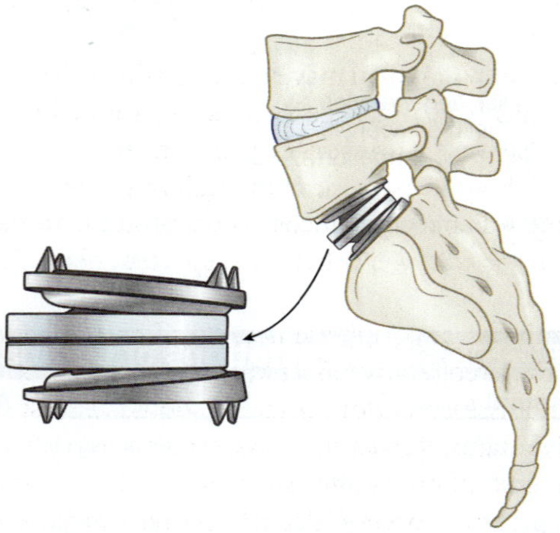

Fig. 68.5 The Charité artificial disc, used to replace a damaged intervertebral disc in degenerative disc disease of the lumbar spine. A movable high-density plastic core is placed between 2 cobalt-chromium alloy end plates. The disc's design helps realign the spine and preserve movement.

TABLE 68.10 NURSING MANAGEMENT

Care of the Patient After Spine Surgery

- Perform frequent peripheral neurologic and cardiovascular assessments.
- Monitor vital signs, intake and output.
- Maintaining proper spinal alignment:
  - Advance activity as ordered
  - Help patent with changing positions
  - Apply any immobilizers, braces, orthotics as ordered
- Assess for the presence of CSF leakage. If suspected, place the patient flat.
- Assess pain and give analgesics as ordered. Assess response.
- Administer IV fluids and antibiotics as prescribed.
- Provide wound care as ordered and assess for signs of infection.
- Assess for constipation and paralytic ileus. Give stool softeners or laxatives as ordered.
- Implement measures to promote elimination. Perform intermittent catheterization as needed.
- Implement prevention measure for VTE and CAUTI (if the patient has an indwelling catheter).
- Immediately report to the HCP:
  - Severe headache
  - Hypotension, tachycardia, fever
  - Suspected CSF leakage
  - Any new muscle weakness or paresthesia
  - Onset of bowel or bladder problems
  - Pain not responsive to analgesics
  - Signs of wound infection

Collaborate With Physical Therapist

- Assess patient's mobility and need for aid.
- Teach safe ambulation with assistive device based on patient's restrictions.
- Establish exercise plan, and teach patient to perform exercises safely.
- Coordinate PT so that patient can receive timely analgesia.

the patient logroll when changing position in bed. Have enough staff available to move the patient without undue pain or strain for the patient or staff. Reassure the patient that proper technique is being used to maintain body alignment.

After surgery, most patients need opioids, such as morphine IV, for 24 to 48 hours. Once the patient receives oral fluids, they can transition to oral drugs. Diazepam (Valium) may be prescribed for muscle relaxation.

Because the spinal canal may be entered during surgery, cerebrospinal fluid (CSF) leakage is possible. Immediately report leakage of CSF on the dressing or if the patient reports a severe headache. CSF appears as clear or slightly yellow drainage on the dressing. It has a high glucose concentration and tests positive for glucose with a dipstick. If suspected, place the patient flat.

Frequently assess peripheral neurologic condition and compare with the preoperative assessment. Movement of the arms and legs and assessment of sensation should at least equal the preoperative status. Repeat these assessments every 2 to 4 hours during the first 48 hours after surgery. Paresthesia may not be relieved right after surgery. Report any new muscle weakness or paresthesia at once. Assess extremity circulation using skin temperature, capillary refill, and pulses.

Paralytic ileus and interference with bowel function may occur for several days. Opioids can slow bowel elimination. Assess if the patient is passing gas, has bowel sounds, and has a flat, soft abdomen. Stool softeners (e.g., docusate) and laxatives may prevent and relieve constipation.

Emptying the bladder may be hard due to activity restrictions, opioids, or anesthesia. Encourage men to dangle the legs over the side of the bed or stand to urinate if allowed by the HCP. Urge patients to use a bedside commode or ambulate to the bathroom when allowed, to promote bladder emptying. Intermittent catheterization or an indwelling urinary catheter may be needed by patients with problems urinating. Loss of sphincter tone or bladder tone may indicate nerve damage. Monitor for incontinence or problems with bowel or bladder elimination. Immediately report problems to the HCP.

With cervical spine surgery, be alert for signs of spinal cord edema, such as respiratory distress and a worsening neurologic condition of the upper extremities. After surgery, the patient's neck may be immobilized in a soft or hard cervical collar.

If the patient also had a spinal fusion, a bone graft is usually involved. Healing time will be prolonged compared with a laminectomy. Activity limitations may be needed for an extended time. A rigid orthosis (thoracolumbar sacral orthosis [TLSO] or chairback brace) is often used during this period. Some HCPs want patients to learn to apply and remove the brace by logrolling in bed. Others allow their patients to apply the brace in a sitting or standing position. Verify the preferred method before starting this activity.

Regularly assess the bone graft donor site. The posterior iliac crest is the most often used donor site, although the fibula may be used. The donor site usually causes greater pain than the spinal fusion area. The donor site is bandaged with a pressure dressing to prevent excessive bleeding. If the donor site is the fibula, perform frequent neurovascular assessment of the extremity.

After spinal fusion, the patient may have some immobility of the spine at the fusion site. Teach the patient to use proper body mechanics and avoid sitting or standing for prolonged periods. Encourage activities such as walking and shifting weight from 1 foot to the other when standing. Review any lifting restrictions. Encourage the patient to think through an activity before starting a potentially injurious task, such as bending or stooping. Any twisting movement of the spine is contraindicated. Teach the patient to use the thighs and knees, rather than the back, to absorb the shock of activity and movement. A firm mattress or bed board is essential.

NECK PAIN

Neck pain can result from various cervical spine problems. It is common in both general and workers' compensation populations. Neck pain may result from benign *(cervical strains)* or more serious conditions (spondylosis, or degeneration; disc herniation; stenosis; or fractures) (Table 68.11).[17]

Cervical neck sprains and strains occur from hyperflexion and hyperextension injuries. Patients have stiffness and neck pain with possible radicular pain into the arm and hand. Pain may radiate to the head, anterior chest, thoracic spine region, and shoulders. Weakness or paresthesia of the arm and hand

TABLE 68.11 Causes of Neck Pain

- Degenerative disc disease, including herniation
- Meningitis
- Osteomyelitis
- Osteoporosis
- Poor posture
- Rheumatoid arthritis
- Spondylosis
- Strain or sprain
- Trauma (e.g., fractures, subluxation)
- Tumor

suggests cervical nerve root compression from stenosis, DDD, or herniation.

The cause of neck pain is diagnosed by history, physical assessment, x-ray, MRI, CT scan, and myelogram. An EMG of the upper extremities may show cervical radiculopathy.

Conservative treatment for acute neck pain in patients without serious pathologies includes physical therapy followed by a home exercise program, gentle traction, and cautious manipulation due to possible worsening of symptoms. TENS and acupuncture may be helpful for short-term pain relief. There is no research to support the use of ultrasound. Drug therapy includes acetaminophen and NSAIDs. Opioids should be used only for intractable pain in the short term with close supervision by HCPs.[17] Multimodal strategies are more effective. Most neck pain resolves in about 2 months without surgical intervention.

Patient teaching should emphasize self-management and the importance of an active lifestyle. Preventing neck pain that occurs with everyday activities, such as prolonged sitting at a computer or television, sleeping in nonaligned spinal positions, or making jarring movements during exercise, is important. Cognitive behavioral therapy may assist with psychosocial risk factors.

FOOT PROBLEMS

The foot is the platform that supports the weight of the body and absorbs shock when the person ambulates. It is a complicated structure composed of bony structures, muscles, tendons, and ligaments. The foot can be affected by (1) congenital conditions; (2) structural weakness; (3) traumatic and stress injuries; and (4) systemic conditions, such as diabetes and rheumatoid arthritis. Table 68.12 outlines common foot problems.

Shoes may cause crowding and angulation of the toes and inhibit normal movement of foot muscles. Ill-fitting shoes that increase foot pain affect quality of life. They may increase the odds of falls in older adults.[18] Prolonged use of improper footwear can also cause a *Morton neuroma*. The neuroma compresses an intermetatarsal plantar nerve, resulting in paresthesia and burning. At first, patients may describe feeling as if a sock is rolled up under their toes. Neuromas usually occur between the third and fourth toes.

❖ NURSING MANAGEMENT: FOOT PROBLEMS

◆ Implementation

◆ Health Promotion

Well-made and properly fitted shoes are essential for healthy, pain-free feet. Footwear should provide support, stability, protection, and shock absorption. Footwear provides a foundation for orthotics and can treat some foot problems.

Women's footwear is often influenced by current styles instead of comfort and support. Stress the importance of having a shoe that conforms to the foot rather than to fashion trends. The shoe must be long enough and wide enough to avoid crowding the toes and forcing the great toe into a position of **hallux valgus** (Fig. 68.6). At the metatarsal head, the shoe should be wide enough to allow foot muscles to move freely and toes to bend. The shank (narrow part of sole under the instep) of the shoe should be rigid enough to give good support. The height of the heel should be realistic in relation to the shoe's purpose. Ideally, the heel of the shoe should not rise more than 1 inch higher than the forefoot support. Wearing higher heeled shoes with a narrow toe box will cause hammertoes and corns over time.

◆ Acute Care

Many foot problems require referral to a podiatrist. Depending on the problem, conservative therapies are tried first (Table 68.12). These include NSAIDs, ice, physical therapy, footwear changes, stretching, warm soaks, orthotics, ultrasound, and corticosteroid injections. If these methods do not help, surgery may be needed.

CHECK YOUR PRACTICE

A 53-year-old woman is scheduled for surgical correction of a bunion after a diagnosis of hallux valgus. You are doing her preoperative assessment. She says, "I love shoes and have a whole closet full of fancy ones. Now I have to wear this big ugly shoe. I hope I can wear my nice shoes after surgery."

- How will you respond to the patient?
- What are the priority learning needs related to her self-care after surgery?

Depending on the type of surgery, pins or wires may extend through the toes, or a protective splint may be placed over the end of the foot. The foot is usually immobilized by a bulky dressing (Fig. 68.7), short leg cast, slipper (plaster) cast, or a platform shoe that fits over the dressing and has a rigid sole (also known as a *bunion shoe*).

Elevate the foot with the heel off the bed to reduce discomfort and prevent edema. Assess neurovascular condition frequently during the immediate postoperative period. Inserted devices may interfere with assessment for movement. Be aware that evaluating sensation may be hard because the patient may be unable to distinguish surgical pain from pain caused by nerve pressure or circulatory impairment.

The type and extent of surgery determine the orders for ambulation. Crutches, a walker, or a cane may be needed. The patient may have pain or a throbbing sensation when lowering

TABLE 68.12 **Common Foot Problems**

Problem	Description	Treatment
Forefoot		
Hallux rigidus	Painful stiffness of first MTP joint caused by osteoarthritis or local trauma.	• Intraarticular corticosteroids, passive manual stretching of first MTP joint. • Shoe with a stiff sole decreases pain in the joint during walking. • Surgical treatment is joint fusion or arthroplasty with silicone rubber implant.
Hallux valgus (bunion)	Painful deformity of great toe with lateral angulation of great toe toward second toe, bony enlargement of medial side of first metatarsal head, swelling of bursa and formation of callus over bony enlargement (Fig. 68.6).	• Wearing shoes with wide forefoot or "bunion pocket" and use of bunion pads to relieve pressure on bursal sac. • Surgical treatment involves removal of bursal sac and bony enlargement and correction of lateral angulation of great toe. • May include temporary or permanent internal fixation.
Hammer and claw toes	Hammer toe is a deformity of PIP joint on 2nd to 5th toes causing toe to be permanently bent, resembling a hammer. Mallet toe is a similar condition affecting DIP joint. Claw toe is a similar deformity with dorsiflexion of proximal phalanx on MTP joint combined with flexion of both PIP and DIP joints. Symptoms include burning on bottom of foot and pain and difficulty walking when wearing shoes.	• Passive manual stretching of PIP joint, use of metatarsal arch support. • Surgical correction consists of resection of base of middle phalanx and head of proximal phalanx, bringing raw bone ends together. • Kirschner wire maintains straight position.
Morton neuroma (Morton toe or plantar neuroma)	Neuroma in web space between third and fourth metatarsal heads, causing sharp, sudden attacks of pain and burning sensations.	• Surgical excision.
Midfoot		
Pes cavus	Elevation of longitudinal arch of foot resulting from contracture of plantar fascia or bony deformity of arch.	• Surgical correction needed if condition interferes with ambulation.
Pes planus (flatfoot)	Loss of metatarsal arch causing pain in foot or leg.	• Use of resilient longitudinal arch supports. • Surgical treatment consists of triple arthrodesis or fusion of subtalar joint.
Hindfoot		
Calcaneus stress fracture	Heel pain after moderate walking. Common causes are overtraining, running on hard surfaces, osteoporosis.	• Rest, ice, shoe heel pad, NSAIDs. • See HCP to assess for osteoporosis.
Heel pain	Heel pain with weight bearing. Common causes are plantar bursitis, plantar fasciitis, bone spur.	• Corticosteroids injected locally into inflamed bursa. • Sponge-rubber heel cup. • Surgical excision of bursa or spur. • Stretching exercises, ice, shoe heel cup, shock-wave therapy, NSAIDs, corticosteroids for plantar fasciitis.
Other Problems		
Callus	Localized thickening of skin. Covers wide area and usually found on weight-bearing part of foot.	• Softened with warm water or preparations containing salicylic acid and trimmed with razor blade or scalpel. • Pressure on bony prominences caused by shoes is relieved.
Corn	Localized thickening of skin caused by continual pressure over bony prominences, especially metatarsal head, often causing localized pain.	• Same as with callus.
Plantar wart	Painful papillomatous growth caused by virus that may occur on any part of skin on sole of foot. Warts tend to cluster on pressure points.	• Remedies containing salicylic acid (e.g., Compound W), excision with electrocoagulation, or surgical removal. • Laser treatments. • May disappear without treatment.
Soft corn	Painful lesion caused by bony prominence of a toe pressing against adjacent toe. Usual location is web space between toes. Softness caused by secretions keeping web space relatively moist.	• Pain relieved by placing cotton or spacers between toes to separate them. • Surgical treatment is excision of projecting bone spur (if present).

DIP, Distal interphalangeal; *MTP,* metatarsophalangeal; *PIP,* proximal interphalangeal.

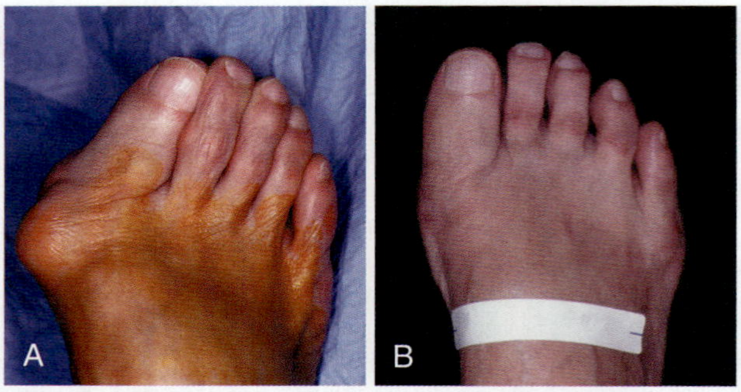

Fig. 68.6 (A) Severe hallux valgus with bursa formation. (B) Postoperative correction. (From Canale ST, Beaty JH: *Campbell's operative orthopaedics,* ed 12, Philadelphia, 2013, Mosby.)

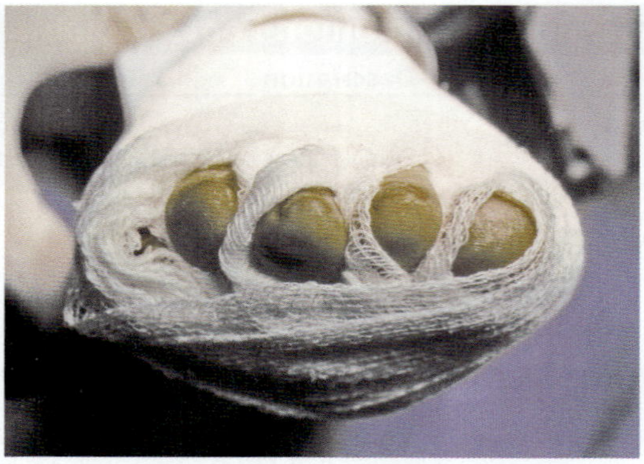

Fig. 68.7 Postoperative supportive dressing for treatment of moderate forefoot deformity. Dressing must be conforming and binding enough to hold toe in exact position. (From Canale ST, Beaty JH: *Campbell's operative orthopaedics,* ed 12, Philadelphia, 2013, Mosby.)

the affected leg. Reinforce instructions from the physical therapist. Teach the patient the importance of walking with an erect posture with proper weight distribution. Report gait problems or continued pain to the HCP. Encourage frequent rest periods with the foot elevated.

◆ Ambulatory Care

Teach the patient to perform daily hygienic foot care and wear clean stockings. Stockings should be long enough to avoid wrinkling and causing pressure areas. Trimming toenails straight across helps prevent ingrown toenails and reduces the risk for infection. Provide instruction to patients with impaired circulation or diabetes to prevent serious complications from blisters, pressure areas, and infection.

Gerontologic Considerations: Foot Problems

The older adult is prone to foot problems because of poor circulation, atherosclerosis, and decreased sensation in the lower extremities. This is especially true for those with diabetes. A patient may develop an open wound but not feel it because of altered sensation from peripheral vascular disease or diabetic neuropathy. Teach older adults to inspect their feet daily and report any open wounds or breaks in the skin to their HCP.

Untreated wounds may become infected, lead to osteomyelitis, and need surgical debridement. If the infection becomes widespread, lower limb amputation may be needed. Teach the caregiver of the older adult who needs help with hygiene practices to assess the feet at regular intervals.

METABOLIC BONE DISEASES

Normal bone metabolism is affected by hormones, nutrition, and genetics. When dysfunction occurs in any of these factors, generalized reduction in bone mass and strength may result. Metabolic bone diseases include osteomalacia, osteoporosis, and Paget disease.

OSTEOMALACIA

Osteomalacia is caused by a vitamin D deficiency that causes bone to lose calcium and become soft. The disease is uncommon in the United States. It is the same as rickets in children, except the epiphyseal growth plates are closed in adults. Vitamin D is required for the absorption of calcium from the intestine. Insufficient vitamin D intake can interfere with normal bone mineralization. With little or no calcification, bones become soft.

Causes include limited sun exposure (ultraviolet rays needed for vitamin D synthesis), GI malabsorption (post weight loss surgery, celiac disease), chronic diarrhea, and pregnancy. Residents of long-term care settings may have inadequate sun exposure and thus poor synthesis of vitamin D. Chronic liver, kidney, and small intestine disease may contribute to vitamin D deficiency. Long-term use of antiseizure drugs (e.g., phenytoin) and phosphate-binding antacids (e.g., Maalox) may decrease calcium and vitamin D absorption.[19]

Common manifestations are bone pain and muscle weakness. The pain is often worse at night and affects the lower back, pelvis, hips, legs, and ribs.[19] Muscle weakness and progressive deformity of weight-bearing bones (e.g., spine, extremities) can lead to problems walking and a waddling gait. Fractures are common and indicate delayed bone healing.

Laboratory findings include decreased serum calcium or phosphorus, decreased serum 25-hydroxyvitamin D, and increased serum alkaline phosphatase. X-rays may show effects of generalized bone demineralization, especially loss of calcium in the bones of the pelvis and associated bone deformity. *Looser transformation zones* (ribbons of decalcification in bone found on x-ray) are diagnostic of osteomalacia. However, significant osteomalacia may exist without x-ray changes.

Treatment is directed toward correcting the vitamin D deficiency. The patient often has a dramatic response when vitamin D_3 (cholecalciferol) and vitamin D_2 (ergocalciferol) supplements are used. Calcium or phosphorus supplements may be prescribed. Encourage a diet rich in eggs, meat, and oily fish (e.g., salmon, tuna). Milk and breakfast cereals fortified with calcium and vitamin D should be part of the diet. Exposure to sunlight and weight-bearing exercise are valuable as well. Assess patients who had weight loss surgery to treat obesity for osteomalacia. Any vitamin D deficiencies should be corrected.[19]

OSTEOPOROSIS

Osteoporosis is a chronic, progressive metabolic bone disease marked by low bone mass and deterioration of bone tissue,

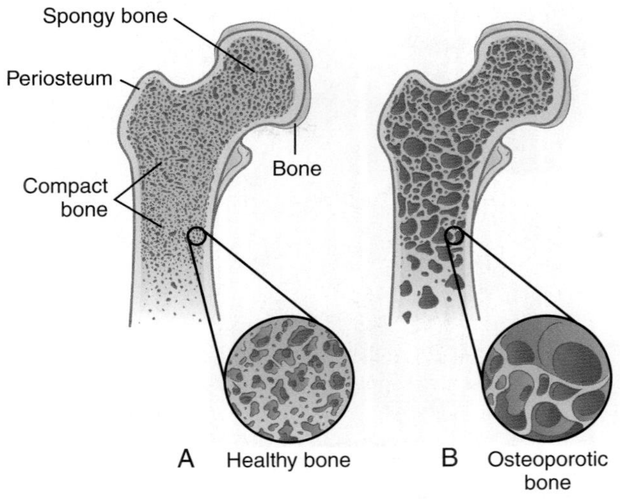

Fig. 68.8 (A) Normal bone. (B) Osteoporotic bone.

BOX 68.2 BIOLOGIC SEX CONSIDERATIONS

Osteoporosis

Men

- Men are underdiagnosed and undertreated for osteoporosis.
- 1 in men older than age 50 will have an osteoporosis-related fracture in his lifetime.

Women

- Osteoporosis is 8 times more common in women than in men.
- 1 in 2 women older than age 50 years will have an osteoporosis-related fracture in her lifetime.

leading to increased bone fragility (Fig. 68.8). More than 54 million persons in the United States have osteoporosis.[20] It is known as the "silent thief" because it slowly robs the skeleton of its banked resources. Bones eventually become so fragile that they cannot withstand normal mechanical stress.

Osteoporosis is more common in women (Box 68.2). There are several reasons why. Women tend to have lower calcium intake than men. Women have less bone mass because of their generally smaller frames. Bone resorption begins at an earlier age in women and becomes more rapid at menopause. Pregnancy and breastfeeding deplete a woman's skeletal reserve unless calcium intake is adequate. Women's longevity increases the risk for osteoporosis.

Current guidelines recommend an initial bone density test in all women older than age 65 years. If results are normal and the person is at low risk for osteoporosis, another test is not needed for 15 years. Women who are younger than 65 and at high risk (e.g., low body weight, smoker, prior fractures) should have a bone density test earlier. Testing should also start earlier and be done more often if a person is at high risk for fractures. Currently there is not enough evidence that shows any benefit for screening men.[21]

Etiology and Pathophysiology

Risk factors for osteoporosis are listed in Table 68.13. Regular weight-bearing exercise and adequate intake of fluoride, calcium, and vitamin D decrease risk. Low testosterone is a major risk factor in men.

TABLE 68.13 Risk Factors for Osteoporosis
• Advancing age (>65 years)
• Asian or White ethnicity
• Diet low in calcium or vitamin D deficiency
• Estrogen deficiency in women (surgical or age-related menopause)
• Excess use of alcohol (>2 drinks/day)
• Family history of osteoporosis
• Female gender
• Low body weight
• Low testosterone in men
• Medications: corticosteroids, thyroid replacement, heparin, long-acting sedatives, antiseizure drugs
• Sedentary lifestyle
• Smoking

Diseases associated with osteoporosis include inflammatory bowel disease, intestinal malabsorption, kidney disease, rheumatoid arthritis, hyperthyroidism, alcohol use disorder, cirrhosis, hypogonadism, and diabetes. Many drugs can interfere with bone metabolism. These include corticosteroids, antiseizure drugs (e.g., divalproex sodium, phenytoin), aluminum-containing antacids, heparin, some chemotherapy drugs, and excess thyroid hormones. When one of these drugs is prescribed, teach the patient about this possible side effect. Long-term corticosteroid use is a major contributor to osteoporosis.

Peak bone mass (maximum bone tissue) is typically achieved before age 20. It is largely determined by 4 factors: heredity, nutrition, exercise, and hormone function. Heredity may be responsible for up to 70% of a person's peak bone mass. Genetic factors also influence bone size, quality, and turnover. Bone loss from midlife (ages 35 to 40 years) onward is inevitable, but the rate of loss varies. At menopause, women have rapid bone loss when the decline in estrogen production is the greatest. The rate of loss then slows and eventually matches the rate of bone lost by men ages 65 to 70 years.

Bone is continuously being deposited by osteoblasts and resorbed by osteoclasts, a process called *remodeling.* Rates of bone deposition and resorption are normally equal, so total bone mass stays constant. In osteoporosis, bone resorption exceeds bone deposition.

Clinical Manifestations

Osteoporosis occurs most often in bones of the spine, hips, and wrists. Early manifestations include back pain and spontaneous fractures. The loss of bone mass causes the bone to become mechanically weaker and prone to spontaneous fractures or fractures from minimal trauma. A person who has a vertebral fracture due to osteoporosis has an increased risk for having a second vertebral fracture within 1 year. Over time, vertebral fractures and wedging cause gradual loss of height and a humped thoracic spine (*kyphosis,* or "dowager's hump") (Fig. 68.9).

Diagnostic Studies

Osteoporosis often goes unnoticed because it cannot be detected by conventional x-ray until 25% to 40% of calcium in the bone is

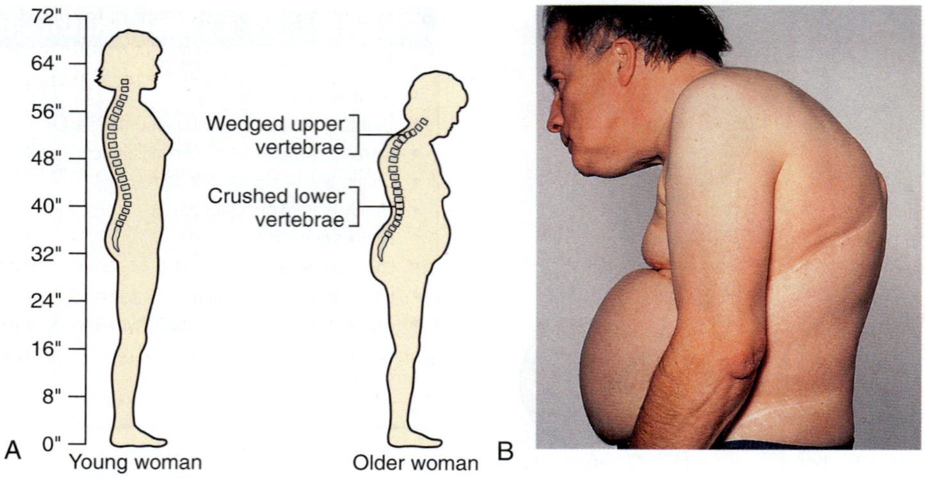

Fig. 68.9 The effects of osteoporosis. (A) Comparison of young woman with an older woman. (B) Severe fixed kyphosis producing a question-mark appearance. (A, From Phillips N: *Berry & Kohn's operating room technique*, ed 12, St Louis, 2013, Mosby. B, Courtesy Mir MA. In Kanski JJ: *Clinical diagnosis in ophthalmology*, St Louis, 2006, Mosby.)

TABLE 68.14 Diagnostic Criteria

Osteoporosis

T-Score	Classification
+1 and −1	Normal
−1 and −2.5	Osteopenia (bone loss that is more than normal but not yet at the level for a diagnosis of osteoporosis)
−2.5 or lower	Osteoporosis
−2.5 or lower with a fracture	Severe osteoporosis

lost. Serum calcium, phosphorus, and alkaline phosphatase levels usually are normal. Alkaline phosphatase may be increased after a fracture.

Bone mineral density (BMD) measurements are typically expressed as grams of mineral per unit volume. BMD is determined by peak bone mass and amount of bone loss (see Table 66.8). BMD may be measured by quantitative ultrasound (QUS) and dual-energy x-ray absorptiometry (DEXA). QUS uses sound waves to measure bone density in the heel, kneecap, or shin. DEXA measures bone density in the spine and hips. These are the most common sites of fragility fractures from osteoporosis. Most treatment guidelines use DEXA to guide the decision on when to start drug therapy to prevent osteoporotic fractures. DEXA studies evaluate changes in bone density over time and assess treatment effectiveness.

BMD test results are compared with the ideal or peak BMD of a healthy 30-year-old adult and reported as T-scores.[22] A T-score of 0 means the BMD is equal to the norm for a healthy young adult (Table 68.14). Differences between the BMD and that of the healthy young adult norm are measured in units called *standard deviations (SDs)*. The greater the negative number, the lower the BMD and the higher the risk for fracture.

Sometimes the HCP uses a Z-score instead of a T-score. In this case a person is compared with someone their own age, gender, and/or ethnic group instead of a healthy 30-year-old person. Among older adults, Z-scores can be misleading

TABLE 68.15 Interprofessional Care

Osteoporosis

Diagnostic Assessment
- History and physical assessment
- Serum calcium, phosphorus, alkaline phosphatase, vitamin D
- Bone mineral densitometry
- Dual energy x-ray absorptiometry (DEXA)

Management
- Adequate diet- calcium (Table 68.16)
- Calcium supplements
- Sun exposure or vitamin D supplements
- Exercise program
- Drug therapy (Table 68.17)
  - Bisphosphonates (recommended)
  - Monoclonal antibodies
  - Recombinant parathyroid hormone
- Minimally invasive procedures
  - Vertebroplasty
  - Kyphoplasty

because decreased bone density is common. If the Z-score is −2 or lower, it may suggest that something other than aging is causing abnormal bone loss.

❖ INTERPROFESSIONAL AND NURSING MANAGEMENT: OSTEOPOROSIS

Management focuses on proper nutrition, calcium and vitamin D supplementation, exercise, prevention of falls and fractures, and drugs (Table 68.15). The National Osteoporosis Foundation recommends treatment for osteoporosis for postmenopausal women with (1) a T-score of less than −2.5, (2) a T-score between −1 and −2.5 with other risk factors (Table 68.13), or (3) prior history of a hip or vertebral fracture.

We can also calculate a patient's risk for fracture from osteoporosis with the Fracture Risk Assessment (FRAX) tool. The

TABLE 68.16 NUTRITION THERAPY

Sources of Calcium

Food	Calcium (mg)
1 cup milk	
• Whole	279
• Skim	299
1 oz cheese	
• Mozzarella	222
• Cheddar	214
• Cottage	138
1/2 cup almonds	152
1 cup ice cream	168
6 oz calcium-fortified orange juice	261
3 oz seafood	
• Salmon	181
• Sardines	325
8 oz yogurt	313–384
Soft serve frozen yogurt	206

FRAX considers BMD and other clinical factors when assessing fracture risk.[23]

The recommended calcium intake is 1000 mg/day for women ages 19 to 50 years and men ages 19 to 70 years and 1200 mg/day in women age 51 years or older and men 71 years or older. Foods high in calcium include milk, yogurt, turnip greens, cottage cheese, ice cream, sardines, and spinach (Table 68.16). If diet intake of calcium is inadequate, calcium supplements calcium may be given.

It is hard to absorb calcium in single doses greater than 500 mg. Teach the patient to take calcium supplements as divided doses to increase absorption. The amount of elemental calcium varies in calcium preparations. Calcium carbonate has 40% elemental calcium. It should be taken with meals because stomach acid is needed to dissolve and absorb this supplement. Calcium citrate has around 20% elemental calcium but is less dependent on stomach acid for absorption. It is better absorbed by patients taking a proton pump inhibitor (e.g., esomeprazole) or histamine receptor blocker (e.g., cimetidine) for acid reflux. Calcium lactate and calcium gluconate are not recommended because they have small amounts of elemental calcium.

Vitamin D is important in calcium absorption and function and may have a role in bone formation. Most people get enough vitamin D from their diet or naturally through synthesis in the skin from exposure to sunlight. Being in the sun for 20 minutes a day is generally enough. However, supplemental vitamin D (800 IU) is recommended for postmenopausal women, older men, persons who are homebound or in long-term care settings, and those in northern climates, due to decreased sun exposure.

Regular physical activity is important to build and maintain bone mass. Exercise increases muscle strength, coordination, and balance. The best exercises are weight-bearing exercises that force a person to work against gravity. These include walking, hiking, weight training, stair climbing, tennis, and dancing. Walking is preferred to high-impact aerobics or running. Both may put too much stress on the bones and cause stress fractures. Encourage patients to walk 30 minutes 3 times a week. Teach patients to quit smoking and decrease alcohol use to lessen negative effects on bone mass.

Encourage patients to remain ambulatory to prevent further loss of bone density due to immobility. Treatment may involve the use of a gait aid to walk safely and protect areas of potential pathologic fractures. For example, a TLSO may be used to maintain the spine in proper alignment after fracture or treatment of a vertebral fracture.

Vertebroplasty and *kyphoplasty* are minimally invasive procedures used to treat osteoporotic vertebral fractures (see Chapter 62). In vertebroplasty, bone cement is injected into the collapsed vertebra to stabilize the spine and improve the patient's pain. This procedure does not restore vertebral height or correct deformity. In kyphoplasty, a small balloon is inserted into the collapsed vertebra and inflated to restore vertebral body height before injection of bone cement. Kyphoplasty is the preferred surgical treatment for vertebral compression fractures.

◆ Drug Therapy

The recommended drug therapies for preventing and treating osteoporosis are the bisphosphonates alendronate, risedronate, zoledronic acid, or denosumab. Bisphosphonates inhibit osteoclast-mediated bone resorption and slow the cycle of bone remodeling. Although a modest increase in BMD is common, bone remodeling may be suppressed to the extent that normal bone formation is impaired and fracture risk increases. Treatment should continue for 5 years (Table 68.17).[24] A rare but serious side effect of bisphosphonates is *osteonecrosis* (bone death) of the jaw. Its cause is unknown. Those with dental disease, cancer, Paget disease, or renal disease are most at risk for this complication.

DRUG ALERT

Bisphosphonates

Teach patient to:

- Take with full glass of water.
- Take 30 min before food or other drugs.
- Stay upright for at least 30 min after taking.

Women no longer routinely use estrogen replacement therapy or estrogen with progesterone after menopause to prevent osteoporosis because of the increased risk for heart disease and breast and uterine cancer. A woman who takes short-term estrogen therapy to treat menopausal symptoms, such as hot flashes, may receive some protection against bone loss and hip and vertebrae fractures.[25] Estrogen may inhibit osteoclast activity, leading to decreased bone resorption.

Patients receiving corticosteroids should receive the lowest effective dose for the shortest possible time. Ensure an adequate intake of calcium and vitamin D, including supplements, when osteoporosis drugs are prescribed. If osteopenia is present in people who are taking corticosteroids, we may start a bisphosphonate.

PAGET DISEASE

Paget disease *(osteitis deformans)* is a chronic skeletal bone disorder in which excessive bone resorption is followed by replacement of normal marrow by vascular, fibrous connective tissue. The new bone is larger, disorganized, and weaker. Areas often affected include the pelvis, long bones, spine, ribs, sternum, and skull. Up to 5% of adults in the United States have

TABLE 68.17 Drug Therapy

Osteoporosis

Drug	Action	Side Effects	Considerations
Bisphosphonates			
alendronate (Fosamax, Binosto) etidronate (Didronel) ibandronate (Boniva) pamidronate (Aredia) risedronate (Actonel) zoledronic acid (Reclast, Zometa)	Inhibit osteoclast-mediated bone resorption and slows cycle of bone remodeling. Increases bone density.	Bone, joint, muscle pain Esophageal irritation Gastritis Osteonecrosis	When taking orally: Take with full glass of water. Take 30 min before food or other drugs. Stay upright for at least 30 min after. Zoledronic acid is once-yearly or every-other-year IV infusion. Monitor kidney function tests and serum calcium. Patients should see a dentist before beginning treatment and then annually.
Monoclonal antibodies			
denosumab (Prolia, Xgeva)	Binds to a protein (RANKL) involved in osteoclast function.	Back and extremity pain Dizziness Hypocalcemia Rash	Subcutaneous injection every 6 months. Give with calcium and vitamin D supplements. Monitor electrolytes.
romosozumab (Evenity)	Inhibits action of sclerostin, a regulatory factor in bone metabolism. Increases bone formation and, to a lesser extent, decreases bone resorption.	Femoral fractures Headache Hypocalcemia Muscle pain Osteonecrosis of jaw	Subcutaneous injection every month for a total of 12 doses. Give with calcium and vitamin D supplements. Monitor electrolytes.
Recombinant parathyroid hormone			
abaloparatide (Tymlos) teriparatide (Forteo)	Increases action of osteoblasts and stimulates new bone formation.	Dizziness GI distress Hypercalcemia Muscle cramps ↑ Uric acid levels	Self-administered daily by subcutaneous injection from preloaded pen. Monitor electrolytes and parathyroid hormone levels. Use for up to 2 years.
Selective Estrogen Receptor Modulator (SERM)			
raloxifene (Evista)	Mimics the effect of estrogen on bone by reducing bone resorption.	Flu-like symptoms Leg cramps VTE, including stroke, pulmonary embolism Weight gain	Reduces risk for vertebral, but not hip, fractures. Discontinue if immobilized; resume only after fully ambulatory. Avoid smoking. Teach symptoms to report to HCP.

Paget disease.[26] Men are affected twice as often. Paget disease is uncommon in people younger than age 40.

We do not know what causes Paget disease. The cause may be viral or genetic. Up to 40% of all patients with the disease have at least 1 relative with the disorder.

In milder forms of Paget disease, patients do not have any symptoms. The disease may be found incidentally through x-ray or serum chemistry findings of high alkaline phosphatase. Bone pain may develop gradually and progress to severe intractable pain. Other early manifestations include fatigue and progressive development of a waddling gait. Patients report becoming shorter or their heads are becoming larger. Headaches, dementia, vision problems, and hearing loss can result from an enlarged, thickened skull. Increased bone volume in the spine can cause spinal cord or nerve root compression.

Pathologic fracture is the most common complication and may be the first sign of Paget disease. Other complications include osteosarcoma, fibrosarcoma, and osteoclastoma (giant cell) tumors.

Serum alkaline phosphatase is very high in advanced disease, showing high bone turnover. X-rays may show curvature of an affected bone. The bone cortex becomes thicker and irregular, especially in weight-bearing bones and the cranium. Bone scans using a radiolabeled bisphosphonate show increased uptake in the affected skeletal areas.

Treatment is usually limited to symptomatic and supportive care, with correction of secondary deformities by surgical intervention or braces. Bisphosphonate drugs (Table 68.17) are used to slow bone resorption. Zoledronic acid is the therapy of choice. It is given specifically to build bone. Calcium and vitamin D can decrease hypocalcemia, a common side effect of drug therapy. Monitor drug effectiveness by regular assessment of alkaline phosphatase.

Calcitonin is an option for patients who cannot tolerate bisphosphonates. Its use is limited in duration as the body's response to this drug quickly decreases. Human calcitonin inhibits osteoclastic activity, prevents bone resorption, relieves acute symptoms, and lowers serum alkaline phosphatase.

Pain is usually managed with NSAIDs. Orthopedic surgery for fractures, hip and knee replacement, and knee realignment may be needed.

A firm mattress can provide back support and relieve pain. The patient may need to wear a corset or light brace to relieve back pain and give support when upright. Teach the patient to correctly apply the device and examine the skin for friction damage. Discourage lifting and twisting. Good body mechanics are essential. Physical therapy may increase muscle strength. A well-balanced diet is important. Vitamin D, calcium, and protein ensure components are available for bone formation. To decrease risk for falls and related fractures, teach the patient to use an assistive device and make environmental changes (e.g., do not use throw rugs).

! SAFETY ALERT

Paget Disease

To reduce the risk for patient harm from falls:

- Assess environment for fall risk factors (e.g., poor lighting, clutter, pets).
- Identify personal risk factors for falls, including drugs and uncorrected vision.
- Take action to address identified risks.

Gerontologic Considerations: Metabolic Bone Diseases

Osteoporosis and Paget disease are common in older adults. Teach patients proper nutrition to decrease risk for further bone loss. Keep the patient as active as possible to slow demineralization of bone from disuse or extended immobilization.

Metabolic bone diseases increase the risk for pathologic fractures. Use caution when turning or moving the patient. Hip fractures, in particular, may decrease quality of life and lead to admission to a long-term care facility. A supervised exercise program is essential to osteoporosis treatment. Encourage ambulation if the patient's condition permits.

Case Study

Osteoporosis/Hip Fracture

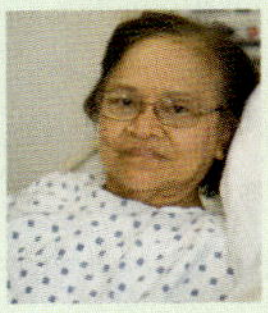

(© azndc/iStock. com.)

Patient Profile

M.K. is a thin 70-year-old Asian woman admitted to the emergency department after falling in her driveway. X-ray shows a left femoral neck fracture. She has a history of hypertension and COPD.

Subjective Data

- Denies hitting her head or loss of consciousness
- Reports significant left hip pain, 9 on the 0–10 pain scale
- States she has never had a bone density test
- Former 2 pack a day smoker who quit 4 years ago
- Takes atenolol every morning and fluticasone propionate/salmeterol (Advair Diskus) inhaler twice a day

Objective Data

- Left lower extremity slightly shorter and externally rotated compared with right lower extremity
- Unable to bear weight on lower extremities
- Moderate edema with bruising on left hip
- 2+ dorsalis pedis and posterior tibialis pulses bilaterally
- Gross motor/sensation intact in affected extremity

Diagnostic Studies

- Normal CBC, metabolic panel, protime/INR and urinalysis
- Chest x-ray shows hyperinflated lung fields
- 12-lead ECG normal sinus rhythm

Interprofessional Care

- Hip arthroplasty for fracture
- Multimodal postoperative pain management
- Physical therapy evaluation and treatment
- Early postoperative mobilization
- Removal of urinary catheter (if applicable) early in postoperative period
- Ambulation using standard walker

Discussion Questions

1. ***Recognize***: Why did a relatively low-energy injury cause M.K.'s fracture?
2. ***Analyze:*** What factors could result in inadequate caloric intake after surgery?
3. ***Plan:*** What postoperative complications are M.K. at risk for developing?
4. ***Prioritize:*** What are M.K.'s priority learning needs?
5. ***Prioritize:*** What is the interprofessional team's top priority at this time for M.K.? What therapy do you expect?
6. ***Prioritize:*** Based on the assessment data, what are the priority clinical problems?
7. ***Act:*** Describe specific actions you would take to promote patient safety.
8. ***Evaluation:*** What outcomes would indicate that care was effective?

Answers available at http://evolve.elsevier.com/Lewis/medsurg.

BRIDGE TO NCLEX EXAMINATION

The number of the question corresponds to the same-numbered outcome at the beginning of the chapter.

1. A patient with acute osteomyelitis is being discharged on antibiotic therapy. What would the nurse include in the teaching plan? *(select all that apply)*
   a. It is important to finish all the antibiotics even if you feel better.
   b. You will need to schedule periodic through bone scans and ESR testing.
   c. If the infection comes back, you must contact the HCP to schedule surgery.
   d. Signs such as fever and night sweats may be present but are usually not severe.
   e. Contact the HCP if signs of infection such as pain and swelling at the site occur.
2. A patient with history of colon cancer is diagnosed with rib fractures, and the HCP orders a bone scan. The nurse determines the patient understands teaching about the purpose of the procedure when they state
   a. "The bone scan will cure my rib fractures."
   b. "The bone scan will see if my colon cancer may have spread."
   c. "My colon cancer was cured so I really don't think this is necessary."
   d. "The results of the bone scan will only just confirm that I have a rib fracture."
3. The nurse provides counseling to a family of a patient with Duchenne muscular dystrophy with the knowledge that
   a. patients are usually female.
   b. all daughters of a carrier will be carriers.

c. genetic testing can help determine treatment.
d. only males can pass the gene to their offspring.

4. Which persons are at high risk for chronic low back pain? *(select all that apply)*
   a. A 63-year-old man who is a long-distance truck driver
   b. A 30-year-old nurse who works on an orthopedic unit and smokes
   c. A 55-year-old construction worker who is 6 ft, 2 in and weighs 250 lb
   d. A 44-year-old female chef with prior compression fracture of the spine
   e. A 28-year-old female yoga instructor who is 5 ft, 6 in and weighs 130 lb
5. When caring for a patient after lumbar spinal surgery, the nurse would immediately report which finding to the HCP?
   a. The patient reports mild low back pain.
   b. The patient has a single episode of emesis.
   c. The patient is nauseated and has not voided in 4 hours.
   d. The patient has loss of sensation to the perineum, buttocks, inner thighs, and back of the legs.
6. A patient who ran his first marathon had heel pain that would not resolve and was diagnosed with calcaneus stress fracture. The nurse will teach the patient to *(select all that apply)*
   a. resume running in 1 week.
   b. rest and refrain from running.
   c. wear a shoe heel pad when ambulating.
   d. walk barefoot to decrease pressure on the heel.
   e. apply ice to the heel and take NSAIDs as directed by HCP.
7. A patient with osteoporosis shows an understanding of appropriate self-care when they state
   a. "I should remove trip hazards such as throw rugs in my house to make it safer."
   b. "I am not using the cane my HCP recommended. I don't want to look that old!"
   c. "I can continue to go downhill skiing as long as I'm careful and don't ever fall."
   d. "I need to take up running to help strengthen my bones. Walking is just not enough."

1. a, b, d, e; 2. b; 3. d; 4. a, b, c, d; 5. d; 6. b, c, e; 7. a.

For rationales to these answers and even more NCLEX review questions, visit http://evolve.elsevier.com/Lewis/medsurg.

EVOLVE WEBSITE/RESOURCES LIST

http://evolve.elsevier.com/Lewis/medsurg
Review Questions (Online Only)
Key Points
Answer Keys for Questions
- Rationales for Bridge to NCLEX Examination Questions
- Answer Guidelines for Case Study

Student Case Study
- Patient With Osteoporosis

Nursing Care Plans
- eNursing Care Plan 68.1: Patient With Osteomyelitis
- eNursing Care Plan 68.2: Patient With Low Back Pain

Conceptual Care Map Creator
Audio Glossary
Content Updates

REFERENCES

1. Hofstee MI, Muthukrishnan G, Atkins GJ, et al.: Current concepts of osteomyelitis: from pathologic mechanisms to advanced research methods, *Am J Pathol* 190:1151, 2020.
2. Schmitt S: Osteomyelitis. Retrieved from https://www.merckmanuals.com/professional/musculoskeletal-and-connective-tissue-disorders/infections-of-joints-and-bones/osteomyelitis#.
*3. Li HK, Rombach R, Zambellas AS, et al.: Oral versus IV antibiotics for bone and joint infection, *N Engl J Med* 380:5, 2019.
*4. Siegel RL, Miller KD, Jemal A: Cancer statistics, *CA Cancer J Clin* 70:1, 2020.
5. American Cancer Society: Osteosarcoma. Retrieved from https://www.cancer.org/cancer/osteosarcoma.html.
6. Brant JM: *Core curriculum for oncology nursing*, ed 6, St Louis, 2020, Elsevier.
7. Muscular Dystrophy Association: Duchenne muscular dystrophy. Retrieved from https://www.mda.org/disease/duchenne-muscular-dystrophy.
8. Mackenzie SJ, Nicolau S, Connolly AM, et al.: Therapeutic approaches for Duchenne muscular dystrophy, *Semin Pediatr Neurol* 37:100877, 2021.
9. Sarepta Therapeutics: Exondys 51. Retrieved from https://www.exondys51hcp.com/.
10. National Institute of Neurological Disorders and Stroke: Low back pain fact sheet. Retrieved from https://www.ninds.nih.gov/disorders/backpain/detail_backpain.htm.
*11. Sun W, Zhang H, Tang L, et al.: The factors of non-specific chronic low back pain in nurses: a meta-analysis, *J Back Musculoskelet Rehabil* 34:343, 2021.
12. American Academy of Orthopedic Surgeons: Cauda equina syndrome. Retrieved from https://orthoinfo.aaos.org/en/diseases–conditions/cauda-equina-syndrome/.
13. Mayo Clinic: Herniated disc. Retrieved from https://www.mayoclinic.org/diseases-conditions/herniated-disk/symptoms-causes/syc-20354095.
14. Mikhail CM, Dowdell III JE, Hecht AC: Adult lumbar spondylolisthesis: interspinous devices, *Semin Spine Surg* 32:100806, 2020.
*15. Vaccaro AR, Fisher CG, Prasad SK, et al.: Evidence-based recommendations for spine surgery, *Spine* 45:21, 2020.
*16. Yue JJ, Garcia R, Blumenthal S, et al.: Five-year results of a randomized controlled trial for lumbar artificial discs in single-level degenerative disc disease, *Spine* 44:24, 2019.
*17. Metzger RL: Evidence-based diagnosis and treatment of cervical spine disorders, *Nurs Pract* 44:30–37, 2019.
18. Oh-Park M, Kirschner J, Abdelshahed D, et al.: Painful foot disorders in the geriatric population, *Am J Phys Med Rehabil* 98:9, 2019.
*19. Minisola S, Colangelo L, Pepe J, et al.: Osteomalacia and vitamin D status: a clinical update, *JBMR Plus* 5:1, 2020.
20. National Osteoporosis Foundation: What is osteoporosis and what causes it? Retrieved from https://www.nof.org/patients/what-is-osteoporosis/.

*21. Screening for osteoporosis to prevent fractures: US preventive services task force recommendation statement, *J Am Med Assoc* 319:24, 2018.
22. Elam REW: Osteoporosis. Retrieved from https://emedicine.medscape.com/article/330598-overview.
23. National Osteoporosis Foundation: Risk assessment (FRAX). Retrieved from https://www.nof.org/patients/diagnosis-information/risk-assessment-frax/.
*24. Camacho PM, Petak SM, Binkley N, et al.: American Association of Clinical Endocrinologists/American College of Endocrinology Clinical Practice Guidelines for the diagnosis and treatment of postmenopausal osteoporosis 2020 update, *Endocr Pract* 26:1, 2020.
*25. Pinkerton JV: Hormone therapy for postmenopausal women, *N Engl J Med* 382:446–455, 2020.
*26. Hsu E: Paget's disease of bone: updates for clinicians, *Curr Opin Endocrinol Diabetes Obes* 26:329, 2019.

*Evidence-based information for clinical practice.

69

Arthritis and Connective Tissue Diseases

Dottie Roberts

http://evolve.elsevier.com/Lewis/medsurg/

CONCEPTUAL FOCUS

Coping
Fatigue
Functional Ability
Inflammation
Mobility
Pain
Self-Management

LEARNING OUTCOMES

1. Outline the sequence of events leading to joint destruction in osteoarthritis and rheumatoid arthritis.
2. Detail the clinical manifestations and interprofessional and nursing management of osteoarthritis and rheumatoid arthritis.
3. Describe the pathophysiology, clinical manifestations, and interprofessional care of gout, Lyme disease, and septic arthritis.
4. Discuss the pathophysiology, clinical manifestations, and interprofessional and nursing management of ankylosing spondylitis, psoriatic arthritis, and reactive arthritis.
5. Describe the pathophysiology, clinical manifestations, and interprofessional and nursing management of systemic lupus erythematosus, scleroderma, polymyositis, dermatomyositis, and Sjögren syndrome.
6. Explain the drug therapy and related nursing management associated with arthritis and connective tissue diseases.
7. Relate possible etiologies, clinical manifestations, and interprofessional and nursing management of fibromyalgia and systemic exertion tolerance disease.

KEY TERMS

ankylosing spondylitis (AS)
arthritis
dermatomyositis (DM)
fibromyalgia (FMS)
gout
Lyme disease
osteoarthritis (OA)
polymyositis (PM)
psoriatic arthritis (PsA)
Raynaud phenomenon
rheumatoid arthritis (RA)
septic arthritis
scleroderma
Sjögren syndrome
systemic exertion intolerance disease (SEID)
systemic lupus erythematosus (SLE)

This chapter discusses *rheumatic diseases,* which mainly affect body joints, tendons, ligaments, muscles, and bones. These diseases are often marked by inflammation, pain, and loss of function in 1 or more of the body's connecting or supporting structures. Limited function and fatigue, loss of self-esteem, altered body image, and fear of disability can challenge the patient's ability to cope. We have found more than 100 kinds of rheumatic diseases.[1] At least 54 million adults in the United States have rheumatic conditions.[2] By 2040, that number is expected to exceed 78 million.

ARTHRITIS

Arthritis involves inflammation of a joint or joints. Most forms of arthritis affect women more often in every age group.[2] Osteoarthritis is the most common chronic condition of the

TABLE 69.1 Causes of OA

Cause	Effects on Joint Cartilage
Drugs	Drugs, such as indomethacin and corticosteroids, may stimulate collagen-digesting enzymes in joint synovium.
Hematologic or endocrine problems	Chronic hemarthrosis (e.g., from hemophilia) may contribute to cartilage deterioration.
Inflammation	Release of enzymes in response to local inflammation may affect cartilage health.
Joint instability	Damage to supporting structures causes instability, placing uneven stress on joint cartilage.
Mechanical stress	Repetitive physical activities (e.g., sports) can cause cartilage deterioration.
Neurologic problems	Pain and loss of reflexes from neurologic disorders, such as diabetic neuropathy and Charcot joint, cause abnormal movements that may contribute to cartilage deterioration.
Skeletal deformities	Congenital or acquired conditions (e.g., dislocated hip) may contribute to cartilage deterioration.
Trauma	Dislocations or fractures may lead to avascular necrosis or uneven stress on cartilage.

joints.[3] Other forms include rheumatoid arthritis (RA), fibromyalgia (FMS), systemic lupus erythematosus (SLE), and gout.

OSTEOARTHRITIS

Osteoarthritis (OA) is a slowly progressive noninflammatory disorder of the diarthrodial *(synovial)* joints. OA affects over 30 million adults in the United States.[2] We expect this number to increase as the population ages.

Etiology and Pathophysiology

OA involves the gradual loss of articular cartilage with formation of bony outgrowths (spurs or osteophytes) at the joint margins. OA is not a normal part of the aging process, but aging is one risk factor for disease development. Cartilage destruction likely begins between ages 20 and 30. Most adults are affected by age 40. Few patients have symptoms until after age 50. By age 65, almost 50% of adults report having arthritis.[4]

OA may be caused by a known event or condition that directly damages cartilage or causes joint instability (Table 69.1). However, we cannot identify a single cause for many persons with OA. In these situations, various genetic traits may contribute to the development of cartilage defects.[5]

Decreased estrogen at menopause may contribute to the increased incidence of OA in aging women (Box 69.1). Obesity contributes to hip and knee OA. It increases mechanical stress on the joints. Regular moderate exercise, which helps with weight, decreases the risk for OA development and progression. Anterior cruciate ligament injury from quick stops and pivoting, as in football and soccer, increase risk for knee OA.[3] Work that requires frequent kneeling and stooping also increases the risk for knee OA.

The development of OA is complex. Genetic, metabolic, and local factors interact to cause cartilage deterioration from damage at the level of the chondrocytes (Fig. 69.1). The normally smooth, white, translucent articular cartilage becomes dull, yellow, and granular as OA progresses. Affected cartilage steadily becomes softer and less elastic. It is less able to resist wear with heavy use.

BOX 69.1 BIOLOGIC SEX CONSIDERATIONS

OA

Men

- Except for traumatic arthritis, men do not have OA as often as women until age 70 or 80 years.
- Hip OA is more common.

Women

- Affects women more often.
- More likely to have hand OA (interphalangeal joints and thumb base).
- Knee OA is more common and likely to be more severe, especially after menopause.

The body's attempts at cartilage repair cannot keep up with the destruction of OA. As the collagen structure in the cartilage changes, articular surfaces become cracked and worn. While central cartilage becomes thinner, cartilage at the joint edges becomes thicker and osteophytes form. Joint surfaces become uneven, affecting the distribution of stress across the joint and causing reduced motion.

Although inflammation is not typical of OA, secondary synovitis may occur when phagocytes try to rid the joint of small pieces of cartilage torn from the joint surface. These changes cause the early pain and stiffness of OA. Pain in later disease occurs when articular cartilage is lost, and bony joint surfaces rub each other.

Clinical Manifestations

Joints

Manifestations range from mild discomfort to significant disability. Joint pain is the main symptom and the typical reason the patient seeks medical care. Pain typically worsens with activity. In early stages of OA, rest relieves the joint pain. However, the patient with advanced OA may have pain at rest or have trouble sleeping due to increased joint pain. Pain may worsen when the barometric pressure falls before the onset of severe weather.

As OA progresses, increasing pain can contribute to disability and loss of function. Pain may be referred to the groin, buttock, or outside of the thigh or knee. It can be hard to sit down or get up from a chair when the hips are lower than the knees. As OA develops in the intervertebral *(apophyseal)* joints of the spine, local pain and stiffness are common.

Joint stiffness occurs after periods of rest or an unchanged position *(gelling phenomenon)*. Early morning stiffness is common. It often resolves within 30 minutes. This distinguishes OA from inflammatory joint disorders, such as RA. Excess activity can cause a mild joint swelling that temporarily increases stiffness. *Crepitation,* a grating sensation caused by loose cartilage particles in the joint cavity, can cause stiffness. Crepitation is common in patients with knee OA.

OA usually affects joints on 1 side of the body *(asymmetric)* rather than in pairs. For example, the left knee may be affected

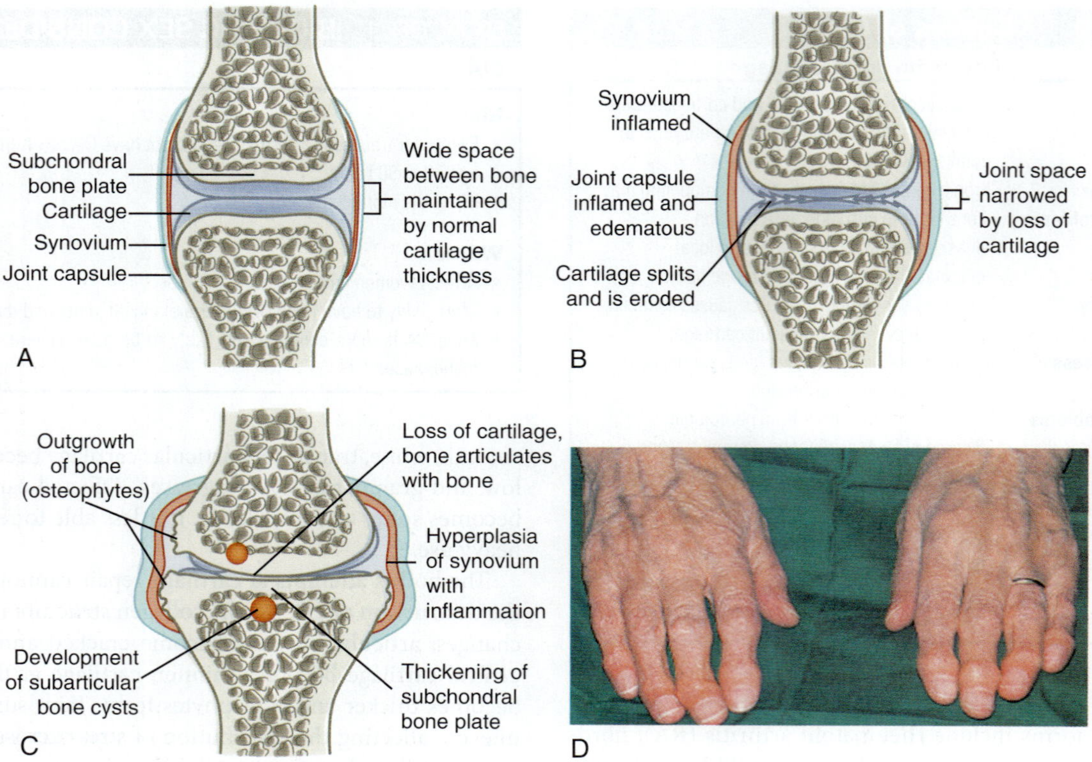

Fig. 69.1 Pathologic changes in OA. (A) Normal synovial joint. (B) Early change in OA is destruction of articular cartilage and narrowing of the joint space. There is inflammation and thickening of the joint capsule and synovium. (C) With time, thickening of subarticular bone occurs, caused by constant friction of the 2 bone surfaces. Osteophytes form around the periphery of the joint by irregular overgrowths of bone. (D) Heberden nodes *(red arrows)* and Bouchard nodes *(yellow areas)* in a patient with OA. (From Forbes CD, Jackson WF: *Color atlas and text of clinical medicine,* ed 3, London, 2003, Mosby.)

and the right knee unchanged. Weight-bearing joints (hips, knees), the metatarsophalangeal (MTP) joint of the foot, and the cervical and lower lumbar vertebrae are often involved (Fig. 69.2). Other affected joints include the distal interphalangeal (DIP) and proximal interphalangeal (PIP) joints of the fingers, and the metacarpophalangeal (MCP) joint of the thumb.

Deformity

Deformity or instability from OA is specific to the involved joint. For example, *Heberden nodes* occur on the DIP joints due to osteophyte formation and loss of joint space (Fig. 69.1D). They can appear as early as age 40. *Bouchard nodes* on the PIP joints indicate similar disease involvement. Heberden and Bouchard nodes are often red, swollen, and tender. They usually do not cause significant loss of function, but the visible deformity may bother the patient.

Knee OA often leads to obvious joint deformity due to cartilage loss in 1 joint compartment. For example, the patient becomes bowlegged *(varus deformity)* from medial joint arthritis. Lateral joint arthritis causes a knock-kneed appearance *(valgus deformity).* In advanced hip OA, 1 leg may become shorter as the joint space narrows.

Systemic

Fatigue, fever, and organ involvement are not present in OA. This is an important distinction between OA and inflammatory joint disorders, such as RA.

Diagnostic Studies

X-rays help confirm disease and stage joint damage. As OA progresses, x-rays often show joint space narrowing and increasingly dense bone. Osteophytes may be visible. However, these changes do not always reflect the degree of pain the patient has. Despite strong x-ray evidence of disease, the patient may have few symptoms. Another patient may have severe pain with only slight x-ray changes. A bone scan, CT scan, or MRI can detect early joint change. They are not typically used for diagnosis due to cost.

Synovial fluid analysis helps distinguish OA from other types of inflammatory arthritis. In OA, the fluid is clear yellow with little or no sign of inflammation. No laboratory tests or biomarkers can be used to diagnose OA. The erythrocyte sedimentation rate (ESR) is normal except for slight increases during acute inflammation. Other routine blood tests (e.g., CBC, liver function tests) are useful only in screening for related conditions or establishing baseline values before starting treatment.

Interprofessional Care

OA has no cure. Care focuses on managing pain and inflammation, preventing disability, and maintaining and improving joint function (Table 69.2). A comprehensive treatment plan may include education and behavioral, psychosocial, and physical interventions. Drug therapy can include topical, oral, and intraarticular agents.[6]

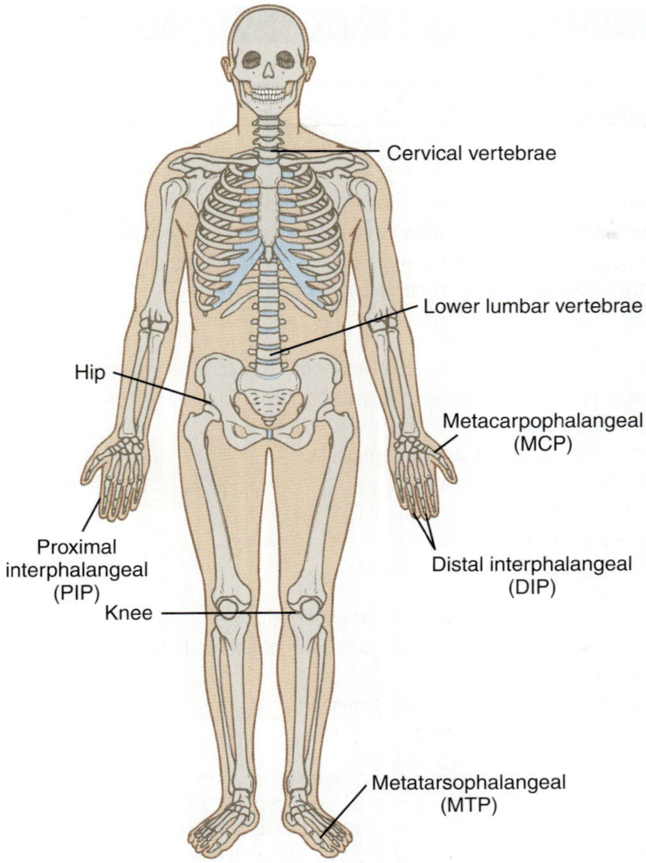

Fig. 69.2 Joints most often involved in OA.

Drugs thought to slow the progression of OA or support joint healing are known as *disease-modifying osteoarthritis drugs (DMOADs)*. To date, no drugs have been approved to modify OA progression despite much research.

Drug Therapy

Drug therapy is based on the joint affected and symptom severity (Table 69.3). Nonsteroidal antiinflammatory drugs (NSAID) are first-line treatment for OA. NSAIDs inhibit the production of cyclooxygenase. When given in equivalent doses, all NSAIDs are comparably effective. They vary widely in cost. Individual responses to NSAIDs also vary. Most NSAIDs are nonspecific, affecting both COX-1 and COX-2.[7] These 2 enzymes convert arachidonic acid into prostaglandins (see Fig. 9.5). COX-2 plays a role in inflammation. COX-1 helps protect the stomach lining. Inhibiting COX-1 causes many of the negative effects of oral NSAIDs, including bleeding and gastrointestinal (GI) irritation.[7]

Some patients start with a topical agent, such as capsaicin cream. It blocks pain by locally interfering with substance P. It is responsible for the transmission of pain impulses. A concentrated product is available by prescription. Creams of 0.025% to 0.075% capsaicin are available over the counter (OTC). Diclofenac gel is another option. OTC products that contain camphor, eucalyptus oil, and menthol (e.g., Bengay, Arthricare) may provide temporary pain relief. Topical salicylates (e.g., Aspercreme) may be an option for some patients. Several applications may be needed daily because topical agents have short-acting effects.

Oral NSAID therapy typically is started in low-dose OTC strengths (e.g., ibuprofen 200 mg up to 4 times daily). The dose may be increased if needed. If the patient is at risk for or develops GI side effects with an NSAID, adding a protective agent, such as misoprostol (Cytotec), may be needed. Arthrotec, a combination of misoprostol and the NSAID diclofenac, is available.

Teach the patient who is taking an oral NSAID to avoid use of a topical NSAID because of increased risk for adverse effects. Patients taking an anticoagulant (e.g., warfarin) and an oral NSAID are at high risk for bleeding. Long-term NSAID treatment may affect cartilage metabolism, especially in older patients who may have poor cartilage integrity. As an alternative to traditional NSAIDs, the COX-2 selective inhibitor celecoxib (Celebrex) may be considered in selected patients.

Some patients still prefer aspirin, but it is no longer a common treatment. It should be used cautiously with NSAIDs because both inhibit platelet function and prolong bleeding time.

Intraarticular corticosteroid injections may be needed for those with local inflammation and swelling. Four or more injections without relief suggest the need for more intervention. Systemic corticosteroids are not used as they may hasten the disease process. Hyaluronic acid injection *(viscosupplementation)* has been a common treatment for knee OA. Neither the American College of Rheumatology (ACR) nor the American Academy of Orthopaedic Surgeons (AAOS) recommends using hyaluronates.[6]

Surgical Therapy

Symptoms are often managed conservatively for many years. Loss of joint function, unmanaged pain, and increased dependence in self-care may lead to consideration of surgery. Reconstructive surgeries (e.g., hip and knee replacements) are discussed in Chapter 67.

TABLE 69.2 Interprofessional Care

OA

Diagnostic Assessment
- History and physical assessment
- Radiologic studies of involved joints (e.g., x-ray, CT scan, MRI, bone scan)
- Possible synovial fluid analysis

Management
- Nutrition and weight management counseling
- Rest and joint protection, use of assistive devices
- Therapeutic exercise
- Heat and cold applications
- TENS
- Reconstructive joint surgery

***Drug Therapy* (Table 69.3)**
- NSAIDs
- Intraarticular corticosteroids

TABLE 69.3 Drug Therapy

OA

Drug	Mechanism of Action	Nursing Considerations
Corticosteroids		
Intraarticular Injections		
methylprednisolone acetate (Depo-Medrol) triamcinolone (Aristospan)	Analgesic Antiinflammatory Inhibit synthesis and/or release of inflammatory mediators	Use strict aseptic technique for corticosteroid injection. Tell patient that joint may temporarily feel worse right after injection. Teach patient to avoid overusing affected joint right after injection. Improvement lasts weeks to months after injection.
Systemic		
dexamethasone hydrocortisone (Solu-Cortef) methylprednisolone (Solu-Medrol) prednisone triamcinolone	Analgesic Antiinflammatory Inhibit synthesis and/or release of inflammatory mediators	Use only in life-threatening exacerbation or when symptoms persist after treatment with less potent antiinflammatory drugs. Give for short time only, taper dose slowly. Abrupt withdrawal of drug worsens symptoms. Monitor BP, weight, CBC, potassium. Limit sodium intake. Report signs of infection.
Nonsteroidal Antiinflammatory Drugs (NSAIDs)		
celecoxib (Celebrex) diclofenac (Voltaren) ibuprofen (Advil) indomethacin (Indocin) ketoprofen meclofenamate meloxicam (Mobic) nabumetone naproxen (Aleve) oxaprozin (Daypro) piroxicam (Feldene) sulindac tolmetin	Antiinflammatory Analgesic Antiinflammatory Inhibit prostaglandin synthesis	Give drug with food, milk, or antacids (as prescribed). Report signs of bleeding, edema, skin rashes, persistent headaches, visual problems. Monitor BP for increases from fluid retention. Use regularly for maximum effect. Monitor for kidney toxicity in older adults.
Salicylate		
aspirin, salicylate	Analgesic Antiinflammatory Inhibit prostaglandin synthesis	Give with food, milk, antacids (as prescribed), or full glass of water. May use enteric-coated aspirin. Report signs of bleeding.
Topical Analgesics		
capsaicin cream	Depletes substance P from nerve endings, interrupting pain signals to the brain	Must be used at regular intervals for maximal effect. Aloe vera cream may decrease burning sensation. Do not use with external heat source (heating pad) because of burn risk. Available in OTC and prescriptive strengths.
diclofenac sodium (Voltaren gel)	Analgesic Antiinflammatory	Avoid sun and ultraviolet (UV) light exposure. Do not use with oral NSAIDs or aspirin due to risk for increased side effects.

Complementary and Alternative Therapies

Complementary and alternative therapies for OA symptom management are popular with patients who have not found relief through traditional medical care. Teach the patient to carefully research any alternative therapies and avoid replacing conventional OA treatments with unproven complementary approaches. Acupuncture may reduce arthritis pain and improve joint mobility.

Some nutrition supplements may have antiinflammatory effects (e.g., fish oil, ginger, SAM-e). However, results of studies on glucosamine and chondroitin are mixed. The ACR and AAOS do not recommend their use.[6] Teach patients to discuss any supplement use with their HCP to identify possible drug interactions.

❖ NURSING MANAGEMENT: OSTEOARTHRITIS

◆ Assessment

Assess and document the type, location, severity, frequency, and duration of the joint pain and stiffness. What makes the pain better or worse? Ask how these symptoms affect the ability to perform activities of daily living (ADLs). Review pain management practices. Ask about success of each treatment. Assess

BOX 69.2 PROMOTING POPULATION HEALTH

Preventing OA

- Avoid smoking.
- Promptly treat any joint injury.
- Maintain healthy weight and eat a balanced diet.
- Use safety measures to protect and decrease risk for joint injury.
- Exercise regularly, including strength and endurance training.

tenderness, swelling, limitation of movement, and crepitation of affected joints. Compare an involved joint with the opposite joint if it is not affected.

Health assessment questionnaires can pinpoint areas of decreased function. They are completed at regular intervals to document disease and treatment progression. Treatment goals can be based on data from the questionnaires and physical assessment, with specific interventions for identified problems.

◆ Clinical Problems

Clinical problems for the patient with OA may include:

- Pain
- Musculoskeletal problems
- Impaired role performance

◆ Planning

Overall goals are that the patient with OA will (1) maintain or improve joint function through a balance of rest and activity, (2) use joint protection measures to improve activity tolerance, (3) achieve independence in self-care and maintain optimal role function, and (4) use drug and nondrug strategies to manage pain satisfactorily.

◆ Implementation

◆ Health Promotion

Prevention of OA is possible in some cases. Focus community education on altering modifiable risk factors (Box 69.2). For example, encourage the patient to lose weight and reduce occupational or recreational hazards. For athletic instruction and physical fitness programs, include safety measures that protect and reduce trauma to the joints.

◆ Ambulatory Care

The patient with OA usually receives treatment as an outpatient. The interprofessional team may include an internal medicine physician or family HCP, a rheumatologist, a nurse, an occupational therapist, and a physical therapist. The patient is usually hospitalized only if having joint surgery (see Chapter 67).

Patient and caregiver teaching related to OA is important. Provide information about the nature and treatment of OA, pain management, body mechanics, correct use of assistive devices (e.g., cane, walker), principles of joint protection and energy conservation (Table 69.4), nutrition choices, weight and stress management, and an exercise program.

Assure the patient that OA is a localized disease and severe deforming arthritis is not the usual course. The patient may gain support and understanding through community resources, such as the Arthritis Foundation's self-help course (www.arthritis.org).

TABLE 69.4 PATIENT & CAREGIVER TEACHING

Joint Protection and Energy Conservation

Include the following instructions when teaching patients with arthritis to protect joints and conserve energy:

- Maintain healthy weight.
- Use assistive devices, if needed.
- Avoid forceful repetitive joint movements.
- Avoid awkward positions that stress joints.
- Use good posture and body mechanics.
- Seek help with needed tasks that may cause pain.
- Organize routine tasks and pace yourself to decrease fatigue and joint pain.
- Modify home and work environment to perform tasks in less stressful ways.

CHECK YOUR PRACTICE

A 54-year-old woman has OA of the left knee. She received an intraarticular corticosteroid injection in the left knee and a prescription for meloxicam 7.5 mg once daily. She has a prescription for physical therapy.

- What self-care information will you reinforce immediately after the injection?
- What information will you provide about meloxicam to ensure safe, effective use?
- What type of exercises would be appropriate?

◆ Heat and Cold Applications

Use of heat or cold is based on symptoms. Ice is not used as often as heat in OA treatment. Ice can help reduce swelling if the patient has acute inflammation. Heat therapy is especially useful for stiffness. It increases flexibility and improves blood flow to the area. Treatments include hot packs, whirlpool baths, ultrasound, and paraffin wax baths.

◆ Nutrition Therapy

If the patient is overweight, a weight-reduction program is a critical part of the treatment plan. Help the patient evaluate the current diet to make needed changes. Chapter 45 discusses ways to help the patient attain and maintain a healthy body weight.

◆ Exercise

Aerobic conditioning, range-of-motion (ROM) exercises, and programs to strengthen muscles around the affected joint help many patients. A physical therapist can help plan an exercise program. Stress the importance of warming up before any exercise to decrease risk for injury. Balance exercises improve the ability to control and stabilize body position. The therapist may recommend an exercise like Tai Chi, which focuses on strength and balance. Tai Chi can be done by patients of all ages and may be done in a wheelchair.

◆ Rest and Joint Protection

Teach the patient to balance rest and activity. Encourage rest of the affected joint during periods of acute inflammation. Keep joints in a functional position with splints or braces if needed. Splints can rest and stabilize painful or inflamed joints. Review ways to modify usual activities to decrease stress on affected joints. Teach the patient with knee OA to avoid standing, kneeling, or squatting for long periods. Work with the physical therapist about the use of assistive devices, such as a cane, walker, or crutches, to decrease joint stress.

◆ Role Performance

Adjust home management goals to meet the patient's needs. Include the caregiver, family members, and significant others in goal setting and teaching. Discuss home and work environment modification for patient safety, accessibility, and self-care. Measures include removing throw rugs, placing rails at the stairs and bathtub, using night-lights, and wearing well-fitting supportive shoes. Assistive devices, such as canes, walkers, elevated toilet seats, and grab bars, reduce the load on an affected joint and promote safety. Urge the patient to continue all prescribed therapies at home and be open to new approaches to symptom management.

Sexual counseling may help the patient and significant other enjoy physical closeness by introducing the idea of alternative positions and timing for sexual activity. Discussion also increases awareness of each partner's needs. Encourage the patient to take analgesics or a warm bath to decrease joint stiffness before sexual activity.

◆ Evaluation

The expected outcomes are that the patient with OA will:

- Have adequate rest and activity
- Achieve acceptable pain management
- Maintain joint flexibility and muscle strength through joint protection and therapeutic exercise

RHEUMATOID ARTHRITIS

Rheumatoid arthritis (RA) is a chronic, systemic autoimmune disease characterized by inflammation of connective tissue in the diarthrodial (synovial) joints. RA is typically marked by periods of remission and exacerbation. RA often has extraarticular manifestations. It is considered one of the most disabling forms of arthritis. Symptoms and outcomes vary greatly. Without adequate treatment, patients may need mobility aids or joint reconstruction. They may have loss of independence and self-care ability.

RA occurs globally, affecting all ethnic groups. It can occur at any time of life. RA most often begins in women between ages 30 and 60 years. It is rare in men under age 45 years. RA affects around 1.5 million adult Americans. Almost 3 times as many women have RA as men.[8]

Etiology and Pathophysiology

We do not know the exact cause of RA. It likely results from a combination of genetics and environmental triggers. An autoimmune cause is the most widely accepted theory. This theory suggests RA begins when a genetically susceptible person has an initial immune response to an antigen. While a bacteria or virus could be the possible antigen, we have not found a specific infection or organism to date.

The antigen, which is probably not the same in all patients, triggers formation of an abnormal immunoglobulin G (IgG). RA is marked by autoantibodies to this abnormal IgG. The autoantibodies are known as *rheumatoid factor (RF)*. They combine with IgG to form immune complexes. At first, the complexes deposit on synovial membranes or superficial articular cartilage in the joints. Complex formation leads to complement activation and an inflammatory response (see Chapter 12).

Neutrophils are attracted to the site of inflammation. They release proteolytic enzymes that damage articular cartilage and cause the synovial lining to thicken (Fig. 69.3). Other inflammatory cells include T helper (CD4) cells, which stimulate cell-mediated immune responses. Activated CD4 cells cause monocytes, macrophages, and synovial fibroblasts to secrete the proinflammatory cytokines interleukin-1 (IL-1), IL-6, and tumor necrosis factor (TNF). These cytokines drive the inflammatory response in RA.

Some patients report a precipitating stressful event, such as infection, work stress, physical exertion, childbirth, surgery, or emotional upset. However, research has not been able to correlate such events with RA onset. Smoking increases the risk for RA. People who smoke are less likely to have disease remission if they have RA. Smoking cessation can reduce the risk of developing RA. The strongest evidence for a genetic predisposition is the role of human leukocyte antigens (HLA), especially the HLA-DR4 and HLA-DR1 antigens. HLA is discussed in Chapter 14.

Clinical Manifestations

Joints

The onset of RA is often subtle. Nonspecific manifestations, such as fatigue, anorexia, weight loss, and general stiffness, may precede the onset of joint symptoms. Stiffness becomes more localized in the following weeks to months.

Specific joint involvement is marked by pain, stiffness, limited motion, and signs of inflammation (e.g., warmth, swelling, pain). Joint symptoms occur symmetrically and often affect the small joints of the hands (PIP, MCP) and feet (MTP). Larger peripheral joints such as wrists, elbows, shoulders, knees, hips, ankles, and jaw may be involved. The cervical spine may be affected. The axial skeleton (spine and bones connected to it) is generally spared. Table 69.5 compares RA and OA.

The patient typically has joint stiffness after periods of inactivity. Morning stiffness may last from 60 minutes to several hours or more, depending on disease activity. MCP and PIP joints are typically swollen. In early disease, the fingers may become spindle shaped from synovial hypertrophy and thickening of the joint capsule. Joints are tender, painful, and warm to the touch. Joint pain increases with motion. It varies in intensity. It may not be related to the degree of inflammation. Tenosynovitis often affects the extensor and flexor tendons around the wrists. This causes symptoms of carpal tunnel syndrome and makes it hard for the patient to grasp objects.

As RA progresses, inflammation and fibrosis of the joint capsule and supporting structures may cause deformity and

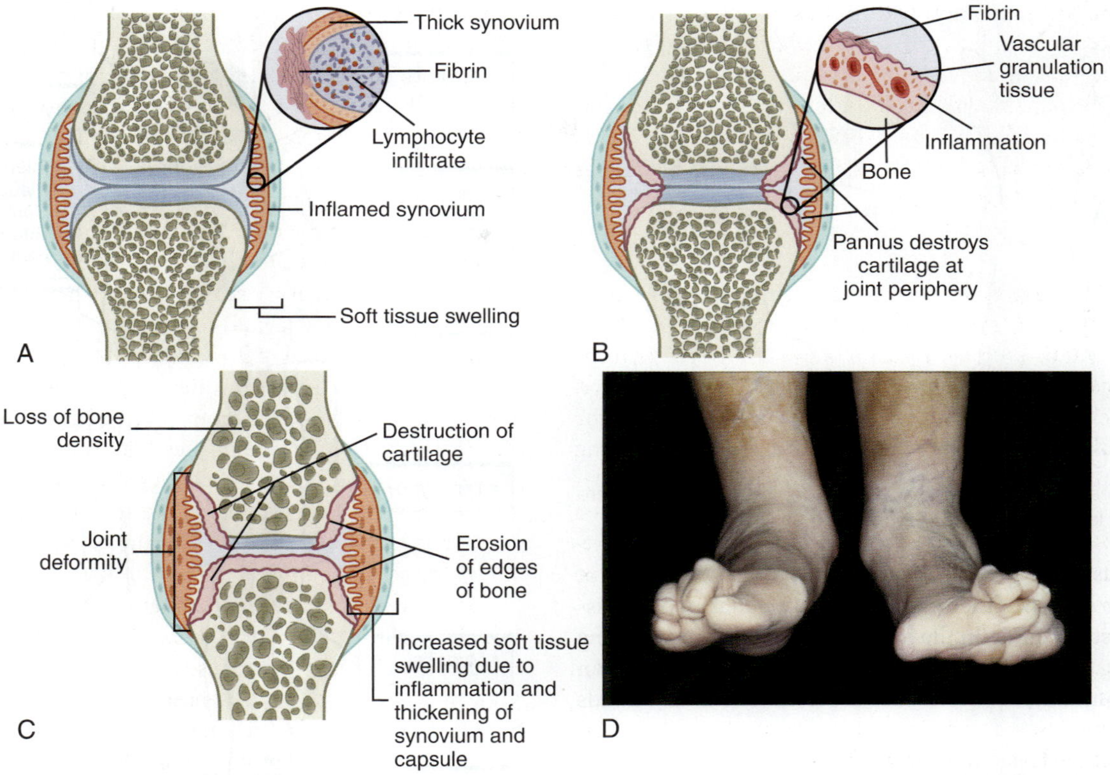

Fig. 69.3 RA. (A) Early pathologic change is rheumatoid synovitis. Synovium becomes inflamed. Lymphocytes and plasma cells increase. (B) Over time, articular cartilage destruction occurs, and vascular granulation tissue grows across the cartilage surface (pannus) from the edges of the joint. Joint surface shows loss of cartilage beneath the extending pannus, most marked at joint margins. (C) Inflammatory pannus causes focal destruction of bone. Osteolytic destruction of bone occurs at joint edges, causing erosions seen on x-rays. This phase is associated with joint deformity. (D) Multiple deformities of the foot from RA. (D, From Canale ST, Beaty JH: *Campbell's operative orthopaedics,* ed 12, Philadelphia, 2013, Mosby.)

TABLE 69.5 Comparison of RA and OA

Parameter	RA	OA
Age at onset	Young to middle age.	Usually older than 40 years.
Gender	Female-to-male ratio is 3:1. Less marked difference after age 60.	Females 2:1 after age 60; except for traumatic arthritis, men less affected until age 70 or 80.
Weight	Lost or maintained weight.	Often overweight or obese.
Disease	Systemic disease with exacerbations and remissions.	Localized disease with variable, progressive course.
Affected joints	Small joints typically affected first (PIPs, MCPs, MTPs), wrists, elbows, shoulders, knees. Usually bilateral, symmetric joint involvement.	Weight-bearing joints of knees and hips, small joints (MCPs, DIPs, PIPs), cervical and lumbar spine. Often asymmetric.
Pain characteristics	Stiffness lasts 1 h to all day and may ↓ with joint use. Pain is variable, may disrupt sleep.	Stiffness occurs on arising but usually subsides after 30 min. Pain gradually worsens with joint use and disease progression, relieved with joint rest but may disrupt sleep.
Effusions	Common.	Uncommon.
Nodules	Present, especially on extensor surfaces.	Heberden (DIPs) and Bouchard (PIPs) nodes.
Synovial fluid	WBC count 5000–60,000/μL with mostly neutrophils; ↓ viscosity.	WBC count < 2000/μL (mild leukocytosis); normal viscosity.
X-rays	Joint space narrowing and erosion with bony overgrowths, subluxation with advanced disease. Osteoporosis related to decreased activity, corticosteroid use.	Joint space narrowing, osteophytes, subchondral cysts, sclerosis.
Laboratory findings	Rheumatoid factor positive in about 80% of patients; negative titers in early disease for about 25%.	Rheumatoid factor negative.
	↑ Antinuclear antibodies (ANAs) titer likely.	ANA negative.
	Positive anti-CCP (anti-citrullinated peptide) in 60%–80%.	Anti-CCP negative.
	↑ ESR, CRP indicative of active inflammation, used to test disease activity. Not specific to RA.	Transient elevation in ESR related to synovitis.

DIPs, Distal interphalangeal joints; *MCPs,* metacarpophalangeal joints; *MTPs,* metatarsophalangeal joints; *PIPs,* proximal interphalangeal joints.

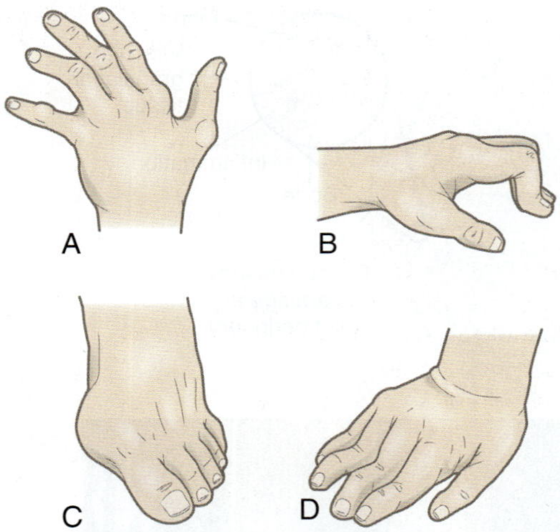

Fig. 69.4 Typical deformities of RA. (A) Ulnar drift. (B) Boutonnière deformity. (C) Hallux valgus. (D) Swan neck deformity.

disability. Muscle atrophy and tendon destruction cause 1 joint surface to slip past the other *(subluxation)*. Metatarsal head dislocation and subluxation in the feet may cause pain and walking disability (Fig. 69.3D). Ulnar drift ("zig-zag deformity"), swan neck, and boutonnière deformities are common in the hands (Fig. 69.4).

Extraarticular Manifestations

RA can affect nearly every body system (Fig. 69.5). Extraarticular manifestations are more likely to occur in the person with high levels of biomarkers, such as RF.

Atherosclerosis can result from chronic inflammation that damages endothelial cells within blood vessels. More cholesterol plaques may be formed. When plaques break loose, they can lead to heart attack or stroke. Risk of heart attack in people with RA is 60% higher than in persons without RA.[9]

Rheumatoid nodules develop in about half the patients with RA.[9] The nodules appear under the skin as firm, nontender masses. They are often found on bony areas exposed to pressure, such as the fingers and elbows. Treatment is usually not needed. However, these nodules can break down, like pressure injuries. Rheumatoid nodules may form in the lungs but are usually harmless.

The patient may develop *Sjögren syndrome*. The inflammation of RA can damage the tear-producing (lacrimal) glands, making the eyes feel dry and gritty.[9] Medications may be needed to prevent damage related to dryness.

Felty syndrome is rare but can occur in those with long-standing RA. It is characterized by an enlarged spleen and low white blood cell (WBC) count. Patients with Felty syndrome are at increased risk for infection and lymphoma.

Flexion contractures and hand deformities cause decreased grasp strength and affect the ability to perform self-care. Depression may occur. However, it is unclear if the patient becomes depressed from struggling with chronic pain and disability or if depression is part of the autoimmune disease process. Levels of C-reactive protein (CRP), a marker of inflammation, are higher in patients with depression compared to those with no symptoms of depression.[10]

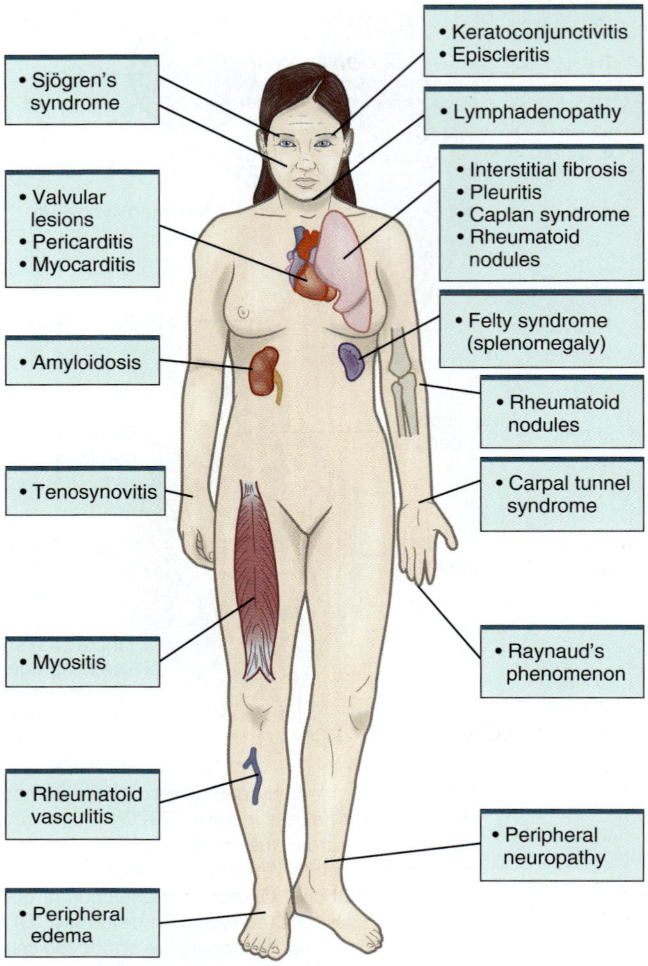

Fig. 69.5 Extraarticular manifestations of RA.

Diagnostic Studies

Accurate diagnosis is important so we can start treatment promptly. A diagnosis is often made based on history and physical findings. Criteria for diagnosis of RA in a newly presenting patient are shown in Table 69.6. Laboratory tests are used to confirm diagnosis and monitor disease progression (Tables 69.7 and 69.8).

Positive RF occurs in about 80% of adults with RA. Negative RF results do not exclude disease. Positive results do not guarantee diagnosis. Titers may rise during active disease. Testing for antibodies to citrullinated peptide (anti-CCP) is more specific than RF for RA. Anti-CCP is present in about 80% of patients with RA. If the patient's symptoms are consistent with RA, the presence of anti-CCP and RF makes a strong case for early, accurate diagnosis. An increase in antinuclear antibody (ANA) titers is a general indicator of autoimmune activity. It is not diagnostic of RA. ESR and CRP are increased as general indicators of active inflammation. Periodic testing can be used to monitor RA activity.

Synovial fluid analysis in early disease often shows slightly cloudy, straw-colored fluid with many fibrin flecks. The WBC count and the enzyme MMP-3 are increased in the synovial fluid. MMP-3 may be a marker of progressive joint damage.

TABLE 69.6 Diagnostic Criteria

Newly Diagnosed Patients With RA

Patients should be tested for RA who initially are seen with:
- At least 1 joint with definite clinical synovitis
- Synovitis not better explained by another disease

Joint Involvement	Score
• 1 large joint	0
• 2–10 large joints	1
• 1–3 small joints (with or without large joint involvement)	2
• 4–10 small joints (with or without large joint involvement)	3
• >10 joints (at least 1 small joint)	5
Serology (at least 1 test result needed for classification)	
• Negative RF *and* negative anti-CCP	0
• Low-positive RF *or* low-positive anti-CCP	2
• High-positive RF *or* high-positive anti-CCP	3
Acute Phase Reactants (at least 1 test needed)	
• Normal CRP *and* normal ESR	0
• Abnormal CRP *or* abnormal ESR	1
Duration of Symptoms	
• <6 weeks	0
• ≥6 weeks	1

Scoring: Add score of categories A–D. Scores range from 0 to 10. A score of ≥6 indicates the definitive presence of RA.

From Aletaha D, Neogi T, Silman AJ, et al.: 2010 Rheumatoid arthritis classification criteria: an American College of Rheumatology/European League Against Rheumatism Collaborative Initiative, *Arthr Rheum* 62:2569, 2010. Retrieved from https://www.rheumatology.org/Portals/0/Files/2010_revised_criteria_classification_ra.pdf.

TABLE 69.7 Stages of RA

Stage	Characteristics
I	• No destructive change on x-ray • X-ray evidence of osteoporosis possible
II	• X-ray evidence of osteoporosis at joint, with or without slight subchondral bone destruction • Slight cartilage destruction possible • Joint mobility may be limited, but no joint deformities noted • Muscle atrophy near joints • Soft tissue lesions (nodules, tenosynovitis) possible near joints
III	• X-ray evidence of cartilage and bone destruction, osteoporosis at joint • Joint deformity without joint fusion • Extensive muscle atrophy near joints • Soft tissue lesions possible near joints
IV	• Criteria from stage III, plus • Fibrous or bony joint fusion

Tissue biopsy can confirm early inflammatory changes in the synovial membrane.

X-rays alone are not diagnostic of RA. They may show only soft tissue swelling and bone demineralization in early disease. A narrowed joint space, articular cartilage destruction, erosion, subluxation, and deformity are seen in later disease. Poor alignment and fusion may be seen in advanced disease. Baseline x-rays may be used to monitor disease progression and treatment effectiveness. Bone scans are more useful in detecting early joint changes and confirming diagnosis so RA treatment can be started.

TABLE 69.8 Interprofessional Care

RA

Diagnostic Assessment
- History and physical assessment
- CBC
- ESR
- C-reactive protein (CRP)
- Rheumatoid factor (RF)
- Antibodies to citrullinated peptide (anti-CCP)
- Antinuclear antibody (ANA)
- X-rays of involved joints
- Synovial fluid analysis, synovial biopsy

Management
- Nutrition and weight management counseling
- Therapeutic exercise
- Psychologic support
- Rest and joint protection, use of assistive devices
- Heat and cold applications
- Reconstructive surgery

Drug Therapy
- Disease-modifying antirheumatic drugs (DMARDs) (Table 69.9)
- Biologic response modifiers (BRMs) (Table 69.9)
- NSAIDs (Table 69.3)
- Intraarticular or systemic corticosteroids (Table 69.3)

Interprofessional Care

A patient-specific treatment plan considers disease activity, joint function, age, sex, family and social roles, and response to previous treatment (Table 69.8). Treatment advances have improved the prognosis for patients with newly diagnosed RA. The progression of joint damage can be decreased and disease activity reduced with aggressive, early treatment.[11] A caring, long-term relationship with the health care team can promote the patient's self-esteem and positive coping.

Drug Therapy

Disease-modifying antirheumatic drugs. Drugs are the cornerstone of RA treatment (Table 69.9). Because irreversible joint changes can occur as early as the first year of RA, HCPs aggressively prescribe disease-modifying antirheumatic drugs (DMARDs). These drugs may slow disease progression and decrease risk for joint erosion and deformity. The choice of drug is based on disease activity, the patient's functional level, and lifestyle considerations, such as the wish to become pregnant.

Methotrexate is preferred for early treatment.[11] It has a lower risk for toxicity than other drugs. Rare but serious side effects include bone marrow suppression and liver toxicity. Therapy requires frequent laboratory monitoring, including CBC and blood chemistry. The patient begins to see therapeutic effects within 4 to 6 weeks. However, not everyone gets adequate relief

TABLE 69.9 Drug Therapy

RA

Drug	Mechanism of Action	Nursing Considerations
Disease-Modifying Antirheumatic Drugs (DMARDs)		
leflunomide (Arava)	Antiinflammatory Immunomodulatory agent that inhibits proliferation of lymphocytes	Monitor liver function. Avoid pregnancy.
methotrexate (Trexall)	Antimetabolite Inhibits DNA, RNA, protein synthesis	Monitor CBC, liver and renal function. Teach patient to report signs of anemia (fatigue, weakness). Keep patient well hydrated. Avoid pregnancy.
sulfasalazine (Azulfidine)	Sulfonamide Antiinflammatory Blocks prostaglandin synthesis	Monitor CBC. Tell patient drug may cause orange-yellow discoloration of urine or skin. Space doses evenly around the clock, taking drug after food with 8 oz water. Treatment may be continued even after symptoms are relieved. Encourage oral fluid intake. Wear sunscreen with sun exposure.
hydroxychloroquine (Plaquenil)	Exact mechanism of action unknown May suppress formation of antigens	Monitor CBC, liver function. Response may not occur for up to 6 months. Teach patient to report vision changes, muscle weakness, ↓ hearing, tinnitus. Have a baseline eye examination with follow-up every 6–12 months because of risk for vision loss. Avoid pregnancy.
Biologic Response Modifiers (Biologics, Immunotherapy)		
B-Cell Depleting Agent		
rituximab (Rituxan)	Monoclonal antibody Binds to CD20, an antigen on B cells, destroying B cells and suppressing immune response	Monitor for infection and bleeding. No live virus vaccines during treatment. Monitor for low BP if taking BP medication. Fatigue is common.
Interleukin-1 Receptor Antagonist		
anakinra (Kineret) canakinumab (Ilaris)	Blocks the action of interleukin-1, ↓ inflammatory response	Do not use with TNF inhibitors. Injection site reaction generally occurs in first month of treatment and decreases with continued therapy. Monitor renal function. Monitor for infection.
Interleukin-6 Receptor Antagonist		
sarilumab (Kevzara) tocilizumab (Actemra)	Blocks action of interleukin-6, thus ↓ inflammatory response	Given to patients for whom other therapies have failed. Monitor BP and for infection. Tell patient of GI effects (e.g., perforation). Monitor liver function, low-density lipoprotein (LDL). Monitor for infection.
JAK (Janus Kinase) Inhibitors		
baricitinib (Olumiant) tofacitinib (Xeljanz) upadacitinib (Rinvoq)	Inhibits action of JAK enzymes, signaling pathways inside the cell with a key role in inflammation of RA	Avoid use in patient with severe liver impairment. Monitor CBC and liver function. Monitor for infection. Avoid pregnancy.
T-Cell Activation Inhibitor		
abatacept (Orencia)	Inhibits T-cell activation, thus suppressing immune response	Do not use with TNF inhibitors. Monitor for infusion reaction if given IV. Assess injection site for reaction. Monitor for infection.
Tumor Necrosis Factor (TNF) Inhibitors		
adalimumab (Humira) certolizumab (Cimzia) etanercept (Enbrel) golimumab (Simponi) infliximab (Remicade)	Bind to TNF, blocking its interaction with cell surface receptors. Decrease inflammatory and immune responses	Monitor CBC, liver function. ↑ Risk for tuberculosis. Teach patient to have yearly PPD. Monitor for infection, bleeding, cancers. No live virus vaccines during treatment. For infliximab: Monitor for infusion reaction. For other TNF inhibitors: SC injection site reaction generally occurs in first month of treatment and ↓ with continued therapy.

from methotrexate alone. It can be given with other DMARDs or biologic response modifiers (BRMs).

Sulfasalazine (Azulfidine) and the antimalarial drug hydroxychloroquine (Plaquenil) may be effective DMARDs for mild to moderate disease. They are rapidly absorbed, relatively safe, and well-tolerated. The synthetic DMARD leflunomide (Arava) blocks immune cell overproduction. Its efficacy and side effects are similar to those of methotrexate and sulfasalazine. Because these drugs are teratogenic, pregnancy must be excluded before starting therapy.

Biologic response modifiers. *Biologic response modifiers* (also called *biologics* or *immunotherapy*) are used to slow disease progression. They can be used alone or in combination therapy with a DMARD, such as methotrexate. BRMs can be used to treat patients with moderate to severe RA who have not responded to DMARDs.

We classify BRMs by their mechanism of action (Table 69.9). These drugs all inhibit the inflammatory response. TNFs bind to TNF in circulation before TNF can bind to the cell surface receptor. Interleukin receptor antagonists block the action of cytokines (IL-1, IL-6) that contribute to inflammation. JAK inhibitors interfere with JAK enzymes involved in joint inflammation in RA. Abatacept (Orencia) blocks T-cell activation. Rituximab (Rituxan) is a monoclonal antibody that targets B cells.

DRUG ALERT

BRM Therapies

- Perform tuberculin test and chest x-ray before starting therapy.
- Monitor for signs of infection. Notify HCP if acute infection develops as therapy may be stopped temporarily.
- Live vaccines should be taken at least 4 weeks before starting drug.
- Report bruising or bleeding.

Other drug therapy. The antibiotics doxycycline (Vibramycin) and minocycline (Minocin) continue to be researched. Any current use of these drugs for RA treatment is not FDA approved. Immunosuppressants (azathioprine) and gold salts are rarely used because they are weak treatments compared to DMARDs and BRMs.

Corticosteroid therapy can be used to manage symptoms during disease flares. Intraarticular injections may temporarily reduce acute pain and inflammation. Low-dose oral corticosteroids may be used for a limited time to decrease disease activity until we see the effects of DMARDs or BRMs. However, they are not used as a sole therapy because they do not affect disease progression. Their long-term use should not be a mainstay of RA treatment. Complications include osteoporosis and avascular necrosis.

Patients use various NSAIDs and salicylates to treat pain and inflammation. They do not alter the course of RA. Aspirin may be used in dosages of 3 to 4 g/day in 3 to 4 doses. We monitor salicylate levels if the patient takes more than 3600 mg daily.[12] NSAIDs have antiinflammatory and analgesic effects. Some relief may be seen within days of starting treatment with NSAIDs. Full effect may take 2 to 3 weeks. The patient may be able to better follow the treatment plan if using an antiinflammatory drug that can be taken only once or twice a day (Table 69.3). Celecoxib (Celebrex), the only available COX-2 inhibitor, is effective in RA. All nonaspirin NSAIDs increase the risk for blood clots, heart attack, and stroke.

Surgical Therapy

Surgery may be needed to relieve severe pain and improve the function of severely deformed joints. Removal of the joint lining *(synovectomy)* is one type of surgery. Total joint replacement *(arthroplasty)* can be done for many different joints in the body. Joint surgery is discussed in Chapter 67.

NURSING MANAGEMENT: RHEUMATOID ARTHRITIS

Assessment

Subjective and objective data you should obtain from the patient with RA are outlined in Table 69.10. Begin with the physical assessment (e.g., joint pain, swelling, ROM, general health status). Assess psychosocial needs (e.g., family support, sexual satisfaction, emotional stress, financial constraints, vocational and career limitations). Are there environmental concerns (e.g., transportation, home or work modifications)? After identifying the patient's problems, plan a program for rehabilitation and education with the interprofessional care team (Table 69.11).

Clinical Problems

Clinical problems for the patient with RA may include:

- Impaired musculoskeletal function
- Pain
- Impaired role performance

Additional information on clinical problems and interventions for the patient with RA is provided in eNursing Care Plan 69.1 (available on the website for this chapter).

Planning

The overall goals are that the patient with RA will (1) have acceptable pain management, (2) have minimal loss of function of affected joints, (3) take part in planning and implementing the treatment plan, (4) maintain a positive self-image, and (5) perform self-care to the maximum amount possible.

Implementation

Care of the patient with RA includes a broad program of drug therapy, self-management strategies, exercise, and patient and caregiver teaching. Nondrug management may include the use of therapeutic heat and cold, rest, relaxation techniques, joint protection (Tables 69.4 and 69.12), biofeedback, transcutaneous electrical nerve stimulation (see Chapter 9), and hypnosis. Allow the patient and caregiver to choose therapies that promote optimal comfort and fit their lifestyle. The Arthritis Foundation offers many publications, classes, and support activities to help persons with RA.

TABLE 69.10 NURSING ASSESSMENT
RA

Subjective Data

Important Health Information

Health history: Recent infections. Precipitating factors, such as emotional upset, infections, overwork, childbirth, surgery. Pattern of remissions and exacerbations

Medications: Aspirin, NSAIDs, corticosteroids, DMARDs, BRMs

Surgery or other treatments: Any joint surgery

Functional Health Patterns

Health perception–health management: Positive family history for RA or other autoimmune disorders. Malaise, ability to take part in treatment plan. Impact of disease on functional ability

Nutritional-metabolic: Anorexia, weight loss, dry mucous membranes

Activity-exercise: Stiffness and joint swelling, muscle weakness, difficulty walking, fatigue

Cognitive-perceptual: Paresthesia of hands and feet, loss of sensation; symmetric joint pain and aching that ↑ with motion or stress on joint, may interfere with rest

Objective Data

Cardiovascular

Symmetric pallor and cyanosis of fingers (Raynaud phenomenon). Distant heart sounds, murmurs, dysrhythmias

General

Lymphadenopathy, fever

GI

Splenomegaly (Felty syndrome)

Musculoskeletal

Symmetric joint involvement with swelling, redness, warmth, tenderness. Deformities (with later disease). Enlargement of PIP and MCP joints. Limitation of joint movement, muscle contractures, muscle atrophy

Respiratory

Bronchiectasis, pleural effusion, tuberculosis, interstitial lung disease

Skin

Scleritis, uveitis, Sjögren syndrome. Subcutaneous rheumatoid nodules on forearms, elbows. Skin ulcers. Shiny, taut skin over involved joints. Peripheral edema

Possible Diagnostic Findings

Positive rheumatoid factor (RF), Antinuclear antibody (ANA), Anti-CCP. ↑ ESR; anemia. ↑ WBCs in synovial fluid. On x-ray evidence of joint space narrowing, bony erosion, deformity, possible osteoporosis

TABLE 69.11 NURSING MANAGEMENT
Caring for the Patient With RA

- Give drug therapy as ordered.
- Teach patient and caregiver about drug therapy, including increased risk for infection with DMARDs and BRMs.
- Assess disease impact on quality of life and joint function.
- Assess pain intensity and give analgesics as ordered. Assess response.
- Develop program for rehabilitation and education with the interprofessional team.
- Teach patient about need for balance of rest and activity, with use of joint protective strategies.
- Supervise AP
  - Aid with passive ROM of affected joints.
  - Help with self-care needs.

Collaborate With Interprofessional Team Members

Physical Therapist

- Assess current mobility and need for help (e.g., walker).
- Develop exercise plan and teach patient to perform exercises safely.
- Coordinate PT with RN so that patient can receive timely analgesia.
- Recommend and apply thermal therapies.

Occupational Therapist

- Assess impact of condition on ability to perform.
- Teach use of assistive devices (e.g., long-handled reacher, long-handled shoehorn) to improve self-care ability without increasing stress on joints.
- Identify modifications to improve role performance (e.g., kitchen modifications for meal preparation).

Social Worker

- Help with obtaining durable medical equipment (e.g., walker).
- Assess psychosocial and financial impact of disease. Arrange vocational retraining if needed.

The patient is usually treated on an outpatient basis. The patient who has systemic complications or needs surgery for decreased functional ability may be hospitalized. Work closely with the HCP, physical and occupational therapists, and social worker to help the patient regain function and adjust to chronic illness.

Teach the patient and caregiver about the disease process and treatment plan. Inflammation may be managed with NSAIDs, DMARDs, and BRMs. Careful timing of drug administration is critical to maintain a therapeutic drug level and reduce early morning stiffness. Discuss the action and side effects of each drug and any needed laboratory monitoring. Many patients take several different drugs, so make the drug regimen as understandable as possible. Encourage patients to develop a way to remember to take their medications (e.g., pill containers).

◆ Rest

Energy conservation requires careful planning. Alternating scheduled rest periods with activity throughout the day (pacing) helps relieve fatigue and pain. The amount of rest needed varies based on disease severity and the patient's limitations. The patient should rest before becoming exhausted. Total bed rest is rarely necessary. It should be avoided to prevent stiffness and other effects of immobility. A patient with mild disease may need daytime rest plus 8 to 10 hours of sleep at night.

Help the patient find ways to change daily activities to avoid overexertion and fatigue, which can worsen disease activity. For example, the patient may be able to prepare meals more easily while sitting on a high stool in front of the sink.

Teach the patient to maintain good body alignment during rest through use of a firm mattress or bed board. Encourage

TABLE 69.12 PATIENT & CAREGIVER TEACHING

Protecting Small Joints

Include the following instructions when teaching the patient with arthritis how to protect small joints:

1. Maintain joint in neutral position to minimize deformity.
   - Press water from a sponge instead of wringing.
2. Use strongest joint available for any task.
   - When rising from chair, push with palms rather than fingers.
   - Carry laundry basket in both arms rather than with fingers.
3. Distribute weight over many joints instead of stressing a few.
   - Slide objects instead of lifting them.
   - Hold packages close to body for support.
4. Change positions often.
   - Do not hold book or grip steering wheel for long periods without resting.
   - Avoid grasping pencil or cutting vegetables with knife for extended periods.
5. Avoid repetitious movements.
   - Do not knit or sew for long periods.
   - Rest between rooms when vacuuming.
   - Use faucets and doorknobs that push rather than turn.
6. Modify chores to avoid stress on joints.
   - Avoid heavy lifting.
   - Sit on stool instead of standing during meal preparation.

positions of extension. Teach the patient to avoid positions of flexion. To decrease the risk for joint contracture, never place pillows under the knees. Use a small, flat pillow under the head and shoulders if needed.

◆ Joint Protection

Protecting joints from stress is important. Help the patient find ways to alter routine tasks to put less stress on joints (Table 69.12). The emphasis is on work simplification. Organize activities to avoid going up and down stairs repeatedly. Use carts to carry supplies. Store frequently used materials in a convenient, easy-to-reach area. Use joint-protective devices (e.g., electric can opener) whenever possible. Teach patients to delegate tasks to other family members.

An occupational therapist helps the patient maintain upper extremity function and encourages use of splints or other assistive devices for joint protection. Lightweight splints can rest an inflamed joint and prevent deformity from muscle spasms and contractures. Remove the splints regularly to assess skin and perform ROM exercises. After assessment and supportive care, reapply splints as prescribed.

Occupational therapy may increase independence with assistive devices that simplify tasks (e.g., built-up utensils, buttonhooks, modified drawer handles, lightweight plastic dishes, raised toilet seats). Encourage the patient to make dressing easier by wearing shoes with Velcro fasteners and clothing with buttons or a zipper in the front instead of the back. Use a cane or a walker for support and decreased pain when walking.

◆ Cold and Heat Therapy

Cold and heat applications can help relieve stiffness, pain, and muscle spasm. They can be used several times a day as needed. Ice is especially helpful during periods of increased disease activity. Cold application should not exceed 10 to 15 minutes at a time. Plastic bags of small frozen vegetables (peas or kernel corn) can easily mold around the shoulder, wrists, or knees to be an effective home treatment. The patient can use ice cubes or small paper cups of frozen water to massage areas on either side of a painful joint.

Moist heat offers better relief for chronic stiffness. Heating pads, moist hot packs, paraffin baths, warm baths, or sitting or standing in a warm shower can relieve stiffness and allow the patient to take part in therapeutic exercise. Heat application should not exceed 20 minutes at a time. Alert the patient to the risk for a burn and the need to avoid using a heat-producing cream (e.g., capsaicin) with an external heat device. Sitting or standing in a warm shower, sitting in a tub with warm towels around the shoulders, or simply soaking the hands in a basin of warm water may allow the patient to perform ADLs more comfortably.

◆ Exercise

Exercise is an important part of the treatment plan. A physical therapist may develop a therapeutic exercise program to improve flexibility and strength of affected joints and increase endurance. Encourage program participation and reinforce correct performance of the exercises. Progressive joint immobility and muscle weakness can occur if the patient does not move the joints. Overaggressive exercise can cause increased pain, inflammation, and joint damage. Emphasize that taking part in a recreational exercise program (e.g., walking, swimming) or doing usual daily activities does not take the place of therapeutic exercise to maintain adequate joint motion.

Gentle ROM exercises daily can help to keep joints functional. The patient should practice exercises with supervision. Exercising in warm water (78° F to 86° F [25° C to 30° C]) allows easier joint movement because of the buoyancy and warmth of the water. Although movement seems easier, water provides 2-way resistance that makes muscles work harder than they would on land. During acute inflammation, limit exercise to 1 or 2 repetitions.

◆ Nutrition

Balanced nutrition is important. Fatigue, pain, and depression may cause a loss of appetite. Limited endurance and mobility may make it hard to shop for and prepare food. Weight loss may result. The occupational therapist can help the patient modify the home environment and use assistive devices for easier food preparation.

Corticosteroid therapy and decreased mobility due to pain may cause unwanted weight gain. Corticosteroids increase the appetite, leading to higher caloric intake. A sensible weight loss program with balanced nutrition and exercise reduces stress on affected joints. The patient taking corticosteroids may become distressed as signs and symptoms of Cushing syndrome (e.g., moon face, redistribution of fatty tissue to the trunk) changes their appearance. Encourage the patient not to change the dose or stop therapy abruptly. Weight will return to normal several months after treatment ends. Remind the patient to continue to eat a balanced diet.

◆ Psychologic Support

For effective self-management, help the patient understand the nature and course of RA and the goals of therapy. Discuss changes in sexuality. Consider the patient's value system and perception of the disease.

Evaluate their support system. Financial planning may be needed. Consider community resources, such as a home care nurse, homemaker services, and vocational rehabilitation. Self-help groups are helpful for some patients.

Chronic pain or loss of function may make the patient vulnerable to claims of false advertising about unproven or even dangerous remedies. Help the patient recognize fears and concerns faced by all people who live with chronic illness.

Living with chronic pain may lead to depression. To decrease depressive symptoms, suggest activities such as listening to music, reading, exercising, and counseling. Hypnosis and biofeedback may be useful.

Gerontologic Considerations: Arthritis

The prevalence of arthritis in older adults is high. The disease is accompanied by problems unique to this age group. Areas of concern for older adults include:

- The high incidence of OA may keep the HCP from considering other types of arthritis.
- Age alone causes changes that make interpretation of laboratory values, such as RF and ESR, more difficult. Drugs taken for comorbid conditions can affect laboratory values.
- Musculoskeletal pain syndromes and weakness may have no physical cause. They may be related to depression and physical inactivity.
- Diseases such as SLE, which often occur in younger adults, can develop in a milder form in older adults.

Physical and metabolic changes of aging may increase the older patient's sensitivity to both therapeutic and toxic effects of some drugs. The older adult who takes NSAIDs has an increased risk for side effects, especially GI bleeding and renal toxicity. Using NSAIDs with a shorter half-life may need more frequent dosing and have fewer side effects in the older patient with altered drug metabolism.

Polypharmacy is a concern. Use of drugs in RA treatment may increase the chance of drug interactions. The drug regimen should be as simple as possible to increase adherence. This is especially important for those who lack regular assistance.

Osteopenia from corticosteroid use can worsen the problem of decreased bone density from aging and inactivity. The risk for pathologic fractures is increased, especially vertebral compression fractures. An age-appropriate exercise program can minimize myopathy from corticosteroid use. The support system for the older adult is critical to the ability to follow a treatment plan.

GOUT

Gout is a type of arthritis characterized by elevation of uric acid *(hyperuricemia)* and the deposit of uric acid crystals in 1 or more joints. Sodium urate crystals may be found in articular, periarticular, and subcutaneous tissues. Unlike other forms of arthritis, gout is marked by painful flares lasting days to weeks followed by long periods without symptoms. More than 9 million Americans have gout. Blacks have a higher incidence compared to Whites.[13] Gout usually develops in men ages 30 to 50. Women rarely develop gout before menopause because estrogen promotes renal excretion of uric acid.

TABLE 69.13 Causes of High Uric Acid Levels

- Acidosis or ketosis
- Alcohol use, especially beer and red wine
- Cancer
- Chemotherapy drugs
- Diabetes
- Drug-induced renal impairment
- Hyperlipidemia
- Hypertension
- Lead exposure
- Metabolic syndrome
- Myeloproliferative disorders
- Obesity
- Renal insufficiency
- Sickle cell anemia
- Starvation
- Use of certain common drugs (aspirin, ACE inhibitors, β-blockers, loop or thiazide diuretics, niacin)

Etiology and Pathophysiology

Uric acid is the major end product of purine catabolism. It is excreted by the kidneys. Gout occurs when either the kidneys cannot excrete enough uric acid or there is too much being made for the kidneys to handle effectively.

We classify hyperuricemia as primary or secondary. *Primary hyperuricemia* is genetic. Accumulation of uric acid may be due to a lack of uricase. Uricase breaks down uric acid into water-soluble products for elimination in urine. A lack of uricase then leads to uric acid retention. *Secondary hyperuricemia* may be caused by conditions that increase uric acid production or decrease uric acid excretion or drugs that inhibit uric acid excretion (e.g., loop diuretics, β-blockers). About 10% of gout cases are due to overproduction of uric acid.[14] Organ transplant recipients receiving immunosuppressive agents are at risk (Table 69.13).

Gout is likely caused by the interaction of several factors. The most important is metabolic syndrome (obesity, insulin resistance, hypertension, hyperlipidemia). Increased intake of foods containing purines (e.g., red and organ meat, shellfish, fructose drinks) can trigger gout. High uric acid may result from prolonged fasting or excess alcohol use because they increase the production of keto acids, which inhibit uric acid excretion. Persons with other forms of inflammatory arthritis (e.g., RA, PsA) are more likely to develop gout.

Not everyone with high uric acid levels develops gout. Two processes are essential for a person to develop gout: crystallization and inflammation. As urate levels increase and saturate the synovial fluid or soft tissues, the excess urate coalesces into crystals. These trigger inflammation. Monocytes and macrophages try to remove the crystals through phagocytosis. This causes the

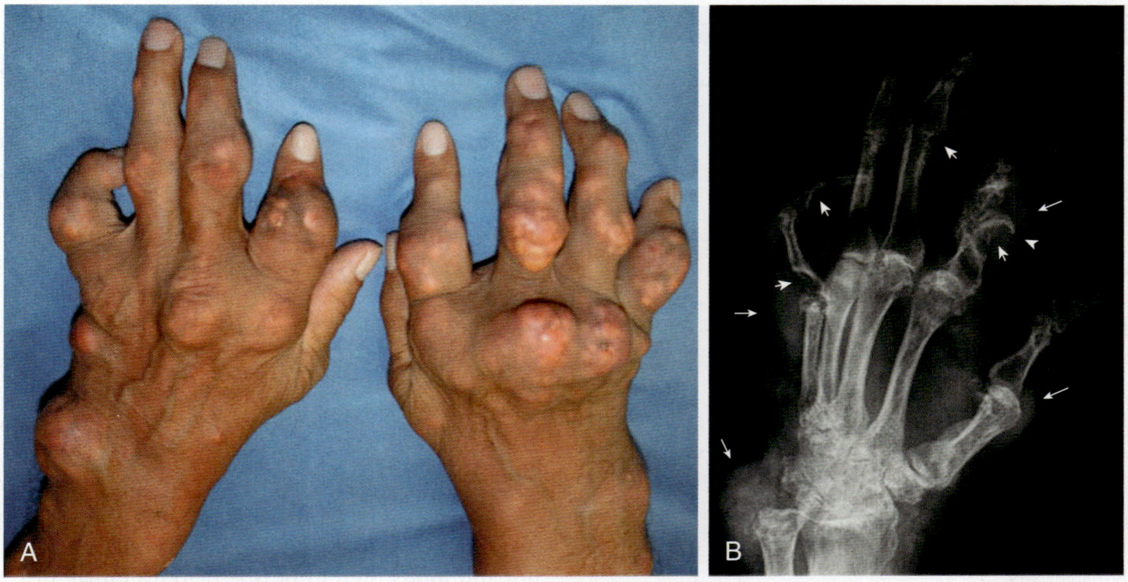

Fig. 69.6 Tophi from chronic gout. Painless nodules are filled with uric acid crystals. (From Barajas-Ochoa A, Castaneda-Sanchez JJ, Ramos-Remus C: Is gout an easy-to-treat disease? *Reumatol Clin* 14:59, 2017.)

release of inflammatory mediators into the surrounding area, causing more inflammation and tissue damage.

Clinical Manifestations and Complications

Gout may occur acutely in 1 or more joints (usually less than 4). Inflammation of the great toe *(podagra)* is the most common initial problem. Other affected joints may include wrists, knees, ankles, and the midfoot. Olecranon bursae may be involved. Affected joints may appear dusky or cyanotic. They are very tender. Acute gout arthritis may be triggered by events such as trauma, surgery, alcohol use, or systemic infection. Symptom onset typically occurs at night with sudden swelling and severe pain peaking within several hours. The painful area is highly sensitive to light touch. Low-grade fever is common.

An attack usually ends in 2 to 10 days with or without treatment. The affected joint returns to normal. Patients have no symptoms between attacks.

Chronic gout is characterized by multiple joint involvement and visible deposits of sodium urate crystals called tophi. Tophi are hard white nodules. They are typically seen in subcutaneous tissue, synovial membranes, tendons, and soft tissues (Fig. 69.6). Tophi often occur many years after the onset of disease.

The severity of gout arthritis varies. The clinical course may involve infrequent mild attacks or multiple severe episodes (up to 12 per year) marked by slowly progressive disability. In general, tophi appear earlier, and the patient has more frequent, severe episodes of gout if serum uric acid is high. Chronic inflammation may cause joint deformity. Cartilage destruction may lead to secondary OA. Large urate crystal deposits may pierce overlying skin, causing draining sinuses that often become infected.

Excess uric acid excretion may lead to stone formation in the kidneys or urinary tract. Pyelonephritis related to sodium urate deposits and obstruction contributes to kidney disease.

Diagnostic Studies

Normal uric acid levels range from 2.7 to 8.5 mg/dL based on gender.[14] The higher the value, the greater the risk for uric acid deposits in joints and future gout attacks. However, hyperuricemia is not specifically diagnostic of gout because serum values may be normal during an acute gout attack. A 24-hour urine uric acid can determine if gout is caused by decreased renal excretion or overproduction of uric acid.

The gold standard for diagnosis of gout is synovial fluid aspiration. Affected fluid contains needle-like monosodium urate crystals. This procedure is done in only a small number of patients because diagnosis can often be made on symptoms alone. However, it is the only reliable way to tell gout from septic arthritis or *pseudogout* (calcium phosphate crystal formation). Aspiration may decrease pain by relieving pressure in a swollen joint capsule.

X-rays appear normal in the early stages of gout. In chronic disease, tophi may appear as eroded areas in the bone.

❖ INTERPROFESSIONAL AND NURSING MANAGEMENT: GOUT

Goals for the care of the patient with acute gout (Table 69.14) include ending an attack with an antiinflammatory agent, such as colchicine. Hyperuricemia and gout are chronic problems that can be controlled with effective patient education and careful adherence to a treatment program. Drug therapy is the primary way to treat acute and chronic gout.

◆ Drug Therapy

Acute gout is treated with oral colchicine (Colcrys, Mitigare) and NSAIDs. Because colchicine has antiinflammatory effects but is not an analgesic, an NSAID is added for pain management. Colchicine often results in pain relief when given within 12 hours of an attack. This helps in diagnosis because good response to this drug is further evidence of gout.

TABLE 69.14 Interprofessional Care

Gout

Diagnostic Assessment
- History and physical assessment
- Family history of gout or other inflammatory arthritis
- Sodium urate crystals in synovial fluid
- ↑ Serum uric acid
- ↑ Uric acid in 24-hr urine
- X-ray of affected joints

Management
- Joint immobilization
- Local application of cold
- Joint aspiration and intraarticular corticosteroids
- Avoid food and fluids with high purine content (e.g., anchovies, liver, wine, beer)

Drug Therapy
- colchicine
- NSAIDs (e.g., naproxen)
- Xanthine oxidase inhibitors: allopurinol (Zyloprim), febuxostat (Uloric)
- Uricosurics: probenecid
- pegloticase (Krystexxa)
- Corticosteroids (e.g., prednisone)
- Intraarticular corticosteroids (methylprednisolone)
- Adrenocorticotropic hormone (ACTH)

Corticosteroids (intraarticular injection or orally by tapered dosing) can be helpful in treating an acute attack. Systemic corticosteroids may be used only if routine therapies are contraindicated or ineffective. Adrenocorticotropic hormone (ACTH) is an option for acute treatment of patients for whom NSAIDs, colchicine, or steroids may be problematic.

Future gout attacks are prevented in part by a maintenance dose of a xanthine oxidase inhibitor. These drugs decrease the production of uric acid. Allopurinol is the drug used most often and the first choice for therapy. It can be used for patients with uric acid kidney stones or renal impairment. Serious adverse effects limit the use of febuxostat (Uloric) to those not treated effectively or having severe side effects with allopurinol.

DRUG ALERT

Febuxostat
- May cause heart-related death and liver failure.
- Encourage patient with cardiovascular disease to take low-dose aspirin therapy.
- Monitor liver function tests before starting therapy and during treatment.
- Teach patient to notify HCP if symptoms of liver or heart problems occur.

A uricosuric agent, which increases uric acid excretion in the urine, may be added with a xanthine oxidase inhibitor if uric acid levels do not decrease. Probenecid is the most common agent. Aspirin inactivates its effect, resulting in urate retention, and must be avoided during treatment. Acetaminophen can be used safely if analgesia is needed.

Uricosurics can cause renal impairment. They are ineffective when creatinine clearance is reduced, as can occur in patients over age 60 years or with renal impairment. They should be taken in the morning with food and water. Teach patients to stay well hydrated and to drink about 2 L of liquid a day when taking the drug.

Patients who cannot take or do not respond to drugs that lower serum uric acid may receive pegloticase (Krystexxa). It is an enzyme that metabolizes uric acid into a harmless chemical excreted in the urine. It is given IV, every 2 weeks, for at least 6 months. Life-threatening anaphylactic and infusion reactions can occur.

The angiotensin II receptor antagonist losartan (Cozaar) may be effective for treating older patients with gout and hypertension. Losartan promotes urate excretion and may normalize serum urate. Combination therapy with losartan and allopurinol may be used.

Serum uric acid is checked regularly to monitor treatment effectiveness. Explain the importance of drug therapy and the need for regular assessment of serum uric acid. Limiting alcohol and foods high in purine help minimize uric acid production. Adequate urine volume with normal renal function (2 to 3 L/day) must be maintained to prevent uric acid precipitation in the renal tubules. Teach obese patients to follow a planned weight-reduction program (see Chapter 45). Teach the patient about other factors that may cause an attack, including fasting, drug use (e.g., diuretics), and major medical events (e.g., surgery, heart attack).

Nursing interventions for the patient with acute gout include supportive care of the inflamed joints. Avoid causing pain by careless handling of an inflamed joint. Bed rest may be needed to immobilize affected joints. Use a cradle or footboard to protect a painful lower extremity from the weight of bed linens. Assess motion limitations and degree of pain.

CHECK YOUR PRACTICE

A patient comes to the primary care office with acute gout. The right great toe is swollen, red, and painful. He is prescribed colchicine.
- What nursing interventions will you teach the patient to protect the foot and decrease pain?
- What will you discuss with the patient about diet changes to decrease risk for future attacks?

LYME DISEASE

Lyme disease is an infection caused by the spirochete *Borrelia burgdorferi*. It is transmitted by the bite of an infected deer tick. The tick typically feeds on mice, dogs, cats, cows, horses, deer, and humans. Person-to-person transmission does not occur. It is the most common vector-borne disease in the United States, with about 35,000 cases annually.[15]

Human infection peaks in summer months. Most U.S. cases occur in the northeastern states from Virginia to northern Maine, and in Wisconsin and Minnesota.[15] Reinfection is common.

Symptoms mimic those of other diseases, such as multiple sclerosis, mononucleosis, and meningitis. The most characteristic symptom of early disease is *erythema migrans* (EM). This

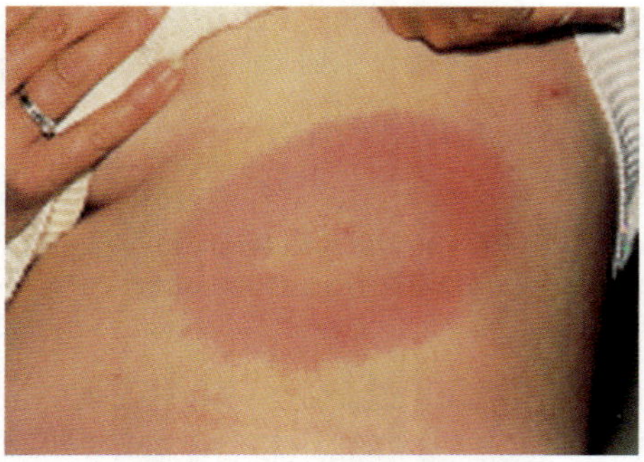

Fig. 69.7 Erythema migrans. Typical skin lesion of Lyme disease occurs at the site of tick bite. (From Marx J, Hockberger R, Walls R: *Rosen's emergency medicine*, ed 7, Philadelphia, 2009, Mosby.)

"bull's-eye rash" occurs in about 80% of infected persons.[15] It appears at the site of the tick bite within 1 month after exposure (Fig. 69.7). It may occur anywhere else on the body as the disease progresses. The EM lesion begins as a central red macule or papule that slowly expands to include a red outer ring of up to 12 in, resembling a bull's eye. It may be warm to the touch but is not itchy or painful. The rash often occurs with acute flu-like symptoms. These include low-grade fever, headache, neck stiffness, fatigue, loss of appetite, and joint and muscle pain. These symptoms generally resolve over weeks or months, even if untreated.

If not treated, the spirochete can spread within several weeks or months to the heart, joints, and central nervous system (CNS). Arthritis is the second most common manifestation of Lyme disease. Many persons with untreated infection develop chronic arthritic pain and swelling in the large joints, mainly the knee. Cardiac symptoms, such as palpitations or irregular heartbeat *(Lyme carditis)*, may require hospitalization.[15] Bell palsy is the most common neurologic effect. Other problems include brain and spinal cord inflammation, dizziness, shortness of breath, and numbness and tingling in the feet.

Diagnosis is often based on the manifestations, especially EM, and a history of exposure in an at-risk area. The CDC recommends a 2-step laboratory testing process to confirm the diagnosis.[15] The first step is the enzyme immunoassay (EIA). It will be positive for most people with Lyme disease. If the EIA is positive or inconclusive, then a Western blot test is done. Results are diagnostic of Lyme disease only if both tests are positive. The CDC does not recommend the Western blot test alone. False-positive results lead to incorrect diagnosis and treatment. Cerebrospinal fluid should be tested in those with neurologic involvement.

Active lesions are treated with oral antibiotics. Doxycycline, cefuroxime, and amoxicillin are often effective in treating early-stage infection and preventing later stages of the disease (see Table 15.8). Short-term therapy of 10 to 14 days of doxycycline is preferred.[15] It treats both Lyme disease and human granulocytic anaplasmosis, which can be transmitted as a co-infection with a single tick bite. While other antibiotics can be used for those who cannot tolerate these drugs, they all are less effective. Patients treated with macrolide antibiotics need close monitoring to ensure symptoms resolve.

A small number of persons treated with antibiotics have lingering fatigue or joint and muscle pain. Antibiotic treatment is extended as needed because the risks of untreated Lyme disease outweigh those of long-term antibiotic therapy.

Reducing exposure to ticks is the best way to prevent Lyme disease. Patient and caregiver teaching for people living in endemic areas is outlined in Table 69.15. No vaccine is available for Lyme disease.

TABLE 69.15 PATIENT & CAREGIVER TEACHING

Prevention and Early Treatment of Lyme Disease

Include the following instructions when teaching patients how to prevent Lyme disease:

- Do not walk through tall grasses and low brush or sit on logs.
- Mow grass frequently. Remove brush around paths, buildings, and campsites to create tick-safe zones.
- Move woodpiles and bird feeders away from your house. Discourage deer (main source of food for adult ticks) from being in the area.
- Keep playground equipment and decks away from yard edges, and in a sunny location if possible.
- Wear long pants or nylon tights of tightly woven, light-colored fabric so that you can easily see ticks.
- Tuck pants into boots or long socks, wear long-sleeved shirts tucked into pants, and wear closed toed shoes when hiking.
- Check often for ticks crawling from pant legs to open skin.
- Thoroughly inspect and wash clothes. Placing clothing in dryer on high heat kills ticks.
- Spray insect repellent containing DEET sparingly on skin or clothing. Apply permethrin to clothing and camping gear; protects for several hours.
- Have pets wear tick collars and inspect them often. Do not allow pets on furniture or beds.

Include the following instructions when teaching patients and caregivers living in endemic areas:

- Remove attached ticks with fine-tipped tweezers (not fingers). Grasp tick's mouth parts as close to skin as possible and pull straight out with steady, even pressure. Do not twist or jerk. Avoid folk solutions, such as painting the tick with nail polish or petroleum jelly.
- Save the tick in a bottle of alcohol (if you need it later for identification). Never crush a tick with your fingers.
- Wash bitten area with soap and water, iodine scrub, or rubbing alcohol. Apply antiseptic. Wash hands.
- See an HCP if flu-like symptoms or a bull's-eye rash appears within 2–30 days after removal of tick.

DEET, N, N-diethyl-m-toluamide.
Adapted from Centers for Disease Control and Prevention: Preventing tick bites on people. Retrieved from https://www.cdc.gov/lyme/prev/on_people.html; and Centers for Disease Control and Prevention: Tick removal. Retrieved from https://www.cdc.gov/lyme/removal/index.html.

SEPTIC ARTHRITIS

Septic arthritis (infectious or bacterial arthritis) is caused by microorganisms invading the joint cavity. These organisms can travel through the bloodstream from another site of active infection, resulting in seeding of the joint. Organisms can be introduced directly through trauma or surgical incision.

Any infectious agent can cause septic arthritis, especially in the immunocompromised patient. *Staphylococcus aureus* is the most common causative organism.[16] Factors that increase infection risk include (1) diseases with decreased host resistance (e.g., RA, SLE), (2) treatment with corticosteroids or immunosuppressive drugs, (3) debilitating chronic illness (e.g., diabetes), (4) joint trauma or an artificial joint, (5) skin conditions (e.g., psoriasis, eczema), and (6) IV drug use.[16]

Large joints, such as the knee and hip, are most often affected. Inflammation of the joint cavity causes severe pain, redness, and swelling. Septic arthritis of the hip can cause avascular necrosis. Because infection has often spread from a primary site elsewhere in the body, fever or shaking chills are often present. Diagnosis may be made by joint aspiration *(arthrocentesis)* and synovial fluid culture. WBC count may be low early in the infectious process, especially in those who are immunosuppressed, so diagnosis is not possible solely based on WBC count. Blood cultures for aerobic and anaerobic organisms should be obtained. X-rays or other imaging tests can assess joint damage or loosening of an artificial joint.

Emergent aspiration or surgical drainage is a cornerstone of treatment. Permanent joint damage can occur without rapid treatment. Sometimes, damage occurs despite treatment. Broad-spectrum antibiotics are often started before we have culture results. Once we identify the organism, more specific treatment can be determined. IV antibiotics are typically transitioned to oral antibiotics, with total treatment of 2 to 6 weeks. If an artificial joint is infected, treatment may involve removing the joint and replacing it temporarily with a joint spacer. The spacer is made with antibiotic cement. If the artificial joint cannot be removed, several months of oral antibiotics will be needed to avoid return of infection.

Assess and monitor joint inflammation, pain, and fever. To manage pain, use resting splints or traction to immobilize affected joints. Local hot compresses can decrease pain. Start gentle ROM exercises as soon as tolerated to prevent muscle atrophy and joint contractures. Explain the need for antibiotics and the importance of their continued use until the infection is resolved (see Table 15.8). Support the patient who needs joint drainage. Use strict aseptic technique when assisting with joint aspiration.

SPONDYLOARTHROPATHIES

The *spondyloarthropathies* are a group of multisystem inflammatory disorders that affect the spine, peripheral joints, and periarticular structures. These disorders include ankylosing spondylitis, psoriatic arthritis, and reactive arthritis. They are all negative for RF, so we call them *seronegative arthropathies.*

Inheriting HLA B27 is strongly associated with these diseases. Both genetic and environmental factors play a role in their development. HLAs and their relationship to autoimmune diseases are discussed in Chapter 14.

Pain in the lower back *(sacroiliitis)* and hips, especially in the morning or after periods of inactivity, is the primary symptom of all spondyloarthropathies. These general symptoms may make it hard to discern among them in early disease. Other related conditions may include peripheral joint involvement (mainly of the lower extremities), pain and redness of the eyes *(uveitis),* intestinal inflammation, and psoriasis.

BOX 69.3 GENETICS IN CLINICAL PRACTICE

Ankylosing Spondylitis (AS)

Genetic Basis
- Inheritance of HLA-B27 increases susceptibility to developing AS.
- We do not know how HLA-B27 increases the risk for AS.

Incidence
- HLA-B27 antigen is found in about 90% of people with AS.
- Inheriting HLA-B27 does not mean a person will develop AS.
- About 80% of those who inherit HLA-B27 do not develop AS.

Genetic Testing
- Testing for HLA-B27 antigen is available.
- Presence of HLA-B27 is not diagnostic for AS.

Clinical Implications
- Diagnosis of AS usually occurs in the third and fourth decades of life.
- Multiple genetic and environmental factors play a role in pathogenesis of disease.

ANKYLOSING SPONDYLITIS

Ankylosing spondylitis (AS) *(axial spondyloarthritis)* is a chronic inflammatory disease that primarily affects the axial skeleton, including the sacroiliac joints, intervertebral disc spaces, and costovertebral articulations. Onset of AS is usually in the third and fourth decades of life, but onset in adolescence is fairly common. Men are more likely to develop radiographic AS, with spine damage that we can see on x-ray. With the nonradiographic form of AS, changes show on MRI rather than x-ray. This form is as common in women as in men. Whites, Asians, and Hispanics are more likely to have AS.

Etiology and Pathophysiology

We do not know the exact cause of AS. HLA-B27 antigen is found in about 90% of all patients with AS, but only 8% of the general population.[17] This suggests genes play a key role in AS (Box 69.3). Families with other diagnosed HLA-B27–positive rheumatic diseases (e.g., psoriatic arthritis, juvenile spondyloarthritis) should be alert to signs of low back pain for early identification of AS.

Inflammation in the joints and adjacent tissue causes the formation of granulation tissue *(pannus)* and dense fibrous scars that can cause joint fusion. Inflammation can affect the eyes, lungs, heart, kidneys, and peripheral nervous system.

Clinical Manifestations and Complications

AS is characterized by symmetric sacroiliitis and progressive inflammatory arthritis of the axial skeleton. Symptoms of inflammatory spine pain are the first clues to AS. The patient often has low back pain, stiffness, and limited motion that is worse during the night and in the morning but improves with mild activity. In women, early symptoms may include pain and stiffness in the neck rather than the lower back. Uveitis is the most common nonskeletal symptom. It can appear as an initial presentation years before arthritic symptoms develop.

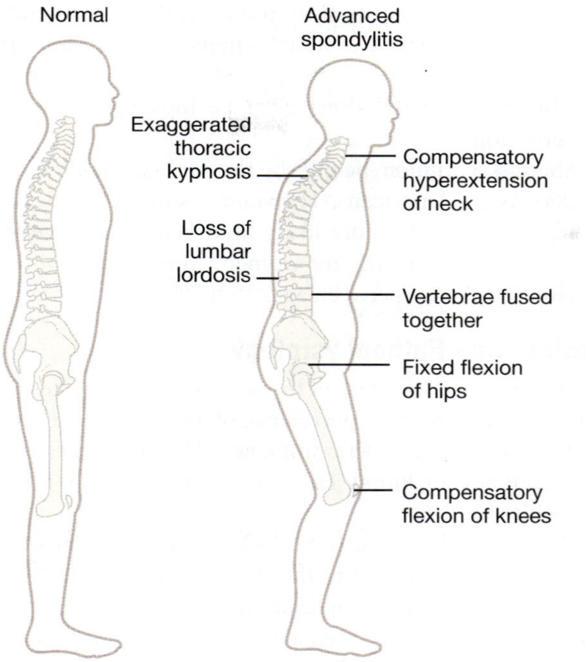

Fig. 69.8 Posture changes in patient with ankylosing spondylitis.

Patients with AS may have chest pain and sternal/costal cartilage tenderness.

Most people with AS stay fully independent or become minimally disabled. Postural abnormalities and deformity can cause disability (Fig. 69.8). Impaired spinal ROM and fusion, along with vision problems, raise concerns about safe ambulation. The patient is at increased risk for aortic insufficiency and pulmonary fibrosis. Cauda equina syndrome (compression of the nerves at the end of the spinal cord) can occur. This contributes to lower extremity weakness and bladder problems. The patient is at risk for spinal fracture from osteoporosis.[17]

Diagnostic Studies

X-rays are the most important technique for the diagnosis and follow up of AS. However, they are limited in detecting early sacroiliitis or subtle changes in posterior vertebrae. MRI is useful in assessing early cartilage changes. CT scan is appropriate in specific situations (e.g., cases with subtle x-ray changes). Changes on later spinal films include the appearance of "bamboo spine," the result of calcifications *(syndesmophytes)* that bridge from one vertebra to another. An increased ESR and mild anemia may be seen. When the suspicion for AS is high, the presence of the HLA-B27 antigen improves the likelihood of the diagnosis.

Interprofessional and Nursing Care

Care goals are aimed at maintaining maximal skeletal mobility while decreasing pain and inflammation. Heat applications can help relieve local symptoms. NSAIDs and salicylates are often prescribed. DMARDs, such as sulfasalazine or methotrexate, have little effect on spinal disease but may help with peripheral joint disease. Local corticosteroid injections may help relieve symptoms.

TNF, which promotes inflammation, is increased in the blood and certain tissues of patients with AS. Etanercept, a BRM, binds TNF and inhibits its action. Etanercept reduces active inflammation and improves spinal mobility. Other anti-TNF inhibitors (infliximab, adalimumab, golimumab) may be effective.

Once pain and stiffness are managed, exercise is essential. Good posture is important to minimize spinal deformity. The exercise plan should include back, neck, and chest stretches. Hydrotherapy (e.g., sauna, steam bath) can decrease pain and facilitate spinal extension. Most patients will not need surgery. Surgery may be done to improve pain and mobility in a severely damaged joint. Spinal osteotomy and total joint replacement are the most common procedures (see Chapter 67).

Teach the patient about the disease and principles of therapy. The home management program should include regular exercise and attention to posture, local moist heat applications, and drug therapy.

Assess chest expansion (using breathing exercises) as part of baseline ROM assessment. Encourage smoking cessation to decrease the risk for lung complications in persons with reduced chest expansion. Ongoing PT includes gentle, graded stretching and strengthening exercises. These preserve ROM and improve thoracolumbar flexion and extension.

Discourage physical exertion during periods of increased disease activity. Proper positioning at rest is essential. Encourage the patient to use a firm mattress. They should sleep on the back with a flat pillow, avoiding positions that encourage flexion deformity. Emphasize the need to avoid spinal flexion (e.g., leaning over a desk); heavy lifting; and prolonged walking, standing, or sitting. Encourage sports that involve natural stretching, such as swimming and racquet games. Family counseling and vocational rehabilitation are important.

PSORIATIC ARTHRITIS

Psoriatic arthritis (PsA) is a progressive inflammatory disease that affects about one-third of people with psoriasis.[18] *Psoriasis* is a common, benign, inflammatory skin disorder characterized by red, irritated, and scaly patches. Although we do not know the exact cause of PsA, we suspect a combination of immune, genetic, and environmental factors. PsA appears to have a genetic link with HLA antigens in many patients.

PsA can occur in different forms. *Asymmetric oligoarthritis* involves different joints on each side of the body. *Symmetric polyarthritis* resembles RA. It affects joints on both sides of the body at the same time. These 2 forms are the most common types of PsA. *Distal interphalangeal predominant PsA* involves the ends of the fingers and toes. The patient often has pitting and color changes in the fingernails and toenails. *Spondylitis* is marked by pain and stiffness in the spine and neck. *Arthritis mutilans* affects less than 5% of people with PsA. It is the most severe form of the disease, causing complete destruction of small joints.

On x-ray, the cartilage loss and erosion are similar to RA. Advanced cases often show widened joint spaces. A "pencil in cup" deformity is common in the DIP joints due to thinning, weakened bone. In this deformity, the narrowed ends of the metacarpals or phalanges insert into the expanded end of the other bone sharing the joint. Some patients have increased ESR and uric acid levels with mild anemia. So, the diagnosis of gout must be excluded.

Treatment includes splinting, joint protection, and PT. Starting NSAIDs early in the course of the disease may help with inflammation. Drug therapy includes DMARDs, such as methotrexate. They are effective for both articular and skin manifestations. Sulfasalazine, cyclosporine, and BRMs (e.g., etanercept, golimumab, adalimumab, infliximab) may be used. Apremilast (Otezla), a phosphodiesterase-4 inhibitor, can treat adults with active PsA.

REACTIVE ARTHRITIS

Reactive arthritis (Reiter syndrome) is associated with a symptom complex that includes urethritis, conjunctivitis, and mucocutaneous lesions. We do not know the exact cause. It appears to be a reaction triggered in the body after exposure to specific genitourinary or GI tract infections. *Chlamydia trachomatis* spreads by sexual contact. Associated GI infections include *Shigella, Salmonella, Campylobacter,* or *Yersinia* species and other pathogens.[19] It occurs more often in young men.

Those who are positive for HLA-B27 are at increased risk for developing reactive arthritis after sexual contact or exposure to certain GI pathogens. This finding supports a genetic predisposition.

Urethritis develops within 1 to 2 weeks after sexual contact or GI infection. Women may have cervicitis. Low-grade fever, conjunctivitis, and arthritis may occur over the next several weeks. Arthritis is usually the last symptom to appear. It tends to be asymmetric. It often involves the toes and the large joints of the lower extremities. Lower back pain may occur with severe disease. Lesions involving the skin and mucous membranes often occur as small, painless, superficial ulcerations on the tongue, oral mucosa, and glans penis. Soft tissue manifestations include Achilles tendinitis or plantar fasciitis. Few laboratory abnormalities occur, although the ESR may be increased.

Most patients recover within a few months of initial symptoms. Because *C. trachomatis* infection can cause reactive arthritis, treatment with doxycycline is recommended for patients and their sexual partners. Antibiotics have no effect on arthritis or other symptoms. NSAIDs are given to treat inflammation. DMARDs may be used if joint symptoms do not resolve. Topical ophthalmic corticosteroids are helpful for uveitis. Conjunctivitis and skin lesions generally do not need treatment. PT may help during recovery.

Most patients have complete remission with return of full joint function. A few develop chronic arthritis, but the condition is often mild. X-ray changes in chronic reactive arthritis closely resemble those of AS. Treatment is based on symptoms.

SYSTEMIC LUPUS ERYTHEMATOSUS

Systemic lupus erythematosus (SLE) is a multisystem inflammatory autoimmune disease. It is a complex disorder of multifactorial origin resulting from interactions among genetic, hormonal, environmental, and immune factors. SLE typically affects the skin, joints, and serous membranes (pleura, pericardium). Renal, hematologic, and neurologic systems are often affected. SLE has a chronic unpredictable course with alternating periods of remission and exacerbation.

About 1.5 million people in the United States have SLE. Blacks, Asian Americans, Hispanics, Native Americans, and Pacific Islanders are more likely than Whites to develop SLE. 90% of those with SLE are women. Most people with lupus develop the disease between ages 15 to 45 years.[20]

Etiology and Pathophysiology

We do not know the cause of the abnormal immune response in SLE. Based on the high prevalence of SLE among family members, we suspect a genetic influence. Multiple genes from the HLA complex, including *HLA-DR2* and *HLA-DR3,* are associated with SLE.

Hormones play a role in SLE. Onset or worsening of disease symptoms may occur after the start of menses, with oral contraceptive use, and during and after pregnancy. SLE tends to become worse in the immediate postpartum period. Infections, including the Epstein Barr virus, may stimulate immune hyperactivity.

Environmental factors can contribute to SLE. These include sun or ultraviolet light exposure, stress, and exposure to some chemicals and toxins. Exposure to silica dust in agricultural or industrial settings can be a factor. Drug triggers include those that make a person more sensitive to the sun (e.g., sulfa drugs, diuretics, tetracycline) and penicillin or similar antibiotics. Drug-induced SLE should not be confused with drug side effects, which typically occur within a few hours or days of short-term drug use. SLE generally occurs months to years after continuous therapy with a causative drug.

In SLE, the body makes various autoantibodies against nucleic acids (e.g., single- and double-stranded DNA), erythrocytes, coagulation proteins, lymphocytes, platelets, and many other self-proteins. Autoimmune reactions (antinuclear antibodies [ANA]) are directed against elements of the cell nucleus, especially DNA.

Circulating immune complexes with antibodies against DNA are deposited in the basement membranes of capillaries in the kidneys, heart, skin, brain, and joints. These complexes trigger inflammation that causes tissue destruction. Overaggressive autoimmune responses are related to activation of B and T cells. Specific disease effects depend on the involved cell types or organs. SLE is a type III hypersensitivity response (see Chapter 14).

Clinical Manifestations and Complications

Severity of SLE varies widely. It ranges from a mild disorder to a rapidly progressive disease affecting many body systems (Fig. 69.9). No characteristic pattern occurs in the progression of SLE. The circulating immune complexes can affect any organ. Common tissues involved are the skin and muscle, lining of the lungs, heart, nervous tissue, and kidneys. General problems, such as fever, weight loss, joint pain, and fatigue, may precede worsened disease activity.

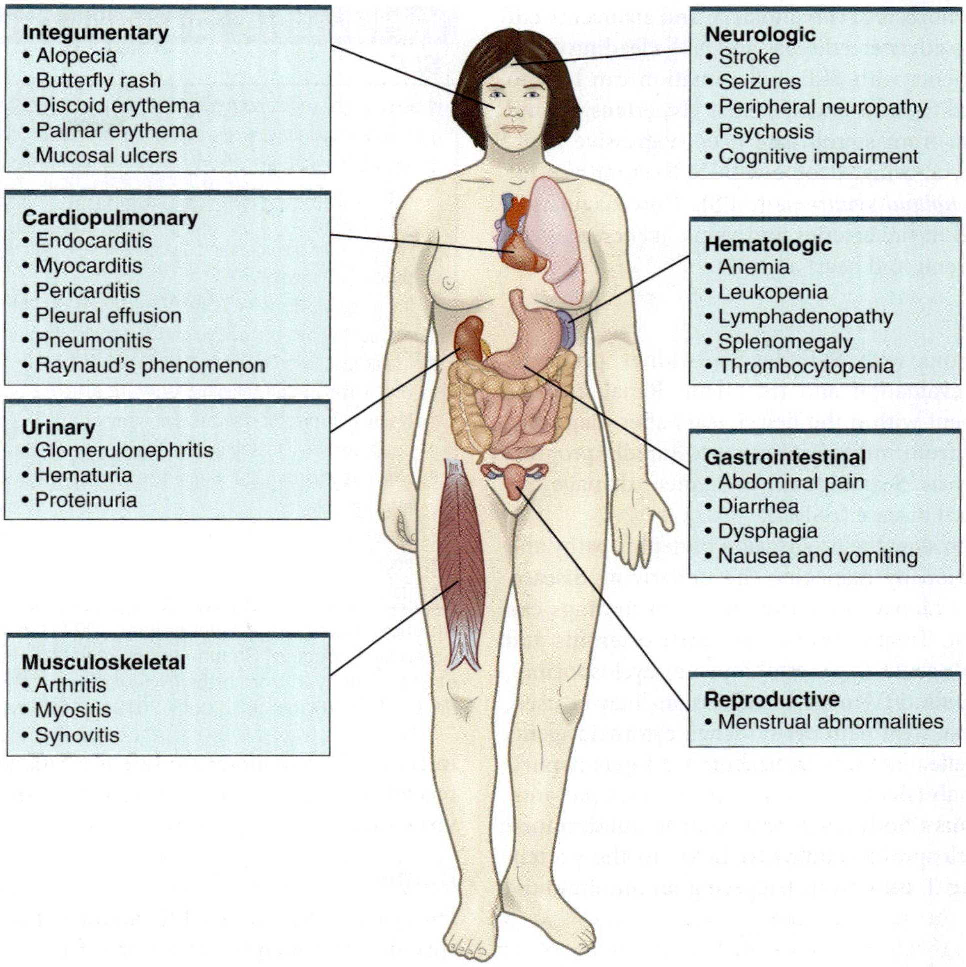

Fig. 69.9 Multisystem involvement in SLE.

Skin Problems

Vascular skin lesions can appear anywhere. Skin lesions are most likely to develop on sun-exposed areas. Severe skin reactions can occur in people who are sensitive to sunlight *(photosensitivity).* For some, the skin rash is the first symptom.

Some patients have a form of lupus limited to the skin. People with *chronic cutaneous lupus erythematosus* (CCLE) have discoid (round, coin-shaped) lesions, usually on the scalp and face. About 10% of patients with CCLE later develop lupus in other organ systems. *Subacute cutaneous lupus erythematosus* (SCLE) is marked by areas of red, ring-shaped lesions. The lesions of *acute cutaneous lupus* appear when the disease is active. The most common form is the classic butterfly rash over the cheeks and bridge of the nose *(malar rash)* that looks like a sunburn (Fig. 69.10). Lesions in SCLE usually do not scar or itch. They are not thick and scaly.[20]

Oral or nasopharyngeal ulcers occur in one-third of patients with SLE. Alopecia is common. The hair may grow back during remission. Hair loss may be permanent over lesions. The scalp becomes dry, scaly, and atrophied.

Musculoskeletal Problems

Arthritis occurs in many patients with SLE. Pain in multiple joints *(polyarthralgia)* with morning stiffness is often the first symptom. It may precede the onset of multisystem disease by

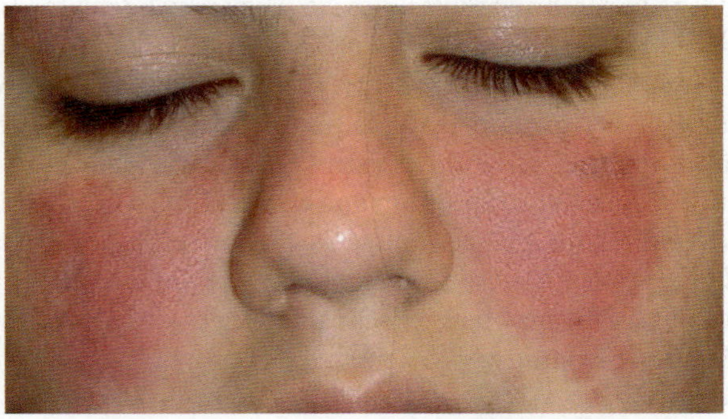

Fig. 69.10 Butterfly rash of SLE. (From Yale Dermatology Residents' Slide Collection. In Bolognia JL, Schaffer JV, Duncan KO, Ko CJ: *Dermatology essentials*, Philadelphia, 2014, Elsevier.)

many years. Diffuse swelling occurs with joint and muscle pain and some stiffness. SLE-related arthritis is often nonerosive. It may cause deformities (e.g., swan neck deformity of the fingers [Fig. 69.4D], ulnar deviation, subluxation with joint laxity). Patients have increased risk for bone loss and fracture.

Cardiopulmonary Problems

Tachypnea and cough suggest the presence of lung disease. Pleurisy is possible. Cardiac involvement may include dysrhythmias due to fibrosis of the sinoatrial and atrioventricular nodes. This shows advanced disease and is the leading cause of death among patients with SLE. Inflammation can lead to pericarditis, myocarditis, and endocarditis. Hypertension and hypercholesterolemia from steroid use need aggressive treatment and careful monitoring. People with SLE are at risk for secondary *antiphospholipid syndrome* (APS). This coagulation disorder causes clots in the arteries and veins. It increases the risk for stroke, gangrene, and heart attack.

Renal Problems

About 40% of persons with SLE develop kidney problems that need medical evaluation and treatment. Renal involvement is usually present within the first 5 years after diagnosis. Manifestations vary from mild proteinuria to rapidly progressive glomerulonephritis. Scarring and permanent damage can lead to end-stage renal disease (ESRD).

The main goal is to slow the progression of nephropathy and preserve renal function by managing the underlying disease. The need for a renal biopsy is controversial, but findings can help guide treatment. Treatments include corticosteroids and immunosuppressive agents (e.g., azathioprine, cyclosporine). Oral prednisone or pulsed IV methylprednisolone may be used, especially in the initial treatment period when cytotoxic agents have not yet taken effect. Newer treatments for lupus nephritis include belimumab (Benlysta), a human monoclonal antibody. It reduces autoantibody levels and controls autoimmune disease activity. Voclosporin (Lupkynis) binds to the protein calcineurin, stopping T cells from triggering an autoimmune response.[21]

Nervous System Problems

Neuropsychiatric manifestations are common. They range from headache to cerebrovascular disease. They may be related to the stress of having a major illness or associated drug therapies. We think that neuropsychiatric SLE (NPSLE) occurs in 1 of 2 ways. *Focal NPSLE* is caused by clots, especially in the presence of antiphospholipid antibodies. A stroke or aseptic meningitis may occur. Headaches are common and can become severe during a disease flare. Small vessel injury in chronic disease may cause vasculopathy. *Diffuse NPSLE* is caused by an inflammatory process. The patient may have psychosis, anxiety, depression, acute confusion, or cognitive problems.

Hematologic Problems

Blood problems are common due to formation of antibodies against blood cells. Anemia, leukopenia, thrombocytopenia, and coagulation disorders (excess bleeding or clotting) are often present. People with SLE are likely to be resistant to the blood-thinning effects of aspirin. Hydroxychloroquine may decrease risk of clots.[22]

Infection

Patients have increased susceptibility to infection. This may be due to impaired ability to destroy invading bacteria, deficient antibody production, and immunosuppressive effects of many antiinflammatory drugs. Pneumonia is the most common infection. Vaccinations are safe for patients with SLE. Patients receiving corticosteroids or cytotoxic drugs must avoid live virus vaccines.

TABLE 69.16 Diagnostic Criteria

SLE

A person is classified as having SLE if 4 or more of the criteria are present, serially or simultaneously, during any interval of observation:

- Antinuclear antibody (ANA): abnormal titer
- Discoid rash: raised patches with scaling follicular plugging; scarring in older lesions
- Hematologic disorder: hemolytic anemia, leukopenia, lymphopenia, or thrombocytopenia
- Immunologic disorder: anti-DNA antibody or antibody to Sm (Smith) nuclear antigen or positive antiphospholipid antibodies
- Malar rash: fixed redness, flat or raised (butterfly rash)
- Oral ulcers: usually painless
- Neurologic disorder: seizures or psychosis (in the absence of causative drugs or known metabolic disorders)
- Nonerosive arthritis: 2 or more peripheral joints with tenderness, swelling, effusion
- Pleuritis or pericarditis
- Photosensitivity
- Renal disorder: persistent proteinuria, cellular casts in urine

American College of Rheumatology: 1997 Update of the 1982 American College of Rheumatology revised criteria for classification of SLE. Retrieved from https://www.rheumatology.org/Portals/0/Files/1997%20Update%20of%201982%20Revised.pdf.

Diagnostic Studies

Diagnosis of SLE is based on distinct criteria (Table 69.16). No specific test is diagnostic for SLE, but a variety of abnormalities may be present in the blood. 97% of persons with SLE have ANA present.[23]

Testing for anti-DNA antibodies, anti-Smith (Sm) antibodies, and antiphospholipid antibodies is expected to identify immunologic disorders typical of SLE. Increased ESR and CRP indicate inflammation but are not diagnostic of SLE. They may be used to monitor disease activity and treatment effectiveness.

Interprofessional Care

A major challenge in the treatment of SLE is managing active disease while preventing complications of treatment. Age, sex, social health determinants, having other problems, and severity influence survival. Prognosis can be improved with early diagnosis, ongoing assessment and prompt recognition of organ involvement, and effective treatment plans.

Drug Therapy

NSAIDs continue to be an important intervention, especially for patients with mild joint pain. The patient may need to try several different NSAIDs to find the most effective one. Monitor the patient on long-term NSAID therapy for GI and renal effects.

Antimalarial agents, such as hydroxychloroquine and chloroquine, are often used to treat fatigue and skin and joint problems. They repress the immune system but do not cause immunosuppression. These drugs may reduce flares. Patients taking hydroxychloroquine should have eye examinations every

TABLE 69.17 Interprofessional Care

SLE

Diagnostic Assessment
- History and physical assessment
- Antibodies (ANA, anti-DNA, anti-Sm, antiphospholipid)
- CBC
- Serum complement
- Urinalysis
- X-ray of affected joints
- Chest x-ray
- ECG to assess cardiac involvement

Management

Drug Therapy
- NSAIDs or acetaminophen for mild disease
- Steroid-sparing drugs (e.g., methotrexate)
- Antimalarials (e.g., hydroxychloroquine)
- Corticosteroids for flares and severe disease
- Immunosuppressive drugs (e.g., cyclophosphamide, azathioprine)

6 to 12 months. Retinopathy can develop over time and with high doses of these drugs. It generally reverses when they are stopped. If the patient cannot tolerate an antimalarial agent, an antileprosy drug, such as dapsone, may be used.

Corticosteroids should be limited to the lowest dose for the shortest possible time. For example, steroids can be used for a few weeks until a slower acting drug becomes effective. Taper the dose of steroid slowly rather than stopping therapy abruptly. High doses of corticosteroids may be appropriate for the patient with severe cutaneous SLE.

Immunosuppressive drugs, such as azathioprine and cyclophosphamide, can suppress the immune system and reduce end-organ damage. Monitor closely to decrease the risk for toxicity and side effects. Because blood clots can be a life-threatening complication of SLE, anticoagulants, such as warfarin or low-dose heparin, may be prescribed.

Topical immunomodulators can be used instead of corticosteroids to treat serious skin conditions. Tacrolimus (Protopic, Prograf) and pimecrolimus (Elidel) suppress immune activity in the skin, affecting the butterfly rash and discoid lesions.

Serial anti-DNA titers and serum complement help us monitor disease management (Table 69.17). ESR or CRP may be helpful.

NURSING MANAGEMENT: SLE

Assessment

Subjective and objective data you should obtain from the patient with SLE are outlined in Table 69.18. Assess the effect of pain and fatigue on ability to perform ADLs.

During a disease flare, the patient may quickly become very ill. Assess fever pattern, joint inflammation, limitation of motion, location and degree of discomfort, and fatigue. Monitor weight, fluid intake, and output. This is especially important if corticosteroids are prescribed because of related fluid retention and possible renal failure. Collect 24-hour urine samples for protein and creatinine clearance as ordered. Observe for signs of bleeding due to drug therapy (e.g., pallor, skin bruising, petechiae, tarry stools).

Carefully assess neurologic function. Observe for vision problems, headaches, personality changes, seizures, and memory loss. Psychosis may result from CNS disease or be an effect of corticosteroid therapy. Nerve irritation of the extremities *(peripheral neuropathy)* may cause numbness, tingling, and weakness of the hands and feet.

Clinical Problems

Clinical problems for the patient with SLE may include:
- Musculoskeletal problems
- Impaired role performance
- Impaired tissue integrity

Additional information on clinical problems and interventions for the patient with SLE is presented in eNursing Care Plan 69.2 (available on the website for this chapter).

Planning

Overall goals are that the patient with SLE will (1) have acceptable pain management, (2) show awareness of and avoid activities that worsen the disease, and (3) maintain optimal role function and positive self-image.

Implementation

The unpredictable nature of SLE presents many challenges for the patient and caregiver. Physical, psychologic, and sociocultural problems linked to long-term management require varied approaches and skills from health care team members. Tell the patient and caregiver that SLE has a good prognosis for most people.

Patient involvement is important for successful self-management. Help the patient understand that adherence to the treatment plan is no guarantee against flares in this unpredictable disease. Several factors may increase disease activity. These include fatigue, sun exposure, emotional stress, infection, drugs, and surgery. Help the patient and caregiver eliminate or reduce exposure to such factors (Table 69.19).

Explain the nature of SLE, treatments, and all diagnostic procedures. Teach patients about their drug therapy. Include indications for use, proper administration, and side effects. Help patients understand that abruptly stopping a drug may worsen disease activity.

Role Performance

The patient with SLE may face many psychosocial issues. Supportive therapies may be as important as medical treatment in helping the patient cope with the disease. Provide emotional support for the patient and caregiver, especially during a disease flare.

Stress the importance of planning recreational and work activities. The young adult may find sun restrictions and physical limitations hard to follow. Help the patient develop and achieve reasonable goals for improving or maintaining mobility, energy, and self-esteem. Those making decisions about marriage and careers worry how SLE will interfere with their plans. Discuss how to approach employers, teachers, and coworkers about the impact of SLE.

TABLE 69.18 NURSING ASSESSMENT

SLE

Subjective Data

Important Health Information

Health history: Exposure to ultraviolet light, drugs, chemicals, viral infections. Physical or psychologic stress. States of ↑ estrogen activity, including early onset of menses, pregnancy, and postpartum period. Pattern of remissions and flares

Medications: Oral contraceptives, procainamide, hydralazine, isoniazid, antiseizure drugs, antibiotics, corticosteroids, NSAIDs

Functional Health Patterns

Health perception–health management: Family history of autoimmune disorders, frequent infections, malaise, impact of disease on functional ability

Nutritional-metabolic: Weight loss, oral and nasal ulcers, nausea and vomiting, dry mouth *(xerostomia),* dysphagia, photosensitivity with rash, frequent infections

Elimination: ↑ Urine output, diarrhea or constipation

Activity-exercise: Morning stiffness, joint swelling and deformity, shortness of breath *(dyspnea),* excessive fatigue

Sleep-rest: Insomnia

Cognitive-perceptual: Vision problems, vertigo, headache, arthralgia, chest pain (pericardial, pleuritic), abdominal pain. Painful, throbbing, cold fingers with numbness and tingling

Sexuality-reproductive: Amenorrhea, irregular menstrual periods

Coping–stress tolerance: Depression, withdrawal

Objective Data

Cardiovascular

Vasculitis, pericardial friction rub, hypertension, edema, dysrhythmias, murmurs. Bilateral, symmetric pallor and cyanosis of fingers (Raynaud phenomenon)

General

Fever, lymphadenopathy, periorbital edema

GI

Oral and pharyngeal ulcers; splenomegaly

Musculoskeletal

Myopathy, myositis, arthritis

Neurologic

Facial weakness, peripheral neuropathies, papilledema, dysarthria, confusion, hallucination, disorientation, psychosis, seizures, aphasia, hemiparesis

Respiratory

Pleural friction rub, ↓ breath sounds

Skin

Alopecia. Dry, scaly scalp. Keratoconjunctivitis, butterfly (malar) rash, palmar or discoid redness, hives, redness at fingernails or toenails, purpura, or petechiae. Leg ulcers

Possible Diagnostic Findings

Presence of anti-DNA, anti-Sm, or antinuclear antibodies. Anemia, leukopenia, thrombocytopenia. ↑ ESR, ↑ serum creatinine. Microscopic hematuria, proteinuria, cellular casts in urine. Pericarditis or pleural effusion on chest x-ray

TABLE 69.19 PATIENT & CAREGIVER TEACHING

SLE

Include the following information in the teaching plan for a patient with SLE and the caregiver:

- Disease process
- Names of drugs, actions, side effects, dosage, administration
- Pain management strategies
- Energy conservation and pacing techniques
- Therapeutic exercise, heat therapy for arthralgia
- Relaxation therapy
- Avoid physical and emotional stress
- Avoid exposure to people with infection
- Avoid drying soaps, powders, household chemicals
- Use sunscreen protection (at least SPF 15) and protective clothing, with minimal sun exposure from 11:00 AM to 3:00 PM
- Need for regular medical and laboratory follow-up
- Marital and pregnancy counseling as needed
- Community resources and health care agencies

◆ SLE and Pregnancy

Because SLE is most common in women of childbearing age, we must consider treatment during pregnancy. Many couples need pregnancy and sexual counseling. They may worry about hereditary aspects and want to know if their children will have SLE.

The HCP and obstetrician should discuss with the woman her desire to become pregnant. For the best outcome, pregnancy should be planned when disease activity is minimal. Some drugs should be stopped (e.g., methotrexate) or switched up to 3 months before the patient tries to become pregnant. Hydroxychloroquine can be safely continued in pregnancy. Infertility may have resulted from renal involvement and use of high-dose corticosteroids and immunosuppressive drugs. The patient should understand spontaneous abortion, stillbirth, and intrauterine growth restriction are common problems. They occur because immune complexes are deposited in the placenta and inflammation occurs in placental blood vessels.

Renal, lung, CNS, and cardiovascular systems may be affected during pregnancy. Women who already show serious effects in these systems should be counseled against pregnancy. Flares are common during the postpartum period. Therapeutic abortion offers the same risk for postdelivery exacerbation as carrying the fetus to term.

◆ Evaluation

The expected outcomes are that the patient with SLE will:

- Use energy-conservation techniques
- Adapt lifestyle to current energy

- Maintain skin integrity with use of topical treatments
- Prevent disease flare with use of sunscreens and limited sun exposure

SCLERODERMA

Scleroderma is a disorder of connective tissue characterized by fibrotic, degenerative, and, sometimes, inflammatory changes in the skin, blood vessels, synovium, skeletal muscle, and internal organs. *Localized scleroderma* mainly affects the skin. It is more common in children. Skin changes of localized disease are usually limited to a few places on the skin or muscle. The prognosis of patients with limited disease is better than for those with systemic disease. *Systemic scleroderma* (or *systemic sclerosis*) is more common in adults.[24] Skin and connective tissue changes progress rapidly during the first months of systemic scleroderma. It is associated with internal organ involvement.

Scleroderma is more common in Blacks, Native Americans, and persons of Japanese descent. The usual age at onset is between 30 and 50 years. Only about 300,000 Americans have the disease.[24] It is more common in women.

Etiology and Pathophysiology

We do not know the cause of scleroderma. We think immunologic and vascular abnormalities play a role in the development of systemic disease. Risk factors include environmental or occupational exposure to coal, plastics, and silica dust.

In scleroderma, the body makes too much collagen (protein that gives normal skin its strength and elasticity) (Fig. 69.11). This leads to progressive tissue fibrosis and occlusion of blood vessels. Collagen overproduction disrupts normal function of internal organs, such as the lungs, kidney, heart, and GI tract. Vascular problems, which involve the small arteries and arterioles, are almost always present. These changes are some of the earliest changes in scleroderma.

Clinical Manifestations

Manifestations range from benign limited skin disease to diffuse skin thickening with rapidly progressive and widespread organ involvement. *Diffuse scleroderma* involves widespread thickening of the skin. This especially occurs in the hands, arms, thighs, chest, abdomen, and face. Blood vessels, heart and lungs, joints and muscles, esophagus, and intestines may be damaged. *Limited scleroderma* affects the face, fingers, hands, and lower arms and legs.

Some patients with limited scleroderma have *CREST syndrome*:

Calcinosis: painful deposits of calcium in skin of fingers, forearms, pressure points

Raynaud phenomenon: intermittent vasospasm of fingertips in response to cold or stress

Esophageal dysfunction: difficulty swallowing due to internal scarring

Sclerodactyly: tightening of skin on fingers and toes

Telangiectasia: red spots on skin from capillary dilation

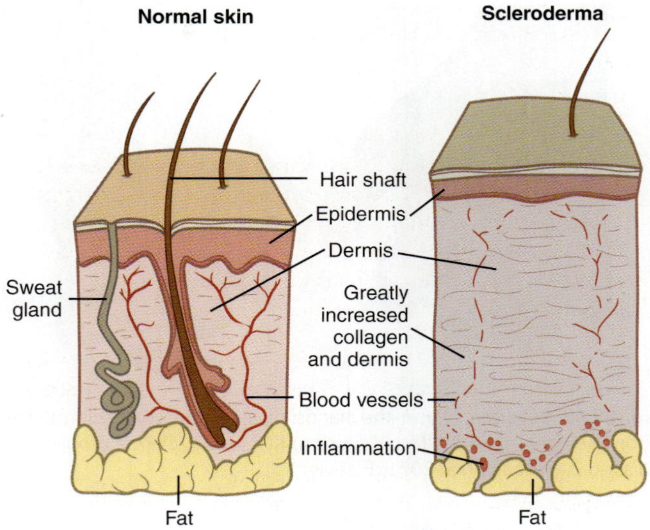

Fig. 69.11 Skin changes in scleroderma.

Raynaud Phenomenon

Raynaud phenomenon (sudden vasospasm of the digits) is the most common first sign in limited scleroderma. Patients have decreased blood flow to the fingers and toes when exposed to cold *(blanching or white phase)*. This is followed by cyanosis as hemoglobin releases O_2 to the tissues *(blue phase)*, then redness during rewarming *(red phase)*. Numbness and tingling often occur. Raynaud phenomenon may precede the onset of systemic disease by months, years, or even decades. Raynaud phenomenon is described in Chapter 41.

Skin and Joint Changes

Symmetric painless swelling or thickening of the skin of the fingers and hands may progress to diffuse scleroderma of the trunk. In limited scleroderma, skin thickening often does not extend above the elbow or knee. The face may be affected. In diffuse disease, the skin loses elasticity and becomes taut and shiny. This causes the typical expressionless face with tightly pursed lips. Skin changes in the face may contribute to reduced ROM in the temporomandibular joint. The fingers may stay in a semiflexed position *(sclerodactyly)*, with tightened skin to the wrist (Fig. 69.12). Reduced peripheral joint function may be an early symptom of arthritis.

Internal Organ Involvement

About 20% of people with systemic scleroderma and a few with localized disease develop secondary Sjögren syndrome, a condition associated with dry eyes and dry mouth.[24] Dysphagia, gum disease, and dental decay can result. Frequent reflux of gastric acid can occur due to esophageal fibrosis. If swallowing becomes difficult, the patient is likely to decrease food intake and lose weight. GI effects include constipation from colonic hypomotility and diarrhea due to malabsorption from bacterial overgrowth.

Lung problems include pleural thickening, pulmonary fibrosis, and abnormal pulmonary function. The patient develops a cough and dyspnea. Pulmonary arterial hypertension and

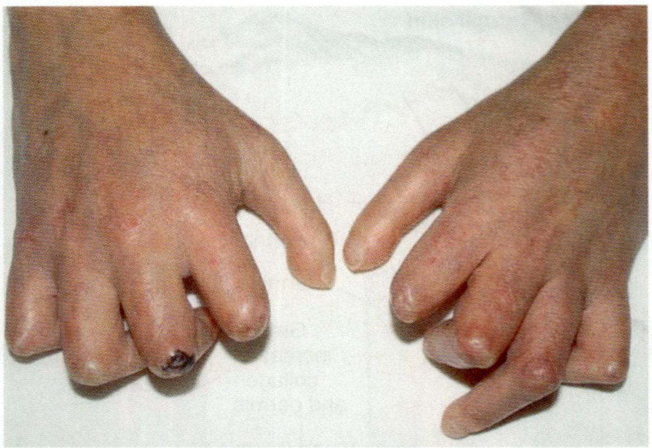

Fig. 69.12 Sclerodactyly in the hands of a patient with scleroderma. (From Bolognia JL, Schaffer JV, Duncan KO, Ko CJ: *Dermatology essentials*, ed 2, Philadelphia, 2021, Elsevier.)

interstitial lung disease may occur. Lung disease is the main cause of death.

Heart disease includes pericarditis, pericardial effusion, and dysrhythmias. Heart failure from myocardial fibrosis occurs most often in patients with systemic disease.

Because malignant hypertension with rapidly progressive, irreversible renal insufficiency can occur, early recognition of renal involvement and initiation of therapy are critical. Dialysis, bilateral nephrectomy in patients with uncontrollable hypertension, and kidney transplant have offered hope to patients with renal failure. Angiotensin-converting enzyme (ACE) inhibitors (e.g., lisinopril) have a marked effect on renal disease.

Diagnostic Studies

Diagnosis is based on the manifestations. No laboratory testing is diagnostic. However, testing is done to rule out other diseases, assess organ involvement, and monitor disease progress. Common tests include CBC, serum muscle enzymes, and ESR. CBC may show mild hemolytic anemia from RBC damage in diseased small vessels. If renal involvement is present, urinalysis may show proteinuria, microscopic hematuria, and casts. Serum creatinine may be increased. Numerous antibodies are related to this condition. Anticentromere antibodies occur in patients with CREST syndrome. Antibodies to topoisomerase-1 are present in about 30% of people with diffuse disease. X-rays may show subcutaneous calcification, distal esophageal hypomotility, or bibasilar pulmonary fibrosis. Pulmonary function studies show decreased vital capacity and lung compliance. Thermography can detect temperature differences between affected and normal tissue. Soft tissue can be assessed with ultrasound and MRI.

Interprofessional Care

There is no specific treatment (Table 69.20). Supportive care is directed toward preventing or treating complications of involved organs. PT helps to maintain joint mobility and preserve muscle strength. Occupational therapy assists the patient in maintaining functional abilities.

TABLE 69.20 Interprofessional Care

Scleroderma

Diagnostic Assessment
- History and physical assessment
- Antibodies to topoisomerase-1
- Anticentromere antibody
- Nail bed capillary microscopy
- Chest x-ray
- Skin or organ biopsy
- Urinalysis (proteinuria, hematuria, casts)
- Pulmonary function tests
- ECG

Management
- Physical therapy
- Occupational therapy

Drug Therapy
- Vasoactive agents: reserpine, bosentan, epoprostenol
- Calcium channel blockers: diltiazem, nifedipine
- ACE inhibitors: lisinopril (Prinivil)
- PDE5 inhibitors: sildenafil, tadalafil
- Immunosuppressive drugs: cyclophosphamide, mycophenolate mofetil

Drug Therapy

Vasoactive agents are often prescribed in early disease.[25] Calcium channel blockers (e.g., nifedipine, diltiazem) and the angiotensin II blocker losartan are common treatments for Raynaud phenomenon. Reserpine, an α-adrenergic blocking agent, increases blood flow to the fingers. Bosentan (Tracleer), an endothelin-receptor antagonist, and the vasodilator epoprostenol (Flolan) may improve blood flow to the lung.

NSAIDs and topical agents may give some relief from joint pain. Capsaicin cream may be useful, not only as a local analgesic but also as a vasodilator. Other therapies prescribed to treat specific systemic problems include (1) tetracycline for diarrhea caused by bacterial overgrowth, (2) histamine (H_2) receptor blockers or proton pump inhibitors (e.g., omeprazole) for reflux, and (3) antihypertensive agent (e.g., captopril, propranolol) for hypertension with renal involvement. Immunosuppressive drugs (e.g., cyclophosphamide) are used in severe cases.

NURSING MANAGEMENT: SCLERODERMA

Nursing interventions often begin during hospitalization for diagnosis. Assess vital signs, weight, intake and output, respiratory and bowel function, and joint ROM regularly to plan care. Stress and cold ambient temperatures may aggravate Raynaud phenomenon. Avoid finger-stick blood testing because of compromised circulation and poor healing.

Teaching is important. Obvious changes in the face and hands often lead to poor self-image and loss of mobility and function. Teach the patient to regularly take part in therapeutic exercises at home to prevent skin retraction and promote vascularization. Mouth excursion (yawning with an open mouth) is a good exercise to help with temporomandibular joint function. Isometric exercises are best if the patient has arthropathy because no joint movement occurs. Encourage the use of moist heat applications or paraffin baths to promote skin flexibility in the hands and feet. Teach the patient to use assistive devices as needed and organize activities to preserve strength and reduce disability.

Teach the patient to protect the hands and feet from cold exposure. Protect against burns or cuts that may heal slowly. Encourage the patient to avoid smoking because of its vasoconstricting effect. Report signs of infection promptly. Use alcohol-free lotions to improve skin dryness and cracking. They must be rubbed in for a long time to be absorbed through the thick skin.

Remind the patient to reduce dysphagia by eating small, frequent meals, chewing carefully and slowly, and drinking fluids. A consultation with a dietitian is helpful. Drugs for GERD and sitting upright for at least 2 hours after eating decrease the risk for heartburn. Using extra pillows or raising the head of the bed on blocks may reduce gastroesophageal reflux during the night.

Job alterations are often needed due to problems with climbing stairs, using a computer, writing, and being exposed to cold. The patient may be socially withdrawn as skin tightening changes the appearance of the face and hands. Dining out may become socially embarrassing because of the patient's small mouth, swallowing difficulty, and reflux. Some persons with scleroderma wear gloves to protect fingertip ulcers and provide extra warmth. Emphasize daily oral hygiene to avoid increased tooth and gum problems. The patient needs a dentist who is familiar with scleroderma and able to adapt care to a small mouth.

Psychologic support, biofeedback training, and relaxation can reduce stress and improve sleeping habits. Sexual problems from body changes, pain, muscular weakness, limited mobility, decreased self-esteem, erectile dysfunction, and decreased vaginal secretions may require sensitive counseling.

CHECK YOUR PRACTICE

A 34-year-old woman hospitalized for aspiration pneumonia has a 5-year history of scleroderma.

- How could scleroderma have contributed to the aspiration pneumonia?
- What strategies will you suggest to decrease the risk for pneumonia recurrence?
- What other self-care strategies will you reinforce with this patient?

AUTOIMMUNE MYOSITIS

Autoimmune myositis is a group of systemic disorders. **Polymyositis (PM)** is diffuse, idiopathic, inflammatory myopathy of striated muscle. It causes bilateral weakness, usually most severe in the proximal or limb girdle muscles. When muscle changes from PM are accompanied by distinctive skin changes, the disorder is called **dermatomyositis (DM)**.[26] These rare disorders can be similar in signs, symptoms, and treatment, but they are 2 distinct diseases. Patients with PM tend to have more severe disease than those with DM.

They typically affect children ages 5 to 15 years and adults ages 40 to 60 years. PM and DM occur twice as often in women.

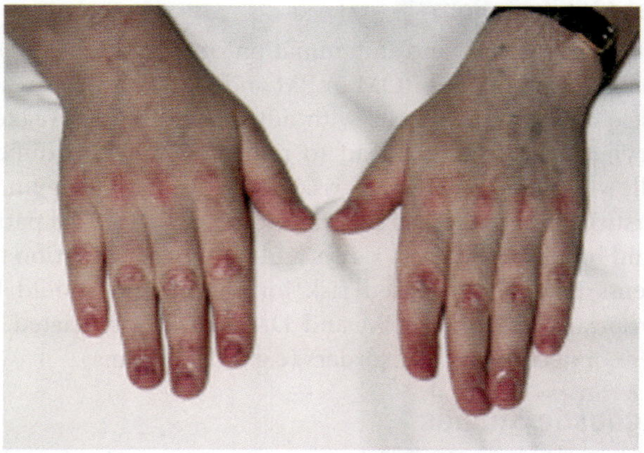

Fig. 69.13 Dermatomyositis skin changes indicating Gottron papules. (From Firestein GS, Budd RC, Gabriel SE, McInnes IB: *Kelley's textbook of rheumatology*, ed 9, Philadelphia, 2012, Saunders.)

Etiology and Pathophysiology

We do not know the cause of PM and DM. We think there is an autoimmune origin with T cell–mediated destruction of unidentified muscle antigens. Environment factors are likely. These include viral and bacterial infection, certain drugs, supplements, vaccines, medical implants, and occupational exposure.

Clinical Manifestations and Complications

Muscular

The patient with PM and DM has weight loss and increasing fatigue, with gradually developing muscle weakness that causes difficulty in performing ADLs. Muscles affected most often are in the shoulders, legs, arms, and pelvis. The patient may have difficulty rising from a chair or bathtub, climbing stairs, combing hair, or reaching into a high cupboard. Repetitive movements are more likely to cause trouble than a single strength exercise. The patient may be unable to raise the head from a pillow as neck muscles weaken. Assessment shows an inability to move against resistance or even gravity. Weak pharyngeal muscles may cause dysphagia and dysphonia (nasal or hoarse voice).[26]

Skin

Rashes are typical with DM. They usually prompt earlier recognition of DM than PM, which has no rashes. Skin changes of DM include a classic red or purple symmetric rash *(heliotrope)* with edema around the eyelids. The typical skin rash is not often found with other disorders. A scaly, smooth, or raised rash may be seen on the knuckles and sides of the hands *(Gottron papules)* (Fig. 69.13).[26] Red, smooth, or scaly patches appear with the same symmetric distribution but sparing the interphalangeal spaces *(Gottron sign)*. The rash can be confused with psoriasis or seborrheic dermatitis. A red, scaling rash *(poikiloderma)* may develop as a late finding on the back, buttocks, and a V-shaped area of the anterior neck and chest.

Hyperemia and telangiectasia are often present at the nail beds. Calcium nodules *(calcinosis cutis)* can develop throughout the skin. They are common in long-standing DM.

Other Manifestations

Joint redness, pain, and inflammation often occur. They contribute to limited joint ROM in PM and DM. Contractures and muscle atrophy may occur with advanced disease. Weakened pharyngeal muscles can lead to poor cough effort, difficulty swallowing, and increased risk for aspiration pneumonia. Interstitial lung disease is a common complication. All patients should have routine chest x-rays and pulmonary function tests. Patients have an increased risk for cancer and should have appropriate screenings. PM and DM may be associated with other connective tissue disorders (e.g., scleroderma).

Diagnostic Studies

Biopsy is the standard for diagnosis. Muscle biopsy shows necrosis, degeneration, regeneration, and fibrosis with pathologic findings distinct for DM or PM. The biopsy should be taken from a muscle with edema found on MRI or weakness. It can also be taken from a contralateral pair of muscles found to be abnormal on EMG.[26] An EMG suggestive of PM shows bizarre high-frequency discharges and spontaneous fibrillation, with positive spikes at rest. Biopsy is not usually needed when skin findings are characteristic of DM. Laboratory tests are helpful, but not diagnostic of either disease. Increased muscle enzymes (e.g., creatine kinase [CK] myoglobin) reflect muscle damage but will decrease to normal or near normal with treatment. Increased ESR or CRP occurs with active disease.

◆ Interprofessional and Nursing Care

PM and DM are treated initially with high-dose oral corticosteroids. We taper the dose based on patient response. Most patients respond well to treatment. Long-term corticosteroid therapy may be needed because relapses are common when the drug is withdrawn. Serial CK values guide treatment effectiveness. When CK values return to normal, we gradually reduce corticosteroid doses. If CK increases, the dose is also increased.

Because the goal is to minimize corticosteroid exposure, a second drug is started at the same time or soon after starting treatment. Immunosuppressive drugs (methotrexate, azathioprine, tacrolimus) may be used in combination with steroids or as a second-line therapy if the patient does not respond to steroids. IV immunoglobulin (IVIG) may be given with corticosteroids or immunosuppressants, but it is not a first-line treatment.

DRUG ALERT

IV Immunoglobulin

- Give slowly to decrease risk for thromboembolic complications.
- Hydrate patient well to decrease risk for thrombosis and renal failure.
- Treat transient adverse effects, such as headache.

Synthetic ACTH injections may help with muscle strength and skin rash. PT can be helpful and is tailored to disease activity. Use massage and passive movement during active disease. Delay more aggressive exercises until disease activity is minimal based on low serum muscle enzymes.

Teach the patient about the disease, therapies, diagnostic tests, and the need for regular medical care. Help the patient understand that the benefits of therapy are often delayed. Patients treated long term with high-dose corticosteroids may become increasingly weak after the initial positive response. This is due to superimposed corticosteroid myopathy.[26] Encourage the use of assistive devices to decrease risk for falls. To prevent aspiration, encourage the patient to rest before meals, maintain an upright position when eating, and choose easily swallowed foods.

Help the patient to organize activities and use pacing techniques to conserve energy. Encourage daily ROM exercises to prevent contractures. When inflammation is decreased, start muscle-strengthening (repetitive) exercises. Home care and bed rest may be needed during acute PM, when the patient may not be able to complete ADLs because of profound muscle weakness.

MIXED CONNECTIVE TISSUE DISEASE

Patients having a combination of clinical features of several rheumatic diseases are described as having *mixed connective tissue disease.* The term describes a disorder with features primarily of SLE, scleroderma, and PM. However, there are no definitive diagnostic features of any one disease. This disease occurs most often in women in their 20s and 30s. People with one connective tissue disease may develop another related disease over the course of several years (known as *overlap syndrome*).

SJÖGREN SYNDROME

Sjögren syndrome is an autoimmune disease that targets the moisture-producing exocrine glands. This leads to *xerostomia* (dry mouth) and *keratoconjunctivitis sicca* (dry eyes).[27] The nose, throat, airways, and skin can become dry. It may affect other glands, including those in the stomach, pancreas, and intestines (extraglandular involvement). This increases the risk for non-Hodgkin lymphoma. The disease is usually diagnosed in people in their 40s and 50s. Most people with Sjögren syndrome are women.

People with primary Sjögren syndrome do not have another rheumatic disease. The secondary form of Sjögren syndrome occurs in combination with another rheumatic disease (e.g., RA, SLE, scleroderma).[27] Autoimmune thyroid disorders, including Graves disease and Hashimoto thyroiditis, are common with Sjögren syndrome.

Sjögren syndrome appears to be caused by genetic and environmental factors. A particular gene predisposes Whites to the disease. Other genes are linked to the disease in people of Japanese, Chinese, and African American ethnicity. The trigger may be a viral or bacterial infection that adversely stimulates the immune system.

In Sjögren syndrome, lymphocytes attack and damage the lacrimal and salivary glands. Decreased tearing causes dry eyes, which leads to a gritty sensation in the eyes, burning, blurred vision, and photosensitivity. Dry mouth causes buccal membrane fissures, changes in taste, dysphagia, and increased mouth infection or dental decay. Dry skin and rashes, joint and muscle pain, and thyroid problems may be present. Other exocrine glands can be affected. For example, vaginal dryness may lead to painful intercourse *(dyspareunia)*. Symptoms may become more generalized and involve the lymph nodes, bone marrow, and visceral organs (pseudolymphoma).

Eye examination (Schirmer test for tear production), measures of salivary gland function, and lower lip biopsy of minor salivary glands aid in diagnosis. Treatment is symptomatic. Instilling preservative-free artificial tears or antiinflammatory eye drops (e.g., cyclosporine [Restasis]) provides adequate hydration and lubrication. Some patients have surgical punctal occlusion.

Encourage increased fluids with meals. Dental hygiene is important. Pilocarpine (Salagen) and cevimeline (Evoxac) can ease the dry mouth and decrease risk of dental caries. Increased humidity at home may reduce respiratory infections. Vaginal lubrication with a water-soluble product, such as K-Y Jelly, may increase comfort during intercourse.

! SAFETY ALERT

Sjögren Syndrome

To help with chewing and swallowing:
- Moisten food with mayonnaise, sauces, gravy, or yogurt.
- Thin foods with skim milk or broth.
- Use a food processor or blender to finely chop or liquefy foods.
- Try soft, creamy foods (e.g., mashed potatoes, macaroni and cheese).
- Drink high-calorie cold liquids (e.g., breakfast drinks).
- Avoid salty, acidic, or spicy foods.

MYOFASCIAL PAIN SYNDROME

Myofascial pain syndrome is a chronic form of muscle pain and tenderness, typically confined to one area in the chest, neck, shoulders, hips, or lower back. Potential but infrequent symptoms include muscle stiffness, fatigue, poor sleep, headaches, and postural abnormalities (e.g., hunching, shoulder rounding, forward head posture). Regions of pain are often within the connective tissue *(fascia)* that covers skeletal muscles. Trigger or tender points are thought to activate a characteristic pattern of pain that worsens with activity or stress.[28]

Myofascial pain syndrome occurs more often in middle-aged adults and in women. Patients report deep, aching pain with a sensation of burning, stinging, and stiffness. It should not be confused with FMS, which is marked by pain and tenderness throughout the body.

Diagnosis is largely by eliminating other conditions that may cause the pain through imaging and tests. The HCP applies gentle pressure to identify tight muscle bands that trigger pain or muscle twitches. We may see posture abnormalities.

Most treatments focus on trigger points. Options include cold laser (low-level light therapy), wet or dry needling, electrical stimulation with electrode application, and transcutaneous electronic nerve stimulation (low-voltage electric signals sent to painful area). Drug therapy includes NSAIDs, lidocaine patch, muscle relaxants, steroids, and the antidepressant duloxetine (Cymbalta).[28] PT, behavior modification, heat, ultrasound, massage, stretching, and acupuncture are helpful.

TABLE 69.21 Common Features of FMS and SEID

Occurrence
Previously healthy, young and middle-aged women

Etiology (Theories)
Infectious trigger, dysfunction in HPA axis, CNS problem

Clinical Manifestations
Generalized musculoskeletal pain, malaise and fatigue, cognitive problems, headaches, sleep problems, depression, anxiety, fever

Disease Course
Variable intensity of symptoms, fluctuates over time

Diagnosis
No definitive laboratory tests or joint and muscle assessments
Mainly a diagnosis of exclusion

Management
Symptomatic treatment may include antidepressant drugs, such as amitriptyline and fluoxetine (Prozac).
Nondrug measures include heat, massage, regular stretching, biofeedback, stress management, and relaxation training

CNS, Central nervous system; *HPA,* hypothalamic-pituitary-adrenal.

FIBROMYALGIA

Fibromyalgia (FMS) is a chronic central pain syndrome marked by widespread, nonarticular musculoskeletal pain and fatigue with multiple tender points. It is a common musculoskeletal disorder and a major cause of disability. FMS affects about 4 million Americans. Women are twice as likely to get FMS.[29] It is the most common cause of musculoskeletal pain in women ages 20 to 55. Symptoms usually appear between ages 30 and 55 years.[30] FMS and systemic exertion intolerance disease (SEID) share many features (Table 69.21).

Etiology and Pathophysiology

FMS involves abnormal central processing of nociceptive pain input in the CNS. PET scans of the brains of people with FMS have shown widespread neuroinflammation. Spinal fluid can contain proteins linked to neuroinflammation. Pain inhibitory pathways do not work effectively. Genetic factors contribute to the development of FMS as a familial tendency exists. People with other autoimmune diseases such as SLE or RA are at risk. Infection or trauma may be a trigger in susceptible people.

Clinical Manifestations and Complications

The patient reports widespread burning pain that fluctuates through the course of a day. The patient often cannot determine if pain occurs in the muscles, joints, or soft tissues. Head or facial pain often results from stiff or painful neck and shoulder muscles. The pain can accompany temporomandibular joint dysfunction, which affects about one-third of patients with FMS.

Assessment usually shows point tenderness at 11 or more of 18 identified tender points (9 pairs) (Fig. 69.14). Patients are sensitive to painful stimuli throughout the body, not just at the identified tender sites. They may have pain in response to

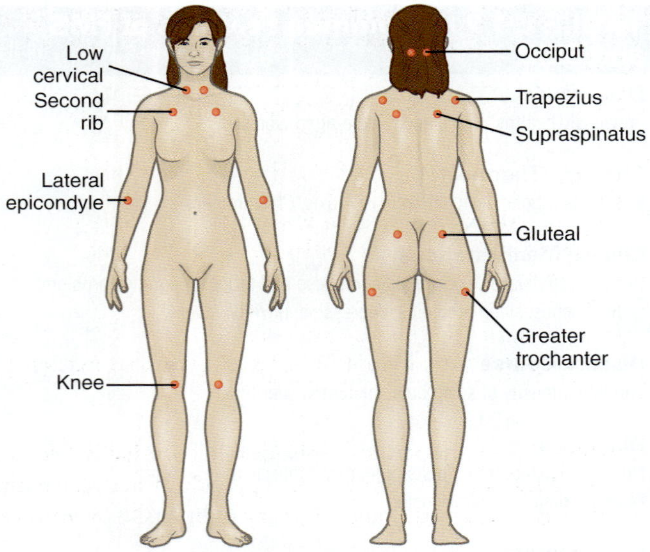

Fig. 69.14 Tender points in fibromyalgia.

a stimulus that does not typically cause pain *(allodynia)*. Point tenderness can vary from day to day. Sometimes, the patient may respond to fewer than 11 tender points. At other times, palpation of all sites may cause pain. Some are very sensitive to pain that would not bother most people.

Cognitive effects range from difficulty concentrating to memory lapses ("fibro fog") and a feeling of being overwhelmed when dealing with multiple tasks. They may be less able to manage stress. Many patients have migraine headaches. Depression and anxiety often occur. Stiffness, nonrefreshing sleep, fatigue, and numbness or tingling in the hands or feet often accompany FMS. Restless legs syndrome is typical. Some describe an irresistible urge to move the legs when at rest or lying down.

Irritable bowel syndrome with constipation and/or diarrhea, abdominal pain, and bloating is common. Patients may have difficulty swallowing, perhaps because of problems in esophageal smooth muscle function. Increased frequency of urination and urinary urgency, in the absence of a bladder infection, may occur. Women may have more difficult menstruation, with disease symptoms worse during this time.

Diagnostic Studies

A definitive diagnosis of FMS is based on 2 elements. First, the Widespread Pain Index (WPI) assesses if (1) pain is experienced in 11 of the 18 tender points on palpation over the past week (Fig. 69.14) and (2) a history of widespread pain is noted for at least 3 months. Widespread pain is defined as pain that occurs on both sides of the body and above and below the waist. Score on the Symptom Severity Index (SSI) is also calculated. To be diagnosed with FMS, the patient must have a WPI score of 7 or more and SSI score of 5 or more, or a WPI score between 3 and 6 and SSI score of 9 or more.[31] Fatigue, cognitive symptoms, and extensive somatic symptoms are considered in establishing a diagnosis.

◆ Interprofessional and Nursing Care

Treatment is symptomatic. Because of the chronic nature of FMS, the patient needs consistent support from the health care team. Encourage the patient to be an active participant in treatment.

Drug therapy for the chronic widespread pain includes pregabalin (Lyrica), duloxetine (Cymbalta), and milnacipran (Savella). Low-dose tricyclic antidepressants, selective serotonin reuptake inhibitors (SSRIs), or benzodiazepines (e.g., diazepam) may be prescribed. SSRI antidepressants (e.g., sertraline, paroxetine) tend to be reserved for patients who also have depression.[32] SSRIs may have to be prescribed at higher doses than when used to treat depression.

Rest can help the pain, aching, and tenderness. In some patients, pain can be managed with OTC analgesics, such as acetaminophen, ibuprofen, or naproxen (Aleve). Nonopioids, such as tramadol (Ultram), may be used. Long-acting opioids are not used unless other therapies are not successful. Short-term use of zolpidem (Ambien) or trazodone can help patients with severe sleep problems. Antidepressants and muscle relaxants have sedative effects that can improve sleep.

Regular, gentle exercise and stretching can help maintain muscle tone and decrease pain. Yoga and Tai Chi are often helpful. Low-impact aerobic exercise, such as walking, can help prevent muscle atrophy. Massage is often combined with ultrasound or use of alternating heat and cold packs to soothe tense, sore muscles and increase blood circulation.

Patients may consider limiting intake of sugar, caffeine, and alcohol because they may be muscle irritants. Vitamin and mineral supplements may help combat stress, correct deficiencies, and support the immune system. Encourage the patient to follow a healthy diet (Box 69.4). Review ways to lose weight with the patient who is obese (see Chapter 45).

Pain and the related symptoms of FMS can cause significant stress. Patients may not cope well with stress. Mental health support is critical. Psychologic counseling (individual, group) and a support group may be helpful. Relaxation strategies include biofeedback, imagery, meditation, and cognitive-behavioral therapy. Patients need initial training for these interventions, but they can continue to practice in their own homes. Stress management is discussed in Chapter 7.

SYSTEMIC EXERTION INTOLERANCE DISEASE

Systemic exertion intolerance disease (SEID), also called *chronic fatigue syndrome* or *myalgic encephalomyelitis,* is a serious, complex, multisystem disease in which exertion of any sort (physical, emotional, cognitive) is impaired and accompanied by profound fatigue. People with SEID are not able to do their usual activities and may even be confined to bed.[33] SEID is a poorly understood condition that can have a devastating impact on the lives of patients and their families.

SEID affects between 800,000 and 2.5 million people in the United States. The condition is 3 times more common in women. The illness is more common in minorities and socioeconomically disadvantaged groups. The true prevalence of SEID is unknown because many people with the disease have not been diagnosed.

BOX 69.4 EVIDENCE-BASED PRACTICE

Nutrition and FMS

You are discharging C.K., a 42-year-old woman who was treated successfully for COVID-19. You note that C.K. was diagnosed with FMS 10 years ago. She has a body mass index of 32 and a history of hypertension. As you discuss C.K.'s home activity orders, she tells you, "I felt terrible even before the COVID. My pain is sometimes so bad that I don't want to get out of bed. It's depressing that I can't lose weight."

Making Clinical Decisions

Synthesis of Best Available Evidence

FMS is a chronic musculoskeletal pain condition characterized by a wide range of symptoms. Osteoporosis has been linked to FMS. Although we do not know exactly how the 2 diseases are linked, research suggests FMS is mediated by common factors. For example, obesity is related to greater pain and disease severity among persons with FMS. Obesity is a risk factor for osteoporosis.

Clinician Expertise

You ask C.K. to describe her usual eating in a 24-hour period. She tells you, "I used to enjoy cooking, but now I can't stand for long periods. My husband hates cooking, so his idea of preparing dinner is bringing home pizza or hamburgers and fries. If I eat breakfast, it is a bowl of cereal. Lunch is often a sandwich and chips." You ask the patient what kinds of food she likes to eat. C.K. says, "I grew up on a farm and used to love fresh vegetables. I also really like fish…but I'm sure I shouldn't be eating fish sticks or fried fish." You ask C.K. if she would be interested in getting information from a dietitian about the Mediterranean diet, a meal plan that includes daily consumption of vegetables, fruits, and grains with weekly intake of fish, poultry, beans, and eggs. You tell C.K. that the Mediterranean diet contributes to improved bone health.

Patient Preferences and Values

C. K. tells you, "Having COVID really scared me. I know I need to eat better and get more active to lose weight. I just need to start with some easy recipes for the right foods." She asks you to schedule her outpatient appointment with the dietitian.

Implications for Nursing Practice

1. In conjunction with the Mediterranean diet, what types of activity should C.K. pursue to lose weight and improve bone health?
2. What might be the benefits of linking C.K. to an FMS support group as she begins the Mediterranean diet?

Reference for Evidence

Correa-Rodriguez M, El Mansouri-Yachou J, Tapia-Haro RM, et al.: Mediterranean diet, body composition, and activity associated with bone health in women with fibromyalgia syndrome, *Nurs Res* 68:358, 2019.

Etiology and Pathophysiology

We do not know the cause or pathology of SEID. Many theories exist about the cause of SEID. Several microorganisms have been researched as causative agents, including herpes viruses (e.g., Epstein-Barr virus [EBV], cytomegalovirus [CMV]), retroviruses, enteroviruses, *Candida albicans,* and mycoplasma. Mental or physical stress may be the cause of SEID. For example, the condition may be triggered by how a patient's immune system responds to stress or illness.

Clinical Manifestations

Severe fatigue is the most common symptom and the problem that causes the patient to seek health care. SEID is often hard to discern from FMS because many clinical features are similar (Table 69.21). In about half the cases, SEID develops slowly, or the patient may have periodic episodes that gradually become chronic. SEID can arise suddenly in a previously active, healthy person. Associated symptoms may vary in intensity over time.

TABLE 69.22 Diagnostic Criteria

SEID

Diagnosis of SEID requires that the patient have the following 3 symptoms:

1. Impaired ability to engage in pre-illness occupational, social, educational, or personal activities lasting at least 6 months and accompanied by profound fatigue
2. Malaise after exertion: total exhaustion after even minor physical or mental exertion that the patient sometimes describes as a "crash"
3. Unrefreshing sleep

At least 1 of the following manifestations is required:

1. Cognitive impairment ("brain fog," confusion)
2. Orthostatic intolerance (lightheadedness, dizziness, imbalance, fainting)

Diagnostic Studies

Physical assessment and diagnostic studies can be used to rule out other possible causes of the patient's symptoms. No laboratory test can diagnose SEID or measure its severity. SEID is a diagnosis of exclusion, based on symptoms (Table 69.22). The patient may become angry and frustrated with HCPs who cannot diagnose a problem.

Interprofessional and Nursing Care

No definitive treatment exists for SEID. Supportive management is essential. Tell the patient what we know about the disease.

NSAIDs can be used to treat headaches, muscle and joint aches, and fever (see Table 12.5). Because many patients with SEID have allergies and sinusitis, antihistamines and decongestants can be used to treat allergic symptoms. Tricyclic antidepressants (e.g., doxepin, amitriptyline) and SSRIs (e.g., fluoxetine, paroxetine) can improve mood and sleep. Clonazepam is an option for sleep problems and panic disorders. Low-dose hydrocortisone to decrease fatigue and disability is being studied.

Teach the patient to avoid total rest because it can create a self-image of the patient as an invalid. On the other hand, strenuous exertion can worsen the exhaustion. Urge the patient to plan a carefully graduated exercise program. Encourage a well-balanced diet, including fiber and fresh dark-colored fruits and vegetables for antioxidant action. Behavior therapy may be used to promote a positive outlook and improve overall disability and fatigue.

The disorder may have a major impact on work and family responsibilities. Some people may need help with ADLs. One major problem facing many patients is loss of livelihood and economic security. When the illness strikes, they cannot work or must decrease the amount of work. Loss of a job often leads to loss of medical insurance. Obtaining disability benefits can be frustrating because of the difficulty of establishing a definitive diagnosis of SEID. Patients with SEID may have severe psychosocial losses, including social pressure and isolation from being labelled as lazy or crazy.

SEID does not appear to progress. Although most patients recover or at least gradually improve, some do not show substantial improvement. Recovery is more common in persons with a sudden onset of SEID.

Case Study

Ankylosing Spondylitis

(© SensorSpot/ iStock.com)

Patient Profile

R.B., a 34-year-old man, comes to the rheumatology clinic with low back pain. He states he has had early morning stiffness that started in the lower back about 6 months ago. He says it is interfering with his work as he "can't move like he used to."

Subjective Data

- Taking acetaminophen, with minimal relief
- Father diagnosed with psoriatic arthritis 15 years ago
- Expresses concern about continued employment due to increasing pain

Objective Data

Physical Assessment

- Severely limited spinal flexion
- Moderate pain over sacroiliac joints
- Mild sternal tenderness

Diagnostic Studies

- Positive ESR, HLA-B27
- Left sacroiliac sclerosis on MRI

Interprofessional Care

- Diagnosed with ankylosing spondylitis
- Started on etanercept subcutaneously once per week, meloxicam once daily

Discussion Questions

1. ***Recognize:*** How will you explain the pathophysiology of AS to R.B.?
2. ***Analyze:*** R.B. asks you if genetic factors are related to AS. How will you respond?
3. ***Plan:*** What referrals may be needed for R.B.?
4. ***Prioritize:*** Based on the assessment data presented, what are the priority clinical problems?
5. ***Act:*** What are some home and work modifications you can suggest to R.B. to facilitate self-care?
6. ***Act:*** Why is an exercise program important in the treatment plan for R.B.?
7. ***Evaluate:*** What outcomes would indicate interprofessional care was effective?
8. Develop a conceptual care map for R.B.

Answers and a corresponding conceptual care map available at http://evolve.elsevier.com/Lewis/medsurg.

BRIDGE TO NCLEX EXAMINATION

The number of the question corresponds to the same-numbered outcome at the beginning of the chapter.

1. In assessing the joints of a patient with osteoarthritis, the nurse understands that Heberden nodes
  a. are often red, swollen, and tender.
  b. indicate osteophyte formation at the DIP joints.
  c. are the result of pannus formation at the PIP joints.
  d. occur from deterioration of cartilage caused by proteolytic enzymes.

2. Assessment findings that the nurse would expect in a patient with rheumatoid arthritis who has articular involvement include *(select all that apply)*
  a. bamboo-shaped fingers
  b. metatarsal head dislocation in feet
  c. noninflammatory pain in large joints
  d. asymmetric involvement of small joints
  e. morning stiffness lasting 60 minutes or more

3. Which drug would the nurse prepare to administer to the patient with acute gout?
  a. Colchicine
  b. Allopurinol
  c. Sulfasalazine
  d. Cyclosporine

4. The nurse should teach the patient with ankylosing spondylitis the importance of
  a. avoiding extremes in environmental temperatures.
  b. regularly exercising and maintaining proper posture.
  c. maintaining the patient's usual physical activity during flares.
  d. applying hot and cool compresses for relief of local symptoms.

5. In teaching a patient with systemic lupus erythematosus about the disorder, the nurse knows the pathophysiology includes
  a. circulating immune complexes formed from IgG autoantibodies reacting with IgG.
  b. an autoimmune T-cell reaction that results in destruction of the deep dermal skin layer.
  c. immunologic dysfunction leading to chronic inflammation in the cartilage and muscles.
  d. the production of a variety of autoantibodies directed against components of the cell nucleus.

6. Which drug would the nurse plan to administer to the patient with Sjögren syndrome with the goal of improving symptoms of dry eyes?
  a. Etanercept (Enbrel)
  b. Pilocarpine (Salagen)
  c. Cyclosporine (Restasis)
  d. Cyclobenzaprine (Flexeril)

7. Teach the patient with fibromyalgia the importance of limiting intake of which foods? *(select all that apply)*
  a. Sugar
  b. Gluten
  c. Alcohol
  d. Caffeine
  e. Red meat

1. b; 2. b, e; 3. a; 4. b; 5. d; 6. c; 7. a, c, d.

For rationales to these answers and even more NCLEX review questions, visit http://evolve.elsevier.com/Lewis/medsurg.

EVOLVE WEBSITE/RESOURCES LIST

http://evolve.elsevier.com/Lewis/medsurg
Review Questions (Online Only)
Key Points
Answer Keys for Questions
- Rationales for Bridge to NCLEX Examination Questions
- Answer Guidelines for Case Study
- Answer Guidelines for Managing Care of Multiple Patients Case Study (Section 12)

Student Case Studies
- Patient With Obesity and Osteoarthritis
- Patient With Rheumatoid Arthritis
- Patient With Systemic Lupus Erythematosus

Nursing Care Plans
- eNursing Care Plan 69.1: Patient With Rheumatoid Arthritis
- eNursing Care Plan 69.2: Patient With Systemic Lupus Erythematosus

Conceptual Care Map Creator
- Conceptual Care Map for Case Study

Audio Glossary
Content Updates

REFERENCES

1. Arthritis Foundation: What is arthritis? Retrieved from https://www.arthritis.org/health-wellness/about-arthritis/understanding-arthritis/what-is-arthritis.
2. Centers for Disease Control and Prevention (CDC): Arthritis-related statistics. Retrieved from https://www.cdc.gov/arthritis/data_statistics/arthritis-related-stats.htm.
3. Arthritis Foundation: Osteoarthritis. Retrieved from https://www.arthritis.org/diseases/osteoarthritis.
4. Arthritis Foundation: Arthritis by the numbers. Retrieved from https://www.arthritis.org/getmedia/e1256607-fa87-4593-aa8a-8db4f291072a/2019-abtn-final-march-2019.pdf.
5. Roberts D: Arthritis and connective tissue disorders. In *Core curriculum for orthopaedic nursing*, ed 7, 2021, National Association of Orthopaedic Nursing.

*6. American Academy of Orthopaedic Surgeons: Treatment of osteoarthritis of the knee: evidence-based guidelines, ed 2. Retrieved from https://www.orthoguidelines.org/topic?id=1005.

7. Arthritis Foundation: NSAIDs. Retrieved from https://www.arthritis.org/drug-guide/nsaids/nsaids.
8. Arthritis Foundation: Rheumatoid arthritis: causes, symptoms, treatments and more. Retrieved from https://www.arthritis.org/diseases/rheumatoid-arthritis.
9. Arthritis Foundation: How rheumatoid arthritis affects more than joints. Retrieved from https://www.arthritis.org/diseases/more-about/how-rheumatoid-arthritis-affects-more-than-joints.
10. Arthritis Foundation: Arthritis and mental health. Retrieved from https://www.arthritis.org/health-wellness/healthy-living/emotional-well-being/anxiety-depression/arthritis-and-mental-health.

*11. Agency for Healthcare Research and Quality: Drug therapy for early rheumatoid arthritis: a systematic review. Retrieved from https://effectivehealthcare.ahrq.gov/sites/default/files/pdf/cer-211-rheumatoid-arthritis_0.pdf

12. Arthritis Foundation: Aspirin. Retrieved from https://www.arthritis.org/drug-guide/nsaids/aspirin.

*13. Butler F, Alghubayshi A, Roman Y: The epidemiology and genetics of hyperuricemia and gout across major racial groups: a literature review and population genetics secondary database analysis, *J Personalized Med* 11:231, 2021.

14. Fields TR: Gout: Risk factors, diagnosis, and treatment. Retrieved from https://www.hss.edu/conditions_gout-risk-factors-diagnosis-treatment.asp.
15. CDC: Lyme disease. Retrieved from https://www.cdc.gov/lyme/index.html.
16. Mayo Clinic: Septic arthritis. Retrieved from https://www.mayoclinic.org/diseases-conditions/bone-and-joint-infections/symptoms-causes/syc-20350755.
17. National Health Service: Ankylosing spondylitis. Retrieved from https://www.nhs.uk/conditions/ankylosing-spondylitis/causes/.
18. Arthritis Foundation: Psoriatic arthritis. Retrieved from https://www.arthritis.org/diseases/psoriatic-arthritis.
19. Arthritis Foundation: Reactive arthritis. Retrieved from https://www.arthritis.org/diseases/reactive-arthritis.
20. Lupus Foundation of America: What is lupus? Retrieved from https://www.lupus.org/resources/what-is-lupus.
21. Huang X, Zhang Q, Zhang H, Lu Q: A contemporary update on the diagnosis of systemic lupus erythematosus, *Clin Review Allergy Immunol* 22:1–9, 2022.
22. Lupus Foundation of America: Antiphospholipid syndrome: evaluating current treatment options. Retrieved from https://www.lupus.org/resources/antiphospholipid-syndrome-evaluating-current-treatment-options.
23. Lupus Foundation of America: The antinuclear antibody (ANA) test. Retrieved from https://www.lupus.org/resources/the-antinuclear-antibody-ana-test.
24. Arthritis Foundation: Scleroderma: Retrieved from https://www.arthritis.org/diseases/scleroderma,
25. American College of Rheumatology: Scleroderma. Retrieved from https://www.rheumatology.org/I-Am-A/Patient-Caregiver/Diseases-Conditions/Scleroderma,
26. Nevares AM: Autoimmune Myositis. Retrieved from https://www.merckmanuals.com/professional/musculoskeletal-and-connective-tissue-disorders/autoimmune-rheumatic-disorders/autoimmune-myositis?query=polymyositis%20dermatomyositis%20prophylaxis.
27. National Institute of Arthritis and Musculoskeletal and Skin Diseases: Sjögren's syndrome. Retrieved from https://www.niams.nih.gov/health-topics/sjogrens-syndrome#tab-overview.
28. American Society of Anesthesiologists: Myofascial pain syndrome. Retrieved from https://www.asahq.org/madeforthismoment/pain-management/types-of-pain/myofascial-pain-syndrome/.
29. CDC: Fibromyalgia. Retrieved from https://www.cdc.gov/arthritis/basics/fibromyalgia.htm.
30. Arthritis Foundation: Fibromyalgia. Retrieved from https://www.arthritis.org/diseases/fibromyalgia.

*31. Galvez-Sanchez CM, Reyes del Paso GA: Diagnostic criteria for fibromyalgia: critical review and future perspectives, *J Clin Med* 9:1219, 2020.

32. National Fibromyalgia & Chronic Pain Association: Fibromyalgia: treatment. Retrieved from https://fibroandpain.org/fibromyalgia/treatment.
33. U.S. National Library of Medicine, Medline Plus: Myalgic encephalomyelitis/chronic fatigue syndrome (ME/CFS). Retrieved from https://medlineplus.gov/ency/article/001244.htm.

*Evidence-based information for clinical practice.

Case Study

Applying Clinical Judgment With Multiple Patients

You are working on the medical-surgical unit and have been assigned to care for the following 4 patients. You have an AP who is helping another nurse and you.

 (© iStockphoto/ Thinkstock.)	J.K. is a 57-year-old woman who had debulking surgery for a temporal-parietal glioblastoma. 4 days ago, she had a hemorrhagic stroke into the site of the tumor bed extending into the thalamus. Has left homonymous hemianopsia. Left arm weakness (3/5) greater than leg weakness (4/5). Vital signs: 150/90, 68, RR 20.
 (© iStockphoto/ Thinkstock.)	M.Y., a 78-year-man, had an ORIF 2 days ago for a fractured left hip. He has a 3-year history of Alzheimer disease and is confused to place and time. He has been pleasant and cooperative. He has a personal alarm and bed alarm on for safety. His hip dressing is dry and intact, and the drainage in the Hemovac drain is minimal.
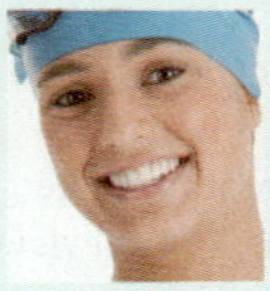 (© iStockphoto/ Thinkstock.)	S.W. is an 18-year-old woman with a C5 cervical spinal cord injury. After spending 1 week in an inpatient rehabilitation facility, she was admitted this morning with severe headaches. She is reporting periodic blurred vision and nausea. Vital signs: 164/94, 84, RR 18.
 (© aronaze/ iStock.com.)	M.C. is a 64-year-old man who had a right proximal femur fracture at the greater trochanter with loss of fixation in the femoral part of a THA he had previously. He had surgery 3 days ago, and discharge is planned today.

1. Highlight all the findings above that require your follow-up.
2. After receiving report, which patient should you see first? Why?
3. Which tasks could you delegate to the AP? *(Select all that apply.)*
   a. Explain discharge instructions to M.C.
   b. Change the dressing on M.Y.'s left hip.
   c. Obtain vital signs on M.C. before discharge.
   d. Assist S.W. with hygienic care and repositioning.
   e. Assess J.K.'s ability to swallow before feeding her breakfast.
4. When you enter the room to assess S.W., you find her diaphoretic with a flushed face and pale extremities. Her BP is 200/102 mm Hg.

Use an X for the nursing actions listed below that are Indicated (appropriate or necessary), Contraindicated (could be harmful), or Nonessential (makes no difference or not necessary) at this time.

Nursing Action	Indicated	Contraindicated	Nonessential
Assess for the presence of any noxious stimuli.			
Direct the AP to stay with S.W. while you contact the HCP.			
Obtain a STAT bladder scan.			
Administer as-needed oral hypertensive medication.			
Place the head of the bed flat.			
Review recent laboratory results.			

Case Study Progression

S.W.'s bladder scan showed 700 mL of urine. Her symptoms subside after you catheterize her. You take this time to teach S.W. about autonomic dysreflexia. You discuss bladder training strategies and how to avoid bladder distention. S.W. is grateful for the information and your caring attitude. As you are finishing, the AP tells you that M.Y. has pulled out his Hemovac drain.

4. What should be your *initial* intervention for M.Y.?
   a. Reinsert the Hemovac drain.
   b. Assess the incision site for a hematoma.
   c. Notify M.Y.'s HCP that the drain was removed.
   d. Apply pressure to the site where the drain was placed.
5. You receive M.Y.'s morning laboratory results and compare them with the day prior.

Laboratory Results

	Postop Day 1	Postop Day 2
RBC	$4.8 \times 10^6/\mu L$	$4.9 \times 10^6/\mu L$
WBC	5000	11,800
Platelets	180,000 μ/L	170,000 μ/L
Hemoglobin	Hgb 10.9 g/dL	Hgb 10.4 g/dL
Hematocrit	Hct 41.2%	Hct 38.2%
Glucose	132 mg/dL	142 mg/dL
INR	1.3	1.4

Choose the most *likely* option for the information missing from statement below by selecting from the lists of options provided.

Based on the laboratory results, you determine M.Y. may be experiencing the priority problem of _____**1**_____. To manage this problem, you expect that the HCP will order _____**2**_____.

Options for 1	Options for 2
Anemia with hypovolemia	Antibiotic therapy
Hyperglycemia	Blood transfusion
Infection	Insulin

6. As you are preparing J.K.'s medications, the EHR system alerts you that patient teaching has yet to be documented for some of her medications. For each medication, select the most likely option for Drug Classification and patient teaching.

Medication	Drug Classification	Patient Teaching
furosemide	Loop diuretic	Take this medication at bedtime
	Potassium-sparing diuretic	Limit oral fluid intake to 1000 mL/day
	Thiazide diuretic	Include foods high in potassium in the diet

Case Study—cont'd

Medication	Drug Classification	Patient Teaching
nimodipine	Calcium-channel blocker	Report a night cough or slowed pulse to health care provider
	ACE inhibitor	This drug may lower blood glucose levels
	Angiotensin receptor blocker	Take on an empty stomach
phenytoin	Serotonin receptor agonist	Maintain good oral hygiene.
	Antiseizure agent	Report the new onset of signs of depression.
	Antineoplastic	Avoid persons who have an infection.

7. Which intervention would be *most* appropriate in caring for J.K.?
   a. Place her left arm in a sling for support.
   b. Arrange the food tray so that all foods are on the right side.
   c. Position her left leg so that the ankle is lower than the knee.
   d. Call the provider to get an order of warfarin to prevent VTE.
8. As you enter M.C.'s room to discuss his discharge plans, you find him all packed up and ready to go. He tells you the AP already told him what he needed to do. What is your *best* initial action?
   a. Ask M.C. if he has any further questions.
   b. Call the AP to M.C.'s room to find out what she told him.
   c. Review discharge instructions with M.C. to ascertain correct understanding.
   d. Give M.C. a telephone number to call in case he has any concerns when he gets home.

Answers and rationales available at http://evolve.elsevier.com/Lewis/medsurg.

A APPENDIX

Basic Life Support for Health Care Providers

Mariann M. Harding

Basic life support (BLS) for HCPs consists of a series of actions and skills performed by the rescuer(s) based on assessment findings. Cardiac arrest is characterized by the absence of a pulse and breathing in an unconscious victim. The current approach for *cardiopulmonary resuscitation* (CPR) is the chest *compressions-airway-breathing* (CAB) sequence.

CARDIOPULMONARY RESUSCITATION

The first action the rescuer performs upon finding an adult victim is assessing for responsiveness. This is done by tapping or shaking the victim's shoulder and asking, "Are you all right?" If the victim does not respond, simultaneously scan the victim's chest for signs of absent or abnormal breathing and perform a pulse check by palpating the carotid pulse for at least 5 but no more than 10 seconds. Remember that gasping and/or irregular or agonal respirations are not considered breathing.

To palpate the carotid pulse, maintain a head-tilt position with 1 hand on the victim's forehead and locate the victim's trachea using 2 or 3 fingers of your other hand. Slide these fingers into the groove between the trachea and neck muscles where the carotid pulse can be felt. The technique is more easily performed on the side nearest you.

If a pulse is felt, give 1 rescue breath every 6 seconds (10 to 12 breaths/min) and recheck the pulse every 2 minutes (Fig. A.1). If no pulse is felt, start CAB.

If the rescuer is alone, the rescuer shouts for help. If someone responds, the rescuer asks them to activate the *emergency response system* (ERS) (if outside of the hospital) or call a code (in the hospital) and get an *automatic external defibrillator* (AED) (if available) or crash cart (in the hospital). If no one responds and the rescuer does not have a mobile phone, the rescuer should leave to activate the ERS, get an AED (if available), and return to the victim before beginning CAB and defibrillation if necessary.

Chest Compressions

The proper technique for providing chest compressions is shown in Fig. A.2. Chest compression technique consists of fast and deep applications of pressure on the lower half of the sternum. The victim must be in the supine position when compressions are performed. The victim must be lying on a flat, hard surface, such as a CPR board (specially designed for use in CPR), a headboard from a unit bed, or, if necessary, the floor. Position yourself close to the side of the victim's chest. More frequently, mechanical chest compression devices are being used to provide chest compressions both prehospital and in the emergency department.

Chest compressions are combined with rescue breathing for an effective resuscitation effort of the adult victim of cardiac arrest. The compression-to-ventilation ratio for 1- or 2-rescuer CPR is 30 compressions to 2 breaths (Table A.1). However, if the patient has an advanced airway (e.g., endotracheal tube, laryngeal mask airway), do not pause between compressions for breaths and deliver 1 breath every 6 seconds (10 breaths/min).

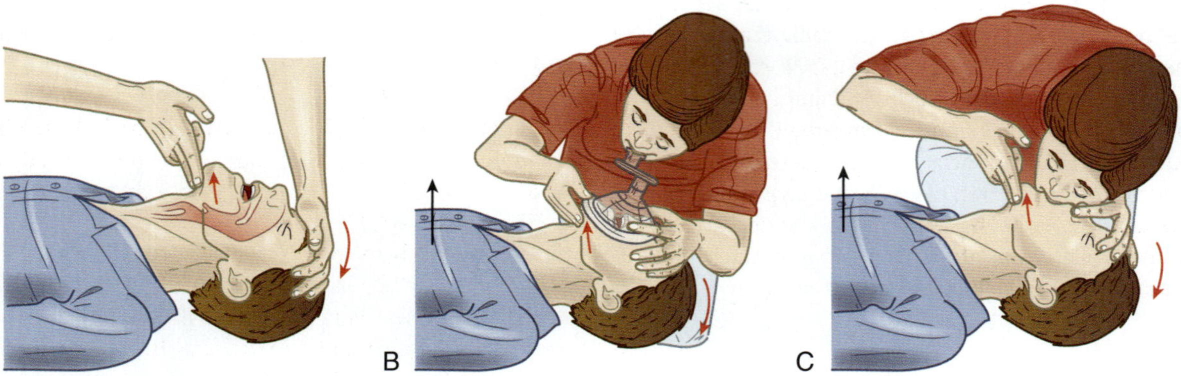

Fig. A.1 The head tilt–chin lift maneuver is used to open the victim's airway to give rescue breaths. (A) Rescuer places 1 hand on the victim's forehead and applies firm, backward pressure with the palm to tilt the head back. The chin is lifted and brought forward with the fingers of the other hand. (B) Mouth-to-barrier device: Rescuer places the device tightly over the victim's mouth and nose and delivers a regular breath. (C) Mouth-to-mouth technique: Rescuer pinches the victim's nostrils, tightly seals mouth over victim's mouth, and delivers a regular breath. NOTE: Rescuer should observe for a rise in the victim's chest *(black arrows)*.

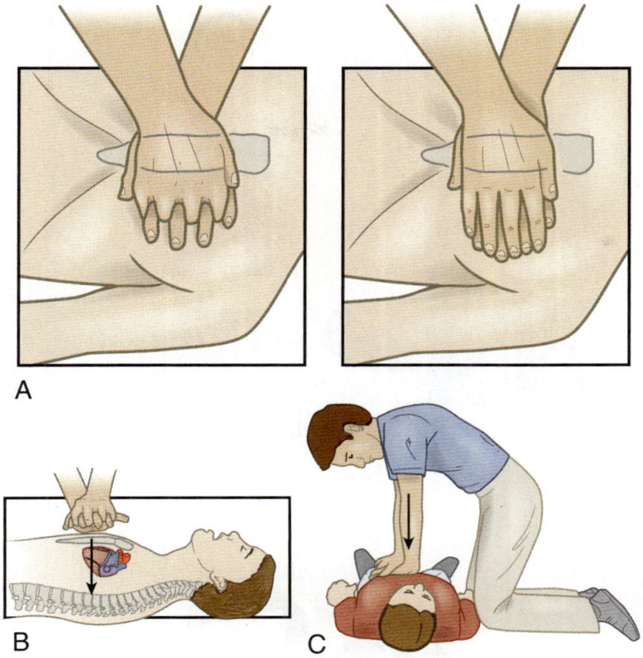

Fig. A.2 CPR. (A) Position of the hands on the lower half of the sternum during chest compressions. (B) When pressure is applied, the sternum is displaced posteriorly with the heel of the hand. (C) Arms are kept straight, and the rescuer pushes deep (at least 2 in [5 cm]) and fast (a rate of 100 to 120 compressions per minute).

If a mechanical chest compression device is not used, it is preferable to have 2 persons performing CPR. One rescuer, positioned at the victim's side, performs chest compressions while the second rescuer, positioned at the victim's head, maintains an open airway and performs ventilations. To maintain the quality and rate of compressions, rescuers should change roles every 2 minutes. Interruptions in CPR should be limited.

Defibrillation

When the AED or advanced cardiovascular life support (ACLS) team arrives, assess the victim's rhythm. If the victim has a shockable rhythm (e.g., ventricular tachycardia, ventricular fibrillation), deliver 1 shock and immediately resume CPR for about 2 minutes before checking the rhythm again. If the rhythm is not a shockable rhythm, immediately resume CPR and recheck the rhythm after 2 minutes. CPR should continue between rhythm checks and shocks and until the ACLS team arrives or the victim shows signs of movement.

The American Heart Association includes training in the use of AEDs with BLS instruction of HCPs and laypersons. Survival from cardiac arrest is the highest when immediate CPR is provided and defibrillation occurs within 3 to 5 minutes. AEDs are found in many out-of-hospital, public settings (Fig. A.3).

Airway and Breathing

If a victim has a pulse but is gasping (e.g., agonal breathing) or not breathing, establish an open airway and begin rescue breathing. Open an adult's airway by hyperextending the head (Fig. A.1). Use the *head tilt–chin lift maneuver.* This involves tilting the head back with 1 hand and lifting the chin forward with the fingers of the other hand. Use the *jaw-thrust maneuver* if you suspect a cervical spine injury. Try to provide ventilation to the victim using a mouth-to-barrier (recommended) device (e.g., face mask or bag-valve mask) or mouth-to-mouth resuscitation (Fig. A.1B and C).

For mouth-to-mouth resuscitation give ventilations with the victim's nostrils pinched. Take a regular (not deep) breath and tightly seal your lips around the victim's mouth. Give 1 breath and watch for a rise in the victim's chest. Continue rescue breaths at a rate of 10 to 12 per minute. When the victim has a tracheostomy, give ventilations through the stoma.

If the victim cannot be ventilated, proceed with CPR. When providing the next rescue breaths, look for any objects in the victim's mouth. If any objects are visible, remove them (Table A.2).

TABLE A.1 Adult 1- and 2-Rescuer Basic Life Support With AED

Assess
Determine unresponsiveness: tap or shake victim's shoulder; shout, "Are you all right?"
Check for no breathing or abnormal breathing (e.g., gasping) while simultaneously performing a pulse check (5–10 sec).
Activate Emergency Response System (ERS)
Activate ERS (e.g., call 911) and get the AED (if available) (outside of hospital).
Call a code and ask for the AED or crash cart (in hospital).
Begin High-Quality CPR
If victim has a pulse but is not breathing or not breathing adequately, begin rescue breathing at a rate of 1 breath every 3–5 sec, or about 12–20/min (Fig. A.1). Recheck the pulse every 2 min.[a]
If there is no pulse, expose the victim's chest and immediately begin chest compressions (Fig. A.2).
Deliver compressions at a rate of 100–120/min.
Compress the chest at least 2 in (5 cm) but not greater than 2.4 in (6 cm).
Allow for complete chest recoil after each compression.
Deliver a compression-ventilation ratio of 30 compressions to 2 breaths.[b]
Minimize interruptions in compressions by delivering the 2 breaths in <10 sec.
Deliver Effective Breaths
Open airway adequately (Fig. A.1A).
Deliver breath to produce a visible chest rise (Fig. A.1B and C).
Avoid excessive ventilation.
Integrate Prompt Use of the AED
Use AED as soon as possible.
If rhythm is shockable, deliver 1 shock and then resume chest compressions immediately after delivery of shock.
If the rhythm is not shockable, resume CPR and recheck rhythm every 5 cycles.
Continue CPR
Continue CPR between rhythm checks and shocks, and until ACLS providers arrive or the victim shows signs of movement.

[a]If possible opioid overdose, give naloxone if available and per protocol.
[b]For patients with ongoing CPR and an advanced airway in place, a ventilation rate of 1 breath every 6 seconds (10 breaths/min) with no interruption in compressions is recommended.
Source: American Heart Association: *Basic life support provider manual,* Dallas, 2020, The Association.

TABLE A.2 Management of the Adult Choking Victim

Conscious Adult Choking Victim

Assess victim for severe airway obstruction.

Look for any of the following signs:

- Poor or no air exchange
- Clutching the neck with the hands, making the universal choking sign
- Weak, ineffective cough or no cough at all
- High-pitched noise while inhaling or no noise at all
- Increased respiratory difficulty
- Possible cyanosis

Ask the victim if he or she is choking. If the victim nods yes and cannot talk or has any of the symptoms noted above, severe airway obstruction is present and you must take immediate action.

Abdominal Thrusts (Heimlich Maneuver) With Standing or Sitting Victim (Fig. A.4)

1. Stand or kneel behind victim and wrap arms around the victim's waist.
2. Make fist with 1 hand.
3. Place thumb side of fist against victim's abdomen. Position fist midline, slightly above navel and well below breastbone.
4. Grasp fist with other hand and press fist into victim's abdomen with a quick, forceful upward thrust.
5. Give each new thrust with a separate, distinct movement to relieve the obstruction. *Caution:* If victim is pregnant or obese, give chest thrusts instead of abdominal thrusts. Position hands (as described) over lower portion of the breastbone and apply quick backward thrusts.
6. Repeat thrusts until object is expelled or victim becomes unresponsive.

Unconscious Adult Choking Victim

If you see a choking victim collapse and become unresponsive:

1. Activate the emergency response system.
2. Lower the victim to the ground and begin CPR, starting with compressions (do not check for a pulse).
3. Open the victim's mouth wide each time you prepare to give breaths. Look for the object. If you see the object and can easily remove it, do so with your fingers. If you do not see the object, continue with CPR using the chest compression–airway–breathing sequence (Table A.1).
4. If efforts to ventilate are unsuccessful, continue with CPR.

Source: American Heart Association: *Basic life support provider manual,* Dallas, 2020, The Association.

Fig. A.3 AED located in an airport.

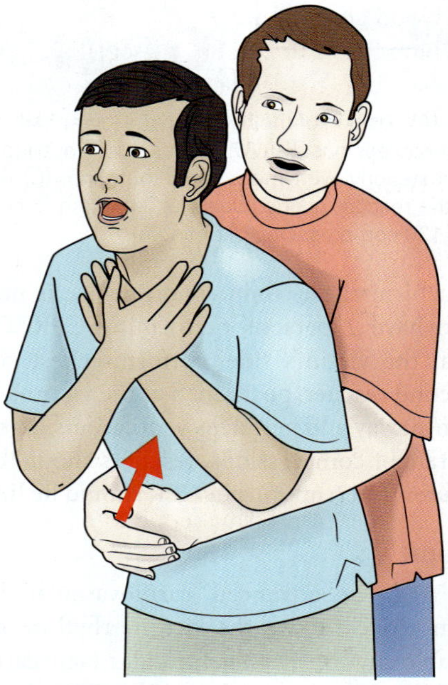

Fig. A.4 Abdominal thrusts (Heimlich maneuver) administered to a conscious (standing) choking victim.

HANDS-ONLY CPR

Hands-only CPR can be used to help adult victims who suddenly collapse from cardiac arrest outside of a health care setting. If an untrained person witnesses the event, the person should provide compression-only CPR. If you are trained and witness the event (as a bystander), you should provide conventional CPR (described previously). If you are unable to do so, provide chest compressions only (push fast and deep in the center of the chest). Both methods are effective when done in the first few minutes of an out-of-hospital cardiac arrest.

APPENDIX B

Clinical Problems With Definitions

1. Acid-Base Imbalance: Imbalance in the state of equilibrium between the acidity and alkalinity of body fluids.
2. Activity Intolerance: Inadequate energy to complete daily activities or desired activities.
3. Allergy: Hypersensitivity induced by exposure to an allergen, resulting in harmful immune responses on subsequent exposures.
4. Altered Blood Glucose Level: Impaired ability to maintain optimal blood glucose levels.
5. Altered Blood Pressure: A force propelling blood through the body at a level inadequate for perfusion.
6. Altered Temperature: Inability to maintain core body temperature from 36.2°C to 37.6°C (97.0°F to 100°F).
7. Anxiety: Feelings of threat, fear, apprehension, danger, or distress.
8. Body Weight Problem: Being either overweight or underweight.
9. Caregiver Role Strain: Distress in performing responsibilities of providing health-related care for a family member or significant other.
10. Continuity of Care Problem: Inadequate coordination across aspects of health care, including a lack of consistency in being able to see the same provider, poor communication and transfer of information across providers and settings, and a lack of follow-up/ongoing monitoring.
11. Cultural Belief Conflict: Differences in values and beliefs that place a person at odds with health care providers or health recommendations.
12. Decisional Conflict: A delay in making a health or treatment choice with accompanying distress and/or uncertainty about the choice.
13. Deficient Knowledge: Lacking information on a specific topic.
14. Depressed Mood: Depressed mood lasting 2 weeks or longer and accompanied by lack of pleasure or interest in most other activities.
15. Difficulty Coping: Inadequate personal ability to manage problems, stress, or responsibilities.
16. Dying Process: Progress toward the end of life.
17. Electrolyte Imbalance: Higher or lower than normal concentrations of an electrolyte.
18. Emotional Problem: An emotional state that interferes with or results in functional impairment.
19. Fatigue: Lack of physical and/or mental energy that interferes with usual and desired activities.
20. Fluid Imbalance: Any change in or modification of body fluid balance.
21. Grief: A pattern of physical and emotional responses to bereavement, separation, or loss.
22. Health Care–Associated Complication: A detrimental patient condition that occurs during the process of providing health care.
23. Health Maintenance Alteration: Impaired ability to manage health and/or access help to maintain health.
24. Impaired Bowel Elimination: Difficulty with formation and evacuation of stool.
25. Impaired Cardiac Function: Inadequate blood pumped from the heart to meet the body's needs.
26. Impaired Cognition: An observable or measurable disturbance in one or more of the thinking processes resulting from an abnormality within the brain or a factor interfering with normal brain function.
27. Impaired Communication: Impediment or blockage to exchanging thoughts, messages, or information.
28. Impaired Endocrine Function: A problem involving the mechanisms that regulate the secretion and action of hormones of the endocrine system.
29. Impaired Family Function: Inability of the family to meet family members' needs.
30. Impaired Fertility: Impaired capacity to reproduce or conceive.
31. Impaired Gastrointestinal Function: Impaired ability of the gastrointestinal system to the ability to ingest, absorb, and/or digest food.
32. Impaired Growth and Development: A delay or decline in growth or one or more areas of development.
33. Impaired Immunity: Impaired ability of the body to resist disease.
34. Impaired Psychologic Status: A state in which there is a loss of contact with reality.
35. Impaired Respiratory Function: Inability to ventilate, clear the airway, and/or diffuse oxygen and carbon dioxide.
36. Impaired Role Performance: Impaired ability to perform normal daily activities required to fulfill usual roles in the family, workplace, and community.
37. Impaired Sexual Function: Presence of a problem with sexual function that prevents the person from experiencing satisfaction from sexual activity.
38. Impaired Sleep: Not obtaining adequate sleep.
39. Impaired Socialization: Insufficient or excessive quantity or ineffective quality of human interaction.

40. Impaired Tissue Integrity: Damage, inflammation, or lesion to the skin or underlying structures.
41. Impaired Urinary Elimination: Difficulty with the collection and discharge of urine.
42. Inadequate Community Resources: Deficiency in environmental support for health.
43. Inadequate Tissue Perfusion: Inadequate blood circulation to a particular area of the body.
44. Increased Intracranial Pressure: A potentially life-threatening situation that results from an increase in brain tissue, blood, and/or cerebrospinal fluid within the skull.
45. Infant Feeding Problem: Any difficulty with the effective feeding of an infant.
46. Infection: Disease caused by the invasion of the body by pathogenic microorganisms.
47. Inflammation: Immunologic response to tissue injury, infection, or allergy.
48. Literacy Problem: Limited ability to obtain and understand basic health information needed to make appropriate health decisions.
49. Musculoskeletal Problem: Impaired ability to move one or more extremities.
50. Negative Self-Image: Negative self-evaluation of oneself.
51. Neurologic Problem: Impaired cognition, motor, sensory, and/or regulatory functions of the central or peripheral nervous system.
52. Nonadherence: An intentional choice to omit or an unintentional overlooking of health-promoting actions.
53. Nutritionally Compromised: Condition of poor nutrition due to intake of unbalanced or insufficient quality of nutrients.
54. Pain: An unpleasant sensory and emotional experience associated with actual or potential tissue damage.
55. Parenting Problem: Inability or change of the parent to provide care that promotes optimal growth and development of the child.
56. Personal Care Problem: Impaired ability to adequately perform personal care.
57. Risk for Disease: A characteristic, condition, or behavior that increases the likelihood of developing a disease or being injured.
58. Risk for Environmental Injury: Risk for adverse health outcomes associated with exposure to environmental contaminants.
59. Risk for Impaired Skin Integrity: At risk for loss of intact skin/tissue barrier.
60. Risk for Infection: Increased risk for a disease caused by the invasion of the body by pathogenic microorganisms.
61. Risk for Injury: State in which a person is at an increased risk for harm.
62. Risk for Perinatal Problems: Increased risk for complications during the perinatal period.
63. Sensory Deficit: Impaired ability to hear, see, taste, smell, or correctly perceive touch.
64. Socioeconomic Difficulty: Challenges to health based on income, educational attainment, financial security, and subjective perceptions of social status and social class.
65. Spiritual Problem: Distress associated with conflicts regarding meaning and purpose in life.
66. Substance Use: Dependence on a substance that leads to detrimental effects to the person's physical or mental health, or the welfare of others.
67. Victim of Violence: Having been harmed or under threat of harm by another person.
68. Violent Behavior: Force, physical or emotional, exerted to cause injury to others or destruction of property.

Laboratory Reference Intervals

The tables in this appendix list some of the most common tests, their reference intervals (formally referred to as *normal values*), and possible causes of abnormal results. Laboratory results may vary depending on different techniques or different laboratories. Abbreviations appearing in the tables are defined as follows:

mEq = milliequivalent
mm Hg = millimeter of mercury
mm = millimeter
mOsm = milliosmole
L = liter
dL = deciliter (10^{-1} liter)
mL = milliliter (10^{-3} liter)
μL = microliter (10^{-6} liter, 10^{-3} milliliter)
fL = femtoliter (10^{-15} liter, 10^{-12} milliliter)
g = gram
mg = milligram (10^{-3} gram)
mcg = microgram (10^{-6} gram)
ng = nanogram (10^{-9} gram)
pg = picogram (10^{-12} gram)
U = unit
μU = microunit
IU = international unit
mU= milliunit
mmol = millimole (10^{-3} mole)
μmol = micromole (10^{-6} mole)
nmol = nanomole (10^{-9} mole)
pmol = picomole (10^{-12} mole)
kPa = kilopascal
μkat = microkatal

Source: Rafai N, Horvath AR, Wittwer CT, Tietz NW: *Tietz textbook of clinical chemistry and molecular diagnostics*, ed 6, St Louis, 2018, Elsevier.

TABLE C.1 Serum, Plasma, and Whole Blood Chemistries

	REFERENCE INTERVALS		POSSIBLE CAUSE	
Test	**Conventional Units**	**SI Units**	**High**	**Low**
Aldolase	22–59 mU/L	22–59 mU/L	Skeletal muscle disease	Muscle-wasting disease
α_1-Antitrypsin	85–213 mg/dL	0.85–2.13 g/L	Acute and chronic inflammation, arthritis	Early-onset emphysema, malnutrition, nephrotic syndrome
α_1-Fetoprotein	<40 ng/mL	<40 mcg/L	Cancer of testes, ovaries, and liver	
Ammonia	10–80 mcg/dL	6–47 μmol/L	Severe liver disease	
Amylase	60–120 Somogyi U/dL	30–220 U/L	Pancreatitis, salivary gland disease, perforated ulcers	Acute alcoholism, cirrhosis, extensive destruction of pancreas
Bicarbonate	21–28 mEq/L	21–28 mmol/L	Compensated respiratory acidosis, metabolic alkalosis	Compensated respiratory alkalosis, metabolic acidosis
b-Type natriuretic peptide (BNP)	<100 pg/mL	<100 pmol/L	Heart failure	
Bilirubin			Biliary obstruction, hemolytic anemia, impaired liver function, pernicious anemia	
• Total	0.3–1.0 mg/dL	5.1–17 μmol/L		
• Indirect	0.2–0.8 mg/dL	3.4–12.0 μmol/L		
• Direct	0.1–0.3 mg/dL	1.7–5.1 μmol/L		

Continued

TABLE C.1 Serum, Plasma, and Whole Blood Chemistries—cont'd

	REFERENCE INTERVALS		POSSIBLE CAUSE	
Test	**Conventional Units**	**SI Units**	**High**	**Low**
Blood gases[a]				
• Arterial pH	7.35–7.45	7.35–7.45	Alkalosis	Acidosis
• Venous pH	7.31–7.41	7.31–7.41		
• $PaCO_2$	35–45 mm Hg	4.66–5.98 kPa	Compensated metabolic alkalosis	Compensated metabolic acidosis
• $PvCO_2$	40–50 mm Hg	5.06–7.32 kPa	Respiratory acidosis	Respiratory alkalosis
• PaO_2	80–100 mm Hg	10.6–13.33 kPa	Receiving high concentration of O_2	Chronic lung disease, decreased cardiac output
• PvO_2	40–50 mm Hg	5.04–5.57 kPa		
Calcium (total)	9.0–10.5 mg/dL	2.25–2.62 mmol/L	Hyperthyroidism, hyperparathyroidism, vitamin D intoxication, multiple myeloma	Pancreatitis, hypoparathyroidism, malabsorption syndrome, renal failure, vitamin D deficiency
Calcium (ionized)	4.5–5.6 mg/dL	1.05–1.3 mmol/L	Acidosis	Alkalosis
Chloride	98–106 mEq/L	98–106 mmol/L	Metabolic acidosis, respiratory alkalosis, corticosteroid therapy, uremia	Addison disease, vomiting, metabolic alkalosis, respiratory acidosis
Cholesterol	<200 mg/dL	<5.2 mmol/L	Biliary obstruction, hypothyroidism, idiopathic hypercholesterolemia, renal disease, uncontrolled diabetes	Extensive liver disease, hyperthyroidism, malnutrition, malabsorption
• High-density lipoproteins (HDLs)	*Male:* >45 mg/dL *Female:* >55 mg/dL	*Male:* >0.75 mmol/L *Female:* >0.91 mmol/L	Excessive exercise	Metabolic syndrome, liver disease
• Low-density lipoproteins (LDLs)	*Recommended:* <130 mg/dL		Chronic liver disease, familial hypercholesterolemia, nephrotic syndrome	Hyperthyroidism
• Very low-density lipoproteins (VLDLs)	7–32 mg/dL		Familial hypercholesterolemia, nephrotic syndrome	Hyperthyroidism
Cortisol	8 AM: 5–23 mcg/dL 4 PM: 3–13 mcg/dL	8 AM: 138–635 nmol/L 4 PM: 83–359 nmol/L	Cushing syndrome, hyperthyroidism	Adrenal insufficiency, panhypopituitary states
Creatine kinase (CK)	20–200 U/L	20–200 U/L	Musculoskeletal injury or disease, myocardial infarction, severe myocarditis, exercise, numerous IM injections	
• CK-MB	<4%–6% of total CK	<0.4–0.6	Myocardial infarction	
Creatinine	*Male*: 0.6–1.2 mg/dL *Female:* 0.5–1.1 mg/dL	*Male*: 53–106 μmol/L *Female:* 44–97 μmol/L	Severe renal disease	Decreased muscle mass, dehabilitation
Ferritin	*Male*: 12–300 ng/mL *Female*: 10–150 ng/mL	*Male:* 12–300 mcg/L *Female*: 10–150 mcg/L	Anemia of chronic disease, sideroblastic anemia	Iron-deficiency anemia
Folic acid (folate)	5–25 ng/mL	11–57 nmol/L	Hypothyroidism, pernicious anemia	Alcoholism, hemolytic anemia, inadequate diet, malabsorption syndrome, megaloblastic anemia

TABLE C.1 Serum, Plasma, and Whole Blood Chemistries—cont'd

Test	REFERENCE INTERVALS: Conventional Units	REFERENCE INTERVALS: SI Units	POSSIBLE CAUSE: High	POSSIBLE CAUSE: Low
γ-Glutamyl transferase (GGT)	*Male and Female >45:* 8–38 U/L *Female <45:* 5–27 U/L	*Male and Female >45:* 8–38 U/L *Female <45:* 5–27 U/L	Liver disease, infectious myocardial infarction, pancreatitis, hyperthyroidism	Hypothyroidism
Glucose (fasting)	74–106 mg/dL	4.1–5.9 mmol/L	Acute stress, Cushing disease, diabetes, hyperthyroidism, pancreatic insufficiency	Addison disease, liver disease, hypothyroidism, insulin overdosage, pancreatic tumor, pituitary hypofunction
Haptoglobin	50–220 mg/dL	0.5–2.2 g/L	Infectious and inflammatory processes, cancer	Hemolytic anemia, malnutrition, chronic liver disease
Insulin (fasting)	6–26 μU/mL	43–186 pmol/L	Acromegaly, adenoma of pancreatic islet cells, Cushing syndrome	Diabetes, hypopituitarism
Iron, total	*Male:* 80–180 mcg/dL *Female:* 60–160 mcg/dL	*Male:* 14–32 μmol/L *Female:* 11–29 μmol/L	Excess RBC destruction, hepatitis, massive blood transfusion	Anemia of chronic disease, iron-deficiency anemia, cancer
(Total) iron-binding capacity	250–460 mcg/dL	45–82 μmol/L	Iron-deficient state, polycythemia	Cirrhosis, chronic infections, pernicious anemia
Lactic acid (L-Lactate), venous	5–20 mg/dL	0.6–2.2 mmol/L	Acidosis, liver disease, sepsis, shock	
Lactic dehydrogenase (LDH)	100–190 U/L	100–190 U/L	Heart failure, hemolytic disorders, hepatitis, metastatic liver cancer, myocardial infarction, pernicious anemia, pulmonary embolus, skeletal muscle damage	
Lactic dehydrogenase isoenzymes				
• LDH1	17%–27%	0.17–0.27	Myocardial infarction, pernicious anemia	
• LDH2	27%–37%	0.27–0.37	Pulmonary embolus, sickle cell crisis	
• LDH3	18%–25%	0.18–0.25	Lymphoma, pulmonary embolus	
• LDH4	3%–8%	0.03–0.08	Systemic lupus erythematosus, pulmonary infarction	
• LDH5	0%–5%	0.00–0.05	Heart failure, hepatitis, pulmonary embolus and infarction, skeletal muscle damage	
Lipase	0–160 U/L	0–160 U/L	Pancreatitis, liver disorders, perforated peptic ulcer	
Magnesium	1.3–2.1 mEq/L	0.65–1.05 mmol/L	Addison disease, hypothyroidism, renal failure	Alcoholism, severe malabsorption
Osmolality	285–295 mOsm/kg	285–295 mmol/kg	Chronic renal disease, diabetes, diabetes insipidus	Addison disease, diuretic therapy, SIADH, hypervolemia
O_2 saturation (arterial) (SaO_2)	>95%	>0.95	Polycythemia	Anemia, cardiac decompensation, respiratory disorders

Continued

TABLE C.1 Serum, Plasma, and Whole Blood Chemistries—cont'd

	REFERENCE INTERVALS		POSSIBLE CAUSE	
Test	**Conventional Units**	**SI Units**	**High**	**Low**
Phosphatase, alkaline	30–120 U/L	0.5–2.0 µkat/L	Biliary system obstruction, bone diseases, marked hyperparathyroidism, rickets	Excess vitamin D ingestion, hypothyroidism
Phosphorus (phosphate)	3.0–4.5 mg/dL	0.97–1.45 mmol/L	Bone cancer, hypoparathyroidism, renal disease, vitamin D intoxication, hypocalcemia	Diabetes, hyperparathyroidism, vitamin D deficiency
Potassium	3.5–5.0 mEq/L	3.5–5.0 mmol/L	Addison disease, diabetic ketosis, massive tissue destruction, renal failure, infection, dehydration	Cushing syndrome, diarrhea (severe), diuretic therapy, gastrointestinal fistula, starvation, vomiting
Progesterone (female)				
• Follicular phase	<50 ng/dL	0.5–2.2 nmol/L	Adrenal hyperplasia, choriocarcinoma of ovary, pregnancy, ovarian cysts	Threatened abortion, hypogonadism, amenorrhea, ovarian tumor
• Luteal phase	300–2500 ng/dL	6.4–79.5 nmol/L		
• Postmenopause	<40 ng/dL	1.28 nmol/L		
Prostate-specific antigen (PSA)	<2.5 ng/mL	<2.5 mcg/L	Prostate cancer, prostatitis, benign prostatic hypertrophy	
Proteins			Burns, cirrhosis (globulin fraction), dehydration	Liver disease, malabsorption
• Total	6.4–8.3 g/dL	64–83 g/L		
• Albumin	3.5–5.0 g/dL	35–50 g/L		
• Globulin	2.3–3.4 g/dL	23–34 g/L		
• Albumin/globulin ratio	1.5:1–2.5:1	1.5:1–2.5:1	Multiple myeloma (globulin fraction), shock, vomiting	Malnutrition, nephrotic syndrome, proteinuria, renal disease, severe burns
Sodium	136–145 mEq/L	136–145 mmol/L	Dehydration, impaired renal function, primary aldosteronism, corticosteroid therapy	Addison disease, diabetic ketoacidosis, diuretic therapy, excessive loss from GI tract, excessive perspiration, water intoxication
Testosterone (total)	*Male:* 280–1080 ng/dL	*Male:* 280–1080 ng/dL	Hyperthyroidism	Hypofunction of testes, hypogonadism
	Female: <70 ng/dL	*Female:* <70 ng/dL	Polycystic ovary, virilizing tumors	
T_4 (thyroxine), total	*Male*: 4–12 mcg/dL *Female*: 5–12 mcg/dL	*Male*: 59–135 nmol/L *Female*: 71–142 nmol/L	Hyperthyroidism, thyroiditis, hepatitis, Graves disease, thyroid cancer	Cretinism, hypothyroidism, myxedema, Cushing syndrome, renal failure
T_4 (thyroxine), free	0.8–2.8 ng/dL	10–36 pmol/L		
T_3 uptake	24%–34%	24%–34%	Hyperthyroidism	Hypothyroidism
T_3 (triiodothyronine), total	*Age 20–50:* 70–205 ng/dL *Age >50:* 40–180 ng/dL	1.2–3.4 nmol/L 0.60–2.8 nmol/L	Hyperthyroidism	Hypothyroidism
Thyroid-stimulating hormone (TSH)	2.0–10 µU/mL	2.0–10 mU/L	Myxedema, primary hypothyroidism	Secondary hypothyroidism, hyperthyroidism
Transaminases				
• Aspartate aminotransferase (AST)	0–35 U/L	0–0.58 µkat/L	Liver disease, myocardial infarction, pulmonary infarction, hepatitis	Acute renal disease, diabetic ketoacidosis

TABLE C.1 Serum, Plasma, and Whole Blood Chemistries—cont'd

	REFERENCE INTERVALS		POSSIBLE CAUSE	
Test	**Conventional Units**	**SI Units**	**High**	**Low**
• Alanine aminotransferase (ALT)	4–36 U/L	4–36 U/L	Liver disease, shock	
Transferrin	*Male*: 215–365 mg/dL *Female*: 250–380 mg/dL	*Male*: 2.15–3.65 g/L *Female*: 2.5–3.8 g/L	Iron-deficiency anemia, polycythemia vera	Cirrhosis, pernicious anemia, sickle cell disease
Transferrin saturation (%)	*Male*: 20%–50% *Female*: 15%–50%	*Male*: 20%–50% *Female*: 15%–50%	Hemolytic anemia, iron overdose	Malnutrition
Triglycerides	*Male*: 40–160 mg/dL *Female*: 35–135 mg/dL	*Male*: 0.45–1.81 g/L *Female*: 0.40–1.52 g/L	Diabetes, hyperlipidemia, hypothyroidism, liver disease	Malnutrition
Troponins (cardiac)			Myocardial infarction, myocardial injury	
• Troponin T (cTnT)	<0.1 ng/mL	<0.1 mcg/L		
• Troponin I (cTnI)	<0.03 ng/mL	<0.03 mcg/L		
Urea nitrogen (BUN)	10–20 mg/dL	3.6–7.1 mmol/L	Increase in protein catabolism (fever, sepsis, stress), renal disease, heart failure, myocardial infarction	Malnutrition, severe liver damage
Uric acid	*Male:* 4.0–8.5 mg/dL *Female:* 2.7–7.3 mg/dL	*Male:* 0.24–0.51 mmol/L *Female:* 0.16–0.43 mmol/L	Gout, gross tissue destruction, high-protein weight reduction diet, leukemia, renal failure	Administration of uricosuric drugs
Vitamin B_{12} (cobalamin)	160–950 pg/mL	118–701 pmol/L	Chronic myeloid leukemia	Strict vegetarianism, malabsorption syndrome, pernicious anemia, total or partial gastrectomy
Vitamin C (ascorbic acid)	0.4–2.0 mg/dL	23–114 µmol/L	Excessive ingestion of vitamin C	Connective tissue disorders, liver disease, renal disease, rheumatic fever, vitamin C deficiency
Vitamin D	25–80 ng/dL	25–80 ng/dL	Excess dietary supplement	Liver disease, malabsorption syndromes, osteoporosis, renal disease

$PaCO_2$, Partial pressure of CO_2 in arterial blood; *PaO_2*, partial pressure of oxygen in arterial blood; *$PvCO_2$*, partial pressure of CO_2 in venous blood; *PvO_2*, partial pressure of oxygen in venous blood; *RBC*, red blood cell; *SaO_2*, arterial oxygen saturation.

[a]Because arterial blood gases are influenced by altitude, the value for PaO_2 decreases as altitude increases. The lower value is normal for an altitude of 1 mile.

TABLE C.2 Hematology

	REFERENCE INTERVALS		POSSIBLE CAUSE	
Test	**Conventional Units**	**SI Units**	**High**	**Low**
Activated partial thromboplastin time (aPTT)	30–40 sec[a]	30–40 sec[a]	Factors I, II, V, VIII, IX, X, XI, XII deficiency; hemophilia, heparin therapy, liver disease	Early DIC, extensive cancer
Bleeding time	1–9 min	60–540 sec	Aspirin ingestion, ineffective platelet function, thrombocytopenia, vascular disease, von Willebrand disease	

Continued

TABLE C.2 Hematology—cont'd

	REFERENCE INTERVALS		POSSIBLE CAUSE	
Test	Conventional Units	SI Units	High	Low
D-Dimer	<250 ng/mL	<250 mcg/L	DIC, myocardial infarction, VTE, unstable angina, cancer	
Erythrocyte sedimentation rate (ESR)	<20 mm/hr (some gender variation)	<20 mm/hr (some gender variation)	*Moderate increase:* hepatitis, myocardial infarction; rheumatoid arthritis *Marked increase:* acute and severe bacterial infections, cancer, pelvic inflammatory disease	Malaria, severe liver disease, sickle cell anemia
Fibrinogen	200–400 mg/dL	2–4 g/L	Burns (after first 36 hr), inflammatory disease, stroke, myocardial infarction	Burns (during first 36 hr), DIC, severe liver disease, malnutrition
Fibrin split (degradation) products	<10 mcg/mL	<10 mg/L	Acute DIC, massive hemorrhage, primary fibrinolysis	
Hematocrit[b] (altitude dependent)	*Male:* 42%–52% *Female:* 37%–47%	*Male:* 0.42–0.52 *Female:* 0.37–0.47	Dehydration, high altitudes, polycythemia, COPD	Anemia, hemorrhage, overhydration, cirrhosis, kidney disease
Hemoglobin[b] (altitude dependent)	*Male:* 14–18 g/dL *Female:* 12–16 g/dL	*Male:* 140–180 g/L *Female:* 120–160 g/L	COPD, high altitudes, polycythemia, dehydration, burns	Anemia, hemorrhage, kidney disease, cancer
Hemoglobin, glycosylated (A1C)	4.0%–5.9%	4.0%–5.9%	Diabetes, pre-diabetes	Sickle cell anemia, chronic renal failure, pregnancy
Platelets (thrombocytes)	150–400 × 10^3/μL	150–400 × 10^9/L	Acute infections, chronic granulocytic leukemia, chronic pancreatitis, cirrhosis, collagen disorders, polycythemia, postsplenectomy	Leukemia, DIC, thrombocytopenic purpura
Prothrombin time (protime, PT)	11–12.5 sec[a]	11–12.5 sec[a]	Deficiency of factors I, II, V, VII, and X; liver disease; vitamin K deficiency; warfarin therapy	
Red blood cell count[b] (altitude dependent)	*Male:* 4.7–6.1 × 10^6/μL *Female:* 4.2–5.4 × 10^6/μL	*Male:* 4.7–6.1 × 10^{12}/L *Female:* 4.2–5.4 × 10^{12}/L	Dehydration, high altitudes, polycythemia vera, severe COPD	Anemia, leukemia, hemorrhage, cancer, chronic illness, kidney disease
Red blood cell indices				
• Mean corpuscular volume (MCV)	80–95 fL	80–95 fL	Alcoholism, liver disease, macrocytic anemia	Microcytic anemia, thalassemia
• Mean corpuscular hemoglobin (MCH)	27–31 pg	27–31 pg	Macrocytic anemia	Microcytic anemia
• Mean corpuscular hemoglobin concentration (MCHC)	32%–36%	32–36 g/dL	Spherocytosis	Iron deficiency anemia, thalassemia
Platelets (thrombocytes)	150–400 × 10^3/μL	150–400 × 10^9/L	Acute infections, chronic granulocytic leukemia, chronic pancreatitis, cirrhosis, collagen disorders, polycythemia, postsplenectomy	Leukemia, DIC, thrombocytopenic purpura

TABLE C.2 Hematology—cont'd

	REFERENCE INTERVALS		POSSIBLE CAUSE	
Test	**Conventional Units**	**SI Units**	**High**	**Low**
Reticulocyte count	0.5%–2.0% of RBC	0.5%–2.0% of RBC	Hemolytic anemia, polycythemia vera	Hypoproliferative anemia, macrocytic anemia, microcytic anemia
White blood cell (WBC) count[b]	5000–10,000/mm^3	$5.0–10.0 \times 10^9$/L	Inflammatory and infectious processes, leukemia	Aplastic anemia, side effects of chemotherapy and radiation
WBC differential				
• Segmented neutrophils	55%–70%	0.55–0.70	Bacterial infections, collagen diseases, Hodgkin lymphoma	Aplastic anemia, viral infections
• Band neutrophils	0%–8%	0–0.08	Acute infections	
• Lymphocytes	20%–40%	0.20–0.40	Chronic infections, lymphocytic leukemia, mononucleosis, viral infections	Corticosteroid therapy, whole body irradiation
• Monocytes	2%–8%	0.02–0.08	Chronic inflammatory disorders, malaria, monocytic leukemia, acute infections, Hodgkin lymphoma	
• Eosinophils	1%–5%	0.01–0.05	Allergic reactions, eosinophilic and chronic granulocytic leukemia, parasitic disorders, Hodgkin lymphoma	Corticosteroid therapy
• Basophils	0.5%–1%	0.005–0.01	Hypothyroidism, ulcerative colitis, myeloproliferative diseases	Hyperthyroidism, stress

[a]Values depend on reagent and instrumentation used.
[b]Components of complete blood count (CBC).

TABLE C.3 Serology-Immunology

	REFERENCE INTERVALS		POSSIBLE CAUSE	
Test	**Conventional Units**	**SI Units**	**High/Positive**	**Low**
Antinuclear antibody (ANA)	Negative at 1:40 dilution	Negative at 1:40 dilution	Chronic hepatitis, rheumatoid arthritis, scleroderma, systemic lupus erythematosus (SLE)	
Anti-DNA antibody	<5 IU/mL	<5 IU/mL	SLE	
Anti-Sm (Smith)	Negative	Negative	SLE	
C-reactive protein (CRP)	<1.0 mg/dL	<10.0 mg/L	Acute infections, any inflammatory condition, widespread cancer	
Carcinoembryonic antigen (CEA)	*Nonsmoker:* <3 ng/mL *Smoker:* <5 ng/mL	*Nonsmoker:* <3 mcg/L *Smoker:* <5 mcg/L	Cancer of colon, liver, pancreas; cigarette smoking; inflammatory bowel disease	
Complement, total hemolytic (CH_{50})	30–75 U/mL	30–75 U/mL	Cancer, ulcerative colitis	Bacterial endocarditis, glomerulonephritis, rheumatoid arthritis, systemic lupus erythematosus

Continued

TABLE C.3 Serology-Immunology—cont'd

Test	REFERENCE INTERVALS Conventional Units	SI Units	POSSIBLE CAUSE High/Positive	Low
Direct Coombs or direct antihuman globulin test (DAT)	Negative	Negative	Acquired hemolytic anemia, drug reactions, transfusion reactions	
Fluorescent treponemal antibody absorption (FTA-Abs)	Negative or nonreactive	Negative or nonreactive	Syphilis	
Hepatitis A antibody	Negative	Negative	Hepatitis A	
Hepatitis B surface antigen (HB_sAg)	Negative	Negative	Hepatitis B	
Hepatitis C antibody	Negative	Negative	Hepatitis C	
Monospot or monotest	Negative	Negative	Infectious mononucleosis	
Rheumatoid factor (RF)	Negative or titer <1:17	Negative or titer <1:17	Rheumatoid arthritis, Sjögren's syndrome, SLE	
RPR	Negative or nonreactive	Negative or nonreactive	Leprosy, malaria, rheumatoid arthritis, SLE, syphilis,	
VDRL	Negative or nonreactive	Negative or nonreactive	Syphilis	

RPR, Rapid plasma reagin test; *VDRL,* Venereal Disease Research Laboratory test.

TABLE C.4 Urine Chemistry

Test	REFERENCE INTERVALS Specimen	Units	SI Units	POSSIBLE CAUSE High	Low
Acetone	Random	Negative	Negative	Diabetes, high-fat and low-carbohydrate diets, starvation	
Aldosterone	24 hr	2–26 mcg/day	6–72 nmol/day	*Primary aldosteronism:* adrenocortical tumors *Secondary aldosteronism:* cirrhosis, heart failure, hyperkalemia, hyponatremia	ACTH deficiency, Addison disease, corticosteroid therapy, hypokalemia
Amylase	24 hr	<5000 Somogyi U/day	6.5–48.1 U/hr	Pancreatitis	
Bence Jones protein	Random	<0.68 mg/dL	<0.68 mg/dL	Multiple myeloma	
Bilirubin	Random	Negative	Negative	Liver disorders	
Catecholamines	24 hr			Heart failure, pheochromocytoma, progressive muscular dystrophy	
• Epinephrine		<20 mcg/day	<109 nmol/day		
• Norepinephrine		<100 mcg/day	<590 nmol/day		
Cortisol	24 hr	<100 mcg/day	<276 nmol/day	Adrenal cancer, Cushing syndrome, hyperthyroidism, obesity, stress	Addison disease, hypothyroidism, liver disease
Creatinine clearance	24 hr	*Male*: 107–139 mL/min *Female:* 87–107 mL/min	*Male*: 1.78–2.32 mL/sec *Female:* 1.45–1.78 mL/sec	Exercise, pregnancy	Cirrhosis, heart failure, renal disease

TABLE C.4 Urine Chemistry—cont'd

	REFERENCE INTERVALS			POSSIBLE CAUSE	
Test	Specimen	Units	SI Units	High	Low
Estrogens	24 hr				
• Female				Gonadal or adrenal tumor	Endocrine disturbance, ovarian dysfunction, menopause
• Nonpregnant		4–60 mcg/day	4–60 mcg/day		
• Postmenopause		<20 mcg/day	<20 mcg/day		
• Male		4–25 mcg/day	4–25 mcg/day		
Glucose	Random	Negative	Negative	Diabetes, pituitary disorders	
Hemoglobin	Random	Negative	Negative	Extensive burns, glomerulonephritis, hemolytic anemia, hemolytic transfusion reaction	
5-Hydroxyindole acetic acid (5-HIAA)	24 hr	2–8 mg/day	10–40 μmol/day	Malignant carcinoid syndrome	
Ketones	Random	Negative	Negative	Diabetes, starvation, dehydration	
Metanephrine	24 hr	<1.3 mg/day	<7 μmol/day	Pheochromocytoma	
Myoglobin	Random	Negative	Negative	Crushing injuries, electric injuries, extreme physical exertion	
Osmolality	Random	50–1200 mOsm/kg	50–1200 mmol/kg	Heart failure, liver disease, shock, SIADH	Aldosteronism, diabetes insipidus, hypokalemia, pyelonephritis
pH	Random	4.6–8.0	4.6–8.0	Urinary tract infection, urine allowed to stand at room temperature	Respiratory or metabolic acidosis
Protein	Random	0–8 mg/dL	0–8 mg/dL	Acute and chronic renal disease, heart failure	
Protein (quantitative)	24 hr	50–80 mg/day	50–80 mg/day	Heart failure, urinary tract inflammation, nephritis, nephrosis, strenuous exercise	
Sodium	24 hr	40–220 mEq/day	40–220 mmol/day	Acute tubular necrosis	Hyponatremia
Specific gravity	Random	1.005–1.030	1.005–1.030	Albuminuria, dehydration, glycosuria, fever	Diabetes insipidus, hypothermia, diuresis
Uric acid	24 hr	250–750 mg/day	1.48–4.43 mmol/day	Gout, leukemia	Nephritis
Urobilinogen	Random	Negative	Negative	Hemolytic disease, liver parenchymal cell damage, liver disease	Complete bile duct obstruction
Vanillylmandelic acid	24 hr	<6.8 mg/day	<35 μmol/day	Pheochromocytoma	

ACTH, Adrenocorticotropic hormone.

TABLE C.5 Fecal Analysis

Test	Reference Intervals: Conventional Units	Reference Intervals: SI Units	Possible Cause
Fecal fat	2–6 g/24 h	7–21 mmol/day	Common bile duct obstruction, malabsorption syndrome, pancreatic disease
Mucus	Negative	Negative	Mucous colitis, spastic constipation
Pus	Negative	Negative	Chronic bacillary dysentery, chronic ulcerative colitis, localized abscesses
Blood[a]	Negative	Negative	Anal fissures, gastrointestinal cancer, hemorrhoids, inflammatory bowel disease, peptic ulcer disease
Color			
• Brown			Various color depending on diet
• Clay			Biliary obstruction, presence of barium sulfate
• Tarry			More than 100 mL of blood in gastrointestinal tract
• Red			Blood in large intestine
• Black			Blood in upper gastrointestinal tract, iron medication

[a]Ingesting meat may produce false-positive results. Patient may be placed on a meat-free diet for 3 days before the test.

TABLE C.6 Cerebrospinal Fluid Analysis

Test	Reference Intervals: Conventional Units	Reference Intervals: SI Units	Possible Cause: High	Possible Cause: Low
Pressure	<20 mm H_2O	<20 mm H_2O	Hemorrhage, intracranial tumor, meningitis	Head injury, spinal tumor, subdural hematoma
Blood cell count (age dependent)	Negative	Negative	Intracranial hemorrhage CNS infection or inflammation	
• WBC	0–5 cells/μL	$0–5 \times 10^6$ cells/L		
• RBC	Negative	Negative		
Chloride	700–750 mg/dL	118–132 mmol/L	Uremia	CNS bacterial infection
Glucose	50–75 mg/dL	2.2–3.9 mmol/L	CNS viral infection, diabetes	Bacterial infection, CNS tuberculosis
Protein				
• Lumbar	15–45 mg/dL	0.15–0.45 g/L	Guillain-Barré syndrome, poliomyelitis, trauma	
• Cisternal	15–25 mg/dL	0.15–0.25 g/L	CNS syphilis	
• Ventricular	5–15 mg/dL	0.05–0.15 g/L	Acute meningitis, brain tumor, chronic CNS infection, multiple sclerosis	

INDEX

Disorder names and key terms are in **boldface.** Page numbers in **boldface** indicate main discussions. Page numbers followed by *b, f,* or *t* indicate boxes, figures, or tables, respectively.

B

H

I

O

V

ABBREVIATIONS

ABG	arterial blood gas
ACE	angiotensin-converting enzyme
ACLS	advanced cardiac life support
ACS	acute coronary syndrome
ACTH	adrenocorticotropic hormone
ADH	antidiuretic hormone
AED	automatic external defibrillator
AIDS	acquired immunodeficiency syndrome
AKA	above-knee amputation
AKI	acute kidney injury
ALI	acute lung injury
ALL	acute lymphocytic leukemia
ALS	amyotrophic lateral sclerosis
AMI	acute myocardial infarction
ANA	antinuclear antibody
ANS	autonomic nervous system
AORN	Association of periOperative Room Nurses
APD	automated peritoneal dialysis
aPTT	activated partial thromboplastin time
ARDS	acute respiratory distress syndrome
ATN	acute tubular necrosis
BCLS	basic cardiac life support
BKA	below-knee amputation
BMI	body mass index
BMR	basal metabolic rate
BMT	bone marrow transplantation
BPH	benign prostatic hyperplasia
BSE	breast self-examination
BUN	blood urea nitrogen
CABG	coronary artery bypass graft
CAD	coronary artery disease; circulatory assist device
CAPD	continuous ambulatory peritoneal dialysis
CAVH	continuous arteriovenous hemofiltration
CBC	complete blood count
CCU	coronary care unit; critical care unit
CDC	Centers for Disease Control and Prevention
CIS	carcinoma in situ
CKD	chronic kidney disease
CLL	chronic lymphocytic leukemia
CML	chronic myelocytic leukemia
CMP	cardiomyopathy
CN	cranial nerve
CNS	central nervous system
CO	cardiac output
COPD	chronic obstructive pulmonary disease
CPAP	continuous positive airway pressure
CPR	cardiopulmonary resuscitation
CRRT	continuous renal replacement therapy
CRNA	certified registered nurse anesthetist
CSF	cerebrospinal fluid
CT	computed tomography
CVA	cerebrovascular accident; costovertebral angle
CVAD	central venous access device
CVI	chronic venous insufficiency
CVP	central venous pressure
D&C	dilation and curettage
DDD	degenerative disk disease
DI	diabetes insipidus
DIC	disseminated intravascular coagulation
DJD	degenerative joint disease
DKA	diabetic ketoacidosis
DM	diabetes mellitus; diastolic murmur
DRE	digital rectal examination
DVT	deep vein thrombosis
ECF	extracellular fluid
ECG	electrocardiogram
ED	emergency department; erectile dysfunction
EEG	electroencephalogram
EMG	electromyogram
EMS	emergency medical services
ENT	ear, nose, and throat
ERCP	endoscopic retrograde cholangiopancreatography
ERT	estrogen replacement therapy
ESKD	end-stage kidney disease
ESR	erythrocyte sedimentation rate
ET	endotracheal
FEV	forced expiratory volume
FRC	functional residual capacity
FUO	fever of unknown origin
GCS	Glasgow Coma Scale
GERD	gastroesophageal reflux disease
GFR	glomerular filtration rate
GH	growth hormone
GI	glycemic index
GTT	glucose tolerance test
GU	genitourinary
GYN, Gyn	gynecologic
HAI	health care–associated infection
HAV	hepatitis A virus
Hb, Hgb	hemoglobin
HBV	hepatitis B virus
Hct	hematocrit
HCV	hepatitis C virus
HD	hemodialysis, Huntington's disease
HDL	high-density lipoprotein
HF	heart failure
HIV	human immunodeficiency virus
H&P	history and physical examination
HPV	human papillomavirus
HSCT	hematopoietic stem cell transplantation
IABP	intraaortic balloon pump
IBS	irritable bowel syndrome
ICP	intracranial pressure
I&D	incision and drainage
IE	infective endocarditis
IFG	impaired fasting glucose
IGT	impaired glucose tolerance
INR	international normalized ratio
IOP	intraocular pressure
IPPB	intermittent positive-pressure breathing
ITP	idiopathic thrombocytopenic purpura
IUD	intrauterine device
IV	intravenous
IVP	intravenous push; intravenous pyelogram
JVD	jugular venous distention
KS	Kaposi sarcoma
KUB	kidney, ureters, and bladder (x-ray)
KVO	keep vein open
LAD	left anterior descending